S0-AZK-736

WHO'S WHO
IN AMERICAN POLITICS
SECOND EDITION 1969-1970

WHO'S WHO IN AMERICAN POLITICS

SECOND EDITION 1969-1970

A Biographical Directory of United States Political Leaders

Edited by PAUL A. THEIS
Public Relations Director, Republican Congressional Committee
and EDMUND L. HENSHAW, JR.
Research Director, Democratic Congressional Committee

R. R. BOWKER COMPANY New York and London 1969

Published by R. R. Bowker Co. (a Xerox company)
1180 Avenue of the Americas, New York, N.Y. 10036

Standard Book Number: 8352-0238-0
Library of Congress Catalog Number: 67-25024

NOTICE: This book has no connection with *Who's Who in America* or its publisher, Marquis-Who's Who, Inc.

Printed and bound in the United States of America

Table of Contents

PREFACE	vii
EDITORIAL ADVISORY COMMITTEE	ix
LIST OF ABBREVIATIONS	xi
BIOGRAPHIES	1
ADDENDA	1275
STATE DELEGATIONS TO THE 91ST CONGRESS	1277
GOVERNORS OF THE STATES	1283
GEOGRAPHICAL INDEX	1285

Editors' Preface

When the 1967-68 edition of WHO'S WHO IN AMERICAN POLITICS was published, we were pleased with its reception and acceptance—particularly since it was the *first* edition of a new and vital and authoritative source of information about the men and women who direct and influence American government at all levels. Generally, the critics who delve into such works saluted the first edition as a valuable source of information about the cast of what one called the "greatest drama of our time—running the American government."

The *Saturday Review* called it "a new and extremely useful reference tool for everyone connected with politics in the United States." *Publisher's Weekly* characterized it as "comprehensive, useful." *Library Journal* labeled it "a unique and invaluable source of current information which should be found in every library." *Editor and Publisher* magazine cited it as "a useful reference book for any newspaper library."

The nation's political leaders who made up the cast of characters in the first edition also had kind words for it. Richard M. Nixon, who was to become his party's presidental candidate and later the President of the United States, commented:

"I believe a directory of America's political leaders has been long needed in this country. It can be a valuable source of information for persons either actively engaged in politics or interested in politics. I believe "Who's Who in American Politics" could well become a must on the bookshelves of Amercans everywhere, no matter what their political faith."

Hubert Humphrey, the then-Vice President of the United States who was to contest Richard Nixon for the presidency, declared: "A resource book on politics is of great value to the public official, the politician, the teacher and the citizen. This political handbook should prove to be very helpful."

In presenting the Second Edition of WHO'S WHO IN AMERICAN POLITICS, we believe we have an even better directory than the first. This edition contains biographical data on approximately 19,000 of America's political leaders and government officials as compared to 12,500 in the first edition. A new dimension has been added this time in the Geographical Index which lists biographees by the states in which they maintain their legal residence. It is hoped that this Index will prove a valuable aid to users of the directory.

To make certain that this edition would be as complete and auhoritative as possible, a blue-ribbon panel of eight of the nation's top political leaders was invited to serve as an Advisory Committee. Members of this group included: Dr. Evron M. Kirkpatrick, Executive Director of the American Political Science Association; Senator Edward W. Brooke, Massachusetts; Governor Richard J. Hughes, New Jersey; Representative Michael J. Kirwan, Ohio, Chairman of the Democratic National Congressional Committee; Senator Warren G. Magnuson, Washington; Governor Ronald Reagan, California, Chairman of the Republican Governors' Association; Richard M. Scammon, Director of the Election Research Center of the Governmental Affairs Institute; and Representative Bob Wilson, California, Chairman of the National Republican Congressional Committee. The interest and contribution of the members of the Advisory Committee was invaluable—and we wish to express a special thanks to these distinguished political leaders.

To ensure a comprehensive coverage of American political leaders at all levels, special criteria were established to govern inclusion in the directory. Categories selected included: the President, Vice President, and Cabinet officers; U. S. Senators and House Members; U. S. Sub-cabinet officials, including key Presidential appointees; Governors, Lieutenant Governors, and State Cabinet officers; State officials of both major parties, including chairmen and members of State Central Committees; *former* Presidents, Vice Presidents,

Presidential and Vice Presidential nominees, Congressmen, Governors and State Chairmen (still living); key staff personnel on Democratic and Republican National, Senatorial and Congressional Committees; delegates to the Democratic and Republican National Conventions; State legislators; Mayors and council members of major cities; county chairmen of both major parties; leaders of minority parties; miscellaneous political leaders, including national and state officials of women's divisions of both parties, of the Young Democratic and Republican Clubs, etc.; plus others nominated by Party National and State Chairmen who are not covered in other categories.

As in the first edition, the information was gathered primarily by questionnaires sent directly to the biographees, specially designed to elicit the most pertinent data such as full name and address, political party affiliation, birthplace and date, education, family data, religion, present and previous political, government and business positions, military service, and so forth.

To obtain addresses so that questionnaires could be sent to people selected for inclusion for the first time and to former biographees for their revisions, state and local party headquarters were combed as well as Congressional sources and the vast resources of the Library of Congress. Every effort has been made to avoid errors in the listings—with the certain knowledge that some have escaped us. The great majority of entries have been edited from information received in questionnaires. If biographical forms were not returned, and the prominence of the biographee warranted inclusion, material was gathered from other sources and a proof prepared and sent to the biographee for verification before it was published. When detailed information was not available, only their name, political or government position, and current mailing address have been given. Biographies of those who did not reply to requests for revision have been repeated; the date in parentheses at the end of these entries indicate they are reprints from the first edition. When more recent information has come to our attention from reliable sources, it has been incorporated into these biographies. When no current addresses could be found, the entries show a notation to this effect. We have used our best effort to include the material submitted within the scope of the established format, but have no legal responsibility for accidental omissions or errors in entries.

We believe we have assembled in this edition of WHO'S WHO IN AMERICAN POLITICS not only the cast of the great drama of politics—but, more importantly, the vital information about these men and women whose activities so vitally affect each of us. By understanding America's political leaders, we are able, in turn, to better understand the political life of the nation itself.

The Editors:

Paul A. Theis, *Public Relations Director*
National Republican Congressional Committee

Edmund L. Henshaw, Jr. *Research Director*
Democratic National Congressional Committee

Editorial Advisory Committee

General Abbreviations

(1967)—No answer to questionnaire. Biography reprinted from first edition with more recent information incorporated when available.

AAONMS—Ancient Arabic Order Nobles of the Majestic Shrine
AASR—Ancient Accepted Scottish Rite
Abstr—Abstracts
acad—academic, academy
acct—account, accountant, accounting
Add—Address
adj—adjunct, adjutant
adjust—adjustment
Adm—Admiral
admin—administration, administrative
adminstr—administrator
adv—advanced, advancement, adviser, advisory, advocate
advert—advertisement, advertising
AEAONMS—Ancient Egyptian Arabic Order Nobles of the Majestic Shrine
AEF—American Expeditionary Force
aeronaut—aeronautic(s), aeronautical
AF&AM—Ancient Free and Accepted Mason
affil—affiliate, affiliation
AFL—American Federation of Labor
agr—agricultural, agriculture
Ala—Alabama
Alta—Alberta
Am—America, American
anal—analysis, analytic, analytical
anat—anatomic, anatomical, anatomy
Ann—Annal(s)
anthrop—anthropological, anthropology
antiq—antiquarian, antiquary, antiquities, antiquity
APO—Army Post Office
app—appoint, appointed
appl—applied
appln—application
Apr—April
apt—apartment(s)
arbit—arbitration
Arch—Archives
archaeol—archaeological, archaeology
archit—architectural, architecture
Ariz—Arizona
Ark—Arkansas
artil—artillery
A/S—Apprentice Seaman
Asn—Association
assoc—associate, associated
asst—assistant
astron—astronomical, astronomy
astronaut—astronautical, astronautics
astronr—astronomer
astrophys—astrophysical, astrophysics
attend—attendant, attending
Aug—August
Ave—Avenue

b—born
bact—bacterial, bacteriologic, bacteriological, bacteriologist, bacteriology
B.C—British Columbia
bd—board
behav—behavioral
bibliog—bibliographic, bibliographical, bibliography
biochem—biochemical, biochemistry
biol—biological, biology
biomet—biometrical, biometric(s), biometry
biophys—biophysical, biophysics
bldg—building
Blvd—Boulevard
BMPIUA—Bricklayers, Masons and Plasterers International Union of America
Bn—Battalion
bot—botanical, botany
br—branch
BRCA—Brotherhood of Railway Carmen of America
Brig. Gen—Brigadier General
Brit—Britain, British
Bros—Brothers
BRT—Brotherhood of Railroad Trainmen
Bul—Bulletin
bur—bureau
bus—business
B.W.I—British West Indies

c—children
C. of C—Chamber of Commerce
Calif—California
Can—Canada, Canadian
cand—candidate
Capt—Captain
cardiol—cardiology
Cath—Catholic
cent—central
cert—certificate, certified
chap—chapter
chem—chemical, chemistry
chmn—chairman
CIO—Congress of Industrial Organizations
clin—clinic, clinical
cmn—commission
cmnr—commissioner
cmt—committee
Co—Companies, Company, County
co-auth—co-author
co-ed—co-editor
Col—College, Colonel
collab—collaboration, collaborative, collaborator
Colo—Colorado
Comdr—Commander
commun—communicable, communication(s), community
comp—comparative
comput—computation, computer(s), computing
conf—conference
cong—congress(es), congressional
Conn—Connecticut
conserv—conservancy, conservation
consol—consolidated, consolidation
consult—consultant, consulting
contrib—contributing, contributor
conv—convention
coop—cooperation, cooperative
coord—coordinating, coordination
corp—corporation
coun—council, councilor
counsr—counselor
CPA—Certified Public Accountant
Cpl—Corporal
CPO—Chief Petty Officer
CWA—Communications Workers of America
CWV—Catholic War Veterans
C.Z—Canal Zone
Czech—Czechoslovakia

d—daughter
D—Democrat
DAR—Daughters of the American Revolution
DAV—Disabled American Veterans
D.C—District of Columbia
Dec—December
Del—Delaware, delegate, delegation
del-at-lg—delegate-at-large
Dem—Democrat(s), Democratic
dent—dental, dentistry
dep—deputy
dept—department
develop—development, developmental
DFL—Democrat-Farmer-Labor
dipl—diploma, diplomate
dir—director, directory
dist—district
div—division, divorced
document—documentation
Dom—Dominion
Dr—Doctor, drive

E—East
East—Eastern
econ—economic(s), economical, economy
economet—econometric(s)
ed—edition, editor, editorial
educ—education, educational
Elec—Election, electric, electrical, electricity
elem—elementary
emer—emeritus
employ—employment
encyclop—encyclopedia
eng—engineering
Eng—England, English
engr—engineer
Ens—Ensign
environ—environment(s), environmental
equip—equipment
espec—especially
estab—established, establishment
ETO—European Theater of Operations
eval—evaluation
Evangel—Evangelical
eve—evening
exam—examination, examiner(s)
exec—executive
exhib—exhibitor(s)
exp—experiment, experimental
exped—expedition(s)
explor—exploration(s), exploratory
expos—exposition
exten—extension

F&AM—Free and Accepted Mason
Feb—February
fed—federal
fedn—federation
fel—fellow, fellowship
FL—Farmer-Labor
Fla—Florida
for—foreign
found—foundation
FPO—Fleet Post Office
Ft—Fort

Ga—Georgia
gen—general
geog—geographic, geographical, geography
geogr—geographer
geol—geologic, geological, geology
geophys—geophysical, geophysics
G.H.Q—General Headquarters
GOP—Grand Old Party
gov—governing, governor(s)
govt—government, governmental
Gr—Greater
grad—graduate
Gt. Brit—Great Britain
guid—guidance

HA—Hospital Apprentice
hist—historical, history
hon—honorable, honorary
hort—horticultural, horticulture
hosp—hospital(s), hospitalization
hq—headquarters
Hwy—Highway

IAMAW—International Association of Machinists and Aerospace Workers
IBEW—International Brotherhood of Electrical Workers
IBT—International Brotherhood of Teamsters, Chauffeurs, Warehousemen & Helpers of America
ILGPNWU—International Leather Goods, Plastics and Novelty Workers Union
ILGWU—International Ladies' Garment Workers Union
Ill—Illinois
Imp—Imperial
improv—improvement
Inc—Incorporated
Ind—Indiana
indust—industrial, industry
Inf—Infantry
info—information
ins—insurance
inst—institute, institution
instnl—institutional
instr—instruction, instructor
int—international
intel—intelligence
introd—introduction
invest—investigation
investr—investigator
Ital—Italian
ITU—International Typographical Union
IUE—International Union of Electrical, Radio and Machine Workers

J—Journal
Jan—January
jg—junior grade
JOUAM—Junior Order United American Mechanics
jour—journal
jr—junior
jurisp—jurisprudence

K. of C—Knights of Columbus
K. of M—Knights of Malta
K. of P—Knights of Pythias
Kans—Kansas
KCCH—Knight Commander of Court of Honor
K.T—Knight Templar
Ky—Kentucky

La—Louisiana
lab—laboratory
lang—language(s)
lect—lecture
lectr—lecturer
legis—legislation, legislative, legislature
L.I—Long Island
lib—liberal
libr—library
librn—librarian
ling—linguistic(s)
lit—literary, literature
Lt—Lieutenant
Lt.(jg)—Lieutenant junior grade
Lt.(sg)—Lieutenant senior grade
Ltd—Limited
LWIU—Leather Workers International Union of America

m—married
mag—magazine
Maj—Major
Man—Manitoba
Mar—March
Mass—Massachusetts
math—mathematical, mathematic(s)
Md—Maryland
mech—mechanic(s), mechanical
med—medical, medicinal, medicine
mem—member, memoirs, memorial
ment—mental
meteorol—meteorological, meteorology
metrop—metropolitan
Mex—Mexico
mfg—manufacturing
mfr—manufacture, manufacturer
mgr—manager
mgt—management
Mich—Michigan
mid—middle
Midn—Midshipman
mil—military
Minn—Minnesota
mkt—market, marketing
Mo—Missouri
mod—modern
monogr—monograph
Mont—Montana
M/Sgt—Master Sergeant
mt—mount, mountain(s)
Munic—Municipal, Municipalities
mus—museum
MWA—Modern Woodmen of America

N—North
NAACP—National Association for Advancement of Colored People
NASA—National Aeronautics and Space Administration
nat—national, naturalized
NATO—North Atlantic Treaty Organization
navig—navigation
N.B—New Brunswick
N.C—North Carolina
N.Dak—North Dakota
Nebr—Nebraska
Nev—Nevada
New Eng—New England
Newf—Newfoundland
N.H—New Hampshire
N.J—New Jersey
N.Mex—New Mexico
North—Northern
Northeast—Northeastern
Northwest—Northwestern
Norweg—Norwegian
Nov—November
N.S—Nova Scotia
N.Y—New York State
N.Y.C—New York City
N.Z—New Zealand

observ—observatory
OCAWIU—Oil, Chemical and Atomic Workers International Union
occup—occupation, occupational
Oct—October
OEEC—Organization for European Economic Cooperation
off—office, official
Okla—Oklahoma
Ont—Ontario
oper—operation, operational, operative
optom—optometric, optometrical, optometry
ord—ordnance
Ore—Oregon
orgn—organization(s), organizational

Pa—Pennsylvania
Pac—Pacific
Pan-Am—Pan-American
path—pathologic, pathological, pathology
P.E.I—Prince Edward Island
Pfc—Private first class
pharm—pharmacy
Phila—Philadelphia
philos—philosophic, philosophical, philosophy
photog—photographic, photography
phys—physical
physiol—physiological, physiology
pkwy—parkway
PO—Petty Officer
polit—political, politics
polytech—polytechnic
pos—position
postgrad—postgraduate
P.R—Puerto Rico
prep—preparation, preparative, preparatory
pres—president
Presby—Presbyterian
prev—prevention, preventive
prfnl—professional
prin—principal
prob—problem
proc—proceedings
prod—product(s), production, productive
prof—professor, professorial
prog—program, programming
proj—project, projectional, projective
prom—promotion
prov—province, provincial
psychiat—psychiatric, psychiatry
psychol—psychological, psychology
PTA—Parent-Teacher Association
pub—public
publ—publication(s), publishing
Pvt—Private

Qm—Quartermaster
Qm. Gen—Quartermaster General
qual—qualitative, quality
quant—quantitative
Quart—Quarterly
Que—Quebec

R—Republican(s)
RAM—Royal Arch Mason
RCIA—Retail Clerks International Association
Rd—Road
R.D—Rural Delivery
ref—refining
registr—registration
Regt—Regiment, Regimental
rel—relation, relative
relig—religion, religious
Rep—Representative, Republican(s)
Repub—Republic
Res—Reserve(s), residence
Ret—Retired
rev—review, revision(s)
R.I—Rhode Island
ROA—Reserve Officers Association of U.S.
RONS—Reserve Officers of the Naval Service
ROTC—Reserve Officers Training Corps
R.R—Railroad, Rural Route
RSM—Royal and Select Master-Masons
rwy—railway

s—son
S—South
S.Africa—South Africa
S.Am—South America
sanit—sanitary, sanitation
SAR—Sons of the American Revolution
Sask—Saskatchewan
S.C—South Carolina
sch—school
sci—science(s), scientific
S.Dak—South Dakota
SEATO—South East Asia Treaty Organization
sec—secondary
sect—section
secy—secretary
sem—seminary
Sen—Senator, Senatorial
Sept—September
serv—service(s), serving
Sgt—Sergeant
SHAEF—Supreme Headquarters Allied Expeditionary Force
soc—social, society
sociol—sociologic, sociological, sociology
South—Southern
Southeast—Southeastern
Southwest—Southwestern
spec—special
Sq—Square
sr—senior
S/Sgt—Staff Sergeant
St—Saint, Street
sta—station
statist—statistical, statistics
struct—structural, structure(s)
subcmt—subcommittee
subj—subject
substa—substation
suppl—supplement, supplemental, supplementary
supt—superintendent
supv—supervising, supervision
supvr—supervisor
supvry—supervisory
surg—surgical, surgery
surv—survey, surveying
Switz—Switzerland
symp—symposium(s)
syst—system(s), systematic(s), systematical

TAR—Teen-Age Republicans
tech—technical, technique(s), technological, technology
tel—telegraph(y), telephone
Tenn—Tennessee
Terr—Terrace
Tex—Texas
theol—theological, theology
theoret—theoretical
trans—transactions, translation(s)
treas—treasurer, treasury
T/Sgt—Technical Sergeant
tuberc—tuberculosis
TV—television
Twp—Township

UAW—United Automobile, Aerospace and Agricultural Implement Workers of America
UDC—United Daughters of the Confederacy
UMW—United Mine Workers of America
UN—United Nations
unemploy—unemployment
UNESCO—United Nations Educational, Scientific and Cultural Organization
UNICEF—United Nations International Childrens Fund
univ—university
UNRRA—United Nations Relief and Rehabilitation Administration
UPW—United Public Workers of America
UPWA—United Packinghouse Workers of America
U.S—United States
USW—United Steelworkers of America

Va—Virginia
v.chmn—vice chairman
vet—veteran(s), veterinarian, veterinary
VFW—Veterans of Foreign Wars
V.I—Virgin Islands
vis—visiting
voc—vocational
vol—voluntary, volunteer(s)
vol—volume
v.pres—vice president
Vt—Vermont

W—West
Wash—Washington
Wash, D.C—Washington, D.C.
West—Western
WHO—World Health Organization
W.I—West Indies
wid—widow, widowed, widower
Wis—Wisconsin
WOW—Woodmen of the World
W.Va—West Virginia
Wyo—Wyoming

YMCA—Young Men's Christian Association
YMHA—Young Men's Hebrew Association
YWCA—Young Women's Christian Association
YWHA—Young Women's Hebrew Association

zool—zoological, zoology

WHO'S WHO IN AMERICAN POLITICS SECOND EDITION 1969-1970

WHO'S WHO
IN AMERICAN POLITICS

A

AALBU, ROY M. D
Chmn, Mineral Co. Dem. Cent. Cmt, Nev.
b. Oslo, Norway, 11/22/91; s. Halvor Aalbu and Johanna Paulsen A; wid; c. Victor H, James N, Roy R, Rose Marie (Mrs. Jack Conely), Dolores (Mrs. E.E. Ottowa) and Sigrid (Mrs. Arnold Cox). Educ: La Salle Exten. Univ, 2 years law; int. correspondence schs, 4 years, archit; Toastmasters Int; Navy League. Polit. & Govt. Pos: Secy. and campaign mgr, Ninth Cong. Dist. Dem-Farmer-Labor Party, Minn, 36-38; asst. chief clerk, Minn. House Rep, 37; supt, Itasca State Park, 37-38; sgt. at arms, Nev. State Sen, 65; chmn, Mineral Co. Dem. Cent. Cmt, Nev, currently. Bus. & Prof. Pos: Ed, Tri-Co. Forum, Thief River Falls, Minn, 32-36; ed, Fergus Falls Tribune, 36; ed, Nev. Dem. Record, 66; columnist and commentator, Spartacus Mineral Co. Independent, Hawthorne, Nev, currently. Publ: Minnesota Kaleidoscope of 1933, Forum Pub. Co; Deadlocked, Coop. Pub. Co. Rel: Non-sectarian. Legal Res: 785 D St, Hawthorne, Nev. 89415. Mailing Add: P.O. Box 757, Hawthorne, Nev. 89415.

AAMOTH, GORDON S. R
N.Dak. State Rep.
b. Valley City, N.Dak, 4/11/14; s. H.C. Aamoth and Claire St. Pierre A; m. 2/4/39 to Margaret Louise McCannel; c. Dr. Gordon McCannel, Bruce, Carolyn, Jane and Archie. Educ: Univ. N.Dak, B.S, 36, LL.B, 38; Phi Delta Phi; Blue Key; Scabbard & Blade; Sigma Chi. Polit. & Govt. Pos: Mem, Fargo Park Bd, N.Dak, 54-64; N.Dak. State Rep, 57-, Speaker, N.Dak. House Rep, 67- Bus. & Prof. Pos: Theater owner, 38-62; trust officer, First Nat. Bank, Fargo, N.Dak, 63- Mil. Serv: Entered as Ens, Navy, 42, released as Lt.(jg), 46, after serv. in Destroyer Escort 536. Mem: Nat. Conf. of Legis. Leaders; Elks; Rotary; Am. Legion; Farm Bur. Rel: Episcopal. Legal Res: 1411 Third Ave. S, Fargo, N.Dak. 58102. Mailing Add: First National Bank & Trust Co, Fargo, N.Dak. 58102.

AAS, LYNN W. R
N.Dak. State Rep.
b. Benedict, N.Dak, 6/4/21; s. George H. Aas and Anna Olson A; m. 7/27/52 to Beverly A. Stockstad; c. David B, Paul W, Daniel G. and Joseph L. Educ: Univ. N.Dak, 41-43; Mass. Inst. Tech, 43-44; Univ. N.Dak, B.S. in commerce, 45 and LL.B, 49; Phi Alpha Delta; Beta Alpha Psi; pres, Intrafraternity Coun; Blue Key; YMCA Bd. Control; Tau Kappa Epsilon. Polit. & Govt. Pos: N.Dak. State Rep, Fifth Legis. Dist, currently. Bus. & Prof. Pos: Spec. agent, Intel. Div, Internal Revenue Serv, 46-60, investr, spec. assignment to King Cmt. of U.S. Cong, 52; bus. mgr, Med. Arts Clinic, Minot, N.Dak, 60-; vis. lectr, Air Force Inst. Tech, Minot, 65. Mil. Serv: Entered Army, 43, served with 17th Airborne Div, ETO, released, 45; Combat Infantryman's Badge; Expert Rifleman's Badge; ETO Medal with 3 Bronze Stars; Bronze Star for Bravery; Purple Heart. Mem: N.Dak. Bar, 49; pres, Fargo Univ, Nat. Asn. Internal Revenue Employees, 55-56 and nat. dir, 57-59; Med. Group Mgt; Minot C. of C, Govt. Affairs Cmt, chmn, 63, Taxation Cmt. and Health, Educ. and Welfare Cmt; dir, Kiwanis, 62-63 and treas, 64-66; Minot Commun. Chest; former cubmaster and dist. v.chmn, Boy Scouts; YMCA; Elks; Minot Country Club. Received second presidential citation for contribution to fel. employees, Nat. Asn. Internal Revenue Employees. Rel: First Lutheran. Mailing Add: 1830 Seventh St, S.W, Minot, N.Dak. 58701.

AASHEIM, MAGNUS S. D
b. Reserve, Mont, 9/21/09; s. S. O. Aasheim and Marthea Akre A; m. 5/36 to Velma Mae Clark; c. Gary L. and Glen H. Educ: Univ. Mont, B.A, 35 and M.E, 41. Polit. & Govt. Pos: Dem. precinct committeeman, Mont, 55-57; Dem. co. chmn, 57-59; Mont. State Rep, 59-65. Bus. & Prof. Pos: Supt, Outlook Pub. Schs, Mont, 37-44; supt, Froid Pub. Schs, 44-45. Mem: President's Cmt. Traffic Safety; Eight-State Proj, Designing Educ. for Future. Rel: Protestant. Mailing Add: Antelope, Mont. 59211.

ABBEY, CLIFFORD ELZA D
V.Chmn, Bourbon Co. Dem. Party, Kans.
b. Bronson, Kans, 3/29/04; s. George Ray Abbey and Myrtle Smith A; m. 5/16/25 to Olive Della Murrow. Educ: Bronson High Sch, Kans, 2 years. Polit. & Govt. Pos: V.chmn, Bourbon Co. Dem. Party, Kans, 60- Bus. & Prof. Pos: Field supvr, Am. Automobile Asn, 32-36; plant employee, Gen. Motors, Kansas City, Mo, 36-43. Mem: Farm Bur; Mason (Dist. Dep. Grand Master, Dist. 8). Rel: Protestant. Mailing Add: R.R. 1, Box 78, Bronson, Kans. 66716.

ABBITT, WATKINS MOORMAN D
U.S. Rep, Va.
b. Appomattox, Va, 5/21/08; s. George Francis Abbitt and Otway C. Moorman A; m. 3/20/37 to Corinne Hancock; c. Anne Culvin, Watkins Moorman and Corinne Hancock. Educ: Univ. Richmond, LL.B, 31 and hon. LL.D, 65; Omicron Delta Kappa; Delta Theta Phi. Polit. & Govt. Pos: Commonwealth's Attorney for Appomattox Co, Va, 32-38; del, Va. State Dem. Conv, 32-; chmn, Dem. Co. Cmt, 37-; Dem. elector, 44; del, Va. State Constitutional Conv, 45; U.S. Rep, Va, 48-, mem, Agr. Cmt; chmn, Va. State Dem. Cent. Cmt, 64- Bus. & Prof. Pos: Lawyer; dir, Farmer's Nat. Bank of Appomattox. Mem: Chmn, Appomattox Am. Red Cross; chmn, Appomattox War Bond Drive, 42-43; Fifth Judicial Circuit Court and Va. Bar Asns; Forestry Asn. (awards cmt, 51-53); Coun. of State Bar; past pres, Ruritan and Lions. Rel: Baptist. Legal Res: Appomattox, Va. 24522. Mailing Add: House Office Bldg, Washington, D.C. 20515.

ABBOTT, ARNOLD PETER D
Mem, Pa. Dem. Exec. Cmt.
b. Beverly, Mass, 4/12/24; s. Melvin M. Rosenbloom and Rebecca Marcy R; m. 6/20/48; c. Pamela Jane, Emily Anne and Robert Craig. Educ: Univ. Pa, A.B, in Journalism, 48, M.A, in Polit. Sci, 65; Fels Inst. of Local & State Govt, Cert, 62; Inter-fraternity Coun; pres, Kappa Nu, 47-48. Polit. & Govt. Pos: Committeeman, Montgomery Co. Dem. Cmt, Pa, 52-, asst. chmn. and registrn. chmn, 64-; police cmnr, Abington Twp, 56-58; cmnr, Abington Twp. Bd. Cmnrs, 56-60; chmn, Abington Twp. Dem. Cmt, 58-62; mem, Montgomery Co. Bd. of Visitors, 58-68; del, Montgomery Co. Exec. Cmt, Seventh Area Dem. Cmt, 60-; chmn, Seventh Area Dem. Cmt, 62-64; del, Dem. Nat. Conv, 64 & 68; dir, Sch. for Cmt. People, Joint Chester, Del. and Montgomery Co. Cmts, 64; mem, Pa. State Dem. Exec. and Policy Cmts, 66-; chmn, Bd. Mgrs. Montgomery Hall Juvenile Home, 68- Bus. & Prof. Pos: Mfrs. rep, A&Z Chain Co, 49-; mem. bd. dirs, Harold G. Knight Found, 58-; pres, Abbott and Co, Inc, 66-; chmn, Eastern Montgomery Co. Housing Cmt, Del. Valley Fair Housing Cmt, 66. Mil. Serv: Entered as Pvt, Army, 42, released as Sgt, 45, after serv. in Fifth Army, 180th Inf, N.Africa and Italy, 43-45; Europe-Africa-Middle East Serv. Medal with Two Bronze Stars; Good Conduct Medal; Victory Medal; Battle Stars of Rome-Arno and Naples-Foggia Campaigns. Publ: Power Structure in a Negro Sub-Community, Univ. Pa, 65; 'Good Bye Commissioner,' In: Anthology of Best Short-Short Stories, Oberfirst Press, 60. Mem: United World Federalist; NAACP; Suburban Coun. of Human Rels; treas, Friends of Freedom in Miss; Seventh Area Dem. Cmt; Am. Civil Liberties Union; Am. Acad. Polit. & Soc. Sci. Pa. Jewelry Salesman of the Year Award, Pa. Retail Jewelers Asn, 69. Rel: Jewish. Mailing Add: P.O. Box 458, Jenkintown, Pa. 19046.

ABBOTT, BARBARA S. R
b. Mannington, W.Va, 11/30/30; d. Ardas Leo Straight and Nellie Starkey S; m. 6/24/61 to George Norman Abbott IV. Educ: Wash. Sch. Secretaries, grad, 49; Rutgers Univ, A.B, 59; Rutgers Women's Club; Student Activities Cmt. Polit. & Govt. Pos: Corresponding secy, Middlesex Co. Young Rep, N.J, 57-58; dist. bd. elec. clerk, Dist. Five, Edison Twp, 58-61; campaign secy, Edison Twp. Cand, 59, hq. mgr, Edison Twp. Elec, 59; campaign secy, Middlesex Co. Freeholder Cand, 60; mem, Metuchen Rep. Club, 61-; committeewoman, Dist. Four, Metuchen, 61-; campaign aid, Rodgers' Cong. Campaign, 62, campaign coordinator, 64; Rep. State Committeewoman, N.J, 65; chmn, Helen DuMont Day, Middlesex Co, 65; mem, State Fedn. Rep. Women, 65-; mem. New Brunswick Rep. Club, 65-; mgr, C. John Stroumtsos Campaign for Cong, 66; asst. in conducting co. wide sem, Co. Rep. Cmt, 66; personal adv. and campaign activities coordinator, Walter J. Duff Mayorality Cand, Metuchen, 67; alternate del, Rep. Nat. Conv, 68; state co-chmn, Nixon Tel. Campaign, 68; v.pres, Middlesex Co. Women's Rep. Club, 69; munic. v.chmn, Rep. Party, Metuchen, 69- Bus. & Prof. Pos: Secy. to v.pres, C. J. Osborn Co, Linden, N.J, 5 years; secy. to Dean Mary Bunting, Douglas Col, 1 year; asst. mgr. catalyst sales, Englehardt Minerals Corp, 3½ years; teacher, Woodbridge Twp. Bd. Educ, 59- Mem: N.J. Educ. Asn; Am. Fedn. Teachers; Eastern Star; Middlesex Co. Women's Rep. Club; Roosevelt Hosp. Auxiliary. Distinguished Alumnus Award, Rutgers Univ. Col; Award for Outstanding Serv, Rep. Party Metuchen, 68. Rel: Presbyterian. Mailing Add: 67 Home St, Metuchen, N.J. 08840.

ABBOTT, GEORGE WILLIAM R
Rep. State Chmn, Nev.
m. 10/1/55 to Marie Micheo; c. Jeanne Marie and George Walter. Polit. & Govt. Pos: Rep. State Chmn, Nev, 65-; del, Rep. Nat. Conv, 68. Mailing Add: P.O. Box 396, Minden, Nev. 89423.

ABBOTT, JAMES CHARLES, JR. R
Mayor, Georgetown, Colo.
b. Corpus Christi, Tex, 5/27/37; s. James Charles Abbott and Helen R. Howell A; single. Educ: Rice Inst, B.A, in geol, 59. Polit. & Govt. Pos: Mem, Georgetown Bd. of Adjust, Colo, 64; state chmn, Youth for Goldwater, 64; Rep. precinct committeeman, Clear Creek Co, 64-; pres, Clear Creek Co. Rep. Club and Denver Young Rep. Speak-Out Club, 65; chmn, Colo. Young Rep. Second

Cong. Dist, 65-66 and Clear Creek Co. Rep. Cent. Cmt, 65-67; mem, Colo. Young Rep. State Bd. of Dirs, 65-; Nat. Committeeman, Young Rep. League of Colo, 66-67, State Chmn, 67-69; mem, Nat. Exec. Cmt, Young Rep. Nat. Fedn, 67-69; mayor, Georgetown, 69- Bus. & Prof. Pos: Building and Land Investments, 64- Mil. Serv: Entered as Ens, Navy, 59, released as Lt.(jg), 61, after serv. in Pac. Barrier Patrol and Pac. Missile Range, 59-61; Lt.(jg), Naval Res, 61- Mem: Bd. dirs, Colo. Rep. Co. Chmns. Asn; Kiwanis Int; Young Americans for Freedom; U.S. Anti-Communist Cong; Am. Conservative Union; United Rep. of Am; Liberty Lobby. Rel: Protestant. Legal Res: 402 11th St, Georgetown, Colo. 80444. Mailing Add: Box 481, Georgetown, Colo. 80444.

ABBOTT, JOSEPH A. D
b. Paterson, N.J, 6/19/05; s. Henry A. Abbott and Mary Roegiers A; m. 8/30/30 to Alice Hughes; c. Joseph A. Educ: Univ. Notre Dame, B.S, 30; Notre Dame Monogram Club. Polit. & Govt. Pos: Pres, Paterson Indust. Cmn, N.J, 56-58; pres, Passaic Valley Water Cmn, 58-66; chmn, Cmn. on efficiency and Econ. in Govt, 65-; alternate del, Dem. Nat. Conv, 68. Bus. & Prof. Pos: Dir. personnel and labor rels, ITT Defense-Space Group, 41-55, dir. pub. rels, 55- Mem: Asn. U.S. Army; Nat. Space Club; Air Force Asn; Pub. Rels. Soc. Am; Elks; Boys Clubs of Am. Rel: Catholic. Mailing Add: 35 Knickerbocker Ave, Paterson, N.J. 07503.

ABBOTT, LONNIE LOWELL D
Okla. State Rep.
b. Ada, Okla, 12/5/25; s. Noah T. Abbott and Willie Francis Smith A; m. 12/20/47 to Willa Dean Walker; c. Tamara Sue. Educ: E. Cent.State Col, B.S, 51; Okla. Univ, M.A, 52; E. Cent. Alumni Asn. Polit. & Govt. Pos: Okla. State Rep, Dist. 25, 60- Bus. & Prof. Pos: Teacher, coach and prin, St. Louis and Tupelo Sch. Syst, 51-64; commun. action dir, Pontotoc Co, 64-65; field rep, Okla. Educ. Syst, 66-69. Mil. Serv: Entered as A/S, Navy, released as Seaman 3/C, after serv. in Asiatic and Okinawa Campaigns, 44-46; Asiatic and Okinawa Ribbons; Good Conduct Medal. Mem: Nat. and Okla. Educ. Asns; Kiwanis; C. of C; Mason; Shrine. Rel: Baptist. Mailing Add: 414 W. Second St, Ada, Okla. 74820.

ABBOTT, RAY GENE R
N.Mex. State Rep.
b. Edinburg, Tex, 12/31/31; s. Chester Barton Abbott and Vivian Louise Cearly A; m. 6/10/51 to June Potter; c. Ray G, Jr, Sandra Louise, Perri Elaine and Charles B. Educ: N.Mex. State Univ, 1 year; Univ. Houston, 50-51. Polit. & Govt. Pos: Precinct chmn, Dona Ana Rep. Party, N.Mex, 58, area co-ordinator, 65; poastmaster, La Mesa, 59-61; mem, Dona Ana Co. Rep. Exec. Cmt, 59-61; N.Mex. State Rep, 69- Bus. & Prof. Pos: Land owner and farmer, La Mesa, N.Mex, 51-61; ins. salesman, Frank O. Papen & Co, Las Cruces, 61- Mem: First dep. dist. gov, dist. 40 M, Lions Int; Farm Bur. Rel: Methodist. Mailing Add: Route 1, Box 265, La Mesa, N.Mex, 88044.

ABBOTT, S. L. R
Dep. State Chmn, Rep. Party, Tex.
b. Fairview, Okla, 7/23/24; s. Aaron Floyd Abbott and Vera Goodwin A; m. 5/5/45 to Arline E. Beahler; c. Alan R. Educ: Tex. West. Col; Pac. Univ, B.S, 52, O.D, 53; Univ. Tex, M.A; Omega Epsilon Phi. Polit. & Govt. Pos: Asst. precinct chmn, Rep. Party, 60; nominee for Tex. State Sen, 62, 64 & 66; mem, Citizen's Adv. Coun, El Paso, 65; chmn, El Paso Co. Rep. Party, 65-66; mem, Rep. Nat. Cmt. Task Force to Study State Constitutional Rev, 66-67; mem, Tex. Rep. Cmt. Fed. Employ, currently; dep. state chmn, Rep. Party, Tex, currently. Bus. & Prof. Pos: Private practice of optom, 53-; ed, El Pasoan, 65-. Mil. Serv: Entered as Pvt, Army Air Force, 44, released as M/Sgt, 52, after serv. in Pac. Theater, 44; Victory and Good Conduct Medals; Bronze Battle Star; M/Sgt, Air Force Res. Mem: C. of C. Testified as expert witness on Chamizal Treaty with Mex, U.S. Senate For. Rels. Cmt, 63. Rel: Catholic. Legal Res: 1316 Mathias Dr, El Paso, Tex. 79903. Mailing Add: 4806 Montana, El Paso, Tex. 78203.

ABBOTT, WILLIAM SAUNDERS R
Mem, Arlington Rep. Town Cmt, Mass.
b. Medford, Mass, 6/2/38; s. Charles Theodoric Abbott and Evelyn Gertrude A; m. 6/24/61 to Susan Ellen Shaw; c. Cathryn Clark and Stephen Shaw. Educ: Harvard Col, A.B, magna cum laude, 60, Law Sch, LL.B, magna cum laude, 66; Phi Beta Kappa; D.U. Club; Hasty Pudding-Institute 1770. Polit. & Govt. Pos: Mem, Watertown Town Meeting, Mass, 64-66; mem, Watertown Rep. Town Cmt, 64-66; White House Fel, Wash, D.C, 66-67; spec. asst. to secy. agr, 67-68; dir, U.S. Agr. Prog. Asia, U.S. Dept. Agr, 67-68; Rep. Cand. U.S. House Rep, 68; mem, Arlington Rep. Town Cmt, Mass, 68-; treas, White House Fellows Asn, 68-; cmnr, Educ. Cmn. of the States, currently. Bus. & Prof. Pos: Attorney, Ropes & Gray, Boston, Mass, 66; spec. asst. to pres, Cabot, Cabot & Forbes, 68-; private practice, 68- Mil. Serv: Entered as Ens, Navy, 60, released as Lt.(jg), 63, after serv. in U.S.S. Barry, Atlantic, Caribbean and Mediterranean Oceans, 60-63; Res, 63-69, Lt; Spec. Letter of Commendation from Area Comdr. Publ: 'The Nonjury Trial,' Harvard Law Rev, 65 & Mod. Practice Commentary, 66; 'Tax Aspects of Restoring the Status Quo,' Boston Univ. Law Rev, 66; 'The Reversed Transaction,' J. Taxation, 67. Mem: Harvard Law Rev; Mass. and Am. Bar Asns; White House Fel. Asn; Harvard Club Boston; VFW; Boy Scouts (exec. bd, Minuteman Coun); Arlington Jaycees. Rel: Unitarian. Mailing Add: 50 Melvin Rd, Arlington, Mass. 02174.

ABDNOR, JAMES R
Lt. Gov, S.Dak.
b. Kennebec, S.Dak, 2/13/23; single. Educ: Univ. of Nebr. B.S, Bus. Admin; Sigma Chi. Polit. & Govt. Pos: Past farm chmn, Young Rep. Nat. Fedn; chmn, Lyman Co. Young Rep, S.Dak, 50-52; first asst. chief clerk, S.Dak. House of Rep, 51, 53 & 55; chmn, S.Dak. State Young Rep, 53-55; S.Dak. State Sen, 56-68; Lt. Gov, S.Dak, 69- Bus. & Prof. Pos: Farming and ranching. Mem: Eastern Star; Am. Legion; Elks; S.Dak. Stock Growers; S.Dak. Crop Improv. Asn; Mason (Past Master); Oriental Consistory; Grange; S.Dak. Wheat Growers Asn. Rel: Methodist. Legal Res: Kennebec, S.Dak. 57544. Mailing Add: State Capitol Bldg, Pierre, S. Dak. 57501.

ABE, KAZUHISA D
Assoc. Justice, Supreme Court of Hawaii
b. Pepeekeo, Hawaii, 1/18/14; s. Manshiro Abe and Matsuyo Fujiwara A; m. 12/9/39 to Haruko Murakami; c. Arnold T. and Clyde T. Educ: Univ. Hawaii, A.B, 36; Univ. Mich. Law Sch, J.D, 39. Polit. & Govt. Pos: Judge, Dist. Courts of North and South Kohala, Hawaii, 40-44; supvr, Co. of Hawaii, 46-52; Sen, Territory of Hawaii, 52-59; Hawaii State Sen, 59-62, v.pres, Hawaii State Senate, 63-64, pres, 65-66; assoc. justice, Supreme Court of Hawaii, 67- Mem: Hawaii State and Hawaii Co. Bar Asns; Hilo Hongwanji Mission. Legal Res: 188 Terrace Dr, Hilo, Hawaii 96720. Mailing Add: P.O. Box 2560, Honolulu, Hawaii 96804.

ABEL, GLENN FREDERICK R
Mem, Ohio Rep. State Cent. Cmt.
b. Milwaukee, Wis, 6/15/32; s. Elmer Charles Abel and Emma Schaefer A; m. 6/25/55 to Alice Ann Schroeder; c. Lori Ann. Educ: Univ. Ill, B.Arch, 55; Alpha Phi Omega; Phalanx; Am. Inst. Architects; Ordance Club; Rifle and Pistol Club. Polit. & Govt. Pos: Mem. equalization bd, Newark, Ohio, 64-65, mem. bldg. code cmt, 65-69; chmn, Licking Co. Rep. Party, 66-; mem, Ohio Electoral Col, 68; mem, Ohio Rep. State Cent. Cmt, 68- Bus. & Prof. Pos: Proj. mgr, Joseph Baker and Assoc. Architects, 57-61, chief of prod, 62-69. Mil. Serv: Entered as 2nd Lt, Army, 55, released as 1st Lt, 57, serv. as unit commander, 46th RCAT Detachment; reentered, 61, released as 1st Lt, 62 after serv. in 150 Armor Cavalry. Mem: Jr. C. of C; Jr. C. of C. Int; Licking Co. Celebrity Speakers Club; mem. bd, Licking Co. Humane Soc; v.pres, Licking Co. Soc. for Mentally Retarded; Young Rep. Club; Lutheran Laymans League. Distinguished Serv. Award, 64-67; Outstanding Nat. Dir. U.S. Jaycees; Cert. of Award, James F. Lincoln Arc Welding Found; Jr. C. of C. Senatorship. Rel: Lutheran. Mailing Add: 1482 Krebs Dr, Newark, Ohio 43055.

ABELE, HOMER E. R
b. Wellston, Ohio, 11/21/16; s. Oscar Abele and Margaret Burke A; m. 1938 to Addie Riggs; c. Terrell Ann, Peter Burke and Andy. Educ: Ohio State Univ. Col. Law, grad, 53. Polit. & Govt. Pos: Ohio State Rep, 49-52; asst. to campaign mgr. for Sen. Robert A. Taft, Rep. Nat. Conv, 52; del, Rep. Nat. Conv, 56; U.S. Rep, Ohio, 62-64; judge, Fourth Dist. Court of Appeals, Ohio, 67- Bus. & Prof. Pos: Mem. staff, Anchor-Hocking Glass, Lancaster, Ohio; mem. staff, Austin Proder Co, McArthur, Ohio, 41; patrolman, Ohio State Hwy. Patrol, Van Wert, 41-43 & 46; legis. counsel, Spec. Transportation Cmt, 53-57. Mil. Serv: Army Air Corps, 43-46. Mem: Am. Legion (exec. officer to Past State Comdr.), Vinton Co. Bar Asn; Lions (past pres, McArthur club). Misc: Prog. chmn, McArthur Develop. Asn; Vinton Co. trustee, Southeast. Ohio Regional Coun. Mailing Add: McArthur, Ohio 45651.

ABELL, TYLER D
b. Washington, D.C, 8/9/32; s. George Abell and Luvie Butler Moore A; m. 1/1/55 to Elizabeth Hughes Clements; c. Dan Tyler and Lyndon. Educ: Amherst Col, A.B, 54; George Wash. Univ. Law Sch, LL.B, 59; Phi Delta Phi; Chi Psi. Polit. & Govt. Pos: Mem, Organizers Cmt, Citizens for Lyndon Johnson for Pres, 60; asst. to exec. asst. to Postmaster Gen, Post Off. Dept, 61-62, spec. asst. to Postmaster Gen, 62-63, assoc. gen. counsel, 63, asst. postmaster gen, 64-67; Chief of Protocol, Dept. of State, 68-69. Bus. & Prof. Pos: Law clerk, Covington and Burling, 58-59, George Wash. Law Sch, 59 and D.C. Circuit Court of Appeals, 59-60; partner, Ginsburg and Feldman, 67-68, McCormack and Bregman, currently. Mil Serv: Entered as Pvt, Army, 55, released as Pfc, 56. Publ: Various law review articles, George Wash. Law Rev, 59. Mem: D.C. and Va. Bar Asns; Big Bros. of Nat. Capital Area; D.C. Health and Welfare Coun. Rel: Episcopal. Mailing Add: 1830 24th St. N.W, Washington, D.C. 20008.

ABERCROMBIE, HOWARD RANDOLPH D
V.Pres, 13th Dist. Dem. Orgn, Mich.
b. Brickyard, Ala, 7/26/16; s. Walter Abercrombie and Mary Alice Johnson A; m. 9/26/42 to Mattie B. Burr; c. Veneda (Mrs. James E. Moreland). Educ: Wayne State Univ. Sch. Bus. Admin, 58-59, Sch. Labor, 66-67. Polit. & Govt. Pos: Mem, Dem. Showboat Orgn, 52-; Dem. precinct del, 13th Dist, 52-, ward chmn, 56-62; zone chmn, Cmt. on Polit. Educ, AFL-CIO, 58-69; mem. civil rights cmt, Trade Union Leadership Coun, Inc, 61-; v.pres, 13th Dist. Dem. Orgn, 63-; mem. housing cmt, Metro. Detroit Labor Coun, 65-68; mem. exec. bd. and chmn. civil rights cmt, Wayne Co. AFL-CIO Cent. Body, 65-69; spec. consult, U.S. Rep. Charles C. Diggs, Mich, 65-; bailiff officer, common pleas court, Wayne Co, Mich, 68- Mem: NAACP; 13th Dist. Bus. and Civic League: South. Christian Leadership Conf; YMCA; Am. Fedn. State, Co. and Munic. Employees, AFL-CIO, elec. cmt, secy-treas, Coun. 77, Local Dept. Pub Works 229, del. and finance cmt. chmn, Pub. Employees Coun; chmn, Fair Employ. Practices Cmt, UAW; trustee, Coop Optical Corp. Commun. and Civic Worker, second runner-up, 42. Rel: Baptist. Mailing Add: 324 Hendrie, Apt. 21, Detroit, Mich. 48202.

ABERCROMBIE, JOHN REID R
Clerk, Alexander Co, Ill.
b. Tamms, Ill, 5/16/22; s. Cryille Herbert Abercrombie and Addie Jan Kendall A; m. 6/16/41 to Mildred Dean Brock; c. John Reid, Jr. Educ: Cape State Col, 38-41. Polit. & Govt. Pos: Rep. precinct committeeman, Tamms, Ill, 54-; chmn, Alexander Co. Rep. Cent. Cmt, 54-; treas, Alexander Co, 50-54 and clerk, 62- Mil. Serv: Entered as Pvt, Air Force, 43, released as S/Sgt, 45; Air Medal with Two Oak Leaf Clusters; ETO Ribbon with Seven Battle Stars. Mem: Mason; Shrine; VFW; R.R. Brotherhood Rwy. Clerks. Rel: Protestant. Mailing Add: Front and Illinois, Tamms, Ill. 62988.

ABERCROMBIE, MARSHALL WEST D
b. Fountain Inn, S.C, 8/25/22; s. Clarence Lewis Abercrombie and Jessie Kellett A; m. 5/28/48 to Linda W. Franks; c. Three. Educ: Clemson Col, 40-42; Presbyterian Col, 45-46; Univ. of S.C, LL.B, 49. Polit. & Govt. Pos: S.C. State Rep, 61-66. Bus. & Prof. Pos: Lawyer. 1967 Legal Res: Laurens, S.C. No mailing address available. (1967)

ABERNETHY, LOUISE R
Rep. Nat. Committeewoman for Ala.
b. Talladega, Ala, 9/23/09; d. Joseph Vann Wallis and Flora Greene W; m. 6/23/32 to Tom Abernethy. Educ: Wesleyan, Macon, Ga; Troy Teachers Col. Polit. & Govt. Pos: Rep. nat. committeewoman, Ala, 56-; del, Rep. Nat. Conv, 60 & 64, mem. Credentials Cmt, 64. Rel: Presbyterian. Mailing Add: 504 S. East St, Talladega, Ala. 35160. (1967)

ABERNETHY, THOMAS GERSTLE D
U.S. Rep, Miss.
b. Eupora, Miss, 5/16/03; s. Thomas Franklin Abernethy and Minnie Agnes Jinkins A; m. 7/5/36 to Alice Margaret Lamb; c. Margaret Gall, Alice Kay. Educ: Univ. of Ala, 20-23; Cumberland Univ, LL.B, 24; Spec. Student, Univ. of Miss. Law Sch, 24-25; Lambda Chi Alpha; honorary, Alpha Kappa Psi. Polit. & Govt. Pos: Mayor, Eupora, Miss, 27-29; Dist. Attorney, Third Judicial Dist, Miss, 35-42; U.S. Rep, Miss, 42- Bus. & Prof. Pos: Lawyer, dir, N.E. Miss. Coun. Mem: Miss. State and Chickasaw Co. Bar Asns; Mason; Shrine; Okolona Exchange Club; Okolona C. of C.(pres). Rel: Methodist. Legal Res: Okolona, Miss. 38860. Mailing Add: U.S. House Office Bldg, Washington, D.C. 20515. (1967)

ABLE, WILLIAM F. R
b. Saluda, S.C, 7/27/33; s. Otis Able and Bertha Riley A; m. 12/29/62 to Carol Ann Heft. Educ: Univ. S.C, A.B, 59 and LL.B, 61; Tau Kappa Alpha; Omicron Delta Kappa; Phi Alpha Delta. Polit. & Govt. Pos: City Judge, Cayce, S.C. Bus. & Prof. Pos: Admin. asst, Am. Bar Asn, 61-63; exec. secy, S.C. Bar Asn, 63-64. Mil. Serv: Entered as Pvt, Army, 53, released as Sgt, after serv. in 33rd Inf. Regt. in Caribbean, 54-56; Nat. Defense Ribbon; Am. Spirit of Honor and Good Conduct Medals. Mem: S.C, Richland Co. and Am. Bar Asns; Commercial Law League; S.C. Traffic Court Conf; DAV; Jaycees; Gr. Columbia C. of C; Textile Workers Union of Am. Rel: Methodist. Legal Res: 3346 Covenant Rd, Columbia, S.C. 29204. Mailing Add: 705 Security Federal Bldg, Columbia, S.C. 29201.

ABLIN, GEORGE D
b. Chicago, Ill, 3/6/23; s. David Ablin and Rose A; m. Mildred Jean Count; c. Pamela Joli, Deborah Sue, Penny Heather, Kip, Lance Craig, Robin Scott and Todd Mark. Educ: Univ. of Mich, B.S. and M.D, 40-48; Univ. of Wis. and Mich, grad. sch, 47-55. Polit. & Govt. Pos: Mem, State Bd. of Pub. Health, Calif, 66; alternate del, Dem. Nat. Conv, 68; chmn, Kern Co. Humphrey-Muskie Cmt, 68; mem, Calif. Dem. State Cent. Cmt, 68-69; trustee, Kern Co. Joint Union High Sch. Dist, Bakersfield, Calif, currently. Bus. & Prof. Pos: Neurological surgeon, 55-; consult, neurological surg, Porterville State Hosp, Calif, 55- Mil. Serv: Sgt, Army, 42-44, with serv. in Inf. Publ: Various articles on neurological surg. Mem: Am. Asn. of Neurological Surgeons; Am. Acad. of Neurology; Cong. of Neurological Surgeons; West. Electroencephalography Soc; Calif. Sch. Bd. Asn; World Federalists; Am. Civil Liberties Union; Rotary; Kern Co. Musical Asn. bd. mem. Legal Res: 4260 Country Club Dr, Bakersfield, Calif. 93306. Mailing Add: 2828 H. St, Bakersfield, Calif. 93301.

ABNEY, BILLY SHAW D
Ga. State Sen.
b. LaFayette, Ga, 10/10/34; s. Jesse A. Abney and Martha Camp Shaw A; m. 8/19/61 to Ann Walker; c. Shaw Walker. Educ: Univ. Ga, J.D, 58; Gridiron; Phi Delta Phi; Sigmi Chi. Polit. & Govt. Pos: Law clerk, Atlanta Judicial Circuit, 59-60; munic. judge, Lafayette, Ga, 60-66; Ga. State Rep, 61-67; Ga. State Sen, 53rd Dist, 67-; juvenile referee, Walker Co, 67-; mem, Ga. Constitutional Rev. Cmn, 69- Bus. & Prof. Pos: V.pres, Ace Vending Co, Inc, 60-; partner, LaFayette Wholesale Co, 60- Mem: Am, Ga. and Lookout Mt. Bar Asns; State Bar of Ga; Fairyland Club; Elks; hon. chap. Future Farmers of Am; Gov. Staff; Optimist Club. Walker Educ. Asn. Sch. Bell Award, 68. Rel: Baptist. Legal Res: South Main, LaFayette, Ga. 30728. Mailing Add: P.O. Box 607, LaFayette, Ga. 30728.

ABOUREZK, JAMES G. D
b. Wood, S. Dak, 2/24/31; s. Charles Abourezk and Lena Mickel A; m. 12/3/52 to Mary Houlton; c. Charles, Nikki June and Paul. Educ: S.Dak. Sch. of Mines, B.S. in Civil Eng, 61; Univ. S. Dak. Law Sch, J.D, 66. Polit. & Govt. Pos: Del, Dem. Nat. Conv, 68; Dem. cand. for Attorney Gen, S.Dak, 68. Bus. & Prof. Pos: Attorney-at-law, James Abourezk Law Offices, currently. Mil. Serv: Entered as Recruit, Navy, 48, released as Fireman, 52, after serv. in Pac. and Far East Theatres, 49-51. Publ: 'South Dakota Indian Jurisdiction,' S.Dak. Law Rev, 66. Mem: Am. Trial Lawyers Asn; Am. and S.Dak. Bar Asns. Rel: Syrian Orthodox. Legal Res: Fairview, Rapid City, S.Dak. 57701. Mailing Add: Box 850, Rapid City, S.Dak. 57701.

ABRAHAM, GEORGE DOUGLAS D
Miss. State Rep.
b. Greenville, Miss, 6/19/37; s. George Abraham and Lily Thomas A; single. Educ: Univ. Miss, B.A, 59, LL.B, 61; ODK; Kappa Alpha order. Polit. & Govt. Pos: Miss. State Rep, 67- Mem: Am, Miss. and Washington Co. Bar Asns; Elks; Moose. Rel: Methodist. Legal Res: Ashburn Plantation, Greenville, Miss. 38701. Mailing Add: Abraham Bldg, Greenville, Miss. 38701.

ABRAHAM, MALOUF R
Tex. State Rep.
b. Canadian, Tex, 7/26/15; s. Nahim Abraham and Ilia Malouf A; m. 3/13/38 to Iris Lewis; c. Malouf, Jr, Betty Lee (Mrs. Cooper) and Bill Ed. Educ: Tex. Tech. Col, 30-33. Polit. & Govt. Pos: Mayor, Canadian, Tex, 53-57; Tex. State Rep, 66-; alternate del, Rep. Nat. Conv, 68. Bus. & Prof. Pos: Owner, Malouf Abraham Co, currently. Mil. Serv: Pvt, Army, 45. Mem: Mason; Shrine; Rotary; Canadian C. of C.(pres, 64-); Am. Legion; W.Tex. C. of C; Am. Asn. of Petroleum Landmen; Independent Petroleum Asn. of Am; Tex. Independent Producers and Royalty Owners Asn; Oklahoma City, Panhandle and Tulsa Landmens Asns; dir, Tex. Tech. Exec. Canadian Man of the Year, 66; hon. awards from Future Farmers Asn. and others. Rel: Presbyterian; Edler, First Presby. Church. Legal Res: 906 Conklin Ave, Canadian, Tex. 79014. Mailing Add: Box 122, State Capitol, Austin, Tex. 78711.

ABRAHAMS, ALBERT EDWARD R
b. Washington Heights, N.Y, 2/17/24; s. J.S. Abrahams and E. Wolff A; m. 12/27/57 to Martha Hildebrandt; c. Amy White (Mrs. Gernsheimer), Anthony G. White, Andrew S. and Mary G. Educ: Cornell Univ, 42-43; Syracuse Univ, A.B, 48; Sigma Delta Chi. Polit. & Govt. Pos: Press and legis. asst. to U.S. Sen, R.C. Hendrickson, 53-54; exec. asst. and legis. asst. to U.S. Sen. Clifford P. Case, 55-64; dir. Wash. off, Gov. Nelson A. Rockefeller, 64; exec. dir, Rep. for Progress, 65-67; campaign mgr, N.J. Legis. Campaign, 67, Mathias for Senate, 68 and Tabor for Mayor, Pittsburgh, 69; exec. dir, Nat. Draft Rockefeller Cmt, 68; admin. asst. to U.S. Sen. Charles McC. Mathias, Md, 69- Bus. & Prof. Pos: With Syracuse Post-Standard, Syracuse, N.Y, 46-48; Newark Star-Ledger, Newark, N.J, 48; Newhouse Newspaper Bur, Wash, D.C, 49-53; A.C. Abrahams Assocs, Inc, 67-69. Mil. Serv: Entered as A/S, Navy, 43, released as PHM 2/C, 46, after serv. in S. Pac. Theatre. Rel: Presbyterian. Mailing Add: 5210 Wapakoneta Rd, Glen Echo Heights, Md. 20016.

ABRAHAMSON, EUNICE F. R
V.Chmn, Delta Co. Rep. Cent. Cmt, Colo.
b. Hallandale, Fla, 10/8/15; d. Arthur L. Peterson and Mabel Matson P; m. 10/17/36 to Eugene L. Abrahamson; c. Wayne and Suzanne (Mrs. Arnold). Educ: Luther Col, 2 years. Polit. & Govt. Pos: Rep. precinct committeewoman, Precinct 2, Delta Co, Colo, 60-69; co. chmn, Delta Co. 1200 Club, 67; v.chmn, Delta Co. Rep. Cent. Cmt, 67- Mem: PTA; Federated Music Club. Rel: Lutheran. Mailing Add: Hotchkiss, Colo. 81419.

ABRAM, MORRIS BERTHOLD D
b. Fitzgerald, Ga, 6/19/18; s. Sam Abram and Irene Cohen A; m. 12/23/43 to Jane McGuire; c. Ruth, Ann, Morris Berthold, Jonathan Adam and Joshua Anthony. Educ: Univ. of Ga, A.B, summa cum laude, 38; Univ. of Chicago, J.D, 40; Oxford Univ, Eng, Rhodes Scholar, & B.A, 48, M.A, 53; Phi Beta Kappa; Omicron Delta Kappa; Phi Kappa Phi. Polit. & Govt. Pos: Mem. prosecuting cmt, Internal Mil. Tribunal, Nuremburg, Germany, 46; asst. to dir, Cmt. for Marshall Plan, 48; counsel and pub. bd. mem, Regional Wage Stabilization Bd. for South, 51; gen. counsel, Peace Corps, 61; chmn, Nat. Exec. Bd. and Mem, Subcmt. on Prev. of Discrimination and Protection Minorities, UN, 63-65; co-chmn, White House Conf. Civil Rights 65; U.S. Rep, UN Cmn. on Human Rights, 65-; mem, Nat. Adv. Coun. Econ. Opportunity, 67- Bus. & Prof. Pos: Partner, Paul, Weiss, Rifkind, Wharton & Garrison, N.Y.C, 62-; pres, Brandeis Univ, currently. Mil. Serv: U.S.A.A.F, 41-45, serv. to Maj; Legion of Merit. Publ: Co-auth, How to Stop Violence in Your Community, 50. Mem: Am. Jewish Cmt.(Nat. Pres); bd. dirs, 20th Century Fund; bd. dirs, Morehouse Col; Afro-Am. Inst; Citizens Cmt. for Children N.Y; Nat. Urban League; Am, N.Y.C, N.Y. State and Atlanta, Ga. Bar Asns; Lawyers Club of Atlanta; pres, Family Serv. Soc. of Fulton, DeKalb, Cobb Co, 57-59; Chmn, Atlanta Citizens Crime Cmt, 58-60; pres, Field Found, Inc, 65-; bd. trustees, Weizmann Inst. of Sci, 66-; bd, Jewish Theological Seminary, 66- Named Hon. Citizen of Atlanta, Ga, 66. Mailing Add: President's Office Brandeis University, Waltham, Mass. 02154.

ABRAMS, MILTON CHARLES D
Secy, State Dem. Cmt, Utah
b. Logan, Utah, 11/22/18; s. George F. Abrams and Nettie Schank A; m. 3/13/56 to Lois Allred; c. Douglas, Kathleen and Sharon. Educ: Utah State Univ, B.S, 48, M.S, 52; Univ. Utah, Ph.D, 63. Polit. & Govt. Pos: Chmn, Cache Co. Dem. Party, Utah, 64-68; bd. mem. and v.pres, Div. State Hist, 64-; secy, State Dem. Cmt, 66- Bus. & Prof. Pos: Prin, Mink Creek High Sch, Idaho, 46-47; librn, Aberdeen High Sch, 48-49; assoc. librn, Utah State Univ, 49-55, Univ. librn, 55- Mil. Serv: Entered as Pvt, Army, 42, released as 1st Lt, 46, after serv. in 88th Reconnaissance Squadron, 8th Armored Div, ETO, 42-45, Korean War, 50-51; Bronze Star. Publ: The Political Philosophy of Christopher St. German, Dissertation, 63; 'Kingship, Equity, and Natural Law in Christopher St. German,' Essays in Legal History in Honor of Felix Frankfurter, Part IV, Bobbs-Merrill Book Co. Rel: Latter-day Saint. Mailing Add: 505 E. Parkview Circle, Smithfield, Utah 84335.

ABRAMS, PINCKNEY N. D
Chmn, Newberry Co. Dem. Party, S.C.
b. Chappells, S.C, 9/25/11; s. N. Pinckney Abrams and Verona Salter A; m. 5/27/41 to Ruby Ruff. Educ: Cross Hill High Sch; Greenwood Bus. Col. Polit. & Govt. Pos: Auditor, Newberry Co, S.C, 37-53; chmn, Newberry Co. Dem. Party, currently. Bus. & Prof. Pos: Exec. v.pres. and secy, State Bldg. & Loan Asn, 53- Mem: Bd, Bank Control of S.C; Mason; York Rite Masonic Bodies; Shrine; Lions. Rel: Methodist. Legal Res: 1224 Walnut St, Newberry, S.C. 29108. Mailing Add: P.O. Drawer 557, Newberry, S.C. 29108. (1967)

ABRAMS, ROBERT D
N.Y. State Assemblyman
b. Bronx, N.Y, 7/4/38; s. Benjamin Abrams and Dorothy Kaplan A; single. Educ: Columbia Col, A.B, 60; N.Y. Univ. Sch. of Law, J.D, 63; pres, Alpha Chap, Phi Sigma Delta. Polit. & Govt. Pos: N.Y. State Assemblyman, 66- Bus. & Prof. Pos: Attorney, Henry H. Abrams, New York, N.Y, 64- Publ: 'Negligent Golfer,' N.Y. Univ. Intramural Law Rev, 3/63. Mem: N.Y. State and Bronx Co. Bar Asns; K. of P; B'nai B'rith; Dayan Club of Pelham Parkway (pres); Zionist Orgn. of Am. Man of Year Award, Rockland Hosp. Guild; Membership Award, Bronx Co. Zionist Orgn. of Am. Rel: Jewish. Mailing Add: 2125 Holland Ave, Bronx, N.Y. 10462.

ABRAMS, ROBERT MARSHALL D
b. Holyoke, Mass, 2/8/33; s. Samuel Abrams and Ida Hoffman A; m. 6/29/61 to Frances Rischin; c. Joshua M, Samuel E. and Annah N. Educ: Amherst Col, B.A, 54; Boston Univ. Sch. Med, M.D, 58. Polit. & Govt. Pos: Alternate del, Dem. Nat. Conv, 68; Dem. ward chmn, Mass, 68. Bus. & Prof. Pos: Pediatrician, Holyoke, Mass, 64-69. Mil. Serv: Capt, Air Force, 61-64, with Med. Corps, Greece, 61-64. Publ: 'Poliomyelitis in Early Infancy,'61 and 'Maple Syrup Urine Disease,' 65, Clin. Proc. Children's Hosp, D.C. Mem: Am. Acad. Pediatrics; Med. Cmt. Human Rights; New Eng. Pediatric Soc; Mass. Med. Soc; Am. Civil Liberties Union; assoc. mem, League Women Voters; Jaycees; Greater Holyoke Commun. Concert Asn.(pres); Holyoke Col. Civic Orchestra. Greater Holyoke Young Man of the Year, 1967. Rel: Jewish. Mailing Add: 28 Dunn Ave, Holyoke, Mass. 01040.

ABRAMS, ROSALIE SILBER D
Md. State Del.
b. Baltimore, Md, 6/2/16; d. Isaac Silber and Dora Rodbell S; m. 10/14/53 to William Abrams; c. Elizabeth Joan. Educ: Sinai Hosp. Sch. of Nursing, Baltimore, Md, grad. with honors, 38; Columbia Univ, grad. study in pub. health admin, 39-40; McCoy Col, Johns Hopkins Univ, B.S. in Soc. Sci. with honors, 63; Johns Hopkins Univ. Grad. Sch, cand. for M.A, currently. Polit. & Govt. Pos: Dem. precinct capt, Fifth Dist, Baltimore, Md, 64-66; Md. State Del, 66-, chmn, Subcmt. on Health and Welfare, Ways and Means Cmt, Md. House of Del, chmn, House of Del. Dem. Study Group, co-chmn, Joint Cmt. on Medicaid; founder and mem. of bd, Fifth Dist. Reform Dem, 67-; mem. bd. of dirs,

City-Co. Dem. Club, 68-; mem, Gov. Cmn. on the Status of Women, Attorney Gen. Cmt. on Transplants, State Comprehensive Health Planning Coun, Regional Planning Coun. and Mayor's Health Serv. Adv. and Planning Coun, currently. Bus. & Prof. Pos: Surg. supvr, operating room, Sinai Hosp, Baltimore, Md, 38-41; pub. health nurse, Baltimore Dept. of Educ, 41-43; mgr. Sequoia Med. Group, Redwood City, Calif, 46-47; asst. bus. mgr, Silber's Bakery, Inc, Baltimore, Md, 47-53. Mil. Serv: Entered as Ens, Nurse Corps, Naval Res, 43, released in 45, after serv. in Naval Hosp, Newport, R.I, 44-45, Victory Medal. Mem: Am. Polit. Sci. Asn; Nat. Order of Women Legislators; Acad. of Polit. Sci; Md. and Am. Nurses Asns; Nurses Alumnae Asn; Johns Hopkins Univ. Alumni Asn; Baltimore Civic Opera Guild; Nat. Asn. of World War Nurses; Jewish War Vet; Baltimore Urban League; Am. Jewish Cong; Nat. Coun. of Jewish Women; United Order of True Sisters; Md. Conf. of Soc. Welfare; Md. Asn. for Ment. Health; Baltimore Heritage, Inc; Baltimore Fellowship, Inc; Citizens Planning and Housing Asn. Louise Waterman Wise Award, 69. Rel: Reform Judaism. Mailing Add: 6205 Wirt Ave, Baltimore, Md. 21215.

ABRAMS, STANLEY PAUL D

b. Brooklyn, N.Y, 5/4/32; s. Gustav Abrams and Jessie Horwitz A; m. 6/16/57 to Barbara Solomon; c. Eric Harlan, Theodore Cameron and Therese Caroline. Educ: Ohio Univ, B.A, 53; Syracuse Univ, 53-54; Univ. Mich, 56-57; Phi Epsilon Pi. Polit. & Govt. Pos: Del, Dem. Nat. Conv, 68; finance chmn, Pima Co. Conf. of Dem, Ariz, 69- Bus. & Prof. Pos: Sales mgr, Beauty Built Homes, Tucson, Ariz, 60-63; regional sales mgr, Larwin Co, Los Angeles, Calif, 64-65; exec. v.pres, P.A.T. Homes, Tucson, Ariz, currently. Mil. Serv: Entered as 2nd Lt, Air Force, 54, released as 1st Lt, 56, after serv. in 442nd Bomb Squadron, Strategic Air Command; Commendation Award, Strategic Air Command, 55. Mem: Nat. Asn. of Homebuilders; South. Ariz. Homebuilders Asn; Develop. Authority for Tucson Expansion; Papago Tucson Develop. Corp. Rel: Jewish. Legal Res: 4540 Cerco Del Corazon, Tucson, Ariz. 85718. Mailing Add: 7301 E. 22nd St, Tucson, Ariz. 85711.

ABRAMSON, JOSEPH D

b. Baltimore, Md, 6/12/00; married. Educ: Baltimore Pub. Schs. Polit. & Govt. Pos: Md. State Del, 63-67. Bus. & Prof. Pos: Merchant. Mem: Pres. of Family Group. Mailing Add: 5012 Windsor Mill Rd, Baltimore, Md. 21207. (1967)

ABRAMSON, MURRAY D

Md. State Del.

b. Baltimore, Md, 12/28/02; s. Abraham Abramson and Sadie Friedlander A; m. 8/20/39 to Helaine Rose Whitehill; c. Alan Carroll. Educ: Grad, Baltimore City Col. Polit. & Govt. Pos: Exam, Baltimore Rent Cmn; bus. analyst, Off. Price Stabilization; Md. State Del, mem, Ways and Means Cmt. and Legis. Coun, currently, chmn, Baltimore City Del, 62-, mem, Budget and Finance Cmt, 67; del, Md. Constitutional Conv. Bus. & Prof. Pos: Exec, retail clothing firm, 20 years; pres, local retail union, 10 years; bus. agent and contract negotiator, Amalgamated Clothing Workers Retail Div, 3 years. Rel: Jewish. Mailing Add: 7304 Park Heights Ave, Baltimore, Md. 21208.

ABSHIER, CHARLES K. D

Polit. & Govt. Pos: Mem. Bd. Trustees, City Redevelop. Cmn, Evansville, Ind, 61-62, City Traffic Cmn, 62-; Ind. State Rep, 63-68. Bus. & Prof. Pos: Machine operator, Whirlpool Corp. Mil. Serv: Army. Mem: Secy, Local 808, IUE, AFL-CIO. Rel: Methodist. Mailing Add: 3320 Hillcrest Terr, Evansville, Ind. 47712. (1967)

ACEVEDO, NICOLAS C. D

Co. Committeeman, Dem. Party, N.Y.

b. Aguadilla, Puerto Rico, 12/6/06; s. Pedro Acevedo and Ramona Castillo A; m. 10/15/33 to Sofia Ruiz; c. Pedro, Jr, Jeanie, Idia and Zaida. Polit. & Govt. Pos: V.pres, Spanish Speaking People in Lower Manhattan, N.Y, 53-65 and Lower East Side Manhattan Club, N.Y.C, 61-; co. committeeman, N.Y. Dem. Party. Rel: Rosicrucian Order. Mailing Add: 950 E. Fourth Walk, New York, N.Y. 10009. (1967)

ACFALLE, JOSE MANALISAY D

Sen, Guam Legis.

b. Merizo, Guam, 1/23/23; s. Juan Babauta Acfalle and Ana Manalisay A; m. 12/30/45 to Jesusa Candosu Chargulaf; c. Mary A.(Mrs. Tainatongo), Eleanor A.(Mrs. Reyes), Ann A.(Mrs. Atoigue), Doris C, Rosie C, Victoria C. and Bertha C. Educ: Los Angeles High Sch, grad. Polit. & Govt. Pos: Rep, Guam Legis, 63-67; Sen, Guam Legis, 67- Mil. Serv: Entered as STD, Navy, 41, released as SD-1, 53, after serv. in World War II and Korean Conflict; Am. Area Campaign and Asiatic-Pac. Area Campaign Medals; Am. Defense Medal with Fleet Clasp; World War II Victory Medal; Presidential Unit Citation. Mem: DAV; Fleet Reserve; Civic Improv. and Develop. Club. Mailing Add: 22 San Dimas St, Merizo, Guam 96910.

ACHESON, DEAN GOODERHAM D

b. Middletown, Conn, 4/11/93; s. Edward Campion Acheson and Eleanor Gooderham A; m. 5/5/17 to Alice Stanley; c. Jane (Mrs. Dudley B.W. Brown), David Campion and Mary Eleanor (Mrs. William P. Bundy). Educ: Yale, A.B, 15; Harvard, LL.B, 18; Delta Kappa Epsilon. Hon. M.A, Yale, 36; LL.D, Wesleyan Univ, 47, Harvard, 50 and Yale, 62; D.C.L, Oxford Univ, 52; L.H.D, Brandeis Univ, 56 and Cambridge Univ, 58. Polit. & Govt. Pos: V.chmn, Cmn. on Orgn. Exec. Br. of the Govt; chmn, Adv. Cmt. on Civil Rules Judicial Conf; Under Secy. of Treas, 33; Asst. Secy. of State, 41-45, Under Secy. of State, 45-47, Secy. of State, 49-53. Bus. & Prof. Pos: Private secy. to Louis O. Brandeis, Assoc. Justice, U.S. Supreme Court, 19-21; with Covington, Burling & Rublee, 21-33; mem, Covington, Burling, Rublee, Acheson & Shorb, 34-41; mem, Covington, Burling, Acheson, O'Brian & Shorb, 47-48; private law practice with Covington & Burling, Wash, D.C, 53- Mil. Serv: Ens, Navy, World War I. Publ: A Democrat Looks at His Party, 55; A Citizen Looks at Congress, 57; Power and Diplomacy, 58; Sketches from Life of Men I Have Known; Morning and Noon, 65. Mem: Am. Acad. Arts and Sci; Scroll & Key; Metrop. Club, Wash, D.C; Century Club, N.Y. Order of Vasa, Sweden; Medal of Merit, U.S; Order of Aztec Eagle, Mexico; Grand Master, Nat. Order of South. Cross, Brazil; Grand Cross Order of Boyaca, Colombia; Grand Cordon, Order of Leopold, Belgium; Order of Rising Sun, Japan; Royal Order Cambodia; Presidential Medal of Freedom, U.S, 64. Rel: Episcopal. Mailing Add: 701 Union Trust Bldg, Washington, D.C. 20005. (1967)

ACHOR, HELEN E. R

Ind. State Rep.

b. Houston, Tex, 3/24/15; d. Earl L. Martin and Blanche L. Williams M; m. 10/11/35 to Judge Harold E. Achor (deceased); c. Patricia Dianne (Mrs. Robert Johnston) and Lana Martin (Mrs. Winston Dean). Educ: Anderson Col, A.B, 60; Sigma Tau Delta. Polit. & Govt. Pos: V.pres, Ind. Fedn. of Women's Rep. Clubs, 45-46; Rep. precinct v.committeeman, Madison Co, 45-69; treas, Nat. Fedn. of Women's Rep. Clubs, 47-51; Rep. v.chmn, Anderson, Ind, 67-68; Ind. State Rep, Madison Co, 68- Bus. & Prof. Pos: Resident dir, Anderson Col, 67-69, dir. of alumni serv, 69- Mem: Ind. State Legislators Club; Nat. Soc. of State Legislators; Girl Scouts (regional cmt, 58-66); State Assembly Women's Club; Anderson Coun. of Women; YWCA; Urban League (mem. bd. of dirs, 69-); Art Club; Tourist Club; Meg March Club. Rel: Church of God. Legal Res: 227 Graceland Ave, Anderson, Ind. 46012. Mailing Add: Anderson Col, Anderson, Ind. 46011.

ACKEL, FRED JOHN R

b. Gloversville, N.Y, 3/28/27; s. Fred Ackel and Anna Azar A; m. 7/15/50 to Mildred Evelyn Krause; c. Debra Ann, Gary Fredric and Kimberly Jean. Educ: Clarkson Col.of Tech, 44-45; U.S. Merchant Marine Acad, 45-46; Hartwick Col, B.S, 50; Georgetown Univ. Sch. of Dent, D.D.S, 54; Delta Sigma Delta; Omicron Pi Omicron. Polit. & Govt. Pos: Pres, Broward Co. Young Rep, Fla, 61-63; chmn, Young Am. for Freedom, 62-65; del, Rep. Nat. Conv, 64; chmn, Citizens for Goldwater-Miller and Nat. Draft Goldwater Cmts, Broward Co, 64; chmn, Rep. Citizens Cmt, Broward Co, 65-67; mem, Fla. State Bd. Health, 67-68; campaign coordinator, Broward Co. Rep. Gen. Elec, 68; mem, Fla. State Racing Cmn, 68- Mil. Serv: Entered as 1st Lt, Air Force, 54, released as Capt, 56. Publ: 'National Dental Service Corporation-Vehicle for Control of Dentistry,' Fla. State Dent. J, 8/65. Mem: Acad. Gen. Dent; Broward Co. Dent. Soc.(pres, 65-66); chmn, Fla. Dent. Asn. del, Am. Dent. Asn. Annual Meeting, 68; trustee, Coral Oaks Med. Dent. Bldg. Enterprises, 63-66; K. of C; C. of C. Rel: Catholic. Mailing Add: 2655 E. Oakland Park Blvd, Ft. Lauderdale, Fla. 33306.

ACKERMAN, LEOPOLD 'LEE' D

b. Clayton, Mo, 10/29/21; s. Melville Ackerman and Ruth Corday A; m. 12/22/43 to Leslie Rogers, div. 1961; c. Mary Lee, Byron W, Carol Rogers and Elizabeth Leslie; m. 2/10/62 to Celia Franco Meyer; c. Douglas and Paul. Educ: Harvard Col, B.A, 47. Polit. & Govt. Pos: Ariz. State Rep, 50-52; mem, Gov. Cmt. Hwy. Safety, 57-58; chmn, Govt. Cmt. Atomic Energy, 58; mem, Pres. Cmt. Traffic Safety, 58; Dem. nominee, Gov, Ariz, 60; Dem. nat. committeeman, Ariz, 64-68. Bus. & Prof. Pos: Pres, Lee Ackerman Investment Co, Inc, 53-; pres, West-Coast Investment Co, 62-; pres. and dir, West. Equities, Inc, 61-63; chmn. bd, Yavapai Hotels Corp, 65-; pres, Lee Ackerman Real Estate, Inc, West. Growth Capital Corp, Diamond Valley, Inc. and Grace and Co, 65- Mil. Serv: Capt, Air Force, 42-45, serv. in Africa, India, Russia, Italy and China; Maj.(Ret), Air Force Res; Citation for Valor in Africa with Two Battle Stars. Mem: Cloud Club; Phoenix Press Club; Kiva Club. Rel: Presbyterian. Mailing Add: 106 W. Mountain Shadows, Scottsdale, Ariz. 85251 (1967)

ACKLEY, (HUGH) GARDNER D

b. Indianapolis, Ind, 6/30/15; s. Hugh M. Ackley and Margaret McKenzie A; m. 9/18/37 to Bonnie Lowry; c. David A. and Donald G. Educ: West. State Teacher's Col, A.B, 36; Univ. Mich, M.A, 37, Ph.D, 40; West. Mich. Univ, LL.D, 64; Kalamazoo Col, LL.D, 67; Kappa Delta Phi; Tau Kappa Alpha; Phi Kappa Phi. Polit. & Govt. Pos: Consult, Nat. Resources Planning Bd, 40-41; economist, Off. Price Admin, 41-43 & 44-46; economist, Off. Strategic Serv, 43-44; econ. adv. and asst. dir, Off. Price Stabilization, 51-52; consult, Dept. Army, 61; mem, Coun. Econ. Adv, Wash, D.C, 62-, chmn, 64-68; U.S. Ambassador, Italy, 68-69. Bus. & Prof. Pos: Consult, Ford Found, Brookings Inst, Nat. Bur. Econ. Research and Mich. Dept. of Finance, various times; instr, Ohio State Univ, 39-40; instr. econ, Univ. Mich, 40-41, asst. prof, 46-47, assoc. prof, 47-52, prof, 52-68, chmn. dept, 54-61 and Henry Carter Adams Distinguished Univ. Prof. of Polit. Econ, 69-; vis. staff mem, Univ. Calif, Los Angeles, 49; Fulbright Research Scholar, Italy, 56-57; Ford Found. Faculty Research fel, 61-62. Publ: Macroeconomic Theory, Macmillan Co, N.Y, 61; Un modello econometrico dello sviluppo italiano nel dopoguerra, A. Giuffre Editors, Milano, 63. Mem: Bd. of Ed, Am. Econ. Rev, 53-56; dir, Soc. Sci. Research Coun, 59-62, chmn, cmt. soc. sci. personnel and mem. exec. cmt, 60-61; Am. Econ. Asn.(cmt. on honors and awards, 59-, chmn. cmt. on research and pub, 59-61, v.pres, 63); Econometric Soc; Am. Asn. Univ. Prof; Mich. Acad. Sci, Arts & Letters; fel. Am. Acad. Arts & Sci. Cavaliere di Gran Croce dell'Ordine 'Al Merito della Repubblica Italiana.' Mailing Add: Dept. of Economics, University of Michigan, Ann Arbor, Mich. 48104.

ACKLIN, JOSEPH CHARLES D

Chmn, Goshen Co. Dem. Party, Wyo.

b. Pontiac, Ill, 1/16/35; s. Joseph C. Acklin and Pauline Finnestad A; m. 8/22/68 to Norma Jean Bates Mahar; c. Bette Gail and John Patrick. Educ: Univ. Colo, 53-57; Alpha Sigma Phi. Polit. & Govt. Pos: Mem, Goshen Co. Libr. Bd, Wyo, 66-68; alternate del, Dem. Nat. Conv, 68; secy, local bd. 8, Wyo. Selective Serv. Supt, 68; chmn, Goshen Co. Dem. Party, 69- Bus. & Prof. Pos: Publisher, Guernsey Gazette, 65-66 and Guide-Rev, 65- Mil. Serv: Entered as Pvt, Army, 57, released as S/Sgt. E-6, 65, after serv. Med. Corps and Active Res. Mem: Wyo. Press Asn; Nat. Newspaper Asn; Elks; Goshen Co. Mental Health Asn. Honored for Best Ed. Written in Wyo. Newspapers, 67 & 68. Rel: Catholic. Mailing Add: P.O. Box 278, Lingle, Wyo. 82223.

ACREE, JOHN WILLIAM D

b. Calhoun, Ga, 5/21/24; s. Marvin Albin Acree; Webbe Hudgins A; m. 8/10/52 to Sara Sue McReynolds; c. Cheryl M, Allen B. and John W. Jr. Educ: W. Ga. Col, Emory Univ, 48-49; Med. Col. of Ga, M.D, 53; Theta Kappa Psi, Interne and G.P. Resident, Macon City Hosp, Macon, Ga. Polit. & Govt. Pos: Ga. State Rep, 63-66. Bus. & Prof. Pos: M.D, Hiawassee, 55-; chief of staff, Towns Co. Hosp; Towns Co. Area Redevelop. Corp, 61-63. Mil. Serv: Armed Forces Med. Dept, 43-46, T/5 Med. Technician to Phillipines and Japan. Rel: Baptist; bd. of trustees, McConnell Mem. Baptist Church. Mailing Add: Hiawassee, Ga. 30546.

ACTON, CHARLES EDWARD R
b. Collison, Ill, 8/19/24; s. Robert Lincoln Acton and Goldie Opal Chesnut A; m. 12/24/44 to Charlotte Ellen Wright; c. Randee Lou (Mrs. Clingan) and Charle Parker. Educ: Armstrong High Sch, 4 years. Polit. & Govt. Pos: Precinct committeeman, Pilot Two Twp. Rep. Party, Ill, 50-69; first v.chmn, Vermilion Co. Rep. Cent. Cmt, 61-69; alternate del, Rep. Nat. Conv, 68; Ill. State Inspector, 69- Bus. & Prof. Pos: Farmer, 46- Mem: Mason (33°); Elks; Young Rep. Club; Farm Bur; Collison Detective Asn. Rel: Church of Christ. Mailing Add: Collison, Ill. 61831.

ADAIR, CHARLES WALLACE, JR.
b. Xenia, Ohio, 1/26/14; s. Charles Wallace Adair and Sarah Torrence Goulard A; m. 11/28/47 to Caroline Lee Marshall; c. Marshall Porter, Caroline and Sarah. Educ: Univ. Wis, A.B, 35; Am. Inst. Banking, 37-38; George Wash. Univ, 38-39; Princeton Univ, 47-48; Phi Gamma Delta. Polit. & Govt. Pos: Entered For. Serv, 40; v.consul, Nogales, Mex, 40-41, Mexico City, 41; detailed to For. Serv. Sch, U.S. Dept. of State, 41; v.consul, Bombay, India, 42-46; India desk officer, 46-47; first secy. to Embassy and Consul, Rio de Janeiro Brazil, 48-51; detailed to Nat. War Col, Wash, 51-52; Counsr. of Embassy for Econ. Affairs, Brussels; dep. dir, U.S. Opers. Mission, Brussels; NATO Adv. Bur. European Affairs, 52-54; U.S. Cmnr. on Tripartite Cmn. for Restitution on Monetary Gold, 54; chmn, Colombo Plans Official Meeting, Seattle, 58; dep. asst. secy. state for econ. affairs, 59-61; dep. secy. gen, Orgn. Econ. Coop. and Develop, Paris, France, 61-63; minister-counsr. dep. chief Mission Am. Embassy, Buenos Aires, Argentina, 63-65; U.S. Ambassador to Panama, 65-69; appointed U.S. Ambassador to Uruguay by the President, 69. Bus. & Prof. Pos: Credit investigator, Chase Nat. Bank, N.Y.C, 35-36 & 37-38, Panama City, 36-37. Mem: Univ. Club, Wash; Royal Bombay Yacht Club, India. Rel: Episcopal. Legal Res: Stuart, Fla. Mailing Add: U.S. Dept. of State Foreign Service, Washington, D.C. 20521.

ADAIR, E. ROSS R
U.S. Rep, Ind.
b. Albion, Ind, 12/14/07; s. Edwin L. Adair and Alice Prickett A; m. 7/21/34 to Marian Wood; c. Caroline (Mrs. David Dimmers) and Stephen Wood. Educ: Hillsdale Col, A.B, 28; George Washington Univ. Law Sch, LL.B, 33; LL.D, Ind. Inst. Tech, 64; Delta Sigma Phi; Phi Alpha Delta. Polit. & Govt. Pos: Former probate cmnr, Allen Co, Ind; mem. exec. cmt. Am. del, Inter-Parliamentary Union, 59, 63-65, 67-; U.S. Rep, Fourth Dist, Ind, 50-, ranking minority mem, For. Affairs Cmt, sr. mem, Vet. Affairs Cmt. and mem, Cmt. on Cmt, U.S. House of Rep. Bus. & Prof. Pos: Mem. law firm, Adair, Perry, Beers, McAlister and Mallers, Fort Wayne, Ind. Mil. Serv: Entered as 2nd Lt, Army, 41, released as Maj, 45, after serv. in 1st Army, ETO; Battle Stars for Normandy, North. France, Ardennes, Rhine and Cent. Europe Campaigns; Lt. Col.(Ret), Judge Adv. Gen. Corps, Army Res. Mem: Bar of Supreme Court of U.S; Am, Ind. and Allen Co. Bar Asns; Elks; Moose; Mason (33°), Shrine; former nat. pres, Delta Sigma Phi; hon. life mem, Amvets, Nat. VFW and Am. Legion; trustee, Hillsdale Col; v.pres, Am. Group Interparliamentary Union. Silver Helmet Award, Amvets; Nat. Asn. State Dirs. Vet. Affairs Award, 65; Distinguished Serv. Award, Ft. Wayne Jr. C. of C, 40, Citizen of Week, 49. Rel: Methodist. Legal Res: 1145 W. Foster Pkwy, Ft. Wayne, Ind. Mailing Add: U.S. House Office Bldg, Washington, D.C. 20515.

ADAIR, NIRA MOORE R
Chmn, Sanilac Co. Rep. Exec. Cmt, Mich.
b. Deckerville, Mich, 1/7/34; m. 11/14/53 to Maurice Adair; c. Michelle Renee. Polit. & Govt. Pos: V.chmn, Sanilac Co. Rep. Exec. Cmt, Mich, chmn, currently; chmn, Co. Bd. of Canvassers, currently. Bus. & Prof. Pos: Secy. Mem: Pres, Sanilac Co. United Fund. Rel: Catholic; mem, Altar Soc, St. Joseph Cath. Church. Mailing Add: 4650 Ubly Rd, Snover, Mich. 48472.

ADAIR, SIDNEY ARTHUR R
Mem, Calif. Rep. State Cent. Cmt.
b. Los Angeles, Calif, 2/16/28; s. Herbert Spencer Adair and Mildred Geneva Gambrell A; m. 8/19/61 to Martha Printup Laugharn; c. Scott Laugharn and Christopher Thompson Dodge (stepson). Educ: Univ. South. Calif, 45-48; Babson Inst. of Bus. Admin, B.S. magna cum laude, 51; Univ. Pa, M.B.A, 54; Univ. South. Calif, J.D, 60; Trinity Univ; Univ. Pittsburgh; Univ. Calif, Los Angeles; Blue Key; Phi Alpha Delta; Alpha Kappa Psi; Chi Phi. Polit. & Govt. Pos: Organizer, mem. and officer, various Young Rep. Clubs, 50-67; victory squad colonel, 15th Cong. Dist, 58, precinct capt, 60; originator, Rep. Town Meetings, 58-59; organizer and adv, Future Rep. of W. Los Angeles and Santa Monica, 59-63; speaker, Shell for Gov, 62; organizer and chmn, Miracle Mile Goldwater Cmt, 64; organizer, Parklabrea Unit, United Rep. of Calif, 64-67, organizer, mem. bd. and del, Wilshire-Crenshaw Unit, 65-67, parliamentarian, Area 11, 66 & 67, organizer and pres, Henry Hazlitt Unit, 66-68; v.chmn, Region III, Ronald Reagan for Gov, 66; mem, Friends of Gov. Reagan, 66-69; assoc. mem, Calif. Rep. State Cent. Cmt, 67-69, mem, 69-; chmn. strategy cmt, Cmt. to Elect Newman, Martin and Ferraro, 68-69; mem, 56th Rep. Assembly Club, 69. Bus. & Prof. Pos: Research consult, Tex. Elec. Serv. Co, Ft. Worth, 54-55; liaison asst, U.S. Steel Corp, Pittsburgh, Pa, 55-57; dep. pub. defender, Los Angeles Co, Calif, 60-61; mem. legal staff and free enterprise dept, Coast Fed. Savings and Loan Asn, Los Angeles, 61-62; part-time prof, Woodbury Col, 62-65; partner, Gaston, Keltner and Adair, 62-65 and Burr, Smith and Adair, 66- Mil. Serv: Entered as Pvt, Air Force, 51, released as 1st Lt, 53, after serv. in Human Resources Research Center, 52-53; Air Force Res, 53-59, Capt.(Ret). Publ: Where do You Stand?, Los Angeles Freedom Club, 56 & 58; 12 Legal Duties and Rights of Parents to Their Children, Coast Fed. Savings and Loan Asn, 62; info. and educ. articles, Los Angeles Co. Young Rep, 62-63. Mem: Los Angeles, Am. and Independent Bar Asns; Calif. Trial Lawyers Asn; Mayor Yorty's Commun. Adv. Cmt; Mason; Los Angeles Univ. Club (Bus. Review Luncheon Cmt, v.pres. of Toastmasters); dist. chmn, Nat. Fed. of Independent Bus; seminar chmn, Opera Assocs. of the Music Center; incorporator, Greater Los Angeles Zoo Asn; Bel Air Bay Club; chmn, Los Angeles Freedom Club; Los Angeles Co. Museum Asn; Los Angeles Navy League; SAR; charter mem. and v.pres, Statler-Hilton Exchange Club; Trojan Club; Jr. C. of C. (feature ed, Pittsburgh Chap); Wellesley Little Theatre Group, Mass; Los Angeles Town Hall; Los Angeles Save Our Sports Found, Inc.(v.chmn and secy). Recipient of Outstanding Trophy, United Fund of Pittsburgh, Pa; Most Outstanding Trophy, Col. of Letters, Arts and Sci, Univ. South. Calif; Outstanding Key, Babson Inst; several speaking awards; Univ. South. Calif. Law Rev. Rel: Unity; church coun. chmn, mem, long range planning cmt. and greeter, First Congregational Church of Los Angeles. Legal Res: 457 S. Arden Blvd, Los Angeles, Calif. 90005. Mailing Add: Suite 310, 530 W. Sixth St, Los Angeles, Calif. 90014.

ADAM, JOSEPH RAYMOND D
Conn. State Rep.
b. Hartford, Conn, 1/4/31; s. Charles L. Adams and Irene Beaulieu A; m. 6/13/53 to Mariette Lavoie; c. Donald and Gerald. Educ: Hartford Pub. High Sch, 4 years. Polit. & Govt. Pos: Conn. State Rep, 69- Mil. Serv: Entered as Pvt, Air Force, 51, released as Airman 1/C, 55, after serv. in Korea, 52-53. Mem: Boy Scouts; Franco-Am. Vet. Rel: Catholic. Mailing Add: 217 Ward St, Hartford, Conn. 06106.

ADAMS, ALFRED O. R
b. Paola, Kans, 1897; m; c. one. Educ: Univ. Mo; Wash. Univ. Med. Sch, St. Louis, Mo, M.D, 24. Polit. & Govt. Pos: Wash. State Rep, 53-68. Bus. & Prof. Pos: Retired physician and surgeon. Mil. Serv: WW I. Mem: Mason. Mailing Add: W. 909 Melinda Lane, Spokane, Wash. 99203.

ADAMS, ALICE E. R
b. Bellows Falls, Vt, 11/26/01; married; c. 2. Educ: Bellows Falls H. S. Polit. & Govt. Pos: N.H. State Rep, 63-67; Town auditor, 20 yrs; former supvr. checklist and Selectmen. Bus. & Prof. Pos: Bookkeeper; Ins. agent. Mem: Ladies Alliance of Unitarian Church; Grange; Past Worthy Matron, Eastern Star; Past Notable Grand Rebekahs. Rel: Protestant. Mailing Add: West St, Charlestown, N.H. 03603. (1967)

ADAMS, ARTHUR F. R
b. Randolph, Vt, 12/16/78; married; c. 1. Educ: Eastman Bus. Col. Polit. & Govt. Pos: N.H. State Rep, 43-67; V.Pres, Rep. & Dir, Twin State Local. Bus. & Prof. Pos: Farmer. Mem: Past master Grange; mem, North. Milk Producers Coop; Dir, Am. Dairy Asn. Rel: Protestant. Mailing Add: W. Lebanon, N.H. 03784. (1967)

ADAMS, BROCKMAN (BROCK) D
U.S. Rep, Wash.
b. Atlanta, Ga, 1/13/27; s. Charles Leslie Adams and Vera Beemer A; m. 1952 to Mary Elizabeth Scott; c. Scott, Dean, Katherine and Aleen. Educ: Univ. Wash, B.A. in Econ, 49; Harvard Univ, LL.B, 52; Phi Beta Kappa; Phi Delta Theta. Polit. & Govt. Pos: U.S. attorney, West. Dist. of Wash. State, 61-64; U.S. Rep, Seventh Cong. Dist, Wash, 65-; del, Dem. Nat. Conv, 68. Bus. & Prof. Pos: Partner, Little, LeSourd, Palmer, Scott and Slemmons, 52-60 and LeSourd, Patten and Adams, 60-61. Mil. Serv: Entered as A/5, Navy 44, released as Electronics Technician's Mate 3/C, 46. Publ: 'Estate and Gift Taxation of the Marital Community,' Univ. Wash. Law Review, 53; 'Dealer Reserves,' Taxes, The Tax Mag, 59. Mem: Seattle, Wash, Am. and Fed. Bar Asns; pres, Puget Sound Chap, Phi Beta Kappa; Seattle Jr. C. of C, Distinguished Serv. Award, 60; Univ. Wash. Alumni Asn. Rel: Episcopal. Legal Res: 1415 42nd Ave. E, Seattle, Wash. 98102. Mailing Add: 3002 Albemarle N.W, Washington, D.C. 20008.

ADAMS, CAMERON R
Supvr, Eau Claire Co, Wis.
b. Cedar Rapids, Iowa, 8/19/32; s. Deane L. Adams and Gertrude Cameron A; m. 6/25/55 to Margaret Ann Johnson; c. Leslie Joan and Julie Johnson. Educ: Univ. Wis, B.S, 54; Psi Upsilon. Polit. & Govt. Pos: Del, Wis. State Rep. Conv, 63-69; supvr, Eau Claire Co, Wis, 66-; asst. exec. dir, Wis. Nixon-Agnew Cmt, 68; alternate del, Rep. Nat. Conv, 68; mem, Eau Claire Co. Rep. Exec. Cmt, Wis, 68-69. Bus. & Prof. Pos: Br. mgr, Adams Machinery, Inc, 58-62; exec. v.pres, Consumers Serv. Co. Inc, 62-69. Mil. Serv: Entered as 2nd Lt, Army, 54, released as 1st Lt, 56, after serv. in Artil, Ft. Sill, Okla. Mem: Kiwanis. Rel: Presbyterian. Mailing Add: 658 Putnam Dr, Eau Claire, Wis. 54701.

ADAMS, CHARLES HARRIS D
b. Ozark, Ala, 2/10/99; s. Joseph Harris Adams and Eura Edwards A; m. 12/14/26 to Willela Milligan; c. Catherine (Mrs. Allen Waid). Educ: Auburn Univ, 19; Spade Soc; Kappa Sigma. Polit. & Govt. Pos: Ala. State Sen, 63-66; Ala. State Rep, 59-63; mem. at large, State Dem. Exec. Cmt. Bus. & Prof. Pos: Dir, 1st Nat. Bank of Dothan; pres, United Warehouse Co; v.pres, Dothan Seed and Supply Co; partner, Segrest Gin and Storage Co. Mil. Serv: Army, WWI. Rel: Methodist. Mailing Add: Box 975, Dothan, Ala. 36301. (1967)

ADAMS, CLYDE BENTON D
b. Easton, Kans, 4/15/06; s. John Bean Adams and Arta Phillips A; m. 4/18/28 to Helen Marie Miller; c. Marianne and James Clyde. Educ: Gen. Signal Officers Sch, N.J; Army-Navy Staff Officers Sch, Va; Command and Gen. Staff Col, Kans. Hon. Alumnus, Kans. State Univ, Manhattan. Polit. & Govt. Pos: Trustee, Quindaro Twp, Kans, 50-52, bus. mgr, 57-62; Kans. State Rep, Ninth Dist, 63-69. Bus. & Prof. Pos: Sales mgr, Various Automobile Agencies; Jewelry Store, Liquor Store and Wholesale Paint dealer. Mil. Serv: Army, 22-23, Marine Corps, 23-31, Army, 31-46, released as Lt. Col.(Ret), after serv. as Dir. of Training, Camp Crowder. Mo; Good Conduct Medal; Marine Corps Expeditionary Medal from Campaign Medal; Am. Defense, Commendation and Victory Medals. Mem: Retired Officers Asn; Am. Legion; DAV; K. of C; C. of C; dir, United Fund; UNESCO; Soil Conservation Asn; Farm Bur; pres, Kans. Dem. Vets. Club; Ex-Rwy Carmans Union; Nat. Asn. Letter Carriers. Rel: Catholic. Mailing Add: 5332 Leavenworth Rd, Kansas City, Kans. 66104.

ADAMS, DON W. R
Committeeman, Ill. Rep. Cent. Cmt.
b. Springfield, Ill, 12/11/35; s. John Adams and Bertha Yates A; m. 8/25/62 to E. Jane Fulkerson; c. Donald Porter, David Yates, Jane E. and Mark Spiro. Educ: Northwest. Univ, 2 years; South. Ill. Univ, 1 year; Theta Xi. Polit. & Govt. Pos: Rep. precinct committeeman, Sangamon Co, Ill, 58-68; chmn, Dist. 10, Sangamon Co, 60-61; mem, Rep. Exec. Cmt, Sangamon Co, 60-; admin. asst, City of Springfield, Ill, 63-69; committeeman, Rep. State Cent. Cmt, 20th Cong. Dist, Ill, 66-; dir, Lincoln Rep. Forum, Springfield, 67-; temporary chmn, Rep. State Conv, 68; chmn, Ill. Electoral Col, 69. Bus.

& Prof. Pos: Secy. of corp, Lincoln Center Shopping Center, Springfield, Ill, 62-; co-owner, Ann Rutledge Pancake House, 62-; pres, Lincoln Depot, Inc, 63- Mil. Serv: Air Nat. Guard and Res. Mem: Springfield Pub. Bldg. Cmn; Am. Publ. Works Asn; Ill. Restaurant Asn; bd. dirs, United Serv. Orgn; bd. dirs, Goodwill Industs, Inc; YMCA; Sangamon Co. Hist. Soc. Rel: Roman Catholic. Mailing Add: 2329 Noble, Springfield, Ill. 62704.

ADAMS, DONALD GILBERT D
Tex. State Rep.
b. Jasper, Tex, 12/18/38; s. Thomas Gilbert Adams and Dess Hart A; m. 8/31/63 to Linda Cullum. Educ: Baylor Univ, B.B.A. & LL.B, 63; Phi Alpha Delta. Polit. & Govt. Pos: Tex. State Rep, 69- Bus. & Prof. Pos: Attorney-at-law, Adams & Adams. Mem: First Judicial Dist. and Tex. Bar Asns; Mason. Rel: Methodist. Mailing Add: 601 Forest Lane, Jasper, Tex. 75951.

ADAMS, EARL CLINTON R
b. San Jose, Calif, 5/12/92; s. John F. Adams and Alice Sinclair A; m. 10/14/22 to Ilse Downey; c. Nancy Camilla (Mrs. Jaquelin Smith Holliday, II) and Robert Pierce. Educ: Stanford Univ, A.B, 16; J.D, 20; Harvard Law Sch, 16-17; Phi Delta Phi; Delta Tau Delta. Polit. & Govt. Pos: Former treas, Rep. State Cent. Cmt, Calif, United Rep. Finance Cmt, Los Angeles Co. and Nixon Fact Finding Cmt, 46. Bus. & Prof. Pos: Partner, Adams, Duque & Hazeltine, Los Angeles, Calif; asst. comnr, Corps, State of Calif, 22-26. Mil. Serv: Entered as Pvt, Army, released as 2nd Lt, 19, after serv. in 107th F.A, 28th Div. and 346th F.A, 91st Div, AEF. Mem: Bd. Counc, Sch. Bus. Admin, Univ. of South Calif; K.T; Shrine; Am. Legion; Town Hall; exec. cmt, March of Dimes Nat. Found, Los Angeles Chap; Calif. Club; Univ. Club; Stock Exchange Club. Rel: Episcopal. Legal Res: 1386 Orlando Rd, San Marino, Calif. 91108. Mailing Add: Suite 1035, 523 W. Sixth St, Los Angeles, Calif. 90014. (1967)

ADAMS, EVA BERTRAND D
Dir, Bur. of Mint, Wash.
b. Wonder, Nev; d. Verner Lauer Adams and Cora Varble A; single. Educ: Univ. of Nev, B.A; Columbia, M.A, 37; Wash. Col. Law, LL.B, 48; Geo. Wash. Univ, LL.M, 50; Wash. Col. Law, Am. Univ, J.D, 68; Cap and Scroll; Kappa Alpha Theta; Phi Kappa Phi; Kappa Delta Pi. Hon. LL.D, Univ. Portland, 66 and Univ. Nev, 67. Polit. & Govt. Pos: Admin. asst. to Sen. Pat McCarran, 40-54, Sen. Ernest Brown, 54- and Sen. Alan Bible, 54-61; dir, Bur. of Mint, Wash, 61- Bus. & Prof. Pos: Teacher, Las Vegas High Sch; instr. Eng. and asst. Dean. of Women, Univ. of Nev, 37-40; Am. Instr. of Mining Engrs. Henry Krumb lectr, 69. Mem: Washoe and St. Mary's Hosp. Guild; bd. mgrs, Graham-Eckes Sch, Palm Beach, Fla; Am, Fed, Nev. and D.C. Bar Asns; Nat. Exec. Secy. Asn.(hon); Am. Newspaper Women; Reno C. of C; Senate Secy. Asn.(pres, 33-34); Wash. Soroptimist; Soc. of Medalists. Mailing Add: 4201 Cathedral Ave. N.W, Apt. 1221W, Washington, D.C. 20016.

ADAMS, FRANK EMIL D
b. Hopkins, Minn, 7/12/15; s. Joseph Adams and Ann A. Bignoski A; m. 6/3/40 to Helen Ann Pauly. Educ: Univ. Minn, B.S, 38. Polit. Pos: Minn. State Sen, 41st Dist, 62-67; sch. bd. dir, Minneapolis Bd. of Educ, 61, 55, 53; pres, Minneapolis Sch. Bd, 56-57. Govt. Pos: Vet. Serv. Officer, Hennepin Co, 47-; dist. supvr, Bur. of Census, 46-47; juvenile probation officer, 42-43; sch. teacher, Minn, 38-42. Mil. Serv: Entered as A/S, Navy, 43, released as Lt.(jg), 46, after serv. in World War II, Asiatic Pac. Theaters; Asiatic Pac, Philippines, Japanese Occupation and Am. Theater Ribbons; World War II Victory Medal; Honor Man in Navy Co; Lt. Comdr, Naval Res, 46-65. Mem: Pres, Minneapolis Joint Vets. Coun, 61-63; dist. comdr, VFW, 49-51; state chmn, Sen. Hubert Humphrey Vets. Cmt, 60; Am. Legion; DAV; Minneapolis Joint Vets. Coun. Selected one of 100 Outstanding Young Men in Minneapolis Metrop. Area, Time Magazine and Minneapolis C. of C, 53. Mailing Add: 2555 Ulysses St, N.E, Minneapolis, Minn. 55418. (1967)

ADAMS, FRANK POLLARD R
Mem. Exec. Cmt, Calif. Rep. State Cent. Cmt.
b. Oakland, Calif, 11/25/08; s. Edson Adams and Jessie Fox A; m. 9/9/50 to Analisa Bosche; c. Edson, Nora, Peter Stewart and Lisa. Educ: Stanford Univ, A.B, 31; Univ. Calif, J.D, 34; Phi Delta Phi; Delta Tau Delta. Polit. & Govt. Pos: V.pres, Calif. Rep. Assembly, 65-66, pres, 67, dir, 69; mem. and treas, Alameda Co. Rep. Cent. Cmt, 67-; mem. exec. cmt, Calif. Rep. State Cent. Cmt, 67-; pres, Lincoln Club Alameda Co, 67-; del, Rep. Nat. Conv, 68; North. Calif. chmn, Rafferty for U.S. Sen. Campaign, 68. Bus. & Prof. Pos: Attorney-at-law, San Francisco, 35-; v.pres, Vacu-dry Co, 41-; pres, Minerals Mgt. Corp, 41-; chmn. bd, The Cyclotron Corp, 65-; chmn. bd, Control Bldg. Systs, Inc, 68- Mem: Am, Calif. and San Francisco Bar Asns; Univ. Club San Francisco; Commonwealth Club San Francisco; SAR. Rel: Protestant. Legal Res: 781 Highland Ave, Piedmont, Calif. 94611. Mailing Add: 1922 Russ Bldg, San Francisco, Calif. 94104.

ADAMS, GEORGE DRAYTON, JR. D
Ga. State Rep.
b. Atlanta, Ga, 4/8/15; s. George Drayton Adams, Sr. and Josephine Adeline A; m. 5/13/39 to Frances Elizabeth Hazelrigs; c. Patricia (Mrs. Sam H. Cann) and Angela (Mrs. Harold J. Smith). Educ: Fulton High Sch, 28-32. Polit. & Govt. Pos: Mem, bd. trustees, Atlanta Pub. Libr, Ga, 62-69; Ga. State Rep, 66- Bus. & Prof. Pos: Sales mgr, Blue Plate Foods, Inc, 39-44; pres, G. D. Adams Co, Atlanta, Ga, 48-69. Mil. Serv: Entered as Pvt, Army, 44, released as Cpl, 46, after serv. in 232nd Field Artil. Bn, 42nd Inf. Div, Rhineland and Cent. Europe Campaigns; two Campaign Ribbons. Mem: Shrine; Lions; Civitan; Am. Legion; VFW; hon. life mem, Ga. Cong, Parent-Teachers Orgn. Rel: Baptist. Legal Res: 532 St. Johns Ave. S.W. Atlanta, Ga. 30315. Mailing Add: 1928 Stewart Ave. S.W. Atlanta, Ga. 30315.

ADAMS, GILBERT TIMBRELL, JR. D
b. Beaumont, Tex, 7/1/42 to Gilbert Timbrell Adams and Viola Mae Joss A; m. 3/22/67 to Marilyn Ann Thornton; c. Angela Ann (deceased). Educ: Lamar State Col, B.S, 64; South Tex. Col. Law, J.D, 68; Delta Kappa Epsilon; Chancery Club; Rodeo Club; Delta Theta Phi; pres. student body, South Tex. Col. Law. Polit. & Govt. Pos: Page to Sam Rayburn, Dem. Nat. Conv, 60, del, 68. Bus. & Prof. Pos: Attorney, Adams & Browne, Beaumont, Tex, 68-; dir, Jefferson Co. Savings & Loan Asn, 69. Mem: Am. & Jefferson Co. Bar Asns; Am. Trial Lawyers Asn; State Bar of Tex; Tex. Trial Lawyers Asn. Recipient of Am. Bar Asn. Silver Key Award; Delta Theta Phi Achievement Award; Board of Governors of South Texas College of Law Award. Rel: Methodist. Legal Res: 995 Thomas Rd, Beaumont, Tex. 77707. Mailing Add: Suite 1012 Goodhue Bldg, Beaumont, Tex. 77701.

ADAMS, H. G. 'JACK' D
S.Dak. State Rep.
b. Galesburg, Ill, 7/5/18; s. Harold Vincent Adams and Merle Edgar A; m. 6/24/39 to Erma Yarian; c. Gerald G, Jaqualine Sue, Michael Ernest, Thomas Edgar, Pamela Kay, Douglas Patrick, David Roy, William Joseph, Paul Vincent and Donald Raymond. Educ: Notre Dame Univ. Polit. & Govt. Pos: Mem. sch. bd, Chamberlain, S.Dak, 60-69; S.Dak. State Rep, 67- Bus. & Prof. Pos: Pres. elect, S.Dak. Independent Mutual Agents, 69- Mem: C. of C; Kiwanis; K. of C. Rel: Catholic. Legal Res: E. Good St, Chamberlain, S.Dak. 57325. Mailing Add: Box 116, Chamberlain, S.Dak. 57325.

ADAMS, HOMER MAT D
b. Galesburg, Ill, 1/14/11; s. Homer Mat Adams and Ethel Allen A; m. 10/21/32 to Catherine Weber; c. Homer Mat III and John Weber. Educ: Univ. Ill, 29-32; Lincoln Col. Law, LL.B, 38; Tumas; Alpha Delta Phi. Polit. & Govt. Pos: Chief of invest, Dept. of Finance, Ill, 33-37, asst. and acting dir, 37-41; trustee, Univ. Ill, 37-43; nat. pres, Young Dem. Clubs of Am, 39-41; Off. of War Info, U.S. Govt, 41-45; secy, N.J. Del, Dem. Nat. Conv, 60; cmnr. of Conserv. and Econ. Develop, N.J, 61-63; chmn, Middlesex Co. Sewerage, Authority, 61-; alternate cmnr. representing N.J, Del. River Basin Cmn, 61-; bd. gov, Rutgers, The State Univ, 63-65; del, Dem. Nat. Conv, 64 & 68; consult. for pub. rels, N.J. State Constitutional Conv, 66; alternate chmn, Governor's Econ. Eval. Cmt. for an Intercontinental Jetport for N.J, 67-; dep. chmn, N.J. Alliance of Businessmen, 68-69; cmnr, N.J. State Open Space Cmn, 69- Bus. & Prof. Pos: Pres, Liberian Roberts Corp, 46-49; spec. asst. to pres, Johnson & Johnson, 50-61, dir. pub. rels, 54-66, spec. asst. to chmn. bd, 61-, dir. pub. affairs, 67- Mil. Serv: Assigned to AFHQ and SHAEF, Psychol. Warfare Div. from Off. of War Info, 43-45; Medal of Freedom. Publ: Numerous articles in prof. journals. Mem: Overseas Press Club; Water Pollution Control Fedn; Players Club; bd, Water Research Found, Inc, N.J. Cmt, Regional Plan Asn; bd. dirs, Middlesex Gen. Hosp. Rel: Presbyterian. Legal Res: 3 Longview Rd, Edison, N.J. 08817. Mailing Add: Johnson & Johnson, New Brunswick, N.J. 08903.

ADAMS, HOOVER D
b. Dunn, N.C, 3/6/20; s. Alexander Benton Adams and Lou Flora Morgan A; m. 9/2/44 to Mellicent Stalder; c. Brent, Maere Kay and Bart Stalder. Educ: Dunn High Sch, Grad; Officer Candidate School, U.S. Army. Polit. & Govt. Pos: Campaign press secy, U.S. Sen. Willis Smith, N.C, 50; secy, Harnett Co. Dem. Conv, on several occasions; mem, Dunn Alcohol Control Bd, currently; del, Dem. Nat. Conv, 68. Bus. & Prof. Pos: Established and founded, Daily Record, a daily newspaper, Dunn, N.C, 50, ed, publisher and owner, 50- Mil. Serv: Entered as Pvt, Army Air Force, 42, released as Capt, 45, after serv. in 101st Airborne Div, Trooper Carrier Command Hq, European Command, London, England. Mem: North Carolina Press Association; Rotary; Am. Legion, Mason; VFW; C. of C; one of founders, Dunn Jr. C. of C. Rel: Christian Church. Legal Res: Lakeshore Dr, Dunn, N.C. 28334. Mailing Add: P.O. Box 811, Dunn, N.C. 28334.

ADAMS, J. M. JR. D
b. Fitzgerald, Ga, 4/12/16; m. to Mary Emerson A; c. J. M. III, Lark E. Educ: Univ. Fla, B.A, 38. Polit. & Govt. Pos: Co. cmnr, Fla, 53-57; Fla. State Rep, 62-66. Bus. & Prof. Pos: Wholesale petrol. distributor. Mil. Serv: Army, 44-45, serv. in Tank Bn, ETO as Lt. and Platoon Leader; Purple Heart. Rel: Methodist. Mailing Add: P.O. Box 538, Avon Park, Fla. 33825. (1967)

ADAMS, JACK R. D
City Councilman, Wheeling, W.Va.
b. Ohio Co, 8/10/95; s. Archie L. Adams and Effie Updegraff A; m. to Frances Grant; c. Jack Richard Jr, Alexander Beall and Frances Grant II. Educ: W. Liberty State Col; Elliott Sch. of Bus; Air Command and Staff Sch. Air Univ. Polit. & Govt. Pos: Mem, W.Va. State Bd. of Aeronauts, 31-33; W.Va. State Rep, 34, 40, 54 & 64-66; Chief Dep. U.S. Marshal, North. Dist. W.Va, 36-39; city councilman, Wheeling, 47, 51, 55 & 67-, mayor, 55-59; pres, W.Va. League of Munic, 56-57; mem, W.Va. Air Pollution Control Cmn, 61-64 & 67-, chmn, 61-62; mem, Ohio-W.Va. Interstate Air Pollution Control Cmn, 68-69. Bus. & Prof. Pos: B. and O. R.R. Mil. Serv: Entered 17; pilot, World War I; pilot and base comdr, World War II, retired Col, 55. Mem: Mason; Farm Bur; Am. Legion (W.Va. Dept. Comdr, 61-62); 40 et 8; Retreads; VFW; Elks. Rel: Presbyterian. Mailing Add: 56 Virginia St, Wheeling, W.Va. 26003.

ADAMS, JAMES H. R
b. W. Haven, 2/17/01; m. to Elsie Best. Educ: Troy Conf. Acad; Poultney; Lyndon Sch. of Agr. Polit. & Govt. Pos: Former Vt. State Rep, constable and tax collector. Bus. & Prof. Pos: Farmer. Mem: Mason; Grange; Farm Bur; del, Metrop. Milk Producers Bargaining Agency. Rel: Baptist. Mailing Add: RFD 1, Fair Haven, Vt. 05743. (1967)

ADAMS, JAMES L. DFL
Minn. State Rep.
m. to Edith Adams; c. Judith, Laura and Douglas. Educ: Dunwoody Inst. Polit. & Govt. Pos: Minn. State Rep, 55- Bus. & Prof. Pos: Electrician; treas, Local 292, AFL-CIO Elec. Workers. Mil. Serv: WWII. Mem: Cdr, Patterson Post VFW; pres, Madison Sch. PTA; Eagles Lodge; Stenbock Swedish Lodge; S. Side Businessmen's Asn; Court House Post, Am. Legion; Cub Scout 55. Rel: Lutheran. Mailing Add: 616 E. 19th St, Minneapolis, Minn. 55404.

ADAMS, JAMES LOWELL, SR. D
Ala. State Sen.
b. Houston Co, Ala, 10/30/15; s. Louis Major Adams and Trudie Harris A; m. 4/14/42 to Broma Phillips; c. James Lowell, Jr, Nancy Jane, Louis Arthur, Margaret Beth and Mary Ann. Educ: High Sch. Polit. Pos: Ala. State Sen, 66- Bus. & Prof. Pos: Pres, Adams Supply Co, Summerlin & Adams,

Inc, Houston Herald Pub. Co. and Perry Co. Stockyards; dir. and mem, finance and exec. cmt, South. United Life Ins. Co. of Montgomery; owner, L&L Farms; v.pres, Adams & Eagle, Inc. Mem: Pres, Southeast Livestock Expos; dir, Am. Quarter Horse Asn; dir. and former pres, Ala. Cattlemen's Asn; Dothan C. of C. Agr. and Ind. Cmt; Ala. Agr. Cent. Bd; Farm Bur; Mason; Dothan Country Club; former dir. and chmn, Dothan C. of C. Agr. Cmt, former pres, Nat. Shorthorn Asn. Rel: Baptist; Deacon; v.pres. Bd. of Trustees, Ala. Baptist Found; former v. moderator and exec. cmt. mem, Columbia Baptist Asn. Legal Res: Route 2, Box 95, Dothan, Ala. 36301. Mailing Add: P.O. Box 490, Dothan, Ala. 36301.

ADAMS, JOHN GIBBONS R
b. Ashland, Ky, 3/23/12; s. Samuel Morton Adams and Helen Gibbons A; m. 6/11/46 to Margaret Paxton Williams; c. Rebecca. Educ: Univ. S.Dak, LL.B, 35; George Washington Univ, LL.M; Sigma Alpha Epsilon. Polit. Pos: V.pres, Young Rep. Nat. Fedn, 41-46. Govt. Pos: Mem, U.S. Civil Aeronaut. Bd, 65-, dir, Bur. Enforcement, 61-65 and mem. staff, 58-61; consult. orgn. and mgt, Atomic Energy Cmn, 56-57; gen. counsel, Dept. Army, 53-55; dep. gen. counsel and dir, Legis. Div, Dept. Defense, 51-53, asst. gen. counsel, 49-51; clerk, Cmt. on Armed Serv, U.S. Senate, 47-49; agent, S.Dak. Dept. Justice, 35. Mil. Serv: Entered as 1st Lt, Army, 42, released as Maj, 46, after serv. In ETO; Bronze Star; N. African, Italian, French and Germany Campaign Ribbons; Col, Army Res. Mem: S.Dak. and D.C. Bar Asns; Army-Navy Club. Rel: Episcopal. Legal Res: S.Dak. Mailing Add: 3415 34th Pl. N.W, Washington, D.C. 20016. (1967)

ADAMS, LUTHER WILEY D
b. Belden, Miss, 6/23/90; m. Polit. & Govt. Pos: Miss. State Rep, 44-52, 56-60 & 64-68. Bus. & Prof. Pos: Farmer, ginner. Mem: Kappa Sigma. Rel: Methodist. Mailing Add: Route 1, Tupelo, Miss. 38801. (1967)

ADAMS, PAUL LINCOLN D
Assoc. Justice, Mich. Supreme Court
b. Sault Sainte Marie, Mich, 4/9/08; s. John Newton Adams and Angela Moloney A; m. 7/28/34 to Ruth Karpinski; c. Mary Louise, Susan E, Katherine W. and Barbara Ann. Educ: Univ. Mich. A.B, M.A. and LL.B; Phi Eta Sigma; Phi Beta Kappa. Polit. & Govt. Pos: Mayor, Sault Sainte Marie, Mich, 38-42; mem, Mich. Soc. Welfare Cmn, 49; chmn, City Charter Cmn, Sault Sainte Marie, 51; regent, Univ. Mich, 56-57; attorney gen, Mich, 58-61; Assoc. Justice, Mich. Supreme Court, 62 & 64- Mem: Elks; Lansing Farmers Club. Rel: Episcopal. Legal Res: R.R. 1, Laingsburg, Mich. 48848. Mailing Add: Michigan Supreme Court, Box 88, Lansing, Mich. 48901. (1967)

ADAMS, PHILLIP WAYNE D
Chmn, Geauga Co. Dem. Exec. Cmt, Ohio
b. Chardon, Ohio, 9/10/27; s. Max Lyle Adams and Lucille Van-Orsdale A; m. 8/25/53 to Geraldine Sorenson; c. Rex Morgan, Victoria Geraldine, Kirk Phillip and Chad Stewart. Educ: Hiram Col, B.A. in Polit. Sci, 52; Delphic Soc. Club. Polit. & Govt. Pos: Dem. precinct committeeman, Geauga Co, Ohio, 51; cand, Ohio House of Rep, 58, Geauga Co. cmnr, 60 and Geauga Co. treas, 68; chmn, Ohio Dem. Party; mem, Geauga Co. Dem. Exec. Cmt, Ohio, 64-, chmn, 68-; chmn, Geauga Co. Dem. Cent. Cmt, 68- Mil. Serv: Entered as A/S, Navy, 45, released as Seaman 1/C, 46, after serv. in Naval Air Transport, U.S; Am. Theatre Ribbon. Publ: Ed. and chmn, Geaugas Prime Reader Monthly, Geauga Co, 69; plus others. Mem: Nat. Asn. Life Underwriters; charter mem, Kiwanis (past v.pres. and past prog. chmn, East Geauga Club, 64); Ohio Asn. Mutual Ins. Agents; F&AM; Claridon Grange; RAM; Amvets; AASR; Consistory. Rel: Methodist; Lay Leader. Mailing Add: P.O. Box 74, East Claridon, Ohio 44033.

ADAMS, ROBERT D
b. Salem, N.J, 6/17/15; m. to Ruth; c. three. Educ: St. Johns Col, Annapolis, N.J; Duke Univ, LL.B. Polit. & Govt. Pos: Cmnr, Cheyenne, Wyo, 52-53; treas, Wyo. State Dem. Party, 55-57; pres, Laramie Co. Libr. Bd, 57; ins. cmnr, 59; Wyo. State Rep, 57-66; Wyo. State Sen, 67-69; alternate del, Dem. Nat. Conv, 68. Bus. & Prof. Pos: V.pres, Key Life Ins. Co. Mem: Shrine; Elks; YMCA (first gov. bd). One of Nation's Outstanding City Officials, Am. Mag, 63. Rel: Presbyterian. Mailing Add: 3916 Dey Ave, Cheyenne, Wyo. 82001. (1967)

ADAMS, ROBERT L. D
b. Joplin, Mo, 10/6/29; m. to Ann G. Educ: Casper Col; Univ. Wyo, B.A, post-grad. work. Polit. & Govt. Pos: Former Wyo. State Rep. Bus. & Prof. Pos: Parks mgr, Natrona Co, Wyo; mem, State Rural Fire Adv. Bd. Mil. Serv: Korean Conflict. Mem: Wyo. Recreation and Parks Asn; Nat. Parks and Recreation Asn; Mason; Elks. Mailing Add: Sunside Sta, Box 4142, Casper, Wyo. 82601. (1967)

ADAMS, RONALD FLETCHER D
Ga. State Sen.
b. Hortense, Ga, 7/23/15; s. Alvah Ray Adams and Nora Middleton A; m. 5/1/47 to Deborah Douglas; c. Anne Douglas, Ronald Middleton and Walter Douglas. Educ: Univ. Ga. Law Sch, LL.B, 40. Polit. & Govt. Pos: Judge of city court, Jesup, Ga, 48-52; Ga. State Sen, 67- Mil. Serv: Entered as Pfc, Marine Corps, 40, released as Maj, 46, after serv. in S.Pac, 41-45; Bronze Star; Purple Heart; 2 Presidential Citations; S.Pac. Ribbon with 5 Battle Stars; Marine Corps Res, 54, Col. Mem: Am. and Ga. Bar Asns; Am. Trial Lawyers Asn; Kiwanis; Am. Legion; Elks; VFW; DAV; Shrine; Purple Heart League; U.S. Marine Corps Res. Officers Asn. Rel: Episcopal. Mailing Add: 1327 Sycamore Ave, Brunswick, Ga. 31521.

ADAMS, RUTH MAY D
V.Chmn, Archuleta Co. Dem. Party, Colo.
b. Kansas City, Kans, 6/22/00; d. Arthur Stonewall Childers and Minnie May Britt C; m. 1/26/25 to Thomas Earl Adams (deceased); c. Mildred Ilene (Mrs. Roy Moore), Margaret Nadine (Mrs. Clark Ford) and Lionel Earl 'Hattie'. Educ: High sch, Papillion, Nebr, 1 year. Polit. & Govt. Pos: Dem. committeewomen and poll watcher, first precinct, Pagosa Springs, Colo, 50-69; v.chmn, Archuleta Co. Dem. Party, 55- Mem: Women's Soc. Christian Serv.(v.chmn); Civic Club; Home Demonstration Club; Copper State Doll Club. Received Awards from Lyndon B. Johnson; co. fair awards. Rel: Methodist. Mailing Add: Star Route Box 5, Pagosa Springs, Colo. 81147.

ADAMS, SALISBURY Conservative
Minn. State Rep.
b. Duluth, Minn, 1925; married; c. four. Educ: Univ. Minn, B.S. in Metallurgical Eng; Harvard Univ. Law Sch. Polit. & Govt. Pos: Mem. bd. and treas, Wayzata Sch. Dist. 284, Minn, 58-62; Minn. State Rep, 62- Bus. & Prof. Pos: Lawyer. Mil. Serv: Navy, 43-46. Mem: Dir, Minn. Family and Children's Serv. Mailing Add: Box 1122, Wayzata, Minn. 55391. (1967)

ADAMS, SHERMAN R
b. East Dover, Vt, 1/8/99; s. Clyde H. Adams and Winnie Marian Sherman A; m. 7/28/23 to Rachel Leona White; c. Marion (Mrs. William Freese), Jean (Mrs. William M. Hallagher), Sarah and Samuel. Educ: Dartmouth Col, B.A, 20, M.A, 40; Sigma Alpha Epsilon. LL.D, Univ. N.H, 50, Dartmouth Col, 53, Bates Col, 54,Bryant Col, St. Lawrence Univ, 54 and Middlebury Col, 57; D.C.L, New Eng. Col, 51. Polit. & Govt. Pos: N.H. State Rep, 41-44, Speaker, N.H. House Rep, 43-44; del, Rep. Nat. Conv, 44 & 52; U.S. Rep, N.H, 45-47; Gov. N.H, 49-53; chmn, Conf. New Eng. Gov, 51-52; asst. to President, 53-58. Bus. & Prof. Pos: Treas, Black River Lumber Co, Vt, 21-22; former dir, Pemigewasset R.R, Concord, N.H; mgr, timberland and lumber opers, Parker-Young Co, Lincoln, 28-45; pres, Loon Mt. Corp, currently. Mil. Serv: Marine Corps, 18. Publ: First Hand Report, 61; Merican Forests, 69; articles in Life and other mags. Mem: Dir, Northeast. Lumber Mfrs. Asn; Soc. Am. Foresters; SAR; N.H. Soc; Mason (33°). Mailing Add: Pollard Rd, Lincoln, N.H. 03251.

ADAMS, THOMAS B. D
b. 1910; m. to Ramelle Cochrane; c. John, Peter, Douglas and Henry Ramelle. Educ: Harvard Univ; Phi Beta Kappa. Polit. & Govt. Pos: Dem. cand. for U.S. Sen, Mass, 66; cand. for Dem. nomination for U.S. Rep. Fifth Cong. Dist, Mass, 68. Bus. & Prof. Pos: Retired hotel exec; former ed. writer, Boston Herald, 32-35; exec, Waltham Watch Co, until 41; Sheraton Hotel Corp, 46, treas, 54-; Harvard Univ. faculty; treas, Am. Acad. Arts & Sci; trustee, Boston Athenaeum, Chapelbrook Fedn. and Neurosci. Research Fedn. Mil. Serv: Air Force, 42-45, Capt. Mem: Pres, Mass. Hist. Soc; past v.pres, Colonial Soc. of Mass; bd. of appeals of Lincoln; fel. Morgan Libr. Mailing Add: Concord Rd. S, Lincoln, Mass. 01773.

ADAMS, THURMAN FREDDIE R
Chmn, Newberry Co. Rep. Party, S.C.
b. Prosperity, S.C, 2/22/38; s. Clarence Freddie Adams (deceased) and Mary Hawkins A; m. 10/9/60 to Erma Jane Cromer; c. Thurman Kevin. Educ: Univ. S.C, Cert. in Hwy. Eng, 56. Polit. & Govt. Pos: Field orgn. chmn, Rep. Party, S.C, 67-68, field finance dir, 68; mem, Third Dist. Rep. Cmt, 68-69; chmn, Newberry Co. Rep. Party, 65- Bus. & Prof. Pos: Owner, vending bus, Newberry, S.C, 68-; treas, security corp, 68- Mil. Serv: Entered as Pvt, S.C. Nat. Guard, 56, released as S/Sgt. E-7, 66, after serv. in Hq. and Hq. Battery, 163rd Artil, Newberry. Mem: Mid-Carolina Country Club, Prosperity, S.C; Newberry Co. Coin Club; Newberry Moose Lodge; S.C. Silver Elephant Club, Columbia. Rel: Methodist. Mailing Add: 8 Player St, Newberry, S.C. 29108.

ADAMS, TOM D
Secy. of State, Fla.
b. Jacksonville, Fla, 3/11/17; s. Thomas Burton Adams, Sr. and Carolyn Hamilton A; m. 7/30/39 to Helen Frances Brown; c. Carolyn (Mrs. James A. DeHaven, Jr), Augusta (Mrs. T. Buckingham Bird) and Frances. Educ: Univ. Mich, A.B, 40; Univ. Fla. Sch. of Law; pres, Sr. Hon. Soc; Alpha Kappa Psi; pres, Phi Delta Theta & Interfraternity Coun. Hon. Dr. Space Educ, Fla. Inst. Tech, 62; hon. L.H.D, Trinity Col, 64. Polit. & Govt. Pos: Fla. State Sen, 29th Dist, 56-60; secy. of state, Fla, 61- Bus. & Prof. Pos: Real estate and property mgr, H. P. Holmes, Inc, Detroit, Mich, 40-42; plant supt, Foremost Dairies, Jacksonville and Daytona Beach, Fla, 42-44; owner, dairy farm, Orange Park, 44-48; lumber dealer and property mgr, Orange Park Properties, 48-60. Mem: Bd, Nat. Waterways Conf.(past pres. and past chmn. bd); bd, Miss. Valley Asn.(past pres, currently chmn. bd); rep. from Fla, U.S. Study Cmn. on Southeast River Basins; Resources Adv. Bd; Southeast Basins Inter-Agency Coun; Nat. Rivers and Harbors Cong; Rotary; Navy League; Newcomen Soc; Moose (state pres, 67). Most Outstanding First-Term Sen, 57, Most Valuable Mem. of Legis, 59 and Most Effective Adminstr. of a State Agency, 61, 63 & 65 (trophy retired, 3 time consecutive winner), Allen Morris Poll of Legis; Sen. Contrib. Most to Agr, Fla. Agr. Coun, 57; Legis. Contrib. Most to Agr, Fla. Fruit and Vegetable Asn, 59; hon. Gold Key mem, Fla. State Univ, 61; Most Outstanding Dem, Fla. Young Dem. Club, 63; hon. Blue Key me, Univ. Fla, 64; hon. mem, Omicron Delta Kappa Leadership Fraternity, 65; Leadership award, Fla. Waterways Asn, 66; Order of San Carlos, 67. Rel: Baptist. Legal Res: 1702 Golf Terr, Tallahassee, Fla. 32304. Mailing Add: The Capitol, Tallahassee, Fla. 32304.

ADAMS, VICTORINE QUILLE D
Campaign Coordinator, Dem. Party, Md.
b. Baltimore, Md, 4/28/12; d. Joseph C. Quille and Estelle Carey Tate Q; m. 7/28/35 to William L. Adams; c. Gertrude (Mrs. Venable). Educ: Coppin State Teacher's Col, 30; Morgan State Col, 40; Phi Delta Kappa; Sigma Gamma Rho. Polit. & Govt. Pos: Chmn, Colored Women's Dem. Club, Md, 46-; del, Dem. Nat. Conv, 64; dir, Register to Vote Campaign and Get Out the Vote Campaign, 64; campaign coordinator, Dem. Party, Md, 64-; Md. State Del, 66-67; mem, Baltimore City Coun, Fourth Dist, 67- Bus. & Prof. Pos: Pub. sch. teacher, Dept. Educ, Baltimore, 30-44; mgr, Charm Centre Inc, 50-63. Mem: Bd. dirs, Advance Savings & Loan Asn. and Provident Hosp; Small Bus. Asn; Nat. Asn. Negro Bus. & Prfnl. Women; Woman Power Inc; United Women's Dem. Clubs of Md; Nat. Coun. Negro Women. Woman of the Year, Zeta Phi Beta Sorority; Afro-Am. Honor Roll. Rel: Catholic. Mailing Add: 3103 Carlisle Ave, Baltimore, Md. 21216.

ADAMS, WAYNE MELVIN R
b. Sonora, Calif, 10/16/29; s. Cecil Merle Adams and Neola Hicks A; m. 9/27/50 to Patricia Ann Junker; c. Rebecca Lu and Wendy Lynn. Educ: South. Calif. Col, 3 years. Polit. & Govt. Pos: Rep. nominee, U.S. House of Rep, Third Cong. Dist, Wash, 68; precinct committeeman, Rep. Party, Clark Co, 68-69; mem. exec. cmt, Clark Co. Rep. Cent. Cmt, 68-69. Bus. & Prof. Pos: Ordained minister, Assemblies of God, 54, state dir. youth, 55-60, sr. minister, Glad Tidings Church, Vancouver, Wash, 60- Mem: Kiwanis Int. Rel: Assembly of God. Mailing Add: 2920 N.E. 45th St, Vancouver, Wash. 98663.

ADAMS, WILHELMINA F. D
b. Key West, Fla; d. Thomas F. Adams and Mary F. Peck A; single. Educ: Hunter Col, 27-30; Pratt Inst. Polit. & Govt. Pos: Supvr, Dept. of Welfare, N.Y.C, 32-40; mem, Legal Cmt, Tammany Hall Dem. Orgn. and state committeewoman, N.Y, 41-51; dist. leader, New Deal Dem. Club, 41-51; court attendent, City Court, N.Y.C, 43-44; co-chmn, Nat. Dem. Campaign for N.Y. State, 44; del, Dem. Nat. Conv, 44; supvr, Dept. of Housing, N.Y.C, 54-58; designer, Dept. of Traffic, N.Y.C, 58-60; investr, Dept. of Finance, N.Y.C, 60-62; dist. leader, United Dem. Club, 62-65; secy, Bd. of Assessors, N.Y.C, 62-66. Bus. & Prof. Pos: Proprietor and mgr, Florist Shop, 39-49; supvr, CARE, 53-54. Mem: Women's City Club of New York; Int. Coun. of Women; Nat. Coun. of Women of U.S; Nat. Coun. Negro Women; Nat. Asn. Negro Bus. & Prfnl. Women's Clubs (pres, N.Y. Club); founder and pres, Nannie Burrough's Club; first pres, Martin Smith Music Asn; secy, Good Hearts Welfare Asn; organizer, Christmas Cheer Cmt; ANVS; life mem. and chmn. of Lifers, NAACP; founder, 1st pres. and mem. commun. rels. cmt, Women's Asn. N.Y. Urban League; Nat. and State Cmn. against Discrimination in Housing; Prince Hall; Eastern Star; YWCA; YMCA; pub. rels. chmn, Nat. Asn. of Colored Women; founder and pres, Aeolian Ladies of Charity; pres, Utopian Neighborhood Club; secy, Friends of Liberian Youth. Achievement Award from Nat. Asn. of Negro Bus. & Prfnl. Women's Asn; Awards from Nat. Asn. of Colored Women and Nat. Coun. of Negro Women; plus many others. Rel: Protestant. Mailing Add: 131 Central Park N, New York, N.Y. 10026.

ADAMS, WILLIAM E. R
N.Y. State Sen.
b. 1923; m. to Jacquela Devlin; c. four. Educ: Ind. Univ; Univ. of Buffalo Law Sch, LL.B; Sigma Nu. Polit. & Govt. Pos: N.Y. State Assemblyman, 56-64; N.Y. State Sen, 64- Bus. & Prof. Pos: Attorney; Falk, Twilvetries, Johnston, & Siemer. Mem: Buffalo Athletic Club; Am. Legion; F.&A.M. Legal Res: 142 Doncaster Rd, Tonawanda, N.Y. 14150. Mailing Add: State Senate, State Capital Bldg, Albany, N.Y. 12224. (1967)

ADAMS, WILLIAM R. 'BILL' R
b. Isom, Ky, 1/27/05; s. James Adams and Sarah Back A; m. 7/23/28 to Janey Wright; c. Lois A.(Mrs. Baker), Douglas G. and James A. Educ: Allice Lloyd Col, 2 years; East. State Univ. Polit. & Govt. Pos: Ky. State Rep, 50-54; elector, 56; del, Rep. Nat. Conv, 60 & 68; chmn, Letcher Co. Rep. Party, 60-69. Bus. & Prof. Pos: Merchant, Jeremiah, 45-; mine operator, 52-60; v.pres, Letcher Mfg. Co, Isom, 64-69. Rel: Baptist. Legal Res: Box 14, Isom, Ky. 41824. Mailing Add: Box 8, Jeremiah, Ky. 41826.

ADAMSON, ELVIN A. R
Nebr. State Sen.
b. Valentine, Nebr, 1/21/20; s. Walter Adamson and Delania Edwards A; m. 6/11/47 to Mabel Gale; c. Cheryl, Janie, Marjorie and Marvin. Educ: Chadron State Teachers Col; Univ. Colo; Univ. Nebr, A.B, 40; Blue Key; Sigma Nu. Polit. & Govt. Pos: Co. cmnr, Cherry Co, Nebr, 51-59; co. chmn, Rep. Party, Nebr, 58; Nebr. State Sen, 61-, speaker, Nebr. Sen, 67-69. Bus. & Prof. Pos: Secy, Sch. Dist. 116, 43-60; dir, Co. Off, 56-59; pres, Nebr. Stock Growers, 62-64; adv. coun, Am. Nat. Cattlemens, 62-; dir, Valentine First Nat. Bank and Independent Col. Found. Mem: Am. Nat. Cattlemen's Asn; Nebr. Stock Growers Asn; Farm Bur; Nebr. Hall Agr. Achievement; Mason; Scottish Rite; Shrine; Elks. Rel: Episcopal. Mailing Add: Country Club Addition, Valentine, Nebr. 69201.

ADCOX, JIMMY DEAN D
Ark. State Rep.
b. Newport, Ark, 5/20/42; s. David W. Adcox, Sr.(deceased) and Lois Nance A; single. Educ: Ark. State Col, Beebe Br, A.A, 62; Ark. State Col, Jonesboro, 62-63. Polit. & Govt. Pos: Ark. State Rep, currently, mem, Pub. Health, Pub. Welfare and State Agency Cmts, Ark. House of Rep. Mem: Lions; Ark. Law Enforcement Asn. Rel: Church of Christ. Mailing Add: 303 Ash St, Newport, Ark. 72112.

ADCOX, JOHN R
Mem, Vance Co. Rep. Cent. Cmt, N.C.
b. Henderson, N.C, 8/13/18; s. Harry Howard Adcox and Effie Louise Horton A; m. 12/31/59 to Irene McPeak; c. Norman C. Roberson. Polit. & Govt. Pos: Chmn. and finance chmn, Vance Co. Rep. Exec. Cmt, N.C, 60-62, mem, 60-; mem, N.C. State Cent. and Exec. Cmts, 63-69; chmn, Second Cong. Dist. Rep. Party, currently. Bus. & Prof. Pos: Owner-mgr, John Adcox Assocs, Advert.-Pub. Rels, 63- Mil. Serv: Entered as Pvt, Army, 39, released as Chief Warrant Officer, W4, 59, after serv. in Civil Affairs and Mil. Govt, European Civil Affairs Div. and ETO, 43-45; Good Conduct Medal; Am. Defense Serv. Medal; Army of Occupation with 4 Overseas Bars; Am. Campaign Ribbon; Nat. Defense Serv. Medal; Europe-Africa-Middle East Campaign Medal with 4 Bronze Battle Stars; Certificate of Merit; Army Res, 60- Mem: N.C. Soc. Co. and Local Historians; chmn. civic affairs cmt, Moose Lodge 1412. Polit. cartooning and Letters to the Editor on polit. subjects; humorous cartoons for The New Yorker magazine. Rel: Methodist. Mailing Add: 574 N. William St, Henderson, N.C. 27536.

ADDABBO, JOSEPH PATRICK D
U.S. Rep, N.Y.
b. Queens, N.Y, 3/17/25; s. Dominick Addabbo and Anna A; m. to Grace Salamone; c. Dominic, Dina and Joseph. Educ: Boys' High Sch, Brooklyn; City Col; St. John's Law Sch, LL.B. Polit. & Govt. Pos: U.S. Rep, N.Y, 60-; del, Judicial Conv. Bus. & Prof. Pos: Gen. Practice Law, Ozone Park, N.Y. Mem: Queens Co. Bar Asn. Mailing Add: 132-43 86th St, Ozone Park, N.Y. 11817.

ADDINGTON, DONNA LORENE R
b. Blockton, Iowa, 7/20/28; d. Willis David McCalla and Nola Older M; m. 3/17/48 to William Hubert Addington; c. Mark Wayne. Polit. & Govt. Pos: Chmn, Morton Co. Rep. Cent. Cmt, Kans, 50-58, v.chmn, 58-60; del, Young Rep. Dist. and State Conv, 51 & 57-63; del, Kans. Dist. and Rep. State Conv, 52, 60 & 64; prog. chmn. and mem. bd. mgt, Kans. Fedn. Rep. Women, 55-64; nat. committeewoman, Kans. Fedn. Young Rep, 57-59, secy, 61-63; del, Young Rep. Nat. Conv, 57-63; mem. exec. bd. and co-dir. region seven, Nat. Fedn. Young Rep, 59-61; treas, Sedgwick Co. Women's Rep. Club, 61-63, first v.pres, 63-65; del, Rep. Nat. Conv, 64; Rep. Nat. committeewoman, Kans, 64-68. Bus. & Prof. Pos: Secy-treas, Moore Co. Grain Co, Dumas, 50-54, Addington Grain Co. of Tex, Amarillo, 59-63 and Addington Grain Co. Inc. of Kans, 59- Mem: Women Kans. Day Club. Rel: Methodist. Mailing Add: 6311 E. English, Wichita, Kans. 67218. (1967)

ADDISON, ROBERT A. R
Treas, Mich. Rep. Finance Cmt.
b. Grand Haven, Mich, 5/7/18; s. Fred J. Addison; m. 9/2/39 to Valaire York; c. Cynthia, Robert A, Jr. and Laurie (Mrs. James W. De Haven). Educ: Univ. Mich, A.B, 39, M.B.A, 41. Polit. & Govt. Pos: Finance chmn, St. Joseph Co. Rep. Cmt, 60-; treas, Fourth Dist. Rep. Cmt, 64-; Finance chmn, Fourth Dist. Rep. Party, 66-68; alternate del, Rep. Nat. Conv, 68; treas, Mich. Rep. Finance Cmt, currently. Bus. & Prof. Pos: V.pres, Kirsch Co, Sturgis, Mich, currently. Rel: Episcopal. Mailing Add: R.R. 1, Sturgis, Mich. 49091.

ADDONIZIO, HUGH J. D
Mayor, Newark, N.J.
b. Newark, N.J, 1/31/14; s. Frank Addonizio and Livia Barasso A; m. 7/6/42 to Doris Goodheart; c. Carol, Frank, Lois, James, Thomas and Joseph. Educ: Fordham Univ, B.S, 39; Student Officers Cand. Sch, Ft. Benning, Ga, 42. Polit. & Govt. Pos: Mayor, Newark, N.J, 62-; U.S. Rep, N.J, 81st -87th Cong. Bus. & Prof. Pos: A&C Clothing Co, Newark, N.J, 39-; v.pres, 46- Mil. Serv: Entered as 2nd Lt, Army, 42, released as Capt, 46, after serv. in 60th Inf, Ninth Div; Bronze Arrowhead with eight campaign stars; Bronze Star Medal; Combat Inf. Badge. Mem: VFW; Am. Legion; Ninth Div. Asn; Elks; Fordham Univ. Club of N.J. Rel: Roman Catholic. Mailing Add: 68 Hazelwood Ave, Newark, N.J. 07106.

ADDONIZIO, VICTOR F. D
s. Frank Addonizio and Livia A; m. to Agnes Russo; c. Victor, Richard, Raymond, Peter. Educ: Seton Hall Col; Augustana Col. Polit. & Govt. Pos: Former N.J. State Assemblyman. Bus. & Prof. Pos: Served in bus. mgt. at Essex Co. Penitentiary. Mil. Serv: Coast Artil, Air Corps; Inf. Bronze Star Medal. Mem: Essex Co. Employees' Asn; K. of C; St. Venantius Holy Name Soc; Orange Valley Parents Athletic Asn; Hugh J. Addonizio Asn. Mailing Add: 318 Carteret Terr, Orange, N.J. 07052. (1967)

ADELSHEIM, MARTHA ANN HENDERSON D
b. Pittsburgh, Pa, 6/28/15; d. Stuart Llewellyn Henderson and Gertrude Alcliffe Mevis H; m. 6/20/42 to Edward Kalman Adelsheim; c. David Brook, Peter Dolf and Michael Wood. Educ: Wellesley Col, B.A, 36. Polit. & Govt. Pos: Asst. economist, Bur. of Labor Statist, U.S. Dept. of Labor, 41-43; chmn, Dollars for Dem. Dr. and other pos. with Dem. Party; v.chmn, Ore. Dem. Party, 62-64, chmn, 64-67; proj. dir, Portland Parent-Child Serv, pre-Head Start, Off. of Econ. Opportunity, 68- Mem: YWCA; League of Women Voters; World Affairs Coun; bd. mem, Commun. Coun. of Portland. Chmn, Oregon's Great Decisions progs, 55-64. Mailing Add: 2755 S.W. Summit Dr, Portland, Ore. 97201.

ADELSTEIN, STANFORD MARK R
Committeeman, S.Dak. Rep. State Cent. Cmt.
b. Sioux City, Iowa, 8/19/31; s. Morris Ezekial Adelstein and Bertha Greenburg A; m. 12/19/52 to Ita Korn; c. Daniel, James David and Jon Stephen. Educ: Univ. Colo, Civil Eng, 53, Bus. Admin, 55. Polit. & Govt. Pos: Alternate del, Rep. Nat. Conv, 60 & 64; pres, State Young Rep. Party, 63-64; secy-treas, Pennington Co. Rep. Orgn, formerly; committeeman, S.Dak. Rep. State Cent. Cmt, currently. Bus. & Prof. Pos: Treas, Humboldt Realty Co; v.pres, Lawrence Realty and Wyo. Improv. Co; pres, Northwest. Eng. Co, S.Dak. Mil. Serv: Entered as Lt, Army, released from Nat. Guard as Capt. Mem: Past mem, Univ. Colo. Eng. Develop. Bd; Beavers; Am. Soc. Civil Engrs; Mil. Engrs; S.Dak. Asn. Engrs; Elks; United Fund; Am. Legion; pres. boys club bd, Rapid City Boys Club; St. John's McNamara Hosp. Bd; Arrowhead Country Club; Rapid City Libr. Bd; Young Pres. Orgn; Nat. Defense Exec. Res. Rel: Jewish; v.pres, Synagogue of the Black Hills. Legal Res: 1999 West Blvd, Rapid City, S.Dak. 57701. Mailing Add: P.O. Box 1392, Rapid City, S.Dak. 57701.

ADKINS, BERTHA SHEPPARD R
b. Salisbury, Md, 8/24/06; d. Frederick Paul Adkins and Edna May Sheppard A; single. Educ: Wellesley Col, A.B, 28; Columbia, A.M, 43. Hon. LL.D, West. Md. Col, 53, Hood Col, 58 and Wheaton Col, 60; hon. L.H.D, Wilson Col, 59. Polit. & Govt. Pos: Rep. Nat. Committeewoman, Md, 48-58; exec. dir, Women's Div, Rep. Nat. Cmt, 50-53; asst. chmn, Rep. Nat. Cmt. and head of Women's Div, 53-58; Undersecy. of Health, Educ. and Welfare, 58-60. Bus. & Prof. Pos: Teacher, private sch, Salisbury, 28-32; secretarial work, 32-34; dean of women, West. Md. Col, 34-42; dean of residence, Bradford Jr. Col, Mass, 42-46; headmistress, Foxcroft Sch, Middleburg, Va, 61-67. Mem: Pi Lamda Theta; Harbor Club (Easton, Md); Sulgrave Club (Wash.). Trustee, Am. Univ. Rel: Methodist. Mailing Add: P.O. Box 396, Oxford, Md. 21654.

ADKINS, JAMES CALHOUN, JR. D
Justice, Supreme Court of Fla.
b. Gainesville, Fla, 1/18/15; s. James Calhoun Adkins, Sr. and Elizabeth Edwards A; m. 7/15/52 to Ethel Fox; c. James C. III and Linda R. Educ: Univ. of Fla, J.D, 38; Pi Kappa Alpha; Phi Delta Phi. Polit. & Govt. Pos: Research aide, Supreme Court of Fla, 38-39, Justice, 69-; asst- attorney gen, Attorney Gen. Off, Fla, 39-41; asst. state attorney, Eighth Judicial Circuit of Fla, 57-59, judge, 64-69; judge, Alachua Co. Court of Record, 59-61. Mil. Serv: Entered as Pvt, Army, 45, released as Pfc, 45, after training. Publ: Florida Criminal Law and Procedure, 54, Florida Real Estate Law and Procedure, 59 and Trials, Florida Law and Practice, 66, Harrison Co. Mem: Fla. Bar; Am. Bar Asn; Am. Judicature Soc; Am. Legion; 40 et 8; Lions; WOW; Elks; Moose; K. of P; Mason. Recipient of Univ. of Fla. James W. Day Award for contribution to legal educ; Good Govt. Award, Jay-Cee's of Gainesville, Fla; Lecturer Award, Acad. of Fla. Trial Lawyers. Rel: Methodist. Legal Res: Fla. Supreme Court, Tallahassee, Fla. 32304. Mailing Add: P.O. Box 427, Tallahassee, Fla. 32303.

ADROUNIE, DOROTHY R
V.Chmn, Barry Co. Rep. Cmt, Mich.
b. Everek, Ankara, Turkey, 9/11/94; d. Tatios Kalaidjian and Rose Minasian

K; m. 8/9/12 to Dr. Harry Adrounie, wid; c. Lt. Col. V. Harry and Zabelle Dorothy (Mrs. Olson). Educ: Armenian Nationalist Sch; American Girls Seminary; Battle Creek Sanitarium, hydrotherapy training. Polit. & Govt. Pos: Del, Rep. State and County Convs, Mich; presidential elector, 60; area chmn, Fourth Dist. Rep. Party, 60-62, mem. exec. bd, Rep. Womens Fedn, 60-64, chmn. ways and means, 62-64; v.chmn, Barry Co. Rep. Cmt, 60-; alternate del, Rep. Nat. Conv, 64. Bus. & Prof. Pos: Sch. teacher, Turkey; chmn, State Conserv. Dept, Land and Water Div, 64- Mem: Barry Co. Rep. Women Club (pres, 58-69); Hastings Literary Club (pres, 56-58); chmn, Hosp. Guild; Mich. Women's Club Fedn.(state chmn. int. affairs, 68-69). Award for Best Adult Educ. Prog, Barry Co. Rep. Women's Club, 58; Silver Tray, Mich. Rep. Party, 69. Rel: Presbyterian. Mailing Add: 126 S. Broadway, Hastings, Mich. 49058.

ADUJA, PETER A. R
Hawaii State Rep.
b. Vigan, Philippines, 10/19/20; s. Dionicio Adjua and Francisca Aquino A; m. 7/31/49 to Melodie Cabalona; c. Jay and Rebecca. Educ: Univ. Hawaii, B.A, 44; Boston Univ. Sch. Law, LL.B, 51; Pre-Legal Club; For. Students Club; Bd. of Debates and Forensics. Polit. & Govt. Pos: Hawaii State Rep, First Dist, 54-56 and Eighth Dist, 66-; Dep. Attorney Gen, Hawaii, 57-60; dist. court magistrate, Honolulu, 60-62; Eighth Dist. del, Constitutional Conv, 68. Mil. Serv: Entered as Pvt, Army, 44, released as I-4, 46, after serv. in First Filipino Inf. Reg, Philippines, 45-46. Mem: Bar Asn. of Hawaii; Hawaii Govt. Employees Asn; Commun. Serv. & Health Asn. Hawaii; Boy Scouts; Am. Legion; Salvation Army Men's Soc. Serv; Honolulu C. of C; State Adult Educ: PTA; YMCA; Big Brothers. Rel: Protestant. Legal Res: 46-445 Holokaa St, Kaneohe, Hawaii 96744. Mailing Add: Room 204, 1136 Union Mall, Honolulu, Hawaii 96813.

AFFLERBACK, C. V. R
Chmn, Bucks Co. Rep. Cmt, Pa.
b. Phila, Pa, 7/23/18; s. Foster Afflerback and Elsie Stickler A; m. 10/5/51 to Lorraine Edgar; c. Carol, Diane, John, Donna, Debra, James and Gerald. Educ: LaSalle Col, 40-41; Univ. Pa, B.A, 48. Polit. & Govt. Pos: Committeeman, Phila. City Cmt, 48-54; pub. chmn, Middletown Twp. Rep. Asn, 57-58, pres, 59; committeeman, Bucks Co. Rep. Cmt, Pa, 58, exec. committeeman, 58-60, asst. chmn, 59-60, exec. dir. and chmn, 66-; chmn, Bristol Twp. Rep. Asn, 59; dir, Lower Bucks Rep. Club, 59; dep. dir, Bucks Co. Indust. Develop. Corp, 60-64; chmn. and exec. dir, Bucks Co. Redevelop. Authority, 62-66; chmn, State Tax Equalization Bd, 66-; del, Rep. Nat. Conv, 68. Bus. & Prof. Pos: Ed, Times Newspapers, 48-53; self-employed, Pub. Rels. Agency, Pa, part time since 48; pub. info. officer, Naval Aviation Supply Depot, 53-58; pub. rels. staff, Gray & Rogers Advert. Agency, 58-59; pub. rels. dir, Am. Cancer Soc, Phila. & Montgomery Co, 59-60. Mil. Serv: Entered as Pvt, Army, 41, released as S/Sgt, 45, after serv. in Ital. Intel. Sect, 133rd Inf. Div, ETO, 41-45; Legion of Merit; Bronze Star; Purple Heart; Combat Inf. Badge; European-African-Middle East. Theater Ribbon with 4 Stars; Am. Defense, Am. Campaign, Victory and Good Conduct Medals. Mem: Northeast and Am. Indust. Develop. Asns; Pa. Asn. of Housing and Redevelop. Authorities; Phila. Chap, Housing and Renewal Conf; Del. Valley Chap, Nat. Asn. of Housing & Redevelop. Officials; Bristol Lodge; hon mem, Bucks Co. Bd. of Realtors; bd. mem, Big Brothers, Inc. and Levittown Pub. Recreation Asn; Int. Asn. Assessing Officers; Elks; Circus Saints and Sinners. Legion of Honor award, Chapel of the Four Chaplains, 64; Commun. Leaders of Am. award, 68. Rel: Episcopal. Mailing Add: 7 Roving Rd, Levittown, Pa. 19056.

AGNEW, ANNE A. D
b. Marlboro Co, S.C; wid; c. 1 son. Educ: Converse Col, B. Mus. Polit. & Govt. Pos: Del, Dem. Nat. Conv, 44-68; parliamentarian, Richland Co. Dem. Women's Club, 64-; Dem. Nat. Committeewoman, S.C, 48-68. Bus. & Prof. Pos: Exec. secy, S.C. State Employee's Asn. Mem: Columbia Commun. Chest; S.C. Pub. Health Asn; adv. bd, S.C. Citizens Cmt. on Children and Youth. Rel: Methodist. Mailing Add: 2829 Blossom St, Columbia, S.C. 29205.

AGNEW, SPIRO THEODORE R
Vice President, United States
b. Baltimore, Md, 11/9/18; s. Theodore Spiro Agnew and Margaret Akers A; m. 5/27/42 to Elinor Isabel Judefind; c. James Rand, Pamela Lee, Susan Scott and Kimberly; grandchild, Michelle Ann Agnew. Educ: Johns Hopkins Univ, 3 years; Univ. Baltimore, LL.B, 47. Hon. LL.D, Univ. Md. and Morgan State Col. Polit. & Govt. Pos: From minority mem. to chmn, Baltimore Co. Bd. Appeals, Md, 57-61; co. exec, Baltimore Co, 62-67; dir, Nat. Asn. Counties, 63, former chmn, transportation cmt; former mem. exec. cmt, Nat. Gov. Conf. and former v.chmn, conf. cmt. on state-urban rels; former mem, Rep. Gov. Asn. Campaign Cmt. and Rep. Coord. Cmt. Task Force on Fed, Fiscal and Monetary Affairs; Gov, Md, 67-69; mem, Adv. Cmn. Intergovt. Rels, 69; Vice President, United States, 69- Bus. & Prof. Pos: Teacher night classes law, Univ. Baltimore, 59-66; former claims adjuster, Lumbermens Mutual Casualty Co; former personnel mgr, Sheiber Food Stores; attorney-at-law. Mil. Serv: 2nd Lt, Army, 42-46, with serv. in Tenth Armored Div, France and Germany, 44-45; recalled for 1 year during Korean Conflict; Bronze Star; Four Battle Stars; Combat Inf. Badge. Mem: Md. and Baltimore Bar Asns; past pres, Loch Raven Kiwanis, Loch Raven Inter-Commun. Coun. and Dumbarton Jr. High Sch. PTA; Am. Legion; Order of the AHEPA. Rel: Episcopal. Legal Res: Towson, Md. 21204. Mailing Add: Office of the Vice President of the United States, Washington, D.C. 20501.

AGNICH, FRED JOSEPH R
b. Eveleth, Minn, 7/19/13; s. John Agnich and Angeleine Germaine A; m. 4/19/41 to Ruth Harriet Welton; c. William F, Richard J. and James R. Educ: Univ. Minn, B.A. in Geol, 37. Polit. & Govt. Pos: Chmn, Dallas Co. for Goldwater, Tex, 64; asst. south. regional dir. in charge of polit. orgn, Wash, D.C, 64; finance chmn, Tower Campaign, 66; chmn, Dallas Co. Rep, Party, 67-69; del, Rep. Nat. Conv, 68. Bus. & Prof. Pos: Exec. v.pres, Geophys. Serv, Inc, Dallas, 51-56, pres, 56-59, chmn. bd, 59-61; v.pres. and dir, Tex. Instruments, Inc, 59-61; dir, Tex. Mid-Continent Oil & Gas Asn, currently; dir, Henderson Co. Savings & Loan Asn, Athens, currently; chmn. bd, Scama Corp, Dallas, currently. Publ: Lead Paper on 'Geophysical Exploration for Lime Stone Reefs,' 55. Mem: Int. Platform Asn; Tex. Rep. Task Force on Job Opportunities and Econ.Growth; Nat. Coun. of Nat. Planning Asn; trustee, Southwest Center Adv. Studies; Univ. Minn. Alumni Asn.(dir); Am. Asn. Petroleum Geophysicists; Soc. Exploration Geophysicists; Dallas Geophys. and Geol. Soc; Dallas Wildcat Cmt; dir, Dallas Mus. Fine Arts, Dallas Civic Opera and Dallas Hist. Soc; Dallas Petroleum Club (dir); Tex. and Southwest. Cattle Raisers Asn; Circle Ten Coun, Boy Scouts; Air Force Asn; Dallas Gun Club; Nat. Wildlife Fedn. Rel: Presbyterian. Legal Res: 5206 Kelsey Rd, Dallas, Tex, 75229. Mailing Add: 4025 First National Bank Bldg, Dallas, Tex. 75202.

AGNOLI, BRUNO D
b. New York, N.Y, 1/6/11; s. Anthony Agnoli and Victoria Anna Gatti A; m. 1/27/38 to Nellie G. Taylor; c. Brenda (Mrs. Perlstein), Tonia (Mrs. Greger), Marena (Mrs. Richardson), Diana (Mrs. Binns), Elissa (Mrs. Monprode), Annetta and Gina. Educ: Toms River High Sch. Polit. & Govt. Pos: Co. committeeman, Dem. Party, N.J, 20 years; policeman, Dover Twp, 32-38; spec. investr, committeeman and co. chmn, Irregular Voting, 32-42; spec. sheriff's dep. and constable Ocean Co, 35-45; cand. for sheriff, 50; chmn, Ocean Co. Elec. Bd, 59-60; munic. chmn, Ocean Co. Dem. Party, 64; del, Dem. Nat. Conv, 64; former pres, Co. Seat Dem. Club; for. mem, Ocean Co. Dem. Orgn; campaign mgr. for many elec; mem, N.J. State Dem. Cmt, 69; mem, Ocean Co. Dem. Exec. Cmt. Rel: Catholic. Mailing Add: 113 James St, Toms River, N.J. 08753.

AGOSTINI, WANDA E. R
Mem, Rep. State Cent. Cmt, Calif.
b. Medford, Ore, 3/16/27; s. Irving L. Eddy and Amelia Owen; m. 3/25/50 to Leo M. Agostini; c. Steven Alan Minor and Ellis Owen. Educ: Sacramento City Col, 46-47. Polit. & Govt. Pos: Pres, Redding Rep. Women's Club, Calif, 59-61; Shasta Co. co-chmn, Shell for Gov. Campaign, 62, Goldwater for Pres. Campaign, 64 and Reagan for Gov. Campaign, 66; mem, Rep. State Cent. Cmt, Calif, 62-; v.chmn, Shasta Co. Rep. Cent. Cmt, 63-; pub. mem. and v.pres, Calif. State Bd. of Nursing Educ. and Nurse Registrn, 68- Bus. & Prof. Pos: Exec. secy, United Crusade of Shasa Co, 54-56. Mem: Nat. and Calif. Fedns. Rep. Women; Calif. Young Rep; Toastmistress Int; Calif. Cong. of Parents and Teachers. Rel: Methodist. Mailing Add: 5401 Elm Lane, Redding, Calif. 96001.

AGUIAR, ANTONE SOUZA, JR. D
Mass. State Rep.
b. Fall River, Mass, 1/2/30; s. Antonio S. Aguiar and Angelina Perry A; m. 6/11/60 to Gertrud Waltraud Kienert; c. Christopher and Stephanie. Educ: Yale Univ, B.A, 52; Georgetown Law Sch, LL.B, 55; Phi Delta Phi; Morris Law Club. Polit. & Govt. Pos: Mem, Bd. of Selectmen, Swansea, Mass, 61-; Mass. State Rep, 64- Bus. & Prof. Pos: Practice of law, Fall River, Mass, 58-; baseball coach, Bradford Durfee Col. of Tech, 59-63. Mil. Serv: Entered as Pvt, Army, 55, released as 1st Lt, 58, after serv. in ETO; Maj, Army Res, 58-65. Mem: Fall River, Bristol Co. and Boston Bar Asns; ROA; Portuguese Am. Civic League; C. of C; Lions. Rel: Roman Catholic. Legal Res: 22 Hetherington Dr, Swansea, Mass. 02777. Mailing Add: State House of Representatives, State Capital Bldg, Boston, Mass. 02133. (1967)

AHART, THOMAS INSELL R
Chmn, Mich. Fedn. Young Rep.
b. Detroit, Mich, 4/3/38; s. Greek Ahart and Eula Reid A; m. 6/26/65 to Menda Britton. Educ: Wayne State Univ, B.A, 62, grad. sch, 68-; Omega Psi Phi. Polit. & Govt. Pos: Chmn, Downtown Detroit Young Rep. Club, Mich, 64-66; del, Young Rep. Nat. Conv, 65 & 67 and chmn, Nat. Del, 69; alternate del, Rep. Nat. Conv, 68; chmn, Mich. Fedn. Young Rep, 67- Mem: Founders Soc; Detroit Inst. of Arts; Asn. for the Study of Negro Life and Hist; NAACP; v.pres, Detroit Jaycees. Rel: Protestant. Mailing Add: 18644 Muirland, Detroit, Mich. 48221.

AHEARN, FRANK EDWARD D
b. Boston, Mass, 8/27/30; s. David Bartholomew Ahearn and Mary O'Callahan A; m. 8/11/56 to Mary McGovern; c. Stephen, Eileen and Elise. Educ: Boston Col, B.S, 55; Georgetown Univ. Law Sch, LL.D, 58. Polit. & Govt. Pos: Corp. Counsel, Town of S. Windsor, 63-; Conn. state rep, 63-67. Mil. Serv: Entered Marine Corps, 50, released as Pfc, after serv. in Korean Conflict; Campaign Ribbons, Korean Conflict. Mem: Lions. Legal Res: 36 Peach Tree Lane, Wapping, Conn. 06087. Mailing Add: 279 Oakland Rd, Wapping, Conn. 06087. (1967)

AHEE, JOE D
b. Scranton, Pa, 2/2/14; s. Solomon Ahee and Sarah Haddad A; m. 12/4/43 to Ann Louise Martin; c. Joseph Edward. Educ: Univ. Ariz, B.S. in Bus. Admin, 38. Polit. & Govt. Pos: Adj. Gen. of Ariz, 65-66. Bus. & Prof. Pos: Mgr, Mgt. Syst, Standards and Data Anal. Dept, Pac. Archit. and Engrs, currently. Mil. Serv: Entered Army 38, retired as Col, 65; asst mil. attache, Egypt, 41-42; comdr, Tank Bn, Europe, 43-47; chief tactics dept, Armored Sch, 48-50; assigned mil. mission to Venezuela, 52-55; chief training div, 5th Army, 55-57; Nat. Guard Bur, 60-63; comdr, Ft. Douglas, Utah, 64-65; Silver Star; Legion of Merit; Bronze Star with oak leaf cluster; Purple Heart with two oak leaf clusters; Commendation Ribbon with oak leaf cluster; Crois de Guerre, Luxembourg and Belgium; various area and campaign ribbons. Mem: Nat. Guard Asn. U.S; Nat. Guard Asn. Ariz; Nat. Rifle Asn; Asn. U.S. Army. Mailing Add: 8480 E. Chaparral Rd, Scottsdale, Ariz. 85251.

AHLERS, JOHN CLARKE R
b. Baltimore, Md, 7/3/27; s. John A. Ahlers and Madeline Clark A; m. 2/20/54 to Katherine C. Smith; c. Clarke Francis, Michael McCardell and Katherine Marie. Educ: Loyola Col, Md, 44-46; Loyola Univ. of South, La, A.B, 48. Bus. & Prof. Pos: Reporter, New Orleans Time-Picayune, 49-50 and Baltimore Evening Sun, 50-55; exec. secy. to U.S. Sen. J. Glenn Beall, Md, 55-63; admin. asst. to Mayor T.R. McKeldin, Baltimore, 63-65; admin. asst. to U.S. Sen. George Murphy, Calif, 65- Mil. Serv: Entered as A/S, Navy, 45, released as Seaman 1/C, 46. Mem: Nat. Press Club; Senate Asn. of Admin. Assts. and Secretaries. Rel: Catholic. Legal Res: 14129 Flint Rock Rd, Rockville, Md. 20853. Mailing Add: 452 Senate Office Bldg, Washington, D.C. 20510.

AHLQUIST, HUGO MAURICE R
b. Denver, Colo, 11/12/02; s. Thure Maurice Ahlquist and Carolyn Lillie Johnson A; m. 10/1/55 to Gussie May Crain; c. John Stribling. Educ: Dartmouth Col, A.B, 25; Lambda Chi Alpha. Polit. & Govt. Pos: Wash. State Rep, 57-65; mem, Pac. Northwest River Basin Cmn. and West. States Water Coun; dir, Wash. State Dept. Water Resources, 65- Bus. & Prof. Pos: Farmer. Mem: Mason; Shrine; Farm Bur; Elks; C. of C. Rel: Christian. Mailing Add: 1929 Forest Hill Dr, Olympia, Wash. 98501.

AIKEN, BENJAMIN OTIS D
Md. State Del.
b. Granville Co, N.C, 7/19/99; s. Rufus Judson Aiken and Nora Hester A; m. 8/12/32 to Hildegarde Miller; c. Barbara (Mrs. Ray S. VanSickle), Martha (Mrs. Best), Margaret (Mrs. Arthur P. Byrne), William Ernest and Amelia (Mrs. Louis Abraham). Educ: Trinity Col, A.B, 22; Duke Univ, M.A, 27. Polit. & Govt. Pos: Md. State Del, Garrett Co, 67- Bus. & Prof. Pos: Prin, Accident High Sch, Md, 30-52; teacher, Poolesville High Sch, 52-54; teacher, Sherwood High Sch, Sandy Spring, 54-62. Mil. Serv: Army, 18, Pvt. Mem: Am. Legion Post 208; Garrett Co. and Md. Farm Burs; Rotary. Medal Valley Forge Found, 60. Rel: Lutheran. Mailing Add: Route 1, Accident, Md. 21520.

AIKEN, GEORGE DAVID R
U.S. Sen, Vt.
b. Dummerston, Vt, 8/20/92; m. to Beatrice M. Howard; c. Mrs. Dorothy Morse, Mrs. Marjorie Cleverly, Howard (deceased), Mrs. Barbara Jones. Polit. & Govt. Pos: Vt. State Rep, 30-34, Speaker, Vt. State House of Rep, 33-34; Lt. Gov, Vt, 33-37, Gov, 37-41; U.S. Sen, Vt, 41- Legal Res: Putney, Vt. 05346. Mailing Add: 358 Old Senate Office Bldg, Washington, D.C. 20510. (1967)

AIKEN, ISAAC MEANS Independent
b. Brunswick, Ga, 8/14/99; s. Franklin Dunwody Aiken and Frances Buford King A; m. to Alice McDonald Harrison; c. Isaac M, Jr. and J.S. Harrison. Educ: Swanee Mil. Acad, 16-17; Ga. Inst. Tech, 17-18; Chi Phi. Polit. & Govt. Pos: Chmn, Brunswick Port Authority, Ga, 50- Bus. & Prof. Pos: From asst. cashier to v.pres, Am. Nat. Bank, 19-41, pres, 41-64, chmn. bd, 64- Mil. Serv: 2nd Lt, Army, 18, serv. in Motor Transport Corps Training Unit, Wentworth Inst. Mem: Kiwanis; Brunswick and Glynn Co. C. of C; Navy League; Elks; dir, Boys Club of Glynn. Rel: Episcopal. Mailing Add: 103 Fraser St, St. Simons Island, Ga. 31522.

AIKEN, RUTH MERLE JONES R
Chmn, Knox Co. Rep. Cmt, Maine
b. Boston, Mass, 2/19/21; d. Frank Poor Jones and Lily Gould Pippy J; m. 7/11/50 to Aubrey William Aiken; c. David Cobb, Susan Poor and Peter Horton-Jones. Educ: Chamberlain Sch, grad, 40; Mus. Sch. Fine Arts. Polit. & Govt. Pos: Rep. State Committeewoman, Maine, 57-; secy, Knox Co. Rep. Cmt, 60-64, v.chmn, 64 and chmn, 64-; pres, Knox Co. Rep. Women's Club, 62-63; mem, Cmt. Voc. Rehab, 64-65; Knox Co. chmn, Citizens for Nixon and Women for Nixon-Agnew, 68; mem. exec. cmt, Rep. State Cmt, 68-69 and chmn. sub-cmt. on Young Rep, 69- Bus. & Prof. Pos: Mem. bd. dirs, Hands Inc, 65- Mem: Girl Scout Leaders; Cub Den Mother, Boy Scouts. Rel: Methodist. Legal Res: Driftwood Farm, Hathorne Point, South Cushing, Maine. Mailing Add: Pleasant Point, Knox Co, Maine 04563.

AINLEY, GRETA M. R
b. 8/14/00; married; c. three. Educ: Univ. Pa, 21. Polit. & Govt. Pos: Del, Constitution Conv, N.H, 56-64; N.H. State Rep, 57-68; alternate del, Rep. Nat. Conv, 60 & 68; mem, Manchester Civic Prog. Cmn, 60-64; pres, Rep. Club. Mil. Serv: Lt, Red Cross Motor Corps, 40-46; Quaker Relief, France, 46. Mem: Founder and life trustee, Libr. Guild, Notre Dame Col, 50, pres, 60-64; YWCA; Manchester Red Cross; Manchester Hist. Soc; New Eng. Women; Francaise of Paris; past pres, Manchester Women's Club. Rel: Catholic. Mailing Add: 1165 Union St, Manchester, N.H. 03104. (1967)

AINSLEY, WILLIAM FRANKLIN D
Chmn, Perquimans Co. Dem. Exec. Cmt, N.C.
b. Wash. Co, N.C, 11/23/14; s. Benjamin Franklin Ainsley and Martha West A; m. 6/1/37 to Doris Gregory; c. William Franklin, Jr. and Margaret Lynne. Educ: Wake Forest Col, 1 year. Polit. & Govt. Pos: Chmn, Perquimans Co. Bd. Elections, N.C, 46-52; mem, Perquimans Co. Cong. Cmt, 52-; mem, Chowan, Pasquetank, Perquimans Hwy. Cmn, 62- and chmn, 65; mem, City Coun, Hertford, N.C, 63-; chmn, Perquimans Co. Dem. Exec. Cmt, currently; del, Nat. Dem. Conv, 68. Bus. & Prof. Pos: Owner, Gregory's 5-10-25¢ Store and Ainsley Realty Co; part owner, Allstate Wholesale Builders Supply, Inc. Mil. Serv: Entered as Pvt, Army, 43, released as Buck Sgt, 45, after serv. in Combat Engrs, Iceland and Europe; Am. & ETO Ribbons; 3 Battle Stars; Presidential Unit Citation; Good Conduct Medal. Mem: Trustee, Col. of the Albemarle; Scottish Rite; Mason; Shrine; master, Perquimans Lodge 106 AF&AM; past pres, secy. & treas, Rotary; chmn, Dept. of N.C. Resolutions Cmt; Dept. of N.C. Civil Defense Cmt. Received Nat. Achievement Award for Serv, Am. Legion. Rel: Baptist, Deacon, Hertford Baptist Church. Legal Res: 108 N. Convent Garden St, Hertford, N.C. 27944. Mailing Add: P.O. Box 22, Hertford, N.C. 27944.

AINSWORTH, WILBURN EUGENE, JR. D
b. Jackson, Miss, 8/2/41; s. Wilburn Eugene Ainsworth and Johnnie Barlow A; m. 7/5/64 to Joy Lynn Williamson; c. Lynn. Educ: Millsaps Col, B.S, 64; Jackson Sch. Law, LL.B, 67; Kappa Alpha. Polit. & Govt. Pos: Admin. asst. to U.S. Congressman G.V. Montgomery, Miss, 67- Rel: Methodist. Legal Res: P.O. Box 123, Florence, Miss. 39073. Mailing Add: 6421 King Louis Dr, Alexandria, Va. 22312.

AITKEN, JOHN WINFIELD R
Md. State Del.
b. Carbondale, Pa, 8/26/35; s. Robert Stark Aitken and Alice Tiffany Spencer A; m. 11/29/58 to Janet Clarissa Hartman; c. John, Jr. and Jennifer Lyn. Educ: Nanzan Univ, Naguya, Japan; Univ. Md. Polit. & Govt. Pos: Del, Rep. State Conv, Md, 64-; Md. State Del, 67- Bus. & Prof. Pos: Prog. chmn, Mid Atlantic Sales Cong, 69. Mil. Serv: Entered as Airman, Air Force, 55, released as A 1/C, 59. Mem: D.C. and Nat. Asn. Life Underwriters; Cmn. on Soc. Concerns (past chmn). Rel: Methodist; Past sponsor Youth Fel. Legal Res: 5700 Annamarie Court, Derwood, Md. 20855. Mailing Add: Suite 208, 414 Hungerford Dr, Rockville, Md, 20850.

AITKEN, WYLIE ARTHUR D
b. Detroit, Mich; s. Jens R. Aitken and Antoinette Elise O'Leary A; m. 9/6/63 to Elizabeth Louise Robb; c. Darren O'Leary and Christopher Robb. Educ: Santa Ana Col, A.A, 61; Calif. State at Fullerton, 61-62; Marquette Univ, J.D, 65; Phi Alpha Theta; Delta Theta Phi; St. Thomas More Scholar; Scholarship Key of Delta Theta Phi. Polit. & Govt. Pos: Pres, Santa Ana Col. Young Dem, 60; chmn, Lawyers For Robert F. Kennedy, Orange Co, Calif, 68; alternate del, Dem. Nat. Conv, 68; pres, Kennedy Club of Orange Co, 69- Publ: 'Jury Instruction Process,' 65 and 'Death Knell For The Misappropriation Theory, 65, Marquette Law Rev. Mem: Orange Co, Calif. and Am. Bar Asns; Calif. and Am. Trial Lawyers Asns; Orange Co. Trial Lawyers Asn. (treas, 68, v.pres, 69). Rel: Catholic. Mailing Add: 1341 Valencia, Placentia, Calif. 92670.

AJELLO, CARL RICHARD D
Majority Leader, Conn. House of Rep.
b. Derby, Conn, 8/22/32; s. Carl R. Ajello, Sr. and Kathryn Flanigan A; m. 6/10/55 to Jacqueline Culmo; c. Michele and Carl III. Educ: Univ. Conn, B.S, 53; N.Y. Univ. Sch. Law, LL.B, 56; Sigma Chi. Polit. & Govt. Pos: Justice of peace, Ansonia, Conn, 60-64, corp. counsel, 64-; Conn. State Rep, 63-, majority leaders, 69- and former asst. majority leader; Conn. mem, Northeast. Forest Fire Protective Asn, 68- Bus. & Prof. Pos: Private law practice, 60-65; partner: Olderman, Winnick, Condon, Ajello & Savitt, 65- Mil. Serv: Entered as 1st Lt, Army, 57, released as Capt, 60. Mem: Rotary; Elks; Am. Trial Lawyers Asn; Am. and Conn. Bar Asns; Naugatuck Valley Bar Asn. (pres, 69-); Am. Judicature Soc; dir, Ansonia Commun. Chest; Naugatuck Valley Mental Health Steering Cmt. Rel: Roman Catholic. Legal Res: 10 John St, Ansonia, Conn. 06401. Mailing Add: 58 High St, Ansonia, Conn. 06401.

AJIFU, RALPH K. R
Hawaii State Rep.
b. Kaneohe, Hawaii, 6/26/26; s. Matsuume Ajifu and Umito Yamashiro A; m. 3/19/49 to Toyoko Takiguchi; c. Laura, Clayton, Sharon, Aileen, Michael and Lois. Educ: Benjamin Parker High Sch, grad. Polit. & Govt. Pos: Mem, Bd. of Agr. and Conserv, State of Hawaii, 59, chmn, Land Use Cmn, 61; Hawaii State Rep, 67- Bus. & Prof. Pos: Owner-mgr, Kaneohe Pork Center, 44- Mem: Hawaii Young Farmers Asn; Farm Bur; Kaneohe Commun. Coun. Rel: Methodist. Legal Res: 45-109 Awele Place, Kaneohe, Hawaii 96744. Mailing Add: P.O. Box 402, Kaneohe, Hawaii 96744.

AKERS, HERBERT S. R
b. Montvale, N.J, 1/7/28; s. Herbert S. Akers and Esther Glaspey A; m. 4/20/50 to Jean Louise Jepsen; c. Herbert S, Edward J, Mark P. and John T. Educ: Del. Col. Sci. and Agr, B.S, 51; class v.pres; A day chmn; pres. and founder, Animal Husbandry Club. Polit. & Govt. Pos: Mo. State Rep, 30th Dist, 67-69. Mil. Serv: Entered as Pvt, Pa. Nat. Guard, released as Sgt, 51, after serv. in 28th Div, 111th R.C.T. Mem: Asst. dist. cmnr, Boy Scouts; Lions. Rel: Methodist. Mailing Add: 3960 Celburne Lane, Bridgeton, Mo. 63042. (1967)

AKERS, ROBERT WOOD
b. Topeka, Kans, 10/7/05; s. Everett B. Akers and Mabel M. Wood A; m. 3/9/56 to Sibylle de l'Epine; c. Margaret Ann. Educ: Washburn Univ, 23-24; Univ. Chicago, 24; Univ. Texas, 25-26; Phi Delta Theta. Polit. & Govt. Pos: Lectr, State Dept, India, Philippines, Japan, Korea, 53; former dep. dir, U.S. Info. Agency. Bus. & Prof. Pos: Reporter, Topeka State J, 22-23, Chicago City News Bur, 24-25, San Antonio Evening News, 25 and Beaumont Enterprise, 26; daily news commentator, Radio Sta. KRIC, 39-42 & 45; city ed, managing ed, ed. and ed-in-chief, Beaumont Enterprise, 53-64; ed-in-chief, Beaumont J, 53-64; v.pres. and secy, The Enterprise Co, Beaumont, 56-64. Mil. Serv: Army Inf, 42-46, serv. in France, 44-45; Purple Heart. Rel: Roman Catholic. Mailing Add: 5319 Potomac Ave. N.W, Washington, D.C. 20016. (1967)

AKESON, HARVEY O. D
Ore. State Rep.
b. Portland, Ore, 11/14/37; m. Polit. & Govt. Pos: Ore. State Rep, Multnomah Co, 69- Rel: Lutheran. Mailing Add: 13034 S.E. Salmon, Portland, Ore. 97233.

AKIN, EDWARD B. D
Chmn, Mason Co. Dem. Party, Ill.
b. Louisville, Ky, 6/30/11; s. Edward Leslie Akin and Addie Rafferty A; div; c. Michael Leslie. Educ: High Sch. grad. Polit. & Govt. Pos: Mem, Selective Serv. Bd. 170, Mason Co, Ill, 49-; supt, Div. Vet. Serv. Ment. Health, 50-52; Dem. committeeman, Precinct One, Mason City, 58-; adminstr, Ill. Vet. Cmn, 60-69; chmn, Mason Co. Dem. Party, 60- Bus. & Prof. Pos: Asst. adj, Dept. of Ill, Am. Legion, 52-60. Mil. Serv: Entered as Pvt, Army, 43, released as T/Sgt, 46, after serv. in Co. F. 328th Regt, 26th Inf. Div, ETO, 44-46; Good Conduct Medal; three battle stars, Bronze Star. Mem: AF&AM; Scottish Rite; Shrine; Eastern Star; Amvets; VFW Post 1232; Am. Legion Post 495; Vet. Asn. Boston. Rel: Methodist. Mailing Add: 116 N. Perry, Mason City, Ill. 62664.

AKINS, GUY BROOKINS, JR. D
Mem, Colo. Dem. State Cent. Cmt.
b. Boulder, Colo, 6/13/30; s. Guy Brookins Akins and Rachel Conda A; m. Jan. 20 to Phyllis Carlson; c. Clark S, Jeffrey A. and Bruce J. Educ: Univ. Colo. Polit. & Govt. Pos: Del, Boulder Co. Dem. Cent. Cmt, Colo, 64, 66 & 68; co. cmnr, Boulder Co, 64-69; mem, Colo. State Asn. of Co. Cmnrs, 65-66, Nat. Asn. of Co. Offs, 65-69 and Interstate Asn. of Pub. Land Counties, 66-68; mem. exec. cmt, Denver Regional Coun. of Govts, 66-69; mem, Colo. Dem. State Cent. Cmt, 68- Bus. & Prof. Pos: Sales mgr, Royal Metal Prod, Arvada, Colo, 64; co-owner, Ov-Ak Quarter Horses, Boulder, 67-; consult, Carl S. Becker Co, Denver, 69- Mil. Serv: Entered as A/S, Navy, 50, released as MM 3/C, 54, after serv. in U.S.S. Rogers DDR-876, Pac. and Korea, 50-53; Korean, China Serv, UN and Good Conduct Medals. Mem: Am. Legion; Lake Valley Golf Club. Rel: Lutheran. Mailing Add: 845 34th St, Boulder, Colo. 80303.

AKIZAKI, CLARENCE YASUO D
b. Honolulu, Hawaii, 5/12/28; s. Rev. Yoshio Akizaki and Hanayo Muramoto A; m. 2/27/54 to Peggy Yaeno Shishido; c. Claudia Tomiko and Vincent Takao. Educ: West. Col. of Radio. Polit. & Govt. Pos: Hawaii State Rep, 63-67. Bus. & Prof. Pos: Mgr, Akizaki Radio & TV Sales, 47-58; pres, Akizaki Enterprises, Inc, 58- Mil. Serv: Entered as Pvt, Army, 51, released as Sgt, 52, after serv. in First Cavalry Div, Korea; Inf. Combat Badge. Mem: Dir, Pawaa-McCully Bus. and Prfnl. Asn. Rel: Shinto. Mailing Add: 2124 S. King St, Honolulu, Hawaii 96814. (1967)

ALAIMO, ANTHONY ALFRED R
Mem, Ga. State Rep. Cent. Cmt.
b. Termini, Sicily, 3/29/20; s. Sam Alaimo and Sandra Granza A; m. 6/11/46 to Jeanne Evelyn Loy; c. Philip Lewis. Educ: Ohio North. Univ, B.A, 40; Emory Univ, J.D, 48; Phi Delta Phi; Delta Sigma Phi. Polit. & Govt. Pos: Del, Rep. Nat. Conv, 60, 64 & 68; mem, Glynn Co. Rep. Exec. Cmt. and Eighth Dist. Rep. Exec. Cmt, Ga, 60-; mem, Platform Cmt, Ga. Rep. Party, 60, Rules Cmt, 64, Credentials Cmt, 66 and gen. coun, 66-68; mem, Rep. Nat. Rules Cmt, 64; chmn, Cmn. Roads & Revenues, Glynn Co, 66-; cmnr, Glynn Co, 65-; mem, Ga. State Rep. Cent. Cmt, 66- Bus. & Prof. Pos: Mem. law firm, Alaimo, Taylor and Bishop, Brunswick, Ga, currently. Mil. Serv: Entered as Aviation Cadet, Air Force, 41, released as 1st Lt, 46; ETO Ribbons; Prisoner of War, Germany, 2 yrs. Mem: Bd. gov, Ga. Bar Asn, 62-, cmt. on rev. of rules of practice and procedure, 65; incorporator, State Bar of Ga. and mem. cmt. for creation and formulation of rules, 64; nat. committeeman, Am. Trial Lawyers Asn, Ga, 59 and 65-66, bd. gov, 66-68; 1st ed, Ga. Plaintiff's Trial Lawyers Asn, 57-58; pres, Brunswick Bar Asn, 65-66; Am. Bar Asn; Atlanta Lawyers Club; chmn, Coastal Area Planning Cmn, 66-69; bd. dirs, Ga. Planning Asn, 67-69. Rel: Methodist. Legal Res: 209 W. Musgrove, Sea Island, Ga. 31522. Mailing Add: Box 705, Sea Island, Ga. 31561.

ALAIMO, CHARLES B. R
Chmn, Enfield Rep. Town Cmt, Conn.
b. Enfield, Conn, 8/29/28; s. Benjamin C. Alaimo and Claudia Lamagna A; m. 3/26/51 to Eugenia Himes; c. Benjamin, Judith, Michael, Peter, Veronica, Elizabeth and Christopher. Educ: Duquesne Univ, B.A, 50; Boston Univ. Sch. Law, L.L.B, 52. Polit. & Govt. Pos: Asst. prosecutor, Town Court, Enfield, Conn, 59-61, town counsel, 61-63, mem. bd. finance, 61-63; chmn, Enfield Rep. Town Cmt, 68- Mem: Am, Conn, Hartford Co. and Enfield Bar Asns; Elks; Enfield Jaycees (secy, 55-57, dir, 55-59); Enfield C. of C.(secy, 67-). Rel: Catholic. Legal Res: 182 Abbe Rd, Hazardville, Conn. 06036. Mailing Add: 709 Enfield St, Thompsonville, Conn. 06082.

ALANSON, ANN D
Mem, Calif. Dem. State Cent. Cmt.
b. San Francisco, Calif, 9/24/26; d. David Wertheim and Eleanor Patek W; m. 4/27/46 to Lionel Mason Alanson, Jr; c. Mary. Educ: Conn. Col. for Women, New London, 44-45. Polit. & Govt. Pos: Former treas. San Francisco Dem. Youth Asn; chmn, Calif. Dollars for Dem, 57-59; women's chmn, Dem. Cent. Cmt, North. Calif, 62-65; women's chmn, President Johnson Campaign North. Calif, 64; Dem. nat. committeewoman, Calif, 65-69; del, Dem. Nat. Conv, 68; mem, Calif. State Dem. Cent. Cmt, 68- Bus. & Prof. Pos: With Books, Inc, San Francisco, 50-56; Book Review, TV Weekly Show Lets Look at Books, 51-54; bd. dirs, Nations, Inc; Youth Camp on For. Affairs. Mem: Calif. Hist. Soc; mem, Auxiliaries, Mt. Zion Hosp, San Francisco, San Francisco Museum of Art and Hebrew Home for Aged. Mailing Add: 65 Montclair Terr, San Francisco, Calif. 94109. (1967)

ALARCON, ANGELITA D
Mem, Calif. Dem. State Cent. Cmt.
b. Los Angeles, Calif, 1/13/24; d. Manuel Alarcon and Antonia Armas A; single. Educ: Bowie High Sch, El Paso, Tex, 40-41. Polit. & Govt. Pos: Dist. rep, Calif. State Assemblyman John Burton, 20th Assembly Dist, 68; co-chmn, U.S. Rep. Philip Burton, Fifth Cong. Dist, 68; mem, Calif. Dem. State Cent. Cmt, currently. Bus. & Prof. Pos: Mem, electronics staff, Lynch Commun. Syst, San Francisco, Calif, 64. Mem: Mex-Am. Polit. Asn; Mission Coalition Orgn; Calif. Dem. Coun; G.I. Forum Womens Auxiliary; VFW; Spanish Speaking Citizen's Found. Rel: Catholic. Mailing Add: 238 San Carlos St, San Francisco, Calif. 94110.

ALARID, MICHAEL D
N.Mex. State Sen.
b. 1924. Educ: Univ. of Mex, B.A; Univ. N.Mex. Col. of Law, 1 year; Delta Sigma Pi. Polit. & Govt. Pos: Mem, Albuquerque Planning Cmn, 56-59; mem, N.Mex. Vet. Serv. Cmn, 57-; N.Mex. State Rep, until 66; N.Mex. State Sen, 67- Bus. & Prof. Pos: Supermarket proprietor and ins. agent. Mem: Charter mem. N. Mex. Boys State; Am. Legion; VFW; Elks. Rel: Catholic. Mailing Add: 1608 Escalante Ave. SW, Albuquerque, N.Mex. 87104.

ALBANESE, VITO A. D
b. Jersey City, N.J, 9/14/17; s. Pasquale Albanese and Colangela Impagliazzo A; m. 2/4/40 to Frances Mary Arcieri, div; c. Loretta Jean and Vito, Jr. Polit. & Govt. Pos: Mem, Ft. Lee Planning Bd, N.J, 59-62; Ft. Lee Dem. Munic. Chmn, 61-66; del, Dem. Nat. Conv, 64; N.J. State Assemblyman, 66-67. Bus. & Prof. Pos: Personnel rels. dir, New Haven Bd. and Carton Co; pres, Pulp, Sulphite and Paper Mill Workers, Union Local 630; exec. secy, Bergen Co. Cent. Trades and Labor Coun; pres, Danny's Excelsior Travel Agency, Annex Inc. and 783 Palisade Ave. Corp; secy-treas, Vito Enterprises, Inc. Mem: Unico; Lions; F&AM. Rel: Episcopal. Mailing Add: 3 Horizon Rd, Fort Lee, N.J. 07024.

ALBANO, VINCENT FRANCIS, JR. R
Chmn, N.Y. Co. Rep. Cmt, N.Y.
b. New York, N.Y, 5/5/14; s. Vincent F. Albano, Jr. and Mary Ann Sullivan A; m. 6/5/37 to Cathleen Claire Cummings; c. Carole (Mrs. DeCandido), Elaine (Mrs. Jefferson), Kathleen (Mrs. Cuttita), JoAnn, Vincent, III and Melanie. Educ: St. Francis Xavier; Pace Col. Polit. & Govt. Pos: Chmn, N.Y. Co. Rep. Cmt, currently. Bus. & Prof. Pos: Personal Property Appraiser, N.Y. State Tax, 53-60; v.pres, Gotham Bank, 60-63; chmn. bd, Century Nat. Bank, 63-65. Mem: Elks; K. of C. Rel: Catholic. Mailing Add: 350 E. 30 St, New York, N.Y. 10016.

ALBEA, WOODROW D
Ala. State Sen.
b. Talladega, Ala, 5/6/18; s. Emmette R. Albea and Lula Limbaugh A; m. 8/30/52 to Joy Cunningham; c. Woodlyn and James Woodrow, Jr. Educ: Jacksonville State Univ. 46-47; Univ. Ala, LL.B, 50; Phi Alpha Delta. Polit. & Govt. Pos: Recorder, Anniston City, Ala; asst. dist. attorney, Calhoun Co; Ala. State Rep, 55-66; Ala. State Sen, Ninth Dist, 67- Mil. Serv: Entered as Pvt, Army Air Force, 41, released as T/Sgt, 45, after serv. in ETO, 42-45. Mem: Calhoun Co. Bar Asn.(pres, 64); Lions; Mason; WOW; United Commercial Travelers; C. of C; VFW; Anniston Quarterback Club. Rel: Baptist. Mailing Add: Suite 401-4, Commercial Bank Bldg, Anniston, Ala. 36201.

ALBERT, CARL BERT D
Majority Leader, U.S. House of Rep.
b. McAlester, Okla, 5/10/08; s. Ernest Homer Albert and Leona Ann Scott A; m. 8/20/42 to Mary Harmon; c. Mary Frances and David Ernest. Educ: Univ. Okla, A.B, 31; Oxford Univ, Eng, Rhodes scholar, B.A, 33 and B.C.L, 34; Kappa Alpha; Phi Beta Kappa. Polit. & Govt. Pos: Legal clerk, Fed. Housing Admin, 35-37; U.S. Rep, Third Dist, Okla, 47-, Majority Whip, U.S. House of Rep, 55-62, Majority Leader, 62-; chmn platform cmt, Dem. Nat. Conv, 64, del. and permanent chmn, 68. Bus. & Prof. Pos: Attorney and acct, Sayre Oil Co, 37-38; mem. legal dept, Ohio Oil Co, 39-40; attorney, Arnote & Arnote, 46-47. Mil. Serv: Entered as Pvt, Army Air Force and Judge Adv. Gen. Dept, 41, released as Lt. Col, 46, after serv. in Pac. Theater; Col, Army Res, 46; Bronze Star. Mem: Am. and Okla. Bar Asns; Okla. Hall of Fame; Mason; Elks: Lions; Am. Legion; VFW; Isaac Walton League; Okla. Cattlemen's Asn. Rel: Methodist. Legal Res: 827 E. Osage, McAlester, Okla. 74501. Mailing Add: 4000 Massachusetts Ave. N.W, Washington, D.C. 20016.

ALBERTS, JOHN MICHAEL R
Wis. State Assemblyman
b. Milwaukee, Wis, 4/24/33; s. John Fred Alberts and Elsie Emma Fritz A; m. 6/11/55 to Elizabeth Ann McDonald; c. Jill Elizabeth, Michael John, Brian Allan and Kevin Charles. Educ: North. Ill. Univ, 2 years; Carroll Col, B.S, 57; Tau Kappa Epsilon; Alpha Kappa Psi; Varsity Club. Polit. & Govt. Pos: Wis. State Assemblyman, Second Dist, Waukesha Co, 69- Bus. & Prof. Pos: Pres, Alberts Serv. Inc, Oconomowoc, Wis, 64- Mem: Jaycees, Kiwanis, Toastmasters. Rel: Lutheran. Mailing Add: 1228 W. Wisconsin Ave, Oconomowoc, Wis. 53066.

ALBERTSON, HOWARD RANDOLPH R
Minn. State Rep.
b. Stillwater, Minn, 1/22/28; s. Walter Albertson and Loretta Nelson A; m. 7/12/58 to Ellen Marie Midthun; c. Martha, Sarah and Laura. Educ: Gustavus Adolphus Col, B.A, 49; Minneapolis Col. Law, B.S.L, 55; William Mitchell Col. Law, LL.B, 57; Pi Kappa Delta; Delta Theta Phi. Polit. & Govt. Pos: Prog. chmn, Minn. State Young Rep. League, 50; v.chmn, Wash. Co. GOP, 52-54; court cmnr, Wash. Co, 58-60; chmn, Standing Cmt. Metrop. and Urban Affairs; Minn. State Rep, 60- Bus. & Prof. Pos: Spec. agent, Northwest. Mutual Life Ins. Co. of Milwaukee, 47-58; sr. partner, Albertson, Morton & Jergens, 58- Mil. Serv: Entered as Pvt, Army, 50, released as Sgt, 52, after serv. in U.S. Mem: Am, Minn. and Wash. Co. Bar Asns. Distinguished Serv. Award, U.S. Jr. C. of C, 61; selected Outstanding Young Man of Year, Stillwater, Jaycees, 62. Rel: Lutheran. Mailing Add: 510 W. Olive St, Stillwater, Minn. 55082.

ALBI, JOE R
b. Denver, Colo, 10/28/31; married; c. three. Educ: Regis Col, grad. Polit. & Govt. Pos: Colo. State Rep, 62-64. Bus. & Prof. Pos: Pres, Cascade Investment Co. and Cascade Westminster Cleaners and Laundry. Mem: V.pres, Denver Better Bus. Bur. Outstanding Young Man of Am, U.S. Jr. C. of C, 65. Mailing Add: 5525 E. Bayaud Ave, Denver, Colo. 80222.

ALBRECHT, HAROLD JOSEPH R
Chmn, Greene Co. Rep. Cmt, Ill.
b. Carrollton, Ill, 8/3/21; s. Joseph D. Albrecht and Anna Banghart A; m. 11/29/50 to Mary Lou Simon; c. Lawrence L, Kenneth J. and Fred J. Educ: Greenfield High Sch, grad, 39. Polit. & Govt. Pos: Rep. precinct committeeman, Precinct 4, Ill, 56-; secy, Greene Co. Rep. Cent. Cmt, 58-66; chmn, Greene Co. Rep. Cmt, 66- Bus. & Prof. Pos: Air Force eng. instr, 43-46. Mailing Add: R.R. 3, Carrollton, Ill. 62016.

ALBRIGHT, ALBION D. D
Second V.Chmn, Snohomish Co. Dem. Cent. Cmt, Wash.
b. Winchester, Ill, 1/14/98; s. John H. Albright and Ida L. Cox A; m. 12/29/28 to Ann K. Anderson; c. John L.D. Educ: Sheldon High Sch, 16-17. Polit. & Govt. Pos: Chmn. of Bd, Snohomish Co. Fire Protection Dist. 1, Wash, 56-69; v.pres, South Co. Dem. Club, 60-64; chmn, Snohomish Co. Dem. Cent. Cmt, 64-68, second v.chmn, 68-; alternate del, Dem. Nat. Conv, 68. Mil. Serv: Entered as Pvt, Army, 17, released as Cpl, 19, after serv. in Battery D, 123rd Field Artil, 33rd Div, AEF France, 18-19; Div. Ribbon. Mem: Mason; York Rite; Shrine; VFW; Vet. of World War I; Am. Legion (past comdr); Rotary; Barbers Int. Union, AFL; Snohomish and Island Co. Fire Cmnr. Asn. (pres, 66-67). Rel: Protestant. Mailing Add: 3611 Serene Way, Alderwood Manor, Wash. 98036.

ALBRO, JOHN I. JR. R
b. Coventry, R.I, 1/10/17; m. to Gertrude L. Gifford A. Educ: W. Greenwich and W. Warwick High Sch. Polit. & Gov. Pos: R.I. State Sen, 64-66; R.I. State Rep, 59-65; mem, W. Greenwich Town Coun, 4 yrs. Bus. & Prof. Pos: Builder. Mil. Serv: 243rd Coast Artil, 3 yrs; 385th Inf. Regt. Div. 76, USAR, 7 yrs. Mem: Lake Mishnock Vol. Fire Co, chief and asst. chief; R.I. Cent. Firefighters League; S. Co. Fire Chiefs and Wardens League; Past Pres, Coventry Lions Club; Zone Chmn, mem. Dist. Gov. Cabinet, 42nd Dist. Lions Int; Trustee, Coventry-W. Greenwich B.P.O.E. No. 2285; Bd. of Inc. of Kent Co. Hosp. Mailing Add: Nooseneck Hill Rd, R.F.D, Coventry, R.I. 02816. (1967)

ALCALDE, HECTOR D
b. New York, N.Y, 10/22/33; s. Armando Alcalde and Amelia Castellano A; m. 6/3/56 to Norma Jean Spoto; c. Cynthia Diane, Richard Allen and Nelson

Bruce. Educ: N.Y. State Tech. Inst, 53-54; Univ. Tampa, B.S, 56; Peabody Col, M.S, 60; Theta Chi. Polit. & Govt. Pos: Admin. Asst. to U.S. Rep. Sam M. Gibbons, Fla, 62- Bus. & Prof. Pos: Teacher, Hillsborough Co. Bd. of Pub. Instr, 56-62. Rel: Roman Catholic. Legal Res: 2914 Aquilla, Tampa, Fla. 33609. Mailing Add: 430 Cannon House Office Bldg, Washington, D.C. 20515. (1967)

ALCARAZ, GERTRUDE ELIZABETH D
Mem, Calif. Dem. State Cent. Cmt.
b. San Francisco, Calif, 6/2/07; d. Harvey William Tammany and Elizabeth Bucholz T; m. 6/14/30 to Ernest Paul Alcaraz; c. Ernest Charles and Frances Elizabeth. Educ: San Diego State Col; Univ. of Calif; Phi Sigma Alpha. Polit. & Govt. Pos: Dir, women's activity div, San Diego Co. Labor Coun, AFL-CIO, 44-; mem, San Diego Co. Welfare Bd, Calif, 63-; mem, Bd. of Library Cmnrs, San Diego, Calif, 65-; mem, Calif. Dem. State Cent. Cmt, 68- Mem: Served on boards of Red Cross, Campfire Girls, Homemakers, Protective Serv. for the Aged, Commun. Welfare Coun, Leadership Conf, United Commun. Serv. and Union of Off. and Prfnl. Employees. Recipient of Several Commun. Serv. Awards. Rel: Unity. Legal Res: 3280 Altadena Ave, San Diego, Calif. 92105. Mailing Add: 339 W. Broadway, San Diego, Calif. 92101.

ALCON, EMILIO S. D
Hawaii State Rep.
b. Lahaina, Maui, Hawaii, 1/27/26; s. Eugenio M. Alcon and Romana Sensano A; m. 7/26/52 to Violeta Miguel; c. Alicia Lynn and William Dean. Educ: Woodbury Col, B.B.A, 50; Univ. Calif, Los Angeles, 56 & 59; Colo. State Col, B.A, 56; Univ. Hawaii, M.Ed, 65; Nat. Defense Educ. Act scholarship in counseling and guid; Pi Omega Pi. Polit. & Govt. Pos: Chmn, Citizen Registrn. Comt. of Kennedy, Maui Co, Hawaii, 60; Hawaii State Rep, 11th Dist, 68-, chmn, House Cmt. Pub. Insts. & Soc. Serv, Hawaii House Rep, currently; pres, Dem. Party, Precinct 1, 11th Representative Dist, 68-; Dem. committeeman, Fourth Sen. Dist, currently. Bus. & Prof. Pos: Ins. salesman, 50-54; teacher, Dept. Educ, 57-64; instr, Kapiolani Community Col, 64-69; real estate broker, Diversified Realty, currently. Mil. Serv: Entered as Pvt, Army, 45, released as S/Sgt, 47, after serv. in Spec. Serv, Pac. Ocean Area. Mem: Phi Delta Kappa; Am. Fedn. Teachers; Am. Legion; Moanalua Commun. Asn; Civic Assocs; Nuuanu YMCA. Rel: Catholic. Legal Res: 1560 Mahiole St, Honolulu, Hawaii 96819. Mailing Add: 329 State Capitol, Honolulu, Hawaii 96813.

ALCORN, HUGH MEADE, JR. R
b. Suffield, Conn, 10/20/07; s. Hugh Meade Alcorn, Sr. and Cora Terry Wells A; m. 4/14/55 to Marcia Elizabeth Powell; c. Thomas Glenn (deceased) and Janet Eileen (Mrs. Van Law). Educ: Dartmouth, A.B, 30; Yale Law Sch, LL.B, 33; Phi Beta Kappa; Corbey Court. Polit. & Govt. Pos: Conn. State Rep, 37-42, Floor Leader, House of Rep, Conn, 39-40 and Speaker, 41-42; chmn, Suffield Town Rep. Cmt, 38-52; mem, Conn. Rep. State Cent. Cmt, Hartford, 48-57; mem, Rep. Nat. Cmt, 53-61, chmn, 57-59 and gen. counsel, 60-61; Rep. floor leader, Constitutional Conv, 65. Bus. & Prof. Pos: Sr. partner, Alcorn, Bakewell & Smith, 33-66; vis. lectr, Ford Found. Course in Polit. Sci, Univ. Mass, 62. Mem: Pres, Conn. Bar Asn, 50-51; Mason (32°), Shrine; Elks; past pres, Rotary. Rel: Congregational. Legal Res: 49 Russell Ave, Suffield, Conn. 06078. Mailing Add: One American Row, Hartford, Conn. 06103.

ALCORN, JANICE CAROL R
b. Washington, D.C, 7/18/36; d. Maxie Howard Dunn and Antionette Borger D; m. 7/1/55 to Raymond Eugene Alcorn; c. Margaret Ann, Mary Katherine, Raymond Eugene, Jr. and John Howard. Educ: Wilson Teachers Col. Polit. & Govt. Pos: Acting polit. educ. chmn, Bowie Rep. Woman's Club, Md. and acting prog. chmn; prog. chmn, Rep. Citizens Orgn, Prince George Co; chmn, Prince George Co. Citizens for Goldwater; chmn. and v.chmn, Bowie Goldwater Club; del, Rep. Nat. Conv, 64. Mem: Belair Woman's Club; Confraternity of Christian Doctrine Teachers. Rel: Roman Catholic, Mailing Add: 2817 Sudberry Lane, Bowie, Md. 20715. (1967)

ALDEN, JOHN TAYLOR R
Vt. State Rep.
b. Cambridge, Mass, 1/6/36; s. John Gail Alden and Evelyn Dynan A; m. 6/6/60 to Patricia White; c. Elisabeth Anne, John Joseph and Richard Taylor. Educ: Boston Univ, 52-55. Polit. & Govt. Pos: Pres, Vt. Young Rep. Fedn, 64-66; v.chmn, Young Rep. Nat. Fedn, 65-67; Vt. State Rep, Dist. 24, 65-, Asst. Majority Leader, Vt. House of Rep, 69-, chmn, House Gen. and Mil. Affairs Cmt, 69-; mem, Rep. State Exec. Cmt, 67- Bus. & Prof. Pos: Ins. broker, Mutual & United of Omaha, 62- Mil. Serv: Entered as Pvt, Army, 55, released as SP-2, 58, after serv. in 54th Missile Bn, Md, 55-58. Mem: Rotary Int; U.S. Jaycees; Vt. Farm Bur; Vt. State Grange. Rel: Episcopal. Legal Res: West Woodstock, Vt. 05091. Mailing Add: P.O. Box 427, Woodstock, Vt. 05091.

ALDHIZER, GEORGE STATTON, II D
Va. State Sen.
b. Broadway, Rockingham Co, Va, 6/15/07; single. Educ: Univ. Va, B.S. and LL.B. Polit. & Govt. Pos: Va. State Del, 50-52; Va. State Sen, 54- Bus. & Prof. Pos: Lawyer. Mil. Serv: Comdr, Naval Res. Mem: Masons; Lions; Elks; past pres, Harrisonburg Bar Asn; Va. and Am. Bar Asns. Rel: Presbyterian. Mailing Add: Broadway, Va. 22815.

ALDRICH, ALEXANDER R
b. New York, N.Y, 3/14/28; s. Winthrop William Aldrich and Harriet Alexander A; m. 8/11/51 to Elizabeth Bayard Hollins; c. Elizabeth, Winthrop, Amanda and Alexander. Educ: Harvard, A.B, 50, LL.B, 53; N.Y. Univ, M.Pub.Admin, 60. Polit. & Govt. Pos: Secy, N.Y.C. Police Dept, 56-58, dep. cmnr, charge youth prog, 58-60; dir, N.Y. State Div. Youth, Albany, 60-63; exec. asst. to gov, State of N.Y, 63-66; formerly exec. dir, Hudson River Valley, N.Y. Bus. & Prof. Pos: Admitted to bar, N.Y.C, 55; practiced law, 55-56; pres, L.I. Univ, Brooklyn Center, 69- Mem: N.Y. Correctional Asn. (bd. dirs); Marist Col; Brooklyn Inst. Arts and Sci; Brooklyn Acad. Music (governing cmt); Am, N.Y. and N.Y.C. Bar Asns; Soc. Cincinnati; Am. Soc. Pub. Admin; trustee, N.Y. Zool. Soc; Porcellian Club, Cambridge, Mass; Tarratine Club, Dark Harbor Maine; Racquet & Tennis Club, N.Y.C. Legal Res: Chatham Center, Valatie, N.Y. 12184. Mailing Add: 1 Pierrepont St, Brooklyn, N.Y. 11201.

ALDRIDGE, GEORGE IRVIN D
Dir, 17th Judicial Dist. Dem. Exec. Cmt, N.C.
b. Caswell Co, N.C, 3/10/34; s. Carlton Huis Aldridge and Edna Rudd A; m. 6/19/55 to Gilmer Lee Lynch; c. George Irvin, Jr. and Sharon Elizabeth. Educ: Elon Col, N.C, A.B. in Hist, 56; Univ. of N.C. Law Sch, Chapel Hill, LL.B, 59; Phi Alpha Delta. Polit. & Govt. Pos: Recorder's Court Solicitor, Caswell Co, N.C, 58-59; chmn, Caswell Co. Bd. of Co. Cmnrs, 60-66; mem, Caswell Person Lake Authority, 67-68; younger voter coordinator, Scott for Gov. Campaign, Raleigh, 67-68; mem, Gov. Inaugural Cmt, 68-69; chmn, 17th Judicial Dist. Dem. Exec. Cmt, presently; mem, Gov. Adv. Cmt. on Beautification and Nat. Gov. Conf. Task Force on Community Develop. and Urban Problems, presently; alternate del, Dem. Nat. Conv, 68; asst. dir, Dept. of Admin, Raleigh, N.C, 69-; dir, Dept. of Local Affairs, 69-; mem, N.C. Cmn. on Interstate Coop. Bus. & Prof. Pos: Gen. mgr, Graphic Syst, Yanceyville, N.C, 59-66; spec. rep, Occidental Life Ins, Raleigh, 66-67; dir, Bank of Reidsville, presently. Mem: 4-H Honor Club; Jaycees (past v.pres. and past pres, Caswell Chap, life mem, past pres. and past nat. dir, N.C. Jaycees); Caswell Young Dem. Club. Distinguished Serv. Award, Caswell Co. Jaycees, 62; Sen, Jr. Chamber Int. Rel: Baptist. Mailing Add: Route 1, Yanceyville, N.C. 27379.

ALEIXO, THEODORE J, JR. D
Mass. State Rep.
b. Taunton, Mass, 8/23/42 to Theodore J. Aleixo and Rose M. Rico A; m. 2/23/63 to Elinor Ruth Soviecke; c. Kara Marie, Theodore Jeffrey, III and Paul Mitchell. Educ: Boston Univ, A.B. in Hist. and Govt, 64; Suffolk Univ. Law Sch, LL.B, 68; Am. Student Bar Asn. Polit. & Govt. Pos: Mass. State Rep, 69- Bus. & Prof. Pos: Ins. Broker, Aleixo Ins. Agency, 64-69; instr. soc. studies, Taunton High Sch, 65-69. Mem: Mass. Teachers Asn; Mass. Legislators Asn; past v.pres. and pres, Taunton Teachers Asn; Mus. of Sci, Boston; Elks; Boston Univ. Alumni Asn; Suffolk Univ. Alumni Asn; chmn, scholarship cmt, Portuguese Am. Civic Club, Taunton; Taunton Boys Club Asn; YMCA; Ward Five Athletic Club. Rel: Roman Catholic. Mailing Add: 136 Broadway, Taunton, Mass. 02780.

ALEX, JOHN MAYNARD R
Mem, Rep. State Cmt, Calif.
b. Lawrence, Mass, 3/27/29; s. Joseph Leonard Alex and Rixie Loretta Maynard A; m. 12/29/51 to Elizabeth Louise Matson; c. Elizabeth Lee, Rebecca Jo, John Matson and Judith Louise. Educ: Colby Col, B.A, 50; Univ. Chicago Law Sch, J.D, 57; Delta Upsilon; Phi Alpha Delta. Polit. & Govt. Pos: Dep. probation officer, Co. of Los Angeles, Calif, 58-60, dep. dist. attorney, 60-69, judge, Citrus Munic. Court, 69-; mem, Rep. State Cmt, Calif, 64- Mil. Serv: Entered as Pvt, Army, 50, released as Sgt, 54, after serv. in Spec. Serv, European Theatre of Occup, 50-54; Good Conduct Medal; Expert Marksman; European Theatre of Occup. Medal. Mem: Dist. Attorneys Asn; Am, Co. of Los Angeles, Pomona Valley and Citrus Bar Asns; State Bar of Calif; Trial Lawyers Asn; Rotary; Rep. Assocs; Rep. League; Calif. Rep. Assocs; Boy Scouts; Girl Scouts; PTA; Humane Rels. Coun. Rel: Unitarian. Mailing Add: 402 N. Cedar Dr, Covina, Calif. 91722.

ALEXANDER, CLIFFORD L. D
b. N.Y.C, 9/21/33; m. 1959 to Adele Logan; c. two. Educ: Harvard, B.A, cum laude, 55; Yale Univ. Law Sch, LL.B, 58; Phi Delta Phi; Alpha chap, Omega Psi Phi. Polit. & Govt. Pos: Asst. Dist. Attorney, New York Co, N.Y, 59-61; exec. dir, Manhattanville Hamilton Grange Neighborhood Conserv. Proj. 61-62; exec. prog. dir, Harlem Youth Opportunities Unlimited, 62-63; for. affairs officer, Nat. Security Coun, Wash, D.C, 63-64; dep. spec. counsel to the President, U.S, 64-67; chmn, Equal Employ. Opportunity Cmn, 67-69. Bus. & Prof. Pos: Attorney, pvt. practice, N.Y.C, 63. Mil. Serv: Army, 58-59. Publ: Contrib, The Newcomers—Negroes and Puerto Ricans in a Changing Metropolis, by Oscar Handlin. Mailing Add: 819 C St. N.E, Washington, D.C. 20003. (1967)

ALEXANDER, DAN C, JR. D
Secy, Mobile Co. Dem. Exec. Cmt, Ala.
b. Mobile, Ala, 8/19/38; s. D. C. Alexander, Sr. and Mary Francis Goodman A; m. to Nancy Fay Southall; c. Dan C, III and Virginia Deann. Educ: Univ. S. Ala, B.S. in Accounting; Univ. Ala, J.D; Phi Alpha Delta. Polit. & Govt. Pos: Secy, Mobile Co. Dem. Exec. Cmt, Ala, 66-, committeeman, 66; del, Dem. Nat. Conv, 68. Bus. & Prof. Pos: Pres, Sports Assoc, Inc, 65; mem, bd. dir, Allied Acceptance Corp, 66; chmn, bd. dir, Jobs Unlimited of Am, 68- Mem: Am. and Ala. Bar Asns; Jr. C. of C; Sertoma. Legal Res: 460 E. Yevonne Curve, Mobile, Ala. 36609. Mailing Add: P.O. Box 334, Mobile, Ala. 36601.

ALEXANDER, DORIS SEARS R
Vt. State Rep.
b. Irasburg, Vt, 7/6/97; m. to Maynard R. Alexander, wid; c. Six. Educ: Irasburg Village Sch; Barton Acad; Johnson Normal Sch, 16. Polit. & Govt. Pos: Justice of the Peace, Vt, 38-; mem, Rep. Town Cmt, Women's Rep. Club, Vt. and Orleans Co. Rep. Cmt; Vt. State Rep, currently. Bus. & Prof. Pos: Librarian. Mem: Eastern Star; PTA; Vt. Libr. Asn; Home Demonstration Group; Am. Legion Auxiliary; Co. Hist. Soc; Vt. Hist. Soc; Irasburg Cemetary Asn; Libr. Trustee, 27- Rel: Methodist; trustee, United Church. Legal Res: Irasburg, Vt, 05845. Mailing Add: State House of Representatives, State House, Montpelier, Vt. 05602. (1967)

ALEXANDER, GEORGE W. R
Pa. State Rep.
b. Clarion, Pa, 10/28/04; s. George W. Alexander and Jennie Maffett A; m. 8/11/25 to Mariam M. Moore; c. Charles and George III. Educ: Pa. State Univ; Denison Univ; Clarion State Col; Lambda Chi Alpha. Polit. & Govt. Pos: Pa. State Rep, 62-; co. chmn, Rep. Party, 4 years; supt, Cook State Forest Park, Pa. Dept. Forests & Waters, 10 years. Mil. Serv: Entered as Pvt, Army, 39, released as 1st Lt, 42. Publ: Outdoor Column, Hits or Misses, for three newspapers, articles for outdoor magazines. Mem: Am. Legion; Outdoor Writers of Am. Managed semi-pro baseball teams. Rel: Presbyterian. Legal Res: 726 Main St, Clarion, Pa. 16214. Mailing Add: State House of Representatives, State Capitol Bldg, Harrisburg, Pa. 17120. (1967)

ALEXANDER, HUGH QUINCY D
Chief Counsel, U.S. Senate Rules Cmt.
b. Moore Co, N.C, 8/11/11; s. Oscar Sample Alexander and Mary Belle Reynolds A; m. 9/25/42 to Myrtle Elizabeth White; c. Elizabeth, Hugh Quincy, Jr, Stephen White and William George. Educ: Duke Univ; Univ. N.C, Chapel Hill. Polit. & Govt. Pos: N.C. State Rep, 47-49; prosecuting attorney, Cabarrus Co. Recorders Court, 50-52; U.S. Rep, N.C, 52-62; Chief Counsel, U.S. Senate Rules Cmt, currently. Mil. Serv: Entered as Ens, Navy, 42, released as Lt, after serv. in Pac; 3 Pac. Campaign Ribbons. Mem: Mason (33°), past master, Cannon Memorial Lodge, Shrine; VFW; Am. Legion; N.C. State, Cabarrus Co. and Am. Bar Asns; state comdr, N.C. Dept, Am. Legion, 50. Distinguished Service Award, Kannapolis Jr. C. of C, 48. Rel: Presbyterian; Elder. Legal Res: 207 S. Main St, Kannapolis, N.C. Mailing Add: 525 Monticello Blvd, Alexandria, Va. 22305.

ALEXANDER, JAMES H. D
b. Memphis, Tenn, 1/2/22; s. E. Marvin Alexander and Lillis McElroy A; m. 12/21/45 to Lola Chesnut; c. Anne, Jean and James H, Jr. Educ: Univ. Tenn, B.S, 43; pres, Delta Sigma Pi, 42-43. Polit. & Govt. Pos: Mem, Tenn. State Bd. Elec, 53-62; alternate del, Dem. Nat. Conv, 56; state campaign mgr, Frank G. Clement for Gov. Tenn, 62 and for U.S. Sen, 64; state treas, Tenn, 63-67; del, Dem. Nat. Conv, 64; governor's staff dir. indust. develop, 67- Bus. & Prof. Pos: Owner, Jim Alexander Ins, 46-; regional v.pres, Insurors of Tenn, 62- Mil. Serv: Entered as Seaman, Navy, 43, released as Lt.(jg), 46, after serv. in ETO; Am. Theater Ribbon; ETO Ribbon with 2 Battle Stars. Mem: Nat. Asn. of State Auditors, Comptrollers and State Treas; Elks; VFW; Am. Legion; Rotary; Richland Country Club; former pres, Tenn. Sch. Bds. Asn; Asn. of State Planning and Develop. Agencies. Rel: Methodist. Legal Res: 714 Stonewall, McKenzie, Tenn. 38201. Mailing Add: 240 Cordell Hull Bldg, Nashville, Tenn. 37219.

ALEXANDER, JANE MARIETTA D
b. Wilkes-Barre, Pa, 11/10/29; d. Isaac C. Lehmer and Marietta Fisher L; m. 6/15/50 to P. Nelson Alexander; c. Nixon, Marstin, Lorinda and Halvard. Educ: Dickinson Col, A.B, 51, Dickinson Sch. of Law, LL.B, 54; Chi Omega; Phi Delta Delta; Delta Kappa Gamma. Polit. & Govt. Pos: Mem. and pres, Dillsburg Borough Coun, Pa, 55-58; mem, North. Joint Sch. Bd, 59-65; Pa. State Rep, 92nd Dist, 65-68; mem-at-lg, Pa. Coun. on Status Women, 67- Mem: Pa, York Co. and Am. Bar Asns; Nat. Soc. of State Legis; past pres, Dillsburg Woman's Clubs (past pres); York Co. Fedn. of Women's Clubs (past pres); Adults and Children's Serv. Adv. Bd.(bd. mem); Planning Cmn, York Co. United Fund; Quota; VFW Auxiliary; PTA; Dickinson Sch. Law Alumni Asn.(secy, 63-69, pres); Pa Fedn. Women's Clubs (state legis. chmn, 67-); York Co. Tuberc. Soc.(bd. mem); Harrisburg Bus. & Prfnl. Women. Legal Res: 148 S. Baltimore St, Dillsburgh, Pa. 17019. Mailing Add: 46 S. Duke St, York, Pa. 17401.

ALEXANDER, JOHN GRANT Independent Republican
b. Willet, N.Y, 7/16/93; s. Edwin H. Alexander and Clara Arbelle Grant A; m. 7/6/49 to Mabel Irene Harrison Peters; c. Ulysses S, Cyrus J, Faith O, Wm. E. and John Harrison Peters. Educ: Cornell Univ, LL.B, 16; Univ. Minn, Minneapolis, postgrad. study; Acacia. Polit. & Govt. Pos: U.S. Rep, Minn, 38-40; former secy, Hennepin Co. Rep. Club, Minn. Mil. Serv: Entered as Pvt, Army, 18, released as Lt, 37, after serv. in 151st Field Artillery. Mem: Past pres, Bldg. Owners and Mgrs. Asn; past pres, Am. Real Property Fedn; past v.pres, Minneapolis Bd. of Realtors; Am. Legion; 40 et 8; Elks; Optimist; past pres, adv. bd, Salvation Army; past pres, adv. bd. Vols. of Am; dir, Izaak Walton League; Nat. Apt. Owners Asn; Independent Fee Appraisers Asn. Rel: Lutheran. Legal Res: 327 Burntside Dr, Golden Valley, Minn. 55427. Mailing Add: 1200 Second Ave. S, Minneapolis, Minn. 55403.

ALEXANDER, JOSEPH D
Mem, Fairfax Co. Dem. Cmt, Va.
b. Fairfax Co, Va, 12/21/29; m. to Davina 'Davie'; c. Cathy Ann and Cheryl Anne. Educ: Va. Polytech. Inst, B.S. in Bus. and Pub. Admin, 51. Polit. & Govt. Pos: Lee Dist. rep, Fairfax Co. Bd. Supvr, Va, 64-; v.chmn, North. Va. Transportation Cmn; mem, permanent cmt. on educ. and urban co. cmt, Va. Asn. of Co; mem, Va. Cmn. for Children and Youth; mem, Fairfax Co. Dem. Cmt, currently; mem, Steering Cmt. Dem. Cmt, chmn, Lee Dist. Dem. Cmt, 4 terms. Bus. & Prof. Pos: Operator, Franconia Hardware, Va; chmn, bd. supvr, Washington-Lee Savings & Loan, one term, v.chmn, four terms, mem, bd. dir, currently. Mil. Serv: Entered as 2nd Lt, Air Force, released as 1st Lt, after serv. in Korea during UN Mil. Opers. Mem: Bd. of control, George Mason Col, Univ. Va; C. of C; VFW; Franconia Vol. Fire Dept. Mailing Add: 6107 Craft Rd, Alexandria, Va. 22310.

ALEXANDER, MYRL EARLY D
Dir, Bur. of Prisons, Dept. of Justice
b. Dayton, Ohio, 8/23/09; s. John Lester Alexander and Florence Early A; m. 1/18/34 to Lorene Shoemaker; c. Nancy (Mrs. Robert A. Hibbs) and John Alexander. Educ: Manchester Col, A.B, 30 and LL.D, 56. Polit. & Govt. Pos: Warden's asst, U.S. Penitentiary, Atlanta, Ga, 31; parole exec, U.S. Bd. of Parole, Wash, D.C, 37-40; assoc. warden, U.S. Penitentiary, Lewisburg, Pa, 40-43; warden, Fed. Correctional Inst, Danbury, Conn, 43-45; chief prisons, Mil. Govt. for German, 45-46; asst. dir, Bur. Prisons, Dept. Justice, Wash, D.C, 57-61, dir, 64-; U.S. rep, v.chmn, of del. to UN Cong. Prevention of Crime and Treatment of Offenders, Stockholm, 65; U.S. Correspondent, UN Sect. on Social Defense; spec. consult, various state correctional systs; mem. bd. dirs. and adv. coun, Nat. Coun. on Crime and Delinquency. Bus. & Prof. Pos: Prof. correctional admin. and dir, Center for Study of Crime, Delinquency and Corrections, South. Ill. Univ, 61-64. Publ: Jail Administration, 57. Mem: Am. Correctional Asn, pres, 56; Am. Soc. Pub. Admin; Am. Acad. Polit. and Soc. Sci; Nat. Jail Asn; bd. dirs, Osborne Asn; bd. dirs, Correctional Serv. Fedn. Rel: Lutheran; mem. exec. bd, Ill. Synod, 61-64. Mailing Add: 310 G St. S.E, Washington, D.C. 20003. (1967)

ALEXANDER, OPAL MANSUR D
Mem, Calif. Dem. State Cent. Cmt.
b. Paris, Mo; d. Henry Jasper Wingate and Emma Johnson W; m. 9/15/15 to Chauncey A. Alexander; c. Elaine (Mrs. McAdams), George W. (deceased); Lt. Col. Kenneth W. and Chauncey A. Educ: Chillicothe Bus. Col, grad. Polit. & Govt. Pos: Pres, Dem. Womens Luncheon Club, Calif, 38-42 & 66-; mem, Los Angeles Co. Dem. Cent. Cmt, 17 years; former alternate del, Dem. Nat. Conv; mem, Los Angeles Co. Cmn. on Obscenity and Pornography, Coord. Coun. Glendale, currently; mem, Calif. Dem. State Cent. Cmt, currently. Bus. & Prof. Pos: Lockhead Aircraft Co, 2 years. Mem: Nat. Asn. Registered Parliamentarians; Delta Unit Registered Parliamentarians; Women's Civic League Glendale; adv. bd, Salvation Army; life mem. PTA. Woman of the Year, Women's Civic League and Tuesday Afternoon Club; special recognition for 27 years as March of Dimes chmn, and for ten years as chmn, Glendale Multiple Sclerosis. Rel: Christian Church. Mailing Add: 1124 San Rafael, Glendale, Calif. 91202.

ALEXANDER, RAYMOND PACE D
b. Philadelphia, Pa, 10/13/98; s. Hilliard Boone Alexander and Virginia Pace A; m. 11/27/23 to Dr. Sadie Tanner Mossell; c. Mary Elizabeth (Mrs. Melvin Frank Brown) and Rae Pace; grandchildren, Virginia Alexander Brown and Raymond Alexander Brown. Educ: Univ. Pa, B.S. with honors, 20; Harvard Law Sch, LL.B, 23; Columbia Univ, 23 & 24; Alpha Phi Alpha; Sigma Pi Phi; hon. mem. Lamba Sigma Kappa. Hon. LL.D, Shaw Univ. and Va. State Col, 40; Litt.D, West. Univ, 47 and Campbell Col, 48. Polit. & Govt. Pos: Nat. chmn, Young Rep, 23; assoc. chmn, Young Dem, 32-36; counsr, Haitian Embassy, D.C, 47-48, hon. consul, Repub. Haiti, Phila, 48-56; spec. adv. to Secy. of Defense, 49; city councilman, Phila, Pa, 52-59, chmn, Cmts. Recreation and Pub. Property and Pub. Works; Judge, Common Pleas Court, Phila, 59-; Am. specialist, Scandinavian Countries, 63, Southeast Asia, 65, Mid. East, 68. Bus. & Prof. Pos: Counsel, Phila. and Pa. NAACP, Am. Civil Liberties Union and Nat. Med. Asn; assoc. counsel, Cmt. Civil Rights, Pa. Fel. Cmn; attorney, Pa. State Baptist Churches, Phila. Episcopal Dist; pres, Crime Prevention Asn. Phila, 67-; bd. mem, Crime Cmn, 69. Publ: 'Selection and Education of the Judiciary—Some Unfinished Tasks,' Pa. Bar Asn. Quart, 10/68; 'Civil Rights, The Negro Protest and the War on Poverty: Efforts to Cure America's Social Ills,' N.Y. State Bar J, 2/69; 'Medicolegal Aspects of Contraception,' (in press); plus others. Mem: Am, Pa. and Phila. Bar Asns; Am. Judicature Soc; hon. mem. Bar of Repub. of Haiti, 49. Plaque of Honor and Citation, Am. Jewish Congress, 50; Outstanding Serv. Awards, Alpha Phi Alpha, Phi Beta Sigma, Pyramid Club, Cotillion Soc, African Methodist Episcopal Church, N.Y.C, 55 and Baptist Ministers Conf, Phila, 59. Rel: Protestant. Legal Res: 700 Westview St, Philadelphia, Pa. 19119. Mailing Add: 536 City Hall, Philadelphia, Pa. 19107.

ALEXANDER, WM. B. D
Miss. State Sen.
b. Boyle, Miss, 12/23/21; s. William Brooks Alexander and Vivien Beever A; m. 3/10/50 to Belle McDonald; c. Brooks, Becky, John and Jason. Educ: Miss. Col, undergrad; Univ. Miss, LL.B, 48; Sigma Nu. Polit. & Govt. Pos: Miss. State Sen, 60- Mil. Serv: Air Force 42-46, served in Pac. Theater; New Guinea, Philippines and Korean Campaign ribbons. Mem: Miss. and Am. Bar Asns; Bolivar Co. Bar Asn.(pres, 63); State Comdr, VFW; Exchange Club; Mason; Shrine. Rel: Baptist. Legal Res: 517 Fayette Davis Ave, Cleveland, Miss. 38732. Mailing Add: 112 N. Pearman Ave, Cleveland, Miss. 38732.

ALEXANDER, WILLIAM HENRY D
Ga. State Rep.
b. Macon, Ga, 12/10/30; s. William Henry Alexander and Elnora Elizabeth A; m. 1965 to Gayle Eileen Jackson; c. Jill Marie. Educ: Ft. Valley State Col, B.S, 51; Univ. Mich, J.D, 56; Georgetown Univ, LL.M, 61; Tau Epsilon Rho; Alpha Phi Alpha. Polit. & Govt. Pos: Legal asst, Soc. Security Admin, 61-63; Ga. State Rep, 66- Bus. & Prof. Pos: Attorney-at-Law, Atlanta, Ga, 63- Mil. Serv: Entered as Pvt, Army, 51, released as Spec. Agent, Counter Intel. Corps, 53; Nat. Defense Serv. Medal. Mem: Am. Atlanta and Gate City Bar Asns; State Bar of Ga; Am. Trial Lawyers Asn; Am. Civil Liberties Union; NAACP; YMCA; Univ. Mich. Alumni Asn; Georgetown Univ. Alumni Asn. Rel: Roman Catholic. Mailing Add: 3725 Dover Blvd. S.W, Atlanta, Ga. 30331.

ALEXANDER, WILLIAM V, JR, 'BILL' D
U.S. Rep, Ark.
b. Memphis, Tenn, 1/16/34; s. William V. Alexander and Eulalia Spencer Buck A; m. 2/5/57 to Gwendolyn Haven 'Gwen'; c. Alyse Haven. Educ: Univ. Ark, 50-51; Southwest. at Memphis, B.A, 57; Vanderbilt Univ. Sch. Law, LL.B, 60; Phi Delta Phi; Kappa Sigma. Polit. & Govt. Pos: Mem, Osceola Port Authority, Civic Center Cmt. and Munic. Planning Cmn; dir, Off. Econ. Opportunity Prog, Miss. Co, Ark; mem, Miss. Co. Quorum Court; dir, Northeast Ark. Econ. Develop. Dist; mem, Ark. Waterways Cmn; legal research asst. to Fed. Judge Marion Boyd; U.S. Rep, Ark. First Dist, 69- Bus. & Prof. Pos: Assoc, Montedonico, Boone, Gilliland, Heiskell, and Loch, 61-62; partner, law firm, Swift & Alexander, 63- Mil. Serv: Entered the Army, 51, released in 53, after serving in Adj. Gen. Corps. Mem: Osceola, Miss. Co, Northeast Ark, Ark, Tenn, and Am. Bar Asns; admitted to practice before all state & fed. courts in Ark. and Tenn, Court of Appeals, Sixth Judicial Court and U.S. Supreme Court. Am. Legion; Mason; dir, E.Ark. Area Coun. Boy Scouts; organized and dir, Miss. Co. YMCA; mem. bd. dir, Southwest. at Memphis; Am. Acad. Polit. & Soc. Sci. Rel: Episcopal. Legal Res: 811 W. Hale Ave, Osceola, Ark. 72370. Mailing Add: 1110 House Office Bldg, Washington, D.C. 20515.

ALFANO, CHARLES THOMAS D
Conn. State Sen.
b. Suffield, Conn, 6/21/20; s. Dominic Alfano and Rose DiMartini A; m. 11/13/54 to Mary Ann Sinatro; c. Diane Elizabeth, Andrea Rose, Charles T, Jr. and Susan Marie. Educ: Univ. Conn, B.A, 43; Univ. Mich, LL.B, 48. Polit. & Govt. Pos: Munic. judge, Suffield, Conn, 49-51 & 54-58; Conn. State Sen, 59-; past pres-pro-tem, Conn. State Senate; alternate del, Dem. Nat. Conv, 68. Bus. & Prof. Pos: Attorney, Alfano & Bumster, 48- Mil. Serv: Entered as A/S, Navy, 42, released as Lt.(jg), 46, after serv. in Pac. Theater. Mem: Hartford Co, Conn. and Am. Bar Asns; Am. Trial Lawyers Asn; K. of C; VFW; Hartford Club; Univ. Club. Rel: Catholic. Legal Res: 50 Marbern Dr, Suffield, Conn. 06078. Mailing Add: 100 Constitution Plaza, Hartford, Conn. 06103.

ALFELD, JACK A. D
Committeeman, Greene Co. Dem. Party, Ill.
b. Livingston, Ill, 8/30/21; s. John Stewart Alfeld and Nancy M. Sawyer A; m. 12/28/45 to Geraldine Bowman; c. Ann Rosalia and Philp L. Educ: Ill.

Col, 39-40 & 46; St. Louis Univ. Sch. Law, LL.B, 48. Polit. & Govt. Pos: Co. judge, Greene Co, Ill, 50-61; committeeman, Greene Co. Dem. Party, 54-, chmn, 64-68; asst. dir. finance, State of Ill, 61-64; extradition counsel, Gov. Ill, 62-64; state's attorney, Greene Co, 64-; del, Dem. Nat. Conv, 68. Mil. Serv: Entered as Pvt, Army, 42, released as T-4, 45, after serv. in 33rd Portable Surg. Hosp, S.Pac and S.W.Pac, 43-45; Bronze Star Medal. Mem: Am, Ill. State and Greene Co. Bar Asns; Am. Judicature Soc; Asn. Am. Trial Lawyers; Ill. Co. Judge's Asn; Ill. State's Attorneys Asn; Nat. Dist. Attorneys Asn; Am. Legion; VFW; Lions Int; C. of C. Rel: Methodist. Legal Res: 821 S. Sixth St, Carrollton, Ill. 62016. Mailing Add: Hodges Office Bldg, Carrollton, Ill. 62016.

ALFONSI, PAUL R. R
Wis. State Assemblyman
b. Pence, Wis, 2/13/08. Educ: Whitewater State Col; Univ. Wis. Polit. & Govt. Pos: Wis. State Assemblyman, 32-40, 58-64 & 66-, Prog. Floor Leader, 35-39, Speaker, 37, Majority Leader, 63, asst. Minority Leader, 65, Minority Leader, 65-, mem. cmts, Tax Compromise, State Bldg, Joint Legis. Orgn, Gov. Cmn. Wis. Water Resources, Interstate Coop. Cmn, Legis. Orgn. and Procedures Cmn, Wis. State Assembly; chmn, Minocqua Rep. Town Cmt, Wis, 35-53; presidential elector, Wis, 60. Bus. & Prof. Pos: Teacher bus. educ, 27-33; supvr. prin, Minocqua schs, 49-55; pres, ins. co, Green Bay, Wis. Mil. Serv: Army, 43-46. Legal Res: Minocqua, Wis. 54548. Mailing Add: State Assembly, State Capitol Bldg, Madison, Wis. 53702. (1967)

ALFORD, ALEXANDER D
b. Georgetown, S.C, 12/13/13; s. Moses Alford and Lula Belle Brown A; m. 6/5/55 to Cleotha Blanding; c. Brenda, Moses Dwayne, Dorian DeWitt and Alexander, Jr. Educ: Fisk Univ, 2 years. Polit. & Govt. Pos: Chmn. local bi-racial cmt, Progressive Dem, 64-; del, Dem. Nat. Conv, 68; Dem. chmn, Precinct Seven, Georgetown, S.C, currently. Rel: African Methodist Episcopal. Legal Res: 514 Merriman Rd, Georgetown, S.C. 29440. Mailing Add: P.O. Box 412, Georgetown, S.C. 29440.

ALFORD, DALLAS L, JR. D
N.C. State Sen.
b. Durham, N.C; s. Dallas Lloyd Alford, Sr. and Sally Kate Pope A; m. 11/17/45 to Margarette Glenn Griffin; c. Dallas L, III, Benjamin G, Margarette G. and Catherine Elizabeth. Educ: Durham High Sch; Duke Univ, 31; Delta Sigma Phi. Polit. & Govt. Pos: Mem. Bd. of Alderman, Rocky Mount, N.C, 39-42; Nash Co. Bd. of Cmnrs, 48-58, chmn, 52-58; chmn, Nash Co. Bd. of Health, 52-58; mem, Cmt. for Study of Revenue Structure of State, 57-58; N.C. State Sen, 59-; chmn, Cmt. to Study Welfare Probs. for State of N.C, 62. Bus. & Prof. Pos: Owner and operator, Alford Ins. & Realty Co. Mil. Serv: U.S. Navy, 42-46, Lt. Comdr. Mem: Past pres, Rocky Mount Realtors Asn; Rocky Mount Mutual Ins. Agents Asn; Lodge 1038, Elks; 40 & 8; Kiwanis; Benvenue Country Club; past pres, N.C. Jr. C. of C; Rocky Mount Jr. C. of C; Rocky Mount C. of C; N.C. Co. Cmnrs. Asn; dir, Peoples Bank & Trust Co, Citizens Savings and Loan Asn; chmn, Twin Co. Law Enforcement Exec. Cmt; comdr, Am. Legion, 1948. Rel: First Methodist Church, mem. off. bd, Rocky Mount, 38-65. Mailing Add: 100 Wildwood Ave, Rocky Mount, N.C. 27801.

ALFORD, ROBERT BRUCE R
b. Hempstead, L.I, N.Y, 9/11/45; s. Lt. Col. W.E. Alford and Ann Menzies A; m. 2/13/69 to Patricia J. Jakoubek. Educ: Stetson Univ, 62-65; Stetson Univ. Col. Law, Ford Grad. Prog, 65-; Pi Kappa Delta (secy-treas. and regional award); S-2 Info. Officer Pershing Rifles; Gamma Delta Iota (pres); Superior Cadet, ROTC and Superior Cadet Hist. Award; writer, col. newspaper. Polit. & Govt. Pos: Treas, Stetson Univ, Young Rep, 62-63, v.pres, 63-64, pres, 64-65; del. for all state bd. meetings and convs, 63-; adv. to TAR, Fla. Dist. Three and Five; del, Vanderbilt Rep. Conv, 64; del, Nat. Young Rep. Conv. Col, 64; v.chmn, Orgn. Cmt, Fla. Col. Young Rep, 64-; chmn, Fla. Fedn. Col. Young Rep, 64, v.pres, Third and Fifth Dist, 66; v.pres, Stetson Univ. Col. Law Young Rep, 65- Bus. & Prof. Pos: Prfnl. actor, stage, radio and TV. Mil. Serv: Entered as 2nd Lt, Army, 68-, serv. in Mil. Intel, Vietnam. Publ: Advertising and the Free World, Advert. Fedn. of Am, 61-62. Mem: Am. Law Student Asn; Actor's Equity Asn; Am. Fedn. of TV and Radio Artists. Received MacLevy Talent Award, 52; trip to Miami, Amateur Actor's Award, 53; trip to Spain, Air Force Reserve Officers Club Award, 60; Orlando Air Force Base Officers Club Award; Nat. Forensics League Award; Optimists Club Speaking Award and Ed. Award, Advert. Club. of Orlando, Inc, 62; Fla. Interscholastic Debate Award, 63. Rel: Presbyterian. Legal Res: 318 W. Hazel Ave, Orlando, Fla. 32804. Mailing Add: 518 S. 20th St, Belleville, Ill. 62221.

ALGER, BRUCE REYNOLDS R
b. Dallas, Tex, 6/12/18; s. David Bruce Alger and Clare Fleeman; div; c. Jill (Mrs. Norman Watts, Jr) and Steven. Educ: Princeton Univ, 40; South. Methodist Univ. Law Sch; Quadrangle Club. Polit. & Govt. Pos: U.S. Rep, 5th Dist, Tex, 55-65. Bus. & Prof. Pos: Owner, Bruce Alger Realtor, Alger Develop. Corp. and Modernaire Const. Co, 47-55; owner, 1st Realty Corp. of Boca Raton, 66. Mil. Serv: Entered as Air Corps Cadet, 41, released as Capt, Air Force, 46, after serv. in 20th Air Force, Marianas; Air Medal with Clusters; Distinguished Flying Cross. Mem: Pres, White Rock C. of C, 53-54; Mason (32°); KCCH. Princeton Silver Anniversary All-Am. Awardee, 65. Rel: Protestant. Mailing Add: 261 N.W. 11th Ave, Boca Raton, Fla. 33432.

ALGER, JAMES PACE D
b. Cleveland, Utah, 1/23/28; s. Edgar Alger and Elna Jensen A; m. 7/21/50 to Merlene Forsyth; c. James P, Jr. and Jack M. Educ: Univ. South. Calif, A.B. in polit. sci, 49; Univ. Utah, J.D, 52; Phi Delta Phi. Polit. Pos: Chmn, Carbon Co. Dem. Cmt, Utah, 60-61; pres, Carbon Co. Young Dem, 58-60. Govt. Pos: U.S. Attorney, Dept. Justice, 62-; asst. attorney gen, Territory of Guam, 61-62; co. attorney, Carbon Co, Utah, 54-61. Bus. & Prof. Pos: Mem, Guam Code Revision Cmt, 65- Mem: Utah State Bar; pres, Guam Bar Asn, 64-65 and East. Utah Bar Asn, 58-59; past pres, Rotary; Jaycees, 56-61, Dist. Serv. Award Winner, 58; Navy League. Legal Res: 103 Bryant St, Agana, Guam 96910. Mailing Add: Federal Bldg, Agana, Guam 96910. (1967)

ALINSKY, SAUL DAVID D
b. Chicago, Ill, 1/30/09; s. Benjamin Alinsky and Sarah Tannenbaum A; m. 6/9/32 to Helene Simon, wid; m. 5/15/52 to Jean Graham; c. Kathryn and David. Educ: Univ. Chicago, Ph.B, 30, grad. work, 30-32; St. Prospectus Col, LL.D, 58. Polit. & Govt. Pos: Mem, State Prison Classification Bd, Joliet, Ill, 33-36; sociologist, Inst. for Juvenile Research, Chicago, 31-39; co-founder, Back of the Yards Neighborhood Coun, Chicago; exec. dir, Indust. Areas Found. and training Inst, 39- Bus. & Prof. Pos: Vis. prof, Vassar Col, 68-69; vis. fel, Mass. Inst. Tech; Willis D. Wood fel, Amherst Col, 69. Publ: Reveille for Radicals, 46; John L. Lewis, A Biography, 49. Authors League Am. Award for Soc. Justice, Cath. Youth Orgn. of Am, 50; Pacem in Terris, Cath. Interracial Coun, Davenport, Iowa, 69. Legal Res: 400 E. Randolph, Chicago, Ill. 60601. Mailing Add: 8 S. Michigan Ave, Chicago, Ill. 60603.

ALIOTO, JOSEPH LAWRENCE D
Mayor, San Francisco, Calif.
b. San Francisco, Calif, 2/12/16; s. Giuseppe Alioto and Domenica Lazio A; m. 6/2/41 to Angelina Genaro; c. Lawrence E, Joseph M, John I, Angela Mia (Mrs. Veronese), Thomas R. and Michael J. Educ: St. Mary's Col, B.A, 37; Cath. Univ. of Am, J.D, 40. Polit. & Govt. Pos: Spec. asst. to the attorney gen, Anti Trust Div, U.S. Dept. of Justice, Wash, D.C, 37-42; mem, Bd. of Econ. Warfare, Wash, D.C, 42-44; pres, Bd. of Educ, San Francisco, Calif, 48-53; pres, Redevelopment Agency, San Francisco, 55-59; mayor, San Francisco, 68- Bus. & Prof. Pos: Attorney, 48-; pres, Rice Growers Asn, 59-69, gen. counsel and bus. consult, 68-; chmn. of the bd, First San Francisco Bank, 65-68; gen. counsel and bus. consult, Charles Krug Winery, 67- Mem: Am. Col. of Trial Lawyers; Salesian Boys Club; C. of C. of San Francisco; Sons of Italy. Justinian Soc. Man of the Year Award, 68; Gran' Ufficiale, Order of Merit of the Italian Repub, 69; Ordre des Arts et des Lettres, French Govt, 69. Rel: Catholic. Legal Res: 34 Presidio Terr, San Francisco, Calif. 94118. Mailing Add: Room 200, City Hall, San Francisco, Calif. 94102.

ALKIRE, ALMA ASENATH R
b. Phoenix, Ariz. Educ: Pomona Col, Claremont, Calif, B.A, 37. Polit. & Govt. Pos: Mem. staff, U.S. Rep. John Rhodes, Ariz, 53-, admin. asst, currently. Bus. & Prof. Pos: Admin. asst, Am. Red Cross, 44-49; secy-librn, Maricopa Co. Med. Soc, Ariz, 49-52. Mem: Jr. League of Phoenix. Legal Res: Phoenix, Ariz. Mailing Add: 4201 Massachusetts Ave. N.W, Washington, D.C. 20016.

ALLAN, STUART B. R
N.H. State Rep.
b. Weymouth, Mass, 12/10/97; married; c. two. Educ: Saugus High Sch. Polit. & Govt. Pos: N.H. State Rep, 61-; selectman, Meredith, N.H, 61-63 & 64-; del, Rep. Nat. Conv, 64; del, Con. Conv. Bus. & Prof. Pos: Ret. invest, U.S. Immigration & Naturalization Serv, Dept. of Justice. Mil. Serv: Army, 16-20; Marine Corps Res, 27-31. Mem: First v.pres, N.H. Munic. Asn; v.pres, N.H. Assessors Asn; Hampden Lodge; AF&AM, Springfield, Mass; Chocorua Lodge No. 83; F&AM, Meredith; All Scottish Rite Bodies. Rel: Congregational. Mailing Add: R.F.D. 1, Old Hubbard Rd, Meredith, N.H. 03253.

ALLARD, AMOS WILSON D
Chmn, Fourth Cong. Dist, Dem. Party, Colo.
b. Walden, Colo, 5/14/20; s. Arthur William Allard and Robena Pearl Wade A; m. 7/15/42 to S. Jean Stewart; c. Alan Wayne and Kermit Lee. Educ: Colo. State Univ, 37-38 and 63; Univ. Mo, Columbia, B.S, 63; Ruf-Nex; Alpha Gamma Rho; Block and Bridle Club; Livestock Club; Livestock Judging Team; Agr. Club. Polit. & Govt. Pos: Chmn, Routt Nat. Forest Adv. Bd, Colo, 49-51; chmn, Farm Home Admin, Jackson Co, 50-54; chmn, North Park Hosp. Dist, 54-61; dir, North Park Soil Conserv. Dist, 56-60; chmn, Ill. River Water Conservancy Dist, 58-61; chmn, Jackson Co. Dem. Cmt, 59-61; chmn, Larimer Co. Dem. Cent. Cmt, 67-69; chmn, Fourth Cong. Dist. Dem. Party, 69- Bus. & Prof. Pos: Mgr, Allard Bros. Ranches, 41-44; mgr, Ill. River Hereford Ranches, 46-54; owner and operator, Allard Cattle Co, 54-61; owner and real estate broker, Loch Lon Homes, 64-; v.pres, I.O.O.F. Develop. Corp. Inc, 68-; v.pres. Ram Construction Co, Inc, 68- Mil. Serv: Entered as A/S, Navy, 44, released as PO 2/C, 45, after serv. as an Athletic Specialist. Mem: Home Builder's Asn. North. Colo; Colo. Cattlemen's Asn; dir, Larimer Co. 4-H Found; dir, Royal Gorge Manor, Sr. Citizens Apt's; dir, Big Thompson Manor, Sr. Citizen Apt's; C. of C; Elks; Odd Fellows (Past Grand Master, jurisdiction of Colo). Rel: Methodist. Mailing Add: 1317 Hazel Court, Loveland, Colo. 80537.

ALLARD, LOU STOCKTON D
Okla. State Rep.
b. Shawnee, Okla, 8/13/09; s. Lou Stockton Allard and Ida May Hayes A; m. 6/18/33 to Wilma Georgia Kincaid; c. Kay Dell (Mrs. Fred Lawson) and Dee Anne. Educ: Okla. State Univ; Sigma Delta Chi. Polit. & Govt. Pos: Co. chmn, League of Young Dem, Okla, 36; dist. dir, Nat. Youth Admin, 40-42; field rep, Off. of Price Admin, 42-43; Okla. State Rep, 46-62 & 64-, asst. majority leader, Okla. House of Rep, 2 terms and former chmn, Appropriations Cmt; chmn, Okla. Semi-Centennial Cmn, 55-57; cand. for Lt. Gov, Okla, 62. Bus. & Prof. Pos: Sports ed, Drumright Derrick, 30-40, bus. mgr, 43-46, publisher, 46- Mem: Dir, Okla. Press Asn, 51- and pres, 58-59; past pres, Drumright Rotary, Drumright C. of C. and Drumright and Okla. Jr. C. of C; Mason (32°), Drumright York Rite Bodies, Okla. Scottish Rite Bodies, K.T, Shrine; Legion of Honor, DeMolay; co. chmn, Nat. Found. for Infantile Paralysis, 45-55; state dir, Nat. Cowboy Hall of Fame. Hon. mem, Chickasaw Indian Nation and Cherokee Indian Tribe; col. of staff of 2 gov. Rel: Methodist. Mailing Add: 421 N. Grand Ave, Drumright, Okla. 74030.

ALLEN, ARIS TEE R
Md. State Del.
b. San Antonio, Tex, 12/27/10; s. James Allen and Maryetta Whitby A; m. 2/28/47 to Faye W, M.D; c. Aris T, Jr. and Lonnie W. Educ: Howard Univ, M.D, 44; Alpha Phi Alpha; Chi Delta Mu. Polit. & Govt. Pos: Md. State Del, currently, minority whip, Md. House of Del, 69-; alternate del, Rep. Nat. Conv, 68. Bus. & Prof. Pos: Physician, 45-66; mem. bd. dirs, Colonial Bank & Trust Co, Annapolis, Md, 69. Mil. Serv: Capt. and Flight Surgeon, Air Force, 51-53. Mem: Am. Med. Asn; Anne Arundel Co. Med. Soc; Acad. of Gen. Practice; Medico Chirurlical Soc; Co. Planning Adv. Bd; YMCA; Ment. Health Bd; Red Cross Bd; Am. Legion; NAACP; Served on Annapolis Annexation Charter Cmt; bd. educ, Ann Arundel Co; Ann Arundel Co. Libr; bd. dirs, C. of C; treas, Staff of Anne Arundel Gen. Hosp. Richard Allen Award for de-

votion to church and state; NAACP State Branches award. Rel: Methodist; Trustee. Mailing Add: 62 Cathedral St, Annapolis, Md. 21401.

ALLEN, BRUCE FRANKLIN R
b. San Jose, Calif, 8/17/16; m. 12/13/43 to Darrella Stewart A; c. Roger Bruce, Richard Stewart and Douglas Blanchard. Educ: San Jose State Col; Univ. of Calif, A.B, 37, LL.B, 40. Polit. & Govt. Pos: Calif. State Assemblyman, 53-62; Superior Court Judge, Calif, 66- Bus. & Prof. Pos: Attorney-at-law. Mil. Serv: Pvt, 41, Army Artil, discharged Capt, 45. Mem: Lions; Eagles; Scottish Rite; Sciots; Am. Legion. Mailing Add: 20130 Thompson Rd, Los Gatos, Calif. 95030.

ALLEN, C. KAY D
b. Heber, Utah, 8/16/25; s. Orson M. Allen and Floretta Simpson A; m. 8/22/49 to Doris Brady; c. Connie, Roger K, Rolayne and Paul B. Educ: Brigham Young Univ, B.S, 53; Univ. Utah, M.S, 55; Phi Delta Kappa. Polit. & Govt. Pos: Chmn, several cmts. for Dem. Party; legis. dist. chmn, Dem. Party, 61-63; Utah State Rep, 63-67, speaker, Utah House of Rep. and chmn, Utah Legis. Coun, 65-67; mem, Little Hoover Cmn, 65-67; chmn, Honors for Utah Cmt, 66; chmn, Coord. Coun. of Health and Welfare, Utah, 67-; del, Dem. Nat. Conv, 68. Bus. & Prof. Pos: Pres, West. Nat. Investment Corp, 59-66; owner, shopping center and apt, 60-; chmn. bd, North Valley State Bank, Denver, 62-; dir, Seven additional corps; teaching staff mem, Adult Educ. Dept, Brigham Young Univ; dir, West. Nat. Bank, Denver, 63- Mil. Serv: Entered as Pvt, Army Air Corps, 43, released as S/Sgt, 46, after serv. as B-24 Radio Operator. Publ: Mental Health Booklet; Learning to Live More Efficiently. Mem: Former v.pres, Jaycees. Rel: Latter-day Saint. Mailing Add: 329 Saunders, Murray, Utah 84107.

ALLEN, CHARLES BRENHAM, JR. D
Miss. State Rep.
b. Rosedale, Miss, 11/19/04; married. Educ: Greenville Mil. Acad, 22; Univ. Miss, LL.B, 27; Sigma Alpha Epsilon, Kappa Beta Phi. Polit. & Govt. Pos: Miss. State Rep, currently. Bus. & Prof. Pos: Retired govt. employee; ins. bus, currently. Mem: Rotary; Golf Club; Nat. Football Rules Cmt. Rel: Episcopal. Mailing Add: Box 344, Amory, Miss. 38821.

ALLEN, CHARLES EDGAR D
b. Windom, W.Va, 2/16/16; s. George E. Allen and Martha Browning A; m. 3/27/37 to Pearl Caldwell; c. Charles Edgar Jr, Jackie Lee, Margaret; Carol Sue, Betty Jo and Barbara Allen Mullens. Educ: Pub. schs, Wyoming Co. Polit. & Govt. Pos: W.Va. State Del, 64-68; former city cmnr, Mullens, W.Va. Bus. & Prof. Pos: Rwy. conductor. Mem: BRT; Mason; Moose. Rel: Baptist. Mailing Add: 902 Poplar St, Mullens, W.Va. 25882. (1967)

ALLEN, CHARLES GICE, JR. R
Mem. Exec. Cmt, Cabarrus Co. Rep. Party, N.C.
b. Raleigh, N.C, 11/3/24; s. Charles Gice Allen, Sr. and Caro McNeill A; m. 12/29/50 to Willie Mae McGuirt; c. Suzanne and Julia Mae. Educ: Concord High Sch, N.C, grad. Polit. & Govt. Pos: Mem. exec. cmt, Cabarrus Co. Rep. Party, 62-; co. tax collector, Cabarrus Co, N.C, 63-; alternate del, Rep. Nat. Conv, 68. Bus. & Prof. Pos: Prfnl. baseball player, Wash. Sen and N.Y. Giants, Farm Systs, 47-54; aircraft plant worker, Douglas Aircraft Co, Charlotte, N.C, 55-62. Mil. Serv: Entered as Seaman, Navy, 43, released as Pharmacist's Mate 2/C, 45, after serv. in Med. Corps, Am. Theater, 43-45. Mem: N.C. State Asn. Tax Collectors; Shrine; Scottish Rite; Mason; VFW; Am. Legion; DAV. Rel: Protestant. Mailing Add: Route 1, Box 151, Midland, N.C. 28107.

ALLEN, CHARLES GUTHRIE D
b. Burlington, N.C, 2/22/22; s. W. Meritt Allen and Mamie Guthrie A; m. 12/28/52 to Mary Claire Bradwell A. Educ: Univ. of N.C, 39-42. Polit. & Gov. Pos: S.C. State Rep, 55-66; City Coun, Dillon, S.C. Bus. & Prof. Pos: Farmer. Mil. Serv: Navy, 42-46; Lt, Res. Mem: Elks; Masons; Shriners; VFW; Am. Legion. Rel: First Baptist Church. Mailing Add: Dillon, S.C. 29536. (1967)

ALLEN, CHARLES HENRY, III D
Mem, 25th Sen. Dist. Dem. Cmt, R.I.
b. Exeter, R.I, 5/1/35; s. Charles Henry Allen, Jr. and Barbara Downs A; m. 8/2/57 to Jane Marie Lyman; c. Sheriann Louise, Charles Henry, IV and Sarah Jane. Educ: Univ. of R.I, 2 years; Univ. of Mass, Amherst, cert, 60. Polit. & Govt. Pos: Town councilman, Exeter, R.I, 62-64; secy, Exeter Dem. Town Cmt, 65-67 and chmn, 67-69; mem, 47th Rep. Dist. Dem. Cmt, 68-; mem, 25th Sen. Dist. Dem. Cmt, 68-; cand, R.I. House of Rep, 47th Dist, 68; exec. secy, Asn. of Dem. Chmn, South. R.I, 69- Bus. & Prof. Pos: Sales mgr, Allen's Seed Store, Slocum R.I, 61- Mil. Serv: Entered as Pvt, E-1, Army, 54, released as Pfc, 56, after serv. in 42nd Armored Field Artil. Bn, 2nd Armored Div, Germany, 55-56. Publ: 'Value of Lime on Putting Green Turf, Turf Clippings, Univ. of Mass, 60. Mem: R.I. Golf Course Supt. Asn; chmn, Exeter Heart Fund. Jr. State Boxing Champion of R.I, 52; Second Armored Div. Light Heavyweight Boxing Champion, Germany, 56. Rel: Baptist; Deacon and mem, Bd. of Trustees, Liberty Baptist Church. Legal Res: South County Trail, Exeter, R.I. 02822. Mailing Add: South County Trail, Slocum, R.I. 02877.

ALLEN, CLAUDE H.
b. Mound City, S.Dak. Educ: St. Paul Col. of Law, LL.B. Polit. & Govt. Pos: Minn. State Rep, 20 years; Minn. State Sen, 58-66. Bus. & Prof. Pos: Sr. partner law firm, Allen, Courtney & Salland. Mailing Add: W. First National Bank Bldg, 332 Minnesota, St. Paul, Minn. 55101. (1967)

ALLEN, CLINTON D. 'SHAG' D
City Councilman, Vinita, Okla.
b. Hallowell, Kans, 2/24/20; s. Walter Scott Allen and Pearl Wright A; m. 11/23/68 to Florence Odell Guy; c. Cheryl Rae (Mrs. Larry Dean Fowler), Jerry Lynn and Debra Diane. Educ: Columbus High Sch, Kans, 34-37. Polit. & Govt. Pos: City councilman, Vinita, Okla, 54- Mem: Mason (32°); Odd Fellows; Am. Legion; Scottish Rite; Tel. Pioneers of Am. Mailing Add: 463 N. Brown, Vinita, Okla. 74301.

ALLEN, CREIGHTON HALE R
Chmn, Lyon Co. Rep. Party, Nev.
b. Ontario, Wis, 8/15/26; s. Alva G. Allen and Irid Bergquist A; m. 6/12/49 to Jane Doris Olsen; c. Jayne Lee, Robin Lyn, Rhonda Susan, Bradford Todd and Craig Hale. Educ: La Crosse State Col, 46-48; Marquette Univ, D.D.S, 52. Polit. & Govt. Pos: Del, Nev. State Rep. Meeting, 64 & 66; chmn, Lyon Co. Rep. Party, Nev, 66- Mil. Serv: Entered as Seaman 3/C, Navy, 45, released as Seaman 1/C, 46, after serv. in S.Pac; Am. and Pac. Theater Ribbons; Victory Medal. Mem: Am, Nev. and Wis. State Dent. Socs; Rotary; C. of C; Am. Legion; VFW; PTA. Rel: Methodist. Legal Res: 6 Austin St, Weed Heights, Nev. 89443. Mailing Add: 1 Austin St, Weed Heights, Nev. 89443. (1967)

ALLEN, DON A, SR. D
b. Iowa; m. to Margaret Rogers A; co Don A, Jr; two grandchildren. Educ: Pub. Schs, Iowa and Nebr; MCI Serv. Schs, grad. Civil Engr; additional courses in eng. sci, mgt. and war training, Univ. of South. Calif. and Calif. Inst. Tech. Polit. & Govt. Pos: Calif. State Assemblyman, 38-46 & 56-66; mem, Los Angeles City Coun, 47-56. Mil. Serv: Marine, Expeditionary, Intel. Sect. Mem: VFW (comdr, Belleau Woods Post 1035); Elks; Boy Scouts (past troop comdr); Ahepa; United Commercial Travelers; Crenshaw Sportsmen; C. of C; life mem, Optimists. 1967 Legal Res: Los Angeles, Calif. No mailing address available. (1967)

ALLEN, DONALD GEORGE R
Chmn, Sprague Rep. Town Cmt, Conn.
b. Norwich, Conn, 1/4/37; s. Donald Carlton Allen and Cecile LaFreniere A; m. 1/7/56 to Lorraine Antonia Fortier; c. Donald G, Jr, Cheryl Ann, George William, III and Barbara Jean. Educ: Norwich Free Acad, 4 years. Polit. & Govt. Pos: Chmn, Sprague Rep. Town Cmt, Conn, currently; bd. selectman, Sprague, Conn, currently. Mil. Serv: Entered as Pvt, Marine Corps Res, 54, released as Sgt, 62, after serv. in Third Spec. Inf. Co. Mem: Nat. Mgt. Asn; Muklak Sportsman Club; Sprague Rod & Gun Club; K. of C.(4°); Int. Order Alhambra; Am. Red Cross (first aid chmn, Norwich Chap). Rel: Roman Catholic. Legal Res: Westminister Rd, Hanover, Conn. 06330. Mailing Add: R.F.D. 1, Box 140 AA, Baltic, Conn. 06330.

ALLEN, ELTON ELLSWORTH R
b. Hurricane, W.Va, 7/17/13; s. Noah R. Allen and Grace Henderson A; m. 4/7/37 to Nancy Roach; c. Don and Ann. Educ: Cincinnati Col. of Mortuary Sci, Embalmer, 38. Polit. & Govt. Pos: Campaign mgr, Putnam Co, Rep. Party, W.Va, 48, finance chmn, 55-56 and chmn, 66-68; mem, Town Coun, Hurricane, W.Va, 14 years. Bus. & Prof. Pos: Owner and mgr, Allen Funeral Home, Hurricane, W.Va, currently. Publ: Articels in various Funeral Dirs. Journals, 66. Mem: W.Va. Funeral Dirs. Asn.(pres, 51-52); mem, W.Va. Bd. of Embalmers and Funeral Dirs, 55-61 and secy, 57-61; mem, Conf. of Funeral Serv. Examining Bds. of U.S.A, 59-62; A.F.&A.M; K. of P; Lions. Ky. Col. Rel: Baptist. Legal Res: 2914 Putnam Ave, Hurricane, W.Va. 25526. Mailing Add: 2837 Main St, Hurricane, W.Va. 25526.

ALLEN, F. MONROE R
R.I. State Sen.
b. Providence, R.I, 8/11/30; s. Frederick W. Allen and Phyllis Lapham A; m. 7/17/54 to Anne Hardman; c. Heidi and David F. Educ: Brown Univ, B.S, 51; Boston Univ. Sch. of Law, LL.B, 54. Polit. & Govt. Pos: Chmn, Smithfield Rep. Town Cmt, R.I, 59-66; R.I. State Sen, 66- Mil. Serv: Entered as Pvt, Army, 55, released 57, after serv. in Heavy Mortar Co, 86th Regt, Tenth Div, Schweinfurt, Germany. Mem: R.I. Bar Asn; Lions. Rel: Protestant. Mailing Add: East Gate Rd, Greenville, R.I. 02828.

ALLEN, GEORGE EDWARD, JR. D
Va. State Del.
b. Victoria, Va, 4/4/14; m. to Elizabeth Stone A. Educ: Va. Polytech. Inst; Univ. Richmond Law Sch, LL.B. Polit. & Govt. Pos: Va. State Del, 54-; past pres, Young Dem. Clubs of Va. Bus. & Prof. Pos: Lawyer. Mem: Am. Bar Asn; Am. Trial Lawyers Asn; Law Sci. Acad. and Found; Co. Club of Va; Commonwealth and Downtown Clubs, Richmond. Rel: Baptist. Legal Res: 213 Lock Lane, Richmond, Va. 23226. Mailing Add: House of Delegates, State Capitol Bldg, Richmond, Va. 23219. (1967)

ALLEN, GOLDEN L. R
State Treas, Utah
b. Portage, Utah, 7/22/12; s. Joseph D. Allen and Elizabeth Naylor A; m. 8/23/35 to Helen Hoffler; c. Joy (Mrs. Gordon S. Purrington), Gay (Mrs. James Farnworth), Bruce L, Ann and Judy. Educ: Utah State Univ, B.S, 35 and summer sch. postgrad, 36-40; Univ. Ariz, 42; Univ. Utah, 46; Phi Kappa Phi. Polit. & Govt. Pos: Auditor, State Bd. Educ, Utah, 41-42; city recorder, Centerville City, 46-68; mem. boxing cmn, Salt Lake City, 59-67; state treas, 69- Bus. & Prof. Pos: High sch. teacher, Kanab, Utah, 35-37 and prin, 38-41; teacher, Latter-day Saint Bus. Col, 46; acct, Universal CIT Credit Corp, 47-68. Mil. Serv: Entered as Lt.(sg), Navy, 42, released as Lt.(sg), 46, after serv. in Pac. Theatre, 43-46; Naval Res, 46-52; Pac. Theatre decorations. Mem: Ambassador Club. Scholastic award, Phi Kappa Phi. Rel: Latter-day Saint. Mailing Add: 120 S. 200 East, Centerville, Utah 84014.

ALLEN, GORDON PHILLIP D
N.C. State Sen.
b. Roxboro, N.C, 4/29/29; s. George Lemuel Allen, Sr. and Sallie Wilkerson A; m. 7/12/52 to Betsy Harris; c. Gordon Phillip, Jr, Katharine Lee, Betsy Reade, George William and Graham Page. Educ: Mars Hill Col, A.A, 49. Polit. & Govt. Pos: Pres, Person Co. Young Dem. Club, N.C, 57; precinct chmn, Person Co. Dem. Party, 58-60; chmn, Person Co. Dem. Exec. Cmt, 60-68; chmn, Roxboro Sch. Bd, 65-66; mem, Airport Authority and Person Co. Exten. Cmt, 65-; N.C. State Sen, 11th Dist, 69- Bus. & Prof. Pos: Partner, Thompson-Allen Agency, 58-; chmn. bd, Home Savings & Loan, Roxboro Br, 63-; secy, Somerset-Hill Co, Inc, 65-; pres, Roxboro Bldg. Co, Inc, currently; dir, People's Bank. Mil. Serv: Entered as Pvt, Army, 51, released as 1st Lt, 53, after serv. in 2nd Inf. Div, Korea, 52-53; Bronze Star Medal; Korean Presidential Citation; Korean Campaign Medal with 2 Battle Stars; Nat. Defense Medal; 1st Lt, Army Nat. Guard, 54-57. Mem: Mason; VFW; pres, Kiwanis, 57-58; Roxboro Country Club. Rel: Methodist. Legal Res: Crestwood Dr, Roxboro, N.C. Mailing Add: Box 100. Roxboro, N.C. 27573.

ALLEN, HARLAN GOLINE SR. D
b. Cullman, Ala, 9/28/12; s. Taswell Nelson Allen and Ada Whatley A; m. 11/10/40 to Percy Weekley; c. Harlan Goline Jr. Educ: St. Bernard Col, Cullman, Ala, 36-37; Howard Col, Birmingham, 37-38. Polit. & Govt. Pos: Ala. State Sen, 54-66; State V.Cmdr, Nat. Exec. Cmt; mem, State Bd. Vets. Affairs, 51-54; chief clerk, Cullman Probate Office, 48-54; City Tax Serv, Cullman, 46-48; Exam. for State Revenue Dept, 39-47. Bus. & Prof. Pos: Ins. Mil. Serv: Army, 43-45. Mem: Mason; Shriner. Rel: Baptist. Mailing Add: Box 28, Cullman, Ala. 35055. (1967)

ALLEN, HENRY BANKS D
b. Omega, Tift Co, Ga, 1/7/16; s. Lyman Banks Allen and Alice Connell A; m. 2/16/51 to Juanita Willis Bryan; stepchildren, William Wheeler and Victoria Anna Bryan. Educ: Mercer Univ, B.A, 39. Polit. & Govt. Pos: Ga. State Rep, 63-66; Tift Co. Forestry Bd, 57-62. Bus. & Prof. Pos: Teacher, 60-62 and 37-41; farmer, 54-62; sch. supt, 49-59. Mil. Serv: Navy, Disbursing Storekeeper, 1/C, NLFED, Norfolk, Va, USS Endymion, ARL 9, 42-46. Mem: Tift Co. Hosp. Bd, 66-; Mason. Rel: Baptist; teacher, Baraca Sunday Sch. class, 1st Baptist Church. Mailing Add: Rt. 1, Chula, Ga. 31733. (1967)

ALLEN, IVAN, JR. D
Mayor, Atlanta, Ga.
b. Atlanta, Ga, 3/15/11; s. Ivan Allen and Irene Beaumont A; m. 1/1/36 to Louise Richardson; c. Ivan, III, Hugh Inman and Beaumont. Educ: Ga. Inst. of Tech, B.S. in commerce, 33; Sigma Alpha Epsilon. Polit. & Govt. Pos: Mayor, Atlanta, Ga, 62- Bus. & Prof. Pos: Dir, Ivan Allen Co. and Nat. Blank Book Co, at present. Mil. Serv: Entered as 2nd Lt, Army, World War II, released as Maj. Mem: Past pres, Atlanta C. of C. Rel: Presbyterian; Deacon. Legal Res: 3700 Northside Dr, N.W, Atlanta, Ga. 30305. Mailing Add: City Hall, Atlanta, Ga. 30303.

ALLEN, J.S. D
b. Doniphan, Mo, 4/4/07; m. 11/16/33 to Grace Oren; c. Mary Louise St. James, Albert Louis, Carol Sue, Opal Jean; grandchildren: James Arthur, Autum Gale. Educ: S.E. Mo. State Col; Univ. of Mo; Ark. State Col; Ark. Univ. Polit. & Govt. Pos: Mo. State Rep, until 66; Supt. of Schs, Carter Co, Mo, 43, 47, 51, 55, 59-63. Bus. & Prof. Pos: Educator. Mem: AF&AM; Scottish Rite; Shriners. Rel: First Baptist Church, Van Buren, Mo. Mailing Add: Box 157, Van Buren, Mo. 63965 (1967)

ALLEN, JACK LEE R
Mem, Nebr. State Rep. Cent. Cmt.
b. Robinson, Kans, 4/2/41; s. Asa Bryan Allen and Ruth Blanche Haney A; single. Educ: Univ. Omaha. Polit. & Govt. Pos: Mem, Young Rep. State Bd, Nebr, 58-59; dep. co. sheriff and chief co. probation officer, Sarpy Co, 65-68; alternate del-at-lg, Rep. Nat. Conv, 68; mem, Sarpy Co. Rep. Cent. Cmt, 68-; mem, Nebr. State Rep. Cent. Cmt, 68- Bus. & Prof. Pos: News ed, Bellevue Press Corp, Nebr, 61-63, ed, 63-65 & 68- Mem. Nebr. Press Asn; Int. Asn. Juvenile Officers; C. of C; Jr. C. of C; DeMolay. Received numerous commun. awards. Rel: Episcopal. Legal Res: 2809 Sandra St, Omaha, Nebr. 68147. Mailing Add: 2217 Franklin St, Bellevue, Nebr. 68005.

ALLEN, JAMES BROWNING D
U.S. Sen, Ala.
b. Gadsden, Ala, 12/28/12; s. George C. Allen and Mary Ethel Browning A; m. 3/16/40 to Marjorie Jo Stephens, wid. 56; m. 1964 to Maryon Pittman Mullins; c. James B, Jr. Educ: Univ. Ala. Polit. & Govt. Pos: Ala. State Rep, 39-45; Ala. State Sen, 47-51; Lt. Gov, Ala, 51-55 & 63-67; U.S.Sen, Ala, 69- Mil. Serv: Entered as Ens, Naval Res, 43, released as Lt.(jg), 46. Rel: Church of Christ. Legal Res: 1321 Bellevue Dr, Gadsden, Ala. 35901. Mailing Add: New Senate Office Bldg, Washington, D.C. 20510.

ALLEN, JAMES E, JR. R
Asst. Secy. for Educ. and Cmnr. of Educ, Dept. of Health, Educ. and Welfare
b. Elkins, W.Va, 4/25/11; m. 4/23/38 to Florence Miller; c. Twins, James E, III and Mrs. John Dolven. Educ: Davis and Elkins Col, A.B, 32; Princeton Univ. Grad. Sch, econ. and pub. finance; Harvard, Ed.M, 42 and Ed.D, 45. Hon. degrees from numerous cols. and univs. Polit. & Govt. Pos: Educ. consult, War Dept, attached to the staff of Commanding Gen. of the Third Air Force, 44-45; consult. and writer, President's Cmn. on Higher Educ, 46-47; exec. asst, N.Y. State Cmnr. of Educ, 47-50, Dep. Cmnr. of Educ, 50-55, Cmnr. of Educ, 55-69; Asst. Secy. for Educ. and Cmnr. of Educ, Dept. of Health, Educ. and Welfare, 69- Bus. & Prof. Pos: With W.Va. State Educ. Dept, 34-39; research assoc, Princeton Surv, 39-41; mem. research staff, Center for Research in Educ. Admin, Harvard, 41-43; secy. to faculty and dir. of placement, Harvard Grad. Sch. of Educ, 43-45; asst. prof. of educ. and dir, Bur. of Sch. Serv, Syracuse Univ, 45-47; pres, Univ. of the State of N.Y, 55-69. Publ: Financing of Higher Education, President's Cmn. on Higher Educ; State School Fiscal Policy for New Jersey; co-author of several monographs and reports in educ. admin. and contrib. to numerous mag. Recipient, Medal for Distinguished Serv, Columbia Univ. Teachers Col, 68. Legal Res: Loudonville, N.Y. 12211. Mailing Add: Dept. of Health, Education and Welfare, 330 Independence Ave. S.W, Washington, D.C. 20201.

ALLEN, JAMES F. R
N.H. State Rep.
b. Boston, Mass, 10/24/85; married. Educ: Suffolk Law Sch. Hon. D.C.L, Franklin Pierce Col, 66. Polit. & Govt. Pos: Town moderator, Rindge, N.H, 48-; chmn, Bd. of Adjust; mem, Chesire Co. Del. to N.H. State Rep. Conv, 58, 60, 62, 64, 66 & 68; v.chmn, Munic. & Co. Govt. Cmt; N.H. State Rep, 59- Bus. & Prof. Pos: Salesman. Mem: Bd. of Trustees of Trust Funds; Grange. Rel: Congregational. Mailing Add: Rindge, N.H. 03461.

ALLEN, JAMES ROBERT R
Mayor, Columbus, Ga.
b. Columbus, Ga, 11/20/30; s. Richard Augusta Allen and Mollie Hutchinson A; m. 10/20/51 to Joyce Ann Ray; c. Gary, Stan and Gwen. Educ: Marsh Bus. Col, Atlanta, Ga, Cert. in Acct; Univ. Ga, Degree in Bus. Admin. Polit. & Govt. Pos: Campaign chmn, Carl Sanders Third Dist. Cmt, 62; mem, Ga. Dem. Exec. Cmt, 62-66; cmnr, Muscogee Co. Cmn, 65-68, chmn, 66-68; mem, Third Dist. Dem. Exec. Cmt, 67-68; Mayor, Columbus, Ga, 69- Bus. & Prof. Pos: Cashier, Coca Cola Co, Columbus, Ga, 51-52, head bookeeper, 52-53; acct, Leonard, West & Favors, CPA, 55-59; comptroller, WRBL-TV-Radio, 59-65; owner-pres, Ky. Fried Chicken, Ga-Ala, 65-69; pres, Signs, Inc, currently. Mem: Columbus Jaycees (past pres. and former sen); Rotary; C. of C; Goodwill Industs; Jr. Achievement; Girls Club of Columbus; United Givers; March of Dimes; Citizens and Mil. Coun, Asn. U.S. Army; U.S. Navy League; Med. Center Bd. Dirs; Ga. Jaycees (secy, 63-64). Columbus Young Man of the Year, 64; One of Five Outstanding Young Men in Ga, 65. Rel: Baptist; Deacon. Legal Res: 2228 Westminster Way, Columbus, Ga. 31904. Mailing Add: P.O. Box 1340, Columbus, Ga. 31902.

ALLEN, JESSE WILLARD R
First V.Chmn, Ariz. Rep. Cmt.
b. Hamilton, Tex, 2/17/17; s. Shoobie Allen and Ethel Lavelle A; m. 3/10/46 to Vivian Zudora Levy. Polit. & Govt. Pos: Co. chmn, Rep. Party, Ariz, 60-63; Ariz. State Rep, 65-66; first v.chmn, Ariz. Rep. Cmt, 66-; bd. mem, Ariz. Dept. Econ. Planning & Develop, 68- Mil. Serv: Entered as A/S, Navy, 35, released as Lt.(jg), 46; World War II Theater Ribbons; Camp Ribbons. Mem: Nat. and Am. Commun. Theatre Asn; Ariz. Oil & Gas Asn; Ariz. Acad. Pub. Opinion (bd. dirs); Elks; VFW; Am. Legion; Rotary; Ariz. Hist Soc. Rel: Roman Catholic. Legal Res: 132 Paseo Contento, Nogales, Ariz. 85621. Mailing Add: P.O. Box 400, Nogales, Ariz. 85621.

ALLEN, JOHN D
Tex. State Rep.
b. Cunningham, Tex, 12/16/26; s. Fred Allen and Lorette Bell A; m. 4/25/47 to Doris Isom; c. Barbara, Peggy, Fred and Jane. Educ: Paris Jr. Col; Univ. of Tex. Polit. & Govt. Pos: Mem, Longview Sch. Bd, Tex, 57-59; Tex. State Rep, 59- Bus. & Prof. Pos: Asst. mgr, Radio Sta. KPLT, 49-51; sales mgr, Radio Sta. KFRO, 51-56, v.pres, 56-66. Mil. Serv: Entered as Pvt, Air Force, 44, released as S/Sgt, 46, after serv. in 20th Air Force, Mariannas. Mem: Mason (32°); Optimists; C. of C; Am. Legion; VFW; Farm & Ranch Club; Adult Leader, R-H; Tex. Asn. of Broadcasters. Named Outstanding Citizen of Longview, 59; Statewide 4-H Alumni Award; many honors in pub. speaking. Rel: Church of Christ. Legal Res: 1003 E. Birdsong St, Longview, Tex. 75601. Mailing Add: State House of Representatives, State Capitol Bldg, Austin, Tex. 78711. (1967)

ALLEN, JOHN JOSEPH, JR. R
b. Oakland, Calif, 11/27/99; s. John Joseph Allen and Catherine Liston Owen A; m. 6/16/26 to Carol Cook (deceased); m. 11/11/57 to Sally Clement; c. Ramona (Mrs. McIntyre), Susanne (Mrs. Harvey), Catherine Clement, Sally Ann and Verna Lucile. Educ: Univ. Calif, A.B, 20; J.D, 22; Theta Chi. Polit. & Govt. Pos: Mem, Oakland Bd. Educ, Calif, 23-43; mem, Alameda Co. Rep. Cent. Cmt, 24-26 & 34-44; v.chmn, Orgn. State Cmn. on Sch. Dists, 46; U.S. Rep, Calif, 47-59; undersecy. transportation, Dept. of Commerce, 59-61. Bus. & Prof. Pos: Attorney-at-law, 22-; dir, Ins. Securities Inc, 54-67. Mil. Serv: A/S, World War I; re-entered Navy, Lt, 43, released as Lt. Comdr, 45, after serv. in Naval Net Depot; Tiburon and various islands in S.Pac. Area; Lt. Comdr, Naval Res.(Ret). Mem: State Bar of Calif; Alameda Co. Bar Asn; Elks; Masons; Kiwanis; Native Sons of Golden West; Am. Legion. Rel: Episcopal. Mailing Add: P.O. Box 721, McCall, Idaho 83638.

ALLEN, JOHN NEVILLE R
Chmn, Kenosha Co. Rep. Party, Wis.
b. Buffalo, N.Y, 7/3/22; s. George Henry Allen and Alice Randall A; m. 5/20/50 to Margery Dixon; c. Holly, Roberta and Leigh. Educ: Wooster Prep. Sch, Conn, grad, 40; Bay Path Bus. Col, Mass, grad, 41. Polit. & Govt. Pos: Precinct committeeman, Rep. Party, Kenosha Co, Wis, 62-64; chmn, Goldwater Cmt, 64-65 and v.chmn, 65-66; chmn, Kenosha Co. Rep. Party, 66- Bus. & Prof. Pos: Various positions, Anaconda Am. Brass Co, 41-59, asst. sales mgr, 59- Mil. Serv: Entered as Pvt, Marines, 42, released as Sgt, 46, after serv. in 1st and 4th Divs, S.Pac. and China Theatres, 44-46; Presidential Unit Citation; Good Conduct Medal; Am. Campaign Medal; Victory Medal; China Serv. Medal; Navy Occup. Serv. Medal; Asia, Asiatic-Pac. Campaign Medal with two bronze stars. Mem: Mason; Elks; Kenosha Country Club; Kenosha Towne Club. Rel: Episcopal. Mailing Add: 406 78th St, Kenosha, Wis. 53140.

ALLEN, JOHN PLATT D
Chmn, Dem. Party, Ore.
b. Brooklyn, N.Y, 9/28/29; s. Harris Hampton Allen and Katharine Whitlock A; m. 3/16/63 to Roxie Anne Sears; c. Karen M, Nancy M, Susan H. and Jeremy J. Educ: Univ. Ore, 48; Portland State Univ, 49; Exten. Schs, Calif, 51 and N.Y, 65. Polit. & Govt. Pos: Precinct committeeman, 18 years; mem. exec. cmt, Clackamas Co. Rep. Cent. Cmt, Ore, 56-58; exec. chmn, Clackamas Co. Dem. Cent. Cmt, 67-68, mem, Gov. Cmn. Taxation, 68; chmn, Dem. Party, Ore, 68-; mem, Cmt. Metro-Planning, 69. Bus. & Prof. Pos: V.pres, Pac. Coast Ins. Agencies, Ltd, Charles W. Sexton Co. Mem: March of Dimes (exec. cmt, 66-68); Ins. Agents Asn; exec. cmt, Exchange Club; Farmers Union; Urban League. Outstanding achievement award, Dem. Party, 68. Rel: Unitarian. Mailing Add: 5350 S.W. Rigert Rd, Beaverton, Ore. 97005.

ALLEN, JOYCE ROSETTA D
Mem, Calif. Dem. State Cent. Cmt.
b. Los Angeles, Calif, 10/14/31; d. Carl Overr and Rosetta Thomas O; m. 8/26/61 to Samuel E. Allen, Jr; c. Daniel K. Tabor, David A. Tabor, Carl G. Tabor and Kathleen J. Allen. Educ: Univ. Calif, Los Angeles; Univ. South. Calif; Delta Sigma Theta. Polit. & Govt. Pos: Exec. secy, New Frontier Dem. Club, Calif, 64-67, v.pres, 67-69, trustee, 69-; mem, Calif. Dem. State Cent. Cmt, 65-; mem. adv. cmt, U.S. Rep. Edward Roybal, Calif, currently; v.pres, Dem. of South. Calif, 69- Rel: Episcopal. Mailing Add: 2708 W. 101st St, Inglewood, Calif. 90303.

ALLEN, KENNETH SETZER R
R.I. State Rep.
b. Gastonia, N.C, 7/7/30; s. Charles F. Allen and Alice Setzer A; m. 8/4/50 to Mona Rose Browne; c. Teresa Mae, Sharon Dawn and Kenneth Charles. Educ: Cent. Wesleyan Col, A.A, 50. Polit. & Govt. Pos: V.chmn, Dist. 3 Rep. Town Cmt, 65-68; chmn, North Kingstown Rep. Town Cmt, 69-; R.I. State Rep, 69- Bus. & Prof. Pos: Real estate broker, Kenneth S. Allen Agency, 67; v.pres, Pipe Line Oil Co, 67; pres, Colony Outdoor Advert, Inc, 68. Mem:

F&AM, Halifax Lodge 81, Daytona Beach, Fla; Gr. Providence C. of C; U.S. Navy League; Palestine Shrine, Providence, R.I. Rel: Southern Baptist. Mailing Add: 57 Ann Lane, North Kingstown, R.I. 02852.

ALLEN, LEM B. D
Chmn, Guadalupe Co. Dem. Party, Tex.
b. Luling, Tex, 3/4/41; s. Louis Fulshear Allen and Frances Gardien A; m. 8/17/63 to Mattie Susan Rogers; c. Lem B, Jr. and Zachary Fulshear. Educ: Tex. Tech. Col, 3½ years. Polit. & Govt. Pos: Chmn, Guadalupe Co. Dem. Party, Tex, 66- Bus. & Prof. Pos: Farmer, 63- Mem: Tex. and Southwest. Cattle Raisers Asns. Rel: Methodist. Mailing Add: Route 1, Box 339, Kingsbury, Tex. 78638.

ALLEN, LESTER J. R
b. Emerson Township, Mich, 5/19/00; married; c. Margaret (Mrs. Garver), Nancy (Mrs. Collins) and Richard. Educ: Alma Col; Mich. State Univ, grad. Polit. & Govt. Pos: Mich. State Rep, 56-68. Bus. & Prof. Pos: Farmer; dir, Fed. Land Bank, St. Paul, Minn; dir, Bank of Alma. Mil. Serv: World War I. Mem: Rotary; Farm Bur; Grange; Elks. Rel: Presbyterian. Mailing Add: RFD 1, Ithaca, Mich. 48847. (1967)

ALLEN, LLOYD M R
Mayor, South Bend, Ind.
b. Bloomfield, Ind, 7/26/19; s. John Frank Allen and Bessie Denny A; m. 11/12/43 to Doris Elaine Hall; c. Ronald Malcolm, Stephen Preston and Richard Denny. Educ: Indiana Univ, LL.B, 48; Phi Delta Phi. Polit. & Govt. Pos: City judge, South Bend, Ind, 59-63; mayor, South Bend, 64- Mil. Serv: Entered as Pilot, Navy, 41, released as Lt. Comdr, 46; Distinguished Flying Cross; Air Medal with two gold stars. Mem: Am. Bar Asn; Ind. State Bar Asn; Elks; Lions; Isaac Walton League; C. of C; Hearing & Speech Soc; Ment. Health Asn. Rel: Presbyterian. Legal Res: 2106 E. Jefferson Blvd, South Bend, Ind. 46601. Mailing Add: City Hall, South Bend, Ind. 46601.

ALLEN, LOUIS J. D
Chmn, State Elec. Cmn, Tenn.
b. Petersburg, Tenn, 12/27/98; s. Sidney H. Allen and Julia Joplin A; m. 11/28/23 to Lorena Randolph. Polit. & Govt. Pos: Chmn, State Elec. Cmn, Tenn; del, Dem. Nat. Conv, 68. Rel: Presbyterian. Mailing Add: 2713 Belmont Blvd, Nashville, Tenn. 37212. (1967)

ALLEN, MARY ELIZABETH D
V.Chmn, Kans. State Dem. Cmt.
b. Lawrence, Kans, 7/10/30; d. John Selig and Agnes Jost S; m. 6/27/53 to Adrian James Allen; c. Roger James and Cynthia. Educ: Univ. of Kans, B.S. in Educ, 52; Pi. Lambda Theta; Omicron Nu. Polit. & Govt. Pos: Women's v.pres, Kans. Dem. Club, 62-63; v.chmn, Second Cong. Dist. Dem. Cmt, 60-64; v.chmn, Shawnee Co. Dem. Cent. Cmt, 60-; secy, Kans. State Dem. Cmt, 64-65, v.chmn, 65-; del, Dem. Nat. Conv, 68. Bus. & Prof. Pos: Teacher voc. homemaking, 52-54. Mem: Treas, Native Daughters of Kans; past pres, Topeka Bar Asn. Auxiliary. Rel: Lutheran. Mailing Add: 5048 Brentwood Dr, Topeka, Kans. 66606. (1967)

ALLEN, NOLA ARLENE R
Chmn, 11th Dist. Rep. Party, Ind.
b. Grand Rapids, Mich, 4/23/33; d. Algion Arnold Allen and Lureatha Scott A; wid; c. Howard Griffin, Jr. Educ: Univ. Mich, B.A. & LL.B; Butler Univ, 58-61; Alpha Phi Alpha. Polit. & Govt. Pos: Chief clerk, Marion Circuit Court, 65-; Rep. ward co-ordinator, Ind, 65-; v.chmn, 11th Dist. Rep. Party, 66-68, chmn, 68-; asst. majority attorney, Ind. House Rep, 67 & 69; Rep. precinct committeeman, 68-; del, Rep. Nat. Conv, 68; chmn. minorities sect, Rep. State Cmt, 69- Mem: Activists. Rel: Methodist. Legal Res: 3318 N. Arsenal Ave, Indianapolis, Ind. 46218. Mailing Add: 321 Illinois Bldg, Indianapolis, Ind. 46204.

ALLEN, NORA ALICE R
Third Dist. Chmn, Rep. Party of Ga.
b. Leesburg, Ga, 8/16/21; d. George Dennis Moreland, Sr. and Nora Davis M; m. 7/5/42 to Carroll Coffey Allen; c. Carol (Mrs. G. Clifford Ranew) and George Dennis. Educ: Womans Col. Ga, 38-41. Polit. & Govt. Pos: State chmn. youth recruitment, Ga. Fedn. Rep. Women, 65; pres, Lee Co. Rep. Women's Club, 65; chmn, Lee Co. Rep. Party, Ga, 65-69; del, Rep. Nat. Conv, 68; Third Dist. chmn, Rep. Party of Ga, 68- Mem: Doublegate Country Club; Radium Country Club. Rel: Baptist. Mailing Add: Box 75, Leesburg, Ga. 31763.

ALLEN, PAUL D
Chmn, Barren Co. Dem. Cmt, Ky.
b. 1910. Educ: West. Ky. State Col. Polit. & Govt. Pos: Mem, Glasgow City Coun, Ky, 53-57; auditor, Barren Co, 57-63; Ky. State Rep, 64-68; chmn, Barren Co. Dem. Cmt, 68- Bus. & Prof. Pos: Ins. agent. Mem: Nat. Asn. Life Underwriters; Lions; C. of C. Rel: Methodist. Mailing Add: 104 JoAnn Dr, Glasgow, Ky. 42141. (1967)

ALLEN, PETER JOHN D
Mem, Calif. State Dem. Cent. Cmt.
b. New York City, N.Y, 5/21/07; s. Carl Aiello and Rose Sapienza A; m. 10/4/45 to Corinne Jane Andrews; c. John Monty and Judi Dominique. Educ: Univ. Santa Clara; Columbia Univ. Ext. Polit. & Govt. Pos: Organizer and dir, Ulster Co. Dem. Clubs, N.Y, 33-37; mem, Ulster Co. Dem. Cent. Cmt, 35-36; supvr, Pub. Works Admin, 35-37; del, Dem. Nat,Conv, 50, 64 & 68; mem, Santa Clara Co. Grand Jury, Calif, 63; chmn, Gov. Edmund G. Brown Finance Cmt, Santa Clara Co, 66; chmn, Dem. Century Club, 67-69; co-chmn, Hubert Humphrey Finance Cmt, North. Calif, 68; chmn, Congressman Don Edwards Campaign, 68; Dem. co-chmn, Ninth Cong. Dist, 69-; mem, Calif. State Dem. Cent. Cmt, 69- Bus. & Prof. Pos: Pres, Peter J. Allen Corp; owner, Allen's Furniture. Mil. Serv: Army Air Force, 42-44. Mem: Calif. Furniture Asn; dir, Santa Clara Co. Heart Asn, 61-62; Santa Clara Univ. Alumni Asn; Kiwanis (exec. bd); DAV (exec. bd. and adv. bd); C. of C; BSA (exec. bd); Multiple Sclerosis (exec. bd); dir, Sumitomo Nat. Bank, San Jose. Legal Res: 1610 Hester Ave, San Jose, Calif. 95128. Mailing Add: 40 S. Second St, San Jose, Calif. 95113.

ALLEN, RALPH WATSON R
Maine State Rep.
b. Nova Scotia, Can, 2/24/99; s. William John Allen and Sarah Welner A; m. 9/24/27 to Dorothy Dansie; c. Robert and Nancy. Educ: Boston Univ, B.B.A, 21, M.B.A, 25; Beta Gamma Sigma. Polit. & Govt. Pos: Maine State Rep, 67- Mil. Serv: Pvt, Army, 18. Rel: Episcopal. Mailing Add: 15 Thomas Ave, Caribou, Maine 04736.

ALLEN, RICHARD JOHN R
Mich. State Rep.
b. Ithaca, Mich, 8/6/33; s. Lester John Allen and Erma Prichard V; m. 8/3/63 to JoAnn Wright; c. Lester James and Carri Jo. Educ: Mich. State Univ, B.S, 55, D.V.M, 57; Sigma Alpha Epsilon. Polit. & Govt. Pos: Mich. State Rep, 69- Bus. & Prof. Pos: Owner and vet, State Road Animal Hosp, Alma, Mich, 58-; assoc. prof, Alma Col, 60-69; v.pres and treas, Bon Accord Farms, Ithaca, 62- Mem: Am. Asn. Adv. Sci; Mich. Vet. Med. Asn; Rotary; Farm Bur. Rel: Presbyterian. Mailing Add: R.R. 1, Ithaca, Mich. 48847.

ALLEN, ROBERT F. D
Founding Chmn, Fifth Dist. New Dem. Coalition, N.J.
b. N.Y.C, 12/26/28; s. Edwin E. Allen and Mary Thompson A; m. 11/21/56 to Elaine Bender; c. Peter and Judd. Educ: State Univ. N.Y, B.S, 49; N.Y. Univ, M.A. and Ph.D, 57; Columbia Univ, post doctoral study, 57-59. Polit. & Govt. Pos: Dem. cong. cand, 12th Dist, N.J, 66 and Fifth Dist, 68; chmn, 12th Dist. Dem. Coalition, 66-67; founding chmn, Fifth Dist. New Dem. Coalition, 68- Bus. & Prof. Pos: Acad. dean, Monmouth Col, N.J, 56-57; dir. grad. study, Newark State Col, Union, N.J, 57-59 and prof, 59-; pres, Sci. Resources, Inc, 64-66 and chmn. bd, 66- Mil. Serv: Entered as Pvt, Marine Corps, 51, released as Sgt, 53. Publ: Delinquency Rehabilitation—The Collegefields Program, U.S. Off. Health, Educ. and Welfare, 66; Educational Training Systems, Macmillan, 68; From Delinquency to Freedom, S C Publ, 69. Mem: Am. Acad. Polit. and Soc. Sci; Am. Psychol. Asn; N.Y. Soc. Clin. Psychologists; Inst. for Appl. Behav. Sci. N.Y. Univ. Founder's Day Award, State Univ. N.Y; Award for Highest Undergrad. Scholastic Rating; Commun. Leaders of Am. Award for Outstanding Commun. Serv. Mailing Add: Tempe-Wick Rd, Morristown, N.J. 07960.

ALLEN, SEWELL ELLYSON D
b. Iowa City, Iowa, 5/4/13; s. George Eugene Allen and Hilda Ellyson A; m. 3/17/43 to Frances Whiting; c. Stephen Whiting and Ellyson. Educ: Compton Jr. Col; State Univ. of Iowa, B.A, 35, Col. of Law, J.D, 39; Delta Chi; Phi Delta Phi. Polit. & Govt. Pos: Iowa State Rep, 41-42; nat. committeeman, Young Dem, 42-45; chmn, Monona Co. Dem. Party, 45-66; mem, State Dem. Cent. Cmt, 54-56; del, Dem. Nat. Conv, 56 & 60, alternate del, 68; attorney, Monona Co, 63-64; spec. asst. attorney gen, Iowa 65-66. Mil. Serv: Entered as Pvt, Army, 42, released as S/Sgt, 45, after serv. in 23rd Sta. Hosp, ETO; Naples-Foggia, Rome-Arno and Rhineland Campaign Ribbons; Good Conduct Medal; Europe-Africa-Middle East Theater Ribbon. Mem: Pres, Onawa Kiwanis, 66; Country Club; Am. Legion; Odd Fellows; Am. and Iowa Bar Asns; pres, Monona Co. Bar Asn, 58 & 68. Rel: Methodist. Mailing Add: 1212 Pearl, Onawa, Iowa 51040.

ALLEN, WALT D
b. Marlow, Okla, 12/4/11; s. Acie Allen and Mettie Stroud A; m. 6/20/36 to Lela Fae Zachary; c. Donald Thomas and Richard Larry. Educ: Cent. State Col, 31-34; George Wash. Univ, J.D, 39; Acacia. Polit. & Govt. Pos: Spec. asst, U.S. Attorney Gen, Wash, D.C, 38-41; del, Dem. Nat. Conv, 56; Okla. State Sen, 50-64; chmn, Grady Co. Dem. Party, 66-69. Bus. & Prof. Pos: Attorney-at-law, Wash, D.C, 38-43, Okla, 43- Mil. Serv: Entered as 2nd Lt, Army, 41, released as Lt. Col, 46, after serv. in Internal War Crimes, Pac, 45-46; Col.(Ret), Judge Adv. Gen. Corps, Army Res. Mem: Okla. Bar Asn; Kiwanis; Elks; Am. Legion; DAV; Farmers Union; Okla. Cattlemen's Asn. Admitted to practice before Okla. Bars, Fed. Courts and U.S. Supreme Court. Rel: Baptist. Mailing Add: 116 N. Fourth, Chickasha, Okla. 73018.

ALLEN, WARREN GEORGE R
N.Dak. State Rep.
b. Deering, N.Dak, 10/10/21; s. Fred Lewis Allen and Clara Holo; m. 8/24/52 to Marjorie Thorpe; c. Fred Lewis and Joellen Clarice. Educ: Minot State Col, B.A, 43; Univ. N.Dak, M.S, 52, Ph.D, 57; Phi Delta Kappa. Hon. L.H.D, Sioux Empire Col, Hawarden, Iowa, 66. Polit. & Govt. Pos: Precinct committeeman, N.Dak. Rep. Part, 62-66; N.Dak. State Rep, Fifth Legis. Dist, 67- Bus. & Prof. Pos: Chmn, Div. Educ. and Psychology, Minot State Col, 57- Mil. Serv: Pvt, Army, 43; Major, Army Res, 66. Mem: Nat. Educ. Asn; Asn. Higher Educ. Rel: Protestant. Mailing Add: 30 Robinwood Estates, Minot, N.Dak. 58701.

ALLEN, WILLIAM GARRISON D
b. Dixon Springs, Tenn, 10/15/19; s. George Webster Allen and Mary Zee Garrison A; m. 10/28/50 to Frances Dale Wallace; c. William W, Barbara Dale and John D. Educ: Univ. Ala, B.S, 41; Cumberland Univ, LL.B, 47; Beta Gamma Sigma; Omicron Delta Kappa. Polit. & Govt. Pos: Admin. asst. to U.S. Sen, Albert Gore, 53- Bus. & Prof. Pos: Attorney, MacFarland & Allen, Columbia, Tenn, 47-51. Mil. Serv: Entered as 2nd Lt, Army, 41, released as Maj, 46, after serv. in 34th Inf. Regt, Pac. Theater, 41-45; reentered as Maj, 51, released in 52; Bronze Star; Purple Heart. Rel: Presbyterian. Legal Res: Dixon Springs, Tenn. 37057. Mailing Add: 1331 Kingston Ave, Alexandria, Va. 22302.

ALLEN, WILLIAM WILSON R
Pa. State Rep.
b. Dayton, Pa, 6/7/08; s. Charles Francis Allen and Luella Maude Wilson A; m. 10/1/28 to Garnet Jewart; c. Robert LaVern. Educ: Dayton Voc. High Sch, 4 years. Polit. & Govt. Pos: Chief clerk, Warren Co, Pa, 57-67; Pa. State Rep, 65th Dist, 67- Bus. & Prof. Pos: Mgr. and specialized pos: The Great Atlantic & Pac. Tea Co, 29-48; ins. agent and broker, 48-57. Mem: Warren Co. Pomona Grange; Mason; Venango Lodge of Perfection and Coudersport Consistory; Garden Club; C. of C; Kinzua Dam Vacation Bur. Rel: United Presbyterian. Mailing Add: 124 Main St, Tidioute, Pa. 16351.

ALLETT, ROBERT G. R
b. Benton Harbor, Mich, 9/24/13; s. John G. Allett and Edith Jewell A; m. 5/28/38 to Dorothy E. Eaton; c. Betsy. Educ: Valparaiso Univ, A.B, 34.

Polit. & Govt. Pos: Sr. staff mem, U.S. House of Rep. Cmt. on Standards of Official Conduct, 69- Mil. Serv: Entered as Ens, Navy, 43, released as Lt.(jg), 46, after serv. as flight instr. Rel: Protestant. Mailing Add: 201 Panorama Dr, Oxon Hill, Md. 20021.

ALLEY, ZEBULON DOYLE D
b. Sylva, N.C, 8/9/28; s. Doyle Davis Alley and Edith Purcell A; m. 11/27/53 to Faye Jones; c. Randall Greer and Doyle David, II. Educ: Univ. N.C, A.B, 53, LL.B, 55. Polit. Pos: Nat. Committeeman, Young Dem. Club, 64-65, v.pres, N.C, 57-58 and pres, Halifax Co, 57-58. Govt. Pos: Co. attorney, Haywood Co. and city attorney, Clyde, N.C, 66-; city attorney, Waynesville, 63-; N.C. Counsel, Fed. Land Bank of Columbia, 58-62; asst. dir, Inst. of Govt, Univ. N.C, 55-56. Mil. Serv: Entered as Pvt, Army, 48, released as Cpl, 51; Korean Campaign Ribbon; UN Ribbon; Far Eastern Ribbon; Bronze Star with V device for valor; Purple Heart. Publn: Rules of the Road in North Carolina, Inst. of Govt, 56. Mem: N.C. State Bar; N.C. Bar Asn; Am. Legion; VFW; Elks. Rel: Methodist. Legal Res: 920 East St, Waynesville, N.C. 28786. Mailing Add: Drawer 1018, Waynesville, N.C. 28786.

ALLGOOD, CLARENCE WILLIAM D
b. Birmingham, Ala, 9/12/02; s. Robert Venable Allgood and Patricia Robertson A; m. 6/27/27 to Marie Maxwell; c. Clarence William. Educ: Howard Col, 21-23; Ala. Polytech. Inst, B.S, 26; Birmingham Sch. Law, LL.B, 41; Pi Kappa Alpha; Sigma Delta Kappa. Polit. & Govt. Pos: Referee in Bankruptcy, U.S. Dist. Court, N.Ala, 37-61; U.S. Dist. Judge N. Dist. Ala, 61- Bus. & Prof. Pos: Dir, Fidelity Mortgage Co. Ala. and Fidelity Fed. Savings and Loan Assoc. Mem: Trustee, Crippled Children's Hosp. and Clinic, 41-, pres, 58; trustee, Ala. Soc. Crippled Children and Adults, 46-48; Counsel Prfnl. Rels, Am. Hosp. Asn, 50-52; chmn, Ala. Hosp. Trustees Asn, 51; chmn. trustees, S. Highland Infirmary, 45-55; Am, Ala. and Birmingham Bar Asns; Elks; Blue Key; Civitan Club. Mailing Add: P.O. Box 155, Birmingham, Ala. 35202.

ALLIGOOD, BOB D
b. Mitchell Co, Ga, 12/5/32; s. Coy Alligood and Gladys L. Thomas A; m. 5/11/56 to Celeste Moore; c. Randall Mark and Robyn Dee. Educ: Univ. Fla, Indust. Eng, 60; Blue Key. Polit. & Govt. Pos: Former Fla. State Rep, Orange and Osceola Co. Bus. & Prof. Pos: Exec. dir, Fla. Eng. Soc, 60-66; gen. mgr, Orlando Div, Watson and Co, and v.pres, Orlando Div, First Data Corp, 66-; dir. develop, Reynolds, Smith & Hill, 68, partner, 69- Mil. Serv: Entered as Pvt, Army, 53, released as Sgt, 56, after serv. in Far East Japan; Cert. of Achievement. Mem: Benton Eng. Soc; Fla. Eng. Soc; Adv. Coun. of Small Bus Admin; Am. Inst. of Indust. Engrs; Orlando Jaycees; Univ. of Fla. Alumni Asn. Baseball Letterman, Univ. Fla; Outstanding Male Leader, Alumni Award. Rel: Baptist. Mailing Add: 7504 Holiday Rd. S, Jacksonville, Fla. 32216.

ALLINGTON, THOMAS B. D
b. Lincoln, Nebr, 4/15/42; s. Tom C. Allington and Margaret Cunningham A; m. 6/7/63 to Marcia Dodge; c. Elizabeth Ann. Educ: Univ. Nebr, B.S, 64, J.D, 66; Beta Gamma Sigma; Order of the Coif. Polit. & Govt. Pos: Alternate del, Dem. Nat. Conv, 68. Bus. & Prof. Pos: Asst. prof. law, Univ. S.Dak, 66-68, assoc. prof, 68-; vis. assoc. prof. law, Univ. Nebr, 69-70. Publ: Ed, The Tasks of Penology, Univ. Nebr. Press, 69. Mem: Am. and Nebr. Bar Asns. Mailing Add: 609 Catalina Ave, Vermillion, S.Dak. 57069.

ALLISON, BETTY VIRGINIA R
V.Chmn, Yuma Co. Rep. Cent. Cmt, Colo.
b. Wray, Colo, 2/5/25; d. Arnold Carl Unger and Thelma Myers U; m. 5/12/43 to Stephen Raymond Allison; c. Virginia Lee, Stephen Louis, Carole Elaine and Barry Raymond. Educ: Wray High Sch. Polit. & Govt. Pos: Rep. precinct committeewoman, Colo, 55-57; pres, Yuma Co. Rep. Club; 58-65; v.chmn, Yuma Co. Rep. Cent. Cmt, 65- Mem: Eastern Star (past Matron); pres, Women's Soc. of Christian Serv; Farm Bur. Rel: United Methodist. Legal Res: Route 1, Wray, Colo. 80758. Mailing Add: Route 1, Box 37, Wray, Colo. 80758.

ALLISON, DAVID LORD R
Ind. State Rep.
b. Washington, D.C, 12/2/42; s. Robert Thomas Allison, Sr. and Patricia Lord; single. Educ: Marian Col, Indianapolis, Ind, B.A, 64; Ind. Univ, Indianapolis Law Sch, J.D, 68; justice and v.justice Hamill Chap, Phi Alpha Delta. Polit. & Govt. Pos: Ind. State Rep, Marion Co, Indianapolis, 68-; mem, bd. of dirs, Marion Co, Ind. Commun. Action Against Poverty, 69- Bus. & Prof. Pos: Court bailiff, Marion Co. Munc. Court Four, Ind, 65-66; caseworker, Marion Co. Dept. of Pub. Welfare, 66-68; mem. staff, Trust Dept, Am. Fletcher Nat. Bank, 68-69; Attorney-at-law, self employed, Indianapolis, 69- Mem: Am, Ind. and Indianapolis Bar Asns; Nat. Soc. of State Legis; Ind. State Legis. Soc; K. of C; Jaycees; Legal Panel, Ind. Civil Liberties Union; Indianapolis Law Sch. Alumni Asns; Nat. Parks Asn; Wilderness Soc; Philatelic Found; Young Am. for Freedom; Indianapolis Zool. Soc; Young Rep. Rel: Catholic. Legal Res: 3024 E. Fall Creek Pkwy. Dr, N, Indianapolis, Ind. 46205. Mailing Add: 3360 N. Meridian St, L.2, Indianapolis, Ind. 46208.

ALLISON, GILBERT J. D
b. Tamaqua, Pa, 11/12/13; s. John L. Allison and Anna Gribbin A; m. to Regina M. Knoblauch. Educ: St. Jerome's High Sch; Lasalle Col, A.B. Polit. & Govt. Pos: Pa. State Rep, 64-67. Bus. & Prof. Pos: Dist. sales mgr. and tax consult; previously internal revenue agent, U.S. Treas. Dept; Westinghouse Elec. Corp; and by Pa. Dept. of Pub. Assistance. Mem: 4° K. of C; past pres, Panther Valley Irish-Am. Asn; Elks; St. Jerome's Holy Name Soc; past pres, PIAA Basketball Chap. Varsity football; officiated PIAA High Sch. football and basketball; Phila. ABC Singles Bowling Champ, 45. Rel: St. Jerome's Catholic Church, Tamaqua. Mailing Add: 449 Arlington St, Tamaqua, Pa. 18252. (1967)

ALLISON, JAMES N, JR. R
Dep. Chmn, Rep. Nat. Cmt.
b. Lincoln, Nebr, 12/4/31; s. James N. Allison, Sr. and Helon Young A; m. 12/27/66 to Carolyn Gaushell; c. Alyson Ann Allison and James N. Allison, III and Tommy Michael Gaushell. Educ: South. Methodist Univ, B.B.A, 53; Blue Key; Sigma Delta Chi; Sigma Iota Epsilon; Sigma Chi. Polit. & Govt. Pos: Asst. campaign dr, George Bush for Sen, Tex, 64; campaign dir, George Bush for U.S. Rep, 66 and Ed. Gurney for Sen, Fla, 68; admin. asst. to U.S. Rep. George Bush, 67; dep. chmn, Rep. Nat. Cmt, 69- Bus. & Prof. Pos: Exec. v.pres, Midland Reporter-Telegram, Tex, 55-64; dir, First Nat. Bank, Midland, Tex, 59-66 and Citizens Savings & Loan, 62-66. Mil. Serv: Entered as 2nd Lt, Air Force, 53, released as 1st Lt, 55, after serv. in 514th Fighter Interceptor Squadron, Royal Air Force Sta, Manston, Eng, 54-55; Capt, Air Force Res; Nat. Defense Serv. Medal. Mem: Midland C. of C.(pres, 63); chmn, Midland Commun. Chest, 62; Midland Jr. C. of C.(pres, 59). Outstanding Young Man of Midland, 59; One of Five Outstanding Young Texans, 61. Rel: Episcopal. Legal Res: Houston, Tex. Mailing Add: 1625 Eye St, N.W, Washington, D.C. 20006.

ALLMON, RAY N. D
b. New Liberty, Mo, 12/11/18; m. 9/21/57 to Ruby Sconce; c. three daughters. Educ: Ariz. State Col, Phoenix; G. Frye Aircraft Sch, St. Louis; Aviation Cadets Pilot Training, West Coast Training Command; GM Acct, Serv. and Tech. Sch. Polit. & Govt. Pos: Mo. State Rep, 64-66. Bus. & Prof. Pos: Chevrolet dealer since 50-; gen. contractor (8 yrs.); oil jobber (12 yrs.); trucking co. (9 yrs.). Mil. Serv: 2nd Lt, USAAF (3 yrs), WW II; Italy, attached to 15th USAF Pilot B-17 Bomber. Mem: AF&AM; Abou Ben Adhem Shrine; Odd Fellows; VFW. Rel: Protestant. Mailing Add: Winona, Mo. 65588. (1967)

ALLOTT, GORDON LLEWELLYN R
U.S. Sen, Colo.
b. Pueblo, Colo, 1/2/07; m. 5/15/34 to Welda Hall; c. Roger Hall and Gordon L, Jr. Educ: Univ. Colo, B.A, 27; Law Sch, LL.B, 29; Phi Gamma Delta. Hon. LL.D. Colo. Col, 64; hon. D.E, Colo. Sch. Mines, 67; hon. LL.D, Colo. State Univ, 68 and Univ. Colo, 69. Polit. & Govt. Pos: Co. attorney, Prowers Co, Colo, 34 & 40-46, dist. attorney, 46-48; chmn, Young Rep. League of Colo, 35-38; chmn, Nat. Fedn. Young Rep, 41-46; lt. gov, Colo, 50-54; U.S. Sen, Colo, 54-; U.S. Rep, UN, 17th Gen. Assembly, 62; v.chmn, U.S. del, Inter-Parliamentary Union; del, Rep. Nat. Conv, 68; chmn, Sen. Rep. Policy Cmt, 69- Bus. & Prof. Pos: Dir. and attorney, First Fed. Savings and Loan, Lamar, Colo. Mil. Serv: Entered as Lt, Army Air Force, 42, released as Major, 46, after serv. in 339th Fighter Sq, S. Pac. Theater; S. Pac. Theater Medal with 7 Battle Stars; Col, Inactive Res. Mem: State Bd. Bar Exam, Colo. Bar Asn, 49-60; secy, Southeast Colo. Livestock Asn, 33-35; Am. Legion; VFW; Rotary; Mason. Mem. All American Track Team in High Hurdles, 27. Rel: Episcopal. Legal Res: Lamar, Colo. Mailing Add: 5229 Senate Office Bldg, Washington, D.C. 20510.

ALLPHIN, JOHN, JR. D
Mayor-Pres. Pro Tem, City and Parish of Baton Rouge, La.
b. Covington, Ky, 6/4/30; s. John Allphin and Stella Davison A; m. 2/4/52 to Johnell Rush; c. Brookie Ann and John R. Educ: La. State Univ, B.S, 51; Sigma Chi; Samurai Interfraternity. Polit. & Govt. Pos: Civil defence dir, East Baton Rouge Parish, La, 54-56; mem, East Baton Rouge Parish Dem. Exec. Cmt, 59-63; councilman, East Baton Rouge Parish, 60-; mayor-pres. pro tem, City and Parish of Baton Rouge, 64-; cmnr. and secy, Greater Baton Rouge Port Cmn, currently. Bus. & Prof. Pos: Owner, Allphin Agency, Real Estate and Ins, 50- Mil. Serv: Entered as 2nd Lt, Air Force, 52, released as 1st Lt, 54, after serv. in Air Training Command, Reese Air Force Base, Lubbock, Tex, 52-54; Capt, Air Force Res, 54-60. Mem: Baton Rouge Bd. of Realtors; La. Realtor Asn; Nat. Asn. of Real Estate Bd; La. Police Jury Asn; Nat. Asn. of Cities; La. Munic. Asn; Odd Fellows; Eagles; Moose; Baton Rouge C. of C. and Jr. C. of C; Amvets; Am. Legion. Outstanding Young Man of the Year in Baton Rouge and La, 59. Rel: Baptist. Legal Res: 7769 Jefferson Hwy, Baton Rouge, La. 70809. Mailing Add: 508 Wiltz Dr, Baton Rouge, La. 70806.

ALLRED, WILLIAM DAVID 'DAVE' D
Tex. State Rep.
b. Austin, Tex, 11/27/33; s. James V. Allred and Joe Betsy Miller A; m. 6/18/60 to Patricia Lee Moyer; c. Rebecca Lee, Stephen David and James Moyer. Educ: Tex. Christian Univ, B.A; Columbia Univ, M.S. Polit. & Govt. Pos: Mem, staff, U.S. Sen. Ralph Yarborough, Tex. and U.S. Rep. Ray Roberts, Tex; investr, House Govt. Activities Subcmt; Tex. State Rep, Wichita Co, 67- Bus. & Prof. Pos: Reporter, Montgomery, Ala. Bur. of The Assoc. Press and Wash. Bur. of the Houston Post, the Wichita Falls Times and the Corpus Christi Caller-Times. Mil. Serv: 2nd and 1st Lt, Army Res; Maj, Army Res, currently. Rel: Disciples of Christ. Mailing Add: 1608 Hayes St, Wichita Falls, Tex. 76309.

ALLSBROOK, JULIAN RUSSELL D
N.C. State Sen.
b. Roanoke Rapids, N.C, 2/17/03; s. William Clemens Allsbrook and Bennie Alice Walker A; m. 6/24/26 to Frances Virginia Brown (deceased); c. Richard Brown, Mary Frances and Alice Harris. Educ: Univ. N.C, 20-24; Univ. N.C. Law Sch, 22-24; Phi Alpha Delta; Golden Fleece; Order of the Grail; Tau Kappa Alpha. Polit. & Govt. Pos: Former mem. bd. trustees, Roanoke Rapids Sch. Dist, bd, City Cmnr. and Munic. Road Cmn; former Secy. of State, N.C; N.C. State Sen, 35-41 & 47-; N.C. State Rep, 41-46; presidential elector, N.C, 36; chmn, Cmn. Platform and Resolutions, Dem. State Conv, 56-58. Bus. & Prof. Pos: Lawyer; dir, Med. Found. of N.C. Inc; N.C. Cmn. on Nursing and Patient Care; trustee, N.C. Symphony, Inc. and Chowan Col, Murfreesboro, N.C. Mil. Serv: Lt, Naval Res, 42-45, Lt. Comdr, Res. Mem: Mason; Widows Son Lodge; WOW; Kiwanis. Distinguished Serv. Citation, N.C. Pub. Health Asn, 65. Rel: Baptist. Legal Res: Roanoke Rapids, N.C. 27870. Mailing Add: State Senate, State Capitol, Raleigh, N.C. 27602. (1967)

ALLSWORTH, EMERSON D
b. Miami, Fla, 8/24/26; m. to Shirley McDowell A; c. Emerson Scott, John Charles, Terrance Gilbert and Mark. Educ: Miami Univ; Univ. of Miami LL.B, 52. Polit. & Gov. Pos: Mem, Fla. House of Rep, 58-66. Bus. & Prof. Pos: Attorney-at-Law. Mil. Serv: Army; Air Force Res. Mem: Elks; Kiwanis; Fraternal Order of Police Assoc; Am. Legion; Jaycees. Award from Mortgage Bankers Asn. for cleaning up mortgage rackets, 57; Jaycee award as one of ten outstanding young men of Broward Co, 58. Rel: Presbyterian. Mailing Add: 412 Blount Bldg, Fort Lauderdale, Fla. 33301.

ALMAND, BOND D
Assoc. Justice, Supreme Court of Ga.
b. Lithonia, Ga, 1/13/94; s. Alexander James Almand and Clara Emily Bond A; m. 6/18/32 to Helen Whitefoot Barnett; c. Bond and Helen (Mrs. Roy F. Morgan, Jr.). Educ: Emory Univ, Ph.B, 13; Columbia, LL.B, 16, M.A, 16; Sigma Nu; Phi Alpha Delta; Omicron Delta Kappa. Polit. & Govt. Pos: Ga. State Rep, 35-38; asst. city attorney, Atlanta, 39-42; solicitor, Criminal Court, Fulton Co, 39-42; judge, Fulton Superior Court, 42-43 & 45-49; assoc. justice, Supreme Court of Ga, 49- Bus. & Prof. Pos: Law practice, Atlanta, 16-42; lectr, Emory Univ. Sch. Law, 51-; lawyer. Mil. Serv: Army, 1st Lt, Inf, World War I, with 82nd and 9th Div, AEF. Mem: Am. Bar Asn. Rel: Episcopal. Mailing Add: 3291 Rilman Rd. N.W, Atlanta, Ga. 30527.

ALMOND, JAMES LINDSAY, JR. D
b. Charlottesville, Va, 6/15/98; s. James Lindsay Almond and Eddie Burgess A; m. 8/15/25 to Josephine Katherine Minter. Educ: Univ. Va. Law Sch, LL.B, 23; Delta Theta Phi; Alpha Kappa Psi; Omicron Delta Kappa. Hon. LL.D, Col. William and Mary. Polit. & Govt. Pos: Asst. Commonwealth's Attorney, Roanoke, Va, 30-33; judge, Hustings Court, Roanoke, 33-45; U.S. Rep, Sixth Cong. Dist, Va. and mem, Mil. Affairs and Post Off. and Civil Serv. Cmts, 46-48; attorney gen, Va, 48-57; gov, Va, 58-62; judge, U.S. Court of Customs and Patent Appeals, 62- Bus. & Prof. Pos: Practice of law, Roanoke, Va, 23-30; former high sch. prin. Mil. Serv: Pvt, Army Inf, 18. Mem: Mason; Scottish Rite (33°); Shrine (Past Potentate, Kazim Temple, Roanoke); Kiwanis Int; Eagles; Moose; United Commercial Travelers. Rel: Lutheran. Mailing Add: 208 Wexleigh Dr, Richmond, Va. 23229.

ALMOND, LINCOLN CARTER R
b. Pawtucket, R.I, 6/16/36; s. Thomas Clifton Almond and Elsie Carter A; m. 10/11/58 to Marilyn Johnson; c. Lincoln Douglas and Amy Elizabeth. Educ: Univ. R.I, B.S, 58; Boston Univ. Sch. Law, LL.B, 61; Lambda Chi Alpha. Polit. & Govt. Pos: Adminstr, Lincoln, R.I, 63-; Rep. nominee, U.S. Rep, First Cong. Dist, R.I, 68; mem, Gov. Cmn. on Crime, 68-69; nominee, U.S. Attorney for R.I. Bus. & Prof. Pos: Attorney, Gunning & Lafazia, 61-63. Mil. Serv: Res, Navy, 53-61. Mem: R.I. Bar Asn; Fed. Bar; Munic. Chief Exec. Asn; Lincoln Rep. Town Cmt; United Fund of R.I; Pawtucket-Blackstone Valley C. of C; dir, Second Pawtucket Area Indust. Found; dir, Blackstone Valley Commun. Action Prog; bd. dirs, Cumberland-Lincoln Boys Club. Outstanding Young Man of the Year, R.I. Jr. C. of C, 68; Distinguished Serv. Award, U.S. Jr. C. of C. Rel: Episcopal. Mailing Add: 12 Hillside Ave, Lincoln, R.I. 02865.

ALONZO, FRANK OLIVER D
b. Mobile, Ala, 3/22/34; s. Reynolds T. Alonzo, Sr. and Myrtle Chamblin A; m. 9/6/58 to Patricia Carey; c. Frank Oliver, Jr, Reynolds Oliver and David Oliver. Educ: Miss. South. Col; McGill Inst; Univ. Ala. Sch. of Law; Sigma Delta Kappa. Polit. & Govt. Pos: Judge, Court of Gen. Sessions of Mobile Co, Ala, 66-; del, Dem. Nat. Conv, 64; pres, Young Dems. of Mobile, 64. Prof. Pos: Attorney, Alonzo and Alonzo, 61- Mil. Serv: Dent. Corps, Navy, 57-59; chosen outstanding recruit at Bainbridge Md. Training Center and received the Am. Spirit of Honor Medal. Mem: Mobile and Ala. Bar Asns; Elks; Jr. C. of C; C. of C; YMCA; Ala. Wildlife Asn. Rel: Catholic. Legal Res: 1610 Dover St, Mobile, Ala. 36608. Mailing Add: 1770 Old Shell Rd, Mobile, Ala. 36608. (1967)

ALPERSON, JOSEPH LIONEL D
b. Poland, 4/10/07; s. Usher Alperson and Rochel Weisman A; m. 3/5/31 to Sadie Horwitz; c. Robert. Educ: Gymnasai in Osowa, Poland; Benjamin Harrison Law Sch, Indianapolis, Ind. Polit. & Govt. Pos: V.chmn, Kefauver for V.Pres, Dem. Party Finance Cmt, 56; v.chmn, Host Cmt. for Dem. Conv, Los Angeles, 60; finance chmn. for Kennedy's 13 West. Regional States; del, Dem. Nat. Conv, 60 & 64; mem, Fed. Adv. Coun, Dept. of Labor and Security. Bus. & Prof. Pos: Pres, Affiliated Metal, Stainless Steel Warehousing Co, 40. Mem: Mason (32°); Shrine; v.pres, Mogen David Temple, 55-57 and mem. bd. of dir, 57-66. Rel: Jewish. Mailing Add: 718 N. Arden Dr, Beverly Hills, Calif. 90210.

ALPERSTEIN, ARNOLD D
Dem. Nat. Committeeman, Colo.
b. New York, N.Y, 9/28/25; s. Herman Alperstein and Ray Schneiderman A; m. 3/25/48 to Pearl Greenblot; c. Donald Wayne and Ellen Sue. Educ: Univ. Mo, LL.B, 50. Polit. & Govt. Pos: Dep. dist. attorney, First Judicial Dist, Colo, 56-60; chmn, Jefferson Co. Dem. Party, 63-67; Dem. chmn, Second Cong. Dist, 67-69; chmn, Colo. Dem. Party Adv. Cmt, 67-69; Dem, Nat. Committeeman, 68- Mil. Serv: Entered as Pvt, Army Air Force, 43, released as Sgt, 46, after serv. in 8th Air Force, ETO, 45-46; Air Medal. Publ: Article in Frontier 50 and Progressive, 51. Mem: Am. Bar Asn; Colo. Bar Asn. (mem. bd. gov, 68-); First Judicial Dist. Bar Asn.(pres, 67-68); Am. Civil Liberties Union. Rel: Jewish. Mailing Add: 12125 W. 20th Ave, Denver, Colo. 80215.

ALPERSTEIN, PEARL D
Mem, State Dem. Cent. Cmt, Colo.
b. Kansas City, Mo, 1/26/27; d. Alex Greenblot and Tillie Kaplan G.(deceased); m. 3/25/48 to Arnold Alperstein; c. Donald W. and Ellen Sue. Educ: Univ. Mo, Columbia, B.J, 47; Univ. Colo, 6 months. Polit. & Govt. Pos: Precinct committeewoman, Jefferson Co. Dem. Party, Colo, 54-64, get out the vote chmn, 60-64, vol. chmn, 64, dist. capt, 64-68 and registrn. chmn, 69-; secy, State Young Dem, 57; del, co. cong. and state conv. and assemblies, 58, 60, 62, 64, 66 & 68; mem, State Dem. Cent. Cmt, 58-60 & 69- and co-chmn, finance drive, 59. Bus. & Prof. Pos: Exec. dir, Am. Jewish Cmt, 67. Publ: Ring Around the World, Farmers Union, 53. Mem: Bd. mem, Ment. Health Asn; bd. mem, Centro Cultural; Am. Civil Liberties Union; Metro Fair Housing Center; Jefferson Co. Human Rels. Coun.(former bd. mem); Wheatridge High Sch. PTA (pres). Dem. Party Serv. Award, 58; Ment. Health Asn. Award, 69. Rel: Jewish. Mailing Add: 12125 W. 20th Ave, Denver, Colo. 80215.

ALPERT, MAXWELL D
b. Baltimore, Md, 1/14/05; married. Educ: Strayer Bus. Col, cum laude; Univ. of Baltimore Law Sch, LL.B, cum laude, 33. Polit. & Govt. Pos: Md. State Del, 65-67. Mem: Baltimore City Coun; B'nai B'rith; Md. Bar Asn. Legal Res: 801 Lake Dr, Baltimore, Md. 21217. Mailing Add: 883 Madison Ave, Baltimore, Md. 21201. (1967)

ALPERT, PAUL EDWIN D
Md. State Del.
b. Baltimore, Md, 9/1/35; s. Simon Alpert and Anne Searies A; m. 2/14/65 to Wilma Sue Newman; c. Evan Braham and Simon Jay. Educ: Univ. Baltimore, A.A, 54, LL.B, 57; Nu Beta Epsilon. Polit. & Govt. Pos: Mem, Dem. State Cent. Cmt, Md, 61-62; Md. State Del, 67-, chmn, Criminal Law Subcmt, Md. House of Del, 69-70. Mil. Serv: Pvt, Army, 57-58, serv. in 104th Med. Bn, Md. Nat. Guard; Sp. 4, Army Res, 58-63. Mem: Cmt, Am, Md, Baltimore and Baltimore City Jr. Bar Asns; Am. Judicature Soc; AF&AM; Golden Eagle Square & Compass Club; Histadrut; Assoc. Jewish Charities. Rel: Hebrew. Legal Res: 3 Leafy Dale Court, Pikesville, Md. 21208. Mailing Add: 353 Equitable Bldg, Baltimore, Md. 21202.

ALSCHULER, BENJAMIN PHILIP D
b. Aurora, Ill, 2/5/33; s. Jacob E. Alschuler and Carolyn Strauss A. m. 12/29/55 to Anne Cockfield; c. John Edward. Educ: Univ. Va, B.A, 55; Univ. Chicago Law Sch, J,D, 60; Phi Beta Kappa; Zeta Beta Tau. Polit. & Govt. Pos: Dem. Cand. U.S. Cong, 15th Dist, Ill, 68. Bus. & Prof. Pos: Partner, law firm, Alschuler, Putnam, McWethy, Weiss & Weiler, Aurora, Ill, 65- Mil. Serv: Entered as Ens, Naval Res, 55, released as Lt. (jg), 57, after serving in Amphibious Forces. Mem: Am, Ill. State and Kane Co. Bar Asns; Aurora Exchange Club; Elks. Rel: Jewish. Mailing add: 32 Water Street, Aurora, Ill. 60506.

ALSOBROOK, HENRY HERMAN R
Mem, First Dist. Rep. Cmt, Ga.
b. Woodland, Ga, 4/27/17; both parents deceased; m. 9/1/39 to Wilhelmina Pool; c. Wilhelmina and Claudette. Educ: Emory Univ, B.S, 38. Polit. & Govt. Pos: Chmn, Effingham Co. Rep. Party, Ga, 64-69; mem, Effingham Co. Sch. Bd, 65-; mem, first Dist. Rep. Cmt, 69- Bus. & Prof. Pos: V.pres, Morgans, Inc, Ga, currently. Mil. Serv: Entered as A/S, Navy, 44, released as Lt.(jg), 46, after serv. in Pac; Lt.(jg), Naval Res; Am. Theater and Asiatic-Pac. Ribbons; Philippine Liberation Medal. Mem: Mason; Scottish Rite. Rel: Christian Church. Mailing Add: Railwood Ave, Guyton, Ga. 31312.

ALSOP, DONALD DOUGLAS R
Chmn, Second Cong. Dist. Rep. Cmt, Minn.
b. Duluth, Minn, 8/28/27; s. Robert Alsop and Mathilda Aaseng A; m. 8/17/52 to Jean Lois Tweeten; c. David D, Marcia Ann and Robert A. Educ: Univ. Minn, B.S.L and LL.B, 52; Order of the Coif; Phi Delta Phi. Polit. & Govt. Pos: Chmn, Brown Co. Rep. Cmt, Minn, 60-62; chmn, Second Dist. LeVander Volunteer Cmt, 66; v.chmn, Second Cong. Dist. Rep. Cmt, 64, chmn, 67-; del, Rep. Nat. Conv, 68. Bus. & Prof. Pos: Partner, Gislason, Reim, Alsop & Dosland, Attorneys at Law, New Ulm, Minn, 54- Mil. Serv: Entered as Pvt, Army, 45, released as Cpl, 46. Mem: Am. and Minn. State Bar Asns; Minn. Defense Lawyers Asn. Jr. C. of C. Distinguished Serv. Award. Rel: Lutheran. Mailing Add: 308 S. Highland Ave, New Ulm, Minn. 56073.

ALSOP, JOHN DE KOVEN R
Rep. Nat. Committeeman, Conn.
b. Avon, Conn, 8/4/15; s. Joseph W. Alsop and Corinne Robinson A; m. 6/19/47 to Augusta Robinson; c. Mary Oliver, Augusta McLane and John De Koven, Jr. Educ: Yale Univ, B.A, 37; Beta Gamma Sigma; Zeta Psi; Scroll and Key. Polit. & Govt. Pos: Mem, Avon Rep. Town Cmt, Conn, 46-49; Conn. State Rep, 47-51; mem, State Bd. Educ, 53-62; Rep. Cand. for Gov, 62; mem, Cmt. Higher Educ, 65-68; del, Rep. Nat. Conv, 68; Rep. Nat. Committeeman, 68- Bus. & Prof. Pos: Pres, Covenant Group, 53- Mil. Serv: Entered as Pvt, Army, 42, released as Capt, 45, after serving in Off. Strategic Serv, ETO and China-Burma-India Theatre, 42-45; Bronze star with cluster; Theatre Medals; Distinguished Unit Citation; Croix de Guerre, France; Cloud Banner, China. Mem: Mason; VFW; Am. Legion; Lions. Rel: Episcopal. Mailing Add: 70 Talcott Notch Rd, Avon, Conn. 06001.

ALSPACH, THOMAS ALAN R
Chmn. Legis. Cmt, Yuma Co. Rep. Cent. Cmt, Ariz.
b. Toledo, Ohio, 5/28/32; s. Don A. Alspach and Florence Witmer A; m. 8/10/56 to Nita Carlson; c. David, Timothy, Sarah and Andrew. Educ: Univ. Toledo, 50-51; Univ. Ariz, B.S. in Pharm, 58. Polit. & Govt. Pos: V.chmn, Yuma Co. Rep. Cmt, Ariz, 63-67, chmn, 67-68; mem, Ariz. Rep. Exec. Cmt, 67-68; chmn, Yuma Co. Gov. Adv. Cmt, 67-68; del, Rep. Nat. Conv, 68; chmn. legis. cmt, Yuma Co. Rep. Cent. Cmt, currently. Mil. Serv: Pvt, Army, 53, released as Cpl, 55, after serv. in 47 Armored Med. Bn, First Armed Div, Ft. Hood, Tex, 53-55. Mem: Ariz. Pharmaceutical Asn.(mem. exec. cmt, 68); Yuma Pharmaceutical Asn.(chmn, 60); Soc. Preservation & Encouragement of Barbershop Quartet Singing in Am; Yuma Symphony Asn; Yuma Fine Arts Asn; Yuma Community Concert Asn; Yuma Baroque Ensemble; Concert Chorale; chmn, Yuma Downtown Merchants Asn, 63; v.chmn, Yuma C. of C, 65. Named Outstanding Co. Chmn, Ariz. State Rep. Cmt, 68. Mailing Add: 1903 18th St, Yuma, Ariz. 85364.

ALSTADT, WILLIAM ROBERT D
b. Thebes, Ill, 10/7/16; s. Henry Lee Alstadt and Gradie Cole A; m. 8/31/62 to Laura May Goodness; c. Richard Lee, Mary Lynn (Mrs. Walker) and Thomas Henry. Educ: Ark. State Col; Wash. Univ; Omicron Kappa Upsilon. Polit. & Govt. Pos: Chmn, Little Rock Civil Serv. Cmn, 49-; alternate del, Dem. Nat. Conv, 60, 64; consult, Ark. State Welfare Dept. and Ark. TV Cmn, 61- Bus. & Prof. Pos: Pres, Am. Dent. Asn, 57-58; regent, Int. Col. of Dentists, 60-66, pres, 68-69; pres, S.W. Soc. Orthodontists, 65-66. Mil. Serv: Entered as 1st Lt, Army, 41, released as Maj, 45; 5 Awards, Decorations and Ribbons; Lt. Col, Dent. Corps Res, 50. Publ: Many articles pub. in dent. and med. publ. Mem: Mason (32°); past pres, Civitan Club. Honorary mem, many foreign dent. asns; 4 honorary degrees. Rel: Methodist. Legal Res: 11 Edgehill, Little Rock, Ark. 77207. Mailing Add: Worthen Motor Bank Bldg, Fourth and Scott Sts, Little Rock, Ark. 72201.

ALSUP, JOHN W. D
Ill. State Rep.
b. Austin Twp, Ill, 1912; m. to Helen Marie Delaney; c. 6 Daughters and 1

Son. Educ: Univ. of Ill. Polit. & Govt. Pos: Former v.chmn, Revenue Cmn, Ill; treas, Macon Co, 54; pres, Co. Treas. Asn. Ill, 55; Ill. State Rep, currently. Bus. & Prof. Pos: Farming, grain elevator mgt, mfg, ins. and real estate. Legal Res: 1712 N. Church St, Decatur, Ill. 62526. Mailing Add: State House of Representatives, State Capitol Bldg, Springfield, Ill. 62706. (1967)

ALTAMORE, MARY D

Mem, Colo. State Dem. Cent. Cmt.

b. Pueblo, Colo, 5/13/03; d. Frank Conty and Rosa Sarlo C; wid; c. John, Jr. Polit. & Govt. Pos: Dept. clerk, assessor's off, Pueblo Co, Colo, 34-60; mem, exec. cmt, Pueblo Dem. Party, 59-69; chief dep. assessor, local and Co, 34-; chief dep. assessor, Pueblo Co, 61-; mem, Colo. State Dem. Cent. Cmt, 69- Bus. & Prof. Pos: Sales lady and dept. head, Montgomery Ward, 27-34. Mem: Fidelity Lodge; CF&T Cmt. on Polit. Educ; Jane Jefferson; Young Dem. Colo; Construction, Maintenance, Prod, and Pub. Serv. Local Union, Cope Steel Workers Auxiliary; Citizens Serv. Orgn. Rel: Catholic. Mailing Add: 939 Box Elder St, Pueblo, Colo. 81004.

ALTIG, DELBERT ROY D

Chmn, Lincoln Co. Dem. Party, Nebr.

b. Ogallala, Nebr, 5/18/33; s. Harry G. Altig and Myrtle Pierce A; m. 10/1/52 to Margaret J. Drost; c. Delbert Roy, Jr, John K, Anthony E, Lisa J, William U, Ruth A, Jean M, Amy T. and April M. Polit. & Govt. Pos: Dem. worker, Lincoln Co. Dem. Party, 63-66, Co. Chmn, 66- Bus. & Prof. Pos: Owner, Men's Clothing Store, 61- and West. Wear Store, 67- Mem: Elks; K. of C; C. of C. Rel: Catholic. Mailing Add: E. Tryon Rt, North Platte, Nebr. 69101.

ALTMAN, J. EUGENE D

b. Aynor, S.C, 2/15/18; s. Jack J. Altman and Celia Grainger A; m. 9/10/48 to Virginia Johnson; c. J. Eugene, Jr. and James Waterman. Educ: Aynor High Sch, grad, 38. Polit. & Govt. Pos: Chmn, Horry Co. ASC Cmt, S.C, 54-55; S.C. State Rep, 55-60 & 62-68; del, S.C. State Dem. Conv, 56, 58, 60, 62 & 64; del, Dem. Nat. Conv, 68; clerk and purchasing agent, Horry Co. Bd. Cmnrs, 68- Bus. & Prof. Pos: Farmer; owner, Gen. Ins. Agency. Mem: Scottish Rite Mason (32°), Past Master, Graddy Lodge; Shrine; Sovereign Camp Rep, WOW; past pres, Aynor Lions Club. Rel: Baptist; Teacher, Young Men's Bible Class, 42-52, secy-treas, Men's Class, 52-57 and supt. of Sunday Sch, 57-60. Mailing Add: Box 55, Aynor, S.C. 29511.

ALTMAN, JAMES ESTON R

Mayor Pro-Tem, Gray, Ga.

b. Manatee, Fla, 1/23/38; s. Eston Altman and Alma Bland A; m. 6/15/58 to Lois Elaine Middlebrooks; c. April Elaine, Allison Leigh and Adriane Ermine. Educ: Ga. Inst. of Tech, B.M.E. Polit. & Govt. Pos: Mayor pro-tem, Gray, Ga, 66-; chmn, Jones Co. Rep. Party, 66- Bus. & Prof. Pos: V.pres, Altman Machine Co, Inc, Gray, Ga, 60-; registered prof. engr, 66-; bus. mgr, Jones Co. Messenger, 69- Mem: Ga. Soc. of Prfnl. Engrs; Jones Co. Jaycees (past pres); Jones Co. Kiwanis Club (past pres); treas, Jones Co. Develop. Cmn, Inc; Moose; Cmt. of 150, Inc. of Macon; pres, Gray Elem. PTA. Rel: Baptist. Legal Res: 501 Fraley St, Gray, Ga. 31032. Mailing Add: P.O. Box 334, Gray, Ga. 31032.

ALTMEYER, ARTHUR JOSEPH D

b. DePere, Wis, 5/8/91; s. John G. Altmeyer and Carrie Smith A; m. 7/3/16 to Ethel M. Thomas. Educ: Univ. Wis, B.A, 14, M.A, 21, Ph.D, 31, hon. LL.D, 39. Polit. & Govt. Pos: Statistician, Wis. Tax Cmn, 18-20; chief statistician, Wis. Indust. Cmn, 20-22, secy, 22-23; chief compliance div, NRA, 33-34; asst. secy. labor, chmn. tech. bd, President's Cmt. Econ. Security, 34-35; mem, U.S. Soc. Security Bd, 35-46, chmn, 37-46; U.S. Cmnr. Soc. Security, 46-53; exec. dir, War Manpower Cmn, 42, mem, 42-45; mem, Exec. Cmt. Nat. Youth Admin, 35; chmn. Am. del, First-Fifth Inter-Am. Cmt. Soc. Security, 42-52; U.S. rep. soc. cmn, UN, 46-53; pres, Nat. Conf. Soc. Work, 54-55; soc. welfare adv. to various foreign govts, 55-; chmn. soc. security cmt, Dem. Adv. Coun, 60. Bus. & Prof. Pos: High Sch. teacher, 14, prin, 16-18; vis. prof, Univ. Utah, Univ. Calif, Los Angeles, Univ. N.C, Univ. Wis, Univ. Chicago and Univ. Salzburg; chmn. bd. trustees, retirement fund, Coat & Suit Indust, 43-65; chief appeals officer, ILGWU Nat. Retirement Fund, N.Y.C, 65-69; chmn. bd. of trustees, Nat. Industs. Group Pension Plan, Wash, D.C, 66- Publ: The Industrial Commission of Wisconsin, 32; co-auth, Economic Study of Peruvian Social Legislation, 57; auth, The Formative Years of Social Security, 65. Mem: Phi Beta Kappa. Decorated D.S.M. Mailing Add: 4728 Regent St, Madison, Wis. 53705.

ALTOBELLO, HENRY D. D

Secy, Dem. State Cent. Cmt, Conn.

b. Meriden, Conn, 10/1/07; s. Antonio Altobello and Agnes Petrucelli A; m. 9/18/30 to Josephine LaMontagne; c. Henrietta (Mrs. Suzio), Lourde (Mrs. Gronback), Daniel, Patricia and Suzanne. Educ: Gettysburg Col; Georgetown Univ. Polit. & Govt. Pos: Selectman, Southwick, Mass, 38-45; Conn. State Sen, 53-55; mayor, Meriden, 54-60; secy, Dem. State Cent. Cmt, currently; del, Dem. Nat. Conv, 68. Bus. & Prof. Pos: Pres, The L. Suzio Const. Co. and the York Hill Trap Rock Co, 49-; chmn. bd, The L. Suzio Concrete Co, 49-, The L. Suzio Asphalt Co, 57; pres, The L. Suzio Sand & Gravel Co, 57- Mem: Elks; Eagles; K. of C; Conn. Road Builders Asn; Conn. Bituminous Concrete Asn; Conn. Ready Mix Concrete Asn. Rel: Catholic. Mailing Add: 165 Brownstone Ridge, Meriden, Conn. 06450.

ALTON, JOSEPH W, JR. R

b. Annapolis, Md, 1/18/19; married. Educ: Annapolis Pub. Schs. Polit. & Govt. Pos: County Exec, 65-; Md. State Sen, 63-65; Sheriff of Anne Arundel Co. for 12 years; Dep. Sheriff of Anne Arundel Co. for 3 years. Mailing Add: 801 Parkwood Ave, Annapolis, Md. 21403. (1967)

ALTORFER, JOHN HENRY R

b. Peoria, Ill, 7/28/20; s. Silas Henry Altorfer and Elizabeth Sauder A; m. 11/17/44 to Harriett Pearson; c. Joanne, Linda and Carol. Educ: Dartmouth Col, B.A, 43; Alpha Delta Phi. Polit. Pos: Mem, Ill. House Reapportionment Cmn, 65; Rep. nominee for Lt. Gov, Ill, 64; alternate del, Rep. Nat. Conv, 64; dir, United Rep. Fund and downstate chmn, United Rep. Fund, Ill, 59-62. Govt. Pos: Trustee, Pleasure Driveway & Park Dist. of Peoria, Ill, 57-64. Bus. & Prof. Pos: Pres, Pioneer Indust. Park, Inc, 65-; secy. & dir, State Life of Ill, 59-; dir, Commercial Nat. Bank, Peoria, 1st Fed. Savings & Loan Asn, Peoria and LaSalle Street Capital Corp, Chicago, presently; v.pres. & dir, Perma Starch, Inc, 49-54 and Radio Station WIRL, Peoria, 46-58; dir, Altorfer Bros. Co, 46-52. Mil. Serv: Entered as Ens, Navy, 43, released as Lt.(jg), 46; Atlantic & Pac. Theater Ribbons. Mem: Zeta Pi, Bradley Univ; Mason; Peoria Consistory, Scottish Rite, Mohammed Temple; VFW; Peoria Asn. of Commerce; Adv. Bd, St. Francis Hosp, Peoria; Trustee, MacMurray Col; Peoria Country Club; Creve Coeur Club; Rotary. Rel: Presbyterian. Legal Res: 7406 Edgewild Dr, Peoria, Ill. 61614. Mailing Add: 1016 Central Bldg, Peoria, Ill. 61602. (1967)

ALVARADO, ARCILIO D

b. Santa Isabel, P.R, 11/7/03; s. Juan Francisco Alvarado and Juana Evangelista A; m. to Adelaida Maldonado Defendini; c. Arcilio, Jr, Carmen Mercedes, Ivette Maria and Edgar. Educ: Univ. P.R, LL.B, 25. Polit. & Govt. Pos: Munic. Judge, P.R, 32-40; prosecuting attorney, Dept. Justice, 40-41; legal adv. to Secy. of Treasury, 41-43; chief legal div, Treas. Dept, 43-44; Superior Court Judge, 44-47; P.R. State Rep, 47-69, chmn, Judiciary Cmn, 49-52, Majority Leader, 53-65 and Speaker, 65-69, P.R. House of Rep. Publ: Several articles in local newspapers and periodicals. Mem: P.R. Bar Asn. Rel: Catholic. Legal Res: Guaynabo, P.R. 00657. Mailing Add: P.O. Box 2981, San Juan, P.R. 00903. (1967)

ALVAREZ, TED, JR. 'MILKMAN' D

Fla. State Rep.

b. Jacksonville, Fla, 9/27/29; m. to Virginia Perry; c. Evelyn Elizabeth, Linda LuAnn and Steve Michael. Educ: Univ. Fla; Student Exec. Coun. Polit. & Govt. Pos; Fla. State Rep, 19th Dist, 66-, Regional Whip, 69- Bus. & Prof. Pos: Co-owner, Holly Hill Dairy and Holly Hill Plastic Container Co; Agr. Consult. Mil: Air Force. Mem: Fla. Dairy Prod. Asn; Cattleman's Asn; C. of C; Boy Scouts; Mason; Farm Bur; Moose. Recipient of Outstanding Young Men of America Award presented by Jr. C. of C. Rel: Methodist. Mailing Add: 13937 Duval Rd, Jacksonville, Fla. 32218.

AMADEI, JAMES ROBERT R

Chmn, 50th Assembly Dist. Rep. Cmt, Kings Co, N.Y.

b. New York, N.Y, 9/13/05; s. Robert Amadei and Mary Maffei A; m. 2/22/31 to Anna Evangeline Fiechter; c. James Robert and Anne Marie (Mrs. McCartney). Educ: St. Lawrence Univ, LL.B, 26; Brooklyn Law Sch, LL.M, 28; Iota Sigma Alpha. Polit. & Govt. Pos: V.pres, Brooklyn Young Rep. Club, N.Y, 32-36; del. and alternate del, Rep. Nat, State and Judicial Convs, 32-64; secy, local sch. bd. dist. 25, Brooklyn, 33-38; govt. appeal agent, Selective Serv. Bd, 40-43; asst. attorney gen, N.Y, 43-44; mem. cmn, Workmen's Compensation Bd, 44-54, trial exam, 54-61; treas, Columbian Rep. League, 48-; mem, N.Y. State Labor Rels. Bd, 61-; chmn, 50th Assembly Dist. Rep. Cmt, Kings Co, N.Y. currently. Mem: Am. and N.Y. State Bar Asns; Brooklyn Bar Asn.(asst. counsel, 62-, exec. secy. and trustee, 28-43); Fed. Bar Coun. of N.Y, N.J. and Conn.(secy, 33-38); Cath. Lawyer's Guild (marshal, Diocese of Brooklyn, 40-42); N.Y.C, Transit Employee's Benevolent Asn.(counsel, 40-43); Lawyers Club of Brooklyn; Am. Judicature Soc; N.Y. State Civil Serv. Employees Asn; Dougan Guild of N.Y. State Cath. Employees (counsel, 54-61); Italian Execs. Am.(v.pres); N.Y. Diabetes Asn.(secy. and dir, 65-); Royal Arcanum; Advocates Int. Trade; Co. East. Travel Club; K. of C; Beaver Dam Lake Asn; Automobile Club of N.Y; Nat. Travel Club; Cong. Club of Kings Co; Am. Asn. Retired Persons; Holy Name Soc. Rel: Catholic. Mailing Add: 204 Washington Ave, Brooklyn, N.Y. 11205.

AMANN, EDWARD J. JR. R

N.Y. State Assemblyman

b. New York, N.Y, 7/17/25; m. 6/27/53 to Joyce Kroplinski ; c. Thomas; Laura and William. Educ: Wagner Col; N.Y. Law Sch. Polit. & Govt. Pos: N.Y. State Assemblyman, 52-, chmn, Joint Cmt. on Unemploy. Ins. and mem, Cmt. on Ment. Retardation and Physically Handicapped, N.Y. State Assembly. Bus. & Prof. Pos: Attorney, private practice. Mil. Serv: Capt, Judge Adv. Gen. Corps, Army Res, World War II. Mem: VFW; Am. Legion; bd. dir, Staten Island Cerebral Palsy Asn; State Island Aid for Ment. Retarded Children; Hillside Swimming Club; K. of C; Elks; Wagner Col. Alumni Asn. Legal Res: 285 Kissel Ave, Staten Island, N.Y. 10310. Mailing Add: State Assembly, State Capitol Bldg, Albany, N.Y. 12224. (1967)

AMANTE, PAUL SAM D

b. Johnstown, N.Y, 5/1/25; s. Girolomo Amante and Josephine Pafumi A; m. 12/27/47 to Mary Petix; c. Jerome, Tina Marie and Paul, Jr. Educ: E. Los Angeles Col, 2 years; Calif. Polytech, Pomona, 1 year. Polit. & Govt. Pos: Field rep, Calif. State Sen. Song, 68- Mil. Serv: Sgt. T-4, Army, 43-46, with serv. in 113th Ord. Corps, Pac. Theatre, 44-46; Pac. Theatre Ribbon; Good Conduct Medal. Mem: Am. Legion (post comdr, Pico Rivera 341); VFW (post comdr, Pico Rivera 6315); Lions Int.(2nd v.pres, Atlantic Square Club); DAV (sgt. at arms, Pico Rivera). Rel: Catholic. Mailing Add: 140 S. Spruce St, Montebello, Calif. 90640.

AMAYA, GEORGE D. D

b. 1922. Educ: Calif. Polytech. Col. of Engrs, degree. Polit. & Govt. Pos: N.Mex. State Rep, 59-60; mem, Colo. State Patrol, 10 years; N.Mex. State Sen, 61-66. Mil. Serv: Mil. Intel. Mem: Elks. Rel: Protestant. 1967 Legal Res: Gallup, N.Mex. No mailing address available. (1967)

AMBLER, WILLIAM EMERSON R

Chmn, DeSoto Co. Rep. Cmt, Fla.

b. Manchester, Tenn, 3/20/10; s. J.C. Ambler and Pauline Brixey A; single. Polit. & Govt. Pos: Chmn, Desoto Co. Rep. Cmt, Fla, currently; former precinct capt. Mil. Serv: Entered as Pvt, Air Force, 42, released as Corporal, 43. Mem: Kiwanis; Am. Legion; Mason. Rel: Methodist. Legal Res: 505 W. Hickory St, Arcadia, Fla 33821. Mailing Add: Box 464, Arcadia, Fla. 33821.

AMBROSE, DANIEL WEBSTER D

Exec. Secy, Dem. Party of the V.I.

b. Pickens, Miss, 9/8/96; s. Daniel Webster Ambrose and Mary Elizabeth Redmond A; m. to Irene M. Miller. Educ: A&M Col, B.S, 18; Howard Univ, LL.B, 24; Kappa Alpha Psi; Tau Delta Sigma. Polit. & Govt. Pos: Asst. state auditor, W.Va, 33-42, 44-50; pres, Cabell Co. Dem. Club, W.Va, 36-40; asst.

state dir, W.Va. Off. of Civil Defense, 42-44; assoc. exec. secy, Young Dem. Clubs of W.Va, 44-50; exec. officer, Tax Exemption Bd, 61-63; mem, V.I. Reapportionment Cmn, 66-68; del, Dem. Nat. Conv, 68; coordinator, Select Cmn. on Reorganization of Govt, 68-69; exec. secy, Dem. Party of the V.I, 68- Mil. Serv: Pvt, Army, 18, with serv. in Student's Army Training Corps, Howard Univ, Wash, D.C. Mem: W.Va. Bar Asn; Bar of the Third Circuit Court of Appeals; Master Mason; Shrine; United Supreme Coun, Kanasha Consistory 73, Charleston, W.Va; V.I. Bar Asn.(bd. of gov, 66-67); Boy Scouts of Am.(chmn, Cmt. on Leadership Training, 68-69); bd. mem. and three term pres, St. Thomas Commun. Chest, 61-69; mem. coun, United Serv. Orgn, 65-69. Rel: Episcopal. Legal Res: Room 12, Palm Passage, Charlotte Amalie, St. Thomas, V.I. 00801. Mailing Add: P.O. Box 194, Charlotte Amalie, St. Thomas, V.I. 00801.

AMBROSE, DELPHIN D. R
Chmn, Lynn Rep. City Cmt, Mass.
b. Lynn, Mass, 1/9/07; s. Peter D. Ambrose and Laura Valeri A; m. to Rita N. Gibbons; c. Gregory Robert, Laura Joan and Sherry Marie. Educ: Boston Univ. Col. of Lib. Arts, Sch. of Law; Delta Sigma Rho; Lambda Alpha. Polit. & Govt. Pos: Mem, Bd. of Pub. Welfare, Mass; V.chmn, Indust. Develop. Cmt; mem, Lynn Housing Authority; del, Mass. Rep. State Conv; chmn, Lynn Rep. City Cmt, Mass, 68- Bus. & Prof. Pos: Pres, Lynn Bd. of Realtors and Assoc. Brokers Corp; dir, Mass. Asn. of Real Estate Bd, Lynn Tuberc. League and Union Hosp. Mil. Serv: Entered as Pvt, Army, 42, released as Sgt. Maj, 45. Mem: Mass. Ins. Brokers Asn; Nat. Asn. Real Estate Bd; Nat. Asn. Housing and Redevelop. Off; Ital. Commun. Center Gr. Lynn; Boston Univ. Alumni Asn; Am. Legion. Mailing Add: 56 Long Hill Rd, Lynn, Mass. 01902.

AMBROSE, JOHN ANTHONY D
b. Brooklyn, N.Y, 9/9/24; s. Joseph Ambrose and Clementina Scandizzo A; m. 5/26/51 to Rose-Marie Sowers; c. Joseph T. and Patricia M. Educ: Brooklyn Col, B.A, 50; St. John's Univ, M.A, 64; N.Y. State War Regents scholarship; Omega Delta Phi. Polit. & Govt. Pos: Dem. Committeeman, Brookhaven Town, Suffolk Co, N.Y, 62-; alternate del, N.Y. State Dem. Conv, 67; secy, Brookhaven Town Dem. Cmt, 67-68; exec. asst. to chmn. of Suffolk Co. Dem. Cmt, 67-; del, Dem. Nat. Conv, 68. Bus. & Prof. Pos: Prod. control analyst, Mergenthaler Linotype Co, Brooklyn, 51-53; prod. control analyst, Am. Machine & Foundry, 53-54; math. teacher, Union Free Sch. Dist. 24, 54- Mil. Serv: Entered as Pvt, Army Air Force, 43, released as Pfc, 46, after serv. in 1969th Ord. Depot Co, Eighth Air Force, Pac. Theatre, Okinawa, 45-46; Asiatic-Pac. Serv. Medal; Am. Serv. Medal; World War II Victory Medal. Mem: Patchogue Fedn. Teachers; Suffolk Co. Math. Teachers Asn; K. of C. Rel: Roman Catholic. Mailing Add: 71 N. Howells Point Rd, Bellport, N.Y. 11713.

AMENTA, PAUL S. D
Conn. State Sen.
b. New Britain, Conn, 9/30/22; s. Salvatore Amenta and Benedette Crisafulli A; m. 2/14/42 to Marion Whitney; c. Joyce, Sharron, Paul Jr, Pamela, Patricia, and Cynthia. Educ: Coe Col, 43-45, Cent. Conn. State Col, B.S, 47; Polit. & Govt. Pos: Mem, sch. bd, 49-62, chmn, 63-; Conn. State Sen, Sixth Dist, 52-56 & 65- Bus. & Prof. Pos: Teacher, 46-47, sales mgr, J.W. Spring Co, 48-50; mfg. rep, Rio Auto Sales and Salvage, 50-52, sales mgr, 52-63; sales mgr, Interpave Corp, Atlantic Cement Co, 63- Mil. Serv: Entered as Aviation Cadet, Army, 43, released as Pvt, 46. Mem: Elks; Lions; Unico; Moose; Italian Am. Vets; Sen. Toga Club (pres). Mailing Add: 80 Cedarwood Dr, New Britain, Conn. 06052.

AMERINE, MERVIN WELLS R
b. Modesto, Calif, 4/21/23; s. Richard Wells Amerine and Lois Thelma Gum A; m. 4/12/47 to Nancy Helen Cavan; c. Barbara and Cavan. Educ: Modesto Jr. Col, 41-42; Ft. Hays State Col, 43. Polit. & Govt. Pos: Dir, Oakdale Irrigation Dist, Calif, 62-; mem, Calif. Aeronaut. Bd, 66-; del, Rep. Nat. Conv, 68. Bus. & Prof. Pos: Partner, Amerine Land Co, 48-; stockholder-exec, Amerine Turkey Breeding Farms, Inc, 62-, Amerine Air, Inc, 64- and Amerine Nat. Corp, 67- Mil. Serv: Entered as Pvt, Army Air Corps, 42, released as 1st Lt, 53, after serv. in Far East Asiatic Pac. and Korean Theatres, 45-46 and 52-53; Air Medal. Mem: F&AM; Scottish Rite; Shrine. Rel: Protestant. Mailing Add: 13242 Hwy. 108, Oakdale, Calif. 95361.

AMES, BOBBIE R
Rep. Nat. Committeewoman, Ala.
b. Washington, N.C, 7/23/30; m. 12/30/50 to John Brewer Ames; c. Elizabeth Acra, John Brewer, II and twins, Laurie and David. Educ: Greensboro Col, N.C, 48-49; E. Carolina Univ, 49-51. Polit. & Govt. Pos: Dir. women's activities, Dallas Co. Rep. Party, 12 years; dir. women's Party to People Prog. under Mary Ellen Miller; pres, Ala. Fedn. of Rep. Women; del, Rep. Nat. Conv, 68; Rep. Nat. Committeewoman, Ala, currently. Bus. & Prof. Pos: Former owner and operator, Antique Shop; prin, Perry Christian Sch, 66- Mem: Ala. Hist. Soc; Blackbelt Antiquarian Soc; past pres, Selma Garden Club and Selma and Dallas Co. Fedn. of Church Women; Girl Scouts; Red Cross; all avenues of commun. serv. Elected Woman of Achievement in 1968, Bus. & Prfnl. Women's Club. Rel: Westminster Commun. Church. Legal Res: Route 2, Marion, Ala. 36756. Mailing Add: S. Washington St, Marion, Ala. 36756.

AMES, EDWARD ALMER, JR. D
b. Onley, Va, 1/22/03; s. Edward Almer Ames and Lena E. Trower A; m. 1/8/36 to Elizabeth Johnson Melson; c. Edward Almer, III. Educ: Randolph Macon Col, 19-21; Wash. and Lee Univ, B.A, 24, LL.B, 25; Phi Beta Kappa; Phi Delta Phi; Order of the Coif. Polit. & Govt. Pos: Commonwealth's attorney, Accomack Co, Va, 43-56; chmn, Accomack Co. Dem. Cmt, 48-; mem, Va. State Dem. Cent. Cmt, 50-; Va. State Sen, First Sen. Dist, 56-68. Bus. & Prof. Pos: Former v.pres. and dir, First Nat. Bank, Onancock, Va, pres, 69- Mem: Accomack Co, Va. State and Am. Bar Asns; Mason; Ruritan; Rotary. Rel: Presbyterian. Legal Res: Accomac, Va. Mailing Add: Onancock, Va. 23417.

AMESBURY, ELIZABETH ELWELL R
Pres, Mass. Fedn. Rep. Women
b. Haverhill, Mass, 10/5/15; d. Clinton Ward Elwell and Frances Kelly E; m. 6/7/37 to Robert R. Amesbury; c. Carol (Mrs. Tedoldi), Robert Clinton and Richard Elwell. Educ: Wheaton Col, Norton, Mass, 33-34; Katharine Gibbs Sch, Boston, Mass, 34-36. Polit. & Govt. Pos: Mem, Wellesley Rep. Town Cmt, Mass, 58-, v.chmn, 60-64; pres, Women's Rep. Club of Wellesley, 60-62; state chmn, Pyramiding for 62, Rep. Nat. Cmt, 61-62; bd. mem, Mass. Fedn. Rep. Women, 63-, v.pres, 68-69, pres, 69-; elected mem, Mass. Rep. State Cmt, 64-, exec. cmt. mem, 64-68, finance chmn, 65-67; v.chmn, 67-68; alternate del, Rep. Nat. Conv, 68. Mem: Wellesley Women's Rep. Club; Wellesley League Women Voters; Village Churchwomen. Rel: Congregational. Mailing Add: 9 Tappan Rd, Wellesley, Mass. 02181.

AMIS, GEORGE CLAYTON D
b. Pueblo, Colo, 3/23/31; s. Gilbert G. Amis and Alice M. Hineman A; m. 12/20/52 to Rosalie M. Ohlsson; c. Michael K, Gilbert G. and Kirk E. Educ: High sch, grad, 50. Polit. & Govt. Pos: Precinct committeeman, Shawnee Co. Dem. Party, Kans, 67-69; del, Dem. Nat. Conv, 68; mem, State Kans. Civil Serv. Bd, 68- Bus. & Prof. Pos: V.pres, Local 307, United Rubber Workers, 59-63, pres. and bus. agent, 63-; int. exec. bd. mem, United Rubber, Cork, Linoleum and Plastic Workers of Am, 66- Mil. Serv: Entered as Pvt, Army, 52, released as Cpl, 54, after serv. in Tenth Inf. Div, Fifth Army, 52-54. Mem: Cmt. Indust. Local Unions in Shawnee Co; Kans. State Fedn. Labor. Rel: Protestant. Mailing Add: 4902 N. Mission Rd, Topeka, Kans. 66618.

AMORY, ROBERT, JR. R
V.chmn, D.C. Rep. Cent. Cmt.
b. Boston, Mass, 3/2/15; s. Robert Amory and Leonore Cobb A; m. 6/17/38 to Mary Armstrong; c. Robert, III and Daniel. Educ: Harvard Col, A.B, 35, Harvard Law Sch, LL.B, 38; Phi Beta Kappa; Spee Club; Hasty Pudding-Inst. of 1770. Polit. & Govt. Pos: V.pres, N.Y. Young Rep. Club, 39-40; mem, City of Cambridge Sch. Cmt, 49-51; dep. dir, Cent. Intel. Agency, 52-62; asst. dir, Bur. of the Budget, 62-65; mem, Task Force on For. Affairs, Rep. Coord. Cmt, 66-68; v.chmn. and mem. finance cmt, D.C. Rep. Cent. Cmt, 67- Bus. & Prof. Pos: Prof. law, Harvard Univ, 46-52; partner, Corcoran, Foley, Youngman & Rowe, Attorneys, Wash. D.C, 65- Mil. Serv: Entered as Pvt, Army, 41, released as Col, 46, after serv. in 533rd Eng. Regt, Southwest Pac. Area, 43-46; Col, Res, Retired; Silver Star; Legion of Merit; Bronze Star. Publ: Surf and Sand, Andover, 47; Materials on Accounting, Found, 49 & 53. Mem: Am. Law Inst; Am. Vet. Cmt; Am. Legion; Cruising Club Am; Cosmos Club; Century Asn. Distinguished Intel. Medal, 62. Rel: Episcopal. Legal Res: 4833 Dexter Terr, N.W, Washington, D.C. 20007. Mailing Add: 1511 K St, N.W, Washington, D.C. 20005.

AMOS, JOHN ELLIS D
b. Charleston, W.Va, 7/16/05; s. John Ellison Amos and Louise Hampton Delaney A; m. 10/5/35 to Edith Johnston; c. John Delaney and Mary Johnston. Educ: Augusta Mil. Acad; W.Va. Univ, LL.B, 29. Polit. & Govt. Pos: W.Va. State Del, 35-47, speaker, W.Va. House Dels, 43-45 & 47; W.Va. Sen, 47-56; Dem. nat. committeeman, 59-68. Bus. & Prof. Pos: Mem, Amos & Brotherton, Attorneys; pres, Bell Lines, Inc, Charleston, W.Va. Terminals and N.C. Terminals; dir, Vulcan Materials Co, Birmingham, Consolidation Coal Co. and Am. Elec-Power Co. Mem: Am. Trucking Asn.(exec. cmt, v.pres. and past pres); pres, W.Va. Bd. of Regents. Mailing Add: 1020 Kanawha Valley Bldg, Charleston, W.Va. 25301.

AMOS, MABEL S. D
Secy. of State, Ala.
b. Brooklyn, Ala; d. James Sanders and Hattie Bethea S. Educ: Ala. Col. at Montavallo; State Teachers Col. at Troy; Peabody Col. Polit. & Govt. Pos: Stenographer, State Tax Cmn, Ala, 31; recording secy. to gov, 39-66; Secy. of State, 67- Bus. & Prof. Pos: Sch. teacher. Mem: Zonta; Bus. & Prfnl. Women's Club (exec. secy, cmn. on status of women). Rel: Baptist. Mailing Add: Office of Secretary of State, State Capitol, Birmingham, Ala. 35202.

AMOS, WILLIAM GEORGE R
b. Columbus, Ga, 2/5/35; s. William G. Amos and Isabel Floyd A; m. 6/8/57 to Patricia LaRue Gunn; c. Evelyn Leigh and Patricia Lynn. Educ: Auburn Univ, B.S. in building construction, 57; pres, Builders Guild and Omicron Delta Kappa; Pi Kappa Phi. Polit. & Govt. Pos: Bd. dirs, Muscogee Young Rep, Ga; admin. asst. to U.S. Rep. Howard H. Callaway, Third Dist, Ga, 64-66; campaign mgr, U.S. Rep. Howard Callaway, 66 Ga. Gov. Race; v.chmn, Third Cong. Dist. Rep. Party, Ga, 66-67; nat. committeeman, Nat. Fedn. of Young Rep, 66-67. Bus. & Prof. Pos: Estimator, Jordan Co, 59-61, asst. proj. mgr, 61-62, proj. mgr, 62-64; innkeeper, Holiday Inn of Callaway Gardens, 68-69; pres, Amos Construction Co, 69- Mil. Serv: Entered as 2nd Lt, Marine Corps, 57, released as 1st Lt, 59, after serv. in Second Bridge Co, Force Troops. One of Outstanding Young Men in America, 64. Rel: Presbyterian. Legal Res: 1502 Slater St, Valdosta, Ga. 31601. Mailing Add: P.O. Box 1184, Valdosta, Ga. 31601.

AMOSA, SOLOFUA
Rep, Am. Samoa House of Rep.
b. Amanaue, Am. Samoa; s. Tauai Amosa and Tuiloa Savali A; single. Educ: Gen. Beadle State Teachers Col, B.A. Polit. & Govt. Pos: Rep, Am. Samoa House Rep, 69- Bus. & Prof. Pos: Teacher, Am. Samoa, 42-58, prin, 62-65; credit officer, Bank of Am. Samoa, 65- Rel: Congregational Christian. Mailing Add: P.O. Box 1153, Pago Pago, Am. Samoa 96920.

AMSBERRY, JEANNE LOUQUET R
Pres, Mont. Fedn. of Rep. Women
b. Wallace, Idaho, 7/17/21; d. Floyd W. Louquet and Violet Waggoner L; m. 10/22/42 to Berton L. Amsberry; c. Barrie Lynne (Mrs. William F. Heinecke). Educ: Helena High Sch, grad, 37; Univ. Mont, 45. Polit. & Govt. Pos: Engrossing clerk, Mont. House of Rep, 51; secy, Mont. State Rep. Cent. Cmt, 51-55, mem. exec. cmt, 68-; enrolling clerk, Mont. State Senate, 55; secy. for Congressman Orvin B. Fjare, 55-57; pres, Park Co. Rep. Womens Clubs, Mont, 58-59, Silver Bow Co. Rep. Womens Club, 60-61 and Flathead Co. Rep. Womens Club, 64-65; dist. dir, Mont. Fedn. of Rep. Women, 61-67, pres, 68-; del, Rep. Nat. Conv, 68. Mem: Shrine, Bozeman, Mont; Toastmistress Club of Gallatin Co; Gallatin Co. Rep. Woman's Club. Nat. Fedn. of Rep. Womens Club Award for Membership Achievement; Mont. Young Rep. Sr. Rep. Award for Distinguished and Outstanding Serv. to Mont. and Nat. Rep. Party. Rel: Presbyterian. Mailing Add: 302 S. Willson Ave, Apt. 102, Bozeman, Mont. 59715.

AMYX, JAY S. R
Mayor, Boise, Idaho
b. Decatur, Tex, 9/27/23; s. James Samuel Amyx and Annie May Stephens A; m. 12/24/45 to Martha Ratts; c. Gordon, Kay, Duane, Lucretia and Donald Scott. Educ: Ponder High Sch, Tex, grad, 42. Polit. & Govt. Pos: Mayor, Boise, Idaho, 66- Mem: Gideon Bible Soc; Horseless Carriage Club. Rel: Baptist. Mailing Add: 1908 Westland Dr, Boise, Idaho 83704.

ANAGNOST, CATHERINE COOK R
b. Tegea, Greece, 2/10/19; d. Peter Cook and Athena Reppas C; m. 8/15/42 to Themis John Anagnost; c. Maria Athena, Alexander Themis and James. Educ: Northwest. Univ, Dipl, 42; Univ. Ill, CPA, 43; Phi Gamma Nu Scholarship Key, Sch. of Commerce, Northwest. Univ, 42. Polit. & Govt. Pres: Cand, Judge Circuit Court, Cook Co, Ill, 64; alternate del, Rep. Nat. Conv, 64. Bus. & Prof. Pos: CPA, 42-48; partner, Anagnost & Anagnost, Attorneys, 48- Mem: Am. Bar Asn.(house of del, 65-67); Nat. Asn. of Women Lawyers (pres, 63-64, past state del, secy. and treas, pres. elect); West Suburban Bar Asn. (pres, 58-59); Hellenic Bar Asn.(pres, 55); Ill. and Chicago Bar Asns; Am. Trial Lawyers Asn; Int. and Nat. Asns. of Women Lawyers; Women's Bar Asn. of Ill; Northwestern Univ. Alumni Asn. and chmn, Founders Day Prog, 66; v.pres. and dir, Beverly Farm Found; past dir, Girl Scouts; Eastern Star, White Shrine of Jerusalem; Nat. Coun. of Women of U.S; Nat. Fedn. of Bus. & Prfnl. Women's Clubs; bd. mem, N.Y. World's Fair Women's Adv. Coun, 64-65; Nat. Woman's Rep. Club; Nat. Rep. Party. Merit Award, Northwest. Univ, 64. Rel: Congregational. Legal Res: 2345 N. Oak Park, Chicago, Ill. 60635. Mailing Add: 11 S. La Salle St, Chicago, Ill. 60603.

ANASTASIO, FRANK D
b. New Haven, Conn, 12/7/33; s. Anthony Anastasio and Emmanuella Chioffi A; m. 10/15/62 to Kathryn Dyal; c. Cort, Alexi and Thomas Anthony Becket. Educ: South. Conn. State Col, B.S, 60; Univ. Conn, M.A, 62. Polit. & Govt. Pos: Del, Dem. Nat. Conv, 68. Bus. & Prof. Pos: Mem, Peace Corps, Philippines, 62-64; instr. Eng, Columbus Col. of Art and Design, 64-65; asst. prof. Eng, Corning Commun. Col, 65- Mil. Serv: Entered as Recruit, Navy, 52, released as Aviation Electronics Technician 1/C, 56, after serv. in VC-33, various bases, U.S. and two cruises aboard aircraft carriers. Mem: Mod. Lang Asn; Cmt. of Returned Vol. Mailing Add: 8 Willow St, Corning, N.Y. 14830.

ANDEEN, BIRGER BALDWIN D
Chmn, Marshall Co. Dem. Party, Minn.
b. Argyle, Minn, 3/31/20; s. Emmanuel Andeen and Hannah Skoglund A; m. 6/27/42 to Doris Evelyn Anderson; c. Diane and Lynette. Educ: High Sch. Polit. & Govt. Pos: Chmn, Marshall Co. Dem. Party, Minn, 63- Bus. & Prof. Pos: Farmer. Mil. Serv: Entered as Pvt, Army, 42, released as T5, 45, after serv. in ETO; Purple Heart. Mem: Farmers Union; Am. Legion. Rel: Lutheran. Mailing Add: Argyle, Minn. 56713. (1967)

ANDERSEN, CHRIS KENNETH R
N.H. State Rep.
b. Chicago, Ill, 12/6/30; s. Carl Martin Andersen and Marie Clausen A; m. 10/4/69 to Susan Elaine Goodwin. Educ: Palmer Col. of Chiropractic, D.C, 59. Polit. & Govt. Pos: N.H. State Rep, Merrimack Co. Dist. 25, 63-; mem, N.H. Bd. Chiropractic Exam, 67- Bus. & Prof. Pos: Pres, N.H. Palmer Col. Alumni Asn, 65-66. Mil. Serv: Entered as Seaman Recruit, Navy, 50, released as Torpedoman 2/C, 54 after serv. in U.S.S. Orion, Sixth Submarine Squadron; Nat. Defense and Good Conduct Medals. Mem: Blazing Star 11 F&AM; N.H. Consistory (32°), Bektash Temple Shrine; Bektash Temple Drum Corps; N.H. Chiropractic Asn; J.F. Grostic Research Asn; Rockley Research Acad. Inc. Rel: Protestant. Mailing Add: 3 South St, Concord, N.H. 03301.

ANDERSEN, ELMER LEE R
b. Chicago, Ill, 6/17/09; s. Arne Andersen and Jennie O. Johnson A; m. 1932 to Eleanor Johnson; c. Anthony, Julian and Emily. Educ: Muskegon Jr. Col, grad, 28; Univ. Minn, B.B.A, 31; Alpha Kappa Psi. Hon. LL.D, Macalester Col, 65. Polit. & Govt. Pos: Del, Rep. Nat. Conv, 48 & 64; Minn. State Sen, 49-59; chmn. coord. cmt, Minn. Rep. Campaign, 52; chmn, platform cmt, Minn. State Rep. Conv, 56, chmn, 58; Gov, Minn, 61-63. Bus. & Prof. Pos: In advert. and sales promotion, H.B. Fuller Co, 34-37, sales mgr, 37-41, pres. and chmn. bd, 41- Mem: Adhesive Mfrs. Asn. Am.(past pres); Rotary Int. (dist. gov; past pres, St. Paul club); Minn. Hist. Soc.(pres); Child Welfare League Am.(past pres; exec. bd, currently); bd. regents, Univ. Minn, Minneapolis; exec. cmt, Boy Scouts; trustee, Augsburg Col; YMCA; Commun. Chest. Outstanding Achievement Award, Univ. Minn, 59. Rel: Lutheran. Mailing Add: 2230 W. Hoyt Ave, St. Paul, Minn. 55108.

ANDERSEN, HANS VERLAN R
Utah State Rep.
b. Logan, Utah, 11/6/14; s. Hans Andersen and Mynoa Richardson A; m. 6/15/43 to Shirley Hoyt; c. Hans Verlan, Jr, Glen Lee, Dale Edwin, LaDawn (Mrs. Jacob), Karen, Lynette, Catherine, Shirley Gay, Elaine, Timothy Hoyt and Dean Andrew. Educ: Brigham Young Univ, B.S. in Acct, 40; Stanford Univ. Law Sch, LL.B, 46; Harvard Univ. Law Sch, LL.M, 48; Order of the Coif. Polit. & Govt. Pos: Utah State Rep, 69- Bus. & Prof. Pos: CPA, Harmon Audit Co, Phoenix, Ariz, 41-42 and H.T. Cuthbert, CPA, 42-43; CPA and attorney-at-law, 48-53; prof, Brigham Young Univ, 53-69; mgr, Cost Plus Ten Mkt, Phoenix, Ariz, 63-64. Publ: Many Are Called But Few Are Chosen, Press Publ. Co, 67. Mem: Ariz, Calif. and Utah Bar Asns. Rel: Latter-day Saint. Mailing Add: 1155 E. 930 N, Provo, Utah 84601.

ANDERSEN, LEONARD CHRISTIAN R
Iowa State Rep.
b. Waukegan, Ill, 5/30/11; s. Lauritz F. Anderson and M. Marie Jacobsen A; m. 6/3/38 to Charlotte O. Ritland; c. Karen (Mrs. Schneider), Paul Raymond, Charlene Kaye (Mrs. Olsson) and Mark Luther. Educ: Huron Col, B.A, 33; Univ. S.Dak, law study, 33 and M.A, 37; Delta Theta Phi. Polit. & Govt. Pos: Iowa State Rep, 61-65 & 67-, chmn, Cities and Towns Cmt, 65-67, mem, Appropriations, Ways and Means, Schs. and Cities and Towns Cmts, currently, ranking mem, Soc. Serv. Cmt, 69- Bus. & Prof. Pos: High sch. teacher, 34; econ. teacher, Waldorf Col, 35-39; ins. salesman, 39-41; econ. teacher, Morningside Col, 42-43; life ins. salesman and mgr, 43-58; owner, Ins. Agency, 58- Mem: Charter Life Underwriters; bd, Iowa Asn. Independent Ins. Agents, Sioux City Chap; Am. Soc. Pub. Admin; Mason (32°); Farm Bur; past v.pres. and Woodburg Co. Campaign chmn, March of Dimes; past bd. mem, Lutheran Welfare Soc; bd. of regents, Augustana Col, S.Dak; bd, Independent Ins. Agents Asn, 67-; bd, Sioux City Rental Asn; City, State and Nat. Life Underwriters Asn.(former bd. mem. and officer); bd, Mid Sioux Opportunities Corp, 4 counties and Siouxland Opportunities Corp, Sioux City, Off. Econ. Opportunity; Shrine; Lions; mem. and v.pres. Investment Adv. Cmt, Iowa Pub. Employee Retirement Syst. Rel: Lutheran, E.L.C. Synod; served 4 terms as chmn. of Morningside Lutheran Church, currently bd. mem. Legal Res: 712 S. Glass St, Sioux City, Iowa 51106. Mailing Add: 604 Security National Bank Bldg, Sioux City, Iowa 51102.

ANDERSEN, STEPHEN DALE R
b. Des Moines, Iowa, 10/4/40; s. William Dale Andersen and Elizabeth Struble A; div. Educ: Buena Vista Col, 58-59; Univ. Nebr, B.S, 63; Beta Theta Pi; Letter Club. Polit. & Govt. Pos: Alternate del, Rep. Nat. Conv, 68. Bus. & Prof. Pos: Syst. analyst, Bendix Corp, Teterboro, N.J, 64; life ins. salesman, Woodman Accident & Life, 64-65; training asst, health, Bankers Life Nebr, 65-69. Mil. Serv: Entered as Pvt, Army, 63, released as Pfc, 64, after serv. in 204th Mil. Police Co, Ft. Sheridan, Ill, 64; 1st Lt, Army Nat. Guard Res, Nebr, 69; 'Number One,' Officer Cand. Sch; Gov. Trophy and Erickson Award, Nat. Guard Bur. Mem: Asn. of Life Underwriters; Elks; Am. Legion; Jaycees. Rel: Presbyterian. Mailing Add: 1025 N. 63rd, Bldg. F, Apt. 16, Lincoln, Nebr. 68505.

ANDERSON, ALVIN BERT 'ANDY' R
Mem, Calif. Rep. State Cent. Cmt.
b. Chicago, Ill, 2/14/24; s. Albert Hilding Anderson and Mary Jenkins A; m. 12/21/47 to Janet Courtney Sersen; c. Michelle Gail and Glenn Fred. Educ: Univ. Ala, 43-44; Univ. Calif, Los Angeles, B.S, Mech. Engr, cum laude, 50; Delta Sigma Phi; Kelp; Gold Key. Polit. & Govt. Pos: Precinct worker, Rep. Party, Van Nuys, Calif, 52; sect. chmn, Small Funds Drive, Rep. Party, Euclid, Ohio, 54; colonel victory squad, Rep. Party, San Fernando Valley, 64, chmn, victory squad, 66, colonel voter registrn, 64, chmn. voter registrn, 66; campaign chmn, GOP Assembly, 68; mem, San Fernando Valley Cent. Cmt, 68-; mem, Calif. Rep. State Cent. Cmt, 68-; mem, Los Angeles Co. Rep. Exec. Cmt, 69-; mem. victory squad and round up chmn, Los Angeles Co. Rep. Party, 69- Bus. & Prof. Pos: Process engr, Fisher Body, Van Nuys, Calif, 53; chief inspector, Euclid, Ohio, 57 & 58; plant engr, Fisher Body, Van Nuys, 59-65, plant supt, 65-66, plant mgr, 66-68, plant mgr, Gen. Motors Assembly Div, 68- Mil. Serv: Entered as Pvt, Army, 43, released as 1st Lt, 46, after serv. in 13th Armored Div, ETO, 44-45; Res, 45-50, Capt; Purple Heart with One Star; Am. Theatre Ribbon; European Theatre Ribbon with Two Battle Stars; Good Conduct and Victory Medals. Mem: Mason; AASR (32°); AAONMS. General Motors Mgr. Quality Award. Rel: Baptist. Mailing Add: 14682 Limedale St, Van Nuys, Calif. 91402.

ANDERSON, AMON RA DFL
Chmn, Mille Lacs Co. Dem-Farmer-Labor Party, Minn.
b. Milaca, Minn, 3/22/26; s. A. Henry Anderson and Anstis Hubbard A; m. 12/22/56 to Betty Wilken; c. Karrie, Aaron and Kala. Educ: Milaca High, grad. Polit. & Govt. Pos: V.chmn, Mille Lacs Co. Dem-Farmer-Labor Party, Minn, 63-66, chmn, 66- Bus. & Prof. Pos: Farmer. Mil. Serv: Entered as Pvt, Army, 50, released as Pfc, 51. Mem: Milaca Farmers Union (past pres); Mille Lacs Co. Fair Bd. Rel: Methodist. Mailing Add: Route 3, Milaca, Minn. 56353.

ANDERSON, ARTHUR BENNETT R
S.Dak. State Sen.
b. Clarkfield, Minn, 5/15/91; s. Gustaf Anderson and Anna Braadtvedt A; m. 10/3/25 to Jennie Elmonde Jackson; c. Dr. Clifford Bennett and Doris Elmonde (Mrs. David Nasby). Educ: Am. Inst. of Banking, night classes for 10 years. Polit. & Govt. Pos: S.Dak. State Rep, 41-47; S.Dak. State Sen, 47-48 & 52-, Pres-Pro-Tem, S.Dak. State Senate, 57-59, chmn, Hwy. and Transportation Cmt, 57-, chmn, Cmt. on Fed. and Interstate Coop, 57-; mem. exec. cmt, Coun. of State Govt, Midwest. Regional Conf, 60-; chmn, S.Dak. Cmn. on Intergovt. Coop, 61-; mem. bd. of mgr, Coun. of State Govt, 61-; mem. exec. cmt, Nat. Legis. Conf, 63-66; mem, Nat. Cmn. on Constitutional Govt, 64-66; chmn. exec. bd, S.Dak. Legis. Res. Coun, 65-66. Bus. & Prof. Pos: Owner, garage, oil jobber and retailer, 23-55. Mil. Serv: Pvt, Army, 18-19; serv. in 56th Inf, AEF, France, Alsace Lorraine, 18; Purple Heart. Mem: Chmn, Sioux Falls C. of C. Hwy. Cmt, 56-; co-chmn, March of Dimes, 60; Mason; Shrine; Hi Twelve Club; Odd Fellows; Kiwanis; Am. Legion; VFW; DAV; life mem, Mil. Order of the Purple Heart; World War I Vet; Farm Bur; Isaak Walton League. Earned title Mr. Highways of S.Dak. Rel: Lutheran. Mailing Add: 1206 W. Seventh St, Sioux Falls, S.Dak. 57104.

ANDERSON, BERNARD McNEIL D
b. Dublin, Va, 10/28/95; s. Jacob Henry Anderson and Lucy Ritter A; m. 2/5/20 to Jennie Lester; c. Carl Wesley and Bernard M, Jr. Educ: High Sch. Polit. & Govt. Pos: Postmaster, Dublin, Va, 34-63; co. chmn, Dem. Party, Va, 63-69. Mil. Serv: Entered as Pvt, Army, 17, released as Cpl, 19, after serv. in 104th Motor Supply Train. Mem: Mason; Dublin Ruritan Club; Am. Legion; Pulaski Co. Fair Inc. Football and Baseball. Rel: Methodist. Mailing Add: P.O. Box 266, Dublin, Va. 24084. (1967)

ANDERSON, BYRON R
Secy. of State, Colo.
Polit. & Govt. Pos: Former pres, Denver Election Cmn; Colo. Secy. of State, currently. Bus. & Prof. Pos: Former pres, Nat. Conf. State Liquor Adminstr; former mem, Colo. Bd. of Realtors; Real Estate Broker, 21 years; Ins. agent, 30 years. Mem: Secy, Nat. Asn. Secy. of State. Mailing Add: State Capitol, Denver, Colo. 80203.

ANDERSON, C. JOSEPH D
Ind. State Rep.
b. West Terre Haute, Ind, 8/4/39; s. Elmer Anderson and Anna L. Ellingsworth A; m. 3/3/62 to Gloria Joyce Bugni; c. C. Joseph, Mark A. and Lisa A. Educ: Ind. State Univ, Terre Haute, A.B; Ind. Univ. Sch. Law, Indianapolis, J.D; Phi Alpha Delta. Polit. & Govt. Pos: Dep. prosecutor, Vigo Co, Ind, 67-68; town attorney, W. Terre Haute, 68-; Ind. State Rep, 69- Bus. & Prof. Pos: High sch. teacher, Govt. and Eng, Indianapolis and Terre Haute. 63-67. Mil.

Serv: Entered as Pvt, Army, 57, released as Specialist 4, 60, after serv. in Army Security Agency, Okinawa and Wash, D.C; Good Conduct Medal. Mem: Ind. State and Terre Haute Bar Asns; K. of C; Rel: Catholic. Mailing Add: 3500 College Ave, Terre Haute, Ind. 47803.

ANDERSON, C. MARIE PINGREY R
V.pres, Turner Co. Rep. Party, S.Dak.
b. St. Augustine, Fla, 6/2/19; d. Douglas Aesop Pingrey and Alberta Smith P; m. 7/7/37 to Berchel Lester Anderson; c. James Douglas, Alberta Kay (Mrs. Strand), Darrell Warren, Duane Lester and Ernest Darwin. Educ: Hurley High Sch, S.Dak, grad, 37. Polit. & Govt. Pos: Rep. committeewoman, Hurley, S.Dak, several years; dep. clerk of courts, Turner Co, S.Dak, 66, dep. registr. of deeds, 67-68, app. registr. of deeds, 68, dep. co. sch. supt, 68-69; v.pres, Turner Co. Rep. Party, 68- Mem: Hurley Commun. Club(secy, 7 years); Royal Neighbors Asn. Rel: United Methodist. Legal Res: Hurley, S.Dak. 57036. Mailing Add: Box 302, Hurley, S.Dak. 57036.

ANDERSON, CARL ALFRED R
Vt. State Rep.
b. Brockton, Mass, 3/2/97; m. to Virginia C. Wilder; c. three. Educ: Univ. of Maine, B.S, 19, M.S, 25; Boston Univ; Univ. of Vt; Kappa Phi Kappa. Polit. & Govt. Pos: Mem. bd. dirs, Thetford Hill Water Supply, Vt; town auditor, Thetford, 39, mem, Budget Cmt, 42; Vt. State Rep, 65- Bus. & Prof. Pos: Retired headmaster, Thetford Acad, 25-61. Mem: Mason; chmn. exec. cmt, trustees of Thetford Acad, 61-; exec. chmn, Orange-Windsor Co. Teachers Asn. Rel: Congregational; Bd. of Deacons, First Congregational Church. Mailing Add: Thetford, Vt. 05074. (1967)

ANDERSON, CARL WILLIAM DFL
Secy, Dodge Co. Dem-Farmer-Labor Party, Minn.
b. Kasson, Minn, 4/7/04; s. Jense Anderson and Ella Leth A; m. 9/6/28 to La Vanche Jeanette Loomis; c. Jane Forrest (Mrs. Watson). Educ: Kasson Pub. High Sch, 2 years. Polit. & Govt. Pos: Dodge Co. co-chmn, Hubert H. Humphrey for Sen, 48, 52 & 56; Dodge Co. co-chmn, Orville Freeman for Gov, 56, 58 & 60; Dodge Co. co-chmn, Hubert H. Humphrey for Pres, 60 & 68; secy, Dodge Co. Dem-Farmer-Labor Party, Minn, 65-; del, Dem. Nat. Conv, 68. Mem: Local 1382, Rochester, Minn. Rel: Methodist. Mailing Add: 304 First Ave. N.W, Kasson, Minn. 55944.

ANDERSON, CARLTON EUGENE D
Liaison Committeeman, Boone Co. Dem. Exec. Cmt, Ky.
b. Hebron, Ky, 1/21/35; s. Henry Anderson and Inell Clayton A; single. Educ: Univ. Ky, B.S, Commerce, 57, B.A, Educ, 58, M.A, Educ, 62; Delta Sigma Pi; Col. of C. of C; Polit. Sci. Club. Polit. & Govt. Pos: Del, Dem. State Conv, 60 &64; treas, Boone Co. Dem. Club, 62, dir, 65-66, pres, 66-68, v.pres, 68-; Rep. committeeman, Airport Precinct, 64-68 and Hebron Precinct, 68-; alternate del, Dem. Nat. Conv, 68; committeeman, Boone Co. Dem. Exec. Cmt, 64-, liaison committeeman, 68- Bus. & Prof. Pos: Teacher, Jr. High Sch, Boone Co. Bd. Educ, 58- Publ: Ed, local Boone Co. Democrat. Mem: Boone Co. Educ. Asn.(past pres); Ky. Educ. Asn.(del, 6 times, Credentials Cmt, 2 times); Nat. Educ. Asn.(del, 3 times); Jr. C. of C; PTA; Boone Co. Athletic Boosters Club (secy, 68-69); Big Bone Lick Hist. Asn; Ky. Hist. Soc; Boone Co. Asn. Retarded Children; Ky. and Nat. Dem. Clubs; past pres, North. Ky. Educ; Asn. Two Ky. Colonel Awards, Gov. Combs and Gov. Brethitt; Young Educ. Year, 68. Rel: Lutheran; Supt. Sunday Sch, Teacher; Mem. Church Coun. Mailing Add: 106 Riverview Dr, Hebron, Ky. 41048.

ANDERSON, CECIL A. D
Chmn, Graves Co. Dem. Party, Ky.
b. Mayfield, Ky, 2/13/17; s. Lewis Anderson and Bessie McClain A; m. 7/4/41 to Martha Dean Chandler; c. John L, Hal C. and Richard A. Educ: Col, 47. Polit. & Govt. Pos: Chmn, Graves Co. Dem. Party, Ky, 59- Bus. & Prof. Pos: Employee, J.C. Penney, 39-41; partner and mgr, Anderson & Son, 46-66. Mil. Serv: Entered as Sgt, Army, 41, released as Major, 46, after serv. in 100th Inf. Div, S. Pac, 44-46; Lt. Col, Army Res, 46-65; Bronze Star; Am. Theater Medal; Victory Medal; Army Commendation Medal; Philippine Liberation Medal; Asiatic-Pac. Theater Medal. Mem: Mason; Farm Bur; ROA. Rel: Protestant. Mailing Add: Star Route, Mayfield, Ky. 42066. (1967)

ANDERSON, CHARLES HILL R
b. Chattanooga, Tenn, 6/16/30; s. Ray Anderson, Sr. and Lois Entrekin A; m. 5/4/56 to Virginia R. Baker; c. Eric Scott, Alicia Lea and Burton Hill. Educ: Univ. Chattanooga; Univ. Tenn. Col. of Law, J.D, 53; Phi Kappa Phi; Phi Delta Phi; ed, Tenn. Law Rev. Polit. & Govt. Pos: Ballot security officer, State Campaign, Tenn, 64; chmn, Davidson Co. Rep. Exec. Cmt, Fifth Dist, 65-66; del, Tenn. Constitutional Conv; U.S. Attorney, Mid. Dist. of Tenn, 69- Bus. & Prof. Pos: Attorney-at-Law, Chattanooga, 53-60; assoc. gen. counsel, Life & Casualty Ins. Co, Nashville, Tenn, 60-69. Mil. Serv: Pvt, Tenn. Nat. Guard, 48; Maj, Army Res, Judge Adv. Gen. Corps, (Ret). Mem: Nashville, Tenn. and Am. Bar Asns; Asn. of Life Ins. Counsel; Am. Judicature Soc; Barristers Club. Rel: Presbyterian. Legal Res: 4704 Granny White Pike, Nashville, Tenn. 37220. Mailing Add: 879 U.S. Courthouse, Nashville, Tenn. 37203.

ANDERSON, CHARLES WILLIAM R
Chmn, Coffee Co. Rep. Cmt, Ga.
b. Hayesville, N.C, 5/14/15; s. Early Lee Anderson and Mamie Miller A; m. 7/11/35 to Virginia Nan Bryan; c. Charles W, Jr, Nancy Carole, James Stephen and Jo Christy. Educ: Hayesville High Sch. Polit. & Govt. Pos: Cmnr, Douglas, Ga, 47-48, v.chmn, Hosp. Authority, 48-54 and mayor, 49-51; mem, Ga. State Dem. Cent. Cmt; chmn, Coffee Co. Rep. Cmt, Ga, currently. Mil. Serv: Entered as Pvt, Marine Corps, 44, released as Pfc, 46, after serv. with 9th Marines; Am. and Asiatic Pac. Theater Ribbons. Mem: W. Master, Douglas Lodge 386, 51, secy, at present; Mason; K.T; Shrine; Elks; VFW; Am. Legion. Rel: Methodist. Mailing Add: 500 W. Peachtree St, Douglas, Ga. 31533. (1967)

ANDERSON, CLIFFORD R, JR. R
Cal Plan Chmn, Calif. Rep. State Cent. Cmt.
b. Alexandria, Minn, 2/6/28; s. Clifford R. Anderson and Capatola Chase A; m. 2/11/50 to Madeline M. Graham; c. Clifford R, III, Alicia Marie, George Maxwell and Eric Preston. Educ: Univ. Calif, Berkeley, B.S, 50; Univ. South. Calif, J.D, 53; Phi Delta Phi; Pi Kappa Alpha. Polit. & Govt. Pos: Admin. asst. to Assemblyman Don Anderson, Calif, 57-58; city councilman, Monterey Park, 58-60; pres, Los Angeles Young Rep, 60; chmn. vol. clubs, Los Angeles Co. Rep. Cent. Cmt, 61-64, chmn. cand. selection cmt, 64-66; state chmn. poll watchers, Goldwater Campaign, 64; chmn. cand. sch, State Calif. Rep. Party, 64, 66 & 68; South. Calif. precinct chmn, Reagan for Gov. Campaign, 66; mem, Calif. Rep. State Cent. Cmt, 66-, state cand. develop. chmn, 66-67, precinct chmn, 67-69, mem. exec. cmt, 67-, Cal plan chmn, 69-; alternate del, Rep. Nat. Conv, 68. Mil. Serv: Seaman, Navy, 45-46, serv. in U.S.S. St. Paul, Pac. Theatre. Mem: Am, Calif, Los Angeles and Pasadena Bar Asns; Am. Judicature Soc; Am. Arbit. Asn; Defense Research Inst; Asn. of South. Calif. Defense Counsel; Appeal Agent-Selective Serv; Rotary; Tournament of Roses Asn; Legion Lex; pres, Calif. Lutheran Homes. Merit Award, Los Angeles Rep. Cent. Cmt. Rel: Lutheran. Mailing Add: 2046 Oak Knoll, San Marino, Calif. 91108.

ANDERSON, CLINTON PRESBA D
U.S. Sen, N.Mex.
b. Centerville, S.Dak, 10/23/95; s. Andrew Jay Anderson and Hattie Belle Presba A; m. 6/22/21 to Henrietta E. McCartney; c. Sherburne Presba and Nancy (Mrs. Ben L. Roberts). Educ: Dakota Wesleyan Univ, 13-15; Univ. Mich, 15-16; Delta Theta Phi; Pi Kappa Delta. Polit. & Govt. Pos: N.Mex. State Treas, 33-34; adminstr, N.Mex. Relief Admin, 35; chmn. and exec. dir, Unemploy. Compensation Cmn, 36; managing dir, U.S. Coronado Exposition Cmn, 39-40; U.S. Rep, N.Mex, 41-45; U.S. Secy. of Agr, 45-48; U.S. Sen, N.Mex, 49-; del, Dem. Nat. Conv, 68. Bus. & Prof. Pos: Reporter, Mitchell Repub, S.Dak, 16-17 and Albuquerque J, 19-22; chmn. bd, Mt. State Mutual Casualty Co. Mem: Rotary Int.(pres, 32-33); Mason; Elks. Rel: Presbyterian. Legal Res: 3621 Camino Alameda S.W, Albuquerque, N.Mex. 87105. Mailing Add: 4215 Senate Office Bldg, Washington, D.C. 20510.

ANDERSON, DAGMAR IRENE R
Chairwoman, Hennepin Co. Rep. Cmt, Minn.
b. Duluth, Minn, 6/21/98; d. The Rev. Carl Oscar Cassel and Ellen Benson C; m. 6/16/26 to Dr. Ernest R. Anderson; c. Judith Ellen (Mrs. Walton). Educ: Gustavus Adolphus Col, B.A, 20; Univ. Minn, post grad. study in eng; Iota Beta. Polit. & Govt. Pos: Finance area chairwoman, Hennepin Co. Rep. Cmt, Minn, 53-55, v.chmn, 61-63, chairwoman, 63-; precinct block capt, Rep. Party, 55-57, chairwoman, 57-59; chairwoman, 11th Ward Rep. Cmt, 59-61; secy, Minn. State Rep. Cent. Cmt, 67-69. Bus. & Prof. Pos: High sch. teacher, Lead, S.Dak, Ortonville, Garden City and Minneapolis, Minn, 21-36 and Roosevelt High Sch, Minneapolis, Minn, 27-36. Mem: Minikahda Club; Minneapolis Athletic Club; Soc. for the Blind; Gustavus Adolphus Twin City Women's Club; Gustavus Adolphus Col. Alumni Asn. and Col. Woman's Club; Minneapolis Citizens League; Methodist Hosp. Auxiliary; personnel chmn, Woman's Club of Minneapolis, 56-57; Eastern Star. Rel: Lutheran. Mailing Add: 5108 Luverne Ave. S, Minneapolis, Minn. 55419.

ANDERSON, DON R
b. Lincoln, Nebr, 5/1/18; s. John M. Anderson and Ida M. Yantzie A; m. 6/15/41 to Elaine W. Jordan; c. Donald A. and Sharon K. Educ: Univ. of Nebr, B.A, 43; Sigma Delta Chi; Phi Mu Alpha, Sinfonia; Phalanx; Gamma Lambda; Sigma Chi. Polit. & Govt. Pos: Pres, 45th Dist. Rep. Assembly, Los Angeles Co, 54-55; mem, Los Angeles Co. Rep. Cent. Cmt, 56-59, orgn. dir, 59-61, exec. secy, 61-64; Calif. State Assemblyman, 45th Dist, 57-59; exec. secy, Orange Co. Rep. Cent. Cmt, 59, mem, 60-62; chief admin. officer, Calif. State Rep. Cent. Cmt, 64-69; exec. officer State Allocation Bd, 69- Mil. Serv: Entered as 2nd Lt, Army, 42, released as Maj, 46, after serv. in 4025th Signal Serv. Group, Asiatic-Pac, 45-46; Lt. Col.(Ret), Army Res, 68; Army Commendation Medal. Mem: F&AM; Optimist Club; ROA; C. of C. (pres, Monterey Park Chap, 54-55). Most Valuable Citizen Award, Monterey Park, 53; Distinguished Serv. Award, Monterey Park C. of C, 59. Rel: Presbyterian. Legal Res: 2972 Tigertail Dr, Los Alamitos, Calif. 90720. Mailing Add: 6204 Gloria Dr, Sacramento, Calif. 95831.

ANDERSON, EDWIN DEWEY, SR. R
Chmn, Starke Co. Rep. Cent. Cmt, Ind.
b. Knox, Ind, 12/12/21; s. Clarence James Anderson and Amanda Sheldon A; m. 12/13/41 to Alberta Marie Smith; c. Edwin Dewey, Jr. and Howard Brian. Educ: Knox High Sch; Reppert Sch. of Auctioning, Decatur, Ind; Ind. Univ. Exten. Real Estate Appraisal Course. Polit. & Govt. Pos: Precinct committeeman, Starke Co. Rep. Cent. Cmt, Ind, 52-66, chmn, 63- Mil. Serv: Entered as Pvt, Army, 45, released as Cpl, 45, after serv. in 5th Army; Marksman Sharpshooter. Mem: Gov, Moose Lodge, 51; North Moose, Moose Legion, 62; Moose fel; adjacent, Am. Legion, 63; Farm Bur; Aviation Club; Nat. and Ind. Auctioneers Asns. Rel: Protestant. Mailing Add: R.R. 2, Knox, Ind. 46534.

ANDERSON, ERIC O. D
Wash. State Rep.
b. New Zealand, 1902; m. to Ida May; c. Two. Polit. & Govt. Pos: Wash. State Rep, 3 terms and 69- Bus. & Prof. Pos: Purchasing agent; store mgr. Mem: Grange; Mason; Eastern Star; IWA Timber Workers. Mailing Add: 627 Grand Ave, Hoquiam, Wash. 98550. (1967)

ANDERSON, ERNEST J. R
Minn. State Sen.
b. Frost, Minn, 11/28/02; s. John Anderson and Louise A; m. 6/12/30 to Olive Alice Olsen; c. James, Marilyn (Mrs. Robert Martinson) and Larry. Educ: Bricelyn High Sch, grad. Polit. & Govt. Pos: Minn. State Sen, Fairbault and Martin Counties, currently, pres. pro tem and chmn, Senate Labor Cmt. and mem, Commerce, Pub. Hwy, Agr, Pub. Welfare, Taxes and Tax Law, Rules and Legis. Expense Cmts, currently. Mem: V.pres, Minn. Farmers Elevator Asn; Jr. Col. Action Cmt; Farm Bur. Rel: Lutheran. Mailing Add: Frost, Minn. 56033. (1967)

ANDERSON, EUGENIE MOORE D
b. Adair, Iowa, 5/26/09; d. Ezekiel Arrowsmith Moore and Flora Belle McMillen M; m. 9/9/30 to John P. Anderson; c. Elizabeth Johanna (Mrs. Ghei) and Hans Pierce. Educ: Stephens Col, 26-27; Simpson Col, 27-28; Carleton Col, 29-30; Julliard Inst. Musical Art, 30-32. Polit. & Govt. Pos: Chmn, Democrat-Farmer-Labor Party, Goodhue Co, Minn, 44-48; del-at-lg,

Minn, Dem. Nat. Conv, 48; mem, Dem. Nat. Cmt, 48-49; ambassador, Denmark, 49-53; U.S. Rep, Third Session UN ad hoc cmt. on POW's, 52; chmn, State Cmn. for FAIR Employ. Practice, 55-60; mem, Dem. Nat. Adv. Cmt. on For. Policy, 57-61; EEMP, Bulgaria, 62-65; alternate U.S. Rep, UN Trusteeship Coun, 65-68; del, Dem. Nat. Conv, 68. Mem: Minn. UN Asn; League of Women Voters. Rel: Methodist. Mailing Add: 'Tower View,' Red Wing, Minn. 55066.

ANDERSON, EUNICE R
S.Dak. State Rep.
b. 12/9/06; m. to Arthur R. Anderson; c. Dr. Courtney Anderson, (Mrs. Catherine Kelley). Educ: Univ. S.Dak, B.A. and M.A. in Chem. Polit. & Govt. Pos: Past asst. S.Dak. State chemist; S.Dak. State Rep, 64- Bus. & Prof. Pos: Florist bus; cattle feeding; farming; chief of Lab and X Ray Dept, Sioux Valley Hosp; asst. prof. chem, Sioux Falls Col; asst. prof. biol, Augustana Col. Mem: Past mem. bd. dirs, Lutheran Soc. Serv. of S.Dak; Am. Asn. of Univ. Women; Sertoma. Rel: Lutheran. Mailing Add: 2112 Spring Ave, Sioux Falls, S.Dak. 57105. (1967)

ANDERSON, FAYNE E. R
N.H. State Rep.
b. Maine, 8/17/03; married; c. 2. Polit. & Govt. Pos: N.H. State Rep, 47-; del, N.H. State Constitutional Conv, 48-64. Bus. & Prof. Pos: Bldg. contractor; pres, Health Center. Mem: Mason (32°); Pemigewasset Valley Fish & Game Club; K. of P. Rel: Protestant. Mailing Add: Warren, N.H. 03279. (1967)

ANDERSON, FORREST H. D
Gov, Mont.
b. Helena, Mont, 1/30/13; s. Oscar A. Anderson and Nora O'Keefe A; m. 1/24/41 to Margaret Evelyn Samson; c. Margaret Louise (Mrs. Gary Templin), Arlee Joan and Newell Burke. Educ: Univ. Mont; Columbus Univ, LL.B, 38; Phi Delta Theta. Polit. & Govt. Pos: Mont. State Rep, 43-45; co. attorney, Lewis and Clark Co, 45-47; spec. counsel, Indust. Accident Fund, Mont, 47-49; assoc. justice, Mont. Supreme Court, 53-57; attorney gen, Mont, 57-69; del, Dem. Nat. Conv, 68; Gov, Mont, 69- Bus. & Prof. Pos: Attorney-at-Law, 38-52. Mem: Mason (32°); Shrine; Elks; Eagles; Moose; Mont. and Am. Bar Asns; Mont. Club; Scandinavian Lodge of Am. Rel: Methodist. Legal Res: 2 Carson St, Helena, Mont. 59601. Mailing Add: Capitol Building, Helena, Mont. 59601.

ANDERSON, GEORGE BANISTER D
Va. State Del.
b. High Point, N.C, 10/30/26; s. Banister Anderson and Margaret Phillips A; m. 9/16/50 to Alice Marie Garrett; c. Margaret Marie, Pamela Sue and Emily Chisholm. Educ: Randolph-Macon Col, B.A, 50; Univ. Richmond Law Sch, LL.B, 54; Omicron Delta Kappa; Phi Delta Theta; Delta Theta Phi. Polit. & Govt. Pos: Chmn, Zoning Bd. of Appeals, Danville, Va, 58-60, city councilman, 60-68, v.mayor, 62-68; Va. State Del, Danville and Pittsylvania Co, 68- Mil. Serv: Entered as Pvt, Army, 45, released as 1st Lt, 46, after serv. in 24th Inf. Div, Asiatic Pac. Theatre; Philippine Liberation Medal; Asiatic Pac. Theatre Medal; Good Conduct Medal; Japanese Occup. Medal; Meritorious Unit Citation. Mem: Va. Trial Lawyers Asn; Am. Judicature Soc; pres, Danville Bar Asn, 61-63; Va. State Bar Asn.(regional v.pres, 66-67); pres, Va. Municipal League, 67-68; Optimist; German Club; Danville Golf Club; Moose. Rel: Methodist. Legal Res: 502 Linden Place, Danville, Va. 24541. Mailing Add: Suite 600, Masonic Bldg, Danville, Va. 24541.

ANDERSON, GERALD EDWARD D
Mem. State Exec. Cmt, Caucus of Conn. Dem.
b. Minneapolis, Minn, 12/7/30; s. George Nathaniel Anderson and Anna Edwardson A; m. 6/15/52 to Martha Ellen Thompson; c. Stanley Karl, Ruth Marie and Freya Nor. Educ: Univ. of Minn, Minneapolis, B.S, 52, M.S, 59. Polit. & Govt. Pos: Town cmt. secy, Andover Dem. Town Cmt, Conn, 63-66; second cong. dist. campaign coordinator and mem. state exec. cmt, Conn. Cmt, McCarthy For Pres, 68; del, Dem. Nat. Conv, 68; mem. state exec. cmt, Caucus of Conn. Dem, 69- Bus. & Prof. Pos: Sr. research engr, Rosemount Aero Labs, Rosemount, Minn, 52-60; heat transfer consult, Rosemount, Minn, 55-56; research engr, United Aircraft Research Labs, East Hartford, Conn, 60-67; research scientist, Travelers Research Corp, Hartford, Conn, 67-; lectr, East. Conn. State Col, 67-; assoc. ed, J. of Appl. Meteorol, 67- Publ: 'Boundary Layer Transition On A Porous Hemisphere With Mass Transfer Cooling At M = 3.7,' Bul. of the Am. Phys. Soc, 59; 'Take-Off And Landing Critical Atmospheric Turbulence (Tolcat), Air Force Flight Dynamics Lab, 68; 'Evaluation of Dispersion Formulae,' Am. Petroleum Inst, 69. Mem: Prfnl. mem, Am. Meteorol. Soc; Am. Inst. of Aeronaut. and Astronaut; Am. Phys. Soc; Am. Geophys. Union; Am. Asn. for the Advancement of Sci; Am. Civil Liberties Union; NAACP. Rel: Congregational. Mailing Add: Long Hill Rd, Andover, Conn. 06232.

ANDERSON, GERALD K R
b. Waupaca, Wis, 4/26/21; m. to Betty Bagan; c. Mary Beth, Kaye Ellen and Jill Ann. Educ: Univ. Wis, B.A, 42, LL.B, 48; Univ. Mo, 43. Polit. & Govt. Pos: Mem, Waupaca Co. Rep. Exec. Cmt, Wis, 62-69; dist. attorney, Waupaca Co, 64; Wis. State Assemblyman, 65-69; mem. rules cmt, Wis. Rep. Party, 67. Bus. & Prof. Pos: Attorney. Mil. Serv: Entered Army, 42, released 45, after serv. as criminal investigator, Mil. Govt. Germany. Mem: State Bar of Wis; DAV; Lions; Am. Legion; VFW. Mailing Add: 703 Demerest St, Waupaca, Wis. 54981.

ANDERSON, GERTIE FEAZEL D
b. Point, La, 8/26/15; d. William Crawson Feazel and Cynthia Day F; m. 1/28/38 to Garnett Murphy Anderson; c. William Garnett and Henry Feazel. Educ: Gulf Park Col, 33-34; Kings Smith Studios, 35; Sigma Psi. Polit. Pos: Co. chmn, Johnson for President, 64. Rel: Methodist. Mailing Add: 6936 Gilbert Dr, Shreveport, La. 71106. (1967)

ANDERSON, GLENN M. D
U.S. Rep, Calif.
b. Hawthorne, Calif, 2/21/13; s. William Anderson; m. Lee Dutton; c. Melinda, Evan and Glenn Michael. Educ: Univ. Calif, Los Angeles, B.A. in Polit. Sci. and Psychol. Polit. & Govt. Pos: Mem, Los Angeles Co. Dem. Cmt, Calif, 38-50, chmn, 48-50; mayor and city councilman, Hawthorne, 40-43; mem, Calif. Dem. State Cmt, 42-; Calif. State Assemblyman, 43-51; chmn, Calif. Dem. State Cent. Cmt, 50-52; Lt. Gov, Calif, 59-67; U.S. Rep, 17th Dist, Calif, 69- Bus. & Prof. Pos: Founder and dir, Hawthorne Savings and Loan Asn, 50- and Hawthorne Financial Corp; pres, Downtown Enterprise Inc, currently. Legal Res: Harbor City, Calif. Mailing Add: 1132 Longworth House Office Bldg, Washington, D.C. 20515.

ANDERSON, GORDON LeROY 'BID' R
Tenn. State Rep.
b. Knoxville, Tenn, 10/21/01; s. Fanning Anderson and Cynthia Roberts A; m. 6/5/20 to Scottie Pilant. Educ: High sch, 16-18. Polit. & Govt. Pos: Tenn. State Rep, 68- Bus. & Prof. Pos: Policeman and Fireman, Knoxville, Tenn, 28-54. Mem: Local Plumbers and Steamfitters 102, UAW. Rel: Baptist. Mailing Add: 3821 Skyline Dr, Knoxville, Tenn. 37914.

ANDERSON, GWEN ADELE R
Rep. Nat. Committeewoman, Wash.
b. Lignite, N.Dak, 6/3/30; d. Adolph Odegaard and Beatrice Shannon O; m. 6/4/51 to Harlan John Anderson; c. Barbara Shannon and Mark Harlan. Educ: Univ. S.Dak, 48-51; Alpha Phi; Radio Guild; Int. Relations Club. Polit. & Govt. Pos: Precinct committeewoman for Hart, Benton Co. Rep. Cent. Cmt, Wash, 58-60, dist. chmn. for Kennewick, 59-60, v.chmn, 60-62, state comitteewoman, 62-65; del, Wash. State Rep. Conv, 60, 62, 64, 66 & 68; treas, Fourth Cong. Dist. Rep. Club, 63-65; v.chmn, Wash. State Rep. Cent. Cmt. and Wash. State Rep. Cent. Cmt. Exec. Bd, 65-68, dir, State Precinct Training Prog, 66; adv. to exec. bd, Wash. State Fedn. of Rep. Women, 65-; del, Rep. Nat. Conv, 68; chmn, Wash. State Women for Nixon, 68; Rep. Nat. Committeewoman, Wash, 68- Bus. & Prof. Pos: Mem, Ed. Bd, Rep. Report, 65-66. Publ: Co-ed, A Guide For Good Political Manners, 1965. Mem: Am. Asn. of Univ. Women; Benton Co. Rep. Women's Club; Tri-City Alpha Phi Alumni Club; Commun. Concert Asn; Mid-Columbia Symphony Guild; Bi-Co. Ment. Health and Ment. Retardation Planning Bd; Tri-City Country Club; Bon Marche Consumer Adv. Bd, 69. Rel: Lutheran. Mailing Add: 2212 S. Vancouver, Kennewick, Wash. 99336.

ANDERSON, HAROLD EARL R
b. Lansing, Mich, 9/6/22; s. Clayton Anderson and Gertrude Moore A; m. 8/24/45 to Geraldine L. Goldammer; c. Catherine and Stephan. Educ: Blackstone, Law degree, 54. Polit. & Govt. Pos: Pres, Bd. of Educ, Reed City, Mich, 55-58, chmn, City Cmt, 58; past chmn, Osceola Co. Rep. Cmt. Bus. & Prof. Pos: Co-partner, Anderson Ins. Agency, 46-; pres, North. Group Writers, 56-58, North. Import Co, 58- and Tasa Wire Corp, 65- Mil. Serv: Entered as Cadet, Air Force, 42, released as 1st Lt, 45, after serv. in 9th Air Force, ETO, 44-45; Air Force Res, 45-52; Air Medal with 3 Clusters. Mem: Rotary; C. of C; VFW; Elks; Moose. Rel: Lutheran. Mailing Add: 466 W. Todd, Reed City, Mich. 49677. (1967)

ANDERSON, HAROLD J. R
Minn. State Rep.
b. Holdrege, Nebr, 9/9/09; s. Swan Anderson and Emily Swanberg A; m. 1/4/50 to Eleanor Owens; c. Margaret Ann, Gary Thomas, Daniel Richard and Mary Lynn. Educ: William Mitchell Col. of Law, LL.B, 36; Univ. Minn. Polit. & Govt. Pos: Spec. agent, Fed. Bur. Invest, 42-46; chmn, Hennepin Co. Young Rep. League, 47; chmn, Minn. Young Rep. League, 48; Minn. State Rep, 51-, chmn, tax cmn, Minn. House Rep, 69- Bus. & Prof. Pos: Attorney-at-law, 36- Mem: Minneapolis Aquatennial Asn.(pres, 54); Elks. Rel: Protestant. Mailing Add: 4919 Colfax Ave. S, Minneapolis, Minn. 55409.

ANDERSON, HARRY DALE D
Mem, Colo. Dem. State Exec. Bd.
b. Barnsdale, Okla, 11/5/20; s. Roy E. Anderson and Edna L. Vance A; m. 8/11/45 to Veda Ione Queen; c. Harold Dale, Jerry Dean, Mike Edward, Leroy A. and Susan Kay. Educ: Pub. schs, 11 years. Polit. & Govt. Pos: Committeeman, Adams Co. Dem. State Cent. Cmt, 67-; mem, Colo. Dem. State Exec. Bd, 67- Bus. & Prof. Pos: Former taxi driver; truck mech, Denver, Colo, 51-57; mech, Commerce Gas & Oil, 57-65 and Hwy. Dept, 66- Rel: Protestant. Mailing Add: 6800 E. 75th Place, Commerce City, Colo. 80022.

ANDERSON, HELEN FUHS R
b. Canton, Mont, 6/3/10; d. Harry Albert Fuhs and Mabel Keene F; m. 4/12/43 to Roswell Hugh Anderson; wid. Educ: East. Mont. Col, 28-30. Polit. & Govt. Pos: Mont. State Sen, 63-65. Mem: Eastern Star; Mont. Farm Bur. Rel: Methodist. Legal Res: Wilbaux, Mont. Mailing Add: Casa Mobil 7-9, Billings, Mont. 59102.

ANDERSON, HENRY H. D
b. Wright, Iowa, 5/9/08; s. Henry Wilbur Anderson; Mary Zollars A; m. 4/14/29 to Minnie Moody; c. Sherill Lee (Mrs. David A. Adkins). Educ: Christian Holiness Univ, Los Angeles Col, D. Chiropractic, Ph.C, 47. Polit. & Govt. Pos: Mayor, Libby, Mont, 51-54; Mont. State Sen, 55-60; mem, Mont. Dem. Cent. Cmt; State Treas,Mont, 65-68; del, Dem. Nat. Conv, 68. Bus. & Prof. Pos: Chiropractor, 47-65. Mem: Nat. Chiropractic Asn; Mason. Mailing Add: Box 38, Libby, Mont. 59923. (1967)

ANDERSON, (NILS) HOLGER R
S.Dak. State Sen.
b. Brandon, S.Dak, 3/23/09; s. John Otto Anderson and Mary Tegstrom A; m. 6/26/30; wid; m. 8/28/68 to Helen Derr; c. Lynore (Mrs. Howard Phillips); Helen Mae (Mrs. Robert Eleeson); Dorothy (Mrs. Harlan Wahde). Educ: Several sales courses; Dale Carnegie. Polit. & Govt. Pos: Mem; Evergreen Dist. 18, Sch. Bd, S.Dak, 51-61, S.Dak. State Rep, 64-66; S.Dak. State Sen, 67- Bus. & Prof. Pos: Petroleum distributor, Truck Stop operator, 30-; farmer and cattle feeder; mem, State Game, Fish and Parks Cmn, 10 years, v.chmn, 58-59 and chmn, 59-60; mem. adv. bd, Northwest. Nat. Bank, Stockyards Br, 60-; mem. bd. dirs, Jobbers-Terminal Warehouse, Minneapolis, 62- Mem: Mason; Shrine; Elks; Odd Fellows; United Commercial Travelers; dir, Salvation Army; dir, Sioux Falls Credit Bur; dir, S.Dak. Petroleum Coun; Independent Oil Men's Asn; C. of C; Sertoma; Crooks Gun Club; Farm Bur; YMCA; Izaak Walton League (dir. and past v.pres). Rel: Swedona Covenant Church. Mailing Add: 5012 N. Cliff Ave, Sioux Falls, S.Dak. 57104.

ANDERSON, HOWARD PALMER D
Va. State Del.
b. Crystal Hill, Halifax Co, Va, 5/25/15; m. to Mildred Webb. Educ: Halifax Co. Pub. Schs; Col. of William and Mary, B.A; Univ. Richmond Law Sch, LL.B; Sigma Pi; Delta Theta Phi; Univ. Richmond Law Sch. Asn. Polit. & Govt. Pos: Former mem, Halifax Co. Sch. Bd; Va. State Del, 58- Bus. & Prof. Pos: Lawyer; former Fed. Bur. of Invest. agent. Mil. Serv: Lt.(sg), Naval Res. Mem: Mason; Lions; Am. Legion; VFW; Va. Farm Bur. Fedn; Sportman's Club of Halifax; Wilson Mem. Ruritan Club; Halifax Co. C. of C; Am, Va. and Halifax Co. Bar Asns; bd. trustees, Patrick Henry Mem. Found; Halifax Co. High Sch. Booster Club. Rel: Baptist. Mailing Add: 1080 Mountain Rd, Halifax, Va. 24558.

ANDERSON, IRVIN NEAL DFL
Minn. State Rep.
b. International Falls, Minn, 6/18/23; s. Albert Eugene Anderson and Agnes Bodway A; m. 12/7/45 to Phyllis J. Peterson; c. Gregory M. and Cynthia J. Educ: Univ. Minn, 47. Polit. & Govt. Pos: Minn. State Rep, 65- Mil. Serv: Entered as Aviation Cadet, Navy, 43, released as Lt.(jg), 47; Air Medal; Asiatic Theater Ribbon. Mem: Am. Legion; VFW; K. of C; Moose. Rel: Catholic. Mailing Add: 909 13th St, International Falls, Minn. 56649.

ANDERSON, JACK Z. R
b. Oakland, Calif, 3/22/04; s. George H. Anderson and Susan Brown A; wid; c. Mrs. James Seay, Mrs. Lonzo Epps and Mrs. Kevin McCray. Educ: High sch. grad. Polit. & Govt. Pos: U.S. Rep, Calif, 38-52; spec. asst. to secy, Dept. Agr, 55-56; admin. asst. to the President of the United States, 56-61. Bus. & Prof. Pos: Mgr, G.H. Anderson Co, 25-38; pres, Calif. Canning Pear Asn, 53-55; mem. bd. dirs, Bank of Am, 53-55. Mem: Elks; Sainte Claire Club. Rel: Protestant. Mailing Add: 535 Anzar Rd, San Juan Bautista, Calif. 95045.

ANDERSON, JESSE THOMAS D
b. Timmonsville, S.C, 10/26/92; s. Ervin Anderson and Frances Thomas A; m. 1/19/21 to Hazel Prickett. Educ: Furman Univ, B.A, 14 (magna cum laude); Univ. S.C, M.A, 42; Furman Univ, LL.D, 51; other Peabody and Univ. Chicago; Phi Beta Kappa. Polit. & Govt. Pos: State Supt. of Educ, 47-67; Florence Co. Supt. of Educ, 29-47. Bus. & Prof. Pos: Sch. teacher and adminstr; Sch. Book Com; Educ. Finance Com; ETV Com; State Com. for Tech. Educ; bds. of trustees of all state insts. of higher learning, except land grant cols. Mil. Serv: WWI. Mem: Pres, SCEA; life mem. NEA, PTA; Lions Club, past pres; past post comdr, Am. Legion; past master Masonic Lodge; past grand comdr, Grand Commandery; bd. dir, Nat. Coun. of State Chief Sch. Officers. Rel: Deacon 1st Baptist Church; Sunday Sch. supt. Mailing Add: 1223 Wellington Dr, Columbia, S.C. 29204. (1967)

ANDERSON, JOE W. D
Chmn, Gaines Co. Dem. Party, Tex.
b. Aspermont, Tex, 11/24/07; s. Hugh W. Anderson and Myrtle Harrington A; m. 10/11/31 to Hazel Voss; c. Nita Joyce (deceased). Educ: Droughns Bus. Col, Abilene, Tex. Polit. & Govt. Pos: Maintenance foreman, Tex. Hwy. Dept, Gaines and Andrews Counties, 34-44; cmnr, Gaines Co, Tex, 46-52; chmn, Gaines Co. Dem. Party, currently; del, Dem. Nat. Conv, 68. Bus. & Prof. Pos: Pres, Anderson Farm Supply, Inc, 38- Mem: Pres, W.Tex. Co. Judges & Cmnr. Asn, 51-52; dir, Plains Cotton Growers Asn; Gaines Co. Livestock Asn; secy. and dir, S.Plains Underground Water Conserv. Dist. 4; Mason; Shrine; Scottish Rite; KT; past pres, Rotary; past pres, C. of C. Rel: Methodist. Legal Res: 503 S.W. 15th St, Seminole, Tex. 79360. Mailing Add: P.O. Box 37, Seminole, Tex. 79360.

ANDERSON, JOHN, JR. R
b. Olathe, Kans, 5/8/17; s. John Anderson and Ora May Bookout A; m. 5/16/43 to Arlene Auchard; c. John, III, King David and Kerry Diann. Educ: Kans. State Univ, 39-40; Kans. Univ, A.B, 43, LL.B, 44; Phi Delta Phi. Polit. & Govt. Pos: Co. attorney, Johnson Co, Kans, 47-53; Kans. State Sen, Johnson Co, 53-56; Attorney Gen, Kans, 56-61; Gov, Kans, 61-65, mem. adv. coun, Intergovt. Rels, Wash, D.C, 61-65, chmn, Gov. Conf, 63-64; pres, Citizens Conf. on State Legis, 65-66. Bus. & Prof. Pos: Attorney, Hodges, Hambleton & Anderson, Olathe, Kans, 53-55; Hackler, Anderson, Chipman, Speer & Vader, currently. Publ: Article in Saturday Rev, 1/9/65. Rel: Methodist. Legal Res: R.R. 1, DeSoto, Kans. 66018. Mailing Add: c/o Hackler, Anderson, Chipman, Speer & Vader, 7500 W. 85th, Olathe, Kans. 66061. (1967)

ANDERSON, JOHN B. R
U.S. Rep, Ill.
b. Rockford, Ill, 2/15/22; m. to KeKe A; c. Eleanora, John Jr. and Diane. Educ: Univ. Ill, A.B, J.D; Harvard Law Sch, LL.M. Polit. & Gov. Pos: Adv. on staff of U.S. High Cmnr. in W.Berlin; mem, U.S. State Dept. Career Dipl. Serv, 52; state's attorney of Winnebago Co, Ill, 56-60; U.S. Rep, Ill, 60-; mem, Joint Cmt. on Atomic Energy; mem, Rep. Policy Cmt; chmn, House Rep. Conf. Cmt, 69-; second ranking mem. of Rules Cmt. Bus. & Prof. Pos: Lawyer; former mem. faculty, Northeastern Univ. Sch. of Law, Boston; admitted to practice law before Supreme Court of Ill, 46. Mil. Serv: Army, 30 months, European Theatre. Publ: Contrib. to We Propose: a Modern Congress and Republican Papers, Doubleday Anchor, 68. Mem: Am. Legion; U. Club of Rockford; Winnebago Co. Bar Asn; served on bd. educ, Trinity Col, Chicago. Rel: First Evangelical Free Church of Rockford (former trustee). Legal Add: Rockford, Ill. Mailing Add: 5616 Ogden Rd, Washington, D.C. 20010.

ANDERSON, JOHN HENRY, JR. D
b. Hawkinsville, Ga, 11/12/36; s. John Henry Anderson and Belle Woods A; single. Educ: Middle Ga. Col, 57-59; Univ. Ga, Col. Bus. Admin, B.B.A, 61. Polit. & Govt. Pos: Ga. State Rep, 71st Dist. Ga, Bleckley and Pulaski Co, 63-66. Bus. & Prof. Pos: Partner, Anderson Oil Co, 59- Mil. Serv: Entered as Seaman Recruit, Navy, 54, released as Sk 2, 57, after serv. aboard the U.S.S. O'Bannon DE 450, 2 years and NAS Jacksonville, Fla, 1 year. Mem: V.pres, Alumni Soc. Middle Ga. Col; v.chmn, Middle Ga. Col. Adv. Cmt; Lions; Bulldog Club; Alumni Soc. Univ. Ga; Pulaski Co. Develop. Bd; Cochran-Bleckley Develop. Corp. Rel: Baptist; Sunday Sch. Teacher. Legal Res: Anderson Rd, Hawkinsville, Ga. 31036. Mailing Add: Box 472, Hawkinsville, Ga. 31036. (1967)

ANDERSON, JOHN HOPE R
Pa. State Rep.
b. New Park, Pa, 5/2/12; s. D. Ross Anderson and Helen Nelson A; m. to Lelia Reed; c. three. Educ: Mercersburg Acad; Gettysburg Col. Polit. & Govt. Pos: Pa. State Rep, 60-; Rep. committeeman; mem. exec. cmt, York Co. Rep. Orgn. Bus. & Prof. Pos: Pres, Stewartstown R.R; served 14 years as sch. dir. in Fawn Twp; mem. bd, York BK & Trust Co. Mem: Dir, White Rose (AAA) Motor Club. Mailing Add: New Park, Pa. 17352.

ANDERSON, JOHN MILTON D
b. San Francisco, Calif, 9/19/36; s. Herman Frederick Anderson and Martha Warneke A; m. 7/1/61 to Jola Lynne Lehds; c. Erika Lina and Edward Milton. Educ: Pomona Col, B.A, 58; Univ. Calif, Berkeley, LL.B, 61; Nu Alpha Phi. Polit. & Govt. Pos: Admin. asst. to chmn, Dem. Nat. Cmt, 64; v.pres, San Francisco Dem. Forum, Calif, 65-67; chmn, Speakers for Gov. Brown, N. Calif, 66; mem, Chmn. Adv. Cmt, Calif, 66-; mem, Calif. Dem. Adv. Cmt, 67-68; advanceman for Sen. Robert Kennedy in Colo, Ore, S.Dak. and Calif, 68; alternate del, Dem. Nat. Conv, 68. Mil. Serv: Entered as Airman Basic, Air Force Res, 62, released as Airman 2/C, 68, after serv. in 631st Hosp. Group, Air Defense Command, 66-68. Publ: 'The Smut Peddlers' (book rev), Calif. Law Rev, 61; 'Working Class Suburb,' Frontier Mag, 62; 'Geneva (Switzerland) Today,' San Francisco Chronicle, 63. Mem: Am, Calif. and San Francisco Bar Asns; Music Libr. Asn. Legal Res: 93 Cazneau Ave, Sausalito, Calif. 94965. Mailing Add: 3300 Crocker Plaza, San Francisco, Calif. 94104.

ANDERSON, JOHN RICHARD R
Chmn, Borden Co. Rep. Cmt, Tex.
b. Midland, Tex, 3/9/29; s. John Robert Balleu (deceased) and Brookie Lee; m. 3/26/51 to Barbara Clayton; c. Sarah, Mary, John Robert and Martha. Educ: Univ. Okla, B.A, 50; Delta Tau Delta. Polit. & Govt. Pos: Finance chmn, Rep. Party, Tex, 62-66, dist. committeeman, 66; chmn, Borden Co. Rep. Cmt, 62- Bus. & Prof. Pos: Rancher. Mem: Univ. Okla. Alumni Club; Am. Quarter Horse Asn; Southwest. Cattle Raisers Asn; Soc. of Range Mgt. Rel: Episcopal. Mailing Add: Box 13, Gail, Tex. 79738. (1967)

ANDERSON, JOHN TRACY NP
Minn. State Sen.
b. 10/29/28; m. 5/7/67 to Lois Elaine Meyer; c. Jevon Todd. Educ: Univ. Minn. Polit. & Govt. Pos: Minn. State Rep, 57-66; Minn. State Sen, 67- Bus. & Prof. Pos: Treas, Geo. J. Grant Construction Co. Mem: AF&AM; Shrine; bd. dirs, St. Paul YMCA. Rel: Presbyterian. Mailing Add: 1048 Van Slyke Ave, St. Paul, Minn. 55103.

ANDERSON, KENNETH THEODORE D
b. Burdick, Kans, 6/22/09; s. Emil Theodore Anderson and Cora Florentine Bjorkback A; m. 2/6/58 to Norma Jean Denny; c. Lisa Nell, Mary Michelle, and Eric Theodore. Educ: Wichita Univ; Univ. of the South, B.S, 31; Phi Gamma Delta. Polit. & Govt. Pos: Kans. State Rep, 48; Dem. Nat. Committeeman from Kans, 52-68. Bus. & Prof. Pos: Hotel mgr, 31-33; employee, prod. dept, Skelly Oil Co, 33-35, sales dept, 35-38; organizer and operator, Universal Butane Corp, Centralia, Ill, 38-40; chmn, Kans. Soya Prod; v.pres, Anderson Cattle Co, Inc, Emporia, Kans; cattle bus, 40- Mil. Serv: Lt.(sg), Gunnery Officer, Navy, 44-46. Rel: Lutheran. Mailing Add: Box 399, Emporia, Kans. 66801. (1967)

ANDERSON, L. ROBERT R
Chmn, San Juan Co. Rep. Cent. Cmt, Utah
b. Provo, Utah, 3/19/29; s. Robert Clair Anderson and Rachel Holbrook A; m. 3/19/51 to Madge Greaves; c. Rachel Gwen, Lynette, Lyle Robert, Peter, Andrew, Samuel, William and Daniel Greaves. Educ: Snow Jr. Col, 46-48; Univ. Utah, LL.B, 54; Order of the Coif. Polit. & Govt. Pos: Chmn, San Juan Co. Rep. Cent. Cmt, Utah, 65- Bus. & Prof. Pos: Attorney, 54- Rel: Latter-day Saint. Legal Res: 260 Blue Mountain Dr, Monticello, Utah 84535. Mailing Add: P.O. Box 1057, Monticello, Utah 84535.

ANDERSON, LeROY HAGEN D
Mont. State Sen.
b. Ellendale, N.Dak, 2/2/06; s. Peter John Anderson and Gena Hagen A; m. 10/19/29 to Jessie Viola Taylor; c. Beverly Jean (Mrs. John Lahr) and Douglas LeRoy. Educ: Mont. State Univ, B.S. in Chem. Eng, 27; Calif. Inst. of Tech, 34-37; Tau Beta Pi; Pi Kappa Delta; Alpha Chi Sigma; Pi Kappa Alpha. Polit. & Govt. Pos: Mont. State Rep, 47-48; Mont. State Sen, 49-56 & 67-; U.S. Rep, Mont, 57-60; alternate del, Dem. Nat. Conv, 68. Mil. Serv: Entered as Capt, Army, 39, released as Col, 45, after serv. in 5th Armored Div, ETO, 44-45; Maj. Gen.(Ret), Army Res; Silver Star; Bronze Star; Croix de Guerre avec Palme; ETO Medal with 5 Battle Stars. Publ: 'Properties of Osmium Tetroxide,' J. Am. Chem. Soc, 37. Mem: Am. Chem. Soc; Mason; Am. Legion; VFW; Lions. Rel: Presbyterian. Legal Res: 118 S. Virginia, Conrad, Mont. 59425. Mailing Add: Box 576, Conrad, Mont. 59425.

ANDERSON, MARCELLUS JACK D
Pres, United Polit. Orgn, Tex.
b. Anderson Co, S.C, 6/21/08; s. Edward Anderson and Mary Morris A; m. 8/14/43 to Ada Cecile Collins; c. Marcellus J, Jr. and Sandra Joy. Educ: Ohio State Univ, A.B, 33; Kappa Alpha Psi. Polit. & Govt. Pos: Pres, United Polit. Orgn, 60-; v.chmn, Tex. Dem. Conv, 62-64; v.chmn, Johnson-Humphrey Campaign, Tex, 64; del, Dem. Nat. Conv, 64 & 68; nat. dir. fraternal orgns, Dem. Nat. Cmt, 68-69; mem. planning cmn, Austin, Tex, 69- Bus. & Prof. Pos: Chmn. div. soc. sci, Huston-Tillotson Col, 46-52, prof. polit. sci, 54-55; gen. agent, Golden State Mutual Life Ins. Co, Calif, 54-; bd. dirs, United Mortgage Bankers of Am, Inc, 62-; pres, Nat. Protestant Brotherhood, 64-; mem. bd. dirs, Tex. South. Univ, 67- Mil. Serv: Entered as Pvt, Army, 42, released as M/Sgt, 45, after serv. in Qm. Corps, Asiatic-Pac. Theater, 44-45; Am. Campaign Medal; Asiatic-Pac. Medal; Victory Medal; Good Conduct Medal. Mem: Nat. Social Sci. Soc; M.W. Grand Master, M.W. St. Joseph Grand Lodge of Tex; Fedn. Masons of the World (pres); Am. Woodman; Boy Scouts; Capitol Area Cerebral Palsy (mem. bd). Rel: Baptist. Mailing Add: 1602 Astor Place, Austin, Tex. 78721.

ANDERSON, MARY DUNN R
Mem, San Diego Co. Rep. Cent. Cmt, Calif.
b. Wooster, Ohio, 11/28/20; d. Waldo Hilary Dunn and Fern Greenwald D; m.

8/22/48 to H. Cuyler Anderson; c. Susan, Daphne, Bruce and Fletcher. Educ: Scripps Col. for Women, B.A, 43; Phila. Sch. of Occup. Therapy, OTR, 46. Polit. & Govt. Pos: Pres, Rancho Santa Fe Rep. Women's Club, Federated, Calif, 64-65 and San Diego Co. Fedn. Rep. Women's Clubs, 66; mem, Calif. Rep. State Cent. Cmt, 67-; second v.pres, South. Div. Calif. Fedn. of Rep. Women, 68-69; mem, San Diego Co. Rep. Cent. Cmt, 69- Rel: Protestant. Legal Res: Via de la Cumbre, Rancho Santa Fe, Calif. 92067. Mailing Add: Box 867, Rancho Santa Fe, Calif. 92067.

ANDERSON, MARY MIZE D
b. Nashville, Tenn, 2/2/21; d. Herman Haslock Mize and Jessie Hartman M; m. 11/9/45 to Kenneth Brown Anderson; c. Gladys Melinda and Kenneth Mize. Educ: Middle Tenn. State Univ, B.S, 42; Univ. Tenn, grad. work, 58 & 65; Alpha Delta Kappa; officer, Sophomore Class and Women's Athletic Asn; Homecoming Queen, sr. year. Polit. & Govt. Pos: Tenn. State Rep, Davidson Co, 63-66, v.chmn, Cmt. on Educ. and mem, Agr, Correctional Insts, Ins. and Banking and Local Govt. Cmts, Tenn. State House of Rep; mem, Tenn. Cmt. on Inter-Govt. Rels; Tenn. State Sen, 66-68; asst. dir, Tenn. Aeronaut. Cmn, 68-69, admin. asst, 69- Bus. & Prof. Pos: Aircraft eng. draftsman, Consol. Vultee Aircraft Corp, Tenn, 42-45; eng. draftsman, Air Utilities, Inc, Murfreesboro, 45-47 and Victor Chem. Co. Nashville, 47-48; pub. rels, Top Flight Instructional Supply, 53-56; Nashville Div. adv, Westmoreland Silver Co, 56-58; teacher, McCann Elem. Sch, 58-61 and Cohn High Sch, 61-65; staff mem, Tenn. Aerospace Educ. Workshop, Middle Tenn. State Univ, summers, 59-64; consult. for NASA, Nat. Aerospace Conf. for Physics Teachers, summer 62; participant, Nat. Aerospace Educ. Coun, Seattle, Wash, 62, Nat. Citizenship Conf, 62 & 63, Inter-Am. Aerospace Conf, Tampa, Fla, 63, Nat. Flight Seminar for Youth, Kitty Hawk, N.C, 63, Nat. Aerospace Physics Conf, Tampa, 64 and Manned Space Flight Center Conf, Houston, Tex, summer 65; commissioned Adm, Flagship Fleet, Am. Airlines, Inc, 63; coordinator, Vol. Serv, Proj. Headstart, Metrop. Bd. Educ, Nashville, summer 65, dir, After Sch. Study Centers, 65-; asst. dir, First Int. Aerospace Educ. Workshop, 67. Mem: Nat, Tenn, Tenn-Mid Sect. and Metrop. Nashville Educ. Asns; Nat. Aerospace Educ. Coun; first pres, Glencliff Elem. Sch. PTA; Ninety-Nines; League Women Voters; Davidson Co. Dem. Womens Club; Int. Platform Asn; mem. reactor panel, Nat. Educ. Asn. Conv, Detroit, Mich, 63; del. South. Regional Educ. Bd. Legis. Conf, Oklahoma City, 63 and Williamsburg, 64; Delta Kappa Gamma; Am. Women in Radio and TV; Teachers in Politics Specialist-Citizenship, Nat. Educ. Asn. Outstanding Civic and Intercultural Leadership Award, Links, Inc; selected one of four Women of the Year, Davidson Co. Bus. and Prfnl. Women's Club, 65; Distinguished Alumni, Middle Tenn. State Univ, 67; Woman of the Year in Govt. in Tenn, 67. Rel: Church of Christ. Mailing Add: 2903 Westmoreland Dr, Nashville, Tenn. 37212.

ANDERSON, MATTHEW GARLAND D
Va. State Del.
b. Louisa Co, Va, 6/28/04; m. to Frederica Mitchell. Educ: Pub. Schs. in Louisa and Goochland Co. Polit. & Gov. Pos: Former chmn, State Bd. of Elec, Va; former treas, Goochland Co, former mem, Bd. of Supvr; treas, Va. Dem. State Cent. Cmt; Va. State Del, 59- Bus. & Prof. Pos: farmer, merchant and lumberman; Pres, Bank of Goochland. Mem: Farm Bur. Fedn; Ruritans; Mason; Acca Temple; Commonwealth Club of Richmond; Soc. of the Cincinnati. Rel: Episcopal. Mailing Add: Oilville, Va. 23129. (1967)

ANDERSON, MILTON JAY R
Dep. State Chmn, Rep. Party of Tex.
b. Eagle Lake, Tex, 6/4/28; s. B.D. Anderson, Sr. and Ruth Clipson A; m. 11/2/51 to Bobbie Fay Dodd; c. Cythina Gay, Sharen Lyn and Milton Jay, Jr. Educ: Eagle Lake High Sch. Polit. & Govt. Pos: State committeeman, Rep. Party of Tex, 65-, dep. state chmn, 67-; del, Rep. Nat. Conv, 68; del, Rep. State Conv. and mem. pre-conv. platform cmt, 68; mem, Tex. State Task Force on Agr; mem, Tex. State Task Force for Revenue & Fiscal. Bus. & Prof. Pos: Pres, Prairie Rice, Inc. and Fireside Mills, Inc; v.pres, Anderson Agr. Chem, Inc; chmn. bd, Sci. Eng. Co, Inc; partner, rice and cattle prod. Mem: Rotary; Farm Bur. Rel: United Methodist; Lay del. to annual and gen. conf. Mailing Add: Route 1, Box 62, East Bernard, Tex. 77435.

ANDERSON, MORINE R. R
Chmn, Carter Co. Rep. Club, Mont.
b. Elgin, Mont, 11/30/16; d. Bob M. Renshaw and Grace Moles R; m. 6/17/37 to Walter Anderson; c. Walter, Jr, Tom and Kay (Mrs. Gundlach). Educ: High Sch. Grad. Polit. & Govt. Pos: Secy-treas, Carter Co. Rep. Women's Club, Mont, 60-64; chmn, Carter Co. Rep. Club, 64- Bus. & Prof. Pos: Owner and mgr, Carter Co. Abstract and Title Co, 35- Mem: Carter Co. C. of C; Mont. Title Asn. Rel: Congregational. Mailing Add: Box 297, Ekalaka, Mont. 59324.

ANDERSON, MYRTA JANE D
b. Osborne, Kans, 6/7/24; d. John Hewitt Anderson and Katherine Anslinger A; single. Educ: Univ. of Kans, B.A, 50, M.A, 56 and cand. Ph.D in philos. at present; Pi Sigma Alpha; Pi Gamma Mu. Polit. & Govt. Pos: V.chmn, Douglas Co. Dem. Cent. Cmt, Kans, 56-68; secy, State Dem. Conv, 58; secy, Kans. State Dem. Cmt, 58-65; del, Dem. Nat. Conv, 64; secy, Third Cong. Dist. Dem. Cmt, 64-68. Bus. & Prof. Pos: Instr. west. civilization and polit. sci, Univ. Kans; instr. polit. sci, Baker Univ. Publ: 'The Older Population and Housing Needs,' 12/66, 'The Kansas Cultural Arts Commission,' 10/67 and 'State Delegations and the National Nominating Conventions,' 3/68, Your Govt, Univ. Kans. Mem: Am. Polit. Sci. Asn; Kans. League of Women Voters; Am. Asn. Univ. Prof; Am. Legion Auxiliary. Rel: Presbyterian. Mailing Add: 1704 W. 24th, Apt. 104, Lawrence, Kans. 66044.

ANDERSON, N. DALE D
Co. Exec, Baltimore Co, Md.
b. Metropolis, Ill, 11/9/16; s. Henry Lee Anderson and Belle Moyer A; m. 11/15/41 to Dorothy Elizabeth Rassa; c. Merridee C.(Mrs. Voelker) and David Lee. Educ: Mt. Vernon Law Sch, East. Col, LL.B, 63. Polit. & Govt. Pos: Co. councilman, Baltimore Co, Md, 58-66, co. exec, 66-; del, Dem. Nat. Conv, 68. Mil. Serv: Entered as Pvt, Air Force, 42, released as Capt, 46. Mem: Am. Legion; Nat. Asn. of Co. Officers (dir); Md. Asn. of Co. Officers (exec. v.pres). Rel: Protestant. Mailing Add: 100 Belhaven Terr, Baltimore, Md. 21236.

ANDERSON, NORA TIDBALL R
V.Chairwoman, Perkins Co. Rep. Party, S.Dak.
b. Isabel, S.Dak, 2/27/28; d. Watson Heston Tidball and Anna M. Paulson T; m. 10/5/46 to James Wallace Anderson; c. Margaret J.(Mrs. Jerry Martin), David Alan, James Watson, Charles William and Daniel Oscar. Educ: Spearfish State Col, Spearfish, S.Dak, 57-69. Polit. & Govt. Pos: Pres, Rep. Women of Perkins Co, S.Dak, 62; v.chairwoman, Perkins Co. Rep. Party, 62- Mem: West River Parents of Speech and Hearing Impaired Children; Domestikates Exten. Club. Rel: Lutheran. Mailing Add: R.R, Meadow, S.Dak. 57644.

ANDERSON, NORMAN CARL D
Wis. State Assemblyman
b. Hammond, Ind, 3/11/28; s. Carl Anderson and Alma Hagstrom A; m. 12/21/54 to Eleanor Shefferman; c. Marie L, Carl D, Ruth C. and Eric W. Educ: Univ. Wis, B.S, 51, LL.B, 54. Polit. & Govt. Pos: Wis. State Assemblyman, 57-59, 61-, asst. majority leader, Wis. State Assembly, currently; cmnr, Madison Redevelop. Authority, 58-65. Mil. Serv: Entered as Pvt, Army, 46, released as T-5, 47, after serv. in 764th Anti-aircraft Artil. Bn, Ft. Sherman, C.Z. Mem: Am. Trial Lawyers Asn; State Bar of Wis; Dane Bar Asn; Dane Co. Conserv. League; Nature Conservancy. Rel: Lutheran. Mailing Add: 5325 Marsh Rd, Madison, Wis. 53716.

ANDERSON, NORMAN H. D
b. St. Louis, Mo, 3/2/24; s. James S. Anderson and Marie Knost A; m. 6/15/46 to Clara Lottman; c. Deborah Lee. Educ: Wash. Univ, B.S, B.A. and LL.B, 51; Tau Kappa Epsilon; Phi Delta Phi. Polit. & Govt. Pos: City Attorney, Jennings, Mo, 52; Magistrate Judge, First Dist, 54; Prosecuting Attorney, St. Louis Co, 58; former Attorney Gen, Mo, 65-69. Mil. Serv: Entered as Pvt, Marine Corps, 43, released as Cpl, 46, after serv. in 5th Div, S.Pac. Opers. Mem: Nat. Asn. Attorneys Gen; Nat. Dist. Attorneys Asn; Am. Legion; VFW. Rel: Presbyterian. Legal Res: 48 Harneywold Dr, St. Louis, Mo. 63136. Mailing Add: 212 S. Central Ave, St. Louis, Mo. 63119. (1967)

ANDERSON, NORVAL AUGUST R
Chmn, Crow Wing Co. Rep. Party, Minn.
b. Osage City, Kans, 12/26/09; s. Evan August Anderson and Augusta Carlson A; m. 7/6/35 to Evelyn M. Brown. Educ: High Sch. Grad; Strickler's Bus. Col, Topeka, Kans, 29. Polit. & Govt. Pos: Chmn, Crow Wing Co. Rep. Party, Minn, 65- Bus. & Prof. Pos: Div. sales mgr, U.S. Tobacco Co, 34-65; retired, 65. Mem: Mason; Elks; Toastmasters Club; Izaak Walton League. Rel: Lutheran. Mailing Add: 305 N. Bluff, Brainerd, Minn. 56401. (1967)

ANDERSON, OSCAR L. R
b. 4/15/97; married; c. 2 sons, 2 daughters. Educ: H. Park Col, Des Moines. Polit. & Govt. Pos: S.Dak. State Sen, 64-66; Kingsbury Co. Cmnr. of ASC; mayor, Erwin, S.Dak, 2 years; assessor, 2 years; Hartland Twp, and Sch. treas, 13 years. Bus. & Prof. Pos: Farmer; dir. of F.L.B, 10 years; dir. of Rea Kings Elec, 10 years. Rel: Lutheran. Mailing Add: Arlington, S.Dak. 57212. (1967)

ANDERSON, QUENTIN V. D
Iowa State Sen.
b. Ellston, Iowa, 5/7/32; s. George Anderson and Lena A; m. 1957 to Rita Hewlett; c. one son. Educ: Am. Inst. of Bus, Des Moines. Polit. & Govt. Pos: Iowa State Rep, until 66; Iowa State Sen, 69- Bus. & Prof. Pos: Owner and operator, 1,320 acre ranch. Mil. Serv: Army, 2 years. Mem: Am. Legion; VFW; Jr. C. of C; Lions; Farm Bur. Rel: Reorganized Latter-day Saint. Legal Res: R.R. 1, Beaconsfield, Iowa 50030. Mailing Add: State Capitol Bldg, E. Tenth and Grand Ave, Des Moines, Iowa 50319. (1967)

ANDERSON, RALPH WILBUR R
Chmn, Grundy Co. Rep. Party, Iowa
b. Jewell, Iowa, 6/2/11; s. Andrew L. Anderson and Annetta Rierson A; m. 6/17/39 to Irene Victoria Humphry; c. Richard C. and Marilyn (Mrs. Estes). Educ: Iowa State Univ, B.S, 33, research assoc, 42-43 & 45-46; Sigma Delta Chi; Alpha Sigma Phi. Polit. & Govt. Pos: Chmn, Grundy Co. Rep. Party, Iowa, 67- Bus. & Prof. Pos: Publisher, Ringsted, Iowa, Dispatch, 34-42; pres. and publisher, Spokesman Press, Grundy Center, 46-69; pres, Agricareers, Inc, New Hampton, Iowa and Kansas City, Mo, 69 and R.W. Anderson Enterprises, 69- Mem: Gamma Sigma Delta; Grundy Center C. of C.(past pres); Grundy Center Rotary Club (past pres); Grundy Center Develop. Cmn.(v.pres); Mason; Elks. Rel: Presbyterian. Mailing Add: 807 12th St, Grundy Center, Iowa 50638.

ANDERSON, RAYMOND E. R
Ill. State Rep.
b. Galesburg, Ill, 12/4/18; m. to Barbara Johnson; c. Joe, Larry and Peter Marshall. Educ: N. Park Col. Polit. & Govt. Pos: Chmn, Mary Davis Home for Delinquent and Dependent Children; mem, Zoning Appeals and Judiciary Cmt; 2nd term, Knox Co. Bd. of Supvr; Ill. State Rep, 62-, asst. majority whip, Ill. House Rep, 75th Gen. Assembly, majority whip, 76th Gen. Assembly. Bus. & Prof. Pos: Owner-operator of dry cleaning estabs, Galesburg; assoc. in ins. bus. and shopping center. Mil. Serv: Army Air Corps, 38 months in ETO, WWII. Mem: VFW; Am. Legion; 40 et 8; past pres, Galesburg Rotary Club; John Ericcson Rep. League (secy, Ill. league); Knox Co. Rep. Vets. League; past dir, C. of C; Ill. Dry Cleaners Asn; Red Cross; Cub Scouts; bd. regents, N. Park Col. Rel: Covenant Church, trustee. Mailing Add: 1606 N. Kellogg St, Galesburg, Ill. 61401.

ANDERSON, ROBERT BERNARD R
b. Burleson, Tex, 6/4/10; s. Robert Lee Anderson and Elizabeth Haskew A; m. 4/10/35 to Ollie Mae; c. James Richard and Gerald Lee. Educ: Weatherford Col, Tex, 27; Univ. Tex, LL.B, 32; Phi Delta Phi. Hon. LL.D, McMurry Col. and Tex. Christian Univ; hon. L.H.D, Midwest. Univ, Tex. Polit. & Govt. Pos: Mem, Am. Coun. on NATO; mem. bus. adv. coun, Dept. Commerce; mem, Tex. Legis, 32; Asst. Attorney Gen, Tex, 32; State Tax Cmnr, Tex, 34; Racing Cmnr, Tex, 34; mem, State Tax Bd, Tex, 34; chmn. and exec. dir, Tex. Unemploy. Cmn, 36; Secy. of Navy, 53-54; Dep. Secy. of Defense, 54-55; Secy. of Treas, 57-61. Bus. & Prof. Pos: Began law practice, Ft. Worth, Tex, 32; prof. of law, Univ. Tex, 33; pres, Ventures, Ltd, and dir. various affiliated and other co, 55-57; trustee, Eisenhower Exchange Fels; dir, Pan-Am. Airways, Goodyear Tire & Rubber Co; ltd. partner, Carl M. Loeb,

Rhoades & Co, 61- Mem: Wash. Nat. Cathedral; Navy League, Am; Am, N.Y.C. and N.Y. State Bar Asns; The Chancellors; Mason (33°); DeMolay (Supreme Coun); Dallas Athletic Club; Links, Metrop. and Univ. Clubs, N.Y.C; Greenwich Country Club; Round Hill Club, Greenwich, Conn; Toronto Club, Toronto, Can. Tex. Award, 54; Cross of the Order of Boyaca, Colombia, 54; Most Exalted Order of the White Elephant, Thailand, 54; Texan of the Year, 55; Medal of Freedom, 55; Navy Distinguished Pub. Serv. Award, 55; Army Exceptional Serv. Award, 55; Air Force Civilian Serv. Award, 55; Grand Cross Court of Honour, 55. Legal Res: 2 E. 67th St, New York, N.Y. 10019. Mailing Add: 1 Rockefeller Plaza, Suite 2700A, New York, N.Y. 10020.

ANDERSON, ROBERT DARROW D
b. Okolona, Miss, 12/20/30; married. Educ: Miss. State Univ, B.A. in Bus. Admin; Kappa Alpha Order; Delta Sigma Pi. Polit. & Govt. Pos: Miss. State Sen, 60-69. Bus. & Prof. Pos: Cattleman; dir, 1st Citizens Nat. Bank; Progressive Citizen Life Ins. Co. Mem: Farm Bur; Miss. Cattleman's Asn; Am. Legion; VFW; C. of C. Rel: Episcopal. Mailing Add: Okolona, Miss. 38860. (1967)

ANDERSON, ROBERT EDWARD 'BOB' D
Miss. State Rep.
b. Hazlehurst, Miss, 11/30/14; m. to Bonnie Drane. Polit. & Govt. Pos: Miss. State Rep, 56- Bus. & Prof. Pos: Farmer and dairyman, currently. Mem: Lions; Touchdown Club; Farm Bur; Miss. Milk Producers' Asn. Rel: Baptist. Mailing Add: Route 3, Box 211, Wesson, Miss. 39191. (1967)

ANDERSON, ROBERT LOWELL R
Committeeman, 44th Representative Dist, Ill. Rep. Cent. Cmt.
b. Burlington, Iowa, 10/12/32; s. Robert Charles Anderson and Evelyn Anderson A; m. 9/14/57 to Roberta Marian Linse; c. Jeffrey Robert and Michael Linse. Educ: Augustana Col, A.B. summa cum laude, 54; Augustana Theol. Sem, B.D. magna cum laude, 58; Union Theol. Sem, S.T.M. summa cum laude, 59; Columbia Univ, 62-63; Phi Beta Kappa; Pi Kappa Delta; Alpha Delta; Alpha Psi Omega; Phi Omega Phi. Polit. & Govt. Pos: Rep. committeeman, Ninth Precinct, South Rock Island Twp, Ill, 64-; committeeman, 44th Representative Dist, Ill. Rep. Cent. Cmt, 66-; admin. asst, Congressman Tom Railsback, 67-68; auditor, South Rock Island Twp, 68-; mem, Libr. Bd, Rock Island, 69- Bus. & Prof. Pos: Pastor, St. Andrew Lutheran Church, West Chicago, Ill, 59-62; asst. prof. relig. and speech, Augustana Col, 63-66, dir. forensics and secy. of faculty, 68-69, registr, 69- Mil. Serv: Army Res, Capt. Mem: Am. Asn. Univ. Prof. Rel: Lutheran. Mailing Add: 2511 35th Ave, Rock Island, Ill. 61201.

ANDERSON, ROBERT ORVILLE R
Rep. Nat. Committeeman, N.Mex.
b. Chicago, Ill, 4/13/17; s. Hugo A. Anderson and Hilda Nelson A; m. 8/25/39 to Barbara Phelps; c. Katherine (Mrs. Thomas K. Denton), Julia (Mrs. Morgan Smith), Maria (Mrs. William Bishop), Robert Bruce, William Phelps, Barbara Burton and Beverley. Educ: Univ. Chicago, B.A, 39; L.H.D, Colo. Col, 65 and Univ. N.Mex, 66; LL.D, N.Mex. State Univ, 68; Psi Upsilon. Polit. & Govt. Pos: Chmn, Rep. Party Crusade for Freedom, N.Mex, 50-53; mem, Rep. State Cent. Cmt, 50-; chmn, Citizens for Eisenhower Cmt, 52; chmn, Chaves Co. Rep. Party, 54-58; chmn, Volunteers for Mechem, 64; mem. finance cmt, Nixon for President, 67-68; Rep. Nat. Committeeman, 68- Bus. & Prof. Pos: Chmn. bd, Aspen Inst. Humanistic Studies, Colo, 60-; owner, Lincoln Co. Livestock Co, N.Mex, 62-; chmn. bd, Atlantic Richfield Co, N.Y, 65-, Lovelace Found, N.Mex, 67 and Eisenhower Exchange Fels, Pa, 69- Mem: Capitol Club; Century Club; Calif. Club. Man of the Year, N.Mex, 66. Rel: Episcopal. Legal Res: 612 N. Kentucky St, Roswell, N.Mex. 88201. Mailing Add: P.O. Box 1000, Roswell, N.Mex. 88201.

ANDERSON, SARAH A. D
Pa. State Rep.
b. Jacksonville, Fla, d. Dr. Henry A. Anderson and Maude Smith A; m. to Dr. A.W. Anderson, Sr, wid; c. Six. Educ: Phila. Normal Sch. Polit. & Govt. Pos: Inspector of elec-committeewoman and legis. consult; chmn, Joint State Govt. Sub-Cmt. on Ment. Health; Pa. State Rep, 54-, chmn. health & welfare cmt, 69-; alternate del, Dem. Nat. Conv, 56, del, 60; mem, Phila. Cmt. Pub. Assistance; secy, Pa. Legistor's Cmt. on First Class Citizenship; Pa. Citizens' Coun; Citizens' Health and Welfare Planning Cmt; Gov. Cmt. on the Handicapped; Gov. Cmn. on the Status of Women; Pa. Hist. and Mus. Cmn. Bus. & Prof. Pos: Former teacher. Mem: Dept. of Vet. Affairs, IBPOEW; Phila.Women's Club (legis. chmn); VFW Auxiliary; Muscular Dystrophy; Am. Legion Auxiliary; Tribune Charities; Auxiliary of Elks of the World; Mercy-Douglas Hosp; Penn Citizens Coun; Harrisburg Bus. & Prfnl. Women's Club; trustee, Citizens Health & Welfare Planning Cmt, Commun. Serv. Pa. Mailing Add: 226 N. 52nd St, Philadelphia, Pa. 19139.

ANDERSON, SCOTT GALE D
b. Dawson, N.Dak, 4/27/37; s. Elmer L. Anderson and Velma Woessner A; m. 12/7/63 to Rosemary Gabriel; c. Heather. Educ: Jamestown Col, B.S, 59; Univ. N.Dak, J.D, 66; Order of the Coif. Polit. & Govt. Pos: Nat. committeeman, Young Dem. N.Dak, 57-59; mem, adv. cmt, orgn, Dem. Nat. Cmt, 59-60; N.Dak. State Rep, 59-61; exec. dir, N.Dak. Dem. Party, 59-61 and secy, 67-68; del. and mem. nat. platform cmt, Dem. Nat. Conv, 60 and del. and mem. rules cmt, 68; cand, U.S. House Rep, 62; spec. asst. to Sen. Quentin Burdick, D.C, 63; N.Dak. coordinator, Sen. McGovern's Cmt. Party Orgn, 69. Bus. & Prof. Pos: City attorney, Fargo, N.Dak, 68-; mem, Am. Food Peace Coun, 61-64. Mil. Serv: Capt, N.Dak. Air Nat. Guard, 61- Mem: Am. and N.Dak. Bar Asns; Am. Judicature Soc; Elks; Am. Legion; Optimist. Rel: Presbyterian. Mailing Add: 2002 Broadway, Fargo, N.Dak. 58102.

ANDERSON, SIGURD R
b. Arendal, Norway, 1/22/04; s. Karl August Anderson and Bertha Broten A; m. 4/3/37 to Vivian Dall Walz; c. Kristin Karen. Educ: Univ. S.Dak, B.A, 31, LL.B, 37; Phi Beta Kappa; Delta Theta Phi; Pi Kappa Delta. Hon. LL.D, Yankton Col, 53 and Gettysburg Col, 58. Polit. & Govt. Pos: Mem, S.Dak. Young Rep, 37-43; state attorney, Day Co, 39-41; pres, Lincoln Club, 40-41; asst. attorney gen, S.Dak, 41-43, attorney gen, 47-51, gov, 51-55; mem, numerous Rep. Orgns, 46-; cmnr, Fed. Trade Cmn, 55-64. Mil. Serv: Entered as Lt(jg), Naval Res, 43, released as Lt. Comdr, 46; Asiatic-Pac. Theater Ribbon; Philippine Liberation Medal; Am. Theater Ribbon and others. Publ: Numerous articles on trade regulation and anti-trust law. Mem: Am, S.Dak. and Fed. Bar Asns; S.Dak. Hist. Soc; Norwegian-Am. Hist. Asn; bd. dirs, Norwegian-Am. Hist. Museum, Decorah, Iowa; Mason, Shrine, Consistory (33°), Chapter Lodge; Farm Bur; Am. Legion; VFW. Freedoms Found. Award, 63; Americanism Medal for achievements by foreign born citizen, DAR. Rel: Lutheran. Mailing Add: 313 W. Seventh Ave, Webster, S.Dak. 57274.

ANDERSON, THOMAS DUNAWAY R
b. Oklahoma City, Okla, 3/9/12; s. Frank Ervin Anderson and Burdine Clayton A; m. 2/21/38 to Helen Louise Sharp; c. Helen Sharp (Mrs. J. David Wright), Lucille Clayton and John Sharp. Educ: Rice Inst, 30-31; Washington and Lee Univ, LL.B, 34; Phi Delta Phi; Sigma Chi. Hon. LL.D, Lambuth Col, 67. Polit. & Govt. Pos: Committeeman, Harris Co. Rep. Party, Tex, 54-56; state treas, Rep. Party of Tex, 56-59. Bus. & Prof. Pos: Assoc, Andrews, Kurth, Campbell & Bradley, Attorneys, 34-47; v.pres, trust officer and dir, Union Nat. Bank of Houston and its successor Tex. Nat. Bank, 47-55; pres, Tex. Fund Mgt. Co, 56-60; dir. and v.pres, Tex. Fund, Inc, 56-60; sr. v.pres. and trust officer, Nat. Bank of Commerce of Houston, 60-65; trustee, Kelsey-Leary Found, Foley Bros. Store Found, Blaffer Found. and Med. Research Found. Tex; pres, Boston Co. of Tex, 66-; partner, Anderson, Brown, Orn & Pressler, Attorneys, 66- Mil. Serv: Entered as Lt.(jg), Navy, 42, released as Comdr, 46, after serv. in Naval Intel, U.S. Gulf Coast and sea duty in Atlantic, 42-46. Mem: Chmn. bd, Cancer Found; Smith Col; Am. and Houston Bar Asns; State Bar of Tex; Coronado Club; Eagle Lake Rod and Gun; Bayou Club; Houston Country Club; Tejas Club; Tex. Corinthian Yacht Club; Financial Analysts Soc. Rel: Episcopal. Mailing Add: 3925 Del Monte; Houston, Tex. 77019.

ANDERSON, THOMAS J(EFFERSON) D
Mich. State Rep.
b. St. Joseph, Mo, 11/21/19; s. Thomas Jefferson Anderson, Sr. and Hazel Shultz A; m. 6/27/42 to Margaret Anderson; c. Laurel Brigitte, Eugene Thomas and Craig Jeffrey. Educ: U.S. Army. Elec. Eng, 43-45 and Marine Corps Elec. Eng, 50-51; Ford Motor Co. Eng. Schs, 46-48. Polit. & Govt. Pos: Precinct del, Dem. Party, Mich, 52-60; supvr, Ecorse Twp, 53-58; mem. bd. supvr, Wayne Co, 53-61; mayor, Southgate, Mich, 58-61, pres, City Coun, 63-64; Mich. State Rep, 65- Bus. & Prof. Pos: Mech. Engr, Ford Motor Co, 46- Mil. Serv: Entered as Pvt, Army, 43, released as T/Sgt, 46, after serv. in Philippine Islands, 45-46; entered as T/Sgt, Marine Corps Res, 46, released as M/Sgt, 52; Good Conduct and Victory Medals; Asiatic Pac. and Am. Theater Ribbons; Philippine Liberation Ribbon. Publ: History of Detroit's Downriver Area, Wayne Co. Pub. Libr, 63. Mem: Am. Soc. for Quality Control; Kiwanis (pres, 65); Marine Corps League. Rel: Protestant. Mailing Add: 13726 Sycamore, Southgate, Mich. 48192.

ANDERSON, THOMAS M. JR. R
Md. State Sen.
b. Washington, D.C, 4/5/30; single. Educ: Haverford Col, B.A, 53; George Wash. Univ. Law Sch, LL.B, 56. Polit. & Govt. Pos: Md. State Del, 63-67; Md. State Sen, 67- Mem: Pres, Montgomery Co. Hist. Soc. Mailing Add: 114 Commerce Lane, Rockville, Md. 20850.

ANDERSON, THOR Conservative
Minn. State Rep.
married; c. 2 sons. Educ: Univ. of Miss, B.A, 58; Univ. of Minn, LL.B, 64. Polit. & Govt. Pos: Minn. State Rep, 63- Bus. & Prof. Pos: Trust admin, Marquette Nat. Bank, 63-65; Lawyer. Mil. Serv: Lt, Navy, 3 years; Naval Res. Mem: Minn. State and Hennepin Co. Bar Asns. Mailing Add: 4012 Xerxes Ave S, Minneapolis, Minn. 55408. (1967)

ANDERSON, VIRGIL ERVIN R
Chmn, Corson Co. Rep. Party, S.Dak.
b. Watauga, S.Dak, 12/8/30; s. Erick Anderson and Charlotte Peterson A; m. 8/13/55 to Shirley; c. Sherry and Clay. Polit. & Govt. Pos: Mem, McIntosh City Coun, S.Dak, currently; chmn, Corson Co. Rep. Party, 68- Bus. & Prof. Pos: Owner, grocery store and farms, 64- Mil. Serv: Entered as Enlisted Man, Air Force, 51, released as Airman 2/C, 54, after serv. in Strategic Air Command, Korea. Mem: Am. Legion; 40 et 8; McIntosh Commun. Club; Corson Co. Wildlife Betterment Club; OAHE Basin Develop. Asn. Rel: Presbyterian. Mailing Add: McIntosh, S.Dak. 57641.

ANDERSON, W. N, JR. 'BILL' D
b. Newhall, W.Va, 2/2/23; s. William N. Anderson and Gace Perry A; m. 3/28/48 to Hallena White; c. William Edward and Robert Michael. Educ: Bowling Green Bus. Univ. Polit. & Govt. Pos: W.Va. State Del, 62-68; alternate del, Dem. Nat. Conv, 68. Bus. & Prof. Pos: Wholesale merchandise and vending machine bus. Mil. Serv: Army, 43-45, ETO. Mem: Elks; Moose; bd. of dirs, Music Operators of Am. Inc; VFW; Am. Legion; former pres. and past dir. of W.Va. Music and Vending Asn. Rel: Protestant. Mailing Add: 202 Second Ave, Logan, W.Va. 25601. (1967)

ANDERSON, WALTER D
Secy, Boone Co. Dem. Cent. Cmt, Ill.
b. Rockford, Ill, 8/1/21; s. Ivar E. Anderson and Elizabeth Gustafson A; m. 7/7/67 to Norma Lee Mitchell; c. Cynthia Hope. Educ: Brown's Bus. Col, Dipl. in Bus. Acct, 42. Polit. & Govt. Pos: Secy, Caledonia Twp, Boone Co, Ill, 60-64; precinct committeeman, Boone Co. Dem. Cent. Cmt, 60-, secy, 62-; secy, Ward One, Precinct Three Dem. Party, Belvidere, 64- Bus. & Prof. Pos: Hog farmer, Caledonia Twp, Ill, 54-61; hwy. maintenance, Ill, 61-69; park supt, Belvidere Park Dist, 69- Mil. Serv: Entered as Pvt, Army, 42, released as Sgt, 45, after serv. in A Co. 745th Tank Bn, First Div, ETO, 43-45; European-African-Mid. East. Theater Ribbon with Four Bronze Battle Stars; Good Conduct Medal; Purple Heart; Bronze Star with Bronze Oak Leaf Cluster; four overseas serv. bars and one serv. stripe. Mem: Alano Club, Rockford. Rel: Protestant. Mailing Add: 960 W. Lincoln Ave, Belvidere, Ill. 61008.

ANDERSON, WARREN MATTICE R
N.Y. State Sen.
b. Bainbridge, N.Y, 10/16/15; s. Floyd E. Anderson and Edna Mattice A; m. to Eleanor C. Sanford; c. Warren David, Lawrence C, Richard S. and Thomas B. Educ: Colgate Univ, A.B, 37; Albany Law Sch, LL.B, 40; Alpha Tau Omega.

Polit. & Govt. Pos: Asst. Broome Co. Attorney, N.Y, 40-42; N.Y. State Sen, 53-, chmn, Senate Finance Cmt, N.Y. State Sen, 66- Bus. & Prof. Pos: Partner, Hinman, Howard and Kattell, Attorneys. Mil. Serv: Entered as Pvt, Army, released as 2nd Lt, after serv. in Judge Adv. Gen. Dept; ETO Ribbon. Mem: Broome Co. Bar Asn; Am. and N.Y. Bar Asns; Fort Orange Club; Binghamton Club; Am. Legion. Rel: Presbyterian. Legal Res: 34 Lathrop Ave, Binghamton, N.Y. 13905. Mailing Add: 7th Floor, Security Mutual Bldg, Binghamton, N.Y. 13901.

ANDERSON, WENDELL RICHARD D
b. St. Paul, Minn, 2/1/33; s. Theodore M. Anderson and Glady Nord A; m. 8/11/63 to Mary C. McKee. Educ: Univ. of Minn, B.A, 54, LL.B, 60; Phi Delta Phi. Polit. & Govt. Pos: Minn. State Rep, 59-63; Minn. State Sen, 63-67. Mil. Serv: Army, 56-57, 2nd Lt. Mem: Minn. Bar Asn; U.S. Olympians. Mem, Olympic Hockey Team, 56 and U.S. Amateur Teams, 55 and 57. Rel: Protestant. Mailing Add: 852 E. Wheelock, St. Paul, Minn. 55106.

ANDERSON, WILLIAM McOWAN, III R
b. Pittsburgh, Pa, 9/8/29; s. William McOwan Anderson, Jr.(deceased) and Margaret Walsh A.(deceased); m. 8/29/53 to Carol Ann Leach; c. William McOwan IV, Patrick John and Susanne Lanahan. Educ: Univ. Miami, B.B.A, 53; Univ. Pittsburgh, 58, grad. work in indust. eng, 57-58; Propellor Club; Nat. Marketing Club; Sigma Phi Epsilon. Polit. & Govt. Pos: Chmn, Hancock Co. Rep. Party, Miss, 68-69. Bus. & Prof. Pos: Dir, youth camp; labor rels. staff, chem. and plastics div, Koppers Co. Inc, Monaca, Pa, 55-58; field engr, indust. diamond div, Elgin Nat. Watch Co, Elgin, Ill, 58-60; sr. staff indust. engr. covering SPRINT activations, Martin-Marietta Corp, Orlando, Fla, and staff asst. to site mgr. and chmn. missile site labor rels. cmt, Denver, Colo. Div, 61-65; sr. proj. engr. test stand activation and proj. control opers, Miss. Test Opers, N.Am. Rockwell, 65-67, supvr. budgets, proposals and financial opers, 67, supvr. computer and configuration opers, 67-68, supvr, Apollo CSM planning and scheduling at Kennedy Launch Opers, Cocoa Beach, Fla, 68- Mil. Serv: Pvt, Marine Corps, 46-48, with serv. in Second Marine Air Wing, Cherry Point, N.C; Good Conduct, Victory and Sharpshooter Medals. Publ: Employee/Employer Relations,' Co. House Organ Publ, 56-58; 'Computer Usage & Applications,' Co.(Div) Manual, 68. Mem: Nat. Mgt. Asn.(treas. and dir); Nat. Personnel Asn; Am. Legion; dir, Miss. Test Opers. Recreation Asn; Co. Boosters Club (pres); Sideliners Club. Named 'BOSS' of the Year, 68, Miss. Jr. C. of C; Recipient of 'Gold Titan Award,' Martin-Marietta Corp, 63, for meritorious serv. during Titan I missile site activations; U.S. Savings Bond Coordinator, 100% of 800 Personnel. Rel: Roman Catholic. Mailing Add: 28 Crystal River Dr, Cocoa Beach, Fla. 32931.

ANDERSON, WILLIAM ROBERT D
U.S. Rep, Tenn.
b. Bakerville, Tenn, 6/17/21; s. David H. Anderson and Mary McKelvey A; m. 6/10/43 to Yvonne Etzel 'Bonny'; c. Michael David and William Robert, Jr. Educ: U.S. Naval Acad, B.S, 42. Polit. & Govt. Pos: Consult. to President for Nat. Serv. Corps, 63-64; U.S. Rep, Tenn, 65- Mil. Serv: Entered as Ens, Navy, 42, released as Capt, 62, after serv. in 11 submarine combat patrols, Pac; Bronze Star with Combat V; 2 Commendation Medals with Combat V; Presidential Legion of Merit and Unit Citation. Publ: Nautilus 90 North and First Under the North Pole, The World Publ. Co, 59, The Useful Atom, 66. Mem: Am. Legion; VFW; Explorers Club. Commanded U.S.S. Nautilus on first under-ice crossing of N.Pole, 58. Rel: Protestant. Legal Res: Waverly, Tenn. 37185. Mailing Add: House of Representatives, Washington, D.C. 20515.

ANDERSON, WILLIS MARTIN D
Va. State Del.
b. Jacksonville, Fla, 11/3/28; s. Willis Carl Anderson and Edna Keister A; single. Educ: Roanoke Col, 46-49; Wash. & Lee Univ, LL.B, 52; Tau Kappa Alpha; Sigma Chi. Polit. & Govt. Pos: Pres, Young Dem. Club, Roanoke, Va, 55-56; mem, city coun, Roanoke, 58-60, mayor, 60-62; Va. State Del, 64- Bus. & Prof. Pos: Attorney-at-law, Va, 51-; gen. counsel, Shenandoah Life Ins. Co, 69- Mil. Serv: Entered as Pvt, Army, 52, released as 1st Lt, 54, after serv. in 5th Inf. Div, 7th U.S. Army, Germany, 53-54. Mem: Roanoke, Va. and Am. Bar Asns; trustee and mem. exec. cmt, Greater Roanoke Valley Develop. Found; Kiwanis (pres, 69). Rel: Methodist. Legal Res: 2118 York Rd. S.W, Roanoke, Va. 24015. Mailing Add: P.O. Box 2421, Roanoke, Va. 24010.

ANDERSON, WILSON R
Treas, W.Va. Rep. Exec. Cmt.
b. Welch, W.Va; s. Luther C. Anderson and Frances Rummel A; m. 6/10/32 to Margaret Richardson. Educ: Ohio Wesleyan Univ, A.B, 27; W.Va. Univ. Col. of Law, LL.B, 30; Phi Delta Phi; Omicron Delta Kappa; Pi Delta Epsilon; Beta Theta Pi. Polit. & Govt. Pos: Prosecuting attorney, McDowell Co, W.Va, 30-36; W.Va. State Sen, Eighth Dist, 56-60; treas, W.Va. Rep. Exec. Cmt, 64- Mem: Am. Bar Asn; W.Va. Bar Asn.(pres, 66-67); Kanawha Co. Bar Asn. (pres, 53); Int. Asn. Ins. Counsel; Charleston Kiwanis (pres, 57). Rel: Methodist. Legal Res: 1600 Loudon Heights Rd, Charleston, W.Va. 25314. Mailing Add: P.O. Box 1588, Charleston, W.Va. 25326.

ANDOLSEK, LUDWIG JOHN D
V.Chmn, U.S. Civil Serv. Cmn.
b. Denver, Colo, 11/6/10; s. Ludvig Andolsek and France Gouze A; m. 11/25/45 to Regina A. Burnett; c. Kathryn M. Educ: St. Cloud State Teachers Col, B.Ed, 35. Polit. & Govt. Pos: With Nat. Youth Admin, 36-42, area dir, North. Minn, 40-42; asst. to personnel officer in charge of Personnel Rels. and Grievance Procedures, Vet. Admin. Hosp, St. Cloud, Minn, 47-50; with Civilian Personnel Off, Ellsworth AFB, Weaver, S.Dak, 50-51; admin. asst. to U.S. Rep. J. A. Blatnik, 51-62; chief clerk, Cmt. Pub. Works, U.S. House of Rep, 63; cmnr, U.S. Civil Serv. Cmn, 63-, v.chmn, currently. Mil. Serv: Army, 42-46, Capt. Mem: Am. Legion; Eagles (dist. dir, Cent. Minn, 48-50). Legal Res: 9609 Bulls Run Pkwy, Bethesda, Md. 20034. Mailing Add: 1900 E St. N.W, Washington, D.C. 20415. (1967)

ANDORA, ANTHONY D. D
Chmn, Bergen Co. Dem. Cmt, N.J.
b. Paterson, N.J, 11/20/20; s. Anthony A. Andora and Theresa Matera A; m. 7/21/62 to Colleen Gill; c. Melissa, Suzanne, Elizabeth and Anthony D, II. Educ: N.Y. Univ, B.S. cum laude, 51; Rutgers Univ. Sch. Law, LL.B, 54; Kappa Phi Kappa; King's Bond. Polit. & Govt. Pos: Dep. attorney gen, N.J, 59-61; pres, Bergen Co. Young Dem, 59-62; asst. prosecutor, Bergen Co, 61-64; pres, Young Dem. Clubs of N.J, 62-64; alternate-at-lg, Dem. Nat. Conv, 64; munic. chmn, East Paterson Dem. Cmt, 64-65; planning bd. attorney, Oakland, N.J. and borough attorney, East Paterson, 65; del, Fourth Conf. of Young Polit. Leaders, NATO Counties Countries, Oxford, Eng, 65; chmn, Bergen Co. Dem. Cmt, 65-; co-chmn, N.J. Reapportionment Cmn, 66-69. Mil. Serv: Entered as Pvt. E-1, Army, 55, released as 1st Lt, 58, after serv. in 10th Inf. Div. and 8th Inf. Div, ETO; Capt, Army Res. Publ: Landlord & Tenant Law of New Jersey, Assoc. Lawyers Publ. Co, 60. Mem: Am. Trial Lawyers Asn; Bergen Co, New Jersey and Am. Bar Asns; Am. Legion; Kiwanis; 1st v.pres, Paterson Jaycees, 61-62. Outstanding Man of the Year, East Paterson, N.J, 66. Rel: Roman Catholic. Mailing Add: 104 Willow St, East Paterson, N.J. 07407.

ANDRADE, CAROLYN MARIE D
b. Rochester, N.Y; d. John Frances and Catherine Ann; div. Educ: Rochester Bus. Inst, 2 years; Univ. Conn, 1 year; George Wash. Univ; Catholic Univ. Polit. & Govt. Pos: U.S. Navy Inspector, Navy and Aircraft Material, Hartford, Conn, 41-42; cryptograph clerk, Cent. Intel. Agency, Wash, D.C, 43-44; secy, Signal Corps, Pentagon, 44-46; secy, Off. Price Stabilization, Wash, D.C, 48-49; personal secy. to U.S. Rep. Kenneth J. Gray, Ill, 57-58; admin. asst. to U.S. Rep. Robert Levering, Ohio, 58-60; exec. secy. to U.S. Rep. Walter Moeller, Ohio, 61; exec. asst. to U.S. Sen. Stephen M. Young, Ohio, 62-63; exec. asst. to U.S. Rep. Seymour Halpern, N.Y, 63; exec. asst. to U.S. Rep. Claude Pepper, Fla, 64; exec. secy. to U.S. Rep. Clair Callan, 65-66; exec. asst. to U.S. Rep. Seymour Haplern, N.Y, currently. Publ: Worked for 1 year on EPIC with Mr. Albert N. Abajian with Harvard Int. Mkt. Inst. Rel: Catholic. Mailing Add: 1334 31st St. N.W, Washington, D.C. 20007.

ANDRE, PEARL ISABELLE D
State Pres, N.Dak. Dem. Non-Partisan League Women
b. East Grand Forks, Minn, 3/16/00; d. Fred J. Shipley and Effie A. Whitney S; m. 1/7/20 to Sen. J. Raymond Andre (deceased); c. Aaron L, Allen R, Robert A. and Georgia B.(Mrs. Seidlitz). Educ: Univ. N.Dak, correspondence courses. Polit. & Govt. Pos: Chmn, Dem. Legis. Women's Cmt, N.Dak, 61; Steele Co. pres, N.Dak. Dem. Non-Partisan League Women, 63-65, state pres, 65-; N.Dak. chmn, Dem. Nat. TV FundCampaign Cmt, 64; mem, N.Dak. State Dem. Non-Partisan League Exec. Cmt, 65-; Dem. precinct committeeman, N.Dak, 67-; state chmn, Women for Humphrey Campaign, 68; del, Dem. Nat. Conv. and mem. Permanent Orgn. Conv. Cmt, 68; publicity chmn, Dist. 23 Dem. Non-Partisan League Exec. Cmt, 68- Publ: Contrib, News of Dem. Women, 65-67 and The Leader, 67. Mem: Past Matron's Club, Farmers Union; State Finance Cmt, Kennedy Mem. Center, Bismarck; Eastern Star (past Matron); Am. Legion Auxiliary (past pres, Hope Auxiliary). Rel: United Methodist. Mailing Add: Hope, N.Dak. 58046.

ANDRE, PETER RICHARD R
Mem, Calif. State Rep. Cent. Cmt.
b. San Luis Obispo, Calif, 1/3/18; s. Joseph Jorge Andre and Lena Wolfsen A; m. 4/6/46 to Carol F. Macmillan; c. James, Katherine, Donald, Jeanne and David. Educ: Santa Clara Univ, B.Sc, 40; Univ. South. Calif, LL.B, 48; Delta Theta Phi. Polit. & Govt. Pos: Pres, San Luis Obispo Co. Young Reps, Calif, 49-50; co. chmn, Richard Nixon Sen. campaign, 50; mem, San Luis Obispo Co. Rep. Cent. Cmt, 50-67, v.chmn, 50-56, chmn, 60-65; co. chmn, Thomas Kuchel Sen. campaign, 52; asst. city attorney, San Luis Obispo, 52-55; co. chmn, Eisenhower-Nixon campaign, 52-56; co. chmn, William F. Knowland Sen. campaign, 56; mem, Calif. State Rep. Cent. Cmt, 58-, mem. exec. cmt, 58-60 & 62-64; chmn. rules cmt, Calif. Asn. Rep. Co. Chmn, 65; chmn, Nixon-Agnew campaign, San Luis Obispo Co, 68. Bus. & Prof. Pos: Adv. bd. mem, Bank of Am, 52-; legal advisor, San Luis Obispo Co. Hist. Soc, 52-; legal counsel, Sinsheimer Bros, 56-, Harmony Valley Creamery Asn, 57- and San Luis Obispo Co. Farm Supply, 60- Mil. Serv: Entered as Pvt, Army, 42, released as 1st Lt, 46, after serv. in 1st, 7th and 9th Armies, ETO; re-entered serv. as 1st Lt, Army, 50, released 51, after serv. in Judge Adv. Off. Hq, Camp Roberts, Calif; Bronze Star; Bronze Arrowhead; N. France Campaign No. 1, Normandy Campaign No. 1, Ardennes Campaign, Cent. Europe Campaign and Rhineland Campaign Ribbons. Mem: Calif, San Luis Obispo Co. and Am. Bar Asns; secy, Caballeros de San Luis Obispo, 54- and pres, 52; pres, Cabrillo Civic Club, 52; dir, San Luis Obispo C. of C, 49-51; pres, San Luis Obispo Chapter Santa Clara Univ. Alumni Asn, 59-64; nat. alumni secy, Univ. Santa Clara, 63-64; Lions; Calif. Cattlemen's Asn; Am. Legion; VFW; Elks; K. of C; Commonwealth Club of Calif; San Luis Obispo Country Club; San Luis Obispo Co. Farm Bur; Native Sons of the Golden West. Rel: Catholic. Legal Res: 1801 Woodland Dr, San Luis Obispo, Calif. 93401. Mailing Add: Suite 210, San Luis Obispo Savings Bldg, 1150 Osos St, San Luis Obispo, Calif. 93401.

ANDRESEN, KARL ADOLF D
Mem-at-Lg, State Admin. Cmt, Wis. Dem. Party
b. Oslo, Norway, 2/3/24; s. Arne J. Andresen and Nanna Annette Helgesen A; m. 12/29/56 to Helen June Primrose; c. Eric Dale, Robert and William. Educ: Luther Col, B.A; Univ. Minn, M.A. and Ph.D; Univ. Hawaii; Oxford Univ. Polit. & Govt. Pos: V.chmn, Eau Claire Co. Dem. Party, Wis, 63-64, chmn, 64-65 & 68; del, Dem. Nat. Conv, 64; co-chmn, Lyndon Johnson for President Cmt, 64; chmn, Bronson LaFollette for Attorney Gen. Cmt, Eau Claire Co, 64; mem-at-lg, State Admin. Cmt, Wis. Dem. Party, 65-; v.chmn, Wis. McCarthy for President Cmt, Wis. Dem. Party, 65-; v. chmn, Wis. McCarthy for President Cmt, 67-68; campaign chmn, Eau Claire Co. Nelson for Senate Cmt, 68; mem. nat. bd, Am. for Dem. Action, 68- Bus. & Prof. Pos: Prof, Wis. State Univ, Eau Claire, 56- Mem: Asn. of Am. Univ. Profs; Am. Fedn. of Teachers. Mailing Add: 327 Lincoln Ave, Eau Claire, Wis. 54701.

ANDREW, JESS CHARLES, JR. R
Ind. State Sen.
b. Chicago, Ill, 1/7/18; s. Jess C. Andrew and Elizabeth Fowler A; m. Sept. 1941 to Muriel Ellen Sharpe; c. Jess, III, James and Elizabeth. Educ: Purdue Univ, 37-38; Ontario Agr. Col, Assoc, 41. Polit. & Govt. Pos: Ind. State Sen, 66- Bus. & Prof. Pos: Dir. and v.pres, Kirtpatrick Grain Co, 43-; dir, Lafayette Bank & Trust Co, 58- Mil. Serv: Entered as Pvt, Air Force, 42, released as Sgt, 46, after serv. in Sixth Air Force, 44-46. Mem: Columbia Club; Am.

Legion; Lions; Fraternal Order of Police; VFW; Mason; Lafayette Country Club; Farm Bur; Conservation Club; Lafayette C. of C; dir, Lafayette YMCA, 68. Rel: Presbyterian. Mailing Add: Box 176, West Point, Ind. 47992.

ANDREW, LESTER M. R
Mem, Rep. State Cent. Cmt, Calif.
b. Buffalo, N.Y, 5/14/28; s. Deane H. Andrew and Siloma Hunt A; div; c. Gary Mitchell and Dayna Lee. Educ: Syracuse Univ. Law Sch, 51-52; Syracuse Univ, A.B, 52; Scabbard & Blade; Psi Upsilon; Kappa Beta Phi. Polit. & Govt. Pos: Assembly dist. chmn, United Rep. of Calif, 63, Lt. Gov, Area 14, 63-64, Gov, 64-66, South. state v.chmn, 66-67, plan chmn, 68-69; mem, Rep. State Cent. Cmt, Calif, 69-70. Bus. & Prof. Pos: Med. serv. rep, Parke, Davis & Co, 53-61, hosp. sales rep, 61-66, med-surg. dressing div. rep, 66- Mil. Serv: Entered as Pvt, Army, 46, released as T/5, 48, after serv. in Seventh Div, 31st Inf, Seoul, Korea, 46-48; Air Force Res, 57, 1st Lt.(Ret); Victory Medal; Good Conduct Medal. Publ: How to be a Successful Hospital Salesman, Parke, Davis & Co, 63. Mem: Elks; Nat. Rifle Asn; Southland Water Cmt; Orange Co. Peace Officers Asn; League of Men Voters. Presidents Coun. Award, 60; Commerce Award, Orange Jr. C. of C, 60-61; Prom-Planning Award, 63. Rel: Protestant. Mailing Add: 17272 Walnut, Apt. 40, Tustin, Calif. 92680.

ANDREWS, ARTHUR GLENN R
b. Anniston, Ala, 1/15/09; s. Roger Lee Andrews and Bess Jones A; m. 1/9/37 to Ethel Jackson; c. Frank Scott, Arthur Glenn, Jr. and Houston (Mrs. Kilby). Educ: Princeton Univ, A.B, 31; Elm Club. Polit. & Govt. Pos: Chmn, Calhoun Co. Rep. Party, Ala, 52-64, regional coordinator, 54-58, dist. chmn, 58-62; del, Rep. State Conv, 52-64; del, Rep. Nat. Conv, 64; U.S. Rep, Fourth Dist, Ala, 65-67; dist. chmn, Fourth Dist. Rep. Party, 69- Bus. & Prof. Pos: Clerk, Nat. City Bank, Ala, summers, 27-31; salesman, Int. Bus. Machines Corp, 32-37; dist. mgr, Eastman Kodak, 37-45; pres, Andrews Advert, Inc, 45- Mem: Rotary, 47-64; YMCA; Friends of Library; C. of C. Rel: Episcopal. Legal Res: 1205 Champaign Ave, Anniston, Ala. 36201. Mailing Add: P.O. Box 1589, Anniston, Ala. 36201.

ANDREWS, ERIN WEBSTER R
Mem, Rep. State Cent. Cmt, Va.
b. Petersburg, Va, 3/9/21; s. Aurelius L. Andrews and Minnie Lee Pritchett A; m. 7/7/43 to Daphne Pate; c. Keith E, Donna J. and Sharon Lee. Educ: Diesel Engine Sch, Richmond, Va, 2 years; Alexander Hamilton Inst, N.Y, 2 years. Polit. & Govt. Pos: Mayor, Colonial Heights, Va, 60-62, councilman, 62-66, v.mayor, 66-68; chmn, Rep. City Cmt, 64-69; chmn, Fourth Dist, Nixon Campaign, 68; secy, Southside, Va. Rep. Cmt, 68-; mem, Rep. State Cent. Cmt, 68- Bus. & Prof. Pos: Mgr, optical lab, Galeski Optical Co, Richmond, 45-62; dispensary mgr, Petersburg Eye Clin, 62- Mil. Serv: Entered as Pvt, Army, 42, released as Sgt, 45, after serv. in 23rd Field Hosp, Pac. Theatre, 43-45. Mem: Am. Bd. Opticianry; Int. Acad. Opticianry; Mason; Royal Arch; Shrine; Am. Legion Post 284. Rel: Methodist. Mailing Add: 212 Ridge Rd, Colonial Heights, Va. 23834.

ANDREWS, FOY RHYNE D
Mem, Ga. State Dem. Exec. Cmt.
b. Walker Co, Ga, 2/18/98; d. William Henry Forney Rhyne, M.D. and Vinnie L. Hawkins R; m. 12/23/21 to Judge M. Neil Andrews; c. A. Rhyne and Ann Elizabeth (Mrs. Clinton J. Morgan). Educ: Ga. State Col. for Women, grad, 18. Polit. & Govt. Pos: Co-chmn, Kennedy-Johnson Campaign, 59; co-chmn, Sanders Campaign, 61; chmn. bd, Walker Co. Dept. Family and Children's Serv, 61-66; mem, State Bd. Family and Children's Serv, 62-66; mem, Walker Co. Jury Revisory Bd, 62-68; del, Dem. Nat. Conv, 62, served on permanent orgn. cmt, 63; co-chmn, Johnson-Humphrey Campaign, Walker Co, 63; mem, Northwest Ga. Econ. Opportunity Authority and State Econ. Opportunity Adv. Bd, 65-66; mem, Ga. State Dem. Exec. Cmt, currently. Mem: League of Women Voters, 54-59; chmn, Walker Co. Chap, Am. Red Cross, 57-63. Rel: Methodist. Mailing Add: 402 S. Cherokee St, La Fayette, Ga. 30728.

ANDREWS, GEORGE ARISTEDES R
Chmn, Phillips Co. Rep. Party, Ark.
b. Alpohorion, Greece, 1/1/92; s. Aristedes Andrews and Paraskeve Darlas A; m. 7/3/22 to Iva Grace Westgate Herrin. Polit. & Govt. Pos: Chmn, Phillips Co. Rep. Party, Ark, currently. Mem: Mason; Kiwanis; Shrine. Rel: Orthodox Christian. Legal Res: 305 Woodland, Helena, Ark. 72342. Mailing Add: Box D, Helena, Ark. 72342.

ANDREWS, GEORGE WILLIAM D
U.S. Rep, Ala.
b. Clayton, Ala, 12/12/06; s. George William Andrews, Sr. and Addie Bell King A; m. 11/25/36 to Elizabeth Bullock; c. Jane M.(Mrs. Thomas M. Hinds) and George W. III. Educ: Univ. of Ala, LL.B, 28; Sigma Nu; Phi Delta Phi; Omicron Delta Kappa. Polit. & Govt. Pos: Circuit solicitor, Third Judicial Circuit, State of Ala, 31-43; U.S. Rep, Ala, 44- Bus. & Prof. Pos: Lawyer. Mil. Serv: USNR, WWII, Lt.(jg). Mem: Third Judicial Circuit and Ala. Bar Asns. Rel: Baptist. Legal Res: Union Springs, Ala. 36089. Mailing Add: 2466 House Office Bldg, Washington, D.C. 20515.

ANDREWS, HUNTER BOOKER D
Va. State Sen.
b. Hampton, Va, 5/28/21; s. Henry Stuart Andrews and Dorothy Booker A; m. 10/21/50 to Cynthia Collings; c. Hunter Booker, Jr. and Bentley Robinson. Educ: Col. of William and Mary, A.B, 42; Univ. Va. Law Sch, LL.B, 48; Kappa Alpha. Polit. & Govt. Pos: Chmn, Hampton Sch. Bd, Va, 58-62; del, Dem. Nat. Conv, 60 & 68; chmn, Hampton Dem. Cmt, 60-63; Va. State Sen, 64- Bus. & Prof. Pos: Partner, Downing, Andrews & Durden, Attorneys, 57- Mil. Serv: Entered as A/S, Navy, 42, released as Lt, 46, after serv. in Pac. Theatre, 42-46; World War II Campaign Ribbon. Mem: Va. State and Am. Bar Asns; Am. Legion; Rotary. Rel: Episcopal. Mailing Add: 4408 Chesapeake Ave, Hampton, Va. 23369.

ANDREWS, IKE FRANKLIN D
N.C. State Rep.
b. Bonlee, N.C, 9/2/25; s. Archie Franklin Andrews and Ina Dunlap A; m. 9/13/47 to Jo Anne Johnson; c. Alice Cecelia and Nina Patrica. Educ: Univ. N.C, B.S, 46, LL.B, 52; Phi Alpha Delta. Polit. & Govt. Pos: N.C. State Sen, 59-60; Superior Court Solicitor, Dist. 10-A, N.C, 61-64; N.C. State Rep, 61-62 & 65- Bus. & Prof. Pos: Mem. bd. dirs, First Union Nat. Bank of N.C, Siler City, 62- Mil. Serv: Entered as Pvt, Army, 43, released as M/Sgt, 45; Bronze Star; Purple Heart; ETO Ribbon; Victory Medal. Mem: Bd. trustees, Univ. N.C. Rel: Baptist. Legal Res: Route 2, Pine Forest, Siler City, N.C. 27344. Mailing Add: P.O. Box 271, Siler City, N.C. 27344.

ANDREWS, JAMES ALLEN D
b. Toccoa, Ga, 1/13/26; s. William Jennings Andrews and Nancy Gibson A; m. 11/5/50 to Margaret Frances Jones; c. James, Jr; Margaret Lee. Educ: Univ. of Ga, B.B.A, 49; Lambda Chi Alpha. Polit. & Govt. Pos: U.S. Rep, Ga, 50-54; Investr. for House Cmt. on Un-Am. Activities. Bus. & Prof. Pos: Merchant; v.pres. Stephens Co. Mil. Serv: Army, s/sgt. in command of Signal Center, Army-Navy Communs. in Pac. Theater, 43-46. Mem: Masons; Elk; Am. Legion; VFW; DAV, past pres; Toccoa Jr. C. of C; past v.pres. Toccoa C. of C; past pres. Toccoa Merchants Asn; Toccoa Kiwanis Club. Rel: Baptist. Mailing Add: Toccoa, Ga. 30577. (1967)

ANDREWS, JOHN STRIKER R
Chmn, Ohio State Rep. Cent. and Exec. Cmts.
b. Cincinnati, Ohio, 4/25/19; s. Burton Richardson Andrews and Cora Striker A; m. 7/4/64 to Marjorie Ann Carney; c. Richard J, Christine C. and Sally J. Educ: Univ. Toledo, B.B.A, 40. Polit. & Govt. Pos: Secy, Toledo Airport Cmn. and mem, Toledo Recreation Cmn, Ohio, 51-55; mem, Lucas Co. Rep. Exec. Cmt, 52-, exec. dir, 55-62, chmn, 62-66; alternate del, Rep. Nat. Conv, 56 & 60, del, 64 & 68; chmn, Lucas Co. Rep. Cent. Cmt, 58-62; chmn, Ohio State Rep. Cent. and Exec. Cmts, 65-; mem, Rep. Nat. Cmt, 65- Bus. & Prof. Pos: Underwriter, Travelers Ins. Co, 40-46; ins. mgr, Owens-Corning Fiberglas Corp, 46-50, admin. asst. to pres, 50-53, dir. pub. rels, 53-55. Mil. Serv: Entered as Pvt, Army Air Corps, 44, realeased as Cpl, 45, after serv. in Aviation Cadet Training Prog, 8th Serv. Command, Tex; Good Conduct Medal; Am. Theater Ribbon. Mem: Mason; Scottish Rite; Shrine; Am. Legion; Univ. Toledo Alumni Asn; trustee, Boys Club of Toledo; Athletic Club of Columbus; Columbus Club; Rockwell Springs Trout Club of Castalia; Toledo Mus. of Art; Toledo Zool. Soc. Outstanding Young Man of the Year, Toledo Jaycees, 53; Distinguished Serv. Award, Ohio Jaycees, 53. Rel: Congregational. Legal Res: 1915 Princeton Dr, Toledo, Ohio 43614. Mailing Add: 50 W. Broad St, Columbus, Ohio 43215.

ANDREWS, MARK R
U.S. Rep, N.Dak.
b. 5/19/26; m. to Mary Willming; c. Mark III, Sarah and Karen. Educ: N.Dak. State Univ, B.S, 49. Polit. & Govt. Pos: Past dir, Garrison Conservancy Dist; Past Rep. Nat. Committeeman, N.Dak; U.S. Rep, 63- Bus. & Prof. Pos: Farmer. Mil. Serv: Enlisted, Army, appointed U.S. Mil. Acad, West Point, 44, discharged, 46. Mem: N.Dak. Crop Improv. Asn.(past pres); Am. Legion; DAV; Elks; Masons; Shrine. Legal Add: Mapleton, N.Dak. 58059. Mailing Add: Room 204 Cannon House Office Bldg, Washington, D.C. 20515.

ANDREWS, MARY ELOISE OKESON D
V.Chmn, Franklin Co. Dem. Party, Kans.
b. Catale, Okla, 7/8/23; d. George Manifold Okeson and Verna Dick O; m. 11/22/41 to Robert Leon Andrews; c. Janith Lea (Mrs. Roger Allen Nearmyer) and George Mark. Educ: Ottawa High Sch, grad, 41. Polit. & Govt. Pos: V.chmn, Franklin Co. Dem. Party, Kans, 68- Bus. & Prof. Pos: Real Estate Broker, Ottawa Real Estate, currently. Mem: Franklin Co. Bd. of Realtors. Rel: Church of Christ. Mailing Add: Route 2, Ottawa, Kans. 66067.

ANDREWS, ROBERT D
Ga. State Sen.
b. Macon, Ga, 6/13/23; m. 1951 to Katherine Perryman; c. Andy, Jones and Clara. Educ: Mercer Univ, LL.B, 49. Polit. & Govt. Pos: One year with the Attorney Gen. of Ga; Ga. State Rep, two terms; Ga. State Sen, 69- Bus. & Prof. Pos: Practiced law in Gainesville, 50- Mil. Serv: Air Force, Europe, 34 combat missions; received Air Medal, 4 Oak Leaf Clusters, Distinguished Flying Cross. Mem: Ga. Bar Asn; Am. Trial Lawyers Asn; Gainesville Bar Asn. Admitted to practice in all superior courts of Ga, Court of Appeals of Ga. Supreme Court of Ga; U.S. Circuit Court of Appeals; U.S. Supreme Court. Rel: Methodist. Mailing Add: 310 Breneau Ave. N.E, Gainesville, Ga. 30501. (1967)

ANDREWS, ROBERT LEON D
b. Ottawa, Kans, 6/30/22; s. Charles E. Andrews and Martha Sluder A; m. 11/22/41 to Mary Eloise O'Keson; c. Janith Lea (Mrs. Roger Nearmyer) and George Mark. Educ: Life Underwriters Col, L.U.T.C. Polit. & Govt. Pos: Committeeman, Ottawa Twp. Dem. Cmt, Kans, currently. Bus. & Prof. Pos: Supvr, Nat. Fidelity Life Ins. Co, currently. Mil. Serv: Entered as A/S, Navy, 42, released as Machinist Mate 2/C, 45, after serv. in U.S.S. Ajay, Pac. Theatre, 2 years. Rel: Church of Christ; Elder, Ottawa, Kans. Mailing Add: Route 2, Ottawa, Kans. 66067.

ANDREWS, THOMAS COLEMAN, JR. American Party
Nat. Chmn, American Party
b. Richmond, Va, 2/15/25; m. to Barbara Jane Ransome. Educ: Dartmouth Col, B.A; Wharton Sch, Univ. Pa. Polit. & Govt. Pos: Former secy, Richmond City Dem. Cmt; Va. State Del, 60-68; nat. chmn, Am. Party, 69- Bus. & Prof. Pos: Owner, T. Coleman Andrews, Jr. Ins. Agency. Mil. Serv: Air Force, combat navigator, auditor gen. Mem: Am. Legion; C. of C; Commonwealth Club. Rel: Episcopal. Mailing Add: 1508 Willow Lawn Dr, Richmond, Va. 23230.

ANDREWS, WILLIAM CLAUD D
Fla. State Rep.
b. Tampa, Fla, 1/24/34; s. Claud Fleming Andrews and Agatha Leeuwenburg A; m. 6/25/55 to Cedora Platt; c. Claudia Lynn, William Claud, Jr. and Suzanne Marie. Educ: Univ. Fla, B.S. and B.A, 55, LL.B, 58; Sigma Alpha Epsilon. Polit. & Govt. Pos: Fla. State Rep, Alachua, Gilchrist and Putnam Counties, 66- Bus. & Prof. Pos: Attorney, individual practice, 59-; dir, Bank of Hawthrone, 66- Mil. Serv: E-2, Army, 58-59; Capt, Army Res, 65. Mem: Am. and Fla. Bar Asns; Jaycees; Kiwanis; Moose. Rel: Methodist. Legal Res: 206 S.E. First St, Gainesville, Fla. 32601. Mailing Add: P.O. Box 1036, Gainesville, Fla. 32601. (1967)

ANDREWS, WILLIAM TAYLOR R
N.H. State Rep.
b. Washington, D.C, 2/4/24; s. John E. Andrews and Dorothy Beuchert A; m. 2/18/49 to Marilyn Ruth Brownfield; c. John Ely, Martha Louise, Robert Bruce and Amanda Bartlet. Educ: George Wash. Univ, B.E.E, 44, LL.M, 51; Albany Law Sch, J.D, 49; Sigma Tau; Sigma Alpha Epsilon; Theta Tau; Soc. Justinian; ed-in-chief, Law Rev. Polit. & Govt. Pos: Del, Rep. State Conv, New London, N.H, 64; mem. zoning bd. of appeals, New London, 64-65, chmn. planning bd, 65-66; del, State Constitutional Conv, New London, 64-; N.H. State Rep, 69-, mem, Judiciary Cmt, Resolutions Cmt, Elec. Cmt. and Asst. Majority Whip. Bus. & Prof. Pos: Attorney, State Marine Lines, 56-61; attorney-at-law, 62-; Justice of the Peace, currently. Mil. Serv: Entered as Seaman, Navy, 44, released as Ens, 46, after serv. in Mine sweepers, Pac. Theatre, 44-46; re-entered as Lt.(jg), 52, released as Lt, 55, after serv. in Naval Intel, London, 52-55; Lt. Comdr, Res, 55-; Asiatic-Pac. and Am. Campaign Medals; Nat. Defense Serv. Medal; World War II Victory Medal; Naval Res. Medal. Mem: N.H. and Merrimack Co. Bar Asns; Lake Sunapee Bd. of Trade; Naval Reserve Asn; New London Vol. Fire Dept; U.S. Naval Inst; N.H. Hist. Soc; New London Hist. Soc. Rel: Protestant. Legal Res: Little Sunapee Rd, New London, N.H. 03257. Mailing Add: Professional Bldg, New London, N.H. 03257.

ANDRINGA, CORNELIUS GEORGE R
Chmn, Waukesha Co. Rep. Party, Wis.
b. Milwaukee, Wis, 3/9/31; s. Cornelius Andringa and Bessie McKenzie A; m. 5/8/54 to Patricia Therese Collins; c. Kathy, Eric, Brian, Barbara, Timothy and Mark. Educ: Univ. Wis, Madison, B.A, 54; LL.D, 58, Sigma Chi. Polit. & Govt. Pos: Chmn, Young Rep. of Waukesha Co, Wis, 59-61; v.chmn, City and town of Waukesha Br. Waukesha Co. Rep. Party, 61-63 and 63-66; chmn, Waukesha Co. Rep. Party, 66- Bus. & Prof. Pos: Claims adjuster, Rural Mutual Ins. Co, 58-61; asst. dist. attorney, Waukesha Co, 61-64; partner, Collins, Collins & Andringa, Attorneys, 64-; asst. family court cmnr, Waukesha Co, 64- Mil. Serv: Entered as 2nd Lt, Army, 54, released as 1st Lt, 56, after serving in 6th Armored Training Div, Fort Leonard, Mo, 54-56; Capt, Army Res, 58-64; Good Conduct Medal. Mem: Farm Bur; chmn, St. Mary's Parish Sch. Bd. Rel: Catholic. Legal Res: 265 Fisk Ave, Waukesha, Wis. 53186. Mailing Add: 300 W. Main St, P.O. Box 234, Waukesha, Wis. 53186.

ANDRUS, CECIL D. D
Idaho State Sen.
b. Hood River, Ore, 8/25/31; s. Hal S. Andrus and Dorothy Johnson A; m. 8/27/49 to Carol M. May; c. Tana Lee, Tracy Sue and Kelly Kay. Educ: Ore. State Univ, 48-49. Polit. & Govt. Pos: Idaho State Sen, Sixth Dist, 61-; Dem. cand. for Gov. of Idaho, 66. Bus. & Prof. Pos: Asst. mgr, Workmen's Compensation Exchange, 63-66; agent, Paul Revere Ins. Companies, 67, agency supvr, 68, field supvr, 69- Mil. Serv: Entered as Recruit, Navy, 51, released as AT2, 55, after serv. in Patrol Squadron 17, Pac. Theatre, 52-55; Korean Serv. Medal. Mem: Mason; Elks; VFW. Man of the Year, VFW, 59. Rel: Lutheran. Mailing Add: 2233 Second St, Lewiston, Idaho 83501.

ANDUJAR, ELIZABETH RICHARDS 'BETTY' R
b. Harrisburg, Pa, 11/6/12; d. Karl Elmer Richards and Katharine Beetem R; m. 8/16/35 to Dr. John Jose Andujar; c. Betty Jo (Mrs. F.D. Shear) and Linda (Mrs. J.F. Meyer, III). Educ: Wilson Col, B.A, 34. Polit. & Govt. Pos: Eisenhower campaign worker, Tarrant Co. Rep. Party, Tex, 52-56, acting precinct chmn, 60 & 64, mem. gubernatorial cmt, 62 & 64, gen. arrangements chmn, 63, 65, 67, 68 & 69, mem. Goldwater Hq. Cmt, 64; educ. chmn, 64 & 68; del, Tex. Rep. Conv, 62, 64, 66 & 68; charter mem. and mem. bd, Ft. Worth Metrop. Rep. Woman's Club, 62-69; committeewoman, Sen. Dist. 22 Rep. Party, 64-; del, Rep. Nat. Conv, 68. Mem: Am, Tex. and Tarrant Co. Med. Asn. Auxiliaries; Tarrant Co. Med. Soc. Auxiliary (past pres); Woman's Club of Ft. Worth (past chmn, speech dept); Planned Parenthood (mem. bd, Tarrant Co. Chap); Int. Good Neighbor Coun. Elected One of the Top Ten Women of Tex. Rep. Party, 65; named Key Rep, Tex, 65,66,67, 68 & 69; Award of Merit, Tarrant Co. Unit, Am. Cancer Soc, 67. Rel: Presbyterian. Mailing Add: 2951 Benbrook Blvd, Ft. Worth, Texas 76109.

ANDUZE, DR. ROY A. D
b. St. Thomas, V.I, 11/19/13; s. Carl Adelbert Anduze and Mildred Veronica Watlington A; m. 5/29/41 to Vivian Irene Kelley; c. Roy Adelbert. Educ: Howard Univ, M.D, 39, fel. in Gen. Surg, 46-47; postgrad. work, Harvard Univ, 50-52. Polit. & Govt. Pos: Mem, Bd. Med. Exam, Govt. V.I, 57-; dir, Surg. Serv, 58-; Hosp. and Med. Serv, 59- and Cmnr. of Health, currently; mem, Territorial Cmt, V.I, 63-; mem, Dem. Nat. Cmt, 64-69. Bus. & Prof. Pos: Trustee, Col, V.I; intern, Freemen's Hosp, Wash, 39-40; asst. resident, 40-41. Mem: Fel, Am. Int. Cols. Surgeons; charter mem, Am. Asn. Pub. Health Physicians; Mason. Distinguished Alumnus Award, Howard Univ, 63. Legal Res: 2 Estate Thomas, St. Thomas, V.I. 00802. Mailing Add: Knud-Hawsen Memorial Hospital, St. Thomas, V.I. 00801. (1967)

ANGEL, NICK D
Treas, Lake Co, Ind.
b. East Chicago, Ind, 11/11/20; s. John Angel and Mary Poppa A; m. 11/30/46 to Darlene Horvath; c. Nikki Lynne and Jack Douglas. Educ: Ind. Univ, B.S. in Bus, 43. Polit. & Govt. Pos: Ind. State Rep, 65-68; del, Dem. State Conv, 66; Treas, Lake Co, Ind, 70- Bus. & Prof. Pos: Int. Revenue Agent, 46-57; owner, Angel Pub. Acct, 57-64; partner, Angel, Kayes & Paterson, Pub. Acct, 64-66. Mil. Serv: Army, 43, Pvt. Mem: Nat, state and local pub. acct. asns. Rel: Presbyterian. Mailing Add: 1411 Kraft Dr, Munster, Ind. 46321.

ANGELL, WAYNE D. R
b. Liberal, Kans, 6/28/30; s. Charlie Francis Angell and Adele Edwards A; m. 8/26/51 to Betty Jean Barnett; c. Patrice, Wynne, Ryan and Wiley. Educ: Ottawa Univ, B.A, 52; Univ. Kans, M.A, 53 and Ph.D, 57; Phi Beta Kappa; Sigma Delta Pi. Polit. & Govt. Pos: Precinct committeeman, Franklin Co. Rep. Cent. Cmt, Kans, 60-, v.chmn, 60-62; Kans. State Rep, 16th Dist, 61-67, v.chmn, water resources cmt, Kans. House Rep, 63-67, chmn, indust. develop. cmt, 65-67; mem. platform cmt, Kans. State Rep. Cmt, 62; permanent chmn, Kans. Rep. Third Dist. Conv, 64; v.chmn, Rep. State Legis. Campaign Cmt, 64-66. Bus. & Prof. Pos: Partner, wheat farm, Meade Co, Kans, 51-; instr. econ, Univ. Kans. Sch. of Bus, 54-56; asst. prof. and assoc. prof, Ottawa Univ, 56-59, prof, 59-, chmn. soc. sci. div, 59-68, dean of the col, 68- Mem: Am. Econ. Asn; Ottawa C. of C; Lions; Franklin Co. Farm Bur; Am. Farm Bur. Rel: Baptist; mem. exec. prog. cmt, Am. Baptist Conv, 65-66; v.pres, Am. Baptist For. Mission Socs. Mailing Add: 1341 S. Mulberry, Ottawa, Kans. 66067.

ANGERS, ROBERT JOHN R
Pub. Rels. Chmn, La. Rep. Party
b. Abbeville, La, 10/20/19; s. Robert J. Angers (deceased) and Anna Mae Nunez A; m. 8/30/41 to Geraldine Beaullieu; c. Gerald, Judith Ann (Mrs. Frank Donaldson), Trent, Stevphen, Thomas, Matthew, Glenn and Jefferson. Educ: La. State Univ, B.A. Journalism; Command & Gen. Staff Col, Ft. Leavenworth, Kans, 49; Sigma Delta Chi, Scabbard & Blade. Polit. & Govt. Pos: Mem, St. Mary Parish Exec. Cmt, La, 63-64; Rep. nominee cong, Third Dist, 64; del, Rep. Nat. Conv, 68; pub. rels. chmn, La. Rep. Party, currently. Bus. & Prof. Pos: Managing ed, Daily Iberian, New Iberia, La, 45-46, co-owner, real estate agency, 46-50; publisher-ed-owner, La. Banner-Tribune, Franklin, 50-65; newspaper columnist-ed. writer, Daily Advertiser, Lafayette, 65-69; pres, Acadian News Agency, 65-69; publisher-ed, Acadiana Profile Mag, 69- Mil. Serv: Entered as 2nd Lt, Army, 42, released as Maj, 45, after serv. in G-3 Sect, XIV Corps, Pac, 42-45; Res, 46-50, Maj; Bronze Star; Combat Infantryman's Badge; D-Day Landing, Pac, Am. Defense and Filipino Liberation Medals. Mem: La. Press Asn.(past pres); Nat. Ed. Asn; La. Printers and Stationers Asn; La. Intracoastal Seaway Asn.(founding secy); bd. trustees, Gulf South Research Inst; Int. Conf. Weekly Ed.(past pres); Coun. Develop. French La; Rotary; Am. Legion; La. Jaycees (past state pres) C. of C; New Iberia Kiwanis (past v.pres); founding mem, Caribbean-Am. Freedom League; life mem. Franklin Jaycees; La. C. of C;(past v.pres third dist). George Wash. Honor Medal for ed. series; Winner of over 150 prizes and awards and cert. and plaques for Banner-Tribune; recipient of numerous awards and cert. from Cuban Exile Orgns. for work with Cuban Exiles; Herrick Award. Rel: Catholic. Mailing Add: 205 River Dr, Lafayette, La. 70501.

ANGLY, MAURICE, JR. R
Tex. State Rep.
b. Houston, Tex, 8/5/40; s. Maurice Angly (deceased) and Virginia Brown A; m. 1/26/62 to Surrenden Hill; c. Maurice, III and Katherine Yvonne. Educ: Univ. Tex, Austin, 58-62; Univ. Tex. Sch. of Law, LL.B, 65; Chi Phi; Praetors. Polit. & Govt. Pos: Tex. State Rep, 67- Bus. & Prof. Pos: Practicing attorney, self-employed, 65-69. Mem: Travis Co, Travis Co. Jr. and Am. Bar Asns; Tex. Trial Lawyers Asn; Town Lake Breakfast Club; Optimists; Travis Co. Farm Bur; Allegro, Houston; Cotillion; Young Adult Rep. Club; Govalle Gardenia Club; Travis Co. Legal Aid and Defender's Soc. Rel: Episcopal. Legal Res: 4301 Balcones Dr, Austin, Tex. 78731. Mailing Add: Suite 810, Scarbrough Bldg, Austin, Tex. 78701.

ANGNEY, ALLAN B, JR. R
b. Pittsburgh, Pa, 5/30/05; m. to Virginia Smith; c. one son, one daughter. Educ: Pa. State Univ, B.S, 27; Alpha Tau Omega. Polit. & Govt. Pos: Vt. State Rep, 61-65; Vt. State Sen, 65-69. Bus. & Prof. Pos: Banker. Mem: Trustee, U.V.M; Dir, Bennington Co. Humane Soc; Dir, Baird Childrens' Center, Burlington; Boy Scouts. Rel: Congregational. Mailing Add: Arlington, Vt. 05250. (1967)

ANGUS, GEORGE W. R
N.H. State Rep.
b. 2/26/97; married; c. 2. Educ: Tufts Col. Polit. & Govt. Pos: Mem, Claremont Indust. Coun, N.H; Unemploy. Compensation Appeals Tribunal; mem. adv. cmt, N.H. Rep. State Cmt; mem, Claremont City Coun; past mayor, Claremont; N.H. State Rep, 43- Bus. & Prof. Pos: Employee, Lambert Supply Co. Mil. Serv: Navy, World War I. Mem: Secy, Vet. Mem. Day Cmn; Dir, Claremont Athletic Club. Rel: Catholic. Mailing Add: 45 Park Ave, Claremont, N.H. 03743. (1967)

ANICH, THOMAS MATTHEW D
V.Chmn, Ashland Co. Dem. Party, Wis.
b. Ashland, Wis, 8/31/18; s. Matt Anich and Cecilia Devcic A; m. 9/20/63 to Beverley Joan Boyle; c. Nina Marie and Mary Katherine. Educ: Northland Col, Ashland, Wis; Univ. of Wis, 40, Law Sch, 42. Polit. & Govt. Pos: Munic. judge, Ashland Co, Wis, 50-61; Dem. chmn, Tenth Dist, 52-54; v.chmn, Ashland Co. Dem. Party, currently. Bus. & Prof. Pos: Attorney. Mil. Serv: Entered as Pvt, Army, 42, released as T/Sgt, 46, after serv. in 248th Signal Radar Maintenance Unit, S.Pac. Area; Asiatic-Pac. Theater Ribbon; Philippine Liberation Medal. Mem: VFW; Elks; Am. and Wis. Bar Asns; Int. Acad. of Law & Scis. Rel: Catholic. Legal Res: 514½ W. Second St, Ashland, Wis. 54806. Mailing Add: Box 388, Ashland, Wis. 54806.

ANNAKIN, V. DEWEY D
b. Akron, Ohio, 6/26/98; s. George Annakin and Linnae Beatty A; m. 6/18/25 to Helen Woody; c. Dorothy (Mrs. Johnson), Virginia (Mrs. Sutch) and Joseph Woody. Educ: DePauw Univ, A.B, 22; Wis. Univ, M.A, 23; Ohio State Univ, Ph.D, 39; Alpha Kappa Delta; Pi Gamma Mu; Tau Kappa Alpha; Phi Delta Kappa; Sigma Phi Epsilon. Polit. & Govt. Pos: Mem. bd. of sch. trustees, Terre Haute, Ind, 51-55; Ind. State Sen. until 66. Bus. & Prof. Pos: Social studies teacher, Tulsa, Okla. High Sch, 24-26; prof. sociol, Ind. State Univ, 26-65, emer. prof. sociol, 66-; vis. prof. sociol, Kent State Univ, 55-56; dean of faculty, Allen Univ, 65-; vis. prof. sociol. and acting chmn. of dept. of anthrop. and sociol, East. Ky. Univ, 66- Mem: Am. Soc. of Hist; Am. Sociol. Soc; Ind. Acad. of Soc. Sci; Am. and Palmetto Educ. Asns; Mason; past dist. gov, Rotary. Rel: Methodist. Mailing Add: 2432 N. Seventh St, Terre Haute, Ind. 47802. (1967)

ANNEAR, GARY D
b. Belfield, N.Dak, 5/27/33; single. Educ: Dickinson State Teachers Col; Univ. of N.Dak. Polit. & Govt. Pos: N.Dak. State Rep, -66. Bus. & Prof. Pos: Lawyer. Mem: Young Dems. Clubs; Elks; Am. Legion; VFW. 1967 Legal Res: Dickinson, N.Dak. No mailing address available. (1967)

ANNENBERG, WALTER H. R
U.S. Ambassador to Gt. Brit.
b. Milwaukee, Wis, 3/13/08; s. M.L. Annenberg; m. 1951 to Leonore Cohn; c. Wallis Weingarten. Educ: Univ. Pa; Phi Sigma Delta; Sigma Delta Chi. Polit.

& Govt. Pos: U.S. Ambassador to Gt. Brit, 69- Bus. & Prof. Pos: Pres, Triangle Publ. Inc, Phila, Pa, 42- Mem: Navy League; Newcomen Soc; Alliance Francaise de Phila; Am. Soc. Newspaper Ed; Int. Press Inst; Inter-Am. Press Asn; mem-at-lg, U.S. Olympic Cmt; Am. Newspaper Publishers Asn; Turf, Bucks and Swinley Forest Clubs; Lyford Cay Club; Bahamas; Nat. Press Club, D.C; Poor Richard Club, Phila. Officer, French Legion of Honor; Comdr, Order of the Lion of Finland; Order of the Crown of Italy and Order of Merit of the Ital. Repub. Legal Res: Wynnewood, Pa. Mailing Add: American Embassy, 24 Grosvenor Square, London, W.1, Eng.

ANNUNZIO, FRANK D
U.S. Rep, Ill.
b. Chicago, Ill, 1/12/15; s. Ralph Annunzio and Rose Malizzio A; m. 12/28/35 to Angeline Alesia; c. Jacqueline (Mrs. Frank Latto), Linda (Mrs. William O'Donnell) and Susan. Educ: DePaul Univ, B.S. and M.Ed. Polit. & Govt. Pos: Regional dir, All Am. Coun; mem. Chicago Cmn. on Human Rels, Ill; chmn, Commun. Serv. Cmt, Chicago; mem. adv. bd, Cook Co. Health and Surv; mem. bd. inspectors, Bridewell Jail, Chicago; mem. adv. cmt, Ill. Indust. Cmn. on Health and Safety and Unemploy. Compensation; chmn, War Ration Bd; dir. Ill. Dept. of Labor; U.S. Rep, Ill, 64- Bus. & Prof. Pos: Pres, Lake Personnel, Chicago; Chicago Temporary Off. Serv; legis. and educ. dir, USW; asst. supvr, Nat. Defense Training Prog, Austin Eve. Sch, Chicago. Mem: Gen. chmn, Villa Scalabrini Develop. Fund; v.pres. lay adv. bd, Villa Scalabrini Ital. Old People's Home; sponsors' cmt, Glenmary Home Missions; bd. trustees, Loretta Col. Fund Drive; Little Flower Soc; bd. dirs, Am. Cmt. on Ital. Migration; Cath. Youth Orgn; chmn, Ital-Am. Dem. Club, Cook Co; K. of C; City Club, Chicago. Legal Res: 400 E. Randolph St, Chicago, Ill. 60601. Mailing Add: c/o Longworth House Office Bldg, Room 1224, Washington, D.C. 20515. (1967)

ANSAI, TOSHIO R
Hawaii State Sen.
b. Wailuku, Maui, Hawaii, 1/5/08; s. Kumataro Ansai and Kesayo Kuroda A; m. 12/24/29 to Ruth Harimoto; c. Carol Mae (Mrs. Ball) and Linda. Polit. & Govt. Pos: Mem, Bd. Supvr, Maui Co, Hawaii, 34-42 & 60-62; Maui mem, Territorial Bd. Agr. & Forestry, 42-43; mem, Kula Sanitorium Managing Bd, 47-48; Territorial Sen, 48-56; Hawaii State Sen, 62-; v.chmn, Hawaii Rep. Party, 65-66. Bus. & Prof. Pos: Mgr, Waihee Dairy and Farm, 34-54; co-owner, Town Construct. Co, 46-65, v.pres, 65-; indust. rel. and pub. rel. supt, Wailuku Sugar Co, 54-66; dir, Waikiki Grand Hotel, 64-66 and N.Am. Mortgage Corp, 66. Mil. Serv: Entered as Pfc, Army, 43, released as 1st Sgt, 45, after serv. in 442nd Regt. Combat Team, ETO; Bronze Star; Mil. Int. Serv. Commendation Award. Mem: Hon. mem, Future Farmers of Am; DVA; Am. Legion; 442 Vet. Club; C. of C; Maui Coun, Boy Scouts (pres). Rel: Catholic. Mailing Add: 229 Awapuhi St, Wailuku, Maui, Hawaii 96793.

ANSELMI, DONALD RAY D
V.Chmn, Wyo. Dem. State Cent. Cmt.
b. Rock Springs, Wyo, 7/17/28; s. John Anselmi and Lillie Malmberg A; m. 11/15/53 to Dora Giovanini; c. Mark, Joseph, Kurt and Gina. Polit. & Govt. Pos: Chmn, Rock Springs Sweetwater Airport Authority, Wyo, 58-69; chmn, bd. of dirs, Sweetwater Mem. Hosp, 59-69; del, Dem. Nat. Conv, 60, 64 & 68, mem, Dem. Nat. Platform Cmt, 68; v.chmn, Wyo. Dem. State Cent. Cmt, 65- Bus. & Prof. Pos: Dir, Am. Hotel Motel Asn, 68-; trustee, Wyo. Blue Cross-Blue Shield, currently. Mil. Serv: Entered as Pvt, Air Force, 50, released as Cpl, 52, after serv. in Fourth Air Force. Mem: Elks; K. of C; Am. Legion. Rel: Roman Catholic. Mailing Add: 422 Fremont, Rock Springs, Wyo. 82901.

ANSELMI, RUDOLPH THEODORE D
b. Rock Springs, Wyo, 5/1/04; s. Joseph Anselmi and Maria Menghini A; m. 7/10/29 to Louise Shuster; c. Mary Lou (Mrs. John Unguren), Lynn (Mrs. Thos. Lockhart) and Jeri (Mrs. Clifford E. Kirk). Educ: Univ. Wyo, B.S, 25; Phi Kappa Phi; Pi Gamma Mu; Sigma Chi. Polit. & Govt. Pos: Chmn. sch. bd, Dist. 4, Rock Springs, Wyo, 36-65; Wyo. State Sen, 37-65, minority floor leader, Wyo. State Senate, 43-63; v.chmn, Wyo. State Dem. Cent. Cmt. 45-65, mem. exec. cmt, 50-65; mem. Legis. Interim Cmt. and chmn, Sweetwater Co. Fair Bd, 50-60; del, Dem. Nat. Conv, 60, 64 & 68; mem, Wyo. State Bd. Equalization, State Tax Cmn, 65-; mem, Gov. Re-orgn. Cmt, 67-68; v.chmn, Wyo. Legis-Exec. Cmn. on Re-orgn. of State Govt, 69- Bus. & Prof. Pos: Dir, N. Side State Bank, Rock Springs, Wyo; secy-treas, Huntley Construct. Co; pres, Miners Mercantile Bldg. Co. Mem: Lions; Elks; Eagles; K. of C; Cheyenne Exec. Club; Int. Asn. of Assessing Officers; Univ. Wyo. Alumni Asn; Cheyenne Serra Club. Hon. Grad, Univ. Wyo. Sch. Commerce, 62. Rel: Catholic. Legal Res: Box 908, Rock Springs, Wyo. 82901. Mailing Add: 2608 House Apt. 17, Cheyenne, Wyo. 82001.

ANSLEY, RUSSELL L. R
b. Frederick, Okla, 2/24/32; s. Leo Ansley and Bessie Johnston A; m. 8/30/58 to Nana M. Childers; c. Gary W. and Barry L. Educ: N.Tex. State Col, B.A. in govt. and hist, 57. Polit. & Govt. Pos: Chmn, Curry Co. Rep. Party, N.Mex, 64; chmn, Pittsburg Co. Rep. Party, Okla, 65-67. Bus. & Prof. Pos: Storeman, Oilwell Supply, USS Div, 57-60; agent, Am. Nat. Ins. Co, 60-61; loan mgr, SW Investment Co, 61-66. Mil. Serv: Entered as Pvt, Marine Corps, 49, released as Cpl, 52, after serv. in H&S Co, Third Bn, Seventh Marines, First Marine Div. FMF Pac, Korea, 51; Korean Serv. Medal with 3 Stars; U.N. Medal. Mem: Toastmaster Int; McAlester Retail Credit Asn. Rel: Presbyterian. 1967 Legal Res: McAlester, Okla. No mailing address available. (1967)

ANSPACH, JOHN HENRY D
Co. Cmnr, Lebanon Co, Pa.
b. Grantville, Pa, 8/21/27; s. Clarence Harvey Anspach and Margaret I. Soliday A; m. 6/24/45 to Laura Mae Witmer; c. Jeanne Louise, Edward Lloyd and Joseph Alfred. Educ: Lebanon Valley Col, night student, 63-65. Polit. & Govt. Pos: Committeeman, East Hanover Twp. Dem. Party, 55-60; tax collector, 57-61; del, Dem. Nat. Conv, 68; co. cmnr, Lebanon Co, 68- Bus. & Prof. Pos: Owner and mgr, Anspach Autos, 51- Mem: Treas. and pres, Pa. Auto and Truck Salvage Asn; dir, East. Pa. Used Auto and Truck Parts Asn; Nat. Auto Truck Wreckers Asn; pres, Jonestown Lions; past pres, East Hanover Twp. PTA; F&AM; Lebanon Co. Shriner's Club; Gideons; chmn, East Hanover Twp. Bd. Authority. Rel: United Methodist. Mailing Add: Route 1, Grantville, Pa. 17028.

ANTHONY, JOSEPH GARNER
b. Phila, Pa, 12/19/99; s. Charles Howard Anthony and Rachel Edith Humphreys A; m. 6/29/26 to Dorothy McClaren; c. Patricia and Garner. Educ: Swarthmore Col, A.B, 23; Harvard Univ, LL.B, 26. Polit. & Govt. Pos: Attorney Gen, Hawaii, 42-43. Bus. & Prof. Pos: Lawyer, admitted to bar Hawaii State Supreme Court, 26 and U.S. Supreme Court, 36. Mil. Serv: Army, World War I. Publ: Articles in legal journals. Mem: Bar Asn. Hawaii (pres, 37-39); Am. Bar Asn.(del, 44). Rel: Episcopal. Legal Res: 3251 Pacific Heights Rd, Honolulu, Hawaii 96813. Mailing Add: P.O. Box 3199, Honolulu, Hawaii 96801.

ANTHONY, PHILIP LaVERN D
V.Chmn, Orange Co. Dem. Cent. Cmt, Calif.
b. Clinton, Iowa, 9/22/35; s. Elmer LaVern Anthony and Emma Marguetta Domann A; m. 7/15/67 to Carolyn Lee Knorzer Bannister; c. Derek S. Bannister (stepson). Educ: Pomona Col, 52-54; Calif. State Col, Long Beach, B.S, 58; Univ. of Hawaii, M.S, 60; Univ. of South. Calif, 60-61; Alpha Gamma Sigma. Polit. & Govt. Pos: Mem. city coun, Westminster, Calif, 62-, mayor pro-tem, 62-64 and 68-; mem, Orange Co. Dem. Cent. Cmt, 66-, chmn, 66-68 and v.chmn, 68- Bus. & Prof. Pos: Group scientist supvr, chem. lab, Autonetics, Div. N. Am. Rockwell, Anaheim, Calif, 61- Publ: 'Solid-Solid Interactions on Active Absorbents,' Nature, 9/60; 'Solid-Solid Interaction Studies by Spectral Reflectance,' Science, 63; 'Galvanic Corrosion on Silver-Plated Copper Wire,' Materials Protection, 3/65. Mem: Nat. Asn. of Corrosion Engr; Am. Electroplaters Soc; Inst. of Printed Circuits; Nat. Mgt. Asn; Lions; Elks. Rel: Methodist. Mailing Add: 13611 Arizona St, Westminster, Calif. 92683.

ANTOINE, WILLIAM ROBERT D
Mo. State Rep.
b. Shawnee, Kans, 1/16/26; s. William L. Antoine and Edith Earnshaw A; m. 9/26/43 to Virginia Garrison; c. Joseph W, Paul R.(deceased) and Christopher Scott. Educ: Univ. Mo; Univ. Kans. Polit. & Govt. Pos: Treas, East. Jackson Co. Dem. Club, Mo; incorporator, Jackson Co. Dem. Club; Dem. committeeman, Blue Twp, 62-64; del, Mo. State Dem. Conv, 64 & 65; treas, Jackson Co. Dem. Club, 65-; Mo. State Rep, 67- Bus. & Prof. Pos: With State Hwy. Dept, formerly; mgr, Antoine Seed Stores, currently. Mil. Serv: Entered as Pvt, Army, 42, released as Pfc, 45, after serv. in 78th Div, Combat Inf, ETO; Cpt, Mo. State Nat. Guard, 41-42; Purple Heart and 1 Oak Leaf Cluster; Combat Inf. Badge; 3 Major Battles; Unit Presidential Citation; French Award. Mem: VFW; DAV; Am. Legion; Sertoma Club; K. of C.(4°); Independence C. of C; Farm Bur; Last Man's Club. Rel: Catholic. Mailing Add: 12101 Newbury Lane, Independence, Mo. 64052.

ANTON, JAMES R
Hearing Exam, Interstate Commerce Cmn.
b. Concord, N.H, 3/22/14; s. Max S. Anton and Helen Lesher A; m. 12/11/54 to Florence A. Morrolf; c. William, Linda and James. Educ: Univ. Ala, A.B, 37; Georgetown Univ, LL.B, 52. Polit. & Govt. Pos: N.H. State Rep, 46-47; treas, Concord, N.H. Sch. Dist, 46-47; asst. jour. clerk, U.S. Sen, 47-53; chmn, N.H. Rep. Cmt. Speaker's Bur, 48-50; spec. counsel, U.S. Sen. Preparedness Cmt, 52-56; chief, off. compliance, Civil Aeronaut. Bd, 56-60; dir, Bur. Enforcement, 60-62; hearing exam, Interstate Commerce Cmn, 62- Bus. & Prof. Pos: Instr, bus. col; newspaper reporter, 39-42. Mil. Serv: Army, 42-45; Air Medal with Clusters; 5 Battle Stars. Mem: Am. Legion; VFW; Eagles. Rel: Episcopal. Mailing Add: 335 Maryland Ave. N.E, Washington, D.C. 20002.

ANTONE, STEVE R
Idaho State Rep.
b. Burley, Idaho, 11/17/21; s. Andrew Antone and Margaret Glover A; m. 8/30/50 to Helen Margaret McKevitt; c. Kathleen (Mrs. Alfred Coccinello) and Steven Kent. Educ: Heyburn High Sch, grad. Polit. & Govt. Pos: Idaho State Rep, 68- Bus. & Prof. Pos: Supvr, Soil Conserv. Dist. Mil. Serv: Entered as Pvt, Air Force, 43, released as T/Sgt, 45, after serv. in 463rd Bomb Group, 15th Air Force, Italy, 44-45. Mem: AF&AM; Elks. Rel: Methodist. Mailing Add: 1141 Link St, Rupert, Idaho 83350.

ANTONELLI, CAMILLO N. D
Md. State Del.
b. W. Va, 8/27/15; married. Educ: Baltimore parochial and pub. schs. Polit. & Govt. Pos: Del, Md. Dem. State Conv, 50; mem, Md. Dem. State Cent. Cmt, Second Legis. Dist, 54; Md. State Del, 65- Bus. & Prof. Pos: Master craftsman. Mem: N.E. Ital-Am. Dem. Club; K. of C. Mailing Add: 525 N. Ellwood Ave, Baltimore, Md, 21205. (1967)

ANTROBUS, RANDALL LEON R
Chmn, Pendleton Co. Rep. Exec. Cmt, Ky.
b. Morgan, Ky. 12/16/20; s. Paul Antrobus and Fannie Harris A; m. 3/14/46 to Elnora Ruth Day; c. Randall L, Jr. and Robert D. Educ: Morgan High Sch. and Laffayette Vocation Sch, Ky. Polit. & Govt. Pos: Precinct chmn, Ky. Rep. Party, 60-68; chmn, Pendleton Co. Rep. Exec. Cmt, 68- Bus. & Prof. Pos: Eng. supvr, Cincinnati Milling Machine Co, 58-66, group mgr, 66- Mil. Serv: Entered as Pvt, Army Signal Corps, 42, released as Sgt, 46, after serving in 3361 Signal Serv. Bn, China, Burma and India, 44-46; Asiatic Theater ribbon with three bronze stars. Mem: Inst. Elec. & Electronic Engrs; Nat. Machine Tool Builders (mem. elec. standards cmt); bd. dirs, Joint Indust. Coun; U.S. adv. cmt. 44, Int. Electro-Tech. Cmn; Nat. Fire Protection Asn.(mem. comt. elec. standards for machine tools); F&AM; RAM; AASR; AAONMS. Rel: Protestant. Mailing Add: R.R. 3, Berry, Ky. 41003.

APKING, WILLIAM TAPPAN R
Chmn, Thayer Co. Rep. Party, Nebr.
b. Daykin, Nebr, 8/31/33; s. Geo. Apking and Ruth Tappan A; m. 7/3/58 to Sharon Anderson; c. David T. and Elizabeth A. Educ: Univ. Nebr. Polit. & Govt. Pos: Treas, Alexandria Sch. Bd, Nebr, 60-63; chmn, Alexandria City Coun, 60-; chmn, Jefferson Co. Young Rep. Club, 64-65; chmn, Thayer Co. Rep. Party, 64- Bus. & Prof. Pos: Chmn, Thayer Co. Bankers Asn, 63- Mil. Serv: Entered as Seaman, Navy, 53, released as PO 2/C, 57. Mem: Am. Legion; Nat. Livestock Feeders Asn, Farmers Bur. Rel: Presbyterian. Mailing Add: Alexandria, Nebr. 68303.

APODACA, JERRY D
N.Mex. State Sen.
b. Las Cruces, N.Mex, 10/3/34; s. Raymond Apodaca and Elisa Alvarez A; m. 8/18/56 to Clara Melendres; c. Cynthia Kay, Carolyn Rae, Gerald Craig, Jeffrey Don and Judith Marie. Educ: Univ. N.Mex, B.S, 57; Phi Delta Theta. Polit. & Govt. Pos: N.Mex. State Sen, Dona Ana Co, 67-; del, Dem. Nat. Conv, 68. Rel: Roman Catholic. Legal Res: 2410 Acoma, Las Cruces, N.Mex. 88001. Mailing Add: 1401-A El Paseo, Las Cruces, N.Mex. 88001.

APONTE, HUMBERTO D
b. Cabo Rojo, Puerto Rico, 9/7/24; s. Jose T. Aponte and Amelia Cofresi A; m. 1/25/47 to Anna Maria Ferrer; c. Anna M. and Roberto. Educ: Metrop. Voc. High Sch, N.Y.C, 4 years. Polit. & Govt. Pos: Leader, Part A, 61st Assembly Dist. Dem. Party, N.Y, 67-; mem, N.Y.C. Coun. against poverty; mem, Bd. of Dirs, N.Y. Urban Coalition; del, Dem. Nat. Conv, 68. Bus. & Prof. Pos: Off. Mgr. for Law firm, Dinkes, Mandel & Dinkes. Mil. Serv: Entered as Pvt, Army, 43, released as PFC, 45, after serv. in 298 Engr. Bn, ETO; Five Bronze Battle Stars, Purple Heart, Victory Medal, Good Conduct Medals, ETO Service Medal. Mem: VFW; Bolivar-Douglas Dem. Club; Coun. of Puerto Rican Orgn; Lower Eastside Neighborhoods Asns. Lane Bryant Volunteer Award, 66-67. Rel: Protestant. Mailing Add: 71 Columbia St, New York, N.Y. 10002.

APPELGET, ERVIN ROY D
Chmn, Fourth Cong. Dist. Dem. Party, Mich.
b. Waldhiem, Sask, 6/15/14; s. George Edward Appelget and Alvina Voth A; m. 12/25/38 to Edith Eulamae Crawford; c. Judith (Mrs. Lohroff), Patricia (Mrs. Jackson), Myron, Richard and Robert. Educ: Benton Harbor High Sch, 30-34. Polit. & Gov. Pos: Worked on campaigns for Roosevelt, Truman, Stevenson, Kennedy, Johnson, Humphrey and co, state and nat. cand. since 1940; organizer, Berrien Co. Dem. Party, Mich, 62-66; mem. registration and voting cmt, Mich. Dem. Party, 64, 66, 68; chmn, Berrien Co. Dem. Party, 66-68; alternate del, Dem. Nat. Conv, 68; chmn, Fourth Cong. Dist. Dem. Party, 69- Mem: IAMAW. Rel: Baptist. Mailing Add: Route 1, P.O. Box 188, Berrien Springs, Mich. 49103.

APPLEGATE, A. EARL D
b. Frankfort, Ind, 12/20/16; s. C. Earl Applegate and Ester Pearl Young A; m. 12/22/40 to Gertrude Fife; c. Donald, Nancy (Mrs. Spitzer), Roberta Sue, Sheldon and Janet. Educ: Ind. Univ, Bloomington, B.S, 38; Ind. Univ, Indianapolis, M.D, 42; Theta Kappa Psi. Polit. & Govt. Pos: City Health Officer, Frankfort, Ind, 47-67; del, Ind. Dem. Conv, 20 years; Dem. precinct committeeman, 20 years; mem, exec. coun, Ind. State Bd. of Health, 60-64; co. health officer, Clinton Co, 66-68; del, Dem. Nat. Conv, 68. Bus. & Prof. Pos: Mem, exec. coun, Ind. Univ, 56-60; chief of staff, Clinton Co. Hosp, 66 & 67. Mem: Am. and Ind. State Med. Asns; Clinton Co. Med. Soc. (pres, 66 & 67); Moose; Frankfort Country Club. Rel: Methodist. Legal Res: 750 Harvard Terr, Frankfort, Ind. 46041. Mailing Add: 1303 S. Jackson St, Frankfort, Ind. 46041.

APPLEGATE, ALBERT AUGUSTUS R
Spec. Asst. to the Secy, Dept. of Housing and Urban Develop.
b. Lawrence, Kans, 12/3/28; s. Albert Angelo Applegate and Grace Robinson A; m. 10/1/54 to Beverly Jane Amann; c. Susan. Educ: Princeton Univ, B.A, 50; Univ. Mich, M.A, 53, Ford Found. fel. in Polit. Behavior Research, 52-56; Princeton Prospect Club. Polit. & Govt. Pos: Secy, Rep. Club, Princeton Univ, 48-49; alternate del, Mich. State Rep. Conv, 51, del, 58-59, mem. pre-conv. resolutions cmt, 60; mem, Ann Arbor Rep. City Cmt, 56; Rep. dir, Ann Arbor Ward, 56; mem, Washtenaw Co. Rep. Cmt, 56-58; del, Washtenaw Co. Rep. Conv, 56-60; mem, Mich. Rep. Research Adv. Cmt, 58-60; adv, Young Rep. Club, East. Mich. Univ, 58-63; Rep. sect. leader, Ann Arbor, 60-61; research consult, Alvin M. Bentley, Congressman-at-lg. Campaign, 62; admin. asst. to the Gov. for prog. develop. and agency liaison, Mich, 63-65 and admin. asst. to the Gov. for commun. research, 65-69; spec. asst. to the secy, Dept. of Housing and Urban Develop, 69- Bus. & Prof. Pos: Instr. polit. sci, East. Mich. Univ, 57-61, asst. prof. polit. sci, 61-63. Publ: Co-auth, Michigan's Recounts for Governor, 1950 and 1952: A Systematic Analysis of Election Error, Univ. Mich, 54. Mem: Am. Polit. Sci. Asn; Midwest Conf. Polit. Scientists. Rel: Presbyterian. Legal Res: Springfield, Va. 22152. Mailing Add: 7629 Tiverton Dr, Springfield, Va. 22152.

APPLEGATE, DOUGLAS D
Ohio State Sen.
b. Steubenville, Ohio, 3/27/28; s. Earl Douglas Applegate (deceased) and Mary Margaret Longacre A; m. 8/25/50 to Betty Jean Engstrom; c. Kirk Douglas and David Allen. Educ: Steubenville High Sch, grad, 47; Aetna Ins, 51. Polit. & Govt Pos: Ohio State Rep, 33rd dist, Jefferson Co, 61-68; del-at-lg, Dem. Nat. Conv, 64; pres, Jefferson Co. Young Dem. Club, 66-67; mem, Ohio Cmn, Interstate Coop; mem, Dem. Policy Making Cmt; del, Nat. Rivers & Harbors Cong, 69; Ohio State Sen, 69- Bus. & Prof. Pos: Salesman, Earl D. Applegate, realtor, Steubenville, Ohio, 50-57; real estate broker and realtor, 57- Mem: Steubenville Bd. Realtors; Ohio & Nat. Asn. Real Estate Bd; Elks; Eagles; Farm Bur; Steubenville Commun. Club; Cath. Commun. Center; PTA; Am. Bowling Cong; Polish Athletic Club; Indian Club; bd. mem, Vol. of Am. Outstanding Young Man of Am, U.S. Jaycees, 65; nominated for John F. Kennedy award for young Dem. of year, 67. Rel: Presbyterian. Mailing Add: 322 Wilma Ave, Steubenville, Ohio 43952.

APPLEGATE, K. EDWIN D
b. Cicero, Ind, 7/21/23; s. Karl Raymond Applegate and Gladys Mae Worley A; m. 6/10/44 to Elizabeth Ann Dilts; c. Eric Edwin, Raymond Alan, Robert Dale and Beth Ann. Educ: Ind. Univ, B.S. in personnel mgt, 46, LL.B, 48; Alpha Kappa Psi; Flame Club; Sigma Delta Kappa; Acacia; v.pres, Independent Asn. Polit. & Govt. Pos: U.S. Cmnr, South. Dist. of Ind, 50-58; dep. prosecutor, Monroe Co, Ind, 59; judge, Bloomington City Court, 60-63; Ind. State Rep, 65-66, mem, Ways and Means, Educ, Judiciary A. and Ins. Cmts, Ind. House of Rep, 65; U.S. attorney, South. Dist of Ind, 67- Bus. & Prof. Pos: Attorney-at-law, 49- Mil. Serv: Entered as Pvt, Army, 43, released as S/Sgt, 44, after serv. in Co. F, 2nd Inf, 5th Div, ETO, 44; ETO Medal with 3 Battle Stars; Combat Inf. Badge; Good Conduct Medal. Mem: Am, Fed. and Ind. Bar Asns; Monroe Co. Bar Asn.(secy, 53-57, pres, Am. Acad. of Polit. and Soc. Sci; Nat. Judicature Soc; Nat. Soc. of State Legislators; Tri-Co. Bar Asn; Nat. Asn. of Munic. Judges; dir, Bloomington Kiwanis, 56-58; dir, United Fund, 4 yrs; Elks; exec. bd, White Rivers Coun, Boy Scouts; exec. bd, Tulip Trace Coun, Girl Scouts; past pres, Varsity Club of Ind. Univ; C. of C; Am. Legion; Mason, RAM, Coun, Knight Templar, Scottish Rite (32°), Shrine, Holy Royal Arch Knight Templar Priest, Red Cross of Constantine, Ind. Grand Officer, Grand Commandery Ind, Grand Comdr, Grand Commandery Knights Templar of Ind, 69-70; trustee & mem. bd, Bloomington Hosp, 68- Outstanding young man of Bloomington, 56; Distinguished Serv. Award, U.S. Jr. C. of C, 56; Good Govt. Award, Ind. State Jr. C. of C, 61; Hon. Ky. Col, 65; Legion of Honor award, Int. Supreme Coun, DeMolay, 69. Rel: Methodist; Treas, mem. official bd. and former trustee, 1st Methodist Church of Bloomington. Mailing Add: 509 S. Swain Ave, Bloomington, Ind. 47401.

APPLETON, WILLIAM MARIS R
Pa. State Rep.
b. Pittsburgh, Pa, 8/23/20; s. Maris Louis Appleton and Kathryn Clarey A; m. 7/4/46 to Louise Mary Biscan; c. William and Louise Kathryn. Polit. & Govt. Pos: Pa. State Rep, 65- Bus. & Prof. Pos: Pres, Nat. Handicapped Industs, 48- and ServiCar of Allegheny Co, Inc, 65. Mil. Serv: Entered as Pvt, Army, 42, released as Cpl, 45, after serv. in Hq. 83rd Inf. Div, ETO; Bronze Star; Normandy, Brittany, Ardennes, Rhineland and Cent. Europe Ribbons. Mem: Am. Legion; past pres, PTA; F&AM; Syria Temple; AAONMS; K.T. Rel: Presbyterian. Mailing Add: Box 176, Ingomar, Pa. 15127.

APPLEWHITE, MARY ELIZABETH R
V.Chmn, Oktibbeha Co. Rep. Party, Miss.
b. El Paso, Tex, 6/28/28; d. Robert Emmett McFadden and Pearl Blackburn M; m. 9/27/52 to Joe Crawford Applewhite; c. Walter Robert, Joe Crawford, Jr. and James Byron. Educ: Christian Col, Assoc. Mus, 47; Northwest. Univ, B.Mus, 49; Miss. State Univ, grad. study, 65. Polit. & Govt. Pos: V.chmn, Oktibbeha Co. Rep. Party, Miss, 63-; del, Rep. Nat. Conv, 68. Bus. & Prof. Pos: Mem. teaching staff, Radford Sch. for Girls, El Paso, Tex, 49-52. Mem: Phi Beta; Oktibbeha Co. Rep. Women; Nat. Guild of Piano Teachers; Nocturne Music Club of Starkville and State Col; Am. Legion Auxiliary. Rel: Protestant. Mailing Add: Route 4, Box 88 A, Starkville, Miss. 39759.

APPLING, HOWELL REEDUS, JR. R
b. Carthage, Tex, 9/5/19; s. Howell R. Appling, Sr. and Arline Howard A; m. 10/16/43 to Jane Elizabeth Jones; c. Janet (Mrs. Robinson), Beverly (deceased), Michael and Beth. Educ: Rice Univ, B.S.Ch.E, 41. Polit. & Govt. Pos: Cmt. chmn, Hatfield for Gov, Ore, 58 & 62, Wyatt for Cong, 60, Burns for Circuit Judge, 64, Parnell for State Supt. of Schs, 68 and Nixon for President, 68; Secy. of State and mem, State Bd. of Control, State Banking Bd. and State Land Bd, 59-64; del, Rep. Nat. Conv, 60, 64 & 68, acting chmn. Ore. Del, 64; chmn, Educ. Endowments Cmn, 60-69; co-founder, Citizens Polit. Action Cmt, Ore, 62-69; mem, State Investment Coun, 67-69; mem, Nat. Water Cmn, 69- Bus. & Prof. Pos: Founder and pres, Independent Distributors, Portland, Ore, 47-69; dir, Redwood Cleaners, Inc, 49-69, Equitable Savings and Loan Asn, 62-69 and JonHop, Inc, 69- Mil. Serv: Entered as Ens, Navy, 43, released as Lt, 46, after serv. in Battle Damage Repair, Puget Sound Naval Shipyard, 43-46. Publ: Five speeches printed in Vital Speeches, 59-64. Mem: V.pres, Nat. Farm Equipment Wholesalers Asn; pres, Portland Tractor and Implement Asn; dir, Assoc. Ore. Indust; bd. overseers, Lewis and Clark Col; chmn. lay adv. bd, Mt. Angel Abbey; hon. life mem, Young Rep. Pub. Figure of the Year, Ore, 60; Trumpeter Award, 64. Rel: Catholic. Legal Res: 1235 S.W. Myrtle Court, Portland, Ore. 97201. Mailing Add: 2355 N.W. Quimby, Portland, Ore. 97210.

AQUILOTTI, SAMUEL D
R.I. State Rep.
b. Clifton, N.J, 4/10/21; s. Augustine Aquilotti and Maria Bonelli A; single. Educ: Cent. High Sch, Providence, R.I, 4 years. Polit. & Govt. Pos: R.I. State Rep, 15th Dist, 69- Bus. & Prof. Pos: Salesman, Shepard Stores, Providence, R.I, 65. Mil. Serv: Entered as Pvt, Army, 42, released as Sgt, 45, after serv. in 877th Heavy Maintenance, ETO, 43-45; Five Major Battle Stars; Marksman Rifle. Mem: Lions; Toscan Club; Italo-Am. War Vet; AFL-CIO; pres, 278 Social Club, 67. Rel: Catholic. Mailing Add: 191 Bridgham St, Providence, R.I. 02909.

ARAGON, MANUEL LEROY D
Pres, Young Dem. of N.Mex.
b. Albuquerque, N.Mex, 3/22/47; s. Manuel C. Aragon and Charlotte Gurule A; m. 6/17/67 to Rosina Barbara Sedillo; c. Gregory Scott. Educ: Univ. of Albuquerque, 65-67; Univ. of N.Mex, 67- Polit. & Govt. Pos: Alternate del, Dem. Nat. Conv, 68; pres, Bernalillo Co. Young Dem, 68- and Young Dem. of N.Mex, 69- Bus. & Prof. Pos: Spec. rep, Jefferson Standard Life Ins. Co, 69 and First Nat. Life Ins. Co, 69- Mem: Optimist Club. Rel: Catholic. Mailing Add: 1213 Truman S.E, Albuquerque, N.Mex. 87108.

ARAGONA, XAVIER ANGELO D
Md. State Del.
b. Brooklyn, N.Y, 11/16/34; s. Angelo A. Aragona and Minnie G. Gatto A; m. 12/16/56 to Marie De Vincentis; c. Edward and Christopher. Educ: Univ. Notre Dame, B.S.C, 56; N.Y. Law Sch, LL.B, 59; Columbia Tech. Inst, Cert. in Construction, 66. Polit. & Govt. Pos: Mem, Cmt. to Rewrite State Constitution, 66-; v.chmn, State Legis. Cmt. for Investigation, 66-; Md. State Del, 67-; mem, Cmt. for Dist. Courts, 69-; chmn, Workmen's Compensation Cmt, 69-; spec. adv. to Gov. of Md. Mil. Serv: 2nd Lt, Army, with serv. in Guided Missles Div, Ft. Bliss, Tex, 56-57; Capt, Army Res. Publ: Weekly columnist, The Bulletin Newspaper. Mem: Md. State and Prince George's Co. Bar Asns; C. of C.(mem. progress and publicity cmt, Prince George's Co. Chap). Named Man of the Year by Columbus Citizens Nat. League, 66; Citation for outstanding contribution to Jewish commun. of Wash, D.C, 66. Rel: Catholic. Mailing Add: 4409 Stardust Place, Oxon Hill, Md. 20022.

ARAKELIAN, HAMPTON D
b. Whitinsville, Mass; m. to Margaret Askikian; c. Eunice, Arthur, David and Karen. Educ: Northbridge Pub. Sch. Polit. & Govt. Pos: Bd. of dir, Worcester Co. Better Bus. Bur, 60-66; v.chmn, bd. of trustees, Worcester State Hosp, 62; dep. sheriff, Worcester Co, 63; court officer. Bus. & Prof. Pos: Pres. and treas, Teddy's Cleansers, Inc. Mem: Pres, Worcester Area Dry Cleaners and Launderers Asn; Cleansing Plant Owners of Mass.(past pres); pres, Worcester Co. Dep. Sheriff's Asn; Elks; Cent. and S. Mass. Police Asn. Mailing Add: Boston Rd, Sutton, Mass. 01603. (1967)

ARBUCKLE, RICHARD DEAN R
Iowa State Sen.
b. Des Moines, Iowa, 4/2/26; s. Charles Martin Arbuckle and Winifred Pettit A; m. 1/3/45 to Anna Catherine; c. Craig Steven, Richard Dean, Jr. and Steve Edward. Educ: George Wash. Univ, 2 years; Iowa State Univ, 2 years. Polit. & Govt. Pos: Campaign chmn, Attorney Gen, Seventh Dist, Iowa, 62; orgn. chmn, Co. Rep. Cent. Cmt, 62-66; campaign event chmn, Gov. Iowa, 64; Iowa State Sen, currently. Bus. & Prof. Pos: Mem. personnel dept, Fed. Bur. Invest, 43-44; bank office mgr, 46-51; businessman, 51-69. Mil. Serv: Entered as Seaman, Navy, 44, released as PO, 46, after serv. in Philippines. Mem: Bus. Asn.(state pres); C. of C.(past pres); Jaycees (state pres, 60); U.S. Jr. C. of C.(Nat. v.pres, 61); Lions Club (past pres); dir, Indust. Develop. Co; Am. Legion; VFW; Elks; fund chmn, Red Cross; proj. chmn, Cancer Soc; dist. chmn, Heart Fund Asn. Rel: Central Christian Church; Elder. Legal Res: Box 55A, S. Elm, Jefferson, Iowa 50129. Mailing Add: R.F.D. 3, Jefferson, Iowa 50129.

ARCARO, HAROLD CONRAD, JR. D
R.I. State Sen.
b. Providence, R.I, 8/9/35; s. Harold Conrad Arcaro and Ines Cicerchia A; m. 7/6/57 to Christine Townsend; c. Harold C. III, Meredith, J. Edward, John T. and Elizabeth. Educ: Brown Univ, A.B, 56; Univ. Va, Charlottesville, LL.B, 59; Boston Univ, LL.M, Taxation, 63; Phi Kappa Psi; Sigma Nu Phi. Polit. & Govt. Pos: R.I. State Sen, 67- Bus. & Prof. Pos: Attorney, U.S. Internal Revenue Serv, 61-65, Arcaro and Swartz, Providence, R.I, 65-69 and Salter, McGowan, Arcaro & Swartz, 69-; v.pres, Golden Gate Corp, 65- Mem: R.I, Am. and Fed. Bar Asns; Am. Judicature Soc; R.I. Tax Forum; ARTS R.I.(pres); R.I. Hemophilia Guild (v.pres); R.I. Civic Chorale and Orchestra (past pres); bd. dirs, Emma Pnedleton Bradley Hosp; bd. Dirs, Providence Child Guid. Clin; bd. dirs, R.I. Philharmonic Orchestra; adv. bd, Marathon House; steering cmt, Family and Children's Div, Coun. of Commun. Serv; legis. cmt, Cath. Diocesan Human Rels. Cmn; chmn, Providence Heart Fund, 69; Mem. Corp, Butler and Lying-In Hosps, R.I. Col. Found, Peoples Savings Bank and Meeting Street Sch; hon. mem. Jaycees; numerous other community organizations. Outstanding Young Man of Providence, Jaycees, 68; One of two R.I. Legislators to participate in Eagleton Inst. Seminar for State Legislators. Rel: Roman Catholic. Legal Res: 27 Rhode Island Ave, Providence, R.I. 02906. Mailing Add: 636 Industrial Bank Bldg, Providence, R.I. 02903.

ARCHAMBAULT, LYLE B. D
b. Morrisville, Vt, 2/10/05; s. Joseph L. Archambault and Catherine Towne A; m. 9/7/31 to Blanche Mureury; c. Douglas P, Jean A. and Cherolyn M. Educ: Brigham Acad, grad, 25. Polit. & Govt. Pos: Zone Dep. collector, U.S. Internal Revenue, 40-48; Vt. State Rep, 66-68; del, Dem. Nat. Conv, 68. Bus. & Prof. Pos: Owner-operator, Archambault Furniture Store, Winooski, Vt, 48-64. Mem: Rotary; K. of C. Rel: Catholic. Mailing Add: 88 Hood St, Winooski, Vt. 05404.

ARCHER, ARDEN FRANK, JR. R
Legal Counsel, Columbia Co. Rep. Cent. Cmt, Wash.
b. Dayton, Wash, 9/30/33; s. Arden Frank Archer and Erma Rogg A; single. Educ: Wash. State Univ, 1 year; Whitman Col, 3 years; Gonzaga Univ, J.D, 67; Sigma Chi. Polit. & Govt. Pos: Chmn, Don Evans for Gov. Cmt, 64; legal counsel, Columbia Co. Rep. Cent. Cmt, 66- Bus. & Prof. Pos: Attorney-at-Law, 63-; mem. bd. trustees, Walla Walla Commun. Col. Mil. Serv: Recruit, Navy, 53, released as Naval Cadet, 54. Mem: Am. and Wash. State Bar Asns; Am. Judicature Soc; Elks; Eagles; Am. Legion; Wash. State Jaycees. Outstanding Local Pres. Under 50, Wash. State Jaycee; Outstanding Man of the State of Wash, Wash. State Jaycee; State Legal Coun, 68; Constitutional Rev. Cmt. Rel: Protestant. Legal Res: 505 S. Sixth St, Dayton, Wash. 99328. Mailing Add: 228 E. Main St, Dayton, Wash. 99328.

ARCHER, FLOY EVELYN R
Mem, Calif. State Rep. Cent. Cmt.
b. White Plains, N.Y; d. Harold Joseph Brennan and Jean Gates B; m. 4/12/47 to Edward P. Archer; c. Marguerite Elizabeth and Nancy Ann. Polit. & Govt. Pos: Third v.pres, Los Angeles Co. Young Rep, Calif, 62-63; del, Rep. Nat. Conv, 64; pres, Whittier Young Rep, 64-65 and Calif. Young Rep, 65-66; v.chmn, 25th Cong. Dist. Rep. Cent. Cmt; mem, Calif. State Rep. Cent. Cmt. and Los Angeles Co. Rep. Cent. Cmt, currently. Rel: Catholic. Mailing Add: 9122 Glenbrook Rd, Fairfax, Va. 22030.

ARCHER, HAROLD LAWRENCE D
b. Adrian, Mich, 7/30/23; s. William L. Archer and Geneva Bell A; m. 7/30/42 to Lorell White; c. Reneé (Mrs. Howard), Sharon (Mrs. Ludlow), Shawn and Lori. Educ: Adrian High Sch. Polit. & Govt. Pos: Past chmn, Lenawee Co. Dem. Cent. Cmt, Mich. Bus. & Prof. Pos: Mgr, Nat. Life Ins. Br. Off, 57-64, Lenawee Hills Mem. Gardens, 64- Mil. Serv: Entered as Pvt, Army, 43, released as 2nd Lt, 46, after serv. in 90th Div. ETO; European Theater Ribbon with 2 Bronze Battle Stars; Infantryman Combat Badge; Presidential Unit Citation. Mem: Elks; Eagles; K. of C; Devils Lake Yacht Club. Rel: Catholic. Mailing Add: 2602 Spielman Rd, Adrian, Mich. 49221. (1967)

ARCHER, ROY ROBERT D
Mem, Calif. Dem. State Cent. Cmt.
b. Parkersburg, W.Va, 3/3/34; s. Roy Ralph Archer and Gladys Schultz A; m. 6/23/67 to Oralee Richardson; c. Kraig, Shawnna and Tomas. Educ: W.Va. Univ, B.A, 56, M.A, 60; Univ. Calif, Berkeley, 61; San Diego State Col, 64; Nat. Polit. Sci. Hon; Nat. Hist. Hon; Kappa Alpha; Nat. For. Serv. Polit. & Govt. Pos: Dem. cand, Calif. State Assembly, 66 & 68; mem, Calif. Dem. State Cent. Cmt, 66 & 68-; mem, San Diego Co. Dem. Cent. Cmt, 66 & 68- Mil. Serv: Entered as 2nd Lt, Army, 56, released as 1st Lt, 58, after serv. in Hq. Garrison, Ft. Dix, N.J; Capt. Calif. Army Nat. Guard, currently. Publ: History of Conflict Between Chinese Communist & Nationalist Parties from 1921 to 1937, W.Va. Univ. Press, 60. Mem: Am. Asn. Univ. Prof; Calif. Jr. Col. Faculty Asn; Calif. Nat. Guard Asn; G.I. Forum; Mexican-Am. Polit. Asn; Calif. Fedn. Teachers. Rel: Methodist. Mailing Add: 1155 Pinecrest, Escondido, Calif. 92025.

ARCHER, WILLIAM REYNOLDS, JR. R
Tex. State Rep.
b. Houston, Tex, 3/22/28; s. William Reynolds Archer and Eleanor Miller A; m. 11/21/53 to Patricia Moore; c. William Reynolds, III, Richard Moore, Sharon Leigh, Elizabeth Ann and Barbara Elise. Educ: Rice Univ, 45-46; Univ. Tex, B.B.A, 49 and LL.B, 51; Phi Delta Phi; Sigma Alpha Epsilon. Polit. & Govt. Pos: Alderman, City of Hunters Creek Village, Tex, 55-62; Tex. State Rep, Dist. 22, Precinct Five, Harris Co, 67- Bus. & Prof. Pos: Pres, Uncle Johnny Mill, Inc, Houston, Tex, 59-61 and W.R. Archer, Inc, 61-; dir, Heights State Bank, 67-; partner, Law Firm of Harris, Archer, Parks & Graul, 67- Mil. Serv: Entered as Pvt, Air Force, 51, released as 1st Lt, 53, after serv. as Instr, Officer Cand. Sch, Lackland Air Force Base, Tex, 51-53; Res, 53-69, Capt. Mem: State Bar of Tex; Houston Bar Asn; dir, Houston Soc. for Prevention of Cruelty of Animals; trustee, Houston Fund for Ment. Research; life mem, Houston Livestock Show and Rodeo. Man of the Year Award, Sigma Alpha Epsilon, 69. Rel: Roman Catholic. Legal Res: 3127 Avalon, Houston, Tex. 77019.

ARCHIBALD, RALPH STRONG R
b. Malden, Mass, 5/6/24; s. Henry Cameron Archibald and Helen Strong A; m. 1/31/48 to Shirley W. Clark; c. David Wm. Educ: Tufts Univ, B.S. in civil eng, 46; Harvard Univ, M.S. in sanit. eng, 47, M.E, 49; Sigma XI; Delta Omega. Polit. & Govt. Pos: Chmn, Ward II, Melrose, Mass, 60-62; chmn, Melrose City Rep. Cmt, 62-66; Melrose-Wakefield coordinator for Richardson-for-Attorney-Gen, 66-67. Bus. & Prof. Pos: Sales mgr, Pipe Founders Sales Corp, 50- Mil. Serv: Entered as A/S, Navy, 42, released as Lt.(jg), 45, after serv. in Atlantic Fleet. Mem: Boston and Am. Socs. Civil Engrs. Rel: Congregational. Mailing Add: 69 Boardman Ave, Melrose, Mass. 02176.

ARCIGA, CARMEN D
Mem, Calif. Dem. State Cent. Cmt.
b. Guanasevi, Durango, Mex, 10/6/14; d. Graciano Gonzalez and Eloisa Diaz G; m. 12/23/29 to Louis Arciga; c. Jeronimo, Isabelle (Mrs. Steger), Marylou (Mrs. Delgado), Robert and Armando A. Educ: Sweetwater High Sch, National City, Calif. Polit. & Govt. Pos: 77th Area coordinator, Dem. Party, National City, Calif, 68-; mem, National City Dem. Club, 68-; mem, Calif. Dem. State Cent. Cmt, 77th Assembly Dist, 69- Bus. & Prof. Pos: Mem. staffs, Mission Packing Co, San Diego, Calif, 29, Sun Harbor Packing Co, 30-51, Essez Wire Corp, 51-53 and Westgate Packing Co, 62-65. Mem: Trustee, Sociedad Progrista Mexicana Lodge 57, San Diego, Calif. Plaque for outstanding serv, Sociedad Progrista Mexicana, Lodge 57, San Diego, Calif, 67; Golden Key award and Outstanding Volunteer, Calif. Dem. State Cent. Cmt, 68. Rel: Catholic. Mailing Add: 1915 Harding Ave, National City, Calif. 92050.

ARDAIZ, ARAN ALTON R
Mem, Calif. Rep. State Cent. Cmt.
b. Monterey, Calif, 3/21/39; s. Severino Ardaiz and Martha Cano A; m. 11/23/63 to Sandra Jane Saleeby; c. Matthew Michael. Educ: Cabrillo Jr. Col; pres. and founder, Assoc. Men's Students of Cabrillo Col. Polit. & Govt. Pos: Chmn, Santa Cruz Co. Latin Am. Rep. Cmt, 69; mem, Calif. Rep. State Cent. Cmt, 69-; struct. chmn, Spanish Speaking Rep. Conf. of Calif, 69-; dist. chmn, Spanish Speaking Rep. Conf. of Santa Cruz Co, 69- Bus. & Prof. Pos: Pres, Las Casitas Reales Corp, Santa Cruz Co, Calif, 66-; sales consult, Unite Unlimited, San Jose, Calif, 69- Mil. Serv: Entered as Pvt, Army Res, 57, released as Pfc, 64, after serv. in 422nd M.P. Co, 15th Corps, Sixth Army. Publ: 'Legal Rights of Tenants,' Las Casitas Reales Corp, 4/69. Mem: Twenty-Thirty Int; Toastmaster Club. Rel: Roman Catholic. Mailing Add: 6996 Soquel Dr, Aptos, Calif. 95003.

ARDOIN, JAMES MADISON D
b. Eunice, La, 10/28/25; s. Eli Ardoin and Lovonia Gary A; m. 6/9/46 to Val Mae Hammon; c. Suzanne and James M, Jr. Educ: La. State Univ, Baton Rouge, 42-43 & 47-48; Univ. Southwest. La, B.S, 50; Univ. Denver, Personnel Guid, cert, 52; Harvard Univ. Grad. Sch.Bus, Sr. Bank Officers Seminar, cert, 65; Blue Key; Mu Sigma Rho; Arnold Air Soc. Polit. & Govt. Pos: Del, Dem. Nat. Conv, 64 & 68. Bus. & Prof. Pos: Pres. and dir, Vernon Bank, Leesville, 61-; pres, Acadian Bank & Trust Co, Eunice, 65-67, dir, 65-; exec. v.pres, Planters Trust & Savings, Opelousas, 67-69, dir, 67-, pres, 69- Mil. Serv: Entered as Seaman, Navy, 43, released as PO 3/C, 46, after serv. in Pac. Fleet, recalled as 1st Lt, Air Force, 50, released as Capt, 54, after Serv. in Air Training Command, Maj, Air Force Res, 64. Mem: Am. Bankers Asn; La. Banking Asn; Pub. Affairs Research Coun. La; United Serv. Orgn. (pres, Leesville Coun, 7 years); Rotary; C. of C; Asn. U.S. Army (v.pres, Leonidas Polk Chap); Am. Legion; VFW; South. Regional Conf. Nat. Coun. on Crime & Delinquency; 1969 Sugar Bowl Parade & Pageant Cmt. Rel: Catholic. Legal Res: 729 Caddo St, Opelousas, La. 70570. Mailing Add: P.O. Box 1271, Leesville, La. 71446.

ARENDS, LESLIE C. R
Minority Whip, U.S. House of Rep.
b. Melvin, Ill, s. George Teis Arends and Talea Weiss A; m. to Betty Tychon A; c. Leslie Talea. Educ: Oberlin Col; Ill. Wesleyan Univ, LL.D. Polit. & Govt. Pos: U.S. Rep, 17th Dist, Ill, 34-, Minority Whip, U.S. House of Rep, 43-; U.S. del. to NATO Parliamentarian Conf, 61-; del, Rep. Nat. Conv, 68. Bus. & Prof. Pos: Banker and farmer, 20-; mem. bd. dirs, Ill. Wesleyan Univ, currently. Mil. Serv: Navy, World War I. Mem: Am. Legion, Post Comdr, Co. Comdr, 17th Dist. Comdr; Ford Co. Farm Bur; Mason (33°). Rel: Methodist. Legal Res: Melvin, Ill. 60952. Mailing Add: 2306 Rayburn House Office Building, Washington, D.C. 20515.

AREY, DONALD LURTON R
Vice Mayor, Danville, Va.
b. Baltimore, Md; s. Ernest C. Arey (deceased) and Martha Rosefink (deceased); m. 8/2/39 to Beverly Jeanne Barclay; c. Linda Lugenia (Mrs. Jack Cooper), Donald L, Jr, Beverly Anne and Holly Marie. Educ: William and Mary Col, 28-30; Wake Forest Univ, B.S. in Med, 34; Jefferson Med. Col, M.D, 36; S.East. Allergy Soc; Am. Col. of Allergy; Lambda Chi Alpha; Phi Rho Sigma. Polit. & Govt. Pos: City councilman, Danville, Va, 58-, vice mayor, 68-; alternate del, Rep. Nat. Conv, 68. Bus. & Prof. Pos: Practice of med, 41- Mil. Serv: Entered as 1st Lt, Air Force, 42, released as Maj, 46, after serv. in Med. Corps; Victory Medal. Danville, Pittsylvania Co. Acad. of Med; Va. State and Am. Med. Socs. Rel: Presbyterian. Legal Res: 411 Maple Lane, Danville, Va. 24541. Mailing Add: 129 S. Main, Danville, Va. 24541.

ARGAZZI, ROBERT ANGELO R
Conn. State Rep.
b. New Britain, Conn, 6/30/38; s. Enzo J. Argazzi and Lena Berti A; m. 4/4/64 to Judith Elizabeth Marra; c. Paul. Educ: Dartmouth Col, A.B, 60; Yale Law Sch, LL.B, 63; Phi Beta Kappa. Polit. & Govt. Pos: Conn. State Rep, 69- Bus. & Prof. Pos: Attorney, Hoppin, Carey & Powell, Hartford, Conn, 64- Mil. Serv: 1st Lt, Army Res, 64. Rel: Catholic. Mailing Add: 92 Bernard Rd, Berlin, Conn. 06037.

ARICO, ANTHONY V, JR. D
Chmn, Barrington Dem. Town Cmt, R.I.
b. Bristol, R.I, 2/14/36; s. Anthony J. Arico and Mary Chellel A; m. 4/19/58 to Joan Grace Tedeschi; c. Janice, Laureen and Anthony. Educ: High Sch. Equivalency Cert, 54; Univ. N.H. Exten. Div, 2 years. Polit. & Govt. Pos: Committeeman, Barrington Dem. Town Cmt, R.I, 60-; chmn, 66- Bus. & Prof. Pos: Asst. off. mgr, Narragansett Lithography Co, Inc, 58-61; cost estimator, Bank Lithograph Co, Inc, 61-67; United Printing, Inc, 67- Mil. Serv: Entered as Airman, Air Force, 54, released as Airman 1/C, 57, after serv. in Strategic Air Command, N.Africa. Mem: K. of C.(Bishop Hickey Coun). Rel: Roman Catholic. Mailing Add: 18 Bosworth St, Barrington, R.I. 02804.

ARIYOSHI, GEORGE RYOICHI D
Majority Leader, Hawaii State Senate
b. Honolulu, Hawaii, 3/12/26; s. Ryozo Ariyoshi and Mitsue Yoshikawa A; m. 2/5/55 to Jean Miya Hayashi; c. Lynn Miye, Todd Ryozo and Donn Ryoji. Educ: Univ. Hawaii; Mich. State Col, grad; Univ. Mich. Law Sch. LL.B; pres, Hawaiian Club, Univ. Mich. Polit. & Govt. Pos: Rep, Territory of Hawaii, 54-58; chmn, Joint House and Senate Health & Welfare Cmts, 54-59; Hawaii State Sen, 58-, chmn, Ways & Means Cmt, Hawaii State Senate, 62-64, Majority Leader, 64- Bus. & Prof. Pos: Attorney, private practice, 52-; dir, First Nat. Bank of Hawaii, 62-; Honolulu Gas Co, Ltd, 64- and Hawaii Ins. Guaranty Co, 66- Mil. Serv: Pvt, Army, 45-46. Mem: M.I.S. Vet. Club; Hawaii Bar Asn; active in various fund drives and commun. asns. Selected as one of top 10 Legislators in Hawaii by Kiwanis Club, 62. Rel: Protestant. Legal Res: 29 Kawananakoa Place, Honolulu, Hawaii 96817. Mailing Add: Suite 1210, First National Bank Bldg, Honolulu, Hawaii 96813. (1967)

ARKLIN, ARAX R
Mem, Calif. Rep. State Cent. Cmt.
b. Del Rey, Calif; d. Haig Arklin and Queenie Abdalian A; single. Educ: Whittier Col, B.A. in Gen. Elem. Teaching, 42; Univ. South. Calif, Sec. Teaching Credential, 46. Polit. & Govt. Pos: Soc. chmn, North Valley Rep. Women, San Fernando Valley, Calif, 66, nationality chmn, 68 and membership chmn, 69-; precinct worker, campaigns for Arklin, Berryhill, Goldwater, Wood, Reagan, Nejedly and Nixon, 68-69; mem, Calif. Rep. State Cent. Cmt, 41st Assembly Dist, 68- Bus. & Prof. Pos: Teacher, sixth grade and boys' phys. educ, Sierra Madre, Calif, 42; elem. teacher, Burbank, 43-53; owner and dir, preschool, San Fernando Valley, 53-69. Publ: 'Who is Educating Your Child,' local press. Mem: San Fernando Valley Private Sch. Asn.(pres, secy, v.pres, past 10 years, legis. chmn, currently); Vol. Worker, World Affairs Coun; C. of C; Granada Hills Tennis Club; San Fernando Valley Antique Doll Club. Tennis, Antique Doll Shows and Chess, awards. Rel: Protestant; Sunday Sch. Supvr, 65. Mailing Add: 16857 San Fernando Mission Blvd, Granada Hills, Calif. 91344.

ARKLIN, HENRY 'HANK' R
Calif. State Assemblyman
b. Albany, Calif, 7/17/28; s. Haig Arklin and Queenie Abdalian A; single. Educ: Los Angeles City Col; Glendale City Col. Polit. & Govt. Pos: Cmnr, Housing and Commun. Develop, State of Calif, 67-68; Calif. State Assemblyman, 41st Assembly Dist, 69- Mem: San Fernando Valley Bus. and Prfnl. Asn; Int. Footprinters Asn; Kiwanis (pres, 68); Pacoima-Arleta Businessmen's Asn.(pres, 67-68); C. of C.(v.pres, Pacoima, 67). Rel: Armenian Apostolic. Legal Res: Pacoima, Calif. Mailing Add: 10640 Sepulveda Blvd, Suite 2, Mission Hills, Calif. 91340.

ARLEDGE, JAMES THURSTON D
b. Saluda, N.C, 7/22/21; s. Hosea Levi Arledge and Alpha Tallant A; m. 3/26/48 to Margaret Cline; c. David Cline and Michael Robert. Educ: Tryon High Sch, grad, 40. Polit. & Govt. Pos: Mem, Gov. Citizen Cmt. for Better Educ, Polk Co. Dem. Exec. Cmt, N.C, 51-56; mem, Inaugural Cmt, for Gov. Stanford; secy. and treas, 11th Dist, N.C. Young Dem. Club, 52, v.pres, West. Dist, 56-57; chmn, Tryon Dem. Precinct Cmt; N.C. State Rep, 57-69. Bus. & Prof. Pos: Mgr, Arledge Hardware Co, Tryon, currently. Mil. Serv: Sgt, Marine Corps, 43-56. Mem: Am. Legion (Comdr. Polk Co. Mem. Post 250, 46, 47, 50 and currently, Comdr, 33rd Dist, 55, Fifth Div. Comdr, N.C. Dept, life mem, Post 250); charter mem, Polk Jr. C. of C; Outboard Motor Club of Am; AF&AM; secy. and treas. Polk Co. Farm Bur. Rel: Baptist. Mailing Add: Vineyard Rd, Tryon, N.C. 28782. (1967)

ARLENE, HERBERT D
Pa. State Sen.
b. Harrison, Ga, 9/5/17; s. Elbert Arlene and Mattie King A; m. to Emma Davis; c. Clara and Herbert Jr. Educ: Phila. eve. and bus. schs. Polit. & Govt. Pos: Mem, Phila. Co. Dem. Exec. Cmt, Pa, 3 terms; former chmn, now co. committeeman, 47th Ward, Phila, currently; Pa. State Rep, 58-67; Pa. State Sen, 67-; del, Dem. Nat. Conv, 68. Bus. & Prof. Pos: Tailor. Mem: Odd Fellows; Mason; Dry Cleaners Local 85, AFL. Rel: Methodist. Mailing Add: 1705 W. Columbia Ave, Philadelphia, Pa. 19121. (1967)

ARMELLINO, JOHN RALPH D
Mayor, West New York, N.J.
b. West New York, N.J, 2/21/21; s. Nicholas Armellino and Emilia DiRito A; m. 11/24/46 to Nina Ritchick; c. Barbara, John and Nicholas. Educ: Va. Mil. Inst, 39-40; Cornell Univ, 41; N.Y. Univ, Sch. Commerce Accounts and Finance, B.S, 50. Polit. & Govt. Pos: Cmnr, N.J, 51-55; mayor, West New York, N.J, 55-; co. freeholder, 59-; alternate del, Dem. Nat. Conv, 68. Mil. Serv: Entered as 2nd Lt, Army, 42, released as Maj, 46, after serv. in ETO; Bronze Star; Silver Star with 2 Oak Leaf Clusters; Combat Infantryman's Badge; Presidential Unit Citation; Distinguished Serv. Cross; ETO Campaign Ribbon; Victory Ribbon. Mem: Elks; K. of C; Moose; Rotary; Kiwanis; VFW; Am. Legion; DAV; Amvets. Rel: Catholic. Mailing Add: 6025 Kennedy Blvd. E, West New York, N.J. 07093.

ARMENTI, CARMEN JOHN D
Mayor, Trenton, N.J.
b. Trenton, N.J, 4/11/29; s. Carmine Armenti (mother deceased); m. 10/1/66 to Hope Vulgaris; c. Melinda. Educ: Trenton Cath. Boys High Sch, 4 years; Pennington Prep. Sch, 2 years. Polit. & Govt. Pos: Mem, Trenton Planning Bd, N.J; spec. asst. for youth unemploy. and retraining of unemployed to State Cmnr. Labor and Indust, 62-66; supvr. recreation, Trenton, 6 years, city councilman, 62-66, mayor, 66- Mil. Serv: Army, 51-53; Mem: U.S. Conf. Mayors; Nat. League Cities; N.J. State League of Municipalities (v.pres, currently); N.J. Conf. of Mayors (v.pres, currently); bd. trustees, Scholarship, Educ. and Travel, Trenton Jr. Col. Free Pub. Library and United Progress Inc; bd. dir, PAL; cmt, Boys Town of Italy; area rep, Boy Scouts; local chmn. for, DVUF, Cancer and Heart Funds, Muscular Dystrophy and Ment. Illness; past pres, Mercer Co. Young Dem; Trenton Polish-Am. Dem. Club; Am. Legion; N.J. State Firemen's Mutual Benevolent Asn; Trenton Police Benevolent Asn; Italian-Am. War Vet. Post 2; Trenton Jaycees; Am-Irish Asn. Mercer Co; Trenton and Carver Br, YMCA; N.Trenton Little League; N.Trenton Italian-Am. Dem. Club; St. James Holy Name Soc; St. James Cath. Youth Orgn. Outstanding Serv. Award, PAL, 61 and St. Francis Hosp. Sch. Nursing. Rel: Catholic. Legal Res: 944 Edgewood Ave, Trenton, N.J. 08608. Mailing Add: Mayor's Office, City Hall, Trenton, N.J. 08608.

ARMIJO, ALEX J. D
State Land Cmnr, N.Mex.
b. Santa Rosa, N.Mex, 5/1/16; s. J. Ignacio Armijo and Manuelita Salazar A; m. Dec. 1938 to Lucy Baca; c. Robert, Camilla (Mrs. Tiny Romero), Raquel (Mrs. Joe Garcia), Cecilia, Dolores and Anthony. Educ: St. Michael's Col, 35-37. Polit. & Govt. Pos: Off. mgr, State Tax Cmn, N.Mex; mgr, State Health Dept; asst. state comptroller; chief local govt div. and budget div, State Dept. Finance & Admin; state auditor; legis. auditor; state land cmnr, 69- Mem: Elks. Rel: Catholic. Mailing Add: 444 Camino De Las Animas, Santa Fe, N.Mex. 87501.

ARMIJO, JOSE ENRIQUE R
Mem, N.Mex. State Rep. Cent. Cmt.
b. Las Vegas, N.Mex, 4/20/01; s. Enrique Armijo and Maria Jaramillo A; m. 5/6/27 to Jane Katherine Sherrill; c. Donna Sherrill (Mrs. Williamson). Educ: N.Mex. Highlands Univ; Univ. Mich; Cumberland Univ. Polit. & Govt. Pos: Spec. asst. to Attorney Gen. of U.S, 29-32; dist. attorney, Fourth Judicial Dist, N.Mex, 45-56; mem. finance cmt, N.Mex. State Rep. Party and mem, N.Mex. State Rep. Cent. Cmt, 66- Mil. Serv: Entered as Yeoman 1/C, Naval Res, 42, released in 45, after serv. in RPIO Saipan, 44. Mem: San Miguel Co. Bar Asn,(pres, 63-65); State Bar of N.Mex; Elks; Am. Legion; VFW; Rotary Int. Name included in plaque of del. to the 1952 Rep. Nat. Conv. dedicated to Dwight D. Eisenhower at Gettysburg. Rel: Catholic. Legal Res: 500 Reynolds Ave, Las Vegas, N.Mex. 87701. Mailing Add: P.O. Box 1150, Las Vegas, N.Mex. 87701.

ARMIJO, ROSALIO D
b. Edinburg, Tex, 8/30/30; s. Manuel Badillo Armijo and Esther Castilleja A; m. 11/15/49 to Carmen Salazar; c. Rosa Linda, Consuelo, Darlene and Jorge Francisco. Educ: Edinburg Jr. High, Tex, 3 years. Polit. & Govt. Pos: Del, Dem. Nat. Conv, 68; precinct committeeman, Franklin Co. Dem. Cent. Cmt, Wash, 69- Bus. & Prof. Pos: Construction laborer, George A. Grant Construction, Inc, 60-69. Mem: Laborers Local 348; Tri-Cities Latin Am. Asn; Wash. Citizen's for Migrant Affairs; Orgn. for Serv. to Agr. Families; Benton-Franklin Commun. Action Cmt; Mexican-Am. Fedn; Dem. Seeking a Newer World; Wash. Dem. Coun; Vol. to Encourage Registrn; 1969 Ad Hoc Cmt. on Human Rels. for the Pasco Sch. Dist. Rel: Catholic. Mailing Add: 1808 N. Jefferson, Pasco, Wash. 99301.

ARMISTEAD, CHARLES S. D
b. Bluefield, W. Va, 7/21/14; s. F. S. Armistead and Anne Aileen Akers A; m. 4/6/38 to Betty Sue Baker; c. Charles S, Jr, George Baker and William Blair. Educ: W.Va. Univ, A.B, LL.B; Sigma Nu; Phi Delta Phi. Polit. & Govt. Pos: Spec. hearing officer conscientious objector matters, Dept. Justice; W.Va. Cmn. Constitutional Rev, 59-63; W.Va. State Del, 59-61 & 65-69; del, Dem. Nat. Conv, 64 & 68. Bus. & Prof. Pos: Lawyer. Mil. Serv: Lt. Col, Army, 40-45. Mem: W.Va. State Bar Asn.(bd. gov, 53-57, pres, 60-61); Monongalia Co, W.Va. and Am. Bar Asns; Am. Judicature Soc; SAR; Am. Legion; VFW. Rel: Methodist. Mailing Add: 168 Chancery Row, Morgantown, W.Va. 26505.

ARMITAGE, CONSTANCE DEAN R
First V.Pres, Nat. Fedn. of Rep. Women
b. San Francisco, Calif, 5/13/20; d. Robert Armstrong Dean and Constance Lawrence D; m. 9/20/41 to Norman Cudworth Armitage; c. Leslie L.(Mrs. Vallhonrat) and Robert D. Educ: Univ. Calif, A.B, 39; grad. studies, Univ. Calif, Los Angeles, Univs. Florence and Perugia, Italy and Columbia Univ; Univ. Ga, M.A, 60. Polit. & Govt. Pos: V.chmn, S.C. Rep, Party, 60-62; second v.pres, Nat. Fedn. of Rep. Women, 62-67, first v.pres, 67-; alternate del, Rep. Nat. Conv, 60, del, 64 & 68. Bus. & Prof. Pos: Prof. art hist, Wofford Col, 61- Mem: Col. Art Asn; Southeast. Col. Art Asn; fel, Am. Coun. of Learned Soc; S.C. Arts Cmn. Adv. Purchasing Cmt. Mem, U.S. Team World Fencing Championships, Paris, France, 39. Rel: Episcopal. Mailing Add: 268 Connecticut Ave, Spartanburg, S.C. 29302.

ARMSTRONG, ANNE LEGENDRE R
Mem. Exec. Cmt, Rep. Nat. Cmt, Tex.
b. New Orleans, La, 12/27/27; d. Armant Legendre and Olive Martindale L; m. 4/12/50 to Tobin Armstrong; c. John Barclay II, Katharine Armant, Sarita Storey and twins, Tobin, Jr. and James Legendre. Educ: Vassar Col, B.A, 49; Phi Beta Kappa. Polit. & Govt. Pos: V.chmn. and chmn, Kenedy Co. Rep. Exec. Cmt, Tex; mem, State Conv. Cmt, 60; Rep. committeewoman, 20th Dist; mem, State Rep. Exec. Cmt, 61-66; del. and mem. platform cmt, Rep. Nat. Conv, 64 and del. and mem. platform cmt. and contests cmt, 68; chmn, state Turn Out Our Vote, 64; mem, State Cand. Cmt, 64-65; dep. state v.chmn, Region III, Rep. Party Tex, 65-66, state v.chmn, 66-68; mem. steering cmt, Women for Nixon, 68; Rep. Nat. Committeewoman, Tex, 68-, mem. exec. cmt, Rep. Nat. Cmt, 69- Bus. & Prof. Pos: Pres, Drink-O-Mat Corp. S.C. Mem: Kenedy Co. Sch. Bd.(trustee, 68-); Coastal Bend Tuberc. Asn.(dir). Rel: Episcopal. Mailing Add: Armstrong Ranch, Armstrong, Tex. 78338.

ARMSTRONG, GORDIAN LEE D
b. Dallas, Tex, 1/19/28; s. Gordon L. Armstrong and Mizpah E. Brown A; single. Educ: Univ. N.Mex, A.B, 53; N.Mex. Highlands Univ, A.M, 61. Polit. Pos: Del, Dem. Nat. Conv, Panama C.Z. Dem. Party, 64. Bus. & Prof. Pos: Teacher, English, Anthropology, N.Mex, 65-; instr, Anthropology, C.Z. Col, 63-64; teacher, Social Sci, English, C.Z, 62-64 and N.Mex, 56-62. Mil. Serv: Entered as Pvt, Marine Corps, 46, released as Pfc, 49, after serv. in 3rd Guard Co, Coco Solo Naval Base, Am. Theater 15th Naval Dist; Am. Theater Medal. Mem: Archaeological Inst. Am; Boy Scout Leadership Prog; Am. Fedn. Teachers; sponsor, Key Club, Kiwanis Affiliate. Lectr; Social Critic; Polit. Theorist. Mailing Add: Old Santa Fe Trail, Santa Fe, N.Mex. 87501. (1967)

ARMSTRONG, HARRY LEON R
Ohio State Sen.
b. Logan, Ohio, 10/15/15; s. Frank Leon Armstrong and Nellie Faye Wyskiver A; m. 1937 to Madaline Kitchen; c. Marvelea, Karen, Maureen and Diane. Educ: High Sch. Polit. & Govt. Pos: Supvr, Soil and Water Conserv. Dist, 42-54; trustee, Starr Twp, 46-52; cmnr, Hocking Co, 53-60; Ohio State Rep, Hocking Co, 63-67; Ohio State Sen, 17th Dist, 67- Mem: Kiwanis; Elks; Eagles; Moose; Farm Bur. Rel: Presbyterian. Legal Res: R.F.D. 3, Logan, Ohio 43138. Mailing Add: Blosser Bldg, Logan, Ohio 43138.

ARMSTRONG, JAKE THOMAS D
b. Knoxville, Tenn, 5/3/26; s. Franklin Spears Armstrong and Norma Polk A; m. 6/14/54 to Opal Jewel McEwen; c. Jake T, Jr, Amy Josephine and Martha Jeanne. Educ: Univ. Tenn, B.S, 46, M.S. 52; YMCA Law Sch, Nashville, LL.D, 61, J.D, 65; Phi Beta Kappa; Sigma Phi Epsilon; Phalanax. Polit. & Govt. Pos: Rep. nominee, U.S. House Rep, 68. Bus. & Prof. Pos: Pres, Commun, Inc, 55-58; pres, Armstrong Enterprises, 59-60. Mil. Serv: Entered as Pvt, Army, 53, released as E-2, 55, after serv. in MRU 8th Army Hq. Mem: Master Mason; Odd Fellows; Jaycees. Rel: Latter-day Saint. Mailing Add: 5410 E. Sunset, Knoxville, Tenn. 37914.

ARMSTRONG, JOHN ALEXANDER R
Asst. Rep. Floor Leader, Mass. House of Rep.
b. Glasgow, Scotland, 6/12/01; s. John Armstrong and Florence McLean A; m. 6/23/28 to Anna E. Raymond; c. Pauline (Mrs. Darsch). Polit. & Govt. Pos: Mass. State Rep, 43-, Asst. Rep. Floor Leader, 64-; mem, Bd. of Selectmen, Plymouth, 40-46, chmn, 46. Mem: Mason; Moose; Old Colony Club. Rel: Episcopal. Mailing Add: 14 Nelson St, Plymouth, Mass. 02360.

ARMSTRONG, JOHN BARCLAY R
b. San Antonio, Tex, 12/23/19; s. Charles Mitchell Armstrong and Lucie Carr A; m. 2/16/44 to Henrietta Alice Larkin; c. Charles Mitchell, Henrietta Julia, Thomas Tobin and Stewart Larkin. Educ: Univ. Tex, B.A, 42; Alpha Tau Omega. Polit. & Govt. Pos: Chmn, Kleberg Co. Rep. Party, Tex, 63-69. Bus. & Prof. Pos: Managing partner, John B. Armstrong Ranch, 51-69; pres, Santa Gertrudis Breeders Int, 57-59; chmn, Beef Indust. Coun. of Nat. Livestock and Meat Bd, 62-69. Mem: Tex. and Southwest. Cattle Raisers Asn; Ala. and Fla. Cattlemen's Asns; Am. Nat. Cattlemen's Asn.(past v.pres. and dir). Rel: Episcopal. Legal Res: Hwy. 141 W, Kingsville, Tex. 78363. Mailing Add: P.O. Box 193, Kingsville, Tex. 78363.

ARMSTRONG, JOSEPH J. D
b. Phila, Pa, 7/17/14; s. Edwin F. Armstrong and Mary G. Donnelly A; m. to Marie M. Crankshaw; c. two sons; one daughter. Educ: Temple Evening Tech; Cent. Realty Board. Polit. & Govt. Pos: Pa. State Rep, 64-67; State Inheritance Tax-Real Estate appraiser, 55-63; 35th Ward committeeman, 45-46. Bus. & Prof. Pos: Real estate bus. Mem: Summerdale Boy's Club; Father Judge Father's Club; LaSalle Col. Assocs; I.U.M.S.W.A; Retail Clerks and Mgrs. 1357. Rel: Roman Catholic. Mailing Add: 958 Marcella St, Philadelphia, Pa. 19124. (1967)

ARMSTRONG, ORLAND KAY R
b. Willow Springs, Mo, 10/2/93; s. Rev. William C. Armstrong and Agnes Brockus A; m. 5/21/22 to Louise McCool (deceased); m. 12/11/49 to Marjorie E. Moore; c. Milton McCool, Orland Kay, Jr, Louise (Mrs. Cattan), William Stanley and Charles Lindbergh. Educ: Drury Col, B.S. in Educ, 16; Cumberland Sch. of Law, LL.B, 22; Univ. Mo. Sch. of Journalism, B.J, 25, M.A, 25; Sigma Delta Chi; Pi Delta Epsilon. Hon. LL.D, 56; hon. J.D, 69. Polit. & Govt. Pos: Exec. secy, Mo. Century of Progress Cmn, 31-32; Mo. State Rep, 33-37 & 43-45; mem, Children's Code Cmn. of Mo, 45-47; chmn, Citizens Cmn. on Reorgn. of Exec. Br, by appointment of the Sen. Cmt. on Post Off. and Civil Serv, 47-48; U.S. Rep, 51-52. Bus. & Prof. Pos: Teacher, Southwest Baptist Col, 16-17; prof. of journalism, Univ. Fla, 25-28; mem. ed. staff, Reader's Digest, 44- Mil. Serv: Entered as Pvt, Army Air Coprs, 17, released as 2nd Lt, 19, after serv. in Taylor Field, Ala, Chanute Field, Ill. and Kelly Field, Tex. Publ: Old Massa's People, story of slavery days, Bobbs-Merrill, 33; The Fifteen Decisive Battles of the United States, McKay Co, 64; The Indomitable Baptists (with Marjorie Armstrong), Doubleday, 66. Mem: Mo. Writers' Guild (past pres); Am. Legion; Net. World War I; Am. War Dads; Mil. Order of World Wars; Kiwanis; Univ. Club. Rel: Baptist. Mailing Add: The Highlands, Republic, Mo. 65738.

ARMSTRONG, ROBERT LANDIS D
Tex. State Rep.
b. Austin, Tex, 11/7/32; s. Robert Cochran Armstrong and Louise Landis A; m. 6/22/62 to Shannon Harrison; c. Martha L, Shannon and Robert L, Jr. Educ: Univ. Tex, B.A. in Govt, 53, LL.B, 59. Polit. & Govt. Pos: Tex. State Rep, 63- Bus. & Prof. Pos: Attorney-at-Law, 58- Mil. Serv: Entered as Ens, Navy, 53, released as Lt.(jg), 55, after serv. in Atlantic-Mediterranean. Mem: State Bar of Tex; Am. Legion; Explorer Chmn, Boy Scouts. Rel: Episcopal. Mailing Add: 4507 Edgemont, Austin, Tex. 78731. (1967)

ARMSTRONG, THOMAS DeBOY D
b. La, 11/11/19; m. to Marguerite Goodwin; c. Thelma D.(Mrs. Hannah) and Thomas D, II. Educ: Tuskegee Inst; Prairie View A&M Col, B.A; Kappa Alpha Psi. Polit. & Govt. Pos: City councilman, Galveston, Tex, 61-63; del, Dem. Nat. Conv, 68. Bus. & Prof. Pos: Partner, B.A.&P. Realty Co, 44-66, owner, 66-; pres, Gold Bond Funeral Benefit Ins. Co, 58-65; pres, Strode-Armstrong Mortuary, 58-; pres, Tyler Life Ins. Co, 65-; dir, Galveston Co. Seawall Bd; mem. bd. dirs, Tex. South. Univ. Mem: United Polit. Orgn. Tex. Rel: Methodist. Mailing Add: 3112 Ave. L, Galveston, Tex. 77550. (1967)

ARNALL, ELLIS GIBBS D
b. Newnan, Ga, 3/20/07; s. Joe Gibbs Arnall and Bessie Lena Ellis A; m. 4/6/35 to Mildred DeLaney Slemons; c. Alvan Slemons and Alice Slemons. Educ: Mercer Univ, 24; Univ. of the South, A.B, 28; Univ. of Ga, LL.B, 31; Atlanta Law Sch, LL.D, 42; Piedmont Col, LL.D, 43; Bryant Col, LL.D, 48; Univ. of the South, D.C.L, 47; Phi Beta Kappa; Phi Delta Phi; Kappa Alpha. Polit. & Govt. Pos: Speaker pro tem, Ga. House Rep, 33-37; attorney gen, Ga, 39-43; Gov. of Ga, 43-47. Bus. & Prof. Pos: Pres, Columbus Nat. Life Ins. Co, Newnan, 46-; pres, Independent Film Producers Export Corp, Beverly Hills, Calif, 48-; chmn. bd, Coastal States Life Ins. Co, Atlanta, 56-; sr. partner, Arnall, Golden & Gregory, Attorneys. Publ: 'The Shore Dimly Seen,' 46; 'What the People Want,' 47. Mem: Trustee, Mercer Univ; fel, Int. Inst. Arts & Sci; Am. Judicature Soc; Nat. Asn. Life Ins. Co.(chmn. bd, 55-); Soc. Motion Picture Arts & Sci; Am, Fed. and Ga. Bar Asns; Atlanta Lawyers Club; Nat. Cmn. UNESCO, 47-51 & 63-, U.S. del, Fifth Conf. UNESCO, Paris, France, 49; U.S. del, Anglo-Am. Film Conf, London, 50, 53-56. Legal Res: 213 Jackson St, Newnan, Ga. 30263. Mailing Add: Fulton Federal Bldg, Atlanta, Ga. 30303.

ARNDT, ELIZABETH MOORE 'BETTY' R
First V.Pres, Mo. Fedn. Rep. Women
b. Newburyport, Mass, 8/25/20; d. Frederick Arnold Moore and Miriam Delano M; m. 5/11/46 to Joseph Manning Arndt, Jr; c. Margaret Anne, Martha Howard, Joseph M, III and Marilyn Delano. Educ: Boston City Hosp. Sch. Nursing, grad, 41. Polit. & Govt. Pos: Pres, Centralia Rep. Women's Club, Mo, 60; treas, Eighth Dist. Rep. Women's Club, 62; campaign activities chmn, Mo. Fedn. Rep. Women, 62-63, recording secy, 63-65, second v.pres, 65-67, first v.pres, 67-; del, Rep. Nat. Conv, 64; committeewoman, Centralia Ward II, Rep. Party, 66-; Mo. del, Nat. Fedn. Rep. Women Conv, 67; v.chmn, 119th Legis. Dist, 68; del, Eighth Dist. Conv. and Mo. State Rep. Conv, 68. Mil. Serv: Entered as 2nd Lt, Army Nurse Corps, 42, released as 1st Lt, 46, after serv. in Camp Crowder Gen. Hosp, Mo; European, African, Middle East. Theater Medal; Victory Medal; Am. Theater Medal. Mem: PTA; Sorosis Fedn. Women's Club; Girl Scouts; pres, Heart of Mo. Girl Scout Coun, 67-; chmn, Centralia United Fund, 67. Girl Scout Leader and Volunteer Trainer of Leaders. Rel: Protestant. Mailing Add: 5 Sunrise Circle, Centr[illegible], Mo. 65240.

ARNE, RICHARD O. R
Chmn, Kandiyohi Co. Rep. Cmt, Minn.
b. Danvers, Minn, 2/20/28; s. Oliver J. Arne and Emma Haugen A; m. 8/8/53 to Mary Louree McDonald; c. Greg W, Erik R, Gretchen M. and Laura J. Educ: St. Olaf Col. Polit. & Govt. Pos: Del, State, Dist. and Co. Rep. Conv, Minn, 64; chmn, Kandiyohi Co. Rep. Cmt, 65- Bus. & Prof. Pos: Student solicitor, St. Olaf Col, 52; ins. adjuster, Mutual Serv. Ins. Co, 53-59, dist. sales mgr, 57-58; mgr, Independent Adjusters, Inc, 60-64, pres, 64- Mem: St. Cloud and Minneapolis Claimmen's Asns; mem, Prfnl. Adjusting Syst. of Am; former pres, Jr. C. of C; former Toastmaster; Willmar C. of C. Lettered in Basketball at St. Olaf Col. Rel: Protestant. Mailing Add: 312 Terrace Dr, Willmar, Minn. 56201. (1967)

ARNEBERGH, ROGER R
City Attorney, Los Angeles, Calif.
b. St. Paul, Minn, 8/17/09; s. Targe Arnebergh and Amelia Graagaard A; m. 5/1/37 to Emilie K. Rogers; c. Patricia Carol (Mrs. Holt). Educ: La Salle Col, LL.B. 35; Phi Delta Phi; Legion Lex, Univ. Southern Calif. Polit. & Govt. Pos: City attorney, Los Angeles, Calif, 53- Bus. & Prof. Pos: Asst. secy. and attorney, Pac. Mutual Life Ins. Co, 37-41. Mem: Am. and Los Angeles Co. Bar Asns; Lawyers' Club; Nat. Inst. Munic. Law Officers; Los Angeles Tennis Club; Jonathan Club. Rel: Protestant. Mailing Add: 2741 Woodstock Rd, Los Angeles, Calif. 90046.

ARNETT, DIXON R
City Councilman, Redwood City, Calif.
b. Trenton, N.J, 2/12/38; s. George Washington Arnett and Annabel Dixon A; m. 2/11/61 to Mary Pavlak; c. John Dixon, Susan Rae and Robert Michael. Educ: Stanford Univ, B.A, 60; Alpha Tau Omega; Walter Army Soc. Polit. & Govt. Pos: On spec. assignment with the U.S. Fed. Bur. of Narcotics, 60-61; exec. dir, San Francisco Bay Area Rep. Alliance, Calif, 62-63, mem. bd. dir, San Mateo Div, 63-67, v.pres, 67-68, pres, 68-69, secy, bd. trustees, 69-; assoc. mem, San Mateo Co. Rep. Cent. Cmt, 62-67, various precinct orgn. and elec. day assignments, 62-68, elected mem, Fourth Supervisorial Dist, 66 & 68, committeeman, 66-; admin. asst, Rep. Minority Caucus, Calif. State Assembly, 63-64; assoc. mem, Calif. Rep. State Cent. Cmt, 63-68, mem, tech. adv. bd, Cal-Plan, 64-66, appointed mem, 68 & 69; co-mgr, Ruhland for Assembly Cmt, 27th Assembly Dist, 64; mem, Tri-City Chap, Young Rep, 64-66, v.pres, 65-66; mem, Live Oak Chap, Calif. Rep. League, 65-68; mem, Younger for Cong. Cmt. and Britschgi for Assembly Cmt, 66; mem, subcmt. on Redwood Shores, Citizens' Cmt. on Park and Recreation, 66-67; mem, steering cmt, Draper for Cong. Cmt, 67; mem, Parks and Recreation Cmn, Redwood City and chmn, sub-cmt, on bond issue priorities, 67-68; chmn, Sequoia High Sch. Dist. Permissive Tax Rate Campaign Cmt, 68; chmn, Redwood City Nixon-Agnew Cmt. and mem, Britschgi for Assembly Cmt, 68; city councilman, Redwood City, 68-, chmn, Marina Cmt. and Redwood City Sch. Dist. Cmt, mem, Legis. Cmt. and Spec. Cmt. on Safety Workers' Benefits. Bus. & Prof. Pos: Partner, Eastman/Arnett Assocs, 64-65; staff assoc, Off. of Gen. Secy, Stanford Univ, 65-66, dir, commun. rels. and assoc. dir, univ. rels, 66- Mil. Serv: Entered as Pvt, Army Res, 56, released as Capt, 69, after serv. in Calif. Army Nat. Guard, 62-68; Capt, Army Res, currently; Fed. Res. Ribbon; Two State Active Duty Awards. Publ: Today's Government Handbook, Curricular Serv. Inst, 64. Mem: Alumni Asn, Fed. Bur. of Narcotics Training Sch, 61-; cong. action cmt, Palo Alto C. of C. 66-; bd. dir. and co-chmn, membership cmt, Sequoia Dist. YMCA, 68-; bd. trustees, Jr. Statesman of Am. Found. 68-, secy. of bd, 69- Rel: Protestant. Mailing Add: 1098 Glennan Dr, Redwood City, Calif. 94061.

ARNETT, HOMER R
Mem, Kalamazoo Co. Rep. Exec. Cmt, Mich.
b. Salyersville, Ky, 1/29/03; m. to Florence L. York; c. Florence Elaine Pegg,

Homer, Jr. and James Edwin. Educ: West. Mich Univ, B.A; Mich. State Univ; Univ. Mich, LL.B. Polit. & Govt. Pos: Former circuit court cmnr; Mich. State Rep, 57-67; mem, Kalamazoo Co. Rep. Exec. Cmt, Mich, 57-; mem, Law Rev. Cmn, 66; supvr, Kalamazoo Co, 67-69. Bus. & Prof. Pos: Lawyer; taught in Mich. pub. schs, 10 years; taught polit. sci, econ. and bus. law, West. Mich. Univ, 12 years. Mem: Former scoutmaster; Coun. of Soc. Agencies; PTA (pres); Coun. Churches (secy); Kalamazoo Methodist Union; Kalamazoo Co. and Mich. State Bar Asns. Rel: Methodist. Mailing Add: 2424 Pine Ridge Rd, Kalamazoo, Mich. 49001.

ARNETT, SHERMAN ROLEN D
Ky. State Rep.
b. Foraker, Ky, 8/31/23; s. Lawrence Arnett and Delia Rowe A; m. 12/21/44 to Mary L. Coffey; c. Brenda Carol, Gerald Maurice and Larry Neil. Educ: Morehead State Univ, A.B. and M.A; Univ. of Ky, grad work. Polit. & Govt. Pos: Ky. State Rep, 71st Dist, 66- Bus. & Prof. Pos: Prin, Clearfield Elem. Sch, 48-66; asst. prin, Rowan Co. High Sch, 66, prin, 67- Mem: Nat, Ky. and Rowan Co. Educ. Asns; Gideon (local v.pres). Rel: Freewill Baptist. Mailing Add: Box 142, Clearfield, Ky. 40313.

ARNICK, JOHN STEPHEN D
Md. State Del.
b. Baltimore, Md 11/27/33; s. John Arnick and Josephine Galliard A; m. 10/15/60 to Joan Nielsen. Educ: Univ. Baltimore, B.S, 56, LL.B, 62. Polit. & Govt. Pos: Magistrate at lg, Baltimore Co, Md, 64-65; Med. State Del, 66- Mil. Serv: Entered as Officer Cand, Marine Corps, 55, released as Capt, 58, after serv. in Third Marine Div, Far E, 56-58. Mem: Md. and Baltimore Co. Bar Ams; Moose; Bear Creek Civic Club; Line Dem. Club. Rel: Catholic. Legal Res: 1619 Gray Haven Court, Dundalk, Md. 21222. Mailing Add: 2 Market Place, Dundalk, Md. 21222.

ARNOLD, ALVA LEE R
Mem, Calif. Rep. State Cent. Cmt.
b. Woodville, Tex, 10/27/19; d. Daniel Louis Cobb and Ida Mae Risinger C; m. 3/6/43 to Ernest Marion Arnold; c. James Bowman, Margaret Mary, Teresa (Mrs. Fredrick Everett Leek, II), Ernest Bernard, David Daniel, Ann Marie and Stephen Francis. Educ: E. Tex. Baptist Col, grad. in Bus. Admin, 42; Calif. State Col, Los Angeles, 3 years; Phi Beta Kappa, secy, Gamma Psi Chap, 39-42; Sigma Iota Chi, pres, Phi Chap, 39-42. Polit. & Govt. Pos: Chmn, Citizens' Freeway Cmt, South Pasadena, Calif, 65-66; co-chmn, Mayor's Freeway Cmt, 67-68; mem, City Freeway Cmn, 69; pres, South Pasadena Rep. Women's Club, Federated, 69; mem, Calif. Rep. State Cent. Cmt, 69- Publ: Series of Freeway Fact articles, South Pasadena Rev, Newspaper, 66-68. Mem: Chmn, South Pasadena serv. team, Girl Scouts; South Pasadena Woman's Club (citzenship chmn); Calif. Roadside Coun; Calif. Planning and Conserv. League; Calif. Tomorrow; Holy Family Cath. Sch. Parent's Guild; PTA. Rel: Catholic. Mailing Add: 1534 Ramona Ave, South Pasadena, Calif. 91030.

ARNOLD, BEN D
m. 8/5/20 to Sara Whitlow; c. Ben, Jr, Sarah Louise (Mrs. Cramer), 6 grandchildren. Polit. & Govt. Pos: Ariz. State Sen, 54-66; Nat. Cmt. for Traffic Safety, 61-; Coolidge mayor, 8 years; Coolidge City Coun; Florence Union High Sch. Bd, pres, 9 years; Florence City Coun; chmn, West. Coun. of State Govts. Cmt. on Traffic Safety. Bus. & Prof. Pos: Rio Grande Oil Co. Agency, 39; Standard Oil Distributor, 35; owner serv. sta, 23; Pinal Co. Hwy. Dept. Mil. Serv: Navy, WWI. Mem: Am. Legion; Coolidge C. of C; Ariz. Munic. League, Ariz. League of Cities And Towns; Ariz. Justices of Peace; Constable Asn. Citations from Ariz. Hwy. Cmn; Ariz. State Hwy. Patrol; hon. by Univ. Ariz, 64, for serv. as outstanding civic leader and dedicated pub. servant. Mailing Add: Box 486, Coolidge, Ariz. 85228. (1967)

ARNOLD, DONALD SPEARE R
Vt. State Sen.
b. Bethel, Vt, 10/22/96; married; c. 1 son and 2 daughters. Educ: Goddard Sem. Polit. & Govt. Pos: Selectman, Bethel, Vt, 49-55; mem, Vt. State Rep. Cmt, 55-59; mem, Windsor Co. Rep. Cmt. Vt; mem, Bethel Rep. Town Cmt; Justice of the Peace; Vt. State Sen, 61- Bus. & Prof. Pos: Formerly mgr, Cent. Vt. Rwy. and Tel. Co, retired. Mil. Serv: Cpl, Army Inf, 18. Mem: Mason (Past Master); Am. Legion (Past Comdr); Bethel Rotary (past pres); Shrine; Hartford Elks. Rel: Congregational. Mailing Add: Bethel, Vt. 05032. (1967)

ARNOLD, EDGAR FRANK, JR. D
Mem, Ky. State Dem. Cent. Exec. Cmt.
b. Madisonville, Ky, 9/29/25; s. Edgar Frank Arnold and Caroline Long A; m. 6/20/48 to Ruby J. Mitchell; div. 6/21/65; m. 3/11/66 to Jeanne Campbell Hannah; c. Frank E, Karen Hannah, Gillis M. and Brian B. Educ: Univ. of Ky, 46-47; Sigma Delta Chi; Sigma Alpha Epsilon. Polit. & Govt. Pos: Dep. sheriff, Hopkins Co, Ky, 54-57; Ky. State Rep, 58-60; state publicity chmn. and speech writer, Wilson W. Wyatt's U.S. Senate Campaign, 62; newsletter ed. and mem. state publicity cmt, Breathitt for Gov. Campaign, 63; ed, Kentucky Democrat, 65-; mem. state-at-lg, Ky. State Dem. Cent. Exec. Cmt, 66-; mem. steering cmt, State Campaign of Henry Ward for Gov, 67; cand. for Ky. State Sen, Sixth Dist, 69. Bus. & Prof. Pos: Reporter-photographer, Madisonville Messenger, 47-50, managing ed, 50-63, ed. and pres, 63- Mil. Serv: Entered as Pvt, Army Air Corps, 43, released as Flight Officer, 45, after serv. in 1st and 3rd Air Force, Am. Theater. Publ: Political Column, 'Broadsides,' Madisonville Messenger, 60- Mem: Associated Press; Assoc. Press Managing Editors' Asn; South. Newspaper Publishers Asn; Nat. Editorial Asn; Ky. Press Asn; Am. Legion; Farm Bur; Rotary; Madisonville C. of C.(first v.pres, 69); Madisonville Commun. Col. Found.(secy, 68-); Madisonville Hosp. Corp. (secy); Country Club. Rel: Christian Church. Mailing Add: 62 E. Broadway, Madisonville, Ky. 42431.

ARNOLD, EDWIN HARRISON R
b. Knoxville, Tenn, 10/18/34; s. James Elisha Arnold and Grace Harrison A; m. 9/1/57 to Sara Evelyn Lewis; c. Monica Lynn, Edwin H, Jr, James Daniel and Diana Suzanne. Educ: Univ. Tenn, B.A, 55; Cumberland Univ, LL.B, 58; Alpha Tau Omega; Delta Theta Phi. Hon. J.D, Samford Univ. Polit. & Govt. Pos: City judge, Loudon, Tenn, 60; Tenn. State Rep, Loudon & Blount Co, 63-67. Mem: Pres, Loudon Co. Bar Asn, 64-65; Tenn. Bar Asn; Am. Trial Lawyers Asn; past pres, Loudon Lions; pres, Loudon Jaycees, 69- Rel: Baptist. Mailing Add: P.O. Box 241, Loudon, Tenn. 37774.

ARNOLD, JIM D
Mo. State Rep.
b. South Bend, Ind, 1/7/35; s. Earl Arnold and Maude Irvine A; m. 5/16/64 to Katherine I. Doyle; c. Bruce Wayne and Earl Bradley. Educ: Tri-State Col, B.S, 57; Alpha Sigma Phi. Polit. & Govt. Pos: Mo. State Rep, currently. Bus. & Prof. Pos: Partner, Arnold & Ichord. Mil. Serv: Entered as Pvt, Army, 58, released as SP-4, 60, after serv. in Comptroller Sect, Ft. Leonard Wood, Mo. Mem: Mason; Scottish Rite Bodies; Shrine; C. of C; Optimist. Rel: Baptist. Mailing Add: Route 1, Waynesville, Mo. 65583.

ARNOLD, JOHN BURLEIGH D
Mem, Mo. State Dem. Cmt.
b. Lewistown, Mo, 5/12/31; s. Egbert F. Arnold and Geneva Madge Harris A; m. 8/10/52 to Mary Carolyn Brookhart; c. Victor John, Charles Andrew and Sharis Leigh. Educ: Northeast Mo. State Teachers Col, bus. educ, 49-52; Univ. Mo. Sch. Law, L.B, 55; Sigma Tau Gamma. Polit. & Govt. Pos: Probate and magistrate judge, Schuyler Co, Mo, 57-58; asst. attorney gen, Mo, 58-60; admin. asst. to Gov. John M. Dalton, Mo, 61-62; chmn, Speaker's Bur, Mo. State Dem. Cmt, 62-64, mem, Mo. State Dem. Cmt, Eighth Cong. Dist, 62-; del-at-lg, Dem. Nat. Conv, 64 & 68. Bus. & Prof. Pos: Instr, Northeast Mo. State Teachers Col, 57-58; v.pres. and trust officer, Cent. Mo. Trust Co, 62- Mil. Serv: 1st Lt, Army, 57, serv. in Judge Advocate Gen. Corps. Mem: Cole Co, St. Louis and Mo. Bar Asns; Mo. and Am. Bankers Asns; Mo. Asn. for Social Welfare; Mo. Good Roads Asn; C. of C; Dem. State Cmt; Cole. Co. Dem. Club; Capitol Young Dem. Club; Mason; Elks; Cole Co. Hist. Soc. Rel: Baptist. Legal Res: 1317 Major Dr, Jefferson City, Mo. 65101. Mailing Add: 238 Madison St, Jefferson City, Mo. 65101.

ARNOLD, JOHN ROBERT R
Chmn, Oktibbeha Co. Rep. Party, Miss.
b. Wattensaw, Ark, 5/17/23; s. Murray Hunter Arnold and Ruth Steele A; m. 8/23/50 to Mary Ann Ficklin; c. Elizabeth, Margaret, Carrie, Hunter and Mary. Educ: Miss. State Univ, B.S, 44. Polit. & Govt. Pos: Chmn, Oktibbeha Co. Rep. Party, Miss, 64- Bus. & Prof. Pos: Owner, John R. Arnold Farms, 44-69; pres, Howard Furniture Mfg. Co, Inc, 57-69, Dodge City, 65-69, Herschede Hall Clock Co, 67-69 and Dodge City Enterprises, 68-69. Mil. Serv: Pvt, Army, 43, serv. in Training Unit, Ft. McClellan. Mem: Farm Bur; Rotary; Sessums Commun. Club. Rel: United Methodist. Mailing Add: Sessums, Miss. 39758.

ARNOLD, LUTHER R
b. Stone Co, Mo, 1903; m. 9/10/24 to Thelma Claybough; c. Wanda, Judith Kay. Educ: Pub. Schs, Stone Co. Polit. & Govt. Pos: Mo. State Rep, 48-66; Rep. caucus chmn, 69th and 73rd Gen. Assemblies; Rep. Committeeman (2 yrs.). Bus. & Prof. Pos: formerly owned and operated grocery store and filling station. Mem: Masonic Lodge. Mailing Add: Reeds Spring, Mo. 65737. (1967)

ARNOLD, LYNWOOD D
Fla. State Rep.
b. Jacksonville, Fla, 10/6/16; m. to Elsie Ferguson; c. Lynwood F, Jr. and Pamela H. Educ: John B. Stetson Univ, B.A, 41. Polit. & Govt. Pos: Fla. State Rep, 63- Bus. & Prof. Pos: Pres, Arnold Sales, Inc, currently. Mil. Serv: Navy, 41-46. Mem: Mason; Shrine; Elks; Lions. Rel: Episcopal. Mailing Add: 859 Edgewood Ave. S, P.O. Box 5062, Jacksonville, Fla. 32207. (1967)

ARNOLD, MARGARET E. D
b. Ft. Wayne, Ind, 7/11/11; d. Patrick J. Sullivan and Johanna Wilkinson S; m. 11/10/34 to Maurice J. Arnold; c. Nan (Mrs. Ryan) and Sister Sharon, O.L.V.M. Educ: St. Catherine's Acad, Ft. Wayne. Polit. & Govt. Pos: Secy, Co. Hwy. Supt, Ind, 30-33; app. by Gov. McNutt of Ind, Bur. of Motor Vehicles, 33-34; Dem. mem, Bd. of Voters Registr, 63-; secy, Fourth Cong. Dem. Cent. Cmt; past v.chmn, Allen Co. Dem. Cent. Cmt. Bus. & Prof. Pos: Mgr, Auto License Bur, Ft. Wayne, Ind, 61-63. Mem: Ft. Wayne-Stellar Concerts; Ind. Dem. Women's Orgn; St. Joseph Hosp. Auxiliary; St. Catherine's Acad. Alumni; Marians; Theresians; Ment. Health; League-of-Women Voters. Rel: Catholic. Mailing Add: 4123 S. Wayne Ave, Ft. Wayne, Ind. 46807. (1967)

ARNOLD, ROBERT ALMERINE D
Chmn, Fourth Dist. Dem. Party, Kans.
b. Latham, Kans, 3/27/21; s. Orville Arnold and Elsie McCullough A; m. 9/18/43 to Doris Jane Klassen; c. Larry Gene and Robert John. Educ: McPherson Col, 40-42. Polit. & Govt. Pos: Chmn, Young Dem. Club, Kans, 52-58, Marion Co. Dem. Club, 62-68, Fourth Dist. Dem. Party, 68- and State Credit Union Dept, 68-; mem, Credit Union Coun, 68- Bus. & Prof. Pos: Chmn, Cuna Mutual Ins. Soc-Policyowners Rep, 64-67 and secy, 67-69. Mil. Serv: Entered as Pvt, Army, 40, released as Sgt, 43, after serv. in Co. F. 137th Inf, 35th Div. Mem: Mutual Ins. Agents; Cues For Credit Unions; Kans. Credit Union League; Kiwanis; C. of C; Lancer Club; N.Cent. Chap. of Credit Unions; Policy Owner Rep. for Credit Unions. Rel: Protestant. Legal Res: 306 S. Kennedy, Hillsboro, Kans. 67063. Mailing Add: Box 3, Hillsboro, Kans. 67063.

ARNOLD, ROGER W. R
b. Braintree, Mass, 1917. Educ: Tufts Univ, Seton Hall Univ, holds A.B, M.A. Polit. & Govt. Pos: Mem, town meeting, Braintree, Mass; mem, Braintree Sch. Cmt, seven terms. Bus. & Prof. Pos: Mem. staff, Emerson Col, 57-, assoc. prof. of math. and sci. and chmn. of dept, currently. Mem: Am. Asn. of Univ. Prof; Am. Asn. for the Adv. of Sci; Braintree Golf Asn; Delta Bowling League; Mass. Asn. of Sch. Cmts. Rel: Unitarian. Mailing Add: Dept. of Mathematics and Science, Emerson College, 130 Beacon St, Boston, Mass. 02116. (1967)

ARNOLD, STANLEY D
b. Indiana, 1903; m. to Almida Lindquist A; c. Stanley D. Educ: Univ. of Calif; Hastings Col. of the Law, LL.B. Polit. & Gov. Pos: Calif. State Sen, 55-66; Dist. Attorney of Lassen Co, 49-55. Mem: State Bar of Calif; Lassen Co. Bar Asn; Elks; Am. Legion; K. of C. Rel: Catholic. Mailing Add: Box 150 Susanville, Calif. 96130. (1967)

ARNOLD, WILLIAM JOSHUA D
Chmn, Independence Co. Dem. Cent. Cmt, Ark.
b. Batesville, Ark, 6/4/27; s. Carl Arnold and Abigail Snapp A; m. 4/12/51 to Bobbye Ann McAlister; c. Martin Blair, Leslie Beth and Robert Brent. Educ: La. State Univ, 44-45; Univ. Okla. and S.Dak. State Col, 45; Univ. Ark, LL.B, 50; Delta Theta Phi; Phi Eta Sigma; Tau Kappa Alpha; Blue Key; Kappa Sigma. Polit. & Govt. Pos: Ark. State Rep, 49-50; prosecuting attorney, Third Judicial Circuit, 51-57; secy, Independence Co. Elec. Cmn, 57-; chmn, Independence Co. Dem. Cent. Cmt, 58- Bus. & Prof. Pos: Partner, law firm, Murphy & Arnold, 56-; secy, Town Plaza, Inc, 62-; pres, Wolf Bayou Dam Asn, 64- Mil. Serv: Entered as Pvt, 44, released as M/Sgt, 47 after serv. in Korea, 46 and Army Specialized Training Prog, 44-45 & 47. Mem: Ark. and Am. Bar Asns; Am. Judicature Soc; Am. Col. Probate Coun; Nat. Asn. Claimants Coun; Independence Co. Bar Asn.(past pres); 8th Chancery Bar Asn. (past pres); Am. Legion; VFW; Kiwanis (past pres, past lt. gov). Rel: Methodist; Past Chmn. Bd, First Methodist Church, Batesville, Ark. Legal Res: 1775 Maple St, Batesville, Ark. 72501. Mailing Add: P.O. Box 360, Batesville, Ark. 72501.

ARNSDORFF, B. FRANK D
b. Clyo, Ga, 7/3/12; s. John L. Arnsdorff and Lillie Edwards A; m. 12/12/36 to Gladys Seckinger; c. O'Neal, B.F, Wayne. Educ: Effingham Pub. Schs. Polit. & Govt. Pos: Cmnr. of Rds. and Revenue, Effingham Co; State Rep, Ga, 59-66. Bus. & Prof. Pos: Farmer; sawmill and planer mill operator. Mem: Masons; WOW. Rel: Methodist. Mailing Add: Springfield, Ga. 31329.

ARON, CARL ROBERT D
b. Brooklyn, N.Y, 11/21/43; s. Paul Harvey Aron and Beatrice Roslyn Feinstein A; single. Educ: Columbia Col, A.B, 65; Harvard Law Sch, LL.B, 68; Phi Beta Kappa. Polit. & Govt. Pos: Alternate del, Dem. Nat. Conv, 68. Mailing Add: 37-16 223rd St, Bayside, N.Y. 11361.

ARONIN, ROBERT MITCHELL D
b. Milwaukee, Wis, 10/25/45; s. Paul Aronin and Mania Ruvinsky A; single. Educ: Univ. Wis, psychol. Polit. & Govt. Pos: Del, Dem. State Conv, Wis, 59-66; mem, Milwaukee Co. Dem. Exec. Bd, 63-65; chmn, Fifth Sen. Dist. and treas, Fifth Cong. Dist, Dem. Party, 63-65; del, Dem. Nat. Conv, 64; pres, Wis. Citizens Legis. Asn, 65- Bus. & Prof. Pos: Pres, Travel Ideas Inc, travel consult, 65- Publ: The Right Way, Empire, N.Y, 62; 'How to Elect a State Legislator, In: Citizens in politics, by Citizens for Better Govt, Milwaukee, 65. Mem: Appointed by mayor to Milwaukee UN Cmt, 63; exec. dir, Wis. Consumers Asn; dir, Wis. Asn. Civic Orgns; E.Town Asn.(pres). Mailing Add: 819 N. Cass St, Milwaukee, Wis. 53202.

ARONOFF, STANLEY J. R
Ohio State Sen.
b. Cincinnati, Ohio, 6/8/32; s. Irwin I. Aronoff and Cecelia Hyman A; m. 6/15/58 to Gretchen Vicky Schwab; c. Tracy, Jay and Leslie. Educ: Harvard Col. and Law Sch; Harvard Glee Club. Polit. & Govt. Pos: Ohio State Rep, 60-66; Ohio State Sen, 66-; mem, Coun. of State Govt, currently. Bus. & Prof. Pos: Arbitrator, Am. Arbit. Asn, 66. Mil. Serv: Cpl, Army, 57; Soldier of Cycle. Publ: J. of Am. Air Law and Commerce. Mem: Am, Ohio and Cincinnati Bar Asns. Rel: Jewish. Mailing Add: 220 Wyoming Ave, Cincinnati, Ohio 45215.

ARONOW, CEDOR BORIS D
b. Odessa, Russia, 9/2/10; s. Boris A.S. Aronow and Anna DeParment A; m. 5/27/36 to Jane Kaster; c. Cedor Boris, II, Marcia Jane (Mrs. Buffandeau) and Natalie Ann (Mrs. Bartschi). Educ: Univ. Wash, A.B, 31, LL.B, 33; Phi Alpha Delta; Phi Delta Sigma; Phi Sigma Kappa. Polit. & Govt. Pos: Pres. and nat. committeeman, Young Dem. of Mont, 36-38; co. attorney, Toole Co, 37-43; Mont. State Rep, 49-53; del, Dem. Nat. Conv, 56. Mil. Serv: Pvt, Marines, 43-45 & 50-51, released as Maj, after serv. in Pac. Theatre; Maj, Marine Corps Res; Presidential Unit Citation. Mem: Am. and Mont. Bar Asns; Judicature Soc; Independent Petroleum Asn. of Am.(dir); pres, Mont. Broadcasters Asn, 47; Elks; Am. Legion; VFW; Shrine; officer and dir, Mont. Jr. C. of C, 40-43; Moose (pres, Mont. Lodge, 47). Rel: Protestant. Legal Res: 153 Main St, Shelby, Mont. 59474. Mailing Add: P.O. Box 651, Shelby, Mont. 59474.

ARONSON, ROBERT SAMUEL R
Mass. State Rep.
b. Boston, Mass, 7/3/20; s. Julius Barnet Aronson and Esther Miller A; m. 7/9/45 to Rita Pearlman; c. Jeffrey B, Randy and Wayne Alan. Polit. & Govt. Pos: Mem, Sch. Bldg. Expansion Cmt, Sharon, Mass, 59, chmn, Warrant Cmt, 59-65, mem, Personnel Bd, 65-68; Mass. State Rep, 12th Norfolk Dist, 69- Bus. & Prof. Pos: Pres, Robert Aronson Assocs, Inc, Boston, Mass, 59-; mem, bd. dir, Sharon Coop. Bank, 65- Mil. Serv: Maritime Serv, 41-46. Mem: Mass. Legislators Asn. Mailing Add: 25 Gannett Terr, Sharon, Mass. 02067.

ARRANTS, JAMES CLATOR D
b. Kershaw Co, S.C, 2/25/17; s. Henry C. Arrants and Ava McLeod A; m. 8/14/63 to Betty Smoak Carter; c. Margaret Brock (by first marriage), Donald Rutledge and Duncan Andrew. Educ: Berry Col, B.S, 39; Univ. S.C, LL.B, 47. Polit. & Govt. Pos: S.C. State Rep, 41-42, 47-48 & 63-66; S.C. State Sen, 51-54. Bus. & Prof. Pos: Teacher, Mt. Pisgah and Iva High Schs; lawyer, currently. Mil. Serv: Navy, 42-46. Mem: Am. Legion; VFW; Kiwanis. Rel: Methodist; Bd. Stewards and Sunday Sch. Teacher, Lyttleton St. Methodist Church. Mailing Add: Springdale Dr, Camden, S.C. 29020.

ARREDONDO, JOE D
Ind. State Rep.
b. E. Chicago, Ind, 3/2/37; s. Miguel Arredondo and Maria Perez A; m. 6/3/61 to Dolores Martinez; c. Felice, Monica and Joseph. Educ: San Diego State Col, B.S, 57; De Paul Univ, M.S, 67. Polit. & Govt. Pos: Ind. State Rep, Lake Co, 68- Bus. & Prof. Pos: Asst. prin, Edison Jr. High Sch, 67-69. Mil. Serv: Entered as Pvt, Army, 57, released as Sgt, 59, after serv. in Third Inf. Div, Germany; Cert. of Achievement for serv. in Third Inf. Div. Honor Guard. Mem: Phi Delta Kappa; Ind. Bus. Educ. Asn; Am. Fedn. of Teachers; Veterans in Politics. Rel: Catholic. Mailing Add: 4917 W. Seventh Ave, Gary, Ind. 46406.

ARRINGTON, JAMES HUGH D
b. Ozark, Ark, 5/23/04; s. William H. Arrington and Laura T. Fulks A; m. 7/5/30 to Veneta C. Berry; c. Harriet V. (Mrs. Griffith), Aneta (Mrs. Davis) and Laura Berry (Mrs. Nigliazzo). Educ: Ark. Polytech. Col; Okla. State Univ; Sigma Nu; Red Red Rose; Okla. State Univ. Hall of Fame; Okla. State Univ. Pres. Club; Ark. Tech Hall of Distinction. Polit. & Govt. Pos: Chmn, Okla. State Dem. Cent. Cmt, 40-46; Okla. State Rep, 42-60; Dem. nat. committeeman, Okla, 56-68; del, Dem. Nat. Conv, 68. Bus. & Prof. Pos: Pres, Jim Arrington Corp, and Amko Corp; dir, Thomas N. Berry & Co. and Okla. Fracturing Serv: Mem: Okla. City Golf and Country Club; pres, Nat. Happy Groundhog Day Asn; Tower Club; Oklahoma City and Stillwater C. of C; pres, Lyndon Johnson's Pres. Club. Ky. Col; Ark. Traveler; Hon. Citizen of Tenn; appointed hon. Colonel by various Okla. governors. Rel: Presbyterian. Legal Res: 1724 Kingsbury Lane, Oklahoma City, Okla. 73116. Mailing Add: 813 Cravens Building, Oklahoma City, Okla. 73102.

ARRINGTON, WILLIAM RUSSELL R
Ill. State Sen.
b. Gillespie, Ill, 7/4/06; s. William Parnell Arrington and Ethel Louise Fanning A; m. 10/8/32 to Ruth Marian Browne; c. Patricia Lee and Michael Browne. Educ: Univ. Ill, A.B, 28, J.D, 30; Phi Beta Kappa; Phi Eta Sigma; Gamma Eta Gamma. Polit. & Govt. Pos: Ill. State Rep, Fourth Sen. Dist, 44-54, chmn, judiciary cmt, Ill. House Rep, 51-54, mem, Ill. Legis. Cmn. Revise Ill. Constitution Revenue Article, 51; mem. Joint Legis. Cmt. to Revise Ill. Constitutional Judicial Article, 51-53; Ill. State Sen, 54-, Pres. Pro Tempore and Majority Leader, Ill. State Senate, 64-, mem, Ill. Legis. Coun, 55-, chmn, Ill. Legis. Audit Cmn, 57-, mem, Ill. Revenue Laws Study Cmn, 61-63. Bus. & Prof. Pos: Admitted to Ill. Bar, 30; v.pres, dir, and gen. counsel, Combined Ins. Co. Am. and related companies, 39-, secy, 62-; Gen. attorney, Ridgeville Park Dist, Ill, 41-57; acting pres. and dir, Soy Bean Prod. Co, 42-45; sr. mem, Arrington and Healy, Chicago, 44-; dir, Bank of Chicago, 54-; chmn. bd. mgr, Robert R. McCormick Chicago Boys Club, 60-; directorships, Chicago Boys Club, 62-, Am. Found. Relig. and Psychiat, 62-, Found. Study of Cycles, Inc, 62-, Found. Research on Nature of Man, 64-, Ment. Health Asn. Gr. Chicago, Inc, 64-, Alberto-Culver Co, 64-, Stone-Brandel Center, 66- and Evanston Hosp, 68-; mem. adv. cmt, Ill. Masonic Hosp, 64- Mem: Nat. Conf. State Legis. Leaders (exec. cmt, 65-); Nat. Soc. State Legislators (bd. gov, 66-); Nat. Legis. Conf. Intergovt. Rels. Cmt, 65-; Gov. Ill. Revenue Study Cmn, 68-; Adv. Cmn. Intergovt. Rels, 69-; Int. Asn. Ins. Counsel; Am. and Ill. Bar Asns; Chicago Bar Asn.(bd. mgr, 52-54); Ins. Fedn. Ill; U.S. C. of C.(ins. cmt); Law Club; Union League; Econ. Club; Chicago Press Club. Rel: Non-Sectarian. Legal Res: 929 Edgemere Court, Evanston, Ill. 60202. Mailing Add: 135 S. LaSalle St, Chicago, Ill. 60603.

ARRIOLA, JOAQUIN CAMACHO D
Speaker, Guam Legis.
b. Agana, Guam, 12/29/25; s. Vicente Fernandez Arriola and Maria Soledad Sablan Camacho A; m. 2/27/54 to Elizabeth Pangelinan Perez; c. Jacqueline Perez, Vincent Perez, Anita Perez, Elizabeth Perez, Franklin Perez, Michael Perez and Joaquin Camacho, Jr. Educ: St. Thomas Col, B.A. cum laude, 50; Univ. Minn. Law Sch, Minneapolis, J.D, 53; Gamma Eta Gamma. Polit. & Govt. Pos: Sen, Guam Legis, 55-, chmn, judiciary cmt, 57-58, legis. counsel and parliamentarian, 59-64, minority counsel, 66, speaker, 67-; disaster counsel, Small Bus. Asn, 62-; chmn, Guam Housing & Urban Renewal Authority, 63-64; chmn, Territorial Planning Cmn, 63-66; chmn. bd. regents, Col. Guam, 63-66. Bus. & Prof. Pos: Partner, Palting & Arriola Law Off, 53-55; attorney-at-law, 56-58; partner, Arriola, Bohn & Dierking Law Off, Agana, Guam, 58- Mem: Guam Bar Asn.(pres, 56-57); Am. Bar Asn; Admitted to Practice: Guam; Minn; U.S. Court of Appeals for Ninth Circuit; Trust Territory of Pac. Islands; U.S. Supreme Court. Cert. of Appreciation from Selective Serv. Syst; Cert. of Appreciation from Univ. Minn. Law Sch. Rel: Catholic. Legal Res: Tamuning, Guam 96910. Mailing Add: P.O. Box X, Agana, Guam 96910.

ARTERBURN, NORMAN F.
Judge, Supreme Court of Ind.
b. Bicknell, Ind, 5/13/02; s. Clay H. Arterburn and Anna Hoover A; wid; c. Faith (Mrs. Nicholson), Linda (Mrs. Ridgley) and Joan. Educ: Ind. Univ, A.B, 23; Univ. of Chicago Law Sch, J.D. Polit. & Govt. Pos: Prosecuting attorney, 12th Judicial Circuit of Ind, 28-30; mem. and pres, Ind. State Bd. of Law Exam, 38-44; mem. bd. of mgrs, Ind. State Bar Asn, 40-42; Judge, Supreme Court of Ind, 55- Bus. & Prof. Pos: Visiting prof. of law, Ind. State Bar Asn; prof. of law, Washburn Col. Law Sch, 28; attorney, Kessinger, Hill & Arterburn, Hill & Arterburn and Arterburn & Hart, 30-54. Publ: Legal publ. in Ill, Mich, Pa. and Ind. Law J. Mem: Mason (32°); Shrine; Elks; Harmony Club; Columbia Club; Kiwanis; C. of C; mem. bd. of gov, Good Samaritan Hosp. Ky. Col. Rel: Methodist. Mailing Add: 1529 Old Orchard Rd, Vincennes, Ind. 47591.

ARTHUR, ALLEN EDWARD D
b. Orwell, Vt, 10/30/07; m. to Marion B. Carragher; c. two sons. Educ: Albany Bus. Col. Polit. & Govt. Pos: Vt. State Rep, 65-67. Bus. & Prof. Pos: Manufacturer, lamps and furniture. Mem: Mason; Grange; Cairo Temple; Rutland. Rel: Congregational. Mailing Add: Orwell, Vt. 05760. (1967)

ARTHUR, CHARLES SHIRK, JR. R
b. Spirit Lake, Iowa, 7/16/17; s. Charles Shirk Arthur and Anna Pearson A; m. 3/29/44 to Mary Ann Bowen; c. Charles Shirk, III, Robert Bowen, Cynthia Ann, Thomas Pearson and Deborah Louise. Educ: Kans. Univ, B.S. in bus, 39, LL.B, 47; Phi Delta Phi; Alpha Tau Omega. Polit. & Govt. Pos: Co. attorney, Riley Co, Kans, 49-53; chmn, Riley Co. Rep. Orgn, 53-55; city cmnr, Manhattan, 53-57, mayor, 56-57; Kans. State Rep, 57-65, speaker, House of Rep, Kans, 63-65; chmn, State Rep. Platform Cmt, 64; Kans. State Sen, 65-69. Bus. & Prof. Pos: Sr. partner, Arthur and Green, Attorneys, 50- Mil. Serv: Entered as Seaman 2/C, Navy Air Force, 41; released as Lt. Comdr, 45, after serv. in Air Group 9, Pac; Purple Heart; Distinguished Flying Cross with Cluster; Air Medal with 6 Clusters. Mem: Pres, Cent. Kans. Bar Asn, 55-56 and Riley Co. Bar Asn, 53-54; Mason (32°); Shrine; past pres, Rotary; Am. Legion; VFW; Elks. Rel: Methodist. Legal Res: 1704 Fairview, Manhattan, Kans. 66502. Mailing Add: Box 248, Manhattan, Kans. 66502.

ARUNDEL, ARTHUR WINDSOR D
b. Wash, D.C, 1/12/28; s. Russell M. Arundel and Marjorie Sale A; m. 5/17/57 to Margaret Crenshaw McElroy; c. Sally Harwood, Peter Windsor, John Howard and Wendy Sale. Educ: Harvard Univ, B.A, 51; Hasty Pudding and Fox Clubs. Polit. & Govt. Pos: Spec. asst. to U.S. Secy of Commerce, 58-59; mem, Fauquier Co. Dem. Cmt, Va, 63-64; cand. for Va. State Sen, 65; Presidential campaign mgr. for Robert F. Kennedy, Va, 68. Bus. & Prof. Pos: Publisher, Loudoun Times-Mirror Newspaper, Va, 60- Mil. Serv: Entered as 2nd Lt, Marine Corps, 51, released as Capt, 55, after serv. in Korea and Vietnam, Pac. Theatre, 53-55; Presidential Unit Citation, Korea; Korean Serv. Medal; Presidential Award, Vietnam. Publ: The Most Political Night, 58 & A Plan for Higher Education in Northern Virginia, 65, Loudoun Times Publ. Co. Mem: Va. Adv. Legis. Cmt. on 200th Anniversary of Va; chmn, Cmt. on Higher Educ. in North. Va; Nat. Asn. of Broadcasters; Nat. Press Club, Wash; Metrop. Club, Wash; Racquet and Tennis Club, N.Y. Rel: Episcopal. Legal Res: Wildcat Mt. Farm, Warrenton, Va. 22186. Mailing Add: 1204 Rosslyn Bldg, 1901 Ft. Myer Dr, Arlington, Va. 22209.

ARVEY, JACOB M. D
Dem. Nat. Committeeman, Ill.
b. Chicago, Ill, 11/3/95; s. Israel Arvey and Bertha Eisenberg A; m. 6/11/16 to Edith Freeman; c. Erwin, Howard and Helen Sue (Mrs. Bresky). Educ: John Marshall Law Sch; hon. LL.D, Jewish Theol. Sem, 66. Polit. & Govt. Pos: Alderman, 24th Ward, Chicago, Ill, 23-41, committeeman, 34-41; cmnr, Chicago Park Dist, 45-67; chmn, Cook Co. Dem. Party, 46-50; Dem. Nat. Committeeman, Ill, 50-; del, Dem. Nat. Conv, 48, 52, 56, 60, 64 & 68. Bus. & Prof. Pos: Sr. mem, Arvey, Hodes and Mantynband & Predecessor Firms, 26- Mil. Serv: Entered as Capt, Army, 41, released as Lt. Col, 45, after serv. in 33rd Inf. Div, Pac. Theater; Bronze Star with Cluster; Legion of Merit. Publ: Politics, U.S.A; As We Knew Adlai. Mem: Am, Fed, Ill. and Chicago Bar Asns; Am. Friends of the Hebrew Univ; Am. Jewish Joint Distribution Cmt; dir, Assoc. Talmud Torahs of Chicago; B'nai B'rith; dir, Douglas Gardens, Jewish Home for the Aged of Gr. Miami; hon. chmn, State of Israel Bonds; Jewish Nat. Fund; Nat. Adv. Coun. Synagogue Coun. of Am; Nat. Jewish Hosp, Denver; Nat. Jewish Welfare Bd; Jewish War Vet; Am. Vet. Cmt; Am. Legion; 33rd Div. Asn; Navy League; Brandeis Univ; Citizens Bd, Cath. Interracial Coun; Elks; AF&AM; Moose; Covenant Club of Ill; civic cmt, DePaul Univ; chmn. bd, Marina City Bank; Nat. Capital Dem. Club; Nat. Dem. Club; Adlai E. Stevenson Mem. Fund; Univ. Chicago Cancer Research Found. and Found. for Emotionally Disturbed Children; Weizmann Inst. of Sci; Bryn Mawr Country Club, Chicago; Westview Country Club, Miami Beach. Rel: Jewish. Legal Res: 2300 N. Lincoln Park W, Chicago, Ill. 60614. Mailing Add: 1 N. La Salle St, Chicago, Ill. 60602.

ARVIN, LESTER CAVE R
Kans. State Sen.
b. East St. Louis, Ill, 7/22/23; s. James Bartley Arvin and Beulah Ann Peery A; m. 5/13/45 to Kay Krehbiel; c. Scott Brentwood and Reed Richardson. Educ: Ottawa Univ, 40-41; Wichita State Univ, A.B, 47; Washburn Law Sch, J.D, 49; Sigma Delta Phi. Polit. & Govt. Pos: Dep. sheriff, Sedgwick Co, Kans, 46-47; asst, Kans. Attorney Gen. and State Tax Attorney, 47-49; chief counsel, Post Off. and Civil Serv. Cmt, House of Rep, 53; cand, Lt. Gov, Kans, 56 and congressman, Fourth Dist, Kans, 60; chmn, Butler Co. Planning Cmn, 63-69; Kans. State Sen, Eleventh Dist, 69-. Bus. & Prof. Pos: Partner, Mullins & Arvin, Wichita, Kans, 49-53; attorney, State Soldiers Home, Dodge City, Kans, 50-54; sr. partner, Arvin, Arvin & Busey, Wichita, Kans, 53-. Mil. Serv: Entered as Pvt, Army, 41, released as S/Sgt, 45, after serv. in Pac, 41-45; Good Conduct Medal. Mem: Bd. of trustees, Wichita State Univ, 64-68 and Golden Gate Sem, Mills Valley, Calif, 66-; Kans, Am. and Wichita Bar Asns; Am. Legion; VFW; Am. Quarter Horse Asn; Bluestem and Am. Charolais Asns; Mason; Wichita Cosmopolitan Club (pres, 49-50); C. of C. Ambassadors Club (v.pres, 62); bd. of dirs, Franchise to Freedom Found, 67-; Cmt. on Bd, South. Baptist Conv, Nashville, Tenn, 69. Rel: Baptist; Deacon and past mem, Bd. of Trustees, Metrop. Baptist Church. Legal Res: Rural Route 1, Rose Hill, Kans, 67133. Mailing Add: 814 Century Plaza Bldg, Wichita Kans, 67202

ARVIZU, ARTHUR A. D
Mem, Kern Co. Dem. Cent. Cmt, Calif.
b. Arvin, Calif, 2/11/27; s. Arthur Ortiz Arvizu and Rachel Vargas A; m. 8/17/50 to Mary Frances Schemmel; c. Arthur Rahe, Anthony James, Robert John, John Thomas, William Scott and Mary Rachel. Educ: Bakersfield Col, A.A. in Bus. Admin, 48; Alpha Gamma Sigma. Polit. & Govt. Pos: Treas, Kern Co. Dem. Cent. Cmt, 62-64, chmn, 64-66, mem, 66-; mem. exec. cmt, Calif. Dem. Cent. Cmt, 64-66; chmn, Kern Co. Dem. Campaign Cmt, 64 Elec. and 64-66; chmn, Viva Brown Cmt, 66; del, Dem. Nat. Conv, 68; chmn, Kern Co. Econ. Opportunity Corp, 68. Bus. & Prof. Pos: Pres, Kern Co. Fire Dept. Benefit & Welfare Asn, 53; organizing pres, Kern Co. Fire Fighters Union 1301, 58, pres, 63-64, v.pres, 65-; legis. rep, Local 1301, 63-64; chmn, Cent. Calif. Action Assocs, Inc, 68. Mil. Serv: Entered as Seaman 2/C, Navy, 44, released as signalman 3/C, 46, after serv. in Commun. Pool, S.Pac; New Guinea and Philippine Theater Ribbons; Okinawa Campaign Ribbon with Bronze Star; Victory Medal. Rel: Catholic. Mailing Add: 509 Telsin Court, Bakersfield, Calif. 93308.

ASBELL, BERNARD D
b. New York, N.Y, 5/8/23; s. Samuel Asbell and Minnie Zevin A; m. 1/2/44 to Mildred Enid Sacarny; c. Paul, Lawrence, Jonathan and Jordis Elizabeth. Educ; Univ. Conn, 43-44. Polit. & Govt. Pos: Mem, Wilton Town Dem. Cmt, Conn, 63-67, chmn, 64-66; consult, U.S. Off. Econ. Opportunity and Secy. of Health, Educ. and Welfare, 65, U.S. Off. Educ, 65-66. Bus. & Prof. Pos: Author, Books and Mag. Articles, 54-66; consult, Univ. Ill, 64, Ford Found, 65-66 & 68-69, Sci. Res. Assocs, 66. Mil. Serv: Entered as Pvt, Army, 43, released as Sgt, 45, after serv. in Inf, 3rd Serv. Command. Publ: When F.D.R. Died, Holt, Rinehart & Winston, 61; The New Improved American, McGraw-Hill Book Co, 65. Mem: Exec. Coun, Soc. Mag. Writers, 64-, pres, 63; Educ. Writers Asn. 1st Prize for best mag. coverage of educ, Educ. Writers Asn, 65. Mailing Add: 1359 Ridge Rd, North Haven, Conn. 06473.

ASBJORNSON, JULIAN O. 'BOOTS' R
Mont. State Rep.
b. Minneota, Minn, 1/18/11; s. Oscar J. Asbjornson, Sr. and Thora E. Strand A; m. 6/2/34 to Dorothy V. Erickson; c. Norman Harold and Raymond Carl. Educ: Winifred High Sch, Mont, grad, 29; William Hood Dunwoody Inst, Minn, 30-31. Polit. & Govt. Pos: Mayor, Winifred, Mont. and sch. bd. mem, Winifred Schs, 12 years; mem, Cent. Mont. Fair Bd, past 15 years; Mont. State Rep, 11th Dist, Fergus Co, 61-, mem, Appropriations Cmt, Mont. House of Rep, 5 sessions, chmn, Univ. Appropriations Subcmt, 67 & 69, chmn, Pub. Health, Welfare and Safety Cmt, 69, chmn, Fiscal Rev. Cmt. and mem, Property Taxation Study Cmt, 69- Bus. & Prof. Pos: Semi-retired from retail farm equip. bus. Mem: Mason (32°), Great Falls; Shrine, Billings; Elks, Lewistown; Eagles; Mont. Pilots Asn; Fergus Co. Farm Bur. Life mem. contributing to support of Shrine Crippled Children's Hosp. Fund. Rel: Lutheran. Mailing Add: Winifred, Mont. 59489.

ASBRIDGE, BERNICE MURIEL R
State Treas, N.Dak.
b. Arena, N.Dak, 9/7/19; d. Sigurd Olaf Wenaas and Nellie Josephine Jacobson W; m. 3/1/42 to Donald Gene Asbridge, wid; c. Donna Jean (Mrs. Joseph O. LaFave) and Darold Adrien; grandchild, Dawnice Jean LaFave. Educ: Bismarck Pub. Schs, 12 years. Polit. & Govt. Pos: Second dep. auditor, Burleigh Co. Auditor's Off, N.Dak, 55-59, co. auditor and co. zoning dir, 59-69; State Treas, N.Dak, 69- Bus. & Prof. Pos: Bookkeeper, A.W. Lucas Co, Bismarck, N.Dak, 37-42; clerk typist, Civil Serv. appointment and various Army Camps, 42-45, Burleigh Co. Auditor's Off, Bismarck, 45-48, machine bookkeeper, 48-55. Mem: N.Dak. Co. Auditor's Asn.(past pres); N.Dak. Co. Auditor's Legis. Cmt.(past chmn); N.Dak. Co. Off. Policy Planning Cmt.(past chmn); Gov. Adv. Cmt. to Govt. Received Fed. Funds; Civil Defense (Burleigh Co. adminstr); assoc. mem, N.Dak. Co. Cmnr. Asn; N.Dak. Water Users Asn; assoc. mem, N.Dak. Assessor's Asn; Nat. Fedn. of Rep. Women (N.Dak. state prog. chmn); Nat. Asn. State Auditors, Treas. and Comptroller's; Nat. Asn. State Liquor Adminstr; Am. Legion Auxiliary; Bus. & Prof. Women (state legis. chmn); Bismarck Elkettes (past pres); Bismarck Cancer Soc. (secy); assoc. mem, Bismarck-Mandan Exec. Club; Bismarck PTA (past pres. and mem. coun). Rel: Lutheran; adv, High League, Trinity Lutheran Church. Mailing Add: 1210 N. Mandan St, Bismarck, N.Dak. 58501.

ASCOLI, GLORIA JEAN R
Recording Secy, St. Louis Co. Rep. Cent. Cmt, Mo.
b. Albuquerque, N.Mex, 2/7/28; d. Walter E. Kemp and Helene G. Berry; m. 11/28/44 to Fred Ascoli; c. Don Mario, Donna (Mrs. Charles Daniels), Dean, Douglas, David, Deborah and Dale. Educ: High Sch. Polit. & Govt. Pos: Airport Twp. committeewoman, St. Louis Co. Rep. Cent. Cmt, Mo, 63-, recording secy, 64-; alternate del, Rep. Nat. Conv, 64, del, 68; state del, Federated Rep. Womens Conv, 64, 66 & 68; bd. mem, exec. cmt, Airport Twp. Regular Rep. Club, 64-; secy, Rep. Womens Club of St. Louis Co, 65-67, first v.pres, 69-; del, Nat. Womens Rep. Conv, 69. Mem: Mo. Fedn. Womens Clubs (secy, 8th dist, 66-67, jr. dir, 8th dist, 68-69, pres, crafts and hobbies club, 68-). Rel: Lutheran. Mailing Add: 12625 Weskan Lane, Bridgeton, Mo. 63042.

ASH, RICHARD A. D
b. Phila, Pa, 11/26/26; s. Benjamin Ash and Rae Peikas A; single. Educ: Lehigh Univ, B.A. & B.S. Elec. Eng, 51; Univ. Mich, M.A, 54; Univ. Pa. Law Sch, LL.B, 64; Pi Lambda Phi. Polit. & Govt. Pos: Del, Dem. Nat. Conv, 68; Consumer Party cand. for dist. attorney, Phila, Pa, 69. Bus. & Prof. Pos: Instr. grad. course data processing, Ariz. State Univ, $1\frac{1}{2}$ years; computer syst. analyst, Univac Div, Sperry Rand Corp, Phila, Pa, 54-61; attorney, Freedman, Borowsky & Lorry, 65-66; staff attorney, Commun. Legal Serv, 66-69; attorney-at-law, 69- Mil. Serv: Entered as Seaman 1/C, Navy, 54, released as Elec. Tech. 2/C, 46, after serv. in Naval Elec. Tech. Prog; Lt.(jg), Naval Res.(Ret); Am. Theatre Medal; World War II Victory Medal. Mem: Phila. and Pa. Bar Asns. Mailing Add: The Plaza, Apt. 12A, 18th and The Parkway, Philadelphia, Pa. 19103.

ASHBACH, ARLENE DELORES 'RONNIE' R
b. Minneapolis, Minn, 12/4/23; d. George Cameron Peterson and Agnes Augusta Martinson P; m. 8/1/42 to Bernard Nickolas Ashbach; c. Sandra, Diana, Bernard, Jr, Steven, Susan, Gregory and Richard. Educ: Central High Sch, St. Paul, Minn, grad, 41; Art courses, exten. and adult educ, 54-63. Polit. & Govt. Pos: Mem, N-T-N Cmt, Roseville, Minn, 58-60; del, Rep. State Conv, 60 & 63-68; ward secy, Roseville Rep. Cmt, 60; v.chairwoman, Wash. Co. Rep. Cmt, 63-65, chairwoman, 65-68; chmn, Washington Co. N-T-N Fund Drive, 63 & 64; alternate del, Rep. Nat. Conv, 68; co-chmn. vol. Minn. Nixon for Pres. Cmt, 68. Mem: Nat. Ceramic Asn.(teacher); Arts and Ceramics League of Minn; Leader, Lake Owasso 4-H Club, 48-53; Eastern Star. 4-H Leader Award; N-T-N Award for Wash. Co, from Minnesota Rep. Cmt, 64. Rel: Lutheran. Legal Res: Green Hill Farm, Route 1, Box 557, Forest Lake, Minn. 55025. Mailing Add: 1004 Shady Lane, Dubuque, Iowa 52001.

ASHBACH, ROBERT O. R
Minn. State Sen.
Polit. & Govt. Pos: Formerly Minn. State Rep; Minn. State Sen, 67- Bus. & Prof. Pos: Pres, construction co. Mailing Add: 1585 Johanna Blvd, St. Paul, Minn. 55113. (1967)

ASHBROOK, JOHN MILAN R
U.S. Rep, Ohio
b. Johnstown, Ohio, 9/21/28; s. William A. Ashbrook and Marie Swank A; m. 7/3/48 to Joan Eilene Needels; c. Barbara, Laura and Madeline. Educ: Harvard Univ, B.S. with honors, 52; Ohio State Law Sch, J.D, 55; Ashland Col, LL.D, 63; Delta Theta Phi; Sigma Delta Chi. Polit. & Govt. Pos: Precinct committeeman, Johnstown Rep. Party, Ohio, 54-; chmn, Licking Co. Rep. Cent. Cmt, 56-60 and Young Rep. Nat. Fedn, 57-59; Ohio State Rep, 57-60; chmn, Ohio League Young Rep, 55; U.S. Rep, 17th Dist, 61- Bus. & Prof. Pos: Publisher, Johnstown Independent, 53-; spec. counsel to Attorney Gen. of Ohio, 55-57; attorney-at-law, 55- Mil. Serv: Navy, 46-48; mem, Byrd Antarctic Exped, 46-47. Mem: Mason (32°); K. of P; Kiwanis; Elks; Lions. Named as one of 15 Outstanding Young Men in Politics in U.S. by Sen. Paul Douglas, Esquire Magazine, 1958. Rel: Baptist. Mailing Add: 87 N. Main St, Johnstown, Ohio 43031.

ASHBY, MILTON D
Constitutional Officer, Ky. House of Rep.
b. Slaughters, Ky, 7/27/90; s. William Finley Ashby and Elizabeth Williams A;

m. 4/4/17 to Augusta May Jackson; c. Derrill S, Ethelyn (Mrs. Streets), Charles, Wendell R. and Frank S. Educ: McLean Col, 08-12. Polit. & Govt. Pos: Councilman, Sebree, Ky; mem, Sebree Springs Park Bd; mem, Sebree Sch. Bd; postmaster, Sebree, 34-60; Ky. State Rep, Webster and McLean Co, 62-66; Constitutional officer, Ky. House of Rep, 66- Mem: Pres, Nat. Postmaster League, 50-54; Farm Bureau; Mason; Dem. Club of Ky. Rel: Christian Church. Mailing Add: 127 S. Church St, Sebree, Ky. 42455. (1967)

ASHE, VICTOR HENDERSON R
Tenn. State Rep.
b. Knoxville, Tenn, 1/1/45; s. Robert L. Ashe and Martha Henderson A; single. Educ: The Hotchkiss Sch, Lakeville, Conn, 61-63; Yale, B.A, 67; Univ. Tenn. Law Sch, student, 69- Polit. & Govt. Pos: Aide to Dan H. KuyKendall, 64; intern under U.S. Rep. Bill Brock, 65; press aide to U.S. Sen, Howard H. Baker, Jr, 66 and legis. aide, 67; Tenn. State Rep, 68- Mil. Serv: Entered as Pvt, Marines, 67, released as Pfc, 68, after serv. in Air Wing, San Diego, Memphis, and Jacksonville; Marine Air Res, 68-, Pfc. Mem: Civitan Club of Knoxville; Dulin Art Gallery. Rel: Baptist. Mailing Add: 3709 Kingston Pike, Knoxville, Tenn. 37519.

ASHEIM, JOHN VERNON R
b. Mohall, N.Dak, 6/13/23; s. John P. Asheim and Serena Dokken A; m. 2/21/45 to Carole Derr; c. John Richard and Donna Jean. Educ: N.Dak. State Univ, 40-43; Alpha Gamma Rho; Saddle and Sirloin; Lutheran Students Asn; N.Dak. State Univ. Mixed Chorus and Men's Glee Club. Polit. & Govt. Pos: Treas, Renville Twp, N.Dak, 48-; clerk, Renville Sch. Dist, 25, 52-63; precinct committeeman, Bottineau Co. Rep. Party, 62-, v.chmn, 62-64 and chmn, 64-68; chmn, Sixth Legis. Dist. Rep. Party, 65- Bus. & Prof. Pos: Farm dir, Greater N.Dak. Asn, 64- Mil. Serv: Entered as Pvt, Army Air Force, 42, released as 1st Lt, 46, after serv. in 89th Fighter Squadron, 80th Fighter Group, China-Burma-India, 45. Mem: Am. Legion; Mason; N.Dak. Stockmen's Asn; U.S. Durum Grower's Asn; legis. cmt, Farm Bur, 63; Farmer's Union; pres, Renville-Bottineau Agr. Improv. Asn, 63, dir. for 6 years; pres, Mohall Band Boosters, 62; pres, Bottineau Co. 4-H Coun, 63, 4-H Club leader, Renville Livestock Farmers, 46-63; state v.pres, Future Farmers of Am, 41; Mohall Country Club; PTA; N.Dak. State Univ. Alumni Asn. Outstanding Young Farmer in N.Dak, Jaycees, 59. Rel: Lutheran. Mailing Add: Mohall, N.Dak. 58761. (1967)

ASHEN, PETE R
Sgt. at Arms, San Francisco Co. Rep. Cent. Cmt.
b. Bakersfield, Calif, 9/20/27; s. Claude Holbert Ashen and Lotta Mae McElroy A; m. 12/28/47 to Catherine Irene Grandin; c. Claude Frank and Mary Catherine. Polit. & Govt. Pos: Pres, Calif. Young Rep, 61; v.chmn, Nat. Fedn. of Young Rep, 61-63; sgt. at arms, San Francisco Co. Rep. Cent. Cmt, 68- Bus. & Prof. Pos: Sales mgr, Milo Harding Co, 52-60; agent, John Hancock Mutual Life Ins. Co, 60-66; dir, disaster serv, Golden Gate Chap, Am. Nat. Red Cross, 66- Mil. Serv: Entered as Seaman, Navy, 45-48 & 50-52, released as Aviation Tech. 1st/C, after serv. in VP-2, Pac. and Far East. Mem: F&AM. Rel: Protestant. Mailing Add: 67 Cityview Way, San Francisco, Calif. 94131.

ASHER, JANICE ALORA D
b. Denver, Colo, 4/26/46; d. Joseph Benjamin Asher and Lucille Sarah King A; single. Educ: Portland State Univ, currently. Polit. & Govt. Pos: Del, Dem. Nat. Conv, 68; exec. asst. to state chmn, Dem. Party, Ore, 68- Mem: Kennedy Action Corps. Rel: Unitarian. Mailing Add: 1426 S.E. 32nd Place, Portland, Ore. 97214.

ASHLER, PHILIP FREDERIC D
b. N.Y.C, 10/15/14; s. Philip Ashler and Charlotte Barth A; m. 6/21/69 to Elise Barrett Duvall; c. Jeffries Duvall, Philip F, Jr, Richard Duvall, Robert Porter and Richard Harrison. Educ: St. John's Univ, B.B.A. cum laude, 35; Harvard Univ, M.B.A, 37; Indust. Col. of Armed Forces, grad, 56; Univ. Fla, grad. work, 64; Delta Mu Delta. Hon. LL.D, Univ. West Fla, 69; Sc.D, Fla. Inst. Tech, 69. Polit. & Govt. Pos: Dir, Off. of Small Bus, Dept. of Defense, 48-51; chmn, Gov. Adv. Cmt, Law Enforcement Educ, Fla, 62-65; Fla. State Rep, 63-68; chmn, Fla. Civil Defense Adv. Bd, 65-69; chmn. Fla. Adv. Cmt, Hospitalization for Indigent, 65-; mem, Gov. cmn. for Qual. Educ, 67-68; vice chancellor, State Univ. Syst. of Fla, 68- Bus. & Prof. Pos: Dir. develop, Pensacola Jr. Col. Found, 61-68, exec. dir, 65-68; consult, Fla. Educ. Asn. and Pensacola Police Dept, 63-; dir, Fla. First Nat. Bank, Pensacola, 64-68. Mil. Serv: Entered as Pvt, Marine Corps Res, 32, retired as Rear Adm, Navy, 59, after 22 years in active duty in all theaters; Bronze Star with Combat V; Korean Presidential Citation with Cluster; Korean Serv. Medal with Marine Corps Combat Distinguished Device; UN Medal; Am, European and Asiatic Theater Ribbons; Am. Defense Medal; Victory Medal. Publ: 'Small Business and Defense Contracts,' Harvard Bus. Rev, 5/51; 'Military Survivors Benefits,' Indust. Col. Armed Forces, 56. Mem: Cmnr, Educ. Cmn. of States; Legis Adv. Coun, Bd. Control South. Regional Educ; past pres, Pan Am. Coun; Fla. Educ. Coun; bd. gov, Pensacola Symphony, 61-62; bd. trustees, Pensacola Art Asn, 61-62; past pres, W.Fla. Heart Asn; secy. and chmn. bd. of dirs, Fla. Heart Asn; bd. of dirs, Escambia Co. Commun. Coun, 61; bd. of gov, Fiesta of Five Flags, 60-63; bd. of dirs, Navy League, 60-63; bd. of dirs, Easter Seal Soc, People to People Prog, Jr. Achievement, United Fund and Pearl S. Buck Found; ed. adv. bd, Fla. Lives; hon. life mem, Nat. Asn. Supvr; Indust. Mgt. Asn; Nat. Asn. Educ. Broadcasters; Mason (32°); Shrine ; Sojourners; Elks; Capitol City Country Club. Most Effective Del, Fla. Legis, 65; Nominated Most Valuable Fla. State Rep, 67. Rel: Episcopal. Mailing Add: Board of Regents, State University System of Fla, 210 Collins Bldg, Tallahassee, Fla. 32304.

ASHLEY, GENE M. R
b. Amma, W.Va, 11/3/20; s. Waitman T. Ashley and Icie Carper A; m. 2/14/47 to Kathleen Harris; c. Mary Jo and Robert Gene. Educ: Morris Harvey Col. Polit. & Govt. Pos: Chmn, Roane Co. Rep. Exec. Cmt, W.Va, 2 years; W.Va. State Del, 60-69. Bus. & Prof. Pos: Employee, chem. plant. Mil. Serv: Army, 301st Engrs, 76th Div, World War II, 3 years. Mem: Mason (32°); Scottish Rite. Rel: Methodist. Mailing Add: Amma, W.Va. 25005. (1967)

ASHLEY, THOMAS LUDLOW D
U.S. Rep, Ohio
b. Toledo, Ohio, 1/11/23; s. Meredith Ashley and Alida A. Educ: Yale Univ, B.A, 48; Univ. Toledo Law Sch; Ohio State Univ, LL.B, 51. Polit. & Govt. Pos: With Toledo Publicity and Efficiency Cmn, Ohio, 48; U.S. Rep, Ninth Dist, 54-; del, Dem. Nat. Conv, 68. Bus & Prof. Pos: Lawyer, Whitehouse, Ohio, 51-52; co-dir. press sect. and then asst. dir. spec. projs, Radio Free Europe, 52-54. Mil. Serv: Entered Army, 42, released as Cpl, 46, after serv. in Pac. Theater, 43-45. Legal Res: South River Rd, Waterville, Ohio 43566. Mailing Add: Rayburn Office Bldg, Washington, D.C. 20515.

ASHMORE, ROBERT THOMAS D
b. Greenville Co, S.C, 2/22/04; s. John Thomas Ashmore and Lena Smith A; m. to Willie Vance Linthicum; c. Nancy Vance. Educ: Furman Univ. Law Sch, 27. Polit. & Govt. Pos: Solicitor, Greenville Co, S.C, 30; solicitor, 13th Judicial Circuit S.C, 36-53; U.S. Rep, S.C, 53-69. Bus. & Prof. Pos: Lawyer, Greenville, 28- Mil. Serv: Army, 42-46; Col, Res. Mem: Dir, v.pres. and pres, Greenville Jaycees; organizer and first pres, State Jr. C. of C; v.pres, U.S. Jr. C. of C; charter mem, past pres, Greenville Exchange Club; Jr. Order United Am. Mech; Elks; Odd Fellows; WOW; Am. Legion; ROA; Men's Garden Club of Greenville. Rel: Baptist. Mailing Add: Manly Dr, Route 9, Greenville, S.C. 29609.

ASHTON, WILLIAM H. R
b. Phila, Pa, 12/24/04; s. Thomas Ashton and Mary Henszey A; m. to Ann Shippen Pepper. Educ: Princeton Univ. Polit. & Govt. Pos: Pa. State Rep, 52-69. Bus. & Prof. Pos: Farmer. Mailing Add: Delchester Farms, Edgemont, Pa. 19028. (1967)

ASHWORTH, KEITH D
Nev. State Assemblyman
b. Kimberly, Nev, 9/4/24; s. John Earl Ashworth and Mary Jane Oxborrow A; m. 4/21/45 to Colleen Christensen; c. Glen Alan, Kenneth Earl and Brian Keith. Educ: Butler Univ, 45-46; Univ. Utah, 46-47. Polit. & Govt. Pos: Pub. adminstr, Clark Co, Nev, 50-54; mem, Las Vegas Youth Adv. Coun, 58-64; secy, State Bd. of Acct, 60-66; Nev. State Assemblyman, Dist. 4, currently. Mil. Serv: Entered as Aviation Cadet, Air Force, 43, released as Flight Officer, 45, after serv. in Pilot Schs, Training Command. Mem: Committeeman, Nat. Soc. Pub. Acct, 65, pres, 57 & 59; past pres, Jaycees; past Exalted Ruler, Elks; Mason, Shrine; Rotary. Outstanding Young Man of Las Vegas and Nev, 1958. Rel: Latter-day Saint. Mailing Add: 674 E. Oakey Blvd, Las Vegas, Nev. 89105.

ASKEW, REUBIN O'D. D
Fla. State Sen.
b. Muskogee, Okla, 9/11/28; m. to Donna Lou Harper; c. Angela Adair and Kevin O'Donovan. Educ: Fla. State Univ, B.S, 51; Denver Univ; Univ. Fla, LL.B, 56. Polit. & Govt. Pos: Asst. co. solicitor of Escambia Co, 56-58; Fla. State Rep, 58-62; Fla. State Sen, 62-, pres. pro tem, Fla. State Senate. Bus. & Prof. Pos: Attorney-at-law. Mil. Serv: Army Paratroopers, Air Force. Mem: York Rite Mason; AAONMS; Hadji Temple; Rotary; past pres, West. Div. of Children's Home Soc. of Fla. and Pensacola Oratorio Soc; YMCA; Am. Legion. One of Fla. Five Outstanding Young Men in 60 selected by state Jaycees; voted by Legis. Press Corps as One of Ten Outstanding House Mem, 61 and One of the Four Outstanding Mem. of the 65 and 67 Senate; runner-up for Most Valuable Mem. of the Senate, 65 & 67. Rel: Presbyterian. Mailing Add: 250 Professional Bldg, Pensacola, Fla. 32501.

ASLETT, LEONA D
Chmn, Jerome Co. Dem. Cent. Cmt, Idaho
b. Cash, Idaho, 8/17/09; d. Raymond G. Leatham and Susan Evelyn Porter L; m. 12/30/25 to David Leon Aslett; c. Marvin and Lorraine (Mrs. Richard Kerruish). Educ: High Sch, Pocatello, Idaho, 1 year. Polit. & Govt. Pos: Pres, Idaho Young Dem, 44-48; secy-treas, Jerome Co. Dem. Cent. Cmt, Idaho, 46-50, committeewoman, 52-56 and chmn, 68-; pres, Jerome Co. Dem. Womens Club, 68- Bus. & Prof. Pos: Office dep, Jerome Co. Sheriff Office, Idaho, 48-50; dent. asst, Dr. F.J. Supple, 50-58; secy-treas. and office mgr, Circle "A" Construction, Inc, 54-68; secy-treas. and office mgr, Triple "A" Construction, Inc, 60- Mem: Dent. Asst. Asn; Bus. & Prfnl. Women; co. chmn, infantile paralysis, 17 years; Civic Club; Neighborhood Club; Jerome Co. Dem. Womans Club. Rel: Latter-day Saint. Mailing Add: Box 68, Jerome, Idaho 83338.

ASPINALL, OWEN STEWART D
b. Grand Junction, Colo, 9/21/27; s. Wayne N. Aspinall and Julia Kuns A; m. 12/24/66 to Taotafa Lutu; c. Robert Stewart. Educ: Univ. Denver, B.A. in Anthrop, 49; Am. Univ, Wash, D.C, LL.B, 55; Beta Theta Pi; Delta Theta Phi. Polit. & Govt. Pos: Dep. dist. attorney, Mesa Co, Colo, 57-61; Attorney Gen, Am. Samoa, 61-62, Territorial Secy, 62-67, Gov, 67-69. Mil. Serv: Army, 44-46, with 504th Parachute Inf. Regt, 82nd Airborne Div. Mem: Am, Wash, D.C. and Colo. Bar Asns; past dist. gov, Lions Int; Am. Legion. Rel: Methodist. Mailing Add: Grand Junction, Colo. 81501.

ASPINALL, WAYNE NORVIEL D
U.S. Rep, Colo.
b. Middleburg, Ohio, 4/3/96; s. Mack Aspinall and Jessie Edna Norviel A; m. to Julia E. Kuns (deceased); c. Wayne Norviel, Owen Stewart, Richard Daniel and Ruth Joanne. Educ: Univ. Denver, B.A, 19; Denver Law Sch, LL.B, 25; Univ. Alaska; Univ. Denver State Univ, LL.D. Polit. & Govt. Pos: App. to Mo. Basin Surv. Cmn. by President Truman; Colo. State Rep, 31-38, Speaker, Colo. House of Rep, 37; Colo. State Sen, 39-48; U.S. Rep, Colo, currently. Bus. & Prof. Pos: Lawyer; Peach Orchard Indust. Mil. Serv: Army, Signal Corps, World War I; Capt, Assigned to Mil. Gov. Serv, World War II, Legal Expert with U.S. and Eng. Forces, participated in Normandy Dr. as Am. Officer with Brit. Second Army. Mem: Am, Colo. and Mesa Co. Bar Asns; Am. Legion; 40 et 8; Mason (33°); K.T; Shrine; Odd Fellows; Elks; Lions. Rel: Methodist. Legal Res: Palisade, Colo. 81526. Mailing Add: 4201 Cathedral Ave. N.W, Washington, D.C. 20016. (1967)

ASPINWALL, JAMES HAMILTON, III D
b. Bridgeport, Conn, 3/10/30; s. James Hamilton Aspinwall, Jr. and Mary McIntyre A; m. 12/29/55 to Marion Elizabeth Hill; c. James H, Charles J,

Timothy P, Mary E. and M. Judith. Educ: Fairfield Univ, B.A, 52; Univ. Conn. Sch. of Law, LL.B, 55. Polit. & Govt. Pos: Chmn, State Claims Cmn, Hartford, Conn, 59-; councilman, Stratford, 61-63; chmn, Stratford Dem. Party, 66-69. Bus. & Prof. Pos: Mem. staff, Paul V. McNamara, Attorney, Bridgeport, Conn, 59-61; attorney-at-law, Stratford, 61- Mil. Serv: Entered as Officer Cand. S/A, Naval Res, 55, released as Lt.(jg), 58, after serv. in Naval Control, Shipping Off, Bahrain Island, Persian Gulf, 1 year and Naval Air Facility, Naples, Italy, 20 months. Mem: Bridgeport and Conn. Bar Asns. Rel: Roman Catholic. Legal Res: 182 Dover St, Stratford, Conn. 06497. Mailing Add: 3589 Main St, Stratford, Conn. 06497.

ASSMAN, JOSEPH JAMES R
b. Winner, S.Dak, 8/9/23; s. William Charles Assman and Isabelle Coyle A; m. 10/18/47 to Esther Elizabeth Einspahr; c. Gregory James, Christopher Joe, Edwin Louis, Bradley Thomas, David Tracy, Michael Scott and Mary Beth. Educ: Winner High Sch, S.Dak. Polit. & Govt. Pos: Committeeman, S.Dak. Rep. State Cmt, 61-62; chmn, Todd Co. Rep. Cent. Cmt, 63-67. Bus. & Prof. Pos: Chmn, Assman Realty Co, Winner, S.Dak, 57-; Producers, Inc, White River, 66-69; treas, Fed. Investment Corp, Rapid City, 66-; chmn, Assman Implement Co, Mission, 69. Mem: Elks; K. of C.(4°); Nat. Farm Orgn; S.Dak. Stockgrowers Asn. Rel: Catholic. Mailing Add: Mission, S.Dak. 57555.

ASTLE, ORRIN WILFORD R
b. Grover, Wyo, 12/3/06; s. William Wilford Astle and Elizabeth Shaw A; m. 12/24/32 to Ruth Whitear; c. Marilyn (Mrs. Peterson), Wilford Bevan, Nedra (Mrs. Peterson), Glen Arthur, Ralph Vernon and Richard Kent. Educ: Utah State Univ, M.Ed. Polit. & Govt. Pos: Past chmn, Morgan Co. Rep. Party, Utah. Mem: Morgan Educ. Asn,(pres); Utah Farm Bur. Silver Beaver, Boy Scouts. Rel: Latter-day Saint. Mailing Add: RFD Box 136, Morgan, Utah 84050.

ASTREDO, JANE ANN R
b. Fullerton, Calif, 1/20/38; d. Ernest H. McCracken and Anna Nielsen M; m. 10/4/57 to Calvin Leo Astredo; c. Ane Kristine and Patrick Michael. Educ: Stephens Col, A.A, 56; student, Calif. State Col, Dominguez Hills, currently. Polit. & Govt. Pos: Mem, Calif. Rep. State Cent. Cmt, until 69. Mem: Paramount Rep. Women's Club; Nat. Cong. of Parents and Teachers. Rel: Episcopal. Mailing Add: 15722 Georgia, Paramount, Calif. 90723.

ATCHISON, JAMES WILBUR D
Chmn, Cooke Co. Dem. Party, Tex.
b. Gainesville, Tex, 3/26/08; s. John Arthur Atchison, Sr. and Katherine Sweeney A; m. 7/4/36 to Lois Usrey. Educ: Tex. Christian Univ, B.S, 30; Univ. Tex. Galveston, M.D, 35; Scholarship Soc. South; Phi Chi. Polit. & Govt. Pos: Chmn, Cooke Co. Dem. Party, Tex, 66- Bus. & Prof. Pos: Med. exam, Cooke Co. Selective Serv. Bd, 26 years; chief of staff, Gainesville Mem. Hosp, Tex, 64- Mil. Serv: Entered as 1st Lt, Army Res, released as Capt, 41, after serv. in 36th Div. Mem: Cooke Co. Med. Soc.(pres); N.Tex. Med. Asn.(pres, 52); Tex. Med. Asn; Am. Med. Asn; Dallas and River Valley Country Clubs; Leeper Lake Club. Rel: Episcopal. Legal Res: 515 Lindsay, Gainesville, Tex. 76240. Mailing Add: 215 S. Commerce, Gainesville, Tex. 76240.

ATCHISON, JEANNINE COWELL D
Mem, Colo. Dem. State Cent. Cmt.
b. Toledo, Ohio, 5/13/29; d. Charles Ellis Cowell and Frances Lindbeck C; m. 8/15/52 to Philip Atchison; c. Timothy and Amy. Educ: Univ. Colo, Boulder, A.B, 51; Univ. Colo, Denver Center, grad. student, 66-; Pi Gamma Mu; Alpha Phi. Polit. & Govt. Pos: Mem, Cmts. to Elect. Stevenson, Robert F. Kennedy and McCarthy, 57-68; del, Colo. and Denver Co. Dem. Conv, 66 & 68; precinct committeewoman, Precinct 13A, Denver Dem. Party, 66-; mem, New Dem. Coalition, Denver, 69; mem, Colo. Dem. State Cent. Cmt; 69- Bus. & Prof. Pos: Sales engr, Pa. Indust. Instruments Corp, Phila, 52-55. Mem: Denver Art Mus; bd, Expanding Opportunities; founding mem. and former bd. mem, Friends of Contemporary Art; human rels. chmn, Ellis Sch. PTA, 68-69; Denver Fair Housing Center. Rel: Episcopal. Mailing Add: 1353 S. Eudora St, Denver, Colo. 80222.

ATCHISON, RAYMOND LEE R
N.Mex. State Sen.
b. 1913. Polit. & Govt. Pos: Mem, Bd. of Educ, N.Mex, 6 years, co. cmnr, 4 years; N.Mex. State Rep, until 66; N.Mex. State Sen, 67- Bus. & Prof. Pos: Contractor in hwy. construction. Mem: Mason; Shrine; Elks; Rotary. Rel: Methodist. Mailing Add: P.O. Drawer D, Aztec, N.Mex. 87410. (1967)

ATHERTON, L. HOWARD, JR. D
Ga. State Rep.
b. Atlanta, Ga, 10/23/26; s. Lucius Howard Atherton, Sr. and Georgia Mary Davis A; m. 9/4/48 to Elizabeth de Garis; c. Jim, Nancy and Mary Frances. Educ: Univ. of Ga, B.S, 49; Sigma Nu; Int. Fraternity Coun. Polit. & Govt. Pos: Former city councilman, Marietta, Ga, mayor, 64-; seventh dist. pres, chmn. of legis. cmt, second v.pres. and pres, Ga. Munic. Asn; pres, Cobb Co. Munic. Asn; v.chmn, Metrop. Atlanta Coun. of Local Govt; assoc. in urban affairs, Nat. Inst. of Pub. Affairs; mem, Atlanta Area Transportation Policy Cmt; Ga. State Rep, Dist. 117, Post 3, 64-. Bus. & Prof. Pos: Registered pharmacist, Ga, 49-; gen. mgr. and pharmacist, retail drug stores, Marietta ans Smyrna, Ga. Mil. Serv: Entered as Seaman 2/C, Navy, 44, released as Radio man 3/C, 46, after serv. in U.S.S. Los Angeles, S.Pac, 44-46; Seventh Fleet Oper. Badges and Citations. Mem: Cobb Co. chmn, Am. Cancer Soc; exec. cmt, Kennestone Hosp. Guild; Cobb Co. Bd. of Health; Ga. Hosp. Adv. Cmn; Metrop. Atlanta Coun. of Health; Ga. Pharmaceutical Asn; Seventh Dist. Pharmaceutical Asn; Kiwanis (pres, Marietta Club); Marietta Country Club (pres); C. of C. (mem. exec. cmt, Cobb Co. Chap); Univ. of Ga. Alumni Soc. (Cobb Co. Chmn); Marietta Touchdown Club; Cobb-Marietta Boys' Club (adv. bd); co-chmn, Joint Tech-Ga. Develop. Fund; exec. cmt, Cobb Co. Youth Mus, united appeal chmn, Marietta City Govt; chmn, City of Marietta Bd. of Lights and Water Works; Cobb-Marietta City Govt; chmn, City of Marietta Bd. of Lights and Water Works; Cobb-Marietta Performing Arts Adv. Bd; bd. of trustees, State of Ga. Joint Munic. Employee's Retirement Fund; adv. bd, YWCA; bd. of dirs, YMCA; Cobb 100 (exec. cmt). Recipient of third annual award for distinguished local govt. serv. in Metrop. Atlanta, Atlanta Region Metrop. Planning Cmn. Rel: Methodist; lifelong mem, bd. of stewards, Marietta First Methodist Church. Mailing Add: 848 Graymont Rd, N.W, Marietta, Ga. 30060.

ATHEY, TYRAS S. D
Md. State Del.
b. Burtonsville, Md, 3/30/27; s. Joseph Tyras Athey and Harriett Dowling A; m. 11/19/50 to Dorothy Norine O'Lexey; c. Darlene, Bryan and Cathleen. Educ: Pub. elem. and high schs, 33-45. Polit. & Govt. Pos: Md. State Del, 67- Bus. & Prof. Pos: Self-employed restaurant bus, Old Farm Inn, Md, 55- Mil. Serv: Entered as HA 2/C, Navy, 43, released as HA 1/C, 45, after serv. aboard U.S.S. Constellation, 44-45. Mem: Optimist Club; Lions; C. of C; Elks; Vol. Fire Dept; Md. Jousting and Tournament Asn. Rel: Protestant. Mailing Add: Box 379F, Route 2, Jessup, Md. 20794.

ATKIN, SIDNEY JOSEPH R
Utah State Rep.
b. St. George, Utah, 7/26/34; s. Rudger C. Atkin and Leona Cox A; m. 6/29/57 to Mary Ann Hunt; c. Shauna, Natalie, Tracy, Maurice, Cory and Kelly. Educ: Dixie Jr. Col, 57-59. Polit. & Govt. Pos: Chmn, Wash. Co. Rep. Party, Utah, 67-69; Utah State Rep, 69- Bus. & Prof. Pos: Pres, Sugar Loaf Cafe, Corp, 58- Mil. Serv: Entered as Pvt, Nat. Guard, 53, released as Sgt. 1/C, 58, after serv. in Battery B 213 FAT. Mem: Utah State Restaurant Asn; Nat. Restaurant Asn; Kiwanis; pres, St. George C. of C, 60-61; Dixie Colonels. Eagle Scout; Outstanding Bus. Student, Dixie Col, 58. Rel: Latter-day Saint. Mailing Add: 46 N. 200 East, St. George, Utah 84770.

ATKINS, Z. D. D
Pub. Serv. Cmnr, Tenn.
b. Weakley Co, Tenn, 11/28/06; m. to Peggy Horne; c. Mrs. Joe Lackey, Jr. Educ: Bethel Col; Memphis State Col; Ohio State Univ; South. Univ. Col. of Law. Polit. & Govt. Pos: Tenn. State Rep, 35; W.Tenn. dist. dir, Nat. Youth Admin, 35-41; Tenn. State Sen, 2 terms; cmnr, Finance and Taxation Tenn, 53-58; pub. serv. cmnr, Tenn, 64- Bus. & Prof. Pos: Lawyer. Mil. Serv: Navy. Mem: Past comdr, Am. Legion Post 35; Mason (32°); Shrine. Rel: Methodist. Mailing Add: Public Service Commission, C-1 110 Cordell Hull Bldg, 436 Sixth Ave. N, Nashville, Tenn. 37219.

ATKINSON, BEVERLY MOON R
Committeewoman, Ohio Rep. State Cent. Cmt.
b. Warren, Ohio, 4/25/24; d. Henry A. Moon and Frances Lehman M; m. 5/13/44 to Charles F. Atkinson; c. Thomas Temple and Amy Allen. Educ: Am. Inst. of Banking, Youngstown, Ohio, 2 years. Polit. & Govt. Pos: Rep. exec. committeeman, Fourth Ward, Warren, Ohio, 60-62; Rep. precinct committeeman, Warren 4-C, 60-64; del, Ohio State Conv, 66 & 68; committeewoman, Ohio Rep. State Cent. Cmt, 66-; chmn, Women for Nixon-Agnew, 19th Cong. Dist, 68; alternate del, Rep. Nat. Conv, 68; Rep. precinct committeeman, Warren 3-B, 68-; Rep. exec. committeeman, Third Ward, Warren, 68- Mem: Trumbull Co. Bar Auxiliary (past pres); Martha Kenney Cooper Ohioana Libr. Asn.(co-chmn); Am. Legion Auxiliary; PTA (past officer); YWCA; Girl Scouts; Vis. Nurses; Women's Rep. Clubs. Rel: Baptist; Deaconess, former Sunday Sch. teacher. Mailing Add: 530 Oak Knoll N.E, Warren, Ohio 44483.

ATKINSON, DOROTHY WRIGHT D
Treas, Dem. Cent. Cmt, Wash, D.C.
b. Wash, D.C, 10/31/11; d. John L. Wright and Mary Letitia Ferguson W; m. 6/23/30 to Judge R. R. Atkinson; c. Richard R, Jr. and Karl S. Educ: Howard Univ, A.B. and M.A; Columbia Univ, grad. study toward a Ph.D; Kappa Mu; Delta Sigma Theta. Polit. & Govt. Pos: Asst. treas, Dem. Cent. Cmt, Wash, D.C, 63-65, treas. and liaison officer, Precincts 73, 74, 75 and 76, currently. Bus. & Prof. Pos: Sr. high sch. teacher, Wash, D.C, 32-48; col. instr, Teachers Col, 48-50. Mem: League of Women Voters; Urban League; Barristers' Wives; Am. Asn. of Univ. Women; Lawyers Wives; Woman's Nat. Dem. Club. Rel: Baptist. Mailing Add: 422 Fifth St. S.E, Washington, D.C. 20003. (1967)

ATKINSON, FRANCES HALL R
Dep. State V.Chmn, Region II, Tex. Rep. Party
b. Lufkin, Tex, 8/17/25; d. Walter Edward Hall and Ida Perry H; m. 6/22/49 to Basil Eric Atkinson, Jr; c. Dennis, Clarinda, Eric and Amy. Educ: Tex. Christian Univ, B.A, 46; Stephen F. Austin Univ, Teacher's Cert. Polit. & Govt. Pos: Worker, Lufkin Nixon Hq, Tex, 60; pres, Lufkin Rep. Women's Club, 62; v.chmn, Angeline Co. Rep. Party, 64; mem, Lufkin City Charter Cmn, 64; del, Rep. Nat. Conv, 64 & 68; committeewoman, Dist. Three Rep. Party, 65; dep. state v.chmn, Region II, Tex. Rep. Party, 67- Bus. & Prof. Pos: Second grade teacher, Lufkin, 49-50. Mem: Commun. Concert; Commun. Playhouse; Lufkin Coun. for Retarded Children; Med. Auxiliary. Rel: Presbyterian. Mailing Add: 1303 Western Dr, Lufkin, Tex. 75901.

ATKINSON, MYRON HILTON, JR. R
N.Dak. State Rep.
b. Bismarck, N.Dak, 9/22/27; s. Myron Hilton Atkinson and Julia Weber A; m. 7/21/52 to Marjory L. Barth; c. Timothy, Kathleen, Thomas, Patrick, Elizabeth, John and Paul. Educ: Bismarck Jr. Col, A.S, 47; Univ. N.Dak, B.S.C, 49, Law Sch, B.S.J.D, 51; Beta-Gamma Sigma; Alpha Tau Omega; Blue Key. Polit. & Govt. Pos: Chmn, Burleigh Co. Rep. Party, N.Dak, 62-63; N.Dak. State Rep, 32nd Dist, 69- Bus. & Prof. Pos: Partner, law firm of Cox, Pearce, Engebretson, Atkinson, Gunnes, 54-63; v.pres, Meyer Broadcasting Co, 64-68; v.pres, Robert James, Inc, 68-69. Mil. Serv: Entered as 2nd Lt, Army, 52, released as 1st Lt, 54, after serv. in Judge Adv. Gen. Corps. Mem: Am. Bar Asn; Am. Legion; Elks; K. of C; Rotary. Rel: Catholic. Legal Res: 106 Ave. B W, Bismarck, N.Dak. 58501. Mailing Add: First National Bank and Trust Co Bldg, Bismarck, N.Dak. 58501.

ATKINSON, WILLIAM P. D
Wis. State Assemblyman
b. Wilkensburg, Pa, 5/14/01; s. Harry Jackson Atkinson and Leonora Heinrich A; m. 9/1/27 to Agnes Hein; c. Catherine, Caroline, Alice, Virginia, Elizabeth and William P, Jr. Educ: Pa. State Univ, B.S. in Civil Eng, 25; pres, student chapter, Am. Soc. Civil Engrs. Polit. & Govt. Pos: Alderman, Fourth Ward, S. Milwaukee, Wis, 51-56; mayor, S. Milwaukee, 56-64; Wis. State Assemblyman, 24th Dist, Milwaukee Co, currently. Bus. & Prof. Pos: Surveyor, chief of party and transitman, Day & Zimmerman Co, 19-21, asst. field engr, 25-28;

mechanic, Bucyrus-Erie Co, 28-32, design engr, 32-39, and proj. engr, 39-64. Mil. Serv: Naval Res, 42-46, Atlantic-Carribean and S. Pac-Okinawa Theaters; Lt.(sg), active Naval Res. Mem: Nat. and Wis. Soc. of Prfnl. Engrs; Eng. Asn. Pa. State Univ; Eagles; ROA; VFW; Am. Legion; Amvets; CWV; Nat. Munic. League; Munic. League of Milwaukee Co. Rel: Catholic. Mailing Add: 1115 16th Ave, South Milwaukee, Wis. 53172. (1967)

ATKISSON, JAMES DOUGLAS D
b. Centerville, Tenn, 3/12/12; s. Phil Atkisson and Olivia Snow Webb A; m. 3/23/40 to Ivy Lee Jones; c. Linda Gayle and James Douglas, Jr. Educ: Hume Fogg High Sch, 32-36. Polit. & Govt. Pos: Del, Dem. Nat. Conv, 68. Mil. Serv: Entered as Pvt, Army, 43, released as Cpl, 45, after serv. in Signal Corps, Europe, 43-45; five Battle Stars; Good Conduct Medal. Mem: Dir, Davidson Co. Cmt. Polit. Educ; IBEW (pres); trustee, Davidson Co. (Bldg.) & Trades Construction; trustee, Labor Temple Asn; Mason; Eastern Star; Royal Arch Mason. Rel: Church of Christ. Mailing Add: 2720 Jones Ave, Nashville, Tenn. 37207.

ATLAS, MORRIS D
Chmn, Dem. Exec. Cmt. Hidalgo Co, Tex.
b. Houston, Tex, 12/25/26; s. Sam Atlas and Bertha Cohen A; m. 8/31/47 to Rita Wilner; c. Scott Jerome, Debra Lynne, Lauren Teri and Lisa Gayle. Educ: Univ. Tex, B.B.A, 49; LL.B, 50; Phi Delta Phi; Alpha Epsilon Pi. Polit. & Govt. Pos: Mem. bd. regents, Pan Am. Col, 65-; del, Dem. Nat. Conv, 68; chmn, Dem. Exec. Cmt. Hidalgo Co, Tex, 68- Bus. & Prof. Pos: Partner, Atlas, Hall, Schwarz, Mills, Gurwitz & Bland, 53- Mil. Serv: Entered as A/S, Navy, 44, released as Seaman 1/C, 46, after serv. aboard U.S.S. Iowa, Pac, 45-46. Publ: 'Settlement of Marital Property Rights,' Tex. Law Rev, 51; reprinted as 'Marital Property Rights,' Tex. Bar J, 51. Mem: Hidalgo Co. Bar Asn.(pres, 59); Tex. and Am. Bar Asns; Asn. Ins. Attorneys; Tex. Asn. Defense Coun.(dir, 64); Tex. Bar Found; Elks; Am. Legion. Rel: Jewish. Legal Res: 1600 Iris, McAllen, Tex. 78501. Mailing Add: 818 Pecan, McAllen, Tex. 78501.

ATTEBERRY, JAMES R. 'JIM' R
b. Mercedes, Tex, 2/20/30; s. Clark Atteberry and Laura Aline Taylor A; m. 10/3/53 to Sara Joy; c. Mark Daniel, Kevan James, David Charles and Janice Irene. Educ: Tex. Col. of Arts and Industs, Kingsville, B.S. in Chem. Eng, 52; Alpha Phi Omega. Polit. & Govt. Pos: Del, King Co. Rep. Conv. and alternate, Wash. State Rep. Conv, 64; Rep. Regional Chmn; del, Rep. 41st Legis. Dist. Caucus and King Co. Rep. Conv, 66 & 68; training chmn, Rep. 41st Legis. Dist. Orgn, 66-68; v.pres, Suburban E. King Co. Young Rep, 68; del, Wash. State Rep. Conv, 68; Wash. State Rep. Elector, 68; precinct committeeman, Rep. Party, 68- Bus. & Prof. Pos: From lead engr. to safety engr, Commercial Airplane Group, Boeing Co, 68-69, mgr. safety sect, 737 Div, 69- Mem: Am. Soc. Safety Engrs; past bd. mem, Newport Hills Commun. Club; past pres, Newport Hills Elem. Sch. PTA. Rel: Methodist. Mailing Add: 4717 24th N.E, Apt. 304, Seattle, Wash. 98105.

ATWELL, BEN JUMBO D
Tex. State Rep.
b. Hutchins, Tex, 8/4/15; s. B.D. Atwell and Margaret Rice A; m. 1/27/56 to Sarah Clark; c. Sandra, Dick Inman and Duke. Educ: Univ. Tex, B.B.A, 38 and LL.B, 41; Theta Xi. Polit. & Govt. Pos: Tex. State Rep, 51- Bus. & Prof. Pos: Attorney. Mil. Serv: Entered as Midn, Navy, 42, released as Lt.(sg), 45, after serv. in Asiatic-Pac; Am. Theater and Asiatic-Pac. Theater Ribbons; Victory Medal. Mem: VFW; Am. Legion; Lions; RONS; Masons; Scottish Rite; Shrine; KCCH. Rel: Christian. Legal Res: 401 First St, Hutchins, Tex. 75141. Mailing Add: Box 542, Hutchins, Tex. 75141.

ATWOOD, ROY FRANKLIN, JR. R
Wash. State Sen.
b. Springfield, Mass, 11/27/26; s. Roy Franklin Atwood and Mertie Hooper Dunn Rogers A; m. 1/15/54 to Marie Louise Matson; c. Deborah Marie, Roy Franklin, III and Suzanne Marie. Educ: Wash. State Univ, B.A. in Polit. Sci, 49; Univ. Wash, LL.B, 51; Scabbard & Blade; Phi Alpha Delta. Polit. & Govt. Pos: Mem, Whatcom Co. Health Bd, Wash, 57-58; councilman sixth ward, City of Bellingham, 57-61, councilman-at-lg, 60-62, mem, Bd. Water Cmnr. pres, Bellingham City Coun, 61-63; Wash. State Sen, 42nd Dist, 63-, Minority Whip, Wash. State Senate, 65-, Minority Floor Leader, 69-; mem, Columbia River Compact Cmn, 65- Bus. & Prof. Pos: Attorney at law for Joseph T. Pemberton, 53-64; gen. practice of law, 64- Mil. Serv: Entered as Pvt, Army, 44, released as T-5, 46, after serv. in Inf, 4th Inf. Div, 37th Inf. Regt, Am; Good Conduct Medal; Am. Theater Victory Medal; Maj, Army Res, 66- Mem: Whatcom Co. Bar Asn; Wash. State Bar Asn; Am. Bar Asn; Lions; Elks; R.O.A; Air Force Asn; Bellingham Yacht Club; State Capitol Hist. Soc; YMCA. Rel: Lutheran. Mailing Add: 317 Park Ridge, Bellingham, Wash. 98225.

AU, BERNARD E. R
b. Kalihi, Hawaii; c. three. Polit. & Gov. Pos: City and Co. Retirement Bd; State Rep. Cent. Cmt. Bus. & Prof. Pos: Wholesale automotive dealer. Mem: Motor Vehicle Dealers' Licensing Bd; Cent. Labor Coun; AFL-CIO Cmt. on Polit. Educ. Mailing Add: 3059 Kalihi St, Honolulu, Hawaii 96819. (1967)

AUBERT, EDWARD JOHN D
Mont. State Rep.
b. Tiber, Mont, 10/1/17; s. John Clarence Aubert and Sophia Rude A; m. 2/23/46 to Fae Henkel; c. Edward George. Educ: Portland Diesel & Elec. Sch, 1 year. Polit. & Govt.Pos: Dem. precinct committeeman, 16 years; chmn, Glacier Co. Dem. Party, Mont, 2 years; mayor, Town of Browning, Mont, 65-71; chmn, City Co. Planning Bd, 66-70; Mont. State Rep, 69- Secy, Browning Develop. Corp, 67-70. Mil. Serv: Entered as Pvt, Air Force, 41, released as T/Sgt, 45, after serv. in 14th Air Force, China, Burma and India, 43-45. Mem: Lions; VFW; Am. Legion; Elks; C. of C.(pres, Browning chap, 65-70). Rel: Catholic. Mailing Add: Box 579, Browning, Mont. 59417.

AUBREY, MARK LEE R
Chmn, Polk Co. Rep. Party, Tex.
b. Joy, Ill, 12/26/01; s. Charles Aubrey (deceased) and Ora Neely A; m. 1/4/23 to Alice Louisa West; c. Robert Mark (deceased). Educ: High sch. Polit. & Govt. Pos: State hwy. policeman, Rock Island Co, Ill, 44-46; tax assessor and constable, Drury Twp, 48-56; head dairyman, E.Moline State Hosp, 55-65, stores clerk, 65-67; chmn, Polk Co. Rep. Party, Tex, 67- Bus. & Prof. Pos: Tel. operator, Chicago, Burlington & Quincy R.R, Duncan, Ill, 21-27, Bushnell, 27-30, New Boston, 30-32, on extra list, 32-36; warehouse foreman, Ill. Wholesale Grocery, Rock Island, 36-39; bulk agent, Skelly Oil Co, Milan, 39-46. Mem: Hon. mem, Dairy Herd Improv. Asn, Ill; Order of R.R. Telegraphers Union; Munic, State and Co. Employees Union; AF&AM. Received Highest Award for Having Highest Producing Dairy Herd, Instnl. Dairy Herd, State of Ill; hon. scholarship, Macomb Normal Sch; Outstanding Policeman, Ill. Rel: Protestant. Mailing Add: Route 2, Box 44-A, Livingston, Tex. 77351.

AUCHINCLOSS, JAMES COATS R
b. New York, N.Y, 1/19/85; s. Edgar Stirling Auchincloss and Maria Sloan A; m. 11/18/60 to Vera Rogers Brown; c. Douglas, Gordon. Educ: Yale, B.A, 08. Polit. & Govt. Pos: U.S. Rep, N.J, 78th-88th Cong; mayor, Rumson, N.J, 3 terms; coun, Borough of Rumson, 12 years; former dep. police cmnr, N.Y.C. Bus. & Prof. Pos: Founder, past treas, pres. and chmn. of bd, N.Y. Better Bus. Bur; N.Y. Stock Exchange, 10-35, bd. of gov, 18 years; Farmers Loan & Trust Co, N.Y.C. Mil. Serv: N.Y. Nat. Guard, 7th Regt, Capt, Mil. Intel. Mailing Add: 300 New Jersey Ave. S.E, Washington, D.C. 20003.

AUCHLY, WILLIAM JOSEPH R
Chmn, Montgomery Co. Rep. Cmt, Mo.
b. Montgomery Co, Mo, 4/26/28; s. Marcus Francis Auchly and Anna Theresa Cunningham A; m. 8/12/67 to Mary Dione Dimond; c. Christopher Marcus. Educ: Montgomery Co. High Sch. Polit. & Govt. Pos: Chmn, Montgomery Co. Rep. Cmt, Mo, 62-; chmn, Ninth Cong. Dist. Rep. Cmt, 66- Bus. & Prof. Pos: Secy-treas-dir, Producers Grain Co, No. 31, Montgomery Co, Mo, 58; secy. and dir, Montgomery Co. Bank, 63. Mem: K. of C; Mo. Farmers Asn; Farm Bur. Rel: Roman Catholic. Mailing Add: R.R. 2, Montgomery City, Mo. 63361.

AUDETTE, MARCEL GRATIEN R
b. Central Falls, R.I, 12/18/21; s. Ernest Audette (deceased) and Laura Fournier A; m. 6/9/42 to Annette Rosalie Langevin; c. Michael and Ronald. Educ: Sanit. Eng, Providence, R.I, 45-47. Polit. Pos: Chmn, Central Falls City Rep. Cmt, R.I, 65-66, mem, 54-66; mem, State Rep. Cent. Cmt, 56-66. Govt. Pos: Mem, R.I. State Bd. Exam. in Plumbing, 64- Bus. & Prof. Pos: Secy, Audette-Plumbing-Heating, Inc, 52-66. Mil. Serv: Entered as Seaman 1/C, Navy, 42, released as PO 2/C, 45, after serv. in Construct. Bn, S.Pac; Asiatic-Pac. Medal with 1 Star; Navy Unit Commendation with 1 Star; Navy Commendation Ribbon; Am. Defense Medal; Good Conduct Medal; Am. Theater Ribbon; Chief Ship Fitter, Naval Res, 45-65. Mem: Past comdr, Am. Legion of R.I; life mem, VFW Post 1271; Am. Legion Post 33; Central Falls Lions Club; N.Eng. Plumbing Inspect. Asn. Semi Prfnl. Football; Prfnl. Hockey. Rel: Catholic. Mailing Add: 85 Jenks Ave, Central Falls, R.I. 02863. (1967)

AUGSBURGER, JOHN FREDERICK R
Ind. State Sen.
b. Gridley, Ill, 6/21/05; s. Daniel Augsburger and Leah Gurtner A; m. 1/20/34 to Dorothy Lucille Bird; c. Carolyn S. (Mrs. Curtis) and John Bird. Educ: Milford High Sch, grad, 24; Bluffton Col, 25; Phi Delta Kappa. Polit. & Govt. Pos: Chmn, Milford Town Coun, Ind, 43-46, mem, 68; trustee, Vanburen Twp, Kosciusko Co, 47-55; chmn, Kosciusko Co. Sch. Reorgn, 59-63; Ind. State Sen, Sixth Dist, 69- Bus. & Prof. Pos: Owner, Augsburger's I.G.A. Mkt, 36-62, pres, Augsburger's Inc. Supermkts, 62-69. Mem: Nat. Asn. State Legislators; Mason (32°); Shrine; C. of C; Milford Lions (charter mem); dir, Kosciusko Co. United Fund; dir, Kosciusko Co. Tuberc. Soc. Rel: Protestant. Legal Res: Henry St, Milford, Ind. 46542. Mailing Add: Box 187, Milford, Ind. 46542.

AUGUST, ROBERT BURTON R
Chmn, Avon Rep. Town Cmt, Conn.
b. Simsbury, Conn, 5/18/21; s. Ferdinand Rudolph August and Mildred Paine A; m. 6/26/48 to Gladys Thompson; c. Betsy, Roberta, Lourie, Ann and Marnie. Educ: Phi Delta Phi. Polit. & Govt. Pos: Conn. State Rep, Avon, 54-60, chmn. cmt. gen. law, Conn. House Rep, 57; chmn, Avon Rep. Town Cmt, 60-; chmn. cmt. suburban town matters, Conn. Rep. State Coun, 63- Bus. & Prof. Pos: Attorney, August and Turner, Simsbury, Conn, 50-; Chmn, Real Properties Section, State Bar Asn, 65. Mil. Serv: Entered as Lt.(jg), Navy, 43, released as Lt.(jg), 46, after serv. in LCFF 504 (Commanding Officer), Pacific. Mem: Hartford Co. and Am. Bar Asns; Conn. State Bar Asn.(chmn. real properties sect, 65); Avon Lions Club (former pres); Curtiss Cemetery Asn.(former pres); YMCA (former state chmn, Hi-Y Youth and Govt. Prog); Yankton Col. Alumni Asn.(former nat. chmn); VFW; former chmn, Avon United Fund. Young Man of the Year Award, Farmington Valley Jr. C. of C, 57. Rel: Congregational. Mailing Add: Old Farms Rd, Avon, Conn. 06001.

AUMAN, TOFFIE CLYDE D
N.C. State Rep.
b. Jackson Springs, N.C, 3/11/09; s. Claude Auman and Lillie Graham A; m. 8/7/36 to Sally Watts; c. two sons and two daughters. Educ: N.C. State Col. Polit. & Govt. Pos: Mem, N.C. Bd. of Juvenile Correction, 50-64; N.C. State Rep, 66- Bus. & Prof. Pos: Dir, N.C. R.R, 49-50; past dir. and pres, N.C. State Col. Agr. Found; past dir, N.C. Farm Bur. Ins. Co; dir, Sandhill Prod. Credit Asn, 50-64; farmer, currently. Mem: Past dir, N.C. Farm Bur; pres-elect, Nat. Peach Coun, 64; Hort. Cmt, Am. Farm Bur, 56-62; pres, N.C. Peach Grower's Soc, 60-63; Adv. to Dean of Agr, N.C. State Col; past dir, N.C. State Col. Alumni Asn; W. End Sch. Cmt, 48-64; N.C. Cmt. for Better Schs, 58. Gamma Sigma Delta Award, N.C. State Col. for contrib. to agr. Rel: Presbyterian; Elder, Cmnr. to Gen. Assembly, 55, v.pres, Synod's Men's Coun, 59; pres, Men of the Church Fayetteville Presbytery. Mailing Add: Route 1, West End, N.C. 27344. (1967)

AURELIO, RICHARD R. R
b. North Providence, R.I, 4/19/28; s. John Aurelio and Anna Savastano A; m. 6/20/58 to Suzanne Berger; c. Jodi and Marco. Educ: Boston Univ, B.S. in journalism, 45; Sigma Delta Chi. Polit. & Govt. Pos: Admin. asst. to U.S. Sen. Jacob K. Javits, N.Y, 61-69, campaign dir, 68; campaign mgr, Mayor John V. Lindsay, 69. Bus. & Prof. Pos: Reporter, several newspapers, 48-50; news ed, Newsday, 50-60; mem. staff, Edward Gottlieb & Assocs, 69- Mil. Serv: Entered as Pvt, Air Force, 45, released as 2nd Lt, 48, after serv. in

Air Force Res. Mailing Add: Edward Gottlieb & Associates, 485 Madison Ave, New York, N.Y. 10022.

AUSICH, JOSEPH L. D
Idaho State Sen.
b. Bisbee, Ariz, 9/19/14; s. Louis Ausich and Eva Butrac A; m. 2/23/37 to Lois E. Hocking; c. Joseph Evon and Mariann. Educ: High sch. grad. Polit. & Govt. Pos: Idaho State Sen, currently. Bus. & Prof. Pos: Theatre bus. and mining bus. Rel: Catholic. Mailing Add: P.O. Box 61, Mackay, Idaho 83251.

AUST, MILDRED GRACE D
State Committeewoman, N.Y. Dem. Party
b. Conewango, N.Y, 1/30/02; d. Perry G. Underwood and Mabel Monroe U; m. 4/27/25 to Arthur James Aust; c. Walter and Albert. Educ: Geneseo State Norman Sch, 20; Buffalo State Normal Sch, 23. Polit. & Govt. Pos: V.chmn, Dem. Rural Women's Committee, Cattaraugus Co, N.Y, 58-63; v.chmn, Cattaraugus Co. Dem. Committee, 67-68. state committeewoman, N.Y. Dem. Party, 68- Bus. & Prof. Pos: Elementary Teacher, Public Rural Sch, Little Valley, N.Y, 20-23, St. Joseph's Sch, Gowanda, N.Y, 59-69; adult educ. teacher, Americanization course, Cattaraugus, 45-47. Mem: Business and Professional Women. Rel: Roman Catholic. Legal Res: Catt-Otto Rd, Otto, N.Y. 14766. Mailing Add: R.D. 3, Cattaraugus, N.Y. 14719.

AUSTIN, ELLEN JANE D
Secy, 18th Dist. Dem. Non-Partisan League Exec. Cmt, N.Dak.
b. Toledo, Ohio, Oct. 15; d. John J. Megivern and Anna O'Neill M; m. 6/4/46 to Alvin E. Austin; c. Suellen and Sheila Ann. Educ: Sacred Heart Acad; Moorhead State Col. Polit. & Govt. Pos: Committeeman, First Precinct Fifth Ward, Grand Forks, N.Dak, 59-; v.pres, Grand Forks Co. Dem. Women, 60-; secy. Grand Forks Co. Dem. Exec. Cmt, 60-67; del, Dem. State Conv, 62, 63, 64, 66 & 68; del, Dem. Women's State Conv, 63, 65, 67 & 69; secy, N.Dak. State Dem. Women, 63-65, dir. news and publ, 65-; mem. bd. dirs, N.Dak. Dem. Women's Club, 63-; del. and publicity coordinator for N.Dak, Dem. Nat. Conv, 64; N.Dak. Publicity Coordinator, Dem. Women's Conf, D.C, 66; dir, Region Four Dem. Women, 66-; mem. adv. cmt, N.Dak. Dem. Non-Partisan League Legislators, 66-; secy, 18th Dist. Dem. Non-Partisan League Exec. Cmt, 67-; Dem. nominee for Presidential Elector, 68; press secy. for U.S. Sen. Campaign, 68; secy, N.Dak. Educ. Broadcasting Coun, 69- Publ: Ed, News, N.Dak. Quart. Publ. of N.Dak. Women; column, 'The Last Word,' The Leader, N.Dak. Off. Dem. Newspaper. N.Dak. Dem. Woman of the Year, 69. Rel: Roman Catholic. Mailing Add: 525 N. 25th St, Grand Forks, N.Dak. 58201.

AUSTIN, IVY FRANK D
Chmn, Pulaski Co. Dem. Cmt, Ga.
b. Cochran, Ga, 12/2/02; s. Benjamin Franklin Austin and Mildred Collins A; m. 2/1/24 to Ora Geraldine Anderson; c. Mildred and Hardy Frank. Educ: Cochran High Sch, grad, 21. Polit. & Govt. Pos: Chmn, Pulaski Co. Dem. Cmt, Ga, 46- Bus. & Prof. Pos: Owner, West. Auto Asn. Store, 36- Mem: Past master, Mt. Hope Lodge 9; past comdr, Rhodes Commandery 34. Rel: Methodist. Mailing Add: 223 Progress Ave, Hawkinsville, Ga. 31036. (1967)

AUSTIN, ROBERT R
b. Davenport, Iowa, 9/10/12; m. 1943 to Marion De Taeye A; c. William, Molly, Mike. Educ: St. Ambrose Col, B.A, 37. Polit. & Gov. Pos: Ill. State Rep, 56-60, 62-64. Bus. & Prof. Pos: Co-owner, Ins, Real Estate and Travel Agency. Mil. Serv: U.S. Navy, 41, cmn. Ensign, 43, released as Lt. (sg), 46. Mem: Sports off. and referee in Nat. Football League (17 years); Rock Island Bd. of Supvrs; Founder of Little League and Babe Ruth summer baseball, E. Moline. Mailing Add: 1218 20th Avenue Way, E. Moline, Ill. 61265. (1967)

AUSTIN, RUSSELL ANDERSON, JR. R
Mem, Rep. State Exec. Bd, Wash.
b. Seattle, Wash, 3/4/30; s. Russell Anderson Austin and Amanda Ficks A; m. 6/23/53 to Barbara Fortnum; c. Russell, III, Katherine Lee, Stephen Fortnum, Tracey Ann and Melissa Ann. Educ: Univ. Wash, B.A, 53, J.D, 64; Wash. Law Review; Order of the Coif; Alpha Delta Phi; Phi Alpha Delta. Polit. & Govt. Pos: Pres, Grays Harbor Co. Young Rep, Wash, 56-60; mem. exec. bd, Grays Harbor Rep. Cent. Cmt, 56-62; councilman, Aberdeen, Wash, 60-62; asst. chmn, King Co. Rep. Cent. Cmt, 66-; mem, Rep. State Exec. Bd, 66-; pres, Seventh Cong. Dist. Rep. Club, 66-; del, Rep. Nat. Conv, 68. Mil. Serv: Entered as A/S, Navy, 50, released as Storekeeper 3/C, 51, after serv. in Fasron 895, Sand Point Naval Air Sta, 50-51, Comdr, Naval Res, 68- Publ: 'Inverse Condemnation in Washington,' Wash. Law Review, 1/65; 'Recreational Rights & Titles to Beds on Western Lakes and Streams,' Natural Resources J, 1/67. Mem: Am, Wash. State and Seattle-King Co. Bar Asns; Am. Trial Lawyers Asn; Mason; Scottish Rite; Shrine. Rel: Protestant. Legal Res: 16220 Maplewild Dr, S.W, Seattle, Wash. 98166. Mailing Add: 609 Norton Bldg, Seattle, Wash. 98166.

AUVIL, KENNETH D
W.Va. State Del.
b. Barbour Co, 2/5/35; s. Dallas Auvil and Goldie Shaffer A; m. 12/27/60 to Laura Davis; c. Kenneth Bradley and Alicia Ann. Educ: Salem Col, B.S, 57; W.Va. Univ; Capt, Salem Col. Football Team, 57; pres, Salem Student Body, 57. Polit. & Govt. Pos: W.Va. State Del, 60- Bus. & Prof. Pos: Bldg. contractor; former teacher; chmn, Barbour Develop. Corp. Mil. Serv: Army, Germany, 57-59. Mem: Pres, Belington Kiwanis Club; instr, Am. Legion Boys' State. Jaycee's Outstanding Young Men in Am, 65. Rel: Methodist. Mailing Add: Box 276, Belington, W.Va. 26250.

AVCOLLIE, BERNARD LINCOLN D
Conn. State Rep.
b. Flushing, L.I, N.Y, 12/14/31; s. Bernard E. Avcollie and Emma Johnson Mahler; m. 8/8/53 to Wanda Klimasieski; c. Mark, Lisa, Neil and Gail. Educ: Univ. Conn, B.A, 60, Sch. Law, LL.B, 61. Polit. & Govt. Pos: Chmn, Naugatuck High Sch. Bldg, Cmt, Conn, 57-61; clerk, Borough Naugatuck, 57-61; mem, Hillside Sch. Bldg. Cmt, 61-62; v.chmn, Naugatuck Sewer Cmn, 64-65; Conn. State Rep, 67- Bus. & Prof. Pos: Contract Mgr, Vickers, Sperry-Rand, 61-65; Attorney, 65- Mil. Serv: Entered as Pvt, Marine Corps, released as Sgt, after serv. in 1st Marine Div, Korean Conflict; Good Conduct, Korean Conflict and UN Medals. Mem: Conn. Bar Asn; Elks; K. of C; Exchange Club; Columbo Soc; Marine Corps League; VFW; Am. Legion; bd. dirs, Am. Red Cross. Rel: Roman Catholic. Legal Res: 111 Partridgetown Rd, Naugatuck, Conn. 06770. Mailing Add: 305 Church St, Naugatuck, Conn. 06770.

AVERY, FRED R
N.H. State Rep.
b. Pittsfield, N.H, 8/24/07; s. Alanson D. Avery and Ida Lyons A; m. 1/23/32 to Helen Dorothy Card; c. Candace C.(Mrs. Maihiot). Educ: Pittsfield, N.H. High Sch, grad; exten. courses. Polit. & Govt. Pos: Town chmn, Robert Taft Presidential Campaign and Ex-Gov. Wesley Powell's Primary Campaign; N.H. State Rep, 69- Bus. & Prof. Pos: Agent, John Hancock Life Ins, Concord, N.H, 33-69, retired. Mil. Serv: Entered as Store Keeper, Seabees, Navy, 43, released as SK 2/C, 45, after serv. in various bur, yards and docks, Hawaiian Area, Pac. Theatre; Good Conduct Medal; Pac. Area Medal. Mem: N.H. Asn. Independent Agents; New Eng. Mutual Agents Asn; Mason. Rel: Protestant. Mailing Add: 20 Manchester St, Pittsfield, N.H. 03263.

AVERY, JOHN BUCHANAN, JR. D
Mem, Tenn. Dem. Exec. Cmt.
b. Alamo, Tenn, 10/7/16; s. John Buchanan Avery and Edwin Efland A; m. 8/4/40 to Beulah Frances James; c. Mrs. Dan S. Arnold, Jr, Mrs. Jerald Wayne White and Ann Buchanan. Educ: Baylor Univ, A.B, 38; Vanderbilt Univ, LL.B, 39. Polit. & Govt. Pos: City attorney, Alamo and Friendship, Tenn, 46-; Tenn. State Rep, 47-49; Tenn. State Sen, 49-51; mem, Tenn. Constitution Conv, 59; mem, Crockett Co. Dem. Primary Bd. Elec, 62-65; mem, Tenn. Dem. Exec. Cmt. and chmn, Crockett Co. Dem. Exec. Cmt, currently. Bus. & Prof. Pos: Dir, Alamo Develop. Corp, 50- Mil. Serv: Entered as Ens, Naval Res, 43, released as Lt.(jg), 45, after serv. in Amphibious Forces, Am, Atlantic, European, Pac. and Philippine Theaters, 43-45; Am, Atlantic, European, Pac. and Philippine Theater Campaign Ribbons; Victory Medal; Naval Res. Ribbon; Lt. Comdr, Naval Res.(Ret). Mem: Bd. of gov, Tenn. Bar Asn, 58-62; Am. Bar Asn; Rotary; Am. Legion; VFW; Farm Bur. Lettered in basketball, track and tennis at Baylor Univ. Rel: Southern Baptist. Legal Res: 404 E. Church St, Alamo, Tenn. 38001. Mailing Add: P.O. Box 127, Alamo, Tenn. 38001.

AVERY, OMER H. D
Mo. State Sen.
b. Troy, Mo, 6/15/00; s. Omer H. Avery and Kate Jefferson A; wid; c. Mrs. Gregory G. McKee. Educ: Univ. Mo, A.B, 22, LL.B, 24; Sigma Nu; Phi Alpha Delta. Polit. & Govt. Pos: Prosecuting attorney, Lincoln Co, Mo, 30-34; city attorney, Troy, 34-42; Mo. State Sen, 57- Mil. Serv: Pvt, Inf, 18; reentered as Capt, Judge Adv. Gen. Dept, 42, released as Maj, 46, after serv. in ETO; Bronze Star. Mem: Odd Fellows. Rel: Methodist. Mailing Add: 103 Troy Bldg, Troy, Mo. 63379.

AVERY, RICHARD MOORE D
b. Heiberger, Ala, 1/17/16; s. William Belcher Avery and Ella Mabel Moore A; m. 8/22/40 to Mildred Glass; c. Mabel Patrice, Richard Moore Jr, William Leland. Educ: Ala. Polytech. Inst, 39 (Voc. Agr.). Polit. & Govt. Pos: Farm Security Admin, 41-42; Ala. State Rep, until 66. Bus. & Prof. Pos: Milk distributor; teacher of voc. agr, 39-40; 43-46; feed bus, 46-47. Rel: Methodist. Mailing Add: Greensboro, Ala. 36744. (1967)

AVERY, THOMAS B(OUSE) R
Tenn State Rep.
b. Memphis, Tenn, 3/13/30; s. Christopher L. Avery and Hester Anderson A; m. 1/28/62 to Elizabeth Anne Dooley; c. Elizabeth Lynne and Thomas Edwin. Educ: Memphis State Univ, 3 years; Vanderbilt Law Sch, LL.B, 55; Kappa Alpha; Phi Alpha Delta. Polit. & Govt. Pos: Tenn. State Rep, 15th Dist, Shelby Co, 66-; majority floor leader, Tenn. House Rep, 69-; alternate del, Rep. Nat. Conv, 68. Bus. & Prof. Pos: Attorney-at-law, 55- Mem: Am, Tenn. and Memphis-Shelby Co. Bar Asns. Rel: Presbyterian. Legal Res: 538 Kinsman Rd, Memphis, Tenn. 38117. Mailing Add: 2112 First National Bank Bldg, Memphis, Tenn. 38103.

AVERY, WILLIAM HENRY R
b. Wakefield, Kans, 8/11/11; s. Herman W. Avery and Hattie M. Coffman A; m. 6/16/40 to Hazel Bowles; c. Bill, Barbara Ann, Bradley Eugene and Martha Sue. Educ: Univ. Kans, A.B, 34; Delta Upsilon. Polit. & Govt. Pos: Dir. sch. bd, Wakefield, Kans, 47-55; Kans. State Rep, 51-55; mem, Legis. Coun. of Kans, 53-55; U.S. Rep, Kans, 55-65; Gov, Kans, 65-67. Bus. & Prof. Pos: Farmer and stockman, 34-; exec, Clinton Oil Co, Wichita, 69- Mem: Kans. Farm Bur; Mason; Lions Int; Kans. Livestock Asn; Kans. Asn. Wildlife. Received Nat. 4-H Award, 67. Rel: Methodist. Mailing Add: 19 Douglas, Wichita, Kans. 67207.

AVEY, ART D
b. Cranbrook, B.C, Can, 1918; m. to Jean A; c. four. Educ: Spokane Jr. Col; Wash. State Univ; Gonzaga Univ. Polit. & Govt. Pos: Washington State Rep, 59-68. Bus. & Prof. Pos: Co-owner, Avey Bros. Lumber Co. Mil. Serv: Pilot, Army Air Force; Capt, Res. Mem: Mason; Shrine; Elks; Eagles; Am. Legion; VFW. Mailing Add: Kettle Falls, Wash. 99141. (1967)

AWERKAMP, THOMAS JAMES D
Supvr, Adams Co, Ill.
b. Quincy, Ill, 5/23/23; s. Arthur A. Awerkamp and Mary J. Wissman A; m. 4/10/48 to Mary Elizabeth 'Bette' McCaughey; c. Lucinda, Mary Jo, Ann, Arthur, Suzanne, Ted, Julia, Beth, James and Ellen. Polit. & Govt. Pos: Co. supvr, Adams Co, Ill, 60-64 & 69-; Ill. State Sen, 65-68. Bus. & Prof. Pos: Real Estate salesman, Bower & Son, 65- Mil. Serv: Entered as Pvt, Air Corps, 42, released as Sgt, 46. Mem: Exchange Club; K. of C; Elks; Quincy Boat Club; Rocky Point Club; Mart Heinen Club. Rel: Catholic. Mailing Add: 2505 Cherry St, Quincy, Ill. 62301.

AXELROD, DANIEL LOUIS D
Mem, Exec. Cmt, Calif. Dem. State Cent. Cmt.
b. Baltimore, Md, 2/6/35; s. Herman William Axelrod and Ida Tossman A; m. 6/14/59 to Phyllis Joy Garfield; c. Dana Lynn, Dean Loren and Paul Scott. Educ: Univ. Calif, Los Angeles, B.A, 60; Harvard Law Sch, LL.B, 63. Polit. & Govt. Pos: Dep. attorney gen, Calif, 64-67; Dem. nominee for Calif. State Assemblyman, 57th Assembly Dist, 66-68; mem, Los Angeles Co. Dem. Cent. Cmt, 66-; mem, Calif. Dem. State Cent. Cmt, 66-, exec. cmt, 68- Bus. &

Prof. Pos: Partner, Niles, Cronin & Axelrod, Los Angeles, Calif. Mil. Serv: Entered as enlisted man, Air Force, 53, released as A/1C, 57, after serv. in Armed Forces Radio Serv, Far E. Network, Japan, 54-57. Mem: Calif. State, Los Angeles Co. and San Fernando Valley Bar Asns; exec. cmt, Anti-Defamation League, Pac. Southwest Region; pres, San Fernando Valley Welfare Planning Coun; bd. dir, San Fernando Valley Child Guidance Clinic; commun. serv. cmt, Los Angeles Jewish Fedn. Coun. Rel: Jewish. Legal Res: 14481 Glorietta Dr, Sherman Oaks, Calif. 91403. Mailing Add: 3460 Wilshire Blvd, Los Angeles, Calif. 90005.

AXELROD, HARRY R
Chmn, Andover Rep. Town Cmt, Mass.
b. Lawrence, Mass, 4/6/16; s. Davis Axelrod and Edith Friedman A; m. 6/11/39 to Evelyn Neumark; c. John, Jane and Nancy. Educ: Syracuse Univ, B.A, 38; Phi Beta Kappa; Sigma Alpha Mu. Polit. & Govt. Pos: Town cmt. mem, Andover Rep. Town Cmt, Mass, 61-, precinct chmn, 61-64, finance chmn, 65 & 66, chmn, 67- Bus. & Prof. Pos: Treas, John Philip Enterprises, Andover, Mass, 46-66; owner, Walbuck Crayon Co, 48-; treas, Greeley Park Homes, Nashua, N.H, 53-62; treas, Sheraton Rolling Green Motor Inn, Andover, 59- Mil. Serv: Entered as Ens, Navy, 43, released as Lt.(jg), 46, after serv. in Third, Fifth and Seventh Fleets, Pac. Theatre, 44-46; Am. Area Campaign Ribbon; Asiatic-Pac. Area Campaign Ribbon with Six Stars; Philippine Liberation Campaign Ribbon with one Star; World War II Victory Ribbon. Mem: Am. Hotel and Motel Asn; Home Builders Asn; Crayon and Color Inst; Kiwanis; Andover Serv. Club. Rel: Jewish. Mailing Add: 27 Alden Rd, Andover, Mass. 01810.

AYCOCK, CLARENCE C. 'TADDY' D
Lt. Gov, La.
b. Franklin, La, 1916; married; c. Six. Educ: Loyola Univ. of the South, LL.B, 37. Polit. & Govt. Pos: La. State Rep. and speaker, La. House of Rep, 52-60; Lt. Gov, La, 60- Mem: La. Bar Asn. Legal Res: 608 Palfrey St, Franklin, La. 70538. Mailing Add: State Capitol, Baton Rouge, La. 70801.

AYCOCK, KENNETH R. R
Chmn, Uintah Co. Rep. Party, Utah
b. Vernal, Utah, 9/29/16; s. Robert L. Aycock and Addie Maud Sowards A; m. 2/17/44 to Alyce Stephenson; c. Stephen Kenneth, Gordon Lee and Rodney James. Educ: Brigham Young Univ, B.S, 39. Polit. & Govt. Pos: City councilman, Roosevelt City, Utah, 52-57, mayor, 57-61; chmn, Duchesne Co. Rep. Party, 54-56; committeeman, Utah Rep. State Cent. Cmt, 56-58; chmn, Uintah Co. Rep. Party, 67- Bus. & Prof. Pos: Prin, Duchesne High Sch, Utah, 46-46-47; asst. mgr, Uintah Power and Light Co, Roosevelt, Utah, 47-51, mgr, 52-61; dist. rep, Utah Power and Light Co, Vernal, Utah, 61-69. Mil. Serv: Entered as Pvt, Army, 41, released as Maj, 46, after serv. in Field Artil, ETO, 44-46; European Theatre Award. Mem: Am. Legion (comdr, Basin Post 64, Roosevelt); Lions (first v.pres, Roosevelt Club); Rotary (past pres, Vernal Club, 64-65); C. of C. (pres, Roosevelt Chap, 58-59 and Vernal Chap, 65-66). Rel: Latter-Day Saint. Mailing Add: 132 N. Sixth W, Vernal, Utah. 84078.

AYCOCK, ROBERT JAMES D
S.C. State Rep.
b. Clarendon Co, S.C, 7/27/93; s. Robert J. Aycock and America Fair Jones A; m. 6/14/16 to Helen B. Geddings. Educ: Clemson Col, 10-11. Polit. & Govt. Pos: S.C. State Rep, 35-36, 49-, Chmn, ways and means cmt, 60- Bus. & Prof. Pos: Merchant, firm of Aycock & Rollings; farmer. Mailing Add: Pinewood, S.C. 29125.

AYERS, J. DOUGLAS D
b. Parkersburg, W.Va, 10/29/17; s. J.D. Ayers and Edna Reighter A; m. 8/24/39 to Beatrice V. Pennybacker; c. Steven, Richard and Penny (Mrs. Steven Moellendick). Polit. & Govt. Pos: Mem, Parkersburg City Coun, W.Va, 50-53; W.Va. State Del, 64-66. Bus. & Prof. Pos: Bldg. contractor, Mem: Elks; Moose. Rel: United Brethren. Mailing Add: 32 Valley View Dr, Vienna, Parkersburg, W.Va. 26101. (1967)

AYERS, JAKE BERTRAM D
b. Glen Allen, Miss, 1/23/20; s. Charley Ayers, Sr. and Maggie Willis A; m. to Lillie Short; c. Henry B, Gwendolyn B, Jake B, Jr, Vernon B, William B, Kennieth B, Hubert B. and Herbert B. Polit. & Govt. Pos: Chmn, Washington Co. Freedom Dem, Miss, 68; del, Dem. Nat. Conv, 68. Bus. & Prof. Pos: Coordinator, Freedom Crafts Coop, 67-; Washington Co. Dir, Citizenship Educ, Delta Ministry. Mil. Serv: Entered as Pvt, Army, 42, released as T/5, 45, after serv. in 374 Engrs, ETO, 44-45. Mem: Bd. dirs, Miss. Human Rels. Coun; Am. Civil Liberties Union (bd, Miss. Chap). Martin Luther King Award, Miss. Coun. on Human Rights; Rural Serv. Award, Off. Econ. Opportunity. Rel: Baptist. Mailing Add: P.O. Box 284, Glen Allen, Miss. 38744.

AYERS, JOHN LAW D
b. Brooksville, Fla, 4/8/02; s. David Ayers and Roberta Sally Lane A; single. Educ: High Sch. Polit. Pos: Fla. State Rep, 56-66; chmn, Hernando Co. Cmn, 35-53, cmnr, 33-53. Govt. Pos: Dir, Soil Conservation, Gulf Ridge Soil Conservation Dist, 44-66; dir, Hernando Co. Aviation Authority, Fla, 57-65 and Hernando Co. Fair Asn, 56-62; mem. bd, Hernando Co. Hosp, 55-65. Bus. & Prof. Pos: Dir, Hernando State Bank, 57-66. Mil. Serv: Fla. Nat. Guard, 20-27. Mem: Farm Bureau; C. of C; Mason, Shrine. Rel: Methodist. Mailing Add: P.O. Box 125, Brooksville, Fla. 33512. (1967)

AYERS, JUDSON FREEMAN, JR. D
b. Greenwood, S.C, 3/17/33; s. Judson Freeman Ayers and Viola Pitts A; m. 4/27/63 to Mildred Ann Smith; c. Jill Melissa, Heidi Lee and Judson Freeman III. Educ: Univ. S.C, B.A, 54; Univ. Va, LL.B, 59; Delta Theta Phi. Polit. & Govt. Pos: Mem, Greenwood City Coun, 61-62; Greenwood Co. Magistrate, 62-65; chmn, Greenwood Co. Young Dems, 64-65; S.C. State Rep, 65-68. Bus. & Prof. Pos: Attorney at Law, 59- Mil. Serv: Entered as Ens, Navy, 54, released as Lt, 56, after serv. in Electronics Unit, Greenwood, S.C and Amphibious Forces, Atlantic; Nat. Serv. Ribbon; European Occup. Ribbon; Lt, Naval Res, 56-58. Mem: Am, S.C. and Greenwood Co. Bar Asns; Am. and S.C. Trial Lawyers Asns; Lions; Moose; Mason, Hejaz Temple; Woodlawn Grange; Jr. C. of C; C. of C. Rel: Baptist. Legal Res: Route 5, Chinguapin, Greenwood, S.C. 29646. Mailing Add: P.O. Drawer 799, Greenwood, S.C. 29646.

AYLWARD, JAMES PATRICK, JR. D
First Asst. Co. Counsr, Jackson Co, Mo.
b. Kansas City, Mo, 6/20/19; s. James Patrick Aylward and Clara Stanley A; m. 7/17/50 to Mary Elizabeth Bourk; c. Mary Susan, James Patrick, III, Timothy Michael, Terence Joseph, Sharon and Shauna. Educ: Univ. Notre Dame, A.B, 41; Univ. Mo, Columbia, J.D. 49; Phi Delta Phi. Polit. & Govt. Pos: Pres, Jackson Young Dem. Club, Mo, 51; chmn, Fifth Dist. Young Dem. Club, Mo, 52; Del, Dem. Nat. Conv, 56, del-at-large, 60 & 68; mem, Mo. Dem. State Cmt, 66-68; first asst. co. counsr, Jackson Co, Mo, 67- Bus. & Prof. Pos: Gen. practice of law, 49- Mem: Am, Mo. and Kansas City Bar Asns; Nat. Conv. Christians and Jews (mem. local bd, 56-60); Am. Legion (comdr, 60); Mayor's Prayer Breakfast Orgn.(secy, 62-, chmn, 67); Friends of the Zoo (one of founding mem); Friends of Art, William Rockhill Nelson Gallery; adv. cmn, Juvenile Insts. Jackson Co, Mo, 64-; spec. gift and bequest coun, Rockhurst Col, Kansas City, 66-; Columns Club and Law Sch. Found, Univ. Mo, Columbia. Hon. Tex. Citizen, Gov. Price Daniel, 57. Rel: Catholic. Mailing Add: 648 W. 68 Terrace, Kansas City, Mo. 64113.

AYLWARD, PAUL L. D
Chmn, First Dist. Dem. Orgn, Kans.
b. Stonington, Ill, 3/1/08; s. Dennis E. Aylward and Via Holben A; m. 10/26/29 to Karma Ellen Golden; c. Paul L, Jr, Patricia (Mrs. Thompson) and Peter G. Educ: Univ. Ill, B.S, 28; Chicago Kent Col. Law, LL.B, 30; Phi Alpha Delta; Phi Kappa Theta. Polit. & Govt. Pos: Co. and city attorney, Ellsworth, Kans, 33-59; spec. attorney, Dept. Justice, 40-53; mem. and chmn, Kans. Park and Resources Authority, 58-62; mem, Nat. Vet. Cmt. for Kennedy, 62; del, Dem. Nat. Conv, 62 & 68; mem, Nat. Adv. Cmt, RAD, Dept. Agr, 63-66; nominee, U.S. Sen, Kans, 64; chmn, First Dist. Dem. Orgn. and Ellsworth Co. Dem. Cmt, Kans, currently and chmn, Kans. Joint Coun. Recreation, 68- Bus. & Prof. Pos: Dir. and v.pres, Citizens State Bank, 40-; dir, Ellsworth Develop. Co, 60-; dir, Spillway Marina, Manhattan, Kans, 63-; dir. and pres, Ellsworth Bldg. Co, 64-68. Mil. Serv: Entered as Lt.(jg), Navy, 43, released as Lt, 45, after serv. in CUE 87 and 103 CIC Officer, Pac; 3 Campaign Ribbons. Publ: 'Separate Trials on Appeals,' Bar J. of Kans, 11/57; 'Eminent Domain in Kansas,' Kans. Law Review, 3/59. Mem: Am. Bar Asn; trustee and past pres, Ellsworth Co. Vet. Mem. Hosp; chmn, Am. Legion Kans. Rehabilitation Cmn; Nat. Legis. Cmt, Am. Legion, 54-57; VFW; Elks; K. of C; C. of C; Kans. Angus Asn; Kans. Livestock Asn; state comdr, Am. Legion, 53. Rel: Roman Catholic. Legal Res: 306 Forest Dr, Ellsworth, Kans. 67439. Mailing Add: Box 83, Ellsworth, Kans. 67439.

AYRES, WILLIAM HANES R
U.S. Rep, Ohio
b. Eagle Rock, Va, 2/5/16; s. William H. Ayres and Loatie Emma Welch A; m. to Mary Helen Coventry; c. Mrs. H.J. James Mount, Frank H. and Judith E. Educ: West. Reserve Univ.(Adelbert Col), B.A, 36. Polit. & Govt. Pos: U.S. Rep, Ohio, 50- Bus. & Prof. Pos: Salesman, 36-44; pres, William H. Ayres, Inc, 46- Mil. Serv: Pvt, Army, released 45. Mem: Am. Legion; Amvets; Eagles; Moose. Rel: Methodist. Legal Res: 158 Edgerton Rd, Akron, Ohio 44303. Mailing Add: 2367 Rayburn House Office Bldg, Washington, D.C. 20515.

AZIM, JAMES N, JR. R
Wis. State Assemblyman
b. Richland Center, Wis, 1/17/36. Educ: St. Thomas Col, St. Paul, Minn; Marquette Univ; Wis. State Col. at Platteville, B.S, 57; Univ. of Wis. Law Sch, 65. Polit. & Govt. Pos: Former chmn, Gov. Coun. Traffic Law Enforcement, Wis; past secy, Blue River Watershed Asn; village trustee, Muscoda, Wis, 60-63; page, Wis. State Assembly, 63rd Session; Wis. State Assemblyman, 64- Bus. & Prof. Pos: Instr. hist, Muscoda High Sch, Wis, 57-62; Attorney, currently. Mem: Wis. Acad. Sci, Arts & Letters; past secy, Muscoda C. of C; founder and past secy, Cmt. to Preserve Rural TV. Legal Res: Muscoda, Wis. 53573. Mailing Add: State Assembly, State Capitol, Madison, Wis. 53702.

AZZOLINA, JOSEPH R
N.J. State Assemblyman
b. Newark, N.J; m. to Roselyn Picone; c. Six. Educ: Drew Univ; Holy Cross Col, B.S; N.Y. Univ. Grad. Sch. Bus, 2 years. Polit. & Govt. Pos: Chmn, Rep. Party, Middletown, N.J; N.J. State Assemblyman, chmn, Cmt. on Commerce, Indust. and Professions and mem, Transportation Cmt, currently. Bus. & Prof. Pos: Mem. bd. of dirs, Middletown C. of C; v.pres, Twin Co. Grocers, Inc; pres, Food Circus Supermarkets, Inc. Mil. Serv: World War II and Korean War: Lt. Comdr, Naval Res, currently. Mem: Past pres, Jersey Shore Coun. Navy League; Rotary; Am. Legion; VFW; past dep. dist. gov, Lions. Mailing Add: Borden Court, Middletown, N.J. 07748.

B

BABB, ROGER SUMNER R
Mass. State Rep.
b. Bridgewater, Mass, 1/7/35; s. Charles Sumner Babb and Ethel L. Hallgreen B; m. 5/7/66 to Judith McKeown Moore; c. Melissa. Educ: Univ. Mass, B.A, 56; Univ. Mich. Law Sch, J.D, 59; Boston Univ. Law Sch. Grad. Tax Prog, currently; Econ. Honor Soc; Adelphia-Men's Honor Soc; Dean's List; pres, Lawyers Club; Univ. senate, senate treas, chmn. finance cmt. and most valuable mem. award; Men's Judiciary; Gen. Court Justice; v.pres, Int. Rels. Club. Polit. & Govt. Pos: Mem. exec. cmt, Plymouth Co. Rep. Club, Mass, 67-; v.chmn, Norwell Rep. Town Cmt, 68; chmn, 68-; Mass. State Rep, Ninth Plymouth Dist, 69-, mem, Joint Legis. Cmt. on Pub. Safety, 69; Freshman representative to Adv. Coun. of Rep. Legislators, 69; lectr-legis. intern, Ford Found. Prog, 69. Bus. & Prof. Pos: House Counsel, Liberty Mutual Ins. Co, Boston, 59-60; trial attorney, law firm Merritt J. Aldrich, 61-64 and law off, James D. Casey, 64-66; trial attorney and head

off, law off, Roger Sumner Babb, Brockton, 66-68; asst. gen. attorney home off. legal dep, Liberty Mutual Ins. Co, 68. Mil. Serv: Recruit, Army Nat. Guard, 60, released as Capt, 67, after serv. in Judge Adv. Gen. Corps, Spec. Staff Commanding Gen, 26th Inf. Div; lectr. in mil. justice. Mem: Phi Alpha Delta; Am, Mass, Boston and Plymouth Co. Bar Asns; Mass. Asn. Defense Counsel; admitted to Fed. practice; Mass. Legislators Asn; Am. Arbitration Asn.(Nat. Panel Arbitrators); Norwell Commun. Coun. Soc. Health (steering cmt); Drug Abuse Coun. Rel: Protestant. Mailing Add: 690 River St, Norwell, Mass. 02061.

BABBITT, WAYNE HUBERT R
V.Chmn, Ark. State Rep. Exec. Cmt.
b. Macedonia, Iowa, 4/21/28; s. Darwin Merritt Babbitt and Francis Charron B; m. 7/16/46 to Eleanor Joan Timmerman; c. Holly Ann, Mark Randall and Maureen Suzanne. Educ: Colo. A & M Univ, B.S, 54 and D.V.M, 56. Polit. & Govt. Pos: V.chmn, Pulaski Co. Rep. Cmt, Ark, 62, chmn, 63; del, Rep. Nat. Conv, 64; v.chmn, Ark. State Rep. Exec. Cmt, 64-; dir, Ark. Livestock & Poultry Cmn, 67- Mil. Serv: Entered as A/S, Navy, 46, released as Seaman 1/C, 48. Mem: Ark. Vet. Med. Asn.(pres. and state secy); Am. Animal Hosp. Asn; Rotary Club; N.Hills Country Club. Rel: Lutheran. Mailing Add: 2 Wayside Lane, North Little Rock, Ark. 72116.

BABCOCK, MILTON D
b. Freeport, Ill, 9/12/06; s. Alexander Lee Babcock and Mary Lillian Reynolds B; m. 12/19/34 to Virginia Derrick; c. Stephen, Martha and David (deceased). Educ: Cornell Univ, B.A, 28; Univ. Mich; London Sch. of Econs, Eng. Polit. Pos: Alderman, 65-; alternate del, Dem. Nat. Conv, 64; precinct committeeman, Dem. Party, 60. Bus. Pos: Advertising, W.T. Rawleigh Co. Mil. Serv: Counseling Serv. with Am. Red Cross in Pac. Theater, World War II. Mem: Rotary; Hist. Soc; Red Cross; Co. Welfare Cmt. Rel: Methodist. Mailing Add: 1006 W. Stephenson, Freeport, Ill. 61032. (1967)

BABCOCK, RICHARD FELT D
b. Evanston, Ill, 11/3/17; s. William Frank Babcock and Gertrude Felt B; m. 6/10/43 to Elizabeth Vaughn Burlingham; c. Rebecca, Richard, Elizabeth, Catherine, David and John. Educ: Dartmouth Col, A.B, magna cum laude, 40; Univ. Chicago, J.D, cum laude, 46 and M.B.A, 50; Phi Beta Kappa; Order of Coif; Lambda Alpha. Polit. & Govt. Pos: Dir, Metrop. Housing and Planning Coun, Chicago; cmnr, Northeast. Ill. Metrop. Planning Cmn; mem, Bd. of Educ, Woodstock, Ill, 59-62, 55-57; assoc. dir, Nat. Vol. for Stevenson, 52; cand, Ill. State Sen. Prof. Pos: Lawyer, Ross, Hardies, O'Keefe, Babcock, McDugald & Parsons, Chicago, 57-, Taylor, Miller, Busch & Wagner, 51-56, Overton & Babcock, 48-51, Sidley, Austin, Burgess & Harper, 46-48; lectr. bus. law, Northwest. Univ. Sch. of Commerce, 51-58; lectr, Univ. Chicago Grad. Sch. of Bus, 53-54; consult. on land use law, Ford Found, 60-62; chmn. research cmt, Am. Bar Found, 65-; chmn. adv. cmn. land use proj, Am. Law Inst. Mil. Serv: Am. Field Serv, 41-43, Brit. 8th Army, West. Desert, 42-43, then with N.Z. Divisional Cavalry. Publns: Contributor of articles to prfnl. reviews. Mem: Am. Inst. of Planners; Am. Soc. of Planning Off, bd. dirs, 65-; Univ. Club, Chicago. Mailing Add: 122 S. Michigan, Chicago, Ill. 60603. (1967)

BABCOCK, ROBERT SHILLINGFORD
b. Chicago, Ill, 7/22/15; s. Oliver M. Babcock and Martha Shillingford B; m. 8/20/40 to Alice-Ann Hanchett; c. Robert Shillingford, Anne, Julie, Peter Trowbridge, Martha Rena. Educ: Univ. Rochester, A.B, 37; Rhodes Scholar, Oxford Univ, 37, B.A, 39, M.A, 43; Northwest. Univ, Ph.D, 49; Marlboro Col, LL.D, 57, Univ. Vt, 69; Phi Beta Kappa. Polit. & Govt. Pos: Econ. analyst, Treas. Dept, 42; mem. bd. Econ. Welfare, 42-43; secy. to Gov, Vt, 55; Vt. State Sen, 51-59, Pres-Pro-Tem, Vt. State Senate, 57-59; Lt. Gov, Vt, 59-61. Bus. & Prof. Pos: Instr. polit. sci, Black Mt. Col, N.C, 40-42; asst. prof, Univ. Vt, 46-54, assoc. prof, 54-59, prof, 61-65; provost, Vt. State Cols, 65- Mil. Serv: Entered Naval Res, 43, released as Lt.(jg), 46. Publ: 'State and Local Government and Politics', 57, rev. ed. 62. Mem: Am. Polit. Sci. Asn. Mailing Add: Office of the Provost, Vermont State Colleges, 322 S. Prospect St, Burlington, Vt. 05401.

BABCOCK, TIM R
b. Little Fork, Minn, 10/27/19; s. Erwin Henry Babcock and Olive Rhinehart B; m. 9/21/41 to Betty Lee; c. Lorna Lee (Mrs. William Kuney) and Marla Kay (Mrs. Mike Fillinger). Polit. & Govt. Pos: Mem. exec. cmt, Mont. Rep. Party; Mont. State Rep, Custer Co, 52 and Yellowstone Co, 56-60; Lt. Gov, Mont, 60-62; Gov, State of Mont, 62-68; del, Rep. Nat. Conv, 64 & 68. Bus. & Prof. Pos: Owner & pres, Mineral Resource Develop, Inc; pres, KBLL Radio & TV; pres, Mont. Motor Transport Asn, 58 & 59 and chmn. bd, 60-61; exec. v.pres, Occidental Int. Corp, D.C, currently. Mil. Serv: Entered as Pvt, Army, 44; released as S/Sgt, 46, after serv. in 99th Inf. Div, ETO; Bronze Star; Three Battle Stars. Mem: Nat. DeMolay Legion of Honor; Rotary; Eagles; VFW; Elks; Mason; Am. Legion. Rel: Presbyterian. Mailing Add: Occidental International Corporation, 1717 Pennsylvania Ave. N.W, Washington, D.C. 20006.

BABIARZ, JOHN EDWARD D
b. Wilmington, Del, 6/6/15; s. Stanley Babiarz and Mary Feret B; m. 6/4/39 to Adele F. Barczuk; c. John E, Jr. and Francis S. Educ: Univ. Del, B.A, 37. Polit. & Govt. Pos: Register in Chancery and clerk of Orphans Court, New Castle Co, Del, 49-53; mem. policy cmt, Dem. City Cmt, 50-; chmn, Ninth Ward Dem. Cmt, 51-57; chief clerk, Del. House Rep, 55-56; Dem. Nat. Conv, 56, 60, 64 & 68; pres, City Coun, Wilmington, 57-61; mem. policy cmt, Dem. State Cmt, 57-; mayor, Wilmington, 61-69. Bus. & Prof. Pos: Treas. and gen. mgr, Del. Bedding Co, Wilmington, 39-69; pres. and chief exec. officer, Better Bus. Bur, Del, 69- Mil. Serv: Entered as Pvt, Army, 45, released as Cpl, 46, after serv. in Hq. and Hq. Co, Africa-Middle East Theatre, 45-46; Africa Middle East Theatre Ribbon; Good Conduct Medal. Mem: Trustee, U.S. Conf. Mayors; chmn, Regional Conf. Elected Officials, 63-66; VFW (comdr, Del, 50-51); Kiwanis; Am. Legion; Pulaski Legion; Polish Falcons; Eagles; K. of C; Mil. Order Cooties. Good Govt. Award, Cmt. of 39, 68 & 69. Rel: Roman Catholic. Mailing Add: 303 Lea Blvd, Wilmington, Del. 19802.

BABIN, WILLIAM ALBERT, JR. D
R.I. State Rep.
b. Providence, R.I, 1/17/29; s. William A. Babin and Marie E. Gaudet B; m. 2/17/51 to Hope F. Stearns; c. Susan L. and Janice A. Educ: La Salle Acad, Providence, R.I. Polit. & Govt. Pos: Mem, Cmt. to Study Probs. of Uninsured Drivers, R.I, 62; mem, R.I. House of Rep. Cmt. of Corp, currently; v.chmn, Joint Cmt. Hwy. Safety, currently; mem, Gov. Cmt. on Crime, currently; mem, R.I. Dem. Exec. Cmt, currently: R.I. State Rep, 66-, Dep. Majority Leader, R.I. House of Rep, currently. Bus. & Prof. Pos: Self employed ins. agent, currently; pres, Mt. Pleasant Credit Union, currently. Mem: Past Grand Knight, Dillon Coun, K. of C.(4th°). Rel: Catholic. Mailing Add: 50 Biltmore Ave, Providence, R.I. 02908.

BABINCSAK, WILLIAM E. D
Ind. State Rep.
Polit. & Govt. Pos: Ind. State Rep, currently, chmn, Minority Caucus, 61 & 67 and Majority Caucus, 65, Ind. State House of Rep; mem. bd. dirs, Commun. Coun, Hammond. Bus. & Prof. Pos: Supvr, Elec. Construction; mem. adv. bd, Lake Fed. Savings and Loan Asn. Mem: Int. Brotherhood Elec. Workers Local Union 697; United Commun. Chest. Legal Res: 1856 S. River Dr, Munster, Ind. 46321. Mailing Add: State House of Representatives, State Capitol Bldg, Indianapolis, Ind. 46204. (1967)

BACA, CLOVIS D
V.Chmn, Valencia Co. Dem. Party, N.Mex.
b. San Fidel, N.Mex, 9/25/24; s. Anselmo Baca and Aurelia Vallejos B; m. June 1942 to Lita Jaramillo; c. Clovis, Jr, Patricia (Mrs. Aragon) and Marvelene (Mrs. Duran). Educ: Grants Union High Sch, grad. Polit. & Govt. Pos: Dem. precinct chmn, N.Mex, 45-65; co. cmnr, 59-62; chmn, Valencia Co. Cmn, 67-; alternate del, Dem. Nat. Conv, 68; v.chmn, Valencia Co. Dem. Party, currently. Mil. Serv: Seaman 1/C, Navy, 43-45, serv. aboard U.S.S. Miss, S.Pac. Theatre. Mem: VFW. Rel: Catholic. Legal Res: 1200 Chavez St, Milan, N.Mex. 87020. Mailing Add: Box 2205, Milan, N.Mex. 87020.

BACCARI, VINCENT JAMES D
R.I. State Sen.
b. Providence, R.I, 11/25/15; s. Tommaso Baccari and Marietta Bellandese B; m. 12/29/45 to Teresa; c. Anna Maria (Mrs. Danny DeAngelis), Vincent J, Jr. and Pia Baccari. Educ: Providence Col, 1 year; R.I. Col. Educ, Ed.B, 40; Boston Univ. Sch. Law, LL.B, 49. Polit. & Govt. Pos: Asst. legal counsel, Providence Redevelop. Agency, 56-61; first asst. trial counsel, State Freeway Acquisition, 61-63; R.I. State Sen, Dist. 8, Providence, 67- Bus. & Prof. Pos: Attorney-at-law, 49- Mil. Serv: Entered as Pvt, Army, 42, released as Capt, 46, after serv. in 36th Inf. Div, Mediterranean Theatre, 43-46. Mem: R.I. Bar Asn; Ital. Am. War Veterans of U.S, Inc; Order Sons of Italy in Am. Rel: Catholic. Mailing Add: 80 Vinton St, Providence, R.I. 02909.

BACHER, EDWARD LEONARD R
Consult, Rep. Nat. Finance Cmt.
b. Gilbertville, Mass, 11/14/89; s. John Michael Bacher and Anna Maria Mueller B; m. 5/24/20 to Corinda La Rocca. Educ: Williams Col, A.B, 11; Phi Beta Kappa. Polit. & Govt. Pos: Del, League of Nations Conf. on Customs Formalities, Geneva, 23; exec. secy, Rep. Nat. Finance Cmt, 44-61, compiler of Rep. Fact Book, 47-50 and consult, presently; exec. dir, Rep. Nat. Cmt, 45-49, asst. treas, 49-61 and comptroller, 52-61; treas, Nat. Recount and Fair Elec. Cmt, 60-61. Bus. & Prof. Pos: For. trader, Java, Sumatra and Straits Settlements, Standard Oil Co, N.Y, 11-15; secy. for. trade course, Bus. Training Corp, N.Y, 16-17; ed. of for. trade course by mail, 16-18; mem. staff, Pac. Commercial Co, 17-18 and Quaker City Corp, Phila, 19-20; asst. mgr, Our World Trade, quart. rev, 20-27, ed, 27-45; lectr, For. Trade Sch, Georgetown Univ, 23-27; former treas. and mem. bd. of trustees, Phi Gamma Delta Educ. Found; mem, Trade Terms Cmt, Int. C. of C, 27-39, Am. sect, Subcmt. to Review Europe-U.S. Trade, 31, mgr, Am. Sect. and U.S. Sect. Inter-Am. Coun. of Commerce and Prod, 43-45; mgr, For. Commerce Dept, U.S. C. of C, 27-45, secy, Nat. Defense Cmt, 33-45, comdr, Nat. For Trade Week, 35-45, secy, Cmt. on Educ, 38-40 and Nat. Policy Coun, 40-41, mem. Spec. Cmt. Int. Postwar Probs, 41-45, mgr, War Serv. Div, 41-45, and mem, Cmt. on Int. Econ. Policy, 44-45; secy, U.S. sect, Can-U.S. Cmt, U.S. and Can. C. of C, 33-45 and Cattleman's Cmt, 37. Publ: Export Technique, 16; Doing Export Business, 27; Foreign Trade Promotion, 30. Mem: Am. Philatelic Soc; Phi Beta Kappa Assocs; Gargoyle, Williams Col; Univ. Club; Cong. Country Club, Wash, D.C; Rehoboth Beach Country Club. Rel: Congregational. Mailing Add: 4523 Hawthorne St. N.W, Washington, D.C. 20016.

BACHMAN, G. CRAIG R
Chmn, Nemaha Co. Rep. Cent. Cmt, Kans.
b. Marion, Kans, 6/4/23; s. George Frederick Bachman and Mary Ann Rathbone B; m. 6/14/47 to Katherine Johanna Lohmuller; c. Bruce Lohmuller, Melissa Jo, Matthew Craig and Johanna Kay. Educ: Kans. State Univ, 41-42 & 45-47; Wichita Univ, 45; Beta Theta Pi. Polit. & Govt. Pos: Farm chmn, Kans. Young Rep. Fedn, 58-59; mem, Gov. Econ. Develop. Cmt, 61-63; mem, Gov. Econ. Research Adv. Cmt, 63-; mayor, Centralia, Kans, 63-; precinct committeeman, Home Twp. Rep. Party, Nemaha Co, 63-; chmn, Nemaha Co. Rep. Cent. Cmt, 66- Bus. & Prof. Pos: Asst. cashier, First Nat. Bank, Centralia, 47-53;v.pres, 53-66 and pres, 66-; v.pres. and treas, Lohmuller-Bachman, Inc, 61- Mil. Serv: Entered as Pvt, Air Force, 42, released as 1st Lt, 45, after serv. in 15th Photo Reconnaissance Squadron, Fifth Group, 15th Air Force, Italy, 44-45; Air Medal with Two Oak Leaf Clusters; Distinguished Unit Citation; Europe-African-Middle East Serv. Medal; Five Battle Participation Awards. Mem: Kans. Bankers Asn.(mem. bank. mgt. cmn, 64-66, statewide advert. cmn, 67-); Kans. State Univ. Endowment Asn.(trustee); Am. Legion; AF&AM; Royal Arch Mason; grand commandery, K.T; Lions; Kans. State C. of C; Boy Scouts of Am. Rel: Congregational. Mailing Add: Centralia, Kans. 66415.

BACHMAN, ILSE D
Mem, Ohio State Dem. Exec. Cmt.
b. Nurnberg, Germany, 5/9/24; m. 10/11/42 to Henry Bachman, M.D; c. David Stanley, Thomas Michael, Barbara June and James Jonathan. Polit. & Govt.

Pos: Co-Chmn, Morgan Co. Jefferson-Jackson Club, Ohio; mem, Dem. State Cent. Cmt, 62-66; del-at-lg, Dem. Nat. Conv, 64, alternate del, 68; mem, State Cand. Screening Cmt, Ohio, 66; mem, State Platform Cmt, 66; mem, Ohio State Dem. Exec. Cmt, 68- Mem: Dir, trustee and secy, Morgan Co. Pub. Libraries, 63-; past pres, PTA; Fedn. Dem. Woman of Ohio; past pres, The Study Club. Mailing Add: 426 E. Union Ave, McConnelsville, Ohio 43756.

BACHMAN, WILLIAM T. D
Pa. State Rep.
b. Eckly, Pa, 1/9/08; s. William Bachman and Harriet M. Aubrey B; m. to Rose Marchetti. Educ: Mining and Mech. Prep. Sch. Polit. & Govt. Pos: Former mem, Foster Twp. Sch. Dist, Pa, former secy, Luzerne Co. Dem. Cmt; former treas, Luzerne Co. Dem. Cmt; former chmn, Dem. Cmt; former revenue agent, Hazleton State Hosp; Pa. State Rep, 60- Mil. Serv: Army Inf, 42 months, serv. in Second Armored Div, ETO; four battle stars; Purple Heart. Mem: United Mine Workers; VFW; DAV; Am. Legion; Moose; Elks; charter mem. Fearnots Fire Co; hon. mem. Hazleton C. of C. and Eckley Soc. and Sports Club. Mailing Add: 125 S. Washington St, Freeland, Pa. 18224. (1967)

BACHRACH, WALTON H. R
b. Cincinnati, Ohio, 12/22/04; s. Fisher Bachrach and Rose Silverglade B; m. 2/4/30 to Ida May Henly; c. Peggy (Mrs. Milton Pockros) and Martha (Mrs. Robert Harris). Educ: Washington & Lee Univ; Univ. Cincinnati Col. of Law, LL.B, 29; Zeta Beta Tau. Polit. & Govt. Pos: Asst. prosecuting attorney, Hamilton Co, Ohio, 33-34, chief dep. clerk of courts, 35-36; city councilman, Cincinnati, 53-, Mayor, 61-68. Bus. & Prof. Pos: Attorney-at-law, 29-37; v.pres, Wheel Cafe Co, 37-66. Mem: Hon. mem, Hotel & Restaurant Employees Union; past gov, Loyal Order of Moose; B'nai B'rith Lodge 4; Miami Lodge 46, F&AM; Ooola Khan Grotto; McMillan Chap. 19, RAM; Scottish Rite; Syrian Temple Shrine; dir, Cincinnati Chap, Am. Red Cross; Dan Beard Coun, Boy Scouts. Rel: Jewish. 1967 Legal Res: Cincinnati, Ohio. No mailing address available. (1967)

BACK, A. G, JR. D
Chmn, Larue Co. Dem. Party, Ky.
b. Drakesboro, Ky, 9/29/23; s. Dr. Adrian G. Back and Ursa Funk B; m. 10/15/49 to Linda Lee Ferrill; c. Mary Donohue and Linda Sue. Educ: Univ. Ky, 40-42; U.S. Naval Acad, B.S.E.E, 45; Sigma Nu; Basketball, Univ. Ky, 2 yrs, U.S. Naval Acad, 3 yrs, named All-Am, 45. Polit. & Govt. Pos: Chmn, Larue Co. Dem. Party, Ky. and elec. cmnr, 60- Bus. & Prof. Pos: Dir, Lincoln Nat. Bank, Hodgenville, Ky, 64-; pres, Donohue Ferrill Motor Co, Inc, 65-; v.pres. and dir, First Nat. Bank, Buffalo, Ky, 66- Mil. Serv: Entered as Ens, Navy, released as Lt.(sg), 53; Comdr, Naval Res; Am, Atlantic and ETO Ribbons. Mem: Naval Acad. Alumni Asn; Rotary; Am. Legion; Farm Bur. Rel: Baptist. Mailing Add: 318 N. Lincoln Blvd, Hodgenville, Ky. 42748 (1967)

BACKES, RICHARD J. D
N.Dak. State Rep.
b. Glenburn, N.Dak, 10/27/25; married; c. three. Educ: Pub. schs. Polit. & Govt. Pos: N.Dak. State Rep, 61- Bus. & Prof. Pos: Farmer. Mil. Serv: World War II. Mem: Am. Legion; Lions; Elks. Mailing Add: Glenburn, N.Dak. 58740. (1967)

BACKMAN, JACK H. D
Mass. State Rep.
b. Saugus, Mass, 4/26/22; s. Saul Backman and Edith Cohen B; m. to Lillian Sagik; c. Steven, Barbara, Marjorie and Judith. Educ: Syracuse Univ, A.B, 43; Harvard Law Sch, LL.B, 48. Polit. & Govt. Pos: Mem, Town Meeting, Brookline, Mass, 59-; mem, Brookline Housing Authority, and Dem. Town Cmt, 60-; Mass. State Rep, 65-; chmn, Mass. Drug Abuse Cmn, 68- Mil. Serv: Entered as Pvt, Army, 43, released as Sgt, 45, after serv. in European, Middle East, Italian and Mediterranean. Mem: Boston Bar Asn; Mass. Trial Lawyers Asn; Harvard Law Sch. Asn; VFW; Jewish War Vets; Am. Legion. Mailing Add: 61 Arlington Rd, Brookline, Mass. 02167.

BACKSTROM, HENRY D
Wash. State Rep.
b. New Britain, Conn, 1897; m. to Elvira; c. three. Educ: Olds Col. of Agr; Edson Inst. Polit. & Govt. Pos: Wash. State Rep. Bus. & Prof. Pos: Ford dealer; owner, truck fabrication plant; ins. and real estate. Mem: Elks; Moose; Lions; Wash. Athletic Club; chmn, trustees of WSADA Ins. Asn. Mailing Add: 516 Olympic Ave, Arlington, Wash. 98223. (1967)

BACKUS, JEAN RAE R
b. Detroit, Mich, 4/24/23; d. Glen Lerch Ettinger and Phebe Wells E; m. 3/18/44 to Ross Allen Backus; c. Ross Allen, Jr. and Pamela Rae. Educ: Albion Col, B.A, 44; Kappa Delta. Polit. Pos: State dir. Mich. Speaker's Bur, GOP State Cent. Cmt; v.chmn, Mich. State Cent. Exec. Cmt; scheduling dir, State Campaign, Spring, 63, Fall, 64; chmn, Oper. Coffee Cup, 62; mem, Mich. State Rep. Cent. Cmt, 6 yrs; v.chmn. Recruit for '60; v.chmn, Shiawassee Co. Rep. Cmt, 56-60; grad, 1st class of Wayne Co. Sch. of Polit. Leadership, 53; pres, Dearborn Women's Rep. Club; v.pres. and bd. mem, Mich. Fedn. of GOP Women. Govt. Pos: Trustee, Cent. Mich. Univ, 64- Mem: Am. Asn. of Univ. Women; United Fund; Memorial Hosp. Auxiliary; Girl Scout Bd. Rel: Christian Science. Mailing Add: 1111 Riverside Dr, Owosso, Mich. 48867. (1967)

BACON, EDGAR D
Va. State Del.
b. Hagan, Va, 12/13/17; m. to Evelyn Colley Edens. Educ: Univ. Tenn; Univ. Va, LL.B, 48; Order of the Coif. Polit. & Govt. Pos: Va. State Del, 66-; del, Dem. Nat. Conv, 68. Bus. & Prof. Pos: Attorney-at-law. Mil. Serv: 1st Lt, Air Force, World War II, serv. as pilot, Four Engine Bomber. Mem: Co. and State Bar Asns; Mason; Lions; Am. Legion; 40 et 8. Rel: Methodist. Mailing Add: Box 236, Jonesville, Va. 24263. (1967)

BACON, MARY ELIZABETH D
Secy, Eighth Cong. Dist. Dem. Party, Mo.
b. El Cajon, Calif, 4/11/98; d. John A. McDonald and Minna J. Roeder M; m. 6/7/19 to Philip A. Bacon; c. Edith Marie, Harry P. and Margaret Ann (Mrs. Smith); 2 grandchildren, Ricki and Vicki Smith. Educ: Southeast State Normal Sch, summer course; Wash. Univ, B.S. in educ, 54; Univ. Mo, exten. course in journalism. Polit. & Govt. Pos: Chmn, Women's Dem. Club Meramec Twp, Mo, 33-36; chmn, Meramec Twp. Dem. Club, 36-50; Meramec Twp. Committeewoman, St. Louis Co. Dem. Cmt, 36-, v.chmn, 36-38, secy, 44-46; secy, 12th Cong. Dist. Dem. Party, 40-42; Mo. State Dem. Committeewoman from Second Cong. Dist, 58-60 & 64-68; del, Dem. Nat. Conv, 64, alternate del, 68; secy, Eighth Cong. Dist. Dem. Party, currently. Bus. & Prof. Pos: Jr. high sch. teacher and sponsor sch. paper, 10 years; elem. sch. teacher for 25 years. Mem: Legis. chmn, charter mem. and former secy, Meramec Bus. & Prfnl. Women's Club; Local, State and Nat. Teachers' Asns; former mem, Co. Teachers' Asn. and Co. Journalism Soc. Rel: Baptist. Mailing Add: Route 1, Box 212, Old Eatherton Rd, Chesterfield, Mo. 63017.

BADEN, JO ANN D
V. Chmn, Montgomery Co. Dem. Cent. Cmt, Kans.
b. Wickes, Ark, 9/20/30; d. Butler James Felts and Florence Gretchen Smith F; m. 2/11/51 to Kenneth Arnold Baden; c. Steven Kenneth and Stanley Joe. Educ: Kans. State Col, Pittsburg, 50-51; Independence Commun. Jr. Col, 60-61; Sigma Sigma Sigma. Polit. & Govt. Pos: Census taker, U.S. Agr. Census, 64; v.pres, Montgomery Co. Young Dem, Kans, 65; precinct committeewoman, Independence Township, 66; mem. invitation cmt, Governor Dockings' Inaugural Cmt, 66; dir, Kans. Dem. Hq, 66-68; vice chmn, Montgomery Co. Dem. Cmt, 66-; census taker, U.S. Civil Defense Surv, 67; secy, Bramble for Cong. Hq, 68; worker campaign materials cmt, S.E. Kans. Citizen's for Humphrey, 68. Rel: Lutheran. Mailing Add: R.R.1, Box 55A, Independence, Kans. 67301.

BADER, GERALD LOUIS R
Secy, Denver Co. Rep. Cent. Cmt, Colo.
b. St. Louis, Mo, 3/15/34; s. Gerald Louis Bader, Sr. and Mable A. Stephens B; m. 8/26/61 to Catherine Louise Ince; c. Gerald Louis, III, Stephanie Anne, Cynthia Anne and Carlie Diane. Educ: Wash. Univ, B.A, 56; Univ. Mich, LL.B, 59; Phi Beta Kappa; Omicron Delta Gamma; Phi Delta Theta. Polit. & Govt. Pos: Asst. capt. and finance chmn, Dist. 12, Rep. Party, Colo, 66-; campaign mgr. and worker, Colo. Rep. Party, 67-68; secy, Denver Co. Rep. Cent. Cmt, Colo, 69- Bus. & Prof. Pos: Attorney, White & Case, N.Y.C, 60-62 & 64-65, Hodges, Silverstein & Harrington, Denver, Colo, 65-68; partner, Friedman, Bader & Moore, 69- Mil. Serv: Entered as 2nd Lt, Army, 62, released as 1st Lt, 64, after serv. in 4th Mil. Intel. Detachment, 6th Army, U.S, 62-64. Mem: Mo, Colo, Denver and Am. Bar Asns; Asn. of the Bar of City of N.Y; Denver Jr. C. of C; Consumer Credit Counseling Serv, Gr. Denver, Inc.(secy. and bd. dirs); Denver Coop. Endeavor Cmt. Rel: Catholic. Legal Res: 859 Cove Way, Denver, Colo. 80209. Mailing Add: 301 Equitable Bldg, Denver, Colo. 80202.

BADER, PALMER WALTER D
Chmn, Deuel Co. Dem. Orgn, S.Dak.
b. Hartley, Iowa, 1/24/03; s. George Bader and Emma Ruwe; m. 4/25/42 to Mabel Anderson; c. Janice. Educ: Common Schs, Iowa and S.Dak. Polit. & Govt. Pos: Chmn, Deuel. Co. Dem. Orgn, S.Dak, 42- Bus. & Prof. Pos: Owner & operator, Clear Lake Lustk. Sales Agency, 43-63. Rel: Am. Lutheran. Mailing Add: Box 41, Clear Lake, S.Dak. 57226.

BADGER, LeMOYNE SMITH R
Mem, Calif. Rep. State Cent. Cmt.
b. Hinckley, Utah, 11/18/24; s. John C. Badger and Mae Smith B; m. 3/23/46 to Lorna Doone Hay; c. Lyle Douglas, Larry Steven, Lynette Ann, Lou Anne and Leo Allan. Educ: Univ. Calif, Los Angeles, A.B, 48; Stanford Sch. Law, LL.B, 52. Polit. & Govt. Pos: Dep. dist. attorney, Riverside Co, Calif, 52-56; dist. dir, Calif. Rep. Assembly, 58; chmn, Riverside Co. Rep. Cent. Cmt, 59; v.chmn, Riverside Calif. Parking and Traffic Cmn, 59-; campaign mgr, several Rep. campaigns, 60-; mem, Calif. Rep. State Cent. Cmt, 66-; Rep. cand, U.S. Rep, Calif, 38th Cong. Dist, 68. Bus. & Prof. Pos: Private practice of law, Badger Biddle & Ensign, 56- Mil. Serv: Entered as Pvt, Army, 43, released as Corp, 46, after serv. in 99th Inf. Div, ETO, 44-46. Mem: Pres, Riverside Co. Bar Asn; dir, Inland Apt. Owners Asn; pres, Riverside Jr. C. of C; dir, Riverside C. of C; pres, Riverside Opera Asn. Mailing Add: 3608 Beechwood Place, Riverside, Calif. 92506.

BADHAM, ROBERT EDWARD R
Calif. State Assemblyman
b. Los Angeles, Calif, 6/9/29; s. Byron Jack Badham, Jr. and Bess Kissinger B. (deceased); div; c. Sharon Ann, Robert E, Jr. and William Arthur. Educ: Occidental Coll, 48-49; Stanford Univ, A.B, 51; Phi Gamma Delta. Polit. & Govt. Pos: Mem. adv. cmt, Nat. Rivers and Harbors Cong; mem, Orange Co. Rep. Cent. cmt, Calif, 63-66; mem. exec. cmt, Calif. Rep. State Cent. Cmt, 63-66; Calif. State Assemblyman, 71st Dist, 63-; alternate del, Rep. Nat. Conv, 64 & 68. Mil. Serv: Entered as Ens, Naval Res, 52, released as Lt.(jg), 54, after serv. as Opers. Officer, Korean War, CIC Instr, Fleet Training Center, Pearl Harbor, 54; China Serv. and Nat. Defense Ribbons; Korean Serv. Ribbon with 2 Stars; UN Medal; Korean Presidential. Unit Citation. Publ: 'Who's an Extremist,' Orange Co. Sun, 9/65, 'Orange County's Coastal Freeway,' 10/65, 'Getting Specific About a Program of Social Welfare,' 5/66. Mem: Am. Soc. of Archit. Hardware Consult; Nat. Builders Hardware Asn; legis. affairs cmt, Orange Co. Assoc. C. of C; Balboa Bay Club; Orange Empire Coun, Boy Scouts; Friends of the Libr, Univ. Calif, Irvine; Friends of the Calif. State Col, Fullerton; Orange Co. Coast Asn; Am. Legion. Rel: Lutheran. Legal Res: 1320 Antigua Way, Newport Beach, Calif. 92660. Mailing Add: 1649 Westcliff Dr, Newport Beach, Calif. 92660.

BADILLO, HERMAN D
Pres, Borough of Bronx, N.Y.
b. Caguas, P.R, 8/21/29; married; c. one. Educ: City Col. N.Y, B.A. magna cum laude, 51; Brooklyn Law Sch, LL.B. cum laude, 54, Class Valedictorian; Beta Gamma Sigma; Alpha Beta Psi. Polit. & Govt. Pos: Dep. cmnr, N.Y.C, 62, cmnr. for relocation, 63-66; pres, Borough of Bronx, N.Y, 66-; chmn, Cmt. Health, Housing and Soc. Serv, N.Y. State Constitutional Conv, 67; del, Dem. Nat. Conv. and mem. credentials cmt, 68; cand. for Dem. nomination for

Mayor of N.Y.C, 69. Bus. & Prof. Pos: With Ferro, Berdon & Co. Cert. Pub. Acct, 51-55; attorney, Permut & Badillo, 55-62. Mem: Nat. Conf. Christians and Jews; chmn, Boy Scouts' Coun. Mailing Add: 405 W. 259th St, Bronx, N.Y. 10471.

BAER, E. D. 'BUSTER' R
Chmn, Walworth Co. Rep. Cent. Cmt, S. Dak.
b. Selby, S.Dak, 6/29/25; s. Emanuel Dale Baer and Mary Schnaible B; m. 6/27/50 to Maxine L. Colborn; c. Tanya Lee, Melanie Dale and Rogene Marie. Educ: North. State Teachers Col, 46-48; Univ. Nebr, B.S. in Bus. Admin, 51. Polit. & Govt. Pos: Chmn, Walworth Co. Rep. Cent. Cmt, S. Dak, 64- Mil. Serv: Entered as Seaman, Navy, 44, released as Storekeeper 2/C, 46, after serv. in Pac; Victory Medal; Am. Theater Medal; Asiatic Pac. Theater Medal and one star; Philippine Liberation Medal and one star. Mem: Am. Legion; Elks; Mason; Selby Commercial Club; S.Dak. Independent Ins. Agents Asn. Rel: Lutheran. Mailing Add: Selby, S.Dak. 57472.

BAER, JOHN MILLER D
b. Blackcreek, Wis, 3/29/86; s. Elizabeth Caroline Riley B; m. 12/28/10 to Estella Gertrude Kennedy; c. John M, Alfred S. and Byron. Educ: Laurence Univ, B.A, 09; Beta Theta Phi. Polit. & Govt. Pos: U.S. Rep, 17-21. Bus. & Prof. Pos: Cartoonist, AFL-CIO and LABOR Newspaper. Mem: Nat. Press Club. Rel: Congregational. Mailing Add: 3809 East West Highway, Chevy Chase, Md. 20015.

BAER, T. JOHN, JR. D
Colo. State Rep.
b. Melvern, Kans, 4/1/23; s. True John Baer and Wilda Carter B; m. 1/17/43 to Laura Marie Oliver; c. Linda Marie (Mrs. Ruth), Peggy Jean (Mrs. Sommerville), Ronald John and James William; granddaughter, Robin Sommerville. Educ: Mesa Col. Polit. & Govt. Pos: Former committeeman, Agr. Conserv. and Stabilization Cmt, Colo; mem, Dem. Patronage Cmt, Mesa Co, 63-64; Colo. State Rep, 65-, mem, Hwy. Cmt, Natural Resources Cmt. and Agr. and Livestock Cmt, Colo. State House of Rep. Bus. & Prof. Pos: Farmer and feeder. Mem: Bd. and past pres, Beet Growers Asn, 50-65; bd, Grand Valley Water Users Asn, 59-64; first pres, Mesa Co. Tomato Growers, 50-57; pres, Loma Commun. Coun, 57-60; Farm Bur; Farmers Union; Odd Fellows; Moose; C. of C. Rel: Loma Commun. Church. Legal Res: 13Q 1/4 Rd, Loma, Colo. 81524. Mailing Add: Box 38, Loma, Colo. 81524. (1967)

BAFALIS, LOUIS A. 'SKIP' R
Fla. State Sen.
b. Boston, Mass, 9/28/29; s. Louis John Bafalis and Vesta Reenstierna B; m. 2/18/56 to Mary Elizabeth Lund; c. Renee Louise and Gregory Louis. Educ: St. Anselm's Col, A.B, 52. Polit. & Govt. Pos: Fla. State Rep, 64-66; Fla. State Sen, 33rd Dist, 67- Bus. & Prof. Pos: Pres. and mem. of bd, First Am. Ins. Co, Miami, Fla; dir. of bd, First Nat. Bank and Trust Co, Riviera Beach. Mil. Serv: Entered as Pvt, Army, 52, released as Capt, 55, after serv. in artil. Publ: Drug Abuse—Like It Is, H. & W. B. Drew Co, 69. Mem: V.chmn, Palm Beach Co. Red Cross; chmn, Muscular Dystrophy; Lions (v.pres, Palm Beach club); North Palm Beach, Palm Beach Gardens, Riviera Beach and Lake Park Jaycees; C. of C; Islanders; dir, S. Fla. Fair; dir, North Co. YMCA; F&AM. Rel: First Christian. Legal Res: 122 N. County Rd, Palm Beach, Fla. 33480. Mailing Add: P.O. Box 1031, Palm Beach, Fla. 33480.

BAFFORD, HALLIE B. D
Chmn, Macon Co. Dem. Party, Ill.
b. Macon, Ill, 4/29/21; s. Benjamin F. Bafford and Ona A. Avis B; m. 2/14/41 to Dorothy M. Aukamp; c. Jerry E, Peggy J.(Mrs. Sprague), Jill D.(Mrs. Snyder), Robin M. and Denna L. Educ: Macon Commun. High, 35-39; Activity Award and Outstanding Student, Macon Commun. High. Polit. & Govt. Pos: Rep. Precinct committeeman, S. Macon Precinct 2, Ill, 50-69; v.chmn, Macon Co. Dem. Party, Ill, 56-58 and chmn, 68-; supvr, S. Macon Twp, 63- Mil. Serv: Entered as Pvt, Army, 44, released as Pfc, 45, after serv. in 506 Combat M.P. Unit, ETO; Good Conduct Medal; Two Battle Stars. Mem: Am. Legion; Mason; Consistory; Shrine; Eastern Star; Musicians Union. Rel: Presbyterian; Elder. Mailing Add: 342 W. Eckhardt, Macon, Ill. 62544.

BAGAGLIA, ALFRED D
b. North Providence, R.I, 5/3/24; s. Antonio Bagaglia and Michelina Cardente B; m. 1/1/51 to Antonetta Croce; c. Beverly A, Alfred A. and Lori A. Educ: Bryant Col, B.S. in bus. admin, 48; Univ. R.I. Exten. Sch. Polit. & Govt. Pos: Mem, North Providence Zoning Bd, R.I, 59-60; R.I. State Rep, North Providence, 61-67. Bus. & Prof. Pos: Off. mgr, Prudential Investment Corp, 49-58; self-employed in acct. and ins, Alfred Bagaglia Agency, 58- Mil. Serv: Entered as Pvt, Army, 43, released as Sgt, 46. Mem: Nat. Asn. Accountants; R.I. and Nat. Asns. Ins. Agents; Marieville Volunteer Fire Dept; Holy Name Soc, Presentation Church; Bouffard Coun, K. of C; troop committeeman, Boy Scouts; Amvets. Rel: Catholic. Legal Res: 32 Cleveland St, North Providence, R.I. 02904. Mailing Add: 1072 Mineral Spring Ave, North Providence, R.I. 02904.

BAGBY, GEORGE TALMADGE D
b. Dallas, Ga, 10/26/20; s. Joel Pinkney Bagby Jr. and Stella Roberson B; m. 4/07/40 to Mamie Ruth Wright; c. Michael Jeffrey, Judith Frances and George Thomas. Educ: W.Ga. Col, 37-39; John Marshall Law Sch, LL.B, 50. Polit. & Govt. Pos: Ga. State Rep, 47-48, 55-60 & 62-66, Speaker-Pro-Tem, Ga. House of Rep, 59-60; dir, State Game and Fish Cmn, Ga, 67- Bus. & Prof. Pos: Attorney. Mil. Serv: Seaman 1/C Navy, serv. in U.S.S. Colorado, Philippine Islands, Okinawa and Japan Occup. Mem: Mason; Shrine. Rel: Methodist. Mailing Add: Dallas, Ga. 30132.

BAGGE, CARL ELMER R
V.Chmn, Fed. Power Cmn.
b. Chicago, Ill, 1/12/27; s. Hjalmar Bagge and Adele Elmquist B; m. 6/25/53 to Margaret Evelyn Carlson; c. Carol Eileen, Barbara Ann, Charles Edward and Beverly Jean. Educ: Uppsala Univ, 47; Augustana Col, B.A. summa cum laude, 49; Northwest. Univ. Sch. of Law, J.D, 52; Univ. South. Calif, 56; Phi Beta Kappa; Pi Kappa Delta; Delta Omega Nu. Polit. & Govt. Pos: Asst. to dir. of publicity, Cook Co. Rep. Cmt, Ill, 48; precinct capt, Eighth Ward Rep. Orgn, 49-52; mem, Zoning Bd. of Appeals, W. Deerfield, 55-58; chmnr, Deerfield Planning Cmn, 58-63; cmnr, Fed. Power Cmn, 65-66, v.chmn, 66-67 & 69-; chmn. working cmt. on utilities, Presidents Coun. on Recreation and Natural Beauty, 68- Bus. & Prof. Pos: Lectr, Stockholm Univ, 47; reporter, Chicago Daily News, 50; attorney, Atchison Topeka & Santa Fe Rwy. Co, 52-62, asst. gen. attorney, 62-63, spec. asst. to pres, 63-64, gen. attorney, 64-65. Mil. Serv: Entered as Seaman, Navy, 45, released as Ens, Naval Res, 51, after serv. in Naval Intel, Submarine Base, Coco Solo, C. Z. Publ: Contrib, The Supreme Court, N.H. Wilson Co, N.Y, 61; 'Compulsory Unionism: An Analysis,' 1/58 and 'Federalism: An Appraisal,' 10/58, Christian Century. Mem: Am. and Chicago Bar Asns; chmn, Pub. Utilities Law Sect, Ill. Bar Asn, 56-58; Am. Judicature Soc; Asn. of Interstate Commerce Cmn. Practitioners; Econ. Club of Chicago; Cong. Country Club, D.C; Capitol Hill Club, D.C; Swedish Club of Chicago; Cmn. on Church and Econ. Life, Nat. Coun. of Churches; trustee, Inst. of Educ. and Ecumenical Rels; mem. exec. cmt, Nat. Asn. Regulatory Utility Cmnr; Coun. of Churches of D.C; Legal Club of Chicago; Lexington Group of Bus. Historians; Ill. State Hist. Soc; Am. Scandinavian Found; trustee, Lutheran Student Found. of Metrop. Chicago and Augustana Col. Rel: Lutheran; church sch. teacher, St. Pauls Lutheran Church, Wash, D.C. Legal Res: 721 Colwyn, Deerfield, Ill. 60015. Mailing Add: 3500 Leland, Chevy Chase, Md. 20015.

BAGGETT, AGNES BEAHN D
Treas, State of Ala.
b. Columbus, Ga, 4/9/05; d. John Richard Beahn and Leila Belle Thomason B; m. 10/14/26 to George Lamar Baggett, wid. Educ: Courses at Jones Law Sch, Montgomery, Ala. Polit. & Govt. Pos: Secy. of state, Ala, 51-55 & 63-67, state auditor, 55-59, state treas, 59-63 & 67- Mem: Eastern Star (past matron, Elizabeth Armstrong Chap); Altrusa Club; Am. Legion Auxiliary; Girls State (chmn, 3 years); past pres, Montgomery and Ala. State Fedn. of Bus. & Prfnl. Women's Club. Rel: Methodist. Career Woman; Ten Top Women. Mailing Add: 3202 Montezuma Rd, Montgomery, Ala. 36106.

BAGGETT, BRYCE A. D
Okla. State Sen.
b. Oklahoma City, Okla, 6/4/32; s. James Everett Baggett and Esther Roberta Tippens B; m. 12/21/53 to Barbara Jean Bolton; c. Bryce Allen, Jr, Breene Everett and Barbara Lynn. Educ: Univ. Okla, A.B, 54, LL.B, 56; Phi Delta Phi. Polit. & Govt. Pos: Okla. State Rep, 58-64; Okla. State Sen, 64- Bus. & Prof. Pos: Partner, Fellers, Snider, Baggett, Blankenship and Bailey, currently. Mailing Add: 2700 First National Bldg, Oklahoma City, Okla. 73102.

BAGGETT, JULIUS HERBERT D
b. Florence, S.C, 2/14/25; s. Julius Herbert Baggett and Myrtis Turner B; m. 3/15/44 to Evelyn Ruth Heacox; c. Stephen Douglas, David Jay, Amy Susan and Judy Kay. Educ: Furman Univ, B.A, 48; Univ. S.C, LL.B, 49; Omicron Delta Kappa; Theta Chi. Polit. & Govt. Pos: Dir, McCormick Co. Civil Defense, S.C, 61-63; mem, McCormick Co. Bd. of Registrn, 62-66; S.C. State Rep, 67-68. Bus. & Prof. Pos: Attorney, U.S. Dept. of Agr, 50-57, McCormick, S.C, 58-, Parksville, 64- and McCormick Co, 66- Mil. Serv: Entered as A/S, Navy, 43, released as Signalman 2/C, 45, after serv. in Armed Guard, Atlantic, Mediterranean, 44-45; ETO Campaign Ribbon; Good Conduct Medal. Mem: S.C. and Am. Bar Asns; Am. Jurisprudence Soc; Am. Legion; Mason; Exchange Club; WOW. Rel: Methodist. Legal Res: Cherry St, McCormick, S.C. 29835. Mailing Add: P.O. Box 8, McCormick, S.C. 29835. (1967)

BAGGETT, W. TATE R
b. St. Stephen, 2/4/11; s. W. T. Baggett (deceased) and Sadie Venning B. Educ: St. Stephen Pub. Sch. Polit. & Govt. Pos: St. Stephen town coun, 2 terms. Bus. & Prof. Pos: Partner, Lane Mfg. Co; farmer and timber broker. Mem: St. Stephen Lions Club; Berkeley Co. Farm Bur. Rel: Presbyterian. Mailing Add: St. Stephen, S.C. 29479. (1967)

BAGGS, THOMAS MARSHALL D
b. Abbyville, Kans, 9/22/12; s. George Franklin Baggs and France Shull B; m. 1/9/41 to Florence Margaret Manwell; c. Frances (Mrs. Syd Delaplane), Betty (deceased), Mary Ann (Mrs. David Olmstead), Michael Clifford, Marshall George and Charles Joseph. Educ: Hutchinson High Sch, grad, 30; Portland State Col, 4 night classes. Polit. & Govt. Pos: Dem. cand, U.S. House of Rep, 68. Bus. & Prof. Pos: Shipping clerk and serv. mgr, Finzer Bus. Machines, Portland, Ore, 45-51, salesman, 51-58, treas, salesman, stockholder and dir, 58- Mil. Serv: Entered as Pvt, Army, 38, released as S/Sgt, 45, after serv. in 603rd TD Bn; ETO, 44-45; Bronze Star Medal; Good Conduct Medal; ETO Ribbon. Mem: Kiwanis Club; Abernethy Grange (master); Sunrise Toastmasters Club (pres). Rel: Protestant; Treas, Harmony Evangelical Church of N.Am. Mailing Add: 12675 S.E. 88th, Portland, Ore. 97266.

BAGLEY, RICHARD MARSHALL D
Va. State Del.
b. Hampton, Va, 5/14/27; m. to Nancy Murray B. Educ: Va. Polytech. Inst, B.S; Omicron Delta Kappa. Polit. & Govt. Pos: Va. State Del, 66-; Hampton Dem. Cmt; Peninsula Indust. Cmt, bd. dirs; Peninsula C. of C, bd. dirs; Citizens and Marine Bank, bd. dirs. Bus. & Prof. Pos: Pres, Bagley Investment Co. Mil. Serv: Coast Guard; Air Force Res, Maj. Mem: James River Country Club; Hampton Rotary Club; Propeller Club; Peninsula V.P.I. Alumni Chap; Am. Legion; Mason (32°), Shrine; Peninsula Arts Asn. Rel: Episcopal; Vestry, St. John's Episcopal Church. Mailing Add: P.O. Box 9, Hampton, Va. 23369.

BAGLEY, WILLIAM D. D
b. Afton, Wyo. 3/28/40; s. William B. Bagley and Della Newswander B; m. 10/30/65 to Margaret Ann Seward; c. William Seward and John Marion. Educ: Univ. Wyo, B.B.A, 62, LL.B, 64; Alpha Kappa Psi; Potter Law Club; Sigma Chi. Polit. & Govt. Pos: Bus. mgr. and co-ed, Wyo. Dem, 59-62; pres, Univ. Wyo. Young Dem. Club, 60-63; mem, Wyo. Dem. Cent. Cmt, 62-64; regional dir, Young Dem. Clubs of Am, 63-64; admin. asst. to U.S. Rep. Teno Roncalio, Wyo, 64-66; asst. prosecuting attorney, Laramie Co, Wyo, 67- Bus. & Prof. Pos: Owner and mgr, WIDBA Enterprises, 58- Publ: 'The 'Ought' and 'Is' of Bad Check Statutes,' Wyo. Law J, 63 and Northwest. Law J, 64; 'Warranty as a Lawyers Tool,' Wyo. Law J, 64. Mem: Wyo, Fed. and Am. Bar Asns; Burro Club. Rel: Latter-day Saint. Legal Res: 920 Western Hills Blvd, Cheyenne, Wyo. 82001. Mailing Add: P.O. Box 467, Cheyenne, Wyo. 82001.

BAGLEY, WILLIAM THOMPSON R
Calif. State Assemblyman
b. Woodacre, Calif, 6/29/28; s. Nino J. Baglietto and Rita V. Thompson B; m. 6/20/65 to Diane L. Oldhan; c. William T, Jr, Lynn L, Walter W, Shana and Tracy. Educ: Univ. Calif, Berkeley, B.A, with honors and Valedictorian, 49; Univ. Calif. Law Sch, LL.B, 52; Phi Beta Kappa, permanent class pres; Bd. Ed, Calif. Law Rev. Polit. & Govt. Pos: Gen. counsel and dir, Calif. Young Rep, 56; chmn, Marin Co. Young Rep, 57; chmn, budget and finance cmt, Calif. Young Rep, 57; v.pres, First Marin Co. Rep. Assembly, 57; regional dir, Calif. Rep. Assembly, 58; chmn, Marin Campaign Cmts, Weinberger and Powers, 58; v.pres, Calif. Rep. Assembly, 59; mem, Marin Co. and State Rep. Cent. Cmt, 60-69; Calif. State Assemblyman, Seventh Dist, 60-, former chmn, Finance and Ins. Cmt. and Judiciary Cmt, Calif. State Assembly, chmn, Revenue and Taxation Cmt, mem, Ways and Means and Govt. Orgn. Cmt; chmn, Spec. Cmt. Open Pub. Records and mem, Select Cmt. Admin. Justice, currently; co-chmn, Marin Co. Nixon for Gov, 62; statewide legis. liason, Nixon Staff, 62; mem, Rep. Legis. Task Force for Nixon, 62; Rockefeller Presidential Del, 64; hon. co-chmn, Marin Co. Goldwater for Pres. Cmt, 64; statewide speakers bur, Murphy for Sen. Cmt, 64; co-chmn, Marin Co. Christopher for Gov. Cmt, 66; North. Calif. staff and speakers bur, Reagan for Gov, 66; statewide campaign cmt, Finch for Lt. Gov, and Flournoy for Controller, 66; chmn, Calif. media rel. cmt, Nixon-Agnew Campaign, 68. Bus. & Prof. Pos: Partner, Bagley, Bianchi & Sheeks. Mem: Marin Co, San Francisco, Calif. and Am. Bar Asns; dir. and chaplain San Rafael, Elks; Native Sons; Commonwealth Club Calif; Redwood Empire Asn; Marin Rod and Gun Club; Tamalpais Conserv. Club; San Rafael C. of C; Marin Coun. Civic Unity; dir, Calif. Alumni Asn; dir, Univ. Calif. Law Sch. Alumni Asn; dir, San Francisco Barristers' Club; chmn, Marin Heart Sunday Drive. Rel: Presbyterian. Legal Res: 1 Fawn Court, San Anselmo, Calif. 94960. Mailing Add: 225 Albert Bldg, San Rafael, Calif. 94901.

BAGNAL, HARRY STROMAN R
N.C. State Sen.
b. Winston-Salem, N.C, 5/5/28; s. Luther Nettles Bagnal and Susie Lofton B; m. 4/4/59 to Anne Elizabeth Broyles; c. Harry S, Jr, David C, Alice Anne, Mary Lofton and Samuel Joseph. Educ: The Citadel, A.B, 49; Univ. N.C, grad. sch, 1 year. Polit. & Govt. Pos: N.C. State Sen, 66-; mem. exec. cmt, Forsyth Co. Rep. Party, N.C, 66-; mem, N.C. State Rep. Cent. Cmt, 69- Bus. & Prof. Pos: Secy-treas, Bagnal Lumber Co, 65- Mil. Serv: Entered as 2nd Lt, Army, 50, released as 1st Lt, 52, after serv. in 3rd Army, ETO, 51-52. Mem: Nat. Hardwood Lumber Asn; Hardwood Dimensions Mgrs. Asn; Am. and N.C. Forestry Asns; C. of C. Rel: Baptist. Mailing Add: 2861 Wesleyan Lane, Winston-Salem, N.C. 27106.

BAGNARIOL, JOHN A. D
Wash. State Rep.
b. Renton, Wash, 1/23/32; s. John M. Bagnariol and Violet Umbinetti B; m. 4/21/51 to Edna M. Kane; c. Michael, Jody, David, Sharon, Teresa, Lori, Gina and Angela. Educ: Franklin High Sch, grad, 49. Polit. & Govt. Pos: Wash. State Rep, 66- Mem: Wash. Ins. Asn; Nat. Asn. of Life Underwriters; Kiwanis. Rel: Catholic. Mailing Add: 10450 61st Ave. S, Seattle, Wash. 98178.

BAGWELL, HARRISON GAREY R
Mem, Rep. State Cent. Cmt, La.
b. Georgetown, La, 12/6/13; s. Arthur D. Bagwell and Birdie Harrison B; m. 6/13/36 to June Sue Ross; c. H. Garey, Jr, Carole (Mrs. John R. Shows, Jr), Janet (Mrs. Donald R. Patt), June (Mrs. Robert C. Oliver), Barry, Bonnie and Martha Sue. Educ: La. State Univ, B.A, 40, LL.B, 42, J.D, 68. Polit. & Govt. Pos: Pres. and founder Sixth Cong. Dist. Rep. Club, 50-60; co-legal counsel La. del, Rep. Nat. Conv, 52; del. or alternate del, Rep. Nat. Conv, 52, 56 & 60; mem. govt. study and recommendation cmt, City of Baton Rouge and Parish E. Baton Rouge, 52-54; chmn. legis. cmt, Rep. State Cent. Cmt, La, 52-60 and mem, 60-; pres. and founder Rep. Orgn. La, 56-60; mem. chmn. and secy. exec. cmt, East Baton Rouge Parish Rep. Party, 56-; chmn, Cong, Sen. and Dist. Rep. Cmt, 60- Bus. & Prof. Pos: Ed, Trumpet Pub. Co, Inc, 54-58. Mem; E. Baton Rouge Bar Asn.(secy, 45-48). Rel: Protestant. Legal Res: 5811 Menlo Dr, Baton Rouge, La. 70808. Mailing Add: 658 St. Louis St, Baton Rouge, La. 70802.

BAHENSKY, LEROY R
b. Merrick Co, Nebr, 2/8/09; m. 8/8/28 to Alice Julia Kotrc; c. Dorothy, Rena, Loretta and Cheryl. Polit. & Govt. Pos: Nebr. State Sen, 59-66. Bus. & Prof. Pos: Land appraiser. Mem: Pres. Spalding Commun. Club; Mason; Flying Farmers. Rel: Methodist. Mailing Add: 417 S. Cotner Bldg, Lincoln, Nebr. 68510. (1967)

BAHNSON, FRED F. JR. D
b. Winston Salem, N.C, 8/26/13; s. Fred F. Bahnson and Bleeker E. Reid B; m. 2/5/42 to Louise Bennett; c. Fred F, III, Bert B. and Bleeker L. Educ: McCallie Sch, Chattanooga, Tenn, 30-31; Univ. of N.C, AB, 1935; Sigma Alpha Epsilon, Chapel Hill. Polit. & Govt. Pos: Chmn, Forsyth Bd. Cmnrs, 56-60; N.C. State Rep, 63-66. Bus. & Prof. Pos: Pres, South. Steel Stampings Inc. Mem: N.C. Cattlemen's Asn.(past pres); past mem. bd. trustees, Salem Col; trustee, East. Carolina Col; Winston-Salem Kiwanis (past pres); trustee, Univ. N.C. Rel: Moravian; Elders, Trustee, Home Moravian Church. Mailing Add: 2035 Georgia Ave, Winston-Salem, N.C. 27104.

BAHOU, VICTOR SAMUEL D
Chmn, Cortland Co. Dem. Cmt, N.Y.
b. Watertown, N.Y, 1/18/21; s. Samuel Bahou and Najiy Abdo B; m. 11/12/44 to Charmotte Mae Ajay; c. Carole and Barbara. Educ: Bard Col, B.A, 51; Syracuse Univ, D.S.Sc, 60. Polit. & Govt. Pos: Chmn, Cortland Co. Dem. Cmt, N.Y, currently. Mem: Am. and N.Y. State Polit. Sci. Asns; Eastern Sociol. Soc; Nat. Munic. League; Am. Sociol. Asn. Mailing Add: 54 Church St, Cortland, N.Y. 13045.

BAILES, E. LAMAR, JR. D
Exec. Committeeman, S.C. Dem. Party
b. Anderson, S.C, 4/10/35; s. E. Lamar Bailes and Margaret Linley B; m. 10/1/60 to Rosemary Fort; c. E. Lamar, III and Carol Susan. Educ: Ga. Inst. Tech, B.I.E, 58; Kappa Sigma; Ga. Tech. T Club. Polit. & Govt. Pos: Alderman, Walhalla, S.C, 63-; pres, Young Dem. of Oconee Co, 65-; alternate del, Dem. Nat. Conv, 68; exec. committeeman, S.C. Dem. Party, 68- Bus. & Prof. Pos: Indust. engr, Eastman Kodak Co, Rochester, N.Y, 57-60; v.pres, Linley Lumber Co, Inc, Walhalla, S.C, 60- Mil. Serv: Capt, S.C. Army Nat. Guard. Mem: Piedmont Urban Policy Conf, Brookings Inst; Past Dist. Dep. Grand Master, S.C. A&FM. Mailing Add: 18 Lovingood Ave, Walhalla, S.C. 29691.

BAILES, GEORGE LEWIS JR. D
Ala. State Sen.
b. Atlanta, Ga, 4/26/19; s. George Lewis Bailes, Sr. and Emilu Fox B; m. 9/23/39 to Rudene Becht Leach; c. Rudene (Mrs. A.L. Crowe), George L. III, Warren L. and Emilu Fox (Mrs. W.C. Brown, Jr). Educ: Mars Hill Col, N.C; Marion Mil. Inst, 34; Univ. Ala, 39. Polit. & Govt. Pos: V.chmn, Dem. State Exec. Cmt, Ala, 58-62; Ala. State Rep, 62-66; Ala. State Sen, 67- Mil. Serv: Capt, Army Air Corps; Maj, Ala. Nat. Guard. Mem: Mason; Shrine; Am. Legion; VFW. Rel: Episcopal. Mailing Add: 600 Euclid Ave, Birmingham, Ala. 35213.

BAILEY, CARL LEROY, JR. D
Mem, N.C. State Dem. Exec. Cmt.
b. Roper, N.C, 6/3/24; s. Carl LeRoy Bailey, Sr. and Vivian Putman B; m. 8/3/57 to Jarahnee Hinson; c. Franklin LeRoy and Trevor Leigh. Educ: Wake Forest Col, 48; Wake Forest Law Sch, 50; Sigma Phi Epsilon; Phi Alpha Delta. Polit. & Govt. Pos: N.C. State Rep, 63-65; mem, Wash. Co. Dem. Exec. Cmt, 66-68; mem, N.C. State Dem. Exec. Cmt, 66-; mem, Platform and Resolutions Cmt, Dem. State Conv, 68- Bus. & Prof. Pos: Attorney, Plymouth, N.C, 50-; chmn. bd. dirs, Home Savings & Loan Asn, 67- Mem: N.C. State Bar; N.C. Bar Asn; Second Judicial Dist. Bar.(pres, 62-63, 69-); Rotary (dir, Plymouth Rotary Club, 68, v.pres, 69). Outstanding Young Man of the Year Distinguished Serv. Award, Plymouth Jr. C. of C, 54. Rel: Baptist. Legal Res: 108 Latham Lane, Plymouth, N.C. 27962. Mailing Add: 202 E. Water St, Plymouth, N.C. 27962.

BAILEY, CONSUELO NORTHROP R
Secy, Rep. Nat. Cmt.
b. Fairfield, Vt, 10/10/99; d. Peter Bent Brigham Northrop and Katherine Fletcher N; wid. Educ: Univ. Vt, Ph.B, 21; Boston Univ. Law Sch, LL.B, 25; Phi Beta Kappa; Sigma Gamma; Kappa Beta Pi; Phi Sigma Pi. Hon. LL.D, Univ. Vt, Am. Int. Col. and Cedar Crest Col, 56. Polit. & Govt. Pos: States attorney, Chittenden Co, Vt, 26-28; White House Mem, Cmt. Refugees; mem, U.S. Civil War Centennial Cmn; mem. at lg, Civil Defense Womens Adv. Cmt; del, Rep. Nat. Conv, 36, 44 & 68, mem. final draft cmt, 44, secy, 69; mem, Rep. Nat. Cmt, 36-, v.chmn, 52-56, first woman chmn, Cmt. of Call, 60, secy, 64-; Vt. State Rep, 50-52, speaker, Vt. House of Rep; mem. adv. bd, U.S. Post Office, 53; Lt. Gov, Vt, 54; mem, state, co. and town Rep. cmt; Presidential Elector, 56; Nat. Committeewoman Vt, 9 times; mem, Vt. Hist. Sites Cmn, 69. Bus. & Prof. Pos: Teacher, Latin and hist, high sch, Shelburne, Vt, 21-22; former dir, Iroquois Light and Power Co; mem, Bd. Womens Med. Col, Phila, Pa; mem, Peter Bent Brigham Corp; attorney, Burlington, 26-66; mem. bd. dirs, Tuttle Law Print Co, 57-; owner and operator, Vt. Farm, Fairfield. Publ: Primary and Election Laws of Vermont 1928. Mem: Zonta Int.(pres, Burlington br, 30-32); admitted to Vt. Supreme Court, 26, U.S. Dist. Court 27, U.S. Supreme Court, 33 and U.S. Customs Court 42; Vt. Bar Asn; Vt. Asn. Blind (former dir); Univ. Vt. Alumni Coun.(former rep); Vt. Order of Women Legislators (former pres); hon. mem, Daughter of Vt, Boston; Champlain Valley Grange; Calvin Coolidge Found.(trustee); Vt. Rose Soc.(former pres); Vt. Hist. Site Cmn, 69- Official observer for Vt. at Las Vegas detonation of atomic bomb, 54; visited Free German Republic as Guest of that country with Women in Public Life, 56. Rel: Episcopal. Legal Res: 1317 Spear St, South Burlington, Vt. 05401. Mailing Add: 203 Main St, Burlington, Vt. 05401.

BAILEY, DANIEL A. R
Pa. State Sen.
b. Pike Twp, 6/5/94; s. Lewis E. Bailey and Jennie Adams B; m. 4/27/27 to Sarah Melba Wells; c. Barbara Wells (Mrs. Filbert E. Spinelli). Educ: Am. Inst. Banking; Pa. State Univ, 46-47. Polit. & Govt. Pos: Dist. twp. engr, Pa. Dept. Hwys, 39-43, chief twp. engr, 44-55; cmnr, Centre Co. Rep. Party, 60-62; Pa. State Sen, 62- Mil. Serv: Army, 18-19; serv. in 320th Inf. Regt, France. Mem: Legis. Cmt, State Asn. Co. Cmnrs; Centre Co. Child Welfare Bd; Nat. and State Socs. Prfnl. Engrs; Am. Legion; VFW; Elks; Rotary; Mason. Mailing Add: 21 N.Second St, Philipsburg, Pa. 16866.

BAILEY, EDWARD RISTON R
Tenn. State Rep.
b. Reagan, Tenn, 5/19/19; s. Dorsie Green Bailey and Betty Cricket Stewart B; m. 5/20/39 to Mableen Overman; c. Betty Carol. Educ: Freed-Hardeman Col, 36-37 & 38-39. Polit. & Govt. Pos: Mem, City Coun, Lexington, Tenn, 49-53 & 55-67, mayor, 53-55; Tenn. State Rep, 66-; chmn, Tenn. Rep. State Exec. Cmt, 69- Bus. & Prof. Pos: Teacher, Henderson Co. Dept. Educ, Tenn, 39-41; clerk, U.S. Govt, Panama Canal Zone, 41-42; foreman, Proctor and Gamble Co, Milan, 43; self employed, Retail Food Sales, 44-50, Mfg. and Wholesale Hardwood Lumber, 50-69. Mem: Lions; Mason (32°); Shrine; Farm Bur. Rel: Baptist. Legal Res: N. Broad St, Lexington, Tenn. 38351. Mailing Add: P.O. Box 296, Lexington, Tenn. 38351.

BAILEY, ELSIE C. D
b. Sunapee, N.H, 1/10/96; single. Educ: Kimball Union Acad. Polit. & Govt. Pos: Sullivan Co. Rural Areas Develop; N.H. State Rep, until 67. Bus. & Prof. Pos: Partner, The Flower Shop; bd. dirs, Newport Industs, Inc; Newport Hosp. Corp. Mem: Bus. & Prfnl. Women's Club; Crescent Rebekah Lodge; N.H. Fedn. Bus. & Prfnl. Women's Club,(past pres); N.H. Order of Women Legislators (past pres). Rel: Episcopal. Mailing Add: 10 South St, Newport, N.H. 03773.

BAILEY, ELVIN LOUIS D
Chmn, Judith Basin Co. Dem. Cent. Cmt.
b. Peabody, Kans, 10/22/06; s. James Riley Bailey and Lillie Landry B; m. 7/3/43 to Cecelia Krier; c. Willis James. Educ: Windham Pub. Schs, Mont, 11 years; Stanford Pub. Sch, Mont, 27. Polit. & Govt. Pos: Sheriff, Judith Basin Co, Mont, 43-47; chmn, Judith Basin Co. Dem. Cent. Cmt, 54-; election judge, Stanford Precinct Number 9, Mont, 56 & 58. Bus. & Prof; Pos: Rancher, Mont, 28- Mem: Mont. Farmers Union; Nat. Farmers Orgn; Live-

stock Producers; Farmers Coop. Oil Co.(bd. dirs, 30 years). Rel: Presbyterian. Mailing Add: Stanford, Mont. 59479.

BAILEY, GENE W. D
Chmn, Kanawha Co. Dem. Cmt, W.Va.
b. Charleston, W.Va, 11/26/26; s. Simon Bailey and Frances Greer B; m. 9/5/48 to Juanita Manning; c. Gene W, II, Jeffrey A. and Jennifer F. Educ: W.Va. Univ, A.B, 49, LL.B, 52; Phi Alpha Delta. Polit. & Govt. Pos: Former city attorney, Belle, W.Va; legal asst. to State Tax Cmnr, 52-56; pres, Kanawha Co. Young Dem, 53-56; W.Va. State Del, 62-65; chmn, Kanawha Co. Dem. Cmt, 69- Bus. & Prof. Pos: Lawyer. Mil. Serv: Army, 44-45. Mem: W.Va. State Bar; Am. Legion. Rel: Methodist. Mailing Add: 307 39th St. S.E, Charleston, W.Va. 25304. (1967)

BAILEY, HARLEY EVAN D
Committeeman, Wood Co. Dem. Party, W.Va.
b. Cedarville, W.Va, 7/16/15; s. Herbert Jefferson Bailey and Ervie Stoneking B; m. 6/29/35 to Helen Catherine Kirkpatrick; c. Carolyn Sue and Lynn Louise. Educ: Ohio Univ, B.A. in philos, 45; Bible Baptist Sem, B. Bibliology, 48, Dr. Bibliology, 49; Burton Col, Dr. Divinity, 52; Ohio Univ. Alumni Asn. Polit. & Govt. Pos: Dep. sheriff, Wood Co, W.Va, 57-58; welfare worker, W.Va, 63-65; del, Rep. Nat. Conv, 64 & 68; committeeman, Wood Co. Dem. Party, W.Va, 64-; housing inspector, City of Parkersburg, 65- Bus. & Prof. Pos: High sch. teacher, Belpre Sch. Syst, Ohio, 57-58; minister, Jefferson Baptist Temple, 57-; Rep, Waddell & Reed, Inc, 59-; high sch. teacher, Calhoun Bd. of Educ, W.Va, 63-64. Mil. Serv: Chaplain (Capt), Civil Air Patrol, W.Va. Wing, 53- Mem: Nat. Educ. Asn; Mason (32°); Eastern Star; WOW. One of 300 in U.S. selected for honor of tape recording in John F. Kennedy Mem. Mus, Boston, Mass. Rel: Baptist. Mailing Add: P.O. Box 3103, Parkersburg, W.Va. 26101.

BAILEY, HOWARD TAFT D
b. Lexington, Miss, 11/21/13; s. Washington S. Bailey and Mary Jane Olds B; m. 7/11/37 to Lillie B; c. Bertha M.(Mrs. Charles E. Jefferson), Barbara J.(Mrs. Sylvester Davis), Lillian D.(Mrs. James Moore), George W, Stephen, Bettee J, James, Elmer V. and Mary J. Educ: Ambrose Voc. High Sch, Lexington, Miss, 4 years. Polit. & Govt. Pos: Del, Dem. Nat. Conv, 68; chmn, Holmes Co. Elec. Cmn, Miss, 69- Bus. & Prof. Pos: Coop. organizer, Mileston Farmers Coop, 67- Mem: Farm Bur; Farmers Coop; NAACP. Sweepstake Winner in Home Improv, 67. Rel: United Methodist. Legal Res: Route 3, Box 57, Lexington, Miss. 39095. Mailing Add: P.O. Box 445, Lexington, Miss. 39095.

BAILEY, J. J. D
Educ: Phi Kappa Phi. Pol. & Govt. Pos: Ind. State Sen, 61-66; Ind. State Rep, 59-60, 55-56, 49-52; Treas, Madison Co. Sch. Employees Credit Union 25 yrs. Bus. & Prof. Pos: Teacher of Civics. Mem: Vice-Chmn, Ind. Civil War Centennial Comm; Comm. to Study Facilities at Penal Inst; Ind. Sch. Bldg. Constr. Study Comm; Gov. Comm. on Natural Resources; Fed. of Teachers; Nat. Educ. Asn; Ind. Schoolmen's Club; Mason; Scottish Rite; Ind. Acad. of Soc. Sci. Rel: Methodist. Mailing Add: 2941 George St, Anderson, Ind. 46014. (1967)

BAILEY, JAMES RUFFIN D
N.C. State Sen.
b. Jacksonville, N.C, 4/13/19; s. Isaac Mayo Bailey and Ida Thompson B; m. 1/18/45 to Nelle Rousseau; c. James Ruffin, Jr. and Jane Rousseau. Educ: Univ. N.C, A.B, 41, Law Sch, LL.B, 48; Pi Kappa Alpha; Phi Delta Phi. Polit. & Govt. Pos: N.C. State Sen, 65- Bus. & Prof. Pos: Lawyer. Mil. Serv: Army Air Force, 41-45; Lt. Col, Air Force Res. Mem: Wake Co. and N.C. Bar Asns; N.C. State Bar. Mem. of Vestry, 50-52, 54-56, 61-63; Jr. Warden, 53, 56. Rel: Episcopal. Mailing Add: 924 Cowper Dr, Raleigh, N.C. 27608. (1967)

BAILEY, JOHN MORAN D
Chmn, Conn. Dem. State Cmt.
b. Hartford, Conn, 11/23/04; s. Michael Bailey and Louise Moran B; m. 8/1/33 to Barbara Leary; c. Louise (Mrs. Conrad Kronholm), Barbara (Mrs. James Kennelly) and twins, Judith and John Michael. Educ: Catholic Univ, A.B. in Sci, 26; Harvard Univ, LL.B, 29. Polit. & Govt. Pos: Exec. secy. to mayor, Hartford, Conn, 31-33; mem, Conn. Dem. State Cmt, 32-, chmn, 46-; judge, Munic. Court, Hartford, 33-35 & 39-41; law clerk, judiciary cmt, Conn. State Legis, 37 and cmnr, statute rev, 41-46; exec. secy. to Gov. of Conn, 46; v.chmn, Metrop. Dist. Cmt. within Hartford, 51; mem, Gr. Hartford Flood Cmt, 55, Conn. Econ, Planning and Develop. Cmt, 56 and Conn. Fiscal Study Cmt, 57; chmn, Dem. Nat. Cmt, 61-68; del, Dem. Nat. Conv, 68. Bus. & Prof. Pos: Dir, New Amsterdam Casualty Co. and South End Bank; sr. partner, Bailey & Wechsler, 46- Mem: Am, Conn. State and Hartford Bar Asns; mem. founders cmt, Univ. Hartford; bd. dir, St. Francis Hosp; Harvard Univ. Alumni Asn; Catholic Univ. Alumni Asn; co-chmn. adv. cmt, Who's Who in American Politics; Wethersfield and Wamdanoag Country Clubs; Burning Tree Club; Hartford C. of C; K. of C.(4°); Elks; cmnr, Promotion Uniformity of Legis. in U.S, 57. Rel: Roman Catholic. Mailing Add: 150 Scarborough St, Hartford, Conn. 06105. (1967)

BAILEY, JOHN W, JR. R
Finance Chmn, Johnson Co. Rep. Party, Ind.
b. Southport, Ind, 4/16/21; s. John W. Bailey and Katherine Rypma B; m. 1/12/46 to Alice C. Schafer; c. Allan and Bruce. Educ: Ind. Univ, B.S. in bus, 43; Blue Key; Alpha Kappa Psi; Bd. of Aeons. Polit. & Govt. Pos: Johnson Co. chmn, Ind. Almanac and Govt. Guide, 63-66; finance chmn, Johnson Co. Rep. Party, Ind, 63-; finance chmn, Goldwater Campaign, Seventh Cong. Dist, 64; alternate del, Rep. Nat. Conv, 64, del, 68; mem. exec. cmt, Ind. Rep. Citizens Finance Cmt. and finance chmn, Sixth Cong. Dist, 66- Bus. & Prof. Pos: Ins. agent, Bailey & Hill Ins. Serv, 46- Mil. Serv: Entered as Pvt, Army, 43, released as Capt, 46, after serv. in Hq, Ninth Army, ETO. Mem: C. of C; Ind. Univ. Alumni Asn. Rel: Methodist. Mailing Add: 605 Valley Lane Court, Greenwood, Ind. 46142.

BAILEY, JOSEPH NATHANIEL, JR. D
b. Coffeeville, Miss, 4/25/13; married. Polit. & Govt. Pos: Miss. State Rep, 1952-68. Bus. & Prof. Pos: Farmer; merchant; lumberman. Mem: Shrine; C. of C; Am. Legion; VFW; Delta Kappa Epsilon; Mason. Rel: Methodist. Mailing Add: Box 296, Coffeeville, Miss. 38922. (1967)

BAILEY, MANSON HARVEY, JR. D
Mem, City-Co. Planning Bd, Glasgow, Mont.
b. Billings, Mont, 3/3/20; s. Manson Harvey Bailey and Addie May Michael B; m. 8/7/46 to Betty Jean Hansen; c. Mari Vawn, Manson Harvey, III, Tana Jean and Kim Marie. Educ: High Sch. Polit. & Govt. Pos: Mem. bd. supvrs, Valley Co. Soil and Water Conserv. Dist, Mont, 51-57; mem, Mont. Fish and Game Cmn, 52-56, chmn, 55; mem, City-Co. Planning Bd, Glasgow, 63-; Mont. State Rep, Valley Co, 63-67 and Valley and Daniels Co, 67-69; pres, Valley Co. Develop. Coun, 69- Bus. & Prof. Pos: Farmer and rancher, 46-; field engr. and safety engr, E.V. Lane Corp, Eagle-West. Construct, 57-60; archit. inspector, Kurk Assocs, Archit. Engrs, 61-62; rep, Financial Prog, Inc, 63-66; rep, Ehli & Hughes, Inc, 66- Mil. Serv: Entered as Pvt, Army, 42, released as S/Sgt, 46, after serv. in 908th Field Artil. Bn, 83rd Inf. Div, Cent. Europe Campaign, 45; European-African-Middle Eastern Campaign Ribbon with 1 Bronze Battle Star; Am. Theater Ribbon; Victory and Good Conduct Medals with 1 Serv. Stripe and 4 Overseas Bars. Publ: 'Administrative Relationships Between Commissions and Departments,' Proceedings of 35th Annual Conf, Western Asn. of State Game and Fish Cmnrs, 6/55. Mem: Nat. Asn. Security Dealers; bd. dirs, State Asn. Soil and Water Conserv. Dist, 55; past pres. and dir, Valley Ridgerunners Saddle Club; Valley Co. Stockgrowers Asn; Boy Scouts (exec. bd, Yellowstone Valley Coun, 68-). Distinguished Serv. Award, Jr. C. of C; two Good Year Awards for Soil Conserv. achievement; Presidents Award, Mont. Wildlife Fedn, 68. Rel: Latter-day Saint; Branch Pres, 56-63 & 69- Mailing Add: Box 743, Glasgow, Mont. 59230.

BAILEY, RAY V. D
b. Royal, Iowa, 12/14/13; s. George L. Bailey and Marie Albers B; m. 6/18/38 to Maxine Sheldon; c. Theron S. and George Bryan. Educ: Univ. Iowa, B.A, cum laude, 35, J.D. cum laude, 37. Polit. & Govt. Pos: Past chmn, Pub. Affairs Cmt, Wright Co. Exten. Coun, Iowa; Iowa State Rep, Wright Co, 65-69, mem, Departmental Rules Rev, Ethics, Appropriations, Commerce, Judiciary, Ways and Means, Steering and Sifting Cmts. and Non-Con Subcmt, Iowa House of Rep; mem, State Bd. of Regents, Iowa, currently. Bus. & Prof. Pos: Research patent counsel, U.S. Gypsum Co, Chicago, 37-39; investr, U.S. Civil Serv. Cmn. and patent adv, War Dept, Warld War II; dir, Clarion Commun. Develop. Cmn; owner of farms; dir, Colonial Homes, Inc; lawyer, patent attorney and property mgr, currently. Mem: Lions; Univ. Iowa Alumni Coun; past pres, Univ. Iowa Dads Asn; Iowa State Bar Asn; Am. Bar Asn.(mem, patent syst. policy planning cmt, Patent, Trademark and Copyright Sect). Silver Beaver Award, Boy Scouts. Rel: Methodist and Christian Science. Mailing Add: 518 First St. N.W, Clarion, Iowa 50525.

BAILEY, ROBERT C. D
Wash. State Sen.
b. Raymond, Wash, 1918; m. to Lee Bailey; c. one son. Polit. & Govt. Pos: Wash. State Sen, currently; West. admin. asst. to Julia Butler Hansen, U.S. Rep, Wash, currently. Mil. Serv: Navy, WWII. Mem: Eagles; VFW; Am. Legion; Mason; Boy Scout Coun. Mailing Add: 602 W. First St, South Bend, Wash. 98586.

BAILEY, ROBERT D. D
b. Baileysville, W.Va, 10/12/12; s. Robert D. Bailey and Sue Starkey B; m. 12/4/44 to Jean Hickman; c. Robert D, III. Educ: Wash. & Lee Univ, LL.B, 34; Phi Delta Phi. Polit. & Govt. Pos: Asst. prosecuting attorney, Wyo. Co, W.Va, 38-49, prosecuting attorney, 49-61; del, Dem. Nat. Conv, 64; Secy. of State, W.Va, 65-68. Bus. & Prof. Pos: Pres, Castle Rock Bank of Pineville, Inc, Radio Sta. WWYO, Independent Herald and Pineville Gas Co; assoc, Bailey, Worrell and Bailey, Attorneys, Pineville, 34-38 and Bailey, Worrell & Camper, Attorneys, 61- Mil. Serv: Entered as Pvt, Army, 43, released as M/Sgt, 46, after serv. in 7th Army, ETO; Three ETO Campaign Ribbons. Mem: Am. and W.Va. Bar Asns; pres, Wyo. Co. Bar Asn, 62-63; Shrine; Mason (32°); John W. Morris Consistory; Elks; Army and Navy Club; charter mem. and past pres, Pineville Rotary; VFW; Am. Legion; Moose; former mem, Gov. Conflict of Interest Cmn, W.Va. Hon. Ky. Col. Rel: Methodist. Mailing Add: Pineville, W.Va. 24874. (1967)

BAILEY, TROY SAMUEL D
b. Princeton, W.Va, 10/21/15; s. Raymond E. Bailey and Mamie Wright B; m. 4/20/43 to Mary Weis; c. Kathleen C. and Richard S. Polit. & Govt. Pos: Del-at-lg, Dem. Nat. Conv, 68. Rel: Catholic. Mailing Add: R.D. 3, Box 35, Bridgeport, W.Va. 26330

BAILEY, WESLEY D
b. Winston-Salem, N.C, 6/20/31; s. Cicero England Bailey and Olivia Shurley B; m. 4/28/56 to Joanna Ray; c. David, Jr. and Cheryl. Educ: Wake Forest Col, B.S, 53, Law Sch, LL.B, 55; Phi Alpha Delta. Polit. & Govt. Pos: Pres, Wilsonian Dem. Club, 58-60; secy, Forsyth Co. Dem. Exec. Cmt, 62-64; N.C. State Rep, 67-69. Mil. Serv: Sgt, Army Res, 10 years. Mem: Forsyth Co. Jr. Bar Asn.(secy, 56-57); Am. and N.C. Bar Asns; N.C. State Bar; Forsythe Co. Sr. and Jr. Bars; Optimists; PTA. Rel: Methodist. Legal Res: 707 Ransom Rd, Winston-Salem, N.C. 27106. Mailing Add: P.O. Box 52, Winston-Salem, N.C. 27102.

BAILEY, WILLIAM DISHAROON D
Treas, Dem. State Cent. Cmt, Caroline Co, Md.
b. Quantico, Wis. Co, Md, 12/7/22; s. Marion Cadmus Bailey and Sarah Emma Disharoon B; separated; c. Karen (Mrs. Gibb). Educ: State Teachers Col, Salisbury, Md; Beacom Bus. Col, Wilmington, Del. Polit. & Govt. Pos: Chmn, Dem. State Cent. Cmt, Caroline Co, Md, 62-66, treas, 66- Bus. & Prof. Pos: Exec. v.pres, The Caroline Co. Bank, Greensboro, Md, 47. Mil. Serv: Entered as Pvt, Army, 43, released as Sgt, 45, after serv. in Pac. Mem: AF&AM (master, Temple Lodge 128, 60). Rel: Methodist. Mailing Add: Main St, Greensboro, Md. 21639.

BAILIN, HAROLD A. D
Mem, Calif. Dem. State Cent. Cmt.
b. Los Angeles, Calif, 5/1/30; s. Isaac John Bailin and Bessie Abrams B; m. 11/30/57 to Joan Gilbert; c. Marguerite, Victoria and Alison. Educ: Univ. Calif. Los Angeles, B.A, 51; Univ. Calif, Berkeley Sch. of Law, J.D, 55. Polit. & Govt. Pos: Dep. attorney Gen, State of Calif, 56; mem, San Bernardino Co. Dem. Cent. Cmt, Calif, 62-68, v.chmn, 2 years; mem, Calif. Dem. State

Cent. Cmt, 64- Bus. & Prof. Pos: Partner, Thorne & Bailin, Attorneys, 56-59, Crowe, Bailin & Gladson, Attorneys, 64-68 and Covington & Crowe, Attorneys-at-law, 68- Mil. Serv: Entered as Cpl, Army Nat. Guard, 50, released as Sgt, 52, after serv. in Japan, 51-52; Japan Theatre Ribbon. Publ: 'Family Law: Separate Maintenance: Integrated Property and Support Agreement,' Calif. Law Rev, 55; 'Fundamentals of Criminal Discovery,' Calif. Trial Lawyers Asn. Annual Seminars, 68. Mem: Calif, Am, San Bernardino Co. and West. San Bernardino Co. Bar Asns; Am, Calif. and local Trial Lawyers Asns; Upland C. of C.(pres, 67-68, dir, 61-63 & 65-68); Upland Rotary Club (dir, currently). Outstanding Young Man of the Year, Ontario-Upland Commun, 65. Rel: Unitarian. Legal Res: 300 W. 22nd St, Upland, Calif. 91786. Mailing Add: P.O. Box 990, Upland, Calif. 91786.

BAILLARGEON, WILFRED J. D
R.I. State Rep.
b. Woonsocket, R.I, 2/6/18. Educ: Woonsocket High Sch, 37. Polit. & Govt. Pos: Mem. bd. of canvassers, 1 term; R.I. State Rep, 61- Bus. & Prof. Pos: Bus. rep, Int. Asn. of Machinists; dir, Taft-Peirce Employees' Credit Union. Mem: K. of C. Rel: Catholic. Mailing Add: 104 Hemond Ave, Woonsocket, R.I. 02895. (1967)

BAILY, THOMAS S. R
Secy, Greene Co. Rep. Cmt, Pa.
b. Waynesburg, Pa, 6/28/10; s. Harry Francis Baily and Lucy Sayers B; m. 9/7/40 to Inis Slaugenhaupt; c. Thomas S, II. Educ: Carnegie-Mellon Univ, B.S, 33; Sigma Nu. Polit. & Govt. Pos: State committeeman, 46 State Sen. Dist. Rep. Party, Pa, 62-; secy, Greene Co. Rep. Cmt, 63-; alternate del, Rep. Nat. Conv, 68. Bus. & Prof. Pos: Partner, Baily Ins. Agency, 56; pres, Greene Co. Indust. Develop. Corp, 66. Mil. Serv: Entered as Pvt, Army, 43, released as S/Sgt, 45, after serving in 136th Infantry Regt. Pac, 44-45; Bronze Star. Mem: Elks; Moose; Mason (32°); Shrine; Isaac Walton League. Rel: Protestant. Mailing Add: R.D. 5, Waynesburg, Pa. 15370.

BAIN, CARL EDGAR R
Chmn, Richmond Rep. City Cmt, Va.
b. Roanoke Co, Va, 1/23/27; s. Milton Albert Bain and Martha Kate Barton B; m. 3/3/51 to Irene Estelle White; c. Patricia Ann, Sarah Collie and Catherine Irene. Educ: Med. Col. of Va, B.S, Pharm, 51; Alpha Sigma Chi; Phi Delta Chi. Polit. & Govt. Pos: Mem, Richmond Rep. City Cmt, Va, 66-, chmn, 68-; Rep. cand, Va. House Rep, Richmond-Henrico, 67 & 69. Bus. & Prof. Pos: Bd. of Dirs, Retail Merchants Asn, Richmond, 69- Mil. Serv: Entered as Seaman, Navy, 45, released as PhM 3/C, 47. Mem: Richmond and Am. Pharmaceutical Asns; Va. Asn. of the Professions (treas, 68-); Nat. Asn. of Retail Druggists; Va. Pharmaceutical Asn.(pres, 66-67); Rotary Int; Willow Oaks Country Club; Bull and Bear Club. Rel: Baptist. Mailing Add: 109 Maple Ave, Richmond, Va. 23226.

BAIN, JEAN KNIGHT R
Colo. State Rep.
b. Denver, Colo, 9/27/09; d. Roger Davis Knight and Nelle Hoop K; m. 6/12/33 to Francis Marion Bain; c. Donald Knight and Lawrence Joseph. Educ: Univ. Colo, A.B, 31; Katherine Gibbs Sch, Boston, 31-32; Kappa Kappa Gamma. Polit. & Govt. Pos: Mem, Cmn. Commun. Rels, City and Co. of Denver, 58-69; mem. defense adv. cmt. on women in serv, Dept. Defense, 60-63; Colo. State Rep, Denver, 61- Bus. & Prof. Pos: Trustee, Doane Coll, 64- Mem: Hon. mem, Delta Kappa Gamma; Altrusa Int; League Women Voters; Am. Asn. Univ. Women; Nat. Order Women Legislators; Rep. Roundtable. Kiwanis award of month; Cosmopolitan Club Award. Rel: United Church of Christ. Mailing Add: 755 Gaylord St, Denver, Colo. 80206.

BAIN, LAURENCE DIXON, JR. D
Mem. Exec. Bd, Bergen Co. New Dem. Coalition, N.J.
b. Salt Lake City, Utah, 2/2/32; s. Laurence Dixon Bain and Rena Bosker B; m. 8/11/56 to Elizabeth Jean MacDonald; c. Jonathan Sargent, Mark MacDonald and Elise Dixon. Educ: Dartmouth Col, B.A. cum laude, 54; Union Theol. Sem, 58-59; Columbia Univ, 1 year; Rufus Choate Scholar in Philos, Dartmouth Col, 52-54; Rockefeller Bros. Fel. in Relig, Union Theol. Sem, 58-59. Polit. & Govt. Pos: Del, Dem. Nat. Conv, 68; founding chmn, Bergen Co. New Dem. Coalition, 68 and mem. exec. bd, 68-; mem. nominating cmt, N.J. New Dem. Coalition, 68 and conv. del, 68-69; mem, Bergen Co. Dem. Cmt, 69. Bus. & Prof. Pos: Educ. rels. mgr, West. Elec, N.Y.C, 62-64 and commun. rels. mgr, 64-65; pub. rels. mgr, Am. Tel. & Tel, 65-67; exec. v.pres, Westbeth Corp, 67-; spec. consult. on housing and urban affairs, Kaplan Found, 67- Rel: Episcopal. Mailing Add: 282 Shadyside Rd, Ramsey, N.J. 07446.

BAINBRIDGE, EUGENE HENRY D
Ind. State Sen.
b. East Chicago, Ind, 2/20/11; s. Thomas Henry Bainbridge and Ruby Mae Harper B; m. 6/3/39 to Stella Krakowiak; c. Phillip Eugene, David Keith and Carol Lynn. Educ: Ind. Univ, Calumet Region Campus, three years. Polit. & Govt. Pos: Ind. State Sen, 52-61 & 62-; cmnr, Dept. of Admin, State of Ind, 62. Bus. & Prof. Pos: Employee, Cities Serv. Oil Co, East Chicago, Ind, 33-53; secy-treas, Oil Dealers, Inc, Hammond, Ind, 53-; pres, E. H. Bainbridge Supply, 65- Mem: K. of P; Moose. Rel: Methodist. Mailing Add: 8309 Northcote Ave, Munster, Ind. 46321.

BAIR, DONALD O. R
Pa. State Rep.
b. Pittsburgh, Pa, 5/9/03; s. Joseph Oliver Bair and Etta Beebe B; c. Donald O, Jr. and Janet B.(Mrs. Ashmun). Educ: Univ. Pittsburgh; Sigma Alpha Epsilon. Polit. & Govt. Pos: Committeeman, State Rep. Party, Pa, 10 years; chmn, Dormont Rep. Party, 8 years; Dormont Borough councilman, 4 years; pres, 45th Sen. Dist. Orgn, 8 years; chmn, Allegheny Co. Rep. Adv. Cmt, 60-61; mem, Allegheny Co. Young Rep; Pa. State Rep, 63-; hon. mem, Bethel Park Young Rep; pres, Upper St. Clair Rep. Club, 3 years; chmn, Mgt. Manpower Prog; pres, 40th Legis. Asn. Bus. & Prof. Pos: Right of way rep, eng. dept, Bell Telephone Co.(Retired). Publ: Pennsylvania Municipal Directory, 56-57. Mem: Mason; charter pres, Dormont Lions; former pres. and mem. bd. trustees, Dixmont State Hosp. Rel: Protestant. Legal Res: 425 Clair Dr, Upper St. Clair, Pa. 15241. Mailing Add: Box 11603, Pittsburgh, Pa. 15228.

BAIRD, RAYMOND RENFRO D
Tenn. State Sen.
b. Jellico, Tenn, 7/6/14; s. Orlando L. Baird and Alice Gallaway B; m. 11/25/38 to Martha Louise Cagle; c. Ray R, Jr. and Nancy Louise. Educ: Hiwassee Col; E.Tenn. State Univ; Ed, col. newspapers. Polit. & Govt. Pos: Mem, Dem. Exec. Cmt, Tenn, 46-; Tenn. State Rep, 54-60; Tenn. State Sen, 60- Bus. & Prof. Pos: Ed-publisher, The Rockwood Times, 41-; treas, Tenn. Press Asn, 56-60, pres, 61-62, dir, 62- Mil. Serv: Entered as Pvt, Army, 44, released as Sgt, 46, after serv. in 61st Signal Bn, S.Pac. and Japan; Good Conduct Medal; S.Pac. Campaign and Japan Occupation Ribbons; Two Battle Stars; Expert Rifleman's Badge. Mem: Am. Legion; VFW; DAV; past pres, Civitan; 40 et 8; Mason, Shrine, Scottish Rite; K. of P; life mem, Jr. C. of C; Tenn. Cong. of Parents and Teachers. Named Most Outstanding Legislator for 57 & 65. Rel: Baptist; Sunday Sch. Teacher. Legal Res: 132 N. Kingston Ave, Rockwood, Tenn. 37854. Mailing Add: P.O. Box 297, Rockwood, Tenn. 37854.

BAIRD, ROSE D. D
b. Burke, Vt, 9/15/02; m. to Earl Baird; c. Five. Educ: Lyndon Inst. Polit. & Govt. Pos: Former town clerk and treas; asst. town clerk, 60-62; Vt. State Rep, 65-66. Mem: Farm Bur. Rel: Catholic. Mailing Add: West Burke, Vt. 05871 (1967)

BAIRD, RUSSELL MILLER
Mem, Chicago Crime Cmn, Ill.
b. Chicago, Ill, 8/4/16; s. Frederick Rogers Baird and Ruth Miller B; m. 3/28/42 to Martha Steere; c. Lindsay Ruth, Scott Rogers and Frederick Rogers II. Educ: Univ. Chicago, A.B, 38; Harvard Univ, LL.B, 41. Polit. & Govt. Pos: Mem. citizens bd, Univ. Chicago, 58-; mem, Chicago Crime Cmn, Ill, 60- Bus. & Prof. Pos: Admitted to Ill. Bar, 41; partner, Leibman, Williams, Bennett, Baird & Minow, 41- Mil. Serv: Lt, Naval Res, 42-46. Mem: Vis. cmt, col, Univ. Chicago, 61-, Divinity Sch, Univ. Chicago, 63-; pres, Ment. Health Asn. Greater Chicago, 62-64; Am, Ill. and Chicago Bar Asns; Legal Club of Chicago, pres, 62-63; Law Club of Chicago; Wine and Food Soc. Chicago; Clubs: Univ, Racquet, Execs, bd. gov, Int. House, Nat. Lawyers (Wash, D.C); River Forest, Tennis, Oak Park Country, Crystal Downs and Country (Frankfort, Mich). Mailing Add: 727 Keystone Ave, River Forest, Ill. 60305.

BAKER, ALVA SAYRS, JR. D
b. Baltimore, Md, 6/22/17; s. Alva Sayrs Baker and Florence Ewell Johnson B; m. 6/17/39 to Dorothy Elizabeth Airey; c. Catherine Ways (Mrs. Mattheiss), Alva Sayrs, III and Susan Deborah. Educ: Univ. Md, B.S, 39; Alpha Gamma Rho; Block and Bridle Club. Polit. & Govt. Pos: Del, Md. Dem. State Conv, 58; chmn, Md. Dem. State Cent. Cmt, 62-68. Bus. & Prof. Pos: Secy-treas, Howard Co. Farm Bur, Inc, 49-; treas. and supvr, Howard Soil Conserv Dist, 50- Mem: Md. Soc. of SAR; Patmos Lodge 70, AF&AM; Patapsco Grange 403. Rel: Methodist. Mailing Add: Albee Farm, Marriottsville, Md. 21104. (1967)

BAKER, BENNIE WADE D
b. Langley, S.C, 12/13/09; s. Walter E. Baker, Sr. and Sally Eidson B; m. 4/4/31 to Helen Timmerman B; c. Arthur L, Wade W. Educ: Langley, S.C, high sch. Polit. & Gov. Pos: S.C. State Rep, 61-66: former mem, Aiken Co. Bd. of Educ; former trustee, Aiken Co. Hosp. Bus. & Prof. Pos: Retail merchant. Mil. Serv: Army, 44-45. Mailing Add: Box 7, Langley, S.C. 29834. (1967)

BAKER, BERT D
b. 5/31/23; married; c. 1 son. Educ: W. Franfkort Ill. High Sch, 40. Mil. Serv: Army, 36th Inf. Div, Awarded Bronze Star Medal with Cluster; Purple Heart with Cluster. Mem: Am. Legion; VFW. 1967 Legal Res: 205 W. Fifth, Benton, Ill. 61516. No mailing address available. (1967)

BAKER, BERTRAM L. D
N.Y. State Assemblyman
b. Nevis, B.W.I, 1/10/98; m. to Irene L; c. Two daughters. Educ: Cambridge Univ. Prep Sch, St. Kitts, B.W.I; LaSalle Exten. Univ. Polit. & Govt. Pos: N.Y. Dem. State Committeeman; Registered Dem. Organizer, Sixth Assembly Dist, Kings Co; exec. mem, United Action Dem. Asn; U.S. Dep. Collector of Internal Revenue, 39-41; mem, local sch. bd, 41-44; confidential inspector to pres. of Borough of Brooklyn, 44-48; N.Y. State Assemblyman, 48- Bus. & Prof. Pos: Acct. Mem: YMCA; Acct. Asn. of N.Y; NAACP; F&AM; Brooklyn Br, Urban League of Gr. N.Y; exec. secy, Am. Tennis Asn; bd. dirs, Brooklyn Div, Protestant Coun. of N.Y.C; chmn. bd. dirs, N.Y. Tennis Asn. Mailing Add: 399 Jefferson Ave, Brooklyn, N.Y. 11221. (1967)

BAKER, BETTY H. D
b. Thomas, W.Va, 9/18/19; d. Harry D. and Kathryn Agnes Higgins Head B; m. 11/22/45 to Donald J. Baker (deceased); c. Martha Louise, Donald J. Jr, Susan Taylor and Stephen Clark. Educ: W.Va. Univ, B.S; Phi Beta Kappa. Polit. & Govt. Pos: W.Va. State Sen, 65-69; del, Dem. Nat. Conv, 68. Mem: Active in local and state Women's Clubs. Rel: Presbyterian. Mailing Add: 212 Winchester Ave, Moorefield, W.Va. 26836.

BAKER, CARROLL WILLIAM R
b. Burleigh Co, N.Dak, 3/19/15; married; c. 5. Educ: Pub. schs. Polit. & Govt. Pos: N.Dak. State Sen, 61-66; N.Dak. State Rep, 47-57; N.Dak. Bd. of higher Educ, 57-60. Mailing Add: Minot, N.Dak. 58701. (1967)

BAKER, CHARLES ALDEN D
b. Damascus, Va; s. Charles Alden; Effie Wyckoff B; m. to Frances Gaskins Educ: Princeton, N.J. High Sch. Polit. & Govt. Pos: N.C. State Rep, 63-67. Bus. & Prof. Pos: Owner and mgr, Radio Sta. WGAI. Mem: Dir, N.C. Asn. of Broadcasters; Rotary; Dist. Committeeman, Boy Scouts; trustee, Museum of Albemarle; South. Regional Educ. Bd; Carolina Soc. of Asn. of Execs; exec. dir, N.C. Educ. Coun. on Nat. Purpose; dir, Roanoke Island Heart Asn; Raleigh Pub. Rels. Soc. Rel: Methodist. 1967 Legal Res: Elizabeth City, N.C. No mailing address available. (1967)

BAKER, DR. CHARLES CURTIS R
b. Hamilton, Tex, 3/5/02; s. Dr. Charles Curtis Baker, Sr. and Alma Nickolson B; m. 10/30/26 to Marjorie Duffie; c. Charles Curtis, III, Stella

Gretchen and Joffin Duffie. Educ: N.Mex. Mil. Inst, 18-22; Tex. Dent. Col, Houston, 22-26. Polit. & Govt. Pos: Chmn, Leon River Dist, Hamilton Co, Tex; chmn, Hamilton Co. Rep. Cmt, 42-66; state committeeman, 12th Dist, Rep. Party, Tex, 48-66. Mem: Am. Dent. Asn; Tex. Dent. Soc; Silver Beaver, BSA; Kiwanis; Lions; Mason; Scottish Rite; Shrine; C. of C; 281 International Hwy. Scoutmaster; Track, N.Mex. Mil. Inst. Rel: Episcopal. Legal Res: 116 Baker St, Hamilton, Tex. 76521. Mailing Add: P.O. Box 472, Hamilton, Tex. 76531.

BAKER, CHARLES DUANE R
Dep. Under Secy, Dept. of Transportation
b. Newburyport, Mass, 6/21/28; s. Charles Duane Baker and Eleanor Little B; m. 6/4/55 to Alice Elizabeth Ghormley; c. Charles D, Jonathan C. and Alexander K. Educ: Harvard Col, A.B, 51; Harvard Grad. Sch. Bus. Admin, M.B.A, 55; PiEta Club; Hasty-Pudding Inst. of 1770. Polit. & Govt. Pos: Dep. Under Secy, Dept. of Transportation, 69- Bus. & Prof. Pos: Buyer, Westinghouse Elec. Corp, N.Y, 55-57, purchasing sect. supvr, N.J, 57-61; v.pres, United Research, Inc, Cambridge, Mass, 61-65; v.pres, Harbridge House, Boston, 65-69. Mil. Serv: ARM3, Navy, 46-48, with serv. in NAS Coco Solo; re-entered as AL3, 51, released as Lt.(jg), 53, after serv. in VP 10 and VC 4. Publ: Balance of Payments and Merchant Marine, 67 and Intermodal Transport Through the NW Corridor, 68, Harbridge House. Mem: Brae Burn Country Club; Needham Pool & Racquet Club; Luncheon Club of Boston; Harvard Club of Boston; Harvard Club of Wash. Rel: Congregational. Legal Res: 21 Cleveland Rd, Needham, Mass. 02192. Mailing Add: 6110 Welborn Dr, Bethesda, Md. 20016.

BAKER, CLEONA TATRO R
b. Boston, Mass, 11/9/06; m. to Alban S. Baker; c. Three sons. Educ: Walnut Hills High Sch, Cincinnati, Ohio. Polit. & Govt. Pos: Vt. State Rep, 57, 59 & 65. Mem: Past pres, PTA and Ladies Aid; Eastern Star; trustee, Concord Libr. Rel: Universalist; Supt, Sunday Sch; trustee, Commun. Church. Mailing Add: P.O. Box 216, Concord, Vt. 05824. (1967)

BAKER, DAVID MARTIN R
V.chmn, W.Va. Rep. State Exec. Cmt.
b. Clarksburg, W.Va, 10/11/23; s. Nathan Robert Baker and Edna Brown B; m. 6/15/48 to Janet Susan Rubin; c. John David, Susan Rachel and Emily Ann. Educ: Marshall Col, 40-42; Univ. Mich, 42; W.Va. Univ, B.A, 48, J.D, 50; Pi Lambda Phi; Phi Delta Phi. Polit. & Govt. Pos: Mem, Huntington City Coun, W.Va, 51-52; W.Va. State Rep, 53-54 & 57-58; spec. legis. counsel to Gov, W.Va, 59-60; v.chmn, Rep. State Exec. Cmt, 66- Bus. & Prof. Pos: Practicing attorney, Huntington, W.Va, 50- Mil. Serv: Entered as Pvt, Army Air Force, 43, released as S/Sgt, 46, after serv. in Training Command. Mem: Am, W.Va, Cabell Co. and Lawyer-Pilots Bar Asns; W.Va. State Bar; Elks; Am. Legion; student ed. bd, W.Va. Law Quart. Rel: Reform Jewish. Mailing Add: 66 Oakwood Rd, Huntington, W.Va. 25701.

BAKER, DONALD E. D
Iowa State Rep.
b. Boone, Iowa, 11/9/30; m. 7/5/52 to Margaret Nowels; c. Becky Lynn and Daniel. Educ: Boone Jr. Col. Polit. & Govt. Pos: Iowa State Rep, currently. Mil. Serv: Korean War. Mem: Am. Legion; Elks; 40 et 8. Mailing Add: 1517 Boone St, Boone, Iowa 50036.

BAKER, E. LaMAR R
Tenn. State Sen.
b. Chattanooga, Tenn, 12/29/15; s. Rush Emmons Baker and Sarah Beall B; m. 8/21/45 to Sue Batey; c. Edward L, Jr. and Sarah Susan. Educ: David Lipscomb Col, 36-38; Harding Col, B.S. in bus. admin, 40. Polit. & Govt. Pos: Rep. precinct chmn, 14th Ward, Hamilton Co, Tenn, 62-63; coordinator, Hamilton Co. Precincts in Chattanooga, 63-64; campaign mgr, Kuykendall for U.S. Senate, 64; chmn, Hamilton Co. Exec. Cmt, 65-66; Tenn. State Rep, Dist. Two, Hamilton Co, 67-68; Tenn. State Sen, 69-, chmn, Senate Rep. Caucus and Hamilton Co. Del, 69- Bus. & Prof. Pos: Pres, Commercial Janitors, Inc, Chattanooga, 62- Mil. Serv: Entered as Pvt, Army Air Force, 42, released as Maj, 46, after serv. in 560th Bomb Squadron H, 388th Bomb Group H, ETO, 43-45; ETO Ribbon with 3 Oak Leaf Clusters; Good Conduct Medal. Mem: C. of C; Am. Legion; Citizens Good Govt. League; Civitan; Chattanooga Safety Coun. Rel: Church of Christ; Elder. Mailing Add: 76 S. Crest Rd, Chattanooga, Tenn. 37404.

BAKER, ETHEL BOWDEN R
Maine State Rep.
b. Orrington, Maine, 5/21/06; d. Ferd D. Bowden and Ellen Lewis B; m. 6/18/27 to Victor M. Baker; c. Alan L. and Gladyce (Mrs. Stais). Educ: Gilman Commer. Sch. Polit. & Govt. Pos: Town clerk, Orrington, Maine, 31-53; Maine State Rep, 59-60, 61-62, 65-66, 67-68 & 69-; mem, Legis. Research Cmt, 67- Bus. & Prof. Pos: Sch. lunch supvr, Bucksport, Maine, 47-58, Orrington, 47-61. Mem: Milwee Chap. 198, Eastern Star; Orrington Garden Club; mem. bd, Garden Club Fedn. of Maine; past. pres, Maine Town and City Clerks Asn. Rel: Methodist. Mailing Add: Center Dr, Orrington, Maine 04474.

BAKER, GEORGE TONE D
Exec. Secy, Dem. Party, Ariz.
b. Minneapolis, Minn, 12/18/31; s. Col. Roy Charles Baker, U.S.A.(Ret) and Marian Bingham B; m. 8/15/59 to Ann Marie Perry; c. Scott Anthony and Gregory Roy. Educ: Univ. of Md, B.S, 60; Phi Kappa Sigma. Polit. & Govt. Pos: Spec. asst. to chmn, Dem. Nat. Cmt, 62-63, off. mgr, 63, field rep, 65; exec. secy, Dem. Party, Ariz, 65- Bus. & Prof. Pos: Asst. dir, D.C. Chap, Nat. Found, 60-61; Alumni Fund Dir, Univ. Md, 61-62. Mil. Serv: Entered as Airman 3/C, 53, released as Airman 1/C, 57, after serv. in Alaskan Air Command, 55-57; Am. Defense Citation; Good Conduct Medal. Mem: Am. Col. Pub. Rels. Asn. Rel: Episcopal. Mailing Add: 3948 W. Lawrence Lane, Phoenix, Ariz. 85021. (1967)

BAKER, HAYDEN BURNICE R
Tenn. State Sen.
b. Pennington Gap, Va, 8/21/23; s. Thomas Franklin Baker and Emma Pearl Rogers B; m. 7/17/43 to Marie Cecelia Holland; c. Hayden Bryan, David Lee, James Paul and Gary Lynn. Educ: Morris Harvey Coll, Univ. Tenn. and Int. Correspondance Sch. Polit. & Govt. Pos: Justice of the peace, Sullivan Co, Tenn, 66-69; Tenn. State Sen, 68- Bus. & Prof. Pos: Designer, Tenn. Eastman Co, 48-; dir, Baptist Childrens Home, 54- Mil. Serv: Entered as A/S, Navy, 44, released as Seaman 2/C, 45. Mem: Instrument Soc. Am; Nat. Asn. Power Engrs; Optimist Int.(Lt. Gov. and state membership chmn, Tenn. Dist); Farm Bur; United Commercial Travelers; hon. mem, Tenn. Law Enforcement Officers Asn; pres, Lynn Garden Optimist Club; charter pres, Morrison City Serv. Club. Rel: Baptist. Mailing Add: 256 Fletcher Ave, Kingsport, Tenn. 37665.

BAKER, HERMAN MERLIN R
Chmn, Darke Co. Rep. Exec. Cmt, Ohio
b. Arcanum, Ohio, 1/19/17; s. Glen C. Baker and Ruth Myers B; m. 11/22/39 to Lucille Fenstermaker; c. Jerrlyn (Mrs. Kent Myers) and Merlin. Educ: Int. Bus. Col, Ft. Wayne, Ind, 36-39. Polit. & Govt. Pos: Mem, Co. Bd. Elec, 66-; committeeman, Ohio Rep. Cent. Cmt, 50-; alternate del, Ohio State Conv, 66 and del, 68; mem. exec. cmt, Darke Co. Rep. Exec. Cmt, 67- and chmn, 68- Bus. & Prof. Pos: Mem, Franklin-Monroe High Sch. Bd. Educ, 59-67 and chmn, 66; Twp. clerk, 61- Mem: Farm Bur; Rotary. Rel: Protestant. Mailing Add: R.R. 2, Arcanum, Ohio 45304.

BAKER, HOWARD, JR. R
U.S. Sen, Tenn.
b. Huntsville, Tenn, 1925; m. to Joy Dirksen. Educ: Univ. of the South, Sewanee; Tulane Univ; Univ. Tenn, LL.B, 49. Polit. & Govt. Pos: U.S. Sen, Tenn, 67-; del, Rep. Nat. Conv, 68. Bus. & Prof. Pos: Attorney. Mil. Serv: USNR, World War II; discharged as Lt.(jg). Mailing Add: c/o Senate Office Bldg, Washington, D.C. 20510.

BAKER, INEZ De GRAW D
b. Baltimore, Md, 1/6/21; m. to Barnabas William Baker. Educ: Woodrow Wilson High Sch, grad, 38. Polit. & Govt. Pos: Mem, Dem. Women's Club, Va; Va. State Del, 58-59 & 66-67. Bus. & Prof. Pos: Housewife. Mem: Bus. & Prfnl. Women's Club; Grove Park Garden Club; March of Dimes; Eastern Star; Portsmouth Woman's Club; Portsmouth Hist. Soc; Portsmouth Gen. Hosp. Auxiliary; Portsmouth Exec. Club; Tidewater Dist. Va. Fedn. of Garden Clubs. Rel: Episcopal. Mailing Add: 81 Kansas Ave, Portsmouth, Va. 23701.

BAKER, J. FREDERICK R
Chmn, LaSalle Co. Rep. Party, Ill.
b. Waterman, Ill, 8/27/37; s. N. Orrin Baker and Garda Holther B; m. 3/23/62 to Barbara Ann Ade; c. Suzanne Gail and Laurel Ann. Educ: Univ. Ill, Champaign, 2 years. Polit. & Govt. Pos: Chmn, LaSalle Co. Rep. Party, Ill, 67- Bus. & Prof. Pos: Pres, JFB Dist. Co, 65-; pres, Baker & Assoc. Publ. Co, 67- Mil. Serv: Entered as Pvt, Air Force Res, 60, released as Sgt, 66, after serv. in Med. Corps, 60-66. Mem: Specialty Advert. Asn; Nat. Asn. Advert. Publishers; Mason; Elks. Rel: Lutheran; Trustee of Church. Mailing Add: 425 Lundy Lane, Leland, Ill. 60531.

BAKER, JAMES HOWARD R
V.Chmn, Rep. State Cent. Cmt, Md.
b. Salem, W.Va, 8/11/21; s. Harley P. Baker and Elisebeth M. Payton B; m. 5/13/50 to Catherine L. Ryan; c. James Harley and Carrol Lee (Mrs. Keller). Educ: Doddridge Co. High Sch, grad. Polit. & Govt. Pos: V.chmn, Rep. State Cent. Cmt, Md, 58-62 & 66-; pres, 12th Dist. Rep. Club, currently; del, Rep. Nat. Conv, 68. Bus. & Prof. Pos: Owner, several county cab co, 14 years; supvr, taxicab bur, Baltimore Co. Police Dept, 62- Mailing Add: 6941 Belclare Rd, Baltimore, Md. 21222.

BAKER, JAMES WILLIE D
b. Lacey Springs, Ala, 12/5/22; s. Emmett Bert Baker and Ida Bell Duff B; m. 6/15/64 to Sue Charline Roach. Educ: Univ. of Ala, LL.B, 50. Polit. & Govt. Pos: Judge of Madison Co. Court, Ala, 52-60; Ala. State Rep, 63-66. Bus. & Prof. Pos: Law practice, 60. Mil. Serv: Navy. Mem: Shriner; WOW; Elks; VFW (judge advocate of the Ala. Dept); Mason. Rel: Protestant. Mailing Add: 205 Uptown Bldg, Huntsville, Ala. 35801.

BAKER, JOE M, JR. R
b. Asheville, N.C, 2/10/27; s. Joe M. Baker (deceased) and Julia Williams B; m. 7/21/50 to Bernice Maupin; c. Joe M, III, Rebecca L, Cynthia L. and Robert L. Educ: U.S. Merchant Marine Acad, B.S, 47; Georgetown Univ. Sch. of For. Serv, 48-49; Univ. Tenn. Sch. of Bus. Admin, B.S. in Bus. Admin, 50; Univ. Tenn, chap. pres, Delta Sigma Pi, secy, Lambda Chi Alpha and pres, Canterbury Club. Polit. & Govt. Pos: Rep. nominee for U.S. Cong, Fifth Dist, Md, 62; chmn, Rep. State Cent. Cmt, Anne Arundel Co, 62-66; del, Rep. State Conv, 64; alternate del, Rep. Nat. Conv, 64. Mil. Serv: Entered as Cadet-Midshipman, Naval Res, 45, released as Lt, 49, after serv. in Merchant Marine; Atlantic, Mediterranean and Pac. Theater Ribbons; Merchant Marine Victory Medal. Mem: Asn. Cmt, U.S. C. of C, 62-65; Am. Soc. of Asn. Exec, 55- and Chartered Asn. Exec, 62; Mason; Elks; former nat. v.pres, U.S. Merchant Marine Acad. Alumni Asn. Named Outstanding Alumnus of the Year of the U.S. Merchant Marine Acad, 57. Rel: Episcopal. Mailing Add: 1870 Lindamoor Dr, Annapolis, Md. 21401.

BAKER, JOHN EDWARD R
Chmn, Orange Rep. Town Cmt, Conn.
b. East Norwalk, Conn, 5/25/17; s. William Henry Baker and Clara Wallin B; m. 2/22/46 to Eleanor Brown; c. Christie (Mrs. Robt. Smith) and John A. Educ: New Haven Col, 2 years. Polit. & Govt. Pos: Mem, Orange Rep. Town Cmt, Conn, 60-, chmn, 67-; Conservation cmnr, Orange, Conn, 64-67. Bus. & Prof. Pos: Plant Foreman, 55-60, Splicing Foreman, 60-67, Plant Staff, Training, South. New Eng. Tel. Co, 67-68, Maintenance Foreman, 67- Mil. Serv: Entered as BM 2/C, Navy, 42, released as CBM, 45, after serv. in Mine Sweeping, S. Atlantic Area, 43-45. Mem: Indust. Mgt. Club of New Haven (pres, 68-69); Mason; Am. Legion. Rel: Episcopal. Mailing Add: 296 Fairlea Rd, Orange, Conn. 06477.

BAKER, KEITH GLOSSON D
b. Concord, N.C, 12/4/38; s. Maurice Dewitt Baker and Jessie Mae Glosson B; m. 5/30/62 to Renate Ilona Kuehne. Educ: Univ. N.C, Charlotte, B.A, 65; Ind. Univ, Bloomington, M.P.A. cand. Polit. & Govt. Pos: Admin. asst, U.S.

Rep. Wm. L. Hungate, Mo, 66- Mil. Serv: Entered as Pvt, Army, 59, released as SP-5, 62, after serv. in Security Agency, West Germany, 60-62. Rel: Protestant. Mailing Add: 7304 Byeforde Court, Springfield, Va. 22150.

BAKER, LINN C. D
b. Thatcher, Utah, 10/31/13; s. Clarence Henry Baker and Bertha Marie Jensen B; m. 6/9/39 to Cyrene Marie Worley; c. Linn J, Jerry W, Colleen Bertha and Diane Marie. Polit. & Govt. Pos: City councilman, North Ogden, Utah, treas, Weber Co. and Utah State Rep, formerly; Utah State Treas, 65-67. Mem: V.pres, Co. Off. Orgn; chmn, Tourist & Conv. Cmt, Ogden C. of C; pres, Utah Bldg. Off. Conf, Ogden Area Motel Asn, Weber Co. Watershed Protective Corp, Civic Clubs of North. Utah and Kiwanis. Rel: Latter-day Saint. Mailing Add: 457 W. 3400 S, Bountiful, Utah 84115. (1967)

BAKER, LLOYD J. (L. J.) D
Mo. State Rep.
b. Jacksonville, Mo, 9/6/31; m. 6/1/52 to Bonnie Janet Sarbaum; c. Michael Jay. Educ: Moberly Jr. Col, 58; Univ. of Mo. Polit. & Govt. Pos: Mo. State Rep, Dist. 97, 64-, v.chmn. cmt. atomic energy and indust. develop. and mem. appropriations and govt. orgn. cmts, Mo. House Rep. Bus. & Prof. Pos: Nat. Detective Agency, mgr. Baltimore Office; Wabash R.R.(Eng. Dept), 2 years; co. surveyor, Randolph Co, 61-65; Field Eng. for Moberly Medium Security Prison, 65. Mil. Serv: Marine Corps, 51-56; two meritorious promotions, spec. guard at NATO Anniversary Meeting and at Camp David. Mem: Brotherhood (past pres); ASCS Commun. Cmt; 4-H Livestock Leader; Cubmaster; Kiwanis Club (v.pres, past pres); Huntsville Commun. Club; PTA; Mo. Dem. Club; Higbee Commun. Club; Mo. Asn. Registered Land Surveyors; Travelers Protective Asn; Moberly Quarterback Club; Marine Legis. Club; Salvation Army Bd. Dirs.(chmn); Randolph Co. Tuberc. Asn. Bd. Dirs; Cerebral Palsy Bd. Dirs; Cancer Soc. Bd. Dirs; Randolph Co. Red Cross (disaster chmn); Randolph Co. Dem. Club; Cole Co. and Boone Co. Young Dem. Rel: Baptist, Sunday Sch. teacher. Mailing Add: RFD 3, Box 150, Moberly, Mo. 65270.

BAKER, MAXINE ELDRIDGE D
Fla. State Rep.
b. Berwyn, Md; d. Maurice Owen Eldridge and Bertha Stier E; m. 6/25/21 to John Adams Baker; c. Grover Eldridge, Douglas Allen and Martha Anne (Mrs. E.F. Hoegger). Educ: Radcliffe Col, A.B, 20. Polit. & Govt. Pos: Mem, 'Blue Ribbon' Grand Jury, Dade Co, Fla, 52; mem, State Welfare Bd, Dist. 9, 53-62; mem, Metrop. Charter Bd, Dade Co, 55-57; mem, Gov. Cmt. on Constitutional Rev, 58-59; mem, Fla. Capitol Bldg. Cmt, 59-61; Fla. State Rep, 90th Dist, 63- Bus. & Prof. Pos: Secy-treas, Baker's Carpet Co, Inc, 61- Mem: Am. Asn. Univ. Women (past pres, Miami Br); Radcliffe Club of Dade Co; League of Women Voters (past pres. of Miami and of Fla); bd. mem, Children's Psychiat. Center; Nat. Order Women Legislators; Ment. Health Asn; Hist. Asn; of South. Fla; Grand Jury Asn. of Dade Co. Received Pub. Serv. Award of Dem. Women's Club of Dade Co. and Commun. Headliner Award of Theta Sigma Phi. Rel: Episcopalian. Mailing Add: 1782 Opechee Dr, Miami, Fla. 33133.

BAKER, NORVAL SANDERS, JR. D
b. Gallatin, Tenn, 3/23/31; s. Norval Sanders Baker, Sr. and Adelaide Haggard B; m. 2/9/61 to Carrie Leone Dismukes; c. Carrie Elizabeth and Adelaide Sanders. Educ: Univ. N.Mex, 50; Pi Kappa Alpha. Polit. Pos: Tenn. State Rep, Sumner Co, 64-65. Bus. & Prof. Pos: Distributor, Sinclair Refining Co. Prod, 57- Mil. Serv: Entered as Airman, Air Force, 50, released as S/Sgt, 54, after serv. in 6910th Security Group, ETO, 52-54; Nat. Defense Serv. Medal; Occup. Medal, Germany; Good Conduct Medal. Mem: Rotary; VFW; Am. Legion. Rel: Presbyterian. Legal Res: Nashville Pike, Gallatin, Tenn. 37066. Mailing Add: P.O. Box 989, Gallatin, Tenn. 37066. (1967)

BAKER, RALPH A. R
Chmn, Cherry Co. Rep. Party, Nebr.
b. Gordon, Nebr, 10/2/95; s. Lee R. Baker and Adelina Celestenia B; m. 8/30/19 to Mary Cole; c. Cole D. and Geneva J.(Mrs. Johnson). Educ: S.Dak. Sch. of Mines, B.A. Polit. & Govt. Pos: Chmn, Drouth Cmt, Cherry Co, Nebr, 30-36 and Welfare Cmt, 31-42; co. cmnr, 32-49; finance chmn, Nebr. Rep. Party, 40-50; regional dir, USO and Civilian Defense, 42-46; mem. adv. bd, Nebr. Bd. of Control, 46-49; mem, Nebr. State Hwy. Cmn, 55-57; chmn, Cherry Co. Rep. Party, Nebr, 56-; del, Rep. Nat. Conv, 60 & 64; chmn, U.S. Govt. Savings Bonds, Cherry Co, 66. Bus. & Prof. Pos: Owner and mgr, Baker Ranch, 20-; pres, Sandhills Cattle Asn, 54-56; mem. exec. cmt, Nebr. Stock Growers Asn, 58-62; dir, Life Investors of Nebr, 62-; pres, Sandhills Investment Syndicate, 66. Mil. Serv: Em. Exped. Force, Coast Artil. Corps, 17-18. Mem: Sesostries AAONMS, Lincoln; Am. Livestock Asn; Am. and Nebr. Hereford Asns; Club 66; VFW; Am. Legion; Farm Bur. Rel: Methodist. Mailing Add: 575 N. Main, Valentine, Nebr. 69201. (1967)

BAKER, RAYMOND EXCELL D
b. 3/31/18; s. John Hiram Baker and Lora Bell Hearn; m. 1/16/42 to Ella Jane Gann; c. John Martin, Jane Maxell, Thomas Ray. Educ: Jacksonville State Col, B.S, 48; Univ. of Ala, M.A, 51. Polit. & Govt. Pos: Ala. State Rep, 62-66. Bus. & Prof. Pos: Teacher, 46-; Football coach at Plainview High Sch, Rainsville. Mil. Serv: Army, 42-46. Mem: Mason. Rel: Baptist. Mailing Add: Box 64, Crossville, Ala. 35962. (1967)

BAKER, RAYMOND L. R
Mich. State Rep.
b. Lake Orion, Mich, 9/10/06; married; c. Mrs. Nancy Simon, Mrs. Carol Sue Hutchinson, Raymond L, Jr, and Gary P. Educ: Detroit Inst. of Tech, Col. of Pharm, grad; Phi Delta Chi. Polit. & Govt. Pos: Mem, Oakland Co. Rep. Cmt, Mich; mem, Berkley City Coun; Mich. State Rep, 60-, chmn, Conserv. Cmt, Mich. State House of Rep. Bus. & Prof. Pos: Registered Pharmacist. Mem: Exchange Club; Elks; Co, State and Nat. Pharmaceut. Asns; Legis. Exec. Coun, Am. Pharmaceut. Asn. Recipient Bowl of Hygeia Award, a nat. honor; Mich. Pharmacist of the Year, 68; Mich. Conservationist Legislator of the Year, 68. Rel: Protestant. Mailing Add: 32718 Grand River Ave, Farmington, Mich. 48024.

BAKER, ROBERT DONALD R
Chmn, Rockingham Co. Rep. Party, Va.
b. Charlottesville, Va, 12/15/26; m. 6/10/44 to Jeanette K. Wenger; c. Mrs. A. Keith Liskey, Donna M. and Cynthia D. Educ: High sch. grad, 44; Mich. State Col, cert, 51. Polit. & Govt. Pos: Chmn, Rockingham Co. Rep. Party, Va, 67- Bus. & Prof. Pos: Operator, Celanese Corp. of Am, Verona, Va, 46-48; route salesman, Toms Products, Harrisonburg, Va, 50-51; asst. mgr. and dispatcher, Smith's Transfer Corp, 51- Mil. Serv: Entered as Pvt, Army Air Force, 45, released as Sgt, 46, after serv. in 26th S.C.U, ETO. Mem: Ruritan Club. Rel: United Methodist. Mailing Add: Box 84, McGaheysville, Va. 22840.

BAKER, ROBERT WILLIAM D
b. Brookline, Mass, 7/30/24; s. Chauncey William Baker (deceased) and Marion Power B; m. 12/29/51 to Rita Agnes Knox; c. Cheryl Alison, Jeffrey Clark and Susan Knox. Educ: Hobart Col, A.B, 47; Clark Univ, Ph.D, 53. Polit. & Govt. Pos: Staff clin. psychologist, Vet. Admin. Hosp, Northampton, Mass, 53-54; field selection officer, Peace Corps, part time, 64-67; alternate del, Dem. Nat. Conv, 68. Bus. & Prof. Pos: Asst. prof. psychol, Clark Univ, 54-57, assoc. prof, 57-66, prof, 66-, dir. psychol. clinic, 54-55 & 56-65, dean students, 65-68, asst. provost student affairs, 69- Mil. Serv: Entered as Aviation Cadet, Navy, 43, released as Seaman 2/C, 44, after serv. in U.S. Publ: 'Incidence of Psychological Disturbance in College Students,' J. Am. Col. Health Asn, 65; 'Susceptibility to Distraction in Academically Underachieving and Achieving Male College Students,' J. Consult. Psychol, 65; 'Students, Parents and the College: Responsibilities and Prerogatives in Grade-Reporting, Lib. Educ, 53: 325-335, 67. Mem: Diplomate in clin. psychol, Am. Bd. Exam. Prfnl. Psychol; fel. Am. and Mass. Psychol. Asns; Am. Asn. Univ. Prof; Am. Civil Liberties Union; Am. Humanist Asn. Mailing Add: 398 May St, Worcester, Mass. 01602.

BAKER, TED R. D
b. Dierks, Ark, 10/25/03; s. Joseph Monroe Baker and Mary Emma Turrentine B; m. 3/22/42 to Louise Newton; c. Raymond Don. Educ: Stephensville A&M Jr. Col, Tex. Polit. & Govt. Pos: Past co. chmn. for George McGovern, 62; chmn, Sully Co. Dem. Party, S.Dak, 64-68. Mem: Onida Lodge 173, AF&AM; v.chmn, Rocky Mt. Lodge 161; Br. S. of A, 51; Sully Co. Sports; Sully Co. Country Club. Rel: Presbyterian. Mailing Add: Onida, S.Dak. 57564.

BAKER, TOM F, III D
b. Sikeston, Mo, 2/25/18; m. 12/9/43 to Wille Marguerite Burks; c. Thomas Frazier IV, Susan Burks and Andrew Norfleet. Educ: Monmouth Col; Southeast Mo. State Col; Murdocho Cotton Sch. Polit. & Govt. Pos: Mo. State Rep, 60-66. Bus. & Prof. Pos: Pres. and owner of Trailback Plantation, Inc. Mil. Serv: Air Force, Capt, 45 months. Mem: Am. Legion; Mason (32°); Elks; Am. Vet. of WWII; VFW; Shrine. Rel: First Christian Church. Mailing Add: Baker, Mo, 63846.

BAKER, WILLIAM D. R
Chmn, Maricopa Co. Rep. Cmt, Ariz.
b. St. Louis, Mo, 6/17/32; s. Harold Griffith Baker and Bernice Kraft B; m. 5/23/55 to Kay Stokes; c. Mark William, Kathryn Xymena, Beth Christie and Frederick Martin. Educ: Colgate Univ, A.B, 54; Boalt Hall Sch. Law, Univ. Calif, Berkeley, LL.B, 60; Sigma Chi. Polit. & Govt. Pos: Dep. co. attorney, Pinal Co, Ariz, 61-63; spec. legal counsel, Rep. State Cmt, 64, legal counsel, 65-69; honorary asst. sgt. at arms, Rep. Nat. Conv, 68; mem, Gov. Adv. Coun, 69; chmn, Maricopa Co. Rep. Cmt, 69- Bus. & Prof. Pos: Attorney, McBryde, Brumage, Vincent & Baker, Florence, Ariz, 61-63 and Rawlins, Ellis, Burrus & Kiewit, Phoenix, 63-; juvenile court referee, Maricopa Co. Superior Court, 66- Mil. Serv: Entered as 2nd Lt, Air Force, 54, released as 1st Lt, 57, after serv. in 5th Bomb Wing, Strategic Air Command, 55-57. Mem: Phi Delta Phi; Am. Bar Asn; Pinal Co. Bar Asn.(v.pres, 62-63); State Bars of Calif. & Ariz; F&AM; York Rite; Shrine; Colo. River Water Users' Asn. Rel: Episcopal. Legal Res: 5309 N. 34th St, Phoenix, Ariz. 85018. Mailing Add: 733 Security Bldg, Phoenix, Ariz. 85004.

BAKER, WILLIAM HOWARD D
Committeeman, Mass. Dem. State Cmt.
b. Holyoke, Mass, 7/22/13; s. William F. Baker and Mary McGrath B; m. 5/20/46 to Cecile Hamel; c. Patricia Gvenette, David Baker and Gail (Mrs. Dygon). Educ: Sacred Heart High Sch, Holyoke, Mass, 3 years. Polit. & Govt. Pos: Ward chmn, Chicopee City Dem. Cmt, Mass, 54, v.chmn, 59 and chmn, 60; committeeman, Mass. Dem. State Cmt, 60-, v.chmn, 61, committeeman, Second Hampden Dist, 69- Mem: Recording secy, Local 45, Holyoke Printing and Pressmans Union. Rel: Catholic. Mailing Add: 11 Charbonneau Terr, Chicopee, Mass. 01013.

BAKEWELL, CLAUDE I. R
Postmaster, St. Louis, Mo.
b. St. Louis, Mo, 8/9/12; s. Paul Bakewell, Jr. and Mary Fullerton B; m. 2/22/36 to Helene Brown; c. Helene B. Educ: Georgetown Univ, A.B, 32; St. Louis Univ. Sch. of Law, LL.B, 35; Alpha Sigma Nu; Delta Theta Phi. Polit. & Govt. Pos: Mem, Bd. of Aldermen, St. Louis, Mo, 41-45, U.S. Rep, 47-48, 51-52; postmaster, St. Louis, 58- Mil. Serv: Entered as Lt.(jg), Navy, 44, released as Lt.(jg), 46, after serv. in Armed Guard, Asiatic-Pac. Theater. Rel: Roman Catholic. Legal Res: 7148 Maryland Ave, St. Louis, Mo. 63130. Mailing Add: 1720 Market St, St. Louis, Mo. 63155.

BAKKEN, ALBERT C. D
Secy, Griggs Co. Dem. Cmt.
b. Sharon, N.Dak, 12/19/20; s. Albert O. Bakken and Martha A. Strand B; m. 6/5/47 to Shirley Ann Gran; c. Gary C, Glenn O. and Gay Ann. Educ: Mayville State Teachers Col, 39-42; Univ. Wis, 43-44; Univ. N.Dak, Ph.B. & LL.B, 48. Polit. & Govt. Pos: State attorney, Steele Co, 49-51; legal counsel, N.Dak. Tax Dept, 53-54; first asst. attorney gen, State of N.Dak, 55-56; state attorney, Griggs Co, 59-66; mem, N.Dak. State Dem. Exec. Cmt; state cent. committeeman; secy, Griggs Co. Dem. Cmt, currently; Dist. Court Judge, First Judicial Dist, 67- Mailing Add: Box 1476, Grand Forks, N.Dak. 58201.

BALABAN, THOMAS R. D
b. Loyalhanna, Pa, 10/9/16; s. Frank Balaban and Anna Belank B; m. to Margaret Mosier; c. Twelve. Educ: Duquesne Univ, B.A. and LL.B. Polit. & Govt. Pos: Parliamentarian, Pa. State House Rep, 65-67; alternate del, Dem. Nat. Conv, 64; Nat. chmn, Yugoslav Div, Dem. Nat. Cmt; Child Welfare Bd, Green Co. Bus. & Prof. Pos: Attorney; Chief Dep. Ins. Cmnr, 55-63; pub. interest dir, Pittsburgh Fed. Home Loan Bank. Mil. Serv: Army, M/Sgt,

Intel, ETO, 42-45. Mem: K. of C; Elks; Am. Bar Asn; Am. Legion; Croation Fraternal Union of Am. Rel: Catholic. Mailing Add: 31 Circle Dr, Camp Hill, Pa. 17011 (1967)

BALCH, RICHARD H. D
b. Brooklyn, N.Y, 3/2/01; s. Burton M. Balch and Mary Horrocks B; m. 9/15/28 to Elizabeth S. Prescott; c. Cynthia Barns, James P, Barbara (Mrs. Colt) and Richard H, Jr. Educ: Williams Col, B.A, 21; Hartwick Col, LL.D, 55; Delta Sigma Rho; Phi Delta Theta. Polit. & Govt. Pos: Chmn, Utica City Dem. Cmt, N.Y, 48-50; chmn, N.Y. State Dem. Cmt, 52-55; cmnr, N.Y. Pub. Serv. Cmn, 55-60. Bus. & Prof. Pos: V.pres, Horrocks Ibbotso Co, 27-42, pres, 42- Publ: Various articles in Sporting Goods Dealer, 27- Mem: F&AM; Ft. Schuyler Club, Utica; Ft. Orange Club, Albany; Manhattan Club, N.Y.C; Williams Club, N.Y.C. Rel: Presbyterian. Mailing Add: 1202 Parkway, Utica, N.Y. 13501.

BALDRIGE, MALCOLM R
Chmn, Conn. State Rep. Finance Cmt.
b. Omaha, Nebr, 10/4/22; s. Howard Malcolm Baldrige and Regina Connell B; m. 3/31/51 to Margaret Trowbridge Murray; c. Megan Brewster and Mary Trowbridge. Educ: Yale Univ, B.A, 44. Polit. & Govt. Pos: Chmn, Waterbury Mayor's Citizens Adv. Cmt, Conn; mem, Woodbury Town Rep. Cmt; del, Rep. Nat. Conv, 64 & 68; del, Conn. Constitutional Conv, 65; mem, Conn. State Rep. Budget Cmt, 66-; mem, Conn. State Rep. Finance Cmt, 66-,chmn, 69-; mem. adv. cmt. on Labor, Conn. State Rep. Cent. Cmt, 67-; co-chmn, Conn. United Citizens for Nixon-Agnew, 68; mem, Conn. Citizens Cmn. on State Legis, 68-; mem, Conn. State Rep. Platform Cmt, 68-; mem, Nat. Rep. Finance Cmt, 69- Bus. & Prof. Pos: Mem. exec. cmt, Yale Univ. Develop. Bd; dir, Univ. of Conn. Found; trustee, Post Jr. Col. and Swiss Re-Ins. Co; pres. and dir, Scovill Mfg. Co, Waterbury, 63-; dir, Northeast Utilities, Hartford, Conn. Mutual Life Ins. Co, Waterbury Savings Bank, Colonial Bank & Trust Co, Waterbury, Lewis Eng. Co, Naugatuck, The East. Co, Am. Chain & Cable Co, New York, N.Y, Copper Develop. Asn, Torin Corp, Torrington, Conn, 69-, Madeira Sch, Greenway, Va, 69-, corporate bd, Am. Sch. for Deaf, Hartford, Conn, 68-; adv. bd, Rodeo Info. Found, Denver, Colo, 69- Mil. Serv: Entered as Pvt, Army, 43, released as Capt, 46, after serv. in Field Artil, 27th Inf. Div, Pac. Theatre. Mem: Dir, Waterbury Red Cross and Chmn, Red Cross Drive, 66; dir, Pearl St. Neighborhood House; incorporator, Easter Seal Soc; trustee, Waterbury Hosp. Hobby: Steer roping. Rel: Congregational. Legal Res: Tomlinson Rd, R.F.D. 2, Woodbury, Conn. 06798. Mailing Add: Scovill Manufacturing Co, 99 Mill St, Waterbury, Conn. 06720.

BALDUS, ALVIN D
Wis. State Assemblyman
b. Boone, Iowa, 4/27/26; s. Leo F. Baldus and Mildred Corbin B; m. 9/26/59 to Lorayne Reiten; c. Deborah, Bruce, Rebecca and Erick. Educ: Austin Jr. Col, Minn, A.A. Polit. & Govt. Pos: Wis. State Assemblyman, Dunn Co, 67- Bus. & Prof. Pos: Dist. rep, Allis Chalmers Mfg. Co, 53-64; zone mgr, Investors Diversified Serv, 64- Mil. Serv: Entered as Pvt, Army, 51, released as Sgt, 53, after serv. in 2nd Div, Korea, 52-53; Bronze Star; Infantryman's Combat Badge. Mem: Rotary Int; Disabled Am. Vet. Rel: Catholic. Legal Res: 1901 S. Broadway, Menomonie, Wis. 54751. Mailing Add: 324 North, State Capitol, Madison, Wis. 53702.

BALDWIN, DAVID RAWSON D
b. New Haven, Conn, 11/2/23; s. Albert A. Baldwin and Hilda Rawson B; m. 6/19/48 to Dorothy E. Sonstrom; c. Dwight R, Brian M. and James A. Educ: Univ. Conn, B.S. in Govt, 47; Wayne Univ, M.P.A, 49; Theta Xi. Polit. & Govt. Pos: Chief assessor, Fayette Co, Pa, 52-56; consult. to Gov-Elect, Pa. Dem. State Cmt, 54; budget secy. and dep. secy. admin, Commonwealth of Pa, 59-63, exec. asst. state treas, 63-65; housing chmn, Pa. Del. to Dem. Nat. Conv, 63; adv. to Dem. mem, Pa. Gen. Assembly, 63-65; asst. secy. of commerce, U.S. Dept. of Commerce, 65-69. Bus. & Prof. Pos: Research asst, Conn. Pub. Expenditure Coun, 48-50; co. exec. secy, Pa. Econ. League, 50-52, research assoc, 56-59; v.pres, Wayne State Univ, 69- Mil. Serv: Entered as A/S, Naval Res, 43, released as Lt.(jg), 46, after serv. with Convoy duty Pac. Theatre. Mem: Am. Soc. for Pub. Admin; Gov. Res. Asn. Rel: Presbyterian. Mailing Add: 2452 Devon Lane, Birmingham, Mich. 28009.

BALDWIN, DOUGLAS PARKS R
b. Lander, Wyo, 10/22/36; s. Melvin Baldwin and Shirley Jeffers B; m. 7/17/60 to Janet LaVerne Curtis; c. Clifford Steven. Educ: Am. Univ, 66. Polit. & Govt. Pos: Pres, Park Co. Young Rep, Wyo, 62; press secy. to U.S. Sen. M.L. Simpson, Wyo, 63-66 and U.S. Sen. C.P. Hansen, Wyo, 67; spec. asst. to U.S. Rep. W.H. Harrison, Wyo, 67-68; news ed, United Citizens for Nixon-Agnew, 68; admin. asst. to U.S. Rep. John Wold, Wyo, 69- Bus. & Prof. Pos: News dir, radio stas, Wyo, 58-62. Mil. Serv: Entered as Pvt, Marine Corps, 55, released as Sgt, 58, after serv. in First and Second Marine Div. and Third Marine Div, Okinawa, 56-58. Publ: 'Cody Called Him Frank,' Denver Post, 61; 'Political Preference Prevails in Congressional Liaison,' Washington Sunday Star, 1/68; 'William Henry Harrison,' Bits and Pieces, 7/68. Mem: U.S. Senate Press Secy. Asn.(v.pres, 66); Toastmasters Int; Capitol Hill Club; Eng. Speaking Union; Nat. Press Club. Recipient of Hungarian Freedom Fighters Asn. Freedom Award, 65. Rel: Methodist. Legal Res: Cody, Wyo. 82414. Mailing Add: 3743 Donnell Dr, Washington, D.C. 20028.

BALDWIN, FRANK EUGENE, JR. D
S.C. State Rep.
b. Ravenel, Ind, 4/10/24; s. Gene Baldwin and Louise Bivens B; m. 4/14/48 to Ruth Thomas Smith B; c. Gene, Tom and Sherry. Educ: Clemson Col, B.S, Agr, 44. Polit. & Govt. Pos: S.C. State Rep, 57- Bus. & Prof. Pos: Voc. agr. teacher, 46-54; farmer. Mailing Add: Drawer J, Ridgeland, S.C. 29936. (1967)

BALDWIN, HOWARD STANLEY R
Ariz. State Sen.
b. New Haven, Conn, 12/15/34; s. Clarence Baldwin and Janie Curry B; m. 7/28/62 to Catherine Mary Huie; c. Lisa and Kendall. Educ: Univ. Conn, 52-54; L.U.T.C, Nat. Asn. of Life Underwriters. Polit. & Govt. Pos: Pres, Scottsdale-Paradise Valley Young Rep. Club, Ariz, 64; Rep. precinct committeeman and dep. registrar, St. Gregory Precinct, Dist. 8-H, 64-; chmn, Maricopa Co. Young Rep. League, 65; Rep. chmn, Dist. 8-H, 68-; transportation chmn, Trunk 'N Tusk Cmt, Rep. Party, 69; Ariz. State Sen, Dist. 8-H, 69-, mem, Rules, Educ. and Agr, Livestock and Finance & Revenue Cmts, Ariz. State Senate, 69- Bus. & Prof. Pos: Supvr, Bus. Men's Assurance Co, Phoenix, Ariz, 67-, sr. dir, Life Club, 67 & 68. Mem: Cent. Ariz. Asn. of Life Underwriters; Intergovt. Coord. Cmt, Phoenix Forward. Awarded membership, Leaders Club, Ariz. Asn. of Life Underwriters. Rel: Episcopal. Legal Res: 1622 W. Clarendon Ave, Phoenix, Ariz. 85015. Mailing Add: Arizona State Senate, Capitol Bldg, Senate Wing, Phoenix, Ariz. 85007.

BALDWIN, ROBERT FREDERICK D
b. Norfolk, Va, 1/22/00; m. to Myra Skinner Carr. Educ: Norfolk Acad; Maury High Sch; Univ. Va, B.A, 19; Phi Beta Kappa. Polit. & Govt. Pos: Va. State Del, 38-47; Va. State Sen, 48-68. Bus. & Prof. Pos: Real estate and ins. agent. Mil. Serv: World War I. Mem: Bd. of trustees, Norfolk Acad; Izaak Walton League; pres, Tidewater AA; Elks; Norfolk Yacht & Country Club; Princess Anne Co. Club; Commonwealth Club; Raven Soc; Am. Legion. Rel: Episcopal. Mailing Add: 116 Brooke Ave, Norfolk, Va. 23510. (1967)

BALEN, MARK LOUIS D
Mayor, Lackawanna, N.Y.
b. Lackawanna, N.Y, 10/9/34; s. Stephen A. Balen and Anne S. Juran B; m. 6/16/56 to Helen F. Przewlocki; c. Mark John and Alan Robert. Educ: Niagara Univ, B.B.A. in Acct, 57; Canisius Col, M.S. in Educ, 60; scholarship, 4 years; treas, St. Class; Scabbard and Blade (treas). Polit. & Govt. Pos: Committeeman, Lackawanna Dem. Party, N.Y, 57-; councilman, Lackawanna, 62-67; del, Dem. Nat. Conv, 68; mayor, Lackawanna, 68- Bus. & Prof. Pos: Teacher, Lackawanna Bd. Educ, 57-68. Mil. Serv: 2nd Lt, U.S.A. Mem: Lackawanna and Erie Co. Teachers Fedns; N.Y. State Conf. Mayors; N.Y. State Teachers Asn; Jr. C. of C; K. of C; Croation Cath. Union. Rel: Catholic. Mailing Add: 108 Shannon Dr, Lackawanna, N.Y. 14218.

BALERUD, BERT A. R
b. Sacred Heart, Minn, 8/3/92; married; c. 4. Educ: Augsburg Acad. and Augsburg Col, Minn, Minn. Polit. & Govt. Pos: N. Dak. State Rep, 55-66. Mem: Farm Bur; Am. Legion; Elks; Sons of Norway. Rel: Lutheran. 1967 Legal Res: Minot, N.Dak. No mailing address available. (1967)

BALES, JANE ALEXANDER R
Mem. Exec. Cmt, Arapahoe Co. Rep. Party, Colo.
b. Phoenix, Ariz, 1/3/14; d. Joseph Lancaster Brent Alexander and Grace Maye Forbes A; m. 11/3/34 to Stuart Franklin Bales; c. Ellen Anne and Stuart Brent. Educ: Phoenix Col. Polit. & Govt. Pos: V.chmn, Arapahoe Co. Rep. Party, Colo, 56-58, mem. exec. cmt, 68-; co. chmn, Sen. Campaign, 60 and Cong. Campaign, 62 & 64; del, Rep. Nat. Conv, 64; second cong. dist. dir, Colo. Fedn. Rep. Women, 63-65, state legis. chmn, 66-68; pres, Cherry Creek Rep. Women, 68-69. Past Mem: League of Women Voters; Denver Symphony Guild; Home Demonstration Clubs of Am; Mile-Hi United Fund; 4 H Club leader; Cherry Creek High Sch. PTA. Rel: Episcopal. Legal Res: 5280 S. University Blvd, Greenwood Village, Colo. Mailing Add: Rt. 3, Littleton, Colo. 80120.

BALES, POLLY ROTH R
V.Chmn, Phillips Co. Rep. Cent. Cmt, Kans.
b. Whitewater, Kans, 6/30/20; d. John P. Roth and Anna Rutschman R; m. 11/29/41 to Dane Gray Bales; c. Dane Gray, Jr. Educ: Univ. Kans, 3 years. Polit. & Govt. Pos: Pres, Logan Women's Rep. Club, Kans, 46-52; Rep. precinct committeewoman, Logan, 48-; pres, Phillips Co. Women's Rep. Club, 50-54; v.chmn, Phillips Co. Rep. Cent. Cmt, 50-; secy-treas, Dist. Women's Rep. Club, 54-55; sixth dist. v.chmn, Rep. State Cmt, 57-59 and first cong. dist. v.chmn, 65-68; alternate del, Rep. Nat. Conv, 60, del, 68. Bus. & Prof. Pos: Organist, United Methodist Church, Logan, Kans, 52- Mem: Logan Bus. & Prfnl. Women's Club (charter mem, 60-, pres, 64-65); Logan Women's Club (pres, 56-57). Rel: Methodist. Mailing Add: Box 185, Logan, Kans. 67646.

BALES, ROBERT H. R
Ind. State Rep.
Educ: Ind. Univ; Alpha Kappa Psi; Sigma Iota Epsilon; Phi Delta Kappa. Polit. & Govt. Pos: Ind. State Rep, currently. Bus. & Prof. Pos: Pub. rels. rep, Eli Lilly & Co. Mil. Serv: Air Force, Korean War. Mem: Masonic Lodge, Royal Arch Masons; Scottish Rite; Shrine; Ind. Univ. Alumni Asn; Soc. of Friends. Mailing Add: P.O. Box 34, Danville, Ind. 46122. (1967)

BALESTRIERI, EDWARD ANTHONY D
b. Hartford, Conn, 7/14/40; s. Anthony Balestrieri and Florence Ann Masi B; single. Educ: Univ. of Bridgeport, B.S. in acct, 64; Univ. Miami, spring 69. Polit. & Govt. Pos: Committeeman, Ward B Dem. Cmt, Conn, 62-67; Justice of the Peace, State of Conn, 63-67; city councilman, Norwalk, 63-67; del, Conn. Fourth Cong. Dist. Conv, 64 & 66. Bus. & Prof. Pos: Jr. acct, Hat. Corp. Am, 63; off. mgr. & acct, Seven-up Bottlers of Fairfield Co, Inc, 64-67; staff acct, Luby Leasing Syst, Inc, Miami, Fla, 67, Arision Shipping Co, Miami, 67-68 and Bloom, Engel, & Schinder, CPA, North Miami Beach, 68- Mem: Sons of Italy; K. of C; NAACP; Holy Name Soc; Biscayne Park Civic Club; Cath. Alumni Club of Miami. Moly Sherman Award, Col. of Bus. Admin, Univ. of Bridgeport. Rel: Roman Catholic. Mailing Add: 664 N.E. 114th St, Miami, Fla. 33161.

BALKCOM, JAMES C, JR. D
b. James, Ga, 4/14/18; s. James C. Balkcom, Sr. and Bessie Ethridge B; m. 2/14/60 to Betty Jean Asbell. Educ: Mercer Univ, A.B, 38; Pi Kappa Alpha. Polit. & Govt. Pos: Chmn, Jones Co. Dem. Exec. Cmt, Ga, formerly. Publ: Columnist, Jones Co. News. Mem: Farm Bur; pres, Jones Co. Boosters Club; Mason; Kiwanis; Am. Legion. Rel: Baptist. Mailing Add: James, Ga. 31043. (1967)

BALKE, RAYMOND E. R
Vt. State Sen.
b. Derby, Vt, 10/9/96; m. to Julia W. Leavens; c. two sons; four daughters. Educ: Stanstead Col, Que; Bugbee Bus. Col, 15. Polit. & Govt. Pos: Mem. sch. bd, Derby, Vt, 15 years; Newport Bd. of Aldermen, 43-49; mem, Newport Airport Cmn, 45-; mayor, Newport, 3 terms; Vt. State Rep, 2 terms; Vt. State Sen, 65- Bus. & Prof. Pos: Retired automobile and marine prods. dealer; adv. bd. of Newport Branch, The Chittenden Trust Co; former dir,

Nat. Bank of Newport. Mem: Masons (32°); Oriental Shrine; Odd Fellows; Rotary. Rel: United Church of Christ. Mailing Add; 927 E. Main St, Newport, Vt. 05855.

BALL, DONALD RAY R
Ky. State Rep.
b. Henderson Co, Ky, 7/27/36; s. James Chester Ball and Marjorie Bryant B; m. 12/20/55 to Mira Lou Snider; c. Donald Ray, Jr, Michael Bryant and Lisa Hays. Educ: Univ. of Ky. Polit. & Govt. Pos: Pres, Univ. Ky. Young Rep. Club, 54; alternate del, Rep. Nat. Conv, 64; dir, Blue Grass Lincoln Club, Ky, 64-; Ky. State Rep, 64-; cand. procurement chmn, Ky. Young Rep. Fedn, 65-; chmn, Rep. Caucus and Rep. Policy Cmt, Ky. House of Rep, 66-, Minority Leader, 68-69; chmn, Nat. Rep. Legislator's Conf, 69; mem, Rep. Coord. Cmt, Nat. Rep. Cmt, 69. Bus. & Prof. Pos: Pres, Ball Homes, Inc, 59-; managing dir, Ky. News Media, Inc, 64-; dir, Cent. Investors Life Ins. Co, 64-. Mem: Pres, Lexington Homebuilders Asn; dir, Ky. Homebuilders Asn. and Nat. Asn. Homebuilders; chmn, Citizens Asn. for Planning Open Space Cmt; C. of C; Lexington Real Estate Bd; Jr. C. of C; pres, Meadowthorpe Optimists; Gardenside Little League Baseball Coach; Young Rep. Club. Outstanding Young Man Award of Lexington-Fayette Co, Jaycees, 68. Rel: Baptist. Mailing Add: Route 8, Old Frankfort Pike, Lexington, Ky. 40504.

BALL, GEORGE WILDMAN D
b. Des Moines, Iowa, 12/21/09; s. Amos Ball and Edna Wildman B; m. 9/16/32 to Ruth Murdoch; c. John Colin and Douglas Bleakly. Educ: Northwest. Univ, B.A, 30 and J.D, 33. Polit. & Govt. Pos: Gen. Counsel's Off, U.S. Treas. Dept, 33-35; assoc. gen. counsel, Lend-Lease Admin, then For. Econ. Admin, 42-44; dir, U.S. Strategic Bombing Surv, London, 44-45; gen. counsel, French Supply Coun, Wash, 45-46; Under Secy. of State for Econ. Affairs, 61; Under Secy. of State, 61-66. Bus. & Prof. Pos: Counsel, Cleary, Gottlieb, Steen & Ball, 46-61 and Cleary, Gottlieb, Stein & Hamilton, 66-; chmn, Lehman Bros. Int, Ltd, 66- Legion of Honor, France; Medal for Freedom, U.S. Mailing Add: 1250 Connecticut Ave. N.W, Washington, D.C. 20036. (1967)

BALL, JUDSON CHARLES D
b. Evergreen Park, Ill, 7/2/41; s. Charles Condon Ball and Anne Clarkin B; m. 9/1/68 to Nancy Sue Lewis. Educ: Valparaiso Univ, B.A, 64; Chicago-Kent Col. Law, J.D, 67; Phi Delta Phi; Phi Delta Theta. Polit. & Govt. Pos: Dem. precinct canvasser, Porter Co, Ind, 62-63; secy-treas, Ind. State Collegiate Young Dem, 62-63; admin. asst. to U.S. Rep. Dan Rostenkowski, Ill, 69- Bus. & Prof. Pos: Partner, Schiller and Ball, 68- Mem: Ill. State Bar Asn; Lakeshore Club Chicago. Am. Jurisp. Award for Excellence in Agency. Rel: Catholic. Legal Res: 2004 McLean Ave, Chicago, Ill. 60647. Mailing Add: 1900 S. Eads St, Arlington, Va. 22200.

BALL, LOIS HELEN R
V.Chmn, La Plata Co. Rep. Party, Colo.
b. Topeka, Kans, 9/11/26; d. Clarence J. Vawter and Marguerite Nelson Merrill V; m. 12/19/47 to William Perry Ball Jr, M.D; c. Amy (Mrs. Wood), William Perry, III, John David and Joseph Edwin. Educ: Hermann Hosp. Sch. Nursing, Houston, R.N, 46; Univ. Houston, B.A, 45. Polit. & Govt. Pos: Precinct committeewoman, La Plata Co. Rep. Party, Colo, 60-68; del, La Plata Co. and Colo. State Rep. Conv, 60-68; pres, Rep. Women's Club, Durango, 67-68; v.chmn, La Plata Co. Rep. Party, 68. Bus. & Prof. Pos: Supvr, med. ward, John Sealy Hosp, Galveston, Tex, 46; operating room surg. nurse, Indianapolis Gen. Hosp, Ind, 47. Mem: Med. Auxiliary, La Plata Med. Soc; Durango Civic Players; Durango Fine Arts Coun. Rel: Methodist. Mailing Add: 100 Mesa Ave, Durango, Colo. 81301.

BALL, ROBERT MYERS D
Cmnr, Soc. Security Admin.
b. N.Y.C, 3/28/14; s. Archey Decatur Ball and Laura Elizabeth Crump B; m. 6/30/36 to Doris Jacqueline McCord; c. Robert Jonathan and Jacqueline Elizabeth. Educ: Wesleyan Univ, B.A, 35, M.A, 36; Phi Beta Kappa; Delta Kappa Epsilon. Polit. & Govt. Pos: Various positions, Bur. of Old-Age & Survivors Ins, 39-46; staff dir, Adv. Coun. Soc. Security to U.S. Senate Finance Cmt, 47-48; asst. dir, Bur. of Old-Age & Survivors Ins, 49-52, dep. dir, 53-62; cmnr, Soc. Security Admin, 62- Publ: 'Social Security: A Changing Program for a Changing World,' St. Louis Univ. Law Journal, 65; 'Health Insurance for People Aged 65 and Over; First Steps in Administration,' U.S. Dept. of Health Educ. & Welfare, Social Security Bul, 2/65. Mem: Am. Pub. Welfare Asn; Am. Soc. for Pub. Admin; Nat. Conf. Social Welfare; Int. Social Security Asn; Int. Labor Orgn; Asm. Pub. Health Asn; Int. Club. of Wash. Rockefeller Pub. Serv. Award, 61; Career Serv. Award, Nat. Civil Serv. League. Rel: Unitarian. Legal Res: 4009 Villa Nova Road, Baltimore, Md. 21207. Mailing Add: Social Security Administration, Washington, D.C. 20201. (1967)

BALL, STEADMAN R
Kans. State Sen.
b. Hiawatha, Kans, 9/20/04; s. Luke Steadman Ball and Frances Wilson B; m. 10/26/29 to Eleanor Margaret Campbell; c. Mary Louise (Mrs. James C. Estes), Susan Jean (Mrs. Harley W. Brown) and Nancy Eleanor (Mrs. William M. Youngman). Educ: Washburn Univ, A.B, 26, J.D, 28; Tau Delta Pi; Phi Delta Theta; Delta Theta Phi. Polit. & Govt. Pos: City attorney, Atchison, Kans, 42-44; Kans. State Sen, 45-49 & 61-, chmn, Judiciary Cmt. and mem, Kans. Judicial Coun, 63-, mem, Legis. Coun, 61-65; Kans. State Rep, 57-59. Publ: 'Americanism vs. Hysteria,' Kans. Teacher, 5/54; 'Education for American Citizenship,' 11/54 and 'King or People,' 11/61, J. Kans. Bar Asn. Mem: Am. and Kans. Bar Asns; pres, Atchison Co. Bar Asn, 60; Mason; Kiwanis; nat. coun, YMCA, 40-55. Rel: Presbyterian. Mailing Add: 1101 N. Fifth St, Atchison, Kans. 66002. (1967)

BALLAM, LOUIS S. R
N.H. State Rep.
b. Walpole, N.H, 8/26/04; married. Polit. & Govt. Pos: Dir, N.H. and Cheshire Fair Asns. and N.H.A.D.A; N.H. State Rep, 55- Bus. & Prof. Pos: Farmer. Mem: Elks; Mason; past pres, Walpole Lions. Rel: Protestant. Mailing Add: Walpole, N.H. 03608. (1967)

BALLARD, DAVID GEORGE D
Chmn, Blount Co. Dem. Exec. Cmt, Tenn.
b. Maryville, Tenn, 7/17/34; s. Fred R. 'Barney' Ballard and Georgia Dykes B; m. 10/17/64 to Judith Jones; c. David G, Jr. Educ: East. Ky. State Col, B.A, 61; Univ. Tenn, Knoxville, LL.B, 64; Phi Alpha Delta. Polit. & Govt. Pos: Chmn, Blount Co. Dem. Exec. Cmt, Tenn, 66-; co-chmn, Humphrey-Muskie Campaign, Blount Co, 68. Bus. & Prof. Pos: Attorney, Maryville, Tenn, 64- Mil. Serv: Entered as Aviation Cadet, Navy, 55, released as Lt.(jg), 59, after serv. in Airborne Early Warning Squadron 2, Patuxent River, Md, 57-59; Res, Lt.(jg); Lebanese Campaign Ribbon. Mem: Kiwanis. Rel: Methodist. Legal Res: Route 1, Rockford, Tenn. 37853. Mailing Add: Box 325, Maryville, Tenn. 37801.

BALLARD, GRADY CECIL D
b. Tucapau, 8/4/15; s. Hose Thomas Ballard and Minnie Davis B; m. 8/1/37 to Etta Mae Hayslip; c. Glenn C. Johnson, Terry Lynn and Sandra Warlick; two grandchildren. Educ: Spartanburg Co. and city schs, adult night sch, 39-40. Polit. & Govt. Pos: S.C. State Rep. until 66; S.C. State Sen, 66-68. Bus. & Prof. Pos: Ballard Sales Co, Gen. Salvage Dealer and owner, Glenn Springs Mineral Water Co. Mil. Serv: Pilot, 25th Wing Anti-Submarine Patrol Command, 30 months, discharged, 44; Air Medal. Mem: Adv. bd, Salvation Army, 60-63; Spartanburg Optimist Club; v.pres, Spartanburg Aviation Asn; pres, Cleveland Jr. High Sch, 59-60; PTA, 16 years. Rel: Baptist; Deacon, Calvary Baptist Church. Legal Res: 8521 Fairforest Rd, Spartanburg, S.C. 29303. Mailing Add: 104 Cleveland Park Dr, Spartanburg, S.C. 29303. (1967)

BALLARD, JOHN STUART R
Mayor, Akron, Ohio
b. Akron, Ohio, 9/30/22; s. Irby S. Ballard and Sarah McCormick B; m. 10/22/49 to Ruth Frances Holden; c. Susan, Karen, John, II, Mark and Ward. Educ: Univ. Akron, A.B, 43; Univ. Mich, LL.B, 48. Polit. & Govt. Pos: Spec. agent, Fed. Bur. Invests, 49-52; mem, Summit Co. Rep. Exec. Cmt, Ohio, 56-; prosecuting attorney, Summit Co, Ohio, 57-64; cand, U.S. Senate, Ohio, 62; mayor, Akron, 66- Bus. & Prof. Pos: Attorney-at-law, Akron, 52-56 & 64-65. Mil. Serv: Inf, Army, 43-46. Mem: Am, Ohio and Akron Bar Asns; Am. Judicature Soc. Recipient, Distinguished Serv. Award, Akron Jr. C. of C, 57. Rel: Episcopal. Legal Res: 107 Kenilworth Dr, Akron, Ohio 44313. Mailing Add: Municipal Bldg, High St, Akron, Ohio 44308.

BALLARD, LEONARD HARRISON R
b. Clover Bottom, Ky, 1/25/93; s. Sheridac Riley Ballard and Elizabeth Harrison B; single. Educ: Berea Col, 08-12; East. Ky. Teachers Col, 13-14; Univ. Ky. Commercial Col, 15-16. Polit. & Govt. Pos: With Emergency Fleet Corp, 18; Ky. State Rep, Madison Co, 19-20; Madison Co. campaign chmn. for Alf Landon, 36 and Louie B. Munn, 63; chmn, Madison Co. Rep. Cmt, 64-68. Bus. & Prof. Pos: Teacher, 12-16. Mem: Mason, F&AM; Shrine. Rel: Baptist. Mailing Add: 905 W. Main St, Richmond, Ky. 40475. (1967)

BALLARD, REECE D
Councilman, Garden Grove, Calif.
b. Olympus, Tex, 11/2/14; s. Horace G. Ballard and Nellie Mae Gipson B; m. 6/17/57 to Emma Jo Albini; c. Thomas Dale. Educ: Riverside City Col; Am. Exten. Sch. of Law. Polit. & Govt. Pos: Chief of police, N. Sacramento, Calif, 55-57 and Garden Grove, 57-62; city councilman, Garden Grove, 64- Mil. Serv: Entered as Pvt, Army, 43, released as Capt, 46; Asiatic-Pac. and Am. Theater Ribbons. Mem: Am. Legion; VFW; Elks; Optimists; Boy Scouts; United Fund; Boy's Club; Calif. Asn. of Private Investrs. Rel: Church of Christ; Bd. Mem. and Sunday Sch. Teacher. Legal Res: 9712 Shannon St, Garden Grove, Calif. 92641. Mailing Add: 12570 Brookhurst St, Garden Grove, Calif. 92640. (1967)

BALLARD, WADE HAMPTON, II R
b. Peterstown, W.Va, 7/26/04; s. Wade Hampton Ballard and Lillie Williams B; m. 10/11/41 to Alice Hamilton; c. Harry Hampton. Educ: W.Va. Univ, A.B, 27, Law Sch, LL.B, 33; Scabbard & Blade; Sigma Nu; Fi Batar Capper; Mountain Club. Polit. & Govt. Pos: V.pres, W.Va. Young Rep. Clubs, 48; del, Rep. Nat. Conv, 56, 60, 64 & 68; circuit court judge, McDowell Co, W.Va, 58; Presidential Elector, W.Va, 64. Bus. & Prof. Pos: Attorney-at-law, 33-; dir, Lynch Realty Co. and Lynch Shopping Center, Inc. Mil. Serv: Entered as Capt, Chem. Warfare Serv, 42, released as Lt. Col, Air Force, 46, after serv. in Nat. Hq. Chem. Warfare Serv. and Air Force, Wash, D.C; Lt. Col.(Ret), Air Force Res; 2 Letters of Commendation. Mem: Am. and W.Va. Trial Lawyers Asns; W.Va. State Bar; W.Va. and McDowell Co. Bar Asns; Commercial Law League of Am; Mason; K.T; Shrine; Moose (Pilgrim); Am. Legion; 40 et 8; Univ. Club. Rel: Episcopal. Legal Res: 532 Riverside Dr, Welch, W.Va. 24801. Mailing Add: 8 Bank St, Carter Hotel Bldg, Welch, W.Va. 24801.

BALLARD, WILLIAM DONALDSON D
Ga. State Rep.
b. Covington, Ga, 3/15/27; s. Robert Hershell Ballard and Eva Dominey B; m. 10/6/51 to Mary McCullough; c. Rebecca Anne, William Donaldson, Frankie Jannelle, Mary Kathryn, Thomas Waters and Susan Kay. Educ: Univ Ga, 45-50, A.B, LL.B, 50; Kappa Sigma. Polit. & Govt. Pos: City attorney, Oxford, Ga, 54-, Mansfield, 55-, Newborn, 55- and Porterdale, currently; Ga. State Rep, 57-; mem. bd. dirs, Upper Ocmulgee Econ. Opportunity Cmn, 67-69, chmn. bd. drs, 67-68. Mil. Serv: Entered as Seaman, Naval Res, 44 released as Seaman 1/C, 46, after serv. in U.S.S. L.S.T. 1076, Pac, 44-46; Pac. Theatre Medal; Invasion of Japan Medal. Mem: Ga. and Stone Mt. Bar Asns; Lions; Am. Legion; Farm Bur; Rotary; VFW; Elks; Gridiron; Newton Co. C. of C; Newton Co. Jr. C. of C.(past pres). Legal Res: 405 Haygood St, Oxford, Ga. 31701. Mailing Add: 1122 Monticello St, Covington, Ga. 30209.

BALLENGER, LOUIS E. R
Ky. State Rep.
b. 1909. Educ: Univ. Pa, degree. Polit. & Govt. Pos: Ky. State Rep, 62-, minority caucus chmn, Ky. House of Rep, 64. Bus. & Prof. Pos: Indust. engr. Rel: Presbyterian. Mailing Add: 1850 Princeton Dr, Louisville, Ky. 40205. (1967)

BALLENGER, THOMAS CASS R
Chmn, Catawba Co. Rep. Party, N.C.
b. Hickory, N.C, 12/6/26; s. Richard Edmonds Ballenger and Dorothy Collins

B; m. 6/14/52 to Donna Jean Davis; c. Lucinda Garrison, Melissa Jane and Dorothy Davis. Educ: Univ. N.C, 44-45; Amherst Col, B.A, 48; Kappa Alpha; Delta Kappa Epsilon. Polit. & Govt. Pos: Precinct chmn, Rep. Party, N.C, 60-64; chmn, Catawba Co. Rep. Party, N.C, 65-; co. cmnr, 66- Bus. & Prof. Pos: Sales mgr, Hickory Paper Box Co, 48-58, pres, 58-; pres. and founder, Plastic Packaging Inc, 57- Mil. Serv: Entered as A/S, Naval Air Corps, 44, released as Aviation Cadet, 45, after serv. in U.S. Mem: Rotary. Rel: Episcopal. Legal Res: 867 20th Ave. Dr, Hickory, N.C. 28601. Mailing Add: Box 2029, Hickory, N.C. 28601.

BALLENGER, WILLIAM S, III R
Mich. State Rep.
b. Flint, Mich, 3/28/41; s. William Sylvester Ballenger and Marie Elizabeth Daley B; m. 6/20/64 to Virginia Lee Woodard. Educ: Princeton Univ, A.B. magna cum laude, 62; Univ. Cottage Club; Triangle Club; Polit. & Govt. Pos: Dir. of Res, Mich. State Rep. Cent. Cmt, 65-; chmn, Shiawassee Co. Rep. Exec. Cmt, 66-68; Mich. State Rep, 87th Dist, 69- Bus. & Prof. Pos: Reporter, Evansville Press, Ind, 63-64. Publ: Many newspaper articles. Mem: Princeton Univ. Alumni Asn; SAR. Rel: Presbyterian. Mailing Add: 8450 W. Hibbard Rd, Ovid, Mich. 48866.

BALLENTINE, BESSIE BANGERT D
d. Edward Duguid Bangert and Kate Alice Morton B; m. 12/14/44 to Lynton Yates Ballentine (deceased); c. Julius W. Phoenix, Jr. and step children, Rebecca (Mrs. Scoggin), Lynton Yates, Jr. and Mrs. Boyd Elliott. Educ: Meredith Col. Polit. & Govt. Pos: Dir, N.C. Gov. Traffic Coun, several years; pres, Wake Co. Young Dem. Club, 34; pres, N.C. Young Dem. Club, 35-36; pres, Sir Walter Cabinet, 47-49, prog. chmn, 65-67; secy, N.C. Dem. Exec. Cmt, 65-69; del. and mem, Credential Cmt, Dem. Nat. Conv, 68. Bus. & Prof. Pos: Exec. secy, N.C. Automobile Dealers Asn, Raleigh, 35- Mem: Bd. dirs, Automotive Trade Asn. Mgrs, 52-53 & 68-, Wake Co. Tuberc. Asn; Raleigh Garden Club, N.C. Traffic Safety Coun, Home Econ. Found, Univ. N.C, 65-69 and YWCA, 2 terms; Raleigh Women's Club (chmn. jr. civic coun. and silver bowl award for best youth proj, 48, chmn. citizenship dept, 49-51, pres, 53-55); N.C. Fedn. Women's Clubs (dist. pres, 56-58, chmn, Conserv. Natural Resources, 58-60, chmn. scholarship fund, 60-62, bd. trustees, 61-66 and chmn, 62-66, treas, 68-); bd. dirs, and former pres, Raleigh Commun. Ambassador Proj; bd. mem, Neusiok Girl Scout Coun, 5 years; United Fund (chmn, Women's Div, 58, treas, 59, v.pres, 60-61); Raleigh Concert Music Asn.(pres, 61); adv. bd, Salvation Army, 59-63; bd. dirs. and secy. Peace Col. Found. Raleigh, Inc, 62-66; Alumnae Asn. Peace Col.(v.pres); Raleigh Little Theatre (v.pres. and mem. bd. dirs, 64, pres, 65-66); Hon. Cmt. for Symphony Ball; bd. trustees, N.C. Mus. of Art, 68-; chmn, Chapel Fund Cmt. for Correctional Center for Women Raleigh, 65; N.C. Tercentenary Celebration Cmn.(art cmt, 62-63); Roanoke Island Hist. Asn.(chmn. membership cmt, 64). N.C. Best Dressed Woman, 57; Tar Heel of Week, Raleigh News and Observer, 59; Woman of Year, Pilot and Quota Clubs, Raleigh, 61; Cert. of Merit, Carol Lane Award, Nat. Safety Coun. and Shell Oil Co, 62. Rel: Presbyterian. Legal Res: 3939 Glenwood Ave, Raleigh, N.C. 27601. Mailing Add: 19 W. Davie St, Raleigh, N.C. 27601.

BALLETTA, VINCENT R, JR. R
N.Y. State Assemblyman
b. Brooklyn, N.Y, 7/7/27; m. to Maria Sottosanti; c. Stephen Vincent, Michele Irene, Andrea Marie and Richard Michael. Educ: Columbia Univ, A.B; St. John's Univ. Law Sch, LL.B, 51. Polit. & Govt. Pos: Pres. and v.pres, Port Wash. Rep. Recruits, N.Y; chmn, Port Wash. Rep. Cmt, 6 years; from town councilman to sr. councilman, N.Hempstead, Nassau Co, N.Y, 59-; N.Y. State Assemblyman, 18th Dist, 66- Bus. & Prof. Pos: Attorney, Balletta & Weintraub, Esquires, 51- Mil. Serv: Warrant Officer, Maritime Serv. and Merchant Marine, 45-47 and Army Counter-Intel. Corps, 51-53. Mem: Nassau Co. Bar Asn; Columbian Lawyers' Asn; Catholic Lawyers' Guild; Nassau Lawyers' Asn. L.I; Exalted Ruler, Elks; v.pres, Columbia Univ. Alumni Asn. L.I; Nat. Conf. Christians and Jews; gen. bus. chmn, Nassau Heart Asn; bd. dirs, Port Wash. Commun. Servs; Nassau Chap, Boys' Towns of Italy; chmn, Am. Cmt. Italian Migration; dist. chmn, Cerebral Palsy Asn; Am. Legion; Lions; K. of C; Eagles Scouts Bd. Review; Sons of Italy; Italian Charities; Holy Name Soc. Rel: Catholic. Legal Res: 112 Country Club Dr, Port Washington, N.Y. 11050. Mailing Add: 114 Main St, Port Washington, N.Y. 11050.

BALLEW, ROBERT KING D
Mayor, Blue Ridge, Ga.
b. Copperhill, Tenn, 3/1/26; s. Robert Fulton Ballew and Helen King B; m. 7/3/49 to Nanette Talley; c. Sara Kay and Robert K, II. Educ: North Ga. Col; Univ. Tenn, LL.B; Phi Delta Phi. Polit. & Govt. Pos: City attorney, Blue Ridge, Ga, 53-; mem, Ga. State Dem. Exec. Cmt, 62-; Ga. State Sen, 50th Dist, 65-66; mayor, Blue Ridge, 68- Bus. & Prof. Pos: Attorney-at-Law, 53. Mil. Serv: Entered as Pvt, Army Air Force, 44, released as Sgt, 46, after serv. in ETO. Mem: Tenn. and Ga. Bars; Am. Bar Asn; Mason, Shrine; VFW. Rel: Methodist. Legal Res: E. Second St, Blue Ridge, Ga. 30513. Mailing Add: P.O. Box 636, Blue Ridge, Ga. 30513.

BALLOU, JOHN WALDO R
b. Bangor, Maine, 9/29/25; s. William Rice Ballou and Gladys Lowell B; single. Educ: Univ. Maine, B.A, 49; Yale Univ, LL.B, 52; Phi Beta Kappa; Phi Kappa Phi; Phi Gamma Delta. Polit. & Govt. Pos: Trustee and former chmn, Bangor Water Dist, Maine, 63-; alternate del, Rep. Nat. Conv, 64; mem, Maine Adv. Cmt. on Ment. Health and Bangor Fine Arts Adv. Cmt, 64-; mem, Penobscot Co. Rep. Cmt, 66-68. Bus. & Prof. Pos: Partner, Mitchell & Ballou, 53- Mil. Serv: Entered as Pvt, Army, 43, released as Cpl, 46, after serv. in 87th Inf. Div, ETO; European-African-Mid.East. Theater Campaign Ribbon with 3 Battle Stars; Am. Theater Campaign Ribbon. Mem: Gen. cmt, Penobscot Co. Bar Asn; Cmt. on Workmen's Compensation and Employers Liability Ins. Law, Am. Bar Asn; Maine State Bar Asn; ex-pres, East. Maine Guidance Center; bd. of dirs, Penobscot Co. Chap, Am. Red Cross; pres, Bangor Savoyards; bd. of dirs, Bangor Commun. Concert Asn; Bangor Symphony; Bangor Civic Theater; Bangor City Club; Penobscot Valley Country Club. Actor and dir, local prfnl. and non-prfnl. dramatic and musico-dramatic prods. Rel: Unitarian. Mailing Add: 52 Montgomery St, Bangor, Maine 04401. (1967)

BALLOUN, CHARLES F. R
Iowa State Sen.
b. Dardanelle, Ark, 9/21/04; s. Van Balloun and Vlasta B; m. 1/1/29 to Mary Delores Matula; c. Gerald and Eugene, (both deceased); grandchildren, Linda, Diana, Jane and Gerald. Educ: Tama High Sch, 24; Iowa State Univ, 29. Polit. & Govt. Pos: Dist. corn storage supvr, 2 years; Iowa State Rep, 59th, 60th and 60th Extra Gen. Assemblies; chmn, Tama Co. Agr. and Stabilization Cmn, $2\frac{1}{2}$ years; Iowa State Sen, 65- Bus. & Prof. Pos: Owner and operator, farm, Toledo, Iowa; co-owner and mgr, Tama Co. Grain Co; supt, Alaska Exp. Farm, 2 years; with U.S. Dept. of Agr, 9 years; sch. teacher and adminstr, 10 years. Mem: Tama Co. Farm Bur; West. Grain & Feed Asn. of Iowa. Rel: Catholic. Mailing Add: Toledo, Iowa. 52342. (1967)

BALOMENOS, SANDRA JEAN R
b. Rochester, N.H, 4/9/42; d. Costas A. Balomenos and Velma L. Van Buskirk B; single. Educ: Univ. N.H, B.A. in govt, 65. Polit. & Govt. Pos: Mem, Young Rep; v.chmn, Rep. City Cmt, Rochester, N.H, 64-66; del, N.H. Rep. State Conv, 64 & 66; N.H. State Rep, 66-68; clerk, Strafford Co. Del, 67. Mem: N.H. Coun. of World Affairs; Univ. N.H. Alumni Club; Nat. Rep. Women's Club; Red Cross Blood Prog. Organized TAR's in Rochester, N.H. Mailing Add: 61 Hanson St, Rochester, N.H. 03867. (1967)

BALTZ, MEADE R
Ill. State Sen.
b. Troy Twp, Will Co, Ill, 1912; m. 1939 to Lydia Beeling; c. Four sons, three daughters. Educ: Joliet High Sch. Polit. & Govt. Pos: Asst. supvr, Co. Bd, 51-52; supvr, Joliet Twp, 53; Ill. State Sen, 62- Bus. & Prof. Pos: Retail paint and wallpaper bus. Mem: Will Co. Commun. Chest; Am. Red Cross; Northeast. Ill. Local Govt. Serv. Cmn; C. of C; Kiwanis; Ill. Pub. Welfare Asn; Ill. Twp. Off. Asn. Mailing Add: 600 Buell Ave, Joliet, Ill. 60435. (1967)

BALZANO, MICHAEL J, JR. R
R.I. State Rep.
b. 1927; m. to Doris L. Ridolfi; c. Three. Educ: Bryant Col. Polit. & Govt. Pos: Past mem, Bristol Police Dept. and Police Reserves, R.I; R.I. State Rep, 67- Bus. & Prof. Pos: Founder of Bristol Colts; asst. dist. mgr, John Hancock Life Ins. Co, East Providence, Mil. Serv: Navy, World War II. Mem: Pres, Elmwood Terr. Improv. Asn; mem, March of Dimes Cmt; C. of C; 50th Jubilee Cmt. of Mt. Carmel Church. Mailing Add: 40 Elmwood Dr, Bristol, R.I. 02809. (1967)

BAMBERG, DANIEL FRANCIS D
Mem, Calif. Dem. State Cent. Cmt.
b. Los Angeles, Calif, 12/23/45 to Francis Lowell Bamberg and Anne Conlon B; single. Educ: Creighton Univ; 63-64; San Diego State Col, A.B. in Soc. Sci, 68; Univ. San Diego Law Sch, 69-; Oceotl; Sigma Alpha Epsilon. Polit. & Govt. Pos: San Diego Co. precinct and 'Get out the Vote' chmn, R.F. Kennedy, Calif. Primary, 68; campaign mgr, dem. cand. 36th Cong. dist, Calif, 68; mem, Calif. Dem State Cent. Cmt, 68- Mem: Downtown Dem; IBT. Fraternity Man of the Year, San Diego State Col, 68, Man of the Month, Feb, 68. Rel: Roman Catholic. Legal Res: 4814 Zelzah Ave, Encinco, Calif. 91316. Mailing Add: 6557 Tait Ave, Apt. 6, San Diego, Calif. 92111.

BAMBERGER, CARL A. R
Ky. State Rep.
b. Bellevue, Ky, 8/27/03; s. Frank J. Bamberger and Clara Ann Meier B; m. 2/4/33 to Ruth Elizabeth Brinkman; c. Janet, Ruth and Mary Martha. Educ: St. Xavier High Sch, 4 years. Polit. & Govt. Pos: City Councilman, Bellevue, 60-63; Ky. State Rep, 68- Bus. & Prof. Pos: Pres. & treas, Addison Sponge & Chamois Co, Inc, 47-; pres, Bellevue Fed. Savings & Loan Asn, 63- Mem: K. of C. Rel: Catholic. Mailing Add: 1216 Wilson Rd, Bellevue, Ky. 41073.

BAMBERGER, THOMAS A. D
Okla. State Rep.
b. Massillon, Ohio, 5/28/26; s. Titus Bamberger and Hester Kegerries B, div; c. Diana, James, Thomas and Kathryn. Educ: Ohio State Univ, B.A, 48; Okla. City Univ, LL.B, 53; Phi Delta Theta. Polit. Pos: Okla. State Rep, currently. Bus. & Prof. Pos: Partner, Bamberger & Baer, Attorneys. Mil. Serv: Entered as Seaman, Navy, 43, released as PO, 46, after serv. in Pac. Theater. Mailing Add: $132\frac{1}{2}$ S.W. 25th St, Oklahoma City, Okla. 73109.

BANCROFT, HOBART DAVID D
b. Talmage, Nebr, 3/4/97; s. William D. Bancroft and Helen Blanche O'Hara B; m. 4/15/28 to Irene Hastings; c. Eleanor (Mrs. Yoakam) and Catherine (Mrs. Sloan). Educ: Univ. Nebr, B.S, 23; Alpha Kappa Psi. Bus. & Prof. Pos: Pres, Commercial State Bank, 47-63. Mil. Serv: Entered as Pvt, Army, 18, released as Sgt, 18, after serv. in Chem. Warfare Serv. Mem: AF&AM; Odd Fellows. Rel: Methodist. Mailing Add: Elsie, Nebr. 69134.

BANDOUVERIS, HARRY R
b. Racine, Wis, 5/22/32; s. Nicholas Bandouveris and Evangeline Kallas B; m. 5/19/57 to Alveda Faye Barbee; c. George Nicholas and Harold Christopher. Educ: Univ. Wis, Madison, B.S, 54. Polit. & Govt. Pos: Ariz. State Rep, 64-66. Bus. & Prof. Pos: Pres, Bandouveris Co. Mailing Add: 3509 Cherokee Rd, Mountain Brook, Ala. 35223.

BANDSTRA, BERT ANDREW D
b. Iowa, 1/25/22; m. 8/24/50 to Theressa Van Wyngardern; c. Bruce Alan and Thomas Anno. Educ: Cent. Col.(Iowa), B.A, cum laude, 50; Univ. Mich, LL.B, 53. Polit. & Govt. Pos: Attorney, Marion Co, Iowa, 55-59; asst. to Congressman Neal Smith, 59-64; U.S. Rep, Iowa, 64-66; Dem. Cand, U.S. House Rep, 68. Mil. Serv: Entered as Seaman, Navy, 42, released as PO 2/C, 45, after serv. in Solomon Islands and Okinawa; Presidential Unit Citation. Mem: Marion Co. and Iowa State Bar Asns; Am. Legion. Rel: Christian Reformed Church. Mailing Add: 1010 Franklin St, Pella, Iowa 50219.

BANE, CORA D
b. Pineville, Ky, d. L.J. Percival and Electa Howard P; m. to Robert C. Bane. Polit. & Govt. Pos: Admin. Asst. to Rep. Watts, Ky, 63-; secy, John Watts, Cmnr, Motor Trans, Frankfort, Ky. Rel: Methodist. Legal Res: Lexington, Ky. Mailing Add: 1001 Wilson Blvd, Arlington, Va. 22209.

BANE, DAVID MORGAN
b. Uniontown, Pa, 9/12/15; m. to Patricia Miller; c. Patricia. Educ: Duke Univ, A.B, 38; Univ. Pa, LL.B, 41. Polit. & Govt. Pos: Career officer, U.S. Dept. of State For. Serv, 47-; v.consul. and second secy, Tokyo, 47-49 and Seoul, Korea, 49-50; consul, Bordeaux, 50-52; first secy, Paris, 53-56; Nat. War Col, 57-58; dep. dir, Off. of N.E. Asian Affairs, 58-59, dir, 59-61; consul gen, Lahore, Pakistan, 61-64; U.S. Ambassador to Gabon, 65-69. Mil. Serv: Col, Army, 41-46, overseas. Mem: Pa. Bar Asn; Univ. Exchange Prog, Univ. Iowa, 64-65. Mailing Add: c/o U.S. Dept. of State Foreign Service, Washington, D.C. 20521. (1967)

BANEN, ABRAHAM THEODORE DFL
Chmn, Koochichina Co. Dem-Farmer-Labor Party, Minn.
b. Eveleth, Minn, 9/30/09; s. Peter Banen and Marian B; m. 2/15/49 to Blanche Bachinski; c. Wendy Ann, Thomas and Terrance. Educ: Aibbing Jr. Col, 27-29; Univ. Wis, B.A, 31; Univ. Minn, D.D.S, 34; Phi Sigma Delta. Polit. & Govt. Pos: Del, Dem. Nat. Conv, 68; chmn, Koochichina Co. Dem-Farmer-Labor Party, Minn, currently. Mil. Serv: Entered as 1st Lt, Army, 42, released as Capt, 45, after serv. in 8th Inf. Div, ETO, 43-45; 2 Bronze Stars; Purple Heart; Combat Med. Badge; 5 campaign ribbons. Mem: Lions (past pres); Jr. C. of C; Mason. Legal Res: 100 Park Ave, International Falls, Minn. 56649. Mailing Add: 216 Third Ave, International Falls, Minn. 56649.

BANG, OTTO T. JR. Conservative
Minn. State Rep.
b. Madelia, Minn, 1931; m; c. four. Educ: Maryville N.D. Sch; Univ. of Minn, B.A. Polit. & Govt. Pos: Chmn, Edina Rep. Cmt, Minn, 60-62; Minn. State Rep, 62- Bus. & Prof. Pos: Pres, Consumers Casualty Co; dir, Consumers Financial Corp, Prfnl. Financial Serv. Mem: AF&AM; Scottish Rite; Shrine; Exchange Club, Minneapolis. Rel: Lutheran. Mailing Add: 5200 Duggan Plaza, Edina, Minn. 55435.

BANISTER, BETTE R
Vice chairwoman, Tenth Cong. Dist. Rep. Party, Ga.
b. Athens, Ga, 11/30/35; d. Dr. Walter F. McLendon and Marguerite Ward M; m. 5/3/58 to Dr. Royce Estes Banister; c. Brian James, Laura Elaine and Marguerite Elizabeth. Educ: Stephens Col, A.A, 54; Univ. Ga, B.S.H.E, 56; Phi Upsilon Omicron; Chi Omega. Polit. & Govt. Pos: Secy, Clarke Co. Rep. Cmt, Ga, 66-; tenth dist. dir, Ga. Fedn. Rep. Women, 67-69; alternate del, Rep. Nat. Conv, 68; mem, Ga. Rep. State Cent. Cmt, 68-; v.pres, Clarke Co. Fedn. Rep. Women, 68-; vice chairwoman, Tenth Cong. Dist. Rep. Party, 68-; Ga. chmn, Nat. Fedn. of Rep. Women's Educ. Adv. Cmt, currently. Mem: Archaeol. Inst. Am; Athens Jr. Assembly; Crawford W. Long Med. Auxiliary; League Women Voters; Athens Gen. Hosp. Auxiliary; Heritage Garden Club; Clarke Co. Fedn. Rep. Women. Rel: Episcopal. Mailing Add: 40 Pine Valley Dr, Athens, Ga. 30601.

BANKS, DAVID OWEN D
Asst. Dir. Pub. Affairs, Dem. Nat. Cmt.
b. Huntington Park, Calif, 12/9/40; s. Willard Louis Banks and Winifred Regan B; m. 8/10/63 to Lyneth Diane Soinski; c. Matthew David, Michael Joseph and Joseph Stephen. Educ: Univ. Dayton, B.S, 64. Polit. & Govt. Pos: Legis. asst, U.S. Sen. Stephen M. Young, 65; exec. secy, Young Dem. Clubs of Am, 65-67; asst. dir. pub. affairs, Dem. Nat. Cmt, currently. Bus. & Prof. Pos: Sports ed, Fostoria Rev. Times, 60-62 and Dayton Jour. Herald, 62-64. Mem: Sigma Delta Chi; K. of C. Rel: Roman Catholic. Legal Res: 709 W. North St, Fostoria, Ohio 44830. Mailing Add: 8123 Heatherton Lane, Vienna, Va. 22180.

BANKS, DORIS NININGER D
Dem. Nat. Committeewoman, Colo.
b. McPherson, Kans, 10/3/21; d. Harvey Harlow Nininger and Addie Delp N; m. 3/17/54 to John Clement Banks; c. Nancy, James and stepchildren, Carolyn Ivey and John Robert. Educ: Grinnell Col, B.A, 43; Phi Beta Kappa; Mortar Board. Polit. & Govt. Pos: Precinct committeewoman, Dem. Party, Denver, Colo, 52-54; captain-at-lg, Denver Co. Dem. Party, 60-63, secy, 63-65, v.chmn, 65-68; Denver Elec. Cmnr, 67; cmnr, Cmn. on Commun. Rels, 67-, chmn, 69-; dem. Nat. Committeewoman, Colo, 68- Bus. & Prof. Pos: Reporter, Denver Post, 45-49; Info. writer, City and Co. of Denver, 52-54. Rel: United Church of Christ. Mailing Add: 1220 Olive St, Denver, Colo. 80220.

BANNER, DOROTHY BERTHA R
Secy, Rio Blanco Co. Rep. Cent. Cmt, Colo.
b. Meeker, Colo, 1/18/14; d. William Henery Cotten and Grace Egan C; m. 1/20/57 to Thomas Richard Banner; c. William Dallas Miller and Jon Kemis Miller. Educ: Meeker High Sch, Colo, 12 years. Polit. & Govt. Pos: Secy, Rio Blanco Co. Rep. Cent. Cmt, Colo, 68- Bus. & Prof. Pos: Clerk, Sommer & Kughman Shoe Store, San Francisco, Calif, 43-45, Meeker Economy Store, Colo, 45-54 and A. Oldland & Co. Inc, 54-63; asst. ed, White River Press, 63-64; clerk, Meeker Hotel, 64-66; Kitchen asst, Pioneer Hosp, currently. Mem: St. James Auxiliary; PTA. Rel: Episcopal. Legal Res: 223 Main St, Meeker, Colo. 81641. Mailing Add: P.O. Box 655, Meeker, Colo. 81641.

BANNISTER, TILLMAN ARTHUR D
b. Lawton, Okla, 5/20/08; s. Lawrence Ward Bannister and Henrietta Hughes B; m. 2/28/32 to Veta Mae Vick; c. Adron Vick and Gary. Educ: Southwest Inst. Tech, B.A, 45; Okla. Univ; Univ. of Ind; N.Mex. West. Univ; Denver Univ. Polit. & Govt. Pos: Precinct chmn, Co. Dem. Cmt, N.Mex, 54-66; mem, State Platform Cmt, 60; mem, Dem. Co. Exec. Cmt, 62-66; del, Dem. Nat. Conv, 64; del, Constitutional Conv, 69. Bus. & Prof. Pos: Prin, Leedy Okla. Sch, 40-41, Otis Elem. Sch. and Carlsbad City Schs, 41-; pres. bd. dirs, Otis Water Users Coop, 64-66; elem. teacher for 5 yrs. Mem: Nat, N.Mex. and Carlsbad Educ. Asns; N.Mex. Coun. for the Improvement of Educ; N.Mex. Br, Asn. for Supervision & Curriculum Develop; Elem. Prin. Asn; hon. dir. of Carlsbad, N.Mex. C. of C; Farm Bur; Mason; AF&AM. Outstanding Educator of the Year Award, Jr. Chamber of Commerce, Carlsbad, N.Mex, 64. Rel: Baptist. Mailing Add: R.R. 1, Box 242, Carlsbad, N.Mex. 88220.

BANNON, EDMOND JOSEPH D
b. Kansas City, Kans, 3/9/12; s. Edmond James Bannon and Rose Goebel B; m. 11/11/41 to Patricia Nan Peters; c. Peter Fredric. Educ: Kansas City Sch. Law, 31-35. Polit. & Govt. Pos: Mem, Bd. Pub. Harbors & Terminals, State Ind, 55-56; mem. bd. trustees, Purdue Univ, 56-59; regional dir, region five, Asn. Gov. Bd. State Univ. and Allied Insts, 58-59; mem, U.S. Trade Develop. Mission to S.Africa, 62; financial adv. Ind. Dem. State Cent. Cmt, 62; mem, World's Fair Cmt. for Ind. Days, 64; treas, Branigin for Gov. Cmt, 64; del, Dem. Nat. Conv, 64 & 68; mem. nat. adv. cmt, U.S. Cmnr. Gen. for U.S. Participation in World Exhibition at Montreal, Can, EXPO 67, 67; mem, Ind. Trade Mission to Orient, 68; mem, State Policy Cmn. Post High Sch. Educ, 68; mem. Cmn. Med. Educ, State Ind, 69; dir. Old Hickory Dem. Club, 69. Bus. & Prof. Pos: Various dept, Liberty Nat. Bank; Fidelity Nat. Bank & Trust Co. and bond dept, Union, Nat. Bank, Kansas City, Mo, 26-35; asst. nat. bank exam, Comptroller of the Currency, 35-41, nat. bank exam, 41-47; first v.pres, Purdue Nat. Bank Lafayette, 47-49, pres, 49-56, chmn. bd. & pres, 57- Mil. Serv: Entered as Pvt, Army, 43, released as 1st Lt, 46, after serv. in staff work, Cent. Pac. Base Command & Mid. Pac, 45-46. Mem: Am. Bankers Asn; Ind. Bankers Asn; Robert Morris Assoc; U.S. C. of C; Ind. State C. of C; Gr. Lafayette C. of C; Am. Inst. Mgt.(pres. coun); Ind. Soc. Chicago; Newcomen Soc. N.Am; Rotary Club; Indianapolis Athletic Club; Indianapolis Press Club; Lafayette Press Club; Am. Legion; Elks; Lafayette Country Club; Ponte Vedra Club, Fla. 200 Club, N.C. Rel: Roman Catholic. Legal Res: 30 Maryhill Rd, Lafayette, Ind. 47905. Mailing Add: Purdue National Bank of Lafayette, P.O. Box 380, Lafayette, Ind. 47902.

BANSMER, GUSTAV D
b. N.Y.C, 1/21/17; s. Adolf G. Bansmer and Emma Bobsien B; m. 1/2/42 to Kathleen Joyce Gibbons; c. Michael K, Peter W. G. and Kathleen A. M. Educ: Columbia Col, A.B, 38, Col. of Physicians & Surgeons, Columbia Univ, M.D, 42. Polit. & Govt. Pos: Chmn, Yakima Co. Dem. Cent. and Exec. Cmts, Wash, formerly; del, Dem. Nat. Donv, 68. Bus. & Prof. Pos: Chief, Dept. of Surg, Group Health Clin, Seattle, Wash, 50-54, chief of staff, 52-54; staff surgeon, Yakima Valley Clin, Grandview, 54- Mil. Serv: Entered as 1st Lt, Army, 43, released as Capt, 46, after serv. in Manhattan Proj. and Med. Corps, Asiatic-Pac. & Am. Theaters. Publ: 'America with Medicare,' Dem. J, 1/65, 'The Unicameral Legislature,' 9/65; numerous sci. articles in Tech. Jours. Mem: Am. Med. Asn; fel, Am. Col. Surgeons, Pan-Am. Med. Soc. and Am. Col. Geriatrics; dipl, Am. Bd. of Surg; Am. Field Serv; Am. Legion; Am. Physicians Art Asn. Oil painting and metal sculpture. Mailing Add: Sandhill Rd, Grandview, Wash. 98930.

BANTA, PARKE M. R
b. Berryman, Mo, 11/21/91; s. Cyrus N. Banta and Susan Learned B; m. 4/13/18 to Gladys Nichols; c. Doris Jean (Mrs. J. Roe Pree), Carol (Mrs. Scott R. Brewer) and Mary Elizabeth (Mrs. James R. McHaney). Educ: William Jewell Col, Mo; Northwest. Univ. Law Sch, LL.B, 14; Delta Theta Phi. Polit. & Govt. Pos: Mem, Co. Cent. and State Rep. Cmts. in '20's; chmn, Wash. Co. Rep. Cent. Cmt, Mo, 24-25; mem. bd. of trustees, Arcadia, several terms in '30's; mem, Arcadia-Ironton Sch. Bd, 31-33; adminstr, Mo. State Social Security Cmn, 41-45; U.S. Rep, Mo, 47-49; gen. counsel, Dept. Health, Educ. and Welfare, 53-61; mem, State Reorgn. Cmn, 63; chmn, finance cmt, Wash. Co. Rep. Cent. Cmt, Mo, 65-66; chmn, Rep. Finance Cmt, 70. Bus. & Prof. Pos: Attorney-at-law, 14- Mil. Serv: Entered as Pvt, Army, 17, released as 1st Lt, 19, after serv. in Adj. Gen. Dept. Mem: Mason, Scottish Rite; Capitol Hill Club of Wash, D.C; hon. mem, Ironton Rotary Club and Rotary Int; Am. Legion. Rel: Methodist. Mailing Add: 204 North Mine St, Potosi, Mo. 63664.

BAPTISTA, MARY ELSIE D
Social Secy, Calif. Dem. State Cent. Cmt.
b. Gloucester, Mass, 12/31/26; d. Joaquin Euzebio Codinha and Lucinda Serra C; m. 9/12/41 to Arnold Nunes Baptista; c. Arnold Frank, Sr, Joseph Joaquin, MaryAnn, Jeanne Lynn and Daniel Wayne. Educ: San Diego City Schs. Polit. & Govt. Pos: Social secy, Sen. James R. Mills, Calif, 66-, San Diego Co. Dem. Cent. Cmt, 67- and Calif. Dem. State Cent. Cmt, 68-; chmn, Housewives for Humphrey-Muskie, San Diego Co, 68. Mem: Sociadade Portugesa Rainha Santa Isabel, San Diego; Cabrillo Club, San Diego; Young Ladies Inst. Madona, Chula Vista-Nat. City; San Diego Co. Health Dept. Vol, San Diego U.S.O. Rel: Catholic. Mailing Add: 760 Beech Ave, Chula Vista, Calif. 92010.

BARANELLO, DOMINIC JOSEPH D
Chmn, Suffolk Co. Dem. Orgn, N.Y.
b. Brooklyn, N.Y, 9/25/22; s. Angelo Baranello and Josephine Belmonte B; m. 11/25/55; c. Dominic, Jr, Stephen and Christiana. Educ: Brooklyn Law Sch, LL.B, 50; Brooklyn Col, 2 years. Polit. & Govt. Pos: Chmn, Brookhaven Dem. Orgn, N.Y, 56-60; alternate del, Dem. Nat. Conv, 60 and del, 68; dep. co. attorney, Suffolk Co, N.Y, 60-62; chmn, Suffolk Co. Dem. Orgn, 66-; mem. exec. cmt, N.Y. State Dem. Cmt, 66-; presidential elector, State of N.Y, 68. Bus. & Prof. Pos: Attorney, 52- Mil. Serv: Entered as Pvt, Air Force, 43, released as Pfc, 46. Mem: Suffolk Co. Bar Ans; Columbian Lawyers Asn; charter mem, Elks (Lodge 2138); Am. Legion; Medford Fire Dept. Rel: Catholic. Mailing Add: 27 Robinson Ave, Medford, N.Y. 11763.

BARBAR, RAYMOND D
b. 1922. Educ: West. Ky. State Col, B.A. and M.A. Polit. & Govt. Pos: Ky. State Rep, 64-68. Bus. & Prof. Pos: Prin, Allen Co. Elem. Sch. Mil. Serv: Army; Maj, Army Res. Mem: Ky. and Nat. Educ. Asns. Rel: Methodist; Off, Church Bd. Mailing Add: R.D. 1, Scotsville, Ky. 42164. (1967)

BARBATO, PASQUALE ANGELO D
Conn. State Sen.
b. Hamden, Conn, 1/14/25; s. Ernest V. Barbato and Amelia Pastena B. Educ: N.Y. Univ, B.S. in Acct. and Finance, 53. Polit. & Govt. Pos: Conn. State Rep, 63-66; Conn. State Sen, 66- Bus. & Prof. Pos: Off. mgr, Fox Steel Co, Orange, Conn, 58- Mil. Serv: 5th Air Force, World War II. Mem: Chmn, Bd. of Tax Rev, Hamden, Conn, 55-59. Mailing Add: 3071 Whitney Ave, Hamden, Conn. 06514. (1967)

BARBEE, ALLEN CROMWELL D
N.C. State Rep.
b. Spring Hope, N.C, 12/18/10; s. John Lucian Barbee and Deborah Vester B; m. 3/7/42 to Mabel McClellan Dixon; c. Rebecca Barnes and Allen Cromwell,

II. Educ: Univ. N.C, 31-32. Polit. & Govt. Pos: Cmnr, Spring Hope, N.C, 47-49, mayor, 50-58; N.C. State Rep, 60- Bus. & Prof. Pos: Ed-publisher, Spring Hope Enterprise; sales exec. and mfrs. rep, 38-50; owner, Barbee Agency, 50-66. Mil. Serv: Entered as Pvt, Army, 42, released as Capt, Air Force, 46, after serv. in Ferrying Div, Air Transport Command, ETO, 43-45; ETO and Normandy Invasion Ribbons. Mem: Am. Legion; Elks; Shrine; Sphinx Club; Benvenue and Peachtree Hills Country Clubs. Rel: Methodist. Mailing Add: Spring Hope, N.C. 27882. (1967)

BARBEE, JUANITA E. D

b. Los Angeles, Calif, 4/23/12; d. Woodford Henry Terry and Louise Sayers T; m. 5/29/54. Polit. & Govt. Pos: Secy, U.S. Rep. Helen G. Douglas, 47-50, U.S. Sen. Humphrey, 51-56 and U.S. Rep. Roosevelt, 56-62; admin. asst. to U.S. Rep. Hawkins, Calif, 63- Mem: Nat. Coun. of Negro Women, NAACP. Accompanist for prfnl, amateur musicians and singers; hobbies; bridge, reading, theater. Mailing Add: 1830 16th St. N.W, Washington, D.C. 20009.

BARBEE, LLOYD AUGUSTUS D

Wis. State Assemblyman

b. Memphis, Tenn, 8/17/25; s. Ernest Aaron Barbee and Adlina Gillian B; div; c. Finn, Daphne and Rustam. Educ: LeMoyne Col, B.A. in Soc. Sci, 49; Univ. Wis, Madison, Law Cert, 55 and J.D, 56. Polit. & Govt. Pos: Nat. v.chmn, student div, Am. for Dem. Action, 48-49, nat. field secy, 51; law exam, Unemploy. Compensation Dept, Indust. Cmn. of Wis, 57-62; mem, Mayor's Cmn. on Human Rights, Madison, 57-62, chmn, 59-61; legal consult, Gov. Cmn. on Human Rights, 59; mem, Gov. Cmn. for UN, 63; Wis. State Assemblyman, Sixth Dist, 65-, mem, Cmt. Joint Finance and chmn, Enrolled Bills Cmt, 65-66, mem. Commerce and Mfg. Cmt, 65-67, mem, Cmt. on Transportation and commerce & Mfr. Cmt, Wis. State Assembly; del, Milwaukee Co. Dem. Coun, 67; chmn, Sixth Ward Dem. Unit, Milwaukee, 67-69; del, Dem. Nat. Conv, 68. Bus. & Prof. Pos: Attorney, Barbee and Jacobson, Madison, Wis, 56-57, Milwaukee, 62; v.chmn, Educ. Film Assocs, 62; bd. dirs, Wis. Film Assocs, Inc, 63; bd. mem, E.B. Phillips Day Care Center, 64-66; team teacher summer law practice course, Univ. Wis. Law Sch, 68 & 69. Mil Serv: Entered as A/S, Navy, 43, released as SM 2/C, 46. Mem: Pres, Wis. Conf. NAACP Br, 61-64, legal redress chmn, 64-65; chmn, Region III NAACP, 58-59, v.chmn, 63-64; v.chmn, Wis. NAACP, 58-60, legal redress chmn. and polit. action chmn, 57-58 and for Madison NAACP, 60-62; chmn, Labor and Indust. Cmt, Milwaukee NAACP, 63-64; spec. consult, Benton Harbor, Mich. NAACP Br, 63; chmn, Milwaukee United Sch. Integration Cmt, 64-; Negro Am. Labor Coun, 64; Milwaukee Citizens for Equal Opportunity, 63; adv. cmt, Northside Inventory Conf, 63; Milwaukee Gen. Semantics Soc, 63-; v.chmn, Wis. Citizens for Fair Housing, 62; chmn, Citizens' Film Cmt. Against Discrimination in Housing, 61-62; steward, Local 145, Wis. State Employ. Asn, 57-62; counselor and resource for Dane Co. Citizens Planning Cmt, Human Rights Sect, 61; Am. Vet. Cmt, 48-50; Elks; pres, Freedom Through Equality, Inc, 69-; bd. consultants, Afro-Urban Inst, 69-; adv. counsel to bd. dirs, Opportunities Industrialization Center-Greater Milwaukee, 69-; We-Milwaukeeans, 67-; chmn, Housing Enterprises, Inc, 69-; Mil. Black Econ. Develop. Inst; Univ. Black Enterprises; bd. dirs, Wis. Metrop. Alliance, Inc, 69- Milwaukee Man of Year Award, Delta Chi Lambda Chap, Alpha Phi Alpha, 65; leader, State Capitol Sit-in for Fair Housing Legis, 61; invited to planning session of White House Conf. To Fulfill These Rights, 65; Cert. Merit in recognition of dedicated serv. to human brotherhood, Ill-Wis. State Asn. of the Int. Elks, 69. Legal Res: 321 E. Meinecke Ave, Milwaukee, Wis. 53212. Mailing Add: 110 E. Wisconsin Ave, Milwaukee, Wis. 53202.

BARBER, ARTHUR NEWELL D

Chmn, Cherokee Co. Dem. Exec. Cmt, Tex.

b. Jacksonville, Tex, 6/25/98; s. Clyde Herbert Barber and Ethel Ewing B; m. 10/13/22 to Mady Ellen Barnes; c. Merle Fay (Mrs. McBee) and John Robert. Polit. & Govt. Pos: Enumerator, Bur. of Census, Wash, 20-50; chmn, Precinct Three, Dem. Exec. Cmt, 32-50; chmn, Cherokee Co. Dem. Exec. Cmt, Tex, 50- Bus. & Prof. Pos: Farmer and rancher. Mem: WOW (secy-treas, 40 years); Tex. Farm Bur.(pres, 40-50, secy-treas, 50-56); Odd Fellows. Rel: Baptist. Mailing Add: R.D. 2, Jacksonville, Tex. 75766. (1967)

BARBER, ARTHUR WHITING D

b. Meriden, Conn, 7/4/26; s. Arthur Leslie Barber and Winifred Viola Whiting B; m. 8/26/49 to Margaret Shorey; c. Jeffrey Whiting, Christopher David, Jonathan Scott, Kimberly Susan and Cynthia Abigail. Educ: Harvard Univ, B.A, 50. Polit. & Govt. Pos: Dep. asst. secy. of defense, Dept. of Defense, 62-67. Bus. & Prof. Pos: With Air Force Cambridge Research Center, 50-61 and Mitre Corp, 61-62; pres, Inst. Polit. and Planning, 67- Mil. Serv: Entered Navy, 44, released as Signalman 3/C, 46, after serv. in Armed Guard, Pac. Rel: Unitarian. Mailing Add: 7600 Hemlock St, Bethesda, Md. 20034.

BARBER, JACK McWHORTER (MAC) D

Ga. State Rep.

b. Banks Co, Ga; m. to Janet Adair McGarity. Educ: Univ. Ga, B.A. Polit. & Govt. Pos: Dir, Housing Authority, Commerce, Ga; chmn, Commerce Chap, Am. Red Cross, 46-; mem, bd. educ, Commerce Pub. Schs, 49-, chmn, 53-54; Ga. State Rep, 49- Mil. Serv: Air Force, World War II. Mem: Past pres, Kiwanis; C. of C.(pres, 53-54). Rel: Methodist; Supt, First Methodist Church Sch, 50-; mem, Bd. of Stewards. Mailing Add: Box 224, Commerce, Ga. 30529. (1967)

BARBER, JAMES DAVID D

Pa. State Rep.

b. Columbia, S.C, 8/16/21; s. Howard Barber and Sallie Whitaker B; m. to Rebecca; c. Diane. Educ: Allen Univ. Polit. & Govt. Pos: Pa. State Rep, 190th Dist, Wards 6 and 27, 69- Mem: Mason; NAACP; W.Phila. Crusade and United Civic Asns; YMCA; ADA. NAACP; Asn. for Retarded Children and Am. Cancer Soc. Awards. Legal Res: 802 N. 40th St, Philadelphia, Pa. 19104. Mailing Add: Room 617, Main Capitol Bldg, House of Representatives, Harrisburg, Pa. 17120.

BARBER, JESSE B, JR. D

b. Chattanooga, Tenn, 6/22/24; s. Jesse B. Barber, Sr. and Mae Fortune B; m. 6/14/48 to Constance Bolling; c. Clifton J, Jesse B, III, Charles R. and Joye. Educ: Lincoln Univ, Pa; Hampton Inst, Va; Yale Univ, 41-44; Howard Univ. Med. Sch, M.D, 48; Alpha Phi Alpha. Polit. & Govt. Pos: Del, Dem. Nat. Conv, 68. Bus. & Prof. Pos: Chief, Div. Neurosurg, Howard Univ. Med. Sch, 61-, assoc. prof. surg, 67- Mil. Serv: Entered as Pvt, Army, 43, released as Pfc, 46, after serv. in Army Specialized Training Prog, Continental U.S, re-entered as Capt, 54, released in 56, after serv. in Med. Corps, Okinawa. Mem: Nat. Med. Asn; Am. Neurosurg. Asn; D.C. Med. Soc; Medio-Chirurgical Soc. of D.C. Rel: Presbyterian. Mailing Add: No. 38 Longfellow St. N.W, Wash, D.C. 20001.

BARBER, MERRILL P. D

b. Marshall, Mo, 12/18/10; m. to Helen Meredith Clarkson; c. Helen (Mrs. Stabile), Carolyn (Mrs. Bacal) and Merrill Jean. Educ: Univ. Fla; Sigma Phi Epsilon. Polit. & Govt. Pos: Mem, Fla. Dem. State Exec. Cmt, 38-40; mayor, Vero Beach, 47-49; mem, State Rd. Bd, 49-53; Fla. State Sen, 54-58 & 63-66. Bus. & Prof. Pos: Banking; investments; pres, Indian River Citrus Bank. Mem: Past pres, Rotary; Shrine; ambassador-at-lg, Mahi Shrine Temple; Scottish Rite Mason (32°); Elks; Fla. State C. of C.(dir, dist. v.pres, 62-63); past pres, Vero Beach Jr. C. of C. Vero Beach Jr. C. of C. Award, 52; U.S. C. of C. Award, 56. Rel: Episcopal. Mailing Add: 625 Royal Palm Place, P.O. Box 936, Vero Beach, Fla. 32960. (1967)

BARBER, RICHARD J.

Dep. Asst. Secy. for Policy and Int. Affairs, Dept. of Transportation

Educ: Wayne State Univ, A.B, 53 and J.D, 55; Univ. Mich, M.A. in Econ, 58; Yale, LL.M, 59; ed-in-chief, Wayne Law Rev, 54-55. Polit. & Govt. Pos: Asst. to the dir, Mich. Tax Study, 58; economist, staff of the Joint Cong. Econ. Cmt, 61-62; consult, House Select Small Bus. Cmt, 63; spec. counsel, Senate Subcmt. on Antitrust and Monopoly, 65-67; Dep. Asst. Secy. for Policy and Int. Affairs, Dept. of Transportation, currently. Bus. & Prof. Pos: Asst. prof. law, Rutgers Univ, 59-61; assoc. prof, South. Methodist Univ, 61-64; ed, J. of Air Law and Commerce, 63-64; vis. prof, Yale, 64-65. Mil. Serv: Army, 55-57. Publ: 'Technological Change in American Transportation: the Role of Government Action,' Va. Law Rev, 64; The Politics of Research, 66; plus other articles in prfnl. and gen. periodicals. Mem: Am. Econ. Asn; Mich. Bar; hon. socs. Legal Res: Mich. Mailing Add: Dept. of Transportation, 800 Independence Ave. S.W, Washington, D.C. 20590.

BARBER, ROBERT J. R

b. Detroit, Mich, 8/26/06; m. 8/31/31 to Gladys Wilkie; c. Susan Ann (Mrs. Uridge) and Robert F. Educ: Detroit Col. of Law, LL.B. and J.D. Polit. & Govt. Pos: Holder of every pos. within the Rep. Party of Kalamazoo Co. commencing with 1947; friend of the court, prosecutor, probate judge, spec. attorney gen. and assoc. munic. judge. Bus. & Prof. Pos: Spec. agent, Fed. Bur. Invest, formerly; attorney-at-law. Mil. Serv: World War II. Mem: United Cerebral Palsy Asn; Kalamazoo Soc. for Crippled Children; Kalamazoo Asn. for Retarded Children; chmn, Kalamazoo Safety Cmn; attorney for Girl Scouts; Boy Scouts; Crippled Childrens Asn; Safety Cmn; Traffic Safety Chmn; dir, State Soc. for Crippled Children; K. of C; Vis. Nurses Asn; Friends of the Coldwater Children; incorporator, Ft. Custer Handicapped Children. Rel: Roman Catholic. Legal Res: 8430 Tumbleweed, Portage, Mich. 49081. Mailing Add: 317 Michigan Bldg, Kalamazoo, Mich. 49001.

BARBERG, WILLIAM WARREN R

Chmn, Eau Claire Co. Rep. Club, Wis.

b. Minneapolis, Minn, 10/12/28; s. Wayne R. Barberg and Lillian Lantto B; m. 10/3/59 to Doreen A. Sieg; c. Lynn Marie, William Warren and Ann Denise. Educ: Stout State Univ, B.S, 51; Epsilon Pi Tau; Sigma Tau Gamma; Alpha Phi Omega. Polit. & Govt. Pos: Col. chmn, Stout State Univ. Young Rep, 50-52; chmn, Dunn Co. Young Rep, Wis, 53-56; chmn, Eau Claire Co. Young Rep, 56-58; dist. chmn, Tenth Dist. Young Rep, 57; v.pres, Wis. Young Rep, 58; mem. exec. cmt, Eau Claire Co. Rep. Club, 60-, chmn, 68-; mem. adv. cmt. and ins. laws rev. cmt, Wis. Legis. Coun, 66-69. Mem: Eau Claire Co. Taxpayers Asn.(chmn); Eau Claire Lions Club (past pres); First Wis. Toastmasters Club (past pres); Wis. Asn. Life Underwriters (past pres); pres, Stout State Univ. Found; pres, Sigma Tau Gamma Found; Chartered Life Underwriters (v.pres, Eau Claire Chap); Chippewa Valley Asn. Life Underwriters (legis. chmn); Zor Shrine Drum and Bugle Corps (secy, currently). Outstanding Alumnus, Sigma Tau Gamma; Distinguished Serv. Award, Wis. Asn. Life Underwriters. Rel: Lutheran; Past Pres, Bd. Deacons: Chmn. Congregation, currently. Mailing Add: 3606 Pine Place, Eau Claire, Wis. 54701.

BARBOSA, PEDRO JUAN New Progressive, P.R.

b. San Juan, P.R, 11/1/92; s. José Celso Barbosa, M.D. and Beleñ Sañchez B; wid; c. Gloria P.(Mrs. de Beyda), Pedro A. Viñas, Mary Jo (Mrs. de Garcia), Maj. José Celso Coloñ and Pedro J. Coloñ. Educ: Armstrong Tech, D.C, B.S; Univ. Mich. Polit. & Govt. Pos: Del, Rep. Conv, 24-; majority floor leader, Munic. Assembly, P.R, 25-29; mem, Racing Cmn, 29-34; asst. cmnr. commerce, 40-43; pub. rels. off. to Mayor of San Juan, 43-46; counsr. & mem, Rep. Cent. Territorial Cmt; treas, P.R. Rep. Party; publicity dir, Accion Politica; P.R. State Sen, 65-69. Bus. & Prof. Pos: Managing ed, El Tiempo, P.R, 23-31; managing ed. of Eng. sect, Revista de Agricultura y Comercio, 40-43; mgr, Barbosa Publishing Co, Inc, 41-46; managing ed, El Sol, 49- Mil. Serv: Entered as Cadet, Army, released as 1st Lt, 19, after serv. in 375th Inf, U.S. Publ: The Political Destiny of Puerto Rico; Puerto Rico 51st State of the Union; The Commonwealth of Puerto Rico; Post Umbra (After Death). Mem: Asn. of Legis. Leaders; Asn. for Statehood; Odd Fellows; Am. Legion. Gold Medal from Post 1, Am. Legion for fight in favor of Americanization of P.R; received Cong. Medal for Meritorious Serv. as Mem. of Selective Serv. Rel: Roman Catholic. Mailing Add: 914 Calle Alcazar Villa Granada, Rio Piedras, P.R. 00923.

BARBOUR, ROBERT TAYLOR R

Chmn, Md. State Rep. Cent. Cmt, Charles Co.

b. Rock Point, Md, 11/22/11; s. Robert Guy Barbour and Charlotte May Twiford B; m. 12/7/41 to Phyllis Buckley; c. Rosemary, Lorena, Lucy and Victoria A. Educ: George Wash. Univ, A.B, 38; Univ. Md, LL.B, 41. Polit. & Govt. Pos: State's attorney, Charles Co, Md, 51-54; chmn, Md. State Rep. Cent. Cmt, Charles Co, 62- Bus. & Prof. Pos: Practicing attorney, La Plata, Md, 47-, present firm name, Barbour and Zverina, Attorneys; hold unlimited license as Master of Ocean Steamships. Mil. Serv: Entered as Pvt, Army,

41, released as Warrant Officer, 45, after serv. in 12th Coast Artil. Mine Planter Battery, Am. Theater; Am. Theater Army Serv. Ribbon; Atlantic, Pac. and Mediterranean Merchant Marine Serv. Ribbons; mem, Exec. Res. Maritime Admin. Dept. of Commerce. Mem: Md. and Charles Co. Bar Asns; Am. Trial Lawyers Asn; Charles Co. Hist. Soc; Soc. for Restoration of Port Tobacco; Int. Order of Masters, Mates and Pilots. Rel: Episcopal. Mailing Add: Port Tobacco, Md. 20646.

BARBOUR, WALTER HARRIS R
Ind. State Sen.
b. Indianapolis, Ind, 7/1/09; s. John Miles Barbour and Effie Askin B; m. 8/10/35 to Ethel Margaret Garrison; c. Clifford Harris, Walter Dean, John Raymond and James Edgar. Educ: Curtis Wright Aeronaut. Eng, grad, 31. Polit. & Govt. Pos: Young Rep. chmn, Lawrence Twp, Ind, 40-44; served on Selective Serv. Bd, 53 & 54; Ind. State Rep, Marion Co, 53, 55, 57, 61, 63 & 67, chmn. hwy. study cmt, Ind. House of Rep, 63 & 64, co-chmn. hwy. needs study cmt, 67 & 68; Rep. precinct committeeman, Lawrence Twp, Ind, 59-; Ind. State Sen, Marion Co, 68- Bus. & Prof. Pos: Owned and operated Barbour Farms, Marion Co, Ind, 35-55; owner and mgr, Barbour Farms, Decatur Co, Ind, 45-; owned and operated Barbour Orchards, Marion Co, 47-55 and Lawrence Material & Supply, 53-66; owner and mgr, North Lawrence Shopping Center, 59- Mem: Ind. Hort. Soc; Ind. Hist. Soc; life mem, Nat. Soc. State Legislators; Ind. State Legislators Club; Farm Bur.(chmn, Marion Co. Club, chmn, Lawrence Twp. Club, mem, Ind. Club); pres, Lawrence Twp. Businessmen's Asn; Optimist. App. to Sagamore of the Wabash by Gov. Harold W. Handley, 60. Rel: Methodist. Mailing Add: 5105 N. Shadeland Dr, Indianapolis, Ind. 46226.

BARBOUR, WALWORTH
U.S. Ambassador to Israel
b. Mass, 6/4/08. Educ: Harvard Univ, A.B, 30. Polit. & Govt. Pos: Career ambassador, U.S. Dept. of State For. Serv, 31-; Naples, 31-32, Athens, 33-36, Baghdad, 36-39 and 42 and Sofia, 39-41; second secy. for Greece and Yugoslavia in Egypt, 43-44; second secy, Athens, 44-45; asst. chief and chief, div. of Southeast. European Affairs, 45-49; counsr, Moscow, 49-51; Dep. Asst. Secy. for European Affairs, 54-55; Dep. Chief of Mission, London, 55-56, minister and counsr, 56-58 and minister, 58-61; U.S. Ambassador to Israel, 61- Legal Res: 14 Grapevine Rd, Gloucester, Mass. 01930. Mailing Add: U.S. Embassy, Tel Aviv, Israel.

BARCLAY, H. DOUGLAS R
N.Y. State Sen.
b. 7/5/32; s. Hugh Barclay and Dorothy B; m. 8/15/59 to Sara Seiter; c. Kathryn, David, Dorothy, Susan and William. Educ: Yale Univ, B.A, 4 years; Syracuse Univ. Col. Law, D.J, 3 years. Polit. & Govt. Pos: N.Y. State Sen, 43rd Dist, 65-; del, Rep. Nat. Conv, 68. Bus. & Prof. Pos: Attorney-at-law. Mil. Serv: Entered as 2nd Lt, Army, released as 1st Lt. Mailing Add: 7377 Bentley Rd, Pulaski, N.Y. 13142.

BARCO, JAMES WILLIAM
b. Benton Harbor, Mich, 4/5/16; s. William John Barco and Maude Bryan B; single. Educ: Univ. Mich, A.B, 38; Harvard, LL.B, 41; Delta Upsilon. Polit. & Govt. Pos: With U.S. Dept. State, 46-61; mem, U.S. Del. to Indonesia, 48; mem, U.S. Del. UN Conciliation Cmn, Palestine, 48-49; acting dep. rep, Palestine, 49; counsr. U.S. Del, UN Gen. Assembly, 55-59; dep. counsr. mission, 54; minister, Mission, 55-60, dep. rep. U.S. on UN Security Coun, 56-60, dep. rep. U.S. Del. UN Conciliation Cmn, Palestine, 54-61, alternate rep, UN Cmn. Peaceful Uses Outer Space, 59-61; dep. permanent rep. U.S, UN and UN Security Coun, 60-61; mem, UN Admin. Tribunal, 62-66. Bus. & Prof. Pos: Asst. to Legis. Counsel HOLC, Fed. Home Loan Bank Bd. & Fed. Savings and Loan Ins. Corp, Wash, D.C, 41-42; spec. asst. to Pres, Times, Inc, 61-62; v.chmn, Atlantic Coun. U.S, Inc, 61-62; trustee, v.chmn. bd, Am. Univ, Cairo; sr. partner, Barco, Cook and Palton, Wash, D.C. and N.Y.C. Mil. Serv: Army, 42; Naval Res, 42-46; Staff Officer to Allied Naval Comdr-in-Chief Exped. Forces, 44, Staff Officer to Comdr, U.S. Naval Forces Europe, 44-46 and Staff Officer to Judge Adv. Gen. Navy, 46. Mem: Am. Bar Asn; Coun. For. Rels; France-Am. Soc; Pilgrims of U.S; River Club; Hemisphere Club; The Brook Club, N.Y.C; Int. Club, Wash, D.C. Rel: Episcopal. Legal Res: Hare Forest, Orange, Va. 22960. Mailing Add: 1200 17th St. N.W, Washington, D.C. 20036. (1967)

BARCUS, G. DOUGLAS, JR. R
Mem. Exec. Cmt, Montcalm Co. Rep. Party, Mich.
b. Miami, Fla, 10/13/22; s. George Douglas Barcus and Irene Walker B; m. 12/31/47 to Shirley Gallagher; c. Christine, Jeff and Mary. Educ: Univ. Fla, B.E.E, 49; Phi Gamma Delta. Polit. & Govt. Pos: Supvr, Montcalm Co, Mich; chmn, Greenville Rep. Party, 62-64; chmn, Montcalm Co. Rep. Party, 64-69, mem. exec. cmt, 69- Bus. & Prof. Pos: Appln. engr, Gen. Elec. Co, Edmore, Mich, 56-60, supvr. quality lab, 60-68, mgr, Alnico Foundry, 68- Mil. Serv: Entered as Pvt, Marines, 42, released as S/Sgt, 46 after serving in First Marine Air Wing, S.Pac, 43-44. Publ: 'The Use of Permanent Magnets in Motors and Generators', Cobalt, 12/60. Mem: Instrument Soc. Am; K. of C. Rel: Catholic. Mailing Add: 418 W. Cass St, Greenville, Mich. 48838.

BARD, E. RONALD R
Conn. State Rep.
b. Norwalk, Conn, 3/20/37; s. Charles E. Bard and Irene Charette B; m. 4/30/60 to Gail Gustafson; c. Gretchen Marie. Educ: Fairfield Univ, B.B.A, 59; Fordham Law Sch, LL.B, 62. Polit. & Govt. Pos: Conn. State Rep, 145th Dist, currently. Mem: South Norwalk Boat Club; K. of C; Kiwanis. Rel: Catholic. Mailing Add: Bissell Lane, Norwalk, Conn. 06850. (1967)

BARDANOUVE, FRANCIS R
Mont. State Rep.
b. Harlem, Mont, 12/10/17; s. John Pete Bardanouve and Alice Miller B; m. 6/25/67 to Venus Tretsven Potts. Polit. & Govt. Pos: Mont. State Rep, 59-, formerly chmn, Appropriations Cmt, Mont. State House of Rep, mem, Legis. Coun, 63-, v.chmn, currently; secy-treas, Ft. Belknap Housing Authority, 63- Bus. & Prof. Pos: Pres. and dir, Equity Coop. Asn, 53-; owner, ranching and farming interests. Mem: Farmers Union. Rel: Protestant. Mailing Add: Harlem, Mont. 59526.

BARDEN, BRYCE R
b. Penn Yan, N.Y, 4/8/07; m. to Martha E. Johnson; c. Richard, Thomas, grandchildren: Mark, Kris, Stephen. Educ: Colgate, B.A, 29; Harvard, B.B.A, 31. Polit. & Govt. Pos: N.Y. State Sen, 64-67. Bus. & Prof. Pos: Pres, The Barden & Robeson Corp, Penn Yan, N.Y. Mem: Past pres, Penn Yan Rotary; trustee, Trust Fund Finger Lakes Coun. Boy Scouts; Soldiers & Sailors Mem. Hosp; former bd. of dir, Empire State C. of C. Rel: Presbyterian; Elder. Mailing Add: Penn Yan, N.Y. 14527.

BARDEN, JOEL RAY D
b. Jamestown, N.Dak, 3/21/46; s. Ward Francis Barden and Helen McManus B; single. Educ: George Wash. Univ, 65-66; Univ. N.Dak, B.A, 68, M.A, 69; Phi Eta Sigma; Alpha Kappa Delta; Blue Key. Polit. & Govt. Pos: V.pres, N.Dak. Teen Democrats, 62-63, pres, 63-64; pres, Tioga, N.Dak. Teen Democrats, 62-64; mem. exec. cmt, N.Dak. Young Democrats, 64-69; asst. to U.S. Rep. Rolland Redlin, 65-66; chmn, 18th Dist. Citizens for McCarthy, N.Dak, 68; conv. orgn. dir, N.Dak. Citizens for McCarthy, 68; del, Dem. Nat. Conv, 68; spec. activities co-ordinator, 18th Dist. N.Dak. Dem. Non-Partisan League, 68; v.pres, Univ. N.Dak. Young Democrats, 68-69. Bus. & Prof. Pos: Teacher aide, South Jr. High Sch, Grand Forks, 67; grad. teaching asst. polit. sci. and sociol, Univ. N.Dak, 68-69. Publ: Regional Facilities for State Government, Bur. Govt. Affairs, Univ. N.Dak, 68. Mem: Midwest Sociol. Soc; Grand Forks Citizens Against Vietnam War; N.Dak. Citizens Against Anti-ballistic Missiles. Chester Fritz Scholar. Rel: Roman Catholic. Mailing Add: 1011½ University Ave, Apt. 2, Grand Forks, N.Dak. 58201.

BARGER, HAZEL KATHLEEN R
b. Batetount Co, Va, 3/26/11; d. William E. Doss and D. Ellen Rubles D; wid, 9/1/34; c. Laurence Ray and Bonnie Ellen. Educ: Lewis Gale Sch. of Nursing, 34; Univ. Va. Polit. & Govt. Pos: Chmn, Rep. City Cmt. of Roanoke, Va, 56-58; del. and mem. platform cmt, Rep. Nat. Conv, 56 & 60, mem. arrangements cmt. and chmn, Va. for Rockefeller for President Cmt, 68; Rep. Nat. Committeewoman, Va, 58-68; mem, President's Adv. Cmt. on Aging, 59-60; del, White House Conf. on Aging, 61; mem, Defense Adv. Cmt, 61- and United Serv. Orgn, Inc, 69- Bus. & Prof. Pos: Owner and mgr, Barger Coal & Oil Co, 51-56. Mem: Bd. dirs, Ment. Health Soc; Crippled Children's Soc; YMCA; Girl Scouts; League of Women Voters; bd, cent. coun, PTA; bd, Dist. Va. Fedn. of Women's Clubs; bd. and dist. off, Va. Fedn. Garden Clubs; Int. Forum; pres, Women's Club; Bus. & Prfnl. Women's Club; bd, Thursday Morning Music Club. Rel: Baptist. Mailing Add: 3642 Sunrise Ave, Roanoke, Va. 23455.

BARHAM, CHARLES CLEM D
La. State Sen.
b. Ruston, La, 4/20/34; s. Charles Emmett Barham and Carice Hilburn B; m. 8/10/54 to Jo Ann Frasier; c. Karla Ann, Charles Emmett II and Lori Elizabeth. Educ: La. Polytech. Inst, B.A, 56; La. State Univ. Law Sch, J.D, 58; Legal Fraternity. Polit. & Govt. Pos: La. State Sen, 28th Sen. Dist, 64-68, Third Sen. Dist, 68- Bus. & Prof. Pos: Attorney-at-law, Barham, Wright, Barham & Dawkins, Ruston, 58- Mem: Lincoln Parish, La. and Am. Bar Asns; La. Trial Lawyers Asn; Jaycees; C. of C; Wildlife Fedn; Cattlemen's Asn; Farm Bur. Rel: Presbyterian. Legal Res: Northwood Terrace, Ruston, La. 71270. Mailing Add: P.O. Drawer K, Ruston, La. 71270.

BARHAM, ERLE EDWARDS R
Chmn, Morehouse Parish Rep. Exec. Cmt, La.
b. Detroit, Mich. 7/10/37; s. Erle McKoin Barham and Rosalie Smith B; m. 8/24/58 to Bennie Faye Berry; c. Ben Edwards, II, Erle West and Amy Weadon. Educ: La. State Univ, B.S, 59; Sigma Chi. Polit. & Govt. Pos: Del, Rep. Nat. Conv, 64 & 68; chmn, Morehouse Parish Rep. Exec. Cmt, La, 64-; mem, Rep. Polit. Action Coun, 65- Bus. & Prof. Pos: Farm mgr, Barham Inc, 59-63; pres, Barham Bros, Inc, 64- Mem: Lions; La. Farm Bur. Fedn. Rel: Episcopal. Mailing Add: Oak Ridge, La. 71264.

BARING, WALTER S. D
U.S. Rep, Nev.
b. Goldfield, Nev, 9/9/11; s. Walter Stephen Baring and Emily Froehlich B; m. 1/31/42 to Geraldine Buchanan; c. Walter Stephan III, William Robert, John Buchanan and Thomas Jefferson. Educ: Univ. Nev, B.S, B.A, 34. Polit. & Govt. Pos: Chmn, Washoe Co. Dem. Cent. Cmt, 36; Nev. State Assemblyman, 36 & 42; city councilman, Sixth Ward, Reno, 47; U.S. Rep, Nev, 48-54 & 56-; del, Dem. Nat. Conv, 68. Bus. & Prof. Pos: Furniture bus, Reno. Mil. Serv: Navy, 42-45. Mem: F&AM; Scottish Rite (32°); Shrine; Eastern Star; Eagles; Sertoma Club; Am. Legion. Rel: Protestant. Legal Res: 580 Casazza Dr, Reno, Nev. 89502. Mailing Add: U.S. House of Representatives, Washington, D.C. 20515.

BARINGER, MAURICE E. R
Treas, State of Iowa
b. Arkansas City, Kans, 12/4/21; s. George Baringer and Ada B; m. 1948 to Dorothy Schlensig; c. Sandra, James, Debra and David. Educ: Univ. of Kans, B.S. in Bus, 1943; Iowa State Univ, B.S, M.S, 1948, 1949. Polit. & Govt. Pos: Iowa State Rep, 61-68; speaker, Iowa House Rep, 67-68; treas, State of Iowa, 69- Bus. & Prof. Pos: Teacher animal husbandry, Iowa Univ; dir. and past pres, Nat. Feed Ingredients Asn; dir. nutrition, Occo Feeds, Oelwein, Iowa, 56-67. Mil. Serv: WWII, 45 months, including two years as antiaircraft artil. officer in S.W. Pac. Mem: Nutrition Coun; Am. Feed Mfg. Asn; Elks; Lions; Farm Bur; Am. Legion; Farm House. Rel: Presbyterian; Elder, Sunday Sch. Teacher. Legal Res: 9 Hillside Dr. E, Oelwein, Iowa 50662. Mailing Add: 1408 Pleasant Dr, West Des Moines, Iowa 50265.

BARITZ, LOREN D
b. Chicago, Ill, 12/26/28; s. Joseph H. Baritz and Helen Garland B; m. 12/26/48 to Phyllis L. Handelsman; c. Anthony G. and Joseph J. Educ: Univ. Wis, Ph.D, 56. Polit. & Govt. Pos: Del, Dem. Nat. Conv, 68. Bus. & Prof. Pos: Asst. prof, Wesleyan Univ, 56-62; assoc. prof, Roosevelt Univ, 62-63; prof, Univ. Rochester, 63-69; prof, State Univ. N.Y, Albany, 69- Publ: Servants of Power, Wesleyan Univ. Press, 60; City on A Hill, 64 and Sources of the American Mind, 66, John Wiley and Sons. Mem: Am. Hist. Asn; Am. Asn. Univ. Profs. Soc. Sci. Research Coun. Research Training fel; Soc. Sci. Research Coun. grant-in-aid; Am. Coun. Learned Socs. grant-in-aid. Mailing Add: R.D. 2, Hawes Rd, Altamont, N.Y. 12009.

BARKAN, ALEXANDER ELIAS
b. Bayonne, N.J, 8/9/09; s. Jacob Barkan and Rachel Perelmen B; m. 5/10/42 to Helen Stickno; c. Lois and Carol. Educ: Univ. Chicago, Ph.B, 33. Bus. & Prof. Pos: Textile Workers Union Am, 37-55; asst. dir, Cmt. on Polit. Educ, AFL-CIO, Wash, D.C, 55-57, dep. dir, 57-63, dir, 63- Mil. Serv: Naval Res, 42-45. Legal Res: 6515 E. Halbert Rd, Bethesda, Md. 20034. Mailing Add: 815 16th St. N.W, Washington, D.C. 20006.

BARKER, AUSTIN E. D
Ind. State Rep.
Polit. & Govt. Pos: Ind. State Rep, currently. Bus. & Prof. Pos: Automobile dealer. Mil. Serv: Inf, Army, World War II; Bronze Star; Purple Heart. Mem: Am. Legion; VFW; Mason; Scottish Rite; Eagles. Rel: Methodist. Mailing Add: 106 W. Main St, Attica, Ind. 47918. (1967)

BARKER, CHRISTOPHER SYLVANUS, JR. D
N.C. State Rep.
b. Trenton, N.C, 9/7/11; s. Christopher S. Barker, M.D. and Ruth Jane Henderson B; m. 12/30/49 to Jean Kouwenhoven; c. C.S, III, Marie-Anne and Gary Cornelius. Educ: U.S. Naval Acad, B.S, 33. Polit. & Govt. Pos: N.C. State Rep, 69- Bus. & Prof. Pos: Broker, McDaniel Lewis & Co, Greensboro, N.C, currently. Mil. Serv: Entered as Midn, Navy, 28, released as Rear Adm, 59, after commanding U.S.S. Courage, Edmonds, Bristol, Stanton and Caloosahatchee; Bronze Star; Legion of Merit; Am, European, African and Pac. Theatre Medals; World War II Victory Medal. Mem: Mason; Elks; Moose; Am. Legion; VFW; ROA. Rel: United Methodist. Legal Res: 711 Broad St, New Bern, N.C. 28560. Mailing Add: Box 988, New Bern, N.C. 28560.

BARKER, HARRY C, JR. R
b. Thermopolis, Wyo, 3/6/25; s. Harry Barker Sr; m. to Margaret; c. four. Educ: Jackson, Univ. of Wyo, 4 yrs. Polit. & Govt. Pos: Wyo. State Rep, 4 terms; Chief Clerk House, 55; Wyo. State Sen, -67. Bus. & Prof. Pos: Dude rancher. Mem: Dude Ranchers' Asn; Farm Bur; Wyo. Develop. Asn; Jackson Hole C. of C; Jackson Fine Arts Festival (Exec. Bd.). Misc: Grandson of Dora McGrath, 1st woman Senator of Wyo. Rel: Episcopalian. Mailing Add: Circle H. Ranch, Moose, Wyo. 83012. (1967)

BARKER, HELEN A. R
N.H. State Rep.
b. Derry, N.H, 5/4/98; m; c. 2. Educ: Pinkerton Acad, Derry Village, N.H. Polit. & Govt. Pos: N.H. State Rep, currently, mem, Exec. Dept. and Admin. Cmt, N.H. State House of Rep; mem, Co. Exec Bd. Mem: State Am. Legion Auxiliary (past state pres); N.H. Vet. Asn. Auxiliary (past state pres); Nashaway Women's Club; Navy Mothers; League of Women Voters. Rel: Protestant. Mailing Add: 10 Dartmouth St, Nashua, N.H. 03060.

BARKER, JESSE S. D
b. Ashford, W.Va, 11/22/05; s. William Cumberland Barker and Bernie Myrtle Atkins B; m. 3/14/37 to Eleanor E. Baber; c. David Allen, Joseph Charles, Jessica Lenor and Deborah Harriet. Educ: Col. Sch. of Mines. Polit. & Govt. Pos: W.Va. State Del, 58-66. Bus. & Prof. Pos: Wholesale distributor. Mem: United Commercial Travelers of Am; Kanawha Valley Retail Gasoline Dealers Asn.(former pres); Int. Garage Owners Asn. of W.Va.(former pres). Rel: Methodist. 1967 Legal Res: Charleston, W.Va. No mailing address available. (1967)

BARKER, JIM L. D
Okla. State Rep.
b. Muskogee, Okla, 6/20/35; s. Fred A. Barker and Pearl G. Hill B; m. 6/5/55 to Leonia Hodges; c. Janet Lee and Brad Alan. Educ: Northeast. State Univ, 2 years, B.S, Business and Accounting; Deans Honor Roll. Polit. & Govt. Pos: Okla. State Rep, Dist. 13, 69-, mem, Rds. and Hwy, Revenue and Taxation and Govt. Affairs Cmts, Okla. House Rep; mem, Constitutional Rev. Cmt; mem, Task Force Cmt. Bus. & Prof. Pos: Pres, Muskogee Restaurant Supply Inc, 59-; Bd. Dirs, Tamale Shacks, Inc. Mil. Serv: Entered as 1st Lt, U.S. Army, 57, released 59, after serv. as Tank Platoon Leader 69th Armor Tank Bn. Mem: Nat. Restaurant Asn; C. of C. Rel: Baptist. Legal Res: 101 Rodman Circle, Muskogee, Okla. 74401. Mailing Add: P.O. Box 1390, Muskogee, Okla. 74401.

BARKER, LAWRENCE D
b. Columbia, Tenn, 7/14/12; s. Louie Barker and Eunice Schotts B; m. 8/18/34 to Oeda Coleman; c. Lawrence, Jr. and Louis Allen. Educ: Ala. Mil. Inst, 1 year; Columbia Mil. Acad, 2 years. Polit. & Govt. Pos: Mayor and city mgr, Dunbar, W.Va, 57-61; cmnr. labor, State of W.Va, 61-69; del-at-lg, Dem. Nat. Conv, 68. Bus. & Prof. Pos: Bus. mgr. and pres, Local Union 1890, IBEW, 53-59; area manpower dir, Human Resources Develop. Inst, 69- Mem: Lions; Moose; Jr. Order of United Am. Mech; Kanawha Juvenile Coun; Goodwill Indust; IBEW. Rel: United Methodist. Legal Res: 330 23rd St, Dunbar, W.Va. 25064. Mailing Add: 1624 Kanawha Blvd, East Charleston, W.Va. 25311.

BARKER, ROBERT R
Chmn, Estill Co. Rep. Exec. Cmt, Ky.
b. Locust Branch, Ky, 1/17/01; s. Elias Barker and Fannie Durbin B; m. 6/17/26 to Helen Cloyd. Polit. & Govt. Pos: Chmn, Estill Co. Rep. Exec. Cmt, Ky, 52- Bus. & Prof. Pos: Secy, Estill Co. C. of C, 47- Mem: Treas, Irvine-Ravenna Kiwanis, past master, Irvine Lodge 137 F&AM; past high priest, Irvine Chap, 42, RAM; past illustrious master, Irvine Coun. 92 RSM; past patron, Irvine Eastern Star, Irvine White Shrine. Rel: Baptist. Legal Res: 602 Elm St, Ravenna, Ky. Mailing Add: 139 Broadway, Irvine, Ky. 40336.

BARKER, THOMAS WAYNE D
b. Mt. Vernon, Tex, 7/16/24; s. Thomas Albert Barker and Foye Lee B; m. 5/24/41 to Barbara F. Jaggers; c. Thomas Wayne, Jr, Lynda Joyce, Robert Louis and Michael Eugene. Educ: Mt. Vernon High Sch, grad. Polit. & Govt. Pos: Dem. precinct chmn, 45th Precinct, Galveston Co, Tex, 56-65; chmn, Galveston Co. Dem. Party, 66 & 67. Bus. & Prof. Pos: Employee, Union Carbide Corp, 47- Mil. Serv: Entered as Pvt, Air Force, 42, released as T/Sgt, 45, after serv. in U.S. Air Force Training Command. Mem: Bus. rep, Texas City Munic. Employees, Local 1498 and Galveston Co. Employees, Local 1521, 56- Rel: Church of Christ. Mailing Add: 419 Robbie St, La Marque, Tex. 77568.

BARKS, MARION EMMETT R
Chmn, Bollinger Co. Rep. Cent. Cmt, Mo.
b. Greenville, Mo, 7/8/28; s. Floyd Hershel Barks and Nellie Hill B; m. 2/24/61 to Shirley Lou Hoxworth. Educ: Southeast Mo. State Col, summer, 47. Polit. & Govt. Pos: Committeeman, Rep. Party, Wayne Co, Mo, 8 years; chmn, Bollinger Co. Rep. Cent. Cmt, 68- Bus. & Prof. Pos: Teacher, Upper Turkey Creek Sch, Wayne Co, Mo, 48; foreman, Voc. Footwear, Lutesville, 50-63; foreman, Sport Specialty Shoemakers, Chaffee, 64-65; plant mgr. and supt, Marble Hill Hat Co, Lutesville, 65-; self-employed electrician; farmer. Rel: Baptist. Mailing Add: P.O. Box 44, Glen Allen, Mo. 63751.

BARLAND, THOMAS HOWARD Nonpartisan
b. San Francisco, Calif, 3/3/30; s. George C. Barland and Lois M. B; m. 5/10/64 to Ann M. Johnson; c. David. Educ: Univ. Wis, B.A, 51; Univ. Wis. Law Sch, LL.B, 56; Order of the Coif; Phi Kappa Phi; Artus; Phi Delta Phi. Polit. & Govt. Pos: Chmn, Eau Claire Co. Young Rep, Wis, 56-59; Wis. State Assemblyman, 61-67; Rep. caucus chmn, Wis. State Assembly, 63-64; mem, Wis. Bd. on Govt. Opers, 63-67; co. trustee, Eau Claire Co, Wis, 65-67, co. judge, 67- Bus. & Prof. Pos: Mem. bd. curators, Wis. State Hist. Soc, 61-, pres, 67-; past secy, Wis. Bar Taxation Sect, dir, 62-67. Mil. Serv: Entered as 2nd Lt, Army, 53, released as 1st Lt, 55, after serv. in Mil. Police, Ft. Crowder, Capt, Res. Mem: State Bar of Wis; Am. Bar Asn; Wis. Ballet Co; past chap. chmn, Red Cross. Private pilot; received Wis. Jaycees Outstanding Young Man of Year Award, 63. Rel: Presbyterian. Mailing Add: 1616 State St, Eau Claire, Wis. 54701.

BARLOW, BOCE WILLIAM D
Conn. State Sen.
b. Americus, Ga, 8/8/15; s. Boce William Barlow and Ethel Lee Green B; m. 7/19/46 to Catherine Louise Swanson; c. Cathy Annette and Bryon Swanson. Educ: Howard Univ, A.B, 39; Harvard Law Sch, LL.B, 49; Kappa Alpha Psi. Polit. & Govt, Pos: Ward chmn, Hartford Dem. Party, Conn, 55-59; del, Dem. Nat. Conv, 68; Conn. State Sen, 69- Bus. & Prof. Pos: Hearing examiner, State Civil Rights Cmn, Conn, 50-55; prosecutor, Hartford Munic. Court, 55-57 and judge, 57-60; bd. of dirs, State Prison, 59-67. Mil. Serv: Entered as Pvt, Army, 43, released as Sgt, 46, after serv. in Qm, S.W. Pac, 44-46. Mem: Hartford Co, Am. and Conn. Bar Asns; subscribing life mem, NAACP; mem. and P.E.R, Charter Oak Lodge of Elks No. 67; Grand Legal Adv. New Eng. and East. Canada, Int. Elks; mem. and former pres, Hartford Negro Dem. Club and Conn. State Fedn. of Negro Dem. Clubs; Hartford Chap, Conn. Civil Liberties Union. Rel: Protestant. Mailing Add: 31 Canterbury St, Hartford, Conn. 06112.

BARLOW, HAVEN J. R
Pres, Utah State Senate
b. Clearfield, Pa, 1/4/22; s. Jesse D. Barlow and Asdora Beck B; m. 11/23/44 to Bonnie Rae Ellison; c. Jesselie E, Heidi E, Haven B, Jr, Duncan E, Stewart E. and Rachael E. Educ: Utah State Univ, B.A, 44; Univ. Utah Law Sch, 47-48; Pi Kappa Alpha. Polit. & Govt. Pos: V.pres, Utah Young Rep, 50; Utah State Rep, 53-57; mem, Gov. Adv. Cmt. Handicapped Children, 60-66; Utah State Sen, and Pres, Utah State Senate, 66-, chmn, Legis. Coun, 66-68, v.chmn, 68- and chmn, Joint Legis. Oper. Cmt, 68; mem, West. Conf. Coun. State Govt. Exec. Cmt, 67-69, chmn, govt. oper. cmt, 68-70. Mil. Serv: Entered as Seaman, Navy, 43, released as Lt.(jg), 46, after serv. in Supply Corps, Atlantic, S.Pac. and Philippines; Philippines Liberation Medal; Pac. and Atlantic Theater Campaign Ribbons. Mem: Am. Soc. of Appraisers; Nat. Prfnl. Appraisal Soc; Am. Right of Way Asn; Utah State Realty Asn; Utah Asn. of Ins. Agents; Nat. Soc. of State Legislators; Rotary. Rel: Latter-day Saint. Mailing Add: 552 Elm St, Layton, Utah. 84041.

BARLOW, HUBERT RAMPTON R
Chmn, Madison Co. Rep. Cent. Cmt, Idaho
b. Salt Lake City, Utah, 5/19/31; s. Hubert Rampton Barlow and Ethyle Watkins B; m. 12/30/57 to Marilyn Moyes; c. Bonnie Marie, Mary Louise, Hubert Rampton, III and Katharine Ann. Educ: Univ. Utah, B.A, 57; Sigma Chi. Polit. & Govt. Pos: Committeeman, Rep. State Cent. Cmt, Idaho, 65-68; chmn, Madison Co. Rep. Cent. Cmt, 68- Bus. & Prof. Pos: Mgt. trainee, Employers Liability Assurance Corp, 57-60; underwriter, Watkins Ringholz Agency, 60; salesman, Snake River Equip. Co, 60-62; mgr-owner, Upper Valley Equip. Co, 63- Mil. Serv: Entered as Pvt, Army, 53, released as SP-5, 55, after serv. in Counter Intel. Corp, Continental Command. Mem: Lions; C. of C; Jaycees. Rel: Latter-day Saint. Mailing Add: 237 Mohawk, Rexburg, Idaho 83440.

BARLOW, JOHN LELAND R
Chmn, Moultrie Co. Rep. Cmt, Ill.
b. Charleston, Ill, 2/6/28; s. Roscoe Leland Barlow, M.D. and Genevieve Tiffin B; m. 8/20/55 to Margaret Campbell; c. John Campbell, Todd Leland and Mary Anne. Educ: Univ. Ill, B.S, 55; St. Louis Col. of Pharm, B.S. in pharm, 61; Phi Delta Chi. Polit. & Govt. Pos: Precinct committeeman, Rep. Party, Moultrie Co, Ill, 62-; chmn, Moultrie Co. Rep. Cmt, 66-; asst. supvr, Sullivan Twp, 69- Bus. & Prof. Pos: Salesman, The Upjohn Co, 55-58; employee, various drug stores, 58-61; pharmacist, Reisacher Drug, 61-64; owner and pharmacist, John's Pharmacy, 64- Mil. Serv: Entered as Pvt, Army, 46, released as Sgt. 3/C, 49, after serv. in Korean Theater; Korean Occup. Ribbon. Mem: Mason; Kiwanis; Ill. Farm Bur; Sullivan Country Club. Rel: Methodist. Mailing Add: 418 S. Washington, Sullivan, Ill. 61951.

BARNARD, AURORA CARO R
Budget and Finance Chmn, Calif. Fedn. of Rep. Women
b. Burke, Idaho, 10/15/08; d. Frank Caro and Chiara Restelli C; m. 12/31/35 to Russell Barnard (deceased); c. Annette Caro (Mrs. Frank Wetherbee) and Roger Keith. Educ: Univ. Calif, 2 years. Polit. & Govt. Pos: Auditor, Eureka Rep. Women, Calif, 55-63, parliamentarian, 64-68; secy, Eureka Rep. Assembly, 56-58, first v.pres, 58-60; Humboldt Co. Women's campaign mgr. for cand, First Cong. Dist, 58; regional v.pres, North. Div, Calif. Fedn. Rep. Women, 59-64; mem, Calif. Rep. State Cent. Cmt, 62-64, 68-; sgt-at-arms state bd, Calif. Fedn. Rep. Women, 64-66, budget and finance chmn, 68-, v.pres, North. Div, 70-; state chmn, Secy. of Nixon-Agnew, 68. Mem: Auditor, San Francisco Credit Womens Breakfast Club, 35-37; Eureka Bus. and Prfnl. Womens Club (pres, 59-60, currently chmn. for legis. and parliamentarian); parliamentarian, Redwood Empire Bus. and Prfnl. Women's Club, 62; Order

of Eastern Star; Order of White Shrine; Eureka Women's Club. Named Woman of the Year for civic participation, 68. Legal Res: 5535 Ocean Vista St, Eureka, Calif. 95501. Mailing Add: P.O. Box 3285, Eureka, Calif. 95501.

BARNARD, DRUIE DOUGLAS, JR. D
b. Augusta, Ga, 3/20/22; s. Druie Douglas Barnard and Lucy Burns B; m. 12/15/46 to Naomi Holt; c. Pamela, Lucy and D. Douglas, III. Educ: Mercer Univ, A.B. and LL.B; Blue Key; Phi Alpha Delta; Phi Delta Theta. Polit. & Govt. Pos: Chmn, Richmond Co. Dem. Exec. Cmt, Ga, 58-62; exec. secy. to Gov. Carl E. Sanders, Ga, 63- Bus. & Prof. Pos: Sr. v.pres, Ga. Railroad Bank & Trust Co, Augusta, Ga, 49-62; dir, Peoples Am. Bank, Atlanta, Ga. and First Railroad & Banking Co, Augusta, Ga. Mil. Serv: Entered as Pvt, Army, 43, released as Sgt. 1/C, 45, after serv. in 57th Financial Disbursing Unit, ETO; ETO Ribbon with 2 Battle Stars. Mem: Nat. Asn. Bank Auditors & Comptrollers; Am. Inst. Banking; Financial Pub. Rels. Asn; Am. Legion; C. of C; Kiwanis. Rel: Baptist. Legal Res: 2819 Ingleside Dr, Augusta, Ga. Mailing Add: Governor's Office, State Capitol, Atlanta, Ga. 30334.

BARNARD, KEITH W. R
Chmn, Ventura Co. Rep. Cent. Cmt, Calif.
b. Ventura, Calif, 12/30/26; s. Morris Hall Barnard and Ruth Dennis B; m. 7/22/50 to Ruth Virden Shutt; c. Stephen James and Teresa Ann. Educ: Univ. Calif, Berkeley, 47-48; Univ. Calif, Los Angeles, B.S, 50; Pi Kappa Alpha. Polit. & Govt. Pos: Mem, exec. cmt, 24th State Sen. Dist. Rep. Cmt, Calif, 63-69; mem, 13th Cong. Dist. Rep. Cmt, 65-69; mem, Rep. State Cent. Cmt, 67; chmn, Ventura Co. Rep. Cent. Cmt, 69- Bus. & Prof. Pos: Chmn, Ventura Co. Gen. Hosp. Adv. Cmt, 60-69; v.chmn, Fillmore Irrigation Co. and San Cayetano Water Co, 63-69; v.chmn, Ventura Co. Agr. Stabilization Cmt, 64-69; bd. mem, Briggs Lemon Asn. Santa Paula, 69-; chmn, Santa Paula Orange Asn, 69- Mil. Serv: Aviation Cadet, Army Air Corps, 44-45. Mem: Pres, Ventura Co. Taxpayers Asn; Ventura Co. Mounted Sheriffs Posse; Navy League; Fillmore Am. Legion; Ventura Co. Farm Bur; Los Rancheros Visitadores. Mailing Add: 757 Central Ave, Fillmore, Calif. 93015.

BARNARD, ROLAND A. D
b. Weare, N.H, 1/5/98; married; c. 5. Educ: Pinkerton Acad, 16. Polit. & Govt. Pos: N.H. State Rep, 63-67; former mem, Sch. Bd; Budget Cmt; Tax Collector. Bus. & Prof. Pos: Carpenter; builder U.S. Dept. of Agr, several years; supvr, Farm Security Admin. and sr. relocation officer, U.S. Dept. of Interior. Mem: N.H. Asn. for Better Schs; Grange; F&AM; Goffstown Men's Club. Rel: Protestant. Mailing Add: 26 N. Mast St, Goffstown, N.H. 03045.

BARNES, BEN F. D
Lt. Gov, Tex.
b. Gorman, Tex, 4/17/38; s. B.F. Barnes and Ina B. Carrigan B; m. 2/22/57 to Martha Jane Morgan; c. Greg and Amy. Educ: Tex. Christian Univ; Tarleton State Col; Univ. Tex, Austin, B.B.A, 60. Hon. LL.D, McMurray Col. and Tex. Tech. Col. Polit. & Govt. Pos: Tex. State Rep, 60-68, Speaker, Tex. House of Rep, 65-68, chmn, Rules Cmt, 63; mem, Nat. Legis. Conf. Cmn. Fed-State Rels, 65-66; v.chmn, Tex. Legis. Coun. and Legis. Budget Bd, 65-68; pres, Nat. Legis. Conf; mem. exec. cmts, Nat. Conf. of State Legis. Leaders and Coun. of State Govt; immediate past chmn, South. Conf. of Coun. of State Govt; mem, President Johnson's Adv. Cmn. on Intergovt. Rels; mem. bd. dirs, States' Urban Action Center; spec. rep. of U.S. Dept. of State, Cmt. on Agr. of UN Econ. Cmt. for Europe in Geneva and NATO Civil Defense Cmt. Conf. in Brussels, 68; del, Dem. Nat. Conv, 68; Lt. Gov, Tex, 69- Bus. & Prof. Pos: Businessman in farming, ranching, radio broadcasting, construction and motels, currently. Mem: State chmn, Easter Seal Campaign, 68; Elks; Jr. C. of C; Southwest. Cattle Growers Asn. One of Five Outstanding Young Texans, Jr. C. of C, 65. Rel: Methodist. Legal Res: DeLeon, Tex. 76444. Mailing Add: Lieutenant Governor's Office, Texas State Capitol, Austin, Tex. 78711.

BARNES, BETTY LOU D
b. Ottawa, Kans, 3/7/29; d. Harris Murray and Rosa Steinman M; div; c. Rodney and Jed. Educ: Ottawa Univ, 47; Kans. State Teacher's Col, B.S.E, 67; Alpha Beta; Pi Lambda Theta. Polit. & Govt. Pos: Dem. committeewoman, third ward, Council Grove, Kans, 68-; polit. action dir, Kans. State Teacher's Asn, 68; legis. chmn, Council Grove Teacher's Asn, 68- Mem: Council Grove and Kans. State Teacher's Asn; Nat. Educ. Asn; Entrepreneur's Club; Neota Club. Rel: Episcopal. Mailing Add: 28 N. Neosho, Council Grove, Kans. 66846.

BARNES, DORIS MARIAN R
Mayor, Wrangell, Alaska
b. Portland, Ore, 8/27/91; d. Oakes M. Plummer and Jessie B. Kribs P; wid, 3/20/12; c. Frank P, Marian E.(Mrs. Clarence E. Henning) and Dorianne(Mrs. Arthur C. Salonek). Educ: Univ. Ore, 10-12; Beta Sigma Phi. Polit. & Govt. Pos: Mem. city coun, Wrangell, 44-46, mayor, 46-48 & 60-, chmn, Charter Cmt, 60; mem, Alaska House of Rep, 49-53; Alaska State Sen, 53-57; mem, First Alaska Interim. Legis. Coun; Rep. Nat. Committeewoman, 55-57 & 64-68; mem, Alaska Rep. State Cmt, 59-62, v.chmn, S.E. Dist, 60-64. Bus. & Prof. Pos: Mem. adv. cmt, Sheldon Jackson Jr. Col; ins. agent, Wrangell, 40- Mem: Charter assoc, Arctic Inst. of N.Am; Alaska Ins. Agents Asn.(exec. bd, 55); past pres, Wrangell C. of C. and Alaska Fedn. of Women's Clubs; Alaska Fedn. of Bus. & Prfnl. Women's Clubs (pres, 55-57). Rel: Presbyterian; V.moderator, Presby. Church, Wash. Synod, 58-59. Mailing Add: Box 20, Wrangell, Alaska 99929. (1967)

BARNES, DWIGHT H. D
b. Cambridge, Mass, 4/16/20; s. Dwight F. Barnes and Mary Baker B; m. 9/13/41 to Marian Tobey; c. Dwight Tobey, Benjamin Lewis and Madge Laurie. Educ: Fresno State Col, B.A, 45; Alpha Phi Gamma; Theta Chi. Polit. & Govt. Pos: Admin. asst. to U.S. Rep. Harold T. Johnson, 59- Bus. & Prof. Pos: Sports ed, Turlock Daily Journal, Calif, 45-46; ed, Merced Express, 47-48; polit. ed, Modesto Bee, 48-59. Mil. Serv: Entered as Midn, Navy, 41, released as Lt. Comdr, 45, after serv. in U.S.S. Pensacola and U.S.S. Springfield, Pac, 41-45; Capt, Naval Res, 63. Publ: Seapower, And Its Meaning, Franklin Watt, 66. Mem: U.S. Naval Inst; U.S. Naval Res. Asn; Cong. Secy. Club; Burros Club. Rel: Protestant. Legal Res: Twain Harte, Calif. 95383. Mailing Add: 1204 Highland Dr, Silver Spring, Md. 20910.

BARNES, EARL THOMAS R
Mem. Exec. Cmt, Hamilton Co. Rep. Orgn, Ohio
b. Sheridan, Wyo, 5/14/21; s. Earle D. Barnes and Beulah Nott B; m. 8/1/42 to Lucy Keen; c. Peter, Christopher, Lucinda, Susan, Sara and Ellen. Educ: Marietta Col, 39-41; Univ. Cincinnati, 41-43, 45; Univ. Cincinnati Col. of Law, LL.B, 47; Delta Upsilon; Phi Alpha Delta. Polit. & Govt. Pos: Asst. campaign chmn, Taft for Senate Cmt, 49-50; nat. coordinator, Taft for President Cmt, 51-52; campaign chmn, First Cong. Dist, Ohio, 52-62; asst. to chmn, Rep. Nat. Conv, 60 & 64, del, 64 & 68; mem. exec. cmt, Hamilton Co. Rep. Orgn, currently. Bus. & Prof. Pos: Attorney, Barnes & Alsfelder, 48-61; dir. pub. rels, The Kroger Co, 61-; mem. bd. of trustees, Univ. Cincinnati, 64- Mil. Serv: Pvt, Air Force, 42-44. Mem: Chmn, Ohio World Trade Asn, 66-; mem. bd. dirs, Gr. Cincinnati C. of C; chmn. of the bd, Mariemont Police Pension Fund. Rel: Protestant. Mailing Add: 700 Walnut, Cincinnati, Ohio 45202. (1967)

BARNES, GEORGE FRANCIS R
Va. State Sen.
b. Pocahontas, Va, 5/25/19; m. to Grace Gillespie. Educ: Va. Polytech. Inst, B.S, 41. Polit. & Govt. Pos: Va. State Sen, 66- Bus. & Prof. Pos: Farmer, coal operator. Mil. Serv: Navy. Mem: Tri-Co. Independent Coal Operators Asn; Nat. Independent Coal Operators Asn; Farm Bur. Rel: Presbyterian. Mailing Add: Box 506, Tazewell, Va. 24651. (1967)

BARNES, INA F. R
b. Chester, Vt, 8/7/01; m. to Lewis Barnes, wid; c. One son and one daughter. Educ: U.V.M. Polit. & Govt. Pos: Town Auditor, 10 years; Vt. State Rep, 65-66. Bus. & Prof. Pos: Teacher, retired. Rel: Baptist. Mailing Add: R.D. 1, Chester, Vt. 05143. (1967)

BARNES, JOHN BREARTON D
Dem. State Cent. Committeeman, Conn.
b. Hartford, Conn, 3/1/10; s. Peter J. Barnes and Mary Brearton B; m. 3/27/31 to Antonina J. Baker; c. Antoinette E. (Mrs. Donald Clerkin) and Mary C.(Mrs. Robert Sheeran). Polit. & Govt. Pos: Dem. chmn, Town of East Windsor, Conn, 55-; Dem. State Cent. Committeeman, Conn, 56- Mem: K. of C; Lions; Newspaper Printing Pressman's Union. Rel: Roman Catholic. Mailing Add: 25 Dean Ave, Warehouse Point, Conn. 06088.

BARNES, RALPH ANTHONY D
Exec. Secy, Maine Dem. State Cmt.
b. Fall River, Mass, 12/28/27; s. Guy U. Barnes and Mae E. McCullough B; m. 7/4/45 to Marion Corgino; c. Stephen G. and Michael P. Educ: Coyle High Sch, Taunton, Mass, grad, 45. Polit. & Govt. Pos: Exec. secy, Maine Dem. State Cmt, 66-; admin. asst. to U.S. Rep. Peter N. Kyros, 1st Dist, Maine, 67-68. Bus. & Prof. Pos: News dir, Radio Sta. WLOB, Portland, Maine, 59-60; State News Mgr. for United Press Int, 60-66. Mailing Add: 547 Blackstrap Rd, Falmouth, Maine. 04105. (1967)

BARNES, RICHARD WILSON D
b. Wellsburg, W.Va, 10/4/17; s. Charles Roy Barnes and Nancy Wilson B; m. 9/5/48 to Magdalene J. Rasz; c. Damian Joseph. Educ: Col. Steubenville, 2 years; W.Va. Univ, LL.B, 51; Law Quart. Polit. & Govt. Pos: City Solicitor, Wellsburg, W.Va, 53-54; asst. prosecuting attorney, Brooke Co, 55-60; del, Dem. Nat. Conv, 60 & 68; presidential elector, 68. Bus. & Prof. Pos: Lawyer, Pinsky, Mahan, Barnes and Watson, 51- Mil. Serv: Entered as Pvt, Army, 62, released as 2nd Lt, 65, after serv. in Signal Corps, Persian Gulf Command, 62-65. Mem: W.Va, Brooke Co. and U.S. Bar Asns; W.Va. State Bar Asn; VFW; Am. Legion; Moose; Elks; K. of C; St. John's Holy Name Soc. Rel: Catholic. Mailing Add: 168 Sycamore St, Wellsburg, W.Va. 26070.

BARNES, ROBERT FIELD R
Chmn, Hidalgo Co. Rep. Cmt, Tex.
b. Danville, Ill, 4/27/20; s. Eugene Field Barnes and Gladys Dye B; m. 8/3/41 to Kathryn Jane Nelson; c. Robert Field, Jr. and Barbara Jean. Educ: Univ. Ill, A.B, 42, LL.B, 48; Phi Delta Phi; Sigma Chi. Polit. & Govt. Pos: Del, Rep. Nat. Conv, 60 & 64; mayor, McAllen, Tex, 61-63; chmn, Hidalgo Co. Rep. Cmt, Tex, 64- Bus. & Prof. Pos: Owner, Robert F. Barnes Custom Broker, 52-; partner, Barnes & Elick, Attorneys, 60-; dir, McAllen C. of C, 61. Mil. Serv: Entered as 2nd Lt, Army, 42, released as 1st Lt, 45, after serv. in 28th Inf. Div, 348th Fighter Group, Pac, 46; Asiatic Pac. Theater Medal, Three Battle Stars; Maj, Air Force, Res, 60-68. Publ: Doing Business in Mexico, San Antonio Bar Asn, 67. Mem: Mason; State Bar of Tex; State Bar of Ill; Col. Confederate Air Force, Rebel Field, Mercedes, Tex; past pres, Rio Grande Valle Customs Brokers Asn. Rel: Protestant. Legal Res: 912 S. First, McAllen, Tex. 78501. Mailing Add: 206 First National Bank Bldg, McAllen, Tex. 78501.

BARNES, THELMA PALMER D
b. Grace, Miss, 8/19/25; d. Andrew Palmer and Ruby Scott P; m. 6/7/45 to Mike Cornelius Barnes, Sr; c. Peter Calvin, III, Paula Michele, Mike Cornelius, Jr. and Ila Annette. Educ: Alcorn A&M Col, 42-43; Henderson Bus. Col, Memphis, Tenn, 44. Polit. & Govt. Pos: Del, Dem. Nat. Conv, 68. Bus. & Prof. Pos: Secy, Baptist Ministerial Alliance, Greenville, Miss, 45-46 and part time secy, 47-48; clerk-payroll, U.S. Army, Tuskegee Army Air Field, Ala, 46-47; part time bookkeeper, Snow White Laundry, Greenville, Miss, 47-48; secy. to bus. mgr, Miss. Valley State Col, 52; clerk typist & mgt. analyst, Greenville Air Force Base, 53-63; secy, Methodist Bishop, Nashville, Tenn, 63-64; proj. dir, Delta Ministry, Nat. Coun. Churches U.S, Miss, 64- Rel: United Methodist. Mailing Add: 217 Trilby St, Greenville, Miss. 38701.

BARNES, WALLACE R
Conn. State Sen.
b. Bristol, Conn, 3/22/26; s. Harry Clarke Barnes and Lillian H. B; m. 9/29/62 to Dorothy D; c. Thomas O, Jarre Ann and Frederick H. Educ: Deerfield Acad; Williams Col, B.A, 49; Yale Law Sch, LL.B, 52; Phi Beta Kappa; Chi Psi. Polit. & Govt. Pos: Chmn, Bristol Rep. Town Cmt, Conn, 53-55; chmn, Rules Rev. Cmt, Rep. State Cent. Cmt, 55; del, Rep. Nat. Conv, 56, 60 & 68; chmn, United Rep. Dinner, 58; Conn. State Sen, Fifth Dist, 59-61, Eighth Dist, 67-, mem, Clean Water Task Force Cmt. and Gov. Cmt, Equal Employ. Opportunity, Ranking Minority Mem, Senate Appropriations Cmt, mem, Gov. Finance Adv. Cmt, 67-68 and Minority Leader, Conn. State

Senate, 69- Bus. & Prof. Pos: Pres, Nutmeg Air Transport, Inc, 51; asst. to treas, Northeast Airlines, 52; assoc, Beach & Calder, 53 and partner, Beach, Calder & Barnes, 57; secy, Assoc. Spring Corp, Bristol, Conn, 57, exec. v.pres, 60 and pres, 64- Mil. Serv: Cadet, Army Air Corps, 44-45. Publ: 'Federal Control of Airline Competition,' and 'Going Concern Valuation of Stock Purchase Warrants,' Yale Law Jour, 51. Mem: Soc. Automotive Engrs, Inc; Hartford Co, Conn. and Am. Bar Asns; secy. exec. cmt, Yale Law Sch, 66-68; Wings Club; Yale Club and Williams Club, N.Y.C; Econ. Club of N.Y; Elks; Farmington and Chippanee Country Club; Nantucket Yacht Club. Keystone Award, Nat. Boys Club Am, 68. Rel: Episcopal. Mailing Add: 50 High St, Farmington, Conn. 06032.

BARNESS, HERBERT R
b. Phila, Pa, 12/1/23; s. Joseph Barness and Mary Silverstein B; m. 6/27/48 to Irma Susanne Shorin; c. Lynda and Nancy. Educ: Bucknell Univ, B.S. in Mech. Engr. Polit. & Govt. Pos: Del, Rep. Nat. Conv, 68. Bus. & Prof. Pos: Partner, Joseph Barness & Son, 48-; pres, Barnsel, Inc, 61-, pres, Water & Sewer Utilities Services, Inc, 63- and pres, Penn Overseas Develop. Corp, 68- Mil. Serv: Entered as 1st Lt, Air Force, 42, released as Capt, 46, after serv. in 70th Army Airways Commun. Gr. and 147th Airways Commun. Squadron, Pac. Mem: Soc. Am. Mil. Engr; Nat. and Bucks Co. Soc. Prfnl. Engr; Mason (32°); Philmont Country Club; trustee, Pop Warner Little Scholars; Am. Technion Soc.(pres, Phila. chap); dir, Welcome House; Bucks Co. Bd. Realtors; dir, Buch Co. Indust. Develop. Corp; Boy Scouts (mem. exec. cmt. Bucks Co. Coun); Bucks Co. Playhouse (dir); Pa. Soc; U.S. Trotting Asn; World Affairs Coun. Phila; Locust Club Phil. Mailing Add: 1334 Easton Rd, Warrington, Pa. 18976.

BARNETT, GEORGE M. D
b. Birmingham, Ala, 12/9/42; s. Dallas Melvin Barnett and Mary Jane Nicholson B; m. 7/6/68 to Ann Cox. Educ: Univ. Ala, B.S, 64, LL.B, 67; Polit. & Govt. Pos: Admin. asst, U.S. Rep. Tom Bevill, Ala, 69- Bus. & Prof. Pos: Pres, Barnett Auto Supply, Inc, 67-; partner, Smith, Wilkes & Barnett, 67- Mem: Ala. and Marshall Co. Bar Asns; Jaycees; C. of C. Rel: Methodist. Legal Res: 2015 Dunlap Ave, Guntersville, Ala. 35976. Mailing Add: 2000 Huntington Ave, Alexandria, Va. 22303.

BARNETT, GWEN HUGHES R
Rep. Nat. Committeewoman, Idaho
b. Dallas, Tex, 10/8/25; d. Palmer Hughes and Marian Taylor Rogers H; m. 8/24/46 to Steele Barnett; c. Carol Jean, Susan Kay and Lawrence Steele. Educ: Stanford Univ; Univ. Tulsa. Polit. & Govt. Pos: Rep. precinct committeewoman, Boise, Idaho, 56-; Rep. committeewoman for Ada Co, 58-60; mem, Young Rep. of Idaho, 59-; Rep. Nat. Committeewoman, Idaho, 60-; secy, West. State Rep. Conf, 61-63. Mem: Nat. Trust for Hist. Preservation. Rel: Episcopal. Mailing Add: 6525 Robertson Dr, Boise, Idaho 83705.

BARNETT, JAMES ARDEN R
Miss. State Sen.
b. Jackson, Miss, 8/4/24; s. Arden Barnett and Vera Turner B; m. 3/4/45 to Lucy Owen; c. Ruth Elizabeth, James Arden, Jr. and Vera Susan. Educ: Univ. Miss, B.B.A, 48, LL.B, 49; Univ. of Miss. Hall of Fame; Omicron Delta Kappa; pres. of student body, Univ. Miss, 47. Polit. & Govt. Pos: Mem, Fourth Dist. Hinds Co. Sch. Bd, Miss, 54-63; city attorney, Clinton, 58-62; Miss. State Rep, Hinds Co, 64-68; Miss. State Sen, 27th Dist, 68-; mem. exec. cmt, Hinds Co. Rep. Party, 69-; mem, Rep. exec. cmt, City of Clinton, 69-; Miss. chmn. for Nat. Conf. of Rep. State Legislators, 69- Bus. & Prof. Pos: Lawyer and assoc, Barnett, Montgomery, McClintock & Cunningham, 49-65; lawyer and partner, Barnett & Barnett, 65- Mil. Serv: Entered as Air Cadet, Naval Air Res, 42, active duty, 43-45, comdr, Naval Res. Law Unit 6-21, currently; Distinguished Flying Cross; Air Medal; Asiatic-Pac. Ribbon with 3 Battle Stars; Philippine Liberation Ribbon with 2 Battle Stars; Am. Theater Ribbon; Victory Medal; Naval Res. and Armed Forces Res. Ribbons. Mem: Am, Miss. and Hinds Co. Bar Asns; Am. Legion; VFW; Lions. Rel: Baptist; Deacon and Trustee, 1st Baptist Church of Clinton. Mailing Add: 710 E. Leake St, Clinton, Miss. 39056.

BARNETT, JOSEPH H. R
S.Dak. State Rep.
b. Sioux Falls, S.Dak, 11/3/31; s. William H. Barnett and Julia Ruth Gurtel B; m. 2/23/54 to Kathleen D. Bolger; c. Joseph P, Sheila Ann, William M, John D, Rita Marie, Paul T, Teresa Jane and James Richard. Educ: Augustana Col, Sioux Falls, S.Dak, 50-51; Col. St. Thomas, B.A. magna cum laude, 53; Univ. S.Dak. Law Sch, LL.B, 57; Phi Delta Pi. Polit. & Govt. Pos: Law clerk to U.S. Dist. Judge George T. Mickelson, Dist. of S.Dak, 57-58; S.Dak. State Rep, Brown Co, 67- Bus. & Prof. Pos: Mem, S.Dak. Bd. Bar Exam, 63-, chmn, 68- Mil. Serv: Entered as Pvt, Army, 53, released as Cpl, 55, after serv. in 74th Armored Signal Co, Third Army Div, Ft. Knox. Mem: Brown Co. Bar Asn.(pres, 66-67); S.Dak. Bar Asn; State Bar of S.Dak; Am. Bar Asn; Kiwanis Club; K. of C; Elks; Y's Men's Club. Rel: Catholic. Legal Res: 1422 N. First St, Aberdeen, S.Dak. 57401. Mailing Add: 500 Capitol Bldg, Aberdeen, S.Dak. 57401.

BARNETT, RALPH EDWARD D
W.Va. State Sen.
b. Roanoke, Va, 6/1/10; s. George Sim Barnett and Emma Zink B; m. 10/2/25 to Nell Margaret Harlow B; c. (Mrs. James P. Eddy), George David, (Mrs. Arnold Day), Ralph Edward, (Mrs. William M. Crockett), Richard Ray, (Mrs. Bobby Surface) and Carolyn. Educ: Obrig Labs. and Am. Bd. of Opticians. Polit. & Govt. Pos: Mem, Mercer Co. Bd. Educ, 12 years; W.Va. State Sen, 60- Bus. & Prof. Pos: Optician. Mem: Mason; Elks; Salvation Army Bd; Bluefield Auditorium Cmt; Mercer Co. Bd. of Health. Rel: Baptist. Mailing Add: 433 Parkway, Bluefield, W.Va. 24701. (1967)

BARNETT, ROSS ROBERT D
b. Carthage, Miss, 1/22/98; s. John William Barnett and Virginia Ann Chadwick B; m. 8/28/28 to Mary Pearl Crawford; c. Ouida (Mrs. Atkins), Ross Robert, Jr. and Virginia (Mrs. Branum). Educ: Miss. Col, B.S, 22; Univ. Miss, LL.B, 26; hon. mem, Kappa Alpha. Polit. & Govt. Pos: Gov, Miss, 60-64. Bus. & Prof. Pos: Cmnr, Miss. Bar. Mil. Serv: Pvt, Army, 18-19; award for serving as attorney for Selective Serv. Bd, Jackson, Miss. Mem: V.pres, Miss. Bar Asn.(pres, 43-44); pres, Jackson Hinds Co. Bar Asn; Nat. Exchange Club; Jackson Exchange Club; Miss. Farm Asn; Univ. Miss. Alumni Asn; Miss. Col. Alumni Asn; Vanderbilt Alumni Asn; Elks. Rel: Baptist; Deacon, First Baptist Church, Jackson. Mailing Add: Barnett Bldg, 200 S. President, Jackson, Miss. 39201. (1967)

BARNETT, ROY ALEXANDER D
b. Sprott, Ala, 4/8/05; s. James Washington Barnett and Anna J. Taylor B; m. 8/10/35 to Emma L. Harrison; c. Roy Alexander. Educ: Livingston State Univ, 2 years. Polit. & Govt. Pos: Ala. State Rep, 59-66; Perry Co. legis. agent, Ala. House Rep, 66- Mem: Mason; Shrine; WOW; pres, Automobile Dealers Asn. Ala, 66-67; dist. judge adv. cent. Ala. dist, Civitan Club, 67. Rel: Baptist. Legal Res: Green St, Marion, Ala. 36756. Mailing Add: P.O. Box 89, Marion, Ala. 36756.

BARNETT, WILLIAM CURLESS R
b. Hanceville, Ala, 6/24/04; s. William Harrison Barnett and Repsie Edwards B; m. 4/13/24 to Wease Martin; c. George Leon. Polit. & Govt. Pos: Alternate del, Rep. Nat. Conv, 68. Bus. & Prof. Pos: Agent, Standard Oil Co, Warrior, Ala, 30-44; owner, Barnett Motor Co, Warrior, Ala, 34-41 and Ononenta, Ala, 44-45; pres, Carbon Hill Motor Co. Inc, Carbon Hill, 47-50; owner, W.C. Barnett Oil Co, Cullman, 51-59; Retired, 60. Mem: Mason (32°). Rel: Missionary Baptist. Mailing Add: Route 6, Cullman, Ala. 35055.

BARNETT, WILMER L. R
Utah State Sen.
b. Payson, Utah, 12/12/15; s. Owen L. Barnett and Genevieve Colvin B; m. 4/3/36 to Nellie Hughes; c. Owen Lee and Mary Lynn (Mrs. McCardell). Educ: Brigham Young Univ, B.S, 39; Phi Delta Kappa. Polit. & Govt. Pos: Utah State Sen, 67- Bus. & Prof. Pos: Cashier and off. mgr, Lincoln Nat. Life Ins. Co, 44-60; state mgr, W.Coast Life Ins. Co, 60-63; counsr, Hillcrest High Sch, 63-66. Mem: Jr. C. of C; Murray Lions. Rel: Latter-day Saint. Mailing Add: 5992 Fontaine Bleu Dr, Salt Lake City, Utah 84121.

BARNHART, HUGH ARTHUR D
b. Rochester, Ind, 7/14/92; s. Henry A. Barnhart and Louretta Leffel B; m. 6/25/28 to Martha Anspaugh. Educ: Univ. Notre Dame, one semester; Ind. Univ, B.A. in econ, 15; Delta Tau Delta; Sigma Delta Chi; Ind. Univ. Union Bd; pres, sr. class; varsity football and basketball teams. Polit. & Govt. Pos: Mem, Gen. Pulaski Cmn, 29; mem. Ind. State Hwy. Cmn. and dir, Cmn. Bd, 31-33; cand. cong, Second Dist, Ind, 36; excise dir, 37-41; dir, Ind. State Conserv. Dept. and mem, State Soil Conserv. Cmt. and Stream Pollution Control Bd, 41-45; mem, Ind. Econ. Coun, 41-45; bus. and defense serv. admin. reservist for indust. mobilization, Dept. Commerce and dir, Dept. Commun, Bus. and Defense Admin, D.C, 6 months; mem, U.S. Defense orientation Conf. Asn; mem, Adv. Cmt. on Ind. Univ, 50-52; mem, Little Hoover Cmn, 55-56. Bus. & Prof. Pos: Advert. dept, Holcomb and Hoke Mfg. Co, Indianapolis, 16; dir, Pub. Serv. Co. Ind, Inc, 43-68, Midwest Co, Inc, Ft. Wayne; publisher, Rochester Sentinel, 19-24; pres, Sentinel Corp, 24-; pres, Rochester Tel. Co, Inc, 34-68. Mil. Serv: Entered as 2nd Lt, Army, 17, released as Capt, Army Res, 10 years. Mem: Ind. del, Coun. State Govt, 39-43; Ind. Sesquicentennial Adv. Cmt; dir, Ind. Tel. Asn; dir, U.S. Independent Tel. Asn, 52-69 and pres, 58-59; former dir, Independent Tel. Pioneers Asn; Ind. State C. of C.(dir, life mem. bd. and former v.pres); Rochester C. of C.(past pres); Isaak Walton League; Mason; Odd Fellows; Moose; Elks; Indianapolis Athletic Club; Indianapolis Press Club; Hoosier State Press Asn; Inland Press Asn; Ind. Soc. Chicago; Rochester Kiwanis (first pres); Rochester Country Club (past pres); Ind. Dem. Ed. Asn.(past pres); Ind. Circus Corp.(past v.pres). Commissioned Sagamore of Wabash by Gov. Harold Handley; Tel. Man of Year, Ind. Tel. Asn, 59. Rel: Baptist; former trustee, First Baptist Church of Rochester. Legal Res: Route 2, Rochester, Ind.46975. Mailing Add: P.O. Box 570, Rochester, Ind. 46975.

BARNHILL, EARL STANTON D
b. Junction City, Kans, 4/3/32; s. Frank Barnhill and Bernetha B; m. 6/10/53 to Dianne Brown; c. William David. Educ: Kans. State Univ, B.S, 56; Washburn Univ. Sch. of Law, LL.B, 59; Sigma Alpha Epsilon. Polit. & Govt. Pos: Asst. city attorney, Junction City, Kans, 62-65 and city attorney, 65-; asst. co. attorney, Geary Co, 65; Kans. State Rep, 65-67. Bus. & Prof. Pos: Secy-treas, H. & B. Invest. Co, Inc, 56-; private practice of law, 59- Mil. Serv: Entered as Pvt, Air Force, 51, released as Sgt, 52, after serv. in U.S. Air Force Security Serv. Mem: Am, Kans, Cent. Kans. and Geary Co. Bar Asns; Nat. Asn. of Dist. Attorneys; Kans. Peace Officers Asn; Mason; Shrine; Am. Legion; C. of C. Rel: Methodist. 1967 Legal Res: Junction City, Kans. No mailing address available. (1967)

BARNHORST, HOWARD JOSEPH R
b. Indianapolis, Ind, 7/31/21; s. August H. Barnhorst and Nellie K. Mullen B; m. 9/7/46 to Helen N. Killilea; c. Howard J, II, Noreen P, Nancy E, Beth A. and Brian A. Educ: West. Carolina Col, B.S, 48. Polit. & Govt. Pos: Ind. State Rep, 67-68. Bus. & Prof. Pos: Agency mgr, Farm Bur. Ins, 48. Mil. Serv: Entered as Pvt, Air Corps, 42, released as Sgt, 45, after serv. in ETO, 43-45. Mem: Elks; K. of C; Am. Legion; Kokomo Country Club; Nat. Asn. Life Underwriters; YMCA; C. of C; Farm Bur. Rel: Catholic. Mailing Add: 3301 Tally Ho Dr, Kokomo, Ind. 46901. (1967)

BARNHOUSE, THOMAS DYE D
Mem, Ohio Dem. Finance Cmt.
b. Belle Valley, Ohio, 10/26/09; s. William Day Barnhouse and Jessie Pearl Archer B; m. 12/24/32 to Florence Mabel 'Sally' King; c. Gloria Kay. Educ: Ohio Univ, B.S.E.E, 33; Command & Gen. Staff Col; The Artil. Sch; Chi Sigma Chi. Polit. & Govt. Pos: Dep. co. engr, Nobile Co, Ohio, 33-35; engr, Ohio Dept. of Highways, 35-45, admin. asst. to dir, 46-47, dep. dir. of hwy, 59-62; cmnr, Boxing and Wrestling Cmn, Columbus, Ohio, 65-; mem, Ohio Dem. Finance Cmt, 66-; del, Dem. Nat. Conv, 68. Bus. & Prof. Pos: Registered prfnl. engr. and registered surveyor, Ohio; v.pres, Newark Concrete, Newark, Ohio, 56-59; pres, Barnhouse Assocs, Inc, Columbus, Ohio, currently. Mil. Serv: Entered as 1st Lt, Army, 40, released as Maj, 46, after serv. in 37th Inf. Div, S.Pac, 41-43; Col, Field Artil, Ohio Nat. Guard, 56; Col.(Ret), Army, 69. Mem: Ohio and Nat. Soc. Prfnl. Engrs; Engrs. Club of Columbus, Ohio; Mason (32°); Shrine. Rel: Protestant. Mailing Add: 2472 Dover Rd, Columbus, Ohio 43209.

BARNING, ELSIE CHRISTENE D
b. Evansville, Ind, 3/24/05; d. Christian Martin Seiler and Carrie Emma Seifert S; m. to Carl Phillip, Sr, wid; c. Carl Phillip, Jr, David Lee and Jerry Ralph. Polit. & Govt. Pos: Ind. State Rep, 49-50, 55-56, 61-64 and 67-68; mem. staff, Dep. Twp. Assessor's Off, 50-55; mem. staff, Chief Dep. Twp. Trustee's Off, 57-66. Mem: Legis. chmn, Evansville Bus. & Prfnl. Clubs, Inc, 66-67; state Legis. chmn, Ind. Fed. Bus. & Prfnl. Clubs, Inc, 64-66; Ind. Cong. of Parents & Teachers; Gen. Assembly Club; Nat. Order of Women Legislators; Ind. Dem. Women's Clubs, Inc; Ind. Fedn. of Dem. Women. Rel: Church of Christ. Mailing Add: 1703 S. Helfrich Ave. Evansville, Ind. 47712.

BARNUM, C. ROBERT R
Mem, Calif. Rep. State Cent. Cmt.
b. Eureka, Calif, 11/26/27; s. Charles Robert Barnum and Helen Wells B; m. 8/13/49 to Patricia Boyle; c. Patricia A, Charles R, III, William F, Cathleen H. and Janet L. Educ: U.S. Merchant Marine Acad, 45-47; Humboldt State Col, 47; Univ. Calif, 48; Alpha Delta Phi. Polit. & Govt. Pos: Chmn, Young Rep. of Humboldt Co, Calif, 57; chmn, Humboldt Co. Reagan for Gov. Cmt, 66; mem, Calif. Rep. State Cent. Cmt, 68- Bus. & Prof. Pos: Pres, Barnum Investment Co, 55- Mil. Serv: Cadet-Midshipman, U.S. Merchant Marine Acad, 45-47. Rel: Protestant. Legal Res: 2039 William St, Eureka, Calif. 95501. Mailing Add: 207 Fifth St, Eureka, Calif. 95501.

BARNWELL, RICHARD BRANTLEY R
b. Burlington, N.C, 8/25/28; s. Robert William Barnwell, Sr. and Willard Smith B; m. 10/4/52 to Cornelia Ditto; c. Richard B, Jr, Holton Ditto, Kenneth Murchison and Beverly Ann. Educ: Davidson Col, B.S, 51; Beta Theta Pi. Polit. & Govt. Pos: Pres, Alamance Co. Young Rep. Club, N.C, 60; mem, N.C. Rep. Exec. Cmt, 62; secy, Alamance Co. Rep. Exec. Cmt, 62-64, chmn, 64-66; del, Rep. Nat. Conv, 64 & 68; Rep. cand. for U.S. Rep, Sixth Cong. Dist, N.C, 66. Mil. Serv: Entered as Seaman Recruit, Naval Res, 52, released as Lt, 57; Nat. Defense Medal; Lt, Naval Res, 57-66. Mem: Burlington Bd. Realtors (secy, 60, v.pres, 61, pres, 62); N.C. Asn. Realtors; Nat. Asn. Real Estate Bds; Jr. C. of C; Moose; adv. bd, Salvation Army; Am. Bus. Club; bd. dirs, United Fund Alamance Co; past chmn, Alamance Co. Indust. and Adv. Cmt. Rel: Presbyterian. Legal Res: 1618 Ridgecrest Ave, Burlington, N.C. 27215. Mailing Add: P.O. Box 393, Burlington, N.C. 27215.

BARNYAK, MARY A. R
Mem, Calif. Rep. State Cent. Cmt.
b. Franklin, Kans, 9/21/23; d. August Kranker and Julia Kramer K; m. to Frank E. Barnyak. Educ: Valley Jr. Col, Van Nuys, Calif, Spanish course, 65. Polit. & Govt. Pos: Mem, Calif. Rep. State Cent. Cmt, 69- Bus. & Prof. Pos: Secy, Ft. Wayne Army Ord. Depot, Detroit, Mich, 41-44, U.S. Air Corps, Lockheed, Calif, 44-49, Reconstruction Finance Corp, Jones & Whitlock and Dwyer-Curlett & Co, Los Angeles; self-employed, 55-67. Mem: Secy, Burbank-Anglers Club. Rel: Catholic. Mailing Add: 4204 Elmer Ave, Studio City, Calif. 91602.

BARONE, ANTHONY JOHN D
b. Providence, R.I, 6/30/06; s. John Barone and Victoria Campanini B; m. 5/14/36 to Rose Marie Rotelli; c. Judith Anne (Mrs. Aiello) and Joan. Educ: Bryant Col. of Bus. Admin, B.B.A, 28. Polit. & Govt. Pos: Unit instr, Civil Defense, World War II; chmn, Gasoline Bd, Chad Brown Rationing Bd, Off. Price Admin, World War II; pres, Fourth Ward Dem. Club, 6 terms; R.I. State Rep, 53-68. Bus. & Prof. Pos: V.pres, treas. and secy, Rotelli Liquor Co, 55-66. Mem: K. of C; founder and past pres, Wanskock Bus. Men's Asn; exec. mem, St. Ann's Holy Name Soc. Rel: Catholic; Trustee, St. Ann's Church, Providence, R.I. Mailing Add: 305 Langdon St, Providence, R.I. 02904. (1967)

BARONE, RALPH PETER D
Mayor, Woodbridge Twp, N.J.
b. West Pittston, Pa, 7/10/21; s. Joseph Barone and Anna Lepore B; m. 6/7/52 to Marie A. Rigato; c. Dianne, Joseph and Michael. Educ: Newark Col, Rutgers Univ, B.A, 49; Univ. Pa, M.S, 50, Ph.D, 53; Sigma Xi; Alpha Chi Sigma. Polit. & Govt. Pos: Mem, Bd. of Educ, N.J, 57-61; councilman, Woodbridge Twp, 62-67, mayor, 67-; del, Dem. Nat. Conv, 68. Bus. & Prof. Pos: Chemist and group leader, Am. Cyanamid, Bound Brook, 52-59, chief chemist, 59-65, gen. supvr, 65-66; mem. bd. mgrs, Roosevelt Hosp, Edison, 63-67; asst. tech. coordinator, Interchem. Corp, Hawthorne, 66-68; mem. bd. trustees, J.F.K. Commun. Hosp, 68- Mil. Serv: Entered as Pvt, Army Air Force, 42, released as Sgt, 45, after serv. in ETO, 42-45; Soldier's Medal. Publ: Doctoral Thesis. Mem: Am. Chem. Soc; Asn. Consult. Chemists & Chem. Engrs; Am. Mgt. Asn; VFW; Am. Legion; Elks. Rel: Catholic. Legal Res: 171 Devon Rd, Colonia, N.J. 07067. Mailing Add: Township of Woodbridge, 1 Main St, Woodbridge, N.J. 07095.

BARONIAN, LEO P. D
R.I. State Rep.
b. Providence, R.I, 6/17/12. Educ: Bryant Col, exten. courses. Polit. & Govt. Pos: R.I. State Rep, 64-; del, Dem. Nat. Conv, 68. Bus. & Prof. Pos: Payroll clerk, Railway Express Agency, currently. Mil. Serv: Navy. Mem: Elks; VFW; BRCA. Mailing Add: 43 Rutherglen Ave, Providence, R.I. 02907.

BAROODY, WILLIAM J, JR. R
Asst. to the Secy. of Defense, Dept. of Defense
b. Manchester, N.H, 11/5/37; s. William J. Baroody and Nabeeha Ashooh B; m. 4/23/60 to Mary M. Cullen; c. William J, III, Mary Nabeeha, David Michael, Jo Ellen, Christopher William, Andrew Thomas, Philip Francis and Thomas Michael. Educ: Holy Cross Col, B.A, Eng, 59; Georgetown Univ, 61-63. Polit. & Govt. Pos: Staff asst, U.S. Rep. Melvin R. Laird, Wis, 61-64, legis. and press asst, 65-69; mem. staff, House Appropriations Cmt, 62-64 and research dir, House Rep. Conf, 68-69; asst. exec. dir. cmt. on resolutions, Rep. Nat. Conv, 64; Asst. to the Secy. of Defense, Dept. of Defense, 69- Mil. Serv: Entered as Ens, Naval Res, 59, released as Lt(jg), 61, after serv. in U.S.S. Chilton, Atlantic Fleet, Phibron Two, 59-61. Rel: Melkite Catholic. Mailing Add: 7910 Bolling Dr, Alexandria, Va. 22308.

BAROODY, WILLIAM JOSEPH R
b. Manchester, N.H, 1/29/16; s. Joseph Assad Baroody and Helen Hasney B; m. 10/15/35 to Nabeeha Marion Ashooh; c. Anne Mary (Mrs. John G. Gallagher), William J, Jr, Joseph David, Helene (Mrs. Michael Payne), Michael E, Mary Frances and Katherine Jane. Educ: St. Anselm's Col, B.A, 36, Hon. LL.D, 65; Univ. N.H, grad. study, 37-38 and Am. Univ, 38. Polit. & Govt. Pos: Asst. statistician, N.H. Unemploy. Compensation Div, 37-40, supvr. of fiscal, research and legis. planning sect, 41-44; research assoc, N.H. Legis. Cmn. on Disability Benefits, 40-44; dir. statist. div, N.H. War Finance Cmt, 43-44; chief of research and statist. div, readjustment allowance serv, Vets. Admin, 46-49. Bus. & Prof. Pos: Exec. secy, Cmt. on Econ. Security and assoc. ed, Am. Econ. Security, U.S. Chamber of Commerce, 50-53; exec. v.pres, Am. Enterprise Inst, 54-62, pres, 62- Mil. Serv: Entered as Ens, Navy, 44, released as Lt.(jg), Naval Res, 45, after serv. in Atlantic Area, 44-45. Mem: Acad. Polit. Sci; trustee and treas, Inst. for Social Sci. Research, 56-; trustee, St. Anselm's Col, 57-; adv. bd, The Hoover Inst, Stanford Univ, 60-; founding mem, Exec. Bd. of Georgetown Univ. Center for Strategic Studies, 62-65; K. of C; John Carroll Soc; pres, St. Basil's Sem. Men's Guild; dir, Melkite Asn. N.Am, Herbert Hoover Birthplace Found, Cambridge Center for Soc. Studies and Near East Found; adv. coun, De Sales Sch. of Theol; Newcomen Soc. Rel: Catholic. Mailing Add: 1111 Francis Hammond Pkwy, Alexandria, Va. 22302.

BARR, BASIL DUKE D
N.C. State Rep.
b. Jefferson, N.C, 11/4/94; s. Felix Barr and Blanche Duke B; m. 1922 to Mabel Phillips; c. Mrs. Robert E. Shepherd, Winfred F. and Basil D, Jr. Educ: Jefferson High Sch, 14-17; N.C. State Col, B.S, 21. Polit. & Govt. Pos: N.C. State Rep, currently. Bus. & Prof. Pos: Retired. Mil. Serv: World War I; World War II; retired as Lt. Col, 54, Corps Engrs. Mem: Mason; Am. Legion. Rel: Baptist. Mailing Add: West Jefferson, N.C. 28694. (1967)

BARR, BRUCE REID R
Mem. Prfnl. Staff, Senate Rep. Policy Cmt.
b. Flint, Mich, 2/2/35; s. Charles Arthur Barr and Jean Hynds B; m. 6/6/59 to Patricia Kiermas; c. Jennifer Ann, Christopher Reid and Jean Marie. Educ: Am. Univ, B.A, 60; London Sch. Econ, Eng, 67-68; Am. Econ. Asn. Polit. & Govt. Pos: Pub. rels. staff, Rep. Cong. Campaign Cmt, 60; mem. prfnl. staff, Senate Rep. Policy Cmt, 62- Bus. & Prof. Pos: Reporter, Dun & Bradstreet, Inc, 56-59; asst. ed, Human Events Newsletter, 61. Mil. Serv: Pvt, Army, 55-56, serv. in 16th Inf. Regiment, 1st Div. Mem: Am. Polit. Sci. Asn; Am. Econ. Asn; Scottish Econ. Soc. U.S. Cong. Staff Fel, 67-68. Rel: Roman Catholic. Mailing Add: 7024 Tilden Lane, Rockville, Md. 20852.

BARR, H. J, II 'JACK' R
b. Larned, Kans, 12/10/24; s. Herbert John Barr and Eula M. Sippel B; m. 10/6/52 to Ann G. Spear; c. Herbert John, III, Stephanie Lynn, Matthew David and Jennifer Ann. Educ: Kans. State Univ, Manhattan. Polit. & Govt. Pos: Mem, State Banking Syst. Study Cmt. and Kans. Bankers Asn. Cmt. on Fed. Legis; Kans. State Rep, 61-62; mem, Kans. Legis. Coun; Kans. State Sen, 64-68. Bus. & Prof. Pos: Active in farming, cattle raising and oil interests; dir, Nat. Sugar Co, AGCO, Inc, Mid-West Financial Corp, Hi-Plains Enterprises, Inc. and Investors Reserve Life Ins. Co; pres. and chmn. of the bd, First State Bank, Leoti, 62- Mil. Serv: Entered as Aviation Cadet, Navy, 42, released as Ens, 45. Mem: Shrine; Elks; Eastern Star; VFW; Am. Legion; Ahepa; exec. bd, Boy Scouts; Garden City Country Club; bd. mem, Agr. Stabilization & Conserv, U.S. Dept. Agr; dir, Wichita Co. Irrigation Asn; High Plains Beet Growers Asn; farm dir, Kans. Young Rep. Mem, Kans. Del. of Bankers Goodwill People-to-People Tour, Moscow, 66. Rel: Presbyterian. Legal Res: Imperial Route, Garden City, Kans. 67846. Mailing Add: First State Bank, Leoti, Kans. 67861. (1967)

BARR, HAROLD A. R
b. Lancaster, Pa, 9/2/94; s. Christian E. Barr and Lulu Shober B; m. 9/15/18 to Mary Staffer; c. Samuel, John and William. Educ: Franklin & Marshall Col, B.S, 16; Pa. State Col, B.S, 17; Phi Sigma Kappa. Polit. & Govt. Pos: Mem, Lancaster City Sch. Bd, Pa, 37-51 and City Council, 63-67. Bus. & Prof. Pos: Chemist, Grasselli Chem. Co, 18-20; teacher, Lancaster High Sch, 20-25; salesman, Pa. Stone, Cement & Supply Co, 25-36; salesman, J.C. Budding Co, 36-40, mgr, 40-68; retired. Mil. Serv: Entered as Pvt, Chem. Warfare Serv, Army, 18. Mem: Mason; Am. Bus. Club. Rel: Evangelical United Methodist Church. Mailing Add: 654 N. President Ave, Lancaster, Pa. 17603.

BARR, JOSEPH M. D
b. Pittsburgh, Pa, 5/28/06; s. James Patrick Barr and Blanche Elizabeth Moran B; m. 6/4/49 to Alice White; c. Alice Elizabeth and Joseph M, Jr. Educ: Univ. Pittsburgh, B.S. in Bus. Admin, 28; Omicron Delta Kappa; Phi Kappa Theta. Polit. & Govt. Pos: Dem. Nat. Committeeman, Pa; mem, Pa. State Dem. Cmt, 36-38, chmn, 54-59; state pres, Young Dem. Clubs, Pa, 38-39; del, various Dem. Nat. Conv, del, 68; Pa. State Sen, 40-60; Mayor, Pittsburgh, Pa, 59-69. Mem: Pres, U.S. Conf. of Mayors; adv. cmt, Off of Econ. Opportunity; President's Cmn. on Civil Defense; trustee, Univ. Pittsburgh and Carnegie Inst. of Tech; adv. bd, Duquesne Univ; Am. Red. Cross; Buhl Planetarium; dir, Action-Housing and mem. of bd, Mercy Hosp; Pittsburgh Athletic Asn. and Field Club. Rel: Catholic. Legal Res: 6839 Juniata Place, Pittsburgh, Pa. 15208. Mailing Add: 514 City-County Bldg, Pittsburgh, Pa. 15219.

BARR, ROBERT LINCOLN D
b. Kingfisher, Okla, 10/8/39; s. Robert Lincoln Barr and Barbara Lucile Will B; m. 6/4/60 to Sandra June Stone; c. Melinda Leigh, Robert Lincoln, IV and Melissa Lee. Educ: Univ. Okla, B.A, 61; Yale Univ, M.A, 62; Phi Eta Sigma; Phi Beta Kappa; Beta Theta Pi; Xi Mu. Polit. & Govt. Pos: Okla. State Rep, 64-68. Bus. & Prof. Pos: Farmer, 62- Mem: Lions; Farm Bur; Farmers Union. Rel: Christian. Mailing Add: Dover, Okla. 73734. (1967)

BARRELL, CHARLES ALDEN D
Mem, Wood Co. Dem. Cent. and Exec. Cmts, Ohio
b. Buckingham, Va, 3/21/09; s. Charles Martin Barrell and Fannie Hall B; single. Educ: Hampden Sydney Col, B.A, 31; Univ. Va, M.A, 32; Ohio State Univ, Ph.D, 38; Pi Sigma Alpha; Sigma Nu. Polit. & Govt. Pos: Alternate del, Dem. Nat. Conv, 64; councilman-at-lg, Bowling Green, 66-; mem, Wood Co. Dem. Cent. and Exec. Cmts, Ohio, currently. Bus. & Prof. Pos: Instr, Wash. & Lee Univ, 36-38, Ohio State Univ, 38-39 and Oberlin Col, 39-40; from asst. prof. to prof, Bowling Green State Univ, 40- Mil. Serv: Entered as Pvt, Army,

42, released as 2nd Lt, 46. Publ: Representation: Its Numerical and Functional Forms, Ohio State Univ. Press, 39; 'Democracy,' In: An Introduction to American Government, Stackpole, 54; 'Metropolitan Government,' Topic, Vol. 4, No. 8. Mem: Am. Polit. Sci. Asn; Nat. Munic. League; Am. Asn. Univ. Prof; Kiwanis. Rel: Presbyterian. Mailing Add: 722 N. Grove St, Bowling Green, Ohio 43402.

BARRETT, ESTHER SCOTT R
V.Chmn, Harrison Co. Rep. Exec. Cmt, Miss.
b. Gulfport, Miss, 2/15/11; d. John Thomas Scott and Lavinia Jager S; m. 6/29/40 to William Earl Barrett; c. William Earl, Jr, Mary Elizabeth, Peter Hickman and Ashton Scott. Educ: Miss. State Col. for Women, 27-28; Gulf Park Col, 28-29; Jefferson Davis Jr. Col, 65-66. Polit. & Govt. Pos: Pres, Gulfport Rep. Women, 63-64; co-chmn, Fifth Cong. Dist. Miss. Rep. Women, 63-64; state co-chmn, Goldwater in Miss, 64; del, Miss. Rep. State Conv, 64 & 68; alternate del-at-lg, Rep. Nat. Conv, 64 & 68, mem. hospitality cmt, south. region, 64; treas, Gulfport Rep. Women, 64-65; del, Miss. Rep. Women State Conv, 67; del-at-lg, Rep. Nat. Women Conv, 67; v.chmn, Harrison Co. Rep. Exec. Cmt, 68-; mem, Gulfport Munic. Exec. Cmt, 69- Bus. & Prof. Pos: Secy, Harrison Co. Planning Cmn, 68- Rel: Episcopal. Mailing Add: 806 Second St, Gulfport, Miss. 39501.

BARRETT, FRANK A. R
Wyo. State Sen.
b. Omaha, Nebr, 6/29/20; s. Frank A. Barrett and Alice Catherine Donoghue B; m. 12/27/43 to Harriett Permelia Holland; c. James, Laurence, Michael, Francis, Patrick, Joseph, Alice and Mary. Educ: Creighton Univ, 38-41; Univ. Wyo, 41; Univ. Mich, M.D, 44; Providence Hosp, Wash, D.C, surgery residency, 47-51; Phi Chi. Polit. & Govt. Pos: Wyo. Cmnr, West. Interstate Cmn. on Higher Educ, 62-; Wyo. State Sen, 67- Mil. Serv: Entered as 1st Lt, Army, 45, released as Capt, 47, after serv. in Med. Corps. Publ: Numerous scientific articles. Mem: Dir, Wyo. Div, Am. Cancer Soc, 62-, Cheyenne C. of C, 65-66 and Laramie Co. United Fund, 60-66; dir, Wyo. Med. Serv, 54-61 and pres, 56-61; Am. Bd. Surg; Am. Med. Asn; Am. Col. Surgeons; Southwest. Surg. Col; K. of C; Am. Legion. Rel: Catholic. Legal Res: Cheyenne, Wyo. 82001. Mailing Add: 1616 E. 19th, Cheyenne, Wyo. 82001.

BARRETT, FRED E. D
b. Missoula, Mont, 11/22/19; s. Simeon Allen Barrett and Emily Bates B; m. 9/28/41 to Ruth Ellen Plank; c. Carolyn. Educ: Univ. Mont, B.A. and Teaching Cert, 41. Polit. & Govt. Pos: Mont. State Rep, Liberty Co, 51-61; chmn, Mont. Dem. State Cent. Cmt, 62-68. Bus. & Prof. Pos: Teacher, High Sch, Cutbank, Mont, 46-48; wheat rancher, Chester, 48-; mem. bd. dirs, Liberty Co. Develop. Corp, 63-66. Mil. Serv: Entered as 2nd Lt, Army, 42, released as Maj, 45, after serv. in 83rd Inf. Div, ETO, 44-45; Bronze Star Medal with one cluster; Combat Inf. Badge; Cent. European Campaign Ribbon with five clusters. Mem: VFW; Rotary; Mason. Rel: Methodist. Mailing Add: Box 367, Chester, Mont. 59522.

BARRETT, JAMES E. R
Attorney Gen, Wyo.
Mailing Add: State Capitol, Cheyenne, Wyo. 82001.

BARRETT, JAMES LUTHER D
b. Mayesville, Okla, 3/3/34; s. George Washington Barrett and Cora Webb B; m. 1/28/61 to Gloria Jeanne Cragg; c. Tanyala Kay, Hollye Jeanne and James Gregory. Educ: Oklahoma Baptist Univ, B.A; American Univ, J.D. Polit. & Govt. Pos: Precinct chmn, Dem. Party, Oklahoma Co, Okla; chmn. subcmt. constitutional rev, Dem. State Conv; Dem. nominee, Okla. State Sen, 66; chmn. credentials cmt, Okla. Co. Dem. Cent. Cmt; former legis. asst. to Sen. Robert S. Kerr and Sen. J. Howard Edmondson; alternate del, Dem. Nat. Conv, 68. Mil. Serv: Air Force, 54-57, Airman 1/C, serv. in Retraining Group, Amarillo, Tex; Good Conduct Medal. Mem: Okla. Co. Bar Grievance Cmt; Okla. Co, Okla. State, Am. and Fed. Bar Asns; Am. Judicature Soc; Kiwanis; Okla. Baptist Univ. Alumni Asn.(pres); gen. chmn, Westside YMCA Fund Drive; Outstanding Young Man of Oklahoma City, 65; Outstanding Young Man of Am, 67. Rel: Baptist. Legal Res: 8116 N.W, 29th, Bethany, Okla. 73008. Mailing Add: 1005 Cravens Bldg, Oklahoma City, Okla. 73102.

BARRETT, JOHN P. D
b. St. Louis, Mo, 11/17/15; m. 8/29/34 to Delores Mabel Miller; c. Robert E, Constance Ann, Mary Michele. Educ: St. Louis Pub. and Parochial schs. Polit. & Govt. Pos: Mo. State Sen, 54-66. Bus. & Prof. Pos: Salesman. Mil. Serv: USN, WWII, South Pac. Mem: De Andres K. of C; Louis Optimist Club; Amvets. Rel: Catholic. Mailing Add: 1627 Veronica St, St. Louis, Mo. 63115. (1967)

BARRETT, RALPH ROLAND D
Chmn, Licking Co. Dem. Cent. Cmt, Ohio
b. Newark, Ohio, 8/19/30; s. Robert A. Barrett and Juanita L. Baker B. Polit. & Govt. Pos: Treas, Licking Co. Dem. Cent. Cmt, Ohio, 56-58, chmn, 62-; mem, Recreation Cmn, City of Newark, 59-60; chmn, Licking Co. Dem. Exec. Cmt, 62-; State Cent. Committeeman, 17th Cong. Dist, 62-68; bd. mem, Licking Co. Bd. of Elec, 62-64, chmn, 64-; del-at-lg, Dem. Nat. Conv, 68. Mil. Serv: Entered as Pvt, Army, 52, released as Sgt, 53, after serv. in 5th AAA Bn, ETO, 7th Army; Good Conduct Medal; Army of Occup. Medal; ETO Medal. Mem: Bd. dirs, Newark C. of C, 59-60; hon. mem, Newark Jr. C. of C.(v.pres, 58-59, pres, 59-60); pres, Newark Exchange Club, 63; bd. mem, Licking Co. Chap, Am. Red Cross, 59-62; Eagles. Rel: Presbyterian. Mailing Add: 59 Pearl St, Newark, Ohio 43055.

BARRETT, THOMAS EDWIN D
Mayor, Homestead, Pa.
b. Homestead, Pa, 9/17/04; s. Edward Jerome Barrett and Elizabeth McCarthy B; m. 9/10/29 to Marie R. Cloherty; c. Edward Martin, Marie Rita, Eileen Elizabeth, Elizabeth Ann and Thomas Edwin, Jr. Educ: Duquesne Univ. Eve. Sch. Polit. & Govt. Pos: Pa. State Rep, 42-48; Pa. State Sen, 49-52; clerk of courts, Allegheny Co, 54-; mayor, Homestead, Pa, 63-; del, Dem. Nat. Conv, 68. Mem: Eagles; Elks; Moose; K. of C; Hibernians; Knights of Equity. Rel: Roman Catholic. Legal Res: 310 E. 11th Ave, Homestead, Pa. 15120. Mailing Add: 115 Court House, Pittsburgh, Pa. 15219.

BARRETT, WILLIAM A. D
U.S. Rep, Pa.
married; c. Three. Educ: St. Joseph's Col, Phila, Pa. Polit. & Govt. Pos: U.S. Rep, Pa, 44-46, 48- Bus. & Prof. Pos: Real estate broker. Legal Res: 2324 Reed St, Phila, Pa. 19146. Mailing Add: U.S. House of Rep, Washington, D.C. 20515.

BARRETTE, EMERY GEORGE R
b. St. Paul, Minn, 6/30/30; s. Gordon Emery Barrette and Clara Emma Kromschroeder B; m. 8/6/49 to Audrey Marie Svendsen; c. Grant Emery, Michelle Marie and Scott Brentley. Educ: Hamline Univ, B.A, 54; Drew Univ, B.D, 57. Polit. & Govt. Pos: Minn. State Rep, Dist. 44A, 67-68; cand. for U.S. Rep, Minn, 68; exec. dir, Gov. Cmn. on Crime Prev. and Control, 68- Bus. & Prof. Pos: Minister, Minn. Conf. of Methodist Church, 57-64; juvenile court chaplain, St. Paul Area Coun. of Churches, 61-69; chaplain, Ramsey City Juvenile Court, 61-69. Mem: Bd. of dirs, Minn. Coun. on Family Life; bd. of trustees, Children's Serv. Inc; St. Paul Jr. C. of C. Initiated and developed Church delinquency Prev. Prog, East Side Proj, and Children and the Law Proj; Selected Outstanding Young Man of Year in St. Paul and One of Ten Outstanding Young Men of Minn, 65; Liberty Bell Award, Ramsey Co. Bar Asn, 66; Serv. to Freedom Award, Minn. Bar Asn, 66; Harry Brucker Award for Commun. Serv, 68. Rel: Methodist; minister. Mailing Add: 718 E. Arlington Ave, St. Paul, Minn. 55106.

BARRINGER, BENJAMIN LANG R
b. New York, N.Y, 12/20/10; s. Benjamin Stockwell Barringer and Emily Dunning B; m. to Anne Wynne Allen; c. Wynne (Mrs. Rogg), Benjamin S, Emily Allen and Henry Allen. Educ: Cornell Univ, A.B, 33, LL.B, 35. Polit. & Govt. Pos: Conn. State Rep, 47-51 & 63-69; mem, Conn. Bd. of Agr, 50-55; pub. prosecutor, New Milford, 51-55; Conn. State Sen, 32nd Dist, 55-59, asst. majority leader and chmn, Judiciary Cmt, Conn. State Senate, 57; chmn, Litchfield Co. Rep. Orgn, 59-68 and New Milford Town Rep. Cmt, 60- Bus. & Prof. Pos: Farmer and attorney-at-law, 36- Mem: Conn. and Litchfield Co. Bar Asns; Conn. Crime Study Cmn; former mem. Conn. Legis. Coun; pres, Litchfield Co. Farm Bur, 57-60. Rel: Protestant. Mailing Add: 586 Danbury Rd, New Milford, Conn. 06776. (1967)

BARRINGER, RUSSELL NEWTON R
Treas, N.C. Rep. Party
b. Newton, N.C, 3/1/03; s. Hamilton Belton Barringer and Jasey McKenzie B; m. 8/16/26 to MaeLee Page; c. Amerylis (Mrs. Alfred N. Costner), Norma (Mrs. David A. Nichols), Russell N. Jr. and David M. Polit. & Govt. Pos: Mem, N.C. Rep. Exec. Cmt, 32-; treas, N.C. Rep. Party, 66-; alternate del, Rep. Nat. Conv, 68. Bus. & Prof. Pos: Pres, West Durham Lumber Co, 25-; v.pres, Barringer-Whitfield Furniture Co, 45-; pres, Calbar Invest. Co, 50-; pres, Dealers Supply Co, 52-; dir, N.C. Nat. Bank, 60- Mem: Dir. and past pres, N.C. Lumber and Bldg. Material Dealers Asn; Kiwanis; Mason; Shrine; Hope Valley Country Club. Kiwanian of the year, 61; N.C. Lumberman of the decade, Nat. Lumber and Bldg. Material Dealers Asn, 63. Rel: Presbyterian. Mailing Add: 3620 Dover Rd, Durham, N.C. 27707.

BARRON, CHARLES LEE R
State Chmn, Idaho Young Rep.
b. Twin Falls, Idaho, 5/14/38; s. Lloyd Francis Barron and Lenore Ennis B; m. 2/12/67 to Gladys Ann Smith; c. Lloyd Edgar. Educ: Univ. Idaho, B.S. in Geol. Eng, 60. Polit. & Govt. Pos: Co. chmn, Idaho Young Rep, 60-67, state chmn. and region IX dir, 67-; del, Idaho State Rep. Conv, 62, 64, 66 & 68; del, Rep. Nat. Conv, 68. Bus. & Prof. Pos: V.pres, Sun Valley Ranches, Inc, Fairfield, 60- Publ: Monthly column, 'The Young Rep. Report,' The Idaho Rep, 67- Mem: Mason (3°). Rel: Methodist. Mailing Add: Corral, Idaho 83322.

BARRON, DEMPSEY JAMES D
Fla. State Sen.
b. Andalusia, Ala, 3/5/22; s. Jessie Carl Dempsey Barron and Minnie Brown B; m. 1/27/52 to Louverne Hall; c. Stephen C. and Stuart J. Educ: Fla. State Univ, B.S. in bus; Univ. Fla, LL.B. Polit. & Govt. Pos: Fla. State Rep, 56-60; Fla. State Sen, 60- Bus. & Prof. Pos: Attorney, Barron & Redding, 54-; rancher, D Bar Ranch. Mil. Serv: Entered as A/S, Navy, 42, released as GM 1/C, 47, after serv. in Pac. Theater & ETO. Mem: Bd. dirs, Panama City and Bay Co. C. of C; bd. dirs, Boys Club of Am; Farm Bur. Selected as one of two outstanding mems. of Fla. Senate, 65; Consistently selected by Press since 1957 as one of ten outstanding mems. of legis. Rel: Methodist. Legal Res: 224 Woodlawn Dr, Panama City, Fla. 32401. Mailing Add: P.O. Box 1638, Panama City, Fla. 32401.

BARRON, FRANCIS R. D
Ill. Dem. State Cent. Committeeman
b. Ottawa, Ill, 1/23/22; s. Arthur W. Barron (mother deceased); m. 8/5/44 to June M. Dietman; c. Leslie Margaret, Sally B. and Mark C. Educ: Colby Col. Polit. & Govt. Pos: Field supvr, Ill. Dept. of Revenue, 61; Ill. Dem. State Cent. Committeeman, 15th Cong. Dist, 62-; supt, Ill. Parole & Pardon Bd, 63-; del, Dem. Nat. Conv, 68. Mil. Serv: Entered as Pvt, Army, 42, released as Lt. Col, Active Army Res. Mem: K. of C; Am. Legion; VFW; Nat. Asn. Paroling Authorities. Rel: Catholic. 1967 Legal Res: Ottawa, Ill. No mailing address available. (1967)

BARRON, GEORGE PINCKNEY D
b. Iola, Tex, 9/19/93; s. John Marion Barron and Johnnie Frances Gilbert B; m. 12/23/32 to Catherine Hudson; c. George P, Jr, Mary Frances and Betsy Catherine. Educ: Sam Houston State Teachers Col; Univ. Tex. Polit. & Govt. Pos: Chmn, Lavaca del. to State Dem. Conv, Tex, 64; del, Dem. Nat. Conv, 64. Bus. & Prof. Pos: Sch. supt, Yoakum, Tex, 27 years, retired. Mil. Serv: Entered as Pvt, Army, 17, released as Lt, 19, after serv. in 90th Div. Mem: Am. Legion. Gave Lyndon B. Johnson his first job as teacher of speech and govt. in Pearsall, Tex. Schs, 30. Rel: Baptist. Mailing Add: 418 E. Hugo, Yoakum, Tex. 77995.

BARROW, LETHA JEWELL D
Committeewoman, Macon Co. and Macon City Dem. Parties, Mo.
b. LaPlata, Mo, 8/26/08; d. William S. McNeely and Mattie Johnson M; m. 11/28/37 to Robert Wilson Barrow; c. Jeanne (Mrs. Ben Marshall, III). Educ:

Droughous Bus. Col, 29; Beta Sigma Phi. Polit. & Govt. Pos: Secy. and audit clerk to Mo. State Auditor, 33-37; v.pres, Young Dem. Club Mo, 38; alternate del, Dem. Nat. Conv, 40, 48, 52, 56 and secy. to Mo. del, 64; committeewoman, Macon Co. and Macon City Dem. Parties, 50- pres, Ninth Cong. Dist. Women's Club. Mem: Anti Rust Club (pres, 52-54); Macon Band Boosters (pres, 55); Macon PTA (v.pres); Macon Girl Scouts (v.pres, 48-58); Mo. Farmers Asn. Rel: Christian Church. Mailing Add: 905 Jackson St, Macon, Mo. 63552.

BARROW, WILLIAM DEAN D
Fla. State Sen.
b. Pensacola, Fla, 8/20/31; s. George William Barrow, Sr. and Opal Colvin B; m. 8/26/51 to Marguerite Engelke; c. Kimberlea Ann. Educ: Univ. Fla. Law Sch, B.A. and LL.B. with honors, 52; valedictorian high sch, 47; Phi Eta Sigma; Phi Kappa Phi. Polit. & Govt. Pos: Co. prosecuting attorney, Okaloosa Co, Fla, 54-68, co. cmnrs. attorney, 54-68; Fla, State Sen, Third Dist, 66-, chmn, Commerce & Licensed Bus. Cmt, Fla. House of Rep, currently. Bus. & Prof. Pos: Sr. partner, Barrow & Holley, Attorneys; v.pres, Jr. Food Stores of W.Fla; secy, Liveoak Park Mem. Cemetery, Inc, Dogwood Acres, Inc. and Crestview Bowling Lanes, Inc. Mil. Serv: Air Force, Strategic Air Command, Lt. Mem: Kiwanis; Mason; Bar Soc.(past pres); First Judicial Circuit. Outstanding Young Man, Crestview Jaycees, 66; Outstanding Young Man of Am, 67. Rel: Methodist. Legal Res: U.S. Hwy. 85, N, Crestview, Fla. 32536. Mailing Add: P.O. Box 486, Crestview, Fla. 32536.

BARROWS, RAYMOND EDWIN R
Chmn, St. Clair Co. Rep. Party, Mo.
b. Clinton, Mo, 11/21/17; s. Charley Williams Barrows and Martha Griffin B; m. 12/7/43 to Georgia Frances Callison; c. Virginia Lee. Educ: Clinton High Sch, 4 years. Polit. & Govt. Pos: City alderman, Appleton City, Mo, 65; chmn, St. Clair Co. Rep. Party, 68- Bus. & Prof. Pos: Owner, Barrows Chevrolet Co, 55- Mil. Serv: Entered as Pvt, Army, 49, released as S/Sgt, 45, after serv. in 231st AFA, ETO, 44-45; Bronze Star. Mem: Optimist; Mason; Scottish Rite; Shrine. Rel: United Methodist. Mailing Add: 715 N. Poplar, Appleton City, Mo. 64724.

BARRY, DAVID MICHAEL D
Conn. State Sen.
b. Manchester, Conn, 11/7/30; s. John Francis Barry and May D'Arcy B; m. 9/12/59 to Judith Ann Leclerc; c. Joan, David M, Jr, Michael and Mark. Educ: Georgetown Univ, 48-50; Trinity Col, B.A, 52; Boston Univ. Law Sch, LL.B, 55. Polit. & Govt. Pos: Conn. State Rep, 59-61; pres, Manchester Young Dem. Club, 60-61; mem, Manchester Dem. Town Cmt, 60-; mem. bd. dirs, Manchester, 62-66, dep. mayor, 64-66; Conn. State Sen, Fourth Dist, 66- Bus. & Prof. Pos: Partner, Bieluch, Barry & Ramenda, 58-68 and Barry & Ramenda, 68- Mil. Serv: Army, 55-57, serv. in Counter Intel. Corps. Mem: Am, Conn. and Hartford Co. Bar Asns; K. of C; Elks; Army-Navy Club. Rel: Roman Catholic. Mailing Add: 473 E. Center St, Manchester, Conn. 06040.

BARRY, FRANK JOSEPH, JR. D
b. Nogales, Ariz, 2/5/13; s. Frank J. Barry and Molly Dunne B; m. 11/25/49 to Martha Procter; c. Michael, Francis and William. Educ: Univ. Calif. at Los Angeles, B.A, 34; Loyola Univ. Sch. of Law, LL.B, 41; Phi Alpha Delta. Polit. & Govt. Pos: Co. attorney, Santa Cruz Co, Ariz, 49-50; mem, Pima Co. Dem. Cent. Cmt, Ariz, 52-60, v.chmn, Co. Cmt, 55-56; mem, exec. cmt, Ariz. State Dem. Cent. Cmt, 55-56, mem, Cent. Cmt, 55-60; del, Dem. Nat. Cmt, 56; chmn, Ariz. Adv. Cmt, U.S. Cmn. on Civil Rights, 60; solicitor, U.S. Dept. of Interior, 61-68. Bus. & Prof. Pos: Private practice of law. Mil. Serv: Entered as Yeoman 2/C, Navy, 42, released as Lt.(sg), 45, after serv. in 3rd & 5th Fleets, Pac. Theater; Am. Theater and Western Pac. Philippines Ribbons. Mem: Fed, Am, Ariz. State and D.C. Bar Asns; Lions; VFW; Am. Legion; Am. Civil Liberties Union; Tucson Coun. for Civic Unity. Rel: Unitarian. Legal Res: Eugene, Ore. Mailing Add: 2705 Emerald St, Eugene, Ore. 97403.

BARRY, HILARY D. D
s. Bernard D. Barry and Fern Donely B; m. 8/22/52 to Cheryl Teske; c. Scott, Mark, Cindy, Carla, Tamara, Teresa, Bruce, Amy, Patrick and Kimberly. Educ: W.Cent. Sch. of Agr; Univ. Minn, Morris, dipl. Polit. & Govt. Pos: Del, State Dem. Conv, 62, 64, 66 & 68; Murray Co. chmn, Second Dist. Dem. Cent. Cmt, 62-68; del, Dem. Nat. Conv, 68. Bus. & Prof. Pos: Owner, Barry Construction Co, Lake Wilson, Minn, 56- Mem: K. of C; pres, Southwest Minn. Contractors Asn. Rel: Catholic. Mailing Add: Lake Wilson, Minn. 56151.

BARRY, JAMES J. R
Dep. Asst. Secy. for Commun. and Field Serv, Dept. of Health, Educ. and Welfare
Educ: St. Anselm's Col, A.B; Boston Col, M.S, 41; Univ. Pittsburgh Sch. Appl. Soc. Sci, M.A. in Pub. Welfare Admin. Polit. & Govt. Pos: Caseworker, N.H. Dept. of Pub. Welfare, former cmnr. of health and welfare; dep. asst. secy. for commun. and field serv, Dept. of Health, Educ. and Welfare, 69- Bus. & Prof. Pos: Lectr, N.Y. State Inst. for Pub. Welfare Training at Cornell Univ. Mem: Chmn, Gov. Cmt. on Children and Youth; dir. and mem, Policy Cmt, Am. Pub. Welfare Asn; charter chmn, N.H. Chap, Nat. Asn. of Soc. Workers; bd, N.H. Tuberc. Asn; bd. dirs, N.H. Soc. Welfare Coun; hon. mem, Co. Cmnr. Asn; State Coun. on Probs. of the Aging; Reciprocal Enforcement of Support Cmt; Coun. of State Govt; past bd. mem, N.H. Distributing Agency; N.Y. Cancer Cmn. Mailing Add: Office of the Assistant Secretary for Community and Field Services, Dept. of Health, Education and Welfare, Washington, D.C. 20203. (1967)

BARRY, JAMES J. D
b. Syracuse, N.Y, 10/31/16; m. to Elizabeth Nielson. Educ: Cent. City Bus. Sch. Polit. & Govt. Pos: Trustee, North Syracuse, N.Y. and mayor, five terms; N.Y. State Assemblyman, 64-68; del, Dem. Nat. Conv, 68. Bus. & Prof. Pos: Off. mgr, Syracuse Constructors, Inc, Syracuse. Mem: Syracuse Liederkranz, Inc; Pastime Athletic Club Inc; K. of C 3717; Cath. Bd. of Charities; St. Rose of Lima Holy Name Soc. Mailing Add: 111 Single Dr, Syracuse, N.Y. 13212. (1967)

BARRY, JOHN D. R
b. Chicago, Ill, 9/17/17; s. Joseph William Barry and Margaret Beckett B; m. 9/26/52 to Jane Powell. Educ: Univ. of Calif, Los Angeles, 35-38. Polit. & Govt. Pos: Admin. asst. to U.S. Rep. Hamilton Fish Jr, N.Y, 69- Bus. & Prof. Pos: Ed, Lehman Publ, Catskill, N.Y, 58-61; pres, John Barry Assocs. Inc, N.Y, 61-69. Mil. Serv: Entered as Pvt, Army, 39, released as M/Sgt, 45, after serv. in Field Artil, Pac. Theatre of Opers, 39-45; Pearl Harbor, Guadalcanal, New Georgia and Good Conduct Medals. Mem: Am. Legion; Survivors of Pearl Harbor; Rotary Int; C. of C. Legal Res: RD 1, Catskill, N.Y. 12414. Mailing Add: 630 E. Capitol St, Washington, D.C. 20002.

BARRY, JOHN JOSEPH D
b. Norfolk, Conn, 10/5/02; s. Michael Thomas Barry and Katherine Dillon B; m. 10/27/36 to Frances W. Gill; c. John M. Polit. Pos: Chmn, Norfolk Town Dem. Cmt, Conn, 42-66. Govt. Pos: Tax Collector, Norfolk, Conn, 58-65, mem. and chmn, Norfolk Sewer Cmn, 42-65; Conn. State Rep, 30-32. Bus. & Prof. Pos: Partner, J.W. Dillon Store, 19-57. Mem: Winchester Coun. 22, K. of C, Father Leo Assembly K. of C. (4°). Rel: Roman Catholic. Mailing Add: Greenwoods Rd, Norfolk, Conn. 06058. (1967)

BARRY, MARTIN JOSEPH D
Chmn, Dickinson Co. Dem. Cmt, Iowa
b. Nemaha, Iowa, 1/7/14; s. Joseph Barry and Ann Foley B; m. 1/7/36 to Marguerite Ellen Cushman; c. Ruth Marie (Mrs. Brinkmann) and Mildred Ann (Mrs. Muehlegger). Polit. & Govt. Pos: Trustee, Estherville, Iowa, 56-66; chmn, Dickinson Co. Dem. Cent. Cmt, 57-66, finance chmn, 58; committeeman, Agr. Stabilization & Conserv. Serv, Estherville, 59-61; chmn, Dickinson Co. Dem. Cmt, 69- Mem: K. of C; Farmers Union; Nat. Farmers Orgn. Rel: Catholic. Mailing Add: R.R. 1, Lake Park, Iowa 51347.

BARRY, RAY HENRY, SR. D
b. Belvidere, Vt, 5/27/06; m. to Maefred Carpenter; c. Four. Polit. & Govt. Pos: Overseer of poor; tax collector; constable; lister; justice of peace; former road cmnr; selectman; Vt. State Rep, 51, 55-57 & 65-66. Bus. & Prof. Pos: Former sales mgr, retired. Rel: Protestant. Mailing Add: Belvidere Center, Vt. 05442. (1967)

BARRY, ROBERT R. R
b. Omaha, Nebr, 5/15/15; s. Ralph Barry and Ethel Thomas B; m. 7/19/45 to Anne Rogers Benjamin; c. Cynthia Herndon and Henry Rogers. Educ: Hamilton Col, 33-36; Tuck Sch. of Bus. Admin, Dartmouth Col, 36-37; N.Y. Univ, 38, 45-46, Law and Grad. Finance; Nat. Journalistic Fraternity; Alpha Delta Phi. Polit. & Govt. Pos: Regional chmn, New Eng. and Cent. States, Wilkie Clubs of Am, 40; financial analyst, Under-Secy. of Navy Off, 45; personnel dir. and asst. to chmn, Dewey for Pres, Rep. Nat. Campaign Cmt, 48; W.Coast and Rocky Mt. mgr, Eisenhower Campaign Cmt, 51; mem, Eisenhower's personal staff, Denver and Chicago, 52; chmn. bus. groups, Co. Rep. Mayoralty Campaign Cmt, N.Y, 49 and mem. finance cmt, 52; chmn. finance cmt, N.Y. State Citizens for Eisenhower, 54; chmn, Yonkers Citizens for Eisenhower, 56; U.S. Rep, N.Y, 59-65, mem, For. Affairs Cmt, Post Off. and Civil Serv. Cmt, Govt. Oper. Cmt, U.S. Del. to NATO 3 times, to UNESCO and to Can. Parliamentary Conf, U.S. House of Rep; Rep. cand. for U.S. Rep, Calif, 66. Bus. & Prof. Pos: With Kiddes Peabody & Co, 37 and Mfg. Trust Co, 38-40; contract mgr. and statistician, Bendix Aviation Corp, 40-44; asst. to Pres, Yale & Towne Mfg. Co, N.Y.C, 45-50; land develop, mining and farming interest, 50-; pres, Calicopia Corp, 65- Mem: Friendly Sons of St. Patrick; nat. coun. and Eagle Scout, Boy Scouts; founder, U.S. Capitol Hist. Asn; Riverside Co. Farm Bur; Int. Seaman's Union. Grand Cross, Eloy Alfaro Found; Man of Year Award, Captive Nations Assembly and Citation for Meritorious Serv, Nat. Asn. Retired Civil Employees. Rel: Presbyterian. Mailing Add: 6108 Olivewood Rd, Riverside, Calif. 92506. (1967)

BARRY, THOMAS J. R
Treas, Rep. City Cmt. Boston, Mass.
b. Wilmington, Del, 8/5/36; s. Arthur Joseph Barry and Sally R. Jeffery B; m. 11/11/66 to Sylvia F. Myrbeck. Educ: Am. Inst. of Banking, cert, 68; Boston Univ, B.S.B.A, cand. Polit. & Govt. Pos: Treas, Gr. Boston Young Rep. Club, Mass, 63-64 & 65-66; chmn, Ward 22 Rep. Cmt, Boston, 65-; Treas, Rep. City Cmt. Boston, 68- Bus. & Prof. Pos: Electronic Data Processing Programmer and syst. analyst for various co, 58- Mil. Serv: Army Nat. Guard, 58, E-1; Air Force Res, 59-64, E-3. Mem: Allston Brighton Citizens Council (dir). Rel: Roman Catholic. Mailing Add: 45 Rogers Park Ave, Brighton, Mass. 02135.

BARRY, TOBIAS D
Ill. State Rep.
b. Chicago, Ill, 4/12/24; s. Tobias F. Barry and Mary Castagnari B; m. 6/5/48 to Janet Bruno; c. Tobias Mark, Patrick Alan, Michele Beth and Daniel Sean. Educ: Marquette Univ, Ph.B, 49; Univ. Notre Dame, LL.B, 52. Polit. & Govt. Pos: Ill. State Rep, 60-; chmn, Bureau Co. Dem. Party, 63- Bus. & Prof. Pos: Attorney-at-law. Mil. Serv: Navy, World War II, serv, in Pac. Theatre. Rel: Roman Catholic. Mailing Add: Ladd, Ill. 61329.

BARRY, WILLIAM H, JR. D
b. Nashua, N.H, 2/3/30; s. William H. Barry and Mabel Monica B; m. 8/12/58 to Nancy R. Collins; c. William H, III, Julia E. and Maura J. Educ: Holy Cross Col, B.S, 56; Suffolk Univ, LL.B, 60. Polit. & Govt. Pos: Chmn, Nashua City Dem. Cmt, N.H, 60-62; mem, N.H. Dem. State Cmt, 62-65; del, Dem. Nat. Conv, 64; regional counsel, Small Bus. Admin, 65-; Dem. cand. for U.S. Rep, Second Cong. Dist, N.H, 66; Asst. U.S. Attorney, 67-69; clerk of U.S. Dist. Court, 69- Mil. Serv: Entered as Pvt, Army, 50, released as M/Sgt, 52, after serv. in 3rd Inf. Div, Korea. Mem: N.H. Bar Asn; Am. Bar Asn; Am. Legion; DAV; Elks; Optimists. Rel: Roman Catholic. Legal Res: 2 Denise St, Nashua, N.H. 03060. Mailing Add: 255 Main St, Nashua, N.H. 03060.

BARRY, WILLIAM LOGAN D
b. Lexington, Tenn, 2/9/26; s. Henry Daniel Barry and Mary Logan B; m. 8/8/66 to Elizabeth Coffman. Educ: Vanderbilt Univ, B.A, 48; B.L, 50; Phi Beta Kappa. Polit. & Govt. Pos: Mem, Lexington Bd. Aldermen, Tenn, 53-55; Tenn. State Rep, 55-67, Majority Leader, Tenn. House of Rep, 59-63, Speaker,

63-67; mem, Tenn. Legis. Coun, 57-67, chmn, 65-67; exec. asst. to Gov. of Tenn, 67- Mil. Serv: Entered as Pvt, Army, 50, released as 1st Lt, 53, after serv. in Far East. Theater. Mem: Tenn. Bar Asn; Lions; Elks; K. of P; Am. Legion; Farm Bureau; VFW. Rel: Baptist. Mailing Add: Natchez Trace Dr, Lexington, Tenn. 38351.

BARTEL, JOHN W, JR. R
V.Chmn, Kern Co. Rep. Cent. Cmt, Calif.
b. Hillsboro, Kans, 7/2/27; s. John Bartel and Elma Brandt B; m. 5/7/51 to Betty L. Knoy; c. John Charles and Jeffrey Michael. Educ: Bakersfield Jr. Col, 2 years; Calif. Col. Mortuary Sci, Los Angeles, grad, 50. Polit. & Govt. Pos: V.chmn. and mem. exec. bd. dirs, Kern Co. Rep. Cent. Cmt, Calif, 67-; mem, Calif. Rep. State Cent. Cmt, 69- Bus. & Prof. Pos: Apprentice embalmer and embalmer, Loyd Funeral Serv, Porterville, Calif, 50-53; embalmer, Sneider & Sullivan Mortuary, San Mateo, 53-56; funeral dir-mgr, J.T. Oswald Mortuary, Reseda, 56-60, Daly & Bartel Mortuary, Anaheim, 60-66 and Hillcrest Mem. Park and Mortuary, Bakersfield, 66- Mil. Serv: Entered as Seaman 2/C, Navy, 44, released as PHM 3/C, 46, after serv. in Hosp. Corps; Nat. Defense Medal; Victory Medal. Mem: Calif. Funeral Dirs. Asn.(mem. ethics cmt, 68-69, clergy rels. cmt, 69-); Nat. Funeral Dirs. Asn; Elks; Bakersfield Kiwanis (bd. dirs); C. of C.(bd. dirs); Cath. Social Serv. (bd. dirs); United Fund (bd. dirs); Presbyterian Men's Club (bd. dirs); Calif. Col. Mortuary Sci. Alumni Asn. Distinguished Serv. Award, Anaheim Jaycees, 62. Rel: Protestant. Mailing Add: 2720 Panorama Dr, Bakersfield, Calif. 93306.

BARTELS, MILLARD R
Mem, Conn. Finance and Budget Cmts.
b. Syracuse, N.Y, 2/24/05; s. Herman Bartels and Jane Millard B; m. 6/1/34 to Eulalia Stevens; c. Millard Stevens, Chester Bruce and Jane (Mrs. Stephenson). Educ: Cornell Univ, A.B, 27; Cornell Law Sch, LL.B, 29; Phi Delta Theta; Phi Delta Phi. Polit. & Govt. Pos: Mem. and chmn, Dist. Cmt, West Hartford, Conn, 35-49, mem, Town Coun, 39, 41, 43 and pres, 43-45; mem. real assets div, comptroller's dept, State of Conn, 49-53; dir, Conn. State Prison and mem, State Bd. of Parole, 53-55; mem, Conn. Finance and Budget Cmts, currently. Bus. & Prof. Pos: Dir, Travelers Ins. Co, 52-, chmn. ins. exec. cmt. and gen. counsel, 55-; dir, Conn. State C. of C, 55-; dir, Conn. Bank & Trust Co, 55-; dir, Inst. of Living, 58. Mem: Hartford Club; Hartford Golf Club; Tunxis Club; Metrop. Club, Wash, D.C. Rel: Episcopal. Mailing Add: 29 Westwood Rd, West Hartford, Conn. 06117.

BARTH, FRANCIS PHILLIP D
Chmn, Dist. 35, N.Dak. Dem. Non-Partisan League
b. Flasher, N.Dak, 4/2/30; s. Phillip F. Barth and Katherine Leingang B; m. 6/5/51 to Burnetta Gerhardt; c. Dwight, Geisele, Elwood, MaDonna and Leland. Educ: High sch, 2 years. Polit. & Govt. Pos: Dem. committeeman, 18th Dist, Morton Co, N.Dak, 51-66; dir, Sch. Bd, 53-62, chmn, 7 years; mem, Morton Co. Dem. Non-Partisan League Exec. Cmt, 60; del, Dem. State Conv, 62, 64, 66 & 68; secy, Dist. 35 N.Dak. Dem. Non-Partisan League, 65-66, chmn, 66-; del, Dem. Nat. Conv, 68. Bus. & Prof. Pos: Farmer-rancher, 1400 Acre Ranch, breeding registered Hereford cattle. Publ: Articles concerning speeches and comments about politics, The Morning Pioneer, Newspaper, Mandan, N.Dak. Mem: Bd. adv, Assumption Col, 64-; Elks; K. of C. (Grand Knight, 61-64, State Dep, 64-, del, Supreme K. of C. Conv, 69); Farmers Union; Nat. Farmers Orgn; life mem, Am. Hereford Asn; N.Dak. Hereford Asn. Rel: Catholic. Mailing Add: Solen, N.Dak. 58570.

BARTHELMES, WES D
b. Winchester, Mass, 5/10/22; s. Albert Wesley Barthelmes and Irma McDevitt B; m. to Dorothy Chase; c. Lisa and Victoria. Educ: Tufts Col, B.A, 47; Middlebury Col, summer 47; L'Institut des Hautes Etudes Internationalies, Geneva, Switz, 47-48; Columbia Univ. Grad. Sch. Journalism, M.S, 49; Zeta Psi. Polit. & Govt. Pos: Admin. asst. to U.S. Rep. Edith Green, Ore, 62-65; press secy, U.S. Sen. Robert F. Kennedy, N.Y, 65-66; campaign coordinator, U.S. Rep. Robert Duncan, Ore, 66; admin. asst. to U.S. Rep. Richard Bolling, Mo, 69- Bus. & Prof. Pos: Reporter and asst. city ed, Telegram, Worcester, Mass, 49-53 and Wash. Post, 53-62. Mil. Serv: Entered as Pvt, Army, 43, released as Cpl, 46, after serv. in Paratroopers 82nd Airborne Div, ETO, 43-46; Presidential Unit Citation. Publ: 'George Wallace is Alive and Well,' Washingtonian Mag, 2/69. Mem: Caucus for a New Polit; Alliance for Dem. Progress. Nat. Honor Soc; Wash. Newspaper Guild's Guildsman of the Year; Washingtonian Mag. Ten Best Admin. Asst. Mailing Add: 6006 Welborn Dr, Washington, D.C. 20016.

BARTHOLOMEW, CLYDE R
b. Benson, Vt, 5/26/06; m. to Florence Munger; c. Eleven. Polit. & Govt. Pos: Town moderator; sch. dir. and chmn, Fair Haven Union Sch. Bd. Vt; selectman, Fair Haven, 47-60; Vt. State Rep, formerly. Bus. & Prof. Pos: Farmer and lumberman. Mem: Benson Fish & Game Club; North Farmers Coop; State Bd. of Dirs. Rel: Protestant. Mailing Add: R.D. 1, Fair Haven, Vt. 05743. (1967)

BARTLESON, THOMAS LEES R
b. Chester, Pa, 8/16/94; s. Edward Evans Bartleson, Jr. and Jennie Rhoades Lees B; m. 9/11/18 to Helen Eugenie Ickes; c. Thomas Lees, Jr. and Janet Marie (Mrs. Mochel). Educ: Swarthmore Col, B.S. in Chem. Eng, 16. Polit. & Govt. Pos: Del. State Rep, 57-67, Rep. Whip, Del. House of Rep, 63-64, Rep. House Leader, 65-67 and chmn, Joint Finance Cmt, 67. Bus. & Prof. Pos: Research chemist, Du Pont Exp. Sta, 16-30, plant engr, 30-50 and asst. to opers. mgr, 50-59. Rel: Episcopal. Mailing Add: 105 North Rd, Wilmington, Del. 19809. (1967)

BARTLETT, CLARENCE EDWARD R
N.H. State Rep.
b. Concord, N.H, 2/23/03; s. Edward Elbridge Bartlett and Maude Kelley B; m. 11/26/21 to Amy Frances Kaime; c. Frances (Mrs. Marston) and Robert Edward. Educ: Palmer Col, D.C, 22; N.Y. Univ, Traffic Safety Mgt course; Acacia Fraternity. Polit. & Govt. Pos: Financial Responsibility Admin, N.H, 61-66; N.H. State Rep, 69- Mem: Mason (32°). Rel: Protestant. Legal Res: Epsom, N.H. 03234. Mailing Add: Box 7, Gossville, N.H. 03239.

BARTLETT, DEWEY FOLLETT R
Gov, Okla.
b. Marietta, Ohio, 3/28/19; s. David A. Bartlett and Jessie B; m. 1945 to Ann C. Smith; c. Dewey, Jr, Joan and Michael. Educ: Princeton Univ, B.S.E, 42. Polit. & Govt. Pos: Okla. State Sen, 62-66; Gov, Okla, 67-; del, Rep. Nat. Conv, 68. Bus. & Prof. Pos: Pres, Dewey Supply Co; partner, Keener Oil Co. Mil. Serv: Entered as 2nd Lt, Marine Corps, 42, released as Capt, 45 after serv. as Combat Divebomber Pilot; Air Medal. Mem: Tulsa C. of C; bd. dir, Salvation Army; dir, Tulsa Co. Chap, Am. Red Cross; dir, Independent Petroleum Asn. of Am; dir, Okla. Independent Producers Asn. Rel: Catholic. Mailing Add: 820 N.E. 23rd St, Oklahoma City, Okla. 73105.

BARTLETT, JOHN WESLEY D
b. Harlowton, Mont, 10/12/25; s. John Bartlett and Eliza Hughes B; m. 4/22/44 to Edith Mae Welch; c. John Clifton, James Craig and Jan Colleen. Educ: Univ. Mont, B.S. in Pharm, 49; Kappa Psi. Polit. & Govt. Pos: Dem. precinct committeeman, Whitefish, Mont, 50-69, city councilman, 56-60; cong. committeeman, Flathead Co. Dem. Party, 58-62, chmn, 62-69; mem, Area Redevelop. Cmt, Flathead Co, 58-65; del, Dem. Nat. Conv, 60; mem, Small Bus. Adv. Coun, Mont, 60-66; Presidential elector, Mont, 68; mem, State Bd. of Health, 69- Bus. & Prof. Pos: Pharmacist and partner, Neville Drug, Whitefish, 49-66; pres, Chalet City Pharm, 66- Mil. Serv: Entered as a Pvt, Army, 43, released as S/Sgt, 45, after serv. in 87th Inf. Div, Third Army, ETO; Bronze Star; Combat Infantryman Badge; Purple Heart with Clusters. Mem: Nat. Asn. Retail Druggists; C. of C; Am. Legion; Moose; Mason; Lions; VFW; Jaycees; Flathead Co. Dem. Club. Life membership, VFW; life membership, Whitefish Jaycees. Rel: Methodist. Mailing Add: 144 Montana Ave, Whitefish, Mont. 59937.

BARTLETT, KENNETH G. R
N.Y. State Assemblyman
b. Plymouth, Mich, 3/13/06; s. Wyman J. Bartlett and Alta Mae Gill B; m. 9/6/30 to Bernice V. Kleinhans; c. Elizabeth (Mrs. John Weinheimer) and John G, M.D. Educ: Albion Col, A.B, 27, LL.D, 55; Syracuse Univ, M.A, 31; Phi Kappa Phi; Alpha Epsilon Rho; Alpha Delta Sigma; Sigma Nu. Polit. & Govt. Pos: Mem, State of N.Y, The Moreland Cmn. on Welfare, 61-63; chmn, cmt. appointed by State Cmnr. of Educ. for Statewide study of educ. TV; v.chmn, Onondaga Co. Rep. Cmt, N.Y, 62-66; N.Y. State Assemblyman, 119th Dist, 67- Bus. & Prof. Pos: V.pres, Syracuse Univ, 53-; pres, Univ. Hill Corp, 62-66, pres, 66-; lectr, Salzburg Seminar, Salzburg, Austria, for study of Pub. Commun, 64; dir, Onondaga Savings Bank, WCNY-TV and Metrop. Develop. Asn. Publ: 'Radiobroadcasting, 1947,' Syracuse Univ. Press. Mem: Syracuse Symphony. Selected, Man of Year, Herald-Journal, 63; received Annual Commun. Serv. Award, Syracuse Rotary, 66. Rel: Presbyterian. Mailing Add: 11 Bradford Dr, Syracuse, N.Y. 13224.

BARTLETT, MARTIN HANDLEY R
b. Stillwater, Okla, 12/21/07; s. Harry Ulyses Bartlett and Eva Maud Whitehead B; div; c. Barbara (Mrs. Benedict), Diane (Mrs. Wellar), Margaret (Mrs. McNatt), Deborah (Mrs. Ackerman), John and Will. Educ: Okla. City Univ, 24-26; Univ. Tex, 40; Univ. Tex. Sch. Med, M.D, 41; Nu Sigma Nu. Polit. & Govt. Pos: Mem, Otero Co. Rep. Cent. Cmt, 52-69; mem, N.Mex. State Rep. Cent. Cmt, 62-69; del, Rep. Nat. Conv, 68. Mil. Serv: Entered as 2nd Lt, Army, 42, released as Lt, 46. Mem: Otero Co. and N.Mex. State Med. Socs; Am. Med. Asn; Am. Acad. Gen. Practice; bd. dirs, Otero Co. Farm & Livestock Bur; Soc. Preservation & Encouragement Barber Shop Quartet Singing in Am; Methodist Men's Club. Rel: Methodist. Legal Res: 414 San Andreas, Alamogordo, N.Mex. 88310. Mailing Add: P.O. Box 593, Alamogordo, N.Mex. 88310.

BARTLETT, RICHARD JAMES R
Chmn, Crime Control Coun, N.Y.
b. Glens Falls, N.Y, 2/15/26; s. George W. Bartlett and Kathryn McCarthy B; m. 8/18/51 to Claire Kennedy; c. Michael and Amy. Educ: Georgetown Univ, 45; Harvard Law Sch, 49. Polit. & Govt. Pos: N.Y. State Assemblyman, 59-66, Rep. Whip, N.Y. Assembly, 66; chmn, Temporary Cmn. Revision Penal Law & Criminal Code, N.Y, 61-, chmn, Crime Control Coun, 67- and chmn, Crime Control Planning Bd, 68-; del, Constitutional Conv, N.Y, 67. Bus. & Prof. Pos: Practicing attorney, Glens Falls, N.Y, 49-; partner, Clark, Bartlett and Caffry. Mil. Serv: Entered as 1st Lt, Air Force, 51, released as Capt, 53. Mem: Am. and N.Y. Bar Asns; N.Y. State Bar Asn.(secy, 69-); Am. Law Inst; Am. Judicature Soc. Rel: Catholic. Mailing Add: 10 Harlem St, Glens Falls, N.Y. 12801.

BARTLEY, DAVID MICHAEL D
Speaker, Mass. House Rep.
b. Holyoke, Mass, 2/9/35; s. James Bartley and Mary Kennedy B; m. 6/27/64 to Elizabeth Ann Keough; c. David Kennedy and Myles Keough. Educ: Holyoke Jr. Col, 52-54; Univ. Mass, Amherst, B.A. in Govt, 56, M.Ed, 61. Polit. & Govt. Pos: Mass. State Rep, 63-, speaker, Mass. House Rep, 69-; del, Dem. Nat. Conv, 68. Mil. Serv: Army. Mem: K. of C; Elks; Boys Club Am. Rel: Catholic. Mailing Add: 25 Hillcrest Rd, Holyoke, Mass. 01040.

BARTLEY, WILLIAM MAURICE D
b. Calhoun, Ill, 9/7/12; s. William Oscar Bartley and Clara Durbin B; m. 8/31/42 to Evelyn Maria Lofgren; c. Susan Diane (Mrs. Barré) and Stephen Nils. Educ: High Sch. grad. Polit. & Govt. Pos: Councilman, City of Alameda, Calif, 65-68. Bus. & Prof. Pos: Equip. mgr, Utah Construct. & Mining Co, 57-59; equip. salesman, Boothe Equip. Co, 59-61; opers. supvr, Am. Machine & Foundry, Inc, 61-62; v.pres, Boothe Radiant Heat, Inc, 62-63; real estate salesman, Agnew & Copeland, Inc, 63-65; real estate broker, Investment Properties, 65- Mil. Serv: Entered as A/S, Navy, 37, released as Comdr, 57, after serv. in Naval Air Force; many campaign ribbons. Mem: Rotary Int; Elks; Navy League of U.S; C. of C; Real Estate Bds. and Socs. Rel: Catholic. Mailing Add: 1507 Gibbons Dr, Alameda, Calif. 94501.

BARTO, RAYMOND N. R
b. Seatonville, Ill, 3/15/11; s. Nato Barto and Julia Chiavario B; m. 8/27/35 to Eileen Lillian Grotti. Educ: High Sch. Polit. & Govt. Pos: Village clerk, Seatonville, Ill, 32-42; Rep. precinct committeeman, Hall Five, 32-66; chmn, Bureau Co. Rep. Cent. Cmt, Ill, 54-66; treas, Bureau Co, Ill, 66-69; sheriff,

Bureau Co, Princeton, Ill, 66- Bus. & Prof. Pos: With Dept. of Conservation, 18 yrs, supt, State Parks and Memorials, Ill, 58-61. Mil. Serv: Entered as Pvt, Air Force, 43, released as Sgt, 46. Mem: Elks; Volunteer Fireman; Mason (32°); Shrine; Am. Legion. Judge of Bird Dog Field Trials, U.S. and Can; played football, baseball and basketball in High Sch. and semi-professionally. Mailing Add: Box 57, Seatonville, Ill. 61359.

BARTOLI, SERGIO D
City Councilman, Shickshinny, Pa.
b. Shickshinny, Pa, 11/6/13; s. Torquato Bartoli and Gemma B; m. 11/25/37 to Ruth Elizabeth Franklin; c. Susan (Mrs. Mailey) and Robert. Educ: Penn State Univ. Exten, 1 year. Polit. & Govt. Pos: Del, Dem. Nat. Conv, 68; city councilman, Shickshinny, Pa, currently. Bus. & Prof. Pos: Pres, Bart's Cleaners Inc, 40-69; real estate broker, S. Bartoli Real Estate, 61-69; dir, First Nat. Bank, Mocanaqua, 64-69. Mem: Rotary (pres, Shickshinny Club, 47); Elks. Rel: Presbyterian. Mailing Add: 103 W. Union, Shickshinny, Pa. 18655.

BARTON, HAROLD BRYAN R
Mem, Ky. Rep. State Finance Cmt.
b. Madison Co, Ky, 11/1/26; s. Clyde Tye Barton and Lula Marie Brown B; m. 5/11/51 to Nelda Lambert; c. Barbara Lynn, Harold Bryan, Jr, Stephen Lambert and Suzanne. Educ: Univ. of Ky, 44, 46-48; Univ. of Louisville Sch. of Med, M.D, 52; post-grad. work, Gen. Surg. Residency, Univ. of Louisville Hosps, 52-57. Dipl, Am. Bd. of Surg. Polit. & Govt. Pos: City campaign chmn, Rep. Party, Ky, 60, 62 & 64; mem. bd. Dirs, Ky. Educ. Med-Polit. Action Cmt, 62-66 and chmn, 65-; del, Rep. Nat. Conv, 64 & 68; chmn, Fifth Cong. Dist. Rep. Fund Raising Dinner, 65; mem, Ky. Rep. State Finance Cmt, currently. Bus. & Prof. Pos: Secy, Corbin Airport Bd, 64-; mem. bd. dirs, Am. Bus. Mens Life Ins. Co, 65-66; chief of surg, S.E. Ky. Baptist Hosp. Mil. Serv: Entered as A/S, Navy, 44, released as Seaman 1/C, 46, after serv. in Commun. Intel, Pac. Theatre; Unit Citation; Presidential Unit Commendation. Mem: Ky. Med. Asn. (v.pres, 65); Am. Med. Asn; Southeast. and Ky. Surg. Socs; C. of C. (bd. dir, Corbin, 64-66); Mason; Lions; Jaycees; Farm Bur; Tri County Club (pres, 64-68); fel. Am. Col. Surg, 58. Corbin Distinguished Citizen Award, 66. Rel: Protestant; Elder and chmn. finance cmt, First Christian Church. Mailing Add: 1311 Seventh St. Rd, Corbin, Ky. 40701.

BARTON, JERRY D
b. Dallas, Tex, 2/7/29; s. Homer H. Barton and Grace Simmans B; m. 8/18/49 to Lometa Wann; c. Laurie Lou, Jerry Dean and Belinda Lea. Educ: Tex. A&M Univ, B.S, 53. Polit. & Govt. Pos: Del, Dem. State Conv, Tex, 64-; precinct chmn, Dem. Party, Brazos Co, 66-; chmn. co. del, Dem. State Conv, 68; del, Dem. Nat. Conv, 68. Bus. & Prof. Pos: Dist. mgr, Nat. Farm Life Ins. Co, cent. Tex, 53-60; gen. agent, State Reserve Life Ins. Co, 60-; owner-mgr, Jerry Barton Ins. Agency, 60- Mil. Serv: Entered as A/S, Navy, 46, released as Seaman 1st Class, 48; 2nd Lt, Air Force Res, 53-56. Mem: Cent. Tex, Tex. and nat. asns. Life Underwriters; mem, Tex. Leaders Round Table; past pres, Bryan Jr. C. of C; past pres, Bi-City Coun. of Serv. Clubs; past pres, Gr. Bryan United Fund, Inc; bd. of dirs, Brazos Valley Rehabilitation Center; Lions; mem, Brazos Co. A&M Club; PTA; Bryan-College Sta. C. of C. Rel: Protestant; Trustee, First Baptist Church, College Station, Tex. Legal Res: 2401 Wayside Dr, Bryan, Tex. 77801. Mailing Add: P.O. Box 3883, Bryan, Tex. 77801.

BARTON, JOHN JOSEPH D
b. Indianapolis, Ind, 6/23/06; s. Patrick Barton and Nora B; m. 1944 to Louise Fitzgerald; c. Mary Ellen, John, Jr. and Margaret. Educ: Purdue Univ, B.S.M.E, 30; Fed. Bur. Invest. Acad, 49; Harvard Invest. Seminar, 58. Polit. & Govt. Pos: Mem. dept, Ind. State Police, 35-63, supt, 61-63; mayor, Indianapolis, 63-68. Bus. & Prof. Pos: Engr, Indianapolis Power and Light Co, 24-26, Babcock and Wilcox, Ohio, 30-32 and Midwest Tank and Mfg. Co, Ind, 57-60. Mil. Serv: Entered as Lt.(jg), Navy, 43, released as Lt. Comdr, 53, after serv. in P.R. and Admiralty Islands, 43-45; Asiatic-Pac. Theater Ribbon; Victory and Occupation Medals. Mem: K. of C; Gr. Indianapolis Progress Cmn; State Symphony Soc; Purdue Alumni Asn; dir, Ind. Munic. League. Rel: Catholic. Mailing Add: 5719 Broadway Terr, Indianapolis, Ind. 46220. (1967)

BARTON, NELDA ANN LAMBERT R
Rep. Nat. Committeewoman, Ky.
b. Providence, Ky, 5/12/29; d. Eulis Grant Lambert and Rubie Lois West L; m. 5/11/51 to Harold Bryan Barton, M.D; c. William Grant (deceased), Barbara Lynn, Harold Bryan, Jr, Stephen Lambert and Suzanne. Educ: West. Ky. Univ, 47-49; Norton Mem. Infirmary Sch. Med. Tech, grad. 50; pres, Beta Omega Chi, 48-49; West. Ky. Univ. scholarship, 47. Polit. & Govt. Pos: Fifth dist. gov, Ky. Fedn. Rep. Women, 63-67; mem, Am. and Ky. Educ. Med. Polit. Action Cmts, 63-; Rep. dist. campaign chairwoman, 67; pres, Corbin Rep. Woman's Club, 68; Whitley Co. Campaign Chairwoman, 68; chairwoman, Whitley Co. Rep. Party, 68-; second v.pres, Ky. Fedn. Rep. Woman's Club, 68-; mem, Ky. State Rep. Cent. Cmt, 68-; Rep. Nat. Committeewoman, Ky, 68-; conf. chmn. for Ky. Nat. Rep. Women's Conf, D.C, 69. Bus. & Prof. Pos: Med. Technologist, 50-53. Mem: Newcomers Club New Albany, Ind. (v.pres, 53); PTA (dist. chmn, 58-59); Ninth Dist. Ky. Fedn. Women's Club (v.gov, 62-64); Women's Auxiliary to South. Med. Asn. (Ky. coun, 65-66, Southeast. U.S. coun, 66-67); Woman's Auxiliary to Ky. Med. Asn. (health career chmn, 65-68); Woman's Auxiliary to Whitley Co. Med. Soc. (pres, 59-60); Ossoli Woman's Club (pres, 61-62); PTA (pres, Corbin Cent. Elem, 63-65); Cub Scout Den Mother, 66-67; Ky. Hist. Soc; charter mem, South East Ky. Fine Arts Asn; Gov. Nunn's Ky. Cmn. Women, 68- Ky. Colonel, 68; PTA Life Mem. Award: Ky. Rep. Woman of the Year, 68-69. Rel: Protestant; Chmn, youth fellowship, Circle Chmn, First Christian Church. Mailing Add: 1311 Seventh Street Rd, Corbin, Ky. 40701.

BARTON, TERRY ALLEN R
Mem, Calif. Rep. State Cent. Cmt.
b. Columbus, Ohio, 9/11/35; s. Albert Jack Barton and Inez Smith B; m. 6/29/57 to Barbara Ellen Watts; c. Gregory Allen. Educ: Ohio State Univ, B.A, 59; Loyola Univ. Sch. of Law, 60-63; Phi Eta Sigma. Polit. & Govt. Pos: Civil Serv. cmnr, Seal Beach Civil Serv. Bd, Calif, 66-67; planning cmnr, Seal Beach Planning Cmn, 67-69; mem, Nat. Defense Exec. Res, 68-69; pres, Seal Beach Rep. Assembly, 69-; mem, Calif. Rep. State Cent. Cmt, 69- Bus. & Prof. Pos: Quality control analyst, Gen. Motors Corp, Columbus, Ohio, 58-59; supvr. contracts and pricing, N.Am. Rockwell Corp, Downey, Calif, 63- Mil. Serv: Entered as 2nd Lt, Air Force, 59, released as 1st Lt, 62, after serv. in 18th Dist. Off, Spec. Invest. Hq, 60-63; Capt, Air Force Res, 67. Mem: Nat. Contract Mgt. Asn; pres, Col. Park Homeowner's Asn. of Seal Beach; Long Beach Elks Club; Seal Beach C. of C; Old Ranch Country Club. Rel: Methodist. Mailing Add: 3840 Sunflower St, Seal Beach, Calif. 90740.

BARTRAM, PHILIP HOYT R
b. Kalamazoo, Mich, 7/27/22; s. Earl Ward Bartram (deceased) and Helen Rockwell B; m. 6/2/65 to Sally Gellerson; c. Stepsons, Greg and Gilman Glover. Educ: Tilton Jr. Col. and Univ. N.H. Polit. & Govt. Pos: Chmn, Dover-Foxcroft Town Cmt, Maine, 56-; treas, Piscataquis Co. Rep. Cmt, 59-62, chmn, 62-68. Bus. & Prof. Pos: Buyer, Great North. Paper Co, Bangor, Maine, 47-; dir, Squaw Mt. Ski Corp, Greenville and dir-treas, Sebec Shores, Inc, 59- Mil. Serv: Entered as Ens, Navy, 43, released as Lt, 46, after serv. in ETO. Mem: Kiwanis; dist. comnr, Boy Scouts. Rel: Catholic. Mailing Add: 34 Autumn Ave, Dover-Foxcroft, Maine 04426. (1967)

BARTRON, G. ROBERT R
S.Dak. State Sen.
b. 11/12/20; m. 1942 to Jean Potticary; c. Lynn Ann (Mrs. Roger Fox); Stephanie (Mrs. James Smith) and Greg. Educ: B.S, M.B, M.D. Polit. & Govt. Pos: S.Dak. State Sen, 64-, Pres-Pro-Tem, S.Dak. State Senate, 69- Bus. & Prof. Pos: Physician-surgeon, Barton Hosp. & Clinic, 46-52, dir, Bartron Clinic, 55-; v.pres-md. dir, Midland Nat. Life Ins. Co, Watertown, S.Dak, 56-; secy, State Bd. Med. Exam, Sioux Falls, 58-; bd. dirs, Farmers & Merchants Bank, Watertown, 59- Mil. Serv: Med. Officer, Air Force, Japan and Korea, 53-55. Publ: 'A Clinical Evaluation of the Everted Intestinal Anastomosis', 68 and 'A Large Duodenal Mass', 68, S.Dak. J. Med. Mem: Dipl. Am. Bd. Abdominal Surg; Int. Col. Surgeons; Int. Bd. Proctology. Boss of the Year Award, Watertown Jaycees, 66; Commun. Serv. Award, S.Dak. State Med. Asn, 67. Rel: Episcopal. Legal Res: 426 S. Lake Dr, Watertown, S.Dak. 57201. Mailing Add: 320 Seventh Ave. S.E, Watertown, S.Dak. 57201.

BARTUNEK, ALLEN JOHN R
Ohio State Rep.
b. Cleveland, Ohio, 6/12/28; s. Clarence Joseph Bartunek and Leona Fricker B; m. 4/23/61 to Susan King Bates; c. Kathryn and Nancy. Educ: Brown Univ, B.A, 52; Boston Univ. Sch. of Law, 52-54; West. Reserve Univ. Sch. of Law, LL.B, 55; Delta Tau Delta; Phi Delta Phi. Polit. & Govt. Pos: V.pres, Polit. Action Cmt. of Gr. Cleveland Young Rep, 62-63; asst. state attorney gen, Ohio, 63-66; Ohio State Rep, 67- Bus. & Prof. Pos: Assoc, Law Firm of Ziegler, Graham & Metzger, Cleveland, 66- Mem: Bd. of dirs, Glenville Neighborhood Commun. Center; Citizens League; Commun. Planning and Develop. Div, Welfare Fedn; Ohio and Cleveland Bar Asns; Urban League of Cleveland; YMCA. Rel: Protestant. Legal Res: 3367 Ormond Rd, Cleveland Heights, Ohio 44118. Mailing Add: 1670 Union Commerce Bldg, Cleveland, Ohio 44115.

BARTUNEK, JOSEPH W. D
b. Cleveland, Ohio, 2/16/24; s. Otto J. Bartunek and Anna Hlavin B; m. 1/15/45 to Pauline Evans; c. Kenneth, Roderick, Deborah and Donna. Educ: Adelbert Col, West. Reserve Univ, B.S, 48; Cleveland Marshall Law Sch, LL.B, 55; Alpha Delta Phi; Delta Theta Phi. Polit. & Govt. Pos: Ohio State Sen, 49-58 & 61-64, minority leader, Ohio State Senate, 51-58, clerk, 59-60; mem, Co. Charter Cmn, 59-60; precinct committeeman; v.chmn, Cuyahoga Co. Dem. Party, Ohio; del, Dem. Nat. Conv, 64; judge, Probate Court, Cuyahoga Co, Ohio 65- Bus. & Prof. Pos: Partner, law firm of Bartunek, Krenzler, Williams & Welf, 60-64; instr, West. Reserve Univ. Law Sch, 65- Mil. Serv: Entered as Pvt, Army, 43, released as T/Sgt, 46, after serv. in Med. Corps, Am. Theater. Mem: Am, Ohio, Cuyahoga Co. and Cleveland Bar Asns; Ohio Asn. of Probate Judges; bd. of trustees, St. Luke's Hosp, Cleveland State Univ, Cleveland Zool. Soc, Cleveland Community Chest and Cleveland Hosp. Coun; Hudson Asn; Cleveland Ment. Health Asn; Citizens League; Parent's Volunteer Asn. for Retarded Children; Cleveland Athletic Club; Columbus Athletic Club; Hermit Club; Canterbury Golf Club. Rel: Roman Catholic. Mailing Add: 2463 Snowberry Lane, Pepper Pike, Ohio 44124.

BASBAS, MONTE GEORGE R
Mayor, Newton, Mass.
b. Manchester, N.H, 5/6/21; s. George Basbas and Rose Economou B; m. 1/10/48 to Audrey Ann Vagiates; c. John T, Monte G, Jr. and Audrey Ann. Educ: Dartmouth Col, A.B. in Govt, 44; Boston Univ. Law Sch, LL.B, 49; Phi Delta Phi; Chi Phi. Polit. & Govt. Pos: Asst. city clerk, Newton, Mass, 51-53, city clerk, workmen's compensation agent, clerk, Bd. of Aldermen and chmn, Elec. Cmn, 53-, mayor, 66-; mem, State Hwy. Study Cmn, Munic. Probs. Cmn, Munic. Police Training Coun, Gov. Cmt. on Law Enforcement and Admin. of Criminal Justice, Gov. Adv. Cmt, Dept. of Commun. Affairs, chmn, The Select Cmt. of One Hundred of Mass. Coun. on Crime and Correction and mem, Attorney Gen. Adv. Cmt. on Conflict of Interest. Bus. & Prof. Pos: Attorney-at-law, 49- Mil. Serv: Entered as Aviation Cadet, Army Air Force, 42, released as Capt, 45, after serv. in 25th Photo Reconnaissance Squadron, S.Pac; Air Medal with Clusters; Distinguished Flying Cross; Seven Battle Stars; Capt, Air Force Res, Judge Adv. Gen. Dept. Mem: N.H. and Mass. Fed. Bars; Boston Bar Asn; Waltham, Watertown, Weston and Newton Bar Asns; Mass. City Clerks Asn. (past pres); Int. City Clerks Asn; dir, Garden City Trust Co. and Newton S. Coop. Bank; chmn, Newton Highlands Adv. Gifts and munic. chmn, United Fund; indust. chmn, Salvation Army; gen. chmn, Newton Citizens Oral Polio Immunization Cmt; Newton gen. chmn, Retarded Children Drive, 62 & 63; Action for Ment. Health in Newton (v.pres); v.chmn, Newton Halloween Parties; campaign chmn, Medic Alert, Newton; area chmn, Cancer Drive; dir, Newton Tuberc. and Health Asn; bd. dirs, Hellenic Col, Mass. Safety Coun, B.U. Law Sch. Alumni Asn. and Parker Hill Med. Center; Norumbega Coun. Boy Scouts (exec. bd); past comdr, Am. Legion Post 48; VFW; Elks; past master, BU Lodge, AF&AM; Langley Breakfast Club. Rel: Protestant. Legal Res: 178 Kirkstall Rd, Newtonville, Mass. 02160. Mailing Add: Newton City Hall, 1000 Commonwealth Ave, Newton Centre, Mass. 02159.

BASFORD, BILL D
b. Jacksonville, Fla, 8/28/30; m. to Patricia Credle; c. Michael and Jeffrey. Educ; Univ. Fla, B.S, B.A, 55, LL.B, 58; pres, Fla. Blue Key; Univ. Fla. Hall of Fame; secy-treas, Student Body; Alpha Gamma Rho. Polit. & Govt. Pos: Fla. State Rep, 63-65; mem, Duval Co. Cmn, 67-68, chmn, 68; mem, Jacksonville City Coun, 68; nat. chmn. air and water pollution cmt, Nat. Asn. Co, 68; pres, Jax Charities Inc. Bus. & Prof. Pos: Attorney. Mil. Serv: Navy, 47-49 and 50-52; Lt.(jg), Intel, Naval Res. Mem: Mason; Shrine; Jaycees; Little League; Quarterback Club; YMCA. Rel: Episcopal. Mailing Add: 7144 Jubal Lane, Jacksonville, Fla. 32210.

BASGALL, WENDELIN E. D
Kans. State Rep.
b. Pfeifer, Kans, 12/3/07; s. Martin E. Basgall (deceased) and Anna Mary Burgardt B; m. 11/27/33 to Julitta Kuhn; c. Rita M. (Mrs. Harold L. Birzer) wid. Educ: LaSalle Exten, Chicago, Ill, Correspondence Course; Univ. Wis, Madison, grad, Sch. of Banking, 58. Polit. & Govt. Pos: With Agr. Adjust. Agency, U.S. Dept. Agr, Wash. D.C, 33-39; dep. co. treas, Ellis Co, Kans, 39-43, co. treas, 43-47; Kans. State Rep, 111th Dist, Ellis Co, 67- Bus. & Prof. Pos: Teacher, Ellis Co, Kans, 28-32; cashier, Farmers State Bank, Hays, 47-63, Hays Nat. Bank, 64-66. Mem: City Planning Cmn, Hays, Kans; lay adv. bd, St. Anthony Hosp, secy. and treas, St. Anthony Hosp. Bldg. Found; bd. dirs, Hays C. of C; Lions; K. of C. Rel: Catholic. Mailing Add: 415 E. 14th St, Hays, Kans. 67601.

BASILE, JAMES CHARLES D
b. Pa, 6/10/25; s. James Basile (deceased) and Mary Spolidore B. (deceased); single. Educ: Univ. Calif, Berkeley, A.A. and B.A. cum laude, 51, LL.B, 55; Phi Alpha Delta. Polit. & Govt. Pos: Asst. dist. attorney and dep. dist. attorney, Ventura Co, Calif, 56-62; treas, Ventura Co. Cmt. to Re-Elect Gov. Brown, 62 and chmn, Cmt. to Elect President Johnson, 64; rep, 37th Assembly Dist, Calif. Dem. Coun, 62-64; chmn, 13th Cong. Dist. Dem. Coun, 64; v.chmn, Ventura Co. Dem. Cent. Cmt, 64-66; dist. counsel, Fairview Co. Water Dist, 64-; mem, Calif. State Dem. Cent. Cmt, 66-68. Mem: Ventura Co. Bar Asn. (secy-treas, 61, trustee, 62-64 & 69- and state bar del, 64-68); mem. credentials cmt, State of Calif. Bar Conf, 65; Am. Bar Asn; State Bar of Calif; Am. Arbitration Asn; Am. Trial Lawyers Asn; Ventura Co. Coun. Boy Scouts; Ventura Co. Forum Arts. Rel: Catholic. Legal Res: 1111 Black Canyon Rd, Santa Susana, Calif. 93063. Mailing Add: 1197 Los Angeles Ave, Simi, Calif. 93065.

BASKIN, GORDON D
b. Albany, N.Y, 2/10/24; s. Harry Baskin and Anna Silberg B; m. 1/2/66 to Adriana Van Dun; c. Betty, Kim, Paula, Mark and Philip. Educ: State Teachers Col, Albany, N.Y, 41-42; Univ. Calif, Los Angeles, B.S. in econs. & bus. admin, 48; Freshman Debate Team; Assoc. Ed, Col. Newspaper; Freshman Class Treas. Polit. & Govt. Pos: Mem; Small Bus. Admin. Adv. Coun, Calif, 64-66, Calif. State Finance Cmt, 63-66; Presidents Club, 64-65; chmn, Sub Cmt. on Banking & Finance, Western States Dem. Conf, 63-65; alternate del, Nat. Conv, 64. Bus. & Prof. Pos: Pres. & bd. chmn, Continental Bank, Los Angeles, Calif, 61-65. Mil. Serv: Entered as Pvt, Air Force, 42, released as Pfc, 46, after serv. in U.S. Mem: Bd. of Dir, Op.5, Calif. Bankers Asn; Bd. of Dir, Vista Del Mar Child Health Center; Bd. of Dir, W. Hollywood C. of C; Beverly Hills Stock Exchange Club. Rel: Jewish. Mailing Add: 3437 Serra Rd, Malibu, Calif. 90265. (1967)

BASMAJIAN, WALTER D
Chmn, St. Lawrence Co. Dem. Party, N.Y.
b. Massena, N.Y, 7/22/22; s. John Basmajian and Virginia Bochalian B; m. 12/26/49 to Marie Billingham; c. David W. and Gina Marie. Educ: Cent. City Bus. Inst, 41-42. Polit. & Govt. Pos: Bldg. and zoning inspector, Massena, N.Y, 56-67; chmn, Massena Dem. Cmt, 56-; del, Dem. State Conv, 58-62; del, Dem. Nat. Conv, 64 & 68; first v.chmn, St. Lawrence Co. Dem. Party, chmn, 68- Bus. & Prof. Pos: Secy. and pres, Massena Bd. Trade, 47-48; asst. mgr, Seaway Int. Bridge Corp, Ltd, 62-65; broker, Basmajian Real Estate, N.Y. and chmn, Massena Neighborhood Center, currently. Mil. Serv: Entered as Pvt, Army, 43, released as T/5, 46, after serv. in 9th Army, 4th Signal Corps, 13th Army Corps, ETO, 44-46; Rhineland-Cent. European and African-Middle East. Theater Campaign Medals; Good Conduct Medal; Victory Medal; Signal Corps, Army Res, 42-43. Mem: Dir, St. Lawrence Co. United Fund, 63-64; pres, Am-Armenian Commun. Center, 63-64; dir, Massena C. of C, 48-66; pres, 64-65; dir, St. Lawrence Co. Commun. Develop. Prog, Inc, 65-; pres, Massena Mourad A.R.F. Club, 62-65; pres, St. Lawrence Co. Real Estate Bd, 66-; Am. Legion; VFW; Moose; F&AM; Lions; hon. mem, Massena Rescue Squad. Rel: Protestant. Legal Res: 10 Sherwood Dr, Massena, N.Y. 13662. Mailing Add: 182 Main St, Massena, N.Y. 13662.

BASON, SAMUEL MURPHEY D
b. Swepsonville, N.C, 12/3/94; s. William Henry Bason and Flora Green Murphey B; m. 10/18/21 to Martha E. Hatchett; c. Carolyn Elizabeth, William Hatchett and Mrs. John J. Burke. Educ: Univ. N.C. Polit. & Govt. Pos: Mem, State Hwy. Cmn, N.C, 37-41 and N.C. Gasoline and Oil Inspection Bd, 42-45; N.C. State Sen, 47-66. Bus. & Prof. Pos: Pres, Bank of Yanceyville, N.C; owner, Caswell Ins. & Realty Co; pres, Caswell Hardware and Implement Co. Mil. Serv: World War I, 22 months, discharged as Color Sgt. Mem: Yanceyville Rotary Club; Caswell Brotherhood Lodge No. 11, AF&AM, Master, 25, 27, 33; bd. dirs, N.C. R.R, 56-57; first pres, Caswell Co. C. of C, 26. Rel: Presbyterian; chmn, Bd. of Deacons, 25-45; supt, Sunday Sch, 35-43. Mailing Add: Yanceyville, N.C. 27379. (1967)

BASS, BOB D
b. Hutchins, Tex, 9/16/21; s. Allie Bass and Stella Smith B; m. 9/28/40 to Joann Sheppard; c. Portia (Mrs. Davis), Penny (Mrs. Kerr) and Pam. Educ: N.Tex. Agr. Col. Polit. & Govt. Pos: Tex. State Rep, 61-68; v.chmn, Textbook Invest. Cmt, 61, mem, Banks and Banking Claims and Accounts, Motor Traffic, Conserv. and Reclamation and Livestock and Stockraising Cmts, 64-65 and chmn, Cmt. to Study Probs. of Deaf and Hard of Hearing, 66. Bus. & Prof. Pos: Businessman and rancher. Mem: Lions; Wildlife Asn; Farm Bur; Texarkana Little Theater. Rel: Baptist. Mailing Add: R.R. 1, De Kalb, Tex. 75559. (1967)

BASS, HARVEY LEE D
Chmn, Bailey Co. Dem. Party, Tex.
b. Anson, Tex, 10/11/18; s. Henry Isom Bass and Mary Evaline Jones B; m. 7/24/46 to Willie Marie Bingham; c. Carolia Marie and Vina Jeanette. Educ: Meadow High, Meadow, Tex; correspondence course, Univ. Tex. Polit. & Govt. Pos: Chmn, Bailey Co. Dem. Party, Tex, 56- Bus. & Prof. Pos: Co-owner and ed, Aspermont Star, Tex, 46-47; chmn, retail activities, C. of C, 66, chmn. bus. activities cmt. bd, 68-70; West Plains Mus. Bd. and West Plains Memorial Hosp. Bd, 68- Publ: Primitive Baptist Doctrine: Banner of Love, 48. Mem: Rotary (former dir. and commun. serv. chmn, v.pres. currently). Man of Year. Rel: Primitive Baptist. Legal Res: 1903 Ave. D, Muleshoe, Tex. 79347. Mailing Add: P.O. Box 488, Muleshoe, Tex. 79347.

BASS, HERBERT EDWARD R
Chmn, Chowan Co. Rep. Exec. Cmt, N.C.
b. Edenton, N.C, 2/19/20; s. Herbert V. Bass and Artie White B; m. 11/22/44 to Lola Allan; c. William E, James H. and Robert L. Educ: U.S. Air Force Inst. of Tech; U.S. Air Force Command & Staff Sch; Debating Soc. Polit. & Govt. Pos: Chmn, Chowan Co. Rep. Exec. Cmt, N.C, 64- Bus. & Prof. Pos: Partner, Bass Bros. Sunoco Sta, 62-65. Mil. Serv: Entered as Pvt, Army, 40, released as Lt. Col.(Ret), Air Force, 62, after serv. in Asiatic Pac. Theater and Korea; Soldiers Medal; Bronze Star; Commendation Ribbon; Am. and Asiatic Pac. Theater Ribbons; Am. Defense and Victory Medals; Korean Serv. Medal; UN Serv. Ribbon; Japanese Occup. Medal; Nat. Defense Serv. Ribbon; Guided Missile Insignia. Mem: Rotary; VFW (comdr. Post 9280, 68-69); Boy Scouts; C. of C. Hobbies: High sch. football and baseball; Silver Beaver Award, Boy Scouts. Rel: Baptist. Mailing Add: W. Queen St. Extended, P.O. Box 175, Edenton, N.C. 27932.

BASS, PERKINS R
b. E. Walpole, Mass, 10/6/12; s. Robert Perkins Bass and Edith Bird B; m. 6/6/41 to Katharine Jackson; c. Alexander, Katharine, William J, Charles F. Roberta. Educ: Dartmouth, B.A, 34; Harvard, LL.B, 38. Polit. & Govt. Pos: N.H. State Rep, 39-43 & 47-49; pres, N.H. State Senate, 49-51; U.S. Rep. N.H. 84th-87th Cong; Rep. Nat. Cmt. Mem. from N.H, 64-68. Bus. & Prof. Pos: Lawyer; dir, mem. exec. cmn, Bird & Son, Inc; trustee, N.H. Savings Bank, Concord, N.H; mem. firm, Sheehan Phinney, Bass and Green, 46- Mem: SAR; Am. Legion; VFW; Mason. Legal Res: Peterborough, N.H. 03101. Mailing Add: Office, 875 Elm St, Manchester, N.H. 03458.

BASS, ROBERT P, JR. R
Chmn, N.H. Rep. State Cmt.
b. Peterborough, N.H, 9/23/23; s. Robert P. Bass and Edith H. Bird B; m. 9/10/55 to Patricia May; c. Timothy P. and Kate P. Educ: Harvard Col, B.A, 48, Law School, LL.B. 51. Polit. & Govt. Pos: Finance chmn, N.H. Rep. State Cmt, 67-68, chmn, 69- Bus. & Prof. Pos: Partner Cleveland, Waters & Bass, Lawyers, Concord, N.H, 60-; Dir. & Mem. Exec. Comm. Bird & Son, Inc, East Walpole, Mass. 62- Mil. Serv: Entered as Pvt. Army, 42, released as 1st Lt. on 46 after serving in 25th Infantry Div, Far East Theatre, 45-46. Mem: Council on Foreign Relations; trustee, Franklin Pierce Col, 66- Rel: Protestant. Legal Res: Hopkinton, N.H. 03301. Mailing Add: 16 Centre St, Concord, N.H. 03301.

BASS, ROSS D
U.S. Sen, Tenn.
b. Giles Co, Tenn, 3/17/18; s. W.A. Bass (deceased) and Ethel Shook B; m. to Avanell Keith, div. Educ: Martin Col, Tenn. Polit. & Govt. Pos: Postmaster, Pulaski, Tenn, 48-54; U.S. Rep, Tenn, 54-64; U.S. Sen, Tenn, 64- Bus. & Prof. Pos: Owner, Ross Bass Assocs, Wash, D.C, 67-; chmn. of bd, Pet-Mart, Springfield, Va, 69- Mil. Serv: Entered as Pvt, Army Air Corps, released as Capt, after serv. in Eighth Air Force, ETO. Mem: Tenn. Asn. of Postmasters (pres); C. of C; Am. Legion; VFW; Elks; LaGorce Country Club, Miami, Fla; Burning Tree Club, Bethesda, Md. Rel: Methodist. Legal Res: East Jefferson St, Pulaski, Tenn. 38478. Mailing Add: 1120 Connecticut Ave. N.W, Washington, D.C. 20036.

BASS, THOMAS HUTCHESON 'TOM' D
Tex. State Rep.
b. Houston, Tex, 1/11/27; s. T.H. Bass and Mary Lee Scoggins B; m. 9/2/50 to Mary Ann King; c. Patricia Marie, Martin Gerard, Paul Joseph, Rita Ann, Amy Louise, Mary Victoria, Robert Allen, Daniel Thomas, Laura Ellen and David Samuel. Educ: Univ. Tex, B.A, 50; Univ. Houston, M.Ed, 54 and cand. Ed.D. at present; Phi Delta Kappa; Kappa Delta Pi; Newman Club. Polit. & Govt. Pos: Tex. State Rep, Harris Co, 62-; chmn, Harris Co. Del. and chmn, Interim Activities Cmt, Tex. State House of Rep, currently. Bus. & Prof. Pos: Asst. mgr. and mgr, West. Auto Supply Co, 51-52; teacher, Houston Independent Sch. Dist, 52-60; assoc. prof, Dominican Col, 60-68; part time instr, Tex. South. Univ, 60-; asst. prof, Univ. of St. Thomas, 68- Mil. Serv: Entered as Pvt, Army, 45, released as Cpl, 47, after serv. in 319th Combat Group in U.S; Lt. Col, Army Res, 63-; Good Conduct Medal; Am. Theater Medal; Victory Medal. Mem: ROA; Am. Asn. Univ. Prof; Am. Polit. Sci. Asn; secy. adv. cmt. on hist, Nat. Cath. Educ. Asn; mem. supv. cmt, Houston Teacher Credit Union, 64- Rel: Catholic. Mailing Add: 3437 N. Parkwood, Houston, Tex. 77021.

BASSETT, CLEMENT R. D
Cmnr, Dept. of Employ. Security
b. Welch, W.Va, 3/15/21; s. Eli A. Bassett and Najla Khoury B; m. to Mary Elizabeth Peak; c. Mary Anne and Margaret Lucile. Educ: W.Va. Univ, A.B, 41; Univ. Mich. Law Sch, LL.B, 48; Kappa Sigma; Phi Beta Kappa; Phi Alpha Delta. Polit. & Govt. Pos: Attorney exam. with the Fed. Trade Cmn, Chicago, Ill, 48-53; trial exam. with the Pub. Serv. Cmn, 54-57; asst. attorney gen, W.Va, 57-61; dir. of Employ. Security, 61-65; cmnr, Dept. of Employ. Security, 65- Mil. Serv: Army Air Force, 42-45; Maj, Air Force Res. Mem: W.Va. State Bar; Mason; Scottish Rite Bodies; Shrine; A.L. Rel: Presbyterian. Mailing Add: State Office Bldg. 2, 112 California Ave, Charleston, W.Va. 25305. (1967)

BASSETT, LEE GARDNER D
Ala. State Rep.
b. Troy, Ala, 6/10/00; s. John H. Bassett and Sarah Ellafair Meredith B; m.

to Gennie Mozell; c. Ruth Ferry (Mrs. H.R. Collins). Polit. & Govt. Pos: Mem. bd. cmnrs, Pike Co, Ala, 34; Ala. State Rep, 55- Bus. & Prof. Pos: Merchant; farmer. Mem: Mason. Rel: Missionary Baptist. Mailing Add: 206 Orange St, Troy, Ala. 36081. (1967)

BASSMAN, C. M. R
Mo. State Rep.
b. Tuscumbia, Mo, 4/7/04; m. 10/8/28 to Mary Elizabeth Williams. Educ: St. Louis Univ, Mo. Polit. & Govt. Pos: Mo. State Rep, 62-, asst. minority leader, Mo. House of Rep, 69- Bus. & Prof. Pos: Clerk, U.S. Post Office, Union, Mo, 25-34; owner and operator of the Hermo Theatre, 34-39; West. Auto Store, 40-59 and Cap Bassman Elec. Contractor, 59-63. Mil. Serv: Corps Engrs; instr, Air Force Tech. Training Command. Mem: Mason; past pres. Hermann C. of C; Lions; Hermann Indust. Develop. Corp; Hermann Libr. Asn; Eagles; Hermann Sharpshooters; Historic Hermann; Exten. Coun, Mo. Univ. Sr. Citizen Award, Hermann Jaycees, 62. Rel: United Church of Christ. Mailing Add: Ninth and Gutenberg, Hermann, Mo. 65041.

BASSO, ROMEO JAMES R
Mem, Ill. Rep. Cent. Cmt.
b. Athens, Ill, 7/11/05; s. John B. Basso and Mary M. Eastin B; div. Educ: High Sch, Athens, Ill, 12 years. Polit. & Govt. Pos: Supported all Rep. cand. throughout Menard Co, Ill, 30-; campaign mgr. for Joseph Meek, 54; mem. adv. bd. for Paul Findley; Rep. precinct committeeman, Menard Co, 64-66; assisted campaign mgrs. for Rep. Robert Michel, 64-68, Rep. William K. Cavanagh, and Gov. Richard B. Ogilvie, Menard Co, 68; mem, Ill. Rep. Cent. Cmt, 66- Bus. & Prof. Pos: Owner, restaurant and tavern, 05- Mem: K. of C. Moose. Rel: Catholic. Legal Res: S. Main, Athens, Ill. 62613. Mailing Add: P.O. Box 133, Athens, Ill. 62613.

BASTIEN, THOMAS D
Colo. State Rep.
b. Denver, Colo, 1/25/37; m; c. 4. Polit. & Govt. Pos: Former Dem. committeeman and capt; Colo. State Rep, currently; mem. Joint Budget Cmt, currently. Mailing Add: 2310 Hudson St, Denver, Colo. 80207.

BASTOVICH, JOHN DFL
Educ: Univ. Minn, B.S. and M.A; Fulbright Grant to India, 64. Polit. & Govt. Pos: Chmn, Anoka Co. Sheriff's Civil Serv. Cmn; mem, Gov. Adv. Coun. on Children and Youth; Minn. State Rep, 67-68. Bus. & Prof. Pos: Instr. soc. studies, Edison High Sch, Minneapolis, Minn. Mil. Serv: Army, 2 years. Mailing Add: 4135 Jefferson St. N.E, Columbia Heights, Minn. 55421. (1967)

BATCHELDER, ANNE STUART R
Nat. Rep. Committeewoman, Nebr.
b. Lake Forest, Ill, 1/11/20; d. R. Douglas Stuart and Harriet McClure S; m. 5/26/45 to Clifton Brooks Batchelder; c. Edward, Lucia, Anne and Mary. Educ: Lake Forest Col, 41-43. Polit. & Govt. Pos: Mem, Douglas Co. Rep. Cent. Cmt, 56-60; mem, Nebr. State Rep. Cent. Cmt, 56-62; mem, Douglas Co. Finance Cmt, 56-63; mem, Nebr. State Rep. Party Finance Cmt, 56-66; pres, Omaha Women Rep. Club, 59-; state v.chmn, Nebr. Rep. Party, 59-64; Nat. Rep. Committeewoman, Nebr, 64- Bus. & Prof. Pos: Dir, U.S. Check Book, 60- Mil. Serv: Am. Red Cross, ETO, 43-45. Mem: PEO; Colonial Dames. Rel: Presbyterian. Mailing Add: 6875 State St, Omaha, Nebr. 68152.

BATCHELDER, MERTON K. R
Chmn, Rep. Town Cmt, Conway, Mass.
b. Conway, Mass, 5/19/21; s. Carlos F. Batchelder and Lillian Schneck B; m. 9/17/55 to Eleanor A. Sears; c. William K. and Edward D. Educ: Arms Acad, 39. Polit. & Govt. Pos: Mem. finance cmt, Conway, Mass, 55-60, selectman, 60-63; del, Mass. Rep. State Conv, 60-66; chmn, Rep. Town Cmt, Conway, currently, moderator, 65- Bus. & Prof. Pos: Agent, Union Nat. Bank, New Eng. and New York and wholesale distributor, Dairy Equip, 56-66. Mem: Morning Sun Lodge; Mason; Commun. Develop. Orgn. Rel: Protestant. Mailing Add: New Hall Rd, Conway, Mass. 01341. (1967)

BATCHELDER, WILLIAM GEORGE R
Ohio State Rep.
b. Medina, Ohio, 12/19/42; s. William George Batchelder, Jr. and Eleanor Dice B; m. 8/13/66 to Alice Moore. Educ: Ohio Wesleyan Univ, B.A, 64; Ohio State Univ. Col. Law, J.D, 67; Omicron Delta Kappa; Phi Alpha Theta; Delta Sigma Rho. Polit. & Govt. Pos: Admin. aide to Lt. Gov. John W. Brown, Ohio, 67; Ohio State Rep, 23rd Dist, 69- Bus. & Prof. Pos: Assoc. attorney, Williams & Batchelder, Medina, 67- Mil. Serv: Entered as Pvt, Army, 68, released as Pfc, 68, after serv. in Hq, Third Army, Judge Adv. Gen. Off, 68. Mem: Medina Co, Ohio and Am. Bar Asns; F&AM; Royal Arch Mason; Jaycees; Young Rep; Am. Legion; Farm Bur; Medina Co. and Ashland Co. Asns. of Twp. Trustees and Clerks. Rel: Episcopal. Legal Res: 446 E. Washington St, Medina, Ohio 44256. Mailing Add: P.O. Box 394, Medina, Ohio 44256.

BATCHELET, WILLIS K. R
Polit. & Govt. Pos: Ind. State Sen, 49-67; City Attorney, Angola, Ind, 30-55; Town Attorney, Fremont. Bus. & Prof. Pos: Attorney. Mem: Charter mem, Angola Lions Club; Past Dir, 4-H Club, Steuben Co; Steuben Co. Bar Asn; Odd Fellows; Masons; Shrine, Scottish Rite of Ft. Wayne; Alpha Sigma Phi. Rel: Pleasant View Church of Christ. Mailing Add: RR 1, Fremont, Ind. 46737. (1967)

BATCHELOR, NORMAN FREDERICK R
Chmn, Orange Rep. Town Cmt, Mass.
b. Orange, Mass, 5/8/22; s. Frederick George Batchelor (deceased) and Emily Tortensen B; m. 2/3/47 to Carolyn Marie Venette. Educ: St. Petersburg, Fla. High Sch, grad, 40. Polit. & Govt. Pos: Selectman, Orange, Mass, 55-58, mem. sch. cmt, 60-65; dep. sheriff, Franklin Co, 61-; chmn, Orange Rep. Town Cmt, Mass, 61- Bus. & Prof. Pos: Trustee, Orange Savings Bank, Mass, 60-; dir, Franklin Co. Trust Co, Greenfield, Mass, 64- Mil. Serv: Entered as Pvt, Air Force, 43, released as Cpl, 45, after serv. in 487th Bomb Group, ETO, 44-45; Am. Theatre Ribbon, Europe-Africa-Middle East Ribbon; Good Conduct Medal; World War II Victory Medal. Mem: Am. Legion; Kiwanis (past pres). Rel: Protestant. Legal Res: 40 Wheeler Ave, Orange, Mass. 01364. Mailing Add: P.O. Box 147, Orange, Mass. 01364.

BATEMAN, FRED W. D
b. Roper, N.C, 9/18/16; s. Nicodemus Bateman and Eloise Tarkenton B; m. 6/12/44 to Frances Marie Sondag; c. Michael Stuart. Educ: Wake Forest Col, B.A, 39; Univ. N.C. Law Sch, 39-42; Gamma Eta Gamma. Polit. & Govt. Pos: Chmn, Newport News Electoral Bd, Va, 56-59; Va. State Sen, 60-68; mem, Jamestown Cmn, 60-69; chmn, Jefferson-Jackson Day, 64; mem, Magna Carta Cmn, 64- Bus. & Prof. Pos: Admitted to practice State and Fed. Courts, Ill. and Va. Mil. Serv: Entered as Seaman, Navy Res, released as Lt.(jg), 46; Comdr.(Ret), 64; U.S. and Pac. Theater Ribbons. Publ: 'Our Professional Responsibility with Respect to Economics,' Tenn. Law Rev, spring 64. Mem: Va. State Bar Asn; pres, Va. State Bar, 64-65, New Newport News Bar Asn, 64; past pres, Asn. Am. Bar Asn, 64-; Va. and Am. Trial Lawyers Asn, 60-; Va. State Bar Coun, 59-64; AF&AM; Mason (32°); past lt. gov, Ruritan Nat; Kiwanis; Elks; Downtown Club, Richmond; James River Country Club. Rel: Baptist. Mailing Add: 23 Cedar Lane, Newport News, Va. 23601.

BATEMAN, HERBERT HARVELL D
Va. State Sen.
b. Elizabeth City, N.C, 8/7/28; s. Elbert E. Bateman and Edna Buffkin B; m. 5/29/54 to Laura Ann Yacobi; c. Herbert H, Jr. and Laura Margaret. Educ: Col. of William & Mary, B.A, 49; Georgetown Univ. Law Center, LL.B, 56; Omicron Delta Kappa; Pi Kappa Alpha. Polit. & Govt. Pos: Va. State Sen, 68-; mem, Peninsula Ports Authority Va, 68-, Study Cmn. Va. Judicial Syst, 68- and Study Cmn. Pub. Sch. Fund Allocation Formula, 68- Bus. & Prof. Pos: Partner, Jones, Blechman, Woltz and Kelly, Attorneys-at-law, 64- Mil. Serv: Entered as Airman, Air Force, 51, released as 1st Lt, 53, after serv in Off. Spec. Invest. Mem: Am. Judicature Soc; Am, Va. and Newport News Bar Asns; Am. Legion; Torch Club of Hampton Roads; U.S. Jr. C. of C.(past gen. legal counsel); Va. Jr. C. of C.(past pres). Distinguished Serv. Award, Hampton Roads Jaycees. Rel: Protestant. Legal Res: 223 Shoe Lane, Newport News, Va. 23609. Mailing Add: P.O. Box 78, Newport News, Va. 23607.

BATEMAN, OLIVER CROMWELL R
Minority Leader, Ga. State Senate
b. Macon, Ga, 8/29/23; s. Dewey Cromwell Bateman and Edna Watson B; m. 12/29/67 to Mary Jane Gosline; c. Bryan Malone. Educ: Citadel, B.S, 48; Harvard Bus. Sch, M.B.A, 50. Polit. & Govt. Pos: Ga. State Sen, 55-, minority leader, Ga. State Senate, 64-; del, Rep. Nat. Conv, 68. Bus. & Prof. Pos: V.pres, Bateman and Co, 60; sales mgr, Inland Container, 54. Mil. Serv: Entered as Pvt, Air Force, 42, released as 1st Lt, 46, after serv. in 14th Air Force, China-Burma-India; recalled as 1st Lt, 51-53. Mem: Rotary; Am. Legion. Rel: Presbyterian. Mailing Add: 247 Candler Dr, Macon, Ga. 31204.

BATEMAN, RAYMOND HENRY R
N.J. State Sen.
b. Somerville, N.J, 10/29/27; s. Charles Palmer Bateman, Sr. and Lydia Coene B; m. 10/10/53 to Joan Speer; c. Caren Palmer, Raymond, Jr. and Christopher Speer. Educ: Wesleyan Univ, B.A, 50; Woodrow Wilson Sch. of Pub. & Int. Affairs, Princeton, grad. work, 50-51; Delta Kappa Epsilon. Polit. & Govt. Pos: N.J. State Assemblyman, Somerset Co, 58-68, Asst. Majority Leader, N.J. State Assembly, 64, Majority Leader, 64-68; mem. bd, Eagleton Inst. Seminar for Young Legislators, 66; del, Rep. Nat. Conv, 68; N.J. State Sen, 68-, Majority Leader, N.J. State Senate, 69- Bus. & Prof. Pos: Pres, Bateman & Assocs, Pub. Rels. & Advert, 58-; pres, Midland Sch. for Brain Injured Children; mem. bd, Somerset Trust Co, Somerset Press, Inc. and Cent. Jersey Press, Inc. Mil. Serv: Entered as Pvt, Army, 46, released S/Sgt, 47, after serv. in 8th Army, Japan. Publ: 'How to Lose an Election,' N.Y. Times Mag, 10/62. Mem: Bd, Somerset Valley YMCA. Rel: Dutch Reformed. Mailing Add: R.D. 3, Somerville, N.J. 08876.

BATES, OREN WARNER R
b. Sherburne, Vt, 7/3/12; m. to Helen Scruton; c. One son and four daughters. Educ: Vt. Sch. of Agr. Polit. & Govt. Pos: Past v.pres. and pres, fire dept; town auditor and agent, sch. dir, fire chief, road cmnr, health officer, justice of the peace, cemetary cmnr. and spec. dep. sheriff; Vt. State Rep, 51-67. Bus. & Prof. Pos: Gen. construction, sand and gravel; owner and operator of sch. bus. Mem: Grange; several fish and game clubs; Farm Bur; Vt. State Firefighters Asn; pres, Alumni Asn, Vt. State Agr. and Tech. Sch. Rel: Episcopal. Mailing Add: P.O. Box 42, Killington, Vt. 05751. (1967)

BATESON, CORNELIUS CHARLES D
Ins. Cmnr, Ore.
b. Portland, Ore, 3/11/30; s. Cornelius Bateson and Mildred Gilbert B; m. 6/16/51 to Janis Carlsen; c. Charles Michael, Allen Thomas and Sarah Ann. Educ: Stanford Univ, B.A, 51. Polit. & Govt. Pos: Chmn, Marion Co. Dem. Cent. Cmt, Ore, 56-58; Ore. State Rep, 61-67; Ore. State Sen, 67-69; del, Dem. Nat. Conv, 68; Ins. Cmnr, Ore, currently. Bus. & Prof. Pos: Farmer, 54-; dir, Ore. Wash. Fruit & Vegetable Growers, 61-68; pres, Blue Lake Packers Inc, 64-67; dir, Ore. Agri-Bus. Coun, 66- Mil. Serv: Entered as 2nd Lt, Marine Corps, 51, released as Capt, 54, after serv. in Third Marine Div, U.S. and Japan, 51-54. Mem: Ore. Hort. Soc.(past pres); Elks; Rotary (past pres); Farm Bur; Grange; Farmers Union; C. of C. Outstanding Young Farmer, Ore. Jaycees, 60. Rel: Congregational. Mailing Add: 9374 Sunnyview Rd. N.E, Salem, Ore. 97301.

BATJER, CAMERON McVICAR R
Justice, Nev. Supreme Court
b. Smith, Nev, 8/24/19; s. Robert W. Batjer and Mary Belle McVicar B; m. 5/16/42 to Lura Gamble; c. Lura, Christina and Marybel. Educ: Univ. Nev, B.A, 41; Univ. Utah, J.D, 50; Phi Alpha Delta; Lambda Chi Alpha. Polit. & Govt. Pos: Dist. attorney, Ormsby Co, Nev, 54-60; city attorney, Carson City, Nev, 54-60, Justice, Nev. Supreme Court, 67- Mil. Serv: Entered as Seaman 2/C, Navy, 42, released as Lt.(jg), 45, after serv. in S.Pac, 43-44; Naval Res, Lt.(Ret). Mem: Am, Utah and Nev. Bar Asns; mem. bd. of gov, Nev. State Bar, 64-67; Am. Judicature Soc; Elks; Rotary; Am. Legion; Int. Footprinters Asn. Rel: Presbyterian. Mailing Add: 7 Circle Dr, Carson City, Nev. 89701.

BATLLE, JOSEFINA OJEDA D
b. Fajardo, P.R, 6/1/10; d. Juan Ojeda and Baudilia Treviño O; m. 6/1/28 to Salvador Batlle; c. Josefina, Carmen, Salvador, Teresita, José Agustin and Jorge Fernando. Educ: Univ. P.R, grad. Polit. & Govt. Pos: Mem, bd. cmnrs,

San Juan, P.R, 48-52, v.pres, city coun, 52-64; mem, Popular Dem. Party Cent. Cmt; Sen-at-lg, P.R. Senate, 64-69; pres, Educ. Cmt, v.pres, Pub. Order Cmt, secy, Work and Labor Cmt. and mem, Cmts. on Health, State and Munic. Govt. and Nominations. Bus. & Prof. Pos: Teacher, P.R. Schs, Dept. of Educ, 4 years. Mem: Nat. Order of Women Legislators; pres. and hon. pres, InterAm. Alliance, P.R. Chap; Women's Civic Club; United Women of Am; YWCA; Red Cross Chap, P.R; Zonta Club Int; UN Asn, P.R; plus others and diplomas and recognitions from many of these societies. Rel: Catholic. Mailing Add: Rampla del Admirante 61, Santurce, P.R. 00911. (1967)

BATSON, RUTH MARION D
b. Boston, Mass, 8/3/21; d. Joel R. Watson and Cassandra Buchanan B. (both deceased); m. 1/3/41 to John Christopher Batson; c. Cassandra, Susan and Dorothy. Polit. Pos: Del, Dem. Nat. Conv, 64; committeeman, Ward 12, Mass, 56-64; del. and mem, platform and resolution cmts, State Conv, 54-62; committeeman, State Cmt, 54-56. Govt. Pos: Mem, Mass. Cmt. on Children & Youth, 65-; mem. adv. bd, Mass. Dept. Pub. Welfare, 63-; cmnr. and secy, Mass. Cmn. Against Discrimination, 63- Bus. & Prof. Pos: Mem, Mass. Conf. on Soc. Work, 66. Mem: Bd. mem, New England Regional Conf, NAACP and Boston Branch, NAACP; Anti Bias Cmn; Mass. Coun. of Churches. Rel: Protestant. Mailing Add: 160 Ruthven St, Roxbury, Mass. 02121. (1967)

BATT, GEORGE KENNETH
b. New Albany, Ind, 10/18/94; s. George McClelland Batt and Hattie Markland B; m. 10/11/21 to Margaret Robinson Dugan; c. Peggy and Mary. Educ: Purdue Univ, 13-15; Bloomfield Col. and Sem, LL.D; Beta Gamma Sigma; Theta Xi. Polit. & Govt. Pos: Mem, Nat. War Labor Bd. and indust. mem, President Roosevelt's Cost of Living Invest, 43-44; v.chmn, Gov. Cmn. War Transport and Human Resources, N.J; mayor, Montclair, N.J, 44-48; chmn, N.J. Rep. Finance Cmt, 45-48. Bus. & Prof. Pos: Mem. exec. staff, R.H. Macy Co, N.Y.C, 19-25; v.pres. and treas, Dugan Bros, 25-62; dir. and mem. exec. cmt, N.J. Bell Tel. Co. and dir, Montclair Nat. Bank & Turst Co. Mem: Pres. and dir, N.J. C. of C, 41-43. Man of Year, Notre Dame Alumni Asn, N.J, 46; Man of Year in N.J. Agr. and Indust, 62. Rel: Presbyterian. Mailing Add: 7711 Hillside Dr, La Jolla, Calif. 92037.

BATT, WILLIAM LOREN, JR. D
b. Cleveland, Ohio, 12/30/16; s. William Loren Batt and Ruby Burroughs B; m. 6/1/46 to Jane Dothard Read; c. Karen Read and Jane Read. Educ: Harvard Univ, A.B. cum laude, 38. Polit. Pos: Mem, Kennedy Task Force on Area Redevelop, 60; res. dir, Dem. Nat. Cmt, 48; chmn, Vets. for Dilworth, Dem. City Cmt, 47; Dem. Nominee for Cong, 17th Dist, Pa, 46. Govt. Pos: Admin, Area Redevelop. Admin, 61-65; secy, Pa. Dept. of Labor and Indust, 57-61; spec. asst. to Secy. Tobin, U.S. Dept. of Labor, 49-53; asst. to W.A. Harriman, Lend Lease Admin, U.S. Embassy, London, 41; asst. to Dep. Dir, War Prod. Bd, 40; res. asst. Temporary Nat. Econ. Cmt, 38-39. Bus. & Prof. Pos: Consultant, 66-; exec. secy, Toledo Indust. Develop. Coun, Ohio, 53-57; salesman, Motor Parts Co, 47-49; res. asst, Robert R. Nathan Assocs, 46. Mil. Serv: Entered as Pvt, Army, 42, released as Maj, 45, after serv. in Gen. Staff Corps, 15th Army Group and 7th Army, Africa and Europe, 42-45; Bronze Star; Medaille de la Reconnaissance Francaise; African-European Theater Ribbon. Publns: 'How Your Town Can Avoid a Recession' Colliers, 1954. Mem: Am. Vets. Cmt; Am. for Dem. Action: Nat. Adv. Cmt. on Farm Labor. Rel: Unitarian. Mailing Add: 6425 31st St. N.W, Washington, D.C. 20015. (1967)

BATTISTA, VITO PIRANESI R
N.Y. State Assemblyman
b. Bari, Italy, 9/7/09; s. Vincenzo Battista and Sabina Caputo B; m. 6/30/41 to Josephine Palermo; c. Sabina (Mrs. John Anselmo) and Vincent Charles. Educ: Carnegie Inst. Tech, B.Arch; Mass. Inst. Tech, M. of Arch; Ecole de Beaux Arts, Fontannebleau, France; Beaux Arts Inst, Columbia Univ; Alpha Phi Delta. Polit. & Govt. Pos: N.Y. State Assemblyman, 38th Assembly Dist, 69; mem, United Taxpayers Party. Bus. & Prof. Pos: Archit. designer, N.Y. World's Fair 1939, Inc, 36-37; archit, N.Y.C. Dept. of Pub. Works, 37-43, Henry V. Murphy, 41-47 and Vito Battista & Assoc, 47-; dir. and founder, Inst. Design & Construction, 47- Mil. Serv: N.Y. Nat. Guard, Engr. Corps, 44-46, 1st Lt. Mem: Am. Inst. Architects (past pres, Brooklyn Chap); N.Y. Soc. Architects (dir); N.Y. State Asn. Architects (dir); Kiwanis; Unico Nat; Hornbostel Prize; Am. Inst. Architects Prize; M.I.T. Prize. Rel: Roman Catholic. Legal Res: 290 Highland Blvd, Brooklyn, N.Y. 11207. Mailing Add: 141 Willoughby St, Brooklyn, N.Y. 11201.

BATTISTI, FRANK JOSEPH D
U.S. Dist. Judge, North. Dist. of Ohio
b. Youngstown, Ohio, 10/4/22; s. Eugene Battisti and Jennie Dalesandro B; m. 8/10/63 to Gloria Joy Karpinski. Educ: Ohio Univ, B.A, 47; Harvard Law Sch, LL.B, 50. Polit. & Govt. Pos: Asst. attorney gen, Ohio, 50; attorney adv, Corps of Engrs, Dept. of the Army, 51-52; first asst. dir. of law Youngstown, Ohio, 54-58; judge, common pleas court, 59-61; U.S. Dist. Judge, North. Dist. of Ohio, 61- Bus. & Prof. Pos: Instr. of law, Youngstown Univ. Law Sch, 52-54. Mil. Serv: Entered as Pvt, Corps of Engrs, Army, 43, released as Pfc, 45; 1st Lt, Army Intel. Res, 49-54; Distinguished Unit Badge; Victory Medal; Am. Theater Medal; ETO Medal with Five Bronze Stars. Mem: Am. Bar Asn; Am. Judicature Soc; Inter Am. Bar Asn; Mahoning Co. Bar Asn; K. of C. Rel: Catholic. Legal Res: 13900 Shaker Blvd, Cleveland, Ohio 44120. Mailing Add: U.S. Dist. Court, Cleveland, Ohio 44113.

BATTLE, LUCIUS D.
b. Georgia, 6/1/18; married. Educ: Univ. Fla, B.A, 39, LL.B, 46. Polit. & Govt. Pos: Mem. staff, War Dept, 42-43; Dept. of State Positions, 46-51; Spec. Asst. to Secy. of State, 51-52 & 61-62; first secy, Copenhagen, 54-55 and NATO, Paris, 55-62; Asst. Secy. of State for Educ. and Cultural Affairs, 62-64; Ambassador to United Arab Repub, 64-67; Asst. Secy. for Near East. and S.Asian Affairs, 67-69. Bus. & Prof. Pos: Mgr, student staff, Univ. Fla, 40-42; v.pres, Hist. Restoration Educ. Found, 56-61; v.pres. for corp. rels, Commun. Satellite Corp, currently. Mil. Serv: Lt, Navy, 43-46. Mailing Add: 3200 Garfield N.W, Washington, D.C. 20008.

BATTLE, WILLIAM CULLEN D
b. Charlottesville, Va, 10/9/20; s. John Stewart Battle and Mary Jane Lipscomb B; m. 11/14/53 to Frances Barry Webb; c. William Cullen, Robert Webb and Jane Tavernor. Educ: Univ. of Va, B.A, 41, LL.B, 47. Polit. & Govt. Pos: U.S. Ambassador to Australia, 62-64; mem, State Dept. Adv. Panel Int. Law & For. Policy, 67- Bus. & Prof. Pos: Mem. law firm, Battle, Neal, Harris, Minor & Williams, Charlottesville & Richmond, Va; mem. law firm, Caplin, Battle & Harris, Wash, D.C; bd. dirs, Va. Nat. Bank; predecessor, Charlottesville & Richmond, 51-62. Mil. Serv: Naval Res, Lt.(sg), 41-45; Silver Star. Mem: Am, Va. and W.Va. Bar Asns; chmn, budget cmn, Charlottesville-Albermarle Co. Commun. Chest; Va. Adv. Bd, Salvation Army. Rel: Baptist. Mailing Add: Charlottesville, Va. 22202.

BATTLES, EVERETT DFL
b. Watkins, Minn, 1900; m; c. four sons, three daughters. Educ: Cokato, Minn. High Sch. Polit. & Govt. Pos: Minn. State Rep, 55-66; Sch. Bd; Warroad Sch. Dist. 12; Co. Cmt. of Prod. and Mkt. Admin, Roseau. Bus. & Prof. Pos: Farmer; pres, Warroad Coop. Creamery; dir. Roseau Co. R.E.A; pres. Farmers Union Oil Co; pres. Minn. Dairy Prods. Asn, Inc. Mem: Masonic Lodge; Shrine. Rel: Union Congregational Church. Mailing Add: Warroad, Minn. 56763. (1967)

BATTLES, GEORGE HERBERT R
b. Braintree, Vt, 12/4/00; m. to Marjorie L. Flint; c. Two daughters. Educ: Randolph High Sch. Polit. & Govt. Pos: Mem, Gov. State Aid Adv. Cmt; chmn. and dir, Braintree-Randolph Union Sch. Dist, Vt; town sch. dir, Braintree, 35-; Vt. State Rep, formerly. Bus. & Prof. Pos: Farmer; v.pres. and dir, White River Dairies, Inc; dir, Cent. Vt. Dairy Herd Improv. Asn. Mem: Farm Bur; Vt. Maple Sugar Makers Asn; Vt. Dairymen's Asn; dir, Randolph Fish and Game Club; Rel: Congregational. Mailing Add: Randolph, Vt. 05060. (1967)

BATTLES, JOHN LEO D
b. West Rutland, Vt, 2/16/93; m. to Cecelia F. Davine; c. One daughter. Educ: West Rutland High Sch. Polit. & Govt. Pos: Moderator, West Rutland, 35-, selectman, 41-46, civil defense chmn, lister and auditor; Vt. State Rep, 65-67. Bus. & Prof. Pos: Former plant off. mgr, Staso Milling Co; retired. Mem: West Rutland Rotary Club. Rel: Catholic. Mailing Add: 96 Clarendon Ave, West Rutland, Vt. 05777. (1967)

BATTLES, LYNN F, SR. R
Iowa State Rep.
b. Haynes, N.Dak, 12/14/10; s. Dana C. Battles and Moloa Taubman B; m. 12/14/37 to Helen Gisel; c. Lynn F, Jr. and Gary Owen. Educ: Maquoketa High Sch, grad, 28. Polit. & Govt. Pos: Iowa State Rep, 67- Bus. & Prof. Pos: Founder and dir, Maquoketa State Bank. Mem: Past Pres. and secy, Jackson Co. Farm Bur. and Jackson Co. Fair Asn. Rel: Methodist. Mailing Add: R.R. 1, Maquoketa, Iowa 52060.

BATUYIOS, JAMES HARRY D
Councilman, Wilmington, N.C.
b. Island Icaria, Greece, 9/14/19; s. Harry James Batuyios and Catherine Spanos B; m. 11/24/46 to Frances Fronista; c. Harry James, Louis James and William James. Educ: Second Pub. Col. of Econ, Athens, Greece. Polit. & Govt. Pos: Councilman, Wilmington, N.C, 58-; state rep, Nat. Rivers and Harbors Cong. and For. Students Rels. Cmt, 60-64; chmn, New Hanover Co. Dem. Exec. Cmt, 64-66. Bus. & Prof. Pos: Jimmy's Produce and Frozen Food Co, Wholesale, 44-65; Int. Shipping Co, 55-; J.H. Batuyios Ins. and Realty Co, 57- Mem: Optimists; Elks; Ahepa. Rel: Greek Orthodox. Legal Res: 2127 Klein Rd, Wilmington, N.C. 28401. Mailing Add: P.O. Box 1693, Wilmington, N.C. 28401. (1967)

BAUER, BURNETT CALIX D
Ind. State Rep.
b. Underwood, N.Dak, 7/23/16; s. Calix F. Bauer and Theresa Reuter B; m. 4/14/41 to Helene Cryan; c. Elizabeth Ann, Burnett Patrick, Teresa, Margaret, Barbara, Matthew, Bernadette, Mary Frances and Brenda. Educ: Univ. of Notre Dame, Ph.B. in Commerce, 38 and M.A, 44. Polit. & Govt. Pos: Ind. State Rep, 64- Bus. & Prof. Pos: Ed, Red Ball Mag, U.S. Rubber Co, Mishawaka, Ind, 46-49; owner and founder, Lindsay Soft Water Co, South Bend, Ind, 50-; pres. and founder, Bauer Distributing Co, 61- Mil. Serv: Entered as Pvt, Marine Res, 36, released as 2nd Lt, 39. Publ: Blue Print for Catholic Family Action, Ave Maria Press, Notre Dame, 50. Mem: Int. Water Conditioning Asn; past mem, Nat. Bd. Dirs, Water Conditioning Found; Nat. Bd. Dirs, Citizens for Educ. Freedom; State Pres, Ind. Citizens for Educ. Freedom; Lions; K. of C; Isaac Walton League; Serra Club; co-founder, Christian Family Movement, 47; Notre Dame Monogram Club; Mil. Affairs Cmt, South Bend-Mishawaka C. of C; Dem. Vol, Former Eagle Scout and Scoutmaster. Rel: Catholic. Legal Res: 16045 Cleveland Rd, Route 1, Granger, Ind. 46530. Mailing Add: 1139 Western Ave, South Bend, Ind. 46625.

BAUER, EDITH J. R
b. West Orange, N.J, 4/21/96; m. to August F. Bauer, wid; c. One son (deceased) and one daughter. Educ: LeMasters Bus. Inst. Polit. & Govt. Pos: Mem, Rep. Town Cmt. and Women's Rep. Cmt. of Vt; tax collector, Landgrove, Vt, 51-; Vt. State Rep, formerly. Bus. & Prof. Pos: Housewife. Mem: Past matron, Laurel Chap. 30, Eastern Star, Orange, N.J; Vt. Hist. Soc; 251 Club; State and Nat. OWLS. Rel: Presbyterian. Mailing Add: Londonderry, Vt. 05148. (1967)

BAUER, FREDERICK T. D
Ind. State Rep.
Educ: Ind. Univ; Ind. Univ. Law Sch. Polit. & Govt. Pos: Past state chmn, Col. Young Dem. Clubs of Ind; Ind. State Rep, currently. Bus. & Prof. Pos: Attorney-at-law. Mil. Serv: Judge Adv. Gen. Corps, Army; Commendation Medal. Mem: Bd. of dir, Vigo Co. Chap. of Nat. Found; exec. cmt, Wabash Valley Coun, Boy Scouts; City, State and Am. Bar Asns; Scottish Rite; Shrine; bd. dirs, Union Hosp. Goodwill Indust; ex-mem, Teamster's Union Local 144. Rel: Episcopal. Mailing Add: 525 Ohio St, Terre Haute, Ind. 47801.

BAUER, HAL WILLIAM D
b. Lincoln, Nebr, 4/7/27; s. William W. Bauer and Nellie May Schultz B; m. to Ethel Louise Sindelar; c. Diane Sue and Dawn Louise. Educ: Univ. Nebr, B.S, 49; Univ. Nebr. Col. of Law, LL.B, 57; Delta Theta Phi; Phi Delta Theta. Polit. & Govt. Pos: Dir, Salt Waltoo Watershed Dist, 63-65; Nebr.

State Sen, 65-66. Bus. & Prof. Pos: Lawyer, Bauer & Galter, 57- Mem: Elks; Mason; Scottish Rite; Shrine; YMCA. Rel: Methodist. Legal Res: 1211 S. 47th, Lincoln, Nebr. 68510. Mailing Add: 511 Anderson Bldg, Lincoln, Nebr. 68508. (1967)

BAUER, M. C. 'MIKE' R
Mo. State Rep.
b. Belvidere, Ill, 3/19/15; m. 2/11/43 to Deva May Coleman; c. Suzanne, Cynthia and Jack. Educ: Univ. Wis; Univ. Ill, Chicago. Polit. & Govt. Pos: Mo. State Rep, 65- Bus. & Prof. Pos: Self-employed retail merchant. Mil. Serv: Navy, World War II, 4 years. Mem: Past pres, Bethany Jr. C. of C; past pres, Bethany C. of C; past pres, Harrison Co. Develop. Corp; VFW; Am. Legion; AF&AM; Shrine; Farm Bur; Kiwanis. Rel: Methodist. Mailing Add: 2100 Wilson Ave, Bethany, Mo. 64424.

BAUER, RICHARD L. R
Chmn, Power Co. Rep. Party, Idaho
b. Lehi, Utah, 5/20/34; s. Benjamen Bauer and Sophia B; m. 2/5/57 to Lois Saathoff; c. Barbara, James and Danial. Educ: Westminster Col, Utah, 4 years. Polit. & Govt. Pos: Rep. precinct committeeman, Power Co, Idaho, 64-67; finance chmn, Power Co. Rep. Party, 64, chmn, 68-; chmn, Legis. Dist. 26, Rep. Party, 66-68; alternate del, Rep. Nat. Conv, 68. Bus. & Prof. Pos: Partner, Gateway Motor Co, Salt Lake City, Utah, 57-63; pres. and gen. mgr, Bauer Chevrolet Co, Am. Falls, Idaho, 63- Mil. Serv: Entered as Pvt, Army, 54, released as Sgt, 56, after serv. in Corps of Engrs, European Theatre, Germany, 54-56. Mem: AF&AM. Rel: Lutheran. Mailing Add: 745 Fillmore, American Falls, Idaho 83211.

BAUGH, JAMES EMORY D
Chmn, Baldwin Co. Dem. Exec. Cmt, Ga.
b. Milledgeville, Ga, 5/19/20; s. Wyatt E. Baugh and Lillian Evelyn Womble B; m. June 20 to Betty George Clark; c. Patricia Ann. Educ: Ga. Mil. Col, Dipl, 39; Ga. Col. Milledgeville, B.S. in Pre-Med, 41; Univ. Ga, A.B, 42; Theta Kappa Psi. Polit. & Govt. Pos: Chmn, Baldwin Co. Dem. Party, 62-; chmn, Baldwin Co. Dem. Exec. Cmt, Ga, currently. Bus. & Prof. Pos: Chief of staff, Baldwin Co. Hosp, 60-61; mem. bd. trustees, Ga. Mil. Col, Milledgeville, currently. Mil. Serv: Entered as 2nd Lt, Army, 42, released as 1st Lt, 46, after serv. in 82nd Airborne Div, World War II, throughout all campaigns of that div. from Casablanca to Berlin; Presidential Unit Citation; 5 Combat Stars; 2 Arrowhead Insignia indicating Beachhead and Airborne Landings; Purple Heart. Mem: State and Dist. Med. Socs; Baldwin Co. Med. Soc.(pres, 54); Mason; Shrine. Recipient of Good Citizenship Award. Rel: Protestant. Legal Res: 1650 Pine Valley Rd, Milledgeville, Ga. 31061. Mailing Add: P.O. Box 669, Milledgeville, Ga. 31061.

BAUGH, PHILIP J. 'JACK' D
N.C. State Sen.
b. Charlotte, N.C, 1932; m. to Patricia Jean Meyers; c. four. Educ: N.C. State Col; Duke Univ, B.A. Polit. & Govt. Pos: N.C. State Rep, 67-69; N.C. State Sen, 69- Bus. & Prof. Pos: Pres, P.J. Baugh Industs, Inc. and Almahurst Farm, Inc, Lexington, Ky; Charlotte Dir, N.C. Nat. Bank. Mil. Serv: Air Force, Jet Fighter Pilot. Mem: Nat. coun. exec. cmt. and v.pres. alumni asn, Duke Univ; dir, Lexington Trot Breeders Asn; dir, Charlotte Downtown Asn; Charlotte City Club; Charlotte Country Club; N.Y. Athletic Club; Soaring Soc. Am. Rel: Presbyterian; Sunday sch. teacher, Deacon, chmn. finance cmt, Presbyterian Church. Mailing Add: 2018 Sharon Rd, Charlotte, N.C. 28207.

BAUGHMAN, FRANK JOHN D
Chmn, Potter Co. Dem. Party, Tex.
b. Connellsville, Pa, 9/21/22; s. Charles Frederick Baughman and Bertha Augusta Karle B; m. 5/8/50 to Lucille Quinto; c. Luann. Educ: Univ. Tex, Austin, B.B.A, 44, LL.B, 55; Delta Theta Phi. Polit. & Govt. Pos: Asst. dist. attorney, 47th Dist, Amarillo, Tex, 57-59, dist. attorney, 61-63; chmn, Potter Co. Dem. Party, 64- Bus. & Prof. Pos: Tax attorney, City Tax Off, Amarillo, Tex, 55-57; partner, Ochsner, Nobles & Baughman, 63- Mil. Serv: Entered as A/S, Navy, 42, released as Seaman 1/C, 46; Good Conduct Medal; S.Pac. Theatre Ribbon. Mem: Tex. and Amarillo Bar Asns; Amarillo Jr. Bar; Lions Int; Mason; Big Bros; Boy Scouts; Fine Arts chmn, Amarillo Ballet Theater; Amarillo Aquatic Club. Rel: Lutheran. Legal Res: 106 N. Beverly, Amarillo, Tex. 79106. Mailing Add: 702 Vaughn Bldg, Amarillo, Tex. 79101.

BAUGHMAN, LEON HODGES D
b. Dothan, Ala, 4/18/95; s. J.W. Baughman and Sallie Hodges B; m. 2/1/18 to Jessie L. Bradford; c. Leon Edward. Educ: Dothan High Sch. Polit. & Govt. Pos: Early Co. cmnr, 37-49. Mil. Serv: Sgt. 1st Class. Mem: Mason; Shriner; Am. Legion. Rel: Methodist. Mailing Add: Cedar Springs, Ga. 31732. (1967)

BAUM, ELMER CARL D
Chmn, State Dem. Exec. Cmt, Tex.
b. Culbertson, Nebr, 9/15/13; s. Emil Baum and Mary Heldt B; m. 8/4/32 to Virginia Kuns; c. Cynthia (Mrs. Gerhardt) and Alan. Educ: Kans. City Col. Osteopathy and Surgery, D.O, 34; Phi Sigma Gamma. Polit. & Govt. Pos: Dem. chmn, Precinct 229, Austin, Tex, 39-69; secy, State Bd. Health, 42-69; chmn, State Dem. Exec. Cmt, 68- Mem: Tex. Asn; Osteopathic Physicians and Surgeons (pres, 52-53); Kiwanis. Gen. practitioner of the Year. Rel: Methodist. Legal Res: 2510 Wooldridge Dr, Austin, Tex. 78703. Mailing Add: 908 Nueces, Austin, Tex. 78701.

BAUM, GLEN FREDERICK R
Chmn, Johnson Co. Rep. Cent. Cmt, Nebr.
b. Tecumseh, Nebr, 2/11/29; s. Fred W. Baum and Mary E. Leuenberger B; m. 5/29/65 to Mary Lou Wood; c. William Charles; Thomas Wayne, Sharon Suzanne and John Dana. Educ: Univ. Nebr, B.Sc. in Agr, 51 and M.Sc, 57; Alpha Zeta; Voc. Agr. Club. Polit. & Govt. Pos: Precinct committeeman, Johnson Co. Rep. Cent. Cmt, Nebr, 66-67, chmn, 68- Bus. & Prof. Pos: V.pres, Bd. of Educ. Serv. Unit Four, 69. Mil. Serv: Entered as Pvt, Army, 51, released as Cpl, 53, after serv. in Signal Corps, Far East Command, 52-53; Korean Serv. Medal; UN Serv. Medal. Mem: VFW; Farm Bur. Rel: United Church of Christ. Mailing Add: R.R. 2, Tecumseh, Nebr. 68450.

BAUM, SHERRY LISS D
Secy, Calif. Dem. State Cent. Cmt.
b. Dearborn, Mich; d. Anthony Ralph Sansone and Victoria Selwa S; m. 5/19/61 to Morton Alex Baum; c. Randall Max and Jason Anthony Liss, Christopher Joseph and Geoffrey Leo Baum. Educ: Univ. Calif, Irvine, 1 year. Polit. & Govt. Pos: Secy, Calif. Dem. State Cent. Cmt, 32nd Cong. Dist, 68- Mem: Marina Dem. Club; Robert Kennedy Mem. Soc; Democ. Women of Orange Co; Dem. Women's Study Club of Long Beach; Kennedy Club of Orange Co; Long Beach Regional Arts Coun; League of Woman Voters; Seal Beach PTA; Dem. of South. Calif; Family Serv. Guild of Long Beach. Mailing Add: 815 Catalina Ave, Seal Beach, Calif. 90740.

BAUMAN, ROBERT EDMUND R
Secy, Am. Conservative Union
b. Bryn Mawr, Pa, 4/4/37; s. John Carl Bauman and Florence House B; m. 11/19/60 to Carol Gene Dawson; c. Edward Carroll, Eugenie Marie and Victoria Anne. Educ: Capitol Page Sch, Libr. of Cong, 55; Georgetown Univ. Sch. of Foreign Serv, B.S. in int. affairs, 59, Law Centre, J.D, 64. Polit. & Govt. Pos: Page, U.S. House Rep, 53-55 and U.S. Sen, spec. session, 54; staff, House Judiciary Cmt, 55-59; asst. sgt. at arms and asst. doorkeeper, Rep. Nat. Conv, 56 & 60; pres, Georgetown Univ. Young Rep. Club, 59-60; asst. minority mgr, House Rep. Cloakroom, 59-65, mgr, 65-68; nat. chmn, Youth for Nixon, 60; mem. bd. dirs. and past. nat. chmn, Young Am. for Freedom, Inc, 60-66; del, Rep. Nat. Conv, 64; secy. and mem. bd. dirs, Am. Conservative Union, 64-; prog. cmt. chmn. and mem. nat. exec. cmt, Young Rep. Nat. Fedn, 65-67; exec. dir, Md. Citizens for Nixon-Agnew Campaign, 68. Bus. & Prof. Pos: Attorney-at-law, 68- Publ: Articles published in Nat. Rev, Human Events and New Guard. Mem: Am. and Md. Bar Asns; Capitol Hill Club, Wash, D.C. Rel: Roman Catholic. Mailing Add: Glebe House, Route 4, Easton, Md. 21601.

BAUMANN, ALBERT F. D
Md. State Del.
b. Baltimore, Md, 8/2/13; married. Educ: Brooklyn Pub. Schs. Polit. & Govt. Pos: Md. State Del, 59- Bus. & Prof. Pos: Draftsman. Mailing Add: 1505 Jackson St, Baltimore, Md. 21230. (1967)

BAUMANN, CAROL EDLER D
b. Plymouth, Wis, 8/11/32; d. Clarence Henry Edler and Beulah Weinhold E; m. 2/28/59 to Richard Joseph Baumann; c. Dawn Carol and Wendy Katherine. Educ: Univ. Wis, Madison, B.A, 54; London Sch. Econ, Univ. London, Ph.D, 57; Fulbright scholarship, 54-55; hon. Woodrow Wilson fel, 54-55; Marshall scholarship, 54-57; Phi Beta Kappa; Phi Kappa Phi; Phi Eta Sigma; Gamma Phi Beta. Polit. & Govt. Pos: V.chmn, N.Shore Dem. Unit, Wis, 67; Dem. nominee, U.S. Rep, Wis, 68. Bus. & Prof. Pos: Instr, Dept. Polit. Sci, Univ. Wis, Madison, 57-61, proj. assoc, Nat. Security Studies Group, 58-61; asst. prof, Dept. Polit. Sci, Univ. Wis, Milwaukee, 62-67, assoc. prof, 67-; dir, Inst. World Affairs, Univ. Wis-Milwaukee and Univ. Exten, 64- Publ: Western Europe: What Path to Integration?, D.C. Heath & Co, 67; 'Britain Faces Europe, Polit. Sci. Quart, Vol. LXXIV, No. 3; 'Political Co-operation in NATO,' Nat. Security Studies Group, Univ. Wis, Madison, 60. Mem: Am. Polit. Sci. Asn; Midwest Conf. Polit. Scientists; Adult Educ. Asn. U.S.A; Nat. Univ. Exten. Asn; Nat. Cmt. Commun. World Affairs Orgns; Soc. Citizen Educ. World Affairs; UN Asn. U.S.A; Int. Inst. Milwaukee Co; World Affairs Coun. Milwaukee (bd. dirs). Rel: Lutheran. Legal Res: 5109 N. Woodburn St, Whitefish Bay, Wis. 53217. Mailing Add: University of Wisconsin-Milwaukee, Bolton 668, Milwaukee, Wis. 53201.

BAUMGART, MERLE DAVID D
b. Buffalo, N.Y, 9/18/34; s. Dewey F. Baumgart and Borghild Quarum B; m. 1/25/55 to Beverly J. Young; c. Martin Dewey and Kirsten Rachel. Educ: Portland State Col, B.A, 59; George Wash. Univ, M.A, 61, study, 61-64. Polit. & Govt. Pos: Staff mem, Sen. Maurine B. Neuberger, 61-63; dist. leader, Wash, D.C. Dem. Party, 64-68; admin. asst. U.S. Rep. Peter W. Rodino, 66- Bus. & Prof. Pos: Lectr, hist, George Wash, Univ, 62-64; instr. hist, D.C. Teachers Col, 63-66. Mil. Serv: Entered as Pvt, Army, 53, released as Sgt, 56, after serv. in Army Mobile Surg. Hosp, Seventh Army, ETO, 54-56. Mem: Am. Hist. Asn; bd. trustees, Friendship House, Wash, D.C. Rel: Protestant. Mailing Add: 604 South Carolina Ave. S.E, Washington, D.C. 20003.

BAUMGARTNER, STEPHEN ELDON D
Chmn, Adams Co. Dem. Party, Wis.
b. Adams, Wis, 10/11/27; s. Steve Baumgartner and Caroline Lamphere B; m. 7/23/55 to DeAnn Van Tassel; c. Bruce, Craige, Janalynn and Darcie. Educ: Adams Friendship High. Polit. & Govt. Pos: Chmn, Adams Co. Dem. Party, Wis, 64-; alderman, City of Adams, 64- Bus. & Prof. Pos: Owner, Mobil Filling Station, 57. Mil. Serv: Entered as Pvt, Air Force, 46, released as Pfc, 47; Am. Theater & Victory Medals. Rel: Protestant. Mailing Add: 151 N. Grant St, Adams, Wis. 53910.

BAUMUNK, LAWRENCE DALE R
Chmn, Sullivan Co. Rep. Cmt, Pa.
b. Forksville, Pa, 4/13/30; s. Lawrence L. Baumunk and Caroline Little B; m. 7/6/52 to Lucy Lindley; c. Ann, Mary and Emily. Educ: Lycoming Col, 1 year. Polit. & Govt. Pos: Sullivan Co. Sch. Dir, Pa, 55-67; committeeman, Fox Twp. Rep. Party, 60-62 & 68-; chmn, Sullivan Co. Rep. Cmt, 62-; alternate del, Rep. Nat. Conv, 64. Bus. & Prof. Pos: Assoc, L.L. Baumunk & Son Lumber Co, Shunk, 55- Mil. Serv: Entered as SR, Navy, 48, released as SN, 49, after serv. in aircraft carrier U.S.S. Leyte, 48-49, recalled as SN, 52-54. Mem: F&AM; Am. Legion Post 452; Sullivan Co. C. of C. Rel: Methodist. Mailing Add: Shunk, Pa. 17768.

BAXLEY, HENRY L. D
Chmn, Fauquier Co. Dem. Cmt, Va.
b. Markham, Va, 9/30/98; s. James Leroy Baxley and Emily Hirst B; m. 6/2/23 to Mamie Maxfield Yates; c. Henry Little, Jr. Educ: Randolph Macon Acad, grad, 17. Polit. & Govt. Pos: Chmn, Fauquier Co. Dem. Cmt, Va, 64- Bus. & Prof. Pos: Farmer, 19-40; Gen. Ins. Agency, 35-63. Mil. Serv: Pvt, Army Air Force, 18-19. Mem: AF&AM; Royal Arch Mason. Rel: Episcopal. Mailing Add: Hume, Va. 22639.

BAXTER, J. STERLING R
Chmn, Pitkin Co. Rep. Party, Colo.
b. Hutchinson, Kans, 6/8/27; s. Wilber David Baxter and Helen Sterling B;

m. 4/9/50 to Peggylee Butler; c. Sarah, Rachel, Ruth, Nancy and Margaret. Educ: Univ. Kans, B.A, M.D; Phi Chi. Polit. & Govt. Pos: Chmn, Pitkin Co. Rep. Party, Colo, 66-; co-cmnr, Pitkin Co, 67- Bus. & Prof. Pos: Physician, Aspen, Colo, 54- Mil. Serv: Entered as A/S, Naval Res, 45, released A/S, 46, recalled as 1st Lt, Army Med. Corps, 53, released as 1st Lt, 54. Publ: 'Open Reduction Tibial Fractures,' Rocky Mt. Med. J, 57. Mem: Am. Med. Asn; Am. Acad. Gen. Practice; Mason; Lions. Rel: Methodist. Mailing Add: Snow Bunny Lane, Aspen, Colo. 81611.

BAYARD, ALEXIS IRENEE duPONT D
b. Wilmington, Del, 2/11/18; s. Thomas F. Bayard and Elizabeth duPont B; m. 4/24/44 to Jane Brady Hildreth (deceased); c. Alexis Irenee duPont, Eugene Hildreth, Richard Henry, Jane Hildreth, John Francis and William Bradford. Educ: Princeton Univ, B.A, 40; Univ. Va, LL.B, 47. Polit. & Govt. Pos: Pres, Young Dem. Del, 48-49; Lt. Gov, Del, 49-53; chmn, Dem. State Campaign, 54; chmn, Citizens for Kennedy-Johnson, 60 and Johnson-Humphrey, 64; chmn, Del. Dem. State Cmt, 67; chmn, Del. River and Bay Authority, 67- Bus. & Prof. Pos: Attorney-at-law, 48; sr. partner, Bayard, Brill & Handelman, 65- Mil. Serv: Entered as Pvt, Marine Corps Res, 42, released as 1st Lt, 45, after serv. in 28th Regt, Fifth Marine Div, Asiatic Theatre; Purple Heart; Navy and Presidential Unit Citations. Mem: Am. and Del. Bar Asns; Am. Judicature Soc; Del. Soc. Mayflower Descendants; Am. Acad. Polit. and Soc. Sci; Wilmington Club; Wilmington Country Club; Greenville Club; Univ. Club; Am. Legion; VFW; Del. Swedish Colonial Soc. Jr. C. of C. Young Man of the Year Award, 51. Rel: Episcopal. Legal Res: 500 Continental Am. Bldg, Wilmington, Del. 19801. Mailing Add: 1006 Overbrook Rd, Westover Hills, Wilmington, Del. 19807.

BAYER, GARY GRAY R
b. St. Louis, Mo, 10/29/42; s. Leslie Aubry Bayer and Virginia Schieble B; single. Educ: Yale, B.A, 64; Stanford Univ, LL.B, 67. Polit. & Govt. Pos: Admin. asst, U.S. Rep. Clarence J. Brown, Ohio, 68-; campaign mgr, Brown for Cong. Cmt, 68. Bus. & Prof. Pos: Regional chmn, Stanford Law Fund, 68- Mil. Serv: Entered as E-1, Army, released as E-2, 67. Mem: Calif, Fed. and Am. Bar Asns; bd. of visitors, Stanford Law Sch. Legal Res: 1117 Spoede Rd, St. Louis, Mo. 63131. Mailing Add: 201 Eye St. S.W, Apt. 705, Washington, D.C. 20024.

BAYH, BIRCH D
U.S. Sen, Ind.
b. Vigo Co, Ind, 1/22/28; s. Birch Evans Bayh, Sr. and Leah Ward Hollingsworth B; m. 8/24/52 to Marvella Hern; c. Birch Evans, III. Educ: Purdue Univ, B.S. in Agr, 51; Ind. Univ, J.D, 60; Ceres; Alpha Zeta; Gimlet; Ind. Law J. Bd. of Eds; Order of the Coif; Alpha Tau Omega; light-heavyweight boxing champion; varsity baseball team, Purdue Univ; pres, senior class; hon. LL.D, Purdue Univ. and Anderson Col; hon. L.H.D, Salem Col, W.Va. Polit. & Govt. Pos: Ind. State Rep, 54-62, Speaker, Ind. House of Rep, 59, Minority Leader, 57 & 61; U.S. Sen, Ind, 63-; del, Dem. Nat. Conv, 68. Bus. & Prof. Pos: Attorney; farmer, 340 acre family farm, Vigo Co, Ind. Mil. Serv: Entered as Pvt, Army, 46, released as Pfc, 48, after serv. in Occup. Forces in Europe. Publ: One Heartbeat Away, Bobbs-Merrill, 66; Remedies Available to Penal Inmates While Incarcerated, summer 59 and Suggested Improvements in the Indiana Legislative Process, winter 60, Ind. Law J. Mem: Bd. of visitors, U.S. Merchant Marine Acad; Purdue Alumni Asn; Ind. Univ. Alumni Asn; Am, Ind. State and Vigo Co. Bar Asns; Isaac Walton League; Jr. C. of C; Farm Bur; Farmers Union; Wabash Valley Asn; Red Cross; Vol. of Am; Elks; Mason; Wabash Valley Fair Bd; Ind. Soc. of Wash; chmn, Ind. Easter Seals, 65-67. Named One of Nations Ten Outstanding Young Men, Nat. Jr. C. of C, 64. Rel: Methodist. Legal Res: Route 2, Terre Haute, Ind. 46602. Mailing Add: 363 Senate Office Bldg, Washington, D.C. 20510.

BAYLEY, NED DUANE R
Dir. Sci. and Educ, Dept. of Agr.
b. Battle Creek, Mich, 12/29/18; s. Howard G. Bayley and Beulah Sperry B; m. 6/5/43 to Lillian Joyce Safstrom; c. Gwen Ellen, Will Douglas and Fred Wallace. Educ: Mich. State Univ, B.S, 40; Univ. Minn, 1 year; Univ. Wis, Ph.D, 50; Harvard Univ, 1 year. Polit. & Govt. Pos: Asst. head, Breeding and Mgt. Sect, Dairy Cattle Research, Agr. Research Serv, Dept. of Agr, Beltsville, Md, 55-56, leader, 56-61, asst. dir, Animal Husbandry Research Div, 61-67, dep. dir, Sci. and Educ, Dept. of Agr, Wash, D.C, 67-68, dir, Sci. and Educ, Off. of the Secy, 68- Bus. & Prof. Pos: Mem. staff, Dairy Husbandry Dept, Univ. Wis, 48-53; assoc. prof, Dairy Dept, Univ. Minn, 53-55. Mil. Serv: Entered as Pvt, Army, 42, released as T/Sgt, 46, after serv. in ETO, 44-45. Publ: 28 tech. publ. in field of animal sci. and research admin. Mem: Am. Dairy Sci. Asn; Am. Soc. of Animal Sci; Am. Asn. for the Adv. of Sci; active in commun. affairs in Colesville and Montgomery Co, Md. Outstanding Performance Rating, U.S. Dept. of Agr, 65. Rel: Protestant. Mailing Add: 13907 Overton Lane, Silver Spring, Md. 20904.

BAYS, KENNETH BRUCE R
Ind. State Rep.
b. Indianapolis, Ind, 1/11/32; s. Byrd Lovell Bays and Cleo Chambers B; m. 12/29/49 to Barbara Jean Miller; c. Bradley Kent, Brian David, Amelia Ann, Jennifer Jean and Bruce Thomas. Polit. & Govt. Pos: Ind. State Rep, 67- Bus. & Prof. Pos: Electronics supvr, Willys Motors, 52-53; experimental engr, Delco-Remy, 54- Mil. Serv: Entered as Basic Airman, Air Force, 49, released as S/Sgt, 52; Good Conduct Medal; European Occupation Ribbon. Mem: Mason; Boy Scouts; Little League Baseball. Rel: Free Methodist. Mailing Add: 5425 Lewis Dr, Anderson, Ind. 46103. (1967)

BAYS, SONDRA KAY D
Secy, Warren Co. Dem. Exec. and Cent. Cmts, Ohio
b. Middletown, Ohio, 6/2/37; d. John Charles Gordon and Ora Lillie Stewart G; m. 1956 to Ralph J. Bays; c. Sherry Kay, Cynthia Rae and Robert Jay. Educ: Lemon-Monroe High Sch, Monroe, Ohio, grad; Univ. Cincinnati Evening Col, currently. Polit. & Govt. Pos: Secy, Warren Co. Dem. Womens Club, Ohio, 63-67; Dem. precinct committeeman, Franklin Twp, S.E, 64, 66 & 68; secy, Warren Co. Dem. Exec. and Cent. Cmts, 65- Bus. & Prof. Pos: Reporter and church ed, Middletown J, Ohio, 55-56; assoc. ed, Warren Co. Reporter, 66-67, managing ed, 67- Mem: Commun. Day Hosp, Middletown, Ohio (former vol. worker); Beta Sigma Phi. Placed first in short story contest, sponsored by Beta Sigma Phi, 64; placed 70th of 200 winners in short story contest sponsored by Writers Digest, 66; received second place in columns div. of news media awards given by Ohio Dept. of Hwy. Safety, 69. Rel: Methodist; Sr. High Youth Sunday Sch. Teacher, Hunter Commun. United Methodist Church. Mailing Add: 3700 Beatrice Dr, Franklin, Ohio 45005.

BAZELL, MICHAEL PHILIP D
Asst. Co. Attorney, Suffolk Co, N.Y.
b. New York, N.Y, 6/8/25; s. Jack Bazell and Frieda Kirschner B; m. 4/12/49 to Anne Feiner; c. Jacalyn, Andrew and Fredrika. Educ: N.Y. Univ, B.A, 48; N.Y. Univ. Sch. Law, LL.B, 50; Phi Sigma Delta. Polit. & Govt. Pos: Committeeman, Smithtown Dem. Cmt, N.Y, 57-, chmn, 65-68; alternate del, Dem. Nat. Conv, 68; asst. co. attorney, Suffolk Co, currently. Mil. Serv: Entered as Pvt, Army, 43, released as Tec 5, 46, after serv. in Coast Artillery and Signal Corps, North. Pac, 44-46. Mem: Am, N.Y. State and Suffolk Co. Bar Asns; N.Y. Co. Lawyers Asn; Am. Legion; Nat. Rifle Asn; Nat. Sheriff's Asn; Mensa. Rel: Jewish. Legal Res: 265 Kohr Rd, Kings Park, N.Y. 11754. Mailing Add: 1008 Jericho Turnpike, Smithtown, N.Y. 11787.

BAZELON, DAVID L. D
b. Superior, Wis, 9/3/09; s. Israel Bazelon and Lena Krasnovsky B; m. 6/7/36 to Miriam M. Kellner; c. James A. and Richard Lee. Educ: Univ. Ill, 28-29; Northwest. Univ, B.S. in law, 31; Colby Col, hon. LL.D, 66. Polit. & Govt. Pos: Asst. U.S. attorney for North. Dist, Ill, in charge of fed. tax matters, 35-40; asst. attorney gen, U.S. Lands Div, 46-47 and Off. of Alien Property, 47-49; judge, U. S. Court Appeals, D.C. Circuit, 49-, chief judge, 62-; chmn. task force on law and pub. awareness, President's Panel Ment. Retardation, 61-62; nat. consult. forensic med. to Surgeon Gen, Air Force, 64- Bus. & Prof. Pos: Sr. mem, Gottieb and Schwartz, 40-46; lectr. law and psychiat, Univ. Pa. Law Sch, 57-58, 58-59; Sloan vis. prof, Menninger Found, Topeka, 60-61; Isaac Ray Award lectr, Univ. Chicago, 61; Lowell Inst. lectr, 64; Edward Douglass White lectr, Georgetown Univ, 64; regent's lectr, Univ. Calif, Los Angeles, 64; lectr. psychiat, Johns Hopkins Univ. Sch. Med, 64-; clin. prof. psychiat, George Wash. Univ, 66-; David K. Niles Mem. lectr, Hebrew Univ, Jerusalem, 66; sesquicentennial, Univ. Cincinnati, 69. Mem: Trustee, Salk Inst. Biol. Studies, 61-; Nat. Asn. Ment. Health Prog. Dirs.(adv. coun, 63-); chmn, Steering Cmt. Model Sch. Subsyst, Washington, 64-66; bd. dirs, Joint Cmn. Ment. Health Children, 65-; Inst. Criminal Law and Procedure, Georgetown Univ; Harvard Univ. Prog. on Tech. and Society (adv. cmt. 66-); Nat. Adv. Ment. Health Coun, Pub. Health Serv; John F. Kennedy Center Research Educ. and Human Develop.(nat. adv. cmt, 68-); Am. Orthopsychiat. Asn.(dir, pres, 69-70); hon. fel. Am. Psychiat. Asn; Cosmos Club. Isaac Ray Award, Am. Psychiat. Asn, 60. Rel: Jewish. Legal Res: 2700 Virginia Ave. N.W, Washington, D.C. 20037. Mailing Add: U.S. Court of Appeals, Washington, D.C. 20001.

BAZETT, SIDNEY R
Ore. State Rep.
b. Hampton, Va, 9/5/01; s. Arthur Edward Bazett and Bertha Eastwood B; m. to Marjorie Pike; c. Sidney Arthur, Barbara Anne, Bruce Allen and Bettina Lynn. Educ: Inst. Chartered Accts, Can, 20-24; Univ. B.C, 25; Golden Gate Col, 26-30; Univ. Calif, Berkeley, 31-33; Chi Pi Alpha. Polit. & Govt. Pos: Mem, State Park Adv. Bd, Ore, 61; Ore. State Rep, 18th Dist, Josephine Co, 61-, chmn, Hwy. Cmt, 6 years and v.chmn, Interim Fiscal Cmt, Ore. State House of Rep. Bus. & Prof. Pos: Acct, Ernst & Ernst, 26-30; controller, Transamerica Corp. and pres. of subsidiaries, 34-36; v.pres, Bank of Am. Co, pres, Franklin Wulff Co, 34-36, dir, 38-42; financial dir, Columbia Pictures Corp, 36-38; dir, Am. Invest. Co, Bankamerica Co, Grand Canyon Boulder Dam Co. and Grand Canyon Airlines, 38-42; founder-pres, Valley Finance Co, Grants Pass, 47-; pres, Northwest Finance Co, Bend, Ore, 64-; founder-pres, Valley Finance of Phoenix, Inc, Phoenix, Ore, 66- Mil. Serv: Entered as Capt, Air Force, 42, released as Lt. Col, 46; Army Air Force Res, 24 years; Liaison officer for U.S. Air Force Acad, Colo. for South. Ore; Navy and Air Force Commendations. Mem: Dir, Assoc. Ore. Industs; Ore. Consumer Finance Asn. and Redwood Empire Asn; Rotary; San Francisco Family Club; founder, Indust. Develop, Inc; dir, Josephine Develop. Co, Inc; past pres. and dir, Grants Pass C. of C. Elected to Exec. and Prfnl. Hall of Fame, 66. Rel: Presbyterian. Mailing Add: P.O. Box 126, Grants Pass, Ore. 97526.

BEACH, STEPHEN LEEDS, III D
Miss. State Rep.
b. Chicago, Ill, 7/3/42; s. Stephen Leeds Beach and Aldona Chipas B; single. Educ: Univ. Miss, B.A. and J.D; Phi Kappa Phi; Omicron Delta Kappa; Pi Sigma Alpha; Eta Sigma Phi; Sigma Nu; Alpha Phi Omega. Polit. & Govt. Pos: Miss. State Rep, 68-; Dem. chmn, Precinct 19, Jackson, 68- Bus. & Prof. Pos: Attorney, Davidson & Beach, 67- Mem: Miss. Bar Asn; Jr. C. of C; Mason; Scottish Rite; York Rite; Shrine. Rel: Methodist. Legal Res: 957 Meadow Heights Dr, Jackson, Miss. 39206. Mailing Add: P.O. Box 663, 614-616 Barnett Bldg, Jackson, Miss. 39205.

BEACH, WILBUR LEWIS R
Chmn, Crawford Co. Rep. Exec. Cmt, Ohio
b. Arlington, Ohio, 5/9/17; s. John A. Beach and Wilhemina Kramer B; m. 6/30/40 to Kathryn A. Gibson; c. Sue Elaine. Educ: Ohio State Univ, B.Sc, 39; Nat. Agr. Honor Soc; Lutheran Students Asn. Polit. & Govt. Pos: Village clerk, Chatfield, Ohio, 52-69; secy, Crawford Co. Rep. Cent. Cmt, 58-66, chmn, 66-68; precinct committeeman, Chatfield Rep. Party, 58-; mem, Crawford Co. Child Welfare Bd, 62-69; vol. fire chief, Chatfield, 62-69; chmn, Crawford Co. Rep. Exec. Cmt, 68-; co. cmnr, Crawford Co, 69- Bus. & Prof. Pos: Pres, Chatfield Hardware Co, Inc, 61-; chmn, Retarded Children, Inc, Crawford Co, 64-67. Mil. Serv: Entered as Pvt, Air Force, 44, released as Cpl, 46, after serv. in Commun, ETO, 45-46; Good Conduct Medal; ETO Ribbon. Mem: Ohio Hardware Asn.(chmn, Crawford Co. Chap, 64-68); Am. Legion; United Commercial Travelers; Crawford Co. Conserv. League (dir, 41-69); Am. Lutheran Church (pres, Ohio Dist. Brotherhood, 53-59). Rel: Lutheran. Mailing Add: Box 1, Chatfield, Ohio 44825.

BEADLE, FRANK D. R
b. Melvin, Mich; married; c. James S. Educ: High Sch. grad. Polit. & Govt. Pos: Justice of the Peace, formerly; Mich. State Sen, 50-68. Bus. & Prof. Pos: Ins. and real estate. Mil. Serv: World War I. Mem: Mason; Am. Legion; Lions Club, dist. gov, 41-42, life mem. Rel: Congregational. Mailing Add: 150 Brown St, St. Clair, Mich. 48079. (1967)

BEADLESTON, ALFRED N. R
N.J. State Sen.
b. Rumson, N.J, 2/20/12. Educ: Yale Univ, B.A, 34. Polit. & Govt. Pos: Dir, Monmouth and Ocean Co, World War II; area adminstr, N.J. Off. of Civilian Defense; councilman, Shrewsbury, N.J, 39-40, mayor, 41-52; pres, Shrewsbury Rep. Club, 41-50; treas, Affiliated Rep. Club of Monmouth Co, 48-49, first v.pres, 50-51; N.J. State Assemblyman, 51-67, majority leader, N.J. State Assembly, 58 & 59 and speaker, 64; N.J. State Sen, 68- Bus. & Prof. Pos: Former pres. and dir, Beadleston & Woerz, Real Estate Operating Co, N.Y.C; retired. Mailing Add: 12 Broad St, Room 400, Red Bank, N.J. 07701. (1967)

BEAGLE, GAIL JOYCE D
b. Beaumont, Tex, 11/25/35; d. Victor Leroy Beagle, Sr. and Hazel Jane Block B; single. Educ: Tex. Woman's Univ, B.S, 58; Univ. Tex. Grad Sch, summer, 59; Theta Sigma Phi; day ed, soc. ed. and church ed, Daily Lasso; pres, Tex. Woman's Univ. Methodist Student Movement. Polit. & Govt. Pos: Jefferson Co. campaign mgr, Gonzalez for Gov, Tex, 58; staff asst. to U.S. Sen. Ralph W. Yarborough, Tex, 59; staff asst. and press secy. to Tex. State Sen, Gonzalez, 59, staff dir. and press secy, 61; dist. committeewoman, Tex. Young Dem. Club, 59-60; secy, Travis Co. Precinct, 60; press secy, Gonzalez for U.S. Sen. Campaign, Tex, 61; off. mgr. and press secy, to U.S. Rep. Henry B. Gonzalez, Tex, 61-63, admin. asst. and press secy, 63- Bus. & Prof. Pos: Staff asst, Tex. Coun. Churches, 58; ed, Methodist Student Movement News, 59-61; admin. asst, Tex. Methodist Student Movement, 60-61. Mem: Theta Sigma Phi Alumni Chap; Tex. Soc. to Abolish Capital Punishment; Austin Cmn. on Human Rels.(ed. newsletter, 60-61). Headliner Award, Theta Sigma Phi, San Antonio, 68. Rel: Methodist. Legal Res: 2943 W. Ashby Place, San Antonio, Tex. 78228. Mailing Add: 220 Second St. S.E. 204, Washington, D.C. 20003.

BEAGLEY, RONALD FRANCIS D
Mem, Calif. Dem. State Cent. Cmt.
b. Chicago, Ill, 10/22/37; s. Thomas Leonard Beagley, Sr. and Josephine M. Fris B; m. 5/7/60 to Georgianne Ruth Brill; c. Kevin Patrick and Timothy David. Educ: Rio Hondo Jr. Col, 67-68; Univ. Calif. Los Angeles exten. courses, 68-69. Polit. & Govt. Pos: Mem, Calif. Dem. State Cent. Cmt, 66-; chmn, Soto for Assembly Cmt, 68; mem, Los Angeles Co. Dem. Cent. Cmt, Calif, 69- Bus. & Prof. Pos: Telephone installer, Ill. Bell Tel. Co, Oak Park, 55-56 & 60-62, Pac. Tel. & Tel, Los Angeles, 62-64, commun. consult, 64-66, area staff asst, 66-68, regional staff supvr. regional pub. affairs, 68- Mil. Serv: Entered as Airman Basic, Air Force, 56, released as Airman 1/C, 60, after serv. in Strategic Air Command, U.S. Air Forces in Europe, Saudi Arabia, 57-58; Good Conduct Medal; Presidential Unit Citation. Mem: Pres, La Puente Dem. Club; K. of C; past pres, Workman Mill Asn, Inc. Rel: Roman Catholic. Mailing Add: 1567 Coleford Ave, Whittier, Calif. 90601.

BEAHRS, JOHN VICTOR R
Councilman, Palo Alto, Calif.
b. Eufaula, Ala, 10/19/12; s. Elmer Charles Beahrs and Elsa Katheryn Smith B; m. 9/10/38 to Virginia Whitty Oakley; c. John Oakley, Richard Hewlett and William Whitty. Educ: Univ. Calif, Berkeley, B.S, 35; Am. Inst. Property & Liability Underwriters, C.P.C.U. Polit. & Govt. Pos: Pres-dir, Palo Alto Stanford Hosp. Center, Calif, 56-60 and Bay Area Hosp. Coun, 58-64; councilman, Palo Alto, 63-; dir, Bay Area Health Facilities Planning Asn, 64-65; mem, War Risk Adv. Cmt, U.S. Maritime Cmn, 66- Bus. & Prof. Pos: Pac. Dept. Marine mgr, The Home Ins. Co, N.Y, 46-61; asst. v.pres, Marsh & McLennan, Inc, 61-65; Ins-Gen. Claims mgr, Matson Navigation Co, 65- Mil. Serv: Entered as Ens, Navy, 41, released as Lt. Comdr, 46, after serv. in Amphibious Forces, Pac; Letter of Commendation, Adm. R.K. Turner. Mem: Univ. Club, Palo Alto, Calif. Rel: Episcopal. Mailing Add: 1830 Guinda St, Palo Alto, Calif. 94303.

BEAL, JOSEPH BURNS R
b. Richfield, Utah, 11/11/16; s. Erin Thorpe Beal and Elva Johnson B; m. 9/23/41 to Iola Tew; c. Camilla, Olani, Christine, Angela, Eloise and David. Educ: Ricks Col, 2 yrs. Polit. & Govt. Pos: Idaho State Sen, 63-67; mem, Gov. Cmt. of Fifty, 59-60; Idaho State Rep, 55-59. Mem: Former mem, Farm Bur. and Rotary. Chaplain, Nat. Jamboree, Boy Scouts, 60. Rel: Latter-day Saints. Mailing Add: Moore, Idaho 83255. (1967)

BEAL, THADDEUS R. R
Under Secy. of the Army
b. N.Y.C, 3/22/17; m. to Katharine Putnam; c. Katharine, Thaddeus, Alice and George. Educ: Yale Col, grad, 39; Harvard Law Sch, grad, 47. Polit. & Govt. Pos: Under Secy. of the Army, 69- Bus. & Prof. Pos: Assoc, Herrick, Smith, Donald, Farley & Ketchum, Attorneys, Boston, Mass, 47-56, partner, 56-57; v.pres, Harvard Trust Co, Cambridge, 57-62, pres, 62- Mil. Serv: Entered Navy, 41, released as Lt. Comdr, 45. Mem: Trustee, Cambridge Savings, Boston Personal Property Trust and Radcliffe Col; dir, Middlesex Mutual Ins. Co; Cambridge Redevelop. Authority; exec. coun, Am. Bankers Asn. Mailing Add: Dept. of the Army, Pentagon, Washington, D.C. 20310.

BEALE, WILSON THOMAS MOORE
b. Salisbury, Md, 7/22/09; div. Educ: Princeton Univ, A.B, 31; Univ. Pa, M.B.A, 33; London Sch. Econ, 33-35; Nat. War Col, 48-49. Polit. & Govt. Pos: Career officer, U.S. Dept. of State For. Serv, 46-67; adv. on Brit. Empire and Commonwealth Commercial Affairs, 46-48; mem, Commercial Policy Staff, 50-52; United Kingdom and Ireland Affairs, 52-55 and Off. Brit. Commonwealth and N.European Affairs, 55-56; For. Serv. Inspector, 56-57; Dep. Asst. Secy. of State for Econ. Affairs, 57-60; Econ. Minister, London, 60-64; Dep. Asst. Secy. of State for Admin, 64-65; U.S. Ambassador to Jamaica, 65-67. Bus. & Prof. Pos: Economist, U.S. Tariff Cmn, 36-42. Mil. Serv: Lt. Comdr, Navy, 42-45. Mailing Add: 1135 16th St. N.W, Washington, D.C. 20036.

BEALL, ALBERT CREASY R
b. Wilmington, N.C, 9/7/29; s. Thomas Edward Beall and Emerald Alberta Creasy B; m. 12/27/50 to Mary Katheryn Davis; c. Kathi, Annelle, Albert C, Jr, Kenneth Edward and James Matthew. Educ: Auburn Univ, B.S, 51. Polit. & Govt. Pos: Chmn, New Hanover Co. Rep. Exec. Cmt, N.C, formerly. Mil. Serv: Entered as 2nd Lt, Marine Corps, 51, released as Capt, 60; Medal of Commendation; Korean Conflict. Mem: Life mem. and past pres, Wilmington Jaycees; past state v.pres, N.C. Jaycees. Rel: Presbyterian. Mailing Add: P.O. Box 455, Wilmington, N.C. 28401. (1967)

BEALL, GEORGE R
Chmn, Third Dist. Baltimore Rep. Nat. Cent. Cmt, Md.
b. Frostburg, Md, 8/17/37; s. J. Glenn Beall and Margaret Schwarzenbach B; m. 12/30/64 to Nancy Stewart Roche; c. Rebecca Stewart and Katharine Barton. Educ: Princeton Univ, A.B; Va. Law Sch, LL.B; Omicron Delta Kappa. Polit. & Govt. Pos: Chmn, Third Dist. Baltimore Rep. Nat. Cent. Cmt, Md, 66-; del, Rep. Nat. Conv, 68; mem, Md. Criminal Injuries Compensation Cmn, 68- Mil. Serv: Entered as 2nd Lt, Army, 59, released as 1st Lt, 60, after serv. in Ft. Benning, Ga; Paratrooper Award. Mem: Baltimore City Jr. Bar Asn.(exec. bd, 68-69). Rel: Episcopal. Mailing Add: 112 Bellemore Rd, Baltimore, Md. 21210.

BEALL, J. GLENN, JR. R
U.S. Rep, Md.
b. Cumberland, Md, 6/19/27; s. J. Glenn Beall and Margaret Schwarzenbach B; m. 8/25/59 to Nancy Lee Smith; c. Victoria Lee. Educ: Yale Univ, B.A, 50. Polit. & Govt. Pos: Chmn, Allegany Co. Rep. State Cent. Cmt, Md, 58-62; Md. State Del, 62-68, Minority Floor Leader, Md. House of Del, 63-68; U.S. Rep, Md, 69-, mem, Banking and Currency Cmt, Ad Hoc Subcmt. Home Financing Practices and Procedures and Rep. Policy Cmt, U.S. House of Rep. Bus. & Prof. Pos: Prin, Beall, Garner & Geare, Inc, 50-; mem. bd. dirs, First Nat. Bank & Trust Co. Mil. Serv: Entered as A/S, Navy, 45, released as SHD 3/C, 46; Lt.(jg) Res. Mem: Past Potentate, Ali Gian Temple Shrine; Past Master, Mt. Lodge 99 AF&AM. Rel: Episcopal. Legal Res: Frostburg, Md. 21532. Mailing Add: 1527 House Office Bldg, Washington, D.C. 20515.

BEALL, RUSSELL G. D
b. Burnt House, W.Va, 3/10/22; s. Roscoe C. Beall and Bessie Cox B; m. 1/1/48 to Mary Margaret Morris; c. Dana and Donna. Educ: W.Va. Univ, B.S. Polit. & Govt. Pos: W.Va. State Del, 64-66. Bus. & Prof. Pos: Real estate developer; livestock dealer; oil and gas driller and producer. Mil. Serv: Capt, Army, 11th Airborne Div, Pac. Theatre. Rel: Baptist. Mailing Add: 2102 Maxwell St, Parkersburg, W.Va. 26101. (1967)

BEAM, JACOB DYNELEY
U.S. Ambassador to U.S.S.R.
b. Princeton, N.J, 3/24/08; s. Jacob Newton Beam and Mary Prince B; m. to Margaret Glassford; c. Jacob Alexander. Polit. & Govt. Pos: Career officer, U.S. Dept. of State For. Serv, 31-; v.consul, U.S. Consulate, Geneva, 31-34; secy, U.S. Embassy, Berlin, 34-40; div. asst, Dept. of State, 40-41; secy, U.S. Embassy, London, 41-45; polit. officer, Hq, U.S. Forces in Germany, 45-47; chief, Div. Cent. European Affairs, 47-48; consul, Batavia, 49; counselor, U.S. Embassy, Djakarta, 49-51 and Belgrade, 51-52; acting head, U.S. Embassy, Moscow, 52-53; dep. dir. policy planning staff, 53; mem. bd. exam. for For. Serv, 54-55; dir, Office of E.European Affairs, 55; dep. asst. secy. of state for European affairs, 55-57; U.S. Ambassador to Poland, 57-61; asst. dir, Int. Rels. Bur, U.S. Arms Control and Disarmament Agency, 62-66; U.S. Ambassador, Czech, 66-69 and U.S.S.R, 69- Legal Res: Princeton, N.J. Mailing Add: U.S. Embassy, Moscow, U.S.S.R.

BEAMAN, JAMES ADDISON R
Mem, Ariz. Rep. State Cent. Cmt.
b. Sidney, Ohio, 9/10/00; s. John Beaman and Anna Irene Pruden B; m. 7/7/24 to Kathryn Madeline Walker; c. James A, Jr. and Nancy (Mrs. McMahon). Educ: Univ. Cincinnati, Com. Eng, 24; Delta Tau Delta; Sigma Sigma. Polit. & Govt. Pos: Del, Rep. Nat. Conv, 48, alternate del, 64; mem, Ariz. Rep. State Cent. Cmt, 48-; chmn, Ariz. Employ. Security Cmn, 51-54 & 59-64. Bus. & Prof. Pos: Acct. controller and asst. treas, S.A. Gerrard Co, 30-37; owner, Gen. Ins, 37-39; controller, O'Malley Co, 39-61, gen. mgr, Investment Div, 61- Mem: Financial Exec. Inst; Maricopa Taxpayers Asn; past pres. and dir, Scottsdale Boys Club. Rel: Protestant. Mailing Add: 6616 Jackrabbit Rd, Scottsdale, Ariz. 85251. (1967)

BEAME, ABRAHAM DAVID D
b. London, Eng, 3/20/06; s. Philip Beame and Esther Goldfarb B; m. 2/18/28 to Mary Ingerman; c. Edmond Morton and Bernard Walter. Educ: City Col. of N.Y, B.B.A, 28; Beta Gamma Sigma. Polit. & Govt. Pos: Asst. budget dir, N.Y.C, 46-52, budget dir, 52-61, comptroller, 62-65, dem. cand. for Mayor, N.Y.C, 65; del. and chmn, Inter-governmental Relations Cmt, Const. Convention N.Y. State; del, Dem. Nat. Conv, 68. Bus. & Prof. Pos: Partner, Beame & Greidineer CPA's, 25-45; chmn, Bd. Dirs, Arrow Lock Corp, Brooklyn, 66-69; owner, Abraham D. Beame Associates, Financial Consultants, N.Y.C, 66-; dir. and chmn, Finance Comn, American Bank & Trust Co, N.Y.C, 66- Mem: N.Y. State Soc. of CPA; Mu Gamma Tau; Tau Phi Sigma; Small Business Advisory Council; trustee, Fedn. of Jewish Philanthropics; bd. dirs, United Jewish Appeal; treas, N.Y. Israel Bond Orgn; Brooklyn bd, Nat. Conf. of Christians and Jews; treas, City Col. Fund; Townsend Harris Medal, City College; Citizen's Budget Cmn. Rel: Jewish. Mailing Add: 60 Plaza St, Brooklyn, N.Y. 11238.

BEAMER, GEORGE N. D
b. Bowling Green, Ind, 10/9/04; s. Jasper F. Beamer and Frances Roush B; m. 5/14/32 to Charlotte L. Hoover; c. George N, Jr. and Judith Ann (Mrs. Roempagel). Educ: Notre Dame Univ, LL.B, 29. Polit. & Govt. Pos: City judge, South Bend, Ind, 33-34, city attorney, 39-41; prosecuting attorney, St. Joseph Co, 37-38; attorney gen, Ind, 41-42; chmn, Pub. Serv. Cmt, Ind, 43-44; U.S. Dist. judge, North. Dist. of Ind, 62- Bus. & Prof. Pos: Partner Crumpacker, May, Beamer, Levy and Searer, South Bend, Ind, 38-40 & 44-62. Mem: Mason (33°) Shrine; Optimist. Rel: Brethren. Legal Res: 1043 Elliott Dr, Munster, Ind. 46321. Mailing Add: U.S. District Court, Hammond, Ind. 46420.

BEAN, ARTHUR E, JR. R
b. Concord, N.H, 11/11/18; s. Arthur E. Bean and Beulah Sargent B; m. 6/29/41 to Alice E. Whipple; c. David W. Educ: Univ. N.H, 40; Boston Univ. Sch. Law, 51. Polit. & Govt. Pos: Asst. attorney gen, N.H, 51-57; del, Rep. Nat. Conv, 64. Mil. Serv: Entered as Flying Cadet, Army Air Force, 40, released as Lt. Col, 46, after serv. in 384th Bomb Group, ETO; Distinguished

Flying Cross with Cluster; Air Medal with 4 Clusters; Croix De Guerre; ETO Theater Ribbon with 4 Battle Stars; Pre Pearl Harbor and Am. Theater Ribbons; Res. Ribbon with Hour Glass Cluster; Col, Air Force Res. Mem: Am. and N.H. Bar Asns. Rel: Protestant. Legal Res: 9 Vernon St, Concord, N.H. 03301. Mailing Add: 1662 Elm St, Manchester, N.H. 03104.

BEAN, CANDACE M. E. R
b. Derby, Vt, 3/24/06; m. to Chester Bean; c. two sons, three daughters. Educ: Derby Acad. Polit. & Govt. Pos: Former town auditor, Troy, Vt, 7 years; Vt. State Rep, 65-69; Justice of the Peace, 69- Bus. & Prof. Pos: Correspondent, Newport Daily Express, 8 years. Mem: Tri-Town Club; v.pres, Busy Trojan Home Demonstration Club; Civil Defense. Rel: Congregational; Deaconess, clerk and treas, 66-, pres, Church Soc. Union, 3 years. Mailing Add: R.D. 2, North Troy, Vt. 05859.

BEAN, JOSEPH EDWARD D
Chmn, St. Mary's Co. Dem. Party, Md.
b. St. Mary's Co, Md, 6/4/29; s. James Lloyd Bean, Sr. and Catherine Tennyson B; m. 4/12/50 to Betty Jeanne Knupp; c. Edward Vernon, Mary Elizabeth and Richard Wayne. Educ: St. Michael's High Sch, 4 years. Polit. & Govt. Pos: Chmn, St. Mary's Co. Dem. Party, Md, 64- Bus. & Prof. Pos: Route mgr, Washington Star Newspaper Co, 53- Mem: K. of C.(Grand Knight, St. Michael's Coun, 2 years); Lexington Park Rescue Squad (vol, pres, 2 years); Elks. Rel: Catholic. Mailing Add: Chancellors Run Rd, Great Mills, Md. 20634.

BEAN, ROBERT RAY D
Co. Attorney, Pinal Co, Ariz.
b. Corona, Calif, 5/4/35; s. Kenneth Ray Bean (deceased) and Madeline Jewel Roberts B; m. 2/18/59 to Joyce E. McFarland; c. Susan E. and Kimberly Ann. Educ: Univ. Calif. Los Angeles, 54; Univ. Ariz, B.A, 57, LL.B, 63; Arnold Air Soc; Kappa Alpha; Phi Alpha Delta; Inter-Fraternity Coun. Polit. & Govt. Pos: Dep. co. attorney, Pinal Co, Ariz, 63-66; chmn, Coolidge Dem. Party, 64-66; v.chmn, Pinal Co. Dem. Party, 66-67, chmn, 67-68; town attorney, Florence, 67-68; del, Dem. Nat. Conv, 68; mem, Coolidge City Planning & Zoning Cmn, 68-; co. attorney, Pinal Co, 69-; mem, Ariz. Dist. 13 Judicial Planning Agency, 69. Mil. Serv: Entered as 2nd Lt, Air Force, 58, released as 1st Lt, 60, after serv. in 58th Fighter Interceptor Squadron, Air Defense Command, Roswell, N.Mex, 59-60; Capt, Air Force Res, 66. Mem: Pinal Co. Bar Asn.(pres, 67); Ariz. State Bar Asn; Am. Judicature Soc; past Exalted Ruler, Elks Lodge 2350; Am. Legion; chmn, Pinal Co. Chap. March of Dimes; Coolidge Indust. Develop. Corp; v.pres, Cent. Ariz. Col. Found; Rotary. Rel: Presbyterian, Ruling Elder. Mailing Add: 865 W. Central, Coolidge, Ariz. 85228.

BEAN, WOODROW W. 'WOODY' D
b. Cascade, Idaho, 11/2/18; s. Willie A. Bean and Mary O. Williams B; m. 9/17/50 to Nivena Monson; c. Jo Lou and Mary Lin. Educ: High Sch. Polit. & Govt. Pos: Mem, City Coun, Village of Cascade, Idaho, 54-58; Idaho State Rep, 58-62; Idaho State Sen, Dist. 9, 64-68. Bus. & Prof. Pos: Grocery store mgr, 40-42; dept. store mgr, CC Anderson Co, 46-48; owner, Cascade Cash Grocery Mkt, 48-68. Mil. Serv: Entered as Pvt, Army, 42, released as T/Sgt, 45, after serv. in 1808th Ord. Co, Europe; 4 Battle Stars; ETO and Victory Ribbons; Unit Citation. Mem: Odd Fellows, Mason; Eastern Star; Grange; Am. Legion. Rel: Christian Church. Mailing Add: Box 28, Cascade, Idaho 83611.

BEANE, ARTHUR E, JR. R
Chmn, Kingston Rep. Town Cmt, Mass.
b. Cambridge, Mass, 9/26/18; s. Arthur E. Beane and Susan Louise White B; m. 6/3/44 to Mary Elizabeth Clarke. Educ: Brown Univ, A.B, 42; Psi Upsilon. Polit. & Govt. Pos: Mem, Kingston Zoning Cmt, Mass, 58; mem, Kingston Planing Bd, 58-69; chmn, Kingston Rep. Town Cmt, 66- Bus. & Prof. Pos: Mem. advertising dept, John Hancock Mutual Life Ins, 44-61; printing coordinator, Boston Univ, 61- Mil. Serv; Entered as SK 2/C, Maritime Serv, 43, released, 44, after serv. in Boston Harbor. Mailing Add: 2 Linden St, Kingston, Mass. 02360.

BEARD, FRED J. R
b. Gwinnette Co, Ga, 9/14/95; s. William James Beard and Josephine Cook B; m. 12/8/20 to Maude Isabel Guess; c. Agnes (Mrs. C.B. Garrett) and Tommy L. Educ: Bethel Sch, Turner Co, Ga. Polit. & Govt. Pos; Justice of Peace, 50-66; chmn, Turner Co. Rep. Cmt, Ga, 32-64. Bus. & Prof. Pos: Farmer, 18-65. Mil. Serv: Pvt, Army, 18-19. Mem: Mason; Odd Fellows; Am. Legion; Farm Bur. Fedn; Vets. World War I. Rel: Missionary Baptist. Mailing Add: Route 1, Box 126, Sycamore, Ga. 31790. (1967)

BEARD, ROBERT QUINCY R
N.C. State Rep.
b. Statesville, N.C, 12/7/29; s. Robert Ezekiel Beard and Nola Hoover B; m. 8/12/50 to Carrie Felicity Stewart; c. Kathryn Ann, Janet Lynne and Mary Faith. Educ: Lenoir Rhyne Col, A.B, cum laude, 55; Lutheran Theol. South. Sem, B.D, 58; Mu Sigma Epsilon. Polit. & Govt. Pos: Exec. committeeman, N.C. Rep. Party, 68-; N.C. State Rep, 40th Dist, 68- Bus. & Prof. Pos: Minister, Grace Lutheran Church, Liberty, N.C, 58-59, Faith Lutheran Church, Conover, 60-62 and St. Paul's Lutheran Church, Newton, 63- Mil. Serv: Entered as Pvt, Marine Corps, 48, released as S/Sgt, 52, after serv. in Second Marine Air Wing, Cherry Point, N.C; Good Conduct Medal, 51; Nat. Defense Serv. Medal, 52. Mem: Catawba Valley Lutheran Ministers' Asn; Catawba Valley Marine Corps Asn; Lions; Startown Elem. PTA; Foard High Sch. PTA; Startown Area Develop. Asn. Rel: Lutheran. Mailing Add: Route 3, Box 416, Newton, N.C. 28658.

BEARDSLEY, HARRY WINFRED D
b. Tuttle, Okla, 6/8/20; s. Pearl Beardsley and Mae Burba B; m. 6/6/44 to Winifred Divine; c. Harriet Winifred and Robert Alan. Educ: Oklahoma City Univ, A.B, 42; Boston Univ, A.M, 47; Lambda Chi Alpha; Alpha Phi Omega. Polit. & Govt. Pos: Civil Serv. Cmnr, West Des Moines, Iowa, 64-66; Iowa State Rep, 67-68; chmn, State Adv. Coun. Adult Educ, 68-69. Bus. & Prof. Pos: Dir, Marietta Johnson Sch, 51; asst. prof, Tex. State Col. Women, 48-51; Simpson Col, 52-54; lectr. philos, Univ. Col, Drake Univ, 58-; pub. rels. mgr, Preferred Risk Mutual Ins. Co, 68- Mil. Serv: Entered as Aviation Cadet, Naval Res, 42, released as Lt, 45, after serv. in Pac. Area, 43-45; Res, until 66. Rel: Methodist. Mailing Add: 544 32nd St, West Des Moines, Iowa 50265.

BEARDSLEY, WALTER RAPER R
b. Elkhart, Ind, 10/23/05; s. Andrew Hubble Beardsley and Helen Brown B; m. 11/20/29 to Marjory Anna Buchanan; c. Robert Buchanan. Educ: Princeton Univ, B.S. in Polit, with honors, 28; Babson Inst, grad. study, 28; London Univ. Sch. Econ, 29. Polit. & Govt. Pos: Co. chmn, Rep. Jr, Ind, 28-30; chmn, Elkhart Co. Rep. Party, 30-34; del, Ind. Rep. Conv, 30-68; finance chmn, Elkhart Co. and Ind. State Rep. Finance Cmts; mem, Elkhart Co. Coun, 34-36; Ind. State Sen, 36-40; del, Rep. Nat. Conv, 48, 52, 56, 60, 64 & 68, mem, Cmt. on Arrangements and chmn, subcmt. Transportation, 64, mem, Rules Cmt, 68; Rep. nat. committeeman, Ind, 61-68. Bus. & Prof. Pos: Admin. asst. to pres, Miles Labs, Inc, Elkhart, Ind, 30-36, v.pres, 36-47, pres, 47-61, chmn. bd, 61-; dir, Hotel Elkhart Corp, First Nat. Bank of Elkhart Co. and Truth Publ. Co; pres. bd. trustees, Elkhart Gen. Hosp. Mil. Serv: Entered as 1st Lt, Air Force, 42, released as Lt. Col, 45, after serv. in Hq. Gulf Coast Training Command, San Antonio, Tex, 42, Hq. Army Air Force, Wash. D.C, 42-43 and XX Bomber Command, China-Burma-India Theater, Kharagpur, India, 44-45; Am. Campaign Ribbon; Asiatic-Pac. Campaign Ribbon with three Battle Stars; Victory Medal. Mem: Bd. dirs, Proprietary Asn.(pres, 48-50); Nat. Indust. Conf. Bd; Princeton Clubs of N.Y; Sky Club, N.Y.C; SAR; art gallery adv. coun, Univ. Notre Dame; Columbia Club, Indianapolis; Univ. Club, N.Y.C; Capitol Hill Club, Wash, D.C. Rel: Presbyterian. Legal Res: 2233 Greenleaf Blvd, Elkhart, Ind. 46514. Mailing Add: 1127 Myrtle St, Elkhart, Ind. 46514.

BEASLEY, DELMAR OTIS
b. Rockport, Miss, 10/13/07; s. James Bascom Beasley anf Floyd Catherine Fox B; m. 6/20/34 to Virginia Macklin Shell B; c. Elizabeth and Nancy. Educ: George Wash. Univ, B.A, 34, LL.B, 41; Phi Sigma Kappa. Polit. & Govt. Pos: Clerk typist, War Dept, 28-30; clerk, bookkeeper, asst. chief, Div. of Acct, 30-41; budget officer, Geol. Surv, 41-42; asst. budget officer and asst. dir, Div. Budget and Admin. Mgt. and dir, Div. of Budget and Finance, 42-52; asst. secy, Admin. Div, Dept. of Interior, 52-65. Bus. & Prof. Pos: Off. boy, W.P. Brown & Sons Lumber Co, Zama, Miss, 27-28; chmn, Oil Import Appeals Bd, 61-62; staff, Gov. Off; attorney-at-law, 66- Mem: Adv. bd, Marine Heart Research Found; dir, Int. Light Tackle Tournament Asn; Am, Fed. and Inter-Am. Bar Asns; Univ. Club; Touchdown Club Wash; Recipient Interior Dept. Distinguished Serv. Award. Legal Res: 4716 44th St. N.W, Washington, D.C. 20016. Mailing Add: 1000 16th St. N.W, Washington, D.C. 20036.

BEASLEY, GERALD LeROY, JR. R
b. Tulsa, Okla, 4/6/26; s. Gerald LeRoy Beasley, Sr. and Lottie Laura Bell B; m. 9/2/49 to Mary Evelyn Burke; c. Gerald LeRoy, III, Donald Edward, Elizabeth Ann and Robert Lawrence. Educ: Univ. Tulsa, 46-49; Univ. Okla, Sch. of Med, M.D, 53. Polit. & Govt. Pos: Rep. cand, U.S. Rep, 3rd Dist, Okla, 68. Mil. Serv: Entered as Aviation Cadet, Air Force, released as Aviation Student, 45. Mem: Am. Asn. Physicians & Surgeons; Am. Med. Asn. Rel: Baptist. Mailing Add: 1005 Cedar, Duncan, Okla. 73533.

BEASLEY, JOHN GERALD D
b. Lamar, S.C, 9/30/34; s. Gerald Beasley and Thelma Joye B; m. 8/10/57 to Mary Delleney Ruff; c. John Gerald, Jr. and Mary Joye. Educ: Univ. S.C, B.S. in Bus. Admin, 57; Blue Key; Kappa Sigma Kappa; Kappa Alpha; pres, Cotillion Club; German Club; head cheerleader, 57 & 68. Polit. & Govt. Pos: Legis. asst. to U.S. Rep. William J.B. Dorn, S.C, 67-; v.pres, Capitol Hill Young Dem, 69-; treas, Capitol Hill Toastmaster, 69- Bus. & Prof. Pos: Dist. sales dir, Swift & Co. Agr. Chem. Div, 57-61; sales mgr, Am. Oil Co, Atlanta, Ga, 61-65; spec. asst. to regional dir, Off. of Econ. Opportunity, 66-68. Mil. Serv: Cpl, Army Res, 54-57. Mem: The Burro Club; charter mem, Capitol Hill Toastmaster Club; S.C. Dem. Party. Received recognition for outstanding serv. as Rotarian. Rel: Episcopal. Mailing Add: 5914 Kingsford Rd, Springfield, Va. 22152.

BEASLEY, KERN GRANT R
b. Linton, Ind, 7/20/03; s. Alfred Milton Beasley and Anna Gertrude Morgan B; m. 7/30/61 to Harriet Clark. Educ: Ind. Univ, A.B, 24; Harvard Univ, 25-26; George Wash. Univ, LL.B, 26, J.D, 28; Acacia; Phi Delta Phi. Polit. & Govt. Pos: Asst. secy, interstate commerce cmt, U.S. Sen, 26-28; prosecuting attorney, 63rd Judicial Circuit Court, Greene Co, Ind, 32-36 & 58-60; del, Rep. Nat. Conv, 68. Bus. & Prof. Pos: Secy, Miller Construction Co, Ind, 43-; pres, Citizens Nat. Bank of Linton, 68. Mil. Serv: 1st Lt, Army Res. (Ret). Mem: Am. and Ind. Bar Asns; Mason (32°); Shrine; Royal Order of Jesters; Elks. Meritorious Pub. Serv. Citation, Navy. Rel: Methodist. Mailing Add: 590 N. Main St, Linton, Ind. 47441.

BEASLEY, RICHARD LEE D
b. Lamar, S.C, 10/14/30; s. J. Wesley Beasley and Lois Long B; m. 8/5/50 to Jacqueline Blackwell B; c. Richard Lewis, Henry Wesley, David Muldrow. Educ: The Citadel, B.A, 51. Polit. & Gov. Pos: S.C. State Rep, 61-64. Bus. & Prof. Pos: Cashier, Carolina Bank & Trust Co; Pres, Beasley & Beasley Ins. Agency, Inc; real estate. Mil. Serv: Army, 8th Cavalry Regt. Combat Team, 51-53. Mem: Pres, Lamar Civitan Club, 59-60. Rel: Off. Bd, Lamar Methodist Church. Mailing Add: Lamar, S.C. 29069. (1967)

BEASLEY, THOMAS WOODROW D
b. Gleason, Tenn, 12/18/18; s. Thomas Guy Beasley and Avie Hawley B; div; c. Jan Leah and Ginger Van. Educ: Toler's Bus. Col, Paris, Tenn. Polit. & Govt. Pos: Inspector, U.S. Corps Engrs, 40-42; field secy, Gov. Frank G. Clement, Tenn, 63-64, spec. asst, 64-66. Bus. & Prof. Pos: Pres, Nashville Auto Auction Inc, 53-; pres, South. Auto Asn, 57; v.pres, Nat. Auto Auction Asn, 57-58, pres, 58-59, mem, bd. of dirs, currently. Mil. Serv: Entered as Pvt, Army, 42, released as S/Sgt, 44, after serv. in Signal Corps, 5th Army, N.Africa, 43-44. Mem: Am. Legion; VFW; Country Music Asn; Bluegrass Country Club; Nashville City Club. Rel: Methodist. Legal Res: Windsor Towers, West End, 4215 Harding Rd, Nashville, Tenn. 37205. Mailing Add: 1406 Lebanon Rd, Nashville, Tenn. 37210. (1967)

BEATON, FRANKLYN GEORGE R
b. Canada, 1/9/93; m. to Cora M. George; c. One son and three daughters. Educ: Cabot High Sch. Polit. & Govt. Pos: Selectman, Marshfield, Vt, Dan-

ville, 35-46; Vt. State Rep, formerly. Bus. & Prof. Pos: Farmer; livestock dealer. Mil. Serv: Cpl, Army, 18-19. Mem: Farm Bur; Vt. Cattlemen's Asn. Rel: Congregational. Mailing Add: Marshfield, Vt. 05658. (1967)

BEATTIE, CATHERINE M. D
Mem, Vt. Dem. State Cmt.
b. Danville, Vt, 4/5/21; m. to Harold Beattie; c. Three sons and seven daughters. Educ: Danville High Sch. Polit. & Govt. Pos: Secy and mem, Co. Bd. of Trustees, Farm Bur; Vt. State Rep, 65-67; mem, Vt. Dem. State Cmt, currently. Bus. & Prof. Pos: Farming. Mem: Eastern Star; Danville Woman's Club; Pythian Sisters; Danville Parent-Teachers Group; Caledonia Co. Farm Bur; Danville Hist. Soc. Rel: Protestant. Mailing Add: Danville, Vt. 05828. (1967)

BEATTIE, CHARLES KENNETH R
Exec. Secy, Harford Co. Rep. Cent. Cmt, Md.
b. Whiteford, Md, 7/19/23; s. Simon Beattie and Susie Hughes B; single. Educ: Strayers Bus. Col, Baltimore, Md, 42; Univ. Baltimore, pre-law, 44. Polit. & Govt. Pos: Precinct chmn, Rep. Party, Md, 45-; assoc. judge of elec, 47-62; pres, Harford Co. Young Rep. Club, 49, 50, 53 & 60, membership chmn, 66, 67, 68 & 69, past treas. and v.pres, assoc. mem, currently; Harford Co. del, Md. State Rep. Conv, 52, 56, 60 & 68; alternate del, Rep. Nat. Conv, 52, 56, 60 & 68; alternate del, Rep. Nat. Conv, 52, 56 & 68; state dir, Md. Fedn. Young Rep, 55-59; chmn. nominating cmt, Md. Fedn. Young Rep. Officers, 57; campaign mgr, Harford Co. Rep. Party, 66; exec. secy, Harford Co. Rep. Cent. Cmt, 66-; co-organizer, Cecil Co. Young Rep. Club, 68. Bus. & Prof. Pos: Clerk, Bainbeidge Naval Training Sta, 42-43; clerk, Edgewood Arsenal, Md, 44-46; sr. customer rels. cler, Baltimore Gas & Electric Co, Bel Air, 46- Mil. Serv: Entered as Recruit, Army, 48, released as Pvt, 49, after serv. in Commanding Off, Aberdeen Proving Grounds, Md. Mem: Mason; Odd Fellows (past Master, York Co. Lodge, Pa); Harford Co. Tuberc. Asn.(v.pres. and mem. bd. dirs); Harford Co. Cancer Bd.(v.pres. and mem. bd. dirs); Hawks Endzone Club (v.pres); Harford Co. Christmas Seal Chmn, 67-69; Moose; Am. Legion; Delta-Cardiff Fire Co; Lions; Presby. Youth (past adv, York Co. Club, Pa); Delta Teen Club (past pres). Rel: Presbyterian; Past youth adv, mem. choir, Sunday Sch. teacher and trustee, Slaterville Presbyterian Church. Mailing Add: Chestnut St, Whiteford, Md. 21160.

BEATTIE, JACK ROBERT R
Chmn, Orange Co. Rep. Exec. Cmt, Fla.
b. Bay City, Mich, 10/2/34; s. Aaron Joseph Beattie (deceased), stepfather, Owen Randolph Colley and Sadie Young Beattie C; m. 6/27/59 to Ernestine Linda Johnson; c. John Robert, Jeffrey Lind and Kimberly Young. Educ: Mich. State Univ, B.A, 56; Univ. Mich, D.D.S, 60; West. Reserve Univ, M.S, orthodontics, 63; Sigma Nu; Porpoise Fratenity; Nat. Collegiate All Am. Swimming Team. Polit. & Govt. Pos: Committeeman, Orange Co. Rep, Exec. Cmt, Fla, 65-, chmn, 68-; alternate del, Rep. Nat. Conv, 68. Bus. & Prof. Pos: Fla. Del, Am. Dent. Asn, 68- Mem: Am, Cent. Dist. and Orange Co. Dent. Asns; Kiwanis; C. of C. Nat. Competition recipient, Milo Helman Research Award, Am. Asn. Orthodontists, 64. Rel: Congregational. Legal Res: 561 Via Lugano, Winter Park, Fla. Mailing Add: 618 E. South St, Orlando, Fla. 32801.

BEATTY, JAMES WARD D
Chmn, Marion Co. Dem. Cmt, Ind.
b. Fort Wayne, Ind, 8/30/31; s. Harry Beatty and Viola Schumann B; m. 8/6/55 to Phyllis Bettmann; c. Lynn, Jay and Leann. Educ: Univ. Mich, A.B, 53; Univ. Mich. Law Sch, J.D, 55; Order of the Coif. Polit. & Govt. Pos: Chmn, Marion Co. Dem. Cmt, Ind. and chmn, 11th Dist. Dem. Cmt, Ind, currently; del, Dem. Nat. Conv, 68. Mem: Am, Ind. and Indianapolis Bar Asns; Commercial Law League; Ind. Civil Liberties Union. Mailing Add: 220 E. Ohio, Indianapolis, Ind. 46204.

BEATTY, JIM D
N.C. State Rep.
b. N.Y.C; m. to Barbara Ann Harmon. Educ: Univ. N.C, 57. Polit. & Govt. Pos: Past dir, N.C. Vols; N.C. State Rep, 67- Bus. & Prof. Pos: Nat. sales mgr, Radio Sta. WAYS, Charlotte. Mil. Serv: Army, 57-58; Nat. Guard. Mem: U.S. Olympic Track Team, 60. Named one of the 10 Outstanding Young Men of the Year by the U.S. Jr. C. of C, 62. Rel: Catholic. Mailing Add: 3716 Rhodes Ave, Charlotte, N.C. 28210. (1967)

BEATY, JEANNE KELLAR D
b. Grand Rapids, Mich, 7/10/22; d. Francis Anthony Kellar and Lula Shaver K; m. 12/28/47 to Chester Broomell Beaty; c. Katherine and Anne. Educ: Grand Rapids Jr. Col, A.A, 41; La. State Univ, B.A, 43; Alpha Xi Delta. Polit. & Govt. Pos: Precinct committeewoman, Missoula Co. Dem. Cent. Cmt, Mont, 62-66 and publicity chmn, 64; chmn, Dollars for Dem, Missoula Co, 62; publicity dir, Cmt. for Paradise Dam, 63; publicity chmn, Missoula Co. Dem. Club and Missoula Co. Dem. Women's Club, 64; publicity dir, Mont. State Dem. Women's Club, 64 and second v.pres, 65-66; mem. state rules cmt, Mont. State Dem. Cmt, 65-67; chmn, Mont. Dissenting Dem, 67; publicity dir, Mont. Dem. for McCarthy, 67-68 and New Reform Party, 68; del, Dem. Nat. Conv, 68. Bus. & Prof. Pos: News reporter, Grand Rapids Herald, Grand Rapids, Mich, 44-45; field correspondent, World Outlook, N.Y.C, 46-47; free lance writer and travel correspondent, N.Y. Times and Good Housekeeping Mag, 47- Publ: Lookout Wife, Random House, 53; 'In Defense of the Wise Housewife,' Good Housekeeping Mag, 6/61, reprinted in Reader's Digest and current Thinking and Writing, 64; 'Let's Talk Facts,' Mont. State Dem. Women's Club, 66. Missoula Co. Dem. Woman of the Year, 65; Mont. Woman-Doer, 66. Rel: Unitarian. Mailing Add: W. Rattlesnake, Missoula, Mont. 59801.

BEATY, ORREN, JR. D
b. Clayton, N.Mex, 6/13/19; s. Orren Beaty and Edith Mason B; m. 12/30/44 to Mary Ethel Turner; c. Orren, III, Laura Leigh and Susan Ray. Educ: N.Mex. State Univ, B.A, 41; Univ. Houston. Polit. & Govt. Pos: Admin. asst. to U.S. Rep. Stewart L. Udall, 56-61; asst. to U.S. Secy. of Interior, 61-68; fed. co-chmn, Four Corners Regional Cmn, 67-69. Bus. & Prof. Pos: Managing ed, Sun-News, Las Cruces, N.Mex, 46-47; reporter, polit. writer and columnist, The Ariz. Republic, 48-55. Mil. Serv: 1st Lt, Army, 42-46; Maj, Air Force, 50-52. Mailing Add: 1784 Proffitt Rd, Vienna, Va. 22100.

BEAUCHAMP, CAROLE ANN R
b. Thurmont, Md, 2/27/38; d. Frank C. Long, Sr. and Ruth Elizabeth Troxwell L; m. 12/9/67 to Dan E. Beauchamp. Educ: Strayer Bus. Col, 56-57. Polit. & Govt. Pos: Admin. asst, U.S. Rep. Silvio O. Conte, Mass, 59- Rel: Protestant. Mailing Add: 110 Maryland Ave. N.E, Washington, D.C. 20002.

BEAUCHAMP, DONALD WAYNE D
Okla. State Rep.
b. Lawton, Okla, 3/1/37; s. Theodore William Beauchamp and Muriel Logan B; single. Educ: Univ. Okla, B.B.A, 60, LL.B, 64. Polit. & Govt. Pos: Okla. State Rep. and asst. majority floor leader, Okla. House Rep, currently. Bus. & Prof. Pos: Attorney. Mil. Serv: Entered as Airman, Air Force Res, 60, released as Airman 1/C, 66; Lt.(jg); Naval Res, 66- Legal Res: 14 N. 28th St, Lawton, Okla. 73501. Mailing Add: 518 D Ave, Suite 102, Lawton, Okla. 73501.

BEAUCHAMP, ISAAC EMERSON D
Chief Clerk, Ky. State Senate
b. Russellville, Ky, 6/14/99; s. Isaac Beauchamp and Ella Offutt B; m. 4/4/22 to Margaret Elizabeth Orndorff; c. Russell Clark and Isaac Emerson, Jr. Educ: Bethel Col, Ky, 20-21; Sigma Alpha Epsilon. Polit. & Govt. Pos: Clerk, Logan Co. Court, Ky, 26-33, sheriff, 37-40; mem, Ky. State Tax Cmn, 33-35, state personnel dir, 48, rural roads cmnr, 49-51, lt. gov, 52-55, cmnr. agr, 60-63 and state treas, 64-68; chief clerk, Ky. State Senate, 44-46 & 68- Mil. Serv: Pvt, Army, 18, reentered, 41, released as 1st Lt, 43, after serv. in ETO. Mem: Mason; life mem. Am. Legion and VFW; DAV. Rel: Methodist. Mailing Add: 108 W. Seventh St, Russellville, Ky. 42276.

BEAUCHAMP, JEAN M. R
Mem, Calif. Rep. State Cent. Cmt.
b. Redding, Calif, 12/10/17; d. Wade Greening Moores and Mabel Lowdon M; m. 5/30/41 to David Dohrmann Beauchamp; c. Mark and Carrie. Educ: Univ. of Calif, Berkeley, A.B. and Gen. Sec. Teachers Credentials, 39. Polit. & Govt. Pos: Mem, Calif. Rep. State Cent. Cmt, 62-63 & 69-; pres, Redding Coun. Rep. Women, 63-64; regional v.pres, Calif. Fedn. of Rep. Women, 66- Bus. & Prof. Pos: Teacher, Shasta Union High Sch, Redding, Calif, 39-41; mgr, Dorothy Wright Liebes Handweaving Studio, San Francisco, 44-48; instr. adult div, Stockton Col, 48-52. Mem: John Birch Soc. Rel: Episcopal. Mailing Add: 830 Overhill Dr, Redding, Calif. 96001.

BEAUDOIN, LEO E. D
N.H. State Rep.
b. Rochester, N.H, 8/14/94; married; c. Seven. Educ: Rochester High Sch. Polit. & Govt. Pos: Mem, Sch. Bd, N.H, 25 years; dir, Pub. Welfare; N.H. State Rep, 63- Bus. & Prof. Pos: Ins. Mem: Elks; dir, Victory Club; 1st pres, Rochester Little League Baseball. Rel: Catholic. Mailing Add: 10 Wash. St, Rochester, N.H. 03867. (1967)

BEAULIEU, ERNEST ROBERT R
Chmn, Burrillville Rep. Town Cmt, R.I.
b. Pawtucket, R.I, 2/7/28; s. Ernest H. Beaulieu and Lillian I. Moreau B; m. 9/25/50 to Adele G. Payette; c. Paula, Sylvia, Roxanne, Michele and Ernest. Educ: Our Lady of Providence Sem, 2 years. Polit. & Govt. Pos: Del, Rep. Nat. Conv, 68; chmn, Burrillville Rep. Town Cmt, R.I, 68-; mem-at-lg, R.I. Rep. State Cent. Cmt, 69- Bus. & Prof. Pos: Mgr, Seaboard Finance Co, 58-63; pres, Beau-Lieu Rest Home, Inc, 63-; pres, Golden Oaks Manor, Inc, 68-; owner, Beau-Lieu Manor, Inc, 68- Publ: 'President Speaks,' Bay State Bul, 3/69; 'Administrators and Inspections,' Patience, 5/69. Mem: Am. Nursing Home Asn.(gov. coun. mem); R.I. State Nursing Home Asn.(pres, 69); New Eng. Regional Nursing Home Asn.(bd. mem); Lions (bd); Jaycees; R.I. Jr. C. of C.(Int. dir. and sen). Burrillville Jaycees Outstanding Citizen, 66. Rel: Roman Catholic. Legal Res: 10 Steere St, Harrisville, R.I. 02830. Mailing Add: P.O. Box 311, Harrisville, R.I. 02830.

BEAUMONT, WILLIAM EUSTACE, JR. D
Ark. State Rep.
b. Little Rock, Ark, 4/3/33; s. William Eustace Beaumont and Mary Elizabeth Hocott B; m. 7/16/51 to Elli Karoline Heinrich; c. William Eustace, III, Mary Elizabeth, Karoline Ann and Suzanna Marie. Educ: Univ. Ark, B.S.B.A, 56; Alpha Tau Omega. Polit. & Govt. Pos: Mem, Health Ins. Benefits Adv. Coun, U.S. Dept. of Health, Educ. and Welfare, 65-67; mem, Ark. Hosp. Adv. Coun, 65-; Ark. State Rep, 69- Bus. & Prof. Pos: Pres, Ark. Nursing Home Asn, 63, Am. Nursing Home Asn, 65-66; chmn, Joint Coun. to Improve Health of the Aging, 64-66. Mem: Fellow, Am. Col. Nursing Home Admins; Mason (33°). Rel: Methodist. Legal Add: 5 Pamela Dr, Little Rock, Ark. 72207. Mailing Add: 516 Rodney Parham, Little Rock, Ark. 72205.

BEAUPRE, JACK RAYMOND D
b. Kankakee, Ill, 7/21/36; s. Sylvester John Beaupre and Mardell Wools B; m. 9/8/62 to Faith Eljean Friberg; c. Susan and Nancy. Educ: Univ. Ill, B.S. in finance, 58; John Marshall Law Sch, LL.B, 66; Alpha Kappa Lambda. Polit. & Govt. Pos: Recorder of deeds, Kankakee Co, Ill, 60-64; secy, Kankakee Co. Dem. Cmt, 61-63; alternate del, Dem. Nat. Conv, 64; state chmn, Young Citizens for Johnson-Humphrey, 64; clerk, Circuit Court, Ill, 64-68; pres, Young Dem. of Ill, 64- Mil. Serv: Entered as 2nd Lt, Army, 58-59; 1st Lt, Army Nat. Guard. Mem: Elks; K. of C. Rel: Catholic. Mailing Add: R.R. 1, 22 Linda Dr, Bourbonnais, Ill. 60614. (1967)

BEAUVAIS, JOHN PAUL D
b. Haverhill, Mass, 8/30/31; s. John Paul Beauvais and Lena Bellemare B; m. to Yvonne Tremblay; c. Phyllis Elaine and Daniel Paul. Educ: St. Anselms Col, 54-56. Polit. & Govt. Pos: Del, Dem. Nat. Conv, 68 & Dem. State Conv, N.H, 68. Bus. & Prof. Pos: Asst. mgr, furniture dept, Sears Roebuck & Co, Manchester, N.H, 56-60; mfrs rep, Gift & Art Assoc, Milford, N.H, 60-68, N.E. sales mgr, 68- Mil. Serv: Entered as Pvt, Army, 53, released as Pfc, 54, after serv. in Inf, Ninth Div, Occup. of Germany, 53-54. Mem: Manchester Jr. Hockey League (bd. dirs); Manchester South Little League (umpire); Can. Club. Rel: Catholic. Mailing Add: 51 Newbury Rd, Manchester, N.H. 03103.

BEAVER, JACK ALDRED R
b. Portland, Ore, 12/1/18; m. 10/10/41 to Mary Margaret English; c. Meredith, Timothy, Patrick. Educ: Univ. of Calif, Los Angeles, A.B. Polit. & Govt. Pos: Calif. State Assemblyman, 54-62; cmnr, Constitutional Rev. Cmn,

Joint Cmt. Calif. Legis. Spec. Cmn, 63-; mem. water resources research adv. coun, Univ. Calif, 64-; mem. bd. dirs, Santa Ana Watershed Planning Agency, 68- Bus. & Prof. Pos: Gen. Mgr, San Bernardino Valley Munic. Water Dist; agriculture. Mil. Serv: Air Force, World War II, Lt. Col, Squadron Comdr, China-India; Korea, dir. of opers, Air Force Intel; Bronze Star, Korea. Publ: 'The Computer and Management,' J. Am. Water Works Asn, 11/68; 'Analytical Resources Management,' Int. Asn. Sci. Hydrology, UNESCO, 12/68. Mem: Am. Water Works Asn; South. Calif. Water Conf; del. water contractors coun, Dept. Water Resources, Calif; Irrigation Dist. Asn. Calif; Mason. Rel: Episcopal; Sr. Warden, Trinity Parish. Mailing Add: 419 Marcia, Redlands, Calif. 92373.

BEAVER, JAMES RAYMOND R

b. Indianapolis, Ind, 5/27/41; s. Dr. Ernest Raymond Beaver and Jeanette Frances Chapman B; m. 11/24/62 to Carole Jean Courtright. Educ: Ind. Univ, Bloomington, A.B. in Govt, 66, Sch. of Law, J.D, 68; Phi Alpha Delta; Student Bar Asn. Polit. & Govt. Pos: Probation officer, Monroe Co. Circuit Court, Ind, 67-68; campaign coordinator, Landgrebe for Cong, 68; off. mgr, U.S. Rep. Earl F. Landgrebe, 68, admin. asst, 68- Bus. & Prof. Pos: Attorney, Ind, 68- Mem: Ind. State Bar Asn; admitted to practice in Fed. Court, South. Dist, Ind; Farm Bur. Rel: Protestant. Legal Res: 111 Thompson St, Rensselaer, Ind. 47978. Mailing Add: 6437 Spring Terr, Falls Church, Va. 22042.

BEAVER, ROBERT F. R

Treas, Calif. Rep. State Cent. Cmt.

b. Columbus, Ohio, 7/5/07; s. William C. Beaver and Elizabeth Ferguson B; m. 9/3/33 to Dorothy Evelyn Brent; c. Gary E and Vicki E. Educ: Univ. Calif, Los Angeles, B.A, 32; Univ. South. Calif, Gen. Sec. Credential, 33; Delta Sigma Phi. Polit. & Govt. Pos: V.chmn. and treas, Orange Co. Rep. Cent. Cmt, Calif, 62-; treas, Lincoln Club Orange Co, 63-; foreman pro-tem, Orange Co. Grand Jury, 64; chmn, subcmt, Orange Co. Rapid Transit Cmt, 66; v.chmn, Cmn. for Develop. Commerce and Indust, 67-; del, Rep. Nat. Conv, 68; treas, Am. Revolution Bicentennial Cmn. Calif, 68-; treas, Calif. Rep. State Cent. Cmt, 69- Bus. & Prof. Pos: Col. trainee, opers. mgr, West. Div, asst. controller and asst. mgr, West. Div, Firestone Tire & Rubber Co, Calif, 33-53; pres, Willard-Brent Co, Inc, Los Angeles, 53- Mil. Serv: Entered as 1st Lt, Army-Inspector Gen, 42, released as Maj, 46, after serv. in Trinidad Sector, Base Command and War Dept. Price Adjust. Bd, Pentagon. Mem: Calif. C. of C; assoc, Gen. Contractors Am; Los Angeles C. of C; Merchants and Mfrs. Asn; Elks; Hacienda Golf Club; Equestrian Trails, Inc; U.S. Power Squadron; Navy League U.S; United Fullerton Fund; adv. bd, Boy Scouts; Cultural Groups Found, N.Orange Co; Chapman Col. Pres. Coun; Childrens Hosp, Orange Co. Rel: Protestant. Mailing Add: 1235 Margarita Dr, Fullerton, Calif. 92633.

BEAVERS, RUTH JONES D

Chmn, Worth Co. Dem. Cent. Cmt, Mo.

b. Grant City, Mo, 12/14/01; d. Abner Marshall Jones and Alice Maupin J; m. Judge Ellis Beavers, wid; c. Joe and Wade. Educ: North-West Teachers Col, 41. Polit. & Govt. Pos: Auditor, recording secy. and v.pres, Dem. Women's Federated Club, Sixth Cong. Dist, Mo, 59-69; twp. committeewoman, Dem. Cent. Cmt; chmn, Worth Co. Dem. Cent. Cmt, 62-; del, Dem. State Conv; mem. cmt, Farmers for Symington, Campaign for Sen. Symington; mem. campaign cmt. for Sen. Edward Long. Bus. & Prof. Pos: Owner, Dry-Goods & Ready to Wear, 55-65; owner and operator, 1420 acre farm, currently. Mem: Bus. & Prfnl. Women; Eastern Star; Am. Legion Auxiliary. Rel: Disciples of Christ; Deaconess, 31- Legal Res: 501 E. Third St, Grant City, Mo. 64456. Mailing Add: P.O. Box 453, Grant City, Mo. 64456.

BECHTEL, WILLIAM RUSSELL D

b. Superior, Wis, 9/19/23; s. Rev. Leslie A. Bechtel and Gertrude Egert B; m. 6/21/47 to Dorothy Wilhelm; c. David Wm. Educ: Univ. Wis, B.A, 47. Polit. & Govt. Pos: Admin. asst. to U.S. Sen. Gaylord Nelson, Wis, 63-69; staff dir, Senate Subcmts. on Employ, Manpower and Poverty, 69- Bus. & Prof. Pos: News ed, Grant Co. Independent, 47-50; reporter, Milwaukee Jour, 50-63. Mil. Serv: Entered as A/S, Navy, 43, released as Ens, 46, after serv. in ETO & Pac. Mailing Add: 3110 Aberfoyle Pl. N.W, Washington, D.C. 20015.

BECHTOLD, CHARLES HARRISON R

b. Brooklyn, N.Y, 3/14/19; s. August Charles Bechtold and Ella Harrison B; m. 1/7/67 to Barbara Mae Allen; c. Charles H, Jr, Andrea Jackson, Emily Perry, David Wells (deceased) and stepchildren, Theodore J. and Suzanne M. Demer. Educ: Brown Univ, A.B, 41; Sigma Chi. Polit. & Govt Pos: Mem, South Kingston Town Coun, R.I, 47-51, pres, 49-51; pres, R.I. Young Rep, 51; chmn. Bd. Assessors, Kingston Fire Dist, 56; R.I. State Rep, 57-62; R.I. State Sen, 62-66; chmn. bd, New Eng. Bd. Higher Educ, 62-63; prog. officer loans, Student Financial Aid, Dept. Health Educ. and Welfare, Boston, 66- Bus. & Prof. Pos: Mgr, Am. Surety, N.Y, 61-; pres-treas, Charles H. Bechtold, Inc. and v.pres, Raphael Paola, Inc, Gen. Insurance, 61-66. Mil. Serv: Entered as Pvt, Marine Corps, 43, released as 2nd Lt, 46, after serv. in Fourth Marine Div, Pac, 44-56; Col, Marine Corps Res, 46- Publ: 'A Pattern for Production,' Casualty and Surety J, 1/51; 'Set Your Sights on Higher Education,' Marine Corps Gazette, 2/68. Mem: Salvation Army Drive, South Kingstown, 50; v.pres, South Kingstown C. of C, 50; chmn, South Kingstown-Narragansett Br, Am. Red Cross, 52-55; Marine Corps Statewide Toys for Tots Campaign, 55-56; R.I. Coun. Hwy. Safety; R.I. Cmt. on Children and Youth; Wash. Co. Heart Fund, 58; Legis. Cmt, R.I. Asn. Insurance Agents; Lions; VFW; Elks; Fraternal Order of Police; chmn, 4-H Driver Prog; Mil. Order For. Wars. Rel: Baptist. Mailing Add: 2 Copper Kettle Lane, Barrington, R.I. 02806.

BECHTOLD, JOHN A R

Ohio State Rep.

b. Cincinnati, Ohio, 9/2/24; s. Clarence F. Bechtold and Margaret Lee Sweeney B; m. 9/24/49 to Mary Evelyn Naish; c. Timothy J, Mary N, Frances M, Connie A, Jean M, Gail J, Paul J. and Peter M. Educ: Xavier Univ, 2 years; Salmon P. Chase Law Coll, J.D, 50; Kappa Xi Delta. Polit. & Govt. Pos: Councilman, Madeira, Ohio, 58; Ohio State Rep, 67- Bus. & Prof. Pos: Attorney-at-law, currently. Mil. Serv: Entered as Pvt, Army, 42, released as Bn. Sgt. Maj. 46, after serv. in 69th and Eighth Inf. Div, ETO, 44-45; Combat Inf. Badge with two Battle Stars; Div. Commendations. Mem: Ohio and Cincinnati Bar Asns; Lawyers Club Cincinnati; Hamilton Co. Rep. Club; Sycamore Twp. Rep. Club. Xavier Legion of Honor. Rel: Catholic. Mailing Add: 7521 Glenover Dr, Cincinnati, Ohio 45236.

BECK, AUDREY PHILLIPS D

Conn. State Rep.

b. Brooklyn, N.Y, 8/6/31; d. Gilbert Wesley Phillips, Sr. and Mary Reilly P; m. 8/4/51 to Curt Frederick Beck; c. Ronald Pierson and Meredith Wayne. Educ: Univ. Conn, B.A, High Honors, 53, M.A, Distinction in Economics, 55; Phi Kappa Phi; Artus; Gamma Chi Epsilon; Delta Sigma Rho. Polit. & Govt. Pos: Mem. bd. finance, Mansfield, Conn, 65-, town govt. study cmt, 67-68, Mansfield-Univ. Liaison cmt, 67-68 and commun. develop. action prog, 68-; Conn. State Rep, 50th Dist, 69- Bus. & Prof. Pos: Teacher econ, Univ. Conn, 60-68, planning economist, Windham Regional Planning Agency, 68. Publ: Mansfield Town Government, 60, Connecticut School System, 62 and State Aid to Education in Connecticut, 63, League of Women Voters Conn. Mem: League of Women Voters; Conn. Fedn. of Dem. Women's Club; Tolland Co. Dem. Asn.(v.pres). Rel: Protestant. Mailing Add: Dunham Pond Rd, Storrs, Conn. 06268.

BECK, CARLA WETZSTEON D

b. Hamilton, Mont, 7/20/33; d. Carl William Wetzsteon and Daisy Tucker W; m. 11/24/62 to Rev. Jacob David Beck; c. Mary Kathryn Hewett and Anne Theresa. Educ: Univ. Mont, B.A, 55; Theta Sigma Phi; Spurs. Polit. & Govt. Pos: Alternate del, Dem. Nat. Conv, 68; Dem. committeewoman, Precinct 42, Cascade Co, Mont, 68- Bus. & Prof. Pos: Reporter, Missoulian, Missoula, 53-57, women's ed, 60-62; reporter, Great Falls Tribune, 66- Mem: Great Falls Newspaper Guild, Am. Newspaper Guild. Rel: Episcopal. Mailing Add: 608 48th St. S, Great Falls, Mont. 59401.

BECK, CLIFFORD WALLACE 'RED' D

Wash. State Rep.

b. Bloomington, Ind, 8/12/07; s. Walter C. Beck and Augusta E. Brummett B; m. 12/1/35 to Hope G. Etchings. Educ: Stanford Univ, bus. admin. Polit. & Govt. Pos: Wash. State Rep, 23rd Dist, Position 1, 61- Bus. & Prof. Pos: Mgr. property holdings, Kitsap Co, Wash, at present. Mil. Serv: Navy for 10 years. Mem: C. of C; Fleet Reserve Asn; Eagles; Kiwanis; Elks; DAV. Rel: Baptist. Mailing Add: Route 5, Box 15, Port Orchard, Wash. 98366.

BECK, JAMES EDWARD D

b. Wilkinson, Ga, 5/18/14; s. Malankthun Newton Beck and Mattie Williams B; m. 10/1/39 to Margaret Eolyne Wall; c. Sarah Eolyne, James Edward Jr. Educ: Gordon High Sch. Polit. & Govt. Pos: Ga. State Rep, 63-66; Twiggs Co. Bd. of Educ, 49-60; city councilman, Jeffersonville, 52-53. Bus. & Prof. Pos: Owner retail furniture and hardware store, 45- Mem: Past master Gordon Lodge 240 F&AM; past master Jeffersonville Lodge 133 F&AM; rep. Grand Lodge of Ga, F&AM from Grand Lodge of Ohio; past patron, Danville Chap. 318 OES; Scottish Rite, Shriner; WOW; Twiggs PTA; Twiggs Band Booster Club; Jeffersonville Men's Civic Club; charter mem. and dir. Twiggs Co. Develop. Corp, 52-54; pres. ibid, 54-55. Rel: Deacon, 1st Baptist Church, Jeffersonville, Ga. Mailing Add: Jeffersonville, Ga. 30549. (1967)

BECK, JAMES N. 'GATOR' D

b. Oinecastle, Fla, 11/4/23; m. to Nellie Law; c. Jan Audie. Educ: Univ. of Fla, B.A.E, 59. Polit. & Govt. Pos: Fla. State Rep, 54-68, speaker pro tempore, Fla. House of Rep, 59. Bus. & Prof. Pos: Former soc. studies teacher, owner, Gator Beck Ins. Agency, Palatka, Fla, currently. Mailing Add: 115 St. Johns Terr, East Palatka, Fla. 32077. (1967)

BECK, JOHN KEITT D

Chmn, Navarro Co. Dem. Exec. Cmt, Tex.

b. Kerens, Tex, 12/28/20; s. John Caleb Beck and Clyde Daniel B; m. 4/25/59 to Cornelia Anne Watson; c. Nancy Clyde and John Keitt, Jr. Polit. & Govt. Pos: Dem. chmn, Precinct 17, Navarro Co, Tex, 50-62; councilman, Kerens, Tex, 58-66; chmn, Navarro Co. Dem. Exec. Cmt, 62- Bus. & Prof. Pos: Farmer and rancher, 37-; acct. and bookkeeper, E.K. Howell Motor Co, 53-56; pres, Kerens Develop. Fund, Inc, 63- Mem: Masons; Tex. Forestry Asn; Friends of the Land. Rel: United Presbyterian. Legal Res: 106 N. Donaldson, Kerens, Tex. 75144. Mailing Add: P.O. Box 143, Kerens, Tex. 75144.

BECK, LESLIE VERNON D

Appellate Court Clerk, Ill.

b. Chicago, Ill, 11/7/10; s. Alvin Henry Beck and Mary Williams B; m. 6/5/29 to Helen Marie Broscious; c. Barbara Therese, Gladys Ann and Gertrude Mary. Polit. & Govt. Pos: Gen. Secy, Bur. of Eng, Ill, 32-46; dep. purchasing agent, City of Chicago, 46-54; Dem. committeeman, Ninth Ward, Chicago, 48-; appellate court clerk, First Dist, 54- Mem: Elks; Rosegrove Civic Asn; Moose; Ninth Ward Safety Coun. Chicago; Porcupine Club of Chicago; Cook Co. Dem. Cent. Cmt; Chicago Motor Club; Lions; Tornado Athletic Club of Chicago; Chicago Civil Defense Corp. Rel: Episcopal. Mailing Add: 10832 S. Forest Ave, Chicago, Ill. 60628.

BECK, RALPH JAMES R

b. Deer Lodge, Mont, 2/13/18; s. Frank C. Beck and Jennie Kramer B; m. 1/3/41 to Marjorie Ross Beck; c. Mary Louise (Mrs. Gillis). Educ: Worsham Col. Mortuary Sci, 40-41. Polit. Pos: Mont. State Sen, 66-67; Mont. State Rep, 63-65; co. coroner, 46-62. Mil. Serv: Entered as Pvt, Air Force, 42, released as S/Sgt, 45, after serv. in 5th Air Force, S.Pac; Asiatic-Pac. Theater Ribbon. Mem: Pres, Mont. Funeral Dirs. Asn, 56; pres, Deer Lodge C. of C, 49; Mason (32°), potentate of Bagdad Shrine Temple; Odd Fellows; K. of P; Elks; Moose; Am. Legion; VFW; Rotary. Rel: Episcopal. Mailing Add: Ross Funeral Home, 601 Missouri Ave, Deer Lodge, Mont. 59722.

BECK, WILLIAM MORRIS D

Ala. State Rep.

b. Hamilton Co, Tenn, 10/12/36; s. W.M. Beck, Sr. and Vera Isbell B; m. 12/3/57 to Ramona Blanche Dodd; c. William Morris, III and John Eugene. Educ: Univ. Ala, B.S. and LL.B, 61; Delta Sigma Pi; Theta Xi. Polit. & Govt. Pos: Ala. State Rep, Dist. 8, Place one, 66- Bus. & Prof. Pos: Partner, Beck and Beck Attorneys, Ft. Payne. Mem: DeKalb Co, Ala. and Am. Bar Asns; Rotary; Mason; Odd Fellows; Jaycees; WOW; C. of C. Outstanding Young Man of DeKalb Co, 67; Nominee, One of Four Outstanding Young Men of Ala, 69. Rel: Baptist. Mailing Add: 1600 Forrest Ave. N, Ft. Payne, Ala. 35967.

BECKER, ANITA M. R
Mem, Wis. State Rep. Exec. Cmt.
b. Port Washington, Wis, 3/6/20; d. Allie N. Kultgen and Florence B. Conter K; m. 5/6/41 to Arnold H. Becker; c. Victoria Ann. Educ: Port Wash. High Sch. Polit. & Govt. Pos: Mem, Wis. State Rep. Exec. Cmt. and v.chmn, Sixth Cong. Dist; Clerk of Courts, Ozaukee Co, 62-64; del, Rep. Nat. Conv, 64. Mem: State recorder-receiver, Royal Neighbors of Am; VFW; Ozaukee Co. Hist. Soc. Rel: Roman Catholic. Mailing Add: Route 1, Box 478, Northwood Rd. N, Port Washington, Wis. 53074. (1967)

BECKER, DANIEL R
N.Y. State Assemblyman
b. Newburgh, N.Y, 2/1/05; s. Wolf Becker and Bessie Freese B; m. 12/20/34 to Marguerite E. Davis. Educ: Newburgh Free Acad, N.Y, 19-22; N.Y. Univ. Law Sch, 22. Polit. & Govt. Pos: Justice of Peace, Newburgh, N.Y, 28-32; city judge, 33-45; corp. counsel, 45-50; counsel to Lee B. Mailler, Majority Leader, N.Y. State Assembly, 53-54; N.Y. State Assemblyman, 59-66 & 69- Bus. & Prof. Pos: Lawyer. Mem: Am. and N.Y. Bar Asns; past pres, Newburgh City Bar Asn; past pres, Orange Co. Bar Asn; past dep, southeast dist. N.Y. State, Elks; F&AM; past dist. dep. grand master, Mason, Orange-Rochland Co, N.Y. Mailing Add: Dogwood Lane, Newburgh, N.Y. 12550.

BECKER, EDWIN CHARLES R
N.Dak. State Sen.
b. Willow City, N.Dak, 1/4/28; father (deceased), mother, Ida Loiselle B; single. Educ: St. John's Univ, Minn, B.A. Polit. & Govt. Pos: Campaign-orgn. dir, N.Dak. Rep. Party, 55-60; N.Dak. State Sen, Sixth Legis. Dist, 58-, mem, N.Dak. Sen. Rep. Policy Cmt, 58-69, chmn, N.Dak. Sen. Finance & Taxation Cmt, 63-; pres, N.Dak. Young Rep, 60; chmn. tax cmt, Midwest. Conf. of Coun. of State Govt, 65-67, v.chmn, 67, chmn, 68; chmn, Gov. Bd. of Nat. Coun. of State Govt, 69. Bus. & Prof. Pos: Farmer. Mil. Serv: Vet. Mem: N.Dak. Farm Bur; Nat. Durum Growers Asn; Elks, Minot, N.Dak. Rel: Catholic. Mailing Add: Willow City, N.Dak. 58384.

BECKER, EUGENE M. R
Asst. Secy. of the Army for Financial Mgt.
b. St. Paul, Minn, 9/1/30. Educ: Colgate Univ, grad, 52; Fulbright scholar, Univ. Paris; Princeton Univ, Ph.D. in Cult. Hist. and Archaeol, 59; Phi Beta Kappa. Polit. & Govt. Pos: Asst. Secy. of the Army for Financial Mgt, 67- Bus. & Prof. Pos: Dir. of info. on munic. securities, Investment Bankers Asn. of Am, 60-61; asst. v.pres, First Nat. City Bank, N.Y.C, 61-66; Dir. of the Budget, N.Y.C, 66-67. Mil. Serv: Army, 54-56, with serv. as press analyst, U.S. European Command Hq. near Paris. Mem: Trustee and v.pres, Carnegie Hall Corp, N.Y.C. Mailing Add: Dept. of the Army, Pentagon, Washington, D.C. 20310.

BECKER, FRANK J. R
b. Brooklyn, N.Y, 8/27/99; m. to Anne Claire Ferris; c. Frances, Betty Ann (Mrs. Jack Myers) and Robert. Polit. & Govt. Pos: N.Y. State Assemblyman, 45-53; U.S. Rep, 83rd-88th Cong, N.Y. Bus. & Prof. Pos: Ins. broker, 45-; dir. Lynbrook Fed. Savings and Loan Asn. Mil. Serv: Army, 18. Mem: VFW; Holy Name Soc; Am. Legion; Elk; K. of C; dir, Nassau Co. Tuberc. & Pub. Health Asn. Rel: Catholic. Mailing Add: 54 Forest Ave, Lynbrook, L.I, N.Y. 11563.

BECKER, HENRY TIMOTHY D
Mem, Manchester Dem. Town Cmt, Conn.
b. Hartford, Conn, 2/5/17; s. Henry M. Becker and Nellie A. Conners B; m. 8/21/41 to Marie Elizabeth De La Chevrotiere; c. Thérèse, Elaine and Timothy. Educ: George Wash. Univ, 50-51; Duquesne Univ, 51-52. Polit. & Govt. Pos: Mem, Manchester Pension Bd, Conn, 56-60, chmn, 62-66; Dem. chmn, Dist. Two, Manchester, 58-62; Conn. State Rep, until 68; mem, Manchester Dem. Town Cmt, currently. Bus. & Prof. Pos: Dist. organizer Int. Asn. Machinists, 47-49; nat. rep. union label dept, Amalgamated Clothing Workers of Am, 50-60, regional dir, 60-; nat. organizer, Am. Fedn. Teacher, 56-58. Mil. Serv: Entered as Pvt, Army Air Corps, 43, released as Pfc, 45, after serv. in N.Am. Theatre; Cpl, N.Y. Nat. Guard, 165th Inf. Regt, 34-38; Good Conduct Medal. Mem: K. of C; Am. Legion; Army-Navy Club. Rel: Roman Catholic. Mailing Add: 736 Center St, Manchester, Conn. 06040.

BECKER, JEROME BILL D
b. Chicago, Ill, 2/25/24; s. Joseph Becker and Hazel Feldman B; m. 2/11/53 to Norma Hunt; c. Hunt, Hazel, Paul, Heidi and Preston. Educ: Univ. Ill, B.S, 49. Polit. & Govt. Pos: Pres, Ark. State AFL-CIO, 60-; del, Dem. Nat. Conv, 68. Legal Res, 125 Winnwood, Little Rock, Ark. 72207. Mailing Add: 1408 Rebsamen Park Rd, Little Rock, Ark. 72202.

BECKER, MARTIN STANLEY D
Md. State Del.
b. Washington, D.C, 6/3/26; s. David Becker and Esther Oscar B; m. 9/7/52 to Etta Nezin; c. Leslie Ann and Nancy Lee. Educ: George Wash. Univ, ½ year; Emory and Henry Col, 2 years; Univ. Va, 1½ years; George Wash. Univ. Law Sch, LL.B, 50; Phi Sigma Delta. Polit. & Govt. Pos: Md. State Del, 67- Bus. & Prof. Pos: Mem. of the Bar, D.C, 50- and State of Md, 56- Mil. Serv: Entered as A/S, Navy, 44, released as Ens, 47, after serv. in Seventh Fleet, U.S. Naval Port Facilities, Shanghai, China, 46-47; Naval Res, 47-59, Lt.(jg); Am. Theater and Victory Medals. Mem: Am, Md, D.C. and Montgomery Co. Bar Asns; C. of C; Jaycees; Wheaton Rescue Squad; Young Dem. Club; East. Montgomery Dem.Club. Rel: Jewish. Mailing Add: 9511 Bruce Dr, Silver Spring, Md. 20901.

BECKER, RICHARD T. R
Chmn, Wash. Co. Rep. Orgn, Wis.
b. Hartford, Wis, 7/24/35; s. Raymond R. Becker and Loretta Cotter B; m. 6/29/59 to Catherine E. Boorman; c. Jerome M, Thomas B, Gregory R, Ann L, and Joseph W. Educ: Marquette Univ, B.S, 57, LL.B, 59; Alpha Phi Omega; Phi Delta Phi. Polit. & Govt. Pos: Dist. attorney, Wash. Co, Wis, 61-66; chmn, Wash. Co. Rep. Orgn, 67- Mem: Am. and Wis. Bar Asns; Wash. Co. Bar Asn.(pres, 58-59); Jaycees; Hartford C. of C; K. of C. Distinguished Serv. Award, Hartford Jaycees, 62. Rel: Roman Catholic. Mailing Add: 827 N. Main St, Hartford, Wis. 53027.

BECKER, ROBERT WILLIAM DFL
Chmn, Stearns Co. Democrat-Farmer-Labor Orgn, Minn.
b. Minneapolis, Minn, 2/24/35; s. Charles Becker and Marjorie Camp B; m. 6/13/58 to Mary B. Baab; c. Elizabeth Anne and David Charles. Educ: Hamline Univ, B.A, 59; Mich. State Univ, M.A, 62, grad. study, 62-; Tozer Fel, 58; Woodrow Wilson Nat. Fel, 59; Nat. Center Educ. in Polit. Fel, 62; Pi Gamma Mu; Hamline Univ. Vet. Asn; Hamline Univ. Young Dem-Farmer-Labor Club. Polit. & Govt. Pos: Spec. asst. to Gov. of Mich, 62; mem, Stearns Co. Dem-Farmer-Labor Cent. Cmt, Minn, 65-, chmn, 68-; mem, Stearns Co. Dem-Farmer-Labor Exec. Cmt, 65-; del, Minn. Dem-Farmer-Labor State Conv, 65, 66 & 68, chmn. Platform Cmt, 66 and Credentials Cmt, 68; del, Dem. Nat. Conv. and mem. Credentials Cmt, 68; mem, Minn. Dem-Farmer-Labor State Cent. Cmt, 68-; mem, St. Cloud Metrop. Planning Cmn, 69- Bus. & Prof. Pos: Asst. instr, Mich. State Univ, 61-62 & 63; asst. prof. polit. sci, St. Cloud State Col, 63- Mil. Serv: Entered as Pvt. E-1, Army, 53, released as Cpl, E-4, 55, after serv. in 1903 Engr. Aviation Bn, Far East Command, Korea, 53-54; Good Conduct Medal; Nat. Defense Medal; United Nations Korean Serv. Medal. Publ: 'Corelates of Legislative Behavior,' Midwest J. Polit. Sci, 62. Mem: Am. Polit. Sci. Asn; Midwest Polit. Sci. Asn; St. Cloud Area Dem-Farmer-Labor Club; St. Cloud Area Citizens Adv. Group. Rel: Methodist. Mailing Add: 320 Third Ave, S, St. Cloud, Minn. 56301.

BECKERLE, JOSEPH W. D
Mo. State Rep.
b. St. Louis, Mo, 6/30/21; m. 11/25/48 to Dorothy E. Doedli; c. Mary Elizabeth and Anne Marie. Educ: St. Louis Parochial schs. Polit. & Govt. Pos: Mo. State Rep, 48- Mil. Serv: Air Corps, World War II, 42-45. Rel: Catholic. Mailing Add: 6145 S. Grand Ave, St. Louis, Mo. 63111. (1967)

BECKHAM, ROBERT CULP R
Chmn, Richmond Co. Rep. Exec. Cmt, Ga.
b. Darlington, S.C, 4/6/32; s. Paul Thurlow Beckham and Leona Culp B; m. 3/1/68 to Susan Hooper; c. William C.D. and Paul T. Educ: Univ. S.C, 2 years. Polit. & Govt. Pos: Elec. day chmn, Richmond Co. Rep. Party, Ga, 64, treas, 64 and campaign chmn, spec. reapportionment elec, 65; area v.chmn, Tenth Cong. Dist. Rep. Cmt, 66; mem, Rep. State Cent. Cmt, 66; chmn, Richmond Co. Rep. Exec. Cmt, 66-; del, and mem. credentials cmt, Rep. Nat. Conv, 68. Bus. & Prof. Pos: Marketer, BP Oil Corp, 69. Mil. Serv: Entered as Pvt, Army, 55, released as SP-3, 57, after serv. in 1st Med. Bn, 1st Inf. Div, Fort Riley, Kans, 55-57. Mem: Ga. Oil Jobbers Asn; Richmond Co. Petroleum Coun; Elks; Augusta C. of C; Augusta Jaycees (past pres, 62-63). Rel: Baptist. Mailing Add: 3020 Fox Spring Rd, Augusta, Ga. 30904.

BECKIUS, JOHN LAWRENCE D
Mayor, Stapleton, Nebr.
b. Stapleton, Nebr, 7/14/98; s. Nick P. Beckius and Eva Schrader B; m. 2/1/21 to Faye A. Hildenbrand; c. Robert L. and James T. Polit. & Govt. Pos: Councilman, Stapleton, Nebr, 28-; chmn, Logan Co. Dem. Cmt, 38-68; Mayor, Stapleton, 45- Bus. & Prof. Pos: Farmer and rancher; owner, billiard parlor, 19-25; owner, Gen. Merchandise Store, 25- Mem: K. of C; Elks; C. of C; Farm Bur. Rel: Catholic. Mailing Add: Stapleton, Nebr, 69163. (1967)

BECKLIN, ROBERT C. Conservative
Minn. State Rep.
b. Braham, Minn, 1926; m. to Joyce; c. Three. Educ: Cambridge High Sch. Polit. & Govt. Pos: Minn. State Rep, 62- Bus. & Prof. Pos: Pres, Rum River Charcoal Co, Isanti, Minn. Mil. Serv: World War II, Pac. Theatre. Mem: Am. Legion; VFW. Rel: Lutheran. Mailing Add: 447 N.W. Fourth, Cambridge, Minn. 55008. (1967)

BECKMAN, JOHN WELLS R
N.Y. State Assemblyman
b. Jamestown, N.Y, 11/3/30; s. Arden Edward Beckman and Julia McClelland B; m. 1/2/52 to Alice Miller; c. Jeanne E, Judy M, Barbara J, John W, Jr, Janet A. and William A. Educ: Syracuse Univ, B.S, 52; Jamestown Commun. Col, non credit, 64-66; Univ. Buffalo, adult-non credit, 67-68; pres, Kappa Sigma, 52. Polit. & Govt. Pos: N.Y. State Assemblyman, 150th Assembly Dist, 69- Bus. & Prof. Pos: Various positions with ins. co, 52-56; owner, Beckman Agency, 56-61; partner, Beckman-Brace Agency, 61-69; sr. v.pres. and secy, Chautauqua Gen. Group, Inc, 69- Publ: Excerpt from speech on ins. legis, Triangle Mag, 4/69. Mem: N.Y. State Conserv. Coun.(past dir, chmn. int. fish and wildlife cmt); Chautauqua Co. Fedn. Sportsmen's Clubs (pres); chmn, Int. Sportsmen's Workshop, 69; Jaycees (past pres); C. of C.(past dir, Westfield Br); Syracuse Univ. Alumni Asn; F&AM; Moose. Rel: Presbyterian. Legal Res: 98 S. Portage St, Westfield, N.Y. 14787. Mailing Add: 67 E. Main St, Westfield, N.Y. 14787.

BECKMAN, VINCENT H. D
b. Cincinnati, Ohio, 12/28/15; s. Vincent H. Beckman, Sr. and Irene Hummel B; m. 12/13/43 to Elizabeth Desloge; c. Vincent, III, Peter H, L. Christopher, Edward D, Betsy D. and Julie M. Educ: Xavier Univ, A.B, 38; Harvard Law Sch, LL.B, 41, Harvard Sch. Bus. Admin, I.A, 43. Polit. & Govt. Pos: Councilman, Cincinnati, Ohio, 54, 55, 57, 59; cmnr, Hamilton Co, Ohio, 61-68; chmn. Dem. party, Cincinnati and Hamilton Co, Ohio, 64-68. Bus. & Prof. Pos: Dir, First Fed. Savings & Loan Asn, Cincinnati, South. Ohio Bank and Cincinnati Ins. Co; guest lectr, Univ. Cincinnati. Mil. Serv: Entered as Pvt, Army, 42, released as Capt, 46, after serv. in Transportation Corps. Mem: Am, Ohio and Cincinnati Bar Asns; Cincinnati Lawyers Club; Xavier Natural Law Soc; lay adv. bd, St. George Hosp, Mt. Alverno Sch. for Boys and St. Xavier High Sch; past chmn, Mayor's Friendly Rels. Cmt; past dir. and secy, Am. Red Cross; past pres, Queen City Asn. and Xavier Alumni Asn; Cincinnati C. of C; Cincinnatus Asn; Harvard Club of Cincinnati; Cath. Interracial Coun; Boy Scouts; Cincinnati Civic Club; Am. Legion; West. Hills Country Club; Harvard Law Sch. Asn. Rel: Catholic. Legal Res: 1 N. Cliff Terr, Cincinnati, Ohio 45220. Mailing Add: 1714 First National Bank Bldg, Cincinnati, Ohio 45202.

BECKSTEAD, LUCY R
Mem, Colo. State Rep. Cent. Cmt.
b. Hazelton, Idaho, 10/28/20; d. Hyrum Johnson and Rilla Shepherd J; m.

8/8/43 to Frank L. Beckstead. Educ: Idaho State Univ, 37-40; Univ. Colo, B.A, 69. Polit. & Govt. Pos: Del, Wash. State Rep. Conv, 54; pres, Valley Women's Rep. Club, Spokane, 60-62; dist. leader, Fourth Legis. Dist, Wash, 61-62; co-chmn, Jefferson Co. Goldwater for Pres. Cmt, Denver, Colo, 63-64; mem, Colo. State Exec. Bd, Goldwater for Pres. Cmt, 63-64; precinct committeewoman, Precinct 501, Jefferson Co. Rep. Party, 66-67; del, State Rep. Conv. and Assembly, 66 & 68; del, Jefferson Co. Rep. Conv, 66 & 68; dist. capt, Jefferson Co. Rep. Party, 67; mem, Colo. State Rep. Cent. Cmt, 69- Bus. & Prof. Pos: Secy. & off. mgr, United Air Lines, Inc, Spokane and Seattle, Wash. and Boise, Idaho, 46-56; free-lance writer, 66- Rel: Latter-day Saint. Mailing Add: 3505 Miller Court, Wheat Ridge, Colo. 80033.

BECKWITH, FLORENCE HESS R
Chmn, Hillsdale Co. Rep. Cmt, Mich.
b. Clinton Co, Mich, 6/11/09; d. John Jacob Hess and Elizabeth Rumbaugh H; m. 6/8/35 to Robert Edgar Beckwith; c. Robert Edgar, Peter Hess and Jon Gardner. Educ: Olivet Col, A.B, 31; Alpha Lambda Epsilon. Polit. & Govt. Pos: Chmn, Hillsdale Co. Rep. Cmt, Mich, 69- Mem: Pres, Hillsdale Co. Rep. Women; regent, DAR; Hillsdale Golf and Country Club. Rel: Episcopal. Mailing Add: Route 2, Hillsdale, Mich. 49242.

BECKWITH, ROBERT JAMES D
b. Toronto, Can, 3/21/21; s. Clarence James Beckwith and Marguerite Keena B; m. 1/10/51 to Alice Karash; c. Robert Warren. Educ: Cent. State Teachers Col, B.S. in educ, 42. Polit. & Govt. Pos: First selectman, City of Hartford, Conn, 48-54 and Justice of the Peace, 54-66; senate clerk, Conn. Gen. Assembly, 55; Property and Procurement Officer, Conn, 57; exec. aide to Gov. Ribicoff and Gov. Dempsey, 57-66; mem, Gov. Mil. Staff, State Bldg. Prog. Cmt. & Med. Affairs Reference Cmt, currently. Bus. & Prof. Pos: Teacher, Hartford, Conn, 48; salesman, Diebold, Inc, 50-54; bus. mgr, John P. Kelly Ins. Co, 55-57; commandant, Vet. Home and Hosp, 66- Mil. Serv: Entered as Pvt, Marine, 42, released as 1st Lt, 47, after serv. in Fourth and 29th Marines, Pac, 43-45; two Purple Hearts. Mem: VFW; Am. Legion; DAV; Elks; K. of C; Purple Heart Asn; Conn. Hosp. Asn; Wethersfield Country Club. Rel: Catholic. Mailing Add: 287 West St, Rocky Hill, Conn. 06067.

BECKWORTH, LINDLEY D
b. Kaufman Co, Tex, 6/30/13; s. Otis Jefferson Beckworth and Josie Slaughter B; m. to Eloise Carter; c. Gary, Carter, Mary, Linda and John Barney. Educ: Univ. Tex; Baylor Univ; South. Methodist Univ; E.Tex. State Teachers Col; Sam Houston State Teacher Col. Polit. & Govt. Pos: Tex. State Rep, 36-38; U.S. Rep, Third Dist, Tex, 38-52 & 56-66. Bus. & Prof. Pos: Sch. teacher, 3 years; admitted to Tex. Bar, 37. Mem: Mason; Odd Fellows. Rel: Baptist. Mailing Add: R.F.D, Gladewater, Tex. 75647. (1967)

BECNEL, BENOIT PAUL D
Chmn, St. James Parish Dem. Exec. Cmt, La.
b. Vacherie, La, 9/27/25; s. Placide Jean Becnel and Antonia Brack B; m. 6/15/46 to Lydia Rita Roussel. Educ: High Sch. Polit. & Govt. Pos: Chmn, St. James Parish Dem. Exec. Cmt, Ward Nine, La, currently. Bus. & Prof. Pos: Salesman, coffee co, 46-48; salesman, furniture co, 48-50; dist. mgr, life ins. co, 50- Mil. Serv: Entered as A/S, Navy, 43, released as PO 1/C, 46, after serv. in Pac. Theater, 43-45; 5 Campaign Ribbons; Good Conduct Medal. Mem: VFW; Am. Legion; Lions; K. of C. Rel: Catholic. Legal Res: 604 N. Airline, Gramercy, La. 70052. Mailing Add: P.O. Drawer J, Gramercy, La. 70052.

BEDELL, GEORGE NOBLE D
b. Harrisburg, Pa, 5/1/22; s. George Harold Bedell and Elsie Noble B; m. 11/4/50 to Betty Jane Goldzier; c. David, Mark, Barbara and Bruce. Educ: DePauw Univ, B.A, 44; Univ. Cincinnati, M.D, 46; Delta Chi. Polit. & Govt. Pos: Treas, Johnson Co. Dem. Cent. Cmt, Iowa, 58-64; precinct committeeman, Iowa City, 58-; del. Dem. Nat. Conv, 68. Bus. & Prof. Pos: Asst. prof, Univ. Iowa, 54-58, assoc. prof, 58-68 and prof, 68-; vis. colleague, Univ. London, 64-66. Mil. Serv: Entered as Pvt, Army, 43, released as Capt, 50, after serving in Okinawa and Japan, 48-50. Publ: 25 articles regarding lung disease and pulmonary physiology, 53-68. Mem: Am. Soc. for Clin. Invest; Am. Physiol. Soc; Cent. Soc. for Clin. Res. Rel: Unitarian. Mailing Add: 327 Blackhawk, Iowa City, Iowa 52240.

BEDELL, J(OEL) F(ERREE) D
b. Charleston, W.Va, 7/20/05; s. Joel Ferree Bedell and Cora W. Kiger B; m. 9/6/24 to Dorothy Jane Courtney (deceased); c. Joel F. III, Barbara (Mrs. James F. Sinnett), Martha (Mrs. John D. Rathbone), Lynn (Mrs. Andrew D. Truslow) and Mary (Mrs. James M. Stewart). Educ: Charleston High Sch. Polit. & Govt. Pos: Pos: W.Va. State Del, 60-66. Bus. & Prof. Pos: Pub. affairs rep, Va, W.Va. area, Humble Oil & Refining Co. Mem: Mason; Shrine; Scottish Rite; K.T; bd. of trustees, Marmet Found. and Charleston Gen. Hosp; bd. of dirs, Kanawha Chap, March of Dimes; W.Va. Petroleum Asn. Rel: Presbyterian. Mailing Add: Box 713, Charleston, W.Va. 25301. (1967)

BEDFORD, HENRY WARD R
Vt. State Rep.
b. Houghton, N.Y, 10/6/06; s. Henry Clark Bedford and Nelle Crow B; m. 8/12/29 to Mary Louise Bates; c. Henry F. and Crayton W. Educ: Earlham Col, A.B, 27; Westminster Choir Col, Mus.B, 33; Univ. Pittsburgh, M.A, 36; Univ. Vt, hon. LL.D, 65. Polit. & Govt. Pos: Treas, Addison Co. Rep. Cmt, Vt, 59-; Vt. State Rep, 59-67 & 69-; chmn, Vt. State Cols. Bd. and acting pres, 61-65; mem, Vt. State Libr. Bd, 65-; moderator, Town of Cornwall, 65-; chmn. appropriations cmt, Vt. House Rep, 66-; mem. exec. cmt, Vt. State Rep. Cmt, 68-; mem, Vt. Legis. Coun, 69; mem. New Eng. Bd. Higher Educ, 69. Bus. & Prof. Pos: Chmn. music dept, Middlebury Col, 36-53; owner, Milaway Farm, 38-; secy, treas, Middlebury Coop. Freeze Lockers, 42-; treas, Porter Hosp, Middlebury, 58- and pres, 66-; treas, Vt. Symphony Orchestra, 63- Mem: Rotary; dir, Ayrshire Breeders Asn, 67-; trustee, East. State Expos, 67-; trustee, Westminster Choir Col, 67- Rel: Episcopal. Mailing Add: R.F.D. 2, Middlebury, Vt. 05753.

BEDGOOD, WILLIAM RANDALL, JR. D
b. Athens, Ga, 5/26/17; s. William Randall Bedgood and Melba McGowan B; m. 12/9/39 to Eleanor Louise Banks; c. William Randall III, Diane Banks, Richard Coe, James David, Glyn Parmelee and Robert Eugene. Educ: Univ. Ga, B.S.C, 37; Sigma Chi. Polit. & Govt. Pos: Chmn, N.E. Ga. Area Planning and Develop. Cmn; mem, Clarke Co. Bd. Educ, 57-59, chmn, bd. cmnrs, 61; Ga. State Rep, 63-66. Bus. & Prof. Pos: Pres, Circle B Ranch, 48-; Owner, Univ. Hotel Court, 54- Mil. Serv: Entered as 1st Lt, Army, 37, released as Lt. Col, 40; Lt. Col, Army Air Force, 40-45; Silver Star; Distinguished Flying Cross with One Cluster; Air Medal with Four Clusters; East. and Middle East. Theater Ribbons; Ten Battle Stars; Am. Defense Medal; Victory Medal; Res. Medal; Longevity Award; UDC Medal of Hon; Distinguished Unit Citation; Air Force Res, Comdr. Mem: Kappa Delta Pi; Elks; Rotary; Am. Legion; VFW. Rel: Baptist; Deacon, Beech Haven Baptist Church. Mailing Add: 375 West View Dr, Athens, Ga. 30601.

BEDINGFIELD, JAMES B. R
b. Bandon, Ore, 1924; married; c. Sally, Janet, Scott and Jeff. Educ: Univ. of South. Calif; Univ. of Ore; Williamette Univ. Col. of Law, LL.B. Polit. & Govt. Pos: Ore. State Rep, 65-69; chmn, Coos Co. Juvenile Court Adv. Cmt; mem, Ore. Coun. on Crime and Delinquency. Bus. & Prof. Pos: Attorney-at-law; former dir, Waverly Baby Home; attorney, Southwest Ore. Commun. Col; chmn, Coos Co. Cmt. of Col. for Oregon's Future. Mil. Serv: Marine Corps. Mem: Former pres, Coos-Curry Bar Asn; Coos Co. United Good Neighbors; Rotary. Mailing Add: 1893 Kingwood Ave, Coos Bay, Ore. 97420. (1967)

BEDNAR, JOHN M. D
N.H. State Rep.
b. Bridgeport, Conn, 3/9/13; married; c. Three. Educ: N.Y. Univ, B.S, Acct. and Pre-Law. Polit. & Govt. Pos: N.H. State Rep, 63-; Town moderator; Supvr. of checklist; mem, Town Budget Cmt. Bus. & Prof. Pos: Tool and die maker; acct, credit and collections. Mem: Exec. dir, Hudson Taxpayers Asn; dir, N.H. Taxpayers Fedn. Rel: Catholic. Mailing Add: 153 Ferry St, Hudson, N.H. 03051. (1967)

BEDNAREK, STANLEY MICHAEL R
b. Philadelphia, Pa, 4/7/04; s. Michael Bednarek and Helen Strzelecki B; m. 10/13/34 to Lucy Bielawski; c. Ronald S. Educ: Roman Cath. High Sch, grad, 23. Polit. & Govt. Pos: Magistrate, Philadelphia, Pa, 51; del, Rep. Nat. Conv, 68. Rep. Leader, 45th ward exec. cmt; currently. Bus. & Prof. Pos: Treas, Kazimierz Wielki S.&L. Asn, 26-; realtor and ins. broker, 45- Mem: Nat. Asn. Real Estate Bds; N. Philadelphia Realty Bd; Philadelphia Real Estate Bd; Northeast Realty Bd; Port Richmond Lions (pres. and organizer, 52-53); Point No Point Rep. Asn.(pres, 62-); Polish Am. Asn; Richmond Polish Asn; Pilsudski Fraternal Asn; United Rep. Club; Westmoreland Rep. Club; United Polish Am. of Pa; Rep. City Cmt. Man of the Year award, Am. Legion; Businessman, Sportsman, Port Richmond Lions Club. Rel: Catholic. Mailing Add: 2607 E. Allegheny Ave, Philadelphia, Pa. 19134.

BEDROSSIAN, ROBERT HAIG R
b. Philadelphia, Pa, 8/31/24; s. Edward Hagop Bedrossian and Sirvart Adourian B; m. 7/9/48 to Carolyn Mary Head; c. Diane Louise, Robert Charles and Karen Lynn. Educ: Haverford Col, A.B, 46; Temple Univ. Med. Sch, M.D, 47; Univ. Pa. Grad. Sch. of Med, M.Sc. in med, 54; Phi Chi. Polit. & Govt. Pos: V.chmn, Clark Co. Rep. Cent. Cmt, Wash, 63-64, asst. v.chmn, 65-66; mem, Gov. Adv. Coun. Comprehensive Health Planning, 68- Bus. & Prof. Pos: Private practice, 52-54 & 57- Mil. Serv: Entered as Capt, Army Med. Corps, 54, released, 57, after serv. in Beaumont Army Hosp, El Paso, Tex. Publ: Twenty-two articles in med. jours. related to diseases of the eye. Mem: Am. Acad. Ophthal. and Otolaryngol; Pac. Coast Otolaryngol. and Ophthal. Soc; Am. Med. Asns. Rel: Presbyterian. Mailing Add: 3200 Main St, Vancouver, Wash. 98663.

BEDSAUL, E. CLIFFORD R
Chmn, Galax City Rep. Party, Va.
b. Galax, Va, 7/22/21; s. Charles Curren Bedsaul and Bessie Walker B; m. 7/7/48 to Louise Amburn; c. Linda Sheryl and Larry Emmett. Educ: Benjamin Franklin Univ. Polit. & Govt. Pos: Clerk, Fed. Bur. Invest, Wash, D.C, 40-42; chmn, Galax City Rep. Party, Va, currently. Bus. & Prof. Pos: Asst. mgr, Porter Furniture Co, Galax, Va, 47-49; resident agent, State Farm Ins. Co, 49-69. Mil. Serv: Entered as Pvt, Air Force, 42, released as Sgt, 46, after serv. in 20th Air Force, Guam. Mem: VFW (past Comdr); Guidans. Rel: Methodist; Treas, First Methodist Church. Legal Res: 108 Front St, Galax, Va. 24333. Mailing Add: Box 758, Galax, Va. 24333.

BEE, CARLOS D
Calif. State Assemblyman
b. Berkeley, Calif, 5/5/17; m. 6/28/46 to Jean Anderson B; c. Diane Elizabeth, Rita Cecelia, Carla Jean, Lori Marie, Allan Carlos. Educ: Santa Barbara State Col, A.B; two years grad. work, Univ. of Calif. Polit. & Govt. Pos: Mem, Dem. State Cent. Cmt, Calif; city councilman, Hayward, 48-54; Calif. State Assemblyman, 54-, Speaker-Pro-Tem, 59-69. Bus. & Prof. Pos: High sch. instr. Mil. Serv: Army. Mem: Calif. Teachers Asn; Nat. Educ. Asn; Eagles; Native Sons of the Golden West. Mailing Add: Suite 1, 22734 Main St, Hayward, Calif. 94541.

BEEBE, ALLISON STANLEY R
Chmn, Holden Rep. Town Cmt, Mass.
b. Whitehall, N.Y, 2/27/17; s. Elbert George Beebe and Florence Pike B; m. 8/12/40 to Barbara Wilson; c. Stephen G, David C. and Janet L. Educ: Middlebury Col, B.A, 38; Alpha Sigma Phi. Polit.& Govt. Pos: V.pres, Erie Co. Young Rep, N.Y, 49-50; finance chmn, Holden Rep. Town Cmt, Mass, 62-65, chmn, 65- Bus. & Prof. Pos: Various pos. including asst. buyer, Jordan Marsh Co, 38-41; asst. dir. group sales, John Hancock Mutual Life Ins, Co, 41-52; v.pres. group dept, Paul Revere Life Ins. Co, 52- Mil. Serv: Entered as Ens, Naval Res, 42, released as Lt, 45, after serv. in Caribbean and Pac. Theaters. Rel: Protestant. Mailing Add: 151 Highland St, Holden, Mass. 01520.

BEEBE, MARGARET SCHERF D
b. Fairmont, W.Va, 4/1/08; d. Charles Henry Scherf and Miriam Fisher S; m. 12/9/65 to Perry Elon Beebe. Educ: Antioch Col, 25-28. Polit. & Govt. Pos: Mont. State Rep. until 67. Publ: The Diplomat and the Gold Piano, The Corpse in the Flannel Nightgown and The Banker's Bones, 68, Doubleday & Co, Inc; plus 21 others. Rel: Episcopal. Mailing Add: 737 First Ave. W, Kalispell, Mont. 59901.

BEECHER, ROBERT J. D
Chmn, Union Co. Dem. Cmt, Iowa
b. Lorimor, Iowa, 6/25/25; s. James A. Beecher and Gladys L. Weitgenant B; m. 6/24/48 to Carolyn J. Askey; c. James William and Mary Anne. Educ: Creston Commun. Col. Polit. & Govt. Pos: Councilman, Creston City Coun, Iowa, 56-58; chmn, Union Co. Dem. Cmt, 60-64 & 66-; mem, Third Dist. Judicial Nominating Cmt, Dem. Party, 63-; pres, Southwest Commun. Col. Sch. Bd, 66- Mem: Pres, Jr. C. of C, 48; chmn, Creston Bd. of Dirs, United Fund, 54; pres, Creston C. of C, 55; chmn, Union Co. Independent Ins. Agents, 65-66 and Southwest. Commun. Col. Scholarship Fund, 66; secy, Creston Industs, Inc, 66 and Crestmoor Golf Club, 66; Elks; K. of C; Holy Name Soc. Rel: Catholic. Legal Res: 702 W. Devoe St, Creston, Iowa 50801. Mailing Add: Box 288, Creston, Iowa 50801. (1967)

BEEDLE, ERNEST ARNOLD D
b. St. Paul, Minn, 8/31/33; s. Ernest A. Beedle, Sr. and Carrie B. Warner B; m. 3/31/62 to Patsy Evelyn Davis; c. Brian K, Ernest III and Stephen P. Educ: Hamline Univ, B.A, 55; St. Paul Col. Law, B.S. in law, 57; William Mitchel Col. Law, LL.B, 59; Delta Theta Phi. Govt. Pos: Minn. State Rep, 58-66. Bus. & Prof. Pos: Pres, Beedle Law Firm Ltd. and Writing Toys Corp; mem. bd, Minn. Brakes, Inc; pres, Oak-Crest, Inc. and Int. Finance Co; secy-treas, Award Homes, Inc. Mil. Serv: 47th Inf. Div, Air Force Reserve, 53-55. Mem: Am. Acad. Soc. & Polit. Sci; Am. Bar Asn; Minn. State Bar Asn; Am. Judicature Soc; The Inter-Am. Bar Asn; Cmt. on Int. Law; Eagles; Mendakota Country Club. Stamp collecting; swimming; skiing. Rel: Baptist. Legal Res: 868 Delaware Ave, St. Paul, Minn. 55107. Mailing Add: 221 W. Grand Ave, South St. Paul, Minn. 55075. (1967)

BEEDON, FRANCIS W. D
b. Forester Twp, Sanilac Co, Mich, 9/26/02; s. Rev. Arthur Beedon and Keturah Weyeneth B; m. 6/23/27 to Georgine C. Ray; c. Francis W, Jr, Charles A, Richard R, and Joyce G. (Mrs. Higgins). Educ: Albion Col, A.B; Univ. Wis, M.A. Polit. & Govt. Pos: Mem. bd. dirs. and pres, Mich. Educ. Asn, 56-57; dir, Nat. Educ. Asn, Mich, 57; Mich. State Rep, 63-68; research analyst, Mich. House Educ. Cmt, 69- Bus. & Prof. Pos: Retired instr, Muskegon Co. Commun. Col. Publ: 'United States Historical Stamp Album,' 32; ed, stamp column, Muskegon Chronicle, 33- Mem: K. of P; Muskegon Y's Men's Club; Gr. Muskegon YMCA; Torch Club; Stamp Club; active in teachers' prfnl. orgn; Muskegon Teachers Club (pres, 41-43); Mich. State Teachers Club (bd. dirs, 43-64, pres, 48-53); Nat. Educ. Asn.(exec. cmt, 58-60, and bylaws and rules cmt). Rel: Methodist. Mailing Add: 2165 Denmark St, Muskegon, Mich. 49441.

BEEMAN, JOSIAH HORTON D
b. San Francisco, Calif, 10/8/35; s. Josiah Horton Beeman and Helen Virginia Hooper B; single. Educ: City Col. San Francisco, 53-54; Reed Col, Portland, Ore; San Francisco State Col, A.B, 57; Pi Sigma Alpha; Alpha Phi Omega. Polit. & Govt. Pos: Claims exam, Soc. Security Admin, 57-58; pres, Calif. Fedn. Young Dem, 63-65, nat. committeeman, 65-67; admin. asst, U.S. Rep. Phillip Burton, Calif, 64-67 & 68-69; chmn. bd. dirs, Young Dem. Clubs of Am, 65-67; mem. bd. supvr, City and Co. of San Francisco, Calif, 67-68; v.pres, Calif. Dem. Coun, 67-69; del, Dem. Nat. Conv, 68. Bus. & Prof. Pos: Dir. of educ, North. Calif-Nev. Coun. of Churches, 61-63; secy. for int. affairs, United Presby. Church in the U.S.A, 69- Mem: West. Govt. Res. Asn; Am. Polit. Sci. Asn; SAR; Sierra Club; NAACP; Am. Civil Liberties Union; Knights of Dunamis. Rel: Presbyterian. Legal Res: 140 Riverside Dr, Apt. 2-J, New York, N.Y. 10024. Mailing Add: 475 Riverside Dr, Room 918B, New York, N.Y. 10027.

BEERMANN, ALLEN JAY R
Dep. Secy. of State, Nebr.
b. Sioux City, Iowa, 1/14/40; s. Albert Beermann and Amanda Schoenrock B; single. Educ: Midland Col, 58-62; Creighton Univ. Sch. Law, J.D, 65; Pi Kappa Delta; Phi Alpha Delta; Kappa Phi (pres); German Club; Creighton Univ. Student Bar Asn.(pres). Polit. & Govt. Pos: Pres, South Sioux City High Sch. TAR, Nebr, 58; pres, Midland Co. Young Rep, 60; mem. campaign staff, Beermann for Cong, First Dist, Nebr, 62; admin. asst. to secy. of state, Nebr, 65-67; dep. secy. of state and legal counsel, Nebr, 67- Mil. Serv: Entered as Pvt, Nebr. Nat. Guard, 65, released as Specialist 4/C, 68; 1st Lt, Army Nat. Guard Judge Adv. Gen. Corps, assigned to Selective Serv, 68-; Spec. Citation of Merit; second in class at basic training; Meritorious Serv. Award, Nebr. Nat. Guard. Publ: Contrib. ed, Nebraska State Government, 68; auth, 'Would You Trade Your Name,' Nebr. Real Estate Cmn. Comment, 68; 'Travel Nebraskaland,' Newspapers of Nebr, 68. Mem: Am. Interprfnl. Inst.(ethics cmt, 68-); Nebr. Bar Asn.(legal-aid cmt, 67-); Am. Bar Asn; Am. Judicature Soc; Nebr. Press Asn; Nebr. Farm Bur. Fedn; Am. Cancer Soc.(bd. dirs, Lancaster Unit, 69); Boy Scouts (bd. dirs, Cornhusker Coun, 69); bd. dirs, Tabitha Home, 68-; bd. dirs, Nebraskaland Found, 68-; v.pres, Int. Rels. Clubs, 61; Elks; Young Rep. Club; Nebr. Nat. Guard Asn; Esquire Club. Distinguished Serv. Plaque, Omaha Legal Aid Soc; gov. del, People-to-People Conf; admiral, Great Navy of the State of Nebr. Rel: Lutheran. Legal Res: 1641 J St, Lincoln, Nebr. 68508. Mailing Add: Dept. of State, Suite 2300, State Capitol, Lincoln, Nebr. 68509.

BEERMANN, RALPH FREDERICK R
Chmn, Dakota Co. Rep. Cent. Cmt, Nebr.
b. Dakota City, Nebr, 8/13/12; s. Fred W. Beermann and Agnes Ellen Ralph B; m. 3/1/38 to Marjorie Louise Smythe. Educ: Morningside Col. Polit. & Govt. Pos: Chmn, Dakota Co. Young Rep, Nebr, 46-48; chmn, Dakota Co. Rep. Cent. Cmt, 54-60 & 66-; U.S. Rep, Third Dist, 61-62 and First Dist, 63-64. Bus. & Prof. Pos: Partner, Beermann Bros, 46-; stockholder and dir, Beermann Meadowview, Inc. and Beermann Farm, Inc, 49- Mil. Serv: Entered as T-3, Army, 42, released as M/Sgt, 45, after serv. in 601st Ord. Bn, African and ETO. Mem: VFW; life mem, Am. Legion; Farm Bur; C. of C; Am. Dehydrators Asn; Flying Farmers and Ranchers; Aircraft Owners & Pilots Asn; Kiwanis Int; Nebr. Alfalfa Dehydrators Asn; Ak-sar-ben. Rel: Lutheran. Legal Res: 20th and Broadway, Dakota City, Nebr. 68731. Mailing Add: P.O. Box 98, Dakota City, Nebr. 68731.

BEERS, ORVAS E. R
Chmn, Allen Co. Rep. Cent. Cmt, Ind.
b. Noble Co, Ind, 8/11/18; s. Orvas Edward Beers and Marjorie Adair B; m. to Margaret Helen Roethlisberger; c. Richard Edward. Educ: Hillsdale Col, A.B. cum laude; Univ. Mich, LL.B. Polit. & Govt. Pos: Dep. prosecuting attorney, City of Ft. Wayne, Ind, 52-57; city chmn, Ft. Wayne Rep. Party, 58; co. attorney, Allen Co, 61-64; chmn, Allen Co. Rep. Cent. Cmt, 61-; chmn, Ind. Nixon for President, 68; del, Rep. Nat. Conv. and chmn. credentials cmt, 68. Mil. Serv: Entered as Pvt, Army, 41, released as Capt, 46, after serv. in ETO; five battle stars; one arrowhead for invasion. Mem: Trustee, Allen Co. Ind. Bar Asn; VFW; Am. Legion; Elks; 100% Club; Friars Club. Rel: Episcopal. Legal Res: 4425 Highwood Dr, Ft. Wayne, Ind. 46805. Mailing Add: 1700 Lincoln Tower, Ft. Wayne, Ind. 46802.

BEERS, ROBERT O. R
Pa. State Sen.
b. Scranton, Pa, 2/29/16; s. Fred E. Beers and Mazie Davis B; m. to Edith Close; c. Four. Educ: Bucknell Univ, A.B; Harvard Law Sch, LL.B; Delta Upsilon. Polit. & Govt. Pos: Mem, Bd. of Pub. Assistance, Pa, 50-54; prothonotary, York Co, 52-56; mem, York Co. Rep. Exec. Cmt, chmn, 59-61; mem, Interstate Commerce Cmn; mem, Spring Garden Twp. Zoning Bd. of Adjust; solicitor, York Suburban Sch. Dist. and N. York Borough; Pa. State Sen, 62- Bus. & Prof. Pos: Asst. gen. attorney, York Corp, 46-49; lawyer; dir, Superior Wire Cloth Co. Mil. Serv: Lt.(sg), Naval Res, 42-46. Mem: Chmn, Retarded Children's Dr, 54; United Fund Budget Cmt, 56; York Co, Pa. and Am. Bar Asns; past pres, Mt. Rose Lions Club; Supreme Court of Pa; York Co. and Fed. Courts; Mason; Isaak Walton League; York Conserv. Soc; Rotary; Moose; past pres, Bucknell Alumni Club, York Co; past comdr, York Post 127 Am. Legion. Rel: Presbyterian. Legal Res: 145 E. Market St, York, Pa. 17401. Mailing Add: 1660 Hillock Lane, York, Pa. 17403. (1967)

BEERY, JOHN THOMAS D
Committeeman, Clinton Co. Dem. Cmt, Mo.
b. Platt Co, Mo, 5/31/84; s. William Beery and Mary Elizabeth Redden B; m. 1/22/03 to Sally M. Rails; c. Raymond, Ronald and Thalma (Mrs. Bowlin). Polit. & Govt. Pos: Committeeman, Clinton Co. Dem. Cmt, 55-, chmn, 60-66. Bus. & Prof. Pos: Farmer, 03-25; supvr, Quaker Oats Co, 25-49; treas, Gower Sch. Dist, Mo, 54- Mem: Mason; charter mem, Gower Lions Club; fund chmn, Clinton Co. Red Cross; pres, Gower Fire Asn; bd. mem, W. Cent. Mo. Fire Asn; mem. legis. cmt, Mo. State Fire Asn. Rel: Baptist. Mailing Add: R.F.D. 1, Gower, Mo. 64454. (1967)

BEESON, ANNA MAE D
b. Castana, Iowa, 6/12/14; d. Arthur Welch and Rachel Neumann W; m. to Edward Junius Beeson; c. Thomas Edward, Julia Ann, Geraldine Rose, John Arthur, Anna Mae, Jr, James Bernard, Mary Kathleen, Joseph Michael and Patricia Susan. Educ: Coburg Consol. High Sch, Valedictorian; Debate Team. Polit. & Govt. Pos: Advisor, Humboldt Co. Dem. Cent. Cmt, Iowa, 65-, chmn, 61-64, v.chmn, 50-61; precinct committeewoman, 48-62. Mem: Organizor and financial chmn, Humboldt Co. Soc. for Crippled Children & Adults. Rel: Catholic. Mailing Add: Gilmore City, Iowa 50541. (1967)

BEESON, TRAVIS N. R
b. Holly Springs, Ark, 1/11/27; s. Joe Abb Beeson and Sarah Elizabeth Evans B; m. 5/29/49 to Doris Smith; c. Bobbie Doris and Travis Gordon. Educ: Ouachita Baptist Univ. Polit. & Govt. Pos: Rep. nominee for Lt. Gov, Ark, 64 and for Ark. State Sen, 66; co-chmn, Ark. Rep. State Cmt, 64-65; del, Rep. Nat. Conv, 68. Mil. Serv: Entered as Pvt, Air Force, 44, released as Sgt, 46, after serv. in Korea; Asian Theater Ribbon; Korean Liberation Medal. Mem: Farm Bur; Ark. Consistory, Camden Shrine Club; Lions; Saharah Temple; Odd Fellows; Am. Legion; C. of C. Rel: Baptist. Mailing Add: 304 Berg Ave. N.W, Camden, Ark. 71701. (1967)

BEGAY, WILBERT C. R
N.Mex. State Rep.
b. Shiprock, N.Mex, 3/22/39; s. Jim Curley Begay and Nannie Bainbridge B; m. to Marietta Simpson; c. Warren. Educ: Ft. Lewis Col, 2 years; Utah State Univ, 1 year. Polit. & Govt. Pos: N.Mex. State Rep, 67- Mil. Serv: Entered as Pvt E-1, Army, 63, released as Pfc E-3, 65, after serv. in Missile Unit, Seventh U.S. Army, Germany, 64-65; Good Conduct Medal; Transportation Medal; Sharp Shooters Medal. Mem: Ft. Lewis Col. Alumni Club. Rel: Latter-day Saint. Mailing Add: P.O. Box 96, Fruitland, N.Mex. 87416.

BEGG, WILLIAM VINCENT D
Conn. State Rep.
b. Waterbury, Conn, 10/5/32; s. William Vincent Begg and Loretta O'Brien B; m. 6/16/62 to Claire Moran; c. William Vincent, III, Thomas Moore and Michael Moran. Educ: Fairfield Univ, A.B, 54; N.Y. Law Sch, L.L.B, 59. Polit. & Govt. Pos: Conn. State Rep, 86th Dist, 67- Bus. & Prof. Pos: Attorney, 59- Mil. Serv: Entered as Pvt, Army, 54, released as Sp-3, 56, after serv. in Medical Dispensary. Mem: Waterbury and Conn. Bar Asns; K. of C.(past Grand Knight); Elks. Rel: Roman Catholic. Legal Res: 245 Columbia Blvd, Waterbury, Conn. 06710. Mailing Add: 29 Leavenworth St, Waterbury, Conn. 06702.

BEGGS, JAMES MONTGOMERY R
Under Secy. of Transportation
b. Pittsburgh, Pa, 1/9/26; s. James Andrew Beggs and Elizabeth Mikulan B; m. 10/3/53 to Mary Elizabeth Harrison; c. Maureen Elizabeth, Cathleen Louise, Teresa Lynn and James Harrison. Educ: U.S. Naval Acad, B.S, 48; Harvard Univ, M.B.A, 55; Sigma Tau. Polit. & Govt. Pos: Assoc. adminstr. adv. research and tech, NASA, 68-69; Under Secy. of Transportation, 69- Bus. & Prof. Pos: Div. mgr, underseas div, Westinghouse Elec. Corp, Baltimore, Md. and Pittsburgh, Pa, 55-61, div. mgr. syst. opers, 61-63, v.pres. defense and space center, surface div, 63-67, dir. purchases and traffic, 67-68. Mil. Serv: Entered as Midshipman-Ens, Navy, 44, released as Lt. Comdr, 54, after serv. in submarines, Atlantic Submarine Force, 50-54; Lt. Comdr, Naval Res, 54-66; various theater ribbons. Mem: Am. Inst. Aeronaut. and Astronaut; Am. Soc. Naval Engrs; v.chmn, Howard Co. Charter Cmn, 67-68. Rel: Roman Catholic. Legal Res: 10000 Carmelita, Potomac, Md. 20854. Mailing Add: 800 Independence, Washington, D.C. 20590.

BEGGS, MARY HARRISON R
b. East Orange, N.J, 6/3/30; d. Charles C. Harrison and Hazel Edwards H; m. 10/3/53 to James Montgomery Beggs; c. Maureen Elizabeth, Kathleen Louise, Teresa Lynn and James Harrison. Educ: Conn. Col. for Women,

B.A, 52; Phi Beta Kappa. Polit. & Govt. Pos: Party worker, Precinct, Dist. Level, Rep. Party, Howard Co, Md, 58-62; mem, Fifth Cong. Dist. Rep. Cmt, 62-66; chmn, Rep. State Cent. Cmt, Howard Co, 62-66; mem, Howard Co. Planning Cmn, 66- Bus. & Prof. Pos: Eng. teacher, Bloomfield High Sch, N.J, 52-53; asst. personnel mgr, Mass. Mem. Hosp, 54-55. Mem: Conn. Col. Alumnae Coun; Turf Valley Country Club. Rel: Congregational. Mailing Add: 10000 Carmelita Dr, Potomac, Md. 20854.

BEGLEY, ELMER R
Secy. of State, Ky.
Mailing Add: State Capitol, Frankfort, Ky. 40601.

BEGLEY, OWEN M. D
b. Schenectady, N.Y, 5/16/06; m. 4/15/63 to Helen Hein Smith; c. Nancy. Educ: Union Col; Albany Law Sch. Polit. & Govt. Pos: Asst. attorney gen, N.Y, 35-42; Mayor, Schenectady, 47-52; N.Y. State Sen, 57-66. Bus. & Prof. Pos: Lawyer, Begley, Moynihan & Quinlan, Schenectady. Mil. Serv: Army, Corps of Engrs, WWII, Capt, China-Burma-India, 42-46, Lt/Col. Mem: N.Y. State and Am. Bar Asns; VFW; 40 et 8; Am. Legion. Mailing Add: 1322 Hawthorn Rd, Schenectady, N.Y. 12309.

BEGOVICH, JOHN C. D
b. Jackson, Calif, 1/17/16; m. to Lorraine M. Love B; c. John. Educ: Sacramento City Col. Polit. & Gov. Pos: Calif. State Sen, 60-66; Judge, Amador Co. Judicial Dist; Vet. Serv. Officer, 5 years; Amador Co. Dem. Club, Cent. Cmt. Mil. Serv: Army. Mem: Am. Legion; VFW; Disabled Officers Asn; Soc. of 3rd Inf. Div; Native Sons; E Clampus Vitus; Druids; Mountain Men; Sportsmen; Lions. 1967 Legal Res: 413 Main St, Placerville, Calif. No mailing address available. (1967)

BEHR, LAWRENCE VAN der POEL R
b. Patterson, N.J, 11/9/40; s. John Henry Behr and Beatrice Vanderpool B; m. 7/7/66 to Melinda F. Hague. Educ: E. Carolina Col, 59-63; E. Carolina Playhouse; Radio-TV Soc. Polit. Pos: Nat. Committeeman, N.C. Young Rep, 65-66 and 1st dist. dir, 59-65; del, Rep. Nat. Conv, 64; mem, Pitt Co. Rep. Exec. Cmt, N.C, 63-66; del, Young Rep. Nat. Conv, 63; pres, E. Carolina Young Rep. Club, 60-63; pres, Pitt Co. TAR's, 57-58. Bus. & Prof. Pos: Mgr. special projs, Multronics Inc, 65-; secy-treas, V.W.B. Inc, 65-; v.pres. eng, Farmville Broadcasting Co, 64-; partner, The Drumstick, 62-63; pres, Lawrence Behr Asn. Inc, 61-; chief engr, E. Carolina Col. Radio-TV; 57-61. Articles: 'Engineering Proficiency—Operational & Economic Aspects,' Jour. of Soc. of Broadcast Engrs, 64; 'RF. Grounding Techniques on Airborne Platforms,' Limited, 66; Book Reviews, Jour. of Soc. of Broadcast Engrs, 65- Mem: Founding mem, Soc. Broadcast Engrs. Inc; Inst. Elec. and Electronic Engrs; Audio Eng. Soc; N.C. Asn. Broadcasters; Aircraft Owners & Pilot Asn; Armed Forces Commun. & Electronics Asn; Am. Ordnance Asn; Moose, Lodge 885; Greenville Optimist Club; Pitt Co. Civil Defense. Amateur Radio Operator, K4JRZ; Pilots License. Legal Res: 2501 E. Fourth St, Greenville, N.C. 27834. Mailing Add: 5712 Frederick Ave, Rockville, Md. 20852. (1967)

BEHRENS, E. FREDERICK R
Exec. Asst. to Secy, U.S. Dept. of Agr.
b. Bryant, S.Dak. 4/8/23; s. Ernest H. Behrens and Catherine Kaucher B; m. 7/1/49 to Wanda Deviney; c. Christopher Frederick. Educ: S.Dak. State Univ, B.S, 49; Am. Univ, 55; Phi Gamma Mu. Polit. & Govt. Pos: Exec. secy, Sen. Karl E. Mundt, S.Dak, 49-58; minority consult, Exec. Reorgn. Subcmt, U.S. Senate Govt. Opers. Cmt, 67-69; exec. asst. to secy, U.S. Dept. Agr, 69- Bus. & Prof. Pos: Mgr, intra-indust. rels, Nat. Forest Prod. Asn, Wash. D.C, 58-67. Mil. Serv: Entered as Pvt, Army, 43, released as Sgt, 46, after serv. in 648th Tank Destroyer Bn, ETO, 44-46; Europe-Africa-Middle East Serv, Good Conduct and Am. Theater Serv. Medals. Mem: Am. Legion; Mason. Rel: Episcopal. Legal Res: Spearfish, S.Dak. 57783. Mailing Add: 1910 Shannon Court, Alexandria, Va. 22306.

BEIJER, ARTHUR R
b. Stockholm, Sweden, 8/11/85; s. Andrew P. Beijer and Amelia B; m. 11/11/08 to Carroll V. Purdy, wid; c. Albin and Donald Arthur. Educ: Aemu Col, Sweden, M.E, 02. Polit. & Govt. Pos: Chmn, Price Co. Rep. Orgn, Wis, 64-69. Bus. & Prof. Pos: Owner, foundry and machine shop, 10-24; teacher, Milwaukee Voc. and Adult Schs, 24-56. Mem: F&AM; RAM. Rel, Presbyterian. Mailing Add: Harmony Lodge, Phillips, Wis. 54555. (1967)

BEILENSON, ANTHONY C. D
Calif. State Sen.
b. New York State, 1932; m. to Dolores Martin; c. two sons, one daughter. Educ: Harvard Col, A.B, 54, Harvard Law Sch, LL.B, 57. Polit. & Govt. Pos: Calif. State Assemblyman, 63-66; Calif. State Sen, 67- Bus. & Prof. Pos: Attorney. Mailing Add: 1122 S. Robertson Blvd, Los Angeles, Calif. 90035.

BEILFUSS, BRUCE F.
b. Withee, Wis, 1/8/15; s. Walter William Beilfuss and Elsie Dodte B; m. to Helen Hendrickson (deceased); m. 10/17/61 to De Ette Knowlton; c. Mark. Educ: Univ. Wis, B.A. and LL.B. Polit. & Govt. Pos: Supvr, Clark Co, Wis, 40-41, dist. attorney, 41-48 and circuit judge, 48-64; assoc. justice, Wis. Supreme Court, 64- Bus. & Prof. Pos: Chmn, Bd. Circuit Judges, 56; chmn, Gov. Cmn. on Law Enforcement and Crime, 65-66. Mil. Serv: Entered as A/S, Navy, 43, released as Lt.(jg); S.Pac. Ribbon; Philippine Liberation Medal. Mem: Mason; Elks; Am. Legion; VFW; Big Brothers of Am. Rel: Protestant. Legal Res: 702 Oneida Place, Madison, Wis. 53711. Mailing Add: Supreme Court Chambers, State Capitol, Madison, Wis. 53702.

BELANGER, JOSEPH A. D
married; c. Mrs. W. Charles Cannon, Mrs. Robert Meuse, Mrs. Ken Perry. Polit. & Govt. Pos: Postmaster, Madison, Maine, 42-46; Maine State Rep, 67-68. Bus. & Prof. Pos: Operated Belanger's Restaurant, 44 years. Mil. Serv: World War II. Mem: Past Comdr, Am. Legion Post and Legion Co. Coun; past pres, Lions; zone dir, Lions Int. Mailing Add: 10 E. Houghton St, Madison, Maine 04950. (1967)

BELAVAL MARTINEZ, EUGENIO S. New Progressive, P.R.
Rep, P.R. House of Rep.
b. Santurce, P.R, 11/13/25; s. Eugenio S. Belaval and Olympia Martinez B; m. 6/27/48 to Virginia Carmen Tranum; c. Eugenio, III, Edvardo, Manuel and Jorge. Educ: Univ. P.R, LL.B; Harvard Law Sch, LL.M; Phi Sigma Alpha. Polit. & Govt. Pos: Rep, P.R. House of Rep, 69- Bus. & Prof. Pos: Mgr. and treas, La Nueva Placita, Inc, Santurce, P.R, 49-61; asst. prof. law, Univ. P.R. Sch. Law, 62- Mil. Serv: Entered as Pvt, Army, 44, released as Capt, 57, after serv. in P.R. Nat. Guard, Am. Theatre, 49-57; Capt.(Ret), Inf, Army Res; Am. Theatre Serv. Medal. Mem: P.R. Bar Asn; Rotary. Rel: Catholic. Legal Res: Calle Amarillo 4, Urb De Diego, Rio Piedras, P.R. 00926. Mailing Add: The Capitol, San Juan, P.R. 00901.

BELCHER, PAGE R
U.S. Rep, Okla.
b. Jefferson, Okla, 4/21/99; married; c. Page, Jr. and Carol (Mrs. Clyde V. Collins). Educ: Friends Univ, Wichita, Kans; Univ. Okla. Hon. LL.D, Okla. City Univ. Polit. & Govt. Pos: Campaign mgr. and secy, former U.S. Rep. Ross Rizley, Okla; court clerk, Garfield Co, Okla; mem, Bd. of Educ; chmn, Eighth Cong. Dist. Rep. Party, ten years; exec. secy, Rep. Party of Okla; U.S. Rep, Okla, 50-; del, Rep. Nat. Conv, 68. Bus. & Prof. Pos: Attorney-at-law. Mem: Garfield Co. and Okla. Bar Asns; C. of C; Kiwanis; Am. Legion; Odd Fellows; mem-at-lg, Nat. Coun. Boy Scouts; former pres, United War Chest of Okla; past chmn, Red Cross. Recipient, Silver Beaver Award, Boy Scouts. Rel: Methodist. Legal Res: 1638 S. Carson, Tulsa, Okla. 74119. Mailing Add: Dorchester House, Washington, D.C. 20009.

BELCHER, TAYLOR GARRISON
U.S. Ambassador, Lima, Peru
b. New York, N.Y, 7/1/20; s. Taylor Belcher and Miriam Frazee B; m. 10/22/42 to Edith Anthony; c. Anthony Wayne and Taylor, III. Educ: Brown Univ, A.B, 41. Polit. & Govt. Pos: Career officer, U.S. Dept. State, For. Serv, 45-, consul, Glasgow, 49-54, v.consul and diplomatic secy, Mexico City, 46-49, consul and consul gen, Nicosia, Cyprus, 57-60, with Can. Nat. Defense Col, 60-61, dir, Off. W.Coast Affairs, 61-64, U.S. Ambassador to Cyprus, 64-69, Lima, Peru, 69- Bus. & Prof. Pos: Mgr, coal co, 41-42. Mil. Serv: Entered as Ens, Naval Res, 42, released as Lt, 45, after serv. in N.Atlantic and S.Pac. Theatres; 13 Battle Stars and various Theatre Ribbons. For. Serv. Asn. Distinguished Honor Award, Dept. of State, 68. Rel: Protestant. Legal Res: Garrison-on-Hudson, N.Y. 10524. Mailing Add: U.S. Embassy, Lima, Peru.

BELCHIC, HARRIET CAMERON R
V.Chmn, Caddo Parish Polit. Action Coun, La.
b. Tiffin, Ohio, 8/17/28; d. Wheelock Hubbell Cameron and Edna Wells C; m. 6/15/49 to George Belchic, Jr; c. Katherine, Cameron, Ellen and Martha. Educ: La. State Univ, B.S, 48, M.S, 49; Geol. & Mining Soc. Polit. & Govt. Pos: Mem, La. Platform Cmt, 62, v.chmn, 64 & 67; v.chmn, La. Rep. State Cent. Cmt, 62-64; del. and mem. cmt. on resolutions, Rep. Nat. Conv, 64 & 68; v.chmn, Caddo Parish Polit. Action Coun, La, 68- Mem: Assoc. mem, Am. Asn. Petrol. Geol, 49-65; Jr. League. Rel: Episcopal. Mailing Add: 6500 Gilbert Dr, Shreveport, La. 71106.

BELCOURT, AGENOR D
N.H. State Rep.
b. LaBaie du Febre, Que, 5/25/01; married; c. One. Polit. & Govt. Pos: N.H. State Rep, 45-; Constitutional Conv, 48, 56 & 64; chmn, Hillsborough Co. Del, 57. Bus. & Prof. Pos: Retired Johns Manville employee, 40 years. Mil. Serv: Mil. Police Bn. Mem: Moose; Sacred Heart; Loyal and Soc. Club; state trustee, CWV; John Manville Quarter Century Club. Rel: Catholic. Mailing Add: 38 Perham St, Nashua, N.H. 03060. (1967)

BELEN, FREDERICK C(HRISTOPHER) D
b. Lansing, Mich, 12/25/13; s. Christopher Frederick Belen and Elizabeth Lehman B; m. 2/7/43 to Opal Marie Sheets; c. Frederick C, Jr. Educ: Mich. State Univ, A.B, 37; George Wash. Univ, LL.B, 42; Delta Chi. Polit. & Govt. Pos: Admin. asst. to U.S. Rep. Andrew Transue, Mich, 37-39 and U.S. Rep. George D. O'Brien, Mich, 40-41; counsel and chief counsel, Post Off. and Civil Serv. Cmt, 46-61; secy, 13th Cong. Dist. Dem. Orgn, Mich, 48; del, Wayne Co. Dem. Conv, 48, Ingham Co. Dem. Conv, 60, 62, 64 & 66; asst. postmaster, Bur. of Opers, Wash, D.C, 61 and Dep. Postmaster Gen, 64-68. Bus. & Prof. Pos: Attorney, Wash, D.C, currently. Mil. Serv: Entered as 1st Lt, Army Res, 41, released as Lt. Col, 46, after serv. as Dep. Chief of Intel. & Security Div, Off. of Chief of Transportation; Army Commendation Award. Publ: Author various Cong. cmt. reports and studies. Mem: Chmn, bd. of trustees, William A. Jump Mem. Found; Am. Soc. for Pub. Admin; State Bar of Mich; Fed. Bar Asn; George Wash. Univ. Law Sch. Alumni Asn; Mich. State Univ. Alumni Asn; Nat. Defense Transportation Asn; bd. of dirs, Multiple Sclerosis Soc; Am. Legion; DAV; Nat. Dem. Club; v.pres, Grand Isle Tarpon Rodeo, La; Commodore of Wa-Vi-Mar Fishing Club. Recipient Benjamin Franklin Award, 63; Mich. State Univ. Distinguished Alumni Award, 63 and Interfraternity Coun. Alumnus Award for outstanding achievement in field of pub. serv, 64; Nat. Bus. Publ. Silver Scroll for outstanding contributions to improved mail serv. and postal efficiency, 64. Rel: Presbyterian. Legal Res: 626 W. Kalamazoo St, Lansing, Mich. 48915. Mailing Add: 2658 N. Upshur St, Arlington, Va. 22207.

BELHUMEUR, ARTHUR A. D
Mem, R.I. Dem. State Exec. Cmt.
b. Central Falls, 4/26/04; m. to Jeanne. Educ: Bryant Col, 34. Polit. & Govt. Pos: R.I. State Sen, 55-66, Dep. Majority Leader, R.I. State Senate, 63-66; Dem. city chmn, Central Falls, currently; mem, R.I. Dem. State Exec. Cmt, currently. Bus. & Prof. Pos: Comptroller, pub. acct. Mil. Serv: Navy, 22-26. Mem: LeFoyer; Cercle Canadien; Sullivan Coun; K. of C; French Fedn. of R.I; Nat. Dir. of L'Union St. Jean Baptiste D'Amerique; Dir. of Franco-Am. Cmt. of R.I; Dexter Credit Union of Central Falls. Rel: Catholic, Trustee of St. Mathieu Parish. Mailing Add: 250 Shawmut Ave, Central Falls, R.I. 02863. (1967)

BeLIEU, KENNETH EUGENE
Dep. Asst. to the President for Cong. Rels.
b. Portland, Ore, 2/10/14; s. Perry Gordon BeLieu and Ilia Jean Rood B; m. 12/22/51 to Margaret Katherine Waldhoff; c. Kenneth Eugene and Christopher Michael. Educ: Univ. Ore, B.A, 37; Adv. Mgt. Prog, Harvard, grad, 55. Polit. & Govt. Pos: Mem. prfnl. staff, Senate Armed Serv. Cmt, 55-58; staff dir, Preparedness Invest. Subcmt. and Senate Cmt. on Aeronaut. and

Space Sci, 58-61; Asst. Secy. of the Navy, Dept. of Defense, 61-65, Under Secy. of the Navy, 65; mem, Defense Sci. Bd, 66-69; Dep. Asst. to the President for Cong. Rels, 69- Bus. & Prof. Pos: Bus. exec. Portland, Ore, 37-40; exec. v.pres. and pres, Leisure World Found, 65-66, mem. bd, 65-; mem. bd. dirs, Inst. Strategic Studies, Georgetown Univ, 65-69; mem. adv. bd, Ryan Aeronaut. Co. and Continental Motors, 65-69; mem. bd. Babcock Electronics Corp, 66-68; mem, Radio Corp. Am. Adv. Bd, 68-69. Mil. Serv: Army, 40-55, Col. Mailing Add: 1214 Westgrove Blvd, Alexandria, Va. 22307.

BELILES, RICHARD VINCENT D
Dir. of Orgn, Jefferson Co. Dem. Party, Ky.
b. Louisville, Ky, 1/31/34; s. Neal Alton Beliles and Mary Buck B; m. 9/27/63 to Beatrice Elizabeth; c. Sherry, Mark Alton and Joseph Hunt. Educ: Univ. Louisville, B.S, 68; Tau Kappa Epsilon. Polit. & Govt. Pos: Dir. of orgn, Jefferson Co. Dem. Party, Ky, 66- Bus. & Prof. Pos: Aetna Casualty Co, 60-64; St. Paul Ins. Co, 64- Mem: Urban League; Mason; Jr. C. of C; Louisville Human Rels. Cmn. Rel: Methodist. Mailing Add: 5412 Danny Boy Lane, Louisville, Ky. 40214.

BELIVEAU, SEVERIN M. D
Chmn, Maine Dem. Party
Mailing Add: 150 Congress St, Rumford, Maine 04276

BELK, IRWIN D
b. Charlotte, N.C, 4/4/22; s. William Henry Belk and Mary Leonora Irwin B; m. 9/11/48 to Carol Grotnes; c. William Irwin, Irene Grotnes, Marilyn and Carl Grotnes. Educ: Davidson Col; Univ. N.C, Chapel Hill, grad, 46; Kappa Alpha; Delta Sigma Pi. Polit. & Govt. Pos: Former mem, Urban Redevelop. Cmt, Charlotte, N.C; N.C. State Rep, 59-62; del, Dem. Nat. Conv, 56, 60, 64 & 68; mem, N.C. Legis. Coun, 63-64 and Legis. Research Cmn, 65-66; N.C. State Sen, Mecklenburg Co, 63-66, chmn, Hwy. Safety Cmt, v.chmn, Appropriations Cmt. and mem, Banking, Higher Educ, Ins, Local Govt, Penal Insts, Pub. Health and Rules Cmts, N.C. Senate, 65-66. Bus. & Prof. Pos: Pres, Belk Enterprises, Inc, Charlotte, N.C; v.pres. and dir, Belk Group of Stores, v.pres. and treas, Belk Stores Serv, Inc. and chmn. of the bd, The Belk Found, Charlotte; pres, Brothers Investment Co, Charlotte and Monroe Hardware Co, Monroe; v.pres. and dir, Randolph Mills, Franklinville and Pilot Mills, Raleigh; dir, Adams-Millis Corp, High Point, First Union Nat. Bank and Highland Park Mfg. Co, Charlotte, Park Yarn Mill, Kings Mountain, Pilot Realty Co, Raleigh, Security Fire & Indemnity Co, Winston-Salem, Stonecutter Mills, Spindale, Union Mills Co, Monroe, Hatteras Yacht Co, High Point, Lumbermen's Mutual Casualty Co, Chicago, Ill. and Fidelity Bankers Life Ins. Co, Richmond, Va. Mil. Serv: Sgt, 491st Bomber Group, 8th Air Force, World War II, 2½ years overseas. Mem: Past pres. and statewide dir, N.C. Merchants Asn; N.C. Div, Am. Cancer Soc; state chmn, Businessmen-for-Heart, N.C. Heart Asn; bd. dirs, N.C. Bur. for Employ. of the Blind, N.C. Educ. Coun. on Nat. Purposes, N.C. Med. Adv. Coun, Univ. N.C, Chapel Hill and N.C. Chap, Nat. Soc. for Prev. of Blindness; Cmn. to Study the Cause and Control of Cancer; N.C. Symphony Ball Cmt; Edenton and Chowan Co. Hist. Cmn; Carolina Charter Corp; v.pres, Eighth Cong. Dist. of N.C. for the N.C. Soc. for Preservation of Antiquities, Inc; dir, Nat. Amateur Athletic Union Adv. Coun, N.Y; Nat. Coun. on Crime and Delinquency, N.Y; dir, Carolinas Carrousel, Charlotte, Mecklenburg Asn, Am. Cancer Soc. and Charlotte and Mecklenburg Am. Heart Asn. and Ment. Health Asn; dir. and finance bd, Charlotte Opera Asn; past pres. and dir, Charlotte Exec. Club; legis. cmt, Charlotte C. of C. and dir. for six years; Charlotte Merchants Asn; first v.pres, Charlotte Cent. Lions Club; F&AM; Shrine; Scottish and York Rite Mason; trustee and mem. finance cmt, Univ. N.C, Chapel Hill; trustee, Queens Col, Charlotte; trustee, v.chmn. bd. and mem. finance cmt, St. Andrews Presby. Col, Laurinburg; chmn. bd. adv, Chowan Col, Murfreesboro; adv. coun, Wingate Col; bd. vis, Appalachian State Teachers Col, Boone; bd. assoc, Meredith Col, Raleigh; bd. counselors, Erskine Col, Due West; chmn. vis. cmt, Univ. N.C, Charlotte; first v.pres, Cmt. on Univ. Develop, Univ. N.C; dir, Home Econ. Found. of N.C, Greensboro, N.C. State Col. Found, Inc, Bus. Found. of N.C. and Educ. Found, Inc, Chapel Hill; pres, Presby. Men's Coun, Synod of N.C; chmn. exec. cmt, Hist. Found. of the Presby. and Reformed Churches, Montreat; bd. dirs, Montreat Retreat Asn. and chmn, Admin. Conf. Bldg. Cmt; bd. dirs, YMCA World Serv. Cmt; finance cmt, N.C. Coun. of Churches, Raleigh; second v.pres, N.C. Presby. Hist. Soc; Sesqui-Centennial Cmt. and Inter-Church Rels. Cmt, Presby. Synod of N.C. Selected 1 of 10 Outstanding Young Men in Charlotte, 54-57. Rel: Presbyterian; Deacon, Myers Park Presby. Church, Charlotte. Legal Res: 400 Eastover Rd, Charlotte, N.C. 28207. Mailing Add: 308 E. Fifth St, Charlotte, N.C. 28202.

BELKER, LOREN B. D
Chmn, Lancaster Co. Dem. Cent. Cmt, Nebr.
b. Quincy, Ill, 6/23/26; s. Bernard John Belker and Verna Leach B; m. 5/1/52 to Darlene K. Tracy; c. Jeffrey Belker and Kendra K. Land. Educ: Univ. Nebr, 57-58; St. Joseph's Col, Ill, 42-43; Quincy Col, 44. Polit. & Govt. Pos: Mem. bus. and commerce cmt, Nebr. Dem. Party, 67 and banking, commerce and indust. cmt, 69-; chmn, Lancaster Co. Dem. Cent. Cmt, 68-; chmn, State Dem. Jefferson-Jackson Day Dinner, 69. Bus. & Prof. Pos: Mgr, Agency Acct. Div, Bankers Life Nebr, Lincoln, 57 and mgr, agency and premium acct. and group acct. Div, 64; v.pres, Midwest Chap, Ins. Acct. & Statist. Asn, 65-66 and pres, 69. Publ: 'Common Sense and Supervision,' Interpreter, 63; 'The Telephone and Conservation,' Best Ins. News, 65; 'Some Second Thoughts on Pre-Authorized Checks,' Life Off. Mgr. Asn. Educ. Prog, 67. Mem: Fel, Life Mgt. Inst; able toastmaster, Toastmasters Int; C. of C. Educ. Cmt; v.chmn, Madonna-Tabitha Trust Drive; chmn, Commun. Chest Budget Cmt, Commun. Chest Exec. Cmt. and Bd. Dirs; former pres, PTA; former v.pres, treas. and chmn, Finance Cmt. Malone Commun. Center; hon. mem, State Young Dem; Knolls Country Club. Cited, Lincoln J. and City of Lincoln; Cum Laude, Health Ins. Asn. Am. Rel: Episcopal; Former Sr. Warden, Jr. Warden and Vestryman. Mailing Add: 2631 Sewell, Lincoln, Nebr. 68502.

BELL, ALPHONZO R
U.S. Rep, Calif.
b. Los Angeles, Calif, 9/19/14; s. Alphonzo Bell and Minnewa B; m. to Sally B; c. Stephen, Matthew, Robert, Anthony Edward and Fonza. Educ: Occidental Col, B.A. Polit. & Govt. Pos: Chmn, Rep. Nat. Cmt. and Rep. State Cent. Cmt, Calif, 56-58; chmn, Los Angeles Co. Rep. Cent. Cmt, 58-60; U.S. Rep, Calif, 60- Bus. & Prof. Pos: Chmn. bd. of dir, Bell Petroleum Co. (prior to elec). Mil. Serv: Army Air Corps. Legal Res: Los. Angeles, Calif. Mailing Add: 113 Cannon House Office Bldg, Washington, D.C. 20515.

BELL, CLARENCE D. R
Pa. State Sen.
b. Upland, Delaware Co, Pa, 2/4/14; s. Samuel R. Bell and Belle Hanna B; m. to Mary Isabel James; c. Clarence D, Jr. and Mary D. Educ: Swarthmore Col; Harvard Law Sch; U.S. Army Command and Gen. Staff Col. Polit. & Govt. Pos: Former v.pres, State Hwy. and Bridge Authority, Pa; Pa. State Rep, 54-60; Pa. State Sen, 60- and chmn, Judiciary Cmt, Pa. Senate; mem, Pa. Bicentennial Cmn, currently. Bus. & Prof. Pos: Attorney-at-law. Mil. Serv: Brig. Gen, Pa. Nat. Guard, assigned as Asst. Adj. Gen; 34 years in active army, Nat. Guard, Res; 62 months active duty, WWII. Mem: Mil. Govt. Asn. (nat. pres, 63); ROA (chmn, Nat. Army Affairs Cmt, 60-61, past state pres); Pa. Exchange Clubs (past pres); Am. Legion (past comdr, Stevenson Post 190); Mason; B'nai B'rith; K. of C; Delco Bd. Realtors; Polish Am. Eagle Citizens; Nat. Guard Asn. of Pa. Awards from DAV, Jewish War Vet, VFW, B'nai B'rith; K. of C, Delco Real Estate Bd, Polish Am. Eagle Citizens Club and Nat. Guard Asn. of Pa. Mailing Add: 400 W. 24th St, Chester, Pa. 19013.

BELL, CLARENCE E. D
Ark. State Sen.
b. Camden, Ark, 2/1/12; s. Joseph Dudley Bell, III and Dona Massengale B; m. 8/16/36 to Hope Raney; c. Joseph Dudley, IV, Beverly Jane and Barbara Ann. Educ: Ouachita Col, A.B; Univ. Ark, M.A. Polit. Govt. Pos: Ark. State Sen, 57- Bus. & Prof. Pos: High sch. prin. and coach, Parkin, Ark, 35-41, supt. sch, 41-63; pub. rels. rep, Ark-La. Gas Co, 63- Mem: Rotary; Farm Bur; Ark. Educ. Asn. Selected on All-State Football Team in High Sch. and Col. Rel: Baptist. Mailing Add: 26 Church St, Parkin, Ark. 72373.

BELL, CORRIE LEE D
Co-Chmn, Portsmouth Dem. Exec. Cmt, Va.
b. Bainbridge, Ga, 4/22/13; d. John Bell and Mamie William B; div. Educ: Hutto High Sch, Bainbridge, Ga. Polit. & Govt. Pos: Co-chmn, Portsmouth Dem. Exec. Cmt, Va, 64-; alternate del, Dem. Nat. Conv, 68. Mem: F&AM. Cert. of Merit, Cent. Civic Forum, Voter Registration, Portsmouth Redevelop. and Housing, NAACP and Naval Air Sta. Rel: Baptist. Mailing Add: 1500 Green St, Portsmouth, Va. 23704.

BELL, DAVID ELLIOTT
b. Jamestown, N.Dak, 1/20/19; s. Reginald Bell and Florence Boise B; m. 11/17/43 to Mary Louise Barry; c. Susan, Peter. Educ: Pomona Col, Calif, B.A, 39, hon. LL.D, 61; Harvard, M.A. in Econ, 41, hon. LL.D, 65; Univ. of Vt, hon. LL.D, 65; Phi Beta Kappa. Polit. & Govt. Pos: Staff mem, Bur. of Budget, 42, 45-47 & 48-49, dir, 61-62; spec. asst. to White House, 47-48 & 49-51; admin. asst. to President Truman, 51-53; adminstr, Agency Int. Develop, 62-66. Bus. & Prof. Pos: Adv. gen. econ, Govt. Pakistan Planning Bd. and proj. field supvr, Harvard Adv. Group, 54-57; lectr. econ, Harvard Grad. Sch, 57-61, secy, Grad. Sch. Pub. Admin, 59-61; v.pres, The Ford Found, 66- Mil. Serv: Marine Corps, 1st Lt, 42-45. Publ: Author, 'Allocating Development Resources: Some Observations Based on Pakistan Experience', 59. Mem: Am. Econ. Asn; Am. Soc. Pub. Admin. Received Rockefeller Pub. Serv. Award, 53. Legal Res: 5801 Bent Branch Rd, Washington, D.C. 20016. Mailing Add: The Ford Foundation, 320 E. 43rd St, New York, N.Y. 10017.

BELL, DONALD ALFRED R
Kans. State Rep.
b. Wichita, Kans, 7/13/28; s. Alven H. Bell and Klotilda Beat B; m. to Eleanor Harriet Van Gieson; c. Carol Anne, Teresa Louise, Catherine Marie, Susan Joann, Steven Francis, David Paul and Jennifer Lynn. Educ: Friends Univ, 50; Creighton Univ, B.S, 53, LL.B, 55; Phi Alpha Delta; Alpha Sigma Nu; Nat. Jesuit Honor Soc. Polit. & Govt. Pos: Kans. State Rep, 65-, Majority Floor Leader, Kans. House of Rep, 69- Bus. & Prof. Pos: Partner, Weigand, Curfman, Brainerd, Harris and Kaufman, Wichita, Kans, 55- Mil. Serv: Entered as Pvt, Marine Corps, 46, released as Cpl, 48. Mem: Wichita, Kans. and Am. Bar Asns. Rel: Roman Catholic. Mailing Add: 1475 Lieunett, Wichita, Kans. 67203.

BELL, E. R. R
b. Perryton, Tex, 12/25/28; s. Roy E. Bell and Lola Hood B; m. 6/15/52 to Joan Sims; c. Terri Lynn and Vicki Ann. Polit. & Govt. Pos: Former chmn, Sherman Co. Rep. Party, Tex. Mil. Serv: Entered as Pvt, Army, 51, released as 2nd Lt, 53, after serv. in Korea. Mem: Lions; Am. Legion; Farm Bur. Rel: Methodist. Mailing Add: 1001 Maple, Stratford, Tex. 79084. (1967)

BELL, EDWIN GRAHAM D
b. Gastonia, N.C, 4/16/39; s. John Clyde Bell and Thelma Henley B; m. 2/8/57 to Gayle Walker; c. E. Graham, Jr, John Chris, Martin Craig, Ann Margaret and Patrick Henley. Educ: IBM Training Center, Atlantic, Ga, Programmer, 61. Polit. & Govt. Pos: Secy, Gaston Co. Young Dem. Club, N.C, 65, pres, 66; pres, Tenth Cong. Dist, Young Dem. Club, 67; alternate del, Dem. Nat. Conv, 68; Young Dem. Nat. Committeeman of N.C, 68- Mil. Serv: Entered as Airman 2/C, Air Force, 57, released as Airman 2/C, 60, after serv. in Mil. Air Transport Serv, Europe, 58-59. Mem: Mason. Rel: Lutheran. Legal Res: 610 Brookgreen Dr, Dallas, N.C. 28034. Mailing Add: Box 593, Dallas, N.C. 28034.

BELL, ELVIN CHARLES D
City Councilman, Fresno, Calif.
b. Merced, Calif, 3/1/37; s. Albert Lloyd Bell and Lucille Spears B; m. 2/20/60 to Viola Frances Bland. Educ: Ft. Benning Inf. Leadership Sch, Ga; Fresno State Col, B.A, 59; Santa Clara, adv. study, summers, 62-64; Sigma Chi. Polit. & Govt. Pos: Pres, Fresno State and Co. Young Dem, Calif, 58; city councilman, Fresno, 65- Bus. & Prof. Pos: Owner, Elvin C. Bell Pub. Rels. and Advert. Agency, Fresno; dir, Fresno Advert. Club, 63; pres, Fresno Chap, Pub. Rels. Soc. Am, 65. Mil. Serv: Entered as Pvt, Calif. Army Nat. Guard, 54, currently Maj; Calif. State Commendation Award with Pendant; Watts Serv. Award; Calif. Meritorious Award. Publ: 'Newspaper Expansion,' Ed. and Publisher, 58; 'Civic Participation,' Grid Mag, 59; 'Playthings and Toys',

Playthings Mag, 59. Mem: Bus. adv. coun, Fresno City Unified Sch. Dist, 63; dir, Fresno Kiwanis; exec. bd, Calif. State Fair; dir, Fresno State Col. Alumni; by-laws cmt, Nat. Guard Asn; Am. C. of C. Execs; Fresno Press Club. Outstanding Young Man of Year, Fresno Co, 63 & 66. Rel: Congregational. Mailing Add: 2908 E. Garland Ave, Fresno, Calif. 93726.

BELL, H. CLARK R
N.Y. State Assemblyman
b. Washington, D.C, 11/18/33; s. H. Clark Bell, Sr. and Margaret Thomas B; m. 11/17/62 to Joy Anne Kieran; c. Kieran O. and Bridget Anne. Educ: Georgetown Univ, B.S. Soc. Sci, 57; George Wash. Law Sch, LL.B. and J.D, 61. Polit. & Govt. Pos: Del, Constitutional Conv, 67; N.Y. State Assemblyman, 69- Mem: Ulster Co. Bar Asn.(dir, 63-68); N.Y. State Trial Lawyers Asn; N.Y. State and Am. Bar Asns. Rel: Roman Catholic. Mailing Add: Box 734, Woodstock, N.Y. 12498.

BELL, HALCYON ALSUP 'CHON' R
Mem, Ga. State Rep. Cmt.
b. Dublin, Ga, 9/8/15; d. Angus Dillon Alsup and Jessie Rice Alsup Williams; m. 2/23/35 to Robert Crittenden Bell; c. Halcyon (Mrs. Robert E. Lamb), Mae Crittenden and Bobbie Marsha. Educ: Wesleyan Col, 33-34; Univ. Ga, 35. Polit. & Govt. Pos: Acting postmaster, Shellman, Ga, 53-54; mem, Bur. Census, Dept. of Commercer, Third Cong. Dist, 59 & 60; pres, Ga. Fed. Rep. Women, 60-62; mem, Ga. State Rep. Cmt, 66-; chmn, Randolph Co. Rep. Party, 67-; alternate del, Rep. Nat. Conv, 68; chmn, Second Cong. Dist, Oper-Lend-an-Ear, Rep. Educ. Surv, 69- Mem: Life mem. PTA; life mem. Women's Soc. Christian Serv. Rel: Methodist. Mailing Add: Route 2, Shellman, Ga. 31786.

BELL, HOOVER FAY D
S.C. State Rep.
b. Wampee, S.C, 2/22/21; s. Oree Jerome Bell and Retha Carter B; m. 1/10/48 to Carolyn McElveen; c. Elizabeth, Suzanne and William G. Educ: Clemson Col; Univ. S.C, LL.B; Phi Delta Phi. Polit. & Govt. Pos: Chmn, Chesterfield Co. Dem. Party, S.C, 54-60; Town of Chesterfield, 55-57; S.C. State Rep, Chesterfield Co, 60- Mil. Serv: Entered as Seaman, Navy, 39, released as Aviation Cadet, 42. Mem: Mason; Civitan; Green River Country Club. Rel: Presbyterian. Mailing Add: Ivy Ave, Chesterfield, S.C. 29709.

BELL, JAMES D.
b. Lebanon, N.H, 7/1/11; m. to Stephanie Mathews. Educ: Univ. of N.Mex, B.A, 34; Univ. of Chicago, Ph.D, 41. Polit. & Govt. Pos: Chief statistician, N.Mex. Dept. of Pub. Welfare, 36-37; analyst, Off. of Coord. of Inter-Am. Affairs, 41-42; spec. asst, U.S. Dept. of Justice, 43-44; labor attache, Bogota, 44-46; career officer, U.S. Dept. of State For. Serv, 47-, 2nd secy, Santiago, 47-50, 1st secy, Manila, 50-53, supvr, Int. Rels. Officer, 53-55, dep. dir, Off. of Philippine and S. E. Asian Affairs, 55-56; dir, Off. of S. W. Pac. Affairs, 56-57 & 60-64, dep. chief, Djakarta, 57-58, U.S. Ambassador to Malaysia, 64-69. Bus. & Prof. Pos: Reporter, Albuquerque J, 33-34; instr, Gary, Ind. Col, 39-41; asst. prof, Hamilton Col, 46-47; Diplomat-in-residence, Univ. of Calif, Santa Cruz, 69- Legal Res: Washington, D.C. Mailing Add: University of California, Santa Cruz, Calif. 95060.

BELL, JOHN WILLIAM R
Fla. State Sen.
b. New York, N.Y, 9/16/16; s. George William Bell and Ethel Ryder B; div; c. Douglas R, Susan Heather and Holli Lei. Educ: Columbia Col, B.A, 38; Columbia Univ. Law Sch, LL.B, 41; Phi Delta Phi; Sigma Alpha Epsilon. Polit. & Govt. Pos: Mem. and chmn, Broward Co. Port Authority, Fla, 53-57 and Broward Co. Cmn, 57-60; Fla. State Rep, 63-64 & 66-67; Fla. State Sen, 67- Bus. & Prof. Pos: Attorney-at-Law, self-employed, 46- Mil. Serv: Entered as Ens, Navy, 43, released as Lt. Comdr, 46, after serv. in Atlantic and Pac. Theaters, 43-46; Invasion Ribbon, Philippine Islands; Lt. Comdr, Navy Res.(Ret), 64. Mem: Am. Bar Asn; Kiwanis; Propeller Club of U.S; Am. Legion; ROA; Navy League. Rel: Episcopal. Legal Res: 2512 Barcelona Dr, Ft. Lauderdale, Fla. 33301. Mailing Add: 100 S.E. Sixth St, Ft. Lauderdale, Fla. 33301. (1967)

BELL, L. CLAUDE R
b. McDonald, Kans, 9/18/13; s. Joseph Bell and Clara Florence Lafollette B; m. 5/29/37 to Marie R. Appel; c. Ronald Claude and Mary Esther. Educ: Kans. State Univ, B.S, 37; Phi Delta Kappa. Polit. & Govt. Pos: Kans. State Rep, 56-60; Kans. State Sen, 39th Dist, 63-67. Bus. & Prof. Pos: Teacher, math and sci, Kans. Schs, 37-42; owner and operator, Broken Bar B Ranch, 40- Mailing Add: R.R, McDonald, Kans. 67745. (1967)

BELL, LLOYD B. D
b. Horry Co, S.C, 12/12/09; m. 6/10/33 to Sylvia Lily Cinner. Polit. & Govt. Pos: S.C. State Rep, 55-60 & 63-68. Bus. & Prof. Pos: Owner and operator, Bel-Aire Motel and Bel-Aire Realty Co. Mem: V.pres. and dir, Gr. Myrtle Beach C. of C. Mailing Add: Box 628, Ocean Drive Beach, S.C. 29582. (1967)

BELL, NANCY BALLANTINE D
b. Calhoun, Ky, 1/16/23; d. Tilden Hendricks Ballantine and Wilmot Bewley B; m. 4/23/44 to John Peay Bell; c. Jane Holloway, John Peay, Jr.(deceased), Walter Flippin, David Ballantine and Victor Holloway. Educ: Bowling Green Bus. Univ, 40-42; Univ. Louisville, 42-69; N.Y. Univ; Catherine Spalding Col. Polit. & Govt. Pos: Worked at Dem. Hq. primarily with vol. and also in individual campaigns, Ky, 63-69; del, Dem. Nat. Conv, 68. Rel: Presbyterian. Mailing Add: 1639 Spring Dr, Louisville, Ky. 40205.

BELL, PAUL MAXWELL R
Mem, Calif. Rep. State Cent. Cmt.
b. N.Y.C, 8/29/37; s. Joseph Lander Bell and Mildred Cohen B; m. 8/29/58 to Barbara Hubbard; c. Ellen and Jennifer. Educ: Wagner Col, B.A, 59; N.Y. Law Sch, J.D, 62; Phi Sigma Kappa. Polit. & Govt. Pos: Assoc. mem, Calif. Rep. State Cent. Cmt, 68; mem, 69. Mem: Orange Co. and West Orange Co. Bar Asns; Nat. Exchange Club. Mailing Add: 1775 E. Lincoln Ave, Anaheim, Calif. 92805.

BELL, RICHARD D. D
Educ: Chem. and eng, Purdue Univ. Polit. & Govt. Pos: Dem. precinct committeeman, Ind, 14 years; mem, Center Twp. Bd, 58-64; former Ind. State Rep. Bus. & Prof. Pos: Quality control inspector, Modine Mfg. Co. Mem: Asst. dist. cmnr, Boy Scouts; Past Master, Mason; pres, Hailmann PAT; past pres, Co. Employees Credit Union; Scottish Rite; UAW-CIO; Grange. Silver Beaver Award, Boy Scouts. Rel: Methodist. Mailing Add: 524 Allen St, LaPorte, Ind. 46350. (1967)

BELL, ROBERT DAVID R
Mem. Finance Cmt, Marion Co. Rep. Cent. Cmt, Ore.
b. Portland, Ore, 5/15/36; s. Vinnie John Bell and Mary Elizabeth Reinhard B; m. 3/9/58 to Patricia Mae Shantz; c. Jeannie Kathleen, John David and James Robert. Educ: Willamette Univ, 54-55; Lewis & Clark Col, 59-61; Pershing Rifles; Chevalier, DeMolay. Polit. & Govt. Pos: Chmn, Young Rep. Fedn. of Ore, 63-64; chmn, 1st Voter Cmt, Young Rep. Nat. Fedn, 63-65; mem. finance cmt, Marion Co. Rep. Cent. Cmt, Ore, currently; tech. asst. to dir. of polit. educ. and training, Rep. Nat. Cmt, 64; alternate del, Rep. Nat. Conv, 64; direct mail coordinator, Ore. for Nixon Cmt, 64. Bus. & Prof. Pos: Consult, electronic data processing, self-employed, 61-65; account exec, Am. Data Servs, 65; real estate consult. specializing in estate bldg. and tax shelter. Mil. Serv: Entered as Pvt, Army, 55, released as SP-5, 57. Mem: AF&AM. Rel: Presbyterian. Mailing Add: 370 Leffelle, South Salem, Ore. 97302.

BELL, ROBERT HUDSON R
Ga. State Rep.
b. Atlanta, Ga, 2/1/29; s. Ernest Lawson Bell and Mattie Lou Richardson B; m. 2/15/58 to Betty Anne Rouse; c. Kathryn Leigh and Allison Gaye. Educ: Univ. Ga, Atlanta Div, 46-48; Erskine Col, 48-49; Ga. State Col, B.B.A, 54; Sigma Kappa Chi. Polit. & Govt. Pos: Pres, DeKalb Co. Young Rep. Club, Ga, 67-68; mem. exec. cmt, DeKalb Co. Rep. Party, currently; Ga. State Rep, 69- Bus. & Prof. Pos: Pres, R.H. Bell & Co, Atlanta, Ga, 62- Mil. Serv: Entered as Recruit, Army, 50, released as Sgt, 52, after serv. in Inf, Europe, 51-52. Mem: Henderson Mill Civic Asn.(pres); Atlanta Athletic Club; Young Rep. Club. Rel: Presbyterian. Mailing Add: 2535 Henderson Mill Rd, Atlanta, Ga. 30329.

BELL, ROBERT MORSE R
Rep. State Committeeman, Ohio
b. Steubenville, Ohio, 1908; s. Charles Dallas Bell and Jessie G. James B; m. 2/20/44 to Mary Magdeline Strickler; c. Robert Terry and James Melvin. Educ: High Sch, 4 years; Preparatory Sch, 1 year; College, 2 years. Polit. & Govt. Pos: Precinct committeeman, Ohio Rep. Party, 30-42; city councilman, Steubenville, 32-54; Rep. state committeeman, 18th Cong. Dist, 58-; del, Rep. Nat. Conv, 64, alternate del, 68; chmn, Ohio Rep. State Conv. Cmt, currently. Bus. & Prof. Pos: Jr. exec, Weirton Steel Co, Weirton, W.Va, 40-66. Mil. Serv: Pvt, Army, 42-44. Mem: Moose; Eagles; Am. Legion. Rel: Protestant. Mailing Add: Weirton Steel Co, Weirton, W.Va. 26062.

BELL, SARA JO R
Vice-chairwoman, Boone Co. Rep. Cmt, Ark.
b. Leslie, Ark, 9/14/41; d. John Franklin Fendley and Inez Jo Hensley F; m. 4/29/65 to Thomas Edward Bell. Educ: Hendrix Col, 59-60; State Col. Ark, B.S.H.E, 63; Univ. Ark, 63-64; Alpha Sigma Alpha. Polit. & Govt. Pos: Secy, State Col. Ark. Young Rep. Club, 62-63; aide & entertainer, Winthrop Rockefeller's Campaign for Gov, Ark, 64; alternate del, Rep. Nat. Conv, 68; mem, Ark. Beautification Cmn, 68; v.pres, Boone Co. Rep. Women's Club, 68, 69; vice-chairwoman, Boone Co. Rep. Cmt, 68-; secy-treas, Boone Co. Rep. Club, 68-; regional dir, Ark. Fedn. Rep. Women, 68- Bus. & Prof. Pos: Dietitian, Boone Co. Hosp, Ark, 67-69. Mem: Boone Co. Rep. Women's Club; Boone Co. Rep. Club; Apollo Club; Ark. Cattleman's Asn; Am. Polled Hereford Asn; Boone Co. Med. Auxiliary; Boone Co. Hosp. Auxiliary. Rel: Methodist. Mailing Add: Route 4, Harrison, Ark. 72601.

BELLANCA, ALFONSO V. R
Chmn, Erie Co. Rep. Cmt, N.Y.
b. Buffalo, N.Y, 6/27/12; s. Philip Bellanca and Mary Gimbrone B; m. 7/17/43 to Marie Barone; c. Carol (Mrs. Bruce), Maryanne (Mrs. La Penna) and Alan. Educ: Univ. Buffalo, 3½ years; Kappa Psi. Polit. & Govt. Pos: Mem, bd. of assessors, Buffalo, N.Y, 52-69; chmn, Erie Co. Rep. Cmt, 68- Bus. & Prof. Pos: Certified assessor, 65-; N.Y. State Assessors, Inst. of Assessing Officers, 67- Publ: Author, several papers on assessments on file at Int. Asn. of Assessing Officers, Chicago, Ill. Mem: Int. Asn. of Assessing Officers (N.Y. State Chmn, 60-65); Buffalo Athletic Club, Buffalo Launch Club, Transit Valley Country Club; N.Y. State Assessors Asn; N.Y. State Soc. of Appraisers. Named Outstanding Rep. of Erie Co, 67; Hall of Fame Award, Chairman's Club, 68. Rel: Roman Catholic. Mailing Add: 566 Richmond Ave, Buffalo, N.Y. 14222.

BELLI, FRANK D
Mayor, Lodi, N.J.
b. Lodi, N.J, 8/10/21; s. Anthony Belli and Edna Luciano B; m. 12/3/50 to Marie Polito; c. Edna, Felicia, Anthony, Maria and Anna. Educ: High Sch. Polit. & Govt. Pos: Trustee, Sch. Bd, Lodi, N.J, 58-64, pres, 61-62; v.chmn, Bergen Co. Dem. Cmt, 62-63; munic. chmn, Lodi, 62-66; Mayor, Lodi, 63-; supt. transportation and equip, Passaic Valley Sewerage Cmt, 64- Bus. & Prof. Pos: Supvr, cutting room, Josephine Dress Co, 15 years. Mil. Serv: Entered as Pvt, Army, 43, released as Tech. 5th Grade, 45, after serv. as Radio Operator, 789th F.A. Bn, Southwest Pac. and Philippines; S. Pac. Theater and Good Conduct Ribbons. Mem: Elks; VFW; Moose; Lions Int; Unico; Local 10 ILGWV. Numismatics. Rel: Catholic. Mailing Add: 385 Westervelt Pl, Lodi, N.J. 07644. (1967)

BELLINO, CHARLOTTE LEE D
b. Colorado Springs, Colo, 12/5/19; d. Frank G. Hughes and Emma B. Maddox H; m. 10/27/46 to John P. Bellino; c. Shirley (Mrs. Proctor), Mrs. Jerold LaQuey, Beverly Jean and John David. Educ: High Sch. Polit. & Govt. Pos: Precinct chairwoman, San Juan Co. Dem. Party, N.Mex, 56-; v.chairwoman, State Dem. Party, 60. Bus. & Prof. Pos: Co-owner and asst. funeral dir, Basin Mortuary, Farmington, N.Mex. Mem: Altrusa Club (recording secy, 61);

charter mem, San Juan Co. Pilot Club; Bus. & Prfnl. Women's Club, Jr. High PTA (pres). Rel: Episcopal. Mailing Add: 1105 N. Buena Vista, Farmington, N.Mex. 87401.

BELLMON, HENRY L. R
U.S. Sen, Okla.
b. Tonkawa, Okla, 9/3/21; s. George D. Bellmon and Edith Eleanor Caskey B; m. 1/24/47 to Shirley Osborn; c. Patricia, Gail and Ann. Educ: Okla. Agr. & Mech. Coll, B.S, 42. Polit. & Govt. Pos: Okla. State Rep, 46-48; state chmn, Rep. State Cmt, 60-62; Gov. of Okla, 63-67; U.S. Sen, 69- Bus. & Prof. Pos: Farmer and rancher; mem. bd. dirs, Williams Bros. Pipeline, Tulsa, 67-68; part owner, Rush Metals Co, Billings, 68- Mil. Serv: Entered Marines, 42, released as 1st Lt, 46, after serving in 4th Marine Div, Pac. Theatre; Legion of Merit; Silver Star. Mem: Okla. Health Sci. Found; rep, Okla. Med. Research Found. Rel: Presbyterian. Legal Res: Route 1, Red Rock, Okla. 74651. Mailing Add: 4203 New Senate Office Bldg, Washington, D.C. 20510.

BELLOMINI, ROBERT E. D
Pa. State Rep.
b. Erie, Pa, 6/1/25; s. Joseph Bellomini and Victoria Oligeri B; m. to Virginia Nesi. Educ: Gannon Col. Night Sch. Polit. & Govt. Pos: Mem, Young Dem. of Erie Co, Pa; Pa. State Rep, 64- Bus. & Prof. Pos: Owner, tavern-restaurant bus. Mem: Bartender's Union, AFL-CIO; K. of C, Coun. 278; v.pres, Wolves Den 8; Ital. Sons and Daughters - Nuova Aurora Soc; Charitable Scholarship Grants Orgn. Rel: Catholic. Mailing Add: 1161 W. 21st St, Erie, Pa. 16502. (1967)

BELLOTTI, FRANCIS XAVIER D
b. Boston, Mass, 5/3/23; s. Peter Vincent Bellotti and Mary Petrocelli B; m. 2/22/49 to Margarita E. Wang; c. Francis Xavier, Kathleen Anne, Mary Elizabeth, Nina Maria, Peter Vincent, Therese Ann, Patricia, Margarita, Joseph Raymond, Thomas, Michael Gerard and Sheila. Educ: Tufts Univ, A.B, 47; Boston Col, LL.B, 52. Polit. & Govt. Pos: Chmn, S.Shore Adv. Coun, Mass. Transit Authority, 60; Lt. Gov, Mass, 63-66; del, Dem. Nat. Conv, 68. Bus. & Prof. Pos: Attorney, Quincy, Mass. Mil. Serv: Lt(jg), Naval Res, 42-46, Pac. Theatre. Mem: Fed. Mass. Boston, Norfolk Co, Quincy Bar Asns; Am. Judicature Soc; Justinian Law Soc; Nat. Asn. Def. Lawyers; Order of Ahepa; Elks; Am. Legion; K. of C; Eagles; chmn. Norfolk Co. Chap, Am. Cancer Soc. Dr, 61; hon. co-chmn, Int. Student Employ. Cmt, 62; hon. bd. of dir, Kiddie Camp, Boston, 63; hon. dinner cmt. mem, 26th annual dinner, Mass. Cmt. Catholics, Protestants and Jews, 63. Annual Citizenship Award, Yeshiva Ohel Torch, Dorchester, Mass, 63; Enrico Fermi Man-of-the Year Award, Italo-Am. War Vets, Mass, 63. Rel: Catholic. Mailing Add: 803 Hancock, Quincy, Mass. 02114. (1967)

BELMONTE, ROBERT A. R
Mass. State Rep.
b. Framingham, Mass, 7/2/30; s. Arcangelo Belmonte and Carmela Millefiore B; m. 6/20/54 to Eleanor DeStefano; c. Dru Theresa and Marcia Lyn. Educ: Yale Univ, B.A, 52; Harvard Law Sch, LL.B, 55. Polit. & Govt. Pos: Mem, Framingham Sch. Cmt, Mass, 58-; asst. attorney gen, Mass, 63-64; Mass. State Rep, 64-; Rep. cand, Attorney Gen, Mass, 69; chmn, Framington Rep. Town Cmt. Mem: S. Middlesex and Middlesex Co. Bar Asns; K. of C. Rel: Catholic. Mailing Add: 27 Linda Ave, Framingham, Mass. 01721.

BELOFF, LELAND M. R
Pa. State Rep.
b. Phila, Pa, 4/17/42; s. Emanuel W. Beloff and Jean Rosenwald B; div. Polit. & Govt. Pos: Pa. State Rep, 66- Bus. & Prof. Pos: Dir, Harlee Manor, Inc. Mem: Chapel of the Four Chaplains; B'nai B'rith; Rabbi Louis Parris Lodge; Nat. Maritime Union. Legion of Merit Award, Chapel of the Four Chaplains. Rel: Jewish. Legal Res: 2330 S. Eighth St, Philadelphia, Pa. 19148. Mailing Add: Main Capitol Bldg, Harrisburg, Pa. 17125.

BELOTTI, FRANK P. R
Calif. State Assemblyman
m. 1934 to Delphine Moranda B. Educ: Dodges Inst. of Railway Acct. and Tel; Univ. of Valparaiso. Polit. & Govt. Pos: Calif. State Assemblyman, 50-; mem, Humboldt Co. Planning Cmn; mem, Calif. Rep. State Cent. Cmt, currently. Bus. & Prof. Pos: Fur Farming, 26- Mem: Past pres, Eureka Kiwanis Club; past master, Humboldt Grange; Farm Bur. Fedn; Moose; Commonwealth Club of Calif; Redwood Empire Asn; dir, Calif. Marine Parks and Harbors Asn. Mailing Add: Box 1025, Eureka, Calif. 95501. (1967)

BELQUIST, RUSSELL L. D
b. Windthorst, Sask, Canada, 4/24/07; married; c. Three. Educ: Minot State Teachers Col; Univ. Mont. Polit. & Govt. Pos: N.Dak. State Rep, until 66. Bus. & Prof. Pos: Farmer. Mil. Serv: WWII. Mailing Add: New Rockford, N.Dak. 58356.

BELSER, CLINCH HEYWARD D
S.C. State Rep.
b. Columbia, S.C, 11/7/18; s. Irvine Furman Belser and Mary Campbell Heyward B; m. 1/31/43 to Elizabeth Anne Albright. Educ: Univ. of S.C, A.B, magna cum laude, M.A, 40; Yale Law Sch, LL.B, 48; Phi Beta Kappa; Omicron Delta Kappa. Polit. & Govt. Pos: S.C. State Rep, 59-, chmn, Judiciary Cmt, 65- Bus. & Prof. Pos: Lawyer, firm of Belser, Belser & Baker. Mil. Serv: Army, 30th Inf. Div, 40-42; pilot, Army Air Corps, 42-46. Mem: V.pres, Fifth Judicial Circuit, Univ. of S.C. Alumni Coun; pres, bd. trustees, Columbia Mus. of Art; asst. treas, Family Serv. Asn; Am. Legion (v.comdr, 56-57); 40 et 8; exec. cmt, Richland Co. Bar Asn. Rel: Episcopal; Secy of the Vestry, Trinity Episcopal Church. Mailing Add: 307 Barringer Bldg, Columbia, S.C. 29201.

BELT, RONALD MADISON R
b. Sue City, Mo, 3/13/31; s. Madison Earl Belt and Hazel Wilson B; m. 8/12/55 to Phyllis Jean Bragg; c. Ellen, Susan, Madison D. and Julia. Educ: Washington Univ, A.B, 52, LL.B, 57. Polit. & Govt. Pos: Floor Leader, Mo. House Representatives, 63-67; del, Rep. Nat. Conv, 68. Mil. Serv: Entered as Pvt, Army, 52, released as M/Sgt, 54, after serv. in 45th Inf. Div. in Korea. Mem: Jaycees; Lions; Mason; Shrine; Am. Legion. Rel: Christian. Mailing Add: 1015 N. Jackson, Macon, Mo. 63552.

BELT, WILLIAM SCOTT R
b. Marion, Ohio, 5/4/08; s. Jacob Milroy Belt and Mae Postel B; m. 4/11/36 to Vivian Ruthella Hipsher; c. Michael Lynn. Educ: Marion Bus. Col. Polit. & Govt. Pos: Clerk, Co. Cmnr, Ohio, 37-41; clerk, Common Pleas Court, 41-65; Ohio State Rep, 65-67; rep. of Roger Cloud, Auditor of State, currently. Bus. & Prof. Pos: Dir, Peoples Bank, 57-, mem. exec. cmt, 61- Mem: Kiwanis; Grange; Farm Bur; C. of C. Rel: Methodist. Mailing Add: RFD 1, Edison, Ohio 43320.

BELTER, WESLEY PAUL R
N.Dak. State Rep.
b. Davenport, N.Dak, 10/5/13; s. Paul Robert Belter and Hulda Marie Buchholz B; m. 8/24/39 to Rachel Elizabeth Dittmer; c. Charles Wesley, Wesley Robert, John Paul and Elizabeth Ann (Mrs. Harvey Larson); Educ: Univ. N.Dak, 31-32; Valley City State Col, 32-33; N.Dak. State Univ, 36-37. Polit. & Govt. Pos: Chmn, Cass Co. Sch. Reorgn. Cmt, N.Dak, 47-66; N.Dak. State Rep, 22nd Dist, 67- Bus. & Prof. Pos: Dir, Lynchburg Farmer's Elevator Co, 49-, chmn, 54-; lay-mem, Provincial Elders Conf. of Moravian Church, North. Province, 56-66; mem. bd. of trustees, Moravian Col, Bethlehem, Pa, 56-66. Mem: Farm Bur; Farmer's Union; Lions. Outstanding Laymans Award, Moravian Col. and Theol. Sem, Bethlehem, Pa. Rel: Moravian. Mailing Add: Leonard, N.Dak. 58052.

BELTING, GEORGE BEMIS R
Wis. State Assemblyman
b. Wis, 7/15/14; s. George William Belting, M.D. and Grace Bemis B; m. 8/12/40 to Elizabeth Kuhl. Educ: Univ. Wis, B.A, 36 and LL.B, 38. Polit. & Govt. Pos: City attorney, Ripon, Wis, 40-43; mem, Rock Co. Bd, 51-57; Wis. State Assemblyman, 57- Bus. & Prof. Pos: Instr, Univ. Wis, 38-39; Law Practice, 39-; bd. dirs, Beloit Better Bus. Bur, 55-; bd. dirs, Beloit Savings Bank, 64- Mil. Serv: Entered as Seaman, Navy, 43, released as Lt, 46, after serv. in Amphibious Forces, Pac; Pac. Theater Medal with Battle Stars. Publ: Belting Genealogy, 59, Grace P. Bemis Ancestry, 61 and Leach Van Dyke Wolfe Ancestry, 63, Grimm. Mem: Past pres, Kiwanis and Beloit Hist. Soc; Past Master, F&AM. Legal Res: 2041 E. Ridge Rd, Beloit, Wis. 53511. Mailing Add: 540 E. Grand Ave, Beloit, Wis. 53511.

BELTON, ACIE JULIOUS D
b. Converse, La, 1/9/16; s. George Washington Belton, Sr. and Leana Diggs B; m. 8/6/39 to Sallie Brown; c. Wesley Julious. Educ: South. Univ, 2 years. Polit. & Govt. Pos: Del, Dem. Nat. Conv, 68. Mil. Serv: Entered as Pvt, Army, 43, released as Cpl, 46, after serv. in 172nd Inf. Rel: Protestant. Legal Res: 10570 Tallow Dr, Baton Rouge, La. 70807.

BELZER, JOHN HENRY R
Chmn, Grayson Co. Rep. Party, Tex.
b. Burkburnett, Tex, 3/2/27; s. John Belzer and Effie Olla Large B; m. 2/19/54 to Venetta Elizabeth Tully; c. Jonetta Leigh and Kermit Edward. Educ: Tex. Christian Univ, $1\frac{1}{2}$ years; Univ. Tex, B.S. Elec. Eng. Polit. & Govt. Pos: Finance chmn, Grayson Co. Rep. Party, 65-66, v.chmn, 67-68 and chmn, 68- Bus. & Prof. Pos: Sales engr, Johns-Manville Sales Corp, 51-61 and dist. sales mgr, 61- Mil. Serv: Entered as A/S, Navy, 44, released as PO 2/C, 46, after serv. in Pac. Theatre, 45-46; Good Conduct Medal; Pac. Theatre and Philippine Independence ribbons. Mem: Am. Mgt. Asn; Nat. Asn. Corrosion Engrs; Am. Waterworks Asn; dir, Denison Boy's Club; Grayson Co. Crime Cmn. Rel: Methodist. Mailing Add: 1000 Balboa, Denison, Tex. 75020.

BEMBRY, PAYTON, JR. D
b. Jasper, Fla, 8/24/38; m. to Alma Fouraker; c. Roger and Theresa. Polit. & Govt. Pos: Fla. State Rep, formerly. Bus. & Prof. Pos: Farmer. Mailing Add: Route 3, Jasper, Fla. 32052. (1967)

BEMISS, FITZGERALD D
b. Richmond, Va, 10/2/22; m. to Margaret Page; c. Margaret Wickham and Samuel Merrifield, II. Educ: Univ. Va. Polit. & Govt. Pos: Va. State Rep, 55-59; Va. State Sen, 60-67; mem, Cmn. Legis. Process, 68-69. Bus. & Prof. Pos: Pres. and treas, Fitzgerald & Co, Inc. of Va, D.D. Fitzgerald, Inc, Va. Sky-Line Co, Inc. and Railway Supply Co. of Ala, Inc; v.pres, secy. and treas, Woodstock Home and Land Co, Inc; dir, United Virginia Bank/State Planters. Mil. Serv: Navy. Mem: Chmn, Va. Cmn. of Outdoor Recreation; pres, Richmond James River Asn; dir, Sheltering Arms Hosp, Va. Inst. for Sci. Research, Atlantic Rural Exposition, Great Books Found. and Richmond Prfnl. Inst. Found; bd, Va. Hist. Soc; bd. trustees, Nat. Recreation & Park Asn; bd. advs, Nat. Trust for Historic Preservation; Taylor Murphy Inst. Coun, Univ. Va; chmn, Woodberry Forest Alumni Coun; trustee, Woodberry Forest Sch; Raven Soc, Univ. Va; bd. gov, Gr. Richmond Commun. Found; men's adv. cmt, Va. Home. Rel: Episcopal. Mailing Add: Box 1156, Richmond, Va. 23209.

BENDA, CAROL JOYCE R
V.Chmn, Marshall Co. Rep, S.Dak.
b. Britton, S.Dak, 7/24/32; d. William Schneider and Hannah Eikamp S; m. 6/1/51 to Chan A. Benda; c. Kathryn M, Alan F. and Robyn Renae. Educ: Britton High Sch, grad. Polit. & Govt. Pos: V.chmn, Marshall Co. Rep. Party, S.Dak, 66-; clerk of courts, Marshall Co, 69- Bus. & Prof. Pos: Legal secy, part time, 20 years; cashier, local theater. Mem: Homemakers Exten. Club (former officer); Farmers Union. Rel: Presbyterian. Mailing Add: Britton, S.Dak. 57430.

BENDA, KENNETH JOHN R
Iowa State Sen.
b. Brooklyn, Iowa, 11/9/18; s. James T. Benda and Rose Posekany B; m. to Lucille Roudabush; c. Barbara (Mrs. Paul R. Jenkins) and James. Educ: Iowa State Univ, B.S, 40. Polit. & Govt. Pos: Chmn, Poweshiek Co. Rep. Party, Iowa, 58-60; state finance dir, Rep. Party, 60-62, mem, Nat. Finance Cmt, 60-; mem, Legis. Research Cmt, currently, Iowa State Sen, currently. Mil. Serv: Entered as A/S, Navy, 42, released as Lt, Naval Res, 64; Presidential Unit Citation. Mem: Fed. Legis. Cmt, Independent Bankers of Am; State Legion Comdr, 56-57. Rel: Protestant. Mailing Add: Hartwick, Iowa 52232.

BENDER, H. G. TOM D
m. to Helen; c. Duane E. and Karen R. Polit. & Govt. Pos: Secy. to U.S. Rep. Will Rogers, Okla, 35-43, U.S. Rep. Sheppard, Calif, 43-47, U.S. Rep, Frank Wilson, Tex, 47-55, U.S. Rep. Gray, Ill, 55-59; asst to Rep. Shipley, Ill, 59-69, secy, 69- Mailing Add: 1320 N. Stuart St, Arlington, Va. 22201.

BENDER, STANLEY B. D
Committeeman, Colo. Dem. State Cent. Cmt.
b. Dorchester, Nebr, 11/19/26; s. Paul E. Bender and Margaret Barton B; m. to Jeanne W. Educ: Univ. Denver, B.S, 54, LL.B, 56; Phi Alpha Delta. Polit. & Govt. Pos: Precinct committeeman, Precinct 302, Adams Co, Colo, 64-69; chief dep. dist. attorney, 17th Judicial Dist, Adams Co, 68; committeeman, Colo. Dem. State Cent. Cmt, 69- Bus. & Prof. Pos: Lawyer, self-employed, 56-69. Mil. Serv: Army, 44-46. Mem: Colo. Juvenile Conf; Adams Co. Peace Officers Asn; Am. Civil Liberties Union; legal panel, Colo. Civil Liberties Union. Rel: Protestant. Mailing Add: 8200 Penn Way, Denver, Colo. 80229.

BENDHEIM, LEROY S. D
Va. State Sen.
b. Alexandria, Va, 2/12/06; s. Charles Bendheim and Edith Schwarz B; m. 6/10/34 to Ethel Colman. Educ: George Wash. Univ, A.B, 28, LL.B, 29. Polit. & Govt. Pos: Staff mem, Nat. Recovery Admin. Rev. Bd, 35-36; city councilman, Alexandria, Va, 48-52, v.mayor, 52-55, mayor, 55-61; Va. State Sen, currently; del, Dem. Nat. Conv, 68. Bus. & Prof. Pos: Dir, First Fed. Savings and Loan Asn. Alexandria; pres. and chmn. bd, Va. Land Title Agency, Inc; dir, Park & Shop Alexandria Corp; dir, Downtown Garage, Inc; instr. commercial law, George Wash. Univ, 49 & 50; former pres. & chmn. bd, Colonial Nat. Bank, Alexandria, 63-68; dir, First Va. Bank, 68- Mil. Serv: Entered as Pvt, Army, 43, released as Sgt, 45, after serv. in Third and First Armies, European Theater; Good Conduct Medal; Victory Medal; four campaign battle stars. Publ: Contrib. ed, State of Va. Probate Law Digest. Mem: Am, D.C. and Va. State Bar Asns; Am. Judicature Soc; Mason (32°); Odd Fellows; Elks; Eagles; Lions; Am. Legion; VFW; Jewish War Vet; Downtown Club; Am. Pub. Works Asn; past chmn, Alexandria Bd. Ed; U.S. Power Squadron; North. Va. Power Squadron (past comdr); Alexandria Sportsmans' Club; Windjammer Club; Lafayette Yacht Club. Rel: Jewish. Legal Res: 309 Mansion Dr, Alexandria, Va. 22302. Mailing Add: 124-126 S. Royal St, Alexandria, Va. 22313.

BENEFIEL, PHILIP BAKER D
b. Lawrenceville, Ill, 6/25/23; s. Ross J. Benefiel and Amanda J. Baker B; m. 11/7/58 to Mary K. Smith; c. Ann Claire, Philip Ross and Daniel. Educ: Univ. Ill. Col. of Law, LL.B, 49; Alpha Chi Rho. Polit. & Govt. Pos: State's Attorney, Lawrence Co, Ill, 49-52; chmn, Lawrence Co. Dem. Orgn, 58-59; city attorney, Lawrenceville, 61-65; Ill. State Sen, 65-67; Assoc. Judge Circuit Court, Second Judicial Circuit of Ill, 68- Mil. Serv: Entered as Pvt, Army, 42, released as T-5, 45, after serv. in 667th Field Artil. Bn, ETO; Three Battle Stars. Mem: Am, State and Local Bar Asns; Elks; Am. Legion; VFW; Eagles; Mason; Shrine; Moose. Received Best Legislators Award by Independent Voters of Ill. for 1965 session of Ill. Legis. Rel: Christian Church. Mailing Add: 333 Lincoln Dr, Lawrenceville, Ill. 62439.

BENEKE, DONALD G. R
b. Laurens, Iowa, 3/14/16; s. Anton Beneke and Theresa Mefferd B; m. 1939 to Mardell Sell; c. Don Jr, Ann, Mary. Educ: Univ. of Iowa, B.A, 1937, J.D, 1939. Polit. Pos: Iowa State Sen, 1961-66; Laurens Sch. Bd, 47-61, Secy, Pres; Co. Attorney, Pocahontas Co, 51-54. Bus. & Prof. Pos: Lawyer. Mil. Serv: U.S. Army, 43-45. Mem: Am. Legion; VFW; Masonic Lodge. Rel: Methodist. Mailing Add: Laurens, Iowa 50554. (1967)

BENEKE, GEORGE FRANK R
b. Wheeling, W.Va, 1/9/14; s. George Claus Beneke and Nada C. Peterson B; m. 4/1/47 to Sarah E. Emblen; c. George R, Lisa R. and Nada C. Educ: Duke Univ, A.B, 36; W.Va. Univ, LL.B, 38; Phi Delta Phi; Lambda Chi Alpha. Polit. & Govt. Pos: W.Va. State Del, 46-56 & 67-69; chmn, Ohio Co. Rep. Exec. Cmt, 58-65. Bus. & Prof. Pos: Partner, Beneke, Callahan and John, 62- Mil. Serv: Entered as Ens, Naval Res, 42, released as Lt, 46. Mem: Dir, Bank of Warwood and Commun. Savings Bank; dir, Radio Wheeling, Inc, WBZE; Mason, Shrine; Jester; Nat. Sojourner; Elks; Moose; Order of Symposiarchs; Am. and Ohio Co. Bar Asns; W.Va. State Bar; Wheeling Country Club; Preston Co. Country Club; Am. Legion. Rel: Lutheran. Legal Res: Box 89, R.D, 4, Wheeling, W.Va. 26003. Mailing Add: 308 Board of Trade Bldg, Wheeling, W.Va. 26003. (1967)

BENEVILLE, WALTER JOHN D
Ind. State Rep.
b. Jersey City, N.J, 9/15/13; s. Robert John Beneville and Florence Elizabeth Ahrens B; m. 8/30/40 to Juanita Mae Heathcote Brubaker; c. Helen (Mrs. Robert Grimes) and Julia (Mrs. Erik Spencer). Educ: N.Y. Univ, 30-32; East. Chiropractic Inst, 33-36; Nat. Chiropractic Col, D.C, 67. Polit. & Govt. Pos: Ind. State Rep, 53-, chmn, Med. Educ. Study Cmt, Ind. House of Rep, 65-67, asst. minority floor leader, 69- Bus. & Prof. Pos: Practicing chiropractor, 40- Mem: Am. and Ind. State Chiropractic Asns; Mason; Elks; Scottish Rite. Chiropractor of the Year Award, Ind, 68. Rel: Episcopal. Mailing Add: 402 Kewanna Dr, Jeffersonville, Ind. 47130.

BENGRY, ELLSWORTH RAY D
Chmn, Iron Co. Dem. Exec. Cmt, Mich.
b. Caspian, Mich, 1/15/29; s. Ray Milton Bengry and Adelia Axelson B; m. 6/18/49 to Florence Frances Pieragostini; c. Marlane, Brian, Shelly, Tracee Lynn, Christine, Diane and Carrie Joy. Educ: Stambaugh High Sch, Mich, 4 years. Polit. & Govt. Pos: Mem, Iron Co. Dem. Exec. Cmt, Mich, 68-69, chmn, 69- Mil. Serv: Entered as Pvt, Air Force, 48, released as Cpl, 50, after serv. in Strategic Air Command. Mem: United Steelworkers Am; Stambaugh Volunteer Fire Dept; Stambaugh Athletic Asn; Eagles. Rel: Lutheran. Mailing Add: 501 Second St, Stambaugh, Mich. 49964.

BENGTSON, L. H, JR. D
Okla. State Rep.
b. Stillwater, Okla, 6/8/26; s. Leroy H. Bengtson and Mildred Horner B; div. Educ: Tulane Univ, B.B.S, 46; Okla. State Univ, M.S, 48; Okla. Univ; Cent. State Univ; Okla. City Univ; Beta Alpha Psi; Alpha Kappa Psi; Kappa Tau Pi; Oak Leaves; Pi Kappa Alpha; Punchers; Men's Glee Club. Polit. & Govt. Pos: Okla. State Rep, 64-, v.chmn, research and invest, Okla. House Rep, 65, v.chmn, Okla. Co. Del, 65-67; v.chmn, banks and banking, 67-68, v.chmn, subcmt. pub. schs, 69, chmn, parks and recreation, 69 and v.chmn, task force indust. develop. and parks, 69. Mil. Serv: Entered as A/S, Navy, 44, released as Ens, 46; Res, 46-50, Lt.(jg); Victory Medal; Am. Theatre Ribbon. Mem: Capitol Hill Alumni Asn.(past pres, 2 years); Lions; Capitol Hill C. of C; Red, Red, Rose (pres); Phi Delta Kappa; Okla. Educ. Asn; PTA; Commun. Action Prog.(bd.dirs); Okla. City Classroom Teachers Asn; Mayors Out Reach Prog. Rel: Disciples of Christ. Mailing Add: 1812 S.W. 16th, Oklahoma City, Okla. 73108.

BENITZ, MAX EDWARD R
Wash. State Rep.
b. Wathena, Kans, 10/9/16; s. Alto Richard Benitz and Nellie Willard B; m. 6/9/40 to Marie Fern Wilson; c. Norma June (Mrs. Fortner), Eileen Marie (Mrs. Bishop), Alvin Ray, Max, Jr, and Ronnie. Educ: Wathena High Sch, 4 years. Polit. & Govt. Pos: Wash. State Rep, 69- Bus. & Prof. Pos: Pres, Wash. State Farm Bur, 60-68; mem, bd. of dirs, Am. Farm Bur, 64-68. Mem: Farm Bur. Rel: Lutheran. Mailing Add: Route 2, Prosser, Wash. 99350.

BENJAMIN, ADAM, JR. D
Ind. State Rep.
b. Gary, Ind, 8/6/35; s. Adam Benjamin and Margaret Marjanian B; m. 7/30/66 to Patricia Ann Sullivan; c. Adam Benjamin, III. Educ: U.S. Mil. Acad, West Point, B.S, 58; Valparaiso Univ. Law Sch, J.D, 66; Phi Alpha Delta. Polit. & Govt. Pos: Zoning Adminstr, Gary, Ind, 64-65; exec. secy. to Mayor, City of Gary, 65-67; Ind. State Rep, 67- Bus. & Prof. Pos: teacher math. and physics, Gary Sch. Syst, 61-62; electronics comput. programmer, Continental Casualty, 62-63; attorney-at-law, 66- Mil. Serv: Entered as Pvt, Marine Corps, 52, released as Cpl, 54, after serv. in Third Div, Far East Command, 53-54; reentered as 2nd Lt, Army, 58, released as 1st Lt, 61, after serv. in 101st Airborne Div; UN, Korean Theater and Nat. Defense Serv. Ribbons; Sr. Parachutist Wings; Ranger Tab. Mem: Ind, Gary and Am. Bar Asns; Nat. Soc. State Legislators; Marine Corps League; Am. Legion; VFW; Elks; Exchange Club; Mason; C. of C; Nat. Rivers and Harbors Cong. Outstanding Freshman Dem. Rep; Jaycee Good Govt. Award; Outstanding Am. of Assyrian Descent. Rel: Catholic Church of the East. Legal Res: 800 Madison St, Gary, Ind. 46402. Mailing Add: 504 Broadway, Gary, Ind. 46402.

BENNER, BARBARA YOUNG R
Dir. Pa. Coun. Rep. Women
b. Allentown, Pa, 8/18/24; d. Robert A. Young and Eleanor Soleliac Y; m. 6/6/44 to Nolan P. Benner, Jr; c. Joan and Carol. Educ: Pine Manor Jr. Col, 44. Polit. & Govt. Pos: V.chmn, Lehigh Co. Young Rep, Pa, 52-53, dir, 52-60; committeewoman, Rep. Party, 52-; dir, Lehigh Co. Coun. Rep. Women, 53-, prog. chmn, 61-62 and legis. chmn, 63-65; dir, Pa. Coun. Rep. Women, 59-64 & 67-, second v.pres, 64-65 and pres, 65-67; alternate del, Rep. Nat. Conv, 60 & 64, del, 68; v.chmn. campaign cmt, Nat. Fedn. Rep. Women, 68- Mem: Girl Scouts (dir, Great Valley Coun, 60-); Lehigh Co. Commun. Coun.(dir, 58 & 59); Allentown Civic Little Theater (dir, 54-58); Lehigh Country Club; campaign chmn. and mem. adv. cmt, Lehigh Valley Heart Asn; legis. chmn, Allentown Women's Club. Rel: Presbyterian. Mailing Add: 225 N. Broad St, Allentown, Pa. 18104.

BENNER, ROBERT WILLIS R
Md. State Del.
b. Doylestown, Pa, 6/17/01; s. Emma Sieger B; m. 9/17/24 to Mildred Rose Appleby; c. Barbara (Mrs. Clericuzio) and Patricia (Mrs. Haynie). Educ: George Wash. Univ, 2 years; Am. Inst. of Banking; Wis. Sch. of Accountancy; Kappa Alpha. Polit. & Govt. Pos: Retired Staff asst. to U.S. Secy. of Treas. and econ. adv. to U.S. Small Bus. Admin; Md. State Del, 63-; Bus. & Prof. Pos: Real estate broker. Mem: AF&AM; Lions; chmn, Calvert Co. Area Redevelop. Cmt; C. of C; Calvert Co. Bd. Trade; chmn, Calvert Co. Blood Prog; adv. bd. dirs, Maryland Nat. Bank of Baltimore; chmn. bd. dirs, Calvert Co. Nursing Center; Md. State Cmn. on Aging; Calvert Co. Indust. Park Authority. Rel: Episcopal; Vestryman. Mailing Add: The Willows, Chesapeake Beach, Md. 20732.

BENNET, AUGUSTUS WITSCHIEF R
b. N.Y.C, 10/7/97; s. William Stiles Bennet and Gertrude Witschief B; m. 10/19/29 to Maxine Layne; c. Linda (Mrs. Lynch), William Stiles, II and Susanna (Mrs. Christopher Humphreys). Educ: Amherst Col, B.A, 18; Columbia Univ. Law Sch, LL.B, 21; Phi Beta Kappa. Polit. & Govt. Pos: U.S. Referee in Bankruptcy, South. Dist. of N.Y, 23-44; U.S. Rep, N.Y, 45-46. Mil. Serv: Chief Qm, Naval Res. Flying Corps, 18-19. Mem: Pres, Orange Co. Bar Asn, 60; past dist. dep. Grand Master, Orange-Rockland Dist, F&AM; past pres, Newburgh YMCA; C. of C; Rotary. Rel: Presbyterian. Legal Res: Balmville Rd, MD 16, Newburgh, N.Y. 12550. Mailing Add: Box 792, Newburgh, N.Y. 12550.

BENNET, DOUGLAS JOSEPH, JR. D
b. Orange, N.J, 6/23/38; s. Douglas J. Bennet and Phoebe Benedict B; m. 6/27/59 to Susanne Klejman; c. Michael Farrand and James Douglas. Educ: Wesleyan Univ, B.A, 59; Univ. Calif, Berkeley, M.A, 60; Harvard Univ, Ph.D, 68; Phi Beta Kappa. Polit. & Govt. Pos: Program analyst, Agency for Int. Develop, 63-64; spec. asst. to Ambassador Bowles, U.S. Dept. of State, 64-66; staff asst. to Vice President Humphrey, 67-69; admin. asst. to Sen. Thomas Eagleton, Mo, 69- Legal Res: Lyme, Conn. 06371. Mailing Add: 3811 Argyle Terr. N.W, Washington, D.C. 20011.

BENNETT, BOB E. D
Chmn, Pontotoc Co. Dem. Cent. Cmt, Okla.
b. Holdenville, Okla, 2/13/30; s. Henry Frank Bennett (deceased) and Lula Hill B; m. 4/2/55 to Sally Jane Farr. Educ: E. Cent. State Col, Okla, B.S, 55; Univ. Okla, LL.B, 58; Delta Theta Phi; Pi Kappa Alpha. Polit. & Govt. Pos: Chmn, Fourth Dist. Okla. Young Dem, 60; mem, Fourth Dist. Nominating Cmt. for Dels. to Dem. Nat. Conv, 64; chmn, Pontotoc Co. Dem. Cent. Cmt, currently. Bus. & Prof. Pos: Pres, Pontotoc Co. Bar Asn; mem, Ada Airport Cmn; former instr, govt, E. Cent. State Col. Mil. Serv: M/Sgt, Army,

50-53; Japanese Occupation Medal; Korean Serv. Ribbon, Second Korean Winter; Bronze Star; Capt. Nat. Guard and Res. Mem: Okla. Bar Asn; Rotary; Am. Legion; VFW. Rel: Presbyterian. Mailing Add: 404 American Bldg, Ada, Okla. 74820. (1967)

BENNETT, BOYD D
Chmn, Moody Co. Dem. Cmt, S.Dak.
b. 11/17/18; m. 5/15/47 to Catherine Hetland; c. Bryan, Craig and Dale. Educ: Aircraft and Mech. Sch, Army. Polit. & Govt. Pos: Former Twp. supvr, Flandreau, S.Dak. and former treas. sch. bd; twp. clerk, 8 years; S.Dak. State Rep, until 66; chmn, Moody Co. Dem. Cmt, currently. Bus. & Prof. Pos: Farmer. Mil. Serv: Army, 41-45. Rel: Lutheran. Mailing Add: Route 3, Flandreau, S.Dak. 57028. (1967)

BENNETT, CHARLES E. D
U.S. Rep, Fla.
b. Jacksonville, Fla, 12/2/10; m. to Jean Fay B; c. Bruce, Charles, James and Lucinda. Educ: Univ. of Fla, B.A, J.D, 34; Univ. of Tampa, Dr. of Humanities, 50; honoris causa. Polit. & Govt. Pos: Fla. State Rep, 41-42; U.S. Rep, Fla, 48- Bus. & Prof. Pos: Attorney-at-law. Mil. Serv: Army Inf, 42-47; discharged as Capt, awarded Silver Star, Bronze Star, Combat Inf. Badge, Inf. Hall of Fame, Ft. Benning Officer Cand. Sch, 58. Publ: Laudonniere and Fort Caroline, 64 and Settlement of Florida, 68, Univ. Fla. Press. Mem: Jr. C. of C.(pres, Jacksonville, 39); DAV; Am. Legion; VFW; Mason; Lions; SAR; bd. trustees, Lynchburg Col. Awarded Cert. by Freedoms Found. for outstanding achievement in bringing about a better understanding of the Am. way of life, 51, 56; Good Gov. Award, Jacksonville and U.S. Jr. C. of C, 52; missed no roll call votes since 6/4/51. Rel: Christian Church. Mailing Add: 3421 Rusticway Lane, Falls Church, Va. 22044.

BENNETT, CLINTON EUGENE R
b. Hardwick, Vt, 9/17/02; wid; c. One. Educ: Sheffield and Lyndon Schs. Polit. & Govt. Pos: Town auditor, Vt, 48-53; lister, 56-64; former Vt. State Rep. Bus. & Prof. Pos: Dairy farmer. Rel: Congregational. Mailing Add: West Charleston, Vt. 05872. (1967)

BENNETT, DONN R
Chmn, Harding Co. Rep. Cmt, S.Dak.
b. Rapid City, S.Dak, 7/19/22; s. Wynn Millard Bennett and Anne Sparks B; m. 12/20/46 to Anita Jane Crockett; c. David, Michael, Kim, Robert, Kristin and Megan. Educ: Univ. Colo, B.A, 46, LL.B, 49; Univ. N.Mex; Phi Delta Phi; Delta Tau Delta. Polit. & Govt. Pos: Del, Rep. State Conv, S.Dak, 54, 56, 58 & 66; mem, Natural Resources Cmn, S.Dak, 55-59; states attorney, Harding Co, 55-; chmn, Harding Co. Rep. Cmt, S.Dak, 56-; cmnr, S.Dak. State Vet. Cmn, 67- Bus. & Prof. Pos: Lawyer, 49-50 & 53- Mil. Serv: Entered as A/S, Navy, 43, released as Lt.(jg), 46, Amphibious Forces in Pac, 44-46; recalled 50, released as Lt, 53, after serv. in Korea, 51, and as Mil. Law Instr, 51-53; Lt, Naval Res.(Ret); Am. Theater Medal; Asiatic-Pac. Medal with 3 stars; Philippine Liberation Medal with 2 stars; Victory Medal; China Serv. and Am. Defense Medals; Korean Serv. Medal with 2 stars; UN Serv, Naval Reserve, Nat. Defense and Philippine Serv. Medals. Publ: 'Oil & Gas Leases in South Dakota,' S.Dak. Bar Jour, 59. Mem: Am. Trial Lawyers Asn; Am. Bar Asn; cmnr, S.Dak. Bar Asn, 60-63; trustee, Rocky Mountain Mineral Law Found, 64-; Aircraft Owners & Pilots Asn; Mason; Elks; Am. Legion; VFW; Buffalo C. of C; dir, West River Ment. Health Asn, 59-; pres, S.Dak. Asn. of Ment. Health Centers, 66-; dir. and gen. counsel, Sky Ranch for Boys, Inc, N.Y. Mailing Add: Box 45, Buffalo, S.Dak. 57720.

BENNETT, EARL D
b. Holland Island, Md, 6/24/94; s. William C. Bennett and Emily Fisher B; m. 11/4/23 to Evelyn Andrews; c. Elaine (Mrs. Chas. E. Day), Dr. Earl, Jr, John W. and Charles T. Polit. & Govt. Pos: Md. State Del, 35-38 & 55-66; Md. State Sen, 39-47. Bus. & Prof. Pos: Second v.pres, United Sanitary Chem. Corp, Baltimore, Md, 66-69. Mil. Serv: Naval Aviation Recruit, 19. Mem: Am. Legion; World War I Vets. Rel: Methodist. Mailing Add: 305 Talbot Ave, Cambridge, Md. 21613.

BENNETT, FRANK B. D
b. Zanesville, Ohio, 6/4/20; s. Walter Lee Bennett and Mary Bell B; m. 12/27/47 to Annabell Lee; c. Jeffrey Lee and Patricia Diane. Educ: Babson Univ. Bus. & Prof. Pos: Chmn. of bd, Bennett Chevrolet Co. Mil. Serv: Entered as Cadet, Navy Air Corp, 42, released as Lt, 46, after serv. in Pac. Mem: Rotary; Eagles. Mailing Add: 671 Vernon Heights Blvd, Marion, Ohio 43303.

BENNETT, HOMER LAMPSON R
Chmn, Rep. State Cent. Cmt, Md.
b. Elkins, W.Va, 9/22/32; s. Homer Lampson Bennett and Mary Drake Naylor B; m. 1/20/65 to Lee Ann Nelson; c. Drake Courtney, Geoffrey Kerr, Phillip Crane and Lee Nelson. Educ: Bethany Col, B.A; Univ. W.Va, 1 year; Univ. Va. Law Sch, 1 year; Alpha Sigma Phi. Polit. & Govt. Pos: Chmn, Rep. State Cent. Cmt, Md, 64- Bus. & Prof. Pos: V.Pres, Rolyans Inc, Oakland, Md, 60; pres, Mitchell Manor Inc, 64; pres, Manor Plaza Inc, 65; dir, First Nat. Bank, 65. Mil. Serv: Entered as 2nd Lt, Marines, 53, released as 1st Lt, 55, after serv. in 7th Marine Regt, Korea; Korean Serv. Medal; UN Serv. Medal. Mem: Pub. Rels. Soc. Am; Lions; Izaak Walton Club; K. of P; Am. Legion. Rel: Methodist. Mailing Add: 422 Alder St, Oakland, Md. 21550.

BENNETT, J. RICHARDSON, JR. R
Chmn, Ala. State Rep. Exec. Cmt.
b. Georgiana, Ala, 10/12/22; s. Julius Richardson Bennett and Jennie Brock B; m. 8/25/47 to Margery Cameron Carey; c. Jean Cameron and Bruce. Educ: Marion Mil. Inst; Univ. Ala. Polit. & Govt. Pos: Mem, Ala. State Rep. Exec. Cmt, 54-, v.pres, 62-66 and chmn, currently; del, Rep. Nat. Conv, 56 & 62, mem. platform cmt, 62; chmn, Policy & Issues Coun, Ala; state campaign mgr, U.S. Sen. Race. Bus. & Prof. Pos: Pres, Bennett Timber Co. Mil. Serv: Entered as Aviation Cadet, Army, 43, released as 2nd Lt, 45. Mem: Rotary; chmn, Greenville Indust. Develop. Bd. Commercial pilot, single and multi engine, Instrument Ratings. Rel: Presbyterian. Legal Res: 725 Ft. Dale Rd, Greenville, Ala. 36037. Mailing Add: P.O. Box 188, Greenville, Ala. 36037.

BENNETT, JAMES DEAN R
b. Bartlesville, Okla, 9/7/23; s. Marion Bennett and Florence Breese B; m. 1/15/46 to Betty Lou Stephenson; c. Bruce, Elizabeth and Dee Ann. Educ: LaSalle Univ. Polit. & Govt. Pos: Former chmn, Washington Co. Rep. Orgn, Okla; precinct chmn, Ward Leader, chmn. of Wards and Precincts Cmt. Mil. Serv: Entered as Aviation Cadet, Navy Air Corps, 42, released as Lt, 52, after serv. in Eighth Naval Dist. Mem: Mason; Am. Legion. Rel: Church of Christ. Mailing Add: R.R. 2, Box 28, Bartlesville, Okla. 74003. (1967)

BENNETT, JIM T, JR. D
Ga. State Rep.
b. Fort Gaines, Ga, 5/4/20; s. Jim T. Bennett and Helen Ward B; m. 9/16/41 to Mayme Sheppard; c. James Thomas, III, Michael Sheppard, Charles Buchanan and Gregory McAllister. Educ: Young Harris Col; John Marshall Col, LL.B. Polit. & Govt. Pos: Ga. State Rep, currently. Bus. & Prof. Pos: Sr. partner, Bennett, Moon & Davis. Mil. Serv: Entered as Pvt, Army Air Force, released as Capt. Mem: Am. and Ga. Bar Asns; Mason; VFW; Am. Legion. Rel: Presbyterian. Legal Res: RFD, Smithbriar Dr, Valdosta, Ga. 31601. Mailing Add: P.O. Box 1211, Valdosta, Ga. 31601. (1967)

BENNETT, JOHN D
Mich. State Rep.
b. Ohio, 5/15/12; married: c. Linda, Carol and Barbara. Educ: Wayne State Univ; Walsh Inst. of Accountancy; Texas A&M Col, Army spec. prog; correspondence course from Dun & Bradstreet in credit and financial anal. Polit. & Govt. Pos: Treas, Redford Twp, Mich, 10 years; Mich. State Rep, 64- Bus. & Prof. Pos: Acct. Mil. Serv: Vet. Mem: Past pres, Wayne Co. Twp. Treas. Asn; dir, Redford Twp. Lions Club; Am. Soc. for Pub. Admin; Munic. Finance Officers Asn; DAV; Wayne Co. Treas. Asn; Pub. Personnel Asn. Rel: Methodist. Mailing Add: 10052 Mercedes St, Detroit, Mich. 48239. (1967)

BENNETT, JOHN MIRZA, JR. R
b. San Antonio, Tex, 6/26/08; s. John Mirza Bennett and Jamie Armstrong B; m. 12/18/46 to Eleanor Freeborn; c. Eleanor (Mrs. Marlow), Carolyn (Mrs. Wood), Davis Graves and John Stephen. Educ: Phillips Acad, Andover, Mass, dipl; Princeton Univ, 2 years; Univ. Tex, Austin, B.A, 31; Cottage Club; Kappa Alpha. Polit. & Govt. Pos: Finance chmn, Rep. Party, Tex, 65 & 66; alternate del. Rep. Nat. Conv, 68. Bus. & Prof. Pos: Chmn. bd, Nat. Bank Commerce, San Antonio, Tex, 50- Mil. Serv: Entered as 2nd Lt, Air Force, 40, released as Maj-Gen, Res, 58; Silver Star; Legion of Merit; Distinguished Flying Cross with one cluster; Bronze Medal; Air Medal with three oak leaf clusters; Groix de Guerre avec Palm. Publ: Letters from England, privately publ, 46. Mem: Dir, Tex. & Southwest. Cattle Raisers Asn. Rel: Episcopal. Legal Res: 417 W. Dewey Place, San Antonio, Tex. 78212. Mailing Add: 411 National Bank of Commerce Bldg, San Antonio, Tex, 78205.

BENNETT, LORA MARIE R
Chmn, Unit 109, United Rep. of Calif, Sacramento
b. St. John, Kans, 3/9/02; d. G. LaFayette Bryant and Sarah Elizabeth Shank B; m. 12/28/36 to John Kerns Bennett. Educ: Univ. Calif, Berkeley. Polit. & Govt. Pos: Mem, Rep. State Cent. Cmt, Calif, 46-52 & 64-; pres, Rep. Women's Club, San Gabriel Valley, 47; mem, Rep. Co. Cent. Cmt, 48-58; del, Rep. Nat. Conv, 64; chmn, Unit 109, United Rep. of Calif, Sacramento, 66- Rel: Christ Unity. Mailing Add: 4500 Whitney Ave, Sacramento, Calif. 95821.

BENNETT, LOWELL E. R
Chmn, Clark Co. Rep. Cent. Cmt, Ill.
b. Martinsville, Ill, 2/28/26; s. Ernie Olin Bennett and Jessie Marie Husted B; m. 1/5/48 to Gwendolyn Jean Hart; c. Scott A. Polit. & Govt. Pos: Committeeman, Clark Co. Rep. Cent. Cmt, Ill, 54-, chmn, 57-; twp. supvr, Martinsville, Ill, 61- Bus. & Prof. Pos: Dir, Martinsville Agr. Fair Asn, 60- Mil. Serv: Entered as A/S, Navy, 44, released as Yeoman 2/C, 46, after serv. in S.Pac; Iwo Jima and Okinawa Medals with Invasion Stars. Mem: Dir, Ill. Poland China Asn, 64-66 and Clark Co. Swine Improv. Asn, 60; Am. Legion; Farm Bur. Rel: Protestant. Mailing Add: R.R. 3, Martinsville, Ill. 62442.

BENNETT, MARION T. R
Chief Cmnr, U.S. Court of Claims
b. Buffalo, Mo, 6/6/14; s. Phil A. Bennett and Mary Bertha Tinsley B; m. 4/27/41 to June Young; c. Ann (Mrs. Paul Guptill) and William Philip. Educ: Southwest Mo. State Col, A.B, 35; Wash. Univ. Sch. of Law, St. Louis, Mo, LL.B, 38; Delta Theta Phi. Polit. & Govt. Pos: Mem, Green Co. Rep. Cent. Cmt, Mo, 38-42; U.S. Rep, Mo, 43-49; chief cmnr, U.S. Court of Claims, 49- Mil. Serv: Capt, Air Force Res, 50; Col, Air Force Res, 65- Publ: American Immigration Policies—A History, Pub. Affairs Press, 63. Mem: Nat. Coun, Fed. Bar Asn; Exchange Club. Outstanding Alumnus Award, Southwest Mo. State Col, 64. Rel: Methodist. Mailing Add; 3715 Cardiff Rd, Chevy Chase, Md. 20015.

BENNETT, MARK LYLE, SR. R
Chmn, Shawnee Co. Rep. Cent. Cmt, Kans.
b. Topeka, Kans, 2/20/07; s. Clarence B. Bennett and Lula Hill B; m. 1/16/32 to Lucile Louise Steves; c. Mark L, Jr. Cicely (Mrs. Glaze) and Stephen A. Educ: Washburn Univ, LL.B, 31; Alpha Delta; Delta Theta Phi. Polit. & Govt. Pos: City attorney, Topeka, Kans, 39-41; mem. and chmn, Topeka Police and Fire Civil Serv. Cmn, 41- and Kans. State Cmn. Revenue and Taxation, 43-48; mem, Kans. State Bd. of Law Exam, 65-; chmn, Shawnee Co. Rep. Cent. Cmt, 68- Mil. Serv: Entered as Seaman, Navy, 44, released as PO 1/C, 45, after serv. in Pac, 44-45. Mem: Am. and Kans. Bar Asns; Topeka Bar Asn. (pres, 69-); Elks; Am. Legion; VFW; Lions; Odd Fellows; C. of C. Rel: Methodist. Mailing Add: 1243 Warren, Topeka, Kans. 66604.

BENNETT, MARK WILSON D
Chmn, Yancey Co. Dem. Party, N.C.
b. Bald Creek, N.C, 11/7/14; s. Dr. W.L. Bennett and Nell Byrd B; m. 8/9/38 to Elizabeth Fleetwood; c. Julia Byrd, Amanda Blanche and Mark Wilson, Jr. Educ: Weaver Col, 32. Polit. & Govt. Pos: Mayor, Burnsville, N.C, 48-51; N.C. State Rep, 55 & 63-66; chmn, Yancey Co. Dem. Party, currently. Bus. & Prof. Pos: Automobile bus. Mil. Serv: Sgt, Army, 43-45. Mem: Burnsville Men's Club; Am. Legion (Comdr, Earl-Horton Post 122, 46-47, Dist. Comdr, 31st Dist, 48). Rel: Methodist. Mailing Add: Box 781, Burnsville, N.C. 28714. (1967)

BENNETT, OTIS BEE D
Miss. State Rep.
b. French Camp, Miss, 6/22/25; s. Otis Bee Hennings and Minnie Dismuke Bennett H; m. 3/30/52 to Esther Browning; c. Richard A. and David B. Educ: Sunflower Jr. Col, 2 years; Miss. State, Starkville, $4\frac{1}{2}$ months; Draughons Bus. Col, Jackson, 7 months. Polit. & Govt. Pos: Miss. State Rep, 68- Mil. Serv: Entered as Pvt, Air Force, 43, released as Sgt, 46, after serv. in 20th Air Force, Pac, 27 missions over Japan, 44-45; Good Conduct and Several Theatre Medals; Air Medal with 3 Oak Leaf Clusters; Distinguished Flying Cross. Mem: Shrine; O.L.McKay Lodge (master, 64); Sunflower Co. Farm Bur.(v.pres, 62-63, pres, 64-65); Delta Coun; Am. Legion; VFW; Sunflower Co. Shrine Club. Rel: Methodist. Mailing Add: Route 1, Box 100, Sunflower, Miss. 38778.

BENNETT, RALPH JULIAN D
b. Panama City, Fla, 3/3/29; m. to Agatha Peeples; c. Michael, Neel, Clark and Derrick. Educ: Stetson Univ, LL.B, 51 (second in Sr. Law Class); Pi Kappa Phi. Polit. & Govt. Pos: Fla. State Rep, 60-66; mem. sch. bd, Dem. Exec. Cmt. and Young Dem. Bus. & Prof. Pos: Attorney; dir, Beach State Bank, Panama City, 68- Mil. Serv: Pvt, Army Inf, 51-52; 1st Lt, Judge Adv. Gen. Corps, 52-54. Mem: Elks; Bay Co. Bar Asn.(former secy, pres, 60); 14th Circuit Bar Asn.(secy); Bay Co. Children's Cmt.(chmn, 59-60); Bay Co. Guid. Clin.(v.pres, 59-60); Am. Legion. Rel: Presbyterian; Deacon, Bible Class Teacher. Legal Res: 911 Degama Ave, Panama City, Fla. 32401. Mailing Add: P.O. Box 1177, Panama City, Fla. 32401.

BENNETT, REID L. D
Pa. State Rep.
b. 2/7/29; s. William H. Bennett and Mary Ruth Thompson B; m. to Mary Ellen Templeton; c. one. Educ: Hartford, Ohio Pub. Schs. Polit. & Govt. Pos: Pa. State Rep, 64- Bus. & Prof. Pos: Acct. exec; Red Cross swimming instr. Mil. Serv: Army, 48-51; Five Battle Stars. Mem: Past pres, Mercer Co. Tourist Prom. Agency; Lions; Mason; Am. Water Skiing Asn. Mailing Add: Orangeville Rd, Sharpsville, Pa. 16150. (1967)

BENNETT, ROBERT FREDERICK R
Kans. State Sen.
b. Kansas City, Mo, 5/23/27; s. Otto Francis Bennett and Dorothy Bess Dodds B; m. 6/10/49 to Mildred Joan Gregory; c. Robert F, Jr, Virginia Lee, Cathleen Kay and Patricia Ann. Educ: Univ. Kans, A.B, 50 and LL.B, 52; Phi Alpha Delta; Delta Sigma Rho. Polit. & Govt. Pos: Councilman, Prairie Village, Kans, 55-57, mayor, 57-65; Kans. State Sen, 65- Bus. & Prof. Pos: Sr. partner, Bennett & Lytle, Attorneys-at-law, 59-68, Bennett, Lytle & Wetzler, Attorneys-at-law, 68-; dir. and secy, Kans. State Bank, 62-68. Mil. Serv: Entered as Pvt, Marine Corps, 45, released as Pfc, 46, after serv. in First Marine Div. and Third Marine Amphibious Corps, Pac. and China Theaters; recalled to active duty, 50-51 and served in Seventh Marine Regt, First Marine Div, Korea. Mem: Am, Johnson Co. and Mo. Bar Asns; Bar Asn. of State of Kans.(secy, 62-68); pres, Kans. League of Munic, 59; Univ. Kans. Alumni Asn; pres, Prairie Village Optimist Club, 55; AF&AM. Rel: Protestant. Mailing Add: 4815 W. 80th St, Prairie Village, Kans. 66208.

BENNETT, ROSALIE B. R
Chmn, Plainville Rep. Town Cmt, Mass.
b. Boston, Mass, 8/31/16; d. George W. Davis and Selina A. Smith D; m. to Harold James Bennett; c. Carol A.(Mrs. Parmenter). Polit. & Govt. Pos: Chmn, Plainville Rep. Town Cmt, Mass, 60-; del, Mass. Rep. State Conv, 62, 64 & 66; del, Rep. Nat. Conv, 64. Bus. & Prof. Pos: Degree day clerk, Attleboro & Plainville Coal Co, 57- Mem: Plainville Grange; bd. of dirs, Plainville United Fund, 5 years. Mailing Add: 94 W. Bacon Sq, Plainville, Mass. 02762.

BENNETT, THOMAS S. R
Chmn, Carteret Co. Rep. Cmt, N.C.
b. Morehead City, N.C, 1/26/34; s. Jessie Gelbert Bennett and Neta Merrill B; m. 10/7/61 to Virginia Lou Thompson; c. Thomas S, Jr. and Ruth Thompson. Educ: Univ. of N.C, A.B, 56; Univ. of N.C. Law Sch, LL.B, 58; Phi Alpha Delta. Polit. & Govt. Pos: N.C. State Rep, 63-66; chmn, Carteret Co. Rep. Cmt, currently. Bus. & Prof. Pos: Lawyer, N.C. State Bar. Mem: N.C, Am. and Carteret Co. Bar Asns; Past Exalted Ruler, Elks. Selected One of America's Outstanding Young Men, U.S. C. of C, 64. Rel: Baptist. Mailing Add: Duncan Wheatly Bldg, Beauford, N.C. 28516. (1967)

BENNETT, VERNA Z. R
Chmn, Ind. Co. Rep. Cmt, Pa.
b. Clearfield Co, Pa. 7/6/02; d. David H. Zartman and Mima Jane Rupert Z; m. 4/12/23 to Boyd D. Bennett; c. Victoria Jane (Mrs. Wadas); grandchild, Vance Shannon. Educ: Ind. Univ. Pa, 20-22, 25, 49 and 55; Stroudsburg State Teachers Col, 24; Pa. State Univ, 42. Polit. & Govt. Pos: Pres, Ind. Coun. Rep. Women, Pa, 54-58, mem, State Conv, State Membership, Legis, Chaplain and Prog. Cmts; v.chmn, Ind. Co. Rep. Cmt, 58-62, chmn, 62-; state dir. bd, Pa. Coun. Rep. Women, 59-; dep. secy, Commonwealth of Pa, 66- Bus. & Prof. Pos: Sch. teacher, 20-46; elem. prin, Pa, 30-46. Mem: Pa. State Educ Asn; Nat. Educ. Asn; Eastern Sar; Hist. Soc. of Ind; Elks Auxiliary; Garden Club Fedn; New Century Women's Civic Club; Roadside Coun; Daughters of 1812. Rel: Presbyterian. Mailing Add: 230 N. Sixth St, Indiana, Pa. 15701.

BENNETT, VERNON NILE D
Iowa State Rep.
b. Winterset, Iowa, 8/18/36; s. Harry Ward Bennett and Helen Francis Kaufman B; m. 7/1/56 to Charlene May Kirschbaum; c. Bobette Gay, Tammy Ruth, Nancey Sue, Belinda May, Bobby Ray, Vernon Nile, Jr. and Pamela Lynn. Educ: Univ. Iowa, 66. Polit. & Govt. Pos: Iowa State Rep, Polk Co, 66- Bus. & Prof. Pos: Bus. rep. and v.pres, IBT Local 147, Des Moines, Iowa, 59- Mem: Iowa Rehabilitation Prog; Young Dem; IBT Local 147. Rel: Protestant. Mailing Add: 1022 Hoffman Ave, Des Moines, Iowa 50316.

BENNETT, DR. W. F. R
Mont. State Sen.
b. Webster, Kans, 1920; m. to Martha; c. Gary and Steven. Educ: Univ. Kans. Polit. & Govt. Pos: Mont. State Sen, 67-; chmn, local sch. bd; former mayor, Columbia Falls, Mont. Mil. Serv: Navy, World War II. Mailing Add: Columbia Falls, Mont. 59912. (1967)

BENNETT, W. TAPLEY, JR.
U.S. Ambassador to Portugal
b. Griffen, Ga, 4/1/17; m. to Margaret White; c. five. Educ: Univ. Ga, B.A, 37; Freiburg Univ, Germany, 37-38; George Wash. Univ, LL.B, 48; fel, Inst. of Int. Educ, 37-38. Polit. & Govt. Pos: Career officer, U.S. Dept. of State For. Serv, 41-; econ. analyst, Dominican Repub, 41-44 and Panama, 44; officer in charge, Dept. of Cent. Am. and Panama Affairs, 46-47, Div. of Cent. Am. and Panama Affairs, 48-51; dep. dir, Off. of S.Am. Affairs, 51-54; Nat. War Col, 54-55; spec. asst. to Dep. Under Secy. of State, 55-57; Counsr. of Embassy, Vienna, 57-60, Rome, 60-61 and Athens, 61-64; U.S. Ambassador to Dominican Repub, 64-66 and Portugal, 66- Bus. & Prof. Pos: Mem. staff, Inst. of Pub. Affairs, 39-40 and Off. for Emergency Mgt, 40-41. Mil. Serv: Army, 1st Lt, 44-46. Mem: Ga. Bar Asn. Dept. of State Commendable Serv. Award, 52. Legal Res: 719 Delaware Ave. S.W, Washington, D.C. 20024. Mailing Add: U.S. Embassy, Lisbon, Portugal.

BENNETT, WALLACE FOSTER R
U.S. Sen, Utah
b. Salt Lake City, Utah, 11/13/98; m. 1922 to Frances Grant B; c. Wallace Grant; Rosemary (Mrs. Robert C. Fletcher), Davis Wells, Frances (Mrs. Lawrence S. Jeppson) and Robert Foster. Educ: Utah, A.B, 19. Polit. & Govt. Pos: U.S. Sen, Utah, 50- Bus. & Prof. Pos: Bd. chmn, Bennett's, Salt Lake City, Bennett Motor Co; prin, San Luis State Acad, Manassa, Colo, 19-20. Mil. Serv: Army Inf, 2nd Lt, 18. Mem: V.pres, Nat. Paint, Varnish & Lacquer Asn, 35-36; pres, Nat. Glass Distributors Asn, 37; pres, Salt Lake Rotary, 40; pres, Salt Lake Commun. Chest, 44-45; pres, Nat. Asn. of Mfgs, 49; Salt Lake Country Club; Alta Club; Timpanogos Club. Publ: Author, 'Faith and Freedom,' 50; 'Why I am a Mormon' 58. Rel: Latter-day Saint. Legal Res: Salt Lake City, Utah 84105. Mailing Add: 4201 Massachusetts Ave. N.W, Washington, D.C. 20016.

BENOIT, JOHN KOLL, SR. 'JACK' D
b. Yetter, Iowa, 7/13/17; s. Valentine Matthew Benoit and Grace Marie Koll B; m. 8/7/39 to Jeanette Kathryn Schultes; c. Linda Clare, John K, Jr, Victor Marc, Jeanette K. and Brian Tom. Educ: Capital Commercial Col, Des Moines; Drake Commun. Col; Northwest. Univ. Sch. Commerce. Polit. & Govt. Pos: Mem, Polk Co. Dem. Party, 36-66; chmn, Iowa's Fifth Cong. Dist. Iowans for Kennedy, 60; alternate del, Dem. Nat. Conv, 64; mem. bd. dirs, Fed. Crop Ins. Corp, 66- Bus. & Prof. Pos: Acct. real estate sect, Equitable of Iowa, 37-44 & 46-49, city loan supvr, 49-54, investment acct. mgr, 54-64 and asst. controller, 64- Mil. Serv: Entered as A/S, Navy, 44, released as Yeoman, 46, after serv. in Asiatic-Pac. Theatre; Asiatic-Pac. Theatre Ribbon. Mem: Trustee, Broadlawns Co. Hosp, Des Moines, Iowa, 62-63; past chmn, Loan Admin. Mortgage Bankers of Am; past pres, Iowa Mortgage Bankers; dist. dep, K. of C; past pres, Exec. Toastmasters 335; past pres, Equiowa Men's Club; Urbandale Country Club. Attended Air War Col. Nat. Security Forum, 66; Cert. of Merit Award, Sch. Commerce of Northwest. Univ. Rel: Roman Catholic. Legal Res: 7205 Oakbrook, Urbandale, Iowa 50322. Mailing Add: Equitable of Iowa, 604 Locust, Des Moines, Iowa 50306.

BENS, RALPH JOSEPH, JR. R
Chmn, Middlesex Co. Rep. Coun, Mass.
b. Quincy, Mass, 10/21/26; s. Ralph J. Bens and Retha Herman B; m. 5/9/55 to Alice Proctor; c. Amy, Beth and Ralph III. Educ: Colby Col, 47-49; Boston Univ, B.S, 51; Delta Kappa Epsilon. Polit. & Govt. Pos: Chmn, Reading Bd. of Selectmen, Mass, 60-64; town constable and chmn, Reading Rep. Town Cmt; chmn, Middlesex Co. Rep. Coun, currently. Bus. & Prof. Pos: Salesman, Atlantic Ref. Co, 51-55; field mgr, Pervacel Tape Corp, 55-61; dist. mgr, Avildsen Tools and Machines, Inc, 61- Mil. Serv: Entered as A/S, Naval Res, 44, released as fire controlman 3/C, 46, after serv. in Asiatic Pac. Theater, 45-46. Mem: Am. Soc. Tool and Mfg. Engrs; Am. Legion; Middlesex Club; Mass. Selectman's Asn; Mass. Constable's Asn; dir, Reading YMCA; dir, Reading Taxpayer's Asn. Rel: Protestant Episcopal. Legal Res: 144 Oak St, Reading, Mass. 01867. Mailing Add: P.O. Box 311, Reading, Mass. 01867.

BENSON, C. J. DFL
Minn. State Sen.
b. Browns Valley, Minn; m; c. Steven. Educ: Macalester Col; Univ. of Minn. Law Sch. Polit. & Govt. Pos: Co. attorney, Big Stone Co, 20 years; Minn. State Sen, 58- Bus. & Prof. Pos: Lawyer, 33- Mem: State Asn. of Co. Attorneys (former pres. and secy). Mailing Add: Ortonville, Minn. 56278. (1967)

BENSON, DANIEL LEROY D
Chmn, Fairfield Co. Dem. Exec. Cmt, Ohio
b. Carroll, Ohio, 6/29/09; s. James O. Benson and Vernia Alspach B; m. 2/16/33 to Mary Martha Black; c. Robert Lee and David A. Educ: Canal Winchester High Sch, grad, 29. Polit. & Govt. Pos: Precinct committeeman, Dem. Party, Ohio, 37-69; chmn, Fairfield Co. Dem. Exec. Cmt, 38- Rel: United Methodist. Mailing Add: 8004 Winchester Rd. N.W, Carroll, Ohio 43112.

BENSON, DAVID B. R
Asst. Majority Floor Leader, Maine House of Rep.
b. Southwest Harbor, Maine, 4/12/28; s. Peter T. Benson (Deceased) and Katharine Gatcomb B; m. 11/23/54 to Anne Foster; c. William D. and Thomas W. Educ: Aurora Col, 3 years. Polit. & Govt. Pos: Maine State Rep, 63-, asst. majority floor leader, Maine House Rep, 67-, speaker pro tem, 67-; mem, Legis. Research Cmt, 65-; chmn, Hancock Co. Rep. Cmt, 66-68; treas, Southwest Harbor Rep. Cmt, 66-; del, Rep. Nat. Conv, 68. Bus. & Prof. Pos: Agent, Paul Revere Life Ins. Co, Southwest Harbor, 58- Mil. Serv: Entered as Pvt, Army, 53, released as Sgt, 55, after serv. in 508th Airborne Inf. and 82nd Airborne Div. Mem: Pres, Mt. Desert Island Hosp; Maine Hosp. Asn; bd. dirs, Pine Tree Crippled Childrens Home; Mason; Scottish Rite; Shrine. Rel: Episcopal. Mailing Add: Freeman Rd, Southwest Harbor, Maine. 04679.

BENSON, DAVID S. R
Del. State Rep.
b. 1900. Educ: Purdue; Ohio Univ; Nat. RR Police Acad, grad. Polit. & Govt. Pos: Del. State Rep, 65-, chmn, Revised Statutes Cmt, mem, Judiciary Cmt and mem, Revenue and Taxation Cmt, Del. House Rep. Bus. & Prof. Pos:

Retired Capt. of Police, Penn. R.R. Legal Res: 1019 Graylyn Rd, Graylyn Crest, Wilmington, Del. 19803. Mailing Add: State House of Representatives, State Capitol Bldg, Dover, Del. 19901.

BENSON, EZRA TAFT R
b. Whitney, Idaho, 8/4/99; s. George Taft Benson and Sarah Dunkley B; m. 9/10/26 to Flora Smith Amussen; c. Reed, Mark, Barbara, Beverly, Bonnie and Flora Beth. Educ: Utah State Agr. Col, Logan, 18-21; Brigham Young Univ, B.S, 26; Iowa State Col, M.S. in Agr. Econ, 27; Univ. Calif, 37-38; Delta Nu; Alpha Zeta. Hon. H.H.D, Col. Osteopathic Physicians; Dr. Agr, Iowa State Col, 53; Dr. Pub. Serv, Brigham Young Univ, 55. Polit. & Govt. Pos: Co. agr. agent. Univ. of Idaho Exten. Serv, 29-30, exten. economist and mkt. specialist in charge of econ. and mkt. work for State of Idaho, 30-38; mem, Nat. Farm Credit Cmt, 40-43; mem, Nat. Agr. Adv. Cmt, World War II; U.S. Del, First Int. Cong. of Farm Orgn, London, Eng, 46; Secy. of Agr, 53-61. Bus. & Prof. Pos: Ordained apostle, Church of Jesus Christ of Latter-day Saints, missionary, Brit. Isles and Europe, 21-23, pres, Newcastle Dist, 21-23, mem, Boise Stake Presidency, Idaho, 33-37, pres, 38-40, first pres, Wash, D.C. Stake, mem, Coun. of the Twelve, 43-, pres, European Mission, 46, supvr, Asian Missions, currently; farmer, 23-30; organizer and secy, Idaho Coop. Coun, 33-38; exec. secy, Nat. Coun. Farmers Coop, 39-44; mem, exec. cmt. and bd. trustees, Am. Inst. Coop, 42-52, v.chmn, bd. trustees, 42-49, chmn, 52; dir, Farm Found, 46-50; mem, nat. exec. bd, Boy Scouts of Am, 48-; dir, Olsen Bros, Inc, Corn Prod. Co. and Corn Refiners Asn, Inc; mem. and gen. chmn, Bd. of Educ; mem, bd. trustees, Brigham Young Univ. Mem: Am. Mkt. Asn; Farm Econ. Asn. Testimonial for distinguished serv. to agr, Univ. Wis, 53. Rel: Latter-day Saint. Mailing Add: 2300 S. 22nd St. E, Salt Lake City, Utah 84109.

BENSON, HARRY EDDIE R
Mem, Pub. Rels. Cmt, Harris Co. Rep. Party, Tex.
b. Port Arthur, Tex, 12/13/25, s. William H. Benson and Eddie A. Rhea B; m. 8/20/49 to Mary Nell Harwell; c. Elizabeth Ann and David Harwell. Educ: Lamar Jr. Col, A.S, 47; Univ. Houston, B.S, 53. Polit. & Govt. Pos: Alternate del, Rep. Nat. Conv, 64; precinct committeeman, Harris Co. Rep. Party, 64-65; del, Rep. State and Co. Conv, 64, 66 & 68; chmn, Neighbor to Neighbor Fund Dr, 65-66; dir, Pub. Rels, Harris Co. Rep. Party, 66-69, mem, Pub. Rels Cmt, 69- Bus. & Prof. Pos: Estimator prod. man, Gulf Printing Co, 52-59; prod. mgr, Marsteller, Rickard, Gebhardt & Reed, 59; typographer, Naylor Type & Mats, 59-60; estimator-prod. man, West. Lithograph Co, Tex, 60-61; purchasing rep. and Graphic arts buyer, TENNECO, Inc, 61- Publ: Former ed, 'The Banner,' monthly publ, Harris Co. Tex. Rep. Party. Mem: Int. Graphic Arts Ed. Asn; Mason (32°); Scottish Rite; K.T; RAM; Nottingham Civic Asn; PTA. Parents League Houston. Rel: Methodist. Mailing Add: 13930 Barryknoll Lane, Houston, Tex. 77024.

BENSON, ROBERT ARTHUR D
b. Lewiston, Maine, 4/14/40; s. Arthur Bensen and Ada Pearl B; m. 6/2/62 to Judith Lorrabee; c. David and Wendy Lee. Educ: Univ. Maine, 62; Beta Theta Pi. Polit. & Govt. Pos: Maine State Rep, 65-67; chmn, Town Dem. Coun, 64-66. Bus. & Prof. Pos: Tech. Spec, S.D. Warren Paper, 63. Mil. Serv: Marine Corps. Rel: Protestant. Legal Res: Mechanic Falls, Maine. 04256. Mailing Add: RFD 2, Gorham, Maine 04038. (1967)

BENSON, TAYLOR D
b. Milwaukee, Wis. Educ: Univ. of Notre Dame, B.A. Polit. & Govt. Pos: Wis. State Sen, 64-68, former Asst. Minority Leader and Dem. Caucus Secy, Wis. State Senate. Bus. & Prof. Pos: Former reporter-writer, sr. pub. rels. rep. for electronics firm. Mil. Serv: Air Force, World War II and Korean War. Mem: Air Force Asn; ROA; Army-Navy Union; SAR; Christian Family Movement; Confraternity of Christian Doctrine; Holy Name Soc; Milwaukee Press Club; Cape Canaveral Press Club; Caledonia Bus. & Prfnl. Men's Asn. Mailing Add: 6729 Hwy. 38, Franksville, Wis. 53126. (1967)

BENT, JAMES EDWARD R
Chmn, Budget Cmt, Conn. Rep. State Finance Cmt.
b. Lee, Mass, 8/15/05; s. James F. Bent and Elizabeth Collins B; m. 9/26/36 to Frances Patricia Williams. Educ: Trinity Col, 3 years; Univ. Conn, 1 year; Psi Upsilon. Polit. & Govt. Pos: Founder and first chmn, Conn. Rep. State Key Man Cmt, 59-60; chmn, budget cmt. and comptroller, Conn. Rep. State Finance Cmt, 59-; alternate del, Rep. Nat. Conv, 60, del, 64 & 68; chmn, West Hartford Rep. Town Cmt, 60-62; chmn, Hartford Rep. Finance Cmt, 63-69; mem, Conn. Constitutional Conv, 64; justice of the peace, Hartford, 66-; cmnr, Hartford Charter Revision Cmn, 67; mem, savings and loan adv. cmt, Treas. Dept, currently; mem, adv. cmt. on coop. to admin. and savings and loan tech. adv, Agency for Int. Develop, Dept. of State, currently; dir, Nat. Fed. Home Loan Bank Bd. Cmt. on Emergency Preparedness, currently. Bus. & Prof. Pos: Dir, Fed. Home Loan Bank of Boston, 55-59; chmn. bd. dir. and chief exec. officer, Hartford Fed. Savings and Loan Asn, currently; chmn. bd. and pres, JEB Corp, currently; dir, Security Ins. Co. of Hartford, Conn. Indemnity Co, Security-Conn. Life Ins. Co. and Fire and Casualty Ins. Co. of Conn, currently; savings and loan tech. adv, Inter-Am. Develop. Bank, Wash, D.C. and Banco de Guatemala, Cent. Am. Mil. Serv: Entered as 1st Lt, Air Force, 43, released as Maj, 46, after serv. as Army Air Force Air Commun. Officer, Am. and European Theatres; Commendation Medal. Mem: Pres, Fed. Savings League of New Eng, Inc, 49-50; pres, New Eng. Conf. of Savings and Loan Asns. and Coop. Banks, 57-58; Fed. Savings and Loan Adv. Coun, 57-59; pres, Nat. League of Insured Savings Asns, 58-59; Soc. of Residential Appraisers; pres, Hartford Alumni Asn, Trinity Col, 49-50; bd. trustees, Hillyer Col, 49-62; state chmn, United Serv. Club Flood Relief Cmt, 55; Rotary (pres, Hartford Club, 55-56); bd. regents, Univ. Hartford, 58-64; mem-at-lg, Hosp. Coun. of Gr. Hartford, Inc, 62-66; pres, Gr. Hartford C. of C, 63-65; Mason (32°); Shrine, Hartford Club; Univ. Club; Hartford Golf Club; Tunxis Club; officers Club of Conn; Newcomen Soc; Colt Trust Asn; Air Force Asn, Officers Reserve; Founders Soc, Trinity Col; Univ. Hartford Assocs; Ft. Lauderdale Yacht Club; trustee, Hartford Sch. for the Blind; corporator, Hartford Hosp. and Inst. for the Living and St. Francis Hosp; Defense Orientation Conf. Asn; chmn, housing cmt, Regional Adv. Cmt. for the Capitol Region; exec. cmt. and bd. trustees, Cent. Conn. Commun. Cult, Civic and Charitable Corp; Conn. State Adv. Coun. on Banking; Conn. State Bldg. Code Amendment Rev. Cmt; v.pres, Conn. State C. of C; Cmt. for Hartford; Hosp. Coun. of Gr. Hartford; adv. Gr. Hartford Commun. Ambassador Proj; Neighborhood Planning Assocs; trustee, Open Hearth Asn; dir, Gr. Hartford Housing Develop. Fund, Inc; Model Cities Cmt. Medal of Excellence, Trinity Col, 63; first recipient of the Most Distinguished Salesman of the Year, Sales and Mkt. Execs. of Hartford, Inc, 65; Commendation for State Dept. Serv. in Guatemala; Charter Oak Leadership Medal, 65. Rel: Methodist. Legal Res: 50 State St, Hartford, Conn. 06101. Mailing Add: 343 N. Steele Rd, West Hartford, Conn. 06117.

BENTLEY, ALVIN M, JR. R
Chmn, Shiawassee Co. Rep. Party, Mich.
b. Washington, D.C, 5/27/41; s. Alvin M. Bentley and Arvilla Duecher B; m. 10/7/61 to Sue Ann Meiers; c. Susan and Marianne. Educ: Staunton Mil. Acad, Va, 4 years. Polit. & Govt. Pos: Chmn, Shiawassee Young Rep, 66-67; finance chmn, Shiawassee Co. Rep. Party, 67-68, chmn, 68-; alternate del, Rep. Nat. Conv, 68; finance chmn, Mich. Citizens for Nixon, 68; chmn, Sixth Cong. Dist. for Nixon, 68. Mil. Serv: Entered as Seaman Apprentice, U.S. Coast Guard, 60, released as Seaman, 64. Mem: Legis. Cmt, Owosso C. of C; charter mem, Owosso Area Human Rel. Cmt; bd. trustees, Alvin M. Bentley Found; Farm Bur; Mich. Partners of the Alliance; Shiawassee Co. Jr. Achievement; YMCA. Rel: Episcopal. Legal Res: 701 W. Oliver St, Owosso, Mich. 48867. Mailing Add: Matthews Bldg. Annex, Owosso, Mich. 48867.

BENTLEY, CHARLES DYER, JR. R
b. Arlington, Vt, 7/1/23. Educ: Burr and Burton Seminary, 42. Polit. & Govt. Pos: Lister; selectman, 6 years; former Vt. State Rep. Bus. & Prof. Pos: Farmer. Rel: Methodist. Mailing Add: RFD 1, Arlington, Vt. 05250. (1967)

BENTLEY, GEORGE EDWARD D
b. Marietta, Ga, 10/6/28; s. James William Bentley and Ruby Hill B; m. 4/26/53 to June White; c. George Edward, Jr. and Elizabeth June. Educ: West Georgia Col, grad. Polit. & Govt. Pos: Chmn, Cobb Co. Dem. Exec. Cmt, Ga, 62-66; Senator's Adv. Cmt, 62-66; v. pres, Young Dems. of Cobb Co, 61-62; Mem, 7th Dist. Dem. Cong. Cmt; Lt. Governor's Adv. Cmt. Bus. & Prof. Pos: Asst. supt, Cobb Co. Water Syst, 60-; owner and operator, Cattle Farm and Horse Ranch, 48- Mem: Past local pres, Marietta Jr. C. of C; Tri-County Nat. Found. Dir; past state cmt. chmn. and mem. President's Adv. Cmt, Ga. Jr. C. of C. Rel: Methodist. Mailing Add: 1018 Ridgeview Lane, Marietta, Ga. 30060. (1967)

BENTLEY, JAMES LYNWOOD D
Comptroller Gen, Ga.
b. Thomaston, Ga, 6/15/27; s. J. Lynwood Bentley and Clarice Abercrombie B; m. 7/22/51 to Gwendolyn Mincey; c. Nina Elizabeth; James Lynwood, III and Samuel Jackson. Educ: Emory at Oxford; Univ. Ga, LL.B, 50; campus leader, Univ. Ga, jr. and sr. years; mem, Demosthenian Literary Soc. and winner, Gold Speaker's Key; pres, Sphinx and Gridiron; Omicron Delta Kappa; Blue Key; Phi Alpha Delta. Polit. & Govt. Pos: Page, Ga. Gen. Assembly; exec. aide. to Gov. Talmadge, Ga, 50, exec. secy, 51; mem, Ga. State Dem. Exec. Cmt; Comptroller Gen, Ga, 63-, ex-officio state ins. cmnr, state indust. loan cmnr. and state fire safety cmnr, 63- Bus. & Prof. Pos: Organizer, United Family Life Ins. Co. and Talmadge Farms Country Cured Sausage Co; owner and operator, farm, Upson Co. Mil. Serv: Aerial Gunner, Navy, World War II. Mem: V.pres, Nat. Asn. Ins. Cmnrs; exec. secy, R.R. Asn. Ga, 55-61; pres, Ga. Ment. Health Asn, 65; Farm Bur; Am. Legion; July Foxhound Asn; Scottish Rite; Mason; Shriner; Kiwanis. Rel: Baptist; Deacon, Morningside Baptist Church of Atlanta. Legal Res: Thomaston, Ga. 30286. Mailing Add: 1649 Lady Marion Lane, N.E, Atlanta, Ga. 30309.

BENTLEY, LUTHER DANIEL JR. D
b. Snead, Ala, 12/10/25; s. Luther Daniel Bentley and Bertha Mae Smith B; m. 6/9/47 to Rachel Bynum; c. Luther Daniel, III, Teresa Annette, Deborah Elaine, James Robert. Educ: Gulf Coast Mil. Acad; Howard Col; Univ. of Ala, B.A, 49. Polit. & Govt. Pos: Oneonta City Bd. of Educ, 54-55; Ala. State Sen, -66. Bus. & Prof. Pos: Owner, Oneonta Radio Sta; part-owner, Boaz Radio Sta. Made a good will tour of Russia, 60. Rel: Methodist. Mailing Add: P.O. Box 481, Oneonta, Ala. 35121. (1967)

BENTON, GEORGE OLIVER D
Mem, State Dem. Exec. Cmt, Tenn.
b. Jackson, Tenn, 6/22/15; s. Oliver Benton and Lucy Wilkerson B; m. 11/6/43 to Theresa Anderson; c. Jane Anderson, George Oliver, Jr. and Hu Anderson. Educ: Lambuth Col, 33-34; Vanderbilt Univ, Law Sch, B.A, 38, LL.B, 40; Sigma Chi. Polit. & Govt. Pos: Tenn. State Sen, 47-51, Speaker, Tenn. Senate, 47-49; mem. and chmn, Madison Co. Elec. Cmn, 53-69; mem, State Dem. Exec. Cmt, 54-; del, Dem. Nat. Conv, 56, del. and mem. credentials cmt, 68. Bus. & Prof. Pos: Partner, Moss & Benton, Attorneys, Jackson, 40-; dir, Nat. Bank of Commerce, 46- Mil. Serv: Entered as 2nd Lt, Marine Corps, 41, released as Maj, 45, after serv. in Southwest Pac. and U.S. Theaters, 41-45, Marine Res, until 60, Lt. Col.(Ret); usual theater ribbons. Mem: Am, Tenn. and local Bar Asns; Am. Legion; VFW; Lions. Rel: Methodist. Mailing Add: 809 First National Bank Bldg, Jackson, Tenn. 38301.

BENTON, MORRIS CAREY, JR. D
Mayor, Winston-Salem, N.C.
b. Kenansville, N.C, 10/25/17; s. Morris Carey Benton and Mattie Grady B; m. 12/25/39 to Elizabeth Holmes; c. William Grady, Kathryn Stuart (Mrs. Broadhurst), Carey Elizabeth and Alice Holmes. Educ: Univ. N.C, Chapel Hill, B.S, Commerce, 38. Polit. & Govt. Pos: Chmn, Winston-Salem Bd. Educ, 57-63; mayor, Winston-Salem, N.C, 63-; past pres. and dir, N.C. League of Munic, 65- Bus. & Prof. Pos: CPA, W.M. Russ & Co, Raleigh, N.C, 39; exec. v.pres, treas. and dir, McLean Trucking Co, 39-; dir, Winston-Salem and Forsyth Co. Indust. Develop. Corp, 52, Winston-Salem Hotel Corp, 54-, Hercules Steel Corp, Fayetteville, 55, N.C. Nat. Bank, 61- and Integon Corp, 69- Mil. Serv: Entered as Aviation Cadet, Air Force, 43, released as 1st Lt, 45, after serv. in Eighth and Third Air Force, ETO, and Southeast. U.S, 43-45; Air Medal with Three Oak Leaf Clusters; Distinguished Flying Cross; 31 Combat Missions. Mem: Am. Trucking Asn.(past pres. and mem. bd. dirs, nat. acct. and finance coun); N.C. Motor Carrier's Asn.(dir); Better Bus. Bur. (past pres); Am. Nat. Red Cross (past chmn. and dir); Salvation Army Adv. Bd, (past chmn); dir, United Fund Winston-Salem and Forsyth Co; Winston-Salem Lions Club (past pres); Gen. Alumni Asn. Univ. N.C.(past pres); bd. trustees, St. Andrews Presby. Col; YMCA; Forsyth Country Club; Pine

Brook Co. Club; Twin City Club; Elks; Moose. Rel: Presbyterian; Elder, Highland Presbyterian Church; Past Pres. Bd. Regents, Barium Springs Home Children. Mailing Add: 2901 Country Club Rd, Winston-Salem, N.C. 27104.

BENTON, WILLIAM D
b. Minneapolis, Minn, 4/1/00; s. Charles William Benton and Elma Caroline Hixson B; m. 6/12/28 to Helen Hemingway; c. Charles, Helen (Mrs. John Nicholas Boley), Louise Hemingway and John Hemingway. Educ: Carleton Col, 17-18; Yale Univ, B.A, 21. Hon. LL.D, Univ. Louisville, 48, Bard Col, 51, Mont. State Col, 57, Knox Col, 60, Carleton Col, 61, Univ. Notre Dame, 68, Brandeis Univ, 68 and Dartmough Col, 68. Polit. & Govt. Pos: Coordinator adv. cmt, Inter-Am. Affairs, 39-45; v.chmn. bd. trustees, Cmt. Econ. Develop, 42-45, exec. cmt. bd. trustees, 58-63 and bd. dir, Fair Campaign Practices Cmt; U.S. del, Inter-Am. Conv. War and Peace, Mex, 45; U.S. del, Constitutional Conv, UNESCO, London, 45, chmn, U.S. Del, First Gen. Conf, Paris, 46, Second Gen. Conf, Mexico City, 47, mem, U.S. Nat. Cmn. and Ambassador, U.S. Exec. Bd, Paris, 63-68; Asst. Secy. of State, 45-47; chmn, U.S. Del, UN Conf. Freedom of the Press, Geneva, 48; U.S. Sen, Conn, 49-53; U.S. Cong. Rep. Consultative Assembly of Europe, Strasbourg, 51; del. and mem. Platform Cmt. and Drafting Subcmt, Dem. Nat. Conv, 52, 56, 64 & 68. Bus. & Prof. Pos: Advert. agency bus. with Lord and Thomas until 29; co-founder and pres, Benton and Bowles, N.Y. Advert. Agency, 29-35, chmn. bd, 29-35; v.pres, Univ. Chicago, 37-45, asst. to chancellor, 45; chmn. bd, Encyclop. Britannica and Encyclop. Britannica Films, 43-67, Encyclop. Britannica Educ. Corp, 67- Publ: This is the Challenge, 58; The Voice of Latin America, 61; The Teachers and the Taught in the U.S.S.R, 66. Mem: Bd, Benton Found.(chmn), Fair Campaign Practices Cmt, Cmt. For Econ. Develop, Am. Assembly, Columbia Univ, Cradle Soc, Inst. Int. Educ, Aspen Inst, Eleanor Roosevelt Mem. Found, Franklin D. Roosevelt Found, Kennedy Libr. Corp, Am. Shakespeare Festival Theatre and Acad. and Friends of Whitney Mus. Am. Art; trustee, Univ. Conn, Univ. Bridgeport and Brandeis Univ; life trustee, Univ. Chicago; hon. trustee, Hampton Inst. and Carleton Col; Am. Legion; Cleveland Conf; Coun. For. Rels; hon. mem, Yale Polit. Union and Am. For. Serv. Asn; Adv. Cmt. Arts, Nat. Cult. Center; Chicago Club; Fairfield Country Club, Conn; Yale Club; Univ. Club; River Club, N.Y.C; Pequot Yacht Club, Conn; Metrop. Club, Wash; Paradise Valley Country Club, Phoenix; Union Interalliee Club, Paris. HIAS Annual Award of Honor, 52; Order of the Star of Solidarity, First Class, Italy, 52; Distinguished Serv. Medal, Sch. Jour, Syracuse Univ, 60; Grand Cross, Nat. Order South. Cross, Brazil, 64; Key to Freedom Award, Hadassah, 66; Distinguished Honor Award, U.S. Dept. State, 67; William Benton Medal for Distinguished Serv, Univ. Chicago, 68; Human Rels. Award, Am. Jewish Cmt, 68; Nat. Human Rels. Award, Nat. Conf. Christians and Jews, 69. Legal Res: Southport, Conn. 06490. Mailing Add: 342 Madison Ave, New York, N.Y. 10017.

BENTSEN, BERYL ANN D
Dem. Nat. Committeewoman, Tex.
b. 1922; m. to Lloyd Bentsen, Jr; c. Lloyd III, Lan and Tina. Educ: Univ. Texas; Pi Beta Phi. Polit. & Govt. Pos: Dem. Nat. Committeewoman, 66-; del, Dem. Nat. Conv, 68. Mem: Area chmn, Cancer Crusade; bd. mem, Mus. of Fine Arts, Houston Symphony and YWCA; River Oaks Garden Club; chmn, Mus. of Fine Arts Annual Benefit; pres, St. John's Sch. Mothers Club; 81st Cong. Club of Wash, D.C.(pres). Rel: Presbyterian. Mailing Add: 3330 Inwood, Houston, Tex. 77019.

BENTSEN, LLOYD MILLARD, JR. D
b. Mission, Tex, 2/11/21; s. Lloyd M. Bentsen and Edna Ruth Colbath B; m. 11/27/43 to Beryl Ann Longino; c. Lloyd M, III, Lan C. and Tina Ann. Educ: Univ. Tex. Sch. of Law; Sigma Nu. Polit. & Govt. Pos: U.S. Rep, Tex, 48-55. Bus. & Prof. Pos: Pres, Lincoln Consolidated, Inc, Houston, 68-; chmn. bd, Lincoln Liberty Life Ins. Co, 68-; dir, Lockheed Aircraft Corp, Continental Oil Co, Panhandle East. P.L. Co, Trunkline Gas Co and Bank of the Southwest Co. Mil. Serv: Entered as Pvt, 42, Air Force, released as Col, 45; Distinguished Flying Cross; Air Medal with three Oak Leaf Clusters. Mem: Tex. Bar Asn; River Oaks Country Club; Ramada Club, Houston, Brook, N.Y. Rel: Presbyterian. Legal Res: 3330 Inwood Dr, Houston, Tex. 77019. Mailing Add: 711 Polk, Suite 1234, Houston, Tex. 77002.

BEOUGHER, ETHEL M. D
V.chmn, Gove Co. Dem. Party, Kans.
b. Healy, Kans, 7/31/20; d. William H. Anderson and Pauline Haverfield A; m. 1/22/39 to Clellan O. Beougher; c. William O, James E, Shirley (Mrs. Walker), Judy (Mrs. Zerr), Philip, Steven and Susan. Polit. & Govt. Pos: Gove. Twp. committeewoman; v.chmn, Gove Co. Dem. Party, Kans, 68- Rel: Methodist. Legal Res: Box 95, Gove, Kans. 67736.

BEPPU, TADAO D
Hawaii State Rep, Speaker, Hawaii House of Rep.
b. Maui, Hawaii, 3/26/19; s. Teizo Beppu and Tora Handa B; m. to Alice Nobu Aoki; c. William J. and Anita M. Educ: Univ. Hawaii, B.A; Northwest. Univ. Polit. & Govt. Pos: Nat. committeeman, Young Dem. Clubs, Hawaii, 57; del, Dem. Nat. Conv, 60 and mem. cmt. Permanent Orgn, 60, del, 68; secy, State Dem. Cent. Cmt, 56-60, campaign chmn, 60 and v.chmn, 60-62; Hawaii State Rep, 65-, V.Speaker, Hawaii House of Rep, 65-67, Speaker, 67- Bus. & Prof. Pos: Dir, Makaha Hand Print, Inc, 62; dir, Honolulu Stadium, 66. Mil. Serv: Entered as Pvt, Army, 43, released as T/Sgt, 45, after serv. in 442nd Regiment Combat Team, ETO; Soldiers Medal; Bronze Star; Purple Heart; Combat Infantryman's Badge; Asiatic-Pac. and ETO Ribbons; Am. Defense and Victory Medals; Presidential Unit Citation with 2 Battle Stars. Mem: life mem, DAV; 442nd Vet. Club; Nat. Legs. Leaders Conf; Hawaii State Planning Cmn. on Ment. Retardation. Rel: Congregational. Legal Res: 3350 Sierra Dr, Honolulu, Hawaii 96816. Mailing Add: 62 Funchal St, Honolulu, Hawaii 96813.

BERBERICK, FREDERICK CHARLES, JR. R
Conn. State Rep.
b. Norwich, Conn, 10/25/33; s. Frederick C. Berberick and Mary Fitsgerald B; m. 7/14/56 to Winifred Mellor; c. Sharon and Sheila. Educ: St. Bonaventure Univ, B.S, 55; Univ. Conn. Sch. Law, LL.B, 63; St. Thomas More Law Soc. Polit. & Govt. Pos: Alderman, Norwich City Coun, Conn, 65-67, Rep. minority leader, 68; Conn. State Rep, Hartford, 69- Bus. & Prof. Pos: Attorney, 63-; instr. bus. law, Mitchell Coll, Conn, 64-68; writer commercial law, Bur. Bus. Practice, 65- Mil. Serv: Entered as Pvt, Army, 55, released as Sp-4, 57, after serving in Missile Co. Mem: Conn. Bar Asn; New London Co. Bar Asn; Norwich C. of C; St. Peter & Paul's Holy Name Soc. Rel: Catholic. Legal Res: 30 Will Rd, Norwich, Conn. 06360. Mailing Add: 16 Franklin St, Norwich, Conn. 06360.

BERDES, GEORGE RAYMOND D
b. Milwaukee, Wis, 2/12/31; s. Frank Raymond Berdes and Johanna Galubinski B; m. 6/27/53 to Jane Louise Berdes; c. Celia Marie, Beth Mary, John Patrick and Mary Madelyn. Educ: Marquette Univ. Col. of Journalism, B.A, 53, M.A, 59; Sigma Delta Chi. Polit. & Govt. Pos: Admin. asst. to U.S. Rep. Clement J. Zablocki, Fourth Dist, Wis. Bus. & Prof. Pos: Reporter, Appleton Post-Crescent, Wis, 55-57; ed. dir, Marquette Univ. Press, 57-63; asst. prof, Marquette Univ. Col. of Journalism, 57-65. Mil. Serv: Entered as Pvt, Army, 53, released as SP-4, 55. Publ: Up from Ashes (Study and Impressions of Mod. Germany); Friendly Adversaries: The Press and Government (Study of Wash. Press Corps on Coop. with Center for Study of the Am. Press) 69. Mem: Am. Asn. Univ. Prof; The Burro Club; Cong. Secretaries Club; Milwaukee Press Club; Wis. Hist. Soc; Marquette Univ. Alumni Asn. Study and Travel grant from W. German Govt, 63 & 67; winner, Milwaukee Press Club, Outstanding Reporting in Int. Affairs Award. Rel: Roman Catholic. Mailing Add: 6025 Berkshire Dr, Bethesda, Md. 20014.

BEREN, DANIEL E. R
Pa. State Rep.
b. Philadelphia, Pa, 11/3/29; s. Arthur Beren and Frances Shapiro B; m. 7/7/56 to Joan Cranmer; c. Day Cranmer, Sandra Elizabeth and Jane Sylvia. Educ: Baldwin-Wallace Col, B.A, 52; Temple Univ. Law Sch, LL.B, 55; Omicron Delta Kappa; Alpha Phi Gamma. Polit. & Govt. Pos: Judge of elec, Rep. Party, Pa, 61-62, committeeman, 62-67; solicitor, Montgomery Co. Inst. Dist, Pa, 63-66; chmn, Montgomery Co. Young Rep, 65-66; Pa. State Rep, 67-, mem, Consumer Protection and State Govt. Cmts, Pa. House of Rep; originator of the Neighborhood Assistance Act; testified on behalf of the Neighborhood Assistance Act before Rep. Nat. Conv. in 1968 and was successful in having the concept included in the 1968 GOP Nat. Platform; chief sponsor of Pa. Consumer Protection Laws; co-leader in fight to reform Pa. Elec. Code. Bus. & Prof. Pos: Partner, Beren & Clancy, Attorneys, Abington, Pa, 64- Mil. Serv: Entered as Pvt, Army, 55, released as Cpl, 57, after serv. in North. Area Command, Germany; Good Conduct Medal. Mem: Am. Trial Lawyers Asn; Pa. and Am. Bar Asns; Am. Judicature Soc; legal aid cmt, Montgomery Co. Bar Asn; Jr. C. of C; Boy Scouts; bd. mgrs, Abington Br, YMCA; hon. tech. orgns. Letterman, Capt, col. track and cross-country teams. Rel: Jewish. Legal Res: 1765 Sharpless Rd, Meadowbrook, Pa. 19046. Mailing Add: 1217 Old York Rd, Abington, Pa. 19001.

BERENTSON, DUANE R
Wash. State Rep.
b. Anacortes, Wash, 1928; m. to Joanne; c. Five. Educ: Pac. Lutheran Univ, B.S; Univ. of Wash. Polit. & Govt. Pos: Wash. State Rep, currently. Bus. & Prof. Pos: Broker-dealer in securities. Mil. Serv: Naval Air Res. Mem: Sigma Nu. Mailing Add: Box 426, Burlington, Wash. 98233. (1967)

BERG, HARRIS ODELL R
N.Dak. State Rep.
b. Grafton, N.Dak, 11/4/35; s. Clifford S. Berg and Hazel Brekke B; m. 11/2/58 to LaVonne Ardell Peterson; c. Scott, Lynn, Brenda and Jodi. Educ: Concordia Col, 2 years; N.Dak. State Univ, 1 year. Polit. & Govt. Pos: N.Dak. State Rep, Dist. 16, 69- Bus. & Prof. Pos: Prfnl. farmer, Berg Farms, 57- Mil. Serv: Entered as SA, Navy, 55, released as RM 3/C, 57, after serv. in Ninth and 12th Naval Dist, U.S.S. Thomaston, 55-57. Mem: Walsh Co. Crop Improv. Asn.(pres); N.Dak. Young Farmers & Ranchers Asn.(past pres); Mason; Shrine; VFW; Am. Legion; Gr. N.Dak. Asn; Farm Bur; Aircraft Owners & Pilots Asn; Lions. Rel: Protestant. Mailing Add: Nash, N.Dak. 58264.

BERG, JOSEPH M. D
R.I. State Rep.
b. Providence, R.I, 3/19/14; single. Educ: Providence Col; Boston Univ. Sch. of Law, LL.B, 40. Polit. & Govt. Pos: R.I. State Rep, currently. Bus. & Prof. Pos: Attorney-at-law, currently. Mil. Serv: Army Signal Corps, 32-34; Air Force, 42-46. Mailing Add: 1451 Broad St, Providence, R.I. 02905. (1967)

BERG, LARRY LEE D
b. Ft. Dodge, Iowa, 7/30/39; s. Carl O. Berg and Zene M. Anderson B; m. 6/12/60 to Mary Ellen Randall; c. Andrea Lee and Mary Michelle. Educ: Iowa State Univ, 57-59; Univ. Iowa, B.A, 62 and M.A, 63; Univ. Calif, Nat. Defense Educ. Act fel, 63-65, Ph.D, 69; Polit. Sci. Discussion Club, Univ. Iowa. Polit. & Govt. Pos: Campaign mgr, minority leader, Iowa House of Rep, 62; alternate del, Iowa State Dem. Conv, 62; precinct committeeman, Johnson Co. Dem. Cent. Cmt, Iowa, 62-63; asst. to dist. dir, Oper. Support Pres. Kennedy, 62-63; pres, Johnson Co. Young Dem, 62-63; exec. asst, U.S. Rep. John R. Schmidhauser, 65-67; campaign coordinator for Assemblyman Winfield Shoemaker, 68; del, Dem. Nat. Conv, 68. Bus. & Prof. Pos: Teaching Asst, Univ. Iowa, 62, research asst, 63; teaching asst, Univ. Calif, Santa Barbara, 64-65, lectr. Am. Polit, 67-69; consult, Gen. Research Corp, 67; asst. prof, Univ. South. Calif, Los Angeles, 69-70. Publ: Co-auth, Evaluation of the Indian Community Project, Gen. Research Corp, 67 and Supreme Court and Congress, Free Press, 69; 'Review of The Lawmakers,' Am. Sociol. Rev, 10/65. Mem: Am. and West. Polit. Sci. Asns; Univ. Iowa Alumni Asn; Nat. Wilderness Soc; Sierra Club; GI Forum; Am. Civil Liberties Union; Asn. Am. Indians. Rel: Lutheran. Mailing Add: 5101 Verdun Ave, Los Angeles, Calif. 90043.

BERG, MARY ELIZABETH DeBARDELEBEN D
Chmn, Door Co. Dem. Party, Wis.
b. Dutton, Mont, 9/11/19; d. John Arthur DeBardeleben and Antoinette Merselis D; m. 5/28/42 to William Gerald Berg; c. John Conrad, William Gerald, Jr, Robert Alan and Elizabeth Ann. Educ: Univ. Wis, Madison, B.S, 41; Spencerian Bus. Col, cert, 41; Hon. Bus. Sorority; Schoolmasters Club. Polit. & Govt. Pos: Dem. committeeman, 7th ward, Sturgeon Bay, Wis, 64-66 & 68- and city chmn, precinct committeeman, 68-; v.chmn, Door Co. Dem.

Party, 64-66, & 68, membership chmn, 67 and chmn, 69-; del, Dem. Nat. Conv, 68; mem, Comprehensive Health Regional Planning Cmt, Door Co, Green Bay Region, 69- Bus. & Prof. Pos: Secy, Bassett's Drug Store Inc, 63-; mem. Continuing Educ. Cmt, Univ. Wis, 64-69. Mem: Chmn. bd, Spec. Day Care Serv. for Handicapped; Ment. Health Asn; Asn. for Retarded Children; charter mem, League Women Voters (prov. pres); Wis. Alumni Asn. Rel: United Church of Christ. Mailing Add: 842 Louisiana St, Sturgeon Bay, Wis. 54235.

BERG, OSCAR W. D
Chmn, Kewaunee Co. Dem. Party, Wis.
b. Algoma, Wis, 5/30/91; s. Charles P. Berg and Louise Mueller B; m. 3/7/17 to Ellen Larson; c. Doris (Mrs. Robert Beetz), Bonnie (Mrs. Gene Sturchio), Marion (Mrs. Julius Hafeman), Venice (Mrs. James Gigstead), Beverly (Mrs. Fred DePrey), Marvel (deceased) and Owen W. Educ: Algoma High Sch, grad, 10; N.Dak. State Normal Sch, summer, 14. Polit. & Govt. Pos: Mem, Dist. Sch. Bd, Ahnapee, Ohio, 23-42 and town clerk, 37-47; secy, La Follette Club, 28-38; mem, War Bd. and Ration Bd, Kewaunee Co, 41-45; v.chmn. and chmn, Co. Sch. Cmt, 48-52; dir, Second Libr. Bd, 48-52; chmn, Kewaunee Co. Dem. Party, 55-66 & 67-; mem, Fed. Housing Admin, 63-66; mem, Unified Sch. Bd, Algoma, 64-66. Mem: Nat. Farm Loan Asn.(dir, 24-48); two co. Guernsey Breeders Asn.(secy, 48-56). Rel: Lutheran; chmn, 4 years and secy, 2 years. Mailing Add: 960 Flora Ave, Algoma, Wis. 54201.

BERG, WILLIAM JR. D
b. Chehalis, Wash, 11/15/07; s. William P. Berg and Cora M. Monaghan B; m. 8/31/35 to Dorothy Helen Shaw B; c. William III, Thomas Miles. Educ: Univ. of Ore, A.B, J.D, 26-31; Univ. of Calif, J.S.D, 37-38; Phi Delta Phi; Order of the Coif; Newman Honor Soc; Phi Sigma Kappa. Polit. & Gov. Pos: Admin. Asst, Sen. Morse, Ore; Asst. to Chmn. William H. Davis, NWLB, Wash; Asst, Wayne Morse, NWLB, 42-46. Bus. & Prof. Pos: Assoc. Prof, Prof. of Law, Univ. of Colo, Boulder, Colo, 46-52; Assoc. Prof. of Law, Univ. of S.Dak, Vermillion, 38-42; Attorney, Portland, Ore, 31-37. Contrib. to Law Reviews. Author: Treatise entitled 'Long-Term Options and the Rule Against Perpetuities' - Calif. Law Review - Vol. 37, 1949. Legal Res: Montgomery, Md. Mailing Add: 5906 Onondaga Rd, Glen Echo, Md. 20016. (1967)

BERGEMANN, LAWRENCE ALFRED DFL
Chmn, Martin Co. Dem-Farm-Labor Party, Minn.
b. Milnor, N.Dak, 1/24/06; s. Rudolph C. Bergemann and Mathilda Luedtke B; m. 10/9/29 to Sadie M. Een; c. Dorothy, Delano, Shirley and Larry. Educ: Jr. Col, 24-25. Polit. & Govt. Pos: Mem. bd. of educ, Sch. Dist. 459, Welcome, Minn, 50-62; mem, Martin Co. Dem-Farm-Labor Exec. Cmt, 55-; chmn, Martin Co. Dem-Farm-Labor Party, 58-; mem, Minn. Dem-Farm-Labor State Cent. Cmt, 59-; mem, Jr. Col. Cmt, Fairmont Area, 66. Mem: Bd. mem, Martin Co. Breeders Asn, 46-58 and Southwest Minn. Hereford Breeders Asn, 48-58; chmn, Martin Co. Farmers Union, 51-57; Minn. Farmers Union. Rel: Lutheran. Mailing Add: R.F.D, Welcome, Minn. 56181.

BERGER, BILL L. R
Mem, Nebr. Rep. State Cent. Cmt.
b. Nebraska City, Nebr, 8/20/21; s. Roy L. Berger and Sarah Brower B; m. 4/28/45 to Lois Grundman; c. Michael Lee, William Thomas and Jamey Robin. Educ: Peru State Teachers Col; Univ. Nebr. Grad. Div; Phi Delta Kappa. Polit. & Govt. Pos: Chmn, Otoe Co. Rep. Cent. Cmt, Nebr, 42-68 and finance chmn, 54-60; mem, Nebr. Rep. State Cent. Cmt, 60-62 and currently. Bus. & Prof. Pos: Supt. of Schs, Nebr, 46-51; owner, Nebr. City Furniture & Appliances, 51- Mil. Serv: Entered as Aviation Student, Air Force, 42, released as 1st Lt, 45, after serv. in Eighth Air Force, ETO; 3 Battle Stars; Air Medal and 6 Clusters. Mem: Shrine; asst. chief, Vol. Fire Dept; Am. Legion; VFW; United Commercial Travelers; City Civil Defense Dir; Sch. Bd; Co. Vets. Serv. Cmt. Rel: United Church of Christ. Legal Res: 523 N. 16th, Nebraska City, Nebr. 68410. Mailing Add: 609 Central, Nebraska City, Nebr. 68410.

BERGER, GERTRUDE MARIBELLE R
Secy, Adams Co. Rep. Party, Colo.
b. Lexington, Nebr, 3/10/22; d. Albert Edward Buchholz and Cecil Chadwick B; m. 8/6/41 to William Casper Berger; c. Patricia (Mrs. Eugene Erickson), Sharon (Mrs. Harry Ranney), William and Linda. Polit. & Govt. Pos: Committeewoman, Adams Co. Rep. Party, Colo, 66-, secy, 68- Rel: Protestant. Mailing Add: 2095 Nome, Aurora, Colo. 80010.

BERGER, HAROLD D. D
Mem. Exec. Cmt, Nassau Co. Dem. Cmt, N.Y.
b. Brooklyn, N.Y, 6/7/21; s. Philip Berger and Sarah Arnoff B; m. 1/31/44 to Eleanor Suvalsky; c. Robert, Lee, Judith and Suzan. Educ: Brooklyn Col, A.B, 42; Polytech. Inst. Brooklyn, 46-48; St. John's Univ, LL.B, 65. Polit. & Govt. Pos: Committeeman, Nassau Co. Dem. Cmt, N.Y, 53-, leader, Green Acre Zone, 63-, mem. exec. cmt, currently; v.pres, Valley Stream Dem. Club, 56-58, pres, 58-60; chmn. legis. cmt, Nassau Co. Youth Bd, 64-; alternate del, Dem. Nat. Conv, 68. Bus. & Prof. Pos: Chief chemist, Stein-Hall & Co, N.Y.C, 48-53; pres, Berco Industs. Corp, 55-; v.pres, Charell Consult. Co, 66- Mil. Serv: Entered as Aviation Cadet, Air Force, 64, released as Capt, 66, after serv. in Ninth Photo Tech. Squadron, Guam, 65-66. Mem: Rubber Div, Rubber Group, Am. Chem. Soc; Soc. Plastic Engrs; Civic Asn. Green Acres (mem. bd). Rel: Hebrew. Mailing Add: 30 Eastwood Lane, Valley Stream, N.Y. 11581.

BERGER, HENRY WEINBERG D
b. Frederick, Md, 7/12/37; s. Ernest Berger and Leah Frances Weinberg B. (deceased); m. 10/8/66 to Mary A. Blistein; c. David Aaron. Educ: Ohio State Univ, B.A, 59; Univ. Wis, M.S, 61, Ph.D, 66; Phi Beta Kappa; Pi Sigma Alpha; Phi Alpha Theta. Polit. & Govt. Pos: V.pres, Ohio State Univ. Young Dem, 58-59; mem, Dane Co. Dem. Party, Wis, 60-65; chmn, Univ. Wis. Young Dem, 61-62; alternate del, Dem. Nat. Conv, 64. Bus. & Prof. Pos: Villas grad. fel, Univ. Wis, 64-65; instr. hist, Univ. Vt, 65-66, asst. prof, 66-70; asst. prof. hist, Wash. Univ, 70- Publ: 'Senator William Borah and Latin America,' Idaho Yesterdays, 65; 'American Labor Overseas,' Nation, 1/67; 'A Conservative Critique of Containment: Senator Taft on the Early Cold War Program' in Containment and Revolution, Beacon Press, 67. Mem: Am. Asn. Univ. Prof; Am. Hist. Asn; Orgn. Am. Historians; NAACP; Am. Civil Liberties Union. Rel: Jewish. Mailing Add: Dept. of History, Washington University, St. Louis, Mo. 63130.

BERGER, JAMES STANLEY R
b. Warren, Pa, 1/3/03; s. C. A. Berger and Harriet Stanley B; m. to Georgianna J. Daniels; c. two. Educ: Kenyon Col; Dickinson Law Sch, LL.B. Polit. & Govt. Pos: Pa. State Sen, 44-67, Senate majority leader, 59-60 & 63-64, minority leader, 61-62, pres. pro tempore, 65-66, dir, Legis. Reference Bur, 67-68; alternate del, Rep. Nat. Conv, 68. Bus. & Prof. Pos: Attorney, admitted to practice before Potter Co. Courts, Supreme Court and Superior Courts, Pa; attorney, private practice, 69- Mailing Add: 2 S. East St, Coudersport, Pa. 16915.

BERGERON, BELVIN FRANCIS D
Chmn, West Baton Rouge Parish Dem. Exec. Cmt, La.
b. West Baton Rouge Parish, La, 10/5/24; s. Willie Joseph Bergeron and Hester Mary Allain B; m. 7/15/50 to Claire Lefebvre; c. Lynette Claire, Debra Anne, David Francis, Amy Geralyn, Yvette Marie, Brian Joseph and Brett Joseph. Educ: La. State Univ, B.S. in bus. admin; Beta Alpha Psi. Polit. & Govt. Pos: Mem, West Baton Rouge Parish Dem. Exec. Cmt, La, 56-, chmn, 64-; sheriff, West Baton Rouge Parish, 60- Mil. Serv: Entered as A/S, Navy, 43, released as Yeoman 1/C, 45, after serv. in Pac. Theater; S.Pac. Campaign Ribbon with One Star. Mem: K. of C; Jr. C. of C; WOW; Am. Legion; VFW; Nat. Sheriffs' Asn; La. Peace Officers Asn; La. Juvenile Officers Asn; Int. Asn. for Identification. Rel: Catholic. Mailing Add: 250 Seventh St, Port Allen, La. 70767. (1967)

BERGERON, LUCIEN E. D
b. Rochester, N.H, 12/26/09; married; c. Ten. Educ: Boston Univ. of Bus. Admin. Polit. & Govt. Pos: N.H. State Sen, 57-68, former Minority Leader, N.H. State Senate. Bus. & Prof. Pos: Gen. ins. agency. Mem: Elks; Moose; K. of C; A.C.A; St. Jean. Rel: Catholic. Mailing Add: 48 Chestnut St, Rochester, N.H. 03867. (1967)

BERGERON, RAYNALD EDWARD D
Chmn, Canton Dem. Town Cmt, Conn.
b. Biddeford, Maine, 9/12/21; s. Edward Andrew Bergeron and Obline Beaupré B; m. 11/28/48 to Eleanor Ann Rasinski; c. Denise Ann and Daniel Edward. Educ: Canton High Sch, 4 years. Polit. & Govt. Pos: Selectman, Canton, Conn, 60-68, pres, Young Dem, Canton; chmn, Canton Dem. Town Cmt, 60. Mil. Serv: Entered as Seaman, Navy, 42, released as CPO, 46, after serv. in Seventh Fleet, Asiatic Theatre, 42-46; Good Conduct Medal; Citation from Secy. Frank Knox; Asiatic Bar with 5 Stars. Mem: Canton Fire Dept; Red Men; Am. Legion. Rel: Catholic. Mailing Add: 66 Bridge St, Collinsville, Conn. 06022.

BERGERUD, ALF L.
Minn. State Sen.
b. Aastad, Minn, 2/2/99. Educ: St. Olaf Col; Univ. of Minn. Polit. & Govt. Pos: Minn. State Rep, 41 & 45-58; Minn. State Sen, 58- Bus. & Prof. Pos: former pres, Red Owl Stores, Inc, Hopkins, Minn; lawyer, firm of Cant, Haverstock, Gray, Plant & Mooty, Minneapolis. Mailing Add: 5100 Ridge Rd, Edina, Minn. 55436.

BERGH, ARNIE D
b. Seattle, Wash, 1931; m. to Shirley B; c. four. Educ: U. of Wash, B.A. Polit. & Gov. Pos: Wash. State Rep, until 66. Bus. & Prof. Pos: Commercial real estate and ins. Mil. Serv: Capt, jet pilot, Air Defense Command, 4 yrs. Mailing Add: 15215 Aurora Ave, Seattle, Wash. 98133. (1967)

BERGHUIS, HENRY EDWIN R
Chmn, Douglas Co. Rep. Party, Minn.
b. Clara City, Minn, 6/29/19; s. Jacob Peter Berghuis and Johanna Elizabeth Nieuwenhuis B; m. 4/1/66 to Ruth Mae Page; c. Daryl Jay and Mary Lou (Mrs. Mulder). Polit. & Govt. Pos: Mayor, Prinsburg, Minn, 51-62; mem, Kandiyohi Co. Rep. Cmt, 54-62; chmn, Douglas Co. Rep. Party, 68- Bus. & Prof. Pos: Partner-mgr, Berghuis Construction Co, 46-; pres. & treas, Alley Construction Co, 68- Mil. Serv: Entered as A/S, Navy, 44, released as Motor Machinist 3/C, 66, after serv. in S.Pac. Mem: Am. Legion. Rel: Protestant. Legal Res: Lake Darling, Alexandria, Minn. 56308. Mailing Add: P.O. Box 652, Alexandria, Minn. 56308.

BERGLAND, BOB SELMER DFL
b. Roseau, Minn, 7/22/28; s. Selmer Bennett Beryland and Mabel Evans B; m. 6/24/50 to Helen Elaine Grahn; c. Dianne, Linda, Stevan, Jon, Allan, Billy and Franklyn. Educ: Univ. Minn, 2 years; Sears Roebuck scholarship. Polit. & Govt. Pos: Secy, Roseau Co. Dem-Farmer-Labor Party, Minn, 51-52, chmn, 53-54; chmn, Minn. State Agr. Stabilization & Conserv. Serv. Cmt, U.S. Dept. Agr, 61-62, dir. Midwest Area Agr. Stabilization & Conserv. Serv, 63-68; cand, U.S. House Rep, 68. Bus. & Prof. Pos: Field Rep, Minn. Farmers Union, 48-50; farmer, 50- Mem: Mason; Lions; Minn. Farmers Union; Nat. Farmers Orgn. Gold Letter A, Univ. Minn. Rel: Lutheran. Mailing Add: Route 3, Roseau, Minn. 56751.

BERGMAN, IRVIN LESTER R
Iowa State Rep.
b. Harris, Iowa, 1/5/11; s. John Albert Bergman and Tena Miller B; m. 2/25/33 to Vera Lucille Donnenwerth; c. John Harvey, Judith Ann (Mrs. Carrico) and Mary Kathryn. Educ: Harris Consolidated Sch, Harris, Iowa, 12 years. Polit. & Govt. Pos: Pres, Harris Consolidated Sch. Bd, Iowa, 40-57 and Osceola Co. Sch. Bd, 57-65; mem, Town Coun, Harris, 57-67; Iowa State Rep, Lyon and Osceola Counties, 67- Bus. & Prof. Pos: Farmer; mem. adv. bd, Area Voc. Sch. at Sheldon at time of orgn; mem, Rural Area Develop. Bd, Osceola Co; dir, Osceola Co. Farmers Mutual Ins. Asn; dir, Osceola Co. Fair Bd; secy, Harris Vol. Fire Dept; pres, secy. and treas, Harris Commun. Club, 60- Mem: Farm Bur; PTA. Rel: Lutheran. Mailing Add: Box 116, Harris, Iowa 51345.

BERGMAN, NELL JOSEPHINE D
V.Chmn, Second Cong. Dist. Dem. Orgn, Colo.
b. Glenwood Springs, Colo, 3/19/09; d. Lawrence Walgenbach Lawless and

Katherine Schultz L; m. 4/3/29 to Ralph Edwin Bergman (deceased); c. Edwin and Robert. Educ: Parks Sch. of Bus, Denver, Colo, grad, 28. Polit. & Govt. Pos: Charter mem, Colo. Dem. Century Club, Adams Co. Adem Club and Adams Co. Jane Jefferson Club; del, state, cong. and co. conv, 20 years; precinct committeewoman, Adams Co. Dem. Party, 50-69; Dem. representative dist. chmn, 60-66; mem, Colo. Dem. State Cent. Cmt, 60-69; Adams Co. chmn, Rural Am. for Johnson and Humphrey, 64 and Volunteers for 66; chmn, first John Fitzgerald Kennedy Birthday Dinner for fund raising, 66; pres, Adams Co. Jane Jefferson Club, 67; nat. del, Womens Conf, Wash, D.C, 67; del, Colo. State Janes Seminar, 67, 68 & 69; area chmn, Dem. Party, 68; chmn, Campaign Conf. Womens Activities, Wash, D.C, 68; del, Victory for 68, Utah; conducted four Janes Workshops for pres, 69; v.chmn, Second Cong. Dist. Dem. Orgn, Colo, 69- Mem: Bd. dirs, Adams Co. Ment. Health Asn, secy-treas, 68; bd. trustees, Adams Co. Ment Health Center Found, secy-treas, 69; leader, Home Demonstration Club, 35-37; pres, Brighton Parents and Teachers, 40, parent teacher health chmn, 40-42; vol. Grey Lady for Red Cross, Fitzsimons Hosp, 42-45; bd. dirs, House of Neighborly Serv; bd. trustees, Adams Co. Libr, 62-63, secy, 67-68; regional chmn, Cath. Rural Life, 64; State Fedn. of Janes rep, Colo. Coord. Coun. of Womens Orgn, 68-69; perpetual mem, Altar and Rosary Soc, Brighton; hon. life mem, Green Valley Grange, Brighton; Farmers Union; Wheat Growers Asn. Mother Award, Future Farmers of Am; Regional Farm Homemaker of the Year, 66. Rel: Catholic; Mem. bd. dirs, Local Cath. Church Coun, 69, mem, Commun. Serv. Cmt. Legal Res: 19251 E. Bridge St, Brighton, Colo. 80601. Mailing Add: Route 1, Box 253, Brighton, Colo. 80601.

BERGMAN, PATRICIA ZOE D
b. Challis, Idaho, 1/5/41; d. Walt H. Hill and Hazel Hamblen H; m. 3/21/60 to Sterling Chase Bergman; separated; c. Valerie Hope. Educ: Westminster Col. Polit. & Govt. Pos: Secy-receptionist, House Educ. and Labor Cmt, 61-62; legis. asst. to U.S. Rep. Robert L. Leggett, 63-65; exec. secy. to U.S. Rep. Frank E. Evans, 65-66; secy. to Dir. Cong. Rels, Off. Econ. Opportunity, 66-68. Bus. & Prof. Pos: Bookkeeper, Bldg. & Construct. Trades Dept, AFL-CIO, 62-63. Rel: Episcopal. 1967 Legal Res: Falls Church, Va. No mailing address available. (1967)

BERKE, FRED H. DFL
b. Corona, S.Dak, 1911; m; c. two. Polit. & Govt. Pos: Acct, City of Litchfield, Minn; Mayor of Litchfield, 60-62; Minn. State Rep, 62-66. Bus & Prof. Pos: Printer, publisher. Mil. Serv: Navy, 42-45. Mailing Add: 236 N. Sibley, Litchfield, Minn. 55355.

BERKES, MILTON D
Pa. State Rep.
b. Phila, Pa, 9/29/24; s. Morris Berkes and Rose Latinsky B; m. 6/8/46 to Ethel Weintraub; c. Marcy, Eileen, Howard and Alan. Educ: Temple Univ, B.S. in educ, 49, M.Ed, 53. Polit. & Govt. Pos: Committeeman, Dem. Party, Pa, 54-62; chmn. bd. supvr, Falls Twp, Pa, 56 & 58-65, supvr, 56-, supt, 63-; founder and former chmn, Regional Coop. Coun, 58-60; campaign mgr, Michener for Cong. Cmt, 62; del, Dem. Nat. Conv, 64; mem. exec. cmt, Bucks Co. Dem. Party, 64-66, co. chmn, 68-69; Pa. State Rep, currently; mem, State Policy Cmt, Pa. State Cmt, 68-69. Bus. & Prof. Pos: Teacher and sch. guidance counselor, Phila. Sch. Dist, 49-62. Mil. Serv: Entered as Pvt, Army, 43, released as T/3, 46, after serv. in Signal Corps, Asiatic Pac. Theater, 44-46; Phillippine Liberation Ribbon with 2 Bronze Stars; Asiatic Pac. Theatre Serv. Medal with 3 Bronze Stars; Meritorious Unit Award; Am. Theater Serv, Victory and Good Conduct Medals. Publ: 'We Can Work Together,' Pa. Mag, 62. Mem: Regional Conf. Elected Officials; v.pres, Bucks Co. Asn. of Twp. Officials, 59-60; bd. dirs, United Fund; Am. Legion; Jewish War Veterans; v.pres, YMHA, Levittown; former dir, Regional Pub. Libr. Rel: Jewish; Dir, Temple Shalom of Levittown. Mailing Add: 56 Palm Lane, Levittown, Pa. 19054.

BERKING, MAX D
b. N.Y.C, N.Y, 7/27/17; m. to Dorothy Noyes, wid; c. Charles, Peter, Laurence and Charlotte. Educ: Williams Col, 39; Univ. Ariz. Bus. Sch. Polit. & Govt. Pos: Asst. to chmn, Fair Employ. Practice Cmt, World War II; campaign dir, Int. Rescue Cmt; bd. of the Am. Cmt. on Africa; Dem. chmn, Rye, N.Y; N.Y. State Sen, 65; Dem. nominee for co. exec, Westchester Co, 69. Bus. & Prof. Pos: Pres, Max Berking, Inc, indust. advert. and mkt, N.Y.C. Publ: Strengthening the Wisconsin Legislature, Rutgers Univ, 69. Mem: Am. Mkt. Asn; Williams Club of N.Y; Manursing Island Club; bd. of Urban League of Westchester; founder and co-chmn, Rye Coun. of Human Rights. Rel: Congregational. Mailing Add: Drake-Smith Lane, Rye, N.Y. 10580.

BERKLEY, RICHARD L. R
Chmn, Jackson Co. Rep. Cmt, Mo.
b. Kansas City, Mo, 6/29/31; s. Walter J. Berkowitz and Erni Stulz B; m. 9/11/58 to Janis Elaine Doppler; c. Elizabeth Claire. Educ: Harvard Col, B.A, 53, Harvard Grad. Sch. of Bus. Admin, M.B.A, 57; Hasty-Pudding Inst. of 1770. Polit. & Govt. Pos: Gov, Citizens Asn, 63-66; pres, Jackson Co. Young Rep, Mo, 64-65; alternate del, Rep. Nat. Conv, 64, del. and secy. Mo. del, 68; chmn, Jackson Co. Rep. Cmt, 65-; mem, Mo. Rep. State Cmt, 66-68; mem, City Coun, Kansas City, Mo, 69- Bus. & Prof. Pos: Dir, Mercantile Bank & Trust Co, 61-67; treas. and dir, Tension Envelope Corp, 66- Mil. Serv: Entered as Seaman Recruit, Navy, 53, released as Lt.(jg), 55, after serv. in Iceland. Mem: Dir. Mus. of Sci. & Indust; Kansas City C. of C; former chmn, Gr. Kansas City Tennis Patrons; bd. mem, Urban League; chmn, 1969 Multiple Sclerosis Hope Chest Gr. Kansas City; Oakwood Country Club; Rockhill Tennis Club; Kansas City Athletic Club; Tower Tennis Club; N.Y. Harvard Club; Capitol Hill Club. Rel: Jewish. Legal Res: 5318 Locust St, Kansas City, Mo. 64110. Mailing Add: c/o Tension Envelope Corporation, 19th and Campbell Sts, Kansas City, Mo. 64108.

BERLA, MICHAEL J. D
b. 7/18/30; s. Julian E. Berla and Freda Hauptmann B; m. 8/23/52 to Nancy Ruth Turner; c. Timothy Scott, Susan, Julie Ann, Tobias Michael. Educ: Oberlin Col, B.A, 48-52; Univ. of Mich, M.A, econ, 52-54. Polit. & Govt. Pos: Admin. asst, Rep. Vivian, Mich. Bus. & Prof. Pos: Film supvr, Univ. of Mich. TV, 56-64. Mil. Serv: U.S. Army, 54-56. Legal Res: 3135 Dolph Dr, Ann Arbor, Mich. 48103. (1967)

BERLE, ADOLF AUGUSTUS D
Hon. Chmn, Liberal Party, N.Y.
b. Boston, Mass, 1/29/95; s. Adolf A. Berle and Mary Augusta Wright B; m. 12/17/27 to Beatrice Bend Bishop; c. Alice (Mrs. Crawford), Beatrice (Mrs. Meyerson) and Peter A.A. Educ: Harvard Univ, A.B, 13, A.M, 14 and LL.B, 16. Polit. & Govt. Pos: Expert on staff, Am. Cmn. to Negotiate Peace with Germany, Versailles Peace Conf, 18-19; financial adv, Am. Embassy, Havana, Cuba, 33; spec. counsel to Reconstruction Finance Corp, 33-38; chamberlain, N.Y.C, 34-38; U.S. Del, Interam. Conf. for Maintenance Peace, Buenos Aires, Argentina, 36-37; U.S. Del, Eighth Interam. Conf, Lima, Peru, 38; Asst. Secy. of State, 38-44; mem. U.S. Del, Spec. Interam. Conf, Havana, Cuba, 40 and Chapultepec, Mex, 45; chmn. U.S. Del. to and pres, Int. Conf. on Civil Aviation, Chicago, 44; U.S. Ambassador to Brazil, 45-46; chmn, Liberal Party, N.Y, 47-55, hon. chmn, 55-; spec. asst. to Secy. of State, U.S, 61; chmn, President Kennedy's Task Force on Latin Am, 61. Bus. & Prof. Pos: Clerk, Brandeis, Dunbar and Butter, Mass, 17 and Round, Hatch, Dillingham and Debevoise, N.Y, 20-24; partner, Lippitt and Berle, 24-29; from prof. to emer. prof, Columbia Univ, 27-; sr. partner, Berle and Berle and predecessor companies, 29-; dir, Savings Banks Trust Co, 32-38, counsel, 38-; trustee and chmn. bd, Twentieth Century Fund, 35-; dir, treas. and chmn. bd, SuCrest Corp, 46-65; dir, Nationwide Corp. and Mich. Life Ins. Co, 56- Mil. Serv: Entered as Pvt, Army, 17, released as 1st Lt, 19, after serv. in inf. Publ: American Economic Republic; The Twentieth Century Capitalist Revolution; The Modern Corporation and Private Property. Mem: Asn. of Bar, City of N.Y; N.Y. State Bar Asn; Am. Acad. of Arts and Sci; Am. Philos. Asn; Am. Philos. Soc; Army and Navy Club; Century Asn; Coun. on For. Rels; Harvard Club of N.Y.C; Pan Am. Soc. of U.S; Players. Hon. mem, Phi Beta Kappa. Rel: Congregational. Legal Res: 142 E. 19th St, New York, N.Y. 10003. Mailing Add: 70 Pine St, New York, N.Y. 10005.

BERLE, PETER ADOLF AUGUSTUS D
N.Y. State Assemblyman
b. N.Y.C, 12/8/37; s. Adolf A. Berle and Beatrice Bishop B; m. 5/30/60 to Lila Wilde; c. Adolf Augustus, Mary Alice and Beatrice Lila. Educ: Harvard Col, B.A. cum laude, 58; Harvard Law Sch, LL.B, 64; Fly Club. Polit. & Govt. Pos: White House staff asst, Food for Peace, Nat. Security Coun, summers, 62-63; consult, Econ. Opportunity, Wash, D.C, 65; N.Y. State Assemblyman, 64th Assembly Dist, N.Y. Co, 69- Bus. & Prof. Pos: Teaching fel. in econ, Harvard Univ, 63-64; Attorney-at-law, Paul, Weiss, Goldberg, Rifkind, Wharton & Garrison, 64- Mil. Serv: Entered as 2nd Lt, Air Force, 58, released as 1st Lt, 61, after serv. in 13th Air Force, Pac. Air Force, 59-61; Capt. Master Parachutist, Air Force, Res, at present; Air Force Commendation Medal Vietnam Serv. Ribbon. Publ: 'The Role of the Advisor in South Vietnam,' Reporter Mag, 2/68. Mem: Asn. of the Bar of the City of N.Y. (mem, spec. cmt. on constitutional conv, 67). Rel: Protestant. Mailing Add: 530 E. 86th St, New York, N.Y. 10028.

BERLINER, HENRY A, JR. R
Gen. Counsel, D.C. Rep. Cmt.
b. Washington, D.C, 2/9/34; s. Henry A. Berliner and Josephine Mitchell B; m. 9/16/61 to Bodil Iversen; c. Tina, John and George. Educ: Univ. Mich, A.B, 56; George Wash. Univ. Law Sch, J.D. with honors, 64; Phi Eta Sigma; Sigma Chi. Polit. & Govt. Pos: Mem. exec. cmt, Young Rep. Nat. Fedn, 61-63; mem, D.C. Rep. Cmt, 64-, gen. counsel, 68-; Asst. U.S. Attorney, D.C, 66-67; VIP tour dir, Nixon-Agnew Campaign Cmt, 68; asst. to chmn, Presidential Inaugural Ball, 69. Bus. & Prof. Pos: Secy-treas, Prototypes, Inc, 62-; partner, Berliner & Ward, 67- Mil. Serv: Entered as Ens, Navy, 56, released as Lt, 59, after serv. in Atlantic Fleet Squadron; Lt, Naval Res, 59- Publ: 'State "Buy American" Policies,' George Wash. Law Rev, 3/64; 'Amendments to Federal Tort Claims Act,' 2/67 and 'Stop the War in Washington—the Nixon Anti-Crime Program,' 5/69, D.C. Bar J. Mem: Phi Delta Phi; D.C. Bar Asn.(chmn, young lawyers sect, 68-69); Judicial Conf, 68- Rel: Episcopal. Mailing Add: 2870 Upton St, Washington, D.C. 20008.

BERLINER, HENRY PAUL D
b. Los Angeles, Calif, 6/15/29; s. Josel Berliner and Concepción Paúl B; m. 12/30/50 to Margaret Del Real; c. Cynthia Susan, Leslie Ann, Henry P. Jr. and John Ralph. Educ: Polytech. Inst. Mex, 1 year; Univ. of Calif, Los Angeles, 2 years. Polit. & Govt. Pos: Pub. rels. secy, Machinist Non-Partisan Polit. League, Los Angeles Co, 67-68; legis. chmn, dist. 727 Machinist IAMAW Lodge B, 67-68; first v.pres, Echo Park Dem. Club, 67, third v.pres, 68; labor chmn, Calif. State Assemblyman David Roberti, 68; mem, Calif. Dem. State Cent. Cmt, 68-69; 48th Assembly dist. chmn, AFL-CIO Cmt. on Polit. Educ, 68-69. Mil. Serv: Entered as Pvt, Army, 51, released as Pfc, 54, after serv. in 8055th Div, Korea; Korean, Nat. Defense and UN Serv. Medals. Mem: IAMAW. Rel: Catholic. Mailing Add: 2125 Echo Park Ave, Los Angeles, Calif. 90026.

BERLO, DAVID KENNETH R
Chmn, Ingham Co. Rep. Party, Mich.
b. St. Louis, Mo, 3/28/29; s. Raymond Leo Berlo and Audrey Mary Brucher B; m. 7/28/53 to Patricia Alice Dennis; c. Sandra, David Todd, Maryellen and Andrea. Educ: Univ. Ill, B.A. in Psychol, 53, Ph.D. in Commun, 56; Delta Sigma Rho; Phi Sigma Phi; Alpha Epsilon Rho. Polit. & Govt. Pos: Chmn, Ingham Co. Rep. Party, Mich, currently; v.chmn, Mich. State Cmt. Arts, Professions and Sci, currently. Bus. & Prof. Pos: Prof. and chmn. dept. commun, Mich. State Univ, 56- Mil. Serv: Entered as Basic Airman, Air Force, 61, released as S/Sgt, 64, after serv. in Human Resources Research Center Training Command, 61-64. Publ: The Process of Communication, Holt, 60; Communication Within the University, Ill. State Univ, 64; Berlo Managerial Communication Film Series, five films, Bur. Nat. Affairs, 66. Mem: Am. Psychol. Asn; Am. Sociol. Asn; Am. Asn. for Pub. Opinion Research; Asn. for Educ. in Journalism; Speech Asn. Am; Am. Asn. Adv. Sci. Rel: Protestant. Mailing Add: 828 Tanglewood Dr, East Lansing, Mich. 48823.

BERMAN, ARTHUR LEONARD D
Ill. State Rep.
b. Chicago, Ill, 5/4/35; s. Morris Berman and Jean Glast B; m. 6/22/60 to Sondra; c. Adam Elliott and Marcy Ellen. Educ: Univ. Ill, Urbana, B.S, 56; Northwest. Univ. Sch. Law, LL.B, 58; Phi Epsilon Pi; Tau Epsilon Rho. Polit. & Govt. Pos: Spec. attorney, Ill. Dept. Ins, 64-67; spec. asst. to Ill. Attorney Gen, 67-68; Ill. State Rep, 69- Bus. & Prof. Pos: Gen. practice of law, 58-

Publ: 2 articles, Northwest. Univ. Law Rev. Mem: V.pres, 50th Ward Regular Dem. Orgn; dir, North Town Commun. Coun; dir, Bernard Horwich Jewish Commun. Center; past pres, West Rogers Park B'nai B'rith; past pres, 50th Ward Young Dem. Rel: Jewish. Legal Res: 2701 W. Sherwin Ave, Chicago, Ill. 60645. Mailing Add: 188 W. Randolph St, Chicago, Ill. 60601.

BERMAN, FREDERIC SANFORD D
b. N.Y.C, 3/7/27; m. to Joan H. Berman, wid; c. James Ronald and Anthony Roger. Educ: Columbia Col, A.B, 49; N.Y. Law Sch, LL.B, 51. Polit. & Govt. Pos: Asst. counsel, N.Y.C. Housing and Redevelop. Bd, 60-62; gen. counsel, N.Y.C. Dept. of Real Estate, 62-64; N.Y. State Sen, 64-65; Cmnr. of Rent and Housing Maintenance, N.Y.C, 66- Bus. & Prof. Pos: Lawyer; asst. prof. of law, N.Y. Law Sch, 58. Mem: Asn. of the Bar of N.Y.C.(mem. spec. cmt. housing and urban develop); Am. and N.Y. State Bar Asns; Commun. Serv. Soc; Horace Mann Alumni Asn.(past pres); Grand Street Boys Asn. Mailing Add: 1085 Park Ave, New York, N.Y. 10028.

BERMAN, HOWARD LAWRENCE D
Pres, Calif. Fedn. Young Dem.
b. Los Angeles, Calif, 4/15/41; s. Joseph M. Berman and Eleanor Schapiro B; single. Educ: Univ. Calif, Los Angeles, B.A, 62, Sch. Law, LL.B, 65. Polit. & Govt. Pos: Citizenship Clearing House polit. intern, Calif. Dem. Coun, summer 61; pres, Univ. Calif, Los Angeles Young Dem, 61-62; legal intern, Dept. Labor, summer 64; Ford Found. legis. intern, Calif. State Assembly, 65-66; VISTA Vol, Baltimore and San Francisco, 66-67; mem. exec. cmt, Calif. State Dem. Cent. Cmt, 67-; pres, Calif. Fedn. Young Dem, 67-; del, Dem. Nat. Conv, 68; chmn, Youth for Bradley for Mayor, 68-69; mem. steering cmt, South. Calif. Am. for Dem. Action, 68- Bus. & Prof. Pos: Attorney, Levy & Van Bourg, 67- Rel: Jewish. Mailing Add: 1255 N. Harper Ave, Apt. 203, Los Angeles, Calif. 90046.

BERMAN, MALCOLM IRVING R
Maine State Rep.
b. Houlton, Maine, 11/27/24; s. Meyer B. Berman and Kate E. Knabenhoff B; single. Educ: Bowdoin Col; Yale Univ, A.B. in Am. Hist, 48; Oxford Univ; Univ. of N.Mex, LL.B, 52, J.D, 68. Polit. & Govt. Pos: Mem, Town Rep. Cmt, Maine, 56-66; Maine State Rep, 61- house chmn, Cmt. on Judiciary, Maine State House of Rep, 67-; mem, Co. Rep. Cmt, 66. Mem: Am. Bar Asn, sections on Criminal Law, Ins. & Negligence and Gen. Practice; Selden Soc, London; Int. Bar Asn; Elks; Mason. Rel: Jewish. Legal Res: 6 Leonard St, Houlton, Maine 04730. Mailing Add: 40 Court St, Houlton, Maine 04730.

BERMAN, MURIEL M. D
m. to Philip I. Berman; c. Nancy, Nina and Steven. Educ: Univ. Pittsburgh; Cedar Crest Col; Muhlenberg Col; Carnegie Tech. Univ; Pa. State Univ. Col. of Optometry, O.D; Aspen Inst. Humanistic Studies, Colo, 65, Tokyo, Japan, 66. Polit. & Govt. Pos: Non-govt. orgn. del, UNICEF, UN, Thailand, 64, Ethiopia, 66, mem. ad hoc cmts. on Latin Am. and Africa; fact-finding ambassador with advice and consent of U.S. State Dept. to Brazil, Argentina, Chile and Peru with subsequent lectures on probs. and prospects of people there; lectr, UN activities and anal; participant, Art in the Embassies Prog; Dem. Presidential Elector, Pa, 68. Bus. & Prof. Pos: Lectr, series on art; chmn. prog. cmt, Lehigh Valley Educ. TV, producer, Col. Speak-In, weekly series; curator and researcher, Berman Circulating Art Exhib. Publ: Art catalogues. Mem: Trustee, Kutzman State Col.(former v.chmn. bd); trustee and secy. bd. dirs, Lehigh Co. Commun. Col; Conf. for Women Trustees, Col. and Univ. Gov. Bds; founder and donor, Carnegie-Berman Col. Art Slide Lbr. Exchange; co. chmn, Allentown Bi-Centennial, 62; chmn. Great Valley Coun, Girl Scouts; v.pres. and fine-arts chmn, Woman's Club; prog. chmn, For. Policy Asn, Lehigh Co, Pa; nat. bd, Hadassah; art appreciation dir. and lectr, Allentown Art Mus. Auxiliary; treas, Annual Symphony Ball; mem. bd, Baum Art Sch; League of Women Voters; YWCA; hon. chmn, Bucks Co. Collectors Art Show, New Hope, 66; sponsor, Lehigh Co. Cultural Center; Dieruff High Sch. Art Adv. Cmt; Wellesley Club; bd. of Phila. Chamber Symphony; Art Collectors Club of Am; Am. Fedn. of Art; Friends of Whitney Mus; Archives of Am. Art; Mus. of Primitive Art; Allentown Art Mus; Lehigh Co. Hist. Soc; Reading Art Mus; Jewish Mus; Metrop. Opera Guild; Lincoln Center. Woman of Valor citation from Bonds for Israel. Mailing Add: 20 Hundred Nottingham Rd, Allentown, Pa. 18103.

BERMAN, PHILIP I. D
b. Pennsburg, Pa, 6/28/15; s. Joseph Berman and Dora Feingold B; m. 10/20/42 to Dr. Muriel Mallin; c. Nancy, Nina and Steven. Educ: Ursinus Col, 32-33; Beta Gamma Sigma. Hon. LL.D, Ursinus Col, 68; hon. L.H.D, Lehigh Univ, 69. Polit. & Govt. Pos: Rep, Small Bus. Asn, Pa. Region, 64-68, mem. nat. adv. coun, 68-70; Presidential Elector, Pa, 64; U.S. State Dept. del, 43rd UN Econ. and Soc. Coun. Meeting, Geneva, Switz, 67; alternate del, Dem. Nat. Conv, 68. Bus. & Prof. Pos: Pres, Hess's Allentown, Pa, 68-; underwriting mem, Lloyd's of London, 68-; chmn. bd, Commonwealth Indust, 69- Mil. Serv: Entered as Pvt, Marine Corps Res, 42, released as Chief Warrant Officer, 45; Unit Decoration. Mem: Soc. Automotive Engrs. Outstanding Civic Leader of Am, 68. Rel: Jewish. Mailing Add: 20 Hundred Nottingham Rd Allentown, Pa. 18103.

BERMINGHAM, JOHN RUTLEDGE R
Colo. State Sen.
b. Chicago, Ill, 11/7/23; s. Edward J. Bermingham and Katherine Carpenter B; m. 12/11/54 to Marcia Dines, div; c. John R, Jr, Katherine D. and Andrew W. Educ: Yale Univ, B.E, 44; Columbia Univ, LL.B, 49; Phi Gamma Delta. Polit. & Govt. Pos: Spec. asst. attorney gen, N.Y.C, 52-53; GOP precinct committeeman, Denver, Colo; Colo. State Sen, 65- Mil. Serv: Entered Navy, 43, released as Ens, 46. Mem: Am. Bar Asn. Rel: Episcopal. Mailing Add: 601 Franklin St, Denver, Colo. 80218.

BERNABUCCI, JOHN ROGER, JR. R
N.Dak. State Rep.
b. Jamestown, N.Dak, 8/9/30; s. John Roger Bernabucci and Mary Schwader B; m. 11/8/52 to Geraldine Isabelle DesJardins; c. Mary Therese and Paul Anthony. Educ: Univ. of N.Dak, B.S, 52; Tau Kappa Epsilon, UND Letterman's Club. Polit. & Govt. Pos: Precinct committeeman, Stutsman Co. Rep. Cmt, N.Dak, 56-66, finance chmn, 57-60, chmn, 61-; del, N.Dak. Rep. Conv, 60, 62 & 64; del. and mem. credentials cmt, Rep. Nat. Conv, 64; N.Dak. State Rep, 66- Mem: Am. Bottlers of Carbonated Beverages; Stutsman Co. Fair Asn. (dir, 62-); N.Dak. Bottler's Asn.(dir, 60-); C. of C.(dir, Jamestown Chap, 62-64, pres, 64); Lions; Elks; Mason; Shrine; Jamestown Country Club; Aircraft Owners & Pilots Asn. Rel: Lutheran. Mailing Add: 709 Fourth Ave. S.E, Jamestown, N.Dak. 58401.

BERNAL, JOE J. D
Tex. State Sen.
b. 1927. Educ: Trinity Univ, B.A; Our Lady of the Lake Col, M.Ed; Tex. Tech; N.Mex. A&M. Polit. & Govt. Pos: Tex. State Rep, 59th Legis; Tex. State Sen, 67- Bus. & Prof. Pos: Former teacher; exec. dir, Guadalupe Commun. Center. Mailing Add: 1801 Durango, San Antonio, Tex. 78207.

BERNARD, BETTY HILL R
First V.Pres, Ark. Fedn. Rep. Women
b. Atlanta, Tex, 2/11/32; d. Troy David Hill and Mary Sparkman H; m. 11/26/53 to Charles Taylor Bernard; c. Sallie Hill, Mary Troy, Charles Taylor, Jr. David Wesley and John Harbert. Educ: Baylor Univ, A.B; Wash. & Jefferson Col; Centenary Col; Athenean Club. Polit. & Govt. Pos: Committeewoman, Ark. State Rep, Party, 66-; mem, Crittenden Co. Rep. Recommendations Cmt, 66-; mem, Crittenden Co. Rep. Cmt, 66-; first v.pres, Ark. Rep. Fedn. Women, 67-; alternate del, Rep. Nat. Conv, 68; pres, Earle Rep. Women's Club, 68- Bus. & Prof. Pos: Pres, Bernard One Hour Martinizing Corps. Rel: Southern Baptist. Mailing Add: Bernard Farms, Earle, Ark. 72331.

BERNARD, CHARLES TAYLOR R
Finance dir, Ark. State Rep. Party.
b. Helena, Ark, 9/10/27; s. Charles LaFayette Bernard and Sallie McGhee B; m. 11/26/53 to Betty Ann Hill; c. Sallie Hill, Mary Troy, Charles Taylor, Jr, David Wesley and John Harbert. Educ: Baylor Univ, B.A; Delta Sigma Pi; Tryon Coterie; Baylor C. of C. Hon. LL.D, Shorter Col. Polit. & Govt. Pos: Mem, Crittenden Co. Welfare Bd, Ark, 54-56; mem. city coun, Earle, Ark, 56-62; Chmn, Crittenden Co. Rep. Party, 66-68; mem, Ark. State Rep. Party Exec. Cmt, 66-; treas, Ark. State Rep. Party, 66-68 and finance dir, 69-; Cand. U.S. Sen, 68; mem. Ark. State Banking Cmn, currently. Bus. & Prof. Pos: Mem. bd. and secy, South. Baptist Col, Ark, 60- and secy, 60-66. Mil. Serv: Entered as Seaman 1/C, Navy, 45, released as Seaman 1/C, 46. Mem: Exec.bd. and v.pres, East. Ark. Area Boy Scout Am; exec. cmt. region 5, Boy Scouts Am; Nat. Coun. Boy Scouts Am; exec. bd, Baptist Conv. Ark; dir, Earle State Bank; Mason (32°); past pres, Earle Rotary Club; past pres, Southern Cotton Ginners Asn. Rel: Baptist. Mailing Add: 1000 Main St, Earle, Ark. 72331.

BERNARD, DONALD JOSEPH D
Maine State Sen.
b. Floral Park, N.Y, 9/6/35; s. L. Bernard and Yvonne M. Cloutier B; m. 4/25/59 to Anita Clemence Shaw; c. Troy Donald and Glenn George. Educ: Miss. South. Univ; Fla. State Univ, currently. Polit. & Govt. Pos: Maine State Rep, 67-68; Maine State Sen, 69- Bus. & Prof. Pos: Pres, Skin Divers Paradise, Salvage Diving Co, 59-66. Mil. Serv: Entered as Pvt, Air Force, 53, released as S/Sgt, 57; S/Sgt, Air Force Res; Nat. Defense, 2 Korean and Good Conduct Medals. Publ: 'Oyster Hunt,' Underwater Naturalist, 62; 'Annex-Civil Defense,' State Civil Defense, 66. Mem: Am. Littoral Soc.(past pres, Maine Chap); Maine Marine Explorers Scuba Club.(pres); bd. exam. for Northeast. U.S. for certifying prfnl. scuba instrs, 68- and Nat. Bd. of Educ, Nat. Asn. of Skin Diving Schs; AF&AM. U.S. Air Force Swimming Team Coach, 54-57. Mailing Add: R.F.D. 3, Turner Rd, Auburn, Maine 04210.

BERNARD, MARY ELIZABETH D
N.H. State Rep.
b. Dover, N.H, 9/20/05; d. Arthur Peter O'Gorman and Margaret Donnelly O; m. 6/29/35 to Albert O. Bernard. Educ: McIntosh Bus. Col, Dover, N.H, 23; Carney Hosp. Sch. of Nursing, Boston, Mass, R.N; Carney Hosp. Alumnae. Polit. & Govt. Pos: Supvr. check lists, Dover, N.H, 63-; mem, Dover City Dem. Cmt, 63-; mem, N.H. Order Women Legislators, 67-; N.H. State Rep, 67-, mem. pub. health cmt, N.H. House Rep, mem. pub. health and welfare cmt, 69-; mem, Strafford Co. Home and Bldg. Cmt, 69; clerk, Dover Co. Dem. Del, 69- Bus. & Prof. Pos: Bookkeeper, A.O. Bernard, Bldg. Contractor, 35-52; real estate agent, 35-; writer, Women's Pages, Boston Globe, 56. Mem: Cath. Daughters Am.(trustee); Sacred Heart (court); St. Mary's Altar and Rosary Socs; Hibernians Ladies Auxiliary (pres); Dover Point Commun. Club (treas); collector, Cath. charities and cancer drives. Rel: Catholic. Mailing Add: 121 Portland Ave, Dover, N.H. 03820.

BERNARD, PETER D
b. Ashland, Maine, 5/20/05; s. Mitchell Bernard and Sophia Clark B; m. Feb. 1946 to Hilda H. Ames; c. Edward Beesley, Mary McGinn, Harold Beesley and Joan Ranks. Educ: Northeast. Univ, $1\frac{1}{2}$ years; Rutgers Univ, 1 year. Polit. & Govt. Pos: Dir, Sch. Bd, SAD, 31, 62-; mem, Enfield Sch. Bd, 60-62, chmn, 62-63; former Maine State Sen, Penobscot Co, former chmn, Senate Legis. Cmt. on Bus, Legis. Interim Senate Apportionment Cmt. and Interim Corridor Rd. Cmt. and former mem, Legis. Cmt. on Towns and Counties. Bus. & Prof. Pos: Owner, Bernard's Hardware, 45; mem, Bd. of Trade, Enfield Howland, 46-; dir, Howland Enfield Develop. Corp, 55- Rel: Catholic. Mailing Add: Box 18, West Enfield, Maine 04493. (1967)

BERNARD, SPENCER THOMAS D
Okla. State Rep.
b. Rush Springs, Okla, 2/5/15; s. Cicero Edgar Bernard and Gertrude Sperling B; m. 8/3/35 to Vivian Opal Dorman; c. Kay Ann. Educ: High Sch, Rush Springs, Okla, 33. Polit. & Govt. Pos: Mem, Wheat Adv. Cmt. to the Secy. of Agr, Wash, D.C; Okla. State Rep, 61- Mem: Lions; Am. Bus. Club; Okla. Cattlemen Asn; Farmers Union; Red Red Rose. Rel: Church of Christ. Mailing Add: Box 158, Rush Springs, Okla. 73082. (1967)

BERNASCONI, FIDELE JOSEPH R
Treas, Souhegan Young Rep, N.H.
b. Milford, N.H, 3/18/31; s. Pierre John Bernasconi and Eva Liberty B; div; c. Michael Charles, Kim Elizabeth, Troy Jay and Todd Russell. Educ: Northeast. Univ. Polit. & Govt. Pos: Pres, Milford Young Rep, N.H, 54-58; mem. adv. cmt, Milford Rep. Town Cmt, 58-60, dist. chmn, 64-; alternate del, Rep.

Nat. Conv, 64; treas, Souhegan Young Rep, 66-; mem, Citizens Adv. Cmt. for N.H. Gov. Coun, Fourth Dist, 69- Mil. Serv: Entered as Pvt, Army, 53, released as Sgt, 55, after serv. in Artillery, ETO; Korean Nat. Defense Ribbon; German Occupation Ribbon; Good Conduct Medal; Sharpshooter MI Rifle Expert Medal 45 Pistol. Mem: Pres, Milford PTA, 59-60; Sportsmans Clubs; coach, Babe Ruth League. Rel: Congregational. Mailing Add: 22 Adams St, Milford, N.H. 03055.

BERNAT, LEO ALLEN DFL
b. St. Paul, Minn, 4/13/23; single. Educ: Univ. Minn, B.Chem, 44, Ph.D, 57; A.C.A.S, Casualty Actuarial Soc. Polit. & Govt. Pos: Chmn, land use cmt, Second Ward Dem-Farmer-Labor Club; cand. for Minn. State Rep; cand. for alderman, Second Ward, Minneapolis; staff mem, Cmn. on Human Develop; employee and consult, Minneapolis Fair Employ. Practices Cmn; consult. to Ramsey Co. Attorney; consult. to Minn. Dept. Employ. Security. Bus. & Prof. Pos: Research asst. in agronomy, Univ. Minn, 47-68, instr, 62-67; research analyst, Minn. Dept. of Employ. Security, 49-56; consult, Minn. Research Assocs, 55-; bus. rep, Univ. of Minn. Employees Local 1958, 61-66. Publ: Should I as a Public Employee Coordinate My PERA Program with Social Security: An Analysis of Relevant Factors, Int. Union Operation Engrs. Local 967, 67; 'From Guild to Labor Union,' Guthrie Theatre play guide for The Shoemaker's Holiday; 'Riot, Baby, Riot,' Minnesota Teacher, 3 part series, 67-68; plus others. Mem: Am. Statist. Asn; Indust. Rels. Research Asn; Am. Asn. Adv. Sci; Minn. Acad. Sci; Int. Asn. Personnel in Employ. Security; Int. Actuarial Asn; Biometrics Soc; Nat. Planning Asn; Am. Acad. Polit. & Soc. Sci; Am. Risk and Ins. Asn; Ins. Soc. of N.Y; Labor Historians; Midwest. Actuarial Forum; adv, Holmes Area Residents and Property Owners Asn; consult, Motley Area and S. E. Minneapolis Residents and Property Owners Asns; bd. mem, Univ. Dist. Improv. Asn; assoc. mem, S. E. Minneapolis Planning and Coord. Cmt; alternate del, Coun. of Commun. Coun; second ward trustee, United Neighbors; Minn. Citizens Cmt. for Pub. Educ; S. E. All Sports; v.pres, Minn. YMCA Table Tennis Asn; Minn. chapter, Am. Civil Liberties Union; Minneapolis Urban League; NAACP; Am. Contract Bridge League; Minneapolis Capital Long-Range Improv. Cmt. Parks Task Force; treas, Minn. Self-Surv, 55-56; Minn. Fedn. Teachers. Mailing Add: Apt. 2, 503 15th Ave. S.E, Minneapolis, Minn. 55414.

BERNBAUM, MAURICE MARSHALL
b. Chicago, Ill, 2/15/10; m. to Elizabeth Hahn; c. Edwin M. and L. Marcia. Educ: Harvard Univ, S.B, 31; Univ. Chicago, summer, 31; Northwest. Univ, 31-32. Polit. & Govt. Pos: Acct, Dept. Treas, 35; economist, U.S. Tariff Cmn, 35-36; v.consul, For. Serv, 36; v.consul, Vancouver, B.C, 36-37; For. Serv. Sch, 38; v.consul, Singapore, 38-41; v.consul, third and second secy, Caracas, Venezuela, 42-45; second secy. and v.consul, Managua, Nicaragua, 45-48; first secy. and consul, Quito, Ecuador, 48-50; Nat. War Col, 50-51; officer in charge, N. Coast Affairs, 51-53; counsr, Caracas, 53-59; dir, Off. S.Am. Affairs, Dept. of State, 55-59; minister counsr. of embassy, Buenos Aires, Argentina, 59-60; U.S. Ambassador to Ecuador, 60-65 and to Venezuela, 65-69. Bus. & Prof. Pos: Soc. worker, 32-35. Mem: Harvard Club, Wash; Int. Platform Asn. Legal Res: Chicago, Ill. Mailing Add: c/o Mrs. Florentine Hahn, 2401 Calvert St. N.W, Washington, D.C. 20008.

BERNER, ALICE VIOLA D
Secy, Mont. State Dem. Women's Club
b. Wolf Point, Mont, 12/10/28; d. Cleo Reese Cahill and Hazel Nail C; m. 6/25/47 to Harvey F. Berner; c. Jerry Ross, Bonnie Lea, Colleen Kay and Allan Lane. Polit. & Govt. Pos: Regional dir, Mont. State Dem. Women's Club, 60-64, secy 65-; precinct committeewoman, Dem. Party, McLone Co, Mont, 60-69; secy, McLone Dem. Club, 65-69, pres, 69-; del, Dem. Nat. Conv, 68. Mem: Mont. Farmers Union; VFW Auxillary. Rel: Presbyterian. Mailing Add: Star Route 231, Box A25, Wolf Point, Mont. 59201.

BERNING, WILLIAM A. R
Educ: Valparaiso Univ. Polit. & Govt. Pos: Legis, Adv, Cmt, 61-64; Ind. House-66; Rep. Caucus Chmn, 65. Bus. & Prof. Pos: Attorney, Berning & Berning. Mem: Co, State and Am. Bar Asns; Kiwanis Club. Rel: Lutheran Church, Missouri Synod. Mailing Add: 4522 Wilmette, Ft. Wayne, Ind. 46806. (1967)

BERNSTEIN, ABRAHAM D
N.Y. State Sen.
b. New York, N.Y, 5/1/18; m. to Ruth Schub; c. David, Barbara. Educ: City Col. New York, B.S.S; Brooklyn Law Sch, LL.B. Polit. & Govt. Pos: Mem, Affiliated Young Dem; appeal agent, Local Draft Bd; N.Y. State Sen, 60- Bus. & Prof. Pos: Lawyer, Bernstein & Koenigsberg. Mil. Serv: World War II, Army Commendation Ribbon. Mem: Bronx Bar Asn; dir, Pelham Pkwy. Jewish Center; Columbus-Evander Youth & Adult Center; Dis. 11, Bronx House and Zionist Orgn. Am; hon. chmn, Pelham Pkwy. Citizens Coun; Grand Street Boys Asn; Am. Jewish Appeal; N.Y. Fedn. Sr. Citizens Orgn, exec. cmt. officer, Bronxboro Citizens Cmt. on Aging; adv. cmt, Soc. for Children with Emotional Disturbances; past pres, Bernard Mogilesky Lodge B'nai B'rith; United Jewish Appeal; Fedn. of Jewish Philanthropies; Joint Defense Appeal; Muscular Dystrophy. Mailing Add: 660 Thwaites Place, Bronx, N.Y. 10467.

BERNSTEIN, GEORGE KASKEL R
Fed. Ins. Adminstr, Dept. of Housing and Urban Develop.
b. N.Y.C, 9/17/33; s. Herman William Bernstein and Annette Kaskel B; c. James A. and Susan. Educ: Cornell Univ, B.A, 55; Cornell Univ. Law Sch, LL.B, 57; Phi Epsilon Pi; Phi Delta Phi. Polit. & Govt. Pos: Asst. Attorney Gen, N.Y. State Dept. of Law, 57-61; dep. supt. and gen. counsel, N.Y. State Ins. Dept, 64-67, first dep. supt. of ins, 67-69; Fed. Ins. Adminstr, Dept. of Housing and Urban Develop, 69- Bus. & Prof. Pos: Attorney-at-law, 61-64. Mem: N.Y. State Dist. Attorneys' Asn; Asn. of the Bar of the City of N.Y; Leadership Coun, United Jewish Appeal. Rel: Jewish. Legal Res: 2575 Palasades Ave, Riverdale, N.Y. 10463. Mailing Add: 430 M St. S.W, Washington, D.C. 20024.

BERNSTEIN, MYRON RONALD R
Chmn, East Haddam Rep. Town Cmt, Conn.
b. Middletown, Conn, 5/25/32; s. Charles Bernstein and Frances B; single. Educ: Univ. Conn, B.S, 55; Boston Univ. Law Sch, LL.B, 60; Tau Epsilon Phi. Polit. & Govt. Pos: Chmn, East Haddam Rep. Town Cmt, Conn, 61-; del, all legis. dist, state senatorial dist, cong. dist. and state conv, 61- Bus. & Prof. Pos: Dir, Nat. Bank of New Eng, 65- Mil. Serv: Entered as 2nd Lt, Army, 55, released as 1st Lt, 57, after serv. in Far East. Mem: Middletown, Middlesex Co, Conn. and Am. Bar Asns; Lions Int; Mason (32°); Shrine; B'nai B'rith; Am. Legion; Vet. Club. Rel: Jewish. Legal Res: North Moodus Rd, Moodus, Conn. 06469. Mailing Add: Plains Rd, Moodus, Conn. 06469. (1967)

BERRA, PAUL M. D
b. St. Louis, Mo, 2/2/25; m. 6/25/50 to Elizabeth Catherine Gilroy; c. Paul Gerald, Richard Lawrence and Ann Marie. Educ: St. Louis Univ. Sch. Commerce and Finance. Polit. & Govt. Pos: Mo. State Rep, 53-64; Mo. State Sen, 64-66; former committeeman, 24th Ward Dem. Party; del, Dem. Nat. Conv, 68. Bus. & Prof. Pos: Bookkeeper; operator Howard Johnson restaurant; dir, Southwest Bank. Mil. Serv: Army, 43-46, ETO. Mem: Am. Legion; post commander, 48-49; 40 et 8; VFW; Past Commanders Club; Improved Order of Red Men; Prfnl. and Bus. Men of the Hill. St. Louis Globe-Dem. Award, Third Most Valuable Legislator, 62; St. Louis Globe-Dem. Award, Second Most Valuable Legislator, 64; Speaker's Award, Most Outstanding Dem, 63. Rel: Catholic, St. Ambrose Church, dir. sch. bd. Mailing Add: 4945a Daggett Ave, St. Louis, Mo. 63110. (1967)

BERRINGER, ST. CLAIR A. R
N.H. State Rep.
b. Lunenburg, Nova Scotia, Can, 8/3/02; married. Educ: Lunenburg Acad; Northeast. Univ, Boston. Polit. & Govt. Pos: N.H. State Rep, currently. Bus. & Prof. Pos: Retired. Mem: Parker Lodge No. 97; Pemigewasset Chap. No. 13; Omega Coun. No. 9 RSM. Rel: Protestant. Mailing Add: P.O. Box 304, N. Woodstock, N.H. 03262.

BERRONG, ED D
Okla. State Sen.
b. Hinton, Okla, 4/17/15; s. Jesse H. Berrong and Alma Jane Dodd B; m. 5/28/38 to Winnie Ola Post; c. Ed, Jr, Mark D. and Brad. Educ: Southwest. State Col, 33-37, A.B, 37; Univ. Okla, 37-38; Okla. City Col. Law, 43-44. Polit. & Govt. Pos: Mayor, Weatherford, Okla, 49-58; Okla. State Sen, Sixth and 27th Dist, 59- Bus. & Prof. Pos: Pres, two corp, Weatherford and Elk City, Okla, 59- and 64-; mem. bd, several corp; pres, two indust. found, Weatherford, 66- Mil. Serv: Entered as A/S, Naval Res, 44, released Lt.(jg), 46, after serv. in S.W. Pac, 45-46. Mem: Okla. Bar Asn; Independent Ins. Agent's Asn. Mem: Am. Legion; VFW; C. of C. Rel: Methodist. Legal Res: 507 N. 5th, Weatherford, Okla. 73096. Mailing Add: Box 268, Weatherford, Okla. 73096.

BERRY, CHARLES EDWARD D
Ga. State Rep.
b. Columbus, Ga, 7/16/08; s. Turner Edmonds Berry and Annie Belle Lynch B; m. 4/28/34 to Martha Louise Bartlett (deceased), m. Mildred Hogan Holleman, 10/13/68; c. Charles Edward, Jr, William Turner Mary Patricia. Educ: Univ. of the South, A.B, 29; Delta Tau Delta; Red Ribbon Soc, Univ. of the South. Polit. & Govt. Pos: Mayor pro tem, Columbus, Ga, 54, mayor, 55, city cmnr, 54-60, exec. bd. emer. of City of Columbus for life; mem, State Dem. Exec. Cmt, Ga; Ga. State Rep, 65-, v.chmn, Gen. Banking, Banks and Banking and Civil Defense, Defense and Vet. Affairs Legis. Cmt, currently; mem. ways & means cmt, Lt. Col. Gov. Staff of Ga. and Ala, currently; v. chmn, Ga. Cmn. for Develop. of Chattahoochee River Basin, currently. Bus. & Prof. Pos: Merchandise mgr, Kirven's 31-42; partner.mgr, Columbus Fixture Mfg. Co, 43-63, v. pres-treas, 63-67, retired; v.pres, Trust Co. of Columbus, Ga, 69- Mil. Serv: Entered as A/S, Navy, 44, released as Seaman 2/C, 44. Mem: Hon. life mem, Ga. Munic. Asn; Lt. Col, Gov. Staff; Mason; Elks; Moose; Lions; trustee, Ga. Hosp. Serv. Asn; mem. bd. mgt, Armed Serv. YMCA, 54-66, chmn, 55; dir, Cerebral Palsy Asn; life mem. and past dir. comdr, Am. Legion; 40 et 8; past dir, C. of C; Assoc. Industs. of Ga; Am. Numismatic Asn; former dir, Chattahoochee Valley Fair Asn; former trustee, Trinity Sch, Inc. Rel: Episcopal; Former Vestryman and Jr. Warden, St. Thomas Episcopal Church. Legal Res: 2516 Harding Dr, Columbus, Ga. 31906. Mailing Add: P.O. Box 1422, Columbus, Ga. 31902.

BERRY, CHARLES FREDERICK R
Mem, Calif. Rep. State Cent. Cmt.
b. San Jose, Calif, 5/13/30; s. Clifford Bell Berry and Mary Elizabeth Clark B; m. 9/4/55 to Ellen Carol Baird; c. Gregory Charles and Douglas Robert. Educ: Univ. of Md. Exten, 53; San Jose State Col, B.A, 56; Univ. of Calif. Exten, 63. Polit. & Govt. Pos: Precinct capt, Co. Rep. Precinct Orgn, 64, area chmn, 65 and regional chmn, 66; assoc. mem, Co. Rep. Cent. Cmt, 66-67; assoc. mem, Calif. Rep. State Cent. Cmt, 67, mem, 68-; mem, Rep. State Precinct Cmt, 67- and Assemblyman Crandall's Exec. and Steering Cmts, 67-; chmn, 25th Assembly Dist. Rep. Precinct Orgn, 67-; co-chmn, Santa Clara Co. Rep. Precinct Orgn, 69-; assemblyman's rep, Santa Clara Co. Rep. Cent. Cmt, 69- Mil. Serv: Entered as Pvt, Air Force, 51, released as S/Sgt, 54, after serv. in Training and Tactical Air Commands, U.S, N.Africa and Middle East, 51-54; Good Conduct and Nat. Defense Serv. Medals. Mem: Am. Nuclear Soc; Am. Soc. for Metals; Pac. Asn. of Gen. Elec. Scientists and Engrs; Webelos Den (leader); Cub Scout Coordinating Cmt; YMCA; Indian Guides; Pee Wee Baseball League (coach); Home and Sch. Club. Recipient of Gov. Award for Top Ten Precinct Leaders in Calif; Rep. State Cent. Cmt. Award for Top 50 Precinct Workers in Calif; Rep. Co. Cent. Cmt. Award, Outstanding Serv. Award for Precinct Work; YMCA Award, Outstanding Performance Award for Bldg. Fund Drive Leadership; Am. Legion Award for Scholarship and Citizenship. Rel: Methodist. Mailing Add: 4052 Jan Way, San Jose, Calif. 95124.

BERRY, DOROTHY B. R
b. Exeter, N.H, 10/22/05; married; c. 2 sons. Educ: Univ. of N.H. Polit. & Govt. Pos: N.H. State Rep, 57-67; formerly, Barrington Sch. Bd. Bus. & Prof. Pos: Housewife. Mem: Officer, Rochester, Barrington Woman's and Garden Clubs; N.H.F.G.C. Rel: Congregationalist. Mailing Add: R.F.D. No. 1, Rochester, N.H. 03867. (1967)

BERRY, E. Y. R
U.S. Rep, S.Dak.
b. Larchwood, Iowa, 10/6/02; m. 1928 to Rose Hartinger; c. Robert E, Nila

Lee and Berry McCracken. Educ: Morningside Col; Univ. of S.Dak. Law Sch, LL.B, 27. Polit. & Govt. Pos: States attorney, co. judge, Corson Co, S.Dak; S.Dak. State Sen, 39-43; mem, Mo. River States Cmt, 40-43; mem, State Bd. of Regents of Educ, 46-50; U.S. Rep, S.Dak, 50- Bus. & Prof. Pos: Lawyer; newspaper ed. and publisher; ed, S.Dak. Bar Asn. J, 38-50. Mem: Pres, S.Dak. Press Asn, 44-45; Lambda Chi Alpha; Delta Theta Phi; Sigma Delta Chi; Mason; Commandery; Consistory; Shrine. Legal Res: McLaughlin, S.Dak. Mailing Add: 118 Schotts Court N.E, Washington, D.C. 20002.

BERRY, FRED OGLE, SR. R
Tenn. State Sen.
b. Knoxville, Tenn, 11/6/12; s. Ralph Lawson Berry and Myrtle Henderlight B; m. 12/26/43 to Ruth Amealia LeCoultre; c. Fred O, Jr, Nancy (Mrs. Scott), George Edward, Dr. David Andrew and six grandchildren. Educ: Gupton-Jones Mortuary Col, M.S, 35; Field Med. Sch, Navy, 44. Polit. & Govt. Pos: Tenn. State Rep, 61-62 & 63-64; Tenn. State Sen, 65- Bus. & Prof. Pos: V.pres. and dir, Tenn. Life & Serv. Ins. Co, 51-58; pres, Berry Morticians, Inc, 51- Mil. Serv: Entered as PhM 3/C, Navy, 43, released as PhM 1/C, 45, after serv. in 16th Naval Air Force Aviation Med. Corps, 45; Capt, Army Res. Mem: Health adv. cmt, U.S. Civil Defense Coun, 61-; pres, Tenn. Funeral Dirs. Asn, 51-52; Civil Defense Cmt; nat. defense cmt, Nat. Funeral Dirs. Asn, 65-; Rotary Int; Eagles; Elks; Senators Club; Gatlinburg Ski Club; E. Tenn. Sportsman Club; Tenn. Bear & Boar Club; Tenn. Conserv. League; Nat. Rifle Club; Top of 100 Club; F&AM (past master); Scottish Rite and York Rite (32°); Shrine; Eastern Star; Am. Legion; WOW; United Commercial Travelers; C. of C; pres, E. Tenn. Wildlife Coun; S. Knoxville Rep. Club; Tenn. Law Enforcement Asn; Travelers Protective Asn; past dir, Better Bus. Bur. Hon. fire chief, Knoxville; hon. capt, Tenn. Hwy. Patrol; Pfizer Award, U.S. Civil Defense Coun, 63. Rel: Methodist. Legal Res: 301 Mayflower Rd, Knoxville, Tenn. 37920. Mailing Add: 3704 Chapman Hwy, Knoxville, Tenn. 37920.

BERRY, LELAND L. D
b. Fairview, Mo, 10/26/05; m. 10/8/27 to Crystal L. Early; c. (Mrs. Robert Langston), James; grandchildren, Cynthia and Mark Langston, Craig and Scott Berry. Educ: Fairview High Sch. Polit. & Govt. Pos: Mo. State Rep, 64-66; Fairview Twp. Cmt. (12 years); Newton Co. Finance Cmt, (12 years); mayor of Fairview (2 years); pres, past pres. Fairview Sch. Bd. (8 years), Newton Co. Rd. Cmn. Bus. & Prof. Pos: Grocery and gen. merchandising bus. (38 years); mgr, Fairview Farmers Exchange (5 years). Mem: Neosho C. of C. Rel: Methodist. Mailing Add: 632 Oakridge Dr, Neosho, Mo. 64850. (1967)

BERRY, LeROY D
Mem, Calif. Dem. State Cent. Cmt.
b. Birmingham, Ala, 10/20/26; s. Lester Berry and Lubertha Foster B; m. 7/28/49 to Ruth Brothers. Educ: Univ. Calif, Los Angeles, B.A; Calif. State Col, Los Angeles, M.A. and Admin. Credential; Kappa Alpha Psi. Polit. & Govt. Pos: Pres, Leimert Dem. Club, Calif, 58-61; rep, 63rd Assembly Dist. Dem. Coun, 60-64; south. credentials chmn, Calif. Dem. Coun, 64-66, region two v.pres, 66-68; mem, Dem. Co. Cmt, 63rd Assembly Dist, 67-; mem, Calif. Dem. State Cent. Cmt, 67- Mil. Serv: Entered as Pvt, Army, 41, released as Cpl, 45, after serv. in Coast Artillery Engineers, Air Force, Western Defense Command, 42-44; Marksman Sharpshooter; Good Conduct Medal. Mem: Life mem, Univ. Calif, Los Angeles Alumni Asn; New Frontier Democratic Club; Am. Fedn. of Teachers. Rel: Protestant. Mailing Add: 3801 Welland Ave, Los Angeles, Calif. 90008.

BERRY, LOREN MURPHY R
b. Wabash, Ind, 7/24/88; s. Charles D. Berry and Elizabeth Murphy B; m. 6/9/09 to Lucile Kneipple (deceased); c. Loren Murphy, Jr, Martha Sue (Mrs. J.P. Fraim), John William and Elizabeth Anne (Mrs. Don Fox); m. 8/28/38 to Helen Anderson Henry; c. Leland Henry. Educ: Northwest. Univ, 09-10; hon. LL.D, Rio Grande Col. Polit. & Govt. Pos: Finance chmn, Montgomery Co. Rep. Finance Cmt, Ohio, 44-50; state finance chmn, Fla. Rep. Finance Cmt, 56-60; mem, Rep. Nat. Finance Cmt, 68-69. Bus. & Prof. Pos: Newspaper reporter, Wabash, Ind, Joliet, Ill, Chicago; sold tel. dir. advert, Marion, Ind, 10, St. Louis, Louisville, Indianapolis; chmn. bd. and chief exec. officer, L.M. Berry & Co, currently; dir, United Utilities, Inc, Kansas City, Fla. Tel. Corp, Ocala, Edison Nat. Bank, Ft. Myers, Fla, Third Nat. Bank & Trust Co, Dayton, Ohio, Laughter Corp, Dayton, Hulman Realty Co, Dayton, Super Food Serv, Inc, Dayton and Mutual Broadcasting Corp, Los Angeles; trustee, Jr. Achievement, Dayton and Rio Grande Col. Mem: U.S. Ind. Tel. Pioneers (pres, 38-39); Bell Tel. Pioneers Asn.(v.pres, N.C. Kingsbury Chap, 39-40); Mason (32°); Shrine; Capitol Hill Club, Wash, D.C; Dayton City Club; Engr. Club; Kiwanis; Dayton Country Club; Dayton Bicycle Club; Surf Club (gov); Cmt. of 100; Indian Creek Club, Miami Beach; Bohemian Club, San Francisco. Rel: Episcopal. Legal Res: 1155 Ridgeway Rd, Dayton, Ohio 45419. Mailing Add: 3170 Kettering Blvd, Dayton, Ohio 45401.

BERRY, LOUISE SPAULDING R
Chmn, Killingly Rep. Town Cmt, Conn.
b. Danielson, Conn, 11/9/27; d. Jacob Lindhurst Spaulding and Frances Upham S; m. 6/9/51 to Richard Chisholm Bliss Berry; c. Donald Spaulding, Pamela Chisholm, Robin Lee, Christopher Warren and Judith Hastings. Educ: Adelphi Col, Dipl. Nursing, 48; Univ. Conn, B.A, 52, M.A, 61; Univ. Conn. Concert Band. Polit. & Govt. Pos: Mem, Killingly Rep. Town Cmt, Conn, 63-, chmn, 65-; mem, Killingly Bd. Educ, 66- Bus. & Prof. Pos: Sch. nurse, Killingly Schs, Danielson, 52-55; sch. nurse, Brooklyn Sch, 58-, dir. guid, 61- Publ: 'The Problem of the Dropout,' 64. Mem: Am. Sch. Health Asn; Conn. Personnel and Guid. Asn; Quinebaug Valley Health and Welfare Coun.(bd. dirs); bd. dirs, Windham Area Commun. Action Prog. First Prize for The Problem of the Dropout, from Westab, Inc. Rel: Congregational. Mailing Add: Mashentuck Rd, Danielson, Conn. 06239.

BERRY, MARY LUCILE R
Chmn, Roberts Co. Rep. Party, Tex.
b. Higgins, Tex, 5/26/11; d. Tullie Roark Saxon and Annie Elizabeth Roach S; m. 1/24/51 to Laurence Raymond Berry. Educ: Miami Pub. Sch, grad, 30. Polit. & Govt. Pos: Chmn, Roberts Co. Rep. Party, 68- Bus. & Prof. Pos: Cashier and bookkeeper, Miami Gas Co, Tex, 34-36; cashier and bookkeeper, Southwest. Pub. Serv. Co, 36- Mem: DAR; treas, Am. Red Cross, Tex, 42-47; auditor, Boy and Girl Scout Drives, 60-64. 30 year serv. award, Southwest. Pub. Serv. Co, 66. Rel: Methodist. Legal Res: 219 W. Commercial, Miami, Tex, 79059. Mailing Add: Box 203, Miami, Tex. 79059.

BERRY, MICHAEL D
Chmn, 16th Cong. Dist. Dem. Orgn, Mich.
b. Highland Park, Mich, 5/8/20; s. Charles Berry and Mary Sayed B; m. 11/26/43 to Vivian Carol Weine; c. Laura Jean, Carol Ann, Gail Marie and Cynthia Michele. Educ: Dearborn Jr. Col, grad; Wayne State Univ; Detroit Col. Law, LL.B, 50; Sigma Nu Phi. Polit. & Govt. Pos: Former attorney, Cooper Sch. Dist, Nankin Twp, Mich; state v.chmn, Elec. Study Cmt. and chmn, Metrop. Area Elec. Study Cmt; chmn, Human Rels. Coun, Wayne Co. Dem. Party, mem. exec. bd, 8 years, precinct del, 12 years and mem, 16 years; Wayne Co. Pub. Adminstr, 56-; attorney, Cent. Wayne Co. Sanit. Authority, 58-; city attorney, Riverview, 61- and Garden City, 63-; twp. attorney, Dearborn, 5 years, Romulus, 62-, Van Buren, 63- and Huron, 66; Presidential Elector, 60; del, Dem. Nat. Conv, 64 & 68; campaign chmn, four consecutive gubernatorial elec, 16th Cong. Dist. Dem. Orgn; former chmn, Bldg. and Teen Dems; chmn, 16th Cong. Dist. Dem. Orgn, presently. Bus. & Prof. Pos: Gen. practice of law, Berry, Hopson, Francis & Mack, Detroit, Mich. Mil. Serv: Air Force, World War II. Mem: Am, Mich. and Detroit Bar Asns; pres, Cedars of Lebanon Bar Asn; Am. Trial Lawyers Asn; Nat. Inst. of Munic. Law Officers; Am. Legion; Amvets; Rotary; past dir, Dearborn United Commun. Servs: hon. pres, S. E. Dearborn Civic Asn; former mem, Dearborn Twp. Goodfellows, City Dir, Aid to Leukemia Stricken Am. Children, Dearborn and Nat. Trustee; Wayne Co. Citizens Cmt. on Juvenile Delinquency. Admitted to practice before U.S. Supreme Court; sponsored by U.S. Dept. of State, Bur. of Educ. and Cultural Affairs, for speaking tour of Near East, 66. Rel: Moslem. Legal Res: 232 N. Vernon, Dearborn, Mich. 48128. Mailing Add: 2015 Cadillac Tower, Detroit, Mich. 48226.

BERRY, RICHARD NATHANIEL R
Maine State Sen.
b. Malden, Mass, 11/4/15; s. Edward Robie Berry and Maude Henneberry B; m. 7/9/38 to Katherine Bunker; c. Andrew B, Richard N, Jr. and Thomas A. Educ: Univ. Maine, B.S, 37; Tau Beta Pi; Beta Theta Pi. Polit. & Govt. Pos: Mem. common coun, City of Malden, Mass, 38-39, fire cmnr, 47-48; Maine State Rep, 61-66; Maine State Sen, 104th Legis, 66- Bus. & Prof. Pos: Consult. engr. Mil. Serv: Entered as 1st Lt, Army, 42, released as Maj, 46, after serv. in Engrs. Corps, Col, Army Res, 66. Mem: Maine Water Utilities Asn; New Eng. and Am. Water Works Asn; Am. Soc. Civil Engrs. Rel: Congregational. Mailing Add: Spring Cove, Cape Elizabeth, Maine 04107.

BERRY, THORNTON GRANVILLE, JR. D
b. Sutton, W.Va, 12/13/04; s. Thornton Granville Berry and Mamie Newlon Kawalska B; m. 6/4/34 to Rita Crockett Brewster. Educ: Va. Mil. Inst, A.B, 28; Wash. & Lee Univ, LL.B, 34; Phi Delta Phi; Phi Kappa Psi. Polit. & Govt. Pos: Cmnr. in Chancery and cmnr. of Accounts, McDowell Co, W.Va, 37-40, prosecuting attorney, 40-42; asst. U.S. attorney, South Dist, W.Va, 39-40; judge Eighth Judicial Circuit of W.Va, 52-58, Supreme Court of Appeals of W.Va, 58- Mil. Serv: Entered as Lt, Navy, 42, released as Lt. Comdr, 46, after serv. in North Pac, 44-45; Am. and Pac. Theater Ribbons; Victory Medal; Navy Res. Medal; Armed Forces Medal; Lt. Comdr. (Ret), Naval Res, 64. Publ: South Eastern Reports, West Publ. Co. Mem: Am. and W.Va. Bar Asns; W.Va. Judicial Asn; Am. Judicature Asn; Am. Law Inst; W.Va. State Bar; Moose; Elks; Am. Legion; Army-Navy Club; Edgewood Country Club; Mason (32°); Shrine; SAR. Hobby: Golf. Rel: Presbyterian. Legal Res: Southwood, Welch, W.Va. 24801. Mailing Add: 1612 Virginia St. E, Charleston, W.Va. 25311.

BERRY, V. E. D
Tex. State Sen.
b. 1899. Polit. & Govt. Pos: Tex. State Rep, 61-66; Tex. State Sen, 67- Bus. & Prof. Pos: Former operator of bar and restaurant; thoroughbred horse-breeding and racing. Mem: Sheriff's Posse; Hermann Sons; Elks; VFW; Am. Legion. Mailing Add: 856 Gembler Rd, San Antonio, Tex. 78219. (1967)

BERRYHILL, GRAILEY HEWITT R
b. McKenzie, Tenn, 8/17/96; s. Adam Douglas Berryhill and Hattie Costeu B; m. 6/20/21 to Thelma Harwood, wid; c. Grailyn (Mrs. Leslie L. Brooks, Jr.) and Ann (Mrs. James Boswell). Educ: Vanderbilt Univ, M.D, 21; Alpha Omega Alpha; Alpha Tau Omega; Alpha Kappa Kappa; Nemo Club; Owl Club; Commodore Club; Eve Club. Polit. & Govt. Pos: Chmn, Co. Dem. Cmt, 6 years; mem, Rep. Exec. Cmt, 65-69; Tenn. State Rep, 66-68. Mil. Serv: Students Army Training Corps, Army, 18, released as Pvt. Mem: Co, State and Am. Med. Asns; Mason; Elks. Rel: Christian Church. Mailing Add: 517 Westmoreland, Jackson, Tenn. 38301.

BERRYMAN, WILLIAM ANDERSON D
Ala. State Rep.
b. Cherokee, Ala, 7/3/10; s. William Howard Berryman and Lillie Ayers B; m. 2/2/30 to Maudie; c. Elbert. Polit. & Govt. Pos: State livestock inspector, Ala, 57-61; Ala. State Rep, 67- Mem: Farm Bur; Ala. Cattlemen Asn; Bear Creek Watershed Asn, Inc; Tri-Cities Cheer Club; Russellville Booster Club. Rel: Baptist. Mailing Add: Route 5, Russellville, Ala. 35653. (1967)

BERRYMAN, WILLIAM ROBERT D
b. St. Louis, Mo, 10/13/42; s. Virgil L. Berryman and Geraldine Carroll B; m. 6/11/67 to Nancy Carol Rasley, wid. 11/7/68. Educ: Univ. Nebr, B.A, 68. Polit. & Govt. Pos: Nat. Committeeman, Nebr. Young Democrats; Campaign mgr, J.B. Dean for Cong, Third Cong. Dist. Nebr, 68; alternate del, Dem. Nat. Conv, 68. Mailing Add: 1618 N. 72nd St, Omaha, Nebr. 68114.

BERSANI, LEONARD F. R
N.Y. State Assemblyman
b. Syracuse, N.Y, 11/21/32; s. Amedeo Bersani (deceased) and Christina Variano B.(deceased); m. 2/1/65 to Maria Wimmer; c. Theresa. Educ: St. Bernard's Col, B.A, 55; Syracuse Univ. Col. of Law, LL.B, 61; Phi Alpha Delta. Polit. & Govt. Pos: Assoc. coun, Syracuse Urban Renewal Agency, 67-68; N.Y. State Assemblyman, 118th Dist, 69- Mem: Onondaga Co, N.Y. State and Am. Bar Asns; Ital-Am. Athletic Club; Sons of Italy; Lincoln Rep. Club. Rel: Roman Catholic. Mailing Add: 128 Rugby Rd, Syracuse, N.Y. 13206.

BERSON, NORMAN S. D
Pa. State Rep.
b. N.Y.C, 11/19/26; s. Joseph A. Berson and Theresa Levinsky B; m. 8/26/55 to Lenora Ersner; c. Peter and Erica. Educ: Temple Univ, A.B, 50; Univ. Pa. Law Sch, LL.B, 53. Polit. & Govt. Pos: Pa. State Rep, 67-; alternate del, Dem. Nat. Conv, 68. Bus. & Prof. Pos: Partner, Freedman, Berson & Freedman, 66. Mil. Serv: Entered as Pvt, Army, 44, released as Sgt, 46, after serv. in 116th Combat Engrs, Pac, 44-45; Pac. Theater Ribbon; Philippine Liberation Medal. Mem: Phila. Bar Asn; Phila. Housing Asn; Am. Jewish Cmt; Phila. Fel. Cmn; Citizens Coun. Pub. Educ. Rel: Jewish. Legal Res: 2421 Spruce St, Philadelphia, Pa. 19103. Mailing Add: 1214 One East Penn Square, Philadelphia, Pa. 19107. (1967)

BERTIER, THEODORE, JR. D
Md. State Sen.
b. Anne Arundel Co, Md, 4/23/28; married. Educ: Univ. of Baltimore, B.S, 53; Johns Hopkins Univ, CME, 54. Polit. & Govt. Pos: mem, Anne Arundel Co. Recreation Cmn, 56-62; Md. State Del, 63-67; Md. State Sen, 67- Bus. & Prof. Pos: Project engineer. Mil. Serv: Army, 45-47. Mem: Am. Soc. of Mech. Engrs; Anne Arundel Soc. of Engrs. and Land Surveyors. Mailing Add: St. Stephens Rd, Millersville, Md. 21108. (1967)

BERTONAZZI, LOUIS PETER D
Mass. State Rep.
b. Milford, Mass, 10/9/33; s. Peter John Bertonazzi and Concetta Rossi B; m. 6/8/57 to Barbara Szymanski; c. Gregg, Lisa and David. Educ: Tufts Univ, B.A, 55; Suffolk Univ, M.A. in Ed, 60; Boston Col, adv. grad. study; Sigma Nu. Polit. & Govt. Pos: Mem. bd. of selectmen, Milford, Mass, 64-69, chmn. bd, 65-68; chmn, Blackstone Valley Econ. Opportunity Coun, 65-66; first dep. dir, Mass. Div. of Youth Serv, 66-69; Mass State Rep, 69- Bus. & Prof. Pos: Teacher govt. & lang, Medway High Sch, 58-60, guid. coun, 60-62, dir. guid, 62-66. Mil. Serv: Entered as Pvt, Army, 56, released as Pfc, 58, after serv. in Fourth Regt. Combat Team, First Army, 56-58; Expert Rifleman Award. Mem: Medway Teachers Asn.(past pres); Norfolk Co. Teachers Asn.(past first v.pres); Mass. Teachers Asn; Nat. Educ. Asn; Mass. Coun. Asn; N.E. and Am. Personnel and Guid. Asns; Nat. Coun. on Crime and Delinquency; N.E. Conf. on Crime and Delinquency; K. of C. Jimmy Fund Award, 64; Hon. Membership Award, Milford Young Dem, 66; Man of the Year Award, Milford Area Heart Fund Asn, 68. Rel: Catholic. Mailing Add: Coolidge Rd, Milford, Mass. 01757.

BERTORELLI, JOSEPH A. D
Md. State Sen.
b. Baltimore, Md, 6/10/11; married. Educ: Baltimore Col. of Commerce. Polit. & Govt. Pos: Former mem, Baltimore City Coun, Md; former spec. asst. to mayor, Baltimore; Md. State Del, 47-55; Md. State Sen, 55- Bus. & Prof. Pos: Prfnl. musician. Mil. Serv: Navy, 44-45; Asiatic-Pacific. Mem: Past v.pres, Musicians Local No. 40, Baltimore City; pres, Ital—Am. Civic Club of Md, Inc; past pres, Southeast. Commun. Coun; Eagles; K. of C; past comdr, Am. Legion Post 177; CWV. Mailing Add: 314 S. High St, Baltimore, Md. 21202. (1967)

BERTSCH, MARIAN N. R
V.Chmn, 32nd Dist. N.Dak. Rep. Party
b. New England, N.Dak. 11/13/11; d. Thomas Christian Nelsen and Johanna Christensen N; m. 9/22/35 to Harold Schafer; c. Haroldeen Anne (Mrs. Robert Heskin), Joanne Bee (Mrs. James Kack), Dianne Margaret, Edward Thomas and Pamela Rikki; m. 5/11/67 to Albert C. Bertsch. Educ: Aberdeen Bus. Col, 29. Polit. & Govt. Pos: Mem, Rep. Nat. Cmt, N.Dak, 61-; mem. arrangements cmt, Rep. Nat. Conv, 64, alternate del, 68; v.chmn, 32nd Dist. N.Dak. Rep. Party, 68- Bus. & Prof. Pos: Mem, bd. dirs, City Center Hotel Asn. and Women Med. Col, Pa. Mem: Pres, Shrine Auxiliary Crippled Children Hosp; pres, Girl Scouts Coun; Zonta Int; Eastern Star. Thanks Badge, Girl Scouts. Rel: Presbyterian. Mailing Add: 1256 N. Parkview Dr, Bismarck, N.Dak. 58501.

BERTSCHE, FAITH BROWN R
Secy, Richmond Co. Rep. Exec. Cmt, Ga.
b. New York City, N.Y, 1/14/17; d. Henry Collins Brown and Clara B; m. 11/23/39 to Edwin Carl Bertsche; c. Susan (Mrs. Newell), David Carl and Virginia; granddaughter, Virginia Newell. Educ: Barnard Col, Columbia Univ. Polit. & Govt. Pos: Secy, Richmond Co. Rep. Exec. Cmt, Ga. Mem: Augusta Country Club; Augusta Authors Club. Rel: Society of Friends. Mailing Add: 2258 Overton Rd, Augusta, Ga. 30904. (1967)

BERTZ, RALPH HARRISON R
Chmn, Presque Isle Co. Rep. Cmt, Mich.
b. Fond du Lac, Wis, 7/30/23; s. Benjiman H. Bertz and Maude Stafford B; m. 7/24/48 to Jessie Taylor Little; c. Douglas R. and Kathryn L. Educ: Univ. Chicago, 43-44; Univ. Wis, B.S. in Mech. Eng, 49; Pi Tau Sigma; Tau Beta Pi. Polit. & Govt. Pos: Chmn, Presque Isle Co. Rep. Cmt, Mich, 67-; chmn, 11th Cong. Dist. S. Rep. Party, 69- Bus. & Prof. Pos: Mech. engr, U.S. Steel Corp, Va, Minn, 49-56, supvr, maintenance planning and eng, 56-61, gen. engr, Rogers City, Mich, 61-63, asst. supt. maintenance, 63- Mil. Serv: Entered as Pvt, Army Air Corps, 42, released as Sgt, 46, after serv. in 15th Weather Squadron, Asiatic-Pac. Theatre, 45-46; Philippine Liberation Medal; Asiatic-Pac. Serv. Medal with One Battle Star. Mem: Huron Shores Chap, Mich. Soc. Prfnl. Engrs; Am. Soc. Mech. Engrs; Northeast. Mich. Eng. Soc; Boy Scouts (Scenic Trails Coun); Rogers City Servicemen's Club. Silver Beaver Award, Scenic Trails Coun, Boy Scouts, 65. Rel: Presbyterian. Mailing Add: 276 S. Lake St, Rogers City, Mich. 49779.

BERUBE, PHILIP D
N.Dak. State Sen.
b. Belcourt, N.Dak, 4/6/05; s. Arthur Berube and Victorine Mongeon B; m. 11/28/29 to Alma Casavant; c. Leonel, Vivian (Mrs. Hurben Cote), Delima (Mrs. James Grossal); Lorette (Mrs. William Leanard), Harvey, Julian (Mrs. Donald Lentz), Adrien and Jackie. Educ: Maryville Pub. Sch, 8 years. Polit. & Govt. Pos: Mem, Co. Sch. Reorgn. Cmt, N.Dak, 47-69; mem, Capitol Bldg. Cmn; N.Dak. State Sen, 52- Bus. & Prof. Pos: Farmer; Gen. Store and Post Off, 27-30. Mem: Commercial Club; co. pres, Farmers Union, 42-68. Rel: Catholic. Mailing Add: 315 Main Ave. E, Rolla, N.Dak. 58367.

BESS, JODA LEE R
Chmn, Butler Co. Rep. Cent. Cmt, Mo.
b. Blodgett, Mo, 11/20/27; s. Joda William Bess and Mary Margret Smith B; m. 10/1/60 to Charlotte Arlene Fureh; c. Kathy Lea and Joda David. Educ: S.E. Mo. State Col, 1 year. Polit. & Govt. Pos: Treas, Howell Co. Rep. Cent. Cmt, Mo, 65-66; chmn, Butler Co. Rep. Cent. Cmt, 68- Mil. Serv: Entered as Pvt, Army, 50, released as Sgt. 1/C, 52, after serv. in 150 Engr. Pontoon Bridge Co. Mem: C. of C.(pres); Kiwanis (pres). Rel: Protestant. Mailing Add: 1320 Susan St, Poplar Bluff, Mo. 63901.

BESSEY, CAROL D
Chmn, Van Buren Co. Dem. Cmt, Mich.
b. Glenn, Mich, 12/24/13; m. to Boyd G. Bessey; c. Boyd T. and Carol Joy (Mrs. Grudecki). Educ: South Haven High Sch. Polit. & Govt. Pos: V.chmn, Van Buren Dem. Cmt, 64-67, chmn, 67-; chmn, Van Buren Co. Dem. Conv. Bus. & Prof. Pos: Shipping clerk, Arthur Arens. Mem: Bus. & Prfnl. Womens Club; Am. Legion; Coterie; DAV. Rel: Methodist. Mailing Add: R.R. 4, Paw Paw, Mich. 49079.

BETENSON, GLEN R
Chmn, Piute Co. Rep. Party, Utah
b. Circleville, Utah, 11/18/99; s. Joseph Arthur Betenson and Elizbeth M. James B; m. 3/28/24 to Nellie Synethlia Whittaker; c. Druce, Beven Whittaker, Eugene H. Bult and Lajauna (Mrs. Riddle). Educ: Col. South. Utah, B.S, 24; Blackstone Col. of Law. Polit. & Govt. Pos: Rep. Party worker, 49 years; co. attorney, Piute Co, Utah, 43-; mayor, Circleville, currently; chmn, Piute Co. Rep. Party, currently; chmn, Dist. Rep. Party, currently; mem, Utah Rep. State Cmt, currently. Bus. & Prof. Pos: Play producer, Gay Nineties Revue, East Lynne, Ten Nights in a Bar Room, Hazel Kirt, On the Bridge at Midnight, The Cabin in the Hills, plus others. Rel: Latter-day Saint. Mailing Add: 390 North First East, Circleville, Utah 84723.

BETENSON, SCOTT PARKER D
Chmn, Kane Co. Dem. Party, Utah
b. Circleville, Utah, 6/15/17; s. Joseph Delbert Betenson and Lula Parker B; m. 2/5/35 to Mariam Brinkerhoff; c. Wade, Elaine (Mrs. Roney Pratt), Nancy Ann and Helen Jill. Educ: Piute High Sch. Polit. & Govt. Pos: Chmn, Kane Co. Dem. Party, Utah, 67- Bus. & Pros. Pos: Mgr, Kanab Theatre, 46-; agent, Palmer Bros. Truck Line, 63- Mil. Serv: Entered as Pvt, Army, 45. Mem: Comdr, Am. Legion; IBT. Rel: Latter-day Saint. Mailing Add: Kanab, Utah 84741.

BETHEA, ALFRED WILLIAM D
b. Dothan, S.C, 6/20/16; s. Fitzhugh Lee Bethea and Bonnie Keen B; m. 2/23/52 to Joan Dellinger B; c. Kitty Lee, Alfred W, Jr, Shannon Marie, Lesa, Camille, Fitzhugh. Educ: Clemson Col, B.A, A.H. & Agr. Econ, 38; Colo. A&M, B.S, Agronomy, 45. Polit. & Govt. Pos: S.C. State Rep, 61-64-66. Bus. & Prof. Pos: Farmer; Bd. of Dir, Dillon Co. Farm Bur. Mil. Serv: Air Force, 39-45, 363rd Fighter Group, 52nd Fighter Group, 9th Tactical Air Force, 19th Tactical Air Force GHQ; Lt. Col, S.S.S. Columbia, S.C. Res. Unit. Mem: Dist. Comdr, VFW, 53-54; Post. Comdr, Post No. 6091, 52; S.C. Rep. Agr. Cmt, U.S. C. of C, 59-60; Rotary. Cand. for Cmnr. of Agr, 58. Rel: Methodist. Mailing Add: R.F.D. 1, Dillon, S.C. 29536.

BETHEA, BARRON D
b. Birmingham, Ala, 5/20/29; s. Malcolm Bethea and Wilma Edwards B; single. Educ: Univ. Ala, B.S. in Law, 51, LL.B, 53; Scabbard and Blade; Arnold Air Soc; Phi Alpha Delta; Phi Gamma Delta. Polit. & Govt. Pos: Mem, State Dem. Exec. Cmt, Ala, 58-66; Ala. State Rep, 62-66. Bus. & Prof. Pos: Pres. & owner, Barron Bethea Co, Inc, 57- Mil. Serv: Entered as 2nd Lt, Air Force, 54, released as 1st Lt, 56. Mem: Assoc. Industs. of Ala; Ala. C. of C; Birmingham C. of C; Bessemer C. of C; Southern Indust. Coun; Pac. Coast Elec. Asn. Rel: Methodist. Legal Res: 2052 Lancaster Rd, Homewood, Ala. 35209. Mailing Add: P.O. Box 2202, Birmingham, Ala. 35201.

BETHEA, MALCOLM R
b. Beaumont, Tex, 9/10/20; s. Malcolm Bethea and Wilma Edwards B; m. 5/24/47 to Sue Ambler Bethea; c. Susan Ambler, Elizabeth Anne, Mary Virginia, Malcolm Smith. Educ: Birmingham-South. Col; Ala. Polytech. Inst; Ga. Inst. of Tech, B.S, 47. Polit. & Govt. Pos: Ala. State Rep, 62-66. Bus. & Prof. Pos: Pres, Bethea Co, Inc. Mil. Serv: Aviator, WWII; Maj, USMCR. Rel: Methodist. Mailing Add: 1606 Wellington Rd, Homewood, Ala. 35209. (1967)

BETLESKI, ADRIAN FRANCIS D
b. Cleveland, Ohio, 7/9/17; s. Frank Betleski and Eufemia Bartosewicz B; m. 9/7/46 to Eileen Curran; c. Clinton A, Rosanne, Adrian F, Jr, Philip S. and Mark A. Educ: Ohio State Univ, B.A. and J.D, 49; Polit. Sci. Hon; Delta Theta Phi. Polit. & Govt. Pos: Asst. co. prosecutor, Lorain Co, Ohio, 54-60; city solicitor, Lorain, 60-66; Dem. nominee, U.S. Rep, Ohio, 68. Mil. Serv: Entered as Aviation Cadet, Navy Air Corps, 42, released as Lt.(sg), 45, after serv. in Air Transport Serv, Atlantic and Pac. Theaters, 42-45, Naval Res, 45-54; Am, Atlantic and Pac. Theater Ribbons. Mem: Ohio State Bar Asn; Lorain Co. Bar Asn.(v.pres, 69-); K. of C; VFW; Polish Legion Am. Vet; Grange. Rel: Catholic. Legal Res: 1723 E. Erie Ave, Lorain, Ohio 44052. Mailing Add: 120 W. 20th St, Lorain, Ohio 44052.

BETTS, BERT A. D
Mem, Calif. Dem. State Cent. Cmt.
b. San Diego, Calif, 1923; c. Terry Lou, Linda Sue, Sally, Bert Alan, Randy and Le Ann. Educ: San Diego State Col; Calif. West. Univ; Int. Acct. Soc. Polit. & Govt. Pos: Pres, Lemon Grove Sch. Dist. Bd. of Trustees, Calif; state treas, Calif, 62-67; mem, Calif. Dem. State Cent. Cmt, currently. Bus. & Prof. Pos: CPA; prin. partner, acct. firm. Mil. Serv: Air Force, B-24 pilot; received Four Air Medals; Distinguished Flying Cross. Mem: 1st V.Pres, San Diego Chap, Calif. Soc. of CPA; past Vice Comdr, Air Force Asn; Am. Inst. of CPA; Nat. Asn. of Acct; Mason; Eagles; Lions; Foresters; VFW; Am. Legion; spec. 3-men cmt, Nat. Asn. of Auditors, Comptrollers and Treasurers to work for continuation of tax exemption on munic. bonds. Mailing Add: 8701 E. Levee Rd, Elverta, Calif. 95626. (1967)

BETTS, JACKSON EDWARD R
U.S. Rep, Ohio
b. Findlay, Ohio, 5/26/04; s. John Edward Betts and Elizabeth Fisher B; m. 6/12/34 to Martha Neeley; c. Nancy Lou (Mrs. David C. Bowman). Educ: Kenyon Col, A.B. cum laude, 26, hon. M.A, 53; Yale Sch. Law, LL.B, 29; Delta Tau Delta; Phi Delta Phi. Hon. LL.D, Ohio Northern, 59, Heidelberg Col, 62 and Findlay Col, 65. Polit. & Govt. Pos: Prosecuting attorney, Hancock Co, Ohio, 33-37; Ohio State Rep, 37-47; Speaker of the House of Rep, Ohio, 45 & 46; U.S. Rep, Ohio, 51- Mem: Am, Ohio and Hancock Co. Bar Asns; Mason (32°); Rotary; Elks; K. of P; Odd Fellows. Rel: Episcopal. Legal Res: 3309 Briarcliff Dr, Findlay, Ohio 45840. Mailing Add: Room 2310 Rayburn House Office Bldg, Washington, D.C. 20515.

BETZ, FRANK HERBERT, III R
Dist. Cmt. Leader, Union Co. Rep. Cmt, N.J.
b. Plainfield, N.J, 5/21/33; s. Frank H. Betz, Jr. and Elsie Teunon B; m. 1955 to Carolyn M. Schoder; c. Brian Cameron, Brooks Hamilton and Catherine Cameron. Educ: Gettysburg Col, A.B, 55; N.Y. Univ. Grad. Sch. Bus. Admin, M.B.A, 63; Phi Sigma Kappa. Polit. & Govt. Pos: Various local appointive positions; dist. cmt. leader, Union Co. Rep. Cmt, N.J, 61-; state platform chmn, N.J. Young Rep, 62-63; alternate del, Rep. Nat. Conv, 64; co. chmn, Union Co. Young Rep, 64-65; chmn, Union Co. Nixon Now Cmt, 68. Bus. & Prof. Pos: Asst. v.pres, Chem. Bank, N.Y.C. Mem: Bd. dirs, Fanwood-Scotch Plains YMCA, 63-65; Fanwood-Scotch Plains Jaycees. Rel: Protestant. Mailing Add: 605 E. Broad St, Westfield, N.J. 08690.

BETZ, FRED McLEAN D
b. Liberal, Mo, 6/2/96; s. John Betz and Margaret McLean B; m. 6/5/17 to Lennie Maud Coffman; c. Fred M, Jr. Polit. & Govt. Pos: Mem. and chmn, bd. dirs, Wichita Farm Credit Admin, 35-38; state supvr, Farm Security Admin, 36-40; chmn, State Bd. for Voc. Educ, 47-67; chmn, Colo. Dem. Party, 55-58 & 62-64; del, Dem. Nat. Conv, 68. Bus. & Prof. Pos: Pres, Betz Publ. Co, 20-; regent, Univ. Colo, 65- Mil. Serv: Entered as Pvt, Colo. Nat. Guard, 22, released as Pfc, 25. Mem: Sigma Delta Chi; Elks; Eagles; Odd Fellows; Rotary. Rel: Methodist. Legal Res: 8 Cedar Hills, Lamar, Colo. 81052. Mailing Add: P.O. Box 930, Lamar, Colo. 81052.

BETZ, VERNON ELWOOD R
Mo. State Rep.
b. Grundy Co, Mo, 1/21/18; m. 8/20/40 to Gertrude L. Koon. Educ: Abesville High Sch.(Stone Co.), scholarship honors. Polit. & Govt. Pos: Trustee, Lincoln Twp, Grundy Co, Mo, 57-58; assoc. judge, Grundy Co. Court, Second Dist, 59-60; Mo. State Rep, 60- Bus. & Prof. Pos: Farmer. Mem: Odd Fellows; AF&AM; Eastern Star; RAM; RSM; K.T; Elks. Rel: Deacon, South Evans Christian Church. Mailing Add: RFD 1, Trenton, Mo. 64683. (1967)

BEVERLY, ROBERT GRAHAM R
Calif. State Assemblyman
b. Belmont, Mass, 7/1/25; s. William James Beverly and Helen Graham B; m. 5/17/46 to Elizabeth Louise Weisel; c. William J, Barbara L, Robert G, Jr. and Brian C. Educ: Univ. Pittsburgh, 43; Univ. Calif, Los Angeles, 46-48; Loyola Univ. Los Angeles, LL.B, 51. Polit. & Govt. Pos: Mayor and city councilman, Manhattan Beach, Calif, 58-67; Calif. State Assemblyman, 46th Dist, 67-; mem, Calif. Rep. State Cent. Cmt, currently. Bus. & Prof. Pos: Attorney at law, 52- Mil. Serv: Entered as Pvt, Marines, 43, released as Cpl, 46, after serv. in Am. Theatre. Mem: Calif. State Bar; Am. Legion; YMCA. Rel: Protestant. Mailing Add: 2700 Highland Ave, Manhattan Beach, Calif. 90266.

BEVILACQUA, FRANCIS J. D
Mass. State Rep.
m. to Agnes Conti; c. Five. Polit. & Govt. Pos: Dem. State Committeeman; has worked for a new Cent. Dist. Courthouse and North. Essex Commun. Col; Mass. State Rep, 59-, chmn, Cmt. on Counties, Mass. State House of Rep, 65-68. Bus. & Prof. Pos: Pres-treas, Country & Town Ins. & Real Estate, 67- Mem: Holy Name Soc; St. Rita's Holy Name Soc; K. of C; Elks; Am. Legion; Essex Co. Dem. Club; Michael Bucuzzo Post; St. James Convent Assocs; Friends of Don Orione. Mailing Add: 15 Day St, Haverhill, Mass. 01830.

BEVILACQUA, JOSEPH A. D
R.I. State Rep.
b. Providence, R.I, 12/1/18; m. to Josephine. Educ: Providence Col, B.A, 40; Georgetown Law Sch, LL.B, 48. Polit. & Govt. Pos: Mem, Dem. State Cmt, R.I, 50-54; asst. adminstr. of charitable trusts, Dept. of Attorney Gen, 50-54; R.I. State Rep, currently, Dep. Majority Leader, R.I. State House of Rep, 65; del, Dem. Nat. Conv, 68. Bus. & Prof. Pos: Attorney-at-law. Mil. Serv: Army, 1st Lt, 41-46. Mailing Add: 125 Pocasset Ave, Providence, R.I. 02903. (1967)

BEVILL, TOM D
U.S. Rep, Ala.
b. Townley, Ala, 3/27/21; s. Herman Bevill and Fannie Fike B; m. 5/24/43 to Lou Betts; c. Susan B, Donald H. and Patricia Lou. Educ: Univ. Ala, B.S. in Bus. Admin, 43, LL.B, 48. Polit. & Govt. Pos: Ala. State Rep, 58-66; U.S. Rep, Seventh Cong. Dist, Ala, 67- Bus. & Prof. Pos: Attorney-at-law, 48- Mil. Serv: Entered as Cpl, Army, 43, released as Capt, 46; Army Res, 46-66, Lt. Col; Rhineland Campaign Ribbon with Battle Star; Army Commendation Ribbon; ETO Ribbon with Bronze Star. Mem: Lions,(past pres, Jasper Chap); Lions Int.(past dep. dist. gov); past pres, United Fund Drive; bd. of trustees, Walker Col; Moose. Rel: Baptist. Legal Res: 1600 Alabama Ave, Jasper, Ala. 35501. Mailing Add: Jasper, Ala. 35501.

BEYDLER, RAYMOND R
b. Jerico Springs, Mo, 11/17/18; m. 6/4/40 to Virginia Gilpin; c. Clayton, Rayma, Barbara, Carolyn, Judith, Arlene, Lynnete, Colleen, Garrett. Educ: Colby Col. Polit. & Govt. Pos: Mo. State Rep, 64-66. Bus. & Prof. Pos: Contractor, engaged in rd. bldg. and conserv. work. Mil. Serv: Army Air Force, pilot, commissioned officer, 26 months. Rel: Protestant. Mailing Add: El Dorado Springs, Mo. 64744. (1967)

BEYER, BETTY D
b. Sacramento, Calif, 3/24/23; d. Alexander W. Browne and Esther Evans B; div; c. Ann (Mrs. D'Angelo), Kelly Brian and Casey Kevin. Educ: Storey Co. High Sch, Virginia City, Nev. Polit. & Govt. Pos: Exec. secy, Nev. State Dem. Cent. Cmt, 61-64; secy, Washoe Co. Dem. Cent. Cmt, 64-68; secy, Dem. Women's Club, West Dist, Nev, 65-68, pres, 68-69; mem. staff, U.S. Sen. Howard W. Cannon, currently. Mem: Past Noble Grand, Colfax Rebekah Lodge 1, Virginia City, Nev. Rel: Protestant. Legal Res: 2250 Andromeda, Reno, Nev. 89502. Mailing Add: P.O. Box 2744, Reno, Nev. 89505.

BEYER, WILLIAM HENRY
Mayor, Racine, Wis.
b. Racine, Wis, 5/23/19; s. Henry W. Beyer and Edna Schoening B; m. 10/4/42 to Jane Witek; c. Susan, Nancy and Mark. Educ: Colo. State Univ, 37-40; U.S. Navy, Pensacola, 40-41. Polit. & Govt. Pos: Supvr, Third Ward, Racine Co, Wis, 55-60; chmn, Racine Co. Bd, 60-63; Mayor, Racine, 63- Mil. Serv: Entered as Ensign, Navy, 40, released as Lt.(sg), 45, after serv. in Atlantic; Am. and Pac. Theater Ribbons. Mem: VFW; Mason; Elks; Eagles; Kiwanis; Boy Scouts; Big Brothers. Rel: Methodist. Legal Res: 902 Perry Ave, Racine, Wis. 53406. Mailing Add: City Hall, Racine, Wis. 53405. (1967)

BEYMER, JAMES ELTON R
Chmn, Kearny Co. Rep. Party, Kans.
b. Santa Fe, Kans, 3/24/14; s. Clyde E. Beymer and Ethel Jones B; m. 2/22/36 to Evelyn Dean Thorne; c. Deanne (Mrs. Frank Husted) and Judith (Mrs. Richard Rohlf). Educ: Kans. Univ, 2 years; Delta Upsilon. Polit. & Govt. Pos: Mem, city coun, Lakin, Kans, 47 & 48, mem, sch. bd, 64-66; chmn, Kearny Co. Rep. Party, 68- Mil. Serv: Entered as Seaman 2/C, Navy, 44, released as Yeoman 1/C, 46. Mem: Mason; Elks. Rel: Methodist. Legal Res: 503 N. Main, Lakin, Kans. 67860. Mailing Add: Box 191, Lakin, Kans. 67860.

BIAGGI, MARIO D
U.S. Rep, N.Y.
b. N.Y.C, 10/26/17; s. Salvatore Biaggi (deceased) and Mary Campari B; m. 4/20/41 to Marie Wassil; c. Jacqueline, Barbara, Richard and Mario, II. Educ: N.Y. Law Sch, LL.B, 63. Polit. & Govt. Pos: Detective Lt, N.Y.C. Police Dept, 42-65; commun. rels. specialist, N.Y. State Div. of Housing, 61-63; asst. to Secy. of State, N.Y, 63-65; U.S. Rep, N.Y, 69-, mem, cmt. on merchant marine and fisheries and cmt. on sci. and astronaut, U.S. House of Rep. Bus. & Prof. Pos: Sr. partner, Biaggi, Ehrlich and Lang, N.Y.C, 66-; consult, Meadowbrook Nat. Bank, 67; former consult, Cent. State Bank. Mem: Am. and Bronx Co. Bar Asns; Trial Lawyers Asn; pres, Nat. Police Officers Asn. of Am, 67; First v.pres. and acting pres, Patrolmen's Benevolent Asn, 6 years; former dir, Police Widows Relief Fund, Police Recreation Center, Police Pension Fund and Munic. Credit Union; pres, grand coun, Columbia Asns. in Civil Serv, Inc, currently; K. of C; Navy League of the U.S. Recipient, Medal of Honor, N.Y.C. Police Dept, 60; Medal of Honor, nat. cmt, Can-Ital. Centennial, 61; Star of Solidarity, Govt. of Italy, 61. Rel: Catholic. Legal Res: 100 E. Mosholu Pkwy, Bronx, N.Y. 10471. Mailing Add: 1221 Longworth Bldg, Washington, D.C. 20013.

BIANCARDI, JOSEPH G. D
b. Newark, N.J, 7/7/06; m. to Helen Noble; c. Arlene (Mrs. Panullo); three grandchildren. Educ: Rutgers Univ, labor exten. courses; St. Peter's Col. Polit. & Govt. Pos: Mem, Adv. Bd, Robert Bruce House, N.J. Reformatory, Bordentown, N.J; mem, Essex Co. Welfare Bd, 64-65; past chmn, Belleville Cmn. on Civil Rights; mem, Essex Co. Dem. Exec. Cmt; former N.J. State Assemblyman. Bus. & Prof. Pos: Pres, Teamsters Indust. & Allied Workers Local Union 97; exec. bd. Joint Coun, 73, Int. Brotherhood Teamsters; v.pres, United Cerebral Palsy Rehabilitation Inst. of N.J; trustee, Cerebral Palsy Rehabilitation Inst; former trustee, Essex Co. Children's Emergency Shelter; adminstr, Amalgamated Welfare Funds. Mem: Belleville INICO. Awarded plaques in recognition of outstanding work and support in aiding civic welfare and charitable endeavors. Mailing Add: 16 King Place, Belleville, N.J. 07109. (1967)

BIANCHI, CAROL ANN R
Mem, Washington Co. Rep. Party Cmt, Vt.
b. Montpelier, Vt, 10/2/42; d. Bruno Bianchi and Mary B. B; single. Educ: Montpelier High Sch, grad, 60. Polit. & Govt. Pos: Secy. to Lt. Gov, Vt, 64-65; secy. to exec. secy, Vt. Rep. State Cmt, 65-66; dir, Washington Co. Young Rep, 65-; mem, Montpelier Rep. Cmt, 65-; secy. to Vt. Speaker of the House, 66-68; exec. secy, Vermonters for Rockefeller, 68; alternate del, Rep. Nat. Conv, 68; justice of the peace, 69; mem, Bd. of Civil Authority, 69; secy. to Secy. of State, 69-; mem, Washington Co. Rep. Party Cmt, 69-; nat. committeewoman, Vt. Young Rep, 69- Bus. & Prof. Pos: Vt. regional dir, Nat. Ins. Women's Asn, 63-64. Rel: Congregational. Mailing Add: 191 River St, Montpelier, Vt. 05602.

BIANCHINI, ROBERT VINCENT D
b. Providence, R.I, 7/25/40; s. Vincent Anthony Bianchini and Antonette La-Fauci B; m. 11/24/62 to Jean Miriam Paventy; c. Lori and Brenda. Educ: Bryant Col, B.B.A, 62; Phi Sigma Nu. Polit. & Govt. Pos: V.pres, Dem. Men's Club, Cranston, R.I, 58-; alternate del, Dem. Nat. Conv, 68; bank cmnr, State of R.I, 69- Bus. & Prof. Pos: Asst. loan officer, Columbus Nat. Bank, R.I, 63-67; asst. treas, Citizens Savings Bank, Citizens Trust Co, 67-69. Mil. Serv: Entered as Recruit, Naval Res, 57, released as Airman, 61, after serv. in U.S.A. Parle, South Weymouth, Mass, 57-60. Mem: Am. Inst. of Banking (holds basic, standard and grad. cert); United Fund; Fifth Ward Dem. Club; West End Dem. Club; Cranston YMCA; Jr. Achievement; Westwood Area Asn. Rel: Catholic. Mailing Add: 136 Westfield Dr, Cranston, R.I. 02920.

BIBBY, JOHN E. R
S.Dak. State Rep.
b. Brookings, S.Dak, 11/21/20; s. I.J. Bibby and Ruth Erwin B; m. 6/18/47 to Jean Starksen; c. Steven J, Mary Jo and Nathan C. Educ: S.Dak. State Univ, B.S, 42. Polit. & Govt. Pos: S.Dak. State Rep, 63- Bus. & Prof. Pos: Pres, Bibby-Kallemegn Dairy, 60- Mil. Serv: Entered as 2nd Lt, Marine Corps, 42, released as Capt, 46, after serv. in Pac, 44-46; Bronze Star. Mem: Rotary; Mason; Shrine; Am. Legion; Brookings C. of C. Rel: Methodist. Mailing Add: 822 Eighth Ave, Brookings, S.Dak. 57006.

BIBBY, JOHN FRANKLIN R
b. La Crosse, Wis, 8/26/34; s. Joseph W. Bibby and Mildred M. Franklin B; m. 8/16/58 to Lucile H. Hanson; c. John Franklin, Jr. and Peter Mark. Educ: Wis. State Col, La Crosse, B.S, 56; Univ. of Ill, M.A, 57; Univ. of Wis, Madison, Ph.D, 63. Polit. & Govt. Pos: Dir. arts & sci. div. Rep. Nat. Cmt, 65-66, admin. aide to the nat. chmn, 66; res. assoc, House Republican Conf, U.S. House of Rep, 67 & 68, res. dir, 69-; staff specialist, Cmt. on Resolutions, Rep. Nat. Conv, 68. Bus. & Prof. Pos: Fel. in govt, The Brookings Inst, Wash, D.C, 61-62; asst. prof. of polit. sci, Univ. of Wis-Milwaukee, 62-63 & 66-68, assoc. prof, 68-69; asst. prof. of polit. sci, North. Ill. Univ, 63-65. Mil. Serv: Entered as Pvt. E-1, Army, 57, released as Pvt. E-2, 58, after serv. in Field Artil, Six Mo. Res. Prog. Publ: On Capitol Hill: Studies in the Legislative Process, Holt, Rinehart & Winston, 67; The Politics of National Convention Finances and Arrangements, Citizens' Research Found, 68; 'Congress' Neglected Function' in the Republican Papers, Doubleday, 68; plus others. Mem: Am. and Midwest Polit. Sci. Asns. Rel: United Church of Christ. Legal Res: 5507 N. Kent Ave, Whitefish Bay, Wis. 53217. Mailing Add: 706 26th Pl. S, Arlington, Va. 22202.

BIBER, SAMUEL L. D
b. Paterson, N.J. Educ: Rutgers Law Sch; Columbia Univ; City Col, N.Y; Seton Hall. Polit. & Govt. Pos: Former N.J. State Assemblyman. Bus. & Prof. Pos: Lawyer. Mil. Serv: Vet. Mem: Past Comdr, Jewish War Vet; past judge advocate of Aigonne Chap; counsel to United Vet. Mailing Add: 64 Hamilton St, Paterson, N.J. 07505. (1967)

BIBLE, ALAN D
U.S. Sen, Nev.
b. Lovelock, Nev, 11/20/09; s. Jacob H. Bible and Isabel Welsh B; m. 11/17/39 to Loucile Jacks; c. Paul Alfred, William Alan, David Milton and Mrs. Robert Watkins. Educ: Univ. Nev, B.A, 30; Georgetown Univ. Sch. Law, LL.B, 34; Phi Alpha Delta; Lambda Chi Alpha. Hon. LL.D, Rider Col. and Georgetown Univ; Order of Merit, Lambda Chi Alpha. Polit. & Govt. Pos: Dist. attorney, Storey Co, Nev, 35-38; Dep. Attorney Gen, Nev, 38-42, Attorney Gen, 42-54; U.S. Sen, Nev, 54-; Del, Dem. Nat. Conv, 68. Mem: Nat. Asn. Attorneys Gen.(past pres); Univ. Nev. Alumni Asn.(past pres); Am. and Nev. State Bar Asns; Eagles; Mason. Rel: Methodist. Legal Res: Reno, Nev. Mailing Add: 145 Senate Off. Bldg, Washington, D.C. 20510.

BIBLE, ROBERT JOSEPH R
Tenn. State Rep.
b. Mohawk, Tenn, 8/4/34; s. Robert Estil Bible and Lula Mae West B; m. 9/12/59 to Elizabeth Anne Hansel; c. Jeffrey Lynn and Roger Alan. Educ: Univ. Tenn, B.S, 61; Alpha Chi Sigma. Polit. & Govt. Pos: Tenn. State Rep, Sullivan Co, 67- Bus. & Prof. Pos: Chem. engr, Tenn. Eastman Co, 61- Mem: Am. Inst. Chem. Engrs; Instrument Soc. Am; Mason; Eastern Star; Moose; Farm Bur; Jaycees. Rel; Baptist. Mailing Add: 1504 Pineola Ave, Kingsport, Tenn. 37664.

BICE, RAYMOND C. R
b. La Crosse, Wis, 4/5/96. Educ: Univ. of Wis. Ext. Div. Polit. & Govt. Pos: Mem, Gov. Coun. on Traffic Law Enforcement, Wis; chmn, Co. Park Cmt; past officer, Co. Bd; chmn, bd. of trustees, Oak Forest Sanatorium; Wis. State Assemblyman, 47-53; Wis. State Sen, 53-68, former chmn, Senate Cmt. on Cmts. Bus. & Prof. Pos: Retired contractor and lumber retailer. Mil. Serv: Army, overseas. Mem: Am. Legion; past pres, La Crosse Co. C. of C. and Businessmen's Club. La Crosse Civic Duty Award, 57; auth, 65/55 Wis. Speed Limit Law and Commun. Day serv. for the Mentally Handicapped Law. Mailing Add: 2406 State St, La Crosse, Wis. 54601. (1967)

BICKFORD, FRANCIS EDWARD D
La. State Rep.
b. Genessee, La, 6/24/16; s. Eddie Robert Bickford and Dolly Sutherland B; m. 6/10/39 to Sarah Ann Imbraguglio; c. Francis E, Jr, Robert Laborde, Peter Larry, Richard Eugene, John Patrick and Cynthia Ann. Educ: Southeast. La. Col, B.A; La. State Univ, M.Ed. Polit. & Govt. Pos: La. State Rep, 14th Dist, 60-64 & 68- Bus. & Prof. Pos: Teacher, pub. sch, Hammond, La, 37-40, prin, 40-42; supvr, pub. sch, Tangipahoa Parish, 49- Mem: Phi Delta Kappa; La. Teachers Asn; Am. Sch. Food Serv. Asn; Am. Red Cross (chap. chmn); La. Sch. Food Serv. Asn.(legis. chmn); Floridana Econ. Develop. Asn. (pres. of bd). Rel: Catholic. Legal Res: Oak St, Amite, La. 70422. Mailing Add: Route 1, Box 13, Hammond, La. 70401.

BICKLEY, CHARLES HENRY D
Chmn, El Paso Co. Dem. Party, Colo.
b. Greenville, Tex, 3/29/18; s. John Samuel Bickley and Bessie Alice Duffer B; m. 6/24/39 to Dora Doris Reynolds; c. Charles Edward and Bonnie Jean (Mrs. Harold Edmondson). Educ: High sch, Sanger Tex; high sch, Springfield, Colo. Polit. & Govt. Pos: Mem. bd. co. cmnr, El Paso Co. Colo, 64-; welfare cmnr, El Paso Co, 65-69; chmn. welfare cmt, State Asn. of Co. Cmnr, 68-69; chmn, El Paso Co. Dem. Party, Colo, 69- Bus. & Prof. Pos: Laborer and ironworker, construction co, 39; mem. staff, Frankoma Pottery Co. and Liberty Glass Co, Sapulpa, Okla; carpenter, Okla, Tex. and Utah, 40-43; brakeman, Union Pac. R.R, Denver, Colo, 43-46; carpenter, Leftwich Construction Co, Greeley, Pueblo & Colorado Springs, Colo, 46-47; carpenter foreman, Bonforte Construction Co, 47-48 and Alexander Construction Co, Colorado Springs, 48-49; construction supt, Whisenant Construction Co, Colorado Springs, 50-56; partner, Bickley-Digman Construction Co, Colorado Springs, 56-58; owner, Bickley Construction Co. Inc, Colorado Springs, 59- Mil. Serv: Civilian Conserv. Corps, 37-39, Supply Sgt. Mem: El Paso Co. Contractors Asn.(pres); Izaak Walton League of Am.(past mem. exec. bd, past pres. bd. and past state pres, Pikes Peak Chap); Home Builders Asn; Int. Footprinters Asn; Air Force Asn; Int. Platform Asn; Sales and Mkt. Exec. of Colorado Springs; Asn. of the U.S. Army; Quarterback Club of Colorado Springs; C. of C; Moose; Civitan; Urban League; NAACP; G.I. Forum; Colorado Springs Fine Arts Center; Big Bros. of Colorado Springs; past bd. mem, United Fund; past bd. mem, Commun. Planning and Research Coun; past pres. and past mem. labor negotiating cmt, Colorado Springs Div. and Past chmn, cmt. of contractors, Pueblo and Colorado Springs, Asn. Gen. Contractors Am; United Brotherhood of Carpenters and Jointers of Am.(past mem. and past chmn, negotiating cmt, Local Union No. 515). Legal Res: Gold Camp Rd, Colorado Springs, Colo. 80904. Mailing Add: 2315 Bott St, Colorado Springs, Colo. 80904.

BIDDINGER, FRANK JAMES R
Ind. State Sen.
b. Marion, Ind, 12/30/35; s. Thurman A. Biddinger and Florence McKaughan B; m. 6/10/56 to Mary Lou Liepse; c. Jennifer Sue and Nancy Ann. Educ: Ind. Univ, B.S, 57, LL.B, 63; Phi Delta Phi. Polit. & Govt. Pos: Ind. State Sen, 67- Bus. & Prof. Pos: Attorney at Law, Biddinger & Johnson, 63- Mil. Serv: Entered as Pvt, Army, 59, released as Specialist 5, 62, after serv. in Adv. Weapons Support Command, Pirmasens, Germany; 1st Lt, Army Res, currently; Army Commendation Medal. Mem: Am, Ind. and Grant Co. Bar Asns; Mason; Scottish Rite; Shrine; v.pres, Grant Co. Mental Health Clinic; Exchange Club. Rel: Christian Church. Mailing Add: 3 Prairie Court, Marion, Ind. 46952. (1967)

BIDDLE, W. CRAIG R
Calif. State Assemblyman
b. Pasadena, Calif, 7/4/31; s. Charles J. Biddle and Helen B. Raitt B; m. 12/28/68 to Sue Johnson; c. Nancy Louise, Eric Collier and Lisa Ann. Educ: Occidental Col, grad; Univ. South. Calif. Sch. Law, LL.B. Polit. & Govt. Pos: Dep. dist. attorney, Riverside Co, Calif, 58-62, Riverside Co. Pub. Defender, 62-64; chmn, Riverside Co. Rep. Cent. Cmt, 64; Calif. State Assemblyman, 74th Dist, 64-, chmn, Criminal Procedure Cmt, 2 years, Govt. Admin. and Intergovt. Rels. Cmt, Select Cmt. Assembly Reorgan. and Select Cmt. Admin. Justice in Calif. and Majority Floor Leader, Calif. State Assembly. Bus. & Prof. Pos: Partner, Badger, Biddle and Ensign, Riverside, Calif. Mem: Kiwanis, Elks; Farm Bur; Boy Scouts. Most Improved Legislator, Sacramento Press Corps, 67; Most Effective Assemblyman, 68. Rel: Presbyterian. Legal Res: 6370 Magnolia Ave, Riverside, Calif. 92506. Mailing Add: State Capitol, Sacramento, Calif. 95814.

BIDWELL, ARLINE M. D
Dem. State Cent. Committeewoman, Conn.
b. Simsbury, Conn, 8/6/17; d. James Anthony Bidwell and Margaret Quinn B; single. Educ: Simsbury High Sch; Univ. Conn, Col. of Ins. Polit. & Govt. Pos: V.chmn, Simsbury Dem. Town Cmt, 42-60, town chmn, 61-66; pres, Simsbury Dem. Women's Club, 52-56; Dem. State Cent. Committeewoman, Eighth Sen. Dist, Conn, currently; del, Dem. Nat. Conv, 68. Bus. & Prof. Pos: Asst. treas, L. Holzman & Son, Inc, 40- Mem: Town Meeting for Tomorrow; Farmington Valley Watershed Asn; Simsbury Grange; Simsbury Vis. Nursing Asn; Simsbury Recreation Cmn; Simsbury League of Women Voters; Simsbury War Mem. Pool, Inc. Rel: Roman Catholic. Mailing Add: 24 Elm St, Tariffville, Conn. 06081.

BIDWELL, EVERETT V. R
b. Houston, Minn, 10/22/99. Educ: Univ. of Minn. Polit. & Govt. Pos: Wis. State Assemblyman, 52-66; past dir, Portage C. of C; Co. bd, 10 years; Gov. Thomson's Adv. Coms. on Indust. Develop, on Problems of Land Acquisition, and on Oper. of the Eminent Domain Law. Bus. & Prof. Pos: Ice cream mfr; bank v.pres; formerly salesman; farmer. Mem: Wis. Ice Cream Mfr's Asn. Mailing Add: 612 W. Edgewater St, Portage, Wis. 53901. (1967)

BIDWILL, ARTHUR JOHN R
Ill. State Sen.
b. Chicago, Ill, 6/24/03; s. Joseph Edward Bidwill and Mary O'Sullivan B; m. 4/20/27 to Mildred Rose Dowdall; c. Neal McGarry, Rev. Joseph E. Bidwill, O.P. and Mrs. William H. Maus, Jr. Educ: Notre Dame, LL.B, 26; Chicago Club of Notre Dame; Blue Circle. Polit. & Govt. Pos: Committeeman, River Forest Twp, Ill, 35-66; Ill. State Sen, currently, chmn, exec. cmt, 35-, pres. pro-tem, 55-65; chmn, Suburban Rep. Cmt, 36-66; mem. cmt, Nat. Conf. Legis. Leaders, 59-, pres, 63. Bus. & Prof. Pos: Pres, Chicago Stationers, Inc, 37-; pres, The Pacific Co, 50- Mem: K. of C; Union League; K. of M; River Forest Serv. Club; Lake Geneva Yacht Club; Big Foot Country Club. Rel: Roman Catholic. Mailing Add: 1403 Bonnie Brae, River Forest, Ill. 60305. (1967)

BIDWILL, NEAL M. R
b. Chicago, Ill, 5/23/30; s. Arthur J. Bidwill and Mildred Dowdall B; m. 1952 to Patricia Moran; c. Joseph, Martin and Mary. Educ: Loyola Univ, 2 years. Polit. & Govt. Pos: Village trustee, River Forest, Ill, 60-66; Rep. twp. committeeman, River Forest, 66- Bus. & Prof. Pos: Pres, Pac. Paving Co. Mil. Serv: Entered Air Force, 50, released as Cpl, 52, after serv. in 433 Troop Carrier, U.S. Mem: Am. Legion (past comdr, River Forest Chap); River Forest Serv. Club; Operating Engrs. Local 150; Union League Club. Rel: Catholic. Mailing Add: 301 Thatcher, River Forest, Ill. 60305.

BIEBER, DONN K. R
b. Osborne, Kans, 1/27/35; s. August J. Bieber and Elise Chapman B; single. Educ: Kearney State Col, B.A, 64; Univ. Nebr, Col. Law, J.D, 66; Pi Kappa Delta; Pi Gamma Mu; Delta Theta Phi. Polit. & Govt. Pos: Treas, Nebr. Young Rep, 60-61; alternate del, Rep. Nat. Conv, 68. Mem: State of Nebr. and Am. Bar Asns; Colfax Co. Bar Asn.(pres, 66-68); Elks; Sertoma; Jaycees. Rel: Presbyterian. Legal Res: Box 203, Schuyler, Nebr. 68661.

BIEBER, OWEN F. D
Chmn, Kent Co. Dem. Cmt, Mich.
b. Byron Center, Mich, 12/28/29; s. Albert F. Bieber and Minnie Schwartz B; m. 11/25/50 to Shirley Van Woerkom; c. Kenneth, Linda, Michael, Ronald and Joan. Educ: Cath. Cent. High Sch, Grand Rapids, Mich. Polit. & Govt. Pos: Precinct del, Dem. Party, Mich, 62-; chmn, Kent Co. Dem. Cmt, 64-; del, Dem. Nat. Conv, 68. Bus. & Prof. Pos: Pres, Local 687, United Auto Workers, 56-61; int. rep, United Auto Workers, currently. Mem: Cath. Order of Foresters; Civil Liberties Union. Kent Co. AFL-CIO Labor's Man of the Year, 1965. Rel: Catholic. Legal Res: 1132 De Boer S.W, Wyoming, Mich. 49509. Mailing Add: Box H, Grand Rapids, Mich. 49506.

BIEGELMEIER, FRANK D
b. Yankton, S.Dak, 9/9/01; s. Frank Joseph Biegelmeier and Marie Blazek B; m. 8/4/29 to Maude Frances McKenna; c. Jean Ann, Mary Lee and Fran D. Educ: Univ. S.Dak. Sch. Law, LL.B. magna cum laude, 26; Tau Kappa Alpha; Phi Delta Phi. Polit. & Govt. Pos: States attorney, Yankton Co, S.Dak, 31-34; city attorney, Yankton, 53-59; mem, S.Dak. Tax Study Cmn, 59; judge, S.Dak. Supreme Court, currently. Mem: Elks; K. of C. Rel: Catholic. Legal Res: Yankton, S.Dak. 57078. Mailing Add: Capitol Bldg, Pierre, S.Dak. 57501.

BIEGERT, MAURINE D
Dem. Nat. Committeewoman, Nebr.
b. Shickley, Nebr, 6/6/29; d. Willard Hiner and Marie Kolar Steyer H; m. to John Richard Biegert; c. Jeffrey Lynn, Deborah Ann and Beth Marie. Educ: Univ. Nebr, 46-47 & 48-49. Polit. & Govt. Pos: Pres, Fillmore Co. Teachers Asn, Nebr, 47-48; pres, Fillmore Co. Exten. Bd, 52-54; organizer, Fillmore Co. Dem. Women's Group, 58; co-chmn, Citizens for Kennedy, Fillmore Co, Nebr, 60; Dem. Nat. Committeewoman, Nebr, 60-; del, Dem. Nat. Conv, 64 & 68. Bus. & Prof. Pos: Rural sch. teacher, 47-48; 4-H camp counselor, 48; frozen foods demonstrator, Int. Harvester Co, 49-50. Mem: Nebr. Homemakers Asn.(pres, 57-58); bd. dirs, Nebr. Crippled Children's Asn; Federated Women's Club. Named 4-H Pub. Speaking Winner, Nebr. and Nat. 4-H Girls Record Winner, 45; Nat. 4-H Achievement Winner, 46. Mailing Add: Shickley, Nebr. 68436.

BIELAWSKI, ANTHONY F. D
Chmn, Bay Co. Dem. Party, Mich.
b. Grand Rapids, Mich, 9/6/13; m. to Sophie; c. Jerome, Lawrence and Mary. Educ: Univ. Mich. and Univ. Mich. Law Sch. Polit. & Govt. Pos: Chmn, Bay Co. Dem. Party, Mich, 54-; del, Dem. Nat. Conv, 68. Bus. & Prof. Pos: Attorney-at-law. Mailing Add: 205 Shearer Bldg, Bay City, Mich. 48706.

BIEMILLER, ANDREW J. D
Dir, Dept. of Legis, AFL-CIO
b. Sandusky, Ohio, 7/23/06; s. Andrew F. Biemiller and Pearl Weber B; m. 12/20/29 to Hannah Perot Morris; c. Andrew J, Jr. and Nancy Barbara. Educ: Cornell Univ, A.B, 26; Delta Kappa Epsilon. Polit. & Govt. Pos: Mem. exec. cmt, Farmer-Labor Progressive Fedn, 35-41; secy, Progressive Party, State Conv, 37, 39 & 41; Wis. State Assemblyman, 37-42, majority leader, Wis. State Assembly, 37-38, minority leader, 39-42; spec. asst. to labor v.chmn, War Prod. Bd, 41-44; U.S. Rep, Wis, 45-46 & 49-50; del, Dem. Nat. Conv, 48; labor consult. to Secy. Interior, 51-52; legis. rep, AFL-CIO, 53-55 and dir, Dept. of Legis, 56-; mem, Atomic Energy Cmn. Labor-Mgt. Adv. Cmt, 63- Bus. & Prof. Pos: Instr. hist, Syracuse Univ, 26-28 and Univ. Pa, 30-31; instr. econ, Bryn Mawr Summer Sch. for Workers, 30-31; educ. dir, Socialist Party, Milwaukee, 33-36; ed, Wis. Leader, 34-36; gen. organizer, Wis. Fedn. of Labor, 37-41; polit. educ. dir, Upholsterers Int. Union, 47-48. Mem: Nat. Press Club; Kenwood Country Club; Cornell Club. Rel: Quaker. Mailing Add: 6805 Glenbrook Rd, Bethesda, Md. 20016.

BIER, HOWARD F. R
N.Dak. State Rep.
b. Bismarck, N.Dak, 8/20/19; married; c. 3. Educ: State Sch. of Sci, elec. eng. Polit. & Govt. Pos: N.Dak. State Rep, 59-, mem, Legis. Research Coun, N.Dak, 65-67, chmn, House Agr. Cmt, 67-69, chmn, House Educ. Cmt, 69-; mem, Midwest. States Coun. of State Govt. Cmt. on Agr, 65-69. Bus. & Prof. Pos: Farmer; dir, Bank of Hazelton, N.Dak, 56- Mil. Serv: Vet, World War II. Mem: Am. Legion; Elks; Lions; K. of C; Farm Bur. Rel: Roman Catholic. Mailing Add: Hazelton, N.Dak. 58544.

BIERBAUM, MAY PEARL R
b. Litchfield, Ill, 6/11/00; d. James Gillespie Steele and Priscilla Eastwood S; m. 9/22/22; c. Helen (Mrs. Karl Coatney), Ruth (Mrs. Melvin Baker), Leroy and Carl. Educ: Litchfield High Sch. Polit. & Govt. Pos: Pres, Litchfield Rep. Club, Ill, several terms; chmn, Montgomery Co. Rep. Party, 65. Mem: Past matron, Eastern Star. Rel: Lutheran. Mailing Add: 804 N. State St, Litchfield, Ill. 62056.

BIERLY, GEORGE REMY D
b. Elizabeth, Ind; s. Frederick Bierly, Sr. and Louise Englert B, both deceased; m. 6/18/13 to Florence C. Fink; c. Florence Marie (Mrs. Robert C. Price), Fern Elizabeth (Mrs. Don M. Wait), George Remy M.D, Frederick E. and Joan Louise (Mrs. Thomas A. Terveer). Educ: Marion Normal Col, B.S, 11; Ind. State Univ, life cert, 13; Ind. Univ, A.B, 15; Univ. Chicago Grad. Sch, summers 15 and 16; Phi Kappa Theta; Phi Alpha Delta. Polit. & Govt. Pos: Ind. State Rep, Harrison Co, 12-14 & 22-24, Crawford Co, 22-24 and Adams and Wells Co, 50-52; clerk, Adams Circuit Court, 37-40; chmn, Adams Co. Dem. Cent. Cmt, 40-44; prosecuting attorney, 26th Judicial Circuit, 44-46; judge, Ind. Appellate Court, 59-63 and 65-69; del, Dem. Nat. Conv, 60 and alternate del, 64. Bus. & Prof. Pos: Attorney-at-law, Decatur, currently. Mem: Pres, Adams Co. Bar Asn.(secy. for two years); del, Ind. Bar Asn. for ten years; Am. Bar Asn; C. of C; Adams Co. Dem. Club; K. of C.(3° and 4°, past Dep. Grand Knight); Ind. Univ. Alumni Asn; Ind. State Univ. Alumni Club; St. Mary's Holy Name Soc. John W. Foster prize for essay, 'America's Rights as a Neutral,' Ind. Univ, 15; Hon. Ky. Col; Hon. Sagamore of Wabash; practice before U.S. Supreme Court and Immigration Appeals Bd. Rel: Roman Catholic. Legal Res: 110 S. Third St, Decatur, Ind. 46733. Mailing Add: 107 S. Second St, Decatur, Ind. 46733.

BIERMANN, FRED D
b. Rochester, Minn, s. Ewald Elliott Biermann and Martha Christopher B; wid. Educ: Valder Col; Univ. Minn, B.A, 05; Columbia Univ. Polit. & Govt. Pos: Mem, Decorah Park Cmn, Iowa, 22- and Decorah Planning Cmn, 60-65; U.S. Marshal, North. Iowa, 40-53; U.S. Rep, Iowa, 33-39; postmaster, Decorah, 13-23. Mil. Serv: Lt, Army, 17-19, serv. in U.S. and France. Mem: Elks; Am. Legion; VFW; pres, Decorah C. of C, 38. Rel: Agnostic. Legal Res: 408 Mechanic, Decorah, Iowa 52101. Mailing Add: Box 224, Decorah, Iowa 52101. (1967)

BIESTER, EDWARD G, JR. R
U.S. Rep, Pa.
b. Phila, Pa, 1/5/31; m. to Elizabeth Lauffer; c. Ann Meredith, Edward G. III, James Paul and David Robertson. Educ: Wesleyan Univ, B.A, 52; Temple Univ, LL.B, 55. Polit. & Govt. Pos: Mem, Various Finance Cmts, Rep. Party, Pa; mem, Primary and Gen. Election Campaign Cmt; asst. dist. attorney, Bucks Co, 6½ years; U.S. Rep, Pa, 67-, mem, Judiciary Cmt, U.S. House of Rep. Bus. & Prof. Pos: Formerly lawyer, Duane, Morris & Hechscher, Phila, I.J. and D.W. VanArtsdalen, Doylestown and Biester & Ludwig, Doylestown. Mem: Past pres, Kiwanis; bd. dirs, Big Bros. of Bucks Co; Am, Pa, Phila. and Bucks Co. Bar Asns; hon. bd. dirs, Bucks Co. Asn. for the Blind. Rel: Reformed Church. Legal Res: Lower Mountain Rd, Furlong, Pa. 18925. Mailing Add: 1214 Longworth Office Bldg, Washington, D.C. 20515.

BIGBEE, JOHN FRANKLIN, JR. R
b. Mountainair, N.Mex, 6/18/34; s. John Franklin Bigbee and Mildred Penry B; m. 11/5/55 to Povy La Farge; c. Amy, Diane and Franklin Mathews. Educ: Colo. State Univ, B.S. with distinction, 55; Alpha Zeta; Omicron Delta Kappa; Alpha Gamma Rho; Livestock Club; pres, Assoc. Students, Colo. State Univ. Polit. & Govt. Pos: N.Mex. State Rep, Torrance Co, 65-66, mem. interim sch. study cmt, N.Mex. House of Rep, 65-66; chmn. revenue cmt, State Constitutional Conv, 69. Bus. & Prof. Pos: Rancher; mgr, Bigbee Bros. Cattle Co, 55- Mem: Second v.pres, N.Mex. Farm & Livestock Bur, Torrance Co, 64-65, bd. dirs, 67-; mem, N.Mex. State Livestock Bd, 67-; bd. dirs, N.Mex. Cattle Growers, 69-; Torrance Co. & Vicinity Livestock Protective Asn. Conserv. Award, N.Mex. Bankers Asn. Rel: Baha'i Faith. Mailing Add: Encino, N.Mex. 88321.

BIGBY, WALTER OLIVER D
La. State Rep.
b. Slagle, La, 4/10/27; s. Harvey Madison Bigby and Ethel Swindle B; m. 6/30/62 to Flo Whittington; c. Walter O, Jr. Educ: La. State Univ, Baton Rouge, LL.B, 52; Phi Delta Phi; Delta Kappa Epsilon. Polit. & Govt. Pos: Alderman, Benton, La, 54-62; La. State Rep, Bossier Parish, 68- Bus. & Prof. Pos: Partner, Wallace, Bigby & Wallace, Attorneys, Bossier City, La, 52- Mil. Serv: Entered as A/S, Navy, 44, released as Yeoman 2nd, 45, after serv. in Naval Repair Base, San Diego, Calif. Mem: Bossier and La. State Bar Asns; Am. Legion; 40 et 8; C. of C; Lions. Rel: Presbyterian. Mailing Add: 2300 Arlington Place, Bossier City, La. 71010.

BIGELOW, CHARLES DeFORREST R
Mem, Calif. Rep. State Cent. Cmt.
b. El Paso, Tex, 10/24/30; s. Roy Vincent Bigelow and Adele Ann Fuess B; m. 8/14/60 to Jennifer Ann Jaquette; c. Bruce Charles, Elisabeth Ann and Keith DeForrest. Educ: Univ. Tex, B.S, 54; Univ. Ill, Champaign, M.S, 64; Stanford Univ, 3 years, Doctoral Cand; Tau Beta Pi; Chi Epsilon. Polit. & Govt. Pos: V.pres. and pres, Menlo Park-Atherton Young Rep, Calif, 62-65; area chmn, San Mateo Co. Rep. Cent. Cmt, 64; assoc. mem, Calif. Rep. State Cent. Cmt, 67-68, mem, 69-; co-chmn, Menlo Park McCloskey Vol. Orgn, 67-; mem. bd. dirs, Calif. Rep. League, 69-; bd. dirs, Santa Clara Co. Cmt. for Green Foothills, 69- Bus. & Prof. Pos: Research asst, Univ. Ill, Urbana, 55-57; engr, Bechtel Corp, San Francisco, 57-60; research engr, Larsen & Nielsen, Copenhagen, Denmark, 60-61; opers. analyst, Stanford Research Inst, 61-68; sr. systs. analyst, URS Systs. Corp, 68- Mil. Serv: Army Res, 54-61, Lt. Publ: Highway Cost Allocation and Tax Policies, 67 and Middle Africa Transportation Survey, 68, Stanford Research Inst; Regional Transportation Planning, URS Systs. Corp, 68. Mem: English-Speaking Union; Commonwealth Club San Francisco; Sigma Xi; Sci. Research Soc. Am. Mailing Add: 1342 Garden Lane, Menlo Park, Calif. 94025.

BIGELOW, L. WALDO JR. R
N.H. State Rep.
b. Portland, Ore, 3/6/12; married; c. 2. Educ: N.E. Inst. of Embalming. Polit. & Govt. Pos: Moderator, Secy, N.H. Passenger Tramway Safety Bd; dept. fire chief and fire warden; selectman, Warner, N.H, town auditor; N.H. State Rep, 55-; del, Constitutional Conv, 56. Bus. & Prof. Pos: Chmn. adv. bd. of Bank; pres-treas, Henniker Crutch Co, Inc; pres, N.H. Slipper Coop, 68-69. Mem: Mason; Eastern Star; Lions; N.H. Fire Chief's Club; Merrimack Co. Fire Warden's Asn. Mailing Add: Roslyn Ave, Warner, N.H. 03278.

BIGLEY, A. DONALD D
b. Magnolia, N.J, 7/6/26. Educ: St. Joseph's Col, Pa; Rutgers Univ. Law Sch, S.Jersey Div. Polit. & Govt. Pos: N.J. State Assemblyman, 62-65; N.J. State Sen, 65-67; prosecutor, Camden Co, 67- Bus. & Prof. Pos: Attorney. Mem: Camden Co, and N.J. Bar Asns; K. of C; St. Joseph's Col. Alumnae; Elks; bd. dir, Visiting Nurse Asn. Mailing Add: 309 Market St, Camden, N.J. 08102.

BIGWOOD, ROBERT MAURICE R
V.Chmn, Minn. Rep. State Cent. Cmt.
b. St. Thomas, N.Dak, 12/5/18; s. William Henry Bigwood and Alta Lydia Young B; m. 5/7/49 to Barbara Ione Barr; c. Charles, Janet, Patricia, Robert and John. Educ: Univ. Minn, B.B.A, 47; Beta Gamma Sigma; student chap, Soc. for the Adv. of Mgt. Polit. & Govt. Pos: Chmn, Young Men of Minn, 57, Lincoln Club, 58-59, Seventh Dist. Rep. Platform Cmt. and Minn. Rep. State Conv. Platform Cmt, 60; v.chmn, Otter Tail Co. Rep. Cmt, 57-61; del. and mem. credentials cmt, Rep. Nat. Conv, 64, del. and mem. rules cmt, 68; v.chmn, Seventh Cong. Dist. Rep. Orgn. Cmt, 61-62, chmn, 63-69; v.chmn, Minn. Rep. State Cent. Cmt, 69- Bus. & Prof. Pos: Asst. personnel dir, Otter Tail Power Co, 48-49, personnel dir, 49-60, mgr. employee rels, 60-65, v.pres. mgt. serv, 65-; v.pres. and dir, Fergus Falls Savings and Loan Asn, 60- Mil. Serv: Entered as Pvt, Army, 42, released as Meteorologist, Weather Squadron, S.W. Pac, 46. Mem: Jaycees (past pres); Kiwanis (past pres); C. of C.(past pres); Minn. Asn. Commerce & Indust.(dir. and officer); Am. Legion; JCI Senator. Rel: Methodist; layleader, Grace Methodist Church, Fergus Falls, Minn. Mailing Add: Hoot Lake Rd, R.R. 1, Fergus Falls, Minn. 56537.

BIKEL, THEODORE D
b. Vienna, Austria, 5/2/24; U.S. citizen; s. Josef Bikel and Miriam Riegler B; m. 4/2/67 to Rita Weinberg. Educ: Habimah Theatre, Tel Aviv, 43-44; Univ. London, 46; Royal Acad. Dramatic Art, 46-48, fel, 48. Polit. & Govt. Pos: Dem. co. committeeman, Manhattan, N.Y, 63 & 69; del, Dem. Nat. Conv, 68. Bus. & Prof. Pos: Founder, Tel Aviv Chamber Theatre, 44; founder and mem. bd. trustees, Newport Folk Festival, Newport, R.I; founder and pres. of arts chap, Am. Jewish Cong, 61, nat. v.pres, 64-; first v.pres, Actors' Equity Asn, 64-, chmn. cmt. aliens and chmn. cmt. legis, 64-; mem. bd. dir, Amnesty Int. of the U.S.A, 68- Publ: Folksongs and Footnotes, Meridian Bks, 60; 'Freedom Songs—From Egypt to Mississippi,' Hootenany, Mar, 64; 'Report on Jewish College Youth,' Am. Jewish Cong-Cong. Bi-Weekly, 68. Mem: Acad. TV Arts and Sci; Acad. of Motion Picture Arts and Sci; Mensa; Nat. Cmt. for Recording Arts; UN Asn. of N.Y; Nat. Cmt. for Sane Nuclear Policy; Nat. Coun. on Arts and Govt; Actors' Equity Asn; Am. Fedn. TV Arts and Sci; Am. Fedn. of Musicians; Screen Actors Guild; Am. Jewish Cong; Village Independent Dem. Citizen of the World and Friend of Humanity Award, Brandeis

Univ, 60; Man of the Year, Mt. Sinai Hosp, 60; Distinguished Serv. in the Cause of Human Rights, Anti-Defamation League, 61; Leader in Americanism and Human Rights, N.Y. Jewish War Vet, 61; Man of the Year, B'nai B'rith, 67; Man of Conscience Award, Am. Jewish Cong, 67. Rel: Jewish. Mailing Add: 25 Bank St, New York, N.Y. 10014.

BILD, FRANK R
Mo. State Rep.
b. Romania, 9/30/11; s. Anton Bild and Katherine Schiebel B; m. 9/18/37 to Flora H. Huss; c. Brian Alan, Norman Anton, Karen Ann and Kathleen Ann. Educ: Normal Col. Am. Gymnastic Union, B.P.E, 34; Ind. Univ, B.S, 34; St. Louis Univ, LL.B, 42; Phi Delta Kappa; Phi Epsilon Kappa. Polit. & Govt. Pos: Mo. State Rep, 13th Dist, 63-64, 47th Dist, currently. Mil. Serv: Entered as 2nd Lt, Army, 42, released as Capt, 46, after serv. in 478th Qm. Group, China-India-Burma. Mem: Lions; Gardenville Affton Mem. Post 300. Rel: Lutheran. Mailing Add: 7 Meppen Court, St. Louis, Mo. 63128.

BILGOR, IRVING J. D
b. Providence, R.I, 1/31/10; m. to H. Myrtle. Educ: Boston Univ. Col. of Bus. Admin; Boston Univ. Sch. of Law, LL.B, 35. Polit. & Govt. Pos: Former treas. and dir, Young Dem. of R.I; former mem, World War II Vet. Bonus Bd; former mem, Coun. on Hwy. Safety; former mem, Motor Vehicle Study Cmn; R.I. State Rep, 49-51 & 53-60; former chmn, Cmn. to Study Probs. Caused by Uninsured Drivers, 62; former secy, Cmn. to Study Aid to Non-pub. Schs, 62; former R.I. State Sen; former chmn, Joint Cmt. Hwy. Safety. Bus. & Prof. Pos: Attorney-at-law. Mil. Serv: Army, 1st Lt, 41-46. Mem: R.I, Mass. and Barnstable Bar Asns; Am. Trial Lawyers Asn. Rel: Congregation Temple Beth-El. Mailing Add: 78 Homer St, Providence, R.I. 02905. (1967)

BILHEIMER, STEPHEN CHARLES R
b. Arkadelphia, Ark, 6/22/03; s. Charles William Bilheimer and Edna Carpenter B; m. 5/5/28 to Jeanne Summerfield; c. Flave (Mrs. David J. Reed, II) and Peter C. Educ: Univ. South. Calif. Bus. Sch, 24-25; Univ. Ore. State, B.S, 27; Beta Theta Pi. Hon. D.B.A, Woodbury Col. Polit. & Govt. Pos: Chmn, Bd. Rep. Assocs. South. Calif, 67; mem. bd. dirs, Calif. Mus. Sci. and Indust; mem, Los Angeles Mem. Coliseum Cmn. and Los Angeles Co. Southeast Gen. Hosp. Authority Cmn; alternate del, Rep. Nat. Conv, 68. Bus. & Prof. Pos: Dir. and mgr, Phelps-Terkel, Inc, 28-54; pres, Silverwoods, 54-67, chmn. bd, 67- Mem: Mason; Los Angeles Country Club; Calif. Club; Bel-Air Bay Club; Rotary. Outstanding Alumnus Award, Univ. South. Calif. Sch. Bus. Admin, 63, Gen. Alumni Asn. Award for Outstanding Serv, 68. Rel: Episcopal. Mailing Add: 142 S. Rockingham Ave, Los Angeles, Calif. 90049.

BILLINGS, BERNARD E. D
b. 1928. Polit. & Govt. Pos: Regional chmn, Ky. Welfare Asn; chmn, Region 10 Tourism Promotion Cmt; dir, Co. Fair Bd; mem, Ky. Foothills Conf; mem, Powell Co. Area Redevelop. Asn; Ky. State Rep, 64-68. Bus. & Prof. Pos: Ins. agent. Mil. Serv: Army, Korean War. Mem: Mason; DAV; Am. Legion; RAM; Ky. and Nat. Asn. of Independent Ins. Agents; PTA; Red River Dam Asn; v.pres, Powell Co. Lions Club; pres, Natural Bridge Park Asn; pres, Powell Co. Alumni Asn; Stanton Vol. Fire Dept. Rel: Christian. Mailing Add: Stanton, Ky. 40380. (1967)

BILLINGS, CLAUDE ELLEDGE, JR. R
b. Hays, N.C, 8/2/33; s. Claude E. Billings and Laura Elledge B; m. to Betty Miner; c. Sandra, Kathy, Jimmy and Bill. Educ: Draughon Bus. Col, 42. Polit. & Govt. Pos: Sheriff, Wilkes Co, N.C, 50-58; state exec. mem, Rep. Party, 54-56 & 60-66; chmn, Wilkes Co. Rep. Party, 60-66; del, Rep. Nat. Conv, 64. Bus. & Prof. Pos: Off. mgr, Barber-Somers Motor Co, 46-50; Gen. mgr, Stroud Ins. Agency, 58- Mil. Serv: Entered as Pvt, Army, 44, released as Sgt, 46, after serv. in Pac. Theater; Phillippine Liberation Medal. Mem: Jaycees; Wilkesboro Bus. & Prfnl. Men; Mason; Elks; VFW; Am. Legion. Rel: Baptist. Legal Res: 106 S. Cherry St, Wilkesboro, N.C. 28697. Mailing Add: 103 Bridge St, Wilkesboro, N.C. 28697.

BILLINGS, FRANKLIN SWIFT, JR. R
b. Woodstock, Vt, 6/5/22; m. to Pauline R. Gillingham; c. Franklin, III, Jireh Swift and Ann. Educ: Harvard Col, B.S, 43; Univ. of Va, LL.B, 47. Polit. & Govt. Pos: Village trustee, Woodstock, Vt, town agent, selectman, mem, Planning Cmn, sch. dir. and libr. trustee; asst. secy, Vt. State Senate, 49 & 51-53, exec. clerk, 55, secy, 57-59; judge, Hartford Munic. Court, 55-62; clerk, Woodstock Union High Sch. Dist, 58-62; mem, Woodstock Planning Cmn, 58-62; Secy. of Civil and Mil. Affairs, 59-60; Vt. State Rep, 61-66, chmn, Judiciary Cmt, Vt. State House of Rep, 61-63, Speaker of House, 63-66; mem, Legis. Coun, 63-67; moderator, Town, Village and Sch. Dist, 66-; Superior Court Judge, 66-; mem, Gov. Cmn. on Crime, Vt, 67- Bus. & Prof. Pos: Attorney-at-law. Mil. Serv: Brit. Eighth Army, Sixth Armored Div, 43-46. Mem: Grange; Mason; Shrine; Am, Vt. and Windsor Co. Bar Asns. Rel: Episcopal. Mailing Add: 5 The Green, Woodstock, Vt. 05091.

BILLINGS, GUY EARL D
Mem, Calif. Dem. State Cent. Cmt.
b. McCallsburg, Iowa, 2/18/17, s. Harry E. Billings and Edna Jorstad B; m. 6/6/40 to Nelda Jean Price; c. Linda Jean (Mrs. Lyons) and Becky Earlene. Educ: Compton Jr. Col, 36-37. Polit. & Govt. Pos: Mem, bd. dirs, Great West. Dairy and Livestock Show—City of Commerce Los Angeles, Calif, 7 years; chmn, Planning Cmn, City of Compton, 50-; mem, Calif. Dem. State Cent. Cmt, 69- Mem: Rotary (pres, Compton Club, 59-60). Rel: Lutheran. Mailing Add: 1403 S. Atlantic Dr, Compton, Calif. 90221.

BILLINGS, HAROLD CARLTON R
Vt. State Rep.
b. Mt. Holly, Vt, 3/15/93; m. to Gladys L. Lawrence; c. One son and one daughter. Educ: Univ. Vt, B.S, 18. Polit. & Govt. Pos: Selectman, 36-58; former chmn, Town Planning Bd; former dir, Civilian Defense, World War II; former mem, Rationing Bd; Vt. State Rep, currently. Bus. & Prof. Pos: High sch. prin, 18-25; retired inspection engr, Jones and Lamson Machine Co. Mil. Serv: Nat. Guard, Mexican border, 16. Mem: F&AM; Windsor Lodge of Perfection, Frank J. Martin Chap. of Rose Croix, Mt. Calvary Coun; Princes of Jerusalem, Vt. Consistory; Mason (32°); Kappa Sigma; U.V.M. Trustee. Rel: Methodist. Mailing Add: 35 Woolson Ave, Springfield, Vt. 05156. (1967)

BILLINGTON, OWEN D
b. 1912. Educ: Murray State Col, B.S. Polit. & Govt. Pos: Ky. State Rep, 52-58; Ky. State Sen, 64-67; chmn Murray Planning Cmn, Ky, until 68. Bus. & Prof. Pos: Pres. and dir, Murray Investors, Inc, Murray, Ky. and Billington-Roberts Industs, Hopkinsville, v.pres. and dir, Billington Finance & Investment Co, Murray and Lakeway Shores, Inc, dir, Fulton Investors, Inc, Fulton, Fulton Inns, Inc, Am. Businessmen's Life Ins. Co, Lexington, Ky. Investors, Inc, Frankfort and Murray Shopping Centers, Inc, Murray, currently. Mil. Serv: Navy, World War II. Mem: Am. Legion; VFW; Ky. Asn. of Ins. Agents; Murray Rotary. Rel: Baptist; Bd. of Deacons, Sunday Sch. Teacher, First Baptist Church, Murray, Ky. Mailing Add: 509 N. Seventh St, Murray, Ky. 42071.

BILLION, DAVID HENRY R
S.Dak. State Rep.
b. Sioux Falls, S.Dak, 6/29/43; s. Henry A. Billion and Evelyn Heinz B; m. 7/3/65 to Marlene Ann Rance; c. Julie Ann and Margaret Evelyn. Educ: Loras Col, 1 year; Carroll Col, B.A, 65. Polit. & Govt. Pos: S.Dak. State Rep, 69- Bus. & Prof. Pos: V.pres. and gen. mgr, Billion Motors, Sioux Falls, S.Dak. Mem: Bd. of Control, Greater Sioux Falls Safety Coun; bd. dirs, Minnehaha Co. Red Cross. Rel: Catholic. Mailing Add: 3108 S. Williams, Sioux Falls, S.Dak. 57105.

BILOWZ, WALTER GREGORY R
Chmn, North Reading Rep. Town Cmt, Mass.
b. Chelsea, Mass, 11/19/29; s. Walter Bilowz and Helen Czarniawksi B; single. Educ: Harvard Univ, A.B, 52; Boston Univ. Sch. of Law, LL.B, 56. Polit. & Govt. Pos: Town counsel, North Reading, Mass, 60; del. and mem, Platform Cmt, Rep. State Conv, 62 & 64; chmn, North Reading Rep. Town Cmt, 64-; mem, Bd. of Selectmen, North Reading, 59-68, chmn, 68-; mem, Issues Cmt, State Rep. Cmt, 66, aide, 63-66; spec. asst. attorney gen, Mass, 68. Bus. & Prof. Pos: Practicing attorney, 59- Mem: First Dist. East. Middlesex Bar Asn; Middlesex Co. Bar Asn; Moose; K. of C. Rel: Roman Catholic. Mailing Add: 47 Central St, North Reading, Mass. 01864.

BILYEU, CHARLES EDWARD 'CHICK' D
Chmn, Bannock Co. Dem. Cent. Cmt, Idaho
b. Tonopah, Nev, 3/9/17; s. Hiram Bilyeu and Valencia Bawden B; m. 10/8/56 to Diane Thelma Falter; c. Brigette A, Clark P. and Valencia Jo. Educ: Univ. Redlands, B.A. in Speech, 40; Pasadena Playhouse Col. Theatre, Calif, Master of Theatre Arts, 49; Alpha Psi Omega; Pi Kappa Delta. Polit. & Govt. Pos: Dem. precinct committeeman, 62-64 & 66-; chmn, Bannock Co. Dem. Cent. Cmt, Idaho, 62- Bus. & Prof. Pos: Assoc. Prof, Speech and Drama, Idaho State Univ, 50- Mil. Serv: Entered as Pvt, Army, 41, released as Capt, 46, after serv. in 190th Ordnance Bn, ETO & Pac; ETO Ribbon with 2 Battle Stars, Pac. Theater Ribbon and 1 Battle Star. Mem: Elks; Am. Asn. Univ. Prof. Featured speaker throughout Idaho; Master of Ceremonies for State Convs; co-producer, full length theatrical feature motion picture, Don't Cry Wolf; dir. and actor, Upper N.Y. Summer Theater; owner and dir, Summer Theater, Pocatello, Idaho. Rel: Episcopal. Mailing Add: Route 1 N, Box 48, Pocatello, Idaho. 83201.

BILYEU, DIANE F. D
Idaho State Sen.
b. Pocatello, Idaho, 2/11/35; d. Leslie L. Falter and Afton Chilton F; m. 10/8/56 to Charles E. 'Chick' Bilyeu; c. Brigette A, Clark P. and Valencia Jo. Educ: Idaho State Univ, B.A. in Speech and Drama, 68; Alpha Psi Omega; Pi Kappa Delta; Spurs; Alpha Omicron Pi. Polit. & Govt. Pos: Precinct committeeman, Pocatello Dem. Party, Idaho, 64-66; chmn, Dist. 35 Dem. Party, 66-68; Idaho State Sen, Dist. 35, 68-, mem. educ, indust, labor and econ. develop, irrigation and judiciary cmts, Idaho State Senate, currently; mem, Gov. Cmn. Status Women, currently. Rel: Episcopal. Mailing Add: Route 1 N, Box 48, Pocatello, Idaho 83201.

BINDEMAN, JACOB EDWARD R
Mem, D.C. Rep. State Cent. Cmt.
b. Baltimore, Md, 3/24/13; s. Isaac Bindeman and Sarah Drobis B; m. 3/22/42 to Julia Paul; c. David Paul and Stuart L. Educ: Georgetown Univ, LL.B, 37, LL.M, 39; Phi Sigma Delta. Polit. & Govt. Pos: Chmn, Pub. Welfare Adv. Coun. of the Dist. of Columbia, 57-63; mem, D.C. Rep. State Cent. Cmt, 67-; chmn, Bd. of Elections of the Dist. of Columbia, 69- Bus. & Prof. Pos: Partner, Bindeman & Burka, Wash, D.C, 37-; pres, Landmark Realty, Inc, Wash, D.C, 67- Mem: Bar Asn. of the Dist. of Columbia; Am. Bar Asn. Man of the Year, Washington Hebrew Congregation; Meritorius Public Service Award, Dist. of Columbia; Distinguished Service Award, Georgetown Univ. Rel: Jewish. Mailing Add: 3020 Brandywine St. N.W, Washington, D.C. 20008.

BINDER, JAMES SHIRLEY R
b. St. Paul, Minn, 7/3/00; s. James Binder and Nettie Singer B; m. 2/17/25 to Laura Heilbron. Educ: Cent. High Sch, St. Paul, Minn; S. St. Paul High Sch. Polit. & Govt. Pos: Mem, Pulaski Co. Rep. Cmt, Ark, 62-66 & 69, treas, 66-68; del, Rep. Nat. Conv, 68; co-chmn, finance cmt, Cent. Ark. Rep. Campaign, 68; mem, Ark. State Rep. Cmt, 69. Bus. & Prof. Pos: Sales mgr, footwear div, Firestone Tire & Rubber Co, Minneapolis and Boston, 27-29; salesman and asst. sales mgr, Converse Rubber Co, Malden, Mass, 29-42, Chicago, Ill, 46-49; pres, Pfeifer Plumbing & Heating Co, Little Rock, Ark, 49-68, chmn. bd, 69- Mil. Serv: Entered as Capt, Air Force, 42, released as Lt. Col, 46, after serv. in Training and Materiel Commands, 42-46; Army Commendation Ribbon, Secy. of War. Mem: Little Rock C. of C; U.S. C. of C; Mason (32°); Scottish Rite; chmn, Metrop. Planning Cmn; Ark. Indust. Develop. Cmn; Ark. Enterprises for the Blind (past pres). Man of the Year Award, Assoc. Plumbing and Heating Contractors of Ark, 54-55. Rel: Jewish. Legal Res: 6705 Waverly Place, Little Rock, Ark. 72207. Mailing Add: P.O. Box 1656, Little Rock, Ark. 72203.

BINGHAM, DONALD WILLIAM R
b. Randolph Co, N.C, 2/3/25; s. Thomas William Bingham and Effie Johnson B; m. 11/27/49 to Sarah C. Smith; c. Debbie E, Betsy J. and Tommi L. Educ: Farmer High Sch. Polit. & Govt. Pos: N.C. State Rep, 63-66. Bus. & Prof. Pos: Lumber Bus. Mil. Serv: Vet, World War II, 43-46. Mem: Clemmons Stock Club. Rel: Methodist; Church Bldg. Cmt; Bd. of Stewards, 61-64. Mailing Add: Route 1, Advance, N.C. 27006. (1967)

BINGHAM, JAMES C. R
b. Littleton, N.H, 9/30/95; wid; c. One daughter; Two granddaughters. Educ: Dartmouth Col. Polit. & Govt. Pos: N.H. State Rep, 61-68. Bus. & Prof. Pos: Retired. Mil. Serv: Vet, World War I. Rel: Episcopal. Mailing Add: 124 Warren St, Concord, N.H. 03301. (1967)

BINGHAM, JONATHAN B. D
U.S. Rep, N.Y.
b. New Haven, Conn, 4/24/14; s. Hiram Bingham; m. to June Rossbach; c. Sherrell (Mrs. Bland), June Mitchell (Mrs. Esselstyn), Timothy W. and Claudia R.(Mrs. Hall). Educ: Groton; Yale, A.B, 36, LL.B, 39; Phi Beta Kappa. Polit. & Govt. Pos: Spec. asst. to Asst. Secy. of State, 45-46; asst. dir, Off. of Int. Security Affairs, 51; dep. and acting adminstr, Tech. Coop. Admin, 51-53; secy. to Gov. Averell Harriman of N.Y, 55-58; U.S. Rep. on Econ. and Soc. Coun. of UN with rank of Ambassador and prin. adv. to Ambassador Adlai E. Stevenson in econ. and soc. affairs; mem, U.S. del. to four UN Gen. Assemblies, 61-63; U.S. Rep. on UN Trusteeship Coun. with rank of Minister, 61, pres. of Coun, 62; U.S. Rep, N.Y, 65-; del, Dem. Nat. Conv, 68. Bus. & Prof. Pos: Spec. correspondent for N.Y. Herald Tribune, 35 & 38 in Europe, USSR and Far East; lawyer. Mil. Serv: Enlisted as Pvt, World War II; discharged as Capt. of Mil. Intel. Mem: Various bar asns; Judiciary Cmt. of N.Y.C. Bar Asn. Legal Res: Bronx, N.Y. Mailing Add: 133 Cannon House Office Bldg, Washington, D.C. 20515.

BINGLE, JAMES DOUGLAS R
Rep. Representative Committeeman, Ill.
b. Fremont, Ohio, 7/20/30; s. Rev. Bert J. Bingle and Mabel Morrison B; m. 3/25/51 to Marjorie L. Higley; c. Christine Ann, Donald James, Richard Paul and foster child, Belinda Kay Arnett. Educ: N.Cent. Col, Naperville, Ill, B.A, 52; Honors Soc. Polit. & Govt. Pos: Rep. precinct committeeman, Will Co, Ill, 59-; v.chmn, Will Co. Rep. Cent. Cmt, 64-68; mem. sch. bd, Will Co. Elem. Sch. Dist. 96, 66-; Rep. representative committeeman, 41st Dist, Ill, 66-; v.chmn, Will Co. Sheriff's Police Merit Cmn, 69-; twp. assessor, DuPage Twp, 70- Bus. & Prof. Pos: Scientific assoc, Argonne Nat. Lab, 53- Publ: Several scientific articles in professional journals. Mem: Ill. Asn. Sch. Bds; Co. Merit Cmn. Asn. Ill; Twp. Officials of Ill; Int. Asn. Assessing Officers; Hampton Park Lions; Will Co. Young Rep. Orgn. Outstanding Rep. Precinct Committeeman, Will Co, Ill, 65. Rel: Presbyterian. Mailing Add: R.R. 2, Lindenwood Lane, Plainfield, Ill. 60544.

BINKLEY, MARGUERITE HALL R
Secy, Harris Co. Rep. Party, Tex.
b. Greenville, N.C, 5/22/26; d. Lannie Pope Hall and Glenna Eleanor Nobles H; m. 8/4/45 to Warren Haskins Binkley; c. Richard Warren (deceased) and Suzanne. Educ: Va. Intermont Jr. Col, 43-45. Polit. & Govt. Pos: V.chmn, Brooks Co. Rep. Party, Tex, 56-57; alternate del. or del, Rep. State Conv, 62, 64, 66 & 68; supvr, numerous campaign hq, Harris Co, 62-; contrib. ed, Rep. Banner, Houston, 64 & 65; pres, West Univ. Rep. Women's Club, 67; alternate del, Rep. Nat. Conv, 68; secy, Harris Co. Rep. Party, 68- Mem: Nat. Asn. of Parliamentarians. Rel: Episcopal. Mailing Add: 6523 Buffalo Speedway, Houston, Tex. 77005.

BIRD, DANIEL WOODROW D
Va. State Sen.
b. Bland, Va, 7/6/12; m. to Elizabeth Kegley Dunn. Educ: Nat. Bus. Col; Emory Col; Henry Col. Polit. & Govt. Pos: Mem, Ninth Cong. Dist. Dem. Cmt; dir, Co. Farm Bur; Va. State Rep, 48-55; Va. State Sen, 56- Bus. & Prof. Pos: Dairyman and farmer; pres, Va. Safety Appliance Corp. Mem: Kiwanis (past pres); Mason; AF&AM; RAM; Ceres Ruritan Club; Co. Dairyman's Asn; Tri-State Milk Producers Asn. Rel: Methodist; Mem, Bd. of Stewards. Mailing Add: Bland, Va. 24315. (1967)

BIRD, JORGE Popular Dem, P.R.
Rep-at-Lg, P.R. House of Rep.
b. Guayama, P.R, 8/23/10; s. Agustín Bird Elías and Angélica Fernández Cintrón E; m. 12/23/34 to Victoria L. Vilella; c. Luisa Angélica (Mrs. Roberto Inclán), Victoria Josefina (Mrs. José Antonio Sáenz de Ormijana), Nellie Aurora, Agustín Jorge and Jorge Pablo. Educ: Univ. P.R; Phi Eta Mu. Polit. & Govt. Pos: Mem, adv. cmt, P.R. Develop. Bank, bd. dirs, Popular Dem. Party, P.R. and P.R. Police Cmn; committeeman, Nat. Dem. Party (on leave); mem, Sch. Bd. of P.R. Voc. Training Courses, Citizens Cmt. on improvement of rels. between P.R. citizenship and govt; adv, Secy. of Commerce, P.R; rep-at-lg, P.R. House of Rep. and mem. finance and planning cmts, currently; mem, Tourism Adv. Cmt, Econ. Develop. Admin, P.R, currently. Bus. & Prof. Pos: Pres. and owner, Bird Restaurants, Inc, Jorge Bird Elect. Appliances, Inc. and P.R. Airways; dir, Amstell Brewery Corp, P.R. and Int. Investment Corp; founder and first pres, P.R. Conv. Bur; dir, Marriott Corp, currently; pres. and owner, Jorge Bird Travel Serv, Inc; Bird Gasoline Sta; Real Estate and Farming. Publ: 'Relato de Un Viaje a España y Niza' (Spanish booklet); co-sponsor, 'Man in the City of the Future,' Columbia Univ. Grad. Sch. Bus, 68; 'Apuntes de Mis Viajes Por el Mundo,' Ed. Madrid, Spain, 69. Mem: Pres, P.R. C. of C; dir, Inter-Am. C. of C; Sales Exec. Club; Elks; U.S. Navy League; YMCA; Lions (past pres, Lions Int, 67-68); pres, P.R. Travel Agents Asn. and Hotel and Restaurant Asn; former mem. bd. of trustees, P.R. Jr. Col; pres. coun, Interam. Univ. of P.R; consult. group bd. dirs, Found. of Sch. Med, Univ. P.R; bd. trustees, Int. Inst, Am. World Univ. of P.R. Man of the Year, P.R. C. of C; P.R. Patriot Eugenio María de Hostos Award; Good Will Ambassador-at-lg, Lions Int; Award of the Cross of the Gentlemen of the Equator of the Repub. of Gabón (Africa) and Comendador of the Order of Christopher Columbus of the Dominican Repub; Hon. Tex. Citizen, 69. Rel: Catholic. Legal Res: Ramírez de Arellano 1-5, Garden Hills, Bayamón, P.R. 00619. Mailing Add: P.O. Box BA, Río Piedras, P.R. 00928.

BIRD, LLOYD CAMPBELL D
Va. State Sen.
b. Valley Center, Va, 8/1/94; m. to Lucille Crutchfield Phinney. Educ: Med. Col. of Va. Polit. & Govt. Pos: Va. State Sen, 29th Sen. Dist, 44- Bus. & Prof. Pos: Pharmacist and farmer; Pres, Phipps & Bird, Inc; Pres, Allied Sci. Corp. Mil. Serv: W.W. I, Base Hosp. 45, McGuire Unit. Rel: Methodist. Mailing Add: 8847 Riverside Dr, Richmond, Va. 23235.

BIRD, MARY LOUISE R
Treas, Okla. Fedn. Rep. Women
b. Bunker Hill, Kans, 7/29/07; d. Eugene Oscar Humes and Alberta Markley H; m. 11/21/31 to Lloyd Phillip Bird; c. Alberta (Mrs. Phillip Royal), Lloyd Phillip, Jr, and James Markley. Educ: Univ. Kans, A.B, 29; Botts Bus. Col, Okla, 30; Polit. & Govt. Pos: Various Rep. precinct off; treas, Ponca City Rep. Women's Club, Okla, 67-68 and mem. bd. dirs, 69; secy, Kay Co. Rep. Cmt, 67-; secy, Kay Co. Rep. Exec. Bd, 67-; alternate del, Rep. Nat. Conv, 68; treas, Okla. Fedn. Rep. Women, 69- Mem: Eastern Star. Rel: Methodist. Mailing Add: 214 Virginia Ave, Ponca City, Okla. 74601.

BIRD, RICHARD ALAN R
Fla. State Rep.
b. Lansing, Mich, 6/16/40; s. Samuel Richard Bird and Esther Grace Coan B; m. to Duchess Williamson. Educ: Mich. State Univ, B.A, 62; Univ. Fla, LL.B, 64; Phi Delta Phi; Alpha Gamma Rho. Polit. & Govt. Pos: Fla. State Rep, 66- Bus. & Prof. Pos: Attorney with Watson, Hubert & Davis, 64, private practice, 67- Mem: Am, Fla, Mich. and Broward Co. Bar Asns; Am. Judicature Soc; Lawyers Title Guaranty Fund; Broward Co. Young Rep; Jaycees; Touchdown Club; Dolphins 100. Rel: Methodist. Mailing Add: 3450 N.E. 19th Ave, Ft. Lauderdale, Fla. 33306.

BIRK, RAYMOND JULE R
Mo. State Rep.
b. Gridley, Kans, 3/17/32; s. Phillip Birk and Bertha Knapp B; m. 9/4/54 to Julia Agnes Robohn; c. Philip Walter, Peter Michael and Ann Margaret. Educ: Univ. Kans, B.S. in Bus, 54 and LL.B, 58; Phi Delta Phi; Alpha Kappa Lambda. Polit. & Govt. Pos: Asst. prosecuting attorney, Jasper Co, Mo, 61; asst. city attorney, Joplin, 62-66; Mo. State Rep, 67- Mil. Serv: Entered as 2nd Lt, Army, 55, released as 1st Lt, 57, after serv. in Army Field Artil, U.S. and P.R, 55-57. Mem: Am, Mo. and Jasper Co. Bar Asns; Am. Trial Lawyers Asn; Elks; Twin Hills Golf & Country Club; K. of C; Kiwanis; C. of C; Jasper Co. Unit, Am. Cancer Soc. Rel: Catholic. Legal Res: 930 N. Moffet, Joplin, Mo. 64801. Mailing Add: 312 W. Sixth St, Joplin, Mo. 64801.

BIRKELAND, ARTHUR C. R
Chmn, Day Co. Rep. Cent. Cmt, S.Dak.
b. Pierpont, S.Dak, 8/7/04; s. Christ H. Birkeland and Anna Askvold B; m. 2/19/49 to Verna Dorothy Thompson. Educ: North. State Col, S.Dak, B.S, 30; Univ. S.Dak; Univ. Wis; Sigma Delta Epsilon; Pi Kappa Delta. Polit. & Govt. Pos: Chmn, Day Co. Rep. Cent. Cmt, S.Dak, 58-; alternate del, Rep. Nat. Conv, 64; v.pres, N.E. S.Dak. Econ. Opportunity, 65-66. Bus. & Prof. Pos: Pres. of bd, Coop. Elevator, Pierpont, S.Dak, 64-66. Mem: Mason, Scottish Rite, Shrine; Farm Bur; bd. mem, Bristol Bowling Asn; Twp. Supvr, Twp. Union. Rel: Lutheran; Secy, Church Board, Lutheran Church, Pierpont, S.Dak, 56-66. Mailing Add: Pierpont, S.Dak. 57468.

BIRKENHOLZ, CARROLL MERLE R
Chmn, Jasper. Co. Rep. Cent. Cmt, Iowa
b. Newton, Iowa, 10/22/23; s. Henry C. Birkenholz, Sr. and Mima C. Montgomery B; m. 7/22/47 to Agnes Lorene Keating; c. Janet (Mrs. Comer) and David. Educ: Univ. Iowa, 41-42; Moorhead State Teachers Col, 43. Polit. & Govt. Pos: Chmn, Newton City Bd. of Rev, Iowa, 64-69; chmn, Jasper Co. Rep. Cent. Cmt, 65- Bus. & Prof. Pos: V.pres, United Fed. Savings & Loan Asn, Des Moines, Iowa, 58-62. Mil. Serv: Entered as Pvt, Air Force, 43, released as Capt, 52, after serv. in 307th Bomb Wing, Pac. Theatre, World War II and Korea, 44-45 & 51-52, Res, Maj, 52-69; Purple Heart; Distinguished Flying Cross; Air Medal with two Clusters; Presidential Unit Citation. Mem: Chmn, Bd. of Realtors City Beautification Proj, Newton, 66-69; Elks. Rel: Methodist. Mailing Add: 305 E. 28th St. S, Newton, Iowa 50208.

BIRKHEAD, KENNETH MILTON D
b. St. Louis, Mo, 11/15/14; s. Leon Milton Birkhead and Agnes Schiereck B; m. 5/17/43 to Barbara Belwood; c. David Keehn and Scott Belwood. Educ: Mo. Valley Col, A.B, 49; Univ. of Mo, M.A, 50. Polit. & Govt. Pos: Asst. to chmn, Dem. Nat. Cmt, 48 & 50-52, finance dir, 57-59; staff dir, Dem. Sen. Campaign Cmt, 52-53; asst. to the Majority Whip, U.S. Senate, 53-55; secy, Nat. Capital Dem. Club, 59-64; confidential asst. to the Secy. of Agr, Dept. of Agr, 61-66, adminstr, Rural Commun. Develop. Serv, 66-68; nat. exec. dir, Citizens for Johnson-Humphrey, 68; nat. exec. dir, Citizens for Humphrey, 68; nat. exec. dir, Citizens for Humphrey-Muskie, 68; spec. asst. to U.S. Sen. Thomas J. McIntyre, 69- Bus. & Prof. Pos: Asst. to dir, Friends of Democracy, 37-48; nat. dir, Am. Vets. Cmt, 55-57; consult, Albert and Mary Lasker Found, 59-61. Mil. Serv: Entered as Pvt, Air Force, 42, released as 1st Lt, 46, after serv. in Air Transport Command. Mem: Am. Acad. of Polit. and Soc. Sci; Int. Town and Country Club, Falls Church, Va. Distinguished Serv. Award, U.S. Dept. of Agr, 64. Rel: Protestant. Mailing Add: 6445 Queen Anne Terr, Falls Church, Va. 22044.

BIRT, WALTER ARTHUR R
Maine State Rep.
b. New Haven, Conn, 9/22/15; s. Walter Howard Birt and Mary Jane MacNevin B; m. 2/15/46 to Dorothy Fern Larlee; c. Walter Howard and Douglas Edward. Educ: Garret Schench High Sch, East Millinocket, Maine. Polit. & Govt. Pos: Mem, Penobscot Co. and East Millinocket Rep. Cmts, 63-; Maine State Rep, 63- Bus. & Prof. Pos: Power sta. operator, Great North. Paper Co, 34- Mil. Serv: Entered as Pvt, Air Force, 42, released as Sgt, 46, after serv. in Fourth Air Force. Mem: Mason (Past Master); C. of C.(past pres); IBEW. Eagle Scout; mem, Maine Sisquicentennial Cmn. Rel: United Church of Christ. Mailing Add: 33 Pine St, East Millinocket, Maine 04430.

BISCHOFF, BARNEY (BERNARD J) DFL
Minn. State Rep.
b. Hibbing, Minn, 1/27/31; s. Bernard Herman Bischoff and Agnes Pauline Russ B; m. 9/20/58 to Grace Elinor Erickson; c. Bernard Joe, Gail Frances, Anita Marie, Nancy Kay, Mari Lynette, LeAnn Grace and Jerome Steven. Educ: Hibbing Jr. Col, Minn, 50-51; Iowa State Univ, B.S. in Chem. Engr, 54; Univ. Minn. Law Sch, Minneapolis, LL.B, 59; Gamma Eta Gamma. Polit. & Govt. Pos: V.chmn, 63rd Dist. Dem-Farmer-Labor Party, Minn, 64-66 and chmn, 66-68; del, Dist. and Co. Dem-Farmer-Labor Party Conv, 66 & 68 and State Dem-Farmer-Labor Party Conv, 66; mem, State Dem-Farmer-Labor

Cent. Cmt, 66-68 & 69; Minn. State Rep, 63rd Dist, 69- Mil. Serv: Entered as Pvt, Army, 54, released as Specialist, 56, after serv. in 82nd Airborne Div, N.C. Mem: Hibbing Jr. C. of C.(v.pres, 64-65, pres, 65-66); C. of C; Range Bar Asn.(secy-treas, 66-67, v.pres, 67-68, pres, 68-69); Am, Minn. and Wis. Bar Asns; Am. Trial Lawyers Asn; Elks; Rotary; K. of C. Rel: Roman Catholic. Legal Res: 3802 Third Ave. E, Hibbing, Minn. 55746. Mailing Add: 2011 Third Ave. E, Hibbing, Minn. 55746.

BISCHOFF, DOUGLAS GEORGE R
Chmn, Salt Lake Co. Rep. Cent. Cmt, Utah
b. Salt Lake City, Utah, 10/19/26; s. Carl Bischoff and Gertrude Kirchoff B; m. 10/7/54 to Cohleen Jensen; c. Tamara and James Douglas. Educ: Columbia Univ, B.S. and M.S, 53; Univ. Utah, B.A, 58; Phi Kappa Phi. Polit. & Govt. Pos: Chmn. pub. rels. and mem. exec. cmt, Salt Lake Co. Rep. Cmt, Utah; del, Rep. Nat. Conv, 68; chmn, Salt Lake Co. Rep. Cent. Cmt, currently. Mil. Serv: Entered as A/S, Navy, 43, released as Pharmacists Mate 1/C, 46; Am. Theater Ribbon; Asiatic Pac. Medal; Victory Medal. Mem: Lions Int. Rel: Latter-day Saint. Mailing Add: 3838 Ruth Dr, Salt Lake City, Utah 84117.

BISHOP, CECIL W. 'RUNT' R
b. Johnson Co, Ill, 6/29/90; s. William C. Bishop and Belle Zada Ragsdale B; m. 12/24/11 to Elizabeth Hutton; c. Jack Hutton, Sr. Educ: Anna High Sch, Ill; Union Acad, Anna, Ill. Polit. & Govt. Pos: U.S. Rep, 25th Dist, Ill, 40-54; asst. postmaster gen, U.S, 55-56; supt. of Indust. Prog. for Ill, 57-58; asst. to dir, Dept. of Labor, Ill, 59-60. Bus. & Prof. Pos: Merchant-tailor, Ladies and Gents, 10-23; city clerk, Carterville, Ill, 16-18; served as mem. of local draft bd. during World War I; postmaster, Carterville, 23-33; crusade chmn, Williamson Co, 60-66. Mem: Spec. rep, Lions Int, Lions Club, Dist. Gov.1-C of Ill, 32-33; Elks; Odd Fellows; Crab Orchard Golf Country Club; Boat and Yacht Club; Big Brothers Sunday Sch. Class of Christian Church. Played semi-pro baseball and football; winner of several golf tournaments, including 2nd place trophy at South. Ill. Sr. Golf Tournament, 66. Mailing Add: 210 Olive St, Carterville, Ill. 62918. (1967)

BISHOP, CLAY MASSEY R
b. Manchester, Ky, 8/3/12; s. Hugh Bishop and Janie Massey B; m. 7/15/34 to Jessie Mae Marcum; c. William H, Georgia Isabelle (Mrs. Bailey) and Clay Massey, II. Educ: Berea Col, 28-30; Univ. Ky, 44-46; Univ. Ky. Law Sch, LL.B, 48. Circuit clerk, Clay Co, Ky, 34-43; R.R. cmnr, Third Dist, Ky, 43-47; mem, Ky. Rep. State Cent. Cmt, 43-47; co. attorney, Clay Co, Ky, 58-61; alternate del, Rep. Nat. Conv, 68; circuit judge, 41st Judicial Dist. of Ky, Clay, Jackson and Leslie Co, 70- Pres, Claymont Coal Co, 47-, Bishop Coal, Stoker & Fuel Co, 48-58; secy. & treas, Continental Coal Co, 64-, Bane Coal Co, 67-; secy-treas, McCreary Co. Coal Co, 68- Mem: F&AM; Mason (32°); charter mem, Manchester Kiwanis Club (past pres). Rel: Presbyterian. Legal Res: 217 Main St, Manchester, Ky. 40962. Mailing Add: P.O. Box 215, Manchester, Ky. 40962.

BISHOP, DONALD E. R
Mich. State Rep.
b. Almont, Mich, 2/27/33; s. G.C. Bishop and Jane W. B; m. 8/6/55 to Nancy Michael; c. Rebecca, Susan, Judith, Martha and Michael. Educ: Oberlin Col, B.A, 55; Detroit Col. of Law, J.D, 66. Polit. & Govt. Pos: Mich. State Rep, 67- Bus. & Prof. Pos: Attorney, Martin & Bishop, Rochester, currently; secy, Litex, Inc, 69-; dir, Nat. Bank of Rochester, Mich, 69- Mil. Serv: Entered as Pvt, Army, 55, released as Sp-3, 57, after serv. in 532nd Field Artil. Observation Bn, ETO, 56-57. Mem: Mich. and Oakland Co. Bar Asns. Rel: Congregational. Mailing Add: 2332 W. Avon Rd, Rochester, Mich. 48063.

BISHOP, JAMES ALDEN D
b. Presque, Isle, Maine, 7/3/14; s. Orrin Joshua Bishop and Grace Chandler B; m. 3/1/42 to Frances Willard Hamilton; c. James A, Jr, Frank H. and Elizabeth J. Educ: Bowdoin Col, A.B, 38; Columbia Univ. Sch. of Law, LL.B, 41; Zeta Psi. Polit. & Govt. Pos: City solicitor, Presque Isle, Maine, 48-; mem. bd. of dirs, Sch. Admin. Dist. One, 58-62; Maine State Rep, Presque Isle, 65-67; mem. bd. of trustees, Maine Maritime Acad, 65-; mem, Maine Transportation Cmn, 65- Bus. & Prof. Pos: Partner, Bishop & Stevens, 58- Mil. Serv: Entered as Ens, Navy, 42, released as Lt, 45, after serv. in Motor Torpedo Boat Squadron, 28, Solomons, Philippines. Mem: Am, Maine and Aroostook Co. Bar Asns; Am. Legion; VFW; Nat. Aviation Club; Aircraft Owners and Pilots Asn. Private Pilot. Rel: Episcopal. Legal Res: 101 Baiton St, Presque Isle, Maine 04769. Mailing Add: P.O. Box 311, Presque Isle, Maine 04769. (1967)

BISHOP, JOHN J, JR. R
Md. State Sen.
b. Baltimore, Md, 12/5/19; s. John Joseph Bishop, Sr. and Mary Lillian Freshline B; m. Doris Lee Anderson; c. John J, III, Suzanne Mary, Karen Lee, Patricia Ann, Michael Raymond and Paul Francis. Educ: Univ. Baltimore, A.A, 49, LL.B, 52. Polit. & Govt. Pos: Md. State Sen, 66- Mil. Serv: Entered as Seaman, Coast Guard, 46, released as Seaman 1/C, 47, after serv. in Am. Theatre of Operations. Mem: Md. State Bar Asn.(chmn, Ethics Cmt, 67); Baltimore Co. Bar Asn; Soc. State Legis; assoc. Eagleton Inst. Politics; Loch Raven Kiwanis; Catholic War Vet. Award, Md. Asn. Retarded Children. Rel: Catholic. Legal Res: 6671 Loch Hill Rd, Baltimore, Md. 21212. Mailing Add: 606 Loyola Fed. Bldg, Towson, Md. 21204.

BISHOP, MARY GERTRUDE R
b. Boston, Mass, 6/3/15; d. John McLaughlin and Clementina P. Jenkins; m. 9/15/45 to Harold Morgan Bishop; c. Harold Morgan, Jr. Educ: Boston Clerical Sch, Exec. Secy. Training. Polit. & Govt. Pos: Mem, East Lyme Rep. Town Cmt, Conn, 57-, v.chmn, 62-64; pres, East Lyme Rep. Women's Club, 60-62; pres, New London Co. Rep. Women's Asn, 61-66; Conn. State Rep, East Lyme, 61-67; pres, Shoestring Rep. Club, 20th Sen. Dist, 62-64; treas, Conn. Coun. Rep. Women's Clubs, 62-64; mem, East Lyme Econ. Develop. Cmn, 62-, exec. secy, 63-; prog. chmn, Conn. Munic. Develop. Cmn, 63-64, secy, 64-65, v.pres, 65-66, pres, 66-; justice of the peace, East Lyme, 64-; pres, Second Cong. Dist. S.Rep. Women's Asn, 66- Bus. & Prof. Pos: V.pres, East Lyme Indust. Found, Inc, 65-; dir, Southeast. Conn. Econ. Develop. Corp, 66- Mem: Secy, East Lyme C. of C; Zonta Int; Lawrence & Memorial Hosp. Auxiliary, New London; Am. Legion Auxiliary; East Lyme Garden Club, Hist. Soc; Conn. and Nat. Orders of Women Legis; Niantic Bay Yacht Club. Auerbach Scholarship to Foreign Policy Conf, Colgate Univ, 59. Rel: Roman Catholic. Mailing Add: 8 Jo-Anne St, Niantic, Conn. 06357. (1967)

BISHOP, ROBERT GRANVILLE R
b. Jamaica, N.Y, 7/20/35; s. William F. Bishop and Mildred Hutchinson B; m. 7/1/56 to Carol Margaret Sharpe; c. Judith Lynn and Sharon Elizabeth. Educ: Mass. Inst. Tech, B.S, 57; Nu Delta, Phi Mu Delta. Polit. & Govt. Pos: Chmn, Hopewell Rep. City Cmt, Va, 64-67. Mem: Am. Inst. Chem. Eng; Jr. C. of C. Rel: Presbyterian. Mailing Add: Route 2, Box 464 H, Chester, Va. 23831. (1967)

BISPO, NAOMI MARIE R
Assoc. Mem, Calif. Rep. State Cent. Cmt.
b. Seattle, Wash, 11/23/02; d. Jesse Anderson Allred and Josephine L. Moss A; m. 6/15/23 to William Lawrence Bispo; c. Frances A.(Mrs. Lewis) and Robert L. Educ: Univ. Calif, Los Angeles, 2 years. Polit. & Govt. Pos: Treas, Southwest Women's Rep. Club, 57-59, secy, 59 and pres, 60-61; v.chmn, Nixon for Pres, Southwest Hq, 60; co-chmn, Nixon for Gov, 31st Cong. Hq, 62; mem. and treas, 63rd Assembly Dist. Rep. Party, 62-64 & 64-66, alternate mem, 67-69; treas, 31st Cong. Dist. Rep. Party, 62-66; mem, Crenshaw-Ladera Rep. Women, Federated, 62-; mem. rules cmt, Los Angeles Co. Cent. Cmt, 64-66; secy, Southwest and Centinela Valley Rep. Club, 68 and treas, 69; supvr, Neighbors for Nixon-Agnew, Southwest, Inglewood, Hawthorne & South Bay Area, 68; sustaining mem, Nat. Hq. Rep. Party, assoc. mem, Calif. Rep. State Cent. Cmt, currently. Bus. & Prof. Pos: Dir. of dramatics, El Retiro Girls Sch, San Fernando, Calif, 22; clerk, Los Angeles Water & Power, 23; sales rep, Avon Prod, Ind, Pasadena, Calif, 41- Mem: Life mem. Am. Legion Auxiliary (past secy, pres, dist. pres. and held past state chairwomanships); 8 et 40 (past pres. and held several state chairwomanships); Int. Toastmistress Club (past pres. and coun. chmn); S. Ebell Club; Am. Cancer Soc. Vol. Ten Year Award, Los Angeles Am. Cancer Soc. Rel: Catholic. Mailing Add: 7710 Brighton Ave, Los Angeles, Calif. 90047.

BISPO, WILLIAM LAWRENCE R
Mem, Calif. State Rep. Cent. Cmt.
b. Danville, Calif, 1/26/97; s. Edward Lawrence Bispo (deceased) and Mary Lewis B. (deceased); m. 6/15/23 to Naomi Marie Allred; c. Frances Ann (Mrs. Lewis) and Robert Lewis. Educ: Univ. South. Calif. Sch. Pub. Admin, B.S.P.A, 52, mem, Student Body. Polit. & Govt. Pos: Vol. polit. work, Rep. Party, Calif, 63-69; assoc. mem, Calif. State Rep. Cent. Cmt, 63-68, mem, 69-; alternate co. cent. committeeman, 63rd Assembly Dist. Rep. Party, Calif, 65-68. Bus. & Prof. Pos: Bills payable acct, Zellerbach Paper Co, Los Angeles, Calif, 20; from stock record clerk to acct. receivable acct, White Auto Co, 20-27; from clerk-typist to sr. clerk of assessments, Civil Serv, City of Los Angeles, 27-64; retired. Mil. Serv: Entered as Seaman, Navy, 18, released as Yeoman 1/C, 19, after serv. at Submarine Base, San Pedro, Calif, 12th Naval Dist; Naval Res, 18-22. Mem: Univ. South. Calif. Alumni Asn. and Sch. Pub. Admin. Alumni Asn; Am. Legion; Los Angeles Civic Center Speakers Club (past secy-treas); Los Angeles City Employees Asn.(off. rep, 3 years); Southwest and Centinela Valley Rep. Club (from treas. to pres); Retired Los Angeles City Employees Asn. Award and Spec. Citation, Bd. of Pub. Works, City of Los Angeles, Spec. Citation, Retirement Bd. Rel: Catholic. Mailing Add: 7710 Brighton Ave, Los Angeles, Calif. 90047.

BISSONNETTE, OSCAR D
N.H. State Rep.
b. Nashua, N.H, 6/23/89; married; c. Four. Educ: Nashua High Sch. Polit. & Govt. Pos: N.H. State Rep, 59- Bus. & Prof. Pos: Retired real estate agent. Rel: Catholic. Mailing Add: 15 Euclid Ave, Nashua, N.H. 03060. (1967)

BITTLE, R(USSELL) HARRY R
Pa. State Rep.
b. Pottsville, Pa, 3/27/38; s. Russell B. Bittle and Margaret A. Gaffney B; m. 3/31/62 to Mary Jane Bietsch; c. Russell B, Jr. and Timothy B. Educ: Gettysburg Co. A.B, 60; Univ. Fla. Col. Law, 61-62; Dickinson Sch. of Law, LL.B, 64; Kappa Delta Rho; Phi Alpha Delta; Reed Law Club; Corpus Juris Soc. Polit. & Govt. Pos: Asst. dist. attorney, Franklin Co, Pa, 65-68; Pa. State Rep, Franklin and Cumberland Counties, 68- Bus. & Prof. Pos: Attorney-at-law, with James A. Strite, 65-68; private practice, 68- Mem: Franklin Co, Pa. and Am. Bar Asns; Mason; Chambersburg Rod & Gun Club; C. of C; Franklin Co. Farmers Asn. Rel: Lutheran. Mailing Add: 811 Woodlawn Circle, Chambersburg, Pa. 17201.

BITTNER, FREDERICK WARREN R
Utah State Rep.
b. Lyndhurst, N.J, 7/9/22; s. Frederick Joseph Bittner and Dorothy Kiefer B; m. 8/1/45 to Florence Black; c. Carol Jean, Frederick Warren, Jr. and Jonathan Chester. Educ: Nichols Jr. Col, A.B.A, 41. Polit. & Govt. Pos: Utah State Rep, Dist. 11, 67- Bus. & Prof. Pos: Salesman, Zellerbach Paper Co, 50-60; mgr. and partner, Printers, Inc, Salt Lake City, 60; pres, Salt Lake Club of Printing House Craftsman, 65; v.pres, Printing Indust. Utah, 66. Mil. Serv: Entered as Pvt, Air Force, 42, released as S/Sgt, 45, after serv. in Eighth Air Force, Eng. and 15 months as prisoner of war, Germany; Air Medal with 2 Oak Leaf Clusters. Mem: Rotary. Rel: Latter-day Saint. Mailing Add: 885 N. 13th West, Salt Lake City, Utah 84116.

BIXEL, C. ERNEST D
Chmn, Marshall Co. Dem. Cmt, Ind.
b. Marshall Co, Ind, 9/21/11; s. Charles Bixel and Hattie C. Shadel B; married to Louise Elsesser. Educ: Plymouth High Sch. Polit. & Govt. Pos: Mayor, Plymouth, Ind, 56-63; former cmnr, Bur. of Motor Vehicles, State of Ind; chmn, Third Dist. Dem. Cmt, Ind; chmn, Marshall Co. Dem. Cmt, currently. Bus. & Prof. Pos: Partner, Sporting Goods Store. Mem: Former pres, Plymouth Rotary Club; Mason. Rel: Protestant. Mailing Add: R.R. 5, Box 286, Plymouth, Ind. 46563.

BIXLER, DENNY JAMES D
Pa. State Rep.
b. Johnstown, Pa, 11/1/40; s. Densel Bixler and Catherine Blackford B; m. 2/14/66 to Beverly Jean Bainbridge. Polit. & Govt. Pos: Pa. State Rep, 79th

Dist, 68- Bus. & Prof. Pos: V.pres, Blair Co. Broadcasters Corp, 66- Mem: Elks; Big Bros. of Am.(bd. dirs); Boy Scouts (bd. dirs). Rel: Protestant. Mailing Add: 1801 Logan Ave, Altoona, Pa. 16602.

BJORLIE, LIV BERGLIOT D
Dem. Nat. Committeewoman, N.Dak.
b. Tolna, N.Dak, 12/30/32; d. Frederick T. Lundeby and Anna Samuelson L; m. 4/4/52 to Elmer Peder Bjorlie; c. Peter, Anna, John, Paul and Laura. Educ: Valley City State Teachers Col, 50-51 & 69. Polit. & Govt. Pos: Pres, Barnes Co. Dem. Women, N.Dak, 58-59; dist. dir, N.Dak. Dem. Non-Partisan League, 58-61, state chmn, 61-64; secy, N.Dak. State Dem. Women, 59, regional dir, 60, pres, 61; campaign mgr, Barnes Co. Dem. Party, 60; mem, exec. cmt, D.Dak. Dem. Party, 61-69, cong. campaign dir, 63 & 66; Dem. Nat. Committeewoman, N.Dak, 64-; chmn, Dem. Mid West Conf. Session, 65, mem. exec. cmt, 67-69; mem, President's Coun. on Youth, 67; mem, Nat. Site Cmt. & Credentials Cmt, Dem. Nat. Cmt, 67-68, mem, Rules Cmt, 69; del, Dem. Nat. Conv, 68. Bus. & Prof. Pos: Teacher, 51-52; off. mgr, Valley Realty, N.Dak, 66; off. mgr, Farmers Union Ins, 67, pres, cmt. on facilities, 67-68. Mem: Int. Platform Asn; N.Dak. Judicial Cmn; Peace Corps Adv. Coun; Nat. Farmers Union; Zonta. Rel: Lutheran. Mailing Add: 1380 C Ave. N, Valley City, N.Dak. 58072.

BJÖRNSON, VAL R
State Treas, Minn.
b. Lyon Co, Minn, 8/29/06; m; c. three daughters, two sons. Educ: Univ. of Minn, 30. Polit. & Govt. Pos: State treas, Minn, 50-54, 56-; Rep. nominee for U.S. Sen, 54. Bus. & Prof. Pos: Radio, newspaper fields; assoc. ed, St. Paul Pioneer Press and Dispatch, 47-50, 55-56. Mill Serv: Navy, 42-46. Mem: Past pres, Nat. Asn. of State Auditors, Comptrollers and Treas. Mailing Add: 2914 46th Ave. S, Minneapolis, Minn. 55406.

BLACHLY, QUENTIN A. R
b. Hammond, Ind, 9/10/34; s. Glenn M. Blachly and Viola Albert B; m. 7/20/57 to Joanne Rogan; c. David, Mary Kathryn and Gregory. Educ: Valparaiso Univ, A.B, 56; Valparaiso Univ. Sch. Law, LL.B, 59; Phi Alpha Delta; Theta Chi. Polit. & Govt. Pos: Attorney, Valparaiso Zoning and Planning Cmns, Ind; attorney, Kouts; Ind. State Rep, 67-68. Mem: Past pres, Porter Co. Bar Asn; Ind. State Bar Asn; bd. dirs, Rotary; bd, Porter Co. YMCA; bd, Valparaiso C. of C. Rel: Protestant. Mailing Add: R.R. 4, Joliet Rd, Valparaiso, Ind. 46383. (1967)

BLACHLY, WILLIAM D
b. Montclair, N.J, 4/13/24; m. to Alice Clifford; c. One son and one daughter. Educ: Oberlin Col, 47-50; Goddard Col, B.A, 56; Putney Grad. Sch, M.A, 57. Polit. & Govt. Pos: Vt. State Rep, 65-66. Bus. & Prof. Pos: Farmer. Mil. Serv: Navy, 42-46. Mailing Add: Marshfield, Vt. 05658. (1967)

BLACK, BEULAH D
Mem, Calif. Dem. State Cent. Cmt.
b. Dallas, Tex, 8/13/99; d. Frank Walker and Roxie Williams W; div; c. Carl Large. Educ: Auberry High Sch, 12 years. Polit. & Govt. Pos: Mem. adv. cmn, Co. Hosp, Los Angeles, Calif, 10 years; mem, Dist. Attorneys Adv. Coun; mem. adv. coun, Assemblyman Jack R. Frenton, 51st Dist, Calif; mem, Calif. Dem. State Cent. Cmt, currently. Mem: World War I Barrax 5 (past pres); Pvt. Alex Burger Auxiliary (past pres); Am. Legion (past pres, Post 323); E. Los Angeles Coord. Coun.(past pres. and scholarship chmn, 10 years); soc. worker, Vet. Serv, officer 5 years; secy, Montebello and E. Los Angeles Breakfast Club; secy, Montebello Park Taxpayers' Asn; Montebello and E. Los Angeles Chap. for Mt. Sinai Hosp. and Clin.(past pres); pres, Eastmont Golden Agers Sr. Citizens, 69; soc. worker for the commun. for the past 20 years. Two Citations, PTA; Plaque, E. Cent. Welfare Assembly. Rel: Baptist; Pub. Rels. Mailing Add: 6028 Hereford Dr, Los Angeles, Calif. 90022.

BLACK, CHARLES EDWIN R
Committeeman, Mass. State Rep. Party
b. Quincy, Mass, 4/29/30; s. Clarence Edgar Black and Emmie Peaslee B; m. 10/20/56 to Norma Arlene Smith; c. Karen Arlene and Diane Louise. Educ: Northeast. Univ, A.B, 52, Law Sch, 51-53; Boston Univ, LL.B, 54. Polit. & Govt. Pos: Mem, Rockland Rep. Town Cmt, Mass, 60-62; mem, Rockland Zoning Bd. Appeals, 61-62; chmn, Rockland Citizens Better Town Govt, 62; pres, Hingham Young Rep. Club, 64-65; asst. town moderator, Hingham, 65; chmn. rules cmt, Mass. Young Rep. Asn. First Annual Conv, 65; mem. rules cmt. and del, Rep. State Conv, 66; chmn. credentials cmt, Mass. Young Rep. Conv, 67; committeeman, Mass. State Rep. Party, 67-, chmn, Hingham Rep. Town Cmt, 68-69. Bus. & Prof. Pos: Attorney, law dept, John Hancock Mutual Life Ins. Co, 60-64 and asst. counsel, 65- Mil. Serv: Entered as Pvt, Army, 55, released as 1st Lt, 60, after serv. in U.S, 55-60, Maj, Res; Army Commendation Medal with Oak Leaf Cluster, Army Res. Medal. Mem: Am. Bar Asn; Am. Life Conv; AF&AM; Ancient and Hon. Artillery Co. Mass; ROA. Outstanding Young Rep, Mass, 65. Rel: Baptist. Mailing Add: 41 Winthrop Rd, Hingham, Mass. 02043.

BLACK, CREED CARTER R
Asst. Secy. for Legis, Dept. of Health, Educ. and Welfare
b. Harlan, Ky, 7/15/25; s. Creed Carter Black and Mary Cole B; m. 12/28/47 to Catherine Davis; c. Creed Carter, Jr, Steven Davis and Douglas Stuart. Educ: Medill Sch. Journalism, Northwest. Univ, B.S, 49; Univ. Chicago, M.A, 52; Lambda Chi Alpha. Polit. & Govt. Pos: Asst. secy. for legis, Dept. of Health, Educ. and Welfare, 69- Bus. & Prof. Pos: Copy ed, Chicago Sun-Times and Chicago Herald Am, 49-50; ed. writer, Nashville Tennessean, 50-59; exec. ed, Savannah Morning News and Savannah Eve. Press, 59-60; v.pres. and exec. ed, Wilmington Morning News and Eve. J, 60-64; managing ed, Chicago Daily News, 64-68, exec. ed, 68-69. Mil. Serv: Entered as Pvt, Army, 43, released as Pfc, 46, after serv. in 100th Inf. Div, ETO, 44-46; Bronze Star; Combat Infantryman's Badge. Mem: Former pres, Nat. Conf. of Ed. Writers; secy. and mem. bd. dirs, Am. Soc. of Newspaper Ed; v.pres, Northwest. Alumni Asn; Sigma Delta Chi; Kappa Tau Alpha; Am. Cmt. of Int. Press Inst; Capitol Hill Club, Wash, D.C. 1962 Merit Award, Northwest. Univ; Outstanding Medill Grad. Award, Chicago Headline Club. Rel: Methodist. Legal Res: 141 Kenilworth Ave, Kenilworth, Ill. 60043. Mailing Add: 2301 E St, N.W, Apt. 610, Washington, D.C. 20037.

BLACK, DAVID C. D
Chmn, St. Francois Co. Dem. Cent. Cmt, Mo.
b. Flat River, Mo, 9/15/22; s. Emmett B. Black and Mary Bremner B; single. Educ: Washington Univ, A.B; Harvard Law Sch, LL.B. Polit. & Govt. Pos: Probate judge, Francois Co, Mo, 54-; del, Dem. Nat. Conv, 56 & 60; mem, Dem. State Cmt, 60-62; chmn, St. Francois Co. Dem. Cent. Cmt, 64- Mil. Serv: Entered as Pvt, Air Force, 42, released as S/Sgt, 46, after serv. in 20th Air Force. Mem: Mo. and Am. Bar Asns; Mo. Asn. of Probate Judges (state pres); Am. Judicature Soc; Am. Legion; VFW; Elks; Kiwanis. Rel: Presbyterian. Mailing Add: 105 McIlvane, Farmington, Mo. 63640.

BLACK, DAVID STATLER D
b. Everett, Wash, 7/14/28; s. Lloyd Llewelyn Black and Gladys Statler B; m. 7/26/52 to Nancy Haskell B; c. David Lloyd, Andrew Haskell and Kathleen Louise. Educ: Stanford Univ, B.A, 50; Univ. of Wash, LL.B, 54; Phi Delta Phi; Delta Kappa Epsilon. Polit. & Govt. Pos: Asst. Attorney Gen, Wash. State, 57-61; counsel, Wash. Pub. Serv. Cmn, 57-61; gen counsel, Bur. Pub. Rds, U.S. Dept. Commerce, D.C, 61-63; v.chmn, Fed. Power Cmn, 63-66; adminstr, Bonneville Power Admin, 66-67; Under Secy. of the Interior, 67-69. Bus. & Prof. Pos: Lawyer, Preston, Thorgrimson and Horwitz, Seattle, Wash, 54-57; v.pres. and adminstr, Dreyfus Corp, N.Y.C, 69- Mem: Wash. State Bar Asn. Legal Res: 114 Woodland Ave, Summit, N.J. 07901. Mailing Add: Dreyfus Corporation, 767 Fifth Ave, New York, N.Y. 10004.

BLACK, ERNEST F. R
Secy, Lucas Co. Rep. Cent. Cmt, Ohio
b. Whitehouse, Ohio, 4/17/15; s. William Gerard Black and Nettie Elliott B; m. 11/12/34 to Evelyn Viola Vitello; c. Carolyn (Mrs. Roger Kosch). Educ: Monclova High Sch, Ohio, grad, 33. Polit. & Govt. Pos: Twp. constable, Ohio, 43-57; twp. trustee, Monclova Twp, Lucas Co, 57-; secy, Lucas Co. Rep. Cent. Cmt, Ohio, 63- Bus. & Prof. Pos: Stationary engr, Toledo Edison Co, 41. Mem: Mason. Rel: Protestant. Mailing Add: 7465 Maumee-Western Rd, Maumee, Ohio 43537.

BLACK, HARRY GORDON R
Chmn, Hancock Co. Rep. Party, Ky.
b. Lexington, Ky, 11/2/07; s. Henry Gordon Black and Nancy Walters B; m. 9/7/34 to Dorothy Carr; c. Gordon Carr. Educ: Univ. Ky. Col. of Law, LL.B, 32; Lambda Chi Alpha. Polit. & Govt. Pos: City attorney, Hawesville, Ky, 40-49; chmn, Hancock Co. Rep. Party, 46-; co. attorney, Hancock Co, 49-; alternate del, Rep. Nat. Conv, 52. Mem: Am. Bar Asn; Ky. State Bar Asn; Co. Attorney's Asn. of Ky; Univ. Ky. Alumni Asn; F&AM; RAM; Owensboro Commandery 15; K.T; R&SM. Rel: Methodist; Trustee. Mailing Add: Hawesville, Ky. 42348. (1967)

BLACK, HUGO LaFAYETTE
Assoc. Justice, U.S. Supreme Court
b. Harlan, Ala, 2/27/86; s. William LaFayette Black and Martha Ardellah Toland B; m. 1921 to Josephine Patterson Foster, wid. 12/7/52; c. Hugo, Jr, Sterling Foster and Martha Josephine; m. 9/11/57 to Elizabeth Seay DeMerritte. Educ: Univ. Ala, LL.B, 06. Polit. & Govt. Pos: Police judge, Birmingham Ala, 10-11; solicitor, Jefferson Co, 15-17; U.S. Sen, Ala, 27-37; assoc. justice, U.S. Supreme Court, 37- Bus. & Prof. Pos: Attorney-at-law, Birmingham, 19-27. Mil. Serv: Second Officers Training Corps, Ft. Oglethorpe, Ga, 17; Commanding Capt, Field Artil; serv. in 81st Field Artil, Adj, 19th Artil. Brigade. Mailing Add: 619 S. Lee St, Alexandria, Va. 22314.

BLACK, JAMES LUCIUS D
b. Preston, Ga, 7/27/15; s. William Liston Black and Dee Everette B; m. 7/24/37 to Myra Nell Chambers; c. Linda Arlene and Anthony Lucius. Educ: Union High Sch, 35. Polit. & Govt. Pos: Ga. State Rep, 45-48 & 51-68. Bus. & Prof. Pos: Farmer. Mil. Serv: Lt, Ga. State Guard. Rel: Baptist. Mailing Add: Preston, Ga. 31824. (1967)

BLACK, JOHN D. D
b. Bristol, Va, 12/19/33; m. to Jan Knippers; c. John D, II and Marc Joaquin. Educ: Univ. Tenn, LL.B, 59; Phi Delta Phi. Polit. & Govt. Pos: Attorney, Dept. of Labor, 60-63; legis. asst, U.S. Sen. Ross Bass, Tenn, 64-67; admin. asst, U.S. Sen. H.A. Williams, Jr, N.J, 67-69. Bus. & Prof. Pos: Attorney-at-law, Knoxville, Tenn, 63-64. Mil. Serv: Entered as Pvt, Air Force, 51, released as Airman 1/C, 55, after serv. in U.S. and Far East. Legal Res: Lawrenceburg, Tenn. 38464. Mailing Add: 201 I St. S.W, Washington, D.C. 20001.

BLACK, JOHN WOODLAND
Dir, U.S. Travel Serv.
b. Spokane, Wash, 9/22/25; s. Hugh James Black and Margaret Woodland B; m. 9/3/59 to Iryne Codon; c. John McKenzie, Catherine Louise, Bridget Dianne, James Joseph, Ian Matthugh and Timothy Andrew. Educ: Colo. Univ, 44-45; Univ. Wash, A.B, 47; Columbia Univ, M. in Int. Affairs, 49; George Wash. Univ, J.D, 59. Polit. & Govt. Pos: With State Dept, 49-50; for. serv. officer, 50-55; U.S. Sen, 55-61; spec. asst. to Secy. of Commerce, 61; dep. dir, U.S. Travel Serv, 61-64, dir, 65- Mil. Serv: Naval Res, 45-46. Mem: Am. Bar Asn. Mailing Add: 7025 31st St. N.W, Washington, D.C. 20015. (1967)

BLACK, KENNETH M. R
b. Roswell, N.Mex, 8/22/28; s. G. Paul Black and Zula Simms B; m. 8/11/67 to Marian Griffith; c. Shelly, Rhonda, Linda, Bill and Stacy. Educ: N.Mex. State Univ, B.S, 50; Alpha Zeta; Theta Chi. Polit. & Govt. Pos: Cmnr, Sierra Co, N.Mex, 58-62; cmnr, N.Mex. State Fair, 60-62; N.Mex. State Rep, 63-67, minority leader, N.Mex. House of Rep, 65-67; v.pres, Bd. Regents, N.Mex. State Univ, 67- Bus. & Prof. Pos: Dir. and v.pres, Price-Black Farms, 63-; dir, Hot Springs Nat. Bank, 67 and Dona Ana Co. Bank, 68; dir, v.pres. and gen. mgr, Price's Producers, 68- Mil. Serv: Army Res. Mem: State dir, N.Mex. Farm Bur. Rel: Episcopal. Mailing Add: P.O. Box 143, Arrey, N.Mex. 87930.

BLACK, KENNETH WALLACE R
V.Chmn, Tazewell Co. Rep. Cent. Cmt, Ill.
b. Peoria, Ill, 12/10/12; s. Wallace J. Black and Margaret Robinson B; m. 8/10/38 to Edith Adele Lowry; c. Barbara (Mrs. Robert Walker Brown);

Kenneth L. and Bruce W. Educ: Bradley Univ, B.S, 34; Univ. of Chicago, J.D, 37; Sigma Chi. Polit. & Govt. Pos: Rep. precinct committeeman, Third Precinct, Wash. Twp, Ill, 53-; v.chmn, Tazewell Co. Rep. Cent. Cmt, 53-; pub. administrator, Tazewell Co, 56-60; alternate del, Rep. Nat. Conv, 68. Bus. & Prof. Pos: Dir, First Nat. Bank of Washington, Ill; city attorney, Washington, 41-53 & 57-; pres, Washington Twp. Libr. Bd, 51-; chmn, activities cmt. and second v.pres, bd. of trustees, Bradley Univ, 57-; pres. and dir, Ill. Valley Libr. Syst, 66- Mem: Peoria Co. and Tazewell Co. Bar Asns; Am. Judicature Soc; Ill. State Bar Asn; Am. Bar Asn; Mason; Shrine; Creve Coeur Club; Peoria Country Club; Rotary Int. Rel: Lutheran. Legal Res: 501 S. Main St, Washington, Ill. 61571. Mailing Add: P.O. Box 157, Washington, Ill. 61571.

BLACK, LILA R
Secy, Rep. State Cmt, Ohio
b. Centerton, Ohio, 12/18/97; d. Mason D. Smith and Grace Barber S; m. 5/26/18 to Wayne C. Black; c. Phyllis (Mrs. G.V. Collister), Patricia and David. Educ: Col. Wooster, 17-18; West. Reserve Univ, B.S, 45, M.A, 48. Polit. & Govt. Pos: Chairwoman, Lorain Co. Rep. Exec. Cmt, Ohio, 44-48, later secy-treas; legal asst. to Attorney Gen, 51-57; supvr, Sales Tax Audits, 58-59; dir. elec, Lorain Co, Ohio, 59-; Rep. precinct committeewoman, Avon Lake, currently; secy, Rep. State Cmt, Ohio, currently; alternate del, Rep. Nat. Conv, 68; second v.pres, Elyria Woman's Club. Mem: Bus. and Prfnl. Women; Am. Asn. Univ. Women; DAR. Rel: Protestant. Legal Res: 33266 Lake Rd, Avon Lake, Ohio 44012. Mailing Add: 115 Cedar St, Elyria, Ohio 44035.

BLACK, ROY HERBERT D
b. Nettleton, Miss, 11/28/14; married. Polit. & Govt. Pos: Former Miss. State Rep. Bus. & Prof. Pos: Merchant. Mem: Mason; Lions. Rel: Methodist. Mailing Add: Drawer P, Nettleton, Miss. 38858. (1967)

BLACK, SHIRLEY TEMPLE R
U.S. Del. to the UN
b. Santa Monica, Calif, 4/23/28; d. George Francis Temple, Sr. and Gertrude Cregier T; m. 12/16/50 to Charles Alden Black; c. Linda Susan, Charles Alden, Jr. and Lori Alden. Educ: Westlake Sch, Los Angeles, grad, 45. Polit. & Govt. Pos: Mem, numerous Rep. financial and campaign cmts. at all levels from co. to nat, Calif. and U.S, 52-; mem, Hosp. Adv. Coun, Calif, 67; mem, Women's Adv. Cmt, Nixon-Agnew, 68; mem, Calif. Rep. State Cent. Cmt, 68-; mem, Calif. Coun. on Criminal Justice, 69; chmn, Youth Week Golden Gate Centennial, San Francisco, 69; U.S. del. to the UN, 69- Mem: Acad. of Motion Picture Arts and Sci; Acad. of TV Arts and Sci; exec. cmt, Zeta Phi Eta; Int. Fedn. of Multiple Sclerosis Socs, Vienna and Health Facilities Planning Coun, San Francisco Mid-Peninsula; bd. trustees, Inst. for Study of Econ. Syst, Wash, Nat. Multiple Sclerosis Soc, N.Y, Health Facilities Planning Asn, San Francisco Bay Area, Bay Area Educ. TV Asn, San Francisco, Regional Adv. Bd. for Criminal Justice, Bay Area and Civic Light Opera Asn, San Francisco; World Affairs Coun, San Francisco; Asia Found; San Francisco Symphony Asn; San Francisco Int. Film Festival; Childrens' Theatre Asn, San Francisco Peninsula; Childrens' Health Coun, Palo Alto; Jr. Leagues of Palo Alto, Inc. and San Francisco, Inc; Theta Sigma Chi. Kiwanis Int. Award, Houston, 67; Dame, Order of the Knights of Malta, Paris, France; Hon. Gov, Acad. of TV Arts and Sci; John Swett Award, Calif. Teachers Asn; Annual Laymans Award, Alameda Educ. Asn. Rel: Episcopal. Mailing Add: Lakeview Dr, Woodside, Calif. 94062.

BLACK, STERLING F. D
N.Mex. State Sen.
b. 1926. Educ: Dartmouth; George Washington Univ; Univ. of Ariz; Columbia Law Sch, LL.B. Polit. & Govt. Pos: Attorney, Atomic Energy Cmn, Los Alamos and Albuquerque, N.Mex, chief counsel, Los Alamos; N.Mex. State Sen, 61-; del, Dem. Nat. Conv, 68. Bus. & Prof. Pos: Lawyer. Mil. Serv: Army Air Force, Admin. Officer, Capt, 43-46. Mem: Kiwanis; Elks. Mailing Add: P.O. Box 1087, Los Alamos, N.Mex. 87544. (1967)

BLACK, THOMAS ANDREW R
Mem, Calif. Rep. State Cent. Cmt.
b. Fresno, Calif, 10/25/32; s. Andrew Joseph Black and Leone Mahoney B; m. 5/5/63 to Barbara Jo Ward; c. Andrew Joseph, Anne Marie and Sarah Elizabeth. Educ: Univ. Santa Clara, A.B, 54, J.D, 59. Polit. & Govt. Pos: Mem, bd. supvr, Santa Cruz Co, 65-69, chmn, 66 & 67; mem, Calif. Rep. State Cent. Cmt, 66-; chmn, State Redwood Parks Spec. Study Cmn, 69- Bus. & Prof. Pos: Dep. dist. attorney, Alameda Co, Calif, 60-61; attorney, Santa Cruz, Calif, 61- Mil. Serv: Entered as 2nd Lt, Army, 54, released as 1st Lt, 66, after serv. in Second Inf. Div, Continental U.S. Mem: Santa Cruz and Calif. Bar Asns; Am. Judicature Soc; Elks; Sierra Club; Dominican Hosp. Bd. of Dir. Rel: Roman Catholic. Mailing Add: 362 Danube Dr, Aptos, Calif. 95003.

BLACK, THOMAS L. D
b. 3/14/34; s. Benjamin F. Black and Margaret Estep B; m. 3/4/54 to Ethel Kluge; c. Thomas Barry, Paul Alan, Patricia Lynn and Wilhelmina Rachele. Educ: W.Va. Inst. of Tech, B.S. Polit. & Govt. Pos: W.Va. State Del, 60-66; Mayor, East Bank. Bus. & Prof. Pos: Rwy. clerk. Mil. Serv: Air Force, 51-55. Mem: Mason; AF&AM; RAM; Am. Legion; Lions; W.Va. Football and Basketball Asn; Magic Valley Lodge 388. Rel: Methodist. Mailing Add: Box 106, East Bank, W.Va. 25067. (1967)

BLACK, WALTER EVAN, JR. R
b. Baltimore, Md, 7/7/26; s. Walter Evan Black and Margaret Rice B; m. 6/30/51 to Catharine S. Foster; c. Walter Evan, III, Charles F. and James R. Educ: Harvard Col, A.B, 47; Harvard Law Sch, LL.B, 49; Speakers Club. Polit. & Govt. Pos: Asst. U.S. attorney, Dist. of Md, 53-55, U.S. attorney, 56-57; chmn, Bd. of Munic. and Zoning Appeals, Baltimore, Md, 63-67. Bus. & Prof. Pos: Assoc, Hinkley & Singley, 49-53, partner, 56-67; partner, Clapp, Somerville, Black & Honemann, 68- Publ: 'The Effect of Renunciations and Compromises on Death and Gift Taxes', Vanderbilt Law Rev, Vol. 3, pages 241-269, 50. Mem: Am, Md. State & Baltimore City Bar Asns; Harvard Club of Md. and of N.Y.C; Merchant's Club. Rel: Baptist. Mailing Add: 1114 Bellemore Rd, Baltimore, Md. 21210.

BLACK, WAYNE L. D
Dem. Nat. Committeeman, Utah
b. Cowley, Wyo, 6/17/19; m. to Bettina; c. Six. Educ: Univ. Utah, J.D. Polit. & Govt. Pos: Asst. co. attorney, Salt Lake Co, Utah, 2 years; asst. dist. attorney, Third Judicial Dist, 3 years; mem, Cmn. on Uniform State Laws, Utah, currently; chmn, Salt Lake Co. Dem. Party, 4 years; alternate del, Dem. Nat. Conv, 68; Dem. Nat. Committeeman, Utah, currently. Bus. & Prof. Pos: Attorney-at-law. Mil. Serv: Lt, Navy, World War II, with serv. as Commun. Officer, U.S.S. Lunga Point; Participated in Leyte, Lingayan Gulf, Iwo Jima, Okinawa and Yellow Sea Opers; Presidential Unit Citation. Mem: Phi Alpha Delta; Univ. Club; Bonneville Knife and Fork Club. Appeared before U.S. Supreme Court, Circuit Court of Appeals, Fed. and State Courts as trial and appellate attorney. Rel: Latter-day Saint. Legal Res: 3941 Mt. Olympus Way, Salt Lake City, Utah 84117. Mailing Add: 530 Judge Bldg, Salt Lake City, Utah 84111.

BLACKBURN, BEN B, III R
U.S. Rep, Ga.
b. Atlanta, Ga, 2/14/27; m. to Mary Pandora; c. Michael James, Robert Bentley, Kathryn Ann and David Thomas. Educ: Emory Univ, Atlanta, 44-45; Univ. N.C, Chapel Hill, A.B, 47; Emory Univ. Law Sch, LL.B, 54. Polit. & Govt. Pos: Rep. precinct worker, 54-64; with State Attorney Gen. Off, Ga, 55-56; secy, Fourth Cong. Dist. Rep. Exec. Cmt; gen. counsel, DeKalb Co. Rep. Exec. Cmt, 64-; chmn, DeKalb Co. Conv, 66; U.S. Rep, Ga, 67- Bus. & Prof. Pos: Dept. store supvr, W.T. Grant Co, Richmond, Va, 49; salesman, Union Carbide Nat. Carbon Div, 49-50; attorney, 56- Mil. Serv: Navy, V-12 Training, 44-46, Lt.(jg), 50-52. Mem: Am, Atlanta and Ga. Bar Asns; Lawyers Club; Peachtree Optimist; C. of C. Rel: Episcopal. Legal Res: 1410 Fama Dr. N.E, Atlanta, Ga. 30329. Mailing Add: 1019 Longworth House Office Bldg, Washington, D.C. 20515.

BLACKBURN, JAMES B. D
Chmn, Savannah Dem. Exec. Cmt, Ga.
b. Dover, Ga, 10/18/25; s. James F. Blackburn and Lillian Boddiford B; m. 9/21/47 to Mercer Griffith; c. James B, Jr. and John F. Educ: Univ. Ga, LL.B, 50; Phi Alpha Delta. Polit. & Govt. Pos: Chmn, Savannah Dem. Exec. Cmt, 55-; legal counsel, Ga. Jaycees, 57-60; city attorney, Savannah, 57-66; Col, Staff of Gov. Ernest Vandiver, Ga, 58-62 and Staff of Gov. Carl Sanders, 62- Bus. & Prof. Pos: Chmn, Legis. Adv. Cmt, Ga. Munic. Asn. 63-66, mem. bd, 64-65. Mil. Serv: Entered as A/S, Navy, 43, released as Lt, Naval Res; Pac. Theater Ribbon. Mem: City Attorneys of Ga.(pres, 64-65); Ga, Savannah and Am. Bar Asns; Mason; Shrine; Elks, Kiwanis. Rel: Baptist. Legal Res: 228 Washington Ave, Savannah, Ga. 31405. Mailing Add: P.O. Box 8501, Savannah, Ga. 31401.

BLACKBURN, ROBERT ED, JR. D
Fla. State Rep.
b. Tampa, Fla, 12/5/12; s. R. Ed. Blackburn and Mary Edmondson B; m. 8/30/40 to Frances Catherine Bishop; c. Barbara (Mrs. Cook). Educ: Univ. Fla, $2\frac{1}{2}$ years; Univ. Tampa, $\frac{1}{2}$ year. Polit. & Govt. Pos: Mem, Hillsborough Co. Port Authority, 49-52; sheriff, Hillsborough Co, Fla, 53-65; Fla. State Rep, 69- Bus. & Prof. Pos: Merchant, Tampa, Fla, 43-50; real estate broker, 50-52; spec. agent, Bankers Life Co, 65- Mem: Hon. life mem, Fla. Sheriffs Asn.(past pres, 64); trustee emer, past chmn. bd. trustees, organizer and first exec. dir, Fla. Sheriffs Boys Ranch; hon. life mem, Future Farmers of Am. Rel: Methodist. Legal Res: 5710 Suwanee Ave, Tampa, Fla. 33604. Mailing Add: P.O. Box 10595, Tampa, Fla. 33609.

BLACKHAM, ANN ROSEMARY R
Secy, Nat. Fedn. of Rep. Women
b. New York, N.Y, 6/16/27; d. Frederick Alfred DeCain and Letitia Stolfe D; m. 8/18/51 to James William Blackham, Jr; c. Ann Constance and James William, III. Educ: Ohio Dominican Col, A.B, 49; Ohio State Univ, M.A, 50; Lincoln Filene Sch. Mgr, cert, 51; Nat. Poetry Award Soc; Eng. Honors Soc; Debating Soc; Jr. League of Cath. Women; Rho Sigma Beta; Drama Soc; Fashion Inst; Lit. Guild; Merry Masquers. Polit. & Govt. Pos: Chmn. precinct III, Winchester Rep. Town Cmt, Mass, 56-65; chmn, Winchester Rep. Finance Cmt, 59-64; membership chmn, Mass. Fedn. Rep. Women, 60-62 and finance chmn, 62-64; pres, Women's Rep. Club Winchester, 60-62; v.chmn, Winchester Rep. Town Cmt, 64-65; pres, Mass. Fedn. Rep. Women, 64-69; assoc. mem. exec. cmt, Mass. Rep. State Cmt, 64-69 and dep. chmn, 65-66; mem, Mass. State Civil Defense Coun, 65-; secy. and New Eng. regional dir, Nat. Fedn. Rep. Women, 67-; alternate del, Rep. Nat. Conv, 68. Bus. & Prof. Pos: Store mgr, Filene's Dept. Store, Winchester, 51-53; sales mgr. and corporate dir, James T. Trefrey, Inc, Realtor, 66-68; pres. and founder, Ann Blackham & Co, Realtors, 68- Mem: Gr. Boston Real Estate Bd; Brokers Inst; Nat. Asn. Real Estate Bd; Mass. Asn. Real Estate Bd; League Women Voters; Doric Dames; Florence Crittenton League; Capitol Hill Club; Heart Fund; Mass. Fedn. Women's Clubs; Friends Winchester Hosp; Rep. Club, Mass; Winchester Country Club; Winchester Boat Club. Broadcaster's award, Civic Leadership, 62; Mass. Order Paul Revere Patriots; Outstanding Young Woman, Am. Rel: Catholic. Mailing Add: 33 Canterbury Rd, Winchester, Mass. 01890.

BLACKMER, MARGARET COUTURE D
Mem, Calif. Dem. State Cent. Cmt.
b. Modesto, Calif, 10/24/21; d. Edward Arnold Couture and Lula Dodson C; div; c. Anne, Carol and Joan. Educ: Modesto Jr. Col, A.A, 40; Univ. Calif, Berkeley, A.B, 42, Sec. Credential, 43; Kappa Delta. Polit. & Govt. Pos: V.pres, Stanislaus Co. Coun. of Dem. Clubs, Calif, 56-57; chmn, E. Stanislaus Dem. Club, 56-68; area precinct chmn, Stanislaus Co. Dem. Campaign Cmt, 56-62; co-chmn, Campaign to Re-elect Gov. Edmund G. Brown, 66; field rep. and legis. asst. to State Sen. Stephen P. Teale, Calif. State Legis, 67-; mem, Calif. Dem. State Cent. Cmt, 68- Bus. & Prof. Pos: Teacher, Richmond City Schs, 47-49. Mem: Ment. Health Asn; Family Serv. Agency; Bus. and Prfnl. Dem. Club; Regional Health Planning Coun; Friends Cmt. on Legis; Grange. Rel: Unitarian. Mailing Add: 416 Stewart Rd, Modesto, Calif. 95350.

BLACKMON, JACK RUSSELL D
Mayor, Corpus Christi, Tex.
b. Leesville, La, 2/5/18; s. Robert Franklin Blackmon and Mamie Edna

Wisenbaker B; m. 7/14/40 to Margaret Lucinda McGlaun; c. Robert Max, Margaret Diane and Deborah Claire. Educ: Wesley College, AA, 36; South. Methodist Univ. Sch. of Law, LL.B, 39; Phi Alpha Delta. Polit. & Govt. Pos: Cmnr, Corpus Christi, Tex, 63-65, Mayor Pro Tem, 65-67, Mayor, 67- Bus. & Prof. Pos: Partner, Berger, Swearingen & Blackmon, 46-49, partner, North & Blackmon, 49-51 and North, Blackmon & White, 51-69; secy-treas, NBW Building Corp, 55-69; Pres, Municipal Gas Corp, 67-69. Mil. Serv: Entered as Ens, U.S. Navy, 43, released as Lt.(jg), 46, after serv. in Security and Legal Invest. Staff, Naval Air Training Command, Corpus Christi, Tex, 44-46; Res, 46-69, Capt; Am. Theater, World War II Victory, Naval Res, and Armed Forces Reserve Medals. Mem: Mem. State Bar of Tex; licensed to practice in all State courts of Tex, U.S. Dist. Court South. Dist. of Tex, Corpus Christi Div, U.S. Court of Appeals, Fifth Circuit, U.S. Supreme Court and U.S. Court of Military Appeals; AF&AM; Scottish Rites; Alzafar Temple; Am. Legion; Nueces Co. Bar Asn; Charter Mem. Corpus Christi Civitan Club; Civitan Int. (past Gov. of the Tex. Dist). Civitan of the Year 65-66; Press Club "Most Panned Man" 67. Rel: Baptist. Legal Res: 101 Alta Plaza, Corpus Christi, Tex. 78411. Mailing Add: P.O. Box 2087, Corpus Christi, Tex. 78403.

BLACKMUN, HARRY ANDREW
b. Nashville, Ill, 11/12/08; s. Corwin M. Blackmun and Theo H. Reuter B; m. 6/21/41 to Dorothy E. Clark; c. Nancy Clark, Sally Ann and Susan Manning. Educ: Harvard Univ, B.A, summa cum laude, 29, LL.B, 32; Phi Beta Kappa. Polit. & Govt. Pos: U.S. Circuit Judge, 8th Circuit Court of Appeals, 59- Bus. & Prof. Pos: Law clerk, Hon. John B. Sanborn, U.S. Court of Appeals, 32-33; assoc, jr. partner and partner, Dorsey, Colman, Barker, Scott and Barber, and predecessor firms, Minneapolis, Minn, 34-50; gen. counsel and mem. sect. of admin, Mayo Clinic, Rochester, 50-59. Publ: Miscellaneous articles in legal and medical publications. Mem: Trustee, Hamline Univ. William Mitchell Col. Law; dir, Kahler Corp, 58-63; dir. and mem. exec. cmt, Rochester Methodist Hosp, 54-; mem, Bd. of Members, Mayo Asn, Rochester, Minn, 53-61; dir, Rochester Airport Co, 52-60; Am. and Minn. Bar Asns; Olmsted Co. 3rd Judicial Dist. Bar Asn; pres, Rotary Club Rochester, 55-56; pres, Harvard Club Minn, 40; mem, Adv. Cmt. on Research to Fed. Judicial Center, 68-; mem, Adv. Cmt. on the Judge's Function to Am. Bar Asn. Spec. Cmt. on Minimum Standards for the Admin. of Criminal Justice, 69- Rel: Methodist; trustee and mem. bd. publ, Methodist Church. Legal Res: 38 Skyline Dr, Rochester, Minn. 55901. Mailing Add: Box 500, Rochester, Minn. 55901.

BLACKORBY, LILA ROSE R
Committeeman, Ill. Rep. Cent. Cmt.
b. Jerseyville, Ill, 6/17/67; d. Arthur William Dabbs and Lora Reed D; m. 9/30/46 to Harold Richard Blackorby; c. Peggy (Mrs. Paul Wheaton) and David. Educ: High Sch, grad. Polit. & Govt. Pos: Committeewoman, Jersey Co. Rep. Party, Ill, 51-60, dep. registr, 51-; del, Ill. Rep. Women's Conv, 52, 54, 56, 58, 60, 62, 64, 66 & 68; v.pres, Jersey Co. Rep. Women's Club, 56-60 & 66-, membership chmn, 60-69; del, Judicial Cmn, 59 & 64; precinct committeeman, Ninth Precinct, Jersey Co. Rep. Cent. Cmt, 60-, secy, 63-69; del, Rep. State Conv, 62, 64 & 66; del, Appellate Judicial Conv, 64; chmn, Gov. Ogilvie's Campaign, 68; committeeman, Ill. Rep. Cent. Cmt, currently. Rel: Methodist. Mailing Add: 205 Walton, Jerseyville, Ill. 62052.

BLACKSHEAR, MARMADUKE HARDEMAN D
b. Dublin, Ga, 10/12/09; s. Marmaduke Hamilton Blackshear and Annie Hardeman B; m. 8/5/37 to Elizabeth Anne Blanchard; c. Pamelea Ann (Mrs. Charles Kenneth Shippey, Jr), David Marion, Margaret Carol and Lucy Elizabeth. Educ: Emory Univ, A.B, 30; Lamar Sch. Law, Emory Univ; Alpha Tau Omega. Polit. & Govt. Pos: Attorney, Sr. Attorney, rationing div, Off. Price Admin, 42-44; Asst. Attorney Gen, Ga, 48; Litigation Attorney, Off. Housing Expediter, 48-49; Dep. Asst. Attorney Gen, Ga, 49-53; Dep. Comptroller Gen, 63-67. Bus. & Prof. Pos: Mem, Blackshear and Blackshear, 30-42; Referee in Bankruptcy, U.S. Court, South. Dist. Ga, 38-42; partner, Haas, Holland & Blackshear, 53-58; King & Spalding, 58-63; attorney-at-law, currently. Mil. Serv: Naval Res, Lt.(jg) and Lt, Supply Corps, 44-46; Liaison Officer Navy Dept, Off. Price Admin. Mem: Decatur-DeKalb, Ga, Am. and Fed. Bar Asns; Atlanta Lawyers Club; Am. Judicature Soc. Rel: Methodist. Mailing Add: 201 Trust Bldg, Decatur, Ga. 30030.

BLACKWELL, CHARLES GRAY D
Miss. State Rep.
b. Ellisville, Miss, 3/4/39; s. Excell Montgomery Blackwell and Ina Rie Napier B; m. 8/29/59 to Julia Ann McDavid; c. Charla Geri and Charles Gray, Jr. Educ: Jones Co. Jr. Col, A.A, 59; Univ. Miss, B.B.A, 61; Univ. Miss. Law Sch, LL.B, 64; Campus Senate, 3 years; Ole Miss Patriotic Youth; Sci. Club; Debating Team; Youth Congress. Polit. & Govt. Pos: Miss. States Rep, Jones Co, 64- Mil. Serv: Specialist, Nat. Guard, 57-62. Mem: Jones Co, Miss. and Am. Bar Asns; Asn. Nat. State Legis; Lions; Civitan; Patriotic Am. Youth; Future Farmers of Am; 4-H. Rel: Baptist; deacon. 1967 Legal Res: Laurel, Miss. No mailing address available. (1967)

BLACKWELL, EARL R. D
Mo. State Sen.
b. Blackwell, Mo, 12/12/23; m. 12/24/48 to Dorothy Henderson; c. Sharon, James, William and Earl Jr. Educ: Univ. of Mo; Univ. of Cincinnati; Wash. Univ, A.B, LL.B. Polit. & Govt. Pos: Mo. State Sen, 58- Bus. & Prof. Pos: Lawyer, 14 years. Mil. Serv: Army, 3 years, World War II. Mem: Sixth consecutive term, Bd. of Gov, Mo. Bar Asn; Am. Bar Asn; Elks; VFW. Rel: Hillsboro Methodist Church. Mailing Add: Hillsboro, Mo. 63050. (1967)

BLACKWELL, MORTON CLYDE R
Mem, La. State Rep. Cent. Cmt.
b. La Jara, Colo, 11/16/39; s. William George Blackwell and Rebecca Barbara Blissard B; single. Educ: La. State Univ; Phi Eta Sigma; Alpha Chi Sigma; Phi Gamma Delta; Varsity Debate Sq; Young Rep, La. State Univ; Young Am. for Freedom. Polit. & Govt. Pos: Pres, Baton Rouge Young Rep, 62-63; state col. chmn, La. Young Rep. Fedn, 63-64, chmn, 64-66; mem. from East Baton Rouge Parish, La. State Rep. Cent. Cmt, 63-; del, Rep. Nat. Conv, 64; mem, Nat. Steering Cmt, Youth for Goldwater, 64; dir, Sparky Hall for Cong. Campaign, Sixth Dist, La, 66; Young Rep. Nat. Committeeman, La, 66-; student activities coordinator, Louie Nunn Ky. Gubernatorial Campaign, 67; alternate del, Rep. Nat. Conv, 68; exec. dir, Col. Rep. Nat. Cmt, 68- Bus. & Prof. Pos: Pres, Admin. Co, 64- Rock hound; Youngest del, 1964 Rep. Nat. Conv. Rel: Episcopal. Mailing Add: 4935 Newcomb Dr, Baton Rouge, La. 70808.

BLADES, BEN C. R
Ill. State Rep.
b. Wayne Co, Ill, 5/21/08; m. 1926 to Alene Crews; c. Ben Jr. and Norma Jean (Mrs. Royce Laycock). Educ: Fairfield Commun. High Sch. Polit. & Govt. Pos: Lt, Ill. State Police, 41-49; former mem. staff, Drivers License Div, Ill; Ill. State Rep, 62- Bus. & Prof. Pos: Self-employed until 41. Mem: Mason; Mississippi Valley Consistory; Shrine. Rel: Presbyterian. Mailing Add: 503 N.E. Fourth St, Fairfield, Ill. 62837. (1967)

BLADES, ORLAND BEVERLY D
b. Seaford Del, 8/29/01; s. Alva Blades and Lillian Thompson B; m. 6/16/29 to Mildred Stevens; c. Beverly Stevens and Robert Stuart. Educ: Wash. Col. Polit. Pos: Md. State Del, 50-66. Mem: Past master. Preston Lodge Masons; past dist. gov, Dist. 22 B, Lions. Mailing Add: Preston, Md. 21655. (1967)

BLADES, RAY R
Mem, State Rep. Cmt, Mo.
b. Holliday, Mo, 11/10/17; s. Ira Jean Blades and Susie Krembs B; m. 7/4/41 to Lucille Fisher; c. Joy and Kent. Educ: Holliday High Sch, Mo, grad. Polit. & Govt. Pos: Sgt-at-arms, Rep. Nat. Conv, 68; chmn, Monroe Co. Rep. Party, Mo, 68-; mem, Mo. State Rep. Cmt, 68-; mem, Mo. State Rep. Adv. Cmt, Ninth Dist, 69- Bus. & Prof. Pos: Farmer and cattle raiser, N.Mo. Mem: Progressive Club, Paris, Mo. (past pres); Moose, Moberly; Mrk Twain Country Club, Paris. Attended Inauguration of President Nixon, Wash, D.C, 69. Rel: Disciples of Christ. Mailing Add: Route 1, Paris, Mo. 65275.

BLAINE, RICHARD ALLAN R
R.I. State Rep.
b. Newton, Mass, 3/26/28; s. Irving E. Blaine and Hope Woodmansee B; m. 6/23/51 to Charlotte Eldredge; c. Susan Elizabeth, Robin Ann and Richard A, Jr. Educ: Univ. R.I, B.S, 49. Polit. & Govt. Pos: Mem, Scituate Zoning Bd. of Rev, R.I, 65-68; mem, Scituate Rep. Town Cmt, 66-; R.I. State Rep, 54th Dist, 68- Mil. Serv: Pvt, Army, Specialized Training Res. Prog, 45-46. Mem: R.I. Asn. Ins. Agents; F&AM; Scituate Lions (past pres); Am. Legion; Scituate Libr.(bd. dirs); Scituate Rep. Club. Rel: Congregational. Legal Res: Rockland Rd, North Scituate, R.I. 02857. Mailing Add: Box 155, North Scituate, R.I. 02857.

BLAIR, CHARLES STANLEY R
Admin. Asst. to Vice President
b. Kingsville, Md, 12/20/27; s. Charles Edward Blair and Beulah Gibson B; m. 6/27/64 to Opal Whiteford. Educ: Univ. Md, B.S, 51, LL.B, 53. Polit. & Govt. Pos: Mem, Harford Co. State Rep. Cent. Cmt, Md, 59-62; secy-treas, Harford Co. Metrop. Cmn, 59-63; Md. State Del, 63-67; Secy. of State, Md, 67-69; del, Rep. Nat. Conv, 68; Admin. Asst. and Chief of Staff to Vice President, 69- Mil. Serv: Entered as Pvt, Army, 53, released as 1st Lt, 56, Capt, Res. Mem: Am, Md. and Co. Bar Asns. Mailing Add: Box 91, Darlington, Md. 21034.

BLAIR, JAMES B. D
Chief Legal Counsel, Dem. Party, Ark.
b. Elkins, Ark, 10/27/35; s. William Joe Blair and Mildred Woolsey B; m. 8/24/57 to Margaret Gibson; c. Heather Elaine, Arden Sue and James Rufus. Educ: Univ. Ark, B.A, 55, J.D, 57; Blue Key, Delta Theta Phi Scholarship Key; Phi Eta Sigma; Acacia. Polit. & Govt. Pos: Campaign mgr, Wash. Co. Young Dem, Ark, 64 and pres, 65; legal counsel, Young Dem. of Ark. Clubs, 65-66; del, Dem. Nat. Conv, 68; chief legal counsel, Dem. Party, Ark, 68- Bus. & Prof. Pos: Ed. and chief, Ark. Law Rev, 56-57; lawyer, Fayetteville, 57; partner, Crouch, Jones & Blair, Springdale, 59, Crouch, Jones, Blair & Cypert, and Crouch, Blair, Cypert & Waters, 69. Mem: Wash. Co, Ark. and Am. Bar Asns; Motor Carrier Lawyers Asn. Rel: Baptist. Legal Res: Route 2, Fayetteville, Ark. 72701. Mailing Add: P.O. Box 88, Springdale, Ark. 72764.

BLAIR, JOHN ELLIS R
Pa. State Rep.
b. Sandy Lake, Pa, 1/1/12; s. Frank P. Blair and Flora Ellis B; m. 2/6/33 to Bessie Amon; c. Sanford Ellis and Carolyn Jean (Mrs. Pasquale). Educ: Grove City Col, B.S, 35. Polit. & Govt. Pos: Finance chmn. and chmn, Area 2, Mercer Co. Rep. Party, Pa, 63-66; Pa. State Rep, 67- Bus. & Prof. Pos: Shop supt, Cooper Bessemer Co, 50-55, supt. of erection, 55-57, mgr, indust. rels, 57-69, dir, wage and salary admin, 69- Rel: Protestant. Legal Res: Box 61, Dunn St, Sandy Lake, Pa. 16145. Mailing Add: R.D. 4, Mt. Vernon, Ohio 43050.

BLAIR, ROBERT EARL R
b. Bentonville, Ark, 7/17/36; s. Earl Harvey Blair and Mary C. Pratt B; m. 1/11/57 to Isabelle Grace Gross; c. Janet Lee, Lorna Kay and Lorraine Day. Educ: East. Okla. Agr. & Mech. Col; Calif. State Polytech. Col. Polit. & Govt. Pos: Chmn, Lassen Co. Rep. Cent. Cmt, Calif, 66-68. Bus. & Prof. Pos: Owner, R.E. Blair Const. Co, at present. Mem: Elks; Farm Bureau; Rotary Int. All-state in high sch. football; bareback champion, East. Okla. Agr. & Mech. Col. Rel: Episcopal. Mailing Add: Richmond Rd, P.O. Box 324, Susanville, Calif. 96130. (1967)

BLAIR, RUSSELL JENKINS D
Pa. State Rep.
b. Perryopolis, Pa, 10/1/07; s. Ira Blair and Luvada Jenkins B; m. 5/29/69 to JoAnn Falcone; c. James D. and Richard. Educ: Calif. Teachers Col, 2 years. Polit. & Govt. Pos: Mayor, Perryopolis, Pa, 53-69; Pa. State Rep, Harrisburg, 67- Bus. & Prof. Pos: Funeral dir, self-employed, 36- Mem: Nat. and Pa. Funeral Dirs. Asns; Pa. Mayors Asn; Mason; Consistory; Shrine. Rel: Protestant. Mailing Add: Independence St, Box 155, Perryopolis, Pa. 15473.

BLAIR, STANLEY L. R
b. Albion, Pa, 10/8/06; s. Claude Blair and Lottie Peters B; m. to Faust Metcalf; c. Two. Polit. & Govt. Pos: Pa. State Rep, 48-68. Mem: F&AM. Rel: Methodist. Mailing Add: 19 West Avenue, Albion, Pa. 16401. (1967)

BLAIR, W. ROBERT R
Ill. State Rep.
b. Clarksburg, W.Va, 11/22/30; s. William Robert Blair and Eleanor Price B; m. 6/28/52 to Patricia Louise Gochenour; c. Steven, Mark and Susan. Educ: W.Va. Univ, A.B, 52, LL.B, 54; Phi Kappa Psi; Phi Delta Phi; Mountain; Sphinx; Coun. of Fraternity Pres; Fi Bator Capor; comdr, Arnold Air Soc; Mountaineer Week Team; Greater W.Va. Week-end Cmt. Polit. & Govt. Pos: Legal consult, Park Forest Planning Cmn, Ill, 59-61; Rep. precinct committeeman, Monee Twp, Will Co, 59-; v.chmn. and mem. exec. cmt, Will Co. Rep. Cent. Cmt, 62-; mem, Will Co. Pub. Bldg. Cmn, 63-; Ill. State Rep, 64-, chmn, Personnel and Pension Cmt, Vet. Affairs, mem, Exec. Cmt, chmn, Consumer Credit Sub-Cmt. and Pension Laws Cmn; mem, Ill. Hwy. Study Cmn, 65- Bus. & Prof. Pos: Attorney-at-law, 54-; pres, Fairfax Realty Co, 60-; asst. to pres, Swift & Co, 61-63. Mil. Serv: Entered as 2nd Lt, Air Force, 54, released as 1st Lt, 56, after serv. as a Judge Advocate in Tech. Training; Nat. Defense Serv. Medal. Mem: Will Co, Ill. State and Am. Bar Asns; South Suburban, Ill. State and Nat. Asn. Real Estate Bd. Rel: Methodist. Legal Res: 124 Shabbona Dr, Park Forest, Ill. 60466. Mailing Add: 2410 Western Ave, P.O. Box 273, Park Forest, Ill. 60466. (1967)

BLAIR, WILLIAM EVANS R
b. Glynn County, Ga, 8/2/32; s. James Raymond Blair and Floy Crocker B; m. 3/22/53 to Dana Futrelle Hendricks; c. Dana Futrelle and Jincy Winifred. Educ: Baylor Sch. for Boys, grad, 50; Univ. Ga, grad, 55; Sigma Chi; Sigma Delta Chi. Polit. & Govt. Pos: Ga. State Rep, 63-66. Bus. & Prof. Pos: V.pres, Americus Times-Recorder, 58, Metalux Corp, 64 and Gibson Lighting Corp, 66; pres, Times-Recorder Printers, 65. Mil. Serv: Entered as 2nd Lt, Army, 56, released as Capt, also serv. in 48th Armored Div, Ga. Nat. Guard, 64. Selected Young Man of Year, Americus and Sumter Co, Ga, 60. Rel: Methodist. Mailing Add: 22 Laudig Lane, Americus, Ga. 31709.

BLAISDELL, CLESSON J. D
b. Keene, N.H, 9/18/26; married; c. three. Educ: Keene High Sch. Polit. & Govt. Pos: N.H. State Rep, -67; Ward Checklist Supvr; former Selectman; State Softball Cmn; State Athletic Cmt. Bus. & Prof. Pos: Sporting goods salesman, Keene. Mil. Serv: USN, 44-46. Mem: Kiwanis; K. of C, fourth degree; Am. Legion; Basketball Off, I.A.A.B.O. and C.B.O.A; Little League Cmn. Rel: Catholic. Mailing Add: 10 Avalon Place, Keene, N.H. 03431. (1967)

BLAISDELL, NEAL SHAW R
b. Honolulu, Hawaii, 11/6/02; s. William Wallace Blaisdell and Malia K. Mersberg B; m. to Lucy Thurston; c. Marilyn (Mrs. Charles Ane, Jr.) and Velma (Mrs. James Clark). Educ: Univ. Hawaii, 21-23; Bucknell Univ, B.A, 26; Sigma Chi. H.H.D, Chaminade Col, Hawaii. Polit. & Govt. Pos: Hawaii State Rep, 44-45; Hawaii State Sen, 46-50; dir, State Dept. of Welfare, 53-54; mayor, City and Co. of Honolulu, Hawaii, 55-69; mem, President's Adv. Cmn. on Intergovt. Rels, 62-; mem, President's Adv. Cmt. for Commun. Rels, 64-; mem, Pub. Officials Adv. Coun. to Off. of Econ. Opportunity, 65- Bus. & Prof. Pos: Teacher and athletic dir, McKinley High Sch, Honolulu, Hawaii; in property mgt, Bishop Trust Co, 30-35; dir. of athletics and coach, Roosevelt High Sch, 35-37; with Dole Corp, Honolulu, 37-53. Mem: Former pres, U.S. Conf. of Mayors; chmn, Am. Exec. Cmt, Japan-Am. Conf. of Mayors and C. of C. Presidents. Rel: Episcopal. Legal Res: 749 16th Ave, Honolulu, Hawaii 96816. Mailing Add: City Hall, Honolulu, Hawaii 96816.

BLAKE, MILTON J. R
b. Denver, Colo, 11/27/05. Polit. & Govt. Pos: Rep. committeeman and block worker, Colo; Colo. State Rep, 47-49; Secy, Colo. Cmt. on Interstate Coop, 47-49; co-chmn, Denver Citizens for Eisenhower, 52; campaign mgr, U.S. Sen. Gordon Allot, 54; Denver regional adminstr. of the Securities and Exchange Cmn, 55-61. Bus. & Prof. Pos: Attorney. Mem: Bd. of Rep. Assoc, 63- Mailing Add: 656 Albion St, Denver, Colo. 80220.

BLAKE, RAYMOND R
Vt. State Sen.
b. Derby, Vt, 9/9/96; m. to Julia W. Leavens; c. Two sons and four daughters. Educ: Stanstead Col, Que; Bugbee Bus. Col, 15. Polit. & Govt. Pos: Vt. State Rep, 37-39 & 59; mem, bd. of aldermen, Newport, Vt, 43-49, mayor, 3 terms; Vt. State Sen, 65-; alternate del, Rep. Nat. Conv, 68. Bus. & Prof. Pos: Mem, Newport Airport Cmn, 45; mem, adv. bd, Chittenden Trust Co; dir, Nat. Bank of Newport; automobile and marine prod. dealer. Mem: Mason (32°); Shrine; Odd Fellows; Rotary. Rel: United Church. Mailing Add: 927 E. Main St, Newport, Vt. 05853. (1967)

BLAKELEY, JAMES GARY D
V.Pres, N.Mex. Young Dem. Clubs
b. New Orleans, La, 9/2/47; s. Jess Chancey Blakeley and Dorothy Brown B; single. Educ: East. N.Mex. Univ, 3 years; Univ. N.Mex, currently. Polit. & Govt. Pos: Permanent page-boy, N.Mex. State Senate, 63-64, student intern, 66-67; legis. aide, Off. Lt. Gov, N.Mex, 64-66; pres, N.Mex. Teen Dem, 64-66; pres, Roosevelt Co, Young Dem. Clubs, 66-68; v.pres, N.Mex. Young Dem, 68- and mem. exec. cmt, 66-, chmn, 68-69; student intern, staff aide, Off. N.Mex. Secy. State, 68-69. Bus. & Prof. Pos: Legis. Adv, Radio Sta KCLV, Clovis, N.Mex, 67-68. Mem: Nat. Asn. Col. Student Govt; Mason; Order of DeMolay; N.Mex. Boy's State Prog; Key Club Am. Outstanding DeMolay of N.Mex, 65; Outstanding Young Citizen of N.Mex, DAR and Am. Legion, 66. Rel: Baptist. Legal Res: 317 S. Ave. F, Portales, N.Mex. 88130. Mailing Add: Box 4155 Portales, N.Mex. 88130.

BLAKEMORE, MURRAY G. D
Tenn. State Rep.
b. Franklin, Tenn, 3/5/12; s. William Blakemore and Cynthia Berry B; m. 4/11/36 to Lucile Patton; c. Gloria (Mrs. Walker). Educ: A. & I. State Univ, B.S, 36; Meharry Med. Col, D.T, 45; YMCA Law Sch, LL.B, 58; Omega Psi Phi. Polit. & Govt. Pos: Tenn. State Rep, 66- Mem: Mason; NAACP; Tenn. Coun. Human Rels; S. St. Commun. Center; State and Fed. Dem. Party. Rel: Presbyterian. Mailing Add: 1404 South St, Nashville, Tenn. 37212.

BLAKEMORE, RICHARD EUGENE D
Mem, Nye Co. Dem. Cent. Cmt, Nev.
b. Parsons, Kans. 9/21/22; s. John Butler Blakemore and Carolyn Fox B; m. 11/6/58 to Angela Catherine Majerus; c. Brian Fox and John Russell. Educ: Pasadena Jr. Col, 2 years. Polit. & Govt. Pos: Chmn, Nye Co. Dem. Cent. Cmt, Nev, 62 & 64, mem, 68-; mem, Nev. Dem. State Cent. Cmt, 62 & 64; del, Dem. Nat. Conv, 68. Mil. Serv: Entered as A/S, Navy, 40, released as Chief PO, 46, after serv. in Torpedo Squadron 12, Air Group 12, S. and Southwest Pac, 42-44; Personal Citation; Air Medal. Mem: C. of C.(pres, Tonopah Chap, 62-63); Lions (pres, Tonopah Club, 64-65); Nev. Aviation Trades Asn. (pres, 68-69); Elks; Shrine; VFW; Mason; mem, Nev. Civil Defense Adv. Bd; Nev. Exec. for Econ. Develop. Rel: Protestant. Mailing Add: Tonopah Airport, Box 672, Tonopah, Nev. 89049.

BLALOCK, DANIEL BRAXTON D
Ga. State Rep.
b. Fayetteville, Ga, 7/20/87; s. Aaron O. Blalock and Dannie Ferguson B; m. 12/28/45 to Eleanor Orr Roan; c. D. Braxton, Jr. and Emma Belle (Mrs. Millard Farmer); grandchildren Mary Estelle, Daniel Braxton, III, Eleanor Catherine Farmer and Millard Courtney Farmer III. Educ: Fayette Co. schs. Polit. & Govt. Pos: First v.chmn, Ga. State Dem. Exec. Cmt; chmn, Jekyll Island Authority; secy. to Gov. Hardwick, both terms; mayor, Fayetteville, Ga, 09; cmnr, Fayette Co, 25-28; Ga. State Sen, 49-50 & 55-56; Ga. State Rep, 53-54, 57-60 & 63- Bus. & Prof. Pos: Pres, Blalock Machinery & Equip. Co. Inc, Atlanta. Mem: Mason; Shrine. Rel: Baptist; Mem, Ga. Baptist Exec. Cmt; trustee, deacon and chmn, Baptist Village Bd. Mailing Add: Nimmons St, Newnan, Ga. 30263. (1967)

BLALOCK, EDGAR D
b. Culloden, Ga, 9/12/01; m. 1/17/33 to Blanche Gaffney; c. Edgar, Jr. and Herbert Gaffney. Educ: Ga. Mil. Col, 18; Univ. Ga, 21; Nat. Univ. Law Sch, 37; Sigma Chi. Polit. & Govt. Pos: Ga. State Sen, 51-52; Ga. State Rep, 55-64. Bus. & Prof. Pos: Cmn. distributor, Pure Oil Co; owner, Blalock Hauling Co. Mil. Serv: Univ. Ga, ROTC. Rel: Methodist. Mailing Add: Jonesboro, Ga. 30236. (1967)

BLANC, DONALD RICHARD D
Chmn, Gem Co. Dem. Cent. Cmt, Idaho
b. Melba, Idaho, 8/10/21; s. Joseph Murrey Blanc and Edith Chapin B; m. 6/25/45 to Margaret Afton Harvey; c. Richard George, Trennis Jack, Barbara (Mrs. Jerry Walton) and Ann (Mrs. Robert Teeter). Educ: Kings Point U.S. Maritime Acad, Sci, 42-45; Boise State Col, 67-69; Col. Idaho, 69; Polaris camera staff. Polit. & Govt. Pos: Dem. precinct committeeman, Letha Precinct, Idaho, 66-67; state committeeman, Idaho Dem. Party, 67-68; chmn, Gem Co. Dem. Cent. Cmt, 68- Bus. & Prof. Pos: Land owner, Black Canyon, Caldwell, Idaho, 47-; mgr, fruit ranches for Brigham Young Univ, Rolling Hills Orchard and Bowman Ranch, Emmett, Idaho, 65-69; teacher, Bur. Indian Affairs, Alaska, 69- Mil. Serv: Entered as A/S, Maritime Serv. and Naval Res, 42, released as Ens, 46, after serv. in S.Pac. Theater, 43-46. Mem: Caldwell Flyers (pres, 54-56); Christian Flying Club; Middleton Ornithology Asn; Nat. Rifleman; Middleton Athletic Boosters; Nat. Farmers Union; Idaho Horticulture Asn. Safe Pilot Award. Rel: Latter-day Saint; Elder, Church of Jesus Christ of Latter-day Saints, 45- Mailing Add: Route 1, Caldwell, Idaho 83617.

BLANCETT, THOMAS JOSEPH R
Chmn, Neosho Co. Rep. Cent. Cmt, Kans.
b. Pittsburgh, Kans, 7/13/25; s. Thomas J. Blancett and Josephine Yartz B; m. 1/14/50 to Pearl Alford; c. Thomas J, III and Rick M. Educ: Pittsburg State Col, 3 years. Polit. & Govt. Pos: Chmn, Neosho Co. Rep. Cent. Cmt, Kans, 66- Mil. Serv: Entered as Pvt, Marine Corps, 43, released as Cpl, 46, after serv. in 5th Marine Div, Pac. Theater, Iwo Jima, 44-46. Mem: Am. Legion (dist. comdr); VFW; Elks. Rel: Protestant. Mailing Add: 11 E. Eighth, Chanute, Kans. 66720.

BLANCHARD, CAROLYN J. R
Wis. State Assemblyman
b. Cambridge, 6/13/21; m. to David Blanchard, wid. Educ: Univ. of Wis, B.S, 43. Polit. & Govt. Pos: Wis. State Assemblyman, 63- Mailing Add: 506 Chamberlain St, Edgerton, Wis. 53534. (1967)

BLANCHARD, HORACE J. D
Tex. State Sen.
b. Denison, Tex, 12/21/23; s. Charley H. Blanchard (deceased) and Lera Phillips B; m. 4/12/47 to Mary Thomas; c. Adrienne (Mrs. Robertson), Jeffrey Paul, John Ben, Robert Henry and William Clifton. Educ: Tex. Tech. Col, B.A, 51; South. Methodist Univ, LL.B, 51; Barristers; Phi Alpha Delta; Kappa Sigma. Polit. & Govt. Pos: Tex. State Rep, Lubbock Co, 57-60; Tex. State Sen, 28th Dist, 63- Bus. & Prof. Pos: Partner, Blanchard, Clifford, Gilkerson & Smith, 64- Mil. Serv: Entered as Pvt, Army, 43, released as 1st Lt, 46, after serv. in 1399th Eng. Bn, Pac. Theater, 45-46; Army Res, 55-, Capt; Theater Ribbon; Good Conduct Medal. Mem: Nat. Motor Carrier Lawyers Asn; Tex, Lubbock Co. and Am. Bar Asns; Tex. Bar Found; Mason; Scottish Rite; Am. Legion; VFW; Lions. Ed, Southwest. Bar J, South. Methodist Univ. Rel: Methodist. Legal Res: 4504 17th St, Lubbock, Tex. 79414. Mailing Add: 1607 Broadway, Lubbock, Tex. 79401.

BLANCHETTE, ALICE FRANCES D
N.H. State Rep.
b. Dover, N.H, 4/19/04; d. Michael M. Madden and Mary E. Nugent M; wid; c. Robert F. Educ: St. Mary's Acad, Dover, N.H, 11 years; Wilfred Acad, Boston, Mass, 1 year. Polit. & Govt. Pos: Chmn, Bd. Supvr, Dover, N.H, 47-69; mem, Dem. City Cmt, Dover, 47-69; mem, Strafford Co. Exec. Cmt, 57-69; clerk, Dover Del, N.H. House of Rep, 57-69; N.H. State Rep, 57- Bus. & Prof. Pos: Former bookkeeper, J.A. Grimes Co; former stenographer and clerk of Strafford Co. Court House; former Mayor's secy; with surv, Manchester, N.H, 68. Mem: Order of Women Legislators; charter mem, Cath. Daughters of Am; Am. Legion Auxiliary. McIntosh Bus. Col. Order of Gregg Artists Award, Remington Typewriting Co. Rel: Catholic. Mailing Add: 22 Sixth St, Dover, N.H. 03820.

BLANCHFIELD, NINA MARIE D
b. Paterson, N.J, 9/25/14; d. Joseph Marchese and Maria Retiro M; m. 7/9/33 to James Joseph Blanchfield; c. Thomas J. and Joseph P. Polit. & Govt. Pos: Dem. committeeman, First Ward, Second Dist, Beacon, N.Y, 40-46; v.chmn, Beacon Dem. Cmt, 45-59; v.chmn, Dutchess Co. Dem. Cmt, 50-

65; v.cmnr. recreation, Beacon, 57-60; del, State Conv, 58 & 62; hon. v.pres, Dutchess Co. Women's Dem. Club, N.Y, 60-66; alternate del, Dem. Nat. Conv, Atlantic City, 64. Bus. & Prof. Pos: Eng. secy, IBM Corp, Poughkeepsie, N.Y, 53-56, ed. asst, IBM-Poughkeepsie News, 56-64, assoc. ed, 64-67. Mem: Beacon Jr. Soc. League; Franklin D. Roosevelt Home Club; Cath. Daughters Am. (Court Liberatta). Rel: Catholic. Mailing Add: 3 Deerfield Place, Beacon, N.Y. 12508.

BLANDFORD, DONALD JOSEPH D
Ky. State Rep.
b. Detroit, Mich, 4/4/38; s. Joseph Ellis Blandford and Maude Merrimee B; m. 5/28/61 to Mary Jane O'Bryan. Educ: Owensboro Cath. High Sch, grad. Polit. & Govt. Pos: Ky. State Rep, 68- Bus. & Prof. Pos: Raiser, purebred cattle, currently. Mem: Farm Bur; Nat. Farmers Orgn; Am. Polled Hereford Asn. Rel: Catholic. Mailing Add: R.R. 1, Philpot, Ky. 42366.

BLANDFORD, JOHN RUSSELL R
b. Buffalo, N.Y, 2/20/18; s. Raymond S. Blandford and Mary Jennie Pooley Perkins B; m. 7/28/44 to Barbara Jane Waterhouse; c. Marcia Ann (Mrs. Irwin R. Hoener). Educ: Hobart Col, B.A, 39; Yale Law Sch, LL.B, 46; Phi Beta Kappa; Tau Kappa Alpha. Polit. & Govt. Pos: Counsel, U.S. House of Rep. Armed Serv. Cmt, 42-63, chief counsel, 63- Mil. Serv: Entered as 2nd Lt, Marine Corps, 41, released as Maj, 46, after serv. in First Marine Div, Pac. Theater, Guadalcanal and New Britain, 42-44; Brig. Gen, Res; Presidential Unit Citation; Theater Ribbons with Stars. New York and D.C. Bars; U.S. Supreme Court; Sojourners Lodge. Rockefeller Pub. Serv. Award, for Law and Legis, 66. Rel: Methodist. Legal Res: 4520 N. 39th St, Arlington, Va. 22207. Mailing Add: 2120 Rayburn Bldg, Washington, D.C. 20515.

BLANEK, FRANK JOSEPH, JR. D
Committeeman, Ill. Dem. Cent. Cmt.
b. Panama C.Z, 1/7/35; s. Frank Blanek, Sr. and Betty Drosdova B; m. 9/21/58 to Sally Ann Miller; c. Michael, Betty Lynn, Debbie and Donna. Educ: St. Procopious Col, B.A, Pol. Sci; v.chmn, Student Govt. Assoc. Polit. & Govt. Pos: Chmn, Dem. Orgn. Lisle Twp, Ill, 68-; Dem. committeeman, Lisle Seventh Precinct, Lisle Twp, currently; mem, Dupage Co. Dem. Cent. Cmt, currently; committeeman, Ill. Dem. Cent. Cmt, 67- Bus. & Prof. Pos: Supvr, Int. Harvester Co; pres, Benet Realty Co, currently. Mil. Serv: Entered as E-2, Army Nat. Guard, 56, released as Sgt, 62, after serv. in 133rd Signal Bn; Top Honor Student, Ft. Leonard Wood, Mo. Mem: Homeowners Orgn.(past pres, 3 years); Ill. Youth Cmn.(regional adv. bd). Chicago Tribune Outstanding Achievement Award, Army Nat. Guard, 61. Rel: Catholic. Mailing Add: 1606 Burlington Ave, Lisle, Ill. 60532.

BLANEY, WALTER EDWIN R
b. Dallas, Tex, 2/11/28; s. Wm. H. Blaney, Sr. and Harriet Jane Silvus B; m. 1/29/50 to Joyce L. Sefcik; c. Rebecca, Carol and Shannon. Educ: Univ. Tex, B.F.A, 51; Phi Eta Sigma. Polit. & Govt. Pos: Rep. cand, U.S. House Rep, 22nd Dist, Tex, 68. Bus. & Prof. Pos: Pres, Show Stoppers of Tex, Inc, 66- Mem: Sales Prom. Exec. Asn; Am. Guild Variety Artists. Mailing Add: 8343 Dover, Houston, Tex. 77017.

BLANGERS, NELL ELIZABETH D
Dem. Nat. Committeewoman, Kans.
b. Kansas City, Mo, 6/18/09; d. Roy Cleveland Solomon and Mary Elizabeth Hanson S; m. 2/26/47 to Clement John Blangers. Educ: St. Joseph's Acad, Fontbonne, St. Louis, Mo. Polit. & Govt. Pos: V.chmn, Sixth Dist. Kans. Dem. Fedn. Womens Clubs, 58-60; v.chmn, Saline Co. Dem. Cent. Cmt, 58-60, chmn, 60-; v.chmn, Kans. Sixth Cong. Dist, 58-62; v.chmn, First Dist. Kans. Dem. Fedn. Womens Clubs, 62-64; v.chmn, Kans. Dem. State Cmn, 64-65; Dem. Nat. Committeewoman, Kans, 65-; del, Dem. Nat. Conv, 68. Bus. & Prof. Pos: Mem, Saline Co. Adv. Coun, Kans. Health Facilities Information Serv, 64 & 65. Mem: Saline Co. Adv. Coun, Kans. Health Facilities Information Club; Womens Kans. Day Club. Rel: Catholic. Mailing Add: 113 S. Connecticut, Salina, Kans. 67401. (1967)

BLANKENAU, FRANCIS JOSEPH R
Chmn, Sarpy Co. Rep. Cent. Cmt, Nebr.
b. Dodge, Nebr, 8/14/40; s. Herman Blankenau and Christina Lienen B; m. 12/26/66 to Christina Darlene Hemmingson; c. Christina Darlene. Educ: Wayne State Univ, B.A.E; Young Americans for Freedom (state chmn, 62-63); Young Rep; Int. Rels. Club; Neuman Club. Polit. & Govt. Pos: Chmn, Sarpy Co. Rep. Cent. Cmt, 66- Bus. & Prof. Pos: Del, Nebr. Educ. Asn. Del. Assembly, 68-69; pres, Papillion Educ. Asn, Papillion, Nebr, 69- Rel: Roman Catholic. Mailing Add: 306 E. Sixth, Papillion, Nebr. 68046.

BLANKENSHIP, C. A. D
Clerk, W.Va. State House of Del.
b. Baileysville, W.Va, 1/5/03; s. James H. Blankenship and Tenn. Frances Cole B; m. 11/28/28 to Inez Mae Perry; c. Carolyn (Mrs. Masson), Barbara (Mrs. Anderson), Patti (Mrs. Wells) and Mary Sue (Mrs. Adams). Educ: Davis-Elkins Col; Marshall Univ; Concord Col, B.A; W.Va. Univ, M.A. Polit. & Govt. Pos: Wyo. Co. supt. of schs, W.Va, 31-35, asst. supt, 45-54; W.Va. State Del, 44-50; clerk, W.Va. State House of Del, 54-; mem. exec. cmt, W.Va. Dem. State Cmt, 60; del-at-lg, Dem. Nat. Conv, 64. Bus. & Prof. Pos: Teacher, elem. prin, high sch. prin. Rel: Baptist. Mailing Add: Pineville, Wyo. Co, W.Va. 24874. (1967)

BLANKENSHIP, GEORGE TONY R
Attorney Gen, Okla.
b. Oklahoma City, Okla, 3/11/28; s. George Tony Blankenship and Daisy Dean B; m. 6/8/51 to Elizabeth Katherine Warren; c. Matthew Steven, Elizabeth Ann and Julie Kay. Educ: Univ. Okla, B.A, 51, LL.B, 54; Phi Alpha Delta; Sigma Nu. Polit. & Govt. Pos: V.chmn, Okla. Young Rep, 57-59, nat. committeeman, 59-61; Okla. State Rep, 60-66; attorney gen, Okla, 67-; del, Rep. Nat. Conv, 68. Bus. & Prof. Pos: Owner, Blankenship Properties, 56-; partner, Lampkin, Wolfe and Blankenship, 61-65. Mil. Serv: Entered as 2nd Lt, Air Force, 54, released as 1st Lt, 56, after serv. in 23rd Fighter Group, Judge Adv. Mem: Okla. and Am. Bar Asns; Mason (32°); Shrine. Rel: Methodist. Mailing Add: 1600 Elmhurst, Oklahoma City, Okla. 73120. (1967)

BLANTON, JACK D
Tex. State Rep.
b. Kansas City, Mo, 1/29/21; s. Lester Franklin Blanton and Lena Smith B; m. 9/4/42 to Marian Good; c. Stephen Franklin, Joan Marion and Mary Elizabeth. Educ: South. Methodist Univ, B.A; Alpha Tau Omega. Polit. & Govt. Pos: Mayor, Carrollton, Tex, 46-48; Tex. State Rep, Austin, 67- Bus. & Prof. Pos: Self-employed. Mem: Mason; Shrine; Nat. Coun. Serv. Int. Visitor; Dallas Co. Red Cross (dir. and mem. bd). Rel: Methodist. Mailing Add: 1501 Francis St, Carrollton, Tex. 75006.

BLANTON, JOHN H. D
Ala. State Rep.
b. Selma, Ala, 2/28/18; s. Robert H. Blanton and Zada Davis Reynolds B; m. 9/16/50 to Mary Hontas Hutchings; c. Barry Scott, John Hutchings and Mary Margaret. Educ: Univ. Ala, B.S, LL.B, 42. Polit. & Govt. Pos: Ala. State Rep, currently. Bus. & Prof. Pos: Lawyer, 46- Mil. Serv: Naval Res, 42-46, Lt. Comdr. Rel: Methodist. Mailing Add: 902 Alabama Ave, Selma, Ala. 36701.

BLANTON, L. RAY D
U.S. Rep, Tenn.
b. Hardin Co, Tenn, 4/10/30; s. Leonard A. Blanton and Ova Delaney B; m. 7/23/49 to Betty Jane Littlefield; c. Debbie, David and Paul. Educ: Univ. Tenn, B.S, 51. Polit. & Govt. Pos: Tenn. State Rep, 64-66; U.S. Rep, Tenn, 67- Bus. & Prof. Pos: V.Pres, Tenn. Plant Mix Asphalt Asn, 65-66. Mem: Adamsville Lions; Moose; Shrine; Mason; Area Coun, Boy Scouts; Univ. Tenn. Alumni; Century Club. Rel: Methodist. Mailing Add: P.O. Box 96, Adamsville, Tenn. 38310.

BLANTON, WILLIAM NEAL, JR. D
b. Waco, Tex, 12/24/15; s. William Neal Blanton, Sr. and Vivian Tressider B; m. 3/31/46 to Elizabeth Putnam; c. Jane (Mrs. R.H. Espy, Jr), William Neal III and Thomas Putnam. Educ: Rice Univ, B.A, 37; Univ. Tex, Austin, J.D, 40; Yale Univ, 43-44; Chi Phi. Polit. & Govt. Pos: Asst. attorney gen, Tex, 46-47; del, Dem. State Convs, 48-68; elec. judge, Bellaire, Tex, 51-54; chmn, Harris Co. Dem. Conv, 52; mem, Harris Co. Dem. Exec. Cmt, 52-56 and chmn, 66 & 68; chmn. and presiding elec. judge, Precinct 234, 54-66; del, Dem. Nat. Conv, 60; co-chmn, Johnson-Humphrey Campaign, Harris Co, 64; dist judge, 11th Dist, 68- Bus. & Prof. Pos: Attorney, Tex. Co, Houston, 40-41; trial attorney, Butler & Binion, 41-42; partner-trial attorney, Butler, Binion, Rice, Cook & Knapp, 47-68. Mil. Serv: Entered as Pvt, Army, 42, released as Capt, 46, after serving in I-357 Co. D, 3rd Mil. Govt. Regt, 19th Brit. Army Group and Europe Civil Affairs Div, SHAEF, 44-46; Capt, Mil. Intel. Res, 46-53; Europe-Africa-Middle East Campaign Medal with four Bronze Stars; Am Theatre Campaign Medal; Victory Medal. Mem: Am, Tex. and Houston Bar Asns; Am Judicature Soc; Fedn. Ins. Counsel; Tex. Asn. Defense Counsel; U.S. Supreme Court, Fifth Circuit Court Appeals; Dist. Court South. Dist. Tex; Tex. Supreme Court; SAR; first v.pres. gen, Sons Repub. Tex; Am Legion; Houston Racquet Club; Inns of Court; past pres, R.E. Lee Sr. High PTA; Briarcroft Civic Club. Rel: Methodist; mem. official bd, St. Luke's United Methodist Church. Legal Res: 5643 Piping Rock Lane, Houston, Tex. 77027. Mailing Add: 305 Civil Courts Bldg, Houston, Tex. 77002.

BLASE, NICHOLAS B. D
Committeeman, Ill. Dem. State Cent. Cmt.
b. Chicago, Ill, 6/8/28; s. Nickolas A. Blase and Toussa Sarris B; wid; c. Marcella and Mari Jo. Educ: Notre Dame Univ, LL.B, 51. Polit. & Govt. Pos: Mayor, Village of Niles, Ill, 61-; committeeman, Ill. Dem. State Cent. Cmt, 66-; del, Dem. Nat. Conv, 68. Bus. & Prof. Pos: Attorney-at-law. Mil. Serv: V5 Naval Officers Training Sch, Notre Dame, 43-45. Mem: Am, Ill. and Northwest Bar Asns; Ill. Munic. League; Cook Co. Coun. Govt; Elks; Lions; Am. Judicature Soc; Hellenic Am. Asn. Distinguished Pub. Serv. Award, Hellenic Am. Soc; Serv. to Youth Award, Boy Scouts; Appreciation Award for Outstanding Serv, Ill. Munic. League. Rel: Greek Orthodox. Legal Res: 8554 Clara Dr, Niles, Ill. 60648. Mailing Add: 8074 Milwaukee Ave, Niles, Ill. 60648.

BLASER, WILLIAM LAWRENCE R
b. Chicago, Ill, 12/10/23; s. William John Blaser and Antoinette Fuka B; m. 6/25/45 to Marion Louise Roos; c. Glenn William, Steven Robert and Joan Louise. Educ: Northwest. Univ, B.S, 47; Harvard Law Sch, 47-48; Alpha Tau Omega. Polit. & Govt. Pos: Trustee, Park Forest Libr. Bd, Ill, 60-64; precinct capt, Rep. Party, 62-69; Ill. State Rep, 65-66. Bus. & Prof. Pos: Pres, EverSweet Foods, Inc, 57-63; v.pres, Capitol Food Indust, 59-67; pres, Bowey's, Inc, 63-65; pres, Mosaic Tile Co, 67-68; pres, Blaser, Andersen & Co, 69- Mil. Serv: Entered as A/S, Naval Res, 42, released as Lt.(jg), 46, after serv. in Pac. Theater; Bronze Star Medal; Navy Unit Commendation; Pac. and Am. Theater Ribbons. Mem: Young Pres. Orgn; Am. Legion; past pres, Nat. Soc. State Legislators. Rel: Unitarian. Mailing Add: 24 Bay Ridge, Springfield, Ill. 62707.

BLASIER, JOHN WILBER R
Mem, Calif. Rep. State Cent. Cmt.
b. Glendale, Calif, 4/20/32; s. Herbert E. Blasier and Miriam Hattery B; m. 12/19/53 to Edith Derryberry; c. Robert and Mary Theresa. Educ: Univ. South. Calif, B.S, 55; Sigma Nu. Polit. & Govt. Pos: Pres, La Canada Young Rep, Calif, 67; v.pres, Los Angeles Co. Young Rep, 68; mem, Calif. Rep. State Cent. Cmt, 67- Bus. & Prof. Pos: Pres, Monitor Prod. Co, Inc, South Pasadena, Calif. Mil. Serv: Entered as Pvt, Army, 55, released as SPC-3, 57, after serv. in Signal Corps. Mailing Add: 5088 Fallhaven Lane, La Canada, Calif. 91011.

BLASKA, JEROME LYLE D
b. Marshall, Wis, 7/4/19; s. John M. Blaska and Rose Schuster B; m. 2/7/48 to Helen Curl; c. David J, Michael, Elizabeth, William, Jane and Richard. Educ: Sun Prairie High Sch, grad. Polit. & Govt. Pos: With Sch. Bd, 12 years; committeeman, Agr. Conserv. Serv; Wis. State Assemblyman, 59-66, chmn, Assembly Hwy. Cmt. and Hwy. Adv. Cmt, 65-66, mem, Legis. Interstate Coop. Cmn, 12 State Midwest Area, 65-66. Bus. & Prof. Pos: Farmer; canning co. field mgr, 39-42; sch. clerk since 50. Mil. Serv: En-

tered as Pvt, Army, 42, released as Corp, 46, after serv. in Detachment 355th Port Co. and 382nd Automatic Weapons Bn, South Pac. Theatre, 42-46. Mem: Lions; Am. Legion; VFW; Cath. Order of Foresters; K. of C; Wis. Farmers Union. Rel: Catholic. Mailing Add: Route 2, Sun Prairie, Wis. 53590.

BLATNIK, JOHN A. DFL
U.S. Rep, Minn.
b. Chisholm, Minn, 8/17/11; m. 1955 to Gisela Hager; c. Thomas H, Stephanie and Valerie. Educ: Winona State Teachers Col, Minn, B.E, 35; Univ. of Chicago; Univ. of Minn, 41-42, grad. work in Pub. Admin. Polit. & Govt. Pos: Minn. State Sen, 40-44; U.S. Rep, 46-; del, Dem. Nat. Conv, 68; mem, Dem. Nat. Cmt, currently. Bus. & Prof. Pos: Teacher and sch. adminstr, 8 years. Mil. Serv: Army Air Corps Intel. and Off. of Strategic Servs, 42-46, discharged as Paratrooper Capt; Bronze Star Medal with Oak Leaf Cluster; Air Medal. Legal Res: 417½ Fourth St. S.W, Chisholm, Minn. 55719. Mailing Add: 2449 Rayburn House Office Bldg, Washington, D.C. 20515.

BLATT, GENEVIEVE D
Secy, Pa. State Dem. Cmt.
b. East Brady, Pa, 6/19/13; d. George F. Blatt and Clara Laurent B; single. Educ: Univ. Pittsburgh, A.B, 33, M.A, 34, J.D, 37; Phi Beta Kappa; Pi Sigma Alpha; Delta Sigma Rho; Pi Tau Phi; Mortar Bd; Women's Debating Asn; Quill Club; Women's Athletic Asn; Women's Self-Govt. Asn; Cwens; hon. degrees from St. Francis Col, Villanova Univ, St. Joseph's Col, Barry Col. and Seton Hill Col. Polit. & Govt. Pos: Secy. and chief exam, Civil Serv. Cmn, Pittsburgh, Pa, 38-42; nat. committeewoman, Young Dem. Clubs of Pa, 40-42, pres, 42-50; mem. exec. bd, Pa. Fedn. of Dem. Women, 40-; asst. city solicitor, Pittsburgh, 42-45; dep. state treas, Pa, 45-49; secy. International Affairs, 55-67; secy, Pa. State Dem. Cmt, 48-; Dem. nominee for Auditor Gen, 52; Dem. nominee for U.S. Sen, Pa, 64; asst. dir, Off. Econ. Opportunity, Exec. Off. of President, 67-68; dir. dept. audits, Auditor Gen. Dept, 69- Bus. & Prof. Pos: Mem. faculty, Univ. Pittsburgh, 34-38; attorney-at-law, 38-55 & 68- Mem: Am, Pa. and Allegheny Co. Bar Asns; Nat. Asn. of Women Lawyers; Am. Soc. Pub. Admin; Am. Asn. Univ. Women; League of Women Voters; Bus. & Prfnl. Women's Club; Nat. Coun. Cath. Women; CWV Auxiliary; bd. dirs, Pa. and Tri-Co. United Funds; bd. mgr, Holy Spirit Hosp, Harrisburg; bd. dirs, La Roche Col, Allison Park; pres. coun, Mt. Mercy Col, Pittsburgh; bd. trustees, St. Francis Col, Loretto and St. Joseph's Col, Emmittsburg, Md; chmn, Cent. Pa. Arthritis Found. Distinguished Daughter of Pa, 56; Named Woman of Year in Govt, 63, Who's Who Among Am. Women. Rel: Catholic. Legal Res: 384 S. Highland Ave, Pittsburgh, Pa. 15206. Mailing Add: Grayco Apt, Harrisburg, Pa. 17101.

BLATT, SOLOMON D
Speaker, S.C. House of Rep.
b. Blackville, S.C, 2/27/96; s. Nathan Blatt and Mollie B; m. 3/18/20 to Ethel Green; c. Soloman, Jr. Educ: Univ. S.C, LL.B, 17. Hon. LL.D, Univ. S.C. and Lander Col. Polit. & Govt. Pos: Trustee, Barnwell Sch, 34 years; mem, Gov. Blackwood's Staff; S.C. State Rep, 33-, Speaker, S.C. House of Rep, 35-47 & 51-; trustee, Univ. S.C, 36-48. Bus. & Prof. Pos: Attorney-at-law, 17-; lawyer, Firm of Blatt & Fales. Mil. Serv: Sgt, Army, 18-19, with 323rd Inf, 81st Div. Mem: Am. Legion; Mason. Mailing Add: Barnwell, S.C. 29812.

BLATZ, JEROME V. Conservative
Minn. State Sen.
b. Bloomington, Minn, 1923; married; c. Seven. Educ: Notre Dame Univ, B.A; Harvard Univ, LL.B. Polit. & Govt. Pos: Minn. State Sen, 62- Bus. & Prof. Pos: Lawyer. Mailing Add: 7701 Harriet Ave. S, Minneapolis, Minn. 55423. (1967)

BLAU, EDWARD JOHN D
b. Newport, Ky, 3/20/13; s. Edward John Blau and Frances Pelzer B; m. 12/29/37 to Mary Ann Meyer; c. Edward B, Bernard J, Rose Ann (Mrs. Henry Dabek), Mary Frances (Mrs. Edward Brieling), Caroline (Mrs. Kurt Meier), Ruth Clare, James R. and Robert E. Educ: Univ. of Cincinnati, A.B, 36; Phi Chi. Polit. & Govt. Pos: Campaign chmn, Campbell Co. Dem. Party, Ky, 56, 62 and 64 and exec. chmn, 64-68; master cmnr, Campbell Co. Circuit Court, 58- Bus. & Prof. Pos: Owner, Blau's Food Market, 31- Mem: Jr. C. of C. (pres, Campbell Co. Chap); Boy Scouts (mem. exec. bd); Rotary (bd. mem, Newport Chap); mem. exec. bd, Cerebral Palsy. Rel: Catholic. Legal Res: 103 Riverside Pkwy, Ft. Thomas, Ky. 41075. Mailing Add: Court House, Newport, Ky. 41071.

BLAYLOCK, CHESTER MERLE D
Chmn, Mont. State Dem. Cent. Cmt.
b. Joliet, Mont, 11/13/24; s. De Witt Blaylock and Iva Nichols B; m. 6/20/47 to Mildred Marie Poznanovic; c. Bruce, Wendelle, Mike, Kathryn and Barbara. Educ: Eastern Mont. Col, 46-48; Univ. Mont, B.A, 51 and M.A, 57. Polit. & Govt. Pos: Pres, Yellowstone Dem. Club, Mont, 62-64; chmn, Yellowstone Co. Dem. Cent. Cmt, 62-67; chmn, Mont. State Dem. Cent. Cmt, 67-; del, Dem. Nat. Conv, 68. Bus. & Prof. Pos: Mem, state ethics cmt, Mont. Educ. Asn, 55-64, pres, Laurel Unit, 60-61. Mil. Serv: Entered as A/S, Navy, 43, released as PO 3/C after serv. on board Battleship U.S.S. West Virginia in Southwest Pac; Letter of Commendation from Admiral of our task force; Philippine Liberation Medal with two stars; Am. Area Campaign Medal; Asiatic-Pac. Area Campaign Medal with four stars. Mailing Add: 502 Third Ave, Laurel, Mont. 59044.

BLAYLOCK, LEN EVERETTE R
Cmnr, Ark. Dept. Pub. Welfare
b. Little Rock, Ark, 12/8/18; s. David Penn Blaylock and Minnie Bradford B; m. 7/7/41 to Melba Winona Wright; c. David Robert, Len E, Jr, Melvin James, Betty Louise and Dale Alan. Educ: Baylor Univ, 51-52; Ark Polytech. Col, B.A, 62; Ark. State Teachers Col, 63. Polit. & Govt. Pos: Field representative, Rep. Nat. Committeeman Ark, 64-67; twp. committeeman, Perry Co. Rep. Cmt, 65-67; cmnr, Ark. Dept. Pub. Welfare, 67- Bus. & Prof. Pos: Owner, Nimrod Trading Post, Nimrod, Ark, 59-61; prin, Perry Sch, 61-64. Mil. Serv: Entered as Pvt, Air Force, 39, released as Maj, 59, after serv. in Strategic Air Command as Navigator-Bombardier and Radar Observer, 52-59, Maj, Res; Theatre Campaign Ribbon; Unit Citations; Legion of Merit. Mem: AF&AM. Rel: Baptist. Mailing Add: Route 1, Perryville, Ark. 72126.

BLEAKLY, JOHN L. D
b. Waterloo, Iowa, 3/12/34; s. John R. Bleakly and Virginia Pierce B; single. Educ: Univ. Iowa, B.A. in Polit. Sci, 59. Polit. & Govt. Pos: Admin. asst. to U.S. Rep. Bert Bandstra, Fourth Dist, Iowa, 65-68; admin. asst. to U.S. Rep. Neal Smith, Iowa, 68- Bus. & Prof. Pos: Reporter, Des Moines Tribune, Iowa, 59-64. Legal Res: 2806 Woodland Ave, Des Moines, Iowa 50312. Mailing Add: 101 G St. S.W, Washington, D.C. 20024. (1967)

BLEDSOE, LAMAR D
b. Atlanta, Ga, 11/4/03; c. Nancy (Mrs. L.A. Kavanaugh), Jane (Mrs. Lawrence Voorhies). Educ: Fla. State Col. for Women; Gamma Alpha Chi. Polit. & Govt. Pos: Secy, Fla. Indust. Cmn, 43-45; off. mgr, State Advert. Cmn, 45-49, asst. to dir. and secy, 49-55; chief clerk, Fla. House of Rep, 45-66; asst. admin. dir. advert. div, State Develop. Cmn, 55-56. Mem: UDC; Altrusa Int. (past pres, Tallahassee Chap); Stephen Foster Mem. State Cmn, 49-67. Allen Morris Award for meritorious pub. serv, 47. Rel: Catholic. Mailing Add: 644 Ingleside Ave, Tallahassee, Fla. 32303.

BLEDSOE, STEWART R
Wash. State Rep.
b. Long Beach, Calif, 1922; m. to Betsy; c. four. Educ: Univ. Calif, Los Angeles; Wash. State Univ, grad. Polit. & Govt. Pos: Wash. State Rep. and majority leader, Wash. State House of Rep, currently. Bus. & Prof. Pos: Cattle rancher. Mem: Phi Delta Theta; Elks; Wash. Cattlemen's Asn. Mailing Add: Route 3, Box 60-B, Ellensburg, Wash. 98926.

BLEDSOE, WILLIAM E. R
b. Aroya, Colo, 7/27/19; s. Carl Bledsoe and Josie Main B; m. 47 to Helen Rooney; c. Mary Ann, Bonnie Lynn, Sara O'Tillia and William E, III. Educ: Colo. State Univ, B.S, 42; Alpha Gamma Rho. Polit. & Govt. Pos: Colo. State Rep, 52-54; Colo. State Sen, 54-66. Bus. & Prof. Pos: Rancher. Mem: Local, State and Nat. Cattlemen's Asn; pres, Lincoln Co. Cattlemen's Asn, 51; legis. bd, Colo. Cattlemen's Asn; Quarter Horse Asn; Farm Bur; Mason; Lions; Univ. Club of Denver. Legal Res: Bledsoe Ranch, Hugo, Colo. 80821. Mailing Add: Box 186, Hugo, Colo. 80821.

BLEICHER, MICHAEL N. D
Mem. Exec. Bd, Dane Co. Dem. Party, Wis.
b. Cleveland, Ohio, 10/2/35; s. David B. Bleicher and Rachel Faigin B; m. 6/4/57 to Betty M. Isack; c. Helene Carol, Laurence Aaron and Benjamin Daniel. Educ: Calif. Int. Tech, B.S, 57; Tulane Univ, M.S, 59, Ph.D, 61; Univ. Warsaw, Ph.D, 61. Polit. & Govt. Pos: Del, Wis. State Dem. Conv, since 64, chmn, resolutions cmt, 68; ward orgn. chmn, Dane Co. Dem. Party, 64-66, chmn, 66-68 and mem. exec. bd, 68-; del, Dem. Nat. Conv, and mem. credentials cmt, 68; state chmn, New Dem. Coalition, 68-69; mem, party reform cmt, Wis. Dem. Party, 69. Bus. & Prof. Pos: Teaching asst. math, Tulane Univ, 57-60; exchange fel, Univ. Warsaw, 60-61; Nat. Sci. Found. fel, Univ. Calif, Berkeley, 61-62; asst. prof, Univ. Wis. Madison, 62-66, assoc. prof, 66-69, prof, 69- Publ: Excursions into Mathematics, Worth, 69; plus others. Mem: Am. Civil Liberties Union; Am Fedn. Teachers; Sigma Xi; Am. Math. Soc; Math. Asn. Am. Rel: Jewish. Mailing Add: 5133 Flad Ave, Madison, Wis. 53711.

BLEIKAMP, BARBARA LEOTA R
b. Lancaster, Ohio, 7/1/33; d. Paul Louis Hershfield and Savilla Dwiggins H; m. 4/10/54 to Chester Edward Bleikamp, Jr; c. Paul Edward and Sherrill Savilla. Educ: Wash. Univ, A.B; Phi Beta Kappa; Delta Gamma. Polit. & Govt. Pos: Del, Rep. Nat. Conv, 68; Nixon Campaign mgr, N. St. Louis Co, Mo, 68; fund raising chmn, newsletter ed, precinct capt, secy, and precinct organizer, Spanish Lake Rep. Orgn, 68-69. Bus. & Prof. Pos: Teacher, Normandy, Mo, 53-54; teacher, Ferguson-Florissant, 68-69; co-owner, Sir Speedy Printing, Scottsdale, Ariz, 69- Mem: Campus Speakers Forum (pres); Florissant Jr. High Mothers Club (pres); rep, Sch. Dist. Planning Cmn. Rel: United Church of Christ. Mailing Add: 8701 E. Sells Dr, Scottsdale, Ariz. 85251.

BLENDT, CARLTON, JR. D
Chmn, State Soil Conserv. Cmn, Del.
b. 1929. Educ: John Bassett Moore High Sch. Polit. & Govt. Pos: Del. State Rep, 61-69; chmn, State Soil Conserv. Cmn, currently. Bus. & Prof. Pos: Dairy farmer, currently. Mem: Former chmn, Del. Dairy Adv. Cmn; Wilmington Milk Mkt. Cmt; former master, Smyrna Grange; Farm Bur; former pres, Del. Crop Improv. Asn. Rel: Presbyterian; Elder, First Presbyterian Church, Smyrna. Mailing Add: Townsend, Del. 19734.

BLESSING, ELIZABETH D
b. Dallas, Tex, 3/6/19; d. Arza James Cupples and Willie Johnson Cupples; m. 12/21/41 to William Blessing; c. James William; Gail Ann; William Scott; and David Brian. Educ: Hockaday Jr. Col, 36-38. Polit. & Govt. Pos: City Councilwoman, Dallas City Council, 61-65. Mem: Dallas Real Estate Bd; Women's Coun. of the Nat. Asn. of Real Estate Bds; Zonta Int; Dem. Women of Dallas Co. Rel: Methodist. Mailing Add: Preston Tower, Apt. 701, 6211 W. Northwest Hwy, Dallas, Tex. 75225. (1967)

BLICK, GEORGE LEONARD R
b. Sedgewick, Colo, 3/10/10; s. John J. Blick and Clementyne Goff B; m. 7/10/37 to Marie C. Senften; c. Gary, Benny and Philip. Educ: Idaho State Normal, 34; Univ. Nev, summer, 37. Polit. & Govt. Pos: Former Co. Agr. advisor, Idaho; Idaho State Rep, 50-56; Idaho Rep, Coun. State Govt, 52-58; v.chmn, State Bldg. Fund Coun, 60-66; Idaho State Sen, Twin Falls Co. and Majority Leader, Idaho State Senate, 63-66; alternate del, Rep. Nat. Conv, 68. Bus. & Prof. Pos: Coach and teacher, 37-43; chmn. bd. dirs, Idaho Frozen Foods; partner, Blick Seed Co. and Blick & Reese Produce; chmn. bd. dirs, Blick Inc, farms. Mem: Mason; Bohl Country Club; Castleford Men's Club; Grange. Rel: Methodist. Mailing Add: Castleford, Idaho 83321. (1967)

BLICKHAN, EDITH M. D
b. Camp Point, Ill, both parents deceased. Educ: High sch. and bus. col, Quincy, Ill. Polit. & Govt. Pos: Employee, State of Ill, 36-42; secy. to chmn,

Ill. State Dem. Cent. Cmt, 42-57; del. and worker, Ill. Dem. State Conv, 42-; worker, Dem. Nat. Conv, 44, 48, 52 & 56, alternate del, 64 & 68; personal secy. to Lt. Gov. Samuel H. Shapiro, Ill, 61-68 and Gov. Samuel H. Shapiro, 68; admin. secy. to Nicholas D. Ciaccio, admin. aide to Ill. Secy. of State Paul Powell, 69- Bus. & Prof. Pos: Claims secy, State Farm Mutual Automobile Ins. Co, 57-60; policy underwriter, Jones-McIntire-Stuches Ins. Co, 60-61. Mem: Dem. Club; chap. chmn, Mariama Club, 50-54. Rel: Catholic. Mailing Add: 2619 S. Park Ave, Apt. 1, Springfield, Ill. 62704.

BLISS, BRUCE JAMES R
Chmn, N. Attleboro Rep. Town Cmt, Mass.
b. Providence, R.I, 5/18/35; s. Carlton H. Bliss and Ethel McKechnie B; m. 6/17/57 to Phebe Ann; c. Karen Lee, Bruce James, Jr, Judith Ann and Susan Jane. Educ: Brown Univ, A.B. in chem, 57; Lambda Chi Alpha. Polit. & Govt. Pos: Del, Mass. State Rep. Conv, 64 & 66; chmn, N. Attleboro Rep. Town Cmt, Mass, 64-; mem, Selective Serv. Bd. 56, Mass, 65-; mem, N. Attleboro Bd. of Water Cmn, 67-, chmn, 68-; mem, N. Attleboro Elec. Cmn, 67-, chmn, 68- Bus. & Prof. Pos: Metallurgist, Tex. Instruments, 58-66 and Gorham Corp, 66-68; mfg. engr, Engelhaul Industs, 68- Publ: Paper in 6th Symposium on Vacuum Techniques. Mem: Am. Chem. Soc. Rel: Universalist. Mailing Add: 156 Raymond Hall Dr, North Attleboro, Mass. 02760.

BLISS, ELLEN ELIZABETH R
S.Dak. State Rep.
b. Vermillion, S.Dak, 1/3/05; d. Alvey Franklin Bliss and O'Lina Lewison B; single. Educ: Univ. S.Dak, 23-27; Univ. Colo, summer, 29. Polit. & Govt. Pos: Supt. schs, Clay Co, S.Dak, 35-39; v.chmn, Clay Co. Rep. Cmt, 37-39; off. mgr, State Welfare Off, Pierre, 39-41; precinct committeewoman, Minnehaha Co. Rep. Cmt, 41-42; mem, Exec. Bd. Legis. Research Coun, 62-66; co. welfare worker, Minnehaha Co, 65-66; dir, Minnehaha Co. Welfare Dept, 66-; mem, State Pub. Welfare Cmn, 69- Mem: Eastern Star; Bus. & Prfnl. Women's Club (pres, Vermillion, S.Dak, 37-39, Sioux Falls, 42-44); Boys Club (bd mem, 58-66). Rel: Lutheran. Mailing Add: 520 N. Menlo Ave, Sioux Falls, S.Dak. 57104.

BLISS, RAY CHARLES R
Rep. Nat. Committeeman, Ohio
b. Akron, Ohio, 12/16/07; s. Emil Bliss and Emilie Wieland B; m. 11/26/59 to Ellen Palmer. Educ: Univ. Akron, A.B, 35; Phi Kappa Tau. Hon. L.H.D, Univ. Akron, 69. Polit. & Govt. Pos: Precinct committeeman and mem, Summit Co. Rep. Exec. Cmt, Ohio, 32-; del, Ohio State Rep. Conv, 32-68; mem, Summit Co. Bd. of Elections, 36-, chmn, 45-46 & 49-50; chmn, Summit Co. Rep. Cent. Cmt, 42-64; mem, Ohio Rep. State Cent. and Exec. Cmt, 44-, chmn, 49-65; del-at-lg, Rep. Nat. Conv, 52, 56, 60, 64 & 68, mem, Rules Cmt, 52, chmn, Ohio del, 56, v.chmn, 60, chmn, Site Cmt, 60 & 68, adv. to exec. cmt, Arrangements Cmt, 64, chmn, 68; Rep. Nat. committeeman, Ohio, 52-; mem, Nat. Rep. Exec. Cmt, 52-, v.chmn, 60-65; chmn, Midwest Rep. State Chmn. Asn, 53-65; chmn, Rep. Nat. Subcmt. on Big City Politics, 61; chmn, Rep. State Chmn. Adv. Cmt. to Rep. Nat. Chmn, 62-65; chmn, Rep. Nat. Cmt, 65-69; presiding officer, Rep. Coord. Cmt, 65-69; presiding officer, Rep. Joint Leadership of Cong, 65-69. Bus. & Prof. Pos: Secy-treas, Wells & Bliss, Inc, 33-37; pres, Tower Agencies, Inc, Akron, Ohio, 47- Publ: 'The Role of the State Chairman' in Politics USA, Doubleday, Inc, 60. Mem: Kiwanis; Akron City Club; Union Club of Cleveland; 1925 F Street Club, Inc, Wash, D.C; Mason (32°); Shrine; Columbus Club, Columbus, Ohio; Portage Country Club. Rel: Episcopal. Univ. Akron Alumni Honor Award, 65. Legal Res: 2535 Addyston Rd, Akron, Ohio 44313. Mailing Add: 2315 First National Tower, Akron, Ohio 44308.

BLISS, ROBERT LANDERS R
b. Binghamton, N.Y, 11/19/07; s. George Calvin Sherwood Bliss and Katherine Barbara Scheider B; m. 5/16/42 to Friede Smidt; c. John Smidt and Friede Sherwood (Mrs. Thomas M. Brayton). Educ: Cornell Univ, A.B, 30, grad, 31; Sigma Delta Chi; Psi Upsilon; Beth L'Amed; Sphinx Head; Aleph Samach. Polit. & Govt. Pos: Mem, New Canaan Town Rep. Cmt, Conn, 48-51, chmn, 51-62; state Rep. cent. committeeman from 26th Sen. Dist, 54-56; chmn, Fairfield Co. Rep. Cmt, 62-64; Conn. State Sen, 26th Dist, 62-67; spec. dep, sheriff, Fairfield Co. Bus. & Prof. Pos: Owner, Vegaline Kennels, purebred show beagles, 45-, judge and exhibit 13 in. beagles; pub. rels. dir, Nat. Asn. of Ins. Agents, 47-49; asst. to publisher, PM Newspaper, 40; exec. v.pres, Pub. Rels. Soc. of Am, Inc, N.Y, 49-56; pres, pub. rels. counsel, Robert L. Bliss & Co, Inc, N.Y.C, 56- Mil. Serv: Entered as 2nd Lt, Army Air Corps, 42, released as Maj, 46, after serv. as Chief, Pub. Affairs Sect, Air Serv. Command, Wright Field, Ohio. Publ: Articles on int. pub. rels, Communiqué, 64-; articles on nat. pub. rels, numerous Am. publ, including Pub. Rels. J. and Pub. Rels. Quart, 50- Mem: Founding charter mem, Int. Pub. Rels. Asn, 55, chmn, research cmt, 58-61, v.chmn. 60-62, v.pres, 63-64, pres, 65-67; chmn, Arden House Conf. on Bus. and Polit, 59 and Am. Bus. Conf. on Practical Polit, 60; Cornell Univ. Coun, Admin. Bd. Pres, Class of 1930, 60-65; gen. rapporteur, Second Pub. Rels. World Cong, Venice, 61, prog. chmn, Third Pub. Rels. World Cong, Montreal, 64, presided over Fourth Pub. Rels. World Cong, Rio de Janeiro, 67; pres, N.Y.C. Chap, Pub. Rels. Soc. Am, 62-63; founding charter mem, 1st life mem. and 1st v.pres, Nat. Soc. State Legislators, 65-; former mem, Newspaper Guild; hon. mem, New Canaan Vol. Fire Dept; Univ. Club; Wings Club; Down Town Asn, N.Y; SAR. Rel: Baptist. Mailing Add: 734 Ponus Ridge, New Canaan, Conn. 06840.

BLIZARD, MARGARET MURRAY D
Mem, Exec. Cmt, Mass. State Dem. Cmt.
b. Boston, Mass, 8/23/19; d. John H. Murray and Mary Connor M; m. 8/10/46 to Frederick J. Blizard; c. Janet Louise, Carol Marie and Christine Ann. Educ: Teachers Col. of City of Boston, B.S, 40, Ed.M, 41; Mass. Inst. Tech, M.P.H, 43; Suffolk Univ. Law Sch, LL.B, 63; chmn. bd. of gov. and treas, Student Bar Asn; Am. Pub. Health Asn. fel; ed, The Brief Case. Polit. & Govt. Pos: Organizer and adv, Norfolk Co. Dem. Women's Club, Mass, 56; dir, Mass. Dem. Women on Wheels, 57, state parliamentarian, 57-58, state first v.pres, 58-59, state pres, 59-61; mem, Cmt. Orgn. of Dem, 60-64; mem, Norwood Dem. Town Cmt, 60-; mem, steering cmt, Gov. Adv. Cmt. on Ment. Health, 63-65; trustee, Medfield State Hosp, 63-; mem, Commonwealth Serv. Corps Study Cmn, 64; legal counsel and mem. exec. cmt, Mass. State Dem. Cmt, 64-; alternate del, Dem. Nat. Conv, 64, del-at-lg, 68; co-chmn, Second Norfolk Dist, Dem. Town Cmt. Coun, 65-; dir, Mass. Fedn. Dem. Women's Clubs, 66. Bus. & Prof. Pos: Teacher high sch. biol, Boston Pub. Schs, 42; health educ. coordinator, Boston Health Dept, 43-45; spec. lectr. in sex guid. in family life educ, Mass. Soc. for Social Hygiene, 43-59; acting exec. dir. & dir. health educ, Cambridge Tuberc. and Health Asn, 45-46; coordinator, Mass. Chest X-Ray Prog, Mass. Dept. Pub. Health, 49, chief coordinator of health educ, 50-56, admin. and legal asst. to Cmnr. of Pub. Health, 65-; attorney, assoc. with Kathleen Ryan Dacey, Boston, 63- Publ: 'Radio Listening Habits of Women who Attend Well-Baby Clinics' (with C.E. Turner), Am. J. Pub. Health, 8/43; ed. chaps. in Health in the Schools, School and Community Health by C.E. Turner. Mem: Fel, Am. Pub. Health Asn. and Soc. Pub. Health Educators; Mass. Pub. Health Asn.(mem. exec. cmt); Mass. Asn. Ment. Health (dir); Norfolk Ment. Health Asn.(dir); pres, Medfield Found. Ment. Health Res, 69-; Mass. Health Coun.(pres-elect, 69); Mass. Bar Asn.(mem. family law cmt); Mass. Trial Lawyers Asn.(trustee); Mass. Asn. of Women Lawyers; Mass. Coun. for Constitutional Reforms; bd. trustees, Norwood Hosp; Ladies Cath. Benevolent Asn. Rel: Roman Catholic. Mailing Add: 8 Wood Dr, Norwood, Mass. 02062.

BLOCH, STUART FULTON R
Chmn, Finance Cmt, Ohio Co. Rep. Party, W.Va.
b. Wheeling, W.Va, 4/23/33; s. Thomas Moffatt Bloch and Nancy Fulton B; m. 6/27/59 to Stephanie Hawkins; c. Karen Fulton, Stuart Stephenson and Caroline Bennett. Educ: Phillips Exeter Acad, 48-52; Princeton Univ, A.B, cum laude, 56. Polit. & Govt. Pos: Chmn, W.Virginians for Goldwater for Pres, 64; alternate del, Rep. Nat. Conv, 64 and del, 68; mem, Finance Cmt, Ohio Co. Rep. Party, W.Va, 68- and chmn, currently. Bus. & Prof. Pos: Sales rep, Whitehall Prod, Inc, 59, advert. mgr, 60 and advert. mgr and v.pres, 61-; dir, The Bloch Bros. Tobacco Co, Wheeling, 62; dir, Whitehall Pipe Co, Richmond Hill, N.Y, 64. Mil. Serv: Entered as 2nd Lt, Air Force, 57, released as 1st Lt, 59. Mem: Nat. Asn. Tobacco Distributors (dir. young exec. div); Assoc. Tobacco Mfrs, Inc.(dir); Half Dollar Trust & Savings Bank (dir. and mem. exec. cmt); Salvation Army (adv. bd); Wheeling Symphony Soc, Inc.(exec. cmt); YMCA (dir); Jr. Achievement (dir). Rel: Protestant. Legal Res: 40 Orchard Rd, Wheeling, W.Va. 26003. Mailing Add: 4000 Water St, Wheeling, W.Va. 26003.

BLOCK, ETHEL LASHER R
Committeewoman, N.Y. State Rep. Cmt.
b. Tivoli, N.Y, 9/9/19; d. Harold Lasher and Emma Du Bois L; m. 9/6/42 to Dr. David Edgar Block; c. Ann M, David E, III and Harold M. Educ: St. Francis Hosp. Sch. of Nursing, Poughkeepsie, N.Y, R.N, 39. Polit. & Govt. Pos: First pres, Red Hook Womens Rep. Club, 62, 63 & 64; secy, Dutchess Co. Rep. Cmt, 63-64, v.chmn, 65-; committeewoman, N.Y. State Rep. Cmt, 67- Bus. & Prof. Pos: Surg. nurse, N.Dutchess Hosp, Rhinebeck, N.Y, 39-42; off. nurse, Red Hook, 45-57. Mem: DAR; Eastern Star; Nat. Fedn. Garden Clubs; Fedn. Rep. Women; PTA; Womans Auxiliary, Am. Med. Soc; lay adv. bd. mem, Marist Col. and Astor Home Child Guid. Clin, Rhinebeck, N.Y. Rel: Episcopal. Mailing Add: 19 North Rd, Tivoli, N.Y. 12583.

BLOCKER, GEORGE D
N.Mex. State Rep.
b. 1915. Polit. & Govt. Pos: Co. Cmnr, 4 years; N.Mex. State Rep, 57- Bus. & Prof. Pos: Oil distributor. Mem: C. of C; Lions; Mason; Consistory; Shrine. Rel: Methodist. Mailing Add: P.O. Box 580, Jal, N.Mex. 88252. (1967)

BLOMEN, HENNING ALBERT Socialist Labor Party
Mem. Nat. Exec. Cmt, Socialist Labor Party
b. New Bedford, Mass, 9/28/10; s. Gustav A. Blomen and Clara E. Magnuson B; m. 4/27/45, div; m. 2/17/69 to Constance Zimmerman; c. Frances (Mrs. Tripp). Educ: Somerville High Sch, Mass, grad, 28. Polit. & Govt. Pos: Cand. for Gov, Mass, Vice President of U.S, 64, and President of the U.S, 68. Bus. & Prof. Pos: Machine assembler, Dewey & Almy Chem. Co, Div. of W.R. Grace, Inc, 38-39. Rel: Brotherhood of Man. Mailing Add: 25 County St, Ipswich, Mass. 01938.

BLOMQUIST, GLENN A. DFL
b. Princeton, Minn, 1906; married. Educ: Princeton High Sch. Polit. & Govt. Pos: Minn. State Rep, 62-66; village clerk, Onamia, 47-49; former secy, Onamia Hosp, Inc. Bus. & Prof. Pos: Proprietor, jr. dept. store; pres, Onamia Bus. Industs, Inc. Mil. Serv: Air Force, 43-45. Mem: Secy, Onamia Civic Asn. Mailing Add: Onamia, Minn. 56359. (1967)

BLONDES, LEONARD SAUL D
Md. State Del.
b. Cleveland, Ohio, 5/7/29; s. Samuel Blondes and Sarah Goldman B; m. 9/10/50 to Shelly Bresler; c. Cliff, Jeffrey and Stacy. Educ: Adelbert Col, West. Reserve Univ, B.A, 51; George Wash. Univ, LL.B. & J.D, 53; Alpha Epsilon Pi; past pres. and V.Grand Chancellor, Nu Beta Epsilon. Polit. & Govt. Pos: Md. State Del, 62-, past chmn, Labor Cmt. and chmn, Judiciary Cmt, Md. House of Del; chmn, Montgomery Co. Dem. Del, currently. Bus. & Prof. Pos: Attorney, 55- Mil. Serv: Entered as Pvt, Army, 46, released as Sgt, 48. Mem: Montgomery Co. and Md. State Bar Asns; past pres, Isadore Gudelsky Lodge, B'nai B'rith, Optimist Club, Silver Spring and Plyers Mill Citizens Asn; past bd. mem, Silver Spring C. of C, Young Dem. Club, Allied Civic Group, Norbeck Country Club, Jewish War Vet, Camp Echo Lake and Jr. C. of C. Rel: Jewish. Legal Res: 7100 Crail Dr, Bethesda, Md. 20034. Mailing Add: Maryland National Bank Bldg, Silver Spring, Md. 20910.

BLOODWORTH, BURNETT SAUNDERS D
V.Chmn, Lee Co. Dem. Exec. Cmt, Fla.
b. Chattanooga, Tenn, 4/9/22; d. Hal Gholson Saunders and Lucy Burnett Wilson S; m. 9/18/45 to Allan Rabun Bloodworth; c. Margaret and Caroline. Educ: Univ. of Chattanooga, 40-43; Univ. of Minn, 43-44; Chi Omega. Polit. & Govt. Pos: Pres, Dem. Women's Club of Lee Co, Fla, 62-63; chmn, Lee Co. Ladies for Lyndon, 64; del-at-lg, Dem. Nat. Conv, 64 and del, 68; recording secy, Dem. Women's Club of Fla, 66-68, pres, 68-69; v.chmn, Lee Co. Dem. Exec. Cmt. and Dem. State Committeewoman, Fla, 66-; asst. to U.S. Rep. James A. Haley, Seventh Cong. Dist, Fla, currently. Bus. & Prof. Pos: Jr. engr, Curtiss-Wright Corp, 44; eng. draftsman, Fla. State Rd. Dept, 46-51. Mil. Serv: Entered as Cadette in Officers' Training, Coast Guard, 44, released as Ens, Women's Res, 45, after serv. as Commun. Officer, U.S. Mem: PTA; DAR; Cancer Soc. Bd; Migrant Mission Bd; Women's Commun. Club. Rel: Episcopal. Mailing Add: 1441 Maravilla Ave, Ft. Myers, Fla. 33901.

BLOODWORTH, JAMES NELSON D
Assoc. Justice, Supreme Court of Ala.
b. Decatur, Ala, 1/21/21; s. Benjamin McGowan Bloodworth and Marguerite Nelson B; m. to Jean Gregg Shelton; c. Catherine, Sandra and Jean Marguerite. Educ: Athens Col, 38-39; Univ. Ala, Sch. Commerce, B.S, 42, Sch. Law, LL.B, 47; Omicron Delta Kappa; Kappa Alpha Order. Polit. & Govt. Pos: Judge, Recorder's Court, City of Decatur, Ala, 48-51; co. solicitor, Morgan Co, Ala, 51; assoc. mem, Bd. Pardons and Paroles, Montgomery, 51-52; circuit judge, Eighth Judicial Circuit, 59-68; chmn, Ala. Dem. Steering Cmt, 61-63; assoc. justice, Supreme Court of Ala, Montgomery, 68- Bus. & Prof. Pos: Attorney-at-law, Calvin and Bloodworth, Attorneys-at-law, Decatur, Ala, 47-58. Mil. Serv: Entered as Pvt, Army, 43, released as Capt, 46, after serv. in 12th Armored Div. and First Armored Div, Am. and European Theaters, 43-46; Res, 46-64, Lt. Col.(Ret); Three Combat Battle Stars; Combat Infantryman's Badge; Bronze Star. Publ: Index to Official Proceedings of the Constitutional Convention of 1901 of the State of Alabama, Univ. Ala, 48. Mem: Morgan Co, Montgomery Co, Ala. and Am. Bar Asns; Am. Legion; VFW; Rotary; Mason; K.T; Shrine. Rel: Presbyterian; Ruling Elder. Legal Res: 1834 Shoreham Dr, Montgomery, Ala. 36106. Mailing Add: Supreme Court, Judicial Bldg, P.O. Box 218, Montgomery, Ala. 36101.

BLOOM, ALLAN R
Ind. State Sen.
b. Ft. Wayne, Ind, 11/16/32; s. A. Everett Bloom and Velma Lenwell B; m. 6/5/54 to Norma Jean Meyer; c. Linda Sue and Laura Jean. Educ: Valparaiso Univ, B.A, 54, Law Sch, LL.B, 56; Delta Theta Phi; Dean of Rentner Senate, 55. Polit. & Govt. Pos: Ind. State Rep, 61-62; Ind. State Sen, 62-, Minority Leader, Ind. State Sen, 65-67, Pres-Pro-Tempore, 69-; chmn, Ind. Legis. Coun, currently. Bus. & Prof. Pos: Mem. bd. of dirs, Anthony Wayne Bank, Waterfield, Colby & Wahl Ins. Co. and Penny Pitch, Inc, currently. Mil. Serv: Entered as Pvt, Marine Corps Res, 52, commenced active duty as 2nd Lt, Marine Corps, 56; organized Marine Corps Res. Medal; Maj. and Commanding Officer, 9th Rifle Co, Marine Corps Res, Ft. Wayne, Ind, at present. Mem: Am, Ind. and Allen Co. Bar Asns; pres. and mem. bd. of dirs, Ind. Soc. Nat. Hist, Inc; bd. of dirs, Parkview Mem. Hosp; merit badge counselor, Boy Scouts. Rel: Methodist; Treas, Wayne Street Methodist Church Found. Legal Res: 2915 Charlotte Ave, Ft. Wayne, Ind. 46805. Mailing Add: 1514 Anthony Wayne Bank Bldg, Ft. Wayne, Ind. 46802.

BLOOM, GEORGE I. R
Chmn, Pa. Pub. Utility Cmt.
b. Burgettstown, Pa, 9/2/98; s. Charles Bloom and Tilly Caplan B; m. 12/8/59 to Luella Hawkins Boeschen. Educ: Univ. Pittsburgh, B.S, 20, LL.B, 22; Lambda Phi. Polit. & Govt. Pos: Mem, Pa. Rep. State Cmt, 39-, chmn, 56-63; secy. to Gov. Martin, Pa, 43-47; admin. asst. to U.S. Sen. Martin, Pa, 47-56; mem, Rep. Nat. Cmt, 56-63; chmn, Cmt. Supervising TV, Radio and News Reel Coverage, Rep. Nat. Conv, 60; mem, Pa. Athletic Cmn, Pa. Pardons Bd, Pa. Bd. of Finance & Revenue and Adv. Cmt. Elec. and Elec. Laws; chmn, Pa. Employees Retirement Bd, Pa. Munic. Employees Retirement Bd. and Gov. Pa. Tax Cmt; secy, Commonwealth of Pa, 63-65; chmn, Pa. Pub. Utility Cmt, currently. Bus. & Prof. Pos: Partner, Firm of Bloom, Bloom, Rosenberg & Bloom, Washington, Pa, 22- Mil. Serv: Navy, World War I. Mem: Am, Pa. and Washington Co. Bar Asns; Order of Coif; Mason; Carlisle Country Club, Pa; Nemocolin Country Club, Wash; West Shore Country Club, Camphill; Concordia Club, Pittsburgh; Variety Club. Cited by Pa. Legis. Corr. Asn. for Coop, 46; Named Pitt Letterman of Year, 63- Legal Res: 406 Leonard Ave, Washington, Pa. 15301. Mailing Add: North Office Bldg, Harrisburg, Pa. 17120.

BLOOM, JEREMIAH B. D
N.Y. State Sen.
b. N.Y.C, 5/25/13; s. Samuel Bloom and Celia Anderman B; m. 2/9/41 to Dorothy Sotland; c. Barton William. Educ: St. John's Univ. and St. John's Law Sch, N.Y. Polit. & Govt. Pos: Mem, City Coun, N.Y.C, 50-57; N.Y. State Dem. committeeman, 58-; N.Y. State Sen, 58- Bus. & Prof. Pos: Secy. and dir, No-Cal Corp, 51-; asst. secy. and dir, Kirsch Beverages, Inc, 51-; partner, Bloom & Crupe Law Firm. Mil. Serv: Entered as A/S, Navy, 43, released as CPO, 45, after serv. in Am. Theater. Mem: Brooklyn, New York State and Am. Bar Asns; Unity Club of Brooklyn; Am. Legion; Jewish War Vets; Mason. Rel: Jewish. Legal Res: 350 Sterling St, Brooklyn, N.Y. 11225. Mailing Add: 110 E. 42nd St, New York, N.Y. 10017.

BLOOM, ROBERT KENNETH R
b. Saegertown, Pa, 1/14/26; s. Maurice M. Bloom and Beatrice Roberts B; m. 8/12/53 to Jane Esther Twichell; c. Robert and William. Educ: Edinboro State Col, B.S. in Educ, 49. Polit. & Govt. Pos: Chmn, Crawford Co. Young Rep, Pa, 60-62; committeeman, Meadville First Ward, 62, 63; former chmn, Crawford Co. Rep. Cmt; secy. to Gov, Pa, 68- Mil. Serv: Entered as A/S, Navy, 43, released as Electrician's Mate 2/C, 46; Pac. Theatre Ribbon. Rel: Presbyterian. Mailing Add: 435 Wood Crest Dr, Mechanicsburg, Pa. 17055.

BLOOM, SAM O. D
b. Pennock, Minn, 6/18/15; married; c. 3. Educ: Pub. Schs. Polit. & Govt. Pos: N.Dak. State Rep, until 66; mem, sch. bd. and twp. bd; co. sch. officer. Bus. & Prof. Pos: Farmer; rancher. Rel: Lutheran. Mailing Add: Grenora, N.Dak. 58845.

BLOSSER, CLARENCE R
Exec. Chmn, Hocking Co. Rep. Party, Ohio.
b. Logan, Ohio, 5/16/01; s. William Calvin Blosser (deceased) and Anna Myers B; m. 7/10/35 to Mary Christine Keller; c. Clarence William and Charles Jacob. Polit. & Govt. Pos: Finance chmn, Hocking Co. Rep. Party, Ohio, 58-62; field rep. for U.S. Rep. Homer Abele, 62-64; finance chmn, Tenth Cong. Dist, Ohio, 62-; mem, Ohio State Rep. Finance Cmt, 62-; exec. chmn, Hocking Co. Rep. Party, 68- Bus. & Prof. Pos: Owner, Blossers Restaurant, Logan, Ohio, 30-66; dir, Farmers & Merchants Bank, 47-; treas, Clover Enterprise Corp, 66- Mem: Pres, Cent. Ohio Restaurant Asn, 43-44; pres, Ohio State Restaurant Asn, 44-45; Mason (32°); York Rite; Shrine; past pres, Rotary; past pres, C. of C. and Trade Club, Logan; charter mem, Isaac Walton League; Hocking Hills Country Club; Southeast. Ohio Regional Coun. Rel: Protestant. Mailing Add: 264 Midland Place, Logan, Ohio 43138.

BLOSTEIN, HAROLD LEON D
Mem, Nebr. Dem. State Exec. Cmt.
b. Chicago, Ill, 9/22/28; s. Joseph Harry Blostein and Charlotte Piel B; single. Educ: Univ. Ill, Chicago, 46-48; Chicago-Kent Col. Law, LL.B, 51, J.D, 69; Roosevelt Univ, B.A, 52; Univ. Va, M.A, 53; Univ. Kans, 63-64; Pi Gamma Mu; Theta Chi; Helen Lee Wessel fel, Woodrow Wilson Sch. For. Affairs, Univ. Va, 52. Polit. & Govt. Pos: Chmn, Buffalo Co. Dem. Cent. Cmt, Nebr, 66-; mem, Nebr. Dem. State Cent. Cmt, 68-; mem, Nebr. Dem. State Exec. Cmt, 68- Bus. & Prof. Pos: Instr. econ, La. State Univ, Baton Rouge, 55-56; polit. ed, Moore Newspapers, Skokie, Ill, 56; from instr. to asst. prof. polit. sci, Washburn Univ, 56-63; asst. prof, Northwest Mo. State Col, 64, Kearney State Col, 64-, head dept, 69- Mil. Serv: Entered as Pvt, Army, 53, released as Pfc, 55, after serv. in Fifth Army Area, Fr. Riley, Kans, 53-55; Good Conduct Medal. Publ: 'The Constitutionality of Compulsory Loyalty Oaths as a Prerequisite for the Acquisition of Public Benefits and Public Employment', Chicago-Kent Law Rev, 6/51; contrib, 'Utah', In: Presidential Nominating Politics in 1952: The West, Johns Hopkins Press, 54. Mem: Am. Soc. Int. Law; Am. Polit. Sci. Asn; Am. Acad. Polit. & Soc. Sci; Am. Asn. Univ. Prof; Nat. Educ. Asn; Am. Asn. Higher Educ; Ill. Bar Asn; B'Nai B'rith. Rel: Jewish. Mailing Add: 3907 Pony Express Rd, Kearney, Nebr. 68847.

BLOUIN, MICHAEL THOMAS D
Iowa State Rep.
b. Jacksonville, Fla, 11/7/45; s. Harold J. Blouin and Alice Berry B; m. 7/15/67 to Suzanne Diers. Educ: Loras Col, B.A, 66; Delta Sigma; Forensics Squad; v.pres, Inter-Club Coun. Polit. & Govt. Pos: Second Dist. committeeman, Iowa Young Dem, 65, nat. committeeman, 66-68; pres, Loras Col. Young Dem, 65-66; task force chmn. for Reorganizing Iowa Dem. Party, 69; Iowa State Rep, Sub Dist. Two, Dubuque Co, 69- Bus. & Prof. Pos: Mgr, Safety Equip. Co, Dubuque, Iowa, 66; field underwriter, N.Y. Life Ins, 67; teacher, Nativity Elem. Sch, 67-69. Mem: K. of C; Optimists Int; Jr. C. of C. Rel: Catholic. Legal Res: 955 N. Booth, Dubuque, Iowa 52001. Mailing Add: State Capitol Bldg, Tenth & Grand, Des Moines, Iowa 50139.

BLOUIN, ROBERT RICHARD R
Committeeman, Cook Co. Rep. Cent. Cmt, Ill.
b. Chicago, Ill, 7/16/26; s. Joseph Blouin and Florence Schuit B; m. 8/30/47 to Marie Louise Szymanski; c. James Robert and Sharon Marie. Educ: St. Willibrord High Sch, grad. Polit. & Govt. Pos: Campaign mgr, Ill. State Sen. Ron Swanson, 62-66 and Alderman Yausic, 67; treas, Ninth Ward Regular Rep. Orgn, Ill, 62-68; committeeman, Cook Co. Rep. Cent. Cmt, 68- Bus. & Prof. Pos: Pres, Bob Blouin Ins. Agency and Blouin Builders Inc, 47-63; pres, All-craft Inc. and Edge-Rite Inc, 63- Mil. Serv: Entered as A/S, Navy, 44, released as 3/C PO, 46, after serv. in Armed Guard, Europe. Mem: Nat. Asn. Plastic Fabricators; Am. Legion; VFW; Lions; Moose; C. of C; K. of C. Rel: Catholic. Mailing Add: 12510 S. Stewart Ave, Chicago, Ill. 60628.

BLOUNT, WINTON M. R
Postmaster Gen. of the U.S.
b. Union Springs, Ala, 2/1/21; s. Winton M. Blount and Clara Belle Chalker B; m. 9/2/42 to Mary Katherine Archibald; c. Winton M, III, Thomas A, S. Roberts, Katherine and Joseph W. Educ: Univ. Ala, 39-41; Sigma Nu. Hon. L.H.D, D.H, LL.D. and D.C.L. Polit. & Govt. Pos: State chmn, Ala. Citizens for Eisenhower-Nixon, 52; Southeast. dir, Vol. for Nixon and Lodge, 60; pres, Ala. C. of C, 64-66; pres, U.S. C. of C, 68-69; Postmaster Gen. of the U.S, 69- Bus. & Prof. Pos: Founder, Blount Bros. Corp, Montgomery, Ala, 46, pres. and chmn. bd, 46-68; chmn. bd, Benjamin F. Shaw Co, Wilmington, Del, 67-68; past dir, Gulf Am. Fire and Casualty Co, Montgomery, Ala, Cent. of Ga. Rwy. Co, Savannah, First Nat. Bank of Montgomery, Ala, Kershaw Mfg. Co, Montgomery, Ala. and Jackson-Atlantic, Inc, Atlanta, Ga. Mil. Serv: 1st Lt, Army Air Corps, 42-45. Mem: Trustee, Univ. Ala; Omicron Delta Kappa; chmn. exec. cmt, treas. and past dir, Young Pres. Asn, N.Y.C; past dir, South. States Indust. Coun, Nashville, Tenn, South. Research Inst, Birmingham, Ala, Nat. Asn. of Mfrs, Nat. Coun. on Crime and Delinquency and United Appeal of Montgomery; YMCA; Rotary. One of Four Outstanding Young Men in Ala, 56; Man of the Year, Montgomery, 61; Golden Knight of Mgt. Award, Ala. Coun. of Nat. Mgt. Asn, 62; Court of Honor Award, Montgomery, Ala. Exchange Club, 69. Rel: Presbyterian. Legal Res: Wynfield, Vaughn Rd, Montgomery, Ala. 36106. Mailing Add: Post Office Department, 1200 Pennsylvania Ave. N.W, Washington, D.C. 20260.

BLUE, BRANTLEY R
Cmnr, Indian Claims Cmn.
b. Pembroke, N.C, 10/11/25; s. D.L. Blue (deceased) and Ada Lowry B; m. 12/16/50 to Dorothy Milam; c. Janet and Patricia. Educ: Pembroke State Col, 43-44 & 46; Cumberland Univ, LL.B, 49; Blue Key; Phi Alpha Delta. Polit. & Govt. Pos: Judge, Kingsport, Tenn, 55-59; mem, judicial cmt, Sullivan Co. Rep. Party, Tenn, 64-68; cmnr, Indian Claims Cmn, Wash, D.C, 69- Mil. Serv: Entered as Seaman, Navy, 44, released as Seaman 1/C, 46, after serv. in a destroyer, Atlantic and Pac. Theatres. Mem: Kingsport Bar Asn.(pres, 56); Kingsport Exchange Club; Am. Legion; VFW; Moose; Gideons Int. Recipient of Distinguished Alumnus Award, Pembroke State Col, 69. Rel: Christian Church of N.Am. Mailing Add: c/o Indian Claims Commission, 726 Jackson Place N.W, Room 5001, Washington, D.C. 20506.

BLUE, FRED O, II R
Mem, W.Va. Rep. Exec. Cmt.
b. Charleston, W.Va, 6/6/26; s. William F. Blue (deceased) and Elizabeth Pratt B; m. 2/28/59 to Mary Eleanor Baker; c. William F, II, John Baker and Kellianne. Educ: Princeton Univ, A.B, 49; Univ. Va. Law Sch, LL.B, 52; Phi Alpha Delta. Polit. & Govt. Pos: Pres, Young Rep. League of W.Va, 57-59; chmn, Mercer Co. Rep. Exec. Cmt, 57-65; mem, Young Rep. Nat. Fedn. Exec. Cmt, 58-59; v.chmn, W.Va. Rep. Exec. Cmt, 58-62, mem, 65- Bus. & Prof. Pos: Attorney, 52-; bd. of govs, W.Va. State Bar, 62-65. Mil. Serv: Entered as Pvt, Army, 45, released as T/3, 47, after serv. in Europe. Mem: Rotary; Am. Legion; Nat. Acad. of Arbitrators of Am. Arbitration Asn. and Fed. Mediation & Conciliation Serv. Rel: Baptist. Mailing Add: 1323 Whitethorn St, Bluefield, W.Va. 24701. (1967)

BLUE, GEORGE D
Chmn, S.Dak. State Dem. Party
b. Huron, S.Dak, 2/12/27; m. to Belva Meyer; c. Thomas, Kathleen and James.

Educ: Huron Col; Univ. of S.Dak. Law Sch, LL.B. Polit. & Govt. Pos: Beadle Co. States Attorney, S.Dak; S.Dak. State Sen, until 66; chmn, S.Dak. State Dem. Party, 69- Bus. & Prof. Pos: Lawyer. Mem: Exec. bd, Legis. Research Coun, 63; Izaak Walton League; K. of C; Elks; Am. Legion. Rel: Catholic. Mailing Add: Box 1414, Huron, S.Dak. 57350.

BLUE, GEORGE RIEBEL D
La. State Rep.
b. Houston, Tex, 12/10/16; s. Kaa Frank Blue and Eulalie Leonard B; m. 3/15/44 to Elizabeth Lida Beard; c. Kaa Frank, II, Leslie R. and George R, Jr. Educ: Soule Col, New Orleans, 33; Tulane Univ, B.A, 37, LL.B, 39; Univ. Miss, 54. Polit. & Govt. Pos: Spec. agent, Fed. Bur. Invest, U.S. Dept. Justice, D.C, 40-45; U.S. Attorney, East. Dist. La, 52-56; finance chmn, Rep. Party La; chmn, Jefferson Parish Rep. Exec. Cmt, 57-61; mem. adv. cmt. on rules of criminal procedure, U.S. Supreme Court, 61-; La. State Rep, Jefferson Parish, 64-; mem. Nixon Task Force on Crime and Law Enforcement, 68- Bus. & Prof. Pos: Partner, Beard, Blue, Schmitt & Treen, 47-; nat. v. pres, Soc. of X-FBI Agents, 61. Mil. Serv: Entered as Pfc, Marine Corps Res. 35, released as 2nd Lt, 41. Mem: New Orleans Bar Asn.(mem. exec. cmt, 64-65); La. and Am. Bar Asns; Am. Judicature Soc; La. Cmn. on Law Enforcement and Admin. of Justice; Metairie Country Club (bd. governors, six years); South. Yacht Club; Plimsol Club; adv. bd, Salvation Army; bd. dir, La. Asn. for Mental Health. Rel: Episcopal. Legal Res: 301 Cuddihy Dr, Metairie, La. 70005. Mailing Add: 833 Howard Ave, New Orleans, La. 70113.

BLUE, JOHN EDWARD D
Mem, Madison Co. Dem. Exec. Cmt, Ala.
b. Anniston, Ala, 4/29/31; s. Joe Albert Blue and Katie Scoggins B; m. 12/17/67 to Judith Fann; c. John Edward, II, Rebecca Carole and Elaine Sanderson. Educ: Auburn Univ, B.S, 53; Delta Sigma Pi; Arnold Air Soc; Scabbard & Blade; Kappa Alpha. Polit. & Govt. Pos: Chmn, Anniston Civil Serv. Bd, Ala, 63; mem, Madison Co. Dem. Exec. Cmt, 66-; del, Dem. Nat. Conv, 68. Bus. & Prof. Pos: Sales rep, Sherwin-Williams Paint Co, Anniston, 58-60; sales rep, Interstate Chem. Co, 60; owner and mgr, Blue's Clothing Co, 60-63; prog. mkt. mgr, Brown Engr. Co, Huntsville, 63-68; sales mgr, Formador Inc, 69- Mil. Serv: Entered as 2nd Lt, Air Force, 54, released as 1st Lt, 56, after serv. in 712 Aircraft Control & Warning Squadron, Alaskan Air Command, 54-55, Capt. Res, 56-; Nat. Defense Serv. Medal. Mem: Nat. Contract Mgt. Asn; Mason; VFW Post 2702; state v.pres, Ala. Jr. C. of C, 60- Outstanding Young Man of the Year Nominee, Anniston, Ala, 59. Rel: Baptist. Mailing Add: 7903 Westhaven Dr, Huntsville, Ala. 35802.

BLUE, JULIAN HUBERT, JR. R
Chmn, Martin Co. Rep. Exec. Cmt, N.C.
b. Lumberton, N.C, 10/23/31; s. Julian Hubert Blue and Katherine Floyd B; m. 8/13/65 to Alice Lilley. Educ: N.C. State Univ, 49-51; Univ. Ga, 57-58. Polit. & Govt. Pos: Chmn, Hoke Co. Rep. Exec. Cmt, N.C, 64-65; co-chmn. orgn. cmt, N.C. Fedn. of Young Rep. Clubs, 66-67; v.chmn, Wake Co. Young Rep. Club, 66-67; chmn, Martin Co. Rep. Exec. Cmt, 68- Bus. & Prof. Pos: Homebuilder, Raeford, N.C, 61-65; materials engr, RAE, Brown & Root, Aurora, 65; plant engr, Payne & Assocs, Raleigh, 65-66; prod. planner, Beaunit Textiles, Hamilton, 66-67; engr-draftsman, Weyerhauser Corp, Plymouth, 67- Mil. Serv: Entered as Pvt, Army, 53, released as Cpl, 55. Mem: Kiwanis; PSPMW. Rel: Episcopal; mem. vestry, Church of the Advent, Williamston. Mailing Add: 401 E. Simmons Ave, Williamston, N.C. 27892.

BLUE, VIRGINIA NEAL R
Colo. State Treas.
b. Meeker, Colo; m. to James Blue. Educ: Colo. Univ, grad. Polit. & Govt. Pos: Colo. State Treas, 67-; regent, Colo. Univ; chmn, Colo. Cmn. on Status of Women; White House Conf. on Children and Youth. Bus. & Prof. Pos: Realtor. Named Denver Realtor of the Year, 62. Mailing Add: State Capitol, 200 E. Colfax Ave, Denver, Colo. 80203.

BLUE, WILLIAM ROY D
Mem, Exec. Cmt, Genesee Co. Dem. Party, Mich.
b. Flint, Mich, 2/8/33; s. Albert O. Blue and Marion Wotzka B; m. 11/6/54 to Marilyn Marie Anderson; c. James Albert, Diane Marie, Robert William, Daniel Scott and Thomas Patrick. Educ: Flint Commun. Jr. Col, Mich, Assoc. Bus, 56; Flint Col, Univ. Mich, B.A. in Bus, 58. Polit. & Govt. Pos: Mem, Flint Bd. Educ, Mich, 65-68; Dem. nominee, U.S. House Rep, Seventh Dist, 68; chmn, Mich. Seventh Dist. Citizens for Kennedy, 68; mem, Mich. Dem. Polit. Reform Cmn, 69-; mem. exec. cmt, Genesee Co. Dem. Party, 69-; mem, Mich. Dem. Cmt. Opposed to Antiballistic Missiles, 69- Bus. & Prof. Pos: Sales rep, Standard Register Co, 58-62; Int. Bus. Machines Corp, 62-64 and Perry Printing Co, 64- Mil. Serv: Entered as Pvt, Army, 54, released as SP-3, 55. Mem: Flint Jr. C. of C.(pres, 63-64); Elks; Dollars for Scholars (v.pres); Jr. Achievement of Flint (bd. dirs). Flint's Outstanding Young Man, Flint Jr. C. of C, 66. Rel: Roman Catholic. Mailing Add: 6908 Orange Lane, Flint, Mich. 48505.

BLUECHEL, ALAN J. R
Wash. State Rep.
b. Edmonton, Alberta, Can, 8/28/24; s. Joseph Harold Bluechel and Edith Daly B; m. 11/2/57 to Aylene Loughnan; c. Gordon Blaire and Turner Farllon. Educ: Univ. B.C, B.A.Sc. and B.A, 48; Beta Theta Pi. Polit. & Govt. Pos: Wash. State Rep, 67-; mem, 1st Dist. Rep. Club, Wash. State Expo 70 Worlds Fair Cmn. and King Co. Flood Control Adv. Bd, currently. Bus. & Prof. Pos: V.pres, Loctwall Corp, 48-65, pres, 65; pres, C.I.C, 64; mem, Wash. State Oriental Trade Mission & Trade Fair, 65 & 66; pres, CM Inn Co, 66. Rel: Presbyterian. Mailing Add: 12534 68th Ave. N.E, Kirkland, Wash. 98033.

BLUMBERG, THELMA NAGLER D
b. N.Y.C, 2/26/19; d. Julius Nagler and Frieda Salz N; m. 2/2/41 to Armond Blumberg; c. Robert and S. Mark. Educ: Brooklyn Col, B.A, 39; Pi Mu Epsilon; Propylea. Polit. & Govt. Pos: Alternate del, Dem. Nat. Conv, 68. Bus. & Prof. Pos: Jr. acct, N.Y.C. Housing Authority, 53-54; asst. acct, Queens Col, 54-56; math. teacher, high schs, N.Y.C. Bd. Educ, 56- Mem: Nat. Coun. Teachers Math; United Fedn. Teachers; Am. Fedn. Teachers; Nat. Cmt. for Sane Nuclear Policy; B'nai B'rith. Mailing Add: 220-55 46th Ave, Queens, N.Y. 11361.

BLUME, JOYCE CAMPBELL D
Chairwoman, Women's Div. Dem. State Cent. Cmt, Ill.
b. Keokuk, Iowa, 12/11/32; d. Peyton Campbell and Nelle Davis C; m. 12/3/50 to Robert Edward Blume; c. Robert Peyton, William Jeffrey, Helene Campbell and Hollis Christine. Polit. & Govt. Pos: Chairwoman, Cass Co. Dem. Cent. Cmt, Ill, 62-66; pres, Dem. Women's Orgn, 64-66; alternate del, Dem. Nat. Conv, 64 & 68; chairwoman, Cent. Dist. Women's Div, Dem. State Cent. Cmt, 65-; secy, Cmn. Employ. of Handicapped, Ill, 65- Bus. & Prof. Pos: Chief probation officer, Cass Co, Ill, 64- Mem: Past v.pres, Young Dems; DAR; Women's Club; bd. dirs, Pub. Libr. Asn; Ill. Probation and Parole Asn. Rel: Methodist. Mailing Add: 17 Woody Ave, Beardstown, Ill. 62618.

BLUME, NORBERT D
Ky. State Rep.
b. 1922. Educ: Univ. of Louisville; Univ. of Ky. Polit. & Govt. Pos: Mem, 12th Ward Dem. Club, Ky; Ky. State Rep, 64- Bus. & Prof. Pos: Labor Rep. Mil. Serv: Navy, World War II. Mem: St. Columba Men's Club; VFW; Shawnee Golf Club. Rel: Catholic. Mailing Add: 4224 Northwestern Pkwy, Louisville, Ky. 40212. (1967)

BLUMENTHAL, ALBERT HOWARD D
N.Y. State Assemblyman
b. N.Y.C, 10/13/28; s. Bennet M. Blumenthal and Matilda B; m. 5/18/58 to Joel Marie Winik; c. Daniel J, Ann Marie, Peter A. and David M. Educ: Col. of William & Mary, B.A, 49; N.Y. Univ. Law Sch, LL.B, 51, Grad. Sch, LL.M, 56. Polit. & Govt. Pos: N.Y. State Assemblyman, 63- Bus. & Prof. Pos: Partner, Blumenthal, Barandes, Moss, Matson & Arnold, 69- Mil. Serv: Entered as Pvt, Army, 51, released as Cpl, 53. Mem: Am. and N.Y. State Bar Asns; adv. cmt, Manhattan Borough Commun. Col; bd. dirs, Metrop. Center for Ment. Health and League for Indust. Dem. Legal Res: 90 Riverside Dr, New York, N.Y. 10024. Mailing Add: 18 E. 48th St, New York, N.Y. 10017.

BLUMER, ARLO R. R
Chmn, Freeborn Co. Rep. Party, Minn.
b. Beresford, S.Dak, 6/6/29; s. Fred Blumer and Mae Mundall B; m. 3/3/56 to Mary Ann Redmond; c. Jody Lynn, Karen Sue, John Redmond, Barbara Mae and Elizabeth Anne. Educ: Westmar Col, 47-50; Univ. S.Dak, B.S. in med, 52; Temple Univ, M.D, 54; Alpha Kappa Kappa. Polit. & Govt. Pos: Dir, Minn. Young Rep, 61-62; mem, Freeborn Co. Rep. Coun, 62-69; chmn, Freeborn Co. Rep. Party, 66- Bus. & Prof. Pos: Physician, Butka Med. Clin, Alhambra, Calif, 55-56, Med. Arts Clin, Albert Lea, Minn. and Med. & Surg. Center Ltd, 62-; chief staff, Naeve Hosp. Med. Staff, 66-67. Mil. Serv: Entered as Capt, Army, 56, released as Capt, 58, after serv. in ASA, Asmara, Eritrea, East Africa Theatre, 56-58. Mem: Freeborn Co. Med. Asn.(chmn, 66); Am. Med. Asn; Am. Acad. Gen. Practice; Kiwanis; Mason. Rel: Presbyterian. Mailing Add: 638 E. Park Ave, Albert Lea, Minn. 56007.

BLY, BELDEN G, JR. R
Mass. State Rep.
Educ: Harvard Univ; Dartmouth Col; Boston Univ; Northeastern Univ, B.A, LL.B. and M.Ed. Polit. & Govt. Pos: Mass. State Rep, currently; bi-partisan selection as legis. del. to attend the White House Conf. on Educ; alternate del, Rep. Nat. Conv, 68. Bus. & Prof. Pos: Teacher, 22 years; attorney-at-law. Mem: Past pres, Essex Co. Teachers' Asn. A winner of Nat. Sci. Found. Award in Bact. at Univ. of Colo. Mailing Add: 46 Auburn St, Saugus, Mass. 01906.

BLYSTONE, ROSE A. L. D
Treas, Crawford Co. Fedn. of Dem. Women, Pa.
b. Youngstown, Ohio, 1/18/91; d. Charles John Lundmark and Hannah Anderson L; m. 12/26/17 to George Everett Blystone; c. Charles L. and Peter E. Educ: Jamestown High Sch. Polit. & Govt. Pos: Precinct committeewoman, Pa, 34-; jury cmnr, Crawford Co, 53-; del, Dem. Nat. Conv, 64; treas, Crawford Co. Fedn. of Dem. Women, Pa, 64- Mem: Grange; Grass Roots Dem. Club; past pres, Dem. Women's Fedn; past pres, Am. Legion. Rel: Presbyterian. Mailing Add: 432 Venango Ave, Cambridge Springs, Pa. 16403. (1967)

BLYTHE, COY DANIEL, SR. R
Rep. Committeeman, Ill. Rep. Cent. Cmt.
b. Shelbyville, Ill, 1/8/18; s. Harold M. Blythe and Ada Reeder B; m. 6/22/41 to Evelyn Marie Arthur; c. Coy Daniel, Jr. Educ: Univ. of Ill, 1 year. Polit. & Govt. Pos: Rep. precinct committeeman, Precinct One, Shelbyville, Ill, currently; secy, Shelby Co. Rep. Cent. Cmt, Ill, 6 years; Rep. Committeeman, Ill. Rep. Cent. Cmt, currently. Bus. & Prof. Pos: City policeman, Shelbyville, Ill, 3 years; salesman, Kaskaskia Co, 18 years; security officer, Oliver Corp, currently. Mil. Serv: Entered as Pvt, Air Force, 42, released as Sgt, 46, after serv. in U.S. Mem: Am. Legion; Moose; Several Awards and Honors, Moose. Rel: Protestant. Legal Res: 117 E. N. Seventh St, Shelbyville, Ill. 62565. Mailing Add: P.O. Box 206, Shelbyville, Ill. 62565.

BLYTHE, E. BRUCE, JR. R
Ky. State Rep.
b. 1927. Educ: Univ. Ky. Polit. & Govt. Pos: Ky. State Rep, currently. Bus. & Prof. Pos: Advert. and pub. rels; pres, Blythe Advert; pres, Swing Image Corp. Mil. Serv: Maj, Ky. Air Nat. Guard. Mem: Past dir, Louisville Jaycees; Univ. Ky. Alumni Asn. Rel: Presbyterian. Mailing Add: 210 Hillcrest, Louisville, Ky. 40206. (1967)

BOAL, LaVERNE C. R
b. Vivian, S.Dak, 10/31/19; m. to Ellen; c. Three. Educ: Univ. of Wyo, grad. and grad. work. Polit. & Govt. Pos: Mem, Upton Sch. Bd, Wyo; former Wyo. State Rep. Bus. & Prof. Pos: Owner, Dept. Store. Mem: Upton Commercial Club; VFW; Mason; Shrine; Am. Legion. Rel: Protestant. Mailing Add: Upton, Wyo. 82730. (1967)

BOARD, PAT, JR. D
b. Clay, W.Va, 3/7/08; s. Pat Board Sr. and Cora Carr B; m. 6/18/32 to Mary Amelia Kincheloe, wid; c. Elsie K.(Mrs. Harrison M. Markley, Jr.) and Pat III. Educ: Univ. of Cincinnati. Polit. & Govt. Pos: W.Va. State Rep, 44, 48, 52 & 54; mem, Kanawha Co. Planning and Zoning Cmn; W.Va. State Del,

58-66. Bus. & Prof. Pos: Bldg. construction; ins. bus. Mem: Charleston Contractors Asn; state chmn, March of Dimes, 5 years; Sigma Chi. Rel: Methodist. Mailing Add: Box 1721, Charleston, W.Va. 25326. (1967)

BOARDMAN, ROBERT EMMETT D
Vt. State Sen.
b. Burlington, Vt, 5/20/32; s. Ivr Munn Boardman and Dorothy McMahon B; m. 8/20/55 to Nancy Katherine Chandler; c. Carla Marie, Robert Emmett, Jr, Kevin Michael and Joanne McMahon. Educ: Col. Holy Cross, B.S, 54. Polit. & Govt. Pos: Mem, Dem. State Exec. Cmt, Vt, 66-; Vt. State Sen, Chittender-Grande Isle Dist, 69- Bus. & Prof. Pos: Treas, Hickok & Boardman, Inc, 60-; trustee, Burlington Savings Bank, 68- Mil. Serv: Entered as Pvt, Army, 54, released as Sp-3/C, 56, after serv. in Counter Intel. Corp. Mem: Pres, United Fund, 69; C. of C.(pres, 65-66). Vt. and New Eng. Jaycee Distinguished Serv. Awards, 67; Freshman Sen. Award, Vt. Legis, 69. Rel: Roman Catholic. Legal Res: 85 Glen Rd, Burlington, Vt. 05401. Mailing Add: 160 College St, Burlington, Vt. 05401.

BOAS, ROGER D
Chmn, Calif. Dem. State Cent. Cmt.
b. San Francisco, Calif, 8/21/21; s. Benjamin Boas and Larie Klein B; m. to Nancy; c. Three sons. Educ: Stanford Univ, grad, 42. Polit. & Govt. Pos: Past mem, Calif. Welfare Study Cmn. and Gov. Traffic Safety Conf; mem, Health and Welfare Cmt, Govt. Serv. Cmt. and Gov. Bus. Adv. Coun; chmn, Cmt. on Planning and Develop, South of Market Adv. Cmt. and Mayor Shelley's South of Market Develop. Cmt; state chmn, UN Day Activities; supvr, City and Co. of San Francisco, 61-; del, Dem. Nat. Conv, 68; chmn, Calif. Dem. State Cent. Cmt, 68- Bus. & Prof. Pos: Producer and moderator, TV progs, San Francisco, Calif; automobile dealer, 45- Mil. Serv: Officer, Army; serv. in 3rd Army, ETO; Silver Star; Bronze Star; Campaign Ribbon and 5 Battle Stars. Mem: Dir, Outer City YMCA, San Francisco Homemakers' Serv, North Calif. Region, Nat. Conf. Christians and Jews and World Affairs Coun. of North. Calif. Mailing Add: Apt. 304, 1182 Market St, San Francisco, Calif. 94102.

BOATWRIGHT, MARY HOWARD R
b. Houston, Tex, 4/8/20; d. Arch Franklin Howard and Mary Dorothy Bennett H; m. 8/29/46 to Victor Taliaferro Boatwright, Jr; c. Mary Dorsey, John Lord, William Howard and Mary Taliaferro. Educ: Trinity Col, B.A. Polit. & Govt. Pos: Conn. State Rep, 62-67; burgess, Bd. of Warden & Burgesses, Stonington, 60-66. Rel: Roman Catholic. Mailing Add: 16 Denison Ave, Stonington, Conn. 06378. (1967)

BOBBITT, JOHN MAXWELL R
b. Huntington, W.Va, 1/20/27; s. Ray Maxwell Bobbitt and Beatrice Wrenn B; m. 6/24/50 to Jeanne Ann Hunt; c. Mary Elizabeth, Martha Hunt and Sarah Maxwell. Educ: Dartmouth Col, 48; Univ. Mich. Med. Sch, M.D, 52; Phi Beta Kappa; Nu Sigma Nu; Phi Chi. Polit. & Govt. Pos: Chmn, Physicians for Underwood for Gov, 64; mem, Rep. State Platform Cmt, 64; W.Va. State Del, 67-69. Bus. & Prof. Pos: Partner, Bobbitt-Harwood Urological Clin, 57- Mil. Serv: Entered as HA 1/C, Navy 45, released as Pharmacist Mate 3/C, 46. Publ: 'Let's Help Our Senior Citizens,' W.Va. State Med. J, 10/62 and articles of tech. interest. Mem: Cabell Co. Med. Soc; W.Va. and Am. Med. Asns; Mid-Atlantic Sect, Am. Urological Asn; Dipl, Am. Bd. of Urology; City Club of Huntington; bd. dirs, United Commun. Serv, 63-65. Rel: Episcopal. Legal Res: 2106 Holswade Dr, Huntington, W.Va. 25701. Mailing Add: 1139 Fourth Ave, Huntington, W.Va. 25701.

BOBBITT, WILLIAM HAYWOOD
Assoc. Justice, N.C. Supreme Court
b. Raleigh, N.C, 10/18/00; s. James Henry Bobbitt and Eliza May Burkhead B; m. 2/28/24 to Sarah Buford Dunlap (deceased); c. Sarah (Mrs. John W. Carter), William Haywood, Buford (Mrs. Ekkehart Sachtler) and Harriet (Mrs. Dan S. Moss). Educ: Univ. N.C, B.A, 21, LL.D, 27; LL.D, Davidson Col, 53. Polit. & Govt. Pos: Trustee Brerard Col, 33-52; Judge, 14th Judicial Superior Court, N.C, 39-54; mem, N.C. Judiciary Coun, 49-54 and Cmn. to Study Improv. Admin. Justice in N.C, 47-49; Assoc. Justice, N.C. Supreme Court, 54- Bus. & Prof. Pos: Lawyer, Charlotte, N.C, 22-38. Mem: Am. and N.C. Bar Asns; Am. Judicature Soc; Univ. N.C. Alumni Asn.(pres, 54-55); Civitan Club (past pres). Rel: Methodist. Legal Res: P.O. Box 1841, Raleigh, N.C. 27602. Mailing Add: Justice Bldg, Raleigh, N.C. 27602. (1967)

BOBROFF, HAROLD D
N.Y. State Dem. Committeeman
b. New York City, N.Y, 4/29/20; s. Max Bobroff and Mary Platofsky B; m. 11/24/45 to Marion Hememdinger; c. Caren Kay and Fredric Jon. Educ: City Col. N.Y.C, B.B.A, 47; N.Y. Law Sch, LL.B, 51. Polit. & Govt. Pos: Committeeman, Nassau Co. Dem. Party, N.Y, 52-; zone leader, Woodmere, 55-58; N.Y. State Dem. committeeman and chmn, 15th Assembly Dist, Nassau Co, 58-; chief dep. attorney, Nassau Co, N.Y, 62-63; chief counsel, Joint Legis. Cmt. Ins. Rates and Regulation, 65- and counsel, Joint Legis. Cmt. on Villages, 68- Bus. & Prof. Pos: Partner, Bobroff & Olonoff, CPA, 49-; partner, Bobroff, Olonoff & Scharf, Attorneys at Law, 53-; Gen. counsel and dir, South Nassau Develop. Corp, 66- Mil. Serv: Entered as Pvt, Army, 42, released as Capt, 46, after serv. in Field Artil, Second Armored Div, ETO, 42-45; ETO, N.African and Sicilian Ribbons; Bronze Star with Cluster; Distinguished Unit Citation with Cluster; Belgian Fouraggere. Mem: Nassau Co. and N.Y. Co. Bar Asns; Masons; B'nai B'rith; trustee, Nassau Community Col, 68- Rel: Jewish; V.pres. and trustee, Temple Sinai of Laurence. Mailing Add: 795 Hampton Rd, Woodmere, N.Y. 11598.

BOCCHINO, JOHN R
R.I. State Rep.
b. Providence, R.I, 7/1/15; m. to Josephine Pascal. Educ: Barrington High Sch. Polit. & Govt. Pos: R.I. State Rep, 58-, Dep. Minority Leader, R.I. House Rep, currently; alternate del, Rep. Nat. Conv, 68. Bus. & Prof. Pos: Pres. and treas, Supreme Ice Cream Co. Mem: Past pres, New England Ice Cream Mfrs. Asn; v.pres, Warren C. of C; officer, K. of C; Coun. 1112; chmn, exec. cmt, PTA; Narragansett Coun. of Boy Scouts. Rel: Catholic. Mailing Add: 570 S. Water St, Warren, R.I. 02885.

BOCK, GREGOR J. R
Wis. State Assemblyman
b. Muscoda, Wis, 11/2/07. Educ: Univ. of Wis. Polit. & Govt. Pos: Dep. sheriff, Wis, 32-; village pres, 38-43; postmaster, Highland, 41-51; sch. bd. pres, 50-59; mem, Co. Bd. Supvr, 61-; Wis. State Assemblyman, currently. Bus. & Prof. Pos: Formerly employed by tel. co. and as farm hand; Sand and Gravel Producer, currently. Mem: Charter mem, Highland Lions Club; K. of C. Church trustee. Mailing Add: 575 Diaednal St, Highland, Wis. 53543.

BOCKELMAN, JAMES F. D
b. Chicago, Ill, 6/7/34; m. to Jessie Mae Mock; c. Zoe R. and Jimmie E. Educ: Tex. West. Col. Polit. & Govt. Pos: Fla. State Rep, 64-66. Bus. & Prof. Pos: Electronics engr. Mil. Serv: Army, 1st Guided Missile Brigade, Cpl; Guided Missile Specialist. Mem: Rotary; Mason. Rel: Methodist. Mailing Add: P.O. Box 214, Carrabelle, Fla. 32322. (1967)

BOCKHORST, ESTELLE WILFERTH R
V.Chmn, Rep. Cent. Cmt, Mo.
b. Jefferson City, Mo, 10/22/96; d. Nichalos Wilferth and Mary Knernschield W; m. to Diedrich Soloman Bockhorst, wid. Polit. & Govt. Pos: Cert. copy clerk, State Bd. of Health Dept, Mo, 20; elector, Rep. Nat. Conv, 60, alternate del, 64 and del, 68; v.chmn, Rep. Cent. Cmt, Eighth Cong. Dist, Mo, currently; mem, Mo. State Rep. Cmt, currently, mem, Budget Cmt, 67-; mem, Eighth Cong. Dist. Rep. Cmt, currently; del, Nat. Fedn. of Rep. Women, Wash, D.C, 67; co-chmn, Eighth Cong. Dist. Nixon-Agnew Campaign Cmt, Mo, 68. Mem: Rep. Fedn. Women's Club; church and farm orgn. Nominated Commun. Leader of Am, 68; Dipl. for One of Two Thousand Women of Distinguished Achievement, London, 69. Rel: Evangelical and Reformed Church. Mailing Add: Star Route 2, Jefferson City, Mo. 65101.

BOCKO, STANLEY J. D
Mass. State Rep.
b. Lowell, Mass, 8/26/20; s. Adolf Bocko and Alice Jaroma B; m. 5/25/47 to Dorothy Alice DuQuesnay; c. Heather Mary (Mrs. Fereira), Stanley Michael, John Raymond and twins, Marcelle and Rosalie. Polit. & Govt. Pos: Selectman, Billerica, Mass, 56-59; chmn, Area Dem, 62; Mass. State Rep, 27th Middlesex Dist, chmn. agr. cmt. and v.chmn. counties cmt, Mass. House of Rep, 59- Bus. & Prof. Pos: Ed. and publisher, The Billerica Pub. Co. Inc, 47- Mil. Serv: Entered as A/S, Navy, 42, 47, released as Chief PO, 47, after serv. in U.S. and Pac; Am. and Pac. Theater Ribbons. Mem: Nat. Ed. Asn; Mass. Press Asn; New Eng. Press Asn; K. of C; Elks; Am. Legion; VFW. Rel: Catholic. Mailing Add: 32 Mt. Pleasant St, North Billerica, Mass. 01862.

BODE, CARL JAMES D
Mayor, Geary, Okla.
b. Topeka, Kans, 10/5/23; s. William Bartholomew Bode and Marie Therese Schumacher B; m. 4/7/51 to Frances E. Murphy; c. John William, Carl James, Jr, Jeffrey Edward and Jane Therese. Educ: Kansas City Col. of Commerce. Polit. & Govt. Pos: Chmn, Blaine Co. Dem. Party, Okla, 59-; Mayor, Geary, 67- Mil. Serv: Pvt, Air Force, 43. Mem: Geary Merchants Asn.(past pres); C. of C.(past. pres, Geary Chap); Kiwanis(charter pres, Geary Club); VFW; Am. Legion; K. of C. Rel: Roman Catholic. Mailing Add: Box 187, Geary, Okla. 73040.

BODGER, RICHARD ALAN R
b. Minneapolis, Minn, 9/23/25; s. Henry Clifford Bodger and Emma Tourangeau B; m. 10/26/46 to Mary Patricia Barney; c. Suzanne Marie and Jacqueline Ann. Educ: Univ. of Minn, B.S.L. and J.D. Polit. & Govt. Pos: City attorney, Benson, Minn, 57-69; committeeman, Swift Co. Rep. Party, 58-60, chmn, 66-68; govt. appeal agent, U.S. Selective Serv, 67-; probate and juvenile judge, Swift Co, 69- Bus. & Prof. Pos: Attorney-at-law, 52-; attorney, Benson Housing & Redevelop. Authority, 66- Mil. Serv: Entered as A/S, Navy, 43, released as Seaman 1/C, 46, after serv. in Pac. Mem: Minn. State and Twelfth Judicial Dist. Bar Asns; N.Am. Munic. Judges Asn; Am. Judicature Soc; Nat. Coun. on Crime & Delinquency; Nat. Coun. of Juvenile Court Judges; K. of C.(4°); Am. Legion; C. of C. Rel: Catholic. Legal Res: 301 Sanford Rd, Benson, Minn. 56215. Mailing Add: Breen's Ramp, Benson, Minn. 56215.

BODINE, RICHARD CLAY D
Educ: Ind. Univ. Sch. of Bus; Ind. Univ. Law Sch. Polit. & Govt. Pos: Ind. State Rep, 63-68. Bus. & Prof. Pos: Attorney-at-law. Mil. Serv: Air Force, Korea. Mem: Co, State and Am. Bar Asns; Am. Legion; Phi Delta Phi; St. Joseph Co. and Mishawaka Young Dem. Rel: Protestant. Mailing Add: 208 1st National Bank Bldg, Mishawaka, Ind. 46544. (1967)

BODRON, ELLIS BARKETT D
Miss. State Sen.
b. Vicksburg, Miss, 10/25/23; s. Ellis Barkett Bodron and Helen Ellis B; m. 7/30/60 to Jane Workman; c. Helen Estelle and Lawrence Ellis. Educ: Univ. Miss, LL.B. and B.A, 46; Phi Delta Phi; Omicron Delta Kappa; Phi Eta Sigma; Phi Kappa Alpha. Polit. & Govt. Pos: Miss. State Rep, 48-52; Miss. State Sen, 52-, chmn, Finance Cmt, Miss. State Senate. Bus. & Prof. Pos: Partner, Law Firm of Ramsey, Bodron & Thames, 57- Mem: Warren Co, Miss. State, and Am. Bar Asns; Nat. Conf. of State Legis. Leaders; Legis. Adv. Cmt; South. Regional Educ. Bd; Lions; C. of C; former mem, Jr. C. of C. Legal Res: 2209 Cherry St, Vicksburg, Miss. 39180. Mailing Add: Room 708, First National Bank Bldg, Vicksburg, Miss. 39180.

BODY, RALPH C. D
b. Yellow House, Pa, 2/18/03; s. Howard W. Body and Mary Alice Esterly B; m. 7/26/30 to Ruth C. Sproesser; c. R. William, Howard E. and Ruth Eleanor (Mrs. Fetterman). Educ: Pa. State Univ, A.B, 25; Univ. Pa, LL.B, 28; Scabbard & Blade; Hare Law Club; Phi Delta Phi; Phi Kappa Psi. Polit. & Govt. Pos: Solicitor for recorder of deeds, Berks Co, Pa, 34-36, asst. co. solicitor, 36-38; local attorney, sales and foreclosure, Home Owners Loan Corp, 34-41; solicitor schs, rd. and boroughs, 46-59; chmn, Berks Co. Dem. Party, 50-52; del, Dem. Nat. Conv, 52; judge, Common Pleas Court, Berks Co, 60-62; judge, U.S. Dist. Court, East. Dist, Pa, 62- Bus. & Prof. Pos: Assoc. Stevens & Lee, 28-36; partner, Body, Muth & Rhoda, 36-60. Mil.

Serv: Entered as 1st Lt, Army, 41, released as Lt. Col, 46, after serv. in Asiatic-Pac. Theater; Pre-Pearl Harbor Ribbon; Am. Theater Ribbon; Asiatic-Pac. Theater Ribbon with Star; Meritorious Serv. Citation. Publ: 'Trial Lawyer Looks at Comparative Negligence.' Mem: Fel, Am. Col. Trial Lawyers and Am. Col. Probate Counsel; Int. Asn. Ins. Counsel; Fed, Am, Pa. and Berks Co. Bar Asns; Berks Co. Bd. Law Exam, 46-60; Rotary; Mason; Consistory; Shrine; VFW; Am. Legion; local fire companies and lodges; v.pres, Pottstown Mem. Hosp; exec. bd, Boy Scouts. Rel: United Church of Christ. Legal Res: 56 N. Reading Ave, Boyertown, Pa. 19512. Mailing Add: 3012 U.S. Court House, Philadelphia, Pa. 19107.

BOE, CARL E. D
b. 2/28/02; m. 1/1/34 to Genevieve Determan; c. Mrs. Barbara Anne Osborn, John D. Educ: Augustana Col, B.A, 26; grad. work, Univ. of Wis. Polit. & Govt. Pos: S.Dak. State Sen, 64-66; Dir. of Finance and Dir. of the Budget, 59-60; Govt. Acct; Acting Postmaster; Relief Adminstr; State Auditor. Bus. & Prof. Pos: Abstractor; owner of Custer Title Co; Instr, Ottawa Jr. Col. Rel: Lutheran. Mailing Add: Custer, S.Dak. 57730. (1967)

BOE, JASON DOUGLAS D
Ore. State Rep.
b. Los Angeles, Calif, 3/10/29; s. Christian J. Boe and Lillian Eggers B; m. 6/1/52 to Kathryn Reule; c. Eric, Peter and Brian. Educ: Pac. Lutheran Univ, B.A, 51; Univ. Wash, 51-52; Pac. Univ, O.D, 55. Polit. & Govt. Pos: City councilman, Reedsport, Ore, 58-64; Ore. State Rep, Douglas Co, 64-, Minority Whip, Ore. House of Rep, 67, Minority Leader, 69; alternate del, Dem. Nat. Conv, 68. Bus. & Prof. Pos: Optometrist, Reedsport, 56-; partner and pres. bd. dirs, Delta Pac. Inc, construction firm, 67- Publ: Various articles on taxation and educ. in The Portland Oregonian and The Ore. J. Mem: Ore. and Am. Optom. Asns; Rotary; C. of C; Jr. C. of C. Rel: Lutheran. Mailing Add: 2078 Hawthorne Ave, Reedsport, Ore. 97467.

BOE, NILS A. R
Dir, Off. of Intergovernmental Affairs
b. Baltic, S.Dak, 9/10/13; s. Rev. N. Boe and Sissel C. Finseth B; single. Educ: Univ. Wis, B.A, 35, LL.B, 37; Phi Alpha Delta. Polit. & Govt. Pos: S.Dak. State Rep, 51-59, Speaker of the House, 55-57; Lt. Gov, S.Dak, 63-65, Gov, 65-69; dir, Office of Intergovernmental Affairs, D.C, 69- Bus. & Prof. Pos: Attorney, May, Boe and Johnson, 46-65. Mil. Serv: Entered as Ens, Navy, 42, released as Lt.(sg), 45. Mem: Minnehaha Co. Farm Bur; Elks; Am. Legion; VFW; Odd Fellows; S.Dak. and Am. Bar Asns. Rel: Lutheran. Legal Res: 504 S. Duluth, Sioux Falls, S.Dak. 57104. Mailing Add: Director, Office of Intergovernmental Affairs, Executive Offices of the President, White House Office, Wash, D.C. 20500.

BOECKMAN, DUNCAN EUGENE R
Gen. Counsel, Rep. State Exec. Cmt, Tex.
b. Houston, Tex, 9/17/26; s. Eugene Frank Boeckman and Nancy Duncan B; m. 4/30/55 to Elizabeth Ann Mayer; c. Nancy Kathryn, Daniel Duncan and Caroline Albert. Educ: Univ. Tex, B.B.A, Law Sch, LL.B; Phi Delta Phi. Polit. & Govt. Pos: Legal counsel, Dallas Co. Rep. Party, Tex, 62-64; chmn, Dallas Co. Rep. Conv, 64; alternate del, Rep. Nat. Conv, 64 & 68; gen. counsel, Rep. State Exec. Cmt, 64-; chmn. justice cmt, Tex. Coun. Fed. Employ, 69- Bus. & Prof. Pos: Partner, Golden, Burrow, Potts & Boeckman, 57- Mil. Serv: Entered as Seaman, Navy, 44, released as Seaman 1/C, 46. Mem: Am, Tex. and Dallas Bar Asns; Am. Judicature Soc; Dallas Country Club; Dallas Petroleum Club; Dallas Hunting & Fishing Club; Salesmanship Club. Rel: Methodist. Legal Res: 5380 Nakoma Dr, Dallas, Tex. 75209. Mailing Add: 2330 Republic National Bank Tower, Dallas, Tex. 75201.

BOECKMANN, VERNON R. D
Wis. State Assemblyman
b. Sheboygan, Wis, 4/16/27; s. Anton C. Boeckmann and Mabel M. Schwartz B; m. 5/13/50 to Audrey June Mehre; c. Cheryl Lynn, Roger Lee, Diane Faye, Dawn Denise and Karen Jean. Educ: Various agr. short courses and F.B.I. Training Seminars in Law Enforcement. Polit. & Govt. Pos: Co. traffic officer, Sheboygan Co, Wis, 55-63; criminal invest, Sheboygan Sheriff Off, 63, under sheriff, 64-66; sheriff, Sheboygan Co, 67-68; Wis. State Assemblyman, Second Dist, 69- Mil. Serv: Entered as Pvt, Army, 45, released as Cpl, 48, after serv. in 2164 ASU Ft. Eustis. Rel: Lutheran Church- Mo. Synod. Mailing Add: Route 2, Plymouth, Wis. 53073.

BOEDECKER, LOUIS GIMMELL D
Cmnr, Mont. R.R. and Pub. Serv. Cmn.
b. Deer Lodge, Mont, 1/7/22; s. Louis G. Boedecker and Bertha Normandin B; m. 7/20/46 to Patricia McRae; c. Michele (Mrs. Hutton), Brett, Brooks, Brice, Blair and Mary. Educ: Carroll Col, Mont, B.S, 47. Polit. & Govt. Pos: Dir, Vet. Bonus Progs, Mont, 58-60; cmnr, Mont. R.R. and Pub. Serv. Cmn, 61- Bus. & Prof. Pos: Govt. rep, Pharmaceutical Co, Wash, D.C, 48-56. Mil. Serv: Entered as Air Cadet, Marines, 41, released as 1st Lt, 46, after serv. in First Marine Air Wing, Pac. Theatre, 43-45, Capt, Marine Res; Distinguished Flying Cross; Air Medal with 5 Oak Leaf Clusters. Mem: Nat. Asn. R.R. and Utility Cmnr. Rel: Catholic. Mailing Add: 221 Adams St, Helena, Mont, 59601.

BOEHLER, CONRAD JOSEPH D
Chmn, Harlan Co. Dem. Party, Nebr.
b. Orleans, Nebr, 1/16/30; s. Joseph John Boehler and Lorette Marie Fuller B; m. 7/23/53 to June Elaine Karlson; c. John Burton, Barbara June, Bryce Conrad and Michael Shawn. Educ: Kearney State Teachers Col, 1 year. Polit. & Govt. Pos: Precinct Committeeman, Orleans Twp, Nebr, 63; chmn, Harlan Co. Dem. Party, 65- Bus. & Prof. Pos: Farmer, 53- Mil. Serv: Entered as Seaman Apprentice, Navy, 51, released as PO3/C, after serving in Atlantic Theatre, 51-53; Presidential Unit Citation. Mem: Am. Legion; K. of C; C. of C; Nat. Farmers Orgn; Lions. Rel: Catholic. Mailing Add: Route 1, Orleans, Nebr. 68966.

BOEHLERT, SHERWOOD LOUIS R
b. Utica, N.Y, 9/28/36; s. Sherwood J. Boehlert and Elizabeth M. Champeaux B; m. 9/19/58 to Jean Bone; c. Mark Christopher, Tracy Ann and Leslie Jane. Educ: Utica Col; Syracuse Univ, B.S, 56-61; Tau Mu Epsilon; Pi Delta Epsilon; Alpha Delta Epsilon. Polit. & Govt. Pos: Exec. asst, Rep. Alexander Pirnie, N.Y, 64- Bus. & Prof. Pos: Staff asst, Wyandotte Chem. Corp, 61-63; mgr, Pub. Rels, 63-64. Mil. Serv: Army, Specialist 3/C, 56-58. Publ: 'Telling the Congressman's Story' in The Voice of Govt, John Wiley & Sons, 68. Mem: Pub. Rels. Soc. of Am. Rel: Catholic. Mailing Add: 8109 Bullock Lane, Springfield, Va. 22151.

BOEHM, DAVID O. R
b. Philadelphia, Pa, 5/3/22; s. Bertha Weinblatt (father deceased); m. 1/12/47 to Elaine Biben; c. Barbara Ellen and Susan Emilie. Educ: St. Joseph's Col; Temple Univ. Law Sch, grad, 46. Polit. & Govt. Pos: Mem, Rep. Speaker's Bur, N.Y, past chmn, Rep. Forum; past chmn, Seventh Judicial Dist. Asn. Young Rep. Clubs; past pres, Monroe Co. Young Rep. Clubs; chmn, Monroe Co. Rep. Adv. Reapportionment Cmt; alternate del, Rep. Nat. Conv, 64; mem. campaign cmt, U.S. Rep. Frank Horton, N.Y; past committeeman, Brighton Town Rep. Cmt; co. judge, Monroe Co, 69- Bus. & Prof. Pos: Former instr. ins. and bus. law, Univ. Rochester. Publ: Illusion and Disillusion, 50; 'Our Freedom Based on Law,' Am. Bar Asn. J, 5/60 and reprinted in Bill of Rights Speakers' Digest and Congressional Record. Mem: Am. Bar Asn; past chmn, Lawyer Referral Cmt, N.Y. Bar Asn; past pres, Monroe Co. Bar Asn. and past v.pres, trustee and chmn. various cmts; N.Y. and Am. Trial Lawyers Asns; chmn, Monroe Co. Penitentiary Study; past mem, Legal and Ment. Health Panel and Monroe Co. Charter Cmn; bd. Dirs, Monroe Co. Ment. Health Asn; bd. dirs, East House Corp; past mem, bd. dirs, Jewish Young Men's & Women's Asn; past v.pres, bd. dirs, Rochester Jr. C. of C; past mem, bd. dirs, Jewish Family Serv; past leader, Great Books Discussion; past pres, Rochester Chap, Am. Jewish Cong; past mem, Speaker's Bur, United Jewish Appeal; life mem, Genesee Conserv. League; Orpheus Lodge F&AM 1087; Myopia Pistol Club; Rochester-Brooks Gun Club; Rochester Club; Irondequoit Country Club; Nat. Rifle Asn; Circus Saints & Sinners; Friars Club. Achievements: Admitted to practice before U.S. Dist. Court, U.S. Circuit Court of Appeals and U.S. Supreme Court; Key-man award, Jr. C. of C, 57; Outstanding Cmt. Serv. Award, Monroe Co. Bd. Supvrs, 65; producer and author of libretto of musical comedy, Sweet Executive, produced in Rochester, 57; author of many published short stories, one listed in Book of Best Am. Short Stories, 50. Rel: Jewish. Mailing Add: 418 Oakdale Dr, Rochester, N.Y. 14624.

BOEHNING, RICHARD ALLEN R
Majority Leader, Ind. House Rep.
b. Renssalaer, Ind, 7/2/37; s. Virgil Allen Boehning and Catherine Hoeferlin B; m. 12/23/56 to Phyllis L. Albrecht; c. Vincent, Anita, Jennifer, Beverly and Stuart Philip. Educ: Ind. Univ, B.S, 59, LL.B, 61; Phi Delta Phi. Polit. & Govt. Pos: City attorney, mem. bd. works and safety, mem. water works trustees and traffic cmn, City of Lafayette, Ind, 64-66; Ind. State Rep, Tippecanoe Co, 67-, majority leader, Ind. House Rep, currently. Mem: Tippecanoe Co, Ind. and Am. Bar Asns; Elks; Jr. C. of C. Rel: Protestant. Mailing Add: 630 Central St, Lafayette, Ind. 47905.

BOEHRS, C.E. D
b. Perkins Co, S. Dak, 10/5/07; m. to Elsie Harris; c. Stuart, Shawn. Educ: Common Sch. Polit. & Govt. Pos: S. Dak. State Sen, 62-64; Sch. Bd, Eagle Butte Independent Sch. Dist; Secy, Eagle Butte Cooperative Asn; former V. Chmn, Dewey Co. A.S.C.S. Cmt. Bus. & Prof. Pos: Farmer, rancher. Mil. Serv: U.S. Army, 41-46, Corregidor, won Am. Defense Serv. Medal with Bronze Star, Asiatic Pacific Campaign Medal, Phillipine Defense Medal with two Bronze Stars, Distinguished Unit Medal with two Oak Leaf Clusters, Purple Heart, WW II Victory Medal. Mem: Mason; Shriner. Rel: Congregationalist. Mailing Add: Eagle Butte, S. Dak. 57625. (1967)

BOEKE, RICHARD FREDERICK D
b. Atlanta, Ga, 3/2/31; s. Eugene H. Boeke and Lillian Rogers B; m. 5/1/65 to Johanna Baarslag; c. Elinore Elizabeth and Diana Irene. Educ: Ga. Inst. Tech, 47-49; Iowa State Univ, B.S, 51; Yale Divinity Sch, B.D, 54; Teachers Col, Columbia Univ, 67-68. Polit. & Govt. Pos: Del, Dem. Nat. Conv, 68. Bus. & Prof. Pos: Minister, Chico Unitarian Church, Calif, 59-61, First Unitarian Church, Flushing, N.Y, 61-68 and United Liberal Church, St. Petersburg, Fla, 68- Mil. Serv: Entered as 1st Lt, Chaplains Corps, Air Force, 55, released as Capt, 58, after serv. at McCoy Air Force Base, Fla, 55-58; Letter of Commendation from Base Comdr. Publ: Universe of Common Freedom, Church Gate Press, Leicester, Eng, 68; plus articles in J. Liberal Ministry, UUA Now and The Churchman. Mem: Unitarian Universalist Ministers Asn; Int. Asn. Relig. Freedom; Greater St. Petersburg Ministers Asn; Rotary; adv. bd, St. Petersburg YWCA. Award for outstanding commun. serv, Northshore Dem. Club, 66. Rel: Unitarian Universalist. Mailing Add: 2300 Seventh St. N, St. Petersburg, Fla. 33704.

BOESE, ELSIE JEAN R
Rep. Nat. Committeewoman, La.
b. New Orleans, La, 1/19/25; d. John Roderick McGivney and Elsie Buist M; m. 5/20/46 to Dr. H. Lamar Boese, M.D; c. Robert Lamar. Educ: Sophie Newcomb Col, Tulane Univ, B.A, 45; Alpha Delta Pi. Polit. & Govt. Pos: Pres, Eighth Dist. Rep. Women's Club, 62-63 & 67-68; del, Rep. Nat. Conv, 64 & 68; mem, La. Rep. State Cent. Cmt, 64-, v.chmn, 64-68; mem, Rapides Parish Rep. Cmt, 64-; pub. rels. dir, Eighth Dist. Rep. Party, 64- Bus. & Prof. Pos: Social worker, Am. Red Cross, 45-46; teacher, retarded children, 53-55; script writer, educ. TV, 53-55. Mem: Orientation chmn, St. Frances Cabrini Hosp. Auxiliary; Poet's Circle (treas); Woman's Auxiliary, Rapides Parish Med. Soc.(past pres); Our Lady of Prompt Succor Altar Soc; Matinee Musical Club. La. Farm Bur. Freedom Award, 65 & 69; Distinguished Serv. Award, 12th Dist. Dept. La. VFW, 67. Rel: Roman Catholic. Mailing Add: 831 City Party Blvd, Alexandria, La. 71301.

BOESE, H. LAMAR R
Rep. Finance Chmn, Eighth Cong. Dist, La.
b. Ardmore, Okla, 6/28/24; s. W.H. Boese and Wynoma McGill B; m. 5/20/46 to Jean McGivney; c. Robert Lamar. Educ: Tulane Univ, B.S, 45, M.D, 47; Pi Kappa Alpha. Polit. & Govt. Pos: Rep. Finance Chmn, Eighth Cong. Dist, La, 64- Mil. Serv: 1st Lt, Army, 50-52; Paratrooper Jump Master Badge. Publ: 'Sjorgen's Syndrome,' Ochsner Clinic Reports, 57; 'Carcinoids of the GI Tract,' Annals of Internal Med, 56; 'Gastro-colic fistula,' Annals of Surg, 56.

Mem: Am. Med. Asn; Am. Col. Surgeons; Southeast. Surg. Cong; Am. Proctologic Soc; Alton Ochsner Surg. Soc; La. Surg. Soc; Kiwanis. Rel: Catholic. Legal Res: 831 City Park Blvd, Alexandria, La. 71303. Mailing Add: P.O. Box 5086, Alexandria, La, 71301.

BOGARDUS, O. A. R
b. Warsaw, Ky, 12/5/03; s. O.A. Bogardus, Sr. and Nancy Ballard B; m. 3/29/29 to Sarah Carroll; c. Graves C. and O.A, III. Educ: Hanover Col, 22-23; Ohio State Univ, 23-24; Phi Gamma Delta. Polit. & Govt. Pos: Chmn, Gallatin Co. Rep. Cmt, Ky, 43-69; mayor, Warsaw, 56-68; dep. cmnr, Ky. State Hwy. Dept, 68- Bus. & Prof. Pos: Pres, Gallatin Sand & Gravel Co, Ky, 46-61. Mem: Mason (32°); Shrine; Lions. Rel: Protestant. Legal Res: 104 E. Pearl, Warsaw, Ky. 41095. Mailing Add: 901 Leawood Dr, Frankfort, Ky. 40502.

BOGART, MARY CONSTANCE D
V.Chmn, Phillips Co. Dem. Cent. Cmt, Kans.
b. Penokee, Kans, 5/27/19; d. Frank Henry Gripp and Mary McCoy G; m. 7/29/39 to Hubert William Bogart; c. Marilynn (Mrs. Harvey Schuster), Linda (Mrs. Roger McCullough), Shirley (Mrs. Eddie McDowell), Hubert, Jr, Mary K. and Deidre. Educ: High Sch, grad, 37. Polit. & Govt. Pos: Committeewoman, Kirwin Twp. Dem. Party, Kans, 68-; v.chmn, Phillips Co. Dem. Cent. Cmt, 68- Bus. & Prof. Pos: Off. employee, Phillipsburg Sales Co, Inc, Phillipsburg, Kans, 65- Mem: Eastern Star (Past Worthy Matron); Farmers Union; Phillips Co. Dem. Womens' Club; Phillips Co. Ment. Health Asn; Jobs Daughters (Past Guardian). Rel: Methodist. Mailing Add: P.O. Box 58, Kirwin, Kans. 67644.

BOGART, VINCENT L. D
b. Kirwin, Kans, 6/8/22; s. Leroy Lindsay Bogart and Maude Wickwar B; m. 8/23/52 to Julia Ruth Henry; c. Candace, Lee, Celeste and Cynthia. Educ: Kans. State Univ, B.S, 53; Washburn Law Sch, LL.B, 55; Sigma Nu. Polit. & Govt. Pos: Committeeman, Dem. Precinct Cmt, Kans, 56-62; mem, Co. Dem. Cent. Cmt, 56-64; mem, Dist. Dem. Cmt, 56-64; Kans. State Rep, 57-59; mem, Kans. State Dem. Coun, 57-61 & 66-69; off. parliamentarian, Co. Dem. Cmt, 58-60, chmn, 60; mem, Kans. State Dem. Cmt, 60; cmnr, Wichita City Cmn, 63-67; mayor, Wichita, 64-65; key-note speaker, Kans. State Dem. Party Coun, 66; chmn, Kans. State Dem. Platform Cmt, 66-67; legis. rep. to Gov. of Kans, 67-69; trustee, Wichita State Univ. Bd. of Trustees, 68; del. and mem, platform cmt, Dem. Nat. Conv, 68; cmnr, Wichita Pub. Bldg. Cmn, Kans, 68-; regent, Kans. Bd. of Regents, 69- Mil. Serv: Entered as Aviation Cadet, Army Air Force, 43, released as 1st Lt, 46, after serv. in 11th Air Force, Asiatic-Pac. Theatre, 45-46; Asiatic-Pac. Theatre Ribbon; Victory Medal. Mem: Wichita Bar Asn; Kans. and Am. Bar Asns; Kans. and Am. Trial Lawyers Asns; Am. Judicature Soc; VFW; Lions. Rel: Catholic. Legal Res: 227 N. Belmont, Wichita, Kans. 67208. Mailing Add: 501 One Twenty Bldg, Wichita, Kans. 67202.

BOGDAN, ALBERT ALEXANDER D
Mem. Planning Cmt, Mass. Dem. Coun.
b. N.Y.C, 2/28/36; s. Alexander Vincent Bogdan and Blanche Capp B; m. 6/6/59 to Edwina Helena Schachinger; c. Andrea Elizabeth, Albert Edward and Stephan Alexander. Educ: City Col. N.Y, B.E.E, 58; Univ. Mass, Amherst, M.B.A, 69. Polit. & Govt. Pos: Alternate del, Dem. Nat. Conv, 68; mem, Berkshire Coun, Mass. Cmn. Against Discrimination, 68-; mem, planning cmt, Mass. Dem. Coun, 69- Bus. & Prof. Pos: Appln. engr, Radio Receptor, Brooklyn, N.Y, 57-58; syst. engr, Sperry Gyroscope, Great Neck, 58-59; prog. engr, Lehigh Design Co, Newark, N.J, 59-61, prog. mgr, Gen. Elec. Co. Ord. Syst, Pittsfield, 61-69; exec. dir, Pittsfield Urban Coalition, 69- Mem: Inst. Elec. and Electronic Engrs; Elfun Soc; bd. mem, Micah; pres, Egremont PTA; mem. adv. cmt, Pittsfield Big Brother; NAACP; v.pres, Pittsfield Citizens' Scholarship Found; Pittsfield Area Coun. of Churches Soc. Action Cmt; Berkshire Co. Ecumenical Asn. Rel: Unitarian; mem. Unitarian-Universalist Church of Pittsfield Exec. Cmt. Mailing Add: 49 Lucia Dr, Pittsfield, Mass. 02101.

BOGENRIEF, MATTIE B. D
b. Duluth, Minn, 10/26/12; m. to Carl Bogenrief; c. Donald, D'Annette. Educ: Northwest Mo. State Teachers Col. Polit. Pos: Iowa State Rep-66. Bus. & Prof. Pos: Farming. Mailing Add: 3211 Cottage Grove, Des Moines, Iowa 50311. (1967)

BOGER, GILBERT LEE R
N.C. State Rep.
b. Cana, N.C, 5/22/27; s. Clyde Houston Boger and Lula Richie B; m. 4/20/52 to Maxine Smith; c. Ronald Lee, Cynthia Lynn and Warren Smith. Educ: High Sch, grad, 43. Polit. & Govt. Pos: N.C. State Rep, 67-; alternate del, Rep. Nat. Conv, 68. Bus. & Prof. Pos: Owner-operator, Gilbo Farm, 52- Mem: Farm Bur; Mason. Rel: Methodist. Mailing Add: Route 3, Mocksville, N.C. 27028.

BOGGINI, N. CHARLES D
Conn. State Rep.
b. Italy, 3/16/10. Educ: N.Y. Univ, B.A. Polit. & Govt. Pos: Formerly with, Dept. of Welfare, New York City; asst. prosecutor, Manchester Town Court, Conn; mem, Manchester Bd. Tax. Rev. and chmn, two years; mem, Manchester Bd. Educ; Conn. State Rep, 69- Bus. & Prof. Pos: Pres. & owner, beverage flavor co. Mem: Conn. Soft Drink Indust. Serv. Club (past pres); State, Co. Munic. Workers Am.(past pres). Mailing Add: 71 Spencer St, Manchester, Conn. 06040.

BOGGIS, DONALD EARL D
b. Nashua, N.H, 3/7/32; s. Edward Joseph Boggis and Dorris Nichols B; m. 6/24/52 to Pauline Claire Bedard; c. Donald Earl, Jr, Ivy Marie, Vint Robert, Martin Thomas, Carl Emil and Greg Paul. Educ: Nashua High Sch, N.H, 4 years. Polit. & Govt. Pos: Alternate del, Dem. Nat. Conv, 68. Bus. & Prof. Pos: Unit engr, Raytheon Co, Andover, Mass, 57- Mil. Serv: Entered as Airman Basic, Air Force, 51, released as Airman 1/C, 55; Good Conduct Medal. Rel: Roman Catholic. Mailing Add: 26 Blanchard St, Nashua, N.H. 03060.

BOGGS, (THOMAS) HALE D
Asst. Majority Leader, U.S. House of Rep.
b. Long Beach, Miss, 2/15/14; s. William Robertson Boggs and Clare Josephine Hale B; m. 1/22/38 to Corinne Claiborne; c. Barbara Rowena (Mrs. P. Sigmund, Jr), Thomas Hale, Jr. and Corinne M. (Mrs. S.V. Roberts). Educ: Tulane Univ, B.A, 35 and LL.B, 37; Phi Beta Kappa; Omicron Delta Kappa; Beta Theta Pi. Polit. & Govt. Pos: U.S. Rep, Second Dist, La, 41-43 & 47-, mem, House Ways and Means Cmt. and Joint Econ. Cmt. and chmn, Subcmt. on For. Econ. Policy, U.S. House of Rep, Asst. Majority Leader, currently; counsel, La. Dept. Conserv, 43; cand. for gov, La, 52; v.chmn, Dem. Nat. Cmt, 56-; parliamentarian, Dem. Nat. Conv, 64, del. and chmn. platform cmt, 68; mem, President's Cmn. on the Assassination of President Kennedy and President's Cmn. to Study the Causes and Prev. of Violence. Bus. & Prof. Pos: Gen. practice of civil law, La, 43 & 46. Mil. Serv: Entered as Ens, Navy, 43, released as Lt. Comdr, 46, after serv. in Maritime Command. Mem: Am, La. and New Orleans Bar Asns; Am. Judicature Soc; hon. mem, Int. Asn. of Ports and Harbors; New Orleans C. of C; SAR; Am. Legion; Amvets; K. of C; gen. mgr, Tulane Univ. Alumni Asn, 37-40; Family Serv. Soc. New Orleans; Cong. Club. Recipient, Miss. Valley World Trade Award, 56 and Cunningham Award of Int. House, 58. Rel: Roman Catholic. Legal Res: 2801 St. Charles Ave, New Orleans, La. 70130. Mailing Add: 2207 Rayburn House Office Building, Washington, D.C. 20515.

BOGGS, J. CALEB R
U.S. Sen, Del.
b. Kent Co, Del, 5/15/09; m. to Elizabeth Muir; c. James Caleb Jr, Marilu. Educ: Univ. of Del, A.B; Georgetown Univ, LL.B; Del. State Col, LL.D, honoris causa. Polit. & Govt. Pos: Judge of Family Court, New Castle Co, Del; U.S. Rep. at Large from Del. to 80th, 81st & 82nd Cong; Gov. of Del, 52-60; chmn, Nat. Gov. Conf, 59; pres. coun, State Govt, 60; U.S. Sen, Del, 61- Bus. & Prof. Pos: Lawyer, mem. of bar, State of Del, U.S. Supreme Court. Mil. Serv: Army Res, Col, retired; Brig. Gen, Del. Nat. Guard, enlisted 26, retired; 5 campaigns ETO; Legion of Merit; Bronze Star with Cluster; French Croix de Guerre with Palm. Cmt. assignments: Appropriations, Pub. Works, Post Off. and Civil Serv. Rel: Methodist. Legal Res: Del. Mailing Add: U.S. Senate, Washington, D.C. 20510.

BOGGUS, FRANK NELSON R
Mem, Tex. State Rep. Hq. Cmt.
b. Brownsville, Tex, 8/16/28; s. James Lewis Boggus, Sr. and Maudie Nelson B; m. 12/19/49 to Peggy Jeanne Long; c. Barbara Sue, Robert Frank and Jack Nelson. Educ: Tex. A&M Univ, B.S, 50. Polit. & Govt. Pos: Mem, Harlingen Sch. Bd, Tex, 59-; mem, State Rep. Finance Cmt, 61-65; alternate del, Rep. Nat. Conv, 64; finance chmn, Cameron Co. Rep. Party; mem, Tex. State Rep. Hq. Cmt. Bus. & Prof. Pos: Partner, Boggus Motor Sales, Ford Dealer, 56-66; pres, Auto and Truck Leasing Co, 60; dir, Tropical Savings & Loan, 65. Mil. Serv: Entered as 2nd Lt, Air Force, 53, released as 1st Lt, Air Training Command, Amarillo AF Base, 55. Mem: Pres, McAllen Jr. C. of C, 52; dir. Harlingen C. of C, 66; Rotary; Elks; Harlingen Country Club. Co-chmn. of what is thought to be first mass switch over of Dem. to the Rep. Party in the South, 61. Rel: Methodist. Mailing Add: 315 E. Washington, Harlingen, Tex. 78550. (1967)

BOGLE, ROBERT STOVER R
Chmn, Cabarrus Co. Rep. Exec. Cmt, N.C.
b. Concord, N.C, 8/20/27; s. William Stover Bogle and Myrtle Taylor B; m. 5/26/54 to Mary Kay Patterson; c. Margaret and William. Educ: Duke Univ, 1 year; Lenoir Rhyne Col, 2 years. Polit. & Govt. Pos: Chmn, Cabarrus Co. Rep. Exec. Cmt, N.C, 68- Mil. Serv: Entered as Pvt, Army, 50, released as Sgt, 52, after serv. in 185th Combat Eng. Bn, Korea, 51-52. Rel: Methodist. Legal Res: 71 Patton Court S.E, Concord, N.C. 28025. Mailing Add: P.O. Box 69, Concord, N.C. 28025.

BOHLEN, CHARLES E.
b. Clayton, N.Y, 8/30/04; m. to Avis Thayer; c. Avis T, Charles E. and Celestine E. Educ: Harvard Univ, B.A, 27. Polit. & Govt. Pos: Career officer, U.S. Dept. of State For. Serv, 29-69, v.consul, Prague, 29-31 and Paris, 31-34, v.consul, Moscow, 34, secy. in diplomatic serv, 34, third secy, 34-35, second secy, 37-38, consul, 38-39, Dept. State, 36 & 42, secy, U.S. del, Int. Sugar Conf, London, 37 and Conf. of Brussels, 37, second secy, Tokyo, 40-41, first secy, Moscow, 42-44, asst. chief, Div. of European Affairs, 43, accompanied Secy. of State to Moscow Conf, 43, attended Tehran Conf, 43, chief, Div. of East. European Affairs, 44, area adv, U.S. Group, Dumbarton Oaks Conversations on Int. Orgn, Wash, D.C, 44, asst. to Secy. of State for White House Liaison, 44, accompanied President Roosevelt to Crimea Conf, 45, polit. and liaison officer, U.S. Del, UN Conf. on Int. Orgn, San Francisco, 45, polit. adv, U.S. Del, Berlin Conf, 45, asst. to U.S. mem, Meeting of Coun. For. Ministers, London, 45, detailed to Meeting of For. Secy, Moscow, 45, polit. adv, U.S. Del, Second Session, Conf. For. Ministers, Paris, 46, polit. adv, U.S. Del, Paris Conf, 46, spec. polit. adv, U.S. Del, Paris Conf, N.Y, 46, spec. asst. to Secy. of State, 46; polit. adv, U.S. Del, Fourth Session, Conf. For. Ministers, Moscow, 47, counsr, Dept. State, 47-51, adv, U.S. Del, Gen. Assembly, UN, N.Y, 47, adv, U.S. Del, Coun. For. Ministers, London, 47, adv, U.S. Del, Gen. Assembly, UN, Paris, 48, minister, Paris, 49, Ambassador to U.S.S.R, 53-57, Ambassador to Philippines, 57-59, spec. asst. to Secy. of State for Soviet affairs, 59-61, Ambassador to France, 62-68, Dep. Under Secy. of State for polit. affairs, 68-69. Mailing Add: 2811 Dumbarton Ave, Washington, D.C. 20007. (1967)

BOHLKE, LLOYD ELMER R
Chmn, Adams Co. Rep. Party, Nebr.
b. Kenesaw, Nebr, 6/27/27; s. Elmer Martin Bohlke and Marie Jacobitz B; m. 6/15/52 to Zella LaVonne Phillips; c. Stephanie LaVonne, Michele Susan and Timothy Lloyd. Educ: Hastings Col, B.S, 50. Polit. & Govt. Pos: Clerk, Wanda Twp, Nebr, 58-62; chmn, Adams Co. Rep. Party, 68- Bus. & Prof. Pos: Teacher, Fullerton Pub. Schs, 50-52, Hastings Pub. Schs, 53-54. Mem: Farm Bur; Lions. Rel: Protestant. Mailing Add: Kenesaw, Nebr. 68956.

BOHN, ERNEST JOHN R
b. Austria-Hungary, 5/12/01; s. Frank J. Bohn and Julianna Kiry B; single. Educ: Adelbert Col, A.B, cum laude; West. Res. Univ, 24, LL.B, 26, LL.D,

51. Polit. & Govt. Pos: Mem, Cuyahoga Co. Rep. Exec. Cmt; League Rep. Clubs, Cuyahoga Co; Nat. Adv. Com. White House Conf. on Aging, 61; Panel on Phys. Environment Pres's. Cmn. Nat. Goals, 60; Nt. Com. White House Conf. Children & Youth, 60; U.S. Del, Housing Com, UN Econ. Cmn. For Europe, Geneva, Switzerland, 59; Forum for Commun. Develop, Citizen's Action Com. on Nursing Homes; Bd. Dirs, Past Pres, Ohio Planning Conf, Cleveland; Mem, Cuyahoga Co. Govtl. Consol. Com. (Past Pres.); Chmn, Develop. Cou. Greater Cleveland; Mem, Coun. of Civil Defense; Mem, Cleveland Met. Servs. Cmn; Trustee, Better Homes & Neighborhoods, Cleveland; Mem, Ohio Cmn. on Aging, panel consultants on aging, Dept. HEW; Cons. Subcmt, Problems Aged & Aging, U.S. Sen; Mem, Com. on Housing for Elderly; Adv. Com. Housing & Commun. Develop. & Housing for Sr. Citizens, HHFA; Exec. Cmt, Am. Coun. to Improve our Neighborhoods; Exec. Cmt, Pres. Eisenhower's Adv. Cmn, Housing Policies; Mem, Int. Fedn. Housing & Town Planning, The Hauge; Bd. Dirs, Nat. Com. on Housing, 45; Mem, Regional Planning Cmn; Cuyahoga Co; Mem, Cleveland Welfare Fedn; Mem, Ohio Urban Develop. Cmn; Midwest Regional Planning Cmn; Adv. Bd, Urban Renewal Agency; Chmn, City Planning Cmn, Cleveland; Dir, Organizer, Regional Asn, Cleveland; Dir, Cleveland Metrop. Housing Authority; Mem, Pub. Housing Admin; Cons. U.S. Housing Authority, Resettlement Admin, Def. Housing Div; Archtl. Adv. Com. Fed, Pub. Housing Authority, 39; Mem, Int. Housing Cmn, 34; Mem, Cleveland City Coun, 34-40; Mem, Ohio Gen. Assembly, 29-30. Bus. & Prof. Pos: Trustee, Vis. Nurses Asn; Bd. Dirs, Golden Age Center; Roadside Coun; Trustee, Goodrich Soc. Settlement House; Mem, Vis. Com. Harvard Grad. Sch. Design & West. Res. Univ. Sch. Applied Soc. Scis; Adv. Com. Notre Dame Col; Garden Center of Clubland; Adv. Bd, St. Vincent's Charity Hosp; Citizen's Adv. Com, Cuyahoga Co. Hosp. Bd; Bd. of Trustees & Mem, Exec. Com, Cath. Charities Corp; Adv. Bd, Past Chmn, Cath. Bur; Dir, 2nd Fed. Savings & Loan Asn; Law practice, Cleveland, 26-38; Adv. Com. on retired workers UAW, Detroit; admitted Ohio Bar, 26. Mem: Nat. Asn. Housing ofcls. (founder, 1st pres.); Am. Soc. Planning Ofcls. (pres, 51); Adult Educ. Asn; Consumers League; Nat. Conf. Soc. Welfare; Cleveland Bar Asn; C. of C; West. Res. Univ. Law Sch. Alumni Asn. (pres, 52); K. of C; Mid-Day Club. Misc: Archbishop Edward F. Hoban medal for distinguished serv, 64; recipient of numerous other awards; co-author: A Housing Program for the U.S, 34. Rel: Roman Catholic. Mailing Add: 12700 Lake Ave, Lakewood, Ohio 44107. (1967)

BOIARSKY, IVOR F. D
W.Va. State Del.
b. Charleston, W.Va, 4/7/20; s. Mose Boiarsky and Rae D. B; m. 12/23/48 to Barbara Faith Polan; c. Marc Edward and Robert Polan. Educ: Language Sch. of Middleburg Col; Brown Univ, B.A, 41; Univ. of Va, LL.B, 47; Coast Guard Acad. Polit. & Govt. Pos: W.Va. State Del, currently. Bus. & Prof. Pos: Lawyer; past pres, Charleston Fed. Savings and Loan Asn. Mailing Add: Box 2189, Charleston, W.Va. 25328. (1967)

BOILEAU, GERALD JOHN Non-Partisan
b. Woodruff, Wis, 1/15/00; s. John R. Boileau and Sophia Daigle B; m. 8/31/25 to Monica McKean; c. Nancy (Mrs. Nirschl) and Mary (Mrs. Bailey). Educ: Marquette Univ. Law Sch, LL.B, 23; Alpha Sigma Nu; Delta Theta Phi. Polit. & Govt. Pos: Dist. Attorney, Marathon Co, Wis, 26-31; U.S. Rep, Seventh Dist, 31-39; circuit judge, 16th Judicial Circuit, 42- Mil. Serv: Entered as Pvt, Army, 18, released as Cpl, 19, after serv. in 11th Field Artil, A.E.F; Muese Argonne Offensive Ribbon. Mem: K. of C.(4°); Elks; Am. Legion; VFW. Rel: Roman Catholic. Legal Res: 914 Grand Ave, Wausau, Wis. 54401. Mailing Add: Box 726, Wausau, Wis. 54401.

BOIRE, HENRY D
N.H. State Rep.
b. St. Malo, Can, 3/22/01; married; c. Four. Educ: Can. Schs. Polit. & Govt. Pos: N.H. State Rep, currently. Bus. & Prof. Pos: Barber. Rel: Catholic. Mailing Add: 17 Second St, Somersworth, N.H. 03878. (1967)

BOISSON, AUGUSTA NELLIE D
V.Chmn, Wabash Co. Dem. Party, Ind.
b. Lansing, Ohio, 2/8/11; d. John Debin and Daisy Scory D; m. 8/16/37 to Hamlet Victor Boisson; c. Diana N. (Mrs. Theodore Nering) and Hamlet V, Jr. Educ: Correspondence Col; Kappa Kappa Kappa. Polit. & Govt. Pos: V.chmn, Wabash Co. Dem. Party, Ind, 60-; precinct committeeman, Wabash Co, 60-; mgr, Wabash License Bur, 61-; del, Dem. Nat. Conv, 68; pres, Wabash Co. Dem. Club, 69. Mem: Wabash Co. Garden Club; Wabash Co. Women's Club; Farm Bur; Organized Wabash Co. Dem. Women's Club; v.pres. of League of Women Voters. Rel: Methodist. Mailing Add: R.R. 2, Wabash, Ind. 46992.

BOISVERT, RALPH W. D
N.H. State Rep.
b. Nashua, N.H, 4/10/01; married. Educ: Trade Sch. Polit. & Govt. Pos: Former ward clerk, Ward Seven, N.H; N.H. State Rep, 59- Bus. & Prof. Pos: Grocer, currently. Mem: Royal Arcanum. Rel: Catholic. Mailing Add: 1 Thomas St, Nashua, N.H. 03060.

BOISVERT, ROMEO T. D
Maine State Sen.
b. Can, 11/15/16; s. Theophile Boisvert and Beatrice Phenix B; m. 5/27/39 to Cecile Doucette; c. Mae Therese (Mrs. Hebert) and Lorette (Mrs. Smith). Educ: St. Joseph Prep Sch, Que, 3 years. Polit. & Govt. Pos: Mayor, Lewiston, Maine, 58-60; Maine State Sen, 61-, Minority Asst. Leader, Maine State Senate, 63-64 & 67-, Majority Asst. Leader, 65-66. Bus. & Prof. Pos: Mill worker, Hill Mfg. Co, Lewiston, Maine, 35-54; ed. and mgr, Le Messager (French newspaper), 54-66; ins. agent, Equitable Life, 66- Mem: Société L'Assomption (v.pres, 55-67). Chevalier de L'Académie Française de France, French Consul, Boston, Mass, 67. Rel: Catholic. Mailing Add: 190 Pine St, Lewiston, Maine 04240.

BOIVIN, HARRY DOLAN D
Ore. State Sen.
b. Ashland, Ore, 2/7/04; s. Henry Boivin and Nellie Dolan B; m. 6/26/34 to Vivian McCauley; c. Robert D. and Kathleen D. Educ: Univ. Santa Clara, Ph.B. and J.D. Polit. & Govt. Pos: City attorney, Klamath Falls, Ore, 30-32; Ore. State Rep, 35-43, speaker of the house, Ore. House Rep, 37-39; chmn, Ore. Liquor Control Cmn, 49-50; mem, State Bd. Educ, 50-51; Ore. State Sen, 55-, pres, Ore. State Senate, 61-63 & 65-67. Bus. & Prof. Pos: V.pres. and dir, Bank of Klamath Falls, 60- Mem: Elks; K. of C. Rel: Catholic. Legal Res: 612 Conger Ave, Klamath Falls, Ore. 97601. Mailing Add: 210 Boivin Bldg, Klamath Falls, Ore. 97601.

BOLAND, EDWARD P. D
U.S. Rep, Mass.
b. Springfield, Mass, 10/1/11. Educ: Boston Col. Law Sch. Polit. & Govt. Pos: Mass. State Rep, 35-40; register of deeds, Hampden Co, Mass, 41-52; U.S. Rep, Mass, 53- Mil. Serv: U.S. Army, Pac. Theatre of Opers, Capt, 46. Mailing Add: 326 Post Off. Bldg, Springfield, Mass. 01103.

BOLDEN, MELVIN REED D
Chmn, Merrimack Co. Dem. Party, N.H.
b. Baltimore, Md, 1/28/19; s. Jacob Percy Bolden and Mary C. Reed B; m. 12/3/49 to Gwyndolyn Claire Hale. Educ: Philadelphia Col. Art, 37-41. Polit. & Govt. Pos: Chmn, Loudon Dem. Party, N.H, 64-69; chmn, Merrimack Co. Dem. Party, 66-; mem. bd. dirs, N.H. Coun. Better Schs, 66-, N.H. Artists Asn, 67- and N.H. Soc. Welfare Coun, 67-; cmnr, N.H. Cmn. Human Rights, 67-; chmn, Gov. Adv. Bd. Off. Econ. Opportunity, 68- Bus. & Prof. Pos: Supvr. installation mech, Glenn Martin Aircraft Co, Baltimore, 41-44; staff artist, Afro-Am. Newspapers, 43-45; staff artist and layout designer, Our World Mag, N.Y.C, 45-47; art dir, Detecto Scales Co, Brooklyn, 48-50; free lance illustrator and cover artist, Saturday Rev, 49-55; advert. illustrator, Reynolds Aluminum, Revere Copper Brass, Ginn and D.C. Heath; illustrator and designer, Grolier Soc, McGraw Hill and World Publ. Co. Publ: Illustrations published in Boy's Life Mag, Fortune, Bus. Week, Wall Street J. and New York Times. Mem: New Eng. Elec. Rwy. Hist. Soc. Rel: Unitarian. Legal Res: Beck Rd, Loudon, N.H. 03301. Mailing Add: R.R. 8, Concord, N.H. 03301.

BOLE, RUTH MARIE D
V.chmn, Fifth Dist. Ind. Dem. Party
b. Grant Co, Ind, 6/25/26; d. Lewis Lester White and Mary Ester Bragg White Jones; m. 3/11/44 to Gerald Leroy Bole; c. Penny Elaine (Mrs. Eric Welch), Brenda Diane and Gary Lee. Educ: Van Buren High Sch, dipl, 44. Polit. & Govt. Pos: V.chmn, Van Buren Dem. Precinct, Ind, 58-61; v.chmn, Grant Co. Dem. Party, 60-64, 66-68; field officer, Ind. Dem. Cent. Cmt, 66; v.chmn, Fifth Dist. Ind. Dem. Party, 66-; treas, Ind. Fedn. Dem. Women's Clubs, 67-; del, Dem. Nat. Conv, 68. Bus. & Prof. Pos: Driver exam, Bur. Motor Vehicles, 61-66, off. mgr, license br, 66-67; field invester, Dept. of Revenue, 68- Mem: Am. Legion Auxiliary (vol. hosp. worker); Eight & Forty Salon; Black Creek Conserv. Club Auxiliary; Marion Gen. Hosp. Auxiliary; Amicae Filae; Grant Co. Women's Dem. Club; govt. counsr, Hoosier Girls' State, 6 years. Rel: Methodist. Mailing Add: 108 E. Park, Box 256, Van Buren, Ind. 46991.

BOLENDER, LAURA LOU D
Sec, Montgomery Co. Dem. Cent. Cmt, Ohio
b. Dayton, Ohio, 3/2/14; d. Herman A. King and Theresa K. Cron K; m. 12/12/36 to Clifford W. Bolender. Educ: Sinclair Bus. Col, 1 year. Polit. & Govt. Pos: Clerk, Montgomery Co. Bd. Elec, Ohio, 48-; financial secy, Federated Dem. Women Ohio, 50-; treas, Kettering Women's Dem. Club, 63-65 & 67-69, secy, 65-67, pres, 69-; secy, Montgomery Co. Dem. Cent. Cmt, 68- Bus. & Prof. Pos: Assembler, Nat. Cash Register Co, 34, 35 & 36; asst. buyer, Rike's Dept. Store, 37-45; buyer, Elder-Johnson Dept. Store, 45-48. Mem: Nat. Dem. Cmt; State Dem. Cmt; Federated Dem. Women Ohio; Kettering Women's Dem. Club; Am. Legion Auxiliary. Achievement Award, Women's Int. Bowling Cong; First and Second Place Winners, Canoe Races; Medals, Women's Basketball Tournaments. Rel: Protestant. Mailing Add: 1541 Constance Ave, Kettering, Ohio 45409.

BOLGER, WILLIAM J. D
b. McHenry, Ill, 4/16/25; s. Thomas A. Bolger and Grace Doherty B; m. 10/1/49 to Carol D. Murray; c. Kathleen, Murray, William and Candace. Polit. & Govt. Pos: Del, Dem. Nat. Conv, 56, 60, 64 & 68; Dem. precinct committeeman and alderman, First Ward, McHenry, Ill, 57- Mil. Serv: Entered as Pvt, Marine Corps, 44, released as Cpl, 46, after serv. in First Marine Div, S.Pac, Okinawa, China, 44-45; Purple Heart; Letter of Commendation with Ribbon. Mem: Pres, McHenry Pub. Libr, 60-; secy, McHenry Little League, 54-; VFW; Am. Legion; Catholic Order of Foresters. Rel: Catholic. Mailing Add: 906 N. Allen Ave, McHenry, Ill. 60050.

BOLIN, GROVER CLEVELAND, JR, M.D. R
Mem, N.C. Rep. Exec. Cmt.
b. Orangeburg, S.C, 11/4/24; s. Grover Cleveland Bolin, M.D. and Lou Ella Sheppard B; m. 6/19/45 to Mae Bradbury; c. Galen and Paula. Educ: Clemson Col, 40-43; Washington Univ, 43-44; Med. Col. of S.C, M.D, 48; Phi Rho Sigma. Polit. & Govt. Pos: Mem, Johnston Co. Rep. Exec. Cmt, N.C, 60-64, treas, 64-65; campaign mgr, Johnston Co, Jim Gardner for Cong. Campaign, 64; asst. treas, John Shallcross for U.S. Sen. Campaign, 66; chmn, Johnston Co. Rep. Party, 66-; mem, N.C. Rep. Exec. Cmt, 66- Bus. & Prof. Pos: Physician, Radiologist, 48- Mil. Serv: Pvt, World War II, 43; re-entered serv. as 1st Lt, Army, 50, released as Capt, 54, after serv. in 8th Army, Korea. Mem: Am. Col. Radiology; Am. Med. Asn; Med. Soc. of N.C; past pres, Civitan Club, Smithfield, N.C; cmnr, Tuscarora Coun, Boy Scouts and 3 Bead Woodbadger; Am. Legion; Am. Rifle Asn; New River Grape Growers Asn. Rel: Presbyterian. Legal Res: 709 Crescent Dr, Smithfield, N.C. 27577. Mailing Add: Box 178, Smithfield, N.C. 27577.

BOLIN, WESLEY H. D
Secy. of State, Ariz.
b. Butler, Mo, 7/1/08; s. D.S. Bolin and Margaret B; m. to Marion Knappenberger; c. Wesley, Jr, Tom, Bill, Steven and Bruce. Educ: Phoenix Jr. Col. Polit. & Govt. Pos: Constable, W. Phoenix Precinct 38, Ariz, 3 terms; justice of peace, 44; Secy. of State, Ariz, currently. Mem: Nat. Secretaries of State (pres, 53); Elks; Moose; Jr. C. of C. Outstanding work with Boy Scouts. Rel: Protestant. Legal Res: 2920 W. Manor Dr, Phoenix, Ariz. 85014. Mailing Add: State House, Phoenix, Ariz. 85007.

BOLLARD, ROBERT D. D
b. Fort Dodge, Iowa, 10/22/22; s. Fred J. Bollard and Idella Strickler B; m. 5/23/44 to M. Roberta Wiegert; c. Barbara Kay. Educ: Eve. classes, Univ. of Chicago, Roosevelt Univ. and Ohio State Univ. Polit. & Govt. Pos: Del, Dem. Nat. Conv, 64. Bus. & Prof. Pos: Employee, Tobin Packing Co, 40-46; asst. ed-educ. dir, UPWA, 46-48; ed. and educ. dir, Ill. CIO Coun, 48-56, rep, USW, 56-66; secy-treas, Ohio AFL-CIO, 63-66, dir, Dept. of Legis. and Commun. Affairs, Am. Fedn. State, Co. and Munic. Employees, AFL-CIO, 67-, mem, Operating Cmt, Cmt. on Polit. Educ. and Legis. Admin. Cmt, currently; mem, Consumer Fedn. of Am, currently. Mil. Serv: Entered as Pvt, Air Force, 43, released as S/Sgt, 45, after serv. in 456 Bomb Group, ETO, Oct. 45; Prisoner of War, Germany; Air Medal; Five Battle Stars; Good Conduct Medal. Rel: Presbyterian; Elder. Legal Res: 1007 Downs Dr, Silver Spring, Md. 20904. Mailing Add: 1155 15th St. N.W, Washington, D.C. 20005.

BOLLE, EVERETT E. D
Wis. State Assemblyman
b. Kossuth, Wis, 8/29/19. Educ: Univ. of Wis. Ext. Div. Polit. & Govt. Pos: Former town supvr; former pres, Local Labor Union; Wis. State Assemblyman, 60- Bus. & Prof. Pos: Former factory worker, worker in gen. merchandise store, trucker and farmer; real estate salesman and auctioneer. Mem: Past pres, Holy Name Soc; K. of C; local fish and game protective asn; former dist. chmn, Heart Fund. Mailing Add: Francis Creek, Wis. 54214. (1967)

BOLLING, BRANTLEY LAMBERD D
Dem. Nat. Committeeman, Va.
b. Ashville, N.C, 12/1/27; d. Charles Ellsworth Lamberd, Jr. and Brantley Carter L; m. 9/3/49 to Albert Stuart Bolling, Jr; c. Brantley Carter and Mary Stuart. Educ: Sweet Briar Col, B.A, 49. Polit. & Govt. Pos: Co-chmn, Portsmouth Women's Campaign Cmt. for Gov. Albertis Harrison, Va, 61; mem, Gov. Cmt. for Youth, 62-; v.chmn. in charge of women's activities, Jefferson-Jackson Day Dinner, Va. Dem. Party, 63; women's chmn, Johnson-Humphrey Campaign, Va. and alternate del-at-lg, Dem. Nat. Conv, 64; co-chmn, Portsmouth Women's Campaign Cmt. for Gov. Mills E. Godwin, 65; mem, Va. Cmn. Visually Handicapped, 65-; dep. dir, Va. Primary Campaign for U.S. Sen. Harry F. Byrd, Jr, 66; former mem. exec. cmt, Va. Dem. State Cent. Cmt, del. and mem. drafting sub-cmt, Platform and Resolutions Cmt, Dem. Nat. Conv, 68; Dem. Nat. Committeewoman, Va, currently. Mem: Pres. bd. dirs, Portsmouth Child Care Center; bd. trustees, Patrick Henry Hosp, Newport News and Portsmouth Historic Found; bd. dirs, Norfolk Civic Ballet; Elizabeth River Garden Club(pres, 64-66); Sweet Briar Col. Alumnae Asn; Portsmouth Dem. Women's Club; Cedar Point Country Club; Portsmouth Hist. Asn. Rel: Episcopal. Mailing Add: 110 Park Rd, Portsmouth, Va. 23707.

BOLLING, CECIL WINTON 'JACK' R
Chmn, Wise Co. Rep. Party, Va.
b. Pound, Va, 6/25/25; s. Cecil Bolling and Winnie Jane Mullins B; m. 3/30/46 to Loretta Jackson; c. Sharon Cecile, Paula Dawn (Mrs. Mullins) and Jessica. Educ: Va. Polytech. Inst, B.S. in Bus. Admin, 47; Lonesome Pine Club; Alpha Kappa Psi. Polit. & Govt. Pos: Chmn, Wise Co. Rep. Party, Va, 68- Bus. & Prof. Pos: Owner, Pound Esso Sta, Va, 47-56; partner, Branham and Bolling Coal Co, 56-61; pres, Universal Coals, Inc, 61-63; partner, Ambrose Br. Coal Co, 63-; pres, Camp Creek Coal Co, 67- Mem: Charter mem, Pound Lions Club (past pres); charter mem, C. of C. Rel: Missionary Baptist. Mailing Add: Box 398, Pound, Va. 24279.

BOLLING, RICHARD WALKER D
U.S. Rep, Mo.
b. New York, N.Y, 5/17/16; s. Richard Walker Bolling and Florence Easton B; m. 1/13/64 to Jim Grant; c. Andrea. Educ: Univ. of the South, B.A, 37, M.A, 39; Vanderbilt Univ, grad. study, 40; Phi Beta Kappa. Polit. & Govt. Pos: U.S. Rep, Fifth Dist, Mo, 48-, mem, Joint Econ. Cmt. and House Cmt. on Rules, currently, chmn, Urban Affairs Subcmt, currently. Bus. & Prof. Pos: Teacher and coach, Sewanee Mil. Acad, Tenn; vet. adv. and dir. student activities, Univ. of Kansas City, Mo. Mil. Serv: Entered as Pvt, Army, 41, released as Lt. Col, 46, after serv. more than 5 years, over 4 of which were overseas in Australia, New Guinea, Philippines and Japan, last assignment was as asst. to Gen. McArthur's Chief of Staff; Legion of Merit; Bronze Star. Publ: Author, House Out of Order, 65 and Power In The House, 68, E.P. Dutton Co, Inc. Received Cong. Distinguished Serv. Award, Am. Polit. Sci. Asn. Rel: Episcopal. Legal Res: Walnut Towers, 722 Walnut St, Kansas City, Mo. 64108. Mailing Add: 307 Warrenton Dr, Silver Spring, Md. 20904.

BOLLINGER, EARL A. D
b. Madison Co, Mo, 11/4/25; m. 12/24/45 to Carleda E. Johnson; c. Carla Ann, Andrea Elizabeth. Educ: Flat River Jr. Col; Southeast Mo. State Col, B.S; Wash. Univ. Polit. & Govt. Pos: Mo. State Rep, 58-66; Col. on the staff of Gov. James T. Blair, Jr; Circuit Clerk of Madison Co. Mil. Serv: Army, scout for 5th Inf. Div, discharged 46 with cert. of disability from wounds received in action. Mem: Am. Legion; VFW; DAV. Rel: Sunday Sch. supt. and deacon, Baptist Church. Mailing Add: 604 Buford Blvd, Fredericktown, Mo. 63645. (1967)

BOLLINGER, GORDON EDWARD D
Mont. State Sen.
b. Piepot, Sask, Can, 7/6/15; s. Carl Bollinger and Magdalena Craig B; m. 7/15/37 to Marie A. Hanggi; c. Gordon Francis, Lt. David Carl and Renee A. Educ: Nashua High Sch, grad. Polit. & Govt. Pos: Mayor, Glasgow, Mont, 53; pres, Glasgow City Coun, 55; Mont. State Rep, Valley Co, until 67, mem. and sub-chmn, Legis. Coun, Mont. State House of Rep, 65 & 66; mem, City-Co. Airport Bd, 62-; Mont. State Sen, 69- Bus. & Prof. Pos: Mem, State Food Bd, Mont, 62-66, legis. chmn, 66. Mil. Serv: Yeoman, 3/C, Navy, 45; serv. in S.Pac. Mem: VFW; Am. Legion; Elks; past grand knight, K. of C; gov, Mont. Dist, Kiwanis Int, 63. Rel: Catholic. Mailing Add: 207 Klein Ave, Glasgow, Mont. 59230. (1967)

BOLTON, ANN D. R
b. Stamford, Conn, 4/4/30; d. Frank D'Elia and Paula Pepe D; m. 9/3/54 to James P. Bolton; c. Jamie Lynn and Keith Patrick. Educ: Merrill Bus. Sch, Stamford, Conn, 48-50. Polit. & Govt. Pos: Personal secy, U.S. Rep. Albert P. Morano, 52-58 and to U.S. Rep. Hastings Keith, 59; govt. liaison to U.S. Rep. Edward J. Derwinski, 60- Bus. & Prof. Pos: Legal secy, Moore & Epifanio, Attorneys at Law, 50-52. Mem: Congressional Secy. Club. Rel: Catholic. Legal Res: Stamford, Conn. Mailing Add: 6031 N. 22nd Rd, Arlington, Va. 22205.

BOLTON, ARTHUR KEY D
Attorney Gen, Ga.
b. Griffin, Ga, 5/14/22; s. Herbert Alfred Bolton and Eunice Maddox B; m. 9/30/46 to Marion Lee Cashen; c. Arthur Key, Jr. and Marian Lee. Educ: N.Ga. Col, 39-41; Univ. Ga. Law Sch, LL.B, 43; Univ. Ala. Law Sch; Phi Delta Phi. Polit. & Govt. Pos: Ga. State Rep, 49-65, chmn, Tax Equalization Cmt, 59-65, chmn, Spec. Judiciary Cmt, 61-62, mem, Constitutional Revision Cmt, 63-64, v.chmn, Rules Cmt. and Floor Leader, 63-65, Ga. House of Rep; c. adminstr, Spalding Co, 50-65; Judge, Criminal Court, Griffin, 52-65; Attorney Gen, Ga, 65- Bus. & Prof. Pos: Attorney-at-Law, 47- Mil. Serv: Entered as 2nd Lt, Army, 43, released as Capt, 46, after serv. in 97th Inf. Div, Mo, 43-44, 118th Inf. Regt, Eng, 44 and 36th Armored Inf. Regt, Third Armored Div, Germany, 44-45; ETO Ribbon with 3 Campaign Stars; Purple Heart; Silver Star; Combat Inf. Badge; Am. Defense Medal; Victory Medal. Mem: C. of C; Kiwanis; Elks; VFW; Am. Legion. Active Voters of Ga. Statesmanship Award; Man of the Year Award, Griffin, Ga, 62; Pub. Serv. Award, Ga. Munic. Asn, 65. Rel: Baptist. Legal Res: Griffin, Ga. 30223. Mailing Add: State Law Dept, 132 State Judicial Bldg, Atlanta, Ga. 30334.

BOLTON, EDGAR SIMPSON Constitution
Chmn, Constitution Party, La.
b. Waynesboro, Miss, 9/22/05; s. James Franklin Bolton and Mary Doby B; m. 2/11/45 to Jewell Lamar Roberts. Educ: High Sch. Polit. & Govt. Pos: Dir. of prog, Constitution Party, La, 65-66 and chmn, 66- Mailing Add: 5213 Blanks St, Monroe, La. 71201. (1967)

BOLTON, FRANCES P. R
b. Cleveland, Ohio, 3/29/85; d. Charles William Bingham and Mary Perry Payne B; m. to Chester C. Bolton, wid; c. Charles Bingham, Oliver Payne, Kenyon Castle and Elizabeth (deceased). Educ: Miss Spence's Sch. for Girls, N.Y; Alpha Iota; Beta Sigma Phi; Delta Kappa Gamma; Phi Delta Gamma; Theta Sigma Phi. Polit. & Govt. Pos: Former U.S. Rep, Ohio. Mem: Trustee, Lakeside Hosp, Cleveland, Lake Erie Col, Tuskegee Inst. and Meharry Med. Col; vice regent from Ohio, Mt. Vernon Ladies' Asn; League of Rep. Women; Soc. of Women Geographers; League of Women Voters; Women's Advert. Club; Women's Nat. Rep. Club; Am. Social Health Asn; Pen and Brush, Cosmopolitan, Bath and Tennis, Everglades, Sulgrave and Int. Clubs; City Tavern Asn; City Club of Cleveland. Rel: Presbyterian. Mailing Add: 2490 Lee Blvd, Cleveland Heights, Ohio 44118.

BOLTON, JAMES CARROLL R
b. Chicago, Ill, 7/8/12; s. Jarvis Arthur Bolton and Elizabeth Carroll B; m. 1942 to Jean Stevens Garlick; c. James C, Jr, David Murray. Educ: Univ. Ill, B.S, 35; Sigma Alpha Epsilon. Polit. & Govt. Pos: Admin. asst. to Rep. Davis, Wis, 65-; mem, President's Cmt. on Employ. Physically Handicapped; mem, President's Conf. Occupational Safety. Bus. & Prof. Pos: Br. mgr, Gen. Motors Acceptance Corp, 38-42; sales mgr, Pyle Chevrolet & Cadillac, 45-52; field dir, Wis. Mfrs. Asn, 52-65. Mil. Serv: Navy, 42-45, Lt. Comdr, Res, 45-55. Mem: Elks; ROA; Am. Legion. Hobbies: Hunting, trap shooting, fly fishing. Legal Res: Whitefish Bay, Wis. Mailing Add: 8513 Cyrus Place, Alexandria, Va. 22308.

BOLTON, LYNDOL D
Ala. State Rep.
b. Millerville, Ala, 1/27/32; s. James Wesley Bolton and Eva Monroe B; m. 5/26/56 to Dorothy Dale; c. Lynn Dale and William Lyndol. Educ: Jacksonville State Col, B.A; Univ. of Ala, LL.B. Polit. & Govt. Pos: Ala. State Rep, 62- Bus. & Prof. Pos: Lawyer. Mil. Serv: Navy. Mem: Mason; Shrine. Rel: Presbyterian. Mailing Add: Ogletree Bldg, Sylacauga, Ala. 35150.

BOLTON, OLIVER P. R
Rep. State Cent. Committeeman, 11th Dist, Ohio
b. Cleveland, Ohio, 2/22/17; s. Chester C. Bolton and Frances Payne Bingham B; m. 10/4/40 to Adelaide Brownlee; c. Charles P, Barbara and William B. Educ: Harvard Univ, A.B, 39; Western Reserve Univ. Law Sch, LL.B, 47; Phi Delta Phi; Delphic Club. Polit. & Govt. Pos: Chmn, Ohio League of Young Rep, 48-51; v.pres, Young Rep. Midwest Coun; nat. committeeman, Young Rep. Party, 51; U.S. Rep, 11th Dist, 52-56 & 62-64; Dir. of Commerce, Ohio, 57; Rep. state cent. committeeman, 11th Dist, 58-61 & 66- Bus. & Prof. Pos: V.pres, Payne-Bingham Co; publisher, pres. & dir, Lake Pub. Co, Tuscarawas Publishers, Inc. and A.B.C. News, Inc, 52-63; Limited partner, Prescott, Merrill, Turben & Co, Investment Bankers, 65- Mil. Serv: Entered as Pvt, 107th Cavalry, Ohio Nat. Guard, 39 and active serv, Army, 41, released as Maj, 46; after serv. in Asiatic-Pac. Area; Asiatic-Pac. Serv. Medal with Iwo Jima Campaign Star; Am. Defense Serv. Medal. Mem: Am. Legion; Mason (33°); Elks; Boy Scouts (pres, Northeast Ohio Coun, chmn, Region Four, mem, Nat. Exec. Bd); bd. of trustees, Lake Erie Col. and Kent State Univ. Rel: Protestant. Legal Res: 8021 S. Center St, Mentor, Ohio 44060. Mailing Add: 900 National City Bank Bldg, Cleveland, Ohio 44114.

BOLTON, RICHARD HALL R
Chmn, Richmond Co. Rep. Cmt, N.Y.
b. New Bedford, Mass, 12/19/23; s. Albert Edward Bolton and Charlotte Hall B; m. 9/6/47 to Helen Wigand; c. Richard H, Jr, Priscilla H. and Tenley A. Educ: Dartmouth Coll, B.A, 47; Phi Gamma Delta. Polit. & Govt. Pos: Pres, Young Rep. Club, Staten Island, N.Y, 54-55; second ward chmn, Richmond Co. Rep. Cmt, 56-60, v.chmn, 60-68, chmn, 68- Bus. & Prof. Pos: Advert. mgr, Great Atlantic & Pac. Tea Co, Ann Page Div, N.Y.C, 60- Mill Serv: Entered as A/S, Naval Res, 43, released as Ens, 46, after serv. as Commun. Officer, Pac. Theatre, 45-46. Mem: Richmond Co. Country Club. Rel: Episcopal. Mailing Add: 630 Victory Blvd, Staten Island, N.Y. 10301.

BOLTON, ROXCY O'NEAL D
Pres, Coral Gables Dem. Women's Club, Fla.
b. Miss, 6/3/26; d. William Bedford O'Neal and Lula L. Gordon O; m. 2/25/60 to David Bolton; c. Randy and Bonnie D. Polit. & Govt. Pos: Co-

chmn, Women's Div, Dade Co. Vols. for Stevenson, Fla, 56; dir. women's activities, Young Dem. Clubs Fla, 58-59, nat. committeewoman, 58; exec. asst, Dem. Senatorial Campaign Cmt, D.C, 60; alternate del, Dem. Nat. Conv, 64; state coordinator, Fla. Women's Activities for Johnson-Humphrey, 64; pres, Coral Gables Dem. Women's Club, 65- Mem: Woman's Nat. Dem. Club; United Daughters of Confederacy; staff aide and Grey Lady, Am. Red Cross. Woman Doer award in polit. leadership and responsibility, Coral Gables Dem. Women's Club, 65. Rel: Baptist. Legal Res: 1302 Alhambra Circle, Coral Gables, Fla. 33134. Mailing Add: P.O. Box 734, Coral Gables, Fla. 33134. (1967)

BOLTZ, RICHARD ALAN R
Chmn, Eighth Cong. Dist. Rep. Party, Wis.
b. Scholfield, Wis, 8/1/32; s. Frank A. Boltz and Victoria Kulick B; m. 7/4/59 to Ann Carlisle; c. Paul, Tom and John. Educ: Univ. Wis, B.S, 55, LL.B, 57; Gamma Eta Gamma. Polit. & Govt. Pos: Secy, Brown Co. Rep. Party, Wis, 59-63, chmn, 64-67; chmn, Eighth Cong. Dist. Rep. Party, 67-; alternate del, Rep. Nat. Conv, 68; mem, Wis. State Cmn. of Uniform State Laws, currently. Mem: State of Wis. Bar Asn; Brown Co. Bar Asn; Am. and Wis. Trial Lawyers Asns; Secy, Brown Co. Rep. Men's Club, 61-63, chmn, 63-64; Elks; Mason (32°), Shriner, Tripoli Temple; Izaak Walton League; mem. bd. dir, Red Cross, United Fund and Girl Scouts. Recipient Distinguished Serv. Award, Brown Co, 65. Rel: Protestant. Mailing Add: 2607 Oakwood Ave, Green Bay, Wis. 54301.

BOMAR, JAMES LA FAYETTE, JR. D
b. Bedford Co, Tenn, 7/1/14; s. James L. Bomar and Aetna Hix B; m. 6/27/40 to Edith Dees; c. James La Fayette, III and Louis Wayne. Educ: Cumberland Univ, A.B, 35, LL.B, 36. Polit. & Govt. Pos: Tenn. State Rep, 43-44, 49-50 & 53-63, speaker, Tenn. House of Rep, 53-63; Tenn. State Sen, 47-48 & 63-64, speaker, 63-64; Lt. Gov, Tenn, 63-65. Bus. & Prof. Pos: Mem. faculty, Castle Heights Mil. Acad, 35-40; law practice, Shelbyville, 40-69. Mil. Serv: Naval Res, Lt.(jg), 44-45. Mem: Fund raising chmn. in Tenn. for Am. Cancer Soc, 59-61, pres, 60-61; Fed, Am. and Tenn. Bar Asns; Int. Soc. of Barristers; Am. Legion; VFW; Tenn. Farm Bur; Tenn. Livestock Asn; Elks; Moose; Rotary (gov, Dist. 678, 69-70); bd. trustees, Cumberland Col, 65- Rel: Presbyterian; Elder. Mailing Add: Route 5, Shelbyville, Tenn. 37160.

BOND, CHRISTOPHER S. 'KIT' R
Asst. Attorney Gen, Mo.
b. St. Louis, Mo, 3/6/39; s. Arthur Doerr Bond and Elizabeth Green B; m. 5/13/67 to Carolyn Ann Reid. Educ: Princeton Univ, cum laude, 60; Univ. Va. Law Sch, LL.B, 63; Omicron Delta Kappa; Cottage Club; Order of Coif. Polit. & Govt. Pos: Law clerk, Fifth U.S. Circuit Court of Appeals, Ga, 63-64; Rep. nominee, U.S. Rep, Mo, 68; Asst. Attorney Gen, 69- Bus. & Prof. Pos: Attorney, Covington & Burling, Wash. D.C, 65-67; attorney, Mexico, Mo, 67- Mem: Bar of Mo; Bar of the U.S. Supreme Court; Jaycees; Optimists Club; bd. dirs, Audrain Cerebral Palsy Sch. Most Outstanding Graduating Student, Univ. Va. Law Sch, 63. Rel: Presbyterian. Legal Res: 1515 Kentucky Rd, Mexico, Mo. 65265. Mailing Add: P.O. Box 472, Mexico, Mo. 65265.

BOND, (HORACE) JULIAN D
Ga. State Rep.
b. Nashville, Tenn, 1/14/40; s. Dr. Horace Mann Bond and Julian Washington B; m. June, 1961 to Alice L. Clopton; c. Horace Mann, II, Phyllis Jane, Michael Julian and Jeffrey Alvin. Educ: Morehouse Col, Atlanta, Ga, completed $3\frac{1}{2}$ years. Polit. & Govt. Pos: Dem. v.chmn. precinct, City of Atlanta, Ga; Ga. State Rep, 67- Bus. & Prof. Pos: Mem. bd, Student Voice, Inc. and South. Educ. & Research Assocs, currently. Publ: Poetry in 5 anthologies, 2 languages besides English. Mem: Mem. bd, South. Conf. Educ. Fund, Inc, Robert Kennedy Mem. Fund, Martin Luther King, Jr. Mem. Center and Highlander Research & Educ. Center. Mailing Add: 162 Euharlee St. S.W, Atlanta, Ga. 30314.

BOND, L. JEAN R
Mem, Ind. State Rep. Cent, Cmt.
b. Portland, Ind, 11/6/06; d. David M. Baker and Lena Burkett B; m. 5/23/42 to Clayton Bond. Educ: DePauw Univ, A.B, 29; Univ. Colo, grad. study, 32; Miami Univ, grad. study, 48-54; Alpha Gamma Delta. Polit. & Govt. Pos: V.chmn, Ind. Tenth Dist. Rep. Party, 6 terms and Union Co. Rep. Party, Ind, 3 terms; mem, Ind. State Rep. Cent. Cmt, 56-; clerk, Supreme and Appellate Courts, State of Ind, 63-67. Mem: Kappa Delta Phi; Eastern Star. Rel: Protestant. Mailing Add: 209 E. Union, Liberty, Ind. 47353.

BOND, ROBERT H. D
Mayor, Pleasant Hill, Ohio
b. Owenton, Ky, 1/9/06; s. Robert C. Bond and Nina Glass B; m. 12/23/33 to Helen Landis; c. Barbara (Mrs. Finfrock) and Janet (Mrs. Hiser). Educ: Univ. Ky, B.A. Polit. & Govt. Pos: Dem. chmn. and mem, bd. of elec, Miami Co, Ohio, 60-64; del, Dem. Nat. Conv, 64; precinct committeeman, Miami Co. Dem. Party, Ohio, 56-; Mayor, Pleasant Hill, 68- Bus. & Prof. Pos: Fed. Govt, 35-42; operator, Soft Drink Bottling Co, 46-49; claims examiner, Ohio, 49-56; operator, Gen. Ins. Agency, 56-; ed. writer and broadcaster, WPTW Radio, Piqua, Ohio, 64- Mil. Serv: Entered as Lt.(jg), Navy, 43, released as Lt, 46, Lt. Comdr.(Ret), Naval Res. Mem: F&AM; Am. Legion; 40 et 8. Rel: Christian Church. Legal Res: 106 S. Church St, Pleasant Hill, Ohio 45359. Mailing Add: Box 314, Pleasant Hill, Ohio 45359.

BONDI, GENE L. D
State Committeeman, Wyo. Dem. Party
b. Acme, Wyo, 5/20/13; s. Bert Bondi and Mary Realon B; m. 2/1/41 to Elizabeth Poynter; c. Bert Roger and Harry Gene. Educ: Sheridan Co. High Sch, grad. Polit. & Govt. Pos: Dem. precinct committeeman, Dist. 3, Ward 3, Sheridan Co, Wyo, 56-; state committeeman, Wyo. Dem. Party, Sheridan Co, 60-; mem. finance cmt. and exec. cmt, Dem. State Cent. Cmt, 62-; alternate del, Dem. Nat. Conv, 68. Mem: Elks; Eagles; K. of C; Kiwanis; Sheridan Co. C. of C.(mem. agr. cmt, 62-68, auditing cmt, 69-); Wyo-Colo. Oil Jobbers. Rel: Catholic. Legal Res: 320 Sherman Ave, Sheridan, Wyo. 82801. Mailing Add: P.O. Box 383, Sheridan, Wyo. 82801.

BONDS, ROBERT ALEXANDER, JR. D
b. Holly Springs, Miss, 3/22/20; s. Robert Alexander Bonds and Anne Hastings B; m. 8/29/48 to Virginia McCoy; c. Robert A, III and William Dow. Educ: Univ. of Miss, B.A. in Bus. Admin, 47 and LL.B, 49; Phi Eta Sigma; Omicron Delta Kappa; Delta Sigma Pi; Delta Kappa Epsilon. Polit. & Govt. Pos: Co. Judge, Adams Co, Miss, 55- Mil. Serv: Entered as Seaman, Navy, 41, released as Aviation Radioman, 43. Mem: Miss. State and Adams Co. Bar Asns; Kiwanis Int. Rel: Baptist. Legal Res: 27 Oakhurst Dr, Natchez, Miss. 39120. Mailing Add: P.O. Box 1371, Natchez, Miss. 39120.

BONDSHU, ROBERT EUGENE R
Chmn, Mariposa Co. Rep. Cent. Cmt, Calif.
b. Chico, Calif. 5/28/29; s. Harold H. Bondshu and Anita B; m. 8/21/56 to Rachel Ann Dunnington; c. William Harold, Coby Ann, Frank Albert and Krista Sue. Educ: Col. of the Pac, A.A, 50; Omega Phi Alpha. Polit. & Govt. Pos: Secy-treas. co. cmt, Mariposa Co. Rep. Cent. Cmt, 58-62; chmn, Mariposa Co. Rep. Cent. Cmt, Exec. Cmt. and Rep. State Cmt, 62- Mil. Serv: Entered as Pvt, Air Force, 50, released as 1st Lt, 56, after serv. in Air Training Command and Cadet Pilot Training Prog, Strategic Air Command, duty in Alaska, Japan and Korea. Mem: Independent Ins. Agents Asn; Lions; VFW; Air Force Asn; chief, Volunteer Fire Dept, Mariposa; Nat. Left Handed Golfers Asn. Rel: Methodist. Mailing Add: Box 808, Mariposa, Calif. 95338.

BONDURANT, JAMES E. D
b. 1929. Educ: Univ. Ky, A.B, LL.B. Polit. & Govt. Pos: City attorney, Hodgenville, Ky, 63; former Ky. State Rep. Bus. & Prof. Pos: Attorney-at-law. Mil. Serv: Naval Res, 52-58. Mem: Jr. C. of C; Ky. Bar Asn; past pres, Elizabethtown Club. Rel: Methodist; v.chmn. of bd, Methodist Church. Mailing Add: Hamilton Heights Ave, Hodgenville, Ky. 42748. (1967)

BONDURANT, KEITH P.
b. Great Bend, Kans, 6/3/14; m. 1940 to Jane Fox; c. Ann (Mrs. Carroll), William, Helen. Educ: Col. of Emporia, A.B, 35, cum laude; Univ. of Mich. Law Sch, 38, J.D. Polit. & Govt. Pos: Mo. State Sen, 62-65 (resigned). Bus. & Prof. Pos: Lawyer, admitted to Ill. Bar, 38, Tenn. Bar, 46, Mo. Bar, 47. Mil. Serv: USN, 42-46, Lt. Comdr, S. Pac. Theater. Mem: Am. Bar Asn; Mo. Bar Asn; Lawyer's Asn. of Kans. City; Dir. and Former Pres, Naturalization Coun. of Gr. Kans. City; Chancery Club; Carriage Club; Trustee, St. Luke's Hosp; Mil. Order of World Wars. Rel: Episcopal; Vestryman, St. Paul's Episcopal Church. Mailing Add: 1249 Stratford Rd, Kansas City, Mo. 64113. (1967)

BONENFANT, GERALD LEO D
b. Central Falls, R.I, 4/23/23. Educ: Sacred Heart Acad. Polit. & Gov. Pos: R.I. State Rep, 57-66; City Coun, 4 yrs. Bus. & Prof. Pos: Driver-salesman. Mil. Serv: W.W. II, Korean War. Mem: K. of C, No. 2700, Sullivan Coun; Am. Legion Post No. 75; St. Jean Baptiste Soc. of Am. Rel: Catholic. Mailing Add: 15 Chestnut St, Central Falls, R.I. 02863. (1967)

BONETTO, JOSEPH F. D
b. Allegheny Co, Pa, 4/20/21; s. Frank Bonetto and Maria Franco B; m. to Helene Kropelak; c. four. Educ: Turtle Creek High Sch. Polit. & Govt. Pos: Pa. State Rep, 64-68; chmn. bd, Plum Borough Munic. Authority; Dem. chmn, Plum Borough, 17 years. Bus. & Prof. Pos: Equip. supvr. Mil. Serv: Army, T/Sgt, topographical engr; S.Pac. Theater. Mem: United Mine Workers of Am. Mailing Add: 1115 Keith Dr, Renton, Pa. 15239. (1967)

BONEY, GEORGE FRANK R
Assoc. Justice, Alaska Supreme Court
b. Savannah, Ga, 7/3/30; s. Clark Howell Boney and Evelyn Anderson B; m. 2/21/55 to Sarah Estelle Boozer; c. Catherine Lynn, George Frank, Jr. and Angela Carol. Educ: Univ. Ga, A.B, 51; Harvard Univ. Law Sch, LL.B, 54; Phi Beta Kappa; Phi Kappa Phi, Phi Eta Sigma; Kappa Sigma; Chancery Club. Polit. & Govt. Pos: Asst. U.S. Attorney, Anchorage, Alaska, 58-59; law mem, Alaska Judicial Coun, 65-68; gen. counsel, Rep. Party, Alaska, 66-68; mem, Gov. Hickel's Adv. Cmt. to Attorney Gen, 67-68; chmn. S.Cent. Dist. Cmt, Rep. Party Alaska, 68; mem, Alaska State Rep. Cent. Cmt. 68; assoc. justice, Alaska Supreme Court, 68- Bus. & Prof. Pos: Partner law firm, Burr, Boney & Pease, Anchorage, 59-68; pres. and dir, Marine, Inc, 62-; v.pres. and dir. Sixth K Corp, 63-; dir, Grocers Wholesale, Inc, 66-68. Mil. Serv: Entered as 2nd Lt, Air Force, 54, released as 1st Lt, 58, after serv. in Air Univ, Air Command and Staff Col, Air Training Command, Lackland Air Force Base and Alaskan Command, Elmendorf Air Force Base, 54-58; Res, 58-67, Maj. Publ: 'Tax Consequences of Marital Dissolution,' 12/66 and 'Plea of Guilty and Plea of Nolo Contendere,' 3/67, Alaska Law J. Mem: Am, Fed, Alaska, Anchorage and Fla. Bar Asns; Am. Trial Lawyers Asn; Alaska Acad. Trial Lawyers; Mason; Scottish Rite; Shrine. Rel: Methodist. Legal Res: 1707 Sunrise Dr, Anchorage, Alaska 99504. Mailing Add: Alaska Supreme Court, 941 Fourth Ave, Anchorage, Alaska 99501.

BONGARTZ, FERDINAND A. R
Chmn, Bennington Co. Rep. Party, Vt.
b. Orange, N.J, 11/5/23; s. Ferdinand A. Bongartz and Laura Pressler B; m. 7/20/48 to Joan Bowen; c. Dulce, Lauren, Seth, Jennifer and Melissa. Educ: Pa. State Univ, 43-44; Susquehanna Univ, B.S, 47; Phi Mu Delta. Polit. & Govt. Pos: Mem, Manchester Town Rep. Cmt, Vt, 58-; selectman, Town of Manchester, 63-69, chmn. bd, 65 & 68; mem, Vt. Rep. State Cmt, 65-; chmn, Bennington Co. Rep. Party, Vt, 65-; mem, Sch. Bd, Manchester, 69- Bus. & Prof. Pos: Owner and operator, Manchester Woodcraft, Manchester Center, Vt, 50- Mil. Serv: Entered as A/S (V-12), Navy, 42, released as Lt.(jg), 46, after serv. in U.S. Foss, Destroyer Escort 59, Atlantic Destroyer Fleet, 44-46. Mem: Boy Scouts. Silver Beaver Award, Ethan Allen Coun, Boy Scouts. Rel: Congregational. Legal Res: Manchester, Vt. 05255. Mailing Add: Manchester Center, Vt. 05255.

BONILLA, TONY Independent
b. Calvert, Tex, 3/2/36; s. Ruben Bonilla (deceased) and Maria Ramirez B; m. 6/18/60 to Olga Garcia; c. Tony, Jr, John Edward, Maria Teresa and Anna Patricia. Educ: Del Mar Col, A.A, 55; Baylor Univ, B.A. in Educ, 58; Univ. Houston, LL.B, 60; Delta Theta Phi. Polit. & Govt. Pos: S.Tex. chmn, Viva Kennedy Group, 60; state organizer, Polit. Asn. Spanish-Speaking orgns, 61-

62; Tex. State Rep, 64-67, auth, Harrison-Bonilla and Bernal-Bonilla Bills, Tex. State House of Rep; mem, Charter Amendment Adv. Cmt, Corpus Christi; founder, Human Rels. Cmn, Crime Cmn. and Teenage Workers Orgn. and Cmt. for Youth Develop, Commun. Action Prog; southwest coordinator, United Citizens for Nixon-Agnew, 68. Bus. & Prof. Pos: Sr. mem, Bonilla, De Pena, Read & Bonilla, Attorneys. Mem: State Bar Tex; Am. and Nueces Co. Bar Asns; Am. Judicature Soc; Nueces Co. Jr. Bar Asn. (past v.pres); Corpus Christi Arts Coun; Boys Club Am; Boys City, Goodwill Indust; C. of C. (cmt. on higher educ, sports cmt, good neighbor cmn. and indust. cmt); League United Latin Am. Citizens (past dir, exec. secy, Dist. II); Del Mar Col. Ex-Students Asn. (past pres, co-chmn, Inter Racial Coun, currently); pres, United Married Couples Club. Rel: Catholic. Legal Res: 327 Baycliff, Corpus Christi, Tex. 78412. Mailing Add: 2590 Morgan, Corpus Christi, Tex. 78405.

BONILLA, WILLIAM DAVID D
b. Calvert, Tex, 8/6/30; s. Ruben Bonilla and Maria Ramirez B; m. 3/10/50 to Evelyn O. Richey; c. Mary Helen, William David, Jr, Elizabeth, Jonathan and Martha S. Educ: Baylor Univ, B.A, 51; Tex. Univ. Sch. of Law, LL.B, 53. Polit. & Govt. Pos: Mem, Nat. Adv. Coun. to Off. of Econ. Opportunity, 66-; del, Tex. Dem. Conv, 66 and Dem. Nat. Conv, 64; mem, Tex. Good Neighbor Cmn, 62; pres, Nueces Co. Young Dems, 55-56. Mil. Serv: Nat. Guard, 47-53. Mem: Am. and Tex. Bar Asns; past mem, bd. dirs, Nueces Co. Bar Asn; Tex. Trial Lawyers Asn; bd. mem, Local Commun. Action Prog. and Corpus Christi Human Rels. Cmn; v.pres, Pan Am. Golf Asn. of Tex; immediate past nat. pres, League of United Latin Am. Citizens; past pres, L'Avenir Club and Mexican C. of C. Articles published in Tex. Law Rev. Rel: Catholic. Legal Res: 5449 Ocean, Corpus Christi, Tex. 78411. Mailing Add: Box 907, Corpus Christi, Tex. 78412. (1967)

BONIN, GARLAND L. D
Cmnr. of Welfare, La.
b. St. Martinville, La, 4/2/12; s. Luke Bonin and Blanche Durand B; m. 6/13/36 to Aline Lallande; c. Yvette (Mrs. Hargett). Educ: Univ. Southwest. La, 33; Tau Sigma Delta; Inter-Fraternity Coun. Polit. & Govt. Pos: Mem. sch. bd, Lafayette Parish, La, 50-62; La. State Sen, 62-65; Cmnr. of Welfare, La, 65- Rel: Catholic. Mailing Add: 143 Parduton, Lafayette, La. 70501.

BONITT, EDWARD JOHN D
b. Woodbine, N.J, 9/1/18; s. John Bonitt and Anne Dickey B; m. 1/10/48 to Sara Ann McIntire; c. Jay E, Jeffrey J. and Murray M. Educ: Woodbine High Sch, grad. Polit. & Govt. Pos: Dem. nominee, U.S. House Rep, Mo, 68. Bus. & Prof. Pos: Union rep, Amalgamated Clothing Workers of Am, 38-; pres, S.W. Mo. Cmt. on Polit. Educ, 66-; pres, S.W. Mo. Labor Coun, 68- Mil. Serv: Entered as Pvt, Army, 42, released as 2nd Lt, 45, after serv. in 324th Inf. Regt, 44th Div, ETO, 44-45; Purple Heart; Bronze Star; Battlefield Cmn. Mem: Gen. Adv. Cmt. for Voc. & Tech. Educ. Progs, Mo. South. Col; VFW; Am. Legion; K. of C. Rel: Roman Catholic. Mailing Add: 220 W. 45th St, Joplin, Mo. 64801.

BONN, BERNARD J, SR. D
b. 1894. Polit. & Govt. Pos: Ky. State Rep, 46-48; Ky. State Sen, 48-53 & 56-68; former chmn, 43rd Legis. Dist. Dem. Party; former dep. co. clerk; former supt. construction, Park Bd; former housing mgr; former mem, Munic. Housing Cmn; former sr. architect, Bur. Valuation, Wash, D.C. Bus. & Prof. Pos: Retired caterer. Mem: K. of C; Mose Green Dem. Club; Holy Name Soc. Rel: Catholic. Mailing Add: 110 Valley Rd, Louisville, Ky. 40204. (1967)

BONNER, DONALD R. R
R.I. State Rep.
b. Westerly, R.I, 1/6/13. Educ: Univ. of R.I, 35. Polit. & Govt. Pos: Past chmn, Westerly Rep. Town Cmt, R.I; mem, Rep. State Cent. Cmt; mem, Zoning Bd; mem, Westerly Sch. Cmt; mem, L.I. Bridge Study Cmn; R.I. State Rep, 63-; mem, Legis. Cmn. on Libr; alternate del, Rep. Nat. Conv, 68. Bus. & Prof. Pos: Granite Mfr. Mil. Serv: Navy, Lt, 42-46, ETO and Pac. Theatre. Mem: Westerly Lions Club; Past Comdr, Narragansett Commandery Number 27, K.T. Mailing Add: P.O. Box 407, Avondale, R.I. 02891. (1967)

BONNER, MERLINE D
b. Bentley, Okla, 1/25/24; d. Jefferson David Case and Lizzie Hill C; m. 8/5/47 to Jerry J. Bonner; c. Frances, Jerry, Robert and Charles. Educ: Okla. Col. for Women, B.A, 44; Univ. Iowa, M.A, 45; Univ. Okla, LL.B, 64; Zeta Phi Eta. Polit. & Govt. Pos: Chmn, Atoka Co. Dem. Party, Okla, 67-69. Mem: Atoka Co. Bar Asn.(secy, 67-68); Okla. Bar Asn. Rel: Christian Science. Legal Res: 11th & Choctaw, Atoka, Okla. 74525. Mailing Add: Box 8, Atoka, Okla. 74525.

BONNEY, EDWARD MAYSON D
Exec. Secy, Maine Dem. State Cmt.
b. Buckfield, Maine, 4/5/33; s. Mayson Turner Bonney and Beatrice Dean B; m. 9/21/57 to Betty Joyce Smith; c. Kerry David, Edward Mayson, Jr. and Brian Everett. Educ: Emerson Col, ½ year; Austin Col, ½ year. Polit. & Govt. Pos: Chmn, Freeport, Maine Dem. Town Cmt, 63-66; mem. and chmn, Freeport Sch. Cmt, 64-67; chmn, Cumberland Co. Dem. Cmt, 66-67; exec. secy, Maine Dem. State Cmt, 67- Bus. & Prof. Pos: Asst. air traffic controller, Fed. Aviation Agency, N.Y.C, 57-59; dept. mgr, W.T. Grant Co, Portland, Maine, 59-67. Mil. Serv: Entered as Airman, Air Force, 52, released as Airman 1/C, 56, after serv. in 3555th Troop Combat Crew Training Wing, Air Training Command, 54-56; Nat. Defense Serv. Medal; Good Conduct Medal. Mem: Elks. Rel: Protestant. Mailing Add: 4 Nathan Nye St, Freeport, Maine 04032.

BONSELL, WILLIAM RICHARD R
Minority Doorkeeper, U.S. House of Rep.
b. Huntington, Pa, 10/1/18; s. Carl Scott Bonsell and Ruth Prindle B; m. 11/10/62 to Katie Rosenthal; c. William Dailey, Susan Lynn, Thomas Alexander and Mark Joseph. Educ: Juniata Col, B.S, 41; Thompson Bus. Col. Polit. & Govt. Pos: Asst. bill clerk, U.S. House of Rep, 47-49; exec. asst. auditor gen, Pa, 50-51; prfnl. staff mem, Senate Cmt. on Appropriations, 51-52; Sgt. at Arms, U.S. House of Rep, 52-54, Minority doorkeeper, 54- Mil. Serv: Entered as Pvt, Army, 41, released as S/Sgt, 45; Presidential Unit Citation. Mem: Am. Legion; Mason. Legal Res: Huntington, Pa. 18622. Mailing Add: 4213 Kingsmill Lane, Annandale, Va. 22003. (1967)

BONTEMPO, SALVATORE D
Chmn, N.J. Dem. Party
Mailing Add: 31-33 N. Willow St, Trenton, N.J. 08608.

BOOKER, EDWARD HAMILTON D
La. State Rep.
b. Lake Charles, La, 12/22/38; s. H.H. Booker, Jr. and Margaret Elisabeth Donohue B; m. 6/20/69 to Luce Marie Robert Lutgen. Educ: Loyola Univ, New Orleans, La, B.A; Tulane Univ, J.D; Alpha Delta Gamma; Phi Delta Phi. Polit. & Govt. Pos: La. State Rep, 68- Mem: La. State and Criminal Courts Bar Asns; Jr. C. of C; Young Democrats. Rel: Roman Catholic. Mailing Add: 2833 General Pershing, New Orleans, La. 70115.

BOOKHAMMER, EUGENE DONALD R
Lt. Gov, Del.
b. Lewes, Del, 6/14/18; s. William H. Bookhammer and Winifred H. Jenkins B; m. 1/31/42 to Katherine Williams; c. Joy and Jean. Educ: Lewes High Sch, 36; Am. Tech. Soc, 38. Polit. & Govt. Pos: Del, Rep. Nat. Conv, 52, 56 & 60; Del. State Sen, 62-68; chmn, Sussex Co. Rep. Party, Del, 64-66; Lt. Gov, 69- Bus. & Prof. Pos: Owner, Bookhammer Lumber Mills, 40-, Joy Beach Develop. Co, 50-; pres, Rehoboth Bay Dredging Co, currently. Mil. Serv: Entered as Pvt, Army, 43, released as M/Sgt, 46, after serv. in 1st, 3rd and 9th Army, ETO, 44-46; Purple Heart; 5 Campaign Ribbons. Mem: Am. Banking Inst; bd. dirs, Beebe Hosp; dir, Farmers Bank, State of Del; Am. Legion; C. of C; Tall Cedars of Lebanon; VFW; life mem, Boy Scouts; Mason (32°); Lions; AF&AM; Shrine. Rel: Protestant. Legal Res: R.D, Lewes, Del. 19958. Mailing Add: Legislative Hall, Dover, Del. 19901.

BOOKSON, PAUL P. E. D
N.Y. State Sen.
b. New York, N.Y, 1/25/33; s. Leo Bookson and Anna B; m. to Tova Heller; c. Bryna, Rochel and Shoshana. Educ: L.I. Univ, B.A; Fordham Univ. Sch. of Law, honor student, LL.B; N.Y. Univ. Grad. Sch. in Pub. Admin; N.Y. Univ. Grad. Law Sch. Polit. & Govt. Pos: Mem, Local Sch. Bd, Dist. Two, N.Y; asst. departmental dir. of admin, First Dept, Judicial Conf; N.Y. State Sen, 64- Bus. & Prof. Pos: Attorney-at-law; past secy, Inter-Prfnl. Cmt. of Physicians and Lawyers. Mem: Asn. of Bar of City of New York; Am. Bar Asn; N.Y. Co. Lawyers Asn; Asn. of Lawyers of Criminal Courts of Manhattan; mem-at-lg, Boy Scouts; Fordham Law Sch. Alumni Asn; B'nai B'rith, Warsaw Ghetto Resistance Orgn; v.pres, Young Israel Synagogue of Manhattan; admitted to practice N.Y. State, U.S. Dist. Courts, South. and East. Dist. of N.Y, U.S. Court of Appeals, Second Circuit and U.S. Supreme Court. Mailing Add: 215 Park Row, New York, N.Y. 10038. (1967)

BOONE, ALEXANDER GORDON, JR. D
Mem: Md. Dem. State Cent. Cmt.
b. Baltimore, Md, 8/21/33; s. A. Gordon Boone and Edith Marion Flint B; m. 12/8/56 to Sylvia Jane Hayes; c. A. Gordon, III, Anne Gordon Herbert and John Rawlings Marshall. Educ: Univ. Md, 56-60; Univ. Baltimore, LL.B, 63; Phi Kappa Sigma. Polit. & Govt. Pos: Pres, Univ. Baltimore Young Dem, 62-63; exec. secy, Nat. Legis. Leaders Conf, 63; pres, Baltimore Co. Young Dem, Md, 66-67; nat. committeeman, Md. Young Dem, 66-67; mem, Md. Dem. State Cent. Cmt, 66-; del, Dem. Nat. Conv, 68. Mil. Serv: Entered as Airman 1/C, Air Force, 53, released as S/Sgt, 56, after serv. in Air Defense Command, Far East. Mem: Md. and Am. Bar Asns; Am. Judicature Soc; Jr. C. of C; Elks. Rel: Roman Catholic. Legal Res: Oak Hill House, Bellona Ave, Baltimore, Md. 21212. Mailing Add: 11 W. Pennsylvania Ave, Towson, Md. 21204.

BOOS, WM. A. JR. D
b. Detroit, Mich, 9/27/22; married; c. Mary Ellen, Charles. Educ: Mich. State Univ, A.B, 47; Detroit Col. of Law, LL.B, 51. Polit. & Govt. Pos: Mich. State Rep, 60-66; Asst. city attorney, housing comnr, mem. Bd. of supv. Bus. & Prof. Pos: Attorney. Mil. Serv: WW II, Pac. Theatre. Mem: Am. Legion Post 22; VFW; Optimist Club; Mich. State Bar Asn. Rel: Congregationalist. Mailing Add: 6 Holland Court, Saginaw, Mich. 48601. (1967)

BOOT, ARMOUR D
b. Jasper Co, Iowa, 7/9/03; s. William Boot and Alice Rietveld B; m. 12/24/29 to Susie Zwank; c. Nola (Mrs. Lloyd Vander Streek). Educ: Rural Schs. Polit. Pos: Iowa State Rep-66; Pella City Coun. Bus. & Prof. Pos: Past Farm Operator; Assoc. with Implement Bus. 17 Years and other Bus. Enterprises. Rel: Reformed Church in America. Mailing Add: 1321 Broadway St, Pella, Iowa. 50219.

BOOTH, CHARLES ROCKWELL 'ROCKY' R
Mem, Calif. Rep. State Cent. Cmt.
b. Beverly Hills, Calif, 1/3/47; s. Charles Gorden Booth and Lillian Lind Booth Foley; m. 8/23/69 to Carolyn Kelly. Educ: Univ. Calif, San Diego, 4 years. Polit. & Govt. Pos: Pres. and founder, Young Rep, Univ. Calif, San Diego, 67-68; chaplin, Calif. Young Rep. Col. Fedn, 67-68, treas, 68-69; assoc. mem, Calif. Rep. State Cent. Cmt, 67-69, mem, 69-; campaign mgr, Bill Ayers, 77th Assembly Dist, 68. Bus. & Prof. Pos: Eng. aide, Scripps Inst. of Oceanography. Publ: 'The Measurement of Adenosine Triphosphate in the Ocean and Its Ecological Significance,' Limnology & Oceanography, 10/66. Rel: Protestant. Mailing Add: 2124 Garnet Ave, Apt. A, San Diego, Calif. 92109.

BOOTH, JOHN THOMAS D
Chmn, Carroll Co. Dem. Exec. Cmt, Ky.
b. Carrollton, Ky, 1/3/14; s. Patrick J. Booth and Mollie Dempsey B; m. to Marilyn Bryant; c. John Thomas, II. Educ: Carrollton High Sch, grad, 33. Polit. & Govt. Pos: Chmn, Carroll Co. Dem. Exec. Cmt, Ky, currently. Bus. & Prof. Pos: Sales mgr, OK Supply Co, 45-60. Mil. Serv: Entered as Pvt, Army, 42, released as Cpl, 45, after serv. as 677th Mil. Policeman, ETO; Europe-Africa-Middle East Theater Ribbon with four Bronze Stars; Good Conduct Ribbon; Distinguished Unit Citation. Mem: Former mem, Am. Legion; Moose; bd. dirs, Kiwanis. Rel: Baptist. Mailing Add: 1009 Seventh St, Carrollton, Ky. 41008. (1967)

BOOTH, MARY BENSON R
Secy-Treas, Eagle Co. Rep. Cent. Cmt, Colo.
b. Bryn Mawr, Pa, 6/19/40; d. Richard Benson and Mary Pew B; m. 4/10/65

to Frederick Roberts; c. Frederick Benson. Educ: Univ. Colo, Boulder, degree, 62; Cosmopolotin Club. Polit. & Govt. Pos: Del, Colo. State Rep. Conv, 64, alternate del, 68; secy-treas, Eagle Co. Rep. Cent. Cmt, 69- Mem: Farm Bur. Rel: Episcopal. Legal Res: Star Route, P.O. Box 215, Gypsum, Colo. 81637. Mailing Add: Gypsum Creek Ranch, Gypsum, Colo. 81637.

BOOTH, WALLACE GORDON D
b. Newbury, Vt, 9/13/03; m. to Beatrice Pacquet; c. Three sons: three daughters. Educ: Barre City High Sch. Polit. & Govt. Pos: Selectman, 42-48 & 58-64; Vt. State Rep, 63-65; v.pres, Barre Area Develop. Corp. Bus. & Prof. Pos: Farmer. Mil. Serv: Nat. Guard, 43rd Div, 22-25. Rel: Catholic. Mailing Add: RFD 3, Allen St, South Barre, Vt. 05670.

BOOTHE, ARMISTEAD LLOYD D
b. Alexandria, Va, 9/23/07; s. Gardner Lloyd Boothe and Eleanor Harrison Carr B; m. 6/30/34 to Elizabeth Ravenel Peelle; c. Julie Ravenel (Mrs. Charles S. Perry), Eleanor Harrison (Mrs. John M. Smith) and Elizabeth Armistead (Mrs. Lee F. Davis, Jr). Educ: Univ. Va, A.B, 28; Oxford Univ, B.A. in jurisprudence, 31, M.A, 46; Phi Beta Kappa; Beta Theta Pi. Polit. Pos: Chmn, 10th Dist. Dem. Cmt, 60-66; chmn, Alexandria City Dem. Cmt, 36-48. Govt. Pos: Va. State Sen, 56-64; Va. State Del, 48-56; city attorney, Alexandria, Va, 38-43. Mil. Serv: Entered as Lt.(jg), Naval Res, 43, released as Lt, after serv. in Carrier Air Groups 2 and 96, Pac, 3rd and 5th Fleets, 44-45; Commendation Ribbon with Combat Device; Presidential Citation U.S.S. Hornet. Publn: 'Civil Rights in Virginia,' Va. Law Review, 11/49. Mem: Pres, Alexandria Bar Asn, 51; State and Am. Bar Asns; Col. Trial Lawyers; Am. Bar Found; Lions; Eagles; VFW; Am. Legion. Rel: Episcopal. Mailing Add: 711 Princess, Alexandria, Va. 22314. (1967)

BOPP, LEONARD A. D
b. Sargent Co, N.Dak, 1901; m. to Ethel Randol; c. 5. Educ: State Sch. of Sci. Polit. & Govt. Pos: Soil conserv. dir, Fed. Wild Rice Dist, 49-69; N.Dak. State Rep, 59-61; N.Dak. State Sen, 61-66; mem, Dem. Adv. Bur, Bismarck, N.Dak, 65-69; co. cmnr, Sargent Co-Forman, 68-69; mem, Local and Co. Bds. Bus. & Prof. Pos: Farmer; teacher. Distinguished Serv. Award for Meritorious Serv. to the Commun, 69. Rel: Catholic. Mailing Add: Cogswell, N.Dak. 58017.

BORAH, DAN V. R
Chmn, Richland Co. Rep. Cmt, Ill.
b. Olney, Ill, 10/8/22; s. O.C. Borah and Margaret Vernor B; m. 9/9/44 to Betty Glover; c. Dan, Jr, James E, Kathryn E, Julie Y, Sally J. and Chris R. Educ: Univ. Ill, 2 years. Polit. & Govt. Pos: Precinct committeeman, Rep. Party, Ill; chmn, Richland Co. Rep. Cmt, 66- Bus. & Prof. Pos: Pres, Borah & Bolunder, Inc, 56-; dir, Olney Trust & Banking Co, 60-; v.pres, Olney Homes, Inc, 61- Mem: Rotary; Elks. Rel: Methodist. Legal Add: 31 Willow Dr, Olney, Ill. 62450. Mailing Add: Box 267, Olney, Ill. 62450.

BORCHERS, ALBERT WEBBER R
Ill. State Rep.
b. Decatur, Ill, 7/1/06; s. Charles Martin Borchers and Alice Bowman B; m. Margaret Stevens (deceased); c. Margret (Mrs. Dean Cuttill) and Elizabeth (Mrs. Herbert Hawkins). Educ: Univ. Ill, B.A, 31; Sigma Delta Kappa; Alpha Phi Omega; Cavalry Club. Polit. & Govt. Pos: Asst. Supvr, Macon Co. Bd. Supvrs, Ill, 12 years; Ill. State Rep, 69- Bus. & Prof. Pos: Pres, Bath Inc, Decatur, 35-59; chmn. bd, 59- Mil. Serv: Entered as Pvt, Army, 25, released as Cavalry Sgt, 46, after serv. in 80th Inf. Div. Cavalry Regt, ETO, 44-45; Four Battle Stars; Purple Heart; Liberation of France Cruix dé Guere with Palm; Good Conduct, European Theatre, Victory, Pearl Harbor, Occup. of Germany and Reserve Serv. Medals; European and Am. Theater Ribbons. Mem: VFW; Macon Co. Regional Planning Cmn; Decatur and Macon Co. Hist. Cmt. Rel: Protestant. Mailing Add: 695 S. Crea, Decatur, Ill. 62522.

BORCHERS, DONALD EARL R
City Councilman, Berlin, N.H.
b. Scranton, Pa, 10/4/20; s. Ulrich W. Borchers and Louise Canova B; m. 6/26/43 to Harriett Brewster Whitney; c. Kenneth A, David W, Dorothy L, Gordon W. and Timothy B. Educ: Syracuse Univ, B.S, 42; Alpha Phi Omega; Phi Gamma Delta. Polit. & Govt. Pos: City councilman, Berlin, N.H, 62-, chmn. educ. study cmt, 66-68, mem. sch. bldg. cmt, 69-; field representative for Congressman James C. Cleveland, 63-; Rep. sen. cand, N.H. State Senate Dist. One, 66 & 68; chmn, Coos Co. Rep. Party, 66-68; mem. airport authority, Berlin Munic. Airport, 68- Bus. & Prof. Pos: Research chemist, Celanese Corp. Am, Cumberland Md, 42-45; develop. chemist, Brown Co, Berlin, N.H, 46-53, supvr. qual. and process control, 54-56, tech. supt, 57-63 and supvr. tech. data processing, 63- Mem: Tech. Asn. Pulp and Paper Indust; Rotary; Eagles. Silver Beaver, Boy Scouts. Rel: Methodist. Mailing Add: 509 Norway St, Berlin, N.H. 03570.

BORCHERS, LOUIS F. R
b. Great Falls, Mont, 8/15/31; s. L. F. Borchers and Leonta Carnall B; m. 9/12/53 to Caryl Wickes; c. Randall, William and Brenda. Educ: Univ. Mont, B.A, 54; Psi Chi; Sigma Nu. Polit. & Govt. Pos: Former chmn, Lake Co. Rep. Cent. Cmt, Mont. Mil. Serv: Entered as 2nd Lt, Army, 54, released as 1st Lt, 66, after serv. in 4th and 9th Divs, Europe. Mem: Elks; Jaycees; C. of C; Flathead Labers. Rel: Presbyterian. Mailing Add: Finley Point, Polson, Mont. 59860. (1967)

BORCHERS, ROGER F. D
Co. Engr, Clark Co, Ohio
b. Springfield, Ohio, 6/8/19; s. Rupert F. Borchers and Elizabeth M. Walters B; m. 8/26/50 to Sylvia P. Sanderson; c. Cynthia Ann. Educ: Ohio State Univ, 46-49; Univ. Dayton, 62; Registered Prfnl. Engr. and Registered Surveyor in State of Ohio. Polit. & Govt. Pos: Co. engr, Clark Co, Ohio, 64-; chmn, Reams for Gov. Cmt, Clark Co, 66; pres, Clark Co. Dem. Men's Club, 66-67; v.chmn, Clark Co. Dem. Cent. and Exec. Cmts, 66-67; Dem. precinct committeeman, Precinct 3VM, Clark Co, 66-; chmn, Cecile for Cong. Cmt, 68; mem, Ohio Dem. Finance Cmt, 68; del, Dem. Nat. Conv, 68. Bus. & Prof. Pos: Partner, Borchers and Borchers Eng. Serv, 50-65. Mil. Serv: Entered as Pvt, Army Air Corps, 39, released as T/Sgt, 45, after serv. in 509th Composite Group, 20th Air Force; Air Force Res, 48-53; Am. Defense Medal; Good Conduct Medal; Am. Theater Ribbon; World War II Victory Medal. Mem: Ohio and Nat. Socs. of Prfnl. Engrs; Co. Engr. Asn, Ohio; Nat. Asn. Co. Engrs; Am. Rd. Builders Asn; Nat. Asn. Co. Off; Springfield Breakfast Optimist Club; Eagles; Moose; Regional Planning Cmn, Clark Co; Springfield-Clark Co. Transportation Coord. Cmt; Clark Co. Park Bd. Hon. V.Chmn, Ohio Dem. Party; Col, Ky. Col. Rel: Roman Catholic. Mailing Add: 2629 Casey Dr, Springfield, Ohio 45503.

BORDALLO, MADELEINE MARY D
Dem. Nat. Committeewoman, Guam
b. Graceville, Minn, 5/31/33; d. Christian Peter Zeien and Mary Evelyn Roth Z; m. 6/20/53 to Ricardo Jerome Bordalle; c. Deborah Josephine. Educ: St. Mary's Col, South Bend, Ind, 52; St. Katherine's Col, A.A. in Music, 53. Polit. & Govt. Pos: Dem. nat. committeewoman, Guam, 64-; pres, Women's Dem. Party and mem. exec. bd, Dem. Party, 65-; mem. exec. bd, Dem. Campaign Cmt, 66; del, Dem. Nat. Conv, 68. Bus. & Prof. Pos: Local news ed, traffic mgr. and prog. dir. sales dept, KUAM Radio-TV, 54-59, women's dir, 59-63. Publ: Fashion and travel articles for local newspapers. Mem: Pres, Marianas Asn. Retarded Children and Brodie Mem. Sch. Exceptional Children, 63-64; assoc. mem. bd. dirs, Guam Rehabilitation Asn, 63-64; pres, Guam Women's Club, 58-59; Fedn. Asian Women's Asns. (1st v.pres, 64-66, pres, 67-); bd. dirs, Guam Theater Guild, 63-66; pres, Guam Symphony Soc, 67-; secy, Am. Red Cross, 63-66; Spanish Club of Guam. Frequent commentator for fashion shows. Rel: Catholic. Mailing Add: P.O. Box 1458, Agana, Guam 96910.

BORDALLO, RICARDO JEROME D
Sen, Guam Legis.
b. Agana, Guam, 12/11/27; s. Baltazar Bordallo and Josephine Pangelinan B; m. 6/20/53 to Madeleine Mary Zeien; c. Deborah. Educ: Univ. San Francisco, 47-50. Polit. & Govt. Pos: Sen, Guam Legis, 56-, Minority Leader, 64-66; chmn, Fifty-Star Flag Raising Ceremony, Guam, 59; del, Statehood Celebration, Hawaii, 59; chmn, Liberation Celebration, Guam, 60; del, Nat. Legis. Conf, Ill, 60 and N.J, 64; charter chmn, Dem. Party Guam, 60-63; chmn, Tuberc. Dr. Gov. Ball, 61; del, Fifth S.Pac. Conf, Am. Samoa, 62; del, Second Inaugural Salute, President Kennedy and Nat. Conf. Dem. State Chairmen, Wash, D.C, 63; del, Dem. Nat. Conv, 64 & 68; del, Legis. Leaders Conf, P.R, 65. Bus. & Prof. Pos: Dealership, Toyota Motor Co. on Guam, 56-; chmn. bd. dir, Family Finance Co, Inc, 59-; dealership, Guam Chrysler Motor Sales, 66-; incorporator and chmn. bd, Am. Enterprises and publisher of daily newspaper, Pac. J, 66-68. Mil. Serv: Army, 53, Pvt. Mem: Marianas Lions Club (pres, 56-57); Marianas Asn. for Retarded Children (bd. dirs, 62-64); assoc. mem. and bd. dirs, Guam Rehabilitation Center, 62-65; Young Men's League of Guam; Navy League of Guam; Guam C. of C; Am. Red Cross (bd. dirs, 65-). Rel: Catholic. Mailing Add: P.O. Box 1458, Agana, Guam 96910.

BORDEN, WINSTON WENDELL DFL
b. Brainerd, Minn, 9/1/43; s. Ralph Waldo Borden and Hazel Converse B; single. Educ: St. Cloud State Col, B.A, 65; Univ. Minn, M.A. and J.D, 68; Student Body Pres; pres, debate team. Polit. & Govt. Pos: Chmn, Minn. Young Dem-Farmer-Labor Party, 64; State Dem-Farmer Labor Internship, 64; mem, Minn. State Dem-Farmer-Labor Cent. Cmt, 65-69; del-at-lg, Dem. Nat. Conv, 68; charter mem, Nat. Citizens for Humphrey Cmt, 68; mem, Minn. Humphrey Campaign Cmt, 68; mem. tech. rev. bd, Gov. Coun. Aging, 68-69. Bus. & Prof. Pos: Counsr, Univ. Minn, 66-68; consult, Upper Midwest Res. & Develop. Coun, Minn, 67-68; attorney, 68-; instr. polit. sci, Wis. State Univ, Superior, 68- Mem: Am. Asn. Univ. Prof; Am. and Minn. Bar Asns; Am. Judicature Soc; Am. Civil Liberties Union. Legal Res: Box 35, Merrifield, Minn. 56465. Mailing Add: 514 Grove, Brainerd, Minn. 56401.

BOREK, JO ANNE R
Mem. Exec. Bd, Mass. Fedn. Rep. Women
b. Bridgeport, Conn, 7/12/33; d. Roland E. Reid (deceased) and Helen H. Hall R.(deceased); m. 2/19/54 to Gordon S. Borek; c. William D, James E. and Scott G. Educ: Katharine Gibbs Secretarial Sch, grad, 51. Polit. & Govt. Pos: Pres, Swampscott Women's Rep. Club, Mass, 66-68, mem. exec. bd, 66-; del, Mass. Rep. State Conv, 66; del, Rep. Nat. Conv, 68; del, Nat. Fed. Rep. Women, 68 & 69; v.chmn, Swampscott Rep. Town Cmt, 68-; mem. exec. bd, Essex Co. Women's Rep. Club, 68-; mem. exec bd, Mass. Fedn. Rep. Women, 69- Bus. & Prof. Pos: Treas, Borek Assocs, Inc, Boston, 64- Mem: Swampscott Youth Hockey Asn.(registr. and dir, 67-); Swampscott Youth Center (recording secy, 66-69); Swampscott Parent-Teachers Coun.(past pres, local PTA, chmn, scholarship drive, 3 times). Swampscott Women Civic Leader of the Year, Daily Evening Item, 66. Rel: Protestant. Mailing Add: 27 Reid Terrace, Swampscott, Mass. 01907.

BORELLI, FRANK PETER, JR. R
Mem, Calif. Rep. State Cent. Cmt.
b. Hollister, Calif, 7/27/35; s. Frank Borelli and Clara La Macchia B; m. 8/26/62 to Josephine Filice; c. Carla, Gia and Frank P, III. Educ: Univ. of Santa Clara, B.S, 56, LL.D, 60. Polit. & Govt. Pos: Mem, San Benito Co. Rep. Cent. Cmt, Calif, 68-; mem, Calif. Rep. State Cent. Cmt, 69- Bus. & Prof. Pos: Attorney-at-law, O'Brien & Borelli, Hollister, Calif, 61- Mil. Serv: Entered as Pvt. E-2, Army, 58, released as Pvt E-2, 59, Army Res, 59-68. Mem: Calif. and San Benito Co. Bar Asns; pres, San Benito Co. C. of C, 69-; Elks; Farm Bur; San Benito Co. Jaycees. Rel: Catholic. Mailing Add: 1025 San Benito St, Hollister, Calif. 95023.

BOREN, DAVID LYLE D
Okla. State Rep.
b. Washington, D.C, 4/21/41; s. Lyle H. Boren and Christine McKown B; m. 9/7/68 to Janna Lou Little. Educ: Yale Univ, B.A, 63; Oxford Univ, M.A, 65; Univ. Okla. Col. of Law, J.D, 68; Phi Beta Kappa; Am. Asn. of Rhodes Scholars; Phi Delta Phi; Delta Sigma Rho; Distinguished Mil. Grad, ROTC, 63; mem. staff, Okla. Law Rev. Polit. & Govt. Pos: Asst. to liaison dir, Off. of Civil and Defense Mobilization, Wash, D.C, 59-62; propaganda analyst, U.S. Info. Agency, 62-63; prog. chmn, Yale Young Dem, 62-63, coordinator, Yale Conserv. Asn, 62-63 and speaker, Yale Polit. Union, 62-63; mem, Speakers Bur, U.S. Embassy, London, Eng, 63-65; Okla. State Rep, Seminole Co, 66-, mem, Okla. Ethical Practices Cmn, Okla. House of Rep, 67-, mem, Okla. Law Center Cmn, 69-; del, Dem. Nat. Conv, 68. Bus. & Prof. Pos: Counsr. for Freshman, Univ. Okla, 65-66; attorney at law, private practice, Seminole and Wewoka, Okla, 68-; asst. prof. polit. sci, Okla. Baptist Univ, 69- Mil. Serv:

1st Lt, Okla. Army Nat. Guard, currently; Army Medal. Mem: Okla. Bar Asn. (Law Schs. Cmt); Am. Bar Asn; Jucicial Conf. of U.S. Tenth Circuit Court of Appeals; Wewoka C. of C.(bd. dirs); Yale Club of Okla; Seminole C. of C; Jaycees; Seminole Sportsmans Club; class agent, Yale Alumni Asn; ROA; Seminole Quarterback Club. Bledsoe Prize as Outstanding Okla. Univ. Law Grad, 68; One of Three Outstanding Young Oklahomans, Okla. State Jr. C. of C, 69. Rel: Methodist; Assoc. Dist. Lay Leader. Legal Res: 917 Wilson St, Seminole, Okla. 74868. Mailing Add: Box 1338, Seminole, Okla. 74868.

BOREN, JAMES HARLAN D
b. Wheatland, Okla, 12/10/25; s. James Basil Boren and Una Lee Hamilton B; m. 8/16/46 to Irene Clark; c. Richard Vincent and James Stanley. Educ: Hardin Col, 43-46; Univ. Tex, A.B. in Econ, 48, grad. student, 52-54; Long Beach State Col, A.B. in Educ, 50; Univ. South. Calif, A.M. in Econ, 50; pres, Univ. Tex. Young Dem, 52; Phi Delta Kappa. Polit. & Govt. Pos: Chmn, World Tapes for Educ; chief acct. div, Tex. Dept. Agr, 52-54; campaign mgr. for Gov. Tex, 56; campaign mgr. for Ralph Yarborough for U.S. Sen, 57; admin. asst, Sen. Yarborough, Tex, 57-61; dep. dir, U.S. Opers. Mission to Peru, 61; dep. dir, U.S. Agency Int. Develop. Mission to Peru, 61-63, dir, Partners of The Alliance Progs, 63-, spec. asst. to U.S. Coordinator, Alliance for Progress, 63- Bus. & Prof. Pos: Teacher and night dir. recreation dept, James Stanley High Sch, Oxnard, Calif, 50-52; prof. educ. and head dept, Arlington State Col, Tex, 54-56; pres, Boren Oil & Gas Corp, 56-57. Mil. Serv: Army Res; Naval Res, 43-46. Mem: Am. Polit. Sci. Asn; Am. For. Serv. Asn; founder and pres, Nat. Asn. of Prfnl. Bureaucrats, Inc; U.S. Senate Admin. Asst. Asn; Burro Club, U.S.(pres, 60); Order Artus; charter mem. and past secy. North Austin Exchange Club; Recipient Outstanding Alumnus Award, Long Beach State Col, 61. Legal Res: 1803 Paul Spring Pkwy, Alexandria, Va. 22313. Mailing Add: State Dept. Bldg, Washington, D.C. 20520.

BOREN, LYLE H. D
b. Waxahachie, Tex, 5/11/09; s. Mark Latimer Boren and Nanie Mae Weatherall B; m. 12/26/36 to Christine McKown; c. David Lyle and Susan Hope. Educ: East Cent. Col, B.A, 28; Okla. State Univ, M.A, 36; Pi Kappa Delta; Eugene Field Soc. of Authors & Writers. Polit. & Govt. Pos: Pres, Okla. Dem. Fraternity, 34-36; U.S. Rep, Okla, 37-47. Bus. & Prof. Pos: Pres, Okla. Cattle Co, 46-55 and Seminole Petroleum Co, 48-57; Wash. rep, Asn. of West. Rwys, 53-; pres, Bodrain Co, 65- Mil. Serv: Entered as Ens, Navy, 36, released as Lt. Comdr, 55, after serv. in Eighth Naval Dist. Publ: Who is Who in Oklahoma, Harlow Pub, 35; Fables in Labels, Nat. Capitol Press, 40; 'History of the Santa Fe Trail,' East. Cent. J, 35. Mem: Okla. Cattlemen's Asn.(founder and past pres); Elks; Odd Fellows; Rotary; Am. Legion. Rel: Church of Christ. Legal Res: General Delivery, Seminole, Okla. 74868. Mailing Add: Apt. 2 G-A, 3900 Watson Place N.W, Washington, D.C. 20016.

BORES, JEROME CLARENCE D
b. Milwaukee, Wis, 4/18/30; s. Max Bores and Anna O'Dea B; m. 7/19/58 to Sylvia Doris Kunzler; c. Linda Marie and Debra Ann. Educ: Riverside High Sch, grad, 48. Polit. & Govt. Pos: Del, Wis. State Dem. Conv, 64-68; chmn, Fifth Ward Unit Dem. Party, 66-68; mem. exec. bd, Milwaukee Co. Dem. Party, 66-68; del, Dem. Nat. Conv, 68; commun. orgn. specialist, 69- Mil. Serv: Entered as Pvt, Army, 51, released as Cpl, 53, after serv. in 176th A.F.A, Korea, 52-53; Korean Serv. Medal with Two Bronze Serv. Stars; UN Serv. Medal; Meritorious Unit Citation; Distinguished Unit Citation. Mem: Eagles. Rel: Catholic. Mailing Add: 2340 N. 45th St, Milwaukee, Wis. 53210.

BORG, GEORGE M. R
b. Colorado Springs, Colo, 10/4/34. Educ: Univ. of Wis. Polit. & Govt. Pos: Alderman, Delavan, Wis, 59-61; Wis. State Assemblyman, 60-66; mem, Gov. Cmt. on Wis. Water Resources; chmn, Health and License Cmt; mem, Civil Defense Cmt, Finance, Ins, Fire and Police Cmts; former Wis. State Sen. Bus. & Prof. Pos: Former plant mgr. for mfg. co; v.pres, local savings and loan asn. Mil. Serv: Army, Korean War. Mem: V.pres, Delavan Sportsman Club; Elks. Mailing Add: 454 Borg Road, Delavan, Wis. 53115. (1967)

BORST, LAWRENCE MARION R
Ind. State Sen.
b. Champaign Co, Ohio, 7/16/27; s. Lawrence M. Borst and Mary Waldeck B; m. 3/21/47 to Eldoris; c. Philip, Elizabeth and David. Educ: Ohio State Univ, D.Journ, 50. Polit. & Govt. Pos: Ind. State Rep, 67-68; del, Rep. Nat. Conv, 68; Ind. State Sen, 69- Mailing Add: 1725 Remington Dr, Indianapolis, Ind. 46227.

BORT, JOSEPH PARKER R
Supvr, Alameda Co Bd. of Supvr, Calif.
b. Avalon, Calif, 7/23/15; s. Milo C. Bort and Mary Parker B; m. 5/14/42 to Jacklyn Taylor; c. Samuel P, Daniel C. and Peggy Jo. Educ: Univ. Calif, Berkeley, B.S; Boalt Hall of Law, Univ. Calif, LL.B; Tau Beta Pi. Polit. & Govt. Pos: Councilman, City of Berkeley, Calif, 63-67; supvr, Alameda Co. Bd. of Supvr, 67- Bus. & Prof. Pos: Life ins. salesman, 46-60; attorney, 60- Mil. Serv: Entered as Ens, Navy 43, released as Lt, 46, after eng. duty, Brooklyn Navy Yard. Mem: Calif. State Bar; Alameda Co. Bar Asn; Estate Planning Coun; Am. Soc. Chartered Life Underwriters. Rel: Christian Science. Legal Res: 615 San Luis Rd, Berkeley, Calif. 94707. Mailing Add: Room 703 Central Bldg, Oakland Calif. 94612.

BOSCH, ALBERT H. R
b. New York, N.Y, 10/30/08; s. Henry Bosch and Margaretha Hamburger B; m. 7/19/36 to Theresa Hoenig; c. Marilyn M, Alice A. Educ: St. John's Univ, LL.B, 33. Polit. & Govt. Pos: Former mem, Woodhaven Rep. Asn, N.Y. and Richmond Hill Rep. Club; committeeman, Queens Co. Rep. Party, 49-52; U.S. Rep, Fifth Dist, 83-86 Cong; co. Judge, Queens Co, 61-62; State Justice, N.Y. Supreme Court 11th Judicial Dist, N.Y. Supreme Court, 62-68. Bus. & Prof. Pos: Lawyer, firm, Archer, Bosch and Engeler, 45-60; trustee, Hamburg Savings Bank. Mem: Am. and Queens Co. Bar Asns; past nat. chmn, Steuben Soc. Am, 52; Mason; Elks; Moose; Blackstone Ridgeway; Bushwick. Mailing Add: 8780 98th St, Woodhaven, N.Y. 11421. (1967)

BOSCH, LOVINNA, 'PAT' D
b. Mesa, Ariz, 2/19/30; d. Azel Lorenzo Mortensen and Ruth C. Bush M; m. 7/6/57 to Dries Bosch; c. Cheryl Lynn, Randall A, Karen Ruth, Roderick Dries, Pamela Ann and Kelley Diane. Educ: Phoenix Col. Polit. & Govt. Pos: Ariz. State Dem. Committeewoman and Dem. Precinct Committeewoman, 54-68; alternate del, Dem. Nat. Conv, 56 & 60; pres, Phoenix Young Dem, 56-57; first v.pres, Ariz. Young Dem, 57 and nat. committeewoman, 58-59; v.chairwoman, Maricopa Co. Dem. Cent. Cmt, 61-62; del, Dem. Nat. Conv. and mem. credentials cmt; secy-treas, Citizens for Johnson-Humphrey Cmt, 64. Bus. & Prof. Pos: Mem, Cent. Ariz. Proj. Asn, 47-51 secy, Registrar of Contractors, 52-53; secy, Gov. Ernest W. McFarland, Ariz, 54-57; owner and operator, Pat Borsch Secy, 58-; pub. rels. dir, Mesa Lutheran Hosp, 63-66; pub. rels. and advert, Legend City Amusement Park, 65-66. Mem: Am. Hosp. Asn. for Pub. Rels. Dirs; hon. mem, Hundred Club; Mesa Lutheran Hosp. Auxiliary; Lioness; charter mem, Phoenix Am. Bus. Women's Asn; PTA; bd. dirs, Nat. Found. March of Dimes, 62-66; Mesa chmn, Ment. Health Asn. Ariz, 66; Organized The Hundred Club in Phoenix to help families of policemen or firemen killed in line of duty with assistance from Troy Browning of Detroit, Mich. Rel: Presbyterian. 1967 Legal Res: Coolidge, Ariz. No mailing address available. (1967)

BOSCH, ROBERT D. R
Chmn, Muscatine Co. Rep. Party, Iowa.
b. Muscatine, Iowa, 5/22/22; s. Glenn Bosch and Freda Schmiekel B; m. 8/24/47 to Miriam Kopf; c. Amy and Kathryn. Educ: Muscatine High Sch, 4 years. Polit. & Govt. Pos: Alderman, Muscatine, Iowa, 58-60 and mayor, 60-65; chmn, Muscatine Co. Rep. Party, 65- Bus. & Prof. Pos: Draftsman, Grain Processing Corp, 47-56; owner, Bosch Pest Control Co, 49-; pres, Rid-A-Bird, Inc, 59-; pres, Am. Chem. Co, 62-; v.pres, Discount Sales Co, Inc, 62- Mil. Serv: Entered as Pvt, Army, 44, released as Pvt, 46, after serv. in 103rd Div, 44-46. Mem: Nat. and Iowa Pest Control Asns; Am. Soc. Appraisers; Iowa Real Estate Brokers; Moose; Shrine; Elks; Mason. Rel: Protestant. Legal Res: 517 Roscoe Ave, Muscatine, Iowa 52761. Mailing Add: P.O. Box 22, Muscatine, Iowa 52761.

BOSCHETTO, LOUIS D
b. Italy, 9/23/98; s. John Boschetto and Mabel Bazzanella B; m. 11/7/25 to Rose Rio; c. Louis Jon and Sibyl (Mrs. John Love). Polit. & Govt. Pos: Chmn, Sweetwater Co. Dem. Cent. Cmt, Wyo, 41-43; Wyo. State Rep, 45-50 & 67-69; Wyo. State Sen, 51-58. Bus. & Prof. Pos: Owner and operator, tailoring dry cleaning bus, 21-51 and motel, 47- Mem: C. of C; K. of C; Eagles; Elks; Improved Order of Redmen; WOW; Am. Italian Lodge. Rel: Roman Catholic. Mailing Add: 817 Seventh, Rock Springs, Wyo. 82901.

BOSCIA, IDA B. D
V.Chairwoman, Huerfano Co. Dem. Party, Colo.
b. Atwood, Kans, 6/6/10; d. Charles Clyde Packard and Minnie Boston P; m. 7/29/26 to Lee Boscia; c. Jacquelyn Boscia (Mrs. Russell Vickers). Educ: Walsenburg High Sch, 2 years. Polit. & Govt. Pos: V.chairwoman, Huerfano Co. Dem. Party, Colo, 69- Bus. & Prof. Pos: Exten. serv. secy, Walsenburg, Colo, 51- Mem: Walsenburg Golf Club; Exten. Homemakers Club; Walsenburg Bowling Asn. Rel: Protestant. Legal Res: 605 Penn, Walsenburg, Colo. 81089. Mailing Add: Box 484, Walsenburg, Colo. 81089.

BOSCO, JOSEPH ANGELO Independent
Spec. Asst. to the Secy, Dept. of Transportation
b. Boston, Mass, 3/25/38; s. Joseph Bosco and Emma Pacillo B; m. 4/19/69 to Carol Whitten Beebe. Educ: Harvard Col, A.B. cum laude, 60; Harvard Law Sch, LL.B, 65; house cmt, Phillips Brooks House; Pre-law Soc; Lincoln's Inn Soc; Howe Club. Polit. & Govt. Pos: Law clerk to U.S. Attorney, Mass, summer 64; law clerk to Chief Justice and Assoc. Justices, Mass. Superior Court, 65-67; legal counsel to Gov, Mass, 67-68; mem. transition team, Dept. of Transportation, 68-69, Spec. Asst. to the Secy, 69- Mil. Serv: Entered as Ens, Navy, 60, released as Lt.(jg), 62, after serv. in U.S.S. Hancock, Far East; Lt. Comdr, Naval Res; Commanding Officer's Commendation, U.S.S. Hancock, 61; Naval Res. Intel. Div. Award, 65, 66 & 68. Mem: Boston, Mass. and Am. Bar Asns; Harvard Club; Navy League. Honors Paper, Harvard Law Sch, 65. Rel: Catholic. Legal Res: Boston, Mass. Mailing Add: 490 M St, S.W, W304, Washington, D.C. 20024.

BOSCO, RUBEN OTERO R
Rep, P.R. House of Rep.
b. Arecibo, P.R, 3/1/19; s. Francisco Otero Bosco and Isabel B; married; c. Elba Otero Cancel and Ruben Otero Font. Educ: High Sch, grad; Col, 1 year. Polit. & Govt. Pos: Chmn, Socialist Party, 49-52; chmn, Statehood Rep. Party, Arecibo, P.R, 56-; Rep, P.R. House of Rep, 61-; chmn, Rep. Munic. Cmt, 68- Bus. & Prof. Pos: V.pres. and mgr, Arecibo Loan Corp, 59-63; ed, Revista Accion, 65-; owner, Arecibo Printing Co, 65- Publ: Monthly editorials in mag, Accion. Mem: Odd Fellows. Rel: Catholic. Legal Res: Urb. Martell E. No. 10, Arecibo, P.R. 00612. Mailing Add: P.O. Box 878, Arecibo, P.R. 00612. (1967)

BOSMA, CHARLES EDWARD R
Ind. State Sen.
b. Beech Grove, Ind, 4/8/22; s. Mitchell C. Bosma and Emma Rodert B; m. 10/24/45 to Margaret Pauline Hagge; c. Janice Irene, Rhonda Jeanne and Brian Charles. Educ: Purdue Univ, 40-43; Beta Sigma Psi. Polit. & Govt. Pos: Rep. precinct committeeman, Marion Co, Ind, 61-66, Rep. ward chmn, 62-66; city chmn, Beech Grove Rep. Campaign, 65; Ind. State Rep, 62-64 & 66-68; Ind. State Sen, 68- Bus. & Prof. Pos: Gen. mgr. and pres, Bosma Dairy, Inc, 46-66. Mil. Serv: Entered as Pvt, Army, 43, released as Capt, 46, after serv. in Field Artil, ETO, 45; Am. Theater Ribbon and European Theater Ribbon with 2 Battle Stars. Mem: Am. Legion; Optimist; Beech Grove Businessmen's Asn; dir, Lutheran Child Welfare Asn. of Ind. Rel: Lutheran, Missouri Synod. Mailing Add: 95 S. 17th Ave, Beech Grove, Ind. 46107.

BOSONE, REVA BECK D
d. Christian Mateus Beck and Zilpha Chipman B; div; c. Zilpha (Mrs. Crouch). Educ: Univ. Calif, Berkeley, B.A, 19; Univ. Utah, J.D, 30. Polit. & Govt. Pos: Utah State Rep, Majority Floor Leader and chmn. sifting cmt, 33-35; judge, Salt Lake City Munic. Court, 36-48; Utah State dir, Educ. on Alcoholism, 47-48; U.S. Rep, Utah, 49-52, legal counsel, labor subcmt, U.S. House of Reps, 57-61; judicial officer, U.S. Post Off. Dept, 61- Bus. & Prof. Pos: Former high sch. teacher, Ogden, Utah. Mem: Utah and Fed. Bar Asns; Soc. of Mayflower Descendants; hon. mem, Soroptimists and Am. Civic League. Mailing Add: 930 Fairway Dr. N.E, Vienna, Va. 22180.

BOSSERT, WILLARD MAX R
Pa. State Rep.
b. Mill Hall, Pa, 7/9/06; s. John Smith Bossert and Minnie Holmes B; m. 10/24/31 to Edythe Hoy; c. Jane (Mrs. Schwab), Thomas Hoy, Willard Max, Jr, Bethany Ann and Barbara Susan. Educ: Lock Haven State Col, B.S. in Educ, 32; Columbia Univ, M.A. in Health and Phys. Educ, 40; Univ. Pa, adv. study; Phi Kappa Sigma. Polit. & Govt. Pos: Mayor, Mill Hall, Pa, 40-47; chmn, Clinton Co. Cmnr, 48-60; sch. dir, Bald Eagle Nittany High Sch, 58-59; Pa. State Rep, 76th Dist, 61- Bus. & Prof. Pos: Dean of men, Lock Haven State Col, 35-40, head football coach, 35-46, dir. of athletics and prof. of health and phys. educ, 39-46; owner and operator, Hardware Store, 46-61 and Dairy Farm, 50- Mem: V.pres, Pa. State Asn. Co. Cmnr, 56-60; pres, Lock Haven State Col. Alumni Asn; Elks; Eagles; F. of M.A; Grange. Rel: Presbyterian; Elder. Mailing Add: Old Beech Creek Rd, Beech Creek, Pa. 16822.

BOSSHARD, JOHN R
b. La Crosse, Wis, 9/28/20; s. John Bosshard and Effie Kremmer B; m. 6/15/44 to Rylla Hattan; c. John, Sabina, William and Kurt. Educ: Univ. Wis. Law Sch, LL.B, Univ. Wis, Ph.B; Harvard Grad. Sch. Bus, M.B.A; Order of the Coif; Phi Delta Theta; Alpha Kappa Lambda. Polit. & Govt. Pos: Clerk, Bangor Area Schs, Wis, 49-; dist. attorney, Small Claims Court, La Crosse Co, 50-54, judge, 55-60; mem, Wis. Gold Ribbon Cmt, 64-65; chmn, Minn-Wis. Boundary Area Cmt, 65-; mem, Fed. Reserve Bd, Minneapolis Dist, 67; Rep. Third Dist. Coordinator. Bus. & Prof. Pos: Partner, law firm, Bosshard, Sundet & Nix, secy, Twin City Ready Mix Concrete, Inc, and exec. v.pres, First Nat. Bank of Bangor, Wis, currently; exec. v.pres, LaFarge State Bank, 69-; dir, West. Concrete Prod. Inc, 69- Mil. Serv: Entered as Pvt, Army, 43, released as 1st Lt, 46, after serv. in Philippines. Mem: Wis. and La Crosse Co. Bar Asns; Kiwanis; Holstein Breeders Asn; Elks. Rel: Baptist. Mailing Add: Bangor, Wis. 54614.

BOSSHARD, RYLLA JANE R
Mem, Wis. State Rep. Exec. Cmt.
b. Clatskanie, Ore, 5/3/23; d. Loyd Stanley Hattan and Gertrude Anne Phillips H; m. 6/16/44 to John Bosshard; c. John III, Sabina, William Hattan and Kurt Robert. Educ: Stanford Univ, B.A, 44; Theta Sigma Phi; Delta Delta Delta. Polit. & Govt. Pos: Del, Wis. Rep. State Conv, 48-; area v.pres, La Crosse Co. Rep. Women, 52-62, pres, 62-64; v.chmn, Third Dist. Rep. Party, 63-; mem, Wis. State Rep. Exec. Cmt, 63-, chmn, Hqs, 67-; mem, Higher Educ. Aids Bd, 65-, chmn, student financial aids cmt, 68-; mem, constitutional Rev. Cmt, 67-; mem. steering cmt, Rep. Party Wis, 67-; alternate del, Rep. Nat. Conv, 68. Bus. & Prof. Pos: Dir, First Nat. Bank, Bangor, 64-; dir, La Farge State Bank, 69- Mem: Am. Asn. Univ. Women; PEO, Stanford Alumni Asn; Delta Delta Delta Alumni; Am. Legion Auxiliary; PTA; Lawyer's Wives of Wis; Rep. Party Wis; Bangor Women's Civic Club. Rel: Baptist. Mailing Add: Box 247, Bangor, Wis. 54614.

BOSSLE, FRANCIS X. D
b. Baltimore, Md, 4/12/13; married. Educ: Loyola Col. Polit. & Govt. Pos: Md. State Del, 63-67; Pres, Catonsville Dem. Club, Inc; Dist. Exec. Cmt, 1st Dist. of Baltimore Co. Bus. & Prof. Pos: Accountant. Mil. Serv: WW II, U.S. Army. Mem: Men's Club of St. Mark's; K. of C; past pres, Catonsville Lions; Mt. St. Joseph Col. Alumni Asn; Loyola Col. Alumni Asn. Mailing Add: 5 Seminole Ave, Catonsville, Md. 21228. (1967)

BOSTIAN, TERAL THOMAS R
N.C. State Rep.
b. Taylorsville, N.C, 1/30/04; s. Charles Lon Bostian and Sibinna Ingram B; m. to Exie Mae Bowman (deceased); c. Nina (Mrs. Jerry Windsor). Educ: Alexander Co. Schs, Taylorsville, N.C, 8 years. Polit. & Govt. Pos: N.C. State Rep, 69- Rel: Lutheran. Mailing Add: Route 1, Box 429, Taylorsville, N.C. 28681.

BOSTON, EUGENE ALFRED R
Mem, Calif. Rep. State Cent. Cmt.
b. Fresno, Calif, 10/15/28; s. Kevork Nerses Boston and Agnes Thompson B; m. 12/17/55 to Eva Stella Bielecka; c. Diane, Kenneth and Margo. Educ: Univ. Calif, Los Angeles, B.A; McGill Univ, M.D; Nu Sigma Nu. Polit. & Govt. Pos: Co-chmn, Goldwater for President Cmt, Fullerton, Calif, 64; mem, Calif. Rep. State Cent. Cmt, 68- Mil. Serv: Entered as 2nd Lt, Air Force, 51, released as 1st Lt, 53, after serv. as Personnel Officer, U.S. Mem: Am. and Orange Co. Med. Asns; Asn. of Am. Physicians and Surgeons; Am. Acad. of Gen. Practice (pres, 67); Kiwanis Int; Los Coyotes Country Club. Rel: Protestant. Mailing Add: 8370 Waverly Circle, Buena Park, Calif. 90620.

BOSTON, HUGH CHESTER D
b. Florence, Ala, 6/15/12; s. Monroe Hugh Collins Boston and Bertha Malinda Easter B; m. 11/1/63 to Sara Dozier; c. Sandra Janet (Mrs. James Rufus Dockery), Hugh Chester, Jr. Educ: Pub. schs, Lauderdale Co. Polit. & Govt. Pos: Ala. State Rep, 63-66; Asst. State Finance Dir, 60-61. Bus. & Prof. Pos: Wholesale produce bus. Rel: Church of Christ. 1967 Legal Res: 601 Cherry St, Florence, Ala. No mailing address available. (1967)

BOSWELL, PAUL P. R
b. Pittsburgh, Pa, 6/12/05; s. Noah W. Boswell and Marie Prince B; m. 7/1/56 to Arnita L. Young; c. Bonnie B. Educ: Lincoln Univ, Pa, A.B, 30; Univ. Minn. Med. Sch, M.B, 39, M.D, 40; Rosenwald Fel, 41-44; Omega Psi Phi; Frogs. Polit. & Govt. Pos: Ill. State Rep, 65-67. Bus. & Prof. Pos: Intern, Provident Hosp, 39-40; assoc, Dr. T.K. Lawless, Chicago, Ill; resident and instr, Univ. of Ill. Research and Educ. Hosp, Dermatology Dept, 47; lectr, Michael Reese and Provident Hosp. Nurses Schs; sr. attending physician, Provident and Mich. Ave. Hosps; sr. dermatologist, Michael Reese Hosp, 50; dermatology consult, Union Health Serv, 56, Toni Co, 63 and Drexel Home for Aged; asst. prof, Univ. of Ill, Chicago Circle, 65. Publ: Observation on Occupational Dermatoses, Nat. Safety Cong, 61; Diagnostic Features of Drug Eruptions; Review of Warts and their Treatment. Mem: Nat, Am. and Pan Am. Med. Asns; Chicago Dermatology Soc; Am. Acad. Dermatology; Int. Soc. Tropical Dermatology; Urban League; NAACP; dir, Ill. Coun. for Ment. Retardation, Chicago Asn. Retarded Children and Woodlawn Ment. Health Serv; Hyde Park-Kenwood and Southside Commun. Cmts; YMCA; Joint Negro Appeal. Man of Year Award, Lincoln Univ; Polit. Activity Award, Ill. Med. Soc; Best Freshman Citation and Best Legislators Award. Rel: Unitarian. Legal Res: 5217 S. University, Chicago, Ill. 60615. Mailing Add: 841 East 63rd St, Chicago, Ill. 60637. (1967)

BOTELER, EDGAR LEE JR. D
Miss. State Rep.
b. Grenada, Miss, 2/4/20; married. Polit. & Govt. Pos: Miss. State Rep, currently. Bus. & Prof. Pos: Farmer. Mem: Rotary; Farm Bur. Rel: Presbyterian. Mailing Add: Riverdale Farms, Grenada, Miss. 38901. (1967)

BOTTIGER, R. TED D
Wash. State Rep.
b. Tacoma, Wash, 1932; m. to Darlene B; c. Three. Educ: Univ. of Puget Sound, B.A; Univ. of Wash. Law Sch, LL.B. Polit. & Govt. Pos: Wash. State Rep, currently. Bus. & Prof. Pos: Attorney-at-law. Mailing Add: 8849 Pacific Ave, Tacoma, Wash. 98444.

BOTTOM, CURTIS HOBBS R
Chmn, Washington Co. Rep. Cmt, Ky.
b. Mackville, Ky, 7/15/06; s. Robert Calvin Bottom and Nelle Hobbs B; m. 3/16/46 to Bernice Marie Miller; c. Robert Curtis and David Alan. Educ: Centre Col, Ky; Northwest. Univ; Sigma Alpha Epsilon. Polit. & Govt. Pos: Chmn, Washington Co. Rep. Cmt, Ky, 48- Mil. Serv: Entered as Lt.(jg), Navy, 42, released as Lt. Comdr, 47, after serv. in Atlantic & Pac. Theaters. Rel: Presbyterian. Legal Res: Lincoln Park Rd, Springfield, Ky. 40069. Mailing Add: P.O. Box 426, Springfield, Ky. 40069.

BOTTORFF, JOHN DAVID D
b. Cortland, Ind, 8/2/37; s. Thomas Marshall Bottorff and Lillian Witeford Claycamp B; m. 2/13/65 to Michael Carolyn Walter. Educ: Franklin Col, A.B, 59; Blue Key; Phi Delta Theta. Polit. & Govt. Pos: Pres, Franklin Col. Young Dem, 58-59; pres, Ninth Dist. Young Dem, Ind, 61-63; chmn, Mid-West Young Dem, 63-65; pres, Ind. Young Dem, 63-65; Secy. of State, Ind, 64-66. Bus. & Prof. Pos: Basketball coach, Reelsville High Sch, 61-63 and Culver High Sch, 63-64. Mil. Serv: Entered as Airman Basic, Air Force Res, 59, released as Airman 1/C, 65. Mem: Ind. State Teachers Asn; Nat. Educ. Asn; Ind. Coaches Asn; Jaycees; Mason; Lions; Moose. Wil B. Nelp Outstanding Athlete Award, Franklin Col, 59. Rel: Christian Church. Legal Res: R.R. 4, Seymour, Ind. 47274. Mailing Add: Old State Road East, Nashville, Ind. 47448.

BOTTORFF, LEWIS MADISON D
b. Gretna, Nebr, 9/13/11; s. Arthur Madison Bottorff and Georgia Campbell B; m. 11/26/36 to M. Pauline Rodgers; c. Judith P.(Mrs. Moore) and William Arthur. Educ: Univ. Nebr, B.S. in agr, 35, M.A, 37; Alpha Zeta; Gamma Sigma Delta; Palladian Literary. Polit. & Govt. Pos: Mem, Nebr. Dem. State Cent. Cmt, 58-62; v.chmn, Sarpy Co. Dem. Cent. Cmt, 59-61, chmn, 62-68; v.chmn, Sarpy Co. Zoning Cmn, 61- Bus. & Prof. Pos: Pres. of bd, South Omaha Prod. Credit Asn, 39-41 and Pioneer Tel. Coop, Philomath, Ore, 49-51. Mil. Serv: Entered as 1st Lt, Army, 41, released as Maj, 46, after serv. in ETO 70th Inf. Div, 274th Inf. Div. and European Theater Mil. Govt, 45-46; Combat Inf. Medal; Bronze Star. Mem: Pres, Sarpy Co. Farm Bur, 60-61; Mason; Scottish Rite; Tangier Shrine; Farm Bureau; Farmer's Union; National Farmer's Orgn. Rel: Methodist. Mailing Add: Rt. 1, Papillion, Nebr. 68046. (1967)

BOTTUM, JOSEPH HENRY R
b. Faulkton, S.Dak, 8/7/03; s. Joseph Henry Bottum and Sylvia Grace Smith B; m. 8/20/29 to Nellie Bergita Bang; c. Mary Jo. Educ: Yankton Col, 20; Univ. Mich, LL.B, 23; Univ. S.Dak, 27; Lambda Chi Alpha. Polit. & Govt. Pos: States attorney, Faulk Co, S.Dak, 33-36; chmn, S.Dak. Young Rep. League, 34-42; dir. taxation, S.Dak, 37-43; chmn, S.Dak. Rep. Cent. Cmt, 46-48; Lt. Gov, S.Dak, 60-62; U.S. Sen, S.Dak, 62-63. Bus. & Prof. Pos: Attorney-at-Law, St. Paul, 28-30; Jacobs & Bottum, Faulkton, 30-36; partner, Bottum & Beal, Rapid City, 55- Mem: Am. and S.Dak. Bar Asns; pres, Black Hills Area Coun, Boy Scouts, 52; Lions; Elks; Mason (33°); Scottish Rite, Chap. Commandry, Red Cross of Constantine; Past Potentates, Shriner; Jesters; Odd Fellows. Rel: Congregational. Legal Res: 910 St. Charles St, Rapid City, S.Dak. 57701. Mailing Add: P.O. Box 1785, Rapid City, S.Dak. 57701.

BOUCHARD, ARTHUR A. D
b. Berlin, N.H, 8/1/13; married; c. One. Educ: Berlin, N.H. Schs. Polit. & Govt. Pos: N.H. State Rep, 45-55 & 59-67; mem, Constitutional Conv, 48, 56 & 64. Bus. & Prof. Pos: Brown Co, Lubrication Co. Mil. Serv: Navy, World War II. Mem: Eagles; Am. Legion. Rel: Catholic. Mailing Add: 610 Burgess St, Berlin, N.H. 03570. (1967)

BOUCHARD, BERTRAND J. D
Alderman-at-Lg, Nashua, N.H.
b. Nashua, N.H, 5/17/28; s. Alfred E. Bouchard and Emelia Durocher B; m. 6/6/51 to Simonne Caron; c. Marc G. and Suzanne. Educ: Northeast. Univ, B.A, 61; Riviere Col, Grad. Sch. of Educ, 1 year. Polit. & Govt. Pos: Various polit. campaign pos; alderman, Nashua, N.H, 66-69, alderman-at-lg, 69-; del, Spec. Dem. Conv, Nashua, 67; del, Dem. Nat. Conv. and Dem. State Conv, 68; chmn, Nashua River Water Pollution Cmn. Bus. & Prof. Pos: Soc. worker, State of N.H, 57-59; acct. exec, Slawsby Ins, 59- Mil. Serv: Entered as Pvt, Army, 51, released as Pfc, 53, after serv. in 28th Inf. Div, Eucom, 51-53. Mailing Add: 102 Lock St, Nashua, N.H. 03060.

BOUCHER, GEORGE VICTOR R
b. Grand Rapids, Mich, 5/4/29; s. George Farquhar Boucher and Hazel Louise Sarsfield B; single. Educ: Univ. Mich, A.B, 51; Harvard Law Sch, LL.B, 56; Phi Beta Kappa; Phi Eta Sigma; Phi Kappa Phi; Pi Sigma Alpha; Scabbard and Blade; Druids; Mimes. Polit. & Govt. Pos: Pres, Kent Co. Young Rep. Club, Mich, 59; chmn, Kent Co. Rep. Cmt, 65-66; chmn, Fifth Dist. Rep. Cmt, 67-68; del, Rep. Nat. Conv, 68; judge, 17th Judicial Circuit, State of Mich, 69- Bus. & Prof. Pos: Partner, Wheeler, Upham, Bryant & Uhl, law firm, 56-68. Mil. Serv: Entered as 2nd Lt, Army, 51, released as 1st Lt, 53, after serv. in 2nd Logistical Command, Korea, 52-53, Maj, Res, 65-; Army Commendation Medal; Am. Defense, Korean Serv, UN Serv. and Armed Forces Res. Ribbons. Mem: Am, Mich. State and Grand Rapids Bar Asns; Am. Judicature Soc; French Soc. Mich; Peninsular Club, Grand Rapids.

Rel: United Church of Christ. Legal Res: 2060 Frances Ave. S.E, Grand Rapids, Mich. 49507. Mailing Add: 454 J Hall of Justice, Grand Rapids, Mich. 49502.

BOUCHER, MAYO TERRY D
b. Stephenville, Tex, 7/15/18; s. Terry Sherman Boucher and Henrietta Turley B; m. 7/31/42 to Mary Catherine Lake; c. Phillip Larry and Terri Sue. Educ: Tex. Tech. Col, 37-41; Univ. N.Mex. LL.B, 52 and J.D, 68; Pi Sigma Alpha; I.R.S. Polit. & Govt. Pos: Treas, Dem. Party, Valencia Co, N.Mex, 53-56; city attorney, Belen, N.Mex, 56-57; N.Mex. State Rep, 57-67, mem, Interim Criminal Law Study Cmt, N.Mex. State House of Rep, 57-63, chmn, House Judiciary Cmt, 61-65; del, Dem. Nat. Conv, 64; attorney, Appeal Bd, Selective Serv, 67- Bus. & Prof. Pos: Attorney-at-law, Belen, N.Mex, 52-; dir, First Nat. Bank of Belen, 60- Mil. Serv: Entered as A/S, Navy, 42, released as Lt.(jg), 45, after serv. in Pac. Theater; Aleutian Islands and S.Pac. Ribbons. Mem: Am. Judicature Soc; N.Mex. and Valencia Co. Bar Asns; AF&AM (Past Master, Bethlehem Lodge 56); Scottish Rite; Eastern Star (Past Patron); pres, Rotary Club, 61-62; pres, Belen C. of C, 55-56. Rel: Baptist; chmn, Bd. of Deacons, First Baptist Church, Belen. Legal Res: El Chapparel De La Mesa, Belen, N.Mex. 87002. Mailing Add: P.O. Box 227, Belen, N.Mex. 87002.

BOUCHER, RAYMOND L. R
b. Rochester, N.H, 9/17/17; married; c. 3. Educ: Gerwick, Maine schs. Polit. & Govt. Pos: N.H. State Rep, -67. Bus. & Prof. Pos: Life and Health Ins. Mem: Rochester Sch. Bd; Kiwanis; Rochester Country Club. Mailing Add: 30 Charles St, Rochester, N.H. 03867. (1967)

BOULEY, ARTHUR D
N.H. State Rep.
b. Nashua, N.H, 6/28/87; married; c. Two. Educ: Parochial and pub. schs. Polit. & Govt. Pos: N.H. State Rep, 57-67 & 69- Bus. & Prof. Pos: Retired salesman, Cudahy Packing Co. Mil. Serv: Sgt, Army 103rd Inf. Regt, World War I; Purple Heart; French Croix de Guerre with Palm; Nat. Guard, Mex. border, 16. Mem: VFW; DAV; World War I Vet; United Commercial Travelers of Am. Rel: Catholic. Mailing Add: 14 Sawyer St, Nashua, N.H. 03060. (1967)

BOULOUS, LILA NEBHAN D
V.Chmn, Broome Co. Dem. Cmt, N.Y.
b. Lebanon, Broummana, 8/15/04; d. Ladlalah Nebhan and Joutine Simsu N; m. 4/8/23 to Peter Boulous; c. Yvonne Yamen, Renee Behlog, Marcell Mansoun and Joyce Stento. Educ: Pub. Sch. 78, Brooklyn, N.Y. Polit. & Govt. Pos: Second v.chmn, Broome Co. Dem. Cmt, N.Y, currently. Mem: Ladies of Lebanon Club (past pres); secy, Am. Civic Asn; Cath. Daughters of Am; pres, Broome Co. Dem. Womens Club (past secy, treas. and bd. dirs). Rel: Catholic. Mailing Add: 915 Front St, Binghamton, N.Y. 13905.

BOURG, EMILE JOSEPH D
b. Mark, La, 8/8/98; s. Henry Joseph Bourg and Corinne Landry B; m. 5/10/22 to Mabel Thompson; c. Emile Joseph, Jr, George James, Jean Marie (Mrs. Ellis); John Ronald and Jerry Henry. Educ: La. State Univ, 16-17. Polit. & Govt. Pos: Mem. Dem. State Cent. Cmt, La, 56-60; del, Dem. Nat. Conv, 68. Bus. & Prof. Pos: Secy, La. AFL-CIO, 37-; supt, Div. of State Bldg, La, 48-60. Mil. Serv: Pvt, Marine Corps, 18-19, with serv. in Second Co, First Reg, Cuba, Haiti, W.I; Victory Medal; Haitian Campaign Badge. Mem: Am. Legion; VFW; Marine Corps League; K. of C; La. Soc. Welfare Asn; Int. Brotherhood of Elec. Workers. Rel: Catholic. Mailing Add: 816 W. Johnston St, Baton Rouge, La. 70802.

BOURGOIN, EMILE J. D
Maine State Rep.
b. Frenchville, Maine, 12/8/00; s. Joseph L. Bourgoin and Flavie Sirois B; m. 6/19/22 to Laura D. Guimond; c. Bernard, Robert, Lewella, Mary Ellen, Roger and James. Educ: Madawaska Training Sch, class of 18. Polit. & Govt. Pos: U.S. Customs inspector, 24-57; Maine State Rep, 63- Mem: Lions; Nat. Customs Serv. Admin. Fishing and hunting. Rel: Roman Catholic. Mailing Add: 50 E. Main St, Ft. Kent, Maine 04743. (1967)

BOUTELLE, PAUL BENJAMIN Socialist Workers Party
b. N.Y.C, 10/13/34; s. Anton Charles Boutelle and Anna May Benjamin B; div; c. Daryl. Educ: Jr. High Sch. 120, $3\frac{1}{2}$ years. Polit. & Govt. Pos: Mem, Young Socialist Alliance, 60-61, Fair-Play-for-Cuba Cmt, 61-63, Cmt. to aid the Monroe Defendents, 62-63, Freedom Now Party and Malcolm X's Orgn. of Afro-Am. Unity, 64, and Socialist Workers Party, 65-; cand, Manhattan Boro pres, 65, attorney-gen. of N.Y, 66, Vice President of U.S, 68 and mayor, N.Y.C, 69; founding chmn, Afro-Am. Against the War in Vietnam, 65; secy, Black United Action Front of Harlem, 66-67; an organizer, Black contingent in the mobilization against the Vietnam war at the UN; off. coordinator and asst. to Rev. James Bevel, leader of the spring mobilization cmn. to end the war, 67. Bus. & Prof. Pos: Salesman, Mar-Rahman Real Estate Brokers, 58; educ. rep, Field Enterprises Educ. Corp, 59-61; dir, Pan-African Book Distributors and sales rep, The Negro Book Club, 61-63; sales rep, Encyclop. Brittannica, 63, 64, 66 & 69; part time taxi driver, currently. Publ: Columnist, The Militant, 67. Rel: Atheist. Mailing Add: 873 Broadway, Second Floor South, New York, N.Y. 10003.

BOUTON, CHARLOTTE ELDREDGE D
b. Cape May, N.J, 2/18/14; d. Henry H. Eldredge and Charlotte L.W. Lindsay E; m. 3/9/63 to James O. Bouton. Educ: Wilson Col, A.B, 35. Polit. & Govt. Pos: Exec. secy, U.S. House of Rep, 37-55, exec. secy. to U.S. Rep. Frank Thompson, Jr, 55-69; committeewoman, N.J. State Dem. Cmt, 46-51. Mem: DAR. Rel: Presbyterian. Legal Res: 52 Tuckahoe Rd, Dennisville, N.J. 08214. Mailing Add: 2857 Monroe St. N.E, Washington, D.C. 20028.

BOUTWELL, ALBERT BURTON D
b. Montgomery, Ala, 11/13/04; s. Clarence C. Boutwell and Lydia Sweatt B; m. 11/23/34 to Helen Balfour Drake; c. Helen Linder, Albert Burton and Charles Drake. Educ: Univ. of Ala, LL.B, 28; Sigma Delta Kappa; Alpha Kappa Psi. Polit. & Govt. Pos: Secy, Joint U.S. Cong. Cmt. Forestry, 39-40; del-at-lg, Dem. Nat. Conv, 44; Ala. State Sen, 46-58; Lt. Gov, Ala, 58-62; mayor, Birmingham, 63-67. Bus. & Prof. Pos: Admitted to Ala. Bar, 28; attorney-at-law, Birmingham, 28-; exec. v.pres. and dir, Merit Oak Flooring Co, Inc, 56-; co-founder and dir, Vulcan Life & Accident Ins. Co. Mem: U.S. Jr. C. of C.(nat. v.pres, 35-36); Am. Bar Asn; Blue Key; Elk (past Exalted Ruler); Eagles; Mason; Shrine; Jester; Lions; Vestavia Country Club; The Club, Birmingham. Rel: Methodist; Steward. Mailing Add: First National Bldg, Birmingham, Ala. 35203.

BOVE, FIORE LOUIS D
Vt. State Sen.
b. Burlington, Vt, 5/17/20; s. Louis Bove and Victoria Falco B; m. 3/5/46 to Mildred Merle Sweet; c. Diane Victoria and Louis Fiore. Educ: Cathedral High Sch, Burlington, Vt, 4 years. Polit. & Govt. Pos: Vt. State Sen, 66, 67-68 & 69- Bus. & Prof. Pos: Restauranteur, Bove's Restaurant, Burlington, Vt, 41- Mil. Serv: Entered as Pvt, Marines, 42, released as Pfc, 46, after serv. in First Marine Div, Guadalcanal and Brit. Solomon Islands, 42-43; Presidential Unit Citation for participation in the defense of Guadalcanal and Brit. Solomon Islands. Mem: Vt. Sportswriters and Sportscasters Asn; charter mem, Essex Junction Am. Legion; charter mem, Burlington Vet. Club; DAV; VFW; Elks; charter mem. and dir, Burlington Downtown Athletic Club. Rel: Roman Catholic. Mailing Add: 23 Bittersweet Lane, Burlington, Vt. 05401.

BOW, FRANK T. R
U.S. Rep, Ohio
b. Canton, Ohio, 2/20/01; m. 5/12/23 to Caroline C. Denzer; c. Robert Lee and Joseph Withrow. Educ: Culver Mil. Acad; Ohio North Univ. Hon. LL.D, Ohio North. Univ, 61 and Mt. Union Col, 63. Polit. & Govt. Pos: Gen. counsel, Subcmt. on Expenditures and Select Cmt. to Investigate the Fed. Communs. Cmn, U.S. Cong, 46-47; regent, Smithsonian Inst; U.S. Rep, Ohio, 50- Bus. & Prof. Pos: Lawyer. Mil. Serv: War Correspondent with the Ohio 37th Div, World War II. Legal Res: 1718 Market Ave. N, Canton, Ohio 44714. Mailing Add: 2182 Rayburn House Office Bldg, Washington, D.C. 20515.

BOWDEN, LAWRY J. D
b. Salt Lake City, Utah, 7/10/34; s. George C. Bowden and Shara Ann Rosson B; m. 1/15/54 to Mary Ellen Hill; c. Chris J, Nancy Ellen and James J. Educ: Univ. Utah, 60- Polit. & Govt. Pos: Voting dist. chmn, Salt Lake Co. Dem. Party, Utah, 14 years, legis. v.chmn, 2 years and sen. v.chmn, 2 years; mem, Salt Lake Co. Dem. Cent. Cmt, 14 years. Bus. & Prof. Pos: Chemist, Kennecott Copper Co, Magna, 53- Mem: USW (pres, 64); Coalition for Dem. Action; Nat. Cong. Parents and Teachers; Young Dem. Rel: Latter-day Saint. Mailing Add: 1898 N. 2450 W, Salt Lake City, Utah 84116.

BOWDON, WILLIAM GEORGE D
Mayor, Alexandria, La.
b. Alexandria, La, 10/18/21; s. William George Bowdon and Mary L. Middleton B; m. 2/24/47 to Ina Smith; c. William George, III. Educ: La State Univ, B.S, 43; Kappa Alpha. Polit. & Govt. Pos: La. State Rep, 48-52; Mayor, Alexandria, La, 53- Bus. & Prof. Pos: Real Estate Broker, La, 46-53. Mil. Serv: Entered as Pvt, Marine Corps, 43, released as Capt, 46, after serv. in Fleet Marine Force, Pac, 44-46. Mem: Elks; Lions; Am. Legion; VFW; Amvets; C. of C; Moose; Alexandria Golf and Country Club. Rel: Methodist. Legal Res: 3131 Elliott St, Alexandria, La. 71301. Mailing Add: City Hall, Alexandria, La. 71301. (1967)

BOWE, JOHN EDWARD 'ED' R
Mem, Calif. Rep. State Cent. Cmt.
b. Los Angeles, Calif, 7/3/18; s. John Edward Bowe and Inez DeCandia B; m. 11/17/51 to Ruby Louise Thiesen. Educ: Stockton High Sch, Calif, grad, 36. Polit. & Govt. Pos: V.pres, Tulare Co. Rep. Assembly, 64, pres, 65; campaign chmn, Tulare and Kings Co. for Sen. George Murphy, 64 and Dinuba City for Calif. Assemblyman Gordon Duffy, 64 & 66; mem, Tulare Co. Rep. Cent. Cmt, 64-67; mem, Calif. Rep. State Cent. Cmt, 65-; v.pres, Tulare Co. Rep. Cent. Cmt, 66; campaign chmn, Tulare Co. for Gov. Ronald Reagan, 66; chief, Calif. State Div. of Housing and Commun. Develop, 67- Bus. & Prof. Pos: Optician, Riggs Optical Co, Stockton, Calif, 36-38; asst. off. mgr, Nat. Biscuit Co, Sacramento, 38-41; dist. mgr, Half Moon Fruit & Produce Co, Dinuba, 46-56; owner, Dinuba Hardware Co, 56-67. Mil. Serv: Entered as Pvt, Army, 41, released as Capt, 46, after serv. in D Squadron, 112th Army Air Force, Continental U.S. Mem: Am. Legion; Lions Int; Commonwealth Club of San Francisco; Dinuba C. of C; Dinuba Merchants Asn. Rel: Roman Catholic. Mailing Add: 1500 Seventh St, Sacramento, Calif. 95814.

BOWEN, A'DELBERT 'DELL' R
b. Tuscumbia, Ala, 11/13/19; s. A'Delbert Bowen and Gertrude Willett B; m. 7/25/45 to Rebecca Proctor; c. A'Delbert III, Lanny, Montez Eliz. Educ: State Teachers Col, 2 years; Atlanta Law Sch, LL.B, 54. Polit. & Govt. Pos: Ga. State Rep, 59-64; Randolph Co. Attorney, Ga, 60- Bus. & Prof. Pos: Attorney-at-law; gen. ins. agent. Mil. Serv: Maj, Army Air Force, 41-47; Lt. Col, Air Force Res, at present. Mem: Masons; Am. & Ga. Bar Asns; Am. Legion. Rel: Methodist. Mailing Add: Cuthbert, Ga. 31740.

BOWEN, CHARLES BENJAMIN D
Exec. Committeeman, Greenville Co. Dem. Party, S.C.
b. Piedmont, S.C, 9/15/27; s. Elmo Arnstein Bowen and Irene Guess B; m. 1/7/47 to Vera Trammell; c. Charles B, Jr. and Bryan Trammell. Educ: Furman Univ, 54; Univ. of S.C, B.S, 57, LL.B, 59. Polit. & Govt. Pos: Del, Dem. Nat. Conv, 60 & 68; chmn, Greenville Co. Dem. Party, S.C, 62-66, exec. committeeman, 66- Bus. & Prof. Pos: Partner, Bolt & Bowen, Attorneys, 60-65, Abrams, Bowen & Townes, 65- Mil. Serv: Entered as Pvt, Army, 51, released as S/Sgt, 53, after serv. in 40th Inf. Div, 160th Inf. Regiment, Korean War; Korean Campaign Medal with Three Bronze Stars; Commanding Officer's Leadership Award; Hawaiian Inf. Training Center Leadership Sch, 52. Mem: Am. Trial Lawyers Asn; pres, S.C. Trial Lawyers Asn; S.C, Am. and Greenville Co. Bar Asns; Am. Judicature Soc; Am. Legion (past post comdr, 62, judge advocate for S.C. Dept, 68-); first v.pres and pres, Greenville Co. Cancer Soc, 60; nat. bd. dir, United Cancer Coun, 67- Rel: Methodist. Mailing Add: 9 Windmere Dr, Greenville, S.C. 29607.

BOWEN, KENNETH L. R
Nebr. State Sen.
b. Red Cloud, Nebr, 1/25/12; m. 5/31/42 to Kathryn V. Kirkbride; c. Marilyn

Kay, Phillip J, Richard L. and Jack Randolph. Educ: Pub. Schs. in Kans. Polit. & Govt. Pos: Past chmn, City Hosp. Bd; past pres, Bd. of Educ; past mayor of Red Cloud, Nebr; past exec. secy, League of Nebr. Munic; Nebr. State Sen, currently; dir, Farmers Home Admin, State of Nebr, currently. Bus. & Prof. Pos: Real estate, ins. and loans bus; owner and operator of farms. Mem: Past pres. and past secy, Red Cloud C. of C; Mason (32°); Shrine. Rel: Methodist. Mailing Add: 534 N. Walnut, Red Cloud, Nebr. 68970

BOWEN, MAURICE RICHARD, JR. D
b. Vicksburg, Miss, 11/21/39; s. Maurice Richard Bowen and Frances Seymour B; m. 6/4/61 to Mary Keith Hampton; c. Jane Hampton. Educ: Univ. Tenn 57-58; Mid. Tenn. State Univ, B.S, 61; Vanderbilt Univ, LL.B, 64, J.D, 69; Young Dem. Polit. & Govt. Pos: Chattanooga-Hamilton Co. Mgr, Humphrey-Muskie Campaign, Tenn, 68; alternate del-at-lg, Dem. Nat. Conv, 68; mem, United Dem. Coun, 68-; secy, Hamilton Co. Young Dem. Club, 68- Bus. & Prof. Pos: Partner, Duncan, Bowen and Breazeale, Attorneys, 67- Mem: Chattanooga, Tenn. and Am. Bar Asns; Chattanooga Trial Lawyers Asn; Sertoma Int. Rel: Cumberland Presbyterian. Mailing Add: 2512 Mahala Lane, Chattanooga, Tenn. 37421.

BOWEN, OTIS R. R
Speaker, Ind. House of Rep.
b. Rochester, Ind, 2/26/18; s. Vernie Bowen and Pearl Wright B; m. 2/25/39 to Elizabeth Steinmann; c. Rick, Judy, Tim and Rob. Educ: Ind. Univ, A.B. in Chem, 39; Ind. Univ. Med. Sch, M.D, 42; Alpha Omega Alpha; Phi Beta Pi; Delta Chi. Polit. & Govt. Pos: Coroner, Marshall Co, Ind, 52-56; Ind. State Rep, Marshall Co, 57-58, 61-62, 63-64, Fulton and Marshall Counties, 65-66, Marshall and Starke Counties, 67-68 & 69-, Minority Leader, Ind. House of Rep, 65-66, Speaker, 67-68 & 69-, chmn, Pub. Health Cmt, 61-62 & 63-64, mem. of several other cmts. during each session, chmn, Cmn. to Study Aid to Dependent Children in Ind, 63-64, mem, Legis. Adv. Cmn, 65-66, mem, Ind. Recreation Coun, Cmt. for Eradication of Tuberc. in Ind, Adv. Coun. of Ind. State Dept. of Pub. Welfare for Med. Care to Aged under Kerr-Mills, Cmt. to Study Med. Educ. in Ind. and Cmt. to Study Needs of Mentally Retarded; cand. for nomination for Gov, State Rep. Conv, 68. Bus. & Prof. Pos: Intern, Mem. Hosp, South Bend, Ind; private practice of med, Bremen, Ind, 46-; mem. staff, Bremen Commun, Parkview, St. Josephs of South Bend, St. Josephs of Mishawaka and Mem. Hosp. Mil. Serv: Entered as 1st Lt, Army, 43, released as Capt, 46, after serv. in Med. Corps, Pac. Theater and Okinawa Campaign. Publ: Several articles in medical journals. Mem: Marshall Co. Tuberc. Asn. (v.pres); Marshall Co. Med. Soc.(past pres); 13th Dist. Med. Soc.(past pres); 13th Dist. Gen. Practice Asn; Ind. State Med. Asn.(legis. cmn, 58-, 13th Dist. coun, 65-69); Am. Med. Asn; Am. and Ind. Acad. of Gen. Practice; Ind. Ment. Health Asn; Trudeau Soc; Bremen Kiwanis (past pres, past v.pres. and past dir); C. of C; Ind. Univ. Alumni Asn; Am. Legion; VFW; Farm Bur; Marshall Co. Civil Defense (dir, health serv, 59-62); Tri Valley Coun, Boy Scouts. Rel: Lutheran; Past v.pres, Congregation and past chmn. bd. finance, Lutheran Church Sch. Bd, St. Paul's Lutheran Church, Bremen, Ind. Mailing Add: 304 N. Center St, Bremen, Ind. 46506.

BOWEN, RALPH W. D
b. Henry Co, Ga, 3/11/13; s. James David Bowen and Sarah Morris B; m. 5/29/38 to Ludya Elizabeth Williams; c. David Rudolph, Ralph Millard, Horace Woodford, Carol Elizabeth. Educ: Monroe A&M, 32; Oglethorpe Univ, 33-36; Alpha Lambda Tau. Polit. & Govt. Pos: Ga. State Rep, 63-64. Bus. & Prof. Pos: Timber cruiser and buyer; poultry and livestock farmer. Mem: Mason; Dawsonville Lions, v.pres, 59-60, pres, 62-63. Rel: Methodist. Mailing Add: Dawsonville, Ga. 30534. (1967)

BOWEN, ROONEY L. D
Ga. State Rep.
b. Lilly, Ga, 7/25/33; s. Rooney L. Bowen, Sr. and Jewell Joiner B; m. 7/28/57 to Marian G. Chandler; c. Judy Elline, Rooney Lilly III. Educ: Univ. Ga. Polit. & Govt. Pos: Councilman and Mayor Pro Tem, Vienna, Ga, 62-63; Ga. State Rep, 63- Bus. & Prof. Pos: Auto dealer; funeral dir. Mem: Mason; Shrine; v.pres, Kiwanis, 63; Elks. Rel: Methodist. Mailing Add: Vienna, Ga. 31092.

BOWEN, ROSS P. D
b. Lyons, Ga, 4/30/13; m. 8/13/48 to Carolyn E. Palmer; c. William Michael, Ross Daniel, Beverly Alice, Carolyn Michelle. Educ: Lyons High Sch. Polit. & Govt. Pos: Ga. State Rep, 61-64. Bus. & Prof. Pos: Farmer. Mil. Serv: Navy, 42-45. Mem: Mason. Rel: Methodist. Mailing Add: Lyons, Ga. 30436. (1967)

BOWEN, WILLIAM F. D
Minority Whip, Ohio House of Rep.
b. Cincinnati, Ohio, 1/30/29; s. William F. Bowen and Henrietta R. Washington B; m. 3/30/56 to Dolores Lee Freeman; c. William F, Kevin Braxton and Terrence Samuel. Educ: Xavier Univ, 52-55. Polit. & Govt. Pos: Alternate del, Dem. Nat. Conv, 68; v.chmn, Hamilton Co. Dem. Party, Ohio, currently; mem, Hamilton Co. Dem. Exec, Steering and Cent. Cmts, currently; mem, Dem. State Cent. Cmt, Ohio, currently; Ohio State Rep, currently, Minority Whip, Ohio House of Rep, currently. Mem: Mason; Wayfarers Club of Cincinnati. Rel: Protestant. Mailing Add: 3494 Reading Rd, Cincinnati, Ohio 45229.

BOWER, ADAM T. R
b. Sunbury, Pa, 2/11/05; s. William Bower and Emma Indrote B; m. to Elizabeth Diehl. Educ: Sunbury High Sch. Polit. & Govt. Pos: Pa. State Rep, 50-67. Mailing Add: 138 Bainbridge St, Sunbury, Pa. 17801. (1967)

BOWER, JOHN DAVID R
Kans. State Rep.
b. McLouth, Kans, 12/17/11; s. David Earl Bower and Mabel Kimmel B; m. 6/13/36 to (Maude) Agnes Black; c. Ronald David and Ruth Ann. Educ: McPherson Col, A.B, 38. Polit. & Govt. Pos: Dir, McLouth Rural High Sch, Kans, 49-55; Kans. State Rep, 53-; dir, Watershed Dist, 56-59. Mem: Farm Bureau; Kiwanis. Rel: Church of the Brethren; Ordained Minister. Mailing Add: Route 1, McLouth, Kans. 66054.

BOWERS, ARTHUR ROBERT D
Ohio State Rep.
b. Steubenville, Ohio, 2/16/19; s. Robert W. Bowers and Helen Foreman B; m. 12/10/43 to Betty Jane Wright; c. Robert, Karen (Mrs. David Gargano), Rebecca, Melissa and Kathryn. Educ: Steubenville Cath. Cent. Col, Ohio, grad; Serv. Schs. Polit. & Govt. Pos: City councilman, Steubenville, Ohio, 3 terms; Ohio State Rep, 33rd Dist, 69- Bus. & Prof. Pos: Owner, Bower's Tile & Marble Contracting Co, currently. Mil. Serv: Entered as Pvt, Army, 42, released as Platoon Sgt, 45, after serv. in 101st 17th Airborne Div. with Parachute Regt, ETO, 44-45; Two Purple Hearts; Bronze Star; Four Campaign Stars. Mem: Elks; Eagles; Am. Legion; DAV; Polish Athletic Club; Mingo Turtle Club; Mingo Slovak Club; C. of C; Tile Setters and Marble Setters Union; VFW. Rel: Catholic. Mailing Add: Eft's Lane, Steubenville, Ohio 43952.

BOWERS, F. WESLEY D
Polit. & Govt. Pos: Attorney for Evansville Air Bd, Ind, 56-59; attorney for Evansville Redevelop. Cmn, 59-; Ind. State Sen, 63-66. Bus. & Prof. Pos: Instr. law and govt, Univ. Evansville, 53-69; lawyer. Mil. Serv: Army Inf, World War II. Mem: Local, State and Am. Bar Asns. Rel: Unitarian. Legal Res: 4519 Bellmeader, Evansville, Ind. 47714. Mailing Add: Permanent Savings Bldg, Evansville, Ind. 47708.

BOWERS, GROVER FORD, JR. D
b. Luray, S.C, 11/20/19; s. Grover F. Bowers and Corrine Fitts B; m. 6/15/50 to Macie Tison B. Educ: Univ. of S.C, A.B, 43. Polit. & Govt. Pos: S.C. State Sen, 63-67. Bus. & Prof. Pos: Dealer, processor in Farm Commodities; partner, firm of Harper & Bowers. Mil. Serv: Marines, 1st Lt. Mailing Add: Estill, S.C. 29918. (1967)

BOWERS, JACK E. R
b. Warsaw, Ind, 8/28/25; s. Bert Bowers and Blanche Orcutt B; m. 3/19/46 to Selma L. Fopay; c. Douglas and David. Educ: Manchester Col, B.S, 49; Univ. Chicago Law Sch, J.D, 50. Polit. & Govt. Pos: Ill. State Rep, 65-66; attorney, DuPage Co. Forest Preserve Dist, 60-66, Village of Oakbrook, 58-66 and Village of Lombard, 60-65; state attorney, DuPage Co, 58-59, asst. state attorney, 52-54. Bus. & Prof. Pos: Partner, Law Firm of Hooper, Bowers, Calkins & Carney, 57- Mil. Serv: Entered as Pvt, Army Air Corps, 43, released as Sgt, 46. Mem: Pres, DuPage Co. Bar Asn, 61; Ill. Bar Asn; Elks; Kiwanis Int; Am. Legion; v.chmn. bd. trustees, Bethany Brethren Hosp. Rel: Methodist. Legal Res: 806 Maple Ave, Downers Grove, Ill. 60515. Mailing Add: 4915 Main St, Downers Grove, Ill. 60515. (1967)

BOWERS, QUINTON R. D
Ala. State Rep.
b. Samson, Ala, 3/20/21; s. William E. Bowers and Mary Aplin B; m. 12/5/53 to Betty Jewel Mathews; c. Lita Kay. Educ: Univ. Ala, B.S, 49; Birmingham Sch. Law, LL.B, 55; Sigma Delta Kappa. Polit. & Govt. Pos: Ala. State Rep, Jefferson Co, 63-, mem. Bus. and Labor and Mil. Affairs, Local Legis. Standing Cmt, chmn, Cmt. Local Legis. Two, mem, Rules Cmt. and Mil. Affairs Cmt. and Floor Leader, Ala. House Rep; spec. asst. attorney gen, State of Ala, 66- Bus. & Prof. Pos: Salesman, Goodyear, 50-51; adjuster, Universal C.I.T. Credit Corp, 51-52; adjuster, Am. Fore Ins. Groupe, 53-57; attorney at law, 57- Mil. Serv: Entered as Pvt, Marine Corps, 39, released as Sgt, 45, after serv. in First Marine Div, Pac. Theatre, 42-44; Am. Campaign Ribbon; Victory and Good Conduct Medals; Am. Defense and Asiatic Pac. Campaign Ribbons; Presidential Unit Citation. Mem: Am. and Ala. Bar Asns; Birmingham Bar Asn. (judicial and legal reform cmt), State of Ala. Employees' Asn; Ala. Peace Officer's Asn; life mem, Ala. League of Aging Citizens; Gov. George Wallace's Cmt. on Employ. of Physically Handicapped, 64; C. of C; Am. Legion (state legis. cmt); assoc. dir, Nat. Vet. Day Cmt, Birmingham; Ala. Vet. Affairs Cmt; VFW (nat. legal cmt, 60, comdr. Kelly Ingram Post 668, mem. All State Team of Post Comdrs, 61-62, comdr, Dept. of Ala, mem. All Am. Team of Dept. Comdrs, 63-64 and nat. legis. cmt, 64-66); Univ. Ala. Alumni Asn; Jefferson Co. Sportsman Asn; Eagles; N. Birmingham Sertoma (past pres); F&AM (Worshipful Master, Lodge 384, 63-64); Shrine. Dept. Comdr. of Year Award, VFW, 64; Hon. State Trooper; Hon. Dept. Sheriff; Hon. Lt. Col. on staff of S. Ernest Vandiver, Ga, 59; Hon. Adm, Ala. Navy, 62. Rel: Methodist; Past pres, George R. Stuart Bible Class and mem. off. bd, First Methodist Church of Birmingham. Legal Res: 1300 Chester St, Birmingham, Ala. 35226. Mailing Add: 915 Frank Nelson Bldg, Birmingham, Ala. 35203.

BOWERS, THEODORE MARKER R
W.Va. State Sen.
b. Point Marion, Pa, 2/1/07; s. Frank L. Bowers, Sr. and Asia L. Sadler B; m. 6/16/31 to Myra Llewelyn; c. Nancy (Mrs. Harry A. Jackson) and Betsy (Mrs. James L. Bobo). Educ: Univ. Pittsburgh; Sigma Alpha Epsilon. Polit. & Govt. Pos: Town Councilman, New Martinsville, W.Va, 38-40; W.Va. State Sen, 42- Mem: Mason, Elks; Moose; Shrine; Eagles; Rotary; Jesters. Rel: Christian. Mailing Add: 391 Long St, New Martinsville, W.Va. 26155.

BOWERSOX, ROBERT JOSEPH D
Mem, Steering Cmt, Calif. Dem. State Cent. Cmt.
b. Youngstown, Ohio; s. John J. Bowersox and Katherine Flask B; m. 6/10/47 to Edith P. Popwell; c. Robert J, Jr, Kathleen, S. Scott and Kim C. Educ: Mich. State Univ; Univ. Mich. Med. Sch. Polit. & Govt. Pos: Mem, 17th Dist. Agr. Asn. Calif, 58-; chmn, Monterey Co. Dem. Cent. Cmt, 64-68; mem, Monterey Co. Hosp. Adv. Cmt, 65; mem, steering cmt, Calif. Dem. State Cent. Cmt, 65-; chmn, Medicare Adv. Cmt, Monterey Co, 66-; del, Dem. Nat. Conv, 68. Bus. & Prof. Pos: Obstetrician and gynecologist, Cent. Med. Clin, Calif, 58-; pres, Gilmed, Inc, currently. Mil. Serv: Pfc, Army, 43-46, re-entered as chief dept. obstetrics and gynecology, Army Hosp, Ft. Stewart, Ga, 56, released as Maj, 58. Mem: Am, Calif. and Monterey Co. Med. Asns; Am. Col. of Obstetricians and Gynecologists; Elks; Pacheco Club. Mailing Add: 1156 Alameda, Monterey, Calif. 93940.

BOWIE, FRANK MOREY R
Chmn, Androscoggin Co. Rep. Party, Maine
b. Durham, Maine, 2/5/23; s. Leon Roy Bowie and Alemeda Libby B; m. 4/15/50 to Lucille Gurtrude Williams; c. Jeffrey W, Betsy A. and Eric C. Educ: Edward Little High Sch, Auburn, Maine, 4 years. Polit. & Govt. Pos:

Pres, Androscoggin Co. Young Rep, Maine, 52-53; Maine State Rep, 55-56 & 60; chmn, Durham Town Rep. Cmt, 56-69; moderator, Town Meetings, 12 years; chmn, Durham Budget Cmt, several years; dir, Durham Indust. Develop, 60-65; Durham Tax Assessor, 63; chmn, Androscoggin Co. Rep. Cmt, 68-69; chmn, Androscoggin Co. Rep. Party, 68- Bus. & Prof. Pos: Dir, Concord Ins. Co, 14 years; dir, State Mutual Ins. Co, 6 years; farmer and contractor, 40- Mem: Mason (past Master); Grange; Fish and Game Asn; Farm Bur.(v.pres, Androscoggin Chap). Rel: Protestant. Legal Res: Durham, Maine 04210. Mailing Add: R.R. 1, Auburn, Maine 04210.

BOWIN, DONALD ALBERT R
b. Roseland, Kans, 9/24/29; s. Elmer Frederick Bowin and May Welcher B; m. 12/13/59 to Mary Elisbeth Cotton; c. Keith, Bryon, Donnie and Lisa. Educ: Kans. State Col; Parsons Jr. Col. Polit. & Govt. Pos: Former Iowa State Rep. Mil. Serv: Entered as Pvt, Air Force, 47, released as Sgt, 48. Mem: Amvets; Lions; Elks; C. of C. Rel: Assembly of God. Mailing Add: 4031 Scenic Dr, Waterloo, Iowa 50704. (1967)

BOWLBY, HAROLD V. R
Chmn, St. Louis Co. Rep. Cmt, Mo.
b. Purcell, Okla, 5/6/14; s. Lee Bowlby and Dorothy Hanson B; m. 11/25/37 to Holland Petty. Educ: Ark. City Jr. Col.(Kans), 2 years. Polit. & Govt. Pos: Twp. committeeman, Rep. Party, Meramec, Mo, 63-; treas, Second Cong. Dist, 64-66; chmn, St. Louis Co. Rep. Cmt, 66-; mayor, Eureka, Mo, 67-; treas, Eighth Cong. Dist, 68- Legal Res: 125 West Ave, Eureka, Mo. 63025. Mailing Add: P.O. Box 95, Eureka, Mo. 63025.

BOWLEN, WAYNE THOMAS D
N.H. State Rep.
b. Portsmouth, N.H, 1/24/45; s. Kenneth James Bowlen and Florence Lemerise B; single. Educ: Univ. N.H, B.A, 68. Polit. & Govt. Pos: N.H. State Rep, 67-68 & 69- Bus. & Prof. Pos: Asst. mgr, Harbour Shoppe, Portsmouth, N.H, 68- Mem: Moose. Mailing Add: 143 Profile Ave, Portsmouth, N.H. 03801.

BOWLER, ANN R
Mem, Calif. Rep. State Cent. Cmt.
b. Batesville, Ark, 4/7/18; m. 1946 to John D. Bowler, Jr. Educ: Univ. Detroit, B.A. Polit. & Govt. Pos: Mem, Calif. Rep. State Cent. Cmt, 56-; dist. supvr, Bur. of Census, 60; del, Rep. Nat. Conv, 64 & 68; Rep. Presidential elector, 64; former mem, Exec. Cmt, Rep. Nat. Cmt. Mem: Red Cross. Mailing Add: 177 Rizo Alto Canal, Long Beach, Calif. 90801. (1967)

BOWLER, JAMES J. D
Mass. State Rep.
b. 1923. Educ: Springfield Col. Polit. & Govt. Pos: Mass. State Rep, 66-; Springfield Parks & Recreation Dept; Dist. Recreation Supvr. Recreation Div, (Civil Serv. status). Mil. Serv: Vet. World War II, Asiatic-Pac. Theater. Mem: Chmn, Springfield Muscular Dystrophy Campaign; Am. Legion; Liberty Post No. 430; K of C, Coun. 160; Van Horn Parents' Asn. (founder and permanent pres); Springfield Boys' Club Alumni Asn; Springfield Playground Supvr. Asn; John L. Sullivan Pee Wee Leagues (past secy, pres. and dir); Youth Organizer and Recreation Dir. of Athletic Prog. Rel: Catholic. Mailing Add: 195 Mildred Ave, Springfield, Mass. 01104.

BOWLER, ORSON LLOYD R
Chmn, Teton Co. Rep. Cent. Cmt, Idaho
b. Salt Lake City, Utah, 12/17/31; s. Orson Cuttler Bowler and Sarah Lloyd B; m. 6/8/60 to Janice Wilde; c. Suzanne, Janalyn, Orson Paul and Matthew Wilde. Educ: Univ. Utah, B.S, 59, Ed.D, 66; Univ. Idaho, M.N.S, 63; research asst, 62-63, research fel, 64-65. Polit. & Govt. Pos: Chmn, Teton Co. Rep. Cent. Cmt, Idaho, 68- Bus. & Prof. Pos: Teacher math. and sci, Soda Springs High Sch, Idaho, 59-62; supt, Teton Co. Sch. Dist. 401, Driggs, 64-69; supt, Eastside Sch. Dist. 201, Preston, 69- Mil. Serv: Entered as Pvt, Army, 53, released as SP-3, 56, after serv. in Detachment 3, 6400 SU USA Regt, Portland, Ore. Publ: 'A History of Federal Activities in Education,' In: School Organization & Administration for Utah Teachers, Univ. Utah, 64; 'A Cost of Education Index for Idaho as Related to Teton County Schools,' Ed.D. Dissertation, 66. Mem: Am. Asn. Sch. Adminstr; Phi Delta Kappa; Lions; C. of C. Rel: Latter-day Saint. Mailing Add: 58 South Third East, Preston, Idaho 83263.

BOWLES, CHESTER D
b. Springfield, Mass, 4/5/01; s. Charles Bowles and Nellie Harris B; m. 2/22/34 to Dorothy Stebbins; c. Barbara B.(Mrs. Coolidge), Chester, Jr, Cynthia, Sarah and Samuel. Educ: B.S, Yale, 24. Hon. LL.D. Law, Am. Univ, 46, Howard Univ, 56, Oberlin Col, 57, Bard Col, 57, Univ. R.I, 59, Univ. Mich, 61 and Yale Univ, 68. Polit. & Govt. Pos: Conn. elector for Franklin D. Roosevelt, 40; del, Dem. Nat. Conv, 40, 48, 56, 60, chmn. Dem. Nat. Platform, 60; dir, Off. Price Admin, 42-45; dir, Econ. Stabilization Cmn, 45-46; Am. del, UNESCO Conf, Paris, 46, mem. nat. cmt, 46-47; asst. of dir. gen, UN, 47-48; gov, Conn, 49-51; Ambassador to India, 51-53 & 63-69; U.S. Rep, Second Dist, Conn, 58-59; Under Secy. of State, 61-62; spec. asst. to President Kennedy on Asia, Africa and Latin Am. Affairs, 62-63. Bus. & Prof. Pos: Reporter, Springfield Rep, 24-25; mem. staff, George Batten Co, 25-29; established Benton & Bowles, Inc, N.Y.C, 29, chmn. bd, 36-41; Shaw lectr, Bryn Mawr Col, 53-54; Berkeley lectr, Univ. Calif, 56; Godkin lectr, Harvard, 56; Chubb lectr, Yale, 57. Publ: The Coming Political Breakthrough, 59; The Conscience of a Liberal, 62; The Makings of a Just Society, 63; plus seven others. Mem: Fletcher Sch. Law and Diplomacy; trustee, Franklin D. Roosevelt Found, Eleanor Roosevelt Mem. Found, Rockefeller Found. and Inst. African-Am. Rels; Asia Soc; Conn. State Grange; Essex Yacht Club. Rel: Unitarian. Mailing Add: Hayden's Point, Essex, Conn. 06426.

BOWLES, HARGROVE, JR. D
N.C. State Sen.
b. Monroe, N.C, 11/16/19; s. Hargrove Bowles and Kelly Bess Moneyhun B; m. 6/29/41 to Jessamine Woodward Boyce; c. Hargrove, III, Erskine Boyce, Mary Holland and Martha Thomas. Educ: Univ. N.C; Beta Theta Pi. Polit. & Govt. Pos: Dir. and chmn. bd, N.C. Dept. of Conserv. & Develop, 60-64; N.C. State Rep; N.C. State Sen, currently. Bus. & Prof. Pos: Dir, First Union National Bank, First Mortgage Ins. Co, Am. Hog Co. of Colo, Capri Indust. and Jewel Box Stores, Inc. Mil. Serv: Entered as Pvt, Army, 43, released as Cpl, 45. Mem: Nat. coun. Boy Scouts; state chmn, N.C. Partners of Alliance; chmn. bd, N.C. Heart Asn; bd. trustees, Methodist Col; bd, Greensboro Cerebral Palsy Sch. Rel: Methodist. Legal Res: 700 Country Club Dr, Greensboro, N.C. 27408. Mailing Add: Piedmont Blvd, Greensboro, N.C. 27406.

BOWLES, LAWRENCE LEONARD R
b. North Tarrytown, N.Y, 10/14/40; s. Leonard Turner Bowles and Catherine Mulligan B; single. Educ: Univ. N.C, Chapel Hill, B.A. with honors, 62; Harvard Law Sch, LL.B, 65; Rotary Found. fel, Law Col, Univ. Calcutta, India, 66-67. Polit. & Govt. Pos: Co-chmn, Harvard Students for Goldwater-Miller, Cambridge, Mass, 64; research dir, Stickley for Gov. Cmt, Charlotte, N.C, 67-68; exec. dir, Osteen for Cong. Cmt, Greensboro, 68-; treas, Nixon Rally Cmt, 68; admin. asst, U.S. Rep. Charles R. Jonas, Wash, D.C, 68- Bus. & Prof. Pos: Personal trust administr, Chase Manhattan Bank, N.Y.C, 65-66; commercial loan analyst, First Union Nat. Bank, Charlotte, N.C, 67. Mem: Ripon Soc; Harvard Law Sch. Asn, Wash, D.C. Rel: Episcopal. Legal Res: 3401 Shamrock Dr, Charlotte, N.C. 28205. Mailing Add: 2133 House Office Bldg, Washington, D.C. 20515.

BOWLING, JOHN HARRISON JR. D
W.Va. State Sen.
b. White Sulphur Springs, W.Va, 8/15/30; s. John H. Bowling and Urzula Coffman B; m. 8/2/52 to Barbara Massey; c. Connie Ann, John H, III, Bruce M, Richard C. and Martha Lynn. Educ: W.Va. Univ, A.B. Polit. & Govt. Pos: Mem, W.Va. State Dem. Exec. Cmt, 60-64; W.Va. State Del, 64-66; W.Va. State Sen, 66- Bus. & Prof. Pos: Hardware bus. Mem: Elks; Rotary Int; Jaycees; Kappa Alpha. Rel: Methodist. Mailing Add: Box 428, White Sulphur Springs, W.Va. 24986. (1967)

BOWMAN, DALE MERDITH D
Chmn, Cass Co. Dem. Party, Nebr.
b. Mahaska, Kans, 9/13/19; s. Max Harry Bowman and Velma V. Smith B; m. 2/1/42 to Maxine Faye Nielsen; c. Charles D. and Mike C. Polit. & Govt. Pos: Chmn, Plattsmouth Dem. Party, Nebr, 64-66; mayor, Plattsmouth, 66-68; chmn, Cass Co. Dem. Party, 68-; city councilman, Third Ward, Plattsmouth, 69- Bus. & Prof. Pos: Private bus, real estate, cafe, bus depot and barber shop, 61- Mil. Serv: Entered as Pvt, Army, 42, released as S/Sgt, 45, after serv. in Hq. Eighth Armored Div, ETO, 44-45, Admin. Warrant Officer, Res, 51-; Good Conduct, Victory, Am. Defense, Occup. and Res. Medals; ETO Medal with Three Battle Stars; Bronze Star. Mem: Master Barber Asn; C. of C.(mgr, 56-61); VFW (state Comdr, 58-59); Odd Fellows; Eagles; Am. Legion; Nebr. N Club. Am. Citizenship Award, 57; Commendation John J. Pershing Award, 59. Rel: Protestant. Mailing Add: 1636 Thayer, Plattsmouth, Nebr. 68048.

BOWMAN, FLETCHER C. JR. D
b. 1936. Educ: McMurry Col, B.S; grad. work, N.Mex. West. Univ. Polit. & Govt. Pos: N.Mex. State Rep, -66. Bus. & Prof. Pos: Mimbres Valley Bank. Mil. Serv: Army, Third Armored Div, NATO Forces, 55-57. Mem: C. of C; Methodist Men; Luna Co. Hist. Soc; Am. Legion's Boys' State, 50. Rel: Methodist. Mailing Add: 1403 S. Silver, Deming, N.Mex. 88030. (1967)

BOWMAN, GEORGE McKINLEY R
Chmn, Grand Forks Co. Rep. Party, N.Dak.
b. Osakis, Minn, 12/23/25; s. William McKinley Bowman and Eve Sieler B; m. 4/19/58 to Darlene Joanne Toby; c. George Toby and Victoria Eve. Educ: Univ. Minn, B.S. in Agr. Eng, 50; Plumb Bob Key; Engrs' Day Key; Award of the Gopher Key; Tau Kappa Epsilon; Bookstore Bd; Tech. Cmn; Sr. Cabinet. Polit. & Govt. Pos: Rural area coordinator, Grand Forks Co. Rep. Party, N.Dak, 64, precinct committeeman, 66, chmn, 66-; alternate del, N.Dak. Rep. State Conv, 66, del, 68. Bus. & Prof. Pos: Sales engr, Tart Ide Corp, Minneapolis, Minn, 50; sales engr, Kaiser Aluminum & Chem. Sales, Inc, Chicago, Ill, 52-53; dist. sales mgr, FMC Corp, Osakis, Minn, 53-59; engr, Lockwood Corp, Grand Forks, N.Dak, 59-63; mgr, N.Am. Pump Corp, 63- Mil. Serv: Entered as Recruit, Army, 50, released as Pfc, 52, after serv. in Engr. Research and Develop. Labs, Ft. Belvoir, Va, 50-52. Mem: Am. Soc. Agr. Engrs; Am. Legion; Elks; C. of C. Rel: Catholic. Legal Res: S. Belmont Rd, Grand Forks, N.Dak. 58201. Mailing Add: Box 1322, Grand Forks, N.Dak. 58201.

BOWMAN, JOHN T. D
Mich. State Sen.
b. Monterey, Tenn, 7/19/21; m. 1940 to Mary Elizabeth Broderick; c. Darryl Joyce. Educ: Wayne State Univ; Univ. of Detroit. Polit. & Govt. Pos: Justice of the Peace, Roseville, Mich, 39-43; Mich. State Rep, 54-60; Mich. State Sen, 62-; del, Dem. Nat. Conv, 68. Bus. & Prof. Pos: Pub. rels. Mil. Serv: Navy, World War II. Mem: Amvets; Am. Legion; F&AM; Shrine. Rel: Baptist. Mailing Add: 26816 Oakland, Roseville, Mich. 48066. (1967)

BOWMAN, LAWRENCE G. R
b. Basswood, Minn, 8/3/03; married; c. 5. Educ: Black Hills Teachers Col. Polit. & Govt. Pos: N.Dak. State Rep, 61-66; Twin Butte Sch. Bd, 41- Bus. & Prof. Pos: Farmer. Mem: Masons. Rel: Methodist. Mailing Add: Bowman, N.Dak. 58623. (1967)

BOWMAN, RICHARD HATCHER D
W.Va. State Del.
b. Roanoke, Va, 7/14/03; s. J. Price Bowman and Blanch Obenshain B; m. 9/19/23 to Emma Hunt Taylor. Educ: Hargrave Mil. Acad; LaSalle Exten. Univ; Univ. Richmond; Pa. State Univ. Polit. & Govt. Pos: Councilman, Rainelle, W.Va, for 15 years, mayor, 50-56; W.Va. State Del, 53- Bus. & Prof. Pos: Owner, R.H. Bowman Distributing Co. and Meadow River Plumbing Co, W.Va, 35-60; owner, Greenhead Farms, 40-66; pres, Royal Crown Bottling, 40-66, Forthill Enterprise, 52-66 and Nichol Funeral Home, 60-66; pres. and chmn. bd, Hargrave Mil. Acad, 50-; dir, Rainelle TV Corp, 55-66; v.pres, West. Greenbrier Bank, 60- Mil. Serv: Entered as 2nd Lt, W.Va. Nat. Guard, 42, released as Capt, 46. Mem: Am. Inst. Mgt; pres, Farm Bureau; past pres, Lions; Elks; Mason, Shrine; Moose; dir, Rainelle Vol. Fire Dept. and Greenbrier Co. Develop. Cmn. Rel: Baptist. Mailing Add: Box 306, Rainelle, W.Va. 25982.

BOWMAN, VERA ANDERSON R
Chmn, Atchison Co. Rep. Cent. Cmt, Mo.
b. Coin, Iowa, 9/15/97; d. Emory Anderson and Anna Mitchell A; m. 6/22/18 to Jess McKinley Bowman; c. Donald A. Educ: Tarkio Col, 1 year; Maryville State Col, 1 year; Citation for Outstanding Serv. and Achievements, Tarkio Col, 53. Polit. & Govt. Pos: Mem, Atchison Co. Cent. Cmt, Mo, 22-30, v.chmn, 30-62, chmn, 62-; v.chmn, Dist. Rep. Club, 64-69. Bus. & Prof. Pos: With Mo. State Farm Bur. Bd, Jefferson City, Mo, 41-67; v.chmn, Woman's Adv. Bd, Tarkio Col, 68, chmn, 69. Mem: Past pres, local Am. Legion Auxiliary; past pres, Co. Exten. Clubs; pres, Local Exten. Club. Rel: Methodist; mem, Church Bd. Mailing Add: Fairfax, Mo. 64446.

BOWMAN, WILSON SHELBY D
b. Booneville, Ky, 12/7/02; s. John T. Bowman and Sally Ann Abshear B; m. 5/21/25 to Fannie Hazel Gabbard; c. John Edward and Anna Frances (Mrs. Joe Marshall). Educ: Greenhill Sch, Booneville, Ky, 8 years. Polit. & Govt. Pos: Chmn, Ousley Co. Dem. Party, Ky, 60-69. Mem: Farm Bur; Sportsman's Club. Rel: Methodist. Mailing Add: Route 2, Box 216, Booneville, Ky. 41314.

BOWNES, HUGH HENRY D
b. N.Y.C, 3/10/20; s. Hugh G. Bownes and Margaret Henry B; m. 12/30/44 to Irja Catherine Martikainen; c. Barbara Ann, David Hugh and Ernest Malcolm. Educ: Columbia Col, A.B, 41; Columbia Law Sch, LL.B, 48. Polit. & Govt. Pos: Mem, N.H. Dem. State Exec. Cmt, 50; Dem. city chmn, Laconia, N.H, 53-55; chmn, Belknap Co. Dem. Party, 58; Mayor, Laconia, 63-65; Dem. Nat. Committeeman, N.H, 63-68. Mil. Serv: Entered as Pvt, Marine Corps, 41, released as Maj, Res, 46, after serv. in Third Marine Amphibian Tractor Bn, S.Pac, 43-44; Silver Star; Purple Heart. Mem: Past pres, Laconia Lions; past pres, Laconia Hosp. Asn; past pres, Laconia Red Cross. Rel: Protestant. Mailing Add: 507 Main St, Laconia, N.H. 03246. (1967)

BOWNES, IRJA CATHERINE D
b. Harrison, Maine, 9/13/17; d. Wester Martikainen and Emma Heikkinen M; m. 12/30/40 to Hugh Henry Bownes; c. Barbara Ann and Twins, David Hugh and Ernest Malcolm. Educ: Bryant & Stratton Bus. Col; Roosevelt Hosp. Sch. of Nursing, New York, N.Y; Teachers Col, Columbia Univ. Polit. & Govt. Pos: Belknap Co. rep, N.H. Dem. State Cmt, 54-60, v.chmn, 60-66; co-chmn, City Dem. Cmt, 56-59; councilwoman, Laconia, 61-63; state co-chmn, Operation Support, 62-65. Bus. & Prof. Pos: Mem, Bd. of Laconia Hosp. Trustee, Laconia, N.H, 61-63; bd. of dirs, N.H. Coun. on World Affairs, 63-; Bd. of Libr. Trustees, Laconia, 63-; mem, Defense Adv. Cmt. on Women in the Serv, U.S. Defense Dept, 64- Mem: Former dir, N.H. Music Festival; League of Woman Voters; Red Cross; United Fund; Cancer Crusade; Heart Fund; Dollars for Scholars Cmt; Hosp. Aid Asn; N.H. Social Welfare Coun; exec. cmt, N.H. Libr. Trustees Asn, 64-65. Rel: Congregational. Mailing Add: 898 N. Main, Laconia, N.H. 03246.

BOWRING, EVA
b. Nevada, Mo, 1/9/92; d. John F. Kelly and M. Belle Hinkes; m. 1911 to T.F. Forester, wid; remarried 4/13/28 to Arthur Bowring, wid; c. Frank H, James Harold, Jo Donald. Polit. & Govt. Pos: U.S. Sen, Nebr, 54; mem. Fed. Parole Bd, 56-64. Bus. & Prof. Pos: Cattle rancher, operator Bar 99 Ranch, Merriman, Nebr, 28-; registered Hereford breeder. Mailing Add: Bar 99 Ranch, Merriman, Nebr. 69218.

BOWSHER, CHARLES ARTHUR D
Asst. Secy. of the Navy for Financial Mgt.
b. Elkhart, Ind, 5/30/31; s. Matthew A. Bowsher and Ella M. West B; m. 12/14/63 to Mary C. Mahoney; c. Kathryn M. and Stephen C. Educ: Univ. Ill, Urbana, B.S, 53; Univ. Chicago, M.B.A, 56; Pi Kappa Alpha. Polit. & Govt. Pos: Asst. Secy. of the Navy for Financial Mgt, 67- Bus. & Prof. Pos: Mem. corporate audit staff, Chrysler Corp, Highland Park, Mich, 53; partner, Arthur Andersen & Co, Chicago, Ill, 56-67. Mil. Serv: Army, 54-55. Mem: Ill. Soc. CPA; Am. Inst. CPA; Univ. Club, Chicago. Distinguished Pub. Serv. Award, Navy, 69. Rel: Protestant. Legal Res: 7800 S. Shore Dr, Chicago, Ill. 60649. Mailing Add: 2801 New Mexico Ave. N.W, Washington, D.C. 20007.

BOWYER, EDNA L. R
Recorder, Warren Co, Ohio
b. King Mills, Ohio, 4/30/17; d. Perry Leroy Bowyer and Clara Belle Arnold B; single. Educ: The Miller Sch. of Bus, 36-37. Polit. & Govt. Pos: Pres, Warren Co. Rep. Women's Club, Ohio, 63; clerk of bd. of co. cmnr, Warren Co, Ohio, 63-64; recorder, Warren Co, 64-; secy-treas, Warren Co. Rep. Exec. and Cent. Cmts, 64- Mem: Treas, Ohio Recorders Asn, 68 and secy, 69; trustee, Warren Co. Hist. Soc, 64-67 and v.pres, 69; Franklin Area Hist. Soc; Kings Mills Civic Club. Mailing Add: 61 Walnut St, Kings Mills, Ohio 45034.

BOYCE, CHARLES WAYNE D
Ark. State Rep.
b. Dardanelle, Ark, 11/18/17; s. Rube Thomas Boyce and Lillian Hearn B; div; c. Charles Clay. Educ: Russellville Schs, 12 years. Polit. & Govt. Pos: Ark. State Rep, Yell, Logan and Franklin Co, Dist. 13, Position One, 67- Bus. & Prof. Pos: Gen. sales mgr, Ark. Valley Industs, 46-65; mgr, Dardanelle Boat Dock & Marina Restaurant, 65-67; owner, Boyce Advert. Supply Co, 67- Mil. Serv: Entered as Pvt, Army, 43, released as S/Sgt, 46, after serv. in Ninth Army, ETO, 45-46; Two Battle Stars. Mem: VFW; Am. Legion; C. of C. Rel: Presbyterian. Mailing Add: Box 309, Dardanelle, Ark. 72834.

BOYCE, MERLE HUNTER R
Mem. Exec. Cmt, Los Angeles Co. Rep. Cent. Cmt, Calif.
b. Wilmington, Calif; s. Ben Owen Boyce and Elma Crosby B; m. to Joanne; c. Lisa, Shaunna, Randall, Holly, James and Maureen. Educ: Compton Col, A.A; Pepperdine Col; Univ. South. Calif; Calif. Col. Med, M.D. Polit. & Govt. Pos: Organizer and first pres, Harbor Young Rep, Calif, 51; former mem, S. Bay Young Rep; Rep. Cand. for U.S. Rep, 62; mem, Steering Cmt. and Speakers Bur, Rafferty campaign, 62; chmn, Dodger Stadium Rallies for Goldwater, 63 & 64; former chmn, Speakers Bur, Los Angeles Co. Rep. Cent. Cmt, chmn, Membership Cmt, 66, mem. exec. cmt, currently; mem, Calif. Rep. State Cent. Cmt, 62-66 & 69-, chmn, Hospitality Cmt, 65-66; chmn, Coun. of Rep. Vol, 63-66; mem, United Rep. Finance Cmt, Los Angeles Co, 63-66, mem, Exec. Cmt; chmn, Los Angeles Co. 9th Inning Rally, 64; del, Rep. Nat. Conv. 64; chmn, Bill Miller for V.Pres. Campaign, 64; gen. chmn, Calif. State Rep. Conv, 65; mem, S.Bay Cmt. for Reagan for Gov, 66; panel mem, Big City Conf, Rep. Nat. Cmt, 66, sustaining mem; mem, Rep. Assocs; state campaign dir, Jud Leetham for Attorney Gen. of Calif, 66; chmn, Sixth Assembly Dist. Rep. Cent. Cmt, 67-; mem, Local Area Planning Cmt. for Calif. Rehabilitation Planning Proj. Cmt, 68 & 69; pub. mem, Calif. Coun. on Intergovt. Rels, 68- Bus. & Prof. Pos: Lab. instr. chem, Pepperdine Col; intern lectr. and faculty mem, Pac. Hosp, Calif. Col. of Med; staff mem, Pac. Hosp, Long Beach and Physicians and Surgeons Hosp, Compton; chmn, Pub. Rels. Cmt, Bay Harbor Hosp, former chief of staff. Mil. Serv: Serv. as Ball Turret Gunner, B-17, 8th Air Force, 42-46; 1st Lt, Air Force Res; Air Medal with Three Clusters. Mem: Am. and Calif. Med. Asns; past pres, Bay Harbor Div. Med. Soc; Redondo Beach C. of C; Fund Raising Cmt, Calif. Col. of Med; former mgr. and drum major, State Champion Drum and Bugle Corps; Air Force Asn; Elks; former mem, Wilmington Am. Legion and West. States YMCA; adv. Youth in Govt. Prog, YMCA Model Legis; chmn, Personnel Cmt, S.Bay YMCA, past pres, Bd. Dirs, chmn, Fund Drive, 62 and spec. gifts chmn, Fund Drive, 63. Recipient Merit Award, Los Angeles Co. Rep. Cent. Cmt, 63; Leadership Award, ITS Fraternity, 62; YMCA Serv. Award, Los Angeles; Nat. Found. March of Dimes Award; nominated Citizen of Year, Redondo Beach, 58. Rel: Presbyterian; Sunday Sch. Teacher. Legal Res: 28220 Ella Rd, Palos Verdes Estates, Calif. 90274. Mailing Add: 1615 Pacific Coast Highway, Redondo Beach, Calif. 90277.

BOYCE, VAUGHAN FIELD R
Vt. State Rep.
b. Proctor, Vt, 12/18/98; s. Guy Herbert Boyce and Maye Ina Field B; m. 6/25/25 to A. Louise Lewis; c. Charles Riford. Educ: Norwich Univ, 4 years, B.S; Phi Kappa Delta. Polit. & Govt. Pos: Village pres. & trustee, Proctor, Vt, 29; secy, Rep. Party, Vt, 40-50; Vt. State Rep, 53-54 & 69-; mem, State Emergency Bd, 54. Bus. & Prof. Pos: Elec. engr, Westinghouse E. & M. Co, 21-23; supvry. positions, Vt. Marble Co, 28-51, prod. mgr, 51-67. Mil. Serv: 2nd Lt, Army, Students Army Training Corps, Norwich Univ, 18; 2nd Lt, Army Res, 21-23. Mem: F&AM; Am. Legion; Am. Bowling Cong; Vt. Hist. Soc; Proctor Pub. Libr.(pres. & trustee). Rel: Protestant; Deacon and Sunday Sch. Supt, Union Church of Proctor, 19 years. Mailing Add: 47 Oak St, Proctor, Vt. 05765.

BOYD, ELIZABETH COBB D
b. Carrollton, Ga, 1/23/13; d. Hiram Felix Cobb and Betty Reynolds C; m. 6/2/34 to Dr. James Emory Boyd; c. Betty (Mrs. David Thomas, Jr) and James Fortson; grandchildren, Elizabeth and Laurie Thomas. Educ: Agnes Scott Col, B.A, 33; French Club; Creative Writing Club; Modern Dance Group. Polit. & Govt. Pos: Aide to chmn, Fifth Dist. Kennedy-Johnson Hq, 60; del, Dem. Nat. Conv, 64 & 68; chmn, Carroll Co. Johnson-Humphrey Campaign, 64; chmn, Carroll Co. Dem. Women, 65-68; mem. exec. cmt, Ga. Dem. Party Forum, 66-69; chmn, Carroll Co. Serv. Coun, 69- Mem: League Women Voters (past pres, Carrollton, Ga, consult, Dalton, 65-66); exec. bd, Ga. Coun. Human Rels. Ga. Woman Doer Oper. Head Start Award, 65. Rel: Episcopal. Mailing Add: West Georgia College, Carrollton, Ga. 30117.

BOYD, ELOISE AGUSTA METZGER R
Chmn, Sumter Co. Rep. Party, Ala.
b. San Bernardino, Calif, 6/28/22; d. Edward Delos Metzger and Ella Papenhausen M; m. 12/22/45 to Clarence Addison Boyd; c. Clarence Pierce and Smith Delos. Educ: Univ. Redlands, B.A. cum laude, 44; Radcliffe Col, 1 year; Mortar Bd; Beta Lambda Mu. Polit. & Govt. Pos: Chmn, Sumter Co. Rep. Party, Ala, 59- Bus. & Prof. Pos: Teacher, Jr. High Sch, Bakersfield, Calif, fall 45; instr. Eng, Livingston Col, Ala, 48. Mem: Am. Asn. Univ. Women (pres, Livingston, Ala, 52-54); Women of the Church Presbyterial Pres.(pres, 66-68); hon. life mem, Tuscaloosa Presbytery, 68. Rel: Presbyterian. Mailing Add: Box 102, Emelle, Ala. 35459.

BOYD, JOSEPH ARTHUR, JR. D
Justice, Fla. Supreme Court
b. Hoschton, Ga, 11/16/16; s. Joseph Arthur Boyd and Esther Puckett B; m. 6/6/38 to Ann Stripling; c. Joanne (Mrs. Robert Goldman), Betty Jean (Mrs. David Jala), Joseph, James and Jane. Educ: Piedmont Col, 36-38, hon. LL.D, 63; Univ. Miami Law Sch, J.D, 48; Pi Kappa Psi; Phi Alpha Delta. Polit. & Govt. Pos: City attorney, Hialeah, Fla, 51-58; co. cmnr, Dade Co, 58-68, vice mayor, 67; chmn, Dade Co. Cmn, 63; dir, State Asn. of Co. Cmnr, 64-68; justice, Fla. Supreme Court, 69- Mil. Serv: Entered as Pvt, Marines, 43, released as Sgt, 46, after serv. in First, Second, Third, Fifth and Sixth Marine Corps Div, S.Pac. Theatre; Good Conduct Medal; Pac. Theatre, Am. Theatre, World War II Victory Medal; Japanese Occup. Medal with one campaign star. Mem: Hialeah-Miami Springs Bar Asn.(pres, 55); Fla, Am. and Dade Co. Bar Asns; pres, Hialeah-Miami Springs C. of C, 56; Miami Scottish Rite; York Rite; Mahi Shrine; Grotto; Am. Legion (past state Comdr, 53); Lions Int; Elks; Moose; VFW; PTA. Top Hat Award, Bus. & Prfnl. Women's Clubs of U.S. for advancing the status of women, 67. Rel: Baptist. Mailing Add: 2210 Monaghan Dr, Tallahassee, Fla. 32302.

BOYD, McDILL R
Rep. Nat. Committeeman, Kans.
b. Phillipsburg, Kans, 1907; s. Frank W. Boyd and Mamie Alexander B; m. 6/11/30 to Marie Kriekenbaum; c. Patricia (Mrs. W. L. Hiss) and Marcia (Mrs. Tom Krauss). Educ: Kans. State Univ, 25-27; Phi Delta Theta. Polit. & Govt. Pos: Publicity dir, Rep. State Cmt, Kans, 38, 40, 46 & 50; coordinator, Eisenhower Campaign, Kans, 52; mem, Kans. Bd. Regents, 53-57, chmn, 57; admin. asst, Gov. Edward F. Arn, 54; chmn, First Dist. Rep. Party, 62-66; Rep. Nat. Committeeman, 66-; Nixon Coordinator, Kans, 68; del, Rep. Nat. Conv, 68. Bus. & Prof. Pos: Partner, Boyd Family, Editors and Publishers, 30- Mem: Sigma Delta Chi; Kans. State C. of C.(former dir); State Hwy. Asn.(former pres); Kans. Press Asn.(former pres); bd. dirs, Nat. Newspaper Asn; Kans. Asn. Ment. Health (former pres); bd. dirs, Nat. Asn. Ment. Health; Kans. Citizens Coun. Educ.(pres); Rotary (former pres); Phillipsburg C. of C; chmn, Salvation Army. Rel: Presbyterian. Mailing Add: 451 F St, Phillipsburg, Kans. 67661.

BOYD, NANNETTE D
Mem, Tex. Dem. State Exec. Cmt.
b. Nevada, Tex, 5/17/15; d. James Maston Gay and Olive Brundidge G; m.

9/6/35 to Roland Boyd; c. William M. and Betty. Educ: Southern Methodist Univ; Chi Omega. Polit. & Govt. Pos: Del, Dem. Nat. Conv, 64 & 68, mem. exec. cmt, Platform Cmt, 64; chmn, State Conf. of Dem. Women, Tex, 66; mem, Tex. Dem. State Exec. Cmt, Ninth Sen. Dist, currently. Mem: Collin Mem. Hosp. Auxiliary; Red Cross; Cancer Crusade; President's Club. Rel: Baptist. Mailing Add: 616 Finch, McKinney, Tex. 75069. (1967)

BOYD, OBIE DALE R

b. Pilot Point, Tex, 7/28/25; s. Tilmon Henson Boyd and Julia Elizabeth Standley B; m. 11/20/54 to Ruby Alice Simmons. Educ: Tex. Christian Univ, 46-50. Polit. & Govt. Pos: Precinct chmn, Rep. Party, Ft. Worth, Tex, 64-; del, Rep. State Conv, 66 & 68; standing cmt. chmn, Tex. Rep. Exec. Cmt, 66-; alternate del, Rep. Nat. Conv, 68. Bus. & Prof. Pos: Salesman, Tex. Elec. Serv. Co, Ft. Worth, Tex, 52-69; sales engr, Westinghouse Elec. Supply Co, 69- Mil. Serv: Entered as A/S, Navy, 43, released as PO 2/C, 46, after serv. in Postal Serv, S.Pac, 43-46, recalled 50-51 as S/Sgt, Marine Corps, serv. in Air Intel, Second Air Wing; Presidential Unit Citation. Mem: Ft. Worth C. of C.(govt. study gr). Rel: Baptist. Mailing Add: 7248 Ellis Rd, Ft. Worth, Tex. 76112.

BOYD, ROBERT DUNLEIGH D

Chmn, First Cong. Dist. Dem. Party, Miss.

b. Gulfport, Miss, 3/8/45; s. Hugh Valentine Boyd and Rosamond Allyne B; m. 7/14/68 to Rebecca Sitton Thackston; c. Rebecca Jane. Educ: Perkinston Jr. Col, A.S; Univ. Miss, 2 years. Polit. & Govt. Pos: Secy, Young Dem. Clubs Miss, 65-68; del, Young Dem. Clubs Am. Conv, 65 & 67; del, Dem. Nat. Conv, 68; mem. press cmt, Dem. Party Miss, 69-; chmn, First Cong. Dist. Dem. Party, Miss, currently. Bus. & Prof. Pos: Staff writer and educ. ed, Delta Dem-Times, Greenville, Miss, 68-, managing ed, currently. Mem: Sigma Delta Chi; Am. Civil Liberties Union (v.pres, 69-); NAACP; Miss. Coun. Human Rels. Rel: Presbyterian. Mailing Add: 323 Central St, Greenville, Miss. 38701.

BOYD, ROBERT STEWART R

b. N.Y.C, 5/17/08; s. Robert J. Boyd and Esabel Bole B; m. 6/25/36 to Evelan Allan Power; c. Lee Allan. Educ: Columbia, bus. admin, 32; Wesleyan Univ, 33; Delta Kappa Epsilon. Polit. Pos: Rep. campaign mgr, 7th Cong. Dist, N.J, 51-52; treas, N.J. for Eisenhower, 51-52; pres, Ridgewood, N.J. Rep. Club, 51-52. Bus. Pos: V.pres, Curtis Pub. Co, 56-; advert. mgr, Nat. Biscuit Co, 47-55; acct. exec, Young & Rubicam, 45-46; dist. sales mgr, Gen. Foods, Inc, 35-41; East. Air Lines, 33-35. Mem: Dir, Nat. Analysis, Inc; pres, Grocery Mfrs. Asn, 40-41, Advert. Club Syracuse, 42. Legal Res: Corey Lane, Brookside, N.J. 07926. Mailing Add: 641 Lexington Ave, New York, N.Y. 10022. (1967)

BOYD, ROBERT W. R

b. McMinnville, Tenn, 4/22/19; s. Fernando C. Boyd, Sr. and Sarah Maxwell B; m. 4/30/41 to Elinor Elizabeth Barker; c. Elizabeth Lawrence (Mrs. Myers) and Robert W, Jr. Educ: Univ. Tenn, B.S, 41. Polit. & Govt. Pos: Mem, city coun, McMinnville, Tenn, 49-51; elec. cmnr, Warren Co, 53-57; co-chmn, Rep. Campaigns, Warren Co, 56-62; campaign dir, Goldwater-Miller Campaign, Fourth Cong. Dist, Tenn, 64; alternate del, Rep. Nat. Conv, 64; chmn, Warren Co. Rep. Exec. Cmt, Tenn, 64-68. Bus. & Prof. Pos: Pres, Globe Nurseries, McMinnville, Tenn, 48- Mil. Serv: Entered as Yeoman 3/C, Naval Res, 41, released as Yeoman 1/C, 45, after serv. in Atlantic Theater, 41-45. Mem: Jaycees (pres, McMinnville Br, 47, v.pres, Mid. Tenn. Br, 48); bd. of gov, Am. Asn. of Nurserymen, 49, 51, 53, 57 & 60; pres, Mid. Tenn. Nurserymen's Asn, 50, Tenn. Nurserymen's Asn, 52-, South Nurserymen's Asn, 62-63 and South Nurserymen's Protection Asn, 65-66. Rel: Church of Christ. Mailing Add: P. O. Box 249, McMinnville, Tenn. 37110. (1967)

BOYD, THOMAS HILARY D

Chmn, Greene Co. Dem. Party, Pa.

b. Munson, Pa, 1/14/06; s. Frank X. Boyd and Jane White B; m. March, 1940 to Pearl Lopes; c. Thomas H, Jr, Samuel W. and Mary Jane. Educ: Waynesburg Col; Delta Sigma Phi. Polit. & Govt. Pos: Chief of Police, Waynesburg, Pa, 47-54; sheriff, 54-62; auditor, Auditor Gen. Dept, Pa. Dept. of Revenue, 62-63; chmn, Greene Co. Dem. Party, currently. Mil. Serv: Army, 41-44. Mem: Elks; Eagles; Pa. Sheriffs Asn; Nat. Sheriff Asn; Am. Legion. Rel: Catholic. Mailing Add: 45 W. Lincoln St, Waynesburg, Pa. 15370. (1967)

BOYD, WILBUR HARRISON D

Fla. State Sen.

b. Terra Cia, Fla, 2/6/27; s. Hugh Edgar Boyd and Flosie Mills B; m. 10/10/48 to Iris Fay Tuten; c. Daphne, Brenda, Valerie and Wilbur, Jr. Educ: Stetson Univ; Univ. Fla. Polit. & Govt. Pos: City councilman, Palmetto, Fla, 54-58; Fla. State Rep, 58-67; Fla. State Sen, 67- Mem: Twice chmn, Co. United Appeal; past chmn, Bd. of Stewards; past pres, Jr. C. of C. and Kiwanis; past v.pres, Manatee Co. Boys Club and C. of C; Cmt. of 100. Phi Delta Kappa Award for Outstanding Serv. in Pub. Educ, Sarasota and Manatee; Distinguished Serv. Award, Jr. C. of C. and Good Govt. Awards, Palmetto and Bradenton Jr. C. of C. Rel: Methodist. Mailing Add: 2117 Seventh St, Palmetto, Fla. 33561. (1967)

BOYER, ELROY G. D

Md. State Del.

b. Baltimore, Md, 5/5/20; married. Educ: Univ. of Md; Washington Col, A.B, 42; Univ. of Md. Sch. of Law, LL.B, 45. Polit. & Govt. Pos: Md. State Del, 59-; past pres, Md. Young Dem. and Kent Co. Young Dem. Bus. & Prof. Pos: Attorney, Rock Hall and Betterton, Md. Mem: Am. Bar Asn; v.pres, Md. State Bar Asn; past pres, Kent Co. Bar Asn. Mailing Add: Chestertown, Md. 21620.

BOYER, JAMES GAMBRELL D

Mem, State Dem. Cent. Cmt, La.

b. Fort Benning, Ga, 12/22/28; s. Emile James Boyer and Louise Gambrell B; m. 11/9/63 to Helen Margaret House; c. William Richard and Catherine Gambrell. Educ: La. State Univ, B.A, 49 and J.D, 51; Lambda Chi Alpha, Phi Delta Phi. Polit. & Govt. Pos: City attorney, Lake Charles, La, 58-60; mem, State Dem. Cent. Cmt, 64-; chmn, Calcasieu Parish Dem. Exec. Cmt, 68-; del, Dem. Nat. Conv, 68. Bus. & Prof. Pos: Mem. bd. dirs, Gulf Nat. Bank, Lake Charles, 68-; mem. bd. dirs, Speech & Hearing Center of Southwest La, Inc, 69- Mil. Serv: Entered as Pvt, Air Force, 51, released as 2nd Lt, 53; Capt, Res, currently. Mem: Southwest La. and Am. Bar Asns; La. State Bar Asn.(mem. house del, 62-); State Bar Tex; Young Mens Bus. Club; Am. Legion; past judge advocate, La. dept, ROA. Rel: Methodist. Legal Res: 330 Drew Park Dr, Lake Charles, La. 70601. Mailing Add: P.O. Box 910, Lake Charles, La. 70601.

BOYER, MAX WAYNE D

b. Garland, Kans, 10/17/06; s. Irma Staff Boyer and Olive McMillan B; m. 8/27/32 to Addye Hicks; c. Don Wayne. Educ: Cumberland Univ, LL.B, 29; Sigma Delta Kappa. Polit. Pos: Alternate Nat. Dem. Conv, 64-; del. State of Tex. Dem. Conv, 36-64; permanent chmn, West Tex. Young Dem. Conv, 34. Govt. Pos: Dist. judge, Tex, 57-; city attorney, City of Perryton, Tex, 54-57; appeal agent, U.S. Selective Serv. Bd. of Ochiltree Co, Tex, 42-48; Tex. State Rep, 37-41; Co. attorney, Ochiltree Co, Tex, 31-37. Bus. & Prof. Pos: Exec. Cmt, Judicial Sect, State Bar of Tex, 65; v.pres, Perryton Savings & Loan Asn, 57-; chmn, Grievance Cmt, 18th Cong. Dist. of State Bar of Tex, 55-57; mem, Grievance Cmt, 18th Cong. Dist. of State Bar of Tex, 52-57. Mem: Am. Bar Asn; State Bar of Tex; pres, North East Panhandle Bar Asn, 51-52; Mason; Lions. Rel: Methodist. Mailing Add: 601 S. Eton, Perryton, Tex. 79070. (1967)

BOYHAN, CYNTHIA ANNE D

State Committeewoman, Wyo. Dem. Party

b. Elbert Co, Ga, 6/23/34; d. John Wayne McCalla and Flo Haynes M; m. 11/8/58 to John H. Boyhan; c. Wayne Michael, Leslie Anne and Stephen Kelly. Educ: Col. William and Mary, B.A, 56; Alpha Chi Omega. Polit. & Govt. Pos: Justice of the Peace, Dubois, Wyo, 68-; state committeewoman, Wyo. Dem. Party, Fremont Co, 68- Bus. & Prof. Pos: Reporter, Wyo. Eagle, Cheyenne, 56; soc. worker, Laramie Co. Welfare Dept, 57 and Fremont Co. Welfare Dept, 57-59; teacher, Dubois Sch, 67-69. Rel: Quaker. Mailing Add: Box 571, Dubois, Wyo. 82513.

BOYKIN, ELIZABETH JOSEPH R

Mem, Montgomery Co. Rep. Exec. Cmt, Ala.

b. Montgomery, Ala, 4/2/24; d. William Francis Joseph and Alice Pelzer B; m. 1/23/45 to Raymond C. Boykin; c. Edna Frances, Alice Chollet and Raymond C, Jr. Educ: Sweet Briar Col, A.B, 45. Polit. & Govt. Pos: V.pres, Montgomery Women's Rep. Club, Ala, 62-63; mem, Montgomery Co. Rep. Exec. Cmt, 63-; alternate del, Rep. Nat. Conv, 64. Mem: Montgomery Junior League; cmts. in YMCA. Rel: Presbyterian. Mailing Add: Rt. 4, Box 48, Montgomery, Ala. 36106. (1967)

BOYKIN, ULYSSES W. R

b. Knoxville, Tenn, 10/17/14; s. Ulysses S. Boykin and Curtis Heard B; m. 4/21/65 to Nancy Merritt; c. Ulysses W, III. Educ: Wayne State Univ, 36-38, and 62. Polit. Pos: Mem. bd. dirs, Wayne Co. Rep. Precinct Orgn, Mich, 45- and v.chmn, Wayne Co. Rep. Educ. Coun; publicity chmn, Wolverine Rep. Orgn; del. and resident chmn, 1st Cong. Dist. Rep. Orgn, 64-66; mem. bd, 13th Cong. Dist. Rep. Orgn, 50-64; pres, Rep. Voters League, 50-55; exec. secy, Nonpartisan Voters League, 38. Govt. Pos: Cmnr, Detroit Metrop. Area Planning Cmn, Mich, 45-55; mem, Bd. of Supvrs, Wayne Co, 51; inspector, Street Railway Cmn, Detroit, 37-38, clerk, City Elec. Cmn, 36-37. Bus. & Prof. Pos: Pub. rels. counsel and ed, Mich. Herald, at present; ed. & publisher, Press-Facts, 61-66; Mich. Ed, Pittsburgh Courier, 62-63; ed, Detroit Metrop, 60; ed. & publisher, Detroit Tribune, 45-51; city ed, Mich. Chronicle, 36-37. Mil. Serv: Mem, Off. Price Admin. Appeal Bd, Mich, World War II. Publn: Handbook on the Detroit Negro, Minority Study Associates, 1943. Mem: Int. Elks; Scottish Rite, Masons. Rel: Baptist. Legal Res: 2009 Orleans, Detroit, Mich. 48202. Mailing Add: 1346 Broadway, Detroit, Mich. 48226. (1967)

BOYLE, EARL E. D

b. Syracuse, N.Y; m. to Catherine Meuller; c. Earl P, Ronald, Sally, Patricia (Sister M. Erlinda, O.S.F.), Mary Catherine. Educ: Christian Bros. Acad; won honors in regional elocution. Polit. & Govt. Pos: N.Y. State Sen, 64-66; Dem. Chmn, Onondaga Co; Exec. Comm. Onondaga Dem. Co. Cmt; Committeeman, 16th Dist, Clay; Past Chmn, Town of Salina, 20 yrs; V.Chmn, Co. Cmt; Pres, Lyncourt Sch. Bd. Bus. & Prof. Pos: Pres, proprietor Factory Printing C; printing trade learned on 'Syracuse Post Standard'; Asst. Chemist, Crucible Steel Co. of Am, Sanderson plant. Mem: Syracuse Typographical Union 55; Syracuse Craftsmen Club, Inc; Syracuse Turn Verein & Arion Singing Soc, Inc; Syracuse Liederkranz, Inc; Greater Syracuse C. of C; K. of St. John Commandary 350, K. of C; Coun, K. of St. John 4th Nobel degrees; Nocturnal Adoration Soc; Christian Bros. Men's Club. Mailing Add: 102 Riverine Rd, Liverpool, N.Y. 13088. (1967)

BOYLE, EDWARD C. D

b. Pittsburgh, Pa, 12/24/04; s. Frank J. Boyle and Mary Gertrude Freyvogel B; m. 2/21/33 to Ellen Veronica Young; c. Sally Ann (Mrs. Heupler) and Carol Jane (Mrs. McGinnis). Educ: Duquesne Univ, B.S, 26, LL.B, 28; Tau Delta Phi; Gamma Phi. Polit. & Govt. Pos: Attorney, Dept. of Justice, 44-54; dist. attorney, Allegheny Co, Pa, 56-64; solicitor, Allegheny Co. Sheriff, 61-63; solicitor, Rankin Borough, 64- Publ: Election Practices in the Commonwealth, 58. Mem: Variety Club; Moose; Elks; Eagles; Dapper Dan. Rel: Roman Catholic. Mailing Add: 5600 Fifth Ave, Pittsburgh, Pa. 15232.

BOYLE, JAMES PHILIP D

Secy, Mass. Dem. State Cmt.

b. Peabody, Mass, 11/25/04; s. Michael Andrew Boyle and Catherine Frances Rahilly B; m. 6/7/30 to Gladys LeCain; c. Mary (Mrs. William F. Doody) and Ann (Mrs. Richard L. Flynn). Polit. & Govt. Pos: Elected mem, Mass. Dem. State Cmt, 52-56, 60 & 64, v.chmn, 52-56, treas, 56, secy, 64-; mem, Mass. Emergency Finance Bd, 60-; pres. elector, Commonwealth of Mass, 64; alternate del, Dem. Nat. Conv, 64 and del, 68; chmn, Essex Co. Dem. Cmt, 64-68. Bus. & Prof. Pos: Notary Public, real estate broker and auditor, currently. Mem: K. of C; Holy Name; Elks; Eire Soc. of Boston; Charitable Irish Soc. of Boston; Essex Co. Dem. Club; State, Co. and Municipal Workers AFL-CIO; Tara Club Northampton. Rel: Catholic. Legal Res: 1 Clement Ave, Peabody, Mass. 01960. Mailing Add: Massachusetts Democratic State Committee, 11 Beacon St, Boston, Mass. 02108.

BOYLE, JUNE D
Wyo. State Rep.
b. Greeley, Colo, 9/30/17; m. to James M. Boyle; c. Two. Educ: Univ. of Colo, B.F.A. Polit. & Govt. Pos: Chmn, Albany Co. Dem. Party, Wyo; Wyo. State Rep, currently; Dem. Nat. Committeewoman, Wyo, currently; del, Dem. Nat. Conv, 68. Mem: S.E. Wyo. Ment. Health Center; Laramie United Fund; Laramie Woman's Club; past pres, Laramie Camp Fire Coun; Univ. of Wyo. Faculty Women's Club; League of Women Voters. Mailing Add: 706 S. 14th St, Laramie, Wyo. 82070. (1967)

BOYLE, ROCHELLE D
Chmn, Union Co. Dem. Party, S.C.
b. Gaffney, S.C, 10/9/06; s. Alie Boyle and Lula Burgess B; m. 9/3/32 to Mary Spencer. Educ: Gaffney High Sch, S.C. Polit. & Govt. Pos: With S.C. Hwy. Patrol, 30-44 & 49-52; sheriff, Union Co, S.C, 44-56; with S.C. Law Enforcement Div, 57-59; chmn, Union Co. Dem. Party, 58-; tax collector and investr, Union Co, 59- Bus. & Prof. Pos: Poultry raising and farming, until 30. Mem: Nat. and S.C. Sheriffs Asns; S.C. Law Enforcement Asn; S.C. Asn. of Counties; Co. Auditors, Treas. and Tax Collectors Asn; Union Co. Police Club; Shrine. Rel: Methodist. Legal Res: 307 Pine St, Union, S.C. 29379. Mailing Add: P.O. Box 254, Union, S.C. 29379.

BOYLSTON, EMILY MASON R
b. Buffalo, N.Y, 5/2/23; d. Charles Payne Mason and Lois Bartlett Howland M; m. 11/25/44 to Arthur Gray Boylston; c. Hope Mason and Lois Howland. Educ: Bradford Jr. Col, grad. third in class, 43. Polit. & Govt. Pos: Pres, Women's Rep. Club: Grosse Pointe, Mich, 55-56; mem, Mich. Rep. State Cent. Cmt, 56-59; v.pres, Mich. Fedn. Rep. Women, 57-58; mem, Broward Co. Rep. Exec. Cmt, Fla, 60-69, v.chmn, 62; founding pres, Women's Rep. Club, Ft. Lauderdale, Fla, 62, prog. chmn. and v.pres, currently; legis. chmn, Fla. Fedn. Rep. Women, 63-67; del, Rep. Nat. Conv, 68. Bus. & Prof. Pos: Asst. to mgr. advert. dept, Greenwich Time, Conn, 43-44; mem. tracing dept, Off. of Cable and Radio Censorship, N.Y.C, 44; v.pres, Fla. Broadcasting Syst, Ft. Lauderdale, currently. Publ: Article on 1943 Bradford Jr. Col. Commencement, Bradford, 11/43. Mem: Coral Ridge Yacht Club; Key Largo Angler's Club. Rel: Presbyterian. Legal Res: 663 Middle River Dr, Ft. Lauderdale, Fla. 33304. Mailing Add: 325 S.E. Sixth St, Ft. Lauderdale, Fla. 33300.

BOYNTON, MARJORIE CHASE R
Asst. Secy, Rep. State Cent. Cmt, Calif.
b. Grand Forks, N.Dak, 2/3/25; d. Victor Newton Chase and Lucy Beatt C; m. 8/6/49 to Searles R. Boynton, D.D.S; c. Paige, Kevin and Tammy. Educ: Univ. N.Dak, Ph.B, 46; Phi Beta Kappa; Sigma Upsilon Nu; Matrix; Delta Gamma. Polit. & Govt. Pos: Pres, Ukiah Rep. Women, Calif, 60-62; women's v.chmn, Rep. Cent. Cmt, 62-64; mem, Rep. State Cent. Cmt, Calif, 62-, asst. secy, 69-; chmn. women's div, First Cong. Dist. Rep. Party, 62-64; secy, Rep. Calif. Co. Chmn. Assoc, 66-; chmn, Mendocino Co. Rep. Cent. Cmt; currently; alternate del, Rep. Nat. Conv, 68. Mem: Am. Cancer Soc; Am. Asn. Univ. Women; PTA; PEO; Am. Contract Bridge League. Rel: Protestant. Mailing Add: 711 Willow Ave, Ukiah, Calif. 95482.

BOZARTH, HORACE W. D
Wash. State Rep.
b. Fairfield, Wash, 1894; m. to Christine B. Educ: Gonzaga Univ, B.A. Polit. & Govt. Pos: Wash. State Rep, currently. Bus. & Prof. Pos: Farmer. Mem: Officer, Wash. State Grange; Eagles. Mailing Add: Mansfield, Wash. 98830. (1967)

BOZZUTO, VICTOR J. D
State Dem. Committeeman, Idaho
b. Waterbury, Conn, 9/1/21; s. John Bozzuto and Louise Laudate B; m. 12/25/44 to Rae L. Anderson; c. William, Robert, Vicky and Anthony. Educ: High Sch. Polit. & Govt. Pos: Chmn, Lincoln Co. Dem. Cent. Cmt, Idaho, 63-68; mayor, Shoshone, Idaho, 66-; dir, Idaho Munic. League, 66-; State Dem. Committeeman, 68- Bus. & Prof. Pos: Owner, Shoshone Furniture Co, 61- Mil. Serv: Entered as A/S, Navy, 42, released as Seaman 1/C, 45, after serv. in Pac. Mem: 1st v.comdr, Am. Legion Post 11, Shoshone; Lions; C. of C; treas, Lincoln Co. Mental Health; Shoshone PTA, 64-65. Rel: Roman Catholic. Mailing Add: 318 West B, Shoshone, Idaho 83352.

BRAATHEN, CLAYTON ARNOLD R
Mem, 14th Cong. Dist. Rep. Cmt, Mich.
b. Suttons Bay, Mich, 1/8/13; s. Carl N. Braathen (deceased) and Anna M. Mork B; m. 5/9/34 to Esther Louise Campbell; c. Clifford A. and James A; 5 grandchildren. Educ: Detroit Inst. Tech, Mich, A.A; Detroit Col. Law, 2½ years; Southeast Univ, LL.B. & LL.M; Alpha Gamma Upsilon, Alpha Sigma Phi. Polit. & Govt. Pos: Publicity mgr, Youngblood Cong. Cmt, 46; mem, Wayne Co. Rep. Cmt, Mich, 46-47; precinct del, Detroit Rep. Party, 56-57; mem, 14th Cong. Dist. Rep. Cmt, Detroit, 56-62 & 64-; mem, 14th Cong. Dist. Exec. Cmt, 56-62; del, State Rep. Convs, 56-69; mem, State Goldwater for Pres. Cmt, 64; mem, State Nixon-Agnew Campaign Cmt, 68; chmn, 14th Cong. Dist. Nixon-Agnew Cmt, 68; del, Rep. Nat. Conv, 68. Bus. & Prof. Pos: Fingerprint classifier and analyst, Fed. Bur. Invest, 34-39 and spec. agent, Tenn, N.C, Wash, N.Y. and Mich, 39-42; invest, supvr. invest. and supvr. plant security, Ford Motor Co, Dearborn, 42-63; asst. v.pres, Detroit Mortgage & Realty Co, 63- Mem: Soc. Former Spec. Agents Fed. Bur. Invest, chmn, Mich. chap, 65-66. Rel: Lutheran. Mailing Add: 929 Westchester, Grosse Pointe Park, Mich. 48230.

BRACHTENBACH, ROBERT F. R
b. Sidney, Nebr, Jan, 31; m. to Nancy; c. Five. Educ: Univ. Wash, B.S, LL.B. Polit. & Govt. Pos: Wash. State Rep, 63-67, Minority Whip, mem, Legis. Coun, 65-67 and mem, Judicial Coun, 63-65, Wash. State House of Rep; del, Rep. Nat. Conv, 68. Bus. & Prof. Pos: Lawyer, Felthous, Brachtenbach & Peters, 55- Mem: Local, State and Am. Bar Asns; Elks; C. of C. One of Ten Outstanding Young Men in Wash, 63. Mailing Add: Route 2, Box 785, Selah, Wash. 98942. (1967)

BRACKEN, FRANK ALEXANDER R
Legis. Counsel, Dept. of the Interior
b. Indianapolis, Ind, 3/29/34; s. Alexander McKnight Bracken and Rosemary Ball B; m. 7/25/59 to Judith Mary Purdy; c. Ann, Tom, Margaret and Jane. Educ: Carleton Col, B.A, 56; Univ. Mich, J.D, 60; Beta Theta Pi; Phi Delta Phi. Polit. & Govt. Pos: Legis. counsel, Dept. of The Interior, 69- Mem: Delaware Co, Ind. and Am. Bar Asns; Delaware Country Club; Indianapolis Athletic Club; Kenwood Golf and Country Club. Rel: Episcopal. Legal Res: Muncie, Ind. Mailing Add: 5151 Palisade Lane, Washington, D.C. 20016.

BRACKIN, J. O. D
b. Headland, Ala, 8/15/06; s. Joseph V. Brackin and Minnie Tiller B; m. 5/25/26 to Eliz. Kirkland. Educ: Headland High Sch. Polit. & Govt. Pos: Ga. State Rep, 57-66. Bus. & Prof. Pos: Farmer. Rel: Baptist. Mailing Add: Iron City, Ga. 31759. (1967)

BRADDOCK, LeROY ILDEFONZE D
Committeeman, Philadelphia Co. Dem. Party, Pa.
b. Altoona, Pa, 9/12/25; s. Joseph Andrew Braddock and Mary Katharine Itinger B; m. 6/26/54 to Eleanor Shaheen; c. Thomas Andrew, Mary Elizabeth, Joseph Michael and Stephen Robert. Educ: Pa. State Univ, B.S, 48, M.S, 49 and Ph.D, 52; Phi Lambda Upsilon; Sigma Xi. Polit. & Govt. Pos: Committeeman, Philadelphia Co. Dem. Party, Pa, 66-; alternate del-at-lg, Dem. Nat. Conv, 68. Bus. & Prof. Pos: Laborer, mailing dept, Altoona Mirror Printing Co, Altoona, Pa, 41-43; teaching asst, chem. dept, Pa. State Univ, University Park, 49-53; research chemist, Pittsburgh Plate Glass Co, Creighton, 52-55 and Mine Safety Appliances Co, Pittsburgh, 55-56; sr. group leader, Callery Chem. Co, Callery, 56-59; asst. prof, chem. dept, Seton Hall Univ, South Orange, N.J, 59-63, assoc. prof, 63-64; res. consult, St. Michael Hosp, Newark, N.J, 62-64; asst. prof, anesthesia dept, Univ. of Pa. Med. Sch, 64-66, dept. pediatrics, 66-67; consult, research staff, Children's Hosp. of Phila, 67-; assoc. prof, pediatrics dept, Hahnemann Med. Col, Phila, 67- Mil. Serv: Entered as A/S, Navy, 44, released as Sonarman 2/C, 66, after serv. in U.S.S. Sturdevant DE239, Atlantic, European and Pac. Theatres, 44-46; Lt(jg), Navy Res, 51-; Theatre ribbons; World War II Victory Medal. Publ: 'Use of the 1931 C.I.E. System of Color Measurement for the Quantitative Study of Spot Test Reactions,' Microchem J, 67; 'Catecholamines in Cystic Fibrosis,' Lancet, 7/15/67; 'A Physical Chemical Study of the Van de Kamer Method for Fecal Fat Analysis,' Gastroenterology, 68. Mem: Am. Chem. Soc; Am. Asn. for the Advancement of Sci; Am. Asn. Univ. Prof; E. Mt. Airy Neighborhood Asn, Philadelphia, Pa; Pa. State Alumni Asn. Rel: Catholic. Mailing Add: 447 E. Mt. Pleasant Ave, Philadelphia, Pa. 19119.

BRADEMAS, JOHN D
U.S. Rep, Ind.
b. Mishawaka, Ind, 3/2/27. Educ: Harvard Univ, B.A, magna cum laude, 49; Oxford Univ, Ph.D, 54, Rhodes Scholar for Ind; Phi Beta Kappa. Hon. LL.D, Univ. Notre Dame, St. Mary's Col, Ind, Middlebury Col. and Columbia Col; hon. L.H.D, Brandeis Univ. Polit. & Govt. Pos: Admin. asst. to U.S. Rep. Thomas Ludlow Ashley, Ohio, 55; legis. asst. to U.S. Sen. Pat McNamara, Mich, 55; exec. asst. to Adlai E. Stevenson, 55-56; U.S. Rep, Ind, 58-; del, Dem. Nat. Conv, 68. Bus. & Prof. Pos: Asst. prof. polit. sci, St. Mary's Col. Mil. Serv: Navy, 45-46. Mem: F&AM; Ahepa; Am. Legion. Rel: United Methodist. Fel, Am. Acad. of Arts and Sci. Legal Res: 750 Leland Ave, South Bend, Ind. 46616. Mailing Add: 2134 Rayburn Bldg, Washington, D.C. 20515.

BRADEN, MARGARET MIZE R
Rep. Nat. Committeewoman, Ariz.
b. Emporia, Kans, d. Robert H. Mize, D.D. and Margaret Moore M; m. 5/15/37 to Forrest Clifford Braden; c. Barbara Louise, Robert Mize and Forrest Arthur. Educ: Univ. Kans, B.A; Pi Beta Phi. Polit. & Govt. Pos: Pres, Yuma Co. Rep. Women, Ariz, 56-57; precinct committeewoman, 58-; secy, Yuma Co. Rep. Cent. Cmt, 58-59; v.chairwoman, Ariz. Rep. Cent. Cmt, 60-61; Rep. Nat. Committeewoman, Ariz, 62-; chmn, Thirteen West. States Rep. Conf, 68-69; mem. exec. cmt, Rep. Nat. Cmt, currently. Mem: Bd. dirs, Ariz. Conf. for Soc. Welfare and San Pablo Home for Youth, Phoenix; bd, Found. of Col. Youth Centers, Episcopal Church in Ariz; welfare bd, Yuma Co; Human Rels. Cmn, Yuma; bd, Yuma City-Co. Libr. and Yuma Co. Econ. Opportunity Coun. Rel: Episcopal. Mailing Add: 700 Second Ave, Yuma, Ariz. 85364.

BRADFORD, MARION TILLSON R
Mem, Calif. Rep. State Cent. Cmt.
b. Modesto, Calif, 4/6/20; d. Warren S. Tillson and Adele Downey T; m. 2/21/43 to Clarkson Beem Bradford, Jr; c. David Tillson and John Scott. Educ: Modesto Jr. Col, Modesto, Calif, 1 year. Polit. & Govt. Pos: Hospitality chmn, Rep. Women Modesto, Calif, 67 & 68, v.pres, 69-; co-chmn, Women for Nixon, Stanislaus Co, 68; mem, Calif. Rep. State Cent. Cmt, 69- Mem: Modesto Symphony Guild; Stanislaus Co. Guide for Blind; Am. Field Serv; People to People. Rel: Protestant. Mailing Add: 1240 N. Magnolia Ave, Modesto, Calif. 95350.

BRADFORD, ROBERT EDWARD R
Exec. Dir, Rep. Party of Ill.
b. Roanoke, Va, 6/27/31; s. Miller Hughes Bradford and Helen Boyd Gardner B; m. 12/29/56 to Margaret Ruth Strader; c. Joseph Charles and Stephen Frederick. Educ: Washington and Lee Univ; Sigma Delta Chi; Scabbard and Blade; Lambda Chi Alpha (pres, 53-54). Polit. & Govt. Pos: Admin. asst. to U.S. Rep. Richard Poff, Va, 58-68; regional dir, Nat. Young Rep. Fedn, 63-65; chmn, Bull Elephants, 65-68; exec. dir, Rep. Party of Ill, 68- Bus. & Prof. Pos: News dir, WRAD, Radford, Va, 54-56; news ed, WMAL-TV, Wash, D.C, 57-58. Mil. Serv: Entered as 2nd Lt, Army, 57, released as 1st Lt, 57; Capt, Army Res, 57-62. Mem: Am. Fedn. TV and Radio Artists; Nat. Defense Transportation Asn; Jaycees; PTA; Westgate Civic Asn; Sangamo Club; Surf Club; pres, Mansion House Club, 67-68. Rel: Methodist. Mailing Add: 1031 N. Seventh St, Springfield, Ill. 62702.

BRADFORD, ROBERT FISKE R
b. Boston, Mass, 1902. Educ: Harvard, A.B, 23, LL.B, 26, LL.D, 48. Polit. & Govt. Pos: Gov, Mass, 42-49. Bus. & Prof. Pos: Partner, Palmer & Dodge; dir, Cambridge Trust Co; hon. dir, Olivetti Underwood Corp; trustee, Boston Five Cents Savings Bank, Investment Trust of Boston and Simmons Col; Sr. Warden, King's Chapel. Mailing Add: 28 State St, Boston Mass. 02109.

BRADLEY, (AGNES) ALBERTA 'ANGEL' R
Sustaining Mem, Rep. State Exec. Cmt, Fla.
b. Boston, Mass, 4/3/21; d. John I. Barnes and LyVonie I. Bamford B; m. 12/19/42 to Charles Vernon Bradley; c. Pamela Bamford. Educ: Quincy High Sch, grad, 39; Katharine Gibbs Sch, Boston, grad. and cert, 41; New York Flyers Club Sch, private pilot, 50. Polit. & Govt. Pos: Corresponding secy, Biscayne Women's Rep. Club, Fla, 66-69; vol. and campaign worker, Dade Co. Rep. Exec. Cmt, 66-69; vol. and campaign worker, Rep. State Exec. Cmt, Fla, 66-69, sustaining mem, 67-; mem, Fla. Fedn. Rep. Women, 66-69, Nat. Fedn. Rep. Women, 66-69; sponsor, Young Rep. Dade Co, 67-69; Miami Springs Women's Rep. Club, 69 and Riviera Women's Rep. Club, 69; del, Rep. Nat. Conv, 68; coordinator, Women for Nixon-Agnew, 68; area dir, Nixon for Pres, Anti-Wallace Div, Dade Co, 68; secy-treas, Rep. Women's Action Coun, currently; sustaining mem, Rep. Nat. Cmt, 69; co-chmn, Dade Co. Skip Bafalis for Gov. Campaign, 69-70; mem, Dade Co. Educ. Asn; chmn, Juvenile Court Observers Prog, Miami Crime Cmn. Bus. & Prof. Pos: Exec. secy, President-Merchants Coop. Bank, Boston, 41-46; off. mgr, R.E. Bradley & Sons, Inc, N.Y, 46-50; off. mgr, Judy Olson Cosmetics, Inc, Fla, 54-57; real estate saleswoman, Miami, 53-; secy-treas. and corp. officer, Diversified Rep. Inc, 55-; secy-treas. and corp. officer, Power Equip. Sales Corp, 62- Mem: Katharine Gibbs Sch. Alumnae Asn. Dade Co.(pres); Aircraft Owners and Pilots Asn; Varsity Club; Rep. Women's Action Coun; Riviera Women's Rep. Club; Miami Springs Women's Rep. Club; Humane Soc; Pkwy. Gen. Hosp. Auxiliary (recording secy); Racquet Club; Palm Bay Club; Runnaway Bay Club; Jockey Club. Vol. Awards for Serv. from Variety Club, Pkwy. Gen. Hosp. Auxiliary and Dade Co. Rep. Exec. Cmt. Rel: Episcopal. Mailing Add: 12855 Hickory Rd, Keystone Islands, North Miami, Fla. 33161.

BRADLEY, CARTER WALLACE D
b. Ada, Okla, 2/24/19; s. Robert William Bradley and Lottie Lea Wallace B; m. 5/29/42 to Loretta Groothouse; c. Teresa Lea and Louis Carter. Educ: Univ. Okla; Sigma Delta Chi. Polit. & Govt. Pos: Chief clerk, U.S. Senate Aeronaut. Sci. Cmt, 61-63; admin. asst. to U.S. Sen. A.S. Mike Monroney, 63-69. Bus. & Prof. Pos: Ed, Okla. Daily, Univ. Okla, 39-40; reporter, Ponca City Daily News, 40-41 and Okla. City Times, 41-42; state mgr, United Press Int, 47-61; dir. commun. rels, Sequoyah Indust, Inc, Oklahoma City, 69- Mem: Oklahoma City Gridiron Club; Oklahoma City Press Club; Nat. Press Club; Sigma Delta Chi; Rotary Int. Rel: Protestant. Mailing Add: 224 N.W. 35th St, Oklahoma City, Okla. 73118.

BRADLEY, CLARK LYNN R
Calif. State Sen.
b. Topeka, Kans, 7/18/08; s. Glenn D. Bradley and Mae E. Clark B; m. 8/19/67 to Della Bradfield; c. Lyn T, Roger C, Sherill M. (Mrs. Hellman) and Maureen C. (Mrs. Jones). Educ: Hastings Law Col, Univ. Calif, LL.B, 31. Polit. & Govt. Pos: City councilman, San Jose, Calif, 38-42 & 48-50, mayor, 50-52; Calif. State Assemblyman, 53-62; Calif. State Sen, 62- Bus. & Prof. Pos: Practice of law, San Jose, Calif, 31- Mil. Serv: Entered Naval Res, 42, released as Lt. Comdr, 45. Mem: Calif. and Santa Clara Co. Bar Asns; past pres, San Jose Kiwanis; bd. dirs. and past pres, Santa Clara Coun. Boy Scouts; bd. dirs, Salvation Army, Red Cross and Cancer Soc; bd. mem. and past v.pres, Good Samaritan Hosp, Santa Clara Valley. Rel: Methodist. Legal Res: 156 Dana Ave, San Jose, Calif. 95126. Mailing Add: 509 First National Bank Bldg, San Jose, Calif. 95113.

BRADLEY, GERALD ALLEN D
Ill. State Rep.
b. Chicago, 10/15/27; s. Gerald F. Bradley and Marie Ryan B; m. 12/19/51 to Mary Margaret Condon; c. David A, Michael E, Kathryn M. and Margaret M. Educ: Ill. Wesleyan Univ, Ph.B, 50; Phi Gamma Delta. Polit. & Govt. Pos: Pres, McLean Co. Young Dem, Ill, 54-58; treas, McLean Co. Cent. Cmt, 62-66, precinct committeeman, 68-69; Ill. State Rep, 69- Bus. & Prof. Pos: Owner, Bloomington Tent and Awning Co, 56- Mil. Serv: Entered as Pvt, Army, 50, released as Sgt. 1/C, 52, after serv. in Sixth Armored Div. Mem: K. of C; Am. Legion; Elks; Order of Titans. Rel: Catholic. Mailing Add: 508 E. Walnut St, Bloomington, Ill. 61701.

BRADLEY, GORDON ROY R
Wis. State Assemblyman
b. Utica, Wis, 7/9/21; s. Roy Carl Bradley and Mayme Thrall B; m. 10/26/46 to Bettylou Hazel Fisher; c. LuAnn Marie. Educ: Univ. Wis, Madison, 1 year. Polit. & Govt. Pos: Sch. clerk, Oshkosh, Wis, 46-62, town clerk, 62-67, town supvr, 67-; Wis. State Assemblyman, 69- Rel: Protestant. Mailing Add: 2644 Elo Rd, Oshkosh, Wis, 54901.

BRADLEY, HAROLD WHITMAN D
Tenn. State Rep.
b. Greenwood, R.I, 7/9/03; s. Harold E. Bradley and Lillian Whitman B; m. 12/5/47 to Pearle E. Quinn; c. Anne Elizabeth and David Whitman. Educ: Pomona Col, B.A, 25, M.A, 26; Stanford Univ, Ph.D, 32; Phi Beta Kappa. Polit. & Govt. Pos: Tenn. State Rep, 64- Bus. & Prof. Pos: From instr. to assoc. prof. hist, Stanford Univ, 30-45; dean, Claremont Grad. Sch, 45-53; prof. hist, Vanderbilt Univ, 54- Publ: The American Frontier in Hawaii, Stanford Univ. Press, 42; contrib. of articles on U.S. hist. to Encyclopedia Britannica and annual article, 'Pacific Islands,' to Collier's Yearbook. Mem: Am. Hist. Asn; Orgn. of Am. Historians. Rel: Methodist. Mailing Add: 2109 Hampton Ave, Nashville, Tenn. 37215.

BRADLEY, JAMES D
Mich. State Rep.
b. Hope, Ark, 1/9/14; s. Samuel and Bessie Bradley; m. 7/7/35 to Ethel Mallory; c. Four sons and four daughters. Educ: Pub. schs, Detroit, Mich. Polit. & Govt. Pos: Constable, Wayne Co, Mich, 53; Mich. State Rep, 54- Bus. & Prof. Pos: Real estate. Mem: Active in civic and church groups. Mailing Add: 3750 Concord St, Detroit, Mich. 48207. (1967)

BRADLEY, JOSEPH GERARD D
b. Cambridge, Mass, 6/14/30; s. George M. Bradley and Elizabeth Mullen B; m. 8/18/51 to Jacquelyn Beverly Maynard; c. Joseph, John, Mary, Elizabeth, Richard, Geralyn and Laurie. Educ: Portia Law Sch, LL.B, 68. Polit. & Govt. Pos: Alderman, Newton, Mass, 58-63; Mass. State Rep, 63-68; legis. secy, Mass. State House of Rep, 69. Mil. Serv: Entered as Seaman 1/C, Naval Air Force, 51, released as PO 2/C, 53, after serv. in Korea. Mem: Ins. Brokers Asn; Mass. Legislators Asn; K. of C; Am. Legion; DAV; NAACP; Elks; Moose; Hibernians. Outstanding Man of Year, Newton Jr. C. of C. and Mass. Jr. C. of C, 65. Rel: Roman Catholic. Mailing Add: 33 Maple Ave, Newton, Mass. 02158.

BRADLEY, MARGUERITE LORRAINE R
V.Chmn, Garfield Co. Rep. Cent. Cmt, Colo.
b. Denver, Colo, 9/27/19; d. John Adam Remick and Grace Marie Ponte R; m. 4/27/41 to Francis Owen Bradley; c. Dennis Owen, Sharon Kay and Laurence Ried. Educ: Barnes Bus. Col, 36-37; Konovsky Sch. Music, Dipl, 37; Emily Griffith Opportunity Sch, 38-39. Polit. & Govt. Pos: Pres, Garfield Co. Rep. Womens Club, 54-59 & 60-62, membership chmn, 59-60 & 62-69; v.pres, 59-60 and treas, 62-64; co. and receiving judge, Garfield Co. Primary and Gen. Elec, 54-68; treas, Garfield Co. Rep. Cent. Cmt, 61-63, v.chmn, 63- Bus. & Prof. Pos: Clerk and personal shopper, Denver Dry Goods, 34-40; teacher private piano lessons, 50-69; clerical asst, F.O. Bradley, Acct. Off, 54-68; bookkeeping and clerk, Chase Pharm, 68-69. Mem: Bus. & Prfnl. Womens Club; Instru-Vocal Music Club; Commun. Concert Asn; Garfield Co. Hist. Soc. Rel: Baptist. Mailing Add: 1614 Grand Ave, Glenwood Springs, Colo. 81601.

BRADLEY, MICHAEL JOSEPH D
b. Philadelphia, Pa, 5/24/97; s. Dennis J. Bradley and Hannah McCarthy B; m. 7/6/19 to Emily Angiuli; wid; c. Raymond J, Marian T, Catharine B.(Mrs. Arter) and Edward J. Educ: High Sch. Polit. & Govt. Pos: Dep. ins. cmnr, Commonwealth of Pa, 35-37; U.S. Rep, Pa, 37-47; chmn, Dem. Co. Exec. Cmt, Phila, 45-48; collector of customs, Port of Phila, U.S. Treas. Dept, 48-53; dep. managing dir, City of Phila, 53-55; mem, Bd. of Rev. of Taxes and Bd. of Viewers, Phila, 55- Bus. & Prof. Pos: Investment, security and brokerage bus, Phila, 20-35. Mil. Serv: Entered Navy, 17, released as chief radio electrician, 20, after serv. in Europe, 17-20. Mem: Independence Nat. Park Adv. Cmn, 45-; K. of C; Am. Legion; VFW. Rel: Roman Catholic. Mailing Add: 9737 Redd Rambler Dr, Philadelphia, Pa. 19115.

BRADLEY, PAUL R
married; c. Two sons and one daughter. Educ: Univ. of Colo, B.A, 33. Polit. & Govt. Pos: Colo. State Sen, 65-68; Rep. cand. for U.S. Rep, Colo, 68. Bus. & Prof. Pos: Asst. football coach, Univ. of Colo, 40-41, 45-47. Mil. Serv: Navy, Lt. Mem: Former pres, Colo. Petroleum Marketers Asn; former pres, Univ. of Colo. Alumni Club. Mailing Add: 2617 Holiday Lane, Colo. Springs, Colo. 80909. (1967)

BRADLEY, RUSSELL WALLEN D
b. Hermansville, Mich, 8/12/21; s. Martin R. Bradley and Jennie Wallen B; m. 1947 to Alice Marian Knapp; c. David Russell, Peter Alan, Robert William, Elizabeth Ann, Karl John and Richard Walter. Educ: Univ. of Mich; Cornell Univ; Wayne State Univ. Polit. & Govt. Pos: Field examiner, Nat. Labor Rels. Bd, 46-55; prosecuting attorney, Menominee Co, Mich, 59-68; chmn, Menominee Co. Dem. Cmt, 64-65; judge, Dist. Court 95, Div. I, 68- Bus. & Prof. Pos: Del, Constitutional Conv, 62. Mil. Serv: Entered as Pvt, Army, 43, released as S/Sgt, 46, after serv. in China; China Theater Ribbon. Rel: Presbyterian. Mailing Add: 1103 First St, Menominee, Mich. 49858.

BRADLEY, THOMAS D
City Councilman, Los Angeles, Calif.
b. Calvert, Tex, 12/29/17; s. Lee Thomas Bradley and Crenner Hawkins B; m. 5/4/41 to Ethel Mae Arnold; c. Lorraine and Phyllis. Educ: Southwest. Univ. Law Sch, LL.B, 56; Univ. Calif, Los Angeles; Kappa Alpha Psi, former Grand Polemarch; Student Bd, Univ. Religious Conf. Polit. & Govt. Pos: Mem, Los Angeles Police Dept, Calif, 40-62; mem, Los Angeles Co. Dem. Cent. Cmt; mem, Calif. State Dem. Cent. Cmt; city councilman, 10th Dist, Los Angeles, 63-, chmn, State, Co. and Fed. Affairs Cmt; treas, city del. and chmn, Legis. Liaison Cmt, Los Angeles Co. Div, League of Calif. Cities; del, Dem. Nat. Conv, 68; cand. for mayor, Los Angeles, 69; chmn, Pub. Works Priority Cmt; chmn, Cmt. Proposed Legis; mem. bd. dirs, Joint Cmn. Ment. Health Children; app. mem, Peace Corps Adv. Coun; mem, Coun. Intergovt. Rels. Bus. & Prof. Pos: Admitted to Bar, 57; attorney-at-law, 62- Mem: Bd. dirs, Avalon-Carver Commun. Center; cmnr, Boy Scouts; Los Angeles Urban League (bd. dirs); Intergovt. Coun. on Urban Growth; Govt. Pre-emption Cmn; NAACP; bd. dirs, South. Calif. Conf. on Commun. Rels; chmn, Los Angeles Co. Conf. of Negro Elected Off; bd. dirs, Bank of Finance, 64-; bd. dirs, UN Asn. of Los Angeles; South. Calif. Asn. Govt, 68-69; Nat. League Cities (mem. several cmts). Letterman, Track Team, Univ. Calif, Los Angeles; All City and South. Calif. Champion, 440 Yards, Polytech. High Sch, Los Angeles. Rel: African Methodist Episcopal; Trustee. Legal Res: 3807 Welland Ave, Los Angeles, Calif. 90008. Mailing Add: 240 City Hall, Los Angeles, Calif. 90012.

BRADLEY, WAYNE W. R
b. Washington, D.C, 11/2/29; s. Wayne W. Bradley and Clare Jayne B; m. 8/5/55 to Marilyn Krueger; c. Jill, David and Paul. Educ: Univ. Mo, B.A, 51; Sigma Delta Chi; Delta Upsilon. Polit. & Govt. Pos: Admin. asst. to U.S. Rep. Glenn Cunningham, Nebr, 57-63; asst. dir, Nat. Rep. Cong. Cmt, 63-68. Bus. & Prof. Pos: Owner, Manpower, Inc, 53-54; reporter, WOW, Omaha, Nebr, 54-56. Mil. Serv: Entered as 2nd Lt, Air Force, 51, released as 1st Lt, 53, after serv. in Strategic Air Command. Mem: Past pres, Omaha Press Club and Edsall Park Civic Asn; Air Force Aid Soc; Capitol Hill Club; Springfield Country Club. Rel: Methodist. Mailing Add: 6707 Bellamy Ave, Springfield, Va. 22150.

BRADLEY, WILLIAM EDWARD D
Ore. State Rep.
b. Jackson, Mich, 7/11/25; s. Elige Albert Bradley and Louise Crostic B; m. 6/4/66 to Laura Albright; c. Peggy Marie and Patricia Louise. Educ: Portland State Col; Nat. Radio Inst, grad. Polit. & Govt. Pos: Ore. State Rep, 59-63 & 67-; chmn, Multnomah Co. Dem. Party, 63-64; alternate del, Dem. Nat. Conv, 68. Bus. & Prof. Pos: V.pres, United Steelworkers Local 330, 55-56. Mil. Serv: Entered as A/S, Navy, 43, released as Gunner Mate 2/C, 46, after serv. in S.Pac, 45-46; Asiatic Pac. Area Campaign Medal with 2 Battle Stars;

Am. Area Campaign Medal; Philippine Liberation Medal with 2 Battle Stars; Victory Medal. Mem: USW; Elks. Rel: Protestant. Mailing Add: 1806 N.E. 113th Ave, Portland, Ore. 97220.

BRADLEY, WILLIAM RANDOLPH R
V.Pres, Calif. Rep. Assembly
b. Loveland, Colo, 3/2/19; s. William Homer Bradley and Irene McBride B; m. 5/27/44 to Ethel Chambers; c. Billie Lee (Mrs. Myron Brown) and Randy Kay. Educ: Univ. of South. Calif, B.S, 57; San Jose State Col, M.A, 67. Polit. & Govt. Pos: Acting asst. city engr, Santa Clara, Calif, 60-67, street supt, 67-69; cand, Calif. State Sen, 66 & 68; ex-officio mem, Santa Clara Co. Rep. Cent. Cmt, 66 & 68; del. mem, Calif. State Rep. Assembly, 66 & 68, v.pres, 69-; pres, Santa Clara Rep. Assembly, 68; dir. of pub. works, Coronado, Calif, 69- Mil. Serv: Entered as A/S, Navy, 44, released as Seaman 3/C, 46, after serv. in Aviation Wing, U.S. and Philippines, 44-46. Mem: Am. Pub. Works Asn; Int. City Mgrs. Asn; Nat. Munic. League; Engrs. Club of San Jose; Commonwealth Club of Calif. Rel: Baptist. Mailing Add: P.O. Box 363, Coronado, Calif. 92118.

BRADNER, MICHAEL DRAKE D
Alaska State Rep.
b. Washington, D.C, 3/1/37; s. George H. Bradner and Alice Abbott B; m. to Janet Ann Kruse; c. Michelle, Bonnie and twins Hiede and Heather. Educ: Univ. Alaska, B.A, 64, grad work, 68. Polit. & Govt. Pos: Field rep, Off. Gov, 65-66; Alaska State Rep, 66-, chmn. House Rules Cmt. and mem, Finance Cmt. and Alaska Legis. Coun, Alaska House of Rep. Bus. & Prof. Pos: River pilot, Yutana Barge Lines, 57-62; night ed, Fairbanks News-Miner, 62-65; ed, Jessen's Daily, 67-68; writer, currently. Young Man of the Year Award, Jaycees, 68. Mailing Add: 915 Kellum St, Fairbanks, Alaska 99701.

BRADSHAW, CHARLES JACKSON R
Finance chmn, S.C. Rep. Party.
b. Lake City, Fla, 7/15/36; s. James William Bradshaw and Florence Synthia Sanders B; m. 6/13/59 to Julia Brewer; c. Charles J, Jr, William B. and Julia Dargan. Educ: Univ. Ga, 1½ years; Wofford Col, A.B, math, 59; Blue Key; Scabbard & Blade; Kappa Alpha. Polit. & Govt. Pos: Nominee, U.S. House Rep, Fourth Dist, S.C, 68; finance chmn, S.C. Rep. Party, 69- Bus. & Prof. Pos: Mgt. trainee, Pierce Motor Co, Spartanburg, S.C, 59-61; pres, Spartan Food Syst, Inc, 61-69, chmn. of bd, 69- Mil. Serv: 2nd Lt, Army, 60, serv. in artil, Ft. Sill, Okla. Mem: Nat. Restaurant Asn; dir, Nat. Bank Commerce, Spartanburg; C. of C; YMCA; dir, Wofford Eleven Club; dir, Spartanburg Country Club; Piedmont Club. All-Am. Football, Assoc. Press, 57; Outstanding Serv. Award, S.C. Rep. Party. Rel: Presbyterian. Legal Res: 609 Crystal Dr, Spartanburg, S.C. 29302. Mailing Add: P.O. Box 3168, Spartanburg, S.C. 29302.

BRADSHAW, JOHN ROGERS R
Majority Leader, N.H. State Sen.
b. Sudbury, Mass, 4/17/30; s. Forrest D. Bradshaw and Katherine Rogers B; m. 11/9/67 to Bess Nichols; c. John R, Jr, Betsy A. and Peter D. Educ: Northeast. Univ; Clark Univ; Boston Univ. Polit. & Govt. Pos: N.H. State Rep, 65-66; N.H. State Sen, 67-, Majority Leader, N.H. State Sen, 69- Bus. & Prof. Pos: Sales engr, R.H. White Sales Co, Auburn, Mass, 52-54, sales engr, Hilco Supply Co, Sudbury, 54-57; partner, Bramil Pump & Supply Co, Keene, N.H, 57-59, owner and gen. mgr, 59- Mil. Serv: Pfc, Marine Corps, 51-52. Mem: N.H. Water Works Asn; Maine Water Utilities Asn; New Eng. Water Well Drillers Asn; Mason; Scottish and York Rite; Shrine; dir, Keene YMCA. Rel: Congregational. Mailing Add: Nelson, N.H. 03457.

BRADSHAW, JUNIE LEROY D
Va. State Del.
b. Erwin, N.C, 1/30/30; m. to Deirdree Eagle. Educ: Norfolk Div, William and Mary Col, A.A; T. C. Williams Sch. of Law, LL.B. Polit. & Govt. Pos: Va. State Del, 62-; v.pres, Va. State Young Dem. Bus. & Prof. Pos: Lawyer. Mil. Serv: Navy, Korean War. Mem: Phi Alpha Delta; Am. Legion Post 361 (legal officer); Phi Theta Kappa; Tuckahoe Lodge, A.F.&A.M; Shrine; Acca Temple. Rel: Baptist. Mailing Add: 201 North Blvd, Richmond, Va. 23220.

BRADSHAW, LESTER JOSEPH, JR. R
b. Brooklyn, N.Y, 1/5/15; s. Lester J. Bradshaw and Helen Theresa Donovan B; m. 4/3/40 to Lilyan Helen Schaeffer. Educ: Marquette Univ, B.A. and M.A. Polit. & Govt. Pos: Page boy, Rep. Nat. Conv, 32; chmn, Citizens Cmt. for Walter Roegers for Mayor, White Plaines, N.Y, 35 and Citizens Ins. Cmt. for Wendel Wilkie, 40; nat. chmn, John W. Bricker Vice Presidential Cmt, 44; chmn, Motion Picture Cmn, Wis, 45-49; in charge Midwest. Pre-Conv. Campaign for Gov. Thomas E. Dewey, 48; former asst. to Len Hall, Rep. Nat. Chmn; mem. exec. cmt, Westchester Co. Rep. Cmt, 49-62; advance mgr, Sen. Richard M. Nixon, Vice Presidential Campaign, 52; in charge del. pub. rels. for Sen. Robert A. Taft, Rep. Nat. Conv, 52; exec. secy. to U.S. Rep. E.B. Dooley, 56-63; mem. prog. cmt, Nat. Rep. Club, 65; First pres. and emer. pres, Mens' Rep. Club, White Plains, N.Y. Bus. & Prof. Pos: Formerly, instr. pub. speaking and parliamentary law, Marquette Univ, dean faculty, Dale Carnegie Inst. and mem. faculty, Life Underwriters; auditor, spec. agent, dist. mgr. and agency supt. in charge, Mid West, Am. Fore, 39; sales mgr, N.Y. Off, Ter Bush-Powell Agency, 49; agency supvr. in charge, Ohio and Wis, Continental Ins. Co; pres, L. & L. Realty, B. & B. Holding Co. and Southold Realty Co; asst. to pres, Prfnl. Ins. Co, 64-; pres, Berkeley-Bradshaw Ins. Agency, currently. Publ: How to Make A Speech, Marquette Univ, 45. Mem: Pres, Ins. Fedn. N.Y, Inc; prog. chmn, Sales Execs. Club N.Y; bd. mem, N.Broadway Civic Asn; past pres, St. John's Holy Name Soc, Speakers Forum, Dale Carnegie Alumni and Wis. Soc. N.Y; House Cmt, YMCA. Received citation for training salesmen to sell war bonds, U.S. Treas; awarded Navy E for training Navy personnel; has made over 1000 speeches in 43 states. Rel: Roman Catholic. Mailing Add: 222 E. 19th St, New York, N.Y. 10003.

BRADY, CARL FRANKLIN R
b. Chelsea, Okla, 10/29/19; s. K.A. Brady and Pauline Doty B; m. 3/29/41 to Carol Elizibeth Sprague; c. Carl Franklin, Jr, Linda Kathryn and James Kenneth. Educ: Univ. Wash, 40. Polit. & Govt. Pos: Alaska State Rep, 65-66; Alaska State Sen, 67-68. Bus. & Prof. Pos: Pres, ERA Helicopters Inc, 60-; dir, Alaska State Bank and trustee, Alaska Mutual Savings Bank, currently. Mil. Serv: Entered as 2nd Lt, Army Air Corps, 43, released as Capt, 46, after serv. in Air Transport Command, Am. Theater. Mem: Pres, Helicopter Asn. Am, 53 & 57, Petroleum Club Anchorage, 63, Alaska Crippled Children's Asn. and Anchorage C. of C, 64; Platform Asn; Rotary Int; Elks; Am. Legion. Rel: Protestant. Mailing Add: 2727 Iliamna Ave, Anchorage, Alaska 99501.

BRADY, EDWIN FRANCIS R
Chmn, Benton Co. Rep. Cmt, Mo.
b. Warsaw, Mo, 5/26/15; s. F.M. Brady and May Sands B; m. 9/12/37 to Juanita Porter; c. Robert Francis. Educ: William Jewell Col, 32-34; Univ. Mo, 34-37; Univ. of Tex, Law Sch, summer 37; Kappa Alpha Order. Polit. & Govt. Pos: Prosecuting attorney, Benton Co, Mo, 49-54; chmn, Benton Co. Rep. Cmt, 68- Mil. Serv: Entered as Ens, U.S. Naval Res, 44, released as Lt, 46, after serving in Amphibious Forces, Pac. Ocean, invasion of Okinawa and second invasion of Philippines, 45-46; ribbons and one battle star. Mem: 29th Judicial Circuit Bar Asn.(pres, 43-); Warsaw C. of C.(pres, 47-); 30th Judicial Circuit Bar Asn.(pres, 65-); Benton Co. Hist. Soc.(pres, 69); Lions; Am. Legion. Rel: Southern Baptist. Legal Res: 716 W. Jackson St, Warsaw, Mo. 65355. Mailing Add: Box 277, Warsaw, Mo. 65355.

BRADY, KENNETH ANDERSON R
Utah State Rep.
b. Sandy, Utah, 3/16/01; s. Lindsay Anderson Brady and Ellen Cathrine Anderson B; m. 8/19/30 to Jessie Amelia Madsen; c. K. Madsen, Rodney Howard, Joanne (Mrs. Frandsen) and Lindsay Anderson. Educ: Univ. of Utah, B.S. in Geol. Eng, 28; 65 hours grad. work at Univ. of Utah, Brigham Young Univ. and Utah State Univ. Polit. & Govt. Pos: Shop supvr, post schs, Hill Air Force Base, Ogden, Utah, 42-44; del, Salt Lake Co. Rep. Conv. and Utah State Conv, 64; Utah State Rep, 67-; chmn, Agr. and Irrigation Cmt, 69- Bus. & Prof. Pos: Teacher of math, Jr. High Schs, Jordan Sch. Dist, Utah, 28-41; partner, Brady-Milne Appliance Co, Murray and Midvale, 45-55; teacher of math, Jordan and Hillcrest High Schs, Jordan Dist, 55-65. Mem: Jordan Educ. Asn.(pres, 38-39); Intermt. Elec. Asn.(v.pres, 52-53); Lions Int.(zone chmn, 47-48); Lions(charter pres, Union Club, 44-46 and pres, 44-54). Rel: Latter-day Saint; Bishop, 5 years; Stake Patriarch. Mailing Add: 8395 S. 1000 East, Sandy, Utah 84070.

BRADY, MAURICE V. D
b. Bayonne, N.J. Educ: Sisters of St. Joseph Home. Polit. & Govt. Pos: Former N.J. State Assemblyman, Majority Leader, N.J. State Assembly, 57 & 59, Speaker, 60 & 61; acting gov, N.J, several times, 60. Mailing Add: 47 Duncan Ave, Jersey City, N.J. 07304. (1967)

BRADY, THOMAS FLOYD D
b. Urania, La, 7/9/38; s. Floyd Lee Brady and Lucille McCarroll B; m. 4/15/69 to Cullyne Scott; c. Roderick Edward and Cecelia Helaine. Educ: Northwest. State Col, B.A, 62. Polit. & Govt. Pos: Admin. asst, U.S. Rep. Speedy O. Long, La, 65- Rel: Baptist. Mailing Add: 1219 Virginia Ave, Natchitoches, La. 71457.

BRADY, THOMAS PICKENS D
Assoc. Justice, Miss. Supreme Court
b. New Orleans, La, 8/6/03; s. Thomas Brady, Jr. and Jane Tullia Smith B; m. 7/23/29 to LaVerne Holmes; c. Thomas Pickens, Jr. and Bruce Holmes. Educ: Yale Univ, A.B, 27; Univ. Miss, LL.B, 30; Sumner Club; Phi Delta Phi; Eta Sigma Phi; Omicron Delta Kappa; Sigma Phi; Zeta Psi. Polit. & Govt. Pos: Del, Miss. State Dem. Conv, 30-; mem, Brookhaven Dem. Exec. Cmt, 32-53; cmnr, Pub. Safety, Miss. and dir, Hwy. Safety Patrol, 40-43; chmn, Hwy. Traffic Adv. Cmt. to War Dept, 42-43; del, Dem. Nat. Conv, 43, 48, 60 and 64; Circuit Judge, 14th Dist. Miss, 50-63; chmn. Speakers' Bur, States' Rights Dem. Party, 58-62; Dem. Nat. Committeeman, Miss, 60-64; assoc. justice, Miss. Supreme Court, 63- Bus. & Prof. Pos: Instr. sociol, Univ. Miss, 29-30; mem. firm, Brady, Dean & Hobbs, 30-38; dir, Brookhaven Bank and Trust Co, Miss, 30-; pres, Brookhaven Investment Co, 34-44 and Brookhaven Leader Co, 42-57; v.pres, Arcade Theatre Inc, 35; attorney, 47-50; dir, Miss. Compress Co, 47-61; mem. bd. dirs, Whitworth Col, 62. Publ: South at Bay, 48; Black Monday, 54. Mem: V.pres, Miss. State Bar Asn, 54-55; dir, Univ. Miss. Alumni Asn, 62-64; Am. Judicature Soc; Abraham Lincoln Asn; Am. Newcomen Soc; Co. Mil. Collectors and Historians; SAR; Mason (32°); K.T; Shrine; New Orleans Athletic Club; Boston Club New Orleans; Jackson Country Club; 1st pres, Miss. Gun Collectors' Asn, 57. Distinguished Serv. Award, Miss. Legis, 56. Rel: Baptist. Legal Res: 730 S. Church St, Brookhaven, Miss. 39202. Mailing Add: The Capitol, Jackson, Miss. 39205.

BRADY, TULLIUS D
Miss. State Rep.
b. Brookhaven, Miss, 6/18/06; married. Polit. & Govt. Pos: Miss. State Rep. Bus. & Prof. Pos: Attorney. Mem: Psi Upsilon; Mason; Civitan; Lions; Brookhaven Country Club; Jackson Country Club; Am. Numismatic Soc; Sons of the Confederacy; SAR. Rel: Presbyterian. Mailing Add: Box 115, Brookhaven, Miss. 39601.

BRAGDON, ORSON H. R
N.H. State Rep.
b. Wells, Maine, 8/27/02; married; c. 3 boys, 3 girls. Educ: Amherst High Sch. Polit. & Govt. Pos: Auditor, Amherst, N.H, 16 years; treas, Hillsborough Co. Soil Conserv. Dist; former pres, N.H. Soil Conserv. Dist. Supvrs. Asn; pres, Hillsborough Co. Farm Bur; N.H. State Rep, 57- Bus. & Prof. Pos: Dairy farmer. Mem: Amherst Men's Club (past pres); Hillsborough Co. Fire Wardens Asn. Rel: Congregational. Mailing Add: R.F.D, Mt. Vernon, N.H. 03057.

BRAGG, JOHN THOMAS D
b. Woodbury, Tenn, 5/19/18; s. Minor Elam Bragg and Luree B; m. 6/29/45 to Annie Lee McElroy; c. John T, Jr. and David McElroy. Educ: Middle Tenn. State Univ, B.S; Univ. Tenn, grad. study in hist; Kappa Alpha. Polit. & Govt. Pos: Foreman, Rutherford Co. Grand Jury, Tenn, 58-66; chmn, Rutherford Co. Elec. Cmn, 60-63; Tenn. State Rep, 65-68; Dem. cand, U.S. Rep, Tenn, 68; dir, Mid. Tenn. Citizens for Court Modernization, 68. Bus. & Prof.

Pos: Publisher, Rutherford Courier, Tenn, 46-58; pres, Courier Printing Co, 58- Mil. Serv: Entered as Pvt, Air Force, 42, released as S/Sgt, 46. Mem: Exec. secy, Tenn. Press Asn, 40-42, pres, 58; Am. Legion; Farm Bureau; Printing Industry of Am; pres, Printing Industry Tenn, 66; Stones River Country Club; Rotary; Mental Health Asn; C. of C; Sportsman's Club; Blue Raider Quarterback Club; trustee, Middle Tenn. State Univ. Scholarship & Develop. Corp; pres, Good Sheperd Childrens Home. Rel: Baptist. Legal Res: 1530 Mercury Blvd, Murfreesboro, Tenn. 37130. Mailing Add: 320 South Church St, Murfreesboro, Tenn. 37130.

BRAKE, BETTY HESS R
V.Chmn, Oklahoma Co. Rep. Party, Okla.
b. Oklahoma City, Okla, 5/14/20; d. Moore C. Hess and Rae Malone H; m. 11/25/43 to Charles Murray Brake; c. Charles Michael, Richard Joseph, Deborah Jane and Peggy Ann. Educ: Mt. Vernon Jr. Col, Wash, D.C, 38-39; Univ. Okla, B.A, 42; Chi Omega. Polit. & Govt. Pos: Precinct v.chmn, Oklahoma Co. Rep. Party, Okla, 61-67, precinct chmn, 65, v.chmn, 66-; asst. state campaign chmn, Okla. Citizens for Goldwater, 64; off. mgr, Patterson for U.S. Senate Campaign, 66; del, Rep. Nat. Conv, 68. Rel: Episcopal. Mailing Add: 3610 N.W. 46th, Oklahoma City, Okla. 73112.

BRAKE, ROBERT MERLE D
b. Detroit, Mich, 9/30/26; s. Merle Eric Brake and Edna LeBrun B; m. 11/15/52 to Eileen Murphy; c. Daniel Katrina and Christopher. Educ: Wayne Univ, 44-47; Univ. Chicago, 47-48; Univ. Mich, LL.B, 50; Delta Theta Phi. Polit. & Govt. Pos: Cmnr, Dade Co. Cmn, Fla, 62-64; Fla. State Rep, 67-69. Mil. Serv: Entered as Pvt, Army, released as Sgt, after serv. in Pac. Theater; Maj, Air Force Res. Mem: Coral Gables, Dade Co, Fla. and Am. Bar Asns; Kiwanis; K. of C. Rel: Catholic. Mailing Add: 1300 Coral Way, Coral Gables, Fla. 33134.

BRAKKE, THOMAS JEROME D
b. Aneta, N.Dak, 7/24/22; s. Helmer C. Brakke and Minnie Fredrikson; wid, 66; second m. 1/6/68 to Joan M. Koenigswald; c. Timothy A, Bradley K. and Kari R. Educ: Mayville State Col, 41-43; Lambda Sigma Alpha; Letterman's Club. Polit. & Govt. Pos: N.Dak. State Rep, 69. Bus. & Prof. Pos: Owner and operator, farm, Aneta, N.Dak, 48-; partner, Ettco Distributing Co, Covina, Calif, 54-60. Mil. Serv: Pvt, Army, 46-47, Photo Lithography, Army Engrs, Ft. Belvoir, Va. Mem: Elks; Am. Legion; Nat. Farmers Orgn; Farmers Union. Rel: Lutheran. Mailing Add: Aneta, N.Dak. 58212.

BRAMAN, JAMES D'ORMA R
Asst. Secy, U.S. Dept. of Transportation
b. Lorimor, Iowa, 12/23/01; s. Jacob Wesley Braman and Susie Mae Huntzinger B; m. 11/27/20 to Margaret V. Young; c. James D'Orma and Robert C. Polit. & Govt. Pos: Mem. city coun, Seattle, Wash, 54-64, mayor, 64-69; mem, Japan-Am. Conf. of Mayors; asst. secy, U.S. Dept. of Transportation, 69- Bus. & Prof. Pos: Pres, Braman Millwork Supply Co, 20-29; pres, Braman Mill & Mfg. Co, Inc, Bremerton, 29-43; pres, Braman Lumber & Hardware Co, Inc, Seattle, 46-56; chmn. bd, Shoreline Savings & Loan Asn, Seattle, 52-; trustee, Pac. Sci. Cent. Found; trustee and mem. steering cmt, Century 21 Corp, 59-62. Mil. Serv: Naval Res, 42-46, Comdr. Mem: Nat. League Cities (chmn. cmn. transportation and commun); rep, Seattle and Wash. State World's Fair Cmn, 57-62; mem, Seattle Cent. Adv. Cmn; Nat. Coun. Exec. Bd; chief, Seattle Coun. Boy Scouts; C. of C. Pres.(exec. cmt); Seattle C. of C; Mason; Kiwanis. Silver Beaver Award, Boy Scouts, 49. Legal Res: Seattle, Wash. Mailing Add: Dept. of Transportation, Washington, D.C. 20590.

BRANCA, ERNEST O. D
b. Italy, 11/17/99; s. Ralph Branca and Antoinette Palatucci B; m. to Agnes E. Corcoran; c. Ralph, Regina. Educ: Pub. schs. Polit. & Govt. Pos: Pa. State Rep, 54, 58-67; 41st Ward Dem. Exec. Cmt. Bus. & Prof. Pos: Salesman, Snellenburg's. Mem: Retail Clerks Union, Local 1390, AFL-CIO, Negotiation and Exec. Bd, 2 terms, pres. and v.pres; St. Leo Coun. 1294, K. of C. Rel: Catholic. Mailing Add: 4734 Sheffield Ave, Philadelphia, Pa. 19136. (1967).

BRANCATO, JASPER M. D
Mo. State Sen.
b. Kansas City, Mo, 11/26/07; m. 4/23/42 to Zaira Follina; c. Jo Ann. Educ: Kansas City Sch. of Law. Polit. & Govt. Pos: Dem. ward leader, Jackson Co, Mo; Mo. State Sen, 56- Bus. & Prof. Pos: Real estate investor; v.pres, A.B.C. Super Mkt, Inc; v.pres, Zaira Realty Corp. Mil. Serv: Army, Qm. Corps, World War II, 2 years. Mem: K. of C.(4°); Kansas City C. of C; Mo. Peace Officers Asn; Am. Legion; co-capt, Red Cross and Commun. Chest drives. Rel: Catholic. Mailing Add: 601 W. 12th, Kansas City, Mo. 64116. (1967)

BRANCH, ELWOOD L. D
b. Smithdale, Miss, 11/30/09; married. Polit. & Govt. Pos: Former Miss. State Rep. Bus. & Prof. Pos: Construction contractor. Mem: United Commercial Travelers. Rel: Baptist. Mailing Add: 414 Michigan Ave, McComb, Miss. 39648. (1967)

BRANCH, KENNETH GORDON D
b. Vernon, B.C, 9/2/14; s. Bertram Henry Branch and Amy F. Moore B; m. 6/2/39 to Genevieve Marr Kohler; c. Beatrice (Mrs. Griffith); Quentin M. and Courtney C. Educ: Univ. of Wash, B.Archit, 39. Polit. & Govt. Pos: Former chmn, Kitsap Co. Dem. Cent. Cmt, Wash. Mem: Am. Inst. of Architects; Lions; Eagles. Rel: Unitarian Universalist. 1967 Legal Res: Bremerton, Wash. No mailing address available. (1967)

BRANCH, TURNER WILLIAMSON R
N.Mex. State Rep.
b. Houston, Tex, 8/22/38; s. James Alexander Branch, Sr. and Juanita Wilson B; m. 8/8/59 to Vicki Brooks; c. Brian Kern and Rebecca Claire. Educ: Univ. N.Mex, B.A, 60; Baylor Univ. Sch. Law, J.D, 65; Omicron Delta Kappa; Pi Sigma Alpha; Chaaka; Phi Delta Phi; Pi Kappa Alpha. Polit. & Govt. Pos: Dir, alcoholic beverage control dept, State of N.Mex, 66-68; N.Mex. State Rep, 69- Mil. Serv: Entered as 2nd Lt, Marine Corps, 60, released as 1st Lt, 63, after serv. in Second Bn, Fifth Marine Regt. Publ: Published 5 articles in Baylor Law Rev, 63-65. Mem: N.Mex, Albuquerque and Am. Bar Asns; N.Mex. and Am. Trial Lawyers Asns; Elks; Mason; PTA (pres); Kiwanis Int; Boy Scouts (packmaster); Jaycees; C. of C. Rel: Presbyterian. Mailing Add: 4308 Avenida La Resolena N.E, Albuquerque, N.Mex. 87110.

BRANCH, W. FRANK D
b. Hampton, Fla, 1/6/09; s. George W. Branch and Maude Thompson B; m. 8/27/36 to Sibyl Blitch; c. Sibyl Frances. Educ: Mercer Univ, 30. Polit. & Govt. Pos: Ga. State Rep, 59-66. Bus. & Prof. Pos: Cotton buyer, broker and merchant. Mil. Serv: Navy, Lt. (j.g.); Armed Guard Comdr, Eng, Scot, France and Russia; European, Asiatic and Am. Theaters. Rel: Methodist. Mailing Add: Tifton, Ga. 31794. (1967)

BRANCHFIELD, EDWARD R
b. Macomb, Ill, 10/30/14; s. Paul Ernest Branchfield and Bertha Garman B; m. 5/17/46 to Edith Blanche Niebuhr; c. Paul Edward, Anne Christine, David Curtiss and Scott Eric. Educ: Univ. Mich, A.B, 39; Univ. Mich. Law Sch, LL.B, 42. Polit. & Govt. Pos: Mem, Sch. Bd, Medford, Ore, 51-61; Ore. State Rep, 63-68; cmnr, Interstate Compact for Educ, 66- Mil. Serv: Entered as Pvt, Army, 42, released as 1st Lt, 46, after serv. in 36th Inf. Div, ETO; Purple Heart; ETO Ribbon. Mem: Am. Bar Asn; Fed. Bar Asn; DAV; Am. Legion; VFW; Elks. Rel: Methodist. Legal Res: 711 E. Main St, Medford, Ore. 97501. Mailing Add: P.O. Box 518, Medford, Ore. 97501. (1967)

BRAND, EDWARD CABELL D
Mem, Salem Dem. City Cmt, Va.
b. Salem, Va, 4/11/23; s. William Fitzgerald Brand and Ruth Cabell B; 2nd m. June, 1964 to Shirley Hurt; c. Sylvia Cabell, Miriam Holmes, Edward Cabell, Jr, Marshall Cabell, Ruth Elison Pence 'Liza,' Richard Franklin Pence and John Wilson Pence. Educ: Va. Mil. Inst, B.S.E.E, 44. Polit. & Govt. Pos: With Mil. Govt. and Dept. of State, Europe, 2 years; mem, Salem Dem. City Cmt, Va, currently; alternate del, Dem. Nat. Conv, 68. Bus. & Prof. Pos: Mem. staff, Ortho-Vent Shoe Co, now Stuart McGuire Shoe Co, 49-, pres, 62-; chmn. of bd, Brand-Edmonds Advert; part-time instr, bus. admin. and sales mgt, Roanoke Col. Mil. Serv: Army, 70th Inf. Div, Europe, 4 years, Capt. Mem: Pres. Asn. of Am. Mgt. Asn; Young Pres. Orgn; Int. Platform Asn; Bus. Leadership Adv. Coun; bd. of gov, VMI Sportsmen's Club; exec. coun, Nat. Indust. Conf. Bd; Newcomen Soc. N.Am; pres, Roanoke Valley Torch Club, 60, Roanoke Touchdown Club, 62 and Salem Rotary Club, 63; dir, Roanoke Sales Exec. Club, 61; dir. and v.chmn, Direct Selling Asn; dir, Roanoke Valley Coun. of Commun. Serv; C. of C.(mem, Manpower Cmt); pres, Total Action Against Poverty in Roanoke Valley, 65-; bd. of dirs, Opportunities Industrialization Center; chmn, Task Force on Employ; initiated Local Bus. Adv. Coun. Outstanding Citizen Award, Dist. 10, Va. Coun. of Soc. Welfare, 67; Urban Serv. Award, Off. of Econ. Opportunity, 67. Rel: Presbyterian. Legal Res: 701 W. Main St, Salem, Va. 24153. Mailing Add: P.O. Box 551, Salem, Va. 24153.

BRAND, GEORGE G. D
b. 1904. Polit. & Govt. Pos: Ky. State Sen, 60-68. Bus. & Prof. Pos: Motel and restaurant owner, operator; retail clothing; real estate. Rel: Christian. Mailing Add: P.O, Mayfield, Ky. 42066. (1967)

BRAND, JAMES HENRY R
Chmn, Crawford Co. Rep. Cent. Cmt, Mo.
b. St. Clair, Mo, 7/29/30; s. Harold G. Brand and Marjory Kemberlin B; m. 3/2/57 to Wanda Leona Williams; c. Janet Michele, La Donna Jean, Gary James and Larry David. Educ: Steelville High Sch, grad. Polit. & Govt. Pos: Chmn, Crawford Co. Rep. Cent. Cmt, Mo, 68- Mil. Serv: Entered as Airman Basic, Air Force, 51, released as A 1/C, 55. Mem: Farm Bur. Rel: Protestant. Mailing Add: Route 2, P.O. Box 4, Steelville, Mo. 65565.

BRAND, W. CALVERT R
Ind. State Rep.
b. Brown Co, Ind, 2/14/18; s. Jesse Sherman Brand and Calcie Irene Carmichael B; m. 1/14/39 to Betty L. Ballard; c. D. Calvert, Joan Carole (Mrs. David B. Dalton), John Scott and Jesse Robert. Educ: Ill. State Normal Univ, 1 year; Purdue Univ, spec. courses; Ind. Univ, grad. exec. develop. prog. Polit. & Govt. Pos: Del, Ind. Rep. State Conv, 52-62; Rep. precinct committeeman, Columbus, Ind, 52-63; mem, Plan Cmn, Columbus, 55-62, City Coun, 55- and Police Cmn, 59-64; chmn, Bartholomew Co. Rep. Finance Cmt, 59-60; chmn, Ninth Dist. Rep. Finance Cmt, 61-65; mem, Batholomew Co. Elec. Bd, 64-67; Ind. State Rep, 67-; chmn, State Budget Cmt, 69- Bus. & Prof. Pos: Mgr, Dunlap & Co, Inc, Seymour, Ind, 39-45, advert. and sales mgr, Columbus, Ind, 46-50, v.pres, 50-64 and exec. v.pres, 64-65; pres, Brands, Inc, 67- Mil. Serv: Entered as Pvt, Army, 45, released as Pfc, after serv. in Training Units. Mem: Ind. and Nat. Lumber Dealers Asns; Nat. Soc. of State Legislators; Nat. Lumber Dealer Research Coun; Am. Legion; Mason; Scottish Rite; Shrine; York Rite; Elks; Kiwanis; Columbia Club; C. of C; Harrison Lake Country Club; Fraternal Order of Police. Distinguished Serv. Award, Jr. C. of C; Sagamore of the Wabash, Ind; Commun. Serv. Award, Columbus C. of C; Named Dealer of the Decade 1954 through 1963, Nat. Lumber Dealers Asn. Rel: Presbyterian. Legal Res: 906 Franklin St, Columbus, Ind. 47201. Mailing Add: P.O. Box 111, Columbus, Ind. 47201.

BRANDL, JOHN EDWARD D
Consult, Dept. of Health, Educ. and Welfare
b. St. Cloud, Minn, 8/19/37; s. Edward Joseph Brandl and Mercedes Hiemenz B; m. 12/29/60 to Rochelle Ann Jankovich; c. Christopher John, Mary Katherine and Amy Frances. Educ: St. John's Univ, B.A, 59; Harvard Univ, M.A, 62 and Ph.D, 63. Polit. & Govt. Pos: Syst. analyst, Off. of the Secy. of Defense, 63-65, consult, 65-68; consult, Dept. of Commerce, Off. of Econ. Opportunity and Civil Serv. Cmn, 65-68; consult, Dept. of Health, Educ. and Welfare, 65-68 & 69-, dep. asst. secy. for educ. planning, 68-69. Bus. & Prof. Pos: Lectr, econ, Boston Col, 61-62; research assoc, Univ. Minn, summer 62, dir, Sch. of Pub. Affairs, 69-; teaching fel, Harvard Univ, 62-63; asst. prof. econ, St. John's Univ, Minn, 65-67; dir. educ. prog, asst. prof. and research assoc, Univ. Wis, 67-68; vis. lectr, Univ. of the Philippines, summer 68. Mil. Serv: Entered Army, 63, released as 1st Lt, 65; Joint Serv. Commendation Medal. Publ: Damage Limiting: A Rationale for the Allocation of Resources by the U.S. and the U.S.S.R, classified mongr. in Off. of Dir. of Defense Research,

64; Education Program Analysis at HEW, Joint Econ. Cmt. Compendium, 69; 'On the Treatment of Incommensurables in Cost-Benefit Analysis,' Land Econ, 11/69. Mem: Am. Econ. Asn; Cath. Econ. Asn.(coun. dir, 68); Econometric Soc; Delta Epsilon Sigma; bd. dir, Tri-Cap, Inc. Named one of Outstanding Young Men of Am, U.S. Jr. C. of C, 67. Rel: Catholic. Mailing Add: School of Public Affairs, University of Minnesota, Minneapolis, Minn. 55455.

BRANDON, JAMES WILLIAM D
b. Poplar Bluff, Mo, 7/19/32; s. James Alexander Brandon and Gerine Marshall B; m. 11/30/57 to Phyllis Louise Dillaha; c. James Alexander, II and Philip Dillaha. Educ: Vanderbilt Univ, 50-52; Univ. Ark, B.S.B.A, 56; Blue Key; Alpha Kappa Psi; grand master, Kappa Sigma Xi Chap. Polit. & Govt. Pos: Nat. chmn, Youth for Kefauver, 52; alternate del, Dem. Nat. Conv, 56; pres, Pulaski Co. Young Dem, Ark, 58 & 67; Ark. State Rep, Pulaski Co, 61-65; Ark. State Sen, 15th Dist, Pulaski Co, 65-67; del, Ark. Seventh Constitutional Conv, 69. Bus. & Prof. Pos: Student working in summer jobs for Sen. Kefauver, Tenn. & Gov. McMath, Ark; acct. exec, Ted Lamb & Assocs, Inc, 56-61; owner-operator, Brandon Advert. Agency, 62- Mil. Serv: Entered as 2nd Lt, Army Inf, 57, released as 1st Lt, Ret. Res, after 6 months active duty at Ft. Benning & Riley. Pres, Pulaski Co. Ment. Health Asn, 68-70; President's Club (mem. exec. cmt. bd. of dirs,66 & 67). Rel: Episcopal; former vestryman and Sunday sch. teacher at Trinity Episcopal Cathedral Parish. Legal Res: 14 Wingfield Circle, Little Rock, Ark. 72205. Mailing Add: 721 Pyramid Bldg, Little Rock, Ark. 72201.

BRANDON, PHYLLIS DILLAHA D
Committeeman, Pulaski Co. Dem. Cmt, Ark.
b. Little Rock, Ark, 7/31/35; d. Calvin Arthur Dillaha and Vera Burt D; m. 11/30/57 to James William Brandon; c. James Alexander, II and Philip Dillaha. Educ: Univ. Ark, B.A, 57; Mortar Bd; Kappa Kappa Gamma. Polit. & Govt. Pos: State chmn, Housewives for Humphrey/Muskie, Ark, 68; del, Dem. Nat. Conv, 68; committeeman, Pulaski Co. Dem. Cmt, 68- Bus. & Prof. Pos: Camera woman and reporter, KTHV TV Sta, 56; reporter, Ark. Dem, 57; assoc. ed, Home and Garden Sect, Ark. Gazette, 58-59. Publ: Many articles concerning Little Rock, when fed. troops were sent there to open schs. in 57; plus others. Mem: Leawood Garden Club (pres, 69). Rel: Episcopal; Sunday Sch. Teacher, Trinity Episcopal Cathedral Parish. Mailing Add: 14 Wingfield Circle, Little Rock, Ark. 72205.

BRANDON, ROBERT FRANKLIN R
b. Bellevue, Pa, 11/20/11; s. Benjamin F. Brandon and Laura Tyler B; m. 5/10/42 to Ione L. Barker; c. Franklin and Debra. Educ: Univ. Ala; Univ. Iowa, D.D.S; Phi Kappa Sigma. Polit. & Govt. Pos: Councilman, Burbank, Calif, 59-66; former mayor, Burbank. Mil. Serv: Entered as Lt, Army, 42, released as Capt, 45, after serv. in ETO. Rel: Methodist. Mailing Add: 912 N. Hollywood Way, Burbank, Calif. 91505. (1967)

BRANDOW, GEORGE WILLIAM R
Chmn, Ottawa Co. Cent. and Exec. Cmt, Ohio
b. Elmore, Ohio, 9/28/14; s. Albert A. Brandow and Emma S. Croll B; m. 9/14/35 to Emeline Bahnsen; c. Robert Henry and Jean Louise. Polit. & Govt. Pos: Secy, U.S. Rep, Ohio, 48 & 49; chmn, Ottawa Co. Cent. and Exec. Cmt, 51-; mem, Ottawa Co. Elec. Bd, 58-62; del, Rep. Nat. Conv, 60. Bus. & Prof. Pos: Owner, George W. Brandow Agency, 45-; pres, Bank of Elmore Co, 62-; v.pres, Walbridge-Lake Ins. Agency, 63- Mil. Serv: Entered as Pvt, Army, 43, released as S/Sgt, 45, after serv. in 5th Serv. Command; Pvt, 148th Inf. Ohio Nat. Guard, 32-35. Mem: Ottawa Co. Ins. Agents Asn; F&AM; Scottish Rite; Grotto; Shrine; Kiwanis (pres, Elmore Club, 58); Am. Legion (Comdr, 46, Co. Comdr, 48); Harris-Elmore Libr. Bd, 46-65; Toledo Area Red Cross Cmt; Toledo Area Coun, Boy Scouts; Ottawa Co. Draft Bd. and Real Estate Bd. Rel: United Church of Christ. Mailing Add: South River Rd, Elmore, Ohio 43416.

BRANDT, EDWARD R. R
Minn. State Rep.
b. Satanta, Kans, 11/17/31; s. Abraham U. Brandt and Anna Reimer B; m. 10/24/53 to Marie Schmidtke; c. Rosemarie, Eileen, Douglas and Bruce. Educ: Univ. Minn, Minneapolis, B.A, 54, grad. study, 67-69; Vanderbilt Univ, 54-55; George Wash. Univ, M.A, 65; Phi Beta Kappa. Polit. & Govt. Pos: Various admin. pos, Tenn. State Dept. Ment. Health, Nashville, 54-58; for. serv. career reserve officer, U.S. Info. Agency, Germany, Pakistan and Wash, 58-67; Minn. State Rep, 69- Bus. & Prof. Pos: Elem. sch. teacher, Woodlea (New Hirsch) Sch. Dist, Camper, Man, 49-50. Publ: 'The German-American Institute: An Experiment in International Cultural Cooperation,' GW: The George Wash. Univ. Mag, winter 65. Mem: Am. Polit. Sci. Asn; Can. Polit. Sci. Asn; Minneapolis Urban League; Minn. Asn. Ment. Health. Recipient of numerous scholarships and fels. Mailing Add: 162 Emerald St. S.E, Minneapolis, Minn. 55414.

BRANDT, LORRAINE HELEN R
V.chmn, Mesa Co. Rep. Party, Colo.
b. Pittsburgh, Pa, 3/8/23; d. Joseph Henry Kagle and Caroline Meyer K; m. 6/7/45 to John Henry Brandt; c. Janet Helen (Mrs. Larry McNally), Barbara Anne, John Henry III and Bruce Alan. Educ: Univ. Pittsburgh, 4 years. Polit. & Govt. Pos: Committeewoman, Mesa Co. Rep. Party, Colo, 60-68, dist. capt, 62-68, v.chmn, 68- Bus. & Prof. Pos: With Gulf Oil Corp, Pittsburgh, Pa, 44-46; with Treas. Off, Mesa Co, Colo, 64-66; secy, law off. of Harry F. Claussen, 69- Mem: Am. Legion Auxiliary; Am. Bus. Women's Asn; March of Dimes. Rel: Protestant. Mailing Add: 1335 Gunnison Ave, Grand Junction, Colo. 81501.

BRANDT, NEILL MATTESON R
b. Orange, N.J, 5/12/15; s. Neill O. Brandt and Dorothy Matteson B; m. 4/17/41 to Dorothy Elizabeth Engelmann; c. Mary Kathleen and Elizabeth Krista. Educ: St. Lawrence Univ, B.S, 37; Graduate study, Univ. Rochester, Univ. Pittsburgh and Worcester Polytech. Inst. Polit. & Govt. Pos: Chmn, Sturbridge Rep. Town Cmt, Mass, 64-67. Bus. & Prof. Pos: Sci. instr, Richfield Springs, N.Y, 37-42; chemist, Bausch & Lomb, 42-46; fel. Mellon Inst, 47-53, and sr. fel, 53-59; sr. staff physicist, Am. Optical Co, 59-64 and chief physicist, 64- Mem: Am. Chem. Soc; Am. Ceramic Soc; fel, Glass Div; British Soc. Glass Tech. Rel: Catholic. Mailing Add: Cedar St, Sturbridge, Mass. 01566. (1967)

BRANDT, WILLIAM B. R
b. Unadilla, Nebr, 12/4/24; m. 8/10/47 to Rose Marie Stoner; c. Robert W, Karen Sue, Joan Marie, Jane Elizabeth. Educ: Nebr. State Teachers Col; Univ. of Idaho; Univ. of Nebr, B.S, 49, J.D, 52. Polit. & Govt. Pos: Nebr. State Sen, 61-64. Bus. & Prof. Pos: Dir, Unadilla First Nat. Bank and The American Bank, Burr, Nebr. Mil. Serv: USAR. Mem: Am. Legion; VFW. Mailing Add: Unadilla, Nebr. 68454.

BRANDWEIN, CARL O. D
b. Walnut Grove, Mo, 1/7/29; m. 12/20/52 to Elaine Wilhelm; c. Carleen Ann, Helen E, Brian L, Mark C. Educ: Rockhurst Col. Polit. & Govt. Pos: Mo. State Rep, 64-66; Dem. Coun. of Jackson Co. Bus. & Prof. Pos: Assoc. with Prudential Ins. Co. Mil. Serv: Navy Air Corps. Mem: Southside Asn. of Independent Dems; Ins. Workers Int. Union, AFL-CIO, Local 109. Rel: Southern Baptist Church. Mailing Add: 11413 Oakland, Kans. City, Mo, 64134. (1967)

BRANHAM, LESTER PROVINCE, SR. D
b. Lugoff, S.C, 7/10/03; s. William Branham and Elizabeth Peake B; m. 12/28/28 to Roberta Hinson. Educ: Clemson Col, 19-20. Polit. & Govt. Pos: Dir, Co. Farm Bur, S.C, 50; P.M.A. Committeeman, 51-53; mem, Co. Hosp. Bd, 53-54; former S.C. State Rep. Bus. & Prof. Pos: Elec. operator, Duke Power Co, 23-48; farmer, merchant, Lugoff Supply Co. Third Place, Nat. Judging Team, 18; Hon. State Farmers Degree, Future Farmers of Am, Clemson Col, 52. Rel: Baptist; Deacon, Spring Vale Baptist Church, treas, 36-50, teacher, Adult Men's Bible Class. Mailing Add: Route 1, Lugoff, S.C. 29078. (1967)

BRANIGIN, ROGER DOUGLAS D
b. Franklin, Ind, 7/26/02; s. Elba L. Branigin and Zula Francis B; m. 11/2/29 to Josephine Mardis; c. Roger D, Jr. and Robert M. Educ: Franklin Col, A.B, 23; Harvard Univ, LL.B, 26; Phi Delta Phi; Theta Alpha Phi; Alpha Phi Omega; Phi Delta Theta. Hon. LL.D, Franklin Col, 56, Butler Univ, 65 and Ind. Univ, 69. Polit. & Govt. Pos: Gen. counsel, Fed. Land Bank, Louisville, Ky, 30-38 and Farm Credit Admin. of Louisville and Related Banks, 33-38; chmn, Tippecanoe Dem. Co. Cent. Cmn, Ind, 38-56; permanent chmn, Dem. State Conv, 48; chmn, Conserv. Cmn, Ind, 48-50; Gov. of Ind, 65-69; del, Dem. Nat. Conv, 68. Bus. & Prof. Pos: Dir, Lafayette Life Ins. Co, Lafayette Nat. Bank and Duncan Elec. Co, 50-, Gen. Tel. Co. of Ind, 58-, Peerless Wire Goods Co, 60-, Nat. Home Corp, 66- and Erie Lackawanna R.R. Co, 69-; partner, Stuart, Branigin, Ricks & Schilling, Lafayette, 69- Mil. Serv: Entered as Capt, Judge Adv. Gen. Dept, Army, 42, released as Lt. Col, 46, after serv. in legal div, Transportation Corps, Wash, D.C, 44-46; Legion of Merit; Army Commendation Medal. Mem: Am. Col. of Trial Lawyers; Am. Law Inst; Am. Col. Probate Coun; Am. Judicature Soc; Ind. State Bar Asn.(pres, 51-52 & 56-60); hon. fel, Lilly Libr; hon. life mem, Chicago Legal Club, Indianapolis Press Club and Ind. Univ. Alumni Asn; Ind. Soc. of Chicago; Am. Legion; Elks; Mason (32°); Shrine; Indianapolis Athletic Club; Lafayette Country Club; Athenaeum Turners; trustee, Franklin Col, 36-, Purdue Univ, 50-52 and 56-60 and Harvard Law Sch. Asn, 65-69. Rel: Baptist; Am. Baptist Conv. Legal Res: 611 S. Seventh St, Lafayette, Ind. 47901. Mailing Add: Eighth Floor, Life Bldg, Lafayette, Ind. 47902.

BRANNAN, CHARLES F. D
b. Denver, Colo, 8/23/03; s. John B. and Ella Louis Street B; m. 6/29/32 to Eda V. Seltzer. Educ: Univ. of Denver, LL.B, 29, LL.D, 48; hon. D.Sc, Colo. Agr. & Mech. Col, 48; Sigma Alpha Epsilon. Polit. & Govt. Pos: Asst. regional attorney, resettlement admin, U.S. Dept. Agr, Denver, 35-37, regional attorney, solicitor's off, Denver, 37-41, regional dir, Farm Security Admin, 41-44, assoc. adminstr, 44, Asst. Secy. of Agr, 44-48, Secy. of Agr, 48-53. Bus. & Prof. Pos: Attorney, 29-35; gen. counsel, Nat. Farmers Union, Denver, 53- Mem: Athletic Club, Denver; Int. Club of Wash, Inc, Wash, D.C; Nat. Lawyers Club, Wash, D.C. Mailing Add: 3131 E. Alameda, Denver, Colo. 80209.

BRANNAN, LOUIE WESLEY D
Ala. State Rep.
b. Grand Bay, Ala, 6/4/04; s. Lewis Webster Brannan and Annie North B; m. 8/14/31 to Mary Katherine Foster; c. Annie Sue. Educ: Univ. Mil. Sch; Vanderbilt Univ; Univ. Ala, A.B, LL.B. Polit. & Govt. Pos: Mem. City Coun, Foley, Ala, 41-; Ala. State Rep, 46-58 & 66-; Ala. State Sen, 63-66. Bus. & Prof. Pos: Lawyer. Mem: Mason. Rel: Baptist. Mailing Add: Foley, Ala. 36535. (1967)

BRANNEN, ROBERT F. 'BOB' D
Fla. State Rep.
b. Lakeland, Fla, 7/27/27; s. Robert Fulton Brannen and Jeanette Moyers B; m. to Barbara J. Baggett; c. Thomas F, Lynnette Marie (Mrs. Geiger) and Timothy C. Educ: Am. Tech. Soc, civil eng. cert, 54. Polit. & Govt. Pos: Chmn, Seventh Cong. Dist. Dem. Exec. Cmt, Fla, 67-69; Fla. State Rep, 56th Dist, 68- Bus. & Prof. Pos: Pres, Blue Seal Excavating & Paving Co, Lakeland, 63-, Lakeland Asphalt Co, 65-, Branco, Inc, 66- and Imp. Develop. Corp, 67- Mil. Serv: Entered as A/S, Merchant Marine, 44, released as Third Mate, 46, after serv. in Atlantic and Pac. Theaters. Mem: F&AM; Elks; Scottish Rite; Moose; Sesame Grotto; Optimist Club; Shrine; Fla. State Grotto Asn; Civitan Club; Cerebral Palsy Asn.(bd. dirs); bd. dirs, Polk Co. Hosp. Rel: Protestant. Legal Res: 600 Brannen Rd, Lakeland, Fla. 33803. Mailing Add: P.O. Box 2457, Lakeland, Fla. 33803.

BRANOM, ROBERT H. D
Mo. State Rep.
b. St. Louis, Mo, 6/19/35; s. Volley B. Branom and Wilma L. O'Briant B; m. 3/20/59 to Teddy M. Merritt; c. Robert H, Jr. and Rebecca L. Educ: Wash. Univ, A.B, 57 and J.D, 59; Eta Sigma Phi; Phi Alpha Delta; Kappa Sigma. Polit. & Govt. Pos: Pres, Normandy Twp. Regular Dem. Club, Mo, 66; Mo. State Rep, currently. Bus. & Prof. Pos: Attorney, 60- Mil. Serv: Entered as 2nd Lt, Army Res, 57, released as 1st Lt, 64, after serv. in Qm. Sch, Ft. Lee, Va, XI Corps. Mem: Am, St. Louis Co, Mo. and St. Louis Bar Asns; bd. dirs, Evangel. Childrens Home; adv. cmt, St. Louis Co. Child Welfare; Boy Scouts; Khoury League. Rel: United Church of Christ. Mailing Add: 2151 69th St, Hillsdale, Mo. 63121.

BRANSCOMB, ANNE WELLS D
b. Statesboro, Ga, 11/22/28; d. Guy Herbert Wells and Ruby Hammond W; m. 10/13/15 to Lewis McAdory Branscomb; c. Harvie Hammond and Katharine Capers. Educ: Univ. N.C, Chapel Hill, B.A, 49; London Sch. Econ, 50-51; Radcliffe Col, M.A, 51; George Wash. Univ. J.D, 62; Rotary Found. fel, 50; Order of the Coif; Phi Beta Kappa; Pi Gamma Mu; Valkyries; Alpha Psi Omega; Pi Beta Phi. Polit. & Govt. Pos: Intel. Officer, Cent. Intel. Agency, Wash, D.C, 51; secy, West. Suburban Dem. Club, Montgomery Co, Md, 56-57; law clerk, U.S. Dist. Court, Colo, 62-63; Dem. Precinct committeewoman, Boulder Co, 64; pres, Dem. Women of Boulder, 64-65; secy, Boulder Co. Dem. Cent. Cmt, 65-67; del, Co, Cong. and State Dem. Conv, 66; historian, Colo. Gen. Assembly, 66; v.chmn, Colo. Dem. State Cent. Cmt, 67-69; Colo. coordinator for citizens groups, Humphrey-Muskie Presidential Campaign, 68; del, Dem. Nat. Conv, 68; chmn, Colo. State Dem. Cmn. to Study Elective Processes, 69; cmnr, Boulder Housing Authority, 69- Bus. & Prof. Pos: Research assoc, Pierson, Ball & Dowd, Attorneys, Wash, D.C, 62; assoc, Williams & Zook, Attorneys, Boulder, Colo, 63-66; lawyer, 66-69; attorney, Arnold & Porter, Wash, D.C, 69- Publ: 'An Analysis of Attempt to Prohibit Racial Discrimination in the Sale or Rental of Publicly Assisted Private Housing,' 4/60 and 'Should Political Broadcasting Be Fair or Equal?,' 10/61, George Wash. Law Rev. Mem: Am. and Colo. Bar Asns; Am. Polit. Sci. Asn; League of Women Voters; Am. Asn. of Univ. Women. Rel: Protestant. Legal Res: 205 Abbey Place, Boulder, Colo. 80302. Mailing Add: 405 N St. S.W, Washington, D.C. 20024.

BRANSON, DALE R. D
Chmn, Lewis Co. Dem. Cent. Cmt, Idaho
b. Craigmont, Idaho, 6/21/24; s. D. Lester Branson and Helen Houchens B; m. 10/5/46 to Arleen Johnson; c. George N, James L, Susan K, Patsy A, Robert D. and David W. Educ: Santa Monica Bus. Col, 43. Polit. & Govt. Pos: Mayor, Nezperce, Idaho, 60-62; chmn, Lewis Co. Dem. Cent. Cmt, 67- Bus. & Prof. Pos: Asst. Mgr, Dokken Import Co, Nezperce, 48- Mem: Lewis Co. Wheatgrowers Asn; Lions; Elks. Rel: Lutheran. Mailing Add: 502 Walnut, Nezperce, Idaho 83543.

BRANSON, FRED R
b. Salem, Ill, 8/31/16; m. to Jane Wilson. Educ: Univ. Ill; Drake Univ. Law Sch, 41. Polit. & Govt. Pos: Ill. State Rep, 62-64. Bus. & Prof. Pos: Lawyer, bd. of dirs. and Secy, City Bldg. and Loan Asn, Centralia. Mil. Serv: Army, 5th Inf. Div, Counter-Intel, World War II. Mem: Am. Legion; VFW; Elks; Rotary. Rel: Christian Church N. Am. Mailing Add: 406 Cedar St, Centralia, Ill. 62801.

BRANTLEY, HASKEW HAWTHORNE, JR. R
Ga. State Rep.
b. Birmingham, Ala, 9/28/22; s. Haskew Hawthorne Brantley and Maggie Lee Hicks B; m. 9/11/48 to Miriam Laughlin; c. Jaquelyn Marie, Margaret Lynn, Susan Elizabeth and Michael David. Educ: Ga. Inst. of Tech, B.S, 48; Sigma Alpha Epsilon. Polit. & Govt. Pos: Ga. State Rep, 14th Dist, 66- Bus. & Prof. Pos: Pres, Am. Tire Co, 58-66; v.pres, Brantley-Katz Co. Inc, 66- Mil. Serv: Entered as Cadet, Navy, 42, released as Lt, 46, after serv. as Naval Aviator. Mem: Dir, Ga. Asn. of Retarded Children; Atlanta and Decalb Real Estate Bds; Atlanta and Cherokee Country Clubs. Rel: Episcopal. Mailing Add: 6114 Riverside Dr, N.W, Atlanta, Ga. 30328.

BRANTLEY, HINES L. D
Ga. State Rep.
b. Johnson Co, Ga, 3/28/11; s. Tom Watson Brantley and Devida Wheeler B; m. 12/27/36 to Edna Myrle Brown; c. Pamela McLendon and Wanda E. Educ: Metter High Sch, 31. Polit. & Govt. Pos: Metter City Councilman, Ga, 55-56; Mayor, Metter, 57-60; Ga. State Rep, 61- Bus. & Prof. Pos: Merchant; retail furniture and farm operator. Mil. Serv: World War II, 43-44. Rel: Primitive Baptist. Mailing Add: Metter, Ga. 30439.

BRANTON, PAREY PERSHING D
La. State Rep.
b. Shongaloo, La, 11/17/18; s. Marion Matthew Branton and Attie Mae Martin B; m. 8/30/43 to Georgia Lusby; c. Parey P, Jr. and Daniel M. Educ: La. State Univ; Univ. Tex. Polit. & Govt. Pos: Mem, Sch. Bd, 52-58; La. State Rep, 60- Mil. Serv: Entered Signal Corps Res, released as Radio Technician. Mem: Ark-La-Tex. Asn. Petrol. Landman; Citizen Coun; C. of C; Lions. Rel: Baptist. Mailing Add: Route 2, Shongaloo, La. 71072. (1967)

BRANYON, JAMES ALEXANDER II D
Ala. State Sen.
b. Fayette, Ala, 4/16/07; s. Dr. Arthur Curtis Branyon, Sr; m. 8/17/35 to Edwyna Walker; c. James Walker. Educ: Univ. of Ala, 27. Polit. & Govt. Pos: Ala. State Rep, 51-66; Ala. State Sen, 67- Bus. & Prof. Pos: Oil distributor; pres, Capital Fire and Casualty Co. Mil. Serv: Air Force, 18 months during World War II, 12 months Berlin Crisis; Col, Ala. Air Nat. Guard. Mem: Mason; Shrine; Am. Legion; 40 et 8. Mailing Add: Box 600, Fayette, Ala. 35555. (1967)

BRASCO, FRANK J. D
U.S. Rep, N.Y.
b. Brooklyn, N.Y, 10/15/32; m. 1959 to Linda Gralla; c. Lauren, Arthur, Meredith and Jennifer. Educ: Brooklyn Col, B.A, 54; Brooklyn Law Sch, LL.B, 57; Brooklyn Col. and Law Sch. Alumni Asns. Polit. & Govt. Pos: Mem, Kings Co. Dem. Exec. Cmt, N.Y, exec. mem, Kings Co. Young Dem. and asst. dist. attorney, Kings Co, formerley; U.S. Rep, N.Y, 67- Bus. & Prof. Pos: Attorney-at-law. Mil. Serv: Army, Inf, 58, Army Res; 4th Judge Adv. Gen. Detachment Unit, N.Y, Capt; USA Res. Officers' Asn. Mem: Bd. of dir, Old Mill Civic Asn; Kings Co. Criminal Bar Asn; Police Athletic League; Brownsville Boys' Club; bd. mem, Abe Stark Philanthropies, Inc. and Brooklyn Women's Hosp. Rel: Roman Catholic. Legal Res: Brooklyn, N.Y. Mailing Add: 1723 Longworth House Office Bldg, Washington, D.C. 20515.

BRASSELL, BOWEN HILL D
Ala. State Rep.
b. Montgomery, Ala, 4/29/22; s. J.W. 'Jabe' Brassell and Bertie Mae Bolton B; m. 8/14/58 to Dorothy J. Williams; c. Bowen H. Brassell, Jr. Educ: Auburn Univ, B.S. in Educ; Univ. Ala. Law Sch, LL.B; Phi Alpha Delta. Polit. & Govt. Pos: Chmn, Russell Co. Young Dem, Ala, 53-54; judge, Juvenile Court of Russell Co, 53-59; Ala. State Rep, 66- Bus. & Prof. Pos: Partner, Brassell & Brassell, Attorneys, 52-62, attorney-at-law, private practice, 62- Mil. Serv: Pvt, Army, 42-43, U.S. Serv. Mem: Ala. and Russell Co. Bar Asns; Mason; Shrine; Civitan Club; Russell Co. Farm Bur. Rel: Methodist. Legal Res: 714 31st St, Phenix City, Ala. 36867. Mailing Add: P.O. Box 573, Phenix City, Ala. 36867.

BRASSIE, RALPH A. R
Polit. & Govt. Pos: Mem, Lafayette City Coun, Ind, 25-29 & 52-56, pres, 52-53; Ind. State Rep, 57-66. Bus. & Prof. Pos: Retired Elect. foreman, Aluminum Co. of Am. Mem: Past pres, Wabash Valley Elect. League; past pres, Indust. Mgt. Club. Rel: Lutheran. Mailing Add: 718 Tenth St, Lafayette, Ind. 47904. (1967)

BRASWELL, HENRY GORDON D
b. Paris, Tex, 2/18/29; s. C. S. Braswell and Mildred Pharis B; m. to Rachel Clark; c. Lauren and Amy. Educ: Paris Jr. Col, A.A, 48; Univ. of Tex, B.A, 50, Law Sch, LL.B, 53; Phi Alpha Delta; Friars; Cowboys. Polit. & Govt. Pos: Judge, Lamar Co, Tex, 55-58; Asst. Attorney Gen, Tex, 58-62; chmn, Lamar Co. Dem. Party, 63-68; judge, sixth judicial dist, Tex, 69- Rel: Methodist. Mailing Add: 3555 Audubon Rd, Paris, Tex, 75460.

BRATAAS, NANCY OSBORN R
Chairwoman, Minn. Rep. Finance Cmt.
b. Minneapolis, Minn. 1/19/28; d. John Draper Osborn and Flo Warner O; m. 11/27/48 to Mark Gerard Brataas; c. Mark Gaylord and Anne Draper. Educ: Univ. Minn, 2 years, Alpha Phi. Polit. & Govt. Pos: Pres, Olmsted Co. Rep. Workshop, Minn, 57-59; city chairwoman, Olmsted Co. Rep. Party, 58-59, co. chairwoman, 59-61; del, Rep. Nat. Conv, 60, del-at-lg, 64 & 68; v.chairwoman, Minn. Rep. Party, 61-63, chairwoman, 63-69; instrumental in planning, writing and implementing organizational prog. for Minn. Rep. Party; chairwoman, Minn. Rep. Finance Cmt, 69- Mem: Am. Asn. Univ. Women; League Women Voters. Testimonial Dinner, 69. Rel: Episcopal. Mailing Add: 839 $10\frac{1}{2}$ St. S.W, Rochester, Minn. 55901.

BRATCHER, I. E. R
b. Millwood, Ky, 10/5/89; married. Educ: Teachers Col, Clarkson, Ky; Boyels Bus. Col, Omaha, Nebr. Polit. & Govt. Pos: Former mem, Sch. and Twp. Bd, N.Dak; N.Dak. State Rep, 51-66. Bus. & Prof. Pos: Farmer; rancher. Mailing Add: Mott, N.Dak. 58646. (1967)

BRATCHER, RHODES R
b. Morgantown, Ky, 12/23/17; s. A.J. Bratcher and Fannie Farris B. (deceased); m. 8/12/46 to Martha Guffy; c. Thomas Rhodes, Suzanne, Sarah and William. Educ: West. Ky. Univ, 36-38; Jefferson Sch. Law, LL.B, 47. Polit. & Govt. Pos: Co. attorney, Butler Co, Ky, 50-53; chief asst. U.S. attorney, West. Dist. Ky, 53-54; mem, Ky. Elect. Cmn, 62; del, Rep. Nat. Conv, 68. Bus. & Prof. Pos: Dir, Lincoln Fed. Savings & Loan Asn, Owensboro, Ky, 62-69. Mil. Serv: Entered as Pvt, Army, 41, released as Sgt, after serv. in China-Burma-India Theatre, 41-45. Mem: Daviess Co, Ky, and Am. Bar Asns; Am. Trial Lawyers Asn; Windridge Country Club. Rel: Baptist. Mailing Add: 2138 N. Stratford, Owensboro, Ky. 42301.

BRATHWAITE, YVONNE WATSON D
Calif. State Assemblyman
b. Los Angeles, Calif, 10/5/32; d. James T. Watson and Lola Moore W; div. Educ: Univ. Calif, Los Angeles, A.B, 52; Univ. South. Calif, LL.B, 56; Pi Sigma Alpha; Alpha Kappa Alpha. Polit. & Govt. Pos: Dep. Corp. Cmnr, Calif, 58-60; Calif. State Assemblyman, 63rd Dist, 67-; del, Dem. Nat. Conv, 68; mem, Coun. on Criminal Justice, Calif, 69. Mem: Women Lawyers; Nat. Asn. Negro Bus. & Prfnl. Women; Langston Law Club; Legion Lex; Leimert Park Dem. Club. Rel: Methodist. Mailing Add: 4036 Buckingham Rd, Los Angeles, Calif. 90008.

BRATTON, RICHARD WALDO R
Chmn, Custer Co. Rep. Cent. Cmt, S.Dak.
b. Basin, Wyo, 2/28/33; s. Ralph Waldo Bratton and Madeliene Baker B; m. 2/8/59 to Alice Walk Peckham; c. Richard John, Randall James and Beth Imogene. Educ: Mont. State Univ, B.S, 60; M-Club; Varsity Basketball. Polit. & Govt. Pos: Finance chmn, Custer Co. Rep. Cent. Cmt, S.Dak, 66, chmn, 68-; city councilman, Custer City, 66-67, mayor, 68; mem. bd. trustees, S.Dak. Munic. League, 69. Bus. & Prof. Pos: V.pres, Custer Develop. Corp, 67-69. Mil. Serv: Entered as Pvt, Marines, released as Sgt, 59, after serv. in Ninth Marine Regt, Third Marine Div, Japan and Okinawa, 56-59; Good Conduct Medal; Bn. Honorman; Marine Recruit Depot, San Diego. Mem: Bus-Indust. Polit. Action Cmt; S.Dak. Elec. Coun; Rotary Club (bd. dirs); Boy Scouts (bd. mem, Black Hills Area Coun); Kiwanis; Toastmasters; C. of C. (pres, Custer, 66-67). Presidential Award of Honor, Newcastle Jaycees, Newcastle, Wyo. Rel: Episcopal. Mailing Add: 1104 Sherman St, Custer City, S.Dak. 57730.

BRAULT, ADELARD LIONEL D
Va. State Sen.
b. Winsted, Conn, 4/6/09; m. to Clarice Louise Covington. Educ: Columbus Univ. Sch. of Law, LL.B. Polit. & Govt. Pos: Mem, Fairfax Bd. Co. Supvr, 62-63; Va. State Sen, 66- Bus. & Prof. Pos: Lawyer. Mil. Serv: Lt. Comdr, Navy. Mem: Fairfax Co. Bar Asn. (pres, 62-63); Am. and Va. State Bar Asns; Va. State Bar. Rel: Catholic. Mailing Add: P.O. Box 248, Fairfax, Va. 22030.

BRAUN, REX D
Tex. State Rep.
b. Kenner, La, 5/2/21; s. Leon Braun and Jeanette Diamond B; m. 11/10/46 to Ruth Hannah Sacks; c. Mike, Debby and Leonard. Educ: Southwest. La. Inst, B.S, 46; Epsilon Pi Alpha; S Club; pres, Inter-fraternity Coun. Polit. & Govt. Pos: Tex. State Rep, 66- Bus. & Prof. Pos: Chmn. bd, Gulfgate Shopping Center, 63-64, Northline Shopping Center, 65-66. Mil. Serv: Entered as Pfc, Marines, 42, released as Cpl, 46, after serv. in 1st Div, Pac. and China, 44-46; Presidential Citation; Marine Corps Medal. Mem: VFW; Am. Legion; Elks; Eagles. Rel: Jewish. Mailing Add: 303 Kings Court, Houston, Tex. 77015.

BRAUN, VIRGINIA MARY R
Assoc. mem, Calif. Rep. State Cent. Cmt.
b. Detroit, Mich. 12/5/17; d. Judson Bradway (deceased) and Florence Elizabeth Michell D; m. 6/7/40 to Henry August Braun; c. Henry Michael, Barbara Michell (Mrs. Telford Alander Walker), Judson and Cynthia Gilbert. Educ: Briarcliff Jr. Col, 1 year; Garland Jr. Col: Alumna Garland Col; pres, freshman class, Briarcliff Jr. Col. and Garland Jr. Col. Polit. & Govt. Pos: Precinct capt, Rep. Hq, Pasadena and Los Angeles, Calif, 50-69; mem. bd, San Marino Rep. Women's Club Federated, 61-66, prog. chmn, three years; del, State and Nat. Conv. Rep. Federated Women, 64-68; mem, Los Angeles Co. Rep. Finance Cmt, 64-69; mem. Women's Div, Freedoms Found. Valley Forge Los Angeles, 64-69; founder and pres, Pasadena Rep. Women's Club Federated, 67-69, adv. bd, 69-; registr. of voters, 67-; alternate del, Rep. Nat. Conv, 68. Bus. & Prof. Pos: Dance teacher, Arthur Murray Studio, Detroit, Mich, 39. Mem: Pasadena Jr. League; Pasadena Guild Childrens Hosp; Nine O'Clock Players; Civic League of Pasadena; Costume Coun. Los Angeles Art Mus; Pro-Am. Club; Pasadena Garden Club; Pasadena Rep. Club; UROC; Capitol Hill Club, Wash, D.C; Calif. Club; Balboa Bay Club; pres, Pasadena Guild Childrens Hosp, 2 years. Rel: Congregational. Mailing Add: 1585 Orlando Rd, Pasadena, Calif. 91106.

BRAUN, WALTER W. R
Chmn, Gage Co. Rep. Cent. Cmt, Nebr.
b. Virginia, Nebr, 2/18/30; s. Frederick W. Braun and Viola Snyder B; m. 4/4/51 to Louise Woltemath; c. Judith Ann, Kathryn Jean and Shauna Lee. Educ: Commercial Exten. Sch. of Commerce, 2 years. Polit. & Govt. Pos: Secy, Beatrice Park Bd, Nebr, 65-; chmn, Gage Co. Rep. Cent. Cmt, 68- Bus. & Prof. Pos: Nat. bank exam, comptroller of currency, U.S. Treas. Dept, 55-58; v.pres, Beatrice Nat. Bank, Nebr, 68- Mil. Serv: Entered as Pvt, Air Force, 50, released as S/Sgt, 54, after serv. in 566th Air Defence Group, 50-54. Mem: Jaycees (past pres); Sertoma Club (dir); C. of C.(first v.pres); Beatrice Outstanding Young Man Award, 63; Nebr. Distinguished Serv. Award, 64, Jr. Chamber Int. Senatorship. Rel: Lutheran. Mailing Add: 400 Morton Dr, Beatrice, Nebr. 68310.

BRAUNER, WILLIAM JESS D
Idaho State Rep.
b. Nampa, Idaho, 9/22/32; s. William Raymond Brauner and Juanita M. Hicks B; m. 6/10/56 to Leila R. Randall; c. William Randall, Jess Charles, Bradley Vincent and Robert Joseph. Educ: Col. Idaho, Caldwell, degree in econ; Univ. Idaho, Moscow, LL.B; Phi Alpha Delta. Polit. & Govt. Pos: Prosecuting attorney, Owyhee Co, Idaho, 56-57; dep. prosecuting attorney, Ada Co, 57; prosecuting attorney, Canyon Co, 59-60; Idaho State Rep, Canyon Co, Dist. 11, 65-66 & 68- Bus. & Prof. Pos: Sr. partner, Law Firm of Brauner, Fuller & Doolittle, 59- Mem: Idaho and Am. Bar Asns; Am. Trial Lawyers Asn; Canyon Co. Lawyers Club; Elks; Kiwanis Int. Outstanding Freshman Legislator, House of Rep, Idaho Legis. Session, Idaho Press Club, 65. Rel: Catholic. Legal Res: 2323 S. Ohio Ave, Caldwell, Idaho 83605. Mailing Add: P.O. Box 130, Caldwell, Idaho 83605.

BRAWLEY, HIRAM WILKS 'BILL' D
b. Lockart, S.C, 4/12/17; s. Wilks Hiram Brawley and Bernice Pendergrass B; m. 9/12/40 to Hazel Townsend; c. Frederica (Mrs. Adkinson) and Carol Lee. Educ: Univ. of the South, 36-40; Sigma Nu. Polit. & Govt. Pos: Acct, Off. Price Admin, Wash, D.C, 41-43 & 46-47; inspector, Fed. Trade Cmn, 47-49; chief staff, Senate Cmt. Post Office and Civil Serv, 49-61; asst. nat. campaign mgr, Adlai Stevenson, 56; nat. dem. coordinator, Kennedy for Pres, 60; dep. postmaster gen, Post Off. Dept, D.C, 61-62; exec. asst. to chmn, Dem. Nat. Cmt, 62-65; regional campaign mgr, Johnson-Humphrey, 64; del, Dem. Nat. Conv, 68. Bus. & Prof. Pos: Personnel dir, Spring Mills, Chester, S.C, 40; v.pres. and mem. bd. gov, Genesco, Inc, 65- Mil. Serv: Entered as Cadet, Air Force, 43, released as 2nd Lt, 46. Mem: Nat. Capital Dem. Club.(pres, 61-62); v.chmn, St. Stephens Sch. Boys, 68-; Wash. Athletic Club (v.chmn, 69-); v.pres, Bryce Mt. Resort, Mt. Jackson, Va, 69- Rel: Episcopal. Mailing Add: 1313 Bishop Lane, Alexandria, Va. 22302.

BRAY, ELZA R
b. Kitzmiller, Md, 8/20/94; married. Educ: Kitzmiller Pub. Schs. Polit. & Govt. Pos: Md. State Del, 59-67; past City Councilman, Lock Lynn Heights. Bus. & Prof. Pos: Life ins. salesman. Mil. Serv: WW I. Mem: Past Chancellor Cmdr, K. of P. Lodge No. 113; past Cmdr, Am. Legion Post No. 71; Garrett Co. Hist. Soc. Mailing Add: 729 E. Oak St, Oakland, Md. 21550. (1967)

BRAY, JAMES HOUSTON 'JAMIE' D
Tex. State Rep.
b. Louisville, Miss, 11/29/26; s. McKinley Charles Bray and Irnie Mae Miller B; m. 8/28/48 to Joveda Murphy; c. Deborah Jo (Mrs. Smith), James Houston, Jr. and Monroe LaMonte. Educ: High Sch. Polit. & Govt. Pos: Tex. State Rep, 24th Legis. Dist, Pos. Six, 69- Bus. & Prof. Pos: Pres. and chmn. bd, Ascot, Inc, 55- Mil. Serv: Entered as Seaman, Merchant Marine, 43, released as Lt.(jg), 51, after serv. in various theatres, 43-51. Mem: Nat. Burglar and Fire Alarm Asn.(past regional v.pres); Rotary; Mason; Shrine; Pasadena Rodeo Asn.(dir); Pasadena C. of C.(dir); Pasadena Mayor's Adv. Coun. Rel: Methodist; Bd. Stewards, First Methodist Church. Legal Res: 601 Brook Lane, Pasadena, Tex. 77501. Mailing Add: P.O. Box 6647, Pasadena, Tex. 77502.

BRAY, WILLIAM GILMER R
U.S. Rep, Ind.
b. Mooresville, Ind, 6/17/03; s. Gilmer Bray and Dorcas Mitchell B; m. 8/16/30 to Esther Debra; c. Richard D. Educ: Ind. Univ, A.B, 27; Tau Kappa Alpha; Acacia. Hon. LL.D, Vincennes Univ. Polit. & Govt. Pos: Prosecuting attorney, Morgan Co, 27-31; temporary chmn, Rep. State Conv; precinct committeeman, Rep. Party, Ind; v.chmn, Rep. Cong. Cmt; U.S. Rep, Ind, 51- Bus. & Prof. Pos: Attorney-at-law, private practice. Mil. Serv: Entered as Capt, Army, 41, released as Col, 46, after serv. in 193rd and 767th Tank Bn, Fourth Armored Group, Mil. Govt, Korea, Asiatic-Pac. Theater; Col, Army Res, 46-63; Silver Star. Publ: Russian Frontiers: From Muscovy to Khrushchev, Bobbs-Merrill Co, Inc, 63. Mem: Dir, Armor Asn; Ind. Bar Asn; Am. Legion; VFW; Amvets; Mason, Scottish Rite, Shrine, K.T; Moose; Elks; Eagles. Rel: Quaker. Legal Res: 489 N. Jefferson St, Martinsville, Ind. 46151. Mailing Add: 2305 Rayburn Office Bldg, Washington, D.C. 20515. (1967)

BRAZIER, DONALD HAY, JR. R
Chief Dep. Attorney Gen, Wash.
b. Seattle, Wash, 3/14/31; s. Donald Hay Brazier and Elzey Skinner B; m. 12/27/58 to Marilyn Lee Search; c. Bruce Donald and Thomas Richard. Educ: Whitman Col, 48-49; Univ. of Wash, B.S, 47, J.D, 54; Phi Gamma Delta; Phi Delta Phi. Polit. & Govt. Pos: Dep. prosecuting attorney, Yakima Co, Wash, 59-60; asst. U.S. attorney, East. Dist, Wash, U.S. Dept. of Justice, 60-61; mem, exec. cmt, Yakima Co. Young Rep, Wash, 61-62; city councilman and asst. mayor, Yakima, 62-66; Wash. State Rep, 14th Dist, 67-69; chief dep. attorney gen, Wash, 69- Bus. & Prof. Pos: Assoc, Halverson, Applegate & McDonald, Attorneys, 57-59; partner, Walters, Whitaker & Brazier, Attorneys, 61-64; indust. rels. and pub. affairs, Timber & Wood Products Group, Boise Cascade Corp, 64-69. Mil. Serv: Sgt, Army, 54-56, serv. in 855th Engr. Bn, Camp Wolters, Tex. Mem: Am, Wash. State and Yakima Co. Bar Asns. Selected as Young Man of the Year, Yakima Jr. C. of C, 65. Rel: Protestant. Legal Res: Yakima, Wash. 98902. Mailing Add: Route Ten, Box 556, Olympia, Wash. 98501.

BREATHITT, EDWARD THOMPSON, JR D
Dem. Nat. Committeeman, Ky.
b. Hopkinsville, Ky, 11/26/24; s. Edward Thompson Breathitt and Mary Jo Wallace B; m. 12/20/48 to Frances Holleman; c. Mary Fran, Linda, Susan and Edward, III. Educ: Univ. Ky, LL.B. and B.A. in commerce; pres, Lamp and Cross; sr. men's honorary; Omicron Delta Kappa. Hon. LL.D, Univ. of Ky, Marshall Col. and Ky. Wesleyan. Polit. & Govt. Pos: Mem. state campaign staff, former V.Pres. Alben W. Barkley's successful campaign for reelection to U.S. Senate; chmn, State Speakers Bur, Adlai Stevenson's Presidential Campaign, 52; pres, Young Dem. Clubs of Ky, 52; mem, State Pub. Serv. Cmn; State Personnel Cmnr; Ky. State Rep, 3 terms; Gov. of Ky, 63-67; Dem. Nat. Committeeman, 67-, mem. cmn. on rules, Dem. Nat. Cmt, 69- Mil. Serv: Entered Army Air Force, 43, released as Aviation Cadet, 45. Mem: Jaycees; Kiwanis; Elks; dir, Hopkinsville C. of C. Lincoln Key Award, 66; seconded nomination of Lyndon B. Johnson for President of U.S. Rel: Methodist. Mailing Add: P.O. Box 24, Hopkinsville, Ky. 42240.

BREAUX, JOHN RICHARD D
La. State Rep.
b. Breaux Bridge, La, 12/16/38; s. Joseph Wade Breaux and Marie Louise Thevenet B; m. 8/25/57 to Judith Ann Sherville; c. Desiree Frances, Denise Ann, John Richard, Jr. and Brett Allen. Educ: Univ. Southwest La, 2 years. Polit. & Govt. Pos: V.pres, Eighth Ward Rep. Dist, Dem. Party, La, 61; council-at-lg, Jeanerette, La, 63-67; La. State Rep, 68- Bus. & Prof. Pos: Sales mgr, Evengeline Food & Pepper Prod, Inc, 66-67; sales mgr, Jeanerette Motor Co, 67-69; banker, Sugarland State Bank, 69. Mil. Serv: Entered as Yeoman 3/C, Naval Res, 56, released 64. Mem: Rotary; Jaycees; K. of C. Outstanding Young Men in Am, 67. Rel: Roman Catholic. Legal Res: 310 Doll St, Jeanerette, La. 70544. Mailing Add: P.O. Box 311, Jeanerette, La. 70544.

BREAZEALE, HAROLD DELOIS D
S.C. State Rep.
b. Pickens, S.C, 5/28/20; s. Ed Breazeale and Doshia Chappell B; m. 8/17/41 to Evelyn Winchester B; c. Danny, Edwin, Elaine, Marion and Harold D, Jr. Educ: Univ. S.C, A.B, 46. Polit. & Govt. Pos: Chmn, Ed. and Pub. Works Cmn; app. by Gov. Hollings to Legis. Adv. Coun, South. Regional Educ. Bd; S.C. State Rep, 55- Bus. & Prof. Pos: Life ins. agent, Calhoun Life. Mil. Serv: Air Force, 43-45, with serv. in 454th Bomb Group (H), 15th Air Force. Rel: Baptist. Mailing Add: R.F.S. 3, Pickens, S.C. 29671. (1967)

BRECKINRIDGE, JOHN BAYNE D
Attorney Gen, Kentucky
b. Wash, D.C, 11/29/13; s. Dr. Scott Dudley Breckinridge and Gertrude Ashby Bayne B; m. 7/5/54 to Helen Congleton; c. Knight (Mrs. Dietrich) and John Bayne. Educ: Univ. Ky, A.B, 37, LL.B, 39; Kappa Alpha. Polit. & Govt. Pos: Spec. attorney, anti-trust div, U.S. Dept. Justice, 40-41; chief indust. and projs. licensing div, Bd. Econ. Warfare, 41-42; Ky. State Rep, 56-59; del, White House Conf. Children and Youth, 60; mem. rules cmt, Dem. Nat. Conv, 60; mem, Ky. Constitution Rev. Cmt, 60-62; Attorney Gen, Ky, 60-64, & 68-; mem, Ky. Cmn. Children and Youth, 60-64 & 68-; mem, South. Interstate Nuclear Bd, 62-, past chmn. and v.chmn; chmn, Ky. Adv. Cmt. Nuclear Energy, 60-66; past chmn, Ky. Sci. and Tech. Coun; dir, Ky. Atomic Energy and Space Authority, 66-67; chmn, Ky. Water Pollution Control Cmn, 68, mem, 68-; mem, Ky. Health and Geriatric Authority, Ky. Turnpike Authority, Ky. Pub. Sch. Authority, Ky. State Property and Bldg. Cmn, Ky. State Archives and Records Cmn, Ky. Employee's Retirement Syst. and Ky. Teachers Retirement Syst, 68- Bus. & Prof. Pos: Attorney, 46- Mil. Serv: Entered as 1st Lt, Army, 41, released as Col, 46, after serv. in Joint U.S-United Kingdom Commanding Officer, Military Liaison Hqs, Albania; Asst. Chief Int. Div, USAFIME Hqs; Joint U.S-United Kingdom Chief Econ. and Supply Officer, Mil. Liaison Hq, Balkan, 46; Secy. of Army Commendation medal for Performance of Duties in Connection with Int. Security Affairs. Publ: Articles for Ky. Law J. 63-64 and spec. issue, 63. Mem: Am, Ky, Fayette Co. and Franklin Co. Bar Asns; Am. Judicature Soc; Ky. Hist. Soc.(pres, 62-64); Civil War Round Table; Atlantic Union Coun.(past pres, Ky. Chap); State Law Libr.(bd. trustees); Ky. Law Enforcement Coun.(past chmn); Nat. Asn. Attorneys Gen.(chmn, South. Regional Conf, mem. exec. cmt, v.chmn. cmt. state constitutions; chmn. cmt. off. of attorney gen); past v.pres. and mem. exec. cmt, United Cerebral Palsy Asn; Dem. Club Ky; Frontier Nursing Serv. (bd. trustees); Ky. Welfare Asn.(bd. dirs, v.pres, 62-63); VFW. Wyman Award, Nat. Asn. Attorneys Gen. Rel: Presbyterian. Legal Res: 1100 Fincastle Rd, Lexington, Ky. 40502. Mailing Add: Capitol Bldg, Frankfort, Ky. 40601.

BREECE, EDWARD JOHN R
Wyo. State Rep.
b. Bloomsburg, Wyo, 7/28/98; s. Daniel W. Breece and Clara Jane Lawton Breece; m. 6/19/28 to Christine Latshaw; c, Daniel E. and John L. Educ: Pa. State Teachers Col, 2 years. Polit. & Govt. Pos: Controller, Chester Co,

Pa, 29-33; Wyo. State Rep, 59- and five time chmn, ways & means cmt. Bus. & Prof. Pos: Newspaper publisher, Pa. & Wyo; radio sta. owner and broadcaster, Wyo. Mil. Serv: Navy, 17-18. Mem: Mason; Elks; Am. Legion. Rel: Episcopal. Mailing Add: 291 Cascade St, Lander, Wyo. 82520.

BREED, WILLIAM JACK R
Chmn, Hinds Co. Rep. Exec. Cmt, Miss.
b. Poplarville, Miss, 6/27/21; s. William Jack Breed and Mary Elma Smith B; m. 8/28/45 to Ellen Rose Batson; c. Nell Inda and Mary Ellen. Educ: U.S. Maritime Service Officers Training Sch, Engr. License Steam-Diesel, 43. Polit. & Govt. Pos: Chmn, Miss. Cand. Cmt, 62-68; Del. Rep. Nat. Conv, 68; Chmn, Hinds Co. Rep. Exec. Cmt, 68- Bus. & Prof. Pos: V.pres, Capitol Hardware Co, Inc, Jackson, Miss, 54-; owner, Breed Sales Co, 58-; owner, Dunrovin Cattle and Timber Farm, Leesburg, 61-; dir, Dixie Nat. Life Ins. Co, Jackson, 68- Mil. Serv: Entered as Midn, Naval Res, 42, transferred to Maritime Serv, released as 2nd Eng. Officer, 45, after serv. in Troop Carrier and Ammunition Ships, European, Mediterranean, Near East and Far East, 42-45; European, Mediterranean, Near East and Far East Campaign Ribbons. Mem: Nat. and Am. Wholesale Lumber Asns; Aircraft Owners and Pilots Asn; Mason; Country Club Jackson; River Hills Club; Jackson Yacht Club; Jackson Knife & Fork Club; C. of C; Am. Angus Asn. Gold Key Fund Raising Award, Miss. Rep. Party; Maywood Nat. Sales Winner, 5 years. Rel: Baptist. Legal Res: 1030 Cedal Hill Dr, Jackson, Miss. 39206. Mailing Add: P.O. Box 4827, Jackson, Miss. 39216.

BREEDEN, EDWARD L, JR. D
Va. State Sen.
b. Norfolk, Va, 1/28/05; m. to Virginia C. Hurt. Educ: Hampden-Sydney Col; George Washington Univ. Polit. & Govt. Pos: Va. State Rep, 36-42; Va. State Sen, 44-; chmn, Second Dist. Dem. Cmt, 50-60; del, Dem. Nat. Conv, 68. Bus. & Prof. Pos: Lawyer; dir. and bd. chmn, South. Bank of Norfolk; dir, The First Va. Corp; trustee, Hampden-Sydney Col, Jamestown Found, Norfolk Gen. Hosp. Mem: Lions; Mason, Shrine, Khedive Temple; Elks; Kappa Sigma; Commonwealth; Norfolk Yacht & Country Club; Princess Anne Country Club; Va. Club. Rel: Presbyterian. Mailing Add: Virginia National Bank Bldg, Norfolk, Va. 23501.

BREEDING, J. FLOYD D
b. Robinson, Kans, 9/28/01; s. Robert M. Breeding and Fannie Victoria Miller B; m. 3/18/21 to Mary Sevilla Tevis; c. Charles M. and Ralph E. Educ: Kans. State Univ, 20-21. Polit. & Govt. Pos: Kans. State Rep, 47-49, Minority Leader, Kans. House of Rep, 49; cand. for Lt. Gov, 50; U.S. Rep, Kans, 56-63, mem, House Banking and Currency Cmt, 57-58, mem. House Cmt. on Agr. and Subcmts. on Conserv. and Credit, Family Farms, Dairy and Poultry, Livestock and Feed Grains and chmn, Wheat Subcmt; expert consult. to Secy. of Agr. with Grain and Feed Div, For. Agr. Serv. and Off. Gen. Sales Mgr, Commodity Credit Corp, 63-; cand. for U.S. Sen, 66. Bus. & Prof. Pos: Farmer-stockman, Morton Co, Kans; dir, KTVC TV Sta, Ensign and Farmers Alliance Ins. Co, McPherson; bd. mem, Rural Tel. Asn, 54-55. Mem: Pres, West. Kans. Develop. Asn, 51; dir, Am. Automobile Asn, Topeka and Wichita, Southwest Royalty Asn, 51-52 and Kans. Asn. Wheat Growers; local bd, Agr. Adjustment Agency and Prod. & Mkt. Admin, 36-46; Southwest Irrigation Asn, Liberal; Rotary; Lions; Eagles; Elks; Moose; Mason; Shrine; Grange; Kans. Livestock Asn; Farm Bur; Farmers Union; C. of C. Rel: Methodist. Legal Res: Rolla, Kans. 67954. Mailing Add: 540 N St. S.W, Apt. S-304, Washington, D.C. 20024.

BREEN, EDWARD D
b. Dayton, Ohio, 6/10/08; s. John Breen and Katherine Beckman B; m. 10/10/56 to Constance Focke; c. Edward, Robert and Cindy Ward. Educ: Ohio State Univ. Polit. & Govt. Pos: Mayor, Dayton, Ohio, 45-48; U.S. Rep, Ohio, 48-51; mem, Montgomery Co. Cmn, 56-60. Bus. & Prof. Pos: Mgr, Dayton Biltmore Hotel, 30-38 and Van Cleve Hotel, 38-40. Mil. Serv: Entered as 1st Lt, Army, 41, released as Lt. Col, 45, after serv. in Mediterranean Theater; Army Res, 28. Rel: Catholic. Mailing Add: 3521 Echo Springs Trail, Dayton, Ohio 45429. (1967)

BREEZE, EVELYN LOUISE COX R
Parliamentarian, Orange Co. Rep. Exec. Cmt, Fla.
b. Lebanon, Ky, 10/24/22; d. Albert Lee Cox and Rosa Raley C; m. 11/25/44 to Robert Carey Breeze; c. Marshall Hall, II, Philip Raley and Robin (Mrs. Windham). Educ: Sch. Nursing, St. Elizabeth's Hosp, Youngstown, Ohio, R.N, 43. Polit. & Govt. Pos: Precinct committeewoman, Orange Co, Rep. Party, Fla, 63-; parliamentarian, Orange Co. Rep. Exec. Cmt, 64-; v.chmn, 68; del, Rep. Nat. Conv, 68; mem, Orange Co. Sch. Bd, 67-, chmn, 69- Bus. & Prof. Pos: Staff nurse, St. Elizabeth's Hosp, Youngstown, Ohio, 43, private duty nurse, Hosp, Ramey Air Force Base, P.R, 53-55; Hosp, Barksdale Air Force Base, La, 56-58; staff nurse, St. Joseph's Hosp, Savannah, Ga, 59-; consult. infant dept, J.C. Penny, 60; staff nurse, Winter Park Hosp, Fla, 62. Mil. Serv: Army Nurse Corps, 44-45, 2nd Lt. Mem: Am. Legion; Coun. Continuing Educ. Women Cent. Fla; Cent. Fla. Rep. Club; Maitland Duplicate Bridge Club; Am. Contract Bridge League; Fla. and Nat. Sch. Bd. Asns. Rel: Protestant. Mailing Add: 250 W. Reading Way, Winter Park, Fla. 32789.

BREHM, WILLIAM KEITH
Asst. Secy. of the Army
b. Dearborn, Mich, 3/29/29; s. Walter Elmer Brehm and Lucille Hankinson B; m. 6/28/52 to Delores Soderquist; c. Eric and Lisa. Educ: Univ. Mich, B.S, 50, M.S, 52; Phi Eta Sigma. Polit. & Govt. Pos: Dep. asst. Secy. of Defense, Off. of Asst. Secy. of Defense, 67-68; Asst. Secy. of the Army, 68- Bus. & Prof. Pos: Research assoc, Eng. Research Inst, Univ. Mich, 50-52; design specialist, Eng. Dept, Convair, San Diego, Calif, 52-57, chief of opers. anal, Convair Astronautics, 58-59, exec. staff asst. to v.pres. planning, Convair Div, Gen. Dynamics Corp, 60-62; corporate dir, develop. planning, N.Am. Aviation, Inc, El Segundo, Calif, 62-64. Mem: Opers. Research Soc. Am. Secy. of Defense Meritorious Civilian Serv. Medal. Rel: Protestant. Mailing Add: 8957 Colesbury Place, Fairfax, Va. 22030.

BREITBACH, ALFRED P, SR. D
b. Balltown, Iowa, 4/26/97; m. 1924 to Anna Rettenmeier; c. Two sons, three daughters. Educ: Iowa State Univ. Polit. & Govt. Pos: Former Iowa State Rep; mem. Farley Sch. Bd. Bus. & Prof. Pos: Retired dairy herd improvement asn. supvr, fieldman for Dubuque-Delaware Dairy Prods. Improvement Asn. Mil. Serv: Navy, Vet, World War I. Mem: K. of C; Am. Legion; Vets. of World War I; 40 et 8; Farley Commercial Club. Rel: Catholic. Mailing Add: Farley, Iowa 52046. (1967)

BREITEL, CHARLES DAVID R
Assoc. Judge, N.Y. Court of Appeals
b. N.Y.C, 12/12/08; s. Herman L. Breitel and Regina D. Zuckerberg B; m. 4/9/27 to Jeanne S. Hollander; c. Eleanor B.(Mrs. William C. Zabel) and Vivian. Educ: Univ. Mich, A.B, 29; Columbia Univ, LL.B, 32. Hon. LL.D, L.I. Univ, 52. Polit. & Govt. Pos: Dep. asst. dist. attorney, N.Y. Co, 35-39; asst. dist. attorney, 39-41, mem, chief indictment bur, dist. attorney's off, 41; counsel to Gov, N.Y, 43-50, mem, several state cmns, 44-50; justice, N.Y. Supreme Court, 50-52, justice, appellate div, first dept, 52-66; mem, Fed. Cmn. on Int. Rules and Judicial Procedure, 59-64, and Nat. Crime Cmn, 65-67; assoc. judge, N.Y. Court of Appeals, 67- Publ: Co-auth, Counsel on Appeal, McGraw-Hill, 68; auth, 'Courts and Lawmaking,' In: Legal Institutions Today and Tomorrow, Columbia, 59; 'The Lawmakers,' Cardozo Lecture, Asn. of the Bar of the City of N.Y, 65. Mem: Am. and N.Y. State Bar Asns; Asn. of the Bar of the City of N.Y; N.Y. Co. Lawyers' Asn; Am. Law Inst.(mem. coun); Inst. of Judicial Admin; Am. Jewish Cmt; B'nai B'rith. Columbia Univ. Fedn. Alumni Medal, 59. Rel: Jewish. Legal Res: 146 Central Park W, New York, N.Y. 10023. Mailing Add: 74 Trinity Place, New York, N.Y. 10006.

BREITKREUTZ, VERNON EDGAR R
Chmn, Goliad Co. Rep. Party, Tex.
b. Lavaca Co, Tex, 8/21/34; s. Edgar Breitkreutz and Ella Pietsch B; m. 2/9/64 to Aline Fay Ressmann. Educ: Tex. Lutheran Col, B.A, 54; Univ. Tex, Austin, summer, 53; Pac. Lutheran Theol. Sem, B.D, 57; Phi Theta Kappa. Polit. & Govt. Pos: Chmn, Goliad Co. Rep. Party, Tex, 68- Bus. & Prof. Pos: Pastor, St. John's Lutheran Church, Goliad, Tex, 57- Mem: Lutheran Soc. for Worship, Music and the Arts. Rel: Lutheran. Legal Res: 600 W. North St, Goliad, Tex. 77963. Mailing Add: P.O. Box 518, Goliad, Tex. 77963.

BREKKE, LOLA M. R
Mem, Calif. Rep. State Cent. Cmt.
b. Scobey, Mont, 5/1/31; d. Roger Von Kuster and Ragnhild Veis V; m. 7/22/56 to George O. Brekke, Jr; c. Charlotte Sue and Lisa Ann. Educ: Minot State Col, standard teaching credential, 52; Sigma Sigma Sigma. Polit. & Govt. Pos: Precinct chmn, Federated Rep. Women's Club of Sacramento, 65, 1st v.pres, 66, pres, 67, legis. chmn. and parliamentarian, 69; assoc. mem, Calif. Rep. State Cent. Cmt, 67-68, mem, 69-; assoc. mem, Sacramento Co. Rep. Cent. Cmt, 67- Bus. & Prof. Pos: Elem. sch. teacher, Conrad, Mont, 52-53, Billings, Mont, 53-55 and Grand Forks, N.Dak, 55-56. Mem: Nat, Mont. and N.Dak. Educ. Asns; PTA; Girl Scouts. Rel: Lutheran. Mailing Add: 7016 Trabert Court, Carmichael, Calif. 95608.

BREMMER, EDWARD D
b. Beaver, Okla, 12/30/29; s. Joseph Bremmer and Nellie B; m. 8/8/59 to Marylyn Seidl; c. Stephen and Andrew. Educ: St. Mary's Univ, San Antonio, Tex; Creighton Univ, M.A; Notre Dame, South Bend, Ind. Polit. Pos: Iowa State Rep-66; Bus. & Prof. Pos: High Sch. Teacher; Am. Govt, Hist. and Debate. Mil. Serv: U.S. Army, Korean War, 2nd Lt. Mem: Carter Lake Jaycees; K. of C; Am. Fedn. of Teachers, Pres, Local 738. Rel: Catholic. 1967 Legal Res: 1112 Cachelin Dr, Carter Lake, Iowa. No mailing address available. (1967)

BRENDA, GUST GOTTLIEB, JR. D
W.Va. State Del.
b. Rush Run, Ohio, 9/4/20; s. Gust G. Brenda Sr. and Ella Ellis B; m. 7/28/40 to Marrietta May Lewis; c. Ronald Keith and Bruce Kevin. Educ: Weir High Sch, 39. Polit. & Govt. Pos: W.Va. State Del, 68- Bus. & Prof. Pos: Planner and work coordinator, Weirton Steel Co, 30 years. Mil. Serv: Entered as Seaman, Navy, 44, released as 3/C PO, 46. Mem: Am. Rifle Asn; Life mem, Am. Ord. Asn; Am. Legion; Hancock Co. Sportsman Asn; Hancock Co. Conserv. Cmt; Moose; Dapper Dan; Weirton Steel 25 Year Club. Rel: Protestant. Mailing Add: 322 Culler Rd, Weirton, W.Va. 26062.

BRENNAN, BERT C. R
Mich. State Rep.
b. Saginaw, Mich, 12/27/14; s. Charles William Brennan, Sr. and Mina Warner B; m. 9/4/37 to Helen Jeanne Brown; c. Anne (Mrs. Ernie Moon), Jackie (Mrs. Jerry Meyer), Bertie C. and Timothy C.(deceased). Educ: Ferris State Col, B.S, 39. Polit. & Govt. Pos: Mem, Human Rels. Cmt, Saginaw, Mich, 58-61; city supvr, 61-68; Mich. State Rep, 69- Bus. & Prof. Pos: Pres, Mich. State Pharmaceutical Asn, 59; pres, Mich. Bd. Pharm, 66-68. Publ: 'The Ships That Go Down to the Sea,' Great Lakes Hist. Soc; 'History of the Michigan Colleges of Pharmacy,' Mich. J; 'Waveys on James Bay,' Can. Nat. Rwy. Mem: Am. Pharmaceutical Asn; Nat. Asn. Retail Druggists; Nat. Bd. Pharm; Mason; Optimist. Rel: Presbyterian. Mailing Add: 2306 N. Morson, Saginaw, Mich. 48602.

BRENNAN, DOROTHY TERESA D
b. Phila, Pa, 4/30/16; d. Murray S. Oliver and Sarah Cannon O; m. 7/3/33 to Melvin George Brennan, Sr; c. Melvin George, Jr, Sarah E. (Mrs. McCullough) and Arlene F; grandchildren, Dennis McCullough, Jr. and Darcel McCullough. Educ: High Sch, 30-33. Polit. & Govt. Pos: Committeewoman, Dem. Party, Pa, 50-, ward leader, 65-68; clerk, Marriage Bur, 64-68; del, Dem. Nat. Conv, 68; chief probate clerk, Register of Wills, 68- Mem: Commun. Action Dem. Women's Forum (v.pres); Concern Women Group (chmn); Phila. Cmt. for Aid to Biafran Children (co-chmn); dir, Commun. Nursing Serv. Bd; YMCA. Rel: Methodist Episcopal. Mailing Add: 5917 Osage Ave, Philadelphia, Pa. 19143.

BRENNAN, FRANK MICHAEL D
Co. Treas, Cuyahoga Co, Ohio
b. Cleveland, Ohio, 1/24/96; s. Michael J. Brennan and Anne Lanagan B; m. 6/25/19 to Agnes C. Bohrer; c. Robert F. Educ: Lake Erie Sch. of Law, LL.B, 32. Polit. & Govt. Pos: Dep. treas, Cuyahoga Co, Ohio, 33-49, chief dep. treas, 49-55 and treas, 55-; committeeman, Cuyahoga Co. Dem. Exec. Cmt, 48-55; committeeman, Cuyahoga Co. Dem. Cent. Cmt, 50-55. Mil. Serv: Entered as Pvt, Army, 18, released as acting Sgt, Spec. Duty, 19.

Mem: Kiwanis; Am. Legion; Treasurer's Club of Cleveland; Mortgage Bankers Asn; Elks; WOW. Rel: Catholic. Mailing Add: 14317 Bidwell Ave, Cleveland, Ohio 44111. (1967)

BRENNAN, JAMES FRANCIS D
Mayor, Somerville, Mass.
b. Sligo, Ireland, 7/23/16; s. Patrick J. Brennan and Catherine A. Davey B; m. 4/17/38 to Ruth L. McAvoy; c. James F, Jr. and Thomas M. Educ: Northeast. Univ, 2 years. Polit. & Govt. Pos: Exec. secy, Somerville Dem. Party, Mass, 58-59; del, Dem. Nat. Conv, 68; mayor, Somerville, 68- Bus. & Prof. Pos: Pres. and treas, Brennan Ins. Agency, Inc, 53- Mil. Serv: Entered as A/S, Naval Res, 44, released as PO 2/C, 46, after serv. in H.S.D. Mechanicsberg, Am. Theater, 44-46. Mem: Auto Ins. Asn; Ins. Brokers Asn; Boston Col. Fire Underwriters; Lions; Elks; Moose; Charitable Irish Soc; Am. Legion. Distinguished Serv. Award, DAV, 69. Rel: Roman Catholic. Mailing Add: 235 School St, Somerville, Mass. 02145.

BRENNAN, WILLIAM J, JR.
Justice, U.S. Supreme Court
b. Newark, N.J, 4/25/06; s. William J. Brennan and Agnes McDermott B; m. 5/5/28 to Marjorie Leonard; c. William Joseph, Hugh Leonard and Nancy. Educ: Univ. Pa, B.S, 28; Harvard Univ, LL.B, 31. Polit. & Govt. Pos: Superior Court Judge, 49-50; appellate div. Judge, N.J, 50-52; justice, N.J. Supreme Court, 52-56; assoc. justice, U.S. Supreme Court, 56- Bus. & Prof. Pos: Attorney, Pitney, Hardin, Ward & Brennan. Mil. Serv: Gen. Staff Corps, Army, 42-45; Legion of Merit. Mailing Add: U.S. Supreme Court, Washington, D.C. 20543.

BRENNER, JOHN SKONING R
b. Elgin, Ill, 1/2/11; s. Henry White Brenner and Mary Skoning B; m. 9/6/34 to Frances Marshall Ford; c. Elizabeth Ford. Educ: N.Mex. Mil. Inst, 25-28; Mont. State Col, 28-29; Univ. Pa, 30-32; Phi Kappa Psi. Polit. Pos: Mont. State Sen, Beaverhead Co, 53-67; minority leader, Mont. State Senate, 63; Mont. State Rep, 49-51. Govt. Pos: Mem, Legis. Coun. Mont, 63-65. Mem: Mem, Exec. cmt, Am. Nat. Cattlemens Asn, 62-63; mem, exec. cmt, Nat. Livestock Sanit. Asn, 61-62; pres, Mont. Stock Growers Asn, 56-57; Mont. Farm Bureau; Reclamation Asn; Elks. Rel: Episcopalian. Mailing Add: Grant, Mont. 59734. (1967)

BRENT, EDWIN LEA R
Chmn, Wash. Co. Rep. Party, Miss.
b. Vicksburg, Miss, 11/6/32; s. Jesse Edwin Brent and Ruth Hayes B; m. 4/24/52 to Ann Eason; c. Ruth Ann, Jesse Edwin, II, Collins Eason, Margaret Elizabeth and Belinda Lea. Educ: Miss. State Univ, B.S. in mech. eng, 54. Polit. & Govt. Pos: Wash. Co. campaign mgr, Rubel Phillips, Miss, 63 and Barry Goldwater, 64; del, Rep. State Conv, 64; mem, Wash. Co. Rep. Exec. Cmt, 64-66; Rep. chmn, First Cong. Dist; chmn, Wash. Co. Rep. Party, currently; del, Rep. Nat. Conv, 68. Mem: Am. Soc Mech. Engr; Soc. Naval Architects & Marine Engrs; Elks. Rel: Methodist. Legal Res: Golding Acres, Greenville, Miss. 38701. Mailing Add: P.O. Drawer 8, Greenville, Miss. 38701.

BRENTON, FONNIE L. R
Mo. State Rep.
b. Petersburg, Ind, 1/26/99; m. 5/29/26 to Elinor Harrison; c. Don and Mrs. John Scott. Educ: Oakland City Col; Valparaiso Univ. of Mo; A.B, M.E, LL.B. Polit. & Govt. Pos: Mo. State Rep, 56-; mem, State Reorgn. Cmn, Mo, until 65; del, Rep. State Conv, 68; mem, Interim Cmt. Mining Probs, 68. Bus. & Prof. Pos: Teacher; high sch. prin; supt. of schs. Mem: Kappa Alpha Phi; Phi Delta Kappa. Rel: Presbyterian. Mailing Add: 806 E. Washington Blvd, Cuba, Mo. 65453.

BRENTON, MARIANNE WEBBER R
b. Freeport, Maine, 2/25/33; d. Milton L. Webber and Leah Hamilton W; m. 3/4/55 to Richard Preble Brenton; c. Anne Elizabeth, Joan Carole and Peter Hamilton. Educ: Bates Col, A.B, 55; Bates Outing Club; Jordan Ramsdell. Polit. & Govt. Pos: Voter surv. chmn, Burlington Rep. Town Cmt, Mass, 64, secy, 64-65, v.chmn, 65-66 and chmn, 66-68; mem. bd. registr, Burlington, 65-; alternate del, Rep. Nat. Conv, 68; dist. chmn, Women for Nixon-Agnew Campaign, 68; trustee, Tewksbury State Hosp, 69- Bus. & Prof. Pos: Head, sci. dept, Southboro High Sch, Mass, 56-57; tech. librn, Trans-Sonics, Inc, 57-59. Mem: League of Women Voters. Rel: Protestant. Mailing Add: 16 Nelson Rd, Burlington, Mass. 01803.

BRENTS, ALVIN LEE D
Secy, Wyandot Co. Dem. Cent. and Exec. Cmts, Ohio
b. Stark, La, 8/1/10; s. William A. Brents and Lissie McCubrins B; m. 6/3/30 to Helen G. Bink; c. Joan (Mrs. Morral), Sharon K.(Mrs. Clark), Gary E. and Marcia L. Educ: Smithville Sch, Sycamore, Ohio, Eighth grade grad. Polit. & Govt. Pos: Committeeman and secy, Wyandot Co. Dem. Cent. and Exec. Cmts, Ohio, 40- Bus. & Prof. Pos: Salesman, I.H. Co. Machinery, 33-42; grocer, 42- Mem: Elks; Sportsmans Club (pres, 20 years). Rel: Protestant. Mailing Add: 111 Main St, Harpster, Ohio 43323.

BRESHEARS, CAROL ANN D
b. Cleveland, Ohio, 8/12/36; d. Melville Herman Behrendt and Helen Dorothy Cudnick B; m. 8/4/56 to Robert R. Breshears; c. Robert, Jr, Ann Marie, Susan Lynn and Linda Christine. Educ: Univ. of Calif, Berkeley, 56-58, Citrus Col, 60-61 and Glendale Col, 64-66, working toward B.S. Polit. & Govt. Pos: Chmn, The Kennedy Girls Campaign Orgn, Robert F. Kennedy's Calif. Primary Campaign, 68; alternate del, Dem. Nat. Conv, 68; mem. women's cmt, Calif. Humphrey-Muskie Presidential Campaign, 68; mem. exec. cmt, Issues of The 70's Conf, Calif, 69; v.chmn, Sacramento Legis. Seminar, 69; mem, Dem. Women's Forum, Los Angeles, currently; mem, Speakers Bur, Calif. Dem. State Cent. Cmt, 69. Mem: Calif. Dem. Women's Div.(South. Div); Women For; third v.pres, Oak Grove PTA, La Canada, Calif, 66-67; first v.pres, Paradise Canyon PTA, 68-69. Rel: Catholic. Mailing Add: 5709 Evening Canyon Dr, La Canada, Calif. 91011.

BRESLER, CHARLES S. R
b. Philadelphia, Pa, 7/11/27; married. Educ: Univ. Md; George Wash. Univ. Polit. & Govt. Pos: Md. State Del, 63-67; asst. to Gov. Agnew, Md, 67-69; asst. chief of staff, V.Pres. Agnew's Campaign, 68-69. Bus. & Prof. Pos: Real estate developer, builder; pres, S.W. Develop. Co; bd. mem, Nat. Union Ins. Co. Mil. Serv: Army, World War II. Mem: B'nai B'rith; chmn. cmt, Hebrew Home for Aged; Mason; Shrine; Montgomery Co. Hist. Soc; Soc. Sponsors; Symphony Asn; Camp Echo Lake; U.G.F; Red Cross; Toastmasters Club. Mailing Add: 3217 Farmington Dr, Chevy Chase, Md. 20015.

BRESLIN, ROBERT HENRY, JR. R
R.I. State Rep.
b. Providence, R.I, 7/20/28; s. Robert Henry Breslin and Kate E. Grimmett B; single. Educ: Brown Univ, A.B, 50; Boston Col. Law Sch, LL.B, 54; Sigma Nu. Polit. & Govt. Pos: Pres, Warwick Young Rep, R.I, 59-60; pres, R.I. Young Rep, 60-61; R.I. State Rep, 61- Bus. & Prof. Pos: Partner, Gnys & Breslin, 56-58 and Saxon, Butler & Breslin, Providence, R.I, 58- Mil. Serv: CT-3, Naval Res. Mem: Am, R.I, Kent Co, Mass. and Boston Bar Asns; Elks; Rotary; bd. dir, Warwick, R.I. Arts Found; C. of C. Rel: Catholic. Mailing Add: 400 Narragansett Pkwy, Warwick, R.I. 02888. (1967)

BRETT, JOSEPH E. D
Mass. State Rep.
b. Washington, D.C, 1907. Educ: Dean Acad, Franklin. Polit. & Govt. Pos: Former mem, Quincy City Coun. and Quincy Conserv Cmn; Mass. State Rep, currently; del, Dem. Nat. Conv, 68. Bus. & Prof. Pos: Pres, Treas, Brett Package Store, Quincy. Mem: Elks; Eagles; K. of C; Moose; United Commercial Travelers. Rel: Catholic. Mailing Add: 254 Fenno St, Quincy, Mass. 02170.

BREUM, OLE D
b. Bellingham, Minn, 2/25/03; m. to Clara Giske. Polit. & Govt. Pos: Soil Conserv. Supvr; Dist. Water Conserv. and Flood Control Supvr; N.Dak. State Rep, 59-66, 53-54. Bus. & Prof. Pos: Farmer. Mem: Farmers Union. Rel: Lutheran. Mailing Add: Rutland, N.Dak. 58067. (1967)

BREUNINGER, LEWIS TALMAGE R
Mem, Rep. Nat. Finance Cmt.
b. Washington, D.C, 7/23/94; s. Lewis E. Breuninger and Sadie Love B; wid; c. Lewis T, Jr. Educ: Johns Hopkins Univ, A.B; George Wash. Univ, LL.B. Hon. LL.D, Southeast. Univ. Polit. & Govt. Pos: Mem, Rep. Nat. Finance Cmt, 48-, v.chmn, 56-69; Rep. Nat. Committeeman for D.C, 60-68. Bus. & Prof. Pos: Pres, L. E. Breuninger & Sons, Inc, 28-; mem, D.C. Bar. Mil. Serv: Entered as Ens, Navy, 17, released as Lt.(jg), 21. Mem: Am. Bar Asn; Capitol Hill Club; Army-Navy Club; Metrop. Club; Nat. Press Club; Kiwanis. Rel: Methodist. Legal Res: 2701 Foxhall Rd. N.W, Washington, D.C. 20007. Mailing Add: 1825 F St. N.W, Washington, D.C. 20006.

BREWER, ALBERT PRESTON D
Gov, Ala.
b. Bethel Springs, Tenn, 10/26/28; s. Daniel Austin Brewer and Clara Yarber B; m. 1/31/51 to Martha Helen Farmer; c. Rebecca Ann and Beverly Alison. Educ: Univ. of Ala, B.A, LL.B; Jacksonville State Univ, L.H.D; Samford Univ, hon. LL.D. Polit. & Govt. Pos: Mem, Decatur City Planning Cmn, 56-63; Ala. State Rep, 55-67, Speaker, Ala. House of Rep, 63-67; mem, Ala. Dem. Exec. Cmt, 64-; Lt. Gov. Ala, 67-68, Gov, 68- Bus. & Prof. Pos: Lawyer. Mem: Phi Alpha Delta; Delta Sigma Phi; Co, State and Am. Bar Asns; Mason; Am. Legion. One of Four Outstanding Young Men of Ala, Ala. Jr. C. of C. Rel: Baptist. Mailing Add: Executive Mansion, Perry St, Montgomery, Ala. 36104.

BREWER, CLYDE BARKLOW R
b. Lincoln, Nebr, 12/7/09; s. Albert L. Brewer and Leone Emminger B; m. 11/10/30 to Elizabeth Zaharko; c. M.D, Clyde, Jr, Sharon (Mrs. Harold Anderson), Beverly (Mrs. Wayne Ward) and Duane. Educ: Melstone and Polson, Mont. high schs, 4 years. Polit. & Govt. Pos: Mem, Sch. Bd, Melstone, Mont, 40-51; mem, Town Coun, 45-51; Mont. State Sen, Musselshell Co, 52-56; mem, Sch. Bd, Roundup, 63-69; mem, Mont. Oil and Gas Conserv. Cmn, 64-69. Bus. & Prof. Pos: Owner, trucking bus, 36-56; pres, C. Brewer, Inc, 56- Mem: Shrine; C. of C; Moose; Petroleum Club; Am. and Mont. Pilots Asns. Rel: Methodist. Legal Res: 424 Second W, Roundup, Mont. 59072. Mailing Add: Box 294, Roundup, Mont. 59072.

BREWER, DAVID S. D
b. Bozeman, Mont; s. Dr. and Mrs. A. D. Brewer; m; c. five. Educ: Mont. State Col, 32. Polit. & Govt. Pos: Cand, Mont. State Sen, 66; 5 years Flathead High Sch. Bd. of Trustees; Pres, Rural Sch. Bds. Asn; Chmn, Sch. Bd. of Dist. 8; Bd. of Supv. of Soil Conserv. Dist, 7 years. Bus. & Prof. Pos: Owns Grade A dairy; raised turkeys for several years; taught in several Mont. high schs. Mil. Serv: World War II. Mem: Served 3 years as Master of Stillwater Grange; Secy. of the Flathead Pomona Grange; Kalispell C. of C. Rel: Presbyterian. Mailing Add: Kalispell, Mont. 59901. (1967)

BREWER, JOE OLIVER R
b. N. Wilkesboro, N.C, 12/26/31; s. Gordon Justus Brewer and Ada Grace Johnson B; m. 7/22/55 to Lillie Dean Bryan; c. Gregory Joseph and Tonya Alisa. Educ: Catawba Col, 51, Detroit Conservatory of Music, 52; Wake Forest Col, N.C. State Col, 56; Univ. of N.C, B.S, 57; Univ. of N.C. Sch. of Law, LL.B, 62. Polit. & Govt. Pos: N.C. State Rep, 63-66. Bus. & Prof. Pos: Lawyer. Mil. Serv: 2nd Lt, Army, 52-54. Mem: Am, N.C. State and Wilkes Co. Bar Asns; C. of C; pres, Wilkesboro Bus. & Prfnl. Men's Club, 69- Rel: Church of Christ; trustee, Wilkesboro Church of Christ, 62- Mailing Add: 208 Cowles St, Wilkesboro, N.C. 28697.

BREWER, OBY T. D
b. Atlanta, Ga, 12/19/93; s. William David Brewer and Dora Elizabeth Jackson B; m. 5/22/17 to Jewell Folks; c. Betty, Oby T. Jr. Educ: Atlanta and Marietta Pub. Schs. Polit. & Govt. Pos: Ga. State Sen, 63-64. Bus. & Prof. Pos: Pres. Geo. Muse Clothing Co; clothing bus, 09- Mil. Serv: Served Draft Bd. Mem: Mason; Elks; Shrine; past pres. Atlanta Humane Soc; past chmn. Atlanta Chap. Am. Red Cross; past pres. Atlanta Civitan Club; past potentate YAARAB Temple Shrine; past pres. Retail Merchants Asn; Better Bus. Bur; Nat. Asns. Retail Clothiers and Furnishers. Rel: Methodist. Legal Res: 199 Robin Hood Rd. N.E, Atlanta, Ga. 30329. Mailing Add: 52 Peachtree Rd. N.W, Atlanta, Ga. 30303. (1967)

BREWSTER, DANIEL BAUGH D
b. Baltimore Co, Md, 11/23/23; married; c. Daniel B. Jr. and Gerry Leiper. Educ: Princeton Univ; Johns Hopkins Univ; Univ. of Md. Law Sch, LL.B, 49. Polit. & Govt. Pos: Md. State Rep, 50-58; U.S. Rep, Md, 58-62; U.S. Sen, Md, 62-69; del, Dem. Nat. Conv, 68. Bus. & Prof. Pos: Owns and operates grain and cattle farm near Glyndon, Md. Mil. Serv: Marine Corps, troop comdr, 42-44; wounded; awarded Purple Heart; Gold Star in lieu of second Purple Heart; Bronze Star; Col, Marine Corps Res. Mem: Am, Md. State and Baltimore Co. Bar Asns; past pres, Md. State Fair and Agr. Soc. Mailing Add: Towson, Md. 21204.

BREYFOGLE, JOHN WILLIAM, JR. R
Mem, Johnson Co. Rep. Exec. Cmt, Kans.
b. Olathe, Kans, 8/12/06; s. John William Breyfogle and Kate O. Taylor B; m. 11/26/32 to Arlene Elizabeth Galloway; c. John W. III, Robert T. and Ann E. Educ: Univ. Kans, LL.B; Phi Gamma Delta; Phi Delta Phi. Polit. & Govt. Pos: Rep. cent. committeeman, Johnson Co, Kans, 46-58; mem, Johnson Co. Rep. Cent. Cmt, 48- and chmn, 48-58; mem, Johnson Co. Rep. Exec. Cmt, 48-; del, Rep. Nat. Conv, 48 & 68. Bus. & Prof. Pos: Dist. chmn, Jr. Am. Bar Conf, Kans, 48; pres, Olathe Commun. Hosp. Found, Inc, 62-64. Mil. Serv: Entered as Lt.(jg.), Navy, 43, released as Lt, 45, after serv. in Pac. Theatre, 44-45. Mem: Am. Bar Asn; Kans. Bar Asn; Johnson Co. Bar Asn.(pres, 50); Am. Col. or Probate Counsel; AF&AM; VFW; Am. Legion; Johnson Co. Farm Bur. Rel: Methodist. Legal Res: 504 E. Cedar, Olathe, Kans. 66061. Mailing Add: Patrons Bldg, Olathe, Kans. 66061.

BRICKER, DALE EUGENE R
Secy, Richland Co. Rep. Exec. Cmt, Ohio
b. Dover, Ohio, 1/29/25; s. Franklin Benjamin Bricker and Beatrice Mae Rodd B; m. 4/23/49 to Elinor Irene Downs; c. Barry Owen. Educ: Furman Univ, 44. Polit. & Govt. Pos: Clerk, Mansfield City Coun, Ohio, 58-63; secy, Richland Co. Exec. Cmt, 58-; pres, Richland Co. Young Rep. Club, 59; secy, Richland Co. Rep. Cent. Cmt, 61-62; dir. elec, Richland Co, 64-; pres, Richland Co. Rep. Club, 68- Bus. & Prof. Pos: Cataloging and standardization technician, Shelby Air Force Depot, 49-58. Mil. Serv: Entered as Pvt, Army Med. Training Detachment, 43, released as Cpl, 46, after serv. in 410th Qm. Depot Co, Cent. Asiatic-Pac. Theatre, 44-46; Am. Theatre Ribbon; Asiatic-Pac. Theatre Ribbon with One Bronze Star; U.S. Victory Medal; Good Conduct Medal; Cent. Pac. Area Unit Citation. Mem: Ohio Asn. Elec. Off.(bd. trustees, 66-69); Shelby Fed. Employees Credit Union (first v.pres, 56-58, bd. dirs); life mem, Mansfield Stamp & Coin Club (pres, 56-58, bd. gov, 59-62 & 64-66); Toastmasters (admin. v.pres, Mansfield Club, 61, 63, 64, 65 & 66, pres, 62 & 69, Area Ten gov, 63); F&AM; Am. Legion; Boy Scouts (counsr, Mansfield Johnny Appleseed Dist, 58-). Young Rep. of the Year, Richland Co. Young Rep. Club, 59; Toastmaster of the Year, Mansfield Toastmasters Club, 62; Spec. Ed. Excellence Award for T.M. Tiding Bul, 66 & 67. Rel: Christian Church of N.Am. Legal Res: 274 Wood St, Mansfield, Ohio 44903. Mailing Add: 7 S. Diamond St, Mansfield, Ohio 44902.

BRICKER, JOHN WILLIAM R
b. Madison Co, Ohio, 9/6/93; s. Lemuel S. Bricker and Laura King B; m. 9/4/20 to Harret Day; c. John Day. Educ: Ohio State Univ, A.B, 16, LL.B, 20, LL.D, 40; Delta Chi; Order of the Coif. Polit. & Govt. Pos: Pres, Buckeye Rep. Club, Ohio, 23-24; asst. attorney gen, Ohio, 23-27, attorney gen, 32-36; mem, Utilities Cmn. Ohio, 27-32; gov. of Ohio, 38-45; Rep. cand, v.pres. of the U.S, 44; U.S. Sen, Ohio, 47-59; former mem, Exec. Cmt, Rep. Party. Bus. & Prof. Pos: Trustee, Ohio State Univ, 47-; mem. bd, Repub. Steel Corp, 59-, Buckeye Savings & Loan Co, 60-, Buckeye Steel Castings Co, 61- Mil. Serv: 1st Lt, Army, 18. Mem: Pres, Columbus Bar Asn, 36-37; Ohio and Am. Bar Asns; Univ. Club; Athletic Club; Rotary; Ohio State Faculty Torch Club; Am. Legion; Mason (32°), K.T, Scottish Rite, Supreme Coun. Rel: Congregational. Mailing Add: 2407 Tremont Rd, Columbus, Ohio 43215.

BRICKLEY, JAMES H.
b. Flint, Mich, 11/15/28; s. J. Harry Brickley and Marie E. Fischer B; m. 6/16/50 to Marianne E. Doyle; c. Janice Marie, James T, William J, Brian J, Kathleen Mary and Kelle Ann. Educ: Univ. Detroit, Ph.B, 51, LL.B, 54; N.Y. Univ, LL.M, 58; Delta Theta Phi; Ed, Univ. Detroit Law J, 53-54. Polit. & Govt. Pos: Chief asst. prosecuting attorney, Wayne Co, Mich, 67-; pres, pro tem, Common Coun, City of Detroit, 66-67, councilman, 62-65; mem, Gov. Cmt. on Local Govt, 65; cmnr, Detroit Metrop. Area Regional Planning Cmn, 62; spec. agent, Fed. Bur. of Invest, 54-58. Bus. & Prof. Pos: Lectr. in Govt, Univ. of Detroit, 59- Mem: Am. and Mich. State Bar Asns; Soc. of Former Spec. Agents of the Fed. Bur. of Invest. Rel: Catholic. Legal Res: 17537 Fairfield Dr, Detroit, Mich. 48221. Mailing Add: 1300 Beaubien, Detroit, Mich. 48226. (1967)

BRIDENBAUGH, HAL R
b. Dakota City, Nebr, 11/26/91; m. 4/19/16 to Ruth V. Kline; c. two. Educ: Iowa State Col. Polit. & Govt.Pos: Rep. co. chmn, Nebr; mem, Sch. Bd. and Exten. Bd; chmn, bd. mgrs, Coun. of State Govt; Nebr. State Sen, 49-66. Bus. & Prof. Pos: Farming and livestock bus. Mem: AF&AM; York and Scottish Rites; Shrine; Eastern Star; South Sioux City C. of C; Kiwanis. Rel: Presbyterian. Mailing Add: Dakota City, Nebr. 68731. (1967)

BRIDGES, DUANE N. R
Chmn, Norton Co. Rep. Party, Kans.
b. Colorado Springs, Colo, 5/21/14; s. Mark Bridges and Nell Harmonson B; m. 4/28/40 to Claudia Manning. Educ: Univ. Kans, B.S, 37; Kappa Sigma. Polit. & Govt. Pos: Chmn, Norton Co. Rep. Party, Kans, 65- Bus. & Prof. Pos: Purchasing agent, Folger Coffee Co, 37-42; owner and operator, Bridges Ins. Agency, 46- Mil. Serv: Entered as 1st Lt, Army, 42, released as Maj, 46, after serving in 84th Inf. Div, ETO, 44-46; Col, Kans. Air Nat. Guard Res, 54-; Bronze Star; ETO ribbon with three battle stars; Occup. Medal; Reservist Medal; Am. Victory Medal Combat Inf. Badge. Mem: Kans. Asn. Independent Ins. Agents (pres, 68); Nat. Asn. Independent Ins. Agents; Rotary; Asn. U.S. Army; Am. Legion; past pres, C. of C; past pres, Kans. Nat. Guard Asn. Rel: Protestant. Legal Res: 610 W. Woodsfield, Norton, Kans. 67654. Mailing Add: 110 W. Main, Norton, Kans. 67654.

BRIDGES, HENRY LEE D
State Auditor, N.C.
b. Franklin Co, N.C, 6/10/07; s. John Joseph Bridges and Ida Loraine Carroll B; m. 12/12/36 to Clarice Hines; c. Joseph Henry and George Hines. Educ: Mars Hill Jr. Col, N.C, A.B, 29; Wake Forest Univ, B.A, 31; Wake Forest Law Sch, 33. Polit. & Govt. Pos: State auditor, N.C, 47- Bus. & Prof. Pos: Mem. bd. trustees, Wake Forest Univ, 42-52, 55-58, 60-63 & 65-; exec. dir, Nat. Asn. State Auditors, Comptrollers & Treas, 58-69; mem. bd. trustees, Southeast. Baptist Theol. Sem, 67- Mil. Serv: Entered as Pvt, Nat. Guard, 34, released as Army Maj, 45. Mem: K.T; AF&AM (past Master, Greensboro Lodge 76); Choraz, Chap. 13 RAM; AAONMS; Societas Rosecrucians in Civitatibus Foedaratis; Lions. Rel: Baptist. Mailing Add: 2618 Grant Ave, Raleigh, N.C. 27608.

BRIDGES, RONALD WAYNE D
Tex. State Sen.
b. Breckenridge, Tex, 4/17/32; s. Leroy Knox Bridges and Vivian Ozelle Conlee B; m. 2/26/55 to Kathleen Doris Schluze; c. Kimberly LeAn, Kathryn Lyn and Kamara Lee. Educ: Del Mar Jr. Col, 50-51; Univ. of Tex, B.A, 54; Univ. of Tex. Law Sch, 54; St. Mary's Law Sch, 55; Lambda Chi Alpha. Polit. & Govt. Pos: Aide to Sen. Lyndon B. Johnson, 55-56; Tex. State Rep, 59-64 & 67-68; Tex. State Sen, 20th Dist, 69- Mil. Serv: Counter Intel, Army, 54-55; Expert Rifleman, Good Conduct and Nat. Defense Medals. Publ: Texas Political Coloring Book; plus others. Mem: C. of C; Better Bus. Bur; Mason; Navy League; Army Aviation Asn. Runner-up for the outstanding young man of Corpus Christi, (three times). Rel: Methodist; mem. and former steward, Off. Bd, South Bluff Methodist Church. Legal Res: 4601 Coventry, Corpus Christi, Tex. 78412. Mailing Add: 866 Petroleum Tower, Corpus Christi, Tex. 78401.

BRIDGES, WEBSTER E, JR. R
Asst. Majority Leader, N.H. State House of Rep.
b. Concord, N.H, 12/21/33; s. Webster E. Bridges and Hazel Brown B. (deceased); m. 5/12/56 to Helen Dunn; c. Webster E, III and James Edward. Educ: Univ. N.H, B.S. in bus, 55. Polit. & Govt. Pos: Dir, Souhegan Young Rep, N.H, 64; del, Rep. State Conv, 64, 66 & 68; chmn, Brookline Rep. Cmt, 64-; N.H. State Rep, 67-, Asst. Majority Leader, N.H. State House of Rep, 69-; alternate del-at-lg, Rep. Nat. Conv, 68; Hillsborough Co. chmn, Nixon for President Campaign, 68. Bus. & Prof. Pos: Rep, The Sperry & Hutchinson Co, 63-68; New Eng. sales mgr, Hoffman Motors Corp/BMW, 68- Mil. Serv: Cpl, Army Res, 54-56, serv. in Hon. Guard, 1st Regt. Combat Team, U.S. Mil. Acad, West Point; Good Conduct Medal; Sharpshooter Award; Expert Rifleman Award. Mem: Campaign mgr. for State Jaycee Pres, 66-67; chmn, Local Heart Fund, 65-67; exec. v.pres, N.H. Jaycees, 66-67; dir, Souhegan Valley Jaycees, 66-67; dir, Merrimack Valley Region Asn, 67-68. Holder, Nat. Competition Drivers License, Sports Car Club of Am; Sperry & Hutchinson Co. Citizenship Award, 67. Rel: Episcopal. Mailing Add: Milford St, Brookline, N.H. 03033.

BRIDGEWATER, WILLIAM KENNETH D
b. Jeffersonville, Ind, 9/17/08; s. William Burkett Bridgewater and Gertrude Lester B; m. to Bernice Henderson; c. Bobby L. and John W. Educ: Little York High Sch. Polit. & Govt. Pos: Del, Dem. State Conv, Ind, 66; chmn, Washington Co. Dem. Party for 2 yrs; precinct committeeman for 12 yrs. Mem: Mason; Steel Workers Union. Mailing Add: Little York, Ind. 47017. (1967)

BRIDWELL, ROBERT VERN D
b. Kokomo, Ind, 7/9/23; s. Vern Ray Bridwell and Mary Leona Kuntz B; m. 2/18/51 to Helen Ruth Hoss; c. Barbara Louise and William Allan. Educ: Ind. Univ, A.B, 48, Sch. of Law, LL.B, 51; Sigma Delta Kappa. Polit. & Govt. Pos: Chmn, Non-Partisans for Better Schs, 68; Ind. State Rep, 64-66, ranking mem, House Cmt. on Legis. Apportionment, Ind. Gen. Assembly, 65-66; chmn, Marion Co. House Del, 65; secy, Ind. Judicial Study Cmn, 65-66; precinct committeeman, Marion Co. Dem. Cmt, 56-61; mem, exec. cmt, Marion Co. Young Dem, 50-51. Bus. & Prof. Pos: Lawyer and partner, Haymaker, Bridwell & Fink, 65-66, Money, Orr, Bridwell & Fink, 62-65 and Orr & Bridwell, 56-62; lawyer and assoc, Dix, Dix, Patrick & Ratcliff, 52-56. Mil. Serv: Entered as Pvt, Army, 43, released as Cpl, 46, after serv. in 94th Inf. Div, 301st Regt, ETO; ETO Ribbon with 4 Stars; Good Conduct Medal; Bronze Star. Mem: Am, Ind. and Indianapolis Bar Asns; Indianapolis Lawyers Asn; Indianapolis Legal Aid Soc. Rel: Methodist. Legal Res: 4108 N. Pennsylvania St, Indianapolis, Ind. 46205. Mailing Add: 322 Circle Tower, Indianapolis, Ind. 46204.

BRIGGS, BRUCE BURRY R
N.C. State Sen.
b. Mars Hill, N.C, 6/20/37; s. Clarence W. Briggs and Eula Burry B; m. 11/26/67 to Jean Elizabeth Miller. Educ: Mars Hill Col, N.C, A.A, 58; West Carolina Univ, 58-59; Wake Forest Univ. Law Sch, LL.B, 62; Student Bar Asn; Phi Alpha Delta. Polit. & Govt. Pos: Chmn, Madison Co. Rep. Exec. Cmt, N.C, 64-66; mem, N.C. Rep. Exec. Cmt, 64-; v.chmn, 11th Dist. Young Rep. Club, 65; chmn, 11th Cong. Dist. Rep. Party, N.C, 66; Mem, N.C. Rep. Cent. Cmt, 66; N.C. State Sen, 31st Dist, 67-; Asst. U.S. Dist. Attorney, 69- Bus. & Prof. Pos: Cmnr-treas, Upper French Broad Develop. Cmn, N.C, 66-67; co. attorney, Madison Co, 68-69. Mil. Serv: Entered as E-1, Army, 62, released as E-4, 68, after serv. in Army Res. Mem: Am. Trial Lawyers Asn; N.C. State Bar; Buncombe Co. and Madison Co. Bar Asns; WOW; N.C. Farm Bur. Rel: Baptist. Legal Res: Mars Hill, N.C. 28754. Mailing Add: P.O. Box 81, Mars Hill, N.C. 28754.

BRIGGS, FRANK P. D
b. Armstrong, Mo, 2/25/94; s. Thomas H. Briggs and Susan Almira Pyle B; m. 5/28/16 to Catherine Allen Shull; c. Thomas Frank, Eugene Allen, Darlene Ruth, Betty Barbara and Dorothy Catherine. Educ: Cent. Col, Fayette, Mo, 11-14; Univ. of Mo, B.J, 15; Sigma Delta Chi. Hon. D.Sc, Cent. Col, 61. Polit. & Govt. Pos: Mayor, Macon, Mo, 30-33; Mo. State Sen, 33-45, pres, Mo. State Senate, 41-45; U.S. Sen, Mo, app. to fill unexpired term of Harry S Truman, 45; mem, Mo. Conserv. Cmn, 47-; Asst. Secy. of Interior for Fish and Wildlife, 61-68; mem, Int. Cmn. for N.Atlantic Fisheries, 61- Bus. & Prof. Pos: Ed, Fayette Dem-Leader, Mo, 15; city ed, Moberly Monitor-Index, 16-17; ed, Trenton Times, 17-18; city ed, 19; night ed, Shawnee Morning News, Okla, 19-23; ed. and owner, Macon Chronicle-Herald, Mo, 24- Mem: Mason, grand master Mo, 57-58; Elks; Rotary; Nat. Press Club, Wash. Distinguished Pub. Serv. Award, Sch. of Journalism, Univ. of Mo, 58. Mailing Add: Box 15, Macon, Mo. 63552.

BRIGGS, JOHN VERN R
Calif. State Assemblyman
b. Alpena, S.Dak, 3/8/30; s. Leslie Richard Briggs and Jessie Ray Snedaker B; m. 12/28/51 to Carmen Nicasio; c. Kathleen, Daniel and Ronald. Educ: Fullerton Jr. Col, A.A. in bus. admin, 54; Long Beach State Col, B.S. in bus. admin, 56. Polit. & Govt. Pos: Pres, Walter Knott Young Rep, 60; Calif. State Assemblyman, 67- Bus. & Prof. Pos: Owner, John Briggs Ins. Group, 65- Mil. Serv: Entered as Pvt, Air Force, 48, released as S/Sgt, 52, after serv. in Mil. Air Transport Serv, Korea, 50; Presidential Unit Citation. Mem: Pres, Buena Park C. of C, 65-66; pres, Buena Park Jr. C. of C, 59; Rotary; Elks; VFW. Rel: Catholic. Mailing Add: 1400 N. Harbor Blvd, Fullerton, Calif. 92632.

BRIGGS, ROBERT ALVIN, JR. R
Bonus Mem, Colo. Rep. Cent. Cmt.
b. Greeley, Colo, 12/24/37; s. Robert Alvin Briggs and Leta Edison B; m. 9/8/57 to Shirley Christine Abbott; c. Robert Reuben and Christy Lynn. Educ: Colo. State Univ, B.S, 59, M.S, 61. Polit. & Govt. Pos: Del, Co. and State Rep. Assemblies, Colo, 68; dist. capt, Adams Co. Rep. Party, 68-69; mem. agr. adv, Cmt. Colo. Dept. Agr, 69; bonus mem, Colo. Rep. Cent. Cmt, 69- Bus. & Prof. Pos: Pres, Briggs Greenhouse Inc, 61- Mem: Colo. Flower Growers Asn.(pres, 68-69); Westminster Jaycees (pres, 65); Westminster Lodge; Rotary; C. of C.(pres, Westminster Br, 68). Man of the Year, Westminster, 63 & 68; One of Three State Chaplains Honored by U.S. Jaycees, 67. Rel: Presbyterian. Mailing Add: 6851 N. Pecos, Denver, Colo. 80221.

BRIGHTMAN, SAMUEL CHARLES D
b. Lancaster, Mo, 6/22/11; s. Samuel Charles Brightman and Alberta Steele B; m. 7/26/47 to Lucy Kirk Cleaver; c. Samuel Charles, Jr, Elizabeth Cleaver, George Forsha and David Sherwood. Educ: Washington Univ, A.B, 32; Univ. Mo, B.J, 33; Sigma Delta Chi; Alpha Tau Omega. Polit. & Govt. Pos: Dep. asst. adminstr, Surplus Property Admin, 45; spec. asst. to Housing Expediter, 46; asst. dir. publicity, Dem. Nat. Cmt, 47-52, dir. publicity, 52-57, dep. chmn. pub. affairs, 57-65; managing ed, Dem. Orgn, 52-57. Bus. & Prof. Pos: Reporter, St. Louis Star-Times, 33-35; copy ed, Cincinnati Post, 35, chief copy ed, 35-40; news ed, Radio Sta. KSD, St. Louis, 37; Wash. correspondent, Louisville Courier-Journal, 40-42, spec. writer and copy ed, 47. Mil. Serv: Entered as Pvt, Army, 42, released as Capt, 45; after serv. in publicity and psychol. warfare in Europe; in charge news coverage for First Army, Omaha Beach, Normandy Invasion; participated in Liberation of Paris, Exec. Officer, Pub. Rels. Detachment for Allied Forces in occupation of Berlin. Mem: Nat. Press Club; Nat. Capital Dem. Club; Kenwood Country Club. Rel: Episcopal. Mailing Add: 6308 Crathie Lane, Bethesda, Md. 20016.

BRIGHTON, HOWARD D
b. Jackson, Mich, 8/22/25; s. Howard William Brighton (deceased) and Eva Elizabeth Campbell B; m. 4/16/48 to Patricia Ann Larson; c. Cheryl Lee, Susan Kay, Lori Jo and Todd Alan. Educ: Cent. Mich. Univ, B.S, 54; Univ. Mich, M.S, 55; Univ. Okla, Ph.D, 64; Phi Delta Kappa. Polit. & Govt. Pos: Mem, Calhoun Co. Dem. Exec. Cmt, Mich, 66-68, St. Joseph Co. Exec. Cmt, and Kalamazoo Co. Dem. Exec. Cmt, 66-68; chmn, Calhoun Co. Dem. Party, 66-68; del, Dem. Nat. Conv, 68. Mil. Serv: Navy, 43-46, Pac; 51-52, Asiatic, Res, 46-51. Mem: Mason. Rel: Baptist. Mailing Add: 4376 Okemos Rd, Apt. 201C, Okemos, Mich. 48864.

BRIGHTON, WILLIAM J. D
Clerk, Vigo Co. Circuit Court, Ind.
b. Gosport, Ind, 4/17/29; s. John William Brighton and Esther Pauline Wampler B; m. 12/24/49 to Betty Jo Brasier; c. John Joseph, William Curtis, Mark Edson, Katherine Ann and Edward Douglas. Educ: Ind. State Univ, B.S, 59. Polit. & Govt. Pos: Ind. State Rep, Vigo, Vermillion and Sullivan Co, Ind, 63-69; dir, Pub. Opinion and Research, Ind. Dem. State Cent. Cmt, 64-69; clerk, Vigo Co. Circuit Ct, 69- Bus. & Prof. Pos: Printer, Tribune-Star Publ. Co, 51-64. Mem: Mason; Int. Typographical Union; Press Club; Farmers Union. Rel: Protestant. Mailing Add: R.R. 32, Box 554, Terre Haute, Ind. 47802.

BRIGIANI, GUIDO J. D
b. New York, N.Y, 1/24/10; m. to Ann Giacalone; c. three. Educ: Rutgers Univ. Law Sch, LL.B. Polit. & Govt. Pos: Magistrate, Perth Amboy, N.J, 20 years; magistrate, Jamesburg, 13 years; secy, Bd. of Adjustment, Perth Amboy; borough attorney, Jamesburg; mem, Jamesburg Bd. of Educ, 5 years; borough attorney, Helmetta, 60-; secy, Jamesburg Planning Bd; former N.J. State Assemblyman. Bus. & Prof. Pos: Attorney, 34-; counselor at law, 37-; mem, adv. bd, 1st Nat. Bank of Middlesex Co, N.J; dir. and counsel, Jamesburg Mutual Savings & Loan Asn. Mem: Middlesex Co. Magistrates Asn; past pres, Jamesburg Lions; Perth Amboy Elks; K. of C. Mailing Add: 175 Smith St, Perth Amboy, N.J. 07505. (1967)

BRILES, JAMES E. R
Iowa State Sen.
b. Prescott, Iowa, 3/31/26; m. to Lorene Tindall; c. Three sons and two daughters. Educ: Prescott High Sch. Polit. & Govt. Pos: Iowa State Sen, 64-; Iowa State Rep, 4 terms. Bus. & Prof. Pos: Assoc. with father in auction bus. Mil. Serv: Asiatic-Pac. Theater, 44-46. Mem: Am. Legion; VFW. Rel: Methodist. Mailing Add: State Capitol, E. Tenth St. and Grand Ave, Des Moines, Iowa 50319. (1967)

BRILEY, CLIFTON BEVERLY D
Mayor, Metropolitan Nashville and Davidson Co, Tenn.
b. Nashville, Tenn, 1/11/14; s. Clifton Weaver Briley and Willie Withorne Vaughan B; m. 7/3/34 to Dorothy Gordon; c. Clifton Beverly, Jr. and Martha Diane (Mrs. Easterling). Educ: Vanderbilt Univ; Cumberland Univ, LL.B. Polit. & Govt. Pos: Secy, Tenn State Dem. Exec. Cmt, 48-50; judge, Davidson Co, 50-63; mayor, Metrop. Nashville and Davidson Co, Tenn, 63-; del, Dem. Nat. Conv, 68. Bus. & Prof. Pos: Partner in Law Firm of Atkinson & Briley. Mil. Serv: Entered as A/S, Navy, 43, released as Navigational Quartermaster 1/C, 45; Pac. and Am. Theater Ribbons and Seven Bronze Stars; Presidential Unit Citation; Commanding Officer Citation. Publ: Author of articles and contrib. to books on local govt. and reformed govt. structure. Mem: Shrine; Scottish Rite, Mason; Am. Legion; DAV; VFW; Tenn. and Nashville Bar Asns; past pres, Nat. Asn. Counties; bd, U.S. Conf. Mayors; pres, Nat. League Cities, 69-; pres, Tenn. Co. Serv. Asn; v.pres, Tenn. Munic League. Football player and mem. track and swimming teams. Rel: Baptist. Legal Res: 1406 Winding Way, Nashville, Tenn. 37216. Mailing Add: 107 Courthouse, Nashville, Tenn. 37201.

BRILEY, JOHN MARSHALL R
Mem, Rep. Nat. Finance Cmt.
b. Monmouth, Ill, 1/10/05; s. Lewis Henry Briley and Mary Frances Ryan B; m. 9/8/31 to Dorothy Louise DeWolf; c. Suzanne (Mrs. René H.M. Gimbrere), Millicent (Mrs. Clifford E. Rader), John Marshall, Jr. and Michael Marshall. Educ: Monmouth Col, Ill, A.B, 27; Harvard Univ, LL.B, 30; Tau Kappa Alpha; Alpha Tau Omega. Polit. & Govt. Pos: Mem. exec. cmt, Lucas Co. Rep. Cmt, Ohio, 58-; del-at-lg, Rep. Nat. Conv, 60 & 64; chmn, Ohio Rep. Finance Cmt, 61-62, life mem, 62-; Rep. cand. for U.S. Sen, Ohio, 62; mem, Rep. Nat. Finance Cmt, 63-; chmn, Citizens for Goldwater-Miller, Ohio, 64; mem, Fed. Prison Bd, chmn, Ohio Bd. Regents, 64-; treas, Citizens for Nixon-Agnew, Ohio, 68; chmn, Presidential Task Force on Prisoner Rehabilitation, 69. Bus. & Prof. Pos: Partner, Shearman & Sterling, 30-51; dir, Hotel Pierre, N.Y.C. pres, Owens-Corning Fiberglas Int; sr. v.pres, Owens-Corning Fiberglas Co, 52- Mem: Am, Ohio and N.Y. State Bar Asns; Asn. of the Bar of New York City; Am. Soc. Int. Law; life mem. Moose; Master Knight, K. of M; Int. Club, Wash, D.C; Harvard Club of N.Y; Toledo Club; Links Club, N.Y; Toledo Country Club; Belmont Country Club; Ohio Soc. of N.Y; Carranor Hunt and Polo Club, Toledo; chmn. bd, Mercy Hosp, Toledo; trustee, Jr. Achievement of Northwest. Ohio; chmn. bd, Philadelphia Nat. League Baseball Team, 43-45. Rel: Roman Catholic. Legal Res: West River Rd, Perrysburg, Ohio 43551. Mailing Add: Box 901, Toledo, Ohio 43601.

BRILEY, MELVIN D
Tenn. State Rep.
b. Mitchellville, Sumner Co, Tenn, 5/19/31; s. Willard Hise Briley and Gladys Hinton B; m. 12/20/54 to Jean Jernigan; c. Hal Overton and Tab Melvin. Educ: Peabody Col. and Univ. Tenn, 54-57. Polit. & Govt. Pos: Page boy, U.S. House of Rep, 46; v.mayor and city councilman, Portland, Tenn, 65-; co. co-chmn, campaigns for U.S. Rep. William R. Anderson, Tenn. and Gov. Buford Ellington, 68; Tenn. State Rep, 68- Bus. & Prof. Pos: Co-owner, Briley & Jernigan Ins, & Real Estate, Portland, Tenn, 58-; dir, Peoples Bank, 67- Mil. Serv: Entered as Pvt, Air Force, 50, released as T/Sgt, 54, after serv. in Far E. Air Command, 51-54; Korean Serv. Medal. Mem: Portland Lions Club(past pres); Portland C. of C;(past pres); VFW; Am. Legion; Mason. Rel: Church of Christ. Mailing Add: Portland Blvd, Portland, Tenn. 37148.

BRILL, NEWTON CLYDE R
Chmn, Howell Co. Rep. Cmt, Mo.
b. Mt. Grove, Mo, 3/10/36; s. Newton Clyde Brill and Marie Young B; m. 6/10/58 to Margaret Carolyn Saunders; c. Julia Elizabeth, Margaret Ann and Joel Newton. Educ: Univ. of Mo, A.B. in Polit. Sci, 58, LL.B, 64; Phi Eta Sigma; Order of the Coif; Phi Delta Phi. Polit. & Govt. Pos: Chmn, Howell Co. Rep. Cmt, Mo, 64- Bus. & Prof. Pos: Partner, Law Office of Moore and Brill, 64- Mil. Serv: Entered as 2nd Lt, Marine Corps, 58, released as 1st Lt, 61, after serv. in 3rd Bn. 11th Marines, 1st Marine Div, Camp Pendleton, Calif; Capt, Marine Corp Reserves, 63. Publ: 'Voir Dire Examination of Jurors,' Law Review, Univ. Mo. Law Sch, 64. Mem: Howell Co. Bar Asn; Mo. Bar Asn; Kiwanis. Rel: Southern Baptist. Mailing Add: 1327 N. Broadway, West Plains, Mo. 65775.

BRILLIANT, MOLLIE WEXLER D
V.Chmn, Dade Co. Dem. Exec. Cmt, Fla.
b. Chelsea, Mass, 12/22/14; d. Jacob Wexler and Bertha Rathman W; m. 8/22/48 to Judge Meyer Mack Brilliant; c. Cynthia Beth and Joni Fern. Educ: Emerson Col, 1 year; Boston Univ, 2 years; Harvard Univ, one course. Polit. & Govt. Pos: Committee mem, Dade Co. Dem. Exec. Cmt, Fla, 58-62, area chmn, 62-66, v.chmn, 66-; pres, Dem. Women's Club Dade Co, 64-66, pres. and co-chmn. coun, 66; 12th Cong. Dist. v.pres, Dem. Women's Clubs Fla, 66-; del, Dem. Nat. Conv, 68. Publ: 'Jewish Women in American History,' under Mollie Williams, Am. Jewish Forum, 43. Mem: Flagler Granada Jewish Commun. Center (former pres); Gr. Miami Jewish Commun. Center Bd; Hadassah; Nat. Coun. Jewish Women (v.pres); Technion (v.pres); Leukemia Soc.(bd. mem); Combined Jewish Appeal (bd. gov); Temple Beth Am (v.pres); assoc. Nat. Coun. Negro Women; Students of Books; Jr. Am. Jewish Cong. (v.pres). Pres. Award, Dem. Women's Clubs Dade Co; Citation of Merit, Leukemia Soc; Cert. of Appreciation, Dem. Exec. Cmt, Dade Co; Cert. of Appreciation, Vol. Unlimited; Golden Donkey Award, Dem. Exec. Cmt; Cert. of Appreciation Coral Gables Dem. Women's Club; Women Doer Award, Dem. Party; Outstanding Dem. Award, Young Dem. Dade Co; Combined Jewish Appeal Award for Outstanding Serv. Rel: Hebrew. Mailing Add: 5835 S.W. 50 Terr, Miami, Fla. 33155.

BRIMMER, ANDREW FELTON
b. Newelton, La, 9/13/26; s. Andrew Brimmer and Vellar Davis B; m. 7/18/53 to Doris Millicent Scott; c. Esther Diane. Educ: Univ. of Wash, B.A, 50, M.A, 51; Univ. of Bombay, India, Fulbright Fel, 51-52; Harvard Univ, Ph.D, 57. Polit. & Govt. Pos: Economist, Fed. Reserve Bank, N.Y.C, 55-58; mem, Fed. Reserve Cent. Banking Mission to Sudan, 57; consult, Securities Exchange Cmn, 62-63; dept. asst. secy, Dept. of Commerce,63-65 and Asst. Secy. of Commerce, 65-69; mem, bd. of gov, Fed. Reserve Syst, 69- Bus. & Prof. Pos: Asst. prof, Mich. State Univ, 58-61, Wharton Sch. of Finance and Commerce and Univ. of Pa, 61-, on leave at present. Mil. Serv: Army, 45-46. Publ: Life Insurance Companies in Capital Marketing, 62; Survey of Mutual Funds Investors, 63. Mem: Am. Econ. Asn; Am. Finance Asn. Named Govt. Man of the Year, Nat. Bus. League, 63. Mailing Add: 4930 30th St, Washington, D.C. 20008. (1967)

BRIMMER, CLARENCE ADDISON R
Chmn, Wyo. Rep. Party
b. Rawlins, Wyo, 7/11/22; s. Clarence A. Brimmer and Geraldine Zingsheim B; m. 8/2/53 to Emily Docken; c. Geraldine, Phillip, Andrew and Elizabeth. Educ: Univ. Mich, B.A, 44; Univ. Mich. Law Sch, J.D, 47; Sigma Delta Chi; Sigma Phi Epsilon; Phi Delta Phi. Polit. & Govt. Pos: Munic. judge, Rawlins, Wyo, 48-54; chmn, Carbon Co. Rep. Party, 48-56; Rep. State committeeman, 61-62; mem, Gov. Water Stud. Cmt, 65-66; chmn, Wyo. Rep. Party, 67- Bus.

& Prof. Pos: Dir, Rocky Mt. Mineral Law Found. Mil. Serv: Entered as Pvt, Air Force, 45, released as Sgt, 46. Mem: Am. and Wyo. State Bar Asns; Rawlins Lions Club (past pres); AF&AM (past master); Elks (Past Exalted Ruler); Rawlins Jr. C. of C.(past dir); C. of C.(past dir); Korein Temple Divan. Rel: Episcopal; Sr. Warden Vestry, St. Thomas Episcopal Church. Legal Res: 1665 Park Dr, Rawlins, Wyo. 82301. Mailing Add: P.O. Box 999, Rawlins, Wyo. 82301.

BRINCK, ADRIAN D
Iowa State Rep.
b. West Point, Iowa, 10/31/13; s. Ben Brinck and Loretta C. B; m. 2/5/44 to Arlowine Arie; c. seven. Educ: St. Mary's High Sch, 32. Polit. & Govt. Pos: Mem, Sch. Bd, West Point, Iowa, 52-65; councilman, 54-58 & 60-62; mayor, 62-63; Iowa State Rep, 59-65 & 69- Bus. & Prof. Pos: Outdoor advert. Mil. Serv: Marine Corps, four years. Mem: K. of C; Elks; Moose; Am. Legion; C. of C; pres, Outdoor Asn. Iowa. Rel: Catholic. Mailing Add: 217 Fourth St, West Point, Iowa 52656.

BRINER, EUGENE MURRAY D
b. Newman, Ill, 5/12/21; s. Purvis T. Briner (deceased) and Georgia Murray B; m. 10/25/40 to Marcella Bunnell. Educ: Rose Polytechnic Inst, 39-41. Polit. & Govt. Pos: Field auditor, Ind. Dept. State Revenue, 48-51; treas, Gibson Co, 57-64; chmn, Gibson Co. Dem. Cent. Cmt, 64-66; mgr, Princeton Auto License Br, Bur. Motor Vehicles, 65- Bus. & Prof. Pos: Treas, Burnett's, Inc, 51-57. Mem: Mason (32°); Shrine; Elks. Rel: Methodist. Legal Res: R.R. 1, Box 30, Hazleton, Ind. 47540. Mailing Add: 221 N. Main St, Princeton, Ind. 47570. (1967)

BRINGHAM, WILLIAM TALBERT R
b. Normal, Ill, 12/16/24; s. Russell Wilson Bringham and Sarah Talbert B; m. 1/10/47 to Ruth Irene Jaeger; c. William Talbert, Jr. Educ: Ill. Wesleyan Univ, Ph.B, 48; Vanderbilt Univ, LL.B. and J.D, 51; Phi Delta Phi; Sigma Chi. Polit. & Govt. Pos: Rep. precinct capt, Proviso Twp, Ill, 52-54; v.pres, Young Rep. of Proviso Twp, 53-54; dir, Proviso Twp. Rep. Party, 53-54; Rep. precinct capt, Evanston Twp, 55-65; dir, Evanston Goldwater Orgn, 60; del, Ill. Rep. State Conv, 60-65; Rep. precinct capt, Northfield Twp, 65-68, area chmn, 68-; cmnr, Fire and Police Cmn, 66-; prog. chmn, Northfield Twp. Rep. Party, 67-69; dir, United Wilmette Party, 69- Bus. & Prof. Pos: Dir, Prudential Savings & Loan Asn, 63- Mil. Serv: Entered as A/S, Naval Res, 42, released as Aero.M. 2/C, 46, after serv. in Pac. Theatre, 44-46; Good Conduct, Pac. Theatre and Atlantic Theatre Medals. Publ: Chap. in Advisor Manual, Sigma Chi Fraternity, 57; Visitation Manual, Nat. Interfraternity Conf, 60. Mem: Nat. Interfraternity Conf; Am. Alumni Coun; Mason; Consistory; K.T; Shrine; Am. Legion; VFW; SAR; Kiwanis; Int. Platform Asn; Navy League; Chartered Asn. Exec; co-chmn, Kendall Col. Fund Dr, 67; dir, Evanston C. of C, 67-; co-chmn, YWCA Fund Dr, 69; dir, Univ. Club of Evanston, 69- Rel: Methodist; Assoc. Trustee, First Methodist Church, Evanston, Ill, 67- Mailing Add: 4020 Bunker Lane, Wilmette, Ill. 60091.

BRINK, LYMAN ARNOLD R
Co. Attorney, Kittson Co, Minn.
b. Duluth, Minn, 9/8/09; s. Andrew A. Brink and Ida Elvira Wedin B; m. 12/22/35 to Esther L. Johnson; c. Mary Lynn and Maureen Linda. Educ: Concordia Col, Moorhead, Minn, 26-27 & 29-30; Univ. N.Dak, LL.B, 34; Order of the Coif; Sigma Nu; Phi Alpha Delta. Polit. & Govt. Pos: Co. attorney, Kittson Co, Minn, 35-50, 52-62 & 63-; Judge, Ninth Judicial Dist, Minn, 62-63; chmn, Kittson Co. Rep. Party, 20 years. Bus. & Prof. Pos: Univ. Regent, Univ. Minn, Minneapolis; trustee, Gustavus Adolphus Col. Mem: Ninth Dist. Bar Asn; Minn. State and Am. Bar Asns; Am. Trial Lawyers Asn; Minn. Trial Lawyers Asn; Int. Soc. of Barristers; Mason; RAM; Shrine; Lions; Modern Woodmen; Elks; Eagles; Farm Bur; Nat. Farm Orgn. Rel: Lutheran. Mailing Add: Hallock, Minn. 56728.

BRINKHAUS, ARMAND JOSEPH D
La. State Rep.
b. Sunset, La, 11/7/35; s. Dr. Armand L. Brinkhaus and Julia Thoms B; m. 11/28/57 to Margaret Bellemin; c. Armand, Michelle, Celeste, Julia, André and Reneé. Educ: Springhill Col, 54; Univ. Southwest. La, 54-56; Loyola Law Sch, La, LL.B, 60, J.D, 68; pres, Delta Theta Phi; bus. mgr, Loyola Law Rev. Polit. & Govt. Pos: La. State Rep, St. Landry Parish, 68- Bus. & Prof. Pos: Private practice, Judge Kalieste J. Saloom, Jr, Lafayette, 61-62; private practice, John L. Olivier, Sunset, 62- Mem: St. Landry Parish, La. and Am. Bar Asns; Am. Judicature Soc; Am. Trial Lawyers Asn; La. Sweet Potato Asn; La. Asn. Young Men's Bus. Clubs (second and first v.pres, and then pres, 62-); WOW (head auditor La. Jurisdiction); St. Landry Parish Red Cross.(bd. dirs); St. Landry Parish Libr. Demonstration (bd. dirs); bd. dirs, Southwest. La. Rehabilitation Center; Boy Scouts (bd. dirs, Parish Finance Cmt, local cmnr); K. of C.(4°, advocate, trustee and Grand Knight); Sunset Lions Club (second v.pres); Sunset Young Men's Bus. Club (pres); Sunset High Sch. Boosters Club; Elks; La. Land and Royalty Owners; Pub. Affairs Research Coun. La; Nat. Rice Growers Asn; St. Landry Cattlemen's Asn; La. Farm Bur. Distinguished serv. award, La. Third Circuit Court Appeal, 61. Rel: Roman Catholic. Mailing Add: P.O. Box 282, Grand Coteau, La. 70541.

BRINKLEY, ARTHUR SUMNER, JR. R
Chmn, Third Cong. Dist. Rep. Party, Va.
b. Richmond, Va, 11/14/25; s. Arthur Sumner Brinkley and Mary Rayner B; m. 4/16/55 to Elizabeth Pollard Parkinson; c. Elizabeth Hopkins, Arthur S, III, Whitfield Rayner and Susan Major. Educ: Princeton Univ, B.A. Polit. & Govt. Pos: Chmn, Third Cong. Dist. Rep. Party, Va. and mem, Henrico Co. Rep. Cmt, 61-; campaign chmn, Third Dist, 62-64; del, Rep. Nat. Conv, 64 & 68; mem, Va. State Rep. Cent. Cmt, 64- Bus. & Prof. Pos: Asst. v.pres, State Planters Bank of Commerce & Trusts, 50-58; sr. v.pres. & treas, Va. Capital Corp, 59- Mil. Serv: Entered as Pvt, Army, 43, released as Sgt, 46, after serv. in 87th Inf. Div, ETO, 44-45. Mem: Kiwanis; C. of C; mem. bd, United Givers Fund, Sheltering Arms Hosp, Richmond Mem. Hosp, Retreat for the Sick Hosp, Collegiate Schs. and Va. Mus. of Fine Arts; mem. bd. and treas, Va. Coun. on Health and Med. Care and Richmond Br, Eng-Speaking Union; Country Club of Va; Rotunda Club; Downtown Club. Rel: Episcopal. Legal Res: Glenbrooke Hills, Richmond, Va. 23226. Mailing Add: 908 State Planters Bank Bldg, Richmond, Va. 23219.

BRINKLEY, JACK THOMAS D
U.S. Rep, Ga.
b. Faceville, Ga, 12/22/30; s. Lonnie E. Brinkley and Pauline Spearman B; m. 5/29/55 to Alma Lois Kite; c. Jack Thomas, Jr. and Fred Alen II. Educ: Young Harris Col, 47-49; Univ. Ga, LL.B, 59; Phi Alpha Delta; Blue Key. Polit. & Govt. Pos: Ga. State Rep, 112th Dist, 65-67; U.S. Rep, Ga, 67- Bus. & Prof. Pos: Attorney, Young, Hollis & Moseley, 59-61; attorney, Coffin & Brinkley, 61-66. Mil. Serv: Entered as Pvt, Air Force, 51, released as 1st Lt, 56. Mem: Columbus, Ga. and Am. Bar Asns; Mason. Rel: Baptist. Mailing Add: 4108 Appalachian Way, Columbus, Ga. 31907.

BRINKMAN, BERNARD J. DFL
Minn. State Rep.
b. Farming, Minn, 1926; married; c. Five. Educ: Albany High Sch. Polit. & Govt. Pos: Minn. State Rep, 64-; past chmn, Local Sch. Bd. Bus. & Prof. Pos: Owner and operator of 'Brinky's,' Richmond, Minn; farmer. Mil. Serv: Navy, 44-46. Mem: Civic and Commerce Club; Lions; Am. Legion; Cath. Order of Foresters. Rel: Catholic. Mailing Add: Richmond, Minn. 56368. (1967)

BRINSON, LELAND VIRGIL D
b. Arapahoe, N.C, 5/6/29; s. Jarvis V. Brinson and Bessie Cahonn B; single. Educ: Kings Bus. Col, 49-50. Polit. & Govt. Pos: V.pres, Pamlico Co. Farm Bur, N.C, 59-61; co. cmnr, 61-62; Pamlico Co. fire cmnr, 62-64; dir, Civil Defense, Pamlico Co, 63-64; N.C. State Rep, 63-66. Bus. & Prof. Pos: Farmer. Mil. Serv: Cpl, Army, 50-52. Rel: Christian; Sunday Sch. supt, Amity Christian Church, 62-64, Deacon. Mailing Add: Arapahoe, N.C. 28510. (1967)

BRIONES, JOSEPH MAGDALENO D
Secy-Treas, Greater Juneau Dem. Precinct Cmt, Alaska
b. Mercedes, Tex, 7/22/20; s. Mauro Briones and Maria Severa Zamora Villegas B; m. 4/27/62 to Marjory Jeanette Orcutt; c. Benita Maria. Educ: Mission High Sch, 39; Army Admin. Sch, Ft. Logan, Colo; Army Admin. Sch, Univ. Miss; Univ. Liverpool, Eng, soc. sci, during serv; Univ. Tex, 46-49; Alpha Phi Omega. Polit. & Govt. Pos: Mem, Kenai Dem. Precinct Cmt, Alaska, 50; working mem, Anchorage Dem. Party, 52-56; mem, Gr. Juneau Dem. Precinct Cmt, 58-62, secy-treas, 62-; bd. mem, State Athletic Cmn, 59-; mem, Southeast Dist. Dem. Cmt, 62-64; del, Dem. Nat. Conv, 64. Bus. & Prof. Pos: Engr. aide, Dist. Engrs, 51; dist. mgr, Alaska Housing Authority, 51-52; instrument man, Ryall Eng. Co, 52-53; engr. inspector, Anchorage, 54-56. Mil. Serv: Entered as Pvt, Army Air Force, 42, released as Cpl, 45, after serv. in 128th Replacement Depot, ETO; Good Conduct Medal; Meritorious Citation, ETO and Atlantic Theater Medals; Victory Medal. Mem: Am. Legion, adj, Alaska Dept, 56-; VFW; Lions; Moose; 40 et 8; Juneau Dem. Club; Steivos; past nat. pres, Serv. Officers Asn; Am. Legion Press Asn; secy, PALS. Football, Mission High Sch, Tex; Am. Legion Baseball Chmn. for Alaska, 53- Rel: Catholic. Legal Res: 839 Dixon St, Juneau, Alaska 99801. Mailing Add: P.O. Box 215, Juneau, Alaska 99801.

BRISCOE, JAMES PRICE D
b. Detroit, Mich, 10/23/94; s. Benjamin Briscoe and Lewis Snyder Price B; m. 6/19/20 to Frances Webster (deceased); c. Jane (Mrs. Harry A. Robertson) and Polly (Mrs. Otto H. Werlin). Educ: Cornell Univ. Agr. Col; Theta Delta Chi. Polit. & Govt. Pos: Mem, sch. bd, Fairplay, Colo, 32-37 and city coun, 34-37; co. cmnr, Park Co, Colo, 37-38; Colo. State Sen, 39-42 and 47-50; cand, Lt. Gov, Colo, 42; mem, Colo. Dem. State Platform Cmt, 46; chmn, Clear Creek Co. Dem. Party, 47; dir, State Insts, Colo, 51-54; secy. and mem, bd. of control, State Homes for Aged, 54-67; mem, State Mineral Resources Bd, 62-65; mayor, Idaho Springs, 56-57 and 60-61; chmn, Clear Creek Co. Planning Cmn, 64. Bus. & Prof. Pos: mem, bd. of dirs, Rocky Mt. Natural Gas Co, 58-69; mining research; ore sampling works; sales and erection, precut aluminum housing. Publ: 'Let's Wake Up,' The Mines Mag, Sch. of Mines, Colo, 1/67. Mem: Colo. Mining Asn; pres, Colo. Prison Asn, 58-62; pres, House of Hope, Denver, Colo, 58-63; chmn, State Metal Mining Fund, 59-62; pres, Park and Clear Creek Co. Metal Mining Asn; adv. bd, Arapaho Nat. Forest; RAM; Sibley Club; acting treas, Red Cross and Heart Fund Drives; Elks; Denver Press Club; C. of C; Lions; Gold Rush Days. Rel: Episcopal. Legal Res: 930 Colorado Blvd, Idaho Springs, Colo. 80452. Mailing Add: P.O. Box 250, Idaho Springs, Colo. 80452.

BRISCOE, JOHN HANSON D
Md. State Del.
b. Leonardtown, Md, 4/10/34; s. John Henry Thomas Briscoe and Hilda Maddox B; m. 8/11/56 to Sylvia Weiss; c. Lisa, Janice, John Hanson, Jr. and Dana. Educ: Mt. St. Mary's Col, A.B, 56; Univ. Baltimore, LL.B, 60. Polit. & Govt. Pos: Md. State Del, 62- Mem: St. Mary's Co. and Md. State Bar Asns; Lions; K. of C. Rel: Catholic. Mailing Add: Court House Dr, Leonardtown, Md. 20650. (1967)

BRISCOE, JOSEPH R, JR. R
Councilman, St. Charles, Mo.
b. St. Louis, Mo, 1/31/37; s. J. Randolph Briscoe and Helen Litteken B; m. 10/8/60 to Joan Gay Foltz; c. Louis R, Valerie A. and James J. Educ: St. Louis Prep Sem, A.A, 56; St. Louis Univ, B.S, 58. Polit. & Govt. Pos: Councilman, St. Charles, Mo, 62-; chmn, St. Charles Co. Rep. Cent. Cmt, 65-68. Bus. & Prof. Pos: Advert. salesman, Radio Sta. KWRE, Warrenton, Mo, 59-61 and St. Charles J, 61-64; field underwriter, Home Life Ins. Co. N.Y, 64-68; supvr. publ. and publicity, Gen. Am. Life Ins. Co, 69- Mil. Serv: Sgt, Marine Corps Res, until 66. Mem: Dir, St. Charles Kiwanis; past pres, St. Charles Jaycees; merit badge coun, Boy Scouts; K. of C.(4°); St. Charles Co. Rep. Club. Rel: Catholic. Mailing Add: 11 Ridgeview Court, St. Charles, Mo. 63301.

BRISTER, MILTON E. D
b. Montgomery Co, Miss, 4/6/17; married. Polit. & Govt. Pos: Miss. State Rep, 60-68. Bus. & Prof. Pos: Asst. cashier; cattle farmer. Mem: Am. Legion; Farm Bur; Aberdeen Angus Breeders Asn; Mason; C. of C; Lions. Rel: Baptist. Mailing Add: Kilmichael, Miss. 39747. (1967)

BRISTLEY, CALVIN WESLEY, JR. R
Chmn, Sandusky Co. Rep. Cent. Cmt, Ohio
b. Fremont, Ohio, 4/28/26; s. Calvin Wesley Bristley, Sr. and Helen Eliza-

beth Fuzesy B; m. 11/29/50 to Patricia Rose Huntzinger; c. Rebecca Kay, Eric David and Rachael Ann. Educ: Ohio Univ, 46-48; Univ. Cincinnati, LL.B, 51; Phi Alpha Delta. Polit. & Govt. Pos: City solicitor, Fremont, Ohio, 56-; mem, Sandusky Co. Rep. Cent. Cmt, 56-, v.chmn, 62-67, chmn, 67- Bus. & Prof. Pos: Secy-treas, Sandusky Co. Law Libr. Asn, Ohio, 59-69; dir, Sandusky Co. YMCA, 69. Mil. Serv: Pvt, Air Force, 44-45. Publ: 'Validity of Municipal Ordinances Prescribing Penalties Greater Than State Laws,' Univ. Cincinnati Law Review, 5/51. Mem: Am. and Ohio State Bar Asns; Kiwanis. Rel: Lutheran. Legal Res: 1017 Franklin St, Fremont, Ohio 43420. Mailing Add: 323 S. High St, Fremont, Ohio 43420.

BRISTOL, GEORGE LAMBERT D
b. Denton, Tex, 8/11/40; married; c. Two. Educ: Univ. Tex, B.A. in Econ. and Govt, 63. Polit. & Govt. Pos: Worked on Sen. race for U.S. Rep. Jim Wright, 61; col. and youth dir. for re-elec. of U.S. Rep. Homer Thornberry, 62; mem. off. staff, U.S. Rep. Homer Thornberry, 63; Dem. doorman, 63; worked in Presidential campaign and for re-elec. of U.S. Rep. J.J. Pickle, Tex, 64; legis. asst. and dist. coordinator, off. of U.S. Rep. J.J. Pickle, 64-65; worked for U.S. Rep. Pickle's re-elec, 66; field rep. for Vice President Humphrey, Mont. and Ky. and 16 state coordinator, Humphrey-Muskie Campaign, 68; floor leader and South. and border state coordinator, Dem. Nat. Conv, 68; spec. asst. to chmn, Dem. Nat. Cmt, 69- Bus. & Prof. Pos: Acct. exec, mgt. consult. firm, Austin, Tex, 65-68. Mailing Add: 3518 35th St. N.W, Washington, D.C. 20008.

BRISTOW, WALTER JAMES, JR. D
S.C. State Sen.
b. Columbia, S.C, 10/14/24; s. Dr. Walter J. Bristow and Caroline Belser Melton B; m. 9/12/52 to Katherine Stewart Mullins; c. Katherine M. and Walter J, III. Educ: Va. Mil. Inst, 41-43; Univ. N.C, A.B, 47; Univ. S.C. Law Sch, LL.B. cum laude, 49; Harvard Law Sch, LL.M, 50; Pi Gamma Mu. Polit. & Govt. Pos: Asst. counsel, U.S. Sen. Subcmt. on Privileges and Elec, 56; S.C. State Rep, 57-58; S.C. State Sen, 59- Bus. & Prof. Pos: Assoc, Marchant, Bristow & Bates, Attorneys. Mil. Serv: Army, 43-46, 292nd Field Observ. Bn; Lt. Col, S.C. Nat. Guard. Mem: Past Exalted Ruler, Lodge 1190, Elks; Nat. Dep. Chief of Staff, Regular Vet. Asn. of the U.S; Am. Legion; VFW; Mil. Order of World Wars; Exchange Club; S.C. Wildlife Asn; Alpha Tau Omega; Wig and Robe. Rel: Presbyterian; Deacon, First Presby. Church. Mailing Add: 1306 Main St, Columbia, S.C. 29201.

BRITSCHGI, CARL A. R
Calif. State Assemblyman
b. Menlo Park, Calif, 1/24/12; m. 8/8/34 to Violet Schaller; c. Brenton. Educ: Santa Clara Univ, B.B.A. Polit. & Govt. Pos: Mayor, Redwood City, Calif, 14 years; councilman; Calif. State Assemblyman, 56-; mem, Calif. Rep. State Cent. Cmt, currently. Bus. & Prof. Pos: Farming, real estate bus. Mem: Lions; Elks; Native Sons of the Golden West. Mailing Add: 2025 Broadway, Redwood City, Calif. 94063. (1967)

BRITT, DAVID MAXWELL D
b. McDonald, N.C, 1/3/17; s. Dudley H. Britt and Martha Mae Hall B; m. to Louise Teague; c. Nancy, Martha Neill, Mary Louise, David Jr. Educ: Wake Forest Univ, 33-35, LL.D, 67; Wake Forest Univ. Sch. Law, 35-37. Polit. & Govt. Pos: Mem, State Dem. Exec. Cmt, N.C, two terms; solicitor, Fairmont Recorder's Court, 40-44; attorney, Fairmont, 46-67; chmn, Fairmont Bd. Educ, 54-58; chmn, Robeson Co. Dem. Exec. Cmt, 56-58; bd. trustees, Southeast. Gen. Hosp, pres, 58; N.C. State Rep, 59-67, Speaker, House of Rep, 67; judge, N.C. Court Appeals, 67- Bus. & Prof. Pos: Lawyer. Mil. Serv: Pvt, Army, 43. Mem: Am. and N.C. Bar Asns; pres, Wake Forest Col. Alumni Asn, 52-53; Pi Kappa Alpha; Gov. Dist. 279, Fairmont Rotary Club, 51-52. Man of the Year Award, Robeson Co, 57. Rel: Baptist; Deacon, Teacher Men's Bible Class; Gen. Bd. Baptist State Conv, N.C. Legal Res: 617 Glen Eden Dr, Raleigh, N.C. 27609. Mailing Add: P.O. Box 888, Raleigh, N.C. 27602.

BRITT, HENRY MIDDLETON R
Permanent Mem, Ark. State Rep. Cmt.
b. Olmstead, Ill, 6/9/19; s. Henry Middleton Britt, Jr. and Sarah Theodosia Roach B; m. 10/29/42 to Barbara Jean Holmes; c. Nancy Marsh, Sarah Barbara and Melissa. Educ: Univ. Ill, Urbana, A.B. in Polit. Sci, 41, Col. Law, J.D, 47; Phi Alpha Delta; Delta Phi; Phalanx. Polit. & Govt. Pos: Former pres, Young Rep. Club, Univ. Ill; asst. U.S. Attorney, West. Dist, Ark, 53-58; cand. for Gov, Ark, 60; gen. counsel, Rep. Party, Ark, 62-64; Rep. mem, Garland Co. Bd. Elec. Cmnrs, 62-66; chmn, Garland Co. Rep. Cent. Cmt, 62-66; circuit judge, 18th Judicial Dist, 67; permanent mem, Ark. State Rep. Cmt; alternate del, Rep. Nat. Conv, 68. Bus. & Prof. Pos: Private practice of law, Hot Springs, Ark. Mil. Serv: Entered Army, 41-46, serv. in Persian Gulf Command, 42-44; Capt.(Ret), Judge Adv. Gen. Corps, Army Res. Mem: Am, Ill. State and Ark. Bar. Asns; Garland Co. Bar Asn.(pres, 61-62, secy-treas, 50-53); Am. Judicature Soc; Ark. Trial Lawyers Asn; Ark. Jr. C. of C.(v.pres, 50-51, pres, 51-52); life mem, Hot Springs Jr. C. of C.(pres, 51-52); v.pres, Commun. Coun. Hot Springs, 59-60; past dir, United Fund; Kiwanis (pres, Hot Springs Club, 69-); U.S. Navy League, (pres, Hot Springs Coun, 66-68); life mem, Univ. Ill. Alumni Asn; Am. Legion; VFW; Elks; Mason; United Commercial Travelers. Nat. Col. State Trial Judges fel. Rel: Presbyterian; Elder and Trustee. Mailing Add: 126 Trivista, Hot Springs, Ark. 71901.

BRITT, MAURICE L. 'FOOTSIE' R
Lt. Gov, Ark.
b. Carlisle, Ark, 6/29/19; s. Maurice L. Britt and Virgie B; m. to Pat B; c. Andrea, Nancy Lea, Mike, Timmy and Patty. Educ: Univ. Ark, B.A; Phi Eta Sigma; Blue Key; Sigma Chi. Polit. & Govt. Pos: Lt. Gov, Ark, 67-; alternate del, Rep. Nat. Conv, 68. Bus. & Prof. Pos: Owner, Beautyguard Mfg. Co, 63-; pres. and sales mgr, Furniture Mfg. Co. Mil. Serv: Entered as 2nd Lt, Army, 41, released as Capt; Cong. Medal of Honor; Distinguished Serv. Cross; Silver Star. Mem: Am. Legion; Rotary; Kiwanis. Rel: Baptist. Mailing Add: 4805 Crestwood Dr, Little Rock, Ark. 72207.

BRITT, WILLIAM ROSS D
N.C. State Rep.
b. Bentonville Battleground, N.C; s. Rufus Kirby Britt and Mary Rebecca Woodall B. Educ: Univ. of N.C, A.B, 44; Univ. of N.C, LL.B, 48. Polit. & Govt. Pos: Solicitor, Johnston Co. Recorder's Court, N.C, 50-58; asst. superior court solicitor, 52-58; N.C. State Rep, 63- Bus. & Prof. Pos: Lawyer. Mil. Serv: 1st Lt, Marines, 43-45; Capt, Marine Corps Res, 51-52. Mem: N.C. State Bar; N.C. and Am. Bar Asns; Am. Judicature Soc; fel, Masonic Lodge 84; Wilmington Consistory, South. Jurisdiction, Scottish Rite; Sudan Temple; comdr, Pou-Parrish Post 132, Am. Legion, 64. Rel: Methodist; Sunday Sch. teacher and mem, off. bd, Centenary Methodist Church. Mailing Add: 408 Hancock St, Smithfield, N.C. 27577. (1967)

BRITTAIN, JACK OLIVER D
b. Greenwood, La, 9/24/28; s. Clarence Lafayette Brittain and Irene Geneva Humphries B; m. 11/25/55 to Ann Marie Williams; c. Jack Oliver, Jr, Marguerite Ann, Rebecca Ann, Lala Elizabeth Ann, Eliza Ann, John Arthur and Mary Jane Ann. Educ: La. Polytech. Inst, B.A, 49; La. State Univ, LL.B and J.D, 59; Omicron Delta Kappa; Lambda Chi Alpha. Polit. & Govt. Pos: Attorney, Natchitoches, La, 59-, Village Provencal, 60-, Natchitoches Area Econ. Develop. Asn, 62-, Waterworks Dist. 2, Natchitoches Parish, 65-, Village Powhatan, 66- and Gas Dist. 2, Natchatoches Parish, 67-; del, Nat. Dem. Conv, 68. Bus. & Prof. Pos: Partner, Watson, Brittain & Murchison, Natchitoches, 59-; partner, Brittain & Watson, 61- Mil. Serv: Entered as Pvt, Army, 51, released as Maj, 68, after serv. in Qm.C. and Judge Adv. Gen. Corps. Publ: Louisiana Model Municipal Code, 65. Mem: Am. and La. State Bar Asns; Am. Trial Lawyers Asn; Defense Research Inst; Rotary Int; La. Farm Bur; Mason; Methodist Men. Rel: Methodist. Legal Res: 919 Parkway Dr, Natchitoches, La. 71457. Mailing Add: P.O. Box 226, Natchitoches, La. 71457.

BRITZ, HARLAND MARSHALL D
Secy, Lucas Co. Dem. Cent. Cmt, Ohio
b. Toledo, Ohio, 7/2/31; s. Morris J. Britz and Lillian Pintis B; m. 10/12/62 to Nancy Gould. Educ: Univ. Mich, B.A, 53, M.A, 56, LL.B, 56; Pi Lambda Phi. Polit. & Govt. Pos: Precinct committeeman, Toledo Dem. Party, Ohio, 58-; asst. U.S. attorney, 62-64; ward chmn, Ottawa Hills Dem. Party, 64-; secy, Lucas Co. Dem. Cent. Cmt, 65-; alternate del, Dem. Nat. Conv, 68. Bus. & Prof. Pos: Chmn, Constitutional Rights Cmn, Toledo Bar Asn, 64-66. Mem: Lucas Co, Ohio and Fed. Bar Asns; Toledo Bar Asn.(chmn. constitutional rights cmt, 64-66); Am. Civil Liberties Union; NAACP; B'nai B'rith; Toledo Tennis Club; Toledo Racquet Club. Rel: Jewish. Mailing Add: 4751 W. Central Ave, Toledo, Ohio 43615.

BRIZENDINE, THOMAS M. D
b. 1917. Educ: Univ. Iowa. Polit. & Govt. Pos: Mem, Franklin City Coun, Ky, 2 terms; Ky. State Rep, 60; Ky. State Sen, 64-68. Bus. & Prof. Pos: Farmer; automobile dealer. Mil. Serv: Navy, World War II; five Air Medals; World War II Victory Medal. Mem: VFW; Ky. Farm Bur; former dir, Civitan Club; past pres. and chmn. bd, C. of C; former post comdr. and dist. comdr, Am. Legion; former dir, UGF. Rel: Baptist. Mailing Add: 501 W. Cedar, Franklin, Ky. 42134. (1967)

BROAD, ELI D
b. N.Y.C, 6/6/33; s. Leon Broad and Rebecca Jacobson B; m. 12/19/54 to Edythe Lois Lawson; c. Jeffrey Alan and Gary Stephen. Educ: Mich. State Univ, B.A. cum laude, 54; Beta Alpha Psi. Polit. & Govt. Pos: State chmn. for U.S. Sen. Alan Cranston, Calif, 68; del, Dem. Nat. Conv, 68. Bus. & Prof. Pos: Acct, Goldman & Golman, CPA, Detroit, 54-55; asst. prof. acct, Detroit Inst. Tech, 55-56; chmn. and pres, Kaufman and Broad Bldg. Co, 57-69, chmn, Kaufman and Broad, Inc, 69-; dir, Bank of the Commonwealth, Detroit, 69- Mem: Nat. Asn. Housing Producers; Coun. Housing Producers (dir); dir, Mich. State Univ. Develop. Fund; mem. adv. bd, Col. Law, Orange Univ; trustee, City of Hope. Man of the Year, City of Hope, 65; Prfnl. Builder of the Year, Prfnl. Builder Mag, 67; Distinguished Alumni Award, Mich. State Grad. Sch. Bus. Admin, 68. Rel: Jewish. Legal Res: 121 N. Rockingham Ave, Los Angeles, Calif. 90049. Mailing Add: 10889 Wilshire Blvd, No. 640, Los Angeles, Calif. 90024.

BROCK, DAVID ALLEN R
b. Stoneham, Mass, 7/6/36; s. Herbert J. Brock and Margaret Morris B; m. 9/3/60 to Sandra Ford; c. Kimberly, Deborah, Tammy and Margaret Ann. Educ: Dartmouth Col, grad, 58; Univ. Mich. Law Sch, grad, 63; Phi Gamma Delta. Polit. & Govt. Pos: Del, N.H. Rep. State Conv, 66 & 68 and mem, State Platform Cmt, 66; chmn, Manchester Rep. City Cmt, 67-68; v.chmn, N.H. Rep. State Cmt, 68-69; mem, Mayor's Citizens' Adv. Cmt, 68-; mem, Manchester Indust. Coun, 68-; U.S. attorney, Dist. of N.H, 69- Bus. & Prof. Pos: Attorney, Devine, Millimet, McDonough, Stahl & Branch, Manchester, N.H, 63-69. Mil. Serv: Entered as 2nd Lt, Marine Corps, 58, released as 1st Lt, 61, after serv. in Fourth Counter Intel. Corps, team comdr, Second Marine Div, Camp Lejeune, N.C, 60-61; Capt, Marine Corps Res, 63; Letter of Commendation from Commandant of the Marine Corps, 60. Mem: Manchester, N.H. and Am. Bar Asns; ROA; pres, Manchester Commun. Guidance Center; trustee, Manchester Boys Club. Third Place Award, Freedom Found. Armed Forces Essay Contest, 60. Rel: Congregational. Mailing Add: 142 Peak St, Manchester, N.H. 03104.

BROCK, H. BURT D
b. Mt. Hermon, La, 8/31/01; s. J. Vol Brock and Henry McClendon B; m. 3/3/31 to Mabel Burns; c. H. B, Jr, Jay V. and Louis B. Educ: Miss. Col, 3 years. Polit. & Govt. Pos: Chmn, Franklin Co. Dem. Party, Miss, 55-65. Bus. & Prof. Pos: State Bank exam, La. State Banking Cmn, 34-40; owner, Chevrolet Dealership, 40-53; v.pres, bank, Coushatta, La, 43-53; owner, West. Auto, 53-67. Mem: Lions (pres, Coushatta, La. Club, 49); Franklin Co. Develop. Asn; Vol. Fire Dept; Civil Defense dir, Red River Parish, La; Mason; Eastern Star. Rel: Baptist. Mailing Add: P.O. Box 248, Meadville, Miss. 39653.

BROCK, LeROY R
Chmn, Bryan Co. Rep. Party, Okla.
b. Brystol, Tex, 11/23/98; s. Benjiman Franklin Brock and Annie Rebeca Hunt B; m. 8/17/21 to Ella Smith; c. Anna Pauline (Mrs. Easley), Ruby Mae and William LeRoy. Educ: Southeast. State Col, 19. Polit. & Govt. Pos: Mem, Co. Fair Bd, Okla, 25-30; clerk, Sch, Bd, 25-35; bd. mem, Co. Ration Bd, 42-45; alternate del, Rep. Nat. Conv, 64; chmn, Bryan Co. Rep. Party, Okla, 65- Bus. & Prof. Pos: Owner and mgr, Brock's Jersey Farm Dairy &

Creamery, 22-53 and Brock's Real Estate Agency, 55-66. Mem: Past pres. and mem, Bryan Co. Farm Bur; Rotary; C. of C. Rel: Presbyterian; Elder, First Presbyterian Church, U.S. Mailing Add: P.O. Box 25, Durant, Okla. 74701.

BROCK, MARGARET MARTIN R
Mem, Rep. Nat. Finance Cmt.
b. Los Angeles, Calif; d. James R. Martin and Pauline Cornwell M; m. 5/1/33 to George C. Brock, wid. Educ: Mt. Vernon Sem, 25. Polit. & Govt. Pos: Trustee, Rep. Assocs, Los Angeles; chmn, women's div. United Rep. Finance Cmt, Los Angeles Co; mem, Rep. Nat. Finance Cmt, 52-; mem, President's Cmt. on Aging, 56-60; del, Rep. Nat. Conv, 68. Mem: Founding mem, Jr. League of Los Angeles; Federated Rep. Women's Clubs; Rep. Assocs. of Los Angeles; Capitol Hill Club, Washington, D.C; Women's Nat. Rep. Club, N.Y; Pro America. Rel: Protestant. Mailing Add: 1404 Century Towers West, 2220 Ave. of the Stars, Los Angeles, Calif. 90067.

BROCK, R. BUCKMAN R
Dist. Chmn, Polk Co. Rep. Cent. Cmt, Iowa.
b. Oakland, Iowa, 12/11/40; s. Virgil Marion Brock and Alma Day McLaughlin B; m. 8/30/64 to Linda Lea Estle. Educ: Drake Univ, B.A, 65; Alpha Delta Sigma. Polit. & Govt. Pos: Former chmn, Appanoose Co. Rep. Cent. Cmt, Iowa; dist. chmn, Polk Co. Rep. Cent. Cmt, currently. Bus. & Prof. Pos: V.pres, Hope Co, Inc, 65-; prog. dir, KCBC Radio, 68. Mem: Radio/TV News Dirs. Asn; Advert. Fedn. of Am; Nat. Sportsbroadcaster's Asn; Elks; Jaycees. Mailing Add: 1300 47th,Des Moines, Iowa 50311.

BROCK, ROBERT LEE D
Chmn, Second Cong. Dem. Dist, Kans.
b. Pawnee Rock, Kans, 12/27/24; s. Eddie Ray Brock and Vivian Crawford B; m. 6/28/52 to Mary Louise Heim; c. Robert, Jr. Eddie, Alan, Steven,and Darin Crawford. Educ: Univ. Kans, A.B, 50 and LL.B, 51; Phi Beta Kappa; Phi Delta Phi; Tau Kappa Epsilon. Polit. & Govt. Pos: Asst. city attorney, Topeka, Kans, 53; campaign mgr. cand. local off. and co. campaign mgr. state cand, 54-64; pres, Shawnee Co. Young Dem, 55-59; mem. exec. cmt, Shawnee Co. Dem. Cent. Cmt, 55-; attorney, Securities Cmnr, Kans, 58; pres, Young Dem. Clubs, Kans, 59-60; mem. exec. cmt, Dem. State Cmt, 59-60 & 66-; alternate del, Dem. Nat. Conv, 60; mem. adv. coun, Kans. Small Bus. Admin, 62-; campaign mgr, Montgomery for Cong, 64; del, Dem. Nat. Conv, 64 & 68; chmn, Second Cong. Dem. Dist, Kans, 66- Bus. & Prof. Pos: Chmn. advert. cmt, Int. Asn. Holiday Inns, 63-64, pres, 64-65, dir, 64-66 and mem. exec. and conf. cmts, 65-66; dir, Fidelity State Bank, 65-; pres, Inn Operations, Inc, 69- Mil. Serv. Aviation Electronic Technician's Mate 3/C, Navy, 43-46. Mem: Dir, Kans. Hotel-Motel Asn, 61, Topeka C. of C, 64-65 and Topeka Flood Control & Conserv. Asn, 64-; Kans. State C. of C; Dem. Action Cmt; Elks. Rel: Congregational. Legal Res: 5041 W. 23rd St, Topeka, Kans. 66614. Mailing Add: 3802 Topeka Ave, Topeka, Kans. 66609.

BROCKE, GEORGE FRANK D
Idaho State Rep.
b. Kendrick, Idaho, 10/8/04; s. Frank Brocke and Julia Otto B; m. 6/8/29 to Emma Rennick; c. George Fred, Morris Eugene and Darrel James. Educ: Kendrick High Sch, Idaho, 21-24. Polit. & Govt. Pos: Idaho State Sen, 49-50, chmn, Forestry and Pub. Lands Cmt, Idaho State Sen, 49-50; Idaho State Rep, 59-, chmn, Agr. Cmt, Idaho House of Rep, 59-60, mem, Forest Lands Tax Study Cmt, 67-, mem, Fire Study Cmt, 67-, mem, States Pub. Lands. Cmt, 69-; mem, Idaho Legis. Coun, 69- Bus. & Prof. Pos: Dir, George F. Brocke & Sons, Inc, 59- Mem: Elks; Latah Co. C. of C. Rel: Protestant. Legal Res: Kendrick, Idaho 83537. Mailing Add: P.O. Box F, Kendrick, Idaho 83537.

BROCK, WILLIAM EMERSON III R
U.S. Rep, Tenn.
b. Chattanooga, Tenn, 11/24/30; s. William Emerson Brock, Jr. and Myra Kruesi B; m. 1/11/57 to Laura Handly; c. William E, IV, Oscar Handly, Laura Hutcheson and John Kruesi. Educ: Wash. and Lee Univ, B.S. in commerce, 53; Sigma Alpha Epsilon. Polit. & Govt. Pos: Nat. committeeman, Tenn. Young Rep, 61-; chmn, Nat. Teen Cmt, 61-; U.S. Rep, Third Dist, Tenn, 62-; mem, Banking and Currency, Joint Econ, Rep. Coord. and Cong. Campaign Cmts, mem, Rep. Cmt. on Research and Planning, Rep. Task Force on Labor Law Reform and regional asst. to Rep. Whip; del, Rep. Nat. Conv, 68. Bus. & Prof. Pos: V.pres. mkt, Brock Candy Co, 60-61. Mil. Serv: Entered as Ens, Navy, 53, released as Lt.(jg), 56, after serv. in 7th Fleet, Far East, 54-56; Korean War and UN Serv. Ribbons; Lt, Naval Res, 61- Mem: C. of C; Jr. C. of C; Am. Legion; Chowder and Marching Soc; Area Literacy Movement; 365 Club for Handicapped. Outstanding Young Rep, 63; Outstanding Young Man of the Year, Tenn. Jaycees, 65; Distinguished Serv. Award, Chattanooga Jaycees, 66; Award for Outstanding Serv. to Teen Age Rep, 67; Award for Outstanding Serv. to Cong. Adv. Coun. of Young Rep. Nat. Fedn; Distinguished Legislator, Young Am. Inaugural Cmt, 69. Rel: Presbyterian; former Sunday Sch. teacher. Legal Res: Dogwood Dr, Lookout Mountain, Tenn. 37350. Mailing Add: 115 Cannon House Office Bldg, Washington, D.C. 20515.

BROCKER, NAIDA LOUISE R
Secy, Jackson Co. Rep. Party, Colo.
b. Laramie, Wyo, 4/15/44; d. William Andrew Simson and Naida Cox S.(deceased); m. 6/16/62 to Gordon Ernest Brocker; c. Kelli Lea and John Gordon. Educ: La Salle Col. Exten. Polit. & Govt. Pos: Alternate del, Colo. State Rep. Conv, 67 & 68; secy, Jackson Co. Rep. Party, Colo, 68- Mem: Colo. Fedn. Womens Clubs; Colo. State Cowbelles; North Park Cowbelles; Rocky Mt. Snowmobile Asn; North Park Snowmobile Club; secy, North Park Roping Club, 62-66; adv, Snowbird Theta Rho Girls Club, 64-67; North Park Womens Club (pres, 69); Rebekah (treas, Walden Lodge 42, 64-69); North Park Auxiliary to Post 2371. Rocky Mt. Snowmobile Powder Puff Champion, 67 & 68; queen of various rodeos. Rel: Presbyterian. Mailing Add: P.O. Box 644, Walden, Colo. 80480.

BROCKINGTON, WILLIAM JOHN D
S.C. State Sen.
b. Helena, Ark, 9/16/17; s. William John Brockington and Daisie O. B; m. 4/27/46 to Elizabeth Townsend Breitling. Educ: The Citadel, 34-37; Northwest. Univ, D.D.S, 42; Univ. Pa. Grad. Sch. Med, 47-48. Polit. & Govt. Pos: S.C. State Rep, until 66; S.C. State Sen, 67- Bus. & Prof. Pos: Orthodontist; businessman; cattle rancher. Mil. Serv: Lt. Comdr, Navy, 42-46. Mem: Pres, Richland Co. Dent. Soc, 58; v.pres, South. Asn. of Orthodontists, 62; pres, cent. dist, Boy Scouts, 58; pres, Columbia Rotary Club, 60; bd. trustees, Columbia Art Mus, 60-62. Mailing Add: 2827 Millwood Ave, Columbia, S.C. 29205. (1967)

BROCKLEBANK, DANIEL R
N.H. State Rep.
b. Grafton, Mass, 4/11/96. Educ: Grafton pub. schs. Polit. & Govt. Pos: N.H. State Rep, 61- Bus. & Prof. Pos: Retired salesman. Mailing Add: Box 206, Hollis, N.H. 03049. (1967)

BROCKMAN, EUGENE EARL 'GENE' R
Chmn, Quay Co. Rep. Cent. Cmt, N.Mex.
b. Mills, N.Mex, 4/7/31; s. W.D. Brockman and Lucille Purcell B; m. 6/15/57 to Jo Ann Bagby; c. Patti Jo, Donald Mark and Stancel Kirk. Educ: East. N.Mex. Univ, 54-57; Univ. N.Mex, J.D, 60. Polit. & Govt. Pos: Mem, Bd. Regents, East. N.Mex. Univ, 62-64, v.chmn, 64-; mem, N.Mex. Rep. Exec. Cmt, 64-69; chmn, Tucumcari Housing Authority, N.Mex, 67-69; chmn, Quay Co. Rep. Cent. Cmt, 68- Bus. & Prof. Pos: Partner, Hart & Brockman, 61-65; owner, E.E. Brockman Law Off, 65- Mil. Serv: Army, 52-54, serv. in U.S. and Korea. Mem: State Bar of N.Mex; Am. and Plains Bar Asns; Kiwanis. Rel: Baptist. Legal Res: 2101 S. Tenth, Tucumcari, N.Mex. 88401. Mailing Add: Box 974, Tucumcari, N.Mex. 88401.

BRODE, FREDA JEAN D
Memphis, Tenn, 8/28/43; d. Sol Cohn and Lena Bachman C; m. 6/24/65 to Marvin Jay Brode; c. William Howard. Educ: Stephens Col, A.A, 63; Memphis State Univ, B.S, 65; Sigma Delta Tau. Polit. & Govt. Pos: Int. rels. chmn, Tenn. State Fedn. of Dem. Women, 67-68; alternate del, Dem. Nat. Conv, 68; pres, Greater Memphis Dem. Women's Club, Tenn, 68-69. Mem: V.pres, Memphis Hadassah; Memphis Bar Auxillary; Brandeis Univ. Club; Stephens Alumni Club; Nat. Coun. of Jewish Women; B'nai B'rith; Sigma Delta Tau Alumni. Rel: Jewish. Mailing Add: 2944 Tishomingo, Memphis, Tenn. 38111.

BRODE, MARVIN JAY D
Mem, Shelby Co. Dem. Exec. Cmt, Tenn.
b. Memphis, Tenn, 8/26/31; s. Howard Moe Brode and Erneice Jacob; m. 6/24/65 to Freda Jean Cohn; c. William Howard. Educ: Vanderbilt Univ, B.A, 53; Vanderbilt Law Sch, LL.B, 54; Tau Kappa Alpha; Phi Alpha Delta; Zeta Beta Tau. Polit. & Govt. Pos: Acting spec. city judge, Memphis, Tenn, 57-64; asst. city attorney, 65-66; Tenn. State Rep, 63-67; hon. mem, Gov. Staff, 66-; mem, Shelby Co. Dem. Exec. Cmt, 66- Bus. & Prof. Pos: Attorney, Brode and Dunlap, 65-66. Mem: President's Cmt. on Traffic Safety; Tenn, Am, Memphis and Shelby Co. Bar Asns; Tenn. Cmn. on the Performing Arts; Mayor's Commun. Action Cmt, mem.bd.dirs, West. Tenn. Arthritis Found. and Memphis, Shelby Co. Safety Coun; Shrine; Mason (32°). Auth, Tenn. Seat Belt Law and worker in the field of motor traffic safety. Rel: Jewish. Legal Res: 2944 Tishomingo Lane, Memphis, Tenn. 38111. Mailing Add: Suite 3116, 100 N. Main Bldg, Memphis, Tenn. 38103.

BRODERICK, FAY LEONE D
Dem. Nat. Committeewoman, Maine
b. Gardiner, Maine, 6/3/33; d. Paul C. Willett and Ruth E. Markham W; m. 12/24/57 to Richard Howard Broderick; c. Michael K, Richard H. and Paul J. Polit. & Govt. Pos: Mem, Maine Dem. State Cmt, 63-64; Dem. Nat. Committeewoman, Maine, 64-; del. and chmn. Permanent Orgn. Cmt, Dem. Nat. Conv, 68. Mem: Dem. Womans Club. Singing. Rel: Episcopal. Mailing Add: Transalpine Rd, Lincoln, Maine 04457.

BRODERICK, RAYMOND JOSEPH R
Lt. Gov. of Pa.
b. Philadelphia, Pa, 5/29/14; s. Patrick J. Broderick and Catharine Burns B; m. 10/2/45 to Marjorie Eileen Beacom; c. Patrick J, Timothy B, Tara M, Deirdre C. and Brian X. Educ: Univ. Notre Dame, A.B,(magna cum laude), 35; Univ. Pa, LL.B, 38. Polit. & Govt. Pos: Cmnr, Plymouth Twp, Pa, 52-54; chmn, Rep. Policy Cmt, Phila, 65-66; pres, Pa. Constitutional Conv, 67-68; mem, Pa. Rep. State Exec. Cmt, 67-69; Lt. Gov. of Pa, 67-; del. and v.chmn. Pa. Del, Rep. Nat. Conv, 68; mem. exec. cmt, Lt. Gov. Conf, 69; chmn, Nat. Conf. Lt. Gov, 69- Bus. & Prof. Pos: Attorney, Broderick, Schubert & Fitzpatrick, 38-41 & 46-66. Mil. Serv: Entered as Lt.(jg), Navy, 41, released as Lt. Comdr, 46, after serv. in Amphibious Forces, Asiatic, Pac. and European Theatres, 42-46; Lt. Comdr, Naval Res. Publ: Formerly, ed, Law Review, Univ. Pa. Mem: Phila, Pa. and Am. Bar Asns; Am. and Phila. Trial Lawyers Asns; Notre Dame Law Asn.(dir. & pres, 65-66); St. Thomas More Soc; Whitemarsh Valley Country Club; Seaview Country Club; Friendly Sons of St. Patrick; Notre Dame Club Phila; Overbrook Farms Club; state chmn, United Serv. Orgn, 69- Rel: Roman Catholic. Mailing Add: 6408 Church Rd, Philadelphia, Pa. 19151.

BRODERICK, RICHARD HOWARD D
b. Portland, Maine, 3/26/25; s. John H. Broderick and Dorothy Giles B; m. 12/24/57 to Fay Leon Willett; c. Michael, Richard and Paul. Educ: Univ. Maine; Portland Univ. Law Sch. Polit. & Govt. Pos: Maine State Rep, 57-58; chmn, Gov. Exec. Coun, Maine, 65-66; del, Dem. Nat. Conv, 68. Bus. & Prof. Pos: Attorney-at-law, 50- Mil. Serv: Navy, 42-46, after serv. in Underwater Demolition Unit 23, Europe and Pac. Mailing Add: Lincoln, Maine 04457.

BRODERSEN, ROBERT JAMES D
b. Herman, Nebr, 5/27/21; s. James C. Brodersen and Sadie Cameron B; m. 5/23/48 to Pearl A. Lang; c. Joan L, Mikel R. and Sara K. Educ: Wayne State Col. Polit. & Govt. Pos: Pres, Sch. Dist. 21, Nebr, 63-69; mem. steering cmt, Co. Sch. Reorgn, 66-; former chmn, Burt Co. Dem. Cmt. Bus. & Prof. Pos: Bd. mem, Farmers Elevator Bd, 66-; owner, Livestock-grain Farm. Mil. Serv: Entered as Pvt, Air Force, 39, released as 1st Lt, 45, after 37 Missions as B-17 Bomber Pilot, Eighth Air Force, ETO; Air Medal with 4 Clusters; Distinguished Flying Cross. Mem: Farmers Union; Am. Legion; Nat. Farmers Orgn; VFW. Rel: Lutheran; Mem, Church Coun. Mailing Add: Tekamah, Nebr. 68061. (1967)

BROIDE, MACE IRWIN D
b. Burlington, Vt, 5/21/24; s. Abraham A. Broide and Ida Rosenberg B; m. 12/24/43 to Gloria Leah Goldsholl; c. Cheryl Ruth, Beverly Elaine and Sandra Pat. Educ: Ind. Univ, Ernie Pyle scholar, 45-46, B.A, 47; pres, Sigma Delta Chi, 45-46; Flame Club. Polit. & Govt. Pos: Campaign coordinator, Hartke for Sen, 58 & 64; admin. asst. to U.S. Sen. Vance Hartke, Ind, 59-68; secy, Nat. Dem. Sen. Campaign Cmt, 61-62; mem. exec. bd, Ind. Dem. Campaign, 64. Mil. Serv: Entered as Pvt, Army, 43, released as Cpl, 46, after serv. in Third Inf. Div, ETO, 44-45; ETO Ribbon with 5 Battle Stars; Silver Star; Bronze Star. Mem: Asn. Admin. Assts. and Exec. Secys, U.S. Senate (v.pres, 65-66, pres, 66-67); Nat. Press Club; Press Club, Evansville, Ind. (v.pres, 55); Nat. Capital Dem. Club; B'nai B'rith. Rel: Jewish. Legal Res: 600 Walnut St, Evansville, Ind. 47708. Mailing Add: 4515 Burlington Place N.W, Washington, D.C. 20016.

BROMBERG, MICHAEL D. D
b. Providence, R.I, 5/4/38; s. Morris H. Bromberg (deceased) and Frances Mittleman B; m. 7/30/68 to Marlys Olson; c. Marjorie Hope, Susan, Cherise and Carrie. Educ: Columbia Col, B.A, 59; N.Y. Univ. Law Sch, LL.B, 62; pres, Tau Epsilon Phi. Polit. & Govt. Pos: Admin. asst. to U.S. Rep, Herbert Tenzer, 65-68; speechwriter for U.S. Rep, Joseph P. Addabbo, 69-; Wash. Legis. Rep. for Nassau Co, N.Y, 69- Bus. & Prof. Pos: Wash. Res. Assoc, Tenzer, Greenblatt, Fallen & Kaplan Esquires, 62-; Wash. rep. for Fedn. Am. Hosp, Inc. Publ: Co-auth, 'New York Civil Practice Act Forms,' Practicing Law Inst, 64. Mem: D.C. Bar Asn; N.Y. Co. Lawyers Asn. Rel: Jewish. Legal Res: Woodmere, N.Y. Mailing Add: 5807 Cherrywood Lane, Greenbelt, Md. 20770.

BROMFIELD, BETSY BYRON R
Chmn, Speakers Bur, Rep. State Cent. Cmt, Calif.
b. Boston, Mass, 6/30/14; d. Walter Harwood Byron and Helen Marie Annis B; div; c. Sally (Mrs. Robert Bruce Whitney) and Ann Cameron. Educ: Miss. Porter's Sch, Farmington, Conn; Leland Sch. Drama, Boston, Mass, 1 year. Polit. & Govt. Pos: Precinct capt, Eisenhower Campaign, Los Angeles, Calif, 52 and precinct div. chmn, Santa Monica Canyon, 56; precinct area chmn, Nixon Campaign, Pac. Palisades, 60; assoc. mem, Rep. State Cent. Cmt, 62-64; precinct chmn, Goldwater-Miller Campaign, Santa Barbara, 64; registrn. precinct chmn, Santa Barbara Co. Rep. Cent. Cmt, 65, co-chmn. precinct, 65-66; precinct coordinator, Friends of Gov. Reagan, Santa Barbara Co, 66; mem, Rep. State Cent. Cmt, 66-, chmn, speaker's bur, 67-, mem, exec. bd, 69-; del, Rep. Nat. Conv. and secy. Calif. Favorite Son Del, 68. Bus. & Prof. Pos: Actress, summer stock, Kennebunk, Maine, 33-34; comparison shopper, R.H. Macy & Co, New York, 37-38. Mem: Jr. League, Boston, Mass. and Syracuse, N.Y; Vincent Club, Boston. Rel: Protestant. Mailing Add: 1933 Tollis Ave, Santa Barbara, Calif. 93103.

BROMLEY, JAMES ROBERT R
Mem, Bd. of Rep, Stamford, Conn.
b. Stamford, Conn, 4/9/36; s. Stanley Willard Bromley and Helen Jean Brown B; single. Educ: Yale Univ, B.A, 58 and LL.B, 62. Polit. & Govt. Pos: Pres, Young Rep, Stamford, Conn, 65; mem, Bd. Rep, Stamford, 66-, asst. minority leader and chmn. legis. and rules cmt, 68- Bus. & Prof. Pos: Attorney with Durey and Pierson, Stamford, 63-68; partner, Pierson, Duel, Holland and Bromley, Darien, 68- Mem: Stamford and Conn. Bar Asns; trustee, Stamford Home for the Aged and Long Ridge Cemetery Asn; dir, Bartlett Arboretum Asn. and Stamford Leukemia Soc; Woodway Country Club. Rel: Congregational; Deacon, North Stamford Congregational Church. Mailing Add: 73 Hoyclo Rd, Stamford, Conn. 06903.

BROMWELL, JAMES EDWARD R
b. Cedar Rapids, Iowa, 3/26/20; s. Max T. Bromwell and Olive MacDuff B; m. 9/10/46 to Dorothy Bennett; c. Maxwell Thomas, Helen Kirk, Catherine MacDuff and James Edward, Jr. Educ: Univ. of Iowa, B.A, 42; Harvard Univ, M.B.A, 47; Univ. of Iowa, LL.B, 50; Phi Delta Phi; Omicron Delta Kappa. Polit. & Govt. Pos: U.S. Rep, 2nd Dist, Iowa, 61-65; asst. co. attorney, Linn Co, Iowa, 56-59. Bus. & Prof. Pos: Owner and Operator, farm, Center Point, Iowa. Mil. Serv: Entered as Pvt, Army, 42, released as Capt, 45, after serv. in Europe. Mem: Am. Legion; Elks; Linn Co. Farm Bur; Mason; Kiwanis; VFW. Mailing Add: 1920 Ridgeway Dr. S.E, Cedar Rapids, Iowa 52403. (1967)

BROMWICH, ELROY WILLIAM R
b. St. Louis, Mo, 10/21/99; s. George Bromwich and Pauline Binder B; m. 4/21/19 to Mary Jane Fearing; c. Jane Pauline (Mrs. Grass), Jean Dorcas (Mrs. Provost) and June Marilyn (Mrs. Domermuth). Polit. & Govt. Pos: Treas, Mo. Rep. State Cmt; treas, Mo. Rep. Finance Cmt; committeeman, Rep. Nat. Cmt; del, Rep. Nat. Conv, 68; chmn, Nixon for President Cmt, Mo, 68-69. Bus. & Prof. Pos: Pres, Tools and Supplies, Inc, Mo, 32-69 and Ind, 38-69. Mil. Serv: Entered as Pvt, Army, 18, released as Sgt, 19. Mem: Glen Echo Country Club; Mo. Athletic Club; Noonday Club. Legal Res: 4548 Nadine Court, St. Louis, Mo. 63121. Mailing Add: Box 8044, St. Louis, Mo. 63156.

BRONSON, BOYD CLINTON R
b. Salt Lake City, Utah, 4/9/24; s. Arch Valjean Bronson and Hyacinth Nielsen B; m. 7/21/48 to Gladys Lee; c. Ann, Cynthia, Barbara, Elaine and Jonathan. Educ: Utah State Univ, B.S. in civil eng, 50; Phi Kappa Phi; Sigma Tau. Polit. & Govt. Pos: Rep. dist. chmn, Utah, 64; legis. chmn, Dist. 19 Rep. Orgn, 64-; former Utah State Rep. Bus. & Prof. Pos: Structural engr, Latter-day Saint Bldg. Cmt, 53-55; design eng, U.S. Steel Corp, Geneva Works, 55-65, sr. design engr, 65- Mil. Serv: Entered as Pvt, Air Force, 43, released as S/Sgt, 45; Air Medal with two Oak Leaf Clusters; Distinguished Flying Cross; Pac. Theater of Operations Ribbon; Good Conduct Medal; 1st Lt, Air Force Res, 50-58. Mem: Lions. Rel: Latter-day Saint. Mailing Add: 6324 Glenoaks St, Murray, Utah 84107. (1967)

BRONSON, LEISA GRAEME D
b. St. Paul, Minn, 1/3/99; d. Albert Wilson and Mabel Nicols W; m. 10/26/22 to Hiram S. Bronson; c. Leisa (Mrs. Royal Sturtevant), Mary C. and Nancy. Educ: Vassar Col, A.B, 21; Franklin Col. of Law; Am. Univ. Polit. & Govt. Pos: Gen. attorney, Off. Field Solicitor, Dept. Interior; mem, Gov. Adv. Cmt. Research on Ment. Health, Ariz; mem. exec. bd, Ariz. Coun. Civic Unity; del, Dem. Nat. Conv, 52, 56 & 60; mem, Dem. Nat. Cmt, Ariz, 56-60. Bus. & Prof. Pos: Pub. affairs chmn, YWCA, Ohio and Calif, 34, 36; mem. staff, Legis. Reference Dept. Libr. Cong, 42-43 & 46-47. Mem: Claremont League Women Voters; North. Ariz. Mus; life mem, San Gabriel Valley YWCA; past pres, Pomona Valley Indian Affairs Asn. Rel: Episcopal. Legal Res: 900 E. Harrison St, Apt. A-9, Pomona, Calif. 91767. Mailing Add: P.O. Box 508, Claremont, Calif. 91711.

BRONSTEIN, HERBERT D
b. Cincinnati, Ohio, 3/1/30; s. Lillian B; m. 6/12/54 to Tamar Blumenfield; c. Deborah, Miriam and Daniel. Educ: Univ. Cincinnati, B.A. and M.A; Hebrew Union Col, B.H.L. and M.H.L; Phi Beta Kappa. Polit. & Govt. Pos: Alternate del, Nat. Dem. Conv, 68. Bus. & Prof. Pos: Rabbi, Temple B'rith Kodesh, 57- Publ: 'In Defense of Kevah,' Cent. Conf. Am. Rabbis J, 1/67; 'Ethical and Religious Issues in Heart Transplants,' Reconstructionist, 5/68; 'Shakespeare, the Jews, and The Merchant of Venice,' Shakespeare Quart, winter 69. Mem: Cent. Conf. Am. Rabbis; Am. Acad. Relig; Omicron Delta Kappa. Rel: Jewish. Mailing Add: 196 Oakdale Dr, Rochester, N.Y. 14618.

BRONSTON, JACK E. D-L
N.Y. State Sen.
b. Plainfield, N.J, 1/10/22; m. to Adele; c. Deena, Rhoda, David. Educ: Harvard, A.B. magna cum laude, 42; Harvard Law Sch, LL.B, 48; N.Y. Univ. Sch. of Law, LL.M, 48; Phi Beta Kappa. Polit. & Govt. Pos: N.Y. State Sen, currently. Bus. & Prof. Pos: Lawyer, Weiss, Bronston and Rosenthal, N.Y.C. Mil. Serv: 1st Lt, Marines, 42-46. Mailing Add: 184-37 Hovenden Rd, Jamaica, N.Y. 11432.

BROOK, JOHN ROBERT R
b. New York, N.Y, 3/26/05; s. John Thomas Brook and Fannie Dean B; m. 7/19/28 to Elizabeth Munro Waters; c. John Robert, Jr, Munro Spalding, Lowell Bigelow (Mrs. Pierce) and Kedron Dudley. Educ: Amherst Col, A.B, 28; Fordham Univ. Law Sch, LL.B, 31; pres, Class of 28, Amherst Col. Polit. & Govt. Pos: N.Y. State Assemblyman, 44-64, chmn, Judicary Cmt, 60-64 and N.Y.C. Cmt, N.Y. State Assembly, 48-60; mem, N.Y. State Judiciary Conf. and N.Y. State Law Revision Cmn, 60-64. Prof. Pos: Attorney-at-Law, Woodstock, Vt, 65- and White Plains and Pelham, N.Y, 31-36; partner, Breed, Abbott & Morgan, N.Y.C, 47-65 and assoc, 44-47; assoc. and partner, Reddy, Greeley & O'Shea, 36-44. Mem: Fordham Univ. Law Sch. Alumni Asn; Ft. Orange Club, Albany, N.Y; Am, N.Y.C. and Vt. State Bar Asns. Rel: Episcopal. Mailing Add: 27 The Green, Woodstock, Vt. 05091. (1967)

BROOKE, ALBERT BUSHONG, JR. R
Mem, Fed. Power Cmn.
b. Paducah, Ky, 6/23/21; s. Albert Bushong Brooke, Sr.(deceased) and Ruth Crawford B; m. 3/1/47 to Virginia Joyce Rogers; c. Albert B, III, Susan Rogers, Roger W. and Virginia Joyce. Educ: Univ. Ky, A.B. in journalism, 47; Phi Beta Kappa; Epsilon Chapter. Polit. & Govt. Pos: Admin. asst. to U.S. Sen. Thruston B. Morton, Ky, 58-68; mem, Fed. Power Cmn, 68- Bus. & Prof. Pos: Reporter, Grand Rapids Press, Mich, summer 40; bookkeeper, Elk Horn Coal Corp, Wayland, Ky, 41-42; reporter and asst. city ed, The Herald, Lexington, Ky, 46-57; acct. exec. pub. rels, Van Sant, Dugdale & Co, Baltimore, Md, 57-58. Mil. Serv: Entered as Pvt, Army Air Force, 42, released as 1st Lt, 46, after serv. in 9th Tactical Air Command, 9th Air Force, ETO; ETO Ribbon with 6 Battle Stars. Hobbies: Basketball, tennis, golf. Mailing Add: 821 Fairway Dr, Towson, Md. 21204.

BROOKE, EDWARD WILLIAM R
U.S. Sen, Mass.
b. Washington, D.C, 10/26/19; s. Edward William Brooke and Helen Seldon B; m. 6/7/47 to Remigia Ferrari-Scacco; c. Remi Cynthia and Edwina Helene. Educ: Howard Univ, B.S, 41; Boston Univ. Law Sch, LL.B, 48, LL.M, 50; Alpha Phi Alpha; ed, Boston Univ. Law Rev, 46-48. Hon. D.P.A, Northeast. Univ, 64; hon. Dr. Sci, Worcester Polytech. Inst, 65; hon. LL.D, Am. Int. Col. and Emerson Col, 65; hon. J.D, Portia Law Sch, 63; hon. degrees from Cath. and Johns Hopkins Univs, 68; Bowdoin Col, 69 and Suffolk Univ, 69. Polit. & Govt. Pos: Rep. nominee, Secy. of State, Mass, 60; chmn, Boston Finance Cmn, 61-62; mem, Rep. Club Mass; mem, President Johnson's Cmn. for Civil Rights Under Law; Attorney Gen, Mass, 63-66; del, Rep. Nat. Conv, 46 & 68; U.S. Sen, Mass, 67- Bus. & Prof. Pos: Lawyer, private practice, Mass, 50- Mil. Serv: Entered as 2nd Lt, Army, 42, released as Capt, 45, after serv. in 366th Inf. Regt, ETO and with Partisans, Italy; Bronze Star; Combat Infantryman's Badge. Publ: The Challenge of Change, Little-Brown, 66; articles for Bar J. and Forum Magazine. Mem: Nat. Asn. Attorneys Gen; Nat. Asn. Dist. Attorneys; Mass. and Boston Bar Asns; fel, Am. Bar Asn. and Am. Acad. Arts and Sci; adv. cmt, Who's Who in Am. Politics, 67 & 69; chmn. bd, Opera Co. Boston; chancellor, Old North Church; trustee, Boston Univ; Nat. Boston Univ. Alumni Coun; Nat. Coun. Boy Scouts; Huntington Sch. for Boys; New Eng. Hosp; Boston Coun. for Int. Visitors; Mass. Dept. Comdr, Amvets, 54-55, Nat. Judge Adv, 55-57. Selected One of Ten Outstanding Young Men of Gr. Boston, Jr. C. of C, 52; Distinguished Serv. Award, Amvets. Rel: Episcopal. Legal Res: 535 Beacon St, Newton Centre, Mass. 02159. Mailing Add: 232 Old Senate Office Bldg, Washington, D.C. 20510.

BROOKHART, SAMUEL HENRY R
Chmn, Lawrence Co. Rep. Cent. Cmt, Ill.
b. Sumner, Ill, 5/2/14; s. William Lee Brookhart and Carrie Alice Legg B; m. 12/25/39 to Martha Cunningham; c. Carol Ann. Educ: East. Ill. Univ, 4 years. Polit. & Govt. Pos: Twp. supvr, Christy Twp, Ill, 54-58; Rep. precinct committeeman, Christy Twp, Precinct 1, 58-; chmn, Lawrence Co. Rep. Cent. Cmt, 67- Bus. & Prof. Pos: Teacher, Clark Co. Sch. Syst, 35-37, Lawrence Co. Sch. Syst, 37-43 & 46-47, prin. and teacher, Petrolia Sch, 47-69, prin, Petty Sch, 69- Mil. Serv: Entered as Pvt, Army, 43, released as 1st Lt, 46, after serv. in 45th Div, 157th Inf. Regt, ETO, 44-45; Bronze Star. Mem: Lawrence Co. Teachers Orgn; Ill. and Nat. Educ. Asns. Rel: United Church of Christ; Deacon. Mailing Add: R.R. 3, Sumner, Ill. 62466.

BROOKING, JOHN R. S. R
Chmn, Kenton Co. Rep. Exec. Cmt, Ky.
b. Louisville, Ky, 11/27/31; s. Harry K. Brooking and Margaret Sampson B; m. 10/30/54 to Charlotte Jarvis; c. John Sampson and Susan King. Educ: Centre Col. Ky, B.A, 53; Cincinnati Law Sch, LL.B, 60; Alpha Phi Omega; Beta Theta Pi. Polit. & Govt. Pos: City attorney, Parkhills, Ky, 66-; chmn, Kenton Co. Rep. Exec. Cmt, Ky, 66- Bus. & Prof. Pos: Partner, Adams &

Brooking, attorneys. Mil. Serv: Entered as Ens, Navy, 53, released as Lt, 57, after serving in U.S.S. Benar, Korea; China Service Medal. Mem: Am, Ohio, Ky. and Kenton Co. Bar Asns; Dir, C. of C; Optimist; YMCA. Rel: Episcopal. Mailing Add: 1132 Audubon Rd, Park Hills, Ky. 41011.

BROOKMAN, EILEEN B. D
Nev. State Assemblyman
b. Denver, Colo, 10/25/21; m. to George G. Brookman; c. Michael L. and Deborah L. Educ: Los Angeles City Col. Polit. & Govt. Pos: Nev. State Assemblyman, 67-; mem, Gov. Cmt. on Status of Women; app. to serve on cmt. selected by Gov. Laxalt; app. by Secy. of Interior Walter Hickel to study allocation of water from Truckee-Carson Basin. Mem: Human Rels. Cmn; planning cmt, Clark Co. Tech. and Voc. High Sch; Nat. Cmt. Support Pub. Schs; Nev. Indian Cmn, N.C.C.J; co-chmn, Nev. State Cmt. Nat. Coun. Crime & Delinquency; subcmt. Welfare Problems; past pres, Coun. Women's Club Sr. Citizens; B'nai B'rith; residential co-chmn, Cancer Drive; v.pres, Sisterhood Temple Beth Sholom; regional bd. West Coast Anti-Defamation League; St. Jude's Auxiliary; Rose DeLima Hosp. Auxiliary; exec. bd, NAACP; adv. bd, Sr. Citizen Resource Center. Woman of the Year, Clark Co, 69; Outstanding Woman of the Year, B'nai B'rith; Outstanding Serv. Recognition, Indians of Nev; Ky. Col, 68. Mailing Add: 1900 Cochran St, Las Vegas, Nev. 89105.

BROOKS, AUSTIN D
Chmn, Curry Co. Dem. Party, N.Mex.
b. Melrose, N.Mex, 12/19/10; s. Sylvester Wyatt Brooks and Ella Frances Page B; m. 1/1/33 to Theo Eldridge; c. Peggy Jo (Mrs. Gene E. Green), Frank Austin and Janet. Educ: N.Mex. State Univ, 29-31. Polit. & Govt. Pos: Clerk, N.Mex. Hwy. Dept, 33-35; comput. clerk, N.Mex. State Eng, 35-37; closing clerk, Fed. Housing Admin, 37; contract clerk, N.Mex. Land Off, 37-39; precinct chmn, Dep. Party, 40-42; mem, State Exec. Cmt, Dem. Party of N.Mex, 54-56; chmn, Curry Co. Dem. Party, 62-; dist. mgr, N.Mex. Bur. Revenue, 64-67; N.Mex. dir, U.S. Savings Bonds Div, U.S. Dept. Treas, 68- Bus. & Prof. Pos: Asst. mgr, Stockmen's Mfg. Co, 41-45; gen. mgr, El Rancho Milling Co, 45-63. Mem: N.Mex. Grain and Feed Dealers Asn.(pres, 53-56); Am. Feed Mfrs. Asn.(dir, 53-59); regent, N.Mex. State Univ, 47-51; C. of C.(pres, Clovis Chap, 54-56); Rotary Int; Rotary (pres, Clovis Club, 47-48). Rel: Church of Christ. Mailing Add: P.O. Box 261, Albuquerque, N.Mex. 87103.

BROOKS, CAROLYN ELIZABETH R
V.Chairwoman, Ga. Rep. Party
b. Macon, Ga, 5/16/17; d. Walter Franklin Thames and Elizabeth Hartness T; m. 12/19/37 to Charles Lewis Brooks; c. Betsy (Mrs. William Charles Boswell, Jr). Educ: Georgia-Alabama Bus. Col, 33-34. Polit. & Govt. Pos: Del, Precinct, Co, Dist. and State Rep. Conv, 64 & 66; mem, Sixth Dist. Rep. Exec. Cmt, 64-65; mem, Bibb Co. Rep. Exec. Cmt, 64-65; pres, Bibb Co. Fedn. of Rep. Women, 64-65; v.chairwoman, Ga. Rep. Party, 64-; Ga. Conf. chmn, Nat. Conf. of Rep. Women, 65; mem, Seventh Dist. Rep. Exec. Cmt, 65-66; historian, South Conf. of V.chmn, Rep. Party, 65-66; vice chairwoman, Whitfield Co. Rep. Party, 66-67. Bus. & Prof. Pos: Secy, Bibb Mfg. Co, 35-37. Mem: Capitol Hill Club, Wash, D.C; Dalton Golf and Country Club; Idle Hour Golf and Country Club; Ponte Vedra Golf and Country Club. Rel: Methodist; mem, Woman's Soc. Christian Serv. Mailing Add: 1304 Lakemont Dr, Dalton, Ga. 30720. (1967)

BROOKS, CHET EDWARD D
Tex. State Sen.
b. Prescott, Ariz, 8/18/35; s. C.E. Brooks, Sr. and Julia Deats Biddle B; m. 6/6/59 to Fay Lamar; c. Laura Lea and Tracie Lynn. Educ: San Jacinto Col. & San Angelo Col, A.A; Univ. Tex, B.A; Sigma Delta Chi. Polit. & Govt. Pos: Mem. steering cmt, Nat. Dem. Campaign, Harris Co, Tex, 60, 64 & 68; Tex. State Rep, 62-66; Tex. State Sen, 66- Bus. & Prof. Pos: Owner, Brooks Agency, 58-; real estate ed, Houston Post, Tex, 59-63; pres, Guardian Security, Inc and Bayou Agency, 64- Mil. Serv: Entered as Seaman Recruit, Navy, 54, released as Ens, 56, after serv. in Officers Cand. Sch, and Res; Army Res, 56-62; Korean War Serv. Ribbon. Mem: Eagles. Numerous serv. awards from educ. asns. and civic groups. Rel: Methodist. Legal Res: 1603 Blackburn Dr, Pasadena, Tex. 77502. Mailing Add: P.O. Box 1302, Pasadena, Tex. 77502.

BROOKS, DORIS L. R
V.Chmn, Broome Co. Rep. Cmt, N.Y.
b. Towando, Pa, 3/20/12; d. Ira I. Steele and Ada L. Green S; m. 10/2/36 to James A. Brooks; c. Richard A. Educ: Lowell Bus. Sch, 32; Broome Tech. Commun. Col. Polit. & Govt. Pos: Committeewoman, Broome Co. Rep. Party, Dist. 45, N.Y, 40-66; pres, Endicott Woman's Rep. Club, 50-52; chmn, Union Town Rep. Cmt, 54-56; v.chmn, Broome Co. Rep. Cmt, 60-; dep. clerk, Broome Co, 63-66, elec. cmnr, 66- Bus. & Prof. Pos: Bookkeeper, Hatchkiss Wallpaper & Paint, 33-40; teller, Maine Midland Trust Co, 42-44; salesman, La Stella's Real Estate, 52-60; broker, Doris Brooks Real Estate, 60- Mem: Zonta Club Binghamton; Cmnr. Asn. N.Y. State; Woman's Soc. United Methodist Church; Rebekah; Grange; Monday Afternoon Club; Harmony Circle of Ideal Hosp. Bronze Plaque for Distinguished Serv. to Rep. Party, 61. Rel: Methodist. Mailing Add: 110 Birdsall St, Endicott, N.Y. 13760.

BROOKS, GARY HAROLD D
b. McCome, Miss, 6/19/46; s. Joe Brooks and Alma Hilbun B; div. Educ: Southwest Miss. Jr. Col, 64-65; Millsaps Col, B.A, 68; Tulane Univ. Grad. Sch, 68-69; Nat. Defense Educ. Act fel, Tulane Univ, 68-69. Polit. & Govt. Pos: Del, State Dem. Conv, Miss, 68; alternate del, Nat. Dem. Conv, 68. Mailing Add: 3720 Mosley, Jackson, Miss. 39206.

BROOKS, GEORGE B. D
Ga. State Rep.
b. Lexington, Ga, 7/20/05; s. William Wynne Brooks and Mary Adkins B; m. 10/29/34 to Dorothy George Little; c. George B, Jr. Educ: Univ. Fla; Univ. Ga, LL.B, 27; Phi Delta Phi; Phi Kappa Phi; Pi Kappa Phi. Polit. & Govt. Pos: Ga. State Rep, 37-42, 51-54, 57-66 & 69-, mem, Sibley Cmn. and Cmn. on Schs, Ga. State House of Rep; attorney, Fed. Govt, 42-46; Ga. State Sen, 49-50 & 55-56; former co. attorney and former mem, South. Regional Educ. Bd; mem, Crawford City Coun, 59; mayor, Crawford, 60-61. Bus. & Prof. Pos: Attorney; chmn. bd. dirs, Commercial Bank, Crawford; dir, Crawford Garment Co. Mem: Elks. Mailing Add: Crawford, Ga. 30630. (1967)

BROOKS, GEORGE HENRY D
Mem, Colo. Dem. State Exec. Cmt.
b. Pittsburgh, Pa, 11/28/17; s. James Clemer Brooks and Elizabeth Leith B; m. 5/15/42 to Georgia Mildred Milligan; c. Bryan Leith, Janet Helen, Margie Ruth and Roger Hunt. Educ: Sterling Col, B.A, 41; Univ. Kans, M.Ed, 52; Colo. State Col, currently. Polit. & Govt. Pos: Precinct committeeman, Weld Co. Dem. Party, Colo, 62-; mem, Weld Co. Dem. Cent. Cmt, Colo, 63-; chmn, Fourth Cong. Dist, Colo, 65-69; mem, Colo. Dem. State Exec. Cmt, 65-; del, State Dem. Assembly and Conv, 66 & 68; del, Nat. Dem. Conv, 68. Bus. & Prof. Pos: Asst. mgr, Campus Center, Univ. Exten, Univ. Kans, 52-55; dist. Scout exec, Long's Peak Coun, Boy Scouts, 55-59, asst. scout exec, 59-61; asst. to dean, Grad. Sch, Colo. State Col, 66- Mil. Serv: Entered as Ens, Navy, 42, released as Lt, 45, after serv. in Motor Torpedo Boat Squadron Six and Subchaser Training Center, S.Pac. and Miami, Fla, 42-45; Res, Lt. Comdr; Am. Theatre Ribbon; S.Pac-Asian Theatre Ribbon with Star; Good Conduct Medal; Expert Pistol Shot; Expert Rifleman. Mem: Phi Delta Kappa; Kiwanis (past treas, past dist.Key Club chmn). Rel: Presbyterian; Ruling Elder, 46- Mailing Add: 1726 19th Ave, Greeley, Colo. 80631.

BROOKS, JACK D
U.S. Rep, Tex.
b. Crowley, La, 12/18/22; m. 12/15/60 to Charlotte Collins; c. Jack Edward. Educ: Lamar Jr. Col; Univ. Tex, B.J, 43, LL.B, 49. Polit. & Govt. Pos: Mem, Tex. Legis, 46-50; U.S. Rep, Tex, 52- Bus. & Prof. Pos: Lawyer. Mil. Serv: Marine Corps. Legal Res: Beaumont, Tex. Mailing Add: 2239 Rayburn Office Bldg, Washington, D.C. 20515.

BROOKS, JOHN D
Treas, North. Calif. Dem. State Cent. Cmt.
b. Oakland, Calif, 9/16/23; s. John Brooks and Marie Besser B; m. 5/10/50 to Barbara Mathews; c. William Mathews and John, Jr. Educ: U.S. Merchant Marine Acad, $2\frac{1}{2}$ years; Heald Eng. Col, B.S. in Mech. Engr, 48; Lincoln Univ, LL.B, 52. Polit. & Govt. Pos: Del, Dem. Nat. Conv, 68; treas, North. Calif. Dem. State Cent. Cmt, currently. Bus. & Prof. Pos: Partner, Besco, San Leandro, Calif, 54-; dir, Bank Fremont, present. Mil. Serv: Entered as Ens, Navy, 44, released as Lt, 46, after serving in Attack Transport, Pac. Theatre, 44-46. Mem: Engr. Club of South. Alameda Co; Commonwealth Club. of Calif; past pres, Fremont C. of C; dir, Boy's Club of Am, San Leandro and Fremont; past dir, First Agr. Dist, Calif; Gov. Cmt. Calif. Beauty; nat. panelist, Am. Arbit. Asn. Rel: Catholic. Legal Res: 1816 Sylvan Circle, San Leandro, Calif. 94577. Mailing Add: 2777 Alvarado St, San Leandro, Calif. 94577.

BROOKS, MARIETTA MOODY D
b. Saratoga, Tex, d. Martin Luther Moody and Artie Mewhinney Applin M; m. 6/29/35 to Robert Max Brooks; c. Robert Johnson and Carole Louise (Mrs. Doherty). Educ: Univ. Tex, 28-32. Polit. & Govt. Pos: Committeewoman, Tex. Dem. State Exec. Cmt, 46 & 48, v.chmn, 56 & 60; mem, Defense Adv. Cmt. on Women in Armed Serv, 51-56, chmn, Defense Ad Hoc Housing Cmt. for Women in Armed Serv, 55; chmn, Cmt. on Nominations for Nursing Serv, State Grad. Nurses Asn, 54-55; mem, Gov. Citizens' Adv. Coun. for State Position Classification, 54-57; del. and chmn. housing cmt, Tex. State Dem. Conv, 56 & 60, del, 64; del. and mem. platform cmt, Dem. Nat. Conv, 56 & 60, alternate del, 64; mem, Citizens' Adv. Cmt. for Austin Pub. Schs, 59, 64 & 69; mem, Tex. Conf. of Judicial Selection, Tenure and Admin, 64; mem, Del. of Outstanding Am. Women to Russia, Hungary and Czech, 68; alternate del. to UNESCO Gen. Conf, Paris, France, 68. Mem: An organizer and pres, Austin Woman's Forum; charter mem. and past pres, Women's Archit. League; Jr. Helping Hand; Am. Legion Auxiliary 76; Univ. Tex. Ex-Students Asn; bd. mem, Austin Symphony Soc, Inc, 50-65, pres, 55-58; charter mem. and mem. adv. cmt, Women's Symphony League; Austin Country Club; Austin Club; Forty Acres Club; Headliners' Club; Citadel Club; bd. dirs, Tex. Fine Arts Asn. and Tex. Youth Conf; Int. Platform Asn. Three Star Award for serv. to United Serv. Orgns; Marietta Brooks Class of Army Nurses at Brooke Army Med. Center named for her, 54; Cert. of Recognition for contrib. to prestige of Women in Serv. stationed within the Fourth Army Area, 54; Hon. Citizen of Dallas, New Orleans and Honolulu; Patroness of Austin Chap, Mu Phi Epsilon, 64; Commun. Leader of Am. Award, 68. Rel: Baptist. Mailing Add: Brooks Aerie, 1500 W. 24th St, Austin, Tex. 78703.

BROOKS, MARY ELIZABETH R
Dir, Bur. of the Mint, Dept. of Treas.
b. Colby, Kans; d. Sen. John Thomas and Florence Jessie Johnson; m. first to Arthur J. Peavey, Jr. and second to C. Wayland Brooks; wid; c. John Thomas and Elizabeth Ann (Mrs. Eccles). Educ: Mills Col; Univ. Idaho, B.A; Kappa Kappa Gamma. Polit. & Govt. Pos: Exec. secy. to U.S. Sen. John Thomas, 42-45; mem, Rep. Nat. Cmt, 57-63, v.chmn, 60-63, asst. chmn, 65-69; official hostess, Rep. Nat. Conv, 60; Idaho State Sen, 21st Dist, 64-69; dir, Bur. of the Mint, Dept. of Treas, 69- Bus. & Prof. Pos: Owner and mgr, Flat Top Livestock Co, Muldoon, Idaho; banker's asst, First Security Corp. Mem: Ill. Ment. Health Bd; Children's Home and Aid, Chicago; Lighthouse for the Blind; Immigrant Serv. League; Defense Adv. Cmt. on Women in Serv; Am. Asn. of Univ. Women; bd. dirs, Idaho Youth Ranch; v.chmn, Red Cross; Arden Shore Asn; bd, Ill. Fedn. of Rep. Women; Am. Legion Auxiliary. Rel: Presbyterian. Legal Res: Carey, Idaho 83320. Mailing Add: Watergate West, 2700 Virginia Ave. N.W, Apt. 1110, Washington, D.C. 20037.

BROOKS, OLIVE D
b. Mobile, Ala, June 23; d. Stewart Brooks (deceased) and Emma Conner B. (deceased); single. Educ: Shorter Col, Randolph Macon Woman's Col, Univ. Ariz, Columbia Univ. and New Sch. for Soc. Res, Undergrad. Work; Phi Mu. Polit. & Govt. Pos: Dep. clerk, U.S. Dist. Court, Mobile, Ala, 18-19; chief, Pub. Rels. Unit, U.S. Army Dist. Engrs, Panama Canal Dept, Ancon, C.Z, 41-46; writer-ed, The Panama Canal Co. and C.Z. Govt, Balboa Heights, 62, 63 & 64; v.chmn, C.Z. Regional Dem. Party, Ancon, 68; del, v.chmn. C.Z. del. and C.Z. rep, Platform Cmt, Dem. Nat. Conv, 68. Bus. & Prof. Pos: Socioecon. writing, Mobile, Ala. and N.Y.C; asst. ed, Shell Progress mag, Shell Oil Co, N.Y.C, 35-40; part-time correspondent for various U.S. newspapers and news mag, also U.S. and Brit. wire serv, 44-; reporter and copyreader, The Nation, Panama City, Rep. of Panama, 47-49; part-time copyreader, reporter and later desk ed, The Panama Am, 49- Publ: Panama Quadrant, (poetry book), Bookman Assocs, N.Y.C, 60-61; various articles in bus, econ. and related subjects. Mem: Overseas Press Club of Am, N.Y.C;

Friends of Nat. Mus. of Panama; Nat. Asn. of Retired Civil Employees, Wash, D.C. Legal Res: Hotel Van Rensselaer, 15 E. 11th St, New York, N.Y. 10003. Mailing Add: Box 374, Balboa Heights, C.Z.

BROOKS, WILLIAM HENRY D
b. Columbus, Ohio, 1/12/12; s. Oberlin G. Brooks and Helen Reid B; m. 6/27/58 to Mary Adams; c. William H, II. Educ: Ohio State Univ, A.B, 33, LL.B, 37, J.D, 67; Pi Sigma Alpha; Alpha Phi Alpha. Polit. & Govt. Pos: Dep. co. auditor, Franklin Co, Ohio, 41-43; admin. asst, Columbus Gen. Depot, 43-44; mem, Civil Serv. Cmn, Columbus, 54-60 and chmn, 2 years; spec. counsel to Attorney Gen. of Ohio, 60-62; Columbus Munic Judge, 62-63; dir, pub. utilities, Columbus, 64-; alternate del, Dem. Nat. Conv, 68. Mil. Serv: Entered as Pvt, Army, 44, released, 45, after serv. in 372nd Inf. Mem: Columbus, Ohio and Nat. Bar Asns; Robert B. Elliott Law Club; Eastside YMCA (bd. mgt. and bldg. cmt); former v.pres, Frontiers Am; former pres, Columbus Br, NAACP and former pres, Ohio State Conf. of Branches; Mason (32° and past potentate, St. Marks Lodge); Shrine (past potentate, Alla Baba Lodge); trustee, Columbus Commun. Coun; bd. dirs, St. Anthony Hosp; v.pres, Columbus Chap, UN Asn. U.S; Franklin Co. Planning Cmt. Ment. Health; re-employ. committeeman, Selective Serv; trustee, House of Hope; bd. dirs, United Serv. Orgn. Coun. Bd. Dir; tech. policy adv. cmt, Comprehensive Regional Plan Franklin Co; charter mem, Wash. World Conf. World Peace Through Law. Rel: Protestant. Mailing Add: 729 N. Nelson Rd, Columbus, Ohio 43219.

BROOKS, WILSON D
b. College Park, Ga, 11/11/24; s. Samuel Leroy Brooks and Camille Wilson B; m. 1/20/45 to Audrey Crane; c. Bonnie Gayle, Bradley Wilson. Educ: Atlanta Law Sch, LL.B, 49; Univ. Ga; Knox Col, Ill. Polit. & Govt. Pos: Ga. State Rep, 57-66. Bus. & Prof. Pos: Attorney, 49- Mil. Serv: Air Force, Lt, pilot B-17, ETO. Mem: Mason; Shriner; Am. Legion. Rel: Methodist. Legal Res: 4532 Club Circle N.E, Atlanta, Ga. 30319. Mailing Add: 44 Broad N.W, Atlanta, Ga. 30303.

BROOKSHIRE, STANFORD RAYNOLD D
b. Troutman, N.C, 7/22/05; s. James C. Brookshire and Effie Perry B; m. 6/12/34 to Edith Mitchell; c. Carolyn (Mrs. Daivd F. Sachsenmaier) and Stanford R, Jr. Educ: Duke Univ, A.B. Hon. L.H.D, Pfeiffer Col. Polit. & Govt. Pos: Mayor, Charlotte, N.C, 61-69. Bus. & Prof. Pos: Pres, Eng. Sales Co, Charlotte, N.C, 32- Mem: Charlotte Engrs. Club; N.C. Soc. of Engrs; Kiwanis; Silver Medalion, Nat. Conf. Christians and Jews; Charlotte News Man of the Year. Rel: Methodist. Legal Res: 900 Huntington Park Dr, Charlotte, N.C. 28207. Mailing Add: P.O. Box 68, Charlotte, N.C. 28201.

BROOME, DEAN CARL D
Chmn, Pierce Co. Dem. Exec. Cmt, Ga.
b. DeKalb Co, Ga, 7/5/18; s. Carl Jackson Broome and Exie Lurline Cunard B; m. 11/26/47 to Janie Kate Hice; c. Dean Carl, Jr, Amelia Janet and Alice Lurline. Educ: Ga. Evening Col, Atlanta, Ga, B.S. in Commerce, 42; Col. Speakers Club. Polit. & Govt. Pos: Spec. writer, Ord. Dept, Qm. Corps, 42; mem, Selective Serv. Bd, Pierce Co, Ga, 52-54; dir, Civil Defense, Pierce Co, 56-58; chmn, Pierce Co. Dem. Exec. Cmt, 58- Bus. & Prof. Pos: Reporter, The Atlanta Constitution, Atlanta, Ga, 41-42. Mil. Serv: Entered as Pvt, Army, 42, released as Technician 3/C after serv. on Stars & Stripes, Mid. East, 45; Mid. East Ribbon. Mem: Rotary; Ga. Press Asn. Rel: Baptist. Mailing Add: 123 Marion St, Blackshear, Ga. 31516.

BROOMFIELD, CHARLES S. D
Mo. State Rep.
b. Clay Co, Mo, 6/11/37; m. 8/11/62 to Charlene Leist. Educ: William Jewell Col, A.B, teacher's cert. Polit. & Govt. Pos: Mo. State Rep, 64-, asst. majority floor leader, Mo. House Rep, 68- Bus. & Prof. Pos: Taught Am. govt. and Am. hist, North Kansas City High Sch. Mem: Sigma Nu; North Kansas City Jaycees; pres. S.W. Unit, Am. Cancer Soc; AF&AM. Rel: Methodist. Mailing Add: 4801 N. Lister Ave, Kansas City, Mo. 64119.

BROOMFIELD, WILLIAM S. R
U.S. Rep, Mich.
b. Royal Oak, Mich, 4/28/22; s. Dr. S.C. Broomfield and Fern B.(deceased); m. 1951 to Jane Thompson; c. Susan, Nancy and Barbara Ann. Educ: Mich. State Univ. Hon. LL.D, Dongguk Univ, Seoul, Korea, 68. Polit. & Govt. Pos: Mich. State Rep, 48, 50 & 52, speaker pro tem, Mich. House of Rep, 53; Mich. State Sen, 54; U.S. Rep, Mich, 56-; U.S. Ambassador, 22nd UN Gen. Assembly, 67. Mem: U.S. del, NATO Parliamentarians' Conf, Paris, 60; cong. del, U.S. Nat. Cmn. for the U.S. Educ, Sci. & Cultural Orgn, Boston, 61-62; U.S. del, Can-U.S. Interparliamentary Conf, 61-64 & 67-69; U.S. del, U.S.-U.K. Parliamentary Conf, Bermuda, 62 and Interparliamentary Conf, 69. Rel: Presbyterian. Legal Res: Royal Oak, Mich. Mailing Add: 2435 Rayburn House Office Bldg, Washington, D.C. 20515.

BROSCO, ANTHONY J. D
b. Providence, R.I, 6/12/28; m. to Angela Archetto. Educ: Mount St. Mary's Col, A.B, 50; Georgetown Univ. Sch. of Law, LL.B, 53. Polit. & Govt. Pos: R.I. State Rep, 64-68. Bus. & Prof. Pos: Lawyer. Mil. Serv: Judge Adv. Gen. of the Navy, 55-57; Maj. and Commanding Officer of local Marine Res. Units, Fields Point, R.I. Mem: K.of C; Ital-Am. War Vet; Am, Fed. and R.I. Bar Asns; Holy Name Soc. Rel: Catholic. Mailing Add: 811 Hartford Ave, Johnston, R.I. 02919. (1967)

BROTHERTON, W. T. JR. D
W.Va. State Sen.
b. Charleston, W.Va, 4/17/26; s. W.T. Brotherton and Kathryn Slack B; m. 6/17/50 to Ann Jourdan Caskey; c. Elizabeth Ann, William T. III, and Laura Jane. Educ: Wash. and Lee Univ, A.B. and LL.B. Polit. & Govt. Pos: Investr, Kanawha Co. Prosecuting Attorney's Off, W.Va, 50-53; W.Va. State Del, 52-64; W.Va. State Sen, 64-, chmn, Judiciary Cmt; alternate del, Dem. Nat. Conv, 68. Bus. & Prof. Pos: Attorney-at-law, currently. Mem: Mason; Kappa Alpha; Phi Alpha Delta; Am. Bar Asn; bd. mem, W.Va. Unit, Am. Cancer Soc. (pres, Co. Unit, 62-64); Action for Appalachian Youth (dir, 63 & 65). Rel: Episcopal. Mailing Add: 1020 Kanawha Valley Bldg, Charleston, W.Va. 25301.

BROTSLAW, IRVING D
b. Buffalo, N.Y, 6/28/29; s. Sam Brotslaw and Yetta Mastman B; m. 5/3/53 to Elaine Doris Reisner; c. Amy Susan and Daniel Jeffrey. Educ: Univ. Buffalo, B.A, 51; Univ. Wis, Madison, M.S, 52, Ph.D, 64; Sigma Alpha Mu. Polit. & Govt. Pos: V.chmn, Third Ward Unit, Milwaukee Co. Dem. Party, Wis, 65-66, chmn, 66-68; del, Wis. Dem. Conv, 65, 66, 67, 68 and Dem. Nat. Conv, 68. Bus. & Prof. Pos: Teaching asst. econ, Univ. Wis, Madison, 54-56; res. dir, United Papermakers, Albany, N.Y, 56-60; assoc. prof, Univ. Wis. Exten, Milwaukee, 61- and assoc. dir, Sch. for Workers, 64- Mil. Serv: Entered as Pvt, Army, 52, released as Cpl, 54, after serving in Med. Corps, U.S, 52-54; 2nd Lt, Army Finance Corps Res, 54- Publ: Struggle to Unite, Univ. Wis. Exten, 64; 'A Philosophy of Labor for Apprentices,' Am. Federationist, 8/63; 'Attitude of Retail Workers Towards Union Organization,' Labor Law J, 3/67. Mem: Univ. Labor Educ. Asn; Indust. Relat. Res. Asn; AFL; Am. Civil Liberties Union; Milwaukee Urban League. Rel: Jewish. Mailing Add: 3258 N. Shepard Ave, Milwaukee, Wis. 53211.

BROTZMAN, DONALD G. R
U.S. Rep, Colo.
b. Logan Co, Colo, 6/28/22; s. Harry Brotzman and Priscilla Ruth Kittie B; m. 4/9/44 to Louise Love Reed; c. Kathleen L. and Donald G.(Chip). Educ: Univ. Colo, B.B.S. and LL.B, 49; Beta Theta Phi; Phi Delta Phi. Polit. & Govt. Pos: Colo. State Rep, 50-52; Colo. State Sen, 52-56; mem, Colo. Crime Cmn, 52-56; cmnr, Uniform State Laws from Colo, 54-; Rep. Cand, Gov. of Colo, 56; U.S. Attorney, Dist. Colo, 59-61; U.S. Rep, Colo, 63-64 & 67-, former mem, Interstate and For. Commerce Cmn, U.S. House of Rep; del, Rep. Nat. Conv, 68. Bus. & Prof. Pos: Attorney-at-law, Boulder, Colo, 49- Mil. Serv: Army, 1st Lt, Inf, Pac. Theatre, 42-46. Mem: Elks; Rotary; Mason; Am, Fed, Colo. and Boulder Co. Bar Asns; Am. Legion; VFW; Reserve Officers Asn; C. of C; Colo. chmn, Easter Seal and Highlander Boys Club Drives and Youth in Govt. Prog, YMCA, 58-62. Chosen by Colo. Press as Outstanding Freshman Mem. of House, 51; Outstanding Freshman Sen, 53; received Distinguished Serv. Award from Colo. Jr. C. of C, 54. Rel: Methodist; Trustee. Legal Res: 735 Highland St, Boulder, Colo. 80302. Mailing Add: 413 Cannon House Office Bldg, Washington, D.C. 20515.

BROUGH, RICHARD M. R
b. Nephi, Utah, 1/1/37; s. Yale Brough and Kathleen Mansfield B; single. Educ: Univ. of Utah, B.S, 59 and grad. work, 63; Phi Alpha Theta. Polit. & Govt. Pos: Precinct chmn, Millard Co. Rep. Party, Fillmore, Utah, 62-65, chmn, 65-66; former Utah State Rep, Juab and Millard Co. Rel: Latter-day Saint. Legal Res: 30 S. Main, Fillmore, Utah 84631. Mailing Add: P.O. Box 283, Fillmore, Utah 84631. (1967)

BROUGHTON, BERLIN ARTHUR R
b. Eldred, Pa, 4/13/96; s. Richard Henry Broughton and Alma Kelsey B; m. 6/19/19 to Hazel Emily Grierson; c. Leone Rose and June Hazel. Educ: Pa. State Univ, B.S. in Elec. Eng, 17. Polit. & Govt. Pos: Precinct committeeman, Rep. Party, 46-54; cmnr. of jurors, Geauga Co, Ohio, 50-54; mem, Geauga Co. Rep. Exec. Cmt, 50-66; clerk, Newbury Twp, Geauga Co, 52-54; Ohio State Rep, 55-66, chmn. educ. cmt, Ohio House of Rep, 65-66. Bus. & Prof. Pos: Tech. writer, Gen. Elec. Co, 19-26; advert. mgr, Willard Storage Battery Co, 26-40; copy writer, Meldrum & Fewsmith Advert. Agency, 40-44; sales promotion, Nat. Petroleum News, 44-51; owner, Off. Supply Store, 51-57. Mil. Serv: Entered as Pvt, Army Air Force, 17, released as 2nd Lt, 17. Mem: Asn. Nat. Advertisers; Mason (32°); Rotary; bd. trustees, Geauga Commun. Hosp; pres, Geauga Co. Tuberc. Asn. Ohio Man of the Year in Voc. Educ, 63. Rel: Protestant; chmn. bd, Newbury Community Church. Mailing Add: 127 Wilson Mills Rd, Apt. 8, Chardon, Ohio 44024.

BROUILLET, FRANK B. D
Wash. State Rep.
b. Puyallup, Wash, 5/18/28; s. Vern F. Brouillet and Doris Darr B; m. June, 1956 to Marge Ellen Sarsten; c. Marc and Blair. Educ: Col. Puget Sound, B.A, B.E, M.A, 47-51; Univ. Mont, 52; Univ. Wash, Ed.D, 66; Phi Gamma Mu; Phi Delta Kappa; Sigma Chi. Polit. & Govt. Pos: Wash. State Rep, 56-, chmn, Joint House-Senate Interim Cmt. on Educ, Wash. State Legis, 65-, cmnr, Interstate Compact for Educ, 66- Bus. & Prof. Pos: Dir. overseas progs, Am. Heritage Asn, 64-65; asst. coordinator col. rels, Univ. Wash, 65- Mil. Serv: Entered as Pvt, Army, 53, released as Spec. Agent, 55, after serv. in Counter Intel. Corps, Alaska. Publ: 'Coordinator of Higher Education,' Col. of Educ. Record, Univ. Wash, 64; 'International Education,' Wash. Educ, 65. Mem: Pres, Wash. Educ. Asn, 64-65; Mason (32°); Grange; Elks. Rel: Presbyterian. Mailing Add: 619 Seventh Ave. S.W, Puyallup, Wash. 98371.

BROUILLET, HECTOR A. R
b. Chicago, Ill; m. to Ethel K. Starr (deceased), m. 1954 to Lona Schmook B; c. Marijane (Mrs. J. H. DeWeird) by first marriage. Educ: Chicago Kent Col. of Law. Polit. & Gov. Pos: Asst. City Attorney; Chicago Police Dept. Inspector; Trial Attorney; First Asst. and Attorney for the Sanitary Dist. of Chicago; Asst. Attorney Gen; Del. to Rep. Nat. Conv; Rep. precinct Capt. Bus. & Prof. Pos: Lawyer. Mem: 22nd Ward Regular Rep. Club. Rel: McKinley Park Methodist Church. Mailing Add: 3532 S. California Ave, Chicago, Ill. 60632. (1967)

BROUILLETTE, FRANCIS DELORE D
Chmn, Dickinson Co. Dem. Party, Mich.
b. Iron Mountain, Mich, 12/3/31; s. William Brouillette and Julia Groh B; m. 12/26/56 to Pauline Andreini; c. Mary, Joseph, Ann and Lisa. Educ: Marquette Univ, 49-55, B.S. & LL.B; Delta Theta Phi. Polit. & Govt. Pos: City attorney, Iron Mountain, Mich, 58-60; prosecuting attorney, Dickinson Co, 60-; chmn, Dickinson Co. Dem. Party, 61-; Dem. campaign chmn, 68; del, Dem. Nat. Conv, 68. Mil. Serv: Entered as Pvt, Army, 55, released as Pfc 57, after serv. in radio opers, France. Mem: Dickinson Co. and Mich. Bar Asns; Mich. Prosecuting Attorneys Asn; Elks; United Commercial Travelers; bd. dirs, Dickinson Co. Area C. of C; bd. dirs, K. of C. Rel: Catholic. Mailing Add: 507 Quinnesec St, Iron Mountain, Mich. 49801.

BROUN, PAUL C. D
Ga. State Sen.
b. Shellman, Ga, 3/1/16; s. Leroy Augustus Broun and Annie Edwards B; m. 6/16/38 to Gertrude Margaret Beasley; c. Paul Collins Jr, Conway Castleman, and Michael Shannon. Educ: Univ. of Ga, B.S. (AE), 37. Polit. & Govt. Pos: Ga. State Sen, 63- Bus. & Prof. Pos: Merchant. Mil. Serv: Lt. Col, Army Inf, World War II. Mem: Elk; Moose; VFW; DAV; Am. Legion; pres, Athens C. of C, 58. Rel: Episcopal. Mailing Add: 287 W. Broad St, Athens, Ga. 30601. (1967)

BROUSE, ROBERT O. R
Chmn, Union Co. Rep. Cmt, Pa.
b. Mifflinburg, Pa, 6/1/19; s. George M. Brouse and Elsie Erdley B; m. 6/13/38 to Geraldine Logan; c. Dianne, Denise, Robert, Jr. and Eric. Polit. & Govt. Pos: Councilman, Lewisburg, Pa, 54-58; prothonotary and clerk of courts, Union Co, Pa, 58-; chmn, Union Co. Rep. Cmt, 62- Bus. & Prof. Pos: Mgr. meat dept, Acme Mkts, 41-46; owner, meat & grocery store, 46-59. Mem: Susquehanna Econ. Develop. Asn.(pres); Elks; Moose. Rel: Lutheran. Mailing Add: 136 S. Seventh St, Lewisburg, Pa. 17837.

BROUSSARD, J. B. D
La. State Rep.
b. Kaplan, La, 3/16/20; s. Paulite Broussard and Edmay Clostio B; m. 2/5/44 to Gertrude Sellers; c. Vickie (Mrs. Carney), James Keith, Dianne, Gregory, Stephen and Monique. Educ: Univ. Southwest. La, B.S. in Acct, 40; Newman Club. Polit. & Govt. Pos: Field Auditor, Dept. of Revenue, State of La, 40-49; mem, Parole Bd, 60-64; La. State Rep, 68- Bus. & Prof. Pos: Rice mill exec, Broussard Rice Mill, Inc, 49- Mil. Serv: Entered as Pvt, Army, 42, released as Capt, 45, after serv. in S.Am. and Pac. Theatres, 42-45; Res, 45-50, Capt; Philippine Liberation Ribbon with 1 Bronze Serv. Star; Asiatic-Pac. Campaign Medal with 3 Bronze Serv. Stars; Am. Theatre Campaign Medal; Victory Medal. Mem: Rice Millers Asn.(pres); bd. mem, Rice Coun. for Mkt. Develop; Int. Rice Festival (past pres, now bd. mem); Am. Legion (past state comdr); VFW; Amvets; K. of C; Boosters (past pres). Rel: Catholic. Mailing Add: P.O. Box 8, Estherwood, La. 70534.

BROUSSARD, MARCUS ANSON, JR. D
Chmn, Vermilion Parish Dem. Exec. Cmt, La.
b. Abbeville, La, 2/14/29; s. Marcus Anson Broussard and Muriel Alice Brady B; m. 12/27/51 to Barbara Ann Schlesinger; c. Marcus, III, James George, Edward Brady, Catherine Clare, Patricia Ann and Virginia Lynn. Educ: Univ. Southwest. La, B.A, 52; Loyola Univ. of the South, LL.B, 55; Blue Key; Alpha Sigma Nu; St. Thomas More Law Club. Polit. & Govt. Pos: Judge, City Court of Abbeville, La, 58-; chmn, Vermilion Parish Dem. Exec. Cmt, La, 65- Mem: Am. and La. State Bar Asns; Am. Judicature Soc; Kiwanis. Rel: Catholic. Legal Res: Route 1, Box 241, Abbeville, La. 70510. Mailing Add: P.O. Box 7, Abbeville, La. 70510.

BROVERMAN, ROBERT LEE D
Secy-Treas, Shelby Co. Dem. Cent. Cmt, Ill.
b. Pana, Ill, 7/1/31; s. Harry Broverman and Elizabeth Bradach B; single. Educ: Millikin Univ, 49-51; South. Ill. Univ, B.A, 53; Univ. Ill, Urbana, J.D, 57; Tau Kappa Epsilon; Phi Alpha Delta. Polit. & Govt. Pos: Precinct committeeman, Shelby Co. Dem. Cent. Cmt, Ill, 58- and secy-treas, 68-; Asst. Ill. Attorney General, Shelby Co, 61-64; state's attorney, 64-68; master in chancery, Shelby Co. Mem: Ill. State Bar Asn.(pres, Shelby Co. Chap, 63-65 and past secy); Am. Bar Asn; Am. Judicature Soc; Moose; C. of C.(dir, Shelbyville Chap). Rel: Presbyterian. Mailing Add: 123 W. Main St, Shelbyville, Ill. 62565.

BROWDER, EDWARD CARMACK D
b. Wheat, Tenn, 2/11/09; s. William Hamilton Browder and Margaret Billingsley B; m. 12/23/38 to Wilma Lenice Johnston; c. Margaret Anne (Mrs. Lionel Bryon Wilde). Educ: Wheat High Sch, grad, 28. Polit. & Govt. Pos: Chmn, Roane Co. Elec. Cmn, Tenn, 55-; del, Dem. Nat. Conv, 56, 60, 64 & 68; mem, Tenn-Tombigbee Water Develop. Authority, 63- Bus. & Prof. Pos: Pres, Harriman Oil Co, Inc, 36-69, chmn. bd, currently; pres, Harriman Motor Co, Inc, 46-69; chmn. bd, E.Tenn. Motor Co, Inc, 55-69; v.pres. and secy, Browder Bros, Inc, 56-69; pres, Rockwood Motor Co, Inc, 58-69; v.pres, Cent. Fla. Oil Co, Inc, 59-69. Mem: Tenn. Oil Men's Asn. (pres, 59-61); Lions; Ft. Loudoun Yacht Club; Elks; C. of C. Col. Aide de Camp, Governors Frank G. Clement and Buford Ellington, Tenn, Edward T. Breathitt, Ky, Paul B. Johnson and John Bell Williams, Miss. Rel: Methodist; Mem, Off. Bd. and Bd. Trustees, Harriman United Methodist Church. Legal Res: 507 Circle Dr, West Hills, Harriman, Tenn. 37748. Mailing Add: P.O. Box 262, Harriman, Tenn. 37748.

BROWERS, CLYDE EDWARD D
Okla. State Rep.
b. Dill City, Okla, 12/3/19; s. Rev. John Walter Browers and Sally Messick B; m. 12/26/42 to Lucille Ann Moore; c. Deborah Ann. Educ: Okla. State Univ, B.S, 42 & M.S, 54; Phi Beta Kappa. Polit. & Govt. Pos: Okla. State Rep, Dist. 66, 68- Bus. & Prof. Pos: Voc. agr. teacher, Sand Springs High Sch, 48-66; builder-developer, nursing home investor and real estate broker, 66- Mil. Serv: Entered as Pfc, Marines, 42, released as Capt, 45, after serv. in First Corps Med. Tank Bn, S.W. and Cent. Pac, 43-45; Col, Marine Res, 45-; Navy Unit Citation; Three Battle Stars; Purple Heart. Mem: Mason (32°); Shrine; Am. Legion; Rotary; C. of C. Sand Springs Outstanding Citizen Award, 62. Rel: Methodist. Mailing Add: 150 Osage Ridge Dr, Sand Springs, Okla. 74063.

BROWN, AARON CLIFTON, SR. D
b. Murray, Ky, 10/16/11; s. Ed Brown and Minnie Cotham B; m. 3/11/39 to Viria Alice Bell; c. Aaron Clifton, Jr. and Gerald Bell. Educ: Univ. Tenn, 31-33; Cumberland Univ, LL.B, 36; Sigma Delta Kappa; Sigma Nu. Polit. & Govt. Pos: Chmn, Henry Draft Bd, Tenn, 46-; clerk and master, Chancery Court, 47-53; Mayor, Paris, Tenn, 54-59; pres, Tenn. Sixth Constitutional Conv, 65; Tenn. State Sen, 67-68; chancellor, Eighth Chancery Div, Tenn, 68- Mil. Serv: Entered Navy, 44, released as SP/A, 46, after serv. in Pac, 45; Pac-Asiatic Campaign Ribbons. Mem: Am, Tenn. and Paris Bar Asns; Am. Judicature Soc; Am. Trial Lawyers Asn; VFW (past comdr, Post 1889); Lions (past pres, Paris Club); Am. Legion. Rel: Methodist. Mailing Add: 308 W. Washington, Paris, Tenn. 38242.

BROWN, AARON S.
b. Pontiac, Mich, 4/15/13; m. to Dorothy Park; c. Two. Educ: Princeton Univ, B.A, 35; Georgetown Univ. Sch. of For. Serv. Polit. & Govt. Pos: Career officer, U.S. Dept. of State For. Serv, 37-; v.consul, Mexico City, 37-38; with Dept. of State, 38-43; third secy, Dublin, 43-45; second secy, Bogota, 45-47; with Dept. of State, 47-49; asst. to Dir. of Exec. Secretariat, 49-50; spec. asst. to Dep. Under Secy. of State, 50-51; counsr, Bangkok, 51-53; dep. chief of mission, Lisbon, 53-56; dep. dir, Off. of Personnel, 56-58; Dep. Asst. Secy. of State for Personnel, 58-61; Acting Dir. Gen, For. Serv, 61; U.S. Ambassador to Nicaragua, 61-67. Bus. & Prof. Pos: Reporter, Pontiac Daily Press, 36-37. Mailing Add: Lyme, N.H. 03768. (1967). See Addenda.

BROWN, ARCHIE R
b. 1909. Polit. & Govt. Pos: Judge, McCreary Co, Ky, 50-53; Ky. State Rep, 58-68. Bus. & Prof. Pos: Mortician. Mem: Mason; Shrine; Lions; Southeast. Funeral Dirs. Asn. Rel: Methodist. Mailing Add: c/o The Capitol, Frankfort, Ky. 40601. (1967)

BROWN, ARNOLD E. D
b. 1932; m. to Lydia; c. Crystal, Beverly, Dale and Arnold, II. Educ: Bowling Green State Univ; Rutgers Law Sch. Polit. & Govt. Pos: Former N.J. State Assemblyman. Bus. & Prof. Pos: Lawyer. Mem: N.J, Am. and Bergen Co. Bar Asns; Attorney's Soc. of Bergen Co; pres, Bergen Co. NAACP; v.pres, Englewood Urban League; dir, Englewood Soc. Serv. Fedn; Englewood C. of C; dir, N.J. State Fedn. of Realists; Black Lawyers; Nat. Lawyers Asn. Cert. to practice law before U.S. Dist. Court and N.J. Courts. Mailing Add: 383 Knickerbocker, Englewood, N.J. 07631.

BROWN, ARNOLD IRWIN D
b. Queens Co, N.Y, 9/19/21; s. Harry Brown and Lillian Nadell B; m. 12/25/48 to Janice Helen Heller; c. Jeffrey Scott, Wendy Sue and William Harry. Educ: N.Y. Univ, B.A, 45; N.Y. Univ. Law Sch, LL.B, 49. Polit. & Govt. Pos: Committeeman, Twelfth Dem. Assembly Dist, 54-; pres, Franklin Square Dem. Club, 62 & 63, zone leader, 63-64; leader, First Assembly Dem. Assembly Dist, Nassau Co, 64-65; chmn, N.Y. State Legis. Research Cmt, 66-68, cmnr, A.B.C. Bd, 66-68; Dem. leader, West Hempstead and Garden City South, currently; alternate del, Dem. Nat. Conv, 68; cmnr, Alcoholic Beverage Control Bd, Nassau Co, currently. Bus. & Prof. Pos: Attorney, Isidore Halpern, 50-62; partner, Halpern & Brown, 62- Mil. Serv: Entered as Pfc, Army, 46, released as Cpl, 47, after serv. in 63rd Inf, Korea. Mem: Brooklyn Bar Asn.(mem. cmt, Supreme Court for Civil Matters); Nassau Co. Bar Asn.(mem, subcmt, Cmt. Courts); arbitrator, Am. Arbitration Asn; trustee, Franklin Square Libr; past pres, Oakwood Gardens Civic Asn; Elks. Rel: Jewish; past pres, Garden City Jewish Center. Mailing Add: 336 Oxford Blvd. S, Garden City, N.Y. 11530.

BROWN, B. MAHLON D
Majority Floor Leader, Nev. State Sen.
b. Shreveport, La, 1/21/14; s. Bert Mahlon Brown and Pearl Sells B; m. 4/20/38 to Lucille Cummings; c. B. Mahlon, III and Stephen Cummings. Educ: Univ. Calif, Los Angeles, 31-34; George Wash. Univ, LL.B, 37; Sigma Alpha Epsilon. Polit. & Govt. Pos: Justice of Peace, Las Vegas Twp, Nev, 41 & 42; Nev. State Sen, 50-, minority floor leader, Nev. State Sen, 55-65, majority floor leader, 65-, pres-pro-tem, 67-68; Nev. coordinator, Johnson-Humphrey Campaign, 64. Bus. & Prof. Pos: Attorney, Brown & Matteucci, 47- Mil. Serv: Entered as Ens, Navy, 42, released as Lt, 46, after serv. in S.Pac, 44-45. Mem: Am. Judicature Soc; Am, Nev. and Clark Co. Bar Asns; Rotary; Elks; Variety Club; Press Club; Am. Legion; VFW. Rel: Presbyterian. Legal Res: 60 Country Club Lane, Las Vegas, Nev. 89109. Mailing Add: First National Bank Bldg, Suite 904, 302 E. Carson, Las Vegas, Nev. 89101.

BROWN, BASIL W. D
Mich. State Sen.
b. Vandalia, Mich, 3/20/27; m. 6/8/50 to Ermajeanne Seeger; c. Lisa Denise. Educ: West. Mich. Univ, A.B; Univ. of Mich, LL.B. Polit. & Govt. Pos: Mich. State Sen, 56- Bus. & Prof. Pos: Attorney. Mil. Serv: Navy; 3 decorations. Rel: Episcopal. Mailing Add: 43 Connecticut, Highland Park, Mich. 48203. (1967)

BROWN, BEN HILL, JR.
U.S. Ambassador, Liberia
b. Spartanburg, S.C, 2/8/14; s. Ben Hill Brown and Clara Twitty Colcock B; div; c. Ben Hill, III, Barbara Middleton, Clara Colcock and Hardy Bart. Educ: Wofford Col, A.B, 35; George Wash. Univ, J.D, 39. Polit. & Govt. Pos: Asst. to legal adv, Dept. State, 46-49; dep. asst. secy. state, Cong. Rels, 49-55; dir, U.S. Oper. Mission, Iraq and Libya, 56-60; counsul gen, Istanbul, 60-64; U.S. Ambassador, Liberia, 64- Bus. & Prof. Pos: Attorney, 39-41. Mil. Serv: Army, 41-46, Lt. Col. Legal Res: 352 Twin Dr, Spartanburg, S.C. 29302. Mailing Add: American Embassy, P.O. Box 98, Monrovia, Liberia.

BROWN, BENJAMIN D. D
Ga. State Rep.
b. Montezuma, Ga, 11/14/39; s. General Lee Brown, Sr. and Nattie Mitchell B. (deceased); m; c. Benjamin Kennedy. Educ: Clark Col, A.B; Howard Univ, LL.B, 64; nat. v.pres, Am. Law Students Asn, 63-64; Phi Beta Sigma; Sigma Delta Tau. Polit. & Govt. Pos: Mem. exec. cmt, Fulton Co. Dem. Club; v.pres, Fulton Co. Young Dem. Club; mem, Ga. Young Dem. Del, Dem. Nat. Conv, 64; mgr, Horace T. Ward Campaign for Ga. State Senate; mem, All Citizens Registrn. Cmt; Ga. State Rep, 135th Dist, currently; mem, Rules Cmn, Dem. Nat. Cmt; mem. bd. dirs, Atlanta Commun. Coun. Bus. & Prof. Pos: Boys counselor, Butler YMCA, 56-60; recreation staff coordinator, N.Y.C. Welfare Dept, 61; guest lectr, Dartmouth Col. and Harvard Univ, 63; law clerk, Hollowell, Ward, Moore and Alexander, 64; instr. bus. admin, Clark Col; co-founder and v.pres, Wright, Jackson, Brown, Williams, Stephens and Bond, Inc, 69- Mem: Exec. secy, Atlanta Br, NAACP; v.pres, Atlanta Clark Col. Alumni Club; boys work cmt. and Westside Adv. Bd, Butler YMCA; Big Bros. of Am; bd. mem, Grady Homes Boys Club and Girls Club. Young Man of Year, Atlanta Y's Men Club, 65; cited by Clark Col. Faculty for outstanding leadership to Col. and Atlanta Commun, 61; prominent leader in Atlanta Student Movement, 60-61. Rel: Christian Methodist Episcopal. Mailing Add: 250 Mathewson Place, Atlanta, Ga. 30310.

BROWN, BYRON TERRELL 'BUD' D
b. Wichita, Kans, 10/25/29; s. Terrell H. Brown and Maybelle Kendrick B; m. 11/23/50 to Carol Esther Becker; c. Michael and Rhonda Sue. Educ: Wichita Univ; Alpha Gamma Gamma. Polit. & Govt. Pos: Chmn, Custer Co. Dem. Cmt, 64-66. Bus. & Prof. Pos: Res. mgr, world's largest buffalo ranch; pres, Brown Copters, Inc, 58-66 and Big Rock Mt. Corp, 61-63. Mil. Serv: Entered as Pvt, Marine Corps, 46, released as Sgt, 49, after serv. in

2nd Marine Div; Victory Medal; Good Conduct Ribbon. Mem: Dir, S.Dak. Wildlife Fedn, 64-66; pres, Custer C. of C, 63-64; VFW; Am. Legion; Masons; Farmers Union. Commercial pilot. Rel: Protestant. Mailing Add: P.O. Box 306, Gillette, Wyo. 82716. (1967)

BROWN, CHARLES HARRISON D
b. Coweta, Okla, 10/22/20; s. Sherman Brown and Frankie C. Harrison B; m. 9/26/42 to Jean M. Vinyard; c. Ann M. and Robert H. Educ: Drury Col, 37-38; George Wash. Univ, 39; Lambda Chi Alpha; Seven Sages. Polit. & Govt. Pos: U.S. Rep, Mo, 85th and 86th Cong. Bus. & Prof. Pos: Asst. prog. dir, Radio Sta. KWTO, Springfield, Mo, 37-38; radio publicity dir, Mo. Conserv. Cmn, 40; alumni secy, Drury Col, 41-42; acct. exec, Gardner Advert. Co, 43-45; pres, Brown Radio-TV Prod, Inc, Springfield, 45-; partner, Brown Bros. Advert. Agency, Nashville, St. Louis and Springfield, 45-; pres, Charles H. Brown, Inc, Pub. Rels Counselors, 61- Mem: Elks; past pres, Nashville Lions. Rel: Presbyterian. Legal Res: Los Angeles, Calif. Mailing Add: Suite 400, 1250 Connecticut Ave. N.W, Washington, D.C. 20036.

BROWN, CLARENCE EBBERT D
Chmn, Gove Co. Dem. Cent. Cmt, Kans.
b. Fruita, Colo, 8/10/07; s. John Fredrik Brown and Anna Barbra Ebbert B; m. 3/31/38 to Ida May Ashworth; c. Clarice Jean (Mrs. Kruschwitz), Carolyn Mae (Mrs. Regier), Annetta Jane (Mrs. Cowart) and Ruth Eileen. Educ: McPherson Col, 29-31; Ft. Hays Kans. State Col, B.S. in Agr, 38. Polit. & Govt. Pos: Asst. state weed supvr, Gove Co. and State Bd. Agr, Kans, 40-43; conserv. technician, Gove Co. Agr. Stabilization & Conserv. Cmt, 46-47; dist. supvr, Gove Co. Soil Conserv. Dist, 49-56; dir, State Assoc. Soil Conserv. Dist. Supvrs, 50-54; mem, State Soil Conserv. Cmt, 52-56; mem, Gov. Watershed Rev. Bd, 54-56; chmn, Gove Co. Dem. Cent. Cmt, 68-; chmn, Gove Co. Exten. Coun. Mem: Kans. Nurserymans Asn; West. Kans. Develop. Asn; Rotary; High Plains Paint Horse Asn; Kans. Farmers Union; Gove Co. Farm Bur. Asn; Mens Fel. Rel: Church of the Brethren; Mem. Dist. Cabinet, Kans, Nebr. and Colo. Dist; Rep, State C.R.O.P. Bd, Mem, Friendship Acre Cmt. Mailing Add: Box 155, Quinter, Kans. 67752.

BROWN, CLARENCE J, JR. R
U.S. Rep, Ohio
b. Columbus, Ohio, 6/18/27; s. Clarence J. Brown (deceased) and Ethel McKinney B. (deceased); m. 6/11/55 to Joyce Eldridge; c. Elizabeth Ellen (deceased), Clarence J, III, Catherine Helen McKinney and Roy Eldridge. Educ: Duke Univ, B.A. in econ, 47; Harvard Grad. Sch. Bus. Admin, M.B.A, 49; Omicron Delta Kappa; pres, Phi Kappa Sigma. Polit. & Govt. Pos: Mem, Champaign Co. Rep. Exec. Cmt, Ohio, 60-; U.S. Rep, Ohio, 65- and mem, Govt. Opers, For. and Interstate Commerce and Joint Econ. Cmts, U.S. House of Rep. Bus. & Prof. Pos: Ed, Blanchester Star Rep, 49-53; ed. and publisher, Franklin Chronicle, 53-57; ed, Urbana Daily Citizen, 57-65 and publisher, 59-; pres, Brown Publ. Co, 65- Mil. Serv: Entered as A/S, Naval Res, 44, commissioned as Ens, 47, served in Korean War, 51-53, released as Lt.(jg); Am. Defense Medal; Korean Serv. Medal with 2 Battle Stars. Publ: Articles relating to newspaper bus. and govt. Mem: Sigma Delta Chi (pres, Cent. Ohio Prfnl. Chap, 64-65); Nat. Newspaper Asn.(chmn, Govt. Rels. Workshop, 66); Rotary; Farm Bur; C. of C; Boy Scouts; Am. Legion; Mason (33°); Red Cross; Urbana Park Develop. Rel: Presbyterian; Trustee, Nat. Presby. Church. Legal Res: 430 Scioto St, Urbana, Ohio 43078. Mailing Add: 212 Cannon House Office Bldg, Washington, D.C. 20515.

BROWN, CLARK SAMUEL D
V.Chmn, Forsyth Co. Dem. Exec. Cmt, N.C.
b. Roanoke, Va, 6/9/11; s. John Perry Brown and Rosa Clark B; m. 8/21/38 to Macie Brown; c. Clark S, Jr. and John Thomas. Educ: N.Y. City Col, 4 years; Omega Psi Phi. Polit. & Govt. Pos: Del, Dem. Nat. Conv, 64 & 68; v.chmn, Forsyth Co. Dem. Exec. Cmt, N.C, currently. Bus. & Prof. Pos: Pres, Clark Brown & Sons Inc, Winston-Salem, N.C, 30-69. Mem: N.C. and Nat. Funeral Dirs. Asns; Mason; Elks; K. of P; Eastern Star. Rel: Baptist. Legal Res: 1025 N. Cameron Ave, Winston-Salem, N.C. 27101. Mailing Add: 727 N. Patterson Ave, Winston-Salem, N.C. 27101.

BROWN, CLAUDE W. D
b. Coleman Co, Tex, 12/7/04; s. Tom Pinkney Brown and Hattie Hughes B; m. 2/20/26 to Christine McGowan; c. Claudyne Thorp. Educ: Ballinger High Sch. Polit. & Govt. Pos: Del, Dem. State Conv, Tex, 58, 60, 62 & 64, Dem. Nat. Conv, 60 & 64; mem, Tex. State Dem. Exec. Cmt, 60-68; secy, State Indust. Cmt, 64-68, v.chmn, 68; mem, Nat. Cmt. on Harbors and Rivers, 65-, mem, Nat. Petrol. Emergency Bd, 67. Bus. & Prof. Pos: Pres, C.W. Brown Pipe & Supply, Tex, 35-; partner, Brown & Thorp Oil Co, 51-; dir, Tex. Independent Producers & Royalty Owners Asn. and Tex. Mid-Continental Oil & Gas Asn, 60-64; v.pres, Security State Bank, McCamey, 64-; pres, Permian Basin Petroleum Asn, pres, McCamey C. of C. and v.pres, W. Tex. C. of C, 65-; dir, Tex. Mfrs. Asn. and Tex. Good Rd. Asn, 65-; trustee, McMurray Col, 68. Mem: Bd. of Develop, Southern Methodist Univ, 64. Rel: Methodist; Del, Gen. Conf, 64. Mailing Add: Box 1029, McCamey, Tex. 79752.

BROWN, DANIEL R. D
b. Stockbridge, Mich, 3/27/33; s. Kenneth G. Brown and Eva McBride B; m. 8/8/53 to Arlene Powers; c. Garret L, Terise A, Douglas R. and Susan D. Educ: Mich. State Univ, B.A, 54. Polit. & Govt. Pos: Budget exam, Dept. of Admin, Mich, 56-62; dir. licensing div, Mich. Corp. & Securities Cmn, 62-64; exec. asst, Mich. Coun. of State Col. Pres, 64-65; admin. asst. to U.S. Rep. Raymond F. Clevenger, 65-66; budget analyst, Appropriations Cmt, Mich. House of Rep, 67; asst. to dir, Mich. Dept. of Commerce, 67- Mailing Add: 3229 Inverary Dr, Lansing, Mich. 48910.

BROWN, DAVID EMERSON R
V.Chmn, Ill. Rep. State Cent. Cmt.
b. Toledo, Ohio, 1/3/26; s. David Era Brown and Crystal Emerson B; m. 8/19/50 to Marjorie Frey; c. David E, Jr, Judith Anne and Thomas Kiess. Educ: Univ. Ill, Urbana, B.S. in Accounting, 49; Loyola Univ, J.D, 53; Ma Wan Da; Beta Theta Pi. Polit. & Govt. Pos: Area chmn, New Trier Rep. Orgn, 60-64, pres, 60-; founder, Rep. Teens of Ill, 62; v.chmn, mem. exec. cmt. and 13th dist. committeeman, Ill. Rep. State Cent. Cmt, 64-; bd. of gov, United Rep. Fund of Ill, 64-; chmn, Nixon Ticker Tape Parade, Chicago, 68 and Nixon's Mt. Prospect Rally, 68; co-chmn, Finance Cmt. to Elect Richard B. Ogilvie, 68. Bus. & Prof. Pos: Acct, Kamper Ins, New Orleans, La, 49-53, off. mgr, 53-55, asst. counsel, Chicago, Ill, 55-61, asst. gen. counsel, 61-67, assoc. gen. counsel, 67-; asst. secy, Excess Underwriters, Inc, 57- Mil. Serv: Entered as A/S, Navy-Air Force, 44, released as Seaman 2/C, 46, after serv. in V-5 and V-12. Mem: Am. Bar Asn; Pub. Affairs Coun; Glen View Club; Chicago Tennis Patrons, Inc; Ill. Curling Asn; U.S. Men's Curling Asn; The Civic Fedn; C. of C; Int. Ins. Adv. Coun; Chicago Asn. of Commerce & Indust; Nat. Asn. of Mfrs; Nat. Asn. Mutual Ins. Co; Ill. Asn. Mutual Ins. Co. Rel: Methodist. Legal Res: 1209 Greenwood Ave, Wilmette, Ill. 60091. Mailing Add: 4750 Sheridan Rd, Chicago, Ill. 60640.

BROWN, DAVID MILLARD R
Chmn, Pennington Co. Rep. Cmt, Minn.
b. Fergus Falls, Minn, 10/11/18; s. David Lloyd Brown and Elsie Wright B; m. 6/3/41 to Helen Elise Fisher; c. David Lloyd, Helen Eve (Mrs. Donald H. Faes) and Tamara Alexis. Educ: N.Dak. Agr. Col, B.S, 41; Univ. Minn, Minneapolis, M.A, 51; Univ. N.Dak, Ed.D, 57; Phi Delta Kappa. Polit. & Govt. Pos: Secy, Todd Co. Rep. Cmt, Minn, 52-53; pres, Marshall-Pennington Young Rep. League, 58-60; Justice of the Peace, Goodridge, Minn, 58-; chmn, Pennington Co. Rep. Cmt, 68- Bus. & Prof. Pos: Teacher, Wildrose, N.Dak, 41-42; supt, Karlsruhe, N.Dak, 42; elem. prin, Maple Plain, Minn, 46-48; supt. schs, Hewitt, 48-53; secy, Fergus Casket Works, Ind, 50-; supt. schs, Goodridge, Minn, 53- Mil. Serv: Entered as 2nd Lt, Army Air Force, 42, released as 1st Lt, after serv. in Assam Air Depot, China-Burma-India, Upper Assam, 45-46; Res, 46-65, Lt. Col; Theater Medals. Mem: Nat, Minn. and Goodridge Educ. Asn; Phi Delta Kappa; Mason; Am. Legion; VFW; Lions; Farmers Union. Rel: Lutheran. Mailing Add: Goodridge, Minn. 56725.

BROWN, DAVID W. D
b. Evanston, Ill, 8/16/37; s. Lloyd W. Brown and Nancy Coleman B; m. 2/29/64 to Alice Bean; c. Peter Bean. Educ: Princeton Univ, B.A, 59; Univ. Col, Univ. of London, 59-60; Harvard Law Sch, LL.B, 63. Polit. & Govt. Pos: Counsel to U.S. Rep. Edward I. Koch, N.Y, 69- Bus. & Prof. Pos: Assoc. lawyer, Patterson, Belknap & Webb, N.Y.C, 66- Mil. Serv: Entered as 1st Lt, Army Res, 63, released as Capt, 65, after serv. in 562nd Artil, Sixth Missile Bn, West Germany. Mem: Asn. of the Bar of the City of New York; N.Y. and Am. Bar Asns; Princeton Club of New York; Commun. Serv. Soc; Village Independent Dem. Rel: Protestant. Mailing Add: 29 Bethune St, New York, N.Y. 10014.

BROWN, DONALD KENT D
b. San Pedro, Calif, 1/13/30; s. James Brown and Mary Ann Stafford B; m. 8/18/59 to Carol Anne Collins; c. Shawn Kevin and Shannon Kent. Educ: Orange Coast Col, A.A, 58; San Diego State Col, B.A, 61; life mem, Alpha Gamma Sigma; Pi Kappa Alpha. Polit. & Govt. Pos: Asst. state treas, Calif, 62-67; alternate del, Dem. Nat. Conv, 68. Bus. & Prof. Pos: V.pres. and dir, govt. rels, Unionamerica Inc, 67- Mil. Serv: Entered as Recruit, Army, 51, released as Cpl, 52, after serv. in First Cavalry Div, Korea; Korean Serv. Medal with Three Bronze Stars; Combat Infantryman Badge; UN Serv. Medal; Army of Occup. Medal, Japan. Mem: Am. Acad. Polit. & Soc. Sci; Am. Soc. Pub. Admin; Elks. Award for Meritorious Serv, Los Angeles City Coun. Rel: Protestant. Mailing Add: 3539 Carolina St, San Pedro, Calif. 90731.

BROWN, DONALD MacRAE D
b. Walla Walla, Wash, 10/26/17; s. Ben Forrest Brown and Margaret Katherine MacRae B; m. 7/26/46 to Marcia French; c. Duncan MacRae, Christopher Mark, Ross MacRae, Gregory Scott, Lesley Margaret, Margaret Katherine MacRae, Donald MacRae, Jr. Educ: Wash. State Univ, B.A. with honors, 39-43; M.A, 45-47; Alpha Kappa Psi; Kappa Sigma. Polit. & Govt. Pos: Admin. Asst, Rep. Hansen, Wash. Bus. & Prof. Pos: Pub. info. officer, Wash. State Dept. of Hwys, 51-62; research economist, State Legis, Olympia, Wash, 47-51. Mil. Serv: Army, Sgt, 42-45, served in ETO; Awarded Purple Heart. Legal Res: Olympia, Wash. Mailing Add: 2011 R.I. Ave, McLean, Va. 22101. (1967)

BROWN, DWIGHT A. R
Co. Cmnr. & Chmn, Hancock Co. Rep. Party, Maine
b. Ellsworth, Maine, 7/29/18; s. Leon H. Brown and Alta Quinn B; m. 11/8/41 to Lois A. Buckley; c. Holly A, Bonnie A. and Dwight Adams. Educ: Univ. Maine, 38-39; Franklin and Marshall Col, 39-40. Polit. & Govt. Pos: Maine State Rep, 57-60; Maine State Sen, 61-67; co. cmnr. & chmn, Hancock Co. Rep. Party, 69- Bus. & Prof. Pos: Ins. exec. Mem: Independent Ins. Agents Asn. Mailing Add: 67 Main St, Ellsworth, Maine 04605.

BROWN, EARLE V. R
b. Malden, Mass, 10/11/05; m. to Mary Jenks Johnstone; c. three sons; three daughters. Educ: Black River High Sch. Polit. & Govt. Pos: Vt. State Rep, 65-66. Bus. & Prof. Pos: Sch. bus driver. Rel: Protestant. Mailing Add: P.O. Box 8, Plymouth Union, Vt. 05057. (1967)

BROWN, EDGAR ALLAN D
S.C. State Sen.
b. Aiken Co, S.C, 7/11/88; s. Augustus Abraham Brown and Elizabeth Howard B; m. 12/30/13 to Annie Love Sitgreaves B; c. Emily (Mrs. R.M. Jeffries, Jr). Educ: Clemson Col, LL.D; Med. Col. S.C, L.H.D, 64. Polit. & Govt. Pos: Court stenographer, Second Circuit, S.C, 08-18; Col. on Gov. Cooper's staff; chmn, Co. Dem. Exec. Cmt. and mem, State Dem. Exec. Cmt, 14-; S.C. State Rep. & pres. pro tem, S.C. House of Rep, 21-26; state chmn, Dem. Exec. Cmt, 22-26 and 52-53; Dem. Nat. Exec. committeeman; del-at-lg, Dem. Nat. Conv, 24, 32, 40, 44, 48, 52, 56, 60, 64 & 68; Cand. for U.S. Sen, 26 & 38; S.C. State Sen, 29- Bus. & Prof. Pos: Lawyer and businessman. Mem: Past chmn. bd. of mgrs, Coun. of State Govts. Mailing Add: Box 248, Barnwell, S.C. 29812.

BROWN, EDMUND GERALD D
b. San Francisco, Calif, 4/21/05; s. Edmund Joseph Brown and Ida Schuckman B; m. 10/30/30 to Bernice Layne; c. Barbara (Mrs. Charles Edward Casey), Cynthia (Mrs. Joseph Kelly), Edmund Gerald, Jr. and Kathleen (Mrs. George Rice). Educ: San Francisco Col. Law, LL.B, 27; sr. class pres. Hon. LL.D, Univ. San Francisco, 59, Univ. Santa Clara and Univ. San Diego, 61; hon. D.C.L, Calif. Col. Med, 64; hon. L.H.D, Univ. Judaism, 65. Polit. & Govt. Pos: Dist. Attorney, San Francisco, 43-50; Attorney Gen, Calif, 50-58, Gov, 58-66. Bus. & Prof. Pos: Partner, Ball, Hunt, Hart and Brown, Beverly

Hills, Calif, currently. Mem: Adv. cmt, Who's Who in Am. Politics; Calif. State Bar; Am. and San Francisco Bar Asns; chmn, Nat. Cmn. Reform of Fed. Criminal Laws; President's Cmn. on Income Maintenance Progs; fel, Am. Col. Trial Lawyers; Elks; Native Sons of Golden West; Moose; Eagles. Rel: Catholic. Mailing Add: Ball, Hunt, Hart and Brown, 9418 Wilshire Blvd, Beverly Hills, Calif. 90212.

BROWN, EDMUND GERALD, JR. D
Mem, Calif. Dem. State Cent. Cmt.
b. San Francisco, Calif, 4/7/38; s. Edmund Gerald Brown and Bernice Layne B; single. Educ: Univ. Santa Clara, 55-60; Univ. Calif, Berkeley, B.A, 61; Yale Univ. Law Sch, LL.B, 64; Inst. Mexicano Norteamericano de Rels. Culturales, 65. Polit. & Govt. Pos: Law clerk, Justice Matthew O. Tobriner, Calif. Supreme Court, 64-65; private investment consult, Chile-Calif. Prog, Santiago, 66; mem, Calif. Narcotics Rehabilitation Adv. Coun, 66-; del, Dem. Nat. Conv, 68; mem, Calif. Dem. State Cent. Cmt, 68-; mem, Los Angeles Co. Crime Cmn, 69-; trustee, Los Angeles Commun. Cols, 69- Mem: Calif. State and Los Angeles Co. Bar Asns. Los Angeles March of Dimes Cert. of Appreciation, 69. Mailing Add: 609 S. Grand Ave, Los Angeles, Calif. 90017.

BROWN, EDWARD G. D
Ky. State Rep.
b. 1920. Educ: West. State Col. Polit. & Govt. Pos: State dir. of recreation, Ky, 59-60; Ky. State Rep, 64- Bus. & Prof. Pos: Land and home developer. Mil. Serv: Air Force, World War II. Mem: Am. Legion; Optimist Club. Rel: Baptist. Mailing Add: 301 Morgantown Rd, Bowling Green, Ky. 42101. (1967)

BROWN, ELEANOR MAE R
V.Chmn, Los Angeles Co. Rep. Cent. Cmt, Calif.
b. Baton Rouge, La, 8/5/06; d. Joseph Harmon Daigre and Adeline Mitchell D; m. 2/3/30 to Chester Brown (deceased 9/1/65); c. Eleanor Mae, II. Educ: Southern Univ, Baton Rouge, La, 3 years. Polit. & Govt. Pos: Crew leader, Bur. Census, U.S. Govt, 40-; supvr. women, U.S. Naval Sta, Terminal Island, 44-49; foster parent, Los Angeles Co, Calif, 49-; organizer, Brown's Youth Center, Watts, Calif, 43-51; notary public, Los Angeles, Co, 49-; precinct chmn, 21st Cong. Precinct, Rep. Cent. Cmt, Los Angeles Co, 54-58; chmn, 64-68; pres. and organizer, Rep. Women's Fedn. Club, Los Angeles, 56-60; v.chmn, Los Angels Co. Rep. Cent. Cmt, 69-; mem, Mayor's Commun. Adv. Cmt, Los Angeles. Mem: Grand chmn, Bus. & Prfnl. Womens, Knights & Daughters of Labor, Ariz-Calif, 66-; chief perceptress, New Beulah Tabernacle 2 C.P, Los Angeles, 60-; chmn, Ad Hoc Cmt. for Retarded; mem. and past Grand Matron, Eastern Star; Household of Ruth; PTA (past pres, elem, jr. high and high sch PTA); Fedn. Negro Women; West Side Fedn. Women's Club; Cent. Ave. Fedn. Club; Neighborhood Club Parliamentarian. Cert. of Appreciation, War Finance Cmt. War Bond Sales, 45; Civilian Employee Award, U.S. Navy, 45; Cert. of Appreciation, Eisenhower-Nixon South. Calif. Cmt, 56; Meritorious Commun. Serv. Award, City of Los Angeles, 67. Rel: Protestant. Mailing Add: 906 E. 82nd St, Los Angeles, Calif. 90001.

BROWN, ERNEST EUGENE R
b. Clarksville, Tenn, 10/19/34; s. William Brady Brown and Lucy Elinor Moorefield B; m. 8/17/63 to Barbara Rose Kauth; c. Evan Richard. Educ: Paducah Jr. Col, 54; Murray State Col, 55-56; Univ. Ky, B.S. in Civil Eng, 59; Sigma Chi. Polit. & Govt. Pos: Treas, McCracken Co. Young Rep. Club, Ky, 65-67, chmn, 68-69, dir, 69-; Lone Oak 1 Precinct capt, John S. Cooper Campaign, 66; chmn, McCracken Co. Rep. Gubernatorial Campaign, 67; chmn, McCracken Co. Rep. Exec. Cmt, 68-69. Mil. Serv: Entered as Ens, Coast and Geodetic Surv, 59, released as Lt.(jg), 61, after serv. in U.S. Mem: Assoc. mem, Am. Soc. Civil Engrs; Nat. Soc. Prfnl. Engrs; v.pres, Ky. Lake Chap, Ky. Soc. Prfnl. Engrs, 68-69, pres, 69-; Lutheran Layman's League; nat. Rep. sustaining mem, Ky. Young Rep. Fedn; Young Am. for Freedom; Free Soc. Asn. Rel: Lutheran. Mailing Add: 4007 Court Ave, Paducah, Ky. 42001.

BROWN, FRANK D
N.Mex. State Rep.
b. Buncombe Co, N.C, 11/19/24; s. Arnold Bly Brown (deceased) and Velma G. Meadows B; m. 7/3/44 to Mary Lois Brown B; c. Sandra Kay and Lloyd Wayne. Educ: High Sch. Polit. & Govt. Pos: N.Mex. State Rep, 65- Mem: IAMAW, Rel: Baptist. Mailing Add: 604 N. Fifth St, Carlsbad, N.Mex. 88220.

BROWN, FRED R
b. 1905. Polit. & Govt. Pos: Mem, Wilmington City Coun, Del, 33-53; Del. State Rep, 67-68. Mem: Elks; B'nai B'rith. Mailing Add: 109 W. 34th St, Wilmington, Del. 19802. (1967)

BROWN, FRED JAMES D
Chmn, Henry Co. Dem. Cent. Cmt, Ill.
b. Victoria, Ill, 2/5/13; s. James Lewis Brown and Emma Josephine Johnson B; c. Gail Lynn and Fred J, Jr. Educ: Ill. Wesleyan Univ, 32-34; Chicago Kent Col. Law, LL.B, 37; Pi Kappa Delta; Chicago Kent Round Table; Soc. Chicago Kent Honor Men. Polit. & Govt. Pos: City cmnr, Kewanee, Ill, 43-45, mayor, 45-50, city attorney, 55-; asst. attorney gen, State of Ill, 60-; chmn, Henry Co. Dem. Cent. Cmt, 60-; city attorney, Geneseo, 62-65; mem, Ill. Dem. Cent. Cmt, currently. Bus. & Prof. Pos: Gen. practice law, 37-; dir, Kewanee Nat. Bank, Ill, 55-; attorney, Kewanee Commun. Unit Sch. Dist. 230, 59-; dir, Blake's Shoe Co, 60-; attorney, Kewanee Airport Authority, 64- Mil. Serv: Entered as Pvt, Army, 43, released as Sgt, 45, after serv. in Judge Adv. Gen. Dept; recalled to active serv, 50 as Capt, Camp Carson, Colo, released 52; Meritorious Conduct Medal; ETO Ribbon; Victory Medal; five Bronze Stars. Mem: Henry Co. Bar Asn; Ill. Bar Asn; Elks; past pres, Rotary; past comdr, VFW; Am. Legion. Rel: Methodist. Legal Res: 520 Fullerton Court, Kewanee, Ill. 61443. Mailing Add: 110½ W. Second St, Kewanee, Ill. 61443. (1967)

BROWN, GARRY ELDRIDGE R
U.S. Rep, Mich.
b. Kalamazoo, Mich, 8/12/23; s. E. Lakin Brown and Blanche Jackson B; m. 9/10/55 to Frances Esther Wilkins; c. Frances Esther, Mollie Earl, Amelia Logan and Abigail Victoria. Educ: Kalamazoo Col, A.B, 51; George Wash. Univ. Law Sch, LL.B, 54. Hon. degree, Doctor of Humanities, Lawrence Inst. of Tech, 64. Polit. & Govt. Pos: U.S. Cmnr, U.S. Dist. Court for the West. Dist. of Mich, 57-62; del, Mich. Constitutional Conv, 62; Mich. State Sen, 21st Dist, 62-67; U.S. Rep, Mich, 67- Bus. & Prof. Pos: Partner, law firm of Ford, Kriekard, Brown & Staton, 54-67. Mil. Serv: Entered as Pvt, Army, 46, released as 2nd Lt, 47, after serv. in 24th Inf. Div. Mem: Am, Mich. State and Kalamazoo Co. Bar Asns; Am. Legion; Elks. Lettered in football, baseball and basketball at Kalamazoo Col, 48-51. Rel: Presbyterian. Mailing Add: 321 W. Eliza, Schoolcraft, Mich. 49087.

BROWN, GEORGE A. R
b. Tonopah, Nev, 9/25/17; s. Charles Brown and Stella Fairbanks B; m. 5/30/40 to Adah Virginia Herrick; c. George A, Jr, Stanton H, Nancy Virginia and Lucia Louise. Educ: Univ. Calif, Berkeley, B.S, 40; Stanford Univ, J.D, 48; Theta Delta Chi; Phi Phi; Golden Bear; Polit. & Govt. Pos: Kern Co. campaign chmn, Nixon for Pres, 60, Shell for Gov, 62 and Goldwater for Pres, 64; del, Rep. Nat. Conv, 64; mem, Calif. State Bd. Educ, 68; judge, Calif. Superior Court, Kern Co, 69- Bus. & Prof. Pos: Attorney at Law. Mil. Serv: Entered as 2nd Lt, Army, 41, released as Maj, 45, after serv. in Alaska Defense Command; U.S. and ETO; Bronze Star; Pac. & ETO Ribbons; Order of Brit. Empire. Mem: Am. and Calif. Bar Asns. Rel: Episcopal. Mailing Add: 6604 Mt. Hood Dr, Bakersfield, Calif. 93309.

BROWN, GEORGE EDWARD, JR. D
U.S. Rep, Calif.
b. Holtville, Calif, 3/6/20; s. George Edward Brown and Bird Alma Kilgore B; m. to Rowena Somerindyke. Educ: Univ. Calif. at Los Angeles, B.S, 40. Polit. & Govt. Pos: Mayor and councilman, Monterey Park, Calif, 54-58; Calif. State Assemblyman, 59-62; U.S. Rep, Calif, 63-; alternate del, Dem. Nat. Conv, 68. Bus. & Prof. Pos: Eng. personnel, Dept. of Water and Power, Los Angeles, Calif, 47-57; exec. secy, Engrs. & Architects Asn, 57-58. Mil. Serv: Entered as Pvt, Army, 44, released as 2nd Lt, 46. Mem: Adult Educ. Asn; Am. Soc. Pub. Admin; S.Calif. Pub. Personnel Asn; Urban League; IBEW; Kiwanis; Am. Legion; Amvets; G.I. Forum; Friends Cmt. on Legis; Commun. Serv. Orgn; Mexican-Am. Polit. Asn; C. of C. Rel: Methodist. Legal Res: Monterey Park, Calif. 91754. Mailing Add: House of Representatives, Washington, D.C. 20515.

BROWN, GEORGE HAY R
Dir, Bur. of the Census, Dept. of Commerce
b. Denver, Colo, 2/4/10; s. Orville G. Brown and Clara Topping B; m. 6/11/32 to Catherine Smith (deceased); c. Ann Catherine. Educ: Oberlin Col, A.B, 29; Harvard Univ, M.B.A, 31; Univ. Chicago, Ph.D, 45; Delta Sigma Pi. Polit. & Govt. Pos: Consult, War Prod. Bd, 43; dir, Bur. of the Census, Dept. of Commerce, currently. Bus. & Prof. Pos: Divisional sales mgr, Mallin ckrodt Chem. Works, St. Louis, Mo, 31-36; mkt. consult, Armour & Co, Chicago Tribune, Gen. Mills, Inc, Toni Div, Gillett, Inc, Motorola and others, 37-54; instr-prof. mkt, Univ. Chicago, 47-, dir. develop, Biol. Phys. and Soc. Sci. Div, Sch. Soc. Serv. and Sch. Bus, 48-50, dir, Bus. Probs. Bur, 50-54; mgr-dir, Mkt. Research Off, Ford Motor Co, Dearborn, Mich, 54-69. Publ: International Economic Position of New Zealand, Univ. Chicago Press, 46; Readings in Marketing From Fortune, Holt, 53; 'Brand Loyalty: Fact or Fiction,' Advert. Age, 51. Mem: Past mem. exec. cmt, Nat. Mkt. Adv. Cmt, U.S. Dept. of Commerce and Adv. Research Found; past trustee, Mkt. Sci. Inst. and Found. for Research on Human Behavior; past mem, research cmt, Better Bus. Bur. Research and Educ. Found; Am. Mkt. Asn.(past pres); Am. Statist. Asn; affil. by invitation, Consumer Div, Am. Psychol. Asn; Beta Gamma Sigma; Chikaming Country Club, Lakeside, Mich. Rel: Presbyterian. Legal Res: Lakeside, Mich. Mailing Add: Bureau of the Census, Washington, D.C. 20233.

BROWN, GEORGE R. D
Dem. State Cent. Committeeman, Conn.
b. Albany, N.Y. 11/10/12; s. Edmund L. Brown and Katherine L. Hardt B; m. 2/5/38 to Anita Virginia Gustaferri; c. Kathryn Virginia, George R, Jr, and Sara Margaret. Educ: Univ. Pa, B.S. in Econ, 34; N.Y. Univ, M.B.A, 47; Delta Phi Alpha. Polit. & Govt. Pos: Asst. dist. supvr. and personnel supvr, Nat. Youth Admin, Binghamton-Albany, N.Y, 38-41; Dem. town chmn, Brookfield, Conn, 58-66, mem, Brookfield Bd. of Finance, 60-; Dem. State Cent. Committeeman, 32nd Sen. Dist, Conn, 66-; expert exam, N.Y. State Civil Serv. Cmn, 66-; cand, Conn. State Sen, 32nd Dist, 68. Bus. & Prof. Pos: Indust. engr, West. Elec, 41-49; instr, Seton Hall Univ, 49-50; mgr. wage and salary, Am. Air Lines, 49-56; employ. mgr-compensation specialist, McGraw-Hill, Inc, 56-68; owner, Retail Bus, 68- Rel: Roman Catholic. Mailing Add: S. Mountain Rd, Brookfield, Conn. 06804.

BROWN, GLENN WILLIAM D
b. Clyde, N.C, 2/27/26; s. Glenn Dephew Brown and Mary Torrence B; m. 4/12/52 to Evelyn Myralyn Davis; c. Glenn W. 'Bill' Jr. and Robert H. Educ: Mars Hill Col, Liberal Arts Cert, 44; Wake Forest Univ, LL.B, 49. Polit. & Govt. Pos: Mem, Haywood Co. Bd. Elec, 51-52, chmn, 52-54; pres, Haywood Co. Young Dem. Club; West Regional Organizer, Young Dem. Club, 54; solicitor, Haywood Co. Recorders Court, 58-59; superior court solicitor, 20th Solicitorial Dist, 59-66; del, Dem. Nat. Conv, 68. Bus. & Prof. Pos: Partner, Law Firm, Morgan, Ward & Brown, currently. Mil. Serv: Army Air Force, 44-46, Sgt. Mem: Am. Legion; AF&AM; AASR (32°); Shrine; sustaining mem. Boy Scouts (orgn. rep, 67-68); N.C. Bar Asn; Haywood Co. Bar Asn.(secy, pres); Am. Judicature Soc; Phi Alpha Delta; 30th Judicial Dist. Bar Asn.(v.pres, 68-69, bar cand. cmt.); chmn, construction of new children's home, West. Home Cmt, 67-; bd. trustees, N.C. Baptist Children's Home, Inc, 67-; dir, Waynesville United Fund; PTA (pres, Waynesville Jr. High, 68-69, pres, Waynesville Elem. Sch, 67-68). Distinguished Serv. Award, U.S. Jr. C. of C, 54; Young Man of the Year Waynesville, 53. Rel: Baptist; Chmn. and Mem. Bd. Deacons, 3 years, Gen. Sunday Sch. Supt; Sunday Sch. Teacher, First Baptist Church Waynesville; Mem. Gen. Bd, N.C. Baptist Conv, 59. Mailing Add: 240 Highland Rd, Waynesville, N.C. 28786.

BROWN, GLORIA RUTH R
Chmn, Citizens-by-Choice Cmt, Rep. State Cent. Cmt, Calif.
b. San Francisco, Calif, 5/22/28; d. Mervyn David Silbersten and Lillian Ruth Swanson S; div; c. Deborah (Mrs. Lee Stevens) and David. Educ: Univ. of Pac, 1 year; Modesto Jr. Col, ½ year. Polit. & Govt. Pos: Capt, Palo Alto Precinct Orgn, Calif, 52-; v.pres, Palo Alto Young Rep, 61-63; co. chmn, New Citizens Cmt, Santa Clara Co. Young Rep, 62-64; new citizens chmn, Palo Alto Calif. Rep. Assembly, 62-64; chmn, New Citizens Cmt, Palo Alto Rep. Women Fed-

erated, 62-64 and Palo Alto New Citizens Cmt, 62-; v.chmn, Nationalities Cmt, Rep. State Cent. Cmt, Calif, 65-66, chmn, Citizen-by-Choice Cmt, 67- and secy, Ethnic and Nationalities Exec. Cmt, 69-; chmn, Citizens-by-Choice Cmt, Santa Clara Co. Cent. Cmt, 66-; North. Calif. coordinator of nationality groups, United Citizens for Nixon-Agnew, 68; mem, Nationalities Dirs. Cmt, Rep. Nat. Cmt, 68- Bus. & Prof. Pos: Owner, Troutmere Lodge, La Honda, Calif, 55-59. Rel: Religious Science Methodist. Mailing Add: 1766 Fulton St, Palo Alto, Calif. 94303.

BROWN, GRUNDY MORTIMORE R
b. Rich Hill, Mo, 10/22/00; s. George Mithro Brown and Elsie Louella Fenton B; m. 2/21/23 to Ruby June Baggerly; c. Robert J, Norma Jean (Mrs. H. E. Ted Montgomery) and George Richard. Educ: High sch. and bus. col, 5 years. Polit. & Govt. Pos: Idaho State Rep, 60-69; chmn, Transportation & Defense Cmt; mem, Ins. Finance and Banking Cmt, Appropriations, Pub. Insts. and State Affairs Cmts. Bus. & Prof. Pos: Pres, Idaho State Transportation Asn, 52-54. Mem: Farm Bur; C. of C; Rotary; Elks; Masons (past master); Scottish Rite; KCCH (32°); York Rite; Shrine. Rel: Disciples of Christ. Mailing Add: 724 17th Ave. South, Nampa, Idaho, 83651.

BROWN, H. ROSS D
Educ: Univ. Tenn, 49; Purdue Univ, 57. Polit. & Govt. Pos: Ind. State Rep, until 66. Bus. & Prof. Pos: Voc. agr. teacher, W. Wash. High Sch. Mil. Serv: Navy. Mem: Odd Fellows; Masons; Lions Club; Am. Legion; prof. teachers' orgns. Rel: Methodist. Mailing Add: R.R. 2, Campbellsburg, Ind. 47108.

BROWN, H. RUSSELL R
b. St. Paul, Minn, 8/29/03; s. William H. Brown and Anna Herr B; m. 3/1/24 to Ruth Carroll; c. Dr. Russell T, Carroll (Mrs. Richard Guddal), Virginia (Mrs. Gerald E. Tracy), Connie (Mrs. Earle Kinsman), Patricia (Mrs. James D. Hanson), James W. and Mary (Mrs. Jack R. Cunningham). Educ: Univ. Minn, Minneapolis, B.S, B.M. and M.D, 27; Phi Rho Sigma. Polit. & Govt. Pos: Supt, Codington Co. Bd. of Health, S.Dak, 37-; del, S.Dak. State Rep. Conv, 64, 66 & 68; del, Nat. Rep. Conv, 68. Bus. & Prof. Pos: Clin. assoc, Univ. S.Dak. Med. Sch. Mem: Am. Col. Surgeons (past pres, S.Dak. Chap); Am. Bd. Abdominal Surg; Int. Col. Surgeons; Watertown Dist. Med. Soc.(past pres); S.Dak. State Med. Asn.(past pres, 48); Am. Med. Asn.(S.Dak. del, 46-54, chmn. cmt. lay-sponsored vol. health plans, 50-58, cmn. on med. care plans and chmn. cmt. miscellaneous and unclassified plans, 54-59, mem. cmt. ins. and prepayment plans, 58-69 and chmn, 63-68, cmt. to study internships, 52-53, adv. cmt. to bd. trustees, 54); St. Ann and Mem. Hosp. Med. Staffs (past pres); Int. Platform Asn; Nat. Asn. Blue Shield Plans (prfnl. rels. cmt); S.Dak. Develop. Cmn; bd. dirs, S.Dak. Med. Sch. Endowment Fund; past pres, N.Cent. Med. Conf; S.Dak. Pub. Health Asn.(past pres); S.Dak. Blue Shield Plan (bd. dirs, 61-, pres, 65-68); C. of C.(past pres); Rotary (past pres). Recipient of first S.Dak. Distinguished Serv. Award by S.Dak. State Med. Asn, 52. Rel: Roman Catholic. Legal Res: 820 N. Broadway, Watertown, S.Dak. 57201. Mailing Add: 506 First Ave. S.E, Watertown, S.Dak, 57201.

BROWN, HARLOW BILLINGS D
b. Loda Twp, Reno Co, Kans, 4/10/89; s. Willis L. Brown and Sadie J. Blake B; m. 8/27/11 to Amanda Cathern Poff; c. Robert W. Educ: High Sch. Polit. & Govt. Pos: City councilman, Langdon, Kans, 34-36; precinct committeeman, Reno Co. Dem. Cmt, 52-56, co. chmn, 56-60; former Kans. State Rep, 75th Dist. and 102nd Dist. Mem: Masons; Hutchinson C. of C; Reno Co. Chap, Am. Asn. Retired Persons. Rel: United Presbyterian. Mailing Add: 802 W. 20th, Hutchinson, Kans. 67501.

BROWN, HOYTE G, JR. R
b. Wallingford, Conn, 11/18/35; s. Hoyte G. Brown, Sr. and Martha B; m. 1/28/56 to Mary Jane Sanelli; c. Laurie A, David S. and Donald H. Educ: West Haven, High Sch, Conn, grad, 54. Polit. & Govt. Pos: Mem, North Branford Rep. Town Cmt, 64-69, chmn, 68; Justice of the Peace, North Branford, 66-69. Bus. & Prof. Pos: Owner and mgr, Hoyte Brown Agency. Mil. Serv: Entered as A/3C, Air Force, 54, released as S/Sgt, 58, after serv. as Basic Training Instr. Mem: New Haven Life Underwriters Asn.(pres, 68-69); pres, North Branford Friendship Bowling League; coach, North Branford Little League. Rel: Catholic; V.chmn, St. Monica Church Coun. Mailing Add: Woodvale Drive, Northford, Conn. 06472.

BROWN, IDA BALDWIN R
b. Burrillville, R.I, 7/27/99; d. Fred Baldwin and Alice Fuller Foster B; m. 22/11/26 to John Credifer Brown, III; wid; c. Janet B.(Mrs. John Wright Morton, III). Educ: Woonsocket Commercial Sch; Brown Univ. Exten. Courses, German & Italian; Acad. Polit. Sci, Columbia Univ. Polit. & Govt. Pos: Conn. State Rep, 59-67. Bus. & Prof. Pos: Herbalist, Herb Gardens, Old Sturbridge Village, Mass, 55-66. Publ: Herb Chart, Old Sturbridge Village. Mem: Pres, Conn. Order of Women Legislators; Herb Soc. of Am. and Conn. Unit; Royal Horticulture Soc. of England; Episcopal Women's Club. Rel: Episcopal; pres, Episcopal Church Women, Vestry, Christ Church, Pomfret, Conn. Mailing Add: Pomfret Center, Conn. 06259.

BROWN, J. MARSHALL D
Dem. Nat. Committeeman, La.
b. 1924; m. to Ellen McInnis; c. 1. Polit. & Govt. Pos: La. State Rep, 52-60; campaign mgr. and chmn, finance cmt. for elec. of Gov. John J. McKeithen; La. campaign mgr. for President Johnson, 64; mem. and pres, La. State Bd. of Educ, 62-; Dem. nat. committeeman, La, currently; del, Dem. Nat. Conv, 68. Bus. & Prof. Pos: Pres, Marshall Brown Ins. Agency, Inc. Mem: President's Club; Nat. Capital Dem. Club; Plimsoll Club of New Orleans. Mailing Add: Suite 2420, 225 Baronne St, New Orleans, La. 70110. (1967)

BROWN, J. WALTER D
Miss. State Rep.
b. Natchez, Miss, 2/9/39; s. John Walter Brown and Rose Martello B; m. 8/31/63 to Joan Elizabeth Hicks; c. Walter Jeffrey, Patrick Kevin and Melissa Lynn. Educ: Univ. Miss, B.A, 63; Univ. Miss. Law Sch, J.D, 65; Claiborne Soc; Phi Delta Phi. Polit. & Govt. Pos: Legis. asst, Congressman John Bell Williams, 62; Miss. State Rep, 68-, mem, Joint Legis. Study Comn. on Ins, Miss. State Legis, 68-; mem, Law Enforcement Cmn, State of Miss, 69- Bus. & Prof. Pos: Instr. polit. sci, Univ. South. Miss, 65-69; attorney-at-law, 65- Mil. Serv: Entered as Seaman Recruit, Navy, 57, released as Yeoman 3/C, 59, after serv. in Staff, Comdr. Serv. Squadron Four, Res, 59-62. Publ: 'On University of Mississippi,' Student, 62. Mem: Am. and Miss. Bar Asns; Am. Judicature Soc; K. of C; bd. dirs, Adams Co. Ment. Health Asn. Rel: Catholic. Legal Res: 3704 Eastbrook Rd, Natchez, Miss. 39120. Mailing Add: 114 S. Wall St, Box 1047, Natchez, Miss. 39120.

BROWN, JACK ALBERT D
Ariz. State Rep.
b. St. Johns, Ariz, 5/2/29; s. Joseph Albert Brown and Elda Whiting B; m. 6/26/53 to Anna Vee Smithson; c. David, Norman, Cynthia, Douglas, Carol, Michael and Janna. Educ: Brigham Young Univ, B.A, 54. Polit. & Govt. Pos: Chmn, Apache Co. Fair, 60- and Rural Area Develop. Cmt, 61-; Ariz. State Rep, Third Dist, 62- Bus. & Prof. Pos: Pres, Lyman Water Co, 55-57, v.pres, 63-; pres, J. Albert Brown Ranches, Inc, 61- Mem: Kiwanis. Rel: Latter-day Saint. Mailing Add: Box 220, St. Johns, Ariz. 85936.

BROWN, JAMES EDWARD R
b. Hardin Co, Tenn, 11/16/22; s. Dewey Dixon Brown and Myrtle Tucker B; m. 5/18/48 to Betty Weatherford; c. Cherry Ann and Martha Jane. Educ: Univ. Tenn; Miss. State Univ, B.S; Alpha Tau Alpha. Polit. & Govt. Pos: Chmn, Hardin Co. Rep. Cmt, Tenn, 61-65. Bus. & Prof. Pos: State mgr, WOW, 65-, dist. mgr, 54-65. Mil. Serv: Entered as Pvt, Air Force, 43, released as S/Sgt, 45, after serv. in Attack Bomber Group, S.W. Pac, 45; Good Conduct Medal; Air Medal; Purple Heart; S.W. Pac, New Guinea, Philippines and Okinawa Campaign Ribbons. Mem: WOW; DAV; Fraternal Cong. Rel: Methodist. Mailing Add: 5754 Cheena, Houston, Tex. 77035. (1967)

BROWN, JAMES ELMER R
Chmn, Box Elder Co. Rep. Party, Utah
b. Falconer, N.Y, 9/22/27; s. Joseph Sanford Brown and Charity B; m. 3/29/57 to Gloria Gayle Gay; c. C. Richard, C. David, Jennifer Gayle, Christopher James and Kimberly Ann. Educ: Univ. Maine, 49-50; Ricker Jr. Col, Houlton, Maine, 51-52; Univ. Maine Law Sch, LL.B, 54; Kappa Delta Phi. Polit. & Govt. Pos: Mem, Durham Rep. Cent. Cmt, Maine, 50-52; mem, Androscoggin Co. Young Rep, 51, officer, 52-53; del, Rep. State Conv, Maine, 52; precinct chmn, Rep. Party, Tremonton, Utah, 62; chmn, Melich for Gov, North. Utah, 64; finance chmn, Burton for Cong, Utah, 64-68; chmn, Box Elder Co. Rep. Party, 65-; mem, Rep. State Cent. Cmt, Utah, 66-; chmn, Burton Cong. Club, 68-69. Bus. & Prof. Pos: Spec. agent, Fed. Bur. Invest, Wash, D.C, 54-59; staff asst, Thiokol Chem. Corp, Brigham City, Utah, 59-61, legal asst. to v.pres, 61-62, mgr, customer rel, 62-63, mgr, customer/pub. rel, 63- Mil. Serv: Entered as A/S, Navy, 45, released as PO 46, after serv. in Amphibious Forces, U.S. & Cuba. Publ: 'Utah Hunting', Gun World, 67; plus others. Mem: Pub. Rel. Soc. Am; Soc. of Former Spec. Agents, Fed. Bur. Invest; Utah Peace Officers Asn; Elks; Mason; Air Force Asn. Bear River Valley C. of C; Nat. Ski Patrol; adv. coun, Box Elder Co. Sch. Dist. Three letters of commendation from Fed. Bur. Invest. Dir. J. Edgar Hoover; Am. Legion Outstanding Student Award, Lisbon Falls High Sch, Maine, 48. Rel: Mormon. Mailing Add: 469 N. First E, Tremonton, Utah 84337.

BROWN, JAMES HARVEY D
b. Jamestown, N.Dak, 4/22/06; s. James S. Brown and Celia Price B; m. 1/27/34 to Ruth Marguerite Hopkins; c. June Ruth (Mrs. Killion), Dorothy Clinton (Mrs. O'Leary) and Maj. James Harvey, Jr. Educ: Southwest. Univ, LL.B; Phi Delta. Polit. & Govt. Pos: Mem, Cmt. II, Bd. of War Commun, 42-46; v.chmn, Calif. State Dem. Cmt, 48-58; mem, 12th Regional Wage Stabilization Bd, 52-55; cent. committeeman, Los Angeles Co. Dem. Cmt, 56-64; City Councilman, Los Angeles, 59-64. Bus. & Prof. Pos: Eng. supvr, Nat. Broadcasting Co, 36-51; attorney-at-law, 39-64; Judge Munic. Court, Los Angeles Judicial Dist, 64- Mil. Serv: Entered as Lt.(jg), Navy, 44, released as Lt, 66; Commendation Ribbon. Mem: Am. Legion; VFW; Mason, Shrine; Los Angeles Athletic Club; FCC and Los Angeles Bar Asns; Bd. of Gov, Hollywood Bar Asn, 60-; Town Hall; exec. bd, Conf. Calif. Judges, 69-; treas, Munic. Court Judges Asn. of Los Angeles Co, 69- Registered Prfnl. Elec. Engr, 52. Rel: Congregational. Mailing Add: 1802 Redesdale Ave, Los Angeles, Calif. 90026.

BROWN, JAMES MONROE D
b. Pulaski, Tenn, 6/17/28; s. John Tyler Brown and Theola McCollum B; m. 5/20/57 to Anne Elizabeth McKissack. Educ: Bridgeforth High Sch, Pulaski, Tenn, 46-48; Armed Forces Schs, 51-52. Polit. & Govt. Pos: Pres, Giles and Lawrence Co. Voters Coun, Tenn, 63-69; mem. exec. cmt, Giles Co. Dem. Orgn, 68; del, Dem. State Conv, 68; del, Dem. Nat. Conv, 68; co-chmn, Tenn. Voters Coun, 68- Bus. & Prof. Pos: Debit mgr, Union Protective Life Ins. Co, 56-60; asst. mgr, Queen Ann Funeral Home, 60- Mil. Serv: Entered as TN 3/C, Navy, 44, released as TN 1/C, 46, recalled, 51-55, served in U.S.S. McIntyre, Tide Water and Gerring, in Atlantic, Pac, Mediterranean & Caribbean Theatres, 44-46 & 51-55; Good Conduct, Pac. Theatre and UN Medals. Publ: 'A Stranger in My Town Powerless and Black,' Counc. News, 4/69. Mem: Elks; Am. Legion; NAACP. Man of the year, 68. Rel: Methodist. Mailing Add: 726 Childers St, Pulaski, Tenn. 38478.

BROWN, DR. JAMES THOMAS R
Chmn. and Finance Chmn, Beadle Co. Rep. Party, S.Dak.
b. East St. Louis, Ill, 3/21/25; s. Dr. James T. Brown and Cleo Crouch B; m. 1/9/46 to Martha Pat Threadgill; c. Carolee. Educ: Kans. State Univ, D.V.M, 52; Alpha Zeta; Gamma Sigma Delta. Polit. & Govt. Pos: Gov. appointee, S.Dak. State Fair Bd, 64; chmn. and finance chmn, Beadle Co. Rep. Party, S.Dak, currently. Bus. & Prof. Pos: Secy-treas, S.Dak. Vet. Med. Asn, 62-; bd. mem, Huron Country Club and co. chmn. for Radio Free Europe, 64- Mil. Serv: Entered as Seaman 2/C, Navy, 43, released as Ph.M 2/C, 46; 2nd Lt, Vet. Med. Corps Res. Mem: Farm Bur; Isaac Walton; Am. Vet. Med. Asn. (v.pres, Minneapolis, 69); pres, S.Dak. Vet. Med. Asn, 69. Rel: Presbyterian. Mailing Add: 1340 Ohio Ave. S.W, Huron, S.Dak. 57350.

BROWN, JANE PHILLIPS R
V.Chmn, Mass. Rep. State Cmt.
b. Cincinnati, Ohio, 6/7/16; d. Thomas Leonard Phillips and Hazel Hake P; m. 7/2/38 to William Glover Brown, III; c. Judith (Mrs. J.A. Ryan, Jr), Joan (Mrs. C.R. Herrmann), Janice Barry, Carolyn Paige, William G, IV and Melinda Jane. Educ: Smith Col, B.A, 38. Polit. & Govt. Pos: Mem, Gloucester Sch. Cmt, Mass, 44-49; state committeewoman, Third Essex Dist, 61-64; 1st v.pres, Women's Rep. Club, Essex Co, 62-64; pres, Cape Ann Women's Rep.

Club, 64; del, Rep. Nat. Conv, 64; v.chmn, Mass. Rep. State Cmt, 64-; v.pres, Mass. Fedn. of Rep. Women, 64- Bus. & Prof. Pos: Society reporter, Boston Traveler, 35-38; mgr, Brown's Bookshop, Gloucester, Mass, 56- Mem: Am. Bookseller's Asn; Cape Ann Sci, Lit. & Hist. Asn; Gloucester Garden Club; Women's Auxiliary of Addison Gilbert Hosp, Gloucester; Mus. of Fine Arts, Boston; Rockport Art Asn; Bus. & Prfnl. Women's Rep. Club; North Shore Smith Col. Club; Gloucester Col. Women's Club. Rel: Episcopal. Mailing Add: Fort Hills Ave, Gloucester, Mass. 01930. (1967)

BROWN, JEAN ISABELLE R
Co-Chmn, Lake Co. Rep. Cmt, Mich.
b. Sanilac Co, Mich, 8/3/26; d. Otis Shephard and Edith Clark S; m. 6/1/46 to William L. Simonson, widowed; remarried 6/13/64 to Darrell Clayton Brown; c. Rodney Wayne, Richard Dean and Janice Mae Simonson. Educ: East. Mich. Univ, B.S, 60, M.A, 62; Cent. Mich. Univ, Ed.S, 69; Kappa Delta Pi. Polit. & Govt. Pos: Co-chmn, Lake Co. Rep. Cmt, Mich, 68- Bus. & Prof. Pos: Elem. and spec. educ. teacher and consult, Lapeer, Genesee and Mason Co. Schs, Mich, 44-49, 57-61 & 64-68; exec. dir, Saginaw Asn. Retarded Children, 61-63, therapeutic teacher, ment. retarded and emotionally disturbed, Lapeer State Home and Training Sch, 63-64; sch. psychologist, Mason and Lake Co, 68-; part-time instr, West Shore Commun. Col, 69- Mem: Nat. and Mich. Educ. Asns; Coun. Exceptional Children; fel. Am. Asn. Ment. Deficiency; Mich. Asn. Educator Psychologists; Am. Asn. Univ. Women; Flint YWCA; Baldwin Womans Club; secy. and legis. chmn, Baldwin Bd. Educ; trustee, Lake Co. Libr. Bd; instr, Am. Jr. Bowling Cong. Rel: United Methodist. Legal Res: Box 231, Baldwin, Mich. 49304. Mailing Add: 308 E. Loomis St, Ludington, Mich. 49431.

BROWN, JESSE FRANCES D
Chmn, Madison Co. Dem. Exec. Cmt, Ga.
b. Carlton, Ga, 12/27/91; s. Wyley Pink Brown and Sarah Kathrine Power B; m. 8/13/11 to Pearl Mae Moon; c. Reba (Mrs. Bobo), John Allison,and Peggy (Mrs. Hutchen). Educ: Carlton High Sch, Ga. Polit. & Govt. Pos: Substitute mail carrier and temporary carrier, 19-57; ex-officio justice of peace, 203rd Dist, Madison Co, Ga; chmn, Madison Co. Dem. Exec. Cmt, Ga, currently; Lt. Col. aide-de-camp, Gov. Ga. Staff, currently. Bus. & Prof. Pos: Pres. and dir, Free State Coop. Fire Ins. Co. of Danielsville, Ga. Mem: F&AM; Mason. Cert. of recognition, Agr. Adjust. Act, 68. Rel: Baptist, Deacon. Mailing Add: Route 2, Carlton, Ga. 30627.

BROWN, JOE RAYMOND D
Chmn, Waterford Twp. Dem. Party, Iowa
b. Charlotte, Iowa, 3/3/13; s. LeRoy John Brown and Rose B. Maloney B; single. Educ: St. Ambrose Col, 36-37. Polit. & Govt. Pos: Dem. twp. clerk, Waterford Twp, Iowa, 36-65 and sch. dir; chmn, Waterford Twp. Dem. Party, 64-; Justice of Peace, Waterford Twp, 66- Mem: Elks; Moose; K. of C.(4°); Toastmasters; Izaak Walton League of Am; Farmers Orgn; Rodeo Cowboys of Am. Rodeo Rider. Rel: Catholic. Mailing Add: R.F.D, Charlotte, Iowa 52731. (1967)

BROWN, JOHN BURNS D
Chmn, Smith Co. Dem. Exec. Cmt, Tex.
b. Dothan, Tex, 9/29/13; s. Benjamin A. Brown and Eva Williams B; m. 7/8/36 to Wynne Mae Moore; c. Jan Moore (Mrs. Jack M. Brady), John Oliver and David Burns. Educ: Schriener Inst, 1 year; Howard Payne Coll, 2 years. Polit. & Govt. Pos: Del, Tex. State Dem. Conv, 64, del. and chmn. of del, 66 & 68; chmn, Smith Co. Dem. Exec. Cmt, 66-; del, Dem. Nat. Conv, 68. Bus. & Prof. Pos: V.pres, W.W. Wise Drilling, Inc, Wise Operating, Inc, and Watburn Oil Co, 55-65; pres, Wise operating, Inc. and Watburn Oil Co, 65- Mem: Tex. Independent Producers Royalty Owners Asn; Independent Petroleum Asn. Am; Am. Petroleum Inst; Shrine; Mason; K.T; Tyler C. of C; Tyler Petroleum Club; Willow Brook Country Club; YMCA. Rel: Methodist. Mailing Add: 4027 Pinedale Place, Tyler, Tex. 75701.

BROWN, JOHN F. R
N.J. State Assemblyman
b. Lakewood, N.J, 11/15/26; m. to Audrey Clayton; c. Charles, Barbaro Jo, William and Valerie. Educ: Lafayette Col; Glassboro Col; Rider Col. Polit. & Govt. Pos: Mem, Libr. Bd, N.J; chmn, Parks and Recreation Bd; police cmnr; chmn, Rd. and Pub. Works; v.pres. and pres, Bd. of Health; mem, Rep. Twp. Cmt, 61-65; pres, Lakewood Rep. Club, 63-64; v.pres, Ocean City Co. Coun. of Men's Rep Clubs, 64-65; mem, N.J. Conf. of Mayors, 65; mayor, Lakewood, 65; N.J. State Assemblyman, currently. Bus. & Prof. Pos: V.pres. John F. Brown & Son, fuel oil and heating bus; mem, Paul Kimball Hosp. Bd. Mem: Rotary; YMCA; Holy Name Soc; Am. Legion; bd. of rev, Boy Scouts, Lakewood; N.J. Travel and Resort Assoc, Inc. Jaycee Outstanding Man of Year Award, 62; Rep. Mayor for Int. Coop. Year in Ocean City; Legislator of 1969, N.J. Asn. Chosen Freeholders. Mailing Add: Park Ave, Lakewood, N.J. 08701.

BROWN, JOHN RICHARD 'DICK' D
Committeeman, Tex. Dem. Exec. Cmt.
b. Hartley, Tex, 2/24/26; s. Joseph Clifford Brown and Lucille Bishop B; m. 6/22/47 to Phyllis Dean Bircher; c. Karen Lynette, Debra Kay and Richard Kent. Educ: Northwest Mo. State Teachers Col, 44; Colo. Univ, B.S, M.E, 47. Polit. & Govt. Pos: Chmn, Hartley Co. Dem. Exec. Cmt, Tex, 55-; former co. chmn, Kennedy-Johnson and Johnson-Humphrey Campaigns; North Plains coordinator for Gov. John B. Connally, 62; committeeman, Tex. Dem. Exec. Cmt, 66- Bus. & Prof. Pos: Mem, adv. bd, Producers Grain Corp, 59; mem, adv. coun, South. Farm Supply Asn, 61-; dir-secy, Asn. of Tex. Wheat Growers, 62-; dir, Grain Sorghum Producers Asn, 65-; trustee, High Plains Research Found, 66. Mil. Serv: A/S, Navy, 44; Lt, Naval Res. attached to Mobilization Team 8-4, Amarillo. Mem: Am. Soc. of Mech. Engrs; Naval Res. Officers Asn; Aircraft Owners and Pilot Asn; Flying Farmers; Farmers Union; Farm Bur. Rel: Baptist. Mailing Add: Box 51, Hartley, Tex. 79044. (1967)

BROWN, JOHN W(ILLIAM) R
Lt. Gov, Ohio
b. Athens, Ohio, 12/28/13; s. James A. Brown and Daisy Foster B; m. 7/10/43 to Violet A. Helman; c. Rosalie (Mrs. Angelus). Polit. & Govt. Pos: Mayor, Medina, Ohio, 50-53; Lt. Gov, Ohio, 53-57 & 63-; Gov. Ohio, 57; Ohio State Rep, 59-60; Ohio State Sen, 61-62. Bus. & Prof. Pos: Pres, Investors Heritage Life Ins. Co. of Ohio, Columbus; former owner, John W. Brown, Inc, Ins. & Real Estate, Medina; former principal broker, Gerspacher-Lincoln & Assocs, Real Estate and Gerspacher-Block, Real Estate and Ins. Mil. Serv: Entered as 2/C PO, Coast Guard, 42, released as 1/C PO, 45, after serv. in ETO; Lt. Comdr, Coast Guard Res; Good Conduct Medal; Am. Theater Ribbon; ETO Ribbon with two stars; Expert Pistol Medal; Victory Medal. Mem: F&AM; RAM; RSM; K.T; Scottish Rite; Mason (32°); Valley of Cleveland, Tadmor Temple Shrine, Yusef-Kahn Grotto; Am. Legion; VFW; 40 et 8; Ohio Gun Collectors. Professional Speaker. Rel: Methodist. Legal Res: 401 Baxter St, Medina, Ohio 44256. Mailing Add: State Capitol, Columbus, Ohio 43215.

BROWN, JOHN YOUNG D
b. Sturgis, Ky, 2/1/00; s. James Brown and Lucy Keeper B; m. to Dorothy Inman; c. Dorothy (Mrs. Benham Sims), Betty (Mrs. William McCann), Diana (Mrs. Alvin Busby), John Y, Jr. and Pamela (Mrs. Rod Anderson). Educ: Centre Col, A.B, 21; Univ. Ky, LL.B, 26; Omicron Delta Kappa and Phi Alpha Delta. Polit. & Govt. Pos: Ky. State Rep, 30, 32, 46, 54, 62 & 66, Speaker, Ky. House of Rep, 32 and Floor Leader, 66; U.S. Rep, Ky, 33-34; Spec. Asst. Attorney Gen. of U.S, 35-36; mem, Criminal Code Cmn, Ky, 58-60. Bus. & Prof. Pos: Attorney-at-law. Mil. Serv: World War I Vet. Mem: Fayette Co, Ky. State and Am. Bar Asns; Am. Col. Trial Lawyers; Am. Trial Lawyers Asn; Kiwanis; Am. Legion. Selected as Outstanding Lawyer, Ky, 62. Rel: Christian. Legal Res: 1824 Fielden Dr, Lexington, Ky. 40502. Mailing Add: 601 Security Trust Bldg, Lexington, Ky. 40507.

BROWN, JOSEPHINE M. R
Mem, Calif. Rep. State Cent. Cmt.
b. Thayer, Mo, 10/16/09; d. Samuel Lee Sagaser and Mary Emma Faulkner S; m. 5/30/35 to Floyd Greer Brown. Educ: Univ. Ariz, A.B, 30; Univ. South. Calif; Univ. Calif, Berkeley, 52; Sacramento State Col, 54. Polit. & Govt. Pos: Mem, Calif. Rep. State Cent. Cmt, 69- Bus. & Prof. Pos: Teacher, Tucson City Schs, Ariz, 31-35, Miss Preston's Sch. for Girls, 35-36, Pinal Co. Sch, Florence, Ariz, 38-43; teacher and supvr, North Sacramento Sch. Dist, 44-67, dir. spec. serv, 68- Mem: Delta Kappa Gamma; Calif. Adminstr. of Spec. Educ; Calif. Asn. of Supvr. of Child Welfare; Calif. Teachers' Asn; Soroptimist Club (past pres, Sacramento North Chap, 54-55); bd. dirs, United Christian Center, 68-; chmn, Lincoln Christian Center Cmt, 68- Rel: Presbyterian. Mailing Add: 3400 Brockway Court, Sacramento, Calif. 95818.

BROWN, JUANITA MAGGIE DEICH D
b. Eckerty, Ind, 10/11/22; d. John Phillip Deich and Amy Young D; m. 7/20/40 to John Brown, Jr; c. Phyllis (Mrs. Donivan Warren), John Dwight and Stephen Mark. Educ: Springs Valley High Sch, 58. Polit. & Govt. Pos: Secy-treas, Orange Co. Dem. Women's Auxiliary Ind, 61-63 and pres, 64; v.chmn, Orange Co. Dem. Cent. Cmt, 64-68. Mem: Treas, Am. Legion Auxiliary Post 76. Rel: Protestant. Mailing Add: 125 Summit St, French Lick, Ind. 47432. (1967)

BROWN, KATHARINE KENNEDY R
Pres, Ohio Fedn. Rep. Woman's Orgns.
b. Dayton, Ohio; d. Grafton Claggett Kennedy and Louise Achey K; m. to Kleon Thaw Brown (deceased). Educ: Dana Hall, student, 06-08. Polit. & Govt. Pos: Mem, Montgomery Co. Rep. Exec. Cmt, Ohio, 20-; alternate del-at-lg, Rep. Nat. Conv, 28; mem, Rep. State Cmt, 28-; Rep. Nat. committeewoman, Ohio, 32-68, dir, West. Women's Div, 36 and v.chmn, Rep. Nat. Cmt, 44-52; del-at-lg, Rep. Nat. Conv, 32, 44, 48, 52, 60, 64 & 68; pres, Ohio Fedn. Rep. Women's Orgn, 40-; mem. bd. trustees, Wilberforce Univ, 56; mem. bd. dirs, Nat. Fedn. Rep. Women; adv. coun, Women's Nat. Rep. Club, N.Y; mem, League Rep. Women, D.C; Capitol Hill Rep. Club. Bus. & Prof. Pos: V.pres, Ohio Yellow Cab Co, 26- Publ: 'What you Want to Know About the Great Game of Politics'; 'Rudiments of Political Organization.' Mem: Jr. League; DAR; Colonial Dames; v.pres, pres, bd. trustees, Taft Mem. Found; Capitol Hill Club, Wash, D.C; Moraine Country Club. Silver Gala Honoree, Silver Anniversary, Nat. Fedn. Rep. Women, 63. Rel: Presbyterian. Legal Res: Duncarrick, Keowee and Webster Sts, Dayton, Ohio 45401. Mailing Add: P.O. Box 324, Dayton, Ohio 45401.

BROWN, KEITH SPALDING R
b. Hinsdale, Ill, 6/15/13; s. William Bruce Brown and Sara Morgan Gardner B; m. 7/3/37 to Katherine Noyes McKennan; c. Keith Spalding, Julie (Mrs. Parker D. Perry), Katherine M, Stephen G. Educ: Phillips Acad, cum laude; Yale, B.A, 35; Alpha Delta Phi. Polit. & Govt. Pos: Mem, Continental Pub. Sch. Bd, 47-65, pres, 59-65; Ariz. State Rep, 55-58; v.chmn, Ariz. Rep. Cmt, 59-60, chmn, 63-65; mem, Rep. Nat. Cmt, 63-65, mem. exec. cmt, 64-65; v.chmn. Ariz. del, Rep. Nat. Conv, 64, del, Rep. Nat. Conv, 64 & 68. Bus. & Prof. Pos: With Procter & Gamble Co, 25-27; prod. supvr, Lyon Metal Prod. Co, Aurora, Ill, 37-39; staff mem, Booz, Fry & Allen & Hamilton Mgt. Consults, Chicago, 39-42; owner-operator, Santa Rita Ranch, Tucson, 46-; v.pres. and dir, Selective Life Ins. Co, 58-65; v.pres, treas, mem. exec. cmt. and dir, Southwest. Research & Gen. Investment Co, 65; chmn. bd, Am. Atomics Corp, 65-; dir, South. Ariz. Bank and Ariz. Land Title & Trust Co, currently. Mailing Add: 3200 N. Swan Rd, Tucson, Ariz. 85716.

BROWN, KENNETH HAROLD R
Chmn, Harrison Co. Rep. Party, Tex.
b. Brazil, Ind, 1/4/02; s. Simpson Brown and Elizabeth Romas B; m. 7/11/64 to Isabell Llewlyn; c. Paul W. Educ: Purdue Univ, B.S, 31. Polit. & Govt. Pos: Chmn, Harrison Co. Rep. Party, Tex, 68- Bus. & Prof. Pos: Prod. mgr, Beatrice Foods, 31-34; prod. mgr, Borden Inc, 34-67, retired, 67. Mem: Lions (past pres, past zone chmn, dep. dist. gov, currently). Rel: Presbyterian. Mailing Add: 41 Buena Vista Dr, Marshall, Tex. 75670.

BROWN, LARRY ROBERT R
Chmn, Rep. Party of Giles Co, Va.
b. St. Marys, W.Va, 3/30/26; s. Frank Crawford Brown and Ila Evelyn McFarland B; m. 1/30/48 to Virginia Anne Troy; c. Justin Devin, Lance Troy, Melissa Dawn, Bruce Kevin and Christopher Dale. Educ: W.Va. Univ, 46-48; Va. Polytech. Inst, B.S. in Chem. Eng, 53, M.S, 55; Sigma Xi; Sigma Nu. Polit. & Govt. Pos: Recording secy, Giles Young Rep. Club, Va, 63-64, chmn, 65; chmn, Rep. Party of Giles Co, 66- Bus. & Prof. Pos: Engr, Celanese Corp. Am, Narrows, Va, 54-56, instrument engr, 56-59, sr. instrument engr,

59-65; sr. proj. engr, Celanese Fibers Co, Div. Celanese Corp, 65-69, plant coordinator pollution abatement, Celco Plant, Celanese Fibers Co, 67-69. Mil. Serv: Entered as Aviation Student, Army Air Corps, 44, released as Pfc, 45, after serv. in Air Training Command, 44-45; grad. Adv. Air Force Res. Officer's Training, W.Va. Univ, 48; recalled as 2nd Lt, 51-52, served in 122nd Fighter Wing, East. Air Defense Command; Res, 52-63, Capt; Distinguished Mil. Student Air Force ROTC. Mem: Instrument Soc. Am.(Dist. II v.pres, 68-70); Am. Chem. Soc; Am. Inst. Chem. Engrs; Registered Prfnl. Engr. Commonwealth Va; Boy Scouts (mem. exec. bd. Appalachian Coun, 58-65); Giles Life Saving and Rescue Squad (squad treas, 66-68). Silver Beaver Award, Boy Scouts, 67; Sect. Pres. Award, Blue Ridge Sect, Instrument Soc. Am, 65-66, D.W. Larcen Award, 68. Rel: Protestant. Mailing Add: 508 Easton Rd, Pearisburg, Va. 24134.

BROWN, LEWIS FRANK D

b. Cleveland, Miss, 8/4/29; s. Frank Cephas Brown and Lula Armstrong B; m. 3/29/56 to Dorothy Jean Fitzgerald; c. Lewis Gene and Orville Frank. Educ: Solano Col, A.A, 55; San Francisco State Col, A.B; 57; Lincoln Univ. Sch. Law, J.D, 64; Two Mile Record Holder, 53-55, Mile Run Record Holder, 53-59. Polit. & Govt. Pos: Pres, Solano Co. Young Dem, Calif, 54-55; committeeman, Solano Co. Dem. Party, 60-66; planning cmnr, Vallejo, Calif, 63-65, city councilman, 65-67, vice mayor, 67-69; v.chmn, Black Elected Officials, Calif, 67-68, North. Calif. chmn, 68-69; field coordinator, Robert Kennedy for Pres, North. Calif, 68; mem. speakers bur, Humphrey-Muskie Campaign, North. Calif, 68. Bus. & Prof. Pos: Sec. teacher, Vallejo Unified Sch. Dist, 57-65; bus. law teacher, Solano Col, 63; asst. supvr, Greenleigh Research Corp, 66, supvr, 67; prin. consult, Health, Educ. and Welfare, North. Calif, 67- Mil. Serv: Entered as E-1, Army, 51, released as Pfc, 53, after serv. in 802nd Qm. Serv. Co, Korea; Korean and U.S. Serv. Medal; 2 Bronze Campaign Stars; Spec. Commendation Award. Publ: 'New Housing Plan for Vallejo,' 3/66 and 'The Cost of False Fire Alarms,' 5/66, Vallejo Times Herald; 'Report of OEO Delegate Agencies, Contra Costa Report,' 3/69. Mem: Calif. Conf. Black Elected Off; West. States Conf. Black Elected Off; Solano Co. Cmt. Evaluate Co. Courts; chmn. spec. sports event, March Dimes, Laurel, Miss, 49-51. Rel: Protestant. Mailing Add: 400 Lakeside Dr, Vallejo, Calif. 94590.

BROWN, LILLIAN CUNNINGHAM D

Mem, Calif. Dem. State Cent. Cmt.

b. Piedmont, S.C, 3/7/15; d. Joseph L. Cunningham and Nellie Burdion C; m. 2/9/34 to William Lee Brown; c. Donald Lee, Lila M. (Mrs. Fred Sanders) and Gerald Julius. Educ: Pasadena, 12 years. Polit. & Govt. Pos: Secy, F.D.R. Club, Pasadena, Calif, 64-65 and v.pres, 68-69; mem, Calif. Dem. State Cent. Cmt, 68- Mem: League of Women Voters; NAACP. Rel: Baptist. Mailing Add: 300 W. Washington Blvd, Pasadena, Calif. 91103.

BROWN, LOLA W. D

b. Pittsburgh, Pa, 7/13/34; d. Adolf H. Wilken and Adella Bueno W; m. 3/31/63 to Gary Robert Brown; c. Robert. Polit. & Govt. Pos: Off. secy. to Rep. George P. Miller, Calif, 66- Bus. & Prof. Pos: Exec. secretarial work with various firms; secy. and off. mgr, Cent. Labor Coun. of Alameda Co, AFL-CIO, Calif, 7 years. Mailing Add: 1439 Sherman St, Alameda, Calif. 94501.

BROWN, M. J, 'BUCK' D

b. 1930. Polit. & Govt. Pos: Ariz. State Rep, 64-66. 1967 Legal Res: Glendale, Ariz. No mailing address available. (1967)

BROWN, MANNY S. D

Wis. State Assemblyman

b. Chicago, Ill, 11/2/17. Educ: Univ. Wis, B.A, 40; Marquette Univ, LL.B, 52. Polit. & Govt. Pos: Served on Racine City Recreation Cmt, Wis, Nat. Coun. Juvenile Court Judges; mem. bd. educ, Racine Unified Sch. Dist, 53-; mem, Racine Co. Safety Coun, 54-, pres, 57-58; bd. dir, Racine Co. Dem. Party; Wis. State Assemblyman, 64- Bus. & Prof. Pos: Attorney, 52- Mil. Serv: Navy. Mem: Bar Asns; Am. Judicature Soc; Am. Trial Lawyers Asn; Racine Co. Humane Soc. and Art Asn; Children's Serv. Soc. Mailing Add: 2817 Ruby Ave, Racine, Wis. 53402.

BROWN, MARION FULLER R

Maine State Rep.

b. Kansas City, Mo, 5/14/17; d. Charles T. Thompson (deceased) and Marion Moreau T; m. to Henry M. Fuller, wid; m. 7/5/67 to Brooks Brown, Jr; c. Alexandra (Mrs. O. Kelly Anderson, Jr), Martha (Mrs. Selz), Henry Weld and Emily Anne. Educ: Bradford Jr. Col, 36; Smith Col, B.S, 38. Polit. & Govt. Pos: Mem, Rep. Town Cmt, York, Maine, 52-; York Co. Rep. Cmt, 58-66; Maine Rep. State Cmt, 60-66, secy, 62-66; consumer mem, Maine Milk Cmn, 60-66; mem, Women's Div, McIntrie for Sen, 64; del, Rep. Nat. Conv, 64; mem, York Planning Bd, 66-; Rep. Nat. Committeewoman, 66-; Maine State Rep, 67- Mem: York Women's League; Women's Hosp. Cmt; dir, Pine Tree Soc. for Crippled Children and Adults; trustee, Bradford Alumnae Asn. Rel: Protestant. Mailing Add: Ram's Head Farm, York, Maine 03909.

BROWN, MARTIN PARKS D

Ga. State Sen.

b. Hart, Ga, 11/29/14; s. Heber C. Brown and Hattie Parks B; m. 6/21/38 to Joyce Winn; c. Jerry Parks, Sandra Joyce and Martin Boyce. Educ: Hartwell High Sch, 32. Polit. & Govt. Pos: Ga. State Rep, 61-66; Ga. State Sen, 68- Bus. & Prof. Pos: Merchant; cotton farmer; fertilizer dealer. Mil. Serv: Army, 43-46; Battle Star, Cent. European Campaign. Rel: Baptist. Mailing Add: P.O. Box 37, Hartwell, Ga. 30643.

BROWN, MATTHEW R

b. N.Y.C, 3/26/05; s. Jack Goddard Brown and Pauline Roth B; m. 10/8/32 to Edna Goodrich; c. Patricia and Ronald (deceased). Educ: N.Y. Univ, B.S, 25; Harvard Univ, LL.B, 28; Pi Lambda Phi. Polit. & Govt. Pos: Alternate del, Rep. Nat. Conv. Bus. & Prof. Pos: Partner, Brown, Rudnick, Freed & Gesmer; dir, Norfolk Co. Trust Co, Winde-McCormick Lumber Co. Mem: Mass. Bar Asn. and Supreme Court, 28; gen. chmn, Jewish Philanthropies fund raising drive, Boston, 53. Publ: A Manuel on Conditional Sales Contracts; Chattel Mortgages and Trust Receipts. Legal Res: 419 Clinton Rd, Brookline, Mass. 02146. Mailing Add: 85 Devonshire St, Boston, Mass. 02109.

BROWN, MONA KATHERINE R

b. Blue Ridge, Mo, 10/7/17; d. Omer Elgin Marshall and Frankie Leland Wright M; m. 7/30/45 to Jack Edward Brown; c. Mona Marie. Educ: Northwest Mo. State Col. Polit. & Govt. Pos: Pres, Daviess Co. Federated Rep. Women, Mo, 61-69; chmn, Daviess Co. Rep. Party, 62-69; Sixth Dist. mem, Mo. Rep. State Cmt, 64-69. Mem: Eastern Star; Farm Bur; Mo. Farmers Asn; Women's Soc. of Christian Serv; VFW Women's Auxiliary. Rel: United Methodist. Mailing Add: Route 3, Box 126, Jamesport, Mo. 64648.

BROWN, NORMAN KNIGHT D

b. Millry, Ala, 1/15/21; s. Arthur Isom Brown and Beatrice Knight B; m. 1947 to Dorothy Colquitt; c. Dorothy Marie, Julia Knight, Norman Knight. Educ: Univ. of Ala, B.S, 43; LL.B, 49. Polit. & Govt. Pos: Ala. State Rep, 62-66. Bus. & Prof. Pos: Lawyer. Mil. Serv: WWII, Pac, Capt. Mem: Mason; Shriner. Rel: Baptist. 1967 Legal Res: 1731 Fairfax Ave, Bessemer, Ala. No mailing address available. (1967)

BROWN, OLGA JAMISON D

b. Indianapolis, Ind; d. Tull Emmet Brown and Ella Dakin Teetor B; single. Educ: Butler Univ, B.A; K.D.P. Polit. & Govt. Pos: Exec. Secy, Rep. Patten, N.J. Legal Res: Washington, D.C. Mailing Add: 1725 Longworth Building, Wash, D.C. 20515.

BROWN, OMAR R

Head, Rep. Territorial Cmt. of V.I.

b. St. Thomas, V.I, 8/4/09; widower; c. Omar, Jr. Educ: Parochial schs. and pub. schs. of St. Thomas. Polit. & Govt. Pos: V.I. Territorial Rep, 38-52; head, Rep. Territorial Cmt. of V.I, currently; del, Rep. Nat. Conv, 68. Bus. & Prof. Pos: Hotel owner. Mem: Rotary Club. Rel: Catholic. Mailing Add: 1 B Commandant Gade, St. Thomas, V.I. 00801. (1967)

BROWN, OTHA NATHANIEL, JR. D

Conn. State Rep.

b. DeQueen, Ark, 7/19/31; s. Otha Brown, Sr. and Elizabeth B; single. Educ: Cent. State Col, Ohio, B.S. cum luade; Univ. Conn, M.A; Univ. Bridgeport, prfnl. dipl. in admin; N.Y Univ, cert. in counseling; Alpha Kappa Mu; Phi Alpha Theta; Kappa Delta Pi; life mem, Alpha Phi Alpha. Polit. & Govt. Pos: Mem, Dist. Dem. Cmt, Conn, 62-; city councilman, Norwalk, 63-; mem. bd. dirs, Anti-Poverty Bd, Conn, 65-; Conn. State Rep, 67-; Majority Leader Common Coun, 68-, chmn. cmt. Human Rights and Opportunities, mem, Educ. Cmt. and Pub. Personnel Cmt. Bus. & Prof. Pos: Teacher, Stratford, Conn, 57-60, Stamford, 60; guidance counselor bd. educ, Stamford, 62- Mil. Serv: Entered as 2nd Lt, Army, 52, released as 1st Lt, 54, after serv. as Psychological Warfare Officer. Mem: Elks; Mason; NAACP; Young Dem; Jaycees; Am. Personnel & Guidance Asn. Norwalk Young Man of the Year Award, 66; Conn. Outstanding Young Man of the Year Award, 66; Outstanding Young Man of Am, 67; Cert. of Merit, Dictionary Int. Biography, 69. Rel: Methodist. Mailing Add: 208 Flax Hill Rd, Norwalk, Conn. 06854.

BROWN, PAUL EDWARD R

b. Raymond, N.H, 4/27/35; s. Theodore Haywood Brown and Bessie Quimby B; m. 10/21/56 to Amelia Ann Dillon; c. Thomas Edward and Vanessa Ann. Educ: Raymond High Sch, grad. Polit. & Govt. Pos: Mem, State Rep. Cmt, N.H, 64-67; chmn, Greater Derry Young Rep, 66; del, Rep. State Conv, 66 & 68; mem, Town and Co. Rep. Cmts, 66-67; N.H. State Rep, 67-68; Rockingham Co. coordinator, Nixon for President, 67-68; advance man, Nixon Staff, 68; del, Rep. State Conv, N.H, 68; treas, N.H. Fedn. Young Rep. Clubs, 68-69; asst. clerk, N.H. House of Rep, currently. Bus. & Prof. Pos: Sales mgr, Derry Real Estate Agency, 63-68, owner and operator, 68- Mil. Serv: Entered as Basic Airman, Air Force, 55, released as A/1C, 59. Rel: Protestant. Mailing Add: Chester Rd, Derry, N.H. 03038.

BROWN, PAUL EUGENE R

S.Dak. State Sen.

b. Bancroft, S.Dak, 4/7/13; s. Walter Warner Brown and Ella Dunlavy B; m. 8/16/36 to Lillian Greenwood; c. Virginia, Esther, Joyce, Edward Vander Wal, Gary Englehorn and Rodney La Mont. Educ: S.Dak. State Univ, B.S, 35; Alpha Zeta. Polit. & Govt. Pos: Chmn, Sch. Bd, S.Dak, 11 years; pres, Co. Exten. Bd, 15 years; S.Dak. State Rep, 54-64, Speaker-Pro-Tem, 61-62, Speaker, 63-64 and pres. exec. bd, Legis. Res. Coun, S.Dak. State House of Rep; pres, S.Dak. State Fair Bd, 65-69; S.Dak. State Sen, 69- Bus. & Prof. Pos: Farmer, 37- Mil. Serv: Entered as 1st Lt, Army Res, 42, released as Capt, 45. Mem: Gamma Sigma Delta; Nat. Livestock Feeders Asn; Mason; Eastern Star; Shrine; Am. Legion; Izaak Walton League; Farm Bur; Nat. Rifle Asn. Rel: Methodist. Mailing Add: Route 4, Arlington, S.Dak. 57212.

BROWN, PAUL WESLEY R

Attorney Gen, Ohio

b. Cleveland, Ohio, 1/14/15; s. William Brown and Mary E. Foster B; m. 11/8/42 to Helen Louise Page; c. Susan, Julie, Barbara, Mary, Jeffrey, Molly and Daniel. Educ: Ohio State Univ, A.B, 37, LL.B, 39; Phi Kappa Alpha; Phi Delta Phi. Polit. & Govt. Pos: Del, Rep. Nat. Conf, 48; judge, Court of Appeals of Ohio, 60-64; judge, Supreme Court of Ohio, 64-69; Attorney Gen, Ohio, 69- Mil. Serv: Entered as 2nd Lt, Field Artil, 41, released as Maj, 46, after serv. in First Armored Div, ETO; Silver Star; Purple Heart; ETO Medal; 2 Battle Stars. Legal Res: Youngstown, Ohio. Mailing Add: 2396 Wimbledon Rd, Columbus, Ohio 43221.

BROWN, PRENTISS MARSH D

b. St. Ignace, Mich, 6/18/89; s. James J. Brown and Minnie Gagnon B; m. 6/16/16 to Marion E. Walker; c. James J, Prentiss M, Paul W, Mariana (Mrs. Rudolph), Ruth (Mrs. Evanshevski), Barbard (Mrs. Laing) and Patricia (Mrs. Watson). Educ: Albion Col, A.B, 11; Univ. Ill; Phi Beta Kappa; Delta Sigma Rho; Delta Tau Delta. Polit. & Govt. Pos: U.S. Rep, Mich, 33-37; U.S. Sen, 37-43; adminstr, Off. Price Admin, 43-44; mem. adv. bd, Reconstruction Finance Corp, Detroit and Mich, 43-44; State Bd. Law Exam. and various city and co. attorneyships; mem, Mich. Hist. Cmn, 48-65; chmn, Mackinac Bridge Authority, 52- Bus. & Prof. Pos: Pres, First Nat. Bank, St. Ignace, 33-65; chmn. bd, Detroit Edison Co, 44-; dir, Nat. Bank of Detroit, 48-66; dir, Parke Davis & Co, 55-63. Mem: Mason (33°). Rel: Methodist. Mailing Add: 11 Prospect, St. Ignace, Mich. 49781.

BROWN, R. FAY R
b. Bismarck, N.Dak, 3/26/10; married; c. 6. Educ: State Teachers Col. Polit. & Govt. Pos: N.Dak. State Rep, 53-68. Bus. & Prof. Pos: Gen. mgr, A.W. Lucas, Co. Mailing Add: 118 Ave. B, W, Bismarck, N.Dak. 58501. (1967)

BROWN, RALPH D. 'DOC' D
Ala. State Rep.
b. Tuscaloosa, Ala, 2/17/19; married; c. three. Polit. & Govt. Pos: Ala. State Rep, 63- Bus. & Prof. Pos: Chiropractor. Mil. Serv: Army. Mem: Lions Club; Am. Legion; Moose; Masons; Shrine; DAV. Rel: Baptist. Mailing Add: 2210 10th Ave, Tuscaloosa, Ala. 35401. (1967)

BROWN, RALPH J. R
b. Lynn, Mass, 9/3/92; s. James Brown and M. Nettie West B; m. 6/8/18 to H. Mabel Hastie; c. Ralph H, Chester J, Betty M. and Peter R. Educ: Northeastern Univ. and Burdett Bus. Col. Polit. & Govt. Pos: Conn. State Rep, 59-68; del, Conn. Constitutional Conv, 65. Bus. & Prof. Pos: V.pres, Gen. Elec. Supply Corp, Bridgeport, Conn, 40-53; pres, Nat. Asn. Elec. Distributors, 57-58. Mem: Pyramid Shrine. Rel: Episcopal. Mailing Add: 174 Sport Hill Rd, Easton, Conn. 06612.

BROWN, RALPH M. D
b. Somerset, Ky, 9/16/08; m. to Lillan Weber; c. Valerie Pierson. Educ: Univ. of Calif, A.B, 30; Stanford Univ, LL.B, 32. Polit. & Govt. Pos: Calif. State Assemblyman, 42-66; former U.S. Conciliation Cmnr; 38th Agr. Dist. Fair Bd; Regent of the Univ. of Calif; Bd. of Trustees, State Cols. Bus. & Prof. Pos: Lawyer. Mem: Modesto C. of C; Eagles; Masons; Shrine; Elks; Eastern Star; Kiwanis; Knights Templar; Ahepa; Calif. Bar Asn; Am. Bar Asn. 1967 Legal Res: 1007 W. Norwich Ave, Modesto, Calif. No mailing address available. (1967)

BROWN, RICHARD A. R
N.Y. State Assemblyman
b. Bridgeport, N.Y, 7/27/08; s. Richard C. Brown and Ella Andrews B; m. 11/8/56 to Edith Steier. Educ: Rider Col, B.S; Chi Phi Chi. Polit. & Govt. Pos: Supvr, Town of Sullivan, N.Y, 42; N.Y. State Assemblyman, 114th Dist, 68- Bus. & Prof. Pos: Owner, Brown's Store, 42- Mil. Serv: Entered as Pvt, Air Force, 43, released as Staff Sgt, 45, after serv. in 9th Air Force, ETO; 5 Gold Stars. Mem: Lions; Mason; Shrine; Fire Co; Grange; Am. Legion; VFW. Rel: Protestant. Mailing Add: 8985 N. Lake Rd, Bridgeport, N.Y. 13030.

BROWN, RICHARD ARTHUR D
b. N.Y.C, Oct. 22; s. Benjamin Brown and Ruth Halper B; m. 9/20/50; c. Jennifer Jo. Educ: City Col. N.Y, B.B.A, 40. Polit. & Govt. Pos: State orgn. dir, N.Y. Vol. for Stevenson, 52; campaign mgr, Akers for Cong, 54; pub. rels. dir, N.Y. State Stevenson for Pres, 55-56; exec. dir, N.Y. Cmt. for Dem. Voters, 59-65; admin. asst. to U.S. Rep. James H. Scheuer, N.Y, 65-; campaign mgr, Scheuer for Mayor, 69- Mil. Serv: Entered as Pvt, Army, 41, released as T/5, 45. Mem: asst. dir, Nat. Orgn. Dept, Anti Defamation League B'nai B'rith, 47-51; asst. dir. Manhattan, Bonds for Israel, 52. Rel: Jewish. Legal Res: New York, N.Y. Mailing Add: 2030 Allen Place N.W, Washington, D.C. 20009.

BROWN, RICHARD GILBERT R
Chmn, Ward Nine Rep. Cmt, Mass.
b. Crewe, Va, 9/29/15; s. Richard Gaines Brown and L. Gertrude Jackson B; widowed. Educ: Boston Univ, M.Ed, 55. Polit. & Govt. Pos: V.chmn, Ward Nine Rep. Cmt, Mass, 64-68, chmn, 68- Bus. & Prof. Pos: Instr. math, Tuskegee Inst, Ala, 55-61, vis. asst. prof, summer 69; chmn. dept. math, Wayland Jr. High Sch, Mass, 61-68; develop. teacher, Lewis Jr. High Sch, Boston, 68- Mil. Serv: Entered as Pvt, Army, 44, released as Sgt, 46, after serv. in Qm. Corps as Medic, ETO, 44-46; recalled as Col, 50, released as Sgt, 51, after serv. in Field Artil. First Armored Div; Good Conduct Medal; European Theatre Ribbon; Battle of the Bulge Ribbon. Mem: Nat. Coun. Teachers Math; Asn. Teachers Math. New Eng; Nat. Educ. Asn; VFW; Am. Fedn. Teachers. Rel: Baptist. Mailing Add: 1059 Tremont St, Boston, Mass. 02120.

BROWN, RICHARD L. D
Fla. State Rep.
b. York, Pa, 5/25/25; s. Louis H. Brown and Lillian Williams B; m. 5/31/46 to Janice M. Phillips; c. Steven L, Thomas R. and Nancy A. Educ: Univ. Miami. Polit. & Govt. Pos: Fla. State Rep. Bus. & Prof. Pos: Pres, Broward Co. Insurors Asn, 59-60. Mil. Serv: Entered as Seaman, Navy, 43, released as AOM 2/C, 46. Mem: Rotary; Salvation Army Bd; YMCA Bd. Rel: Methodist. Legal Res: 2636 27th Court N.E, Ft. Lauderdale, Fla. 33306. Mailing Add: P.O. Box 11248, Ft. Lauderdale, Fla. 33306.

BROWN, RICHARD ROSS R
City Councilman, El Cajon, Calif.
b. Tracy, Minn, 1/28/33; s. Henry Norvan Brown and Helen McCorquodale B; m. 3/4/51 to Harriet Elaine Hunnewell; c. Richard Douglas, David Ross and Donald James. Educ: Sweetwater High Sch, Calif, 4 years. Polit. & Govt. Pos: Pres, C. of C, El Cajon, Calif, 64-65; mem, Calif. Rep. State Cent. Cmt, 64-; assoc. mem, San Diego Rep. Cent. Cmt, 64-; city councilman, El Cajon, 66-, mayor, 67-68; mem, Revenue and Taxation Cmt, League of Cities, 66-69, mem. transportation cmt, 69-; mem, Gov. Task Force on Transportation, 67; chmn. exec. cmt, Rep. Assoc. San Diego Co, 67-68; alternate del, Rep. Nat. Conv, 68; chmn, San Diego Region Comprehensive Planning Orgn, 68-; legis. chmn, League Calif. Cities, San Diego Div, 68-; chmn. regional cmt, Calif. Coun. Criminal Justice, 69. Bus. & Prof. Pos: Pres. and gen. mgr, Dilaine Corp, DBA, Brown Tool Eng. Co, El Cajon, 56-; v.chmn, San Diego Co. Indust. Asn, 59-60; pres. and gen. mgr, Dilaine Indust. Inc, 61-; mem. bd. dirs, San Diego Employers Asn, 66-69. Mem: Nat. Asn. Mfgs; San Diego Employers Asn; El Cajon, Calif. and San Diego C. of C; Rotary; Elks; Boys Club; Heartland YMCA; Salvation Army (adv. bd). Rel: Protestant. Legal Res: 480 Horizon Hills Dr, El Cajon, Calif. 92020. Mailing Add: 544 Vernon Way, El Cajon, Calif. 92020.

BROWN, ROBERT C. R
b. Oakland, Calif, 5/6/16; married; c. three. Educ: Univ. Calif, Los Angeles; Fordham Univ; Keene State Col. Polit. & Govt. Pos: Air attache, Turkey; former N.H. State Rep. Bus. & Prof. Pos: Math. teacher. Mil. Serv: Air Force, World War II and Korea. Mem: Am. Legion; NHEA; Lions. Rel: Episcopal. Mailing Add: Middle Hancock Rd, Peterborough, N.H. 03458. (1967)

BROWN, ROBERT HENRY D
b. Nashville, Tenn, 8/2/26; s. Warren H. Brown and Libby Forgy B; m. 8/17/63 to Deloris M. Roby. Educ: Univ. Ind, 2 years. Polit. & Govt. Pos: Del, State and Nat. Dem. Conv, 68. Bus. & Prof. Pos: Int. rep, Machinist Union, 10 years. Mil. Serv: Entered as Seaman, Navy, released as Boatswain Mate, after serv. in South Pac. Theatre, 42-45. Mem: Int. Asn. of Machinist and Aerospace Workers, AFL-CIO; VFW; Am. Legion; Elks. Rel: Protestant. Mailing Add: 517 N. Main St, Princeton, Ind. 47570.

BROWN, ROBERT JOHN R
Minn. State Sen.
b. Stillwater, Minn, 6/15/35; s. Lindsay R. Brown and Bertha Fiorito B; m. 8/22/59 to Janet Rae Johnson; c. Anthony, Daniel, Linda, Michael and Andrew. Educ: Col. of St. Thomas, 53-54; Winona State Col, B.S, 57; Univ. of Minn, M.A, 58 and Ph.D, 64; Kappa Delta Pi. Polit. & Govt. Pos: Mem, Dakota Co. Rep. Exec. Cmt, Minn, 60-62; co. chmn, Dakota Co. Young Rep. League and mem, State Bd. of Dirs, Minn. Young Rep. League, 62; city chmn, Stillwater Rep. Party, 63-64; mem, Wash. Co. Rep. Exec. Cmt, 63-; Minn. State Sen, Eighth Dist, 67-; chmn, Fourth Cong. Dist. Rep. Party, 69- Bus. & Prof. Pos: Teacher and counsr, Farmington High Sch, Minn, 58-60; guid. dir, Simley High Sch, South St. Paul, 60-63; instr, Univ. Minn, 63-64; asst. prof, Col. St. Thomas, 64- Mem: Bd. dirs, Minn. Asn. Sec. Sch. Prin; Nat. and State Asn. Sec. Sch. Prin; Jaycees; C. of C.(chmn. recreation cmt, St. Croix); Minn. Educ. Coun. Rel: Catholic. Mailing Add: 106 W. Wilkin St, Stillwater, Minn. 55082.

BROWN, ROLLAND D. R
Chmn, Grant Co. Rep. Party, Ark.
b. Crooksville, Ohio, 10/12/11; s. Herbert H. Brown and Chloe Williams B; m. 6/15/35 to Rhea Dawson; c. Sally L. (Mrs. Birkimer) and Beth D. (Mrs. Heinz). Educ: Ohio Univ, Engr, 32; Phi Kappa Tau. Polit. & Govt. Pos: Mem, Ohio State Rep. Cent. Cmt, 37-52; mem, Conserv. Cmn, 39-48; chmn, Grant Co. Rep. Party, Ark, 67- Bus. & Prof. Pos: Engr, Manhatton Coal Co, Ohio, 32-40; self employed, Sonny Hill Aggregates Corp, 40-42 & 45-58; self employed, Sheridan White Rock Inc, 58- Mil. Serv: Entered as Pvt, Army, 42, released as M/Sgt, 45, after serv. in 18th Cavalry Reconnaissance Squadron, ETO, 43-45; Good Conduct Medal; European-African, Middle East Campaign Ribbon with three bronze stars; one Overseas Bar. Mem: Mason; C. of C; Rotary; Rep. Time Club. Rel: Protestant. Mailing Add: 580 Jones St, Sheridan, Ark. 72150.

BROWN, ROSCOE DELANO D
Ark. State Rep.
b. Viola, Ark, 2/23/15; s. John Madison Brown and Mary Pate B; m. 5/27/49 to Lucy Belle Morris; c. Charlotte Ann, Ramona Kay and stepson, Alfred D. Tripp. Educ: Ark. State, B.S.E, 49; Peabody Col. for Teachers, M.A, 52; Catholic Univ; George Wash. Univ; Univ. of Hawaii. Polit. & Govt. Pos: Ark. State Rep, 11th Dist, 63-; secy, Northeast Ark. Legis. Coun, 65- Mil. Serv: Entered as Pvt, Army, 41, released as S/Sgt, 153rd Inf. of Ark, Alaska. Mem: Nat. Educ. Asn; legis. del, Ark. Educ. Asn; Classroom Teachers Asn; Mason; state legis. chmn, Am. Legion; Farm Bur; Nat. Soc. Legislators; Universal Commercial Travelers; C. of C. Rel: Methodist. Mailing Add: 1107 Holly St, Jonesboro, Ark. 72401.

BROWN, RUSSEL LEROY D
Secy, Alaska Dem. State Cent. Cmt.
b. Palisade, Nebr, 6/26/36; s. James Clark Brown and Helen BloBaum B; div; c. Renee. Educ: McCook Col, 52-54; Univ. Nebr, 54-57. Polit. & Govt. Pos: V.chmn, Alaska Young Dem, 64-65, chmn, 65-68, nat. committeeman, 68- and southeast. dist. chmn, 64-66; founder and pres, Ketchikan Young Dem, Alaska, 64-66; chmn, Ketchikan Harbor Cmt, 65-67; chmn, Ketchikan Consolidated Dem. Cmt, 66-; regional dir, Young Dem. Clubs Am, 67-; secy, Alaska Dem. State Cent. Cmt, 67-; chmn. party orgn. cmt, Dem. State Conv, 68; alternate del, Dem. Nat. Conv, 68. Bus. & Prof. Pos: Field asst. archeologist, River Basin Surv, Kans, Nebr. and S.Dak, Smithsonian Inst, 56-57; chemist, Alaska Fisheries Exp. Cmn, Ketchikan, 57-59; fishery technologist, Alaska Dept. Fish & Game, 59-62; chemist, Ketchikan Pulp Co, 62- Mil. Serv: Entered as Pvt, Army Nat. Guard, 58, released as Sgt. 1/C, 64, after serving in Co. A, 3rd Bn; 297th Inf. Publ: 'Protein Analysis of Shrimp Waste Meal' Commercial Fisheries Rev, 59; 'Paralytic Shellfish Poison in the Alaska Butter Clam,' Proc. Alaska Sci. Conf, 60; 'Frozen King Crab Meat: Effect of Processing Conditions on Fluids Freed Upon Thawing,' Fishery Indust. Res, 65. Mem: V.pres, Eagles 162; Alaska Native Brotherhood; founder and mem. first bd. dirs, Tongass Hist. Soc; dep. dist. dir. chem, biol. and radiological warfare defense, Ketchikan Civil Defense Dist; chmn. supvry. cmt, Ketchikan Pulp Employees Fed. Credit Union. Rel: Lutheran. Legal Res: 1200A Millar, Ketchikan, Alaska 99901. Mailing Add: P.O. Box 1125, Ketchikan, Alaska 99901.

BROWN, STUART BARNETT R
b. St. Louis, Mo, 1/5/34; s. Sid Brown and Sara Dennison B; m. 6/16/62 to Sharon Dale Bryant; c. Glenn M. and Linda M. Educ: Pasadena City Col, A.A, 59; Univ. Calif, Los Angeles, B.S, 61; Theta Delta Chi. Polit. & Govt. Pos: Precinct leader, Newport News Rep. Party, Va, 59-63, v.chmn, 63-64 and chmn, 64-67. Bus. & Prof. Pos: Dist. mgr, CEC, 61-65; mkt. mgr, Midwest. Instruments, 65- Mil. Serv: Entered as ETSN, Navy, 53, released as ETZ (SS), 57, after serv. in submarines, Pac. Theater; Good Conduct Medal; Presidential Award; Japanese Occupation Medal; Korean War Medal; Korean Presidential Citation. Mem: Inst. Elec. & Electronics Engrs; Instrument Soc. of Am; Audio Eng. Soc. Rel: Protestant. Mailing Add: 4772 S. Irvington, Tulsa, Okla. 74135. (1967)

BROWN, STUART ELLETT, JR. D
Mem, Clarke Co. Dem. Cmt, Va.
b. Richmond, Va, 4/25/16; s. Stuart Ellett Brown and Dakota Best B; m. 7/10/48 to Ann Lowe Rieman Barton; c. Ann Barton, Elizabeth L.T. and Stuart E. Polit. & Govt. Pos: Campaign mgr, Wendell Wilkie, Md, William

Preston Lane, Jr, Gov, Md, Charles Fenwick, Gov. Va. and William B. Spong, Jr, U.S. Sen, Va; mem, Clarke Co. Dem. Cmt, Va, 52-; asst. to William C. Battle campaign mgr. for Va. for John F. Kennedy, 60. Bus. & Prof. Pos: Assoc. and partner, Niles, Barton, Morrow and Yost, Baltimore, Md, 41-51; lawyer, Berryville, Va, 51- Mil. Serv: Entered as A/S, Navy, 41, released as Lt. Comdr, 47, after serv. as commanding officer in U.S.S. Vagrant and U.S.S. ATR-53, North Atlantic and North and Cent. Pac, 41-47; mem. instr. staff, Sub Chaser Training Center, Miami, Fla. Publ: Ed, Skyland, 60, auth, The Horses of Arlington, 64 and Virginia Baron, 65, Chesapeake Book Co; plus others. Mem: Md. Bar; Va. Bar; Va. State Bar Asn; Am. Legion; VFW; Va. Hist. Soc; Potomac Appalachian Trail Club. Rel: Episcopal. Legal Res: Poulshot, Millwood, Va. 22646. Mailing Add: Berryville, Va. 22611.

BROWN, TED W(ILLIAM) R
Secy. of State, Ohio
b. Springfield, Ohio, 4/19/06; s. George A. Brown (deceased) and Mabel Rhonemus B. (deceased); m. 4/19/26 to Florence Mitchell; c. Marilyn Ann (Mrs. Bruning), Barbara Lou (Mrs. Larkins) and Sherrie Lucille (Mrs. Rogers). Educ: Wittenberg Col; past pres, Kappa Phi. Polit. & Govt. Pos: Recorder, Clark Co, Ohio, 26-32; admin. post, Ohio Bur. Motor Vehicles, 40-44; Secy. State, Ohio, 51-; del, Rep. Nat. Conv, 68. Bus. & Prof. Pos: Formerly owner of heating and ventilating business. Publ: Columnist, 'Your Election Laws,' Ohio newspapers. Mem: Past pres, Exec. Cmt, Nat. Asn. of Secys. of State; former pres, Ohio Asn. of Co. Records; charter mem, Springfield, Ohio, Jr. C. of C; Blue Lodge, Mason; Scottish Rite; Grotto; Moose; Jr. Order. Three nat. awards for educ. booklets and pamphlets used in educ. prog. as Secy. of State; received Nat. Am. Heritage Award (non-partisan group) three times. Rel: Methodist. Legal Res: 6036 Dublin Rd, Dublin, Ohio 43017. Mailing Add: State House, Columbus, Ohio 43215.

BROWN, THOMAS CLAYTON, JR. D
Ga. State Rep.
b. Tallahassee, Ala, 9/11/13; s. Thomas Clayton Brown and Pauline Stilwell B; m. to Edythe Francine Ennis; c. Clayton, III, Francine Stilwell, David Nelson and Mary Ennis. Educ: Univ. Ga, A.B. in Journalism, 35; Sigma Delta Chi; Chi Psi. Polit. & Govt. Pos: Ga. State Rep, 67- Bus. & Prof. Pos: Owner, Goode-Nichols Furniture Co, Griffin, Ga, 35- Mil. Serv: Entered as Pvt, Air Force, 42, released as Capt, 46, after serv. in ETO, Army Airways Commun. Syst, 44-46; Lt. Col, Army Res, currently; Air Force Commendation and Army Commendation Medals; Unit Citation; Occupation Ribbon; Am. Defense Medal; Victory Ribbon; Good Conduct Medal. Mem: Dir, Ga. Retail Furniture Asn; Gridiron; Elks; VFW; Am. Legion; Rotary (pres, Griffin Chap, 59-60, Dist. Gov. Elect); C. of C.(dir. treas, 60-61); Moose; Ga. Farm Bur. Rel: Episcopal. Mailing Add: 550 S. Hill St, Griffin, Ga. 30223.

BROWN, THOMAS E. D
Dem. Nat. Committeeman, N.Mex.
b. Lampasas, Tex, 9/18/00; s. Thomas P. Brown and Hattie Hughes B; m. 6/10/23 to Anna Cleo Bowers; c. Thomas E, Jr. Educ: High sch. grad, 19. Polit. & Govt. Pos: Dem. Precinct Committeeman, 50-52; v.chmn, Eddy Co. Dem. Cent. Cmt, N.Mex, 52-54; chmn, Dem. Cent. Cmt, 54-56; Dem. Nat. Committeeman, N.Mex, 56-; treas, West. States Dem. Conf, 62-63, chmn. exec. cmt, 65; del, Dem. Nat. Conv, 68. Bus. & Prof. Pos: Dir, N.Mex. Boys Ranch; dir, Baptist Found. N.Mex; mem. Bd. Trustees, Col. of Artesia; pres, Brown Pipe & Supply of Artesia, Inc. Mem: Dir, Southeast. N.Mex. Agr. Research Asn; dir, Artesia C. of C; past pres, Rotary Club; Mason (32°). Rel: Baptist, Deacon. Mailing Add: P.O. Box 68, Artesia, N.Mex. 88210.

BROWN, THOMAS ELZIE, JR. D
N.Mex. State Rep.
b. Coleman, Tex, 10/24/29; s. Thomas Elzie Brown and Anna Cleo Bowers B; m. 11/22/49 to Mary Frances Gandy; c. Mary Ann, Paula Jean and Thomas Elzie, III 'Tracy' Educ: Baylor Univ, B.B.A, 51. Polit. & Govt. Pos: City councilman, Artesia, N.Mex, 56-62, chmn, Planning Cmn, 62-63; N.Mex. State Rep, 67- Bus. & Prof. Pos: Exec. v.pres, Brown Pipe & Supply Co, 51. Mem: Lions; Elks. Rel: Baptist. Legal Res: 2407 Cerro Rd, Artesia, N.Mex. 88210. Mailing Add: P.O. Box 68, Artesia, N.Mex. 88210.

BROWN, THOMAS HENRY D
Mayor, Westland, Mich.
b. Loogootee, Ind, 7/29/17; s. John Sylvester Brown and Emma Mae Draime B; m. 10/10/45 to Helen Catherine Hunter; c. Paul Thomas, Robert Timothy, Judith Ann (Mrs. Bullock), Joanna Catherine, Bonnie Leah and Mary Beth. Polit. & Govt. Pos: Trustee, Nankin Twp, Mich, 61-63, treas, 63-65 and supvr, 65-66; pres, League Nankin Dem. Voters, 63-65; mayor, Westland, Mich, 66-; del, Dem. Nat. Conv, 68; exec. bd. mem, Mich. 15th Dist. Dem. Orgn, currently. Bus. & Prof. Pos: Food prod. salesman; hosp. attend; hardware salesman; operator, Mobilgas Serv. Sta; sales and customer rels, Shell Oil Distributor. Mil. Serv: Entered as Pvt, Army, 40, released as S/Sgt, 45, after serv. in 5th Army, ETO, 42-45; European Theatre ribbon with 5 battle stars. Rel: Catholic. Mailing Add: 1917 Eagle Court, Westland, Mich. 48185.

BROWN, THOMAS L. R
Mich. State Rep.
b. Hillsdale, Mich, 11/10/31; s. Leo K. Brown and Maurine Harris B; m. 9/3/55 to Maria Mercedes Mejia; c. José Thomas, Suzanne Marie, Catherine Elizabeth, Ramôn Thomas, Maria Mercedes and Tomás Leo. Educ: Mich. State Univ, B.A, 57; Univ. Detroit, LL.B, 61; Gamma Eta Gamma. Polit. & Govt. Pos: Precinct committeeman, First Ward, Lansing, Mich, 62-63 and ward chmn, 63-64; asst. prosecuting attorney, Ingham Co, 62-65; asst. city attorney, Lansing, 63-64; mem, Ingham Co. Rep. Exec. Cmt, 64-68; village attorney, Leslie, 66-67; Mich. State Rep, 57th Dist, 67- Mil. Serv: Seaman 1/C, Navy, 53-55. Mem: Mich. and Ingham Co. Bar Asns; Ingham Co. Bench and Bar; Am. Trial Lawyers Asn; Am. Judicature Soc; K. of C. Rel: Roman Catholic. Legal Res: 2604 Heights Ave, Lansing Mich. 48912. Mailing Add: 603 Capitol Savings and Loan, 112 E. Allegan, Lansing, Mich. 48933.

BROWN, TOM FAIRFIELD R
V.Chmn, State Rep. Exec. Cmt, Fla.
b. Lakeland, Fal, 6/20/26; s. Sidney C. Brown and Myra Fairfield B; m. 8/26/50 to Ora Katherine Cannon; c. Tom F, Jr, Clifford, Anna Katherine, Carroll Lynn and Richard Douglas. Educ: Univ. Fla, LL.B, 50; Blue Key; pres, F Club; capt, swimming team; secy. of relig; pres. cabinet; 4 varsity letters in sports. Polit. & Govt. Pos: Chmn, Hillsborough Co. Rep. Cmt, Fla, 51-54; cand, Fla. State Rep, 52; mgr, Eisenhower Campaign, Hillsborough Co, 52; Rep. State Committeeman, Hillsborough Co, 54-66; chmn, Rep. State Speakers' Bur. and mem, Rep. State Finance Cmt, 56-58; alternate del, Rep. Nat. Conv, 56 & 60; asst. gen. counsel, State Rep. Exec. Cmt, 58-62, chmn, 62-66, v.chmn, 66-; mem, Rep. State Chmn. Conf; chmn, Fla. Del. to Rep. Nat. Conv, 64; mem, Rep. Nat. Cmt. Bus. & Prof. Pos: Sr. partner, Brown, Dixon & Shear. Mil. Serv: Navy, 44-46. Mem: Am. Fla. and Tampa Bar Asns; pres, Hillsborough Co. Bar Asn; Am. Trials Lawyers Asn; dir, Lawyers's Title Serv; Fla. Sheriffs Asn; Mason (33°); Shrine; Lions; Am. Legion; DAV; Boy Scouts; PTA; Gideons; dir, Salvation Army, Tampa; life mem, Gr. Tampa C. of C; Christian Businessmans Cmt; past dir, Execs. Club; Dads Club, Chamberlain High Sch; Tampa Men's Garden Club; United Fund; Univ. Club; Tampa Sales Exec. Club; patron, Lyric Theater and Metrop. Theater; dir, U.S. Crusade for Christ. Rel: Baptist. Legal Res: 12202 N. Armenia Ave, Tampa, Fla. 33612. Mailing Add: 18th Floor Exchange National Bank Bldg, Tampa, Fla. 33602.

BROWN, TOT MOFFETT D
b. Pittsburg, Kans, 12/17/16; s. William Archibald Brown and Alene Moffett B; m. 1/20/52 to Pauline McDaniel; c. Randall William. Educ: Kans. State Teachers Col; Tulsa Univ, B.M.E. and M.M. Polit. & Govt. Pos: Okla. State Rep, 64-68. Mil. Serv: Entered as Pvt, Air Force, 42, released as Sgt, 45. Mem: C. of C.(pres, Sand Springs, 66-); Rotary (pres, 63-64); Asn. of Ins. Agents; Mutual of New York Field Club. Rel: Methodist. Legal Res: 1302 McKinley Ave, Sand Springs, Okla. 74063. Mailing Add: P.O. Box 456, Sand Springs, Okla. 74063.

BROWN, VIRGINIA MAE D
Interstate Commerce Cmnr.
b. Pliny, W.Va, 11/13/23; d. Felix Melville Brown (deceased) and Hester Ann Crandall B; m. 4/8/55 to James Vernon Brown; c. Victoria Anne and Pamela Kay. Educ: W.Va. Univ, A.B; W.Va. Col. Law, LL.B, 47. Polit. & Govt. Pos: Asst. Attorney Gen, State of W.Va, 52-61, Counsel to Gov, 61, Ins. Cmnr, 61-62 and mem, Pub. Serv. Cmn, 62-64; Interstate Commerce Cmnr, 64-, chmn, Interstate Commerce Cmn, 69. Mem: Am. and W.Va. State Bar Asns. Rel: Presbyterian. Legal Res: Pliny, W.Va. 25158. Mailing Add: 1200 Olde Towne Rd, Alexandria, Va. 22307.

BROWN, WILLIAM HILL, III R
Chmn, Equal Employ. Opportunity Cmn.
b. Phila, Pa, 1/19/28; s. William Hill Brown, Jr. and Ethel L. Washington B; m. 8/29/53 to Sonya M. Brown; c. Michele. Educ: Temple Univ, B.S, 52; Univ. Pa. Law Sch, LL.B, 55; Alpha Phi Alpha. Polit. & Govt. Pos: Chief of frauds, Dist. Attorney's Off, Phila, Pa, 68, dep. dist. attorney, 68; chmn, Equal Employ. Opportunity Cmn, 69- Bus. & Prof. Pos: Assoc, Norris, Green, Harris & Higginbotham, Phila, Pa, 56-62; partner, Norris, Green, Harris & Brown, 62-64; partner, Norris, Brown & Hall, 64-68; mem. regional bd. dir, First Pa. Bank, 68- Mil. Serv: Entered as Pvt, Army Air Force, 46, released as Cpl, 48, after serv. in 12th Air Ammunition Squadron, Far East. Mem: Phila, Pa, Am. and Fed. Bar Asns; Am. Trial Lawyers Asn. Rel: Episcopal. Legal Res: 4728 Osage Ave, Philadelphia, Pa. 19143. Mailing Add: 4701 Willard Ave, Apt. 1635, Chevy Chase, Md. 20015.

BROWN, WILLIAM HOLMES
Asst. Parliamentarian, U.S. House of Rep.
b. Huntington, W.Va, 9/3/29; single. Educ: Swarthmore Col, B.S, 51; Univ. Chicago, J.D, 54. Polit. & Govt. Pos: Asst. Parliamentarian, U.S. House of Rep. Mil. Serv: Entered as Ens, Naval Res, 54, released as Lt(jg), 57; Lt. Comdr, Res. Mailing Add: 490 M St. S.W, Washington, D.C. 20024.

BROWN, WILLIAM KIRKLAND D
La. State Rep.
b. Dry Prong, La, 1/7/23; s. Richard Ed Brown and Sarah Irene Rhodes B; m. 5/23/53 to Mae Ella Foster; c. Susan Clotilde. Educ: La. State Univ, Baton Rouge, B.S, 49, M.E, 56. Polit. & Govt. Pos: La. State Rep, Grant Parish, 60-64, Grant and Rapides Parish, 36th Dist, 64-, mem. judiciary cmt, sect. C, educ. cmt. and health, welfare and charitable insts. cmt, La. House of Rep, 60-64, mem. judiciary cmt, sect. B, 64-68, mem. house affairs cmt, 64-, chmn. enrollment cmt, mem. ins. and banking cmt. Bus. & Prof. Pos: Ins. agent, W.K. Brown Ins. Agency, 57- Mil. Serv: Entered Navy, 43, released as Pharmacist's Mate 2/C, 46, after serv. in S.Pac. Theater, 43-46; Two Bronze Stars. Mem: Farm Bur.(chmn. nursing home cmt); VFW; Am. Legion; Lions; Grant Parish March of Dimes (chmn); Grant Parish Teacher's Asn.(past pres); C. of C. Rel: Baptist. Legal Res: P.O. Box 27, Pollock, La. 71467. Mailing Add: P.O. Box 326, Alexandria, La. 71301.

BROWN, WILLIE L, JR. D
Calif. State Assemblyman
b. Mineola, Tex, 3/20/34; s. Willie Lewis Brown, Sr. and Minnie Collins B; m. 9/1/57 to Blanche Vitero; c. Susan Elizabeth, Robin Elaine and Michael Elliott. Educ: San Francisco State Col, A.B, 55; Univ. Calif. Hastings Col. Law, LL.B, 58; Phi Alpha Delta; Alpha Phi Alpha. Polit. & Govt. Pos: Committeeman, Co. Dem. Cmt, Calif, 60-62; Calif. State Assemblyman, 65-; mem, Calif. Dem. State Cent. Cmt, currently; del, Dem. Nat. Conv, 68. Mil. Serv: Specialist 3/C, Nat. Guard. Rel: Protestant. Legal Res: 1524 Masonic Ave, San Francisco, Calif. 94117. Mailing Add: 666 Octavia, San Francisco, Calif. 94102. (1967)

BROWN, WINTHROP GILMAN
Dep. Asst. Secy. of State for E. Asian & Pac. Affairs
b. Maine, 7/12/07; m. to Peggy Bell; c. Three. Educ: Yale Univ, B.A, 29, LL.B, 32. Polit. & Govt. Pos: Attorney, Lend Lease Admin, 41; exec. officer, Harriman Mission and Mission for Econ. Affairs, London, 41-45; dir, Office of Int. Trade Policy, 45-48; counselor, London, 52-55; dir, Int. Coop. Admin. Mission, United Kingdom, 55-57; minister-counselor, India and Nepal, 57-60; U.S. Ambassador to Laos, 60-62; dep. commandant, Nat. War Col, 62-64; U.S. Ambassador to Korea, 64-67; dep. asst. secy. of state for E. Asian and Pac. Affairs, 68- Bus. & Prof. Pos: Law clerk, 32-38; lawyer, 38-41. Mem: N.Y. Bar Asn. Superior Serv. Award, 52; Distinguished Fed. Civilian Serv. Award by President Kennedy, 63. Mailing Add: 2435 Tracy Place N.W, Washington, D.C. 20037.

BROWNE, ELIZABETH WINGREENE D
Ore. State Rep.
b. Minneapolis, Minn, 4/4/26; d. William Alexander Wingreene and Margaret Blackwood W; m. 11/13/49 to Colbert Hughes Browne; c. Claudia, Scott, Paula Jane and Christopher. Educ: Univ. Minn, B.A, 48; Univ. Chicago, M.A, 51; Univ. Ore, LL.B, 66. Polit. & Govt. Pos: Dir, Sch. Dist. 76, Ore, 61; dep. dist. attorney, Lane Co, 67-68; referee, Lane Co. Circuit Court, 68-69; Ore. State Rep, 69- Bus. & Prof. Pos: Instr, Dade Co, Fla, 51-58; attorney-at-law, Ore, currently. Publ: 'Gault-Its Impact in Oregon,' Willamette Law Rev, 67; ed, Juvenile Judges Digest and Handbook on Juvenile Law, Ore. State Bar. Mem: Lane Co, Ore. State and Am. Bar Asns; Judicature Juvenile Judges Asn; Bus. & Prfnl. Womens Asn. Rel: Protestant. Mailing Add: Laurel Butte Dr, Oakridge, Ore. 97463.

BROWNE, GLENN GORDON
Dep. Gov. and Dir, Land Bank Serv, Farm Credit Admin.
b. Park City, Utah, 12/17/17; s. Joseph Stacy Browne and Emily Gordon B; m. 9/5/48 to Barbara Ann Jameyson; c. Linda Louise and Daniel Glenn. Educ: Univ. Calif, Berkeley, 34-36. Polit. & Govt. Pos: Asst. v.pres. and regional mgr, Fed. Land Bank, Berkeley, Calif, 36-58; asst. dir. of prog. and econ. policy, Chief Investment and Finance Div, Agency of Int. Develop, Dept. of State, Seoul, Korea, 59-64; spec. consult. to Dept. of State on S. Vietnam; dep. gov. and dir, Land Bank Serv, Farm Credit Admin, Wash, D.C, 64- Mil. Serv: Naval Res, 42-45. Kentucky Colonel. Mailing Add: 5908 Lennox Rd, Bethesda, Md. 20034. (1967)

BROWNE, JAMES BROACH D
Asst. Dist. Attorney, Payne Co, Okla.
b. University City, Mo, 10/4/35; s. D. Henry S. Browne and Willie Myers B; div; c. Henry Allen, James Malone and Christopher Clifton. Educ: Yale Univ, 53-54; Tulsa Univ, B.A, 57; Univ. Okla. Law Sch, LL.B, 59; Kappa Sigma; Phi Alpha Delta. Polit. & Govt. Pos: Asst. co. attorney, Payne Co, Okla, 59-60, asst. dist. attorney, 67-; city cmnr, Cushing, 65-67, v.chmn, 67; chmn, Payne Co. Dem. Cent. Cmt, 67-69; alternate del, Dem. Nat. Conv, 68. Bus. & Prof. Pos: Dir, Cushing Oil & Gas Co, Okla, 65-; dir, Assoc. Petrol and Mining, Inc, 65-; dir. and v.pres, Midwest Line Serv, 66-; dir. and secy, C&G Enterprise, Inc, 67- Mem: Payne Co. Bar Asn.(pres, 65); Okla. and Am. Bar Asns; Am. and Okla. Trial Lawyers Asns; Am. Judicature Soc; Mason(32°); Scottish Rite; York Rite. Rel: Protestant. Legal Res: 1115 E. Sixth, Cushing, Okla. 74023. Mailing Add: Box 1385, Cushing, Okla. 74023.

BROWNE, JAMES HAROLD R
V.Chmn, Kans. State Rep. Party
b. Little Rock, Ark, 4/11/10; s. Felix Browne (deceased) and Phebe Person B; m. 6/16/37 to Lucille Elaine King; c. Elaine (Mrs. Owens) and Rosalyn (Mrs. Welch). Educ: Sumner High Sch, grad, 28. Polit. & Govt. Pos: Cmnr, Civil Serv, Kansas City, Kans, 51-55; v.chmn, Kans. State Rep. Party, 68- Bus. & Prof. Pos: Rwy. mail clerk, 36-45; asst. mgr. and salesman, Atlanta Life Ins. Co, 45-57; v.pres, Douglass State Bank, 47-66, chmn. bd. dirs, 66-; founder and pres, Crusader Life Ins. Co, 57-; U.S. C. of C. Bus. representative for U.S. Govt, ILD Conv, Geneva, Switzerland, 61. Mem: Kiwanis Int; v.pres. govt. affairs, Kansas City C. of C; gen. chmn, United Commun. Fund, 68. B'nai B'rith Award, 62. Rel: Methodist. Mailing Add: 1317 N. 12th St, Kansas City, Kans. 66102.

BROWNE, JEROME FIELDING D
Dem. Statutory Chmn, Dunn Co, Wis.
b. Metropolis, Ill, 1/10/21; s. William Louis Browne and Mary Nellius B; m. 6/18/55 to Virginia Valetta Richartz; c. William Theodore. Educ: High Sch. Polit. & Govt. Pos: Sgt-at-Arms, First Ward Dem-Farmer-Labor Club, Minneapolis, 50-51, v.chmn, 52; secy, Dunn Co. Dem. Party, 59-62, chmn, 63-65; Dem. Statutory chmn, Dunn Co, Wis, 64-; chmn, Dunn Co. Humphrey-Muskie Campaign, 68. Bus. & Prof. Pos: Dock and warehouse foreman, S.J. Groves & Sons, Antigua, B.W.I, 41-42; from order clerk to foreman, Kraft Foods Co, 44-58; parts sales mgr, Richartz Implement, 58- Mem: Dunn Co. Fish & Game Asn; treas, Menomonie Toastmasters. Rel: Congregational. Mailing Add: Rt. 6, Menomonie, Wis. 54751.

BROWNE, KENNETH N. D
b. N.Y, N.Y, 6/25/23; m. to Shirley Ann Session; c. Karen, Kenneth, Jr. Educ: Long Island Univ, B.S; Brooklyn Law Col, LL.B; McGill Univ. Sch. of Engr; A&T Col. of N.C; W.Va. State Col; Columbia Univ. Sch. of Law; earning credits toward Dr. of Judicial Sci. Polit. & Govt. Pos: N.Y. State Assemblyman, 64-66; Asst. Dist. Attorney Queens Co, 61-; Bd. of Dirs, United Dems, 11th Assembly Dist; Criminal Investigator, Bur. of Alcohol & Narcotics, U.S. Treas. Dept; Postal Clerk. Bus. & Prof. Pos: Lawyer; formerly with Caldwell & Browne, Buffalo. Mil. Serv: U.S. Army, WW II, 42-46, M/Sgt; Good Conduct Medal, Purple Heart with Oakleaf Cluster, European, African, Middle East. Medal with 4 battle stars, Am. Serv. Medal, WW II Victory Medal. Mem: Jamaica Br. NAACP; N.Y. State Dist. Attorney Asn; NAACP Legal Redress Cmt; Bd. of Dir, Queens Co. Boy Scouts; St. Albans Improv. Asn; Elks; Erie Co. & Am. & Queens Co. Criminal Bar Asns. Mailing Add: 185-19 Henderson Ave, Hollis, N.Y. 11423. (1967)

BROWNE, MAXINE GERTRUDE R
Rep. Committeewoman, 25th Sen. Dist, Tex.
b. Saskatoon, Sask, Can, 1/17/15; d. Kenneth Abraham Reeder and Zadie Louise Struthers R; m. 8/22/44 to Charles Foster Browne, M.D; c. Brenda Ann, Charles Foster, Jr. and Paul Douglas. Polit. & Govt. Pos: V.chmn, Sutton Co. Rep. Cmt, Tex, 50-54, chmn, 54-55; alternate del, Rep. Nat. Conv, 56 & 65, del, 64; regional v.chmn, Rep. Party, Tex, 56-58; Rep. committeewoman, 25th Sen. Dist, 56- Mem: Past pres, Sonora Woman's Club and Sonora Garden Club; council woman, Tex. Med. Auxiliary. Rel: Episcopal. Legal Res: Old San Antonio Rd, Sonora, Tex. 76950. Mailing Add: P.O. Box 456, Sonora, Tex. 76950.

BROWNE, ROBERT SPAN D
b. Chicago, Ill, 8/17/24; s. William H. Browne, Jr. and Julia Barksdale B; m. to Nguyen Thi Huoi; c. Hoa Nguyen, Mai Julia, Ngo Alexi and Marshall Xuan. Educ: Univ. Ill, B.A, 44; Univ. Chicago, M.B.A, 47; City Univ. N.Y, 64-69; Phi Eta Sigma; Alpha Phi Alpha. Polit. & Govt. Pos: Del, Dem. Nat. Conv, 68. Bus. & Prof. Pos: Instr, Dillard Univ, 47-49; secy, Watchtower Life Ins. Co, Houston, 49-50; indust. field secy, Chicago Urban League, 50-53; economist, Int. Coop. Admin.(stationed in Cambodia and Vietnam), 55-61; asst. prof. econ, Fairleigh Dickinson Univ, 64-69. Mil. Serv: Entered as Pvt, Army, 44, released as Sgt, 46. Publ: Race Relations in International Affairs, Pub. Affairs Press, 61; 'The Civil Rights Movement and the War in Vietnam,' Freedomways, Fall 65; 'The Case for Two Americas,' N.Y. Times Mag, 8/68. Mem: Am. Econ. Asn; Union of Radical Polit. Economists. Mailing Add: 214 Tryon Ave, Teaneck, N.J. 07666.

BROWNE, ROY EDWARD R
Chmn, Summit Co. Rep. Cent. Cmt, Ohio.
b. Barberton, Ohio, 10/16/04; s. Herbert C. Browne and Nellie Neitz B; m. 7/7/33 to Harriet Elizabeth Brooker; c. Walter R, Royce and Carolyn (Mrs. Gay). Educ: Cleveland Marshall Law Sch, LL.B, 29; Univ. Akron, B.A, 37; Pi Kappa Delta; Lambda Chi Alpha. Polit. & Govt. Pos: Asst. attorney gen, Ohio, 36-42; law dir, Akron, 42-53; chmn, Summit Co. Rep. Exec. Cmt, 53-63; chmn, Summit Co. Rep. Cent. Cmt, 53-; mem, Bd. of Elec, Summit Co, 53-; del, Rep. Nat. Conv, 68; mem, Ohio Rep. State Cent. Cmt, currently. Mem: Mason (32°); Shrine; Lions. Rel: Methodist. Mailing Add: 1910 First National Tower, Akron, Ohio 44308. (1967)

BROWNE, RUTH T. D
Secy, Kans. Dem. State Cent. Cmt.
b. Norton, Kans, 3/11/30; d. John W. Hickert and Mary Fink H; m. 4/14/52 to John C. Browne; c. Michael, Charles, Mary Helen, Theresa, James and Daniel. Educ: Lorretto Heights Col, A.B. in soc. sci. Polit. & Govt. Pos: Secy, Kans. Dem. State Cent. Cmt, 65-; chmn. and precinct committeewoman, Clay Co. Dem. Party, 65-68; del, Dem. Nat. Conv, 68. Rel: Catholic. Mailing Add: 1603 Fifth St, Clay Center, Kans. 67432. (1967)

BROWNE, SECOR DELAHAY R
Chmn, Civil Aeronaut. Bd.
b. Chicago, Ill, 7/22/16; s. Aldis Jerome Browne and Elizabeth Cunningham B; m. 8/23/45 to Mary Denise Giles; c. Patrick R. and Giles C. Educ: Harvard Univ, A.B, 38; Signet Soc; Hasty Pudding; Inst. of 1777. Polit. & Govt. Pos: Mem, Lincoln Rep. Town Cmt, Mass, 62-68; Asst. Secy. for Research and Tech, Dept. of Transportation, 69; chmn, Civil Aeronaut. Bd, 69- Bus. & Prof. Pos: Engr. draftsman, Kroeschell Eng. Co, Chicago, Ill, 38-39; engr. salesman, Barber-Colman Co, Rockford, 39-42, mgr. aircraft prod, 46-51; Clifford Mfg. Co, Waltham, Mass, 51-55; pres. and chmn. bd, Browne & Shaw Co, 55-69, Browne & Shaw Research Corp, 63-68; assoc. prof, Mass. Inst. Tech, 58-69; transportation consult, Edwards Browne Assocs, London, Eng, 67-69; v.pres, Bolt, Beranek and Newman, Inc, Cambridge, Mass, 68-69. Mil. Serv: Entered as Aviation Cadet, Army Air Corps, 42, released as Maj, 46, after serv. in 50th Troop Carrier Squadron, 314th Group, First Allied Airborne Army, Europe-Africa-Middle East Theatre, 44-46; Eight Battle Stars; Two Presidential Unit Citations; Bronze Star. Publ: 'The National Interest in Supersonic Transport,' 1/65 and 'National Transportation: A Study in Conflicts,' 3/66, Tech. Rev; 'The Quiet Airport: It Could Mean a Decaying City, Too,' Boston Herald Traveler, 11/29/68. Mem: Soc. of Automotive Engrs; Am. Soc. Heating, Ventilating and Refrigerating Engrs; Am. Helicopter Soc; Harvard Club, Boston; St. Botolph Club of Boston; Wings Club, N.Y.C; Nat. Aviation Club, Wash, D.C; Kittery Point Yacht Club, Kittery, Maine. Rel: Roman Catholic. Legal Res: Trapelo Rd, Lincoln, Mass. 01773. Mailing Add: 4201 Cathedral Ave. N.W, Apt. 1419 E, Washington, D.C. 20016.

BROWNE, STANLEY ROBERT RIEVE R
b. Sioux Falls, S.Dak, 10/13/23; s. Walter Watson Browne and Ida Zelma Rieve B; m. 6/13/48 to Coral Jane Freeman; c. Laurel Sue and Neal Freeman. Educ: Winona State Teachers Col, 46; Augustana Col, 47-48; Drake Univ, LL.B, 51; collegiate pres, Delta Theta Phi. Polit. & Govt. Pos: Rep. precinct committeeman, Iowa, 57; chmn, Jack Miller for U.S. Sen. Cmt, 60; admin. asst, Jack Miller, U.S. Sen, Iowa, 61- Mil. Serv: Entered as Pvt, Army, 43, released as Cpl, 46, after serv. in 13th Airborne Div, ETO, African and Mid. East Theaters. Mem: Iowa State and Polk Co. Bar Asns; past pres, Polk Co. Jr. Bar Asn; past pres, Capitol Hill Admin. Asst. & Secy. Club; past master, New Century Masonic Lodge; past chmn, Central Iowa Multiple Sclerosis Soc; Jr. C. of C.(state legislative chmn). Finished second in Nat. Masters Volleyball Tournament, 58. Rel: Presbyterian. Legal Res: 5523 Grand, Des Moines, Iowa 50312. Mailing Add: River House, 1600 S. Joyce, A-1511, Arlington, Va. 22202.

BROWNE, WILLIAM V. D
Exec. Dir, Dem. State Cmt, N.J.
b. N.Y.C, 11/3/21; s. William S. Browne and Della Curry B; m. 9/24/49 to Kathleen Hannon; c. Colleen and Patricia. Educ: Univ. Calif, Berkeley, 2 years; Fordham Univ, 1 year. Polit. & Govt. Pos: Dem. leader, Hazlet Twp, N.J, 59; chmn, Citizens for Kennedy, Monmouth Co, 60; chmn, Citizens for Hughes, 61; asst. to state treas, N.J, 62-63; asst. to state chmn, Dem. Party, 63-64; exec. dir, Dem. State Cmt, 64-; alternate del, Dem. Nat. Conv, 68. Mil. Serv: Entered as Pvt, Army, 42, released as Warrant Officer, 46, after serv. in CID. Mem: Am. Legion; K. of C; Holy Name Soc. Rel: Catholic. Mailing Add: 13 Bucknell Dr, Hazlet, N.J. 07730.

BROWNELL, HERBERT R
b. Peru, Nebr, 2/20/04; s. Herbert B. and May A. Miller B; m. 6/16/34 to Doris A. McCarter; c. Joan, Ann, Thomas McCarter, James Barker. Educ: Univ. Nebr, B.A, 24; Yale Univ, LL.B, 27. Polit. & Govt. Pos: N.Y. State Assemblyman, 32-37; chmn, Rep. Nat. Cmt, 44-46; U.S. Attorney Gen, 53-57; head, United Serv. Orgn. Campaign, 64-65. Bus. & Prof. Pos: Attorney, Root, Clark, Buckner & Ballatine, 27-29; attorney, Lord, Day & Lord, N.Y.C, 29-53 & 57- Mem: Am, N.Y. State and N.Y.C. Bar Asns; N.Y.C. Century Asn; Downtown Asn. Rel: Methodist. Mailing Add: 25 Broadway, New York, N.Y. 10004.

BROWNING, CHAUNCEY H. D
Judge, Supreme Court of Appeals, W.Va.
b. Chauncey, W.Va, 5/15/03; s. Ballard F. Browning and Mary E. Curry B; m. 2/4/29 to Evelyn Mahone; c. Barbara Ruth (Mrs. Jack Stickman) and Chauncey, Jr. and 8 grandchildren. Educ: W.Va. Univ, A.B, 24, LL.B, 27; Kappa Sigma. Polit. & Govt. Pos: Attorney, City of Logan and secy, State Workmen's Compensation Cmn, W.Va, 25-44; asst. prosecuting attorney and

prosecuting attorney, Logan Co, 44-52; Attorney Gen, W.Va, 52 and judge, Supreme Court of Appeals, 52- Bus. & Prof. Pos: Teacher hist. and govt, Logan High Sch, W.Va, 24-25. Mem: W.Va. State Bar; Am. and W.Va. Bar Asns; former pres, Logan Co. Bar Asn. and W.Va. Judicial Asn; Am. Law Inst; Am. Judicature Soc. Rel: Methodist. Mailing Add: c/o Supreme Court of Appeals, Charleston, W.Va. 25305.

BROWNING, CHAUNCEY H, JR. D
Attorney Gen, W.Va.
b. Charleston, W.Va, 11/21/34; s. Chauncey H. Browning and Eyelyn Mahone B; m. 1954 to May Elizabeth Gallaher; c. Chauncey H, III, Charles Preston and Steven Thomas. Educ: W.Va. Univ, A.B, 56 and LL.B, 58. Polit. & Govt. Pos: Law clerk, U.S. Dist. Court for South. Dist. W.Va, 58; attorney-in-charge, Legal Aid Soc, Kanawha and Putnam Co, 59-60; Cmnr. Pub. Insts, W.Va, 62-69; Attorney Gen, W.Va, 69- Bus. & Prof. Pos: Attorney-at-law, Charleston, W.Va, 58-62. Publ: Former ed, W.Va. Law Quart. Mem: W.Va. Cmn. on Aging; v.pres, W.Va. Ment. Retardation Cmn; Am, W.Va. and Kanawha Co. Bar Asns; W.Va. State Bar; W.Va. Trial Lawyers Asn; Order of the Coif; Phi Delta Phi; Kappa Sigma. Mailing Add: State Capitol, Charleston, W.Va. 25305.

BROWNING, GEORGE MORTIMER D
Mem, Md. Dem. State Cent. Cmt.
b. McHenry, Md, 12/19/14; s. Jessie Frank Browning and May Williams B; m. 10/24/35 to Mary Margaret Kelly; c. Mary Jane and Nathan Criss. Educ: Elec. & Bus. Courses and High Sch. Polit. & Govt. Pos: Forest supt, Md. State Dept. Forestry, 34-41; state trooper, Md. State Police, 41-43; mem. and past chmn, Md. Dem. State Cent. Cmt, 54- Bus. & Prof. Pos: Chief Maintenance, Pa. Elec. Co, 43- Mem: AF&AM; Consistory (32°); Ali Ghan Temple; Ali Ghan Relief Asn; life mem, Moose; Md. State Police Alumni Asn. Inc; Oakland Optimist Club. Rel: Episcopal. Mailing Add: Route 1, Box 358-A, Oakland, Md. 21550. (1967)

BROWNING, JAMES ARTHUR, JR. D
Mem, Ventura Co. Dem. Cent. Cmt, Calif.
b. Kansas City, Mo, 11/20/30; s. James Arthur Browning and Mary Elizabeth Van Arsdall B; single. Educ: Univ. Calif. at Los Angeles, A.B. in polit. sci, 52, Law Sch, LL.B, 57; Theta Delta Chi; Phi Delta Phi. Polit. & Govt. Pos: Pres, Oxnard Dem. Club, Calif, 60; mem. exec. cmt, Calif. State Cent. Cmt, 62-64; chmn, Ventura Co. Dem. Cent. Cmt, 62-64 and mem, currently; del, Dem. Nat. Conv, 64. Bus. & Prof. Pos: Assoc, F. Gile Tiffany, Jr, attorney-at-law, 57-61; partner, Tiffany, Hunt & Browning, Oxnard, 61- Mil. Serv: Entered as 2nd Lt, Air Force, 52, released as 1st Lt, 54, after serv. as Adj, 529th Air Defense Group; Nat. Defense Serv. Medal. Mem: Ventura Co, Calif. and Am. Bar Asns; bd. dirs, Better Bus. Bur. of the Tri-Counties, Inc. Legal Res: 4059 Ocean Dr, Oxnard, Calif. 93030. Mailing Add: P.O. Drawer 792, Oxnard, Calif. 93030.

BROWNING, LEVI MARTIN D
b. Benton, Ill, 9/3/04; s. Thomas Seborn Browning and Juliet Robertson B; married. Educ: Univ. Ill, M.D. Polit. & Govt. Pos: Cmnr, Dept. of Health and Welfare, Alaska, 63- Mil. Serv: Commissioned officer, Med. Corps, Army and Air Force, 36-63; Am. Defense, Am. Campaign, Asiatic-Pac. and Europe-Africa-Middle East Campaign Ribbons; Victory Medal; Army Commendation; Air Force Commendation with Oak Leaf; Nat. Defense Ribbon. Mem: Am. Col. of Hosp. Adminstr; Am. Bd. Prev. Med; Am. Med. Asn; Aerospace Med. Asn; Am. Pub. Health Asn; Asn. Mil. Surgeons. Rel: Protestant. Mailing Add: Birch Hill, Box 88, Palmer, Alaska 99645. (1967)

BROWNLEE, JERRY L.
Mem, Tex. Water Quality Bd.
b. Lawrence, Kans, 7/17/31; s. William Oscar Brownlee and Laverne Sanders B; m. 6/24/55 to Marjorie Woodson; c. Laura, Michael, Susan and John. Educ: Univ. Kans, A.B, 53 and M.P.A, 56; Phi Beta Kappa; Beta Theta Pi. Polit. & Govt. Pos: Mem, City Research and Budget Dept, Kansas City, Kans, 54-58, dir, 58-59; asst. to city mgr, Ft. Worth, Tex, 59-63, city mgr, 63-67; mem, Tex. Water Quality Bd, 68- Bus. & Prof. Pos: V.pres, Kimbell, Inc, Ft. Worth, Tex, 67- Mem: Int. City Mgr. Asn; Nat. Munic. Asn; Am. Soc. Publ Admin. Achievement Award, Munic. Adv. Coun. Tex; Cert. of Merit, Munic. Finance Officers Asn, 61; Outstanding Young Texan, 63; Ft. Worth's Outstanding Young Man, 64. Mailing Add: 3609 Kimberly Lane, Ft. Worth, Tex. 76133.

BROWNSTEIN, IRWIN D
b. N.Y, N.Y, 11/4/30. Educ: LL.B, 53; Iota Theta Law Grad. Asn. Polit. & Govt. Pos: N.Y. State Sen, 63-66; N.Y. State Assemblyman, 59-63; Dem. State Cmt; Legis. Affairs Cmt. of Dem. State Cmt, 63; Dem. Adv. Cmt. on Platform, 62; Asst. Corp. Counsel, NYC Div. of Legis, Opinions, Penalties; Asst, Victor F. Condello, 53; Law Asst. to Chief Judge Albert Conway, Court of Appeals, 53-55. Mem: Founding Mem. of Munic. Lodge, B'nai B'rith; N.Y. State Bar Asn. Mailing Add: 16 Court St, Brooklyn, N.Y. 11201. (1967)

BROWNSTEIN, PHILIP NATHAN D
b. Ober, Ind, 2/14/17; s. Max Brownstein and Anna Katz B; m. 9/14/38 to Esther Savelle; c. Michael. Educ: George Washington Univ, 37; Columbus Univ, LL.B, 40, LL.M, 41. Polit. & Govt. Pos: With Fed. Housing Admin, 34-44; with Vet. Admin, 46-63, dir. loan guaranty serv, 56-61, chief benefits dir, 61-63; asst. secy. for mortgage credit and cmnr. of fed. housing, Dept. of Housing and Urban Develop, 63-69. Bus. & Prof. Pos: Counsel, Parsons, Tennent & Zeidman, Wash, D.C, 69- Mil. Serv: Marine Corps Res, 44-46. Exceptional Serv. Award, Vet. Admin, 60; Top Performer Award, House & Home Mag, 64; Career Serv. Award, Nat. Civil Serv. League, 67. Mailing Add: Parsons, Tennent & Zeidman, 1035 Connecticut Ave. N.W, Washington, D.C. 20036.

BROYHILL, JAMES EDGAR R
Mem. Rep. Nat. Cmt.
b. Wilkes Co, N.C, 4/5/92; s. Isaac Broyhill and Margaret Parsons B; m. 6/21/21 to Satie L. Hunt; c. Allene (Mrs. W. Stevens), Paul H, James T. and Bettie (Mrs. Willard Gortner). Polit. & Govt. Pos: Mem, Rep. Nat. Cmt, 48-; del, Rep. Nat. Conv, 7 times. Bus. & Prof. Pos: Exec. head, Broyhill Furniture Factories, Lenoir Chair Co, Lenoir Furniture Corp, Lenoir Veneer Co, Nat. Veneer Co, Harper Furniture Co, Lenoir Furniture Forwarding Co, Can-over Furniture Co. and Otis L. Broyhill Furniture Co; dir, Wachovia Bank & Trust Co, C&N-N Rwy; mem. adv. bd, Am. Mutual Liability Ins. Co; mem. bd. of gov, Am. Furniture Mart; Mil. Serv. Army. Mem: Trustee Wake Forest Col. and Southeast. Baptist Theol. Sem; Mason; K. of P; Charlotte City, Lenoir, Sedgefield and Forest Country Clubs; Quail Hollow, Boon, Biltmore, Mimosa and Blowing Rock Golf Clubs. Rel: Baptist. Mailing Add: Wilkesboro Rd, Lenoir, N.C. 28645.

BROYHILL, JAMES THOMAS R
U.S. Rep, N.C.
b. Lenoir, N.C, 8/19/27; s. James Edgar Broyhill and Satie Hunt B; m. 6/2/51 to Louise Horton Robbins; c. Marilyn, Eddie and Philip. Educ: Univ. N.C, B.S. in Commerce, 50; Phi Delta Theta. Polit. Pos: U.S. Rep, N.C, 63- Bus. & Prof. Pos: Exec, Broyhill Furniture Factories of Lenoir, N.C, 46-63. Mem: Mason, Shrine. Rel: Baptist. Legal Res: Lenoir, N.C. Mailing Add: House Office Bldg, Washington, D.C. 20515.

BROYHILL, JOEL T. R
U.S. Rep, Va.
b. Hopewell, Va, 11/4/19; m. to Jane Marshall Bragg; c. Nancy Pierce, Jane-Anne and Jeanne Marie. Educ: George Wash. Univ. Polit. & Govt. Pos: U.S. Rep, Va, 52- Bus. & Prof. Pos: Real estate, bldg. exec. Mil. Serv: Army, World War II. Mem: Past pres, Arlington Co, Va. C. of C; Arlington Co. Planning Cmn; Arlington Optimist Club; Am. Legion; VFW; DAV; Amvets; Mason; Moose; Elks; Eagles; Izaak Walton League; Int. Supreme Coun. DeMolay; Friendship Vet. Fire Engine Co; Mt. Vernon Guard; Kappa Alpha Alumni Asn. Rel: Lutheran; Trustee, Resurrection Lutheran Church. Mailing Add: Rayburn House Office Building, Washington, D.C. 20515.

BROYLES, PAUL W. R
Ill. State Sen.
b. McLeansboro, Ill; m. to Olivia Bersche B; c. Mrs. John H. Casey. Polit. & Govt. Pos: Chmn, Draft Bd. 1, Mt. Vernon, Ill, World War II; Ill. State Rep, 42; World War II Bonus chmn; Ill State Sen, 44-; chmn, Seditious Activities Invest. Cmn, 47-49; app. to serve on White House Conf. on Aging, 61. Bus. & Prof. Pos: Investments and farm owner. Mem: Egyptian Shrine Club; Egyptian Past Comdrs. Club; Ainad Temple; Knights Templar; Elks; Moose; Consistory; past dir, Mt. Vernon C. of C; past pres, Mt. Vernon Rotary Club; past comdr, Am. Legion Post 141; Amvets; DAV; DAR. Commended for meritorious serv. by Am. Legion, Dept. of Ill; Mil. Order of the Purple Heart. Rel: Methodist. Mailing Add: 1800 Franklin Ave, Mt. Vernon, Ill. 62864. (1967)

BRUBAKER, ROBERT LEE R
Chmn, Fayette Co. Rep. Exec. Cmt, Ohio
b. Greenfield, Ohio, 7/14/17; s. Kinsey Jerry Brubaker and Louise Leutkemeier B; m. 2/12/42 to Betty Brock; c. John A, Electa J, Robert Loring, Mary Melissa and Susannah. Educ: Vanderbilt Univ, A.B, 37; Vanderbilt Law Sch, LL.B, 39; Omicron Delta Kappa; Chi Phi. Polit. & Govt. Pos: Judge, Washington Court House, Munic. Court, Ohio, 52-55; judge, Fayette Co. Probate and Juvenile Court, 52-61; chmn, Fayette Co. Rep. Cent. Cmt, 64- Mil. Serv: Entered as Chief Specialist, Naval Res, 42, released as Lt, 45, after serv. in Destroyer Div. 25, Cent. Pac, 44-45. Mem: Fayette Co. Bar Asn. (past pres); Ohio State Bar Asn; Washington Court House C. of C.(past dir); Fayette Co. Commun. Chest (past dir. and pres); Scioto-Paint Valley Guid. Center (trustee); Symposiarchs (past pres, Washington Court House Chap). Rel: Episcopal. Legal Res: 315 N. Main St, Washington Court House, Ohio 43160. Mailing Add: 205 N. Fayette St, Washington Court House, Ohio 43160.

BRUCE, DAVID K. E.
b. Baltimore, Md, 2/12/98; m. to Ailsa Mellon 5/29/26 and Evangeline Bell, 4/23/45; c. Audrey (Mrs. Currier, deceased), Alexandra, David Surtees and Nicholas Cabel. Polit. & Govt. Pos: Md. State Del, 24-25; with Dept. of State For. Serv. Off, 25-28; Va. State Del, 39-40; chief rep, Am. Red Cross, Gt. Brit, 40-41; with Off. of Strategic Serv, 41-45, dir. for European Theater 43-45; Asst. Secy. of Commerce, 47-48; chief EC Mission to France, 48-49; U.S. Ambassador to France, 49-52; Undersecy. of State, 52-53; spec. U.S. observer, Interim Comt. of Europe Defense Commun. and U.S. Rep. to Europe High Authority for Coal and Steel, 53-54; U.S. Ambassador, Fed. Rep. of Germany, 57-59 and Gt. Brit, 61-69. Bus. & Prof. Pos: Banker, businessman, lawyer and farmer, 28-40; with Bankers Trust Co. of N.Y. and W.A. Harriman & Co; dir. of numerous corp. Mil. Serv: Army, Field Artil, 2nd Lt, 17-19; Army Air Force, Col, 42-45; mil. decorations for serv. in both wars from U.S, Gt. Brit, France, Poland, Norway, Denmark and Czech. Publ: Revolution to Reconstruction, a History of American Presidents. Mem: Former trustee, Metrop. Opera and Frick Mus, N.Y.C, Va. Mus. of Art, Va. Hist. Soc, Va. State Libr. and Va. Polytech. Inst; past pres, Nat. Gallery of Art, D.C. Rel: Episcopal. Mailing Add: 1405 34th St. N.W, Washington, D.C. 20007.

BRUCE, JAMES EDMOND D
Ky. State Rep.
b. 1927. Educ: Univ. Tenn, B.S. Polit. & Govt. Pos: Former v.pres, Christian Co. Farm Bur, Ky; Ky. State Rep, 64- Bus. & Prof. Pos: Farmer. Mem: Elks. Rel: Methodist. Mailing Add: Route 1, Hopkinsville, Ky. 42240. (1967)

BRUCE, MARION D
Chmn, Randall Co. Dem. Exec. Cmt, Tex.
b. Randall Co, Tex, 3/26/12; s. Robert William Bruce and Ellen Sophia Osgood B; m. to Louise Evans; c. Robert, Barbara (Mrs. Ray Cullin), Sharon (Mrs. Mack Jones), Helen (Mrs. E.J. Moorman) and Matt. Educ: Univ. Tex. Polit. & Govt. Pos: Chmn, Randall Co. Dem. Exec. Dmt, Tex; mem, Randall Co. Bd. Educ. and Tax Equalization Bd; co. del, Dem. State Conv, 20 years; alternate del, Dem. Nat. Conv, twice. Bus. & Prof. Pos: Rancher and shorthorn breeder. Mem: Kiwanis (dist. Lt. Gov, S.Amarillo); Mason; Potter Randall Citizens Cmt.(chmn, group work and recreation coun). Rel: Baptist. Mailing Add: Route 2, P.O. Box 11, Amarillo, Tex. 79105.

BRUCE, WILLIAM ROLAND, JR. D
Tenn. State Sen.
b. Portsmouth, Va, 7/13/35; s. William Roland Bruce, Sr. and Elizabeth Jack B; m. 9/1/56 to Katherine Ely Martin; c. Katherine, William Robert, Elizabeth, Margaret, Andrew and Alexander. Educ: Univ. Va, Charlottesville,

B.A, 56, LL.B, 59; Delta Sigma Rho; Kappa Alpha Order. Polit. & Govt. Pos: Tenn. State Rep, 66-68; Tenn. State Sen, 68- Bus. & Prof. Pos: Assoc, Martin, Tate & Morrow, Attorneys, Memphis, Tenn, 59-62; proprietor, William R. Bruce, Jr, Attorney, 63-65; partner, Bruce & Southern, Attorneys, 65- Mil. Serv: Entered as 2nd Lt, Army, 57, released as Capt, Res, 68. Mem: Am, Tenn, Va. State and Memphis and Shelby Co. Bar Asns; Univ. Club of Memphis; Memphis Press Club; pres. W.Tenn. Easter Sear Soc; pres, Memphis Area Clean Air Asn; Memphis Mental Health Asn; Tenn. TB Asn; Delta Sailing Club. Outstanding Young Man in Tenn, Tenn. Jaycees, 68. Rel: Episcopal. Legal Res: 528 S. McLean Blvd, Memphis, Tenn. 38104. Mailing Add: Suite 1921, 100 N. Main Bldg, Memphis, Tenn. 38103.

BRUECK, KARL ARTHUR D
Chmn, Miami Co. Dem. Cmt, Kans.
b. Paola, Kans, 7/24/10; s. William B. Brueck and Katherine Amelia McGrath B; m. 4/25/64 to Thelma M. Hart. Educ: Univ. Kans, A.B, 32; Sigma Nu. Polit. & Govt. Pos: V.pres, Kans. Young Dem. and pres, Third Dist. Young Dem, 39-40; chmn, Miami Co. Dem. Cmt, 50-; pres, Kans. Dem. Club, 53-54; Kans. State Rep, 55-61; permanent chmn, Second Cong. Dist. Dem. Conv, 56; del, Dem. Nat. Conv, 56, 60 & 64 and alternate del, 68: hwy. cmnr, Fourth Kans. Div, 67-; hygiene cmnr, Fourth Dist. Kans, 67- Bus. & Prof. Pos: Ed, The West. Spirit Newspaper, Paola, 30-42; rep, Equitable Life Assurance Soc, 46-66. Mil. Serv: Entered as S 1/C, Naval Res, 42, released as SK 1/C, 45, after serv. in S.W. Pac. Mem: Leaders Corps, Equitable Life Assurance Soc, 62-66; Kans. Dem. Ex-Serv. Men's Club.(pres, 55-56); C. of C; Elks; VFW; Am. Legion; Paola Country Club; Fin & Feather Club; bd. dirs, Ursuline Convent Guild, 68-; bd. trustees, Miami Co. Hosp, 61-65; U.S. Navy League. Rel: Roman Catholic. Legal Res: 4 Brookside Dr, Paola, Kans. 66071. Mailing Add: 133 S. Pearl, Paola, Kans. 66071.

BRUFF, JOHN BOWMAN D
Chmn, Macomb Co. Dem. Cmt, Mich.
b. Saginaw Co, Mich, 4/29/29; s. Hayward M. Bruff, Sr. and Anna Elizabeth Bowman B; m. 7/8/61 to Alyce M. Briers; c. John Thomas and Jeanne Lynn. Educ: Mich. State Univ, B.A. with honors, 51; Univ. Mich. Law Sch, J.D, 53. Polit. & Govt. Pos: Secy, Macomb Co. Dem. Cmt, Mich, 58-60, chmn, 69-; precinct del, 58-64 & 68-; dist. rep. for U.S. Rep. James G. O'Hara, 59-; chmn, Seventh Cong. Dist. Dem. Cmt, 60-64; circuit court cmnr, Macomb Co, 63-65; chmn, 12th Cong. Dist. Dem. Cmt, Mich, 64-65 & 66-69; counsel, U.S. Senate Labor Subcmt, Wash, D.C, 65-66; chmn, Mich. Dem. Campaign and coordinator Hubert H. Humphrey Mich. Campaign, 68; del, Dem. Nat. Conv, 68. Mil. Serv: Entered as 2nd Lt, Air Force, 53, released as 1st Lt, 55 after serv. in Judge Advocate Gen. Corps, 4706th Air Defense Wing, 53-55. Mem: Macomb Co. Bar Asn; State Bar of Mich; Clinton and Macomb Human Rels. Cmts; Amvets; trustee, Oakland Univ, 57-62; Mich. State Univ. Alumnae Asn. (bd. mem, 67-69). Rel: Unitarian. Mailing Add: 37258 Ingleside, Mt. Clemens, Mich. 48043.

BRUGGENSCHMIDT, JOSEPH G. D
Ind. State Rep.
Educ: Purdue Univ. Polit. & Govt. Pos: Mem, Perry Co. Long Range Planning Cmn, Ind; dist. forester, Ind. Dept. of Conserv, 3 years; Ind. State Rep, 63- Bus. & Prof. Pos: Consult. forester. Mil. Serv: Marine Corps, Korea. Mem: VFW; K. of C; Jaycees. Rel: Catholic. Mailing Add: R.R. 1, Tell City, Ind. 47586. (1967)

BRUGGER, JEANNE DE BOW R
Secy, Montgomery Co. Rep. Cmt, Pa.
b. Phila, Pa, 4/12/16; d. Richard Edgar Adamson De Bow and Alice Griffiths D; m. 7/17/43 to John T. Brugger, Jr; c. Bonnie De Bow (Mrs. John P. Monks, Jr) and Read D. Educ: Smith Col, B.A, 36, M.A, 39; Bryn Mawr Col, fulfilled course requirements for Ph.D; Phi Beta Kappa; Sigma Xi. St. Davids Golf Club; Smith Col. Club of Phila. Polit. & Govt. Pos: Dir, Sch. Bd, Upper Merion Twp, Pa, 63-65; Pa. State Rep, Montgomery Co, 65-66; secy, Montgomery Co. Rep. Cmt, Pa, 66- Bus. & Prof. Pos: Prof, Psychol. and Educ, Smith Col, Mass, 43-47, Bryn Mawr Col, Pa, 50-58 and Drexel Inst. of Tech, 63- Mem: Trustee, Woman's Med. Col, Phila, Pa, Phila. State Hosp, N. Phila. Regional Health Asn. and Upper Merion Twp. Authority, King of Prussia, Pa. Rel: Unitarian. Mailing Add: 1096 Broadview Rd, Wayne, Pa. 19087.

BRUMBAUGH, D. EMMERT R
b. Henrietta, Pa, 10/8/94; s. Moses R. Brumbaugh and Sara Florence Stewart B; m. to Carolyn Acker; c. four. Educ: Martinsburg Summer Normal Sch; Int. Correspondence Sch; Hood Col, citation on 75th Convocation; Franklin and Marshall Col, Dr. in Commercial Sci. (hon.). Polit. & Govt. Pos: Chmn, Blair Co. Draft Bd, World War II; U.S. Rep, Pa, 43-47; State Secy. Banking, Pa, 47-51; del, Rep. Nat. Conv, 51, 55 & 60; Pa. State Sen, 62-67. Bus. & Prof. Pos: Chmn. bd, Cent. Pa. Nat. Bank of Claysburg; partner, Brumbaugh Ins. Agency, Queen Lumber Co; dir, Pa. State Mutual Fire Ins. Co. Mil. Serv: World War I, 58th Brigade Hq, A.E.F. Mem: Past pres. Claysburg Rotary Club; trustee, Altoona Hosp, Claysburg Am. Legion Home Asn; dir, Blair Co. Automobile Asn; Union League, Phila; Blairmont Country Club; past potentate, Jaffa Shrine. Rel: United Church of Christ, Elder, Claysburg United Church of Christ. Mailing Add: Claysburg, Pa. 16625.

BRUMBY, MARY FAYE D
b. Marietta, Ga, 5/11/12; d. William H. Martin and Lillian Truman Grogan M; m. 9/28/34 to Edward Hunt Brumby, Sr; c. Mary Bolan (Mrs. Forrest) and Ida Hunt (Mrs. Townson). Educ: Young Harris Col, A.A, 55; West. Carolina Col, B.S, 62. Polit. & Govt. Pos: N.C. State Rep, 63-66; N.C. State Sen, 66-68. Bus. & Prof. Pos: Mfr. Publ: Poems in newspapers; Anthology of Verse, Christmas Lyrics, Beacon Publ, 39. Mem: Bus. and Prfnl. Women's Club; officer, PTA; pres, Murphy Garden Club, 2 years; pres. Women of the Church, 50; asst. dir, Dist. II Garden Clubs, 64. Woman of the Week of Cherokee Co, Aug. 64. Rel: Presbyterian; Sunday Sch. teacher; dist. chmn, 60; asst. supt, Sunday Sch, 64. Mailing Add: Box 6, Murphy, N.C. 28906. (1967)

BRUMER, GEORGE D
N.H. State Rep.
b. Brattleboro, Vt, 11/27/18; married; c. Nine. Educ: Brattleboro Bus. Inst; Ore. State Col; Seattle Col; Sigma Alpha Epsilon. Polit. & Govt. Pos: First treas, N.H. Young Dem; chmn, Grafton Co. Dem. Cmt, 54-56; selectman, 63-65; dir, Civil Defense; N.H. State Rep, 63- Bus. & Prof. Pos: Contractor. Mil. Serv: CPO, Navy, World War II. Mem: SAR; 40 et 8; Mil. Order of Cooties; VFW; Am. Legion (past comdr). Rel: Catholic. Mailing Add: 351 Main St, Lisbon, N.H. 03585. (1967)

BRUMLEY, CALVIN EDGAR R
Dep. Spec. Asst. to the Secy, Treas. Dept.
b. Hereford, Tex, 3/12/24; s. Bonnie Edgar Brumley and Alma Knox B; m. 9/29/51 to Mary Jayne Keegan; c. Bryan. Educ: Tex. A&M Univ, B.S, 45. Polit. & Govt. Pos: Dep. Spec. Asst. to the Secy, Treas. Dept, 69- Bus. & Prof. Pos: Reporter, Amarillo Globe-News, Tex, 45-48; Assoc. Press, Dallas, 48-49; ed. and co-publisher, Tulia Herald, 49-50; reporter and agr. ed, Lubbock Avalanche J, 50-51; ed, Tex. Hereford, Ft. Worth, 51-52; West. Livestock Mag, Denver, Colo, 52-54; reporter, Wall St. J, Dow Jones & Co, N.Y.C, 54-55, reporter and Southeast news bur. chief, Jacksonville, Fla, 55-61, Northeast. news bur. chief, Boston, Mass, 61-66; news ed, Assoc. Press-Dow Jones Int. Econ. Report, N.Y.C, 66-69. Mil. Serv: Pvt, Army, 42-43. Mem: Sigma Delta Chi (former v.pres, New Eng. Chap); first v.pres, Jacksonville Coun. of the Arts, Fla; Citizens Adv. Cmt. for Passage of Auditorium Bond Issue for Design and Construction of City Auditorium in Jacksonville; Seminole Club, Jacksonville; Union Boat Club, Boston, Mass. Legal Res: Chilmark, Mass. Mailing Add: Room 3415, Main Treasury, 15th and Pennsylvania Ave, Washington, D.C. 20220.

BRUMMETT, CLAUDIA MAE D
State Dem. Committeewoman, Tex.
b. Amarillo, Tex, 2/28/27; d. Claude J. Brummett and Mae Kight B; single. Educ: Amarillo Col, A.S, 46; Univ. Colo, 48; Gamma Theta Chi; Iota Sigma Alpha; Beta Sigma Phi. Polit. & Govt. Pos: Chmn, precinct three, Potter Co. Dem. Exec. Cmt, Tex, 56-62; secy, 58-, chmn, precinct one, 62-; v.chmn, women's activities, Potter Co. Dem. Party, 60; co-chmn, Area Dem. Hq, 62 & 64; gen. chmn, Gov. Day, 63; state Dem. committeewoman, 31st sen. dist, Tex, 63-; del, Dem. Nat. Conv, 64 & 68, mem, Rules Cmt, 64, mem, Credentials Cmt, 68; chmn. poll tax and registrn. subcmt, State Dem. Exec. Cmt, 64-, chmn, publicity subcmt, 68; founder and exec. chmn, League of Dem. Women, 64-; del. and mem, Credentials Cmt, State Dem. Conv, 68; v.chmn, 31st Sen. Dist. Dem. Exec. Cmt, currently. Bus. & Prof. Pos: Stenographer, Panhandle and Santa Fe Rwy, 48-55, claim investr, 55-59; chief diversion and tracer clerk, Santa Fe Rwy, West. Lines, 59-69; rancher and bus. mgr, JAL Ranch, Alvarado, Tex, 68- Mem: Rwy. Bus. Women Asn; Armstrong Co. Hist. Soc; Lodge 1079, Brotherhood of Rwy. and Steamship Clerks; West. Cowpunchers Asn; Panhandle Kennel Club; Panhandle and Santa Fe Credit Union; mem. state affairs subcmt, W. Tex. C. of C; STEP Speakers Bur; v.chmn, Local Housing Authority. Rel: Baptist. Legal Res: 1312 Taylor St, Amarillo, Tex. 79101. Mailing Add: JAL Ranch, Box 308, Alvarado, Tex. 76009.

BRUNERO, STEPHEN D
b. Providence, R.I, 12/8/29; m. to Elizabeth Burns. Educ: Providence Col; Boston Col. Law Sch, LL.B, 52. Polit. & Govt. Pos: R.I. State Rep, 64-66; v.chmn, W. Warwick Minimum Housing Cmt, currently. Bus. & Prof. Pos: Attorney-at-Law. Mil. Serv: Army, 53-55. Mailing Add: 790 Providence St, W. Warwick, R.I. 02893.

BRUNGARDT, KENNETH FLORIAN D
Mem, Gove Co. Dem. Cent. Cmt, Kans.
b. Morland, Kans, 1/9/30; s. Florian A. Brungardt and Agnes Sophie B; m. 4/15/52 to Bernice Ann Korbe; c. Kenneth M, Rene Ann, John T, Kevin M, Stephen B, Gary J. and Sonya K. Educ: Kans. State Col, 48-49. Polit. & Govt. Pos: Mem, Gove Co. Dem. Cent. Cmt, Kans, precinct committeeman, 56 and chmn, 58-69. Bus. & Prof. Pos: Bookkeeper, Peoples State Bank, Grinnell, Kans, 54, dir. and cashier, 66- Mil. Serv: Entered as Pvt, Army, 51, released as 2nd Lt, after serv. in Korean Mil. Adv. Group, 54. Mem: Elks; K. of C; Am. Legion; VFW. Rel: Catholic. Mailing Add: Grinnell, Kans. 67738.

BRUNGOT, HILDA C. F. R
N.H. State Rep.
b. Berlin, N.H, 11/25/86; d. Hans Christian Johnson and Sara Nora Johansdatter J; wid; c. Clarence Jorgin, Clara Constance (Mrs. Martin), Nora Christine (Mrs. Beasley), Norman Stanley and George O. R. Educ: Berlin High Sch, 3 years; Gen. Educ. Develop. Test, 66. Polit. & Govt. Pos: Del, N.H. State Constitutional Conv, 30, 38, 48, 56 & 64; N.H. State Rep, 31-39, 41-59 & 65-, mem, Judiciary Cmt, N.H. State House of Rep, 12 terms, mem, Agr. Revision Statutes Cmt. and Educ. Cmt, Norman Schs. chmn, 43; chmn, City Rep. Club, 41-43; Justice of Peace, 50-; Notary Pub, 50-; telephone attache, N.H. State House of Rep, 61-63. Bus. & Prof. Pos: In real estate. Mem: Grange; Scandinavian Fraternity of Am; Am. Legion Auxiliary; VFW Auxiliary; Women's Relief Corp; Joliette Snow Shoe Club; O.W.L.S. N.H. Fedn. of Bus. and Prfnl. Women's Clubs Citation as Career Woman of the Year, 68. Rel: Lutheran. Mailing Add: 1285 Main St, Berlin, N.H. 03570.

BRUNK, JAMES DON R
b. Berkeley, Calif, 4/30/28; m. to Jo; c. five. Educ: Univ. of Calif. Polit. & Govt. Pos: Wyo. State Sen, until 67. Bus. & Prof. Pos: Indust. rels. consult, Thermopolis C. of C. and pres, Thermopolis Develop. Corp, currently. Mem: Am. Legion; Elks. Rel: Protestant. Mailing Add: 1145 Arapahoe St, Thermopolis, Wyo. 82443.

BRUNNER, JOHN L. D
Pa. State Rep.
b. Langeloth, Pa, 8/18/29; s. John J. Brunner and Violet Riley B; m. 8/14/54 to Frances E. Byrne; c. Mary Margaret, Michael Damian and Monica Jane. Educ: Duquesne Univ, A.B, 53; Georgetown Univ. Law Sch, LL.B, 56. Polit. & Govt. Pos: Pa. State Rep, 65- Mil. Serv: Entered as Pvt, Army, released as S/Sgt. Rel: Roman Catholic. Mailing Add: 15 Frederick St, Burgettstown, Pa. 15021. (1967)

BRUNO, JERRY D
b. Kenosha, Wis, 4/13/26; s. Joseph Bruno and Rose B; m. 1/6/55 to Dorothy Malazhan; c. Carol Ann. Polit. & Govt. Pos: Mem. staff, Sen. William

Proxmire, Wis, 57-59 and John F. Kennedy Campaign, 59-60; spec. asst. to chmn, Dem. Nat. Cmt, 62-65; N.Y. State Rep. to Sen. Robert F. Kennedy, 65-68; del, Dem. Nat. Conv, 68. Mailing Add: 210 Lansdowne Rd, De Witt, N.Y. 13214.

BRUNO, JOSEPH F. D
R.I. State Sen.
b. Bristol, R.I, 4/24/17; m. to Lucy P. Educ: Colt Mem. High Sch, 35. Polit. & Govt. Pos: Pres, Bristol Town Coun, R.I, 53-56; Bristol Dem. Town Cmt; R.I. State Sen, currently. Bus. & Prof. Pos: Ins. agent. Mil. Serv: Navy, World War II; Honor Man, Naval Training Co, 513, Sampson, N.Y, 45. Mailing Add: 39 High St, Bristol, R.I. 02809. (1967)

BRUNSDALE, CLARENCE NORMAN R
b. Sherbrooke, N.Dak, 7/9/91; s. Knute H. Brunsdale and Anna Margaret Nordgaard B; m. 8/30/24 to Carrie Lajord; c. Margaret Marie (Mrs. Larson) and Helen Lucille (Mrs. Williams). Educ: Luther Col, B.A, hon. LL.D, 51. Polit. & Govt. Pos: U.S. sen, by appointment, 59-60; gov, N.Dak, 51-57; N.Dak. state sen, 41-51 and 27-34, floor leader 45-49. Bus. & Prof. Pos: Dir, Goose River Bank, Mayville, N.Dak, 20-66; dir, First Nat. Bank, Portland, N.Dak, 20-33; dir. and pres, First and Farmers Bank, Portland, 33-40; mgr, Brunsdale Farms, 14-31; dir. and 3rd v.pres, Russel Grader Mfg. Co, Minneapolis, Minn, 18-29. Mem: Local Civic Club and similar organizations. Rel: Lutheran. Mailing Add: 235 Second Ave. N.W, Mayville, N.Dak. 58257.

BRUNT, A. W. 'BILL' D
b. Idaho Falls, Idaho, 8/27/09; s. George Brunt and Clara Rasicot B; m. 6/16/37 to Amelia Stevenson; c. Dr. Alfred William, Jr, Roger S, John S, Jane (Mrs. Ball), Alice Anne, Mary (Mrs. Seymour) and Nancy Louise (Mrs. Richards). Educ: Univ. Idaho, 28-29; Brigham Young Univ, 32-33; George Wash. Law Sch, 33- 37. Polit. & Govt. Pos: Statistician, Fed. Deposit Ins. Corp, 33-37; Idaho State Rep, 40-44; asst. adminstr, Off. Price Admin, 43-44; state chmn, Dem. Cent. Cmt, 52-54 & 62; campaign chmn, Northwest. States Harriman for Pres. Cmt, 56; del, Dem. Nat. Conv, 58-; nominee, U.S. Sen, Idaho, 60; nominee, U.S. Rep, Idaho, 66. Bus. & Prof. Pos: Realtor; farm operator. Mem: Secy, Idaho Falls Real Estate Bd, 45, v.pres, 46, pres, 50; dir, Nat. Asn. Real Estate Bds, 50-53 & 62-65; v.pres, Nat. Asn. Homebuilders, 57-58. Rel: Latter-day Saint; Bishop, Idaho Falls, leader and serv. as missionary, France and Belgium. Legal Res: Pinehaven, Ashton, Idaho 83420. Mailing Add: Box 156, Idaho Falls, Idaho 83401.

BRUTON, GEORGE A. D
N.H. State Rep.
b. Manchester, N.H, 1/25/97; married; c. 3. Educ: Columbia Law Sch. Polit. & Govt. Pos: Contact rep, finance officer and loan guaranty officer, U.S. Vet. Admin, 38 years; N.H. State Rep, 61- Mil. Serv: Vet. World War I. Mem: Am. Legion; K. of C. Rel: Catholic. Mailing Add: 632 Belmont St, Manchester, N.H. 03104. (1967)

BRUTON, THOMAS WADE D
b. Capelsie, N.C, 9/10/02; s. David Dudley Bruton and Susan Eleanor Wade B; m. 1928, first wife deceased; m. 12/8/64 to Elizabeth Nelms Flournoy. Educ: Va. Mil. Inst, A.B, 25; Duke Univ. Law Sch, 25-27; Kappa Sigma; Order of the Coif. Polit. & Govt. Pos: Mem, N.C. Dem. State Exec. Cmt; N.C. State Rep, 29-31; asst. attorney gen, 33-60, attorney gen, 60-69. Mil. Serv: Mem. Cavalry Res, 25-40, 2nd to 1st Lt, active duty Army, 42-46, Capt. to Lt. Col; Col, Judge Adv. Gen. Corps, N.C. Nat. Guard, 55-62, Brig. Gen. (Ret); Am. and ETO Ribbons; Bronze Star Medal, 45; Distinguished Serv. Medal, 60. Mem: N.C. Bar Asn; Am. Legion. Rel: Methodist. Legal Res: Troy, N.C. 27371. Mailing Add: 5005 N. Hills Dr, Raleigh, N.C. 27602. (1967)

BRYAN, GROVER L. D
b. Holdenville, Okla, 12/8/27; s. Ollie D. Bryan and Lillie Sisk B; m. 11/25/53 to Dorothy Jean Deckert; c. Michael D, Kathleen Ann, Sean Patrick and Kevin Paul. Educ: Pratt Jr. Col, grad, 49; Wichita State Univ, B.A, 51; Washburn Univ, J.D, 54; Delta Theta Phi. Polit. & Govt. Pos: Dep. co. attorney, Seward Co, Kans, 58-62; city police judge, Liberal, 58-; Dem. precinct committeeman, 58-; chmn, Seward Co. Dem. Party, 66-68. Bus. & Prof. Pos: Pres. and bd. mem, AD & G Enterprises, Inc, Liberal, Kans, 61-; secy. and bd. mem, Tri-State Commun, Inc, 61-; assoc. attorney, Farmers Home Admin, Wash, D.C, 65-69; secy. and bd. mem, United Builders, Inc, Liberal, Kans, 65-; assoc. attorney, Kans. Hwy. Dept, Topeka, 66- Mil. Serv: Entered as Pvt, Army, 45, released as Pfc, 47, after serv. in 123rd Eng. Surv. Bn, Eighth Army, Japanese Occup, 46-47; World War II Victory Medal; Japanese Occup. Medal. Publ: Contrib, American Jurisprudence Pleading and Practice, Lawyers Coop. Publ. Co, 56. Mem: Seward Co. Bar Asn.(pres, 59-62); Kans. and Am. Bar Asns; Am. Trial Lawyers Asn; Am. Legion; K. of C; Elks; PTA; C. of C. Rel: Catholic. Legal Res: 128 W. Wilson, Liberal, Kans. 67901. Mailing Add: P.O. Box 223, Liberal, Kans. 67901.

BRYAN, JOSEPH McKINLEY D
b. Elyria, Ohio, 2/11/96; s. Bart Bryan and Caroline Ebert B; m. 11/19/27 to Kathleen Marshall Price; c. Mrs. Bryan Edwards, Nancy Ann (Mrs. Duncan McLauchlin Faircloth) and Joseph McKinley, Jr. Educ: Mt. Hermon Prep. Sch, Mass; Sigma Chi. Hon. LL.D, Belmont Abbey Col. Polit. & Govt. Pos: Dir, Greensboro Housing Authority, N.C, 41-44; mem. exec. cmt, N.C. Rural Indust. Cmn, 45-46; mem, Guilford Co. Spec. Study Cmn, 46; mem. bd. gov, State Cmt. for Traffic Safety, Inc, 47-49; chmn, N.C. State Bd. Elec, 60-61; mem, Gov. Adv. Cmt. on Low-Income Housing, 66. Bus. & Prof. Pos: Sr. v.pres, Jefferson Standard Life Ins. Co, until 61, dir. and mem. exec. cmt, currently; hon. chmn. bd. dirs. and mem. exec. cmt, Pilot Life Ins. Co; chmn. bd. dirs. and mem. exec. cmt, Jefferson Standard Broadcasting Co; dir, Jefferson-Pilot Corp, Greensboro, N.C; dir. and mem. exec. trust investment and trust cmts, N.C. Nat. Bank, Charlotte; pres. and dir, Carolina Apt. Hotel Corp, Raleigh; pres, Kananjo Investment Corp; v.pres, Bryan Family Found, Inc; dir, N. Elm Apt. Co, Inc. and N.C. Bus. Found; mem. bd. visitors, Davidson Col; N.C. State chmn, Radio Free Europe Fund, 63. Mil. Serv: AEF, 17-18. Mem: Dir, Carolina Motor Club; Rotary; C. of C; adv. coun, Maryfield Nursing Home, Inc, High Point; bd. gov, Shriner's Hosps. for Crippled Children, Greenville Unit; Nat. Coun, Nat. Planning Asn, 55-59; pres, Am. Life Conv, 55-56 and chmn. financial sect, 48-49; Greensboro Rep, Govt. Affairs Inst, 54-55; chmn, Empty Stocking Fund, 51; pres, Med. and Hosp. Fund, 39-41; co-chmn, Cmt. for Econ. Develop. in Guilford Co, 41; 1st pres, Greensboro Chap, Nat. Off. Mgt. Asn, 41-42; treas, Greensboro Cmt, United Serv. Orgn. for Nat. Defense, 41; Greensboro Personnel Adv. Cmt, 40; chmn, Civilian Cmt. for Naval Officer Procurement, 40; C. of C. War Indust. Prod. Cmt, 40 and pres. Birthday Ball, 36; Am. Legion; VFW; AF&AM; RAM; K.T; Scottish Rite (32°); Valley of Greensboro Consistory; AAONMS; Oasis Temple, Potentate, 45-46; pres, Southeast. Shrine Asn, 54-55; Cabiri, Jesters; Sedgefield Hunt Club; Merchants and Mfrs. Club; Piedmont Shooting Club; Greensboro, Starmount Forest and Sedgefield Country Clubs; Lyford Cay Club; Augusta Nat. Golf Club; Rolling Rock Club; Metrop. Club; N.Y. South Soc. Hatteras Marlin Club; Charlotte City Club; String and Splinter Club; N.C. Skeet Asn. Hon. chmn, 18th Annual Gr. Greensboro Open Golf Tournament, 55; Significant Sig Award, Sigma Chi, 59. Rel: Episcopal. Legal Res: 711 Sunset Dr, Greensboro, N.C. 27408. Mailing Add: Jefferson Standard Bldg, Greensboro, N.C. 27402.

BRYAN, RICHARD H. D
Nev. State Assemblyman
b. Washington, D.C, 7/16/37; s. Oscar W. Bryan and Lillie Pleasants B; m. 9/1/62 to Bonnie Fairchild; c. Richard H, Jr, Leslie L. and Blair A. Educ: Univ. Nev, A.B, 59; Univ. Calif. Hastings Col. Law, LL.B, 63; Phi Alpha Theta; Alpha Tau Omega. Polit. & Govt. Pos: Dep. dist. attorney, Clark Co, Nev, 64-66, pub. defender, 66-68, counsel to juvenile court, 68-; Nev. State Assemblyman, Clark Co, 68- Mil. Serv: 2nd Lt, Army, 59-60; Capt, Army Res. Mem: Am. and Nev. Bar Asns; Am. Trial Lawyers Asn; Am. Judicature Soc; Elks; Mason; Las Vegas Jaycees; Clark Co. Legal Aid Soc. Distinguished serv. award, Vegas Valley Jaycees; selected as one of two legislators to attend Nat. Legis. Conf. Rel: Episcopal. Legal Res: 2221 Glen Heather Way, Las Vegas, Nev. 89107. Mailing Add: 401 S. Third St, Las Vegas, Nev. 89101.

BRYAN, ROBERT JENSEN
b. Bremerton, Wash, 10/29/34; s. James Wesley Bryan, Jr. and Vena Jenson B; m. 6/14/58 to Cathy Ann Welander; c. Robert James, Ted Lorin and Ronald Terance. Educ: Univ. Wash, B.A, 56, LL.B, 58; Nat. Col. State Trial Judges, Reno, Nev.(Phila. session), grad, 67; Purple Shield; pres, Oval Club; Scabbard & Blade; Fir Tree; Big W Club; Phi Delta Phi. Polit. & Govt. Pos: Miscellaneous polit. chmnships, cmts, campaigns, etc, 57-; precinct committeeman, Kitsap Co. Rep. Cent. Cmt, Wash, 60-, secy, 60-61, chmn, 61-62; alternate del, Rep. Nat. Conv, 64; superior court judge, State of Wash, 67- Mil. Serv: Entered as 2nd Lt, Army Res, currently Maj. Mem: Kitsap Co. Bar Asn.(secy, 61); Wash. State Bar Asn.(chmn, Cmt. Legal Serv. to Armed Forces, 64-65); Am. Bar Asn; Am. Judicature Soc; Eagles; Lions; bd, YMCA; Jaycees; bd, C. of C; Ft. Lawton Officers' Club. Legal Res: 2137 Madrona Point Dr, Bremerton, Wash. 98310. Mailing Add: Kitsap County Courthouse, Port Orchard, Wash. 98366.

BRYAN, STANLEY GATEWOOD D
Va. State Del.
b. Norfolk, Va, 2/15/30; s. Clarence Gatewood Bryan and Elnora Hadley B; m. 11/7/59 to Marvourneen Elizabeth Albertson; c. Jo Ann and Stanley G, Jr. Educ: Col. of William & Mary, 47-53, B.A. and B.C.L; Sigma Nu (past comdr). Polit. & Govt. Pos: Va. State Del, 66- Bus. & Prof. Pos: Attorney-at-law, Law Firm of Bryan & Griffin. Mil. Serv: Entered Army, 53, released as Pfc, 55, after serv. in 716th MP Bn, Korean War; Good Conduct Medal. Mem: Norfolk, Chesapeake, Va. State and Am. Bar Asns; Elks; Va. Farm Bur. Rel: Methodist. Mailing Add: 801 George Washington Hwy. S, Chesapeake, Va. 23323.

BRYAN, WALKER D
N.Mex. State Rep.
b. 1910. Educ: Tex. A&M. Polit. & Govt. Pos: City Water Cmnr, Carlsbad, N.Mex; Mayor, Carlsbad; N.Mex. State Rep, 59- Bus. & Prof. Pos: Motel operator. Mem: Lions; Masons (all bodies); C. of C. Rel: Methodist. Mailing Add: 302 Riverside Dr, Carlsbad, N.Mex. 88220.

BRYANT, CECIL FARRIS D
b. Ocala, Fla, 7/26/14; s. Charles Cecil Bryant and Lela Margaret Farris B; m. 9/18/40 to Julia Burnett; c. Julie Lovett, Cecilia Ann and Allison Adair. Educ: Univ. Fla, B.S, 35; Harvard Law Sch, LL.B, 38; Phi Delta Phi; Alpha Kappa Psi; Kappa Delta Pi; Alpha Phi Omega; Blue Key; Gold Key; Alpha Tau Omega. Hon. degrees from Fla. South. Col, Rollins Col, Fla. State Univ. and Fla. Atlantic Univ. Polit. & Govt. Pos: Fla. State Rep, 42 & 46-55 and Speaker, Fla. House Rep, 53; chmn. Fla. Del, Dem. Nat. Conv, 52 & 60 and del, 64 & 68; Gov. of Fla, 60-65; dir, Off. of Emergency Planning, Exec. Off. of President, 66-67; mem, Nat. Security Coun, 66-67; chmn. finance cmt, Dem. Policy Cmt, Fla, 68. Bus. & Prof. Pos: Partner, Bryant, Freeman, Richardson & Watson, Attorneys, 65-66; chmn. bd, Nat. Life Ins. Co. of Fla, Nat. Variable Annuity Co. of Fla, and Voyager Life Ins. Co, 65-; chmn. bd, Eagles Life Ins. Co, 67-; pres, Nat. Life of Fla. Corp, 68- Mil. Serv: Entered as Ens, Navy, 42, released as Lt, 46, after serv. in Anti-Submarine Warfare, Atlantic, Pacific, Mediterranean and Caribbean; Lt, Naval Res. Publ: Co-author, Government and Politics in Florida. Mem: Am. and Fla. Bar Asns; VFW; Ocala Rotary(pres, 48); Elks(Exalted Ruler, 48); Mason; Shrine; Navy League; Nat. Coun. and exec. cmt, N.Fla. Coun, Boy Scouts; Am. Legion; C. of C.(pres, Marion Co, 48); Jr. C. of C.(v.pres, Fla, 48); Gold Key Distinguished Serv. Award, Fla. Jr. C. of C, 48 & 50. Rel: Methodist. Legal Res: 1870 Challen Ave, Jacksonville, Fla. 32205. Mailing Add: 1200 Barnett Bank Bldg, Jacksonville, Fla. 32202.

BRYANT, CURTIS CONWAY D
Co-Chmn, Pike Co. Dem. Party, Miss.
b. Tylertown, Miss, 1/15/17; s. Monroe Bryant and Anna Luter B; m. 7/6/41 to Emogene Gooden; c. Gladys Jean (Mrs. Billie Jackson) and Curtis Conway, Jr. Educ: South McComb High Sch, 40-41. Polit. & Govt. Pos: Mem. bd, South West Inc. S.M.O. Bd; del, Dem. Nat. Conv, 68; chmn, Miss. Dem. Party Employ. Cmt, 68-69; co-chmn, Pike Co. Dem. Party, 68- Mem: Mason (Master); Celaks (chmn, chmn. legis. cmt); NAACP (pres, Pike Co). Rel: Baptist. Mailing Add: 333 B McComb St, McComb, Miss. 39648.

BRYANT, FREDERICK BOYCE R
b. Malone, N.Y, 12/5/11; s. Frederick Howard Bryant and Florence Boyce B; m. 2/9/37 to Grace Noble Green; c. Barbara (Mrs. McChesney) and William. Educ: Middlebury Col, A.B, 33; Columbia Law Sch, LL.B, 36; Chi Psi. Polit. & Govt. Pos: Asst. dist. attorney, N.Y. Co, N.Y, 38-39; dist. attorney, Tompkins Co, 47-56; chmn, Tompkins Co. Rep. Cmt, 56-67; supreme court justice, Sixth Judicial Dist, 67- Bus. & Prof. Pos: Pres, Tompkins Co. Bar Asn, 54; pres, Sixth Dist. Fedn. of Bar Asns, 62. Mil. Serv: Entered as Lt. (jg), Navy, 44, released as Lt, Naval Res, 45, after serv. in LST Group 18, Pac. Fleet; Okinawa Campaign Ribbon. Mem: State and Co. Bar Asns; Mason; Shrine; Elks; VFW; Am. Legion; Soc. Am. Magicians; Int. Brotherhood of Magicians; City Club of Ithaca. Performing magician part time. Rel: Episcopal. Legal Res: 107 Northway Rd, Ithaca, N.Y. 14850. Mailing Add: County Courthouse, Ithaca, N.Y. 14850.

BRYANT, GARLAND LEE D
Treas, Newton Co. Develop. Coun, Ark.
b. Mt. Judea, Ark, 7/11/38; s. R.L. Bryant and Gertie Sue Holt B; m. 6/5/63 to Jerlene Villines; c. Jacque Lynn and Jason Scott. Educ: Ark. Tech, B.S.E, 62; Ark. Tech. Illumni Club. Polit. & Govt. Pos: Pres, Young Dem. Newton Co, 64-66; former Ark. State Rep; treas, Newton Co. Develop. Coun, 67- Bus. & Prof. Pos: Teacher, Kingston High Sch, Ark, 62, Jasper High Sch, 63-64; supt, Mt. Judea High Sch, 65-69; supt. of schs, Mt. Judea, 69- Rel: Church of Christ. Mailing Add: Mt. Judea, Ark. 72655.

BRYANT, KELLY D
Secy. of State, Ark.
Mailing Add: State Capitol, Little Rock, Ark. 72201.

BRYANT, PHILLIP DAVIS D
b. Baltimore Md, 4/5/37; s. Kirby Knapp Bryant, M.D. and Lena Ester Davis B; m. Aug, 1962 to Linda Mize. Educ: Univ. Miss, B.S.J, 63, J.D, 66; Beta Theta Pi. Polit. & Govt. Pos: Miss. State Rep, 60-68. Mil. Serv: Entered as Pvt, Army, 55, released as SP-3, 58. Mem: Am, Miss. and Lafayette Co. Bar Asns; Jaycees. Rel: Presbyterian. Legal Res: 918 Jefferson, Oxford, Miss. 38655. Mailing Add: Box 403, Oxford, Miss. 38655.

BRYANT, TED R
Colo. State Rep.
b. Hartshorne, Okla, 4/21/29; married; c. four. Polit. & Govt. Pos: Former block worker and asst. dist. finance chmn; Rep. precinct committeeman; Colo. State Rep, currently. Bus. & Prof. Pos: Flight opers. instr, United Airlines; assoc. ed, Aero West; pres, Flight Training, Inc. Mem: Pres, S.E. Denver Civic Asn; former pres, Ellis Improv. Asn. Mailing Add: 1590 S. Birch St, Denver, Colo. 80222.

BRYCE, OLIN S. R
b. Sheldon, Vt, 10/6/99; m. to Florence Tatro; c. four sons, two daughters. Educ: Sheldon High Sch; Enosburg Falls High Sch. Polit. & Govt. Pos: Cambridge town lister, Vt, 61-; Vt. State Rep, 63-66. Bus. & Prof. Pos: Farmer. Rel: United Church of Cambridge. Mailing Add: Cambridge, Vt. 05444. (1967)

BRYDGES, EARL WILLIAM R
Pres, N.Y. State Senate
b. Niagara Falls, N.Y, 5/25/05; s. William H. Brydges and Margaret McInerney B; m. 4/28/34 to Eleanor Mahoney; c. Mary Lynn (Mrs. William B. Barden); Jerauld, Earl W, Jr, Dennis, Thomas, William and Margaret. Educ: Univ. Buffalo Law Sch, hon. LL.D. Polit. & Govt. Pos: Past pres, Assoc. Sch. Bd, Niagara and Orleans Co, N.Y; N.Y. State Sen, currently, Pres. and Majority Leader, N.Y. State Sen, chmn, Joint Legis. Cmts. to Revise and Simplify Educ. Law and on Ment. Retardation and Physical Handicap, v.chmn, Spec. Cmt. on Integrity and Ethical Standards and State Hwy. Finance Cmn, mem, Joint Legis. Cmts. on Employees Retirement Syst, on Lake Erie-Lake Ontario Canal, on Sch. Financing and on Interstate Coop, mem, Spec. Legis. Cmt. on Rev. and Simplification of Constitution; del, Rep. Nat. Conv, 68. Mem: Past pres, Bar Asn. of the City of Niagara Falls, N.Y, Niagara Frontier Planning Asn. and Niagara Falls Commun. Chest; 1st pres, Niagara Falls Hermes Club, Exchange Club, Wilson Lions Club and dir. and drive co-chmn, Niagara Falls Chap, Am. Red Cross. Rel: Roman Catholic. Legal Res: 82 Lake St, Wilson, N.Y. 14172. Mailing Add: 426 Third St, Niagara Falls, N.Y. 14202. (1967)

BRYDIA, GEORGE S. R
b. Saunemin, Ill; m. 1/31/59 to Pearl Glathart Miller. Educ: Fairbury Schs. Polit. & Govt. Pos: Chmn, Ill. State Miss. Scenic Pkwy. Cmn; Rep. Co. Chmn, 36; Ill. State Rep, 38-63; mayor, Prophetstown, Ill, 20 years; chmn, Ill. del, Rep. Nat. Conv, 56. Bus. & Prof. Pos: Former traveling salesman. Mem: MWA; Mason; K.T; Elks; Lions; Grange. Rel: Methodist. Mailing Add: Prophetstown, Ill. 61277.

BRYE, DAVID L. D
b. Coon Valley, Wis, 5/22/38; s. Emil M. Brye and Alice Stromstad B; single. Educ: St. Olaf Col, B.A, 60; Harvard Univ, M.A, 61; Danforth and Woodrow Wilson grad. fels; Phi Beta Kappa; Pi Gamma Mu; Blue Key. Polit. & Govt. Pos: Del, State & Dist. Dem. Conv, Wis, 65-69; west. Wis. field dir, McCarthy for President Cmt, 67-68; del, Dem. Nat. Conv, 68; Dem. cand. for Wis. State Sen, 32nd Dist, 68. Bus. & Prof. Pos: Asst. prof. hist, Luther Col. (Iowa), 65-69. Mem: Am. Hist. Asn; Orgn. Am. Historians; State Hist. Soc. Wis; Norweg-Am. Hist. Asn. Rel: Lutheran. Mailing Add: Route 1, Coon Valley, Wis. 54623.

BRYSON, THADDEUS DILLARD D
b. Bryson City, N.C, 10/15/03; s. Thaddeus Dillard Bryson and Amy Black B; m. 9/25/28 to Carolyn Forbell; c. Irene Gail (Mrs. Douglas Elliott), Charlotte Ann (Mrs. Wallace Martin), T.D, IV and Frederick Edgar. Educ: Univ. N.C. Polit. & Govt. Pos: Mayor, Bryson City; N.C. State Rep, Swain Co, 39; solicitor, 20th Solicitorial Dist, N.C, 48-58; research Judge Superior Court, 30th Judicial Dist, N.C, 66- Rel: Baptist. Mailing Add: Box 578, Bryson City, N.C. 28713.

BUBB, GEORGE WILLIAM R
Chmn, Elkhart Co. Rep. Party, Ind.
b. Detroit, Mich, 7/22/20; s. Harry G. Bubb and Emma McCollough B; m. 5/18/42 to Billie Jean Schirm. Educ: Butler Univ, 46-47. Polit. & Govt. Pos: Common Coun, Goshen, Ind, 60-64, clerk-treas, 64-68; Rep. chmn, Elkhart Co, Ind, 66-, co. recorder, 68- Mil. Serv: Entered as Pvt, Marine Corps, 40, released as Maj, 46, after serving in 2nd Tank Bn, 2nd Marine Div, Iceland and South Pac, 42-45, recalled as Lt. Col, 50, retired 60, after serving in 1st Tank Bn, 1st Marine Div, Korea, 51-53. Mem: F&AM; Scottish Rite; Shrine; Am. Legion; VFW; Moose; Goshen Chap, Bashor, Coun. and Goshen Commandery, York Rite. Rel: Presbyterian; Deacon & mem. of choir, First Presbyterian Church, Goshen. Mailing Add: 313 E. Jefferson, Goshen, Ind. 46526.

BUBB, HENRY AGNEW R
b. Williamsport, Pa, 3/26/07; s. Harry Agnew Bubb and Marjorie Wheeler B; m. 6/26/29 to Elizabeth Black; c. Betty (Mrs. John C. Dicus). Educ: Univ. Kans, 28; Washburn Univ, D.B.A, 62; Alpha Kappa Psi; Sigma Chi. Polit. & Govt. Pos: Regional dir, Nat. Exec. Cmt, Young Rep. Fedn, 34-38, v.chmn, 35-37, chmn, 37-38, mem, 38-40; del, Rep. Nat. Conv, 64; nat. chmn, Citizens for Reagan Info. Cent, Topeka, 68; mem, adv. cmt, U.S. Treas. and U.S. Senate Banking and Currency Cmt; mem. and former chmn, Kans. State Bd. Regents; chmn, State Higher Educ. Facilities Cmn; mem, Adv. Coun. on Naval Affairs, Ninth Naval Dist. Bus. & Prof. Pos: Chmn. bd, Capitol Fed. Savings and Mortgage Guaranty Ins. Corp, Milwaukee; dir, Security Benefit Life Ins. Co, Topeka; Columbian Title & Trust Co; legis. consult, mem. exec. cmt. and former pres, U.S. Savings & Loan League; v.pres. and mem. exec. cmt. and coun, Int. Union of Bldg. Societies & Savings & Loan Asns; mem. bd, Kans. Research Found; trustee, Kans. Univ. Endowment Asn; mem. and treas, Housing Indust. Coun, N.Y.C; former mem, Fed. Home Loan Bank Bd. Task Force, Wash, D.C. and Fed. Savings and Loan Coun; former pres, Midwest Savings and Loan Conf. and Kans. Savings and Loan League: former chmn, Fed. Home Loan Bank of Topeka; former trustee, Am. Savings and Loan Inst, chmn, MGIC Investment Corp, Milwaukee; Commercial Loan Ins. Corp; v.chmn, N.Y. Guaranty Corp; trustee, Inst. Fiscal and Polit. Educ. Mem: Nat, Kans. and Topeka C. of C; former nat. pres, Kans. Univ. Alumni Asn; SAR; Topeka Country Club; Topeka Press Club; Garden of the Gods Club; Rotary; AF&AM; Scottish Rite; Mason (32°); KCCH, former potentate, Arab Temple, Shrine; former dir, Jesters; The Cabiri; Elks. U.S. Treas. Award for Patriotic Serv, 46; Distinguished Serv. Citation, Univ. Kans, 65; Distinguished Serv. Award, Grand Lodge AF&AM, Kans. Rel: Episcopal. Legal Res: 2701 Fairway Dr, Topeka, Kans. 66611. Mailing Add: 700 Kansas Ave, Topeka, Kans. 66603.

BUCHANAN, CREELEY S. R
N.H. State Sen.
b. Watertown, Mass, 10/4/17; married; c. 4. Educ: Univ. of N.H. Polit. & Govt. Pos: Alternate del, Rep. Nat. Conv, mem. town budget and sch. study cmts, chmn, Amherst Village Dist. Cmn, N.H, and Amherst Sch. Moderator, formerly; del, Rep. Nat. Conv, 68; N.H. State Sen, currently. Bus. & Prof. Pos: Mgr. N.H. Agency, Phoenix Mutual Life Ins. Co. of Hartford. Mil. Serv: Army, 41-45, Capt; Army Res, Lt. Col. Mem: Am. Legion; Mason; Shrine; SAR; ROA; Nat. Asn. Life Underwriters; Hon. Order of Ky. Cols; Univ. N.H. Alumni Asn; Patch Hill Club. Rel: Congregational. Mailing Add: P.O. Box 446, Amherst, N.H. 03031.

BUCHANAN, DONALD WILLIAM R
b. Unionport, Ohio, 5/22/20; s. John Slayter Buchanan and Mary Hazel Orr B; m. 1/20/45 to Ellen Mary McConnell; c. Donald W. Jr, Margaret E. and Elizabeth A. Educ: Col. Wooster, A.B, 42; Univ. Pittsburgh, Pa, B.S. in Eng, 46; Sigma Tau; Sigma Gamma Epsilon. Polit. & Govt. Pos: Chmn, Vol. for Witwer, White Co, Ill, 60; area leader, Area 11, Ward One, Okla. Co. Rep. Party, 62; former chmn, Carter Co. Rep. Party. Bus. & Prof. Pos: Engr, 46-68; instr, Jefferson Co. Tech. Inst, Ohio, 68- Mil. Serv: Entered as A/S, Coast Guard, 42, released as Lt, 45, after serv. in Greenland; Lt. Comdr, Coast Guard Res, 45- Rel: Presbyterian. Mailing Add: 113 Crawford, Wintersville, Ohio 43952.

BUCHANAN, G. SIDNEY R
Mem, Tex. Rep. State Exec. Cmt.
b. Houston, Tex, 11/27/33; s. George Sidney Buchanan and Dorothy Dodds B; m. 7/17/57 to Corrine Adelle Crothers; c. Emily Louise. Educ: Princeton Univ, A.B. in Hist; Univ. Mich. Law Sch, J.D. magna cum laude; Order of the Coif; Phi Delta Phi. Polit. & Govt. Pos: Alternate del, Rep. Nat. Conv, 64; precinct chmn, Harris Co. Rep. Party, Tex, 65-67; mem, Tex. Rep. State Exec. Cmt, currently, mem, State Sen. Dist. 15, 66- Bus. & Prof. Pos: Lawyer-assoc. Vinson, Elkins, Weems and Searls, 59-; mem, bd. dir, Tex. Bill of Rights Found, 66- Mem: Am, Tex. and Houston Bar Asns. Rel: Episcopal. Mailing Add: 4014 Whitman, Houston, Tex. 77027. (1967)

BUCHANAN, HARRY E. D
N.C. State Sen.
b. Sylvia, N.C. Educ: West. Carolina Col; Univ. of N.C. Polit. & Govt. Pos: Mayor, Sylvia, N.C, 31; mem, State Hwy. Cmn, 53-57; N.C. State Sen, 67-; alternate del, Dem. Nat. Conv, 68; mem, N.C. State Dem. Exec. Cmt, currently. Bus. & Prof. Pos: N.C. Theatres, Inc. Mem: Dir, Carolina Motor Club; chmn. of the bd, Cherokee Hist. Asn; Elks. Mailing Add: 1205 Hyman Ave, Hendersonville, N.C. 28739.

BUCHANAN, JOHN HALL, JR. R
U.S. Rep, Ala.
b. Paris, Tenn, 3/19/28; m. to Elizabeth Moore; c. two. Educ: Howard Col, 49; Univ. Va; South. Theol. Sem, Louisville. Polit. & Govt. Pos: U.S. Rep, Ala, 64-; dir. of Finance, Ala. Rep. Party; chmn, Jefferson Co. Rep. Party. Bus. & Prof. Pos: Pastor. Mil. Serv: Navy. Mailing Add: 1212 Longworth House Office Bldg, Washington, D.C. 20515.

BUCHANAN, ROBERT HENRY 'BOB' R
b. Ecru, Miss, 9/16/15; s. Henry Alexander Buchanan and Kitty Stapleton B; m. 7/24/37 to Annie Mae Yancy; c. Bobbie Anne and Freddie Wayne. Polit. & Govt. Pos: Chmn, Calhoun Co. Rep. Party, Miss, 63-69; Presidential Elector, 64. Bus. & Prof. Pos: Temporary rural mail carrier, 44-49, substitute, 49-66; farmer, 49-66; owner and operator, sawmill, 56-66; salesman, Modern Dixie Life Ins, 65-66. Mem: Antioch Masonic Lodge; Miss. Farm Bur; Calhoun City Chap. 152, RAM; J. J. Melton Coun. 50 Lodge; St. Cyr Commandery 6, K.T. Rel: Baptist. Mailing Add: Route 2, Bruce, Miss. 38915.

BUCHANAN, WILLIAM EDWARD R
b. Ocean City, N.J, 8/6/25; s. Ernest Buchanan and Sarah Anna Gold B; m. 6/7/52 to Regina Agnes Ventre; c. Jeaneen, Cheryl, Deborah and Elizabeth. Educ: Iowa State Univ; Delta Sigma Phi. Polit. & Govt. Pos: Dist. Rep, 16th Dist, Stamford Bd. of Rep, Conn, 65- Bus. & Prof. Pos: Comptroller, Sherwood, Mills & Smith, 58-; gen. mgr, F.L. Savage, 52-57; supvr. of Acct, Gen. Elec. Co, 49-52. Mil. Serv: Entered as Pvt, Air Force, 45, released as Sgt, 46, after serv. in Weather Wing, Am. Theater; Am. Theater Ribbon; Good Conduct Medal; Victory Medal. Mem: Chap. pres, asst. dir, New Eng. Region, Admin. Mgt. Soc; Boy Scouts. Rel: Episcopal; former vestryman. Mailing Add: 53 Idlewood Place, Stamford, Conn. 06905. (1967)

BUCHANAN, WILLIAM GEORGE R
b. Home, Pa, 1/27/21; s. Alexander Meade Buchanan and Stella Stear B; m. 12/26/48 to Roberta Jean McLachlan; c. Lana Jo, William George, Jr. and Robert Meade. Educ: Ind. Univ. Pa, B.Ed, 42; Univ. Pittsburgh, Litt.M, 49; Phi Delta Kappa; Phi Alpha Zeta. Polit. & Govt. Pos: Pa. State Rep, 52-54 & 56-68. Mil. Serv: Entered as Pvt, Army Air Force, 43, released as Sgt, 46, after serv. in 4th Air Force. Mem: Nat. Educ. Asn; Pa. Hist. Soc; Pa. Coun. Soc. Studies; Am. Legion; Grange; Mason. Mem, Hall of Fame, Young Rep. of Pa; Alumni Award, Ind. Univ. Pa, 68. Rel: Lutheran. Mailing Add: 380 Poplar Ave, Indiana, Pa. 15701.

BUCHBINDER, LUCIE HAHN D
Mem, Castro Valley Dem. Club, Calif.
b. Vienna, Austria, 5/17/24; d. Hinda Gottlieb; m. 8/30/46 to Egon Buchbinder, M.D; c. Joan, Janet, Ann and Eric. Educ: Univ. Calif. at Los Angeles, A.B; Univ. Calif. at Berkeley, gen. sec; Mills Col, post-grad. study. Polit. & Govt. Pos: Mem, Castro Valley Dem. Club, Calif, 56-, v.pres, 59, chmn, Precinct Orgn, 59-63, pres, 60; mem, Calif. Dem. State Cent. Cmt, 62-65; presidential elector, Eighth Cong. Dist, 64. Bus. & Prof. Pos: Teaching assoc, Subject A, Univ. Calif. at Berkeley, 45-46; dir, Eden Area, Calif. Against Proposition 14, 64; dir, Low-Cost Housing Proj, Econ. Opportunity Orgn, Eden Area, 66; exec. secy, Eden Coun. for Hope and Opportunity, 65- Mem: League of Women Voters; chmn, Bay Area Housing Opportunities Cmt; Coun. for Civic Unity of San Francisco Bay Area. Mailing Add: 5667 Greenridge Rd, Castro Valley, Calif. 94546. (1967)

BUCHELE, JAMES PAUL, JR. D
Kans. State Rep.
b. Cedar Vale, Kans, 9/25/41; s. Paul Buchele and Helen Fettig B; m. 12/28/65 to Bonnie Jean Cadwalader; c. Amy Ann. Educ: Kans. State Univ, B.S, 63; Washburn Univ. Sch. of Law, J.D, 66; Phi Alpha Delta; Alpha Gamma Rho. Polit. & Govt. Pos: V.chmn, Chautaugua Co. Dem. Cent. Cmt, Kans, 64-66; Kans. State Rep, 42nd Dist, 65-; pres, Kans. Dem. Club, 66; precinct committeeman, Shawnee Co. Dem. Cent. Cmt, 68-; city attorney, Topeka, 69- Mem: Kans. and Topeka Bar Asns; Shawnee Co. Ment. Health Asn; Elks; Kiwanis; Kans. Vet. Club (pres, 65); Mason; Farm Bur; C. of C. Rel: Baptist. Mailing Add: 420 W. 33rd St, Topeka, Kans. 66611.

BUCHENHOLZ, JANE JACOBS D
b. N.Y.C, 10/28/18; d. Joseph Jacobs and Sofia Frucht J; div; c. Nancy and Susan. Educ: Hunter Col, A.B, 42; New Sch. for Soc. Research, 47-49; Phi Beta Kappa; Phi Sigma. Polit. & Govt. Pos: Dir. Nat. Roosevelt Day Dinner, Am. for Dem. Action, 61-66, nat. secy, 63-67, mem. nat. bd, 63-; research consult. for voter regis, Nat. Coun. Negro Women, 64; secy-treas, for. policy coun, N.Y. Dem. Party, 66-; nat. adv. coun, Nat. Conf. for New Politics, 66-67; nat. bd, Cmt. for Sane Nuclear Policy, 66-68; exec. dir, Broadway for Peace, 68; campaign mgr, Mel Dubin for Cong, Brooklyn, 68; alternate del, Dem. Nat. Conv, 68; del, New Dem. Coalition N.Y, currently; mem. nat. coun, Nat. Emergency Civil Liberties Cmt, currently; mem. exec. cmt, Ansonia Independent Dem, 68- Bus. & Prof. Pos: Math teacher, control chemist and plant pathologist, 42-46; remedial reading teacher, Reading Clinic, N.Y Univ, 46-49; spec. teacher, emotionally disturbed children, 48-49; pianist and accompanist for mod. dance classes, 55-61; exec. dir, Call for Action, Radio Sta, WMCA, 62-64; spec. consult. for syst. and inventory control, Crown Fabrics Div, Bangor Punta Indust, 66-68; dir. of develop, New Sch. for Soc. Research, 68- Chap. Chmn. Award, Am. for Dem. Action, 63. Rel: Jewish. Mailing Add: 315 W. 70th St, New York, N.Y. 10023

BUCHLI, MILTON S. D
b. Gilmanton, Wis, 8/18/10; s. Sam Buchli and Agnes Senty B; m. 6/4/41 to Erna E. Riesch; c. Byron and Terry. Educ: Buffalo Co. Teachers Col, 28-29. Polit. Pos: Wis. State Assemblyman, until 66; mem, Exec. Cmt, Buffalo Co. Dem, 50-; chmn, Buffalo Co. Dem, 50-56. Govt. Pos: Mem, Sch. Bd, Buffalo Co. Teachers Col, 65-; treas, Town of Montana, 47-; mem, Sch. Bd, Arcadia High Sch, 57-60; mem, Draft Bd, Buffalo Co, 50-54; mem, Sch. Cmt, Buffalo Co, 50-53. Mil. Serv: Entered as Pvt, Army Air Force, 42, released as S/Sgt, 45, after serv. in Southwest Pac; Air Medal; Five Battle Stars; Philippine Liberation Medal; Pac. Theater Ribbons. Mem: Am. Legion; Farmers Union; Nat. Farm Orgn. Rel: Evangelical United Brethren. Mailing Add: Route 1, Independence, Wis. 54747. (1967)

BUCK, ARTHUR L. D
Wyo. State Rep.
b. Wichita, Kans, 1906; married to Irene Sue. Educ: Carleton Col, B.A; Colo. State Col, M.A; Univ. of Wyo; Northwest. Univ. Polit. & Govt. Pos: Wyo. State Rep. and minority whip, Wyo. House Rep, currently. Bus. & Prof. Pos: Teacher. Mil. Serv: Army, WWII; Army Commendation Ribbon. Mem: Elks; Odd Fellows; Pi Delta Epsilon; Phi Delta Kappa; Nat. Adv. Bd; Am. Vets. Cmt. Rel: Congregational. Mailing Add: 3018 Thomes, Cheyenne, Wyo. 82001.

BUCK, ELLSWORTH BREWER R
b. Chicago, Ill, 7/3/92; s. Orlando Jacob Buck and Lillian Louise Brewer B; m. 4/12/19 to Constance Tyler; c. Orlando John (deceased) and Nancy (Mrs. Nancy B. Burger). Educ: Dartmouth Col, B.S, 14, M.A, 39; Wagner Col, LL.D, 41; Delta Tau Delta. Polit. & Govt. Pos: Pres, N.Y. Bd. Educ, 42-44; chmn, Richmond Co. Rep. Cmt, N.Y, 51-52; del, Rep. Nat. Conv, 52; U.S. Rep, N.Y, 43-47; dir, Off. Trade, Investment and Monetary Affairs, For. Oper. Admin, 54; pub. adv. U.S. del. UN Econ. and Soc. Coun, Geneva, 55. Bus. & Prof. Pos: Lab. asst, Wm. Wrigley Jr. Co, Chicago, 14-16, treas, L.A. Dreyfus Co, 20-25, v.pres. and treas, 25, dir, 25-; pres. and treas, 25-32 and chmn. bd, 32-57; bus. exec, v.pres. and dir, Thunder Mt. Ranch Co. Mil. Serv: Navy, Ens. Mem: Trustee Wagner Col; trustee Staten Island Zool. Soc; India House; Richmond Co. Country Club. Mailing Add: 152 Stuyvesant Place, Staten Island, New York, N.Y. 10301.

BUCK, FORREST M. R
W.Va. State Del.
b. Aliquippa, Pa, 3/8/09; s. Luster F. Buck and Katherine Marshall B; m. 5/31/33 to Mary Harrington; c. Lawrence H, Willis R, Barbara Ann (Mrs. William S. Robertson) and Edward F. Educ: Rollins Col; Ohio State Univ. Polit. & Govt. Pos: W.Va. State Del, 62- Bus. & Prof. Pos: Automotive dealer. Mil. Serv: Tech. rep, Air Serv. Command, China-Burma-India Theatre. Mem: Mason; Elks; Sigma Chi; Nemesis Shrine. Rel: Presbyterian. Mailing Add: 116 Hill St, Sisterville, W.Va. 26175.

BUCK, MILDRED REEL D
b. Reelsboro, N.C, 2/20/14; d. Floyd Hines Reel and Lizzie E. Brinson R; m. 6/27/34 to Eugene Buck; wid; c. Emily C, Gene R. and Linda. Educ: High Sch. and Bus. Col. Polit. Pos: Precinct registr, several past elecs; alternate del, Dem. Nat. Conv, 64. Bus. & Prof. Pos: Clerk. Mem: Eastern Star. Rel: Methodist. Legal Res: Reelsboro, New Bern, N.C. 28560. Mailing Add: Route 1, Box 306, New Bern, N.C. 28560.

BUCK, RAYMOND ELLIOT D
b. Ft. Worth, Tex, 7/13/94; m. 12/8/21 to Katharine Camp; c. Raymond Elliot, Jr. and Katharine (Mrs. Roy E. McDermott). Educ: Tex. Christian Univ, 11-13; Univ. Tex, LL.B, 17; Sigma Alpha Epsilon. Polit. & Govt. Pos: Chmn. and organizer, Young Dem. Tex, 31-35; del, Tex. State Dem. Conv, 32-64; chmn, 56; del, Dem. Nat. Conv, 40-; co-chmn, Lyndon B. Johnson for U.S. Sen. Cmt, 41 & 48; Tex. chmn, Jefferson Day Dinner, 41-42; finance chmn, Tex. Dem. Party, 42; co-chmn, Tex. War Bonds Cmt, 42-45; Gov. Post War Planning Cmt. Taxes and Aviation, 44-46; mem, Dem. Adv. Coun, 55; Tex. state chmn, Bus. and Prfnl. Men and Women for Kennedy-Johnson, 60; chmn, Tarrant Co. Dem. Conv. and N.Tex. Bus. Men for LBJ, 64. Bus. & Prof. Pos: Attorney, Buck & Buck, 19-; assoc. gen. counsel, Am. Airlines Inc, 29- and Gen. Dynamics/Ft. Worth, 41-; owner-operator, Raymond F. Buck Ranch & Cattle Co, 38-; dir, Continental Nat. Bank, 43-, v.chmn. bd, 66- and mem. exec. and loan cmts; chmn. and gen. counsel, Commercial Standard Fire and Marine Co, 52- and Commercial Standard Life Ins. Co, 58-; mem. exec. and invest. cmts, Commercial Standard Ins. Group; pres, Tarrant Land Co, 54-; v.pres. and dir, Geyser Corp, 64- Mil. Serv: Capt, Inf, Army, 17-19; AEF, France. Mem: Am, Tex. and Tarrant Co. Bar Asns; President's Club (mem. adv. coun. for Tex, 65-); chmn. N.Tex. area, Presidential Ball, 66 & 67; Nat. Develop. Prog. of Sam Rayburn Found; dir. and mem. exec. cmt, Southwest. Exposition and Fat Stock Show, 48-; Trinity Improv. Asn.(dir, 55-); Better Bus. Bur.(pres. and dir, Ft. Worth, 57-60); C. of C.(dir, Ft. Worth, 57-64, pres, 61-64); dir, Jr. Achievement of Ft. Worth, Inc, 58-; Scott & White Mem. Hosp. Citizen's Coun, 59-; St. Joseph's Hosp. Lay Coun, 58-; Fels. Tex. Bar Found, 66; dir, Tex. Christian Univ. Stadium Asn, 55- and pres, Ex-Students Asn, 52; dir, Tex. Tech. Col. Found, 56-58; emer. mem, Int. Bd. of Electors Ins. Hall of Fame, 65-; chmn. bd. gov, Int. Invitational Ins. Seminars, 64-67; Univ. Tex. Ins. Adv. Coun. and Planning Cmt, 62- and Coun. Bus. Admin. Found, 64-; UN Asn of the U.S.(pres, Ft. Worth Chap, 64-); Ft. Worth, Three Stags, Key, Rivercrest Country and Ridglea Country Clubs. B'nai B'rith Award for Outstanding Serv. to Civic and Commun. Affairs, 64; Spec. Tex. Ranger. Mailing Add: 1500 Alta Dr, Ft. Worth, Tex. 76107.

BUCK, THOMAS BRYANT, III D
Ga. State Rep.
b. Columbus, Ga, 3/2/38; s. Thomas Bryant Buck, Jr. and Violet Burrus Litchfield B; single. Educ: Emory Univ, B.A, 59, LL.B, 62; Alpha Phi Omega; Kappa Alpha Order. Polit. & Govt. Pos: Ga. State Rep, 67- Mil. Serv: Army Res, 63-69, Pfc; Outstanding Basic Trainee. Mem: Am. Bar Asn; State Bar of Ga; Phi Delta Phi; Kiwanis; Green Island Country Club; Columbus Country Club. Rel: Baptist. Legal Res: 2033 Wynnton Rd, Columbus, Ga. 31906. Mailing Add: P.O. Box 196, Columbus, Ga. 31902.

BUCKINGHAM, HAROLD D. R
b. 9/7/10; m. 6/12/32 to Ella N. Eckert; c. five. Educ: Nebr. State Teachers Col, B.S. Colo. State Teachers Col. Polit. & Govt. Pos: S.Dak. State Sen. until 66; Rapid City Bd. Educ; Co. Bd. Educ; dir, pres, assoc, Sch. Bds. of S.Dak; Exec. Cmt. Gov. Lay Conf. on Elem. and Sec. Educ, 61; past pres, Cmt. for Educ. in S.Dak. Bus. & Prof. Pos: Founder of Buckingham Freight Lines; owner, pres, Nat. Sch. of Bus; lumber bus. Mem: Chmn, United Fund Drive, Rapid City and Ellsworth, 64; Mason; Lions, dir. and off, Bennett-Clarkson Mem. Hosp. Rel: Presbyterian. Mailing Add: 2774 Murray, Rapid City, S.Dak. 57701.

BUCKLEY, JAMES P. D
b. Waukesha, Wis, 6/7/33. Educ: Carroll Col, B.S. in hist. Polit. & Govt. Pos: Chief clerk, 65, dep. state chmn, Wis. Dem. Party, 61-64. Mil. Serv: Air Force, 51-55. Mailing Add: 453 N. Washington St, Waukesha, Wis. 53186. (1967)

BUCKLEY, JOHN J. R
m. to Marie Costello; c. 2. Educ: Boston Col, Col. of Bus. Admin, 52, Sr. class pres, 52. Polit. & Govt. Pos: Spec. Asst. to Sen. Leverett Saltonstall; Campaign consult, adv, Lt. Gov. Elliot Richardson 64; former mem. Walpole Rep. Town Cmt. Bus. & Prof. Pos: Founder, Campus Blouse Co, the J.J. Buckley Furniture Co; Former mem, educ. brs. Doubleday and Co, and D.C. Health, a div. of Raytheon. Mil. Serv: USAR, 52-; Lt. Mem: Kiwanis; Precincts, Inc; Cmt. for the Christian Herter Chair in Int. Rels. at Brandeis Univ. Mailing Add: 44 Doncaster, Roslindale, Mass. 02131. (1967)

BUCKLEY, JOHN REED D
b. Kansas City, Mo, 9/9/21; s. Albert Patrick Buckley and Rebecca Grace Skinner B; m. 5/28/40 to Meriam Ruth Mollins; c. John Reed Jr, Stephen M. and Wayne P. Polit. & Govt. Pos: Mem. staff of Rep. Fascell, Fla, 55-, admin. asst, currently. Mem: Jaycees (v.pres, Fla. Chap. and pres, Miami

Springs-Airport chap); Fla. State Soc.(past pres); Burro Club (v.pres); Capitol Hill First Friday Club (pres). Hobbies: Photography, woodwork, fishing, hunting. Legal Res: Miami Springs, Fla. 33166. Mailing Add: 5483 30th St. N.W, Chevy Chase, Md. 20015.

BUCKLEY, JOHN TIMOTHY R
N.Y. State Assemblyman
b. Utica, N.Y, 2/8/36; s. John T. Buckley (deceased) and Catherine Milet B; single. Educ: Georgetown Univ, B.S, 58; Albany Law Sch, LL.B, 61; N.Y. Univ. Grad. Sch. of Pub. Admin, 66; pres, Albany Law Sch. Class. Polit. & Govt. Pos: Past pres, Oneida Co. Young Rep. Club, N.Y; mem. staff, N.Y. State Sen. Fred J. Rath, formerly; coordinator, Youth for Eisenhower, Rep. Nat. Hq, 56; mem, Charter Rev. Cmn, City of Utica, 64-65; v.chmn, Young Rep. State Conv, 66; N.Y. State Assemblyman, 116th Dist, 67- Bus. & Prof. Pos: Attorney, Kernan & Kernan, Utica, N.Y, 61-68; Buckley & Scholl, 69- Mil. Serv: Entered as Pvt, Army, 61, in 322nd Mil. Police Criminal Invest. Detachment and serv. as 1st Lt, Judge Adv. Gen. Corps; Capt, Army, Res, 414th Civil Affairs Co. Mem: Oneida Co, N.Y. State and Am. Bar Asns; E. Utica Rep. Club; New Hartford Rep. Club; chmn, K. of C. Speakers Bur; pres, Friendly Sons of St. Patrick; Dick Mix Mem. Asn; Elks; Utica Jr. C. of C; pres, Georgetown Club of Mohawk Valley; bd. dirs, Foothills Girl Scout Coun. Admitted to practice before the U.S. Supreme Court, 68. Rel: Roman Catholic. Legal Res: 13 Proctor Blvd, Utica, N.Y. 13501. Mailing Add: First Bank Bldg, Utica, N.Y. 13501.

BUCKLEY, JOSEPH B. D
Conn. State Sen.
b. Ansonia, Conn, 7/13/28; s. Batholomew F. Buckley (deceased) and Julia L. Burns B; married. Educ: Fordham Univ, B.S, 48. Polit. & Govt. Pos: Corp. counsel, Ansonia, Conn, 56-64; Conn. State Rep, 61-66; Conn. State Sen, 67- Mil. Serv: Entered as 2nd Lt, Air Force, 52, released as 1st Lt, 55. Rel: Roman Catholic. Mailing Add: 366 Main St, Ansonia, Conn. 06401.

BUCKLEY, T. GARRY R
Vt. State Sen.
b. Albany, N.Y, 9/13/22; s. Christopher H. Buckley and Margaret E. Garry B; m. 4/21/45 to Frances Kingsbury Littlefield; c. T. Garry, Jr, David Gifford, Katherine Frances, Peter Stokes,and Jonathan Blair. Educ: Albany Acad. for Boys; Cheshire Acad; Cranwell Prep; Brown Univ; Flight Officers Training, Union Col, Univ. Scranton and Northeast Airlines Instrument Sch, Univ. Vt; Delta Kappa Epsilon. Polit. & Govt. Pos: Trustee, Village of Old Bennington, Vt, 47-55; selectman, Town of Bennington, 48-56; Vt. State Sen, 55-56, 57-58 & 69-, v.chmn, Judiciary Cmt, Vt. State Senate, 69- Bus. & Prof. Pos: Pres, B&B Theatrical Inc, 48-50, Mem. Theatre Inc, 48-; trustee, Bennington Mus, 55-, chmn. bd, 66 & 67; dir. and founder, Bennington Co. Indust. Corp, 58-; dir, Ben-Mont Paper Co, 69- Mil. Serv: Entered as Aviation Student, Army Air Force, 41, released as Lt, 45, after serv. in First Troop Carrier Command. Mem: Nat. Asn. Real Estate Bd; Vt. and Bennington Co. Real Estate Bd; pres, Continental Asn. Real Estate Appraisers; Am. Legion. Rel: Roman Catholic. Legal Res: Tichenor Place, Old Bennington, Vt. Mailing Add: Buckley Bldg, Bennington, Vt. 05201.

BUCKLEY, WILLIAM FRANK, JR. Conservative
b. New York, N.Y, 11/24/25; s. William Frank Buckley and Aloise Steiner B; m. 7/6/50 to Patricia Taylor; c. Christopher T. Educ: Univ. Mex, 43; Yale, B.A, 50. Hon. L.H.D, Seton Hall Univ, 66, Niagra Univ, 67 and St. Peter's Col, 69. Polit. & Govt. Pos: Cand. for Mayor of N.Y, 65. Bus. & Prof. Pos: Assoc. ed, Am. Mercury, 52; ed-in-chief, Nat. Rev, N.Y.C, 55- Mil. Serv: Army, 44-46, 2nd Lt. Publ: God and Man at Yale, 51; co-auth, McCarthy and His Enemies, 54; auth, Up From Liberalism, 59; contrib, Ocean Racing, 59 and The Intellectuals: A Controversial Portrait, 60; ed, The Committee and its Critics, 62; auth, Rumbles Left and Right, 63; contrib, What is Conservatism?, 63; Dialogues in Americanism, 64; auth, The Unmaking of a Mayor, 66; The Jeweler's Eye, 68 and Did You Ever See a Dream Walking, 69. Mem: N.Y. Yacht Club; Overseas Press Club, N.Y.C; Nat. Press Club, D.C. Order of Lafayette Freedom Award, 66; George Sokolsky Award, Am. Jewish League Against Communism, 66; Distinguished Journalism Achievement Award, Univ. South. Calif, 68; Emmy Award for Outstanding TV Prog. Achievement, 69. Rel: Catholic. Mailing Add: 150 E. 35th St, New York, N.Y. 10016.

BUCKMAN, ERNEST U. R
b. Wilkes-Barre, Pa, 11/15/25; s. Lewis Taylor Buckman and Abbie Lee B; m. 11/16/46 to Katherine Elizabeth Stearns; c. Margaret D, Elizabeth T. and John L. Educ: Mass. Inst. Tech, B.S, 46; Kappa Sigma. Polit. & Govt. Pos: Alternate del, Rep. Nat. Conv, 68. Bus. & Prof. Pos: V.pres. leasing, Oliver Tyrone Corp, 59- Mil. Serv: Entered as A/S, Navy, 43, released as Ens, 46, after serv. in Officer Training, recalled as a Lt, 51-53, Atlantic Fleet. Mem: Rotary. Rel: Protestant. Mailing Add: 661 Canterbury Lane, Sewickley, Pa. 15143.

BUCKMAN, JAMES DAVID 'JIGGS' D
b. Shepherdsville, Ky, 3/13/11; s. James David Buckman, Sr. and Carletta Hatzell B; m. 3/25/44 to Angelina Butera; c. Carletta A. and Ann. Educ: Univ. Louisville, LL.B, 36; Phi Delta Phi. Polit. & Govt. Pos: Circuit court clerk, Bullitt Co, Ky, 31-36; Ky. State Rep, 50-52 & 60-62; pres, Young Dem. Clubs of Ky, 50-52; chmn, 7 Jefferson-Jackson Day Fund Raising Dinners; Attorney Gen, Ky, 52-56; chmn, Bullitt Co. Dem. Cmt, 61-65; Ky. State Sen, 62-68, chmn, Senate Dem. Caucus, 62-64 and majority floor leader. Mil. Serv: Entered as Pvt, Army, 42, released as Sgt, 44. Mem: Ky. and Am. Bar Asns; Mason; Am. Legion; DAV; Ky. and Bullitt Co. Farm Bur. Rel: Baptist. Legal Res: Shepherdsville, Ky. 40165. Mailing Add: 309 Hermitage Dr, Frankfort, Ky. 40601.

BUCKNER, ELMER LA MAR R
Utah State Sen.
b. Provo, Utah, 4/27/22; s. Elmer Ray Buckner and La Vern Maxfield B; m. 10/3/45 to Melba Hale; c. Lynda, Brent La Mar, Terry Hale, Kathy and David La Mar. Educ: Brigham Young Univ, B.S, 46. Polit. & Govt. Pos: Admin. field asst. to Sen. Watkins, 56-58; del, Rep. Nat. Conv, 60; chmn, Weber Co. Rep. Party, Utah, 60-64; Utah State Rep, Fourth Legis. Dist, Weber Co, 65-67; Utah State Sen, 67- Bus. & Prof. Pos: Pres, Buckner Ins. Counsrs, 56; pres, Buckner Hunter Ins. Agency, Salt Lake City, Utah, 66-; mem, bd. of dirs, ZCMI, Salt Lake City, 68. Mil. Serv: Entered as Aviation Cadet, Air Force, 43, released as 1st Lt, 45, after serv. in 490th Bomb Group, 350th Squadron, 8th Air Force, ETO, 45; Air Medal with 3 Oak Leaf Clusters; European Campaign Ribbon; Presidential Unit Citation. Mem: Pres, Brigham Young Univ. Alumni Asn; pres, Ogden Kiwanis; Am. Legion; coun. v.pres, Boy Scouts; bd. dirs, U.S. C. of C; Jr. C. of C.(Utah state pres, 52, nat. pres, 54-55); bd. gov, Am. Nat. Red Cross, 56-62; int. pres, Sigma Gamma Chi, 67-69. Utah State Distinguished Serv. Award, 52; Silver Beaver Award, Boy Scouts, 67. Rel: Latter-day Saint. Mailing Add: 1550 Country Hills Dr, Ogden, Utah 84403.

BUCKRIDGE, MARILYN L. D
V.Pres, Wash. Fedn. Dem. Women
b. Colorado Springs, Colo, 9/5/32; d. Robert E. Lewis and Virginia Manning L; c. Lisa, Eric, Sara, Kurt and Amy. Educ: Col. of Idaho. Polit. & Govt. Pos: Mem, Wash. Dem. State Exec. Cmt, 62-64; del, Dem. Nat. Conv, 64; mem, Wash. Dem. State Rules Cmt, 64; chmn, Snohomish Co. Pub. Asst. Adv. Bd, 64-66; mem. exec. cmt, Referendum 15, 66; v.pres, Wash. Fedn. Dem. Women, 68-; chmn, 38th Legis. Dist. Dem. Party, 68- Mem: Everett League of Women Voters (pres, 62). Rel: Episcopal. Mailing Add: 732 Wetmore, Everett, Wash. 98201.

BUCKSON, DAVID PENROSE R
Attorney Gen, Del.
b. Townsend, Del, 7/25/20; s. Leon J. Buckson and Margaret Hutchison B; m. 2/20/63 to Patricia Maloney; c. Brian, David H, Eric, Kent and Marlee. Educ: Univ. Del, B.A, 41; Dickinson Sch. Law, LL.B, 48; Sigma Nu. Polit. & Govt. Pos: Chmn, Kent Co. Rep. Exec. Cmt, Del, 56; Lt. Gov, Del, 57-60, gov, 60-61, Attorney Gen, 63-; alternate del, Rep. Nat. Conv, 68. Mil. Serv: Entered as 2nd Lt, Army, 41, released as Maj, 46, after serv. in 198th Coast Artil.Regt, Southwest Pac, 42-45. Mem: Del. and Am. Bar Asns; Am. Judicature Soc; Rotary; Del. Vets; Nat. Sojourners, Inc; Am. Legion; VFW; Union Lodge 5; Del. Consistory-Nur Temple: Del.Asn. Chiefs of Police; Smyrna Volunteer Fire Co. Rel: Methodist. Mailing Add: Beech Haven Dr, Dover, Del. 19901.

BUCKWAY, DALLAS HENRY D
b. Ogden, Utah, 11/2/37; s. Henry Buckway and Verba Sessions B; m. 9/16/61 to Carol A. Thompson; c. Dallas, Jr, Cory and Michael. Educ: Weber State Col; Int. Relations Club. Polit. & Govt. Pos: Utah State Rep, until 67; Tax Study Cmt, Weber Co, 66; secy, Utah Young Dem, 62-63. Bus. & Prof. Pos: Owner, U & I Carpet Center, 64- Rel: Latter-day Saint. Mailing Add: 4053 Madison, Ogden, Utah. 84403. (1967)

BUCZKO, THADDEUS JOSEPH D
Auditor, Commonwealth of Mass.
b. Salem, Mass, 2/23/26; s. Ignacy Buczko and Veronica Brzozowska B; single. Educ: Norwich Univ, B.A. with honors, 49; Boston Univ. Sch. of Law, LL.B, 51. Polit. & Govt. Pos: Former postmaster, Salem, Mass; mem, Salem City Coun, 56-59; fourth ward chmn, Dem. City Cmt; second Essex sen. dist. campaign coordinator, Edward M. Kennedy for U.S. Sen; Mass. State Rep, 59-64, mem. pensions and old age assistance, judiciary and munic. finance cmts. and spec. cmn. on munic. home rule, Mass. House of Rep; chmn. cmt. on rules, Dem. State Conv, Springfield, 63; auditor, Mass, 64-; del, Dem. Nat. Conv, 68. Bus. & Prof. Pos: Attorney-at-law, 51- Mil. Serv: Entered as A/S, Navy, 44, released as Fireman 1/C, 46, after serv. in Asiatic-Pac. Theater; re-entered as 2nd Lt, Army, 52, serv. as Unit Tank Comdr. and asst. staff Judge Adv, Third Armored Div, Korean War; at present, LTC, Army Res, 357th CA Area Hq. B, Boston Army Base, Mass; Asiatic-Pac. Theater Campaign Star. Mem: Nat. Asn. of State Auditors, Comptrollers & Treasurers; Am, Salem, Boston, Essex, Mass. and Fed. Bar Asns; Asn. of U.S. Army; Mil. Order of Foreign Wars of U.S; ROA; Mil. Govt. Asn; Amvets; VFW; Am. Legion; Polish Legion Am. Vets; Mass. Legislators Asn; Mass. Trial Lawyers Asn; Norwich Univ. Alumni Asn; K. of C; Century Club; Polish-American Citizens Club; Polish Falcon's Club; St. Anthony's Soc; former chmn, Heart Fund and Ment. Health Fund Drive, Salem; St. Joseph's Polish Roman Cath. Union; Sons of Poland Soc; Ward Two Social Club; Polish-Russian-Lithuanian-Am. Citizens Club; St. Michael's Soc; Gallows Hill Commun. Club. Rel: Roman Catholic. Legal Res: 47 Butler St, Salem, Mass. 01970. Mailing Add: 276 Essex St, Salem, Mass. 01970.

BUDD, HARRELL R
b. 1926. Educ: South. Methodist Univ, B.S, M.S. Polit. & Govt. Pos: N. Mex. State Rep, -66. Bus. & Prof. Pos: Consult. petroleum geologist. Mil. Serv: Navy, 43-46. Mem: Elks; Scouts. Rel: Protestant. Mailing Add: 1613 Camino Rio, Farmington, N.Mex. 87401. (1967)

BUDD, JOSEPH LINCOLN R
b. Salt Lake City, 5/31/11; s. John C. Budd and Lucille McGinnis B; m. 12/27/36 to Ruth Francis Peterson; c. Betty Louis (Mrs. Frank C. Fear), Mary Kaye (Mrs. Stanley Flitner), Nancy Ruth. Educ: Wyo. Univ, 29-30; Utah State Univ, 32-34. Polit. & Govt. Pos: Mem, Rep. Nat. Com, Wyo; mem. Interstate Streams Cmn, 50-; mem. Wyo. House of Reps, 51-63 (minority floor leader, 59; speaker, 61); pres. Wyo. Reclamation Asn, 43-45. Bus. & Prof. Pos: Mgr, partner Budd Hereford Ranch, Big Piney, Wyo, 34-; dir. Pac.-Atlantic Life Ins. Co; chmn, trustees Big Piney Schs; dir. Wyo. Safety Found. Mem: Wyo. Stock Growers Asn, (exec. com.); Am. Cattlemen's Asn, (2nd v. pres.); Elks; Mason; Lions. (past pres, Big Piney). Rel: Presbyterian. Mailing Add: P.O. Box 340, Big Piney, Wyo. 83113. (1967)

BUDD, WILLIAM H, JR. R
Wyo. State Rep.
b. Kemmerer, Wyo, 7/27/30; s. William H. Budd and Thelma Vickrey B; m. 8/27/55 to Carolyn Mockler; c. Robert Wesley, Cynthia Lee, Jennifer Ann, Donald Mockler and Mary Elise. Educ: Univ. Wyo, B.S. in bus. admin, 59; Alpha Kappa Psi. Polit. & Govt. Pos: State chmn, Wyo. Young Rep, 55-57; grad, Young Rep. Leadership Training, 57; state chmn, Cmt. Polit. Educ. and Participation, 63; councilman, Riverton, Wyo, 64-66; Wyo. State Rep, 67- Bus. & Prof. Pos: Spec. agent, Prudential Life Ins. Co. of Am, 58-66; pres, Budd Ins, Inc, 62-66; instr, Life Underwriters Training Coun, 65-; gen. rep, Teton Nat. Ins. Co, 68- Mil. Serv: Entered as Pvt, Air Force, 50, released

as S/Sgt, 54, after serv. in Far East, Japan and Korea; Korean Serv. Medal. Mem: Charter mem, Wind River Asn. Life Underwriters,(pres, 58); Jaycees; Am. Legion; VFW; Elks; Mason; AF&AM. Distinguished Serv. Award from Riverton, Wyo. Jaycees. Rel: Episcopal; past vestryman and sr. warden, lay reader. Legal Res: 829 W. Fremont, Riverton, Wyo. 82501. Mailing Add: P.O. Box 687, Riverton, Wyo. 82501.

BUDGE, HAMER HAROLD R
Chmn, Securities and Exchange Cmn.
b. Pocatello, Idaho, 11/21/10; s. Alfred Budge and Ella Hoge B; m. 8/30/41 to Jeanne Keithly; c. Kathleen. Educ: Col. Idaho, 28-30; Stanford Univ, B.A, 33; Univ. Idaho, LL.B, 36; Sigma Alpha Epsilon. Polit. & Govt. Pos: Idaho State Rep, 39, 41, 49, Majority Floor Leader, Idaho House of Rep; U.S. Rep, Idaho, 82nd-86th Cong; mem, Securities and Exchange Cmn, 64-69, chmn, 69- Bus. & Prof. Pos: Attorney-at-law, Boise, Idaho, 26-42, 46-51. Mil. Serv: Lt. Comdr, Naval Res, 42-45. Mem: Am. and Idaho Bar Asns; Elks; Idaho C. of C; bd, Salvation Army; Lincoln Day Banquet Asn. Rel: Latter-day Saint. Legal Res: Boise, Idaho. Mailing Add: Securities and Exchange Commission, Washington, D.C. 20549.

BUDGE, REED WILLIAM R
Idaho State Sen.
b. Logan, Utah, 1/7/21; s. Thomas B. Budge and Duella Alvord B; m. 4/17/43 to Gweneth Steffensen; c. twins, Reed Douglas and Linda Duella, Randall Christian, Brian William and Suzanne. Educ: Utah State Univ, B.S, 46; Sigma Nu; Intercollegiate Knights; Alpha Epsilon Delta. Polit. & Govt. Pos: Co. cmnr, Caribou Co, Idaho, 63-67; Idaho State Sen, Dist. 32, 68- Bus. & Prof. Pos: Co-mgr, Fish Haven Resort, Bear Lake Co, Idaho, 46-51; pres. and mgr, Budge Land and Livestock Co, 50-61; rancher, Soda Springs, Idaho, 61. Mil. Serv: Entered as Pvt, Army, 43, released as T/Sgt, 45, after serv. in Second Armored Div, 66th Regt, European and Mid. East. Theatres, 44-45; ATO Serv. Ribbon; European-Africa-Middle East. Serv. Ribbon; Good Conduct Medal; Purple Heart Medal; Silver Star Medal; Belgian Fourragere. Mem: Bear River Compact Cmn; Kiwanis; Idaho Cattlemans Asn. Rel: Latter-day Saint. Mailing Add: 231 S. First East, Soda Springs, Idaho 83276.

BUECHLER, EDMUND R
b. Bremen, N.Dak, 3/1/12; married; c. Three. Educ: Pub. schs, Bremen, N.Dak. Polit. & Govt. Pos: Dir, Farm Bur; twp. clerk, N.Dak; N.Dak. State Rep, 61-66. Bus. & Prof. Pos: Farmer. Rel: Lutheran. Mailing Add: Bremen, N.Dak. 58319. (1967)

BUEHL, WILLIAM ANTHONY 'TONY' R
Ariz. State Rep.
b. Brooklyn, N.Y, 12/20/34; s. William Adolph Buehl and Doris Johnson B; m. 4/5/57 to Bobby June Mangels; c. William Sanford. Educ: Univ. Ariz, 56-60; Civitan. Polit. & Govt. Pos: Ariz. State Rep, 65-, chmn. ways and means cmt, Ariz. House Rep, 67- Bus. & Prof. Pos: Salesman, Mangels Reality, Tucson, Ariz, 57-66; owner, Tony Buehl Agency, Ins, 63-69; pres, Henderson Realty, 66-69. Mil. Serv: Entered as Pvt, Marine Corps, 53, released as Cpl, 56, after serv. in Marine Corps Track Team, Japan, 54 and Korea, 55; Good Conduct Medal; Nat. Defense Medal; UN Medal; Korean Medal. Mem: Tucson Bd. of Realtors; Eagleton Inst. Polit; Ariz. Acad. Rel: Protestant. Legal Res: 4926 E. Copper St, Tucson, Ariz. 85716. Mailing Add: 40 N. Swan, Tucson, Ariz. 85716.

BUEHLER, JOHN R
b. Emery, S.Dak, 10/16/02; m. to Helen Guenthner; c. Marjorie, James, Robert, William, Dorothy, Karon. Educ: Emery High Sch. Polit. & Govt. Pos: Assessor; mem, Sch. Bd; S.Dak. State Sen, 40 & 42; chmn, Hanson Co. Soil and Water Conserv. Cmt; S.Dak. State Rep, 48-66. Bus. & Prof. Pos: Farmer, feeder. Rel: Presbyterian. Mailing Add: Emery, S.Dak. 57332. (1967)

BUEHLER, PAUL RICHARD D
V.Chmn, Taylor Co. Dem. Party, Wis.
b. Medford, Wis, 11/24/93; s. William Buehler and Elizabeth Gertz B; m. 9/5/22 to Helen Albertina Resech (deceased); remarried 5/17/69 to Cecilia F. Wolton Williams; c. Armin Paul, Ervin Roland, Phyllis Helen (Mrs. Keith Hutson), Lorraine Elizabeth (Mrs. Richard Peters) and John Williams. Educ: Bus. Col. Night Sch. Polit. & Govt. Pos: Assessor, Wis, 26-27; supvr, Medford, 52-54; secy. and treas, Taylor Co. Dem. Party, 52-54, chmn, 64-69, v.chmn, 69- Mil. Serv: Entered as Pvt, Army, 18; Purple Heart, Campaign Ribbons. Mem: Am. Legion; VFW; DAV; pres, Local Farmers Union; pres, Co. Asn. of Coops; dir, Fed. Land Bank; pres, Taylor Co. Coop. Credit Union. Received Citation for Meritorious Serv. as Post Comdr, Am. Legion. Rel: Lutheran. Mailing Add: Route 2, Medford, Wis. 54451.

BUFFINGTON, HERBERT L, JR. D
b. Nelson, Ga, 1/29/22; s. Herbert Luther Buffington, Sr. and Nancy Cline B; m. 12/16/50 to Sarah Boddie; c. Nancy Ann. Educ: Reinhardt Col, grad; Univ. Ga, A.B; Atlanta Law Sch, Georgia, LL.B; Sigma Delta Kappa; Kappa Chapter. Polit. & Govt. Pos: Chmn, Cherokee Co. Dem. Exec. Cmt, Ga, 58-68. Mil. Serv: Entered as Pvt, Army, 42, released as Technician 3/C, 45, after serv. at Hq. 5th Attachment, 2nd Army. Mem: Canton, Blue Ridge Circuit and Am. Bar Asns; State Bar of Ga; Am. Judicature Soc; Am. Trial Lawyers Asn; Am. Legion; Moose; Burns Club of Atlanta; Lions. Rel: Methodist. Legal Res: 10 Muriel St, Canton, Ga. 30114. Mailing Add: P.O. Box 189, Canton, Ga. 30114.

BUFFINGTON, J. RAYMOND D
b. Baltimore, Md, 5/23/11; married. Educ: Baltimore City Col; William & Mary Col; Am. Univ, A.B, 33; Univ. of Md, LL.B, 57. Polit. & Govt. Pos: Md. State Del, 43-59, 64-67; Md. State Sen, 59-63. Mem: Am. Bar Asn; Shrine; Mason. Mailing Add: 221 Ridgemeade Rd, Baltimore, Md. 21210. (1967)

BUFORD, ROBERT PEGRAM R
Mem, Va. Rep. State Cent. Cmt.
b. Roanoke Rapids, N.C, 9/7/25; s. Robert Pegram Buford and Edith Rawlings; m. 6/26/48 to Anne Bliss Whitehead; c. Robert P, IV, Bliss Whitehead and Anne Peyton. Educ: Univ. of Va, LL.B, 50; Phi Delta Phi. Polit. & Govt. Pos: V.chmn, Henrico Co. Rep. Cmt, Va, 62-64, chmn, 64-67; campaign chmn, Third Cong. Dist, 65; mem, Va. Rep. State Cent. Cmt, 68- Bus. & Prof. Pos: Partner, Hunton, Williams, Gay, Powell & Gibson, 52- Mil. Serv: Entered as A/S, Naval Res, 43, released as Lt.(jg), 46. Mem: Am, Va. and Richmond Bar Asns; dir, Va. State C. of C; Richmond Forward; Richmond First Club; Richmond Forum Club; Country Club of Va; Commonwealth Club. Rel: Episcopal. Legal Res: 7 Ralston Rd, Richmond, Va. 23229. Mailing Add: 700 Bldg, Richmond, Va. 23212.

BUGATTO, B. JOHN R
b. San Francisco, Calif, 7/20/34; s. Mario Bugatto and Lietta De Martini B; m. 12/2/61 to Maria De Martini; c. Barry, Annette and Robert. Educ: St. Mary's Col. of Calif, A.B, 57; Univ. San Francisco Sch. Law, LL.B, 61; Phi Delta Phi. Polit. & Govt. Pos: Mem, Bay Area Transportation Study Cmn, Calif, 68-; alternate del, Rep. Nat. Conv, 68. Mil. Serv: Entered as Airman Basic, Air Force, 58, released as Airman 2/C, 63, after serv. in 631st Res. Unit, Continental Air Command, 58-63. Mem: Calif. and San Francisco Bar Asns; Columbus Civic Club (pres); Lions (pres, North Beach Club); Ital. Fedn. of Calif; San Francisco Athletic Club; K. of C.(Grand Knight, Dante Coun). Rel: Roman Catholic. Legal Res: 2346 Jones St, San Francisco, Calif. 94123. Mailing Add: 470 Columbus Ave, San Francisco, Calif. 94133.

BUGLEWICZ, JOHN VALENTINE R
Chmn, Fremont Co. Rep. Cent. Cmt, Colo.
b. Omaha, Nebr, 6/12/33; s. Valentine S. Buglewicz and Mary F. Piskac B; wid; m. 6/17/67 to Doris Coffee; c. John, Judy, Steve, Pat, Carol, Tim and Diane Buglewicz and Stephen and Dale Coffee. Educ: Creighton Univ. and Med. Sch, M.D, 58; Alpha Sigma Nu; Alpha Omega Alpha; Phi Chi. Polit. & Govt. Pos: Chmn, Fremont Co. Rep. Cent. Cmt, Colo, 68- Mil. Serv: Entered as Sr. Asst. Surgeon, U.S. Pub. Health Serv, 59, released as Surgeon, 61, after serv. in Dulce & Zuni, N.Mex. Mem: Am. Med. Asn; Fremont Co. Med. Soc; Colo. Med. Soc; Elks; Lions; K. of C; C. of C.(pres, Florence, Colo, 64). Rel: Roman Catholic. Mailing Add: 502 E. Fourth, Florence, Colo. 81226.

BUGLIONE, NICHOLAS JOSEPH D
Mass. State Rep.
b. Lawrence, Mass, 9/12/32; s. Nicola Buglione and Battestina Ianonne B; m. 10/10/54 to Joan Shirley Habeeb; c. Suzanne Marie and Lisa Ellen. Educ: Air Force Commun. Sch, cert; Salem State Col, 3 years, part-time. Polit. & Govt. Pos: Mem, Town Meetings, Methuen, Mass, seven years, sch. committeeman, 65-; Mass. State Rep, 15th Essex Dist, 69- Bus. & Prof. Pos: Off. supvr, Avco Corp, Wilmington, Mass, 58-69. Mil. Serv: Entered as Airman Basic, Air Force, 52, released as S/Sgt, 56, after serv. in Commun, Korean Conflict, 53-54; Good Conduct Medal; UN Medal; Korean Medal; one Battle Star; Nat. Defense Medal. Mem: Mass. Legislators Asn; Mass. Asn. Sch. Cmts. New Eng. Sch. Develop. Coun; K. of C; Boosters Club; Methuen Bd. of Trade; Methuen East End Civic Orgn. Award, Cost Reduction Prog, Avco Corp. Rel: Catholic. Mailing Add: 4 Jane Rd, Methuen, Mass. 01844.

BUHL, LLOYD FRANK R
Chmn, Eighth Cong. Dist. Rep. Party, Mich.
b. New Haven, Mich, 1/9/18; s. William C. Buhl and Bessie L. Meier B; m. 10/26/40 to Rosamond Davidson; c. William C, Robert L, Marcia E. and Karl E. Educ: High Sch. Polit. & Govt. Pos: Assessor, Deckerville, Mich, 39-46, trustee, 63-69; justice of the peace, Marion Twp, 46-69; mem, Sanilac Co. Rep. Cmt, 50-51; asst. state chmn. and organizer, Eisenhower Campaign, Mich, 52; mem. ed. and legis. coun, Rep. Farm Coun, 52; mem, Sanilac Co. Rep. Cmt, 56-60; chmn, Sanilac Co. Rep. Party, 67-68; chmn, Eighth Cong. Dist. Rep. Party, 69- Bus. & Prof. Pos: Publisher, Deckerville Recorder and Carsonville Jour, 35-69. Mem: Odd Fellows; DOKK; K. of P.(Past Grand Chancellor); charter mem, Deckerville Lions Club (pres, 39). Rel: Presbyterian. Legal Res: 3665 N. Main St, Deckerville, Mich. 48427. Mailing Add: 2534 Black River St, Deckerville, Mich. 48427.

BUHLER, BETTE-JO SIMPSON R
Mem, Tex. State Rep. Hq. Cmt.
b. Olympia, Wash, 5/2/21; d. Jess Ray Simpson and Blanche Taylor S; m. 7/7/42 to Frank Sibley Buhler, Jr; c. Frank Sibley, III, Leslee Kathryn, Blanche Orbin, Jessica and Bruce Taylor. Educ: Univ. Wash, B.A, 42; Gamma Phi Beta. Polit. & Govt. Pos: V.chmn, Victoria Co. Rep. Cmt, Tex, 52-53; dist. committeewoman, Tex. Rep. Exec. Cmt, 53-56, 59-61 & 62-66, state v.chmn, 56-59; mem, Tex. State Rep. Hq. Cmt, currently. Mem: Seattle Jr. League; Victoria Jr. Serv. League; bd, Gulf Bend Center. Rel: Episcopal. Mailing Add: 11 Spring Creek Rd, Victoria, Tex. 77901. (1967)

BUHLER, ROBERT EARL R
b. Salt Lake City, Utah, 11/19/24; s. Orson Earl Buhler and Florence Emma McAllister B; m. to Phyllis Liddle; c. Susan, David Liddle, Stephen John, Linda Dianne, Kathryn, Douglas Wayne and Janean. Polit. & Govt. Pos: Policeman, Salt Lake City, Utah, 47-59, Sgt, Police Dept, 56-59; del, Utah Rep. State Conv, 64 & 66, Rep. Co. Conv, 66; former Utah State Rep. Bus. & Prof. Pos: Salesman, Prudential Ins. Co, 59-63; owner, Prfnl. Salesmen's Serv. Co, 63-; salesman, Boyd W. Strong, Inc, Realtor, 66- Mil. Serv: Entered Merchant Marines, 43, released as Ens, 46, after serv. in Grad. Officers Sch, Maritime Serv, Alameda, Calif, 45; reentered as Sgt, Army, 701st Mil. Police Bn, 50-51. Rel: Latter-day Saint; Lay Minister; Bishop of the Liberty Ward, 5 years; mem, Liberty Stake High Council; High Priest. Legal Res: 1076 S. Fifth E. St, Salt Lake City, Utah 84105. Mailing Add: P.O. Box 784, Salt Lake City, Utah 84110. (1967)

BUKY, FALLIS VERNON R
b. 1904. Educ: Manual and Clark Bus. Sch. Polit. & Govt. Pos: Ky. State Rep, 62-68. Bus. & Prof. Pos: Retired supvr, South. Bell Tel. & Tel. Co. Mem: Mason; Shrine; Tel. Pioneers of Am. Rel: Baptist. 1967 Legal Res: Louisville, Ky. No mailing address available. (1967)

BULEN, LAWRENCE KEITH R
Rep. Nat. Committeeman, Ind.
b. Pendleton, Ind, 12/31/26; s. Lawrence Elston Bulen and Ople Odell Benefiel B; div; c. Lisa K. and Leslie Kathleen. Educ: Ind. Univ, A.B, 49, J.D, 52; Phi Delta Phi; Sigma Nu; Skull and Crescent; Falcon; Sphinx. Polit. & Govt. Pos: Dist. chmn, Young Rep, Ind, 54; committeeman, Rep. Party, 54-64; del, Rep. State Conv, 54-66; Ind. State Rep, 60-64; chmn, 11th Dist. Rep. Cmt, 66-68

and Marion Co. Rep. Cent. Cmt, 66-; mem, Ind. Rep. State Cent. Cmt, formerly; del, Rep. Nat. Conv, 68; Rep. Nat. Committeeman, Ind, 68-, mem, exec. cmt, Rep. Nat. Cmt, 69; chmn, Ind. Nixon Inaugural Cmt, 69. Bus. & Prof. Pos: Attorney, Bulen & Castor. Mil. Serv: Entered as Pvt, Air Force, 45, released as Sgt. of Guard, 46; Lt, Air Force Res, 49-50; Occupation of Japan Medal; Asia and S.Pac. Ribbons. Mem: Indianapolis Lawyers Asn.(pres, 60); Mason; pres, Great Lakes and Murat Shrine Chanters Asns; Scottish Rite; Columbia Club; Ind. Univ. Varsity Club; pres, Rep. Vets. Rel: Disciples of Christ. Legal Res: 700 N. Alabama, Apt. 100, Indianapolis, Ind. 46204. Mailing Add: 144 N. Delaware, Indianapolis, Ind. 46204.

BULGERIN, LORETTA R
Chmn, Eastland Co. Rep. Party, Tex.
b. Houston, Tex, 8/3/30; d. Donald Morrison Davis and Lillian Harvey D; m. 6/8/53 to Harold James Bulgerin; c. Stephen Mitchell, Donald Lawrence, Curtis Wayne, Keith Edward and Claudia Diane. Educ: Southwest. Univ, B.S. in Biol, 52; Alpha Chi; Cardinal Key; Delta Zeta. Polit. & Govt. Pos: V.chmn, Eastland Co. Rep. Party, Tex, 66-68, chmn, 68- Mem: Am. Soc. Clin. Pathologists; Woman's Auxiliary to Am. Med. Asn; Parent Teacher's Orgn. (pres, 68-69); Women's Soc. of Christian Serv.(pres, Eastland Methodist Church orgn, 64-67). Rel: Methodist. Mailing Add: 1800 W. Plummer, Eastland, Tex. 76448.

BULL, CORALEE KITCHINGS D
b. S.C; d. Boyce Dexter Kitchings and Mary Getzen K; m. to Rear Adm. John Carraway Bull, wid; c. John C, Jr. M.D. Educ: Winthrop Col; Univ. Wash; George Wash. Univ. Polit. & Govt. Pos: Admin. asst, U.S. Rep. Mendel L. Rivers, S.C, 57- Rel: Episcopal. Legal Res: Beaufort, S.C. 29902. Mailing Add: 2205 Rayburn House Office Bldg, Washington, D.C. 20515.

BULLARD, JAMES MARVIN D
Dep. Ins. Cmnr, Okla.
b. Elmore City, Indian Territory, Okla, 4/13/01; s. Sidney A. Bullard and Minnie E. Burns B; m. 3/3/38 to Edith Marion Furst; c. Marion Sue (Mrs. Eddie Lockhart). Polit. & Govt. Pos: Dep. treas, Stephen Co, Okla, 24-26, treas, 34-38; Okla. State Rep, 39-40 & 42-62, speaker of the house, Okla. State House of Rep, 51, chmn, Legis. Coun, 52, majority floor leader, 55 & 57; Okla. Secy. of State, 62-67; former asst. dir, Motor Carrier Div, Okla. Corp. Cmn; dep. ins. cmnr, Okla, 67- Bus. & Prof. Pos: Oil producer, 24-27; owner-operator of ranch, 30-62. Mem: Nat. Secys. of State; Reclamation Asn.(dir); Okla. Med. Research Found; Mason; Elks; Kiwanis; YMCA; pres, Beaver Cow Creek Watershed Develop. Asn. Rel: Baptist. Mailing Add: 8514 Waverly, Oklahoma City, Okla. 73120.

BULLIS, HAROLD OWEN R
b. Robinson, N.Dak, 10/2/23; s. Harold Edward Bullis and Clara Hedahl B; m. 9/7/52 to Dolores Jean Fuhrman; c. Rebecca Ann, John David, James Robert and Mark Edward. Educ: N.Dak. State Sch. Sci, 41-42; Mo. Sch. of Mines, 43-44; Jamestown Col, A.B, 48; Univ. N.Dak, J.D, 54; Order of the Coif; Phi Delta Phi. Polit. & Govt. Pos: Law clerk, Judge Charles J. Vogel, Eighth Circuit Court of Appeals, Fargo, N.Dak, 54-55; exec. secy, U.S. Sen. Milton R. Young, Wash, D.C, 55-59; states attorney, Richland Co, N.Dak, 63-67; N.Dak. State Rep, 25th Legis. Dist, 67-69; U.S. Attorney, Fargo, N.Dak, 69- Bus. & Prof. Pos: Prin. and coach, Litchville High Sch, N.Dak, 48-50; ed-in-chief, N.Dak. Law Rev, 53-54; law practice, Lewis and Bullis, Wahpeton, 59-68. Mil. Serv: Entered as Pvt, Army, 43, released as Pfc, 45, after serv. in Inf. 44 Div, ETO, 44-45; Purple Heart, one Oak Leaf Cluster. Publ: 'North Dakota Dead Man's Statute,' N.Dak. Law Rev, 4/54. Mem: Am. Legion; VFW; Kiwanis (pres, 67); Mason (Worshipful Master); AF&AM; Elks; Eagles. Rel: Methodist. Legal Res: 1331 N. Seventh St, Wahpeton, N.Dak. 58075. Mailing Add: Box 728, Wahpeton, N.Dak. 58075.

BULLOCK, BOB R. D
b. Evanston, Wyo, 7/4/30; s. Leland M. Bullock and Juanita Hagerman B; m. 5/20/61 to Mary Lou Goin; c. Elizabeth Anne and Robert Charles. Educ: Univ. Utah, B.S, 54; Univ. Wyo, LL.B, 59; Am. Law Student Asn, 10th Circuit; Sigma Alpha Epsilon. Polit. & Govt. Pos: Ward leader and precinct committeeman, Natrona Co. Dem. Cent. Cmt, Wyo, 60-64; committeeman, Wyo. State Dem. Cent. Cmt, 64-66; Wyo. State Rep, 65-68. Bus. & Prof. Pos: Private practice of law, Winter, Burgess, Forrister & Bullock, Casper, Wyo, 61- Mil. Serv: Entered as Pvt, Army, 54, released as Pfc, 56, after serv. in Ninth Inf. Div, ETO, 54-56; Army Occupation Medal; Good Conduct Medal; Army Res, 56-62. Publ: 'Law Notes,' Wyo. Law J, 58 & 59. Mem: Am, Wyo. and Natrona Co. Bar Asns; Masons, AF&AM; Elks; Lions Int. Rel: Presbyterian. Legal Res: 2207 Crescent Ave, Casper, Wyo. 82601. Mailing Add: 407 Con Roy Building, Casper, Wyo. 82601. (1967)

BULLOCK, CHARLES LOUIE D
Miss. State Rep.
b. Newhebron, Miss, 6/17/15; married. Polit. & Govt. Pos: Miss. State Rep, 40-44 & currently. Bus. & Prof. Pos: Ins. and investments. Mem: Mason; Civitan; YMCA Bd. of Dirs. Rel: Baptist. Mailing Add: 203 42nd St, Gulfport, Miss. 39501.

BULLOCK, ELMER DAVID R
b. Georgia, Vt, 7/10/08; m. to Charlotte M. Hurlbut; c. Two sons and one daughter. Educ: Vt. State Agr. Sch. Polit. & Govt. Pos: Sch. dir, 6 years; clerk of sch. bd, 3 years; town lister, 7 years; town grand juror, 6 years; fence viewer, 16 years; justice of the peace, 48-; chmn, Rep. Town Cmt, 66-68; Vt. State Rep, 63-68, mem, Health Cmt, Vt. House Rep, 63-64, Gen. and Mil. Affairs Cmt, 65-68 and ranking mem, Gen. Cmt, 66-68. Bus. & Prof. Pos: Dairy farm owner. Mem: Banner Grange 356 (past master); Farm Bur; 1st Franklin D.H.I.(past secy. and treas); Milton Coop. Creamery Asn; Milton Boro Cemetery Asn.(past chmn. and treas). Mailing Add: R.D. 3, Milton, Vt. 05468.

BULLOCK, J. ROBERT R
Mem, Utah State Rep. Cent. Cmt.
b. Provo, Utah, 12/16/16; s. James A. Bullock and Norma Poulton B; m. 8/29/49 to Ethel M. Hogge; c. James R, Jr, Charles Scott, David A. and Steven H. Educ: Utah State Univ, B.S, 38; George Wash. Univ, J.D, 42; Sigma Nu; hon. Order of the Coif, Univ. Utah, 69. Polit. & Govt. Pos: Attorney, Vet. Admin, 46-50; voting dist. chmn, Rep. Party, 50-54; co-chmn, Rep. Party, 61-62; Utah State Rep, 63-66; mem, Utah State Rep. Cent. Cmt, 65-; mem, Utah Legis. Coun; state del, numerous times. Prof. Pos: Partner, Aldrich, Bullock & Nelson, Law Firm, Utah, 50- Mil. Serv: Entered as Ens, Navy, 41, released as Lt. Comdr, 46, after serv. in Am. and Pac. Theaters and ETO, 41-45; Bronze Star; Army Commendation Medal; Philippine Liberation Medal; ETO Ribbon; Pac. and Am. Campaign Ribbons; Victory Medal; Comdr, Naval Res, 46- Publ: 'Judicial Review of Selective Service Board Classification by Habeas Corpus,' George Wash. Law Rev. Mem: Rotary; C. of C. Rel: Latter-day Saint. Legal Res: 1584 Willow, Provo, Utah 84601. Mailing Add: P.O. Box L, Provo, Utah 84601.

BULLOCK, JOSEPH E. D
Md. State Del.
b. Baltimore, Md, 11/21/23; married. Educ: Baltimore parochial, pub. schs. Polit. & Govt. Pos: Mem, Cornwall Dem. Club and United Dem. Club, Ward 26; Md. State Del, 59- Bus. & Prof. Pos: Foreman, street repairs. Mil. Serv: Navy, 43-46. Mem: Our Lady of Pompei Holy Name Soc; K. of C. Mailing Add: 104 N. Highland Ave, Baltimore, Md. 21224. (1967)

BUMGARDNER, DAVID WEBSTER, JR. D
N.C. State Rep.
b. Belmont, N.C, 11/2/21; s. David Webster Bumgardner and Winnifred Ballard B; m. 8/14/48 to Sara Margaret Jones; c. Sharon Inez and Sandra Jo. Educ: Belmont Abbey Col, 38-40; Gupton-Jones Col. of Mortuary Sci, 41-42. Polit. & Govt. Pos: N.C. State Rep, 67- Mem: N.C. and Nat. Funeral Dirs. Asns; Conf. Funeral Serv. Examining Bds. U.S; Am. Legion; VFW; Belmont Masonic Lodge; Gastonia York Rite Masonic Orders; Oasis Temple of Shrine; Elks; Kiwanis; Aircraft Owners & Pilots Asn. Pvt. Pilot. Rel: Baptist. Legal Res: 209 Peachtree St, Belmont, N.C. 28012. Mailing Add: P.O. Box 409, Belmont, N.C. 28012.

BUNCHE, RALPH JOHNSON D
Under-Secy. Gen. for Spec. Polit. Affairs UN
b. Detroit, Mich, 8/7/04; s. Fred Bunch and Olive Agnes Johnson B; m. 6/23/30 to Ruth Ethel Harris; c. Joan Harris, Jane Johnson (deceased) and Ralph Johnson. Educ: Univ. Calif, Los Angeles, A.B, 27; Harvard, A.M, 28, Ph.D, 34; post-doctoral work in anthrop. and colonial policy, Northwest. Univ, London Sch. of Econ. and Univ. Capetown, S.Africa, 36-37; Boston Univ, LL.D; Ozias Goodwin fellow, Harvard, 29; Rosenwald fel, Europe, Eng, N. and W. Africa, 31-32; Soc. Sci. Research Coun. post-doctoral fel. in Europe, S. and E. Africa, Malaya and Netherland Indies, 36-38. Polit. & Govt. Pos: Asst. Secy, U.S. Del, Dumbarton Oaks, 44; with Dept. of State, 44-47; adv, U.S. Del, 27th Session, Int. Labour Conf, Phila. and 28th Session, Paris, 45; and UNCIO, San Francisco, 45; U.S. Del. Exec. Cmt, UN, London, 45; U.S. Del. Gen. Assembly, UN, London, 46; U.S. Cmnr, Caribbean Cmn, 45-47, and W. Indian Conf, Second Session, St. Thomas Virgin Islands, 46; dir, Div. Trusteeship, UN, 46-48; prin. secy, UN Palestine Cmn, 48; acting UN Mediator on Palestine, 48-49; prin. dir, Dept. Trusteeship, 48-54, undersecy, Trusteeship Div, UN, 55; undersecy. for Spec. Polit. Affairs, UN, 54-67, Under-Secy-Gen, 67-; mem. bd. higher educ, N.Y.C, 58-64; UN Spec. Rep. in Congo, 60; UN Mission to Yemen, 63. Bus. & Prof. Pos: Asst. in polit. sci, Univ. Calif, Los Angeles, 25-27; instr, Howard Univ, 28-29, asst. prof, 29-33, assoc. prof, 33-38, prof, 38-, head polit. sci. dept, 29-50, asst. to pres, 30-31; staff mem, Carnegie Corp. Surv. of Negro in Am, 39; sr. soc. sci. analyst in charge of research on Africa and other colonial areas, Brit. Empire Sect, Office of Strategic Servs, 41-44; dep. chief, Near East-Africa Sect, 43; chief, Africa Sect, Off. of Strategic Servs, 43-44; prof. govt, Harvard, 50-52, mem. bd. overseers, 60-65; trustee, Oberlin Col. Mem: Past pres, Polit. Sci. Asn; Am. Philos. Soc; trustee, Rockefeller Found, 55-68. Spingarn Medal, NAACP, 49; Nobel Peace Prize, 50; Theodore Roosevelt Asn. Medal of Honor, 54; Third Order of St. Frances Peace Award, 54; Presidential Medal of Freedom, 60 & 63. Legal Res: 115-24 Grosvenor Rd, Kew Gardens, N.Y. 11415. Mailing Add: United Nations, New York Station, New York, N.Y. 10017.

BUNDLIE, ORDNER T. (JR) DFL
b. Duluth, Minn, 10/24/19; s. Ordner T. Bundlie, Sr. and Olive Egeland B; m. 11/30/46 to Shirley Ann Heikkinen; c. Scott, Barbara, Andrew and Nancy. Educ: Univ. Minn, B.S. in law; Univ. Minn. Law Sch, LL.B; Delta Theta Phi. Polit. & Govt. Pos: Asst. attorney gen, Minn, 56-60; chmn, Pipestone Co. Dem-Farmer-Labor Cmt, 60-66; del, Dem-Farmer-Labor State Conv, 62, 64 & 66, mem, State Constitution Cmt, 64 and State Rules Cmt, 66. Bus. & Prof. Pos: Attorney-at-law, 48-56 & 60- Mil. Serv: Entered as Pvt, Army, 43, released as T-4, 7th Conv. Hosp, ETO, 46; Good Conduct Medal and ETO Ribbons. Mem: Ed, Pipestone Kiwanis Club; United Fund; secy-treas, YMCA; pres, Band Parents; Am. Legion; Dist. and State Bar Asns; Red Cross (co. chmn); 13th Judicial Dist. Bar Asn.(past pres). Rel: Lutheran; mem, secy. and past pres, bd. trustees, First Lutheran Church. Mailing Add: 828 Fourth Ave. S.W, Pipestone, Minn. 56164.

BUNDY, McGEORGE
b. Boston, Mass, 3/30/19; s. Harvey Hollister Bundy and Katharine Lawrence Putnam B; m. 6/10/50 to Mary Buckminster Lothrop; c. Stephen, Andrew, William and James. Educ: Yale, B.A, 40; Phi Beta Kappa. Polit. & Govt. Pos: Spec. asst. to the President for Nat. Security, 61-66. Bus. & Prof. Pos: Polit. analyst, Coun. For. Rels, 48-49; vis. lectr, Harvard, 49-51, assoc. prof. govt, 51-54, dean faculty arts & sci, 53-61, prof, 54-61; pres, Ford Found, 66- Publ: Co-auth, On Active Serv; ed, Pattern of Responsibility; auth, The Strength of Government, 68. Mem: Am. Polit. Sci. Asn. Mailing Add: 320 E. 43rd St, New York, N.Y. 10017.

BUNDY, WILLIAM P. D
Asst. Secy. of State for E. Asian and Pac. Affairs
b. Washington, D.C, 9/24/17; m. to Mary Acheson; c. Michael, Caroline and Christopher. Educ: Yale Col, B.A, 39; Harvard Univ, M.A, 40, LL.B, 47. Polit. & Govt. Pos: Mem. Bd. Nat. Estimates, Cent. Intel. Agency, 51-61; staff dir, Pres. Cmn. on Nat. Goals, 60-61; Dep. Asst. Secy. of Defense for Int. Security Affairs, 61-63, Asst. Secy. of Defense for Int. Security Affairs, 63-64; Asst. Secy. of State for E.Asian and Pac. Affairs, 64- Bus. & Prof. Pos: Attorney-at-law, 47-51. Mil. Serv: Army, 41-46, Maj. Mailing Add: 3500 Lowell St. N.W, Washington, D.C. 20016.

BUNKER, A. G. R
N.Dak. State Rep.
b. Equality, Ill, 4/16/27; s. Warren Sam Bunker and Helen Duty B; m. 6/24/61 to Norene Leverson. Educ: Univ. Wyo, 47-49; N.Dak. State Univ, B.S, 52; Blue Key; Scabbard & Blade; Alpha Tau Omega. Polit. & Govt. Pos: N.Dak. State Rep, 67- Bus. & Prof. Pos: V.pres, Security Int. Ins. Co, 62- Mil. Serv: Entered as Pvt, Army, 45, released as Sgt, 47, after serv. in Sixth Armored Div, recalled 52 as 1st Lt. Mem: Nat. Asn. Life Underwriters; Elks; Am. Legion; N.Dak. State Univ. Alumni Bd. Outstanding Alumni Award, N.Dak. State Univ. Bus. Econ. Club. Rel: Lutheran. Mailing Add: 721 Southwood Dr, Fargo, N.Dak. 58102.

BUNKER, ELLSWORTH
U.S. Ambassador to Vietnam
b. Yonkers, N.Y, 5/11/94; s. George R. Bunker and Jean Polhemus Cobb B; m. to Harriet Butler (deceased); m. 1/3/67 to Carol Laise; c. Ellen B. (Mrs. Fernando Gentil), John Birkbeck and Samuel Emmet; twelve grandchildren. Educ: Yale Univ, B.A, 16. Hon. LL.D, Yale, 59, Mt. Holyoke, 62 and Windham Col, 63. Polit. & Govt. Pos: Ambassador to Argentina, 51, Italy, 52-53, India, 56-61 and Nepal, 56-59; pres, Am. Red Cross, 53-56; del, UN Gen. Assembly, 56; mediator, UN, Indonesian-Netherlands dispute, 62 and Saudi Arabia-Egypt dispute, 63; consult. to Secy. of State, 63; Ambassador, Orgn. Am. States, 64-66; Ambassador-at-lg, Dept. of State, 66; Ambassador to Viet Nam, 67- Bus. & Prof. Pos: Dir, Nat. Sugar Refining Co, 27-40, pres, 40-49, chmn. of the bd, 49- Mem: Trustee, Asia Found; past dir. and trustee, Asia Soc. and Exp. in Int. Living; Bur. Soc. Sci. Research; Educ. and World Affairs; For. Policy Asn; Friends of India Cmt; Hampton Inst; Inst. Int. Soc. Research; New Sch. for Soc. Research; Vt. Coun. on World Affairs; Coun. For. Rels; Am. Acad. Arts and Sci; Acad. Polit. Sci. Grand Cross Knight of the Repub. of Italy, 54; Presidential Medal of Freedom with Spec. Distinction, 63 & 68. Rel: Episcopal. Legal Res: R.F.D. 2, Putney, Vt. 05346. Mailing Add: American Embassy, APO San Francisco 96243.

BUNKER, VERNON E. D
Nev. State Sen.
b. St. Thomas, Nev, 4/23/04; s. Martin A. Bunker and Helen McNeil B; m. to Rose Stewart; c. Patricia Sperry, Bill, Jolene (Mrs. Nance) and Barry Wendell. Educ: Moapa Valley Schs, Nev. Polit. & Govt. Pos: Nev. State Assemblyman, 59-67; Nev. State Sen, 67- Bus. & Prof. Pos: Ins. agent. Mem: C. of C; South. Nev. Ins. Agents Asn. Mailing Add: 511 E. Sahara, C203, Las Vegas, Nev. 89105.

BUNN, GEORGE D
b. St. Paul, Minn, 5/26/25; s. Charles Bunn and Harriet Foster B; m. 7/19/49 to Fralia Suter Hancock; c. Peggy Joan, Peter Wilson and Matthew George. Educ: Univ. Wis, B.S. in Elec. Eng, 46; Columbia Univ, LL.B, 50; Tau Beta Pi; Eta Kappa Nu; Phi Eta Sigma; Order of the Coif. Polit. & Govt. Pos: Attorney, Gen. Counsel's Off, Atomic Energy Cmn, 50-51; mem. staff preparedness subcmt, U.S. Senate, 57; del, Dem. Nat. Conv, 60; counsel to President's Adv. on Disarmament, 61-62; gen. counsel, U.S. Arms Control and Disarmament Agency, 61-69; U.S. del, 18 Nation Disarmament Conf, 62-68; UN Disarmament Cmn, 65; alternate U.S. Rep, Geneva Disarmament Conf, 68; Bus. & Prof. Pos: From assoc. to partner, Arnold, Fortas & Porter, 51-61; vis. prof, Univ. Wis. Law Sch, currently. Mil. Serv: Entered as A/S, Naval Res, 43, released as Ens, 46, after serv. in U.S.S. Logan, Pac, 45-46. Publ: 'Nuclear Nonproliferation Treaty,' 68 and 'Banning Gas and Germ Warfare,' 69, Wis. Law Rev. Mem: Fed. and D.C. Bar Asns; Am. Soc. Int. Law; Nat. Capitol Dem. Club. Legal Res: 5600 Lake Mendota Dr, Madison, Wis. 53705. Mailing Add: Law School, University of Wisconsin, Madison, Wis. 53706.

BUNN, THOMAS DAVIS D
b. Raleigh, N.C, 1/17/25; s. Julian Wilbur Bunn and Maude Davis B; m. 8/10/50 to Rebecca Smith; c. T. Davis, Jr, Rebecca M, W. LeRoy and Nancy E. Educ: N.C. State Col, 43-44; Wake Forest Col, LL.B, 50; Phi Alpha Delta; Pi Kappa Alpha. Polit. & Govt. Pos: Dir, Wake Co. Bar Asn, N.C, 55; pres, Orgn. of Young Dem. Clubs, 59; chmn, Wake Co. Dem. Rally, 64; N.C. State Rep, Wake Co, 63-68. Mil. Serv: Entered as Pvt, Air Force, 41, released as Capt, 46, after serv. in 484th Bombardment Squadron and 505th Bombardment Group, 20th Air Force, Marianas Islands, Asian Theater; Victory, Am. Campaign, Occupancy of Japan and Asian-Pac. Serv. Medals; Air Medal with 103 Oak Leaf Clusters; Distinguished Unit Badge; Capt, Air Force Res, until 52. Mem: Kiwanis; Exec. Club; Toastmasters Club. Rel: Baptist. Mailing Add: 2507 Wake Dr, Raleigh, N.C. 27608. (1967)

BUNNELL, ORVAL E. R
b. Lawrence, Nebr, 7/24/14; m. to Mildred; c. four. Educ: Colo. State Univ, D.V.M. Polit. & Govt. Pos: Wyo State Rep, -67; Chmn, Washakie Co. Hosp. Bd. Bus. & Prof. Pos: Vet. Mem: Chmn, Nat. Found; C. of C; Kiwanis; Farm Bur; Int. Christian Leadership; Wyo. Vet. Med. Asn. (Pres.); Past Pres, Wyo. Jr. C. of C. Rel: Methodist. Mailing Add: 817 Russell, Worland, Wyo. 82401. (1967)

BUNSTINE, EDWARD ROYAL D
Chmn, Ross Co. Dem. Exec. Cmt, Ohio
b. Columbus, Ohio, 11/14/31; s. Royal Buckman Bunstine and Stella Coyne B; m. 9/13/52 to Marjorie Joan Drury; c. Nicholas, Edward, Catherine and David. Educ: Ohio State Univ, B.S, 54, J.D, 59; Acct. Hon. Soc; Phi Beta Phi. Polit. & Govt. Pos: Asst. prosecuting attorney, Ross Co, Ohio, 60-68; chmn, Ross Co. Dem. Exec. Cmt, 68- Bus. & Prof. Pos: Attorney-at-law, 60- Mil. Serv: Entered as 2nd Lt, Army, 55, released as 1st Lt, 57, after serv. in Hq, Armor Center. Mem: Ross Co, Ohio State and Am. Bar Asns; Am. and Ohio Acad. Trial Attorneys; K. of C; Elks; Chillicothe Country Club; YMCA. Rel: Catholic. Mailing Add: 90 Applewood Dr, Chillicothe, Ohio 45601.

BUNTEN, WILLIAM WALLACE R
Kans. State Rep.
b. Topeka, Kans, 4/5/30; s. Robert Muir Bunten and Mary Rock B; m. 1/27/61 to JoAnn Francis Heyka; c. William W, Jr, Sandra and Ann. Educ: Univ. Kans. Polit. & Govt. Pos: Kans. State Rep, 32nd Dist, 62-64, 34th Dist, 64-66 and 47th Dist, 66- Mil. Serv: Entered as Pvt, Marines, 52, released as Capt. 54, after serv. in 1st Marine Div, Far East Theater; Far Eastern Theater, Korean Theater and UN Serv. Ribbons. Mem: C. of C; 20-30 Int; Elks; Farm Bur. Rel: Methodist. Legal Res: 1701 W. 30th St, Topeka, Kans. 66611. Mailing Add: P.O. Box 1098, Topeka, Kans. 66601. (1967)

BUNTING, EUGENE D. R
Secy. of State, Del.
Mailing Add: Legislative Hall, Dover, Del. 19901.

BUNYAN, WILLIAM PRICE, III R
Chmn, Meade Co. Rep. Cent. Cmt, Kans.
b. Los Angeles, Calif, 8/21/38; s. William Price Bunyan, II and Loraine Gregory B; m. 4/18/69 to Susan Fisher. Educ: Col. Emporia, 57-59; Kans. Univ, B.A, 61, post grad. study, 61-62; Pi Sigma Alpha; Delta Chi. Polit. & Govt. Pos: Chmn, Meade Co. Young Rep, Kans, 62-67; precinct committeeman, Fowler Twp, 62-69; committeeman, 36th Sen. Dist. Young Rep, 63-65; chmn, Citizens for Goldwater, 64; treas, Meade Co. Rep. Cent. Cmt, 64-68, v.chmn, 68, chmn, 68-; v.chmn, Kans. Young Rep, 65-67; chmn, First Cong. Dist. Young Rep, 67-69; dir, Region Seven Young Rep, Kans, Nebr, Mo, Iowa and Okla, 69- Bus. & Prof. Pos: Farmer rancher, Bill and Greg Bunyan's Lazy W Bar Ranch, Fowler, 62- Mil. Serv: Entered as Pvt, Army Res, 56, released as SP-4, 64, after serv. in 489th AAA Bn. Mem, Jaycees; Farm Bur; Am. Conservative Union. Key Man Award, Fowler Jaycees, 67. Mailing Add: Fowler, Kans. 67844.

BUNZEL, JOHN HARVEY D
b. New York, N.Y, 4/15/24; s. Ernest Everett Bunzel and Harriet Harvey B; m. 5/11/63 to Barbara Bouvyer; c. Cameron and Reed. Educ: Princeton, A.B, 48; Columbia Univ, M.A. in Sociol, 49; Univ. Calif, Berkeley, Ph.D. in Polit. Sci, 54. Polit. & Govt. Pos: Mem, Calif. Kennedy Del, 68; del, Dem. Nat. Conv, 68. Mil. Serv: Entered as Pvt, Army, 43, released as M/Sgt, 46, after serving in Alaskan Command. Publ: The American Small Businessman, 62 and Anti-Politics in America, 67, Knopf; Issues of American Public Policy, Prentice-Hall, 2nd ed, 68. Mem: Am. Polit. Sci. Asn; West. Polit. Sci. Asn; North. Calif. Polit. Sci. Asn. Presidential award for outstanding serv. in field of polit. sci, North. Calif. Polit. Sci. Asn, 69. Rel: None. Mailing Add: 1519 Escondido Way, Belmont, Calif. 94002.

BURACZYNSKI, ANTHONY C. D
Vt. State Rep.
b. N. Walpole, N.H, 9/23/08; married; c. One daughter. Educ: Hinsdale, N.H. High Sch. Polit. & Govt. Pos: City councilman, Torrington, Conn, 42-50; mem, Motor Vehicle Racing Cmn, 63-64; mem, Vt. Civil Authorities, 63-64; Vt. State Rep, 63- Bus. & Prof. Pos: Proprietor of cabins. Mem: K. of C; Elks; Eagles; Rotary; Polish Nat. Alliance. Rel: Catholic. Mailing Add: RFD 1, 152 Putney Rd, Brattleboro, Vt. 05301. (1967)

BURBACH, JULIUS W.
Nebr. State Sen.
b. Hartington, Nebr, 4/5/12; m. 4/5/37 to Bernice Jensen. Educ: Holy Trinity High Sch. Polit. & Govt. Pos: Mem, Sch. Bd, Nebr; Nebr. State Sen, 57- Bus. & Prof. Pos: Grain and feed dealer, livestock feeder. Mem: Past pres, Crofton C. of C; former dir, Gavins Point Develop. Asn; dir, Knox Co. Agr. Asn; dir, Livestock Feeders Asn; K. of C; Elks; Moose. Rel: Catholic. Mailing Add: Crofton, Nebr. 68730. (1967)

BURBANK, HELEN ELIZABETH R
b. Otego, N.Y, 7/27/98; s. Horace J. Burbank and Edith L. Wicks B; single. Educ: St. Johnsbury Acad. and Bus. Col. Polit. & Govt. Pos: Secy. to Dep. Secy. State, Vt, 24-47, secy. of state, 47-49, Dept. secy. state, 49-65; del, Rep. Nat. Conv, 64; alternate del, Rep. State Conv, 64; mem, Montpelier City and Wash. Co. Rep. Cmts; asst, Legis. Coun, 67-69; Justice of the Peace, 68- Bus. & Prof. Pos: Secy, Vt. Cmnr. Industs, 17-18; secy, Vt. Div. U.S. Employ. Serv, 18-19; cashier and secy. home off, Nat. Life Ins. Co, 19-20. Mem: Rep. State and Nat. Women's Clubs; hon. mem. state and nat. Order Women Legis; charter mem. Women's Soc. Christian Serv. St. Johnsbury-in-Life Award, St. Johnsbury Acad, 60; Career Woman of Year, Vt. Bus. & Prfnl. Women's Club, 61. Rel: Methodist. Mailing Add: 145 Main St, Montpelier, Vt. 05602.

BURCH, CHARLES COWDEN D
Tenn. State Rep.
b. Evanston, Ill, 5/3/28; s. Robert Lee Burch, Jr. and Ruth Cowden B; m. to Wanda Campe; c. Charles C, II. Educ: Univ. Wis, B.S, 51, LL.B, 53; N.Y. Univ, grad. work; Phi Delta Theta. Polit. & Govt. Pos: Tenn. State Rep, 65-; asst. pub. defender. Rel: Episcopal. Legal Res: 100 N. Main Bldg, Memphis, Tenn. 38112. Mailing Add: 751 Hein Park Center Dr, Memphis, Tenn. 38112.

BURCH, CLYDE MONROE D
b. Callao, Mo, 7/4/26; s. Durwood Burch and Isabel Dunseith B; m. 12/24/53 to Marilyn Leathers; c. Mona, Karen, John, James and Rebecca. Educ: Northeast Mo. State Col, B.S.E, 50; Univ. Minn, 51; Univ. Mo, Kansas City, J.D, 54; Am. Polit. Sci. Asn; Mo. Hist. Soc. Polit. & Govt. Pos: City attorney, Fulton, Mo, 55-59; asst. attorney gen, Jefferson City, 61-64; mem, Mo. Gov. Cmn. Local Govt, 67-; del, Dem. Nat. Conv, 68. Bus. & Prof. Pos: Instr, Westminster Col, 59-60; prof. govt, Northeast Mo. State Col, 64- Mil. Serv: Entered as A/S, Naval Res, 45, released as PO, 46. Publ: Missouri Presidential Elections, 1900-1968, Miss. State Teachers Asn, 68. Mem: Mo. Bar Asn; Mo. Hist. Soc; Mo. State Teachers Asn; Mason; Mo. Farmers Asn. Rel: Baptist. Mailing Add: R.R, Bethel, Mo. 63434.

BURCH, DEAN R
b. Enid, Okla, 12/20/27; s. Bert Alexander Burch and Leola Atkisson B; m. 7/7/61 to Patricia Meeks; c. Shelly, Dean and Dianne. Educ: Univ. of Ariz, LL.B, 53; Phi Delta Theta, Blue Key. Polit. & Govt. Pos: Asst. Attorney Gen, Ariz, 53-54; admin. asst. to Sen. Barry Goldwater, 55-59; dep. dir, Goldwater for President Cmt, 63-64; chmn, Rep. Nat. Cmt, 64-65; chmn, Goldwater for Senate Cmt, 68; mem, Bd. Regents, Ariz, 69- Bus. & Prof. Pos: Attorney, Dunseath, Stubbs & Burch, Tucson, 59- Mil. Serv: Lt. Col, Army Res. Mailing Add: 5610 E. Eighth St, Tucson, Ariz. 85711.

BURCH, FRANCIS B(OUCHER) D
Attorney General, Md.
b. Baltimore, Md, 11/26/18; s. Louis Claude Burch and Constance M. B; m.

4/12/47 to Mary Patricia Howe; c. Francis B, Jr, Catherine H, Richard C, Constance B, Edwin H, Robert S. and Mary Patricia. Educ: Loyola Col, Baltimore, Ph.B, summa cum laude, 41; Yale Law Sch, LL.B, 43; Phi Delta Phi; Corbey Court Club. Polit. & Govt. Pos: Mem, Mayor's Cmt. Conflict of Interest, Baltimore, Md, 60, pres, Civil Serv. Cmn, 60-61, chmn, Mayor's Cmt. Mass Transit, 61, chmn, Mayor's Cmt. Scholarship Prog, 61, city solicitor, 61-63, mem, Bd. Estimates, 61-63, mem, Pension Study Cmt, 62; mem, Standard Policy Bd, State of Md, 60-61, ins. cmnr, 65-66, Attorney General, 66-; del, Dem. Nat. Conv, 68. Bus. & Prof. Pos: Dir. various corp; counsel, v.pres. and chmn. exec. cmt, Baltimore Jr. Asn. Commerce, 50-54; secy, v.pres. and pres, Jr. Bar Asn. Baltimore City, 52-54; dir. Legal Aid Bur, 54. Mil. Serv: Entered as Seaman 1/C, Coast Guard, 44, released, 45, after serv. in Vol. Port Security Force, Baltimore. Publ: 'On Calling a Constitutional Convention,' Daily Record, Baltimore, 50. Mem: V.chmn, South. Conf. Attorneys General, 67-; mem. exec. cmt, v.chmn. cmt. transportation and chmn. ins. laws cmt, Nat. Asn. Attorneys General, 67; chmn. legis. cmt, East. Seaboard Conf. Attorneys General, 69; Baltimore, Md. State and Am. Bar Asns; panel mem, Am. Arbit. Asn; dir, Goodwill Indust; first v.pres, Bd. Gov. Paint & Powder Clubs; v.chmn, Alumni Div. Loyola Col. Develop. Prog; pres, Reciprocity Club; pres, Baltimore Safety Coun; Center Club; Tri-State Angler's Asn; Marlin Club; South. Md. Soc; Friendly Sons St. Patrick; chmn, Cancer Crusade Md; trustee, Camp Fire Girls. Spiritum Award, Cardinal Gibbons High Sch, 66; Man of the Year Award, Hibernian Soc. Md, 67; Pub. Servant Award, Dept. Md, CWV, 67; Humanitarian Award, Nu Beta Epsilon Nat. Law Fraternity, 68; Man of the Year Award, Nat. Jewish Hosp, Denver, 69; St. Thomas More Soc. Man of all Seasons Award, 69. Rel: Catholic. Legal Res: 207 Chancery Rd, Baltimore, Md. 21218. Mailing Add: One Charles Center, Room 1200, Baltimore, Md. 21201.

BURCH, KATHERYNE PEREGOY D
Mem, Henrico Co. Dem. Cmt, Va.
b. Baltimore, Md, 11/28/31; d. William Henry Thorn Peregoy and Mary Marguerite Ziegenhein P; m. 10/10/40 to John Thomas Burch; c. John Thomas Jr. and William Henry. Educ: St. Paul's Episcopal Sch, and West. High Sch, Baltimore, Md. Polit. & Govt. Pos: Mem. bd, Dem. Woman's Club, Richmond, Va, 60-65; del, Dem. Nat. Conv, 64; del, Dem. State Conv, 64 & 68; mem, Henrico Co. Dem. Cmt, 66-; pres, Richmond Area Dem. Woman's Club, 69- Mem: Life mem, Va. Fedn. Garden Clubs. Rel: Episcopal. Mailing Add: 8005 Yolanda Rd, Richmond, Va. 23229.

BURCH, PALMER LYLE R
Colo. State Rep.
b. Ordway, Colo, 3/27/07; s. Robert H. Burch and Nancy Robinette B; m. 3/16/46 to Elvera M. Hultquist; c. Susan. Educ: Cent. Bus. Col, Denver, Colo. Polit. & Govt. Pos: Colo. State Rep, 47-48, 51-58 & 61- and majority leader, Colo. House Rep, 69-; mem, Denver Bd. Educ, 59-67 and pres, 63-67. Mem: Denver Asn. Bldg. Owners & Mgrs. Rel: Lutheran. Legal Res: 395 Fairfax St, Denver, Colo. 80220. Mailing Add: 901 Majestic Bldg, Denver, Colo. 80202.

BURCH, WILLIAM ALVA R
Chmn, Bates Co. Rep. Party, Mo.
b. Butler, Mo, 10/19/25; s. Jerry Burch and Mary Edith Searfus B; m. 9/30/50 to Barbara Joan Ehart; c. William Douglas, Larry Dean and Brett Duane. Educ: Butler High Sch, dipl, 43. Polit. & Govt. Pos: Mem, Twp. Bd, Mt. Pleasant, Mo, 54; co. treas-collector, Bates Co, 56-64; Mt. Pleasant Twp. committeeman, 64-; chmn, Bates Co. Rep. Party and Rep. Cent. Cmt, 66- Mil. Serv: Entered as Seaman 2/C, Navy, 45, released as Seaman 1/C, 46, after serving in Navy Air Corps; Naval Res, 46-51. Mem: Odd Fellows; Lions; Am. Legion; IBT; PTA; Am. Field Serv. Rel: Reorganized Latter-day Saint. Mailing Add: Route 4, P.O. Box 11, Butler, Mo. 64730.

BURDEN, EMMETT WYNN D
b. Aulander, N.C, 7/26/23; s. Marion Clyde Burden and Belle Mitchell B; m. to Lila Rook Sumrell; c. Anthony Clyde, Kaye Wynn. Educ: Univ. of N.C, 40-43; Navy V-12 course, Columbia Univ, 43-44. Polit. & Govt. Pos: Bldg. inspector, Aulander, N.C, 50-62; mem, State Adv. Cmt. on Firemanship Training; fire chief, Aulander, 50-62; dir, Civil Defense, 52-62; secy-treas, Bertie Co. Fire Protective Cmt, 59-62; mem, Bd. Cmnrs, Aulander, 61-63; N.C. State Rep, 63-68. Bus. & Prof. Pos: Gen. Ins. Agency, real estate, farming. Mil. Serv: Naval Res, 43-45, released as Lt. Comm. Off. U.S.S. LCI (G) 473, 45. Mem: N.C. Asn. of Ins. Agents Inc; Aulander Ruritan Club (pres, vice-pres, sec,); N.C. Asn. of Rescue Squads (state dir, Area 1, 61-62); Lt. Gov, Roanoke Dist, Ruritan Nat, 59. Rel: Baptist; Finance Comm, Super. Adult Sunday Sch; pres, Young Men's Bible Class. Mailing Add: E. Main St, Aulander, N.C. 27805. (1967)

BURDETTE, LLOYD VERNON D
Chmn, Hill Co. Dem. Party, Tex.
b. Alvarado, Tex, 4/23/87; s. Abner Green Burdette and Isabella Francis Kelley B; m. 9/20/19 to Ethel Ray Smith; c. Frances Laverne (Mrs. Garner) and Dalma (Mrs. Garner). Educ: Hillsboro High Sch, 9 years. Polit. & Govt. Pos: Chmn, Hill Co. Dem. Party, Tex, 60- Bus. & Prof. Pos: Car salesman, Cent. Motor Co, Waco, Tex, 19-28; sales mgr, Beard Motor Co, Hillsboro, 28-69. Mil. Serv: Entered as Pvt, Nat. Guard, released as 1st Lt, 31, after serv. in Sixth Cavalry. Rel: Methodist; Mem. Bd. Stewards. Mailing Add: 311 Smith St, Hillsboro, Tex. 76645.

BURDICK, IRWIN H. R
b. Detroit, Mich, 5/2/13; s. Aaron Burdick and Ida Marcus B; m. 12/25/43 to Jeannette Edelman; c. Alice N, Linda C. and Laura M. Educ: Wayne State Univ, LL.B; Phi Sigma Lambda. Polit. & Govt. Pos: Chmn, Rep. Party 15th Cong. Dist, Mich, 57-64; del, Rep. Nat. Conv, 60, 64 & 68; exec. v.chmn, Wayne Co. Rep. Cmt, Mich, 64-68; judge, Common Pleas Court, 68- Bus. & Prof. Pos: Attorney at Law, 36- Mil. Serv: Entered as Pvt, Army, 42, released as S/Sgt, 45, after serv. in 41st Inf. Div, Pac; Philippine Campaign Ribbon with 1 Battle Star. Mem: B'nai B'rith; Jewish War Veterans; Anti Defamation League. Rel: Jewish. Mailing Add: 19400 Warrington, Detroit, Mich. 48221.

BURDICK, MARGARET CAROTHERS R
Mem. Bd. Dirs, Nat. Fedn. Rep. Women, D.C.
b. Carlisle, Pa, 8/30/09; d. Samuel Henderson Carothers and Sarah Elizabeth Ogle C; m. 7/24/30 to Dr. William Foster Burdick; c. Nancy (Mrs. Galbraith) and William Henderson; eight grandchildren. Educ: Cornell Univ, 3 years. Polit. & Govt. Pos: Del, Rep. Nat. Conv, 52, 56 & 60; mem. exec. cmt. and v.chmn. gov. reception, Presidential Inaugural, 53; nat. prog. chmn, Nat. Fedn. Rep. Women, 54-59, mem. bd. dirs, 55-, nat. protocol chmn, 60-; co-chmn, Inaugural Ball at D.C. Armory, 57; Rep. Platform Cmt, 60; alternate del, Rep. Nat. Conv, 68; nat. chmn, Culture and Fine Arts Campaign Cmt, 68; mem, Rep. State Cmt, D.C, currently; mem. bd. dirs, Capital Hill Club, D.C, gov, currently; former mem, D.C. Women's Rep. Club, currently; mem. bd. dirs, Women's Nat. Rep, N.Y; mem, Speakers Bur; mem, Presidential Campaigns. Bus. & Prof. Pos: Teacher Eng. and pub. speaking, Ardmore High Sch, 28, Bryn Mawr High Sch, 29 & 30. Publ: Goldmine of Facts for Rep. Women, Rep. Nat. Cmt, 56; Program Manual for Nat. Fedn. Rep. Women; Handbook on Political and Social Protocol. Mem: Chevy Chase Club; Women's Nat. Press Club of Wash, D.C; Women's Nat. Rep. Club. Wash, D.C. Citizenship Citation; Awards for Pub. Welfare Work and for Polit. Achievements in Welfare Work. Rel: Episcopal. Mailing Add: 5027 Sedgwick St, Washington, D.C. 20016.

BURDICK, MILDRED MARYA D
b. Cleveland, Ohio, 4/10/08; d. Vincent Ostrowski and Wladyslawa Kaminski O; m. 11/24/26 to Ignace Bernard Burdick; c. Barbara Jean (Mrs. Piechnik), Richard E. and Diana M.(Mrs. Kabacinski). Educ: High Sch. Polit. & Govt. Pos: Dem. precinct committeewoman, Ind, 30-66; v.chmn, La Porte Co. Dem. Party, 64-66; former v.chmn, Mich. City Dem. Party. Mem: Bus. & Prfnl. Women Asn; C. of C; War Mothers 157. Rel: Catholic. Mailing Add: 311 Felton St, Michigan City, Ind. 46360. (1967)

BURDICK, QUENTIN N. D
U.S. Sen, N.Dak.
b. Munich, N.Dak, 6/19/08; s. Usher L. Burdick and Emma Robertson B: m. to Jocelyn Birch; c. Jonathan, Jan (Mrs. Glenn Hill), Jennifer, Jessica, Leslie, Birch and Gage. Educ: Univ. Minn, B.A, LL.B. Polit. & Govt. Pos: U.S. Rep, N.Dak, 58-60; U.S. Sen, N.Dak, 60- Legal Res: 1110 S. Ninth St, Fargo, N.Dak. 58103. Mailing Add: 305 C St. N.E, Apt. B106, Washington, D.C. 20002.

BURDITT, GEORGE MILLER R
Ill. State Rep.
b. Chicago, Ill, 9/21/22; s. George Miller Burditt and Flora Hardie B; m. 2/15/45 to Barbara Helen Stenger; c. Betsey Anne, George M, III, Deborah Jane and Barbara Lee. Educ: Harvard Col, A.B, 44, Harvard Law Sch, LL.B, 48; Pi Eta. Polit. & Govt. Pos: Chmn, Young Rep. Orgn. of Cook Co, Ill, 52-53; v.pres, Young Rep. Orgn. of Ill, 53-54; chmn, West. Springs Plan Cmn, 53-55; exec. v.pres, Regular Rep. Orgn. of Lyons Twp, 54-55; state v.chmn, Ill. Citizens for Eisenhower-Nixon, 56; state chmn, Vol. for Witwer, 60; Ill. State Rep, 65- Bus. & Prof. Pos: Attorney, Swift & Co, 48-54; partner, Chadwell, Keck, Kayser, Ruggles & McLaren, 54-68; partner, Burditt and Calkins, 69- Mil. Serv: Entered as Cadet, Army Air Force, 43, released as 2nd Lt, 45, after serv. in South East Training Command as Twin Engine Pilot Instr. and Air Transport Command as Four Engine Ferry Pilot. Publ: 'The Current Status of Weights and Measures Problems,' Soap and Chem. Specialties, 4/64; 'Weights and Measures, Foods and Drugs, and Uniformity,' Asn. of Food & Drug Officials of the U.S. Quarterly Bul, 10/64; 'Need for New Uses of the Regulatory Power to Establish Food Standards,' Food Drug Cosmetic J, 3/65. Mem: Am, Ill, Chicago and West Suburban Bar Asns; Kiwanis. Rel: Congregational. Mailing Add: 540 S. Park Rd, La Grange, Ill. 60525.

BUREN, JOHN LEONARD D
b. Leland, Iowa, 6/10/13; s. William Pascal Buren and Mary Elizabeth B; m. to Thora M. Berg; c. Kathleen Ann and John Paul. Educ: Loras Col, two years. Polit. Pos: Iowa State Sen, 64-66; Dem. Co. Chmn, six years. Bus. & Prof. Pos: Auto and Farm Machinery Bus; Farm Owner. Mil. Serv: U.S. Navy, WWII, two years. Mem: Elk Club; Lion; Am. Legion. Rel: Catholic. Mailing Add: Clinton St, Forest City, Iowa 50436. (1967)

BURFORD, DOROTHY WRIGHT R
Mem, State Rep. Cmt, Mo.
b. Doniphan, Mo, 10/2/03; d. Thomas Lyon Wright and Clara Robinson B; m. to Peyton Jerome Burford; c. Virginia Jerry (Mrs. William S. McAninch). Educ: Galloway Col, 22-23; Stephens Col, A.A, 24. Polit. & Govt. Pos: Mem, State Rep. Cmt, Mo, 42-; del, Rep. Nat. Conv, 56 and alternate del, 68; chmn, Ripley Co. Rep. Cent. Cmt, 56- Bus. & Prof. Pos: Mgr, gravel div. T.L. Wright Lumber Co, 26-40. Rel: Methodist. Mailing Add: 101 Summit St, Doniphan, Mo. 63935.

BURFORD, ROBERT F. R
Chmn, Eagle Co. Rep. Cmt, Colo.
b. Grand Junction, Colo, 2/5/23; s. Ellery E. Burford and Cleone Fitzpatrick B; m. 3/16/51 to Judith M. Allen; c. Joseph Ellery, Robert Kelley, Richard F. and Joyce. Educ: Colo. Sch. Mines, E.M, 44; Theta Tau. Polit. & Govt. Pos: Chmn, Eagle Co. Rep. Cmt, Colo, currently. Mil. Serv: Entered as Pvt, Marines, 44, released as Cpl, 46, after serv. in 1st Marine Div, Pac. Theatre; Pac. Theatre Ribbon and two Stars. Mem: Mason; Farm Bur. Mailing Add: 113 Mira Monte Rd, Grand Junction, Colo. 81632. (1967)

BURG, MARY LOU D
Dem. Nat. Committeewoman, Wis.
b. Slinger, Wis, 2/10/31; d. Leo R. Burg and Henrietta Loew B. (deceased); single. Educ: Rockford Col. Women, 1 year; Univ. Nev, 2 years; Univ. Wis, Madison, B.S, 52; Delta Delta Delta. Polit. & Govt. Pos: Chmn, Women's Cmt, Wash. Co. Dem. Party, Wis, 60-64, chmn, Wash. Co. Dem. Party, 66-68; precinct committeewoman, 4th ward, West Bend, 64-; member-at-large, Dem. Admin. Cmt, 67-68; Dem. Nat. Committeewoman, 68- Bus. & Prof. Pos: Dir. of continuity & pub. affairs, WEMP Radio, Milwaukee, 58-64, sales rep, Sta. WYLO, Milwaukee, 64-67, gen. mgr, 67- Mem: Milwaukee Advert. Club. Rel: Methodist. Mailing Add: 407 S. Sixth Ave, West Bend, Wis. 53095.

BURGENER, CLAIR W. R
Calif. State Sen.
b. Vernal, Utah, 12/5/21; s. Walter H. Burgener and Nora Taylor B; m. 9/27/41 to Marvia Hobusch; c. Rod, Greg and John. Educ: San Diego State Col, A.B, 50; Blue Key; Sigma Chi. Polit. & Govt. Pos: Councilman, San Diego, Calif, 53-57, v.mayor, 55-56; chmn, San Diego Co. Nixon for Pres.

Campaign, 59; consult. spec. educ, U.S. Dept. Health, Educ. & Welfare, 59-64; Calif. State Assemblyman, 76th Dist, 63-67; Calif. State Sen, 38th Dist, 67- Bus. & Prof. Pos: Pres. and owner, Clair W. Burgener Co, Realtors, 47- Mil. Serv: Entered as Cadet, Army Air Corps, released as 2nd Lt; serv. in Korean Conflict, S.Pac. Theater, 52-53; Air Medal. Mem: Am. Legion; VFW; Old Globe Theater; bd. dirs, United Commun. Serv, Commun. Welfare Coun; gen. chmn, Heart Fund Campaign, San Diego Co, 57; gen. chmn, United Fund, San Diego, 57, pres, 60-61; pres, San Diego Co. Asn. Retarded Children, 57-59; 2nd v.pres, Nat. Asn. Retarded Children, 62-63, Southwest. regional v.pres, 63-64; chmn, Two Year Action Cmt. Reforems in Prog. Dependent and Neglected Children. Rel. Latter-day Saint. Legal Res: 6038 Ridgemoor, San Diego, Calif. 92120. Mailing Add: 8690 Center Dr. Suite Three, La Mesa, Calif. 92041.

BURGES, THEODORE ROOSEVELT R
b. Clara City, Minn, 5/21/02; s. Cornelius Burges and Wilhelmina Bykerk B; m. 7/27/26 to Polina Vern Jones; c. Mary Louise (Mrs. Froiland). Educ: Macalester Col; Sigma Delta Chi. Polit. & Govt. Pos: Chmn, Deuel Co. Rep. Cmt, S.Dak, 55; state chmn, Census Dr, 54 & 59; mem, Clear Lake City Coun, 65-; chmn, Karl Mundt for Sen. Club. Bus. & Prof. Pos: Mem. sch. bd, Clear Lake, S.Dak, 54-64; dir. and secy, Deuel Tel. Coop, 56- Mem: Clear Lake Commercial Club (pres, 45-49); Kiwanis (pres, 56); Mason; Shrine; Eastern Star. Rel: Congregational. Mailing Add: Clear Lake, S.Dak. 57226.

BURGESS, BARBARA ANN D
Del, Calif. Dem. State Cent. Cmt.
b. Hurst, Ill, 11/2/22; d. Arthur Michael Knowles and Lorena McKenzie; m. 2/17/56 to Delbert Jack Burgess; c. Carol Lee (Mrs. Allan Schnur), Linda C. (Mrs. James Johnson), Russell D, Sgt, Marine Corps and William J. Educ: Riverside Jr. Col, A.A, 42; Pasadena City Col, 64. Polit. & Govt. Pos: Publicity chmn, Yucaipa Dem. Club, Calif, 67; secy, James Evans for Assembly Cmt, 73rd Assembly Dist, 68; del, Calif. Dem. State Cent. Cmt, 68- Bus. & Prof. Pos: Asst. cashier, Hills Bros. Coffee, Inc, Los Angeles, Calif, 45-57; off. mgr, Hall Trucking, Montebello, 62-64; off. mgr. and secy, Bodle, Fogel, Julber & Reinhardt, Attorneys-at-law, San Bernardino, 67-68; acct. exec, Coordinated Commun, Inc, Colton, 69. Mil. Serv: Released as A/M 3/C after serv. in Naval Air Corps, 42-45. Mem: Eagle Rock Chap, Royal Order of Amaranth; past pres, Mothers' Club; DeMolay. Rel: Methodist. Mailing Add: 35230 Santa Maria, Yucaipa, Calif. 92399.

BURGESS, BRADLEY FLEET R
b. Fredericksburg, Va, 8/27/38; s. Fleet A. Burgess and Elva Gray Heflin B: m. 5/26/63 to Anita Adams; c. Stephanie Marie. Polit. & Govt. Pos: Chmn, Spotsylvania Co. Rep Party, Va, 66-67. Bus. & Prof. Pos: Owner, Bradley Burgess Ins. Agency, 64- and Brad-Burg Fabrics-Interiors, 66- Mil. Serv: Entered as Airman Basic, Air Force, 56, released as Airman 2/C, 60; Good Conduct Medal. Mem: Jr. C. of C; dir, Fredericksburg Methodist Church. Rel: Methodist. Mailing Add: 406 Powell, Fredericksburg, Va. 22401. (1967)

BURGESS, CARL T. R
b. Lanar, Ark, 4/22/11; m. to Cathryn Riodian. Educ: Nebr. State Teachers Col, A.B. Polit. & Govt. Pos: S.Dak. Rep, 52-66; mem, exec. bd, Legis. Research Coun, 61; v.pres, Nat. Coun. of State Legis. Leaders; S.Dak. State Sen, 67-68. Bus. & Prof. Pos: Concession, Mt. Rushmore Nat. Mem. Mil. Serv: Security-Intel, 4 years 8 months. Mem: Mason. Rel: Protestant. Mailing Add: Box 510, Rapid City, S.Dak. 57701. (1967)

BURGESS, GERALD RAY D
Ala. State Rep.
b. Duke, Ala, 12/13/36; s. Josh Robert Burgess and Willie Pauline Sampler B; m. 6/25/55 to Lavada Ann Carroll; c. Bridget Elaine, Lawanna Raye, Lisa Ann and Gerald Ray, Jr. Educ: Jacksonville State Univ, B.S. in sec. educ, 58; Football, J.Club. Polit. & Govt. Pos: Ala. State Rep, 16th Dist, Place I, currently. Bus. & Prof. Pos: Teacher and football and baseball coach, Headland High Sch, East Point, Ga, 58-59; territory mgr, Wholesale Div, B.F. Goodrich Tire Co, 59-65; partner, City Tire Co, 65- Mil. Serv: Pvt, Nat. Guard, 57-62; Naval Res, 62-66, Naval Air Res, 66- Mem: Mason; Shrine; Anniston Exchange Club. Rel: Baptist. Mailing Add: Box 1363, Anniston, Ala. 36201. (1967)

BURGESS, HUGH D
Md. State Del.
b. Ellicott City, Md, 9/15/29; s. Lionel Burgess and Lenna L. Baker B; m. 2/28/49 to Doris Aileen Royer; c. Sandra Lee, Deborah Ann, Stephan Hugh, Reid Edwin and Holly Ellen. Educ: West. Md. Col, A.B, 49; Univ. Baltimore, LL.B, 63. Polit. & Govt. Pos: Md. State Del, 67- Mem: Am, Md. and Howard Co. Bar Asns; Kiwanis; Mason; Odd Fellows; Grange. Rel: Methodist. Legal Res: 3999 College Ave, Ellicott City, Md. 21043. Mailing Add: Box 126, Ellicott City, Md. 21043.

BURGESS, ISABEL ANDREWS R
b. Cleveland, Ohio; d. William H. Andrews and Alice Ball A; m. 6/15/39 to Richard S. Burgess, div; c. Richard Ball, Thomas H. and Mrs. Allen Cordsen. Educ: Mills Col. and West. Reserve Univ. Polit. & Govt. Pos: Ariz. State Rep, 53-54, 56-58 & 60-66; Ariz. State Sen, 67-69; mem, Nat. Transportation Safety Bd, 69- Mem: Phoenix Press Club; exec. cmt. and bd. dirs, Heard Mus. Rel: Episcopal. Legal Res: 6601 N. 36th St, Phoenix, Ariz. 85018. Mailing Add: National Transportation Safety Board, 726 Jackson Place, Washington, D.C. 20591.

BURGESS, JOHN STUART R
Speaker, Vt. House of Rep.
b. N.Y.C, 5/10/20; s. Frederick Vaughn Burgess and Olive Hornbrook Moore B; m. 6/28/47 to Ronda Helen Prouty; c. Frederick Moore and Helen Prouty. Educ: Univ. of Vt, B.A, 47; Northeast. Univ. Sch. of Law, LL.B, 49; Sigma Delta Psi; Sigma Phi. Polit. & Govt. Pos: Chmn, Brattleboro Rep. Town Cmt, Vt, 49-51 & 53-63 and Windham Co. Rep. Cmt, 50-51; legal counsel, Off. of Price Stabilization 51; town attorney, Brattleboro, 53-; spec. counsel, Vt. Hwy. Dept. 55-58; moderator, Brattleboro Union High Sch. Dist, 58-; Vt. State Rep, Dist. 4-5, 66-, speaker, Vt. House of Rep, 69-, chmn, Constitutional Rev. Cmn, 68-, mem, Civil Defense Cmn. and Legis. Coun, 69- Mil. Serv: Entered as Pvt, Army Field Artil, 41, released as Capt, 46, after serv. in Seventh Fighter Command, Pac. Theatre, 45-52; recalled as 1st Lt, Air Force, 51-53; with serv. in 90th Bomb Squadron, Korean Theatre; Air Force Res, Lt. Col, 62-; Distinguished Flying Cross; Air Medal; For. Decorations. Mem: Windham Co, Vermont and Am. Bar Asns; Nat. Asn. of Munic. Attorneys (state chmn); Nat. Asn. Claimants Compensation Attorneys; Am. Legion (past comdr, Brattleboro Post 5 and mem, Nat. Americanism Adv. Cmn); Am. Civil Liberties Union (v.pres); VFW; Shrine; Elks. Rel: Episcopal. Legal Res: 50 Western Ave, Brattleboro, Vt. 05301. Mailing Add: 67 Main St, Brattleboro, Vt. 05301.

BURGESS, LLOYD ALBERT R
Mem, Rep. Nat. Cmt, Alaska
b. Culver, Ore, 10/4/17; s. Estell Elmer Burgess and Arrista Pearl Ditterline B; m. 12/16/55 to Wanda Marie Gregory; c. Jason McKinley, Gregory Scott, Elizabeth Anne and Jefferey Lloyd. Educ: Ore. State Univ. Polit. & Govt. Pos: Cent. Dist. Finance Chmn, Rep. Party, Alaska, 56-58; Alaska State Finance Chmn, Rep. Party, 58-62; mem, Rep. Nat. Cmt, Alaska, 64-; del, Rep. Nat. Conv, 68. Bus. & Prof. Pos: Engr, Corps of Engrs, 39-40, Douglas Aircraft, 40-41 and Tide Water Assoc. Oil Co, 41-42; pres, Burgess Construction Co, 46- Mil. Serv: Entered as Ens, Navy, 42, released as Lt. Comdr, 46, after serv. in Civil Engr. Corps, Pac. Theatre; Pac. Theatre Ribbon; Philippines Liberation Medal; Marksman's Medal. Mem: Wash. Athletic Club; assoc, Gen. Contractors; Harbor Club; Elks; Am. Legion. Rel: Protestant. Legal Res: 390 Hamilton Ave, Fairbanks, Alaska 99701. Mailing Add: P.O. Box 1410, Fairbanks, Alaska 99701.

BURGESS, WARREN RANDOLPH R
b. Newport, R.I, 5/7/89; s. Isaac Bronson Burgess and Ellen Wilbur B; m. 3/5/55 to Helen Hamilton Woods; c. Leonard Randolph and Julian Ayres. Educ: Brown Univ, A.B, 12, LL.D, 37; Columbia Univ, Ph.D, 20; fel, Brown Univ; Delta Upsilon; Phi Beta Kappa. Hon. LL.D, Univ. Rochester, 48, Bowdoin Col, 59 and Univ. Calif, 62. Polit. & Govt. Pos: Chmn, N.Y. State War Finance Cmt, 43-44; Dep. to Secy. Treas, 53-54; Undersecy. of Treas, 55-57; U.S. Permanent Rep. to NATO, 57-61; chmn, Atlantic Treaty Asn, 61-63, v.chmn, 63- Bus. & Prof. Pos: Became assoc. with Fed. Reserve Bank of N.Y, 20, dep. gov. of bank, 30-36, v.pres, 36-38; v.chmn, Nat. City Bank of N.Y, 38-48; pres, N.Y. State Bankers Asn, 40-41; chmn, Econ. Policy Cmn, Am. Bankers Asn, 40-44, pres, 44-45 and chmn, Pub. Debt Policy Cmt, 46-47; chmn. bd, City Bank Farmers Trust Co; dir, Discount Corp, Int. Banking Corp. and U.P.R.R. Royal-Liverpool Group Ins. Co. in U.S; chmn. exec. cmt, Nat. City Bank, N.Y, 48-52; pres, Per Jacobsson Found. and Reserve City Bankers Asn, 52; trustee, Robert Col. and Teachers Col, Columbia Univ; Regent prof, Univ. Calif, Berkeley, 62. Publ: Trends of School Costs, 20; The Reserve Banks and the Money Market, 27, rev. ed, 36 & 46; ed, Interpretations of Federal Reserve Policy by Benjamin Strong, 30; contrib. of many articles to prfnl. jour. Mem: Am. Econ. Asn; Am. Philos. Soc; Century Asn, Univ, River, Chevy Chase and Cosmos Clubs. Legal Res: Queenstown, Md. 21658. Mailing Add: Atlantic Council U.S., 1616 H St. N.W, Washington, D.C. 20006.

BURGIN, WILLIAM GARMER, JR. D
Miss. State Sen.
b. Rock Hill, S.C, 8/3/24; married. Polit. & Govt. Pos: Miss. State Sen, 52- Bus. & Prof. Pos: Attorney. Mem: Mason; Elks; Lions Club. Rel: Baptist. Mailing Add: 516 Second Ave. N, Columbus, Miss. 39701. (1967)

BURGOON, GARREL R
Ill. State Rep.
b. Grant Co, Ind, 6/15/00; m. to Berniece Webster; c. three. Educ: Purdue Univ. Polit. & Govt. Pos: Ill. State Rep, 69th, 70th, 72nd and 73rd Gen. Assemblies and 66-; Sheriff, 50. Bus. & Prof. Pos: Retired retail businessman. Mil. Serv: Army, 18; Comdr, Army Res, 29; 41-46, Commanding officer, Gun Bn, Third Army; Lt. Col, Army Res; Bronze Star. Mailing Add: 1016 12th St, Lawrenceville, Ill. 62439. (1967)

BURGUM, KATHERINE K. R
Rep. Nat. Committeewoman, N.Dak.
b. Minneapolis, Kans, 2/26/15; m. 4/8/44 to Joseph Burgum; c. Bradley, Barbara and Douglas. Educ: N.Dak. State Univ, B.S, 37; Columbia Univ, M.A, 39; Phi Upsilon Omicron; Gamma Phi Beta. Polit. & Govt. Pos: Past pres, 11th Dist. Federated Womans Club, Cass Co, N.Dak; past secy, 11th Dist. Rep. Party; mem, Arthur Sch. Bd, 66-; alternate del, Rep. Nat. Conv, 68; Rep. Nat. Committeewoman, N.Dak, 68. Bus. & Prof. Pos: Teacher, Sayville, Jr. High and High Sch, N.Y, 37-39; asst. prof, Wayne State Univ, 39-47; N.Dak. rep, McCalls Mag. Cong. for Better Living, 57. Publ: Co-author with Rietz Larsen, Aircargo Potential for Fresh Fruits and Vegetables, 46 and Air Cargo Potential for Sea Food, 47, Wayne State Univ. Mem: Dir, Red River Valley and Cass Co. Fair Asns; past pres, N.Dak. Hosp. Auxiliary Asn, Cass. Co. Homemakers and St. Lukes Hosp. Auxiliary, Fargo; dir, Cass Co. Hist. Soc. Aviation Writers Prize, 49, Outstanding contrib. to commercial aviation through aircargo studies. Rel: Methodist; past secy, Arthur Methodist Church Bd. Mailing Add: Box 57, Arthur, N.Dak. 58006.

BURGUM, LESLIE R. R
b. McLean Co, N.Dak, 1890; m. 1926 to Blanche Gustafson; c. Mary Lois, Thomas Leslie. Educ: Univ. of N.Dak, 27; Univ. of N.Dak. Law Sch. Polit. & Govt. Pos: N.Dak. State Rep, 35, 37; asst. state attorney of Stutsman Co, 44; state's attorney, 52; N.Dak. attorney gen, 54-68. Bus. & Prof. Pos: Lawyer. Mil. Serv: World War II. Mem: Dept. chaplain, Am. Legion, 50-51. Mailing Add: Jamestown, N.Dak. 58401. (1967)

BURHANS, DONALD LUCAS R
Committeeman, Ill. Rep. Cent. Cmt.
b. Peoria, Ill, 3/26/19; s. Levi Alden Burhans and Eda Isabelle Lucas B; m. 8/19/49 to Helen Bobette Lyon; c. Donald L. II, Stephen Lyon and Bobette Lyon. Educ: Knox Col, 37-38; Wabash Col, A.B, 41; Univ. Cincinnati, M.D, 44; Phi Delta Theta. Polit. & Govt. Pos: Committeeman, Ill. Rep. Cent. Cmt, currently. Bus. & Prof. Pos: Mem. staff, Proctor Hosp, currently; sr. med. exam, Fed. Aviation Agency, currently. Mil. Serv: Lt.(jg), Navy, 45-46, with serv. in Farragut, Asiatic-Pac. Theatre; re-entered as Lt, 52, released as Lt. Comdr, 54, after serv. in Bur. of Med. & Surg, Wash, D.C; Lt. Comdr; U.S.N.R.R. Mem: Am. Med. Asn; Ill. State Med. Soc; Am. Acad. Gen. Prac-

tice; VFW; Holland Soc. of N.Y; Chicago Press Club; Creve Coeur Club of Peoria; Chicago Civil War Round Table. Rel: Congregational. Mailing Add: 4716 N. Knoxville Ave, Peoria, Ill. 61614.

BURHANS, ROBERT L. R
b. Peoria, Ill, 1916. Educ: Univ. of Mich, A.B, 37; Juris Dr. (with honors), 39. Polit. & Govt. Pos: Ill. State Rep, 48-64; Ill. Judicial Adv. Coun, 57-61, Chmn; Fed. Attorney, 41-42. Bus. & Prof. Pos: Lawyer, admitted to Ill, U.S. Courts, Asns; Am. Legion; Creve Coeur Club; Alpha Delta Phi. Rel: Congregational. Mailing Add: 5508 N. Mont Clair Ave, Peoria, Ill. 61614. (1967)

BURK, RACHEL IRENE D
Chmn, Branch Co. Dem. Cmt, Mich.
b. Montpelier, Ohio, 3/19/18; d. Dennis Harold Blue and Bertha Walz B; m. 8/5/50 to Chester Lovette Burk; c. Dennis Price and Thomas. Educ: Davis Bus. Sch, Toledo, Ohio, 1 year. Polit. & Govt. Pos: Hospitality chmn, Fourth Dist. Dem. Women, Mich, 69; chmn, Branch Co. Dem. Cmt, 69- Bus. & Prof. Pos: Self-employed, Upholstery Shop. Mem: Am. Legion Ladies Auxiliary; Boy Scouts; Cancer Soc. Rel: Lutheran. Mailing Add: R. R. 3, Coldwater, Mich. 49036.

BURK, ROBERT WILLIAM, JR. R
W.Va. State Sen.
b. Parkersburg, W.Va, 12/16/39; s. Robert William Burk and Evelyn Simonton B; m. 1/30/62 to Susan Coddington; c. Robert William, III and Christopher Barrett. Educ: Duke Univ, A.B, 61; W.Va. Univ. Col. of Law, LL.B, 64; Pi Sigma Alpha; Order of the Coif; Sigma Chi; Old Trinity Club; Phi Delta Phi. Polit. & Govt. Pos: W.Va. State Del, Wood, Co, 66-69; W.Va. State Sen, Third Dist, 69- Publ: Several articles, W. Va. Law Rev, 62 & 63. Mem: Am, W.Va. and W.Va. State Bar Asns; Wood Co. Bar Asn.(secy, 64-66, v.pres, 67-68, pres, 68-69); Rotary; Elks; Farm Bur; past dir, Mid-Ohio Valley Jr. Achievement; Wood Co. Recreation Cmn; Jaycees; dir, Vienna United Appeal; dir, Parkersburg Boys Club. Rel: Presbyterian. Legal Res: 1009 51st St, Vienna, W.Va. 26101. Mailing Add: P.O. Box 287, Parkersburg, W.Va. 26101.

BURK, WALTER O. D
b. Cheney, Minn, 1/2/02; married; c. 4. Educ: Univ. of N.Dak. Polit. & Govt. Pos: N.Dak. State Rep, 57-66; Former Mayor, Williston; States Attorney, Williams Co; alternate del, Dem. Nat. Conv, 68. Bus. & Prof. Pos: Lawyer. Mailing Add: Box 842, Williston, N.Dak. 58801.

BURKARDT, ROBERT F. R
Pa. State Rep.
b. Pittsburgh, Pa, 10/17/23; s. Adolph F. Burkardt and Stella Hibbs B; m. 6/21/41 to Donna Murphy; c. David, Pamela, Robert, Mary Janet, Margaret and Elizabeth. Educ: Univ. of Pittsburgh, A.B. cum laude, 47, Law Sch, J.D, 50; Phi Eta Sigma; Pi Kappa Alpha; Delta Theta Phi. Polit. & Govt. Pos: Pa. State Rep, 69- Bus. & Prof. Pos: Attorney at law, 50-; pres, Belle Fons Chem. Corp, 57-58 and Chem. Serv. Engrs, 68-69; mem. bd. of gov, Univ. of Pittsburgh Law Sch, 69- Mil. Serv: Entered as Pvt, Army, 43, released as 2nd Lt, 45, after serv. in Air Force Res; Lt. Col, Air Force Res, Judge Adv. Gen. Corps, 63-; Good Conduct, Am. Theatre, Victory and Reserve Medals. Mem: Co, State and Am. Bar Asns; Lawyers Club of Allegheny Co.(bd. dirs, past pres); Amvets (comdr, post 73); Allegheny Co. Bar Asn.(founder young lawyers sect, chmn, Jr. sect, 52-53 and mem. exec. cmt, 53-54); Moose; Am. Legion; ROA; Aero Club; St. Thomas More Lawyers Guild; Boy Scouts (troop committeeman, Troop 129 Verona); Young Rep; Mil. Order World Wars (v.comdr. and staff officer). Named 1967 Young Rep. Man of the Year. Rel: Roman Catholic. Mailing Add: 1461 Stanley Dr, Verona, Pa. 15147.

BURKE, ALFRED J. Independent
S.Dak. State Sen.
b. 10/5/97; married; c. six. Educ: Spearfish Normal, 2 years. Polit. & Govt. Pos: Organizer and chmn, N.W. Regional Libr; Butte Co. cmnr, S.Dak, 9 years; mem, Common Sch. Dist, 36 years; S.Dak. State Sen, 64- Bus. & Prof. Pos: Ranching interests. Mem: Mod. Woodmen of Am; Lions Club; Am. Nat. Cattlemen's Asn; S.Dak. and Black Hills Hereford Asns; Nat. Wool Growers Asn; West. S.Dak. Sheep Growers Asn. Rel: Catholic. Mailing Add: Newell, S.Dak. 57760. (1967)

BURKE, BILLY BROWN D
W.Va. State Del.
b. Stouts Mills, W.Va, 3/14/28; s. Roy Hammond Burke and Freda Brown B; m. 12/20/52 to Marjorie Carol Hardman; c. Roberta Diane and Carolyn Sue. Educ: Glenville State Col, 45-48. Polit. & Govt. Pos: W.Va. State Del, 66- Bus. & Prof. Pos: Pres, M & B Coal Co, 48-49; operating engr, Pipeline Indust, 49-58, construction supvr, 58-62; pres, B & F Trucking Co, 55-58; owner and mgr, Hardman Hardware Co, 62-; pres, Gilmer Co. Indust. Develop. Asn, 63-; pres, Gilmer Realty Co, Inc, 64- Mem: Gilmer Co. Lodge 118, AF&AM; Rotary; Gilmer Co. Vol. Fire Dept; United Commercial Travelers of Am, 28; PTA; Farm Bur; Farming for Better Living; Cent. W.Va. Coun, Boy Scouts. Rel: Baptist; Deacon and Sunday Sch. Supt. Legal Res: 22 Sumac Court, Glenville, W.Va. 26351. Mailing Add: P.O. Box 367, Glenville, W.Va. 26351. (1967)

BURKE, DONALD FRANCIS D
Chmn, Lee Co. Dem. Cent. Cmt, Ill.
b. Rockford, Ill, 6/4/40; s. James John Burke and Agnes Donavan B; m. 10/15/60 to Vonna Jean Lee. Educ: North. Ill. Univ, B.S, 67. Polit. & Govt. Pos: Chmn, Lee Co. Dem. Cent. Cmt, Ill, 68-; asst. supvr, Dixon Twp, 69- Bus. & Prof. Pos: Supvr, Canteen Corp, 60-67; co-owner, Coffee Host Co, 67- Mem: K. of C; Optimist Int; C. of C. Rel: Catholic. Mailing Add: 217 Monroe, Dixon, Ill. 61021.

BURKE, FRANK WELSH D
b. Louisville, Ky, 6/1/20; s. Joseph M. Burke and Ann Welsh B; m. 4/6/43 to Evalyne Hackett; c. Lynn (Mrs. Dennis Clare), JoAnn (Mrs. George Schuhmann), Lucy and Frank Jr. Educ: Univ. South. Calif, 38-39; Xavier Univ, Ph.B, 42; Univ. Louisville, LL.B, 48; Alpha Sigma Nu; Phi Kappa Psi. Polit. & Govt. Pos: Asst. city attorney, Louisville, Ky, 50-51, dir. of pub. safety, 52 & exec. asst. to mayor, 52-53; Ky. State Rep, 57; U.S. Rep, Ky, 58-62; del, Dem. Nat. Conv, 68. Bus. & Prof. Pos: Attorney-at-law, 48- Mil. Serv: Entered as Pvt, Army, 42, released as 1st Lt, 46, after serving in various truck co, ETO, 44-45; Europe, Africa and Middle East campaign ribbons with three battle stars. Mem: Phi Alpha Delta; Louisville and Ky. Bar Asns; Am. Legion; VFW; K. of C. Rel: Catholic. Mailing Add: 1234 Eastern Pkwy, Louisville, Ky. 40204.

BURKE, GEORGE GERALD D
Dist. Attorney, Norfolk Co, Mass.
b. Brooklyn, N.Y, 8/3/32; s. John F. Burke and Ruth Joyce B; m. 10/3/59 to Sandra Bachofen; c. Jeanne Marie, Susan Lee, Joanne and George G, III. Educ: Univ. Mass, A.B, 56; Boston Col. Law Sch, LL.B, 59; Adelphia; Owls; Lambda Chi Alpha. Polit. & Govt. Pos: City Councillor, Quincy, Mass, 60-67, pres, city coun, 66-67; Mass. State Rep, First Norfolk Dist, 65-67; dist. attorney, Norfolk Co, 67-; del, Dem. Nat. Conv, 68. Bus. & Prof. Pos: Attorney, Barry & Burke, 59- Mil. Serv: Capt, Armor Unit, Army Res, 51-64. Mem: Am, Mass. Fed, Quincy and Norfolk Bar Asns; Am. and Mass. Trial Lawyers Asns; Dist. Attorney's Asn; Am. Legion; Elks; Moose. Former Rookie of Boston Celtics; selected All Am, All East and All New England in Basketball. Rel: Catholic. Mailing Add: 174 Warren Ave, Quincy, Mass. 02170.

BURKE, HOWARD L. D
B. Cheyenne, Wyo, 7/8/14; m. to Vernice E; c. two. Educ: Univ. Pa; Univ. Wyo. Polit. & Govt. Pos: Mem, State Adv. Coun, Small Bus. Admin, Wyo, formerly; Wyo. State Rep, 59-66. Bus. & Prof. Pos: Pres, Burke Moving & Storage, Inc. and v.pres, Rocky Mt. Area, N.Am. Van Lines, formerly. Mem: Nat. Defense Transportation Asn.(state chmn); dir, Wyo. Trucking Asn; Sertoma; C. of C. Rel: Episcopal. Mailing Add: 2614 Pioneer Ave, Cheyenne, Wyo. 82001.

BURKE, J. EDWARD D
Co. Treas, Berkshire Co, Mass.
b. Pittsfield, Mass, 8/27/10; s. James A. Burke and Margaret Muller B; m. 1/4/42 to Madelyn Fitzgerald; c. Bernadette M. Educ: Pittsfield High Sch, grad, 29. Polit. & Govt. Pos: Co. treas, Berkshire Co, Mass, 68- Mil. Serv: Entered as Pvt, Army, 43, released as Cpl, 45, after serv. in 796th M.P. Batallion, ETO; 2 Battle Stars; Good Conduct Medal. Mem: Am. Legion; VFW; Elks. Rel: Catholic. Mailing Add: 52 Dorchester Ave, Pittsfield, Mass. 01201.

BURKE, J. HERBERT R
U.S. Rep, Fla.
b. Chicago, Ill, 1/14/13; m. to Evelyn Krumtinger; c. Kelly Ann, Michele Kathleen. Educ: Cent. YMCA Col, Chicago, 35; Northwest. Univ, Chicago, 37; Kent Col. of Law, LL.B, 40. Polit. & Govt. Pos: Mem, S.E. adv. bd, Small Bus. Admin; mem, Broward Co. Traffic Asn, Fla; adv, Nat. Rivers and Harbors Bd; Broward Co. Rep. precinct committeeman, 50-56; Broward Co. cmnr, 52-66; Rep. State committeeman, 54-60; U.S. Rep, Fla, 66-; del, Rep. Nat. Conv, 68. Bus. & Prof. Pos: Past law clerk and bond and securities clerk; attorney at law. Mil. Serv: Capt, Army, 42-45; Purple Heart; Bronze Star, Good Conduct, Am. Theatre and German Occup. Medals; European Medal with five Battle Stars. Mem: Past comdr, Post 92, Am. Legion; state dir, Eagles, 60, 61; 40 et 8; VFW; DAV; Elks; Moose; C. of C; Broward Co. and Fla. Bar Asns; Kiwanis; Judge Advocates Asn; Ital-Am. Club. Good Citizenship Award, Civitans; Good Govt. Award, Jaycees; Outstanding Serv. Award, Heart Fund. Rel: Catholic. Mailing Add: 1218 Hollywood Blvd, Hollywood, Fla. 33020. (1967)

BURKE, JAMES A. D
U.S. Rep, Mass.
b. Boston, Mass, 3/30/10; m. 10/29/68 to Aileen A. McDonald. Educ: Suffolk Univ. Polit. & Govt. Pos: Registr. Vital Statist, Boston, Mass; Mass. Gen. Court, 10 years; v.chmn, Mass. Dem. State Cmt, 4 years; U.S. Rep, Mass, 58-; del, Dem. Nat. Conv, 68. Mil. Serv: Army, Spec. Agent, Counter Intel, 77th Inf. Div; 4 Battle Stars. Legal Res: Milton, Mass. 02186. Mailing Add: U.S. House of Representatives, Washington, D.C. 20515.

BURKE, JAMES W. D
b. Sioux City, Iowa, 1934; Single. Educ: Univ. of Iowa. Polit. Pos: Iowa State Rep, 64-66; Admin. Asst. to City Mgr, Sioux City, 7 Years. Bus. & Prof. Pos: Real Estate Salesman. Mil. Serv: U.S. Air Force, Korea. Mailing Add: 1725 W. 3rd St, Sioux City, Iowa. 51101. (1967)

BURKE, JEROME A. D
Mem, Ohio Co. Dem. Exec. Cmt, W.Va.
b. Wheeling, W.Va, 11/25/37; s. Richard Vincent Burke and Elizabeth Greene B; m. 6/25/66 to Janet Ruth Miller; c. Jerome A, Jr. Educ: West Liberty State Col, 1 year. Polit. & Govt. Pos: Mem, Small Bus. Admin. Adv. Bd, W.Va, 62; alternate del, Dem. Nat. Conv, 64 and del, 68; chief dep. clerk, Ohio Co. Court, 65; v.pres, Ohio Co. Young Dem, 66; mem, Wheeling Human Rights Cmn, W.Va, 67; mem, Ohio Co. Dem. Exec. Cmt, 68- Bus. & Prof. Pos: Grocery clerk, Kroger Co, 69. Mem: K. of C.(4°); Jr. C. of C; Amalgamated Food Union. Named Jaycee of the Month and Key Man of the Year, Wheeling Jaycees, U.S. Jaycees Key Club. Rel: Roman Catholic. Mailing Add: 164 E. Cove Ave, Wheeling, W.Va. 26003.

BURKE, JEROME U. R
b. Orange, N.J, 9/30/32; s. Michael E. Burke and Elizabeth Underhill B; single. Educ: Upsala Col. Polit. & Govt. Pos: N.J. State Assemblyman, Essex Co, 64-65; Rep. campaign mgr, 11th Cong. Dist, N.J, 66. Bus. & Prof. Pos: Stockbroker, Francis I. Du Pont & Co, N.J. Mil. Serv: Entered as Pvt, Army, 54, released as Cpl, 56, after serv. in 529th Field Artil, Europe; German Occupation Medal; Good Conduct Medal. Mem: Past pres, N.J. Jaycees; Elks; Am. Legion; Amvets; Ironbound Mfrs. Asn. Rel: Catholic. 1967 Legal Res: Millburn, N.J. No mailing address available. (1967)

BURKE, JOHN PATRICK SHANAHAN D
Dist. Attorney, East. Dist. Mass.
b. Lawrence, Mass, 2/5/15; s. Thomas Burke and Mary Shanahan B; m. 9/22/52 to Patricia Geraldine Twomey. Educ: Villanova Univ, B.A, 37; Boston Col. Law Sch, J.D, 48; class pres, Villanova Univ, 34, 35 & 36. Polit. &

Govt. Pos: Dist. Attorney, East. Dist. Mass, 58-; del, Dem. Nat. Conv, 68. Bus. & Prof. Pos: Teacher, Lawrence High Sch. and Lawrence Eve. High Sch, 37-42; real estate broker, 37-42; attorney-at-law, 48- Mil. Serv: Entered as Seaman, Navy, 42, released as Lt, 46, after serv. in European and Pac. Theatres; Five Battle Stars. Publ: The Posture of Evidence, Sullivan Bros, 65. Mem: Am, Mass, Essex Co. and Lawrence Bar Asns; Nat. Asn. Dist. Attorneys (mem. nominating cmt, 63); trustee, Mass. Trial Lawyers Asn; Cath. Lawyers Guild; Am. Judicature Soc; pres, Mass. Dist. Attorneys Asn, 62-; dir, Bon Secours Hosp. Guild; Men of Merrimack Col. Guild; St. Basil's Sem. Guild; Lawrence Gen. Hosp. Asn; Elks (past exalted ruler and pres, past exalted rulers, Lawrence Lodge); Am. Legion; Mass. State Elks Asn; K. of C; VFW; DAV; Holy Name Soc; Vincent DePaul Soc; Friends of Sisters of Charity of Halifax; Irish Charitable Soc, Boston; Ancient Order of Hibernians; South Lawrence Assocs.(past pres); bldg. fund regional chmn. for Augustinian Sem, Lawrence Boy's Club, Bon Secours Hosp. and Merrimack Col; regional chmn, Commun. Chest and United Fund; trustee, Lawrence Pub. Libr; President Johnson's Nat. Crime Cmn, 67; Gov. Cmn. on Capital Punishment; Legis. Cmn. Study Grand Jury Syst; Criminal Law Rev. Cmn; proposal rev. bd, Gov. Pub. Safety Cmt; Lawrence Youth Cmn. Admitted to practice in U.S. Fed. Court and U.S. and Mass. Supreme Courts. Rel: Catholic. Mailing Add: 72 Salem St, Lawrence, Mass. 08143.

BURKE, JOHN WALTER R
b. Harford Mills, N.Y, 12/24/98; m. to Lois E. Gardiner; c. two sons; two daughters. Educ: LaSalle Inst. (Bus. Exten. Course). Polit. & Govt. Pos: Dep. sheriff, Addison Co, Vt, 32-50; Middlebury Fire Chief, 34-43; Middlebury Village trustee, 38-58; Vt. State Rep, 65-68. Bus. & Prof. Pos: Trustee, Columbus Smith Estate; mem, exec. bd. Chittenden Trust Co, Addison Co. Div, Vt; v.pres, Vt. Milk and Cream Co, Inc; retired dist. mgr, Borden Farm Prod. Co. Mil. Serv: Pvt, Army; Student Training Corps, Cornell Univ, Motor Mech. Mem: Past pres, Rotary; Am. Legion; organizing pres, Twin States Sanitarians Asn; past pres, past dir, Vt. Dairy Indust. Asn; hon. mem, Future Farmers of Am, Middlebury Chap. Rel: Congregational. Mailing Add: Box 268, Middlebury, Vt. 05753. (1967)

BURKE, M. JOSEPH R
b. Casper, Wyo, 4/6/17; m. to Mary; c. 10. Educ: Univ. of Wyo; Creighton Univ. Polit. & Govt. Pos: Wyo. State Rep. until 67; Rep. cand. for Gov. of Wyo, 66; pres. bd. of Pub. Utilities of Casper. Bus. & Prof. Pos: Dir, Wyo. Nat. Bank; rancher; real estate; investment; Shamrock Ranch Co, Secy. and Gen. Mgr; pres. Oil City Corp; pres. shamrock Investment Co; secy. Wyo. Motor Co; secy. West. Co; dir, Guaranty Fed. Savings and Loan. Mem: Pres. Wyo. Wool Growers Asn; v.pres, Am. Sheep Producers Coun; past state dep, K. of C; Stockgrowers; Elks; Phi Kappa; Casper C. of C; Farm Bur; Wyo. Taxpayer's Asn; Am. Irish Hist. Soc. Rel: Catholic. Mailing Add: 109 E. 10th St, Casper, Wyo. 82601. (1967)

BURKE, M. M. 'MARTY' R
Chmn, Fourth Dist. Rep. Finance Cmt, Kans.
b. Ardmore, Okla, 8/19/33; s. Arnold John Burke and Marie K. Martin B; m. 9/7/56 to Datha D. Lauber; c. Marta E, Darla D. 'Dee Dee,' J. Vance and Zane M. Educ: Tex. A&M Univ; Kans. State Univ, B.S; Univ. Kans; Wichita State Univ, 1 year; Theta Zi. Polit. & Govt. Pos: V-chmn, Kans. Young Rep, 65-66; chmn. Fourth Dist. Young Rep, 67-68; chmn, Fourth Dist. Rep. Finance Cmt, Kans, currently; alternate del, Rep. Nat. Conv, 68. Bus. & Prof. Pos: Pres, Consumer Audio, Inc, 57-59, Consumers Farm Gas, Inc, 59-62, M & M Investments, Inc, 62-65 and Petroleum Prod, Inc, 65-69. Mem: Nat. L-P Gas Asn; K. of C; Elks; Rotary. Rel: Catholic. Legal Res: 119 Carlton Rd, Hutchinson, Kans. 67501. Mailing Add: P.O. Box 1055, Hutchinson, Kans. 67501.

BURKE, NANCY AELISHIA R
West. Conf. Chmn, N.Mex. Rep. Party
b. Des Moines, Iowa, 12/2/33; s. Harold Vincent Burke and Aelishia Smith B; single. Educ: Univ. N.Mex, B.A, 56; Univ. Albuquerque, 69; Alpha Delta Pi. Polit. & Govt. Pos: Del, Young Rep. Nat. Fedn, 61, 63, 65,67 & 69, co-dir, Region XI, 61-63 and dir, Region XI, 67-69; precinct secy, Bernalillo Co. Rep. Party, N.Mex, 64-68 and mem. co. cent. cmt, 64-69; nat. committeewoman, N.Mex. Young Rep, 64-69; del, Atlantic Alliance of Young Polit. Leaders, Luxemburg, 68; alternate del, Rep. Nat. Conv, 68; West. Conf. chmn, N.Mex. Rep. Party, 69- Bus. & Prof. Pos: Teacher, Highland High Sch, Albuquerque Pub. Schs, N.Mex, 56-69. Mem: N.Mex. Coun. for Improv. of Educ.(exec. bd); N.Mex. Coun. Teachers of Eng; Nat. Coun. of Teachers of Eng; Albuquerque Classroom Teachers; N.Mex. Educ. Asn; Albuquerque Opera Guild. Rel: Presbyterian. Mailing Add: 5624 Princess Jeanne N.E, Albuquerque, N.Mex. 87110.

BURKE, RAYMOND F. D
b. N. Brookfield; m. to Pearl Hatstat. Educ: N. Brookfield schs. Polit. & Govt. Pos: Mem, Bd. of Selectmen 6 years, now chmn; mem, Dem. Town Cmt; del, Dem. State Conv, Mass. Mil. Serv: World War II, Europe and China-Burma-India Theaters; Purple Heart. Mem: VFW; Past Comdr. of Boulette-Skyten Post, Am. Legion, during his term as comdr. he instituted a membership drive that won a nat. award for the largest gain in post membership. Mailing Add: E. Main St, East Brookfield, Mass. 01515. (1967)

BURKE, ROBERT H. R
Calif. State Assemblyman
b. Des Moines, Iowa, 7/16/22; s. Henry Burke and Mabel Anderson B; m. 6/12/54 to Claire Spencer; c. Bradley, Spencer and Carrie. Educ: Iowa State Col; Univ. of Calif, Berkeley, B.S. in eng, 49. Polit. & Govt. Pos: Trustee, Huntington Beach City Sch. Dist, Calif, 63-66; Calif. State Assemblyman, 70th Dist, 67-, mem, Elec. and Reapportionment, Munic. and Co. Govt. and State Employ, Retirement and Mil. Affairs Cmts, Calif. State Assembly; mem, Calif. Rep. State Cent. Cmt, currently. Mil. Serv: Entered as Pvt, Air Force, 42, released as 1st Lt, 46, after serv. in Pac. Theatre. Mem: Am. Petroleum Inst; Am. Inst. of Mech. Engrs; Kiwanis; Toastmasters; Huntington Beach C. of C. Named Outstanding Man of the Year, Huntington Beach Chap, United Rep. of Calif; received one of the five Outstanding Legislator Awards, Calif. Rep. Assembly, 67. Rel: Protestant. Legal Res: 8362 Malloy Dr, Huntington Beach, Calif. 92646. Mailing Add: 17732 Beach Blvd, Huntington Beach, Calif. 92647.

BURKE, ROBERT JAMES D
Treas, W.Va. Dem. Exec. Cmt.
b. Wheeling, W.Va, 9/3/34; s. Richard Vincent Burke and Elizabeth Greene B; m. 10/4/58 to Dolores Louise Moski; c. Timothy James, Sheila Marie, Patrica Jean, Daniel Martin and Paula Anne. Educ: W. Liberty State Col. night sch, 7 years. Polit. & Govt. Pos: V.chmn, Ohio Co. Dem. Exec. Cmt, W.Va, 64 and chmn, 68; dir, W.Va. Young Dem. Clubs, 64; assoc. campaign mgr, W.Va. Campaign, 66; exec. secy, W.Va. Young Dem, 66; chmn, Citizens for Sprouse for Gov, 67-68; del-at-lg, Dem. Nat. Conv, 68; treas, W.Va. Dem. Exec. Cmt, 68- Bus. & Prof. Pos: V.pres, Warwood Tool Co, 63-65 and pres, 65-; v.pres, Waller Chem, 67-; secy, Warwood Manor, 67- Mil. Serv: Entered as Pvt, Army, 54, released as SP-3, 56, after serv. in Adj. Gen. Corp; Good Conduct Medal. Mem: Am. Hardware Mfg. Asn; K. of C; Elks; Eagles; Am. Legion. Outstanding Small Bus. Man, Nat. C. of C, 69. Rel: Roman Catholic. Mailing Add: R.D. 1 Avalon Estates, Box 106, Wheeling, W.Va. 26003.

BURKE, THOMAS A. D
b. Cleveland, Ohio, 10/30/98; s. Thomas A. Burke and Lillian McNeil B; m. 6/25/24 to Josephine Lyon; c. Jo Ann, Barbara. Educ: Holy Cross Col, B.A, cum laude 20, (hon); LL.D, 54; West. Res. Univ, LL.B, 23; Phi Alpha Delta. Polit. & Govt. Pos: U.S. Sen, Ohio, 53-54; mayor of Cleveland, 45-53; dir. of law, City of Cleveland, 41-44; spec. counsel to attorney gen. of Ohio, 37; prosecuting attorney, Cuyahoga Co, Ohio, 30-36. Bus. & Prof. Pos: Lawyer, partner Burke, Haber & Berick, Cleveland; mem. firm McConnell, Blackmore, Cory & Burke, Cleveland, 37-41. Mem: K. of C; Shaker Heights (O) Country Club; Cleveland Athletic Club. Mailing Add: Union Commerce Bldg, 925 Euclid Ave, Cleveland, Ohio 44115.

BURKE, VINCENT S. D
b. Luverne, Minn, 5/17/20; s. James M. Burke and Marion F. B; m. 4/13/40 to Mary A. Crilly; c. Michael, Alice and JoAnn. Educ: Morningside Col, B.S, 1958; Univ. of N.Y; Univ. of S. Dak. Polit. Pos: Iowa State Sen-66. Bus. & Prof. Pos: Rehabilitation of Physically and Mentally Handicapped and Socially Maladjusted. Mil. Serv: U.S. Army Air Force, Air Transport Command Ferry Div, 42-45. Mem: Nat. Rehabilitation Asn; Am. Inter-Prfnl. Asn; Iowa Welfare Asn; V. Pres, Iowa Wing OX-5 Club of Am. (Aviation Pioneers); Antique Airplane Asn; Exp. Aircraft Asn. Rel: Catholic. Mailing Add: 1017 S. Paxton, Sioux City, Iowa. 51106.

BURKE WILLIAM J. R
b. W. Rutland, Vt, 5/10/90; m. to Teresa F. Hanley; c. Two sons; six daughters. Educ: W. Rutland Pub. Schs. Polit. & Govt. Pos: Vt. State Sen, 49-66; Vt. State Rep, 35, 47; Rutland Liquor Control Bd; Emergency Bd; Rutland Rwy. Study Cmn. Bus. & Prof. Pos: Property appraiser, real estate, part time farmer. Mem: Rutland Co. Farm Bur; K. of C. Coun. 232; A.C.P. Co. Cmt, 38-48. Rel: Catholic. Mailing Add: N. Grove St, RFD 1, Rutland, Vt. 05701. (1967)

BURKHARDT, DOROTHY JEAN R
b. Hebron, Ky, 9/27/11; d. John Chester Hall Hood and Callie Clore H; m. 1/28/55 to George Burkhardt, III; c. Carol (Mrs. John H. Rose) and Raymond K. Poole and George Burkhardt, IV. Educ: The Miller Sch. of Bus, Cincinnati, Ohio, grad, 29. Polit. & Govt. Pos: Mem, Alexandria City Rep. Cmt, Va, 62-, v.chmn, 62-65 & 68-; cand, Va. House Del, 63 and Alexandria City Coun, 64 & 66; mem. Mamie Eisenhower Libr. Proj. Cmt, Nat. Fedn. Rep. Women, 63-64, del, dist. and state conv; co-chmn, Vol. Participation Cmt. for the Inaugural; mem, Women for Nixon Cmt; charter mem. and first pres, Potomac Coun. Rep. Women, Alexandria, Va; chmn. house-to-house canvas cmt, Rep. Party, Va, 64 and asst. coord, MORE Cmt, 65; v.pres, Va. Fedn. Rep. Women, 64-66 and pres, 66-68; mem. adv. cmt, Elem. and Sec. Educ. Act, Alexandria Pub. Schs, 65-66; mem, Va. Rep. State Cent. Cmt, 66-; chmn. credentials cmt, Nat. Fedn. Rep. Women Conv, Wash, D.C, 67; alternate del, Rep. Nat. Conv, 68; assoc. dir, Pres. Cmt. on Consumer Interests, 69- Bus. & Prof. Pos: Mem. women's adv. bd, Fidelity Savings and Loan Asn, Alexandria, Va; stenographer-secy. Treas. Dept, Cincinnati, Ohio and Wash, D.C; mfrs. rep, East Coast Post Exchange; owner, sales showroom, 55-65; secy-treas, Va. Home Loan Corp, Alexandria, 61-; treas, Stag Shops Inc, Arlington, Alexandria and Manassas, Va, 65-; real estate salesman, Robertson & Heck Inc, Arlington and Alexandria, 66-69. Mem: Cub Scouts (den mother, Alexandria Club, 47-48); charter mem, Beverley Hills Women's Club, Alexandria (past pres, 47-48, commun. affairs chmn, 65); C. of C.(chmn. educ. cmt, Alexandria Chap, 64-66); Old Dominion Bus. and Prfnl. Women's Club (legis. chmn, 65); co-chmn, Alexandrians for Econ. Progress, 68; Toastmistress Club (past pres, North. Va. chap); Alexandria Hosp. Corp; North Ridge Citizen's Asn, Alexandria; Alexandria Bd. of Trade. Elected Va. Rep. Woman of the Year, Va. Fedn. Rep. Women, 69. Rel: Presbyterian. Mailing Add: 3400 Russell Rd, Alexandria, Va. 22305.

BURKHARDT, ROBERT JAMES D
Secy. of State, N.J.
b. Chicago, Ill, 6/10/16; s. Ernest Ross Burkhardt and Dale Messinger B; m. 12/29/36 to Lucille Frances Hogan; c. Constance R, Robert J, Jr, Ross M. and Valerie L.(Mrs. Philip R. Tamis). Educ: Purdue Univ. Polit. & Govt. Pos: Chmn, N.Y. Young Dem, 48-49; nat. committeeman, Young Dem. of Am, 50-51; dir. speakers bur. and asst. to chmn, Dem. Nat. Cmt, 51-53, mem. adv. cmt. polit. orgn, 57-60 and mem. campaign planning cmt, 60; campaign dir. for Gov. Robert B. Meyner, N.J, 53, exec. secy. to Gov. Robert B. Meyner, 54-57; exec. dir, Dem. State Cmt, N.J, 57-60 & 64-65, campaign dir, 61-62 and chmn, 65-; exec. dir, Nat. Voter's Registrn. Cmt, 60; exec. dir, Inaugural Cmt, D.C, 60-61; asst. postmaster gen. for facilities, D.C, 61; Secy. of State, N.J, 62-; exec. dir, N.J. Host Cmt, Dem. Nat. Conv. and Citizens for Johnson and Humphrey, D.C, 64; del, Dem. Nat. Conv, 68. Bus. & Prof. Pos: Asst. supt. and construct. supt, Merritt Chapman & Scott Corp. and A.M. Hazell, Inc. Inc, 36-54; v.pres, Hudson Valley Aluminum Co, 47-51. Mil. Serv: Army, 45. Mem: F&AM (past master, Woodbury Lodge 993); AAONMS; Valley of Newark; Scottish Rite; Elks. Rel: Methodist. Legal Res: 27 W. State St, Trenton, N.J. 08608. Mailing Add: Secretary of State, State House, Trenton, N.J. 08625.

BURKHART, JEAN M. D
V.Chmn, Neosho Co. Dem. Cent. Cmt, Kans.
b. Parsons, Kans, 4/19/30; d. Clarence H. Titus and Lyda Carter; m. 6/10/50

to George A. Burkhart; c. Monte Jean. Educ: St. Francis Sch, grad, 48. Polit. & Govt. Pos: Precinct cmt. woman, Lincoln Twp, Neosho Co, Kans, 64-; pres, Neosho Co. Women's Dem. Club, 66-68, v.pres, 68-; secy, Neosho Co. Dem. Cent. Cmt, 66-68, vice committeewoman and v.chmn, 68- Bus. & Prof. Pos: Secy-treas, St. Paul Commercial Club, 58- Mem: St. Paul Commercial Club. Rel: Catholic. Mailing Add: Box 35, St. Paul, Kans. 66771.

BURKHART, STEPHEN R
Chmn, Livingston Co. Rep. Exec, Cmt, Ky.
b. Wallins, Ky, 8/26/31; s. S.B. Burkhart and Serena Long B; m. 4/14/54 to Jean Paul; c. Gregory, Carol and Bruce. Educ: Berea Col, B.A, 51; Univ. W.Va, 51; Univ. Louisville, M.D, 55; Alpha Kappa Kappa. Polit. & Govt. Pos: Chmn, Livingston Co. Rep. Exec. Cmt, Ky, 68- Bus. & Prof. Pos: Mem, Livingston Co. Bd. Health, Ky, 64-; pres, Crittenden Co. Hosp. Med. Staff, 66-; v.chmn. & bd. mem, West. Ky. Regional Ment. Health Bd, 67- Mil. Serv: Entered as 1st Lt, Air Force, 56, released as Capt, 58, after serv. in Strategic Air Command, Ga, 56-58; Capt, Air Force Res. Mem: Ky. Med. Asn; Livingston Co. Med. Asn.(pres, 62-); Am. Asn. Physicians and Surgeons; Nat. Farm Orgn; Livingston Co. Riding Club. Rel: Baptist. Mailing Add: Salem, Ky. 42078.

BURKHEAD, WILLIAM JOSEPH D
Md. State Del.
b. Baltimore, Md, 12/30/11; s. William B. Burkhead and Eleanor Newton B; div; c. Gail S. Educ: Baltimore Inst. Jr. Col; Univ. of Baltimore, Pre-Law. Polit. & Govt. Pos: Md. State Del, 67- Bus. & Prof. Pos: Sales rep, P. Ballantine & Sons. Mil. Serv: Pfc, Army, 29-32; BM 2/C, Navy, 42-46; Good Conduct, Am. Theater and Victory Medals. Mem: Elks; Moose; Am. Legion. Rel: Protestant. Mailing Add: 15 Country Club Dr, Glen Burnie, Md. 21061.

BURKHEIMER, NANCY BROWN D
Md. State Del.
b. Colora, Md, 2/24/40; d. Joseph J. Brown and Margaret Caroline Clemens B; m. 11/28/63 to Robert Carl Burkheimer. Educ: Univ. Md, B.S, 62; Univ. Md. Sch. of Law, 62-64; Pi Sigma Alpha. Polit. & Govt. Pos: V.pres, Md. Young Dem, 62-63; secy, Women's Dem. Club of Cecil Co, Md, 62-; Md. State Del, Cecil Co, 63- Bus. & Prof. Pos: Treas, Gold Medal Develop. Co. Inc, 65- Mem: Bd. dirs. and secy, Nat. Order of Women Legislators; Alumni Asn. Univ. of Md; League of Women Voters; C. of C; Hist. Soc; Col. Club of Cecil Co; Associated Cecil Endeavors, Inc; Md. Cmn. Status of Women; Woman's Col. Club (pres, 66-68); YMCA (bd. dirs, 65-70). Named Outstanding Young Female in Politics in 63 by Mademoisella Mag. Mailing Add: 37 Norman Allen St, Elkton, Md. 21921.

BURKMAN, CAROL LYNN R
Treas, Fifth Dist. Rep. Party, Kans.
b. Ada, Kans, 2/21/30; d. Lee Spence VanMeter and Doris Lambertson V; m. 9/2/51 to Reuben J. Burkman, M.D; c. Ronald Lee, Jeanine Hyacinth and Gary Linn. Educ: Kans. Wesleyan Univ, 48-50; Kans. Univ, 51; Kans. State Univ, B.S, 52; Beta Sigma Chi. Polit. & Govt. Pos: Treas, Neosho Co. Rep. Cent. Cmt, Kans, 64-; co-chmn, Kans. Young Rep. Fedn, 65-67, mem. exec. bd, 67-; del, Nat. Young Rep. Conv, 67; sustaining mem. Rep. Party, Wash, D.C, 68; del, Rep. Nat. Conv, 68; distinguished mem, Rep. Fivescore Club, Kans, 68; treas, Fifth Dist. Rep. Party, 68-; attended 17th Annual Rep. Women's Conf, Wash, D.C, 69. Bus. & Prof. Pos: Typist, Kans. Univ. Med. Ctr, 52; teacher, Kansas City, 52-53 & 54-55; typist-secy, Cent. Packing Co, Kansas City, 53-54. Mem: Am. Asn. Univ. Women; P.E.O; PTA; Woman's Kansas Day Club; United Presby. Women; Neosho Co. Med. Auxiliary; Neosho Co. Hosp. Auxiliary; Am Cancer Soc. (mem. co. educ. cmt); Art & Lit. Club; Chanute Country Club. Invited to President Nixon's Inauguration and Inaugural Ball. Rel: Presbyterian. Mailing Add: 911 S. Highland, Chanute, Kans. 66720.

BURKSTALLER, SARAH RUTH D
Chairwoman, Chaves Co. Dem. Party, N.Mex.
b. Sacramento, Calif, 1/26/34; d. James Edward Stringer and Thelma Casey S; m. 1/28/56 to Dr. Steve Marshall Burkstaller; c. Lisa Blair and Ross Frederick. Educ: Univ. N.Mex, B.A. in hist; Mortar Bd; Phi Alpha Theta; Pi Lambda Theta; Spurs; Pi Beta Phi. Polit. & Govt. Pos: Chairwoman, Chaves Co. Citizens for Kennedy, N.Mex, 60; del, Dem. Nat. Conv, 68; chmn, Chaves Co. Dem. Party, N.Mex, 69- Bus. & Prof. Pos: Teacher, Roswell Pub. Schs, 57-62. Mem: Roswell Assistance League; Roswell Symphony Guild; Am. Asn. Univ. Women; adv. bd, East. N.Mex. Univ; Roswell Libr. Bd; Alumni Bd, Univ. N.Mex. Rel: Unitarian. Mailing Add: 600 N. Lea Ave, Roswell, N.Mex. 88201.

BURLEIGH, JOSEPH R
N.H. State Rep.
b. Franklin, N.H, 10/25/00; s. Harry Walter Burleigh and Nannie Burley B; m. 1/1/27 to Alice Taggart; c. Joseph Harry, Hugh Taggart, Richard Thomas and Peter Gregg. Educ: Dartmouth Col, B.S, 24; Sigma Alpha Epsilon. Polit. & Govt. Pos: N.H. State Rep, Dist. 14, 69- Bus. & Prof. Pos: Mem. staff, West. Elec. Labs, New York, N.Y, 25-26; elec. contractor, Franklin, N.H, 27-29 & 32-35; mem. staff, Sulloway Hosiery Mills, 32-35 and Franklin Sch. Dist, 35-67. Mem: Rotary Int.(gov, dist. 787, 66-67); Boy Scouts. Silver Beaver and Wood Badge Beads, Boy Scouts. Rel: Unitarian. Mailing Add: 921 S. Main St, West Franklin, N.H. 03235.

BURLEIN, LESTER F. R
Chmn, Wayne Co. Rep. Cmt, Pa.
b. Honesdale, Pa, 2/1/07; s. Frederick George Burlein and Carrie Theobald B; m. 4/28/28 to Una Catherine Foster; c. Joan M. (Mrs. Michelotti), Joyce A. (Mrs. Osborne) and John P. Educ: Pa. State Col. Polit. & Govt. Pos: Chmn, Wayne Co. Rep. Cmt, Pa. and Northeast Chmn. Asn, Rep. Party, 53-; asst. chmn, Rep. State Cmt, 62; primary campaign co-chmn, Scranton for Gov, 62; Dep. Secy of Hwy, Pa, 63. Bus. & Prof. Pos: Proj. engr, Pa. Hwy. Dept, 32-36; plant engr, Lummus Co, 55-61; consult. engr, L.F. Burlein Engrs, 61-63; chmn, Pa. Turnpike Cmn, 63- Mem: Soc. Prfnl. Engrs; Am. Soc. Mech. Engrs; Am. Soc. Hwy. Engrs; Am. Ord. Asn; Mason; Shrine. Rel: Lutheran. Mailing Add: 758 Ridge St, Honesdale, Pa. 18431.

BURLESON, DAVID J. D
b. Auburn, Ala, 12/31/19; s. David Burleson and Alice Wesson B; m. 5/5/45 to Lillian Oliver; c. Ann, Clare, Jane and David O. Educ: Univ. Ark, B.S.B.A, 47 and LL.B, 50; Delta Theta Phi; Sigma Chi. Polit. & Govt. Pos: Ark. State Rep, Washington Co, 59-66. Bus. & Prof. Pos: Private law practice, 50- Mil. Serv: Entered as Aviation Cadet, Army Air Corps, 42, released as Capt, 45, after serv. in China-Burma-India Theater, 43-45; Lt. Col, Air Force Res. Mem: Am, Ark. and Washington Co. Bar Asns; Am. Legion; VFW; CBI Vets. Asn. Rel: Methodist. Mailing Add: 1028 Sunset Dr, Fayetteville, Ark. 72702.

BURLESON, OMAR D
U.S. Rep, Tex.
b. 3/19/06; s. J.M. Burleson and Betty B; m. to Ruth. Polit. & Govt. Pos: Formerly, Spec. Agent, Fed. Bur. Invest, Co. Judge, Jones Co, Tex, and Co. Attorney; del, Dem. Nat. Conv, 68; U.S. Rep, Tex, currently. Bus. & Prof. Pos: Attorney-at-law. Mil. Serv: Navy, 3 years. Mailing Add: Anson, Tex. 79501.

BURLING, EDWARD, JR. R
Mem, D.C. Rep. Cmt.
b. Chicago, Ill, 2/5/08; s. Edward Burnham Burling and Louisa Peasley B; m. 4/4/59 to Frida Frazer Winslow; c. Anne (Mrs. Ward Just), Lucinda (Mrs. George B. Doubleday), Belinda (Mrs. Luis F. Moro), Walter Thacher Winslow, Jr. and David L. Winslow. Educ: Yale Univ, Ph.B, 29; Harvard Law Sch, LL.B, 32. Polit. & Govt. Pos: Chmn. finance cmt, D.C. Eisenhower for Pres. Club, 52, D.C. Citizens for Eisenhower Cmt, 54-58, D.C. Cmnrs. Citizens Adv. Coun, 56-62 and D.C. Cmt. for Forward Looking Rep, 64-; mem, D.C. Rep. Cmt, 53-, finance chmn. and mem. exec. cmt, 60-64; mem. exec. cmt, Rep. for Progress, 64-; alternate del, Rep. Nat. Conv, 60, del, 64 & 68. Bus. & Prof. Pos: Partner, Covington & Burling, Attorneys, 35-; dir, United-Greenfield Corp. and predecessor, United Drill & Tool Corp, 37-68; dir, J.H. Williams & Co, 46-58 and Buffalo-Eclipse Corp, 54-58; treas. and dir, Historic Georgetown, Inc, D.C, 51-; dir. and v.chmn, The Cottages Ltd, Jamaica, 60- Mil. Serv: Entered as 1st Lt, Army Air Corps, 42, released as Maj, 45, after serv. in Air Transport Command, U.S. Hq, Mediterranean Theatre and Air Force Hq, D.C; Award of Merit. Mem: Am. Bar Asn; D.C. Bar Asn.(chmn, legal ethics cmt, 59-60); Am. Judicature Soc; Wash. Criminal Justice Asn.(dir, 38-42); charter mem, World Peace Through Law Center; Am. Red Cross (chmn. D.C. Chap, 60-66, v.chmn, 66); Atlantic Coun. of U.S; trustee, Fed. City Coun, D.C; chmn. Wash. Home Rule Cmt; Georgetown Citizens Asn; Yale Club of Wash, D.C; Harvard Law Sch. Asn; Alfalfa Club; City Tavern Asn; Fed. City Club; Metropolitan Club. Rel: Episcopal. Legal Res: 1339 29th St. N.W, Washington, D.C. 20007. Mailing Add: 888 16th St. N.W, Washington, D.C. 20006.

BURLISON, BILL D. D
U.S. Rep, Mo.
b. Wardell, Mo, 3/15/31; s. J. I. Burlison and Lillie Marler B; m. 8/14/55 to Barbara Ann Humphreys; c. James David, Andrew Jefferson and Laura Anne. Educ: Southeast Mo. State Col, B.A, 53, B.S. & Ed, 59; Univ. Mo, LL.B, 56, M.Ed, 64; Phi Alpha Theta; Phi Delta Phi; Pi Kappa Delta; Sigma Chi; Alpha Phi Omega. Polit. & Govt. Pos: Spec. asst. to Attorney Gen, Mo, 61-66; prosecuting attorney, Cape Girardeau Co, 63-69; del, Dem. Nat. Conv, 64; v.pres, Mo. Young Dem. and pres, Cape Girardeau Co. Young Dem, 66; U.S. Rep, 69- Mil. Serv: Entered Marine Corps, 56, released as 1st Lt, 59. Mem: Am, Mo. and Cape Girardeau Co. Bar Asns; Mo. Gov. Colonels Staff; AF&AM. Rel: Baptist. Legal Res: 2306 Jane Dr, Cape Girardeau, Mo. 63701. Mailing Add: 1313 Longworth Bldg, Washington, D.C. 20515.

BURNETT, BENIFIELD R
b. Prince Edward Co, Va, 10/8/30; s. Farris Berkley Burnett and Effie V. Hall B; m. 3/24/51 to Ruth Bethel Fairbanks; c. Robert Lewis, Shirley Rae, Teresa Ann and Sherry Lee. Polit. & Govt. Pos: Campaign mgr, Charlotte Co. Rep. Elec. Cmt, Va, 64; chmn, Goldwater Cmt, 64; v.chmn, Fifth Dist. Rep. Party; chmn, Charlotte Co. Rep. Party, 64-67. Bus. & Prof. Pos: Pres, Keysville Heating, Inc, 60- Mil. Serv: Navy, 48-52. Mem: Keysville AF&AM Lodge 154; dir, Charlotte Co. Red Cross. Rel: Methodist. Mailing Add: RFD 1, Box 378, Keysville, Va. 23947.

BURNETT, BENJAMIN OLIVER D
S.C. State Rep.
b. Rock Hill, S.C, 12/26/37; s. Claude O. Burnett and Vera Edwards B; m. 8/5/61 to Alice A. Drake; c. Allison C. and Drake O. Educ: Newberry Col, B.S, 60. Polit. & Govt. Pos: S.C. State Rep, 68- Bus. & Prof. Pos: Br. mgr, The Macke Co, currently. Mem: Kiwanis; Jaycees; bd. mem, YMCA. Rel: Methodist. Legal Res: 100 Westover Dr, Greer, S.C. 29651. Mailing Add: P.O. Box 213, Greer, S.C. 29651.

BURNETT, GAIL TINER R
Secy, Lake Co. Rep. Party, Colo.
b. Hartshorne, Okla, 4/22/20; d. George Tiner and Sadie Poor T; m. 12/22/56 to John Wesley Burnett, Jr; c. John Wesley, III. Educ: Colo. Mt. Col, 69. Polit. & Govt. Pos: Rep. committeewoman, Precinct One, Colo, 68-; secy, Lake Co. Rep. Party, 69- Mem: Rebekah (past Noble Grand); chmn, United Pilgrimage Trip; Odd Fellow Cemetery Asn. Rel: Christian Church of N.Am. Legal Res: 426 E. Tenth, Leadville, Colo. 80461. Mailing Add: Box 582, Leadville, Colo. 80461.

BURNETT, JAMES H. R
Mont. State Rep.
b. Luther, Mont, 7/1/17; s. James M. Burnett and Eda D. Brickman B; m. 12/12/41 to Alice E. Boggio; c. James D, Dolores J. and Diane A. Educ: Billings Polytech, 36-38. Polit. & Govt. Pos: Rep. committeeman, Precinct 20, Mont, 49-54; chmn, Carbon Co. Rep. Cent. Cmt, 54-58; committeeman, Mont. State Rep. Cent. Cmt, 58-68; Mont. State Rep, Carbon-Stillwater Dist, 69- Bus. & Prof. Pos: Dir. and chmn, West. Ditch Co. Inc, Carbon Co, 50-; owner and operator, Burnett Ranch, Luther, 53-; dir, Salt Lake Producers, 54-, U.S. Nat. Bank, Red Lodge, 58- Mil. Serv: Entered as Pvt. Cadet, Army Air Corps, 42, released as Flight Officer, 45, after serv. in 439th Aircraft Carrier, ETO, 44-45; Maj, Air Force Res, 66; Air Medal with 3 Clusters; Presidential Unit Citation; Victory Medal; ETO Ribbon with 4 Battle Stars and

B2 Army Arrowhead. Publ: 'Where the Cattle Roam',(mag. sect), Billings Gazette, 12/68. Mem: Mason; Am. Legion; VFW; ROA; Mont. Stockgrowers; Mont. Farm Bur. Rel: Methodist. Mailing Add: Luther, Mont. 59051.

BURNETT, ROBERT MOORE D
Tex. State Rep.
b. Sanger, Tex, 1/20/34; s. John Q. Burnett and Bama Draper B; m. 6/18/66 to Sue Reese; c. Lisa Anne and Jeffery William. Educ: Univ. Tex. Sch. Bus, B.B.A, 55; Univ. Tex. Sch. Law, LL.B, 57; Phi Alpha Delta. Polit. & Govt. Pos: Asst. dist. attorney, Tarrant Co, Tex, 59-61; city attorney, Arlington, 62-64; Tex. State Rep, Dist. 52, 69- Mem: Pres, Arlington Bar Asn, 69-; Tarrant Co. and Am. Bar Asns; State Bar of Tex; Kiwanis. Rel: Baptist. Mailing Add: Route 3, Box 2368, Arlington, Tex. 76010.

BURNETT, WAYNE BART D
b. Seymour, Tex, 9/21/36; s. Eugene Sparks Burnett and Laura Bessie Rogers; single. Educ: Univ. Tex, 3 yrs. Polit. & Govt. Pos: Chmn, Baylor Co. Dems, Tex, 62-66. Bus. & Prof. Pos: Mgr, Seymour C. of C, 64- Mem: Tex. C. of C. Mgr. Asn; Tex. Indust. Develop. Coun; C. of C. Exec. Asn. of W.Tex. Rel: Baptist. 1967 Legal Res: Seymour, Tex. No mailing address available. (1967)

BURNEY, CECIL E. D
b. Riesel, Tex, 10/6/14; s. Frank E. Burney and Allye S. Goodman B; m. 1/15/49 to Kara Hunsucker; c. Cecil E, Jr, Karita and Frank B. Educ: Univ. Tex, B.A, LL.B. Polit. & Govt. Pos: Dist. rep, Lyndon B. Johnson, 48; chmn, Speaker's Bur. Dem. Campaign, Tex, 56; dist. dir, Kennedy-Johnson Campaign, 60 and Johnson-Humphrey Campaign, 64; co-chmn, Nat. Citizens for Johnson-Humphrey, 64; dir, Humphrey-Muskie Campaign, Tex, 68; presidential elector Tex, 68; del, Dem. Nat. Conv, 68. Bus. & Prof. Pos: Attorney-at-law, Corpus Christi, Tex, 38-; dir, Brownsville Nat. Bank of Commerce, Parkdale State Bank of Corpus Christi, Mercantile Nat. Bank of Kingsville and First Nat. Bank of Ingleside; mem. bd. dirs, Fed. Nat. Mortgage Asn, 68-69; mem. bd. dirs, Stonewall Bank, Corpus Christi, Tex. Mil. Serv: Entered as Lt.(jg), Naval Res, released as Lt. Comdr, 45. Mem: Del, Am. Bar Asn. and chmn, Membership Cmt, 55-56, chmn, Am. Citizenship Cmt, 58-59, chmn, Sect. of Bar Activities, 59-60, bd. gov, chmn, Finance Subcmt, Joint Cmt. for Effective Admin. of Justice, fel, Am. Bar Found; pres, State Bar Tex, 51-52; pres, Am. Judicature Soc, 60-62; chmn, Nat. Conf. of Bar Pres, 55-56; dir, Nat. Legal Aid and Defender Asn, 53-65; treas. and mem. exec. cmt, Lawyers' Cmt. for Civil Rights; pres, Commun. Cmt. on Youth Educ. and Job Opportunities; pres, Jr. C. of C; chmn, Nueces Co. Red Cross; chmn, Corpus Christi Housing Authority. Distinguished Serv. Award, U.S. Jr. C. of C; Outstanding Young Man in Corpus Christi, 38; Arthur von Briesen Award, Nat. Legal Aid and Defender Asn, 63; St. Thomas More Award, St. Mary's Univ, 64. Rel: Presbyterian, Elder. Legal Res: 4895 Ocean Dr, Corpus Christi, Tex. 78412. Mailing Add: Box 2467, Corpus Christi, Tex. 77703.

BURNEY, DWIGHT WILLARD R
b. Hartington, Nebr, 1/7/92; m. 12/2/14 to Edna (deceased); m. 1/1/65 to Grayce E. Hahn; c. Donald, Dwight, Jr, Willard and Keith. Educ: Univ. S.Dak, 2 years. Polit. & Govt. Pos: Nebr. State Sen, 45-57, Spec. Sessions, 46, 52 & 54; Lt. Gov, Nebr, 57-65, Gov, 60-61. Bus. & Prof. Pos: Dir. rural sch, formerly; farming and livestock business, currently. Publ: 'Nebraska's Farmer Governor,' Hasting Tribune, 67. Mem: Scottish Rite; Mason, KCCH (32°); Eastern Star; Nebr. Ment. Health Bd. Agr. Award for Distinguished Serv, 66; Key Man in Agr, 62; 50 Year Shipper Award, 66; Adm, Nebr. Navy. Rel: Congregational. Mailing Add: Hartington, Nebr. 68739.

BURNEY, JOHN J, JR. D
N.C. State Sen.
b. Wilmington, N.C, 10/5/24; s. Judge John J. Burney and Effie B; m. to Catherine Evans; c. Deborah Salinda, John Jay, III, William Shaw. Educ: Wake Forest Col, B.S, LL.B. Polit. & Govt. Pos: Dist. solicitor, N.C, 9 years; N.C. State Sen, 67- Bus. & Prof. Pos: Attorney. Mil. Serv: U.S. Army, World War II; Bronze Star and two Purple Hearts. Rel: Presbyterian. Mailing Add: 720 Forest Hills Dr, Wilmington, N.C. 28401. (1967)

BURNEY, WILLIAM E. D
b. Hubbard City, Tex, 9/11/93; s. John Joseph Burney and Mary Evans B; m. 10/26/21 to Eunice Latamore; c. William E, Jr, Phillip G. and Isabel (Mrs. Booth). Educ: Univ. N.Mex, 3 years; capt, baseball team; Athletic Club; Kappa Sigma. Polit. & Govt. Pos: U.S. Rep, Colo, 73rd Cong; pres, bd. educ. Mil. Serv: MM 2/C, Navy, 18; also entered as Maj, Army, 42, released as Col, 46, after serv. as Comdr, Camp Ross, Calif; 9 campaign and length of serv. medals. Mem: Pres, Pueblo C. of C, 24-42; pres, Commun. Chest and Kiwanis Club; comdr, Am. Legion; Mason (32°), Consistory, Shrine; Elks; 40 et 8; Denver Press Club; Mt. Vernon Country Club; N.F.W; Alumni Asn. Rel: Protestant. Mailing Add: 1555 Jasmine St, Denver, Colo. 80220. (1967)

BURNHAM, DWIGHT E, SR. R
Vt. State Rep.
b. Bloomfield, Conn, 9/9/05; m. to Bernice Snyder; c. Three sons and one daughter. Educ: Bloomfield High Sch. Polit. & Govt. Pos: Mem, Addison Co. Rep. Cmt, Vt; justice of the peace; selectman, Waltham; dir, Vergennes Union High Sch. Dist; auditor, 58-63; Vt. State Rep, 63- Bus. & Prof. Pos: Dairy farmer. Mil. Serv: Marines, 23-27 & 42-45. Mem: Mason; Grange; Farm Bur; East. Milk Producers Asn. Rel: Congregational. Mailing Add: Waltham, Vt. 05491. (1967)

BURNHAM, HORACE RUPERT D
b. Jacksonville, Ala, 5/25/17; s. Horace Burnham and Annie Cheatwood B; m. 6/30/51 to Jane Elizabeth Self; c. Patrick Self, Anne Danzey, William Robert and Jane Elizabeth. Educ: Jacksonville State Col; Univ. Ala, LL.B, 50. Polit. & Govt. Pos: Ala. State Rep, 62-66. Mil. Serv: Army, 45, Capt, recalled during Korean Conflict; Lt. Col, Army Res, at present. Mem: Mason. Rel: Baptist. Mailing Add: Box 1618, Anniston, Ala. 36201. (1967)

BURNHAM, ROLAND B. R
b. Nashua, N.H, 2/28/96; married: c. Four. Educ: Sch. of Banking, 48. Polit. & Govt. Pos: Former N.H. State Rep. Bus. & Prof. Pos: Banker, secy and dir, Nashua Trust Co. Mil. Serv: Marines, World War I. Mem: Trustee, Suburban Cemeteries; Rotary; N.H. Consistory; Shrine; past gov, Moose; Am. Legion; VFW; World War I Barracks. Rel: Protestant. Mailing Add: 4 Stark St, Nashua, N.H. 03060. (1967)

BURNS, ANDREW JOSEPH, JR. D
Md. State Del.
b. Baltimore, Md, 7/25/27; s. Andrew Joseph Burns, Sr. and Anne Belle Tunstall B; m. 6/27/53 to Shirley Nina Taylor; c. Andrew J, III, Michael T, Raymond B, Richard T, Patrick T. and Christopher T. Educ: Loyola Col, Baltimore, Md, B.S, 50; Univ. Md. Law Sch, LL.B, 60; Dean's List, Loyola Col; Zeta Eta Theta; Gamma Eta Gamma. Polit. & Govt. Pos: Md. State Del, 67- Bus. & Prof. Pos: Attorney-at-law, Baltimore, Md, 60- Mil. Serv: Seaman, Navy, 45-46; re-entered as Ens, 50, released as Lt.(jg), 54, after serv. on U.S.S Putnam; Lt, Naval Res, 47-50 & 54-; N.Atlantic and Am. Defense Ribbons; World War II Victory Medal; Korean and China Serv. Medals; UN and Naval Res. Medals; Japan and German Occupation Medals. Mem: Am, Md. and Baltimore Bar Asns; Asns. of Defense Trial Counsel; K. of C.(4°); Grand Advocate, Order of Alhambra; Friendly Sons of St. Patrick; pres, Bellona Gittings Commun. Asn; Cicha; YMCA Phys. Fitness Cmt; United Third Dist. Dem. Orgn; Assoc. Dem. Rel: Catholic. Legal Res: 6033 Bellona Ave, Baltimore, Md. 21212. Mailing Add: 612 Keyser Bldg, Calvert and Redwood St, Baltimore, Md. 21202.

BURNS, ARTHUR FRANK R
Counsr. to the Pres.
b. Stanislau, Austria, 4/27/04; s. Nathan Burns and Sarah B. Juran B; m. 1/25/30 to Helen Bernstein; c. David and Joseph. Educ: Columbia Univ, A.B, 25, A.M, 25, Ph.D, 34; Phi Beta Kappa. Hon. LL.D, Lehigh Univ, Brown Univ, Dartmouth Col, Oberlin Col, Wesleyan Univ, Swarthmore Col, L.I. Univ, Univ. Chicago, Rikkyo Univ. and Fordham Univ; L.H.D, Rutgers Univ; Sc.D, Univ. Pa. and Univ. Rochester. Polit. & Govt. Pos: Chmn, Pres. Coun. Econ. Adv, 53-56; mem, U.S. Adv. Coun. on Soc. Security Financing, 57-58; mem, N.Y. Temporary State Cmn. on Econ. Expansion, 59-60; mem, Pres. Adv. Cmn. on Labor-Mgt. Policy, 61-66; mem, Gov. Cmt. on Minimum Wage, N.Y, 64; Counsr. to the Pres, 69- Bus. & Prof. Pos: Prof. econ, Columbia Univ, 41-69; pres, Nat. Bur. Econ. Research, N.Y.C, 57-67. Publ: Production Trends in the U.S. Since 1870, 34; Measuring Business Cycles (with W.C. Mitchell), 46; Frontiers of Economic Knowledge, 54; The Business Cycle in a Changing World, 69. Mem: Am. Econ. Asn; Am. Acad. Arts and Sci; Am. Statist. Asn; Acad. Polit. Sci; Am. Philos. Soc; Coun. on For. Rels; Cosmos Club, Wash, D.C; Century Asn, N.Y.C. Rel: Jewish. Legal Res: 45 Sutton Place S, New York, N.Y. 10022. Mailing Add: Sheraton-Park, 2660 Connecticut Ave. N.W, Washington, D.C. 20008.

BURNS, BARBARA LOU
b. Honolulu, Hawaii, 9/23/26; d. Lawrence Reginald Holt and Priscilla Alden H; div; c. Valerie Puanani, Donna Lee and Robert Kalikolehua. Polit. Pos: Nominee, Hawaii State Rep, 66; committeewoman, Rep. Precinct, 59-66; alternate del, Rep. Nat. Conv, 64; state secy, Rep. Cent. Cmt, 62-64. Bus. Pos: Exec. Secy, Hawaii Movie Production, 65; exec. secy. and catering mgr, Ilikai Hotel, 63-64; exec. secy, Hawaii State Legis, 59-64, Am. Factors, Ltd, 60-63 and C. Brewer & Co, 44-57. Mem: Lani-Kailua Bus. & Prfnl. Women; Rep. Women's Club; Hawn Civic Club. Rel: Congregational. Mailing Add: 605 N. Kainalu Dr, Kailua, Hawaii 96734. (1967)

BURNS, BERNARD JOHN R
Chmn, Rep. Town Cmt, Milford, Conn.
b. Waterbury, Conn, 1/29/23; s. Bernard J. Burns and Mary Carroll B; m. 2/22/46 to Kathyrn M. Eustace; c. Bernard, II, Kathleen, Joseph, Christopher and Jeffrey. Educ: Univ. Conn, B.S, 48; Sigma Nu; Sigma Alpha Mu; Newman Club. Polit. & Govt. Pos: Chmn, Rep. Town Cmt, Milford, Conn, currently. Mil. Serv: Entered as Pvt, Army, 42, released as Sgt, 46, after serv. in 84th Inf. Div; Bronze Star; three Purple Hearts; ETO Ribbon; Unit Citation with three Battle Stars. Mem: V.pres, Conn. Asn. Ins. Agents, 65-66, pres, 66-67; Rotary; K. of C; Am. Legion; VFW. Rel: Catholic. Mailing Add: 101 River St, Milford, Conn. 06460. (1967)

BURNS, BRIAN DOUGLAS D
Vt. State Rep.
b. Burlington, Vt, 11/17/39; s. Walter F. Burns and Eugenia Lanctot B; m. 4/1/59 to Linda Jeanne Brouillard; c. Rebecca Anne, Brian Patrick, Jennifer Lynn, Cynthia Jeanne and Brendan Alton. Educ: Univ. Vt. Polit. & Govt. Pos: State pres, Young Dem. Clubs, Vt, 66-68; Vt. State Rep, 67-; v.chmn, Burlington Dem. Party, Vt, 68, chmn, 69; mem. legis. coun, State of Vt, 69- Bus. & Prof. Pos: Pres, Richmond Realty, Vt, 4 years. Mil. Serv: Entered as Pvt, Army-Vt. Nat. Guard, 59, released as Pfc, 59, after serv. in Judge Adv. Gen. Corps. Mem: V.pres, Truax Assocs. of Richmond, 69. Rel: Catholic. Mailing Add: 67 Caroline St, Burlington, Vt. 05401.

BURNS, CLYDE L. D
Miss. State Rep.
b. Alcorn, Miss, 1/28/08; married. Polit. & Govt. Pos: Miss. State Rep, currently. Bus. & Prof. Pos: Businessman; farmer. Mem: Mason; Shrine. Rel: Baptist. Mailing Add: Route 1, Glen, Miss. 38846. (1967)

BURNS, DOROTHAE VIVIAN D
b. Bowie, Tex, 6/23/03; d. Robert L. Gray and Ruby B. Houston G; wid; c. Ouida Ann and John R.(deceased). Educ: N.Mex. Normal Univ; Beta Sigma Phi. Polit. & Govt. Pos: Mem. Exec. Bd. Rep. Assembly Dist, Quay Co, N.Mex, 63-66; mem. credential cmt, Dem. Nat. Conv, 64; mem, Econ. Opportunity Act, 64-66; pres, Quay Co. Dem. Ladies Orgn, 65-66. Bus. & Prof. Pos: Sch. teacher, N.Mex, 25-26; Motion Picture Rep, May Co, Los Angeles, Calif, 29-34; pres, First Nat. Bank, 51-56; owner, John Burns Lumber & Hardware and owner and operator, Burns Cross F Ranch, 51-66; inspector, N.Mex. Livestock Bd, Santa Fe, 67-69; mem, Quay Co. Exten. Adv. Coun, 69- Mem: State and local Garden Clubs; adv. bd. and research cmt, N.Mex. Cattle Growers Asn; N.Mex. Farm Bur. Rel: Catholic. Mailing Add: Cross F Ranch, Nara Visa, N.Mex. 88430.

BURNS, FINDLEY, JR.
Dep. Asst. Secy, Bur. Am. Repub. Affairs, Dept. of State
b. Baltimore, Md, 5/4/17; m. to Martha Lobeck. Educ: Princeton Univ, B.A,

39. Polit. & Govt. Pos: Career officer, Dept. State For. Serv, 42-; third secy, Am. Embassy, Madrid, Spain, 42-44, second secy, Brussels, Belgium, 44-45, Warsaw, Poland, 47-49 and Vienna, Austria, 51-54; for. serv. inspector, 54-56; for. affairs officer, 57-58; personnel officer, 58; asst. dep. chief of mission, Berlin, Germany, 58-60; spec. asst. to Dep. Under Secy. for Admin, 60-61; mem. staff, Nat. War Col, 61-62; counsr. for admin, London, Eng, 62-66; U.S. Ambassador to Jordan, 66-67; Dep. Asst. Secy, Bur. of Am. Repub. Affairs, Dept. of State, 68- Bus. & Prof. Pos: Clerk, commercial firm, 39-41. Legal Res: Del Ray Beach, Fla. Mailing Add: American Republics Affairs-Latin America Mgt, Dept. of State, Washington, D.C. 20520.

BURNS, GARY FRANKLIN D
b. Gadsden, Ala, 4/23/33; s. Henry Walter Burns and Elza Clementine Wright B; m. 9/5/53 to Mary Ellen Bell Burns; c. Gary Franklin, Jr, Warren Alvin, Stewart Earl. Educ: Jacksonville State Col, B.S; Univ. of Ala, LL.B, 58. Polit. & Govt. Pos: Ala. State Rep, 62-66. Bus. & Prof. Pos: Lawyer. Mil. Serv: Army Res, Lt, Field Artil, 59-61. Mem: Mason. Rel: Baptist. 1967 Legal Res: 1000 Forest Ave, Gadsden, Ala. 35901. No mailing address available. (1967)

BURNS, HUGH ALLAN D
Chmn. Denver County Dem. Party, Colo.
b. Denver, Colo, 7/28/30; s. O.H. Burns and Mary Gerkin B; m. 8/29/54 to Beverly Mae Faubion; c. Laurel Elisabeth, Hugh Allan, Jr. and Catherine Mary. Educ: Princeton Univ, A.B, 52; Oxford Univ, B.A.(Juris) 54, M.A, 60; Univ. Chicago Law Sch, J.D, 55; Phi Beta Kappa; Quadrangle Club, Rhodes Scholarship. Polit. & Govt. Pos: Precinct committeeman, Denver Co. Dem. Cent. Cmt, Colo, 58-68, capt, 63-68; del, Dem. Nat. Conv, 68; chmn, Denver Co. Dem. Party, 68-; chmn, First Congressional Dist. Dem. Party, 68- Bus. & Prof. Pos: Assoc, Dawson, Nagel, Sherman & Howard, Attorneys-at-law, Denver, Colo, 55-61, partner, 61- Mil. Serv: Entered as Pvt, Army, 56, released as Sgt, 58, after serv. in Hq. Co, Fourth Army, San Antonio, Tex, 56-58, Res, 58-62, Sgt; Commendation Ribbon with Metal Pendant; Good Conduct Medal. Mem: Denver, Colo. and Am. Bar Asns; Bd. of Trustees, Princeton Univ; Denver Club; International House; United Nations Asn. Rel: Unitarian. Mailing Add: 615 Garfield St, Denver, Colo. 80206.

BURNS, HUGH M. D
Calif. State Sen.
b. Arizona. Polit. & Govt. Pos: Calif. State Assemblyman, 36-43; Calif. State Sen, 16th Dist, Fresno Co, 57-, Pres-Pro-Tem, Calif. State Senate, 57-69. Mem: 20-30 Club; Past Grand Knight, K. of C; past pres, Jr. C. of C; Past Exalted Ruler, Elks. Legal Res: 600 W. Shaw, Fresno, Calif. 93704. Mailing Add: State Capitol Bldg, Sacramento, Calif. 95814.

BURNS, JAMES MacGREGOR D
b. Melrose, Mass, 8/3/18; s. Robert Arthur Burns and Mildred Curry Bunce B; m. 5/23/42 to Janet Rose Dismorr Thompson; c. David MacGregor, Timothy Stewart, Deborah Edwards, Margaret Rebecca Antonia. Educ: Williams Col, B.A, 39; Harvard, M.A, Ph.D, 47; London Sch. Econ, Student, 49; Phi Beta Kappa; Delta Sigma Rho. Polit. & Govt. Pos: Mem, Dem. Town Cmt, Williamstown, Mass. and Am. for Dem. Action; mem, Mass. Del, Dem. Nat. Conv, 64-60, 56 and 52; Dem. Cand. for Cong, 1st Dist, Mass, 58; Berkshire Co. Del, Mass. State Conv, 54; staff mem, Hoover Cmn, 48; exec. secy, Non-Ferrous Metals Cmn, NWLB, 42-43. Bus. & Prof. Pos: Chmn, Dept. Polit. Sci, Williams Col, 62-66; faculty, Salzburg,Seminar in Am. Studies, 61, 54; James Phinney Baxter Prof. Hist. and Pub. Affairs; mem, bd. trustees, Stockbridge Sch; chmn. bd. advs, Berkshire Commun. Col, 63-64; assoc. prof, Williams Col, 50-53; asst. prof, 47-50; instructor, 41-42. Mil. Serv: Entered as Pvt, Army, 43, released as M/Sgt, 45, after serv. in 1st Info. and Hist. Serv, Pa. Theater; Bronze Star and 4 Battle Stars. Publn: Presidential Government: The Crucible of Leadership, 66; The Deadlock of Democracy: Four Party Politics in America, 63; Roosevelt: The Lion and the Fox, 56, plus 5 others. Mem: Am. Polit. Sci. Asn; pres, New Eng. Polit. Sci. Asn, 60-61; Am. Civil Liberties Union; Am. Legion; Recipient Tamiment Inst. Award for Best Biography, 56; Woodrow Wilson Prize, 57. Rel: Congregational. Mailing Add: 115 Park St, Williamstown, Mass. 01267. (1967)

BURNS, JOHN A. D
Gov, State of Hawaii
b. Montana, 3/30/09; c. two sons, one daughter. Educ: St. Louis Col. Polit. & Govt. Pos: Capt, Honolulu Police Dept, Hawaii, 41-45; second v.chmn. and chmn, Oahu Dem. Cmt, 48-52; adminstr, Oahu Civil Defense Agency, 51-55; del, Dem. Nat. Cmt, 52, 56, 60 & 64; del. to U.S. Cong, 56-59; Gov. of Hawaii, 62- Bus. & Prof. Pos: Pres. and mgr, Burns & Co. Mil. Serv: Army, 27-28. Mailing Add: State Capitol, Honolulu, Hawaii 96813.

BURNS, JOHN DAVID D
Ore. State Sen.
b. Portland, Ore, 3/3/36; s. James Dunn Burns and Mary C. O'Rourke B; m. 3/23/63 to Brooke Lee Claridge; c. John David, Nancy Brooke, Molly Frances and James Dunn. Educ: Univ. Notre Dame, A.B, 58; Georgetown Univ. Law Center, J.D, 61; Notre Dame Monogram Club. Polit. & Govt. Pos: Asst. to U.S. Sen, Richard L. Neuberger, 59-60, asst. solicitor, Portland Regional Solicitor, U.S. Dept. of Interior, 61-62; asst. dist. attorney, Multnomah Co, Ore, 62-65; Ore. state sen, Multnomah Co, 67-; legal counsel, Democratic State Cent. Cmt, 68- Bus. & Prof. Pos: Partner, Law Firm, Joss, Bosch & Burns, Portland, Ore, 67- Mem: Ore. State and Multnomah Co. Bar Asns; City Club of Portland; Izaak Walton League; Multnomah Athletic Club; Ore. Hist. Soc. Carnegie Grant to Eagleton Inst. of Politics Seminar, Naples, Fla, July, 1969. Rel: Catholic. Legal Res: 2460 S.W. Broadway Dr, Portland, Ore. 97201. Mailing Add: 909 American Bank Bldg, Portland, Ore, 97205.

BURNS, JOHN HOWARD
Dir. Gen, For. Serv, Dept. of State
b. Pauls Valley, Okla, 12/12/13; s. Arthur Parsons Burns and Susan Elizabeth Matthews B; single. Educ: Denison Univ, 31-32; Univ. Okla, B.A, 35. Polit. & Govt. Pos: Secy. to Mem. of Cong, 40-41; v.consul, Juarez, Mex, 41-43 and Belem, Para, Brazil, 43-44; third secy, Am. Embassy, Rio de Janeiro, Brazil, 44-47; first secy, Haiti, 49-52; for. serv. inspector, 52-54; mem. staff, Nat. War Col, 54-55; consul gen, Frankfurt, 55-57; exec. dir, Bur. European Affairs, 57-58; spec. asst, Dep. Under Secy. of State for Admin, 58-60; couns, Bonn, 60-61; U.S. Ambassador, Cent. African Rep, 61-63; spec. asst. Supreme Allied Comdr, Europe, 63-65; U.S. Ambassador, Tanzania, 65-69; Dir. Gen, For. Serv, Dept. of State, 69- Legal Res: Pauls Valley, Okla. 73075. Mailing Add: Dept. of State, Washington, D.C. 20520.

BURNS, JOHN J. D
Chmn, N.Y. Dem. State Cmt.
b. Binghamton, N.Y. 7/12/21; s. William P. Burns and Marie Hennessey B; m. 10/2/48 to A. Teresa McMahon; c. Patrick, Sheila, John, Joseph, Thomas, Marie, Jean, Ann, Daniel, Vincent, Teresa and Robert. Polit. & Govt. Pos: Exec. asst. to mayor, Binghamton, N.Y, 53-57, mayor, 58-65; chmn, N.Y. Dem. State Cmt, 65-; del, Dem. Nat. Conv, 68. Mil. Serv: Entered serv. in Coast Guard, 42, released as Radarman 1/C, 45, after serv. in Atlantic Theater. Mem: Hon. mem, Police Benevolent Asn, Int. Asn. of Fire Fighters and Am. Fedn. of State, Co. and Munic. Employees; Am. Legion; K. of C; Elks; Interracial Asn. Rel: Roman Catholic. Legal Res: 123 Leroy St, Binghamton, N.Y. 13902. Mailing Add: Democratic State Committee, 150 E. 39th St, New York, N.Y. 10016.

BURNS, JOHN M. R
b. Grosse Pointe Shores, Mich, 2/26/24; s. John McNeil Burns and Hattie Grace B; single. Educ: Syracuse Univ, B.A, 50 and M.S, 51; Psi Upsilon. Polit. & Govt. Pos: Pres, N.Y. Young Rep. Club, 59-60; regional dir, 11 East. states, Rep. Nat. Cmt, 60; consult, N.Y. State Div. for Youth, 61; asst. to chmn, Rep. Cong. Cmt, Wash, 62; N.Y. State Assemblyman, 64th Assembly Dist, until 68. Bus. & Prof. Pos: Sales exec, Nat. Broadcasting Co, 51-57; acct. exec. Young & Rubicam, Inc, 57-60; sales exec, Sperry & Hutchinson Co, 62-66; v.pres. for urban affairs, Westinghouse Broadcasting Co, currently. Mil. Serv: Entered as Aviation Cadet, Army Air Force, 43, released as Pfc, 46. Mem: Am. Acad. of Polit. Sci; Am. Legion Post 1093; City Club of ship rowing crew, N.Y. Athletic Club, 52; plays piano and sings. Rel: Christian Scientist. Mailing Add: 305 E. 72nd St, New York, N.Y. 10021.

BURNS, MARY FRANCES D
Chmn, Daviess Co. Dem. Cent. Cmt, Mo.
b. Gallatin, Mo, 7/30/09; d. Virgil Edward Knight and Julia Nichols K; m. 4/28/31 to Russell Burns; c. Conrad Ray and Julia Kaye (Mrs. Stanley Norris); grandchildren, Paul Russell Norris, Julia Rebecca Norris and Kathryn Frances Burns. Educ: Chillicothe Bus. Col, grad. secy. and bookkeeper, 29. Polit. & Govt. Pos: V.chmn, Daviess Co. Dem. Cent. Cmt, Mo, 62-64, chmn, 64-; mem, State Dem. Cmt, 66- Mem: Rebekah Lodge and Past Noble Grand Club; Mo. State Dem. Club; New Frontier Dem. Women's Club. Awarded Ten Year Gold Pin as 4-H Leader. Rel: Methodist. Mailing Add: Route 3, Gallatin, Mo. 64640.

BURNS, ROBERT H. R
S.Dak. State Sen.
b. Philip, S.Dak, 9/15/28; s. Harry D. Burns and Elizabeth Harvey B; m. 6/12/49 to Doris E. Sorensen; c. James, Deborah and Cynthia. Educ: Philip High Sch, S.Dak, 4 years. Polit. & Govt. Pos: V.chmn, S.Dak. Young Rep. League, 54-56, nat. committeeman, 56-58; chmn, Lyman Co. Rep. Cent. Cmt, 57-62; v.chmn, Young Rep. Nat. Fedn, 58-60; S.Dak. State Rep, 60-64; mem, Co. Sch. Bd, 67-68; S.Dak. State Sen, 68- Bus. & Prof. Pos: Mgr, Tri State Milling Co, Vivian, S.Dak, 50-69; owner and mgr, Vivian Tel. Co, 57-69 and Burns Feed Lots, 61-69; dir, Big Band Bldg. Corp, Pierre, S.Dak, 69. Mem: Mason; Elks; Wheat Growers; Isaak Walton League. Named Jaycee Outstanding Young Am. Rel: American Lutheran. Mailing Add: Vivian, S.Dak, 57576.

BURNS, ROBERT JOHN D
b. Oxford, Iowa, 8/22/22; s. John William Burns and Regina Cash B; m. 6/15/44 to Ada Margaret Wilson; c. Michael, Sheila, Anthony, Stephen, Linda, Margery and Maureen. Educ: Univ. Iowa; Univ. Kans. Polit. & Govt. Pos: Co. committeeman, Dem. Party, Iowa; former Iowa State Sen, 21st Dist. Mil. Serv: Entered as Pvt, Army, 43, released as Sgt, 45, after serv. in Rainbow Div; Purple Heart; Combat Inf. Badge; Battle of Rhineland Ribbon and two Battle Stars. Mem: Am. Legion. Rel: Catholic. Mailing Add: 618 Dearborn, Iowa City, Iowa 52240. (1967)

BURNS, WILLIAM LLOYD R
Finance Dir, Gogebic Co. Rep. Cmt, Mich.
b. Central Lake, Mich, 5/20/94; s. Elias Burns and Mary Ann Wilson B; m. 8/18/19 to H. Mable Williams; c. Robert William (deceased), Dorr Harold, Jeanne Louise (Mrs. Bennett), Mary Margaret (Mrs. Tinder) and Roberta Gayle (deceased). Educ: Central Lake High Sch, grad. Polit. & Govt. Pos: Finance dir, Gogebic Co. Rep. Cmt, Mich, 45-; mem, State Central Cmt. at various times; del. or alternate del, Rep. Nat. Conv, 24 years. Bus. & Prof. Pos: Dir, Gogebic Nat. Bank, Ironwood, 12 years, Lake Superior Dist. Power Co, 25 years and Upper Peninsula Develop. Bur, 30 years; pres, Burns Chevrolet-Cadillac, Inc, 27-55; pres, Cent. Credit Corp, 31- and Upper Peninsula Develop. Bur, 41-43. Mem: Kiwanis; Mason; Shrine; Elks; Planning Cmn; others. Man of the Year, Ironwood C. of C, 49. Rel: Methodist. Mailing Add: 215 E. Arch St, Ironwood, Mich. 49938.

BURNS, WILLIAM THOMAS R
Vt. State Rep.
b. South Dorset, Vt, 7/9/99; m. to Elinor Lawrence Sterling; c. One son and one daughter. Educ: Univ. of Vt, B.S. Polit. & Govt. Pos: Town lister, 61-68; mem, Bennington Co. Tax Appeal Bd, Vt, 63-65 & 67-68; Vt. State Rep, 63- Bus. & Prof. Pos: Retired pub. utility v.pres. Mil. Serv: R.O.T.C, WW I. Mem: Am. Gas Asn; Soc. of Gas Operators; Am. Legion; K. of C; Alpha Tau Omega; N.Y. State, Vt. and Nat. Soc. Prfnl. Engrs; Int. Asn. Assessing Off. Rel: Catholic. Mailing Add: South Dorset, Vt. 05263.

BURNS, WILLIAM VERNON D
Chmn, Lincoln Co. Dem. Cent. Cmt, Ark.
b. Star City, Ark, 10/9/19; s. Joseph Lee Burns, Sr. and Dona Bell Majors B; m. 2/7/42 to Hortense Ann Greenham; c. W.V, Jr, James Aaron and Peggy Louise. Polit. & Govt. Pos: Chmn, Lincoln Co. Dem. Cent. Cmt, Ark, 64- Bus. & Prof. Pos: Carpenter, self-employed, 45- Mil. Serv: Entered as Carpenters Mate 2/C, Navy, 42, released as Carpenters Mate 1/C, 45, after serv. in Navy C.Bee's 52nd, Alaska and S.Pac. Rel: Methodist. Mailing Add: Box 411, Star City, Ark. 71667.

BURNSIDE, MAURICE GWINN D
b. near Columbia, S.C, 8/23/02; s. James Walter Burnside and Olivia America McCants B; m. 5/29/37 to Evelyn Jackson Pell; c. Marilyn McCants. Educ: The Citadel, 19-22; Furman Univ, B.S, 26; Univ. of Tex, M.A, 28; Duke Univ, Ph.D, 38; Lambda Chi Alpha; Pi Gamma Mu. Polit. & Govt. Pos: Mem, Parole and Probation Exam. Bd, W.Va, 39-41; head, Workers Educ, 43-45; head, Citizens Recreation Prog, Huntington, 43-45; regional coordinator, Inter-Am. Affairs, W.Va, East and South. Ohio and East. Ky. Cultural and Bus. Rels; br. chief, Nat. Security Agency, 52; U.S. Rep, W.Va, 81st, 82nd and 84th Cong; del. and mem. platform cmt, Dem. Nat. Conv, 60; former asst. to Secy. Defense. Bus. & Prof. Pos: Instr, Greenville High Sch, S.C, 31-32; purchaser, Duke Libr, 33-35; grad. research in off, Gov, S.C, 35-36; instr, Ala. Polytech. Inst, 36-37; prof. polit. sci, Marshall Univ, 37-48, head dept, 41-45; legal rep, Nat. Educ. Asn; mgrs. rep, 53; pres, Tri-State Tobacco Warehouse Co, 56- Publ: Pardon, Parole and Indeterminate Sentence with Special Reference to South Carolina, 38; co-auth, Union Check List of Newspapers of U.S. and Canada; Government of W.Va, 49. Mem: Pres. W.Va. Soc; Am. Polit. Sci. Asn; Am. Pub. Admin. Asn; a founder, Int. Club Am; Am. Asn. Univ. Prof; Soc. Polit. Sci. Asn; Moose; Rotary. Rel: Presbyterian; Elder. Mailing Add: 800 Crescent Dr, Alexandria, Va. 22302. (1967)

BURR, JAMES M. R.
b. Opelousas, La, 3/18/97; s. Thomas Burr and Louvenia Moore B; m. Aug, 1913 to Fannie Enerstine Brown; c. Vera Lucile (Mrs. Brownlee), deceased. Educ: Leland Univ, B.S. in educ, 14; West Sch. of Journalism, Denver; Univ. La. Polit. & Govt. Pos: Agent, U.S. Dept. Agr, La; del. leader, Rep, Nat. Conv, 28, alternate del, 64; former admin. asst. to Committeeman A.J. Wilson, Sixth Ward Rep. Orgn, Ill; former pres, First Cong. Dist. Rep. Club. Bus. & Prof. Pos: Teacher, Booker T. Washington High Sch, Tulsa, Houston, Tex. High Sch. and La. State Normal Schs; teacher and v.prin, Branch Normal Col, Pine Bluff, Ark; Railway Postal Clerk, 6 years; supvr, Negro Schs. of East Baton Rouge; dir. of advert, Houston Informer; publisher and ed, Houston Sentinel, Galveston Sentinel and Ill. Sentinel; employed by Chicago Eve. Am, Chicago Daily Tribune and Chicago Transit Authority. Publ: 'Chicago Transit Authority and It's Negro Employees,' Chicago Courier, 3/63; 'Negro Editor Tells View on Racial Problems', Chicago Am, 8/65. Mem: F&AM, Mason, Prince Hall Affil, Arabic Temple, Shrine, Ancient Egyptian Arabic Order Nobles of the Mystic Shrine. Rel: Baptist. Mailing Add: 7643 S. Wabash Ave, Chicago, Ill. 60219. (1967)

BURRESS, RICHARD THOMAS R
Dep. Counsel to the President
b. Omaha, Nebr, 12/22/22; s. B.J. Burress and Lea Dickinson B; m. 6/16/51 to Jan Eaton; c. Bonny and Lee. Educ: Univ. Omaha, A.B, 44; Univ. Iowa Law Sch, J.D, 48; N.Y. Univ. Grad. Law Sch, M.L, 53. Polit. & Govt. Pos: Spec. agent, Fed. Bur. Investigation, 48-53; dep. asst. gen. counsel, Nat. Labor Rels. Bd, 56-58; minority counsel, House Educ. and Labor Cmt, 61-63; counsel, House Rep. Conf, 65-69; dir, House Rep. Policy Cmt, 65-69; Dep. Counsel to the President, 69- Bus. & Prof. Pos: Attorney, Lockheed Aircraft Corp, 58-61. Mil. Serv: 1st Lt, Marine Corps, 43-46. Mem: Am. and Calif. Bar Asns; Soc. Former Spec. Agents, FBI. Mailing Add: 5521 Mohican Rd, Washington, D.C. 20016.

BURROUGHS, JOHN D
b. Robert Lee, Tex, 4/7/07; s. James Harley Burroughs and Amertius Ashley B; m. 6/14/35 to Jean Mitchell; c. Jane (Mrs. Downs), Nan, Karen (Mrs. Marchman) and Belinda. Educ: Tex. Tech. Col, B.S, 29. Hon. Doctors Degree, Ark. A&M Col. Polit. & Govt. Pos: N.Mex. State Rep, 57-58; Gov, N.Mex, 59-60; del, Dem. Nat. Conv, 68. Bus. & Prof. Pos: Pres, Portales Valley Mills, Inc, Am. Nut. Corp, Lewisville, Tex, Burroughs Broadcasting Co, Albuquerque, N.Mex, v.pres, Audio Equip. Co, owner, KDCE Radio, Santa Fe-Espanola, owner, KRSY Radio, Roswell and partner, KMUL AM-FM Radio, Muleshoe, Tex, currently. Rel: Presbyterian. Legal Res: 1505 S. Abilene St, Portales, N.Mex. 88130. Mailing Add: P.O. Box 329, Portales, N.Mex. 88130.

BURROUS, KERMIT O. R
Ind. State Rep.
b. Peru, Ind, 1931. Educ: Ball State Univ; Ind. Univ. Polit. & Govt. Pos: Ind. State Rep, 60-64 & 67- Bus. & Prof. Pos: Farmer; salesman, Duane Horst Ford Sales. Mem: Bd. of dir, Kiwanis and Miami Co. United Fund. Rel: Methodist; Kokomo Dist. Leader, Mexico Methodist Church. Mailing Add: Route 3, Peru, Ind. 46970. (1967)

BURROWS, JOHN R
b. Davenport, Iowa, 10/18/12; s. Parke Tunis Burrows and Camilla Simmons Wolcott B; m. 4/12/45 to Margaret Eddowes Morris; c. Margaret Anne. Educ: Amherst Col, B.A, 35; Alpha Delta Phi. Polit. & Govt. Pos: Mem. bd, Davenport Commun. Sch. Dist, Iowa, 52-58; precinct committeeman, Rep. Party, 58-64; chmn, Iowans for Goldwater, 64. Bus. & Prof. Pos: With Ralston Purina Co, 35-45, gen. mgr. Davenport Plant, 45-65; partner, McB Farm Co, 62- Mil. Serv: Entered as Lt.(jg), Naval Res, 43, released as Lt, 45, after serv. in electronic supply, Navy Yard, Pearl Harbor and New York, Naval Supply Depot, Oakland and Floating Supply Base, Pac. Fleet, 43-45. Mem: Rotary; Crow Creek Golf Club, Davenport; Crystal Downs Country Club, Frankfort, Mich; Crystal Lake Yacht Club, Frankfort, Mich; Outing Club; Davenport Club; pres. bd. trustees, St. Luke's Hosp; bd. mem, First Fed. Savings & Loan Asn. Rel: Presbyterian. Mailing Add: 3840 Jersey Ridge Rd, Davenport, Iowa 52807.

BURRUSS, ROBERT S, JR. R
Va. State Sen.
b. Lynchburg, Va, 11/9/14; m. to Margaret Brooks. Educ: Va. Polytech. Inst, B.S. Polit. & Govt. Pos: Va. State Sen, 64- Bus. & Prof. Pos: Former dir, Peoples Nat. Bank & Trust Co; mem. adv. bd, First and Merchants Nat. Bank; dir, Keith Furniture Co. and Royal Crown Bottling Co; owner and operator, Ralco Stores, Inc, and R.S. Burruss Lumber Co; lumber mfr. and farmer. Mil. Serv: Army, Corps of Engrs, 5 years, released as Lt. Col. after serv in ETO. Mem: Izaak Walton League; Boonsboro Co. Club; Willis River Hunt Club; Lumber Mfrs. Asn. of Va. Rel: Methodist. Mailing Add: P.O. Box 270, Lynchburg, Va. 24505.

BURSLEY, GILBERT E. R
Mich. State Sen.
b. Ann Arbor, Mich, 2/28/13; s. Philip Everette Bursley and Flora Peters B; m. 1/15/49 to Vivette Mumtaz; c. Philip Everette II. Educ: Univ. Mich, B.A, 34; Harvard Bus. Sch, M.B.A, 36; George Washington Univ, 53-54, post grad. work in int. rels. Polit. & Govt. Pos: Mil. attache, Istanbul, 46-49; with Joint U.S. Mil. Adv. Mission, Athens, 49-52, Army Psychol. Warfare Hq, Wash, 53 and UN Truce Supvr. Orgn, Palestine; sr. mil. adv, Israel-Jordan and Israel-Egypt Mixed Armistice Cmns, 54; Am. consul. and pub. affairs officer in charge U.S. Info. Agency Prog, Belgian Congo, French Equatorial Africa, Ruanda Urundi, Cameroons and Angola, 55-57; consult, World Wide Broadcasting Found, 57; chmn, Ann Arbor Rep. City Cmt, Mich, 59-60; Mich. State Rep, 60-62; Mich. State Sen, 64-, asst. pres. pro tem, Mich. State Senate, 66, chmn, Corp. and Econ. Develop. Cmt, v.chmn, Educ. Cmt. and mem. cmts, Commerce, Sen. Bus. and Interstate Coop, chmn, Int. Commerce Cmt, Urban Mass Transportation Cmt. and Abortion Law Reform Cmt, currently; mem, U.S. Trade and Investment Mission to Cameroons and Ivory Coast, 68. Bus. & Prof. Pos: Asst. dir, Develop. Coun, Univ. Mich, 57-65; assoc, Conductron Corp, 65-66. Mil. Serv: Army, World War II; 3 Campaign Stars; Lt. Col, Korean War. Mem: Elks; Rotary; VFW; Am. Legion; SAR; Gov. of Mich. Soc. of Mayflower Decendants; Mich. Indust. Ambassador; Econ. Club Detroit; C. of C; Univ. Club; Harvard Bus. Sch. Club Detroit; Univ. Mich. Alumni Club; Am. Inst. Archaeol; For. Policy Asn; YMCA; State YMCA Youth in Govt. Cmn; African Studies Asn; Am. Alumni Coun; Adv, Soc. of Am. Magicians; Int. Platform Asn; Mich. Partners Alliance; Nat. Soc. State Legis. Rel: Episcopal. Mailing Add: 2065 Geddes Ave, Ann Arbor, Mich. 48104.

BURT, ADDISON MOORE R
Chmn, Wilkes Co. Rep. Cmt, Ga.
b. Sharon, Ga, 2/14/19; s. Paul Duffy Burt and Dinah Moore B; m. 12/27/38 to Louise Dunnaway; c. Lavenia (Mrs. Goolsby) and Carol. Educ: Crawfordville High Sch, Ga, 4 years. Polit. & Govt. Pos: Councilman, City of Washington, Ga, 66-70; chmn, Wilkes Co. Rep. Cmt, 67- Mil. Serv: Entered as Pvt, Army, 44, released as S/Sgt, 46. Mem: F&AM; Knights of Columbia; Shrine; Rotary Int; Washington-Wilkes Country Club; Farm Bur; Wilkes Co. C. of C.(dir, 65-66); Ga. Caroline Lumberman's Asn.(dir, 67-68). Plaque for Outstanding Commun. Serv, Washington-Wilkes C. of C. Rel: Methodist. Legal Res: 33 Lexington Ave, Washington, Ga. 30673. Mailing Add: P.O. Box 220, Washington, Ga. 30673.

BURT, WARREN BROOKER R
Del. State Rep.
b. N.Y.C, 5/16/34; s. Dr. Con Amore V. Burt and Mazie Brooker B; m. 6/8/56 to Cynthia Jane Henderson; c. David Henderson and John Warren. Educ: Univ. Nebr, B.S, 56; Univ. Va. Law Sch, LL.B, 59; Phi Delta Theta. Polit. & Govt. Pos: Mem. nat. exec. cmt, Young Rep. Nat. Fedn, 65-67, dir, Mid-Atlantic Region, Young Rep. Nat. Fedn, 65-67; v.pres, Del. State Young Rep; pres, New Castle Co. Young Rep; Del. State Rep, 68- Bus. & Prof. Pos: Law Clerk, U.S. Dist. Court, Wilmington, Del, 59-60; assoc, Prickett & Prickett, Law Offices, 60-65; partner, Prickett, Ward, Burt & Sanders, Law Offices, Wilmington, Del. 65- Publ: 'A Recent Trend in Application of the Collateral Source Doctrine:Elimination of Plaintiff Passenger's Double Recovery for Medical Expenses Under Both Liability and Medical Payments Coverages of Defendant Driver's Insurance Contract,' Fedn. Ins. Counsel Quart, fall 65. Mem: Am. and Del. Bar Asns; YMCA (bd. mgrs). Rel: Presbyterian. Legal Res: 4810 Lancaster Pike, Wilmington, Del. 19807. Mailing Add: 1310 King St, Wilmington, Del. 19801.

BURTCH, JACK LEE D
b. Portland, Ore, 5/11/26; s. Jack L. Burtch and Alice Carpenter B; m. 11/8/52 to Edna Doering; c. John L, Kevin D. and Kathleen. Educ: Whitman Col, B.A, 50; Univ. Wash, LL.B, 55; Phi Delta Phi; Sigma Chi. Polit. & Govt. Pos: Dep. prosecuting attorney, Grays Harbor Co, Wash, 56-61; Wash. State Rep, 61-66; corp. counsel, City of Aberdeen, Grays Harbor Co, 66- Mil. Serv: Entered as Seaman 2/C, Navy, 44, released as Seaman 1/C, 46. Mem: Wash. State and Grays Harbor Co. Bar Asns; past pres, Aberdeen Aerie, Eagles; Elks; Lions; VFW; Am. Legion. Rel: Methodist. Mailing Add: 1319 N. F St, Aberdeen, Wash. 98520. (1967)

BURTON, BEN FRANKLIN D
Ark. State Rep.
b. Magnolia, Ark, 8/12/29; s. Elmer Travis Burton and Evalee Smith B; m. 3/24/51 to LaVerne Bolding; c. Boni Catherine, Bruce Bolding, Brooks Franklin and Bevalee. Educ: Ark. Agr. & Mech. Col, Magnolia, Assoc. Educ, 49; State Col, Ark, B.S. in Educ, 51, Univ. Ark, M.S. in Educ, 55; Sigma Tau Gamma. Polit. & Govt. Pos: Ark. State Rep, Dist. 30, 69- Bus. & Prof. Pos: High sch. football coach, DeQueen, Malvern, Hope & Hot Springs High Schs, Ark, 51-65; training dir, Dierks Forests Inc, DeQueen, 66- Mil. Serv: Army Nat. Guard, 206th Tank Bn, 47-49. Publ: 'The Potential Force of High School Athletics,' Tex. Coach, 4/63; 'The Martydom of Andy,' Am. Educ. Asn. J, 10/66. Mem: Nat. Educ. Asn; Int. Work Simplification Inst; Am. Soc. Training and Develop; Lions. Rel: Methodist. Mailing Add: Route 1, DeQueen, Ark. 71832.

BURTON, DANIEL F(REDERICK) DFL
Mem, Constitution Reform Cmn, Minn. Dem-Farmer-Labor Party
b. Chicago, Ill, 10/3/15; s. Clyde Daniel Burton and Hazel Henthorne B; m. 7/22/50 to Verona Devine; c. John Daniel. Educ: Univ. Chicago, M.S, 40, Ph.D, 47; Phi Delta Theta. Polit. & Govt. Pos: Chmn, Sixth Mankato Precinct, Minn. Dem-Farmer-Labor Party, 62; chmn, Second Cong. Dist. Johnson for President Cmt, 64; chmn, Second Dist, Minn. Dem-Farmer-Labor Cand. Cmt, 64 & 66; v.chmn, Minn. Water Resources Rev. Cmt, 66; chmn, Blue Earth Co, Minn. Dem-Farmer-Labor Party, 66-69; mem, Constitution Reform Cmn, Minn. Dem-Farmer-Labor Party, 69- Bus & Prof. Pos: Instr. botany, Miss. State Col, 46-48; asst. prof. biol, Mankato State Col, 48-50, assoc. prof, 50-60, prof, 60- Mil. Serv: Entered as Pvt, Army, 42, released as 1st Lt, Med. Admin. Corps, 46, after serv. in 6th Army, Pac; Pac. and Am. Theatre Ribbons; Philippine Liberation, Japanese Occupation and Good Conduct Medals. Publ: 'Anatomy of the Cotton Leaf and Effects Induced by 2, 4-dichlorophenoxyacetic Acid' Bot. Gazette 111:325-331, 50; The Absorption of Minerals by Plant Leaves,' In: Research Problems in Biology, Investigations for Students, Doubleday, 63. Mem: Am. Asn. Adv. Sci; Am. Inst. Biol.

Sci; Bot. Soc. Am; Ecol. Soc. Am; Am. Fern Soc; Int. Soc. Plant Morphologists; Soc. Econ. Bot; Soc. Tropical Biol; Am. Soc. Pharmacognosy; Minn. Acad. Sci; past pres. Mankato chap, Am. Asn. Univ. Prof; past pres, Mankato Lions; life mem. C.D. Burton Post 808 Am. Legion. Rel: Episcopal. Mailing Add: 512 Hickory St, Mankato, Minn. 56001.

BURTON, DANNY L. R
Ind. State Sen.
b. Indianapolis, Ind, 6/21/38; s. Kindith A. Kelley (stepfather) and Bonnie L. Hardesty K; m. 10/24/59 to Barbara Jean Logan; c. Kelly Jean. Educ: Ind. Univ; Cincinnati Bible Sem. Polit. & Govt. Pos: Rep. precinct chmn, Marion Co, Ind, 64; ward chmn, Marion Co. Rep. Party, 64-65; chmn, Marion Co. Young Rep, 65; Ind. State Rep, Marion Co, 67-68; Ind. State Sen, Marion Co, 69- Bus. & Prof. Pos: Independent ins. agent, Cleveland-Smith Agency, 65-67, Dan Burton Agency, 68- Mil. Serv: Pvt, Army, 57-58. Mem: Mason; Scottish Rite; Murat Shrine; Jaycees. Rel: Christian Church. Mailing Add: 7180 Twin Oaks Dr, Indianapolis, Ind. 46226.

BURTON, EDNA JOSEPHINE D
b. St. Charles, Mo, 6/24/04; d. Herman Yungbluth and Anna Schroeder Y; m. 8/14/24 to Walter E. Burton; Educ: St. Anthony's High Sch, 1 year. Polit. & Govt. Pos: Co-chmn, Okmulgee Co. Dem. Orgn, Okla, 67-69; alternate del, Dem. Nat. Conv, 68; pres, Second. Dist. Fedn. Dem. Women's Clubs, 69- Bus. & Prof. Pos: Operator, Southwest. Bell Tel. Co, 20-24, instructress, 24-29, eve. chief operator, 29-46, chief operator, 46-69. Mem: VFW Auxiliary; Okla. Heart Asn.(mem. bd); C. of C; Okla. and Okmulgee Bus. & Prfnl. Women's Clubs; Red Cross (bd. dirs); Okmulgee Cancer Crusade. Woman of the Year, Okla. Bus. & Prfnl. Women, 55. Rel: Catholic. Mailing Add: 1636 E. Sixth, Okmulgee, Okla. 74447.

BURTON, GEORGE AUBREY, JR. R
Mem, La. Rep. State Cent. Cmt.
b. Texarkana, Ark, 6/21/25; s. George Aubrey Burton and Theo Simmons B; m. 7/31/47 to Joan Cunningham; c. George Aubrey, III and Sandra. Educ: Centenary Col, La, B.S, 51, Study of La. Law, 53-57; pres, Delta Tau Omicron. Polit. & Govt. Pos: Mem, Caddo Parish Rep. Cmt, La, 54-60, chmn, 60-; mem. citizens adv. cmt, Caddo Parish Sch. Bd, 55-56; rapid learner cmt, 57-59; mem. citizen's adv. bd, Shreveport Housing Rehabilitation, 56-57; alternate del, Rep. Nat. Conv, 60; mem, La. Rep. State Cent. Cmt, 60-; chmn, Lyon's for Cong, 61; mem. citizens adv. cmt, Caddo Parish Police Jury, 67-68. Mil. Serv: Entered as A/S, Navy, 43, released as Seaman 1/C, 46, after serv. in 107 NCB, Sea Bees, Pac, 44-46. Mem: Am. Inst. CPA; La. Soc. CPA (membership chmn, 67-68, prfnl. develop. chmn, 68-69); hon. life mem. Shreveport Jaycees (past pres); Sertoma Club (past secy); hon. life mem. Jr. ROTC Parents Club (past pres). Rel: Methodist. Mailing Add: 4423 Creswell Rd, Shreveport, La. 71106.

BURTON, JOE NELSON D
Asst. to Secy. of State, Ga.
b. Colbert, Ga, 2/09/15; s. Ramie Clyde Burton and Clara Hix B; m. 4/06/35 to Nelle Tucker. Educ: City Schs, Athens, Ga. Polit. & Govt. Pos: Asst. to Secy. of State, Ga, 46- Mil. Serv: U.S. Eighth Air Force, World War II, European Theatre, POW, 1 year; 2 Purple Hearts, 4 Air Medals, 5 Battle Stars & 2 Presidential Citations. Rel: Protestant. Mailing Add: Office of the Secretary of State, Capitol Bldg, Atlanta, Ga. 30334. (1967)

BURTON, JULIA ANN D
V.Chmn, Fulton Co. Dem. Party, Ind.
b. St. Louis, Mo, 3/13/22; d. Elmer D. Gordon and Fay DeMont G; m. 12/15/45 to Bryce McNamee Burton; c. Ann Gilbert (Mrs. Raymond Wootten), Linda Kay (Mrs. Michael Hatch), Nanci (Mrs. Larry Beck), Kathleen, Christine Sue and Rebecca Jane. Educ: Ind. Univ, Bloomington, 1 year. Polit. & Govt. Pos: Del, Dem. Nat. Conv, 68; v.chmn, Fulton Co. Dem. Party, Ind, currently. Rel: Baptist. Mailing Add: R.R. 2, Rochester, Ind. 46975.

BURTON, LAURENCE JUNIOR R
U.S. Rep, Utah
b. Ogden, Utah, 10/30/26; s. Laurence S. Burton and Marguerite Roghaar B; m. 9/16/47 to Janice Shupe; c. Carol, Susan, Sally and Laurence Shupe. Educ: Weber Col, A.A, 48; Univ. Utah, B.S. in Polit. Sci, 51; Utah State Univ, M.S. in Polit. Sci, 56; postgrad. work, Georgetown and George Wash. Univs, 57-58. Polit. & Govt. Pos: Asst. to U.S. Rep. Henry A. Dixon, 57-58; state v.chmn, Young Rep, 59; admin. asst. to Gov. George D. Clyde, Utah, 60-62; U.S. Rep, Utah, 63-; del, Rep. Nat. Conv, 68. Bus. & Prof. Pos: Asst. prof. polit. sci, Weber Col, 58-60. Mil. Serv: Navy Air Corps, 45-46. Publ: Publishers, JUCO Mag, 10 years. Mem: Am. Soc. Pub. Admin; Kiwanis; Am. Legion. Rel: Latter-day Saint. Legal Res: 4170 Edgehill Dr, Ogden, Utah. Mailing Add: Room 1705 Longworth Bldg, Washington, D.C. 20515.

BURTON, LOUIS WYATT R
Del. State Rep.
b. Millsboro, Del, 10/2/34; s. Theodore Burton, Jr. and Olive Brittingham B; m. 4/22/66 to Nanci Holden Radcliffe; c. Kristen C. and Michael L. Educ: Gen. Motors Inst, 55. Polit. & Govt. Pos: Del. State Rep, 35th Dist, 67- Mem: Past pres, Del. Auto Dealers Asn, 63-64; Franklin Lodge 12, AF&AM, Nur Temple; Del. Consistory; Tall Cedars of Lebanon; Ninth Dist. Rep. Club; Kent and Sussex Scottish Rite Club; charter mem, Sussex Co. Country Club. Rel: Episcopal. Mailing Add: R.D. 4, Box 118 A, Georgetown, Del. 19947.

BURTON, MARION B. R
b. Little Rock, Ark, 11/23/30; s. Melven Boyd Burton, Sr. and Helen Tedstrom B; m. 8/27/55 to Ann Bowker Tyler; c. Allyson Leigh, Jenifer Lynne, George Tyler and Amelia Jynkens. Educ: Pa. State Univ, B.S, 52; Univ. Mich. Law Sch, LL.B, 58; Sigma Pi Sigma; Scabbard and Blade; Quarterdeck Soc; Phi Alpha Delta; Phi Gamma Delta. Polit. & Govt. Pos: Clerk to Chief Justice of Ark. Supreme Court, 59-61; campaign mgr, Ricketts for Gov, Ark, 62; asst. to state chmn, Rep. State Cmt, 62-63; chmn, Pulaski Co. Rep. Cmt, 64-66; campaign dir, Rockefeller for Gov, 66; exec. secy, Ark. State Gov, 67. Bus. & Prof. Pos: Jr. engr, Temco Aircraft Corp, 56; attorney, Russell & Hurley, 61-62; Legal Counsel to Rep. Nat. Committeeman, 63- Mil. Serv: Entered as Midshipman, Navy, 48, released as Lt.(jg), 56; Comdr, Naval Res, 60-; Navy Unit Citation; UN Ribbon; Korean Campaign Ribbon with two Campaign Stars; Nat. Defense Medal. Mem: Am. Legion; Naval Res. Officers Asn. Commercial pilot. Rel: Methodist. Legal Res: 8001 Evergreen, Little Rock, Ark. 72207. Mailing Add: 530 Tower Bldg, Little Rock, Ark. 72201.

BURTON, MELVIN MATTHEW, JR. R
Mem, D.C. Rep. Cent. Cmt.
b. Salisbury, N.C, 2/14/29; s. Melvin M. Burton and Ivory Walker B; m. 12/2/55 to Jacqueline Scott. Educ: Howard Univ, A.B, 50, LL.B, 53; Georgetown Univ, 56-58; Phi Beta Sigma. Polit. & Govt. Pos: Precincts co-chmn, D.C. Exec. Cmt. for Rockefeller, 68; mem, D.C. Rep. Cent. Cmt. and ward-coordinator, 68-, chmn. housing cmt, 69-; mem, Speaker's Cmt. Inaugural and Law and Legis. Cmt. Inaugural, 69. Bus. & Prof. Pos: Partner, McDaniel, Burton & Daniels, Lawyers, 56- Mil. Serv: Entered as 2nd Lt, Air Force, 54, released as 1st Lt, 56, after serv. in Judge Adv. Legal Off; Nat. Defense Serv. Medal; Good Conduct Medal. Mem: Nat. and Wash. Bar Asns; Howard Univ. Law Alumni Asn; Am. Civil Liberties Union. Rel: Baptist. Mailing Add: 700 Seventh St. S.W, Washington, D.C. 20024.

BURTON, PHILLIP D
U.S. Rep, Calif.
b. Cincinnati, Ohio, 6/1/26; married; c. one daughter. Educ: Univ. of South. Calif, A.B, 47; Golden Gate Law Sch, LL.B, 52. Polit. & Govt. Pos: Former nat. officer, Young Dem; Calif. State Assemblyman, 56-64; del. to Atlantic Treaty Asn. Conf, France, 59; U.S. Rep, Calif, 64-; del, Dem. Nat. Conv, 68; founder, Calif. Dem. Coun; secy, 88th Cong. Dem. Club; regional v.chmn, Dem. Study Group. Bus. & Prof. Pos: Attorney, admitted to practice before US Supreme Court, 56. Mil. Serv: Korean Vet. Mem: Past pres, George Washington High Alumni Asn; Blue Key. Legal Res: San Francisco, Calif. Mailing Add: U.S. House of Rep, Washington, D.C. 20515.

BURTON, THOMAS LAWSON R
Chmn, Elbert Co. Rep. Cmt, Ga.
b. Bowman, Ga, 8/5/22; s. Joseph Homer Burton, Sr. and Tolver Grimes B; m. 1/13/46 to Mary Jo Johnson; c. Mary Thomas, Margaret Joan and Linda Laine. Polit. & Govt. Pos: Chmn, Elbert Co. Rep. Cmt, 64- Bus. & Prof. Pos: Owner and mgr, Branding Iron Restaurant, Elberton, Ga, 46-66. Mil. Serv: Entered as Pvt, Army Air Corps, 42, released at T/Sgt, 45, after serv. in 15th Air Force, ETO, 44-45; Air Medal with Silver Cluster; Air-Combat Medal, Balkans and Germany; Rome-Arno Campaign Ribbon; South. and North. France Campaign Ribbons. Mem: Elks Lodge 1100; VFW Post 5456; Am. Legion Post 14. Legal Res: 83 Carey St, Elberton, Ga. 30635. Mailing Add: P.O. Box 213, Elberton, Ga. 30635. (1967)

BURTON, WALTER WELDON D
b. Covington, Va, 7/14/34; s. Walter Grant Burton and Florence Hanna B; m. 8/22/53 to Phyllis Hinty; c. Teresa Page, Walter Kirkwood, David Scott, Beth Anne and John Hinty. Educ: Wash. and Lee Univ, B.S. in commerce, 56, LL.B, 59; Phi Delta Phi; Who's Who in Am. Cols. and Univs; Beta Theta Phi. Polit. & Govt. Pos: Pres, Mercer Co. Young Dem, W.Va, 59-60; mem, W.Va. Dem. Exec. Cmt, 60-61; pres, Young Dem. of W.Va, 61-65; alternate del, Dem. Nat. Conv, 68. Bus. & Prof. Pos: Partner, Burton, Griffith, Burton & Burkett, 58-61; Burton & Burkett, 61- Mil. Serv: Entered as 2nd Lt, Army, 57, released as 2nd Lt, 57, recalled to active duty as 1st Lt, 61, released as 1st Lt, 62; Capt, Army Res, discharged, 65. Mem: Am, W.Va. and Mercer Co. Bar Asns; Am. Judicature Soc; Elks; Moose. Rel: Episcopal. Legal Res: City View Heights, Princeton, W.Va. 24740. Mailing Add: Law Bldg, Princeton, W.Va. 24740.

BURTON, WILLIAM SMITH R
b. Salt Lake City, Utah, 10/10/15; s. Harold Hitz Burton and Selma Smith B; m. 12/18/65 to Anne R. Hillman; c. Susan (Mrs. Bruce J. Shapiro), Betsey (Mrs. George C. Wick, Jr) and Dianne (Mrs. George S. Sherwin). Educ: Bowdoin Col, B.S. magna cum laude, 37; Harvard Law Sch, LL.B, 40; Phi Beta Kappa; Delta Kappa Epsilon. Polit. & Govt. Pos: Ohio State Rep, 51-54; mem. bd. educ, Shaker Heights, Ohio, 55-63, pres, 61-63; mem. charter cmn, Cuyahoga Co, 59. Bus. & Prof. Pos: Assoc, Garfield, Baldwin & Jamison, 40-51; partner, Arter & Hadden, 51- Mil. Serv: Entered as Ens, Naval Res, 42, released as Lt, 45, after serv. in Naval Intel, 42-43; Gunnery Officer in Pac. Area, 44-45; Navy Commendation Ribbon; Presidential Unit Citation; Purple Heart; Pac. and Atlantic Theater Ribbons; Philippine Liberation Medal. Mem: Am. Bar Asn.(chmn. standing cmt. aeronaut. law, 54-58 & 63-64); Ohio State and Cleveland Bar Asns; fel. Am. Bar Found. Rel: Unitarian. Mailing Add: 2761 N. Park Blvd, Cleveland Heights, Ohio 44118.

BURTT, THEODORE C. R
b. Deerfield, N.H; married; c. three. Educ: Drake Univ; Northeast. Univ. Polit. & Govt. Pos: Town Sch. cmt. 6 years. Bus. & Prof. Pos: Pres. Gutterson & Gould, Inc; Rowland Industs. Mil. Serv: Air Force, Bomber pilot, World War II. Mem:Civic and fraternal orgns. Mailing Add: 62 Whittier St, Andover, Mass. 01810. (1967)

BURWELL, LINA D
b. Birmingham, Ala, 8/31/90; d. Eugene Weinberg and Emma Rehwaldt W; m. 12/3/12 to Earle G. Burwell; c. Eleanor Borden (Mrs. Maurice L. Snider), Orrin Earle, Jerome Ellis and Robert Randolph. Polit. & Govt. Pos: Active in Dem. Party for 30 years; former precinct committeewoman, Casper, Wyo, State Dem. V.Chmn. and mem, Dem. Nat. Cmt; Dem. Presidential Elector, 48. Mem: Wesleyan Serv. Guild (co-ordinator); Cmt, Nat. Found. Infantile Paralysis. Rel: Methodist. Mailing Add: 1022 S. Wolcott St, Casper, Wyo. 82601.

BUSBEE, GEORGE D. D
Ga. State Rep.
b. Vienna, Ga, 8/07/27; s. Perry Green Busbee and Nell Dekle B; m. 9/05/49 to Mary Elizabeth Talbot; c. Beth Talbot, Jan Guest, George Dekle Jr. and Jeff Talbot. Educ: Duke Univ; Univ. Ga, B.B.A, 49, LL.B, 52; Phi Delta Theta. Polit. & Govt. Pos: Ga. State Rep, 57-, Majority Leader, Ga. House of Rep. Bus. & Prof. Pos: Attorney. Mil. Serv: Navy, World War II. Rel: Baptist. Legal Res: Albany, Ga. Mailing Add: Georgia State House of Representatives, Atlanta, Ga. 30334.

BUSBY, ALLEN JOSEPH R
Wis. State Sen.
b. Chicago, Ill, 3/6/00; s. Joseph Thomas Busby and Ellen Kenny B; m. 7/10/29 to Linda Marie Schubert; c. Dr. Thomas Allen and Judy Lee (Mrs. Coffey). Educ: Milwaukee State Normal Sch, cert, 20; Univ. Wis, B.A, 22, M.A, 25, LL.B, 28, J.D, 28; Gamma Eta Gamma. Polit. & Govt. Pos: Wis. State Assemblyman, 31-32, 33 & 35-37; village attorney, West Milwaukee, 32-67; Wis. State Sen, Eighth Dist, 37- Bus. & Prof. Pos: Sch. prin, 22-24; high sch. teacher, 28-33; attorney, Busby, Dineen & Luehring. Publ: Co-auth, Rosenberry Apportionment Act. Mem: Milwaukee and Wis. Bar Asns; F&AM; RAM; RSM; hon. mem. C. of C; hon. mem. VFW; S.W. Allis Advan. Asn; W.Milwaukee Bus. & Advan. Asn. Outstanding Civic Serv. Trophy, Village of W.Milwaukee; Munic. Off. & Legis. Citations, Wis. Legis; Golden Eagle Award; Dedicated Serv. Plaque, U.S. Olympic Cmt; Distinguished Alumnus Award, Univ. Wis-Milwaukee. Rel: Protestant. Mailing Add: 1673 S. 53rd St, Milwaukee, Wis. 53214.

BUSBY, HORACE D
b. Ft. Worth, Tex; m. to Mary. Educ: Univ. Tex, 47; ed, Daily Texan. Polit. & Govt. Pos: Admin. officer, Senate Preparedness Subcmt, 48-51; secy. to the President's Cabinet; spec. asst. to President Johnson on Appointments, Correspondence, Nat. Security Affairs and Preparedness, 64-65. Bus. & Prof. Pos: Correspondent, Int. News Serv; Am. Int. Bus. Research Corp; ed, Tex. Businessman. Author of LBJ 'Gettysburg Add,' 5/30/63. Rel: Protestant. Legal Res: 121 Ednor Rd, Sandy Spring, Md. 20860. Mailing Add: 1100 Connecticut Ave. N.W, Washington, D.C. 20036. (1967)

BUSCH, HENRY W. R
b. Bristow, Iowa, 1920; s. Henry Busch and Bilda B; m. 1946 to Maurine Busch; c. Beverly, Paul. Educ: Allison High Sch, 37. Polit. & Govt. Pos: Former Iowa State Rep. Bus. & Prof. Pos: Farming, real estate bus. Mil. Serv: Army, 103rd Inf, 38 months. Mem: C. of C; Farm Bur; Amvets; Rotary. Rel: Methodist. Mailing Add: Route 2, Waverly, Iowa. 50677. (1967)

BUSCH, VIRGINIA MARIE D
Secy, Fourth Cong. Dist. Dem. Party, Colo.
b. Greeley, Colo, 6/28/21; d. Robert N.G. Hibler and Della Hood H; m. 12/4/65 to Melvin Frank Busch; c. Bettye (Mrs. Robert F. Paden) and Billy Scott Harrod. Educ: Greeley High Sch, Colo, G.E.D, 64; Aims Col. Adult Div, Ft. Lupton, Colo, 68-69. Polit. & Govt. Pos: Ft. Lupton precinct committeewoman, Weld Co. Dem. Party, Colo, 52-58; justice of the peace, Ft. Lupton, Colo, 58-63; v.chmn, Weld Co. Dem. Cent. Cmt, 59-66 and 69-; secy, Fourth Cong. Dist. Dem. Party, 64-; ex-officio mem, Dem. State Exec. Cmt, 69-; ex-officio mem. exec. cmt, Weld Co. Dem. Cent. Cmt, 69- Bus. & Prof. Pos: Clerk, Assessor's Office, Greeley, Colo, 63-65. Mem: Jane Jefferson Dem. Club; League of Women Voters; Evening Belles Toastmistress Club; Am. Legion Auxiliary (girls state cmt); Ft. Lupton Garden Club (chmn, Blue Star Mem. Highway Cmt). Awarded Grant from Sears, Roebuck & Co. for Blue Star Roadside Park, 3/19/69. Rel: Lutheran. Legal Res: 930 McKinley Ave, Ft. Lupton, Colo. 80621. Mailing Add: P.O. Box 141, Ft.Lupton, Colo. 80621.

BUSH, ALVIN C. R
Pa. State Rep.
b. Philipsburg, Pa, 1/22/24; s. Alvin R. Bush and Lucinda Mattern B; m. to Elizabeth Crooks; c. four. Educ: Univ. of N.C, B.S. Polit. & Govt. Pos: Mem, Williamsport Traffic Cmn, Pa; mem, exec. cmt, Muncy Valley Hosp; past dir, Lycoming Co. Young Rep; Pa. State Rep, 60- Bus. & Prof. Pos: Automobile dealer, farm operator; dir, Lowry Elec. Co; dir, North. Cent. Bank and Trust Co; pres, Wyno Sales Co; pres, Alvin Bush Motors; pres, Loyal Leasing Co. Mem: Phi Gamma Delta; chmn, N.Cent. Div, Pa. Heart Asn; chmn, Lycoming Co. Cancer Dr, 60; chmn, Lycoming Valley March of Dimes, 65; past dir, Lycoming Co. Tuberc. Asn; Red Cross; past pres, Pa. Guernsey Breeders Asn; past dir, Am. Guernsey Cattle Club; dir, Lycoming Co. Consolidated Sportsmen; dir, Pa. Automotive Asn; dir. N.Cent. Automobile Club; F&AM Lodge 755; Williamsport Consistory. Rel: Methodist. Mailing Add: R.F.D. 2, Muncy, Pa. 17756. (1967)

BUSH, BAKER HOSKINS D
Alderman, Helena, Ark.
b. Helena, Ark, 8/1/36; s. Jamer R. Bush and Margaret Hoskins B; m. 8/27/67 to Nicole Dane Holmes. Educ: Memphis State Univ, B.S; Kappa Sigma. Polit. & Govt. Pos: Alderman, Fifth Ward, Helena, Ark, 66- Mem: Memphis State Alumni Asn; Farm Bur. Rel: Roman Catholic. Legal Res: Neil Rd, Helena, Ark. 72342. Mailing Add: 325 York St, Helena, Ark. 72342.

BUSH, DOROTHY VREDENBURGH D
Secy, Dem. Nat. Cmt.
b. Baldwyn, Miss, 12/8/16; d. Will Lee McElroy and Lany Holland McE; m. 1/13/62 to John W. Bush. Educ: George Wash. Univ, 35; Miss. State Col. for Women, B.S, 37; past pres, Beta Sigma Phi. Polit. & Govt. Pos: Asst. secy, Young Dem. of Am, 41, v.pres, 43-48, acting pres, 44; nat. committeewoman, Ala. Young Dem, 41-50; secy, Dem. Nat. Conv, 44-68; secy, Dem. Nat. Cmt, 44- Bus. & Prof. Pos: Dir, Coastal Caribbean Oils & Minerals, Ltd; mem. bd. of adv, Int. Univ. of Commun. Mem: Life mem, Ark. Traveler and Jane Jefferson Nat. Fedn. of Bus. and Prfnl. Women. Rel: Baptist. Mailing Add: 4201 Cathedral Ave. N.W, Washington, D.C. 20016.

BUSH, ELMER OGDEN R
b. DeLancey, N.Y, 9/14/98; s. Clarence A. Bush and Anna Bostwick B; m. 5/9/25 to Ella Vitt; c. Mrs. Robert Lewis, Jr, Mrs. Richard Storrer, Joan Salenda and Elmer Ogden, Jr. Educ: Del. Acad, N.Y; Univ. Buffalo, Dental Sch. Polit. & Govt. Pos: Cmnr, Harness Racing Cmn, 65-; N.Y. State Sen, 56-64; N.Y. State Assemblyman, 33-37. Prof. Pos: Mem, Del. Acad. Sch. Bd, Delhi, N.Y, 5 yr. term. Mil. Serv: Pvt, Army, 18. Mem: Am. Col. of Dentists; pres, 6th Dist. Dental Soc; Am. Legion; Mason; Ft. Orange Club; Farm Bureau. Rel: Presbyterian. Legal Res: DeLancey, N.Y. 13752. Mailing Add: Delaware St, Walton, N.Y. 13856.

BUSH, EUGENE LORIN R
b. Idaho Falls, Idaho, 11/13/28; s. Arthur Harold Bush and Grace Jeppson B; m. 12/4/53 to Ann Marie Eggleson; c. Katherine, Ronald, Elizabeth T, Joan T, Carolyn, John and Emily. Educ: Univ. Idaho, LL.B, 51; Phi Alpha Delta; Beta Theta Pi. Polit. & Govt. Pos: Justice of the Peace, Bonneville Co, Idaho 54-56, prosecuting attorney, 58-62; Idaho State Rep, 64-68. Mem: Am. and Idaho State Bar Asns; Elks. Rel: Latter-day Saint. Mailing Add: 200 11th St, Idaho Falls, Idaho 83401. (1967)

BUSH, GEORGE R
U.S. Rep, Tex.
b. Milton, Mass, 6/12/24; m. 1/6/45 to Barbara Pierce; c. George W, John E, Neil M, Marvin P. and Dorothy W. Educ: Yale Univ, B.A. in econ, 48; Phi Beta Kappa; Delta Kappa Epsilon. Polit. & Govt. Pos: V.chmn, GOP Task Force Job Opportunity; chmn, Harris Co. Rep. Party, Tex; del, Rep. Nat. Conv, 64 & 68; U.S. Rep, Tex, 66-, mem, Ways and Means Cmt, U.S. House of Rep; del, Rep. Nat. Conv, 68. Bus. & Prof. Pos: V.pres, Zapata Petroleum Co, 52-59; pres. and chmn, Zapata Off-Shore Co, 54-66. Mil. Serv: Entered as Ens, Naval Res, 42, released as Lt.(jg), 45, after serv. as Navy Pilot; Distinguished Flying Cross; Three Air Medals. Rel: Episcopal. Legal Res: 5000 Longmont, Houston, Tex. 77027. Mailing Add: 1608 Longworth House Office Bldg, Washington, D.C. 20515.

BUSH, HILARY ASHBY D
b. Excelsior Springs, Mo, 6/21/05; s. Aubrey Charles Bush and Clair Grantham B; m. 7/16/32 to Frances Stromberg; c. Charles R. Educ: William Jewell Col, A.B, 27; Univ. Kansas City, LL.B, 32. Polit. & Govt. Pos: Lt. Gov, Mo, 60-64. Bus. & Prof. Pos: Partner, Johnson, Lucas, Bush & Snapp, 32- Mil. Serv: 42-45, Lt. Col. Mem: Am, Mo. and Kansas City Bar Asns; Mason (32°). Rel: Methodist. Mailing Add: 1006 Grand Ave, Kansas City, Mo. 64106.

BUSH, JOHN WILLIAM D
b. Columbus, Ohio, 9/17/09; s. William Hayden Bush and Esther Brushart B; m. 1/13/62 to Dorothy McElroy; c. Jan Hayden (Mrs. Jennings) and Emily Ann (Mrs. Bennett). Educ: Va. Polytechnic Inst, B.S; v.pres, Cotillion Club; bus. mgr, The Bugle, 31. Polit. & Govt. Pos: Mem, City Coun, Portsmouth, Ohio, 42, 43 & 44; state purchasing supt, Gov. Lausche's Cabinet, 49-57; dir. of commerce, Gov. Di Salle's Cabinet, 59-61; cmnr, Interstate Commerce Cmn, 66- Bus. & Prof. Pos: Pres, Ohio Syst, Inc, 46- and John W. Bush, Inc, 57- Mem: Pres, Nat. Asn. of State Purchasing Officials, 54. Rel: Episcopal. Legal Res: 1551 Kinney's Lane, Portsmouth, Ohio 45662. Mailing Add: 4201 Cathedral Ave, N.W, Washington, D.C. 20016.

BUSH, PRESCOTT SHELDON R
b. Columbus, Ohio, 5/15/95; s. Samuel Prescott Bush and Flora Sheldon B; m. to Dorothy Walker; c. Prescott Sheldon, George Herbert Walker, Nancy (Mrs. Alexander Ellis, Jr), Jonathan James and William Henry Trotter. Educ: Yale, M.A, 17. Polit. & Govt. Pos: Chmn, Nat. War Fund Campaign, 43-44; chmn, Conn. Rep. Finance Cmt, 48; del-at-lg, Rep. Nat. Conv, 48, 56 & 60, chmn, Platform Cmt, 56; U.S. Sen, Conn, 52-63. Bus. & Prof. Pos: Partner, Brown Bros, Harriman & Co, 30-; trustee, Yale Univ; past dir, C.B.S, Prudential Ins. Co. of Am. Mil. Serv: Capt, Army, F.A, AEF, 17-19. Mem: Pres, U.S. Golf Asn, 35. Rel: Episcopal. 1967 Legal Res: Greenwich, Conn. No mailing address available. (1967)

BUSHEMI, MARION J. D
Ind. State Rep.
Educ: Gary Bus. Col, elec. eng. course, $2\frac{1}{2}$ years; grad, Dale Carnegie Course Human Rels; Hazlett Leadership Course. Polit. & Govt. Pos: Ind. State Rep, 59-60 & 63-; app. by President Kennedy as chmn, Cmn. on New Jobs and New Growth in Commun, 61; chmn, Cmn. on Utilization of Available Lake Co. Labor, 63. Bus. & Prof. Pos: Former operator, restaurant bus; steelworker. Mil. Serv: Ind. Nat. Guard, Cpl, World War II. Mem: Life mem. Dale Carnegie Alumni Asn; life mem. Nat. Soc. State Legislators; CIO Local 1014; Moose; Izaak Walton League; Better Boating Asn; Dem. Clubs. Rel: Catholic. Mailing Add: 4101 Fillmore St, Gary, Ind. 46408.

BUSHEY, WALTER O. D
N.H. State Rep.
b. Waterville, Maine, 4/16/89; wid; c. 6. Educ: Morgan Bus. Col. Polit. & Govt. Pos: N.H. State Rep, 55- Bus. & Prof. Pos: Tailor. Mem: Fish & Game Club. Rel: Catholic. Mailing Add: State St, Groveton, N.H. 03582. (1967)

BUSHFIELD, VERA CAHALAN R
b. Miller, S.Dak, 8/9/89; d. Maurice Francis Cahalan and Mary Ellen Conners C; m. to Harlan John Bushfield, wid; c. Mary Janith, John Pearson and Harlan John, Jr. Educ: Univ. of Minn; Dakota Wesleyan Univ; Stout Inst, Wis. Polit. & Govt. Pos: U.S. Sen, S.Dak, 47-48. Mem: Eastern Star; Bus. & Prfnl. Women's Club; PEO; Woman's Club; Garden Club. Rel: Presbyterian. Mailing Add: 209 Third Ave. E, Miller, S.Dak. 57362.

BUSING, EDWARD E. D
b. Denver, Colo, 1929; m. 4/3/50 to Rachel Van Langen; c. Delayne, Edward, Jr, Jody Jane and Janis Ann. Educ: Stanhope Iowa High Sch. Polit. Pos: Iowa State Rep-66; Hamilton Co. Bd. of Supvrs (Past Chmn). Bus. & Prof. Pos: Contractor. Mil. Serv: U.S. Army, 24th Inf. Div, Korea, 50-51. Mem: Lions Club (Past Pres.); Am. Legion. Rel: Lutheran. Mailing Add: Stanhope, Iowa. 50246. (1967)

BUSS, WILLIAM Conservative
b. 1896. Educ: Country Sch. Polit. & Govt. Pos: Cand, Minn. State Rep. Bus. & Prof. Pos: Retired carpenter and builder. Mil. Serv: Vet, WWI. Mem: Carpenters Local 1382; Odd Fellows 13; William T. McCoy Post 92 Am. Legion; Barracks 923 of Vets. of WWI; Olmstead Co. Mem. Asn. Rel: Our Savior's Lutheran Church. Mailing Add: 829 9th St, N.W, Rochester, Minn. 55901. (1967)

BUSSIE, VICTOR D
Chmn, Cmt. on Polit. Educ, La. AFL-CIO
b. Montrose, La, 1/27/19; s. Christopher Bussie and Fannie Lacaze B; m. 4/4/37 to Gertrude Foley; c. Deanna Jeanne (Mrs. Love) and Carolyn Lee (Mrs. Huff). Educ: Shreveport La. Pub. Schs. Polit. & Govt. Pos: Chmn, Cmt. on Polit. Educ, La, AFL-CIO, 57-; mem, Nat. Civil Defense Adv. Coun, Nat. Defense Exec. Res, Labor Adv. Cmt, Off. Emergency Planning, Southwest. Regional Manpower Adv. Cmt, U.S. Dept. Labor, Nat. Budget and Consultation

Cmt; mem, La. Cmn. on Govt. Ethics; mem, Gov. Adv. Cmt. to La. Tax Cmn, Gov. Cmt. on Employ. of Handicapped, Citizens' Adv. Cmt. on La. Educ, Adv. Coun, Div. Employ. Sec, bd. dirs, Coun. for Better La; mem, Caddo Parish Educ. Study Cmt, 50-52, nine-mem. charter cmn. which wrote Home Rule Charter for Shreveport, Gov. Parolee Rehab. Cmt, Gov. Educ. Cmt, La. Reorgn. Study Cmn, Spec. Legis. Cmt. on Cent. Acct, Receipts and Disbursements, State of La; del, Dem. Nat. Conv, 68. Bus. & Prof. Pos: Hoseman, Shreveport Fire Dept, 40-52; chief, Fire Prev. Bur, 52-56; pres, La. AFL-CIO, 56-; chmn. bd. dir, Gulf Union Corp, 57- Mil. Serv: Entered as Seaman, Navy Air Force, 43, released as CPO, 46; Lt, La. Nat. Guard, 50-53. Mem: Pres, Shreveport Cent. Trades and Labor Coun, 47-56; pres, Shreveport Fire Fighters Asn, 46-56; coun. trustees, Gulf South Research Inst; Bus. Sch. Coun, Tulane Univ; Int. Platform Asn; hon. mem, Beta Gamma Sigma, Col. Bus. Admin, La. State Univ; bd. dir, Baton Rouge Red Cross, Speech and Hearing Found, United Cerebral Palsy Asn, Baton Rouge Safety Coun, United Fund, YMCA, Family Counseling Serv. and La. Asn. for Ment. Health; Am. Legion, Nat. Sponsor's Cmt. of United Way in Health. Rel: Church of Christ. Legal Res: 815 S. Acadian Thruway, Baton Rouge, La. 70806. Mailing Add: P.O. Box 58, Baton Rouge, La. 70821.

BUSSIERE, ANDREW JOSEPH R
b. Lowell, Mass, 12/22/00; s. Joseph F. Bussiere and Mary Alice Lagasse B; m. 11/21/27 to Rose Anna Fillion; c. Wilfred G, Louise E, Pauline F, Richard R, Robert E. and Janet M. Polit. & Govt. Pos: N.H. State Rep, 67-68. Bus. & Prof. Pos: Owner, Elite Laundry Co, 37-60. Mem: Eagles; Moose; Jaffrey Rod & Gun Club; Jaffrey Bd. of Trade; Jaffrey Civic Club. Rel: Roman Catholic. Mailing Add: 21 Aetan St, Jaffrey, N.H. 03452. (1967)

BUSSIERE, EMILE R. D
b. Manchester, N.H, 5/16/32; s. Joseph Bussiere and Emerentienne B. Gagnon B; m. 8/16/69. Educ: St. Anselm's Col, N.H, 49-51; Boston Col, LL.B, 54. Polit. & Govt. Pos: U.S. Cmnr, N.H, 60-63; co. attorney, Hillsborough Co, N.H, 63-68; Dem. nominee, Gov. N.H, 68. Bus. & Prof. Pos: Attorney, N.H, 54- Mil. Serv: Entered as Pvt, Army, 56, released in 58, after serv. in Qm.C. Mem: N.H. and Manchester Bar Asns; Nat. Asn. Dist. Attorneys (dir); Elks; K. of C. Rel: Catholic. Legal Res: 585 Lincoln St, Manchester, N.H. 03104. Mailing Add: 1008 Elm St, Manchester, N.H. 03101.

BUSTERUD, JOHN A. R
b. Coos Bay, Ore, 3/7/21; m. 4/18/53 to Anne Witwer B; c. John W, James P. and Mary Holt. Educ: Univ. Ore, B.S; Yale Univ. Law Sch, LL.B; Phi Beta Kappa. Polit. & Govt. Pos: State pres, Young Rep, 55-56; State Assemblyman, Calif, 56-62; Rep. Nominee, State Treas, 62; mem, Calif. Constitution Rev. Cmn, 65- Bus. & Prof. Pos: Attorney-at-law. Mil. Serv: Army, 43-46; Army Res, Lt. Col, Retired. Mem: V.pres, Commonwealth Club of Calif; Bar Asns. of San Francisco; Am. Acad. Polit. Sci; Univ. Club of San Francisco; Chi Psi; Phi Delta Phi. Mailing Add: 102 Mountain View Ave, San Rafael, Calif. 94901.

BUSWELL, DAVID HASTINGS R
Mem, Md. State Rep. Cent. Cmt.
b. Chicago, Ill, 6/25/34; s. Otis Leroy Buswell and Eleanor Haser B; m. 10/15/60 to Susan Rowe; c. Janice and Scott. Educ: Univ. Ariz, 52-53; Univ. Ill, 53-55; North. Ill. Univ, B.S, 57; Alpha Phi Gamma; Phi Kappa Psi. Polit. & Govt. Pos: Pub. rels chmn, Draft Goldwater Cmt, Md, 64; pres, Howard Co. Young Rep. Club, 64-65; mem, adv. coun, Congressman Gilbert Gude, 66; mem, Howard Co. and Md. State Rep. Cent. Cmts, 66-; alternate del, Rep. Nat. Conv, 68. Bus. & Prof. Pos: Sr. ed, Martin-Marietta Corp, 60-62; staff ed, Asphalt Inst, 62-64; spec. asst. to the dir, Hwy. Res. Bd, Nat. Acad. Sci, 64- Mil. Serv: Journalist, Coast Guard, 57-59; Lt, Navy Res, 66-; U.S. Coast Guard Pistol Expert. Mem: Int. Coun. Indust. Eds; Construction Writers Asn; Mid. Atlantic Asn. Indust. Eds; Navy League U.S; Naval Reserve Asn; AF&AM; Nat. Press Club. Ed. of the Year, Mid. Atlantic Asn. of Indust. Eds, 65. Rel: United Church of Christ. Mailing Add: 5617 Old Lawyers Hill Rd, Elkridge, Md. 21227.

BUTCHER, JAKE F. D
Chmn, Union Co. Dem. Exec. Cmt, Tenn.
b. Maynardville, Tenn, 5/8/36; s. Cecil H. Butcher, Sr. and Kate Walters B; m. 4/6/62 to Sonya Wilde; c. Maria Paige, Scarlett Ann and Jacob Bradford. Educ: Univ. Tenn, 53-55 and 59-62; Phi Sigma Kappa. Polit. & Govt. Pos: Chmn, Union Co. Dem. Party, Tenn, 67-; del, Dem. Nat. Conv, 68. Bus. & Prof. Pos: Mem. bd. dirs, Union Co. Bank, Maynardville, 50-; pres, Butcher Oil Co, 64-68; pres, First Union Develop. Corp, 64-; chmn. bd, First Nat. Bank of Anderson Co, Lake City, 68-; pres, JFB Petroleum & Land Co, Maynardville, 68-; cmnr, Powell-Clinch Utility Dist, Lake City, 68-; mem. bd. First Union Finance Corp, Maynardville, currently. Mil. Serv: Marine Corps, 55-58, Korea and Japan. Mem: Nat. Oil Jobbers Coun.(cmt. on mkt. research); Sen. Club; Deane Hill Country Club; Oak Ridge Country Club; Union Co. Young Dem. Club (organizer and past pres); Young Dem. Club Tenn; charter mem, Union Co. Jr. C. of C; E. Tenn. Heart Asn.(bd. dirs); Union Co. Heart Fund (chmn, 68); Elks. Rel: Methodist; Bd. of Trustees, Maynardville United Methodist Church. Legal Res: Route 2, Hwy. 33, Maynardville, Tenn. 37807. Mailing Add: First National Bank of Anderson County, Lake City, Tenn. 37769.

BUTCHER, WILLIAM ARTHUR D
b. Detroit, Mich, 7/30/41; s. Arthur Butcher and Effie Shortinghise B; m. 7/1/63 to Pauline Des Jardins; c. Kristin. Educ: Calif. State Col, Long Beach, B.A, 63. Polit. Pos: Campaign Mgr, Co. Cmt. to Re-elect Gov. Brown, Calif, 66; campaign mgr, Cmt. to elect Richard T. Hanna, Congressman, 64 and 62; admin. asst. to U.S. Rep. Richard T. Hanna, 65-66 and 63-64. Rel: Protestant. Mailing Add: 8081 Westminster Ave, Westminster, Calif. 92683. (1967)

BUTCHKO, JOHN THADDEUS D
Mem, Dem. State Cent. Cmt, Calif.
b. Cleveland, Ohio, 9/13/37; s. John Butchko and Bertha Rybka B; single. Educ: Univ. South. Calif, B.S.L, 60, LL.B, 62, LL.M, 64; Phi Beta Kappa; Phi Kappa Phi; Order of the Coif. Polit. & Govt. Pos: Mem, Los Angeles Co. Dem. Cent. Cmt, 66-68; v.pres, Burbank Dem. Club, 67-68; Dem. nominee, 27th Cong. Dist, Calif, 68; mem, Dem. State Cent. Cmt. Calif, 68- Bus. & Prof. Pos: Assoc. ed, South. Calif. Law Rev, 61-62; law clerk, Judge William M. Byrne, U.S. Dist. Court, 62-63; assoc, Richards, Watson & Hemmerling, Attorneys, Los Angeles, 63-65; attorney at law, Burbank, 66-68; assoc, Dryden, Harrington & Swartz, Attorneys, Los Angeles, 68- Publ: 'Monetary Awards for Unfair Competition in California,' South. Calif. Law Rev, spring 61. Mem: Los Angeles Co. Bar Asn; State Bar Calif; South. Calif. Asn. Defense Counsel; K. of C; Burbank Human Rel. Coun; San Fernando Valley Fair Housing Coun; Burbank Dem. Club. Rel: Catholic. Mailing Add: 123 N. Myers St, Burbank, Calif. 91506.

BUTERA, ROBERT JAMES R
Pa. State Rep.
b. Norristown, Pa, 1/21/35; s. Harry Butera and Anne Constable B; m. to Constance J. Hanson; c. Robert J, Jr. and Nina Hanson. Educ: Univ. Pa, Wharton Sch. Commerce and Finance, B.S. in econ, 56; Dickinson Sch. Law, LL.B, 59; Beta Theta Phi. Polit. & Govt. Pos: Pa. State Rep, 63-, majority whip, Pa. House of Rep, 67-69, minority whip, 69-70. Bus. & Prof. Pos: Attorney, mem. of Montgomery Co. Courts, Pa. Superior and Supreme Courts; partner, Huganir, Butera and Detwiler Law Firm, 60-; ed, Montgomery Co. Law Reporter, 61-66. Mil. Serv: Pa. Nat. Guard, 59, Pfc. Mem: Montgomery Co. and Pa. Bar Asns. Rel: Roman Catholic. Legal Res: 1926 Brandon Rd, Norristown, Pa. 19401. Mailing Add: 516 DeKalb St, Norristown, Pa. 19401.

BUTH, MARTIN D. R
Mich. State Rep.
b. Comstock Park, Mich, 10/18/17; m. 6/10/43 to George Ann Shaw; c. Martin D, III and George S. Educ: Mich. State Univ, grad. Polit. & Govt. Pos: Former trustee, Plainfield Twp, Mich; Mich. State Rep, 59- Bus. & Prof. Pos: Dairy farmer. Mem: Past pres, Mich. Purebred Dairy Cattle Asn; Mich. Farm Bur; Rotary. Rel: Episcopal. Mailing Add: 5531 Skyway Dr, Comstock Park, Mich. 49321.

BUTLER, ALGERNON LEE R
b. Clinton, N.C, 8/2/05; s. George Edwin Butler and Eva Boykin Lee B; m. 6/5/35 to Josephine Lydia Broadwell; c. Eva Josephine (Mrs. Louis B. Daniel, Jr.), Algernon Lee, George Edwin. Educ: Trinity Col; Univ. of N.C. (Assoc. Editor, Law Review, 27-28); Sigma Nu. Polit. & Govt. Pos: U.S. Dist Judge East. Dist, N.C, 59-; Mem, Rep. Exec. Cmt, N.C, 42-59; Asst. Chmn, 46-50; Del, Rep. Nat. Conv, 48, 40, 36; Co. Attorney, Sampson Co, 38-51; Organizer 1st Chmn, Young Rep. Clubs, N.C, 32-34; Mem, N.C. Gen. Assembly, Sampson Co, 31. Bus. & Prof. Pos: Gen. practice, Clinton Co, 28-59; admitted to N.C. Bar, 28. Mem: Am, N.C, Sixth Dist, Sampson Co. Bar Asns; Rotary. Rel: Episcopalian (vestry). Mailing Add: 312 College St, Clinton, N.C. 28328. (1967)

BUTLER, BAYFORD DUNCAN R
Mem, Calif. Rep. State Cent. Cmt.
b. Oakland, Calif, 4/21/38; s. Humphrey Bayford Butler and Mildred Lillie Duncan B; m. 6/27/64 to Nancy Jean Grandin; c. Bayford Duncan, Jr. Educ: Stanford Univ, A.B, 61; Los Arcos Eating Club. Polit. & Govt. Pos: Dir. and Newsletter ed, Monterey Peninsula Young Rep, Calif, 65, pres, 65-66; assoc. mem, Calif. Rep. State Cent. Cmt, 65-69, mem, 69-; First v.pres. and prog. chmn, Monterey Co. Young Rep, 66-67, pres, 67-68; assoc. mem, Monterey Co. Rep. Cent. Cmt, 67-; tri-co. regional coordinator, Rafferty for U.S. Sen. Campaign, Monterey, Santa Cruz and San Benito, 68; chmn, Monterey Co. Welfare Cmn, 68- Bus. & Prof. Pos: Travel agent, Lynden LaVere Travel Agency, San Francisco, Calif, 62 & 63-64; salesman, Equitable Life Assurance Soc, 64; admin. asst, Dudley Swim, Carmel, Calif, 65-; corporate treas. and secy, Butler Prod, Inc, San Francisco, 68- Mil. Serv: Entered as Airman Basic, Air Force Res, 61, released as S/Sgt, 67, after serv. in 349th Troop Carrier Wing. Mem: Newsletter ed, Upper Noe Valley Neighborhood Coun, 64; dir, Monterey Peninsula, Jr. C. of C, 66-67; dir. and corporate secy, Monterey Peninsula Taxpayers Asn, Inc, 65-69; corporate secy, Monterey Co. Found. for Conserv, 66-, Pacific Grove City Study Cmts, Regional Govt, Alcoholic Beverage Control Ord, 67-68. Rel: Christian. Mailing Add: Apt. 26E, Solano Park, Davis, Calif. 95616.

BUTLER, CHARLES FREDERICK R
U.S. Rep, Int. Civil Aviation Orgn.
b. Quincy, Mass, 7/10/33; s. Percy T. Butler and Ethel Sutermeister B; m. 6/21/59 to Alice Ryan; c. Charles F, Jr, Colin M, Christopher R. and Alison F. Educ: Boston Univ, A.A. and A.B, 59; George Wash. Univ. Law Sch, J.D. with honors, 64; Sigma Phi Epsilon. Polit. & Govt. Pos: Air transport exam, Civil Aeronaut. Bd, 59-63; admin-legis. asst, U.S. Rep. Hastings Keith, Mass, 63-65; U.S. Rep, Int. Civil Aviation Orgn, 69- Bus. & Prof. Pos: Wash. rep. for int. proc. and asst. v.pres, East. Airlines, 65-69. Mil. Serv: Entered as E-1, Army, 53, released as E-4, 55, serv. in 1264th Army, Camp Kilmer, N.Y. Mem: Mass. Bar; Nat. Lawyers Club; Capitol Hill Club; Int. and Nat. Aviation Clubs. Cert. of Honor Award, Civil Aeronaut. Bd. Rel: Protestant. Legal Res: 5933 One Penny Dr, Fairfax Station, Va. 22039. Mailing Add: 1323 Redpath Ct, Montreal, Que, Can.

BUTLER, EARL DENNETT D
b. Shelltown, Md, 10/10/18; s. Leroy Charles Butler and Anna Powell B; m. 3/2/39 to Gladys Florence Powell; c. Dennett Lee. Polit. Pos: Register of Wills, 66-; Md. State Del, 61-66. Mem: Elks; Lions; Farm Bureau; Marion Fire Dept; Country Club. Rel: Protestant. Mailing Add: Marion, Md. 21838. (1967)

BUTLER, ELLIOTT ARTHUR R
b. Wood Lake, Nebr, 7/4/12; s. Eli Emmett Butler and Cora Blanche Rider B; m. 10/30/38 to Elizabeth Eleanor DeVoe; c. Dennis Eugene, Kathleen Marie (Mrs. Fox) and Elliott Arthur, II. Educ: Univ. Nebr, Lincoln, 1 year; Iowa State Univ, D.V.M, 38; Cardinal Guild. Polit. & Govt. Pos: Committeeman, Rep. Party, Iowa, 62-64; chmn, Pottawattamie Co. Rep. Party, 66-68; chief, Dir. of Animal Indust, Iowa Dept. of Agr, 68- Mil. Serv: Entered as 1st Lt, Army, 43, released as Capt, 46, after serv. in Vet. Corps, Am. Theatre. Mem: Am. Vet. Med. Asn; Iowa Vet. Med. Asn.(exec. bd, 60-62, legis, cmt, 62-69); Mason; Eastern Star; Farm Bur; Kiwanis; YMCA (pres, local chap, mem. bd, W.Cent. Area). YMCA Century Award; 4-H Proj. Leaders Award. Rel: Presbyterian. Mailing Add: 8835 N. W. Polk City Drive, Ankeny, Iowa 50021.

BUTLER, FRANCIS JESSE R
N.Dak. State Sen.
b. Brocket, Ramsey Co, N.Dak, 10/2/11; s. Matthew Daniel Butler and Alvina

J. Anderson B; m. 9/10/31 to Doris Yvonne Bourassa; c. Judith (Mrs. Wallace R. Nikle), Matthew D, David J. and Gregory F. Educ: Univ. N.Dak, 29-31. Polit. & Govt. Pos: Planning and zoning cmnr, Grand Forks, N.Dak, 45-52; N. Dak. aeronaut. cmnr, Bismark, 59-60; N.Dak. State Sen, 67- Bus. & Prof. Pos: Chmn. bd, Butler Machinery Co, Fargo, currently. Mem: Caterpillar Dealers Asn; Assoc. Equip. Distributors; N.Dak. Water Users Asn; mem. bd, Dakota Med. Found; Minneapolis Athletic Club; K. of C; Elks; Fargo Country Club; U.S. C. of C; Boy Scouts; Fargo C. of C. (mem. bd. & past pres); subcmt. on finance and taxation and subcmt. on transportation, N.Dak. Legis. Coun. Eagle Scout and Silver Beaver Scout, Boy Scouts; Fargo Jaycees Boss of the Year, 67; Outstanding Bus. Leader award, N.Dak. State Univ, 67-68. Rel: Catholic. Mailing Add: 1753 Eighth St. S, Fargo, N.Dak. 58102.

BUTLER, G. HILTON D

b. 5/10/98. Polit. & Govt. Pos: Dir, Selective Serv, Tenn; adj. gen; cmnr. of revenue; cmnr. of safety, 3 terms. Publ: Several books and articles on state govt. Mem: Past comdr, Post 5, Am. Legion; Shrine. Awarded Legion of Merit, World War II. Rel: Methodist. Mailing Add: c/o State Capitol, Nashville, Tenn. 37219. (1967)

BUTLER, JOHN R

b. Boston, Mass, 1/13/36; s. Morris John Butler and Dorothy Ash B; m. 12/30/67 to Nancy Richardson. Educ: St. Lawrence Univ, B.S, 61; Am. Inst. For. Trade, B.F.T, 64; Delta Phi Epsilon; Sigma Chi. Polit. & Govt. Pos: Mem. bd. dirs, Hawaii State Young Rep, 65, asst. treas, 66, chmn, 67 & 68; dir, Hawaii TAR Prog, 65-; Rep. v.chmn, 14th precinct, 15th dist, 67-68; mem, Hawaii Rep. State Cent. Cmt, 67-68; del. and mem. nat. platform cmt, Rep. Nat. Conv, 68; nat. chmn. state publicity cmt, Young Rep. Nat. Found, 68-69. Bus. & Prof. Pos: Pac. area mgr, Allyn & Bacon Publ. Co, Honolulu, 64- Mil. Serv: Entered as Pvt, Army, 54, released as Pfc, 57, after serv. in Second Bn. Combat Team, Iceland, 55-57. Mem: Jr. C. of C; Hawaii Yacht Club; Oahu Young Rep. Club; Capitol Hill Club. Outstanding Young Rep, Hawaii, 67; Bronze, Silver and Gold Awards for Outstanding Serv. to Rep. Party, Young Rep. Nat. Fedn, 68. Rel: Congregational. Mailing Add: 3173 Beaumont Woods Place, Honolulu, Hawaii 96822.

BUTLER, LUNA E. D

b. Siloam, Mo, 12/13/04; m. 1929 to Pauline M. Whittington; c. Eddie, (Mrs. Joan Pool). Educ: Pub. schs, Gentry and Harrison Cos. Polit. & Govt. Pos: Mo. State Rep, 62-66; previous terms, 44-60; Gentry Co. collector and treas, 36-44; city collector of Albany, 32-36. Bus. & Prof. Pos: Blue grass seed operator; automobile salesman. Mil. Serv: Nat. Guard, 8 years. Mem: Field Sec. for Mo. Farmers Asn, 61-62. Rel: Baptist. Mailing Add: E. Clark, Albany, Mo. 64402. (1967)

BUTLER, MANLEY CALDWELL R

Va. State Del.

b. Roanoke, Va, 6/2/25; m. to June Nolde B. Educ: Univ. of Richmond, A.B, 48; Univ. Va. Law Sch, 50; Phi Beta Kappa. Polit. & Govt. Pos: Chmn, Roanoke City Rep. Party, Va, 60-61; Va. State Del, 62-, Minority Leader, Va. House of Del, 66- Bus. & Prof. Pos: Attorney. Mil. Serv: Ens, Naval Res. Mem: Va. State Bar; Roanoke, Va. and Am. Bar Asns; Tau Kappa Alpha; Omicron Delta Kappa; Phi Gamma Delta; Raven Soc; Order of the Coif. Rel: Episcopal; Vestryman, St. John's Episcopal Church. Mailing Add: P.O. Box 2887, Roanoke, Va. 24001.

BUTLER, PAUL CLINTON R

b. Hudson, Ky, 5/29/16; s. Clint Butler and Mary Awbrey B; m. 7/24/48 to Evelyn Amelia Keeffner; c. Brett Dwayne, Deborah Kay and Pamela Gayle. Educ: Univ. of Louisville, 36-37. Polit. & Govt. Pos: Rep. precinct committeeman, Harned, Ky, 59-69; secy, Second Cong. Dist. Rep. Party, 63-69; chmn, Breckenridge Co. Rep. Party, 67-69. Bus. & Prof. Pos: Farmer, 38-52; decorating contractor, 52-67. Mil. Serv: Entered as Pvt, Army, 42, released as Sgt, 46, after serv. in 18th Malaria Surv. Unit, C.B.I, 43-46; Good Conduct, Am. Theater, Asiatic Pac. and North. Burma Campaign Medals. Mem: Mason; VFW; Am. Farm Bur. Rel: Protestant. Mailing Add: Route 1, Box 60, Harned, Ky. 40144.

BUTLER, PERCY R

s. Drury Morton Butler and Naomi Chandler B; m. 6/27/25 to Mary Susan Crittenden; c. Bobby R. (deceased), Marcheta H. (Mrs. Brannon), Naomi Sue (Mrs. Walker), Mae Frances (Mrs. Moore) and Elizabeth Ann. Educ: Okla. Sch. Accountancy, Law and Finance, 27-29 & 58. Polit. & Govt. Pos: Chmn, Mayes Co. Rep. Cent. Cmt, Okla, 50-53; Rep. nominee for U.S. Rep, 54 & 56, for State Treas, 58, and for Corp. Cmnr, 60; Okla. State Rep, Dist. 76, 64-66. Bus. & Prof. Pos: Timekeeper, City of Tulsa Water Line, 24; rural mail carrier, U.S. Post Off. Dept, 28-49; independent oil operator, 50-66. Mil. serv: Entered Home Guards, 17 and 18, Pryor, Okla, World War I. Mem: Mason Lodge 513, Tulsa Consistory, Mason (32°), Akdar Shrine; Indian Territory Cowboys & Pioneers Asn. Received posthumous award of Purple Heart for son Bobby R. Butler killed in Germany, 45. Rel: Methodist. Mailing Add: 4916 East Haskell Place, Tulsa, Okla. 74115.

BUTLER, RICHARD C, JR. R

Mem, Pulaski Co. Rep. Cmt, Ark.

b. Little Rock, Ark, 9/21/37; s. Richard C. Butler and Gertrude Remmel B; single. Educ: Wash. & Lee Univ, B.A, 59; Univ. Mo, Columbia, summer 61; Univ. Ark, LL.B, 62. Polit. & Govt. Pos: Page, Rep. Nat. Conv, 52, asst. sgt-at-arms, 56 & 60, alternate del, 68; pres, Wash. & Lee Univ. Young Rep. Club, 58-59; pres, Univ. Ark. Young Rep. Club, 60-61; Young Rep. Nat. Committeeman, Ark, 61-62; mem, Pulaski Co. Rep. Cmt, 62-; exec. dir, Ark. State Rep. Cmt, 64, chmn. rules cmt, 68; mem, Ark. State Rep. Cmt, Pulaski Co, Ark, 66-68; elec. cmnr, Pulaski Co, 68- Bus. & Prof. Pos: Assoc, House, Holmes & Jewell Law Firm, 63-68; asst. trust officer, Commercial Nat. Bank, Little Rock, 68- Mil. Serv: Entered as Pvt, Army Res, 62, released as Sp-6, 68, after serv. in 431st Civil Affairs Co. Mem: Delta Theta Phi; Am, Ark. and Pulaski Co. Bar Asns; Am. Judicature Soc; Country Club of Little Rock; dir, Big Brothers of Pulaski Co, Inc; dir, Quapaw Quarter Asn; Pres, Ark. State Festival of Arts, 69-70; mem. gen. bd, Ark. Counc. of Churches. Rel: Methodist. Legal Res: 405 E. Tenth St, Little Rock, Ark, 72202. Mailing Add: P.O. Box 624, Little Rock, Ark. 72203.

BUTLER, ROBERT NEIL D

b. New York, N.Y, 1/21/27; s. Fred Butler and Easter Carole B; m. 9/18/50 to Diane McLaughlin; c. Anne Christine, Carole Melissa and Cynthia Lee. Educ: Columbia Col, B.A, 49; Columbia Univ. Col. Physicians and Surgeons, M.D, 53; Nacoms Hon. Soc; Phi Gamma Delta. Polit. & Govt. Pos: Research physician, Nat. Insts. Health, 55-62; sr. surgeon, U.S. Pub. Health Serv, 55-62; del, Dem. Nat. Conv, 68; active mem, D.C. Dem. Party; D.C. Dem. for Peace and Progress; Nat. Pres. Campaign, 68. Bus. & Prof. Pos: Mem. faculty, George Wash. Med. Sch, 59-; research psychiatrist and gerontologist, Wash. Sch. Psychiat, 62-; mem. faculty, Wash. Psychoanalytic Inst, 62-; consult, St. Elizabeths Hosp, 63-, Nat. Inst. Ment. Health, 67- and Dept. Pub. Welfare, 68- Mil. Serv: Entered as Seaman, Merchant Marine, 45, released as Ens, 47, after serv. in Atlantic, Mediterranean, Pac. Theatres; Lt. Comdr, U.S. Pub. Health Serv, 62-; Atlantic, Mediterranean and Pac. Ribbons. Publ: Human Aging, Pub. Health Serv, 63; 'The Life Review,' Psychiatry, 63; 'Life Cycle,' In: Aging and Modern Society, Am. Psychiat. Asn, 68. Mem: Group for the Adv. of Psychiat; Am. Psychiat. Asn; Gerontological Soc; Am. Geriatrics Soc; Bd, Nat. Ballet of Wash, 62-; bd, Nat. Coun. on the Aging, 69- Rel: Episcopal. Mailing Add: 3815 Huntington St, N.W, Washington, D.C. 20015.

BUTLER, WARREN HAROLD R

Spec. Asst. to the Asst. Secy. for Model Cities, Dept. of Housing and Urban Develop.

b. Paterson, N.J, 9/23/36; s. Harold M. Butler and Alice Jahn B; m. 8/29/64 to Kristin Alma Westberg; c. Alison Paige. Educ: Northwest. Univ, B.A. with honors in hist, 58; Yale Univ. Law Sch, LL.B, 61; Univ. Calif, Los Angeles, 61-62; Deru, Northwest. Univ. Polit. & Govt. Pos: Legis. asst. to U.S. Rep. William B. Widnall, N.J, 62-69; spec. asst. to Secy. George Romney, Dept. of Housing and Urban Develop, 69, spec. asst. to the Asst. Secy. for Model Cities, 69- Publ: 'Administering Congress: The Role of the Staff,' Pub. Admin. Rev, 3/66; 'A New Approach to Low and Moderate Income Home Ownership,' Rutgers Law Rev, fall 67. Mem: Am. Polit. Sci. Asn; Fed. Bar Asn; D.C. Bar. Am. Polit. Sci. Asn. Cong. Staff Fel. Rel: Lutheran. Legal Res: 47 Amherst Court, Glen Rock, N.J. 07452. Mailing Add: 4100 W St, N.W, Washington, D.C. 20007.

BUTLER, WENDELL P. D

State Supt. Pub. Instr, Ky.

b. Sulphur Well, Ky, 12/18/12; s. Henry Butler and Pearl Pace B; m. 1/15/47 to Edna Ford; c. Wendell Ford and twins, Rendell and Kendell. Educ: West. Ky. State Col, B.A, 36; Univ. Ky, M.A, 50; Phi Delta Kappa; Kappa Delta Pi. Polit. & Govt. Pos: Ky. State Sen, 47-51; State Supt. Pub. Instr, Ky, 52-55 & 60-; cmnr. agr, Ky. Dept. Agr, 64; del, Dem. Nat. Conv, 68. Bus. & Prof. Pos: Teacher pub. schs, Metcalfe Co, Ky, 31-36; supt. schs, 38-42; pres. and mgr, Sch. Serv. Co. Mil. Serv: Navy. Mem: Nat. and Ky. Educ. Asns; Farm Bur; Am. Legion; VFW; Mason. Rel: Methodist. Mailing Add: 121 Crittendon Rd, Frankfort, Ky. 40601. (1967)

BUTROVICH, JOHN R

Alaska State Sen.

b. Fairbanks, Alaska, 1910; married; c. One. Polit. & Govt. Pos: Alaska Territorial Sen, 44-58; Alaska State Sen, 62- Bus. & Prof. Pos: Owner, ins. agency. Mem: Pioneers of Alaska; Elks. Mailing Add: 1039 Fifth Ave, Fairbanks, Alaska 99703. (1967)

BUTT, BETTIE LOU R

b. Crane, Mo, 12/12/18; d. Andrew Jackson Stephens and Mae Moore S; m. 1/10/42 to Dr. William G. Butt; c. Stephen G. Educ: Green Forest High Sch, Ark. Polit. & Govt. Pos: Del, Rep. State Conv, Mich, 63, 64, 65 & 66; alternate del, Rep. Nat. Conv, 64; chmn, Isabella Co. Rep. Cmt, 65-68. Mem: Am. Cancer Soc; Cent. Mich. Commun. Hosp. Auxillary; Univ. Dames. Rel: Methodist. Mailing Add: Rt. 2, Box 207, Escanaba, Mich. 49829.

BUTTENWIESER, BENJAMIN JOSEPH D

b. N.Y.C, 10/22/00; s. Joseph L. Buttenwieser and Caroline Weil B; m. 10/3/29 to Helen Lehman; c. Lawrence B, Carol (Mrs. Loeb, deceased), Peter L. and Paul A. Educ: Columbia Col, B.A, 19. Polit. & Govt. Pos: U.S. Asst. High Cmnr. for Germany, Dept. of State, 49-51; chmn, N.Y. State-N.Y.C. Fiscal Rels. Cmt, 56; del, Dem. Nat. Conv, 68. Bus. & Prof. Pos: Gen. partner, Kuhn, Loeb & Co, 32-49, limited partner, 52- Mil. Serv: Entered as Lt, Navy Res, 42, released as Comdr, 45, after serv. in Pac. Area; Presidential Unit Citation. Mem: C. of C. (Exec. cmt, N.Y.C.). Rel: Jewish. Legal Res: 450 E. 52nd St, New York, N.Y, 10022. Mailing Add: 40 Wall St, New York, N.Y. 10005.

BUTTERFIELD, ALEXANDER PORTER R

Dep. Asst. to the President

b. Pensacola, Fla, 4/6/26; s. Horace Bushnell Butterfield and Susan Armistead Alexander B; m. 9/9/49 to Charlotte Mary Maguire; c. Leslie Carter (deceased), Alexander Porter, Jr, Susan Carter and Elisabeth Gordon. Educ: Univ. Calif, Los Angeles, 46-48; Univ. Md, European Div. and College Park, B.S. in Int. Affairs, 56; Nat. War Col, 66-67; George Washington Univ, M.S. in Int. Affairs, 67; Sigma Nu. Polit. & Govt. Pos: Dep. Asst. to the President, 69- Mil. Serv: Entered as Aviation Cadet, Air Force, 48, retired as Col, 69, after serv. as fighter pilot and mem. skyblazers, U.S. jet aerobatic team, Europe, 49-53; aide to comdr, Fourth Allied Tactical Air Force, NATO, 54-55; opers. officer, interceptor squadron, 55-56; acad. instr, U.S. Air Force Acad, 57-59; sr. aide to comdr-in-chief, U.S. Pac. Air Forces, 59-62; comdr. jet fighter squadron, S.E. Asia, 62-64; policy planner, Hq, 64-65; mil. asst. to Spec. Asst. to Secy. Defense, 65-66; sr. U.S. mil. rep. and CINCPAC rep, Australia, 67-69; Legion of Merit; Distinguished Flying Cross; Bronze Star; Air Medal with Four Oak Leaf Clusters; Joint Services Commendation Medal; Air Force Commendation Medal; Army Commendation Medal, plus unit awards, and serv. ribbons for Germany, Laos, Vietnam and Antarctica; campaign medals, rated as Command Pilot and Parachutist. Scholastic honors and athletic awards during school years. Mem: Acad. Polit. Sci. Rel: Episcopal. Legal Res: 272 I Ave, Coronado, Calif. 92118. Mailing Add: 7416 Admiral Dr, Alexandria, Va. 22307.

BUTTERFIELD, ALTON 'TONY' D

b. Salt Lake City, Utah, 6/20/10; m. to Lucile; c. four. Educ: Jordan High Sch, Salt Lake City. Polit. & Govt. Pos: Former Wyo. State Rep. Bus. &

Prof. Pos: Locomotive engineer for UP. Mem: Brotherhood of Locomotive Firemen & Engineermen; UP Oldtimers Club; Odd Fellows No. 4; Quarterback Club; Carbon Co. Conserv. Club; mgr, coach, Rawlins baseball clubs. Rel: Latter-day Saint; Sunday Sch. supt, 14 years. Mailing Add: 1113 Alder St, Rawlins, Wyo. 82301. (1967)

BUTTERS, SHIRLEY SUE D
Dem. Nat. Committeewoman, Mo.
b. Pike Co, Mo, 8/11/34; d. William J. Moore, Jr. and Velma S. Simpson M; m. 8/10/52 to David L. Butters; c. David M, Cary L. and Richard L. Educ: Bowling Green High Sch, grad, 52. Polit. & Govt. Pos: Secy, Pike Co. Young Dem, Mo, 53, v.pres, 54 and pres, 65-68; corresponding secy, Mo. Young Dem, 67, admin. v.pres, 68; del, Dem. Nat. Conv, 68; coordinator, Mo. State Dem. Cmt, 68 & 69; Dem. nat. committeewoman, Mo, 68- Bus. & Prof. Pos: Dep. collector revenue, State License Off, 65- Mem: Eastern Star (Past Matron, Bowling Green Chap); VFW Auxiliary. Rel: Baptist. Mailing Add: 311 N. Main Cross, Bowling Green, Mo. 63334.

BUTTERWORTH, JAYNE BURBRIDGE R
Committeewoman, Fla. Rep. State Exec. Cmt.
b. East Liverpool, Ohio, 6/21/18; d. Earl S. Burbridge and Rachel M. Cooper; m. 11/14/41 to J. Donald Butterworth; c. Tim E. Educ: Miami Univ, B.S. in Bus. Admin, 36-40; Chi Omego. Polit. & Govt. Pos: Committeewoman, Fla. Rep. State Exec. Cmt, currently; v.chmn, Co. Exec. Cmt, 62-67; prog. chmn, Fla. Fedn. of Rep. Women, 63-65; del, Rep. Nat. Conv, 64. Bus. & Prof. Pos: Sales prom, Hollywood Maxwell Co, 41-46; sales mgr, Bunny Bear Prod, 46-48; personal shopper, Cohen's, Jacksonville, Fla, 58-61; real estate broker, McKinney-Green, Inc, Gainesville, 63- Mem: Gainesville Bd. Realtors; Fla. Asn. of Realtors, Bus. and Prfnl. Women; League of Women Voters: Gainesville Garden Club; Univ. Faculty Club; dir, Alachua Co. Cancer Soc; Univ. Women's Club. Rel: Presbyterian. Mailing Add: 2244 N.W. Ninth Place, Gainesville, Fla. 32601. (1967)

BUTTERWORTH, MIRIAM BROOKS D
Committeewoman, Conn. Dem. Party.
b. Hartford, Conn, 4/14/18; d. John Lee Brooks and Genevieve Ford B; m. 6/30/40 to Oliver Butterworth; c. Michael, Timothy, Dan and Kate. Educ: Conn. Col. for Women, A.B, 40; Wesleyan Univ, M.A, 59; Phi Beta Kappa; Student-Faculty Policy Cmt; Conn. Col. Outing Club. Polit. & Govt. Pos: Dist. committeewoman, West Hartford Dem. Party, Conn, 53-54; chmn, West Hartford McCarthy for Pres. Orgn, 68; exec. bd. mem, Conn. McCarthy for Pres, 68; chmn. of del, West Hartford Del. to Conn. Dem. Conv, 68; del, Dem. Nat. Conv, 68; exec. cmt. mem, Cmt. to Form an Ongoing Lib. Orgn. Within Dem. Party, 68; founding mem, Caucus Conn. Dem, 68; West Hartford del, Caucus Conn. Dem, 69; exec. cmt. mem, West Hartford Dem. Caucus, 69; committeewoman, Conn. Dem. Party, 69- Bus. & Prof. Pos: Dir. and teacher, Kent Nursery Sch, Kent, Conn, 40-42; trustee, Conn. Col. for Women, 47-52; teacher, hist, Ethel Walker Sch, Simsbury, 59-61, Chaffee Sch, Windsor, 61-69 and Loomis Sch, 67-69. Publ: The Mind and Heart of Georges Sorel, Wesleyan Univ, 59. Mem: League Women Voters (dir, West Hartford League); West Hartford PTA (dir); Conn. Prison Asn.(mem. bd. dirs); Conn. Hist. Soc; Am. Civil Liberties Union; NAACP; Urban League; Am. Dem. Action. One of ten Plaintiffs in Butterworth vs Dempsey, the court case that brought about Conn. reapportionment of both houses of Conn. Gen. Assembly, 65-66. Rel: Protestant. Mailing Add: 81 Sunset Farm Rd, West Hartford, Conn. 06107.

BUTTERWORTH, W. WALTON
b. New Orleans, La, 9/7/03; s. Dr. William Walton and Maud Ravencamp Campbell B; m. 11/10/28 to Virginia Parker; c. Cynthia and John Blair. Educ: Princeton Univ, B.A, 25; Univ. Dijon, France, summer 25; Rhodes Scholar, Worcester Col, Oxford Univ, 25-27. Polit. & Govt. Pos: For. Serv. Officer, Dept. State, 28-29, 32; v.consul, Singapore, 29-31, third secy, Ottawa, 32-33; second secy. and spec. treas. rep, London, 34-41; spec. asst. to under secy. commerce, 41-42; mem. adv. cmt, Lend Lease Trade Policy; first secy, Lisbon and Madrid, 42-44; dir. gen., U.S. Commercial Co, Iberian Peninsular, 42-44; counsellor Madrid, 44-46; minister, Nanking, 46-47; dir, Far East. Affairs, 47-49; asst. secy. state, Far East. Affairs, 49-50; ambassador, Sweden, 50-54; dep. chief missions and minister, London, 54-55; ambassador, European Coal & Steel Commun, 56-59; European Econ. Commun. & Atomic Energy Commun, 58-59; U.S. Rep. European Commun, 59-62; Ambassador, Canada, 62-68. Mailing Add: 50 Battle Rd, Princeton, N.J. 08540.

BUTTON, DANIEL E. R
U.S. Rep, N.Y.
b. Dunkirk, N.Y, 11/1/17; s. Roy Button and Alice Root B; m. 1945; to Rebecca B. Pool; c. Nancy, Sarah, Daniel, Jr, Jefferson and Mary Caroline; second marriage to Rena P. Posner, 1969. Educ: Univ. Del, A.B, 38; Columbia Univ, M.S, 39; Phi Kappa Phi. Polit. & Govt. Pos: U.S. Rep, N.Y, 67- Bus. & Prof. Pos: Reporter, Wilmington News, Del, 39-43 and The Assoc. Press, N.Y.C, 43-46; dir. pub. rels, Univ. Del, 47-51; asst. to pres, State Univ. N.Y, 52-58; exec. ed, Albany Times-Union, 60-66. Publ: Lindsay; A Man for Tomorrow, Random House, 65. Mailing Add: 134 Chestnut St, Albany, N.Y. 12210.

BUTTON, ROBERT YOUNG D
Attorney Gen. of Va.
b. Culpeper Co, Va, 11/2/99; s. John Young Button and Margaret Agnes Duncan B; m. 8/20/31 to Kathleen Antoinette Cheape; c. Robert Y, Jr. and Kathleen Margaret (Mrs. Ginn). Educ: Univ. Va, LL.B, 22; Raven Soc. Polit. & Govt. Pos: Trustee, Jamestown Corp; mem, State Bd. of Accountancy, Va, 36-42; mem, State Parole Bd, 42-45; mem, State Bd. of Educ, 45-60; Va. State Sen, 46-61; attorney, Town of Culpeper, 50-62; mem. and chmn, Va. Adv. Legis. Cmt, 52-61; mem, Cmn. Pub. Educ, 54 & 59; mem, Potomac River Cmn, 58; Attorney Gen. of Va, 62- Bus. & Prof. Pos: Dir, Mutual Fire Ins. Co. of Loudoun, Merchants Grocery of Culpeper, Second Nat. Bank of Culpeper and Cent. Hardware Co, 30- Mem: Fel, Am. Col. Trial Lawyers; Am. and Va. Bar Asns, mem. coun, Va. Bar Asn, 50-56; Mason; Rotary; Commonwealth Club of Richmond. Rel: Baptist. Legal Res: Box 350, Culpeper, Va. 22701. Mailing Add: Prestwould Apt, Richmond, Va. 23220.

BUTZER, HAROLD GODFREY R
b. Mary's Home, Mo, 12/28/21; s. Guido Godfrey Butzer and Elizabeth Angenendt B; m. 6/24/50 to Catherine Louise Markle; c. D'Arcy, Lisa, Vanessa and Nicolette. Educ: Sch. of Mines & Metallurgy, Univ. of Mo; Blue Key; Theta Tau; Nat. Soc. Pfrnl. Engrs. Polit. & Govt. Pos: City councilman, Jefferson City, Mo, 61-63; chmn, Cole Co. Rep. Party, 63-65; committeeman, Jefferson Twp. Rep. Party, currently; Presidential elector, Eighth Cong. Dist, Mo, 68. Bus. & Prof. Pos: Pres, Harold G. Butzer, Inc, 60-; bd. mem, Exchange Nat. Bank, Jefferson City, Mo, 65- Mil. Serv: Entered as Pvt, Army, 42, released as 1st Lt, 46, after serv. in Corp. of Engrs, ETO. Mem: Am. Legion; bd. of dirs, C. of C, Jefferson City, Mo; bd. of dirs, Mo. State C. of C; U.S. C. of C; bd. of dirs, Mo. Asn. of Plumbing-Heating-Cooling Contractors. Rel: Catholic. Mailing Add: 411 Schellridge Rd, Jefferson City, Mo. 65101.

BUTZNER, JOHN DECKER, JR.
b. Scranton, Pa, 10/2/17; s. John Decker Butzner, M.D. and Bess Robison B; m. 5/25/46 to Viola Eleanor Peterson; c. John Decker, III. Educ: Univ. Scranton, B.A, 38; Univ. Va. Law Sch, LL.B, 41. Polit. & Govt. Pos: Assoc. Judge, 15th Judicial Circuit, Va, 58-61; Judge, 39th Judicial Circuit, 61-62; U.S. Dist. Judge, East. Dist, 62-67; U.S. Circuit Judge, Fourth Circuit, 67- Bus. & Prof. Pos: Attorney-at-law, Fredericksburg, Va, 41-42, 46-58. Mil. Serv: Entered as Pvt, Air Force, 42, released as S/Sgt, 45, after serv. in Weather Serv. Rel: Presbyterian. Mailing Add: P.O. Box 2188, Richmond, Va. 23217.

BUZHARDT, J. FRED, JR. R
b. Greenwood, S.C, 2/21/24; s. J. Fred Buzhardt, Sr. and Edna Hardin B; m. 7/15/46 to Imogene Sanders; c. Linda, J. Fred, III, George and Jill. Educ: West Point, B.S, 46; Univ. S.C, LL.B. magna cum laude, 52. Polit. & Govt. Pos: Admin. asst. to U.S. Sen. Thurmond, S.C, 58; alternate del, Rep. Nat. Conv, 68. Bus. & Prof. Pos: Lawyer private practice, 52-57. Mil. Serv: Air Force, 46-59. Mailing Add: P.O. Box 218, McCormick, S.C. 29835. (1967)

BUZHARDT, JOSEPH FRED D
b. Greenwood, S.C, 12/21/03; s. Joseph Cleveland Buzhardt and Sara Terry B; m. 1/29/23 to Edna Elizabeth Hardin. Educ: Furman Univ, 20-21; student, law offices of Thurmond & Thurmond, Edgefield, 31-34. Polit. & Govt. Pos: S.C. State Rep, 63-66; v.chmn. S.C. Bd. of Corrections, 60-64; bd. of dirs, S.C. Penitentiary, 54-60; mem, Assoc. Coun. of Clarks Hill Authority, 47-53; chmn. bd. of McCormick Sch. Trustees, 39-47; co. chmn. McCormick Co. Dem. Exec. Com, 42-; town attorney, 36-; co. attorney, 37- Bus. & Prof. Pos: Lawyer, firm of Buzhardt & Baggett. Mem: Mason (shriner); Moose; Exchange Club; Am, S.C. Bar Asns. Rel: Baptist, bd. of deacons. Mailing Add: Box 8, McCormick, S.C. 29835. (1967)

BYCK, MARY HELEN D
Dem. Nat. Committeewoman, Ky.
b. Louisville, Ky, 6/28/07; d. Cyrus Adler and Alice Goldsmith A; m. to Dann C. Byck, Sr.(deceased); c. Lucy (Mrs. Shapero), Elizabeth (Mrs. Goodman) and Dann C, Jr. Educ: Vassar College, 28. Hon. L.H.D, Catherine Spalding Col. Polit. & Govt. Pos: Chmn, Jefferson Co. Dem. Gubernatorial Campaign, 63; also served as campaign chmn. for several mayoralty campaigns; Dem. nat. committeewoman, Ky, currently; del, Dem. Nat. Conv, 68. Bus. & Prof. Pos: Pres, Byck Bros. & Co, 60-64, chmn. of the bd, 64- Mailing Add: 332 Penruth Ave, Louisville, Ky. 40207.

BYCROFT, RONALD EUGENE R
Chmn, Buffalo Co. Rep. Party, Nebr.
b. Brooks, Iowa, 12/10/32; s. Henry George Bycroft and Gladys Hewitt B; m. 8/20/55 to Jeannetta Mae Schweitzer; c. Barton George and Melanie Joyce. Educ: Iowa State Univ, B.S, 54; Alpha Zeta; Ward System; ISA. Polit. & Govt. Pos: Del, Rep. State Conv, Iowa, 58; village mayor, Gibbon, Nebr, 64; chmn, Buffalo Co. Rep. Party, Nebr, 68- Bus. & Prof. Pos: Pres, Exchange Bank, 65-; chmn. of bd. of dirs, Elm Creek State Bank, 67- Mem: Lions Int; Nebr. Flying Farmers; Aircraft Owners & Pilots Asn; Elks; Buffalo Co. T-Bone Club; Jaycees. Buffalo Co. 4-H Alumni Award, 68. Rel: Lutheran. Legal Res: May Ave, Gibbon, Nebr. 68840. Mailing Add: Box K, Gibbon, Nebr. 68840.

BYE, HOWARD O. R
b. Gilby, N.Dak, 4/16/08; married; c. 2. Educ: Univ. N.Dak. Polit. & Govt. Pos: N.Dak. State Rep, 53-63. Bus. & Prof. Pos: Farmer. Mem: Mason; Scottish Rite; Shrine; Elks; Farm Bur. Silver Beaver Award, Boy Scouts. Mailing Add: Gilby, N.Dak. 58235.

BYERS, FRANCIS ROBERT R
Wis. State Assemblyman
b. Marion, Wis, 3/30/20; s. Elmer S. Byers and Luella DeVaud B; m. 6/19/48 to Florence Marquette; c. Cristy, Tracy and Jamie. Educ: Univ. Wis, Ph.B, 43; Acacia. Polit. & Govt. Pos: Supv, Waupaca Co. Bd, Wis, 50-60; chmn, Waupaca Co. Rep. Party, 56-60; cmnr, Northeast. Wis. Regional Planning Cmn, 67-69; Wis. State Assemblyman, Waupaca Co, 69- Bus. & Prof. Pos: Ed, Marion Advertiser, Wis, 46-67; ed, Manawa Advocate, 56-59; partner, JBM Clothiers, Marion, 59-69; partner, Cinderella Beauty Salon, 62-69; ed, Tigerton Chronicle, 65-67; dir, Marion State Bank, 66-69. Mil. Serv: Entered as A/S V-7, Navy, 43, released as Lt. 46, after serv. in Amphibious Forces, Pac. Theatre, 43-46; Unit Citation; Purple Heart; Phillipine Liberation, Pac. Theatre and Victory Ribbons. Mem: Mason; Rotary; Am Legion; Conserv. Club. Rel: Methodist. Mailing Add: Marion, Wis. 54950.

BYERS, ROBERT KEITH R
b. Stockton, Calif, 11/4/31; s. Paul L. Byers and Laura Dean B; m. 6/16/51 to Peggy Cartier Miller; c. Christine Michele and James Alan. Educ: Univ. Calif, Berkeley, B.A. cum laude, 52; Law Sch, LL.B, 59 and J.D, 68; Phi Alpha Delta; Phi Sigma Kappa; Scabbard and Blade. Polit. & Govt. Pos: V.pres. and bd. mem, Young Rep, 60-69; fire cmnr, Castro Valley, Calif, 64; judge, San Leandro-Hayward Munic. Court, 69- Mil. Serv: Entered as 2nd Lt, Army, 53, released as 1st Lt, 55, after serv. in Mil. Police attached to 12th Ord. Bn, Holloman Air Force Base, N.Mex, 6 months and Germany $1\frac{1}{2}$ years. Mem: Pres, Lambda Alpha Epsilon, 51-52; chmn, Alameda Co. Coun. on Alcoholism, 54; mem. adv. bd, Alameda Co. Ment. Health Asn, 55; mem. bd, South Alameda Co. Bar Asn, 62-; chmn. and pub. mem, Local Agency Formation Cmn, 65-68; v.pres, Alameda Co. Bar Asn, 69-; Elks. Outstanding

Officer, Mil. Police; Various Boy Scout Awards, Castro Valley Orgn; Baseball Mgr. Awards. Rel: Protestant. Mailing Add: 18601 Capricorn Court, Castro Valley, Calif. 94546.

BYERS, WILLIAM H. R
Mem, Los Angeles Co. Rep. Cent. Cmt, Calif.
b. Pasadena, Calif, 5/11/27; s. Paul W. Byers and Kathyrn G. Duff B; m. 6/11/55 to Anita C. Egnew; c. Paul W. and Carol Ann. Educ: Claremont Men's Col, 4 years. Polit. & Govt. Pos: Mem, Los Angeles Co. Rep. Cent. Cmt, Calif, 60-; co-chmn, Cmt. to Re-elect Congressman Glenard P. Lipscomb, Congressman from 24th Dist, 62 & 64, campaign mgr, 66, field rep. to, 67-; mem, Calif. Rep. State Cent. Cmt, 62-69. Bus. & Prof. Pos: Byers-Froeberg, Inc, 53- Mil. Serv: Entered as A/S, Navy, 45, released as Yeoman 3/C, 46, after serv. in 31st Naval Construction Bn, S.Pac. Theater, 45-46. Mem: Kiwanis; Cong. Secy. Club. Rel: Protestant. Legal Res: 1275 Lane Court, Claremont, Calif. 91711. Mailing Add: P.O. Box 351, Claremont, Calif. 91711.

BYINGTON, HOMER MORRISON, JR.
Am. Consul Gen, Naples, Italy
b. Naples, Italy, 5/31/08; s. Homer Morrison Byington and Jeanette Lindsley Gregory B; m. 9/31/32 to Jane Craven McHarg; c. Homer Morrison. Educ: Yale, A.B, 30. Polit. & Govt. Pos: For. Serv. officer and secy, Diplomatic Serv, 30; with Dept. of State, Wash, D.C, 30-32; press officer, U.S. Del. to UN Conf. on Int. Orgn, San Francisco, 45; dep. polit. adv, Supreme Allied Comdr, Allied Force Hq, Mediterranean Theater Oper, 46-47; first secy. of embassy, Am. Embassy, Rome, 45-47, counselor, 47, minister plenipotentiary, 48; dir, Off. West. European Affairs, Dept. of State, 50; counselor embassy, Madrid, 54-57; U.S. Rep. 14th Session Econ. Cmn. for Asia and Far East, 58; Ambassador, Malaya, 57-61; spec. asst. to Dep. Under Secy. of State for Admin, Dept. of State, 61-62; Am. Consul Gen, Naples, Italy, 62- Mem: Metropolitan Club; Chevy Chase Club. Medal of Freedom, 46. Mailing Add: Box 18, FPO, New York 09521.

BYNUM, F. G. R
North. Region Coordinator, Jefferson Co. Rep. Party, Ala.
b. Oneonta, Ala, 5/19/17; s. Dee Bynum and Effie McCuen B; m. 4/14/38 to Avis Deborah Clark; Educ: High sch, grad, 37. Polit. & Govt. Pos: Precinct capt, Jefferson Co. Rep. Party, Ala, 63-67; del, Rep. Co. Conv, 64, 66 & 68; del, Rep. State Conv, 64, 66 & 68; mem, Jefferson Co. Rep. Cmt, 64-, mem. exec. cmt, 67-; north. region coordinator, Jefferson Co. Rep. Party, 67-; alternate del, Rep. Nat. Conv, 68. Bus. & Prof. Pos: Partner, prod, Bymoco Metal Fabricators, Birmingham, Ala, 54- Mil. Serv: Entered as Pvt, Army, 44, released as Cpl, 46, after serv. in 106th Div, ETO, 44-46; Europe-Africa-Middle East. Serv. Medal with 4 Bronze Stars, North. France, Ardennes, Rhineland, Cent. Europe; Good Conduct Medal; World War II Victory Medal; Combat Infantryman Badge; Cert. of Merit. Mem: Mason (Master); C. of C. Rel: Protestant. Mailing Add: 1808 Linthicum Lane, Birmingham, Ala. 35217.

BYNUM, KNOX D
b. Clayton, Ga, 2/03/26; s. Thaddeus Lexington Bynum and Irene Powell B; m. 4/08/56 to Alice Armede Craft; c. Mary Alice, Thad Craft, Roslyn Irene and Rebecca. Educ: Draughton Sch. of Commerce; Piedmont Col; Univ. Ga; Admitted Ga. Bar, 51. Polit. & Govt. Pos: Past secy, Rabun Co. Dem. Exec. Cmt, Ga; committeeman, Clayton Dist; Rabun Co. attorney, 53-; Clayton City attorney, 57-; Ga. State Rep, 59-65. Bus. & Prof. Pos: Attorney; farmer. Mil. Serv: Maritime Serv, 44; Merchant Marine, 44-46. Mem: Past pres, Clayton Rotary Club, 59-60; past pres, Mt. Bar Asn; Am. Bar Asn; Jaycee State dir, 61-62. Ga. Indust. Ambassador. Rel: Methodist. Mailing Add: Clayton, Ga. 30525.

BYNUM, PRESTON C. R
Ark. State Rep.
b. Pryor, Okla, 6/8/39; s. Homer Franklin Bynum and Roma May Hays B; m. 6/30/62 to Linda Sue Allen; c. Leasa Sue and Angela Dawn. Educ: Univ. Ark, 57-60. Polit. & Govt. Pos: Mem, City Coun, Siloam Springs, Ark, 62-68; Ark. State Rep, Benton Co, 69- Bus. & Prof. Pos: Partner, Bynum Motor Co, Siloam Springs, Ark, 60-; bd. dirs, Liberty Savings & Loan, currently. Mil. Serv: Entered as Pvt, Ark. Nat. Guard, 55, released as SP-1/C, 64, after serv. in B Battery, 936 Field Artillery Bn, 142nd Group. Mem: Rotary; C. of C; Sales and Mkt. Execs. Club. Outstanding Young Man of 67, Siloam Springs, Ark. Rel: Baptist. Mailing Add: 1003 S. Maxwell, Siloam Springs, Ark. 72761.

BYRAM, STANLEY HAROLD R
b. North Vernon, Ind, 1/11/06; s. Henry Nelson Byram and Iona Fleming B; c. Beverly (Mrs. William Anderson) and Barbara (Mrs. Leo Jordan). Educ: DePauw, A.B, 28; Beta Theta Pi. Hon. D.Litt, Lincoln Mem. Univ, 64. Polit. & Govt. Pos: Chmn, Rep. Citizens Finance Cmt. of the Seventh Dist, Ind, 58-61; v.chmn. and mem, Exec. Cmt, Rep. Citizens Finance Cmt. of Ind, 58-65; mem, Nat. Rep. Finance Cmt, 59-; del, Rep. Nat. Conv, 60; chmn, Ind. Finance Campaign, 60; chmn, Ind. Rep. Finance Cmt, 60-63; treas, Ind. State Rep. Cent. Cmt, 61-65. Bus. & Prof. Pos: Pres, Grassyfork, Inc, 45- Mem: Am. Fisheries Soc; N.Y. Algernon Sidney Sullivan Asn; Coun. of the Sagamores of the Wabash; Ind. Soc. of Chicago; Columbia Club, Indianapolis; Indianapolis Athletic Club. Rel: Methodist. Legal Res: State Rd. 37 N, Martinsville, Ind. 46151. Mailing Add: Grassyfork, P.O. Box 268, Martinsville, Ind. 46151.

BYRD, GARLAND TURK D
b. Reynolds, Ga, 7/16/24; s. Dozier Eugene Byrd and Mable Gaultney B; m. 8/22/46 to Gloria Elizabeth Whatley; c. Garland F, Jr.(Buster) and Charles Whatley (Chuck). Educ: Univ. of Ga, 46-48; Emory Univ, LL.B, 48; Sigma Chi. Polit. & Govt. Pos: Ga. State Rep, 47-49; asst. dir, Vets. Serv. Dept, 49-52; dir, Ga. Citizens Coun, 52-54; Lt. Gov, Ga, 59-63; Ga. State Sen, 17th Dist, 63-64. Bus. & Prof. Pos: Attorney, farmer, warehouse ginner and real estate dealer. Mil. Serv: Army, 83rd Inf. Div, 42-43, Sgt; grad, Officers Cand. Sch, 43, as 2nd Lt, discharged 45, as Capt; Ga. Nat. Guard, Lt. Col; State Judge Adv; Silver & Bronze Star. Mem: Mason; Moose; VFW; Am. Legion; Kiwanis; Elks. Rel: Baptist. Mailing Add: Reynolds, Ga. 31076.

BYRD, HARRY FLOOD, JR. D
U.S. Sen, Va.
b. Winchester, Va, 12/20/14; s. Harry Flood Byrd and Anne Douglas Beverley B; m. 8/9/41 to Gretchen Bigelow Thomson; c. Harry Flood, III, Thomas Thomson and Beverley Bigelow. Educ: Va. Mil. Inst; Univ. Va. Polit. & Govt. Pos: Va. State Sen, 47-65; U.S. Sen, Va, 65- Bus. & Prof. Pos: Pres. and ed, Winchester Evening Star, Va, 35- and Harrisonburg Daily News-Record, Va, 37- Mil. Serv: Lt. Comdr, Naval Res. Mem: Am. Legion; VFW; Rotary; Elks; Moose; Eagles; Va. Fruit Growers. Rel: Episcopal. Legal Res: 411 Tennyson Ave, Winchester, Va. 22601. Mailing Add: 417 Senate Office Bldg, Washington, D.C. 20510.

BYRD, JOE K. D
b. Morganton, N.C, 12/28/23; s. Edgar Harris Byrd and Elva Leslie Duckworth B; m. 5/11/47 to Gleta Ruby; c. Elaine G, Joe K, Jr, Jane H, Ann L, James E, Philip N. and Eric E. Educ: Berea Col, 41-42; Univ. N.C, A.B, 47, Sch. of Law, LL.B, 50; Delta Theta Phi. Polit. & Govt. Pos: Solicitor, Burke Co. Criminal Court, N.C, 51-54; pres, Burke Co. Young Dem. Club, 52-54; mem, Burke Co. Dem. Exec. Cmt, 55-66; N.C. State Rep, 59-60; mem, N.C. State Dem. Exec. Cmt, 59-64; N.C. State Sen, 63-64 & 67-68. Mil. Serv: Entered as Pvt, Army, 42, released as S/Sgt, 45, after serv. in 84th Inf. Div, ETO, 44-45; Lt. Col, Army Res, 108th Training Div, 50-; Bronze Star with V Clasp; Combat Infantryman's Badge; ETO Ribbon with 3 Battle Stars; Army of Occup; Am. Campaign; WW II Victory and Armed Forces Res. Medals. Publ: 'Unregistered Trade Marks and Trade Names,' N.C. Law Rev, 50. Mem: Pres, Burke Co. Bar Asn, 64-65; 25th N.C. Judicial Bar Asn; N.C. State Bar Asn; N.C. Acad. of Trial Lawyers (mem. bd. gov, 68-); U.S. Supreme Court Bar; Mason; Am. Legion; VFW; Lions. Rel: Baptist. Legal Res: 1 Byrd St, Drexel, N.C. 28619. Mailing Add: Mimosa Bldg, Morganton, N.C. 28655.

BYRD, JOHN THOMAS D
b. Arnold's Institute Community, 12/24/97; s. William R. Byrd (Bird) and Minnie Dial B; m. 2/5/63 to Edna Hasty Jones; c. step-daughter, Mrs. Thomas J. Lee (Frances Jones); grandchildren, Rickey Stephen, Jimmy Thomas; Sam H. Educ: graduated high sch, 17. Polit. & Govt. Pos: Ga. State Rep, 63-67; Dir. Walton Co. Farm Bur, 33; Walton Co. Hosp. Authority, 47, Chmn, 62; Walton Co. Bd. Educ, 39-59, Chmn, 12 yrs; Dir, Sch. Bd. Asn, 50; Cmnr, N.E. Ga. Area Develop. Asn, 62. Bus. & Prof. Pos: Merchant; farmer; real estate; owner, cotton gin, wholesale grocery, Monroe Nursing Home. Misc: Organizer & pres. 'One Variety Cotton' Commun; received trophy. Rel: Christian; Elder Corinth Christian Church; Chmn. Bd, 35. Mailing Add: Loganville, Ga. 30249. (1967)

BYRD, ROBERT BOND, SR. D
b. Morganton, N.C, 5/31/30; s. Edgar Harris Byrd (deceased) and Elva Duckworth B; m. 7/10/54 to Joyce Elaine Gouge; c. Robert Bond, II, Dixon Duckworth and Sara Lou. Educ: Berea Col, A.B. in Hist. and Polit. Sci, 52; Univ. N.C, LL.B, 55; Phi Alpha Delta; pres, Law Sch, Univ. N.C, 54-55. Polit. & Govt. Pos: Mem, Young Dem. Club, Burke Co, N.C, 55-, v.chmn, 60; v.chmn, Burke Co. Dem. Exec. Cmt, 58-62, chmn, 62-66; mem, N.C. State Dem. Exec. Cmt, 60-64; chmn, State Dem. Cmt. to Revise Party Plan of Orgn, 63; mem, State Campaign Cmt, 68. Bus. & Prof. Pos: Partner, Byrd, Byrd and Ervin Law Firm. Mil. Serv: Entered as Pvt, Army Res, 52, released as Sgt, 60, after serv. in Co. H, 518th Inf. Regt, 108th Div. Mem: Am. and N.C. Bar Asns; Trial Lawyers Asn; bd. Dirs, United Fund; past pres, Burke Co. Polio Fund; Lions (past pres, Morganton club). C. of C; past pres, Forest Hill PTA. Varsity tennis player, Berea Col, 49-52; intramural table tennis and volleyball team champions, Univ. N.C, 54-55. Rel: Methodist. Legal Res: 203 Greenwood Place, Morganton, N.C. Mailing Add: Box 832, Morganton, N.C. 28655.

BYRD, ROBERT C. D
U.S. Sen, W.Va.
b. North Wilkesboro, N.C, 1/15/18; s. Cornelius Sale Byrd and Ada Kirby B; m. 5/29/37 to Erma James; c. Mona, Carole and Marjorie Ellen. Educ: Beckley Col, Concord Col, Morris Harvey Col, 50-51; Marshall Col, 51-52; Am. Univ, J.D, 63. Polit. & Govt. Pos: W.Va. State Del, 46-50; W.Va. State Sen, 50-52; U.S. Rep, W.Va, 52-58; U.S. Sen, W.Va, 58-; del-at-lg, Dem. Nat. Conv, 60. Rel: Baptist. Legal Res: Sophia, W.Va. 25929. Mailing Add: 105 Old Senate Office Bldg, Washington, D.C. 20510.

BYRD, WADDELL D
Exec. Committeeman, Marion Co. Dem. Party, S.C.
b. Marion, S.C, 8/26/30; s. Furman B. Byrd and Isabella Dew B; m. 1/3/49 to Mary Sawyer; c. Waddell Dale, Jr. and Ken Elliott. Educ: Woodrow Wilson Sch. of Law; Sigma Delta Kappa. Polit. & Govt. Pos: Precinct chmn, Dem. Party, S.C; chmn, Marion Co. Dem. Party, exec. committeeman, 64-; magistrate, Marion Co, 64-; del, Dem. State Conv, 6 years; del, Dem. Nat. Conv, 68; state pres, S.C. Magistrate Asn, 68-69; state exec. committeeman, S.C. Dem. Party, 69- Bus. & Prof. Pos: Attorney at Law, Marion, S.C. 58- Mem: Am. and S.C. Bar Asns; S.C. State Bar; S.C. Trial Lawyers Asn.(dir); Jaycees (pres); WOW (counsel comdr); S.C. Jaycees (past chmn. pub. affairs). Young Man of the Year, 55. Rel: Methodist. Legal Res: 1201 N. Main St, Marion, S.C. 29571. Mailing Add: P.O. Box 65, Marion, S.C. 29571.

BYRNE, CHARLES DAVID R
Auditor, City and Co. of Denver, Colo.
b. Denver, Colo, 3/24/26; s. Patrick Harry Byrne and Estelle B; m. 8/5/49 to Dorothy Louise Lewis; c. Dorothy E, Tara C, Catherine A, Charleen A. and Mason Lewis. Educ: Univ. of Denver, 47-49; Kappa Sigma. Polit. & Govt. Pos: Pres, Denver Young Rep. League, Colo, 57-58; area leader, Denver Co. Rep. Cent. Cmt, 58-59; clerk and recorder, City and Co. of Denver, 58-59, auditor, 63- ; chmn, Young Rep. Nat. Conv, 59; Colo. State Rep, 60-63; alternate del, Rep. Nat. Conv, 68. Bus. & Prof. Pos: Serv. rep, Mt. State Tel, 52-55; acct, Am. Crystal Sugar Co, 55-58; assoc. Milne Duplicating Co, 58-60. Mil. Serv: Entered as A/S, Navy, 44, released as Seaman 1/C, 46, after serv. in Naval Amphibious, Pac. Theatre, 45-46; Am. and Cent. Pac. Theater Ribbons; Pac. Theater Ribbon and two Battle Stars; Japanese Occup. Medal; Victory Medal. Mem: Munic. Finance Officers Asn; Colo. Munic. League; Kiwanis; Elks; K. of C; VFW; Am. Legion. Rel: Roman Catholic. Legal Res: 75 S. Jasmine St, Denver, Colo. 80220. Mailing Add: 300 City and County Bldg, Denver, Colo. 80202. (1967)

BYRNE, EMMET FRANCIS R
b. Chicago, Ill, 12/6/97; s. James Patrick Byrne and Mary Alice Murphy B; m. 2/14/29 to Mary Margaret Farrell; c. Sally (Mrs. James Martin), Molly (Mrs. Thomas Sikorski), Barbara (Mrs. Richard Brown), Patrice (Mrs. Robert Williams), Emmet F, Jr, Judith (Mrs. Neville Lancaster), Mrs. Robert Kern and Thomas F. Educ: Loyola Univ, 16-17; DePaul Univ. Law Sch, LL.B, 20; Polit. & Govt. Pos: Asst. corp. counsel, Chicago, Ill, 21-23; asst. states attorney, Cook Co, 23-28; chmn. bd. 86, Selective Serv, World War II; hearing officer, Ill. Commerce Cmt, 47-48; U.S. Rep, 56; past mem, Rep. Exec. Cmt, Chicago, Ill. Bus. & Prof. Pos: Attorney, currently. Mil. Serv: Pvt, Army, 18-19, serv. in Ord, Camp Hancock, Ga. Mem: Chicago Bar Asn.(cmt. on cand. and cmt. on criminal law, past justice, Story Chap); Evanston Rep. Orgn; Phi Alpha Delta; Chicago Alumni Asn.(past pres); Lake Shore Club; Am. Legion (past comdr); 40 et 8. Admitted to Supreme Court, Ill, 25. Rel: Catholic. Legal Res: 412 Lee St, Evanston, Ill. 60202. Mailing Add: 33 N. LaSalle St, Chicago, Ill. 60602.

BYRNE, JAMES ALOYSIUS D
U.S. Rep, Pa.
b. Phila, Pa, 6/22/06; m. 6/7/39 to M. Virginia Mullin. Educ: St. Joseph's Col. Polit. & Govt. Pos: Chief disbursing officer for State Treas, Pa; U.S. Marshal for East. Dist. of Pa; Pa. State Rep, 50-52; U.S. Rep, Pa, 52- Bus. & Prof. Pos: Funeral dir. Legal Res: 2315 E. Cumberland St, Philadelphia, Pa. 19125. Mailing Add: U.S. House of Representatives, Washington, D.C. 20515. (1967)

BYRNE, THOMAS ROBERT DFL
Mayor, St. Paul, Minn.
b. St. Paul, Minn, 3/9/23; s. Philip J. Byrne and Mary McMonigal B; m. 6/9/45 to Mary Therese Barrett; c. Mary Ellen, Joseph, Patrick, Thomas and Timothy. Educ: Col. of St. Thomas, B.A, 47; Univ. Minn, M.A, 60; Delta Epsilon Sigma. Polit. & Govt. Pos: Chmn, Minn. Dem-Farmer-Labor Legis. Dist. Club, 63; chmn, Fourth Cong. Dist. Johnson-Humphrey Campaign, 64; v.chmn, Minn. Munic. Cmn, 66-67; mayor, St. Paul, Minn, 66- Bus. & Prof. Pos: Instr, St. Thomas Acad, 47-53, Cleveland Jr. High Sch, 53-58 and Hazel Park Jr. High Sch, 58-64; guid. counsr, Wilson Jr. High Sch, 64-66. Mil. Serv: Entered as Pvt, Army Air Corps, 43, released as 1st Lt, 45 after serv. in 15th Air Force, European-African-Mediterranean, 50 missions as navigator-bombardier; Air Medal with 2 Clusters; European-African-Mediterranean Theater Ribbon with 5 Battle Stars. Mem: St. Paul Fedn. Teachers; Minn. Educ. Asn; Nat. Cong. Parents & Teachers; St. Paul Conf. Human Rels; exec. cmt, Nat. League Cities, 67-; past v.chmn, Minn. Munic. Cmn; past comdr, VFW Ran View Post 6210; Am. Legion; Little League. Rel: Catholic. Legal Res: 2170 Wellesley Ave, St. Paul, Minn. 55105. Mailing Add: Room 347, City Hall, St. Paul, Minn. 55102.

BYRNE, Wm. MATTHEW D
b. Bakersfield, Calif, 7/10/96; s. John Joseph Byrne and Mary Ellen Mills B; m. 6/2/25 to Julia Ann Lamb; Moira (Mrs. Foster) and Wm. Matthew, Jr. Educ: Univ. Loyola, Los Angeles; Alpha Sigma Nu. Polit. & Govt. Pos: Sr. judge, U.S. Dist. Court, Cent. Dist, Calif, 66-, chief judge, 65-66 and judge, 50-; judge, Superior Court, Calif, 46-50; judge, Munic. Court, Los Angeles Co, 43-46; speaker pro tem, Calif. State Legis, 25-30. Bus. & Prof. Pos: Attorney at law, 29-43. Mil. Serv: Entered as A/S, Navy, 17, released as Boatswain Mate, 19. Rel: Catholic. Mailing Add: 520 Cherakee Ave, Los Angeles, Calif. 90004. (1967)

BYRNES, DANIEL MAURICE R
b. Milwaukee, Wis, 7/29/37; s. Maurice Bernard Byrnes and Mary Wilkinson B; m. 6/11/60 to Joan Frances Hudson; c. Robert Daniel, Sheila Anne, John Barry, Mary Bridget, Colleen Frances, Timothy Patrick, Kevin Michael and James Brendan. Educ: Univ. Notre Dame, 55-56; Marquette Univ, A.B, 60; Univ. San Francisco, LL.B, 63; Alpha Phi Omega; Phi Delta Phi. Polit. & Govt. Pos: Dist. attorney, Burnett Co, Wis, 65-69; chmn, Burnett Co. Rep. Party, 66-69. Bus. & Prof. Pos: Partner, Cwayna, Novitzke & Byrnes, Amery, Wis, currently. Mem: Am. and Polk-Burnett Bar Asns; State Bar of Wis; Wis. Dist. Attorneys Asn.(v.pres, 68-69); Inter-Co. Bar Asn.(pres, 68-69); Nat. Dist. Attorneys Asn. Rel: Catholic. Legal Res: 416 Riverside Dr, Amery, Wis. 54001. Mailing Add: Box 847, Amery, Wis. 54001.

BYRNES, JAMES FRANCIS D
b. Charleston, S.C, 5/2/79; s. James Francis Byrnes and Elizabeth McSweeney B; m. 5/2/06 to Maude Perkins Busch. Hon. LL.D, Charleston, Presbyterian Col, John Marshall Col, Yale, Columbia, Pa, Wash. and Lee and others. Polit. & Govt. Pos: Gov, S.C, 51-55; secy. of state, 45-47; dir, War Mobilization, 43-45; dir, Economic Stabilization, 42-43; assoc. justice, U.S. Supreme Court, 41-42; U.S. Sen, 30-41; U.S. Rep, 10-25. Bus. & Prof. Pos: Attorney at Law. Mil. Awards: Distinguished Serv. Medal. Mem: Masons. Rel: Episcopal. Mailing Add: 12 Heathwood Circle, Columbia, S.C. 29201. (1967)

BYRNES, JOHN WILLIAM R
U.S. Rep, Wis.
b. Green Bay, Wis, 6/12/13; s. Charles W. Byrnes and Harriet Schumacher B; m. 2/15/47 to Barbara Preston; c. John Robert, Michael, Bonnie Jean, Charles, Barbara and Elizabeth. Educ: Univ. Wis, B.A, 36; Univ. Wis. Law Sch, LL.B, 38. Hon. LL.D, Lawrence Univ, 62. Polit. & Govt. Pos: Dep. cmnr. of banking, State of Wis, 38-40; Wis. State Sen, 41-44, majority floor leader, 43-44, chmn, Judiciary Cmt, 43-44; U.S. Rep, Wis, 45-, ranking minority mem, Ways and Means Cmt, U.S. House of Rep, 63-, chmn, House Rep. Policy Cmt, 59-65; del, Rep. Nat. Conv, 56, 60, 64 & 68, chmn. Wis. Del, 64. Bus. & Prof. Pos: Gen. law practice, 39-44. Mem: Elks. George Washington Award, Am. Good Govt. Soc, 62; Distinguished Pub. Serv. Award, The Tax Found, 63. Rel: Roman Catholic. Legal Res: 406 N. Washington, Green Bay, Wis. 45301. Mailing Add: 2206 Rayburn House Office Bldg, Washington, D.C. 20515.

BYRNES, LAWRENCE C. R
b. Copenhagen, N.Y, 10/24/26; m. to Laura Varga. Educ: Cortland State Teachers Col. Polit. & Govt. Pos: N.Y. State Assemblyman, 64-66; chmn, Lewis Co. Rep. Cmt, 58-66; mem, Exec. Cmt, N.Y. Rep. State Cmt; chmn, Lewis Co. Bd. Supvr, 59. Bus. & Prof. Pos: Indust. rels, The J.P. Lewis Co, Beaver Falls. Mem: Denmark Grange; Beaver River Fish and Game Club; Lowville Elks; Croghan Lions; Beaver Falls and Copenhagen Fire Dept; Lewis Co. Firemans' Asn; K. of C; Croghan Holy Name Soc. Mailing Add: Beaver Falls, N.Y. 11305. (1967)

BYROADE, HENRY A.
U.S. Ambassador to Philippines
b. Allen Co, Ind, 7/24/13; m. to Jitka Henson; c. Gene, Alan, John and Linda. Educ: U.S. Mil. Acad, B.S, 37; Cornell Univ, M.S. in Eng, 41. Polit. & Govt. Pos: Dep. dir. of the Off. of German and Austrian Affairs, Dept. of State, 49; dir. Bur. of German Affairs and asst. secy. of state for Near East, S.Asian and African affairs, 49-52; U.S. Ambassador to Egypt, 55-56; U.S. Ambassador to Union of S.Africa, 56-59; U.S. Ambassador to Afghanistan, 59-62; chmn. of disarmanent adv. staff, New Arms Control and Disarmament Agency, 62; U.S. Ambassador to Burma, 63-68; State Dept. Adv. to the Industrial Col. of the Armed Forces, Wash, D.C, 68-69; U.S. Ambassador to Philippines, 69- Mil. Serv: World War II, command of Serv. of Supply in East. India, command of Serv. Supply in East. China, responsibility for air base construction in China and a tour of duty Army Gen. Staff responsible for coord. of policy affecting operations in India, China and Southeast Asia; Distinguished Serv. Medal; Legion of Merit with Two Oak Leaf Clusters; Air Medal; Spec. Breast Order of the Yun Hua. Legal Res: 6330 Nicholson, Falls Church, Va. 20011. Mailing Add: U.S. Embassy, Manila, Philippines.

BYRON, GOODLOE EDGAR D
Md. State Sen.
b. Williamsport, Md, 6/22/29; s. William Devereux Byron and Katharine Edgar B; m. 12/20/52 to Beverly Barton Butcher; c. Goodloe Edgar, Jr, Barton Kimball and Mary McComas. Educ: Univ. Va, A.B, 51; George Wash. Univ, J.D, 53; Gamma Theta Upsilon; Kappa Alpha Order. Polit. & Govt. Pos: Co. attorney, Frederick Co, Md, 59-62; pres, Young Dem. Clubs of Md, 61-62; Md. State Del, 63-67; Md. State Sen, currently. Bus. & Prof. Pos: Mem, Md. Hist. Trust, 64-; trustee, Md. Sch. for the Deaf, 65- Mil. Serv: Entered as 1st Lt, Army, 55, released as Capt, 57, after serv. in Judge Adv. Gen. Corps. Publ: 'The Production and Admissibility of Government Records in Federal Tort Claims Cases,' Md. Law Rev, spring 60. Mem: Nat. Capital Dem. Club; Md. Club; Mason; Elks; Ruritan; Optimist. Distinguished Serv. Award, Jr. C. of C, 65. Rel: Episcopal: Vestry, All Saints Episcopal Church. Mailing Add: 306 Grove Blvd, Frederick, Md. 21701.

BYRON, KATHARINE EDGAR D
b. Detroit, Mich, 10/25/02; d. Brig. Gen. Clinton Goodloe Edgar and Mary McComas E; m. to William Devereux Byron, wid; c. William D, Jr, James Edgar, Goodloe Edgar, David Wilson, II (deceased) and Louis McComas. Educ: Liggett Sch, Detroit, Mich; Holton-Arms Sch, Wash; Westover Sch, Middlebury, Conn. Polit. & Govt. Pos: Former U.S. Rep, Sixth Dist, Md; councilwoman, Williamsport, 38-40. Bus. & Prof. Pos: Chmn. flood disaster, Red Cross, Williamsport, Md, 36; former mem. bd, W.H. Edgar & Son, Sugar Brokers, Detroit, Mich. and W.D. Byron & Sons, Tanners, Williamsport, Md. Mem: Woman's Nat. Dem. Club; assoc. mem, Capitol Dem. Club; Cong. Club; Army and Navy Country Club; Arts Club Wash. D.C; Soc. Register Asn; pres, PTA, 36-38. Rel: Episcopal. Mailing Add: 3202 Scott Pl, Washington, D.C. 20007.

BYRON, PHILIP E. D
b. Chicago, Ill, 2/23/11; s. Philip Byron and Anna Bennett B; m. 10/31/36 to Josephine Archbold; c. Thomas A. Educ: Ind. Univ, LL.B, 34; Delta Tau Delta; Phi Delta Phi. Polit. & Govt. Pos: Mem. bd. trustees, City Sch, Elkhart, Ind, 57-60 & 65-66; mem, Ind. Dept. of Financial Insts, 60-62; mem, Ind. Employ. Sec. Bd, 62-65 and pres, 65; gen. counsel, Ind. Toll Rd. Cmn, 62- Bus. & Prof. Pos: Sch. attorney, City Sch, Elkhart, 61-65; mem. bd. trustees, Elkhart Gen. Hosp, 65- Mil. Serv: Entered as Lt.(jg), Navy, 42, released as Lt, 46, after serv. in Central Pac. Mem: City Club of Elkhart; Elks; Indianapolis Athletic Club; Elkhart City, Elkhart Co, Ind, Indianapolis, Seventh Fed. Circuit and Am. Bar Asns. Rel: Catholic. Legal Res: 1225 Greenleaf Blvd, Elkhart, Ind. 46514. Mailing Add: Byron and Daniels, 250 Indiana Bldg, Elkhart, Ind. 46514.

BYSTROM, IRENE NEVILLE D
Chmn, Women's Activities in Nebr. Dem. Party
b. Lincoln, Nebr, 7/1/18; d. Keith Neville (former Gov. of Nebr) and Mary Virginia Neill N; m. 7/25/42 to Roy Victor Bystrom; c. Patricia Margaret, Keith Neville and William Victor. Educ: Stephens Col, A.A, 37; Univ. Nebr, B.S. in Educ, 39; Sawyers Sch. of Bus, 41; Pi Lambda Theta; Kappa Kappa Gamma. Polit. & Govt. Pos: Co-chmn, Women for Kennedy, Nebr, 60; secy, Nebr. Jane Jefferson Club, 60-61; State Cent. Committeewoman, 45th Dist, 60-66 & 68; mem, State Prom. Cmt, 61; Lincoln Co. Chmn, Morrison for Gov, 62-64; mem, Higher Educ. Facilities Act Cmn, 64-66 & 68-69; v.chairwoman, Nebr. Dem. Party, 64-68; leader, Nebr. Del. to Women's Conf, Wash, 66; state coordinator, Robert F. Kennedy primary campaign, Nebr, 68; chmn, Women's Activities in Nebr. Dem. Party, 68-69. Bus. & Prof. Pos: Third Grade teacher, Ashland Sch, Nebr, 39-40; block worker, Am. Heart Fund, 69. Publ: Columnist, 'Party Girls,' Nebraska Democrat, monthly, 69- Mem: PTA; past mem, DAR, PEO and Am. Asn. Univ. Women; former Campfire Leader and Cub Scout Den Mother. Nebr. Ladies Skeet Champion, 57, 59 & 61; Pac. Northwest Ladies Skeet Champion, 64. Rel: Episcopal. Mailing Add: 316 E. Circle Dr, North Platte, Nebr. 69101.

C

CABANAS, HENRY ANTHONY, SR. R
b. Key West, Fla, 1/16/24; s. Julio Cabanas and Caridad Pazos C; div; c. Rita C.(Mrs. Ratliff) and Henry A, Jr. Educ: Univ. Fla, 45-46; Los Picaros; Phi Gamma Delta. Polit. & Govt. Pos: Mem, Monroe Co. Rep. Precinct Cmt, Fla, 67-69; dist. chmn, Monroe Co. Rep. Exec. Cmt, 67-69, chmn, 68-69; chief inspector, Fla. State Racing Cmn, 68-69. Bus. & Prof. Pos: Postal employee, U.S. Post Off, 52-62; real estate broker, Moffat Real Estate, Key West, Fla, 58-61; Cabanas Real Estate, 61-63; ins. adjuster, Freeman Enterprises, 63-64; Arnold & Watts, 64-66; Cabanas Adjusting, 66- Mem: Mail Carriers Union (pres, v.pres). Rel: Baptist. Mailing Add: 2213 Fogarty Ave, Key West, Fla. 33040.

CABELL, EARLE D
U.S. Rep, Tex.
b. Dallas, Tex, 10/27/06; s. Ben E. Cabell and Sadie Pearre C; m. 2/22/32 to Elizabeth Holder; c. Lee (Mrs. Pulley) and Earle, Jr. Educ: Tex. A&M, 25; South. Methodist Univ, 26. Polit. & Govt. Pos: Mem, Gov. Econ. Adv. Cmn, Tex, 52-57; adv. bd, Small Bus. Admin, 53-60; mayor, Dallas, Tex, 61-64; U.S. Rep, Fifth Dist, Tex, 65- Bus. & Prof. Pos: Pres, Tex. Mfrs. Asn, 55; Dairy Prod. Inst. of Tex, 56; Dallas Crime Cmn, 56-57; Dallas Sales Exec. Club, 57. Mem: Legion of Honor; DeMolay; Elks; Dallas Country Club; Dallas City Club; Dallas Athletic Club. Son and Grandson of Former Mayors of Dallas. Rel: Episcopal. Legal Res: Dallas, Tex. Mailing Add: 418 Cannon House Office Bldg, Washington, D.C. 20515.

CABELL, JOHN ALLEN D
Chmn, Harrison Co. Dem. Cent. Cmt, Ind.
b. Kiowa, Okla, 10/25/09; s. George Samuel Cabell and Elizabeth Mildred Winn C; m. 9/29/36 to Norma Ruth Windell; c. James Windell, Richard Allen, Bruce David and Rebecca Ellen. Educ: High sch. grad, 28. Polit. & Govt. Pos: Twp. trustee, Harrison Twp, Ind, 47-54; treas, Harrison Co. Dem. Cent. Cmt, 48-59 and chmn, 59-; clerk, Circuit Court, Harrison Co, 57-64; bridge administr, Ind. State Toll Bridge Cmt, 65-69. Bus. & Prof. Pos: Farm owner and operator, Corydon, Ind, 35- Mem: K. of P; Farmers Union; Nat. Farmers Orgn; Farm Bur. Ind. Rel: Lutheran. Mailing Add: R.R. 3, Box 49, Corydon, Ind. 47112.

CABLE, JOHN LEVI R
b. Lima, Ohio, 4/15/84; s. Davis Joseph Cable and Mary Harnley C; m. 12/9/10 to Rhea Watson; c. Alice Mary (Mrs. Samuel P. Hayes) and Davis Watson. Educ: Kenyon Col, LL.B, 06, hon. M.C.L; George Wash. Law Sch, J.D, 09; Delta Tau Delta. Polit. & Govt. Pos: Prosecuting attorney, Allen Co, Ohio, 16-20; U.S. Rep, Fourth Dist, Ohio, 21-25 & 29-33, auth. act granting independent citizenship to American women, 22, co-auth, Restrictive Immigration Act with Nat. Aliens Quota Syst, 24, auth, Fed. Corrupt Practices Act of 1925 and sponsor of act to present medals to officers and men of the Byrd 'Little America' Anarctic Exploration and drafted report with bill, 30; cand, gov, Ohio; spec. asst. to Attorney Gen. and Reconstruction Finance Corp, Ohio, 33-37; Rep. presidential elector, 36; govt. appeal agent, Selective Serv. Bd, Lima, 48-60. Bus. & Prof. Pos: Dir. and officer, Client Corps, currently. Publ: American Citizenship Rights of Women, U.S. Senate Subcmt. on Immigration, 72nd Cong; Loss of Citizenship; Denaturalization; The Alien in Wartime, Nat. Law Bk. Co, 43; Decisive Decisions of United States Citizenship, Michie Co, 68. Mem: Ohio State and Am. Bar Asns; Allen Co. Bar Asn.(pres, 50); past pres, Lima Kiwanis Club; YMCA (past mem. bd. trustees, Lima YMCA); Mason (32°); Elks; chmn, Red Cross Roll Call, 39-40. John L. Cable Manuscript Collection Established by Syracuse Univ, 65. Rel: Episcopal. Mailing Add: 117 N. Washington Dr, St. Armands Key, Sarasota, Fla. 33577.

CABOT, LAWRENCE A. D
b. Yonkers, N.Y, 5/17/19; m. to Rosalind; c. two. Educ: City Col. N.Y. Polit. & Govt. Pos: Mem. bd. of assessors, chmn, Ardsley Dem. Cmt and v.chmn, Greenburgh Dem. Cmt, formerly; N.Y. State Assemblyman, 64-67. Bus. & Prof. Pos: Pres, J. Ramsey Reese, Inc, dir, Tax Inst, C.W. Post Col. and mem. bd. dirs, Saw Mill River 'Y'. Mil. Serv: Army, 2nd Armored Div. Mem: Pres. 2nd Armored Div. Asn; U.S. Armor Asn; Am. Ord. Asn; Hardware Boosters; Nat. Asn. Mfrs; C. of C; Mfrs. Agents Nat. Asn; Ambulance Corps; Auxiliary Police; 52 Asns; Westchester Co. Civil Defense; N.Y. State Assessors; dir, Nat. Conf. Christians and Jews. Mailing Add: 135 Heatherdell Rd, Ardsley, N.Y. 10502.

CADA, FRANK JOSEPH D
b. Nebr, 10/30/06; s. Rudolph Cada and Emma Novotny C; m. 8/7/33 to Marcelline Pokorny; c. Dean F, Francis Ray, James A. and Mary F. Educ: Boyles Bus. Col, 22. Bus. & Prof. Pos: Pres, Colfax Co. Feeders & Breeders, 61-; bd. mem, Colfax Co. Fair, 40-66; treas, Sch. Dist. 47, 33-60. Mem: Pres, Clarkson Lions, 56; bd. mem, Farm Bureau, 50-66; Farmers Union; K. of C; Clarkson Commercial, Am. Angus Asn; Nebr. Angus Asn. Rel: Catholic. Mailing Add: Rt. 1, Clarkson, Nebr. 68629. (1967)

CADE, LIONEL BRUCE D
City Councilman, Compton, Calif.
b. Port Arthur, Tex, 8/14/18; s. Charles William Cade and Inez Slocum C; m. 1/24/52 to Gladys Louis Breach; c. John E, Frances (Mrs. Eric Wilson), Katherine Taylor and Kevin B. Educ: Univ. San Francisco, B.S, 47; Univ. South. Calif, M.B.A, 53; Alpha Phi Alpha. Polit. & Govt. Pos: Mem, 17th Dist, Dem. State Cmt, Calif, 62-, chmn, 68-; city councilman, Compton, 64-; treas, 17th Dist. Dem. Coun, 64-, v.pres, 67th Assembly Dist. Dem. Coun, 68; field rep, Calif. State Sen, 32nd Dist, 67-69, admin. asst, 69- Bus. & Prof. Pos: Pub. acct, Brooks & Cade, Compton, Calif, 59-; sr. field rep, State Bd. of Equalization, Los Angeles, 55-58. Mil. Serv: Entered as Pvt, Army, 42, released as Lt. Col.(Ret), Calif. Air Nat. Guard, 65, after serv. in various commands. Mem: Am. Soc. of Pub. Adminstr; Am. Legion; Elks; NAACP; bd. dirs, Compton C. of C; Boy Scouts; Camp Fire Girls. Gulick Award, Camp Fire Girls; Resolutions of Commendation for Commun. Serv, Calif. State Senate and Assembly. Rel: Roman Catholic. Mailing Add: 2421 W. 154th St, Compton, Calif. 90220.

CADIGAN, PATRICK J. D
b. Springfield, Ill, 11/1/36; s. Joseph A. Cadigan and Eva Kress C; m. 9/16/67 to Patricia Lock; c. Joseph L. Educ: Wash. Univ, A.B, 58; Univ. Ill, LL.B, 61; Sigma Alpha Epsilon; Phi Delta Phi. Polit. & Govt. Pos: Parliamentarian and legal adv. to Lt. Gov, Ill. State Sen, 65 & 67; circuit court magistrate, Seventh Judicial Circuit, Ill, 65-67; del, Dem. Nat. Conv, 68; asst. to Gov. Ill, 68-69; staff asst. to Sen. Minority Leader, Ill. State Sen, 67-68 & 69- Bus. & Prof. Pos: Assoc, Roberts & Kepner, Springfield, 61-65; assoc, Gillespie, Burke & Gillespie, 67- Mil. Serv: Entered as Airman, Air Nat. Guard, 61, released as Airman 1/C, 66, after serv. in 180th Tactical Fighter Squadron, 61-62. Mem: Sangamon Co, Ill. State and Am. Bar Asns; Ill. Supreme Court; U.S. Seventh Circuit Court Appeals; Sangamo Club; Island Bay Yacht Club. One of Ten Outstanding Young Men, Sangamon Co, Ill, 65. Rel: Roman Catholic. Mailing Add: 2317 Wiggins, Springfield, Ill. 62704.

CADWALLADER, JAMES KERRICK R
Mem, N.Mex. State Rep. Exec. Cmt.
b. Alamogordo, N.Mex, 4/10/27; s. Edgar E. Cadwallader and Allene Blacker C; m. 8/30/55 to Jane Briner; c. Allene Beth, Jan Elaine, Laurel Anne, Gwynn Adele and James Bruce. Educ: Colo. State Univ, B.A; Univ. N.Mex, grad. work, 2 years. Polit. & Govt. Pos: V.chmn, Otero Co. Rep. Party, N.Mex, 65-66, chmn, 66-; mem, N.Mex. State Rep. Exec. Cmt, 66- Bus. & Prof. Pos: Owner, Cadwallader Orchards. Mil. Serv: Entered as A/S, Navy, 45, released as SN, 46, re-entered as SN, 51, released, 52; Am. and Asiatic-Pac. Theater Ribbons; Korean Conflict Medal. Rel: Lutheran-Mo. Synod. Mailing Add: High Rolls, Mountain Park, N.Mex. 88325.

CADWALLADER, WILLIAM RAYBURN R
b. Cincinnati, Ohio, 9/27/31; s. Rayburn Woods Cadwallader and Ruth Windsor C; m. 4/13/57 to Patricia Ann Burch; c. John and Jeanne. Educ: Univ. Cincinnati, B.B.A, 54; Salmon P. Chase Law Sch, LL.B, 59; Delta Tau Delta. Polit. & Govt. Pos: Ohio State Rep, 65-69. Bus. & Prof. Pos: V.pres. New bus, 53rd Bank, 56-63; v.pres, Waldon, Inc, 63-65; commercial mgt. mgr, First Nat. Bank, 65-66. Mil. Serv: Entered as 2nd Lt, Army, 54, released as 1st Lt, 56. Mem: Cincinnati Mortgage Bankers Asn; Ohio Mortgage Bankers Asn; Cincinnati Real Estate Bd; Gr. Cincinnati Jr. C. of C; Ohio C. of C; Cincinnati Club. Rel: Quaker. Mailing Add: 711 Stanton Ave, Terrace Park, Hamilton, Ohio 45174. (1967)

CAEMMERER, JOHN D. R
N.Y. State Sen.
b. Brooklyn, N.Y, 1/19/28; s. Albert John Caemmerer and Helen Rooney C; m. 5/24/58 to Joan Holt; c. Jeanne, John, Matthew, Kathleen and Christine. Educ: Univ. Notre Dame, B.S, 49; St. John's Univ, LL.B, 57; Monogram Club. Polit. & Govt. Pos: Pres, Williston Park Rep. Club, N.Y, 58-60; village attorney, Williston Park, 59; dep. co. attorney, Nassau Co, 60-62; committeeman, North Hempstead Rep. Party, 60-, chmn, 66-; dep. town attorney, North Hempstead, 62-66; N.Y. State Sen, Fifth Dist, 66-; chmn. villages cmt, N.Y. State Legis, 66-68, v.chmn. Sen. judiciary cmt, 67-68, chmn. Sen. sub-cmt. on right of privacy, 68- and chmn. motor vehicles cmt, 69-; del, Rep. Nat. Conv, 68. Bus. & Prof. Pos: Real estate and ins. broker, 54-58; attorney, Pratt, Caemmerer and Cleary, 57- Mem: N.Y. State, Nassau Co. and Am. Bar Asns; Nassau Co. Cath. Lawyer's Guild; Maritime Law Asn; Williston Park Rep. Club; K. of C; Kiwanis; hon. mem, Town-wide Rep. Clubs. Merit award, Village of Williston Park. Rel: Roman Catholic. Mailing Add: 11 Post Ave, E. Williston, N.Y. 11596.

CAESAR, VICTORIA D
Single. Polit. & Govt. Pos: Former Ind. Sen. journey clerk and postmistress, Ind. State House of Rep. and Ind. State Senate; former Dep. U.S. Marshall; former justice of the peace, Calumet Twp; chief dep. to City Clerk, Gary, 59-64; former Ind. State Rep. Bus. & Prof. Pos: Public Relations. Mailing Add: Hotel Gary, Apt. 1008, Gary, Ind. 46402. (1967)

CAFFERTY, MICHAEL J. D
Dep. Asst. Secy. for Urban Systs. and Environ, Dept. of Transportation
b. N.Y.C, 6/7/24; s. Michael J. Cafferty and Bridget Martin C; single. Educ: Univ. Wash, B.A, 48, J.D, 51; Phi Delta Phi. Polit. & Govt. Pos: Counsel to U.S. Sen. Henry M. Jackson, 59-61; spec. asst. to chmn, Civil Aeronaut. Bd, 61-65; consult. to mayor, Seattle, Wash, 65-69; Dep. Asst. Secy. for Urban Systs. and Environ, Dept. of Transportation, 69- Bus. & Prof. Pos: Lawyer, 65- Mil. Serv: Entered as Aviation Cadet, Navy, 42, released as Lt.(jg), 46, after serv. in Naval Air Patrol Squadron in Pac, 44-45; Recalled to active duty during Berlin and Cuban Crisis, 61-62; Comdr, Naval, Res, 60- Publ: 'C.A.B. an Appraisal,' Univ. Wash. Bus. Quart, 12/65. Mem: Participant, 1st Int. Air Cargo Symposium, Atlanta, 62; panel chmn, 2nd Int. Air Cargo Symposium, Motnreal, 64; panelist, Nat. Asn. Railroad & Utility Cmnr, Honolulu, 64. Superior Serv. Award presented by Charles Murphy, Chmn, Civil Aeronaut. Bd, 65. 3000 pilot hours, single and multi-engine. Legal Res: Seattle, Wash. 98104. Mailing Add: Dept. of Transportation, 800 Independence Ave. S.W, Washington, D.C. 20590.

CAFFERY, PATRICK THOMSON D
U.S. Rep, La.
b. Franklin, La, 7/6/32; s. R. Earl Caffery and Letitia Decuir C; m. 1/30/54 to Anne Bercegeay; c. Patrick, Jr, Kevin and Machael. Educ: Univ. Southwest. La, B.A, 55; La. State Univ. Law Sch, J.D, 56; pres. student body, Univ. Southwest. La; Blue Key. Polit. & Govt. Pos: Asst. dist. attorney, 16th Judicial dist, La, 58-62; La. State Rep, 64-68; U.S. Rep, La, 68- Bus. & Prof. Pos: Assoc. and managing ed, La. Law Rev, 55-56; attorney-at-law. Mem: Iberia Parish, La, and Am. Bar Asns; chmn, Atchafalaya Basin Causeway Cmn, 68; Rotary (past pres, New Iberia Chap); Iberia Parish United Givers Fund (past pres); exec. bd, Evangeline Area Boy Scout Coun.(past cmnr); dir, Iberia Crippled Children's Asn. Distinguished Serv. Award, New Iberia Jaycees, 59; House of Del, La. Bar Asn, 62. Rel: Catholic. Legal Res: New Iberia, La. 70560. Mailing Add: 1206 Longworth House Office Bldg, Washington, D.C. 20515.

CAFFREY, JAMES TERENCE D
Iowa State Rep.
b. New York, N.Y, 2/19/09; s. Patrick Caffrey and Ellen Timmons C; m. 9/27/41 to Veronica Adrian; c. Velda Anne (Mrs. Sansaverino) and Veronica Katherine (Mrs. Zenti). Educ: Drake Commun. Col. Indust. Rels, Iowa, 5 years. Polit. & Govt. Pos: Iowa State Rep, Polk Co, 65-; mem, Des Moines Human Rights and Job Discrimination Cmns and Gov. Soc. and Econ. Trends Cmn. Bus. & Prof. Pos: Firestone Tire & Rubber Co, 45- Mem: Int. Exec. Bd, United Rubber Workers, 4 years; past pres, Local 310 United Rubber Workers Am, Des Moines, 12 years; v.pres, S.Cent. Iowa AFL-CIO, 63-; K. of C; labor chmn, U.S. Savings Bonds. Rel: Catholic. Legal Res: 2312 S.W. 12th St, Des Moines, Iowa 50315. Mailing Add: P.O. Box 4034 Highland Park Sta, Des Moines, Iowa 50333.

CAFIERO, JAMES S. R
N.J. State Assemblyman
b. North Wildwood, N.J, 9/21/28; m. to Patricia E. Campbell; c. Jamey, Drew and Stephen. Educ: Princeton Univ, A.B, 50; Univ. Pa. Law Sch, LL.B, 53. Polit. & Govt. Pos: Asst. prosecutor, Cape May Co, N.J, $2\frac{1}{2}$ years; mem. and

past pres, Cape May Co. Young Rep. Club; mem, North Wildwood Men's Rep. Club; solicitor, City of North Wildwood and Boroughs of West Wildwood and Woodbine, currently; solicitor for Bd. of Educ. and Planning Bd, City of North Wildwood, currently; N.J. State Assemblyman, Dist. 1, 68- Bus. & Prof. Pos: Attorney-at-law, Wildwood, N.J, 54-; mem. bd. dir, Marine Nat. Bank and mem. bd. gov, Burdette Tomlin Mem. Hosp, currently. Mil. Serv: Lt. Naval Res.(Ret). Mem: Cape May Co. Bar Asn.(past treas, v.pres, and pres); N.J. State and Am. Bar Asns; past v.pres. and dir, Wildwood Jr. C. of C; past pres, Cape May Co. Commun. Concerts Asn; past chmn, Cape May Co. Red Cross; Kiwanis; Navy League (past judge advocate, Jersey Cape Coun); Order of Sons of Italy. Legal Res: 410 Ocean Ave, North Wildwood, N.J. 08260. Mailing Add: 3303 New Jersey Ave, Wildwood, N.J. 08260.

CAHILL, WILLIAM T. R
U.S. Rep, N.J.
b. Phila, Pa, 6/25/12; m. to Elizabeth B. Murtetus; c. Eight. Educ: St. Joseph's Col, A.B, 33; Rutgers Law Sch, LL.B, 37. Polit. & Govt. Pos: U.S. Rep, N.J, 58-; mem, N.J. State Legis; spec. agent, Fed. Bur. of Invest; dep. Attorney Gen. of N.J; first asst. prosecutor, Co. of Camden; prosecutor, City of Camden. Bus. & Prof. Pos: Counselor at law. Rel: Catholic. Legal Res: 1009 Park Ave, Collingswood, N.J. 08108. Mailing Add: 2443 Rayburn Bldg, Washington, D.C. 20515. (1967)

CAHOON, FRANK KELL R
b. Austin, Tex, 6/20/34; s. Charles Wilbur Cahoon, Jr. and Sibyl Kell C; m. 2/16/57 to Paula Wanda Powers; c. Corrinne Elise and Frank Kell, Jr. Educ: Univ. Tex, B.S. in Geol, 57; Kappa Sigma. Polit. & Govt. Pos: Tex. State Rep, 70th Dist, Tex, 64-67 and mem. cmts, Revenue and Tax, Labor, Pub. Health, Liquor Regulation and Vet. Affairs, Tex. State House of Rep; del, Rep. Nat. Conv, 68. Bus. & Prof. Pos: Independent Oil Operator, Midland, Tex, 66; secy, Hobbs Flare, Hobbs, N.Mex, 66. Mil. Serv: Entered as 2nd Lt, Corps of Engrs, U.S. Army, 57, released as 1st Lt, 59. Mem: Kiwanis; Am. Legion. Rel: Presbyterian. Legal Res: 1615 Ventura, Midland, Tex. 79701. Mailing Add: 620 Commercial Bank Tower, Midland, Tex. 79701. (1967)

CAHOON, PAUL STACY D
b. Walden, Vt, 12/16/22; m. to Elsie B. Fuller; c. One son, three daughters. Educ: Danville High Sch. Polit. & Govt. Pos: Mem, Danville Sch. Bd, Vt, 52-, chmn, 7 years; town agent, Danville, 57 and town grand juror, 57-; former Vt. State Rep. Bus. & Prof. Pos: Dairy farmer. Mem: Caledonia Co. Farm Bur. Rel: Methodist. Mailing Add: R.D. 1, West Danville, Vt. 05828. (1967)

CAIN, CHARLES MARSHALL R
S.C. State Rep.
b. Richmond, Va, 7/20/34; s. Calvin Howard Cain (deceased) and Helen Holley C; m. 6/24/61 to Anne Kennedy Hodges; c. Julia Summerall and John Marshall. Educ: Univ. S.C, B.S, 56, LL.B, 59; Blue Key Hon. Leadership; Kappa Sigma Kappa; Phi Kappa Sigma; Univ. S.C. Inter-Fraternity Coun. Polit. & Govt. Pos: Mem, Aiken Co. Tax Equilization Study Cmn, S.C, 64; mem. and chmn, City of Aiken Planning & Zoning Cmn, 65-68; S.C. State Rep, 68- Mil. Serv: Entered as Airman Basic, Air Nat. Guard, 59, released as Airman 1/C, 65, after serv. in D.C. Air Nat. Guard and 9301st Air Force Res. Recovery Squadron. Publ: 'Right of Privacy,' S.C. Law Quart, 58. Mem: Am. Bar Asn; S.C. Bar Asn.(circuit v.pres, 65); Aiken Co. Bar Asn.(v.pres, 66); dir, Gr. Aiken C. of C, 68-; Rotary. Distinguished Serv. Award of Aiken, S.C. Jaycees, 67. Rel: Baptist. Mailing Add: 9 Belaire Terr. S.W, Aiken, S.C. 29801.

CAIN, ELMO VIRGIL D
b. Lemmon, S.Dak, 8/20/18; s. Wesley Cain and Laura Terrell C; single. Educ: Lemmon High Sch, 4 years. Polit. & Govt. Pos: Chmn, Perkins Co. Dem. Party, S.Dak, 45-68. Bus. & Prof. Pos: Gen. mgr, Farmers Coop. Asn, Thunder Hawk, S.Dak, 45-69 and Lemmon Equity Exchange, Lemmon, S.Dak, 49-69. Mil. Serv: Entered as Pvt, Army, 42, released as S/Sgt, 45, after serv. in 808 T.D. Bn, ETO, 44-45; Good Conduct Medal with 3 Stars. Mem: Lions; VFW; D.H.L. Riding Club; Perkins Co. Fair Bd; C. of C; Farmers Union. Rel: Presbyterian. Mailing Add: 4 Third St. E, Lemmon, S.Dak. 57638.

CAIN, FRANCIS JOSEPH D
Mayor, Burlington, Vt.
b. Burlington, Vt, Dec. 20; s. Leo Andrew Cain and Elizabeth Carpenter C; m. 11/8/47 to Mary Jane Allen; c. Michael, William, Carolyn, Thomas, Martha, Patricia, Karen Elizabeth, Susan, Barbara and Brian. Educ: St. Michael's Col, A.B, 43; Am. Inst. Property and Liability Underwriters, C.P.C.U, 51. Polit. & Govt. Pos: Park Cmnr, Burlington, Vt, 58-62, alderman, Ward I, 62-65, mayor, 65-; del, Dem. Nat. Conv, 68. Mil. Serv: Entered as Midn, Naval Res, 43, released as Lt.(jg), 46, after serv. in European, Mediterranean and Pac. Theatres, 44-46. Mem: Soc. Chartered Property Casuality Underwriters; K. of C.(4°); Am. Legion. Rel: Catholic. Mailing Add: 22 Bilodeau Court, Burlington, Vt. 05401.

CAIN, JAMES CLEMENT D
W.Va. State Del.
b. Canton, Ohio, 4/13/25; s. Emmet Alexander Cain and Wilhelmina Hessee C; m. 9/11/50 to Nancy Lee Caldwell; c. Ray Lee, Lawyer. Educ: W.Va. Bus. Col; Concord Col, B.A; Tulane Univ, LL.B; Phi Alpha Delta. Polit. & Govt. Pos: W.Va. State Del, 64-; trustee in bankruptcy, U.S. Dist. Court, South. Dist, W.Va. Mem: W.Va. State Bar Asn; YMCA; former pres, W.Va. Jaycees. Rel: Presbyterian. Mailing Add: Law & Commerce Bldg, Bluefield, W.Va. 24701.

CAIN, L. JOHN D
b. Colchester, Vt, 4/28/25; s. Leo Andrew Cain and Mary Elizabeth Carpenter C; m. 7/31/48 to Paulina Woodbury Powers; c. John Powers, Stephen James, Paul Rutter, Daniel Nolan, Lawrence Andrew, Constance Mary and Elizabeth. Educ: Univ. Vt, 46-47; Boston Col. Law Sch, LL.B, 50; Alpha Tau Omega. Polit. & Govt. Pos: Vt. State Rep, 53-54; alderman, Burlington, 57-61; city attorney and corp. counsel, Burlington, 63-65; Vt. State Sen, Grand Isle and Chittenden Co, 67-69. Mil. Serv: Entered as Pvt, Army Air Force, 43, released as Tech. Sgt, 45, after serv. in Eighth Air Force, 305th Bomb Group, 422nd Bomb Sq, ETO, 44-45; Purple Heart; Air Medal with 2 Oak Leaf Clusters. Mem: Am. and Vt. Bar Asns; pres, Chittenden Co. Bar Asn, 67; Ethan Allen Club; Burlington Country Club. Rel: Catholic. Legal Res: 56 Cliff St, Burlington, Vt. 05401. Mailing Add: 231 South Union St, Burlington, Vt. 05401. (1967)

CAIRNES, WILLIAM E. R
b. Chicago, Ill, 7/22/09; s. Chauncey Edison Cairnes (deceased) and Ethel McConnell C.(deceased); m. 11/6/37 to Rose Pratscher; c. Nancy (Mrs. C. Lawrence McBurney) and Donna (Mrs. Jerry Mannon). Educ: Univ. Ill, 29-30; Pi Tau Pi Sigma; Phalanx. Polit. & Govt. Pos: Committeeman, Palos Twp, Twp. Rep. Cmt, Ill, 66- Bus. & Prof. Pos: Chief engr, Motorola, Inc, Chicago, Ill, 37-47; pres, Radio Cores, Inc, Oak Lawn, Ill, 47-65; chmn. bd, Am. Bank of Oak Lawn until 63; owner and pres, Roberts Oak Printing, Inc, 68-69; consult. Mem: Sr. mem, Inst. of Elec. & Electronics Engrs; Ill. Soc. Prfnl. Engrs; Registered Prfnl. Engr; Am. Ord. Soc; South. Shores Yacht Club; Oak Lawn Lions Club; Elks; trustee, Buena Vista Col; Southwest YMCA (chmn. bd); Far South Dist. YMCA (chmn. coord. coun). Rel: Presbyterian. Mailing Add: 119 Old Creek Rd, Palos Park, Ill. 60464.

CAIRNS, ROBERT THOMPSON R
b. Hartford, Conn, 12/13/97; s. Edward Thompson Cairns and Elizabeth Allardyce C; m. 6/19/24 to Franceska Fairbanks, wid. 12/8/59; c. Franceska G.(Mrs. Morrison), Robert A. and Pauline C.(Mrs. Murphy). Educ: Yale Col, A.B, 20; Beta Theta Pi. Polit. & Govt. Pos: Del, Rep. State Conv, 50-; Conn. State Rep, 53-69, chmn. pub. personnel cmt, 55, state develop. cmt, 57 and finance cmt, 61-65; mem, spec. cmn. on Long Lane Sch, 55; Conn. Cmn. on Intergovt. Coop, 55-57; mem, Conn. Rep. Finance Cmt, 55-58, v.chmn, 55-57; del, Rep. Nat. Conv, 56 & 64; chmn, Gov. Spec. Cmn. on Maintenance State Employees, 59; mem, Legis. Coun, 59-69; mem, Conn. Transportation Authority, 65-; chmn, Island Ave. Elem. and Daniel Hand High Sch. Bldg. Cmts; mem, Madison Rep. Town Cmt, 60-66 & 69-; mem, Conn. Cmn. Higher Educ, 63-65. Bus. & Prof. Pos: Gen. agent, Providence Ins. Co, Wash, 40-42; dir, Madison Trust Co, Conn, 55-64; columnist, Report from Hartford, Shore Line Times, 59-69; chmn. adv. cmt, Union & New Haven Trust Co, 64- Mil. Serv: Entered as Pvt, Army, 17, released as 1st Lt, 19, after serv. in Field Artil, France; recalled to duty, 42, released as Maj, 46, after serv. as Exec. Officer, War Dept. Personnel Center, Ft. Devens; Army Commendation Medal with Star. Mem: Pres, Conn. Soc. Prev. Blindness; bd. mem, Nat. Soc. Prev. Blindness; Am. Legion; SAR; Elks; pres, Madison Country Club; Madison Beach Club; Grad. Club of New Haven; Hartford Club. Rel: Episcopal. Legal Res: 17 Hotchkiss Lane, Madison, Conn. 06443. Mailing Add: Box 529, Madison, Conn. 06443.

CAJERO, BERNARDO MORENO D
Ariz. State Rep.
b. Morenci, Ariz, 1/30/16; s. Inocencio Cajero and Lupe Moreno C; m. May, 1938 to Carmen Fernandez; c. Olivia Bernadine (Mrs. Martin Bedford) and Monica. Educ: Morenci High Sch, grad, 35; Am. Barber Col, grad, 37. Polit. & Govt. Pos: Mem. exec. bd, Young Dem. of Tucson, Ariz, 69; Ariz. State Rep, Dist. 7A, Pima Co, 69- Bus. & Prof. Pos: Owner and operator of barber shops, 37-; owner, Nayo's Liquor Store, 63-67; owner, Nayo's Barber Shop, Tucson, Ariz, 68- Mem: Young Dem. Gr. Tucson; South Tucson Lions; Sociedad Mutualista Porfirio Diaz, Tucson; WOW. Rel: Catholic. Mailing Add: 104 W. District St, Tucson, Ariz. 85714.

CALABRESE, ANTHONY O. D
Ohio State Sen.
b. Forli Del Sannio, Campobasso, Italy, 7/20/11; s. Raffaele Calabrese and Filomena Giammari C; m. 9/8/31 to Mary Margaret Buzzelli; c. Anthony O, Jr. and Leonard Michael. Educ: West. Reserve Univ, 58-60. Hon. LL.D, Bethany Col. Polit. & Govt. Pos: Nominee, Cleveland City Coun, Ohio, 50; ward leader, 19th Ward Dem. Party, 50; precinct committeeman, Dem. Party, 52-56; Ohio State Rep, 52-56; Ohio State Sen, 63-; del, Dem. Nat. Conv, 68. Bus. & Prof. Pos: Pres, Real Estate Appraisals & Bus. Consults, 50-; pres, Calabrese & Assocs, 50-; mkt. consult, Massillon Savings & Loan Co, 64- Mem: Appraisers Asn, Ohio; K. of C; first asst. pres, Sons of Italy; Boys Town of Italy; Columbus Day Civic Club; Cleveland City Club; del, Local 108, AFL-CIO. Man of Year Award, 62; Cross of Order of Merit, Republic of Italy, 59. Rel: Roman Catholic. Mailing Add: 12618 Fairhill Rd, Cleveland, Ohio 44120.

CALABRESE, ANTHONY O, JR. D
b. Cleveland, Ohio, 6/20/35; s. State Sen. Anthony O. Calabrese and Mary Buzzelli C; m. 4/18/59 to Carolyn Silla; c. Lisa Marie, Carla Marie and Regina Marie. Educ: John Carroll Univ, B.S.S, 57; Cleveland-Marshall Law Sch, LL.B, 61. Polit. & Govt. Pos: Ohio State Rep, 60-66; Dem. Precinct Committeeman, Cleveland, Ohio, 62-63; committeeman, 22nd Dist. State Dem. Cent. Cmt, 65-69; alternate del, Dem. Nat. Conv, 68. Mem: Cleveland, Cuyahoga and Ohio State Bar Asns; Am. Trial Lawyers Asn; Justinian Forum; Citizens League; City Club; K. of C. Rel: Catholic. Legal Res: 12601 Mt. Overlook, Cleveland, Ohio 44120. Mailing Add: 750 Prospect, Cleveland, Ohio 44115. (1967)

CALABRESE, JOSEPH V. D
Colo. State Rep.
b. Denver, Colo, 4/2/11. Polit. & Govt. Pos: Colo. State Rep, serving seventh term. Bus. & Prof. Pos: Exec. dir, Laradon Hall, a sch. for mentally retarded. Mem: Former dir, Nat. Asn. for Retarded Children. Mailing Add: 2707 W. 46th Ave, Denver, Colo. 80211.

CALABRESE, SYLVIA M. D
Recording Secy, 14th Cong. Dist. Dem. Orgn, Mich.
b. Detroit, Mich, 12/31/34; d. Orland J. Calabrese and Ralphine Barretta C; single. Educ: E. Commerce High Sch, diploma, 53. Polit. & Govt. Pos: Recording secy, 14th Dist. Young Dem, Mich, 65-67; recording secy, Fighting Fourteenth Dem. Club, 66-67; exec. bd, Am. Dem. Action, Metrop. Detroit Chap, 67-68; precinct del, Dem. Party, Mich, 66-; recording secy, 14th Cong. Dist. Dem. Orgn, 67-; mem, Citizens for Kennedy, 68; alternate del, Dem. Nat. Conv, 68. Bus. & Prof. Pos: Supvr, Mich. Blue Cross, 58-61, procedure analyst, 61-68, specialist, 68- Rel: Roman Catholic. Mailing Add: 14667 Collingham, Detroit, Mich. 48205.

CALDEN, GERTRUDE BECKWITH R
Mem, Calif. Rep. State Cent. Cmt.
b. Santa Paula, Calif, 4/18/09; d. Ralph Leslie Beckwith and Bernice Hart Hall B; m. 12/16/61 to Guy Cecil Calden, Jr, wid; c. Thad Carlyle MacMillian. Educ: Woodbury Col, grad. in Bus; Santa Barbara City Col; Univ. Calif, Berkeley; Los Angeles and Santa Barbara; Univ. Affiliates; Commun. Coun. Polit. & Govt. Pos: Admin. asst. to Santa Barbara Co. campaign chmn, Nixon-Lodge campaign, Calif, 60; assisted recruitment and strategy, Nixon for Gov, Santa Barbara Co, 62; organizer and charter pres, Montecito Rep. Women's Club, Federated, 63-65; v.pres, Santa Barbara Rep. Assembly, 64-65; organizer, Coldspring, Mission Area, Riviera, Alamar, G.A.L.S. and Santa Maria Rep. Women's Clubs, Federated, 65-68; mem, 13th Cong. Dist. Rep. Cmt, 65-; co. chmn, Robert Finch for Lt. Gov, 66; pres, Santa Barbara Co. Fedn. of Rep. Women's Clubs, 66-; mem. bd. of dirs, Calif. Federated Rep. Women, South. Div, 66-; assoc. mem, Calif. Rep. State Cent. Cmt, 67-68, mem, 69- and mem, Speakers Bur, 67-; del, Nat. Conv, Nat. Fedn. of Rep. Women, 67 & 69 and Rep. Women's Nat. Spring Conf, 68 & 69; co. fedn. coordinator, Women for Nixon-Agnew, 68; mem, State Adv. Cmt. on Continuing Educ. for Calif. Commun. Cols, 69- Bus. & Prof. Pos: Co-founder and pres. of commun. coun, Santa Barbara City Col, Calif, 57-63; mem. bd. of dirs, Santa Barbara Personnel Asn, 57-58; chmn. teacher recognition div, Santa Barbara Co. Selective Teacher Recruitment Coun, 60; pres. adult educ. adv. cmt, Santa Barbara Commun. Col, 67-69; mem. bd. of dirs, Santa Barbara Work Training Prog, Inc, 69- Publ: Contributed various poems, Gossamer Wings, 39. Mem: Zonta Int.(dist. chmn, Amelia Earhart Scholarship, 57-58, bd. dirs. and pres, Santa Barbara Club, currently); Women's Bd. of Santa Barbara Ment. Health Asn; mem. bd. of dirs, Santa Barbara United Serv. Orgn; Channel City Women's Forum; Santa Barbara Scholarship Found; Santa Barbara Coun. of Women's Clubs; Am. Field Serv; Friends of Santa Barbara Libr; Calif. Hist. Soc; Nat. Soc. of Parliamentarians; Calif. Parliamentary Soc; Int. Platform Asn; C. of C.(mem. educ. cmt, Santa Barbara Chap, 55-61); adv. mem, The Marguis Biographical Libr. Soc. Rel: Protestant. Mailing Add: 2700 State St, Apt. 6, Santa Barbara, Calif. 93105.

CALDER, N(ORMAN) BRUCE R
b. Dallas, Tex, 7/21/25; s. Curtis E. Calder and Bennie Glanton C; m. 3/15/68 to Mitzie Lee Crater; c. Christopher Bruce, Curtis Howard, Craig Gordon and Norman Bruce Jr. Educ: Yale Univ, B.S. in Indust. Admin, 46; Univ. Tex, Austin, B.S. in Petrol. Eng, 49; Sigma Gamma Epsilon; Delta Psi. Polit. & Govt. Pos: Campaign chmn, Jim Collins, Tex, 66; finance chmn, Dallas Co. Rep. Party, 67-68; cand. for State Rep, Tex, 68; alternate del, Rep. Nat. Conv, 68. Bus. & Prof. Pos: Petroleum engr, Gulf Oil Corp, West Tex, 49-51; petroleum engr, Woodward & Co, Dallas, 51-56; owner-mgr, Horizon Oil & Gas Co, 56-60, v.pres, 60- Mil. Serv: Entered as Aviation Cadet, Air Force, 43, released as Aviation Cadet, 45, after serving in Air Training Command, 43-45; Good Conduct Ribbon; Am. Theatre Ribbon. Mem: Soc. Petroleum Engrs; dir, Independent Petroleum Asn. Am; past pres, Yale Club Dallas; mem. alumni bd, Phillips Acad, Andover, Mass; pres, Dad's Club St. Mark's Sch, Tex. Rel: Protestant. Legal Res: 8509 Town House Row, Dallas, Tex. 75225. Mailing Add: 1200 Hartford Bldg, Dallas, Tex. 75201.

CALDWELL, HUGH D
b. Paisley, Scotland; married; c. three. Educ: Grad. St. Mungo's Acad, Glasgow, Scotland. Polit. & Govt. Pos: Mem. Union Co. Bd. of Freeholders; four years as city chmn. Bus. & Prof. Pos: Toolmaker. Mem: Pres, Local 260, UAW, AFL-CIO; former 1st v.pres, N.J. CIO. Mailing Add: 1238 Moffett, Plainfield, N.J. 07060. (1967)

CALDWELL, IRENE CATHERINE R
State Committeewoman, Mass. Rep. Party
b. Medford, Mass. 4/30/21; d. Pacifico Antonelli and Emilia Quarato A; m. 2/24/59 to Owen Manson Caldwell. Educ: Somerville High Sch, Mass. Polit. & Govt. Pos: Mem, Mass. Women Fedn. Rep. Club, 52; pres, Women's Columbus Rep. Club, Mass, 60; mem, Boston City Cmt, 60; v.chmn, Rep. Ward Cmt, Jamaica Plain, 68; alternate del, Rep. Nat. Conv, 68; state committeewoman, Mass. Rep. Party, 68- Rel: Catholic. Mailing Add. 50 Lochstead Ave, Jamaica Plain, Mass. 02130.

CALDWELL, J. EDWARD D
Conn. State Sen.
b. Bridgeport, Conn, 6/13/27; married. Educ: Fairfield Univ, B.A. cum laude; Univ. Conn. Law Sch, LL.B. Polit. & Govt. Pos: Conn. State Sen, 59- Bus. & Prof. Pos: Attorney. Mailing Add: 1115 Main St, Bridgeport, Conn. 06603. (1967)

CALDWELL, JAMES CARLTON D
Tenn. State Rep.
b. Decatur, Ala, 9/24/25; s. James Carlton Caldwell, Sr.(deceased) and Jewel Farrar C; m. 8/31/46 to Mary Griswold; c. James Wesley, Carlton Dewitt, Mark Rankin and Bruce Griswold. Educ: Univ. Chattanooga, B.B.A, 50. Polit. & Govt. Pos: Tenn. State Rep, 59- Bus. & Prof. Pos: Pres, Caldwell-Casey & Assoc, Inc, 54-; secy, Nat. Motor Club, Inc, 59- Mil. Serv: Entered as Pvt, Army Air Corps, 43, released as Cpl, 46, after serv. in 160th Liasion Sq. Commando, South Pac, 44-45; Battle Ribbons. Mem: Nat. Asn. of Life Underwriters; bd. mem, United Fund, Orange Grove Center for Retarded, Ment. Health Asn, United Cerebral Palsy and Coun. for Alcoholism; Jr. C. of C; C. of C; Signal Mt. Golf & Country Club. Young Man of the Year, Tenn, 56. Rel: Baptist; Deacon. Mailing Add: 1116 Crownpoint Rd. West, Signal Mountain, Tenn. 37377.

CALDWELL, JAMES H. D
b. Janesville, Wis, 1/13/16; married. Educ: Wis. pub. schs. Polit. & Govt. Pos: Mem. city coun, Salisbury, Md, 51-52; chmn, Wicomico Co. Dem. State Cent. Cmt, 54-58; Md. State Del, 59-67. Bus. & Prof. Pos: Proprietor of ins. agency. Mem: Chmn, Salisbury Dist. Boy Scouts; Youth & Civic Center Fund; dir, United Fund and Red Cross; past pres, Salisbury Jr. C. of C; Salisbury C. of C; Lions; Eastside Men's Club. Rel: Presbyterian; Bd. of Trustees. Mailing Add: 106 W. Circle Ave, Salisbury, Md. 21801. (1967)

CALDWELL, JAMES M. R
b. 1919. Educ: Univ. Ky, A.B.J. Polit. & Govt. Pos: Ky. State Rep, 63-67; past mem. bd. trustees, Fairmeade, Ky. Bus. & Prof. Pos: Sta. mgr, WAVE Radio, Inc. Mil. Serv: Navy Res. Mem: First Magisterial Rep. Club; Cmt. for Shakespeare in Cent. Park; bd. and past pres, Ky. Broadcasters Asn; chmn, Ky. Radio Indust. Adv. Cmt; v.chmn, Louisville Great Decisions Cmt; dir, Louisville Children's Theatre. Rel: Presbyterian. Mailing Add: 606 Fatima Lane, Louisville, Ky. 40207.

CALDWELL, JOHN JAY, JR. R
Chmn, Marengo Co. Rep. Party, Ala.
b. Demopolis, Ala, 7/12/23; s. John Jay Caldwell and Alice Ars C; m. 3/21/47 to Mary Lane Lee; c. Cathy and John Jay. Educ: Auburn Univ, B.S, 47; Alpha Omega Pi; Phi Delta Theta. Polit. & Govt. Pos: Chmn, Marengo Co. Rep. Party, Ala, 68- Bus. & Prof. Pos: Log and timber buyer, Miller & Co, Inc, York, Ala, 48-63 and Demopolis, Ala, 63- Mil. Serv: Entered as A/S, Navy, 43, released as Ens, 46 after serv. in assembly and repair plant, Seattle, Wash, 45-46. Mem: Lions Int.(past dist. gov). Rel: Methodist. Legal Res: U.S. Hwy. 80 E, Demopolis, Ala. 36732. Mailing Add: P.O. Box 148, Demopolis, Ala. 36732.

CALDWELL, JOHNNIE L. D
Ga. State Rep.
b. Taylor Co, Ga, 8/10/22; m. 1/17/42 to Martha Smisson; c. Patricia Ann, Barbara Sue and Johnnie L, Jr. Educ: Woodrow Wilson Law Col. Polit. & Govt. Pos: Ga. State Rep, 55- Bus. & Prof. Pos: Attorney, Thomaston and Zebulon. Mil. Serv: U.S. Army, World War II. Mailing Add: Thomaston, Ga. 31792.

CALDWELL, LEWIS A. H. D
Ill. State Rep.
b. Chicago, Ill, 10/12/05; s. Lewis A.H. Caldwell, Sr.(deceased) and Mary Prince C; m. 1/17/47 to Ruth Stimpson; c. Barbara and Phyllis Y. Educ: Northwest Univ, B.S, 33, M.S, 40; Alpha Phi Alpha. Polit. & Govt. Pos: Case worker, Cook Co. Bur. Pub. Aid, Ill, 33-41; probation officer, Cook Co. Family Court, 41-48; Ill. State Rep, 29th Dist, 67- Bus. & Prof. Pos: Mgr, Baldwin Ice Cream Co, 52-61; sales rep, Hawthorn-Mellody Farms Dairy, 61-67. Publ: The Policy King, New Vistas Publ. Co, 46; Chicago—City of Opportunity and Progress, The Cosmopolitan C. of C, 61. Mem: Financial secy, Cosmopolitan C. of C; exec. dir, Cosmopolitan C. of C, 68-; bd. mem, Chicago Area Proj. Rel: Methodist. Mailing Add: 6518 S. Minerva Ave, Chicago, Ill. 60637.

CALDWELL, MILLARD FILLMORE, JR. D
b. Knoxville, Tenn, 2/6/97; s. Millard Fillmore Caldwell and Martha Jane Clapp C; m. 2/14/25 to Mary Rebecca Harwood; c. Sally Perkins (Mrs. McCord) and Susan Beverly (Mrs. Dodd). Educ: Carson and Newman Col, 13-14; Univ. Miss, 17-18; Univ. Va, 19-22, LL.B; Alpha Kappa Psi; Blue Key; Kappa Sigma; Phi Alpha Delta. Hon. LL.D, Rollins Col, Univ. Fla, Fla. South. Univ. and Fla. State Univ. Polit. & Govt. Pos: Co. attorney, Santa Rosa Co. and City attorney, Milton, Fla, 25-32; mem, Fla. State Legis, 28-32; U.S. Rep, 33-41; Gov, 45-49; chmn. bd. control, South. Regional Educ, 48-51; chmn, Fla. Cmn. Constitutional Govt, 57-65; Chief Justice, Supreme Court of Fla, 62-69. Mil. Serv: Entered as Pvt, Army, 18, released as 2nd Lt, 19. Mem: Newcomen Soc; Huguenot Soc; SAR. Legal Res: Old Bainbridge Rd, Tallahassee, Fla. 32301. Mailing Add: Harwood Plantation, Old Bainbridge Rd, Tallahassee, Fla. 32301.

CALDWELL, NEIL D
Tex. State Rep.
b. Gulf, Tex, 11/13/29; s. Allen Caldwell and Mattye Hester C; m. 2/29/56; to Mary Lou Dorchester; c. Bruce Shelton, Matthew Ray, Leigh Ann and Declan Neil. Educ: Univ. Tex, B.A, 54, LL.B, 57; Phi Alpha Delta; Silver Spurs Serv. Orgn. Polit. & Govt. Pos: Tex. State Rep, Dist. 23, 60- Bus. & Prof. Pos: Prof. Law, S.Tex. Col. Law, 58-59. Mil. Serv: Entered as Pvt, Army, 51, released as Pfc, 53, after serv. in 3rd Army, U.S. Mem: Am. Legion; Tex. Bar Asn; bd. dirs, Brazoria Co. Bar Asn, 63. Photography winner, Houston Div, Nat. Newspaper Snapshot Award. Rel: Baptist. Legal Res: 1810 Meadowview, Alvin, Tex. 77511. Mailing Add: Angleton Savings Annex, Angleton, Tex. 77511.

CALDWELL, PAMELA BUTLER R
Chmn, Westfield Rep. City Cmt, Mass.
b. Westfield, Mass, 2/18/31; d. Alden F. Butler and Florence Quinn B; m. 2/21/53 to Eben Caldwell; c. Candace and Sarah. Educ: Westbrook Jr. Col, Portland, Maine, Assoc. Secretarial Sci. Polit. & Govt. Pos: Del, Mass. Rep. State Conv, 66; v.chmn, Westfield Rep. City Cmt, 66-68, chmn, 68-; mem. and secy, Westfield High Sch. Bldg. Cmt, 68- Mem: Bd. Trustees, Shurtleff Mission. Rel: Protestant. Mailing Add: P.O. Box 312, Carriage Lane, Westfield, Mass. 01085.

CALDWELL, THOMAS DIXON, JR. R
b. Harrisburg, Pa, 10/24/28; s.Thomas D. Caldwell and Martha Shartzer C; m. 6/9/51 to Lenore June Shadle; c. Thomas, IV, Ellen Lee and Suzanne. Educ: Dickinson Col, B.A, 49; Dickinson Sch. of Law, LL.B, 52; Beta Theta Pi. Polit. & Govt. Pos: Pa. State Rep, 65-67. Mil. Serv: Entered as Pvt, Army, 52, released as Pfc, 54. Mem: Dauphin Co. Bar Asn; Pa. Bar Asn; Mason; bd. mem, Dauphin Co. Children's Home; Boys Club of Harrisburg. Rel: Methodist. Mailing Add: 550 Park Terr, Harrisburg, Pa. 17111.

CALHOON, ED LATTA R
Chmn, Beaver Co. Rep. Party, Okla.
b. Beaver, Okla, 12/9/22; s. Walter Lee Calhoon and Wina Rae Latta C; m. 8/19/49 to Felice Hazel Warburton; c. Scott and Lane Felice. Educ: Northwest. State Col, B.S, 47; Univ. Okla. Sch. Med, M.D, 51. Polit. & Govt. Pos: Chmn, Beaver Co. Rep. Party, Okla, 60-; mem. bd. regents, Okla. Col. Lib. Arts, 65. Bus. & Prof. Pos: Dir, Okla. State Cancer Soc, 58-; trustee, Okla. State Med. Asn, 63-, mem, coun. prfnl. educ, 64-, pres. elect, 69; mem, State Ment. Health Planning Bd, 65; pres, Okla. Univ. Med. Sch. Alumni. Mil. Serv: Pvt, Army, 42-43. Mem: Mason. Rel: Methodist. Mailing Add: Box 70, Beaver, Okla. 73932.

CALHOUN, ANNE CARTER R
b. Atlanta, Ga, 3/16/23; d. Edgar Vernon Carter and Lawson Hines C; m. 9/23/44 to William Cozart Calhoun; c. Elizabeth Carter, Patricia Lawson and Catherine Martin. Educ: Univ. Ga, 44; Phi Mu; Glee Club. Polit. & Govt.

Pos: Del, Rep. Nat. Conv. and mem, Platform Cmt, 60 & 64; secy, Ga. State Rep. Exec. Cmt, 66; v.chmn, Tenth Cong. Dist. Rep. Exec. Cmt, 66; first v.pres, Ga. Fedn. Rep. Women; former secy, Ga. State Rep. Party. Mem: V.chmn, Easter Seal Drive, 62; Girl Scout Coun, East. Ga; Jr. League of Augusta. Rel: Episcopal. Mailing Add: 2337 Kings Way, Augusta, Ga. 30904. (1967)

CALHOUN, FRANK ELLINWOOD R
Mem, Cornwall Rep. Town Cmt, Conn.
b. Cornwall, Conn, 4/1/05; s. John Edward Calhoun and Marjorie Ellinwood C; m. 5/9/31 to Mary Everett Swift; c. Susan C. (Mrs. Heminway), Gordon S, Theodore W, Faith Jade and John E. Educ: Yale Univ, B.A, 27; Conn. Agr. Col, 28; Zeta Psi; Litchfield Co. Univ. Club. Polit. & Govt. Pos: Conn. State Rep, 49-67, mem, Cmt. on Agr, Conn. House of Rep, 49-67, chmn, 61-67; mem, Cornwall Rep. Town Cmt, Conn, currently. Bus. & Prof. Pos: Pres, Coltsfoot Farm Inc, 29-66 and Cornwall Water Co, 48-64. Mem: Dir, Conn. Forest and Park Asn; Litchfield Co. Farm Bur. Rel: Congregational. Mailing Add: Cornwall, Conn. 06753.

CALHOUN, FRANK WAYNE D
Tex. State Rep.
b. Houston, Tex, 4/15/33; s. Wilmer Cecil Calhoun and Ruby Edith Willis C; m. 7/5/56 to Doris Lee Wampler; c. Michael Lee and Frank David. Educ: Tex. Tech. Col, B.A, 56; Univ. Tex, LL.B, 59 and J.D, 69; Sigma Alpha Epsilon; Alpha Phi Omega. Polit. & Govt. Pos: Mem, Taylor Co. Dem. Exec. Cmt, Tex, 60-66; precinct chmn, Dem. Party, 60-66; Tex. State Rep, 67- Mil. Serv: Entered as Seaman Recruit, Navy, 52, released as Airman 1/C, 53, after serv. in Naval Air Training Command, Pensacola, Fla. Mem: Am. and Tex. Bar Asns; Rotary; dir, Abilene C. of C. and Abilene YMCA. Outstanding Young Man of Abilene, 68. Rel: Methodist. Legal Res: 2101 Crescent, Abilene, Tex. 79605. Mailing Add: P.O. Box 1834, Abilene, Tex. 79604.

CALHOUN, HARLAN MAYBERRY D
Judge, Supreme Court of Appeals of W.Va.
b. Franklin, W.Va, 10/25/03; s. H. Mayberry Calhoun and Virginia Mullenax C; wid; m. 9/4/54 to Florene Simpson Baker; c. Ann Fredlock (Mrs. G.T. Williams) and Joseph Harlan. Educ: Potomac Jr. State Col, 21-23; W.Va. Univ, LL.B, 26; Phi Delta Phi; Kappa Sigma. Polit. & Govt. Pos: Prosecuting attorney, Hardy Co, W.Va, 33-36; judge, 22nd Judicial Circuit, W.Va, 37-58; judge, Supreme Court of Appeals of W.Va, 58-, pres. court, 62 & 67. Bus. & Prof. Pos: Conduct Practice court, Col. Law, W.Va. Univ, 49-; chmn, Judicial Coun. W.Va, 60- Mem: W.Va. Judicial Asn.(past pres); W.Va. State Bar; W.Va. State and Am. Bar Asns; Am. Judicature Soc; Nat. Coun. Appellate Judges; Mason. Rel: Methodist. Legal Res: 1549 Virginia St. E, Charleston, W.Va. 25311. Mailing Add: Supreme Court of Appeals, State Capitol, Charleston, W.Va. 25305.

CALHOUN, JOHN A.
U.S. Ambassador to Tunisia
b. Berkeley, Calif, 10/29/18; s. George Miller Calhoun and Ellinor McKay Miller C. Educ: Univ. Calif, B.A, 39; Harvard, M.A, 40. Polit. & Govt. Pos: V.consul, Tijuana, Mex, 41-42; third secy. and v.consul, Tehran, Iran, 42-44; for. serv. officer and consul, Berlin, Germany, 46-49; dep. dir, Off. German Polit. Affairs, Dept. State, 50; first secy, Am. Embassy and consul, Seoul, Korea, 53-55; adv, U.S. Del. to Geneva Conf. on Korea and Indo-China, 54; Air War Col, Maxwell Air Force Base, 55-56; first secy, Am. Embassy, Paris and mem, U.S. Del. to NATO, 56-57; from dep. dir. to dir, Exec. Secretariat, Dept. of State, 57-60; counsr, Am. Embassy, Athens, Greece, 60-61; U.S. Ambassador to the Repub. of Chad, 61-63; Am. minister, Berlin, Germany, 63-67; minister-counsr. polit. affairs, Saigon, Vietnam, 67-69; U.S. Ambassador to Tunisia, 69- Mil. Serv: Ens, Supply Corps, Naval Res, overseas duty, 44-46. Mem: Am. For. Serv. Asn; Delta Tau Delta; Univ. Club, D.C. Mailing Add: U.S. Embassy, Tunis, Tunisia.

CALHOUN, NATHAN MEREDITH D
Chmn, Concordia Parish Dem. Exec. Cmt, La.
b. Vidalia, La, 2/10/26; s. Robert D. Calhoun and Anna Perrault C; m. 6/20/51 to Jean Falkenheiner; c. Katharine and Mary Ann. Educ: La. State Univ, LL.B, 50; Delta Kappa Epsilon; Phi Delta Phi. Polit. & Govt. Pos: Chmn, Concordia Parish Dem. Exec. Cmt, La, 64- Bus. & Prof. Pos: Partner, Dale, Richardson & Dale, 50-60; partner, Falkenheiner, Calhoun & McDonough, 60- Mil. Serv: Enlisted, Navy, 43, released as TM 3/C, 46. Mem: K. of C; Holy Name Soc; Am. Legion; La. State and Am. Bar Asns; Am. Judicature Soc. Rel: Catholic. Legal Res: 415 Georgia St, Vidalia, La. 71373. Mailing Add: P.O. Box 308, Vidalia, La. 71373.

CALIFANO, JOSEPH A, JR. D
b. Brooklyn, N.Y, 5/15/31; s. Joseph Anthony Califano and Katherine Gill C; m. 7/4/55 to Gertrude Zawacki; c. Mark Gerard and Joseph Anthony, III. Educ: Holy Cross Col, A.B, 52; Harvard Univ, LL.B, 55. Polit. & Govt. Pos: Spec. asst. to gen. counsel, Dept. of Defense, 61-62; spec. asst. to Secy. of Army, 62-63; spec. asst. to Secy. and Dep. Secy. of Defense, 64-69; spec. asst. to President of U.S, 65-69. Bus. & Prof. Pos: Lawyer, Dewey, Ballantine, Bushby, Palmer and Wood, N.Y.C, 58-61; partner, Arnold & Porter, Wash, D.C, 69- Mil. Serv: Lt.(sg), Naval Res, 55-58. Mem: Am. Judicature Soc; Am. and Fed. Bar Asns. Recipient Distinguished Civilian Serv. Award, Dept. of Army, 64. Legal Res: 3551 Springland Lane, Washington, D.C. 20008. Mailing Add: 1229 19th St, N.W, Washington, D.C. 20036.

CALKINS, JOHN THIERS R
Chmn, Cmt. of Spec. Assts. to Chmn, Rep. Cong. Campaign Cmt.
b. Elmira, N.Y, 5/14/25; s. John Thiers Calkins, Sr. and Laura Westervelt C; m. 12/27/52 to Patricia Painton; c. Sharon Lucille and Carolyn Leigh. Educ: Syracuse Univ, A.B, 49; Univ. London, summer courses, 51; Georgetown Univ. Law Center, J.D, 57; Am. Polit. Sci. Asn. Cong. Staff Fel, Grad. Inst. Int. Studies, Geneva, Switz, 65; Psi Upsilon; Phi Kappa Alpha. Polit. & Govt. Pos: Admin. asst. to U.S. Rep. J.C. Davies, 39th Dist, N.Y, 49-51 and to U.S. Rep. Sterling Cole, 37th Dist, N.Y, 53-57; exec. asst. to U.S. Rep. Howard Robison, 33rd Dist, N.Y, 58-; answer desk, Rep. Nat. Cmt, 60; chmn, Cmt. Spec. Assts. to Chmn, Rep. Cong. Campaign Cmt, 62- Bus. & Prof. Pos: Lectr, Univ. N.H, Conn. Col. and Elmira Col; acct. exec, Mellor Advert. Agency, 52; dir, Elmira Data Processing Corp, N.Y, 64-; dir. & v.pres, Robert N. Pyle, Inc, Severna Park, Md, 69- Mil. Serv: Entered as Pvt, Army, 43, released as S/Sgt, 46, after serv. in Army Disbursing Off, Manila, Philippines and New Guinea, 43-46; S.W. Pac. Theater Ribbon with 2 Battle Stars; Maj, Res, 60-69. Mem: D.C. Bar; Am. Polit. Sci. Asn; Psi Upsilon Alumni Asn; Am. Legion; Order of Lafayette; Capitol Hill Club; Elmira City Club; Bull Elephants Club. Rel: Episcopal. Legal Res: 759 W. Clinton St, Elmira, N.Y. 14905. Mailing Add: 5010 Reno Rd, Washington, D.C. 20008.

CALL, RICHARD A. R
Utah State Sen.
b. Gooding, Idaho, 7/16/20; s. Ambrose Call and Martha Ann Fox C; m. 9/21/44 to June Humpherys; c. Richard Ambrose, II, Mary Ann and Barbara Susan. Educ: Univ. Utah, B.A, 42, M.D, 44; Harper Hosp, Detroit, Mich, internship, 44-45; Univ. Utah Col. Med, path. res, 47-49; Sigma Chi. Polit. & Govt. Pos: Pathologist, Salt Lake Vet. Hosp, 52-54; treas, Utah Co. Rep. Cent. Cmt, 63-65; del, Rep. Nat. Conv, 64; mem, State Rep. Cent. Cmt, 64; del, Rep. State Conv, 64-66; mem, Air Pollution Cmt, Utah State Dept. Health, 64-; chmn, Med. Exam. Cmn, Utah, 66-; Utah State Sen, 16th Dist, 67- Bus. & Prof. Pos: Chief of Staff, Utah Valley Hosp, 67- and dir. of labs and pathologist; consult. in path, Utah State Hosp. Mil. Serv: Entered as Pvt, Army, 43, released as 1st Lt, 47; Col, Army Res, 63. Publ: 'Arsenical Encephalopathy,' Arch. Path, 48:119-128, 8/49; 'Legal Medicine in Utah,' Utah Med. Bul, 9/53; 'Histological and Chemical Studies in Man on Effects of Fluoride,' Pub. Health Reports, 65. Mem: Utah Co. Med. Soc; bd. trustees, Utah State Med. Asn, 60-66; Soc. Utah Pathologists; Am. Med. Asn; WHO; fel. Col. Am. Pathologists; Am. Acad. Forensic Sci; Am. Soc. Clin. Pathologists; Asn. Mil. Surgeons; Calif. Soc. Pathologists; Med. Bd, Utah Div, Am. Cancer Soc; bd. dirs, C. of C; Riverside Country Club. Rel: Latter-day Saint. Legal Res: 510 East 3950 North, Provo, Utah 84601. Mailing Add: 1034 N. Fifth W, Provo, Utah 84601.

CALL, ROBERT TRAIP D
b. Portsmouth, N.H, 3/29/34; s. Thomas Edward Call and Margaret Helen Sardy C; m. 9/20/67 to Barbara J. Wiese. Educ: Univ. N.H, B.A, 65. Polit. & Govt. Pos: Mem, Portsmouth Bd. Registrars, N.H, 65-66; N.H. State Rep, 66-67. Bus. & Prof. Pos: Hotel mgr, Boston, Mass. Mil. Serv: Entered as Pvt, Army, 53, released as Cpl, 56, after serv. in Combat Engrs, European Theatre. Legal Res: 84 Pinehurst Rd, Portsmouth, N.H. 03801. Mailing Add: 464 Huntington Ave, Suite 5, Boston, Mass. 02115.

CALLAGHAN, DAVID COURTNEY D
b. Richwood, W.Va, 9/14/34; s. David Edwin Callaghan and Elelyn Courtney C; div; c. Mike, Mark and Elizabeth. Educ: W.Va. Univ, B.S. in Econ, 61. Polit. & Govt. Pos: Exec. asst. to Gov. of W.Va, 64-66; dep. dir, Dept. Natural Resources, W.Va, 66-68; del, Dem. Nat. Conv, 68. Mil. Serv: Army,54-56. Mailing Add: 314 54th St, Charleston, W.Va. 25304.

CALLAHAN, ARTEMAS KILLIAN D
b. Tuscaloosa, Ala, 5/18/04; s. William Thomas Callahan and Nancy Speed C; m. 1/10/42 to Marguerite Tarwater; c. Nancy Miles and Artemas Killian, Jr. Educ: Univ. Ala, LL.B, 26. Polit. & Govt. Pos: Ala. State Rep, 31-35, 47-51, 55-67. Bus. & Prof. Pos: Lawyer. Rel: Methodist. Mailing Add: 913 First National Bank Bldg, Tuscaloosa, Ala. 35401.

CALLAHAN, CAROLYN BOSSERT D
b Clovis, N.Mex, 4/12/46; d. Walter Callahan and Catherine McCormick C; single. Educ: Fla. State Univ, B.A, 68, working on M.A, 69-; Pres, Garnet Key; Pi Beta Phi (v.pres). Polit. & Govt. Pos: Organizer, Young People in Polit. in High Sch, Homestead, Fla, 63-64; youth worker, Dem. Exec. Cmt, Fla, 68; del, Dem. Nat. Conv, 68. Mem: Nat. Counc. Soc. Stud. Awards from Civic Clubs in School; Pi Beta Phi Nat. Award. Rel: Roman Catholic. Legal Res: 1867 N.W. Ninth Ave, Homestead, Fla. 33030. Mailing Add: 1591 S. Lane Ave, Apt. 36-Strand, Jacksonville, Fla. 32210.

CALLAHAN, EVERETT LAWRENCE 'LARRY' D
b. Marion, Ind, 10/2/09; s. George Morris Callahan and Olive Devannah C; m. 2/15/45 to Irmal Lee Shull; c. Linda Lee, Carol Sue and Jack Morris. Educ: Purdue Univ, 27-29; Debate Team; Theta Chi. Polit. & Govt. Pos: Secy, treas. and pres, Benton Co. Libr. Bd, Ore, 52-62; trustee, Ore. Libr. Asn, 54-55; chmn, Benton Co. Dem. Cent. Cmt, 62-69. Bus. & Prof. Pos: Ed, Marion Observer, Ind, 36-46. Mem: Formerly Elks, Toastmasters and Corvallis Typographical Union. Rel: Unitarian. Mailing Add: 2725 Pilkington Ave, Corvallis, Ore. 97330.

CALLAHAN, JAMES N. D
Mich. State Rep.
b. 1932. Educ: Cent. Mich. Univ. Polit. & Govt. Pos: Mem, Mich. Munic. League Cmt. on Employee Rels. and Gov. Adv. Cmt. on Local Govt, mem. and chmn, Genesee Co. Bd. Supvrs. and mayor, Mt. Morris, 6 years, formerly; Mich. State Rep, 67- Bus. & Prof. Pos: Mgr, D.E. Newcombe Sons, Gen. Ins. Agency. Mailing Add: 3059 Merwood Dr, Mt. Morris, Mich. 48458.

CALLAHAN, JOE D
b. Milford, Ill, 5/30/92; s. Era Eugene Callahan and Frances Fanning C; m. 9/25/19 to Helen Marie Meyer; c. Francis, Josephine (Mrs. Pruitt), Waneta (Mrs. Erdman) and Eugene. Educ: High Sch. Polit. & Govt. Pos: Ill. State Rep, 65-67; precinct committeeman, Dem, 38 years; v.chmn, Iroquois Co. Dem. Cent. Cmt, 20 years. Mil. Serv: Pvt, Army, 18-19; after serv. in 317th Field Artil, France. Mem: Chmn. Bd, Ill. Farmers Union, 53-66; Nat. Chester White Swine Asn, v.pres, 30-52, pres, 52-60; dir, Nat. Pork Producers Asn, 44-52; Comdr, Am. Legion Milford Post, 23-25. Alonzo Stagg World Track Meet, Chicago, 20. Rel: Protestant. Mailing Add: R.R. 3, Milford, Ill. 60953. (1967)

CALLAHAN, VINCENT FRANCIS, JR. R
Va. State Del.
b. Washington, D.C, 10/30/31; s. Vincent F. Callahan and Anita Hawkins C; m. 9/23/60 to Dorothy Budge; c. Vincent F, III, Elizabeth L, Anita M, Cynthia and Robert B. Educ: Georgetown Univ, B.S. in F.S, 57; Am. Univ. Grad. Sch, D.C, 58-59; Kappa Alpha Phi. Polit. & Govt. Pos: Alternate del, Rep. Nat. Conv, 64; chmn, Goldwater for Pres. Cmt, North. Va, 64; pres, Old Dominion Rep. Club, McLean, Va, 64-65; cand, Lt. Gov. Va, 65; chmn, U.S. Senate Campaign, Va, 66; v.chmn, Fairfax Co. Rep. Cmt, 66-68; chmn, Va. Rep. Finance

Cmt, 66-68; mem, Rep. State Cent. Cmt, 66-; Va. State Del, 67-; Sgt-At-Arms, Rep. Nat. Conv, 68; chmn, Nixon for Pres. Cmt, North Va, 68. Bus. & Prof. Pos: Pres, Callahan Publ, Wash, D.C, 58- Mil. Serv: Entered as Pvt, Marine Corps, 50, released as Cpl, 52, after serv. in Third Marine Div; Lt, Coast Guard Res, 59-63. Publ: Underwater Defense Handbook, 63, Military Research Handbook, 64 and Space Guide, 66, Callahan Publ. Mem: Nat. Press Club; Army & Navy Club; Am. Inst. Aeronaut. & Astronaut; Am. Ord. Asn; Aviation/Space Writers Asn; U.S. Naval Inst; Nat. Space Club; Kiwanis (pres, McLean Kiwanis); dir, Va. Asn. Prevention Blindness; mem. exec. coun, Fairfax-Falls Church Health & Welfare Coun; Am. Legion; past dir, McLean Citizens Asn; North. Va. Ment. Health Asn; North. Va. Heart Asn. Rel: Roman Catholic. Legal Res: 6220 Nelway Dr, McLean, Va. 22101. Mailing Add: 1427 Center St, McLean, Va. 22101.

CALLAN, CLAIR ARMSTRONG D
b. Odell, Nebr, 3/29/20; s. John S. Callan and Agnes E. Armstrong C; m. 12/25/42 to Joyce Stark; c. John and Catherine. Educ: Peru State Col, B.A; hon. trustee, Pershing Col. Polit. & Govt. Pos: U.S. Rep, Nebr, until 67; mem, state and local sch. bds; Dem. cand, U.S. Rep, Nebr, 68. Bus. & Prof. Pos: Formerly, owner farm implement sales hardware bus, Ford agency, farmer and owner cattle raising bus. Mil. Serv: Lt, Navy, serv. in Naval Res, Pac. Mem: Gage Co. Fair Bd; Gage Co. Extension Bd; chmn, Gov. Cmt. on State Govt. Reorganization Bd; Nebr. Power Review Bd; Odd Fellows; Elks; Odell Commercial Club; Am. Aberdeen Angus Asn; Am. Legion; VFW; Mason; Shrine; Beatrice Optimists Club; Citizens for Educ. Freedom; Int. Platform Asn. & Nat. Capitol Dem. Club. Rel: Methodist. Mailing Add: Odell, Nebr. 68415. (1967)

CALLANAN, JOHN P. R
b. Buffalo, N.Y, 6/28/27; m. to Charlotte Myers. Educ: Canisius Col, 51; Cornell Univ. Law Sch, 54. Polit. & Govt. Pos: N.Y. State Assemblyman, 64-66. Bus. & Prof. Pos: Attorney; Valent, Callanan, Ruger. Rel: Catholic. Mailing Add: 109 S. Monroe St, Watkins Glen, N.Y. 14891. (1967)

CALLAWAY, HOWARD HOLLIS R
Rep. Nat. Committeeman, Ga.
b. LaGrange, Ga, 4/2/27; s. Cason Jewell Callaway and Virginia Hand C; m. to Elizabeth Walton; c. Elizabeth Walton, Virginia Hand, Howard Hollis, Jr, Ralph Walton and Edward Cason. Educ: Ga. Inst. Tech, 45; U.S. Mil. Acad, 45-49. Polit. & Govt. Pos: Mem. bd. regents, Univ. Syst. of Ga, 53-64; U.S. Rep, Third Dist, Ga, 65-66; Rep. nominee for Gov. of Ga, 66; del, Rep. Nat. Conv, 68; Rep. Nat. Committeeman, Ga, 68- Bus. & Prof. Pos: Pres, Callaway Gardens, Pine Mt, Ga, 53- Mil. Serv: Entered as 2nd Lt, Army, 49, released as 1st Lt, 52, after serv. in 17th Inf. Far East Command, Korea, 50; Combat Infantryman Badge; Korean Serv. Medal with 3 Bronze Stars; Republic of Korea Badge; Presidential Unit Citation Badge; UN Serv. Medal. Mem: Bd. dirs, Nat. 4-H Serv. Cmt; chmn, bd. trustees, Freedoms Found. at Valley Forge, Pa. Rel: Episcopal. Mailing Add: Callaway Gardens, Pine Mountain, Ga. 31822.

CALLAWAY, JULIA BALES NOE R
Mem, Hamblen Co. Judiciary and Chancery Cmt, Rep. Exec. Cmt, Tenn.
b. Morristown, Tenn, 2/10/13; d. Forest Clifford Noe and Dora Bales N; m. 12/25/34 to William Robert Callaway; c. Julia Forrest (Mrs. Black); grandsons: Andrew William and Dwaan Callaway. Educ: Ward Belmont Col, grad. 33. Polit. & Govt. Pos: Dist. dir, Eisenhower-Nixon Campaign, 52 & 56 and Nixon-Lodge Campaign, 60; v.chmn, Hamblen Co. Rep. Orgn, Tenn, 56-60; v.pres, Tenn. Fedn. Rep. Women, 58-62, pres, 62-66; v.chmn, Tenn. Rep. Exec. Cmt, 62-66; state dir, Women's Orgn. Rep. Campaign, 64; v.chmn, South. Regional Asn. Rep. V.Chmn, 66; mem, Hamblen Co. Judiciary and Chancery Cmt, Rep. Exec. Cmt, 66- Mem: Alpha Delta Pi Mother's Club; pres, Am. Legion Auxiliary; chmn. 2 cmts, C. of C; lt. warden, Civil Defense; Hamblen Co. Rep. Women; Friday Bridge Club; Country Club; Ladies Golf Asn; Wednesday Book Club; Somo Sala Circle; pres, Hamblen Co. Asn. Preservation Tenn. Antiquities and dir. state asn; chmn, Centennial Woman of the Year Contest, Nat. Fedn. Rep. Women, 69. First Lady of Morristown Award, 65. Rel: Baptist; Jr. Song Leader and Circle Chmn, First Baptist Church and pres, Day Woman's Missionary Soc, 69. Mailing Add: 1332 E. Hodge Dr, Morristown, Tenn. 37814.

CALLAWAY, LELAND D
Polit. & Govt. Pos: Ind. State Rep, 63-67. Bus. & Prof. Pos: Teacher, real estate. Mem: Pres, LaPorte Coun. of Soc. Studies; past pres. Kiwanis and Mich. City Classroom Teachers Asn; Ind. State Teachers Asn; Nat. Educ; past pres. Ind. Coun. of Geog. Educ; Nat. Coun. of Geog. Educ; Farm Bur; Elks Lodge. Rel: Methodist. Mailing Add: 3620 S. Franklin St, Mich. City, Ind. 46360. (1967)

CALLAWAY, MICHAEL ENGERS D
b. Cleveland, Tenn, 12/11/39; s. Eugene Earl Callaway and Marie Engers C; single. Educ: Univ. Va, B.A, 62, LL.B, 65. Polit. & Govt. Pos: Alternate del, Dem. Nat. Conv, 64. Prof. Pos: Bell, Whitson, Painter, McMurray and Callaway, Attorneys, 65- Mil. Serv: Pvt, Nat. Guard, 66. Mem: Am, Tenn. and Bradley Co. Bar Asns; Elks. Rel: Episcopal. Mailing Add: P.O. Box 1169, Cleveland, Tenn. 37311. (1967)

CALLI, WILLIAM S. R
b. Utica, N.Y, 12/27/23; m. to Ann Dunn; c. Robert. Educ: Utica Free Acad; Dartmouth Col; Albany Law Sch. Polit. & Govt. Pos: N.Y. State Sen, 64-66; N.Y. State Assemblyman, 50-64. Bus. & Prof. Pos: Attorney, Calli, Calli & Palewski. Mem: K. of C; Am. Legion; Elks; Utica C. of C; City Club of Utica; Optimist Club; Oneida Co. Bar Asn; N.Y. State Bar Asn; Upstate Trial Lawyers Asn; Greenfield Fish & Game Club; Commun. Club of Utica. Mailing Add: 215 Highby Rd, New Hartford, N.Y. 13413. (1967)

CALLICOTT, WILLIAM EDWARD D
Miss. State Rep.
b. West Point, Miss, 6/16/24; married. Polit. & Govt. Pos: Miss. State Rep, 60-. Bus. & Prof. Pos: Ins. agent. Mil. Serv: Nat. Guard. Mem: Am. Legion; VFW; 40 et 8; Rotary. Rel: Presbyterian. Mailing Add: Senatobia, Miss. 38668.

CALLISON, PRESTON HARVEY D
S.C. State Rep.
b. Lexington, S.C, 1/22/23; s. T.C. Callison and Margaret Reel C; m. 1/9/49 to Helen Elizabeth Leppard; c. Kathryn E, Helen Rebecca, Dale P, Melissa R. and Preston H, Jr. Educ: Univ. S.C, A.B, 42; Univ. S.C. Law Sch, LL.B, 47; Phi Kappa Sigma. Polit. & Govt. Pos: S.C. State Rep, Lexington Co, 65-66 & 69- Bus. & Prof. Pos: Attorney-at-law, Columbia S.C, 47- Mil. Serv: Entered as Pvt, Army Air Force, 42, released as S/Sgt, 46, after serv. in Army Air Corps, Pac; Pac. Theatre Ribbon. Mem: Lexington, Richland, S.C. and Am. Bar Asns; Soc. Hosp. Attorneys; Lions Int; dir, Columbia C. of C, and W.Columbia-Cayce C. of C. Rel: Baptist; Deacon, bd. dir, South. Baptist Found, 65-67, chmn, Stewardship Cmn, 66-67; pres, S.C. Baptist Conv, 69. Legal Res: 1520 Alpine Dr, West Columbia, S.C. 29169. Mailing Add: 1508 Lady St, Columbia, S.C. 29201.

CALLISTER, LOUIS H, JR. R
b. Salt Lake City, Utah, 8/11/35; s. Louis H. Callister, Sr. and Isabel Barton C.(deceased); m. to Ellen Gunnell; c. Mark Louis, Jane, Isabel and Edward Gunnell. Educ: Univ. Utah, B.S, 58, J.D, 61; Phi Delta Phi; Sigma Chi. Polit. & Govt. Pos: Asst. attorney gen, State of Utah, 61; voting dist. chmn, Rep. Party, 62, legis. dist. chmn, 63-; del, Rep. State and Co. Convs, 62; chmn, Utah Rockefeller for Pres. Cmt, 64, co-chmn, 68; treas. exec. cmt, Utah State Rep. Cent. Cmt, 65-69. Mil Serv: Utah Nat. Guard. Rel: Latter-day Saint. Legal Res: 1421 Chandler Dr, Salt Lake City, Utah 84101. Mailing Add: Suite 800 Kennecott Bldg, Salt Lake City, Utah 84101.

CALLOW, JOHN A. R
b. Oregon, Mo, 7/6/23; m. 2/28/45 to Ruth Ellen Prussman; c. Thomas H, Jean Ellen. Educ: Oregon High Sch. Polit. & Govt. Pos: Mo. State Rep, 64-66; Oregon Sch. Bd. Bus. & Prof. Pos: Real Estate; ins. agency; farmer. Mem: Past Pres, Oregon Kiwanis; AF&AM; Odd Fellows. Rel: Christian. Mailing Add: 135 Nodaway St, Oregon, Mo. 64473. (1967)

CALLOWAY, DeVERNE LEE (MRS.) D
Mo. State Rep.
b. Memphis, Tenn, 6/17/16; m. 1946 to Ernest A. Calloway. Educ: LeMoyne Col; Atlanta Univ; Northwest. Univ; Pioneer Bus. Inst; Quaker Sch; A.B. in Eng. Polit. & Govt. Pos: Mo. State Rep, 62- Bus. & Prof. Pos: Teacher; secretarial and clerical work for Fair Employ. Practices Coun, Jewish Welfare Fund, Health Dept. of Chicago; staff asst, United Serv. Orgn. Club, Ft. Huachuca, Ariz; Am. Red Cross, Calcutta, India. Mem: YWCA; Nat. Coun. of Negro Women; Order of Women Legislators; Am. for Dem. Action; NAACP; Fourth Ward Regular Dem. Orgn. Rel: Congregationalist. Mailing Add: 4309 Enright, St. Louis, Mo. 63108. (1967)

CALLOWAY, JAMES RICHARD D
b. Hot Springs, N.C, 11/2/28; s. Norman Astor Calloway and Kate Hall C; m. 12/17/49 to Helen Gebhart; c. James R, Jr. and Susan Jane. Educ: George Wash. Univ, A.B, 59 and LL.B, 63. Polit. & Govt. Pos: Spec. asst. to U.S. Sen. Allen Frear, Del, 49-61; prfnl. staff mem, cmt. on govt. opers, U.S. Senate, 61-65, chief counsel and staff dir, 65- Mil. Serv: Entered as Pvt, Army, 52, released as Sgt, 54, after serv. in Chem. Corps, Korea. Mem: D.C. and Am. Bar Asns. Rel: Presbyterian. Legal Res: New Castle, Del. Mailing Add: 3111 Savoy Dr, Fairfax, Va. 22030.

CALOGERO, PASCAL FRANK, JR. D
Mem, La. Dem. State Cent. Cmt,
b. New Orleans, La, 11/9/31; s. Pascal F. Calogero, Sr. and Louise Moore C; m. 6/18/55 to Geraldine James; c. Deborah Ann, David, Pascal, III, Elizabeth, Thomas, Michael, Stephen and Gerald. Educ: Loyola Univ, La, Col. of Arts and Sci, 49-51; Loyola Univ. Sch. of Law, J.D, 54; Blue Key; Alpha Sigma Nu; Alpha Delta Gamma; St. Thomas More Law Club. Polit. & Govt. Pos: Mem, La. Dem. State Cent. Cmt, 64-68 & 68-; del, Dem. Nat. Conv, 68. Bus. & Prof. Pos: Partner, law firm, Landrieu, Calogero & Kronlage, 58-; v.pres, Greater New Orleans Trial Lawyers Asn, 67-69. Mil. Serv: Entered as 2nd Lt, Army, 54, released as Capt, 57, after serv. in Judge Adv. Gen. Corps. Mem: Am. and La. State Bar Asns; Gr. New Orleans Trial Lawyers Asn.(v.pres, 67-69). Dean's Award; Number One Graduate, Loyola Univ. Sch. of Law, 54. Rel: Roman Catholic. Legal Res: 3524 Gentilly Blvd, New Orleans, La. 70122. Mailing Add: 4136 Washington Ave, New Orleans, La. 70125.

CALVERT, RICHARD B. R
N.C. State Rep.
b. Portsmouth, Ohio, 1901; m. to Catharine; c. Three; seven grandchildren. Educ: Denison Univ, Granville, Ohio, B.S, 23; Univ. Cincinnati, post grad. work; Sigma Alpha Epsilon. Polit. & Govt. Pos: N.C. State Rep, 67- Bus. & Prof. Pos: Owner and operator of two contract post offices, Charlotte; past pres. and gen. mgr, DOALL Carolina Co, Charlotte, and DOALL Southwest, New Orleans. Mem: Civitan Int; C. of C; Rel: Baptist; Deacon, Myers Park Baptist Church. Mailing Add: 417 Jefferson Dr, Charlotte, N.C. 28211.

CALVERT, WILLIAM BAILEY D
Chmn, Cecil Co. Dem. Cmt, Md.
b. Woodlawn, Md, 9/5/37; s. Wilson Levering Calvert and Erma Bailey C; single. Educ: Univ. Baltimore, A.A, 58, LL.B, 60; Sigma Delta Kappa. Polit. & Govt. Pos: Co. attorney, Cecil Co, Md, 62-; chmn, Cecil Co. Dem. Cmt, 66-; del, Dem. Nat. Conv, 68. Mil. Serv: Entered as Pvt, Marine Corps Res, 60, released as Sgt, 66. Mem: Am, Md. and Cecil Co. Bar Asns; Am. Judicature Soc; assoc. mem, Am. Legion; Kiwanis; Perryville Vol. Fire Co. Rel: Episcopal. Legal Res: Aiken Ave, Perryville, Md. 21903. Mailing Add: 131 E. Main St, Elkton, Md. 21921.

CALVIN, RICHARD WOODLAND, JR. R
Mem. Exec. Cmt, Calif. Rep. State Cent. Cmt.
b. Welsh, La, 3/15/36; s. Richard Woodland Calvin, Sr. and Hazel O'Neal C; m. 3/18/61 to Gladys Virginia Calhoun; c. Reginald. Educ: Dillard Univ, B.A, 57; San Diego City Col, Cert, 67; Kappa Alpha Psi. Polit. & Govt. Pos: Treas, Southeast Rep. Club, San Diego, Calif, 67; mem, Co. Rep. Cent. Cmt, 69; mem, Calif. Rep. State Cent. Cmt, currently, mem. exec. cmt, currently; admin. rep, Calif. Youth Authority, 69- Bus. & Prof. Pos: Police officer, San Diego, 62-68; personnel officer, South. Calif. First Nat. Bank, 68-69. Mil. Serv: En-

tered as Pvt, Marine Corps, 57, released as Cpl. E-4, 61, after serv. in Marine Barracks; Good Conduct Medal. Rel: Methodist. Mailing Add: 6140 Gloria Dr, Apt. 27, Sacramento, Calif. 95831.

CALVO, HORACE LAWRENCE D
Ill. State Rep.
b. Chicago, Ill, 1/4/27; s. Horace L. Calvo, Sr. and Mary C. Drew C; m. 6/28/47 to Josephine E. Beth; c. Larry Alan, Mary Elizabeth, David William and Linda Beth. Educ: Univ. Illinois, Champaign, 44-45; Lincoln Col. Law, 50-51; St. Louis Univ, LL.B, 54. Polit. & Govt. Pos: Asst. Attorney Gen, Ill, 60-68; Ill. State Rep, 55th Dist, 69- Bus. & Prof. Pos: Clerk-off. auditor and internal revenue agent, U.S. Treasury Dept, 47-55; title exam, Title Ins. Corp, St. Louis, Mo, 55-56; attorney-at-law, Granite City, Ill, 56-69. Mil. Serv: Entered as Pvt, Army Air Force, 44, released as Counter Intel. Agent, 47, after serv. in 702nd Counter Intel. Corps, ETO, 46-47. Mem: Am, Ill, Madison Co. and Tri-City Bar Asns; Ill. Trial Lawyer Asn; Am. Right-of-Way Asn; K. of C; Elks; Amvets; Am. Legion; Sunset Hills Country Club. Rel: Roman Catholic. Mailing Add: 3254 Westchester Dr, Granite City, Ill. 62040.

CAMACHO, CARLOS GARCIA R
Gov, Guam
b. Agana, Guam, 11/16/24; s. Felix Martinez Camacho and Antonia Cruz Garcia; m. 5/14/55 to Lourdes Duenas Perez; c. Carlos Anthony, Felix James, Thomas John, Mary Margaret, Ricardo Jose and Francis Gerard. Educ: Aquinas Col, 46-49; Marquette Univ, D.D.S, 54; Delta Sigma Delta. Polit. & Govt. Pos: Sen, Guam Legis, 64-66; Gov, Guam, 69- Bus. & Prof. Pos: Dentist, Govt. of Guam, 54-55 and Cath. Med. Center, 55-56 & 58-69. Mil. Serv: Capt, Dent. Corps, Army, 56-58, with serv. in Camp Zama, Japan. Mem: Am. Med. Asn; K. of C.(4°). Rel: Roman Catholic. Legal Res: Fr. Duenas Dr, Tamuning, Guam 96910. Mailing Add: Office of the Governor, Agana, Guam 96910.

CAMARODA, PAT JOSEPH D
b. Brooklyn, N.Y, 5/4/10; s. Joseph Camaroda and Rose Manduano C; m. 2/22/46 to Queenie Kalian; c. Patrick and Rodney. Educ: High Sch. Polit. & Govt. Pos: Councilman, Dem. Party, Calif. Bus. & Prof. Pos: Owner, Camaroda Press, 30- Mil. Serv: Pvt, Army. Mem: Elks; Verdi Club; Fresno Co. Dem. Bus. Mens Asn; Air Force Asn; DAV; Am. Legion; People to People Coun; Soc. Prev. Cruelty to Animals; Fresno and Edison High Boosters Club; San Joaquin Valley Printing House Craftsman. Rel: Catholic. Mailing Add: 858 E. Home Ave, Fresno, Calif. 93728.

CAMAROT, HENRY J. D
b. New York, N.Y, 5/2/23; s. Henri Camarot and mother (deceased); m. 9/18/48 to Elizabeth Loretta Henry; c. Linda, Gay and Tammy. Educ: George Wash. Univ, LL.B, 51, LL.M, 54; Phi Delta Phi. Polit. & Govt. Pos: Chmn, Fourth Div. Dem. Party, Fairbanks, Alaska, 64-65; mem, Alaska State Dem. Cent. Cmt, 64-65; chmn, Lane Co. Dem. Party, Ore, 67-68; mem, Ore. State Dem. Cent. Cmt, 67-68. Bus. & Prof. Pos: Partner, McNealey, Merdes & Camarot, Fairbanks, Alaska, 59-65, Sanders, Lively, Camarot & Wiswall, 65- Mil. Serv: Capt, Army, serv. in Inf-Paratroopers. Mem: Am, Ore. State, Alaska and D.C. Bar Asns; Elks. Rel: Catholic. Legal Res: 2849 Chateau Place, Springfield, Ore. 97477. Mailing Add: 655 N. A St, Springfield, Ore. 97477.

CAMERA, JOSEPH LEONARD D
Ohio State Rep.
b. Franklin, Mo, 8/14/14; s. Joseph Anthony Camera and Nellie Lowe C; m. 5/16/39 to Laverne Diewald; c. Thomas, Jan, Sandra Shuler, Michael, Mary Lawrence, Leonard, Guy and Shawn. Educ: High sch, 4 years. Polit. & Govt. Pos: Councilman, Lorain City Coun, Ohio, 62-69; Ohio State Rep, 69- Bus. & Prof. Pos: Field supvr, Am. Shipbldg, 42-47; field supvr, Spohn Corp, 50-69. Mem: Elks; K. of C; Pipefitters Local Union; Nat. Soc. State Legislators; C. of C. Rel: Catholic. Mailing Add: 1147 Tenth St, Lorain, Ohio 44052.

CAMERON, CRAWFORD WILLIAMS D
Chmn, Love Co. Dem. Cmt, Okla.
b. Dublin, Tex, 3/29/91; s. Evan Dhu Cameron and Clara Williams C; m. 8/5/19 to Lulabelle Chambers; c. Crawford, Jr. and Clara Louise (Mrs. Hodges). Educ: Okla. Univ. Sch. of Law, LL.B; Kappa Sigma; Phi Delta Phi; Sooner Bar. Polit. & Govt. Pos: Chmn, Love Co. Dem. Cmt, Okla, 41-; city attorney, Marietta, Okla, 41- Bus. & Prof. Pos: Mem. exam. bd, Okla. Bar Asn, 3 years; spec. justice, Supreme Court, 2 cases. Mil. Serv: Entered as Pvt, Army, 18, released as Pfc, after serv. in 90th Div. Mem: Am. and Okla. Bar Asns; Am. Legion; Mason; Lions; C. of C. Rel: Baptist. Legal Res: 108 W. Main St, Marietta, Okla. 73448. Mailing Add: P.O. Box 147, Marietta, Okla. 73448. (1967)

CAMERON, GARY L. D
b. Iowa City, Iowa, 9/9/33; s. Glenn T. Cameron and Opal M. C; m. 1954 to Nan Druet Burchette; c. Druet, Josephine, Streetar. Educ: Northeast Mo. State Teachers Col, 55; Univ. of Iowa, 58; Phi Delta Phi. Polit. & Govt. Pos: Secy. of State, 64-66; Jefferson Co. attorney, 61-64; Fairfield City attorney, 59-60. Bus. & Prof. Pos: Lawyer. Mailing Add: Fairfield, Iowa 52556. (1967)

CAMERON, JAMES WESLEY D
Ala. State Rep.
b. Chatom, Ala, 10/8/28; s. George William Cameron and Floye Strickland C; m. 8/29/53 to Betty Longshore; c. James Wesley, Jr. and Allison Longshore. Educ: Univ. Tenn, 47-49; Huntingdon Col, B.A, 52; Univ. Ala. Law Sch, LL.B, 55; Sigma Nu. Polit. & Govt. Pos: Ala. State Rep, Montgomery Co, 67- Mil. Serv: Entered as 2nd Lt, Air Force, 55, released as 1st Lt, 68, after serv. in Judge Adv. Gen. Corps, Okinawa, 56-58. Rel: Methodist. Mailing Add: 340 Cullen Dr, Montgomery, Ala. 36105.

CAMERON, MARTHA E. R
b. Pittsburgh, Pa; d. John Paul Cameron, Jr. and Martha R. Young C; single. Educ: Univ. Pittsburgh, B.A, 35, M.Litt, 37; Kappa Alpha Theta. Polit. & Govt. Pos: Admin. asst, U.S. Rep. James G. Fulton, Pa, 45- Bus. & Prof. Pos: Legal secy, Alter, Wright & Barron, 37-42; asst. secy, Allegheny Co. Bd. of Law Exams, 42-43; admin. asst, Dist. Attorney, Allegheny Co, 43-45. Mem: Cong. Secy. Club; Nat. Secy. Asn; Bus. & Prfnl. Women; Mt. Lebanon League of Women Voters; Allegheny Co. Coun. of Rep. Women. Rel: United Presbyterian. Legal Res: 700 Osage Rd, Pittsburgh, Pa. 15216. Mailing Add: 2117 New Federal Bldg, Pittsburgh, Pa. 15222.

CAMERON, RONALD BROOKS D
b. Kans. City, Mo, 8/16/27; m. to Constance C; c. Victoria Brooks, Richard Malcolm. Educ: West. Res. Univ; Univ. of Calif. Polit. & Govt. Pos: U.S. Rep, Calif, 62-67; Calif. Legis, 58-62. Bus. & Prof. Pos: CPA, 54. Mil. Serv: Marine Corps, 45. 1967 Legal Res: Whittier, Calif. No mailing address available. (1967)

CAMERON, SALLY FREEMAN R
Asst. Chmn, Fla. Rep. Party
b. Grosse Point, Mich, 6/21/30; d. Frederick James Freeman and Clora Riggs F; div; c. Barbara Glenn. Educ: Univ. Ga, degree, 52; Kappa Alpha Theta; Theta Sigma Phi. Polit. & Govt. Pos: Pub. rels. dir, Gov. Campaign, Fla, 66; asst. chmn, Fla. Rep. Party, 68- Bus. & Prof. Pos: Atlanta Journal-Constitution Atlanta, Ga, 48-50; Columbus Ledger-Enquirer, Columbus, 51-59; Miami Herald, Fla, 59-61; pub. rels. and advert, Jack Drury & Assoc, Ft. Lauderdale, 61-68 and Image Inc, 69- Rel: Episcopal. Mailing Add: 2624 Tortugas Lane, Ft. Lauderdale, Fla. 33312

CAMERON, WARD FRANCIS D
Chmn, Butte Co. Dem. Cent. Cmt, Calif.
b. Flint, Mich, 3/17/21; s. Ward A. Cameron and Francis Brady C; m. 2/19/44 to Joyce A. Howard; c. Howard F, Dane A. and Brady Lee. Educ: Flint Jr. Col, Mich, 1 year. Polit. & Govt. Pos: Co. publicity chmn, Brown for Gov, Calif, 58 & 66, mem, Gov. Brown's Adv. Cmt. on Pub. Info, 62-66; co. publicity chmn, Johnson for President, 64, 'Bizz' Johnson for U.S. Rep, Calif, each elec. year; co. chmn, Cranston for U.S. Sen, Calif, 68; chmn, Butte Co. Dem. Cent. Cmt, 68- Bus. & Prof. Pos: Supermkt. mgr, Millers Mkts, 47-51; radio salesman, K-Pay Radio, Chico, Calif, 52-, sales mgr, 4 years. Mil. Serv: Entered as Pvt, Army, 42, released as Sgt, 45, after serv. in 1st. U.S. Inf. Div, European from N.Africa, Sicily to France and Czech; 8 Battle Stars; 3 Assault Landings; 7 Overseas Time Stripes; Bronze Star Medal; Unit Citations; Div. Decorations. Mem: Chico Exchange Club; North. Travelers Club, Chico; Chico Dem. Club; Paradise Dem. Club; Dem. Nat. Cmt; mem. staff, Region Civil Defense. Rel: Protestant. Mailing Add: 1837 Merrill Rd, Paradise, Calif. 95969.

CAMMACK, BENJAMIN FRANKLIN, JR. D
b. Rockport, Miss, 6/16/08; married. Polit. & Govt. Pos: Former Miss. State Rep. Bus. & Prof. Pos: Farmer; cattleman; merchant. Mem: Copiah Co. Farm Bur.(pres); Farm Bur; Hazlehurst Touchdown Club. Rel: Methodist. Mailing Add: Route 1, Hazlehurst, Miss. 39083. (1967)

CAMMACK, WILBERT D
Idaho State Rep.
b. Spanish Fork, Utah, 1/19/10; s. Francis Cammack and Sarah Atwood C; m. 1/24/30 to Eunice Ward; c. Rodonna (Mrs. Ted Katseanes), Ward W, Elaine (Mrs. McKell Crawford) and Farrell. Educ: High sch. grad. Polit. & Govt. Pos: Precinct committeeman, Dem. Party, Idaho, 60-64; Idaho State Rep, 65- Bus. & Prof. Pos: Self employed, dairy bus. Mem: Rotary. Rel: Latter-day Saint. Mailing Add: 498 S. Fisher, Blackfoot, Idaho 83221.

CAMP, ASHLEY LEONIDAS, JR. D
b. Munford, Ala, 7/19/23; s. Ashley Leonidas Camp and Elise Davenport C; m. 5/17/46 to Leta Mae Knight; c. Ashley L, III, Cary Franklin and Bruce Anthony. Educ: Jacksonville State Univ, 45-47; Palmer Chiropractic Col, D.C, 49. Polit. & Govt. Pos: Ala. State Rep, Talladega Co, 59-67, mem. ins. cmt, Ala. House of Rep, 59-63, v.chmn. health cmt, 59-67, chmn. interim cmt. on ment. health and ment. retardation, 62-65, mem. transportation cmt, 63-67. Mil. Serv: Entered as Pvt, Army Tank Corps, 43, released as Cpl, 45, after serv. in 743rd Tank Bn, ETO, 44-45; Bronze Star; Presidential Unit Citation; Purple Heart and 2 Clusters; 4 Battle Stars. Mem: Boy Scout scoutmaster; Ala. Sch. for Blind, Talladega, 3 years; dist. chmn, Cheaha Dist. Boy Scouts, 2 years; Int. and Ala. Chiropractic Asns; Am. Legion; VFW; Farm Bur; Am. Angus Asn; Ala. Cattleman's Asn; Talladega C. of C; Ala. Asn. for Retarded Children; Patrons of Partlow, Partlow State Sch. and Hosp. Avid hunting and fishing sportsman; farming interest and cattle raising. Rel: Church of Christ. Mailing Add: 305 E. North St, Talladega, Ala. 35160.

CAMP, GEORGE R
Okla. State Rep.
b. Drumright, Okla, 8/15/26; s. Ira Camp and Susie Dittmeyer C; m. 9/1/49 to Lora Lee Atchison; c. Mark Arnold and Cheryl Ann. Educ: Univ. Okla, LL.B, 50; Phi Delta Phi. Polit. & Govt. Pos: Precinct chmn, Major Co. Rep. Party, Okla, 50-51; chmn, 52-54; co. attorney, Major Co, 51-53; del, Rep. State Conv, 52, 63 & 65, mem. resolutions cmt, 52 and rules cmt, 65; del. and mem. rules cmt, Rep. Dist. Conv, 52; del, Rep. Co. Conv, 52, 63 & 65, mem. resolutions cmt, 65; asst. U.S. Attorney, West Dist. Okla, 54-61; precinct chmn, Okla. Co. Rep. Party, 62-64; Okla. State Rep, Okla. Co, 64-; mem, Gov. Select Cmts. on Rev. State Elec. Laws and Judicial Reform, 65; mem, Okla. State Rep. Cmt, 65-66; mem, Spec. State Rules Rev. Cmt, 65-66. Bus. & Prof. Pos: Mem, Love, Camp and Amick, 61; dir. and officer, Mortgage Investors Exchange, Inc, 62-66; chmn, bd. and pres, Serendipity, Inc, 66. Mil. Serv: Entered as Pvt, Army, 45, released as Cpl, 46, after serv. in 81st Inf; South Philippines, Victory, Am. Pac. Theater, Philippine Liberation and Good Conduct Medals; Army Res, 46-48. Mem: Am. Bar Asn.(gen. practice cmt); Okla. State and Okla. Co. Bar Asns; Univ. Okla. Col. of Law Asn; Lions; Sportsman's Club; N.W. C. of C; Okla. City C. of C. Rel: Methodist. Mailing Add: 2411 N.W. 46, Oklahoma City, Okla. 73112. (1967)

CAMP, JOHN NEWBOLD 'HAPPY' R
U.S. Rep, Okla.
b. Enid, Okla, 5/11/08; s. John Roland Camp and Minnie Catherine Newbold C; m. 11/26/30 to Vera Juanita Overman; c. John, III, Kay (Mrs. Dan D. Dillingham), Pat (Mrs. Roy Gilbert Rainey) and Steven Richard. Educ: Phillips Univ, 3 years. Polit. & Govt. Pos: Okla. State Rep, 43-63; chmn, State Bd. Pub. Affairs, 67-68; U.S. Rep, Sixth Dist, 69- Bus. & Prof. Pos: Pres. and chmn. bd, Waukomis State Bank, Waukomis, Okla. Mil. Serv: Pvt, Nat.

Guard, 46 months. Mem: Lions; Mason (32°); Shrine; Jesters; hon. mem, 4-H; Future Farmers Am; bd, Christian Church Found. Silver Beaver, Boy Scouts. Rel: Disciples of Christ. Legal Res: Box 97, Waukomis, Okla. 73773. Mailing Add: 1406 Longworth Bldg, Washington, D.C. 20515.

CAMPBELL, A. HARTWELL D
N.C. State Rep.
b. Buies Creek, N.C, 10/8/16; s. Dr. Leslie Hartwell Campbell and Viola Haire C; m. 10/20/42 to Verda Harris; c. Thomas Hartwell, Vann and Neal. Educ: Campbell Col, A.A, 34; Wake Forest Univ, B.S, 36; Univ. N.C. grad. Sch, 37-38; Yale Univ, B.D, 41; Gamma Sigma Epsilon. Polit. & Govt. Pos: Mem, City Bd. Educ, Greenville, N.C, 57-63; mem, Gov. Cmn. Educ. TV, 62-64; mem, City Coun, Greenville, 63-64; chmn, Wilson Co. Econ. Develop. Cmn, 64-69; N.C. State Rep, 15th House Dist, 69- Bus. & Prof. Pos: Minister, Immanuel Baptist Church, Greenville, N.C, 41-46; builder and mgr, three radio sta, 46-50; organizer, builder and mgr, TV Sta. WNCT, 50-63; organizer and pres, Sentinel Life Ins. Co, 56-59; pres, owner and gen. mgr, Campbell Broadcasting, Inc, WGTM, Wilson, 64-69. Mem: Wilson-Rocky Mt. S.M.E. Club (pres); Rotary; C. of C; Wilson Co. Young Dem. Club; Wilson Co. Dem. Party. Tar Heel of the Week, Raleigh News and Observer. Rel: Baptist. Deacon, First Baptist Church; Sunday Sch. Teacher. Mailing Add: 1709 Wilshire Blvd, Wilson, N.C. 27893.

CAMPBELL, ALBERTA W. 'BERTIE' R
b. Salt Lake City, Utah, 4/17/32; d. Robert L. Warburton and Alvina Riedheim W; m. 11/28/53 to Douglas Gordon Campbell; c. Kimberly Dee, Deanne Jaye, Darcy Lee and Robin Cheyne. Educ: Univ. Utah, 1 year; Univ. Wash, 2 years; Alpha Delta Pi; Univ. Wash. Rally Girls; pres, Univ. Wash. ROTC Sponsors; bd. mem, Univ. Wash. Woman's Asn. Polit. & Govt. Pos: Chmn, Buena Park City Rep. Precinct, Calif, 64; mem, Calif. State Rep. Cent. Cmt, 64-68; chmn, 69th Assembly Dist. Precinct Orgn, 65-; del, Rep. Nat. Conv, 68. Bus. & Prof. Pos: Secy, Boeing Airplane Co, Seattle, Wash, 52-53; secy. to pres, Am. Instrument Corp, 54-55; exec. secy, Joshua Hendy Corp, 55-56. Mem: San Mority Club. Rel: Reformed Church of America. Mailing Add: 5891 Los Angeles Way, Buena Park, Calif. 90620.

CAMPBELL, ALLAN P. R
N.H. State Rep.
b. 6/1/94; married; c. Two. Educ: Wentworth Inst; Hawley Sch. of England. Polit. & Govt. Pos: N.H. State Rep, 61- Bus. & Prof. Pos: Retired Supvry. electrician. Mem: Odd Fellows; Mason R.A.C-K.T. Rel: Unitarian Universalist. Mailing Add: 32 Severance St, Claremont, N.H. 03743. (1967)

CAMPBELL, ALLEN E. R
Wyo. State Rep.
b. Fairview, Wyo, 12/21/12; m. to Ellen; c. Six. Educ: M.S, Educ; LL.B. Polit. & Govt. Pos: Chmn, Lincoln Co. Rep. Party; mem, Wyo. Rep. Cent. Cmt; Wyo. State Rep, currently. Bus. & Prof. Pos: Sch. prin. Mem: Nat. and Wyo. Educ. Asns; Afton C. of C; cmnr, Boy Scouts Dist. Rel: Latter-day Saint. Mailing Add: P.O. Box 187, Afton, Wyo. 83110. (1967)

CAMPBELL, AMBROSE LEO D
R.I. State Sen.
b. Pawtucket, R.I, 12/20/08; s. Joseph Edward Campbell and Anne Farrell C; m. 2/24/36 to Alice M. Branigan; c. Ann Judith (Mrs. Desrosiers), Daniel L, M. Kathleen (Mrs. Furtado) and Henry V. Educ: Pawtucket High Sch, 25-29. Polit. & Govt. Pos: Mem, City Coun, Pawtucket, R.I, 52-62; R.I. State Sen, 62- Bus. & Prof. Pos: Sales mgr, Campbell Auto Supply, 48- Mem: R.I. Asn. Retarded Children; Blackstone Valley Chap. for Retarded Children (pres, 3 terms); Moose; K. of C; New Eng. Chap. Horsemen's Benevolent & Protective Asn. Rel: Catholic. Mailing Add: 513 Walcott St, Pawtucket, R.I. 02861.

CAMPBELL, ANONA JEANNE R
Mem, Calif. Rep. State Cent. Cmt.
b. Calexico, Calif, 10/6/30; d. John William Propes and Norma Anona Cooley P; m. 9/3/50 to Norman Campbell; c. Russell William and Richard Alan. Educ: Fullerton Jr. Col, 48-49; Univ. Calif, Santa Barbara, 50. Polit. & Govt. Pos: Dist. precinct chmn, 70th Assembly Dist, Calif, 64-67; mem, Calif. Rep. State Cent. Cmt, 69- Bus. & Prof. Pos: V.pres. and treas, Magic Carpet Travel Agency, Inc, 68- Mem: Federated Rep. Women of Huntington Beach; Native Daughters of Golden West; Calif. Rep. Assembly. Rel: Protestant. Mailing Add: 10011 Crailet Dr, Huntington Beach, Calif. 92646.

CAMPBELL, ARCHIBALD ALGERNON D
Va. State Del.
b. Wytheville, Va, 7/23/21; m. to Eloise Richberg. Educ: VMI, B.A; Univ. Va, LL.B. Polit. & Govt. Pos: Va. State Del, 66- Bus. & Prof. Pos: Attorney. Mil. Serv: Marine Corps. Mem: Rotary; Southwest Va. Horsemen's Asn; Wytheville Vol. Fire Dept; Wythe Commun. Concert. Rel: Presbyterian. Mailing Add: First National Exchange Bank Bldg, Wytheville, Va. 24382.

CAMPBELL, BLAKE O. D
Chmn, Archer Co. Dem. Party, Tex.
b. Ashland, Ala, 9/13/01; s. Alexander Campbell and Dora C; m. 10/23/29 to Lena Sturm; c. Lavern and Sandra. Educ: High Sch. Polit. & Govt. Pos: Chmn, Archer Co. Dem. Party, Tex, currently. Bus. & Prof. Pos: Self employed. Mem: Mason; Scottish Rite; Shrine; Farm Bur. Mailing Add: R.R. 2, Box 146-B, Wichita Falls, Tex. 76307. (1967)

CAMPBELL, BLAND HAYDEN D
Miss. State Sen.
b. Middlesboro, Ky, 2/7/05; married. Polit. & Govt. Pos: Miss. State Rep, 48-52; Miss. State Sen, 56- Bus. & Prof. Pos: State agent, Mortgage Guaranty Ins. Corp, Milwaukee, Wis. Mem: Hinds Co. Cancer Asn; Old Men's Home; Little Red Sch. House; Miss. Chap, Nat. Soc. for Prevention of Blindness; Miss. Asn. for Retarded Children; Miss. Coun. on Ment. Retardation; Miss. Advert. Club; Sons of Confederate Vet; Miss. Travelers Asn; Jackson Knife and Fork Club. Rel: Methodist. Mailing Add: 3529 Galloway Ave, Jackson, Miss. 39216.

CAMPBELL, CHARLES ARTHUR R
Mem, Calif. State Rep. Cent. Cmt.
b. Cleveland, Ohio, 9/25/24; s. Harry Gordon Campbell and Sarah Wilson C; m. 4/25/53 to Elaine Williams; c. Kathleen W. and Duncan Scott. Educ: Denison Univ, A.B, 48; Phi Delta Theta. Polit. & Govt. Pos: Mem, Santa Barbara Co. Rep. Cent. Cmt, 62-, secy, 62-64, v.chmn, 65-66, chmn, 67-68 and mem. exec. cmt, 69-; mem, Calif. State Rep. Cent. Cmt, 65-; area chmn, Calif. Co. Chmn. Asn, 67-68 and ex officio mem, 69- Mil. Serv: Entered as Pvt, Army Air Corps, 42, released as T/Sgt, 44, after serving in 12th Air Force, African-Italian Theater, 43-44; Air Medal with Seven Oak Leaf Clusters. Mem: Los Angeles Food Indust. Sales Mgr. Club; VFW Post 7139; Farm Bur; Calif. Cattlemen's Asn; Assoc. Farmers; Solvang Bus. Asn. Rel: Episcopal. Mailing Address: 1727 Refugio Rd, Santa Ynez, Calif. 93460.

CAMPBELL, CHARLES EDWARD
b. Atlanta, Ga, 1/12/42; s. Borden Burr Campbell and Bonnie Mae McPherson C; single. Educ: Emory Univ, 60-61; Univ. Ga, A.B. and M.A; Georgetown Univ. Law Center, 66-; Omicron Delta Kappa; Blue Key; Phi Beta Kappa; Pi Sigma Alpha; Independent Party. Polit. & Govt. Pos: Legis. asst, U.S. Sen. Richard B. Russell, Ga, 66-69, exec. secy, 69- Mem: Am. Polit. Sci. Asn; U.S. Senate Staff Club; Cong. Secy. Club; out of state v.pres, Univ. Ga. Alumni Soc. Rel: Baptist. Legal Res: R.R. 3, Jackson, Ga. 30233. Mailing Add: B1114, 1400 Joyce St, Arlington, Va. 22202.

CAMPBELL, CHARLES M. 'CHUCK' R
Ill. State Rep.
b. Danville, Ill, 10/11/21; m. 7/28/43 to Marjorie Barton; c. Con and Randy. Educ: Univ. Ill, B.S. in Bus. Admin, 43; Sigma Chi. Polit. & Govt. Pos: Ill. State Rep, 62-63 & 67-, permanent mem. adv. cmt, Ill. Pub. Aid Cmn. and Toll Rd. Cmn, v.chmn, Water Resources Cmt, 63-64 & 67-68 and chmn, Munic. Cmt, 69-70, Ill. State House of Rep; mem. exec. cmt, Co. Rep. Mil. Serv: Lt.(jg), Navy, 42-46, serv. in Seventh Fleet, Pac. Theatre, 44-46; Silver Star. Mem: Am. Bus. Club; Am. Legion; Elks; YMCA; C. of C. Prfnl. baseball pitcher, 46. Rel: Presbyterian. Mailing Add: 102 N. Logan Ave, Danville, Ill. 61832.

CAMPBELL, CLOVES COLBERT D
Ariz. State Sen.
b. Elizabeth, La, 4/12/31; s. John Campbell (deceased) and L.D. Fisher C. (deceased); m. 10/20/54 to Juanita Burleson; c. Debra, Carol, Cloves, Jr. and Carlton. Educ: Ariz. State Univ, B.A. in Educ, 58; Kappa Alpha Psi. Polit. & Govt. Pos: Ariz. State Rep, 62-66; Ariz. State Sen, 67- Bus. & Prof. Pos: Salesman, Ariz. Light & Gas Co, 54- Mil. Serv: Entered as Pvt, Army, 52, released as Cpl, 54. Mem: Elks; Am. Legion; Big Brothers; Mason; W.Coast Conf. Black Elected Official; bd. dir, Urban Affairs Inst. Rel: African Methodist Episcopal. Mailing Add: 5002 S. 21st Way, Phoenix, Ariz. 85040.

CAMPBELL, COURTNEY WARREN D
b. Chillicothe, Mo, 4/29/95; s. Thomas Courtney Campbell and Ellen Minor C; m. June, 1933 to Henrietta Hisgen. Educ: Westminster Col, Fulton, Mo; Univ. Mo; Beta Theta Pi. Polit. & Govt. Pos: Mem, State Road Dept. Dist. 1, Fla, 43-47; mem, Fla. 83rd Cong. Bus. & Prof. Pos: V.pres, FMC Corp; lawyer. Mil. Serv: 2nd Lt, Army, World War I. Mem: Bd. dirs, First Nat. Bank, Tampa; dir, WLCY Channel 10, St. Petersburg; trustee, Mease Hosp. & Clin, Danedin; Rotary; Mason; Shrine. Rel: Christian Church of N.Am. Mailing Add: 1086 Eldorado Ave, Clearwater, Fla. 33515.

CAMPBELL, DELLA B. R
V.Chmn, Ore. State Rep. Cent. Cmt.
b. Winamac, Ind, 1/16/14; d. Joseph Carlisle Wagerman and Elsie Doyle W; m. 5/2/37 to Charles S. Campbell, M.D; c. Timothy, Mary Ellen, Catherine and Daniel. Educ: Ind. Univ, G.N, 36; Sigma Theta Tau; Phi Mu. Polit. & Govt. Pos: Alternate v.chmn, Marion Co. Rep. Cent. Cmt, 54-56, v.chmn, 56-60; educ. chmn, Ore. State Rep. Cent. Cmt, 60-62, v.chmn, 63- Bus. & Prof. Pos: Staff nurse, Indianapolis Pub. Health Nursing Asn, 36-38. Mem: Womens Auxiliary, Ore. State Med. Soc; Assistance League of Salem. Rel: Presbyterian. Mailing Add: 3603 Westridge Place S, Salem, Ore. 97302. (1967)

CAMPBELL, DONALD A. R
Chmn, Montgomery Co. Rep. Party, N.Y.
b. Amsterdam, N.Y, 8/2/22; m; c. three. Educ: Columbia Univ, honor scholar; Albany Law Sch, 48, cum laude; Columbia Univ. Varsity C Club. Polit. & Govt. Pos: N.Y. State Assemblyman, 51-68, clerk, N.Y. State Assembly, 68-; chmn, Montgomery Co. Rep. Party, 59-; del, Rep. Nat. Conv, 68. Bus. & Prof. Pos: Treas, Amsterdam, Chuctarunda and North. R.R. Co; adv. bd. Amsterdam Br, Marine Midland Nat. Bank of Troy; attorney-at-law, 48-; dir, Commun. Serv. Broadcasting Corp, 69- Mil. Serv: Army, World War II, Lt, three years. Mem: N.Y. State and Montgomery Co. Bar Asn; N.Y. State Agr. Soc; Justinian Nat. Hon. Legal Scholarship Soc; F&AM; AAONMS; C. of C; Am. Legion; adv. cmt, Industs. for Amsterdam Inc; Montgomery Co. Area Redevelop. Cmt; dir, Montgomery Co. Muscular Dystrophy Asn; N.Y. State Legis. Dir. of Amvets; bd. of adv, Amsterdam Children's Home. Amsterdam Jr. C. of C. Young Man of Year, 57; N.Y. State Amvet of the Year, 62; PBA Legis. Award, 64. Rel: Episcopal; Vestryman, Coun. Mailing Add: 20 Market, Amsterdam, N.Y. 12010.

CAMPBELL, DONALD G. R
Co. Chmn. Wahkiakum Co. Rep. Party, Washington
b. Billings, Mont, 6/24/26; s. Alvah D. Campbell and Austa Stockland; m. 8/7/46 to Jeanne E. Kitterman; c. Laurie S. and Christopher S. Educ: Univ. of Mont, B.S. in Forestry, 51. Polit. & Govt. Pos: Co.chmn, Wahkiakum Co. Rep. Party, Wash, 64- Mil. Serv: Entered as Pvt. Army, 44, released as Pfc, 46 after serving in Americal Div, Philippines, 45-46; Combat Infantrymans Badge, Purple Heart. Mem: Soc. of Am. Foresters. Mailing Add: E. Valley, Skamokaua, Wash. 98647.

CAMPBELL, DOROTHY MILDRED R
b. Elloree, S.C, 7/27/19; d. Moses D. Perry and Amanda Lee Anderson P; m. 10/18/43 to Leslie Antonio Campbell; c. Ronald Alleyn and Dwight Carleton. Educ: Haaren High Sch, 4 years. Polit. & Govt. Pos: Mem, Bronx Co. Rep. Cmt, N.Y, 65-69; co-leader, Taft Rep. Club, Bronx, N.Y, 67-; del, Rep. Nat. Conv, 68. Mem: Ladies auxillary, Soundview Little League. Plaque. Mailing Add: 1440 Bronx River Ave, Bronx, N.Y. 10472.

CAMPBELL, E.J. R
b. 2/4/03; m. 12/10/44 to Mariam Olson; c. Three. Educ: High Sch, 2 years. Polit. & Govt. Pos: S.Dak. State Rep, 64-67. Bus. & Prof. Pos: Retired from Northwestern Bell Tel. Co, 63. Mem: Masonic Lodge; Knights Templars; Myrtle Lodge 91; Ivy Chap. 25; Rotary Club; Boy Scouts. Mailing Add: Centerville, S.Dak. 57014. (1967)

CAMPBELL, ETHAN HUBBARD R
b. Eagleville, Mo, 4/7/19; s. Ralph Campbell (deceased) and Goldie I. Hubbard C; m. 4/7/46 to Mary Katherine McCampbell; c. Douglas Alan and Brian Scott. Educ: St. Joseph Jr. Col. Polit. & Govt. Pos: Rep. Cand. for U.S. Rep, 60 & 62; del, Rep. Nat. Conv, 64; chmn, Mo. State Rep. Cmt, 64-66. Bus. & Prof. Pos: Mgr, Gen. Advert, St. Joseph News Press & Gazette, 46-64 & 67-; chmn, Recreation Cmn, St. Joseph, Mo, 56-58; registered rep, Waddell & Reed, Inc, 66-67. Mil. Serv: Entered as Pvt, Army, 40, released as Sgt, 46, after serv. in 194th Tank Bn, Pac; survivor of Bataan Death March; prisoner-of-war, Pac, 3½ years; Am. Defense, Am. Theater, Philippine Defense, Asiatic-Pac. Theater Ribbons; Presidential Unit Citation with 2 Oak Leaf Clusters. Mem: Mason; Shrine; Am. Legion; VFW; 40 et 8; DAV; Rotary Int. (past pres, S.Side, St. Joseph); Nat. Asn. of Securities Dealers; Elks (Past Exalter Ruler St. Joseph Lodge 40). Rel: Methodist. Mailing Add: 2615 Buehler, St. Joseph, Mo. 64506.

CAMPBELL, FRED YOUNG D
b. Haywood Co, N.C, 7/20/11; s. David Crockett Campbell and Harriett Cogdill C; m. 1/27/39 to Ila Green. Educ: West. Carolina Col, 3 yrs. Polit. & Govt. Pos: Chmn, Haywood Co. Dem. Exec. Cmt, N.C, 64-66; del, Nat. Dem. Conv, 64; sheriff, Haywood Co, 50-60. Bus. & Prof. Pos: Supvr, Mats. Handling, Champion Papers, Inc, 60-; dir, Northwest. Bank. Mil. Serv: Entered as Pfc, Army, 42, released as Sgt, 46, after serv. in ETO. Mem: Past comdr, VFW and Am. Legion; Mason; Lions Club; dir, C. of C. Rel: Methodist. Mailing Add: R.R. 5, Maggie Valley, Waynesville, N.C. 28786. (1967)

CAMPBELL, GEORGE W. R
Finance Chmn, Beaver Co. Rep. Cmt, Pa.
b. Connellsville, Pa, 12/4/22; to Clyde Sparks Campbell and Catherine Strawn C; m. 11/18/50 to Lois Katherine Ruff; c. Jill Katherine, Beth Ann and Lynn Ellen. Educ: Westminster Col, Pa, B.B.A, 44; Univ. Pittsburgh, D.D.S, 50; Univ. Tex, Residency in oral surg, 53-55; Alpha Sigma Phi; Psi Omega. Polit. & Govt. Pos: Sch. dir, Rep. Party, 62-; del, Rep. Nat. Conv, 64 & 68; mem, Beaver Co. Rep. Cmt, Pa, 66-, finance chmn, 68-; pres, Highland Sch. Bd, currently. Bus. & Prof. Pos: Mem. bd. trustees, Univ. Pittsburgh, 68- Mil. Serv: Entered as A/S, Navy, 43, released as Lt.(jg), 46, after serv. in Amphibious Forces, Pac. Area; Pac. Campaign Ribbon. Mem: Am. Dent. Asn; Am. Soc. Oral Surgeons; pres, Beaver Co. Dent. Soc. and West. Pa. Soc. Oral Surgeons, 65; Mason; Shrine; bd. dirs, Beaver Co. Cancer Soc, 58- and Tuberc. Asn, 59-; secy, Beaver Co. Pitt Club, 60-; Lakeview Country Club; Beaver Valley Country Club. Rel: Presbyterian. Legal Res: 2 Davidson Dr, Beaver Falls, Pa. Mailing Add: 290 W. Park, Rochester, Pa. 15074.

CAMPBELL, HERBERT LAWRENCE R
Iowa State Rep.
b. Chariton, Iowa, 12/24/10; s. Herbert L. Campbell and Clara Holmes C; m. 2/5/31 to Neva Stacy; c. Linda, Herbert L, III, Bruce and Rodney. Educ: Iowa Wesleyan Col, 1½ years; Sigma Phi Epsilon. Polit. & Govt. Pos: Iowa State Rep, 69- Bus. & Prof. Pos: Pres, Campbell Farms Inc; active in many farm oriented orgn. Mem: Y's Men; Farm Bur. Master Farmer. Rel: Methodist. Legal Res: R.R. 1, Washington, Iowa 52353.

CAMPBELL, HUGH BROWN, JR. D
N.C. State Rep.
b. Charlotte, N.C, 2/19/37; s. Hugh Brown Campbell and Thelma Welles C; m. 11/3/62 to Mary Irving Carlyle; c. Hugh Brown, III and Irving Carlyle. Educ: Davidson Col, A.B, 59; Harvard Law Sch, LL.B, 62; Phi Delta Theta; Lincoln's Inn Soc. Polit. & Govt. Pos: Mem, Mecklenburg Co. Dem. Exec. Cmt, 66-68; N.C. State Rep, 69- Bus. & Prof. Pos: Partner, Craighill, Rendleman & Clarkson, 67- Mil. Serv: Entered as 2nd Lt, Army, 62, released as 1st Lt, 64, after serv. in 115th Intelligence Corps, Seattle, Wash, 62-64; Res, 64-, Capt. Mem: N.C. and Am. Bar Asns; Eng. Speaking Union (bd. dir, Charlotte Br); Olde Providence Raquet & Swim Club. Rel: Episcopal. Mailing Add: 1428 Scotland Ave, Charlotte, N.C. 28207.

CAMPBELL, J. T. D
b. Faucett, Mo, 8/30/03; m. 6/20/31 to Mildred Duncan; c. James Truman. Educ: Buchanan Co. Pub. Sch. Polit. & Govt. Pos: Committeeman, Crawford Dem. Twp, Buchanan Co, Mo; former Mo. State Rep. Bus. & Prof. Pos: Farming; stock raising; supt, Buchanan Co. Farm. Mem: Rebekah; Odd Fellows. Rel: Presbyterian. Mailing Add: Faucett, Mo. 64448. (1967)

CAMPBELL, JACK M. D
b. Hutchinson, Kans, 9/10/16; s. John M. Campbell and Blanche E. Chain C; m. 11/17/45 to Ruthanne DeBus; c. Patty, Terry, Mike and Kathy. Educ: Washburn Col, A.B. magna cum laude, 38 and LL.B, 40; Hon. Doctorate, Col. Santa Fe, 65, N.Mex. State Univ, 65, N.Mex. Inst. Mining & Tech, 66; Tau Delta Pi. Polit. & Govt. Pos: Mem, State Bd. Finance, N.Mex, 55-59; N.Mex. State Rep, 56-62, Speaker House of Rep, 61-62 and chmn. Legis. Coun, 62; Gov, N.Mex, until 67. Bus. & Prof. Pos: Agent, Fed. Bur. Invest, 41-42; exec. secy, N.Mex. Oil & Gas Asn, 46-47; Attorney, Atwood, Malone & Campbell and Campbell and Russell, Albuquerque and Roswell, 48-63 and Stephenson, Campbell and Olmsted, Santa Fe, 67-; dir, Inst. Soc. Res. & Develop, Univ. N.Mex, currently. Mil. Serv: Entered as Pvt, Marine Corps, 42, released as 1st Lt, 45, after serv. in S.Pac; Capt, Marine Corps Res. Mem: Chmn, Inst. for State Prog. in 70's, Chapel Hill, N.C; Rotary; Am. Legion; VFW. Elected hon. mem-at-lg, Delta Sigma Rho-Tau Kappa Alpha Forensic Soc, 65. Rel: Roman Catholic. Mailing Add: Box 877, Santa Fe, N.Mex. 87507.

CAMPBELL, JACQUELINE F. R
Mem, Calif. State Rep. Cent. Cmt.
b. Lidgerwood, N.Dak, 4/2/27; d. Arthur F. Bonzer and Ferne Woodward B; m. 8/20/50 to Robert R. Campbell; c. Jeffrey and Bonnie. Educ: Univ. Calif, Los Angeles; Univ. Calif, Santa Barbara, A.B, 50. Polit. & Govt. Pos: Mem. libr. cmn, City of Long Beach, Calif, 63-; mem, United Rep. of Calif; chmn. Goldwater Campaign, Long Beach, 64; alternate del, Rep. Nat. Conv, 64; membership chmn, 32nd Cong. Dist. Women's Fedn; co-chmn, Reagan for Gov. Cmt, Long Beach, 66; mem, Calif. Rep. State Cent. Cmt, 67-; mem, Co. Rep. Cent. Cmt, 67- Mem: DAR; Assistance League; PTA. Rel: Baptist. Mailing Add: 412 Orlena Ave, Long Beach, Calif. 90814. (1967)

CAMPBELL, JAMES PHILANDER, JR. R
Under Secy, U.S. Dept. Agr.
b. Athens, Ga, 4/9/17; s. James Philander Campbell, Sr. and Lorraine Montez Proctor C; m. 3/20/43 to Elizabeth Ann McCreery; c. Elizabeth Ann (Mrs. Phil Prichard), Vivian Lorraine, J. Phil, III, John Alan, Jennifer Claire and Janice. Educ: George Wash. Univ, 34; studied agr. in Denmark, 38-39; Univ. Ga, B.S.A, 40; Phi Kappa Phi; Kappa Alpha. Polit. & Govt. Pos: Ga. State Rep, 49-54; cmnr, Ga. Dept. Agr, 55-69; Under Secy, U.S. Dept. Agr, 69-, mem. nat. adv. cmts. to Secy. Agr. for Hog Cholera Eradication and for Wholesome Meat and Food Inspection, 69. Bus. & Prof. Pos: Trustee, Univ. Ga. Found, currently. Mil. Serv: Entered as Cadet, Air Force, 42, released as 1st Lt, 45, after serv. in Air Force Training Command, Tex. Mem: Former secy-treas. and chmn. bd, Stone Mt. Mem. Asn, until 69; Univ. Ga. Alumni Soc. (pres, 56); Am. Legion; Farm Bur; Rotary; Athens Country Club; Atlanta Athletic Club. Rel: Baptist. Legal Res: Watkinsville, Ga. 30677. Mailing Add: 8822 Fircrest Place, Alexandria, Va. 22308.

CAMPBELL, JOSEPH R
b. New York, N.Y, 3/25/00; s. Thomas Campbell and Anne Conneil C; m. to Dorothy Bostwick; c. Frederick, Douglas, Robert, Alan, Colin, Mrs. John V.B. Dean, Mrs. Henry A. Rudkin, Jr. and W.T. Sampson Smith, Jr. Educ: Columbia, A.B, 24, LL.D; Colgate Univ, LL.D; Alpha Delta Phi. Polit. & Govt. Pos: Mem, Atomic Energy Cmn, 53-54; Comptroller Gen, U.S, 54-65. Bus. & Prof. Pos: Assoc, Lingley, Baird & Dixon, Accts, 24-27; asst. comptroller, Valspar Corp, 27-29, comptroller, 29-32; partner, R.T. Lingley & Co, 32-33 and Joseph Campbell & Co, Accts, 33-41; asst. treas, Columbia Univ, 49-55, treas. and v.pres, 49-55; emer. trustee, Trinity Col. Mem: Am. Inst. Accts; Conn. State Soc. CPA; Union League and Madison Sq. Garden Clubs; Down Town Asn, New York; Seawanhaka Corinthian Yacht Club, L.I; Chevy Chase Club. Rel: Episcopal. Mailing Add: 3111 Woodland Dr. N.W, Washington, D.C. 20008.

CAMPBELL, JOSEPH BRADBURN R
b. Denver, Colo, 3/21/08; s. Joseph D. Campbell and Naomi Bradburn C; m. 6/8/34 to Dorothy Murphy; c. Susan (Mrs. Law), Sheila (Mrs. Rhoades) and Martha (Mrs. Murphy). Educ: Colby Col; Georgetown Univ, LL.B, 31, LL.M, 32; Zeta Psi. Polit. & Govt. Pos: City solicitor, Hallowell, Maine, 38-47, munic. court judge, 49-53; Maine State Rep, 49-51; co. attorney, Kennebec Co, Maine, 53-54; acting city mgr, Augusta, Maine; Maine State Sen, 63-64; former pres, Maine Senate. Mil. Serv: Entered as 1st Lt, Army Air Force, 42, released as Maj, 45, after serv. in Hq, Mediterranean Theater of Operations; Europe-African-Middle East. Serv. Medal; Air Offensive Ribbon, Europe; Naples Foggia; Rome Arno Stars; Col, Army Res, 61- Mem: Am. Col. of Trial Lawyers; Am. Judicature Soc; Am, Maine and Kennebec Co. Bar Asns; Am. Legion. Rel: Catholic. Legal Res: 76 Willow St, Augusta, Maine 04330. Mailing Add: 284 Water St, Augusta, Maine 04330. (1967)

CAMPBELL, LEHMAN SHELBY 'SAM' R
Rep. State Committeeman, Walton Co, Fla.
b. Newton, Ala, 7/14/07; s. William Alphred Campbell and Alice Scott C; m. 8/2/25 to Liza Lenora Beasley; c. James Lehman, Virginia Dair, Lydia Catherine and Myrtice Carolyn. Educ: Midland City High Sch. Polit. & Govt. Pos: V.chmn, First Dist. Rep. Party, Fla, 62-66; Fla. State Rep, Walton Co, 64-65; Rep. State Committeeman, Walton Co, Fla, currently. Mem: F&AM (Past Dist. Dep. Grand Master, Second Masonic Dist, Past and Present Master); Eastern Star (Past Patron and Present Assoc. Patron). Rel: Methodist. Mailing Add: Route 2, Box 240D, DeFuniak Springs, Fla. 32433. (1967)

CAMPBELL, LESLIE DUNLOP, JR. D
Va. State Sen.
b. Doswell, Va, 1/26/25; s. Leslie Dunlop Campbell and Norine Dickson C; m. 7/18/59 to Eleanor Miller Dickson; c. Sarah Payne, Mary Scott, Leslie Dunlop, III and Virginia Wells. Educ: Randolph-Macon Col, 42 & 46-48; Univ. Richmond Law Sch, LL.B, 51; Phi Alpha Delta. Polit. & Govt. Pos: Substitute Judge, Hanover Co. Court, Va, 54-55; Commonwealth's attorney, Hanover Co, 56-63; Va. State Sen, 26th Dist, 63- Bus. & Prof. Pos: Private law practice, 51-; assoc, Campbell & Ellis, Attorneys, 55- Mil. Serv: Entered as A/S, Navy, 44, released as RM 3/C, 46. Mem: Va. Bar Asn; Va. State Bar; past pres, 15th Judicial Circuit Bar Asn; Montpelier Ruritan Club (past Lt. Gov. for Chesapeake Dist, Ruritan Int); Hanover Jr. C. of C; Am. Legion Post 206; Jamestown Soc; Fishing Bay Yacht Club; Ashland C. of C; Soc. of the Cincinnati, State of Va; Ashland Kiwanis. Sailboat racing, Cougar Mark III Catamaran. Rel: Episcopal. Legal Res: Lochland, Route 2, Doswell, Va. 23047. Mailing Add: 133 Hanover Ave, Ashland, Va. 23005.

CAMPBELL, LESLIE KENNETH R
Mem, Calif. Rep. State Cent. Cmt.
b. Quimby, Iowa, 1/21/04; s. John Abram Campbell and Katherine Amelia Bower C; m. 6/24/39 to Alice Ann Hildebrand; c. Robert A. Miles (stepson). Educ: Buena Vista Col, 24-25; State Univ. Iowa, D.D.S, 29; Omicron Kappa Upsilon; Psi Omega. Polit. & Govt. Pos: Mgr, Nixon Club, Arcadia, Calif, 60; charter mem, bd. dir. and v.pres, Arcadia Rep, Inc, 60-; Rep. precinct chmn, Arcadia Area Precinct, 63-; alternate mem, Calif. Rep. State Cent. Cmt, 66-68, mem, 69-; mem, coord. coun, 54th Assembly Dist. Rep. Party, 69- Bus. & Prof. Pos: Dentist, Newton, Iowa, 29-48 and Alhambra and Arcadia, Calif, 48-59; instr. dent. health educ, Los Angeles, 48-59 & 59-68. Mil. Serv: Entered as Capt, Army, 43, released as Maj, 46, after serv. in Dent. Corps, U.S.A; Army Res, 46-53; Am. Theatre Medal; Sharpshooters Medal. Mem: Am. Dent. Asn and its component socs; Asn. of Sch. Dentists (retired); leader Boy Scouts, 17 years; Kiwanis (pres, Newton, Iowa Club, 42); Mason. Silver Beaver Award, Boy Scouts. Rel: Presbyterian; Elder, Arcadia Presby. Church, Calif. Mailing Add: 957 Kingsley Dr, Arcadia, Calif. 91006.

CAMPBELL, LEVIN HICKS R
b. Summit, N.J, 1/2/27; s. Worthington Campbell and Louise Steele Hooper C; m. 6/1/57 to Eleanor Saltonstall Lewis; c. Eleanor Saltonstall,

Levin Hicks and Sarah Hollyday. Educ: Harvard Col, A.B, 48, Harvard Law Sch, LL.B, 51. Polit. & Govt. Pos: Mass State Rep, 63-64; Asst. Attorney Gen, Mass, 65-67, First Asst. Attorney Gen, 67-68. Bus. & Prof. Pos: Assoc, Ropes & Gray, Boston, Attorneys, 54-64; fel, Inst. Polit, John F. Kennedy Sch. of Govt, Harvard, 68- Mil. Serv: Entered as Pvt, Army, 51, released as 1st Lt, 54, after serv. in Inf. and Judge Adv. Gen. Corps, K COM Z, Taegu, Korea, 53; Army Commendation Medal. Mem: Mass, Boston and Am. Bar Asns; Mass. Legis. Asn; Judge Advocates Asn; VFW; dir, Cambridge Civic Asn. and Cambridge Center Adult Educ; Mayor's Crime Cmn, Cambridge. Rel: Protestant. Mailing Add: 17 Bates St, Cambridge, Mass. 02140.

CAMPBELL, WILLIAM COWDEN R
Chmn, Mercer Co. Rep. Cmt, Pa.
b. West Middlesex, Pa, 3/27/16; s. Thomas Bruce Campbell and Ethel Davis C; m. 4/24/37 to Dorothy Marshall; c. Wm. Bruce, James, Thomas and Richard. Polit. & Govt. Pos: Sch. dir, 50-; mem, Mercer Co. Rep. Cmt, Pa, 50-54, chmn, 54-; del, Rep. Nat. Conv, 68. Bus. & Prof. Pos: Pres, Shenango Steel Bldgs, Inc. Mem: Hon. farmer, Future Farmers of Am; Mason; Grange. Rel: Presbyterian. Legal Res: R.D. 2, Pulaski, Pa. 16143. Mailing Add: West Middlesex, Pa. 16159.

CAMPBELL, WILLIAM DEWEY, JR. D
b. 10/31/28; s. William D. Campbell and Estelle Patton C; m. to Lillian F. Spencer, wid; c. William D. III and Susan Elizabeth. Educ: Univ. of Ala, B.A, 49, LL.B, 54. Polit. & Govt. Pos: Ala. State Rep, until 67. Bus. & Prof. Pos: Used car dealer. Rel: Presbyterian; Deacon. Mailing Add: Tuscaloosa, Ala. 35401.

CAMPBELL, WILLIAM LOY D
b. DeKalb Co, 11/26/27; single. Educ: Univ. Ala. Law Sch. Polit. & Govt. Pos: Ala. State Rep, 63-67; solicitor, Jackson Co. Bus. & Prof. Pos: Attorney. Mailing Add: Box 241, Scottsboro, Ala. 35768. (1967)

CAMPBELL, WILLIAM RICHARDSON R
Mont. State Rep.
b. Missoula, Mont, 6/29/25; s. John Louis Campbell and Mary Tower C; m. 8/30/47 to Hope Moeller; c. Colleen, Constance Ann and Douglas William. Educ: Univ. Mont, B.A, 65, M.A, 68; Phi Delta Theta. Polit. & Govt. Pos: Alderman, Missoula City Coun, Mont, 59-62, 67-; Mont. State Rep, 69- Bus. & Prof. Pos: Salesman, Armour & Co, Spokane, Wash, 50-60; field dir, Mont. Tax Payers Asn, Helena, 61-62; salesman, Liftco, Spokane, 62-64; teacher, Missoula Sch. Dist. I, Mont, 65- Mil. Serv: Pvt, Marines, 43, released as Cpl, 46, after serv. in 3rd Amphibious Corps, Pac. Theatre, 44-45. Mem: Mont. Educ. Asn; Phi Delta Kappa; Elks. Rel: Protestant. Mailing Add: 620 Crestline Dr, Missoula, Mont. 59801.

CAMPBELL, WYMAN D. D
b. Milan Twp, Mich, 2/16/20; s. John Campbell and Winona Lentz C; m. 10/20/46 to Syble B. McConnell; c. Jack Edward. Educ: Albion Col, Mich. Polit. & Govt. Pos: Secy-treas, Milan Twp. Dem. Cmt, Mich, 50-59; del, Dem. State Conv, 50-66; mem, Dem. State Cent. Cmt, Mich, 55-58 & 63-64; clerk, Milan Twp, Mich, 59-66; del, Dem. Nat. Conv, 64; chmn, Monroe Co. Dem. Cmt, Mich. and mem, Second Dist. Cent. Cmt, Dem. Party, 65-66; postmaster, U.S. Post Off, Milan, 67- Mil. Serv: Entered as A/S, Navy, 41, released as CPO, 45, after serv. in Fleet Hosp. No. 103 and 111, Pac. Area; Am. Defense Medal; Pac. and Am. Theaters; Good Conduct Medal; World War II Victory Medal. Mem: Pres, Monroe Co. Clerks Asn, Mich, 65-67; Nat. Dent. Lab. Asn; Mich. State Dent. Lab. Asn; Masonic Lodge 323, Milan, Mich; life mem, VFW; Eastern Star; Nat. Rifle Asn. Rel: Protestant. Mailing Add: 18231 Redman Rd, Milan, Mich. 48160.

CAMPI, P. PAUL D
Chmn, Monmouth Co. Dem. Party, N.J.
b. Pocantico Hills, N.Y, 4/8/08; s. Rocco M. Campi and Theresa Frasca C; m. 10/27/29 to Mildred Helen Frey; c. Gayle. Educ: Rutgers Univ. and Dickinson Sch. Eng. Polit. & Govt. Pos: Chmn, First Regional Sewerage Meeting, Monmouth Co, N.J, undersheriff, Monmouth Co. and mem, Electoral Col, Planning Bd, Bd. Gov, Indust. Develop. Cmt. and Beautification Cmt, formerly; mayor, Little Silver, N.J, 56-60; del, Dem. Nat. Conv, 68; chmn, Monmouth Co. Dem. Party, presently. Bus. & Prof. Pos: V.pres, Ramsey Estates, Inc. and with N.J. Bell Tel, 37 years. Mem: Red Bank Coun, Tel. Pioneers of Am; Transport Workers Union; IBEW. Rel: Roman Catholic. Mailing Add: 51 Queens Dr, Little Silver, N.J. 07739.

CANADAY, ALYCE D.
b. N.Y.C; d. Florence Doherty and Ann Happ D; m; c. Henry T. Educ: Julia Richman High Sch; Grace Inst. Bus. Sch. Polit. & Govt. Pos: Staff asst, U.S. Sen Styles Bridges, N.H, 51-61, U.S. Sen. Kenneth B. Keating, N.Y, 61-63 and U.S. Rep. Richard C. White, Tex, 65-68; admin. asst, U.S. Rep. Peter N. Kyros, Maine, 68- Bus. & Prof. Pos: Personnel staff mem, Shell Oil Co. Mil. Serv: Recruiter, Women's Army Corps, 43-45. Mem: Salvation Army Auxiliary; Capitol Hill First Friday Club. Mailing Add: Apt. 525, 4201 S. 31st St, Arlington, Va. 22206.

CANADAY, PAUL D. R
b. Osceola, Mo, 7/16/20; m. 9/4/44 to Ruth Thompson; c. Stephen Paul, Connie Jean. Educ: Drury Col; Marine Corps Sch. Polit. & Govt. Pos: Mo. State Rep, -66. Bus. & Prof. Pos: Pres, Exec. Security Life Ins. Co. Mil. Serv: U.S.M.C. Mem: Am. Legion; VFW; Elks; Masons. Rel: Christian Church. 1967 Legal Res: Springfield, Mo. No mailing address available. (1967)

CANADAY, TRAVIS D
Chmn, Chester Co. Dem. Exec. Cmt, Tenn.
b. Enville, Tenn, 2/10/18; s. William Victor Canaday and Lucy Lee C; m. 12/24/38 to Margie Bullman. Educ: Morris Chapel, Tenn, 4 years. Polit. & Govt. Pos: Mem, Chester Co. Court, Tenn, 55-, probate officer, Juvenal Judge and Co. Judge, 68-; del, Constitutional Conv, 64-69; chmn, Chester Co. Dem. Exec. Cmt, 58- Rel: Methodist. Mailing Add: Enville, Tenn. 38332.

CANALE, DREW JUSTIN D
Tenn. State Sen.
b. Memphis, Tenn, 8/25/22; s. George Anthony Canale and Arnette Sturla C; m. 5/9/56 to Helen McAdams; c. Drew Justin, William Brooks and Anthony Shane. Educ: South. Law Univ, LL.B. Polit. & Govt. Pos: Tenn. State Sen, Shelby Co, 67- Bus. & Prof. Pos: Pres, Nat. Tobacco, Inc, Memphis, Tenn, 50- Mil. Serv: Entered as Seaman, Navy, 42, released as CPO, 45, after serv. in Destroyer Escort, U.S.S. Mitchell, 42-45; Eight Major Citations aboard the Destroyer U.S.S. Mitchell; Presidential Unit Citation. Mem: Dir, Youth Guid. Cmn; Juvenile Court Adv. Bd. Rel: Catholic. Mailing Add: 620 S. Belvedere, Memphis, Tenn. 38104.

CANDLER, THOMAS SLAUGHTER D
b. Blairsville, Ga, 12/15/90; s. William Ezekial Candler and Mary Elizabeth Haralson C; m. 4/26/16 to Augusta Beulah Cook; c. Sarah (Mrs. Gilliland), Nell (Mrs. McNeil) and Tom, Jr. Educ: Young Harris Col, A.B, 13; Univ. Ga, B.L, 15. Polit. & Govt. Pos: Mayor, Blairsville, Ga, 16-20; chmn, Union Co. Dem. Exec. Cmt, 20-39; U.S. Cmnr, 27-39; judge, Northeast. Circuit, 39-45; assoc. justice, Ga. Supreme Court, 45-65, former presiding justice. Mem: Am, Ga. and Mt. Judicial Bar Asns; Mason; WOW; Blue Key; hon. mem, Peace Officers Asn. of Ga; Future Farmers of Am; Ga. Hist. Soc.(past pres). Rel: Methodist. Mailing Add: P.O. Box 171, Blairsville, Ga. 30512. (1967)

CANFIELD, DAMON R. R
Wash. State Sen.
b. Siloam Springs, Ark, 9/21/97; s. Herbert Howe Canfield and Adelia Laughlin C; m. to Marie Strode; c. Charles D. and Marilyn J. (Mrs. Adler). Educ: Univ. Wash, 14-16; Wash. State Univ, B.S, 21; Alpha Zeta; Phi Kappa Phi; Theta Chi. Polit. & Govt. Pos: Wash. State Rep, 53-66; asst. Rep. leader, 59-64; chmn, Rep. Policy Cmt, 61-64; Wash. State Sen, 67- Mil. Serv: Entered as Seaman 2/C, Navy, 17, released as Ens, 19; Peace Medal. Mem: Past pres, Yakima Classroom Teachers Asn, Wash. State Dept. of Classroom Teachers, Wash. Voc. Asn; Wash. Agr. Teachers' Asn; Wash. Angus Breeders Asn; Yakima Valley Breeders Asn. and Wash. Poultry Asn; Wash. Fruit Cmn; past chmn, Wash. Cherry Mkt. Cmt, Wash. Cherry Inst. and Lower Yakima Valley Soil Conserv. Dist; Hon. State Farmer, Future Farmers of Am; hon. mem, 4-H Coun; trustee, Wash. 4-H Found; past master, Grange; Farm Bur; pres, Cent. Wash. Fair; Am. Legion; Vet. of WW I; Mason; Wash. Cattleman's Asn. Rel: Methodist. Mailing Add: 1368 Upland Dr, Sunnyside, Wash. 98944.

CANFIELD, GORDON R
b. Salamanca, N.Y, 4/15/98; s. Carl A. Canfield and Florence A. Saxton C; m. 11/15/28 to Dorothy E. Greenwell; c. Carl M. and Maj. Allan R. Educ: George Wash. Univ, LL.B; Paterson State Col, L.H.D. Polit. & Govt. Pos: U.S. Rep, N.J, 41-61. Bus. & Prof. Pos: Dir. commun. rels, First Nat. Bank of Passaic Co, N.J. Mil. Serv: Signal Corps, Army, 18; founder, U.S. Coast Guard Res. now having 302 units. Mem: Mason; Rotary. Rel: Protestant. Mailing Add: 317 E. 30th St, Paterson, N.J. 07504.

CANFIELD, JOHN A. 'JACK' D
b. Pittsburgh, Pa, 6/2/41; s. L. Frank Walker and Clydetta Conlon Canfield W; m. 7/22/61 to June Louise Smith; c. John Michael and Christopher Alan. Educ: Potomac State Col, W.Va. Univ, A.A, 61; W.Va. Univ, B.S. in Journalism, 63; Sigma Delta Chi. Polit. & Govt. Pos: Co-founder, Mineral Co. Young Dem, W.Va; cmt. asst. to U.S. Rep. Harley O. Staggers, W.Va, 63-64; press aide in gubernatorial campaign of Hulett Smith, 64-65; admin. asst. to Gov. Hulett Smith, 65-67, press secy, 67-69; del, Dem. Nat. Conv, 68. Bus. & Prof. Pos: News ed, WCLG Radio, Morgantown, W.Va, 61-63 and WCHS-TV, Charleston, 63; contrib. ed, WSAZ-TV, Charleston, currently. Publ: Ed, The Papers and Public Addresses of Gov. Hulett C. Smith, State of W.Va, 69. Mem: W.Va. Partners of the Alliance, Inc. Named Outstanding Male Grad. in Sch. of Journalism at W.Va. Univ. by Sigma Delta Chi, 63. Rel: Roman Catholic. Mailing Add: 205 56th St, S.E, Charleston, W.Va. 25304.

CANFIELD, JOHN LEMUAL D
Chmn, 15th Cong. Dist. Dem. Party, Mich.
b. Senath, Mo, 9/14/17; s. Oda Thomas Canfield and Ethel Hollis C; m. 10/7/39 to Claudene Caldwell; c. Ruth Ann and Glenda Sue. Educ: High Sch. Polit. & Govt. Pos: Precinct del, Dem. Party, Mich, 46-; exec. bd. mem, 16th Dist. Dem. Party, 50-64; chmn, Dearborn Twp. Dem. Club, 55-57; park cmnr, Dearborn, 55-57, trustee, 57-59 and supvr, 59-63; mem. bd. supvrs, Wayne Co, 59-; alternate del, Dem. Nat. Conv, 60, del, 64 & 68; mayor, Dearborn Heights, 63-; chmn, 15th Cong. Dist. Dem. Party, 64- Mil. Serv: Entered as A/S, Navy, 43, released as PO 3/C, 45. Mem: Hon. mem, Jaycees; Lions. Rotary; Elks; Moose; Mason; UAW. Rel: Protestant. Mailing Add: 7026 N. Inkster Rd, Apt. 105O, Dearborn Heights, Mich. 48127.

CANFIELD, ROBERT ROE R
b. Chana, Ill, 5/12/09; s. Isaac F. Canfield and Maude Roe C; m. 5/6/33 to Elizabeth Foard; c. James and Phillips. Educ: Cornell Col, A.B, 31; Northwest. Univ. Law Sch, J.D, 37; Tau Kappa Alpha. Polit. & Govt. Pos: States attorney, Winnebago Co, Ill, 48-56; Ill. State Sen, 56-64; Ill. State Rep, 64-66. Bus. & Prof. Pos: Attorney at Law, 34- Publ: Fat Cat Lobbyists Make Your Laws, Vantage, 69. Mem: Am, Ill. State and Winnebago Co. Bar Asns. Named Mr. State's Attorney of Ill, State's Attorney's Asn, 53. Rel: Methodist. Legal Res: Spring Creek Rd, Rockford, Ill. Mailing Add: 1100 Rfd. Trust Bldg, Rockford, Ill. 61601.

CANGELOSI, THEODORE FRANCIS
b. Baton Rouge, La, 12/14/11; s. Frank Cangelosi and Lily Distefano C; m. 12/18/41 to Daisy Skardon Gore; c. Phyllis Sandra, Theodore Francis, Jr, Cheryl Skardon, Guy Gore, Dale Douglas and Gary Stephen. Educ: La. State Univ, B.A, 32, Law Sch, J.D, 68; v.pres. and rep. sr. class, Student Coun; Varsity Debating Team, Best Debator Award, 30; pres, Newman Club; Tau Kappa Alpha; Theta Alpha Phi; Pi Sigma Alpha; hon. mem, Gamma Eta Gamma. Polit. & Govt. Pos: La. State Rep, E.Baton Rouge Parish, 40-44; gen. counsel, La. Hwy. Dept, 48-50 and Gr. Baton Rouge Port Cmn, 58-59; mem, 100 Man Curriculum Study Cmt, Dept. Educ; chmn, La. State Sci. Found; mem, State Cmn. for Higher Educ. Facilities Act; civilian aide to Secy. Army for La, 61-63. Bus. & Prof. Pos: Lectr, Law Sch, La. State Univ, 49-50, secy, 52-56, v.chmn, 56-58, chmn, 58-60, chmn. emer. and mem. bd. supvr, 50-; gen. real estate investments; attorney-at-law; chmn. bd. dir, Baton Rouge Bank & Trust Co, 67- Mil. Serv: Entered as Pvt, Army,

41, released as Maj, 46, after serv. as Exec. Officer to Judge Adv. Gen, ETO; Lt. Col, Judge Adv. Gen. Dept, Army Res; Legion of Merit; Am. Defense Serv. Medal; European-African-Middle East. Campaign Medal with Bronze Star. Mem: Regional dir, Nat. Asn. Gov. Bd. State Univs. and Allied Insts, 54-56, exec. cmt, 56-; Int, Am. and Baton Rouge Bar Asns; Sixth Cong. Dist. Rep, Standing Cmt. on Selection Judicial Cand. and Exec. Cmt. for Sesquicentennial Celebration of Civil Code, La. Bar Asn; Am. Judicature Soc; pres, La. Educ. Research Asn; bd. dirs, La. State Univ. Found; State Legis. Chmn, Am. Legion, 49-50, Nat. Cmt. on Constitution and By-laws, 49-51; Amvets; K. of C; Elks; charter mem, City Club Baton Rouge. Outstanding Civilian Serv. Medal, U.S. Army. Rel: Roman Catholic. Legal Res: 2644 E. Lakeshore Dr, Baton Rouge, La. 70802. Mailing Add: 617 N. Boulevard, Baton Rouge, La. 70802.

CANN, CARMINE J. D
b. Clarksburg, W.Va, 7/27/30; s. James Cann and Antoinette Oliverio C; m. to Florence Chico; c. James, Samuel Joseph, Antoinette, Judith, Claudia, Carmine and Hilarion. Educ: W.Va. Univ, A.B, LL.B. Polit. & Govt. Pos: Legal draftsman, W.Va. House of Del, 60-; former W.Va. State Del. Bus. & Prof. Pos: Lawyer. Mem: Clarksburg Columbian Club; Moose; K. of C; Elks; Am. Bar Asn. Rel: Roman Catholic. Mailing Add: 512 Prunty Bldg, Clarksburg, W.Va. 26301. (1967)

CANN, WILLIAM FRANCIS R
Dep. Attorney Gen, N.H.
b. Somerville, Mass, 10/10/22; s. William Arthur Cann and Frances E. Hardy C; m. 9/6/58 to Ellen Catherine Hughes; c. Ellen R. Lockhart and Allan C. Watts. Educ: Tufts Univ, 40-42; Boston Univ. Sch. Law, LL.B, 48; Phi Delta Phi. Polit. & Govt. Pos: Attorney, Off. of Attorney Gen, N.H, 60-61, asst. attorney gen, 61-67, dep. attorney gen, 67- Bus. & Prof. Pos: Sr. auto exam, Allied Am. Mutual Fire Ins. Co, Boston, 48-52, sr. fire exam, 52-57; sr. liability claim exam, Am. Mutual Liability Ins. Co, Wakefield, 57-60. Mil. Serv: Entered as Pvt, Army Signal Corps, 43, released as Sgt, 45, after serv. in 324th Army Air Force Base Unit, 486th Bomb Group, ETO, 44-45; Europe-Africa-Middle East Campaign Ribbon with Three Battle Stars; Rhineland, Cent. Europe, Ardennes; Am. Theatre Campaign Ribbons; Good Conduct Medal. Mem: Am. Judicature Soc; Am, N.H. and Merrimack Co. Bar Asns; N.H. Hist. Soc; Audubon Soc. N.H. Rel: Congregational. Mailing Add: 36 Roger Ave, Concord, N.H. 03301.

CANNEY, RALPH W. R.
N.H. State Rep.
b. Durham, N.C, 8/7/96; s. Henry J. Canney and Mary Eleanore Wilson C; m. 9/18/21 to Ethel Maude Hayes; c. Phillip Carl (deceased); Lois Elaine (Mrs. Prisco DePrizio); Ralph Wilson, Paul J, Priscilla Joyce (Mrs. Maurice DuTalle, Carroll and Carolyn E. Educ: Rochester High Sch. Polit. & Govt. Pos: Mem. budget cmt, Farmington, N.H, 53-69; del, State Constitutional Conv, 64; N.H. State Rep, 63-65 & 69- Bus. & Prof. Pos: Motel Owner, poultry, real estate and investments. Mem: Elks; Mason; Past Master Grange. Rel: Protestant. Mailing Add: Route 2, Rochester, N.H. 03867.

CANNON, CALVIN LAWRENCE R
Tenn. State Sen.
b. Riceville, Tenn, 3/8/26; s. William Fred Cannon and Dorothy Medlin C; m. 3/18/50 to Flora Hawkins; c. Carolyn Ann, Marilyn Joan, Nancy Grace and Calvin Fred. Educ: Univ. Tenn, B.S, 53, M.S, 54; Univ. Ga, D.V.M, 58; Omega Tau Sigma. Polit. & Govt. Pos: Sheriff, McMinn Co, Tenn, 62-66; Tenn, State Sen, Ninth Dist, 66- Bus. & Prof. Pos: Asst. instr, Univ. Tenn, 53-54; instr, Univ. Ga, 56-58; private vet. practice, McMinn Co. Animal Hosp, Athens, Tenn, 58- Mil. Serv; Entered as A/S, Navy, 44, released as Seaman 3/C, 46, after serving in amphibious opers, Pac. Theater, 44-46. Mem: Elks; Moose; VFW; Am. Legion; C. of C. Rel: Baptist. Mailing Add: Box 369, Riceville Hwy, Athens, Tenn. 37303.

CANNON, EDWARD M. D
Mo. State Rep.
b. Foley, Mo, 9/4/07; m. 3/29/38 to Louise Hechler (deceased); c. Earl and David; m. 11/28/60 to Mary B. Davis. Educ: Winfield High Sch. Polit. & Govt. Pos: Founder, Young Dem. Club, Lincoln Co, Mo, 32; Mo. State Rep, 56- Bus. & Prof. Pos: Farmer; real estate. Mem: Young Dem. Club. Rel: Baptist. Mailing Add: RFD 2, Troy, Mo. 63379.

CANNON, FARRAR HUFFMAN D
Chmn, Coahoma Co. Dem. Exec. Cmt, Miss.
b. Monticello, Miss, 7/13/96; s. Will Carey Cannon and Mary Lily Huffman C; m. 6/19/20 to Mary Ella Findley; c. Shirley Ann and Betty Lou. Educ: Miss. A&M Col. Polit. & Govt. Pos: Secy-treas, Delta Levee Bd, Yazoo, Miss, 20-24; chmn, Coahoma Co. Dem. Exec. Cmt, 53- Mil. Serv: Entered as Pvt, Army, 17, released as Sgt, 19, after serv. in Co. K, Ninth Inf, Second Div, Europe; Silver Star; Croix de Guerre; Purple Heart. Mem: Am. Legion; 40 et 8; Miss. Farm Bur; C. of C. Legal Res: 501 Pecan, Clarksdale, Miss. 38614. Mailing Add: P.O. Box 818, Clarksdale, Miss. 38614.

CANNON, HOWARD WALTER D
U.S. Sen, Nev.
b. St. George, Utah; s. Walter Cannon and Leah Sullivan C; m. to Dorothy Pace; c. Nancy Lee and Alan Howard. Educ: Ariz. State Teachers Col, B.E, 33; Univ. Ariz, LL.B, 37; hon. LL.D, Ariz. State Col, 62. Polit. & Govt. Pos: U.S. Sen, Nev, 58- Mil. Serv: Maj. Gen, Air Force Res. Legal Res: Las Vegas, Nev. Mailing Add: 5312 Portsmouth Rd, Spring Hill, Md. 20016.

CANNON, HUGH D
b. Albemarle, N.C, 10/11/31; s. Hubert N. Cannon and Nettie Harris C; m. 1/28/56 to Jessie Mercer; c. John Stuart and Marshall. Educ: Davidson Col, A.B, 53; Oxford Univ, B.A, 55, M.A, 60; Harvard Law Sch, LL.B, 58; Phi Beta Kappa; Omicron Delta Kappa; Am. Asn. of Rhodes Scholars; Phi Gamma Delta. Polit. & Govt. Pos: Asst. to Gov, N.C, 61; dir. admin, N.C, 61-65. Bus. & Prof. Pos: Partner law firm, Sanford, Cannon & Hunter, 65-68, Sanford, Cannon, Adams & McCullough, 68- Mil. Serv: Capt, N.C. Nat. Guard, 62- Mem: Am, N.C, and Wake Co. Bar Asns; N.C. State Bar; trustee, N.C. School of Arts and Davidson Col; Parliamentarian; Nat. Educ. Asn. Rel: Methodist. Mailing Add: P.O. Box 389, Raleigh, N.C. 27609.

CANNON, JOE WESLEY R
Committeeman, Ill. Rep. Cent. Cmt.
b. Bowen, Ill, 6/2/23; s. Harry Claud Cannon and Lillian Mae Brown C; m. 12/29/46 to Josephine Gerdes; c. Jill Susanne, Joe David, Jeffrey Lynn, Jonathan Lee and James Gregory. Educ: Ill. Col, A.B, 47; Univ. Ill, B.S, 49, M.D, 51; Gamma Nu; Alpha Kappa Kappa. Polit. & Govt. Pos: Mem, sch. bd, 57-63; alternate del, Rep. Nat. Conv, 64; Committeeman, Ill. Rep. Cent. Cmt, 66- Bus. & Prof. Pos: Del, State Meeting of Ill. Acad. Gen. Practice, 60-65. Mil. Serv: Entered as Pvt, Army Air Force, 43, released as 1st Lt, 45, after serv. in 357th Fighter Group, Eighth Air Force, ETO, 44-45; Eight Air Medals; ETO Ribbon. Mem: Am. Med. Asn; Ill. Med. Soc; Am. Acad. of Gen. Practice; Mason. Rel: Methodist. Mailing Add: 900 Harmony Lane, Lacon, Ill. 61540.

CANNON, JOSEPH NATHANIAL, JR. R
b. Pecos, Tex, 6/6/29; s. Joseph Nathaniel Cannon and Mable Hill C; m. 8/22/50 to Norma Rose Barnett; c. Victor Lee, Rosanne and Michael Joseph. Educ: Baylor Univ, B.S, 50; Baylor Univ. Col. of Med, M.D, 53. Polit. & Govt. Pos: Former chmn, Matagorda Co. Rep. Party, Tex. Mil. Serv: Entered as Lt.(jg), Naval Res, 53, released as Lt, 56. Mem: Matagorda, Jackson, Wharton and Ft. Bend Med. Socs; Tex. and Am. Med. Asns; Tex. Acad. of Gen. Practice; Asn. of Am. Phys. & Surg; Lions Int. Rel: Latter-day Saint. Legal Res: 3121 Dunbar, Bay City, Tex. 77414. Mailing Add: 1413 Ave. G, Bay City, Tex. 77414.

CANNON, PATRICIA ELAINE D
Mem, Alaska State Dem. Cent. Cmt.
b. Whitefish, Mont, 7/11/29; d. Perry Bryce McMurdo and Jean Campell M; m. 9/3/53 to Lloyd Wynel Cannon; c. Carolyn Ann, Susan Elaine (Mrs. Davey) and Michael Wynel (deceased). Educ: Univ. Alaska, 46-47. Polit. & Govt. Pos: Dem. precinct chmn, Kodiak Island, Alaska, 63-; mem, Kodiak Island Sch. Bd, 65-69; mem, Alaska State Dem. Cent. Cmt, 67-; del, Dem. Nat. Conv, 68; mem, Alaska State Voc. Educ. Bd, 68- Mem: Alaska Cripple Children Asn; Alaska Ment. Retarded Asn; League of Women Voters; PTA. Rel: Protestant. Legal Res: 28 Mill Bay Rd, Kodiak, Alaska 99615. Mailing Add: Box 585, Kodiak, Alaska 99615.

CANNON, RALPH S. R
Utah State Rep.
b. Bountiful, Utah, 4/16/12; s. George M. Cannon and Ellen Christina Steffensen C; m. 1/20/50 to Mary Alice Wood; c. Michael Ray, Christina Wood, Wilford Wood, Ralph Wood and George Wood. Educ: Univ. of Utah, B.S, 47. Polit. & Govt. Pos: Utah State Rep, 63 & 67-; state del, Rep. Party, 64 & 66. Bus. & Prof. Pos: Mgr, Cannon's Dance Center, 47-57 and Mt. States Ins. Agency, 58-; pres, Mortgage Security Corp, 64-; field mgr. Salt Lake Branch, Equity Funding Corp. Am, currently; regional mgr, Unity Securities Corp. of Am, currently. Mil. Serv: Served with armed forces in the Pac. Area as Am. Red Cross Field Dir. and Asst. Field Supvr, 42-46. Mem: Nat. Asn. Securities Dealers; Am. Guild Variety Artists; Kiwanis. Formerly prfnl. dancer and teacher, night club work, Radio City Music Hall Corps de Ballet. Rel: Latter-day Saint. Legal Res: 714 W. 3800 S, Bountiful, Utah 84010. Mailing Add: 2525 S. Main, Suite 13, Salt Lake City, Utah 84115.

CANNON, ROSS W. D
Mem, Dem. State Cmt, Mont.
b. Butte, Mont, 5/1/29; s. Paul Cannon and Caroline Duffes C; m. 7/28/57 to Natalie Norby; c. Stephanie S. and Davis S. Educ: Univ. Mont, B.A. and LL.B; George Washington Univ, LL.M; Sigma Chi; Phi Delta Phi. Polit. & Govt. Pos: Mem, Lewis and Clark Co. Dem. Cent. Cmt; asst. attorney gen. and dep. co. attorney, 65-69; mem, Dem. State Cmt, currently; mem, State Planning and Develop. Cmn, currently. Bus. & Prof. Pos: Attorney adv, Interstate Commerce Cmn, Washington, D.C, 57-59; Attorney-at-law, Helena, Mont, 59- Mil. Serv: Entered as 2nd Lt, Air Force, 55, released as 1st Lt, after serv. in 380th Air Refueling Sq, Strategic Air Command, 55; Am. Defense Medal; Maj, Air Force Res. Mem: YMCA (past pres, pres. dir, Helena Chap); Mont. Bar Asn. First Judicial Dist.(v.pres); Mont. Club; First Dist. Bar Asn.(past pres); Am. Trial Lawyers Asn. Rel: Presbyterian. Mailing Add: 2130 Highland St, Helena, Mont. 59601.

CANNON, T(HOMAS) QUENTIN R
Utah State Rep.
b. Salt Lake City, Utah, 4/29/06; s. Jesse Fox Cannon and Margaret Ann McKeever C; m. 8/26/34 to Katherine Bowman; c. Thomas Quentin, Jr, Richard Bowman, Kathleen (Mrs. Roger B. Pinnock) and Jesse Fielding. Educ: Univ. Utah, A.B, 31; George Wash. Univ, LL.B, 35; Georgetown Univ, J.D, 38; Delta Phi; Delta Theta Phi. Polit. & Govt. Pos: Attorney, Reconstruction Finance Corp, 39; law clerk to chief justice, Utah Supreme Court, 41; dep. enforcement attorney & asst. U.S. attorney, Off. Price Admin, 47; reference attorney, U.S. House Rep, 47, 49 & 63; dep. attorney gen, State of Utah, 63-67; dep. co. attorney, Salt Lake Co, 67-69; Utah State Rep, 69- Bus. & Prof. Pos: Pres. & bd. mem, Salt Lake City Bd. Educ. and Salt Lake Co. Recreation Bd, 51-60; v.pres. and bd. mem, Salt Lake Area Vocation Sch, 51-60; gen. counsel, Days of 47, 53-60; European gen. counsel, Church of Jesus Christ of Latter-day Saints, 61-62; pres, Utah State Soc. of Wash, D.C, 39. Mil. Serv: 2nd Lt, Qm. Corps; Lt. Col, Utah State Guard. Mem: Am. & Utah State Bar Asns; D.C. Bar; Am. Trial Lawyers Asn; SAR; Rotary Int; Bonneville Knife & Fork Club. Rel: Latter-day Saint. Legal Res: 5340 Cottonwood Lane, Salt Lake City, Utah 84117. Mailing Add: 619 Continental Bank Bldg, Salt Lake City, Utah 84101.

CANSON, VIRNA M. D
Mem, Calif. Dem. State Cent. Cmt.
b. Bridgeport, Okla; d. William A. Dobson and Eula M. Gross D; m. to Clarence B. Canson, Sr; c. Clarence, Jr. and Faythe. Educ: Tuskegee Inst; Univ. Wis. Sch. for Credit Union Personnel, grad. Polit. & Govt. Pos: Commun. orgn. rep, State Off. Econ. Opportunity, Sacramento, Calif; mem, prog. adv. cmt, State Consumer Coun, 62; past pres, Dem. Women's Club, 63; chmn, Sacramento Co. Coun. Dem. Clubs, 64; mem, exec. cmt, Calif. Dem. State Cent. Cmt. and co-chmn, 3rd Cong. Dist; women's chmn, Alan Cranston for Controller; mem, Steering Cmt, Californians Against Proposition 14; del, Dem. Nat. Conv. and mem, Credentials Cmt, 64; legis. advocate, Negro Polit. Action Asn, Calif, 65; mem, Calif. Dem. State Cent. Cmt, currently. Bus. &

Prof. Pos: Treas-mgr, Credit Union, NAACP, 53- Publ: 'NAACP and the Credit Union,' Crisis Mag; 'Hunt for a Home,' The Progressive, 4/54. Mem: Bd. dir, Sacramento Br, NAACP Credit Union; exec. bd, Sacramento Br, NAACP; Policy and Adv. Cmt, West Coast Region, NAACP and chmn, Credit Union Cmt; regional rep, Adv. Resolution Cmt, Nat. Conv, NAACP, 2 terms; Citizen's Adv. Cmt. to Sacramento Co. Welfare Dept. Job Develop. and Placement Unit; bd. dir, Sacramento Chap, People to People; past secy, Sacramento Coun. of Churches; adv. cmt. on Family Life Educ, Sacramento Unified Sch. Dist; adv. bd. to Domestic Relations Court, Sacramento Co; bd. dir, Asn. Calif. Consumers; bd. dir, Sacramento World Affairs Coun; Founders Club, Credit Union Nat. Asn; dir, Calif. Credit Union League, 4 years, chmn, Mutual Area Meetings Cmt, 2 terms and pres, Sacramento Valley Chap. First winner, D.D. Mattocks Award from Sacramento Br, NAACP for distinguished serv. to commun; received Woman of the Year, Bus. Week Award, Iota Phi Lambda, 57 and 62. Rel: Congregational. Legal Res: 4216 Lotus Ave, Sacramento, Calif. Mailing Add: 1025 Ninth St, Sacramento, Calif. 95814. (1967)

CANTONI, FRANK H. D
b. Charleroi, Pa, 10/19/07; s. Anthony Cantoni and Anna Bigi C; m. to Alma Pater Lini; c. two. Educ: Grove City Col, B.S. Polit. & Govt. Pos: Pa. State Rep, 64-67; mayor, two terms; Water Authority, five years; justice of the peace, ten years. Bus. & Prof. Pos: Sch. teacher. Mem: Lions Club. Mailing Add: 505 Crest Ave, Charleroi, Pa. 15022. (1967)

CANTRELL, BERRY DABNEY LYNCHMORE D
b. Hamilton, Ala; s. William Henry Cantrell and Effie Lona Crane C; m. 6/19/47 to Emogene Victory; c. Berry Dabney Lynchmore, Jr, Martha Jeanne. Educ: Ala. Polytech. Inst; Florence State Col. Polit. & Govt. Pos: Ala. State Rep, 63-66; dep. comm, Bd. of Corrections, 64; Ala. State Sen, 55. Mil. Serv: Marine Corps; Nat. Guard. Mem: Mason. Rel: Methodist. Mailing Add: 1820 Federal Dr, Montgomery, Ala. 36110. (1967)

CANTRELL, E. J. D
Mo. State Rep.
b. St. Louis, Mo, 11/19/28; m. April, 1949 to Lillian Harrison; c. Five. Educ: Cape Girardeau, Mo. pub. & parochial schs. Polit. & Govt. Pos: Mo. State Rep, 58- Bus. & Prof. Pos: Employee, auto mfg. firm, 17 years; past bd. mem, Village of Breckenridge Hills. Mil. Serv: U.S. Army Air Corps, 46. Mem: Midland Twp. Dem. Club (past pres); UAW (past chmn. educ. cmt, local 325, past ed. newspaper). Rel: Catholic. Mailing Add: 3406 Airway, Overland, Mo. 63114. (1967)

CANTRELL, ORBY LEE D
Va. State Del.
b. Pound, Va, 11/10/06; m. to Janie Mullins. Educ: Radford Col. Polit. & Govt. Pos: Mayor, Pound, Va; Va. State Del, 52- Bus. & Prof. Pos: Merchant; bank-dir; past pres, Breaks Interstate Park Asn. Mem: Masons; Lions; Wise Co. C. of C.(past pres); former chmn, Clinch Valley Col. Adv. Cmt; Ky. Col; adv. Cmt. Appalachian Regional Hosp. Mailing Add: Box 188, Pound, Va. 24279. (1967)

CAPALDI, JOHN FIORE D
b. Providence, R.I, 10/2/30; s. John Capaldi and Anna Morelli; m. 6/17/56 to Barbara Ann Stead; c. Patty Ann, John Paul and Betsy Jane. Educ: Providence Col, 48-50; Boston Univ. Law Sch, LL.B, 53. Polit. & Govt. Pos: Dir, Dept. Pub. Works, R.I, 61-63; chmn, R.I. Dem. State Cmt, 65-67; chmn, R.I. Cmn. Racing and Athletics, 67- Mil. Serv: Spec. Agent, Counter-Intel. Corps, 55-57. Mem: R.I. Bar Asn; R.I. Roadbuilders Asn; Utility Contractors Asn; Aurora Civic Asn; Metacomet Country Club. Rel: Catholic. Legal Res: 3 Stephanie Dr, North Providence, R.I. 02911. Mailing Add: P.O. Box 5097, Esmond, R.I. 02917.

CAPANEGRO, MICHAEL J. D
b. Queens Co; married. Educ: N.Y. Univ, B.S; Cornell Law Sch, LL.B, 55. Polit. & Govt. Pos: N.Y. State Assemblyman, 60-66. Bus. & Prof. Pos: Lawyer. Mil. Serv: Army Air Force. Mem: Flushing Boys Club; Ferrini Welfare League; Emerald Asn; Boyside Babe Ruth League; Utopia Improv. Asn; Queens Co. and N.Y. State and Am. Bar Asn; N.Y. State Asn. of Plaintiff Trial Lawyers; Columbia Lawyers; Flushing Lawyers Club; Eagles; Queens C. of C; Elks. Mailing Add: 136-51 37th St, Flushing, N.Y. 11363. (1967)

CAPELLA, ANTONIO New Progressive, P.R.
Rep, P.R. House of Rep.
b. Aguadilla, P.R, 10/1/23; s. Francisco Capella and Epifania Acevedo C; m. 6/17/62 to Adriana; c. Antonio, Jorge and Alejandro. Educ: Polytech. Inst. of P.R, B.A, 45; P.R. Sch. Tropical Med, M.P.H.E, 48; Sch. Med, Mex. City, Mex, 51-55; Sch. Med, Univ. Madrid, M.D, 56; Pre-Med. Club; pres, Student Coun. Polit. & Govt. Pos: Rep, P.R. House of Rep, 69- Bus. & Prof. Pos: Med. dir, Utuado Health Center, 59-61; gen. practitioner, 62-68. Mil. Serv: Entered as Pvt, Army, 46, released as Pfc, after serv. in Inf, Caribbean. Mem: P.R. Med. Asn; Rotary; Am. Legion. Rel: Christian. Legal Res: No. 2, Kennedy Ave, Utuado, P.R. 00761. Mailing Add: House of Representatives, San Juan, P.R. 00903.

CAPEN, RICHARD GOODWIN, JR. R
Dep. Asst. Secy. of Defense
b. Hartford, Conn, 7/16/34; s. Richard Goodwin Capen and Virginia Ann Knowles C; m. 7/13/62 to Joan Lees Lambert; c. Christopher Goodwin and Kelly Lambert. Educ: Columbia Univ, A.B, 56. Polit. & Govt. Pos: Dep. Asst. Secy. of Defense, 69- Bus. & Prof. Pos: Asst. to the dir, Structural Clay Prod. Inst, Wash, D.C, 59-60; mem. staff, Presidential Campaign, 60; San Diego Co. mgr, William Aldrich Co, San Diego, Calif, 61; dir. pub. affairs, Copley Newspapers, La Jolla, 61-69. Mil. Serv: Entered as Ens, Navy, 56, released as Lt.(jg), 59, after serv. in U.S.S. Ernest G. Small, Seventh Fleet. Publ: Various articles. Mem: Exec. cmt, Scripps Clin. and Research Found; Friends of Research; Pub. Rels. Soc. of Am; Nat. Asn. Mfrs; Nat. Asn. Pub. Affairs Officers; dir, San Diego Co. YMCA; U.S. C. of C; Mil. Order of World Wars; Cuyamaca Club; La Jolla Beach and Tennis Club; Navy League; Univ. Club, San Diego. Five Freedoms Found. Awards, Pub. Address Category; San Diego Outstanding Young Man of the Year, 67; Calif. Outstanding Young Man of the Year, 69. Rel: Presbyterian. Mailing Add: 3301 Clearwood Court, Falls Church, Va. 22042.

CAPINERI, JOSEPH A. D
R.I. State Rep.
b. Pawtucket, R.I, 5/2/29; m. to Ethel M. Pierce. Educ: Prov. Col, B.A, 51; Boston Univ. Law Sch, LL.B, 54. Polit. & Govt. Pos: R.I. State Rep, 57- Bus. & Prof. Pos: Attorney-at-law; bd. dirs, Equitable Credit Union. Mem: Elks; Moose; R.I. Hist. Soc; Sons of Italy; Pawtucket and Am. Bar Asns; Ital. Dramatic Independent Polit. Club. Mailing Add: 24 Alexander McGregor Rd, Pawtucket, R.I. 02861.

CAPISTRAN, ARMAND D
b. Manchester, N.H, 11/19/25; married; c. Two. Educ: St. Anselm Col, A.B; L'Université Lavel, A.M; Boston Univ. Law Sch, LL.B. Polit. & Govt. Pos: N.H. State Rep, 63-68. Bus. & Prof. Pos: Lawyer. Mil. Serv: Korean Conflict. Mem: Am. Legion; Jolliet Club; Asn. Canado-Américaine. Rel: Catholic. Mailing Add: 26 Congress St, Manchester, N.H. 03102. (1967)

CAPLAN, MILTON IRVING D
Conn. State Rep.
b. New Haven, Conn, 8/12/33; s. Morris Caplan and Diana Weissman; m. 6/17/56 to Patricia Irene Stein; c. Deborah Lee, Mark Andrew and David Oren. Educ: Yale Univ, B.A, 55; Univ. Conn. Law Sch, LL.B, 58. Polit. & Govt. Pos: Mem, Hamden R.T.M, Conn, 63-65; mem, Hamden Dem. Town Cmt, 66-; Conn. State Rep, 67- Bus. & Prof. Pos: Partner, Merriam, Virshup & Caplan, Attorneys, 63- Mem: New Haven Co. and Conn. Bar Asns; Yale Club of New Haven; Yale Alumni Fund; Grad. Club. Rel: Jewish. Mailing Add: 354 Belden Rd, Hamden, Conn. 06514.

CAPLIN, MORTIMER M. D
b. N.Y.C, 7/11/16; s. Daniel Caplin and Lillian Epstein C; m. 10/18/42 to Ruth Sacks; c. Lee, Mary Ellen, Michael, Jeremy and Catherine. Educ: Univ. of Va, B.S, 37, LL.B, 40; N.Y. Univ, J.S.D, 53; St. Michael's Col, LL.D, 64; Phi Beta Kappa; Omicron Delta Kappa; Order of the Coif; Raven Soc; ed-in-chief, Va. Law Rev, 39-40. Polit. & Govt. Pos: Trustee, George Wash. Univ, law clerk to judge, U.S. Court of Appeals, 40-41; U.S. Cmnr, Internal Revenue, Treas. Dept, 61-64; del, Dem. Nat. Conv, 68. Bus. & Prof. Pos: Overseer, Col. of V.I; dir, Variable Annuity Life Ins. Co, Peoples Drug Stores Inc, Standard Prudential Co, Pueblo Supermarkets, Inc. and Airlie Found; dir. and chmn. finance cmt, Prentice-Hall Inc; with firm of Paul, Weiss, Rifkind, Wharton & Garrison, N.Y.C, 41-50; prof. law, Univ. Va, 50-61; counsel, Perkins, Battle & Minor, Charlottesville, Va, 52-61; attorney, Caplin & Drysdale, 64-; vis. prof. law, Univ. Va, 64- Mil. Serv: Naval Res, 42-45, Lt, ETO. Mem: D.C, N.Y. and Va. Bars; Am. Fed. D.C. and Va. Bar Asns; Am. Law Inst; Nat. Tax Asn; pres. and dir, Nat. Civil Serv. League. Alexander Hamilton Award, U.S. Treas; Distinguished Serv. Award, Tax Execs. Inst. Legal Res: 4536 29th St. N.W, Washington, D.C. 20008. Mailing Add: 1101 17th St. N.W, Washington, D.C. 20036.

CAPOZZOLI, LOUIS J. D
b. Italy, 3/6/01; s. Gabriele Capozzoli and Christina Ciongola C; m. 9/25/27 to Adele M. Valli; c. Louis J, Jr, Christine (Mrs. Raso) and Gloria (Mrs. Barbieri). Educ: Fordham Univ, LL.B, 22. Polit. & Govt. Pos: Asst. dist. attorney, N.Y. Co, 30-37; N.Y. State Assemblyman, 39-40; U.S. Rep, N.Y, 41-44; justice, City Court, N.Y.C, 47-50; judge, Court of Gen. Sessions, 51-57; justice, Supreme Court, N.Y, 57-66; assoc. justice, Appellate Div. N.Y, First Dept, 66- Mem: Asn. Supreme Court Justices; Am, N.Y. State & N.Y.C. Bar Asns; N.Y. Co. Lawyers Asn; Columbian Lawyers Asn; Elks; Fordham Law Alumni; Grand St. Boys Asn; Nat. Dem. Club. Rel: Catholic. Legal Res: 600 W. 11th St, New York, N.Y. 10025. Mailing Add: 27 Madison Ave, New York, N.Y. 10010.

CAPPAERT, LeROY A. D
Mayor Pro-Tem, Ann Arbor, Mich.
b. Moline, Ill, 7/18/23; s. Charles Louis Cappaert and Marguerite LeRoy C; m. 12/18/48 to Lael Regina Pierson; c. Andrea, David, Thomas and Marlys. Educ: Augustana Col, A.B, 49; Univ. Wis, Madison, M.A, 52. Polit. & Govt. Pos: Mem. exec. bd, Washtenaw Co, Mich, 64-68; city councilman, Ann Arbor, 64-; del, Dem. Nat. Conv, 68; mayor pro-tem, Ann Arbor, 68- Bus. & Prof. Pos: Educator, Ann Arbor Schs, 52- Mil. Serv: Entered as Pvt, Army, 43, released as Sgt, 46, after serv. in Army Band and Combat Engrs, ETO and Asiatic Theaters. Mailing Add: 2335 S. Circle, Ann Arbor, Mich. 48103.

CAPPOLA, PASQUALE R
b. N.Y.C, 2/24/06; s. Gennaro Cappola and Maria Greco C; m. 9/17/50 to Sylvia Cannarella. Educ: N.Y. Univ, spec. course, Safety Educ. Polit. & Govt. Pos: Field inspector for Pres. Boro Manhattan, N.Y, 38-45; sr. field inspector indust. safety, N.Y. State Dept. Labor, 46-62; spec. asst. to indust. cmnr, N.Y. State Dept. Labor, 62-; del, Rep. Nat. Conv, 68. Mem: East Harlem Civic Asn; Union Rep. Club. Rel: Catholic. Legal Res: 318 E. 104th St, New York, N.Y. 10029. Mailing Add: P.O. Box 156, New York, N.Y. 10029.

CAPPS, JOHN PAUL D
Ark. State Rep.
b. Steprock, Ark, 4/17/34; s. Edwin H. Capps and Vivian Pinegar C; m. 7/30/55 to Elizabeth Ann Vaughan; c. Paula Ann and Kimberly Kay. Educ: High Sch. and Beebe Jr. Col. Polit. & Govt. Pos: Ark. State Rep, White Co, 62- Bus. & Prof. Pos: Announcer, KWCB, Searcy, Ark, 55-57, asst. mgr, 58-65, sta. mgr, 65-; announcer, KTHV, Little Rock, Ark, 57-58. Mil. Serv: Army Res, 53-61. Mem: Lions; Searcy Jaycees (past pres); adv. bd, Vo-Tech Sch, Searcy, Ark; bd, White Co. Asn. for Mental Health. Rel: Church of Christ. Mailing Add: 10 Dalewood Rd, Searcy, Ark. 72143. (1967)

CAPPS, R. WALTER D
Chmn, Russell Co. Dem. Exec. Cmt, Ala.
b. Opelika, Ala, 8/24/12; s. Robert Tolleigh Capps and Mary Frances Huguley C; m. 2/7/31 to Etta Griffin; c. Hilda (Mrs. Jack P. Kelly) and Jean (Mrs. Robert E. Schooler). Educ: Beauregard High Sch, 29. Polit. & Govt. Pos: Mem, Russell Co. Dem. Exec. Cmt, Ala, 34-, chmn, 58- Bus. & Prof. Pos:

Farmer and cattleman. Mem: Hon. Lt. Col, Ala. State Militia; WOW; Farm Bur; Country and State Cattlemans Asn; C. of C. Rel: Baptist. Mailing Add: Route 1, Opelika, Ala. 36801.

CAPURRO, RANDALL VICTOR R
Nev. State Assemblyman
b. Reno, Nev, 11/30/42; s. Louis J. Capurro and Genevieve Dondero C; m. 1/19/63 to Annette Barbara Compagnoni; c. Gina Louise, Anthony Randall and Christopher. Educ: Univ. Nev, 1 year; Hartford Ins. Co. Adv. Sch, 1 year. Polit. & Govt. Pos: Nev. State Assemblyman, 69- Bus. & Prof. Pos: Partner, Capurro & Voss Ins. Counsr, 63- Mil. Serv: Entered as E-1, Coast Guard Res, 60, released as E-5, 66. Publ: 'Selling Liability Insurance,' Rough Notes, 7/67. Mem; Am. Asn. Independent Ins. Agents; North. Nev. Independent Ins. Agents; Elks; Kiwanis Int; Reno Young Rep. Rel: Catholic. Legal Res: 6450 Longley Lane, Reno, Nev. 89502. Mailing Add: P.O. Box 7575, Reno, Nev. 89502.

CAPUZI, LOUIS F. R
Ill. State Rep.
b. Chicago, Ill, 11/6/20; m. to Geneva R. Flatt; c. Three. Educ: Northwest. Inst. Foot Surg. and Chiropody, D.S.C, 42. Polit. & Govt. Pos: Ill. State Rep, currently. Mil. Serv: Europe, Second Armored Div, 27 months; Bronze Star; Purple Heart. Mem: Am. Legion; VFW; Amvets (Capt, William J. Clark, I Will Post). Mailing Add: 710 N. Rockwell, Chicago, Ill. 60612. (1967)

CARACCIOLA, JOSEPH JOHN R
Vt. State Rep.
b. Whitehall, N.Y, 9/13/15; s. Bruno Caracciola and Francis C; m. 2/16/42 to Anna Smith. Educ: Whitehall High Sch, N.Y, 4 years. Polit. & Govt. Pos: Mem, Rep. Co. Cmt; Vt. State Rep, 63- Bus. & Prof. Pos: Owner, Caracciola Real Estate. Mil. Serv: Entered as Seaman 2/C, Navy, 43, released as Yeoman 2/C, 46, after serv. in Am. & Pac. Theatres. Mem: Am. Legion; Elks; Country Club; Bennington Club; Farm Bur; Vt. Police Asn; Nat. Realtors Asn. Rel: Catholic. Legal Res: Hunt St, Bennington, Vt. 05201. Mailing Add: Box 486, Bennington, Vt. 05201.

CARANCI, ANTHONY BENJAMIN, JR. R
Chmn, North Providence Rep. Town Cmt, R.I.
b. North Providence, R.I, 8/17/30; s. Antonio Benjamin Caranci and Carmella Ciprano C; m. 11/30/57 to Matilda Angeloni; c. Patricia Ann and Maria Susan. Educ: Univ. Mass, Turf Managers School; Univ. R.I. Polit. & Govt. Pos: Mem, North Providence Rep. Town Cmt, R.I, 52-, chmn, 59-; cmnr, Providence Worster R.R, 58-62; mem, R.I. Rep. State Cent. Cmt, 59-; mem. state appeal bd, Automobile Body Repair Shop Hearing Bd, 62- Bus. & Prof. Pos: Chmn, Univ. Mass. Winter Sch. Seminar, 68 & 69. Mil. Serv: Entered as Pvt, Army, 51, released as Cpl, 53, after serv. in 76th Construct. Engrs, Far East Command, Korea, 51-53. Publ: 'Golfdome,' and 'The Golf Course Reporter,' Nat. Mag; 'Turf Clippings,' New Eng. Mag. Mem: New Eng. Golf Course Supt. Asn. (pres, 67-); R.I. Golf Course Supt. Asn.(pres, 56-58); Golf Course Supt. Asn. Am; Am. Forestry Asn; Elks; Lions; North Providence Boosters Asn; Wanskuck Rod and Gun Club; Mass. Tuft Asn; St. Anthonys Holy Name Soc; North Providence High Sch. Bldg. Cmt. Rel: Catholic. Mailing Add: 22 Hill View Dr, North Providence, R.I. 02904.

CARAWAY, WILLIAM JULIUS D
Miss. State Sen.
b. Brookhaven, Miss, 8/23/10; married. Polit. & Govt. Pos: Miss. State Sen, 60- Bus. & Prof. Pos: Chemist; real estate; insurance; banker. Mem: Rotary Club; Lions; Am. Legion; Flying Farmers Delta Coun; Farm Bur; C. of C; Aircraft Owners & Pilot Club; Miss. Auto Club; Twin City Little Theatre; Pi Kappa Alpha. Rel: Methodist. Mailing Add: 105 California Ave, Leland, Miss. 38756. (1967)

CARBAUGH, HARRY CLARKE R
b. Tasso, Tenn, 5/11/95; s. Harry Francis Carbaugh and Bertha Fletcher C; m. 12/10/17 to Alyce Katherine Huffaker; c. Betty Carolyn (Mrs. Fancher). Educ: Univ. Chattanooga, 2 years; Sigma Chi. Polit. & Govt. Pos: Finance chmn, Tenn. State Rep. Party, 44-62, chmn, 64-65; del. and mem. Platform Cmt, Rep. Nat. Conv, 48-68; mem, Nat. Finance Cmt, 50-62; v.chmn, Nat. Finance Cmt. for South. States, 54-60; mem, Budget Cmt, Rep. Party, 56-60; committeeman, Rep. Nat. Cmt, 63-64. Bus. & Prof. Pos: Pres. & dir, Tenn. Egg Co, 27-63; dir, Hamilton Nat. Bank of Chattanooga, 48-; dir, Interstate Fire Ins. Co. and Interstate Life & Accident Ins, 50-; pres, and dir, Scenic City Develop. Corp, 63- Mil. Serv: Entered as 2nd Lt, Army, 17, released as 1st Lt, after serv. in Res, 46th Inf. Mem: Rotary; Am. Legion; Mountain City Club; Fairyland Club. Rel: Baptist. Mailing Add: 219 W. Brow Oval, Lookout Mountain, Tenn. 37350.

CARBONE, EUGENE R. D
b. St. Paul, Minn, 3/2/08; s. Paul Carbone and Marian LePiane C; m. 4/15/34 to Raphaela Felice; c. Marian (Mrs. Cruz) and Paul Emil. Educ: Oak Park and River Forest Twp. High Sch, 4 years. Polit. & Govt. Pos: Chmn, Calif. Dem. State Cent. Cmt, 60-64; dir, 33rd Agr. Dist, 64-66; dir, San Benito Water and Flood Control Dist; del, Dem. Nat. Conv, 68. Bus. & Prof. Pos: Pres, Hollister Canning Co, 54- Mem: Elks; K. of C. Rel: Catholic. Legal Res: 1255 San Benito St, Hollister, Calif. 95023. Mailing Add: P.O. Box 100, Hollister, Calif. 95023.

CARD, ANDREW HILL R
Mem, Holbrook Rep. Town Cmt, Mass.
b. Holbrook, Mass,7/14/29; s. John Henry Card and Elizabeth Platts C; m. 12/29/46 to Joyce-Ann Whitaker; c. Andrew H, Jr, John H, Alison P, Sara W. and A. Bradford. Educ: Boston Univ, B.S. in Educ, 52; Suffolk Univ, LL.B, 58. Polit. & Govt. Pos: Mem, Holbrook Sch. Cmt, Mass, 58-65; Town counsel, Holbrook, 65-69; former chmn, Holbrook Rep. Town Cmt, mem, currently. Bus. & Prof. Pos: Attorney, assoc. with William J. Finton, currently. Mem: Mass. Bar Asn; Mass. Asn. of City Solicitors and Town Counsel; Mass. Asn. of School Cmt; AF&AM; Boy Scouts (exec. bd. Old Colony Coun); Rel: Congregational; Moderator. Mailing Add: 56 Linfield St, Holbrook, Mass. 02343.

CARDIN, BENJAMIN LOUIS D
Md. State Del.
b. Baltimore, Md, 10/5/43; s. Meyer M. Cardin and Dora Green C; m. 11/24/64 to Myrna Edelman; c. Michael. Educ: Univ. Pittsburgh, B.A. in Econ, 64; Univ. Md. Law Sch, LL.B, 67, grad. first in class; Omicron Delta Epsilon; Druids; v.pres, Nu Beta Epsilon; pres, Pi Lambda Phi. Polit. & Govt. Pos: Md. State Del, 67-; mem, Gov. Cmn. Minimum Statewide Housing Standards, 67-68. Mem: Am, Jr. and Md. Bar Asns; AF&AM; Young Dem. of Md; Pi Lambda Phi Alumni Asn; bd, Safety First Club of Md. Rel: Jewish. Mailing Add: 2509 Shelleydale Dr, Baltimore, Md. 21209.

CARDIN, CARL WILLIAM R
b. St. Louis, Mo, 3/28/25; s. William Mervin Cardin (deceased) and Alberta Johnson C; m. 5/29/48 to Marianne Margaret Miller; c. Kristin Deeanne, Julie Anne, William Page and Thomas George. Educ: Knox Col, 42 & 46; Univ. Tulsa, B.A, 49; Tau Kappa Epsilon. Polit. & Govt. Pos: Pres, Univ. Tulsa Young Rep, 48; admin. asst. to U.S. Congressman Errett Scrivner, Kans, 55-58; Rep. precinct chmn, Md, 58-59; departmental asst. to U.S. Congressman E.W. Hiestand, Calif, 59; info. officer and spec. asst. to the cmnr, Fed. Housing Admin, Wash, D.C, 60; mem, Md. Rep. State Cent. Cmt, 63-65; admin. asst. to U.S. Congressman John Paul Hammerschmidt, Ark, 67- Bus. & Prof. Pos: Newsman, Radio Sta. KOMA, Oklahoma City, Okla. and KCMO, Kansas City, Mo, 49-55; mem, prfnl. staff (polit. specialist), U.S. C. of C, 61; news ed, Nat. Broadcasting Co. Three-Star Extra, 62-65, desk supvr, Nat. Broadcasting Co. News, Wash, D.C, 65-67. Mil. Serv: Entered as Pvt, Army, 43, released as Sgt, 45, after serv. in 612th Field Artil, Mule Pack, China-Burma-India, 44-45; Maj, Army Res; four Battle Stars. Publ: They Grade the Congress, U.S. C. of C, 62; 'Communications Satellites,' Army Info. Digest, 4/66. Mem: Nat. Asn. of Radio and TV News Dirs; Nat. Press Club; U.S. House and Senate Radio-TV Gallery; Writers Guild of Am; Cong. Secy. Club. Rel: Episcopal. Mailing Add: 9113 Lindale Dr, Bethesda, Md. 20034.

CARDIN, JEROME S. D
b. Baltimore, Md, 9/7/25; s. Jacob L. Cardin and Florence J. Klein C; m. 8/17/48 to Shoshana Shoubin; c. Steven H, Ilene M, Nina B. and Sanford R. Educ: Loyola Col, Md, 43-45; Univ. Md. Law Sch, LL.B, 48. Polit. & Govt. Pos: Trial Magistrate, Pikesville, Md, 59-61; mem, Adv. Com. on Hosp. Construction, State of Md; mem, Md. Traffic Safety Cmn. Citizen Support Cmt; hon. life chmn. of bd, Citizens Dem. Club of Baltimore Co; del, Dem. Nat. Conv, 68. Bus. & Prof. Pos: Attorney-at-law, Md, 48-; chmn. bd, gen. counsel and dir, Old Court Savings and Loan, Inc; v.chmn. bd. and gen. counsel, Md. Housing Corp; pres. and gen. counsel, Chesapeake Homes, Inc. and Southwest Properties, Inc; v.pres. and gen. counsel, Admiral Construction Corp. and Inter-State Bus. Investment Co; gen. counsel, Sequoia Savings and Loan Asn, Inc; dir, Md. Savings Share Ins. Corp. Mem: Int, Am. and Md. Bar Asns; Nat. Asn. of Home Builders Sales Mgr. Club; past chancellor, Baltimore Chap. and nat. past grand chancellor, Nu Beta Epsilon; Trial Magistrates Asn; v.pres, Boys' Town of Md, Inc; past pres, Jewish Nat. Fund; chmn, ways and means cmt, Golden Eagle Square and Compass Club, Inc; Am. Israel Soc; Baltimore Museum of Art; Safety First Club; Metropolitan Civic Asn; Citizens Planning and Housing Asn; Am. Soc. for Technion; B'nai B'rith; Yedz Grotto; pres, Bonnie View Country Club; past master, St. John's Lodge 34, AF&AM; past patron, Beacon Chap, Eastern Star; Advertising Club of Baltimore; Am. Jewish Cong; AAONMS; AASR. Mailing Add: 233 Equitable Bldg, Baltimore, Md. 21202.

CARDIN, MAURICE D
b. Baltimore, Md, 7/19/09; married. Educ: Univ. Baltimore, LL.B, 29. Polit. & Govt. Pos: Md. State Del, 51-66; cmnr, Workmen's Compensation Cmn. Mil. Serv: World War II, U.S. Army. Mem: Am, Md. and Baltimore Bar Asns; K. of P; Mason; Am. Legion. Mailing Add: 108 E. Lexington St, Baltimore, Md. 21202.

CARDONA, LOIS EILEEN D
b. Sioux Falls, S.Dak, 5/4/29; d. Harold Byllesby and Emily Ross B; m. 8/29/53 to Antonio Cardona; c. Harold and Carol. Educ: Dakota Wesleyan Univ, Teaching Cert, 49; Univ. Calif, Santa Barbara, B.A, 52; Fresno State Col, 68-69, M.S. cand; Delta Phi Upsilon; Kappa Delta Pi. Polit. & Govt. Pos: Campaign co-mgr, Kings Co. Dem. Party, Calif, 68 & 69; mem, Calif. State Dem. Cent. Cmt, 68-69 and Kings Co. Dem. Cent. Cmt, 68-69. Bus. & Prof. Pos: Teacher, kindergarten, Sioux Falls Pub. Schs, S.Dak, 49-50; lectr, early childhood educ, Univ. Calif, Santa Barbara, 52; teacher, kindergarten and first grade, Santa Barbara City Schs, 52-59; asst. dir, nursery sch, Starr King Parent Child Workshop, 66-67; teacher, primary grades, Am. Samoa, 69- Mem: Nat. Educ. Asn; Calif. Teachers Asn; Nat. and Cent. Calif. Asns. for Educ. of Young Children; League Women Voters; PTA; Univ. Calif, Santa Barbara Alumni Asn. Rel: Presbyterian. Legal Res: 529 Brinkerhoff, Santa Barbara, Calif. 93101. Mailing Add: Dept. of Education, Government of American Samoa, Pago Pago, American Samoa 96920.

CAREY, DAVID JAMES D
Pres, Colo. Young Dem.
b. Denver, Colo, 7/25/42; s. James L. Dean and Shirley L. Schelling D; single. Educ: George Wash. Univ, B.A, 65; Univ. Denver Col. Law, J.D, 68; Phi Alpha Delta. Polit. & Govt. Pos: Pres, George Wash. Univ. Young Dem, 62-63; del, Denver Co. & State Dem. conv, Colo, 64, 66 & 68; Democratic precinct committeeman, 65-; mem, Denver Co. Dem. Cent. Cmt, 65-; mem. bd. dirs, Denver Young Dem, 67-68, v. pres, 68-69; pres, John F. Kennedy Dem.Club, 68-; mem, Colo. Dem State Cent. Cmt, 69-; pres, Colo. Young Dem, 69-; Bus. & Prof. Pos: Attorney at law, Eberhardt, Safran and Payne, Denver, 69- Mem: Colo, Denver and Am. Bar Asns; Am. Civil Liberties Union; Colo. Trial Lawyers Asn; Southwest Denver Serv. Orgn; Toastmasters, Int. Rel: Roman Catholic. Legal Res: 2797 S.Fenton St, Denver, Colo. 80227. Mailing Add: 1930 S. Federal Blvd, Denver, Colo. 80219.

CAREY, EDWARD ANTHONY D
Pres, Common Coun, Detroit, Mich.
b. East Pittsburgh, Pa, 1/2/05; s. Anthony Carey and Margaret C; m. 3/24/39 to Beatrice Warren; c. Colleen, Patricia, Sheila Potts (Mrs. Edmund), Edward, Jr, Shannon and Mary Lou. Educ: High Sch. Polit. & Govt. Pos: Mich. State Rep, 45-58 and Admin. Floor Leader, 7 years; mem, Common Coun, Detroit, 58-, pres, 62-; chmn, Wayne Co. Bd. Supvrs, 61-62, chmn, Capitol Improv. Cmt. and Wayne Co. Gen. Hosp. Cmt. and mem, Cmt. for Reorgn. State Govt. Bus. & Prof. Pos: Int. rep, UAW, 14 years. Mem: K. of C. As State Rep, named 'An Outstanding Legis.' by the Press Corps in the House

and Senate. Rel: Catholic. Legal Res: 15626 Parkgrove, Detroit, Mich. 48205. Mailing Add: 1340 City-County Bldg, Detroit, Mich. 48226.

CAREY, HUGH L. D
U.S. Rep, N.Y.
b. Brooklyn, N.Y, 4/11/19; s. Dennis J. Carey and Margaret Collins C; m. to Helen Owen; c. Alexandria, Christopher, Susan, Peter, Hugh, Jr, Michael, Donald, Marianne, Nancy, Helen, Bryan, Paul and Kevin. Educ: St. John's Col; St. John's Law Sch, LL.B, 51; Phi Delta Phi. Polit. & Govt. Pos: U.S. Rep, N.Y, 62-, mem, educ. and labor cmn. and int. and insular affairs cmt, U.S. House Rep. Bus. & Prof. Pos: Lawyer; bd. dirs, Gaullaudet Col; bd. trustees, League Sch; bd. dirs, St. Vincent's Home for Boys. Mil. Serv: N.Y. Nat. Guard, Lt. Col, serv. in 101st Cavalry, Inf, Officer Cand. Sch. and France, Belgium, Holland, Germany; Bronze Star; Croix de Guerre with Silver Star, Combat Inf. Award. Mem: Boy Scouts Finan. Camp; Am. Legion; VFW; CWV; K. of C. Rel: Catholic. Legal Res: 61 Prospect Park W, Brooklyn, N.Y. 11215. Mailing Add: 106 Cannon House Office Bldg, Washington, D.C. 20515. (1967)

CAREY, JACK WESLEY R
Chmn, Legis. Dist. 29 Rep. Party, Idaho
b. Pocatello, Idaho, 10/1/28; s. Farrow Sherman Carey and Esther Walker Harris C; m. 7/7/49 to Peggy Lauree DeValcour; c. Linda Lauree, Steven Wesley, Doreen Jo and Dale DeVal. Educ: Idaho State Univ, B.S. in Pharm, 52; charter mem, Idaho State Univ. Chap, Rho Chi; pres, Student Br, Am. Pharmaceut. Asn. Polit. & Govt. Pos: Idaho Rep, Young Rep. Nat. Fedn. Campaign Cmt, 63; gen. arrangements chmn, Bill Miller Visit to Idaho Falls, Pres. Campaign, 64; del. and gen. arrangements chmn, Idaho State Rep. Assembly, 64; precinct committeeman, Rep. Party, 64; former Idaho State Rep, former mem, House Appropriations and Econ. Affairs Cmts, Idaho House Rep; chmn, Legis. Dist. 29 Rep. Party, currently. Bus. & Prof. Pos: Partner and druggist, Pay'n Save Drug, Idaho, 56- Mil. Serv: Entered as Pvt, Army, 46, released as T-5, 48, after serv. in Transportation Corps, Asian Theater. Publ: The Value of A Survey in a Political Campaign, Idaho Young Rep. League, 64. Mem: Idaho State Pharmaceut. Asn; v.chmn, Eagle Rock Scouting Dist. Hon. mention, All-State Basketball, Pocatello High Sch, 46; Outstanding Senior, Col. of Pharm, Idaho State Univ, 51; Outstanding Young Rep, Idaho, 63-64; Pharmacist of the Year, Idaho, 65. Rel: Latter-day Saint. Mailing Add: 1537 Westland Ave, Idaho Falls, Idaho 83401.

CAREY, JACQUELYN ANN R
Mem, Calif. Rep. State Cent. Cmt.
b. Oakland, Calif, 8/5/37; d. John J. Carey and Mae Reichhold C; div; c. Kimberly Ann Dilbeck and Shannon Liese Dilbeck. Educ: Stephens Col, 55-57; Univ. of Mo, B.A, 59; Jr. League; Sigma Alpha Chi; Hosp. Guild of South. Calif. Polit. & Govt. Pos: Mem, Young Rep. of Calif, 59-63; mem, Calif. Rep. State Cent. Cmt, 69- Bus. & Prof. Pos: Bus. opportunity sales, W.L. Mitchener & Co, Calif, 60-65; asst. adminstr, Calif. Coordinated Health Care Serv. Inc, 67-69; consult, State Tech. Adv. Cmt. for Home Care, 68-69; exec. dir, Am. Home Care Asn, 69. Mem: Am. and Calif. Home Care Asns. Calif. Phys. Therapist Asn; PTA; Bus. and Prfnl. Women's Club; League of Women Voters of Calif; Sierra Club; Archdiocesan Coun. of Catholic Women. Award for outstanding serv. in representation of Calif. Phys. Therapist's Asn, 69. Rel: Catholic. Legal Res: 42 Collins, San Francisco, Calif. 94118. Mailing Add: 450 Sutter St, Suite 511, San Francisco, Calif. 94108.

CAREY, MAY E. D
V.Chmn, Orleans Co. Dem. Party, N.Y.
b. Clarendon, N.Y, 4/21/89; d. Owen McAllister and Maria Murphy M; m. 8/16/24 to Frank L. Carey (deceased). Educ: Rochester Bus. Inst, Bookkeeping, grad. Polit. & Govt. Pos: Dem. committeewoman, Dist. Three, Murray, N.Y, 15-; v.chmn, Orleans Co. Dem. Party, 49-; elec. cmnr, Orleans Co, 56-69; del, N.Y. State Dem. Conv. Bus. & Prof. Pos: Bookkeeper, Duffy Moth Co, Holley, 8 years, Alo Beedon, Albion, 8 years and Box Factory Off, Brockport, 8 years. Received Personal Invitation to President John F. Kennedy's Inauguration. Rel: Catholic. Mailing Add: 115 S. Main St, Holley, N.Y. 14470.

CAREY, PATRICIA JEAN I. R
Secy. Exec. Cmt, Oakland Co. Rep. Orgn, Mich.
b. Mersea Twp, Ont, Can, 5/2/29; d. Albert Edwin Peterson and Madeline Brown P; m. 4/15/49 to James Francis Carey; c. James Edward, Monica Jean, Maureen Bridget, Cheryl Lynn, Mark Edwin and Kathryn Mary (deceased). Educ: Bus. Inst, Detroit, Mich, 2 years, Alpha Iota. Polit. & Govt. Pos: Precinct del, Rep. Party, Troy, Mich, 60-66; held off. of pres, secy, coun. del, prog. chmn. and parliamentarian, Birmingham-Troy Rep. Women's Club, 60-; del, Mich. Rep. State Conv, 60-; dir, Troy Rep. Party, 63-65; cmt. mem, Oakland Co. Rep. Party, 63-; ex officio mem, Oakland Co. Rep. Exec. Cmt, 65-69, mem, 66-67; coun. del, Coun. Rep. Women's Club, 63-64, ex officio mem, 65-69; secy, 18th Cong. Dist. Rep. Cmt, 64-65; mem. budget and finance cmt, Mich. State Rep. Cent. Cmt, 65-67, secy. exec. cmt, 67-69; alternate del, Rep. Nat. Conv, 68; secy. exec. and co. cmts, Oakland Co. Rep. Orgn, 68- Bus. & Prof. Pos: Off. mgr, H.M. Harper Co, Detroit, 48-50; secy. emergency room, Providence Hosp, Southfield, 67-68; exec. secy. and off. mgr, Am. Variable Annuity, Oak Park, 68-69; admin. asst. and secy. to secy-treas, MultiVest Funding Corp, 69- Mem: Beta Sigma Phi; PTA; Girl Scouts; St. Thomas More Altar Soc; Nat. Cong. Cmt, 64-66. Rel: Roman Catholic. Mailing Add: 2691 Binbrooke Dr, Troy, Mich. 48084.

CAREY, PETER JOHN R
Finance chmn, N.Dak. Rep. Party
b. Fertile, Minn, 6/28/97; s. Peter J. Carey, Sr. and Isabell Stephens C; m. 1918 to Katherine Ingeborg Madson; c. Terrence J. (deceased) and Kenneth J. Educ: Fertile and Crookston High Sch, grad, 16. Polit. & Govt. Pos: Precinct committeeman, Rep. Party, Fargo, N.Dak, 62-68; finance chmn, Cass Co, 63; finance chmn, N.Dak. Rep. Party, 63-; del. to 10 state convs; alternate del, Rep. Nat. Conv, 64 and del, 68; state chmn, Oil Indust Info. Cmt. Bus. & Prof. Pos: Sales rep, Standard Oil Co, N.Dak, 29-35, sales mgr, 35-48 and dir. of pub. rels, 48-62; retired; Civic Affairs Consult. Mem: K. of C.(Grand Knight 3°, Faithful Navigator 4°); Lions Int.(pres. & dist. gov. Fargo & State N.Dak); Elks. Rel: Catholic. Mailing Add: 2449 W. Country Club Dr, Fargo, N.Dak. 58102.

CAREY, RALPH P. R
Secy, Lackawanna Co. Rep. Cmt, Pa.
b. Old Forge, Pa, 4/1/25; s. Thomas Carey and Lena Perfilio C; m. 11/24/6 to Teresa Petrocelli. Educ: Bucknell Univ. and Wilkes Col, 46-48, B.A, 48; Dickinson Sch. Law, Carlisle, Pa, J.D, 51; Corpus Juris Soc; Student Coun. Polit. & Govt. Pos: Town chmn, Old Forge, Pa, 58-62 and town solicitor, 63-; secy, Lackawanna Co. Rep. Cmt, 62-; hearing exam, Pa. Liquor Control Bd, 66-; del, Rep. Nat. Conv, 68. Bus. & Prof. Pos: Partner, Casey, Carey and Mazzoni, Attorneys, 62- Mil. Serv: Entered as Pvt, Army, 43, released as 1st Sgt, 46, after serv. in 118th Inf. Div, ETO, 44-46; Lt, Res, 47-50; Good Conduct Medal; ETO Ribbon with North. France Battle Star. Mem: Am, Pa. and Lackawanna Co. Bar Asns; Past Exalted Ruler, Elks; Moose; Lions (past pres); Scranton C. of C; Am. Legion; VFW. Rel: Roman Catholic. Legal Res: 600 Shady Lane Rd, South Abington Township, Pa. 18508. Mailing Add: R.D. 1, Scranton, Pa. 18508.

CAREY, RICHARD JAMES D
Maine State Rep.
b. Waterville, Maine, 1/7/29; s. Augustus Joseph Carey and Alma Vashon C; m. 6/23/52 to Helen Muriel Fortin; c. Michael, Steven, Gregory, Denise, Martha and Peter. Educ: Univ. Maine, 2 years. Polit. & Govt. Pos: Councilman, Waterville, Maine, 62-64, alderman, 64-68; Maine State Rep, 103rd Legis. Dist, 67-69, 104th Legis. Dist, 69- Bus. & Prof. Pos: Chief survey parties, James W. Sewall Co, Old Town, Maine, 55-60; self employed registered land surveyor, 60- Mil. Serv: Entered as Pvt, Air Force, 48, released as Cpl, 52, after serv. as Troop Carrier, 49-52; Presidential Unit Citation. Mem: Am. Cong. Surv. and Mapping; Registered land surveyor, Maine; K. of C; Am. Legion; Little League Coach; Commun. Leaders Am. Rel: Roman Catholic. Mailing Add: 27 Sterling St, Waterville, Maine 04901.

CARGILE, RICHARD FRANKLIN R
Chmn, Irwin Co. Rep. Party, Ga.
b. Ocilla, Ga, 11/15/32; s. (father deceased) Thelma M. C; single. Educ: S.Ga. Col, 49-50; Mercer Univ, 50-51; Ga. State Col, B.B.A, 58. Polit. & Govt. Pos: Chmn, Irwin Co. Rep. Party, Ga, 67-; treas, Eighth Dist. Rep. Party, Ga, 68- Bus. & Prof. Pos: News dir, Ben Hill Broadcasting Co, Fitzgerald, Ga, 60-68; opers. mgr, Sizland Broadcasting Co, Inc, Ocilla, Ga, 68- Mil. Serv: Entered as Pvt, Army Security Agency, 52, released as S/Sgt, 55, after serving in 327 Commun. Reconnaissance Co, Japan, 53-55; Korean Serv. Medal; Far E. Theater Medal; Good Conduct Medal. Mem: Ga. Asn. Broadcasters; Nat. Asn. Broadcasters; Int. Broadcasters Soc; Jr. Chamber-Int; Rotary; Am. Legion Post 100; Irwin Co. Farm Bur. Serv-above-self award, Ocilla Rotary Club; excellent award, Ga. Assoc. Press Broadcasters Asn, 67; Commun. Leader of Am. award, 69; hon. mem, Ga. Future Homemakers Asn, 69. Rel: Baptist. Legal Res: 650 Cargile Rd, Ocilla, Ga. 31774. Mailing Add: P.O. Box 321, Ocilla, Ga. 31774.

CARGO, DAVID FRANCIS R
Gov, N.Mex.
b. Dowagiac, Mich, 1/13/29; s. Francis Clair Cargo and Mary Harton C; m. 9/22/60 to Ida Jo Anaya; c. Veronica Ann, David Joseph, Patrick Michael and Maria Elena Christina. Educ: Univ. Mich, A.B. in Lit, 51, M.A. in Pub. Admin, 53 and LL.B, 57; Delta Sigma Pi. Polit. & Govt. Pos: Asst. dist. attorney, Second Judicial Dist, N.Mex, 58-59; pres, N.Mex. Young Rep, 59; N.Mex. State Rep, 63-66; Gov, N.Mex, 67-; del, Rep. Nat. Conv, 68. Mil. Serv: Entered as Pvt, Army, 53, released as Cpl, 55, after serv. in Finance Corps. Mem: State Adv. Bd, N.Mex. Div, Am. Automobile Asn; Am. Legion; VFW; Elks; Am. Soc. Pub. Admin; Isaac Walton League (past v.pres). Nominated One of the Ten Outstanding Young Men in Am, N.Mex. Jr. C. of C, 64; Man of the Year, Albuquerque Jaycees, 64. Rel: Roman Catholic. Mailing Add: Executive Residence, Mansion Ridge Rd, Santa Fe, N.Mex. 87501.

CARIELLO, MARIO J. D
Pres, Borough of Queens, N.Y.
b. Manhattan, N.Y, 1/23/07; s. Joseph and Mary Cariello; m. 7/5/31 to Lee Palante. Educ: Fordham Univ; N.Y. Law Sch. Polit. & Govt. Pos: N.Y. State Rep, 36-41; munic. court justice, Queens, 41-63; pres, Borough of Queens, N.Y, 63- Bus. & Prof. Pos: Lawyer. Mem: State Boys' Club and Ferrini Welfare League, Queens; Queens Co. Bar Asn; Columbian Lawyers Club; Elks; Ahepa; First Assembly Dist. Regular Dem. Club; K. of C.(Lincoln Coun); Holy Name Soc. Rel: Roman Catholic. Mailing Add: 120-55 Queens Blvd, Kew Gardens, N.Y. 11415. (1967)

CARINO, ANTHONY JACOB D
b. Agrigenti, Sicily, Italy, 4/3/09; s. Domenick Carino and Vincencess Pericone C; m. 7/12/30 to Jennie Rose Roccosanto; c. Jean (Mrs. Jerry Shapiro), Joan (Mrs. Philip Casciano), Joyce (Mrs. Ralph Malanga) and Domenick. Educ: West Side High Eve. Sch, Newark, N.J, dipl; Acad. Adv. Traffic, N.Y.C, 1 year. Polit. & Govt. Pos: Pres, East Orange Dem. Club, N.J, 51-54; Dem. committeeman, 12th Dist, East Orange, 53-58, Dem. chmn, Fourth Ward, 55-58; Dem. chmn, East Orange Dem. Party, 58-69; mem, Bd. of Assessment, 59-62; secy. to speaker, N.J. House Rep, 61-62; cmnr, Hwy. Right of Way Chap. 15, Essex Co, 63-67; del, Dem. Nat. Conv, 64 and alternate del, 68. Bus. & Prof. Pos: Traffic consult, Branch Motor, 33-49, York Motor, 49-59; sales rep, Adley Express, 59- Mem: Nat. Asn. Security Dealers; Newark Traffic Club; Raritan Traffic Club New Brunswick; Delta Nu Alpha; North Jersey Traffic Club; Elks; K. of C.(3°); Ital. Am. Execs. Am. Rel: Roman Catholic. Mailing Add: 162 Oak St, East Orange, N.J. 07018.

CARITHERS, WILLIAM RICHMOND R
Chmn, Shelby Co. Rep. Cent. Cmt, Ind.
b. Shelbyville, Ind, 11/4/07; s. Leondias Bradley Carithers and Cora Mae Bassett C; single. Educ: Ind. Univ, 25-27; Sigma Pi. Polit. & Govt. Pos: Chmn, Young Rep. Club, Ind, 36-40; city chmn, Shelbyville, 51-52; chmn, Shelby Co. Rep. Cent. Cmt, 52-56, treas, 62-63, chmn, currently; investr, Ind. Securities Cmt, State of Ind, 55-57; br. supvr, Bur. Motor Vehicles, 57-62. Bus. & Prof. Pos: Men's clothing salesman, Todd-Bennett, 27- Mem: Elks; Eagles. Rel: Presbyterian. Mailing Add: 17 E. Polk St, Shelbyville, Ind. 46176. (1967)

CARLE, JACKSON T. D
b. Lindsay, Calif, 10/25/02; s. Charles J. Carle and Greta M. Ashley C; married. Educ: Stanford University, 20; University of San Francisco,

LL.B, 29-32; Bancroft-Whitney Prize; Delta Chi. Polit. & Govt. Pos: Exec. Secy. to U.S. Rep. Sisk, D-Calif. Bus. & Prof. Pos: Lawyer, pub. rels, Los Angeles and Fresno, Calif. 1967 Legal Res: 129 E St. S.E, Washington, D.C. No mailing address available. (1967)

CARLENO, HARRY EUGENE D
Mem. Exec. Cmt, Arapahoe Co. Dem. Cent. Cmt, Colo.
b. Denver, Colo, 3/3/28; s. Benjamin Edward Carleno and Elizabeth B. DeRose C; m. 9/14/57 to Ann Marie Kraft; c. Gregory Scott, Paul Christopher and Jennifer Ann. Educ: Univ. Denver, B.S. in Bus. Admin, 51 and LL.B, 55; Phi Delta Phi; Brewer Inn. Polit. & Govt. Pos: Dep. dist. attorney, First Judicial Dist, Colo, 58-60; precinct committeeman, Dem. party, 58-62, dist. capt, 62-66; mem, Arapahoe Co. Dem. Cent. Cmt, 58-65, chmn, 65-68, mem. exec. cmt, 62-; dep. dist. attorney, 18th Judicial Dist, 60-68; chmn, Career Serv. Bd, Englewood, 61-64; mem, exec. cmt, Colo. State Dem. Cent. Cmt, 65-68. Bus. & Prof. Pos: Gen. practice of law, Englewood, Colo, 56-; pres, Accident Report Serv, Inc, 60-62. Mil. Serv: Entered as Pvt, Army Air Force, 46, released as 1st Lt, 53, after serv. in Am. Theater; Am. Defense, Air Force Res. and Victory Medals; Am. Theater and Am. Defense Ribbons; Lt. Col, Asst. Staff Judge Adv, Air Force Acct. & Finance Center, 63. Mem: Colo, Denver and Arapahoe Co. Bar Asns; C. of C; Arapahoe Co. Ment. Health Asn. Rel: Roman Catholic. Mailing Add: 5471 S. Sherman St, Littleton, Colo. 80120.

CARLETON, MARILYN JEAN R
V.Chmn, Logan Co. Rep. Cent Cmt, Colo.
b. Oak Park, Ill, 7/29/26; d. Elmer H. Wirth and Margaret Binder W; m. 6/10/49 to Neil Lamont Carleton; c. Christy A, Cynthia S, Robert B. and Thomas M. Educ: Univ. Colo, B.A, 48, grad. study, 48-49; Alpha Omicron Pi; Young Rep. Polit. & Govt. Pos: Secy, Young Rep, Colo, 45-47; v.pres, Logan Co. Rep. Women, 61-62, pres, 62-63, secy, 63-64; v.chmn, Logan Co. Rep. Cent. Cmt, 66- Rel: Protestant. Mailing Add: 302 Taylor, Sterling, Colo, 80751.

CARLETON, WILLIAM HENRY R
b. Windham, Vt, 6/7/07; m. to Verna L. Westine; c. Two sons. Educ: Londonderry High Sch. Polit. & Govt. Pos: Lister, Vt, 45-; Vt. State Rep, 65- Bus. & Prof. Pos: Farmer; caretaker; carpenter. Mem: Londonderry Fire Compound; Londonderry Credit Union. Rel: Protestant. Mailing Add: Box 136, Londonderry, Vt. 05148. (1967)

CARLEY, DAVID D
Mem, Dem. Nat. Cmt. for Wis.
b. Detroit, Mich, 6/13/28; s. Berndt Carley and Laura Cook C; m. 8/28/49 to Adele J. Kuempel; c. Laurie A, Pamela J, Michael Ann, James A. Educ: West. Mich. Univ, B.A, 50; Kalamazoo Col, M.A, 52; Univ. of Wis, Ph.D, Polit. Sci, 59. Polit. & Govt. Pos: Asst. to city mgr, Kalamazoo, Mich, 50-52; research dir, Wis. C. of C, 54-58; polit. adv. to Gov. Wis, 58-62; dir, Wis. Dept. Resource Develop, 59-62; Dem. cand. for Lt. Gov, 62; mem, Nat. Commun. Rels. Bd, 64-; mem, Dem. Nat. Cmt. Wis, 64-; del, Dem. Nat. Conv, 68. Bus. & Prof. Pos: Pres, Continental Mortgage Ins, Inc, Madison, 63-; dir, Marshall Erdman and Assocs, Inc; dir, Milwaukee Midland Nat. Bank. Publ: Contributions to prfnl. jour. Mem: Am. Polit. Sci. Asn. Mailing Add: P.O. Box 2017, Madison, Wis. 53705. (1967)

CARLEY, ROBERT JOSEPH D
R.I. State Rep.
b. West Warwick, R.I, 5/16/30; s. Edward Linus Carley and Agnes Barrett C; m. 11/8/52 to Nellie Petrarca; c. James C, Roberta L, Darleen R, Robert T, Thomas R. and Edward H. Educ: Bryant Col, B.S. in Acct. & Finance, 50, B.S. in Educ, 53. Polit. & Govt. Pos: Tax assessor, West Warwick, R.I, 60-64; R.I. State Rep, currently. Bus. & Prof. Pos: Partner, acct. off. firm, Nardella, Carley & Petrarca, 54-; officer, ins. off. firm, 63- Mem: Nat. Soc. Pub. Acct; Elks; Sons of Italy Lodge; Holy Ghost Brotherhood; K. of C; Friendly Sons of St. Patrick; Portuguese Am. Sports Club; Natick Dem. Club. West Warwick Man of the Year, West Warwick Jaycees, 64. Rel: Catholic. Mailing Add: 7 Lanphear St, West Warwick, R.I. 02893.

CARLING, RICHARD JUNIUS R
Utah State Rep.
b. Salt Lake City, Utah, 12/6/37; s. Jacob Junius Carling and Reba Olsen C; m. 6/8/61 to Diane Saxey; c. Angela and Cynthia. Educ: Univ. Utah, B.S. in Polit. Sci, 62, J.D, 65; Phi Delta Phi. Polit. & Govt. Pos: Held various voting dist. off. and del. pos, Utah, 61-69; legis. dist. v.chmn, Rep. Party, 62-63; mem, Salt Lake Co. Rep. Cent. Cmt, 62-65, secy, 68; dir, Salt Lake Co. Young Rep, 67-68; Utah State Rep, 67-; chmn, Legis. Coun. Task Force on Econ. Develop, 68; mem, Utah House-Sen. Joint Opers. Cmt, 69-70. Bus. & Prof. Pos: Compiler, water rights sect, Utah State Engrs. Off, 60-62; owner-mgr, Security Credit Asn, 62-65; attorney-partner in firm of Neslen & Mock, 65- Mem: Am. and Salt Lake Co. Bar Asn; Utah State Bar (mem. legis. cmt, Law Day and Am. Citizenship Cmt); trustee, Salt Lake Commun. Action Prog; mem. policy adv. cmt, Salt Lake Proj. Head Start; Explorer Post adv, Boy Scouts. Rel: Latter-day Saint. Legal Res: 523 Douglas, Salt Lake City, Utah 84102. Mailing Add: 1000 Continental Bank Bldg, Salt Lake City, Utah 84101.

CARLISLE, JACK B. D
Chmn, Choctaw Co. Dem. Exec. Cmt, Miss.
b. McCool, Miss, 3/19/08; s. Joe B. Carlisle and Joanna Tomlinson C; m. 9/9/39 to Virginia Dare Patterson; c. Virginia Anne, Mary Jacqueline and William Thomas. Educ: Holmes Jr. Col; Univ. Miss; Cumberland Univ, LL.B, 38. Polit. & Govt. Pos: City attorney, Ackerman, Miss, 47-53 & 61-; attorney, Bd. Supvr, Choctaw Co, 47-; chmn, Choctaw Co. Dem. Exec. Cmt, 48- Bus. & Prof. Pos: Attorney, 38- Mil. Serv: Army, 43-45, Pvt. Mem: Am. and Miss. Bar Asns; Am. Trial Lawyers Asn; Shrine; Mason; Rotary. Rel: Methodist. Legal Res: 302 Cherry St, Ackerman, Miss. 39735. Mailing Add: Box 181, Ackerman, Miss. 39735. (1967)

CARLISLE, LILIAN BAKER D
Vt. State Rep.
b. Meridian, Miss, 1/1/12; d. Joseph H. Baker and Lilian White Flournoy B; m. 1/9/33 to Edgar Grafton Carlisle, Jr; c. Lilian Diana (Mrs. Edward S. Schwerdtle); Penelope Suzanne (Mrs. Leroy G. Meshel); six granddaughters. Educ: Dickinson Col, 29-30; Peirce Col. Bus. Admin, dipl, 31; Chi Omega. Polit. & Govt. Pos: Various cmt. positions in commun. projs; asst. coordinator, Vt. Ment. Retardation Planning Proj, Montpelier, 65; proj. dir, Medicare ALERT, Champlain Valley Off. Econ. Opportunity, four co, 66; asst. ballot clerk, Burlington, 60-67; Vt. State Rep, 69- Bus. & Prof. Pos: Free lance author, writer and lectr. on antiques, health and welfare, 50-; head research and collections, Shelburne Mus, Vt, 51-61; coordinator and exec. secy, Burlington Area Commun. Health Study 63-64. Publ: Carriages at Shelburne Museum, 56, Pieced Work and Applique Quilts at Shelburne Museum, 57 and Hat Boxes and Bandboxes at Shelburne, 60; numerous articles in nat. antique mag, 62- Mem: Am. Pub. Health Asn; Vt. Conf. Soc. Concerns; Burlington Area Commun. Coun.(past pres); Vt. Hist. Soc.(trustee); Chittenden Co. Hist. Soc.(pres); Old Cemetery Asn; Vt. Folklore Soc; Carriage Asn. Am; Embroiderers Guild; Green Mt. Doll Club; Nat. Writers Club; Nat. League of Am. Pen Women; League Vt. Writers (past pres); Zonta Clubs Int.(past pres, Burlington, Vt. Club); PTA (past pres, Burlington Jr-Sr. High Sch); Vt. Cong. Parents & Teachers (recording secy). Rel: Congregational; Past Pres, Women's Fellowship, First Church Burlington, Vt, Clerk of Church. Mailing Add: 117 Lakeview Terrace, Burlington, Vt. 05401.

CARLSON, BERNARD O. DFL
Minn. State Rep.
b. St. Louis Co, Minn, 1913; married; c. Two. Educ: Cloquet Pub. Schs. Polit. & Govt. Pos: Treas, Cloquet Sch. Bd, 58-61; Minn. State Rep, 60- Bus. & Prof. Pos: Maintenance Dept, Northwest Paper Co; bd. dirs, Cloquet Mem. Hosp, 58-61. Mem: Firemen and Oilers Union (pres, Local 939). Mailing Add: 1216 Selmeer Ave, Cloquet, Minn. 55720. (1967)

CARLSON, ELMER GUSTAV D
b. Massena, Iowa, 4/24/09; s. Carl Fredrick Carlson and Christina F. C; div; c. Nancy and Jennifer. Polit. & Govt. Pos: Dem. Nat. Committeeman, Ill, 52; del, Dem. Nat. Conv. and Nat. Platform Committeeman, 64; Dem. Precinct Committeeman, Iowa, 66- Mem: Lions Int.(pres, 44); C. of C.(pres, 46); Nat. Farmers Union; Zig-i-zag; Shrine; 100 Bushel Corn Club (coordinator, 65-66). Worlds Champion Corn Husker, Nat. Corn Husking Contests, 35. Rel: Presbyterian. Mailing Add: 115 Circle Dr, Audubon, Iowa 50025.

CARLSON, FRANK R
b. Concordia, Kans, 1/23/93; s. Charles E. Carlson and Anna Johnson C; m. 8/26/19 to Alice Fredrickson; c. Eunice Marie (Mrs. Ed Rolfs). Educ: Concordia Normal & Bus. Col; Kans. State Col. Hon. LL.D, Bob Jones Univ, 51, Springfield Col, 53, William Jewell Col, 55, St. Benedict's Col, 61, Kans. State Univ, 62, Baker Univ, Southwest. Univ. and Ottawa Univ. Polit. & Govt. Pos: Kans. State Rep, 29-33; chmn, State Rep. Cmt, Kans, 32-34; U.S. Rep, Kans, 6 terms; mem. state & fed. affairs cmn, Hoover Cmn. Reorgn; Gov, Kans, 46-50; chmn, Interstate Oil Compact Cmn, 49; chmn, Nat. Gov. Conf, 49; chmn, Coun. State Govt, 50; v.chmn, Pres. Nat. Safety Conf, 50; U.S. del, UN; U.S. Sen, Kans, 50-69, mem. cmts, Post Off. & Civil Serv, Finance, For. Rels. and joint cmt. Internal Revenue Tax. Bus. & Prof. Pos: Farmer, stockman. Mil. Serv: World War I. Mem: Mason (33°); pres, Int. Coun. Christian Leadership; bd. gov, Menninger Found; Inst. Logopedics. Agr. Hall of Fame, 64. Rel: Baptist. Mailing Add: Concordia, Kans. 66901.

CARLSON, JACK LEWIS R
Chmn, 17th Cong. Dist. Rep. Cent. Cmt, Calif.
b. Long Beach, Calif, 2/11/40; s. Roy Gunnar Carlson and Dorothy Lundy G; m. 8/12/62 to Joan Raycraft; c. Joan Anne. Educ: Woodbury Col, B.B.A, 63; Harbor City Col, 2 years; Univ. Calif. Los Angeles, 1 year; Long Beach State Col; Phi Gamma Kappa. Polit. & Govt. Pos: V.chmn, 68th Assembly Dist. Rep. Cent. Cmt, Calif, 68; v.pres, San Pedro-Peninsula Rep. Assembly, 69; mem, Calif. Rep. State Cent. Cmt, 69-; chmn, 17th Cong. Dist. Rep. Cent. Cmt, 69- Bus. & Prof. Pos: Gen. mgr, Carlson & Assocs, 62-; purchasing agent, Bandachrome, Inc, 63; sr. contract adminstr, Gulton Industs, Inc, 63- Rel: Presbyterian. Mailing Add: 858 Basin St, San Pedro, Calif. 90731.

CARLSON, JACK WILSON
Asst. Dir. for Prog. Eval, U.S. Bur. of the Budget
b. Salt Lake City, Utah, 11/20/33; s. Oscar William Carlson and Gretta Wilson C; m. 3/20/54 to Renee Pyott; c. Catherine, Christine, Steven, Diane, John and David. Educ: Univ. Utah, B.S, 55, M.B.S, 57; Harvard Univ, M.P.A, and Ph.D, 63. Polit. & Govt. Pos: Sr. staff economist, Coun. Econ. Adv, 66-68; dir. Prog. Eval. Staff, U.S. Bur. of the Budget, 68-69, asst. dir. for Prog. Eval, 69- Bus. & Prof. Pos: Instr, Univ. Utah, 55-57. Mil. Serv: Entered as 2nd Lt, Air Force, 57, released as Capt, 66, after serv. in Air Defense Command, Air Training Command, 57-59, assoc. prof, Air Force Acad, 59-65, asst. for spec. studies, Off. of Secy. of Air Force, 65-66; Two Commendation Medals. Mailing Add: 500 Canterbury Lane, Alexandria, Va. 22314.

CARLSON, MARY ELLEN R
Chmn, Fourth Dist. Rep. Party, Wis.
b. Glen Flora, Wis, 12/2/32; d. Paul Wesley Orme and Eleanora Sorenson O; m. 2/23/52 to Laurence Neil Carlson; c. Douglas Wayne, Chris Ellen, Kurt David and Paul Andrew. Educ: Elroy High Sch, Wis, grad; Stout State Univ, 2 years. Polit. & Govt. Pos: Chmn, Fourth Dist. Rep. Party, Wis, 67- Rel: Lutheran. Mailing Add: 6450 S. 18th St, Milwaukee, Wis. 53221.

CARLSON, RAYMOND FRANKLIN R
Kans. State Rep.
b. Clifton, Kans, 6/27/13; s. Frank Carlson and Caroline Holmquist C; m. 12/13/54 to Ethel Laurel Lewis. Educ: High sch. Polit. & Govt. Pos: Kans. State Rep, 47- Bus. & Prof. Pos: Farmer. Mil. Serv: Entered as Pvt, Air Force, 41, released as Cpl, 45, after serv. in Fifth Wing; 301st Gr, 419th Squadron, European Theatre, 42-45; Twelve Battle Stars; Two Presidential Citations. Mem: Farm Bur. Rel: Lutheran. Mailing Add: R.R. 1, Clifton, Kans. 66937.

CARLTON, ARTHUR LEROY D
b. Elmore City, Okla, 7/5/03; s. James Stanford Carlton and Mary Etta Magyourk C; m. 9/18/38 to Velma Lucille Cooper; c. Carolyn (Mrs. Andy Cox) and William Monroe. Educ: E.Cent. State Col, B.A, 39; Okla. Univ, M.Ed, 42. Polit. & Govt. Pos: Garvin Co. mgr, H.C. Jones for Gov, Okla, 48; chmn, Garvin Co. Dem. Party, 62-69. Bus. & Prof. Pos: Sch. prin, Dist. 38,

Wynnewood, Okla, 57-68. Mem: Okla. Teacher's Asn; Blue Lodge; K.T; Scottish Rite; RAM; dist. dep. grand master, AF&AM; leader, Garvin Co. 4-H. Hon. life mem, Future Farmers of Am. Rel: Southern Baptist. Mailing Add: 100 N. Williams, Maysville, Okla. 73057.

CARLTON, DOYLE E, JR. D
b. Tampa, Fla, 7/4/22; m. to Mildred Woodberry; c. Susan and Doyle, III. Educ: Univ. of Fla; Sigma Alpha Epsilon. Polit. & Govt. Pos: Fla. State Sen, 52-60 & 64-66. Bus. & Prof. Pos: Farmer. Mil. Serv: Air Force. Mem: Kiwanis; Am. Legion; Elks. Rel: Baptist; Deacon; Chmn. of Bd. Mailing Add: Box 385, Wauchula, Fla. 33873. (1967)

CARLTON, FRANK ANDERSON JR. D
Miss. State Rep.
b. Los Angeles, Calif; 2/12/35; married. Polit. & Govt. Pos: Miss. State Rep, currently. Bus. & Prof. Pos: Attorney. Mem: Lions; Jaycees; Wash. Co, Miss. State and Am. Bar Asns; Phi Alpha Delta. Rel: Baptist. Mailing Add: P.O. Box 442, Greenville, Miss. 38701. (1967)

CARLTON, LEE MARK D
b. New York, N.Y, 2/13/25. Educ: Hiram Col, Ohio; Fordham Univ; Feagin Sch. of Commun; Acad. of Lighting Arts, Newark. Polit. & Govt. Pos: Former N.J. State Assemblyman. Bus. & Prof. Pos: TV lighting dir. engr, NBC, N.Y.C, 16 years. Mil. Serv: Army Air Force, World War II. Mem: Soc. of TV Lighting Dirs; pres, Northwood Golf Club; pres, Park Investors; v.pres, Old Tappan Rod and Gun Club; Boy Scouts, 29 years. 1967 Legal Res: Trenton, N.J. No mailing address available. (1967)

CARLTON, MILTON AUGUSTUS, SR. D
b. Canton, Ga, 11/10/13; s. Wellborn Chaudoin Carlton and Florence Grace C; m. 6/17/37 to Mary Frances Hatcher; c. Milton Augustus, Jr. Educ: Mid. Ga. Jr. Col, 32; Atlanta Law Sch, LL.B, 35. Polit. & Govt. Pos: Ga. State Sen, 63-66; Judge, City Court of Millen, 1/1/47-8/4/51, resigned; City Coun, Millen, 2/1/39-6/42, resigned; N.P. & Ex. Off, Justice of the Peace, May 37-39. Bus. & Prof. Pos: Attorney. Mil. Serv: World War II with promotions from Pvt. to Capt; European Theater Medal and Six Bronze Stars, three Unit Presidential Citations. Mem: Masons; Screven Lodge No. 248; F&AM; Rotary. Rel: Baptist. Mailing Add: Swainsboro, Ga. 30402. (1967)

CARLTON, VASSAR B. D
Justice, Supreme Court, Fla.
b. Island Grove, Fla, 11/13/12; s. Benjamin Franklin Carlson and Zeffie Ergle C; m. 9/23/59 to Grace Ramer; c. Mary Carol (Mrs. Crispfulli), Martha (Mrs. Fulmer), Barbara and Pamela. Educ: Univ. Fla, 31-33; Stetson Univ, LL.B, 37; Phi Alpha Delta. Polit. & Govt. Pos: Co. Judge, Brevard Co, Fla, 41-54; Circuit judge, Ninth Judicial and 18th Judicial Circuit, 54-69; Justice, Supreme Court, Fla, 69- Mem: Mason (32°); Shrine; Kiwanis (past pres); Elks (Past Exalted Ruler); Jaycees (past pres). Good govt. award, twice. Rel: Baptist. Legal Res: 1103 Gardenia St, Tallahassee, Fla. 32303. Mailing Add: Supreme Court Bldg, Tallahassee, Fla. 32304.

CARMACK, WILLIAM ROSS, JR. D
b. Decatur, Ala, 3/5/29; s. William Ross Carmack and Frances R. Farrar C; m. 8/16/56 to Shirley Dennis; c. David Ross and Scott Dennis. Educ: Abilene Christian Col, B.A, cum laude, 49-51; Fla. State Univ, M.A, 53; Univ. Ill, Ph.D, 58. Polit. & Govt. Pos: Admin. Asst. to U.S. Sen. Fred Harris, Okla, 64-65; asst. cmnr. for commun. serv, Bur. of Indian Affairs, 66-69. Bus. & Prof. Pos: Asst. prof. speech, Okla. Christian Col, 54-56; assoc. prof, Univ. Okla, 58-61, dir. Human Rels. Center, 61-64. Publ: 'Communication and Community Readiness for Social Change,' Am. J. Orthopsychiat, 3/65; co-auth, Dallas Texas: Factors Affecting Community Change. Mem: Nat. Asn. Intergovt. Rels. Officers; Speech Asn. Am. Legal Res: Norman, Okla. Mailing Add: 1503 Audmar Dr, McLean, Va. 22101.

CARMICHAEL, DONALD D
b. Toledo, Ohio, 2/19/12; s. Grey Thornton Carmichael and Edna Earle Jaite C; m. 5/28/40 to Mary Glenn Dickinson; c. Mary Brooke and Pamela Hastings. Educ: Harvard, B.A, 35; Univ. Mich, LL.B, 42; Phi Gamma Delta. Polit. & Govt. Pos: Staff dept. law, Cleveland, Ohio, 38-; chief renegotiation br, Cleveland Ord. Dist, War Dept, 42-46; del, Dem. Nat. Conv, 60 & 64; mem, Cuyahoga Co. Dem. Exec. Cmt; mem, President's Task Force on War Against Poverty, 64. Bus. & Prof. Pos: Law practice, Cleveland, Ohio, 46; asst. secy, Diamond Alkali Co, 46-48, secy, 48-59, gen. counsel, 57-59; v.pres-gen. counsel, Stouffer Corp, 59-60, exec. v.pres, 60-64; chmn, Tower Int. Corp; pres, Tower Industs, Ayer Storage Ltd, Toronto, Montreal, 64-; lawyer and bus. exec, Cleveland, 64- Publ: Ed, 'F.D.R: Columnist,' 47. Mem: Am, Ohio and Cleveland Bar Asns; chmn. bd. trustees, Cuyahoga Co. Hosp, Urban League and Karamu House; pres, Harvard Club, Cleveland and N.Y; Union Club; Chagrin Valley Hunt Club. Mailing Add: Terminal Tower, Cleveland, Ohio 44113.

CARMICHAEL, GILBERT ELLZEY R
b. Columbia, Miss, 6/27/27; s. Calvin Ellzey Carmichael and Clyde Smith C; m. 8/24/54 to Carolyn Dean White; c. Gilbert Scott. Educ: Texas A&M Col, B.S. in bus. mgt, 48. Polit. & Govt. Pos: Formerly chmn, Lauderdale Co. Rep. Party, Miss; formerly pres, Rep. Club of Lauderdale Co; numerous nat. and state offices and co. campaign chmn, Rep. Party, 61-; del, Rep. Nat. Conv, 68. Bus. & Prof. Pos: Pres, Carmichael-Dahlke, Inc, 61- and Gil Carmichael, Inc, 65; dir, Allen Supply, Tucker Steel Corp. and South. Investment. Mil. Serv: Entered as Recruit, Coast Guard Res, 45, released as Seaman 1/C, 46; reentered as Ens, Coast Guard, 51, released as Lt.(jg), 53, after serv. in N.Atlantic; Silver Life Saving Medal; Am. Theater Ribbon; Victory Medal. Mem: Dir, Miss. Auto Dealers Asn; past pres, Sales & Marketing Exec. Club. Rel: Episcopal. Mailing Add: 2009 39th St, Meridian, Miss. 39301.

CARMICHAEL, JACK KEMPER R
Co. Clerk, Delaware Co, Ind.
b. Muncie, Ind, 7/3/30; s. John Kemper Carmichael and Gertie Wray S; single. Educ: Ind. Univ, A.B. in Govt, 58. Polit. & Govt. Pos: Rep. precinct committeeman, Muncie, Ind, 59-; admin. asst. to U.S. Rep. Ralph Harvey, 61-66; admin. asst. to Mayor, Muncie, Ind, 67; co. clerk, Delaware Co. Ind, 68- Bus. & Prof. Pos: Teacher, soc. studies, high sch, Randolph Co, Ind, 58-61. Mil. Serv: Entered as Pvt, Air Force, 50, released as S/Sgt, 54, after serv. in Officer Cand. Sch, Lackland AFB, Air Training Command, 52-54; Good Conduct and Korean Serv. Medals. Mem: Ind. State Hist. Soc; Ind. Univ. Alumni Asn; pres, Northeast Dist. Asn. Ind. Co; Co. Clerks Asn. Ind; Kiwanis (bd. dir, Muncie Kiwanis); SAR (treas. Ind. SAR). Rel: Baptist. Mailing Add: S. 2013 S. Walnut St, Muncie, Ind. 47302.

CARMICHAEL, JAMES A, JR. D
b. Bessemer, Ala, 1/14/25; m. to Barbara Moroski; c. Cathy and David Alan. Educ: McKenie Lunger Sch. of Commerce, Rochester. Polit. & Govt. Pos: Chmn. planning bd, Batavia, N.Y, until 64; N.Y. State Assemblyman, 64-66. Bus. & Prof. Pos: Operates Carmichael Ins. Agency, Batavia, N.Y; publisher, weekly newspaper, Genesee Independent Press. Mil. Serv: Entered Army Air Force, 43, released 46, after serv. with 20th Air Force in China-Burma-India Theatre. Mem: Am. Legion (dir, G. Loomis Post); dir, Batavia Businessmen's Asn; dir. off, Genese Co. Indust. Develop. Corp; dir, Salvation Army; dir, Batavia Chap, March of Dimes; co. chmn, Cancer Crusade, 64; Mutual Agents Asn; Moose; Rotary; dir, Batavia Landmark Asn. Mailing Add: Batavia-Oakfield Townline Rd, Batavia, N.Y. 14020.

CARMICHAEL, OLIVER CROMWELL, JR. R
b. Birmingham, Ala, 3/10/20; s. Oliver Cromwell Carmichael and Ruth Crabtree C; m. 9/28/46 to Ernestine Morris; c. Carmen C.(Mrs. Murphy), Oliver Cromwell, III, Ernestine, II and Stanley Clark. Educ: Vanderbilt Univ, A.B, 40; Duke Univ. Law Sch, LL.B, 42; Columbia Univ, M.A, 51, Ph.D, 52; Phi Beta Kappa, Omicron Delta Kappa and Beta Theta Pi; Order of the Coif. Franklin Col, D.C.L; Univ. Notre Dame, Wabash Col. and Centre Col, LL.D, Polit. & Govt. Pos: Del, Rep. Nat. Conv, 64 & 68; chmn, Ind. Rep. Citizens Finance Cmt, 66-69. Bus. & Prof. Pos: Exec. dir, Vanderbilt Univ. Develop. Found, 55-56; pres, Converse Col, 56-60; chmn, Assocs. Investment Co, First Bank & Trust Co. and Capitol Life Ins. Co, 60- and Marshall Co. Bank & Trust Co, 65- Mil. Serv: Lt.(sg), Naval Res. Publ: New York Establishes a State University. Mem: Morris Park Country Club, South Bend; Pickwick Club, Niles, Mich; Pine Tree Golf Club, Delray Beach, Fla. Rel: Presbyterian. Legal Res: 110 N. Esther St, South Bend, Ind. 46617. Mailing Add: 1700 Mishawaka Ave, South Bend, Ind. 46624.

CARNAHAN, CLEVE L. D
b. Viola, Iowa, 8/16/95; s. William Carnahan and Nancy Anderson C; m. 1924 to Lucille Krumpholtz; c. William, Arlene, Robert, Lois Ann, Harold and James; 16 grandchildren. Educ: Ottumwa High Sch, 15. Polit. & Govt. Pos: Former Iowa State Rep; Sch. Bd, 3 terms. Bus. & Prof. Pos: Switchman, Cent. Mt. & States Pac. R.R, 44 years. Mem: Mason; K. T; Shrine; K. of P; Am. Legion; Vet. of World War I; Brotherhood of R.R. Trainmen; W.End Boosters of Ottumwa; Izaak Walton League. Rel: Congregational. 1967 Legal Res: Ottumwa, Iowa. No mailing address available. (1967)

CARNAHAN, ERNEST BRYAN, JR. D
Chmn, Carter Co. Dem. Cent. Cmt, Mo.
b. Garwood, Mo, 3/12/26; s. Ernest Bryan Carnahan, Sr. and Lillie Boyer C; m. 1/29/49 to Wanda Edwina Roark; c. Ronald Ernest and Donald Edwin. Educ: Ellsinore High Sch, 12 years. Polit. & Govt. Pos: Chmn, Carter Co. Dem. Cent. Cmt, Mo, 66- Bus. & Prof. Pos: With Mo. State Dept. Agr, 66- Mil. Serv: Entered as Seaman 2/C, Navy, 44, released as Ship Fitter 3/C, 46, after serv. in Pac. Theatre, 44-46. Mem: AF&AM, Mason (32°); Eastern Star; Agr. Stabilization & Conserv. Twp. Chmn. Rel: Baptist. Mailing Add: Route 1, Ellsinore, Mo. 63937.

CARNAHAN, MELVIN EUGENE D
b. Birch Tree, Mo, 1/11/34; s. A. S. J. Carnahan and Mary Kathel Schupp C; m. 6/12/54 to Jean Ann Carpenter; c. Roger Andrew, Raymond Russell and Robin Colleen. Educ: George Wash. Univ, B.A, 54; Univ. Mo, LL.B, 59; Mo. Law Review; Order of the Coif; Phi Alpha Delta. Polit. Pos: Majority Leader, Mo. House of Rep, 65-66; Mo. State Rep, Phelps Co, 63-66; police judge, City of Rolla, Mo, 61-62. Bus. & Prof. Pos: Attorney, Rolla, Mo, 61-; attorney, Bruer Northern and Crow, 59-61. Mil. Serv: Entered as 2nd Lt, Air Force, 54, released as 1st Lt, 56, after serv. in Office of Special Investations; Capt, Air Force Res. Mem: Mason; Shrine; Kiwanis; Am. Legion; C. of C. Rel: Baptist. Mailing Add: 49 Laird Ave, Rolla, Mo. 65401. (1967)

CARNEAL, GEORGE UPSHUR, JR. R
Spec. Asst. to the Secy, Dept. of Transportation
b. N.Y.C, 5/31/35; s. George Upshur Carneal and Florence Nutt C; m. 4/19/58 to Susan Muzzey; c. George, III, Scott Hamilton, Erik St. John and Kristen Dahlander. Educ: Princeton Univ, A.B, 57; Univ. Va. Sch. Law, LL.B, 61. Polit. & Govt. Pos: Law clerk to Hon. E. Barrett Prettyman, Judge of the U.S. Court of Appeals, D.C, 61-62; staff asst, Off. of President-Elect Richard M. Nixon, 68-69; Spec. Asst. to Secy. John A. Volpe, Dept. of Transportation, 69- Bus. & Prof. Pos: Attorney, Hogan & Hartson, Wash, D.C, 62-68. Mil. Serv: Entered as Pvt, Army, 58, released as Sgt, 63, after serv. in Army Inf. Res. Publ: 'The Unified Bar Controversy', 9/67 and 'The Unified Bar—A Constructive Proposal', 11/67, D.C. Bar Asn. J. Mem: Am, Fed, Va. State and D.C. Bar Asns; Princeton Club of Wash; River Bend Golf and Country Club; Order of the Coif; Raven Soc. Rel: Protestant. Mailing Add: 1148 Daleview Dr, McLean, Va. 22101.

CARNEAL, RUSSELL MORRIS D
Va. State Del.
b. Fredericksburg, Va, 5/9/18; m. to Vertie Elizabeth Leachman. Educ: Univ. Va, B.A. and LL.B; Delta Upsilon; Delta Theta Phi. Polit. & Govt. Pos: Chmn, Williamsburg Dem. Cmt, Va; city councilman, Williamsburg, 52-53; Va. State Del, 54- Bus. & Prof. Pos: Lawyer; dir, Williamsburg Life Ins. Co. Mil. Serv: World War II, Navy. Mem: Exchange Club; past pres, Va. State Exchange Clubs; Ruritans; Am. Legion; past master, Masons; Shrine; chmn, James City Co. Savings Bond Prog; 7-Up Club; Pulaski Club; VFW; Elks; Commonwealth Club; Va. State and Am. Bar Asns; Va. Trial Lawyers Asn; dir, Jamestown Festival Park. Rel: Presbyterian. Mailing Add: Box 440, Williamsburg, Va. 23185.

CARNES, MRS. JACK D
Dem. Nat. Committeewoman, Ark.
Polit. & Govt. Pos: Dem. Nat. Committeewoman, Ark, 44-; del, Dem. Nat.

Conv, 44- Bus. & Prof. Pos: Prfnl. worker, oil indust. and private investments. Mem: Nat. bd. trustees and state bd, Crippled Childrens Found; Bus. & Prfnl. Women's Club; Camden and Little Rock Country Clubs. Mailing Add: 132 California St. N.W, Camden, Ark. 71701.

CARNEY, CY, JR. R
Ark. State Rep. Committeeman, Washington Co.
b. Rudy, Ark, 12/26/22; s. Cy Carney and Lettie Comstock C; m. 1/7/44 to Clarice Allen; c. Cy, III, Charles Allen and Chere Amie. Educ: Ft. Smith Jr. Col, 41; Chillicothe Bus. Col, B.A. in mkt, 43. Polit. Pos: Ark. State Rep. committeeman, Washington Co, 64-; committeeman, Washington Co. Rep. Party, 62-65; del. & mem, Exec. Cmt, Rep. Nat. Conv, 3rd Dist, Ark, 64; mem, Ark. Young Rep, 60-64; cand, 3rd Dist, 63. Bus. & Prof. Pos: Owner, Cy Carney Propane Co, Ark, 50-65. Mem: Pres. spec. panel, Nat. Liquified Petroleum Gas Asn. and dist. dir, 65; v.pres, Ark. Liquified Petroleum Gas Asn, 60-61 and dir, 54-60; D. Carnegie Masters Speakers Inc; Mason (32°), Shrine; Elks; past pres, Exchange Club; dir, C. of C; bd. of dir, Salvation Army; Fayetteville Country Club; Springdale Country Club; pres, Ark. Bowling Asn; v.pres, Southern Bowling Cong. Rel: Baptist. Mailing Add: 333 E. Prospect, Fayetteville, Ark. 72701. (1967)

CARNEY, GLENN EDWARD D
b. Butte, Mont, 12/22/00; s. Frank Joseph Carney and Marion Sullivan C; m. 2/14/42 to Bernice Winifred Totten; c. Glenda (Mrs. Kivela) and granddaughter Kristen. Educ: Bus. Col, Los Angeles, Calif, 2½ years. Polit. & Govt. Pos: Health inspector, Silver Bow Co, Mont, 32; liquor inspector, Mont. Liquor Control Bd, Butte, 37, mgr. state liquor store, 39; alternate del, Dem. Nat. Conv, 40; del, Mont. State Dem. Conv, 65. Bus. & Prof. Pos: Mgr, identification dept, Pub. Rels, Butte, Mont, 42-45, labor rels, 45-50, pub. rels, 50-69.(Retired). Mem: Mont. Stockgrowers Asn; Mont. Woolgrowers Asn; C. of C; regional fund chmn, Red Cross, 59-60; Elks; Butte Country Club; Mont. Club, Helena; Meadow Lark Country Club, Great Falls. Rel: Catholic. Mailing Add: 1701 Marcia, Butte, Mont. 59701.

CARNEY, JOHN D
Chmn, Maricopa Co. Dem. Party, Ariz.
Polit. & Govt. Pos: Chmn, Maricopa Co. Dem. Party, Ariz, currently; del, Dem. Nat. Conv, 68. Bus. & Prof. Pos: Veterinarian; former pres, Chandler Indust. Develop. Found. Mailing Add: 2144 E. Roosevelt, Phoenix, Ariz. 85009.

CARNEY, JOHN JOSEPH D
V.Chmn, Cuyahoga Co. Dem. Orgn, Ohio
b. Cleveland, Ohio, 6/16/10; s. John J. Carney and Celia McCafferty C; m. 7/28/41 to Virginia M. Dreisig; c. John J, Jr, James A, Jeanne M. and Joseph D. Educ: West. Reserve Law Sch, LL.B, 43; Baldwin Wallace Col; John Carroll Univ; dean, Delta Theta Phi, 43. Hon. LL.D, Wilberforce Univ, 58. Polit. & Govt. Pos: Ohio State Rep, 37-47, Dem. Leader, Ohio House of Rep, 37-41; chmn, Ohio Soldiers and Sailor Cmn, 46; v.chmn, Cuyahoga Co. Dem. Exec. Cmt, 51, mem, 56-; auditor, Cuyahoga Co, 51-63, mem. bd. of elec, 66-, and chmn, currently; Dem. Nat. Committeeman, 52; alternate del, Dem. Nat. Conv, 64, del, 68; v.chmn, Cuyahoga Co. Dem. Orgn, currently. Bus. & Prof. Pos: Dir, Charity Hosp, Ohio, 63-; v.chmn, 64-65; dir, Capital Nat. Bank and Capital Bancorporation, currently. Mil. Serv: Capt, 45; Four ETO Campaign Ribbons. Publ: 'Appraisal Techniques,' Self, 57; 'Income Approach to Value,' The Appraisal J, 65. Mem: John Carroll Univ. Asn; West. Reserve Alumni Culver Fathers' Club; William's Col. Fathers' Club; Kiwanis; bd. of dirs. and bd. trustees, Gilmour Acad, Gates Mills, Ohio; Am. Legion; former Nat. Judge Advocate, Amvets; Ohio, Cleveland and Cuyahoga Co. Bar Asns; v.pres, Ohio State Auditors Asn, 61-62 and Int. Asn. Assessing Officers, 62-63; pres, Ohio Auditors Asn, 63-64; mem. bd, Sisters of the Humility of Mary, Pa. and Magnificate High Sch. Produced First film on Real Estate. Rel: Roman Catholic. Legal Res: 18777 Lookout Circle, Fairview Park, Ohio 44126. Mailing Add: 717 Superior Ave. N.E, Cleveland, Ohio 44114.

CARNEY, PHILIP N. D
Mass. State Rep.
m. to Katherine Muldoon; c. 2. Educ: Bentley Col, Acct. and Finance; Boston Univ, School of Bus. Admin. Polit. & Govt. Pos: Mass. State Rep, currently. Lynn Cent. Labor Union Citation, 61 & 62. Mailing Add: 12 Ward St, Lynn, Mass. 01902. (1967)

CARNEY, ROBERT I. D
b. 1908. Educ: Rutgers Univ. Polit. & Govt. Pos: Former Del. State Sen. Bus. & Prof. Pos: Du Pont Chambers Works. Mem: PTA: Moose; Elks; Kiwanis (former dist. lt. gov); Boy Scouts (former cmnr. and dist. v.chmn). Rel: Asbury Methodist Church; Former Lay Leader. Mailing Add: 215 W. Grant Ave, Wilmington Manor, Del. 19899. (1967)

CAROTHERS, CHARLES G, III
Dep. Asst. Secy. for Fish and Wildlife, Dept. of the Interior
b. Mass, 1929. Educ: Wesleyan Univ, grad. Polit. & Govt. Pos: Dep. Asst. Secy. for Fish and Wildlife, 69- Bus. & Prof. Pos: Officer, Mass. Conserv, Inc. and predecessor orgn, 53-; former dir, Mass. Wildlife Fedn, Inc; mem. exec. cmt, Ducks Unlimited, Inc. of Chicago. Mailing Add: Dept. of the Interior, Washington, D.C. 20240.

CAROTHERS, NEIL, III R
Finance Chmn, D.C. Rep. Party
b. Fayetteville, Ark, 10/11/19; s. Neil Carothers (deceased) and Eileen Hamilton C.(deceased); m. 3/16/55 to Mary Crocker deLimur; c. Neil and Andre Sperry. Educ: Blair Acad, 35-37; Princeton Univ, B.S. in Elec. Eng, 41; Rhodes Scholar, Oxford Univ, B.A, 50, M.A, 55; Cap and Gown Club; Myrmidon Soc. Polit. & Govt. Pos: Consult, Research and Develop. Bd, U.S. Dept. Defense, 51; asst. sci. adv, U.S. Dept. State, 51-53; spec. asst to the dir, Nat. Sci. Found, 53-61, consult. to the dir, 62-63; dep. to mem, Nat. Aeronaut. and Space Coun; rep, Nat. Security Coun. Planning Bd. and Opers. Coord. Bd; mem, D.C. Rep. Cmt, 68-; mem, Rep. Nat. Finance Cmt, 68-; finance chmn, D.C. Rep. Party, 68- Bus. & Prof. Pos: Asst. to dir, guided missiles prog, Johns Hopkins Applied Physics Lab, Md, 46-48; bd. dirs, Provident Securities Co, San Francisco, currently; consult, currently. Mil. Serv: Entered as Ens, Naval Res, 41, released as Lt. Comdr, 45, after serv. as Experimental Test Pilot and Engr, Patuxent River Naval Air Test Unit, 43-45. Mem: Nat. Coun. For. Policy Asn.(chmn, Wash, D.C. Area); Wash. Inst. For. Affairs; Am. Asn. Adv. Sci; Capitol Hill Club; Fed. City Club; Metrop. Club; Chevy Chase Club; Princeton Club N.Y; trustee, Meridian House Found, Int. Student House, Inc, Aspen-East and Multiple Sclerosis Asn; Rel: Episcopal. Legal Res: 3244 Nebraska Ave, Washington, D.C. 20016. Mailing Add: 1701 Pennsylvania Ave, Washington, D.C. 20006.

CARPENTER, DENNIS E. R
Chmn, Rep. State Cent. Cmt, Calif.
b. Minneapolis, Minn, 9/3/28; s. Frank Henry Carpenter and Helen Luedtke C; m. 11/10/68 to Madine; c. Kenneth R, Bruce H, Frank H, II and Scott R. Educ: Univ. Calif, Los Angeles, B.A, 52, LL.B, 58; Alpha Tau Omega; Phi Delta Phi. Polit. & Govt. Pos: Spec. agent, FBI, 54-57; chmn, Orange Co. Rep. Cent. Cmt, 62-67, exec. cmt, 68-; chmn. Calif. Plan Cmt, Rep. State Cent. Cmt, 62-69, v.chmn, Rep. State Cent. Cmt, 67-69, chmn, 69-; del, Rep. Nat. Conv, 68. Bus. & Prof. Pos: Lawyer, Duryea, Carpenter & Barnes, Newport Beach, Calif, 58-; chmn, Orange Co. Airport Cmn, Santa Ana, 67- Mil. Serv: Entered as Pvt, Army, 46, released as 1st Lt, 48. Mem: Am, Calif, Orange Co. and Harbor Area Bar Asns. Rel: Presbyterian. Legal Res: 120 Via Quito, Newport Beach, Calif. 92660. Mailing Add: P.O. Box 1786, Newport Beach, Calif. 92663.

CARPENTER, ELIZABETH SUTHERLAND D
b. Salado, Tex, 9/1/20; d. Thomas Shelton Sutherland and Mary Elizabeth Robertson S; m. 6/17/44 to Leslie Carpenter; c. Scott Sutherland and Christy. Educ: Univ. Tex, B.J, 42; Theta Sigma Phi; Alpha Phi. Polit. & Govt. Pos: Exec. asst. to the Vice President, 61-63; press secy. and staff dir. to the First Lady, 63-69. Bus. & Prof. Pos: Partner with husband, Carpenter News Bur, 47-61; lectr. and auth, 69- Mem: Pres, Women's Nat. Press Club. Rel: Methodist. Legal Res: Austin, Tex. Mailing Add: 4701 Woodway Lane N.W, Washington, D.C. 20016.

CARPENTER, M. JOHN D
Chmn, Barton Co. Dem. Party, Kans.
b. Lawrence, Kans, 5/18/33; s. Miller J. Carpenter and Anna Smith C; m. 5/2/53 to Mary Lee Hadl; c. Chris Ann and Gail Lynn. Educ: Univ. Kans, B.A. & LL.B. Polit. & Govt. Pos: Housing authority comnr, Great Bend, Kans, 67-; chmn, Barton Co. Dem. Party, Kans, 68-; workmen's compensation examiner, Kans, 69- Bus. & Prof. Pos: Libr. trustee, Barton Co. Bar Asn, 69- Mem: Barton Co. Bar Asn; Kans. Bar Asn. Rel: Protestant. Legal Res: Bissells Point, Great Bend, Kans. 67530. Mailing Add: P.O. Box 677, Great Bend, Kans. 67530.

CARPENTER, MARGARET WODTKE D
Co-Chmn, Dem. State Cent. Cmt. Md.
b. Akron, Ohio, 11/15/13; d. Hans von Wodtke and Mathilda Blessman W; m. 11/25/37 to William Echols Carpenter; c. Christopher Lee, Carol (Mrs. Esteban) and Craig Wodtke. Educ: Univ. Akron, A.B, 35; Simmons Col, Cert. Med. Tech, 36. Polit. & Govt. Pos: Precinct chmn, Dem. Party, Montgomery Co, Md, 55-59; secy, Mont. Co. Dem. Cent. Cmt, 58-62, mem, 64-66; del, Dem. Nat. Conv, 68; co-chmn, Dem. State Cent. Cmt. Md, 68. Bus. & Prof. Pos: Med. technologist, Boston and Worcester, Mass, 36-39. Rel: Protestant. Mailing Add: 4103 Woodbine St, Chevy Chase, Md. 20015.

CARPENTER, ROBERT ANDY D
b. Comanche, Tex, 2/13/12; s. David Gilston Floyd Carpenter and Ebbie Louisia Meyers C; m. 3/16/34 to Mildred Barrett; c. Joan (Mrs. Frank G. Couch) and Robert Craig. Educ: Comanche High Sch; correspondence and col. short courses, several inst. Polit. & Govt. Pos: Coordinator for Gov. John Connally, 12th Sen. Dist, Tex. and Comanche Co. Del. Floor Leader, 66; co, dist. and state organizer and campaign worker for several Dem. Officeholders, Tex, 35 years; 17th Cong. Dist. Del, Dem. Nat. Conv, 64. Bus. & Prof. Pos: Prod. supt, The Comanche Chief, printers and publishers, 51-, head, composing room, 29- Mem: Secy-treas, mem. annuity bd. and training co. capt, Comanche Vol. Fire Dept; dir, Comanche Co. and City Civil Defense; active in civic affairs. Authority on early West Texas hist; football, baseball and track in high sch; semi-pro baseball. Rel: Protestant; mem, church bd. Legal Res: 901 E. Highland Ave, Comanche, Tex. 76442. Mailing Add: P.O. Box 332, Comanche, Tex. 76442. (1967)

CARPENTER, SAMUEL EMLEN, III R
Chmn, Rep. Party of Va.
b. Ossining, N.Y, 11/29/25; s. Samuel Emlen Carpenter, Jr. and Evelyn Stone Wallace C; m. 6/18/49 to Lois Waterbury; c. Perry N. and Brien W. Educ: Univ. Va, Charlottesville, B.S. in Commerce, 48; Phi Kappa Psi. Polit. & Govt. Pos: Chmn, Fairfax Co. Rep. Party, Va, 66-68; chmn, Rep. Party of Va, 68-; mem, Rep. Nat. Cmt, 68-; mem, South. Asn. State Chmn, 68- Bus. & Prof. Pos: Sales mgr, Owens Corning Fiberglas, acoustical prod, 56-57; v.pres, A.W. Lee Co, 58-62; pres, Carpenter Oil Co, 62-67; real estate, investments, 62-; v.pres, Wash. Brittanicas, Pro Soccer, 67-69. Mil. Serv: Entered as A/S, Navy, 43, released as Seaman 1/C Aviation Radioman, 66, after serv. in Air Arm, U.S, 43-46. Mem: Acoustical Contractors Asn. (v.pres); Bldg. Owners and Mgrs. Asn; Wash. Bldg. Cong; Chevy Chase Country Club; Univ. Club, D.C; Bd. dirs, McLean, Va. Civic Asn. Award from Owens Corning Fiberglas, 55 and Sales Builders Club. Rel: Episcopal. Mailing Add: 976 Saigon Rd, McLean, Va. 22101.

CARPENTER, TERRY M. R
Nebr. State Sen.
b. Cedar Rapids, Iowa, 3/28/00; m. Sept. 1931 to Hazeldeane Carruthers; 3 children, (1 deceased). Polit. & Govt. Pos: Nebr. State Sen, 1953- Mailing Add: P.O. Box 170, Scottsbluff, Nebr. 69361. (1967)

CARPENTIER, DONALD DEE R
Ill. State Sen.
b. Moline, Ill, 1/21/31; s. Charles Francis Carpentier and Alta Sarginson C; m. 8/24/50 to Marylee Beth Morehart; c. Susan Jane, Charles Jeffrey, Alta Lizabeth, Jane Anne and Christine Dow. Educ: St. Ambrose Col, 49-51. Polit. & Govt. Pos: V.chmn, Ill. Young Rep, 53, chmn. of Speakers Bur, 54; Ill. State Sen, 43rd Dist, 62- Bus. & Prof. Pos: Ins. broker, Carpentier Ins. Agency, 53- Mem: Cath. Order of Foresters; Jaycees; Elks; Sponsor Amvets Post 145. Rel: Catholic. Legal Res: 477 27th Ave, East Moline, Ill. 61244. Mailing Add: 1465 41st St, Moline, Ill. 61265.

CARPER, FRANCES I. D
Chmn, Kit Carson Co. Dem. Cent. Cmt, Colo.
b. Goodland, Kans, 7/26/10; d. Francis James O'Brien and Inez Strom O; m. 5/17/41 to George James Carper, Co. Judge; c. Virginia Carol (Mrs. Roberts) and Billie Frances (Mrs. Busby). Educ: High Sch, Phillipsburg, Kans. Polit. & Govt. Pos: V.chmn, Kit Carson Co. Dem. Cent. Cmt, Colo, 57-61, chmn, 61-; v.chmn, Colo. Fourth Judicial Dist. Dem. Party, 61-; v.chmn, Colo. Third U.S. Cong. Dist, Dem. Party, 63-69; chmn, Colo. 17th Sen. Dist. Dem. Party, 63-; del, Dem. Nat. Conv, 64 & 68, mem. permanent orgn. cmt, 64. Mem: Burlington Zonta Club (past pres). Rel: Catholic. Mailing Add: 372 14th St, Burlington, Colo. 80807.

CARR, ANDREW REMBERT D
Mem. State Cmt, Dem. Party of Miss.
b. Clarksdale, Miss, 7/4/26; s. Oscar Clark Carr, Sr. and Blanche Busby C; m. 10/28/50 to Virginia Erb; c. Andrew R, Jr, Michael E, Susan M, David B. and Virginia E. Educ: U.S. Naval Acad, grad. and commissioned, 49. Polit. & Govt. Pos: Mem. Miss. State Adv. Cmt, U.S. Civil Rights Cmn, 67-; del, Dem. Nat. Conv, 68; mem. state cmt, Dem. Party of Miss, 68- Bus. & Prof. Pos: Pres, Mascot Plantation, Inc, 58-; pres, Carr Gin Co, Inc, 62-; dir, First Nat. Bank of Clarksdale, 65-; pres, Coahoma Opportunities Inc, anti-poverty agency, 65- Mil. Serv: Entered as Seaman, Navy, 44, released as Lt.(jg), 54, after serv. in U.S. Naval Acad, U.S.S. Beatty and U.S.S. Cambria, Atlantic Fleet, 49-54. Mem: Nat. Cotton Coun; Delta Coun.(past v.pres, dir, 64-); Miss. Econ. Coun; C. of C; Nat. Asn. Commun. Develop.(dir, 66-68); Miss. Heart Asn.(state dir. and dist. chmn, 60-64); Clarksdale Country Club; K. of C; Cotton Producers Inst; State and Local Sch. Bd; Miss. Indust. & Spec. Serv; Hurricane Point Hunting Club. Nat. Rural Serv. Award. Rel: Roman Catholic; Bishop's Adv. Cmt, St. Elizabeth Catholic Church. Mailing Add: Route 1, Box 672, Clarksdale, Miss. 38614.

CARR, AUBREY J. D
Ala. State Sen.
b. Walker Co, Ala, 8/21/20; m. to Nell Shepherd; c. Two sons. Educ: Birmingham Bus. Col; Dallas Inst. of Mortuary Sci. Polit. & Govt. Pos: Coroner, Marshall Co, Ala, 12 years; Ala. State Rep, until 66; Ala. State Sen, 67- Bus. & Prof. Pos: Operator, funeral homes. Mil. Serv: Maritime Serv, World War II; Naval Res. Mem: Lions; nat. dir, U.S. Jr. C. of C; chmn, Bd. of Sch. Trustees. Guntersville Man of the Year, 60. Rel: Methodist. Mailing Add: Box 326, Guntersville, Ala. 35976. (1967)

CARR, DELMAN R. R
Chmn, Isle of Wight Co. Rep. Party, Va.
b. Creme, Va. 8/31/18; s. Chester Lloyd Carr and Dollie V. Rhodes C; m. 6/7/38 to Sally Glenn Scott; c. Delman Lew and Chester Glenn. Educ: Carrsville High Sch, 35-36. Polit. & Govt. Pos: Mem, Isle of Wight Co. Agr. Stabilization & Conserv. Serv, U.S. Dept. Agr, 50-55; mem, Va. State Agr. Stabilization & Conserv. Serv, 56-; chmn, Isle of Wight Co. Rep. Party, Va, 68- Mem: Va. Forest Inc; Soil Conserv. Soc. U.S; Va. Farm Bur; Nat. Farmers Orgn; Windsor Ruritan Club. Rel: Baptist; Deacon, Carrsville Baptist Church. Mailing Add: RFD 1, Carrsville, Va. 23315.

CARR, E. MICHAEL D
Chmn, Delaware Co. Dem. Party, Iowa
b. Dubuque, Iowa, 4/25/40; s. Hubert Carr and Iola Johnson C; m. 6/22/69 to Sylvia Louise Lundin. Educ: State Univ. Iowa, B.A, 62, J.D, 64; Omicron Delta Kappa; Delta Tau Delta; Lettermen's Club; Phi Delta Phi. Polit. & Govt. Pos: Chmn, Delaware Co. Dem. Party, Iowa, 66-; co. attorney, Delaware Co, 67-68, 69-; del, Dem. Nat. Conv, 68. Mil. Serv: Entered as 2nd Lt, Army, 64, released as 1st Lt, 66, after serv. in First Bn, Seventh Artillery, First Inf. Div, U.S. and Vietnam, 64-66; Res, 66-, 1st Lt. Mem: Am. Bar Asn; Iowa State Bar Asn.(exec. coun. jr. bar sect, 69-70); Nat. Dist. Attorneys Asn; Mason; Lions; Am. Legion. Rel: Congregational. Legal Res: 108 W. Union St, Manchester, Iowa 52057. Mailing Add: Box 6, Manchester, Iowa 52057.

CARR, GERALD D
b. Rose Hill, N.C, 4/12/25; s. Rufus Carr and Adell Rouse C; m. 11/25/54 to Katherine Waller; c. Norma Daly. Educ: N.C. State Univ, B.S, 49. Polit. & Govt. Pos: Cmnr, Town of Rose Hill, N.C, 58-60, mayor, 60-64; del, Dem. Nat. Conv, 68. Bus. & Prof. Pos: Partner, Coastal Construction Co, 52- Mil. Serv: Entered as Seaman, Navy, 44, released as PO 2/C, 46, after serv. in Amphibious Forces, Pac. Theatre, 45-46. Mem: Am. Soc. Civil Engrs; Lions; Civitan Club. Rel: Presbyterian. Mailing Add: Box 118, Rose Hill, N.C. 28458.

CARR, GLADYS B. R
Councilwoman, Santa Barbara, Calif.
b. Los Animas, Colo; d. Oliver M. Banta and Meta M. Elliott B; wid. Educ: Santa Barbara State Col. Polit. & Govt. Pos: Councilwoman, First Ward, Santa Barbara, Calif, currently. Bus. & Prof. Pos: Escrow officer, First Nat. Bank, 10 years and Bank of Am, Nat. Trust and Savings Asn, 5 years; mgr, Officer Escrow Dept, First Am. Title Co, 58-62; v.pres, Estado Escrow Co, 62-64. Mem: League of Women Voters; Cancer Asn; Toastmistress Club (past pres); Rep. Women; Calif. Escrow Asn.(past pres. and hon. life mem); Santa Barbara Woman Realty Bd; cmt. mem. many civic orgns. Winner of many tennis trophies. Rel: Methodist. Mailing Add: 1112 Quinientos, Santa Barbara, Calif. 93103.

CARR, HARRIET LOUISE D
Vt. State Rep.
b. Canaan, Vt, 11/2/21; single. Educ: Canaan High Sch. Polit. & Govt. Pos: Town auditor, 2 years; Vt. State Rep, 57, 59, 65- Mem: Farm Bur.(women's chmn. of Essec Co); secy-treas, Essex Co. Natural Resources Conserv. Dist. Rel: Protestant. Mailing Add: Canaan, Vt. 05903.

CARR, JAMES DREW R
Mem, Aroostook Co. Rep. Cmt, Maine
b. Houlton, Maine, 7/17/35; s. Wilder Drew Carr and Verna Hall C; single. Educ: Ricker Col, 53-54; Bowdoin Col, 54-55; Babson Inst, B.S, 60; Boston Univ. Law Sch, LL.B, 64; Blue Key Nat. Honor Soc; Beta Theta Pi. Polit. & Govt. Pos: Chmn, Houlton Rep. Town Cmt, Maine, 66-; judge of probate, Aroostook Co, 66-; mem, Aroostook Co. Rep. Cmt, 68-; alternate del, Rep. Nat. Conv, 68. Attorney, James D. Carr Law Off, 65- Mil. Serv: Entered as Pvt. E-2, Army, 56, released as Pvt. 1/C, 57, after serv. in Artil, Ft. Bliss, Tex. Mem: Maine State and Aroostook Co. Bar Asns; Mason; Elks. Rel: Methodist. Legal Res: 67 High St, Houlton, Maine 04730. Mailing Add: Box 301, Houlton, Maine 04730.

CARR, JAMES K. D
Gen. Mgr, Pub. Utilities, San Francisco, Calif.
b. Redding, Calif, 1/15/14; s. Francis Carr and Mary Kennedy C; m. 10/14/39 to Katherine Kergan; c. Mary, Ann, Susan and Margaret. Educ: Univ. of Santa Clara, Calif, B.S, 34. Polit. & Govt. Pos: Consult, WPA, Geol. Survey Dept. Interior, Shasta Co. Surveyor's Off, City Engr. Off, Redding, Calif, 34-36; Bur. Reclamation, Dept. Interior, 36-51; eng. consult. to Cmt. on Interior and Insular Affairs, U.S. House of Rep, 51-53; asst. gen. mgr, Sacramento Munic. Utility Dist, 53-61; chmn, Calif. Water Cmn, 59-61; bd. regents, Univ. of Santa Clara, 59-65; Undersecy, Dept. of Interior, Wash, 61-64; gen. mgr, Pub. Utilities City-Co. of San Francisco, 64- Mem: Calif, D.C. Fel. Am. Soc. Civil Engrs; Sacramento C. of C; Rotary; K. of C. Civil Govt. Award, 64. Rel: Catholic. Mailing Add: 1420 Marlborough Rd, Hillsborough, Calif. 94010.

CARR, JOE C. D
Secy. of State, Tenn.
b. Cookeville, Tenn, 6/20/07; m. 1934 to Mary Oliver Hart; c. Carolyn (Mrs. Welch) and Joe C, Jr. Educ: Nashville Pub. Schs. Polit. & Govt. Pos: Page, Tenn. Senate, 23 and House of Rep, 25; bill clerk, House of Rep, 29 & 31; secy, Orgn. Young Dem. Clubs of Tenn, 32, pres, 34; asst. chief clerk, House of Rep, 33-35, reading clerk, 37 and chief clerk, 39 & 53; pres, Young Dem. Clubs of Am, 41; Secy. of State, Tenn, 41-44 & 45-; del, Dem. Nat. Conv, 68. Bus. & Prof. Pos: Trustee, Belmont Col. and Baptist Hosp. Mil. Serv: 44-45. Mem: Nat. Asn. Secretaries of State (past pres); Scottish Rite Mason (33°); York Rite Mason; Royal Order of Jesters; Elks; Exchange Club (pres, 54); Cumberland Club; Soc. Amateur Chefs; Am. Legion (former V.Comdr, Post 5); 40 et 8; Shrine (Potentate, Al Menah Temple, 55); Tenn. Baptist Brotherhood (past pres). Rel: Baptist; Deacon. Mailing Add: State Capitol Bldg, Nashville, Tenn. 37219.

CARR, MARION P. D
Polit. & Govt. Pos: N.Mex. State Sen, -66; N.Mex. State Rep, 6 years; Mayor, 12 years; secy, Sch. Bd, 16 years. Bus. & Prof. Pos: Lumberman, banker. Mem: Rotary. Rel: Methodist. Mailing Add: 718 Ave. C, Ft. Sumner, N.-Mex. 88119. (1967)

CARR, OSCAR CLARK, JR. D
b. Memphis, Tenn, 8/4/23; s. Oscar Clark Carr and Blanche Rembert Busby C; m. 6/21/50 to Billie Fisher; c. Oscar Clark, III, Blanche Busby, Palmer Scott, John T. Fisher and E'Lane Tucker. Educ: Cornell Univ, 41-42; U.S. Naval Acad, B.S. with distinction, 45; Psi Upsilon. Polit. & Govt. Pos: Chmn, Mississippians for Robert Kennedy, 68; Coahoma Co. chmn, Humphrey Campaign, 68; del, Dem. Nat. Conv, 68. Bus. & Prof. Pos: Pres, Carr Planting Co, Inc, Clarksdale, Miss, 48-; pres, Delta Coun, Stoneville, 61-62; dir, Cotton Coun. Int, Memphis, Tenn, 64-67; chmn, First Nat. Bank, Clarksdale, Miss, 64-; chmn, Samelson Cigar Co, Memphis, Tenn, 67-69. Mil. Serv: Entered as Midn, Navy, 42, released as Lt.(jg), 47, after serv. as asst. gunnery officer, U.S.S. Wisconsin, Pac, 45-47. Mem: Nat. Cotton Coun; Newcomen Soc; Am. Acad. Polit. and Soc. Sci; Naval Acad. Alumni Asn; Coahoma Co. C. of C.(pres, 58); Miss. Econ. Coun; pres, Episcopal Laymen of Miss, 64. Rel: Episcopal. Mailing Add: Route 2, Box 156, Clarksdale, Miss. 38614.

CARR, THOMAS CASWELL D
b. Rhine, Ga, 7/4/12; s. E.F. Carr and Kathleen Ryals C; m. 12/28/41 to Margaret Jordan; c. Margaret Jordan, Kathleen Dorothy. Educ: Mid. Ga. Col; Univ. of Ga; Ga. South, B.S, 38; MIT (grad. work), 42-43. Polit. & Govt. Pos: Ga. State Rep, 63-66; Mayor, City of Sandersville, 52-59. Bus. & Prof. Pos: Fertilizer mfr, seed farmer. Mil. Serv: U.S. Air Corps, WW II, 42-45, 1st Lt. Mem: Mason Shrine; Rotary; Dir, C. of C, 54-58; Sandersville Indust. Develop. Corp, 56. Rel: Methodist. Mailing Add: Sandersville, Ga. 31082. (1967)

CARR, WAGGONER D
b. Fairlie, Tex, 10/1/18; s. Vincent Carr and Ruth Warlick C; m. 12/21/41 to Ernestine Story; c. David William. Educ: Tex. Tech. Col, B.A, 40; Univ. of Tex. Law Sch, LL.B; Delta Theta Phi. Polit. & Govt. Pos: Asst. dist. attorney, 72nd Judicial Dist, 48; attorney, Lubbock Co, 49-51; Tex. State Rep, 51-61, speaker, Tex. House Rep, 57-61; former Attorney Gen, Tex. Mil. Serv: Entered as Pvt, Air Force, 42, released as Aviation Cadet, 45. Mem: Lions; K. of P; Farm Bur; Am. Legion; Tex. and Lubbock Co. Bar Asns; KCCH, Scottish Rite; Nat. and Southern Asns. of Attorneys Gen. Wyman Award as Outstanding State Attorney Gen. in the U.S, Nat. Asn. of Attorneys Gen, 66. Rel: Methodist. Legal Res: 6903 Mesa, Austin, Tex. 78731. Mailing Add: International Life Bldg, Austin, Tex. 78701.

CARRASGUILLO, QUIÑONES ERNESTO D
Sen, P.R. Senate
b. Yabucoa, P.R, 11/7/01; s. Pablo Carrasguillo and Juanita Quiñones C; m. 4/8/33 to Conchita Lopez Lopez; c. Ernesto Luis and Connie Margarita. Educ: Teacher's Diploma. Polit. & Govt. Pos: Pres, Popular Party, Yabucoa, P.R, 38-66; mayor, Yabucoa, P.R, 40-48; mem, Wage Minimum Bd, P.R, 42-44; Rep, P.R. House of Rep, 36-40; Sen, P.R. Senate, 48- Bus. & Prof. Pos: Teacher, Dept. of Educ, Yabucoa, P.R, 21-40. Mem: Pres, Farm and Indust. Worker's Union, 38-66, P.R. Teacher's Asn. Rel: Catholic. Mailing Add: Degetau St. No. 4, Yabucoa, P.R. 00767. (1967)

CARRAWAY, WILSON D
b. Tallahassee, Fla, 10/16/04; m. to Polly Lively; c. Wilson, Jr, Emily (Mrs. Kemp). Educ: Univ. Pa, B.S, 25; Alpha Sigma Phi. Polit. & Govt. Pos: Fla. State Rep, 44-50; Fla. State Sen, 54-66, pres, Fla. State Sen, 63. Bus. & Prof. Pos: Banker; bottler. Mem: Rotary (past pres); C. of C.(past pres). Rel: Episcopal. Mailing Add: P.O. Box 870, Tallahassee, Fla. 33502. (1967)

CARRELL, THOMAS C. D
Calif. State Sen.
b. Cooper, Tex; m. 8/24/29 to Dolphia Carmack; c. Tommy, Jr.(deceased).

Educ: Univ. Calif, Los Angeles, B.A; Univ. South. Calif, M.A. Polit. & Govt. Pos: Los Angeles Co. Dem. Cent. Cmt, 10 years; del, five Dem. Nat. Conv; Calif. State Assemblyman, 59-67; Calif. State Sen, 22nd Dist, 67- Bus. & Prof. Pos: Sch. teacher; owner, auto agency, 38- Mil. Serv: Army, Admin. Serv, World War II, received citations. Mem: Elks; Moose; Toastmasters; Am. Legion; past pres, Kiwanis and San Fernando C. of C; former chmn, Valley Presbyterian Commun. Hosp. Mailing Add: 753 San Fernando Rd, San Fernando, Calif. 91340.

CARRENO, DELORES MAE D
Mem, Calif. Dem. State Cent. Cmt.
b. Ellendale, N.Dak, 6/26/31; d. Eugene Volney Fisk and Lydia Streeter F; div; c. Toni (Mrs. Luis Domondon), JoAnne (Mrs. Donald Norton), David J, Steven Fisk, Jon Fredric, Kelly Jean and Rebecca Lynn. Polit. & Govt. Pos: Pres, John F. Kennedy Dem. Club, 64-65; registrn. chmn, San Joaquin Co. Dem. Campaign Cmt, Calif, 64 & 68; mem, San Joaquin Co. Dem. Cent. Cmt, 64-, secy, 68-; mem, Calif. Dem. State Cent. Cmt, 64-; coordinator, Kennedy Campaign, 68, Humphrey Campaign, 68; treas, Pereira for Calif. State Assembly, 68; San Joaquin Co. coordinator, LaCoste for Calif. State Assembly, 69; regional v.pres, Dem. of Cent. Calif, 69- Mem: NAACP; Stockton Citizens Workable Prog. Cmt, Coun. of Neighborhood Asn; Coun. of Fair Oaks Neighbors, Citywide, Save Our Stockton. Rel: Protestant. Mailing Add: 540 E. Wyandotte, Stockton, Calif. 95204.

CARRIER, J. ROBERT D
Maine State Rep.
b. Lewiston, Maine, 6/29/25; s. Stanislas Carrier (deceased) and Cordelia Vaillancourt C; m. June, 1949 to Marie Therese Arsenault; c. Robert J, Richard A, Michele M. and Ronald A. Educ: Portland Univ, A.A. in Bus. Admin, 59, Law Sch, 60-63; Univ. Maine. Polit. & Govt. Pos: Maine State Rep, 67- Mil. Serv: Entered as A/S, Merchant Marine, 43, released as 2nd Mate, 50, after serv. in European and Pac. Theatre. Mem: K. of C; Holy Name Soc. Rel: Catholic; mem. coun, St. Hyacinthe Parish. Mailing Add: 315 Bridge St, Westbrook, Maine 04092.

CARRIER, JOHN T. Independent R
b. Readsboro, Vt, 7/2/08; m. to Florence Canedy; c. Two sons, one daughter. Educ: Vt. Acad; Bliss Bus. Sch, 1 year. Polit. & Govt. Pos: Town selectman; sheriff; lister, 8 years; twice mem, Windham Co. Appeal Bd; former Vt. State Rep. Bus. & Prof. Pos: Lumberman. Mil. Serv: Vt. State Guard, 2 years. Mem: Mason; Lions. Rel: Baptist. Mailing Add: Whitingham, Vt. 05361. (1967)

CARRIER, MARIA L. D
N.H. State Rep.
b. Washington, D.C, 8/21/20; d. Vito Stefano Lozupone and Maria Colacicco L; m. 3/8/42 to Paul Vernon Carrier; c. Stephan Paul and James G. Educ: Univ. N.H, B.A, 67, grad. sch. govt, M.A. cand, 67-68; Phi Sigma Alpha; Pi Gamma Mu; teaching assistantship. Polit. & Govt. Pos: Del, Dem. Nat. Conv, 68; mem, Dem. Nat. Platform Cmt, 68; N.H. State Rep, 69- Mem: Am. Civil Liberties Union bd. mem, N.H. Br; bd. mem, United Commun. Serv. Greater Manchester; League Women Voters (past bd. mem); Am. Asn. Univ. Women; N.H. Coun. Better Schs; N.H. Coun. World Affairs; United World Federalist; NAACP. Rel: Protestant. Mailing Add: 2125 Elm St, Manchester, N.H. 03104.

CARRIGAN, JAMES D. D
Ill. State Rep.
b. Peoria, Ill, 3/15/05; m. to Dorothy Payne; c. Mary Joanne, Jaicomo, Fulton J. Educ: Spalding Inst. Polit. & Govt. Pos: Mem, Peoria City Coun, Ill, 33-35; co. auditor, Peoria City, 36-44; chmn, Dem. Co. Cmt, 37-46; chmn, Liquor Cmn; Ill. State Rep, currently. Bus. & Prof. Pos: Pres, Carrigan Elec. Co. Mailing Add: 156 E. South Gate Rd, Peoria, Ill. 61614.

CARRIGAN, JOHN E. R
W.Va. State Sen.
b. Glen Dale, W.Va. 8/25/10; s. Charles E. Carrigan and Harriet Davis C; m. to Norma L. Schliff; c. Erin E. Educ: Bethany Col, A.B; W.Va. Univ, LL.B; Kappa Alpha. Polit. & Govt. Pos: W.Va. State Sen, 50-, minority leader, W.Va. State Sen, 53rd-59th Legis. Bus. & Prof. Pos: Lawyer. Mil. Serv: U.S. Navy. Mem: Mason; Elks; Marshall Co. and W.Va. Bar Asns; Am. Legion. Rel: Presbyterian. Mailing Add: Sherrard, Marshall Co, W.Va. 26057.

CARRIGG, JOSEPH L. R
b. Susquehanna, Pa, 2/23/01; s. Thomas J. Carrigg and Ellen Houlihan C; m. 5/11/46 to Catherine E. O'Neill. Educ: Niagara Univ; Albany Law Sch; Dickinson Law Sch; Devils Own; Woolsach; Phi Sigma Kappa. Polit. & Govt. Pos: Dist. attorney, Susquehanna, Pa, 36-48 and mayor, 50-51; U.S. Rep, Tenth Dist, Pa, 51-59; dir. of practice, U.S. Treas. Dept, 60-61; mgr. State Workmen's Ins. Fund, Dept. Labor and Indust, Pa, 63- Bus. & Prof. Pos: Attorney-at-law, 26- Mem: Susquehanna Co, Pa, Am. and Fed. Bar Asns; Moose; K. of C; Serra Int; Lions Int. Rel: Roman Catholic. Mailing Add: 414 Erie Ave, Susquehanna, Pa. 18847.

CARRILLO, OSCAR, SR. D
b. Hebbronville, Tex, 11/22/21; s. David Carrillo Chapa and Emma Peña C; m. 3/23/41 to Evangelina Rebecca Garcia; c. David Homero, Oscar Rene, Diana Hilda (Mrs. Sijifredo Flores), Ludivina (Mrs. Juan M. Benavides), Adriana Lamar, Rebecca Anna, Evangelina, Lucinda, Roberto Mario and Maria Teresa. Educ: Draughns Bus. Col, 39-40. Polit. & Govt. Pos: Mayor, Benavides, Tex, 47-49; Tex. State Rep, 66- Mil. Serv: Entered as Pfc, Army, 44, released as Pfc, 46, after serv. in Sixth Army Group Spec. Troop, ETO, 45-46; Bronze Star. Mem: Rotary; Am. Legion; VFW; K. of C. Rel: Catholic. Mailing Add: P.O. Box 356, Benavides, Tex. 78341.

CARROLL, DONALD FRANCIS D
Chmn, Meriden Dem. Town Cmt, Conn.
b. Meriden, Conn, 1/24/15; s. Charles Neal Carroll and Gertrude R. Brooks C; m. 8/17/35 to Pauline J. La Bonte; c. Valerie (Mrs. Carl R. Blume), David N. and Joan V. (Mrs. Richard M. Correll). Educ: Oxford Col. Admin, B.B.A; Omicron Gamma Alpha; Beta Lambda. Polit. & Govt. Pos: Chmn, Meriden Dem. Town Cmt, Conn, 47-48, 49-53 & 64-; del, Dem. State Conv, 46-68; del, Dem. Nat. Conv, 52; mem. cmt. hosp. costs, Dept. Health, Educ. and Welfare, Wash, D.C. and Dallas, Tex, 62-63; mem, Conn. Legis. Cmt, Ins. Costs, Hartford Conn, 65-67; mem, Gov. Cmt. Hosp. Costs, 65-67. Bus. & Prof. Pos: Owner, Pub. Acct. Firm, Carroll & Co, Meriden, Conn, 38-; pres. and chmn, Broad Manor, Inc, 49-64; chmn. region I, Am. Nursing Home Asn, 61-65; trustee, Mem. Hosp, 64-, chmn. bd. trustees, 64-66 & 68. Mem: Am. Asn. Acct; Nat. Soc. Pub. Acct; Conn. Asn. Pub. Acct; Elks. Mailing Add: 229 Cardinal Dr, Meriden, Conn. 06450.

CARROLL, GEORGE ARTHUR D
Chmn, York Co. Dem. Cmt, Maine
b. Limerick, Maine, 3/3/19; s. William Thomas Carroll and Mary Ann Fox C; m. 4/12/42 to Rita Rose Morin; c. Nancy Lee (Mrs. John H. Weeks), Arthur George and Anthony Robert. Educ: Limerick High Sch, grad; U.S. Army Tel. Carrier Sch, N.Africa; Ins. and Real Estate Courses. Polit. & Govt. Pos: Maine State Rep, 65-69, mem, Ways and Means Cmt, Maine House of Rep, 65-67 and Educ. Cmt, 65-69; mem, New Eng. Bd. Higher Educ, 67; chmn, York Co. Muskie for Pres. in 72 Cmt; chmn, York Co. Dem. Cmt, Maine, currently. Bus. & Prof. Pos: Owner and mgr, Alderwood Farm, 48-; owner, George A. Carroll Ins. and Real Estate Agency, 65-; chmn, Limerick Bd. of Appeals, 69. Mil. Serv: Entered as Pvt, Army, 41, released as 1st Lt, 48, after serv. in Fifth Army, 57th Signal Bd, European Theatre, 43-44; N.Africa and European Campaign Ribbons. Mem: New Eng. Milk Producers Asn; Holstein Friesian Asn. of Am; serv. officer, White-Tibbetts Post 55, DAV; Am. Legion; VFW. Amended Sinclair Law to Encourage Formation of More Sch. Dists; Named Maine Turnpike Gold Star Mem. Hwy. Rel: Catholic. Mailing Add: Elm St, Limerick, Maine 04048.

CARROLL, GEORGE FRANCIS D
Sgt-at-Arms, N.Y. Dem. State Cmt.
b. Corona, N.Y, 6/7/23; s. William H. Carroll, Sr. and Capitolia Greene C; m. 8/21/68 to Catherine L. Miles; c. Joann M. and George E. Educ: Flushing High Sch, 4 years. Polit. & Govt. Pos: Sgt-at-arms, N.Y. Dem. State Cmt, 58-, admin. asst. to chmn, 58-; del, Dem. Nat. Conv, 68. Mil. Serv: Entered as Pvt, Army, 41, released as Sgt, 45, after serv. in Corp. of Engrs; ETO, 43-45. Rel: Roman Catholic. Legal Res: 111-17 Northern Blvd, Apt. C2, Corona, N.Y. 11368. Mailing Add: New York Democratic State Committee, 150 E. 39th St, New York, N.Y. 10016.

CARROLL, HOWARD THOMAS D
Chmn, Albany Co. Dem. Cent. Cmt, Wyo.
b. Laramie, Wyo, 5/20/17; s. Thomas Francis Carroll and Gertrude Noxon C; m. 1/10/47 to Jean Satra; c. Teri and Lori. Educ: Univ. Wyo, B.S, 40; Sigma Alpha Epsilon. Polit. & Govt. Pos: Chmn, Albany Co. Dem. Cent. Cmt, Wyo, 67- Mil. Serv: Entered as 2nd Lt, Army, 40, released as Maj, 46, after serv. in Inf, Asiatic-Pac.Theater, 40-46. Mem: Am. Soc. Rural Appraisers; Elks; VFW; Am. Legion. Rel: Catholic. Mailing Add: 2103 Spring Creek Dr, Laramie, Wyo. 82070.

CARROLL, JAMES FRANCIS R
b. Baldwinsville, N.Y, 8/30/08; s. James F. Carroll and Alice King C; m. 10/3/31 to Helen Irene Gearhart. Educ: Syracuse Univ, B.S. in Journalism, 31; Albany Law Sch, LL.B, 36; Sigma Delta Chi; Pi Delta Epsilon; Justinian; Kappa Sigma. Polit. & Govt. Pos: Chief enforcement attorney, Off. Price Admin, Upstate, N.Y, 42-44; former chmn, Saratoga Co. Rep. Party. Bus. & Prof. Pos: Senior partner, Carroll & Amyot, 38- Mem: Saratoga Co. and N.Y. State Bar Asns; Am. Trial Lawyers; Elks. Rel: Roman Catholic. Mailing Add: 423 Broadway, Saratoga Springs, N.Y. 12866. (1967)

CARROLL, JANE IRENE D
V.chmn, Reno Co. Dem. Cent. Cmt, Kans.
b. Kinsley, Kans, 5/2/21; d. Francis Joseph Bishop and Etta Marie Tolley B; m. 10/5/41 to John Duane Carroll. Educ: Hutchinson Jr. Col, 1 semester. Polit. & Govt. Pos: Precinct committeewoman, Reno Twp, Dem. Party, Kans, 56-; secy, Reno. Co. Dem. Cent. Cmt, 58-60, 60-62 & 64-66 and v.chmn, 69-; secy, Fedn. Women's Dem. Club, 60-62; pres, Reno Co. Women's Dem. Study Club, 67-69. Bus. & Prof. Pos: Off. asst. to co. engr, Edwards Co, Kans, 39-41; machine operator, Cessna Aircraft Co, Wichita, 44-45; bookkeeping machine operator, Farmers & Merchants Life Ins. Co, 45-46; off. asst, Bassett Construction Co, 46-48; off. and lab. helper, Dr. Cramer Reed, 48-50. Mem: Am. Legion Auxiliary. Rel: Methodist. Mailing Add: 1718 W. Blanchard, Hutchinson, Kans. 67501.

CARROLL, JOHN SPENCER D
Colo. State Rep.
b. Boulder, Colo, 6/10/28; s. Earl T. Carroll and Sylvia Petrie C; m. 5/24/52 to Joan Appel; c. Marjorie Dianne, Barbara Lynn, Debra Hunt and John Edward. Educ: Univ. Colo, A.B, 50; Univ. Denver, LL.B, 52; Univ. Philippines, 52-53; Phi Alpha Delta. Polit. & Govt. Pos: Precinct committeeman, Colo, 50-51; mem, Colo. Dem. State Cent. Cmt, 50-51 & 65-; asst prog. officer, U.S. Agency for Int. Develop, 61-62; admin. asst. to Gov. of Colo, 62-63; hearing officer, Colo. Real Estate Cmn, 63-65; Colo. State Rep, 69- Bus. & Prof. Pos: Lawyer admitted to practice in Colo, 52 and Calif, 54. Mil. Serv: Entered as Pvt, Army, 46, released as Pfc, 48, after serv. in Fifth Inf. Div. Mem: Colo, Denver and Adams Co. Bar Asns; State Bar of Calif; Am. and Colo. Trial Lawyers Asns; Elks. Mailing Add: 7240 Newton St, Westminster, Colo. 80030.

CARROLL, JOHN W. R
Ill. State Sen.
b. Omemee, Ont; m. to Carole Weber; c. 2. Educ: Univ. Calif; Antheneo de Manila, Philippines; Sigma Delta Chi. Polti. & Govt. Pos: Mem, Maine Twp. Regional Rep. Orgn. and Maine Twp. Rep. Club, alderman, Park Ridge, Ill. and Ill. State Rep, 5 terms, formerly; Ill. State Sen, 66- Bus. & Prof. Pos: Pres. and publ, Pickwick Newspapers, Park Ridge. Mil. Serv: Army, 3 years. Mem: Ill. Press Asn.(past pres); C. of C; Kiwanis; Cook Co. Suburban Publ. Asn; Surburban Press Found; Elks; Chicago Press Club; VFW. Mailing Add: 29 Fairview, Park Ridge, Ill. 60068.

CARROLL, JULIAN MORTON D
Ky. State Rep.
b. Paducah, Ky, 4/16/31; s. Elvie Beeler Carroll and Eva Heady C; m.

7/22/51 to Charlann Harting; c. Kenneth Morton, Iva Patrice and Bradley Harting. Educ: Univ. Ky, A.B, 54, LL.B, 56; Phi Delta Phi. Polit. & Govt. Pos: Ky. State Rep, Third Dist, 62-, Speaker House of Rep, 68-; del, Dem. Nat. Conv, 68; trustee, Paducah Jr. Col, 69- Mil. Serv: Entered as 2nd Lt, Air Force, 56, released as 1st Lt, 59; Capt, Air Force Res, 62- Mem: Am. Bar Asn; Ky. Bar Asn; charter pres, Optimist Club, 61-62; Nat. Asn. of Home Builders; Ky. State Rep, Nat. Cmt. for Support Pub. Schs. Rel: Cumberland Presbyterian. Legal Res: Route 1, West Paducah, Ky. Mailing Add: 815-817 Citizens Bank Bldg, Paducah, Ky. 42001.

CARROLL, THOMAS CHARLES D
Chmn, Jefferson Co. Dem. Exec. Cmt, Ky.
b. Louisville, Ky, 9/1/21; s. Tarlton Combs Carroll and Irene Crutcher C; m. 4/23/59 to Julianne Kirk. Educ: Harvard Col, B.A, 42; Univ. Ky. Col. of Law, LL.B, 48; Phi Delta Phi; Hasty Pudding Club; Institute of 1770. Polit. & Govt. Pos: Nat. committeeman, Young Dem. Clubs Ky, 52-56, pres, 60-62; orgn. chmn, Dem. State Campaign, 62 & 64, campaign coordinator, 63; legal counsel, Ky. State Dem. Cent. Exec. Cmt; chmn, Jefferson Co. Dem. Exec. Cmt, currently; del, Dem. Nat. Conv, 68. Bus. & Prof. Pos: Attorney-at-law. Mil. Serv: Entered as Pvt, Army, 42, released as Capt, 46, after serv. in Sixth Army Group, ETO; Five Battle Stars. Mem: Am. Trial Lawyers Asn; Am, Ky. and Louisville Bar Asns; Pendennis Club; Louisville Boat Club; Harvard Club of NYC; Nat. Capital Dem. Club. Outstanding Lawyer Award, Ky. State Bar Asn, 57; Del, NATO Conf. in Europe, 61. Rel: Protestant. Legal Res: 1605 Evergreen Rd, Anchorage, Ky. 40223. Mailing Add: 1415 Kentucky Home Life Bldg, Louisville, Ky. 40202. (1967)

CARROLL, THOMAS JAY D
Wyo. State Rep.
b. Wheatland, Wyo, 6/22/24; s. Floyd Eugene Carroll and Grace Parks C; m. 6/21/47 to Vanda Johnson; c. Thomas J, III, Timothy M. and Patricia Ann. Educ: Moorehead State Teacher's Col, Minn; Univ. Wyo. Col. Law, J.D, 49; Sigma Alpha Epsilon. Polit. & Govt. Pos: Dem. precinct committeeman, Wyo, 50-60 & 68-69; pres, Wyo. Young Dem, 51-53; asst. co. and prosecuting attorney, Laramie Co, 57-59 and dep. co. and prosecuting attorney, 59-63; chmn, Laramie Co. Dem. Cent. Cmt, 65; Wyo. State Rep, 67-; munic. judge, Cheyenne, 68- Mil. Serv: Entered as Pvt, Army Air Force, 42, released as 1st Lt, 45, after serv. in 15th Air Force, Mediterranean Theatre, 44-45; ETO Campaign Ribbon with 7 Battle Stars; Air Medal with 3 Oak Leaf Clusters; Distinguished Flying Cross. Mem: Laramie Co, Wyo. and Am. Bar Asns; VFW; Moose; Elks; Am. Legion; K. of C. Rel: Catholic. Legal Res: 3625 Foxcroft Rd, Cheyenne, Wyo. 82001. Mailing Add: 219 E. 20th St, Cheyenne, Wyo. 82001.

CARROW, ROBERT DUANE D
b. Marshall, Minn, 2/5/34; s. Dr. Meddie Joseph Carrow and Estelle Marie Kough C; m. 9/2/60 to Jacqueline Mary Givens; c. Leslie, Tamara, Amelia, Vanessa and Creighton. Educ: Univ. Minn, B.A; Stanford Univ, LL.B; Ed, Minn. Law Rev; Phi Delta Phi. Polit. & Govt. Pos: City councilman, Novato, Calif, 63-64, mayor, 64-66; mem. exec. cmt, Calif. State Cent. Cmt, 59-68; past chmn, Marin Co. Dem. Cent. Cmt. Mil. Serv: Air Force, 58, hon. discharge, 64, after serv. in 349th TCW Res. Mem: Am. and Marin Co. Bar Asns; Am. and Calif. Trial Lawyers Asns; Jaycees; C. of C; Commonwealth Club; Am. Civil Liberties Union; Am. for Dem. Action. Novato Man of the Year, 65. Rel: Roman Catholic. Legal Res: 29 Truman Dr, Novato, Calif. 94947. Mailing Add: P.O. Box 623, Novato, Calif. 94947.

CARRUTH, GEORGE SIMMONS (DOC) D
Miss. State Rep.
b. Summit, Miss, 11/6/06; married. Polit. & Govt. Pos: Miss. State Rep, 52- Bus. & Prof. Pos: Employee, I.C.R.R. Mem: Masons; Shrine; Eastern Star; v.pres, Employ. Serv. Club, I.C.R.R. Rel: Methodist. Mailing Add: R.F.D, Summit, Miss. 39666. (1967)

CARRUTHERS, THOMAS G. R
Chmn, Vernon Rep. Town Cmt, Conn.
b. Worcester, Mass, 5/5/29; s. Thomas G. Carruthers and Maria Rodgers C; m. 2/14/52 to Sandy Marie Comtois; c. Thomas, Scott, Brian, Robert and Lori. Educ: Becker Col, A.S. in acct, 52; Univ. Hartford. Polit. & Govt. Pos: Pres, Young Rep. Club, Vernon, Conn, 61-62, mem. exec. cmt, 62-; treas, Vernon Bd. Educ, 61-64; chmn, Rep. Town Cmt. and mem, Bd. Rep, Vernon, currently. Bus. & Prof. Pos: Acct, Pratt & Whitney Aircraft Div, United Aircraft Corp, 53- Mil. Serv: Entered as Pvt, Air Force, 56, released as Cpl, 59, after serv. in 5th Air Force, Pac. Theatre. Mem: Mason; committeeman, Boy Scouts; bus. adv, Jr. Achievement; pres, Asn. of Informative TV, Inc. Rel: Congregational. Legal Res: 20 Lawler Rd, Vernon, Conn. 06086. Mailing Add: R.F.D. 3, Rockville, Conn. 06066.

CARSON, HOWARD W. D
b. Montgomery, W.Va, 4/30/10; s. Lawrence W. Carson and Alice Montgomery C; m. 11/22/39 to Sunny N. Hill; c. Linda Lee, John Montgomery. Educ: Washington & Lee Univ, A.B, 31, LL.B, 33; Lambda Chi Alpha; Phi Alpha Delta. Polit. & Govt. Pos: Former prosecuting attorney, Fayette Co; former chmn, Fayette Co. Dem. Exec. Cmt; W.Va. State Sen, 56-68, pres, W.Va. State Senate, 55th-57th legis. Bus. & Prof. Pos: Lawyer. Mem: Mason; Moose; Lions; W.Va. and Fayette Co. Bar Asns; W.Va. State Bar. Rel: Methodist. Mailing Add: Fayetteville, W.Va. 25840. (1967)

CARSON, JAMES H, JR. R
N.C. State Rep.
b. Charlotte, N.C, 1935; m. to Beverly; c. Page L, Susanna R, Christina K. Educ: Univ. N.C, B.A, 60, LL.B, 63. Polit. & Govt. Pos: N.C. State Rep, 67- Bus. & Prof. Pos: Partner, Carson & Schwartz, law firm. Mil. Serv: Fighter Pilot, Navy, 5 years active duty; Lt. Cmdr, Naval Res. Mem: C. of C; Jaycee; Kiwanis; Res. Officers Asn. Rel: Presbyterian. Mailing Add: 419 Ellsworth Rd, Charlotte, N.C. 28211. (1967)

CARSON, ROBERT TREBOR R
Hon. Life Chmn, Hawaii Rep. Party
b. Butte, Mont, 12/17/10; s. Robert Stephen Carson and Ethel Jones C; single. Educ: Univ. Calif, 28-29; Stanford Univ, 31-32. Polit. & Govt. Pos: Has held every off. in Rep. Party of Hawaii, was chmn, 44-52 and is now hon. life chmn, Hawaii Rep. Party; campaigner in 36 states for Thomas E. Dewey, 47; mem, Territorial Grand Jury, 49; dir, Fed. Housing Admin, Hawaii and Guam, 54-57; mem. land cmt, Hawaii House of Rep, 59 and Hawaii Senate 59-60; campaigner, West. States, Nixon for Pres, 60 and Calif, Nixon for Gov, 62; admin. asst. to U.S. Sen. Hiram L. Fong, 60- Bus. & Prof. Pos: Newspaperman, Hearst Papers and Honolulu Advertiser, sports announcer and news commentator, NBC and Hawaii Sta. KGU, and for. and war correspondent, 38-49; investment banker, pres, Honolulu Stock Exchange and exec. secy, Honolulu Auto Dealers Asn, 49-54; asst. to Henry J. Kaiser, gen. mgr. of Kaiser TV & Radio Network, 57-58; pres, Distributors of Hawaii, 58-61; chmn. bd, Pan Pac. House, 59-61. Mem: Waialae Country Club; Mason (32°); Shrine (past potentate, Aloha Temple, Hawaii); pres, U.S. Asn. Admin. Assts; U.S. Senate Staff Club; Cong. Secretaries; Nat. Press Club; Elks; hon. life mem. of 148 Shrine Temples in U.S, Can. and Mex. Played first baseman, Pac. Coast League, Sacramento, Calif. Legal Res: P.O. Box 1872, Honolulu, Hawaii. 96805. Mailing Add: 1313 New Senate Office Bldg, Washington, D.C. 20510.

CARSON, WALLACE P, JR. R
Ore. State Rep.
b. Salem, Ore, 6/10/34; s. Wallace P. Carson and Edith Bragg C; m. 6/24/56 to Gloria Stolk; c. Wallace Scott, Carol Elizabeth and Steven Bruce. Educ: Stanford Univ, B.A, 56; Willamette Univ. Law Sch, J.D, 62; Phi Delta Theta; Delta Theta Phi. Polit. & Govt. Pos: Mem, Ore. Rep. State Cent. Cmt, 65-67; Ore. State Rep, 67-, majority leader, 69- Bus. & Prof. Pos: Attorney, Carson, Carson & Carson, Salem, 62- Mil. Serv: Entered as 2nd Lt, Air Force, 56, released as 1st Lt, 59, after serv. in Korea and Far East as Jet Pilot; Capt, Air Force Res, 59- Publ: Writ of Mandamus, Legal Educ. Series, Ore. State Bar, 64; 'Speed at Some Distance from the Scene—Twilight Zone of Admissible Evidence,' Willamette Law J, 61. Mem: Marion Co. Bar Asn. (secy-treas, 65-68); Ore. State Bar Asn.(standards and admissions cmt, 63-66); Am. Bar Asn. Comdr. Trophy, Air Force Flight Sch, 56; Distinguished Serv. Award, Salem Jaycees, 68; one of five, Ore. Outstanding Young Man of the Year, 68. Rel: Episcopal. Mailing Add: 1309 Hillendale Dr. S.E, Salem, Ore. 97302.

CARSTEN, ARLENE DESMET D
Mem, Calif. Dem. State Cent. Cmt.
b. Paterson, N.J, 12/5/37; d. Albert F. Desmet and Ann Greutert D; m. 2/11/56 to Alfred John Carsten; c. Christopher Dale and Jonathan Glenn. Educ: Alfred Univ, 55-56; Univ. Calif. Exten. Courses. Polit. & Govt. Pos: V.pres, San Dieguito Dem. Club, 65-67, treas, 69; 80th Assembly Dist. Rep, Calif. Dem. Coun, 67-69; chmn, San Diego North Co. McCarthy Write-In Campaign, 68; mem, San Diego McCarthy for President Campaign Cmt, 68; mem, Calif. Dem. State Cent. Cmt, 68-; mem. exec. cmt, Unruh for Gov, currently. Bus. & Prof. Pos: Piano teacher, 65- Mem: Women's Int. League for Peace and Freedom, San Diego-La Jolla Chap.(bd. mem); Active Citizens for Racial Equality (bd. mem); Am. Civil Liberties Union; Del Mar Citizens Cmt. for Effective Long-term Sewage Disposal; chmn, Ad Hoc Citizens Cmt. Against the War in Vietnam, 67-68; San Diego Cmt. for a Coalition. Key Woman Award, 68. Rel: Ethical Culture. Mailing Add: 1415 Via Alta, Del Mar, Calif. 92014.

CARSTENSEN, HELENE SIMSON R
Secy, Melrose City Rep. Cmt, Mass.
b. Winthrop, Mass, 12/19/02; d. Fredrick William Simson and Margaret Ethel Douglas S; m. 11/13/26 to Deane Winthrop Carstensen; c. Deane Winthrop, Jr. Educ: Winthrop Pub. Schs; Boston Univ. eve. courses. Polit. & Govt. Pos: Pres. and press correspondent, Melrose Women's Rep. Club, Mass; del, Mass. Rep. Conv; alternate del, Rep. Nat. Conv, 64; former finance chmn, Melrose Rep. City Cmt, secy, currently. Bus. & Prof. Pos: Mem, Am. Trust Co. and United Fruit Co, Boston, Mass. Mem: DAR; Melrose Women's Club (past pres); Melrose Highlands Drama Club. Rel: Methodist. Mailing Add: 110 Woodcrest Drive, Melrose, Mass. 02176.

CARSWELL, CATHERINE IDELLA D
b. Brighton, Mass, 12/7/22; d. John Russell Forbes and Gertrude Stack F; m. 4/5/63 to Charles Gordon Carswell. Polit. & Govt. Pos: Maine State Rep, 57-68. Mem: Maine Cosmetologist Asn; Portland League of Women Voters; Nat. Order of Women Legis; Pineland Parents and Friends Asn; Portland Bus. and Prfnl. Womens Club; Maine Coun. of Social Agencies; Friends of the Blind. Rel: Roman Catholic. Mailing Add: 26 Panoramic View Dr, Portland, Maine 04103. (1967)

CARTAN, GLORIA HARRISON D
Committeewoman, Idaho Dem. Party
b. Helena, Mont, 9/9/31; d. Henry T. Harrison and Eva Milliron H; m. 7/9/55 to Dr. Frederick Owen Cartan; c. John F. and Joan K. Educ: Mont. State Univ, B.S. in Chem, 52; Alpha Lambda Delta; Spurs; Mortar Bd; Kappa Delta. Polit. & Govt. Pos: Precinct committeeman, Bonneville Co. Dem. Cent. Cmt, Idaho, 66, v.chairwoman, 67; alternate del, Dem. Nat. Conv, 68; state committeewoman, Idaho Dem. Party, 68- Bus. & Prof. Pos: Chemist, Vet. Admin. Hosp, Ft. Harrison, Mont, 52-53; chemist, Phillips Petroleum Co, Nat. Reactor Testing Sta, Idaho, 53-55; chemist, Vet. Research, Mont. State Univ, 55-58. Publ: 'A Succinoxidase Inhibitor in Feeds Associated with Muscular Dystrophy in Lambs and Calves,' Am. J. Vet. Research, 3/59. Mem: Sigma Xi; League Women Voters. Rel: Unitarian. Mailing Add: 787 Sonja Ave, Idaho Falls, Idaho 83401.

CARTER, ABE PARKER R
Chmn, Monroe County Rep. Exec. Cmt, Ky.
b. Tompkinsville, Ky, 12/11/07; s. James Clark Carter, Sr. and Idru Tucker; m. 6/12/31 to Evelyn Evans, wid; c. James Evans, M.D, Rebecca (Mrs. Nevius) and Jack Parker. Educ: Western Ky. State Teachers Col, 28-31; Cumberland Univ. Col. of Law, LL.B, 32; Jefferson Sch. of Law, LL.B, 33. Polit. & Govt. Pos: Co. treas, Monroe Co, Ky, 32-35, sheriff, 36-42, judge, 42-46 and co. attorney, 46-; chmn, Monroe Co. Rep. Exec. Cmt, 60- Mem: Mason; F&AM; Ky. State and Am. Bar Asns. Rel: Baptist. Mailing Add: 602 Idru St, Tompkinsville, Ky. 42167.

CARTER, ALLEN H. R
b. Athens, Tenn, 6/26/38; s. L.A. Carter, Jr. and Sue Humphreys C; m. 7/9/67 to Valerie Foster. Educ: Univ. Ga; Univ. Tenn, B.S. and LL.B; Phi

Delta Phi; Sigma Chi. Polit. & Govt. Pos: Chmn. cmt, Bill Brock for Cong, 62-64; chmn, McMinn Co. Rep. Exec. Cmt, 63-66 and McMinn Co. Cmnrs. of Elec; chmn, Howard Baker for U.S. Senate, 64 & 66. Mil. Serv: Entered as Airman, Air Force, 63, released as Sgt, 69, after serv. in 134th Air Refueling Group, Tenn. Air Nat. Guard, 63-69. Mem: McMinn Co. Bar Asn.(secy, 64-65, v.pres, 65-66); C. of C.(bd. dirs, 65-66, 68-69); Am. Legion; Am. and Tenn. Bar Asns; Kiwanis. Rel: Baptist. Legal Res: Madison Ave, Athens, Tenn. 37303. Mailing Add: P.O. Box 6, Athens, Tenn. 37303.

CARTER, ANDERSON R
b. Roswell, N.Mex, 10/10/26; s. Powhatan Carter and Effie Anderson C; m. 7/30/49 to Gerldine Mador; c. Anderson, II, Stuart and Cassius. Educ: Tex. Christian Univ, 3 years; East. N.Mex. Univ, B.A. in econ, 50; Student Body pres, 50. Polit. & Govt. Pos: N.Mex. State Rep, Roosevelt Co, 53-60, creator and 1st chmn, Legis. Finance Cmt, N.Mex. House of Rep; state co-ordinator, State Rep. Party, N.Mex, 62-64; cand. for U.S. Sen, N.Mex, 66; del, Rep. Nat. Conv, 68. Bus. & Prof. Pos: Rancher; oil, wholesale food and investment interests. Mil. Serv: Navy, 44-47. Mem: Cattlegrowers Asn; Mason; Shrine. Rel: Church of Christ. Mailing Add: P.O. Box 725, Lovington, N.Mex. 88260. (1967)

CARTER, CHARLES HILL, JR. D
Chmn, Charles Dem. City Cmt, Va.
b. Charles City, Va, 8/16/19; s. Charles Hill Carter and Emily Harrison C; m. 8/4/60 to Helle Margarethe Klingemann; c. Charles Hill, Robert Randolph and Harriet Emily. Educ: Va. Polytech. Inst, B.S, 43. Polit. & Govt. Pos: Chmn, Charles City Bd. Supv, Va, 52-; chmn, Charles Dem. City Cmt, 58-Mil. Serv: Army, 43, serv. in OCS Anti Aircraft. Rel: Episcopal. Mailing Add: Shirley Plantation, Charles City, Va. 23030.

CARTER, CHESTER CHARLES
Mem, President's Cmt. on UN
b. Emporia, Kans, 2/14/21; s. Chester Charles Carter and Mary Lenore Johnson C; m. 3/9/56 to Claudia June Bernard; c. Chester Charles, Marise Sue and Carol Jill. Educ: Univ. South. Calif, A.B, 49 and M.A, 52; Loyola Univ, LL.B, 58; Skull and Dagger; Blue Key; Kappa Alpha Psi. Polit. & Govt. Pos: Dir, Peace Corps, Africa, 62-63; dep. asst. secy, Dept. of State, 63-64, dep. chief of protocol, 64-; mem, President's Cmt. on UN, 64- Bus. & Prof. Pos: Asst. dir, Los Angeles Bur. Charities, 55-56; probation officer, Los Angeles Co. Court, 56-60; juvenile referee, Los Angeles Co. Superior Court, 60-62. Mil. Serv: 2nd Lt, Army, 42-46, 1st Lt, 50-52. Mem: For. Serv. Asn. Legal Res: 1360 Fourth St. S.W, Washington, D.C. 20024. Mailing Add: Dept. of State, 2100 C St. N.W, Washington, D.C. 20024. (1967)

CARTER, CLAYTON D
b. Sec, Ala, 9/25/23; s. Ulysses Erskine Carter and Nell Rowe C; m. 9/13/47 to Victoria Lynn Podobed; c. Clayton, Jr, Janice Lynn and Charles David. Educ: South. Methodist Univ, 52. Polit. & Govt. Pos: Ala. State Sen, 66; mayor pro tem, Guntersville City Coun, Ala, 68- Bus. & Prof. Pos: Agent, State Farm Ins. Mil. Serv: Navy, Pharmacist Mate, 43-47. Mem: Mason; Shrine. Rel: Baptist. Mailing Add: P.O. Box 519, Guntersville, Ala. 35976.

CARTER, DONALD VICTOR D
Maine State Rep.
b. Waterville, Maine, 11/1/27; s. Fred Carter and Mabel Montminy C; m. 5/30/53 to Wilma Siegmann; c. Linda, Doreen, Donald V, Jr. and Lee. Educ: Univ. Md, Overseas Br; Univ. Maine; Colby Col, B.A. in hist. Polit. & Govt. Pos: Admin. asst, Dept. of Army in Europe, 48-53: first selectman and chmn. bd. of selectmen, Assessors and Overseer of the Poor, 63-64; chmn, Winslow High Sch. Bldg. Cmt, 64; chmn, Winslow Dem. Town Cmt, 64-68; Maine State Sen, Kennebec Co, 65-66; councilman, Winslow, 69-; Maine State Rep, 69- Bus. & Prof. Pos: Proprietor, Donald V. Carter Ins. Agency, 66- Mil. Serv: Entered as Pvt, Army, 45, released as S/Sgt, 48, after serv. in ETO. Mem: Winslow Sportman's Asn; McCrillis-Rousseau Post 8835; Messalonskee Fish and Game Club. Rel: Roman Catholic. Legal Res: 7 Baker St, Winslow, Maine 04901. Mailing Add: P.O. Box 544, Waterville, Maine 04901.

CARTER, ERNEST RAWLS R
Chmn, Bertie Co. Rep. Cmt, N.C.
b. Ahoskie, N.C, 9/1/27; s. Ernest Randolph Carter and Lucie Tayloe C; m. 8/19/56 to Rebecca Edwards; c. Jennifer Kay and Ernest, Jr. Educ: Louisburg Jr. Col; Univ. of N.C; Phi Theta Kappa. Polit. & Govt. Pos: Mem, Powellsville Govt. Town Cmt, 58-66; Chmn, Bertie Co. Rep. Cmt, N.C, 66- Bus. & Prof. Pos: Owner and Partner, E.R. Carter & Son, 50-66. Mil. Serv: Entered as Pvt, Army, 45, released as Cpl, 47, after serv. in Inf; Good Conduct and Victory Medals. Mem: Vol. Fire Chief; Lions. Rel: Methodist. Mailing Add: Box 33, Powellsville, N.C. 27967. (1967)

CARTER, FRANK R
Chmn, Miss. Co. Rep. Cmt, Mo.
b. Emmett, Ark, 2/9/13; s. A.R. Carter and Rena Fennema C; div; c. Ronald. Educ: High Sch. Polit. & Govt. Pos: Mayor, East Prairie, Mo, 57-63; mem, Mo. Rep. State Cmt, Tenth Dist; chmn, Miss. Co. Rep. Cmt, currently. Bus. & Prof. Pos: Self-employed, 44-66; Salesman, Ohio Valley Supply Co, Paducah, Ky, 66- Rel: Christian Church N.Am. Mailing Add: 312 N. Garfield, East Prairie, Mo. 63845. (1967)

CARTER, HALBERT L, JR. R
Tenn. State Rep.
b. McLemoresville, Tenn, 11/21/33; s. Halbert L. Carter, Sr. and Virginia Hillsman C; m. 3/3/62 to Margaret Winchester Heiskell; c. John Heiskell and James Reddick. Educ: Univ. Tenn, B.S, 58; Sigma Chi. Polit. & Govt. Pos: Tenn. State Rep, 65-, chmn, State and Local Govt. Cmt, Tenn. House or Rep. and v.chmn, Cmt. Calendar and Rules, 69-70; exec. dir, Huntingdon Housing Authority, 66; chmn, Rep. Legis. Campaign Cmt, Tenn. Rep. Party and legis. coordinator, Nixon-Agnew Campaign, 68. Bus. & Prof. Pos: Gen. mgr, H.L. Carter & Son, 60-65. Mil. Serv: Entered as Pvt. E-1, Army, 54, released as Specialist 3/C, after serv. in Spec. Detachment, Ammunition Renovation, Third Army, Ft. Campbell, Ky. Mem: Jaycees; Elks; Am. Legion; C. of C. Rel: Methodist. Mailing Add: 292 E. Paris St, Huntingdon, Tenn. 38344.

CARTER, HARVEY D, JR. R
Vt. State Rep.
b. N.Y.C, 11/2/38; s. Harvey D. Carter and Susan J. Stiles C; m. 5/5/62 to Gertrude Cleave; c. Harvey D, III and H. Cleave. Educ: Williams Col, B.A, 60; Duke Univ. Law Sch, LL.B, 63; Delta Sigma Rho; Chi Psi. Polit. & Govt. Pos: Secy, Bennington Co. Regional Planning Cmn, Vt, 65-; staff attorney, Vt. Legal Aid, 67-68; trustee, Bennington-Rutland Opportunity Coun, 68-; Vt. State Rep, 69- Bus. & Prof. Pos: Partner, Williams, Witten & Carter. Mem: Bennington Co. Bar Asn.(secy-treas, 66-68); Vt. and Am. Bar Asns. Rel: Episcopal. Legal Res: R.D, Pownal, Vt. 05261. Mailing Add: P.O. Box 350, Bennington, Vt. 05201.

CARTER, J. C. R
Ky. State Sen.
b. Bowling Green, Ky, 7/26/23; s. Charles Matthew Carter, Sr. and Lassie Steen C; m. 1/10/47 to Evelyn Mitchell; c. Jennifer M.(Mrs. Emery), Joan and Jeffrey. Educ: Univ. Tenn, 1 year; Reppert Auction Sch, 1 year. Polit. & Govt. Pos: Ky. State Sen, Ninth Dist, 68- Bus. & Prof. Pos: Life partner, Carter Realty Auction Co; partner, Carter Motels, 15 years; owner, Carter Motor Co, 20 years, Carter Hardware Stores, 22 years, Carter Ins. Agency, 10 years. Mil. Serv: Entered as Pvt, Army, 43, released as Pfc, 46, after serv. in Field Artil. Mem: Rotary. Ky. Jaycees Outstanding Young Man, 56. Rel: Methodist. Legal Res: Route 1, Scottsville, Ky. 42164. Mailing Add: Carter Realty Auction Co, Carter Bldg, S. Court St, Scottsville, Ky. 42164.

CARTER, JAMES EARL, JR. D
b. Plains, Ga, 10/1/24; s. James Earl Carter and Lillian Gordy C; m. 7/7/46 to Rosalynn Smith; c. John William, James Earl, III, D. Jeffrey and Amy Lynn. Educ: Ga. Southwest. Col, 41-42; Ga. Tech, 42-43; U.S. Naval Acad, grad, 47; postgrad. work nuclear physics, Union Col. Polit. & Govt. Pos: Chmn, Am. & Sumter Co. Hosp. Authority, Ga; chmn, Sumter Co. Bd. Educ, 55-62 and W.Cent. Ga. Area Planning and Develop. Cmn, 64; Ga. State Sen, 63-66. Bus. & Prof. Pos: Pres, Plains Develop. Corp. and Sumter Redevelop. Corp, 63; Ga. Crop Improv. Asn. and Ga. Planning Asn, 68-69. Mil. Serv: Naval Officer until 54; resigned as Lt.(sg). Mem: Lions Int.(dist. gov, 68-69). Rel: Baptist. Mailing Add: Plains, Ga. 31780.

CARTER, JAMES REECE D
Tenn. State Rep.
b. Johnson City, Tenn, 6/16/34; s. Walter Floyd Carter and Margaret Price C; m. 2/14/58 to Juanita Cox; c. James R, Jr, Evelyn Renee and Angelia Kay. Educ: Univ. Tenn, B.S, 58, LL.B, 61; Omicron Delta Kappa; Phi Sigma Kappa. Polit. & Govt. Pos: Mem. exec. cmt, Wash. Co. Dem. Exec. Cmt, Tenn; Tenn. State Rep, 63-; del, Dem. Nat. Conv, 68. Mil. Serv: Entered as 2nd Lt, Army, 58, released as 1st Lt, 60, after serv. in 521st Mil. Police Co, Ft. Belvoir, Va. Mem: Elks. Rel: Presbyterian. Legal Res: 1706 Sunnyview Circle, Johnson City, Tenn. 37602. Mailing Add: 500 Professional Bldg, Johnson City, Tenn. 37601.

CARTER, JAMES Y. D
Ill. State Rep.
b. Raleigh, N.C, 4/20/15; m. to Beatrice Turner; c. Christine, Maudette. Educ: Hampton Inst; Bates Col, A.B, 36; Boston Univ, M.A, 37, LL.B, 40. Polit. & Govt. Pos: Mem, Bd. Local Improv, Chicago, Ill; mem, Hearing Referee Dept. Revenue, 48-52; cmnr, Pub. Motor Vehicles License; Ill. State Rep, currently; alternate del, Dem. Nat. Conv, 68. Bus. & Prof. Pos: Lawyer; Instr. law, N.C. Col, 40-42. Mil. Serv: Air Force Cadet, 42; Air Force, pilot, 43; Oper. Officer, 302nd Fighter Squadron and 332nd Fighter Group, 43; Command Officer, 618th Bomb Squadron, 477th Bomber Group; Relieved active duty, 45. Mem: N.C. Bar Asn; Ill. Bar, 46. Mailing Add: 601 E. 32nd St, Chicago, Ill. 60616. (1967)

CARTER, JOHN ROBERT, JR. D
b. Conway, S.C, 1/31/24; s. John Robert Carter, Sr. and Lula Hardwick C; m. 12/25/42 to Willie Hardee; c. James R, Judy and Deborah. Educ: Loris High Sch, S.C, grad. 42. Polit. & Govt. Pos: S.C. State Rep, 57-60 & 65-66; mem, S.C. Hwy. Cmn, 66-69, chmn, 69-; off. mgr, U.S. Rep. John L. McMillan, 68- Mem: Mason (past master, Lodge 205); Kiwanis. Community Leaders of Am. Award, 68; Intracoastal Waterway Bridge on Hwy. 17 to be dedicated in my honor when completed. Rel: Baptist. Mailing Add: Route 1, Longs, S.C. 29568.

CARTER, MALCOLM M. R
N.H. State Rep.
b. Concord, Mass, 9/27/18; married; c. Four. Educ: Milford & Stearn's Prep. Polit. & Govt. Pos: Selectman, Milford, N.H, 6 years; Chmn. of Bd, 2 years; N.H. State Rep, 63- Bus. & Prof. Pos: Proprietor & oper, Carter's Mobil Serv. Station; former sales rep, Quaker Oats Co. Mem: F&AM. Rel: Unitarian. Mailing Add: Jennison Rd, Milford, N.H. 03055. (1967)

CARTER, MARIAN ELIZABETH R
Mem, Colo. Rep. State Cent. Cmt.
b. Greatbend, Kans, 6/14/35; d. Clarence John Glantz and Ella Bartel G; m. 12/26/57 to J. Braxton Carter; c. J. Braxton, II, David Brian and Carol Elizabeth. Educ: Univ. Colo, B.A, 57; Colo. State Univ, 57-58; Kappa Delta. Polit. & Govt. Pos: V.chmn, El Paso Co. Young Rep, Colo, 66; Rep. precinct committeewoman, El Paso Co, 66 & 68; dir, Third Cong. Dist. Young Rep. League of Colo, 67; secy, Young Rep. League of Colo, 67, Rep. State Representative Dist. 19, 67 & 69; del, Rep. State Conv. and Third Cong. Dist. Conv, 68; pub. trustee, El Paso Co, 69-; mem, Colo. Rep. State Cent. Cmt, El Paso Co, 69- Bus. & Prof. Pos: With Pub. Rels. Dept, Ill. Inst. Technol, 57-58. Mem: Eastern Star; Rep. Women's Roundtable; Young Rep; Assistance Guild of Colorado Springs. Rel: Protestant. Mailing Add: 2521 N. Chelton Rd, Colorado Springs, Colo. 80909.

CARTER, MICHAEL LAVERNE R
Chmn, Lapeer Co. Rep. Party, Mich.
b. Flint, Mich, 6/8/39; s. Laverne Cecil Carter and Agnes Mary Fosdick; m. 11/3/56 to Jan Lee Traver; c. Lisa Anne and Barry Gene. Educ: Gen. Motors Inst, B.M.E, 62; Univ. Mich, LL.B, 66; Phi Sigma Phi; Phi Alpha Delta. Polit. & Govt. Pos: Alternate del, Rep. Nat. Conv, 68; chmn, Lapeer

Co. Rep. Party, 69- Bus. & Prof. Pos: Engr, Buick Motor Div, Gen. Motors Corp, Flint, Mich, 62-64; attorney, Taylor & Carter, Lapeer, Mich, 67- Mem: Am. and Mich. Bar Asns; 40th Judicial Bar Asn; Rotary Int. Rel: Episcopal. Mailing Add: 1488 W. Genesee St, Lapeer, Mich. 48446.

CARTER, PAUL THOMAS R
Del, Calif. Rep. State Cent. Cmt.
b. Gladstone, Mich, 2/7/22; s. Fred J. Carter and Elizabeth Richards C; m. to Majel Louise Wheeler; c. Candace J, Christine Janos, David and Douglas Beach. Educ: Mich. State Univ. Sch. Bus, B.B.A; Univ. South. Calif. Col. Commerce, grad. with honor; N.Am. Ins. Schs, grad; Home Off. Sch. for exec. spec. agent training, Phila, Pa, grad. ranking first, nationwide; Blue Key, Nat. Scholastic Hon. Polit. & Govt. Pos: Del, Calif. Rep. State Cent. Cmt, 69- Bus. & Prof. Pos: Rate clerk, underwriter and spec. agent, Ins. Co. of N.Am, Los Angeles; mgr, San Diego Serv. Off, N.Am. Group and Northwest Serv. Off, N.Am, Portland, Ore; partner, Cosgrove & Dunn Ins. Agency and Cosgrove, Dunn, Carter and Higgins, San Diego, Calif; pres, Carter and Higgins of Calif. Inc, San Diego, San Diego Ins. Corp, and Borrego Valley Ins. Inc, currently. Mil. Serv: Artil. Officer, Army, World War II and Korean Conflict, with serv. in Ital. Campaign, Tenth Mt. Div. and U.S. Counterintel. Corps, Ft. Holibird, Md; Bronze Star for Meritorious Serv. Mem: Former dir, Pac. Homes Corp, Los Angeles and Cmn. on World Serv. and Finance; Lions Int. (past pres); Gr. San Diego Sports Asn.(past pres); dir. bd. of gov, Calif. Brokers Asn; chmn, All Am. Stadium, Inc; bd. dirs, San Diego Stadium Authority; v.pres, Ins. Brokers Asn. of Calif. and Nat. Surety Bond Asn. Rel: Methodist; past chmn. off. bd, Methodist Church, La Mesa. Mailing Add: 5181 Mt. Helix Dr, La Mesa, Calif. 92041.

CARTER, PHILLIP LEROY D
Mem, Calif. Dem. State Cent. Cmt.
b. Oak Park, Ill, 7/11/32; s. Ralph Waldo Carter and Ruth Jones C; m. 6/18/59 to Patricia Kerns; c. Cassandra, Ethan and Leah. Educ: Northwest. Univ, B.S, 54; Univ. Calif, Los Angeles, M.S.W, 58. Polit. & Govt. Pos: Supvr, Calif. Youth Authority, Los Angeles, 60-66; dir, State Serv. Center, Venice, Calif, 66-68; mem, Calif. Dem. State Cent. Cmt, 68-; app. by Los Angeles City Coun. to Los Angeles Human Rels. Adv. Cmt. Bus. & Prof. Pos: Dir. urban progs, Commonwealth United Corp, Beverly Hills, 68- Mil. Serv: Entered as 2nd Lt, Marines, 54, released as Capt, 64, Res. Mem: Nat. Asn. Soc. Workers; bd. of dirs, Santa Monica, Calif. Family Serv. Asn; Venice Health Coun. Off. Econ. Opportunity Urban Affairs Award; West Los Angeles Welfare Planning Coun. Award. Rel: Methodist. Mailing Add: 1344 Glenavon Ave, Venice, Calif. 90291.

CARTER, RALPH C. D
b. Geneva, Ala, 6/25/32; m. 7/25/54 to Joyce Howard; c. Ralph, Jr. and Angela Marie. Educ: Chipola Jr. Col; Univ. Fla. Polit. & Govt. Pos: Fla. State Rep, 60-66; past chmn, Dist. One Welfare Bd. Bus. & Prof. Pos: Livestock farmer; pecan grower; bd. dirs. and past pres, Wash. Co. Rural Area Develop. Coun. Mem: Wash. Co. Farm Bur; bd. dirs, Wash. Co. Sportsman's Club; Cattlemen's Asn. Rel: Presbyterian, Bd. of Deacons. Mailing Add: Chipley, Fla. 32428. (1967)

CARTER, REX LYLE D
S.C. State Rep.
b. Honea Path, S.C, 6/20/25; s. D.B. Carter and Eunice Y. Carter C; m. 11/26/55 to Lucy Florida Gulledge; c. Lucy Coulter and Kimberly Lyle. Educ: Erskine Col, A.B, 50; Univ. S.C, LL.B, 52; Exchequer, Phi Delta Phi; Omicron Delta Kappa; pres, Law Sch. Student Body. Polit. & Govt. Pos: S.C. State Rep, 53-, Speaker, S.C. State House of Rep, 57- Bus. & Prof. Pos: Lawyer, Carter & Hill. Mil. Serv: Coast Guard, 43-46, serv. in Atlantic & Pac. Theatre. Mem: Pres, Int. Rels. Club; pres, Philomathean Lit. Soc. Mailing Add: 123 Broadus Ave, Greenville, S.C. 29601. (1967)

CARTER, ROBERT THOMAS D
b. Cleveland, Ohio, 3/21/38; s. John Bennet Carter and Theresa V. Rowell C; single. Educ: Baldwin-Wallace Col, B.A, 59; Univ. Calif, Los Angeles, Cand. Prfnl. Cert; Lettermans Club; Student Coun. Polit. & Govt. Pos: Del, Dem. Nat. Conv, 68. Bus. & Prof. Pos: Teacher, Cleveland Pub. Sch. Syst, Ohio, 59-64; sales, Shell Oil Co, Long Beach, Calif, 64-66; sales, Hoffman-LaRoche, Nutley, N.J, 66-68; sales exec, KFI Radio Sta, Los Angeles, Calif, 68- Mem: New Frontier Dem. Club; Martha Jennings Found. Teaching Award. Rel: Protestant. Mailing Add: 4431 Don Ricardo Dr, No. 3, Los Angeles, Calif. 90008.

CARTER, TIM LEE R
U.S. Rep, Ky.
b. Tompkinsville, Ky, 9/2/10; s. James Clark and Idru Tucker C; m. 11/15/31 to Kathleen Bradshaw; c. William Starr. Educ: West. Ky. Univ, A.B, 34; Univ. Tenn. Sch. Med, M.D, 37; Alpha Omega Alpha. Polit. & Govt. Pos: Chmn, Monroe Co. Rep. Exec. Cmt, 52-64; U.S. Rep, Ky, 65-; alternate del, Rep. Nat. Conv, 68. Bus. & Prof. Pos: Chief of Staff, War Mem. Hosp, 53-57. Mil. Serv: Entered as 1st Lt, Army, released as Capt, 45, after serv. in 38th Inf. Div, Southwest Pac. Theater; Combat Medic Badge; Bronze Star Medal. Mem: Ky. Med. Asn; Ky. Acad. Gen. Practice; Am. Med. Asn; Am. Acad. Gen. Practice; Farm Bur; VFW; Am. Legion; Amvets. Rel: Baptist. Legal Res: 701 N. Main St, Tompkinsville, Ky. 42167. Mailing Add: 1202 Longworth Office Bldg, Washington, D.C. 20515.

CARTER, TOM M, SR. R
Mo. State Rep.
b. Hartville, Mo, 12/29/10; m. 1954 to Naomi Davis Meador; c. Tom M, Jr. Educ: Southwest Mo. State Col, B.S, 36; Univ. Mo, M.A, 43. Polit. & Govt. Pos: Mo. State Rep, 64-; mem, Hartville City Coun, 8 years. Bus. & Prof. Pos: Teacher, 29-47; supt. sch, Cassville, Mo, 45-47; owner, mgr, operator, auto agency, 47- Mem: Hartville Indust. Develop. Corp; C. of C; Mason; Coun. Chap. and Comdr, Abou Ben Adhem Temple. Rel: Christian Disciples of Christ; Elder, mem, Bd. Trustees, secy-treas, Christian Disciples of Christ Church; mem, Drury Col. Bd. of Rel. Mailing Add: Hartville, Mo. 65667.

CARTER, VINCENT R
b. St. Clair, Pa, 11/6/91; s. William J. Carter and Julia Ann Clarke C; m. 1921 to Helen Carlson (deceased); m. Aug, 1929 to Mary Crowley; c. James (deceased), Helen, Jerome and Roch. Educ: Cath. Univ; Fordham Univ. Polit. & Govt. Pos: Dep. Attorney Gen, Wyo, 19-23; State Auditor and State Purchasing Agent, 23-29; mem, Bd. Charities and Reform, 23-29; U.S. Rep, 29-35; Rep. nominee for U.S. Senate, 34. Bus. & Prof. Pos: Attorney-at-law, Casper, Wyo; retired. Mil. Serv: Lt, Marine Corps, World War I. Mem: Am. Legion; Elks. Mailing Add: 1331 Park Ave. S.W, Albuquerque, N.Mex. 87102.

CARTWRIGHT, ARTHUR D
Mich. State Sen.
b. Madison, Ala, 5/24/09; s. William Cartwright and Catherine Scales C; div; c. Arthur, Jr, Melvin, Everett H, Wade R, Thelma Lee, Thelma Octavier, Henry A, Mary Catherine and Bryan L. Educ: Indust. High Sch, Birmingham, Ala. Polit. & Govt. Pos: Constable, Wayne Co, Mich, 33-43; Bailiff of Commonplace Court, 43-60; Mich. State Rep, 63-64; Mich. State Sen, Fifth Dist, 66- Bus. & Prof. Pos: Real estate dealer, currently. Mem: Life mem, NAACP; Booker T. Washington Bus. Asn; Hotel Owners Asn; Hubbard Beshard Improv. Asn; S.W. Dem. Club; 13th and 16th Cong. Dist. Dem. Orgn; Trade Union Leadership Coun. Rel: Methodist. Legal Res: 5036 Wabash, Detroit, Mich. 48208. Mailing Add: 7541 Linwood, Detroit, Mich. 48206.

CARTWRIGHT, WILBURN D
V.Chmn, Okla. Corp. Cmn.
b. Georgetown, Tenn, 1/12/92; s. J.R. Cartwright and Emma Baker C; m. 6/6/20 to Carrie Staggs (deceased); c. Doralyn Emma (Mrs. Leo Gordon) and Wilburta May (Mrs. Arnold). Educ: Univ. Okla, LL.B, 21; Southeast. State Teachers Col, Durant, Okla, grad, 23; Acacia. Polit. & Govt. Pos: Okla. State Rep, 15-19; Okla. State Sen, 19-23; U.S. Rep, 3rd Dist, Okla, 27-43; Secy. of State, Okla, 47-51, state auditor, 51-55; v.chmn, Okla. Corp. Cmn, 55- Bus. & Prof. Pos: Prin. and supt. of schs, 21-27. Mil. Serv: Serv. as Maj, Army, 43-44, Mil. Govt. N.Africa, Mediterranean Area, Italy, 43-44; N.Africa, Mediterranean and Italy Serv. Ribbons; citation for injury. Mem: Odd Fellows (Past Grand Master); Mason; Lions; Am. Legion; VFW; DAV; Farmers Union. Rel: Baptist. Mailing Add: 801 N.E. 21st St, Oklahoma City, Okla. 73105.

CARTY, MELVILLE A. D
Cmnr, Delaware River Joint Toll Bridge Cmn, N.J.
b. Phillipsburg, N.J, 12/23/01; s. Melville H. Carty and Annie Sigafoos C; m. 9/9/39 to Thelma C. Sloan; c. Geraldine Ann and Melville A, Jr. Educ: Pub. Sch. Polit. & Govt. Pos: Councilman, Borough of Alpha, Warren Co, N.J. and chmn, Planning Bd, 62-66; cmnr, Delaware River Joint Toll Bridge Cmn, 64- Bus. & Prof. Pos: Partner, Phillipsburg Bridge & Equipment Co, 30-66; pres, M.A. Carty & Son Supply Co, Inc, 62-66. Mem: Mason, Miami Consistory, Mahi Temple Shrine; West Jersey Shrine Club; Lehigh Valley Club; Tall Cedars of Lebanon; Elks; Water Gap Country Club. Legal Res: 610 Sigsbee Ave, Alpha, N.J. 08865. Mailing Add: 309 S. Main St, Phillipsburg, N.J. 08865.

CARVEL, ELBERT NOSTRAND D
b. Shelter Island, N.Y, 2/9/10; s. Arnold W. Carvel and Elizabeth Nostrand C; m. 12/17/32 to Ann Valliant; c. Mrs. Charles L. Palmer, Edwin Valliant, Ann Hall and Barbara C.(Mrs. Saviola). Educ: Univ. Baltimore, LL.B, 31; Sigma Delta Kappa; Alpha Zeta. Hon. LL.D, Del. State Col, 64. Polit. & Govt. Pos: Trustee, Univ. Del, 45-; pres, Del. Pardon Bd, 45-49; chmn, Del. State Dem. Cmt, 46-47 & 54-57; Lt. Gov, Del, 45-49, Gov, 49-53 & 61-65; del, Dem. Nat. Conv, 48-64; jointly nominated Adlai E. Stevenson for Pres. on the Dem. Ticket, 52; chmn, Del. Constitutional Revision Cmt, 68-69; mem, Worlds Affairs Coun. of Del, 68-69; trustee, Univ. Baltimore, 68- Bus. & Prof. Pos: Treas, Valliant Fertilizer Co, 36-45, pres, 45-; v.pres, Milford Fertilizer Co, 37-61, chmn. bd, 61-; dir, Sussex Trust Co, 41-49; dir, Peoples Bank & Trust Co, 57-; v.pres, Laurel Grain Co, 65- Mem: Master, Hope Lodge 4, 64-65; Potentate, Nur Shrine, 64-65; Del. Consistory; Lions; Grange; Sussex Co. Soc. of Archaeol. and Hist; Lewes Hist. Soc; Milford and Del. Hist. Socs; Dem. League of Del; Seaford Golf & Country Club; exec. coun, Delmarva Coun, Boy Scouts, 67-; v.pres, Del. Safety Coun, 68-69; Del. Coun. of Churches; Proj. Equality of Del; former mem, Diocesan Coun. of Del; Del. Partners of the Alliance; goals cmt, Episcopal Diocese of Del, 69. Good Citizenship Award, Cmt. of 39, 64; designated Comdr, Order Orange, Nassau by Queen Juliana of the Netherlands, 51; The Vrooman Award, 65; Good Medal for Good Citizenship, SAR, 67; Sussex Co. Serv. Club Award for serv. to Agr, 69. Rel: Episcopal; former Vestryman and former Sr. Warden, St. Philips Episcopal Church. Legal Res: 107 Clayton Ave, Laurel, Del. 19956. Mailing Add: Box 111, Laurel, Del. 19956.

CARVELL, KEVIN Independent
b. Mott, N.Dak, 10/6/45; s. Robert Alfred Carvell and Adeline Svihovec C; single. Educ: N.Dak. State Univ, 63-65 & 67-69; Blue Key. Polit. & Govt. Pos: Alternate del, Dem. Nat. Conv, 68; state campaign mgr, N.Dak. McCarthy for Pres. Orgn, 68; mem. exec. cmt, Fargo, N.Dak. Concerned Dem, 68- Mil. Serv: Entered as Pvt, Army, 65, released as SP-4, 67, after serv. in HHC, 3rd Inf. Div, 7th Army, Germany, 66-67. Mailing Add: 2106 Eighth St. N, Fargo, N.Dak. 58102.

CARVER, JOHN A, JR. D
b. Preston, Idaho, 4/24/18; s. John A. Carver and LaVerne Olson C; m. 6/7/42 to Ruth Patricia O'Connor; c. John A, III, Craig Roger and Candace Elaine. Educ: Brigham Young Univ, A.B; Georgetown Univ, LL.B; Boise Col; George Wash. Univ; Univ. Idaho; Univ. Mont. Polit. & Govt. Pos: Various civil serv. positions, 40-47, including regional dir, civilian personnel div, Off. of Secy. of War, New York, 42-43; asst. attorney gen, Idaho, 47-48; admin. asst. to U.S. Sen. Frank Church, 57-61; asst. secy, Dept. of Interior, 61-64 and under secy, 64-66; cmnr, Fed. Power Cmn, 66- Bus. & Prof. Pos: Attorney, Carver, McClenahan & Greenfield, Boise, Idaho, 48-57. Mil. Serv: Entered as Pvt, Army, 43, released as 1st Lt, Air Force, 46, after serv. in Strategic Bombing Surv, Eng. & Japan; ETO, Asiatic and Am. Theatre Ribbons. Mem: Elks; adv. coun, Center Adv. Study in Orgn. Sci, Univ. Wis, Milwaukee. Legal Res: Boise, Idaho. Mailing Add: 4421 25th St. N, Arlington, Va. 22207.

CARVEY, TOM B, JR. D
Chmn. Cmn. Party Structure and Del. Elec, Calif. Dem. Party.
b. Ft. Worth, Tex, 4/12/22; s. Tom B. Carvey, Sr. and Florence Haney C;

m. 3/11/45 to Dorothea Crile; c. Christopher, Geoffrey, Crile and Tom B, III. Educ: Stanford Univ, A.B. in mech. eng, 43; Phi Beta Kappa; Tau Beta Pi. Polit. & Govt. Pos: Mem, Los Angeles Co. Dem. Cent. Cmt, Calif, 52-64 & 66, secy, 54-56; mem, Dem. State Cent. Cmt, 54-66, secy, 56-58; del, Dem. Nat. Conv, 56, 60, 64 & 68; mem, Gov. Adv. Cmt. on Ment. Health, 59-66; pres, Calif. Dem. Coun, 61-65; mem, Gov. Sci. Adv. Cmt, Calif, 66; mem, Brown for Gov. Steering Cmt, 66; chmn. cmn. party structure and del. elec, Calif. Dem. Party, currently. Bus. & Prof. Pos: Proj. engr, Marquardt Aircraft Co, 43; engr, N.Am. Aviation, Inc, 46-47; mgr. propulsion and power systs. lab, space systs. div, Hughes Aircraft Co, 48-66, mgr. materiel, space and weapons systs, 68- Mil. Serv: Entered as Ens, Navy, 43, released as Lt, 46, after serv. on small aircraft carrier; with Bur. Aeronautics, 45-46; Am. and Pac. Theatre Ribbons. Mem: Los Angeles Exec. Bd. for Great Books (former dir); YMCA Bd.(former local dir); Commun. Coordinating Coun.(past pres); Am. Asn. UN; Commun. Rels. Coun. South. Calif; Am. Civil Liberties Union; Am. Inst. Aeronautics and Astronautics; Am. Soc. Mech. Engrs. Rel: Protestant. Mailing Add: 530 Avenue G Apt. 16, Redondo Beach, Calif. 90277.

CARWILE, ADDISON BROOKS D
b. Cold Spring, S.C, 10/13/96; s. Dr. Preston Brooks Carwile and Leila Kay C; m. 10/12/18 to Alice Frances Callaham; c. Alice Frances (Mrs. L.R. Arrington), Dorothy Ann (Mrs. Stanford Woodhurst), Addison B, Mary Leila (Mrs. R.J. Andrews), John Preston and Sarah Elizabeth (Mrs. H.E. McLeod); seventeen grandchildren. Educ: Clemson Col, B.S, 16; several U.S. Serv. Schs. Polit. & Govt. Pos: Co. agr. agent, S.C, 17-22; mgr, De la Howe State Sch. Farm, 23-24, Antreville schs, 24-28; dir. vet. sch, Abbeville High Sch, 50-62; judge, Probate Court, Abbeville Co, 31-42; supvr, Soil and Water Conserv, Abbeville Dist, 55-; S.C. State Sen, Abbeville Co, 63-66. Bus. & Prof. Pos: Dir. Vet. training, Abbeville Mills, Abbeville, 46-49. Mil. Serv: World War I, 18, 2nd Lt; Army Res, 19-39; S.C. Nat. Guard, 39, Capt. in Artil, mobilized for World War II, serv. with Inspector Gen. Staff in Pac, with Occupation Japan until 46; Col, S.C. Nat. Guard, 47-56, (Ret); World War I Medal; Reservist Medal; Am. and Pac. Theater Medals; Several Battle Stars; Japanese Occupation Medal. Mem: Am. Legion; life mem, State and Nat. Guard; Retired Officers Asn; Mason; Lions Int; Farm Bur; Gov. Agr. Coun; Livestock Asn; Clemson Alumni; develop. bd, Abbeville Co. Soil and Water Conserv. Cert. of Appreciation, Gov. Agr. Coun, 63; Cert. of Award and Cert. of Appreciation as Chmn. of State Cmt, Soil and Water Conserv. and Cert. of Merit, Soil and Water Conserv, 64 & 65; Conserv. Man of Year, 66. Rel: Baptist; Deacon, Trustee and Sunday Sch. Teacher, First Baptist Church. Legal Res: Rt. 1, Abbeville, S.C. 29620. Mailing Add: P.O. Box 725, Abbeville, S.C. 29620.

CARY, ASHTON HALL, (JR) R
Mem. exec. cmt, Troup Co. Rep. Orgn, Ga.
b. LaGrange, Ga, 12/13/23; s. Ashton Hall Cary, Sr. and Edna Freeman C; m. 7/16/49 to Betty Baugh; c. Edna Helen, Ashton Hall, John Huntley, Elizabeth Hanson and Bradley Henry. Educ: Ga. Sch. Tech, B.S. in Ch.E; Alpha Tau Omega. Polit. & Govt. Pos: Del, Precinct, Co, Dist. and State Convs, Ga, 64 & 68; mem. exec. cmt, Sixth Dist. Rep. Party, 64-66; mem. exec. cmt, Troup Co. Rep. Orgn, 64- and treas, 64-67; finance chmn. for G. Paul Jones for cong, Troup Co, 66; del, Rep. Nat. Conv, 68. Bus. & Prof. Pos: Mem. bd. dirs, Am. Red Cross, 50, Dunson Mills, 50, Dunson Sales, 50, United Appeal, 54, La Grange C. of C, 54 and La Grange Welfare Asn, 68; trustee and treas, City Co. Hosp, 60. Mil. Serv: Entered as Pvt, Army, 42, released as Pfc, 46, after serv. in calvary, ETO, 45; two Battle Stars, Rhineland & Cent. Europe. Publ: Several textile articles in Textile World and Textile Indust. Rel: Presbyterian. Legal Res: Cameron Mill Rd, La Grange, Ga. 30240. Mailing Add: Box 1076, La Grange, Ga. 30240.

CASALE, LOUIS JOSEPH, JR. R
b. Stamford, Conn, 3/29/35; s. Louis Joseph Casale and Giacenti Vitti C; single. Educ: Stamford High Sch, grad, 54. Polit. & Govt. Pos: First Dist. Rep, Stamford Bd. of Rep, Conn, 65-67. Bus. & Prof. Pos: Partner, L.J. Casale & Son, 54- Mil. Serv: Entered as Pvt, Nat. Guard, 57, released as Sp4, 63. Mem: K. of C. Rel: Roman Catholic. Mailing Add: 155 Frederick St, Stamford, Conn. 06902.

CASASSA, HERBERT ALFRED R
N.H. State Rep.
b. Fitchburg, Mass, 3/9/97; married; c. One son. Educ: Fitchburg High Sch. Polit. & Govt. Pos: N.H. State Rep, 61-; past chmn, Hampton Munic. Budget Cmn. Bus. & Prof. Pos: Pres, Colt News Store, Inc. Mem: Dir, C. of C; chmn, Hampton Co. March of Dimes, 63; past pres, Hampton Kiwanis; past trustee, Elks. Rel: Catholic. Mailing Add: 7 Thomsen Rd, Hampton, N.H. 03842. (1967)

CASATTAS, PAUL STEVEN R
Mem, Calif. Rep. State Cent. Cmt.
b. San Francisco, Calif, 9/19/26; s. Carl G. Casattas and Assunta Molfino C; m. 6/17/54 to Helen Marie Frank; c. Anne Marie and Sherri Lynn. Educ: San Jose State Col, B.A, 53; Theta Kappa Phi; Newman Club. Polit. & Govt. Pos: Chmn, Sunnyvale Goldwater for Pres. Cmt, Calif, 63-64; chmn, Sunnyvale Rep. Hq, 64; assoc. mem, Calif. Rep. State Cent. Cmt, 64-66, 66-68 and mem, 69-; assoc. mem, Santa Clara Co. Rep. Cent. Cmt, 64-66; treas, Sunnyvale Rep. Assembly, 64-66, pres, 67; exec. dir, Sunnyvale United Rep. Effort, 64-69; spec. events chmn, Sunnyvale Reagan for Gov. Cmt, 65; treas, Sunnyvale Rep. Campaign Hq, 66; Tenth Dist. Dir, Calif. Rep. Assembly, 67-68, state v.pres. and chmn. membership cmt, 68-69, state treas, 69-; chmn, Santa Clara Co. Reagan Favorite Son Cmt, 67; primary chmn, Santa Clara Co. Rafferty for Sen. Campaign, 68; chmn, Bill Bradley for State Sen. Campaign, 68. Bus. & Prof. Pos: Asst. area auditor, Atlas Constructors, Casablanca, French Morocco, 53-54; supt. and coordinator, Bragato Paving Co, Belmont, Calif, 54-69; life underwriter, Equitable Life Assurance Soc, Fanning Agency, Santa Clara, Calif, 69- Mem: Engr. Grading Contractors Asn; Life Underwriters Asn; K. of C.(4°). Rel: Catholic. Mailing Add: 880 Burbank Dr, Santa Clara, Calif. 95051.

CASDIN, JOSEPH CHARLES D
City Councillor, Worcester, Mass.
b. Fiskdale, Mass, 3/10/14; s. Simon Cohen Casdin and Ida Ostroff C; m. 6/20/37 to Miriam Joan Whitman; c. Jeffrey W, Ruth Ann and Deborah Sue. Educ: Boston Univ; Tau Delta Phi. Polit. & Govt. Pos: City Councillor, Worcester, Mass, 56-, Mayor, 59-60, 62 & 67-68; del, Dem. Nat. Conv, 68. Bus. & Prof. Pos: Dir, Home Fed. & Savings Asn, 59-; owner, Casdin Gallery, Worcester, 64- Mem: C. of C.(dir, Worcester Area, 58-63); Mason (32°); K. of P; Probus Club; Kiwanis. Rel: Jewish. Mailing Add: 12 Lenox St, Worcester, Mass. 01602.

CASE, CLIFFORD PHILIP R
U.S. Sen, N.J.
b. Franklin Park, N.J, 4/16/04; s. Clifford Philip Case and Jeannette Benedict C; m. 7/13/28 to Ruth Miriam Smith; c. Mary Jane (Mrs. William M. Weaver), Ann (Mrs. John C. Holt) and Clifford Philip, III. Educ: Rutgers Univ, A.B, 25; Columbia Univ, LL.B, 28; Phi Beta Kappa; Phi Delta Phi; Delta Upsilon. Hon. LL.D, Rutgers Univ, 55, Middlebury Col, 56, Rollins Col, 57, Rider Col, 59, Bloomfield Col, 62, Columbia Univ, 67, Princeton Univ, 67 and Upsala Col, 69. Polit. & Govt. Pos: Mem, Rahway Common Coun, N.J, 38-42; N.J. State Assemblyman, 43-44; U.S. Rep, Sixth Dist, N.J, 45-53; pres, Fund for Repub, 53-54; U.S. Del, 21st UN Gen. Assembly; U.S. Sen, N.J, 54-, mem, Senate For. Rels. and Appropriations Cmts; del, Rep. Nat. Conv, 56, 64 & 68. Bus. & Prof. Pos: Assoc, Simpson Thacher and Bartlett, N.Y, 28-39, mem, 39-53. Mem: Elks; Essex Club; Fed. City Club; Century Asn; trustee, N.J. Soc. for Crippled Children and Adults; Roper Pub. Opinion Research Center, Williams Col; Am. Red Cross, Rahway, N.J; YMCA, Rahway; dir, Columbia Law Sch. Alumni Asn; bd. dirs, Columbia J. of Law & Social Probs, Inc; Am. and N.Y. City, Co. and State Bar Asns; Coun. For. Rels; adv. bd, N.J. Chap, Arthritis and Rheumatism Found; adv. coun, Woodrow Wilson Sch, Princeton Univ; hon. trustee, N.J. Hist. Soc; trustee, N.J. Cmt. to Preserve the Dem. Process; sponsor, Inst. for Am. Dem. Citation, N.J. Regional Bd, Anti-Defamation League and Rutgers Alumni Fedn, 55, NAACP, 60, Coun. for United Civil Rights Leadership, 64, Am. Legion, Dept. N.J, 65, N.J. State AFL-CIO and N.J. Asn. for Adult Educ, 65. Medal of Merit, N.J. Dept, Jewish War Vet, 53 and John F. Kennedy Mem. Award, Elin-Unger Post 273, 66; Speaker of Year in Nat. Affairs, Tau Kappa Alpha, 54; Award, N.J. VFW, 59 and Northeast. Fedn. Women's Clubs, 65; 1 of Senate's 10 Ablest Mem, 50 leading Wash. columnists and correspondents, 60; Meritorious Serv. Award, DAV, 61; Man of the People Award, Union Co. Cent. Labor Union, 61; Citizenship Award, Master Printers Asn. Newark, 64; Cert. of Merit, Gloucester Co. Br, NAACP, 64; Amity Award, N.J. Region, Am. Jewish Congr, 66; Award, N.J. State Asn, Dept. of Civil Liberties, Elks of Wash, 66; Cert. of Merit, Monmouth-Ocean Co, N.J. Br, Jewish War Vet, U.S, 66; Citation and Award, N.J. Recreation and Parks Soc. and N.J. Parks and Recreation Asn, 67; Award, City of Hope, Nat. Med. Center, 67; Justice Louis D. Brandeis Award, N.J. Region, Zionist Orgn. of Am, 69. Rel: Presbyterian. Legal Res: 191 W. Milton Ave, Rahway, N.J. 07065. Mailing Add: 315 Senate Office Bldg, Washington, D.C. 20510.

CASE, GEORGE MILTON D
Miss. State Rep.
b. Canton, Miss; 7/5/34; single. Polit. & Govt. Pos: Miss. State Rep, 60- Bus. & Prof. Pos: Attorney. Mem: K. of P; Mason; Elks; Lions; Jaycees. Rel: Baptist. Mailing Add: 114 W. Center St, Canton, Miss. 39046.

CASE, MERVIN ROY R
Mo. State Rep.
b. Climax Springs, Mo, 1/12/26; m. 8/21/49 to Faye Davis; c. Marsha Rhea and Rebecca Anne. Educ: Southwest Mo. State Col. Polit. & Govt. Pos: Mo. State Rep, 64-66 & 69- Bus. & Prof. Pos: Employee, Ava Produce Co; sales agent, Prog. Sec. Co; operated bulldozer, 16 years. Mil. Serv: Army, 44-46, ETO. Mem: Am. Legion. Rel: Protestant. Mailing Add: RFD 4, Ava, Mo. 65608. (1967)

CASE, ROBERT ELROY R
b. Des Moines, Iowa, 10/19/23; s. Elroy M. Case and Elsie A. Holdiman C; m. 1/15/46 to Abigail Elizabeth Bartlett. Educ: Drake Univ, Des Moines, B.A. in Jour, 49; Sigma Delta Chi. Polit. & Govt. Pos: Admin. asst. to U.S. Rep. H.R. Gross, Iowa, 53- Bus. & Prof. Pos: Reporter and asst. wire ed, Waterloo Daily Courier, Iowa, 49-50 & 51-53. Mil. Serv: Marine Corps, Sgt, 42-46, serv. in Pac; Marine Corps, S/Sgt, 50-51, serv. in Korea with First Marine Div. Inf. in Commun. Pub. Info. Mem: Mason; Am. Vet. World War II; Young Rep. Club; Bull Elephants; Cong. Secy. Club. Rel: Methodist. Legal Res: Cedar Falls, Iowa. Mailing Add: 8817 Stark Rd, Annandale, Va. 22003. (1967)

CASE, STEWART STANTON R
Mem, Calif. Rep. State Cent. Cmt.
b. Yonkers, N.Y, 11/8/29; s. S. Stewart Case and Louise Porth C. (deceased); m. 1/8/56 to JoAn Delleny; c. Larry Stewart, Brian Stanton, Scott Edwin and Douglas Stanford. Educ: N.Y. Univ, B.S, 51; Univ. Calif, Los Angeles, M.S, 55; Alpha Kappa Delta, Gamma Chap. Polit. & Govt. Pos: Pres, Lakewood Young Rep, Calif, 58; admin. asst, State Sen, John A. Murdy, Jr, 61-64; Rep. nominee for Calif. Legis, 69th Assembly Dist, 66; first v.pres, Westminster Area Rep. Assembly, 67-68, mem, bd. dirs, 68-; mem, Orange Co. Rep. Cent. Cmt, Second Dist, 68-; mem, Calif. State Rep. Cent. Cmt, 68- Bus. & Prof. Pos: Newspaperman, Orange Co. Evening News, 55-60; pres, M-R Assocs, Inc, Pub. Rels. and Advert, 64-; dir. commun. serv, Santa Ana Col, 67- Mil. Serv: Entered as Pvt, Army, Mil. Intel, 52, released as Cpl, 54, after serv. in Army Gen. Sch, Ft. Riley, Kans; Res, Army, 54-60; Good Conduct Medal. Publ: Is Your Public Relations Showing?, M-R Assocs, Inc, 65. Mem: Sigma Delta Chi; Orange Co. Press Club; Am. Col. Pub. Rels. Asn; Calif. Jr. Col. Asn; bd. dirs, Garden Grove C. of C; past pres, Garden Grove Jaycees; bd. dirs, Boys Club of Garden Grove; Am. Legion; Kiwanis; Exchange Club; participant, Orange Co. Sci. Fair; life mem, Calif. PTA; Rep. Assocs; Young Rep; Calif. Rep. Assembly. Young Man of the Year in Garden Grove, 64. Rel: Protestant. Mailing Add: 8161 Hynes Rd, Anaheim, Calif. 92804.

CASEY, JACK TULL D
b. San Francisco, Calif, 1909; m. 7/6/35 to Ruth N. McNaughton; c. Sharon Marie. Educ: Univ. of Calif. at Berkeley, B.S, M.A, Ph.D. Polit. & Govt. Pos: Calif. State Assemblyman, 1960 - 66. Bus. & Prof. Pos: Col. Instr. Mem: Commonwealth Club; N.S.G.W; Kern Co. Hist. Soc; Calif. Teachers Asn; Tejon Lodge, F & AM; Am. Asn. of Univ. Profs. Chmn, Off, Concerts & Lects,

Bakersfield Col; Chmn. Juds. Comm, Kern Co. Art Festival, 6 years; past pres. & Adv, Bakersfield Coun, Com. Plan. 1967 Legal Res: 212 Goodman St, Bakersfield, Calif. 93305. No mailing address available. (1967)

CASEY, JOHN PETER 'JACK' D
b. Dorchester, Mass, 11/4/48; s. William Joseph Casey and Anne Helen Koval C; single. Educ: Boston State Col, currently; Boston State Col. Newspaper, Yearbook and Student Govt. Asns. Polit. & Govt. Pos: Youth coordinator for State Rep. O'Leary, S.Boston, Mass, 66 and City Coun. Cand. O'Leary, 67; legis. asst. to City Coun. O'Leary, 68; admin. asst. to City Coun. Pres, O'Leary, 69- Bus. & Prof. Pos: Sports reporter, Boston Globe Newspaper, 65-68; polit. ed, Boston State Col. Newspaper, 67-68, managing ed, 68-; ed, Gazette-Courier-Beacon Newspaper, 68; mgr, Tel-A-Serv, summer, 68. Publ: The Student Government and Beacon Hill, 1/15/69, SDS–An Asset or a Threat, 2/15/69 and The New Generation Offers a Leader, 5/15/69, Boston State Col. Mem: Boston Press Club; Soc. for the Study of Dem. Insts; Mass. Young Dem; Jefferson-Jackson Club; adv, Boy Scouts. Rel: Roman Catholic. Legal Res: 5 Howes St, Dorchester, Mass. 02125. Mailing Add: Pres. Office, New City Hall, Boston, Mass. 02201.

CASEY, JOHN SEARS D
b. Birmingham, Ala, 12/31/30; s. James Lebus Casey and Winnie Sears C; m. 8/1/53 to Mary Carolyn Pounds; c. Sarah Lynne, Carol Leigh and Patrick P. Educ: Jacksonville State Col, 49-50; Auburn Univ, B.S, 53; Univ. Ala, LL.B, 57; Phi Alpha Delta; Phi Kappa Tau. Polit. & Govt. Pos: Ala. State Rep, 59-66. Bus. & Prof. Pos: Legis. rep, Ala. Educ. Asn, 68-69. Mil. Serv: Entered as 2nd Lt, Air Force, 53, released as 1st Lt, 55, after serv. in Northeast Air Command. Mem: Am, Ala. and Calhoun Co. Bar Asns; Ala. Trial Lawyers Asn; Am. Judicature Soc; Am. Legion; Heflin Jaycees; Heflin Lions Club (past pres). Rel: Baptist. Mailing Add: Box 266, Heflin, Ala. 36264.

CASEY, JOSEPH EDWARD R
Chmn, West Haven Rep. Town Cmt, Conn.
b. New Haven, Conn, 10/7/13; s. John E. Casey and Mary E. Cain C; m. 4/6/42 to Marjorie Stone; c. Joseph E, Jr. and Walter S. Educ: Wharton Sch. Finance, Univ. Pa; Conn. Col. Commerce. Polit. & Govt. Pos: Chmn, West Haven Rep. Town Cmt, Conn, currently; former exec. secy. to Mayor, West Haven; legis. bulletin clerk, Conn. Gen. Assembly, 61-66; former mem, U.S. Selective Serv. Adv. Cmt. Mem: Elks. Rel: Catholic. Mailing Add: 145 Church St, West Haven, Conn. 06516. (1967)

CASEY, JOSEPH FRANCIS R
Sgt-At-Arms, N.Y. State Assembly
b. 9/23/32; s. Dennis Casey (deceased) and Mary O'Kelly C; m. 11/17/56 to Lorraine Magill; c. Collenn Beth, Michael William, Joseph Scott, Patricia, David, Mary Erin and Darrell. Educ: Hudson Valley Commun. Col, grad. Polit. & Govt. Pos: With N.Y. State Dept. Pub. Works, 59-60, Troy Engr. Off, 60-61; dep, Rensselaer Co. Hwy, 61-62, supt, Hwys, 63-68; chmn, Rensselaer Co. Rep. Cmt, 66-; del, Rep. Nat. Conv, 68; Sgt-at-Arms, N.Y. State Assembly, 69- Mil. Serv: Air Force, 51-55. Mem: Hudson Valley Commun. Col. Soc; Young Rep. Orgn; Elks; bd. dirs, Hudson Valley Alumni Asn, 60-66 and pres; co. co-chmn, Muscular Dystrophy Asn, 63-64; bd. dirs, Co. Red Cross, 63-65; bd. govs, Country Club, 63-64; bd. dirs, Kiwanis, 63-65; bd. trustees, Hudson Valley Commun. Col, 64-; bd. dirs, Co. Young Rep. Club, 64; chmn, Govt. Serv. Div, United Heart Fund Dr. Man of the Year Award, Troy Jr. C. of C, 62; N.Y. State Man of the Year, 63. Rel: Roman Catholic. Mailing Add: 80 Campbell Ave, Troy, N.Y. 12180.

CASEY, JOSEPH S. D
La. State Rep.
b. New Orleans, La, 9/29/13; s. Joseph A. Casey and Dora Stubbs C; m. 2/5/42 to Lillian K. McGraw; c. Joseph T, Phyllis O. and Roy A. Educ: Loyola Univ, New Orleans, LL.B, 37, A.B, 38. Polit. & Govt. Pos: La. State Rep, 52-56 & 60- Mil. Serv: Entered as Pvt, Army, 41, released as Cpl, 42. Rel: Catholic. Legal Res: 871 Lopaz St, New Orleans, La. 70124. Mailing Add: 415 Maritime Bldg, New Orleans, La. 70130. (1967)

CASEY, LORAN WILLIAM R
Mont. State Rep.
b. Bainville, Mont, 8/31/27; s. Harry W. Casey and Lily Torgerson C; m. 6/6/50 to Bernette Stiff; c. Marty, Miles, Debbie and Dee Ann. Educ: Mont. State Univ, B.S, 50; Sigma Alpha Epsilon; M Club. Polit. & Govt. Pos: City alderman, Wolf Point, 61-65; Mont. State Rep, Roosevelt Co, 63- Mil. Serv: Entered as Seaman, Navy, 45, released as Seaman 1/C, 46, after serv. in Naval Res. Mem: Elks; K. of C; Am. Legion; Farm Bur. Rel: Catholic. Legal Res: 107 Dawson, Wolf Point, Mont. 59201. Mailing Add: Drawer Q, Wolf Point, Mont. 59201.

CASEY, MIKE D
b. Ona, W.Va, 7/29/99; s. William Sinclair Casey and Sidna Lewis C; m. 7/1/20 to Sadie Louise Coffman; c. Robert L. and William A. Educ: Booth's Bus. Col. Polit. & Govt. Pos: W.Va. State Del, 38-68. Bus. & Prof. Pos: Receiving and shipping clerk, rwy. co. Mem: Former Grand Master, Odd Fellows, rep, Sover. Grand Lodge, Phoenix, Ariz, and Montreal, Can, 2 years, Sover. Grand Guardian, Minneapolis, 64, Rebekahs; Red Men; Jr. OUAM; D of A; Brotherhood Rwy. Clerks. Rel: Baptist. Mailing Add: Huntington, W.Va. 25701. (1967)

CASEY, ROBERT P. D
State Auditor, Pa.
b. Jackson Heights, N.Y, 1/9/32; s. Alphonsus L. Casey and Marie Cummings C; m. to Ellen Harding; c. Seven. Educ: Holy Cross Col; George Wash. Univ. Law Sch, A.B, LL.B, J.D; pres. sr. class, Holy Cross Col; athletic scholarship, Holy Cross Col; trustee scholarship, George Wash. Univ; Order of the Coif. Polit. & Govt. Pos: Pa. State Sen, 62-67; alternate del-at-lg, Dem. Nat. Conv, 64, del, 68; State Auditor, Pa, 69- Bus. & Prof. Pos: Attorney. Publ: Author, 'Counter Claims Against the United States,' George Wash. Law Rev, 1/57. Mem: Cancer Drive, Lackawanna United Fund Dr. Admitted to practice before, Lackawanna Co. Courts, Supreme and Superior Courts of Pa; D.C. & Fed. Courts; Middle Dist. of Pa. Court. Legal Res: 2002 N. Washington Ave, Scranton, Pa. 18509. Mailing Add: Capitol Bldg, Harrisburg, Pa. 17120. (1967)

CASEY, ROBERT RANDOLPH 'BOB' D
U.S. Rep, Tex.
b. Joplin, Mo, 7/27/15; s. Sam Russel Casey and Mabel Caywood C; m. 8/13/35 to Hazel Marian Brann; c. Hazel Mary, Bob, Jr, Catherine, Bonnie, Michael, Shawn, Bridget, Eileen, Timothy and Kevin. Educ: Univ. Houston, 34-36; S.Tex. Col. Law, 36-40; Delta Theta Phi. Polit. & Govt. Pos: City attorney, Alvin, Tex, 42-43 and mem. sch. bd, 43; asst. dist. attorney, Harris Co, 43-47, Tex. State Rep, 49-50 and Judge, 51-58; U.S. Rep, 59- Bus. & Prof. Pos: Clerk, Skelly Oil Co, 34-35, Barnsdall Oil Co, 35 and Shell Oil Co, 35-41; attorney-at-law, 42-43 & 47-51. Mem: Tex. and Houston Bar Asns; Am. Soc. Oceanography; Houston Speech and Hearing Center. Rel: Protestant. Legal Res: 2256 Dryden Rd, Houston, Tex. 77025. Mailing Add: 2353 Rayburn Bldg, Washington, D.C. 20515.

CASEY, WILLIAM F. D
Mo. State Rep.
b. Potosi, Mo, 12/3/21; m. 1947; c. James William. Educ: Westminster Col. Polit. & Govt. Pos: Mo. State Rep, 58- Bus. & Prof. Pos: Owner and operator, radio & TV sales-serv. bus, 56- Mil. Serv: Navy, World War II, 4 years, serv. in Pac. Mem: Am. Legion; VFW; Elks; Eagles. Rel: Protestant. Mailing Add: 304 Mineral St, Potosi, Mo. 63664. (1967)

CASH, TOM R
b. Flint, Mich, 8/24/27; s. Ben Cash and Gertrude Green C; m. 12/22/45 to Peggy Jean Bass; c. Carolyn, Connie, Sally, Tommy and Steve. Educ: Kennett High Sch, Mo. Polit. & Govt. Pos: Committeeman, Rep. Party, Pascola Twp, Mo, 54-66; chmn, Pemiscot Co. Rep. Cmt, until 68. Bus. & Prof. Pos: Farmer and co. fieldman, Fed. Crop Ins, U.S. Dept. of Agr. Mil. Serv: Entered as Pvt, Army, 45, released as Pfc, 47, after serv. in Transportation Corp. Mem: Bd. Dirs, Semo Indust. Develop. Cmt, 66-; mem, Kennett Sch. Bd, Mo, 65-; Bragg City Lions Club (bd dirs, 62-); Mo. Cotton Prod. Asn. (twp. committeeman, 58-66). Rel: Christian Church; Supt. Sunday Sch, First Christian Church, Kennett, Mo. Legal Res: Route 2, Bragg City, Mo. 63827. Mailing Add: Box 116, Bragg City, Mo. 63827. (1967)

CASHION, DAVID CARL R
Mem, Calif. Rep. State Cent. Cmt.
b. Los Angeles, Calif, 12/12/35; s. Lawrence John Cashion and Dorothy Beech C; m. 4/9/66 to Grace Gemmill; c. Kimberly Jeanne and Stephen Matthew. Educ: Univ. South. Calif, A.B, 57; Univ. South. Calif. Law Sch, J.D, 60; Phi Gamma Delta. Polit. & Govt. Pos: Pres, South Pasadena Young Rep, Calif, 66, Pasadena Rep. Club, 69-; mem, Calif. Rep. State Cent. Cmt, 69- Mem: Am, Los Angeles Co. and Pasadena Bar Asns; State Bar of Calif; Lawyers Club of Los Angeles; Univ. Club of Pasadena, Oneonta Club of South Pasadena; Kiwanis Club of Greater Pasadena. Rel: Methodist. Mailing Add: 680 Edgeview Dr, Sierra Madre, Calif. 91024.

CASHION, ROY WILSON D
Mem, N.C. State Dem. Exec. Cmt.
b. Sanford, N.C, 10/21/31; s. Lloyd Franklin Cashion and Ethel Wicker C; m. 1/1/66 to Ruth Thomas; c. Stephanie Ruth. Educ: Elon Col, 53; Univ. N.C, Chapel Hill, B.S, 59. Polit. & Govt. Pos: Mem, N.C. State Dem. Exec. Cmt, 68-; del, Dem. Nat. Conv, 68; Lee Co. Campaign mgr, Gov. Robert W. Scott, 68. Bus. & Prof. Pos: Partner, Sanford Transfer & Storage Co; pres, Cashion Moving & Storage, Inc. Mil. Serv: Entered as Pvt, Army, 54, released as Cpl, 56. Mem: Jaycees; Moose; Elks; VFW; Woodmen of World; Kiwanis. N.C. Traffic Safety Award; distinguished serv. award, Lee Co. Rel: Presbyterian. Mailing Add: 506 Sunset Dr, Sanford, N.C. 27330.

CASHMAN, JOSEPH T. R
b. 9/5/31. Educ: Goldey Beacom, A.A, 57; Franklin & Marshall Col, B.S. Polit. & Govt. Pos: Del. State Rep, 67-68; former mem, Citizen's Adv. Coun, New Castle Sch. Dist; budget dir, Del, 69- Bus. & Prof. Pos: Partner, CPA firm of Cashman & Schiaui. Mem: Trustee and secy, Del. Found. Acct. Educ; pres, Stockton Civic Asn. Rel: Catholic; mem. bd. adv, St. Peter's Catholic Church. Mailing Add: 8 Stabler Court, Stockton, New Castle, Del. 19720.

CASHMORE, WILLIAM FRANCIS R
Mont. State Rep.
b. Dillon, Mont, 2/8/05; both parents deceased; m. 1932 to Louise McLaren; c. Sarah (Mrs. Ed. Herold), Robert W. and Lynn (Mrs. James Secrest). Educ: Mont. State Univ, B.S, 28; Univ. Chicago, Rush Med. Col, M.D, 35; Phi Chi; Sigma Alpha Epsilon. Polit. & Govt. Pos: Mont. State Sen, Lewis and Clark Co, 61-63; mem, State Bd. of Med. Exam, Mont, 64-; mem, State Appeal Bd. Selective Serv, 67-; Mont. State Rep, Lewis and Clark Co, 69- Mem: Pres, Mont. Wildlife Fedn, 45-46; chmn. Mont. div, Am. Cancer Soc, 47-48; dir, Mont. Tuberc. Asn, 67-; Mason; Scottish Rite; Algeria Shrine; Jesters. Rel: Protestant. Mailing Add: 10 Montana Ave, Helena, Mont. 59601.

CASILLAS, JOE DAVID R
Mem, Calif. Rep. State Cent. Cmt.
b. Chula Vista, Calif, 5/11/27; s. Felix L. Casillas and Urbana Anton C; m. 3/20/49 to Gloria S. Castillo; c. David Felix and Carol Ann. Educ: San Diego City Col, A.A, 57; Univ. Calif, 56-62; Calif. West. Univ, B.Sc, 62, Sch. Law, 64-65. Polit. & Govt. Pos: Mem, San Diego Co. Civil Serv. Cmn, Calif, 65-; mem, Calif. Rep. State Cent. Cmt, 69- Bus. & Prof. Pos: With U.S. Dept. of Defense, 48-64; Off. of Econ. Opportunity, Exec. Off. of the Pres, 66-67; exec. dir, Manpower Develop. Off, San Diego Mayor's Cmt. for Jobs, Inc, 67- Mil. Serv: Entered as Pvt, Air Force, 45, released as Corp, 48, after serv. in 101st Airways and Air Commun. Squadron, Strategic Air Command, 46-48; World War II Victory Medal. Mem: Am. G.I. Forum of the U.S; Father Junipero Serra Chap, San Diego Pueblo of San Diego Rep. Asn. Rel: Catholic. Mailing Add: 758 Neptune Court, Chula Vista, Calif. 92011.

CASKEY, WILBURN D
Chmn, Boyd Co. Dem. Exec. Cmt, Ky.
b. West Liberty, Ky, 1/5/21; s. Ivory Blankenship Caskey; m. July, 1950 to Dorothy Ann Coonrod; c. Jeff and Pike. Educ: Centre Col, B.A; Sigma Alpha Epsilon; C. Club. Polit. & Govt. Pos: Past mem, Ky. Develop. Coun. and Ky, Adv. Cmts. on Planning and Zoning and on Metrop. Govt; mem, Water Pollution Control Cmt; mayor pro tem, Ashland, 51-53 and mayor, 55-59, mem, City Cmt, 51-55; pres, Ky. Munic. League, 57-58; chmn, Boyd Co. Dem.

Exec. Cmt, 65-; mem, Citizens Cmt. on State Legislatures, currently. Mil. Serv: Entered as Pvt, Marine Corps, 42, released as 1st Lt, 46, after serv. in Pac. Theater; Pac. Theater Ribbon. Mem: Dir, Tuberc. Asn. and Home for the Aged; Elks; Am. Legion; former mem, Bd. of Overseers and Bd. of Dirs, Centre Col. Alumni Asn. Jaycees Outstanding Young Man of Ashland, 53. Rel: Methodist. Mailing Add: 2811 Cumberland Ave, Ashland, Ky. 41101.

CASO, RALPH GEORGE R
V.Chmn, Bd. of Supvr, Nassau Co, N.Y.
b. N.Y.C, 11/26/17; s. George Ralph Caso and Josephine DeNicola C; m. 7/2/55 to Grace Milone; c. Ralph George, Jr. and Jolisa. Educ: Hofstra Univ, 2 years; N.Y. Univ, B.S; N.Y. Univ. Law Sch, J.D; Alpha Tau Omega; Phi Alpha Delta. Polit. & Govt. Pos: Rep. committeeman, Merrick, N.Y, 51-, pres, Rep. Recruits, 51-52; councilman, Hempstead, 53-61, supvr, 61-65 and presiding supvr, 65-; v,chmn, Bd. of Supvr, Nassau Co, 65-; del, Rep. Nat. Conv, 68. Bus. & Prof. Pos: Attorney, private off, Merrick, N.Y, 49- Mil. Serv: Entered as Pvt, Army, 42, released as M/Sgt, 45, after serv. in Y Force, China, 43-45; Three Combat Stars; Bronze Star Medal for Meritorious Serv. Mem: Nassau Co. Bar Asn; Nassau Lawyers Asn; Cath. Lawyers Guild; K. of C; Am. Legion; Elks. Torch of Liberty Award, B'nai B'rith; Annual Achievement Award, L.I. Columbia Asn; Grass Roots Award, Nassau Co. Press Asn; Man of Year Award, Asn. for Help of Retarded Children; St. Francis Col. Charter Award. Rel: Catholic. Mailing Add: 2045 Baldwin Court, Merrick, N.Y. 11566.

CASON, WILLIAM J. D
Mo. State Sen.
b. Higginsville, Mo, 10/1/24; married; c. Brian Austin, William Wilson, Patrick Jennings and Candiss Anne. Educ: Univ. Mo, B.S, LL.B. with honors; Sigma Nu. Polit. & Govt. Pos: Mo. State Sen, 60-; Prosecuting Attorney, Henry Co, 6 years. Bus. & Prof. Pos: Lawyer, 51-; acct; grocery clerk. Mil. Serv: Army Air Corps, World War II, bomber pilot 3 years. Mem: Jr. C. of C; C. of C. Distinguished Serv. Award, Mo. Acad. of Gen. Practice; Citation of Merit, Mo. Hosp. Asn; St. Louis Globe-Democrat Award. Rel: Christian. Mailing Add: 215 E. Franklin, Clinton, Mo. 64735. (1967)

CASS, MILLARD D
Dep. Under Secy. of Labor
b. Norfolk, Va, 11/8/16; s. Sigismund Cass and Ridia Schreier C; m. 7/19/43 to Ruth Claire Marx; c. Sandra Jean (Mrs. Jeffrey A. Burt), Ronald Andrew and Pamela Celeste. Educ: Univ. Va, B.S, 38 and LL.B, 40; Phi Beta Kappa; Omicron Delta Kappa; Order of Coif; Raven Soc. Polit. & Govt. Pos: Attorney, Securities and Exchange Cmn, 41; attorney, Nat. Labor Rels. Bd, 41-45, legal asst. to gen. counsel, 45-46; asst. to Asst. Secy. of Labor, 46-47, asst. to Under Secy. of Labor, 47-50, spec. asst. to Secy. of Labor, 50-55, Dep. Under Secy. of Labor, 55-; Mobilization Planning Coordinator, 62-; exec. officer, Manpower Admin, 63-64; Liaison Officer with State Governors, 69- Bus. & Prof. Pos: Attorney-at-law, Portsmouth, Va, 40-41. Mem: Va. State and Am. Bar Asns; pres, Montgomery Co. Coun. of PTA's, Md, 62-64; bd. mgrs, Md. Cong. Parents & Teachers, 62-64; bd. dir, Montgomery Co. Scholarship Fund, 62-64. Recipient, Arthur S. Flemming Award, 55; Distinguished Serv. Award, U.S. Dept. of Labor, 60; Rockefeller Pub. Serv. Award, 66; Montgomery Co. Educ. Asn. Hornbook Award, 68; Nat. Civil Serv. League Career Serv. Award, 69. Rel: Jewish; bd. mgrs, Wash. Hebrew Congregation, 59-, first v.pres, 68-; bd. dir. which established Int. Synagogue at John F. Kennedy Airport, NYC, 59-64. Mailing Add: 2103 Plyers Mill Rd, Silver Springs, Md. 20902.

CASSADY, HELEN B. D
Md. State Del.
b. Baltimore, Md, 9/28/06; widow. Educ: Md. Bus. Col. Polit. & Govt. Pos: Md. State Del, 65-; asst. supvr. Master Files, Bd. of Elecs; pres, Ital-Am. Women's Dem. Club, of Seventh Ward; United Women's Dem. Clubs, Md. Mem: Exec. secy, Monument St. Businessmen's Asn. Mailing Add: 816 N. Milton Ave, Baltimore, Md. 21205. (1967)

CASSIDY, CLIFTON WILSON, JR. D
Chmn, Pub. Safety Cmn. Tex.
b. San Antonio, Tex, 10/30/27; s. Clifton Wilson Cassidy and Winifred Lynn C; m. 12/13/52 to Sally Otis; c. Elynn, Clifton Wilson, III, Kelly Anne and Michael. Educ: Univ. Tex, Austin, B.B.A, 50; Delta Sigma Phi; Phi Kappa Sigma. Polit. & Govt. Pos: Chmn, Dallas Co. Dem. Exec. Cmt, Tex, 64; del, Dem. Nat. Conv, 64 & 68; cmnr, Pub. Safety Cmn, Tex, 66- Bus. & Prof. Pos: Pres, Richardson Savings & Loan and Cassidy Feed Mills, Inc; chmn. exec. cmt, First Bank & Trust; dir, Tex. Bank & Trust and Dallas Title & Garranty. Mil. Serv: Entered as A/S, Navy, released as Lt; Lt, Res. Mem: Coun. Soc. Agencies; Dallas Summer Musicals; Dallas Assembly; Rotary; Brook Hollow Golf Club; City Club. Distinguished Alumni Award, Univ. Tex, 66. Rel: Methodist. Mailing Add: 10211 Hollow Way, Dallas, Tex. 75229.

CASSIDY, JOHN E, JR. D
b. 1925. Polit. & Govt. Pos: Ill. State Rep, 65-68; past mem, Peoria Pleasure Driveway and Park Dist. Bd; past pres, Ill. Asn. of Parks. Bus. & Prof. Pos: Attorney. Named Outstanding Freshman, 65-66 Gen. Assembly. Mailing Add: 6526 St. Mary Rd, Peoria, Ill. 61614. (1967)

CASSIDY, JOSEPH W. D
b. Waukon, Iowa, 3/26/22; s. James Cassidy; Kathleen; m. 1959 to Nelda E. Stender. Educ: Univ. of Iowa, B.A, M.A; Columbia Univ. Polit. & Govt. Pos: Former Iowa State Sen. Bus. & Prof. Pos: Pub. Sch. Admin. Mil. Serv: U.S. Army. Mem: Izaak Walton; Iowa State Educ. Asn. and Nat. Educ. Asn; Scott Co. Dem. Cent. Cmt; Co-chmn, Scott Co. Cit. Against the Shaff Plan. Rel: Methodist. Mailing Add: Route 2, Walcott, Iowa 52773. (1967)

CASTELLINI, WILLIAM McGREGOR R
Mem-at-Lg, St. Landry Parish Rep. Exec. Cmt, La.
b. Cincinnati, Ohio, 6/29/28; s. William A.A. Castellini and Ruth E. McGregor C; m. 8/20/60 to Helen Louise Oliver. Educ: Univ. Cincinnati, B.B.A, 49; Univ. Southwest. La, 60-61; Alpha Kappa Psi; Scabbard & Blade; Phi Delta Theta. Polit. & Govt. Pos: Pres, St. Landry Parish Rep. Club, La, 64; alternate del-at-lg, Rep. Nat. Conv, 64; mem-at-lg, St. Landry Parish Rep. Exec. Cmt, 64-; committeeman, Fourth Ward Rep. Cmt, Opelousas, currently. Bus. & Prof. Pos: Owner, W.M. Castellini Co, 54-; pres, Calona Farms Inc, 63- Mil. Serv: Entered as 2nd Lt, Army, 49, released as 1st Lt, 53; Ohio Nat. Guard, 147th Inf. Regt. and Army Res, Lafayette, La, until 58; Third Korean War Winter Campaign Ribbon; Nat. Defense Medal; United Nations Medal, Korean Presidential Citation. Mem: 37th Div. Vets. Asn; Opelousas Little Theatre (mem. bd, past pres. and secy); La. Yambilee (mem. bd, past pres, v.pres. and treas); La. Sweet Potato Asn.(bd. dir). Rel: Roman Catholic. Mailing Add: 330 Highland Dr, Opelousas, La. 70570.

CASTILE, GEORGE EDWARD D
b. Minneapolis, Minn, 7/23/15; s. Shepherd Castile and Gertrude Mathias C; m. 11/27/57 to Eleanor Viola Essex; c. Eve-Ann (Mrs. Calvin Wilkinson) and George Pierre. Educ: Wash. Univ, St. Louis, Mo, A.B, 46; Adelphi Col, 55-56, grad. work in applied math; Kansas Univ, Wichita, Kans, 59-63, grad. work in physics. Polit. & Govt. Pos: Pres. and founder, Madison Co. Dem. Club, Ala, 65-67; alternate del, Dem. Nat. Conv, 68. Bus. & Prof. Pos: Research engr, Boeing Co, Wichita and Huntsville, 59-69; sr. staff engr, Sperry-Rand Space Support Div, Huntsville, Ala, 69- Mem: Oper. Research Soc. of Am; Toastmasters Int. Rel: Unitarian. Mailing Add: 1411 Mountainbrook Dr, S.E, Huntsville, Ala. 35801.

CASTILE, ROBERT O. D
Mem, Calif. Dem. State Cent. Cmt.
b. Wortham, Tex, 11/2/29; s. Lee Vance Castile, Sr. and Jessie C; m. 11/27/54 to Dorothy A. Leffall; c. Billye Joyce, Robert O, Jr. and Patrick Allen. Educ: Wortham High Sch, grad. Polit. & Govt. Pos: Mem, Calif. Dem. State Cent. Cmt, 69- Bus. & Prof. Pos: VISTA Supvr, Venice Commun. Improv. Union, Inc, Calif, 66-67 and dir, 67-; dir, Oakwood Wesley House, 69- Mil. Serv: Entered as Pvt, Army, 55, released as Pfc, 57, after serv. in 865 AAA Missile Bn, Ft. McArthur; Good Conduct Medal. Mailing Add: 621 San Juan Ave, Venice, Calif. 90291.

CASTILLO, JOSEPH A. D
Ariz. State Sen.
b. Los Angeles, Calif, 12/26/33; s. Joseph E. Castillo and Feliciana Gallegos C; m. 8/30/52 to Dorothy V. Rios; c. Steven, Dorthina, Karl and Eric. Polit. & Govt. Pos: Councilman, South Tucson, Ariz, 61-66; precinct committeeman, 62-66; Ariz. State Sen, Dist. 7A, 67- Bus. & Prof. Pos: Pres. and owner, Pima Blueprint Co, Inc, Tucson. Mem: Ariz. Firemans Asn; Soc. Reproduction Engrs; Blueprinters Asn. of Ariz.(pres, 64-66); Tucson C. of C; U.S. C. of C. Rel: Catholic. Mailing Add: 320 E. Silverlake, Tucson, Ariz. 85713.

CASTLE, MICHAEL NEWBOLD R
Del. State Sen.
b. Wilmington, Del, 7/2/39; s. James Manderson Castle, Jr. and Louisa Bache C; single. Educ: Hamilton Col, A.B, 61; Georgetown Univ. Law Sch, LL.B, 64; Alpha Delta Phi. Polit. & Govt. Pos: Mem. bd. dirs, Wilmington Young Rep, New Castle Co. Young Rep, Del. Young Rep, 64-; first v.pres, Wilmington Young Rep, 64-; dep. attorney gen, State Attorney Gen. Off, 65-66; Del. State Rep, Sixth Dist, 67-69; Del. State Sen, 69- Bus. & Prof. Pos: Attorney, Connolly, Bove & Lodge, 64- Mem: D.C, Del. and Am. Bar Asns. Rel: Roman Catholic. Mailing Add: 1600 N. Broom St, Wilmington, Del. 19806.

CASTLE, ROBERT MARVIN D
Mem, Calif. State Dem. Cent. Cmt.
b. Lubbock, Tex, 10/21/20; s. Robert Ira Castle and Clara Lillie Hammond C; m. 5/1/53 to Alice Louise Kern; c. Jacqueline Patricia and Stephen Christopher. Educ: Tex. Tech. Col, B.A, 47, M.A, 51; Sigma Delta Pi; Phi Delta Kappa. Polit. & Govt. Pos: Mem, Calif. State Dem. Cent. Cmt, 58-; pres, Bakersfield Dem. Club, 59; secy, Kern Co. Dem. Cent. Cmt, 60-62; co-chmn, 18th Cong. Dist. Cent. Cmt, 62-64; V.pres, 15th Dist. Agr. Asn, 62-66; del, Dem. Nat. Conv, 64 & 68; mem, Electoral Col, 64. Bus. & Prof. Pos: Dean of student activities, Kern Co. High Sch. Dist, 58-69; asst. prof, Fresno State Col. Exten, 62-66. Mem: Calif. Teachers Asn; Calif. Asn. Dirs. of Activities; Nat. Educ. Asn; Calif. Asn. Secondary Sch. Adminstr; Am. Asn. Teachers Spanish & Portuguese; Calif. Asn. of Adult Educ; Mason; Elks; Eagles; DAV; Nat. Order of Trench Rats; VFW; Civil Air Patrol. Rel: Presbyterian. Mailing Add: 3311 Christmas Tree Lane, Bakersfield, Calif. 93306.

CASTLEBERRY, KELLY L. D
b. S. Charleston, W.Va, 1/17/26; s. William Thomas Castleberry and Thelma Stover C; m. 10/27/45 to Lorena Russe; c. Kelly L, II, David, Martin. Educ: Pub. Schs. of Kanawha Co. Polit. & Govt. Pos: W.Va. State Del, 60-66; former mem, Kanawha Co. Dem. Exec. Cmn; del, Dem. Nat. Conv, 68. Bus. & Prof. Pos: Realtor. Mil. Serv: Army, 45-47. Mem: Mason (32°); Nat. Asn. of Real Estate Bds; W.Va. Asn. of Realtors; Charleston Bd. of Realtors; Shrine; Royal Order of Jesters. Rel: Methodist. Mailing Add: 717 Jefferson St, South Charleston, W.Va. 25309. (1967)

CASTLES, RUTH BLAKE R
b. Great Falls, Mont, 5/25/18; d. William H. Blake and Lena Brown B; m. 1939 to Wesley Castles; c. Susan Lynn (Mrs. Billings), Judith Kay (Mrs. Golberg), Deborah Jane. Educ: Col. of Great Falls, 36-37; Mont. State Univ, 37-38. Polit. & Govt. Pos: Mem, Wesley Castles for State Attorney Gen. Campaign, 50; pres, Lewis and Clark Co. Rep. Women, 55-56; mem, Wesley Castle for Mont. Supreme Court Campaign, 58 & 64; campaign mgr, Hinman for State Treas, 60; secy, State Rep. Cent. Cmt, 60-66; precinct committee woman, 64-67; del, Rep. Nat. Conv, 68; co-chmn, Mont. State Nixon Pres. Cmt, 68. Mem: Daughters of the Nile; grand guardian, Job's Daughters, Mont, 60. Rel: Protestant. Mailing Add: York Route, Helena, Mont. 59601.

CASTLES, WESLEY Non-Partisan
Assoc. Justice, Mont. Supreme Court
b. Superior, Mont, 9/26/18; s. William Castles and Catherine Irwin C; m. March, 1939 to Ruth Olive Blake; c. Susan Lynn (Mrs. Billings), Judith Kay (Mrs. Golberg) and Deborah Jane. Educ: Univ. Mont, B.S. in forestry, 39, LL.B, 49. Polit. & Govt. Pos: Co. attorney, Missoula Co, Mont, 52-53; chmn. and exec. secy, Unemploy. Compensation Cmn, Mont, 53-55; exec. secy. to Gov, 55-56; assoc. justice, Mont. Supreme Court, 57- Bus. & Prof. Pos: Chmn, Criminal Law Cmn, Mont, at present. Mil. Serv: Entered as Pvt, Army Air Corps, 44, released as Cpl, 45. Rel: Protestant. Mailing Add: York Route, Helena, Mont. 59601.

CASTRO, RAMON D
Mem, Calif. Dem. State Cent. Cmt.
b. Monolith, Calif, 11/8/26; s. Jose Castro and Arnulfa Esparza C; m. 4/8/67 to Marian Dolores Bonner. Educ: Univ. Calif, Berkeley, A.B, 53; Univ. San Francisco Sch. of Law, LL.B, 59; Univ. Calif. Honor Soc; Nat. Soc. Scabbard and Blade. Polit. & Govt. Pos: Dep. city attorney, San Diego, Calif, 61-63; mem, Sen. Robert Kennedy's Campaign Cmt, San Diego Co, 68; co-chmn, Humphrey for President, San Diego Co, 68; mem, Calif. Dem. State Cent. Cmt, 68- Bus. & Prof. Pos: Attorney, San Diego, Calif, 63-65, Sheela, Lightner, Hughes, Hilmen & Castro, 66-; asst. prof. law, Univ. San Diego, 66- Mil. Serv: Entered as 2nd Lt, Army, Inf, 53, released as 1st Lt, 55, after serv. in 69th and 9th Inf. Div, continental U.S, 54-55, Res, 55-60. Mem: State Bar of Calif; San Diego Co. Bar; Am. Bar Asn; Am. Judicature Soc; Am. Trial Lawyers Asn; Nat. Asn. Defense Attorneys in Criminal Cases; Am. G.I. Forum (San Diego chap); Mexican-Am. Polit. Asn; Chicano Fedn. of San Diego; Fair Employ. Practices Adv. Cmt; Univ. Calif. Alumni Asn; Univ. San Francisco Law Soc. Rel: Catholic. Mailing Add: 1376 La Palma St, San Diego, Calif. 92109.

CASTRO, RAUL HECTOR D
b. Cananea, Sonora, Mex, 6/12/16; s. Francisco D. Castro and Rosario Acosta C; m. 11/13/47 to Patricia Norris; c. Mary Pat; Beth E. Educ: North. Ariz. Univ, B.A, 39; Univ. Ariz, LL.B, 49; Phi Alpha Delta; Phi Sigma Delta. LL.D, North. Ariz. Univ. Polit. & Govt. Pos: Dep. Dist. Attorney, Tucson, Ariz, 50-54, dist. attorney, 54-58, juvenile court judge, 59-61 and superior court judge, 62-64; U.S. Ambassador to El Salvador, 64-68; U.S. Ambassador to Bolivia, 68- Bus. & Prof. Pos: Instr. Spanish, Univ. Ariz, 46-49; sr. partner, Castro & Wolfe, Law Firm, Tucson, 49-51. Mil. Serv: Entered as Pvt, Ariz. Nat. Guard, 37, released as 1st Sgt, 39, after serv. in Inf, U.S. Publ: Several opinions while supreme court judge. Mem: Am, Inter-Am. and Pima Co. Bar Asns; Am. Judiciary Soc; Nat. Coun. Juvenile Court Judges; Am. Soc. Int. Law; Am. For. Serv. Asn. Outstanding Naturalized Citizen Award, Pima Bar Asn, 63; Americanism award, DAR, 64; Distinguished Pub. Serv. Award, Univ. Ariz, 66; Matias Delgado Decoration, Govt. El Salvador. Rel: Catholic. Mailing Add: 3701 E. River Rd, Tucson, Ariz. 85715.

CASWELL, RICHARD W. R
b. New York, N.Y, 1/24/04; m. to Doris Gravenhorst. Educ: Rutgers Univ, B.L, 26. Polit. & Govt. Pos: Mem, War Prod. Bd, 41-45; mem, Defense Transportation Admin, 50-53; town moderator, Narragansett, R.I, 55-58; former, chief, Bus. and Elec. R.R. Br; R.I. State Rep, 59-61 & 63-68, mem, Cmn. Interstate Coop, 59-60 and Pub. Rights of Way Cmt, 63-68, R.I. State House of Rep; v.chmn, Narragansett Planning Bd, 61- Bus. & Prof. Pos: Real estate broker; hwy. transport. consult. Mem: Sports and Recreation Cmn, Narragansett, 54-47. Mailing Add: 48 Kingstown Rd, Narragansett, R.I. 02883. (1967)

CATALÁ, LUIS ENRIQUE D
P.R. State Rep.
b. Yauco, P.R, 11/7/17; s. Francisco Catalá and Rita Maria Mattel C; m. 12/22/45 to Cecilia Franceschini; c. Cecilia Maria, Luis Enrique, Salvador Francisco, Ramón Antonio and Ana Rita. Educ: Peirce Sch. of Bus. Admin. Polit. & Govt. Pos: P.R. State Rep, 65- Bus. & Prof. Pos: Coffee Grower; Salesman, San Miguel Fertilizer Corp, 56-64. Mil. Serv: Entered as Pvt, Army, 42, released as T/Sgt, 45, after serv. in 65th Inf, 7th Army; Rome Arno, Rhine Land and Cent. Europe Campaign Ribbons; Am. Theater Serv. Medal; Victory Medal; 6 Overseas Serv. Bars; Good Conduct Medal; European African Middle East. Theater Serv. Medal with 3 Bronze Stars. Mem: Rotary; Am.Legion; Asn. Agr. P.R; Comité Asesor Lydia de Gallos en P.R. Yauco Volley Ball Team, 40. Rel: Catholic. Legal Res: Comercio 22, Yauco, P.R. 00768. Mailing Add: State House of Representatives, Capitol Bldg, San Juan, P.R. 00903. (1967)

CATALDO, PAUL AMADEO R
b. Franklin, Mass, 5/15/35; s. Joseph P. Cataldo and Irene Brennan C; m. 7/15/62 to Jean M. Phelan; c. John Paul and Joseph Paul. Educ: Trinity Col, Hartford, Conn, grad; Boston Col. Law Sch, Chestnut Hill, Mass, grad. Polit. & Govt. Pos: Town moderator, Franklin, Mass, 62-; Mass. state rep, 63-67. Mem: Mem, Nat. Asn. of Defense Lawyers (Criminal cases), 63- and Mass. Bar Asn, 61-; mem, Exec. Coun, Norfolk Co. Bar Asn, 64-66 and Am. Trial Lawyers Asn, 63-66. Mil. Serv: Pvt, Army Res, 60. Rel: Roman Catholic. Legal Res: 299 Main St, Franklin, Mass. 02038. Mailing Add: Law Offices of Bachner, Roche & Cataldo, 18 Cottage St, Franklin, Mass. 02038. (1967)

CATE, BYRON LEE D
Okla. State Rep.
b. Norman, Okla, 1/18/42; s. Roscoe Simmons Cate, Jr. and Frances Ethel Mitchell C; m. 6/15/63 to Sylvia Sharon Martin; c. Christie Lee and Byron Lee, Jr. Educ: Univ. Okla. Col. Law, 60-; Phi Gamma Delta. Polit. & Govt. Pos: Justice of the Peace, First Dist, Norman, Okla, 64-66; Okla. State Rep, 44th Dist, Cleveland Co, 66-, v.chmn, Engrossed and Enrolled Bills Cmt, Okla. House Rep, 67-68 and chmn, Appropriations and Budget Cmt, Subcmt. on Insts, 69-70. Bus. & Prof. Pos: Pres, Pedigo Builders, Inc, Norman, Okla, 69- Mem: Norman Bd. Realtors; Jaycees; C. of C. Nominated for the Three Outstanding Young Oklahomans by the Norman Jaycees, 69. Rel: Presbyterian. Mailing Add: 1602 Oakwood, Norman, Okla. 73069.

CATE, JEROME JOSEPH D
b. Baker, Mont, 9/19/39; s. Clifford G. Cate and Mary Bradac C; m. 6/18/66 to Mary Katherine McEacheron; c. Kristin. Educ: Carroll Col, B.A. in Bus. Admin, 61; Georgetown Univ, 61-63; Univ. Mont. Sch. Law, J.D, 66; Delta Epsilon Sigma; Delta Theta Phi. Polit. & Govt. Pos: Pres, Carroll Col. Young Democrats, 57-61; mem, Mont. State Dem. Exec. Cmt, 58-59; legis. asst. to U.S. Sen. Lee Metcalf, 61-64; v.pres, Mont. Young Democrats, 65-69; pres, Yellowstone Co. Dem. Club, 66-67; chmn, Mont. Civil Rights Cmt, 66-69; chmn, Yellowstone Co. Dem. Cent. Cmt, 68-69. del, Dem. Nat. Conv, 68. Bus. & Prof. Pos: Attorney at law, Billings, Mont, 66-69. Mem: Yellowstone Co. Bar Asn; Mont. Bar Asn; Mont. Trial Lawyers Asn; Am. Trial Lawyers Asn; Am. Judicature Soc; Am. Civil Liberties Union; Billings C. of C; Billings Commercial Club; Consumer's Coun; Human Rels. Cmt. Outstanding Man of Am, 69. Rel: Roman Catholic. Legal Res: 229 Clark, Billings, Mont. 59101. Mailing Add: P.O. Box 1943, Billings, Mont. 59103.

CATER, DOUGLASS D
b. Montgomery, Ala, 8/24/23; s. Silas D. Cater and Nancy Chesnutt C; m. 12/20/50 to Libby Anderson; c. Silas Douglass, III, Rebecca S, Libby M. and Benjamin W. Educ: Harvard, A.B, 47, M.A, 48; Guggenheim Fel, 55; Eisenhower Fel, 57-58. Polit. & Govt. Pos: Spec. asst. to Secy. of Army, 51; dir, Mutual Security Agency, 52; spec. asst. to President of U.S, 65-68. Bus. & Prof. Pos: Wash. ed, Reporter Mag, 50-63; Ferris vis. prof. pub. affairs, Princeton Univ, 59; vis. prof, Wesleyan Univ, 63; assoc. dir, Center Adv. Studies, 63; vis. scholar, Brookings Inst, 68- Publ: Co-auth, Ethics in a Business Society, Harper, 54; auth, The Fourth Branch of Government, Houghton, 59; Power in Washington, Random, 63. George Polk Mem. Award, 61. Rel: Presbyterian. Legal Res: 4901 Glenbrook Rd. N.W, Washington, D.C. 20016. Mailing Add: 1775 Massachusetts Ave. N.W, Washington, D.C. 20036.

CATER, EUGENE R. D
Mich. State Rep.
b. St. Joseph, Mo, 12/8/23; m. 1948 to Donna Mae Fenner; c. Robert Eugene. Educ: Ludington High Sch. Polit. & Govt. Pos: Mich. State Rep, 64-, asst. finance clerk, Mich. House of Rep, 69- Bus. & prof. Pos: Semi-retired. Mil. Serv: World War II. Mem: Elks; Eagles; Masons; Danish Brotherhood of Am; Am. Legion Post 76; DAV (state comdr, 63-64); U.S. Coast Guard Auxiliary; Mason Co. Conserv. Club; Nat. Order of Trench Rats; Ludington Boat Club; Mich. Laundry Asn.(state pres, 61-62). Rel: Lutheran. Mailing Add: 501 Ressequie St, Ludington, Mich. 49431.

CATES, JOHN LEWIS D
b. Columbiana, Ala, 6/3/28; s. Cecil Watson Cates and Hazel Mooney C; m. 2/10/51 to Jacquelyn Howell; c. John Howell, Jeffry Cecil and James Randolph. Educ: Auburn Univ, B.S; Sigma Pi. Polit. & Govt. Pos: Chmn, Bd. Supvr, Shelby Soil and Water Conserv. Dist, Ala; Ala. State Rep, 59-66. Bus. & Prof. Pos: Cattle and trucking bus. Mil. Serv: Entered as 1st Lt, Army Res, 50, released as Capt, 54, after serv. in 87th Maneuver Area Command. Mem: 1A Master Mason (3°); Scottish Rite; Mason (32°); past pres. Jr. C. of C. Rel: Methodist. Mailing Add: P.O. Box 1097, Columbiana, Ala. 35051.

CATLETT, LEON BIDEZ D
b. Dardanelle, Ark, 3/26/09; s. Samuel Graham Catlett and Alix Bidez C; m. 3/12/36 to Sally Cooper. Educ: Univ. of Ark. Sch. of Law, LL.B, 32; Phi Alpha Delta; Kappa Alpha. Polit. & Govt. Pos: Chmn, Ark. Dem. State Cmt, 63-67; del, Dem. Nat. Conv, 60, 64 & 68. Mil. Serv: Pvt, Army, 44-45. Mem: F&AM; Ark. Consistory; Valley of Little Rock; Shrine; Am. Col. Trial Lawyers; Am, Ark, Pulaski Co. and Fed. Bar Asns; Am. Judicature Soc; Am. Col. Probate Counsel; Am. Legion; Little Rock Country Club; Little Rock Club; Top of the Rock Club; North Hills Country Club. Rel: Presbyterian; Elder. Legal Res: 324 Midland Ave, Little Rock, Ark. 72203. Mailing Add: 727 Pyramid Life Bldg, Little Rock, Ark. 72201.

CATON, EDWARD T, III (NED) D
Va. State Sen.
b. Norfolk, Va, 4/7/28; m. to Patricia Lee Ackiss. Educ: Univ. Va, B.S, LL.B. Polit. & Govt. Pos: Former substitute judge, Princess Anne Co. Court, Va; former councilman, Va. Beach; Va. State Del, 66-69; Va. State Sen, 69- Bus. & Prof. Pos: Lawyer, Caton & Wright. Mil. Serv: Coast Guard Res, Korean Conflict. Mem: Va. State Bar Asn.(mem, First Dist. Cmt, chmn, Jr. Bar Sect). Young Man of the Year, Virginia Beach, 62. Rel: Methodist. Mailing Add: 418 Discovery Circle, Virginia Beach, Va. 23451. (1967)

CATT, VIRGINIA ANN D
Mem, Clark Co. Dem. Cent. Cmt, Nev.
b. Chicago, Ill, 2/18/31; d. Joseph A. Piekut and Anna Formella P; m. 5/11/57 to Charles E. Catt; c. Donald Norman, Julie Ann and Trudy Marie. Educ: John Marshall Law Sch, 3 years. Polit. & Govt. Pos: Secy, Las Vegas Young Dem, Nev, 55-57 and pres, 63-64; clerk of Justice Court, Las Vegas Twp, 55-57; secy, Nev. State Dem. Cent. Cmt, 56-58, mem, 58-68 and treas, 64-66; alternate del, Dem. Nat. Conv, 56-; precinct capt. and mem, Clark Co. Dem. Cent. Cmt, 56- and chairwoman, 60-62; Nat. Committeewoman, Young Dem. of Nev, 57-59, 61-63, 67-69 and state pres, 64-67; mem. coordinating cmt. & chmn. banquet and luncheon, Young Dem. Clubs of Am. Nat. Conv, 63 & 69; campaign secy, Howard W. Cannon Sen. Campaign, 64; state v.chmn, Citizens for Kennedy, 67-68. Mem: Paradise Bus. & Prfnl. Women's Club (treas, 58-59); Las Vegas Legal Secys.(gov, 57-58); Las Vegas Press Club; Clark Co. Parents and Teachers Orgn. Rel: Catholic. Legal Res: 343 Desert Inn Rd, Las Vegas, Nev. 89109. Mailing Add: P.O. Box 757, Las Vegas, Nev. 89101.

CATTERSON, JAMES M, JR. R
b. L.I, N.Y, 7/5/30; s. James M. Catterson and Dorothy Downs C; m. 9/5/55 to Lola Fae Hartwig; c. Lynn Fae and James Michael. Educ: Niagara Univ, A.B. cum laude, 52; St. John's Univ. Sch. Law, LL.B, 58; Delta Alpha Sigma. Polit. & Govt. Pos: Asst. Attorney Gen, State of New York, 58-59; Asst. U.S. Attorney, East. Dist. N.Y, 59-61; Asst. Dist. Attorney, Chief Rackets Bur, Suffolk Co, 63-67; Rep. cand, U.S. House Rep, First Cong. Dist, 66 & 68; counsel to Majority Leader, N.Y. State Assembly, 69- Bus. & Prof. Pos: V.pres. and gen. counsel, Am. Menmax Corp, Port Jefferson, N.Y, 67-; partner, Catterson and Nolan, Attorneys, 68- Mil. Serv: Entered as 2nd Lt, Army, 52, released as 1st Lt, 55, after serv. in 19th Inf. Regt, 24th U.S. Div, Korea, 53-54; Army Res, 54-66, Maj; Korean Serv. Medal; UN Serv. Medal; Am. Defense Ribbon; ROK Presidential Citation. Mem: Suffolk Co. and Fed. Bar Asns; N.Y. State Dist. Attorney's Asn; Ancient Order of Hibernians. Rel: Roman Catholic. Legal Res: Druid Hill Rd, Belle Terre, Port Jefferson, N.Y. 11777. Mailing Add: 314 Main St, Port Jefferson, N.Y. 11777.

CAUBLE, FLORENCE HORKAN (MRS. JOHN A.) R
Rep. Nat. Committeewoman, Ga.
b. Moultrie, Ga, 7/4/29; d. George Arthur Horkan and Martha Olliff H; m. 10/14/50 to Dr. John A. Cauble; c. Sally, Susan and David. Educ: Wesleyan Col, A.B, 50. Polit. & Govt. Pos: Pres, Cherokee Co. Fedn. Rep. Women, Ga, 60-65; dir. women's activities, ninth cong. dist, Prince Cong. Campaign, 64; ninth cong. dist. dir, Ga. Fedn. Rep. Women, 64-65 and treas, 65-68; v.chmn, Cherokee Co. Rep. Party, 64-66; chmn. co. conv. cmt, Ga. Rep. Party, 66, mem. ninth dist. cmt. and state cmt, 66-68 and mem. exec. cmt, 68-; Rep.

Nat. Committeewoman, 68- Bus. & Prof. Pos: Teacher, DeKalb Co, Ga, 50-51. Callaway Award, Outstanding Rep. Woman, Ga, 66. Rel: Methodist. Legal Res: Sunset Dr, Canton, Ga. 30114. Mailing Add: Route 6, Box 51, Canton, Ga. 30114.

CAUBLE, JOHN A. R
Chmn, Ninth Cong. Dist. Rep. Party, Ga.
b. Lupton City, Tenn, 1/1/28; s. George Clifford Cauble and Charlotte Honeycutt C; m. 10/14/50 to Florence Horkan; c. Sally, Susan and David Horkan. Educ: Emory Jr. Col, Oxford, Ga, 44-46; Emory Univ, B.A, 49; Emory Univ. Sch. Med, M.D, 54; Phi Delta Theta. Polit. & Govt. Pos: Chmn, Cherokee Co. Rep. Party, Ga, 64-68; chmn, Ninth Cong. Dist. Rep. Party, 66-; mem. exec. cmt, Rep. Party, Ga, 66-; del, Rep. Nat. Conv, 68. Bus. & Prof. Pos: Physician, Canton, Ga, 56- Mil. Serv: Entered as Pvt, Army, 46, released as Sgt, 47. Mem: Am. Med. Asn; Acad. Gen. Practitioners; Med. Asn. Ga; Ga. Med. Polit. Action Cmt; Cherokee-Pickens Med. Soc; Kiwanis. Rel: Methodist. Legal Res: Sunset Dr, Canton, Ga. 30114. Mailing Add: 200 Marietta St, Canton, Ga. 30114.

CAUCHON, ROBERT V. D
Chmn, Marshfield Dem. Town Cmt, Mass.
b. Lakewood, R.I, 6/21/26; s. Herve P. Cauchon and Lillian Page C; m. 10/22/55 to Betty A. Pederzini; c. Barbara A, Richard R. and Thomas W. Educ: Wesleyan Univ, Yale Univ, B.A; Univ. of Conn. Law Sch; Suffolk Law Sch, LL.B. Polit. & Govt. Pos: Del, Mass. Dem. State Conv, 62 & 66 and Dem. Nat. Conv, 64 & 68; exec. dir, Mass. Dem. State Cmt, 62-65, spec. counsel, 67-68; cmnr. apportionment, Mass. House of Rep, 63; secy, Gov. Cmt. of Mass, 64; chmn, Marshfield Dem. Town Cmt, currently. Bus. & Prof. Pos: Lectr. polit. sci, Am. Int. Col; attorney, Sullivan & Worcester, Boston, 65- Mil. Serv: Lt. Comdr, Naval Res. Mem: Plymouth Co. Dem. League; Yale Club of Boston; Am. Legion; Reserve Officers Asn. Rel: Roman Catholic. Mailing Add: 945 Union St, North Marshfield, Mass. 02059.

CAUSBY, TROY D
b. Calhoun, Ga, 1922; s. G.C. Causby and Zella Wood; m. 4/25/57 to Evelyn Hatcher Brooks; c. Molly Brooks Gallman, William Hartwell Brooks, Susan Rebecca Brooks, Martha Kathleen Brooks, John Holland Brooks, Mary Evelyn. Educ: Calhoun High Sch; N. Ga. Col, 2 yrs. Polit. & Govt. Pos: Ga. State Rep, 63-66. Bus. & Prof. Pos: Farmer, oil distributor. Mem: Gordon Co. Farm Bur. Rel: Methodist. Mailing Add: Calhoun, Ga. 30701. (1967)

CAVANAGH, EDWARD FRANCIS, JR. D
b. N.Y.C, 8/18/06; s. Edward Francis Cavanagh and Mae M. Masterson C; m. 3/26/40 to Nancy Miller; c. Edward Francis, III, Nannette Christine, Roderick Anthony and Mae M. Educ: Georgetown Univ, B.A, 29; Harvard Law Sch, 30-31; Brooklyn Law Sch, St. Lawrence Univ, LL.B, 33; Phi Delta Phi. Polit. & Govt. Pos: Practiced before N.Y. Dist. Courts, 35-36 and Supreme Court, 38; dep. cmnr, Dept. Marine and Aviation, N.Y.C, 47-49, cmnr, 50-54, dep. cmnr. and acting cmnr, Dept. Hosps, 49-50; cmnr, Fire Dept, 54-62; dep. mayor, N.Y.C, 62-66; mem, Gov. Emergency Adv. Cmt; chmn, Mayors Chaplaincy Bd, Mayor's Cmt. on Harlem Affairs and Mayors Task Force on Mkts; chmn, Interagency Relocation Coord. Cmt; v.pres. and dir, Thannawaga Dem. Orgn, N.Y.C; mem. exec. cmt, World's Fair, 64-65; mem, Hudson River Valley Cmn, Albany, 65- Bus. & Prof. Pos: Attorney-at-law, 33-; counsel, Curtiss-Wright Corp, N.Y.C. and Woodbridge, N.J, 45-47; dir, Neighborhood House, Glen Cove, L.I; chmn. bd, Layman's Adv. Cmt, Bellevue Hosp; treas, Mercy Hosp, Hempstead, L.I, 50-56; dir, James Cavanagh Corp; v.pres. and dir, Baker Industs, Inc, 66-; v.pres, Wells Fargo Armored Serv. Corp, 67- Mil. Serv: Lt. Col, Army Air Force, 42-45; Legion of Merit, U.S; Knight Grand Cross Order Holy Sepulchre of Jerusalem; Order St. George, Greece; Order Ruben Dario, Nicaragua; Cavaliere Officiale Order of Merit, Italy. Mem: N.Y. Bar Asn; Nat. Fire Protection Asn; Am. Legion; Racquet and Tennis, Lotos, Piping Rock and Beaver Dam Clubs; Whitehall Club, N.Y.C; Winter Sports Club, Locust Valley. William Randolph Hearst Gold Medal, Downtown Lower Manhattan Asn, 54; Distinguished Serv. Award, N.Y. Dept. Am. Legion, 55; Cath. War Vet. Award; Anti-Defamation League Award, 65; Chevalier, Order of Crown, Belgium; Economienda of Order of Isabella Catolica, Spain; Medal of Merit, Iran. Rel: Catholic. Legal Res: Naghward, Glen Cove, N.Y. 11542. Mailing Add: 205 E. 63rd St, New York, N.Y. 10021.

CAVANAGH, JEROME PATRICK D
Mayor, Detroit, Mich.
b. Detroit, Mich, 6/16/28; s. Sylvester J. Cavanagh and Mary Irene Timmins C; div; c. Mark, Patrick, David, Mary Therese, Christopher, Philip, Jerome Celestin and Elizabeth Angela. Educ: Univ. Detroit, B.S. in Polit. Sci, 50; Univ. Detroit Law Sch, J.D, 54; hon. fel, Kennedy Inst, Harvard Univ. Polit. & Govt. Pos: Chmn, Wayne Co. Young Dem, Mich, 49-50; del, State and Co. Dem. Conv; mem, Detroit Metrop. Airport Bd. of Zoning Appeals, until 62; mayor, Detroit, 62-; del-at-lg, Dem. Nat. Conv, 68. Bus. & Prof. Pos: Attorney-at-law, 55-62. Mem: Pres, U.S. Conf. of Mayors, 66; pres, Nat. League of Cities, 66; Urban Coalition Steering Cmt; Am. Judicature Soc; Am. Polit. Sci. Asn. Rel: Roman Catholic. Legal Res: 9240 Dwight Ave, Detroit, Mich. 48214. Mailing Add: 1126 City-County Bldg, Detroit, Mich. 48226.

CAVANAUGH, JAMES H. R
Dep. Asst. Secy. for Health and Sci. Affairs, Dept. Health, Educ. and Welfare
b. Madison, N.J, 3/3/37; m. to Esther S. Musselman; c. Elizabeth A. & Michael P. Educ: Fairleigh Dickinson Univ, B.S, 59; Univ. Iowa, M.A, 61; Ph.D, 64. Polit. & Govt. Pos: Former dir, Off. Comprehensive Health Planning, Pub. Health Serv. & Off. Planning & Prog. Coordination in Off. of Asst. Secy. Health & Sci. Affairs; Dep. Asst. Secy. Health & Sci. Affairs, 69- Bus. & Prof. Pos: Admin. staff, Princeton Hosp, N.J, 61-62; faculty, col. med, Univ. Iowa, 62-66. Mil. Serv: Lt, Med. Serv. C, U.S.N.R. Publ: 'The Rise of the Areawide Planning Agency,' 8/65 & 'Applying Industrial White Room Design Principles to Operating Room Design,' 8/65, Hospitals; 'The Physician's Role in Areawide Planning,' JAMA, 2/66; plus others. Mem: Am. Pub. Health Asn; Am. Hosp. Asn; Am. Col. Hosp. Adminstr. Recipient, William A. Jump Award for achievement in pub. admin, 69. Rel: Episcopal. Legal Res: 315 Ellis Ave, Iowa City, Iowa 52240. Mailing Add: Dept. of Health, Education & Welfare, 330 Independence Ave. S.W, Washington, D.C. 20201.

CAVANAUGH, PAUL JOSEPH D
Mass. State Rep.
b. Boston, Mass, 2/22/36; s. Matthias Cavanaugh and Charlotte Danca C; single. Educ: Suffolk Univ, A.B, 57, Law Sch, LL.B, 59. Polit. & Govt. Pos: Mass. State Rep, 63- Bus. & Prof. Pos: Lawyer, Medford, Mass, 59- Mem: Am. and Mass. Bar Asns; Elks; Moose; Kiwanis. Rel: Roman Catholic. Mailing Add: 14 Spring St, Medford, Mass. 02155.

CAVENDER, JOHN C. R
b. Manila, Philippine Islands, 1/21/19; s. Alexander C. Cavender and Elizabeth Carpenter C. Educ: Drew Univ, A.B; Jefferson Med. Col, M.D. Polit. & Govt. Pos: Pa. State Rep, 62-66. Bus. & Prof. Pos: Physician. Mil. Serv: U.S. Medical Corps, Maj. Mem: AMA; Pa. Med. Soc; past pres, Susquehanna Co. Med. Soc; VFW, State Surgeon, 54-56, State Comdr, 58-59, Nat. Surgeon Gen, 60-61; Mason. Mailing Add: Hop Bottom, Pa. 18824.

CAVIS, MORTON HASTINGS R
b. Bristol, N.H, 12/31/03; married; c. 1 son. Educ: Bristol and Dartmouth. Polit. & Govt. Pos: N.H. State Rep, until 67. Bus. & Prof. Pos: Retired in retail hardware bus; bd. of dir, Bristol Commun. Center and First Nat. Bank, Bristol. Mil. Serv: World War II. Mem: ATO; F&AM; Eastern Star; Am. Legion; Rotary. Rel: Congregational. Mailing Add: Star Route, Bristol, N.H. 03222.

CAVNAR, SAM R
Mem, Calif. Rep. State Cent. Cmt.
b. Denver, Colo, 11/10/25; m. 1947 to Lenora Woodgate; c. Dona (Mrs. Joseph Hambly) and Judy (Mrs. Ronald Peck). Polit. & Govt. Pos: Gen. chmn, Operation Houseclean and Citizens Cmt. to Elect Rep. Legislators; mem, Calif. and Los Angeles Co. Rep. Cent. Cmts, currently; nat. exec. dir, Proj. Prayer; exec. dir, Proj. Alert; cand, U.S. Rep, 30th Cong. Dist, Calif, 68. Bus. & Prof. Pos: Dist. mgr, U.S. C. of C, 53-58; owner and operator, bus. mgt. firm, 58-; nat. chmn. and bd. dir, Civic Asn. of Am, 8 years; mgr. Nu Orm Plans, Inc; consult. to architect and contractor, 1st U.S. missile site; prin. organizer, Westway Corp. and subsidiaries, South. Calif. Develop. Co. and Continental Am. Video Network Assocs. Reg, Inc; chmn. bd. dir, Boy Sponsors, Inc; v.pres. and treas, Am. Center for Educ, currently. Mil. Serv: Entered Navy, 42, released, 45, after serv. in Amphibious Forces, Atlantic and Pac. Theatres; Air Force Res, Korean War; Comdr, 20th Air Div, Coast Guard Auxiliary Search and Rescue Forces for five states, 59-60. Mem: Am. Legion (Nat. conv. distinguished guest cmt. and past comdr); DAV; VFW; co-chmn, Air Power Mem. Stadium Found. and Air Power Show; U.S. Air Force Acad. Uniform Selection Cmt; gen. chmn, Hungarian Freedom Fighters Tenth Anniversary Commemoration. Mailing Add: P.O. Box 3450, Hollywood, Calif. 90028.

CAVNESS, DON W D
Tex. State Rep.
b. San Antonio, Tex, 4/22/28; s. Charles H. Cavness and Addie Word C; m. 12/25/48 to Wynelle Ray; c. Susan, Randy and Carolyn. Educ: Univ. Tex, B.B.A. with Honors, 51; T Asn; Ex-Students Asn. Polit. & Govt. Pos: Tex. State Rep, Travis Co, 63-; fiscal officer, State Dept. Health; chief clerk, State Bd. Control. Mil. Serv: Entered as Pvt, Marine Corps, 46, released as Pfc, 48, after serv. in Pearl Harbor Marine Base, Marine Garrison Forces; Good Conduct Medal; Pac. Theater Medal. Publ: Fiscal Responsibilities in Public Health, Tex. Hosp, 64. Mem: Bd. dirs, Tex. Pub. Employees Asn, 56-58, v.pres, 57-58; bd. dirs, Univ. Kiwanis Club, 64-67; VFW; Travis Co. Farm Bur. Rel: Baptist. Mailing Add: Box 4807, Austin, Tex. 78751.

CAWLEY, ROBERT LUCIAN D
Mass. State Sen.
b. Boston, Mass, 7/30/34; s. Michael Joseph Cawley and Delia A. Conway C; m. 11/10/62 to Patricia A. O'Sullivan; c. Christopher, Suzanne, and Robert. Educ: Boston Col, B.S.B.A, 60; Northeast. Univ, M.A, 69. Polit. & Govt. Pos: Mass. State Rep, 63-68, committeeman, Fifth Suffolk Dem. Dist, 68-; Mass. State Sen, 69- Bus. & Prof. Pos: Sales promotion mgr, Signet Club Play, 61-63. Mil. Serv: Entered as Pvt, Marine Corps, 52, released as Cpl, 55, after serv. in First Marine Div, Korea, 53; Presidential Unit Citation with two battle stars; Purple Heart; Good Conduct Medal; Korean Presidential Unit Citation. Mem: Mass. Legis. Asn; VFW; Am. Legion; Order of Purple Heart; K. of C; Holy Name Soc. (exec. bd). One of Ten Outstanding Young Men of Greater Boston, 69. Rel: Catholic. Mailing Add: 53 Chesbrough Rd, W. Roxbury, Mass. 02132.

CAWTHORN, MERLE SLOAN D
Mem, La. State Dem. Cent. Cmt.
b. Grand Cane, La, 2/8/19; d. William Oscar Sloan and Birdie Griffin S; m. 7/9/38 to Joe Terrell Cawthorn, wid; c. Melody Merle. Educ: Grand Cane High Sch, La, grad, 35. Polit. & Govt. Pos: Clerk, Agr. Exten. Serv, La, 37-38; mem, La. State Dem. Cent. Cmt, currently; alternate del, Dem. Nat. Conv, 68; Outreach coordinator, De Soto Area Action Asn, local Off. Econ. Opportunity, La, 69- Bus. & Prof. Pos: Owner, Melody Realty Co, Mansfield, La, 60-69. Mem: Past pres, secy. and treas, De Soto Dept. Club; past pres, secy. and treas, Mansfield Elem. PTA; past secy. and treas, Mansfield Garden Club; secy, Mansfield High Sch. Band Boosters Club. Lady Citizen Award, De Soto Dept. Club, Mansfield, 65. Rel: Baptist; Pres, Dorcus Sunday Sch. Class, First Baptist Church. Legal Res: Highland Dr, Mansfield, La. 71052. Mailing Add: P.O. Box 671, Mansfield, La. 71052.

CAYCE, GEORGE L. D
b. Tulsa, Okla, 3/3/19; s. George Alfred Cayce and Cora Broadus C; m. Nov. 22nd to Ana Jane Chambers; c. George Lynn and Urita Ann. Educ: John Brown Univ, M.E.E, 39. Polit. & Govt. Pos: Alternate del, Dem. Nat. Conv, 68. Mil. Serv: Entered as Pvt, Air Force, 42, released as S/Sgt, 45. Mem: Kiwanis; UAW; pres, Kennedale Schs. Rel: Independent Fundamental. Mailing Add: Route 13, Box 290, Ft. Worth, Tex. 76119.

CAYLEY, HUBERT S. D
Chmn, Pembina Co. Dem, N.Dak.
b. Grafton, N.Dak, 6/8/24; s. Michael S. Cayley; m. to Rose Marie Marley; c. Michele, Patricia, John, Mary Jo and Marcia. Educ: Univ. N.Dak, LL.B, 50; Phi Alpha Delta. Polit. & Govt. Pos: Chmn, Pembina Co. Dem, N.Dak, currently; states attorney, Pembina Co, 59-61; mem, Abstracters Bd. of Exam, N.Dak, 63-; del, Dem. Nat. Conv, 64. Mil. Serv: Army, 43-46; Philippines and Okinawa Campaign Ribbons. Mem: N.Dak. Bar Asn. Mailing Add: Cavalier, N.Dak. 58220.

CAYWOOD, DELMAR EUGENE R
Treas, Mo. Rep. State Cmt.
b. Towanda, Kans, 10/12/17; s. Lu Caywood and Myrtle Bess C; m. 10/18/42 to Martha McClure; c. Janet (Mrs. Gary A. Stokes) and Carol. Educ: Med. Group Mgt. Asn. Inst, Mich. State Univ, 54; Drury Col, A.B, 55; Med. Group Mgt. Asn. Inst, Univ. Okla, 58; Med. Group Mgt. Asn. Inst, Tulane Univ, 61. Polit. & Govt. Pos: Chmn, Greene Co. Rep. Cent. Cmt, Mo, 59-64; treas, Mo. Rep. State Cmt, 68- Bus. & Prof. Pos: Mgr, Smith-Glynn-Callaway Clin, Springfield, 53-, secy. and dir, 56-; secy, Springfield Builders, Inc, 54-; exec. v.pres. and dir, Springfield Baptist Hosp, 56-; pres. and dir, The CeCat Co, Springfield, 59-; secy, Springfield Clin. Corp, 61- Mil. Serv: Entered as Pvt, Army, 41, released as Capt, 45, after serv. in 24th Div, Southwest Pac. Theater, 45, Res, 45-62, Maj.(Ret); Am. Defense, Good Conduct, Am. Theater, Victory and Res. Medals; Asiatic Theater Medal with Two Battle Stars; Philippine Liberation Medal with One Star; Occup. Medal with Japan Cluster. Publ: 'A Modified Incentive Plan for Distribution of Income,' 5/64 and 'Productivity and Manpower Utilization in a Group Practice Setting,' 5/68, Med. Group Mgt. Mem: Med. Group Mgt. Asn.(pres. and dir, 64-); fel. Am. Col. Clin. Mgr; Am. Pub. Health Asn; Mason (32°); Scottish Rite; Shrine; Am. Legion; perpetual mem, Mil. Order World Wars; VFW; life mem, Nat. Guard Asn. U.S; Springfield C. of C.(dir); Mo. State C. of C.(dir); U.S. C. of C; Asn. Army U.S; Mo. Pub. Expenditure Surv; Ozark Playground Asn; Nat. Geog. Soc; YMCA; Drury Col. Alumni Asn; Hickory Hills Country Club. Distinguished Serv. Award, Springfield Jr. C. of C, 53. Rel: Methodist. Legal Res: 1445 S. Fairway, Springfield, Mo. 65804. Mailing Add: 1211 S. Glenstone, Springfield, Mo. 65804.

CAYWOOD, MARY EUDORA R
V.Chmn, Archuleta Co. Rep. Party, Colo.
b. Stinnett, Tex, 11/26/17; d. Oliver Wesley Luginbyhl and Cleo Zell Ingram L; m. 12/24/35 to Marian Grover Caywood; c. Grover Clarence, Patricia Adale (Mrs. Petterson) and Ivan Terryle. Educ: Okla. Col. for Women 1 year. Polit. & Govt. Pos: Precinct committeewoman, Rep. Party, Archuleta Co. Colo, 65-67; v.chmn, Archuleta Co. Rep. Party, 67- Bus. & Prof. Pos: Secy, Caywood Inc, Pagosa Springs, Colo, 61- Mem: Rebeka; Farm Bur; Nat. Food Orgn; Cowbells; Home Demonstration Club. Rel: Southern Baptist. Mailing Add: Star Route, Pagosa Springs, Colo. 81147.

CEASER, PAUL G. D
b. Chicago, Ill, 9/20/11; m. 9/14/46 to Luella R. Trombly, M.D. Educ: DePaul Univ; John Marshall Law Sch, LL.B, 34. Polit. & Govt. Pos: Ill. State Rep, 70th-73rd Gen. Assembly; Asst. State's Attorney, 7 yrs; dir, Civil Defense, City of Berwyn. Prof. Pos: Magistrate, Circuit Court of Cook Co, Ill. Mil. Serv: Army, Maj, Europe, Bronze Star; 5 Battle Stars. Mem: Am, Ill. and W. Suburban Bar Asns; Am. Legion Post 422; Berwyn; Elks; Moose; Eagles; 33rd Div Asn. Mailing Add: 3622 Oak Park Ave, Berwyn, Ill. 60402. (1967)

CECCARELLI, DAVID PAUL D
Wash. State Rep.
b. Seattle, Wash, 6/1/33; s. Henry Paul Ceccarelli and Helen Lundberg C; m. 9/5/53 to Lois Ann Mortensen; c. Paul David, John Michael, Daniel Richard and Joseph Andrew. Educ: Seattle Univ, B.C.S. in commerce & finance, 55; Pan Xina. Polit. & Govt. Pos: Wash. State Rep, 34th Dist, 67- Bus. & Prof. Pos: Advert, Gen. Elec. Co, 53-58; dist. mgr, Libby McNeill & Libby, 58- Mem: Past pres, Univ. Toastmasters, 304 Int; bd. mem, West Seattle Coun. on Youth Affairs. Rel: Catholic. Mailing Add: 3823 42nd S.W, Seattle, Wash. 98116.

CECI, LOUIS J. R
b. New York, N.Y, 9/10/27. Educ: Marquette Univ, Ph.B, 51, LL.B, 54. Polit. & Govt. Pos: Former chmn, Youth Opportunity Cmt. UNICO; prosecuting asst. city attorney, Milwaukee, Wis, 58-63; Wis. State Assemblyman, 64-66. Bus. & Prof. Pos: Former brewery worker, taxicab driver and clerk-typist, War Dept; attorney-at-law, currently. Mil. Serv: Navy. Mem: Milwaukee Bar Asn.(mem, Cmn. Children's Court Surv); Milwaukee Bar Speakers Bur; Past Comdr, Am. Legion; former v.chmn, Northwest Civic Adv. Asn. Mailing Add: 8232 W. Winfield Ave, Milwaukee, Wis. 53218. (1967)

CECILE, ROBERT EARL D
Mem, Clark Co. Dem. Exec. Cmt, Ohio
b. Syracuse, N.Y, 11/25/30; s. Earl Francis Cecile and Marie Damico C; m. 3/31/51 to Norma Jean McBurney; c. Robert E, Jr, David J, Karen M, Daniel D, Kathy A, Joseph L, and James H. Educ: Syracuse Univ; Univ. Dayton; Miami Univ; Univ. South. Miss, B.S, 61; Univ. Okla, M.A, 63; Ph.D, 65; Nat. Defense Educ. Act grad. fel, 3 years; Pi Sigma Alpha; Pi Gamma Mu. Polit. & Govt. Pos: Dem. cand, U.S. House of Rep, Seventh Cong. Dist, Ohio, 68; mem, Ohio Cmt. to Revise Struct. of Nat. Conv. & Party Selection, 69; pres, Clark Co. Young Dem. Club, 69; mem, Clark Co. Dem. Exec. Cmt, 69- Bus. & Prof. Pos: Teaching asst. polit. sci, Univ. Okla, 64-65; asst. prof. polit. sci, Winona State Col, 65-66; naval intel. agent, Off. Naval Intel, Wash, D.C, 65; asst. prof. polit. sci, Wright State Univ, 66-69, acting chmn. dept, 67-68; assoc. prof, Cent. State Univ, Wilberforce, Ohio, 69- Mil. Serv: Entered as Pvt, Air Force, 50, released as T/Sgt, 62, after serv. in Strategic Air Command, U.S, Europe and Mid.E, 52-54; Lt, Naval Intel. Res, 64-; Aircrewmember Badge; Nat. Defense Medal; Expert Pistol; Army of Occup, Germany Ribbon; Good Conduct Medal. Publ: 'Frame of Reference for Study of American Foreign Policy,' J. Minn. Acad. Sci, 68; 'Teaching American Foreign Policy in Secondary Schools,' Soc. Stud, 68. Mem: Am. Polit. Sci. Asn; Midwest Polit. Sci. Asn; exec. bd, Dayton Am. Civil Liberties Union; pres, Wright State Univ. Fedn. of Teachers, AFL-CIO; del, Dayton-Miami Valley Labor Coun, AFL-CIO; NAACP; Lions Int. Rel: Catholic. Mailing Add: 3726 Marion Dr, Enon, Ohio 45323.

CEDERBERG, ELFORD A. R
U.S. Rep, Mich.
b. Bay City, Mich, 3/6/18; married; c. two. Educ: Bay City Jr. Col. Polit. & Govt. Pos: Mayor, Bay City, Mich, 49 & 51; U.S. Rep, 52-; del, Rep. Nat. Conv, 68. Bus. & Prof. Pos: Mgr, Nelson Mfg. Co. Mil. Serv: Army, 41-; commissioned Capt, 43; participant in Normandy Invasion, France and Germany; 5 Battle Stars; Bronze Star. Mem: Lions; Elks; Odd Fellows; Mason; Am. Legion; VFW. Rel: Evangelical. Legal Res: Bay City, Mich. 48706. Mailing Add: 7100 Sussex Pl, Alexandria, Va. 22307.

CEFKIN, J. LEO D
Co. Exec, Larimer Co. Dem. Party, Colo.
b. Rochester, N.Y, 3/16/16; s. Mischa Cefkin and Bluma Jacobson C; m. 8/3/49 to Rose Mackanick; c. Judith B, Barbara L, Jonathan S. and Melissa S. Educ: Los Angeles City Col, A.A, 39; Univ. South. Calif, B.A, 48; Columbia Univ, M.A, 49, Ph.D, 54; Pi Sigma Alpha. Polit. & Govt. Pos: Precinct committeeman, Larimer Co. Dem. Party, Colo, 58-; del, Dem. State Conv, 60, 62, 64 & 68; mem. exec. cmt, Larimer Co. Dem. Party, 60-, chmn, 61-63, co. exec, 69-; chmn, Colo. Prof. for Johnson-Humphrey, 64; chmn, Colo. Prof. for Humphrey-Muskie, 68; del, Dem. Nat. Conv, 68. Mil. Serv: Entered as Pvt, Army, 43, released as Pfc, 45, after serv. in 409th Inf. Div, ETO, 44-45; Combat Infantryman's Badge. Publ: Background of Current World Problems, David McKay, 67; 'The New States of Africa: A Troubled Start,' Rocky Mt. Soc. Sci. J, 10/67; 'The Rhodesian Question at the United Nations,' Int. Orgn, Vol. XXII, No. 3. Mem: Am. and West. Polit. Sci. Asns; Int. Studies Asn.(steering cmt); fel. African Studies Asn; Rocky Mt. Soc. Sci. Asn.(second v.pres, 61-62); West. Slavic Asn; Am. Asn. Univ. Prof; Larimer Co. Dem. Men's Club. Harris T. Guard Distinguished Prof. and Top Prof, Colo. State Univ; Nat. Merit Award, Nat. Jewish Welfare Bd. Rel: Jewish. Legal Res: 1932 Sheely Dr, Ft. Collins, Colo. 80521. Mailing Add: Dept. of Political Science, Colorado State University, Ft. Collins, Colo. 80521.

CELEBREZZE, ANTHONY J. D
b. Anzi, Italy, 9/4/10; s. Rocco Celebrezze and Dorothy Marcoguiseppe C; m. 5/7/38 to Anne Marco; c. Anthony J, Jean Ann, Susan Marie. Educ: John Carroll Univ; Ohio North. Univ, LL.B, 36; Hon. D.D, Wilberforce Univ, 55, LL.D, Fenn Col, 62, Boston Col, 63, LaSalle Col, 63, Ohio North. Univ, 63; Ph.D, R.I. Col, 64; D.Pub.Serv, Bowling Green State Univ, 64 and D.H.L, Miami Univ, 65. Polit. & Govt. Pos: Ohio State Sen, 51-53; mayor, Cleveland, Ohio, 53-62; secy, Dept. Health, Educ. and Welfare, 62-65; mem, President's Adv. Cmn. on Intergovt. Rels, 59-; mem, Sixth Circuit Court of Appeals, 65- Mil. Serv: Seaman, Navy. Mem: Am. Munic. Asn.(pres, 58-59). Distinguished Serv. award, Am. Munic. Asn, 60; Brotherhood Award, Nat. Conf. Christians and Jews, 55; Nat. Human Rels, 62; Order of Merit of Rep. of Italy, 55; Citation, United Negro Col. Fund, 56; Nat. Fiorello LaGuardia Award, 61; Nat. Cath. Resettlement Coun, 62; Pub. Serv, YMCA, 62; Gullick Award, Camp Fire Girls, Inc, 62; Peter Canisius Medal, Canisius Col, 63; Gold Medallion City of Rome, 63; Order of Merit; Eleanor Roosevelt Humanities Award. Rel: Catholic. Mailing Add: 17528 Lake Rd, Lakewood, Ohio 44107.

CELEBREZZE, JAMES P. D
Ohio State Rep.
b. Cleveland, Ohio, 2/6/38; s. Frank D. Celebrezze and Mary Delsander C; m. 11/11/67 to Daria Y. Yurkiw. Educ: Ohio State Univ, B.S, 60; Cleveland Marshall Col. Law, Cleveland State Univ, J.D, 67. Polit. & Govt. Pos: Page, Ohio State Legis, formerly; mem, Cuyahoga Co. Dem. Exec. Cmt, currently; Ohio State Rep, 50th Dist, 65- Bus. & Prof. Pos: Teacher, Cleveland Sch. Syst, 62-68; attorney-at-law, 67- Mil. Serv: Entered as Pvt, Army, 60, released as SP-4, 62, after serv. in 2/28 Artil, ETO, 61-62. Mem: Am, Ohio, Cleveland, Cuyahoga Co. and War Vets. Bar Asns; Ital. Sons and Daughters of Am; Ukranian Prfnl. Soc; Citizens League; Delta Theta Phi; Fourth, 22nd and 33rd Ward Dem. Clubs; Brook Park and Middleburg Heights Dem. Clubs; exec. bd, Southwest. Cultural Arts; Am. Fedn. Teachers. Rel: Roman Catholic. Mailing Add: 14612 Sheldon Blvd, Cleveland, Ohio 44142.

CELLER, EMANUEL D
U.S. Rep, N.Y.
b. Brooklyn, N.Y, 5/6/88; s. Henry H. Celler and Josephine Muller C; m. 6/30/14 to Stella B. Baar; wid; c. Judith C. and Jane B. (Mrs. Sydney B. Wertheimer). Educ: Columbia Col, A.B, 10; Columbia Univ. Law Sch, LL.B, 12. Polit. & Govt. Pos: U.S. Rep, N.Y, 22-, chmn, House Cmn. on the Judiciary; mem, Platform and Resolutions Cmts, Dem. Nat. Conv, 44, 48, 52, 56, & 60; del, Dem. State Conv, N.Y; trustee, Jewish Nat. Fund. Bus. & Prof. Pos: Lawyer; dir, Fischbach & Moore and Oppenheimer Fund; organized Brooklyn Nat. Bank; mem, Weisman, Celler, Allan Spett & Sheinberg. Publ: You Never Leave Brooklyn. Mem: Am, Co. and Brooklyn Bar Asns; Am. Jewish Cmt; Am. Jewish Cong; chmn, Am. Red Mogen David; dir, Brookdale Hosp. Center; hon. dir, Jewish Family Welfare Soc; Columbia Univ. Alumni Asn; B'nai B'rith; K. of P; Unity Club. Award and Medallion of Commendatore of the Order Merit of Repub. of Italy. Legal Res: 9 Prospect Park West, Brooklyn, N.Y. 11215. Mailing Add: The Mayflower, Washington, D.C. 20036.

CENARRUSA, PETER THOMAS R
Secy. of State, Idaho
b. Carey, Idaho, 12/16/17; s. Joseph Cenarrusa and Ramona Gardoqui C; m. 10/25/47 to Freda B. Coates; c. Joe Earl. Educ: Univ. Idaho, B.S. in Agr, 40; Tau Kappa Epsilon. Polit. & Govt. Pos: Idaho State Rep, 51-67, speaker, Idaho House of Rep, 63-67; mem, Idaho Bd. Land Cmnrs. and Idaho Bd. of Exam; Parliamentarian, Idaho Rep. State Conv, 62, chmn, 64; chmn, Idaho Legis. Coun, 63 and Idaho Govt. Reorgn. Cmt; Idaho del. mgr. for bd. mgrs, Coun. State Govt, 63-; Secy. of State, Idaho, 67- Bus. & Prof. Pos: Teacher, high sch, Cambridge, Carey and Glens Ferry, Idaho, 40-41 & 46; teacher voc. agr, Vet. Admin, Blaine Co, 46-51; owner, Cenarrusa Livestock and Farming, 48- Mil. Serv: Entered Marine Corps, 42, released as Maj, 46, after serv. as Naval Aviator, VMF 421, El Toro, Calif, VMSB 932, Cherry Point, N.C. and instr. in naval aviation, Corpus Christi, Tex; Maj.(Ret), Marine Corps Res, 46-59; Am. Theatre, Victory and World War II Medals. Mem: Blaine Co. Livestock Mkt. Asn.(dir, 52); Blaine Co. Woolgrowers Asn.(chmn, 54), Carey C. of C.(pres, 52); Univ. Idaho Alumni Asn; Idaho Flying Legislators (pres, 53-63); bd. dirs, Idaho State Arthritis Found; Elks; Kiwanis; Am. Legion. Named Hon. Farmer, Future Farmers of Am, 55. Rel: Catholic. Legal Res: Carey, Idaho 83320. Mailing Add: 2400 Cherry Lane, Boise, Idaho 83701.

CENOTTO, LAWRENCE ARTHUR, IV 'LARRY' R
Mem, Calif. Rep. State Cent. Cmt.
b. St. Louis, Mo, 10/20/31; s. Lawrence A. Cenotto, III and Mary Smith C; m. 6/15/52 to Barbara Mary Grogan; c. Lawrence A, V, Lisa Dawn, Loring Ames, Locke Ashley and Laird Andrew. Educ: Compton Col, A.A, 51; Calif. State Col. Long Beach; Univ. Calif, Berkeley; Univ. Calif, Los Angeles, 1½ years; Beta Phi. Polit. & Govt. Pos: Founder, Amador, Calaveras, El Dorado and Inyo Co. Young Rep, Calif, 67; chmn, Amador Co. Young Rep, 67; mem,

Amador Co. Rep. Cent. Cmt, 67-; field admin. asst. to Calif. State Assemblyman Gene Chappie, 67-; region VI v.pres, Calif. Young Rep, 68, resolutions chmn, 69; mem, Calif. Rep. State Cent. Cmt, 69- Bus. & Prof. Pos: Sports dir, KTMS, Santa Barbara, Calif, 60-63; news ed, KBEE, Modesto, 63-64; reporter and photographer, Sacramento Bee, 64-67. Mil. Serv: Entered as Pvt, Army Mil. Police, 52, released as Cpl, 54, after serv. in 91st Mil. Police Bn, Korea, 53-54; Miscellaneous minor ribbons and unit decorations. Mem: Nat. Sportcasters Asn; Amador Co. Hist. Soc; Kiwanis; Adults for Youth Asn; Jackson Quarterback Club; Ital. Benevolent Soc; Kit Carson Mt. Men; E Clampus Vitus. Mailing Add: 211 W. Sierra View Dr, Jackson, Calif. 95642.

CEPHAS, B. ADDISON, JR. D
Mem, City Coun, Richmond, Va.
b. Newport News, Va, 4/25/08; s. B. Addison Cephas, Sr. and Fannie Blair C; m. 9/21/34 to Marjorie Louise Sircus; c. Gloria (Mrs. Venter) and Marilyn (Mrs. Rozier). Educ: Va. Union Univ, grad. class of 31; Alpha Phi Alpha. Polit. & Govt. Pos: Mem, Richmond City Planning Cmn, Va, 60-64; Mem, City Coun, Richmond, Va, 64- Bus. & Prof. Pos: Owner, B.A. Cephas Real Estate. Mem: Crusade for Voters; NAACP, Richmond Chapter of Guardsmen. Rel: Baptist. Legal Res: 3304 Edgewood Ave, Richmond, Va. 23222. Mailing Add: 537 N. Second St, Richmond, Va. 23219. (1967)

CERMAK, ALBINA ROSE R
Committeewoman, Ohio Rep. State Cent. Cmt.
b. Cleveland, Ohio; d. Frank J. Cermak and Rose Marek C; single. Educ: Cleveland Col, Western Reserve Univ. Polit. & Govt. Pos: V.chmn. and secy, Cuyahoga Co. Rep. Cent. and Exec. Cmts, Ohio, 39-53; chairwoman, Rep. Women's Orgn. Cuyahoga Co, 39-53; del, Rep. Nat. Conv, 40, 44, 52 and 64, mem. resolutions cmt, 44 & 52; bd. mem, Ohio Fedn. Women's Rep. Clubs, 40-53 & 62-; mem, Rep. Cent. and Exec. Cmts, 20th Cong. Dist, 40-53 and 62-; U.S. Collector Customs, Ohio Dist, 41 & 53-61; secy, Ohio Rep. Cent. and Exec. Cmts. and mem, Cuyahoga Co. Bd. Elec, 46-53; cand. for mayor, Cleveland, 61; secy, Ohio Real Estate Cmn, 63; bailiff, Cuyahoga Co. Common Pleas Court, 64-65; State exam, State Auditor's Off, 65-67, admin. specialist, 67-; committeewoman, Ohio Rep. State Cent. Cmt, 23rd Cong. Dist, 66- Mem: Ohio Asn. Elec. Off.(v.pres. and secy, 48-53); League Women Voters; former bd. mem, Women's City Club; bd. mem, Grand Jury Asn, Cath. Sch, Nat. Coun. Cath. Women, Cleveland Diocesan Coun. Cath. Women, Cleveland Cath. Fedn. and Coun. Human Rels; Cath. Daughters Am; Women's Guild, St. Vincent Charity Hosp; Carmelite Guild; Bus. & Prfnl. Women's Club; Citizens League; Cleveland Ment. Health Asn; Cleveland Coun. World Affairs; Cleveland Mus. Art; adv. bd, Depaul Maternity and Infant Home; Our Lady of Angels Guild; Mt. Loretta Guild; former treas, St. Ignatius Altar and Rosary Soc; Consumers League; Christ Child Soc; Cleveland World Trade Asn; past resident chmn, Am. Red Cross; trustee, Nationality Serv. Center; mem, Cath. Bd. of Educ. Diocese of Cleveland. Selected 1 of 10 Outstanding Cleveland Career Women; Life Mem. Award, DePaul Maternity and Infant Home, 69. Rel: Roman Catholic. Mailing Add: 3719 Rocky River Dr, Cleveland, Ohio 44111.

CEROSKY, RICHARD A. R
N.Y. State Assemblyman
b. New York, N.Y, 2/13/27; m. to Edith Glade; c. four. Educ: N.Y. State War Serv. Scholarship, N.Y. Univ. Polit. & Govt. Pos: Pres, Rep. Club and bd. of assessors, Mt. Pleasant, N.Y. and mem, Westchester Co. Rep. Cmt, formerly; N.Y. State Assemblyman, 64- Bus. & Prof. Pos: With Carvel-Dari Freeze Stores, Inc, 49-51, v.pres, 51-57; real estate and ins. bus, currently. Mil. Serv: Army, ETO, discharged 47. Mem: Valhalla Civic Asn; Rotary; Westchester Co. Realty Bd; Westchester Co. Independent Ins. Agents Asn; Commun. Div. of Civil Defense, Westchester; N.Y. State Assessors Asn. Rel: Lutheran. Mailing Add: 50 Galloway Lane, Valhalla, N.Y. 10595.

CERULLI, LOUIS ANTHONY D
b. Rochester, N.Y, 7/2/11; s. Emidio Cerulli and Virginia Bottone C; m. 8/13/33 to Elizabeth Sarah Giglia; c. Carreen Randy (Mrs. Guglielmino). Educ: Univ. Ala, A.B, 35; Hahnemann Med. Col, M.D, 40; Alpha Phi Delta; Lambda Phi Mu. Polit. & Govt. Pos: Cmnr. schs, Bd. Educ, N.Y, 59-, pres, 3 terms; pres, Prfnl. Men's Club, 65; physician, Rochester Post Off, 66-67; del, Dem. Nat. Conv, 68; chmn, Big Six Bd. Educ, N.Y. State, 68-69. Bus. & Prof. Pos: Pres, Delite Dairy Co, Rochester, N.Y, 60; treas. and bd. dirs, Park Ave. Hosp, 64-67, pres. staff, 65; pres, Monroe Co. Gen. Practice, 65; pres, Am. Cancer Soc, 65. Mil. Serv: Navy, 42, Lt.(jg). Mem: Monroe Co, N.Y. State and Am. Med. Soc; jr. fel, Int. Col. Surgeon; fel. Am. Soc. Abdominal Surgeons; Prfnl. Men Club; C. of C; Adclub; Kiwanis; plus other civic orgns. Citizen of the Year, Rochester, 65; Citation, Bd. of Educ, Rochester, Am. Cancer Soc. and Greece, N.Y. C. of C. Rel: Catholic. Mailing Add: 2085 Lake Ave, Rochester, N.Y. 14615.

CERUZZI, MICHAEL JOSEPH D
Chmn, Easton Dem. Town Cmt, Conn.
b. New Haven, Conn, 8/30/12; s. Leonardo Antonio Ceruzzi and Maria Gioscia C; m. 6/26/39 to Mary Assunta Taglino; c. Anne Marie (Mrs. Kenney), Michael L. and Paul E. Educ: Fordham Col, A.B, 33; Harvard Bus. Sch, M.B.A, 35; Alpha Phi Delta. Polit. & Govt. Pos: Mem. Bd. of Educ, Easton, Conn, 50-59, bd. of Tax Rev. and Bd. of Finance, 62-; chmn, Easton Dem. Town Cmt, 66- Bus. & Prof. Pos: Agent, Am. Credit Ind. Co, 46-69; loan reviewer, City Trust Co, 69- Mem: Exchange Club. Rel: Catholic. Mailing Add: 20 Cedar Hill Lane, Easton, Conn. 06612.

CERVANTES, ALFONSO J. D
Mayor, St. Louis, Mo.
b. St. Louis, Mo, 8/27/20; married; c. six. Educ: St. Louis Univ. Polit. & Govt. Pos: Alderman, St. Louis, Mo, 49-59, pres, Bd. of Aldermen, 59-63, mayor, 65- Bus. & Prof. Pos: Pres, Cervantes and Assocs, gen. ins. Recipient, citations for work in field of human rights; nat. recognition for address calling upon indust. to fit long-time unemployed into jobs; Outstanding Man of Year, C. of C, Metrop. St. Louis, 55. Mailing Add: c/o City Hall, 1206 Market, St. Louis, Mo. 63103.

CERVANTES, ALFRED F. D
Committeeman, Santa Clara Co. Dem. Cent. Cmt, Calif.
b. Del Rio, Tex, 12/8/33; s. Epigmenia Fuentes C. and father deceased; m. to Oralia Rios; c. Donna Dorothy, Antionette Marie and Arlene Francis. Educ: Univ. Tex, Austin, 59-60; Tex. West. Col, 60-64. Polit. & Govt. Pos: Del, Dem. Nat. Conv, 68; committeeman, Santa Clara Co. Dem. Cent. Cmt, 68- Mil. Serv: Entered as Pvt, Army, 51, released as Sgt, 54, after serving in 97 AAA Gun Bn; Good Conduct Medal; Nat. Defense Serv. Medal; Korean Serv. Medal with Three Bronze Stars; Syngman Rhee Citation. Mem: Painters local union; Notre Dame Dad's Club; Mex. Am. Commun. Orgn; Mex. Am. Polit. Orgn. Rel: Catholic. Mailing Add: 2630 Gassmann Dr, San Jose, Calif. 95121.

CERVENKA, WILLIAM JOSEPH R
Chmn, Runnels Co. Rep. Party, Tex.
b. Rowena, Tex, 2/5/31; s. E. J. Cervenka and Otillia Gengross C; m. 3/14/53 to Theresa Ann Guilbeau; c. Frank, Annette and Christopher. Educ: Tex. A&M Univ, B.S; Phi Kappa Phi; Alpha Zeta. Polit. & Govt. Pos: Secy-treas, Runnels Co. Rep. Party, Tex, 63-66, chmn, 66- Mil. Serv: Entered as 2nd Lt, Air Force, 52, released as 1st Lt, 54, after serv. in Japan; Maj, Air Force Res; Korean Serv. Medal; UN Serv. Medal; Nat. Defense Serv. Medal. Mem: V.pres, Runnels Co. Farm Bur. Rel: Catholic. Mailing Add: Route 1, Ballinger, Tex. 76821.

CHACON, MATIAS L. D
Educ: Ind. Univ, B.S; Univ. of N.Mex, LL.B. Polit. & Govt. Pos: N.Mex. State Sen, -66; N.Mex. State Rep, 57-64; majority floor leader; State pres, N.Mex. Young Dems. Bus. & Prof. Pos: Lawyer. Mil. Serv: WWII. Mem: Am. Legion; VFW; K. of C; Elks. Rel: Catholic. Mailing Add: P.O. Box RR, Espanola, N.Mex. 87532. (1967)

CHADWICK, OTIS CLIFTON R
Chmn, Randolph Planning Cmn, Vt.
b. Randolph, Vt, 6/9/00; s. Charles Arvil Chadwick and Mary Blodgett C; m. 10/8/23 to Edith Dorothy Clifford; c. Nelson, Charles, Elaine (Mrs. Harold J. Soule) and Mary (Mrs. Stan Poeter). Educ: Vt. State Sch. Agr, 16-18; Cornell Univ, 19-20. Polit. & Govt. Pos: Selectman, Randolph, Vt, 44-53, mgr, 57-62; Vt. State Rep, 57-65; chmn, Town Planning Cmn, 67- Bus. & Prof. Pos: Owner poultry and dairy farm. Mem: Farm Bur; past pres, Vt. Poultry Asn; exec. secy. and treas, Vt. Tech. Col. Alumni Asn. Master Poultryman's Award, Vt. Poultry Asn. Rel: Congregational. Mailing Add: RFD 1, Randolph, Vt. 05061.

CHADWICK, THOMAS ALLEN R
b. Osterville, Mass, 5/31/95; m. to Mabel A. French; c. Three sons; four daughters. Educ: Tabor Acad; 2 years private classes, Prof. A.E. Hinckley. Polit. & Govt. Pos: Vt. State Rep, 65-69; del, Rep. Nat. Conv, 68. Bus. & Prof. Pos: Retired, machinist, 25 years. Mem: Patrons of Husbandry; past Nat. Comdr, Sons of Union Vets, Civil War; Lt. Col, Sons of Vets. Res; Chester Rod & Gun Club; Vt. Civil War Cent. Cmt, 6 years. Rel: Baptist. Mailing Add: R.D. 1, Box 81, Chester, Vt. 05143. (1967)

CHAFEE, JOHN HUBBARD R
Secy. of the Navy
b. Providence, R.I, 8/22/22; s. John Sharpe Chafee and Janet Hunter C; m. 11/4/50 to Virginia Coates; c. Zechariah, Lincoln, John, Georgia and Quentin. Educ: Yale Univ, A.B, 47; Harvard Univ, LL.B, 50; Delta Kappa Epsilon. Polit. & Govt. Pos: R.I. State Rep, 57-61, Minority Leader, R.I. House of Rep, 58-61; Gov, R.I, 63-69; del, Rep. Nat. Conv, 64 & 68; chmn, Compact for Educ, 65; mem, Nat. Rep. Coord. Cmt. and Exec. Cmt, Rep. Gov. Asn; v.chmn, Nat. Rep. Gov. Asn, 67-69; Secy. of the Navy, 69- Mil. Serv: Enlisted Marine Corps, serv. in First Div, 42-46, Guadalcanal, Okinawa and China; 50-52, First Div, Korean War, discharged as Capt. Mem: Am. Legion. Rel: Episcopal. Legal Res: Ives Rd, Warwick, R.I. 02818. Mailing Add: 4E686, Pentagon Bldg, Washington, D.C. 20350.

CHAFFEE, FLORENCE ESTHER R
b. Beaver, Pa, 4/27/04; d. Benjamin Heideger and Nellie T. Camp H; m. 10/3/25 to Lyle LaVerne Chaffee. Educ: Duff's Iron City Bus. Col, grad, 23. Polit. & Govt. Pos: Pres, v.pres and bul. chmn, St. Petersburg Women's Rep. Club, 48-61; dir, Pinellas Co. Rep. Exec. Cmt, 48-69, secy, 66; alternate del, Rep. Nat. Conv, 60, del, 64; treas, Fla. Fedn. Rep. Women, 61-63; v.pres, Pinellas Co. Women's Rep. Club, 65-67, pres, 67-69. Mem: Fla. Fedn. Women's Clubs (credentials chmn, dist. dir, educ. chmn, club news ed, libr. chmn. and mem. scholarship cmt, 58-69); St. Petersburg Woman's Club (pres, v.pres, 2nd v.pres. and treas, 48-69); Toastmistress Club (St. Petersburg Pres. and Roster Chmn, 65-66, v.chmn, chmn. and secy TM-Coun, 66-69); Church Drama Guild (corresponding secy, 62-70); pres, Christian Women's Fel, Mirror Lake Christian Church and Year Book Circle Leader, 56-70; Little Theater of St. Petersburg (active mem, dir, props chmn, producer and actress, 48-69). Rel: Christian Church. Mailing Add: 808 16th Ave. N, St. Petersburg, Fla. 33704.

CHAHARYN, ORIST D. D
R.I. State Rep.
b. Woonsocket, R.I, 5/17/17; m. to Emily M. Educ: Univ. of R.I, B.S, 39; Northeast. Univ, LL.B, 54. Polit. & Govt. Pos: Councilman, Woonsocket, R.I, 50-52; R.I. State Rep, 53-; del, Constitutional Conv, 58 & 65. Bus. & Prof. Pos: Attorney. Mil. Serv: Air Force, World War II; Lt. Col, Air Force Res, formerly liaison officer for Air Force Acad. Mailing Add: 35 Lyman St, Woonsocket, R.I. 02895. (1967)

CHAISSON, JOEL THOMAS D
b. Chaegby, La, 12/9/34; s. Arthur F. Chaisson and Elva Hymel C; m. 6/11/55 to Bobbie Nell Gulledge; c. Joel Thomas, II, Paul Andre, Robert Arthur, Jared Andrew, Walter David and Maria Marlaine. Educ: Southeast. La. Col; La. State Univ; Francis T. Nicholls State Col; Phi Delta Phi. Polit. & Govt. Pos: Former La. State Rep, St. Charles Parish. Bus. & Prof. Pos: Mem, St. Charles-St. John the Baptist Bridge & Ferry Authority, 64- Mil. Serv: Entered as 2nd Lt, Army Res, 59, released as Capt, 66. Mem: Am, La. and 29th Judicial Dist. Bar Asns; K. of C; Lions; dir, United Givers Fund, 64. Rel: Catholic. Legal Res: River Rd, Destrehan, La. Mailing Add: P.O. Box 73, Luling, La. 70070.

CHALUPSKY, HARRY RICHARD R
Chmn, Itasca Co. Rep. Party, Minn.
b. Silver Lake, Minn, 1/5/25; s. Frank A. Chalupsky and Mary Podhrasky C;

m. 10/1/65 to Joyce Hammarbeck; c. Jan Donald and Rosemary Mueller. Educ: Col. of St. Thomas, 3 years; William Mitchell Col. Law, LL.B, 52; Phi Beta Gamma. Polit. & Govt. Pos: Mem, Rep. Finance Drives, Itasca Co, Minn, 60-66; finance chmn, Itasca Co, 63; co. conv. chmn, Itasca Co, 64-65; chmn, Itasca Co. Rep. Party, 67-; Eighth Dist. chmn, Hennen for Cong. Vol. Cmt, 68. Bus. & Prof. Pos: Practicing attorney, Grand Rapids, Minn, 60-; pres, Show Boat, Inc, Grand Rapids, Minn, 61-65. Mil. Serv: Entered as A/S, Navy, 43, released as Yeoman 1/C, 46, after serv. in U.S.S. Ashland and U.S.S. Grand Canyon, S.Pac; World War II Medal; Saipan, Tinian, Leyte and Lingaeyan Gulf, Philippines and Iwo Jima opers. citations. Publ: Author, local newspaper articles. Mem: Minn. State Bar Asn; Itasca Co. Bar Asn. (secy, 61-62, chmn. munic. court cmt, 63-68); Am. Legion, VFW; C. of C; Kiwanis. Rel: Catholic. Legal Res: Route 4, Grand Rapids, Minn. 55744. Mailing Add: Huntley Bldg, Grand Rapids, Minn. 55744.

CHAMBERLAIN, CHARLES E. R
U.S. Rep, Mich.
b. Locke Township, Mich, 7/22/17; m. 1943 to Charlotte Mary Craney; c. Charlotte Ellen, Christine Clark and Charles Jr. Educ: Univ. Va, B.S, LL.B, 49. Polit. & Govt. Pos: Internal Revenue Agent, U.S. Treas. Dept, 46-47; city attorney, East Lansing, Mich, formerly; legal counsel, Mich. Sen. Judiciary Cmt, 53-54; prosecuting attorney, Ingham Co, 55-56; U.S. Rep, Mich, 56-Bus. & Prof. Pos: Attorney-at-law. Mil. Serv: World War II, 4 years; Commanding Officer of Vessels, Pac. and Atlantic; Coast Guard Res. Mem: Mich. State Bar; Am. Bar Asn. Legal Res: East Lansing, Mich. 48823. Mailing Add: U.S. House of Representatives, Washington, D.C. 20515.

CHAMBERLAIN, KENNETH WELLINGTON R
b. Berwick, Maine, 11/30/98; married; c. 7. Educ: Dartmouth Col; Northeast. Univ. Polit. & Govt. Pos: Former N.H. State Rep. and selectman, Alton, N.H. Bus. & Prof. Pos: Retired RR airbrake instr. Mil. Serv: Hon. discharge, Dartmouth S.A.T.C. Mem: Mason (32°); Am. Legion. Rel: Protestant. Mailing Add: Old Wolfeboro Rd, Alton, N.H. 03809. (1967)

CHAMBERLAIN, LESLIE M. R
b. Brookfield, N.H, 7/24/90; married; c. Seven. Educ: Brewster Acad. Polit. & Govt. Pos: Selectman, Wolfeboro Falls, N.H, 23-32; hwy. agent, 32-56; N.H. State Rep, 59-69. Bus. & Prof. Pos: Retired. Mil. Serv: U.S. Army, 18-19. Mem: Masons; Am. Legion; World War I Vet. Rel: Protestant. Mailing Add: Wolfeboro Falls, N.H. 03894. (1967)

CHAMBERLAIN, WILLIAM H. D
b. Springfield, Ill, 1/22/31; s. Don E. Chamberlain and Agnes Kennedy C; m. 4/19/58 to Carolyn Jenot; c. Karen Sue, Lisa Lynn, William and Robert. Educ: Springfield Jr. Col, A.A, 51; Univ. Ill, B.S, 53, Univ. Ill. Law Sch, J.D, 55; Kappa Sigma; Phi Delta Phi. Polit. & Govt. Pos: Legal adv. to Speaker of House. Rep, Ill, 59-61; admin. asst. to Gov, 61-64; secy. of state, 64-65; Circuit Court Judge, Seventh Circuit, Ill, 65- Bus. & Prof. Pos: Lawyer. Mil. Serv: Marine Corps Res, 53-63; serv. in First Marine Air Wing, Japan. Mem: Sangamon Co. and Ill. State Bar Asns; Am. Judicature Soc; K. of C; Springfield Urban League. Rel: Catholic. Mailing Add: c/o County Bldg, Springfield, Ill. 62701.

CHAMBERLIN, GAYLORD BARTLETT R
Chmn, Kootenai Co. Rep. Party, Idaho
b. Bend, Ore, 7/31/26; s. Gaylord Bartlett Chamberlin and Jean Richards C; m. 4/19/68 to Evelyn Boling; c. Ruth Ann, Nancy, Karen Leigh, Kara, Sandra Louise, Kevin, Kurt, James Bartlett and Patricia Lynn. Educ: Univ. Idaho, B.S, 48, M.S, 49; Univ. Calif, Los Angeles, 49-50; Phi Delta Theta. Polit. & Govt. Pos: Chmn, Kootenai Co. Rep. Party, Idaho, 68- Mil. Serv: Entered as Pvt, Army, 45, released as T/4, 49, after serv. in 9th Inf. Div. Finance, ETO, 45-46. Mem: Toastmaster Clubs; Athletic Clubs Univ. Idaho Vandal Boosters; Lions. Rel: Protestant. Mailing Add: Route 1, Box 299-D, Coeur d'Alene, Idaho 83814.

CHAMBERLIN, ROBERT MATHER D
b. Hecla, S.Dak, 6/7/20; s. Merritt Foster Chamberlin (deceased) and Margaret Mather; m. 4/27/45 to Jane Dorothy Pope; c. Deborah Jane and Merritt Pope. Educ: Univ. South. Calif, 37-39; Univ. Wis, B.S, 41, M.S, 48; Theta Chi. Polit. & Govt. Pos: U.S. Civil Serv. job, Ft. Bragg, N.C, 50-52; S.Dak. State Rep, 55-61; chmn, Brown Co. Dem. Party, S.Dak, 64-66, S.Dak. State Dem. Party, 67-68; Dem. nominee, Gov, S.Dak, 68. Bus. & Prof. Pos: Teacher, pub. sch, Orlando, Fla, 48-49; farmer, 52- Mil. Serv: Entered as Aviation Cadet, Navy, 41, released as Lt. Comdr, 46, after serv. in Aircraft, Pac. Fleet, Southwest Pac. Ocean Areas, 43-45, Res, Capt, 57-; Air Medal with 2 Gold Stars. Mem: Am. Legion; Odd Fellows. Rel: Methodist. Mailing Add: Hecla, S.Dak. 57446.

CHAMBERS, JOE REED R
b. Lindrith, N.Mex, 7/4/32; s. Gaston Brock Chambers, Sr. and Ida Bernice Darnaby C; m. 9/8/51 to Georgetta Stolebarger; c. Jo Lynne, Marilyne D. and Steven B. Educ: Tex. A&M Univ; Sigma Delta Chi. Polit. & Govt. Pos: Precinct chmn, Rep. Party, Tex, 64-66; chmn, Grayson Co. Rep. Party, Tex, 66-68. Bus. & Prof. Pos: Instr. Eng, Sherman Pub. Schs, 62-63, asst. prin, 63- Mil. Serv: Tex. Nat. Guard, 48-50; Recruit, Navy, 50, released as Radioman 2/C, 54; Good Conduct, Japanese Occupation and Korean Campaign Medals; UN and China Theater Ribbons; Unit Citation. Mem: Optimist Int; Nat. Educ. Asn; Tex. State Teachers Asn; Scoutmaster, Texoma Valley Coun. Rel: Baptist. Mailing Add: R.R. 2, Sherman, Tex. 75090. (1967)

CHAMBERS, LILLIAN BOYLE R
V.Chmn, 14th Dist. Rep. Cmt, Mich.
b. Rome, Ind, 2/8/08; d. A. Bruce Boyle and Sophia Schove B; m. 7/21/30 to Byron J. Chambers; c. B. Bruce. Educ: Ind. State Univ. Polit. & Govt. Pos: Del, Rep. State Conv, 54-; dir, 14th Dist. Rep. Cmt, Mich, 56-65, v.chmn, 62-; mem, Mich. State Rep. Cent. Cmt, 58-62; alternate del, Rep. Nat. Conv, 60, del, 64. Bus. & Prof. Pos: Teacher, special classes, in the 30's. Mem: Am. Asn. Univ. Women; Int. Platform Asn; Eastern Star; Women's City Club, Detroit. Mailing Add: 183 Lakeview, Grosse Pointe, Mich. 48236. (1967)

CHAMBERS, LOUIS D
b. Lebanon, Tenn, 3/22/90; s. James Louis Chambers and Lula Wharton C; m. 10/10/46 to Lucile Wharton. Educ: David Limpscomb Col; Cumberland Univ; Vanderbilt Univ. Polit. & Govt. Pos: Mem, Tenn. State Dem. Exec. Cmt, 42-52, secy, 50-52; del, Dem. Nat. Conv, 52; chmn, Wilson Co. Dem. Exec. Cmt, 56-66; del, State Constitution Conv, 59 & 65. Bus. & Prof. Pos: Lawyer, 13-; Justice of the Peace, Wilson Co, Tenn, 56-66. Mil. Serv: Army, World War I; Muese-Argonne Sector Ribbon. Mem: Mason; Shrine; Am. Legion. Mailing Add: 133 Public Square, Lebanon, Tenn. 37087.

CHAMBERS, MELVIN THAYER D
Ark. State Sen.
b. Magnolia, Ark, 10/3/05; s. George Charles Chambers and Almeda Elizabeth Nall C; m. 12/24/32 to Myrtle Click; c. Rodney Thayer and Anita (Mrs. Prince). Educ: Univ. Ark, LL.B, 35. Polit. & Govt. Pos: Ark. State Rep, 43 & 45; Ark. State Sen, 60-63 & 67- Mem: Columbia Co. Bar Asn.(pres, 63); Ark. Bar Asn; pres, Southwest Wildlife Asn; Farm Bur.(past pres, Co. Chap); pres, Dorcheat Bayou Asn. Commun. Leaders of Am. Award, 68. Lifelong study of water conserv. Rel: Methodist. Legal Res: 1608 LaCari Ave, Magnolia, Ark. 71753. Mailing Add: P.O. Box 157, Magnolia, Ark. 71753.

CHAMBERS, RAY BENJAMIN R
b. Long Beach, Calif, 4/7/40; s. James R. Chambers and Eileen Cox Chambers; m. 4/3/66 to Mary Alice Kepler. Educ: Univ. Redlands, B.A. magna cum laude, 62; Rutgers Univ, M.A, 63; Omicron Delta Kappa; Alpha Gamma Nu. Polit. & Govt. Pos: Asst. to U.S. Rep. Del Clawson, Calif, 63-65; exec. asst. to U.S. Rep. Robert F. Ellsworth, 65-66; campaign consult, Ruppe for Cong, 66; admin. asst. to U.S. Rep. Philip E. Ruppe, Mich, 67- Mil. Serv: Enlisted in Coast Guard Res, 63, stand by res, 69. Rel: Methodist. Mailing Add: 2211 39th St. N.W, Washington, D.C. 20007.

CHAMBERS, ROBERT EUGENE D
b. Corpus Christi, Tex, 3/5/10; s. R.S. Chambers and Minta Chandler C; m. 3/20/34 to Lollie Dee King; c. Celeste (Mrs. Bohnn), Neva (Mrs. Dawson) and R.E, Jr. Educ: Rice Univ, B.S, 33; Houston Law Sch, 34-35; S.Tex. Sch. Law, 35-36; Univ. Tex, LL.B, 36. Polit. & Govt. Pos: Asst. to Lyndon B. Johnson, Dem. Nat. Conv, 56, del, 60, 64 & 68; mem, State Dem. Exec. Cmt, Tex; mem, Wichita Co. Dem. Orgn. Bus. & Prof. Pos: Attorney, private practice, Houston, 37-42; attorney, J.S. Abercrombie, 42-48; attorney and gen. mgr, Armour Properties, Wichita Falls, 48- Mil. Serv: Retained by War Man Power Cmn. to construct and operate 100-octane plants, World War II. Mem: Wichita Co, Tex. State and Am. Bar Asns; charter mem, Tex. Bar Found; Nat. Petroleum Coun; dir, Brazos River Authority; dir, City Nat. Bank Wichita Falls; trustee, Southwest Found. Research & Educ; Mid-Continent Oil & Gas Asn.(dir); Tex. Independent Producers & Royalty Asn; Farm & Ranch Club. Outstanding Leadership, W.Tex. C. of C, 66. Rel: Church of Christ. Legal Res: 2413 Clayton, Wichita Falls, Tex. 76308. Mailing Add: 1107 Oil & Gas Bldg, Wichita Falls, Tex. 76301.

CHAMBERS, WILLIAM CLYDE R
Chmn, Clay Co. Rep. Party, Ga.
b. Fort Gaines, Ga, 9/13/99; s. I.P. Chambers and Nell Speight C; m. 6/12/21 to Frankie Eoline Grimsley; c. William Clyde, Jr. Polit. & Govt. Pos: Chmn, Clay Co. Rep. Party, Ga, currently. Mem: Mason; Shrine. Rel: Methodist. Legal Add: 204 Jackson St, Fort Gaines, Ga. 31751. Mailing Add: P.O. Box 95, Fort Gaines, Ga. 31751.

CHAMBLESS, CLARENCE G. R
Chmn, Terrell Co. Rep. Party, Ga.
b. Terrell Co, Ga, 8/7/03; s. Wesley G. Chambless and Nannie Kirksey C; m. 11/22/26 to Ercell Hayes; c. Varese (Mrs. Charles Hillis), Harold H, Jack W. and David L. Educ: Graves High Sch, 10 years. Polit. & Govt. Pos: Chmn, Terrell Co. Rep. Party, Ga, 66- Bus. & Prof. Pos: Partner, Stewart Webster Gas Co, Richland, Ga, 48-; pres, Chambless Gas Co, Inc, Dawson, Ga, 56-Mem: Rotary; Farm Bur. Rel: Baptist. Legal Res: 615 E. Lee St, Dawson, Ga. 31742. Mailing Add: P.O. Box 366, Dawson, Ga. 31742.

CHAMBLISS, DONALD R. D
b. Purvis, Miss, 2/10/32; married. Polit. & Govt. Pos: Miss. State Rep, 60-64. Bus. & Prof. Pos: Real estate broker. Mem: Mason; Lions; Farm Bur; DeSoto Co. Planning & Develop. Coun; Miss. Bd. Realtors; Nat. Asn. Bd. Realtors; PTA. Rel: Baptist. Mailing Add: Box 49, Horn Lake, Miss. 38637. (1967)

CHAMPAGNE, EDWARD D
N.H. State Rep.
b. Lowell, Mass, 5/25/89; married; c. 4. Educ: Graniteville, Mass. schs. Polit. & Govt. Pos: N.H. State Rep, 57- Bus. & Prof. Pos: Retired. Mem: Legion of Honor; Cath. Order of Foresters. Rel: Catholic. Mailing Add: 621 Somerville St, Manchester, N.H. 03103.

CHAMPION, WILLIAM J, JR. D
b. Newport, R.I, 12/23/01; m. to Margaret Elizabeth. Educ: Newport Pub. Schs. Polit. & Govt. Pos: R.I. State Rep, 59-69. Bus. & Prof. Pos: Retired. Mem: Past pres, Newport Metal Trade Coun; Wharf and Dock Builders Local AFL-CIO; hon. mem. Waterfront Cmt; Newport Men's Dem. Club; K. of C. St. Mary's Holy Name Soc; Dem. City Cmn. 1st Class State pilot's license since 37; Marine Capt's license for coastal waters, 30 years. Rel: Catholic. Mailing Add: 25 County St, Newport, R.I. 02840. (1967)

CHAMPLAIN, ROBERT ALFRED R
Mem, Rep. Co. Cent. Cmt, San Francisco, Calif.
b. San Francisco, Calif, 10/25/36; s. John Frederick Champlain and Virginia Mastagni C; single. Educ: Univ. Calif, Berkeley, A.B. cum laude in Polit. Sci, 58; Univ. Calif. Law Sch, Berkeley, J.D, 61; Phi Alpha Delta. Polit. & Govt. Pos: Mem, United Rep. Calif, Rep. Co. Cent. Cmt, San Francisco and Calif. Rep. Assembly, 68-; mem, Rep. State Cent. Cmt, 69- Bus. & Prof. Pos: Attorney mkt. dept, Standard Oil Co. Calif, San Francisco, Calif, 65-67. Mil. Serv: Entered as 1st Lt, Army Judge Adv. Gen. Corps, 61, released as Capt, 64, after serv. in Hq. Army Commun. Zone, Orleans, France, 62-64; Capt, Army Res, 64. Mem: State Bar of Calif; Am. Bar Asn; Am. Legion; Commonwealth Club Calif; Parkside Dist. Improv. Club San Francisco (chmn, legis. cmt). Rel: Presbyterian. Mailing Add: 1378 39th Ave, San Francisco, Calif. 94122.

CHAMPLIN, MALCOLM McGREGOR R
b. San Francisco, Calif, 4/13/11; s. Charles Chaffee Champlin and Maude Fraser C; m. 12/2/55 to Virginia Pearson; c. Sarah Jane, William Bradford and Mimi Lizette. Educ: U.S. Naval Acad, B.S, 34; Univ. Calif. Law Sch, D.J, 39; U.S. Naval War Col, grad, 44; Phi Delta Phi. Polit. & Govt. Pos: Spec. agent, Fed. Bur. Invest, Justice Dept, until 41; mem. bd, First Dist. Agr. Asn, Calif, 55-56; vets. chmn, Eisenhower Campaign, Alameda Co. Rep. Party, 52 & 56; del, Rep. Nat. Conv, 60 & 64; cand. for U.S. Rep, 7th Cong. Dist, Calif, 66; assoc. mem, Calif. Rep. State Cent. Cmt, 66-67; Munic. Court Judge, Oakland-Piedmont Judicial Dist, Calif, 67- Bus. & Prof. Pos: Partner, Stark and Champlin, Oakland Calif, 47-67; dir, Ventura Coastal Lemon Co, Inc, 45-53; v.pres, Ventura Processors, Inc, 49-53. Mil. Serv: Entered as Midshipman, Naval Acad, 30, Ens, Navy, 34-37, reentered, 41, released as Capt, 45, after serv. in Philippines, Australia, Aleutian Islands and U.S; Navy Cross; Army Silver Star; 3 Presidential Unit Citations; Asiatic and Pac. Theater Campaign Ribbons; Capt.(Ret), Naval Res. Publ: 3 articles on elements sea power in Bataan Campaign, Sea Power Magazine, 45; 'U.S. Constitution and What It Means to Us,' New Age, 65. Mem: Am. and Alameda Co. Bar Asns; State Bar of Calif; fel. Am. Acad. Matrimonial Lawyers; Soc. Former Spec. Agents Fed. Bur Invest; past comdr, Dept. Calif, Am. Legion; Naval Acad. Alumni Asn; Orinda Lodge 521 F&AM, Oakland Scottish Rite Bodies, Aahmes Temple of Shrine; Elks; Lions; Commonwealth Club Calif; former state chmn, March of Dimes. George Washington Honor Medal Award, Freedoms Found. at Valley Forge, 65. Rel: Congregational; former trustee, 1st Congregational Church of Oakland. Mailing Add: 485 Ellita Ave, Oakland, Calif. 94610.

CHANANAU, ALEXANDER D
N.Y. State Assemblyman
b. Bronx, N.Y, 11/11/15; m. to Adele Housthor; c. Rosalind. Educ: City Col. New York; N.Y. Univ. Law Sch. Polit. & Govt. Pos: N.Y. State Assemblyman, 58-; mem, Dem. State Cmt; exec, N.End Dem. Club of 82nd AD of Bronx Co; del, Dem. State Conv, 58 & 62; del, Dem. Nat. Conv, 64. Bus. & Prof. Pos: Lawyer; former instr, City Col. New York; trustee, Hebrew Inst. of Univ. Heights and Concourse Center of Israel; dir, Hebrew Home for Aged in Riverdale. Mil. Serv: Army, rifleman, 69th Inf. Div; Judge Adv. Gen. Off, discharged 46, Sgt. Mem: Dir, Bronx Co. Bar Asn; dir, N.Y. State Asn. of Trial Lawyers; past comdr, State Adjutant, chief Nat. Aid Jewish War Vets of U.S; past chmn, Bronx Co. Lawyers Conf; Nat. Panel of Arbitrators of Am. Arbitration Asn. Mailing Add: 1833 Loring Place, Bronx, N.Y. 10453.

CHANCE, GENIE D
Alaska State Rep.
b. Dallas, Tex; d. Albert Sidney Broadfoot and Jessie Butler B; m. 8/25/47 to Winston Cash Chance; c. Winston C, Jr, Albert Broadfoot and Jan. Educ: E.Tex. State Teachers Col, 43; South. Methodist Univ, 43-44; Paris Jr. Col, 44; N.Tex. State Univ, B.S, 46; Baylor Univ. Grad. Sch, 47. Polit. & Govt. Pos: Alaska State Rep, 69- Bus. & Prof. Pos: Mem, Defense Adv. Cmt. Women in the Serv, 67-, chmn. pub. rels. cmt, 68, v.chmn, 69- Publ: 'Year of Decision and Action,' U.S. Geol. Surv. Prfnl. Paper, 67. Mem: Alaska State Press Club (v.pres, 65-66); Alaska Press Women (pres, 66-67); Nat. Fedn. Press Women; Bus. & Prfnl. Women; bd. dirs, Jesse Lee Home Children, chmn. develop. cmt; Anchorage Women's Club; Bob Bartlett Dem. Club; NAACP. McCall's Top Golden Mike Award for outstanding women pub. serv; broadcaster, 65; Four First Place Awards and Golden Nugget Award, 67, Alaska Press Women; 11 First Place Awards, Alaska State Press Club; 64-68; First Place Award, Nat. Fedn. Press Women, 67; Lady of the Year Award, Camp Fire Girls, 69; Distinguished Alumnus Award, N.Tex. State Univ, 69. Rel: Protestant. Legal Res: 1101 H St, Anchorage, Alaska 99501. Mailing Add: P.O. Box 2392, Anchorage, Alaska 99501.

CHANCE, SIMON W. R
S.Dak. State Rep.
b. Ewing, Mo, 7/3/09; m. to Elsie M. Hehn; c. Vina and Karen. Polit. & Govt. Pos: S.Dak. State Rep, 58-; former twp. supvr, Scotland, S.Dak; former mem. sch. bd. and bd. of educ. Bus. & Prof. Pos: Farmer, feeder. Mem: Rotary. Rel: Protestant. Mailing Add: Scotland, S.Dak. 57059. (1967)

CHANCEY, C. RAY D
Chmn, Jackson Co. Dem. Cent. Cmt, Ill.
b. Murphysboro, Ill, 12/4/14; s. Walter A. Chancey and Hattie M. C; m. 8/11/40 to Mary Jeannette Richardson; c. Robert Bruce. Educ: South. Ill. Univ, 34-36. Polit. & Govt. Pos: Precinct committeeman, Jackson Co. Dem. Cent. Cmt, Ill, 52-, v.chmn, 62-67, chmn, 67-; v.chmn, 21st Cong. Dist. Dem. Cmt, 68- Bus. & Prof. Pos: Restaurant owner, RayMar Cafe, Murphysboro, Ill, 40-54; retired, 54-61; real estate and ins. partner, Chancey-Ozburn Agency, 61- Mem: Elks; C. of C. Rel: United Methodist. Mailing Add: 1911 Spruce St, Murphysboro, Ill. 62966.

CHANDLER, ALBERT BENJAMIN D
Chmn, Woodford Co. Dem. Exec. Cmt, Ky.
b. Corydon, Ky, 7/14/98; s. Joseph Chandler and Callie Sanders C; m. 11/12/25 to Mildred Watkins; c. Marcella (Mrs. Thomas D. Miller), Mildred (Mrs. James J. Miller), Joseph Daniel and Albert Benjamin, Jr. Educ: Transylvania Col, A.B, 21, LL.D, 36; Harvard, 21-22; Univ. Ky, LL.B, 24, LL.D, 37; Pi Kappa Alpha. Polit. & Govt. Pos: Master cmnr, Circuit Court, Woodford Co, Ky, 28; Ky. State Sen, 29-31; Lt. Gov, Ky, 31-35; Gov, Ky, 35-39 & 55-59; U.S. Sen, Ky, 39-48; chmn, Woodford Co. Dem. Exec. Cmt, currently; former Dem. Nat. Committeeman, Ky. Bus. & Prof. Pos: Receiver officer, Inter-South. Life Ins. Co, Louisville, Ky, 32; organizer, Ky. Home Life Ins. Co, Louisville, 32; high cmnr. of baseball, 45-51; cmnr, Continental Football League, 65; pres, Int. Baseball Cong, Wichita; dir, Coastal States Life Ins. Co. Ga; v.pres. and dir, First Flight Golf, Chattanooga, Tenn, currently. Mil. Serv: Serv. as Capt, Army, 18, Res, Judge Adv. Gen. Dept, one of 5 Sen. designated by U.S. Senate to visit world battlefronts, 43. Mem: Trustee, Ty Cobb Found; chmn. bd. trustee, Univ. Ky; chmn, Transylvania Col. Bd. Trustees and Fund Raising Cmt; Am. Legion; 40 et 8; Lexington and Idle Hour Country Clubs. Named Kentuckian of Year, Ky. Press Asn; one of first ten to Ky. Sports Hall of Fame, 57; received Cross of Mil. Serv, United Daughters of Confederacy, 59. Rel: Episcopal; received Bishop's Medal, 59. Mailing Add: 191 Elm St, Versailles, Ky. 40383. (1967)

CHANDLER, GERALD REID R
b. Albemarle, N.C, 7/8/29; s. Bivens Alfred Chandler and Clara Alma Underwood C; m. 6/14/52 to Margaret Ann Hatley; c. Donald Pritchard and Beverly Ann. Educ: Pfeiffer Col, 47-48; Elon Col, 48-49; Wake Forest Univ, B.A, 51; Wake Forest Univ. Law Sch, LL.B, 54; Pi Kappa Delta; Phi Alpha Delta; Delta Sigma Phi. Polit. & Govt. Pos: Pres, Wake Forest Col. Young Rep. Club, N.C, 50-51; state chmn, N.C. Young Rep. Collegiate Coun, 51; chmn, East. U.S. Young Rep. Collegiate Conf, 51; solicitor, Stanly Co. Court, Albemarle, N.C, 56-60, judge, 60-68; chmn, Stanly Co. Rep. Party, 56-64; del, Rep. Nat. Conv, 68. Mil. Serv: Seaman Recruit, Naval Res, V6, 47-50. Mem: N.C. State Bar; N.C, Stanly Co. and 20th Judicial Dist. Bar Asns; U.S. Dist. Court Bar; Am. Judicature Soc; N.C. Acad. Trial Lawyers; co. chmn, Am. Cancer Soc, 56; co. campaign chmn, 57 March of Dimes Drive; mem. exec. cmt, Stanly Co. Tuberc. Asn. Five Years Serv. Award, Nat. Found. Rel: Baptist. Legal Res: 505 Wesley Heights Dr, Albemarle, N.C. 28001. Mailing Add: P.O. Box 704, Albemarle, N.C. 28001.

CHANDLER, O. SHELDON D
Chmn, Dem. State Cent. Cmt, Md.
b. Mappsville, Va, 10/14/01; s. Oscar M. Chandler and Hattie W. Nock C; m. 11/24/20 to Macon Kathryne Quillin; c. O. Sheldon, Jr. and B. Quillin. Educ: High Sch. Polit. & Govt. Pos: From secy. to chmn, Dem. State Cent. Cmt, Md, 46-; cmnr, State Accident Fund, 60-; alternate del, Dem. Nat. Conv, 64. Bus. & Prof. Pos: Assoc, East. Fedn. Feed Merchants, 21, pres, 64-65; pres, Berlin Milling Co. and Feed Mfg, 48- Mil. Serv: Entered as Pvt, Res. Militia of Md, released as Lt, after serv. in World War II. Mem: Charter mem. Berlin Lions Club (past pres); Gov. Club; Farm Bur. Md. chmn, N.Y. Worlds Fair, 64-65; Ky. Col. Rel: Methodist. Mailing Add: Washington, Berlin, Md. 21811. (1967)

CHANDLER, PHILIP M. D
Ga. State Rep.
b. Milledgeville, Ga, 3/27/20; s. William J. Chandler and Eunice Horton C; m. 5/2/42 to Ruth Clodfelter; c. Elizabeth Ruth and Sally (Mrs. Jones). Educ: Milledgeville High Sch, 38; Ga. Mil. Col, 40. Polit. & Govt. Pos: Ga. State Rep, 59- Bus. & Prof. Pos: Merchant, house builder. Mil. Serv: WW II, 2nd Lt. to Maj, 41-46; Purple Heart; Bronze Star with Cluster; Presidential Unit Citation; Pre-Pearl Harbor Ribbon; 5 ETO Campaign Ribbons. Mem: Moose. Rel: Methodist. Mailing Add: Milledgeville, Ga. 31061.

CHANDLER, RALPH C. R
b. Fla; m. to Nancy; c. Five. Educ: Stetson Univ, grad, 56; Rutgers Univ, M.A; Union, B.D; Princeton, M.Th; pres, Student Govt; Outstanding Sr. Man in Class. Polit. & Govt. Pos: Rep. capt, Princeton Twp, N.J, 62-68; parliamentarian, N.J. Gen. Assembly, 64 & 68. Bus. & Prof. Pos: Minister, 1st Presbyterian Church of Princeton, N.J; teacher, Princeton, lectr. polit, 61; mem. staff, Psychiat. Inst, Yale Univ. Med. Sch, 62; Scandinavian Desk Officer, Off. of Asst. Secy. of Defense for Int. Security Affairs; asst. prof, Faculty of Aeronaut. Systs, Univ. of W. Fla, 69- Mil. Serv: Navy, 4 years; Commissioned, Off. Cand. Sch, Newport, R.I, 56; served aboard combat ships in Second Fleet; Commanding Officer of Naval and Marine Corp Res. Training Center, Kansas City, Mo. Publ: The New Jersey Legislature, Eagleton Inst. of Polit, Rutgers Univ, 63. Rel: Presbyterian. Mailing Add: 2621 Dunsinane Rd, Pensacola, Fla. 32503.

CHANDLER, ROGER CARL R
Mem, Calif. Rep. State Cmt.
b. Marysville, Calif, 10/19/26; s. W. Ray Chandler and Grace Johnson C; m. 6/11/49 to Lois Jacqueline Kofahl; c. Christopher R. and Charles F. Educ: Univ. Calif, B.S, 49; Sutter Co. Bd. Realtors. Polit. & Govt. Pos: Charter mem, v.pres. and pres, Sutter-Yuba Young Rep, 50-53; mem, Calif. Rep. State Cmt, currently; mem, Sutter Co. Rep. Cent. Cmt, 60-, chmn, 62-65; alternate del, Rep. Nat. Conv, 64; area chmn, Rep. Co. Chmn. Asn, 64-65; six co. area chmn, Reagan for Gov. Cmt, 66; mem, Exec. Cmt, Calif. State Rep. Cmt. Bus. & Prof. Pos: Farmer, 49-; realtor, 63- Mil. Serv: Entered as Pvt, Army, 45, released as Cpl, after serv. in U.S, 46. Mem: C. of C, Sutter Co; Sutter Co. Bd. Educ; Farm Bureau; Boy Scouts Cmt. Mailing Add: 919 Ohleyer Rd, Yuba City, Calif. 95991. (1967)

CHANEY, BUENA R
Chmn, Ind. Rep. State Cent. Cmt.
b. Coxville, Ind, 11/16/21; parents deceased; m. 5/6/49 to Betty Jo Williams; c. Tamara and Lisa. Educ: Wabash Col. A.B, 43; Ind. Univ. Law Sch, J.D, 48; Sigma Delta Kappa. Polit. & Govt. Pos: Chmn, Vigo Co. Rep. Party, Ind, 60-69; chmn, Sixth Dist. Rep. Party, 62-66; chmn, Seventh Dist. Rep. Party, 66-; chmn, Ind. Rep. State Cent. Cmt, 67-; del, Rep. Nat. Conv, 68. Bus. & Prof. Pos: Attorney-at-law, 48- Mil. Serv: Entered as Pvt, Army, 43, released as T-4, 46, after serv. in 21st Evacuation Hosp, S.Pac; Capt, Army Res, 52. Mem: Am, Ind. and Terre Haute Bar Asns; Am. and Ind. Trial Lawyers Asns; Elks; Shrine; Lions; VFW; Am. Legion. Rel: Protestant. Legal Res: R.R. 51, Box 615, Terre Haute, Ind. 47805. Mailing Add: Republican State Headquarters, 111 N. Capitol, Indianapolis, Ind. 46204.

CHANEY, ISABELLE CAROLINE R
Mem, State Rep. Cent. and Exec. Cmt, Ohio
b. Cadiz, Ohio; d. William Grant Kent and Margaret Gaines K; m. to G.F. Stevens; wid; m. 2/13/54 to Lawrence Hayden Chaney; c. Naomi (Mrs. Root) and Wayne A, Virginia L. (Mrs. McMaster) and Donald O. Stevens. Educ: Exten. courses, Geneva State Col; private lessons, commercial course, pub. speaking and law. Polit. & Govt. Pos: Dep. clerk, Harrison Co. Probate and Juvenile Court, Ohio, 29-54; secy, Harrison Co. Prosecuting Attorney, 57-65; chairwoman, Harrison Co. Rep. Party, 13 years; mem, Harrison Co. Rep. Cent. and Exec. Cmt, 5 years; pres, Harrison Co. Rep. Women's Club, 9 years; alternate del, Rep. Nat. Conv, 60 & 68; mem, State Rep. Cent. and Exec. Cmt, 66- Bus. & Prof. Pos: Legal secy, Pettay & Mosser, Attorneys, 55-57; researcher and news correspondent, 65- Mem: Past pres. tent and dist, Daughters Union Vet. Civil War, jr. v.pres. state; past pres, Am. Legion Auxiliary; pres. and v.pres, Cadiz Women's Civic Club; dist. chmn. legis. and citizenship, past dist. pres. and state chmn. legis. and citizenship, Ohio Fedn. Rep. Women. Rel: Methodist; Lay speaker, various bds. and cmns, pres, Woman's Soc. Christian Serv. Legal Res: County Rd. 5, Cadiz, Ohio 43907. Mailing Add: P.O. Box 244, Cadiz, Ohio 43907.

CHAPAS, JOHN WILLIAM D
b. Danielson, Conn, 1/20/18; s. William Peter Chapas and Mary Mavroides C; m. 2/1/41 to Helen Carlos; c. Lt. Wm. John and James J. Educ: Duquesne Univ, A.B, 41; Univ. Miami Sch. of Law, LL.B, 54; historian, Phi Alpha Delta; Secy. legal orgns, Univ. Miami, 53-54. Polit. & Govt. Pos: Pres, Hellenic Polit. Alliance, Allegheny Co. and chmn. Greek Div, Allegheny Co. Dem. Party, Pa, 49-; legal investr, Allegheny Co, 54-61; mem. bd, Allegheny Co. Housing Authority, 56-; referee, Workmen's Compensation Cmn, Pa, 61-63; alternate del-at-lg, Dem. Nat. Conv, 64 & 68; mem, Allegheny Co. Dem. Exec. Cmt, 64-69; magistrate, City Court, Pittsburgh, 64- Mem: Bd. of mgrs, Allegheny Br, YMCA; bd. mem, Pittsburgh Coun. of Churches; adv. coun, N.S. C. of C; N.S. Civic Promotion Coun; N.S. Citizens' Action Cmt; chmn, N.S-N. Hills Fund Raising Crusade, Am. Cancer Soc, 61-62; past dir. and past pres, Holy Trinity Greek Orthodox Commun, Pittsburgh, pres, Past Presidents' Cmt; Bishop Theodosios' Diocesan Adv. Coun, 63-; F&AM; RAM; Syria Temple Shrine, Ahepa. Orthodox del, Fourth Nat. Study Conf. on Church and Econ. Life, Nat. Coun. of Churches, Pittsburgh, 62. Rel: Greek Orthodox. Legal Res: 10 Allegheny Center, Pittsburgh, Pa. 15212. Mailing Add: Public Safety Bldg, Grant St. & Blvd. of Allies, Pittsburgh, Pa. 15219. (1967)

CHAPEL, CHARLES EDWARD R
b. Manchester, Iowa; m. to Dorothy Messner Young; c. Joanne (Mrs. Leland Coontz, Jr), Nancy, Charles, Richard Young (stepson). Educ: State Univ. of Iowa; Mo. Univ; U.S. Naval Acad; A.B. and B.S. Polit. & Govt. Pos: Calif. State Assemblyman, 50-66. Bus. & Prof. Pos: Lic. prfnl. mech. engr (aeronaut. & ordinance). Mil. Serv: 2nd Lt, U.S.M.C, 26; 1st Lt, 33; 5th regt, Nicaragua, 27; U.S.S. Calif, 29-31; shore stas, 31-33; 4th regt, Shaghai, 33-35; Judge Adv, 5th U.S.N. Dist, 36-37; retired, 37. Mem: hon. life mem, Nat. Rifle Asn; Inst. Aerospace Sci; VFW; Mason (32°); Shrine; Elks; IOOF; Moose. Misc: Author, more than 3,000 mag. & news articles; 25 published books; Who's Who in Am, since 42; Good Citizen Medal, Sons of Am. Rev, 54. 1967 Legal Res: Redondo Beach, Calif. No mailing address available. (1967)

CHAPIN, EDWARD YOUNG, III R
b. Chattanooga, Tenn, 1/17/23; s. E.Y. Chapin, Jr. and Dorris Carter C; m. 9/28/45 to Mildred Toner; c. E.Y, IV, Garnet, Mary, William H. and James I. Educ: Princeton Univ, A.B, 43. Polit. & Govt. Pos: Del, Rep. State and Dist. Conv, 64; del, Rep. Nat. Conv, 64 & 68. Bus. & Prof. Pos: Pres, Rock City Gardens, Inc, 50- Mil. Serv: Entered as Cpl, Army, 43, released as 1st Lt, 46, after serv. in ETO; Air Medal with Two Clusters; ETO Campaign Ribbon. Rel: Presbyterian. Mailing Add: 1303 Patten Rd, Lookout Mountain, Tenn. 37350. (1967)

CHAPIN, JOHN CARSTEN R
Spec. Asst. to the Secy, Dept. Housing and Urban Develop.
b. Detroit, Mich, 10/1/20; s. Roy Dikeman Chapin and Inez Tiedeman C; m. 8/15/64 to Helen Willard; c. Suzanne (Mrs. Christopher Wilkins), John Jr, Deacon Samuel and David Dwight. Educ: Yale Univ, B.A, 42; George Wash. Univ, M.A, 67; Zeta Psi. Polit. & Govt. Pos: Commun. dir, 14th Dist. Rep. Party, Mich, 58-62; chmn, Citizens for Romney, D.C, 67-68; mem. exec. cmt, Rockefeller for Pres, 68; v.chmn. finance cmt, D.C. Rep. Cmt, 68; spec. asst. to secy, Dept. Housing and Urban Develop, 69- Bus. & Prof. Pos: Acct. exec, MacManus, John and Adams, Detroit, Mich, 46-50; commun. dir, Diocese of Mich, 50-62; commun. warden, Nat. Cathedral, D.C, 62-69. Mil. Serv: Entered as Pfc, Marine Corps, 42, released as Capt, 45, after serv. in Fourth Marine Div, Pac, 43-44; Two Purple Hearts. Mem: Pub. Rels. Soc. Am; trustee, Philatelic Found; Chevy Chase Club. Rel: Episcopal. Mailing Add: 4740 Quebec St. N.W, Wash, D.C. 20016.

CHAPIN, RICHARD U. R
Wash. State Rep.
b. N.Y.C, 7/3/29; s. Samuel M. Chapin and Evelyn Kaplan C; m. 6/6/53 to Hope Redington; c. Cary Ann, Bruce Redington and Nancy Lynn. Educ: Univ. Mich, 46-50; Columbia Univ. Law Sch, LL.B, 53; Phi Delta Phi. Polit. & Govt. Pos: Exec. dir, King Co. Rep. Cent. Cmt, Wash, 61-63; Wash. State Rep, 67- Bus. & Prof. Pos: Partner, Cole, Chapin, O'Connell & Nelson Law Firm, Bellevue, Wash, currently. Mil. Serv: 1st Lt, Army, 54-57, serv. in Judge Adv. Gen. Corps, Ft. Lewis, Wash. Mem: Am, E. King Co. and Wash. Bar Asns; Kiwanis. Rel: Jewish. Legal Res: 4408 95th Ave. N.E, Bellevue, Wash, 98004. Mailing Add: 225 108th Ave. N.E, Bellevue, Wash. 98004.

CHAPLEAU, LOUIS CAREY D
b. Greenfield, Mass, 11/15/07; s. Louis A. Chapleau and Mary Carey C; m. 11/29/33 to Mary Hubbard; c. Adrienne (Mrs. Wolf), Marilyn (Mrs. Barashkoff), Edward A. and Louis Carey. Educ: Univ. Notre Dame, J.D, 30. Polit. & Govt. Pos: chmn, St. Joseph Co. Dem. Orgn, Ind, 42-44; co. attorney, St. Joseph Co, 44-46; del, Ind. Dem. Conv, 53-; proxy del, Dem. Nat. Conv, 60, del, 64 & 68. Bus. & Prof. Pos: Attorney, South Bend Commun. Sch. Corp, 61- Mem: St. Joseph Co, Ind. State and Am. Bar Asns; Bar Asn. Seventh Circuit; Nat. Asn. Univ and Col. Attorneys; Elks; Ind. Club. Rel: Catholic. Legal Res: 605 N. Coquillard Dr, South Bend, Ind. 46615. Mailing Add: 316 First Bank Bldg, South Bend, Ind. 46601.

CHAPMAN, ALFRED FRANCIS D
b. Milwaukee, Wis, 5/19/00; s. John Stephen Chapman and Mary C; m. 1/26/20 to Lucille Elizabeth Palmer; c. Margaret. Educ: Univ. Wis, Exten; Univ. Wis. Alumni. Polit. & Govt. Pos: Dist. del. and del-at-lg, Dem. Nat. Conv, 24, 44, 48, 52, 56, 60, 64 & 68, secy. of W.Va. Del, 64; v.chmn, Milwaukee Co. Dem. Party, 23-26; dist. committeeman, Cook Co. Dem. Party, 23-28; mem, W.Va. State Cmt, First Sen. Dist, 40-56; secy, Human Rels. Cmn, W.Va, 42-45; mem, Indust. Salvage Cmt. of W.Va, 42-45 and Warehouse and Storage Facility Cmns; coordinator, Dem. Young Club, 42-48; state v.chmn. and reg. mem. of Small Bus. Admin, leader, Dem. Party, W.Va; mem, W.Va. Small Bus. Adv. Cmt, 62. Mil. Serv: Mem, Army Mil. Police Force, 42-45. Mem: Ohio Valley Bd. of Trade; charter mem, Ohio Valley Traffic Club; hon. life citation, Warwood's Kain Club and Civitan's Int; President's Club, Wash, D.C; hon. Col, Gov. Staff, Ky, W.Va, Ga. and Md; Am. Acad. of Polit. & Soc. Sci; Ambassador of Good Will for life, Ga, 62; Elks; Moose; Eagles; K. of P; Duqeusne Lodges. Citizen of Month, Jr. C. of C; hon. citizen, Tenn. Rel: Methodist. Mailing Add: 629 Main St, Shady Rest, Wheeling, W.Va. 26003.

CHAPMAN, ALICE HACKETT R
Mem, Calaveras Co. Rep. Cent. Cmt, Calif.
b. Hillsboro, Md, 9/22/02; d. Thomas Cox Hackett and Mary Louise Holt H; wid. Educ: Los Angeles Bus. Col, grad, 18; Univ. exten. courses. Polit. & Govt. Pos: Secy. to city attorney, Los Angeles, Calif, 30-49; mem, Calaveras Co. Rep. Cent. Cmt, 58-, chmn, 67-68. Mem: Soroptimist Club; Bus. & Prfnl. Womens Club Calaveras Co; Ebbetts Pass Wonderland Asn; Nathan B. Forrest chap, UDC; Eastern Star (Worthy Matron, 69-70); Calaveras Co. Hist. Soc. Serv. Award, City of Los Angeles; Outstanding Performance Award, State Rep. Cent. Cmt, 67-68. Rel: Episcopal. Mailing Add: P.O. Box 76, Hathaway Pines, Calif. 95233.

CHAPMAN, CHARLES HICKERSON, JR. R
Mem, Rep. Nat. Cmt, Ala.
b. Dothan, Ala, 4/17/20; s. Charles Hickerson Chapman and Florie Malone C; m. 12/20/43 to Martha Farmer; c. Charles Hickerson, III, Davis F and Florrie Lou. Educ: Wash. and Lee Univ, B.S, 41. Polit. & Govt. Pos: Mem, Rep. Nat. Cmt, Ala, 64-; del, Rep. Nat. Conv, 68. Bus. & Prof. Pos: Pres, Chapman Construction Co, Dothan, 46-; chmn. bd, Malone Industs, Inc; dir, First Nat. Bank, Dothan; Dothan Oil Mill Co. Mil. Serv: Naval Res, 42-45, Lt. Mem: Chmn, Houston Country Heart Fund, 65; Dothan C. of C.(dir, past chmn, indust. cmt, govt. affairs cmt.). Mailing Add: P.O. Drawer 220, Dothan, Ala. 36302. (1967)

CHAPMAN, CYRUS MILLER 'CY' D
Ga. State Sen.
b. Carmi, Ill, 7/22/24; s. John Miller Chapman and Lillian Gentry C; m. 6/7/47 to Pauline McKinney; c. Cheryl Ann, Peggy Lee, Susan Gail, Cyrus McKinney, Ronald Mark, Scott Gentry, Mary Michele and Rebecca Leigh. Educ: Emory Univ, B.B.A, 48; Alpha Tau Omega. Polit. & Govt. Pos: Ga. State Sen, 32nd Dist, currently; mayor pro-tem, Smyrna, Ga, 62-63 and councilman-at-lg. Bus. & Prof. Pos: Salesman, Selig Co, 48-60; gen. mgr, Janitors Unlimited, 60-62; proprietor, Cy's Supplies, 62-66. Mil. Serv: Entered as Pvt, Army Air Force, 43, released as S/Sgt, 45, after serv. in 392nd Bomb Group, Second Div, Eighth Air Force, ETO; Air Medal with Four Clusters. Mem: Elks; Rotary; Am. Legion. Rel: Methodist. Mailing Add: 2871 Stone Creek Rd. S.E, Smyrna, Ga. 30080.

CHAPMAN, EUGENIA SHELDON D
Ill. State Rep.
b. Fairhope, Ala, 1/10/23; d. Chauncey Bailey Sheldon and Rose Donner S; m. 11/24/48 to Gerald M. Chapman; c. George, Andrew, John and Katherine. Educ: Chicago Teachers Col, B.Ed, 44. Polit. & Govt. Pos: Mem. bd. educ, Dist. 214, Cook Co, Ill, 61-64, secy, 62-64; Ill. State Rep, 64- Bus. & Prof. Pos: Pub. Sch. Teacher, Cicero, 44-47, Chicago, 47-51. Mem: Pres, League of Women Voters, 57-59; PTA; Dem. Women's Groups; exec. cmt, Tri Co. Div, Ill. Asn. Sch. Bds, 64. Best Freshman and Best Legislator Awards, Independent Voters of Ill. Rel: Protestant. Mailing Add: 16 S. Princeton Court, Arlington Heights, Ill. 60005.

CHAPMAN, HARRY A. JR. D
S.C. State Sen.
b. Greenville, S.C, 2/9/36; s. Harry A. Chapman and Mildred Marett C; m. 4/27/56 to Mona Ruth Freeman C; c. Karen Camille. Educ: Univ. of S.C, B.A, 58, LL.B, 60; Pres, Lambda Chi Alpha, 56; Phi Delta Phi; Blue Key. Polit. & Govt. Pos: S.C. State Rep, 63-66; S.C. State Sen, 67- Bus. & Prof. Pos: Lawyer, Foster, Johnston, Ashmore & Chapman. Mem: Am. and S.C. Bar Asns; Civitan Club; exec. cmt, S.C. Crippled Children Soc; pres. & v.pres, Greenville Co. Crippled Children Soc, 61-62; pres, S.C. Asn. Future Farmers of Am, 53; pres, Law Sch. Student Body, 59; pres, Clariosophic Lit. Soc, 55. Rel: Baptist. Mailing Add: 2016 Lawyers Bldg, Greenville, S.C. 29601. (1967)

CHAPMAN, JAMES FREDERICK D
Recorder, Madison Co, Ill.
b. Troy, Ill, 1/7/07; s. Thomas Chapman and Nancy Scott C; m. 8/23/30 to Jessie Cherotti; c. Nancy (Mrs. Joseph Willett), Joan (Mrs. Leonard Massa) and James F, Jr. Educ: Brown Bus. Col. Polit. & Govt. Pos: Clerk of bd. of rev, dep. co. clerk, clerk of ciruit court, clerk in treas. off. and asst. to chief dep. in sheriff's off, Madison Co, Ill, 36-57, Recorder, Ill, 57- Bus. & Prof. Pos: Clerk, Chicago Lumber and Coal Co, 23; bookkeeper, Cole Chem. Co, 28; agent, Prudential Life Ins. Co, 29-36. Mem: Ill. State Clerks and Recorders; Nat. Recorders and Clerks; Mason; Collinsville Dem. Club; Ill. Munic. Employees Union. Rel: Presbyterian. Mailing Add: 220 W. Lee, Collinsville, Ill. 62234.

CHAPMAN, JEROME F. DFL
Educ: Univ. Minn, 46-48; Minn. Col. Law, 48-52, B.S, 50, LL.B. Polit. & Govt. Pos: Former Minn. State Rep; Asst. Attorney Gen, Minn, 55-61. Bus. & Prof. Pos: Attorney. Mil. Serv: Air Force, 2 years. Mem: Minn. State and Hennepin Co. Bar Asns; YMCA Indian Guides; Lawyer's Guild of St. Thomas More; Richfield DFL Club. Mailing Add: 6221 12th Ave. S, Richfield, Minn. 55432. (1967)

CHAPMAN, JOSEPH F. D
Fla. State Rep.
b. Brewton, Ala, 8/4/38; s. Joseph F. Chapman, Jr. and Gladys Alford C; m. 7/26/64 to Jeannette Elizabeth Byers; c. Mary Marie Elizabeth and Joseph F, IV. Educ: Univ. Fla, Gainesville; Fla. Blue Key; Sigma Chi. Polit. & Govt. Pos: Former attorney, Gov. Off, Fla; former gen. counsel, State Rd. Bd; Fla. State Rep, currently. Mem: Fla. Bar Asn. Rel: Baptist. Mailing Add: 412 Magnolia Ave, Panama City, Fla. 32401.

CHAPMAN, OSCAR LITTLETON D
b. Omega, Va, 10/22/96; s. James Jackson Chapman and Rosa Archer Blount C; m. 2/24/40 to Ann Kendrick; c. James. Educ: Univ. Denver, B.A, 22-24; Univ. N.Mex, 27-28; Westminster Law Sch, Denver, LL.B, 29; Colo. State Col. Educ, Augustana Col, Howard Univ, LL.D, 49; Univ. Denver, 51; West. State Col. Colo, 61; Phi Alpha Delta. Polit. & Govt. Pos: Asst. chief probation officer, Juvenile Court, Denver, Colo, 22-24, chief probation officer, 24-27; Asst. Secy. of Interior, 33-45, Undersecy. of Interior, 46-49 and

Secy. of Interior, 49-53. Bus. & Prof. Pos: Attorney, Chapman, Di Salle & Friedman, D.C. Mil. Serv: Navy, 18-20. Rel: Methodist. Mailing Add: 4975 Hillbrook Lane N.W, Washington, D.C. 20016.

CHAPMAN, RICHARD F. 'DICK' D
b. London, Eng, 9/13/96; s. Robert Chapman and Emily Francis Banfield C; m. 11/18/27 to Vera Medora Harris. Educ: High Sch. Polit. & Govt. Pos: Ore. State Rep, 55-56; Ore. State Sen, 57-69. Bus. & Prof. Pos: Owner, Coos Bay Paint Co, 20-57; pres, Chapman Homes, Inc, 44-57. Mil. Serv: Entered as Pvt, Canadian Army, 15, released as Acting Major, 19, after serv. in France; Allied Serv. Medals. Mem: Eagles (pres, 54-55); Odd Fellows. Rel: Episcopal. Legal Res: 977 S. Eighth St, Coos Bay, Ore. 97420. Mailing Add: P.O. Box 242, Coos Bay, Ore. 97420.

CHAPMAN, ROBERT FOSTER R
Chmn, Spartanburg Co. Rep. Party, S.C.
b. Inman, S.C, 4/24/26; s. James Alfred Chapman and Martha Marshall C; m. 12/21/51 to Mary Winston Gwathmey; c. Edward Bates, Alfred Foster and Winston Gwathmey. Educ: Univ. S.C, B.S, 45, LL.B, 49; Omicron Delta Kappa. Polit. & Govt. Pos: Gen. counsel, S.C. Rep. Party, 60-61, chmn, 61-63; alternate del, Rep. Nat. Conv, 68; chmn, Spartanburg Co. Rep. Party, currently. Bus. & Prof. Pos: Partner, Butler, Chapman & Parler, 49- Mil. Serv: Entered as Seaman, Navy, 43, released as Ens, 46, recalled to duty, 51, released as Lt, 53. Rel: Presbyterian; Ruling Elder. Legal Res: 837 Glendalyn Ave, Spartanburg, S.C. 29301. Mailing Add: P.O. Box 451, Spartanburg, S.C. 29301.

CHAPMAN, THOMAS E. 'TOM' D
Chmn, Co. Urban Affairs Cmt, Ky.
b. Louisa, Ky, 9/6/22; s. Homer E. Chapman and Mary E. Carey C; m. 7/31/43 to Dorothy Lee Do Nard; c. Patricia Lee (Mrs. Easterling), Linda Kay (Mrs. Griffith) and Pheobe Carey. Educ: Morehead State Univ, 40-41. Polit. & Govt. Pos: Ky. State Rep, 64-67; cand, Ky. State Rep, 69; chmn, Co. Urban Affairs Cmt, 69- Bus. & Prof. Pos: Retail Merchant. Mil. Serv: Army, World War II, 2 Bronze Stars. Mem: Boyd Co. Dem. Club; Young Dem. Ky; Am. Legion; Elks; Lions; dep. gov, Lions Int; F&AM; Scottish Rite; C. of C; co-chmn, United Fund, 63-69; bd. dirs, Ky. Ment. Health Asn, 65-69; Northeast. Fish & Game Asn; Ky. Sportsmen League; Boyd Co. Horse Club; pres, Boyd Co. Athletic Boosters Club, 5 years. Ky. Col; Ky. Admiral; Col. Aide de Camp; Pub. Safety Commendation, State Police; Outstanding Serv. Award, Morehead Univ. Alumnus Asn; Award of Merit, Cmt. Natural Resources, Ky. Rel: Methodist. Mailing Add: Rush, Ky. 41168.

CHAPPELL, WILLIAM VENROE, JR. 'BILL' D
U.S. Rep. Fla.
b. Reddick, Fla, 2/3/22; s. William Venroe Chappell and Laura G. Kemp C; m. 3/26/44 to Marguerite Gutshall; c. Judith Jane (Mrs. Edward Taylor), Deborah Kay, William V, III and Christopher Clyde. Educ: Univ. Fla, B.A, 47, LL.B, 49, J.D, 67; Phi Alpha Delta; Tau Kappa Alpha. Polit. & Govt. Pos: Co. prosecuting attorney, Marion Co, Fla, 50-54; Fla. State Rep, 54-64 & 67-68, speaker Fla. House Rep, 61-63; U.S. Rep, Fla, 69- Bus. & Prof. Pos: Owner, J & J Elec. Co, currently; secy. of bd, Bank of Belleview, currently; attorney, Chappell, Rowland & Curry, until 69; attorney, Law Firm, Chappell, Dickens, Miller, Graham, Linn and Mahorner, 69- Mil. Serv: Entered as Aviation Cadet, Navy, 42, released as Lt.(jg), 47; after serv. in Training Command, 44-46; Capt. Res, 46-69. Mem: Fla. and Am. Bar Asns; Int. Lawyers Asn; Am. Trial Lawyers Asn; Lions; Elks; Mason; Shrine; Moose; Am. Legion; VFW. Allen Morris Award for the Most Valuable Mem. of 1967 Fla. House of Rep. and the Most Effective in Debate. Rel: Methodist. Legal Res: 1818 Edwards Rd, Ocala, Fla. 32670. Mailing Add: 1131 Longworth Office Bldg, Washington, D.C. 20515.

CHAPPIE, EUGENE A. R
Calif. State Assemblyman
b. Sacramento, Calif, 3/28/20; s. Albert Chappie and Irma Sperinde C; m. 10/5/41 to Paula Di Benedetto; c. Susan, Eugene, II, John, Tina and Linda. Educ: Sacramento High Sch, Sacramento; Nat. Sch, Los Angeles. Polit. & Govt. Pos: Supvr, El Dorado Co, Calif, 50-65; Calif. State Assemblyman, until 67, 69-; del, Rep. Nat. Conv, 68. Bus. & Prof. Pos: Rancher, Self employed. Mil. Serv: Entered as Pvt, Air Force, 42, released as Capt, after serv. in Amphibious Tractor Bn, Pac, 46; Am. Defense, Asiatic Pac. and Good Conduct Medals; Bronze Star. Mem: Rotary; Am. Legion; Pilot Hill Grange; Native Sons; Farm Bur; VFW; Elks; Holy Name Soc; Urban Land Inst; E Clampus Vitus. Rel: Catholic. Mailing Add: Cool, Calif. 95614.

CHARDON, FERNANDO New Progressive, P.R.
Secy. of State, P.R.
b. Ponce, P.R, 9/5/07; s. Carlos Félix Chardon-León and Isabel Palacios-Pelletier C; m. Aug, 1931 to Carmín Guyar-Gatell; c. Diana María (Mrs. Rengel), Carmen Isabel (Mrs. Ortiz), Fernando Luis and Marissa. Educ: Cornell Univ, B.S.A; Delta Chi. Hon. LL.D, Interam. Univ, P.R. Polit. & Govt. Pos: Secy. of State, P.R, currently. Bus. & Prof. Pos: Asst. agronomist for research in sugar cane and tobacco, staff of agr. exp. sta, Univ. P.R, 28-39; chief of sect. agr. rehabilitation div, P.R. Reconstruction Admin, 37; field mgr, Constancia Sugar Mill, Toa Baja, P.R, 39-41; dir. appraisal div, P.R. Land Authority, 46-47; v.pres. in charge of opers.and colonos, East. Sugar Assocs. and its successor, Fajardo East. Sugar Assocs, 47-61; secy-treas, P.R. Sugar Producers Asn, 62-; dir. sugar indust. improv. prog, P.R. Dept. of Agr, 1 year. Mil. Serv: 1st Lt, Capt, Maj. and Lt. Col, Inf, Army, Am. and Pac. Theatres, 41-46, Comdr, 296th Regt. Combat Team, 50-58 and head of mil. mission to Peruvian jungle; exec. officer, P.R. Nat. Guard, 46-65, acting Adj. Gen, P.R, 7 months; Col.(Ret), Army Res, 67. Publ: Several papers on P.R. sugar industry. Mem: Chmn, Bd. of Exam. for Agronomists, 47-57; pres, P.R. Technologists Asn, 52 and Penn-Cornell Club, 56; secy. gen, Int. Soc. of Sugar Cane Technologists, 65; Mil. Order of World Wars. Rel: Roman Catholic. Mailing Add: Las Marias St. 1506, Santurce, P.R. 00911.

CHARETTE, ROBERT L. D
Wash. State Rep.
b. Aberdeen, Wash, 1923; m. to Betty; c. Three. Educ: Grays Harbor Jr. Col; Univ. of Wash. Law Sch; Phi Kappa Psi; Phi Delta Phi. Polit. & Govt. Pos: Wash. State Rep, 66- Bus. & Prof. Pos: Lawyer, Schumacher & Charette. Mil. Serv: Army; Purple Heart. Mem: Grays Harbor and Am. Bar Asns; Eagles; Elks; VFW; Am. Legion; Mil. Order Purple Heart. Mailing Add: 100 W. First, Aberdeen, Wash. 98520. (1967)

CHARKOUDIAN, ARPPIE R
Chmn, Mansfield Rep. Town Cmt, Conn.
b. Springfield, Mass, 12/13/25; d. Nishan N. Charkoudian and Azniv Sanjian C; single. Educ: Am. Inst. of Banking, Cert, 46; Tanglewood, Lenox, Mass, summer 47; Springfield Col, 57-58. Polit. & Govt. Pos: Ward cmt. mem, Springfield Rep. City Cmt, Mass, 57-59; state committeewoman, Mass. Rep. Party, 58 & 59; chmn, Mansfield Rep. Town Cmt, Conn, 68-; v.chmn, Mansfield Charter Cmn, 69- Bus. & Prof. Pos: Teller, Springfield Nat. Bank, Mass, 43-47; exec. secy, Springfield Symphony Orchestra Asn, 47-56; east. area rep, Columbia Artists Mgt. N.Y.C, 56-57; girls prog. dir, Springfield YMCA, 57-59; asst. mgr, Jorgensen Auditorium, Univ. Conn, 59- Mem: Zonta Int.(Hartford Area Club pres, 68 & 69); Asn. of Col. and Univ. Concert Mgrs; Univ. of Conn. League (chmn, 69); Hampden Co. Musicians' Asn, Am. Fedn. Musicians; Armenian Relief Soc.(int. treas, 59 & 60). Rel: Armenian Apostolic. Legal Res: N. Eagleville Rd, Storrs, Conn. 06268. Mailing Add: 2 Lakeside Apt, Storrs, Conn. 06268.

CHARLES, ERLAND W. R
Chmn. Sixth Dist, Minn. State Cent. Rep. Cmt.
b. Montevideo, Minn, 12/2/26; s. Ernest H. Charles and Clara Erlandson C; m. 10/3/49 to Joyce Loehr; c. Wayne and Carter. Polit. & Govt. Pos: Rep. precinct chmn, Stevens Co, Minn, 58; chmn, Stevens Co. Rep. Finance Cmt, 59; chmn, Stevens Co. Rep. Cmt, 59-62; chmn, Seventh Cong. Dist. Rep. Cmt, 61-62; chmn. sixth dist, Minn. State Cent. Rep. Cmt, Minn. Exec. Cmt, 61-; del, Rep. Nat. Conv, 64 & 68; chmn, Stevens Co. Nixon Campaign Cmt, 68. Bus. & Prof. Pos: Farmer, Minn, 47-; mem. bd. dirs, DirAction Inc, Minneapolis, 65- Mil. Serv: Entered as Cadet, Army Air Force, 44, released as Pfc, 46, after serv. in Tenth Air Force. Mem: Am. Farm Bur; Am. Legion; Jaycees; Aircraft Owners and Pilots Asn; Flyers Inc; Nat. Rifle Asn; Morris Rifle Club. Rel: Lutheran. Mailing Add: Hancock, Minn. 56244.

CHARLES, ROBERT HORNE
Asst. Secy, U.S. Air Force
b. St. Louis, Mo, 9/14/13; s. Benjamin Hynes Charlés and Nancy McCandless Horne C; m. 7/9/38 to Elizabeth Olive Sewall C.(wid. 7/12/67); m. 2/8/69 to Marion Oates Leiter; c. Robert Horne Jr, Ellena, Summer Sewall, McCandless, Elizabeth. Educ: Yale, B.A, 35, LL.B, 38; Yale Club, N.Y.C; pres, Yale Club, St. Louis. Polit. & Govt. Pos: Consult. to Adminstr, NASA, 62-63; asst. secy, U.S. Air Force, 63- Bus. & Prof. Pos: With Thompson, Mitchell, Thompson & Young, St. Louis, 38-41; asst. secy, McDonnell Aircraft Corp, St. Louis, 43-45, secy, 45-52, dir, 48-60, mem. exec. cmt, 49-60, v.pres, 52-53 and exec. v.pres, 53-60; trustee, St. Louis Co. Day Sch, 53-56, secy. bd, 54; dir, Hamilton Shoe Co, St. Louis Bd. Mgrs. and Cent. Inst. Deaf, 58-62; exec. v.pres, mem. exec. cmt. and dir, Universal Match Corp, 60-61. Mem: Am. and Mo. Bar Asns; past pres, Am. Ord. Asn, St. Louis; Knickerbocker Club; Raquet Club; St. Louis Country Club; Burning Tree Country Club, Wash; past dir, St. Louis C. of C; Chevy Chase Country Club; Metrop. Club, Wash. Rel: Episcopal. Mailing Add: 3259 R St. N.W, Washington, D.C. 20007.

CHARLTON, FRED RUSSELL R
Chmn, Fourth Cong. Dist. Rep. Party, Mich.
b. Virginia, Minn, 12/9/13; s. Demetrius Edward Alexis Charlton (deceased) and Edith Russell C. (deceased); m. 2/21/42 to Elizabeth Jean Robertson; c. Margaret E. and Susan J. Educ: N.Y. Univ, 32-34; Univ. Mich, B.S. Cert. in Journalism, 37; Phi Delta Theta. Polit. & Govt. Pos: Committeeman, St. Joseph Co, Mich, 64-; mem, State Rep. Cent. Cmt, 66-68; chmn, Fourth Cong. Dist. Rep. Party, 68-; city cmnr, Sturgis, 69- Bus. & Prof. Pos: Newspaper reporter, Marquette Mining J. and Iron Mountain News, Mich, 41-42; advert. mgr, Manistee News-Advocate, 46-55, gen. mgr, 55-63; gen. mgr, Sturgis J, 63-64; pub. affairs dir, Kirsch Co, 64- Mil. Serv: Entered as Pvt, Army Air Force, 42, released as Capt, 46, after serv. in 94th Fighter Control Squadron, Seventh Air Force, Pac. Theatre, 45-46; Am Defense, Pac. Theatre and Victory Ribbons. Mem: Elks; Rotary. Rel: Episcopal. Mailing Add: 109 Maplecrest Ave, Sturgis, Mich. 49091.

CHARLTON, THOMAS JACKSON R
b. Savannah, Ga, 7/12/34; s. Thomas Jackson Charlton and Anne Read C; div; c. Thomas J, Jr, William B, Anne Read and Carol Lawton. Educ: Yale Univ, B.E, 56; Chi Psi. Polit. & Govt. Pos: V.chmn, Charlotte Co. Rep. Cmt, Va, 66-68; chmn, Rep. Cmt, Fifth Cong. Dist, Va, 68; chmn, Fifth Cong. Dist. Nixon for Pres, 68; del, Rep. Nat. Conv, 68. Bus. & Prof. Pos: Asst, Yale Univ. Admissions Off, 59-60; engr, F.R. Quible, P.E, Chase City, Va, 60-63; partner, Quible & Charlton, Engrs, 63-68; engr, Williams Bros. Overseas Co. Ltd, Libya, 69. Mil. Serv: Entered as 2nd Lt, Marines, 57, released as 1st Lt, 59, after serv. in Second Marine Div, U.S, 57-59; Res, 59-68, Capt. Mem: Nat. Soc. Prfnl. Engrs; Va. Asn. Surveyors. Rel: Episcopal. Legal Res: Route 1, Saxe, Va. 23967. Mailing Add: Williams Bros, P.O. Box 1023, Tripoli, Libya, Africa.

CHARLTON, WM. STUART R
Chmn, Delaware Co. Rep. Party, Iowa.
b. Manchester, Iowa, 11/19/28; s. Shannon B. Charlton and Etna Barr C; m. 12/26/52 to Lois D. McCord; c. Deborah, Pamela, Barbara, Bruce and Rebecca. Educ: Univ. of Iowa, B.A, 50 and J.D, 52; Phi Kappa Psi; Phi Delta Phi. Polit. & Govt. Pos: Delaware Co. Attorney,Iowa, 55-64; state secy, Young Rep. of Iowa, 56-60, state chmn, 60-64; gen. counsel, Young Rep. Nat. Fedn, 63-65; del, Rep. Nat. Conv, 64; chmn, Delaware Co. Rep. Party, Iowa, 64- Bus. & Prof. Pos: Farm mgr, 54-; attorney, Gilkey, Gould & Charlton, 54-58, Charlton, Charlton & Willey, 58- Mil. Serv: 1st Lt, Air Force, 52-54. Publ: 'Joint Tenancy in Bank Accounts,' Iowa Law Rev, 51. Mem: Cmt. on Income Taxation, Am. Bar Asn; pres, Rotary, 65; pres, Jr. C. of C, 57; Mason; K. of P; Farm Bur. Local Dist. Serv. Award, Jr. C. of C, 58. Rel: Presbyterian. Legal Res: 800 Ridgewood Dr, Manchester, Iowa. Mailing Add: 401 E. Main St, Manchester, Iowa 52057.

CHARRON, SANFORD E. D
b. Crawford Co, Mich, 5/13/17; m. 37 to Loretta V. Sorenson; c. Sandra, Rodney, Diane, Kaye, Rebecca. Educ: High sch. grad. Polit. & Govt. Pos:

Mich. State Rep, 64-66; former township clerk and councilman. Bus. & Prof. Pos: Serv. station operator. Mil. Serv: U.S. Army Engrs. Mem: Lions Club; DAV. Rel: Lutheran. Mailing Add: 823 W. 4th St, Pinconning, Mich. 48650. (1967)

CHARTIER, GLENN DELL D
Chmn, Cloud Co. Dem. Party, Kans.
b. Clyde, Kans, 3/31/93; s. Charles Dunning Chartier and Cora Trussel C; m. 2/2/20 to Dora Istas. Polit. & Govt. Pos: V.pres, Cloud Co. Farm Bur. Kans, 40-42, dir, rural electrification, Belleville, 40-45; chmn, U.S. Dept. Agr. Bd, Concordia, 40-51; chmn, War Bd, Concordia, 41-50 & Defense Bd, 45-50; ins. agent & adjuster, Fed. Crop. Ins. State Kans, 50-53; chmn, Cloud Co. Dem. Party, 64- Mem: Elks; Moose; Kiwanis. Rel: Episcopal. Legal Res: Concordia, Kans. Mailing Add: Clyde, Kans. 66938.

CHASE, ANTHONY GOODWIN R
b. San Francisco, Calif, 2/15/38; s. Goodwin Chase and Gudrun Mack C; m. 6/18/60 to Karen Lynne Zeissler; c. Betsy Marie, Whitney Marie and Goodwin Samuel. Educ: Univ. Wash, B.A, 60; Georgetown Univ. Law Center, J.D, 67; Phi Delta Phi; Georgetown Law J; Beta Theta Pi; Univ. of Wash. Oval Club; mem, Bd. of Control and pres, Inter-Fraternity Coun, Univ. of Wash, 60. Polit. & Govt. Pos: Nat. bank exam, U.S. Treas, 62-65; Asst. U.S. Comptroller Currency, D.C, 65-67; asst. to Gov. for Fed. State Rels, Olympia, Wash, 67-68; cand, U.S. House Rep, Wash, 68; legal counsel, State Wash, 68-69; spec. asst. to U.S. Secy. of Commerce, currently. Bus. & Prof. Pos: Consult, Am. Security & Trust Co, D.C, 67; law practice, currently. Mil. Serv: Entered as 2nd Lt, Marine Corps, 60, released as 1st Lt, 62, after serv. in First Bn; Res, Capt. Publ: 'Bank Holding Company Act and Interstate Expansion,' Bankers Mag, fall 69. Mem: D.C. and Wash. Bar Asns; Am. Bar Asn. (corp, banking and bus. law sect, admin. law sect); Nat. Press Club; U.S. Navy League; bd. trustees, Pierce Co. March Dimes; Univ. Union Club; Tacoma Country and Golf Club; Tacoma Lawn Tennis Club. Outstanding Young Man Award, Wash. State Jaycees, 68; Outstanding Young Man of Am. Award, 69; Am. Jurisp. Award, 67. Rel: Lutheran. Mailing Add: 732 N. Stadium Way, Tacoma, Wash. 98403.

CHASE, CYRIL CHARLES D
b. Athol, Idaho, 10/26/17; s. Fred B. Chase and Sylvia Jane Norman C; m. 1/12/37 to Verdie Jane Shepherd; c. Charles Ray, Dixie Lee and Sylvia Jane (deceased). Educ: High Sch; correspondence courses in elec. eng. Polit. & Govt. Pos: Idaho State Sen, 61-67; chmn, Area Redevelop. Admin, Area Redevelop. Cmt, Benewah Co. and Lower Shoshone Co, 63-65; city councilman, St. Maries, 48-52. Bus. & Prof. Pos: Pres, Chase Chevrolet Pontiac, Inc, St. Maries, Idaho, 54-; partner, Benewah Meat and Locker Co, St. Maries, Idaho, 46-54; partner, Chase Shepherd Lumber Co, Calder, Idaho, 48-54; plant supt, Pot Latch Forests, Inc, 41-46. Mem: Elks; Eagles; Kiwanis; pres, Jr. C. of C; dir, Sr. C. of C, 2 terms. Rel: Methodist. Mailing Add: 1026 College Ave, St. Maries, Idaho 83861. (1967)

CHASE, DeWAYNE ARTHUR NEWTON R
Mem, Kans. State Exec. Rep. Cmt.
b. Omaha, Nebr, 5/4/02; s. D.A.N. Chase and Harriet Annette Ayer C; m. 2/4/26 to Mary Emaline Ramsey; c. D.A.N, III. Educ: Washburn Univ, A.B, 24; Kappa Sigma. Polit. & Govt. Pos: Mayor, Fredonia, Kans, 43-52; chmn, Fifth Dist. Rep. Cmt, Kans, 62-69; chmn, Wilson Co. Rep. Cmt, Kans, 62-; mem, Kans. State Exec. Rep. Cmt, 62-; del, Rep. Nat. Conv, 68. Bus. & Prof. Pos: Store mgr, Montgomery Ward & Co, 28-30; owner, Burke Printing Co, Fredonia, Kans, 30- Mem: Elks; AF&AM; Mason (32°). Tennis letterman in col, 24; Rel: Methodist. Mailing Add: 415 N. 11th, Fredonia, Kans. 66736.

CHASE, HAROLD H. R
b. Springfield, Mo, 3/31/12; s. Fred Lee Chase and Beulah Mary Yowell C; m. 6/15/40 to Marian Caroline Schmitt. Educ: Phillips Univ, 30-31; Kans. Wesleyan Univ, A.B, 34; Washburn Univ, LL.B, 37. Polit. & Govt. Pos: U.S. Cmnr, Kans, 41-42; Lt. Gov, 61-65, chmn, Nat. Conf. Lt. Gov, 63-64; mem, Bd. Mgrs. Coun. State Govt, Chicago; chmn, Kans. Motor Vehicle Reciprocity Bd, Kans. Cmn. Interstate Coop. and Kans. Legis. Coun. Bus. & Prof. Pos: Attorney-at-law, Salina, Kans, 37-; dir, Griffith Provision Co, Inc, Downs. Mil. Serv: Army of U.S, 43-45 & 51-52, Capt; Army Res, Lt. Col. Mem: Am, Kans. and Salina Co. Bar Asns; N.W. Kans. Bar Asn.(pres, 58-59); Am. Legion (dist. comdr); VFW; ROA (Nat. Judge Advocate, 67-); Judge Advocates Asn; Elks; K. of C; Kiwanis. Rel: Catholic. Mailing Add: Great Plains Bldg, Salina, Kans. 67401.

CHASE, JOHN WILLIAM R
Chmn, Lawrence Co. Rep. Cent. Cmt, Ind.
b. Medora, Ind, 3/7/26; s. Maurice Chase and Catherine Hamilton C; m. 5/27/50 to Evelyn M. Nelson; c. Cheryl Lynn and Lisa Ann. Educ: Ind. Univ, 1 year. Polit. & Govt. Pos: Del, Ind. State Rep. Conv, 52-58; chmn, Lawrence Co. Young Rep, 53; driver exam, Bur. of Motor Vehicles, 57-60; clerk, Lawrence Circuit Court, 61-68; chmn, Lawrence Co. Rep. Cent. Cmt, 66-; mgr, Bedford License Br, 69- Mil Serv: Entered as Seaman, Navy, 44, released as Coxswain, 46, after serv. in U.S.S. Pitt, Pac, 44-46; Victory Medal; Am. Area Campaign Medal; Asiatic Pac. Area Campaign Medal with one star. Mem: F&AM; RSM; RAM; K.T; Ind. Consistory S.P.R.S. 32; Am. Legion; Rotary; Farm Bur. Awarded Sagamore of the Wabash. Rel: Methodist. Mailing Add: Route 1, Bedford, Ind. 47421.

CHASE, NANCY BASTIEN R
Chmn, Washtenaw Co. Rep. Cmt, Mich.
b. Chicago, Ill, 5/8/16; d. Alvin E. Bastien and Lena Kelly B; m. 1/25/47 to Charles Borden Chase; c. Charles Borden, III, Barbara Bastien and Peter Bastien. Educ: Art Inst. Chicago, 36-37. Polit. & Govt. Pos: V.chmn, Ann Arbor City Rep. Cmt, Mich, 64-66; chmn, Washtenaw Co. Elly Peterson for U.S. Sen. Campaign, 66; hq. chmn, Washtenaw Co. Rep. Cmt, 66 & 67; mem, Mich. State Rep. Cent. Cmt, 67-68, chmn, 67-68, mem, State Finance Exec. Cmt, 67-68; mem, Second Cong. Dist. Rep. Cmt, 67, 68 & 69; chmn, Washtenaw Co. Rep. Cmt, 68- Mil. Serv: Am. Red Cross Clubmobile, Europe, 44-46. Mem: Commun. Camp Placement Cmt; United Fund and Commun. Serv. Ann Arbor (bd. dirs and secy); Thrift Shop Asn; Red Cross Clubmobile Asn; Jr. League Providence, R.I; Ann Arbor Women's City Club; Rep. Women's Club Ann Arbor. Ford Motor Co. Commun. Serv. Award, 67. Rel: Congregational. Mailing Add: 1 Regent Dr, Ann Arbor, Mich. 48104.

CHASE, NANCY WINBON D
N.C. State Rep.
b. Fremont, N.C, 10/12/03; d. Robert Edward Winbon and Kate Davis W; m. 1/27/22 to John B. Chase (deceased); c. John B. Jr. and Thomas E. Educ: Fremont High Sch, 21. Polit. & Govt. Pos: Mem, sch. bd, Eureka, N.C, 59-60 and Charles B. Aycock Sch. Bd, 60-62; co-chmn, Wayne Co. Dem. Campaign, 60; v.chmn, Eureka Dem. Precinct, 60-61; mem, State Welfare Study Cmn, 61-62; mem, Gov. State Traffic Safety Coun. and State Tobacco Adv. Cmn; N.C. State Rep, 63-; mem, Wayne Co. Exten. Adv. Cmn, 64; del, Dem. Nat. Conv, 68. Bus. & Prof. Pos: Housewife. Mem: Chmn, Legis. Cmt, N.C. Ment. Health Asn; Bus. & Prfnl. Women's Club; N.C. Lit. & Hist. Asn; pres, Women's Soc. Christian Serv; chmn, N.C. Farm Bur.(Women's Cmn, 55-61); treas, N.C. Coun. Women's Orgn, 59-61; hon. mem, Delta Kappa Gamma, 63; Beta Sigma Phi; bd. dirs, Wayne Co. Red Cross; Ment. Health Cmt; Traffic Safety Cmt. Distinguished Serv. to Agr. Award, 56; Woman of the Year, 56, Wayne Co; Dem. Woman of the Year, Wayne Co, 62; Tarheel of the Week, 8/12/62; Commun. Serv. Award, 63, Eureka Ruritan Club. Rel: Methodist, Bd. of Stewards, 59-64; treas, Eureka Church, 59-64; teacher, adult Sunday Sch, 47-64. Mailing Add: Box 226, Eureka, N.C. 27830. (1967)

CHASE, PHILIP R. R
b. Syracuse, N.Y, 10/15/05; m. to Elizabeth Estabrook; c. Philip R, Jr, Stephen E. and Sarah C. Educ: Amherst Col, 27. Polit. & Govt. Pos: Councilman-at-lg, Syracuse, N.Y, 38-42; N.Y. State Assemblyman, 54-66. Bus. & Prof. Pos: Spec. agent, Northwest. Mutual Life Ins. Co; trustee, Syracuse Savings Bank and Gen. Hosp. of Syracuse, Oakwood Cemetery; dir, Merchants Nat. Bank & Trust Co. of Syracuse. Mil. Serv: Army, 42-46, Lt. Col. Mem: C. of C.(past pres, Syracuse, dir); Orondoga Hist. Asn; Syracuse Boys' Club; Burns Supply, Inc; Commun. Chest (past pres); Orondoga Co. War Mem.(past cmnr); N.Y. State Asn. Life Underwriters (past pres). Mailing Add: Hunt Lane, Fayettville, N.Y. 13066.

CHASE, ROBERT LEON R
Chmn, Goffstown Rep. Cmt, N.H.
b. North Conway, N.H, 7/17/29; s. John Leon Chase and Laura M. Clemons C; m. 6/20/53 to Ann Bradford Jones; c. R. Bradford and David W. Educ: Univ. N.H, B.S, 53; Psi Epsilon; Acacia. Polit. & Govt. Pos: Alternate del, Rep. Nat. Conv, 64; v.chmn, Goffstown Rep. Cmt, N.H, 64-66, chmn, 66-; mem. exec. cmt, Hillsboro Co. Rep. Cmt, 65; chmn, Goffstown Young Rep, 65-67; del, Rep. State Conv, N.H, 66 & 68; mem, Rep. State Cmt, 66- Bus. & Prof. Pos: Claim supvr, N.H. Ins. Group, 63; spec. agent, Aetna Ins. Co, 64-67; spec. agent, Employers-Commercial Union Ins. Group, 67-; registered rep, Employers Group Fund, Inc, 67- Mil. Serv: Lt, Coast Guard Res. Mem: Mason. Rel: Episcopal. Mailing Add: 25 N. Mast Rd, Goffstown, N.H. 03045.

CHASE, RUSSELL CUSHING R
N.H. State Rep.
b. Boston, Mass, 2/5/07; s. William Cooledge Chase and Mabel Cushing C; m. to Katherine Elizabeth Owen; c. Barbara (Mrs. Wetherbee) and David Owen. Educ: Northeast. Univ, B.S.C.E, 29. Polit. & Govt. Pos: N.H. State Rep, 69- Bus. & Prof. Pos: Various eng. jobs, Mass, 29-42; from N.E. mgr. asphalt dept. to mgr. of mgt. training, Shell Oil Co, 42-67. Mem: Boston Soc. Civil Engrs; Rotary; Mason. Rel: Unitarian. Mailing Add: Middleton Rd, Wolfeboro, N.H. 03894.

CHASE, SEYMOUR M. D
b. New York, N.Y, 4/14/24; s. Harold Chase and Rhoda Oshrin C; m. 11/12/60 to Janet Schwartz; c. Neil. Educ: Univ. Mich, A.B, 47; Columbia Univ, M.A, 49; Columbus Univ. Sch. Law, LL.B, 52; Phi Sigma Delta. Polit. & Govt. Pos: Attorney-advisor, Fed. Commun. Cmn, 53-54; del, Dem. Nat. Conv, 56, alternate del, 64; mem, Dem. Cent. Cmt, D.C, 61-68; field adv, Dem. Nat. Cmt, Presidential Campaign, 68; campaign dir, Dem. United for Johnson, later Dem. United, D.C. Primary, 68. Bus. & Prof. Pos: Assoc, Law Firm of Segal, Smith & Hennessey, 54-58; Attorney-at-Law, 58- Mil. Serv: Entered as Pvt, Army, 43, released as Cpl, 45, after serv. in 103rd Inf. Div, ETO, 44-45. Publ: 'Closing The Door—The District of Columbia Securities Act,' J. Bar Asn. D.C, 12/64. Mem: Am, D.C. and Fed. Commun. Bar Asns; Broadcast Pioneers; Int. Platform Asn; bd. dirs, Wash. Home Rule Cmt, 63-, v.pres, 65 and legis. chmn, 65; D.C. Securities Adv. Cmt, 65-69; Univ. Mich. Club of Wash, D.C; Tantallon Country Club; Nat. Broadcasters Club; Nat. Lawyers Club. Legal Res: 3015 Stephenson Place. N.W, Washington, D.C. 20015. Mailing Add: Brawner Bldg, Suite 308, Washington, D.C. 20006.

CHASE, THEODORE WILLIS R
Mayor, Sun Prairie, Wis.
b. Sun Prairie, Wis, 8/21/11; s. Benjamin Joseph Chase and Edith Crosse C; m. 2/3/34 to Maecella Dolan; c. Diane (Mrs. Frank Worzala), David, Nancy (Mrs. John McMahon), Susan (Mrs. John Deans), Byron and Theodore, Jr. Educ: Univ. of Wis, 29-30; Ripon Col, B.A, 33; Alpha Sigma Phi. Polit. & Govt. Pos: Mem, Dane Co. Rep. Exec. Cmt, Wis, 60-65; chmn, Second Dist. Rep. Party, 65-69; mem, Wis. State Rep. Exec. cmt, 65-69; del, Rep. Nat. Conv, 68; mayor, Sun Prairie, Wis, 69- Bus. & Prof. Pos: Treas, Wis. Retail Lumber Dealers, 69- Mil. Serv: Entered as Lt.(jg), Navy, 43, released as Lt. Comdr, 45, after serv. in Harbor Entrance Control, N.Y. and Panama; Lt. Comdr.(Ret), Naval Res. Mem: Am. Legion; VFW; Lions; Cath. Order of Foresters; Madison Club. Rel: Catholic. Mailing Add: 206 Windsor St, Sun Prairie, Wis. 53590.

CHASE, WILLIAM ROGER R
b. Winchendon, Mass, 6/25/27; s. Roger Clark Chase and Elmina Eaton C; m. 7/28/47 to Louise Lillian Knowlton; c. Mark Irwin, William Roger, Jr, Jo Ellen and Geoffrey David. Educ: Univ. Colo; Tri-State Col, B.S.M.E, 56. Polit. & Govt. Pos: Mem, Bristol Town Cmt, Conn, 62-68, and secy, 63-65; city councilman, Bristol, Conn, 63-65. Bus. & Prof. Pos: Engr, New Departure-Hyatt Bearings, 56-66. Mil. Serv: Entered as A/S, Navy, 45, released as ADE-3, 46, after serv. in Naval Air Corps; Am. Theater Ribbon; Victory Medal. Mem: Soc. of Automotive Engrs; Am. Soc. of Mech. Engrs; exec. bd. mem. & training cmt. chmn, Bristol Coun, Boy Scouts. Rel: Congregational. 1967 Legal Res: Bristol, Conn. No mailing address available. (1967)

CHASSE, PETER N. D
N.H. State Rep.
b. Somersworth, N.H, 8/27/00; married; c. Two. Educ: Somersworth Schs. Polit. & Govt. Pos: N.H. State Rep, currently. Bus. & Prof. Pos: Health officer. Mem: Holy Name Soc; St. Jean Baptiste; Kiwanis Club. Rel: Catholic. Mailing Add: 115 Franklin St, Somersworth, N.H. 03878. (1967)

CHATALAS, WILLIAM (BILL) D
Wash. State Rep.
b. Constantinople, Turkey, 1907; m. to Goldie; c. Three sons. Educ: Univ. Wash. Exten. Sch. Polit. & Govt. Pos: Wash. State Rep, currently. Bus. & Prof. Pos: Sales and pub. rels. mgr. Mem: Order of Ahepa; Eagles; Rainer Bus. Men's Club; Mt. Baker Improv. Club; C. of C; PTA; Jackson St. Commun. Coun, Scouts. Mailing Add: 2802 33rd St, Seattle, Wash. 98144. (1967)

CHATELAIN, LEON, JR. R
Committeeman, D.C. Rep. Cmt.
b. Washington, D.C, 3/8/02; s. Leon Chatelain and Bertha Ashbacher C; m. 2/14/44 to Mary Wysong; c. Jo Ann, Edward Russell and Leon, III. Educ: George Wash. Univ, B.Arch, 27; Alpha Chi Rho; Scarabs; Theta Delta Chi. Polit. & Govt. Pos: Committeeman, D.C. Rep. Cmt, 64- Bus. & Prof. Pos: Owner, Leon Chatelain, Jr, Architect, 30-39; partner, Chatelain, Gauger & Nolan, 59- Mem: Am. Inst. Architects (past pres); fel. Construction Specification Inst; sr. mem. Nat. Soc. Real Estate Appraisers; past master, Mason; Shriner; Jesters; Red Cross of Constantine; Columbia Country Club; Cong. Country Club; Cosmos Club; Univ. Club; Capitol Hill Club; Arts Club. President's Cmt. Employ. Handicapped distinguished serv. award; Cosmopolitan Club's distinguished serv. medal; Wash. Bd. Trade Man of the Years. Rel: Methodist. Mailing Add: 1823 23rd St. N.W, Washington, D.C. 20008.

CHATTERSON, BERTHA MARIE R
b. Bagley, Wis, 8/13/17; d. Clyde Max Miller and Minnie I. Boldt M; m. 2/7/41 to Clifford Winn Chatterson; c. Aaron Lee. Educ: Wis. State Col, 50; Wis. State Univ. at Eau Claire Area Cmt. Polit. Pos: V.chmn, Eau Claire Co. Rep. Club, Wis. 63-67 and chmn, 61-63; 2nd v.pres, State Women's Fedn, 65-67; mem, Gov.Cmn. on Status of Women, 65-66; secy, 10th Dist, Wis, 63-65; dist.del, Nat. Conv, 64 and 60; State Statutory Cmn, 62-64; State Neighbor-to-Neighbor Chmn, 63-64; 10th Dist. V.Pres. of Rep. Women, 59-65. Govt. Pos: Secy, Western Dairyland Econ. Opportunity Coun, 66-67. Prof. Pos: Teacher. Mem: Eastern Star; Eau Claire Women's Club; County Guidance Clin. Board; United Cerebral Palsy of Chippewa Valley; Chippewa Valley Mus. Bd; State Hist. Soc; Eau Claire Country Club. Rel: Methodist. Mailing Add: 668 Fairford Rd, Grosse Pointe Woods, Mich. 48236.

CHATTIN, CHESTER COLES D
Assoc. Justice, Supreme Court of Tenn.
b. Winchester, Tenn, 11/2/07; s. Edward Walter Chattin and Ellen Shadow C; m. 5/15/35 to Mary Eleanor Kiningham; c. Mary Kay. Educ: Univ. of the South, B.S; Cumberland Law Sch, LL.B; Phi Gamma Delta. Polit. & Govt. Pos: Asst. dist. attorney gen, Tenn, 35-37 & 39-47; Tenn. State Rep, 40-44; dist. attorney gen, 18th Judicial Circuit of Tenn, 47-58, circuit judge, 58-62; Judge, Court of Appeals of Tenn, 62-65; Assoc. Justice, Supreme Court of Tenn, 65- Bus. & Prof. Pos: Dir, Farmers Nat. Bank, Winchester, Tenn, 47- Mil. Serv: Entered as Draftee, Navy, 45, released as Hosp. Apprentice 1/C, 45, after serv. in Hosp. Corps. Mem: Tenn. Judicial Conf; Tenn. and Franklin Co. Bar Asns; Am. Judicature Soc; Mason; Shrine; Am. Legion; C. of C; Franklin Co. Country Club; Boy Scouts (mem. exec. bd. Mid. Tenn. Coun). Rel: Episcopal. Mailing Add: Winchester, Tenn. 37398.

CHAUDOIN, OTIS R. D
b. 1914. Educ: Monmouth Col, 58-64. Polit. & Govt. Pos: Ky. State Rep, until 68. Bus. & Prof. Pos: Ins. and Real Estate Broker. Mil. Serv: World War II, U.S. Army. Mem: Lions (past pres, past zone chmn); Am. Legion; VFW; Pewee Valley Civic Club; Oldham Co. Farm Bur; PTA. Rel: Presbyterian. Mailing Add: 123 Tulip Ave, Pewee Valley, Ky. 40056. (1967)

CHAVEZ, DAVID, JR. D
b. Albuquerque, N.Mex, 11/8/97; s. David Chavez and Paz Sanchez C; m. 10/14/26 to Genevieve Trovillion; c. Caroline T. Educ: Univ. N.Mex; Georgetown Univ. Law Sch, LL.B, 23. Polit. & Govt. Pos: Mayor, Santa Fe, N.Mex, 30-32; dist. attorney, First Judicial Dist, 32-36, Dist. Judge, 36-42; U.S. Dist. Judge, Dist. of P.R, 47-50; Justice, Supreme Court, N.Mex, 60-68. Bus. & Prof. Pos: Private practice of law, Sante Fe, N.Mex, 23-30 & 50-60. Mil. Serv: in 82nd Field Artil, World War I, 18; reentered as Maj, Air Force, 42, released as Col, after serv. in Judge Adv. Gen. Dept, San Bernardino A.D.C.E. Command, 43, Allied Garrison of Sardinia, SOLOC, War Crimes, 43-46; Mex. Border Serv. and World War I Victory Medals; Am. Theater Ribbon; Europe, Africa, Middle East Ribbon with 2 Bronze Serv. Stars; World War II Victory Medal, Croix de Guerre with Palm. Mem: N.Mex. and Am. Bar Asns; Am. Judicature Soc; Am. Legion; VFW; Serra Club, Santa Fe; Papal Knight of St. Gregory. Rel: Roman Catholic. Legal Res: 710 Gildersleave, Santa Fe, N.Mex. 87501. Mailing Add: P.O. Box 1790, Santa Fe, N.Mex. 87501. (1967)

CHAVEZ, JOSE BENITO D
N.Mex. State Rep.
b. Alcalde, N.Mex, 7/6/34; s. Jose Miguel Chavez and Rosarito Barela C; single. Educ: St. Michael's Col, B.A, 60; Highlands Univ, 68. Polit. & Govt. Pos: N.Mex. State Rep, Rio Arriba Co, 67- Mil. Serv: Entered as Pvt, Marines, 53, released as Cpl, 56, after serv. in First Marine Div, 11th Marines, Korea, 54-55. Mem: Am. Legion; K. of C. Rel: Roman Catholic. Mailing Add: Box 40, San Juan Pueblo, N.Mex. 87566.

CHAVEZ, TIBO J. D
N.Mex. State Sen.
b. 1914. Educ: Univ. of N.Mex, A.B; Georgetown Law Sch, LL.B. Polit. & Govt. Pos: Former mem, For. Serv, State Dept, S.Am; Lt. Gov, N.Mex, 51-54; N.Mex. State Sen, 61-, Majority Leader, N.Mex. Senate, currently; del, Dem. Nat. Conv, 68. Bus. & Prof. Pos: Attorney-at-law. Mem: Lions. Rel: Catholic. Mailing Add: 500 Becker Ave, Belen, N.Mex. 87002.

CHAVIS, PATRICK E, JR. D
Educ: Kappa Alpha Psi; Sigma Pi Phi. Polit. & Govt. Pos: Ind. State Sen, 66; former dep. prosecutor, Marion Co; asst. city prosecutor, Indianapolis; pub. defender, Marion Co. Bus. & Prof. Pos: Lawyer. Mem: Masons (33°). Rel: Baptist. Mailing Add: 1753 W. 63rd, Indianapolis, Ind. 46260. (1967)

CHEEKS, DONALD EDWARD D
b. Augusta, Ga, 5/1/31; s. Clarence Cheeks and Johanna Elizabeth McKnight C; m. 9/4/60 to Betty Jo Horne; c. Donna Elizabeth and Deborah Eunice. Educ: The Citadel, 50-51; Univ. Ga, 55-56. Polit. & Govt. Pos: Former mem. sch. bd, Curtis Baptist Sch, Ga; mem, City Coun, Augusta, Ga, 63-; Ga. State Rep, 67-69. Bus. & Prof. Pos: Salesman real estate, 54; pres, Donald E. Cheeks Ins, Inc, 62- and Augusta Putt-Putt, Inc, 65-; treas, Church & Sch. Supply, Inc, 66- Mil. Serv: Entered as Seaman, Navy, 51, released as PO 2/C, 54, after serv. in Far East Command, 52-54; Nat. Defense, Korean Serv, UN, Navy Occupation, Good Conduct and Am. Spirit Honor Medals. Mem: Life mem. Young Men's Libr. Asn; Elks; Civitan Club; Moose; Tenth Dist. govt. affairs chmn, Jaycees, 62; VFW; Am. Legion. Rel: Baptist. Mailing Add: 754 Metcalf St, Augusta, Ga. 30904. (1967)

CHEEVER, GENE G. R
Chmn, Butte Co. Rep. Party, S.Dak.
b. Brookings, S.Dak, 12/30/28; s. Herbert E. Cheever and Margaret Williams C; m. 6/18/52 to JoAnn Coughlin; c. Patrick, Timmothy, Dan and Todd. Educ: S.Dak. State Univ, B.S, 51; Univ. Ill, M.S, 52; Blue Key; Delta Tau Delta. Polit. & Govt. Pos: Chmn, Butte Co. Rep. Party, S.Dak, currently. Bus. & Prof. Pos: Football coach and dir. of phys. educ, Dakota Wesleyan Univ, 52-53; football coach and athletic dir, Watertown High Sch, 54-55; sales mgr, Black Hills Clay Prod. Co, 56-62, mgr, 63- Rel: Catholic. Mailing Add: 1021 Perkins, Belle Fourche, S.Dak. 57717.

CHELF, FRANK, SR. D
b. Elizabethtown, Ky, 9/22/10; s. Judge Weed S. Chelf and Hallie Wrather C; m. to Louise Rash; c. Caroline, Bonnie and Frank, Jr. Educ: St. Mary's Col; Centre Col; Cumberland Univ, LL.B; Phi Delta Theta. Polit. & Govt. Pos: U.S. Rep, Ky, 45-67; prosecuting attorney, Marion Co, 12 years. Bus. & Prof. Pos: Attorney. Mil. Serv: Maj, Army Air Force, World War II. Mem: Am. Legion; VFW; K.T; Eastern Star. Rel: Presbyterian. Mailing Add: Lebanon, Ky. 40033.

CHELSETH, ARCHIE DONALD R
Mem, Gov. Coun. Health, Welfare and Rehabilitation, Minn.
b. Duluth, Minn, 4/18/42; s. Osmund H. Chelseth and Myrtle Ann LaTour C; m. 12/16/67 to Andrea Louise Lundberg. Educ: Univ. Minn, Duluth, B.A. cum laude, 63; M.A. Pub. Admin, 68; U.S. Steelworkers Scholar, 60-61. Polit. & Govt. Pos: Chmn, Duluth Youth for Nixon-Lodge, 60; chmn, Univ. Minn. Young Rep. Club, 60-61; research asst, League Minn. Munic, 63; research asst. to Gov, Min, 64-66; admin. asst, Asn. Minn. Co, 66; research dir, Forsythe for U.S. Sen. Campaign, 66 and for Gov. Harold LeVander, 66-69; mem, Gov. Coun. Exec. Reorgn, 67-68, adv. cmt. mgt. training, 67-68 and coun. Health, Welfare and Rehabilitation, 67- Bus. & Prof. Pos: Teaching asst. polit. sci, Univ. Minn, 62-63, admin. asst. to dean, Inst. Agr, Univ. Minn, 64-65; asst. dir. civic affairs, H.B. Fuller Co, St. Paul, 65-66; instr. polit. sci, Col. St. Thomas, St. Paul, 68; asst. to publisher, Minneapolis Star and Tribune, 69- Mem: Am. Soc. Pub. Admin; coun. mem, Minn. Soc. Pub. Admin; Am. Polit. Sci. Asn; Nat. Munic. League; Minn. Planning Asn; bd. dirs, Voyageurs Nat. Park Asn; Ft. Snelling State Park Asn; Minn. Hist. Soc; Univ. Minn. Alumni Asn; Univ. Minn. Duluth Alumni Asn; Minn. Young Rep. League. Rel: Presbyterian. Legal Res: 2258 Glenridge Ave, St. Paul, Minn. 55119. Mailing Add: 425 Portland Ave, Minneapolis, Minn. 55415.

CHENOWETH, J. EDGAR R
b. Trinidad, Colo, 8/17/97; s. Thomas Beaseman Chenoweth and Esther Rebecca Shamberger C; m. 12/25/19 to Ruth Ollevia Crews; c. William B, Wanda Elizabeth, John Edgar, James Richard and Ruth Anne. Educ: Univ. Colo. Polit. & Govt. Pos: Asst. dist. attorney, Third Judicial Dist, Colo, 29-33; co. judge, Las Animas Co, 33-41; chmn, Rep. State Cmt, 37-40; U.S. Rep, Third Cong. Dist, Colo, 41-49 & 51-65. Mem: Am. Bar Asn; former mem. bd. gov, Colo. Bar Asn; Mason; Elks; Eagles; Rotary (past pres, Trinidad Rotary Club and past dist. gov); Denver Press Club. Rel: Baptist. Legal Res: 315 Alta St, Trinidad, Colo. 81082. Mailing Add: Box 48, Trinidad, Colo. 81082.

CHENOWETH, JOHN CRAIG D
Minn. State Rep.
b. St. Paul, Minn, 5/20/43; s. William Vernon Chenoweth Sr. and Florine Ann Johnson C; single. Educ: St. John's Univ, Minn, B.S, Govt, 65; John Carroll Univ, 65; St. Paul Sem, 65-66; William Mitchell Col. Law, 67-68; student body pres, St. John's Univ. Polit. & Govt. Pos: Cong. campaign dir, Second Dist. Minn, 66; mem, Dem-Farmer-Labor State Cent. Cmt, Minn, 68-; Minn. State Rep, 68- Mil. Serv: Minn. Nat. Guard. Rel: Roman Catholic. Mailing Add: 987 Earl St, St. Paul, Minn. 55106.

CHERBERG, JOHN ANDREW D
Lt. Gov, Wash.
b. Pensacola, Fla, 10/17/10; s. Fortunato Cherberg and Annie Rand C; m. 8/17/35 to Elizabeth Anne Walker; c. James Walker, Kay (Mrs. Ray Cohrs) and Barbara (Mrs. Dean Tonkin). Educ: Univ. Wash, B.B.A. in econs, Mkt. & advert, 33, Col. of Educ, Life Teaching Diploma, 34; Sigma Nu; Oval Club; Fir Tree. Polit. & Govt. Pos: Lt. Gov, Wash, 57-, chmn, Nat. Conf. of Lt. Gov, 68-69, Data Processing Adv. Cmt. and Interim Legis. Cmt. on Govt. Coop, mem, State Capitol Cmt, State Finance Cmt, Oil & Gas Conserv. Cmt. and State Patrol Retirement Bd; mem, World Fair Cmn, 70. Bus. & Prof. Pos: Teacher and football coach, Cleveland High Sch, Seattle, Wash, 34-38 and Queen Anne High Sch, Seattle, 38-46; football coach, Univ. Wash, 46-56. Mem: Seattle Local, Am. Fedn. of TV & Radio Artists; Nat. Asn. of Football Coaches; Nat. Acad. of TV Arts & Sci; U.S. Army Asn; Nat. Educ. Asn; Wash. Educ. Asn; hon. life mem, Seattle Fedn. of Teachers; Warehousemen's Union; Retail Clerks' Union; hon. life mem, Wash. State Asn. Broadcasters; mem. exec. bd, Jerry Lorentson Found; Variety Club of Pac. Northwest; Generator's Lorentson Found; Variety Club of Pac. Northwest; Generator's Club. Man of the Year Award; Seattle Post-Intelligencer, 37; Am. Legion Honor Award; Flaherty Medal, Univ. Wash. Inspirational Award; Hon. U.S. Navy Seabee; Hon. Ky. Col; Honor Achievement Award by Bikur Cholim; VFW Achievement

Award; Hon. Chief, Yakima Indian Nat. Rel: Catholic. Legal Res: 505 Howe St, Seattle, Wash. 98109. Mailing Add: Legislative Building, Olympia, Wash. 98501.

CHERINGTON, PAUL W. R
Asst. Secy. for Policy and Int. Affairs, Dept. of Transportation
b. Cambridge, Mass, 6/16/18; m. to Rita Van Dusen; c. Charlotte, Alexander and Paul. Educ: Harvard Col, B.S, 40; Harvard Bus. Sch, D.B.A, 56. Polit. & Govt. Pos: Econ. analyst, U.S. Senate Mil. Affairs Cmt, 46; liaison to air coordinating cmt, Civil Aeronaut. Bd, 47-48, exec. asst. to chmn, 48-50; Asst. Secy. for Policy and Int. Affairs, Dept. of Transportation, 69- Bus. & Prof. Pos: Opers. clerk, Pan Am. Airways, Africa, Ltd, Brit. W.Africa, 42; mem. faculty, Harvard Bus. Sch, 50-63, James J. Hill Prof. of Transportation, 63-69, dir, Weapons Acquisition Research Proj, 58-65. Mil. Serv: Opers. and Statist. Control Officer, Air Transport Command, Army Air Corps, 43-45. Legal Res: 9 Coolidge Hill Rd, Cambridge, Mass. 02138. Mailing Add: Dept. of Transportation, 800 Independence Ave. S.W, Washington, D.C. 20591.

CHERKASKY, SHIRLEY EVELYN D
b. Marinette, Wis, 10/10/27; d. Frederick Henry Schroeder and Elsie Christensen C; m. 2/4/50 to William Benjamin Cherkasky; c. Mara, Clare and Lisa. Educ: Univ. Wis, B.A, 49, M.S, 68; George Wash. Univ, grad. student, 69; Sigma Epsilon Sigma; Phi Kappa Phi. Polit. & Govt. Pos: Co. secy, Outagamie Co. Dem. Party, Wis, 55, 56 & 57, co. chmn, 57-59; secy-treas, Eighth Dist. Dem. Party, 55-63; mem-at-lg, State Admin. Cmt, Dem. Party of Wis, 61-62; orgn v.chmn, Dem. Party of Wis, 62-67; del, Dem. Nat. Conv, 64; mem, Gov. Cmn. on Status of Women, 64. Bus. & Prof. Pos: Res. assoc, George Wash. Univ, 67- Mem: Am. Sociol. Asn; D.C. Sociol. Soc; Am. Civil Liberties Union; League of Women Voters; PTA. Rel: Unitarian. Mailing Add: 7312 Rebecca Dr, Alexandria, Va. 22307.

CHERKASKY, WILLIAM BENJAMIN D
b. Madison, Wis, 8/11/24; s. Benjamin Cherkasky and Anna C; m. 2/4/50 to Shirley Schroeder; c. Mara, Clare and Lisa. Educ: Northwestern Univ; Univ. Wis, B.B.A, 49; Beta Alpha Psi. Polit. & Govt. Pos: Former legis. dir. for U.S. Sen. Gaylord Nelson, Wis, admin. asst, currently; many and varied polit. positions, Wis, 49-; area supvr, Econ. Develop. Admin, U.S. Dept. of Commerce, 66. Mil. Serv: Entered as Pvt, Army, 43, released as Pfc, after serv. in 89th Inf. Div, ETO; Bronze Star; ETO Ribbon with Three Battle Stars. Rel: Unitarian. Mailing Add: 7312 Rebecca Dr, Hollin Hills, Alexandria, Va. 22307. (1967)

CHERNER, BENNETT LEE 'BEN' D
Ala. State Rep.
b. Bessemer, Ala, 11/5/36; s. Jacob Cherner and Muriel Weiss C; m. 1/24/69 to Barbara Lorraine; c. Stacey Lynn. Educ: Samford Univ, B.S, 61; Sigma Alpha Mu. Polit. & Govt. Pos: Ala. State Rep, 67- Bus. & Prof. Pos: Pres, Cherner Enterprises, Inc. and subsidiaries, 56- Mil. Serv: Entered as Pvt, Ala. Nat. Gurad, 58, released as S/Sgt, 64. Mem: Lions Int; Jaycees; C. of C; Am. Legion; Eagles. Selected Man of The Year, Bessemer, Ala, 66. Rel: Jewish. Legal Res: 613 Melody Lane, Bessemer, Ala. 35020. Mailing Add: P.O. Box 669, Bessemer, Ala. 35020.

CHERRY, DICK D
b. 3/22/28; s. Frank Hanley Cherry and Ruth Helen Dicken C; m. 8/20/49 to Elizabeth A. Davis; c. Mark Davis, Christopher John and Lisa Dawn. Educ: Wabash Col, A.B, summa cum laude; Univ. Chicago, M.A, 52; post grad. work, 52-55; Phi Beta Kappa, 49; Pi Sigma Alpha; Tau Kappa Alpha; Phi Delta Theta. Polit. & Govt. Pos: Tex. State Rep, 62-66; admin. asst. to U.S. Sen. Ralph Yarborough of Tex, 65-67; cong. rels. officer, Model Cities Admin, Dept. of Housing and Urban Develop, 67-69; fed. aids rep, Nat. League of Cities, U.S. Conf. of Mayors, 69-; Wash. Asst, New Orleans, La, 69- Bus. & Prof. Pos: Group worker, Bethlehem Commun. Center, 52-55; acting chmn. and asst. prof, polit. sci. dept, Baylor Univ, 55-65, dir, Center For. Serv. Studies, 58-63; ed, Background on World Politics, quart, 59-62. Publ: Christianity and Communism (with Merriam Cuninggim and Paul Green), 58; The Politics of Reapportionment (with Malcolm Jewell), 62. Rel: Lutheran. Legal Res: 4112 N. 27th St, Waco, Tex. Mailing Add: 307 Cree Dr, Forest Heights, Md. 20021.

CHERRY, FRANK ELLIOTT R
Chmn, Sioux Co. Rep. Party, Nebr.
b. Douglas Co, Nebr, 8/10/13; s. Earl Roe Cherry and Grace Ellen Warren C; m. 11/3/42 to Lucille Caroline Wegehoeft; c. William David and Grace Anne. Educ: Univ. Nebr, B.S, 36; Pershing Rifles; Phi Gamma Delta. Polit. & Govt. Pos: Chmn, Sioux Co. Rep. Party, Nebr, 64- Bus. & Prof. Pos: Dir, First Nat. Bank, Morrill, Nebr, 46-; dir, local Rural Electrification Admin. Coop, 52-68. Mil. Serv: Entered as Pvt, Army, 42, released as T/Sgt, 46, after serv. in Air Force Finance, 42-46. Mem: Nebr. Stock Growers Asn.(exec. coun, 63-66); Nebr. Beef Coun.(pres, 62-68); Am. Nat. Cattlemen's Asn.(beef prom. cmt, 67-); AF&AM (past Master, Sioux Lodge); Am. Legion. Rel: Methodist. Mailing Add: Star Route 6, Box 12, Harrison, Nebr. 69346.

CHERRY, ROBERT E. D
Ill. State Sen.
b. Phila, Pa; married; c. two. Educ: Chicago Law Sch, LL.B. Polit. & Govt. Pos: Spec. cmnr, Circuit Court of Cook Co, Ill; Asst. Attorney Gen, 49-53; Ill. State Sen, 54-; alternate del, Dem. Nat. Conv, 68. Bus. & Prof. Pos: Attorney-at-Law. Mem: Am. and Chicago Bar Asns; Decalogue Soc. of Lawyers; City Club of Chicago; Convenant Club of Ill. Mailing Add: 33 N. LaSalle St, Chicago, Ill. 60602.

CHESNEY, CHESTER ANTON D
b. Chicago, Ill, 3/9/16; s. Anthony Chesney and Anna Stupak C; m. 3/9/43 to Betty Jane Uetrecht; c. Elizabeth Ann. Educ: DePaul Univ, B.S, 39; Northwest. Univ. Grad Sch, 47. Polit. & Govt. Pos: U.S. Rep, 11th Cong. Dist, Ill, 48-50; fed-state liaison officer, Fed. Civil Defense Admin, 50-51; committeeman, Elkgrove Twp. Dem. Orgn, 62-; alternate del, Dem. Nat. Conv, 68. Bus. & Prof. Pos: Asst. v.pres, Advance Mortgage Corp, 53-60; v.pres. and dir, Avondale Savings and Loan Asn, 60- Mil. Serv: Entered as Pvt, Air Force, 41, released as Maj, 46; Am. Defense, Am. Theater, Asiatic-Pac. Theater and ETO Ribbons; Victory Medal. Mem: Northwest Real Estate Bd; Northwest Builders Asn; Soc. of Real Estate Appraisers; VFW; Moose; K. of C. Was Little All American, 38, played for Cincinnati Bengals, 39 and Chicago Bears, 39-40; played with world champions in 40. Rel: Catholic. Mailing Add: 801 E. Golfview Dr, Mt. Prospect, Ill. 60056.

CHESNUTT, JOHN HENRY R
Chmn, DeKalb Co. Rep. Cent. Cmt, Ill.
b. Rushville, Ill, 5/27/12; s. John M. Chesnutt and Bessie Parr C; m. 5/26/35 to Marion L. Boyle; c. William Allen and Chalys Faith. Educ: Cornell Col, 30-31; North. Ill. Univ, 31-34. Polit. & Govt. Pos: Chmn, DeKalb Co. Rep. Cent. Cmt, Ill, 64-; chmn, 33rd Rep. Cmt, 65-; precinct committeeman, Rep. Party; v.pres, Rep. Ill. Co. Chmns. Asn, 69. Bus. & Prof. Pos: Agent, Metrop. Life Ins. Co, 35-40; sales supvr, IEA Ins. Co, 46-47; ins. consult, IAA Ins. Serv, 47-48; agency supvr, Keystone Automobile Club, Phila, Pa, 48-49; sales supvr, Farm Bur. Ins. Co, Nebr, 49-54; owner, Chesnutt Ins. Serv, 54-58; owner and ins. broker, R.B. Paterson Agency, Ill, 58-66. Mil. Serv: Entered as Sgt, Army, 42, released as 1st Lt, 46, after serv. in 301st Ord. Regt. and 184th A.A. Gun Bn, ETO; Silver Star; Six Campaign Ribbons. Mem: Mason; Shrine; VFW; Am. Legion; Elks; Kiwanis; PTA; Moose; YMCA; John Erickson Rep. Club. Rel: Methodist. Mailing Add: 1347 Prosser Dr, Sycamore, Ill. 60178.

CHESROW, FRANK WILLIAM D
b. Chicago, Ill, 3/27/03; s. Frank Cesario Chesrow and Frances Passarelli C; m. 1/24/38 to Ruth Isabel Atwood; c. Charlotte Frances. Educ: Valparaiso Univ, Ph.C, 24. Polit. & Govt. Pos: Trustee, Bd. Trustees, Metrop. Sanit. Dist, Gr. Chicago, Ill, 48-, pres, 58-; alternate del-at-lg, Dem. Nat. Conv, 52, 56 & 60, del-at-lg, 64 & 68. Bus. & Prof. Pos: Pres, F.W. Chesrow and Co, 28-42 and Chesrow Drug Stores, 28-65; dir, Chesrow Mem. Found; v.pres. and dir, Research Found, Chicago, Ill, 56- Mil. Serv: Entered as Lt, Army, 42, released as Col, 46, after serv. in 118th Sta. Hosp, U.S, 42-43 and as Opers. Officer and Chief Spec. Serv, Africa and Italy, 43-46 and Liaison Officer, Royal Family Italy, 43-45; Bronze Star Medal; Distinguished Unit Citation; European-African-Middle East. Campaign Medal and 3 Battle Stars; Am. Campaign, Armed Forces Res. and Victory Medals; Sharpshooters Medals for Carbine and Pistol; Hon. Legionare, French For. Legion; Sovereign Mil. Order of Knights of Malta, Italy, Italian Underground Medal, Partisans Cross, Bronze War Cross of Merit, Star of Solidarity, plus many other orders and decorations of Italy; Instr, Army Res, 32-42 and 46-63, Col. (Ret), 322nd Logistic Command, 46-63. Mem: Am. and Ill. Pub. Health Asns; Ill. State Acad. Sci; Am. Asn. for Adv. Sci; Nat. and Chicago Retail Drug Asns; v.pres, Soc. Am. Mil. Engrs; past pres, Reserve Officers Asn, Ill; dir, Chicago United Serv. Orgn. and Asn. Jewish Blind, Chicago; pres. and dir, Munic. Art League Chicago; hon. dir, Palette and Chisel Acad. Fine Arts Chicago; Citizens Cmt, Univ. Ill, DePaul Univ. and Loyola Univ; Lions; Elks; Kiwanis; Moose; Hektoen Inst. for Med. Research, Cook Co. Hosp; Mrs. Frank J. Lewis Milk Found; Art Inst; founding mem, Boys Towns Italy and Oasis of Santa Rita, Rome; Carmelite and Servite Fathers Seminaries; Crusade of Mercy; Girl Scouts; Boy Scouts; Combined Jewish Appeal; Navy League; Amvets; Am. Legion; VFW; Cath. War Vet; Mil. Order World Wars; K. of C; hon. mem, Interpol; Chicago Drug, Exec, Adventurers, Ill. and Chicago Athletic, South Shore Country, Irish Fel. and Lake Shore Clubs. Achievements: Man of Year Award, Young Dem. Ill, 60 and Nat. Cath. War Vet, 62; V.I.P. Award, Ill. Club for Cath. Women, 64; Little Flower Charitarian's Award, Soc. of Little Flower, 65; Good Am. Award, Chicago Cmt. of 100, 65; Hon. Attorney Gen, 64; Hon. Ky. Col, 65; Hon. Citizen of Tex, 66. Rel: Roman Catholic. Legal Res: 232 E. Walton Place, Chicago, Ill. 60611. Mailing Add: 100 E. Erie St, Chicago, Ill. 60611. (1967)

CHESTER, JOSEPH ARNATHEN, SR. D
Md. State Del.
b. Wilson, N.C, 3/4/14; s. Arthur Chester and Fannie Fasion C; m. 4/29/34 to Pearl V. Brothers; c. Fannie Elzina (Mrs. Wilbur Alston, Jr), Pearl B. (Mrs. Walter B. Mccants), Joseph A, Jr, James A, Julia (Mrs. H. Watkins), William T. and Irvin E. Educ: Wilson High Sch, N.C; Art Soc. Club; Bus. Men's Soc. Club; Pals Soc. Club. Polit. & Govt. Pos: Dist. committeeman, Dem. Club of Baltimore, 34-47; chmn, Fed. Neighborhood Improv. Asn, 58-69; pres, New Area Dem. Club of East Baltimore, 64-69; Md. State Del, 67-; mem. bd, Mt. Royal Dem. Club; mem, City County Dem. and E. Side Dem. Clubs; mem, Nat. Negro Legis. Cmt. Bus. & Prof. Pos: Chmn, Hue Chem. Sales and Hue Janitorial Supply Co. Mil Serv: Entered as Stewart Mate, Navy, 44, released as PO, 45. Rel: Baptist. Mailing Add: 3027 E. Federal St, Baltimore, Md. 21213.

CHESTNUT, WEBSTER ROBERT R
Chmn, Sixth Dist. Rep. Party, S.C.
b. Conway, S.C, 4/12/14; s. William Benjamin Chestnut and Grace Lewis C; m. 7/2/35 to Helen Berniece DuBose; c. Martha Dean (Mrs. Hines) and Helen Rose. Educ: Conway High Sch, grad, 34. Polit. & Govt. Pos: City councilman, Conway, S.C, 50-54; chmn, Horry Co. Rep. Party, 63-67 and state exec. committeeman, 67-68; chmn, Sixth Dist. Rep. Party, 68-; alternate del, Rep. Nat. Conv, 68. Mil. Serv: Entered as Pvt, Army, 43, released as Sgt, 46, after serv. in IRTC Camp Blanding, Fla. and Philippines, 45-46; Theatre and Good Conduct Medal. Mem: Conway Life Underwriters Asn.(pres, 66, secy, 68); v.pres, Conway Swimming Pool; bd. mem, Waccamaw Swim Team Myrtle Beach; bd. dirs, Conway Rotary Club, 47; past comdr, Am. Legion Post III. Rel: Southern Baptist; past chmn. bd. deacons, First Baptist Church. Legal Res: 1007 Snow Hill Dr, Conway, S.C. 29526. Mailing Add: P.O. Box 41, Conway, S.C. 29526.

CHEW, CHARLES, JR. D
Ill. State Sen.
b. Greenville, Miss, 10/9/22; s. Charles Chew, Sr. and Celia Jenkins C; m. 6/25/61 to Carolyn Lawson; c. Lorenzo. Educ: Tuskegge Inst, B.S. in Bus, 42. Polit. & Govt. Pos: Councilman, Chicago, Ill, 63-67; Ill. State Sen, 66- Bus. & Prof. Pos: V.pres, Jackson Mutual Life Ins. Co, 58; v.pres, South Parkway Safe Deposit Corp, currently. Mil. Serv: Entered as Seaman 1/C, Navy, 43, released as PO, 46, after serv. in S.Pac; Philippine Liberation and Good Conduct Medals; 2 Battle Stars. Mem: VFW; Am. Friendship Club; NAACP. Rel: Baptist. Mailing Add: 37 W. 78 St, Chicago, Ill. 60620.

CHICK, JOHN FRANK R
b. Monroe, Ga, 12/29/10; s. John Aldman Chick and Rosa Cross C; m. 10/1/37 to Lillian Browning; c. John Arthur. Educ: Ga. Tech, B.S, in Mech. Eng, 33; Tau Beta Pi; Beta Kappa. Polit. & Govt. Pos: Chmn, Richland Co. Rep. Party, S.C, 66-69. Bus. & Prof. Pos: Owner, John F. Chick, Contractor, 53- Mil. Serv: Entered as 2nd Lt, Army, 41, released as Lt. Col, 46, after serv. in Alaska; Campaign Ribbons. Mem: Lions; C. of C. Rel: Baptist. Mailing Add: 836 Camellia, Columbia, S.C. 29205.

CHICKERING, SHERMAN R
Mem, United San Francisco Rep, Finance and Exec. Cmts.
b. Oakland, Calif, 8/20/11; s. Allen Lawrence Chickering and Alma Sherman C; m. 12/9/38 to Jean Rawlings; c. A. Lawrence, III, Nicholas R. and Nancy. Educ: Univ. Calif, Berkeley, A.B; Harvard Univ, LL.B. Polit. & Govt. Pos: Alternate del, Rep. Nat. Conv, 64; chmn. for San Francisco, Goldwater Primary Campaign, Calif, 64; mem, United San Francisco Rep. Finance and Exec. Cmts, 64-; Gov. Rep, Pub. Land Law Rev. Cmn, 67; alternate del, Rep. Nat. Conv, 68; cmnr, Calif. Fish and Game Cmn, 68- Bus. & Prof. Pos: Partner, Chickering & Gregory; v.pres. and dir, San Diego Gas and Electric Co, 57. Mil. Serv: Entered as Lt.(jg), Navy, 42, released as Lt. Comdr, 45, after serv. in Air Seventh Fleet, Southwest Pac. Rel: Protestant. Legal Res: 3525 Washington St, San Francisco, Calif. 94118. Mailing Add: 111 Sutter St, San Francisco, Calif. 94104.

CHIKASUYE, CLESSON Y. D
Mem. Coun, City and Co. of Honolulu
b. Honolulu, Hawaii, 7/10/19; s. Izumi Chikasuye and Oen Tsuda C; m. 7/22/44 to Lorraine M. Schmoker; c. Clesson William and Kenneth A. Educ: Univ. Hawaii, B.A, 40; Stanford Univ. Law Sch, 41-42; Univ. Colo. Law Sch, LL.B, 44; Tau Kappa Epsilon and Phi Kappa Phi. Polit. & Govt. Pos: Secy, v.pres. and pres, Dem. Precinct Club, Honolulu, Hawaii, 48-54; mem, State Labor and Indust. Rels. Appeal Bd, 51-53; mem, Cent. Cmt, Dem. State Party, 55-56; mem. coun, City and Co. of Honolulu, 57-; del, Dem. Nat. Conv, 68. Mem: Am. and Hawaii Bar Asns; v.pres, Nat. Asn. of Counties; dir, Honolulu Japanese C. of C. and Tarkio Col, Mo; bd. gov, Iolani Sch. Rel: Lutheran. Legal Res: 1350 Ala Moana Blvd, Honolulu, Hawaii 96814. Mailing Add: 510 Bishop Insurance Bldg, 33 S. King St, Honolulu, Hawaii 96813.

CHILDERS, ERASMUS ROY R
Chmn, Wilcox Co. Rep. Exec. Cmt, Ala.
b. Selma, Ala, 3/17/25; s. Erasmus Roy Childers and Margaret Miller C; m. 4/14/56 to Bebe Skinner; c. Nancy and Marcus. Educ: Auburn Univ, B.S, 48; Chi Epsilon; Tau Beta Pi; Kappa Alpha. Polit. & Govt. Pos: Chmn, Wilcox Co. Rep. Exec. Cmt, Ala, 66-; mem, Ala. Rep. State Exec. Cmt, 68- Bus. & Prof. Pos: Owner, Midway Plantation, Catherine, Ala, 49- Mil. Serv: Entered as Pvt, Air Force, 43, released as Flight Officer, 45, after serv. in Troop Carrier Command; Res, 45-66, Capt; Pilot Rating. Mem: Ala. Cattlemen's Asn; Ala. Farm Bur; Camden Exchange Club; Am. Legion. Rel: Reformed Presbyterian; Deacon in Camden Assoc. Reformed Presby. Church. Mailing Add: Route 1, Catherine, Ala. 36728.

CHILDERS, WILSON R. D
b. Thayer, Mo, 9/6/14; m. 11/16/32 to Eva May Preston; c. Keith, Derondia. Educ: Pub. schs, Oregon Co, Mo. Polit. & Govt. Pos: Mo. State Rep, 64-66; city alderman, Thayer, Mo, 62-64; presiding judge of the Oregon Co, Mo. Court, 50-62. Bus. & Prof. Pos: Farmer; auto mech; car salesman. Mem: Past master, Clifton Lodge 463, AF&AM; Royal Arch and Commandery; coun, Mt. Grove; Abou Ben Adhem Temple; Odd Fellows. Rel: Baptist. Mailing Add: 631 Vine St, Thayer, Mo. 65791. (1967)

CHILDRESS, HAROLD NOEL R
Chmn, Scotland Co. Rep. Party, Mo.
b. Memphis, Mo, 12/22/21; s. Lloyd Emerson Childress and Eyvonne Fryrear C; m. to Dorothy Jean Dye; c. Linda Jo, LeAnn, Candice and Michella. Educ: Northeast. Mo. Teachers Col, 2 years. Polit. & Govt. Pos: Mem, Selective Serv. Bd, Mo, 15 years; chmn, Scotland Co. Redistricting Bd. of Educ; chmn, Scotland Co. Rep. Party, currently. Mem: Lions; Mason; Moose. Rel: Methodist. Mailing Add: 539 N. Main, Memphis, Mo. 63555.

CHILDS, JOHN LAWRENCE Liberal
V.Chmn. Liberal Party
b. Eau Claire, Wis, 1/11/89; s. John Nelson Childs and Helen Janette Smith C; m. 7/22/15 to Grace Mary Fowler. Educ: Univ. Wis, B.A, 11; Columbia Univ, M.A, 24, Ph.D, 31; South. Ill. Univ, L.H.D, 68; Sigma Delta Chi; Phi Alpha Tau; Kappa Delta Pi; Delta Sigma Rho. Polit. & Govt. Pos: Founder and first state chmn, Liberal Party, v.chmn, currently. Bus. & Prof. Pos: Grad. secy, Univ. Wis, 11-12; intercollegiate dept, YMCA, 12-16; for. secy. int. cmn, YMCA, Peking, China, 16-27; prof. Philos. of educ, Teachers Col, Columbia Univ, 37-54, emer. prof. educ, 54-; vis. prof, Univ. Mich, 57-58, Univ. Ill, 58-59, South. Ill. Univ, 60-61, 62-63 and adj. prof, 64-; educator and lectr, Univ. Wis, 65. Publ: Education and Morals, 50; American Pragmatism and Education; co-auth, Education in the Age of Science, 59. Mem: Fel. Am. Educ. Asn; Am. Fedn. Teachers; fel, Am. Asn. Arts & Sci; Nat. Cmn. Educ. Reconstruction; Nat. Cmn. Acad. Freedom; Am. Civil Liberties Union; AFL Postwar Cmt; Nat. Coun. Relig. Higher Educ; Am. Philos. Asn; Am. Polit. Sci. Asn. Order of the Abundant Harvest, Chinese Nat. Govt, 21; Nicholas Murray Butler Silver Medal, 51; Wm. H. Kilpatrick Award, 56; Educ. Award, Wayne State Univ, 58; League for Indust. Democracy Award, 59; John Dewey Soc. Award, 65; Nat. Acad. Educ. Award, 66; Distinguished Serv. Medal, Teachers Col, Columbia Univ, 68. Mailing Add: 4141 N. Rockton Ave, Rockford, Ill. 61103.

CHILDS, NANCY JANE D
Mem, Nebr. Dem. Cent. Cmt.
b. Lincoln, Nebr, 1/19/21; d. Paul Rolphe Halligan and Kathleen Doyle H; m. 7/7/45 to Richard Holmes Childs; c. Leslie Craig, Richard H, Jr, Geoffrey, Nancy, Jr, Cyrus and Dana. Educ: Univ. Nebr, 2 years; Manhattanville Col, 1 year; Alpha Phi; Lincoln Jr. League. Polit. & Govt. Pos: Co. chmn, Citizens for Kennedy, 60; del, Co, State & Nat. Convs, 68; mem, Nat. Permanent Orgn. Cmt, 68; mem, Nebr. Dem. Cent. Cmt, 68- Bus. & Prof. Pos: Model, Lily Dache, N.Y, 43-44; fashion coord, Havland-Swanson, Nebr, 59; owner, modeling sch, 59-67; lectr, Nancy Childs Lect. Bur, 67- Publ: 'Importance of Standards in Greek System,' Alpha Phi Quart, 68; 'Here's How,' (in press). Mem: v.pres, Sigma Chi Mother's Club. Outstanding Alumna award, Nat. Alpha Phi Conv, 66. Rel: Catholic. Mailing Add: 1745 Dee, Lincoln, Nebr. 68502.

CHILDS, THEODORE F. D
b. Jamaica, N.Y, 2/17/21; s. Andrew Wesley Childs and Maude Thompson C; m. 5/19/44 to Marie Jackson; c. Sheila and Theodore W. Educ: Shaw Univ, B.S, 44; Univ. Iowa, Cert. R.P.T, 48; Columbia Univ, M.A, 57; Phi Delta Kappa; Alpha Phi Alpha; pres, YMCA. Polit. & Govt. Pos: Del, Dem. Nat. Conv, 68; cand, N.Y. State Sen, Fifth Sen. Dist, 68; cand, North Hempstead Town Coun, 68; first v.pres, Westbury Dem. Club, currently. Bus. & Prof. Pos: Chief, phys. therapy sect, Brooklyn Vet. Hosp, 48-62; coordinator, phys. therapy serv, N.Y. Univ-Goldwater Mem. Hosp, 62-65; asst. prof. and prog. dir. disabled students prog, L.I. Univ, 65-; speaker, First Pan-Caribbean Conf. on Rehabilitation, San Juan, P.R, 65; speaker, Third Symposium on Rehabilitation in Africa, Lusake, Zambia, 69; consult, rehabilitation med. dept, Vet. Admin, Wash, D.C. Mil. Serv: Entered as Pvt, Army, 44, released as Lt, 46, after serv. in 348th Ord. Ammunition Co, Asiatic Pac. Theatre, 44-46; Maj, Army Res, 46-; Expert Rifleman Medal. Publ: 'The Rehabilitation of the Hemipelvectomy,' 59 and 'A Critical Analysis of the Swing-Through Crutch Gait,' 61, Archives Phys. Med; 'Helping The Handicapped Africans,' Int. Soc. Rehabilitation of the Disabled, 62. Mem: Am. Asn. Univ. Prof; Am. Phys. Therapy Asn; Int. Soc. Welfare of the Disabled (secy, U.S. Cmt. Rehabilitation in Africa, 8 years); Brit. Royal Soc. Health; soc. sci. bd, N.Y. chap, Nat. Hemophilia Asn; adult activities cmt, United Cerebral Palsy Asn. of N.Y. State; Am. Registry of Phys. Therapist; charter mem. and former v.pres, Westbury br, NAACP; 369th Vet. Asn; Nat. Cmt. Black Heritage Found, Urban League; Nassau Co. Youth Bd, 68-71; Nassau Co. Econ. Opportunity Cmn, 65-68; adv, Town of North Hempstead Econ. Opportunity, 65-68; chmn. bd, Westbury Commun. Coun. Econ. and Educ. Opportunity, 65-68; mem. adult educ. adv. bd, Westbury Sch. Dist, 65. Westbury Resident of the Year Award, Westbury Times; travel fel, Nat. Found, Europe, Israel and E.Africa, 57. Rel: Episcopal. Mailing Add: 558 Rutland St, Westbury, N.Y. 11590.

CHILES, LAWTON D
Fla. State Sen.
b. Lakeland, Fla, 4/30/30; m. to Rhea Grafton; c. Tandy, Lawton M, III, Edward G. and Rhea Gay. Educ: Univ. Fla, B.S.B.A, 52, LL.B, 55; Alpha Tau Omega; Phi Delta Phi; Fla. Blue Key; Univ. Fla. Hall of Fame. Polit. & Govt. Pos: Fla. State Rep, 58-66; Fla. State Sen, 67- Bus. & Prof. Pos: Attorney-at-law. Mil. Serv: Army Artil, Korean Conflict. Mem: Kiwanis; Jr. C. of C. (past v.pres); past pres, Lakeland Quarterback Club; past chap. chmn, Nat. Found. Infantile Paralysis; campaign chmn, March of Dimes. Rel: Presbyterian. Mailing Add: 221 E. Lime St, Lakeland, Fla. 33801.

CHILSEN, WALTER JOHN R
Wis. State Sen.
b. Merrill, Wis, 11/18/23; s. Walter Burt Chilsen and Margaret Sullivan C; m. 9/20/52 to Roseann Edl; c. Jon, Anna, Kristine, Elizabeth, Paul, Matthew and twins, Peter and Patricia. Educ: Lawrence Univ, B.S, 49; Northwest. Univ, 52; Delta Tau Delta. Polit. & Govt. Pos: Wis. State Sen, 29th Dist, 66-, secy, Rep. caucus, 67-68, chmn, Rep. caucus, 69-, Wis. State Senate; Rep. cand. for U.S. Rep, 69. Bus. & Prof. Pos: News dir, WSAU-TV, Wausau, Wis, 54-64, TV acct. exec, 64- Mil. Serv: Entered as Pvt, Army Air Corps, 43, released as 1st Lt, 45, after serv. as Bombardier on B-24's, Seventh Air Force, Pac. Theater; Purple Heart. Mem: Lions; VFW; Am. Legion; Marathon Co. Workshop for Handicapped (past pres); Friends of Menominees (past pres). Rel: Roman Catholic. Mailing Add: 1821 Townline Rd, Wausau, Wis. 54401.

CHILTON, WILLIAM EDWIN, III D
b. Kingston, N.Y, 11/26/21; s. William Edwin Chilton, Jr. and Louise Schoonmaker C; m. 4/5/52 to Elizabeth Easley Early; c. Susan Carroll. Educ: Yale Univ, A.B, 50; W.Va. State Col, Hon. L.H.D, 66. Polit. & Govt. Pos: W.Va. State Del, 53-60; del-at-lg, Dem. Nat. Conv, 60 and mem, platform cmt, 64; mem, Kanawha Co. Parks and Recreation Cmn, 67-; mem, Citizens Adv. Cmn. on Legis. of W.Va, 68- Bus. & Prof. Pos: Asst. promotion mgr, Charleston Gazette, 50-52, promotion mgr, 52-57, asst. publisher, 57-61 and publisher, 61- Mil. Serv: Entered as Pvt, Army, 41, released as Pfc, 45, after serv. in Army Air Corps; China-Burma-India Theater Ribbon; Good Conduct Medal. Mem: Elks; Edgewood and Berry Hills Country Clubs; Press Club. Rel: Episcopal. Legal Res: 1 Scott Rd, Charleston, W.Va. 25314. Mailing Add: 1001 Virginia St. E, Charleston, W.Va. 25330.

CHIN, RICHARD R
Ky. State Sen.
b. Louisville, Ky, 5/26/32; s. Ming Chin and Florence Beck C; m. 2/8/57 to Mildred Lucille Riddle; c. Sharon Lynn, Richard Wayne and Douglas Paul. Educ: Univ. Louisville, 50-52; Univ. Ky, B.S. in commerce, 54. Polit. & Govt. Pos: Ky. State Sen, 66- Bus. & Prof. Pos: Chinese Restaurant Owner, 54- Rel: Baptist. Mailing Add: 9803 Highcrest Ave, Valley Station, Ky. 40172. (1967)

CHING, DONALD D. H. D
Hawaii State Sen.
b. Honolulu, Hawaii, 1/13/26; s. Dai Sun Ching and Sun Hoo Wong C; m. 9/8/51 to Kazuko Shikuma; c. Donna Rae, Deborah Ann, Sandra Kay, Jeffrey and Melvin. Educ: Univ. of Hawaii, B.A, 50; George Wash. Univ. Law Sch, LL.B, 53. Polit. & Govt. Pos: Hawaii Territorial Rep, 58-59; Hawaii State Rep, 59-66; Hawaii State Sen, 67- Bus. & Prof. Pos: Asst. secy, Bank of Hawaii, 66- Mil. Serv: Entered as Pvt, Army, 45, released as Technician 4/C, 47, after serv. in Hawaiian Med. Depot, Hawaii. Mem: Am. and Hawaii Bar Asns. Rel: United Church of Christ. Mailing Add: 2005 Aamanu St, Pearl City, Oahu, Hawaii 96782.

CHING, WILETTA PARKER R
b. Houston, Tex, 11/6/20; d. Will Thacheray Parker and Marie Black P; wid; c. R. Brooks, Anne, Carol and Mary Margaret. Educ: Univ. Tex, 2 yrs. Polit. Pos: Del, Rep. Nat. Conv, 64; corresponding secy, Women's Rep. Fedn. of La, 56-64, nominated for pres, 64, but declined for reasons of

health; mem-at-lg, Women's Rep. Fedn, 8 yrs, plus various other offices in the Rep. Party. Mem: New Orleans Country Club. Rel: Roman Catholic. Mailing Add: 7307 Burthe St, New Orleans, La. 70118. (1967)

CHIN-LEE, WILLIAM R
Mem, D.C. Rep. Cent. Cmt.
b. Washington, D.C, 4/22/23; s. Ying Hong Chin and Lee Ngon Win C; m. 6/27/48 to Nancy A. Wong; c. William Bruce, Peter E, Sandra L, Cynthia D. and Warren D. Educ: Am. Univ, A.A, 44; George Wash. Univ, M.D, 47; Wash. Hosp. Center, internship and residency, 53; George Wash. Univ. Med. Soc. Polit. & Govt. Pos: Precinct chmn, 63-66; alternate del, Rep. Nat. Conv. and mem, Forward Looking Rep. Cmt, 64; mem, D.C. Rep. Exec. Cmt, 64-, D.C. Rep. Cent. Cmt, 65- Bus. & Prof. Pos: Attend. physician, Wash. Hosp. Center, D.C, 53-; pres, Chin Inc, 58-; v.chmn, Buck Young Inc, 65; dir. and pres, Lee Fed. Credit Union, 66. Mil. Serv: Entered as Pvt, Army, 44, released 46; entered Air Force, 51, released as Capt, 53; Good Conduct Medal; Am. Theater Ribbon; Victory Medal. Mem: D.C. and Am. Socs. of Internal Med; C.C. Med. Soc; Am. Med. Asn; Am. and D.C. Heart Asns; Am. Univ. Alumni Asn; Wash. Urban League; past pres, Chi-Am. Lions; past pres, Chinese Consol. Benevolent Asn; v.chmn. and camp lichtman, camping serv. cmt, YMCA; secy, Lee Family Asn. Rel: Methodist; former mem. bd, Union Methodist Church, D.C; trustee and mem. bd, Chinese Commun. Church. Mailing Add: 5023 Reno Rd. N.W, Washington, D.C. 20008.

CHISHOLM, MARY E. D
b. Peabody, Mass, 9/9/27; d. James J. Brennan and Dorothy Noone B; div; c. Colin A, III and Christopher A. Educ: St. John's Girls Sch; Mansfield Academy. Polit. & Govt. Pos: Maine State Sen, mem, Labor Cmt, chmn, Retirements & Pensions Cmt. and mem, Dairy Industry Interim Study Cmt, 65-66; mem, Dem. Cmt, Cape Elizabeth, 64-66. Prof. Pos: Former teacher of religion, Holy Cross, S. Portland, Maine, 64. Mem: Nat. Cong. of PTA, 57-66; Nat. Legis. Women, 65-66; Cumberland Co. Dem. Club, 65-66; Mothers Club, Boy Scouts, 60-66. Rel: Catholic. Mailing Add: 64 Scott Dyer Rd, Cape Elizabeth, Maine 04107. (1967)

CHISHOLM, SHIRLEY ANITA D
U.S. Rep, N.Y.
b. Brooklyn, N.Y, 11/30/24; d. Charles St. Hill and Ruby Seale S; m. 10/8/49 to Conrad Chisholm. Educ: Brooklyn Col, B.A. in Sociol, 46; Columbia Univ, M.A. in Childhood Educ. Hon. L.H.D, Talladega Col. Polit. & Govt. Pos: N.Y. State Assemblywoman, 55th Dist, 64-68; U.S. Rep, 12th Dist, N.Y, 68-; Dem. Nat. Committeewoman, N.Y, 68- Bus. & Prof. Pos: Nursery sch. teacher, Mt. Calvary Child Care Center, N.Y.C, 46-52; pvt. nursery sch. dir, Friend in Need Nursery, Brooklyn, 52-53; dir, Hamilton-Madison Child Care Center, N.Y.C; educ. consult, Div. of Day Care, N.Y.C, 59-64. Achievement Award, Yeshiva Univ; Alumna of the Year, Brooklyn Col. Alumni Bul, Fall Issue, 57; Recipient of Award for Outstanding Work in the Field of Child Welfare, Brooklyn Women's Coun, 57; Key Women of the Year Award, 63; Cmt. of Friends Plaque for Many Years of Loyal and Dedicated Serv. to Commun, 65; Human Rels. Award, Cent. Nassau Club of Bus. & Prfnl. Women, 65; Citation for Outstanding Serv. in the Field of Early Childhood Educ. and Welfare, Sisterhood of Concord Baptist Church, Brooklyn, 65; Outstanding Serv. in Good Govt. Plaque, Christian Women's Retreat, 65; Cert. of Honor Award for Outstanding Achievement in Serv. to Youth, Jr. High Sch. 271, Brooklyn, 65; Woman of Achievement Award at Waldorf Astoria, Key Women Inc, 65. Rel: Methodist. Mailing Add: 1028 St. Johns Place, Brooklyn, N.Y. 11213.

CHO, MARIA CHUNGSOOK R
Mem, Calif. Rep. State Cent. Cmt.
b. Changnyun, Kyongsang-Pukdo, Korea, 11/17/31; d. Sam Sool Kim and Tae Sun Woo K; m. 5/8/57 to Benjamin Cho; c. Ann Byongsook and Julia Hyonsook. Educ: Seoul National Univ, 47-51. Polit. & Govt. Pos: Assoc. mem, Calif. Rep. State Cent. Cmt, 64-66, mem, 69-, mem. platform cmt, 67-68; v.chmn. nationality cmt, Orange Co. Rep. Women Federated, 65-67; v.chmn, Reagan for Gov. cmt, 66; membership chmn, Buena Park Rep. Women Federated, 67, v.pres, 68; chmn, Woman for Nixon in Buena Park, 68. Bus. & Prof. Pos: Dir, I M B Electronics Inc, Santa Fe Springs, Calif, 68- Mem: Korean Cath. Asn. South Calif. Rel: Roman Catholic. Mailing Add: 8470 Philodendron Way, Buena Park, Calif. 90620.

CHOATE, A. VANCE D
b. Sparta, N.C, 11/24/94; s. S.A. Choate and Laura Ann Edwards C; m. 1921 to Rebecca Osborne; c. two daughters. Educ: Appalachian State Teachers Col. Polit. & Govt. Pos: N.C. State Rep, 61-66. Bus. & Prof. Pos: Farmer, retired U.S. govt. worker. Mil. Serv: Navy, Seaman 2/C, 17-18. Mem: C. of C; VFW; Robert L. Doughton Mem. Cmt; Camp Poke Cmn; dir, Yadkin Valley Dairy Coop. Mailing Add: Sparta, N.C. 28675. (1967)

CHOATE, CLYDE L. D
Ill. State Rep.
b. West Frankfort, Ill, 6/28/20; m. 5/10/47 to Mabel Ross C; c. Elizabeth Ellen, Madonna Kim. Educ: Anna-Jonesboro High Sch. Polit. & Govt. Pos: Ill. State Rep, currently, Minority Whip, 69th and 70th Assemblies and Majority Whip, 71st and 72nd Assemblies, Ill. State House of Rep; del, Dem. Nat. Conv, 68. Mil. Serv: Army, Pvt, World War II; served 31 months overseas in European Theatre, took part in invasion of N. Africa, Sicily, Italy, France and Germany as Sgt; cited for bravery in action on Anzio Beachhead in Italy and twice on battlefields of France, where he refused a battlefield cmn; wounded in action; holder of Purple Heart; French Fourragere; Bronze and Silver Stars President Citation and the Cong. Medal of Honor. Mem: Am. Legion; VFW, Military Order of Purple Heart; DAV; Moose; Elks. Mailing Add: R.R. 1, Anna, Ill. 62906.

CHOINIERE, ULRIC EMELIEN D
b. Farnham, Quebec, Canada, 9/4/96; wid; c. Eight sons; Two daughters. Educ: Farnham, Quebec. Polit. & Govt. Pos: Road cmnr, 31-36; selectman, 40-46; 61-; town auditor, 51-58; town grand juror, 56-59; Former Vt. State Rep. Bus. & Prof. Pos: Retired, previously farmer and carpenter. Mem: Grange; Farm Bur; dir, United Farmers of New Eng, 46-48; Commun. Committeeman for PMA, 43-55. Rel: Catholic. Mailing Add: RFD 2, Box 29, Orleans, Vt. 05860. (1967)

CHOQUETTE, PAUL J, JR. R
Secy, R.I. Rep. State Cent. Cmt.
b. Providence, R.I, 7/24/38; s. Paul J. Choquette and Virginia Gilbane C; m. 8/26/62 to Elizabeth Walsh; c. Jeanne Marie, Denise Elizabeth and Suzanne. Educ: Brown Univ, A.B, 60; Harvard Law Sch, LL.B, 63; Delta Kappa Epsilon. Polit. & Govt. Pos: Chmn, Youth for Gov. Chafee Cmt, 64-68; exec. counsel, R.I, 65-67; mem. town cmt, North Kingston, 68-; secy, R.I. Rep. State Cent. Cmt, 68- Bus. & Prof. Pos: Assoc, Law Firm of Edwards & Angell, 63-69. Mem: Dir, Bus. Opportunities, Inc; dir, Marathon House, Inc; v.pres, Brown Football Asn. Rel: Catholic. Mailing Add: 60 Prospect Ave, North Kingston, R.I. 02852.

CHOWNING, JAMES PAUL R
b. Springfield, Tenn, 11/1/23; s. Richard Emmett Chowning and Helen Richardson C; m. 4/5/52 to Patricia Margaret Lawrence; c. Margaret Ann and Jane Lawrence. Educ: Middle Tenn. State Univ, 41-42; Univ. Ga, 43-44; Miami Univ, B.A, 49. Polit. & Govt. Pos: Co-dir, Davidson Co. Goldwater-Miller Campaign, Tenn, 64; chmn, Goldwater for President Cmt, 64; alternate del, Rep. Nat. Conv, 64; mem, Davidson Co. Steering Cmt, 64; chmn, 34th Coun. Dist, 64-65; mem, Davidson Co. Adv. Cmt, 65-; chmn, Davidson Co. Rep. Club, Fifth Dist, 65-67. Mil. Serv: Entered as Pvt, Army Air Force, 43, released as S/Sgt, 46, after serv. in 1261st Combat Engrs. Bn, Tenth Armored Div, ETO; ETO Ribbon; Good Conduct Medal. Mem: Civitan Int; Am. Legion. Rel: Presbyterian. Mailing Add: 4608 Benton Smith Rd, Nashville, Tenn. 37215. (1967)

CHRISMAN, P. MICHAEL R
Mem, Calif. Rep. State Cent. Cmt.
b. Visalia, Calif, 9/24/44; s. Ira Jackson Chrisman and Charlotte Bequette C; m. 8/22/64 to Barbara Paul; c. Josh Ira. Educ: Menlo Col, 1 year; Univ. Ariz, B.S, 66; Alpha Zeta; Alpha Gamma Rho; Student Senate; Crops and Soils Club. Polit. & Govt. Pos: Assoc. mem, Calif. Rep. State Cent. Cmt, 66-68, mem, 68-; dir, 24th Dist. Agr. Asn, 69- Mem: Am. Soc. Agronomy; Calif. Cattleman's Asn; v.pres, Tulare Co. Cattlemans Asn, 68-; Visalia Jaycees (v.pres); Tulare Co. Farm Bur. Agronomy Student Award, Am. Soc. of Agronomy. Rel: Episcopal. Mailing Add: 1403 W. College Ave, Visalia, Calif. 93277.

CHRISTENSEN, CARL L. D
c. twin sons. Educ: Univ. of Calif, A.B, 31; Boalt Hall, LL.B, 34. Polit. & Gov. Pos: Calif. State Sen, 57-66; Dist. Attorney, Humboldt Co, 47-49; Judge of Superior Court, Humboldt Co, 49-56. Bus. & Prof. Pos: Attorney. Mil. Serv: Navy, Beachmaster, Lt. Comdr. Mem: Past Exalted Ruler, No. 652, B.P.O.E; Kiwanis and Ingomar Clubs; VFW; Am. Legion. Mailing Add: 937 Sixth St, Eureka, Calif. 95501.

CHRISTENSEN, EARL R
Wyo. State Sen.
b. Sheridan, Wyo, 12/20/19; married; c. four. Educ: Univ. Wyo. Polit. & Govt. Pos: Wyo. State Sen. and Pres. of Senate, currently. Bus. & Prof. Pos: Rancher. Mem: Stock Growers Asn; Farm Bur; mem. adv. coun, Future Farmers Am; leader 4-H; mem. adv. coun, Demolay; Mason; Shrine; Eastern Star; Lions. Rel: Methodist. Mailing Add: Newcastle, Wyo. 82701.

CHRISTENSEN, GERALD OTHELLO R
Chmn, Bannock Co. Rep. Cent. Cmt, Idaho
b. Idaho Falls, Idaho 5/28/27; s. Ezra Othello Christensen and Vida Criddle C; m. 8/25/47 to Catherine Scott; c. Gerald Kay, Scott W. and Debra Ilene. Educ: Ricks Col, 43-44 & 46; Weber Col, 49; Lamba Delta Sigma. Polit. & Govt. Pos: Precinct committeeman, Bannock Co, Idaho, 66-; chmn, Bannock Co. Rep. Cent. Cmt, 68- Bus. & Prof. Pos: Chief meter inspector, Intermountain Gas Co, Idaho, 59- Mil. Serv: Entered as A/S, Naval Res, 45, released as Yeoman 3/C, 46, after serving in Naval Air Sta, Calif, 45-46. Mem: Pocatello C. of C. Rel: Latter-day Saint. Mailing Add: 1680 Ammon St, Pocatello, Idaho 83201.

CHRISTENSEN, J. LLOYD D
Chmn, Franklin Co. Dem. Cent. Cmt, Idaho
b. Mink Creek, Idaho, 7/7/18; s. Lars Henry Christensen and Serena Hammersmark C; m. 7/14/40 to Reana Whitehead; c. Lo Ree (Mrs. Robert Gang), Iva Lou (Mrs. John Morgan), Rhonda (Mrs. A.J. Shomas), Sonya (Mrs. Melvin Ray), Paulette, Jay Lloyd, Lee Grand, Mary Ann and John Mark. Educ: Utah State Univ, 37-38. Polit. & Govt. Pos: Chmn, Franklin Co. Dem. Cent. Cmt, Idaho, 60-; alternate del, Dem. Nat. Conv, 68. Rel: Latter-day Saint. Mailing Add: Route 2, Preston, Idaho 83263.

CHRISTENSEN, NELS P. D
b. Wilmot, S. Dak, 1/14/91; m. to Cora Foss; c. one son, one daughter. Educ: Grade sch. and two yr. short course. Polit. & Govt. Pos: S. Dak. State Rep, -66; Commun. Committeeman (6 yrs); Twp. Bd. and Twp. Assessor. Bus. & Prof. Pos: Retired farmer; raising and feeding hereford cattle. Mem: Co. Chmn, P.M.A. (16 yrs.); Dir, Nat. Farm Loan Asn. and Coop Elevator; Pres, Watertown Prod. Credit Asn; Dir, Roberts Co. Mutual Fire Ins. Co; Farmers Union Crop Improv. Asn; Co. Livestock Asn. Rel: Lutheran. Mailing Add: Wilmot, S. Dak. 57279. (1967)

CHRISTENSEN, PERRY LEE R
Iowa State Rep.
b. Creston, Iowa, 8/30/32; s. Oliver M. Christensen and Leola Armstrong C; m. 1/1/54 to Dolores Jane Weber; c. Sandra and Scott. Polit. & Govt. Pos: Iowa State Rep, 67- Mil. Serv: Entered as Pvt, Air Force, 51, released as Sgt, 53, after serv. in Alaskan Air Command. Mem: Pres, Farm Bur, 64-66; VFW; Am. Legion; Lions. Rel: First Christian, Disciples of Christ. Mailing Add: R.R, Kent, Iowa 50850.

CHRISTENSEN, ROBERT F. Conservative
Minn. State Rep.
b. Madelia, Minn, 1914; married; c. 10. Educ: St. Mary's Col. of Winona, B.S, Summa Cum Laude; Univ. of Minn, M.A. Polit. & Govt. Pos: Minn. State Rep, 62- Bus. & Prof. Pos: Personnel Mgr. Mailing Add: 148 S. Wheeler Ave, St. Paul, Minn. 55105. (1967)

CHRISTENSEN, WALTER D
b. Mercer, N.Dak, 4/21/10; married; c. Seven. Educ: Pub. sch. Polit. & Govt. Pos: Former pres, Mercer Sch. Bd, N.Dak; N.Dak. State Rep, 61-66; State Treas, N.Dak, 67-68. Bus. & Prof. Pos: Farmer. Rel: Lutheran. Mailing Add: Mercer, N.Dak. 58559. (1967)

CHRISTENSEN, WILLIAM PATTERSON, JR. D
Chmn, Pacific Co. Dem. Cent. Cmt, Wash.
b. Syracuse, N.Y, 10/15/28; s. William Patterson Christensen and Margaret Butts C; m. 8/16/50 to Doris Irene Roed; c. Darcel and William, III. Educ: Everett Jr. Col, Wash, 1 2/3 years. Polit. & Govt. Pos: Precinct committeeman, Raymond, Wash, 64-; chmn, Pac. Co. Dem. Cent. Cmt, 66- Bus. & Prof. Pos: Frieght agent, CMStP&P RR, 56- Mil. Serv: Entered as Pvt, Army, 52, released as Cpl, 54, after serv. in 303rd Sig. Bn; Sixth and Third Army, 52-54. Mem: Elks; Brotherhood of Railway and Airline Clerks. Rel: Protestant. Mailing Add: 924 Fowler St, Raymond, Wash. 98577.

CHRISTENSON, GERALD WILLIAM D
b. Litchfield, Minn, 4/9/30; s. Lee Christenson and Marguerite Quinn C; m. 8/14/54 to Pearl Jacobson; c. Kathryn, Carol, Michael, Thomas, Rebecca and Karen. Educ: St. John's Univ, B.A, 53; Univ. Minn, M.A, 54. Polit. & Govt. Pos: Chmn, Fourth Cong. Dist, Dem-Farmer-Labor Party, Minn, 63-65; del, Dem. Nat. Conv, 64; admin. asst. to U.S. Rep. Joseph Karth, 65-66; nominee for Lt. Gov. of Minn, Dem-Farmer-Labor Party Primary Elec, 66; exec. dir, President's Coun. on Youth Opportunity, 67- Rel: Roman Catholic. Legal Res: 127 Patton Rd, New Brighton, Minn. 55112. Mailing Add: 8420 Stonewall Dr, Vienna, Va. 22180.

CHRISTENSON, RONALD SIDNEY D
b. Chippewa Falls, Wis, 7/10/37; s. Sigfred Magnus Christenson and Vivian Heatley C; m. 6/25/60 to Kathryn Kidd Christenson; c. Rolf and Abigail. Educ: Wis. State Univ, Eau Claire, B.S, 59; Univ. Minn, M.A, 61, Ph.D, 65; Woodrow Wilson fel, 59; Greater Univ. fel, Univ. Minn, 63-64. Polit. & Govt. Pos: Mem, Cent. Cmt, Winneshiek Co. Dem. Party, Iowa, 66-68; alternate del, Dem. Nat. Conv, 68. Bus. & Prof. Pos: Asst. prof. polit. sci, Luther Col, Decorah, Iowa, 64-69; assoc. prof. polit. sci. & chmn. dept, Gustavus Adolphus Col, 69- Publ: 'The Political Theory of Persecution,' Midwest J. Polit. Sci, fall 68. Mem: Am. Polit. Sci. Asn; Caucus for a New Polit. Sci; Am. Asn. Univ. Prof. Rel: Lutheran. Mailing Add: Gustavus Adolphus College, St. Peter, Minn. 56082.

CHRISTGAU, VICTOR
b. Austin, Minn, 9/20/94; s. Fred Christgau and Adeline Vanselow C; m. 7/30/31 to Muriel Doyle. Educ: Univ. Minn. Col. of Agr, B.S, 24, grad. student, 23-25; Gamma Sigma Delta. Polit. & Govt. Pos: Minn. State Sen, 27-29; U.S. Rep, Minn, 29-33; from asst. dir. to dir. prod. div. and asst. adminstr, Agr. Adjustment Admin, 33-35; adminstr, Minn. Works Prog. Admin, 35-38; dir. and cmnr, Minn. Employ. Security Agency, 39-54; dir, Bur. Old Age & Survivors Ins, 54-63, exec. asst. and asst. to cmnr, Social Security Admin, 63- Mil. Serv: Entered as Pfc, Army, 18, released as Sgt. 1/C, 19, after serv. in Eng. Corps. Mem: Am. Pub. Welfare Asn; Am. Soc. Pub. Admin; Am. Farm Econ. Asn; Am. Legion; VFW. Rel: Lutheran. Legal Res: Route 5, Austin, Minn. 55912. Mailing Add: 3900 16th St. N.W, Washington, D.C. 20011.

CHRISTIAN, ALVIN E. JR. D
b. Rock Springs, Wyo, 8/3/40; Single. Educ: Col. Grad. Polit. & Govt. Pos: Wyo. State Rep, 62-67; Wyo. State COPE Dir. Bus. & Prof. Pos: Radio & TV Announcer; Pres. Continental Broadcasting Co. Mem: Odd Fellows; Masonic Lodge; Eagles; Hon. Thespian; DeMolay; Boys State. Col. State & Nat. Speaking & Debate Champ. of Northwest; Named one of Outstanding Young Men of 1964 by Nat. Jr. C. of C. Head; Named One of Leading Men in the U.S. in Britannia Ltd's. 64-65 Ed. Rel: United Church of Christ. Mailing Add: 1104 McKinley Ave, Rock Springs, Wyo. 82901. (1967)

CHRISTIAN, CLARENCE CARR, JR. D
W.Va. State Del.
b. Princeton, W.Va, 11/24/17; s. Clarence Carr Christian and Lola Mae Cooke C; m. 5/31/38 to Hallie Mae Shupe; c. Lawrence Lee, Geoffrey Wayne. Educ: Concord Col. Polit. & Govt. Pos: W.Va. State Del, 56- Bus. & Prof. Pos: Locomotive engr. Mem: Brotherhood of Locomotive Engrs; Kiwanis; Elks; Mercer Anglers Club. Rel: Presbyterian; Deacon. Mailing Add: Box 282, Princeton, W.Va. 24740. (1967)

CHRISTIAN, GEORGE D
b. Austin, Tex, 1/1/27; m. 1950 to Elizabeth Brown (deceased 1957); m. 1959 to Jo Anne Martin; c. Elizabeth, Susan, George Scott, Bruce, John and Brian. Educ: Univ. Tex, 44 & 46-49. Polit. & Govt. Pos: Asst. to Sen. Price Daniel, 56; press secy. and exec. asst. to Gov. Price Daniel, Tex, 57-63, state campaign mgr, 62; press secy. and admin. asst. to Gov. John Connally, 63-66; admin. asst. to President of U.S, 66-; press secy. to President of U.S, 66-69; polit. pub. rels, currently. Mil. Serv: Entered Marine Corps, 44, serv. in Pac. Theater, Occupation of Japan, 45-46, Sixth Marines, 2nd Div. Rel: Episcopal. Legal Res: Austin, Tex. Mailing Add: 108 First National Life Bldg, Austin, Tex. 78767.

CHRISTIAN, MAUD TRUBY D
Mem, W.Va. Dem. State Exec. Cmt.
b. Christian, W.Va, 7/2/06; d. George Thomas Christian and Martha Ann Duff C; single. Educ: Morris Harvey Acad; Morris Harvey Col; Marshall Univ. Polit. & Govt. Pos: Off. reporter, W.Va. House of Del, 31-33; secy, Gov. of W.Va, 33-36; off. reporter, Criminal & Circuit Courts of McDowell Co, 37-69; mem, W.Va. Dem. State Exec. Cmt, 40-; del, Dem. Nat. Conv, 64. Mem: Nat. Shorthand Reporters Asn; W.Va. Shorthand Reporters Asn; Cert. Shorthand Reporter. Dem. Woman-of-the-Year for W.Va, 63. Rel: Methodist. Legal Res: 4 McClaren Apartments, Welch, W.Va. 24801. Mailing Add: P.O. Box 310, Welch, W.Va. 24801.

CHRISTIAN, TOM TERRILL R
Tex. State Rep.
b. Claude, Tex, 11/27/31; s. William Terrill Christian and Frances Woods Collins C; m. 3/12/58 to Jeanne Anne Thomas; c. Frances Anne; Joe Tom and Richard William. Educ: W.Tex. State Univ, B.S, 55. Polit. & Govt. Pos: Chmn, Armstrong Co. Rep. Party, Claude, Tex; Tex. State Rep, 68- Mil. Serv: Entered as A/S, Navy, 52, released as Seaman, 53, after serv. in Navy Ceremonial Guard. Mem: Panhandle Livestock Asn.(dir, 66-69); Tex. Southwest. Cattle Raisers Asn; Shrine; Mason (32°); Armstrong Co. Med. Asn; Farm Bur. Rel: Methodist. Mailing Add: Figure 3 Ranch, Claude, Tex. 79019.

CHRISTIANSEN, EDWARD WILLIAM, JR. D
Mont. State Rep.
b. Fargo, N.Dak, 2/24/14; s. Dr. Edward William Christiansen and Mabel Claire Cork C; m. 12/26/47 to Hattie James; c. Linda Susan (Mrs. Doane) and Deborah Ann. Educ: Fargo High Sch, N.Dak, grad, 31; N.Dak. State Col, 31-33. Polit. & Govt. Pos: Mont. State Rep, Eighth Dist, 65- Bus. & Prof. Pos: V.pres, Hardin Auto Co, Mont, 47-; pres, Hardin Broadcasting Inc, 63- Mem: Hardin Youth Coun.(pres, 63-68); Campfire Girl's Asn.(pres, Big Horn Co. club, 66); Boy Scouts (finance chmn, 65); Elks; Ft. Custer Golf Club. Rel: Catholic. Mailing Add: 310 N. Crow Ave, Hardin, Mont. 59034.

CHRISTIANSEN, LEE D. D
b. Kenmare, N.Dak, 10/9/24; married; c. Two. Educ: N.Dak. State Univ. Agr. and Applied Sci. Polit. & Govt. Pos: Former N.Dak. State Sen and N.Dak. State Rep. Bus. & Prof. Pos: Farmer. Mil. Serv: World War II. Mailing Add: Kenmare, N.Dak. 58746. (1967)

CHRISTIANSEN, RAYMOND C. D
Chmn, Alaska Dem. Party
Mailing Add: P.O. Box 35, Bethel, Alaska 99559

CHRISTIANSON, GALE EDWARD D
b. Charles City, Iowa, 6/29/42; s. John E. Christianson and Donna Lester C; m. 11/26/65 to Terry Diane Carman. Educ: North Iowa Area Commun. Col, 60-62; Univ. Iowa, B.A. in Polit. Sci, 64; Univ. North. Iowa, M.A. in Soc. Sci, 66; Carnegie-Mellon Univ, Grad. Assistanceship, 69-; Alpha Chap. Polit. & Govt. Pos: Del, Iowa State Dem. Conv, 68; alternate del, Dem. Nat. Conv, 68; mem, Iowa State Dem. Conf, 69. Bus. & Prof. Pos: History instr, N. Iowa Area Commun. Col, Mason City, 66-69. Mem: Am. Asn. of Univ. Prof. Rel: Methodist. Legal Res: 1203 S. Vermont, Mason City, Iowa 50401. Mailing Add: 228½ W. Fourth St, St. Ansgar, Iowa 50472.

CHRISTIANSON, MARVIN E. DFL
Minn. State Rep.
b. Halstad, Minn, 1928; m. to Donna Andrae Pekin; c. Marvin, Jr, Lori Ann. Educ: Halstad High Sch; State Farmer degree F.F.A, 45. Polit. & Govt. Pos: Del, Minn. Dem-Farmer-Labor State Conv, 63; former co. chmn, Dem-Farmer-Labor Cmt; Minn. State Rep, 65- Mem: Future Farmers Am.(former state officer); Ada Toastmasters; PTA; Retarded Children's Asn; Farmers Union. Outstanding Young Farmer, Mower Co, Minn, 61. Mailing Add: Route 2, Halstad, Minn. 56548. (1967)

CHRISTIE, JOE D
Tex. State Sen.
b. Rising Sun, Tex; m. to Tana Horwitz; c. Charles A. and Molly D. Educ: Univ. Tex, B.S. in Geol. and LL.B, 61. Polit. & Govt. Pos: Cand, Tex. legis, 64; former asst. co. attorney, El Paso; Tex. State Sen, 66- Bus. & Prof. Pos: Consult. on water and oil probs, formerly; attorney-at-law, currently. Mil. Serv: Marine Corps, 2 years. Mailing Add: 915 El Paso National Bank Bldg, El Paso, Tex. 79902.

CHRISTIE, JOHN M. R
Treas, Rep. Nat. Cmt.
b. 8/14/10; m. to Dorothy A. Farrell. Educ: George Wash. Univ, 35; Am. Inst. of Banking, 37; Rutgers Univ. Grad. Sch. of Banking, 40. Polit. & Govt. Pos: Asst. treas, Inaugural Cmt, 53, spec. asst. to chmn, 57 & 69; treas, Rep. Nat. Cmt, 69- Bus. & Prof. Pos: Dir, Govt. Employees Ins. and Life Ins. Co, Govt. Employees Corp. and Financial Corp, Criterion Ins. Co. and Cent. Charge Serv, Inc. and pres. Riggs Nat. Bank, D.C, currently. Mem: First v.pres, D.C. Bankers Asn; chmn. finance and budget cmt, Salvation Army Adv. Bd, 68; dir, Boy's Club, dir. and past pres, Metrop. Police; trustee, Fed. City Coun; mem, Investor Panel, Transportation Asn. of Am; dir, Wash. Chap. Am. Red Cross and Wash. Heart Asn, Inc; Rotary Club of D.C; Asn. of Reserve City Bankers; Am. Inst. of Banking; Wash. Bd. of Trade. Legal Res: 9519 W. Stanhope Rd, Rock Creek Hills, Kensington, Md. 20795. Mailing Add: 1625 Eye St. N.W, Washington, D.C. 20006.

CHRISTIE, ROLAND E. JR. R
b. Wakefield, Mass, 6/29/15; married; c. One. Polit. & Govt. Pos: Former N.H. State Rep, v.chmn, Liquor Laws Cmt, chief of police, Mont Vernon, N.H, Cemetery Trustee, naval inspector, U.S. Bur. of Ships. Bus. & Prof. Pos: Food broker. Mem: Grocery Mfgs. Salesmens' Asn; Manchester Press Club; F&AM. Rel: Methodist. Mailing Add: Main St, Mont Vernon, N.H. 03057. (1967)

CHRISTOFFERSEN, PAUL JOHN D
b. Richmond, Utah, 10/29/08; s. John Christian Christoffersen and Ava Sovonia Gregory C; m. 6/5/29 to Elverna M. Gardner; c. Paul, Jr, Verlene, Delwyn, Dixie and LeAnn. Educ: Utah State Univ, grad; grad. study, Univ. Calif, Calif. State Polytech. Col. and Fresno State Col; Alpha Zeta. Polit. & Govt. Pos: Mayor, Chowchilla, Calif, 48-52; chmn, Madera Co. Bd. Supvrs, 58-62; former mem, Calif. State Dem. Cent. Cmt; chmn, Madera Co. Dem. Cent. Cmt, 64-66. Mem: Pres, Madera Co. C. of C, 56; Lions Int. Rel: Latter-day Saints. Legal Res: 23372 Robertson Blvd, Chowchilla, Calif. 93610. Mailing Add: P.O. Box 846, Chowchilla, Calif. 93610.

CHRISTOPHER, ALBERT JOSEPH R
Mayor, Pembina, N.Dak.
b. Aitkin, Minn, 1/1/97; s. Harley H. Christopher and Mary Lemire C; m. 6/20/25 to Helen Henrietta Conmy; c. Albert Melbourne and Catherine Anne. Educ: Denver Engr. Inst, 20-22. Polit. & Govt. Pos: Mayor, Pembina, N.Dak, 31-; city rep, N.Dak. League Munic, 31-; Rep. Co. committeeman, Pembina Co, 50-63; mem, Pembina Co. Selective Serv. Bd, 48-52; 61; pres, Red River Watershed and Flood Control Asn, 50-53; pres, Pembina River Flood Control Asn, 50-; state dir, N.Dak. Water Users Asn, 52-; N.Dak. State Rep, 53-67;

pres, Econ. Develop. Corp, Pembina, 62- Bus. & Prof. Pos: Owner-operator, Christopher's Serv. & Sales, 20-62. Mil. Serv: Pvt, C.E.F. Army, 16-19; Chief PO, Navy, 43-45, serv. in Seabee's, ETO and Pac. Theatre. Mem: N.Dak. State Hist. Soc, Inc.(dir, 65-68); chmn, Pembina Co. Am. Red Cross, 52-53; dir, Pembina Co. Centennial, 67; dir, Pembina State Mus, 62-; Pembina Co. Hist. Soc, 68-69; Pembina Community Club; Farm Bur; charter mem, Am. Legion (past pres, Kern-Thompson Post 77, Am. Legion); comdr, Pembina Co. Barracks 1361 World War I, 68-69. Gov. Leadership Man of the Year Award, N.Dak. Econ. Develop. Cmn, 62; Distinguished Serv. Award, N.Dak. League Munic; Cert. of Appreciation, Selective Serv, 48, 52 & 61. Rel: Methodist. Mailing Add: Pembina, N.Dak. 58271.

CHRISTOPHER, WARREN MINOR D
b. Scranton, N.Dak, 10/27/25; s. Ernest William Christopher and Catharine Anna Lemen C; m. 12/21/56 to Marie Josephine Wyllis; c. Lynn Southgate, Scott Wyllis, Thomas Warren and Kristen Ingrid. Educ: Univ. Redlands, 42-43; Univ. South. Calif, B.S. in finance, 45; Stanford Univ, LL.B, 49; Order of Coif; Phi Kappa Phi; Phi Alpha Delta; Kappa Sigma Sigma. Polit. & Govt. Pos: Chmn. U.S. del, U.S-Japan Cotton Textile Negotiations and Geneva Cong. on Cotton Textiles, Calif, 61; spec. consult. to Undersecy. George W. Ball on For. Econ. Probs, 61-65; co-chmn, Lawyers Cmt. for Stanley Mosk for Attorney Gen, 62; civilian aide, Secy. of the Army for South. Calif, 62; pres, Coord. Coun. for Higher Educ. in State of Calif, 63-65; spec. rep. of Secy. of State, Wool Textile Meeting, Tokyo, London and Rome, 64-65; v.chmn, Gov. Cmn. on Los Angeles Riots, Calif, 65-66; co-chmn, statewide campaign for re-election of Gov. Edmund G. Brown, 66; Dep. Attorney Gen. of U.S, 67-69. Bus. & Prof. Pos: Law clerk to Justice William O. Douglas, U.S. Supreme Court, 49-59; ed-in-chief, Los Angeles Co. Bar Bul, 55-56; partner, O'Melveny & Myers, Attorneys, 58; chmn. standing cmt. on aeronaut. law, Am. Bar Asn, Los Angeles, 66-67; mem. bd. bar exam, Bar of Calif, 66-67. Mil. Serv: Entered as A/S, Naval Res, 43, released as Lt.(jg), 46, after serv. in Pac. Theater, 45-46. Publ: 'The Constitutionality of the Voting Act of 1965,' and 'The Outer Continental Shelf Lands Act: Key to a New Frontier,' Stanford Law Rev; Chap. on 'Trial' (with John P. Pollock) in Manual of Fed. Practice, McGraw-Hill, 67. Mem: Am, Calif. and Los Angeles Co. Bar Asns; Chancery Club; Calif. Club; exec. cmt, Lawyers' Cmt. for Civil Rights Under Law; Los Angeles Cmt. on For. Rels. Rel: Methodist. Legal Res: 455 N. June St, Los Angeles, Calif. 90004. Mailing Add: 611 W. Sixth St, Los Angeles, Calif. 90017.

CHRISTOPHERSON, FRANK W, JR. D
b. Superior, Wis, 5/24/27. Educ: Superior State Col. Polit. & Govt. Pos: Wis. State Sen, 62-66; Gov's. Comm. on Law Enforcement and Crime; Co. Bd. mem, 56-62; v.chmn, 57-62; elected to Assembly 58 and 60. Bus. & Prof. Pos: Locomotive engr. and fireman since 45; newspaper publisher. Mil. Serv: Army Air Corps. Mailing Add: 2414 E. 6th St, Superior, Wis. 54882. (1967)

CHRISTOWE, STOYAN R
Vt. State Sen.
b. Konomlady, Macedonia, 9/1/98; s. Christo Naumoff and Mitra Koteva N; m. 9/30/37 to Margaret Wooters. Educ: Valparaiso Univ, 18-22. Polit. & Govt. Pos: Sr. analyst, Mil. Intel. Div, War Dept, 41-45; Vt. State Rep, 60-64; chmn. bd, Vt. Free Pub. Libr, 62-68; Vt. State Sen, 65- Bus. & Prof. Pos: Ed, House Organ and asst. advert. mgr, Valspar Corp, 26-29; Balkan correspondent, Chicago Daily News For. Serv, 29-31; free lance writer, 31-; mem. Vt. Educ. TV Broadcasting Coun, 69- Publ: Heroes and Assassins, McBride, 35; This is My Country, Lippincott, 38; My American Pilgrimage, Atlantic-Little, Brown, 47. Mem: Nat. Asn. Support Pub. Schs; Windham Co. Rep. Cmt; Educ. Cmn. of States; Farm Bur. Rel: Catholic. Mailing Add: West Dover, Vt. 05356.

CHRISTY, DONALD R
Kans. State Sen.
b. Scott City, Kans, 11/23/09; s. Marion Estes Christy and Effie May Ater C; m. 5/28/33 to Helen Georgia Shedd; c. Donald Owen, Arthur Estes and Alice Alieen. Educ: Kans. State Univ. and Tex. A&M Univ, M.S. Polit. & Govt. Pos: Mem, Area Property Tax Study, Kans, 54; served on U.S. Dept. Agr. Adv. Cmt. on Equip. and Struct, 6 years, Kans. State Bd. Agr, 12 years, Kans. State Fair Bd, 12 years, Scott Co. Fair Bd, Kans, 24 years, Kans. Water Resources Bd, 13 years, Kans. Watershed, 4 years and helped in formation of Soil Conserv. Bd, Scott Co, Kans; Kans. State Sen, 27th Dist, 69- Bus. & Prof. Pos: Teacher of irrigation drainage and soil conserv, Tex. A&M Univ, 9 years; farmer and banker, Scott Co, Kans, currently. Publ: Terracing, 40. Mem: Bd. of Educ; Co. agent and 4-H activity; Lions; Farm Bur; C. of C. Soil Conserv. Award, Kans. Bankers; Chmn Award, Kans. Asn. Soil Conserv. Dist. Supvr. Rel: Christian Church of N.Am; Deacon, First Christian Church and Sunday Sch. Teacher. Legal Res: 1005 Washington, Scott City, Kans. 67871. Mailing Add: Box 103, Scott City, Kans. 67871.

CHRISTY, JOHN GRIER
Mayor, Jefferson City, Mo.
b. Marathon, Ohio, 6/9/97; s. of Grier G. Christy and Carrie Johnson C; m. 8/21/18 to Fern Booker; c. Grace Mary (Mrs. Donald M. Gee). Educ: Ohio Wesleyan Univ, 14-16; Kansas City Dent. Col, D.D.S, 19. Polit. & Govt. Pos: Mo. State Rep, 33-40, speaker, Mo. House of Rep, 35-40; mayor, Jefferson City, 63- Bus. & Prof. Pos: Dentist, Kansas City and Festus, Mo, 19-40. Mil. Serv: Army, 17-19; Lt. Col, Army, 42-47. Mailing Add: 613 E. McCarty, Jefferson City, Mo. 65101.

CHRISTY, WILLIAM D
Ind. State Sen.
Polit. & Govt. Pos: Ind. State Sen, 55-, chmn, Dem. Caucus, Ind. State Sen, 63. Bus. & Prof. Pos: Steelworker, Youngstown Sheet and Tube Co, pres, Lake Fed. Savings & Loan Asn, Hammond, Ind. Mem: Steel Workers Local Union (former pres); Lake Co. Indust. Union Coun.(former v.pres). Rel: Christian Church. Mailing Add: 7106 Grand Ave, Hammond, Ind. 46323. (1967)

CHRONIC, BETTY M. R
Campaign Chmn, Colo. Fedn. Rep. Women
b. Tulsa, Okla, 6/24/25; d. Roland Forest McWilliams and Faye Foster M; m. 4/7/45 to William Lee Chronic; c. Barbara Lee, Jane Ann and Katherine Sue. Educ: Univ. Tulsa, 43-45 & 46; Univ. Colo, B.A, 50; Phi Beta Kappa; Phi Alpha Theta; Phi Mu. Polit. & Govt. Pos: Secy. and exec. dir, Gov. Cmt. Ment. Health, Colo, 54-56; precinct committeewoman, Boulder Co. Rep. Cent. Cmt, 54-58, v.chmn, 58-61; mem, Electoral Col, 60; Colo. State Rep, 60-61; secy, Colo. Rep. Cent. Cmt, 61-64; mem, Colo. Bd. Health, 63-; del, Rep. Nat. Conv, 64; secy, Colo. Water Pollution Control Cmn, 66-; campaign chmn, Colo. Fedn. Rep. Women, 66- Mem: Am. Asn. Univ. Women; Colo. Fedn. Rep. Women; Girl Scouts; PTA. Rel: Presbyterian. Mailing Add: 4705 Shawnee Place, Boulder, Colo. 80302.

CHU, BETTY TOM D
Mem, Calif. Dem. State Cent. Cmt.
b. San Diego, Calif; d. Tom K. Choy and Yee Siu C; m. to Robert W. Chu; c. Brian and Jon Kevin. Educ: Univ. of South. Calif, B.S, 58; Univ. of South. Calif. Law Sch, LL.B, 61. Polit. & Govt. Pos: Mem, Calif. Dem. State Cent. Cmt, 66-; chmn, Monterey Park Commun. Rels. Cmn, 69- Bus. & Prof. Pos: Corp. counsel, Div. of Corp, State of Calif, 64-68; dep. co. counsel, Los Angeles Co. Counsel, 68- Mailing Add: 105 Ladera St, Monterey Park, Calif. 91754.

CHU, SAMUEL EN FON R
Committeeman, Honolulu Co. Rep. Cmt.
b. Waimea, Hawaii, 11/9/08; s. John Yok Hon Chu and Annie Yap C; m. 11/16/30 to Dorothy Alice Aikue; c. Lorna K. Kaeck, Norman K, Sherwin K, Anna K. Willocks and Henridene K. Aluli. Educ: Univ. of Hawaii, Extension Night Courses, 2 years. Polit. & Govt. Pos: City and Co. Liquor Cmnr, Hawaii; past chmn, Honolulu Co. Rep. Cmt, committeeman, currently; del, Rep. Nat. Conv, 68. Bus. & Prof. Pos: Asst. Secy, Hawaiian Trust Co. Ltd, Honolulu, Hawaii, 47. Mem: PTA (past pres); trustee, Palama Settlement; trustee, Kapiolani Hosp; founder and charter mem, Kalihi-Palama Commun. Coun. (past pres. and legis. chmn); Man-of-the-week, Club Hawaii. Rel: Episcopal. Mailing Add: 2004 Kula St, Honolulu, Hawaii 96817.

CHUBB, ELIZABETH LOUISE R
V.Chmn, Cattaraugus Co. Rep. Exec. Cmt, N.Y.
b. Randolph, N.Y, 10/23/22; d. Leslie Aldrich Smith and Pansy Walters S; m. 6/28/39 to Adolph Ernest Chubb; c. Joseph, Patricia (Mrs. Robert Zollinger), Carol Marie and Margaret Ann. Educ: Randolph Cent. Sch, N.Y, 5 years. Polit. & Govt. Pos: V.treas, Cattaraugus Co. Rep. Cmt, N.Y, 62-64, committeeman, 62-69; secy, Randolph Rep. Club, 62-69; v.chmn, Cattaraugus Co. Rep. Exec. Cmt, 66- Mem: Randolph Homemakers; Randolph Garden Club; Grange; Cattaraugus Co. Coop. Exten. Serv. Rel: Catholic. Mailing Add: Bowen Rd, Randolph, N.Y. 14772.

CHUDOFF, EARL D
b. Philadelphia, Pa, 11/16/07; s. Morris Chudoff and Jennye Rubin C; m. 8/31/36 to Bess Cohen; c. Stephen and Diane. Educ: Wharton Sch, Univ. Pa, B.S. in econ, 29; Univ. Pittsburgh Law Sch, LL.B, 32, J.D, 68; Tau Epsilon Rho; Beta Gamma Sigma. Polit. & Govt. Pos: Bldg. and Loan Exam, Pa. State Dept. Banking, 36-39; Pa. State Rep, 41-48; U.S. Rep, Pa, 48-58, mem, House Cmt. Judiciary, chmn, Pub. Works and Resources Subcmt. and Cmt. Govt. Opers; Judge, Court Common Pleas One, Phila. Co, Pa, 58- Mil. Serv: Chief Boatswain's Mate, Coast Guard Res. Mem: Phila, Pa. and Am. Bar Asns; pres, Phila. Chap, Fed. Bar Asn; Fel. Cmn; George B. McCracken Mem. Chap, Coast Guard League; Am. Jewish Cong; 4 Freedoms and Justice Lodges, B'nai B'rith, Mason; Golden Slipper Square Club; 21 Jewel Square Club; 32 Carat Club; Lehigh Consistory; Scottish Rite. Annual Achievement Award, Alpha Lodge, B'nai B'rith, 54; Max Slepin Award, Haim-Parnes Post 1951, Jewish War Vet, 56; Histadrut Humanitarian Award, Parkside Lodge, B'nai B'rith, 57; Humanitarian Awards, Zionist Orgn. Am. and 4 Freedoms Lodge, B'nai B'rith, 58. Rel: Jewish. Legal Res: Kennedy House, 1901 J.F. Kennedy Blvd, Philadelphia, Pa. 19103. Mailing Add: 242 City Hall, Philadelphia, Pa. 19107.

CHUINARD, FRITZI G. R
Ore. State Rep.
b. Ida Grove, Iowa, 6/9/06; d. Dr. Winfield Preston Goff and Dr. Anna Sheldon G; m. 7/5/30 to Dr. Eldon George Chuinard; c. Robert Gary, M.D. and Beverly Ann (Mrs. Garry Forrest). Educ: Wash. State Univ, B.S, 28, grad. work later in Social Case Work; Delta Delta Delta. Polit. & Govt. Pos: Mem, Multomah Co. Planning Cmn, Ore, 53-56, v.chmn, 56-59; Ore. State Rep, Sixth Dist, 61-; former mem, Curriculum Coun, Portland Pub. Schs. Bus. & Prof. Pos: Teacher, Tacoma Pub. Schs, 28-29; social case worker, Am. Red Cross, 33-44, Multnomah Co, Ore, Welfare Dept, 34-36 and Children's Dept, 36-38. Mem: Exec, YWCA, Tacoma, 29-30; Am. Asn. of Univ. Women; Multnomah Co. Med. Soc. Auxiliary; Portland Garden Club; Garden Club of Am; League of Women Voters; Altrusa. Rel: Protestant. Mailing Add: 7307 N.W. Penridge Rd, Portland, Ore. 97229.

CHURCH, CORBETT D
W.Va. State Del.
b. Yukon, W.Va, 7/17/22; s. Rufus C. Church and Pearl Dale C; m. 12/24/45 to Edith Wright; c. Bennett E. Educ: Concord Col, B.S; Marshall Univ, M.A. Polit. & Govt. Pos: W.Va. State Del, 64- Bus. & Prof. Pos: Elem. sch. prin. Mem: Pres, McDowell Co. Educ. Asn; McDowell Co. Chap. Marshall Univ. Alumni Asn; Bradshaw Town Improv. Asn; Berwind Conserv. Club; Bradshaw Lion's Club. Mailing Add: Yukon, W.Va. 24899. (1967)

CHURCH, FRANK D
U.S. Sen, Idaho
b. Boise, Idaho, 7/25/24; m. to Bethine Clark; c. Forrest and Chase. Educ: Stanford Univ, A.B. and LL.B; Phi Beta Kappa. Polit. & Govt. Pos: State chmn, Young Dem. of Idaho, 52-54; U.S. Sen, 56-, chmn, For. Rels. Subcmt. West. Hemisphere Affairs, Interior Subcmt. Pub. Lands and Subcmt. Consumer Interests of Elderly of Spec. Cmt. on Aging; keynoter, Dem. Nat. Conv, 60; U.S. Del, 21st Gen. Assembly of UN. Bus. & Prof. Pos: Attorney-at-law. Mil. Serv: Enlisted as Pvt, Army, World War II, commissioned 44; Mil. Intel. in China, Burma, India. Mem: State chmn, Crusade For Freedom, 54-55. Named Nat. Jaycee Outstanding Young Man, 57. Legal Res: Boise, Idaho. Mailing Add: Room 204, Senate Office Bldg, Washington, D.C. 20510.

CHURCH, JAMES OLIVER R
Chmn, Trumbull Rep. Town Cmt, Conn.
b. Bridgeport, Conn, 12/24/21; s. James O. Church and Mabel Cliffe C; m. 10/30/48 to Kathryn MacNaughton; c. Sally K. Educ: Springfield Col, B.S, 43. Polit. & Govt. Pos: Representative, Trumbull Town Meeting, Conn, 59-61; mem, Trumbull Rep. Town Cmt, 61-66, chmn, 66- Bus. & Prof. Pos: Spec. agent, Northwest. Mutual Life Ins. Co, Conn, 50- Mil. Serv: Entered as Pvt, Army, 42, released as Capt, 46, after serv. in 84th Div, ETO, 42-46, Res, 46-65, Maj.(Ret); Bronze Star. Publ: History of 418 Regiment USAR, Privately Publ, 65. Mem: Northwest Mutual Life Ins. Co. Agents Asn; secy, YMCA, 46-50. Rel: Protestant. Mailing Add: 20 Placid St, Trumbull, Conn. 06611.

CHURCH, MARGUERITE STITT R
b. New York, N.Y, 9/13/92; d. William James Stitt and Adelaide Forsythe S; m. 1918 to Ralph E. Church; wid; c. Ralph Edwin, Jr, William Stitt and Marjory Williams (Mrs. Wood). Educ: Wellesley Col, A.B, 14; Columbia Univ, A.M. in polit. sci, 17; Phi Beta Kappa; Delta Kappa Gamma. Hon. LL.D, Russell Sage Col, 58, Lake Forest Col, 60 and Northwest. Univ, 62; hon. D.H.L, Nat. Col. Educ, 63. Polit. & Govt. Pos: U.S. Rep, 13th Dist, Ill, 51-63, mem, House Cmt. on For. Affairs, 10 years, and Subcmts. on For. Econ. Policy, Far East and Pac, mem, Cmt. on Govt. Opers, 51-55 and Rep. Policy Cmt, 2 terms; House of Rep. del, inauguration of President, Mex, 58; del, White House Conf. on Children and Youth, 60; U.S. Del, UN Gen. Assembly, 61; del, Rep. Nat. Conv, 64. Bus. & Prof. Pos: Consult. psychologist, State Charities Aid Asn, N.Y.C; teacher, Wellesley Col, 1 year. Mem: Ill. Children's Home and Aid Soc; Infant Welfare Soc; pres, Cong. Club. and Nat. Alumnae Asn. Wellesley Col; Bus. and Prfnl. Women's Clubs; Phi Beta Kappa Assocs; Zonta Int; int. hon. mem, Beta Sigma Phi; Nat. Bd. Dirs, Girl Scouts; Woman's Bd, Univ. Chicago. VIP Award, Ill. Club for Cath. Women, 60; Founders' Day Award, Loyola Univ, 62; Merit Award, Civic Affairs Assocs, Inc, 60. Rel: Methodist. Mailing Add: 300 Church St, Evanston, Ill. 60201.

CHURCHILL, WALTER AUGUSTUS R
Chmn, Lucas Co. Rep. Party, Ohio
b. Toledo, Ohio, 11/12/03; s. Joseph Walter Churchill and Bertha V. Ricketts C; m. 6/9/28 to Dorothy Helen King; c. Walter A. Jr. and Carolyn Ann (Mrs. Lynn A. Colwell). Polit. & Govt. Pos: Chmn, Lucas Co. Rep. Party, Ohio, 67-; del, Rep. Nat. Conv, 68. Bus. & Prof. Pos: Pres, Churchills Super Markets Inc, Assoc. Grocers Wholesale Co. and Churchills Bellevue Market Inc; chmn. of the bd. and chief exec. officer, U.S. Marines Youth Found. Inc, 69. Mil. Serv: Entered as Pvt, Marine Corps, 22, released as Maj. Gen, 63; Marine Corps Res.(Ret); Bronze Star; Gold Star. Publ: Marine Corps League Physical Fitness Program Booklet, 68. Mem: Marine Corps League (past nat. commandant); Nat. Asn. of Retail Grocers of the U.S.(past pres). Rel: Protestant. Mailing Add: 3003 Cheltenham Rd, Toledo, Ohio 43606.

CHYTIL, JOE R
b. Aberdeen, Wash, 1909; m. to Jane C; c. Two. Educ: Bus. Col. Polit. & Govt. Pos: Wash. State Rep, 53-59; Wash. State Sen, 60-69. Bus. & Prof. Pos: Radio Broadcaster, 37-; chmn, bd. of dir, Wash. State Asn. of Broadcasters. Mem: Rotary; Elks; Eagles. Mailing Add: 1274 Fifth St, Chehalis, Wash. 98532.

CIANFRANI, HENRY J. D
Pa. State Sen.
b. Phila, Pa, 3/19/23; s. Henry B. Cianfrani and Chinzie C.(deceased); m. 6/29/46 to Rita Ann Marano; c. Mary Ellen, Maria and Elvira. Educ: Temple Univ, 45-46; Univ. Pa. Wharton Sch, 47-48. Polit. & Govt. Pos: Pa. State Rep; committeeman, Dem. Party, Pa, 53-55, ward leader, 55-; del, Dem. Nat. Conv, 60 & 64, alternate del, 68; Pa. State Sen, currently. Bus. & Prof. Pos: Importer, Aurino Frani Inc, 60- Mil. Serv: Entered as Pvt, Army, 42, released as Sgt, 45, after serv. in China-Burma-India; China-Burma-India Ribbon; 3 Battle Ribbons; Served with famed Merrill's Marauders, Burma. Mem: Past comdr, VFW 589; past comdr, Am. Legion, Kater Memorial Post; Sons of Italy; Pa. Civic Liberties League. 10 Letter Man, High Sch. Rel: Catholic. Mailing Add: 747 S. Sixth St, Philadelphia, Pa. 19147.

CIARLONE, ANTHONY MICHAEL D
Conn. State Rep.
b. New Haven, Conn, 5/8/29; s. Gaetano Ciarlone and Carmela Ciarlone C; m. 5/9/53 to Jean Patricia Irons; c. Cynthia, Linda, Jeanmarie and Cathy. Educ: Quinnipiac Col, A.S, 49. Polit. & Govt. Pos: Mem. bd. alderman, New Haven, Conn, 65-68; Conn. State Rep, 67- Bus. & Prof. Pos: Corp. exec. Mem: Wooster Sq. Commun. Asn; Wooster Sq. Renewal Commun; Alpha Club; St. Michaels Holy Name Soc. Rel: Catholic. Mailing Add: 232 St. John St, New Haven, Conn. 06511.

CINA, FRED A. DFL
married; c. 3. Educ: Grad, Univ. of Minn. Polit. & Govt. Pos: Minn. State Rep, 47-69. Mil. Serv: World War II. Mem: Am. Legion. Mailing Add: 11 N. Erie St, Aurora, Minn. 55705. (1967)

CINCOTTA, GEORGE A. D
N.Y. State Assemblyman
b. Brooklyn, N.Y, 12/5/14; s. George A. Cincotta and Lillian Cirina C; m. 9/18/38 to Theresa D'Antonio; c. Lillian (Mrs. Fiore) and George, Jr. Educ: St. Johns Col. Polit. & Govt. Pos: Former mem, N.Y.C. Coun; mem. coord. coun, 71st precinct, N.Y.C. Police Dept; N.Y. State Assemblyman, mem, Joint Legis. Cmt. on State's Commerce, Econ. Develop, Tourism and Motor Boats, ranking mem, Assembly Cmt. on Commerce, Indust. and Econ. Develop. and mem, Assembly Cmt. on Govt. Employees, currently. Bus. & Prof. Pos: Bus. exec. Mem: Pres, Andrew Jackson Club; hon. co-chmn, Yeshivah of Crown Heights and Judea Center Dinner Cmt; hon. mem, Crown Heights Jewish War Vets; hon. trustee, J.F.K. Libr. for Minorities, Inc; trustee, St. Columbia Coun, K. of C; dir, Cath. Guardian Soc. of the Diocese of Brooklyn, Flatbush YMCA and Cath. Charities of the Diocese of Brooklyn; chmn. bd. dirs, Jr. Bluejackets of Am; co-chmn, Fedn. of Christians and Jews Award Dinner; former chmn. adv. bd. of Brooklyn East, N.Y.C. Police Dept; Flatbush Lions; St. Francis of Assisi Holy Name Soc; L.I. Gen. Assembly, K. of C.(4°); hon. mem, AFL Off. Employees; active in boys orgn. in Kings Co. and Gr. N.Y.C. for thirty years. Mailing Add: 96 Maple St, Brooklyn, N.Y. 11225.

CINGCADE, LESTER EARL D
Admin. Dir. of the Courts, Hawaii
b. Eagle Point, Ore, 1/31/34; s. Merrill H. Tozier and Hazel Loretta Hatfield C; m. to Judith Ann. Educ: South. Ore. Col, 51-54; Univ. Ore, B.S. in Hist, 55; Univ. Hawaii, M.Ed, 66. Polit. & Govt. Pos: Mem, Dem. Cent. Cmt, Hawaii, 62-66; admin. dir. courts, Hawaii, 66- Bus. & Prof. Pos: Dean boys, Mid-Pac. Inst, 55-66. Mil. Serv: Entered as Pvt, Army, 59, released as Specialist 5, after serv. in Adj. Gen. Sch; Capt, Res, serv. in 322nd CA Group, Ft. De Russy, Hawaii. Rel: Congregational. Mailing Add: 47-706 Hui Io Place, Kaneohe, Hawaii 96744.

CIOFFI, DOMINICK E. D
b. New Castle, Pa, 7/28/99; s. Samuel Cioffi and Antionette DeGregory C; m. to Violet Frasso; c. Three. Educ: New Castle Bus. Col. Polit. & Govt. Pos: Pa. State Rep, 52-68; secy, Lawrence Co. Dem. Cmt, 14 years. Bus. & Prof. Pos: Hardward buyer. Mailing Add: 25 E. Reynolds St, New Castle, Pa. 16101. (1967)

CIPRIANI, HARRIET EMILY D
Dep. Dir. Women's Activities, Dem. Nat. Cmt.
b. N.Y.C; d. Floyd Stickels and Emily Gaetke S; m. 2/10/45 to Alfred Berne Cipriani. Educ: Flushing High Sch, N.Y, grad; Art Students League, N.Y.C. Polit. & Govt. Pos: Secy, D.C. Dem. Cent. Cmt, 60-64, v.chmn, 64-67; del, Dem. Nat. Conv, 60, 64 & 68, secy. to D.C. del, 60 and sergeant at arms, 64; alternate Dem. nat. committeewoman, D.C, 64-67, committeewoman, 67-68; nat. coordinator Women for Humphrey, 68; dep. dir. women's activities, Dem. Nat. Cmt, 68- Mem: League of Women Voters U.S; Woman's Nat. Dem. Club; D.C. Dem. Woman's Club; Urban League; Family & Child Serv; Mt. Pleasant Neighbors Asn. Rel: Nonsectarian. Mailing Add: 1761 Harvard St. N.W, Washington, D.C. 20009.

CITRINO, ROBERT JOSEPH, JR. R
b. Nutley, N.J, 1/3/30; s. Robert Joseph Citrino, M.D. and Anna Santora C; m. 3/2/57 to Jean M. Coraci; c. Diane, Robert Joseph, III, Mary Ann, Vicki and Suzanne. Educ: Villanova Univ; Columbia Univ, B.S; Boston Univ. Sch. of Med; Georgetown Univ. Law Sch, LL.B. Polit. & Govt. Pos: Nutley Town Attorney, 64-; cmnr, Bd. of Elecs, 63-; alternate del, Rep. Conv, 60, 64; admin. asst. to Essex Co. Rep. Chmn, Rep. Robert W. Kean, 59, 62; personal aide to U.S. Sen. Clifford P. Case, 54. Prof. Pos: Partner, Citrino, Carella & Balsam, Esqs, 58- Mem: N.J. Inst. of Munic. Attorneys; Nutley Rep. Club; Lions Club; Elks Club; Amvets; K. of C. Rel: Roman Catholic. Legal Res: 70 North Rd, Nutley, N.J. 07110. Mailing Add: c/o Citrino, Carella & Balsam, 345 Centre St, Nutley, N.J. 07110. (1967)

CLABAUGH, CHARLES WESLEY R
Ill. State Rep.
b. Lerna, Ill, 8/15/00; s. Thomas Nelson Clabaugh and Patsy Richardson C; m. 3/9/44 to Louise Zimmerman; c. Dorothy Kay (Mrs. Richard McGuire) and Patsy Lee (Mrs. James G. Johansen). Educ: Univ. Ill, 1 year; East. Ill. Univ, B.Ed. Polit. & Govt. Pos: Rep. precinct committeeman, Champaign Co. Cent. Cmt, Ill, 30-34; Ill. State Rep, 48th Dist, 39-, chmn, House Educ. Cmt, 14 years and Sch. Prob. Cmn, 12 years. Bus. & Prof. Pos: Teacher, 5 years. Mem: Elks (state treas, 2 years, v.pres-at-lg, 1 year, state pres, 1 year, Grand Lodge Rep, 1 year, Past Exalted Ruler). Distinguished Pub. Serv. Award, South. Ill. Univ, 56; Man of the Year Award, State Bd. Spec. Educ. Dirs. Rel: Methodist. Mailing Add: 405 W. University Ave, Champaign, Ill. 61820.

CLAFLIN, RUSSELL G. R
N.H. State Rep.
b. Phila, Pa, 10/27/14; wid; c. One son. Educ: Harvard. Polit. & Govt. Pos: Del, N.H. Constitutional Conv, 56-64; N.H. State Rep, 57- Bus. & Prof. Pos: Retired land surveyor. Mil. Serv: Field Artil, Army, ETO, World War II, European Theatre. Rel: Congregational. Mailing Add: Box 577, Wolfeboro, N.H. 03894.

CLAIBORN, JACK DEWEY R
Idaho State Rep.
b. Payette, Idaho, 9/12/99; s. Edward Claiborn and Susie Walker C; m. 12/25/19 to Emily Wall; c. Elaine (Mrs. Burkey), William L, Jack D, Jr. and Edward L. Educ: High sch. grad, 18. Polit. & Govt. Pos: Idaho State Rep, 60-, chmn. agr. cmt, Idaho House Rep, 4 sessions, mem. state affairs cmt; mem, Kimberly Sch. Bd, 12 years, chmn, 11 years. Bus. & Prof. Pos: Pres, Claiborn & Sons, Inc, 56-; owner and operator 500 head cattle oper; v.pres, secy, C & H Murtaugh Inc; v.pres, Twin Falls Co. Mutual Fire Ins. Co; mem. farm ration bd, World War II. Mem: Idaho Beet Growers Asn.(past dir, pres); Nat. Beet Growers Fedn.(pres, 67-68, past v.pres); Elks; Blue Lakes Country Club (dir. several years, past chmn. bd, 3 years); Mason. Rel: Methodist. Mailing Add: Route 3, Twin Falls, Idaho. 83301.

CLAMPITT, BRUCE WILLARD R
Chmn, Hardin Co. Rep. Party, Iowa
b. New Providence, Iowa, 8/31/09; s. Ralph R. Clampitt and Lela Norman C; m. 7/25/38 to Jennye E. Evans; c. Robert B. and Joyce E. Educ: Iowa State Univ, B.S; Life Underwriter's Training Coun, L.U.T.C. Polit. & Govt. Pos: Twp, precinct chmn, Rep. Party, Iowa, 6 years; chmn, Hardin Co. Rep. Party, 66- Bus. & Prof. Pos: Voc. agr. teacher, Sloan Pub. Sch, 38-42; co. exten. dir, Plymouth Co, Iowa, 42-45; ins. fieldman, Farm Bur. Ins, 45-50; ins. agent, Columbus Mutual Ins. Co, 50-55; ins. agent, Mutual of N.Y, 55-; pres, S. Hardin Rural Tel. Coop. Mem: Local, state and nat. Life Underwriters Asns; bd. mem, Iowa Cancer Soc; Mason; Lions; Elks. Rel: Society of Friends. Mailing Add: R.F.D, New Providence, Iowa 50206.

CLANCY, DONALD D. R
U.S. Rep, Ohio
b. Cincinnati, Ohio, 7/24/21; m. 1949 to Betty Jane Mangeot; c. Kathy, Patricia and Danny. Educ: Xavier Univ; Univ. Cincinnati, LL.B, 48. Polit. &

Govt. Pos: Councilman, Cincinnati, Ohio, 51-57, mayor, 57-61; U.S. Rep, Second Dist, Ohio, 61- Rel: Roman Catholic. Mailing Add: 7403 Green Farms Dr, Cincinnati, Ohio 45224.

CLANCY, JEAN THERESA D
Committeewoman, N.Y. State Dem. Orgn.
b. Ellenville, N.Y, 8/4/28; d. Harry L. Clancy and Agnes L. Wilklow C; single. Educ: Ellenville High Sch, grad. Polit. & Govt. Pos: Pres, 12th Ward Dem. Club, N.Y, 58-60; Dem. committeewoman, Fifth Dist, 12th Ward, Schenectady, 58-69; del, N.Y. State Dem. Conv, 66; chmn, Preforum Luncheon for Gubernatorial Cand, 66; mem, Schenectady Co. Dem. Publicity and Pub. Rels. Cmt, 66-67; mem, Schenectady Co. Dem. Planning Bd, 66-69; co-chmn, Dem. Women's Anniversary Luncheon, 67; chmn. prog. and planning cmt, Women's Dem. Club, 67-68; mem, Schenectady League Women Voters, 67-69; rep, N.Y. State Annual Polit. Conv, 67-69; chmn, Dem. Woman of the Year Award, 68; del, Dem. Nat. Conv, 68; mem, N.Y. State Womens Legis. Forum, 68 & 69; committeewoman, N.Y. State Dem. Orgn, 105th Assembly Dist, 68- Bus. & Prof. Pos: Supvry. equip. clerk, N.Y. Tel. Co, 62-65, asst. dial serv. supvr, 65- Mem: Schenectady Mus; Schenectady Co. Hist. Soc; Cath. Daughters of Am.(Court St. Catherine); Schenectady Co. Fedn. Womens Clubs. Rel: Catholic. Mailing Add: 911 McClellan St, Schenectady, N.Y. 12309.

CLAPP, NORMAN MOSES D
b. Ellsworth, Wis, 10/28/14; s. Rufus Newell Clapp and Jane Erdman C; m. 12/26/36 to Analoyce Elkington; c. David Allen, William Reynold and Douglas Edwin. Educ: Lawrence Col, B.A, 37; Phi Beta Kappa; Sigma Delta Chi. Polit. & Govt. Pos: Investigator and mediator, Wis. Labor Rels. Bd, 37-39; staff employee, Nat. Labor Rels. Bd, 39; staff asst. to Sen. Robert M. LaFollette, Jr, 35-37 & 39-42; minority expert, U.S. Senate, Finance Cmt. Staff, 42-44; del, Dem. Nat. Conv, 56; nominee, U.S. Rep, Third Dist, Wis, 56, 58 & 60; exec. dir, Dem. Party Wis, 59-60; adminstr, Rural Electrification Admin, 61-69. Bus. & Prof. Pos: Partner, Muscoda Pub. Co, 53-58; ed. and publisher, Grant Co. Independent, 44-58. Mem: F&AM; Scottish Rite; Eastern Star. Rel: Congregational. Mailing Add: 1305 Lynnbrook Dr, Arlington, Va. 22201.

CLAPSADDLE, R. J. D
b. Rockwell, Iowa, 3/4/04; s. Frank Clapsaddle and Lela C; m. 6/7/27 to Agnes Dillon; c. Betty Lou (Mrs. Francis)Lapointe; Charles. Polit. Pos: Iowa State Rep, 64-66. Bus. & Prof. Pos: P/T Employee, Wadell and Reed Co, Sales of Mutual Funds and Ins; Employee, Standard Oil Co, 34 Years, Retired; Owner and Operator General Store. Mem: K. of C. (Past Grand Knight). Rel: St. Joseph's Catholic Church, Mason City. Mailing Add: 323 Sixth St, Mason City, Iowa 50401. (1967)

CLARDY, GEORGE L. R
Mem, Ga. Rep. State Cent. Cmt,
b. Fayette, Ala, 12/10/27; s. Berry Burlington Clardy and Cora Etta Corbett C; m. 9/27/47 to Helen Joyce Rasberry; c. George Alan and Stanley Wayne. Educ: High Sch. grad. Polit. & Govt. Pos: Chmn, Lee Co. Rep. Party, Ga, 64-65 & 68; mem, Ga. Rep. Cent. Cmt, 64- Bus. & Prof. Pos: Serv. mgr, Lee-land Farms & Equipment, 60. Mil. Serv: Entered as A/S, Navy, 45, released as EM 3/C, 50, after serv. in S.Pac; Victory Medal; Good Conduct Medal; Pac. Theatre Ribbon. Mem: Am. Legion; Commun. Club; Brotherhood. Rel: Baptist; Deacon, First Baptist Church, 8 years. Mailing Add: Route 1, Leesburg, Ga. 31763.

CLARK, ANDREW LEWIS D
b. Mt. Hope, W.Va, 5/19/21; s. Elmer Clark and Hattie Craddock C; m. 9/5/47 to Theresa Caroline Brown; c. Terry Alston; Andrew L. and George W. Educ: W.Va. Univ, B.S.M.E, 47; Tau Beta Pi; Pi Tau Sigma; Beta Theta Pi. Polit. & Govt. Pos: W.Va. State Del, Mercer Co, 54 & 56; del, Dem. Nat. Conv, 64 & 68. Bus. & Prof. Pos: Pres, Princeton Area Develop. Corp; dir, Princeton Bank & Trust Co. Mil. Serv: Entered as Pvt, Army, 42, released as 1st Lt, 46, after serv. in Army Signal Corps, West. Pac. Theater, 44-46. Mem: Past pres, Automobile Dealers Asn. of W.Va; Mason; Elks; Rotary; C. of C.(pres, Princeton Br, 55). Rel: Methodist. Mailing Add: 213 Mahood Ave, Princeton, W.Va. 24740.

CLARK, BUFORD THOMAS R
Ky. State Rep.
b. Corbin, Ky, 9/26/11; s. Thomas V. Clark and Laurinda Mae Flowers C; m. 6/4/36 to Eleanor Randolph Owens; c. Kent Randolph, Lynne Eleanor (Mrs. Douglas Logan) and Thomas Carlisle. Educ: Union Col, A.B, 28; Univ. Ky, 32-36; George Peabody Col. and La. State Univ, 36-37; N.Y. Univ, M.A, 39; Univ. Ill, 45-46. Polit. & Govt. Pos: Ky. State Rep, 86th Dist, 60- Bus. & Prof. Pos: Instr. math. and athletic coach, Corbin High Sch, 32-36; dir. health and safety, Int. Harvestor, Benham, 36-37; instr. and athletic coach, Union Col, 37-40; head dept. Eng, Knox Cent. High Sch, Barbourville, Ky, 57- Mil. Serv: Entered as Aviation Cadet, Air Force, 41, released as Maj, 50, after flying Long Range B 29's and hurricane missions; Commendation from French Govt. Mem: Am. Legion; Farm Bur; Mason; KT; Shrine. Rel: Methodist. Mailing Add: Kenlyn, Box 704, Barbourville, Ky. 40906.

CLARK, CARROLL HERBERT R
Maine State Rep.
b. Ogunquit, Maine, 10/9/97; s. Joseph Boody Clark and Nellie Florence Snow C; div; c. Carroll H, Jr. and Jean (Mrs. Clarence Kimball). Educ: Bowdoin Col, degree, 21; Delta Upsilon. Polit. & Govt. Pos: Town moderator, Wells and Ogunquit, Maine; dir, Civil Defense, Ogunquit, 54-69; chmn, York Co. Rep. Cmt, 57-61; mem, Dist. Rep. Cmt, 57-65; Maine State Rep, 67- Bus. & Prof. Pos: Postmaster, Ogunquit, Maine, 22-33; owner, real estate, stores and houses, 50-69. Mil. Serv: Entered as Pvt, Army, 18, released as Lt. Col, 55, after serv. in Transportation Corps, Am. Atlantic, European, Africa and Far East, 42-55, attache, U.S. Embassy, Paris, France, 50-54; Eight Campaign Bars with four battle stars; Legion of Honor from French President, 53. Publ: Military Manuals, for harbor boats in New York Harbor, 55, In Japan for transfer of U.S. ships and for training German seamen in operation of fishing boats. Mem: State Legislators; Mason (32°); Shrine; Elks; Descendant of Royal Blood; state comdr, Mil. Soc. of World Wars; past gov, Soc. Mayflower Descendants in Maine; Soc. Descendants of Charlemagne; Soc. Descendants Magna Charta; past pres. Maine Soc, SAR; gov, Maine Soc. Colonial Wars; New Eng. comdr. of holders of French Legion of Honor; Bowdoin Col. Alumni Cmt; Soc. First Families of Va; Soc. Founders & Patriots in Maine & Mass. Rel: Episcopal. Legal Res: 12 Berwick St, Ogunquit, Maine 03907. Mailing Add: Legislative Post Office, State House, Augusta, Maine 04330.

CLARK, CLABIE D
Mem, State Dem. Cent. Cmt, La.
b. Kaplan, La, 4/8/20; s. Ovey Clark and Elodie Simon C; m. 2/19/39 to Louella Vallot; c. Kenneth Dale, Daniel Lee, Jeanette Faye and Cheryl Lynn. Polit. & Govt. Pos: Chmn, Parish Dem. Cmt, La, 60; mem, State Dem. Cent. Cmt, La, 64- Bus. & Prof. Pos: Owner, tire and appliance store, 48; farmer, 64. Rel: Catholic. Legal Res: 722 First St, Jennings, La. 70546. Mailing Add: P.O. Box 698, Jennings, La. 70546. (1967)

CLARK, CLOYD ELLSWORTH R
Co. Chmn, Rep. Party, Nebr.
b. McCook, Nebr, 8/7/01; s. Abner F. Clark and Hattie B. Yarger C; m. 8/2/41 to Lucile R. Hanson; c. Cloyd E, Jr, Carlton E. and Kendall H. (deceased). Educ: Univ. of Nebr, LL.B, 25; Phi Alpha Delta; Nebr. Alumni Asn. Polit. & Govt. Pos: Nebr. State Sen, 35; co. chmn, Rep. Party, currently. Bus. & Prof. Pos: Am, Nebr. State and 14th Judicial Dist. Bar Asns. Mem: Mason (32°); Shrine. Rel: Methodist. Mailing Add: Box 104, Elwood, Nebr. 68937.

CLARK, CURTIS LUTHUR R
Exec. Chmn, Morgan Co. Rep. Party, Ohio
b. Richie Co, W.Va, 10/29/05; s. Walter Clark and Blanche Smith C; m. 3/29/29 to Lucille Faye Welch; c. Herman, Edna (Mrs. Pennock), Norman, Cecil, Edward, Gerald and Ronald. Educ: Ohio Univ, B.S, 59. Polit. & Govt. Pos: Twp. trustee, Ohio, 32-34 and clerk, 48-68; precinct cmt. mem, 34-69; exec. chmn, Morgan Co. Rep. Party, 54-; mem, Morgan Co. Bd. Elec, 64-69; alternate del, Rep. Nat. Conv, 68. Bus. & Prof. Pos: Teacher, Center Bd. Ed, 28-39 & 46-59; teacher, Fort Frye Bd. Ed, 59-69. Mem: Mason; Farm Bur; Grange. Rel: Protestant. Mailing Add: Route 1, Beverly, Ohio 45715.

CLARK, DAVID D
b. Lincolnton, N.C, 7/4/22; s. Thorne Clark and Mabel Gossett C; m. 4/18/51 to Kathryn Goode; c. David, Allison Thorne, Walter and Caroline. Educ: Wash. and Lee Univ, 41-43; Univ. N.C, LL.B, 50; Phi Delta Theta. Polit. & Govt. Pos: N.C. State Rep, 51-53 & 55-57; pres, Lincoln Co. Young Dem. Club, 54; chmn, N.C. Reorgn. Cmn, 55-57; N.C. State Sen, 63. Bus. & Prof. Pos: Pres, Lynnwood Court, Inc. and Hope Springs Farm Co and chmn, bd. Clark Pub. Co, currently. Mil. Serv: Entered as Pvt, Air Force, 43, released as 1st Lt, 45, after serv. in 5th Air Force, Pac. Theater; Air Medal. Mem: N.C. and Am. Bar Asns; pres, Lincoln Co. Bar Asn, 61; Rotary; VFW; Farm Bur. Rel: Presbyterian. Legal Res: Route 1, Iron Station, N.C. 28080. Mailing Add: Box 9, Lincolnton, N.C. 28092.

CLARK, DONALD E. D
Cmnr, Multnomah Co, Ore.
b. Silverton, Oregon, 4/25/33; s. Harold Edward Clark and Vera Mary C; m. 9/28/52 to Barbara June Bollen; c. Donna Kim and Donald E, Jr. Educ: Vanport Col, 2 years; San Francisco State Col, A.B, 56; Portland State Univ, 1 year; Theta Nu. Polit. & Govt. Pos: Sheriff, Multnomah Co, Ore, 63-67, co. cmnr, 69-; adv, President's Cmn. on Law Enforcement and Justice, Wash, D.C, 66; mem, Task Force on Order and Justice, 68; del, Dem. Nat. Conv, 68; mem, Criminal Law Rev. Cmt, Ore. State Legis, 68-69. Bus. & Prof. Pos: Consult. and dir, Police Design Assoc, Portland, Ore, 67-68; assoc. dir. of Law Enforcement Programs, Portland State Univ, 67-68. Publ: A Forward Step: Educational Backgrounds for Police, Charles C. Thomas, 66; numerous articles in Police Magazine, Police Chief, Law & Order and others. Mem: Nat. Sheriff's Asn.(life membership); Ore. State Sheriff's Asn; Int. Asn. of Chiefs of Police; Int. Asn. of Police Professors; Mil. Police Asn; Am. Asn. of Univ. Professors; Am. Correctional Asn; Am. Soc. of Criminology; Ore. Educ. Asn; Portland Classroom Teachers Asn; Boy's Club of Portland (bd. dirs); Boys and Girls Aid Soc.(bd. dirs); City Club of Portland; Isaac Walton League; Ore. Hist. Soc; Urban League; Navy League (bd. dirs). Reverence for Law Award for Ore, 69. Rel: Unitarian. Legal Res: 4327 S.W. Tunnelwood Dr, Portland, Ore. 97221. Mailing Add: Room 605, Multnomah Co. Courthouse, Portland, Ore. 97204.

CLARK, EDWARD A.
b. San Augustine, Tex, 7/15/06; m. to Anne Metcalfe C; c. Lelia (Mrs. Douglas C. Wynn); three grandchildren. Educ: Tulane Univ, B.A, 26; Univ. Tex, LL.B, 28. Polit. & Govt. Pos: Attorney, San Augustine Co, Tex, 29-30; Asst. Attorney Gen, Tex, 31-34; secy. to Gov, Tex, 35-36; Secy. of State, Tex, 37-39; U.S. Ambassador to Australia, 65-68. Bus. & Prof. Pos: Sr. partner, law firm, Clark, Thomas, Harris, Denius and Winters, 39-65; pres, First Nat. Bank, San Augustine, 59-; chmn. bd, Capital Nat. Bank, Austin, 60- Mil. Serv: Capt, Army, 42-45. Mem: Am. and Tex. State Bar Asns; trustee, Allen Mil. Acad. Mailing Add: P.O. Box 1148, Austin, Tex. 78767. (1967)

CLARK, ERNEST D. R
N.H. State Rep.
b. Kingston, N.H, 7/23/94; married; c. 2. Educ: Sanborn Seminary. Polit. & Govt. Pos: N.H. State Rep, 61-; former selectman. Bus. & Prof. Pos: Retired Rural Letter Carrier. Mem: Universalist Soc; Odd Fellows; N.H. Rural Carriers Asn. Rel: Protestant. Mailing Add: RFD, East Kingston, N.H. 03827. (1967)

CLARK, EZRA THOMPSON R
Utah State Sen.
b. Farmington, Utah, 12/3/14; s. Nathan George Clark and Cleo Call C; wid; c. Ezra T, Jr, Anne (Mrs. George C. Pingree), James E, Janet (Mrs. W. Robert Wright), Ilene and Mark H. Educ: Brigham Young Univ, B.S, 37; Alpha Kappa Psi. Polit. & Govt. Pos: City councilman, Bountiful, Utah, 45-46; mem, Davis Co. Sch. Bd, Utah, 52-56; mem, Utah State Sch. Bd, Salt Lake City, 59-60; bd. mem. and pres, Bountiful Water Sub-Conservancy Dist, 55-65; bd. mem, chmn. bd. and pres, Weber Basin Conservancy Dist, 65-; Utah State Sen, 67- Bus. & Prof. Pos: V.pres, Bountiful State Bank, 53-62; pres, Growers Mkt. Co, Salt Lake City, 53-; bd. mem. and pres, Davis Co. Bank, Farmington, 62- Mem: Rotary. Rel: Latter-day Saint. Mailing Add: 1106 East 400 North, Bountiful, Utah 84010.

CLARK, FRANK M. D
U.S. Rep, Pa.
b. Bessemer, Pa, 12/24/15; m. 1941 to Patricia Loy; c. Frank, Jr. and Kelly. Educ: Pittsburgh Sch. of Aeronaut. Polit. & Govt. Pos: Chief of police, Bessemer, Pa, 45; U.S. Rep, 25th Dist, Pa, 54-, mem. pub. works and merchant marine and fisheries cmts. and chmn, Coast Guard and Coast and Geodetic Survey Cmts. and navigation subcmt; del, NATO Parliamentary Conf, 56, inspection tour of NATO Bases, 60 & 63, NATO Conf, Paris, 64 & 66 and Brussels, 67 & 68 and NATO Parliamentary Conf, N.Y.C, 65; del. to visit German Govt, 57, Int. Christian Leadership Peace Conf, The Hague, 58, Nat. Roads Conf, S.Am, 59, Int. Hwy. Conf, 61, Int. Roads Conf, Sydney, Australia, 58 and S.Am, 65 and Coast Guard Loran Sta. in Mediterranean, 68 & 69; del, Dem. Nat. Conv, 68. Mil. Serv: Flight Officer and Glider Pilot, Army Air Force, World War II; Maj, Air Force Res. Mem: Am. Legion (past comdr); VFW (past comdr); 40 et 8; Odd Fellow (Past Grand Master); Consistory; Moose; AAONMS; Bessemer Vol. Fire Dept; Chief of Police Asn. of Pa. Rel: Presbyterian. Legal Res: Bessemer, Pa. 16112. Mailing Add: 2238 Rayburn House Office Bldg, Washington, D.C. 20515.

CLARK, GEORGE THOMAS, JR. R
b. Lumberton, N.C; s. George Thomas Clark; Sarah Carlyle C; m. 9/21/57 to Elizabeth Ann Patman; c. George T, III, William Louis. Educ: Univ. of the South, Sewanee, Tenn, 46-48; Univ. of N.C, A.B, 48-50; Univ. of N.C. Law Sch, LL.B, 52. Polit. & Govt. Pos: N.C. State Rep, 63-68. Bus. & Prof. Pos: Lawyer. Mil. Serv: Naval Res, 53, Lt. Comdr; Commun. Officer, Naval Res. Surface Div, Wilmington, N.C.(inactive duty), 62-64. Mem: New Hanover Co. Bar Asn; N.C. State Bar; Maritime Law Asn. of the U.S; Kiwanis Club of Wilmington. Rel: Episcopal. Mailing Add: 1218 Fairway Dr, Wilmington, N.C. 28401. (1967)

CLARK, HARLAND CALVIN R
S.Dak. State Sen.
b. Lane, S.Dak, 2/18/17; s. Nelson M. Clark and Mabel I. Maynard C; m. 6/7/60 to Marjorie Joan Bishop; c. Gloria, Robert, Sherry, Sandra, Richard, Bryce and Steven. Educ: Dakota Wesleyan, B.A, 39. Polit. & Govt. Pos: Mem, Bd. of Educ, 57-66; S.Dak. State Sen, 66- Mil. Serv: Entered as Air Corps Cadet, Navy, 42, released as Lt.(sg), 45, after serv. as Patrol Plane Comdr, S.Atlantic & European Theaters; Distinguished Flying Cross; Presidential Unit Citation; Navy Commendation. Mem: Shrine; Elks; Am. Legion. Rel: Methodist. Mailing Add: 1809 Eisenhower Circle, Aberdeen, S.Dak. 57401.

CLARK, HAROLD B. D
Mich. State Rep.
b. Saskatchewan, Canada, 5/5/27; married; c. Wayne, Karen, Gary and Lynn. Educ: Univ. West Ont, B.A; Univ. Detroit, LL.B; Delta Theta Phi. Polit. & Govt. Pos: Mich. State Rep, 64-; chief trial lawyer, off. of Macomb Co. Prosecuting Attorney; v.pres, East Detroit Bd. of Educ; Dem. precinct del. Bus. & Prof. Pos: Attorney. Mem: Prosecuting Attorney's Asn; Warren Dem. Club; Nat. Asn. of Sch. Bd. Adminstrs; Macomb Co. Bar Asn; Mich. Asn. of Sch. Bds, Inc; Elks. Rel: Protestant. Mailing Add: 23600 Wellington, Warren, Mich. 48089. (1967)

CLARK, HARRY PATRICK D
Mem, Ala. Dem. State Exec. Cmt.
b. Mobile, Ala, 1/30/10; s. John Michael Clark and Margaret Burns C; m. 7/1/34 to Margaret Ellen McDonough; c. Margaret Constance (Mrs. Sweeney), Harry McDonough and James Michael. Educ: McGill Inst. Grad; Univ. St. Louis, 2 years; Phi Delta Kappa. Polit. & Govt. Pos: Ky. Col. under Gov. Chandalor and Mil. Col. under Gov. White, Miss, 34-38; Mil. Col, Gov. Staff, Ala, 34-66; coordinator, Mobile Co. Dem. Party 50-60; Mil. Col. under Gov. Long, La, 56-60; chmn, Mobile Housing Bd. of Cmnrs, 56-; del, Dem. Nat. Conv, 64 & 68; mem, Ala. Dem. State Exec. Cmt, 66- Bus. & Prof. Pos: Committeeman, Mobile Co, Ward 8, 34-38; owner, H.P. Clark Real Estate Co, 39-66; partner, McDonough Brothers Ice and Coal Co, 40-51; pres, B&C Construct. Co, 58-61. Mil. Serv: Served as Licensed Officer, Merchant Marine, 42-45. Mem: Torpedo Club; hon. mem, Sheriff and Peace Officers, State of Pa; hon. fire cmnr; Mobile Co. Wildlife; PTA; Mobile Country Club; Seafarers' Int. Union of N.Am; K. of C, Coun. 666; v.pres, Jr. C. of C; Mobile Downtown Optimist Club; Mayor's Indust. Adv. Cmt. Achieved Southern Welter Weight Championship, Nat. Amateur Asn. Rel: Roman Catholic. Mailing Add: 1353 Springhill Ave, Mobile, Ala. 36607.

CLARK, HUBERT WOODY D
Ark. State Rep.
b. Forrest City, Ark, 8/1/34; s. Hubert Lee Clark and Vera Sulcer C; m. 5/24/51 to Eunita Reed; c. Mikeal and Scheryl. Educ: Forrest City High Sch, grad. Polit. & Govt. Pos: Ark. State Rep, 69- Mem: Mason (32°); Lions; Forrest City Jr. C. of C.(first v.pres. and bd. dirs, 67-69); bd. dirs, Boy's Club, 67-68. Rel: Baptist. Mailing Add: 2311 E. Broadway, Forrest City, Ark. 72335.

CLARK, JAMES ERLE D
Mem, La. Dem. Exec. Cmt.
b. Strong, Ark, 2/10/29; s. Carey Eugene Clark and Mary Braswell C; m. 1/22/50 to Betty Sue Erskine; c. Christopher George, Daniel David and Jeffrey Frank. Educ: La. Polytech. Inst, B.S, 52; La. State Univ, LL.B, 57; Kappa Sigma; Phi Delta Phi. Polit. & Govt. Pos: 4th cong. dist. campaign mgr. for Gov. John J. McKeithen, 63-67; attorney for inheritance tax collector, Caddo Parish, La, 64-; del, Dem. Nat. Conv, 64 & 68; attorney, Red River Waterway Cmn, La, 67-; mem, La. & Caddo Parish Dem. Exec. Cmts, 67- Bus. & Prof. Pos: Sr. partner, Cook, Clark, Egan, Yancey & King, Attorneys, 57- Mil. Serv: Entered as Pvt, Marines, 46, released as Cpl, 48, after serv. in 1st Marine Div, Continental U.S; Air Force Res, 52-66, Capt. Mem: Shreveport, La. & Am. Bar Asn; Am. Judicature Soc; La. Asn. Defense Counsel; exalted ruler, Shreveport Elks; Mason; Scottish Rite; Shrine. Rel: Methodist. Legal Res: 920 McCormick Blvd, Shreveport, La. 71104. Mailing Add: P.O. Box 77, Shreveport, La. 71102.

CLARK, JAMES F, JR. D
Md. State Sen.
b. Ellicott City, Md, 12/19/18; married. Educ: Iowa State Col, B.S, 41. Polit. & Govt. Pos: Md. State Sen, 63-; Howard Co. Soil Conserv. Dist. Supvr. Bus. & Prof. Pos: Farmer. Mil. Serv: Air Force, 41-45. Mem: Rotary; VFW. Mailing Add: Ellicott City, Md. 21042. (1967)

CLARK, JAMES STERLING D
Ala. State Sen.
b. Eufaula, Ala, 10/7/21; s. Edward Ephriam Clark and Stella Lee Floyd C; m. 1/22/49 to Marie Turner Kendall; c. James Sterling, Jr, Jennie Kendall and William Holleman. Polit. & Govt. Pos: Ala. State Sen, 59- Bus. & Prof. Pos: Partner, Johnston-Clark Co, 60-; chmn. bd, The Citizens Bank of Eufala, 65- Mil. Serv: Sgt, World War II, 42-45. Rel: Methodist. Mailing Add: Eufala, Ala. 36027.

CLARK, JOE P. D
Chmn, Simpson Co. Dem. Cmt, Ky.
b. Franklin, Ky, 6/14/02; s. Albert Chesterfield Clark and Sallie Milliken Butler C; m. 3/31/34 to Charleen Jones. Educ: Centre Col, 25; Cumberland Univ. Law Sch, 28; Sigma Delta Kappa. Polit. & Govt. Pos: City attorney, Franklin, Ky, 34-38; master cmnr, Simpson Circuit Court, 34-62; co. attorney, Simpson Co, 41-53; Circuit Judge, Simpson and Allen Co, 62; Circuit Judge, 49th Dist, Ky, currently; chmn, Simpson Co. Dem. Cmt, 69- Mem: Pres, Franklin C. of C, 41 and Lions Club, 39; master, Simpson Benevolent Lodge; Ky. Farm Bur. Legal Res: 418 S. Main, Franklin, Ky. 42134. Mailing Add: Box 226, Franklin, Ky. 42134. (1967)

CLARK, JOE TAYLOR D
b. Ringgold, Ga, 2/12/11; s. James Harvey Clark and Mary Edith Robinson C; m. to Ruth Isadora Hayes; c. William Henry Harrison and Roddy Joseph Hayes. Polit. & Govt. Pos: Ga. State Rep, 61-66; mayor, Ringgold, 55-56; Dem. Exec.Cmt, Catoosa Co, 38-44. Bus. & Prof. Pos: Sausage mfr. Mem: Pres, Civitan, 47; Rotary. Rel: Presbyterian. Mailing Add: Ringgold, Ga. 30736. (1967)

CLARK, JOHN CONRAD D
Dir, Export-Import Bank of U.S.
b. N.Y.C, 2/19/13; s. John C. Clark and Marie A. Sparnecht C; m. 12/17/49 to Lillian Fischer; c. Roger Scott. Educ: N.Y. Univ. Sch. Bus. Admin, 2 years; Univ. N.C, exten. div. Polit. & Govt. Pos: Dir, Export-Import Bank of U.S, 69- Bus. & Prof. Pos: Pres, John C. Clark & Co, Inc, N.Y.C, 47-67; asst. mgr. bond dept, Chase Manhattan Bank, 47-51; mgr. and v.pres. bond dept, Wachovia Bank & Trust Co, Winston-Salem, N.C, 51-67, sr. v.pres. pub. finance, 67-69. Mil. Serv: Entered as 2nd Lt, Army, 41, released as Maj, 45, after serv. in Anti-Aircraft Artillery, C.Z. and ETO; Lt. Col. inactive, Army; ETO Citation for Ardennes, Rhineland and Cent. Europe Campaigns. Publ: The Bankers Handbook and Popular Govt, Univ. N.C. and Am. Banker, Int. Issue, 11/69. Mem: Rotary; Munic. Forum of N.Y; Munic. Finance Forum; Munic. Treas. Asn. of U.S; past mem, Munic. Securities Cmt, Investment Bankers Asn; past v.chmn. and dir, N.C. Munic. Coun; N.C. Educ. Develop. Coun. Cert. of Award as Mem. of Finance Cmt. of the Gov. of N.C. Study Cmn. on the Pub. Sch. Syst, 68. Rel: Presbyterian. Legal Res: 983 Kenleigh Circle, Winston Salem, N.C. 27106. Mailing Add: 2500 Wisconsin Ave. N.W, Washington, D.C. 20007.

CLARK, JOHN R. D
Fla. State Rep.
b. Hancock, Md, 6/9/24; s. John N. Clark and Della Alderton C; m. 11/18/63 to Geneva Rolfe; c. John R, Jr, Douglas, Robert, Sandra, James, Edward and Randall. Educ: Transylvania Col, B.A, 47; Univ. Ky, M.A, 49; Pi Kappa Alpha. Polit. & Govt. Pos: Fla. State Rep, Polk and Sumter Co, 66- Bus. & Prof. Pos: Elem. sch. prin, 49- Mil. Serv: Entered as Pvt, Army, 45, released as T-4, 46, after serv. in Transportation Corps, ETO, 45-46. Mem: Am. Legion. Rel: Protestant. Mailing Add: 3118 E. Henderson Circle, Lakeland, Fla. 33803.

CLARK, JOHNNY R. D
Chmn, Burke Co. Dem. Party, N.C.
b. Morganton, N.C, 12/1/33; s. Robert D. Clark and Anna Keller C; m. 5/28/54 to Nancy Nantz; c. Johnny R, Jr, Joan D, Jeffery A. and Jeanne N. Educ: Caldwell Col. of Commerce and Bus. Sch, 56-57. Polit. & Govt. Pos: Mem, Burke Co. Dem. Exec. Cmt, 64-65; chmn, Burke Co. Dem. Party, 66-; mem, Oak Hill Sch. Bd, 68-69. Bus. & Prof. Pos: Owner, Clark Ins. Agency, 65-; partner-v.pres, Table Rock Investment Corp, 67- Mem: U.S. Life Underwriters Asn; Moose; Elks; Oak Hill Recreation Found; Life Underwriters Asn.(local v.pres); Ruritan Nat.(nat. v.pres). Ruritan of Year, Burke Co, 60; Outstanding Dist. Gov. Ruritan Nat, 64; Winner Ruritan Nat. Expansion Award, 64. Rel: Methodist. Legal Res: Route 5, Morganton, N.C. 28655. Mailing Add: P.O. Box 916, Morganton, N.C. 28655.

CLARK, KIMBALL D
b. St. Louis, Mo, 11/19/28; s. Bennett Champ Clark and Miriam Marsh C; m. 10/31/50 to Adelaide M. Coble; c. Ann Kimball. Educ: Univ. Mo, 46-47; Washington and Lee Univ, 47-49; Sigma Delta Chi; Sigma Chi. Polit. & Govt. Pos: Admin. Asst, U.S. Rep. W.R. Hull, Jr, Mo. Bus. & Prof. Pos: Reporter, Kans. City, 50-57. Mil. Serv: Mo. Nat. Guard, 35th Inf. Div, 51-56. Mailing Add: 3807 N. Abingdon St, Arlington, Va. 22207.

CLARK, LEE HINCHMAN R
Secy, Rep. State Cent. Cmt, Mich.
b. Bryn Mawr, Pa, 10/7/25; s. Lee Hinchman Clark and Margaret Bellows C; m. 9/13/50 to Nancy Covert Wensinger; c. Susan, Elizabeth, Lee, III and Anne. Educ: Marquette Univ, B.M.E, 46; Univ. Mich, M.B.A, 49; Tau Beta Pi; Pi Tau Sigma; Pi Mu Epsilon; Phi Eta Sigma; Alpha Sigma Phi; Alpha Kappa Psi. Polit. & Govt. Pos: Trustee, Grosse Ile Twp, Wayne Co, Mich, 57- and Rep. precinct del, 62-; chmn, Grosse Ile Rep. Club, 62-64; mem. exec. cmt, Rep. State Cent. Cmt, Mich, 63-65 & 69-, secy, 69-; del, Rep. Nat. Conv, 64 & 68; chmn, 16th Cong. Dist. Rep. Cmt, Mich, 64-69; mem. exec. cmt, Southeast Mich. United Rep. Fund, 69- Bus. & Prof. Pos: Realtor, self-employed, Grosse Ile, Mich, 54- Mil. Serv: Entered as A/S, Navy, 43, released as Ens, 46. Mem: Grosse Ile Rotary Club (past pres); South. Wayne Co. C. of C.(dir). Named Realtor of the Year, Down River Bd. of Realtors, 62. Rel: Episcopal. Legal Res: 29719 E. River Rd, Grosse Ile, Mich. 48138. Mailing Add: Box 98, Grosse Ile, Mich. 48138.

CLARK, LYN HENDERSON D
Secy, Montgomery Co. Dem. Cent. Cmt, Md.
b. N.Y.C, 12/15/32; d. Leon Henderson and Myrlie Hamm H; m. 10/9/54 to William Giddings Clark; c. Elizabeth Henderson and William Giddings, Jr. Educ: George Wash. Univ, B.A, 54; Chi Omega. Polit. & Govt. Pos: Off. dir, Citizens for Kennedy, 60; v.chmn, Joseph D. Tydings Senate Campaign, Md, 62; del. and secy, Md. del, Dem. Nat. Conv, 68; secy, Montgomery Co. Dem. Cent. Cmt, currently. Mem: V.pres, George Wash. Univ. Alumni Asn; mem. bd, Montgomery Co. Heart Asn. Rel: Episcopal. Mailing Add: 9810 Summit Ave, Kensington, Md. 20795.

CLARK, MEREDITH P. R
Rep. Nat. Committeewoman, V.I.
b. Oconto Falls, Wis, 1/14/27; m. 6/24/50 to Philip Clark; c. James William and Meriweather Kaye. Educ: Lawrence Univ, B.A, 48; N.Y. Sch. of Soc. Work, courses, 49. Polit. & Govt. Pos: Cand, first elected bd. of educ, V.I; territorial secy, Rep. Party, 64-68, br. treas, St. Croix, 65-67; exec. v.chmn, V.I. Nixon for President Cmt. and mem, V.I. Inauguration Cmt. for Nixon-Agnew; Rep. Nat. Committeewoman, V.I, 68- Bus. & Prof. Pos: Dept. head of stock, Saks Fifth Ave, 48-49; psychiat. social work, 49-50; secy, U.S. Govt, 51-53, V.I. Tel. Co, 56 and law off, 56-57. Mem: Red Cross; den mother, Boy Scouts; Commun. Theatre; Concert Soc; League of Women Voters; pres. Psi Chap, Kappa Delta, 47-48. Rel: Methodist. Mailing Add: Box 788, Christiansted, St. Croix, V.I. 00820.

CLARK, NATHANIEL DOUGLAS D
Utah State Rep.
b. Liberty, Utah, 9/29/94; s. Charles Edward Clark and Sally Ann Barker C; m. 1/26/26 to Nellie Corea Palmer (deceased); c. Nathaniel Palmer, Colleen, Wessley DeWayne and David Leon. Educ: Davis High; Weber Acad. Polit. & Govt. Pos: Mem, Utah Dem. State Cent. Cmt, treas, 4 years; mem, Weber Co. Dem. Cmt; chmn, 33rd and 40th Dists. Dem. Orgn, 40-, and Fifth Dist. Dem. Orgn, 12 years; Utah State Rep, 65-66 & 69-, mem, Hwys, Patronage, Mgt, Polit. Subdiv, Pub. Health, Gen. Affairs and Agr. and Irrigation Cmts, Utah House of Rep; Sgt-at-Arms, Utah State Senate; mem, legis. coun, 20 years; mem, Weber Area Coun. of State Govt; mem, Ogden Improv. Prog. Bus. & Prof. Pos: Sales rep, John Scowcroft Co, 40-44; sales rep, Hewlett Co, 44-62; former health inspector, Ogden. Mem: Sons of Utah Pioneers; Utah State Hist. Soc. Rel: Latter-day Saint; mem, Ogden Stake High Coun, 20 years and Ordinance Worker, 24 years. Mailing Add: 2025 Jefferson Ave, Ogden, Utah 84401.

CLARK, NEWMAN H. R
Wash. State Rep.
b. Hawthorne, N.J. 1899; m. to Marian C; c. two sons. Educ: Univ. of Wash. Law Sch. grad. Polit. & Govt. Pos: Wash. State Rep, 50- Bus. & Prof. Pos: Lawyer. Mil. Serv: Army, World War I; Navy, World War II. Mem: Mason; Shrine. Mailing Add: 1625 IBM Bldg, Seattle, Wash. 98101. (1967)

CLARK, PHILIP CANNADY R
Mem. Territorial Cmt, Rep. Party, V.I.
b. Hutchinson, Kans, 6/4/26; s. Walter Lawrence Clark and Mabel Cannady C; m. 6/24/50 to Meredith Kaye Plier; c. James William and Meriweather Kaye. Educ: Univ. Wisconsin, Madison, 43 & 46-47; Lawrence Col, B.S, 48; Northwest. Univ, B.S, 46; Univ. Colo, 54-55; Tau Beta Pi; Chi Epsilon; Phi Mu Alpha; Delta Tau Delta; Sextant. Polit. & Govt. Pos: Mem, Territorial Cmt, Rep. Party, V.I, 66- and first v.chmn, 66-68; del, Rep. Nat. Conv, 68; mem, V.I. Bd. Elec, St. Croix, 68- Bus. & Prof. Pos: Asst. mgr, Little Harbor Club, Mich, summers, 45-58; asst. mgr, Thunder Mt. Resort, Colo, summer 55; land surveyor, Charles L. Hilbron & Assoc, Inc, Christiansted, St. Croix, V.I, 56-57; v.pres. and gen. mgr, Young-Clark Ins. Ltd, 57-; treas, V.I. Title & Trust Co, 57-66 and pres, 67-; licensed ins. agent, 57-; treas, Pentheny, Ltd, 61- Mil. Serv: Entered as A/S, Naval Res, 44-46 & 48-54, released as Lt, 54, after serv. as Beachmaster, Underwater Demolition, Amphibious Forces, Atlantic Fleet, 48-54, Res, 43-69, Lt; Retired. Mem: Ins. Agents Asn. V.I; charter mem. and former dir, Rotary Club St. Croix; dir, St. Croix C. of C; dir, Island Center of St. Croix; past pres. and former dir, Tennis Club of St. Croix; St. Croix Yacht Club; St. Croix Auditor, Boy Scouts, 64-69; Capitol Hill Club, D.C; Naval Res. Asn; Navy League U.S. Rel: Presbyterian. Legal Res: Estate the Sight, Christiansted, St. Croix, V.I. 00820. Mailing Add: P.O. Box 788, Christiansted, St. Croix, V.I. 00820.

CLARK, RAMSEY D
b. Dallas, Tex, 12/18/27; m. to Georgia Welch; c. Ronda Kathleen and Tom C. Educ: Univ. Tex, B.A, 49; Univ. Chicago, M.A, 50, J.D, 51. Polit. & Govt. Pos: Asst. attorney gen, Dept. Justice, 61-65, dep. attorney gen, 65-66, acting attorney gen, 66-67, attorney gen, 67-68. Bus. & Prof. Pos: Assoc. and partner, Law Firm of Clark, Reed & Clark, 51-61; partner, Paul, Weiss, Goldberg, Rifkind, Wharton & Garrison, Attorneys-at-Law, 68- Mil. Serv: Marine Corps, 45-46. Mem: Fed. Bar Asn.(pres, 64, 65); Am, Tex. and Dallas Bar Asns; Am. Judicature Soc.(dir, 63); Southwest. Legal Found. Alumni Medal, Univ. Chicago Alumni Asn, 69. Mailing Add: 37 W. 12th St, New York, N.Y. 10011.

CLARK, RAYMOND E. D
b. 11/3/19; m. 5/12/43; c. Three daughters. Educ: S.Dak. State Univ, B.S. Polit. & Govt. Pos: S.Dak. State Rep, 64-69; plant quarantine officer, State Dept. of Agr. Bus. & Prof. Pos: Nursery man. Mil. Serv: Army Air Force, pilot, 4 years. Rel: Catholic. Mailing Add: Milbank, S.Dak. 57252. (1967)

CLARK, RICHARD CLARENCE D
b. Paris, Iowa, 9/14/29; s. Clarence Clark and Bernice Anderson C; m. 6/6/54 to Jean Shirley Gross; c. Julie Ann and Thomas Richard. Educ: Upper Iowa Univ, B.A, 53; Univ. Md, Wiesbaden, Germany, 50-52; Univ. Frankfurt, Germany, 51-52; Univ. Iowa, M.A, 56; secy, Phi Alpha Theta; Pi Kappa Delta. Polit. & Govt. Pos: Campaign worker, Hershell Loveless for Gov, 56 & 58 and Harold E. Hughes for Gov, 62; mem. campaign staff, E.B. Smith for U.S. Sen, 62; chmn, Gov. Legis. Cmt, 63; mem, Dem. Platform Cmt, 62 & 64; pres, Fayette Commun. Sch. Bd, 62-65; chmn, Off. Emergency Planning in Iowa and Iowa Civil Defense Admin, 63-65; mem, Gov. Cmn. on State and Local Govt, 64-; admin. asst. to U.S. Rep. John C. Culver, 65-69; campaign mgr, Culver for Cong, 64, 66 & 68. Bus. & Prof. Pos: Eng. teacher, Wadena High Sch, Iowa, 53-54; research asst, Univ. Iowa, 55-56, instr. hist, 56-59; asst. prof. hist, Upper Iowa Univ, 59-64. Publ: Witches Beware, Northwest. Univ. Press, 53; Some Personal Observations on the Russian Economy, Mo. Valley Research & Develop. Coun, 63; Political Implications Mobility in the Public Service, Am. Soc. of Pub. Admin, 66. Mil. Serv: Entered as Pvt, Army, 50, released as Cpl, 52, after serv. in 78th Field Artil, Intel, Germany, 51-52. Mem: Am. Hist. Asn, Conf. on European Hist; Am. Asn. Advancement of Slavic Studies; Am. Asn. Univ. Prof; UN Asn. of the U.S; Iowa Asn. Sch. Bds; Am. Civil Liberties Union; Bd. Int. Educ; Conf. on Slavic and E.European Hist. Named Nat. Oratorical Champion and Nat. Discussion Champion, 53. Mailing Add: 1825 Eighth Ave, Marion, Iowa 52302.

CLARK, RICHARD OWEN D
Mayor, Albany, Calif.
b. Kansas City, Mo, 1/29/31; s. Sterling Howard Clark and Elizabeth C; m. 1/1/69 to Gloria Clare Molina. Educ: St. Mary's Col, Moraga, Calif, B.A, 55; Univ. Calif, 55; Univ. San Francisco, 59-60; Debate Soc; West. All-Stars (Football), 54; St. Mary's Football Championship Team, 54. Polit. & Govt. Pos: Chmn, Albany Dem. Party, Calif, 62 & 64; alternate del, Dem. Nat. Conv, 64 & 68; mem. tax equalization bd, Alameda Co, 65, chmn, Local Agency Formation Cmn, 69 and chmn, Interagency Coun. Waterfront Planning, 69; mayor, Albany, Calif, 66-; mem, Alameda Co. Dem. Cent. Cmt, 66-; mem. cmt. bldg. laws, League Calif. Cities, 67; co-chmn, Alameda Co. for Robert Kennedy Campaign, 68; mem, Calif. State Dem. Cent. Cmt, Seventh Cong. Dist, 68-; mem, Dem. State Cent. Cmt, 69; v.chmn. and chmn, Alameda Co. Mayors Conf, 69; mem, Asn. Bay Area Govt, 69; del, Seventh Cong. Dist. Dem. Coun, 69. Bus. & Prof. Pos: Claims adjuster, Travelers Ins. Co, San Francisco, 62-66; agent, N.Y. Life Ins. Co, 66-68; agent, Farmers Ins. Group, Oakland, 69- Mil. Serv: Entered as 2nd Lt, Marines, 55, released, 59; Maj, Res. Helicopter Squadron, 69. Mem: Albany C. of C; Marine Corps ROA. Outstanding Men of Am. award, Jr. C. of C, 66; Outstanding Commun. Serv. award, Lions, 67. Rel: Roman Catholic. Legal Res: 941 Taylor St, Albany, Calif. 94706. Mailing Add: City Hall, 1000 San Pablo Ave, Albany, Calif. 94706.

CLARK, RICHARD SCHUYLER D
N.C. State Rep.
b. Wadesboro, N.C, 2/12/27; s. H.G. Clark, Sr. and Ruby Lee Hardy C; m. 6/14/53 to Margaret Gerock; c. Connie, Nancy, Mary Margaret and Elizabeth Ann. Educ: Pfeiffer Col, 46-47; Wake Forest Col, 47-48, Sch. Law, LL.B, 51; Phi Delta Phi. Polit. & Govt. Pos: Chmn, Randolph Co. Dem. Exec. Cmt, 58-60; solicitor, Randolph Co. Recorder's Court, 58-60; solicitor, Recorder's Court, Liberty, 59; mem, N.C. Gen. Statutes Cmn, 63-65; N.C. State Rep, 67- Bus. & Prof. Pos: Secy-Treas, 19th Judicial Dist. Bar, N.C, 55-56. Mil. Serv: Entered as Seaman 3/C, Navy, 45, released as Seaman 1/C, 46, after serv. in S.Pac, 45-46. Mem: Am, N.C. and Union Co. Bar Asns; Monroe-Union Co. C. of C; Moose; Optimist. Rel: Episcopal. Legal Res: 702 Kintyre Dr, Monroe, N.C. 28110. Mailing Add: P.O. Box 308, Monroe, N.C. 28110.

CLARK, RICHARD WAYNE D
Fla. State Rep.
b. San Antonio, Tex, 5/9/33; s. Stephen Peter Clark and Gertuide Cecelia C; m. 10/13/56 to Diane LaPrade; c. Lisa Marie, Richard Wayne and Christina Lee. Educ: Loyola Univ, 2 years; Upsilon Beta Lambda. Polit. & Govt. Pos: Fla. State Rep, 68- Bus. & Prof. Pos: Secy-owner, Clark Construction Co. Inc, 55- Mil. Serv: Combat Engrs, Army, Korean War, 53-55, Pfc. Mem: Moose; Elks; Lions; K. of C; AFL-CIO. Rel: Catholic. Legal Res: 6725 S.W. 133rd Terr, Miami, Fla. 33156. Mailing Add: 45 Giralda Ave, Coral Gables, Fla. 33134.

CLARK, ROBERT GEORGE Independent
Miss. State Rep.
b. Ebenezer, Miss; s. Robert Flecher Clark and Julian Williams C; single. Educ: Jackson State Col, B.S, 53; Fla. Agr. & Mech. Univ, study in Health, Phys. Educ. and Recreation, 60; Mich. State Univ, M.A, 61; West. Mich. Univ, study in Math. and Sci, 62. Polit. & Govt. Pos: Pres, Black Elec. Officials of Miss, 67-; Miss. State Rep, 67-; del, Dem. Nat. Conv, 68. Bus. & Prof. Pos: Pres, Miss Dept. of Health, Phys. Educ. & Recreation, 65- Publ: 'Political Power Prelude to Change,' Afro-Am, 68. Mem: Pres, Holmes Co. Teachers Asn, 69- Coach of the Year, 66; Man of the Year Award in Commun. Serv, 68; Man of the Year in State Affairs, 69; Outstanding Serv. & Inspiration to Humanity Award. Rel: Baptist. Legal Res: State Capitol, Jackson, Mississippi 39202. Mailing Add: P.O. Box 184, Lexington, Miss. 39095.

CLARK, ROBERT LYBROOK D
b. Stuart, Patrick Co, Va; single. Educ: Randolph-Macon Col; Lambda Chi Alpha. Polit. & Govt. Pos: Va. State Del, 58-69. Bus. & Prof. Pos: Partner, Clark Bros Co; mem. bd. dirs, Patrick Co. Bank; pres. bd. dirs, R.J. Reynolds-Patrick Co. Mem. Hosp; v.pres, Patrick Henry Br, Univ. Va. Mil. Serv: Navy, $3\frac{1}{2}$ years. Mem: Am. Legion; Downtown Club Richmond; Mason; Scottish Rite; Shrine; Rotary; Eastern Star (bd. gov, Eastern Star Home, Richmond). Rel: Baptist; Deacon, Stuart Baptist Church. Mailing Add: P.O. Box 385, Stuart, Va. 24171. (1967)

CLARK, SHIRLEY M. R
N.H. State Rep.
b. Waterbury, Conn, 5/13/23; married. Educ: Pa. State Col; Univ. of N.H, B.A, M.A; Phi Kappa Phi; Phi Beta Kappa; Pi Gamma Mu; Pi Sigma Alpha. Polit. & Govt. Pos: N.H. State Rep, 61- Mem: Lee Planning Bd; Am. Acad. of Polit. & Soc. Sci; pres, Lee Stompers; N.H. Women's Golf Asn. Rel: Episcopal. Mailing Add: RFD 1, Newmarket, N.H. 03857. (1967)

CLARK, STEPHEN PATRICK D
Mayor, Miami, Fla.
b. Florence, Kans, 11/19/23; s. Stephen Peter Clark and Gertrude Mary Fisher C; m. 6/8/69 to Fay Knowles; c. Peter, James, Theresa, John, Cecile and Paul. Educ: Univ. Miami, $2\frac{1}{2}$ years. Polit. & Govt. Pos: Cmnr, Miami, Fla, 63-67, mayor, 67- Bus. & Prof. Pos: V.pres, Clark Construction Co. of Miami, Inc, 57- Mil. Serv: Entered as Pvt, Army Air Corps, 43 released as Sgt, 46, after serv. in 153rd AACS Squadron, Caribbean Theatre, 45-46. Am. Theatre Good Conduct Medal. Mem: Nat. League of Cities; U.S. Conf. Mayors; Fla. League Munic; Dade League Munic; Greater Miami C. of C; Fla. State

C. of C; Am. Legion Moose; Elks; VFW; Dade Co. Young Dem; Grapeland Heights Civic Asn; Tiger Bay Club; K. of C. Gen. Employees of City of Miami Outstanding Citizen Award; DAV Nat. Commanders Award; Amvets Special Achievement Award; Consolidation Fighter of the Year, Dade League of Munic. Rel: Catholic. Mailing Add: 3051 N. W. 4th St, Miami, Fla. 33125.

CLARK, THEODORE NICHOLS R
Secy, Anne Arundel Co. Rep. Cent. Cmt, Md.
b. Owings Mills, Md, 8/4/26; s. Herbert Bender Clark and Juanita Manger C; m. 6/18/49 to Elsie Jean Heer; c. Deborah Jean, Herbert Christopher and John Stephen. Educ: Glen Burnie High Sch, grad, 44; Baltimore Inst, Assoc. of Acct. and Bus. Admin, 49. Polit. & Govt. Pos: Rep. precinct leader, Third Dist, First Precinct, Anne Arundel Co, Md, 58-64; Rep. dist. leader, Third Dist, 66-69; secy, Anne Arundel Co. Rep. Cent. Cmt, 66-; del, Rep. Nat. Conv, 68; mem, Md. Apprentice and Training Coun, 68- Bus. & Prof. Pos: Chmn, bd, Heer Bros, Inc, Baltimore, 49- Mil. Serv: Entered as Pre-Aviation Cadet, Air Force, 45, released as Aviation Cadet, 46, after serv. in Training Unit. Mem: Assoc. Builders & Contractors, Md, Inc; Bldg. Cong. & Exchange, Baltimore; Kiwanis; Rock Hill Beach Improv. Asn; YMCA; Bus. Men's Club Gr. Baltimore. Rel: Methodist. Mailing Add: Box 530, Route 6, Pasadena, Md, 21122.

CLARK, THOMAS CAMPBELL D
b. Dallas, Tex, 9/23/99; s. William H. Clark and Jennie Falls C; m. 11/8/24 to Mary Ramsey; c. William Ramsey, Mildred (Mrs. Thomas R. Gronlund) and Thomas Campbell Jr.(deceased). Educ: Va. Mil. Inst, 17-18; Univ. of Tex, A.B. 21, LL.B, 22; Phi Alpha Delta; Delta Tau Delta; Order of the Coif. Hon. LL.D, Bethany Col, 45, John Marshall Col, 45, Centre Col, Tex. Tech. Col, Mo. Valley Col, 48, Dickinson Sch. Law, 59, Northwest. Univ, 60, Vincennes Univ, 60, St. Louis Univ, Univ. Mont, 61, Univ. Maine, 62, Boston Univ, Ohio Wesleyan Univ, St. John's Univ, Univ. San Diego, Suffolk Univ, George Wash. Univ, N.Y. Univ. Law Sch, Syracuse Univ, and La Salle Col. Polit. & Govt. Pos: Civil dist. attorney, Dallas Co, Tex, 27; asst. attorney gen. in charge antitrust div, Dept. Justice, 43 and in charge criminal div, 43-45, attorney gen, 45-49; assoc. justice, U.S. Supreme Court, 49-67; dir, Fed. Judicial Center, 68- Bus. & Prof. Pos: Assoc, Clark and Clark, Dallas, 22-27. Mil. Serv: 153rd Inf, Army, World War I. Mem: State Bar Tex; Am, Dallas and Fed. Bar Asns; hon. fel. Am. Col. Trial Lawyers; chmn. bd. dirs, Nat. Col. State Trial Judges; fel. Inst. Judicial Admin.(pres, 66-67); mem. vis. cmt, Univ. Chicago Law Sch; Am. Legion; VFW; Mason (33°); Shrine; Eagles; Univ, Chevy Chase, Exchange, Alfalfa, Burning Tree and Nat. Lawyers Club; mem-at-lg, Nat. Coun. Boy Scouts. Silver Buffalo Award, 60 and Silver Beaver Award, 62, Boy Scouts; Gold Medal, Am. Bar Asn, 62; First Annual Award, Am. Judicature Soc, 62; President Key, Loyola Univ; Distinguished Alumnus Awards, Ex-Students Asn, Univ. Tex, 62 and Univ. Tex. Law Sch, 64. Rel: Presbyterian. Legal Res: Dallas, Tex. Mailing Add: 2101 Connecticut Ave, N.W, Washington, D.C. 20008.

CLARK, WALTER HUGH D
b. Johnston, S.C, 12/4/29; s. W. H. Clark, Sr. and Minnie Jordan C; single. Educ: Johnston High Sch, 47. Polit. & Gov. Pos: S.C. State Rep, 61-66; Johnston City Coun, 53-60. Bus. & Prof. Pos: Cotton Gin, farmer, fertilizer. Mem: Mason; V.Pres. and Dir, Lions Club. Who's Who in the Southland, Outstanding Young Men of Am, 65 eds. Rel: deacon, Johnston Baptist Church. Mailing Add: Box 96, Johnston, S.C. 29832. (1967)

CLARK, WILLIAM GEORGE D
b. Chicago, Ill, 7/16/24; s. John Smith Clark and Ita Kennedy C; m. 11/28/46 to Rosalie Locatis; c. Merrilee, William G, Jr, John S.V, Donald D. and Robert Kennedy. Educ: Loyola Univ, Chicago, 42-43; Univ. Mich, Army Specialized Training, 43-44; Loyola Univ, Chicago, 44; DePaul Univ, LL.B, 46; Delta Theta Phi; Univ. Club of Loyola. Hon. LL.D, John Marshall Law Sch, Chicago, 62. Polit. & Govt. Pos: Attorney for pub. adminstr, Cook Co, Chicago, Ill, 49-52; Ill. State Rep, 53-54; Ill. State Sen, 55-56; Ill. State Rep, 57-60, Majority Leader, Ill. House of Rep, 59-60; Attorney Gen, Ill, 61-69; del, Dem. Nat. Conv, 68. Bus. & Prof. Pos: Attorney-at-law, Crane, Kearney, Korzen & Phelan, 47-49, Crane, Kearney, Phelan & Clark, 49-53 and private practice, 53-61; partner, Arvey, Hodes & Mantynband, 69- Mil. Serv: Pvt, Army, 43-44, serv. in Army Specialized Training. Mem: Am. and Ill. State Bar Asns.(mem, Cmt. on Judicial Ethics, 61-69), Patron Mem, 63-68, mem, Legis. Cmt, Chicago, 53-68, mem, Spec. Consumer Credit Remedies Cmt, 61-62; West Suburban Bar Asn.(mem. bd. gov, 62-63, legis. and judiciary cmts, 53-68); Cath. Lawyers Guild of Chicago; Amvets; Am. Legion; Moose; Ancient Order of Hibernians; Irish Fel. Club of Chicago (pres, 62); Eagles; Elks; K. of C; Cath. War Vet; Chicago Athletic Asn. Field & Stream Magazine Award for catching World Record Arctic Grayling, 59. Rel: Catholic. Mailing Add: 1420 N. Lake Shore Dr, Chicago, Ill. 60610.

CLARK, WILLIAM HENRY, III D
Mem, Tex. State Dem. Exec. Cmt.
b. Dallas, Tex, 12/11/30; s. William Henry Clark, Jr. and Martha Mildred Harral C; m. 1/28/55 to Anne Kerbey Williams; c. Kimberley Anne, William Henry, IV and James Littlefield. Educ: Amherst Col, 48-49; Univ. Tex, Austin, B.A. and LL.B; Phi Delta Theta; Phi Alpha Delta. Polit. & Govt. Pos: Asst. Attorney Gen, State of Tex, 55-56; chmn, Dallas Co. Dem. Exec. Cmt, 63-66; mem, Tex. State Dem. Exec. Cmt, 66-; alternate del, Dem. Nat. Conv, 68. Bus. & Prof. Pos: Assoc, Clark, Reed & Clark, Attorneys, Dallas, 56-63; partner, Clark, West, Keller, Sanders & Ginsberg, Attorneys, 63- Mem: Dallas Bar Asn; Tex. Bar Asn.(secy, Fels. of Tex. Bar Found. and mem. legis. cmt); Am. Bar Asn.(mem. coun, pub. utility law); Newcomen Soc. N.Am; bd. dirs, City Club of Dallas; Dallas Petroleum Club; Brook Hollow Club; Austin Club; mem. bd, Voc. Nurses Asn; Soroptimist Clubs for Crippled Children; United Cerebral Palsy Asn. Dallas(pres. and past chmn. bd); Exec. Toastmasters Club Dallas (past pres). Rel: Methodist; mem. off. bd, Highland Park Methodist Church. Legal Res: 6116 Westwick, Dallas, Tex. 75205. Mailing Add: 2424 First National Bank Bldg, Dallas, Tex. 75202.

CLARKE, BIEHL PATRICK 'BUNDY' R
b. New York, N.Y, 12/1/25; s. Tracy Leeds Clarke and Mary Jeannette Biehl C; single. Educ: Yale Univ, A.B, 48; Columbia and George Washington Univs, post grad. work. Polit. & Govt. Pos: Pres, Larchmont-Mamaroneck Young Rep. Club, N.Y, 50-52; v.pres, Westchester Co. Asn. Young Rep. Clubs, N.Y, 51-55; orgn. dir, Westchester Co. Citizens for Eisenhower, 52; exec. secy, Young Rep. Nat. Fedn, 53-54; pres, Young Rep. Club, D.C, 61-62; secy, Task Force on Fiscal and Monetary Policies, Rep. Coord. Cmt, 65-; chief research assoc, Rep. Nat. Cmt, 65-68. Bus. & Prof. Pos: Mem. research dept, Warwick & Legler Advert. Agency, N.Y, 48-53; asst. mgr, domestic distribution dept, U.S. C. of C, 54-58, asst. mgr. polit. participation prog, 58-59; pres, Civic Affairs Assocs, Inc, 59-; consult, Am. Med. Polit. Action Cmt, 62-64. Mil. Serv: Army Air Force, 44, Pvt. Publ: Action Course in Practical Politics, C. of C. of U.S, 59; Free Citizens Voting Record, Civic Affairs Assocs, 59, 60 & 61; Precinct Action Course, Civic Affairs Assocs. for Rep. Cong. Cmt, 62. Mem: Yale Club Wash.(bd. dirs, 56-59); Am. Acad. Polit. & Soc. Sci; Am. Econ. Asn; Univ. Club of Wash. Rel: Catholic. Mailing Add: 2612 P St. N.W, Washington, D.C. 20007. (1967)

CLARKE, CLIFTON WINTHROP R
Chmn, Chelsea Rep. City Cmt, Mass.
b. Chelsea, Mass, 2/19/10; s. James Douglas Clarke and Mae Wells C; m. 4/12/36 to Jennie Delores Tarlowski; c. Clifton Winthrop, Jr. Educ: Chelsea Sr. High Sch, 4 years. Polit. & Govt. Pos: Del, Mass. Rep. State Conv, 31-; committeeman, Chelsea Sch. Cmt, 32; originator, Suffolk Co. Rep. Club, 39; chmn, Chelsea Rep. City Cmt, Mass, 40-44, 48-52 & 68-; del, Rep. Nat. Conv, 52 & 56; mem, Mass. Rep. State Finance Cmt, 53; mem, Excise Bd, 61 & 65; chmn, Alcoholic Beverage Cmn, 68-; app. to Chelsea Housing Authority by Gov. Sargent, 69- Bus. & Prof. Pos: Gen. contractor, Chelsea and Boston, Mass, 36-62; mem. bd. dirs, Chestnut Credit Union, Chelsea, 40-44; gen. construction inspector-sr, Metrop. Dist. Cmn, 62- Mem: AF&AM. Rel: Protestant. Mailing Add: 167 Central Ave, Chelsea, Mass. 02150.

CLARKE, HAROLD GRAVELY D
Ga. State Rep.
b. Forsyth, Ga, 9/28/27; s. Jack Holman Clarke and Ruby Ray Lumpkin C; m. 6/28/52 to Nora Gordon; c. Lee Ann, Harold Gravely, Jr, Julia Ray and Elizabeth Gordon. Educ: Univ. of Ga, LL.B, 50; Omicron Delta Kappa; Sigma Alpha Epsilon. Polit. & Govt. Pos: Ga. State Rep, 61- Bus. & Prof. Pos: Attorney. Mil. Serv: Army, S/Sgt; Cert. of Merit; Far East. Command; Army Commendation Ribbon. Mem: Flint Circuit Bar Asn, pres, 60; pres, Forsyth Lions Club; pres, Forsyth Touchdown Club. World War II, managing ed. of Pac. Stars and Stripes. Rel: Presbyterian. Mailing Add: Forsyth, Ga. 31029.

CLARKE, HELEN HOPKINS R
V.chmn, Third Cong. Dist. Rep. Party, Nebr.
b. Woodlawn, Pa, 8/18/11; d. Thomas Richard Hopkins and Ellen Edna Bradford H; m. 10/12/35 to Donald Wallace Clarke; c. Holly (Mrs. Robert J. MacKinnon) and Douglas Wallace. Educ: Allegheny Col, A.B, 33; Phi Beta Kappa; Phi Sigma Iota; Alpha Chi Omega. Polit. & Govt. Pos: Mem. Civil Serv. Cmn, Hastings, Nebr, 36-37; Rep. chmn, IIIA, Precinct, Hastings, 48-58; mem. bd. educ, 50-62 and pres, 60-61; zoning cmnr, Adams Co, 57; pres, Adams Co. Rep. Women, 58-61; v.chmn. Adams Co. Rep. Party, 58-61; mem, Adams Co. Rep. Cent. Exec. Cmt, 58-; mem, State Rep. Cent. Cmt, 64-68; del, Rep. Nat. Conv, 68; mem, Nebr. State Exec. Cmt, 68-; v.chmn, Third Cong. Dist. Rep. Party, 68- Mem: Am. Red Cross.(secy, 44-58); PEO; Lochland Country Club. 1954 Nebr. Heart Chmn. Rel: Presbyterian. Mailing Add: 1124 N. Lincoln Ave, Hastings, Nebr. 68901.

CLARKE, HILDA ROSE R
Conn. State Rep.
b. Norwalk, Conn, 5/5/96; d. Henry Schenk and Rose Kiepler S; m. 6/21/17 to Josiah Stuart Clarke; c. Doris Barbara (Mrs. Osguthorpe) and Stuart Henry. Educ: Col. night courses. Polit. & Govt. Pos: Secy, Stamford Rep. Town Cmt, Conn, 8 years; Conn. State Rep, 55-59 & 67-; committeewoman, Conn. Rep. State Cent. Cmt, 56; chmn, Cmt. Educ. and Welfare, 61-63; clerk, Bd. of Rep, Stamford, 65-67. Mem: Nat. and Conn. Order Women Legis; Stamford Rep. Woman's Club; Family and Children's Serv; hon. life mem. Springdale PTA. Rel: Episcopal. Mailing Add: 81 Palmer St, Springdale, Conn. 06879. (1967)

CLARKE, HUGH HAUSER R
Iowa State Sen.
b. Conrad, Iowa, 8/11/18; s. John L. Clarke and Ruth Hauser C; m. to Frances Winter; c. Jeanne Marie (Mrs. Craig Boller). Educ: Iowa State Univ, 37-38; Farmhouse Fraternity. Polit. & Govt. Pos: Iowa State Sen, 67- Bus. & Prof. Pos: V.Pres, Tomco Genetic Giant, Inc, Iowa, 50-67; dir, Belmond Develop. Corp. Mem: Past pres, Iowa Seed Dealers; past chmn. hybrid corn div, Am. Seed Trade Asn; mem. original bd. dirs, U.S. Feed Grain Coun; Lions; Elks; Mason; Elkahir Shrine; Aircraft Owners and Pilots Asn; Clarmond Country Club. Winner, crops judging contest. Rel: Methodist. Mailing Add: 408 Tenth Ave. N.E, Belmond, Iowa 50421.

CLARKE, JACK WELLS D
Mem, State Dem. Cent. Cmt, La.
b. Abingdon, Va, 6/26/14; s. James Sydnor Clarke and Ottie Wells C; m. 3/24/38 to Dorothy Irelan. Educ: Williams Col, A.B, 35; New York Univ. Sch. Bus. Admin, 35-37; Phi Delta Theta. Polit. & Govt. Pos: V.chmn, Caddo Dem. Asn, La, 66-67, chmn, 67-68; del, Dem. Nat. Conv, 68; chmn, La. Fourth Cong. Dist. Dem. Campaign Cmt, 68; La. Dem. Party Elector, 68; mem, State Dem. Cent. Cmt, 39th Representative Dist, 68-; mem. and v.chmn, Caddo Parish Dem. Exec. Cmt, 68- Bus. & Prof. Pos: Bond analyst and statistician, Dubosque & Co, New York City, 35-37; from asst, budget-statist. dept. to mgr, Lion Oil Co, El Dorado, Ark, 38-42, asst. to pres, 46-51; dir. pub. and financial rels, Tex. East. Transmission Corp, 51-55; exec. v.pres, Freestate Indust. Develop. Co, Shreveport, La, 55-56, pres. and dir, 56-68; pres. and dir, N.Shreveport Develop. Co, 56-68; self employed, 68- Mil. Serv: Entered as Ens, Naval Res, 42, released as Lt, 45, after serving in all theatres, 42-45; Lt, Naval Res, Retired; Am. Theatre and Victory Medals; Pac-Asiatic Ribbon with two Battle Stars; African-European Ribbon with one Battle Star; Philippine Liberation Ribbon with two Battle Stars. Mem: Am Indust. Develop. Coun; Am. Ord. Asn; Int. Coun. Assessing Officers; Int. Coun. Shopping Centers, Inc; Urban Land Inst; La. Real Estate Broker; Shreveport-Bossier Bd. Realtors; Nat. Asn. Real Estate Bd; La. Real Estate Asn; life mem, ROA; Navy League Shreveport; Am. Legion; Shreveport Club; former chmn, Ambassadors Club; Holiday-in-Dixie; gov. bd. and bd. dirs, Shreveport YMCA; dir,

Shreveport Ment. Health Center; Shreveport Cmt. One Hundred; Shreveport C. of C; Bossier City C. of C; Round Table Club; Shreveport-Bossier Found; Shreveport Country Club. Cert. appreciation, Am Petroleum Inst. Rel: Episcopal; former vestryman, St. Mark's Episcopal Church, Shreveport. Legal Res: 708 Azalea Dr, Shreveport, La. 71106. Mailing Add: P.O. Box 7776, Shreveport, La. 71107.

CLARKE, JAMES FRANCIS D
b. Pittsburgh, Pa, 11/26/18; s. John W. Clarke and Mary Hughes C; single. Educ: Univ. Pittsburgh, grad; Univ. Pittsburgh Sch. Law, LL.B, 51. Polit. & Govt. Pos: Co. committeeman, Dem. Party; Pa. State Rep, 59-68; del, Dem. Nat. Conv, 68; prothonotary, Court Common Pleas, Allegheny Co, 68-Bus. & Prof. Pos: Partner, Cauley, Birsk & Clarke, 51- Mil. Serv: Entered as Pvt, Army Air Corps, 41, released as S/Sgt, 45, after serv. in 1st Aircraft Assembly Squadron, European, African and Mid. East. Theatre, 43-45. Mem: Allegheny Co, Pa. and Am. Bar Asns; Am. Judicature Soc; Am. Records Mgt. Asn; VFW; Am. Legion; Lions; C. of C. Rel: Roman Catholic. Mailing Add: 3606 Parkview Ave, Pittsburgh, Pa. 15213.

CLARKE, RUSSELL LELAND R
Mem, Calif. Rep. State Cent. Cmt.
b. Selma, Calif, 3/28/23; s. Rozell Frank Clarke and Karen Nelson C; m. 12/8/62 to Jeanne Dausse; c. Judith (Mrs. Gregory Allan Farmer), Stanley Nelson and Janine Dale. Educ: City Col. of San Francisco, AA, 43. Polit. & Govt. Pos: Mem, Mendocino Co. Rep. Cent. Cmt, 58- and chmn, 60-65; mem, Calif. Rep. State Cent. Cmt, 58-, mem. exec. cmt, 60-64 and secy-treas. co. chmn. asn, 61-65; regional v.pres, Young Rep. of Calif, 59, nat. committeeman, 60 and exec. v.pres, 61; state co-chmn, Young Californians for Nixon for Pres, 60; mem, First Cong. Dist. Rep. Cmt, 60- and orgn. chmn, 60; N. Coast Region chmn, Nixon for Gov. Cmt, 62. Bus. & Prof. Pos: Exec. Bd. Calif. Asn. of Employers, Inc, 66- Mil. Serv: Entered as Pvt, Army, 43, released as M/Sgt, 46, after serv. in 97th Inf. Div. European Theater and Asiatic Theater; Army Res, 46-68, Maj; Am, European, Asiatic Theater, Good Conduct, Japanese Occupation, World War II Victory Medals. Mem: Am. Mil. Engrs; Free and Accepted Masons; Royal Arch Mason; Elks; Am. Legion; Toastmasters; Lions Int; C. of C. Rel: Episcopal. Legal Res: 181 Fairview Court, Ukiah, Calif. 95482. Mailing Add: 245 E. Standley, Ukiah, Calif. 95482.

CLARKE, TERREL E. R
Ill. State Sen.
b. 3/11/20; m. to Catherine; c. Three. Educ: Univ. of Colo, B.S; Harvard Grad. Sch. of Bus. Admin, M.B.A. Polit. & Govt. Pos: Committeeman, Lyons Twp. Rep. Cmt, Ill, 54-62; Ill. State Rep. 4 terms; Ill. State Sen, 66- Bus. & Prof. Pos: Teacher, Univ. of Kans, 2 years; ins. broker. Mil. Serv: Army, 43-46, ETO. Rel: Episcopal. Mailing Add: 4070 Cent. Ave, Western Springs, Ill. 60558.

CLARKSON, C. JACK R
Chmn, Rush Co. Rep. Party, Ind.
b. Rushville, Ind, 12/18/30; s. Harold L. Clarkson and Dorothy V. C; m. 8/9/50 to Jacqueline L. Kiplinger; c. Jean, Jon and Ann. Educ: Butler Univ, B.A, 57; Ind. Univ. Law Sch, J.D, 58; Order of Coif; Phi Delta Phi. Polit. & Govt. Pos: Prosecuting attorney, Rush Co, Ind, 59-66; chmn, Rush Co. Rep. Party, Ind, 64- Mailing Add: 127 W. Second St, Rushville, Ind. 46173.

CLARKSON, E. MILTON D
Chmn, Refugio Co. Dem. Exec. Cmt, Tex.
b. Refugio, Tex, 12/2/20; s. Robert P. Clarkson and Iris Catherine Baumgartner C; m. 12/10/42 to Wilma Belle Summers; c. William Edward (Bill). Educ: Mercy Acad, Refugio, Tex, grad, 38. Polit. & Govt. Pos: Chmn, Refugio Co. Dem. Exec. Cmt, Tex, 67- Bus. & Prof. Pos: Newspaper reporter, Refugio Timely Remarks, 37-39; time keeper and clerk, Heard & Heard, Inc, 39-45, truck dispatcher and br. mgr, 46- Mil. Serv: Entered as Pvt, Army, 42, released as Pfc, 45, after serv. in 333rd Ord. Depot Co, 9th Army, ETO, 43-45; ETO Combat Ribbon. Mem: K. of C.(3°); Am. Red Cross (home serv. chmn, Falfurrias Chap, 49-53 and disaster chmn, Refugio Chap, 66-). Rel: Roman Catholic. Legal Res: 505 W. Heard St, Refugio, Tex. 78377. Mailing Add: P.O. Box 429, Refugio, Tex. 78377.

CLAUDON, ROGER KEITH R
Chmn, Porter Co. Rep. Cent. Cmt, Ind.
b. Waukegan, Ill, 10/21/29; s. Joseph H. Claudon and Ida Frey C; m. 6/15/69 to Jane Hays. Educ: Valparaiso Univ, B.A. and LL.B; Delta Theta Phi. Polit. & Govt. Pos: Chmn, Porter Co. Rep. Cent. Cmt, Ind, 67-; co. attorney, Porter Co, 68- Mem: Ind. State Bar Asn; F&AM; Scottish Rite; Shrine. Rel: Methodist. Mailing Add: 500 Indiana Ave, Valparaiso, Ind. 46383.

CLAUSEN, DON H. R
U.S. Rep, Calif.
b. Ferndale, Calif, 4/27/23; m. to Ollie Piper C; c. Beverly, Dawn Marie. Educ: San Jose State Col; V5 Prog, USN; Calif. Polytech; Weber Col, Ogden, Utah; St. Mary's Col. Polit. & Govt. Pos: U.S. Rep, Calif, 63-; past mem, Bd. of Supvr, Del Norte Co. Bus. & Prof. Pos: Clausen Assoc. Ins. Agency, Crescent City, Calif; Clausen Flying Serv, Crescent City, Calif; Air Ambulance Serv. Mil. Serv: Navy Carrier Pilot, Asiatic-Pac. Mem: Del Norte C. of C; Unit Redwood Empire Asn.(supvr). Legal Res: Crescent City, Calif. 95531. Mailing Add: 7777 Maple Ave, Takoma Park, Md. 20012.

CLAUSSEN, PETER H. R
b. Leigh, Nebr, 12/30/94; m. 1/21/19 to Elsie M. Dasenbrock; c. two. Polit. & Govt. Pos: Mem, Nebr. Unicameral Legis, 57-66; Mem, House of Rep, Bicameral Legis, 1935. Bus. & Prof. Pos: Dir, Stanton Co. REA Dist, 19 years; Supvr, Stanton Co. Soil Conserv. Dist; Pres, Norfolk Prod. Credit Asn; Past Secy, Leigh Farmers Ins. Co, 22 years; Past Pres, State Asn. Mutual Ins. Co; Pres-Dir, Farmer Union Coop. Oil Asn, 29 years. Mem: Sch. Bd. Rel: Lutheran. Mailing Add: Route 2, Leigh, Nebr. 68643. (1967)

CLAWSON, DELWIN MORGAN 'DEL' R
U.S. Rep, Calif.
b. Thatcher, Ariz, 1/11/14; m. 1934 to Marjorie Anderson C; c. Larry, James. Educ: Gila Col, Thatcher, Ariz. Polit. & Govt. Pos: with U.S. Employ. Serv. and Fed. Pub. Housing Authority, 41-47; mem, Park and Recreation Cmn, Compton, Calif, 50-53; mem, Compton City Coun, 53-57; dir, Los Angeles Co. Sanit. Dists, 1, 2 & 8, 57-63; mayor, Compton, 57-63; U.S. Rep, 63- Bus. & Prof. Pos: Salesman and bookkeeper, 34-41; mgr, Mutual Housing Asn. of Compton, 47-63. Mem: Kiwanis Int; Exec. Dinner Club; C. of C; Boy Scouts (chmn. Midland Dist, 60); Commun. Chest (city chmn); Red Cross (city chmn). Citizen of the Year Award, Compton C. of C, 60. Rel: Latter-day Saint. Legal Res: Downey, Calif. Mailing Add: 4201 Massachusetts Ave, Washington, D.C. 20016.

CLAWSON, JAMES HOWARD R
Chmn, Columbia Co. Rep. Cent. Cmt, Ore.
b. Redgranite, Wis, 7/19/20; s. Holly Elmer Clawson and Lida Brooks Graves C; m. 7/19/42 to Nancy Lamberson; c. Burrell Edward, Richard James, Carl William and Wendy Sue. Educ: Univ. of Ore, 2 years; Northwest. Col. of Law, 3 years. Polit. & Govt. Pos: Port cmnr, Port of St. Helens, Ore, 52-60; Rep. precinct committeeman, 58-; chmn, Columbia Co. Rep. Cent. Cmt, 64- Bus. & Prof. Pos: Credit mgr, Portland Gen. Elec. Co, 42-47; pres. and mgr, Credit Bur. of Columbia Co, Inc, 48- Mil. Serv: Entered as A/S, Coast Guard, 42, released as Aviation Machinist 3/C, 45, after serv. in Elizabeth City, N.C. Mem: Am. Legion; Elks; Kiwanis; C. of C; Assoc. Credit Burs. of Am; Am. Collectors Asn; Int. Consumer Credit Asn. Legal Res: 17 Crescent Dr, St. Helens, Ore. 97051. Mailing Add: Box 247, St. Helens, Ore. 97051. (1967)

CLAY, CHARLES E. R
S.Dak. State Rep.
b. Stahl, Mo, 8/10/22; s. Jessie William Clay and Iva A. Thompson C; m. 1/26/46 to Clara Mae Hagen; c. Roberta Jean Kennedy. Educ: Eldora Pub. Sch, 12 years. Polit. & Govt. Pos: City councilman, Hot Springs, S.Dak, 54-56, city auditor, 59-61; del, Rep. State Conv, 61, 63 & 65; S.Dak. State Rep, Custer-Fall River Co, 67-, mem, S.Dak. Indian Cmn. and Appropriation Cmt, 67-, Constitutional Revision Cmn, 69 and Asst. Majority Leader, 69- S.Dak. State House of Rep. Bus. & Prof. Pos: Dir, Black Hills Bd. Realtors, 67-69; mem. state bd. dirs, S.Dak. Real Estate Bd, 68-69; second v.pres, S.Dak. Land Title Asn, 69. Mil. Serv: Entered as Pvt, Air Force, 43, released as T/Sgt, 46, after serv. in Eighth and Second Air Forces, Pac, 46; Korean Conflict, 50-52. Mem: Lions (pres, 59); past pres, Kiwanis and C. of C; Sr. Grand Warden, S.Dak. Masonic Lodge; Am. Legion; VFW. Rel: Protestant. Legal Res: 106 S. Third St, Hot Springs, S.Dak. 57747. Mailing Add: P.O. Box 908, Hot Springs, S.Dak. 57747.

CLAY, LUCIUS DuBIGNON R
b. Marietta, Ga, 4/23/97; s. Alexander Stephen Clay and Francis White C; m. 9/21/18 to Marjorie McKeown; c. Lucius D, Jr. and Frank B. Educ: U.S. Mil. Acad, B.S, 18. Polit. & Govt. Pos: Ambassador, personal rep. of President, Berlin, Germany, 61-62; former chmn, Rep. Nat. Finance Cmt. Bus. & Prof. Pos: Sr. partner, Lehman Bros, 63-; trustee, Cent. Savings Bank; dir, Chase Int. Investment Corp, Lehman Corp, Standard Brands, Inc, Allied Chem. Corp, Continental Can Co. and Presbyterian Hosp, N.Y. Mil. Serv: Instr, Officers' Training Camp, 18-19; Engr. Sch. Application, 19-20; asst. prof. mil. sci. and tactics, Ala. Polytech. Inst, 20-21; construction qm. and post engr, Ft. Belvoir, Va, 21-24; instr. civil eng, U.S. Mil. Acad, 24-27; field mapping, 11th Engrs. C.Z, 27-30; asst. to dist. engr. Pittsburgh, in charge construction lock and dam 2, Allegheny River, 30-33; asst. to chief of engrs, River and Harbor Sect, 33-37; consult. on develop. water resources to Nat. Power Corp, Philippine Commonwealth, 37-38; in charge construction Denison Dam, 38-40; asst. to adminstr, Civil Aeronaut. Admin. on airport prog, 40-41; dir. material, Army Serv. Forces, 42-44; comdr, Normandy Base, 44; dep. dir. war mobilization and reconversion, 45; dep. mil. gov, 45-47; comdr-in-chief, European Command and Mil. Gov, U.S. Zone, Germany, 47-49. Publ: Decision in Germany, 50. Mem: Army and Navy Club; Univ. Club; Links Club; Pinnacle Club; Blind Book Club; Augusta Nat. Club; Bohemian Grove Club; Eastward Ho Club. Mailing Add: 1 William St, New York, N.Y. 10004.

CLAY, WILLIAM LACY D
U.S. Rep, Mo.
b. St. Louis, Mo, 4/30/31; s. Irving C. Clay and Luella Hyatt C; m. 10/10/53 to Carol Ann Johnson; c. Vicki Flynn, William Lacy, Jr. and Michelle Katherine. Educ: St. Louis Univ, B.S. in Hist. and Polit. Sci, 53. Polit. & Govt. Pos: Dem. Alderman, 26th Ward, St. Louis, Mo, 59-64, Dem. committeeman, 64-; U.S. Rep. First Dist, 69- Bus. & Prof. Pos: Real estate broker, St. Louis, Mo, 55-59; mgr, Indust. Life Ins. Co, 59-61; educ. coordinator, Steamfitters Local No. 562, 66-67. Mil. Serv: Entered as Pvt, Army, 53, released as Cpl, 55. Publ: 'Anatomy of an Economic Murder,' St. Louis Bd. of Alderman, 63. Mem: Former exec. bd. mem, St. Louis chap. NAACP; CORE; mem. bd, Narcotics Anonymous; Jr. C. of C; dist. chmn, Friends of Scouts. Distinguished Citizens award, Alpha Kappa Alpha, 69; Argus Award, St. Louis Argus Newspaper, 69. Rel: Catholic. Legal Res: St. Louis, Mo. Mailing Add: 1209 Longworth House Office Bldg, Washington, D.C. 20515.

CLAYBURGH, BENNIE JAMES R
Rep. Nat. Committeeman, N.Dak.
b. Scobey, Mont, 1/31/24; s. Mark John Clayburgh and Anna Horvick C; m. 6/26/48 to Mina Tennison (deceased); c. James, Robert, John and Richard. Educ: Univ. N.Dak, B.A, 46, B.S, 47; Temple Univ. Sch. Med, M.D, 49; Mayo Found, Rochester, Minn, M.S. in Orthopaedic Surgery, 56; Blue Key; Beta Theta Pi. Polit. & Govt. Pos: Mem, N.Dak. State Rep. Exec. Cmt; v.chmn, N.Dak. Rep. State Cmt, 52-54, chmn, 54-55; chmn, Grand Forks Dist. Rep. Exec. Cmt, 52-; del, Rep. Nat. Conv, 64 and alternate del, 68; Rep. nat. committeeman, N.Dak, 68- Bus. & Prof. Pos: Orthopaedic surg, Orthopaedic Clin, Grand Forks, N.Dak, 56- Mil. Serv: Entered as 1st Lt, Air Force Med. Corps, 51, released as Capt, 53, after serv. in 28th Strategic Bomber Wing. Mem: Am. Med. Asn; Am. Acad. Orthopaedic Surg; Am. Bd. Orthopaedic Surg; Clin. Orthopaedic Soc. Rel: Lutheran. Legal Res: 729 Reeves Dr, Grand Forks, N.Dak. 58201. Mailing Add: 201 S. Fourth St, Grand Forks, N.Dak. 58201.

CLAYPOOLE, WILLIAM HARVEY R
Pa. State Rep.
b. Worthington, Pa, 3/30/07; s. Charles Claypoole and Annie Elizabeth

Bouser C; m. 3/31/28 to Evelyn Pearl; c. William Reed. Educ: Elem. sch. Polit. & Govt. Pos: Supt, Armsdale Home & Farm, Armstrong Co, Pa, 32-44, cmnr, 44-67; Pa. State Rep, 61st Dist, 67- Bus. & Prof. Pos: Bank dir. and v.pres, Merchants Nat. Bank, Kittanning, Pa, 48- Mem: Elks; Grange; Odd Fellows; Jr. Order United Am. Mech; Moose; Eagles. Rel: Protestant. Mailing Add: 115 Queen St, Kittanning, Pa. 16201.

CLAYTON, BILL W. D
Tex. State Rep.
b. Olney, Tex, 9/11/28; s. William Thomas Clayton and Myrtle F. Chitwood C; m. 3/10/50 to Delma Jean Dennis; c. Brenda Jean and Thomas Wayne. Educ: Tex. A&M Col, B.S. in Agr. Econ. Polit. & Govt. Pos: Tex. State Rep, 62- Bus. & Prof. Pos: Pres, Springlake Enterprises, Inc, 64- Mem: Nat. exec. cmt, Interstate Conf. on Water Probs; Mason; Lions. Award for outstanding Serv. in Water Conserv, Ft. Worth Press. Rel: Baptist. Mailing Add: Box 38, Springlake, Tex. 79082.

CLEARY, PATRICK JAMES R
42nd Dist. Representative Committeeman, Ill. Rep. Party
b. Momence, Ill, 1/20/29; s. James Augustine Cleary and Nellie Liston C; m. 10/1/55 to Alice Marie Duval; c. Mary Elizabeth, James Augustine and Michael John. Educ: Cent. YMCA Col, 46; Univ. Chicago, Chicago Loop Br, 47. Polit. & Govt. Pos: Legis. asst, Ill. Sen, 51-59; pub. adminstr, Kankakee Co, 54-57; city clerk, Kankakee, 55-57; secy, Kankakee Zoning Bd. and Police Cmn, 55-57; mem, Kankakee Pension Bd, 57-61; co. clerk and clerk of the co. and probate courts, Kankakee Co, 58-62; 42nd Dist. representative committeeman, Ill. Rep. Party, 66-; committeeman and mem. exec. cmt, Kankakee Co. Rep. Party, 68-; chmn. bd. rev, State of Ill. Dept. of Labor, 69- Bus. & Prof. Pos: Mem. ed. staff, Kankakee J, 45-52; reporter, Gary Post Tribune, 52, pub. rels. exec, Plumbing Contractors Asn. of Chicago and Vicinity, 56-58; co-publisher and v.pres, Farmers Weekly Rev, Inc, 62- Mem: Chicago Press Club; Ill. Press Asn; Nat. and North. Ill. Ed. Asns; Gabriel Guild; Ill. Co. Clerks Asn; Ill. Munic. League (exec. cmt); Co. Off. Asn. of Ill. (v.pres); bd. adv, The New World Cath. Newspaper, Chicago; Chicago Press Vet. Asn; Nat. Press Club, Wash, D.C; Farm Bur; United Commercial Travelers; Moose; K. of C. (4°). Rel: Roman Catholic. Legal Res: 1905 E. Oak St, Kankakee, Ill. 60901. Mailing Add: 165 N. Canal St, Suite 200, Chicago, Ill. 60606.

CLEATON, C. WILLIAM D
Va. State Del.
b. Crichton, Va, 11/6/99; m. to Alva Bracey C. Educ: Col. of William and Mary. Polit. & Govt. Pos: Former mem. town coun, South Hill, Va; former mayor, LaCrosse, Va; Va. State Del, 48-; del-at-lg, Dem. Nat. Conv, 60. Bus. & Prof. Pos: Hardware, tractor, farm implement and automobile dealer. Mem: Va. Retail Hardware Asn; Mason (32°); Shrine; Eastern Star; Lions; South Hill C. of C. William and Mary Alumni Medallion, 63. Rel: Methodist. Mailing Add: 221 Park Lane, South Hill, Va. 23970. (1967)

CLEAVELAND, BRADFORD IRA R
b. Lakeville, Conn, 1/19/16; s. Paul Bradford Cleaveland and Gladys Traver C; m. 4/4/41 to Lise Graser; c. Paul B. II, Nancy J, Katherine L, Lisa A. and John E. Educ: Yale Univ, 34-38. Polit. & Govt. Pos: Chmn, Caldwell Co. Rep. Party, Tex, 60-66. Bus. & Prof. Pos: Pres, Ellmag Oil Corp, 41-48; owner, Cleaveland Well Serv, 48- Rel: Episcopal. Legal Res, 715 S. Pecan Ave, Luling, Tex. 78648. Mailing Add: P.O. Box 308, Luling, Tex. 78648.

CLEEK, LYMAN McGARVEY D
Mem, Mo. Dem. State Cmt.
b. Bonne Terre, Mo, 3/4/20; s. Alexander Cole Cleek and Stella Mae Carr; m. 12/14/58 to Beverly Charlene Foster; c. Michael Cole, Nancy Lynne and Lynda Sue. Educ: Univ. of Mo, Columbia, A.B, 46; Univ. of Mo. Law Sch, Columbia, LL.B, 48, J.D, 69; Phi Delta Phi. Polit. & Govt. Pos: City attorney, Columbia, Mo, 54-56; mem, Dem. State Cmt, 64-; mem, Mo. State Athletic Cmn, 65-; del, Dem. State Platform Cmt, 68; del, Dem. Nat. Conv, 68. Bus. & Prof. Pos: Attorney-at-law, Mo, 48- Mil. Serv: Entered as Pvt, Air Force, 42, released as 1st Lt. Pilot, 45, after serv. in Combat Cargo, China, Burma and India, 44-45; Capt, Air Force Res, 45; Distinguished Flying Cross with Two Oak Leaf Clusters; Air Medal with Four Oak Leaf Clusters; Three Battle Stars. Mem: V.pres, World Boxing Asn, 67-; pres, Boone Co. Bar Asn, 68-; Mo. Bar Asn; Shrine; Mason; K.T; Royal Arch; White Shrine; Eastern Star; Elks; VFW; Am. Legion. Hon. Col, Mo. and Ky. Rel: Methodist. Legal Res: 712 E. Rockcreek Dr, Columbia, Mo. 65201. Mailing Add: 410 Guitar Bldg, Columbia, Mo. 65201.

CLEETON, ALAN ROBERT D
b. Pittsburgh, Pa, 12/9/26; s. Glen U. Cleeton and Jennie Terry C; m. 5/21/50 to Gloria Leitner; c. Victoria (Mrs. Stephen Ackerman), Deborah Lee, Glen Alan, Timothy Burnham and Sarah Marie. Educ: Univ. Rochester, 44-45; Okla. State Univ, B.S, 49; Boston Univ, S.T.B, 52, S.T.M, 69, doctoral cand, 69-; Alpha Sigma Eta, Sigma Theta Epsilon, Methodist Student Movement. Polit. & Govt. Pos: Consult, Soc. Security Admin, Pa, 66-67; consult, Commun. Action Agency, Pa, 67-68; Dem. nominee, U.S. House Rep, 23rd Dist, 68. Bus. & Prof. Pos: Minister to married students, State Univ, Iowa, 52-55; assoc. exec. secy, Rocky Mt. Methodist Bd. Educ, Denver, Colo, 55-59; dir, Wesley Found, Univ. Colo, 59-64; and Pa. State Univ, State College, 64-68. Mil. Serv: Entered as A/S, Navy, 44, released as Fireman 1/C, 46, after serv. in U.S.S. Dayton, CL 105, Pac. Theater and Atlantic Fleet, 45-46; Am. Theater Ribbon; Pac. Theater Ribbon; Victory WWII Medal. Publ: 'Freedom and a Philosophy of Social Design,' Critique, 3/65; 'Browning and Buneul, A Comparative Review,' Am. Fedn. Film Socs, 4/65; 'Updike Revisited, A Question of Suburban Sex Ethics,' HUB Fine Arts Rev, 10/67. Mem: Faith and order cmn, Pa. Coun. Churches, 66-69; Pa. state bd, Am. Civil Liberties Union, 66-69; Am. Fedn. Film Soc; Am. Acad. Social & Polit. Sci; Student Travel Asn. Am. (v.pres, 68-69); nat. adv, Sigma Theta Epsilon, 54-58. Outstanding Youth Worker, Methodist Church, 59. Rel: Methodist; Ordained Minister, 52- Mailing Add: 1017 Houserville Rd, State College, Pa. 16801.

CLELAND, JACK CYRIL D
Mem, Calif. Dem. State Cent. Cmt.
b. Glendale, Calif, 3/7/16; s. John Williams Cleland (deceased) and Lillian Jensen C. (deceased); m. 7/22/61 to Doris Lorraine Zerby; c. Gerald Roger and Cleo Joy. Educ: Glendale Col, 34-36; Univ. South Calif, 36-38; Beta Phi Gamma; ed, col. paper, year book and handbook; YMCA. Polit. & Govt. Pos: V.chmn, Los Angeles Co. Dem. Cent. Cmt, 58-60, chmn, 60-62; recreation cmnr, Lynwood, Calif, 61; mem, Calif. State Dem. State Cent. Cmt, 62-; sustaining mem, Dem. Nat. Party, 64-; dep. supvr, Co. Los Angeles, 66- Bus. & Prof. Pos: Auth. movie column, Cinematized, 34-; Ed, Glendale Star, 34-41; sr. managing ed, Herald Am. Newspapers, Compton, 45-66; originator of phrases, The Life You Save May be Your Own, Nat. Safety Coun, Fresh up with 7 Up, 7 Up Bottling Co, and Yardbird and Gismo Center, Army Prod. Hey, Rookie. Mem: Gr. Los Angeles Press Club; Carson Rotary Club (v.pres); Gr. Carson-Dominguez C. of C. (dir); Compton C. of C. (dir); life mem, Optimist Int; Lions; Town Affiliation Asn. U.S; Paramount Sister City Cmt, LULAC; Elks; life mem, Amvets; Los Angeles Co. Employees Asn. George Washington Medal, Freedoms Found. Valley Forge, 53. Rel: Protestant. Mailing Add: 4029 Walnut Ave, Lynwood, Calif. 90262.

CLEMENS, ARTHUR J. D
b. Cannelton, Ind, 8/12/28; s. Edward F. Clemens and Anna Hay C; m. 11/6/48 to Joan Robinson; c. Arthur, Jr, Richard, Catherine, Timothy, James and Christopher. Educ: Ind. Univ, Bloomington, 3½ years. Polit. & Govt. Pos: Del, Ind. Dem. Conv, since 56; pres, Perry Co. Coun, 56-60; pres, Perry Co. Air Bd, 63-65; alternate del, Dem. Nat. Conv, 68. Bus. & Prof. Pos: Asst. sales mgr, Cannelton Sewer Pipe, 54-56; sales mgr, CAN-TEX Indust, 56-64, secy, 63-67, v.pres. sales, 67-69, v.pres, 69-; pres, Swiss Boat Builders, 68- Mil. Serv: Entered as Pvt, Army, 46, released as Cpl, 48, after serv. in Seventh Inf. Div, Korea; re-entered as Cpl, 50, released as M/Sgt, 52; Good Conduct, Overseas Marks and Asian Theatre Medals. Mem: Nat. Clay Pipe Inst; Govt. Rels. Cmt; pres, Trickling Filter Floor Inst; Moose; Kiwanis; K. of C; Am. Legion; 40 et 8; Jr. C. of C; Hoosier Heights Country Club. Rel: Catholic. Mailing Add: 2 Visi Lane, Cannelton, Ind. 47520.

CLEMENS, DAVID EDWARD D
b. Cannelton, Ind, 7/17/26; s. E.F. Clemens and Anna Hay C; m. 12/4/47 to Jayne Ann Birchler; c. David, Jr, Stephanie, Al John, Kevin, Elizabeth and Suzie. Educ: Evansville Col, 2 years. Polit. & Govt. Pos: Mem, Palo Pinto Co. Dem. Exec. Cmt, Tex, 62-64; mem, Tex. State Dem. Exec. Cmt, 64-68; del, Dem. Nat. Conv, 68. Bus. & Prof. Pos: Traffic mgr, Tex. Vitrified Pipe Co, 48-51, personnel mgr, 51-53, asst. sales mgr, 53-55, sales mgr, 55-58, asst. gen. mgr, 58-62 and gen. mgr, 62-66; v.pres, Can Tex Industs, 66- Mil. Serv: Entered as A/S, Navy, 44, released as S 1/C, 46, after serv. in Commun. Unit, Am. and Pac. Theatres, 44-46; Am. Theatre and Pac. Ribbons. Mem: Am. Ceramic Soc; Water Pollution Control Fedn; Water Conserv. Asn, Tex; C. of C. Fel. of Col, St. Joseph's Col. Rel: Catholic. Legal Res: 615 N.W. 20th St, Mineral Wells, Tex. 76067. Mailing Add: P.O. Box 340, Mineral Wells, Tex. 76067.

CLEMENS, HAROLD W. R
State Treas, Wis.
b. Milwaukee, Wis, 10/21/18; s. (father deceased) Sue Clemens; single. Educ: Oconomowoc and Milwaukee Sch. Syst, Wis. Polit. & Govt. Pos: Serv. as village trustee, village clerk, health officer, bldg. inspector, civil defense dir; was co. supvr. 8 years; Wis. State Assemblyman, Waukesha Co, 56-68, speaker pro tem, Wis. State Assembly, 63, v.chmn, Munic. Cmt, 57 and mem, 63 & 65, mem, Legis. Coun. Boating Study Cmt, 57, mem, Elections Cmt, 57, 59 & 67 and v.chmn, 63, mem, Cmt. on State Affairs, 59 and Reapportionment Study Cmt, 59 & 63, v.chmn, Educ. and Transportation Cmts, 61, chmn, Vet. and Mil. Affairs Cmt, 63 & 67 and mem, Legis. Coun. and its Urban Probs. Cmt. and v.chmn, Rules and Interstate Coop. Cmts, 63 and secy, Legis. Coun. Local Govt Cmt, 65; State Treas, Wis, 68-, mem, Cmnrs. Pub. Lands, State Bd. of Canvassers and bd. of trustees of the Conserv. Warden Pension Fund. Bus. & Prof. Pos: Former printing compositor and toolmaker; operator of recreation area. Mil. Serv: Navy, 44-46. Mem: Am. Legion; Amvets; VFW; Lions; Eagles; K. of C; Soc. State Legislators; Nat. Asn. of State Treas. Legal Res: 272 Lac La Belle Dr, Oconomowoc, Wis. 53066. Mailing Add: 111 West, State Capitol, Madison, Wis. 53702.

CLEMENT, FRANK GOAD D
b. Dickson, Tenn, 6/2/20; s. Robert Samuel Clement and Maybelle Goad C; m. 1/6/40 to Lucille Christianson C; c. Robert Nelson, Frank Goad, James Gary. Educ: Cumberland Univ; Lebanon, Tenn, 39; Vanderbilt Univ, LL.B, 42; Sigma Alpha Epsilon; Phi Delta Phi. Polit. & Govt. Pos: Past pres, Tenn. Young Dem; past chmn, South. Regional Educ. Bd; former agent, Fed. Bur. Invest, 41-43; chief counsel, Tenn. Utilities Cmn, 46-50; Gov, Tenn, 53-59 & 63-67; past chmn, South. Gov. Conf. and mem. exec. cmt, 56; del, Dem. Nat. Conv, 68. Bus. & Prof. Pos: Attorney-at-law, Nashville and Dickson, Tenn, 46- Mil. Serv: 1st Lt, Army; Lt. Col, Tenn. Air Nat. Guard, 58- Mem: Chmn. bd, Cordell Hull Found. Int. Educ, 55-59; past Comdr, Tenn. Dept. Am. Legion; Dickson Co. Jr. C. of C; Mason (32°); Shrine; Kiwanis. Outstanding Young Man, Tenn. Jr. C. of C, 48; One of Nation's Ten Outstanding Young Men, U.S. Jr. C. of C, 53; Spec. Serv. Award, South. Psychiat. Asn, 59; Spec. Award, Nat. Asn. Ment. Health, 58. Rel: Methodist. Legal Res: Dickson, Tenn. 37055. Mailing Add: 711 J.C. Bradford Bldg, Nashville, Tenn. 37219.

CLEMENT, ROBERT FREDERICK R
Mem, Colo. State Rep. Cent. Cmt.
b. Muskogee, Okla, 7/20/17; s. Robert Caylor Clement and Nell Ann D'Amato C; m. 3/21/42 to Marjorie Elizabeth Lawrence; c. Lawrence Caylor and Elizabeth Ann. Educ: Muskogee Jr. Col, Okla, 35-37; Okla. State Univ, B.A, 40; Blue Key; Kappa Sigma. Polit. & Govt. Pos: Dist. capt, S.E. Jefferson Co. Dist. II, Colo, 66-; mem, Jefferson Co. Planning Cmn, 67-; v.pres, Jefferson Co. Rep. Workshop, 68-; mem. bd. dir, Colo. State Rep. Workshop, 68-; secy, bd. dir, Alameda Water & Sanit. Dist. and mem. designate to Metrop. Sewer Dist, Colo, 69; mem, Colo. State Rep. Cent. Cmt, 69- Mil. Serv: Entered as Aviation Cadet, Air Force, 41, released as Capt, 45, after serv. in 7th Bombardment Group, China-Burma-India, 44-45; Air Force Res, 45-56, Retired; Presidential Unit Citation, 7th Bombardment Group. Mem: Assoc. mem, Jefferson Co. Planning Cmn; AF&AM; Alameda C. of C; Lakewood Country Club. Rel: Methodist. Mailing Add: 470 S. Otis St, Lakewood, Colo. 80226.

CLEMENTE, CELESTINO R
b. Penns Grove, N.J, 6/11/22; s. Ermanno Clemente and Caroline Friozzi C; m. 11/16/46 to Marie Strangio; c. Jeffrey, Roderick, Mark, Laurie and

Jonathan. Educ: Rutgers Univ, B.S, 42; Univ. Pa, M.D, 45; Alpha Kappa Kappa. Polit. & Govt. Pos: Rep. cand, U.S. House Rep, Tenth Dist, N.J, 68. Bus. & Prof. Pos: Chief of Staff, United Hosp. of Newark, N.J, 67-; dir. surg, Babies Hosp, attending surgeon, Presby. Hosp, attending surgeon, St. Vincent's Hosp, Montclair, clin. asst. prof. surg, N.J. Col. Med. and Dent; dir, Montclair Nat. Bank and Trust Co; mem. med. adv. bd, Essex Co. Hosp, Belleville, mdm. adv. bd. Blue Cross Hosp. Affairs to Cmnr. Ins. & Banking N.J. Mil. Serv: Active duty Naval Res. Med. Corps, 46-48, Lt.(jg). Publ: Author of several med. publ. Mem: Dipl, Am. Bd. Surg; Fel, Am. Col. Surgeons; Am. Med. Asn; Essex Co. Med. Soc; Am. Asn. Adv. Sci; Essex Club. Rel: Roman Catholic. Mailing Add: 364 Ridgewood Ave, Glen Ridge, N.J. 07028.

CLEMENTS, CHARLES McCALL, III R
Chmn, Marion Co. Rep. Party, Ga.
b. Columbus, Muscogee Co, Ga, 11/27/41; s. Charles McCall Clements, Jr. and Embelle Thurmond C; single. Educ: Emory Univ, 60-61; Emory at Oxford, 61-62; Univ. Ga, A.B, 65; Pi Kappa Phi (steward, Univ. Ga. chap, 63-65). Polit. & Govt. Pos: Membership dir, Univ. Ga. Young Rep. Club, 64-65; secy, Marion Co. Rep. Party, Ga, 65-68, chmn, 68-; del, Rep. Dist. Conv, 66 & 68; co-chmn. Area III, Third Cong. Dist. Ga, Rep. Exec. Cmt, 66-68, treas, 68-70; del. & mem. resolutions cmt, Ga. State Rep. Conv, 68; city councilman, Buena Vista, 65-68 and chmn, Citizens Adv. Cmt. on Housing Needs, 68- Bus. & Prof. Pos: Partner, Clements Hardware & Furniture Co, Buena Vista, 65-; v.chmn, Marion Co. Re-Develop. Corp, 68- Mem: Lions Int.(secy, Buena Vista Chap, 66-67, third v.pres, 67-68, first v.pres. & chmn. recreation cmt, 68-69, pres. elect, 69-70). Guest at Inauguration of President Richard M. Nixon and related events, 69; Bronze Medallion for Meritorious Service in Fight Against Heart Disease, Am. & Ga. Heart Asns. Rel: Baptist. Mailing Add: Box 56, Baker St, Buena Vista, Ga. 31803.

CLEMENTS, HOMER M. D
b. Jackson Co, Mo, 9/20/00; m. 1926 to Nellie Fae Johnson; c. Carolee Clements (Mrs. Quinlan), Linda Jane Clements (Mrs. Wood). Educ: Univ. of Kans, Lawrence; Univ. of Mo, Columbia, B.A, M.A; Phi Delta Kappa. Polit. & Govt. Pos: Mo. State Rep, 62-66; Jackson Co. supt. of schs, 22 years; city supvr. of schs, 10 years. Mem: Kiwanis; Knife & Fork Club; past secy, Jackson Co. Libr. Bd. and Jackson Co. Sch. Admin; Legis. Comm, Mo. State Teachers Asn. Rel: Presbyterian. Mailing Add: 1234 S. Main St, Independence, Mo. 64054. (1967)

CLEMENTS, JOHN V. R
Chmn, Baraga Co. Rep. Cmt, Mich.
b. Baraga, Mich, 1/14/13; s. J. Edward Clements and Bernardine Vaughan C; m. 6/14/47 to Elizabeth Rees Furbeck; c. Ann Mitchell, Jane Elizabeth, John Vaughan, Jr, Margaret Rees and Miriam Louise. Educ: St. Mary's Col, Minn, 30-32; Cardinal Club; v.pres. of Class. Polit. & Govt. Pos: Secy. bd. educ, L'Anse Schs, Mich, 46-49; chmn, Baraga Co. Rep. Cmt, 54-56 & 64-; mem. bd. rev, Baraga Twp, 56-65; nominee for Mich. State Auditor, 58 & 60; alternate del, Rep. Nat. Conv, 64; mem, Baraga Twp. Sch. Adv. Cmt, 64-66; chmn, Ojibwa Housing Cmn, 65-; secy, 11th Cong. Dist. Rep. Cmt, 64- Bus. & Prof. Pos: State agent, Royal Globe Ins. Group, 53-66; pres, Baraga Co. Agency, Inc, 53- Mil. Serv: Entered as Pvt, Army Air Corps, 41, released as S/Sgt, 45, after serv. in Seventh Ferrying Group of Air Transport Command; Good Conduct Medal; ETO, Pac, China-Burma-India and Am. Theater Ribbons. Publ: Package Auto Insurance, Rough Notes Mag, 64. Mem: Upper Peninsula, Mich. and Nat. Asns. of Ins. Agents; Am. Legion; VFW; K. of C; Third Order St. Francis; v.pres, Upper Peninsula Laymen's Retreat Asn. Rel: Catholic. Legal Res: Box 200 Route 1, Buckland Dr, Baraga, Mich. 49908. Mailing Add: 1 N. Front St, L'Anse, Mich. 49946. (1967)

CLEMENTS, MAHLON THOMPSON R
V.Chmn, St. Lawrence Co. Rep. Cmt, N.Y.
b. Lisbon, N.Y, 12/22/35 to George W. Clements and Dacie E; m. 3/28/59 to Elizabeth Briggs; c. Thomas Gray, Mahlon Christopher George and Douglas Lee. Educ: Univ. Rochester, B.A, 57; Cornell Univ, LL.B, 60; Sigma Chi. Polit. & Govt. Pos: V.chmn, St. Lawrence Co. Rep. Party, N.Y, 65- Bus. & Prof. Pos: Partner, Brown & Clements, Attorneys, 66- Mem: N.Y. State and St. Lawrence Co. Bar Asns; Mason. Rel: Protestant. Mailing Add: Chapman St, Morristown, N.Y. 13664.

CLEMENTS, RICHARD OWEN R
b. Pittsburgh, Pa, 9/20/26; s. Verne Ole Clements and Sylvia Shields C; m. 9/6/46 to Mary Martha Headrick; c. Richard O, Jr, Susan Shields, Carol Bishop and William Headrick. Educ: Rice Univ, 46; Baylor Col. Med, M.D, 51; Alpha Omega Alpha; Phi Beta Pi. Polit. & Govt. Pos: Chmn, Liberty Co. Rep. Party, Tex, 61-68. Bus. & Prof. Pos: Physician, private practice, 51- Mil. Serv: Navy, 44-46, Pac. Theater; Lt, Med. Corps, Army, 51-53, U.S. Mem: Am. Med. Asn; Am. Acad. of Gen. Practice. Rel: Presbyterian. Mailing Add: 1710 Travis, Liberty, Tex. 77575. (1967)

CLEMENTS, RUTH WELCH D
V.chmn, Conway Co. Dem. Cent. Cmt, Ark.
b. Conway, Ark, 11/14/17; d. John Walter Welch and Nancy Jane Waters W; div; c. Rebecca Jane (Mrs. Raymond Bryant) and Frank Benjamin, Jr. Educ: Ark. State Teachers Col, B.S.E, 38; Alpha Sigma Tau. Polit. & Govt. Pos: Secy, Lt. Gov. of Ark, 51-67; v.chmn, Conway Co. Dem. Cent. Cmt, 55-67, chmn, 67-68 and v.chmn, 68- Bus. & Prof. Pos: Legal secy, Gordon & Gordon, Attorneys, Morrilton, 48- Mem: Bus. & Prfnl. Women's Club. Rel: Baptist. Mailing Add: 805 N. Morrill, Morrilton, Ark. 72110.

CLEMENTS, WALLACE DeWITT D
b. Chattanooga, Tenn, 9/21/27; s. Edward DeWitt Clements and Ola Evans C; m. 2/4/47 to Audrey Dean Davis; c. Lana Joyce, Michael Steven, Lisa Ann and Mark Edward. Educ: Soddy-Daisy High Sch, grad. Polit. & Govt. Pos: Del, Dem. Nat. Conv, 68. Bus. & Prof. Pos: Legis. field rep, Int. Brotherhood of Teamsters, Washington, D.C, 62- Mil. Serv: Entered as A/S, Navy, 45, released as S 1/C, 46. Mem: F&AM; Consistory; Shrine; DAV; Am. Legion. Rel: Methodist. Mailing Add: 1604 Chamberlain Ave, Chattanooga, Tenn. 37404.

CLEMONS, A. J. D
Okla. State Rep.
b. Duke, Okla, 11/9/13; s. Olonzo Thomas Clemons and Eva Johnson C; m. 11/25/37 to Floreine Powers; c. Mary Kathryn and Johnny. Educ: Cent. State Col, B.A, 34; Univ. Okla, M.A, 45. Polit. & Govt. Pos: Okla. State Rep, 65- Mem: Okla. and Nat. Educ. Asns; Kiwanis; C. of C; Mason. Rel: Church of Christ. Mailing Add: 3504 N. Idylwild, Midwest City, Okla. 73110. (1967)

CLEMONS, ANCE C, JR. D
La. State Sen.
b. Hobby, Tex, 4/16/21; s. Ance C. Clemons, Sr. and Anabelle Hames C; m. 7/12/41 to Dorothy Vincent; c. Alison and Charlene Sue. Educ: Vinton High Sch. Polit. & Govt. Pos: La. State Sen, 14th Dist, 60-; mem, Commerce and Ins, Conserv, Health and Welfare, Transportation and Pub. Works, Gov. Hwy. Safety Cmts. and v.chmn, Local and Munic. Affairs, La. State Senate. Bus. & Prof. Pos: Pres, V & C Mud & Chem. Co, 48-66; chmn. bd, Serv. Truck Line of Tex, Inc, 66- Mil. Serv: Capt, Air Force, 42. Mem: Bd. dirs, Jennings Asn. of Commerce; bd. mem, Jeff Davis Country Club; Lake Charles Country Club; pres, La. Motor Transportation Asn; life mem, Mason (32°); Shrine. Rel: Methodist; Chmn. of Bd, First Methodist Church. Legal Res: 419 Alice St, Jennings, La. 70546. Mailing Add: P.O. Box 811, Jennings, La. 70546. (1967)

CLEVELAND, HARLAN D
b. New York, N.Y, 18. Educ: Princeton, grad, 38; Oxford Univ, Rhodes Scholarship, 38-39. Ten hon. degrees. Polit. & Govt. Pos: Mgr, For. Econ. Prog, U.S. Govt, 12 years; aid admin. for UN, Italy and China; U.S. Asst. Secy. of State for Int. Orgn. Affairs, 61-65; U.S. Ambassador to NATO, 65-69. Bus. & Prof. Pos: Exec. ed. and publisher, The Reporter, 53-56; dean, Maxwell Grad. Sch. Citizenship and Pub. Affairs, Syracuse Univ, 56-61, prof. polit. sci, until 69; Pres, Univ. Hawaii, 69- Publ: The Obligations of Power, Harper and Row, 66; plus others. U.S. Medal of Freedom; decorated by Govt. of Italy and Repub. of China; Woodrow Wilson Award, Princeton Univ. Mailing Add: Office of the President, University of Hawaii, Honolulu, Hawaii 96822.

CLEVELAND, JAMES C. R
U.S. Rep, N.H.
b. Montclair, N.J, 6/13/20; s. Dr. and Mrs. Mather Cleveland; m. 12/9/50 to Hilary Paterson; c. Cotton Mather, James Colby, David Paterson, Lincoln Mather and Susan Sclater. Educ: Colgate Univ, magna cum laude; Yale Law Sch, 48, Phi Beta Kappa. Polit. & Govt. Pos: N.H. State Sen, 50-62; U.S. Rep, N.H, 62- Bus. & Prof. Pos: Partner, Cleveland & Bass, 60-62; lawyer, Cleveland, Waters & Bass, 62-; organizer, incorporator, off. and dir, New London Trust Co; incorporator, dir, King Ridge Ski Area. Mil. Serv: World War II, Field Artillery, 40th Inf. Div, Pac. Theatre; Bronze Star for Valor; discharged as Capt, 45; recalled active overseas duty, Korean War. Mem: Am. Legion; VFW; Rotary; Mason; Elks; Grange; Eagles; Moose; New London Outing Club. Legal Res: New London, N.H. 03257. Mailing Add: House Office Bldg, Washington, D.C. 20515.

CLEVELAND, MACK N, JR. D
b. Sanford, Fla, 7/9/24. Educ: Univ. of Fla, Stetson Univ, B.S.B.A, 1949, LL.B, 1951; Ye Mystic Krewe, 10 outstanding students award; Student Body Treas; V.Pres, Jr. Class; Phi Alpha Delta; Alpha Tau Omega. Polit. & Govt. Pos: Fla. State Sen, 63-67; Fla. State Rep, 52-62; Speaker Pro Tem, 57-58; City of Sanford Civil Serv. Bd. Mil. Serv: U.S. Air Corps, WWII, Pac. Mem: Kiwanis; C. of C, Past Pres; Jr. C. of C; Masons; Elks; Bahia Shrine Temple; Am. Legion; VFW; 40 et 8. Rel: Baptist. Mailing Add: P.O Drawer Z, Sanford, Fla. 32771. (1967)

CLEVENGER, RAYMOND FRANCIS D
b. Chicago, Ill, 6/6/26; m. 1948 to Francile Corbat; c. Phil, Diane, Jeffrey, John and Sue Ann. Educ: Roosevelt Univ, B.A, 49; Univ. Mich, LL.B, 52; London Sch. Econ. Polit. & Govt. Pos: Former acting Munic. Judge in the Sault, Sault Ste Marie, Mich; cmnr, Chippewa Co. Circuit Court, 58-60; cmnr, Mich. Corp. and Securities Cmn, 61-63; U.S. Rep, Mich, 64-66; Dem. nominee, U.S. Rep, Mich, 68. Bus. & Prof. Pos: Lawyer. Mil. Serv: Army Med. Corps, 44-46. Mem: Sault Indust. Develop. Cmn; Sault Park Cmn; founder, Sault Commun. Coun. for Youth Work. Mailing Add: 213 W. Spruce St, Sault Ste. Marie, Mich. 49783. (1967)

CLIFFORD, CLARK McADAMS D
b. Ft. Scott, Kans, 12/25/06; s. Frank Andrew Clifford and Georgia McAdams; m. 10/3/31 to Margery Pepperell Kimball; c. Margery Pepperell (Mrs. Wm. H. Lanagan, Jr.), Joyce Carter (Mrs. Richard D. Barrett) and Randall (Mrs. Ed. I. Wright). Educ: Wash. Univ, St. Louis, LL.B, 28; Kappa Alpha. Polit. & Govt. Pos: Naval Aide to U.S. President, 46, spec. counsel, 46-50; U.S. Secy. of Defense, 68-69. Bus. & Prof. Pos: Assoc, Holland, Lashley and Donell, 28-33; partner, Holland, Lashley and Lashley, 33-37, Lashley, Lashley, Miller and Clifford, 38; dir, Nat. Bank of Wash. and Phillips Petroleum Co; sr. partner, Clifford and Miller, Wash, 50-68, Clifford, Warnke, Glass, McIlwain & Finney, 69- Mil. Serv: Lt.(jg), Navy, 44, promoted to Capt, 46; awarded Naval Commendation Ribbon. Mem: Fed, Am, Mo, D.C. and St. Louis Bar Asn; Raquet Club, St. Louis; Burning Tree, Chevy Chase, Wash. and Metrop. Clubs; bd. of dir, Wash. Univ, St. Louis, Mo. Medal of Freedom presented by The President of U.S. Legal Res: 9421 Rockville Pike, Bethesda, Md. 20015. Mailing Add: 815 Connecticut Ave, Wash, D.C. 20006.

CLIFFORD, JANE ELIZABETH R
Coordinator for Cities, Mass. Rep. State Cmt.
b. Boston, Mass, 10/15/28; d. Kenneth Eugene Macomber and Aileen Harris M; m. 11/26/50 to John Joseph Clifford; c. Patricia Ann, Peter Alan and Philip Andrew. Educ: Hickox Sch, 2 years. Polit. & Govt. Pos: Mem, Belmont Rep. Town Cmt, Mass, 62-65; mem, Braintree Rep. Town Cmt, 65; area coordinator, Mass. Rep. Finance Cmt, 66; campaign dir, Sargent for Lt. Gov. Cmt, 66; mem, Marshfield Rep. Town Cmt, 66-; spec. asst. to Lt. Gov. of Mass, 67; campaign coordinator, Mass. Rep. State Cmt, 67-69, coordinator for cities, 67- Bus. & Prof. Pos: Ed, 'Target', Mass. Rep. State Cmt, 67- Mem: PTA; Girl Scouts of Am. Legal Res: 69 Flaggler Dr, Marshfield, Mass. 02050. Mailing Add: 73 Tremont St, Boston, Mass. 02108.

CLIFTON, O. K. R
Secy, Mesa Co. Rep. Cent. Cmt, Colo.
b. Collbran, Colo, 1/29/24; s. J. Frank Clifton and Grace Sanders C; m. 6/30/48 to Lois M. Kraai; c. Darrell, Roxann, Gary, Michael and Linda. Educ: Univ. Denver Col. Law, B.S. & LL.B. Polit. & Govt. Pos: Precinct committeeman, Rep. Party, 59; finance chmn, Rep. Party Cong. Race, 61; secy, Mesa Co. Rep. Cent. Cmt, Colo, 67- Bus. & Prof. Pos: Exec. v.pres, Valley Fed. Savings & Loan, 53-; dir, Savings & Loan League of Colo, 53-56; dir, Fed. Home Loan Bank of Topeka, 64-65. Mil. Serv: Entered as A/S, Navy, 43, released as 2/C PO, 46. Mem: Lions; AF&AM; Colo. Heart Asn; Mesa Co. 4-H Found. Rel: Protestant. Mailing Add: 2464 Broadway, Grand Junction, Colo. 81501.

CLINE, ROBERT CORDE R
Mem, Calif. Rep. State Cmt.
b. San Francisco, Calif, 5/6/33; s. John W. Cline, M.D. and Edith Bertha Cordé C; m. 8/24/55 to Betty Clare Robison; c.Bruce and Caren. Educ: Univ. Calif, Berkeley, A.B, 55, M.B.A, 60. Polit. & Govt. Pos: Assoc. mem, Calif. Rep. State Cmt, 62-64, mem, 64-; mem, Los Angeles Co. Rep. Cent. Cmt, 62-65; Rep. nominee, U.S. House of Rep, 22nd Cong. Dist, 64 & 66; South. Calif. campaign dir, Max Rafferty for U.S. Senate, 68; campaign mgr, Donald D. Lorenzen for Los Angeles City Coun, 69; v.pres, Los Angeles Jr. Col. Dist. Bd. of Trustees, 69- Bus. & Prof. Pos: Financial analyst, Litton Industs, Beverly Hills, Calif, 60-64; owner, Robert C. Cline Co, 64- Mil. Serv: Entered as Pvt, Army, 56, released as Sp-4 (Res), 62, after serv. in 513th Antiaircraft Missile Bn, Seattle Defense, Ft. Lawton, Wash, 56-58. Mem: Canoga Park C. of C; Kiwanis; Van Nuys Jaycees, dir. and treas, San Fernando Valley Bus. and Prof. Asn. Rel: Episcopal. Legal Res: 6615 Sausalito Ave, Canoga Park, Calif. 91304. Mailing Add: 20944 Sherman Way, Canoga Park, Calif. 91303.

CLINGAN, LEE D
Educ: Purdue Univ. Polit. & Govt. Pos: Ind. State Sen, 61-66; Fountain Co. Draft Bd, 16 years. Bus. & Prof. Pos: Ins. agent; livestock auctioneer. Mil. Serv: 1st Lt; Bronze Star; Purple Heart; Combat Infantryman's Badge. Mem: Am. Legion; VFW; Kingman Post 384, past comdr; Masons; DAV; Elks; Wabash Valley Asn. Mailing Add: 121 Elm Dr, Covington, Ind. 47932. (1967)

CLINTON, ELLAREE AVANT D
b. Des Moines, Iowa, 1/5/22; d. Thomas Burke Avant and Mattie Bradshaw A; m. 4/9/47 to William James Clinton; c. Michael Allan and David Andrew. Educ: Iowa State Univ, B.S. in Child Develop, 64; Drake Univ, M.S. in Educ, 69; Delta Sigma Theta. Polit. & Govt. Pos: Precinct committeewoman, Polk Co. Dem. Cent. Cmt, Iowa, 64-; secy, John F. Kennedy Dem. Club, 66-69; del-at-lg, Dem. Nat. Conv, 68; mem, exec. bd, Iowa State Dem. Cent. Cmt, 68; precinct committeewoman, dist. chmn. and mem. exec. bd, Iowa Dem. Conf, 69- Bus. & Prof. Pos: Child develop. caseworker, Iowa Children's and Family Serv, 64-; child develop. consult. for teachers, Tiny Tot Day Care Serv, 68- Mem: Nat. and Iowa Asns. for Educ. of Young Children; life mem, Iowa State Univ. Alumni Asn; Iowa Welfare Asn.(exec. bd); Pub. Health Nursing Asn.(exec. bd); Eastern Star; Daughters of Isis; New Frontier Club of Iowa; Jack and Jill of Am; Winthrop Club of Des Moines; Prfnl. Womens League of Des Moines. Rel: Methodist. Mailing Add: 1190 Tenth St, Des Moines, Iowa 50314.

CLINTON, GORDON STANLEY R
b. Medicine Hat, Alta, Can, 4/13/20; s. John Henry Clinton and Gladys Hall C; m. 12/19/42 to Florence Helen Vayhinger; c. Barbara Helen (Mrs. Charles A. Tompkins, Jr), Gordon S, Jr. and Deborah Ruth. Educ: Univ. Wash, B.A, 42, J.D, 47; Pi Sigma Alpha; Phi Delta Phi. Hon. LL.D, Univ. Puget Sound, 57, Seattle Pac. Col, 60. Polit. & Govt. Pos: Spec. agent, Fed. Bur. Invest, 41-43; dep. prosecuting attorney, King Co, Wash, 46-68; judge pro tem, Munic. Court, Seattle, 49-52; mayor, Seattle, 56-64; chmn, Citizens for Dan Evans for Gov, 64; mem, Wash. State Bd. Educ, 68; alternate del, Rep. Nat. Conv, 68; Wash. state chmn, Nixon for President Cmt, 68. Bus. & Prof. Pos: Trustee, Seattle Bar Asn, 50; mem. bd. trustees, Seattle-King Co. Munic. League, 69; pres, Assoc. Methodist Homes, 69; mem. bd. dirs, Town Affil. Asn, 69; bd. trustees, Wash. State Int. Trade Fair, 69. Mil. Serv: Entered as A/S, U.S. Navy, 44, released as Lt.(jg), 46, after serv. in Pac, 44-46; Am. Pac. Theatre Oper. Ribbon. Mem: Seattle-King Co. Bar Asn; Wash. State Bar Asn; Am. Bar Asn; Am. Arbitration Asn; Japan-Am. Soc; Kobe-Seattle Affil. Cmt, chmn, 64-69; Univ. Lodge F&AM, KCCH (32°); Nile Temple Shrine; Red Cross of Constantine; Am. Legion. Methodist Man of the Year, 56; Civic Unity award, Seattle, 63; Outstanding Pub. Off, King Co. Munic. League, 64; distinguished grad. award, Roosevelt High Sch, 64; citation, Japan-Am. Citizens League, 65; citation, Nat. Conf. Christians & Jews; Republican of the Year for King Co, 68. Rel: Methodist. Legal Res: 7733 58th N.E, Seattle, Wash. 98115. Mailing Add: Third Lenora Bldg, Seattle, Wash. 98121.

CLIPSON, JAMES HUGH, JR. R
Chmn, Colo. Co. Rep. Party, Tex.
b. Lissie, Tex, 8/21/38; s. James Hugh Clipson and Ana Mae Causey C; m. 12/5/60 to Jane Katherine Andersen; c. Julie Ruth, Jane Louise, Jerri Lynn and James Wilber. Polit. & Govt. Pos: Mem, Bush Campaign Cmt, Colo. Co, Tex, 64; Rep. chmn, Precinct 17, Eagle Lake, Tex, 64-; chmn, Colo. Co. Rep. Party, Tex, 66- Bus. & Prof. Pos: Operator, Rice Farming and Ranching, 58- Mil. Serv: Entered as Airman, Air Force Res, 58, released as Airman 3/C, 64, after serv. in Alamo and Tater, 446 Troop Carrier Wing, Houston, 56-64, Inactive Res, 64-66. Mem: Elks; Tex. Jaycees; Tex. Farm Bur; Lions. Rel: Presbyterian. Legal Res: 626 Willow, Eagle Lake, Tex. 77434. Mailing Add: Box 832, Eagle Lake, Tex. 77434.

CLOCKSIN, VIRGINIA TEITZEL R
b. Port Townsend, Wash, 7/4/34; d. Frederick G. Teitzel and Nell E. T; m. 12/4/52 to Duane Brown Clocksin; c. William Frederick, Renée La Rae and Jini Linn. Educ: Metrop. Bus. Col; Port Angeles Bus. Col. Polit. & Govt. Pos: Committeewoman, Wash. State Rep. Cent. Cmt, 61, mem. exec. bd, 64-69; pres, Port Townsend Rep. Club, 62; secy, Second Cong. Rep. Club, 65; former Wash. State Rep. Bus. & Prof. Pos: Owner, Flowers by Gini. Mem: PTA; Eastern Star; Soroptimists. Rel: Presbyterian. Legal Res: R.R. 1, Port Ludlow, Wash. 98365. Mailing Add: 901 Water, Port Townsend, Wash. 98368. (1967)

CLOSE, ALBERT STEPHEN R
Mem, Ohio Rep. Cent. and Exec. Cmt.
b. Sandusky, Ohio, 5/10/05; s. Albert C. Close and Walla Young C; single. Educ: Univ. Pa, grad, 26; West. Reserve Law Sch, LL.B, 30; Alpha Tau Omega. Polit. & Govt. Pos: Secy, Erie Co. Rep. Cent. and Exec. Cmt, Ohio, 40-; mem, Ohio Rep. Cent. and Exec. Cmt, 62-; mem, Erie Co, Bd. Elec, 68- Bus. & Prof. Pos: Partner and mem, A.C. Close Agency, gen. ins; partner and mem, Close & Close, Attorneys-at-law. Mem: Erie Co. and Ohio Ins. Agents Asns; Erie Co, Ohio and State of Ohio Bar Asns; Elks (Past Exalted Ruler); life mem, K. of P; Eagles; Odd Fellows; Singara Grotto; AF&AM (32°); Sandusky Yacht Club; Erie Co. Golden Key Club; Richland Co. Rep. Club; life mem, Moose; life mem, United Commercial Travelers Am. Rel: United Presbyterian. Legal Res: 336 E. Adams St, Sandusky, Ohio 44870. Mailing Add: P.O. Box 555, Sandusky, Ohio 44870.

CLOSE, PAT M. D
V.Chmn, Shelby Co. Dem. Cent. Cmt, Ind.
b. Shelbyville, Ind, 2/8/32; d. William C. Ruhlman and Alma M. Jeffries R; m. 1/30/49 to Charles W. Close; c. Connie Lynn (Mrs. Richard Balting). Educ: Shelbyville High Sch. Polit. & Govt. Pos: Pres, Shelby Co. Dem. Club, Ind, 63-64; v.chmn, Shelby Co. Dem. Cent. Cmt, 64-; mgr, Shelbyville Auto License Br, 66- Bus. & Prof. Pos: Treas, Marion Twp. PTA, 56-57, pres, 58-59. Mem: Am. Legion Auxiliary; Nat. 600 Bowling Club. Rel: Catholic. Mailing Add: R.R. 2, Shelbyville, Ind. 46176.

CLOSSEY, CHRISTINA D
Chmn, Sauk Co. Dem. Party, Wis.
b. Spring Green, Wis, 12/9/00; d. Carl L. Peterson and Kathryn Alt P; m. 11/10/25 to Dennis J. Clossey, Sr; c. Dennis J, Jr. Educ: Spring Green High Sch, 2 years; Reedsburg High Sch, 2 years. Polit. & Govt. Pos: Precinct committeeman, Reedsburg Dem. Party, Wis, 32-69; mem, Wis. Dem. State Cent. Cmt, 46-48; chief crew leader for census, Third Dist, Wis, 50; elec. off, Reedsburg, periodically; chmn, Sauk Co. Dem. Party, 67- Mem: Am. Legion Auxiliary; VFW Auxiliary; Cath. Daughters Am.(vice grand regent); Federated Club Reedsburg; Reedsburg Country Club; Am. Red Cross, Sauk Co; Altar Soc, Sacred Heart Cath. Church. Rel: Catholic. Mailing Add: 527 Eighth St, Reedsburg, Wis. 53959.

CLOSZ, HAROLD F, JR. R
Chmn, Muskegon Co. Rep. Finance Cmt, Mich.
b. Muskegon, Mich, 8/16/23; s. Dr. Harold F. Closz and Elizabeth Cox C; m. 3/22/44 to Mary Jean Phipps; c. Michael Charles, Harold F, III, Catherine McCormick, John Chapin and Thomas Murray. Educ: DePauw Univ, B.A, 47; Delta Tau Delta. Polit. & Govt. Pos: Chmn, Muskegon Co. Young Rep, Mich, 48-50; v.chmn, Muskegon Co. Rep. Cmt, 48-50, chmn, 62-68; mem, Rep. State Cent. Cmt, 50-52; alderman, North Muskegon, 58-62; del, Rep. Nat. Conv, 68; chmn, Muskegon Co. Rep. Finance Cmt, 68- Bus. & Prof. Pos: Mgr, Bridgeways Inc, 48-51; mgr. terminal, Roadway Express Inc, 51-66. Mil. Serv: Entered as Pvt, Army Air Force, 43, released as 1st Lt, 45, after serv. in 448th Bomber Squadron, Second Div, Eighth Air Force, European Theater, 44-45; Air Medal with 5 Oak Leaf Clusters; European Theater Ribbon and 4 Battle Stars. Mem: Kiwanis; Transportation Club; West State Press Club; North Muskegon Commun. Club. Rel: Roman Catholic. Mailing Add: 825 Miller Dr, North Muskegon, Mich. 49445.

CLOUD, ROGER R
Ohio State Auditor
Polit. & Govt. Pos: Former Ohio State Rep, 9 terms and Speaker of the Ohio State House of Representatives, 5 two-year terms; alternate del, Rep. Nat. Conv, 68; Ohio State Auditor, currently. Legal Res: R.R. 1, DeGraff, Ohio 43318. Mailing Add: State House, Columbus, Ohio 43215. (1967)

CLOUGH, BARRY LENWOOD R
Mem. Adv. Cmt, N.H. Rep. State Cmt.
b. Rochester, N.H, 11/22/42; s. Eli Lenwood Clough and Melva Kehoe C; m. 5/6/66 to Susan Donna Lawrence; c. Thayne and Heather. Educ: Plymouth State Col, B.Ed, 64; Ball State Univ, M.A. in Polit. Sci, 67. Polit. & Govt. Pos: State chmn, Taft for Gov. Campaign, N.H, 66; coordinator, First Cong. Dist. Rep. Cmt, 66; chmn, Strafford Co. Rep. Party, 67-69; asst. to campaign dir, N.H. Rep. State Cmt, summer 68, mem. adv. cmt, 69- Bus. & Prof. Pos: Am. hist. teacher, Littleton High Sch, N.H, 64-66; prin, Barrington Elem. Sch, 67- Mem: N.H. Educ. Asn; Am. Polit. Sci. Asn; Mason; Kiwanis; Barrington Libr. Asn. Rel: Congregational. Mailing Add: 6 Tappan St, Farmington, N.H. 03835.

CLOWARD, McRAY D
Mem, Utah Dem. State Cent. Cmt.
b. Monroe, Utah, 5/2/24; s. Elwin H. Cloward and Lorene Warenski C; m. 8/10/46 to Marius Larson; c. M. Gregory, Charisse and Krista. Educ: South. Utah State Col, Cedar City, A.S, 49; Utah State Univ, B.S, 50, grad. work, 55-; Univ. of Bridgeport, M.S, 54; Peabody Col, Ed.D, 58; Beloit Col, 63-; Phi Kappa Phi; Kappa Delta Pi; Phi Delta Kappa; Sigma Alpha Epsilon. Polit. & Govt. Pos: Dist. and precinct off, Cedar City Dem. Party, Utah, 62; mem, Iron Co. Dem. Cent. Cmt, 63; mem, Utah Dem. State Cent. Cmt, 64-; chmn, Iron Co. Dem. Party, 64- Bus. & Prof. Pos: Col. prof, Col. South. Utah, 50-; v.pres. and bd. mem, Meadow Lake Estates, 65-; pres. and chmn. of bd, Brian Head Ski Corp, 66- Mil. Serv: Entered as Pvt, Army, 43, released as S/Sgt, 46, after serv. in 137th Evacuation Hosp, ETO, 44-46; European Theatre Ribbon; Unit Citations; Good Conduct Medal. Publ: 'Small Colleges Can Build Adequate Dormitories,' Col. and Univ. Bus, 49; 'My Discovery of the South,' Peabody Reflector, 56; 'Higher Education and Community Serv,' Utah Educ. Asn. Mag, 68. Mem: Nat. and Utah Educ. Asns; Mt. Plains and Utah Adult Educ. Asns; Am. Personnel and Guidance Asn; Am. Asn. of Humanistic Psychol; Adult Educ. Asn. of the U.S; past pres. and lt. gov, Utah Idaho Dist, Kiwanis; Elks; past bd. mem, Cedar City C. of C; bd. mem. and past co. chmn, Iron Co. Chap, Red Cross. Cand. for Outstanding Citizen. Rel: Latter-day Saint. Mailing Add: 328 S. 500 W, Cedar City, Utah 84720.

CLOWE, CHARLES EDWARD, JR. R
b. Ardmore, Okla, 10/28/28; s. Charles Edward Clowe and Betsy Brown C; m. 3/5/60 to Sue Myers; c. Ann and Charles Myers. Educ: Tex. Tech. Col, B.S. in Agr, 49. Polit. & Govt. Pos: State Rep. committeeman, Carter Co, Okla, 58-60; alternate del, Rep. Nat. Conv, 60, del, 64; chmn, Carter Co. Rep. Cmt, 66-68. Mil. Serv: Entered as Seaman Recruit, Navy, 51, released as Lt.(jg), 55, after serv. in Korea. Mem: Secy-treas, South. Okla. Asn. of Petrol. Landmen, 66-67; mem, Phys. Educ. Cmt, YMCA, Ardmore, Okla, 66-67. Rel: Episcopal. Legal Res: 615 R St. S.W, Ardmore, Okla. 73401. Mailing Add: P.O. Box 1488, Ardmore, Okla. 73401.

CLUNIS, WAGER FREDERICK D
b. Elkton, Mich, 8/27/02; s. Frederick E. Clunis and Lavina M. Wager C; m. 5/11/29 to Alice M. Seddon; c. Gail E, Wager F. Jr, and Douglas J. Educ: Cent. Mich. Univ, A.B, cum laude, 32; Univ. Mich, M.A, 34. Polit. & Govt. Pos: Trustee, Elkton-Pigeon-Bay Port Sch. Bd. Educ, Mich, 44-; mem, Huron Co. Dem. Cmt, 61-; mem, Eighth Cong. Dem. Exec. Cmt, 65-; dem. cand. cong, Eighth Cong. Dist, 66; del, Dem. Nat. Conv, 68. Bus. & Prof. Pos: Univ. & pub. sch. teacher, 25 years; mem. bd. dirs, Elton Coop Farm Produce Co. & Elton Petroleum Coop, 44-59. Mem: Mich. Asn. Sch. Bd; Nat. Asn. Sch. Bd; Nat. Educ. Asn; Mich. Educ. Asn; Rotary Int; Mason; K.T; NAACP; Nat. Farm Orgn; PTA. Hon. chap. farmer, Future Farmers Am. Rel: Methodist. Mailing Add: 4204 Pigeon Rd, Elkton, Mich. 48731.

CLYDE, GEORGE DEWEY R
b. Springville, Utah, 7/21/98; s. Hyrum Smith Clyde and Elnora Jane Johnson C; m. 9/10/19 to Ora Packard; c. Ned Packard, Ruth C. (Mrs. Landsaw), Richard Bruce, Jerald Reid and Mary Ann (Mrs. Christensen). Educ: Utah State Univ, B.S. in Agr. Eng, 21; Univ. Calif, M.S. in Civil Eng, 23; Hon. Doctor's Degree, Westminster Col, Univ. Utah and Utah State Univ; Sigma Xi; Tau Epsilon; Phi Kappa Phi. Polit. & Govt. Pos: Chief, Div. Irrigation Research, Soil Conserv. Serv, U.S. Dept. Agr, 45-53; dir, Utah Water & Power Bd, 53-65; Gov, Utah, 57-65. Bus. & Prof. Pos: Mem. faculty and research staff, Utah State Univ, 23-44; consult. engr, Woodward, Clyde & Assoc. and Clyde, Criddle & Woodward, Inc, 65- Mil. Serv: Pvt, Army, 17, serv. in training camp. Publ: Author research and technical publ, 23- Mem: Hon. mem. Am. Soc. Civil Engrs; Am. Soc. Agr. Engrs; Am. Soc. Prfnl. Engrs; Am. Soc. Pub. Works Asn. and Am. Soil Conserv. Soc. of Am; life mem. Nat. Reclamation Asn; Consult. Engrs. Coun; Kiwanis; Utah Water Users Asn. Rel: Latter-day Saint. Mailing Add: 2865 Sherwood Dr, Salt Lake City, Utah 84108.

CLYDE, WILLIAM A. D
Asst. Cmnr, and Exec. Secy, Ga. Labor Dept.
b. Easley, S.C, 12/7/98; s. Charles M. Clyde and Eula Martin C; m. 4/12/26 to Bertha Mae Posey. Educ: High Sch; Bus. Inst. Polit. & Govt. Pos: Asst. cmnr. and exec. secy, Ga. Labor Dept, 38- Bus. & Prof. Pos: Real estate bus, 18-38. Mem: Mason; Shrine; Eastern Star. Rel: Methodist; Trustee, St. Paul's Methodist Church. 1967 Legal Res: Atlanta, Ga. No mailing address available. (1967)

CLYMER, W.B. SHUBRICK D
b. Boston, Mass, 1/20/06; married; c. 3. Educ: Harvard Col; Harvard Bus. Sch. Polit. & Govt. Pos: N.H. State Rep, -67; Chmn, Harrisville Rep. Comm; chmn, Bd. of Adjust; mem, Sch. Bd; former mem, Town Planning Bd. Bus. & Prof. Pos: Retired. Mem: Peterborough Rotary Club; Soc. of the Cincinnati. Mailing Add: Harrisville, N.H. 03450. (1967)

CLYNES, JAMES JOSEPH D
Conn. State Rep.
b. Hartford, Conn, 9/24/23; s. James Henry Clynes and Josephine McAloon C; m. 4/23/49 to Rhoda Mary Leonard; c. Nancy Ann and James William. Educ: New Britain High Sch, 4 years. Polit. & Govt. Pos: Conn. State Rep, 67- Mil. Serv: Entered as A/S, Navy, 42, released as Water Tender 2/C, 46, recalled 50-52. Mem: Am. Legion; Kiwanis (charter mem. and past pres, Southington Club). Rel: Catholic. Mailing Add: 31 Birchcrest Dr, Southington, Conn. 06489.

CMICH, STANLEY A. R
Mayor, Canton, Ohio
b. Glencampbell, Pa. Educ: Ohio State Univ. Polit. & Govt. Pos: Liquor agent in charge for 18 co, Ohio Dept. of Liquor Control, 49-51; safety dir, Canton, Ohio, 52-57 and mayor, 63- Bus. & Prof. Pos: Gen. prod. mgr, A.G. Stafford Co, Canton, Ohio, 58-63; mem. bd. dirs, Stark Co. Construction. Mil. Serv: With AUS, World War II. Mem: Am. Judicature Soc; Elks; Eagles; Moose; K. of C.(4°); Am. Legion; Stark Co. Hist. Soc; Am. Hall of Fame; Libr. Bd. of Gov; hon. mem, Rotary; Admirals Club, Inc; hon. mem, Exchange Club; DAV; Old Timers Asn; VFW; Ex-Newsboys Asn. Named Outstanding Young Man of the Year, U.S. Jr. C. of C, 52; Distinguished Serv. Award, Ohio Jr. C. of C, 52; Man of the Year Award, Canton Jr. C. of C, 52; Young Rep. Orgn. Award, 65; Gold Serv. Award, Canton Kiwanis, 65; VFW World War I Award, 65; plaque, Stark Co. Rep. Coun, 65; Award of Merit, Stark Co. Rep. Cent. and Exec. Cmt; Distinguished Serv. Award, Malone Col, 68; Distinguished Salesman Award, Sales and Mkt. Execs, 68; Golden Gloves Appreciation Award, Canton Boxing Cmn, 68; Recognition Award, Citizens of Canton, 68. Rel: Roman Catholic. Legal Res: 138 20th St. N.E, Canton, Ohio 44714. Mailing Add: 218 Cleveland Ave. S.W, Canton, Ohio 44702.

COAD, PATRICIA M. D
b. Montesano, Wash, 10/8/31; d. Frank Quimby and Mary Walters Q; div; c. Stephanie (Mrs. Seymour), Robert Everett, III, James Skyler and Tygen Lee. Educ: Grays Harbor Jr. Col, 50-51. Polit. & Govt. Pos: Secy, Marinette Co. Dem. Party, Wis, 64-66, chmn, 67-68. Bus. & Prof. Pos: Ins. underwriter, Grange Ins. Co, Seattle, Wash, 52-53; emergency room asst, St. Johns Hosp, Longview, 59; off. mgr, R & G Eng, Inc, Wausaukee, Wis, 65-, purchasing agent, 65- Award, DAR, 49. Rel: Presbyterian. Legal Res: Route 2, Crivitz, Wis, 54114. Mailing Add: Box 245, Wausaukee, Wis, 54177.

COAKLEY, RICHARD WALKER R
Mem. Bd. Supvrs, James City Co, Va.
b. Havre de Grace, Md, 2/28/26; s. William Crothers Coakley and Margaret Walker C; m. 9/19/59 to Martha Hildreth; c. Virginia Hildreth and Janice Frazier. Educ: Franklin and Marshall Col, 43-44; Univ. Md, B.S. in Chem. Eng, 50; Phi Kappa Sigma. Polit. & Govt. Pos: Mem, bd. supvrs, James City Co, Va, 68- Bus. & Prof. Pos: Engnr, E.I. duPont de Nemours & Co, Wilmington, Del, 50-51, prod. supvr, Aiken, S.C, 51-56 and develop. engnr, Niagara Falls, N.Y, 56-59; sr. engnr, Olin-Mathieson Co, Niagara Falls, 59-60; research engnr, Dow-Badische Co, Williamsburg, Va, 60- Mil. Serv: Entered as A/S, Navy Res, 43, released as Lt(jg), 46, after serv. in U.S.S. Vella Gulf (CVE-111), Pac. Theatre, 45-46; Am. Defense, World War II Victory and Pac. Theatre Medals. Mem: Am. Inst. Chem. Engnrs; VFW; Birchwood Civic Asn; bd, C. of C; Jr. C. of C; Am. Philatelic Soc; Elks; Rawls-Byrd PTA; James City Co. Rep. Cmt. Rel: Methodist. Mailing Add: 110 Redbud Lane, Williamsburg, Va. 23185.

COATES, DENNIS FLEET, JR. D
Chmn, Crockett Co. Dem. Party, Tex.
b. Ozona, Tex, 9/16/17; s. Dennis Fleet Coates, Sr. and Effie Gladine Powell C; m. 12/11/43 to Margaret Howard; c. Diana Faye (Mrs. Schreffler) and Cora Kaye. Ozona High Sch, Tex, 12 years. Polit. & Govt. Pos: Chmn, Crockett Co. Dem. Party, Tex, 67- Bus. & Prof. Pos: Rancher, currently. Mil. Serv: Entered as Pvt, Army, 42, released as 2nd Lt, 46, after serv. in Field Artil, ETO, 43-45; Good Conduct Medal; Bronze Star. Rel: Baptist. Mailing Add: 512 Ave. J, Box 716, Ozona, Tex. 76943.

COATS, WILLIAM JEAN R
Mem, Weakley Co. and Eighth Cong. Rep. Exec. Cmts.
b. Greenfield, Tenn, 2/1/06; s. William Andrew Coats and Lockie Hillis C; m. 3/21/31 to Virginia White; c. Betty (Mrs. Zimmerman), Sandra (Mrs. Morrel), Lt. Jere B.(killed in action) and Cathy Ann. Educ: Univ. Tenn; Sigma Phi Epsilon; Orange and White Staff. Polit. & Govt. Pos: Mem, Co. and Dist. Rep. Finance Cmts, Tenn, 48-; mem, Tenn. State Rep. Exec. Cmt, 56-60; del, Rep. Nat. Conv, 56 & 64; acting postmaster, Greenfield, 58-60; mem, Weakley Co. and Eighth Cong. Dist. Rep. Exec. Cmts, 64-; mem, City Coun. and Sch. Bd, Greenfield, 10 years. Bus. & Prof. Pos: Gen. Ins. Agency and Wholesale and Retail Field Seed, 30-53; rice and cattle farming and grain elevator operator, Tenn. and Ark, 50-; dir, Greenfield Banking Co, currently. Mil. Serv: 1st Lt, Home Guard, World War II. Rel: Presbyterian. Mailing Add: 106 W. Main St, Greenfield, Tenn. 38230.

COBB, ANDREW WHITNEY R
Supvr, Clinton Co, Mich.
b. Elsie, Mich, 2/12/11; s. Lyman Jason Cobb and Estella Grenlund C; m. 10/31/36 to Elizabeth Jean Mansfield; c. Lawrence, Lee, Shirley Larsen, Martha and Alan. Educ: Mich. State Univ, B.S, 34; Alpha Zeta; Pi Kappa Phi; Varsity Club. Polit. & Govt. Pos: Justice of the Peace, Duplain Twp, Mich, 45-50; Mich. State Rep, Clinton Co, 50-54 and Eaton Dist, 55-64; supvr, Clinton Co, 69- Bus. & Prof. Pos: Dairy farmer, 36- Mem: Farm Bur; Grange; Centennial Farm Asn; Mich. Milk Producer's Asn; Mich. Artificial Breeders; Dairy Herd Improv. Asn; Lions; Mason. Mich. 4H Alumni Award; Fed. Land Bank 50th Anniversary Medal; Mich. Milk Producer's Asn. Distinguished Serv. Award. Rel: United Methodist. Mailing Add: Route 2, Elsie, Mich. 48831.

COBB, J. C. D
Dem. Nat. Committeeman, Okla.
b. Iowa Park, Tex; m. to Rheba; c. Larry. Educ: N.Tex. State Univ; Capitol Col. of Pharmacy, B.S. in Pharmacy. Polit. & Govt. Pos: Mayor, Tishomingo, Okla, 50-54; secy, State Bd. of Pharmacy, 51-62; precinct, co. and dist. chmn, Dem. Party, 62-68; chmn. rules cmt, two Okla. Dem. State Conv; del, Dem. Nat. Conv, 64 & 68; Dem. Nat. Committeeman, Okla, 68- Bus. & Prof. Pos: Pharmacist; retail drug bus. Mem: Rotary (pres); Nat. Asn. of Retail Druggists (past pres); Shrine. Rel: Presbyterian; Elder, Presby. Church. Mailing Add: 215 W. Main, Tishomingo, Okla. 73460.

COBB, J. WILLIAM, JR. R
b. East Greenwich, R.I, 9/4/22; m. to Mary J. Educ: La Salle Acad; Univ. of R.I. Polit. & Govt. Pos: R.I. State Sen, 64-69; mem, East Greenwich Town Coun, 14 years, pres, 4 years. Bus. & Prof. Pos: Ins. agent. Mil. Serv: World War II, 95th Inf. Div, ETO; Korean Conflict, Seventh Div. 1967 Legal Res: East Greenwich, R.I. No mailing address available. (1967)

COBB, JOHN BYNUM, II D
Mem, Shelby Co. Dem. Exec. Cmt, Tenn.
b. Memphis, Tenn, 10/24/32; s. John Bynum Cobb and Edna Sennett C; m. 4/4/62 to Mary Lee Billingsly; c. Lynn Ann and John Bynum, III. Educ: Memphis State Univ, B.S, 55; Vanderbilt Univ, LL.B. and J.D, 60; Kappa Sigma; Phi Delta Phi. Polit. & Govt. Pos: Mem, Shelby Co. Dem. Exec. Cmt, Tenn, 60-; alternate del, Dem. Nat. Conv, 68. Bus. & Prof. Pos: Attorney-at-law. Mil. Serv: Entered as 2nd Lt, Air Force, 55, released as Capt, 58, after serv. in Strategic Air Command, Alaska; Capt, Res. Mem: Memphis Trial Lawyers Asn.(past pres); Tenn. Club. Rel: Baptist. Mailing Add: 83 W. Walnut Grove Court, Memphis, Tenn. 38117.

COBB, LAWRENCE DEAN D
Tex. State Rep.
b. Marlin, Tex, 5/16/36; s. Lawrence Morgan Cobb and Ruth Day C; m. 7/1/61 to Patricia Grace Threadgill; c. Kendall McKay and Courtney Read. Educ: Univ. Tex, B.A, 58; Baylor Law Sch, LL.B, 62; Tex. Cowboys; Cactus Goodfellow Phi Kappa Sigma; Phi Alpha Delta. Polit. & Govt. Pos: Co. attorney, Moore Co, Tex, 64-68; Tex. State Rep, 69- Mil. Serv: Entered as 2nd Lt, Army, 58, released as 1st Lt, 59, after serv. in QMC Sch, Ft. Lee, Va, 36th Inf. Div, Nat. Guard, 6 years. Publ: 'Common Law Marriages in Texas,' Baylor Law Rev, spring 61. Mem: Tex. and Am. Bar Asns; Tex. and Am. Trial Lawyers Asns; 69th Judicial Dist. Bar Asn; Rotary; YMCA; Am. Cancer Soc; C. of C.(bd. dirs, Dumas Br); Boy Scouts (exec. coun). Rel: Presbyterian. Legal Res: 109 Amherst, Dumas, Tex. 79029. Mailing Add: P.O. Box 477, Dumas, Tex. 79029.

COBB, OWENS TAYLOR, JR. D
b. Columbia, S.C, 2/27/33; s. Owens T. Cobb and Kathryn Williams C; m. 8/15/53 to Jacqueline Oswald C; c. Kathy, Jody, Owens T. III. Educ: Clemson

Col, 51-52; Univ. of S.C, LL.B, 59; Sigma Alpha Epsilon; Phi Delta Phi. Polit. & Gov. Pos: S.C. State Rep, 63-66. Bus. & Prof. Pos: Lawyer. Mil. Serv: Army, 8th Inf. Div, 260th Signal Corps, 53-55. Mem: Columbia Young Lawyers Club; Bd. Dir, Richland Co. Legal Aid Soc; V.Pres, Downtown Optimist Club; Columbia and Am. Bar Asns; WOW. Rel: Off. Bd, Main St. Methodist Church. Legal Res: 1233 Washington St, Columbia, S.C. Mailing Add: 1421 Bull St, Columbia, S.C. 29201. (1967)

COBB, WILLIAM ALLEN R
N.J. State Assemblyman
b. Dover, N.J, 11/24/07; s. Frank Cobb and Mary Ellen Ross C; m. to Willa Frances Headley; c. Nancy Jane and William Allen, Jr. Educ: Dover High Sch, 4 years. Polit. & Govt. Pos: Mem, twp. cmt, Denville, N.J, 36-37, twp. treas, 37-59; N.J. State Assemblyman, Morris Co, 68- Bus. & Prof. Pos: Munic. acct, 44-69. Rel: Presbyterian. Legal Res: Franklin Rd, Denville, N.J. 07801. Mailing Add: 45 E. Blackwell St, Dover, N.J. 07801.

COBBE, MARGARET HAMMETT D
V.Chmn, Pinellas Co. Dem. Exec. Cmt, Fla.
b. Gaffney, S.C, 8/3/20; d. Davis Eugene Hammett and Ava Era Barrett H; m. 11/23/43 to Jerome Francis Cobbe (deceased); c. Jerome Francis, Jr, Sheila (Mrs. Tobin); Michael Timothy and Luane Carol. Educ: Strayer's Bus. Col, Wash, D.C, Secy. Course, 38. Polit. & Govt. Pos: Secy, Gulfport Area Dem. Club, Fla, 61-62; secy, Pinellas Co. Dem. Exec. Cmt, 62-65, v.chmn, 65-; alternate del, Dem. Nat. Conv, 68; first v.pres, St. Petersburg Dem. Women's Club, Fla, 68-; eighth cong. dist. v.pres, Dem. Women's Club of Fla, 68- Bus. & Prof. Pos: Secy, Bur. Old Age & Survivors Ins, Wash, D.C, 40-43; pvt. secy. to pres, Glenn E. McCormick Co, Inc, St. Petersburg, Fla, 55-59. Mil. Serv: Entered as Pvt, Women's Army Corps, Army Air Force, 43, released as Sgt, 45, after serv. in Air Transport Command, ETO, 44-45; Good Conduct Medal. Mem: League of Women Voters, St. Petersburg, Fla. Top Fundraiser Cert, Pinellas Co. Dem. Exec. Cmt, 64, Perfect Attendance Cert, 65; Outstanding Dem. Woman of Fla, 69. Rel: Baptist; Supt, young people's dept, Pasadena Baptist Church. Mailing Add: 901 62nd St. S, Gulfport, Fla. 33707.

COBBS, LYLE RICHARD R
Idaho State Rep.
b. Boise, Idaho, 7/22/30; s. Hartzell Cobbs (deceased) and Edith Miller C; m. 4/9/54 to Donna Lee White; c. Nancy Marie, Diane Elizabeth, Kathryn Ann and Lyla Renée. Educ: Northwest Christian Col, 49-51. Polit. & Govt. Pos: Idaho State Rep, Ada Co, 64- Mil. Serv: Entered as Pvt, Army, 51, released as Cpl, 53, after serv. in Army Res, Inf, Korea, 52; several mil. awards & decorations. Mem: Kiwanis Int, pres, local club; Mason; Rel: Christian Church. Mailing Add: 1346 Tetonia Dr, Boise, Idaho 83705. (1967)

COBEY, JAMES ALEXANDER D
b. Frostburg, Md, 10/3/13; s. James C. Cobey, M.D. and Elizabeth Earle C; m. 8/1/42 to Virginia Joy Branum; c. Hope Branum, Christopher Earle and Lisa Elizabeth. Educ: Princeton Univ, A.B, 34; Yale Univ, LL.B, 38; Harvard Grad Sch. Bus. Admin, cert, 38. Polit. & Govt. Pos: Sr. attorney, Nat. Labor Rels. Bd, Was, D.C, 38-46; chief research attorney, Second Calif. Dist. Court Appeals, Los Angeles, 46-48; dep. counsel, Los Angeles, Co, Calif, 48; Calif. State Sen, 55-66; Assoc. Justice, Calif. Court of Appeals, 66- Bus. & Prof. Pos: Faculty mem, Loyola Univ, 48; assoc. mem. law firm, C. Ray Robinson, 49-60; sr. partner, Cobey & Adams, Merced, Calif, 60-66. Mil. Serv: Entered as Ens, Navy, 42, released as Lt, 46. Mem: V.pres, State Conf. Jr. Bar Mems, 47; past comdr, Dist. 12, Am. Legion; S.E.S; life mem, PTA; F&AM; Scottish Rite; Shrine. Winner, 1st Golden Gavel Award for best legis. cmt. report, Nat. Conf. of State Legis. Leaders, 61-62. Rel: Episcopal; Asst. Vestryman, All Saints Episcopal Church, Pasadena, Calif. Mailing Add: 560 S. Orange Grove Blvd, Pasadena, Calif. 91105.

COBLE, J. KERMIT D
b. Greensboro, N.C, 8/12/25; s. Jerome Bedford Coble and Mary Freshwater C; m. to Marilyn Wentworth; c. Carolyn Dawn and J. Kermit, Jr. Educ: Wake Forest Col, N.C; Stetson Univ. Law Sch, DeLand, Fla; Univ. Miami, LL.B, 53; Phi Delta Phi. Polit. & Govt. Pos: Fla. State Rep, 64-68. Mil. Serv: Sgt, Air-Sea Rescue, Army Air Corps. Mem: Am, Fla. and Volusia Co. Bar Asns; F&AM; Shrine; Past Pres, YMCA; Cmt. of 100 at Daytona Beach C. of C; past pres. and past mem, bd. dirs, Daytona Beach Jr. C. of C; Am. Legion; Kiwanis; bd. dirs, United Fund; Fraternal Order of Police; state dir, Jaycees; asst. city judge, Daytona Beach. Outstanding Young Man of Year, Jaycees, 59; Honored by Daytona Beach for Work on Zoning Bd. of Appeals; Chosen one of three Outstanding Freshman Legislators in 65th session, Fla. State Legis. Rel: Presbyterian. Legal Res: 1150 Florida Ave, Daytona Beach, Fla. 32014. Mailing Add: 136½ S. Beach St, Daytona Beach, Fla. 32014.

COBLE, JOHN HOWARD R
N.C. State Rep.
b. Greensboro, N.C, 3/18/31; s. Joe Howard Coble and Johnnie Holt C; single. Educ: Appalachian State Teachers Col, 49-50; Guilford Col, A.B, 58; Univ. N.C. Sch. Law, Chapel Hill, LL.B, 62; Delta Theta Phi. Polit. & Govt. Pos: Various pos, Young Rep. Club, N.C, 59-62; asst. co. attorney, Guilford Co, 67-69; N.C. State Rep, 69- Mil. Serv: Entered as Seaman Recruit, Coast Guard, 52, released as YN2, 56, after serv. in various Coast Guard units and stas, Lt. Comdr, Res, 60- Mem: Greensboro and N.C. Bar Asns; N.C. State Bar; Am. Judicature Soc; Lions; ROA. Rel: Presbyterian. Mailing Add: Route 10, Box 168, Greensboro, N.C. 27406.

COBLEIGH, MARSHALL W. R
Speaker, N.H. House of Rep.
b. Nashua, N.H, 6/4/30; married. Educ: Boston Univ. Gen. Col; Boston Univ. Col. Bus. Admin, B.S; Sch. for Mutual Ins. Agents; Univ. N.C; Boston Univ. Varsity Club. Polit. & Govt. Pos: Del, Legis. Leaders Conf. Hwy. Safety; past pres, Gr. Nashua Young Rep. Club; v.chmn, Hillsborough Co. Rep. Del; del, N.H. Constitutional Conv, 64; N.H. State Rep, 63-, Majority Floor Leader, N.H. House of Rep, 67-68 and Speaker, 69- Bus. & Prof. Pos: Gen. mgr, Independent Mutual Ins. Agents of New Eng. Mil. Serv: Navy, 51-55; chosen for duty on Pres. Truman's Yacht, U.S.S. Williamsburg (ACC369); first enlisted man to serve as Athletic dir, U.S. Naval Air Sta, Patuxent River, Md. Mem: Past pres, N.H. Jr. C. of C; past pres, N.H. Asn. of Mutual Ins. Agents; past v.pres, U.S. Jr. C. of C; Am. Legion; Nat. Alumni Coun. of Boston Univ; secy-treas, Nat. Rep. Legislators Conf; mem. ethics cmt, Nat. Soc. State Legislators; dir, Nashua C. of C; dir, N.E. Soc. Asn. Exec; legis. cmt, Am. Soc. Asn. Exec. Mailing Add: P.O. Box 606, Nashua, N.H. 03060.

COBLENTZ, ARTHUR PAUL R
Ind. State Rep.
b. Red Haw, Ohio, 9/10/99; s. Herbert W. Coblentz and Cora Kester C; m. 3/5/21 to Bernice Roberts; c. Max E. and Jerry Arlene (Mrs. Schannep). Educ: Park Col, Parkville, Mo. Polit. & Govt. Pos: Cmnr, Wabash Co, Ind, 34-40; Ind. State Sen, 41-48 & 57-61; Ind. State Rep, 65- Bus. & Prof. Pos: Pres. and owner, Coblentz & Son, 21-66; pres, Rittenhouse Am. Corp, 62-66. Mil. Serv: Pvt, Students Army Training Corps, Park Col, Mo, 18. Mem: Mason; Scottish Rite, Shrine; pres, Kiwanis, N. Manchester, Ind; past pres, Ind. Retail Farm Implement Dealers Asn, Indianapolis. Rel: Evangelical United Brethren. Mailing Add: Main St, Liberty Mills, Ind. 46946. (1967)

COBLENTZ, WILLIAM KRAEMER D
b. San Francisco, Calif, 7/28/22; s. Zach Benjamin Coblentz and Fritze Levy C; m. 11/22/52 to Jean Berlin; c. Wendy K. and Andrew S. Educ: Univ. Calif, Berkeley, B.A, 43; Yale Univ, LL.B, 45; Corbey Court. Polit. & Govt. Pos: Spec. asst. to Attorney Gen, San Francisco, Calif, 51-52; spec. counsel to Gov. of Calif, 59-60; trustee, Calif. State Col, 60-64; consult, U.S. Dept. of State, 62; regent, Univ. Calif, 64-; del, Dem. Nat. Conv, 68. Bus. & Prof. Pos: Partner, Jacobs, Sills and Coblentz, Attorneys-at-law, 53- Mil. Serv: Entered as Pvt, Army, 43, released as Lt, 45. Publ: 'The Iron and Steel Community,' Am. Bar Asn; 'Human Rights in a World Community,' Calif. Law Rev; 'Air Law and Admiralty,' Univ. South. Calif. Law Rev. Mem: San Francisco, Calif. and Am. Bar Asns; Asn. of Bar of City of New York; Am. Law Inst; Civic league of Improv. Clubs (dir); Bay Area Educ. TV (dir); Mt. Zion Hosp. and Med. Center (dir); dir, NAACP Legal and Educ. Defense Fund. Rel: Jewish. Legal Res: 10 Fifth Ave, San Francisco, Calif. 94118. Mailing Add: Bank of America Plaza, San Francisco, Calif. 94104.

COBURN, ROSCOE NEWTON R
N.H. State Rep.
b. Milford, N.H, 1/10/98; s. Stephen Carroll Coburn and Ida Belle Goodwin C; m. 6/16/21 to Blanche Lorraine Anderson; c. Sandra (Mrs. Newbold). Educ: Milford High Sch, N.H, grad, 16. Polit. & Govt. Pos: Chmn, N.H. Selective Serv. Bd. 17, Milford, N.H, 48-68; selectman, Milford, 50-52; N.H. Rep, 65- Mil. Serv: Pvt, Army, 18-19, serv. in Co. C 1st U.S. Engrs, ETO. Mem: Rotary; Mason; VFW; Vet. World War I; Am. Legion (past comdr, Ricciardi-Hartshorn Post). Am. Legion Citation. Rel: United Church of Christ. Mailing Add: 78 Elm St, Milford, N.H. 03055.

COCHRAN, ALICE LIDDLE R
b. Flat Rock, Mich, 7/18/36; d. Joseph E. Liddle and Hilda Melke L; m. 6/21/69 to James R. Cochran. Educ: Univ. Mich, A.B, 58, M.A, 61; Mich. State Univ; Circle Hon, Univ. Mich. Polit. & Govt. Pos: Mem, Gratiot Co. Rep Women's Club, Mich, 63-68; dir, Mich. Teen-Age Rep, 65-68; v.chmn, Gratiot Co. Rep. Party, 65-66, chmn, 66-68; mem, bd. of dirs, Mich. Women's Rep. Fedn. and Mich. Young Rep. Fedn, 66-68; dir. of youth activities, Mich. Rep. Party, 67-68. Bus. & Prof. Pos: Jr. high geog. and Eng. teacher, Midland Pub. Sch, 58-59 and Wayne Pub. Schs, 59-60; sr. high Eng. teacher, Alma Pub. Schs, 60-67; teacher, San Rafael, Calif. Schs, 68-69. Mem: Nat. Educ. Asn; Mich. Nat. Coun. Teachers of Eng; past pres, Alma Branch, Am. Asn. Univ. Women; Gratiot Co. League of Women Voters; past mem, Jaycee and Lions Auxiliaries. Named Outstanding Young Educator, Alma Jaycees, 66. Rel: Methodist. Mailing Add: 2422 Thaddeus Dr, Mountain View Calif. 94040.

COCHRAN, DALE M. D
Iowa State Rep.
b. Ft. Dodge, Iowa, 11/20/28; s. Melvin Cochran and Gladys C; m. 1952 to Jeanene Hirsch; c. Deborah, Cynthia and Tamara. Educ: Iowa State Univ, B.S, 50; Pi Kappa Phi. Polit. & Govt. Pos: Iowa State Rep, currently; former staff mem. U.S. Rep. Merwin Coad; former dir, Co. Exten. Bus. & Prof. Pos: Owner and operator 400 acre farm; pub. rels. dir, Hartland, Inc; past farm ed, Ft. Dodge Messenger. Mem: Various farm orgn. Rel: Methodist. Legal Res: Route 3, Eagle Grove, Iowa 50533. Mailing Add: State Capitol, E. Tenth and Grand Ave, Des Moines, Iowa 50319. (1967)

COCHRAN, EUGENE F. D
b. Newport, R.I, 4/22/17; m. to Elizabeth Moran. Educ: Providence Col, B.A, 38; Boston Univ. Law Sch, LL.B, 47. Polit. & Govt. Pos: Former mem, R.I. Young Dem. and 11th Ward Dem. Club; former dep. town solicitor, Bristol, R.I, town solicitor, 49-50; R.I. State Rep, 55-69, Dep. Majority Leader, R.I. State House of Rep, 65-69. Bus. & Prof. Pos: Attorney-at-law. Mil. Serv: Lt. Comdr, Navy, 41-46, serv. in Mediterranean Theatre; Bronze Star; Navy Commendation Medal. Mem: R.I. Bar Asn; Am. Legion; VFW; K. of C; SAR; Hibernians. Mailing Add: 87 Princeton Ave, Providence, R.I. 02907. (1967)

COCHRAN, FRANKLIN DELANO D
Tenn. State Rep.
b. Tiptonville, Tenn, 10/20/37; s. Clarence Ulas Cochran and Essie Berry C; m. 8/10/58 to Patsy Jo Whitfield; c. Kent. Educ: David Lipscomb Col; Univ. Tenn; Univ. Tenn. Col. Law; Alpha Tau Omega; Phi Alpha Delta. Polit. & Govt. Pos: Tenn. State Rep, 62-; co. attorney, 63-; city attorney, 65- Mem: Am. Bar Asn; Tenn. Trial Lawyers Asn; Mason; Kiwanis; Farm Bur. Rel: Church of Christ. Legal Res: 513 Foster, Tiptonville, Tenn. 38079. Mailing Add: 301 Church, Tiptonville, Tenn. 38079. (1967)

COCHRANE, GORDON SWAIN D
Chmn, Benton Co. Dem. Cent. Cmt, Wash.
b. Hudson, Mass, 10/25/15; s. Merlin Cochrane and Ruth Swain C; m. 9/3/40 to Patricia Hart; c. Helen and James. Educ: Lowell Inst, 35-38; Antioch Col, 38-40. Polit. & Govt. Pos: Mem. campaign cmts. for Adlai Stevenson, 52 & 56, Sen. Warren G. Magnuson, 56, Gov. Albert D. Rosellini, 56, 60 & 64, Sen. Henry M. Jackson, 58 & 64, John F. Kennedy, 60 and Lyndon B. Johnson, 64; mem. exec. bd, Fourth Cong. Dist. Dem. Coun. and chmn. coun, 54-56; chmn, Benton Co. Dem. Cent. Cmt, 54-60 & 64-; coordinator, Atomic Develop.

Activities, Wash. State, 58-63; del, Dem. Nat. Conv, 60 & 64; precinct committeeman, 62-66; consult, Gov. Adv. Coun. on Atomic Energy, 63. Bus. & Prof. Pos: Machinist-draftsman, Gen. Elec. Co, 34-38, prod. engr. res. and develop, turbine-gear eng. dept, Lynn, Mass. River Works, 38-47, design engr. design and construction, Hanford Works, 47-53, sr. develop. engr. reactor and fuel develop, Hanford Labs, 53-65; sr. develop. engr. metallurgy dept, Battelle Mem. Inst, Pac. Northwest Labs, 65-68, asst. to div. mgr, chem. and metallurgy div, 68-, div. facility engr, 69- Mem: Am. Civil Liberties Union; Am. Soc. Mech. Engr.(exec. bd, pub. rels. cmt); Am. Little League (coach); Thomson Engrs. Club; licensed Class A amateur radio operator; UN Asn; CORE; Am. Acad. Polit. and Soc. Sci. Rel: Unitarian. Mailing Add: 1636 Howell, Richland, Wash. 99352.

COCHRANE, JAMES GORDON D
b. Salem, Mass, 3/26/46; s. Gordon S. Cochrane and Patricia Hart C; single. Educ: Univ. Wash, B.A. in Econ, 68; Univ. Calif, Davis, summer 67; Omicron Delta Epsilon. Polit. & Govt. Pos: Founding mem, Wash. Dem. Coun; alternate del, Dem. Nat. Conv, 68. Mil. Serv: Entered as Airman, Air Force, 68- currently, trainee, Off. Training Sch, Lackland AFB, Tex. Rel: Episcopal. Legal Res: 1636 Howell, Richland, Wash. 99352. Mailing Add: Sq. 2 Flt. 13 Cmr 7, Lackland AFB, San Antonio, Tex. 78236.

COCHRANE, JOHN CAMPBELL R
Chmn, Islip Rep. Town Cmt, N.Y.
b. Bay Shore, N.Y, 11/16/29; s. John Campbell Cochrane and Helen Spach C; m. 11/29/52 to Elizabeth Cook; c. Susan B, Elizabeth A, John C. and James R. Educ: U.S. Naval Acad, B.S.Eng, 51. Polit. & Govt. Pos: Alternate del, Rep. Nat. Conv, 68; chmn, Islip Rep. Town Cmt, N.Y, 68- Bus. & Prof. Pos: Pres, Cochrane & Craven Agency Inc, 56-; dir, First Nat. Bank of Bay Shore, 57-; trustee, United Fund of L.I, 63- Mil. Serv: Entered as Midn, Navy, 47, released as Lt.(jg), 55, after serv. in U.S.S. Melvin and U.S.S. Antietam; Comdr, Naval Res; Armed Forces Res. Medal; Nat. Defense Award; European Occup. Ribbon. Mem: Past pres, Bay Shore Lions and Bay Shore-Brightwaters United Fund; treas, Bay Shore Yacht Club. Rel: Episcopal. Mailing Add: 131 S. Windsor Ave, Brightwaters, N.Y. 11718.

COCHRANE, PAT D
b. Melville, Mont, 7/27/16; d. John Walker Hart and Eleanor Armstrong H; m. 9/3/40 to Gordon S. Cochrane; c. Helen and James. Educ: Mont. State Col, B.S, 39; Boston Univ, M.A. in biol, 40; Pi Beta Phi; Spartanian; Gridiron Club; Episcopal Youth Group; Int. Rels. Club; Mont. State Col. Chorus, 4 years; Debate Team; assoc. ed, col. paper and staff mem, col. annual, 4 years; off. mgr, Dean Women, Mont. State Col, 3 years; Grad. Sch. Coun; Bios Club; Episcopal Club, Boston Univ. Polit. & Govt. Pos: Pres, Richland Women's Dem. Club, 54-56; legis. chmn, Wash. State Fedn. Dem. Women's Clubs, 54-56, mem. exec. bd, 54-60, chmn, 56-60; mem. exec. bd, Wash. Dem. State Cent. Cmt, 54-58; state committeewoman, Benton Co, Wash, 54-60 and precinct committeewoman, 54-62; Wash. State Fund Chmn. for Adlai E. Stevenson, 56; alternate del, Dem. Nat. Conv, 56 & 64; state chmn, Dollars for Dem, 57-60; del, Wash. State Conf. on Children and Youth, 59 and White House Conf. on Children and Youth, 60; mem, Gov. Cmt. on Youth Employ. and Cmt. on Employed Women, Gov. Cmn. on Status of Women, Wash, 63-64; del, White House Conf. on Int. Coop. Year and U.S. Cmn. for UNESCO Conf, 65. Bus. & Prof. Pos: Lab. instr, pre-med. dept, Mont. State Col, 2 years; teacher chem, Boston Med. Jr. Col, 40; saleswoman, West Auto Stores, Lynn, Mass, 41-43; owner, Columbia Book Store, Richland, Wash, 49-54; exec. dir, Camp Fire Girls, 57-66. Publ: Off. book on Col. Customs and Manners, Mont. State Col. Mem: Am. Acad. Polit. and Soc. Sci; World Peace through World Law Center; nat. cmt, Adlai Stevenson Inst. of Int. Affairs; Region VI Exec. Dirs. Asn. Camp Fire Girls; numerous positions, UN Asn; troop mother, Girl Scouts, 6 years; den mother, Boy Scouts, 2 years; Little League, Pony League, Colt League; March of Dimes; Commun. Chest; United Crusade; PTA and pre-sch. PTA; United Vol. Serv; Am. Asn. Univ. Women; League Women Voters; charter mem, Richland Munic. League; Am. Civil Liberties Union; NAACP; publicity dir, Richland Incorporation Cmt; CORE; Head Start Adv. Cmt, 65; exec. dir, Benton Franklin Commun. Action Cmt, 66-68; finance coordinator, Wash. Dem. Coun, 69- Rel: Episcopal. Mailing Add: 1636 Howell Ave, Richland, Wash. 99352.

COCHRANE, WILLIAM McWHORTER D
b. Newton, N.C, 3/6/17; s. William Daniel Cochrane and Veasey Fillingim C; m. 6/3/45 to Thornton Shirley Graves; c. William Daniel and Thomas McWhorter. Educ: Univ. N.C, A.B, 39, LL.B, 41; Yale Univ, LL.M, 51; Order of the Golden Fleece. Polit. & Govt. Pos: Exec. secy. to the late U.S. Sen. W. Kerr Scott, 54-58; admin. asst. to U.S. Sen. B. Everett Jordan, N.C, 58-; exec. dir, Joint Cong. Cmt. on 1969 Presidential Inaugural Ceremonies, 68. Bus. & Prof. Pos: Asst. dir, Inst. of Govt, Univ. N.C, 40-42 & 45-52, admin. dir. inst, assoc. research prof. pub. law and govt. and managing ed, Popular Govt, 52-54. Mil. Serv: Entered as A/S, Naval Res, 42, released as Lt, 45, after serv. in Atlantic, 43-44 and Mediterranean, 44-45; Lt. Comdr, Naval Res, 45-66; Ready Res. Medal; Am. Theater Ribbon; European-African Ribbon with Star; Victory Medal; Naval Res. Serv. Medal. Mem: N.C. State Bar; N.C. Bar Asn; C. of C. Admitted to practice in N.C. Supreme Court and U.S. Supreme Court. Rel: Methodist. Legal Res: P.O. Box 3, Chapel Hill, N.C. 27514. Mailing Add: 3229 Senate Office Bldg, Washington, D.C. 20510.

COCHRANE, WILLIAM P.
Asst. Parliamentarian, U.S. House of Rep.
b. Charlotte, N.C, 10/18/14; s. Fred Ernest Cochrane and Claudia Babbington C; m. 10/17/36 to Sara Margaret Townsend; c. Sara Margaret. Educ: Nat. Univ.D.C, LL.B, 40; George Wash. Univ, J.D, 68; Sigma Nu Phi. Polit. & Govt. Pos: Asst. parliamentarian, U.S. House of Rep; spec. asst, U.S. Attorney Gen; gen. coun, Philippine Alien Property Admin. Mil. Serv: Col, Air Force Res, Hq. Judge Adv. Gen, 48-55. Mem: Bd. dirs, United Serv. Orgn; pres, Capitol Hill First Friday Club; Nat. Press Club; Int. Club of Wash. Legal Res: Charlotte, N.C. Mailing Add: 9 Ninth St. N.E, Washington, D.C. 20002.

COCKERILL, LEON HERBERT, JR. R
Chmn, Dist. 22 Rep. Party, N.Dak.
b. Omaha, Nebr, 8/25/27; s. Leon Herbert Cockerill, Sr. and Eva Martin C; m. 10/9/49 to Helen Arlene Pederson; c. Pam Nadine, Lon Adair, Randi Allyn, Brian Bruce and Leon Herbert, III. Educ: Mapleton, N.Dak, Dist. 7, 11 years. Polit. & Govt. Pos: Chmn, Dist. 22 Rep. Party, N.Dak, 68- Bus. & Prof. Pos: Farming, 50-69. Mem: AF&AM; Farm Bur. Rel: Presbyterian. Mailing Add: Mapleton, N.Dak. 58059.

COCKRILL, STERLING ROBERTSON, JR. D
Ark. State Rep.
b. Little Rock, Ark, 4/7/25; s. Sterling Robertson Cockrill and Helen Bracy C; m. 9/4/45 to Adrienne S; c. Mary Ashley and Cecilia Ann. Educ: Univ. Ark, B.S. in Bus. Admin. Polit. & Govt. Pos: Ark. State Rep, 57-, Speaker, Ark. House of Rep, 67, Majority Leader, 69- Bus. & Prof. Pos: Pres, Ark. Asn. Ins. Agents, 66-67. Mil. Serv: Entered as A/S, Navy, 43, released as Lt, 46. Rel: Episcopal. Mailing Add: 4801 Crestwood, Little Rock, Ark. 72207.

COCKRUM, CLAUDIA O. D
Chmn, Mills Co. Dem. Party, Tex.
b. Goldthwaite, Tex, 7/20/12; d. Samuel Nathan Carroll and Ola Bare C; m. 2/7/42 to Raymond Kelon Cockrum, wid. 11/21/62. Educ: Draughon Bus. Col, 30. Polit. & Govt. Pos: Chmn, Mills Co. Dem. Party, Tex, 58- Bus. & Prof. Pos: Owner, Mills Co. Hardware, 41-63; Stacy's Ins. Agency. Mem: Past Matron and Grand Officer, Eastern Star. Rel: Baptist. Mailing Add: P.O. Box 100, Goldthwaite, Tex. 76844.

CODINHA, PAUL PHILLIP R
Mem, Gloucester Rep. City Cmt, Mass.
b. Gloucester, Mass, 6/7/39; s. Joequien E. Codinha and Esther Cortina C; single. Educ: N.Y. Inst. of Finance; North Shore Commun. Col, 68-69. Polit. & Govt. Pos: Mem, Gloucester Rep. City Cmt, Mass, 63-, chmn, 65-66; chmn, ways & means cmt, Cape Ann Young Rep. Club, 63-64, pres, 64-65. Mil. Serv: Entered as Pvt, Army, 57, released as Sp/4, 60; recalled to active duty during Berlin Crisis for 9 mos; Good Conduct Medal. Mem: K. of C.(3°); Elks. Rel: Roman Catholic. Mailing Add: 70 Friend St, Gloucester, Mass. 01930.

COE, MARGARET WYMAN R
Chmn, Madison Rep. Town Cmt, Conn.
b. Washington, D.C, 7/8/19; d. William Howard Wyman and Mary Louise Barlup W; m. 1/15/43 to George Hughes Coe; c. Jeanne (Mrs. Lake). Educ: Averett Col, 34-36; Wash. Sch. for Secretaries. Polit. & Govt. Pos: V.chmn, Madison Rep. Town Cmt, Conn, 66-68, chmn, 68- Bus. & Prof. Pos: Secy, Liberty Nat. Bank, Wash, D.C, Mutual Broadcasting Co. and Haloid Co. Mem: Eastern Star; Yale-New Haven Hosp. Auxiliary; Am. Red Cross; Madison Women's Rep. Club. Rel: Congregational. Mailing Add: 48 Stonewall Lane, Madison, Conn. 06443.

COELHO, PETER J. D
R.I. State Rep.
b. East Providence, R.I, 5/10/21; s. Joseph Bernardino Coelho and Eugenia Lopes C; m. 7/15/44 to Julia De Pina; c. Jean A, Carol C. (Mrs. Lopes), Julia A, Sheila J. and Susan Lee. Educ: Inst. of Appl. Sci, Chicago, cert, 45; Univ. R.I. Exten, cert, 62. Polit. & Govt. Pos: Secy, Ward Two Dem. City Cmt, 61-62; R.I. State Rep, Dist. 84, 66- Bus. & Prof. Pos: Owner-operator, Coelho Painting Co, 47-65; spec. agent, N.Y. Life Ins. Co, 65-68; exec. dir, Homes for Hope Found, 68- Mil. Serv: Entered as Pvt, Army Air Force, 42, released as Sgt, 46, after serv. at Tuskegee Army Air Field, 42-46. Mem: Cape Verdean Progressive Center; Diocesan Human Rels. Cmn; Pius X Assembly; K. of C. (4°). Rel: Catholic. Mailing Add: 155 Leonard Ave, East Providence, R.I. 02914.

COERR, WYMBERLEY DeRENNE Independent
b. N.Y.C, 10/2/13; m. to Eleanor Hicks; c. two. Educ: Yale Univ, B.A, 36. Polit. & Govt. Pos: Career officer, U.S. Dept. of State For. Serv, 39-43, 47-, v.consul, Montreal, 40-41, Honduras, 41-43 and Mex, 43-44, second secy, Suva, Fiji Islands, 47-48, Batavia, 48-50 and Indonesia, 50-51; officer in charge of Indonesian Affairs, 51-54; counsr, Honduras, 54-55 and Guatemala, 55-56, Nat. War Col, 56-57 and LaPaz, 57-59, dir, Off. W.Coast Affairs, 59-60, Acting Asst. Secy. of State for Inter-Am. Affairs, 60-61, U.S. Ambassador to Uruguay, 62-65 and Ecuador, 65-67; dir. of res. and anal. for Latin Am, 69- Bus. & Prof. Pos: Mfg. educ. dir, Consumer Coop. Corps, 43-47. Legal Res: McLean, Va. Mailing Add: U.S. Dept. of State, Washington, D.C. 20521.

COFFEE, JOHN MAIN D
b. Tacoma, Wash, 1/23/97; s. William Buckingham Coffee and Anne Rae Main C; m. 11/20/23 to Lillian Mary Slye; c. John Main, Jr. Educ; Univ. Wash, A.B, 18, LL.B, 20; Yale Univ, J.D, 21; Sigma Upsilon; Xi Pi; Alpha Sigma Phi. Polit. & Govt. Pos: Mem, Tacoma Civil Serv. Cmn, Wash, 26; chmn, Co-City Unemploy. Relief Cmt, Tacoma, 30-32; secy, State Recovery Bd. Nat. Recovery Admin, 33-35; U.S. Rep, Wash, 37-47, chmn, Liberal Bloc, U.S. House Rep, 39-45. Bus. & Prof. Pos: Lawyer, at present. Publ: 'Why Not a West Point for Diplomats?' Coronet Magazine, 44; 'A Study of Alcoa,' This Week Mag, 45. Mem: Elks; Eagles; Grange; Yale Club, Wash. D.C. & Seattle; Mason; founder, Young Men's Bus. Club Tacoma; Pierce Co, Wash. and Am. Bar Asn; hon. mem. Am. Fedn. Govt. Employees; Carpenters Union. Hobbies: Philately; swimming. Rel: Unitarian. Legal Res: 4104 Sixth Ave, Tacoma, Wash. 98406. Mailing Add: 811 Washington Bldg, Tacoma, Wash. 98402.

COFFEE, TOM FRANKLIN R
Chmn, Lipscomb Co. Rep. Cmt, Tex.
b. Miami, Tex, 9/9/28; s. Clyde Merwyn Coffee and Abbie Gripp C; m. 10/15/60 to Betty Lou Stanford; c. Walter Clyde and Tom Clay. Educ: Miami High Sch. Polit. & Govt. Pos: Precinct chmn, Rep. Party, 64-65; co. campaign chmn. for Congressman Bob Price, 64-; chmn, Lipscomb Co. Rep. Cmt, Tex, 65- Bus. & Prof. Pos: Cattle rancher, 48-; livestock inspector, First Nat. Bank, Amarillo, Tex, 66- Mil. Serv: Entered as Pvt, Army, 50, released as Cpl, 52, after serv. in Fourth Inf. Div, ETO, 51-52; Good Conduct Medal; Occup. Medal, Germany. Mem: Mason; Am. Legion; C. of C; Baptist Brotherhood. Rel: Baptist. Mailing Add: Box 206, Higgins, Tex. 79046.

COFFEY, BARBARA JEAN D
b. Ft. Fairfield, Maine, 4/9/44; d. Adra P. Hanscomb and Gladys Leavitt H; m. 11/17/62 to John P. Coffey, Jr; c. Kathleen Marie, Thresa Lee, Bar-

bara Jean and John Patrick. Educ: South Portland Pub. Sch. Syst, Maine, grad. high sch, 62. Polit. & Govt. Pos: Former Maine State Rep. Rel: Roman Catholic. Mailing Add: 21 Mallett Dr, Topsham, Maine 04086.

COFFIN, FRED J. D
b. Can, 11/10/96; married; c. 1. Polit. & Govt. Pos: Former N.H. State Rep; formerly, city assessor; former city councilman. Bus. & Prof. Pos: Retired. Mem: Eagles. Rel: Catholic. Mailing Add: 76 Elm St, Somersworth, N.H. 03878. (1967)

COFFING, THOMAS H. R
b. Oxford, Ind, 11/19/23; s. Thomas T. Coffing and Elizabeth Hall C; m. 2/16/63 to Mary Elizabeth Kuykendall; c. John Ramon Gorman, Paul Lee Gorman and Bonnie Elizabeth. Educ: Purdue Univ, B.S. in Chem. Eng, 47; Beta Theta Pi. Polit. & Govt. Pos: Rep. precinct chmn, Tex, 59-63; campaign coordinator, State Rep, 61; campaign mgr, Ninth Cong. Dist, 62; chmn, Galveston Co. Rep. Party, 63-66. Bus. & Prof. Pos: Chem. Engr, Monsanto Co, 47-. Mil. Serv: Entered as Pvt, Army, 43, released as T/5, 46, after serv. in Spec. Eng. Detachment, Oak Ridge, Tenn, 44-46; Victory Medal; Am. Serv. Medal; Good Conduct Medal; Meritorious Unit Award with 1 Bronze Oak Leaf Cluster. Mem: Am. Inst. Chem. Engrs; F&AM; AASR; Nat. Asn. of Parliamentarians; Boy Scouts; Toastmasters Int. Rel: Baptist. Mailing Add: 1511 18th Ave. N, Texas City, Tex. 77590.

COFFMAN, WILLIAM J. R
Iowa State Rep.
b. North English, Iowa, 9/30/18; s. William S. Coffman and Bertha Greenlee C; m. 1940 to Jean Owen; c. Helen Janyce (Mrs. Smock), Kathy Ann (Mrs. Dennis C. Stevens); grandchildren Kevin Allen and Kathy Ann Smock. Educ: North English High Sch. Polit. & Govt. Pos: Iowa State Rep, currently; Rep. precinct committeeman, 4 years; mayor, North English, 1 term; mem, town coun, 4 terms; clerk, Dist. Court, Iowa City, 2 terms. Mil. Serv: Navy, World War II, 5 years. Mem: Mason; Shrine; Consistory; DAV; VFW; Am. Legion (officer, 10 years); Mil. Order Purple Heart. Rel: Methodist. Mailing Add: 108 E. Oak St, North English, Iowa 52316.

COFONE, CHARLES JOSEPH R
Mem, R.I. State Rep. Cent. Cmt.
b. Westerly, R.I, 7/24/16; s. James L. Cofone and Angeline Mary Siciliano C; m. 7/15/39 to Gilda Rose Arnone; c. Carol Ann, Charles Joseph, Jr. and Evelyn Mary. Educ: High Sch; Ins. and Investment Seminars. Polit. & Govt. Pos: Chmn, Westerly Rep. Town Cmt, R.I, 61-62, mem, currently; mem, Westerly Town Coun, 62-64; mem, R.I. State Rep. Cent. Cmt, 64- Bus. & Prof. Pos: Mgr, Life Ins. Dept. and Mutual Fund Dept, Checker, Inc, 61-; registered rep, Renyx, Field & Co, 61- Mem: Italo-Am. Soc, Bradford, R.I; Holy Name Soc; St. Clares Parish; Independent Ins. Group. Rel: Roman Catholic. Mailing Add: Wagner Rd, Shelter Harbor, Westerly, R.I. 02891. (1967)

COGAN, GENE D
Educ: Ball State Teachers Col, B.S, 53, M.S, 63. Polit. & Govt. Pos: Ind. State Rep, -66. Bus. & Prof. Pos: Elem. Sch. Prin. Mil. Serv: 29th Inf. Div. Mem: Lions Club; VFW; Am. Legion; Nat. and Ind. Elem. Sch. Prin's. Asn; E. Noble Classroom Teachers Asn. Rel: Methodist; lay leader, Calvary Methodist Church. Mailing Add: 220 Baum St, Avilla, Ind. 46710. (1967)

COGAN, JOHN FRANCIS, JR. D
State Committeeman, Mass. Dem. Party
b. Boston, Mass, 6/13/26; s. John Francis Cogan and Mary Galligan C; m. to Mary Therese Hart; c. Peter G, Pamela E, Jonathan C. and Gregory M. Educ: Harvard Col, A.B. cum laude, 49; Harvard Law Sch, LL.B, 52. Polit. & Govt. Pos: Mem, Lexington Dem. Town Cmt, Mass, 62-, chmn, 67-68; mem, Lexington By-Law Cmt, 65-66; representative mem, Lexington Town Meeting Mem, 65-; trustee, Lexington Trustee of Pub. Trusts, 66-67; mem, Lexington Capital Expenditures Cmt, 67-; state committeeman, Mass. Dem. Party, 68- Bus. & Prof. Pos: Partner, Hale and Dorr, Boston, Mass, 52-; pres. and dir, Fund Research & Mgt, Ind, Boston, Pioneer Fund Inc, Pioneering Mgt. Corp, Pioneer Enterprise Fund Inc. and Pioneer Plans Corp; sr. v.pres. and dir, Pioneer West. Corp, Fla, 68- and West. Reserve Life Ins. Co, Ohio, 68- Mil. Serv: Entered as A/S, Navy, 44, released as PO, 46, after serv. in CBMU 509, Pac. Theatre, 44-46. Mem: V.pres. and trustee, Univ. Hosp; Boston, Am. and Inter-Am. Bar Asns; past pres, Boston Estate and Bus. Planning Coun; secy, Boston Probate and Estate Planning Forum; treas, Lexington Counseling Serv. Legal Res: 29 Patterson Rd, Lexington, Mass. 02173. Mailing Add: 28 State St, Boston, Mass. 02109.

COGGESHALL, ROBERT ALAN R
N.H. State Rep.
b. Newport, N.H, 7/13/45; s. Theodore Ronna Coggeshall and Katherine Emery C; m. 8/24/68 to Janice Leach: Educ: Youngstown Univ, 64-68; Intercollegiate Soc. of Individualists; Young Am. for Freedom. Polit. & Govt. Pos: Pres, Youngstown Univ. Young Rep. Club, 65-68; mem. exec. bd, Ohio League of Col. Young Rep. Clubs and Mid-West Fedn. of Col. Rep. Nat. Cmt, 66-68; v.chmn, Newport Rep. Town Cmt, N.H, 68-; finance chmn, Young Rep. State Cmt, 69-; N.H. State Rep, 69- Mem: Cmt. for a Better N.H. Rel: Congregational. Mailing Add: 69-C Main St, Newport, N.H. 03773.

COGGIN, FRANK EDWARD D
Ga. State Sen.
b. Madras, Ga, 10/2/27; s. Joseph Terrell Coggin, Sr. and Hattie Rooks C; m. 5/22/49 to Billie Carolyn Smarr; c. Victoria Lee, Frank Edward, Jr. and Ricky. Educ: Univ. Ga, 46-49; Woodrow Wilson Col. Law, LL.B, 54; Sigma Delta Kappa. Polit. & Govt. Pos: City councilman, Hapeville, Ga, 56-59, mayor, 60-64; Ga. State Sen, 63-, Admin. Floor Leader, Ga. State Sen, 67- Bus. & Prof. Pos: Attorney-at-Law, Atlanta, Ga, 55- Mil. Serv: Entered as Pvt, Marine Corps, 45, released as Sgt, 46, after serv. in 2nd Marine Div, re-entered as Pfc, 50, released 51. Mem: Exec. cmt, Ga. Stud. Educ. Fund, Univ. Ga; Mason; Moose; Jr. C. of C; Exchange Club. Rel: Methodist. Legal Res: 201 Victoria Lane, Hapeville, Ga. 30354. Mailing Add: 1001 Virginia Ave, Hapeville, Ga. 30354.

COGGINS, JYLES JACKSON D
N.C. State Sen.
b. Iredell Cty, N.C, 1/10/21; s. James Lee Coggins and Jeanette Arney C; m. 9/24/43 to Frances K. Lyon; c. Frances Rebecca, Anna Katherine, Debra Lyon, Jyles Jacquelyn and Judy Carolyn. Educ: Univ. N.C, 39-40; N.C. State Col, 41, 46, 47. Polit. & Govt. Pos: N.C. State Rep, 63-66; N.C. State Sen, 66- Bus. & Prof. Pos: Gen. contractor. Mil. Serv: Navy, 1st Lt, Marine Corps, 42-46, serv. as Aviator. Mem: Nat. Asn. of Cemeteries; N.C. Cemetery Asn; Raleigh Merchants Bur; Raleigh C. of C; N.C. Asn. of Quality Rests, Inc; N.C. Motel Asn; Mason; Elks; Am. Legion; Raleigh Civitans. Rel: Presbyterian. Mailing Add: 3601 Ridge Rd, Raleigh, N.C. 27609. (1967)

COGHILL, KENNETH LASSITER D
b. Charleston, W.Va, 12/27/23; s. Julain Baxter Coghill, Sr. and Ruth Putney C; m. 10/11/47 to Lee Estill; c. Kenneth L. Jr, David C. and Susan K. Educ: Washington & Lee Univ, A.B, 43; LL.B, 47; Kappa Sigma. Polit. & Govt. Pos: W.Va. State Del, 64-66, legis. draftsman, 56th Legis. Bus. & Prof. Pos: Lawyer. Mil. Serv: Navy, 43-46. Mem: W.Va. and Va. State Bars; W.Va. Trial Lawyers Asn; Army & Navy Club. Rel: Presbyterian. Mailing Add: 12 Capitol St, Charleston, W.Va. 25301.

COHEE, DARWIN DICK R
Mem, Calif. Rep. State Cent. Cmt.
b. Whittier, Calif, 2/7/26; s. William Vincent Cohee and Vesta D. King C; m. 10/8/45 to Nell Arlene Sever; c. Renee (Mrs. Smith) and Evelyn. Educ: Brawley Union High Sch, Calif, grad; Maritime Specialty Sch, Avalon, Calif. Polit. & Govt. Pos: Mem, Calif. Rep. State Cent. Cmt, 68-; mem, Imperial Co. Rep. Cent. Cmt, 68-, exec. bd, 69- Bus. & Prof. Pos: Rancher; bd. mem, Bonanza Chem. Co, Brawley, Calif, 69- Mil. Serv: U.S. Maritime Sch, Merchant Marines, 44-46; Pac. and Atlantic Serv. Ribbons. Mem: Elks; bd. mem, Imperial Co. Chap, Calif. Farm Bur, 68-; Calif. Beet Growers Asn. Rel: Presbyterian; bd. trustees, First Presbyterian Church, Brawley, Calif. Mailing Add: 633 S. Rio Vista, Brawley, Calif. 92227.

COHELAN, JEFFERY D
U.S. Rep, Calif.
b. San Francisco, Calif, 6/24/14; m. 2/10/39 to Evelyn Elizabeth Ellis; c. Pamela Joy (Mrs. David Benson), Catherine Anna, Terrence Daniel and Lt. (jg) Timothy Douglas, U.S.N.R. Educ: Univ. of Calif, A.B; Grad. Sch. of Econ, Univ. of Calif; Fulbright Research Scholar, Leeds and Oxford Univs, 53-54. Polit. & Govt. Pos: Secy-treas, Milk Drivers and Dairy Employees Local 302, 42; mem, Berkeley Welfare Cmn, 49-53; city coun, Berkeley, 55; former mem, Armed Serv. and D.C. Cmts; U.S. Rep, Calif, 58-, mem. appropriations cmt. Bus. & Prof. Pos: Consult, Univ. of Calif. Inst. of Indust. Rels. Mem: Commonwealth Club of Calif. Legal Res: Berkeley, Calif. Mailing Add: 2446 Rayburn House Office Bldg, Washington, D.C. 20515.

COHEN, BERNARD S. D
Committeeman, Alexandria Dem. City Cmt, Va.
b. Brooklyn, N.Y, 1/17/34; s. Benjamin Cohen and Fannie Davis C; m. 12/21/58 to Rae Rose; c. Bennett Alan and Karen Linda. Educ: City Col, N.Y, B.B.A, 56; Georgetown Univ, J.D, 60; Phi Alpha Delta. Polit. & Govt. Pos: Economist, U.S. Dept. Labor, 56-61; committeeman, Alexandria Dem. City Cmt, 63-, v.chmn, 64-67, chmn, 67-68. Bus. & Prof. Pos: Dir, Va. Citizens Consumer Coun, 68-69. Mem: Am. Trial Lawyers Asn; Alexandria and Am. Bar Asns; North. Va. Trial Lawyers Asn. (pres, 67); Lions Int; Am. Fedn. Govt. Employees; Va. Trial Lawyers Asn. (del, 64). Rel: Jewish. Mailing Add: 495 Naylor Place, Alexandria, Va. 22304.

COHEN, DAVID D
City Councilman, Phila, Pa.
b. Phila, Pa, 11/13/14; s. Frank Cohen and Rachel Krangel C; m. 2/9/46 to Florence Herzog; c. Mark B, Denis P, Sherrie J. and Judy L. Educ: Univ. Pa, B.S, 34, LL.B, 37; Order of the Coif. Polit. & Govt. Pos: Dem. committeeman, Phila, Pa, 54-, treas, ward exec. cmt, 56-66, ward leader, 17th ward, 66-, mem, Dem. city cmt, 66-, city councilman, Eighth Dist, 68- and chmn, City Coun. Health and Welfare Cmt, 68-; del, Dem. Nat. Conv, 68; mem, State Cmt. New Dem. Coalition, Pa, 69- Bus. & Prof. Pos: Law practice, 38- Mil. Serv: Entered as Pvt, Army, 43, released as S/Sgt, 46, after serv. in Med. and Eng. Corps, Pac. Theatre, British and Dutch New Guinea, 44-46; Pac. Theatre awards. Mem: Phila, Pa. and Am. Bar Asns; Phila. Patent Law Asn; Urban League; Am. Civil Liberties Union; Jewish War Vet. Various community awards. Rel: Jewish. Legal Res: 5635 N. 16th St, Philadelphia, Pa. 19141. Mailing Add: Room 484, City Hall, Philadelphia, Pa. 19107.

COHEN, EDWIN SAMUEL R
Asst. Secy. for Tax Policy, Treas. Dept.
b. Richmond, Va, 9/27/14; s. LeRoy S. Cohen and Miriam Rosenheim C; m. 8/31/44 to Helen Herz; c. Edwin Carlin, Roger and Susan Wendy. Educ: Univ. Richmond, B.A, 33; Univ. Va, LL.B, 36; Omicron Delta Kappa; Phi Beta Kappa; Pi Delta Epsilon; Order of the Coif; Raven Soc. Univ. Va; Phi Epsilon Pi. Polit. & Govt. Pos: Mem. and counsel, Adv. Group on Subchapter C (Corporate Transactions), Cmt. on Ways and Means, U.S. House of Rep, 56-58; consult, Va. Income Tax Study Cmn, 66-68; mem, Adv. Group to Cmnr. of Internal Revenue, 67-68; Asst. Secy. for Tax Policy, Treas. Dept, 69- Bus. & Prof. Pos: Assoc, Sullivan & Cromwell, N.Y.C, 36-49; partner, Root, Barrett, Cohen, Knapp & Smith, 49-65; prof. law, Univ. Va, 65-68, Joseph M. Hartfield prof. law, 68-69; counsel, Barrett, Knapp, Smith & Schapiro, N.Y.C, 65-69. Publ: Co-auth, 'A Technical Revision of the Federal Income Tax Treatment of Corporate Distributions to Shareholders,' Columbia Law Rev, 52; auth, 'Taxing the State of Mind,' Tax Exec, 60; 'Substantive Federal Tax Reform,' Va. Law Rev, 64. Mem: Am. Law Inst; Am. Judicature Soc; Am, N.Y. State and Va. State Bar Asns; Asn. of the Bar of the City of N.Y; N.Y. Co. Lawyers Asn; Am. Asn. Univ. Prof; Nat. Lawyers Club, Wash, D.C; Broad St. Club; Univ. Va. Club of N.Y.C; Keswick Club; Colonnade Club, Charlottesville, Va. Phi Epsilon Pi Nat. Achievement Award. Rel: Jewish. Legal Res: 194 Stuart Place, Ednam Forest, Charlottesville, Va. 22901. Mailing Add: U.S. Treasury Dept, Room 3430, Washington, D.C. 20220.

COHEN, GERTRUDE S. D
b. Chicago, Ill, 11/1/13; d. J. David Siegel; Bess; m. to Ben Cohen; c. Devra (Mrs. Marcus), Loren. Educ: Univ. of Minn, B.S; Grad. Work, State Col. of Iowa, 62-63. Polit. & Govt. Pos: Iowa State Rep -66. Mem: United World Federalists; League of Women Voters; CLU; NAACP; Life Mem,

Hadassah; Life Mem, Nat. Women's Cmt. of Brandeis Univ. Hon. Citizen, Boys Town, Nebr. Rel: Jewish, Mem, Sons of Jacob Synagogue. Mailing Add: 151 Lovejoy, Waterloo, Iowa 50701. (1967)

COHEN, JOSEPH D
Secy, Bronx Co. Dem. Cmt, N.Y.
b. N.Y.C, 8/8/26; s. Louis Cohen and Belle Lazarus C; m. 11/17/56 to Rosalind Goldstein; c. Marcy Hope and Michael Bennett. Educ: N.Y. Univ, Sch. Commerce, B.S, 48; Columbia Univ, Sch. Law, LL.B, 51. Polit. & Govt. Pos: Secy, Bronx Co. Dem. Cmt, N.Y, 62-; alternate del, Dem. Nat. Conv, 68. Bus. & Prof. Pos: Attorney. Mil. Serv: Entered as Pvt, Army, 44, released as T/4, 46. Mem: Am, N.Y. State and Bronx Co. Bar Asns; Asn. Bar City N.Y; N.Y. Co. Lawyers Asn. Rel: Jewish. Mailing Add: 3850 Hudson Manor Terr, Bronx, N.Y. 10463.

COHEN, LEONARD N. D
b. New York, N.Y, 12/22/20; s. Ralph Cohen and Lillian Saline C; single. Educ: City Col. N.Y, B.Soc. Sci, 42; Columbia Law Sch, LL.B, 49. Polit. & Govt. Pos: N.Y. Co. committeeman, 51-; del, Dem. State Convs, 52, 54, 56, 58, 62 & 64; dist. leader, West Wide Dem. Club, N.Y. Co. Dem. Orgn, 53-; law secy. to N.Y. State Supreme Court Justice, 55-60; small claims court arbitrator, Civil Court, N.Y.C, 58-64; dep. cmnr. and gen. counsel, N.Y.C. Dept. Marine and Aviation, 62-65; first v.chmn, N.Y. Co. Dem. Exec. Cmt, 62-68; alternate del, Dem. Nat. Conv, 64; dep. pres, Borough of Manhattan, N.Y.C, 65- Mil. Serv: Entered as Pvt, Army, 42, released as Cpl, 45; ETO Ribbon with Four Battle Stars. Mem: South Dist. of N.Y. Fed. Bar Asn; Bar Asn. City of N.Y.(munic. affairs cmt, 65-, law reform cmt, 62-65); Columbia Law Sch. Alumni Asn; N.Y. Co. Lawyers Asn.(family court cmt, 65-, law reform cmt, 62-64); City Col. N.Y. Alumni Asn; Planetarium Neighborhood Adv. Cmt; pres, West Side Sch. Commun. Center, 64; Am. Jewish Cong; N.Y. Young Dem.; Zionist Orgn. Am; B'nai B'rith; West Side C. of C; Lions. West Side United Jewish Appeal Man of the Year Award, 60. Rel: Jewish. Mailing Add: 450 West End Ave, New York, N.Y. 10024. (1967)

COHEN, MANUEL FREDERICK D
b. Brooklyn, N.Y, 10/8/12; s. Edward Cohen and Lena Kartzmar C; m. 4/20/40 to Pauline Grossman; c. Susan D.(Mrs. Paul D. Borman) and Jonathan W. Educ: Brooklyn Col, B.S, 33; Brooklyn Law Sch, St. Lawrence Univ, LL.B, 36, LL.D, 66, Philonomic Coun, 36. Hon. LL.D, Brooklyn Col, Babson Inst. of Bus. Admin. and Brooklyn Law Sch, St. Lawrence Univ; hon. D.H.L, Hebrew Union Col. Polit. & Govt. Pos: Lawyer, Securities and Exchange Cmn, 42-52, chief counsel to cmn, 52-59, adv. to cmn, 59-60, dir. Div. of Corp. Finance, 60-61, cmnr, 61-64 and chmn, 64-69. Bus. & Prof. Pos: Research assoc, Twentieth Century Fund, 33-34; lawyer, corporate and real estate, 37-42; lectr. law, George Wash. Univ. Law Sch, 58-; mem, Coun. Admin. Conf. of U.S, Wash, D.C, 61-69; attorney-at-law, Wilmer, Cutler & Pickering, Wash, 69- Publ: 'Federal Legislation Affecting the Public Offering of Securities,' George Wash. Law Rev, 59; 'Investment of Private Capital in Foreign Securities' in A Lawyer's Guide to International Business Transactions, Joint Cmt. on Continuing Legal Educ. of Am. Law Inst. and Am. Bar Asn, 63; 'Importance of Administrative Adjudication in their Development,' Law and Contemporary Probs, 64. Mem: Am, N.Y. and Fed. Bar Asns; Am. Law Inst; Am. Soc. Int. Law; Am. Acad. Polit. and Soc. Sci; Société Royale d'Economie Politique de Belgique; Cosmos Club; Woodmont Country Club. Rockefeller Pub. Serv. Award; Career Serv. Award; Distinguished Alumnus Medal; Distinguished Serv. Award, Securities and Exchange Cmn; Distinguished Alumni Award, Brooklyn Col; Brotherhood Award, Nat. Conf. of Christians and Jews; Hon. Initiate, Order of the Coif. Rel: Jewish. Legal Res: 6403 Marjory Lane, Bethesda, Md. 20034. Mailing Add: Wilmer, Cutler & Pickering, Farragut Bldg, 900 17th St. N.W, Washington, D.C. 20006.

COHEN, MARVIN S. D
b. Akron, Ohio, 10/16/31; s. Norman J. Cohen and Faye Abramovitz C; m. 6/19/53 to Frances E. Smith; c. Samuel D, Jeffrey L. and Rachel A. Educ: Univ. Ariz, B.A. & LL.B; Phi Beta Kappa; Blue Key; Phi Kappa Phi; Chain Gang; Delta Sigma Rho. Polit. & Govt. Pos: Precinct committeeman; pres, Dems. for Better Govt, 64; spec. asst. to the solicitor, Dept. of Interior, 61-63; chmn, Pima Co. Dem. Cent. Cmt, Ariz. and pres, Young Dems. of Ariz, 60. Bus. & Prof. Pos: Attorney, Boyle, Bilby, Thompson & Shoenhair, 63-; 1st asst. city attorney, Tucson, 61; chief civil dep. co. attorney, Pima Co, 58-60. Mil. Serv: Entered as 2nd Lt, Air Force, 53, released as 1st Lt, 55. Mem: Am. Trial Lawyers Asn; B'nai B'rith; Ariz. and Pima Co. Bar Asns; Nucleus Club. Rel: Jewish. Mailing Add: 4645 E. San Carlos Place, Tucson, Ariz. 85716. (1967)

COHEN, MONROE D
City Councilman, N.Y.C.
b. N.Y.C, 3/12/26; s. Jacob Cohen and Eva Leibowitz C; m. 9/26/54 to Evelyn Yanowsky; c. Marleen, Richard and Carole. Educ: Ohio State Univ, B.A, 48; Brooklyn Law Sch, LL.B, 52; Tau Epsilon Phi. Polit. & Govt. Pos: Del, Dem. Nat. Conv, 68; city councilman, N.Y.C, 68- Bus. & Prof. Pos: Attorney. Mil. Serv: Entered as Pvt, Army Res, released as Maj, 60, after serv. in Asia. Mem: B'nai B'rith; Ment. Health Asn; various vet. groups; 13 civic asns. Rel: Jewish. Legal Res: 105-58 Ave. M, Brooklyn, N.Y. 11236. Mailing Add: 16 Court St, Brooklyn, N.Y. 11201.

COHEN, NATHAN D
Mem, Gov. Exec. Coun, State of Maine
b. Bangor, Maine, 2/13/13; s. Jacob Cohen and Alice C; m. 12/29/46 to Miriam Berman. Educ: Univ. of Maine, B.A. Polit. & Govt. Pos: Mem, Wash. Co. Dem. Cmt. and Dem. City Cmt, Maine; mem, Eastport City Coun, 58, chmn, 59-60; Dem. State Committeeman, Wash. Co, 62-65; del, Dem. Nat. Conv, 64, mem, Gov. Exec. Coun, State of Maine, 65- Bus. & Prof. Pos: Pres, Wash. Co. Econ. Develop. Corp, 66- Mil. Serv: Entered as Pvt, Air Force, 43, released as Pfc, 46. Mem: Eastport C. of C.(v.pres, 65-66); treas, Salvation Army, Eastport, 63-66; Am. Legion; C. of C; trustee, Eastport Mem. Hosp; Mason (32°, Past Master); pres, East Develop. Corp. Rel: Jewish. Mailing Add: 39 Boynton St, Eastport, Maine 04631. (1967)

COHEN, WILBUR JOSEPH D
b. Milwaukee, Wis, 6/10/13; s. Aaron Cohen and Bessie Rubenstein C; m. 4/8/38 to Eloise Bittel; c. Christopher, Bruce and Stuart. Educ: Univ. Wis, Ph.B, 34; Artus; Phi Kappa Phi; Athenia. Hon. L.H.D, Adelphia Col, 62, Univ. Wis, 66, Brandeis Univ, 68, Kenyon Col, Univ. Louisville and Univ. Detroit, 69. Polit. & Govt. Pos: Asst. to exec. dir, President Roosevelt's Cabinet Cmt. Econ. Security, 34-35; tech. adv. to cmnr. for soc. security, Dept. Health, Educ. and Welfare, 35-52, dir, div. research and statist, Soc. Security Admin, 53-56, asst. secy. for legis, 61-65, Under Secy, 65-68, Secy, 68-69. Bus. & Prof. Pos: Prof. pub. welfare admin, sch. soc. work, Univ. Mich, 56-61; vis. prof, Univ. Calif, Los Angeles, 57; lectr, Cath. Univ, 61-62; pres, Nat. Conf. Soc. Welfare, 69-70; prof. educ. and dean sch. educ, Univ. Mich, 69- Publ: Co-auth, Readings in Social Security, Prentice Hall, 48; auth, Retirement Policies in Social Security, Univ. Calif, 57; co-auth, Social Security; Programs, Problems and Policies, Irwin, 60. Mem: Nat. Asn. Soc. Workers; Am. Pub. Welfare Asn; Am. Econ. Asn; Ind. Rels. Research Asn; Nat. Dem. Club. John Lendrum Mitchell Gold Medal, 34; Distinguished Serv. Award, Dept. Health, Educ. and Welfare, 56; Distinguished Serv. Award, Group Health Asn, Wash, 56; Nat. Conf. Soc. Welfare Award, 57; Florina Lasker Award, 61; Terry Mem. Merit Award, Am. Pub. Welfare Asn, 61; Blanche Ittelson Award, 62; Asn. Phys. & Ment. Rehabilitation Award, 65; Nat. Asn. Ment. Retarded Children Award, 66; Am. Pub. Health Bronfman Prize, 67. Rel: Jewish. Mailing Add: School of Education, University of Michigan, Ann Arbor, Mich. 48104.

COHN, HAROLD W. D
b. Brooklyn, N.Y, 9/25/13; m. to Lillian Bartell; c. Michele, Steven. Educ: St. Johns Univ, B.S.S, 34; St. Johns Law Sch, 36. Polit. & Govt. Pos: N.Y. State Assemblyman, 59-69; mem, 57th Dist. Assembly Dist. Dem. Orgn. Bus. & Prof. Pos: Lawyer. Mil. Serv: World War II, Field Artil. Off. Europe. Mem: Brooklyn Lawyers Club Fedn; Seneca Club of Kings Co; Boy Scouts; Am. Legion; co-chmn. Williamsburgh Drives Fedn; Bonds for Israel; United Jewish Appeal; YMHA; YWHA. Mailing Add: 171 Heyward St, Brooklyn, N.Y. 11206. (1967)

COHN, MORTON RAY D
b. Toledo, Ohio, 7/19/23; s. Jay Cohn and Martha Lefkowitz C; m. 9/29/60 to Jean Marie Dushane; c. Morton R, Jr. and Laura Ann. Educ: Univ. Mich, B.A, 48; Pi Lambda Phi. Polit. & Govt. Pos: Planning Cmnr, Monroe, Mich, 63-66, mayor, 66-68; del, Dem. Nat. Conv, 68; exec. dir, Port of Monroe, 69- Bus. & Prof. Pos: Dir, Buckeye Furniture Co, Monroe, Mich, 48-; dir:owner, Best Jewelers, 48-; owner, Mort Cohn Indust. Gifts, 68-69. Mil. Serv: Entered as Aviation Cadet, Army Air Corps, 43, released as 1st Lt, 46, after serv. in 397th Bombardment Squadron, Sixth AF, Caribbean Theatre, 44-46; Good Conduct Medal. Mem: Assoc. mem, Am. Gem. Soc; Mason; Shrine; Valley of Detroit Consistory; Am. Legion; VFW; Monroe Co. Rod and Gun Club; Monroe Golf and Country Club. Alumnus of the Year, Monroe High School Alumni Asn, 69. Rel: Reform Judaism. Mailing Add: 302 Crampton Dr, Monroe, Mich. 48161.

COHN, NATHAN D
b. Charleston, S.C, 1/20/18; s. Samuel Cohn and Rose Baron C; c. Norman. Educ: San Francisco Law Sch, LL.B. and J.D, 47. Polit. & Govt. Pos: Cmnr, Calif. Recreation Cmn, 65-66; alternate del, Dem. Nat. Conv, 68. Bus. & Prof. Pos: Attorney. Mil. Serv: 1st Lt, Air Force Res, Judge Adv. Gen.C, 50-55. Publ: Criminal Law Seminar I, 61, II, 62 and III, 63, Cent. Book Co. Mem: Am. Bd. Trial Advocate; Am. Trial Lawyers Asn; Nat. Asn. Defense Lawyers Criminal Cases; Am. Acad. Matrimonial Lawyers; Calif, Fed. and Am. Bar Asns; Am. Judicature Soc; San Francisco Trial Lawyers (pres, 66); nat. judge advocate, Regular Vet. Asn; Irish-Israel Italian Soc; co-pres, F&AM; Shrine; Hibernians; Press Club; Elks; Fryers Club; Calamari Club; Footprinters; Dem. Assembly. Rel: Hebrew. Legal Res: 540 Darien Way, San Francisco, Calif. 94127. Mailing Add: 1255 Post St, San Francisco, Calif. 94109.

COIL, HENRY WILSON, JR. R
City Councilman, Riverside, Calif.
b. Riverside, Calif, 12/27/32. Educ: Univ. Calif, Berkeley; West State Univ. Col. Law; Alexander Hamilton Inst; Skadron Col; Lambleau Real Estate Sch; Theta Tau; Lambda Chi Alpha; Phi Phi; water polo team. Polit. & Govt. Pos: Mem, Riverside Young Rep. Club, Calif, 50-64; spec. dep, Riverside Co. Sheriff's Dept, 62-; pres, League of Calif. Cities, 63-; city councilman, Riverside Calif, 63-, mayor protem, 64-65, mem, youth and commun. cmt. and city hall cmt; mem, Econ. Opportunity Bd. Riverside Co, 64-; mem, Calif. Rep. Assembly, 65- Bus. & Prof. Pos: Civil engr, Calif. Elec. Power Co, 57-58 and summers 49-55; civil engr, C.V. Brown Gen. Contractors and Civil Engrs, 58-59; plant engr, Hydro Conduit Corp, 59-64; consult. engr, Marcus W. Meairs Co, 65- Mil. Serv: Engr, Navy, 55-61, Philippines; Mil. Commendation Ribbon. Mem: Am. Concrete Inst; Am. Pub. Works Asn; Los Angeles Engrs. Club; Assoc. Gen. Contractors Asn; Boy Scout and Scouter, 24 years; Lions; Jaycees; C. of C; Univ. Calif. Alumni Asn; Citizens Univ. Cmt, Univ. Calif. at Riverside, 64-65; United Fund; YMCA; Mason; Shrine; Mo. Lodge of Research. Eagle Scout Award, Boy Scouts, 48, Award of Merit, Silver Beaver, 65 & 67; One of Outstanding Young Men of Am, U.S. Jaycees, 64, One of Ten Outstanding Young Men of Calif, Jaycees, 65. Mailing Add: 3505 Beechwood Place, Riverside, Calif. 92506. (1967)

COKER, GRADY N. D
b. Chappells, S.C, 12/17/94; s. Newton Jasper Coker and Mary Trammell C; single. Educ: Emory Univ. Med. Sch, M.D, 20, Augusta. Polit. & Govt. Pos: Ga. State Rep, 63-67, 55-56; Ga. State Sen, 41, 47-48, 53-54; past mayor of Canton 7 years. Bus. & Prof. Pos: Gen. surgeon. Mil. Serv: WWI, WWII, Selective Serv. Medal, Cert. of Appreciation. Mem: Mason; Shriner; Elk; Moose; Lions; Delta Tau Delta; Alpha Kappa Kappa; Alpha Omega Alpha; Cherokee Med. Soc; Med. Asn. of Ga; Canton C. of C; Southeast. Surgical Cong; Am. Col. of Surgeons. Pubh: ed. Med. Journ, State Med. Asn. of Ga, 3839. Rel: Baptist. Mailing Add: Canton, Ga. 30114. (1967)

COKER, JOSEPH WARREN D
S.C. State Rep.
b. Manning, S.C, 11/10/30; s. Robert Carlisle Coker and Sarah Bradham C; m. 10/30/50 to Mary Frances Heriot; c. Joseph W, Jr. and Robert Heriot. Educ: Univ. S.C, B.S, 56, M.Ed, 60. Polit. & Govt. Pos: Mem. town coun, Turbeville, S.C, 62-66; S.C. State Rep, 67- Mil. Serv: Entered as Pvt, Army, 51, released as 1st Lt, 53, after serv. in 45th Inf. Div, Korea, 52-53; Bronze

Star. Mem: S.C. Educ. Asn; past pres, Clarendon Co. Educ. Asn; S.C. C. of C; Clarendon C. of C.(dir, 64-); Elks; Mason; Am. Legion; past pres, Ruritan. Rel: Presbyterian. Legal Res: Coker St, Turbeville, S.C. 29162. Mailing Add: P.O. Box 226, Turbeville, S.C. 29162.

COKER, ROY N. D
b. Sycamore, Ga, 9/25/22; s. Cone E. Coker and Ruth Bussey C; single. Educ: Turner Co. Schs. Polit. & Govt. Pos: Ga. State Rep, 63-66. Bus. & Prof. Pos: Owner, Coker Gas. Co. Mil. Serv: U.S.M.C, WW II, 42-45; Good Conduct Medal. Rel: Baptist. Mailing Add: Sycamore, Ga. 31790. (1967)

COLAY, HARRY BRADFORD D
Ark. State Rep.
b. Cleveland, Ark, 5/31/08; s. John Henry Colay and Mable Bradford C; m. 10/28/33 to Ruth Marie Aday (deceased); c. Mabel Jo (Mrs. Herbert L. Ray). Educ: Univ. Ark, B.A, 32; Univ. Ark. Law Sch, LL.B, 35; Xi Delta Psi; Univ. Ark. Poetry Club. Polit. & Govt. Pos: Ark. State Rep, Columbia Co, 47-56 & 59-66, 39th Dist, Columbia and Lafayette Co, 67- Bus. & Prof. Pos: Prin, high sch, Wonder View Dist, Conway Co, Ark, 32-34; attorney-at-law, Magnolia, Ark, 38-69. Mil. Serv: Entered as 2nd Lt, Army Res, 32, released as 1st Lt, 42, after serv. in 405th Inf. Res, Command Officer Co. 4739 CCC, 36-37 and Ft. Frances E. Warren, 41-42. Publ: 'A Fountain of Life,' Young Men's Bible Class, 50. Mem: Am, Ark. and Columbia Co. Bar Asns; Am. and Ark. Trial Lawyers Asns; Interstate Commerce Cmn. Practitioners Asn; Am. Judicature Soc; 13th Judicial Dist. Bar Asn; pres, Nat. Soc. State Legislators, 66-67; F&AM; K.T; RAM; AAONMS; Consistory (32°); Shrine; Am. Legion; Magnolia 100 Indust. Club; C. of C. Outstanding Poetry Award, Expression Mag, 67. Rel: Baptist. Mailing Add: 800 N. Jefferson St, Magnolia, Ark. 71753.

COLBERG, SEVERO E. D
b. Cabo Rojo, P.R, 9/16/24; s. Juan Cabrera Colberg and Isolina Ramirez Marini C; m. 7/23/48 to Eva Nilda Toro; c. Yanira, Severo, Jr, Eva, Esther, Nelson and Jorge. Educ: Univ. P.R, B.S, 50; Harvard Univ, M.A. in pub. admin, 54; Univ. P.R. grad. studies in law and social work. Polit. & Govt. Pos: Mem. pres. panel, Popular Dem. Party, P.R, 64-; P.R. State Rep, 64-68. Bus. & Prof. Pos: Prof. pub. admin, Univ. P.R, 54-64, dir, grad. sch, 61-63; consult, Dept. Commerce, Govt. of P.R; mem, Inst. Econ. Studies. Mil. Serv: Entered as Pvt, Army, 43, released as Sgt, 46, after serv. in 342nd Antiaircraft Artil. Searchlight Bn, Caribbean Defense Command. Publ: Weekly Column, Sobre el Yungue, daily P.R. newspaper. Mem: P.R. Soc. Pub. Admin. Rel: Presbyterian. Mailing Add: DX-5, Faculty Residences, University of Puerto Rico, San Juan, P.R. 00903. (1967)

COLBURG, DOLORES D
Supt. Pub. Instr, Mont.
b. Big Timber, Mont, 4/3/32; d. Victor Jerome Erickson and Doris Webb E; div. Educ: East. Mont. Col, 61-62; Univ. Colo, 62-63; Univ. Mont, B.A. with honors, 64; Col. Young Dem. Polit. & Govt. Pos: Secy, Yellowstone Co. Dem. Cent. Cmt, Mont, 56-57; v.pres, Col. Young Dem, Univ. Mont, 63-64; Supt. Pub. Instr, Mont, 69- Mem: Am. Asn. Univ. Women; Coun. Chief State Officers; Nat. Educ. Asn; Am. Asn. Sch. Adminstr; Univ. Mont. Alumni Asn. Rel: Protestant. Legal Res: 301 W. Lawrence, Helena, Mont. 59601. Mailing Add: P.O. Box 992, Helena, Mont. 59601.

COLBURN, MAJORIE D. R
b. Milford, N.H, 6/26/24; married; c. Three. Educ: Milford, New Boston Pub. Schs. Polit. & Govt. Pos: Del, N.H. Constitutional Conv, 64; N.H. State Rep, 65-69. Bus. & Prof. Pos: Feature article writer. Mem: PTA; New Boston Betterment Asn. Rel: Presbyterian. Mailing Add: No. 1 Woods Lane, New Boston, N.H. 03070. (1967)

COLCLESSER, GALEN A. R
Educ: Huntington Col; Lutheran Theol. Sem; Ind. Univ, Ed.D. Polit. & Govt. Pos: Ind. State Sen, 63-66. Bus. & Prof. Pos: Asst. to pres, dir. of pub. rels. and dir. of admissions, Huntington Col; asst. dir. of admissions, Ind. Univ, 64-67; dir, Off. of Extended Serv, Ball State Univ, 67- Mil. Serv: Vet. Mem: Exchange Club; Asn. of Col. Admission Counsr; Am. Col. Pub. Rels. Asn; dir, Bible Lands Visualized Found. Rel: United Brethren in Christ. Mailing Add: P.O. Box 1314, Ft. Wayne, Ind. 46801.

COLDSNOW, ROBERT A. 'BOB' R
Kans. State Rep.
b. Kansas City, Mo, 9/26/24; s. Elmer O. Coldsnow and Edith Allen C; m. 11/20/48 to Dorothy Ainsworth; c. Allen and Jane. Educ: Univ. Kans, A.B, 49 and J.D, 51; Phi Alpha Delta. Polit. & Govt. Pos: Precinct committeeman, Rep. Party, Kans, 60-; Kans. State Rep, 65- Bus. & Prof. Pos: Partner, Alkire, Clausing, Coldsnow & Bradley, 54-; secy Wichita Bar Asn, 59. Mil. Serv: Entered as Pvt, Air Force, 43, released as S/Sgt, 46, after serv. in Weather Wing, Pac; Caribbean Theater Ribbon; Pac. Theater Ribbon; 2nd Lt, Air Force Res, 49-54. Mem: Wichita Bar Asn; Kans. Bar Asn; Am. Bar Asn; Am. Judicature Soc; Am. Trial Lawyers Asn; Mason. Rel: Episcopal. Mailing Add: 8 Linden Dr, Wichita, Kans. 67206.

COLDWELL, COLBERT D
b. El Paso, Tex, 4/30/21; s. Ballard Coldwell and Eleanor Eubank C; m. 3/10/45 to Ida Wesson; c. Carlisle and Ballard Eubank. Educ: Tex. A&M, B.S, 43. Polit. & Govt. Pos: Precinct chmn, Dem. Party, Tex, 57-58; U.S. Cmnr, West. Dist, El Paso Div, Tex, 65-66; co. judge, El Paso Co, 67-; alternate del, Dem. Nat. Conv, 68. Bus. & Prof. Pos: Mgr, H. Schumacher Oil Works, Nauasota, Tex, 46-50; farmer, Coldwell Farms, El Paso Co, 50-; assoc, Collins, Langford & Pine, Attorneys, 61-63; partner, Collins, Langford, Pine & Coldwell, 63-65. Mil. Serv: Entered as Pvt, Army, 43, released as 1st Lt, 45, after serv. in Cavalry. Mem: El Paso, Tex. and U.S. Bar Asns; Farm Bur; El Paso Pub. Libr. Bd; trustee, St. Anne's Sch. Rel: Episcopal. Mailing Add: Route 1, Box 479, El Paso, Tex. 79927.

COLE, BARNEY D
b. Wheatland, Wyo, 7/5/23; m. to Sara; c. Five. Educ: Carleton Col; Univ. of Nebr; Univ. of Wyo, LL.B. Polit. & Govt. Pos: Mem, Laramie Co. Zoning Bd, Wyo; Wyo. State Rep, 57-68; Laramie Co. Attorney, 58-62. Bus. & Prof. Pos: Lawyer; v.pres, Key Life Ins. Co. Wyo. Mem: Am. Legion; Elks; Sertoma Club; Shrine. Rel: Baptist. 1967 Legal Res: Cheyenne, Wyo. No mailing address available. (1967)

COLE, BERT L. D
b. Arlington, Wash, 5/12/10; m. 1937 to Norma Chittick. Educ: West. Wash. Col. Educ; Univ. Wash, B.A. in Sociol, 35. Polit. & Govt. Pos: State cmnr. pub. lands, Wash, 57-; mem. sch. bd, Quillayute Valley Sch. Dist; co. cmnr, Clallam Co; city councilman, Montesano; mem, pub. lands cmt, Interstate Oil Compact Cmn; state coordinator, N.Cascades Study; mem, Interagency Cmt. for Outdoor Recreation; mem, State Adv. Cmt. Rural Area Develop; state coordinator between fed. govt. and univs, McIntire-Stennis Coop. Forestry Research Prog; mem. adv. coun, Pub. Land Law Rev. Cmn. Bus. & Prof. Pos: Owner, logging bus, Forks, Wash; asst. mgr, Nat. Bank of Commerce, Montesano Br; jr. high sch. principal, Montesano; grade sch. principal, Adna. Mil. Serv: Entered as Pvt, Army, 42, released as Capt, 47, after serv. in Signal Corps. Mem: C. of C; Am. Legion; Eagles; Elks; Mason; Consistory, Nile Temple; Grange; PTA; State Sch. Dirs. Asn; past pres, West. State Land Cmnr. Asn; Citizens' Cmt, Outdoor Recreation Resources Rev. Cmn; trustee, Keep Wash. Green Asn; West. forest land use cmt, West. Forestry and Conserv. Asn. Mailing Add: Dept. Natural Resources, P.O. Box 168, Olympia, Wash. 98501.

COLE, CHARLES MORTON R
Chmn, Knox Co. Rep. Cent. & Exec. Cmts, Ohio
b. Topeka, Kans, 11/16/26; s. Ferd Cole and Mary C; m. 11/23/47 to Shirley Ann Hauger; c. Kevin Eugene and Thomas Courtney. Educ: Ohio State Univ, 45-46. Polit. & Govt. Pos: Past treas. and past pres, Knox Co. Young Rep. Club Ohio; chmn, Knox Co. Rep. cent. & exec. cmts, 60-; treas, 17th Cong. Dist. Rep. Cmt, 60-; asst. doorkeeper, Rep. Nat. Conv, 64, del, 68. Bus. & Prof. Pos: Asst. mgr, Sears Roebuck & Co, 50- Mem: Mason; Scottish Rite; Shrine; C. of C. Rel: Congregational. Mailing Add: 711 E. High St, Mount Vernon, Ohio 43050.

COLE, DONALD DENNIS R
b. Phillipsburg, Pa, 6/14/25; s. Raymond Thomas Cole and Marjorie Dennis C; m. 1/27/56 to Donna Marie Albertson; c. Elizabeth Marie, Marjorie Cecelia, Lucinda Grace and Raymond Charles. Educ: Univ. N.C, War Certificate, 45; Columbia Univ, B.S, 48; Cornell Univ. Law Sch, LL.B, 51; Phi Delta Phi. Polit. & Govt. Pos: Mem, Chemung Co. Rep. Cmt, N.Y, 53-62, chmn, 62-69; mem, N.Y. State Senate Research Coun, 55; asst. co. attorney, Chemung Co, 56-; coun. dist. chmn, Elmira Rep. Party, 57-61, city chmn, 61-69. Bus. & Prof. Pos: Attorney and counsellor at Law, 51- Mil. Serv: Entered as A/S, Naval Res, 43, released as Ens, 46. Mem: Chemung Co. Bar Asn; F&AM; Corning Consistory, Scottish Rite; RAM; K.T; Southern Tier Yacht Club; Moose. Rel: Methodist. Legal Res: 651 Euclid Ave, Elmira, N.Y. 14901. Mailing Add: 417-419 Robinson Bldg, Elmira, N.Y. 14901.

COLE, JAMES WILLIAM D
Chmn, Terrell Co. Dem. Cmt, Ga.
b. Preston, Ga, 10/24/96; s. James Henry Cole and Sarah Elizabeth Ball C; m. 8/3/25 to Jesie Pritchard. Educ: Univ. Ga. Polit. & Govt. Pos: Past mayor, Parrott, Ga, 3 terms, councilman, 60-; chmn, Terrell Co. Dem. Cmt, 62- Bus. & Prof. Pos: Farmer, Terrell Co, Ga, 41- Mil. Serv: Entered as Pvt, Army, 18, released as Sgt. 1/C, 19, after serv. in Chief Finance Off, Paris, France. Mem: Am. Farm Bur; Am. Legion; 40 et 8; VFW. Rel: Methodist. Mailing Add: Parrott, Ga. 31777.

COLE, LOUIS V. 'LOUIE' R
Chmn, 53rd Dist. Rep. Cent. Cmt, Calif.
b. Paris, Tex, 7/26/01; s. Vance Murray Cole, Sr. and Martha E. Wood C; div; c. Louie, Jr. Educ: Univ. Calif, Los Angeles, 21-24; Biggers Bus. Col, Los Angeles, Cert, 24; Phi Beta Sigma. Polit. & Govt. Pos: Chmn, 53rd Dist. Rep. Cent. Cmt, Calif, 40-; mem, Area Minority Adv. Cmt, 48-52; chmn, Spec. Cmt. to Elect Dwight D. Eisenhower and Richard M. Nixon, 52; cmnr, Los Angeles Co. Human Rels, 54-62; nominee for Calif. State Assemblyman, 53rd Dist, 62 & 68. Publ: Publisher, Los Angeles Comet, 49-50. Mem: Univ. Calif, Los Angeles Alumni Asn; Mason (32°); NAACP; Los Angeles Urban League; Gr. Cent. C. of C. Hon. Mayor of Cent. Ave, 67-69; City of Los Angeles Meritorious Serv. Award; Co. of Los Angeles Award of Honor; State of Calif. Great Seal; Phi Beta Sigma George Wash. Carver Award; Valiant Knights Benevolent Soc. Achievement Award; 35 Year Serv. Award, Hamilton Methodist Church. Rel: Methodist. Mailing Add: 1363 E. Washington Blvd, Los Angeles, Calif. 90021.

COLE, LUTHER FRANCIS D
b. Alexandria, La, 10/25/25; s. Clem Cole and Catherine Wiley C; m. 3/9/45 to Juanita Barton; c. Frances Jeannette, Jeffrey Martin and Christopher Warren. Educ: La. State Univ, LL.B; Phi Delta Phi, prosecuting attorney for Honor Court. Polit. & Govt. Pos: La. State Rep, 64-66; judge, 19th Judicial Dist, Div. G, La, 66- Mil. Serv: Entered as A/S, Navy, 43, released as Lt.(jg), 46, after serv. in Am. Theater. Mem: Pres, Baton Rouge Bar Asn, 66, v.pres, 65, secy, 64 and treas, 63; Am. and La. Bar Asns; La. Dist. Judges Asn; La. Cmn. on Law Enforcement; Judicial Coun. of La; pres, Exchange Club of Baton Rouge, 54; Am. Judicature Soc; Eagles; Am. Legion. Rel: Baptist. Legal Res: 9525 Donna Dr, Baton Rouge, La. 70815. Mailing Add: E. Baton Rouge Parish Courthouse, Baton Rouge, La. 70801.

COLE, ORVILLE JOHN R
b. Garnett, Kans, 3/4/28; s. Ray Daniel Cole and Edna Mae Reinfield C; m. 12/26/53 to LaVerne K. Klingenberg; c. Kathryn Elizabeth, John William and Thomas Michael. Educ: Washburn Univ, A.B, 49, LL.B, 51. Polit. & Govt. Pos: Co. attorney, Anderson Co, Kans, 56-60; chmn, Anderson Co. Rep. Cent. Cmt, Kans, 59-67. Mil. Serv: Entered as Pvt, Army, 51, released as SFC, 53, after serv. in 28th Inf. Div, ETO. Mem: Am, Kans. State and Anderson Co. Bar Asns; Mason (32°); Regional Dir. of Boy Scouts; dir, Camp Fire Girls; VFW. Rel: First Christian Church. Mailing Add: 111 E. Fourth St, Garnett, Kans. 66032. (1967)

COLE, RALPH A. R
Colo. State Rep.
b. Plattsmouth, Nebr, 3/25/15; married. Polit. & Govt. Pos: Colo. State Rep, currently. Bus. & Prof. Pos: Lawyer. Mailing Add: 10 Wedgeway, Littleton, Colo. 80120. (1967)

COLE, RALPH D, JR. R
b. Findlay, Ohio, 6/12/14; s. Ralph D. Cole and Blanche Davis C; m. 7/21/40 to Mary Ellen Biery; c. Constance K. Educ: Williams Col, A.B, 36, summa cum laude; Western Reserve Univ. Law Sch, J.D, 39; Phi Beta Kappa; Order of the Coif; Phi Delta Phi. Polit. & Govt. Pos: City solicitor, Findlay, Ohio, 48-52; Ohio State Rep, 55-68; Judge, Third Dist. Court Appeals, Ohio, 68- Prof. Pos: Lawyer, 46- Mil. Serv: Entered as Pvt, Army, 42, released as Maj, 46, after serv. in Transportation Corps; recalled to active duty with 408th Mil. Govt. Unit for Korean Crisis, 50. Mem: Am, Ohio and Findlay Bar Asns; Am. Judicature Soc; Am. and Ohio Title Asns; Am. Legion; Mason (32°); Elks; C. of C. Rel: Methodist. Legal Res: 925 Sixth St, Findlay, Ohio 45840. Mailing Add: Third District Court of Appeals, Allen County Court House, Lima, Ohio 45001.

COLE, STACEY WARD R
b. Keene, N.H; married. Educ: Vt. Acad; Thompson Sch. of Agr. Polit. & Govt. Pos: N.H. State Rep, -67. Bus. & Prof. Pos: Farmer; writer; radio farm dir. Mem: Farm Bur; Grange. Rel: Protestant. Mailing Add: Red Crow Farm, W. Swanzay, N.H. 03469. (1967)

COLE, THOMAS DAVID Conservative
Chmn, Niagara Co. Conservative Party, N.Y.
b. New Castle, Pa, 10/31/99; s. Thomas Cole and Elizabeth Hamilton C; m. 12/19/59 to Jeanette Presky. Educ: Univ. Colo, B.S.M.E, 22; Tau Beta Pi; Sigma Chi. Polit. & Govt. Pos: Chmn, Niagara Co. Conservative Party, N.Y, 64- Bus. & Prof. Pos: Pres, Lockport Mills, Inc, 42-66; v.pres, Mill Creek Corp, 60-67. Mil. Serv: Pvt, Army, Inf. in U.S, 18. Mem: Rotary; Bd. of Dir, Salvation Army and YMCA for 20 years. Rel: Presbyterian. Mailing Add: 453 Willow St, Lockport, N.Y. 14094. (1967)

COLE, THOMAS E. R
b. Bath, N.Y, 3/28/33; s. W. Sterling Cole and Elizabeth Thomas C; m. 3/24/59 to Joan Beth Matthews; c. Craig M. Cuthbert, Linda, Thomas E, Jr, Betsy D. and Andrew J. Educ: Colgate Univ, A.B, 54; Sigma Nu. Polit. & Govt. Pos: Spec. asst. to U.S. Rep. Howard W. Robison, N.Y, 65-66; admin. asst. to U.S. Rep. Louis C. Wyman, N.H, 67-69, U.S. Sen. Norris Cotton, N.H, 69- Bus. & Prof. Pos: Plant mgr, Seneca Foods Corp, Dundee, N.Y, 61-63; prod. coordinator, Honeywell Inc, St. Petersburg, Fla, 63-64. Mil. Serv: Entered as Officer Cand, S/A, Navy, 54, released as Lt.(jg), 57, after serv. in U.S.S. Newport News, Atlantic Fleet and Sixth Fleet, Mediterranean; Nat. Defense Medal; European Occup. Medal. Mem: Bull Elephants; Cong. Secy. Club; Asn. Admin. Assts. & Secy; Senate Staff Club. Rel: Protestant. Legal Res: 532 W. Lake Rd, Hammondsport, N.Y. 14840. Mailing Add: 11710 Devilwood Dr, Rockville, Md. 20854.

COLE, TOM C. D
Chmn, Yuma Co. Dem. Cent. Cmt, Ariz.
b. Yuma, Ariz, 9/13/37; s. D.C. Cole and Faye Benton C; m. 8/30/60 to Helen Joyce Edwards; c. Brent Thomas and Scott Benton. Educ: Brigham Young Univ, B.S, 60; Univ. Ariz. Col. of Law, LL.B, 63; Phi Gamma Delta; Phi Delta Phi. Polit. & Govt. Pos: Chmn, Yuma Co. Dem. Cent. Cmt, Ariz, 68-; v.chmn, Ariz. State Dem. Party, currently. Bus. & Prof. Pos: Assoc. law firm, Westover, Keddie & Choules, Yuma, Ariz, 63-; partner, 66- Mem: Am, Ariz. State and Yuma Co. Bar Asns; Elks. Rel: Episcopal. Legal Res: 2240 16th Place, Yuma, Ariz. 85364. Mailing Add: P.O. Box 551, Yuma, Ariz. 85364.

COLE, WILLIAM JENNINGS BRYAN R
Treas, Rep. State Cent. & Exec. Cmts, Ohio
b. South Webster, Ohio, 4/26/97; s. John Wesley Cole and Amelia Charlotte Potts C; m. to Margaret Ethel Hughes; c. Rosemary (Mrs. Williamson), Alice Joan (Mrs. Hess) (deceased), Ronald Caven and William Howard (deceased). Educ: Rio Grande Col, 16-17. Polit. & Govt. Pos: Past pres, Scioto Co. Men's Rep. Club; mayor, South Webster, Ohio, 31-39; exam, Dept. Taxation, Ohio, 39-42; dir, Scioto Co. Bd. Elecs, 42-; del, Rep. State Conv, 56, 58, 60, 62, 64, 66 & 68; treas, Rep. State Cent. and Exec. Cmts, 62-; del, Rep. Nat. Conv, 64. Mil. Serv: Pvt, Army, 18. Mem: Lions (pres, South Webster Lions Club). Rel: Methodist. Mailing Add: Tyrell St, South Webster, Ohio 45682.

COLEMAN, BRUCE RICHARD D
b. Reading, Pa, 10/24/16; s. Samuel Whistler Coleman and Nora Weintraut C; m. 9/22/42 to Violet G. Stoner; c. Charles Bruce. Educ: LaSalle Col, 4 years. Polit. & Govt. Pos: City Acct, Reading, Pa, 42-46, postmaster, 49-52, city controller, 56-60, city councilman, 60-64; mem, Reading Sixth Ward Dem. Cmt, 42-49; chmn, Berks Co. Dem. Party, 60-64; regional supvr, Pa. Dept. Auditor Gen, 66-; del, Dem. Nat. Conv, 68. Bus. & Prof. Pos: CPA, John A. Beard & Co, Reading, 46-49; CPA, self-employed, 52- Mem: Am. and Pa. Insts. of CPA; Nat. Asn. Acct; Wyomissing Club; Elks. Rel: Catholic. Mailing Add: 1800 Olive St, Reading, Pa. 19604.

COLEMAN, C. JOSEPH D
Iowa State Sen.
b. Clare, Iowa, 3/14/23; m. 1954 to Polly Pflanz; c. Joe, Jr, Kevin and Kerry. Educ: Iowa State Univ; Bradley Univ. Polit. & Govt. Pos: Iowa State Sen, 56- Bus. & Prof. Pos: Farmer; former technician, U.S. Dept. Agr. Mem: Pres, Iowa Soybean Asn. Legal Res: Clare, Iowa 50524. Mailing Add: State Capitol, E. Tenth and Grand Ave, Des Moines, Iowa 50319. (1967)

COLEMAN, CAROBEL BLAIR D
Mem. Exec. Cmt, Wichita Co. Dem. Women's Orgn, Tex.
b. Gainesville, Ga, d. William Wiley Blair and Carrie May Merrill B; m. 9/1/21 to Joseph Pickens Coleman; c. Blair Pickens, M.D. and Carolyn (Mrs. W.T. Sanders, Jr). Educ: St. Mary's Dominican Col, B.A. and Valedictorian. Polit. & Govt. Pos: Organizer, Women's Dem. Clubs in Wichita Co, Hardeman Co. and Wilbarger Co, Tex; mem, Tex. State Dem. Exec. Cmt, 60-64; mem. exec. bd, Wichita Co. Dem. Women's Orgn, 61-; chmn, Wichita Co. Women's Participation, Johnson-Humphrey Campaign, 64; alternate del, Dem. Nat. Conv, 64; del, Dem. State Conv, 66. Bus. & Prof. Pos: Secy, Blair & Hughes Co, 19-21. Mem: St. Mary's Dominican Col. Alumnae Asn; Wichita Falls Woman's Forum; Criterion Club; Unity Jr. Club; Wichita Falls Symphony League; Civic Music Orgn; Wichita Ballet Theater League. Rel: Episcopal. Mailing Add: 2004 Avondale St, Wichita Falls, Tex. 76308.

COLEMAN, CHARLES BRUCE D
b. Reading, Pa, 7/30/45; s. Bruce Richard Coleman and Violet Stoner C; single. Educ: George Wash. Univ, B.A, 67; Univ. Tenn. Grad. Sch, 67-69; Pi Sigma Alpha, Beta Zeta Chap. Polit. & Govt. Pos: Alternate del, Dem. Nat. Conv, 68. Bus. & Prof. Pos: Trainee, Reading Develop. Authority, Pa, 69- Mem: Am. and South. Polit. Sci. Asns. Rel: Lutheran. Mailing Add: 1800 Olive St, Reading, Pa. 19604.

COLEMAN, DORIS CATHERINE R
Secy, Allen Co. Rep. Cent. Cmt, Ohio
b. Lima, Ohio, 11/7/12; s. Charles Burtchin (deceased) and Mary Jane Baber B.(deceased); m. 9/22/32 to Reed Coleman; c. Carolyn Elaine (Mrs. Ronald Loudenback) and Wendell Harold. Educ: Shawnee Centralized, Lima, Ohio, 18-30. Polit. & Govt. Pos: Shawnee Twp. mem, Allen Co. Rep. Cent. Cmt, 40-69, secy, 60-; mem, Allen Co. Rep. Exec. Cmt, 52-69; pres, Allen Co. Fedn. Rep. Women, 56-58 & 64-68, mem. state citizenship cmt, 66-68; mem. vacancy and patronage cmt, Allen Co. Rep. Orgn, 60-; asst. clerk, Allen Co. Bd. Elec, 68- Bus. & Prof. Pos: Elected and Served on Charter Cmn. of Ft. Shawnee, Ohio. Mem: Pres, Shawnee Sch. PTA, 46-48; Eastern Star. Rel: Lutheran; pres. and charter mem, Shawnee Methodist Women Soc, 38-42; secy, Women of the Church, Zion Lutheran Church, 60-62. Mailing Add: 1993 Reed Rd, Lima, Ohio 45804.

COLEMAN, EVA LORETTA R
V.Chmn, Oconto Co. Rep. Party, Wis.
b. Appleton, Wis, 12/1/01; d. Harry Henry Predith and Matilda Yahr P; m. to Alvin Andrew Coleman (deceased); c. Harvey and Lorraine (Mrs. Lipinski). Educ: Elem. sch, Lakewood, Wis, 8 years. Polit. & Govt. Pos: V.chmn, Oconto Co. Rep. Party, Wis, 39-; v.chairwoman, Eighth Dist. Rep. Party, 60-64. Bus. & Prof. Pos: Merchant, 16-63; clerk, Bd. Educ. Grade and High Schs, 10 years; secy-treas, Oconto Co. Retail Food Dealers Asn, 59-69; secy-treas, Pres. & Secy. Asn. Wis. Asn. Food Dealers, 63-69; mem. state bd, Wis. Asn. Ford Dealers, 63- Mem: Charter mem, VFW Auxiliary 2119, pres, 12 years; chmn, Salvation Army, 49-; chmn, N.Oconto Co. Wis. Asn. Retarded Children, 65- Rel: Lutheran. Mailing Add: Mountain, Wis. 54149.

COLEMAN, FLOYD BUTLER R
Ind. State Rep.
b. Palmyra, Ind, 12/24/17; s. George Washington Coleman and Kathryn Klinker C; m. 8/18/40 to Eva Lenore Owens; c. David Owen, Janet Sue, Diann Elaine (Mrs. Penland), Anita Nell, Brenda Lynn, Loretta Gail, Stanley Roger and Rachel Marie. Educ: Ind. Univ, Bloomington, B.S, 40; Ind. Univ, Indianapolis, M.D, 45; Nu Sigma Nu. Polit. & Govt. Pos: Dep. coroner, DeKalb Co, Ind, 48-54 and coroner, 54-66; Ind. State Rep, DeKalb and Steuben Counties, 69- Mil. Serv: Entered as Pvt, Army, 42, released as Capt, 48, after serv. in Ind. Univ. Med. Sch, 42-45 and Percy Jones Army Hosp, Battle Creek, Mich, 46-48. Mem: Am, Ind. State and Christian Med. Socs; DeKalb Co. Med. Soc. (former secy-treas, pres, 64-); Am. Acad. of Gen. Practitioners; Ind. Flying Physicians; Lions; Farm Bur; Nat. Farmers Orgn. Rel: Church of Christ. Mailing Add: 425 S. Wayne, Waterloo, Ind. 46793.

COLEMAN, IRWIN WELDON, JR. R
Mem, Mobile Co. Rep. Exec. Cmt, Ala.
b. Austin, Tex, 1/23/34; s. Irwin W. Coleman and Mabel Lucille Gibbs C; m. 6/3/56 to Frances Elizabeth Thompson; c. Elizabeth. Educ: Univ. Tex, B.A, 55, M.A, 56; Univ. Ala, LL.B, 59; pres, Bench and Bar Soc, 59; Kappa Alpha; Phi Alpha Delta. Polit. & Govt. Pos: Del, Mobile Co. Rep. Conv, 64 & 66; del, Ala. State Rep. Conv, 64, 66 & 68, sgt-at-arms and mem. by-laws cmt, 68; mem, Mobile Co. Rep. Exec. Cmt, 65-, chmn, elec. procedures and ballot security cmt, 64-, mem, campaign coord. cmt, 66, cmt. to initiate Mobile Co. Rep. Primary, 67-68 and mem, cand. recruitment cmt, 68; campaign chmn, Bert Nettles for State Senate, 66; chmn, elec. procedures and ballot security, First Cong. Dist, Ala, 66 & 68; del, Ala. State Young Rep. Conv, 67; charter mem, Gulf Coast Young Rep. Club, 67; campaign chmn, Nixon-Agnew, Mobile Co, 68; alternate del, Rep. Nat. Conv, 68; chmn. canvas cmt, Mobile Co. Rep. Cmt, 68; mem. finance cmt. and campaign adv. cmt, Bert Nettles for State House Rep, 69. Bus. & Prof. Pos: Attorney, 59- Publ: 'The Invitee in Alabama', 10: 369-406 & 'Constructive Knowledge of Negligent Condition of Invitor's Premises', 11: 125-138, Ala. Law Rev. Mem: Am, Ala. State and Mobile Co. Bar Asns; charter mem, Mobile Co. Kappa Alpha Alumni Asn. (secy, 61-69). Admitted to bars, U.S. Supreme Court, Fifth Circuit U.S. Court of Appeals, U.S. South. Dist. Court Ala. and Ala. Supreme Court. Rel: Episcopal. Mailing Add: 2256 N. Levert Dr, Mobile, Ala. 36607.

COLEMAN, JAMES M, JR. R
N.J. State Assemblyman
b. Long Branch, N.J, 2/17/24; m. to Dolores Kassak; c. Six. Educ: Dartmouth Col, A.B; Cornell Law Sch, LL.B; Beta Theta Pi; Phi Delta Phi. Polit. & Govt. Pos: Mem, Asbury Park Zoning Bd, N.J, 53-57; mem, Asbury Park Housing Authority, 54-65, chmn, 59-65; councilman, Asbury Park, 57-65, city attorney, 65-; N.J. State Assemblyman, currently. Mem: Monmouth Co. and N.J. Bar Asns; Kiwanis; K. of C. Legal Res: 711 Bangs Ave, Asbury Park, N.J. 07712. Mailing Add: State House, Trenton, N.J. 08625.

COLEMAN, JAMES SAMUEL, JR.
Assoc. Justice, Supreme Court, Ala.
b. Mobile, Ala, 6/8/06; s. James Samuel Coleman (deceased) and Mary Belle Peteet C.(deceased); m. to Eleanor Ruth Montgomery (deceased); c. James Samuel, III; m. to Mary Ruth Morgan Hobbs. Educ: U.S. Naval Acad; Univ. Ala. Law Sch. Polit. & Govt. Pos: Rural mail carrier, Ala; Ala. State Sen, 32nd Dist, 46-50 & 54-56; assoc. justice, Supreme Court, Ala, 57- Bus. & Prof. Pos: Concrete inspector, 27-28; teacher, Marion Inst. and South. Mil. Acad; private practice of law, 34-56. Mil. Serv: Navy, 42-45. Mem: VFW; Am. Legion; Sons Confederate Vet; Lions. Outstanding Mem. and Best Parliamentarian, Ala. State Senate, 55. Rel: Presbyterian; Ruling Elder. Legal Res: 2803 Woodley Rd, Montgomery, Ala. 36111. Mailing Add: Supreme Court of Alabama, Judicial Bldg, Montgomery, Ala. 36104.

COLEMAN, JOHN PATRICK D
Info. Dir, Off. of Emergency Preparedness, D.C.
b. Minneapolis, Minn, 9/11/31; s. James W. Coleman and Marjorie J. Fox

C; m. 6/9/54 to Patricia A. Reding; c. Maureen and Kathleen. Educ: St. Thomas Col, B.A, 53; Univ. Minn, 56-58; Arnold Air Soc. Polit. & Govt. Pos: Press liaison man for U.S. Rep. Joe Karth, Fourth Dist, Minn, 61-64; mem, Minn. Dem. State Cent. Cmt, 61-65; del, Dem. Nat. Conv, 64; Info. Dir, Off. of Emergency Preparedness, Exec. Off. of the President, D.C, 64- Bus. & Prof. Pos: Dem. columnist, Coleman's Corner, and feature writer, St. Paul-Minneapolis Suburban Newspapers, Minn, 60-64. Mil. Serv: Entered as 2nd Lt, Air Force, 53, released as 1st Lt, 55, after serv. in 848th Air Control and Weather Squadron, Hokkaido, Japan, 54-55; Capt, Air Force Res, 60-; Korean Serv, UN and Nat. Defense Medals. Publ: Red Rover, Red Rover. Mem: VFW; Nat. Press Club; K. of C; Lions. Rel: Catholic. Mailing Add: 4233 S. 35th St, Arlington, Va. 22206.

COLEMAN, LEONARD OUTLAR R
Chmn, Grimes Co. Rep. Party, Tex.
b. Navasota, Tex, 12/12/27; s. Solon Douglas Coleman and Mabell Outlar C; m. 7/11/63 to Carole Johnson; c. Leonard Hardison, Solon Douglas, Patricia Elaine, Mary Caren, Mabell Christine and Constance Lynn. Educ: South. Methodist Univ, B.S, 50; Baylor Med. Sch, M.D, 54; Kappa Sigma. Polit. & Govt. Pos: Chmn, Grimes Co. Rep. Party, Tex, 60-; city cmn, Navasota, 63-; alternate del, Rep. Nat. Conv, 68. Bus. & Prof. Pos: Chief of surg, Grimes Mem. Hosp, Navasota, 60-, chief of staff, 66-67. Mil. Serv: Entered as Seaman, Navy, 45 released as Seaman 1st Class, 46 after serving in the Pac. Theatre, 45-46. Mem: Am. Med. Asn; Am. Bd. Surg; Am. Col. Surg; Southwest Surg. Cong; Tex. Surg. Cong; VFW; Am. Legion; Kiwanis; Farm Bur. Rel: Presbyterian. Legal Res: 915 Neal, Navasota, Tex. 77868. Mailing Add: Medical Center, Navasota, Tex. 77868.

COLEMAN, MARION WILFORD D
Chmn, Clay Co. Dem. Cent. Cmt, Ill.
b. Iola, Ill, 11/11/17; s. Elmer Coleman and Sadie Williams C; m. 11/22/47 to Mildred Feldhake; c. Thomas, Charles, William, Richard and James. Educ: East. Ill. Col, Charleston, Ill, 1 year. Polit. & Govt. Pos: Cnmn, Clay Co. Dem. Cent. Cmt, Ill, 68- Mil. Serv: Entered as Pvt, Army, 42, released as S/Sgt, 45, after serv. in 311th Inf, 78th Div, ETO, 44-45; Good Conduct Medal. Mem: Am. Legion; Nat. Farmers Orgn; Farmers Union; Odd Fellows. Rel: Baptist. Mailing Add: R.R. 4, Box 79, Louisville, Ill. 62858.

COLEMAN, NICHOLAS D. DFL
Minn. State Sen.
b. St. Paul, 1925; m. to Bridget Finnegan; c. Nicholas, Patrick, Brendan, Meghan, Christopher. Educ: Col. of St. Thomas, B.A; Univ. of Minn. Polit. & Govt. Pos: Minn. State Sen, 62-; exec. dir, Johnson-Humphrey Vol. Cmt, 64. Bus. & Prof. Pos: Owner, Coleman Advert. Agency. Mil. Serv: Vet. Mem: St. Paul Area C. of C; St. Paul Sales and Mkt. Execs; Ran-View VFW. Mailing Add: 700 Linwood Ave, St. Paul, Minn. 55105. (1967)

COLEMAN, THOMAS WILLIAM R
Chmn, Latimer Co. Rep. Party, Okla.
b. Shady Point, Okla, 9/22/23; s. Aden Arthur Coleman and Amelia Boyken C; m. 8/24/42 to Marie Mashburn; c. Amelia Ann and Tommye Lynn. Educ: High Sch. Polit. & Govt. Pos: Chmn, Latimer Co. Rep. Party, Okla, 65-; del, Rep. Nat. Conv, 68. Bus. & Prof. Pos: Owner, New and Used Automobile agent, 52-69. Mil. Serv: Army, 43, Pvt. Mem: C. of C; Am. Legion. Rel: Baptist. Legal Res: Route 2, Talihina, Okla. 74571. Mailing Add: Box 607, Talihina, Okla. 74571.

COLEMAN, WILLIAM L. D
Mem, Dem. State Exec. Cmt, Ohio
b. Marysville, Ohio, 2/6/14; s. John Henry Coleman and Marie Zacharias C; m. 11/23/40 to Rose Anna Green; c. William Henry, Thomas Hewitt, Charlotte Marie, Stephen G, Rose Anna and Michael S. Educ: Ohio North. Univ, polit. sci; Ohio State Univ. Col. of Law, LL.B, 39; mem. staff, North. Review and pres, Sophomore Class, Ohio North. Univ; Gamma Eta Gamma; Col. of Law Rep, Ohio State Student Senate; mem. staff, OSU Lantern. Polit. & Govt. Pos: Mem, Young Dem. State Exec. Cmt, Ohio; permanent chmn, four State Convs, 40-54; prosecuting attorney, Union Co, 41-49; served as permanent chmn. of Young Dem. Nat. Conv, 47; mem, Union Co. Bd. of Elec, 54-66; chmn, Dem. State Exec. Cmt, 56-66, mem, currently; Dem. cand. for Lt. Gov, 66; del, Dem. Nat. Con., 68; mem, Co. Bd. of Elec, currently. Mem: Am, Inter-Am, Ohio State and Union Co. Bar Asns; Am. and Ohio State Trial Lawyers Asns; Am. Judicature Soc; Kiwanis; Union Co. Tuberc. and Health Asn; Farm Bur; League of Ohio Sportsman; Boy Scouts; Cent. Ohio Area Coun. Rel: Lutheran; Former mem, Bd. Dirs, Trinity Lutheran Church. Mailing Add: R.F.D. 1, Milford Center, Ohio 43045.

COLEMAN, WILLIAM MATTHEW D
Cmnr, Mercer Co, Pa.
b. Sharon, Pa, 3/30/22; s. Patrick Henry Coleman and Mary Purcell C; m. 3/17/51 to Evelyn Desales Driscoll; c. Mary Gertrude and Elizabeth Ann. Educ: Minor Judiciary Procedure Cert, 56, 57 & 58; Shenango Valley Commercial Inst, 60-61; LaSalle Accounting Sch, cert, 67. Polit. & Govt. Pos: Committeeman, Fourth Ward Dem. Cmt, Sharon, Pa, 50-, alderman, 56-; chmn, City Dem. Cmt, 62-66; chmn, Mercer Co. Dem. Cmt, 66-67; cmnr, Mercer Co, 68- Mil. Serv: Entered as Pfc, Army, 42, released as 1st Sgt, 46, after serv. in ETO, 43-46. Mem: Pa. Magistrates Asn; Elks; Am. Legion; Fraternal Order Police Lodge; K. of C. Rel: Catholic. Mailing Add: 272 Cedar Ave, Sharon, Pa. 16146.

COLES, FRANK VAN de VEN R
Chmn, Henry Co. Rep. Party, Iowa
b. Ottumwa, Iowa, 11/26/02; s. William Franklin Coles and Anna Marie Van de Ven C; m. 6/22/61 to Helen; c. Linda (Mrs. Raymond Miller). Educ: Iowa Wesleyan Col, B.A, hon. Dr.Sci, 67; Univ. Iowa, D.D.S; Pi Kappa Delta; Omicron Kappa Upsilon. Polit. & Govt. Pos: Chmn, Henry Co. Rep. Party, Iowa, currently; del, Rep. Nat. Conv, 68. Bus. & Prof. Pos: Practicing dentist, 29-; sr. dent. surgeon, U.S. Pub. Health Serv. Res, 53-66. Publ: Articles in Iowa Dental J. Mem: Mason; Elks; Sigma Phi Epsilon; Xi Psi Phi; Lt. Gov, Kiwanis Int; Iowa-Ill. Boys and Girls Dist. Chmn; Asn. Mil. Surgeons. Rel: Methodist. Mailing Add: 125½ W. Monroe St, Box 463, Mt. Pleasant, Iowa 52641.

COLGROVE, LARRY W. 'CORKY' R
Mem, Colo. Rep. State Cent. Cmt.
b. Mott, N.Dak, 5/25/29; s. Edgar W. Colgrove and Fern Acklin C; m. 8/18/55 to Avis Hoeft; c. Hugh W. Polit. & Govt. Pos: Rep. committeeman, Precinct Six, Weld Co, Colo, 66-; mem, Weld Co. Rep. Cent. Cmt, 66-, mem, Weld Co. Rep. Exec. Cmt, 69-; mem, Colo. Rep. State Cent. Cmt, 69-; chmn, 45th Cong. Dist. Rep. Party, 69- Bus. & Prof. Pos: Maintenance mech, United Air Lines, 52-66, maintenance instr, 66- Mil. Serv: Entered as Pvt, Air Force, 47, released as Sgt, 50, after serv. in Mil. Air Transport Command. Mem: Lions; Am. Legion; C. of C; Boy Scouts. Rel: Congregational. Mailing Add: 1130 Hoover, Ft. Lupton, Colo. 80621.

COLL, MAX R
N.Mex. State Rep.
b. Roswell, N.Mex, 2/26/32; s. Max W. Coll and Lillian Hinkle C; m. 1952 to Martha McGranahan; c. Melanie, Kristi and Max. Educ: Univ. Mo, B.A, Chem, 54; Sigma Nu. Polit. & Govt. Pos: Mem, Young Rep. Nat. Fedn. Exec. Cmt, 66-69; N.Mex. State Rep, 67- Mil. Serv: Entered as 2nd Lt, Army, released as 1st Lt, 57, after serv. in 83rd Reconnaissance, Third Armored Div, Germany, 56-57. Mem: Elks; Landmans Asn. Rel: Episcopal. Legal Res: 1317 W. Third, Roswell, N.Mex. 88201. Mailing Add: Box 1818, Roswell, N.Mex. 88201.

COLLATOS, CHARLES NICHOLAS D
b. Boston, Mass, 3/21/17; s. Nicholas Charles Collatos and Vasiliki Anagnos C; m. 11/26/50 to Florence Koniaves; c. Nicholas Charles and Dianne Florence. Educ: Northeast. Univ, A.B, 41; Suffolk Law Col, LL.B, 64. Polit. & Govt. Pos: Former mem, Mass. Cmn. on Refugees; secy. to Gov. Paul A. Dever, 48-52; del, Dem. Nat. Conv, 48-64; Mass. Labor Rels. Cmnr, 52-57; del, Dem. State Conv, Mass, 56-62; dir, Korean Bonus Div, Vet. Serv, Mass, 54-66 and cmnr, Vet. Serv, 57-; mem, Presidential Appeal Bd, Nat. Selective Serv. Hq, 65-; mem, Mass. Pub. Bequest Cmn, Rehabilitation Cmn, World War II Mem. Cmn, Legis. Cmn. on Vet. Laws, Re-employ. Rights Cmt, Cmn. on Employ. of Handicapped and Inter-Agency Cmt. on Voc. Rehabilitation, President's Cmt. on Employ. of Handicapped and Cmn. Relative to Laws Relating to Convalescent or Nursing Homes. Bus. & Prof. Pos: Dir, Town Bank & Trust Co, Brookline, Mass, 64-; publisher, Greek Am. Newspaper, The Athens. Mil. Serv: Entered as Pvt, Army, 41, released as Chief Warrant Officer, 45, after serv. in First Allied Airborne Army, Mediterranean Theater and ETO and Spec. Duty, Potsdam Conf, Germany. Mem: Mass. and D.C. Bar Asns; Am. Arbitration Asn; Ahepa; VFW; DAV; life mem, Amvets; nat. pres, Nat. Asn. State Dirs. Vet. Affairs, 63-64; nat. exec. committeeman, Am. Legion, 4 years and Mass. State Comdr, 54; Mass. Chmn, Freedom, Inc. and Crusade for Freedom Drive; Mass. Vet. Chmn, Cancer Drive. Rel: Greek Orthodox. Mailing Add: 27 Apple Hill Lane, Lynnfield, Mass. 01940.

COLLETT, BYRON SYLVESTER R
Mem, Rep. State Cent. Cmt, Utah
b. Vernal, Utah, 1/28/02; s. Sylvanus Collett and Sarah Elizabeth Simkins C; m. 9/11/29 to Clela Young; c. Nita Veley (Mrs. Peterson) and Clela Renae (Mrs. Johnstun). Educ: Uintah Acad, Utah, grad, 21. Polit. & Govt. Pos: Construction foreman, U.S. Forest Serv, 31-44; co. assessor, Duchesne Co, Utah, 47-51; chmn, Duchesne Co. Rep. Party, 48-50 & 65-69; mem, Rep. State Cent. Cmt, 50-52 & 69-; chmn, 22nd Sen. Dist. Rep. Party, currently. Bus. & Prof. Pos: Bd. dirs, Moon Lake Elec. Asn. Inc, 44-48; self employed, 52- Rel: Latter-day Saint. Mailing Add: Box 377, Duchesne, Utah 84021.

COLLETT, HAROLD EDWIN D
b. Burley, Idaho, 3/25/30; s. Thomas William Collett and Minnie Peterson C; single. Educ: Univ. Idaho, B.S. in Agr, 53. Polit. & Govt. Pos: Precinct committeeman, Elmore Co. Dem. Cent. Cmt, Idaho, 56-57; pres, Young Dem. Clubs Idaho, 58-59, nat. committeeman, 60-61; dir, Region Eight, Young Dem. Clubs. of Am, 62-63; Idaho State Sen, Elmore Co, 64-69. Mil. Serv: Entered as Aviation Cadet, Air Force, 53, released as Airman 1/C, 55. Mem: Am. Legion; Elks; Lions; Toastmasters; Farm Bur. Rel: Congregational. Mailing Add: Grand View, Idaho 83624. (1967)

COLLETTE, WILFRED D
b. Grafton, N.Dak, 5/21/94; married; c. 6. Educ: Pub. Schs. Polit. & Govt. Pos: N.Dak. State Rep, 41-53, 57-66. Bus. & Prof. Pos: Dir, Grafton Nat. Bank; Grafton Grain Farmers Coop; Modern Potato Storage; Arrowhead Properties, Inc; Retired farmer. Mailing Add: Grafton, N.Dak. 58237. (1967)

COLLIER, CHARLES RUSSELL R
Mem, Calif. Rep. State Cent. Cmt.
b. St. Louis, Mo, 4/10/23; s. Charles Whitfield Collier and Pauline Russell C; m. 6/14/47 to Carol Lineer; c. Constance, Kathleen and Suzanne. Educ: Stanford Univ, A.B. with honors, 43, M.B.A, 48; Delta Chi. Polit. & Govt. Pos: V.chmn, Rep. Alliance, Calif, 66-68, chmn, 68-; finance chmn, San Mateo Co. Rep. Cent. Cmt, 69; mem, Calif. Rep. State Cent. Cmt, 69- Bus. & Prof. Pos: Exec. v.pres, Pac. Plan of Calif, 59- Mil. Serv: Entered as Pvt, Army, 43, released as 1st Lt, 46, after serv. in 69th Div, ETO, 44-46; Bronze Star for Valor with Oak Leaf Cluster; Purple Heart. Mem: Better Bus. Bur.(past pres, San Mateo Co. Br); Peninsula Advert. Club (past pres); Foothills Club (past pres). Rel: Catholic. Mailing Add: 570 St. Francis Court, Menlo Park, Calif. 94025.

COLLIER, CLINT C. D
Chmn, Neshoba Co. Loyalist. Dem. Party, Miss.
b. Philadelphia, Miss, 8/24/10; s. John Collier and Lena Stribling C; m. 3/28/40 to Alaid Johnson; c. Ann, Steve and Helen. Educ: Jackson Col, 40-41; Howard Univ, 41-47. Polit. & Govt. Pos: Del, Dem. Nat. Conv, 68; chmn, Nesholia Co. Loyalist Dem. Party, Miss, currently. Bus. & Prof. Pos: Teacher of math, 52-65; minister, United Methodist Church, 59-69. Mil. Serv: Entered as Seaman 2/C, Navy, 42, released as Seaman 1/C, 45. Mem: Nat. Educ. Asn; Miss. Teachers Asn. Rel: Christian. Mailing Add: Route 7, Box 187, Philadelphia, Miss. 39350.

COLLIER, ERNEST SIMS D
Ala. State Rep.
b. Equality, Ala, 11/19/03; s. Marvin Sims Collier and Annie Mae Johnson C;

m. 4/11/25 to Eleanor Merle Ward; c. Sylvia Dare (Mrs. McConnell) and Eleanor Carolyn (Mrs. Williams). Educ: Auburn Univ, B.S, 35, B.S, 38, M.S, 51. Polit. & Govt. Pos: Agr. educ. technician for U.S. State Dept, Honduras, Cent. Am, 51-56; Ala. State Rep, 67- Bus. & Prof. Pos: Elem. and jr. high teacher, Elmore Co. Bd. of Educ, Wetumpka, Ala, 25-37; voc. educ. teacher, Ala, 38-48, 49-52, 55-; Calif, 48-49. Mem: Ala. and Nat. Educ. Asns; Ala. and Nat. Voc. Asns; Mason; Lions; Kiwanis; Farm Bur; Indust. Develop. Bd, Wetumpka; Ala. Future Farmers. Kappa Delta Pi; Gamma Sigma Delta; Iota Lambda Sigma. Rel: Southern Baptist. Mailing Add: 408 Pine St, Wetumpka, Ala. 36092.

COLLIER, HAROLD R. R
U.S. Rep, Ill.
b. Lansing, Mich, 12/12/15; s. Joseph Howard Collier and Anna Koener C; m. 9/3/38 to Carol Jean Bangert; c. Calvin Joseph, Harold Paul and Lynne Ann (Mrs. Kulp). Educ: J. Sterling Morton Jr. Col, 33-34; Lake Forest Col, 34-37; Quill and Scroll Soc; DiGamma Alpha Epsilon. Polit. & Govt. Pos: Mem, Cook Co. Rep. Cent. Cmt, Ill; Rep. twp. committeeman; secy-treas, Cook Co. Supvr. Asn, 3 years; alderman, Berwyn City Coun, 51; pres, Berwyn Pub. Health Bd; pres, Young Rep. Club; secy, Third Legis. Dist. Rep. Cmt; chmn, First Sen. Dist. Rep. Cmt; mem, Rep. Policy Cmt; U.S. Rep, Ill, 56- Bus. & Prof. Pos: Ed, Berwyn Beacon, 37-38; ed. dept, Life Publ, 38-42; personnel mgr, Match Corp. Am, 39-51; advert. and sales promotion mgr, McAlera Mfg. Co, 51-56. Mem: Riverside Dr. Improvement Asn; Lake Forest Col. Alumni Asn; Berwyn-Cicero Univ. Club. Rel: Methodist. Legal Res: 3819 Howard Ave, Western Springs, Ill. 60558. Mailing Add: 2438 Rayburn House Office Bldg, Washington, D.C. 20515.

COLLIER, HARRY P. R
b. Accident, Md, 11/8/95; s. Tarleton O. Collier and Mary Weller C; m. 6/30/20 to Altha Hockman; c. Helen A.(Mrs. Glotfelly), Leah J.(Mrs. Brenneman) and Joanne E.(Mrs. Durst). Educ: High Sch. Polit. & Govt. Pos: Judge, Orphans Court of Garrett Co, Md, 66-; chmn, Garrett Co. Rep. Cent. Cmt, until 68. Bus. & Prof. Pos: Auctioneer. Rel: Lutheran. Mailing Add: Accident, Md. 21520. (1967)

COLLIER, JAMES BRUCE R
Chmn, Lawrence Co. Rep. Cent. Cmt, Ohio
b. Ironton, Ohio, 9/25/20; s. James W. Collier and Faye Clark C; m. 3/24/43 to Bette Elaine Fawcett; c. James, Jr. and Gretchen J.(Mrs. Randall). Educ: Miami Univ, 38-41; State Univ. Iowa, LL.B, 49; Delta Kappa Epsilon; Phi Beta Phi. Polit. & Govt. Pos: Mem, Lawrence Co. Rep. Cent. Cmt, Ohio, 50-, chmn, 67-; mem, Ironton Sch. Bd, 63-67. Mil. Serv: Entered as Flying Cadet, Army Air Corps, 41, released as Capt, 46, after serv. in 504th Bomb Group, 20th Air Force; Air Medal; Purple Heart. Mem: Lawrence Co. Bar Asn. (pres, 60-62, v.pres, 64-); Ohio and Am. Bar Asns; Elks; Rotary (pres, Ironton Club, 66-67). Rel: Episcopal. Legal Res: 1111 Mastin Ave, Ironton, Ohio 45638. Mailing Add: 411 Center St, Ironton, Ohio 45638.

COLLIER, JOHN L. E. R
Calif. State Assemblyman
b. Wetumpka, Ala, 9/6/04; single. Educ: Occidental Col, A.B, 1932; Army Intel. Sch, Harrisburg, Pa; Prisoner of War Intel. Sch, London, Eng; Kappa Sigma. Polit. & Govt. Pos: Calif. State Assemblyman, 46-, chmn, Rep. Caucus Assembly, chmn, Los Angeles City Del, chmn, Cmt. Educ, v.chmn, Cmt. Water, mem, Way & Means Cmt, Educ. Cmt, Pub. Utilities & Corp. Cmt, Calif. State Assembly and Joint Legis. Budget and Joint Sch. Finance Cmt, Calif. State Legislature. Mil. Serv: Combat Intel. Officer, Army, World War II; in invasion, Sicily, Italy, France and Holland. Mem: F&AM; Am. Legion; VFW; Amvets; Kiwanis Int; Elks; Los Angeles Town Hall. Legal Res: 832 Cooper Ave, Los Angeles, Calif. 90042. Mailing Add: Room 3130, State Capitol, Sacramento, Calif. 95814.

COLLIER, RANDOLPH D
Calif. State Sen.
b. Etna, Calif; m. 1924 to Aida Pillsbury; c. John, Suzanne and Camille. Educ: Univ. Calif. Polit. & Govt. Pos: Police Judge, Yreka, Calif, 25-28; Calif. State Sen, 38-; mem, Calif. Dem. State Cent. Cmt, 68- Bus. & Prof. Pos: Pres, Siskiyou Title Co. Mem: Odd Fellows; Eagles; Grange; Eastern Star; Rebekahs; Mason; Shrine. Rel: Episcopal. Mailing Add: 1057 College Ave, Suite 2, Santa Rosa, Calif. 95404. (1967)

COLLIER, ROBERT ALVIS, JR. D
b. Statesville, N.C, 1/13/31; s. Robert Alvis Collier and Margaret Adams C; m. 9/4/55 to Barbara Ann Stone; c. Robert A, III, James B, Christopher McL, Margaret Paige and Anne Randall. Educ: Univ. N.C, A.B, 57; LL.B, 59; Phi Delta Phi; Phi Delta Theta. Polit. & Govt. Pos: N.C. State Rep, 65-67; Resident Superior Court Judge, 22nd Judicial Dist, N.C, 68- Bus. & Prof. Pos: Pres, Interstate Develop. Co, 64-; dir, First Union Nat. Bank, 63-; partner, Jones-Collier Realty Co, 61- Mil. Serv: Entered as Pvt, Air Force, 51, released as Spec. Agent, 54, after serv. in Off. Spec. Invests, Inspector Gen. Dept, 52-54; Am. Spirit Hon. Medal; Good Conduct Medal. Mem: Iredell Co, N.C. and Am. Bar Asns; Elks; Moose; Mason; Rotary; Shrine; Am. Legion; Statesville Country Club; Statesville City Club; bd. adv, Salvation Army; chmn, Morehead Scholarship Selection Cmt. Rel: Methodist. Legal Res: 306 Valley Stream Rd, Statesville, N.C. 28677. Mailing Add: Courthouse, Statesville, N.C. 28677.

COLLIER, WILMA BERNICE BLENDT R
b. Elk Basin, Wyo, 4/10/23; d. William George Blendt and Ella Vivian Rose B; m. 9/5/44 to John Allen Collier; c. Candace Ellen, Wilma Olivia and John Allen, III. Educ: Wilmington Gen. Hosp. Sch. of Nursing, R.N, 44. Polit. & Govt. Pos: V.chmn, Wash. Co. Rep. Party, Miss, 62-64; mem, Miss. Rep. State Cent. Cmt, 63-65; pres, Miss. Fedn. of Rep. Women, 63-65; mem-at-lg, Nat. Fedn. of Rep. Women Exec. Cmt, 64-68. Mem: Jr. Auxiliary; Deer Creek Garden Club; PTA; Deer Creek Town and Racquet Club. Rel: Southern Baptist. Mailing Add: Route 2, Leland, Miss. 38756. (1967)

COLLIER, WOODROW WILSON D
Chmn, Weakley Co. Dem. Exec. Cmt, Tenn.
b. Martin, Tenn, 11/20/15; s. John Bevley Collier and Fannie Craig C; m. 10/29/33 to Modean Jacobs; c. Shirley Ross and Betty Gail. Educ: Stella Ruth High Sch, Tenn, 2 years. Polit. & Govt. Pos: Mem, Co. Dem. Exec. Cmt, Tenn, 57-; co. chmn, Farmers for Kennedy and Johnson, 60 and Johnson and Humphry, 64; mem. and chmn, Co. Agr. Cmt, 62-68; del. chmn, Dem. State Conv, 68; chmn, Weakley Co. Dem. Exec. Cmt, 68-; chmn, Co. Primary Elec. Cmn, 69- Bus. & Prof. Pos: Livestock farmer, 30-; woodcraft art craftsman, 50-; dir, sta. WCMT Laymen Prog, 68. Mem: Tenn. Livestock Asn; Co. C. of C. Agr. Cmt; bd. dirs, Farm Bur, 56-67; pres, Co. Farm Bur, 62; 4 H Leadership and Training Award; cert. achievement, Univ. Tenn. Col. Agr. Rel: Methodist; lay speaker. Mailing Add: Route 4, Martin, Tenn. 38237.

COLLINGWOOD, ROBERT T. D
b. Elk Point, S.Dak, 1/24/98; m. to Vivian Pennel. Educ: High sch. Polit. & Govt. Pos: Mem, Farm Tenancy Prog, 38-39; auditor, Union Co, S.Dak, 59-62; S.Dak. State Rep, 62-69. Bus. & Prof. Pos: Farmer (retired). Mem: S.Dak. Hist. Soc; Nat. Geog. Soc; Mason (3°); past treas, Union Co. Chap. Am. Red Cross. Rel: Congregational. Mailing Add: Elk Point, S.Dak. 57025. (1967)

COLLINS, CHARLES C. D
Chmn, Latimer Co. Dem. Cent. Cmt, Okla.
b. Colbert, Okla, 7/27/08; s. Dan H. Collins and Nancy Madlyn Colbert C; m. 9/7/29 to Lola Martin; c. Charles M. Educ: Southeast. State Col, B.S, 35; Okla. State Univ, M.S, 47. Polit. & Govt. Pos: Precinct chmn, Dem. Party, Red Oak, Okla, 48; chmn, Latimer Co. Dem. Cent. Cmt, 50- Bus. & Prof. Pos: Teacher and coach, Cameron Pub. Sch, 29-31; high sch. prin, teacher, coach, LeFlore Pub. Sch, 31-48; supt. and prin, Red Oak Sch, 48-49. Mil. Serv: Entered as Pvt, Nat. Guard, 26, released as Pvt, 29, after serv. in Durant Hq. Co. Mem: Nat, Okla. and Latimer Co. Educ. Asns; Okla. Sch. Admin. Asn; Mason; Lions; Sportsman Club; Boy Scouts. Rel: Methodist; Assoc. Dist. Lay Leader. Mailing Add: P.O. Box 35, Red Oak, Okla. 74563.

COLLINS, CHARLES EDWARD D
b. Frederick, Md, 7/19/05; s. Charles Alvin Collins and Frances Brookey C; m. 5/9/39 to Helen Elizabeth James; c. Charles Edward, Jr. Polit. & Govt. Pos: Md. State Del, 59-69. Bus. & Prof. Pos: Self employed. Mem: Optimist; Lions; Elks; Eagles; Moose; New Mkt. Grange; Jeffersonian Dem. Club; New Mkt. Vol. Fire Co; Cent. Md. Implement Dealers Asn. Rel: Lutheran. Mailing Add: 1602 Rock Creek Dr, Frederick, Md. 21701. (1967)

COLLINS, CLARA STONE D
Ala. State Rep.
b. Mobile, Ala, d. George Edwin Stone and Claudia Kirkpatrick S; m. to Edward E. Fields, wid. 9/29/56, m. 7/24/64 to Neal A. Collins; c. Edward E. and George S. Fields. Educ: Univ. Ala, A.B; Am. Col. Life Underwriters, C.L.U; Mortar Bd; Chi Delta Phi; Delta Delta Delta; Beta Sigma Phi. Polit. & Govt. Pos: Secy, Mobile Co. Dem. Exec. Cmt, Ala, 58-66; Ala. State Rep, 62-; secy, Nat. Order of Women Legislators, 64-65, first v.pres, 66-67, pres. elect, 68-69; mem. bd. trustees, Ala. Inst. for Deaf and Blind. Bus. & Prof. Pos: Mem, Estate Planning Coun. of Mobile, Ala, 60- Mem: Delta Kappa Gamma; Mobile, Ala. and Nat. Asn. of Life Underwriters; Am. Soc. Chartered Life Underwriters; Nat. Soc. State Legis; Nat. Women Leaders Round Table; Mobile Wildlife & Conserv. Asn; Mobile Symphony Guild; YWCA; Historic Mobile Preservation Soc; Mobile Auxiliary to Power Squadron; Mobile Area C. of C; Friends of Mobile Pub. Libr; Jr. League of Mobile; Ky. Col. Received U.P.I. Ala. Woman of Year Award, 63; Outstanding Ala. Life Underwriter, 64; Outstanding Alumna, Univ. Ala, 69. Rel: Presbyterian. Mailing Add: 1950 Hunter Ave, Mobile, Ala. 36606.

COLLINS, CLARICIE VISSER R
Chmn, Clay Co. Rep. Cent. Cmt, S.Dak.
b. Hurley, S.Dak, 2/22/27; d. Leonard Visser and Leta Thompson V; m. 9/17/50 to Gerald Morris Collins; c. Lowell Louise, Kimberly Ann, Gerald Leonard, Alex Charles and Andrea Lee. Educ: Univ. of S.Dak, B.A, 49; Pi Delta Epsilon; Eta Sigma Phi; Kappa Alpha Theta. Polit. & Govt. Pos: V.chmn, Clay Co. Rep. Cent. Cmt, S.Dak, 60-65, chmn, 65- Bus. & Prof. Pos: Hostess, Mid-Continent Airlines, 49-50; exec. secy, Univ. S.Dak. Alumni Asn, 67- Mem: PEO; Am. Field Serv. Rel: United Church of Christ, First Congregational. Mailing Add: 812 Canby, Vermillion, S.Dak. 57069.

COLLINS, CONSTANCE SULLIVAN R
Pres, Conn. Fedn. Rep. Women's Clubs
b. Holyoke, Mass, 1/29/24; d. George Wilmer Sullivan and Elizabeth O'Neil S; m. 1/22/49 to James Francis Collins; c. James Barry, Elizabeth Frances, Patricia Alice and Mary Ellen. Educ: Holyoke Sch. Nursing, 42; Boston Univ, Sargent Col, B.S. in Phys. Therapy and Phys. Educ, 50; Univ. Hartford, M.A. in Educ, 69; Veterans Club; Phys. Therapy Club; Basketball Team; Horseback Riding Club. Polit. & Govt. Pos: Co. chmn. ward, Rep. Town Cmt, Conn, 52-61; mem. exec. bd, Hartford Co. Rep. Women's Asn, 55-, chmn. mem. cmt, 59-61, pres, 61-63, counsr, treas. and chmn. nominating cmt, 63-65 and chmn. legis. cmt, 64-66; mem, Nat. Fedn. Rep. Women, 55-; alternate del, Rep. State Conv, 58; mem. exec. bd, Women's Rep. Club Hartford, 58-61; mem. exec. bd, Conn. Coun. Rep. Women, 60-64, mem. rev. by-laws cmt, 62 and mem. nominating cmt; alternate del, Rep. Nat. Conv, 64 & 68; pres, Conn. Fedn. Rep. Women's Clubs, 68- Bus. & Prof. Pos: Teacher, Hartford, Conn, 66- Mil. Serv: Entered as Seaman, W.A.V.E.S, 44, released as PO 1/C, 46, after serv. as Cartographer, Suitland, Md. Mem: Sargent Col. Alumnae; Boston Univ. Alumni; Phys. Therapy Asn; Sargent Club, Hartford; City Club of Hartford; Noah Webster PTA; St. Justins Ladies Guild. Rel: Roman Catholic. Mailing Add: 104 Westerly Terrace, Hartford, Conn. 06105.

COLLINS, COPP R
Asst. to the Secy. for Pub. Affairs, Dept. of Agr.
b. Keokuk, Iowa, 12/31/14; s. Harrie Richards Collins and Elsie Parsons C; m. 9/28/40 to Frances Truax; c. Michael Truax, Nicole Elyse and Copp, Jr. Educ: Univ. Redlands, B.A, 38; Pi Kappa Delta; Alpha Phi Gamma; Kappa Sigma Sigma. Polit. & Govt. Pos: Former mem, United Finance Cmt, Rep. Assembly, Calif; former mem, Los Angeles Young Rep; former chmn, El Cajon Valley Young Rep; co-founder, Young Rep. of San Diego Co; mem, Eisenhower-Nixon Presidential Campaign and Hollywood rep. for Eisenhower-Nixon, 52; mgr, Rep. Selectmen's Campaign, Westport, Conn, 55; mem. public-

ity and pub. rels. staff, N.J. Conf. for Prom. of Better Govt. and Campaign for U.S. Sen. Clifford Case, 59 & 60; mem. publicity, Rep. Campaign Cmt, Westport, Conn. Nixon-Lodge Campaign, 60; mem. campaign staff, Ogden R. Reid for U.S. Rep, N.Y, 62 & 64; campaign coordinator and press aide, U.S. Rep. Romeo Petroni, Conn, 66; supvr. campaign lit. and materials, Nixon-Agnew Campaign Cmt, N.Y, 68; aide to Herbert G. Klein, Asst. Info. Officer, Nixon-Agnew Campaign Cmt. and Nixon for President Cmt, 68; mem, GOP Listening Post, Dem. Nat. Conv, 68; mem, Misson Bay Press Rels. Staff assisting Herbert G. Klein; mem. press rels. staff assisting Herbert G. Klein in releases, news features and biographies, Rep. Nat. Conv, 68; aide to dir. of commun. Herbert G. Klein, Off. of President-Elect, N.Y, 68 and Wash, D.C, 68-69; asst. to the Secy. of Agr. for Pub. Affairs, Dept. of Agr, 69- Bus. & Prof. Pos: Bur. mgr, United Press, San Diego, Calif, 39-40; commercial sales supvr. and flight admin. supvr, Consolidated Vultee, 42-47; owner, Copp Collins, Publicity, Pub. Rels. and Prom, San Diego and Beverley Hills, 48-53; mgr. pub. rels. and W. Coast rep. info, Mutual Broadcasting Syst, 51-55; mgr. pub. rels, Bahrain Petroleum Co, Persian Gulf, 55-58; asst. to exec. v.pres, Burns & Roe, Consult. Engrs, N.Y, 58-60; v.pres. and dir, Chirurg & Cairns, Inc, 61-62 and Friend-Reiss Advert. Inc, 62-63; pres, Collins & Lynge, Ltd. and Copp Collins Assocs, Pub. Rels. Consult, 63-67; dir. mkt, merchandising and prom, N.Am. Soccer League and Nat. Prfnl. Soccer League, 67-68. Publ: Building Better Box Offices, Nat. Prfnl. Soccer League, 67. Mem: Cmt, Boy Scout Troops 36 and 28, Westport, Conn, 53 & 55; chmn. pub. rels, Westport, Conn. Citizens Planning Asn, 54-55; chmn, N.Y. Chap, Univ. Redlands Alumni Asn, 55; chmn, Pub. Rels. Adv. Coun, Red Cross Chap. of South. Conn, 55. Co-capt, Cross Country Team, Univ. Redlands, 38, chmn, Interfraternity Coun; S.Calif. Amateur Middleweight Boxing Champion, 39. Rel: Protestant. Mailing Add: 3410 Mansfield Rd, Falls Church, Va. 22041.

COLLINS, DENNIS J. R
Ill. State Sen.
b. Champaign Co, Ill, 11/15/00; m. June 1944 to Gertrude Kellman; c. Cathleen Sue (Mrs. David Rogers), Carole Kay and Dennis J, III. Educ: Univ. of Ill; Northwest. Univ. Law Sch. Polit. & Govt. Pos: Ill. State Rep, 30-42, chmn, Agr. Cmt, Ill. House of Rep, 38-42; Ill. State Sen, 42-, chmn, Munic. Cmt, Ill. State Sen, 42-54, chmn, Agr. Cmt, 50-; del, Rep. Nat. Conv, 48. Bus. & Prof. Pos: Attorney-at-law, farming, and business interests. Mem: Am, Ill. and DeKalb Co. Bar Asns; Ill. Agr. Asn; Ill. State Grange; DeKalb Co. Farm Bur; Dekalb Bar Asn.(past pres). Mailing Add: 545 Northern Lane, Dekalb, Ill. 60115.

COLLINS, DONALD EUGENE D
Exec. V.Chmn, Winnebago Co. Dem. Party, Wis.
b. Del Norte, Colo, 4/11/37; s. Thomas Aubrey Collins and Loretta Mabry C; m. 12/28/58 to Edith McFadden; c. David Michael, Sara Lynne and John Martin. Educ: Univ. Denver, A.B, 59; Iliff Sch. Theol, B.D, 62; Relig. Coun; Methodist Student Found. Polit. & Govt. Pos: Alternate del, Dem. Nat. Conv, 68; exec. v.chmn, Winnebago Co. Dem. Party, Wis, 68- Bus. & Prof. Pos: Assoc. dir, Methodist Student Found, Univ. Denver, 60-62; dir, Wesley Found, Bemidji State Col, 62-66; Methodist Univ. minister, Wis. State Univ, Oshkosh, 66-69, mem, United Ministries in Higher Educ, 69- Publ: 'A Functional Analysis of Baptism,' Iliff Rev, winter 67. Mem: Nat. Campus Ministry Asn; Am. Civil Liberties Union; Am. Dem. Action. Rel: United Methodist. Mailing Add: 932 Vine Ave, Oshkosh, Wis. 54901.

COLLINS, DONALD L. R
b. Gadsden, Ala, 9/8/29; s. Luther Thomas Collins, Sr. and Mattie Scarbrough C; m. 8/30/52 to Hannah Case Snellgrove; c. Henry C, Cynthia C, Donald L. Jr. Educ: Jacksonville State Coll, B.S, 52; Univ. Ala, LL.B, 57; Omicron Delta Kappa; Phi Alpha Delta. Polit. & Govt. Pos: Ala. State Rep, 62-66, mem, Ins, Rules and State Safety Coord. Cmts; Rep. nominee for attorney gen. Ala, 66; spec. asst. state campaign mgr, Nixon-Agnew Campaign and campaign coordinator, Sixth Cong. Dist, 68; alternate del-at-lg, Rep. Nat. Conv, 68; chmn, Ala, Inaugural Banquet & Ball Cmt. Nixon Inaugural. Mil. Serv: Entered as Pvt. Marine Corps Res, released as Capt, 55, after serv. as intel. officer, 52-55; Res, Maj.(Ret); UN, Am. Defense, Korean and Marine Res. Medals. Mem: Am. and Birmingham Bar Asns; Ala. Bar Asn.(chmn. pub. rels. cmt. jr. sect, 57, chmn. continuing legal educ, 58, exec. coun, 58-59, secy, 60, v. chmn, 61, chmn, 62 and mem. grievance cmt, 62-64); Law Sci. Acad. Am; Am. Legion; VFW; Eagles; Rotary; Touchdown Club. Scholastic Achievement Awards, Sigma Delta Kappa and Bur. Nat. Affairs. Rel: Episcopal. Legal Res: 29 Ridge Dr, Mountain Brook, Ala. 35223. Mailing Add: 1212 Bank for Savings Bldg, Birmingham, Ala. 35203.

COLLINS, ELSON K. D
Miss. State Sen.
b. Jones Co, Miss, 12/17/11; married. Polit. & Govt. Pos: Miss. State Sen, 60- Bus. & Prof. Pos: Attorney-at-law. Mil. Serv: World War II, serv. in War Crimes Prosecution, S.Pac; Bronze Star; Asiatic Pac. Campaign Ribbon with Three Stars. Mem: Judge Adv. Gen; State and Co. Bar Asns; bar cmnr, 18th Circuit Court Dist; chmn, Nat. Legal Cmt, VFW, 67, past state comdr; Mason; Shrine; Am. Legion. Rel: Presbyterian. Mailing Add: Box 732, Waynesboro Dr, Laurel, Miss. 39440. (1967)

COLLINS, EMMETT MARVIN R
b. Corpus Christi, Tex, 4/11/34; s. Bruce Livingston Collins and Lucile Tankersley C; single. Educ: South. Methodist Univ, B.B.A, 54, LL.B, 59; Blue Key; Phi Alpha Delta; Alpha Kappa Psi; Alpha Tau Omega. Polit. & Govt. Pos: Former asst. to U.S. Rep. Bruce Alger, Tex; exec. dir, Dallas Co. Rep. Hq, 60-62; exec. dir, Rep. Party, Tex, 63-67; campaign mgr, Linwood Holton, Rep. Cand. for Gov, Va, 69. Bus. & Prof. Pos: Partner, Collins-Knaggs & Assocs, 67- Mil. Serv: Entered as 2nd Lt, Air Force, 55, released as 1st Lt, 57; Capt, Air Force Res. Rel: Methodist. Legal Res: 505 W. Seventh St, Austin, Tex. 78701. Mailing Add: 1905 N. Lamar, Suite 208, Austin, Tex. 78705.

COLLINS, FRANCIS JAMES R
Conn. State Rep.
b. Danbury, Conn, 11/20/33; s. Thomas Collins (deceased) and Sara Lowe C; m. 8/4/56 to Dora M. Rencsko; c. Kevin J, Keith A, Kathleen A, Kristy and Kyle. Educ: Miami Univ, Oxford, Ohio, B.S, 55; Univ. Conn. Sch. of Law, LL.B, 62. Polit. & Govt. Pos: Mem, Brookfield Rep. Town Cmt, 64-; Conn. State Rep, 165th Dist, 67- Bus. & Prof. Pos: Partner and attorney, Cutsumpas, Collins & Hannafin, Danbury, Conn. Mil. Serv: Entered as Pvt, Army, 56, released as Specialist 4/C, 58, after serv. in Qm. Corps, Ft. Lee, Va. Mem: Dir, Univ. Conn. Law Sch. Alumni Asn, 66; Am. and Conn. Bar Asns; Brookfield Exchange Club; Brookfield Commun. Chest; Brookfield C. of C. Rel: Roman Catholic. Mailing Add: Whisconier Hill, Brookfield, Conn. 06805.

COLLINS, JAMES MITCHELL R
U.S. Rep, Tex.
b. Hallsville, Tex, 4/29/16; s. Carr Pritchett Collins and Ruth Woodall C; m. 9/16/42 to Dorothy Colville Dann; c. Michael James, Nancy Miles and Dorothy (Mrs. Weaver). Educ: South. Methodist Univ, B.Sc, 37; Northwest. Univ. M.B.A, 38; Harvard Bus, M.B.A, 43; Cycen Fjodr; Phi Delta Theta, Blue Key, Alpha Kappa Psi. Polit. & Govt. Pos: U.S. Rep, Tex, 68- Bus. & Prof. Pos: V.pres, Fidelity Union Life Ins. Co, Dallas, Tex, 46-54, pres, 54-64. Mil. Serv: Entered as Pvt, Army, 43, released as Capt, 46, after serv. in 1197 Engineers; ETO, $1\frac{1}{2}$ years; Medal of METZ; Four Battle Stars. Mem: Am. Legion; VFW. Rel: Baptist. Legal Res: Route 1, Box 210, Hard Rock Rd, Grand Prairie, Tex. 75050. Mailing Add: 1512 Longworth House Office Bldg, Washington, D.C. 20515.

COLLINS, JOHN FELTON D
b. Collins, Ga, 12/20/27; s. Horatio Lee Collins and Ida Mae Kennedy C; m. 4/2/45 to Myrtice Braswell; c. John Charles and Cathy. Educ: High Sch. Polit. & Govt. Pos: Ga. State Rep, Dist. 62, until 69. Bus. & Prof. Pos: Pres, United Commun. Inc, 58- Rel: Baptist. Legal Res: 100 Marcliff Rd, Vidalia, Ga. 30474. Mailing Add: Box 407, Vidalia, Ga. 30474.

COLLINS, JOHN FREDERICK D
b. Boston, Mass, 7/20/19; s. Frederick Basil Collins and Margaret Mellyn C; m. 9/6/47 to Mary Cunniff; c. Mary Patricia, John Frederick, Jr, Thomas Francis and Margaret Agnes. Educ: Suffolk Univ. Law Sch, LL.B. Hon. LL.D, Boston Univ; D.C.L, Northeast. Univ; D.P.A, Suffolk Univ; Ph.D, Harvard Univ. and Tufts Univ; D.J.P, Portia Law Sch. Polit. & Govt. Pos: Mass. State Rep, 47-50; Mass. State Sen, 50-54; city councilman, Boston, 56; registrar probate, Suffolk Co, 57-59; mayor, Boston, 60-67; trustee, U.S. Conf. Mayors, mem. exec. cmt, 64-65. Bus. & Prof. Pos: Mem, Nat. Urban Coalition; trustee, Boston Five Cents Savings Bank; former pres, Nat. League of Cities; vis. committeeman, Kennedy Sch. Govt, Harvard Univ; mem. tech. adv. bd, U.S. Dept. Commerce; mem. nat. adv. coun, Voc. Rehabilitation; mem. bd. trustees, Am. Pub. Works Asn. Research Found; corporator, Faulkner Hosp, Jamaica Plain, Mass. prof. urban affairs, Alfred P. Sloan Sch. Mgt, Mass. Inst. Tech, 68- and chief adv, Fel. Urban Affairs Prog, currently; mem. cmt. housing and urban law, Am. Bar Asn, currently. Mil. Serv: Entered as Pvt, Army, 42, released as Capt, 46, after serv. in Intel. Corps. Rel: Roman Catholic. Legal Res: 20 Myrtle St, Jamaica Plain, Boston, Mass. 02130. Mailing Add: 50 Memorial Dr, Cambridge, Mass. 02139.

COLLINS, JOHN JOSEPH D
b. Jackson, Mich, 3/12/35; s. Joseph C. Collins and Martha Bush C; m. 9/6/58 to Carolyn A. Doyle; c. Joseph Michael, John Edward, Patrick James and Kathleen Ann. Educ: Univ. Mich, B.A, 58. Polit. & Govt. Pos: Campaign mgr, John J. Swainson for Gov, 60; chmn, Mich. State Dem. Party, 61-63. Bus. & Prof. Pos: Pres, Wayne Nat. Life Ins. Co, 63-67 and Pac. Am. Life Ins. Co, 66-67; chmn. bd, Wis. Ins. Corp, 65-67; pres, Financial Progs. of Can. Ltd, 69- Mem: Detroit and Nat. Asns. of Life Underwriters; Confrerie de la Chaine des Rotisseurs; Detroit Bd. of Commerce; Presidents Club of Wash. D.C; City Club of Lansing; Econ. Club of Detroit; Detroit Golf Club. U.S. Rep. to World Univ. Seminar, Ghana, 57; Named Outstanding Man of the Year by Mich. State Jr. C. of C, 61. Rel: Roman Catholic. Legal Res: 2339 Jefferson Rd, Clarklake, Mich. 49234. Mailing Add: 505 N. Service Rd. E, Oakville, Ontario, Can.

COLLINS, JON RICHARD D
Chief Justice, Nev. Supreme Court
b. Ely, Nev, 5/7/23; s. Joseph L. Collins, Sr. and Dorothy May Frey C; m. 2/26/49 to Rita Baird; c. Pamela, Candace, Jona and Melissa. Educ: Univ. Pa, B.S. in Econ, 47; Georgetown Univ. Law Sch, J.D, 49; Sigma Alpha Epsilon. Polit. & Govt. Pos: Off. staff mem, Off. U.S. Sen. Patrick A. McCarran, 41-43 & 47-49; Off. Dep. Attorney Gen, Dept. Justice, Wash, D.C, 49-50; dist. attorney, White Pine Co, Ely, Nev, 50-54; dist. judge, Seventh Judicial Dist, Ely, 58-66; chmn, Conf. of Dist. Court Judges of Nev, 61; Justice, Nev. Supreme Court, 66-69 and Chief Justice, 69- Bus. & Prof. Pos: Attorney-at-law, Ely, Nev, 54-58; teacher bus. law, Univ. Nev, Off-campus Sch, 58-62. Mil. Serv: Entered as A/S, Navy, 42, released as Lt.(jg), 46, after serv. in U.S.S. Ajax, AR 6, West. Pac. Theatre, 44-46; Lt.(jg), Naval Res, 46-57. Publ: Opinions, Nev. Supreme Court, 66- Mem: Am. Adjudicature Soc; Am. Bar Asn; Conf. Chief Justices of U.S; Elks. Rel: Episcopal. Legal Res: 20 Moore Lane, Reno, Nev. 89502. Mailing Add: Nevada Supreme Court, Carson City, Nev. 89701.

COLLINS, LEROY D
b. Tallahassee, Fla, 3/10/09; s. Marvin H. Collins and Mattie Brandon C; m. 6/29/32 to Mary Call Darby; c. Leroy, Jane, Mary Call and Darby. Educ: Cumberland Univ, LL.B, 31. Polit. & Govt. Pos: Fla. State Rep, 34-40; Fla. State Sen, 40-54; chmn, South. Regional Educ. Bd, 55-57; mem, Nat. Adv. Coun. Peace Corps; chmn, Nat. Pub. Adv. Cmt. on Area Develop, U.S. Dept. of Commerce; Gov, Fla, 55-60; former chmn. of Nat. Gov. Conf. and South. Gov. Conf; chmn, Cmt. on Goals for Higher Educ. in the South, 61-62; dir, Commun. Rels. Serv, Dept. of Commerce, 64-65, Under Secy. of Commerce, 65-66; Bd. of Gov, Nat. Cathedral Sch; trustee, Randolph-Macon Women's Col; Dem. cand, U.S. Sen, Fla, 68. Bus. & Prof. Pos: Pres, Nat. Asn. of Broadcasters, 61-64. Mil. Serv: Navy, Lt. Mem: Honor corps, Nat. Conf. of Christians and Jews; Am. Bar Asn; dir, Adv. Coun; Int. Radio and TV Soc; Nat. Munic. League; U.S. Int. C. of C. Rel: Episcopal. Mailing Add: Fowler, White, Collins, Gillen, Humkey and Trenam, P.O. Box 1438, Tampa, Fla. 33601.

COLLINS, LOREE R
b. New York City, N.Y, 11/10/27; s. David M. Collins and Louise Loree C; m. 5/13/50 to Sherley Loheke; c. Craig L, Sherley L. and Cynthia L. Educ: Williams Col, 44; U.S. Naval Acad, B.S, 49; N.Y. Univ, M.B.A, 60. Polit. &

Govt. Pos: N.J. Assemblyman, 64-65; chmn, Union Co. Rep. Party, N.J, 66-68 mem, Electoral Col, 68. Bus. & Prof. Pos: Mem. staff, W.R. Grace & Co, 54-58; v.pres, John Wood Co, 58-64; publisher, Rahway News Record and Clark Patriot, 64-66; pres, Publications Ltd, 66. Mil. Serv: Entered as A/S, Navy, 45, released as Lt; Am. Defense and Korean Theater Ribbons with two battle stars. Rel: Catholic. Mailing Add: 19 Essex Rd, Summit, N.J. 08102.

COLLINS, MARY ANN NEUHOFF R
b. Dallas, Tex, 4/16/32; d. Henry Neuhoff, Jr. and Jane Hudson N; m. 6/13/53 to Godfrey M. Collins; c. Nancy Neuhoff, Susan Moora, Stephen Hudson, Ann Shelton, Madeline Moora, Peter Godfrey, Bruce Hutchinson and Shannon Joseph. Educ: Marymount Col, 49-50; Maryville Col, B.S. in Educ, 52. Polit. & Govt. Pos: Hq. chmn, Dallas Co. Rep. Party, Tex, 56, v.chmn, 67-68; coffee chmn, Cong. Bruce Alger, 58 and legis. cand, 60; alternate del, Rep. Nat. Conv, 60 & 68; get out the vote chmn, Dallas Co. Rep, 63 & 66; co-chmn, Dirksen $100 Plate Dinner, Dallas, 66. Bus. & Prof. Pos: Kindergarten Teacher, Holy Trinity Sch, Dallas, 52-53. Mem: Jr. League of Dallas; Christ King Mothers Club. Nominee, Outstanding Young Women of Am, Nat. Coun. Cath. Women, 66. Rel: Catholic. Mailing Add: 3560 Marquette, Dallas, Tex. 75225.

COLLINS, MICHAEL McHALE D
b. Covington, Va, 8/9/01; m. to Eleanor McCoy. Educ: Mt. St. Mary's Col, Md; Univ. of Va, LL.B. Polit. & Govt. Pos: Va. State Del, 48-55; Va. State Sen, 60-66. Bus. & Prof. Pos: Lawyer; pres, Hotel Collins, Inc; dir, First Nat. Exchange Bk. of Va. Mem: Rotary; Elks; Moose; Va. Bar Asn; Covington Fire Dept; Va. C. of C. Rel: Catholic. Mailing Add: Covington, Va. 22426. (1967)

COLLINS, OAKLEY C. R
Ohio State Sen.
b. Lawrence Co, Ohio, 1916. Educ: Ohio Univ, B.S, 38. Polit. & Govt. Pos: Ohio State Sen, 52-; Ohio State Rep, 1 term; mem, Ohio Rep. State Exec. Cmt, 68- Bus. & Prof. Pos: High Sch. Adminstr, 19 years. Legal Res: 1005 Kemp Lane, Ironton, Ohio 45638. Mailing Add: State Capitol, Columbus, Ohio 43215. (1967)

COLLINS, PHIL C. D
b. Cincinnati, Ohio, 4/6/36; s. Philip M. Collins and Laura E. Kienzle C; m. 8/8/59 to Nancy Ann Smith; c. Kathleen Ann and Philip Daniel. Educ: Univ. Cincinnati, B.B.A, 60; Chase Col. Law, J.D, 62; Phi Alpha Delta. Polit. & Govt. Pos: Ohio State Rep, 58-61; city councilman, Cincinnati, Ohio, 61-68; mem. exec. cmt, Hamilton Co. Dem. Party, 64-68. Bus. & Prof. Pos: Attorney at law, 62- Mem: K. of C; Hamilton Co. Good Govt. League. Rel: Roman Catholic. Legal Res: 2083 Raeburn Dr, Cincinnati, Ohio 45223. Mailing Add: 6 E. Fourth St, Cincinnati, Ohio 45220.

COLLINS, PURVIS WESLEY D
S.C. State Rep.
b. Winnsboro, S.C, 7/11/23; s. William Calvin Collins and Lula Player C; m. 12/3/55 to Ila Mae Clamp C; c. Kim. Educ: Univ. S.C, B.S, M.Ed, 48, with Honors. Polit. & Govt. Pos: S.C. State Rep, 59- Bus. & Prof. Pos: Sch. admin; retail merchant; sch. supt, private sch, 53-55. Mil. Serv: Navy, 43-46, Pac. Theatre; Comdr, Navy Res. Mem: Dir, Rotary Club; Mason; Hejaz Shriners; WOW; VFW; Pres, CATAWBA Sch. Conf; Moose; S.C. Athletic Off. Asn; S.C. Sch. Admin. Asn; dir, United Fund; S.C. Coaches Asn. Outstanding Young Man, Fairfield Co, 59. Rel: Methodist; Off. Bd, Gordon Memorial Methodist Church. Mailing Add: Winnsboro, S.C. 29180. (1967)

COLLINS, STANLEY NEWCOMB, JR. R
Ga. State Rep.
b. Alexandria, Va, 1/30/37; s. Stanley Newcomb Collins, Sr. and Mary Elsie Bloxom C; m. 7/18/58 to Joyce Diane Pratt; c. Kendra Ann, Andrew David, Daniel Newcomb and Katie Louise. Educ: Univ. Md, B.S, 62; Col. William and Mary, M.Ed, 65; Iota Lambda Sigma. Polit. & Govt. Pos: Ga. State Rep, Dist. 72, Post 2, 69- Bus. & Prof. Pos: High sch. teacher, Richmond, Va, 62-64; pilot, Delta Air Lines, 65- Mil. Serv: Entered as Naval Air Cadet, Marine Corps, 56, released as 1st Lt, 60, after serv. in First Marine Air Wing, HMR-362 and VMO-2, Far East, 59-60; Maj, Res. Mem: Air Line Pilots Asn; U.S. Marine Corps Reserve Officers Asn; ROA. Rel: Methodist. Mailing Add: 1727 W. Nancy Creek Dr. N.E, Atlanta, Ga. 30319.

COLLINS, WILLIAM MONTGOMERY D
Ala. State Rep.
b. Birmingham, Ala, 7/21/30; s. Neal Glen Collins and Katherine Barfield C; m. 11/27/53 to Euber Roberts; c. William Montgomery, Homer Roberts, Perry Robinson and Mary Katherine. Educ: Univ. Ala, 49-53, Sigma Alpha Epsilon. Polit. & Govt. Pos: Ala. State Rep, 66- Bus. & Prof. Pos: Dist. sales mgr, Ga. Hwy. Express, 59- Mil. Serv: Entered as Pvt, Air Force, 50, released as Sgt, 52, after serv. in Unit. 160th Fighter Squadron, U.S. Mem: Mobile Traffic and Transportation Club; Mason; Am. Legion; Shrine. Rel: Baptist. Legal Res: 4007 Cresthaven Rd, Mobile, Ala. 36609. Mailing Add: P.O. Box 1411, Mobile, Ala. 36601.

COLLISHAW, LYMAN E. R
N.H. State Rep.
b. Exeter, N.H, 5/10/99; married; c. 2. Educ: Exeter schs. Polit. & Govt. Pos: N.H. State Rep, 59- Bus. & Prof. Pos: Retired, co-owner Ice Cream Manufacturer and Retailer. Mil. Serv: Vet, World War I. Mem: Imp. O.R.M; Am. Legion; World War I Vets; Bow Lake Camp Owners Asn; N.H. Seacoast Regional Devel. Asn. Rel: Episcopal. Mailing Add: 57 Portsmouth Ave, Exeter, N.H. 03833. (1967)

COLLUM, THAD L. R
Mem, Rep. State Finance Cmt, N.Y.
b. Corsicana, Tex, 7/24/98; s. Simon C. Collum and Pauline P. Kelly C; m. 9/4/26 to Eleanor Anne Boshart; c. Edward Boshart and Thad Phillips. Educ: Cornell Univ, C.E, 21; Sigma Phi Epsilon; Quill and Dagger; Hon. LL.D, Lemoyne Col, 67. Polit. & Govt. Pos: Mem, Rep. State Finance Cmt, N.Y, 52-; mem, N.Y. State Bd. Regents, 54-67, v.chancellor, 62-67; del, Rep. Nat. Conv, 64 & 68 and N.Y. State Constitutional Conv, 67; chmn, Onondaga Co. Rep. Party, 67-68. Bus. & Prof. Pos: Instr. and civil engr, Cornell Univ, 20-23; struct. engr, private practice, 23-28; treas, Henderson-Johnson Co, 28-68; treas, Collum Acoustical Co, 34-68. Mil. Serv: Entered as Seaman, Navy, 18. Rel: Protestant. Mailing Add: Marvelle Rd, Fayetteville, N.Y. 13066.

COLMER, WILLIAM MEYERS D
U.S. Rep, Miss.
b. Moss Point, Miss, 2/11/90; s. Henry Colmer and Anna S. Meyers C; m. 9/17/17 to Ruth Miner; c. William Meyers, James Henry, Thomas Warren. Educ: Millsaps Col, Jackson, Miss, 10-14; Pi Kappa Alpha. Polit. & Govt. Pos: Co. attorney, Jackson Co, Miss, 21-27; dist. attorney, Second Dist, Miss, 28-33; U.S. Rep, Miss, 32-, sponsor and chmn. spec. cmt, Post-War Econ. Policy and Planning, 78th-79th Cong, mem, Nat. Forest Reservation Cmn. and chmn, House Rules Cmt, 90th Cong. Bus. & Prof. Pos: Sch. teacher, 14; attorney-at-law. Mil. Serv: Entered as Pvt, Army, 18, released as Regt. Sgt. Maj, 19. Mem: Am. Legion; 40 et 8; Mason; WOW; Rotary. Omicron Delta Kappa Leadership Award, Univ. Miss; George Wash. Am. Good Govt. Award, 57; Watch Dog of the Treas. Award, Nat. Asn. Businessmen, 65-66. Rel: Methodist. Legal Res: Pascagoula, Miss. 39567. Mailing Add: 2307 House Office Bldg, Washington, D.C. 20515.

COLOGNE, GORDON R
Calif. State Sen.
b. Long Beach, Calif, 1924; m. 9/28/57 to Patricia R. Regan; c. Steven John and Ann Maureen. Educ: Univ. Calif; B.S, 48; Long Beach City Col; Harvard; Southwest. Univ, LL.B, 51. Polit. & Govt. Pos: Mayor, Indio, Calif, 54-56, city councilman, 57; bd. freeholders, Riverside Co, 57-58; Calif. State Assemblyman, 60-64; Calif. State Sen, 64-, chmn, Sen. Cmt. on Water Resources, 67- Bus. & Prof. Pos: Attorney-at-Law. Mil. Serv: Navy, 44-46. Mem: Jr. C. of C; Am. Legion; Elks; Rotary; Riverside Co. Farm Bur; past secy, Indio Exchange Club; past v.pres, Riverside Co. Coun. Boy Scouts. Jaycee Award, One of Five Outstanding Young Men, 60. Rel: Methodist. Mailing Add: Box 1270, Indio, Calif. 92201.

COLÓN, LUIS ALFREDO D
b. Moca, P.R, 1/24/16; s. Francisco Colón and Artura Velázquez C; m. 1/24/48 to Delia González; c. Luis Felipe, Delia Enid and Víctor Alfredo. Educ: Univ. P.R, B.A. and LL.B. Polit. & Govt. Pos: Munic. judge, P.R, 43; former Sen, P.R. Senate; mem, Constitutional Conv, 51. Mem: Bar Asn. of P.R; Nat. Soc. of States Legis. Rel: Catholic. Legal Res: Bo. Voladoras, Moca, P.R. 00716. Mailing Add: 47 Muñoz Rivera St, Aguadilla, P.R. 00603. (1967)

COLON, RAMIRO LUIS R
b. Ponce, P.R, 8/5/04; s. Ramiro Colon Y Colon and Carlota Castaño C; m. to Josefa Muñoz; c. Irving Josephine, Addy Yolanda, Marlene, Ramiro L, Jr, José R. and Wendell W. Educ: High sch, Ponce, P.R. Polit. & Govt. Pos: Sen, P.R. Senate, 56-69; del, Rep. Nat. Conv, 68. Bus. & Prof. Pos: Gen. mgr, Coop. Cafeterios, P.R, 33-; pres, P.R. Agr. Loans, Inc, P.R. Farmers Ins, Inc, Café Instante de Puerto Rico, Inc. and Colon Brothers, Inc; dir, Revista del Café, Bank Crédito and Ahorro Ponceño. Mem: Dir, P.R. Farm Bur; state finance chmn, Am. Inst. of Coop; dir, United Coop. Rel: Catholic. Legal Res: 36 Roosevelt St, Ponce, P.R. 00731. Mailing Add: P.O. Box 1511, Ponce, P.R. 00731. (1967)

COLOROSO, DOMINIC A. D
Colo. State Rep.
b. Denver, Colo, 9/20/03; married; c. Three. Polit. & Govt. Pos: Colo. State Rep, 35- Mailing Add: 3535 Vallejo St, Denver, Colo. 80311. (1967)

COLSON, NEVEILLE H. D
b. Bryan, Tex; d. Walter Johnson Higgs and Ollie Mamie Jowers H; wid. Educ: Baylor Univ; Tex. A&M Univ; Sam Houston State Col; Univ. of Tex. Polit. & Govt. Pos: Tex. State Sen, 49-67, pres. pro tempore, Senate and acting gov, Tex, 5 days; Tex. State Rep, 38-49; head charter dept, Off. of Secy. of State, 32-35. Bus. & Prof. Pos: High Sch. teacher and prin, 25-27. Mem: Conroe Bus. & Prfnl. Women's Club; Senate Ladies Club; hon. life mem, PTA; hon. mem, Delta Kappa Gamma; Four Co. Develop. Asn; hon. mem, Tex. 4-H Clubs, Girl Scouts, Lions of Conroe, Crockett, Lovelady and Navasota, Conroe and Huntsville Rotary, Navasota Kiwanis and Civic Clubs; Tex. Forestry Asn; United Daughters of Confederacy. Longest girder bridge in Tex. named Neveille H. Colson Bridge in recognition of her contribution in the road field; named Woman of Year by Progressive Farmer mag; received Distinguished Serv. Award for advancing voc. agr. in Tex. Rel: Presbyterian. Mailing Add: 202 Brewer, Navasota, Tex. 77868. (1967)

COLTEN, A. THOMAS R
Chmn, Webster Parish Rep. Cmt, La.
b. Detroit, Mich, 10/21/22; s. Arthur L. Colten and Judith G. C; m. 6/21/47 to Jane H. Kimmel; c. Connie, Craig and Lee A. Educ: DePauw Univ, B.S, 47; Sigma Delta Chi; Pi Sigma Alpha; Delta Upsilon. Polit. & Govt. Pos: V.Chmn, Wash. Parish Rep. Cmt, 48-55; mem, La. State Rep. Cent. Cmt; chmn, Webster Parish Rep. Cmt, 58-; mem, Minden Civic Improv. Cmt, 65-; mayor, Minden, 67- Bus. & Prof. Pos: Pres, Commun. Newspapers Inc, 62-63. Mil. Serv: Entered as Pvt, Army, 43, released as Sgt, 46, after serv. in Eighth Serv. Command, U.S. Mem: Pres, La. Press Asn, 64-65, state chmn, Nat. Educ. Asn, 64-66; Rotary; Lions; Am. Legion; United Fund; Boy Scouts. Rel: Presbyterian. Mailing Add: 1202 Drake Dr, Minden, La. 71055.

COLVER, WARREN C. D
b. Fenton, Mich, 1/19/25; s. Howard Sidney Colver and Esther Cornell C; m. 11/10/49 to Della Elizabeth Kruse; c. John Warren, James Cornell and Jane Della. Educ: Univ. Alaska, 50-52; Willamette Univ, B.A, 54 and LL.B, 56; Pi Gamma Mu; Delta Theta Phi. Polit. & Govt. Pos: Dep. U.S. Cmnr, Anchorage, Alaska, 56-57; first state dist. attorney, Third Dist, Anchorage, 59; co-chmn, Alaska Kennedy for President Cmt, 60; U.S. Attorney for Alaska, 61-64; asst. attorney gen, Alaska; Attorney Gen. Alaska, 64-68. Bus. & Prof. Pos: Lawyer, Moody & Colver, Anchorage, 57-61. Mem: Gr. Anchorage Dem. Club (pres, 58); Am. Fed, Alaska and Anchorage Bar Asns; Commercial Law League of Am; Am. Legion; Anchorage Athletic Round Table; Elks; Lions; Univ. Alaska Alumni Asn.(past pres). Legal Res: 2123 Hilcrest Place, Anchorage, Alaska 99503. Mailing Add: 360 K St, Anchorage, Alaska 99501. (1967)

COLVIN, WILLIAM ALVIN D
Chmn, Beaver Co. Dem. Cmt, Okla.
b. Balko, Okla, 10/5/09; s. Charles Edward Colvin and Birdie Alice Horsman C; m. 7/19/38 to Lorene L. Slater; c. Willis Dwayne, Curtis Dale, Eloyse Kathleen (Mrs. Savely) and Alice Raynelle (Mrs. Jefferis). Polit. & Govt. Pos: Chmn, Beaver Co. Dem. Cmt, Okla, 64- Bus. & Prof. Pos: Balko Sch. Bd; bd. dirs, Ins. Co; Organizing Cmt. for REA Coop; pres, Panhandle Tel. Coop, 50- Mem: Okla. Wheat Growers; Beaver C. of C; Tri-Co. Elec. Coop; Okla. Cattleman's Asn; hon. mem, Okla. Young Dem; Balko Chap, Future Farmers Am; Okla. Peace Officers Asn. Mailing Add: Balko, Okla. 73931.

COMAN, E. REX R
R.I. State Sen.
b. Springfield, Mass, 12/24/11; m. to Eleanor. Educ: Brown Univ; Duke Univ, 35. Polit. & Govt. Pos: Mem, Narragansett Twp. Coun, R.I, 46-52; clerk, Corps, Fisheries, Agr, Spec. Legis, Pardons, Elec. and Pub. Inst, R.I. State Senate, 51-54; town moderator, Narragansett, 52-54; R.I. State Rep, 54-58, Dep. Minority Leader, R.I. State House of Rep, 57-58; R.I. State Sen, 58-, Dep. Minority Leader, R.I. State Senate, 62- Bus. & Prof. Pos: Ins. and real estate. Mil. Serv: Marine Corps, 43-46, serv. in S.Pac. Mem: VFW; Am. Legion; Marine Corps League; Elks; C. of C; pres, Narragansett Commun. Fund, 2 years; Narragansett Coun, Boy Scouts; dir, Animal Rescue League, South. R.I; v.pres, R.I. Golf Asn. Mailing Add: 84 Rodman St, Narragansett, R.I. 02882. (1967)

COMBS, ATIWLDA GERTRUDE BROWN D
V.Chmn, E. Clinton Co. Dem. Party, Ind.
b. Mulberry, Ind, 1/21/92; d. John Gibson Brown and Martha Jane Bryant B; m. 12/25/12 to William Bown Combs; c. Lillian Mae (Mrs. Charles W. Hendricks); William Brown; Martha Gertrude (Mrs. William Albert Richards); John Gordon and James Robert; nine grandchildren and one great-grandchild. Educ: Valparaiso Univ, 09. Polit. & Govt. Pos: Pres, Co. Dem. Woman's Club, Ind, 50; v.chmn, E. Clinton Co. Dem. Party, 60- Mem: Eastern Star; Union Vet. Auxiliary; Farm Bur; Home Demonstration Club; Sr. Citizens Club. One of Two-Thousand Women of Achievement of the World. Rel: United Methodist. Mailing Add: 1159 E. Clinton, Frankfort, Ind. 46041.

COMBS, BERT THOMAS D
b. Manchester, Ky, 8/13/11; s. Stephen Gibson Combs and Martha Jones C; m. 6/15/37 to Mabel Hall C; c. Lois Ann, Thomas George. Educ: Cumberland Col, 29-31; Univ. of Ky, LL.B, 37; Order of the Coif; Phi Delta Phi. Polit. & Govt. Pos: City attorney, Preston, Ky, 50; commonwealth attorney, 31st Judicial Dist, Ky, 50-51; Judge, Court of Appeals, 51-55; Gov, Ky, 59-64; Judge, U.S. Court Appeals, Sixth Circuit, 67- Bus. & Prof. Pos: Attorney-at-law, 38-41, 46-51, 64- Mil. Serv: Capt, Army, serv. in Judge Adv. Gen. Dept, 41-46; Bronze Star. Mem: Am. Bar Asn; past pres, Jr. Bar Asn. Ky; Mason (32°). Rel: Baptist. Legal Res: Prestonburg, Ky. 41653. Mailing Add: 247 Federal Bldg, Louisville, Ky. 40202.

COMBS, JAMES CLINTON R
Co. Clerk and Recorder, Menard Co, Ill.
b. Petersburg, Ill, 4/25/26; s. Virgil Hobart Combs and Bernice Smith C; m. 6/12/48 to Yuvonne Dew; c. Vicki Sue and Debra Kay. Educ: Easton Commun. High Sch, 4 years. Polit. & Govt. Pos: Asst. chief clerk, Shipping Dept, State of Ill, 53-64; village clerk, Oakford, Ill, 60-66; co. clerk and recorder, Menard Co, Ill, 66- Mem: Co. Clerk's Asn; Rotary. Rel: United Methodist. Legal Res: 404 S. Ninth St, Petersburg, Ill. 62675. Mailing Add: Menard County Court House, Petersburg, Ill. 62675.

COMBS, VERA SALYER D
b. Jeff, Ky, 4/3/26; d. Dr. K. N. Salyer and Vera Howard S; div; c. Carl Salyer and Carla Vee. Educ: Univ. Ky, B.S, 48. Polit. & Govt. Pos: Ky. State Women's Chmn. for John Y. Brown for U.S. Sen; mem, Credential Cmt, Nat. Dem. Conv, 64. Rel: Baptist. Mailing Add: 1906 Old Paris Pike, Lexington, Ky. 40505. (1967)

COMER, HARRY R. J. D
Pa. State Rep.
b. Phila, Pa, 1/20/12; s. Linwood Comer and Elizabeth Dickson C; m. to Helen Murphy; c. three. Educ: Bus. Schs. Polit. & Govt. Pos: Pa. State Rep, 52-; chmn, 33rd Ward Dem. Exec. Cmt. Bus. & Prof. Pos: Ins. broker and real estate agent. Mil. Serv: Cpl, Army, Field Artil, 42-45. Mem: AFHW; Boilermakers Local 803, AFL-CIO; IBEW, AFL-CIO. Mailing Add: 2764 N. Howard St, Philadelphia, Pa. 19133. (1967)

COMER, WILLIAM MARSHALL D
S.C. State Rep.
b. Hickory Grove, S.C, 11/15/18; s. William Thomas Comer and Myrtle Sanders C; m. 4/29/44 to Juanita Sanders c. Susan and Billy. Educ: Wofford Col, A.B, 50. Polit. & Govt. Pos: S.C. State Rep, currently; Union City Coun, 62-64. Bus. & Prof. Pos: Textile dyer, Excelsior Woolen Mill. Mil. Serv: Navy, 42-45; W.Coast and Pac; Navy Res, 17 yrs. Mem: Mason; Shrine; VFW; Am. Legion. Rel: Baptist; Deacon, Sunday Sch. teacher, Tabernacle Baptist Church. Mailing Add: 134 Highland Dr, Union, S.C. 29379. (1967)

COMFORT, SYLVIA HAGUE R
b. Norfolk, Va; d. Capt. James Hall Comfort, U.S.N. (deceased) and Grace Hague C. Educ: San Diego State Col; Calif. Scholarship Fedn. Polit. & Govt. Pos: Exec. secy. to U.S. Rep. Gordon L. McDonough, 45-62 and to U.S. Rep. Ed Foreman, Second Dist, Tex, 63-64; exec. and legis. asst. to U.S. Rep. John H. Buchanan, Jr, Ala, 65-68; exec. asst. to U.S. Rep. Ed Foreman, N.Mex, 69- Mem: Charter mem, Rep. Women of Capitol Hill. Rel: Protestant. Legal Res: Hollywood, Calif. Mailing Add: 1721 Longworth House Office Bldg, Washington, D.C. 20515.

COMMONS, DORMAN LELAND D
b. Denair, Calif, 3/5/18; s. Walter F. Commons and Dorothy Rhea Murdy C; m. 3/2/41 to Gerry Barnett; c. David Brian, Leslie (Mrs. Carabas), Stanley Barnett and Spencer Charles. Educ: Stanford Univ, A.B. in Econ, 40; Modesto Jr. Col, 2 years; Univ. Calif, Extension Div, C.P.A, 47. Polit. & Govt. Pos: Mem, State Bd. Educ, Calif, 62-, pres, 67; mem, Nat. Export Expansion Coun, 67-69; del, Dem. Nat. Conv, 68. Bus. & Prof. Pos: Sr. acct, John F. Forbes & Co, Los Angeles, 44-47; sr. v.pres, Douglas Oil Co, Los Angeles, 47-64; sr. v.pres, Finance, Occidental Petroleum Corp, 64- Mil. Serv: Army, 43, Pvt. Mem: Constitutional Rights Found.(Bd. of Dirs); Nat. Cmt. for Support of the Pub. Schs.(Exec. Cmt). Rel: Protestant. Mailing Add: 119 Miramonte Dr, Fullerton, Calif. 92632.

COMPANION, JAMES F. R
W.Va. State Del.
b. McKees Rocks, Pa, 7/29/41; s. Frank D. Compagnone and Mary Ventomiller C; m. 8/12/67 to Linda Blackmon; c. Christine Lynn. Educ: Bethany Col, A.B, 63; Univ. Mich. Law Sch, J.D, 66; Nat. Econ. Hon. Soc; Beta Theta Pi. Polit. & Govt. Pos: W.Va. State Del, 69- Mil. Serv: Res, 2nd Lt, Army, 68. Mem: Ohio Co, W.Va. and Am. Bar Asns; K. of C; Elks; Jr. C. of C; YMCA (membership cmt). Rel: Catholic. Legal Res: 15 Pleasant Dr, Wheeling, W.Va. 26003. Mailing Add: 600 Board of Trade Bldg, Wheeling, W.Va. 26003.

COMPTON, RANULF R
b. Poe, Ind, 9/16/78; s. William Charles Compton and Alice Emily True C; m. 5/20/07 to Florence Jane Mabee; c. William Ranulf, Douglass Mabee and Alice (Mrs. Giffen). Educ: Harvard, 04. Polit. & Govt. Pos: Mil. secy, Gov. of N.Y, 18-20; asst. secy, N.Y, 20-21; U.S. Rep, Third Dist, Conn, 42-45; Staff Major to Gov. of Conn, 46. Bus. & Prof. Pos: Pres, S.Jersey Broadcasting Co, Camden, N.J, 45- Mil. Serv: Capt, 103rd N.Y. Inf, 12, 369th U.S. Inf, 18, released as Maj, 19, after serv. in Tank Corps, U.S. and France, Acting Brig. Gen, Third Brigade, Argonne, 18; Distinguished Serv. Cross, N.Y; Legion of Honor, France; Purple Heart; U.S. Border, St. Miheil, Argonne and Amiens Campaign Ribbons. Mem: Mason, Blue & Commandery; Am. Legion; VFW; Order of La Fayette; C. of C; Harvard Club of N.Y.C; Madison Beach Club, Conn; Quinnipiack Club, New Haven; Bath and Tennis Club, Delray Beach. Rel: Episcopal. Legal Res: 42 Middle Beach Rd, Madison, Conn. 06443. Mailing Add: Box 507, Madison, Conn. 06443.

COMPTON, RICHARD WESLEY R
Chmn, Montgomery Co. Rep. Cmt, Ala.
b. Montgomery, Ala, 9/4/25; s. Robert Emmett Compton and Eloise Parsons C; m. 8/6/49 to Margaret Seay; c. Dale, Ann and Eloise. Educ: Auburn Univ, B.S, 48; Sigma Nu; Alpha Phi Omega. Polit. & Govt. Pos: Mem, Ala. State Rep. Exec. Cmt, 62-; mem, Second Cong. Dist. Rep. Exec. Cmt, 62-; chmn, Montgomery Co. Rep. Cmt, 62-; del, Rep. Nat. Conv, 68; chmn, Ala. Rep. Forum, 68-69. Bus. & Prof. Pos: Estimator and construction supvr, Bear Bros, Inc, 49-64; owner, Richard Compton, Gen. Contractor, 64-; dir, Capitol Nat. Bank of Montgomery, 66- Mil. Serv: Entered as Pvt, Air Force, 43, released as 2nd Lt, 45, after serving in Am. Theatre, 43-45, Maj, Res, 45-69. Mem: Assoc. Gen. Contractors Am; past pres, Montgomery Jaycees; past pres, Capital City Kiwanis Club; past Lt. Gov, Kiwanis; Montgomery C. of C; Ala. C. of C; U.S. C. of C; Montgomery Country Club. Rel: Presbyterian. Legal Res: 2734 Fairmont Rd, Montgomery, Ala. 36111. Mailing Add: P.O. Box 1706, Montgomery, Ala. 36103.

COMSTOCK, KIRKE WHITE D
City Councilman, Palo Alto, Calif.
b. Jackson, Mich, 6/6/30; s. Kirke White Comstock and Marie Harris C; m. 6/14/53 to Dorothy Florence Brand; c. William Louis, Karen Clark and Kristin Brand. Educ: Univ. Mich, B.S. in Aeronaut. Eng, 54; Zeta Psi. Polit. & Govt. Pos: Pres, United Palo Altans, Calif; City Councilman, Palo Alto, currently. Bus. & Prof. Pos: Oper. eng. mgr, United Air Lines, San Francisco, 68- Publ: 'Cost Estimation for Supersonic Transports,' J. Soc. of Automotive Engrs, 64. Mem: United Air Lines Mgt. Club; Nat. League of Cities Cmt. on Airports; Sierra Club; Calif. Tomorrow; Audubon Soc; YMCA; Boy Scouts; NAACP; Am. Civil Liberties Union. Rel: Unitarian. Mailing Add: 265 Coleridge Ave, Palo Alto, Calif. 94301.

COMSTOCK, ROLLAND L. D
b. Springfield, Mo, 11/9/36; m. to Alberta Mae Quick; c. Faith, Rod, Sherry and Michael. Educ: Drury Col, Springfield, A.B; Univ. Mo, Kansas City, M.A, LL.B; St. Andrews, D.Litt; Exeter Col, Oxford Univ, cert; Phi Delta Phi. Polit. & Govt. Pos: Admin. asst. to Greene Co. Dem. Chmn, Mo, 62; Mo. State Rep, 64-66. Bus. & Prof. Pos: Attorney-at-law. Mem: Eagles. Rel: Episcopal. Mailing Add: 2848 Bergman, Springfield, Mo. 65802.

CONABLE, BARBER BENJAMIN, JR. R
U.S. Rep, N.Y.
b. Warsaw, N.Y, 11/2/22; s. Barber Benjamin Conable and Agnes G. Gouinlock C; m. 9/13/52 to Charlotte Elizabeth Williams; c. Anne E, Jane A, Emily C. and Samuel W. Educ: Cornell Univ, A.B, 42, Law Sch, LL.B, 48; Order of the Coif. Polit. & Govt. Pos: N.Y. State Sen, 53rd Dist, 63-65; U.S. Rep, 37th Dist, N.Y, 65- Mil. Serv: Entered as Pfc, Marine Corps, released as Lt. after World War II, Maj. after Korean War; Col, Marine Corps Res; Iwo Jima and Japanese Occupation Medals. Rel: Protestant. Legal Res: Box 155, Alexander, N.Y. 14005. Mailing Add: 230 Cannon House Office Bldg, Washington, D.C. 20515.

CONAGHAN, BRIAN FRANCIS R
Okla. State Rep.
b. Tonkawa, Okla, 2/8/27; s. Billy Frank Conaghan and Letha Siler C; m. 6/10/51 to Dorothy Dell Miller; c. Joseph Lee, Charles Alan and Roger Lloyd. Educ: Univ. Okla, B.A. in Hist, 51; Acacia. Polit. & Govt. Pos: Pres, Kay Co. Young Rep, Okla, 58; Okla. State Rep, 38th Dist, Kay Co, 63- Bus. & Prof. Pos: Owner, Contractors' Bit Serv, 56- Mil. Serv: Entered as Pvt, Army, 44, released as T/4, 47, after serv. in 25th Mil. Police,CID, Korean Occupation, 46-47. Mem: Am. Legion; Elks; C. of C; Mason (32°); Blue Lodge; Chevalier, DeMolay; Eastern Star. Rel: Baptist. Legal Res: 904 E. Grand, Tonkawa, Okla. 74653. Mailing Add: P.O. Box 402, Tonkawa, Okla. 74653.

CONAGHAN, DOROTHY DELL R
V.Chmn, Sixth Cong. Dist. Rep. Party, Okla.
b. Oklahoma City, Okla, 9/24/30; d. John Joseph Miller 'Joe' and Wilhelmina Boyer M; m. 6/10/51 to Brian Francis Conaghan; c. Joseph Lee, Charles Alan and Roger Lloyd. Educ: Univ. Okla, 49-51. Polit. & Govt. Pos: Secy, Okla. State Young Rep, 57; Rep. chmn, Precinct One, Tonkawa, Okla, 60-62; v.chmn, Kay Co. Rep. Party, 61-65; mem, Kay Co. Rep. Exec. Cmt, 61-; chmn,

Tonkawa Rep. Party, 62; mem, Bellmon Belle orgn. for Henry Bellmon, 62; campaign mgr. for State Rep. Brian F. Conaghan, 62-; pres, Tonkawa Rep. Women's Club, 63; mem. inaugural cmt, Gov. Henry Bellmon, 63; mem, Okla. Rep. State Exec. Cmt, 67-; v.chmn, Sixth Cong. Dist. Rep. Party, 67-; mem. Bellmon Belle State Exec. Cmt, 68; del, Rep. Nat. Conv, 68. Mem: Ohoyohoma Club; Eastern Star (Past Matron, Worthy Matron, 59); Delphi Study Club; bd. mem, Tonkawa United Fund, 66-69; Twentieth Century Research Club; PTA (pres, Wash. Elem. Sch, 66-67); Am. Legion Auxiliary; Blackwell Book Rev. Club; Kay Co. Young Rep. Rel: Christian Church of N.Am; Children's Div. Chmn, Sixth Grade Sunday Sch. Teacher. Legal Res: 904 E. Grand, Tonkawa, Okla. 74653. Mailing Add: P.O. Box 402, Tonkawa, Okla. 74653.

CONATSER, RAY D
Chmn, San Bernardino Co. Dem. Cent. Cmt, Calif.
b. Ozark, Ark, 12/24/24; s. Raymond C. Conatser and Rebecca Carter C; m. 6/18/65 to Lella M. Galvani; c. Judith, Carol and John. Educ: Stanford Univ, A.B, 48, A.M, 52. Polit. & Govt. Pos: Dem. nominee, Calif. State Assembly, 73rd Dist, 62 & 64; mem, San Bernardino Co. Dem. Cent. Cmt, 66-68, chmn, 68- Bus. & Prof. Pos: Teacher and counsr, Corning Union High Sch. Dist, 49-51; sch. psychologist, San Bernardino City Sch. Dist, 54- Mil. Serv: Entered as A/S, Navy, 43, released as Ens, 46, after serv. in U.S.S. Otus, Southwest Pac. Theatre, 45-46. Mem: San Bernardino and Calif. Teachers Asns; Nat. Educ. Asn; Am. Personnel & Guid. Asn; Calif. Asn. Sch. Psychologists & Psychometrists. Rel: Methodist. Mailing Add: 25619 Pacific St, San Bernardino, Calif. 92404.

CONCANNON, DONALD O. R
Chmn, Kans. Rep. Party
b. Garden City, Kans, 10/28/27; s. Hugh O. Concannon and Margaret McKinley C; m. 11/23/52 to Patricia June Davis; c. Chris, Debra and Craig. Educ: Garden City Jr. Col, A.A, 48; Washburn Univ, B.A, Washburn Univ. Law Sch, 49-52; Kappa Sigma; Delta Theta Phi. Polit. & Govt. Pos: Attorney, Stevens Co, Kans, 53-57; chmn, Stevens Co. Young Rep, 54-56; attorney, Satanta, 56-62; chmn, Fifth Dist. Rep. Party, 57-59; chmn, Kans. Young Rep, 59-61; chmn, Kans. Presidential Electors, 60; chmn, Kans. Rep. Party, 68- Bus. & Prof. Pos: Dir, State Bank of Satanta, Spikes, Inc, Fidelity Ins. Agency and Fidelity Finance Co, currently. Mil. Serv: Entered as A/S, Navy, 45, released as GM 3/C, 46, after serv. in TCE 84 and 899, Pac. Theatre. Mem: Am. and S.W. Kans. Bar Asns; cmt. mem, Kans. Bar Asn; Kans. Livestock Asn; Am. Legion; VFW; Mason. Rel: Protestant. Legal Res: 129 N. Jackson, Hugoton, Kans. 67951. Mailing Add: Box 759, Hugoton, Kans. 67951.

CONDIE, ANGUS R. R
Idaho State Rep.
b. Preston, Idaho, 10/19/07; s. Gideon Condie and Carrie Clausen C; m. 6/7/35 to Marian Glenn; c. Reed, Boyd, Philip, Keith, Clyde and Clair. Educ: Utah State Univ, M.Ed, 67. Polit. & Govt. Pos: Co. Cmnr, Franklin Co, Idaho, 47-55; Idaho State Rep, 68- Bus. & Prof. Pos: Secy, Preston Whitney Irrigation Co, 37-; prin, Jr. High Sch. Dist. 201, 46- Mem: Rotary; Preston C. of C. (exec. secy, 34-39). Rel: Latter-day Saint. Mailing Add: Route 3, Preston, Idaho 83263.

CONDON, GENE F. D
b. Waterloo, Iowa, 1928; m. 1948 to Carmen Lukes; c. Debra, Kelly, Robin. Polit. & Govt. Pos: Iowa State Sen -66. Bus. & Prof. Pos: Exec. Sec, Black Hawk Co. Union Coun, AFL-CIO. Mem: Local 838, U.A.W; Amvets; VFW; K. of C; Izaak Walton League; C. of C; Eagles Aerie 764. Rel: Catholic; Sacred Heart Catholic Church. Mailing Add: 3211 W. Ninth St, Waterloo, Iowa 50702. (1967)

CONDON, JAMES MATHEWES D
S.C. State Rep.
b. Charleston, S.C, 11/17/30; s. Eugene Luke Condon and Mary Mathewes C; m. 5/10/55 to Caroline Elise Ehrhardt; c. Caroline E, James M, Jr, Ann E, Ellen E, Bernard E. and Mary Louise. Educ: Univ. S.C, 48-50; St. Bernard Col, B.A, 54. Polit. & Govt. Pos: S.C. State Rep, 69- Mil. Serv: Entered as A/S, Navy, 55, released as PN3, 67, after serv. in U.S. Naval Training Center, Bainbridge, Md, 55-56. Mem: Pres, Charleston Bd. of Realtors, 69; S.C. Bd. of Realtors (dir); Nat. Bd. of Realtors: K. of C; Hibernian Soc; James Island Yacht Club; C. of C. Rel: Catholic. Mailing Add: 606 Peoples Bldg, Charleston, S.C. 29401.

CONDON, RICHARD PAUL R
Fla. State Rep.
b. Superior, Wis, 9/14/43; s. Paul Robert Condon and Mary Anderson C; m. 9/2/67 to Ellen McGreevy. Educ: Stetson Univ, Deland, Fla, B.A, 65; Univ. Fla, Gainesville, 65-67; Old Dominion Col, Norfolk, Va, 68-69. Polit. & Govt. Pos: Fla. State Rep, 66- Mil. Serv: Entered as Seaman Recruit, Naval Res, 67; Yeoman 3/C, Naval Res; Nat. Defense Serv. Ribbon. Rel: Unitarian. Mailing Add: 3414 Dover Rd, Pompano Beach, Fla. 33062.

CONE, CHARLES W. D
b. Oakesdale, Wash, 3/8/25; s. Victoria Johnson; m. 11/20/53 to Ruth Ann Gaukroger; c. Cathleen, Charles R. and Frank O. Educ: Whitman Col, 42-46; Mont. State Univ, LL.B, 49; Sigma Chi; Phi Delta Phi. Polit. & Govt. Pos: Prosecuting attorney, Chelan Co, Wash, 55-60, state committeeman, 62-66 and chmn, 66-68; alternate del, Dem. Nat. Conv, 60 and del. and mem. credentials cmt, 68; mem. exec. bd, Wash. State Dem. Cmt, 62-68. Bus. & Prof. Pos: Lawyer, 60-69. Mil. Serv: Entered as Pvt, Army, 43, released as Cpl, 45, after serv. in Off. Strategic Serv, Det. 101, Burma, 44-45. Mem: Am. and Wash. Bar Asns; Am. Trial Lawyers Asn; Eagles; Elks; Am. Legion. Rel: Protestant. Legal Res: 410 N. Miller, Wenatchee, Wash. 98801. Mailing Add: Box 1267, Wenatchee, Wash. 98801.

CONE, JOHN COIT R
N.H. State Rep.
b. Cambridge, Mass, 6/24/18; s. Morris Huntington Cone; m. to Monique F. Denoeu; c. Elizabeth H, John D. and Janet M. Educ: Union Col, B.A, 40; Dartmouth Col, 59; Sigma Phi. Polit. & Govt. Pos: Receiver, U.S. Dist. Court, N.H, 62-; N.H. State Rep, 67- Bus. & Prof. Pos: Pres. and treas, Hartford Woolen Co, 46- and Dodge Davis Co. Inc, 49- Mil. Serv: Entered as Cadet, Air Force, 44, released as Officer Cand, 45. Rel: Congregational. Mailing Add: 5 Choate Rd, Hanover, N.H. 03755.

CONELLY, CARL ROBERT R
Mem. Exec. Cmt, Calif. Rep. State Cent. Cmt.
b. Hawthorne, Nev, 9/30/12; s. Thomas Middleton Conelly and Mabel Ann Finley C; m. 11/23/31 to Jacqueline Jane Eckley; c. Juliann and Robynn. Educ: Univ. Nev, Reno; Univ. Calif, Berkeley. Polit. & Govt. Pos: Trustee, San Lorenzo Valley Unified Sch. Dist, Calif, 47-58; mem. statewide cmt, Eisenhower-Nixon Campaign, 52-56; chmn, Santa Cruz Co. Rep. Cent. Cmt. and Rep. Assembly; dir. and pres, Calif. Asn. Co. Rep. Cent. Cmt. Chmn, 60-65; mem. exec. cmt, Calif. Rep. State Cent. Cmt, 64-; dir. bd, affiliates, Univ. Calif, Santa Cruz, 64-; pres, Santa Cruz Co. Asn. Grand Jurors, 64-; hon. life mem, Santa Cruz Co. Rep. Assembly, 65-; state dir, Calif. Rep. Assembly, 66- Bus. & Prof. Pos: Real estate and ins. broker, Carl Conelly Realty, 44-; trustee, Cabrillo Col, 58- Mem: San Lorenzo Valley Asn. Ins. Agents (pres, 65-66); C. of C.(pres, 62-64, dir); Calif. Real Estate Bd.(dir, Santa Cruz Chap, 63); Cabrillo Music Guild (dir); hon. mem. Vol. Fire Dept; Commonwealth Club San Francisco; Elks; Mason; Univ. Calif. Alumni Asn; Valley Horsemen Asn. Received Santa Cruz Man of Year Award, 58; lectured on Russia following trip in 59. Legal Res: Route 2, Box 36, Ben Lomand, Calif. 95005. Mailing Add: P.O. Box 827, Boulder Creek, Calif. 95006.

CONEY, JACK ARTHUR R
b. Dayton, Ohio, 7/17/18; s. Joseph P. Coney and Ethel Margolis C; m. 7/31/48 to Mercedes Campos; c. Jeffrey. Educ: Northwest. Univ, B.S, 40; J.D, 43; Phi Epsilon Pi; Tau Epsilon Rho. Polit. & Govt. Pos: Asst. corp. counsel, Peoria, Ill, 45; mem, U.S. Bd. Rent Control, 47; representative, 43rd Dist. Rep. Cmt, 48-64; alternate del, Rep. Nat. Conv, 56, 60 & 64. Mem: Am, Ill. State and Peoria Bar Asns; Nat. Trial Lawyers Asn; Creve Coeur Club; Standard Club of Chicago, Am. Bus. Club. Rel: Jewish. Legal Res: 4810 Knoxville, Peoria, Ill. 61614. Mailing Add: First National Bank Bldg, Peoria, Ill. 61602.

CONFAIR, ZEHNDER H. R
Pa. State Sen.
b. Berwick, Pa, 1/11/06; s. Charles H. and Rena Baum C; m. to Arlene S. Hoyt (deceased); c. one. Educ: Wharton Sch, Univ. Pa, B.S. Polit. & Govt. Pos: Pa. State Sen, 58-; mem, Young Men's Rep. Club and Rep. League. Bus. & Prof. Pos: Soft drink bottler; pres, First Fed. Savings & Loan Asn; bd. dir, North. Cent. Bank and Trust Co. Mem: Moose; Elks; Mason; Rotary; Cons. Sportsmen Lycoming Co; pres. Keystone Shortway Asn; bd. dir. C. of C. Mailing Add: 1327 Race St, Williamsport, Pa. 17701. (1967)

CONGER, J. WILLIS D
Ga. State Rep.
b. Bainbridge, Ga, 6/16/17; s. A.B. Conger and Onys Willis C; m. 7/22/42 to Margaret Douglas Ziegler; c. James Willis, Jr, Robert Ziegler, Melinda Douglas and Michael Gaffney. Educ: Mercer Univ, B.A, 38, LL.B, 40; Phi Delta Phi; Phi Delta Theta. Polit. & Govt. Pos: Spec. agent, Fed. Bur. Invest, 43; former city attorney, Bainbridge, Ga; Ga. State Rep, 53-54 & 64-; Ga. State Sen, 61-64. Bus. & Prof. Pos: Lawyer, 40- Mil. Serv: 1st Lt, Air Force, 44-46. Mem: Decatur Co. Bar Asn; Albany Judicial Circuit Bar Asn; Elks; Moose; Am. Legion; VFW; Atlanta Athletic Club. Rel: Baptist. Mailing Add: 940 Pine St, Bainbridge, Ga. 31717. (1967)

CONGER, STEPHEN HALSEY Am. Party
Treas, Am. Party of N.C.
b. Asheville, N.C, 7/14/27; s. Allen Ford Conger and Gwendylon Margery Evans C; m. 6/29/51 to Marian Lansdale Meiere; c. Susan de Camp, Stephen Halsey, Jr, Robert Cody Lansdale and Marian Lansdale Meiere. Educ: Univ. Ga, B.S.F, 49; BIFTAD; Sigma Alpha Epsilon. Polit. & Govt. Pos: Chmn, Halifax Co. Rep. Party, N.C, 61-65 & 67-68; mem. exec. cmt, N.C. Rep. Party, 63-65 & 67-68; del, Rep. Nat. Conv, 64 & 68; treas, Am. Party of N.C, 69- Bus. & Prof. Pos: Pres, Pioneer Lumber Corp, Dailey, W.Va, 64-; secy, Dubarco Inc, Richmond, Va, 67-; v.pres, Caro-Craft, Inc, Sharpsburg, N.C, 68-; exec. v.pres. and secy, Coastal Lumber Co, Weldon, N.C, 68- Mil. Serv: Entered as Pvt, Army, 46, released as T-5, 47, after serv. in 660th Eng. Troop Bn, Caribbean; Good Conduct Medal; Am. Theatre Medal; World War II Victory Medal. Mem: Soc. Am. Foresters; Newcomen Soc; South. Cypress Mfrs. Asn; Chockoyotte Country Club; John Birch Soc. Rel: Anglican. Mailing Add: 509 Sycamore St, Weldon, N.C. 27890.

CONKLIN, CHARLES ROSS D
b. Delta, Colo, 6/23/20; s. George Ross Conklin and Adaline Weeks C; m. 5/7/42 to Marjorie Jane David; c. Marty (Mrs. Thomas Eugene Durlin) and Leslie. Educ: Harvard Col, B.A, 48; Harvard Law Sch, LL.B, 51; Phi Beta Kappa. Polit. & Govt. Pos: Colo. State Rep, 55-60 & 65-66, Speaker, Colo. House of Rep, 57-60; dep. dist. attorney, Seventh Judicial Dist, Colo, 57-58; asst. dir, Pub. Land Law Rev. Cmn, Wash, D.C, 67- Bus. & Prof. Pos: Partner, Conklin, Carroll & Willett, Law Firm, 60-66. Mil. Serv: Entered as Yeoman 3/C, Navy, 42, released as Chief Yeoman, 45. Rel: Episcopal. Legal Res: Delta, Colo. Mailing Add: 4100 Cathedral Ave. N.W, Washington, D.C. 20016.

CONKLIN, GEORGE WILLIAM D
Chmn, Dem. Town Cmt, Woodbridge, Conn.
b. Rome, Italy, 11/14/08; s. William H. Conklin and Iola Schmidlapp C; m. 11/14/44 to Anne P. Thomas; c. Holly Anne and Iola (Mrs. Benedict). Educ: Dartmouth Col, B.A, 31; Princeton Univ, 31-32; Univ. Pa, B.Arch, 34; Sigma Chi. Polit. & Govt. Pos: Selectman, Woodbridge, Conn, 63-67; chmn, Dem. Town Cmt, Woodbridge, 63-; mem, Adv. Cmt, Conn. Zoning Statutes, 66; chmn, Third Cong. Dist. McCarthy for Pres. Campaign, 67-68; del, Dem. Nat. Conv. and mem. Permanent Orgn. Cmt, 68; mem, Nat. Affairs Cmt, Caucus Conn. Dem, 69. Bus. & Prof. Pos: Co-chmn. architect's cmt, New Haven Festival Arts, 62; Chmn. pub. rels. cmt, Am. Inst. Architects, 62-64. Mil. Serv: Entered as Lt.(jg), Navy, 42, released as Lt. Cmdr, 46, after serv. in Naval Oper. Base Oran, N.Africa, 42-44; Lt.Comdr.(Ret), Naval Res, 46; N.Africa, ETO Campaign Ribbons. Publ: 'Politics and Fine Arts,' Podium, 64; 'Master Plan, Chicopee, Mass,' 66; 'New Boroughs Program,' Urban Design, 67. Mem: Conn. Soc. Architects; Am. Inst. Architects; Jamaica Soc. Architects; Conn. Urban Renewal Asn; Conn. Fedn. Planning & Zoning Agencies; Woodbridge Club; Men's Club; Woodbridge Unlimited. Rel: First Church of Christ. Mailing Add: Hickory Rd, Woodbridge, Conn. 06525.

CONKLIN, RUSSEL D
Auditor, Cascade Co, Mont.
b. Winnebago, Minn, 5/31/01; s. Wilfred C. Conklin and Frances Perkins C; m. 1/30/26 to Dorothy Bennington; c. Richard B, William P. and Russel G.W. Educ: Univ. Chicago, 1 year; Univ. Wash, B.B.A; Law schs. of Georgetown Univ, George Wash. Univ. and Gonzaga Univ, 1 year each; Beta Gamma Sigma; Beta Alpha Psi; Sigma Nu. Polit. & Govt. Pos: Off. secy, U.S. Sen, C.C. Dill, Mont, 25-26; chmn, Dem. City Cent. Cmt, Great Falls, 53-54, treas, 68-69; mayor, Great Falls, 55-57; Mont. State Rep, 57-58 & 61-63; precinct committeeman, Great Falls, 64-69; auditor, Cascade Co, 64-; alternate del, Dem. Nat. Conv, 68. Bus. & Prof. Pos: Scout exec, Boy Scouts, 29-35; prin, Wenatchee Bus. Col, 36-44, Great Falls Commercial Col, 44-62. Publ: 'Taxation as a Factor in Property Development,' Am. City Mag, 56; several articles on Land Value Taxation, Henry George News, various times. Mem: Am. Inst. CPA; Mont. State Bar; former treas, Commun. Chest; former treas, Camp Fire Girls; former chmn, Salvation Army; Henry George Sch. of Soc. Sci; Am. Civil Liberties Union. Silver Beaver Award, Boy Scouts; Hon. mem, Mont. Police Protective Asn. Legal Res: 2500 Fourth Ave. S, Great Falls, Mont. 59401. Mailing Add: Box 1143, Great Falls, Mont. 59401.

CONKLIN, WILLA CHARLENE R
Iowa State Sen.
b. Pottawattamie Co, Iowa, 7/10/29; d. Charles Willard DeWitt and Viola Gertrude Turner D; m. 6/7/52 to Dwight Emerson Conklin, M.D; c. Beth Ann, Barbara Jeanne-Anne, Ralph Willard, James Dwight and Robert Charles. Educ: State Col. of Iowa, B.A, 50; Univ. Iowa, M.A, 53; Kappa Delta Pi; Kappa Phi; Math Club; Foreign Language Club; Iowa Future Teachers. Polit. & Govt. Pos: Iowa State Rep, 67-69; Iowa State Sen, 69- Bus. & Prof. Pos: Teacher, Massena High Sch, 50-52; speech therapist, Hosp. Sch. for Handicapped Children, Iowa City, 53-54. Mem: Am. Speech and Hearing Asn; Nat. Educ. Asn; Iowa Educ. Asn; adult leaderships, Girl Scouts, Boy Scouts and Children of the Am. Revolution; Am. Asn. Univ. Women; DAR; bds, YWCA, PTA, Co. Med. Auxiliary and Co. Rep. Women's Coun; Auxiliaries of Goodwill Industs, Schoitz Hosp. and Am. Nursing Home; State Univ. of Iowa Alumni Asn; Co. and State Hist. Socs. in Iowa. Rel: Presbyterian. Legal Res: 141 Woodlawn Rd, Waterloo, Iowa 50701. Mailing Add: State House, Des Moines, Iowa 50319.

CONKLIN, WILLIAM T. R
N.Y. State Sen.
b. Brooklyn, N.Y; m. to Jessie F. Hanrahan; c. Joyce (Mrs. Jack Jarrard), William and Patricia (Mrs. W. Davis). Polit. & Govt. Pos: Mem, Tenure Cmt, N.Y. State Sen, 50 & 53; N.Y. State Sen, 56-, chmn, Senate Cmt. Banks, N.Y. State Senate, currently; chmn, Joint Legis. Cmt. on Ment. and Physical Handicap, 63-69 and Joint Legis. Cmt. to Revise Banking Law, currently. Bus. & Prof. Pos: Mem. bd. dirs, Bay Ridge Savings & Loan Asn. Mem: Dir, Uptown C. of C. of N.Y.C; hon. pres, Guild for Exceptional Children; hon. sponsor, N.Y. Chap. Hemophilia Found; dir, Asn. for Help of Retarded Children; dir, Bay Ridge Day Nursery. Cited by Ambassador J.G. McDonald for Charitable Affairs Leadership. Mailing Add: 7905 Colonial Rd, Brooklyn, N.Y. 11209.

CONLAN, JOHN B, JR. R
Ariz. State Sen.
b. Oak Park, Ill, 9/17/30; s. John B. Conlan and Ruth Anderson C; m. 9/13/68 to Irene Danielson. Educ: Northwest. Univ, B.S, 51; Harvard Law Sch, LL.B, 54; Fulbright scholar, Univ. Cologne, Germany, 54-55; Hague Acad. Int. Law, Netherlands, 58. Polit. & Govt. Pos: Ariz. State Sen, Maricopa Co, 65-; mem, Gov. Crime Cmn. and Coun. Orgn. State Govt, 67- Bus. & Prof. Pos: Attorney-at-law. Mil. Serv: Entered as 1st Lt, Army, 56, released as Capt, 61, after serv. in 24th Inf. Div, ETO. Mem: Ariz. and Ill. Bar Asns. Outstanding Young Man in Ariz. Award, Jaycees, 64. Rel: Christian. Mailing Add: 750 First National Bank Bldg, Phoenix, Ariz. 85004.

CONLEE, PATRICIA ANN R
Secy, Ariz. State Rep. Cmt.
b. Fresno, Calif, 6/17/28; d. Eldor Richard Muller and Susan Aikins M; div; c. Michael William and Cathleen Patricia. Educ: San Diego State Col, B.A, 49; Kappa Alpha Theta. Polit. & Govt. Pos: Ward committeeman, Rep. Party, Tucson, Ariz, 61-; dist. leader, Legis. Dist, Pima Co, 64-65; v.chmn, Pima Co. Rep. Cmt, 65-66; secy, Ariz. State Rep. Cmt, 66-; dist. rep, Sen. Paul J. Fannin, 67-; alternate del, Rep. Nat. Conv, 68. Rel: Protestant. Legal Res: 732 N. Jefferson, Tucson, Ariz. 85711. Mailing Add: Room 236, Federal Bldg, Tucson, Ariz. 85701.

CONLEY, HARRY V. D
Chmn, Logan Co. Dem. Cent. Cmt, Ohio
b. Scioto Co, Ohio 8/23/27; s. Thomas J. Conley and Lola Rigsby C; m. 9/5/53 to Marilyn Brimner C; c. Jeani and Lee Ann. Educ: Ohio State Univ, D.V.M, 56; Alpha Psi. Polit. & Govt. Pos: Committeeman, Ohio Dem. Cent. Cmt, 64-; mem, Logan Co. Dem. Exec. Cmt, 64-; chmn, Logan Co. Dem. Cent. Cmt, 66-; pres, City Coun, Belle Center, currently. Mil. Serv: Entered as Pvt, Army, 46, released as Pfc, 49, after serv. in Med. Corps, 48-49. Mem: Second Ohio Dist, Ohio and Am. Vet. Med. Asns; C. of C; Mason; Shrine; Elks. Rel: Methodist. Legal Res: Belle Center, Ohio 43310. Mailing Add: Box 687, Belle Center, Ohio 43310.

CONLEY, JOHN, JR. D
b. St. Louis, Mo, 3/15/20; wid. 5/25/42; c. Four. Educ: Ark. Baptist Col. Polit. & Govt. Pos: Precinct capt, 22nd Ward Regular Dem. Orgn, St. Louis, Mo; Mo. State Rep, 62-68. Bus. & Prof. Pos: Mem. staff, U.S. Post Off. and Off. of Recorder of Deeds, St. Louis, Mo. Mil. Serv: Navy, 4 years chief PO. Rel: Methodist. Mailing Add: 5852 Wabada, St. Louis, Mo. 63112. (1967)

CONLIN, EDWARD JOSEPH R
Vt. State Rep.
b. Windsor, Vt, 8/22/97; m. to Frances O'Neill. Educ: Windsor High Sch, 15. Polit. & Govt. Pos: Vt. State Rep, 59-; former town and village auditor; former mem, Rutland Rwy. Cmn. Bus. & Prof. Pos: Former asst. mgr, Metrop. Life Ins. Co; retired. Mil. Serv: Cpl, Air Corps, World War I. Mem: Am. Legion; K. of C; chmn, Bd. of Hist. Sites. Rel: Catholic. Mailing Add: 6 Dewey Ave, Windsor, Vt. 05089. (1967)

CONLIN, ROLLO G. R
b. Tipton, Mich, 7/1/03; married; c. Jeane. Educ: Cleary Bus. Col. Polit. & Govt. Pos: Mich. State Rep, 44-66; Bd. of Supvrs; Sch. Bd. Bus. & Prof. Pos: Farmer. Mem: Masons; R.A.M; Elks. Rel: Congregationalist. 1967 Legal Res: Adrian, Mich. No mailing address available. (1967)

CONMEY, LARRY J. D
Chmn, Jones Co. Dem. Party, Iowa
b. Anamosa, Iowa 4/22/40; s. Lawrence J. Conmey and Pearl Allen C; single. Educ: Loras Col, B.A, 62; St. Louis Univ, LL.B, 65. Polit. & Govt. Pos: Chmn, Jones Co. Dem. Party, Iowa, 69- Bus. & Prof. Pos: Attorney-at-law, 65- Mem: Am. Bar Asn; Iowa Bar Asn; v.pres, Jones Co. Bar Asn.(pres, twice). Rel: Catholic. Legal Res: 103 Main, Anamosa, Iowa 52205. Mailing Add: Box 203, Anamosa, Iowa 52205.

CONN, HARRIETTE BAILEY R
Ind. State Rep.
b. Indianapolis, Ind, 9/22/22; d. Robert Lieutenant Bailey and Nelle Hayes B; div; c. Matinel (Mrs. Samuel Brandon), Clifton F, Jr, Robert Bailey, Harriette (Mrs. Glen Sawyer), J. Sidney, Cecil Richardson and Eric Hayes. Educ: Talladega Col, A.B, 41; Ind. Univ. Sch. Law, Indianapolis, J.D, 55; Delta Sigma Theta. Polit. & Govt. Pos: Dep. attorney gen, Ind, 55-64; dep. prosecuting attorney, 19th Judicial Circuit, Marion Co, 65-66; Ind. State Rep, Marion Co, 66-; asst. city attorney, Indianapolis, 68 & 69. Mem: Lawyers' Cmn, Indianapolis Bar Asn; Marion Co. and Am. Bar Asns; bd, Commun. Serv. Coun; bd, Sr. Citizens Center. Sagamore of the Wabash, 63; Cert. of Appreciation for civilian serv. to Ind. Nat. Guard. Legal Res: 308 Northern Ave, Indianapolis, Ind. 46208. Mailing Add: 321 Peoples Bank Bldg, Indianapolis, Ind. 46204.

CONNALLY, BEN C. D
b. Marlin, Tex, 12/28/09; s. Tom Connally and Louise Clarkson C; m. 9/27/37 to Sarah Nell Allen; c. Tom and Louise. Educ: Univ. Tex, B.A, 30, LL.B, 33; Harvard, LL.M, 34. Polit. & Govt. Pos: U.S. Dist. Judge, South. Dist. of Tex, 49- Bus. & Prof. Pos: Lawyer, mem. firm, Sewell, Taylor, Morris and Connally, 34-42, Butler and Binion, 45-49. Mil. Serv: Army, 42-45. Mem: Am, Tex. and Houston Bar Asns; Am. Legion; Houston C. of C. Rel: Methodist. Mailing Add: 9513 U.S. Courthouse, Houston, Tex. 77002.

CONNALLY, JOHN BOWDEN D
b. Floresville, Tex, 2/27/17; s. John B. Connally and Lela Wright C; m. 12/21/40 to Ida Nell Brill; c. John B, III, Sharon (Mrs. Ammann) and Mark. Educ: Univ. Tex. Sch. Law, LL.B, 41. Polit. & Govt. Pos: Admin. asst. to Sen. Lyndon B. Johnson, 49; Secy. of Navy, 61; Gov, Tex, 63-69; del, Dem. Nat. Conv, 68. Bus. & Prof. Pos: Gen. mgr, Radio Sta. KVET, Austin, Tex, 46-49; attorney, Powell, Wirtz & Rauhut, Austin, 50-52 and Richardson & Bass, Ft. Worth, 52-61; partner, Vinson, Elkins, Searls & Connally, Houston, 69- Mil. Serv: Entered Navy, 41, released as Lt. Comdr, 46, after serv. in Atlantic and Pac, 46; Legion of Merit; Bronze Star. Univ. Tex. Ex-Students Asn. Distinguished Alumnus Award, 61. Rel: Methodist. Mailing Add: First City National Bank Bldg, Houston, Tex. 77002.

CONNARN, JOHN PATRICK D
b. Brattleboro, Vt, 7/8/17; s. Frederick Connarn and Margaret Holland C; div; c. Patricia S.(Mrs. Peter F. Young) and Michael J. Educ: Norwich Univ, A.B, 41; Portland Univ. Law Sch, LL.B, 52. Polit. & Govt. Pos: Mem. sch. bd, Northfield, Vt, 54-59, chmn, 56-59; Vt. State Rep, from Northfield, 57-58; Montpelier Munic. Judge, 63-65; Attorney Gen, Vt, 65-67; Judge, Wash. Dist. Court, Montpelier, 67- Bus. & Prof. Pos: Attorney-at-law. Mil. Serv: Entered as 2nd Lt, Army, 41, released as Capt, 47, after serv. in Tenth Mt. Div, Combat Duty, 45th Inf. Div, ETO, 44; Combat Inf. Badge; Purple Heart. Mem: Vt. and Wash. Co. Bar Asns; Elks; Am. Legion; VFW. Allen Winter Rowe Acad. Medal, Norwich Univ, 37. Rel: Catholic. Mailing Add: 11 S. Main St, Northfield, Vt. 05663.

CONNELL, TED C. D
b. Hamlin, Tex, 12/5/24; s. Albert A. Connell, Sr. and Etna Bell Lawrence C; m. 11/5/46 to Edith Juanette Duty; c. Mark Stanley and Carol Juanette. Educ: Army War Col, B.S. in Mil. Sci, 49. Polit. & Govt. Pos: Del. and sgt-at-arms, Tex. State Dem. Conv, 48-, chmn, Bell Co. Del, 60; chmn, Vet. Affairs Cmn, Tex, 58-61; del, Dem. Nat. Conv, 60, 64 & 68, asst. sgt-at-arms, 64 & 68; mayor, Killeen, Tex, 62-66; mem, Am-Philippine Cmn, 63-68; mem, Vet. Land Bd, Tex, 63-69; field dir, Vet. Adv. Cmn, U.S. Vet. Admin, 67-68; mem, Am. Battle Monuments Cmn, 68- Bus. & Prof. Pos: Partner, Connell Used Cars, Killeen, Tex, 46; pres, Connell Chevrolet Co, Inc, 55-; owner, Modern Dry Cleaners & Laundry, Connell Ins. Agency and T.C. & E. Real Estate Co; dir. and v.pres, First State Bank; dir, Cowhouse Motor Hotel and First Nat. Bank; chmn. bd. dirs, Hood Airlines, Inc. and DAL Airlines, Inc. Mil. Serv: Entered as Pvt, Army, 43, released as M/Sgt, 45, after serv. in Field Artil, Tank Destroyer Bn, 98th Inf. Div, S.Pac. Theatre, 43-45; Lt. Col, Army Res, currently; Four Battle Stars; Meritorious Pub. Serv. Award, Dept. of the Navy; Ordre Militaire du Combattant de L'Europe, French Govt. Mem: Planning coun, Chevrolet Motor Div, Gen. Motors Corp; Nat. and Tex. Automobile Dealers Asns; ROA; VFW (State Comdr, 55-56, Nat. Comdr-in-Chief, 60-61); life mem, Lions; Asn. of U.S. Army; bd. dirs, E.Tex. C. of C, 52-62; Gr. Killeen C. of C; Am. Legion; Nat. Coun, Boy Scouts. Named Man of the Year, E.Tex. C. of C, 60; Distinguished Serv. Medal, VFW U.S.A; Outstanding Citizen Award, Killeen, Tex, 60 & 64; Carl L. Estes Award as Outstanding Citizen of Tex, 66; Outstanding Citizen of Tex, Am. Legion, 66. Rel: Baptist. Legal Res: 501 Nolan Ave, Killeen, Tex. 76541. Mailing Add: P.O. Box 666, Killeen, Tex. 76543.

CONNELL, WILLIAM JAMES D
b. Chicago, Ill, 9/2/25; s. Lowell Connell and Bernadette Puff C; m. 3/3/45 to Phyllis Batson; c. Carey Anne, William V. and Thomas J. Educ: Univ. Tex, B.A, 45; Univ. Minn, M.A, 48. Polit. & Govt. Pos: Exec. asst. to U.S. Sen. Hubert Humphrey, 55-64, admin. asst. to V.Pres. Humphrey, 64-69. Bus. & Prof. Pos: Asst. dir, pub. rels, Univ. Minn; producer, radio-TV documentaries; pres, Concept Films, 69- Mil. Serv: Navy, 43-46, 50-52; Naval Res, Comdr.(Ret). Mem: VFW. Rel: Episcopal. Legal Res: 4809 Morgan Dr, Chevy Chase, Md. 20015. Mailing Add: 1510 H St. N.W, Washington, D.C. 20005.

CONNELLEE, DOUGLAS W. D
b. Baltimore, Md, 8/28/13; married. Educ: Univ. of Baltimore. Polit. & Govt. Pos: Md. State Del, 65-67; Commis. Elkton, 58-65; Cecil Co. Draft Bd, 60- Bus. & Prof. Pos: Motion picture exhibitor. Mil. Serv: WW II, Merchant Marine. Mem: Pres, Md. Theatre Owner's Asn; Masons; N.E. River Yacht Club. Mailing Add: 103 Kentmore Ave, Elkton, Md. 21921. (1967)

CONNELLY, BRIAN ROBERT R
Chmn. Campaign Cmt, Mich. State Rep. Cent. Cmt.
b. Evanston, Ill, 8/17/35; s. William Henry Connelly and Jane Kaye C; m. 11/23/58 to Janet Lou Harris; c. Patrick William and Michael Leslie. Educ: Mich. State Univ, 53-58; Pi Kappa Phi. Polit. & Govt. Pos: Chmn. campaign pub. rels. cmt, Ann Arbor Rep. Cmt, Mich, 65, 66 & 67; chmn. pub. rels. cmt, Washtenaw Co. Rep. Cmt, 66, v.chmn, 69; councilman, City of Ann Arbor, 67-69; mem, Washtenaw Co. Nixon for Pres. Cmt, 68; chmn, Ann Arbor City Rep. Cmt, 69-; chmn. campaign cmt, Mich. State Rep. Cent. Cmt, 69- Bus. & Prof. Pos: Prog. dir, WKHM Radio, Jackson, Mich, 59-61; v.pres, Connelly Co, 61-66, pres, Brian Connelly Advert, Inc, 66- Mil. Serv: Entered as Pvt, Army, 58, released as Sp-4, 64, after serv. 6 months active duty, $5\frac{1}{2}$ years active res. Mem: Civitan Int.(gov. elect, Mich. Dist, 69). Rel: Episcopal. Legal Res: 500 Parklake Ave, Ann Arbor, Mich. 48103. Mailing Add: 316 N. Main St, Ann Arbor, Mich. 48104.

CONNER, DOYLE E. D
State Cmnr. of Agr, Fla.
b. Starke, Fla, 12/17/28; s. J. Leon Conner and Ruby Norman C; m. 6/25/53 to Johnnie 'Kitten' Bennett; c. Doyle, Jr, John Bryant and Kimberly Ann. Educ: Univ. of Fla, B.S, 52. Polit. & Govt. Pos: Fla. State Rep, Bradford Co, 50-57; State Cmnr. of Agr, Fla, 61- Bus. & Prof. Pos: Ins. bus, Starke and Miami, Fla, 52; farmer. Mem: C. of C; Farm Bur; Fla. Cattlemen's Asn; Mason; Shrine. One of Nation's Outstanding Youths, Outdoor Writers of Am, 47; One of Five Outstanding Young Men in Fla, Fla. Jaycees, 50; Served as youngest Speaker of Fla. House of Rep, 57; One of Ten Outstanding Young Men in Nation, U.S. Jaycees, 61. Rel: Baptist. Legal Res: 2902 Woodside Dr, Tallahassee, Fla. 32303. Mailing Add: Captiol Bldg, Tallahassee, Fla. 32304.

CONNER, JAMES L. (JIMMY) D
Ga. State Rep.
b. Harlem, Ga, 6/20/30; s. Leon Mitchell Conner, Sr. and Thelma Eaves C; m. 6/5/54 to Jeannine Hinson; c. James L, II and Drew Fletcher. Educ: Ga. Teachers Col, B.S, 49; Univ. Ga, M.A, 53; honor grad. Polit. & Govt. Pos: Ga. State Rep, 59- Bus. & Prof. Pos: Athletic dir. and coach, Hazlehurst, 53-57; Ins. and Real Estate Bus, 56-; farming; banking. Mil. Serv: Marine Corps. Mem: Mason; WOW. Coach of the Year, 57; Outstanding Basketball and Baseball Record, Ga. Teacher's Col; Played with St. Louis Browns in Ga. State League. Mailing Add: Hazlehurst, Ga. 31539.

CONNER, LOUISE THOMPSON R
Del. State Sen.
b. Eau Claire, Wis, 2/19/18; d. Tolleff Hansen Thompson and Ragna Peterson T; m. 11/3/43 to William John Conner; c. Katherine, Daniel James, Herbert Thompson and Bruce Richard. Educ: Worthington Jr. Col, A.A, 38; Univ. Minn. Law Sch, 38-40; Kappa Beta Pi; Int. Rels. Club; Col. Choir; Student Forum Cmt. Polit. & Govt. Pos: Co. chmn, Del. Young Rep, 55-56; dir, Statewide Blocking Prog. Rep. Party, Del, 62; Del. State Sen, 65- Bus. & Prof. Pos: Off. mgr, Capital Transit Co, 43. Mem: Am. Asn. of Univ. Women. Rel: Methodist. Mailing Add: 109 Sunset Dr, Delaire, Wilmington, Del. 19801. (1967)

CONNER, PAUL H. D
Wash. State Rep.
b. Port Angeles, 1925; m. to Thelma; c. four. Educ: Port Angeles Bus. Col; W. Wash. Col; Univ. of Wash. Polit. & Govt. Pos: Wash. State Rep, currently; Wash. State Sen, 57. Bus. & Prof. Pos: Teaching asst. Mem: Eagles; Grange; Lions; Elks; Toastmasters. Mailing Add: Route 3, Box 472, Sequim, Wash. 98382. (1967)

CONNER, WARREN JOHN R
Secy, Pitkin Co. Rep. Cent. Cmt, Colo.
b. Aspen, Colo, 7/25/20; s. Milton G. Conner and Margaret Ann Harrington C; single. Polit. & Govt. Pos: Secy, Pitkin Co. Rep. Cent. Cmt, Colo, 49-; committeeman, Precinct 2, Rep. Party of Colo, 50- Bus. & Prof. Pos: Pitkin Co. Assessor, 47-58, chief appraiser, Pitkin Co. Assessor's Off, 58- Publ: 'Assessment of Ski Areas,' 1/68 and 'Speculative Land,' 6/69, CATAlog. Mem: Assoc. mem, Am. Soc. of Appraisers; assoc. mem, Colo. Assessor's Asn; cert. tax appraiser, grade 1, Colo; Elks. Rel: Catholic. Legal Res: 534 E. Hopkins Ave, Aspen, Colo. 81611. Mailing Add: P.O. Drawer 159, Aspen, Colo. 81611.

CONNOLLY, EUGENE PAUL D
b. New York, N.Y, 11/9/01; s. William A. Connolly and Mabel Nugent C; 1st m. to Frances Seley; 2nd m. 11/7/64 to Marian Fraser Tuthill; c. Jeremy S. and Dennis R. Educ: N.Y. Univ; Columbia Univ. Polit. & Govt. Pos: Mem, Horatio Seymour Dem. Club and New Chelsea Reform Dem. Club; mem, N.Y.C. Coun, 45-49; campaign mgr, U.S. Rep. Leonard Farbstein, 62-66; del, Dem. Nat. Conv, 64. Bus. & Prof. Pos: Pres, Nat. Inst. Surplus Dealers, Inc, 56; pres, Exposition Mgt. Asn, Inc, 60 & 65. Mem: Founding mem, Labor's Non Partisan League; int. organizer, AFL-CIO; Cent. Trades and Labor Coun; founding mem, Nat. Maritime Union, Transport Workers Union; Farmer Labor Party; founding mem. and chmn, N.Y. Co. Cmt, Am. Labor Party; SAR; Commun. Dem. Asn.(pres); Grand St. Boys Tough Club. Rel: Roman Catholic. Mailing Add: 46 Horatio St, New York, N.Y. 10014.

CONNOLLY, JOHN STEVENS D
Chmn, Fourth Dist. Dem-Farmer-Labor Party, Minn.
b. St. Paul, Minn, 2/16/32; s. John Lawrence Connolly and Marie Stevens C; m. 6/7/58 to Carol McLellan; c. John, Kathleen, Ann, William, Shelgh, Ignatius and Brigit. Educ: St. Thomas Col, 51-54; Georgetown Law Center, 54-57. Polit. & Govt. Pos: Pub. defender, Ramsey Co, Minn, 59-61; chmn, Minn. Orgn, McCarthy for Pres, 68; del, Dem. Nat. Conv, 68; chmn, Fourth Dist. Dem-Farmer-Labor Party, Minn, 68-; mem, Minn. Dem-Farmer-Labor State Exec. Cmt. Bus. & Prof. Pos: Attorney-at-law, private practice, St. Paul, Minn, 57- Mem: Am. Bar Asn.(chmn, Cmt. Legal Aid and Judicial Defendants for Minn); Am. for Dem. Action (bd. dirs, Minn. Br). Rel: Catholic. Legal Res: 1382 Summit Ave, St. Paul, Minn. 55105. Mailing Add: 303 Degree of Honor Bldg, St. Paul, Minn. 55101.

CONNOLLY, SELDEN WOLCOTT R
Chmn, Braintree Rep. Town Cmt, Mass.
b. New Bedford, Mass, 7/12/25; s. Harold William Connolly and Constance Selden C; m. 6/21/52 to Ann Louise Arnold; c. Richard Selden, Joan Rosamond and Robert Arnold. Educ: Harvard Col, A.B, 48. Polit. & Govt. Pos: Chmn, Braintree Rep. Town Cmt, Mass, 68-; v.chmn, Bd. Cmnr. Trust Funds, Braintree, 68- Bus. & Prof. Pos: Trust officer, State St. Bank & Trust Co, Boston, 55-; asst. treas, Gr. Boston Charitable Investment Trust, 65-; secy, Braintree Bus. Practices Study Cmt, 67-; treas. & trustee, Thayer Birthplace Endowment Trust, Braintree, 68- Mil. Serv: Entered as trainee, Army Air Force, 44 released as Cadet, 45. Mem: Am. Inst. Banking; Abraham H. Howland Jr. Lodge; Harvard Clubs, Boston and Quincy; entertainment chmn, Neighborhood Club, Quincy. Rel: Protestant. Mailing Add: 32 Windemere Circle, Braintree, Mass. 02184.

CONNOR, EUGENE D
Mem, Dem. Nat. Cmt.
b. Selma, Ala, 7/11/17; s. King Connor and Molly Godwin C; m. 9/29/20 to Beara M. Levens C; c. Dora Jean (Mrs. Jack Vernon). Educ: Pub. schs, Plantersville, Ala. Polit. & Govt. Pos: Ala. State Rep, 35-37; cmnr, Pub. Safety, Birmingham, 37-53 & 57-; Dem. Nat. Committeeman, Ala, 60-; del, Dem. Nat. Conv, 68. Bus. & Prof. Pos: Tel. operator, R.R, West. Union and Postal Tel. Co, 14-25; radio sports announcer, Sta. WBRC, Birmingham, Ala, 26-36; salesman, 53-57. Mem: Mason; Shrine; Elks; Eagles; Lions. Outstanding Radio Sports Announcer of U.S, Sporting News, 33. Mailing Add: 1116 S. 53rd St, Birmingham, Ala. 35222. (1967)

CONNOR, FRANK TIMOTHY D
Wash. State Sen.
b. Seattle, Wash, 9/30/16; s. Michael Connor and Alice Morrisey C; m. 6/21/58 to Arlene Dolores Mayrand. Educ: O'dea High Sch, Seattle, Wash, 4 years. Polit. & Govt. Pos: Wash. State Rep, 51-57; Wash. State Sen, 57- Bus. & Prof. Pos: Self-employed, Connor Sales, until 55; dep. assessor, King Co. Assessor, 55-65; real estate broker, 65- Mem: Eagles; K. of C; Rainier Bus. Mens Club. Rel: Roman Catholic. Mailing Add: 3201 S. Massachusetts, Seattle, Wash. 98144.

CONNOR, FRED, JR. R
b. Eutawville, S.C, 4/25/24; s. Fred Connor and Rose Taylor C; m. 8/8/47 to Jacquelyn Way C; c. Fred, III, Rosalyn Eldis, Thomas Lawton and James Lawrence. Educ: Clemson Col, 42-43. Polit. & Govt. Pos: S.C. State Rep, 61-69. Bus. & Prof. Pos: Farmer; dir, Farmers & Merchants Bank and South. Methodist Col. Mil. Serv: Navy, Pac. Theatre, 43-46. Mem: Dir, Orangeburg Co. United Fund; chmn, Orangeburg Co. Tuberc. Asn; Lions; Holly Hill Young Farmers; Mason; Orangeburg Co. Farm Bur; Am. Legion. Rel: Methodist; trustee. Mailing Add: Route 1, Eutawville, S.C. 29048. (1967)

CONNOR, JAMES E. (NICK) D
b. Gadsden, Ala, 7/7/04; s. Claude Eugene Connor and Rubie Dunklin C; m. to Rachael Allen Barnes; c. Miriam (Mrs. Terry Hancock, II); 4 Grandchildren. Educ: Univ. Fla; Phi Kappa Tau. Polit. & Govt. Pos: City clerk, Inverness, Fla, 5 years; clerk, Circuit Courts for Citrus Co, 13 years; pres, City Coun, Inverness, 14 years; gen. agent, State Bd. of Conserv, $3\frac{1}{2}$ years; chmn, Hernando Co. Libr. Bd; Fla. State Sen, 52-65, pres, Fla. State Sen, 65; co. judge, Citrus Co, 69- Bus. & Prof. Pos: Fuel oil distributor; rancher. Mem: Masons; Scottish Rite; Shrine (past pres); Odd Fellows of Fla.(past grand master); Eastern Star; Kiwanis (past pres); Hernando Co. Fair Asn. (dir); Lions. Rel: Baptist; Trustee. Mailing Add: Route 1, Box 56, Crystal River, Fla. 32629.

CONNOR, JAMES MANKER D
b. Brunson, S.C, 5/26/26; s. Wallace Darlington Connor and Emmie Gooding C; m. 7/11/51 to Lynn Couch; c. James M, Jr. and Laura Lynn. Educ: Clemson Univ, 42-44 & 46-47; Univ. S.C, LL.B, 49; Pershing Rifles. Polit. & Govt. Pos: Chmn, Williamsburg Co. Dem. Party, S.C, 66-68; judge, Munic. Recorder's Court, Kingstree, 68-; mem, S.C. State Bd. of Educ, 68- Bus. & Prof. Pos: Partner, Connor & Connor, Kingstree, S.C, 49- Mil. Serv: Entered as A/S, Navy, 44, released as Seaman 1/C, 46, after serv. in PT Boats, Pac. Theatre, 45-46; Comdr, Naval Res, 66; Am. and Pac. Theatre Medals; World War II Victory Medal; Armed Forces Res. Medal; Philippine Liberation Ribbon; Philippine Presidential Unit Citation. Mem: S.C. and Am. Bar Asns; Nat. Asn. of State Bd. of Educ; ROA; VFW; Moose; Mason. Rel: Methodist. Legal Res: 635 Singleton Ave, Kingstree, S.C. 29556. Mailing Add: P.O. Box 544, Kingstree, S.C. 29556.

CONNOR, JAMES WILLIAM R
Okla. State Rep.
b. Seminole, Okla, 8/21/32; s. William M. Connor and Gertrude Smith C; m. 2/27/60 to Louise Allen Rucker; c. James W, Jr, Laura Louise, Patrick Michael and Andrew Allen. Educ: St. Benedict's Col, Kans, B.S, 54; Okla. Univ, LL.B, 59; Delta Theta Phi; Order of Coif. Polit. & Govt. Pos: Asst. co. attorney, Wash. Co, Okla, 59-60, co. attorney, 61-62; Okla. State Rep, Wash. Co, 63-, asst. minority leader, Okla. State House of Rep, 65-66, Minority Leader, 67- South. Regional Dir, Nat. Asn. Rep. Legislators; del, Rep. Nat. Conv, 68. Mil. Serv: Entered as Pvt, Army, 54, released as Sp-3, 56, after serv. in 9th Signal Co, 9th Inf. Div, Germany, 54-56; Good Conduct, Am. Defense and Army of Occupation Medals. Mem: V.pres, Okla. Co. Attorney Asn, 62; K. of C; Am. Legion; C. of C. Prosecutor, N.B. Johnson Impeachment Trial, Okla, 65; Distinguished Serv. Award, Bartlesville, Jr. C. of C. Rel: Catholic. Legal Res: 522 E. 16th St, Bartlesville, Okla. 74003. Mailing Add: 416 E. Fifth, Bartlesville, Okla. 74003.

CONNOR, JOHN THOMAS D
b. Syracuse, N.Y, 11/3/14; s. Michael J. Connor and Mary V. Sullivan C; m. 6/22/40 to Mary O'Boyle; c. John Thomas, Geoffrey and Lisa Forrestal. Educ: Syracuse Univ, A.B, magna cum laude, 36; Harvard Univ, LL.B, 39;

Phi Beta Kappa; Phi Kappa Psi; Phi Kappa Phi; Phi Kappa Alpha. Polit. & Govt. Pos: Gen. counsel, Off. Sci. Research and Develop, Wash, D.C, 42-44; counsr, Off. Naval Research and spec. asst. to Secy. of Navy, 45-47; U.S. Secy. of Commerce, 65-67. Bus. & Prof. Pos: Admitted to N.Y. Bar, 39; lawyer, Cravatte, de Gersdorff, Swaine & Wood, N.Y.C, 39-42; gen. attorney, Merck & Co, Rahway, N.J, 47, secy. and counsel, 47-50, v.pres, 50-55, pres. and dir, 55-65; dir, Cmt. Econ. Develop; incorporator, Commun. Satellite Corp; dir, Gen. Motors Corp; dir, Gen. Foods Corp; pres. and dir, Allied Chem. Corp, 67-69, chmn. and dir, 69-; dir, Chase Manhattan Bank, 68- Mil. Serv: Entered as 2nd Lt, Marine Corps, 44, released as 1st Lt, 45. Mem: Bus. Coun; Coun. on For. Rels; trustee, Syracuse Univ. and Pingrey Sch. Rel: Roman Catholic. Mailing Add: Blue Mill Rd, R.D. 2, Morristown, N.J. 07960.

CONNOR, ROBERT T. R
Borough Pres, Richmond, N.Y.
b. Washington, D.C, 1919; m. 1947 to Carol Pouch; c. Susan and Robert, Jr Educ: Boston Col; U.S. Naval Acad. Polit. & Govt. Pos: Cent. Intel. Agency, 46-49; staff officer, For. Serv, Dept. State; councilman-at-lg, Staten Island, 63-65; Borough Pres, Richmond, N.Y, 65- Bus. & Prof. Pos: Exec. with Pouch Terminal, Inc. Mil. Serv: Lt. Comdr, Navy, 42-45; Capt, Naval Res, 45- Mem: Bd, Staten Island Ment. Health Soc; K. of C; Naval Acad. Alumni Asn; Am. Legion; VFW; pres, N.Y. Coun. Navy League U.S; mem. bd. trustees, Notre Dame Col. Staten Island. Outstanding Serv. Award, Salvation Army; Distinguished Citizens Award, B'nai B'rith. Legal Res: 88 Coventry Rd, Staten Island, N.Y. 10304. Mailing Add: 120 Borough Hall, Staten Island, N.Y. 10301.

CONNORS, WILLIAM R. 'BILL' D
Mo. State Rep.
b. St. Louis, Mo, 7/17/00; m. to Ann V. Gavigan; c. William H, Robert E. and Glennon. Polit. & Govt. Pos: Auditor, State Dept. of Revenue, 59-62; Mo. State Rep, 62- Bus. & Prof. Pos: Salesman. Rel: Catholic. Mailing Add: 5362 A N. Kingshighway, St. Louis, Mo. 63115. (1967)

CONNORTON, JOHN VINCENT D
b. N.Y.C, 5/29/13; s. Patrick Joseph Connorton and Bridget Durkin C; m. 12/28/40 to Grace Guerin; c. John Vincent, Jr, Mary Grace, Margaret Ann, Kevin Joseph, Jane Marie and Peter Michael. Educ: Fordham Univ, A.B, 34, M.A, 38, Ph.D, 44, J.D, 50. Polit. & Govt. Pos: Research asst. to U.S. Secy. of Navy, 46-47; dep. city adminstr, N.Y.C, 54-55, dep. mayor, City Adminstr, 65-66. Bus. & Prof. Pos: Asst. prof. of hist, Fordham Col, 35-42; exec. v.pres, Gr. N.Y. Hosp. Asn, 47- Mil. Serv: Entered as Ens, Navy, 42, serv. as Spec. Asst. to Dep. Chief of Naval Commun, 42-46; Lt. Comdr.(Ret), Naval Res. Mem: Am. Soc. Int. Law; Am. and N.Y. State Bar Asns; Asn. of Bar of City of New York; Nat. Coun. Juvenile Court Judges; N.Y. Co. Lawyers Asn; Cath. Lawyers Guild; Judge Advocates Asn; Soc. of Med. Jurisp; Cardinal's Cmt. of Laity; Cath. Asn. for Int. Peace; Madison Square Boys Club; Nat. Conf. Christians and Jews; Acad. Polit. Sci; U.S. Cath. Hist. Soc; Pub. Rels. Soc. Am; Am. and Gr. N.Y. Hosp. Asns; Hosp. Asn. N.Y. State; Hosp. Credit Exchange; Hosp. Coun. of Gr. N.Y; Am. Pub. Welfare Asn; Am. Pub. Health Asn; Int. Hosp. Fedn; adv. cmts. educ, nursing, Boy Scouts; citizens cmts. on aging, budget, fire prev; N.Y. City Alcoholism Study; Mayor's Emergency Control Bd. Rel: Roman Catholic. Mailing Add: 20 Stuyvesant Oval, New York, N.Y. 10009.

CONOLLY, JOHN HAMILTON R
Ill. State Rep.
b. Waukegan, Ill, 6/4/35; s. Robert Carhart Conolly and Mary Hardy C; m. to Suzanne Haugan. Educ: Mich. State Univ, B.A. in Econ, 59; Blue Key. Beta Theta Pi. Polit. & Govt. Pos: Rep. precinct committeeman, Ill, 62-; mem. bd, Ill. Young Rep, 62-; Ill. State Rep, 63- Bus. & Prof. Pos: Partner, Robert C. Conolly & Co, Invest. Securities, 59-65; pres, Conolly & Co, Invest. Securities, 65- Mil. Serv: Entered as Pvt, Army, 57, released as Pfc, 58, after serv. in Signal Corps, Missile Agency, Huntsville, Ala. Mem: Security Traders Asn, Chicago, Inc; Street Club; Elks; Amvets; Nat. Legis. Conf; K. of C.(4°); Lake Co. Navy League, Univ. Club; bd. mem, Oak Plain Coun. Boy Scouts and Grove Sch. for the Handicapped; C. of C. Rel: Roman Catholic. Legal Res: 837 N. Sheridan Rd, Waukegan, Ill. Mailing Add: 221 Washington St, Waukegan, Ill. 60085.

CONOVER, EVA W. D
b. Huntington, Utah, 11/2/08; d. George Henry Westover and Alice Ann Leonard W; m. 5/18/33 to Harry L. Conover; c. Carolyn (Mrs. Jack Lewis), George Harry and Linda Elizabeth. Educ: Univ. Utah Sch. of Educ: Utah State Univ. Polit. & Govt. Pos: Mem, Utah Dem. Cent. Cmt. and chairwoman, Emery Co. Dem. Party, 46-60; co-chmn, Emery Co. Campaign for Sen. Moss, 56; chairwoman, First Cong. Dist. Dem. Party, 56-60; chmn, Emery Co. Tourism and Recreation Cmt, 58-62; Utah State Rep, 63-66; del, Dem. Nat. Conv, 68. Bus. & Prof. Pos: Teacher, Emery Co. Sch. Dist, Utah, 29-33, 36-37 & 51-52. Mem: State educ. leader, Utah Farmers Union; Good-will Exchange to Egypt, Farmers and World Affairs and U.S. State Dept; Emery Co. chmn, Am. Cancer Soc, 12 years; twice mem, Rocky Mt. Am. Assembly. Short story winner in high sch; Salt Lake Tribune short story contest; poetry and news articles published. Rel: Latter-day-Saint. Mailing Add: Box 333, Ferron, Utah 84523. (1967)

CONRAD, CHARLES J. R
Calif. State Assemblyman
b. Phila, Pa, 11/28/09; s. Charles Julius Conrad and Anna Beath C; m. 2/10/51 to Grace Odell. Educ: Wharton Sch. Finance and Commerce, Univ. Pa. Polit. & Govt. Pos: Calif. State Assemblyman, 57th Dist, 47-, Minority Leader, Calif. State Assembly, 63-64, Speaker Pro-Tem, 57-58 & 69- Mil. Serv: Entered as A/S, Coast Guard, 42, released as Specialist 1/C, after serv. in Chem. Warfare Serv, S.Pac; S.Pac. Theater Medal with Battle Star. Mem: Am. Legion; Amvets; state exec. cmt, YMCA Youth and Govt; Mason; Legion of Honor, DeMolay; Screen Actors Guild. Rel: Congregational. Legal Res: 13444 Moorpark St, Sherman Oaks, Calif. 91403. Mailing Add: 13440 Ventura Blvd, Sherman Oaks, Calif. 91403.

CONRAD, CHARLES OSCAR D
b. Alton, Ill, 7/23/30; s. Fredrick Richard Conrad and Mildred DeWolfe C; m. 8/23/58 to Charlotte Ann Eary; c. Charles E, Christopher F, John J. and Ann E. Educ: Central Mich. Univ, A.B, 53; Mich. State Univ, 57-60. Polit. Pos: Mich. State Rep, until 67. Prof. Pos: Teacher, Soc. Sci, Jackson Pub. Schs, 58-65. Mil. Serv: Entered as Pvt, Army, 53, released as Sp-3, 56. Mem: Mich. Educ. Asn.(Life). Rel: Unitarian-Universalist. Mailing Add: 1001 W. Michigan Ave, Jackson, Mich. 49202. (1967)

CONRAD, PRISCILLA PAULETTE D
V.Chmn, Denver Co. Dem. Party, Colo.
b. Scottsbluff, Nebr, 8/10/32; d. Carl John Greisen and Jacqueline Gullett G; m. 2/25/63 to Louis Neal Conrad; c. Cynthia J, Randy J and Louis N. Educ: Loretto Heights Col, 1 year; Pa. State Univ, 2 years. Polit. & Govt. Pos: Dem. committeewoman, Precinct 1602, Denver, Colo, 63-67; vice capt, 16th Dist. Dem. Party, 67-68; liaison for Dem. Party and White Buffalo Coun. of Am. Indians, 67-68; v.chmn, Denver Co. Dem. Party, 68-; mem, Cmt. on Party Struct-Del. Selection and Human Rights Cmn, Colo. Dem. Party, 69. Bus. & Prof. Pos: Mgr, basic stock, Gimbels Retail Stores, Phila, Pa, 57-60; mgr, ready-to-wear, Joslins Retail Sotre, Aurora, Colo, 60-62; buyer, coats, May D&F Retail Store, Denver, 62-63. Mem: Jane Jefferson Dem. Club Colo; John F. Kennedy Dem. Club; membership chmn, North East Parkhill Civic Asn; Denver Dem. Club. Merit Award for Contribution to Educ. TV. Rel: Lutheran. Mailing Add: 2870 Magnolia, Denver, Colo. 80207.

CONRADT, ERVIN W. R
Wis. State Assemblyman
b. Bovina, Wis, 10/4/16; m. 9/17/38 to Grace Voight. Educ: Spring Brook Elem. Sch, Outagamie Co, Wis. Polit. & Govt. Pos: Supvr, Town Bd, Wis, 51-52, chmn, 53-67; mem. bd, Outagamie Co, 53-; Rep. precinct committeeman, 56; mem, Rep. Statutory Cmt, 57-58; chmn, Outagamie Co. Hwy. Cmt, 66; Wis. State Assemblyman, 64-, mem, Cmt. Excise and Fees, 67, chmn, Cmt. Printing, v.chmn, Cmt. Hwy and Transportation. Cmt, Wis. State Legislature, 69. Bus. & Prof. Pos: Farmer, Shiocton, Wis; ins. agent, 57-69. Mem: Pres, Church Coun. Mailing Add: Route 2, Shiocton, Wis. 54170.

CONROY, EDWARD THOMAS D
Md. State Sen.
b. N.Y.C, 1/31/29; s. William Conroy and Mary Clifford C; m. 12/29/51 to Mary Ann O'Connor; c. Edward John and Kevin. Educ: Fordham Univ, B.S, 51; Georgetown Law Center, J.D, 56, LL.M, 57; Delta Theta Phi. Polit. & Govt. Pos: State V.chmn, Vet. for Kennedy, Md, 60; state chmn, Vet. for Tydings, 62; Md. State Del, 62-66, chmn, Prince George's Co. Del, 62-65; Md. State Sen, 1st Dist, Prince George's Co, 67-; chmn, Gov. Cmt. to Promote Employ. for the Handicapped, Prince George's Co, 69. Bus. & Prof. Pos: Practicing Attorney, Edward T. Conroy & Assocs, 57- Mil. Serv: Entered as 2nd Lt, Army, 52, released as 1st Lt, 54, after serv. in Inf; Silver Star Medal; 2 Purple Hearts; Special Commendation by Gen. Mark W. Clark. Publ: Eight articles published on legal subjects pertaining to torts, medical-legal practice, etc. Mem: Am. Trial Lawyer's Asn; Md, D.C. and Fed. Bars and Supreme Court of U.S; Prince George's Co. Bar Asn; Int. Platform Asn; bd. dirs, Korean Cultural Found; adv. bd, Edgemeade Rehabilitation Center; 1st pres, Belair Citizens Asn; charter mem, Lions; Elks; C. of C; Young Dem; Am. Legion; VFW; K. Of C.(4°); DAV (past cmdr, Chap. Seven, Bowie, past state cmdr, third jr. nat. cmdr). Holder of Fordham Univ. Encanenia Award, highest award to an alumni; Outstanding Md. Off, Md. Munic. League, 67; Outstanding Disabled Am. Vet. in the U.S, 68. Rel: Catholic. Mailing Add: 12432 Shawmont Lane, Bowie, Md. 20715.

CONROY, RICHARD L. R
Chmn, Jefferson Co. Rep. Cent. Cmt, Ore.
b. Madras, Ore, 3/5/33; s. John E. Conroy and Mary Ann Riley C; m. 4/22/61 to Irene J. Reif; c. Mary Elaine, Sheila Ann and John Daniel. Educ: Univ. Ore; Kappa Sigma. Polit. & Govt. Pos: Chmn, Jefferson Co. Rep. Cent. Cmt, Ore, currently and precinct committeeman, 59-64. Mil. Serv: Entered as Pvt, Army, 56, released as SP-4, 58, after serv. in 17th Signal Bn, Karlsruhe, Germany. Mem: Pres, Cent. Ore. Auto Dealers Asn, 65-66; bd. dirs, Jefferson Co. C. of C, 64; Mason; AF&AM; Elks. Rel: Episcopal; Mem, Bishops Cmt, St. Marks Episcopal Church, 64-67. Mailing Add: Box 48, Loucks Rd, Madras, Ore. 97741.

CONSTANTINI, JAMES K. D
b. Iron Mountain, Mich, 9/24/28; m. 1952 to Florence Pawler; c. Paula. Educ: LaSalle Exten. Univ; Calif. Wine Inst. Polit. & Govt. Pos: Mich. State Rep, 60-66. Mil. Serv: U.S. Coast Guard. Mem: Italian Lodge; Northside Athletic Asn. Rel: Catholic. Mailing Add: 609 Grant St, Iron Mountain, Mich. 49801. (1967)

CONSTANTINO, PATRICK RONALD D
b. Puunene, Maui, Hawaii, 5/6/43; s. Francisco Constantino (deceased) and Felisa Cabacungan C; m. 8/26/61 to Corazon Bio; c. Cary Carl, Darlene Frances, Pamely Christine and Jamie Lynn. Educ: Maui Commun. Col, 61-62; Univ. Calif, Los Angeles, 62-64. Polit. & Govt. Pos: V.pres, Young Dem. Maui, 61-67; secy, 27th Dem. Precinct Maui, 64-; del, Hawaii Dem. Conv, 66; pres, Coun. Polit. Assocs, 67-; del, Dem. Nat. Conv, 68; mgt. asst. to mayor, Co. Maui, Hawaii, 69- Publ: 'Mayor Announces Cabinets,' 11/68, 'Youngest Member of the Cabinet,' 1/69 & 'First Filipino to be Appointed to a Cabinet Position,' 1/69, Maui Newspaper Co. Mem: Maui Jr. C. of C; Kula Commun. Fed. Credit Union; United Pub. Works; Hawaii Govt. Employ. Asn; Maui Filipino Commun. Coun; Wailuku Filipino Cath. Club. Rel: Catholic. Mailing Add: P.O. Box 30, Kula, Maui, Hawaii 96790.

CONTE, SILVIO O. R
U.S. Rep, Mass.
b. Pittsfield, Mass, 11/9/21; s. Ottavio Conte and Lucia Lora C; m. 11/8/47 to Corinne Louise Duval; c. Michelle, Sylvia, John F.X. and Gayle. Educ: Boston Col; Boston Col. Law Sch, J.D, 49; hon. mem, Phi Delta Phi and Pi Sigma Alpha. Polit. & Govt. Pos: Mass. State Sen, 51-58; U.S. Rep, First Dist, Mass, 59-, mem, Treasury and Post Office, Foreign Operations and Transportation Subcmts. of House Appropriations Cmt, U.S. House Rep, mem, Select Cmt. on Small Bus, Migratory Bird Conservation Cmn. and Joint Cmn. Coinage; del. and mem. platform cmt, Rep. Nat. Conv, 60, 64 & 68; v.chmn, Rep. Cong. Campaign Cmt, Wash, D.C. Bus. & Prof. Pos: Law practice, 50-65. Mil. Serv: Entered as Seaman 1/C, Navy, 42, released as Mechanic 3/C, 44. Mem: Fed, Mass. and Berkshire Co. Bar Asns; dir, Hillcrest Hosp. and

Pittsfield Girls Club; VFW; Am. Legion; Elks; K. of C; Eagles; Mazzini Lodge; NAACP; DAV; Mass. Rep. Club; Mass. State Soc; Polish Commun. Club; Sons of Italy. Admitted to practice before the Supreme Court of the U.S; named Outstanding Young Man of Year, Mass. Jr. C. of C, 54; football at Boston Col. Rel: Catholic. Legal Res: Blythewood Dr, Onota Lake, Pittsfield, Mass. 01201. Mailing Add: 239 Cannon House Office Bldg, Washington, D.C. 20515.

CONTRIS, CHARLES MELANCHTHON D
Chmn, Allen Co. Dem. Cent. Cmt, Ohio
b. Lafayette, Ohio, 8/1/12; s. Charles Melville Contris and Hulda Herr C; m. 11/5/45 to Mary Joanna Ackerman. Educ: Lafayette Sch, 11 years. Polit. & Govt. Pos: Mem. bd. elec, Allen Co, Ohio, 66; chmn, Allen Co. Dem. Cent. Cmt, 67- Bus. & Prof. Pos: Owner, Chas. Contris Stockyards, 42- Mem: Ohio Asn. Elec. Off; Elks; Allen Co. Hist. Soc; Nat. Farmers Union; Lima Automobile Club; Lima Farmers Club; Independent Livestock Mkt. Asn; hon. mem, Future Farmers, Boy Scouts and 4-H Farmers. Rel: Protestant. Legal Res: R.F.D. 5, Lima, Ohio 45801. Mailing Add: Box 7172, Lafayette, Ohio 45854.

CONWAY, EARL CRANSTON D
Sen, Guam Legis.
b. Mosinee, Wis, 11/9/03; s. Joseph Conway (deceased) and Janet Green C. (deceased); div; c. Kathleen C.(Mrs. D'Anthony), Earl C, Jr. and Michael C. Educ: St. Peters Col; Univ. Hawaii; Alpha Gamma Phi. Polit. & Govt. Pos: Chief of supply, Atlantic Area, C.Z, 42-43; personnel supvr, Hawaiian Air Depot, Hawaii, 44; head payroll savings div, War Finance, U.S. Treas, Honolulu, 44-46; sr. rep, Trust Territory of Pac. Islands, 46-48; chief procurement and supply, Territory Guam, 51-53; Sen, Guam Legis, 66- Bus. & Prof. Pos: Chmn. bd. trustees, Dept. of Med. Serv. and Guam Mem. Hosp, 56-63; mgr, Scandia, Inc, Agana, Guam, 59- Mem: Soc. Am. Mil. Engrs; Mason (32°); Shrine; Elks. Hon. Citizen, Repub. of Philippines since 62; Resume of Background written into Cong. Record, 11/67; Given key to cities of Manila and Quezon City, Philippines, 68; Chmn. Bd. Judges, Miss Asia Beauty Quest, Manila, 68; First Mainlander and First Caucasian ever elected to Guam Legis. Rel: Methodist. Legal Res: J and G Housing, Maite, Guam 96910. Mailing Add: P.O. Box E C, Agana, Guam 96910.

CONWAY, JAMES FRANCIS D
Mo. State Rep.
b. St. Louis, Mo, 6/27/32; s. Charles Francis Conway and Amelia Buchholz C; m. 6/4/55 to Joan Carol; c. Michael John, Stephen James, Diane Marie, Matthew Joseph and Daniel Francis. Educ: Gen. Motors Inst; St. Louis Univ, B.S, 55 and M.B.A, 64. Polit. & Govt. Pos: Mo. State Rep, 65th Dist, 67- Bus. & Prof. Pos: Pres, ACI Plastics, Inc, 67- Mil. Serv: Entered as Pvt, Army, 55, released as Specialist 3/C, 57, after serv. in 13th Inf. Regt, Eighth Inf. Div, Germany, 57; Soldier of The Day, Ft. Knox, Ky, 55; Hon. Student, Radio Mech. Sch, Ft. Carson, Colo, 56. Mem: Engrs. Club of St. Louis; St. Vincent de Paul Soc; St. Louis C. of C. Breeder and Exhibitor of Oriental Frill & African Owl Pigeons. Rel: Catholic. Mailing Add: 3811 Flora Place, St. Louis, Mo. 63110.

CONWAY, JAMES STEPHEN D
Mass. State Rep.
b. Malden, Mass, 7/4/30; s. Michael Stephen Conway and Beatrice McGonagle C; m. 9/3/51 to Ann Rowena Boudreau; c. Cheryl Ann and Stephen Marc. Educ: Malden High Sch, grad. Polit. & Govt. Pos: Mem. sch. cmt, Malden, Mass, 64-65; city councillor, Malden, 66-69; Mass. State Rep, 69- Bus. & Prof. Pos: Bank Clerk, First Nat. Bank of Malden, Mass, 53-58; ins. agent, John Hancock Mutual Ins. Co, 58- Mil. Serv: Entered as Pvt, Army, 48, released as Pfc, 49, after serv. in 37th Field Artil. Bn, Ft. Lewis, Wash; 26th Inf. Div, Nat. Guard, 49-60. Mem: K. of C; Hibernians; Moose; Eagles; West Side A.A; Holy Name Soc. Rel: Catholic. Mailing Add: 67 Gilbert St, Malden, Mass. 02148.

CONWAY, JOHN R
b. Appleton, Wis, 9/10/24; s. John Conway and Jane Evans C; m. 11/29/66 to Carole M. Steiner; c. John, Jr, Lydia Jane, Vickie and Catherine. Educ: Northwest. Univ, B.S, 49; Delta Upsilon. Polit. & Govt. Pos: Chmn, Outagamie Co. Rep. Party, Wis, 61-63; chmn, Eighth Dist. Rep. Party, 63-67; Wis. Housing Chmn. and Sgt-at-arms, Rep. Nat. Conv, 64, del, 68; mem, Aeronaut. Coun, State of Wis, 68- Bus. & Prof. Pos: Pres, Conway Hotel Co, 52-; sr. v.pres, Air Wis, 66-; pres, Lakeshore Inn, Inc, 68- Mil. Serv: Entered as Pvt, Army Air Forces, 44, released as 2nd Lt, 46, after serv. in 513th Troop Carrier Group, China-Burma-India Theatre, 45-46; Bronze Star. Mem: Cornell Soc. of Hotel Men; Rotary; Am. Legion; Appleton Area C. of C. Rel: Protestant. Mailing Add: 1530 Reid Dr, Appleton, Wis. 54911.

CONWAY, JOHN O'CONNOR D
Chmn, Oswego Co. Dem. Cmt, N.Y.
b. Oswego, N.Y, 7/24/11; s. Daniel H. Conway and Ellen O'Connor C; m. 7/24/62 to Mary Fitzgibbons; c. Ellen. Educ: Harvard Col; Georgetown Univ. Law Sch, LL.B, 38. Polit. & Govt. Pos: Chmn, Oswego Co. Dem. Cmt, N.Y, 58-; mayor, Oswego, 68- Bus. & Prof. Pos: Attorney-at-law, 46- Mil. Serv: Entered Army, 42, released as 1st Lt, 46, after serv. in 13th Cavalry, Tank Co. Comdr, Light Tanks, ETO, 20 months; Bronze Star. Legal Res: 136 E. Sixth St, Oswego, N.Y. 13126. Mailing Add: 11 W. Bridge St, Oswego, N.Y. 13126.

CONWAY, MARTHA BELL D
Secy. State, Commonwealth of Va.
b. Raleigh, N.C, 7/24/17; d. Elijah James Conway and Cora Henderson C; single. Educ: Col. of William and Mary; Univ. of Richmond Law Sch, LL.B, 39. Polit. & Govt. Pos: Cmnr. in Chancery, Hanover Co, Va, 42-52; patent attorney, Va, 45-; dist. counsel, Off. Price Stabilization, 51-52; Secy. State, Commonwealth of Va, 52-; mem, Cmn. Interstate Coop, 58-; chmn, Gov. Cmn. Status of Women, 64-66. Bus. & Prof. Pos: Real estate broker, 51-55; past pres, Nat. Asn. of Secy. of State, 67. Publ: 'Report of the Secretary of the Commonwealth, Laws Relating to Notaries Public, The Seal of Virginia,' Wings over Va, spring 58; 'The Commonwealth's Coat of Arms,' Va. J. Educ, 9/59; The Compacts of Virginia, 64. Mem: Richmond Bar Asn; Va. State Bar; Va. Hist. Soc; Ment. Hygiene Soc. Va; Va. Mus. Arts; Richmond Family & Children's Serv. Soc; Valentine Mus; Third Cong. Dist. Dem. Women's Club; Eng. Speaking Union; Ky. Col; Am. Asn. Univ. Women. Rel: Methodist. Legal Res: 2500 Grove Ave, Richmond, Va. 23220. Mailing Add: Ninth St. Office Bldg, Richmond, Va. 23219.

CONWAY, WALTER I. D
b. Muscatine, Iowa, 7/23/05; m. 7/14/31 to Dorothy C. Boland; c. Jerome, Richard, Thomas, Kathleen, Michael. Educ: St. Ambrose Col, Davenport, Iowa. Polit. Pos: Iowa State Rep, 64-66; State Bd. of Control, 2 1/2 Years; Mayor, Muscatine, 6 Years; Alderman, Muscatine, 5 Years. Bus. & Prof. Pos: Agent for Rwy Express Agency, Muscatine, 30 Years. Mem: Brotherhood of Rwy. Clerks. Good Govt. Award, Muscatine C. of C, 1955. Mailing Add: 214 Clinton St, Muscatine, Iowa 52761. (1967)

CONWAY, WILLIAM RAYFORD D
Fla. State Rep.
b. Green Cove Springs, Fla, 7/25/11; s. James Franklin Conway and Idella Jane Minton C; m. 2/4/50 to Dianne Anger; c. William R, Jr, Robert Fisher, James Marvin, Julia Ann and John Charles. Educ: Univ. Fla, B.S.B.A, 36; Pi Kappa Phi. Polit. & Govt. Pos: Fla. State Rep, Dist. 35, 66- Bus. & Prof. Pos: Pres, Fla. Liquified Gas Asn, 50. Mil. Serv: Entered as Lt.(jg), Navy, 42, released as Lt. Comdr, 45, after serv. in PT Boats, S.W. Pac. Theatre; Commanding Officer, Naval Res. Training Div, 46-50; Bronze Star; numerous battle stars. Mem: Pres, Univ. Fla. Nat. Alumni Asn, 63; chmn, Cancer Crusade, 65; Shrine; Mason; VFW; Kiwanis (pres, N. Orlando Club, 53); Univ. Club. Rel: Episcopal. Mailing Add: 734 John Anderson Dr, Ormond Beach, Fla. 32074.

CONWELL, EVELYN LONA R
Chmn, Northwest. Dist. Rep. Party, Alaska
b. Kotzebue, Alaska, 10/31/30; d. Louis Reich Sr. and Mamie Holland R; m. 6/11/52 to George H. Conwell, Jr; c. May, Marie Loraine, Helen Diane, Georgianna, Camille Dorothy, Louise Sarah, Lenora Rose, Allan Brian and Lucinda Bernice. Educ: High sch. correspondence course, grad, 46. Polit. & Govt. Pos: Nurse's aide, Bur. Indian Affairs Hosp, Kotzebue, Alaska, 46-52; magistare, Kotzebue, 59-60; city clerk, 59-66, food stamp supvr, 68-; cand, Alaska House Rep, Dist. 17, 66; secy, Bur. Indian Affairs Soc. Serv, 67-68; chmn, Northwest. Dist. Rep. Party, 67-; mem, State Cmt. Nutrit, Kotzebue, 69. Mem: Chmn, March of Dimes; chmn, Am. Cancer Soc; Alaska Crippled Children Asn; PTA (v.pres. and secy); Cath. Ladies Alter Soc.(pres, secy. and treas). Rel: Catholic. Legal Res: Kotzebue, Alaska 99752. Mailing Add: Box 125, Kotzebue, Alaska 99752.

CONYERS, JOHN, JR. D
U.S. Rep, Mich.
b. Detroit, Mich, 5/16/29; s. John Conyers and Lucille C; single. Educ: Wayne State Univ, B.A, 57; Wayne State Univ. Law Sch, LL.B, 58. Polit. & Govt. Pos: Secy, 15th Cong. Dist. Dem. Orgn; legis. asst, Congressman John D. Dingell, 58-61; referee, Mich. Workmens Compensation Dept, 61-63; U.S. Rep, 64-, sponsor, Full Opportunity Act, U.S. House Rep, mem. House Judiciary Cmt, supporter, Miss. Challenge, 65, voting rights act, 65, civil rights act, 66, mem. select cmt. to consider seating Adam Clayton Powell, sponsored amendment to fair housing sect. of the civil rights bill, 66; organized fact finding missions, Ala, 65, Miss, 66 & 67; del, Dem. Nat. Conv, 68. Bus. & Prof. Pos: Sr. partner, Conyers, Bell and Townsend, Law Firm, 59-61. Mil. Serv: Entered as Pvt, Army, 50, released as 2nd Lt, 54, after serv. in Korea, 1 year; combat and merit citations. Mem: Cotillion Club (chmn, police rels. cmt); NAACP (exec. bd. mem. Detroit Br); Am. Civil Liberties Union; Wolverine Bar Asn.(exec. bd). Rel: Baptist. Legal Res: Detroit Mich. Mailing Add: 222 Cannon House Office Bldg, Washington, D.C. 20515.

CONZEMIUS, GEORGE ROBERT DFL
Minn. State Sen.
b. Hastings, Minn, 7/23/36; s. George Henry Conzemius and Margaret Driscoll C; m. 8/4/62 to Karen Jeanne Thorson; c. Martha Jane, Anne Marie and Kristin Margaret. Educ: Univ. Minn, B.S, 59; Univ. Oslo, Norway, 59; Delta Theta Sigma; Univ. of Minn. Football Team; Agr. Educ. Club. Polit. & Govt. Pos: Del, Goodhue Co. Dem-Farmer-Labor Party, Minn, 64-65, secy, 65-66; alderman, Cannon Falls City Coun, 65-66; chmn, Co. Dem-Farmer-Labor Conv, 66; del, Minn. State Dem-Labor-Farmer Conv, 66; Minn. State Sen, Sixth Dist, 67- Bus. & Prof. Pos: Farmer owner, 55-; voc. agr. & sci. teacher, Cannon Falls High Sch, 60-67. Mil. Serv: Entered as Pvt, Army Res, 59, released as Airman 2/C, Air Force Res, 65. Mem: Cannon Falls, Minn. and Nat. Educ. Asn; Hon. Degree, Future Farmers of Am; Farmer's Union; Delta Theta Sigma Alumni Corp. Semi-Prfnl. Baseball; Noted Speaker on Travels to Russia. Rel: Catholic. Mailing Add: 800 W. Hoffman, Cannon Falls, Minn. 55009. (1967)

COOK, ALLEN JONES D
Del. State Sen.
b. Kenton, Del, 9/18/19; s. William Jones Cook and Amy Crossley C; 2nd marriage 12/28/63 to Nancy Jean Wilson; c. Allen Jones, Jr, and Thomas Jay. Educ: Goldey Beacom Col, 37-39. Polit. & Govt. Pos: Del. State Rep, 49-52; sheriff, Kent Co, Del, 55-56; Del. State Sen, Kent Co, 57- Bus. & Prof. Pos: Farmer. Rel: Methodist. Mailing Add: Box 127, Kenton, Del. 19955.

COOK, ANNE MILTEER D
V.Chmn, S.C. Dem. Party
b. Franklin, Va, 9/10/21; d. James Vernon Milteer and Katie Estell Edwards M; m. to Claude Preston Cook; c. James Calvin. Educ: Stratford Col, 41. Polit. & Govt. Pos: State chmn, Women of L.B.J. TV Campaign; v.chmn, Laurens Co. Dem. Party, 62-; del, Dem. Nat. Conv, 64 & 68, mem. permanent orgn. cmt, 64; Dem. State Elector, 64; v.chmn, S.C. Dem. Party, 65- Bus. & Prof. Pos: Mgr, Forest Lawn Cemetery, 62- Mem: Bus. & Prfnl. Women's Club; Little Theater; Women League of Voters Laurens Co; PTA (past pres); Magnolia Garden Club (past pres); mem, Laurens Recreation Bd, 58-60; Garden Club Coun.(past secy). Rel: Presbyterian. Legal Res: 1012 W. Main, Laurens, S.C. 29360. Mailing Add: P.O. Box 152, Laurens, S.C. 29360. (1967)

COOK, CECIL W. D
N.Mex. State Rep.
b. Rotan, Tex, 7/18/30; s. Sam Cook and Addie B. Carter C; m. 12/27/53 to

Maxine Nuckols; c. Sammy, Sandra and Jimmy. Educ: East. N.Mex. Univ, grad, 56. Polit. & Govt. Pos: N.Mex. State Rep, currently. Bus. & Prof. Pos: Dir, Roosevelt Co. C. of C, 63-65; secy-treas, Bd. of Educ, Portales, N.Mex, 65-; dir, N.Mex. Asn. Ins. Agents, 66-68. Mil. Serv: Entered as Seaman, Navy, 50, released as Radioman 3/C, 54, after serv. in Task Force 77, Korea. Mem: Lions; Mason. Rel: Baptist. Legal Res: Valley Manor Estates, Portales, N.Mex. 88130. Mailing Add: P.O. Box 630, Portales, N.Mex. 88130.

COOK, CLAYTON HENRY D
Chmn, Oldham Co. Dem. Exec. Cmt, Tex.
b. Moundridge, Kans, 4/21/12; s. Herbert Cook and Bertha Wilkening C; m. 4/13/41 to Margery Maxine Manning; c. Larry Clayton, Ronald Leigh, Michael Craig and Melanie Beth. Educ: Moundridge High Sch. grad, 29. Polit. & Govt. Pos: Co. chmn, Johnson for Senator Campaign, Tex, 48, 54 & 60, Stevenson and Kefauver Campaign, 56, Kennedy & Johnson Campaign, 60, Connally for Gov. Campaign, 64 and Johnson & Humphrey Campaign, 64; mem, Tex. Econ. Cmn, 50-54; chmn, Oldham Co. Dem. Exec. Cmt, 56-58 & 62- Mem: Past Master, Vega Masonic Lodge 899, AF&AM; Int. Platform Asn; Vega Kiwanis Club; bd. dirs, Amarillo Little Theatre. Past Lt. Gov. Div. 6, and presently Dist. Chmn, Past. Lt. Govs, Tex-Okla. Dist, Kiwanis Int. Rel: Methodist. Mailing Add: Box 57, Vega, Tex. 79092.

COOK, CONSTANCE E. R
N.Y. State Assemblywoman
b. Cleveland, Ohio, 8/17/19; d. Walter R. Eberhardt and Catherine Sellmann E; m. 6/24/55 to Alfred P. Cook; c. Catherine and John. Educ: Cornell Univ, B.A, 41, LL.B, 43; Columbia Univ; Univ. Oslo; Hague Acad. Int. Law, Netherlands. Polit. & Govt. Pos: Confidential law asst. to Gov. T.E. Dewey; legal consult, Div. Munic. Affairs, Dept. Audit and Control; research counsel to Law Rev. Cmn; asst. counsel Temporary State Cmn. on Fire Laws; counsel, Joint Legis. Cmt. on Unemployment Ins; counsel Assembly Pub. Health Cmn; N.Y. State Assemblywoman, 63- Bus. & Prof. Pos: Attorney-at-Law. Mem: Am, N.Y. State, N.Y.C. and Tompkins Co. Bar Asns; Bus. & Prfnl. Women's Club; Cornell Women Club of Ithaca; Zonta Int; Tompkins Co. Soc. Planning Coun. Rel: Episcopal. Mailing Add: Coy Glen Rd, Ithaca, N.Y. 14850.

COOK, DENNIS SHELTON D
b. Globe, N.C, 7/28/07; s. Job Filmore Cook and Lula Stroup C; m. 9/24/32 to Annabev Whitmire; c. Dennis Shelton Jr, Carol K. Educ: Univ. of N.C, 27-28; Emory Univ, D.D.S, 28-32; Delta Sigma Delta. Polit. & Govt. Pos: Lenoir City Cmn. on Reapportionment and Redistricting for State, N.C; mem, Lenoir Pub. Health Cmt, 46-55; mem. city coun, Lenoir, 46-55, mayor-pro-tem, 50-55; N.C. State Sen, 55-66. Bus. & Prof. Pos: Dent. Surgeon. Mil. Serv: Maj, Air Force Med. Corps, 41-45; Chief Dent. Surgeon, U.S. Air Force Base Hosp, Barksdale Field, La, 42-44. Mem: Tri Co. Dent. Soc.(pres, 36); pres, First Dist. Dent. Soc. N.C; Fel. Am. Col. Dentists; chmn. first dist. liaison cmn, Old North State Dent. Soc; Am. Dent. Asn.(alternate del); N.C. Dent. Soc.(v.pres, 61, treas, 62-65, mem. indust. cmn. cmt, adv. cmn. sch. health coord. serv. and mem. first dist. house of del); Shrine; Scottish Rite; Mason (32°). Rel: Presbyterian; Deacon. Mailing Add: 210 Norwood St, Lenoir, N.C. 28645.

COOK, DON W. R
N.Y. State Assemblyman
b. Rochester, N.Y, 7/8/19; m. 4/29/44 to Dorothy Yanke; c. Thomas, Kathleen and Susan. Polit. & Govt. Pos: Justice of the Peace, Henrietta, N.Y, 52-56, town supvr, 56-67; mem, Monroe Co. Bd. Supvrs, 56-67; N.Y. State Assemblyman, 135th Dist, 67- Bus. & Prof. Pos: Salesman, William H. Archer Corp. and Clyde Milling Corp; proprietor, Henrietta Poultry Farm, 47-56. Mil. Serv: Entered as Pvt, Marine Corps, 42, released as Sgt, 45. Mem: Am. Legion; Lions; VFW; Shrine; Mason; Rochester Consistory; dir, Monroe Co. Fair; Boy Scouts; dir, Rochester Civic Music Asn. and Monroe Co. Soil Conserv; bd. of trustees, Leukemia Soc; N.Y. State Supvrs. Asn. Rel: Presbyterian. Mailing Add: P.O. Box 181, Henrietta, N.Y. 14467.

COOK, EDNA PEPPER D
Md. State Del.
b. Hamilton, Ohio, 1/1/97; d. Frank E. Pepper and Pauline Laubach P; m. 5/26/23 to Stanley G. Cook (deceased); c. Stanley G, Jr. Educ: West. Col, B.A, 18; Miami Univ. Grad. Sch, 19; Univ. Chicago Grad. Sch, 20. Polit. & Govt. Pos: Mem, Consumer Adv. Cmt, Pres. Econ. Adv, 49-50; mem, Gov. Cmn. Children and Youth, Md, 56-66; Md. State Del, 59-, mem, Ways and Means, Metrop. Affairs and Agr. Natural Resources Cmts, Md. House of Del, 59-67, educ. chmn, 64-, chmn, Bi-Co. Cmt. Rapid Transit Legis. and sponsor, Interstate Compact on Rapid Transit for Metrop. Wash, 65, mem. Legis. Coun. Cmt. on Educ. TV, 65-66, mem. Legis. Coun, 67- and rep, Legis. Cmt. South. Regional Educ. Bd, 69-; mem. bd. dirs, Wash. Metrop. Coun. Govt, 64-66; West. area chmn, United Dem. Women Md, 64-66; v.pres, Montgomery Co. Dem. Women's Clubs, 64-66; pres, Md. Br, Nat. Order Women Legis, 65- Bus. & Prof. Pos: Assoc. prof. math, West. Col, 20-23. Mem: Am. Asn. Univ. Women; League of Women Voters; hon. state pres, Md. Cong. of Parents and Teachers Asn; Hornbook Award, Montgomery Co. Educ. Asn; Ladies Golf Team, Navy Circuit Metrop. Wash, 30-50. Rel: Episcopal. Mailing Add: 8319 Piney Branch Rd, Silver Spring, Md. 20910.

COOK, EVERETT E. D
b. Marion, Ky, 12/27/98; s. Joseph R. Cook and Laura Sue Gilbert C; m. 6/19/26 to Dorothy Putnam Dean; c. Doris Dean (Mrs. K.W. Elliott). Educ: Marion High Sch, Marion, Ky; Bell Tel. and U.S. Govt. Short Courses. Polit. & Govt. Pos: Co. Judge, Livingston Co, Ky, 50-54; Ky. State Rep, Seventh Dist, 56-58 & 62-64. Bus. & Prof. Pos: Trouble shooter and operator, South. Bell and Mich. Bell Telephone Co, 26-30; poultry & groceries, 30-37; hardware dealer, 37-45; farmer, 63- Mem: Elks; Lions; Farm Bur. Rel: Methodist. Mailing Add: Rolling Acres Farm, Burna, Ky. 42028.

COOK, GAYTHER COLEMAN, JR. R
Tenn. State Rep.
b. Norma, Tenn, 4/26/23; s. Gayther Coleman Cook, Sr. and Nova Marcum C; m. 12/31/55 to Margaret Love Cooper; c. David Coleman. Polit. & Govt. Pos: Tenn. State Rep, Anderson and Roane Counties, 68- Mil. Serv: Entered as Pvt, Army, 43, released as Sgt, 45, after serv. in 126th Inf. Div. Mem: Am. Legion; VFW; Pipefitters Union; Roane Co. Rep. Club; Exec. Cmt, Anderson Co. Rep. Club and Oak Ridge Rep. Club; Capitol Club; Civitan. Rel: Methodist. Mailing Add: Route 3, Tacora Hills, Clinton, Tenn. 37716.

COOK, GEORGE A. D
b. Hillsboro, N.H, 6/10/94; wid; c. one; three grandchildren. Polit. & Govt. Pos: Former N.H. State Rep; Chief of Police, 10 yrs; Forest Fire Warden, 42 yrs. Bus. & Prof. Pos: Former Road Agent, 30 yrs. Mil. Serv: World War I, vet. Mem: Charter Mem, Am. Legion; K. of C; Merrimack Co. Forest Fire Warden's Asn; Hooksett Men's Club. Rel: Catholic. Mailing Add: 6 Maple St, Hooksett, N.H. 03106. (1967)

COOK, GEORGE M. D
Mo. State Rep.
b. Hornersville, Mo, 12/16/17; s. H. C. Cook Sr. and Allie Mae Wells; m. 6/26/38 to Julia Catherine Corbett; c. George Wells, William Rollin and Winston Keith. Educ: Caruthersville High School, grad, 36. Polit. & Govt. Pos: Mo. State Rep, 162nd Dist, 69-, mem, Banks and Financial Insts. Cmt. and Agr. Cmt, Mo. State Legis, at present. Bus. & Prof. Pos: Franchised Automobile Dealer and Farmer, 48-69. Mil. Serv: Entered as Pvt, Marine Corps, 44, released as Cpl, 46 after serv. in 4th Marine Div, S. Pac, 45; Expert Rifleman. Mem; Am. Legion; VFW; Mason; Shrine; Mo. Consistory; past mem, Rotary, Lions, Jr. C. of C. and Moose. Rel: Methodist; Mem, Off. Bd, Lodal Methodist Church, 21 years, on occasion, served as Chmn, Finance Cmt. Legal Res: 700 Beckwith, Caruthersville, Mo. 63830. Mailing Add: P.O. Box 37, Caruthersville, Mo. 63830.

COOK, GEORGE WALLACE FOSTER R
b. Shrewsbury, Vt, 5/20/19; married; c. 2 sons; 1 daughter. Educ: Middlebury Col, A.B, 40; Columbia Univ. Law Sch, LL.B, 48; Georgetown Univ. Law Sch, LL.M, 52. Polit. & Govt. Pos: Chmn. sch. bd, Rutland, Vt, 50-; Vt. State Sen, 61-69. Bus. & Prof. Pos: Lawyer; tree farmer. Mil. Serv: Army Air Force, 43-46. Mem: Wallington, Vt. and Am. Bar Asns; Am. Legion; Rotary. Rel: Protestant. Mailing Add: 70 Litchfield Ave, Rutland, Vt. 05701. (1967)

COOK, H. DALE R
Gen. Counsel, Okla Rep. State Cmt.
b. Guthrie, Okla, 4/14/24; s. Harold Payton Cook and Mildred Arvesta Swanson C; m. 10/1/50 to Irene Tarleton Bond; c. Harold Dale, II, Caren Irene and Randall Swanson. Educ: Iowa Wesleyan Col, 43; Univ. Okla, B.S. in Bus, 43, LL.B, 50; Phi Delta Phi; Delta Sigma Phi; Beta Theta Pi. Polit. & Govt. Pos: Pres, Univ. Okla. Young Rep, 48-50; state committeeman, Logan Co. Rep. Party, Okla, 50-54; co. attorney, Logan Co, 51-54; campaign chmn, Fourth Cong. Dist, 52; asst. U.S. attorney, West. Dist, Okla, 54-58; chmn. policy cmt, Okla. Co. Rep. Party, 58-60; mem, Okla. Co. Rep. Exec. Cmt, 58-60; attorney to Gov. Okla, 63-65; gen. counsel, Okla. Rep. State Cmt, 67-; chmn, State Rep. Conv, 69. Bus. & Prof. Pos: Partner, Rhinehart, Morrison & Cook, 58-62, Cook and Ming, 65-66 and Cook, O'Toole and Tourtellotte, 66-; v.pres. and dir, Shepherd Mall State Bank, 67- Mil. Serv: Entered as Pvt, Air Force, 43, released as 2nd Lt, 45, after serv. in West. Flying Training Command. Mem: Am. and Fed. Bar Asns; Okla. Bar Asn. (dir); Mason; Shrine; Scottish Rite; KCCH; Legion of Honor DeMolay; Eastern Star; Quail Creek Golf & Country Club. Rel: Methodist. Mailing Add: 2925 Huntleigh Dr, Oklahoma City, Okla. 73120.

COOK, HENRY BUSHNELL R
b. Abington, Mass, 9/16/92; m. to Grace Cordelia Landon; c. 1 son, 4 daughters. Educ: High Sch, Quincy, Mass. Polit. & Govt. Pos: Underhill town listener, 36-56; Vt. State Rep, 63-69. Bus. & Prof. Pos: Retired; star route carrier; farmer; pharmicist asst. Mil. Serv: Pfc, 302nd Field Artil, Bat. A, 17-19. Mem: Am. Legion. Rel: Methodist; trustee, Underhill Methodist Church. Mailing Add: Box 63, Underhill Center, Vt. 05490.

COOK, HENRY HOLDEN D
Chmn, Ionia Co. Dem. Cmt, Mich.
b. Ionia, Mich, 12/19/10; s. Henry James Cook and Sara Louise Holden C; m. 6/15/31 to B. Hope Wood; c. Louise, H. Douglas, Wallace Wood, Michael James, David Ora and Hollis Treadway. Educ: Ionia High Sch, grad, 30. Polit. & Govt. Pos: Cand, Mich. State Rep, 62 & 64; del, Dem. Nat. Conv, 64; opened and managed Ionia Co. Dem. Hq, Mich, 68; chmn, Ionia Co. Dem. Cmt, 69- Bus. & Prof. Pos: Supvr. criminal insane, Ionia State Hosp, 42-55; union rep, Am. Fedn. of State, Co. and Munic. Employees, AFL-CIO, 55-64, Hotel-Restaurant, Mich, 64-69; Mem: Licensed Private Detective, Mich; former, chmn, Ment. Health Policy Cmt. and commun. serv. chmn, Mich. State Employees Union, AFL-CIO; life mem, Moose, Ionia (Past Master, Lyons Lodge, 54-55); Eastern Star, Lyons; White Shrine, Iona. Given Membership in Mich. Dem. Century Club for serv. to party. Rel: Protestant. Mailing Add: R.R. 1, Ionia, Mich. 48846.

COOK, HOWARD C. R
Ohio State Sen.
b. Oregon Twp, Ohio, 2/20/18; s. Henry D. Cook and Caroline Ackerman C; m. 11/13/43 to Elizabeth Marie Ruch; c. Susan E. and Howard, Jr. Educ: Wittenberg Univ, B.A, 39; Harvard Law Sch, LL.B, 42; Phi Gamma Delta; Tau Kappa Alpha; Theta Alpha Phi. Polit. & Govt. Pos: Del, Rep. Nat. Conv, 48, alternate del, 68; mem, Civil Serv. Cmn, Toledo, Ohio, 48-51; v.mayor, Toledo, 52-53; Toledo Councilman, 52-53 & 59-66; v.chmn, Lucus Co. Charter Cmn, 58-59; Ohio State Sen, 67- Bus. & Prof. Pos: Pres, Riverside Hosp, 62- Mil. Serv: USN Aviator, WW II, 42-45; Naval Air Ferry Command Squadron VRF2. Mem Past State V.Comdr, Amvets; Past State V.Pres, RONS; Toledo Post Am. Legion; Toledo C. of C; Past Trustee, Bd. of Trustees of Buckeye Boy's State; Past Bd. of Trustees, Riverside Hosp; Ohio & Am. Bar Asns; Dir, Greater Toledo Mental Health Asn; Toledo Museum of Arts; Coun. of World Affairs; Zenobia Shrine; Past Pres, Lutheran Men's League, Toledo; Past V.Pres, Brotherhood of Am. Lutheran Church. Rel: Lutheran. Mailing Add: 3818 Beechway Dr, Toledo, Ohio 43614.

COOK, JACK RANDALL, SR. R
Chmn, Andrews Co. Rep. Party, Tex.
b. Caddo, Tex, 5/27/24; s. Joe McMeen Cook and Minnie Jackson C; m.

6/17/50 to Yvonne Gober; c. Jack Randall, Jr. and Robert Owen. Educ: Weatherford Jr. Col, 42-43; Tarleton State Col, 44-46. Polit. & Govt. Pos: Campaign mgr, St. Rep, Andrews Co. Tex, 62; del, Rep. State Convs, 62, 64, 66 & 68; chmn, Andrews Co. Rep. Party, 63- Bus. & Prof. Pos: Subsurface Pressure Analyst, Shell Oil Co, McCamey, Tex, 49-50; pumper, Shell Oil Co, Denver City & Seminole, Tex, 50-54; area subsurface pressure analyst, Shell, Hobbs, N.Mex, 54-60 and Andrews, Tex, 60-65; well tester, Shell Oil Co, 65- Mil. Serv: Entered as A/S, Navy, 43, released as Radio Man 3/C, 46, after serv. in Armed Guard, Pac. Fleet, Honolulu, New Guinea, Pac. Islands, Okinawa, Calcutta, India, 27 months. Mem: Andrews Boys Club of Am.(past off. & dir); "Hoof in Mouth" Toastmaster's Club (officer); C. of C. Rel: Church of Christ; lay teacher in Permian Church of Christ. Mailing Add: 1318 Alpine Dr, Andrews, Texas 79714.

COOK, JAMES CLIFFORD D
Mem, Calif. Dem. State Cent. Cmt.
b. Ely, Minn, 1/24/15; s. Anthony Hilary Cook and Mathilda Butler C; m. 5/17/41 to Kathleen DeLaney; c. Kathleen Rose (Mrs. Longden), Patrick James, Paul DeLaney and Rose Marie. Educ: Univ. of Minn, 2½ years. Polit. & Govt. Pos: Committeeman, Riverside Co. Dem. Cent. Cmt, Calif, 58-66, chmn, 60 & 62-66; dir, West. Munic. Water Dist, Riverside Co, 61-; mem, Calif. Dem. State Cent. Cmt, 62- and exec. cmt, 62-66; state senate nominee, 38th dist, 66-70. Bus. & Prof. Pos: Licensed eng. contractor, class 'A' Calif. Dept. Prfnl. and Voc. Standards, 47-; dir. of eng. and construction, Adv. Maintenance Corp, 67- Mil. Serv: CM 1/C, Navy Sea Bee's, 42-44, with serv. in 26th Sea Bee's Pac. Theatre, Guadalcanal, 42-43; Unit Citation. Rel: Catholic. Mailing Add: 6304 Cinnabar Dr, Riverside, Calif. 92509.

COOK, JAMES DREXEL D
Ala. State Rep.
b. Elba, Ala, 11/13/22; m. Two children. Educ: Jones Law Sch. Polit. & Govt. Pos: Former pres, Ala. Young Dem; Ala. State Rep, 59- Mil. Serv: Navy. Mem: Elks; VFW; Am. Legion; Jaycees. Rel: Baptist. Mailing Add: Box 435, Elba, Ala. 36323. (1967)

COOK, JAMES FOSTER D
b. Springfield, Tenn, 1/23/13; s. Jesse Foster Cook and Mary Patton C; m. to Mary Watkin Brown; c. Maryann, Mrs. Ronald Vanderpool and James Foster, Jr. Educ: Vanderbilt Univ. Polit. & Govt. Pos: Tenn. State Rep. until 67. Mem: Richland Country Club; Cumberland Club. Rel: Presbyterian. Legal Res: 3630 Knollwood Dr, Nashville, Tenn. Mailing Add: 128 15th Ave. N, Nashville, Tenn. 37203. (1967)

COOK, JOHN LEWIS R
b. Natick, Mass, 10/22/18; s. Arthur Rupert Cook and Margaret Dudley Lewis C; m. 9/26/53 to Gretchen Clough; c. Jonathan Clough, Margaret Dudley, Heidi and Polly. Educ: Northeast. Univ, B.S.B.A, 41. Polit. & Govt. Pos: Mem, Charlton Rep. Finance Cmt, Mass, 51-62; mem, Charlton Sch. Cmt, 62-; Charlton Rep. Town Cmt, 68 & 69; Rep. cand, Mass. State Sen, 68; mem, Dudley Charlton, Southbridge Regional Sch. Planning Bd, 68-69. Bus. & Prof. Pos: Owner and operator, Dairy Farm, Charlton, 46-48. Mil. Serv: Entered as Pvt, Army Air Force, 42, released as T/Sgt, 45, after serv. in Hq. Squadron, 13th Army Air Force, Southwest Pac, 43-45; Northern Solomon, Bismark Archipelago and Philippine Liberation Ribbons; Good Conduct Medal. Mem: Worcester Co. Farm Bur. Asn; New Eng. Milk Prod. Asn; Nat. Farmers Orgn. Rel: Protestant. Mailing Add: Stafford St, Charlton, Mass. 01507.

COOK, JOHN W. D
Ala. State Rep.
b. Cullman, Ala, 6/14/34; s. Ocie M. Cook, Sr. and Pearl Herring C; m. 9/7/57 to Mary Patricia Elliott; c. Pamela. Educ: Auburn Univ, B.S, 56; Birmingham Sch. of Law, LL.B, 61; Sigma Pi; Sigma Delta Kappa. Polit. & Govt. Pos: Ala. State Rep, 14th Dist, currently. Mil. Serv: 2nd Lt, Army, 56; Maj, Ala. Nat. Guard, 131st Signal Bn, currently. Mem: Jaycees; Birmingham Traffic and Trasportation Club; Motor Truck Club; Elks; Eagles; Mason; Shrine; Green Valley Country Club; Downtown Club. Rel: Methodist. Mailing Add: 1620 Stonewall Dr, Birmingham, Ala. 35226.

COOK, K. RICHARD D
b. Midwest, Wyo, 8/27/33; s. Glenn Warren Cook and Virginia L. Glenn C; m. 6/26/55 to Arlene Rae Croco; c. Tracey Susan and Valerie Ann. Educ: Univ. of Wyo, B.S, 51-55; Inter-Fraternity Coun; Pi Delta Epsilon; Phi Epsilon Phi; Fourth Estate Club; Sigma Nu. Polit. & Govt. Pos: Admin. asst. to U.S. Sen. Gale McGee, Wyo, currently. Bus. & Prof. Pos: With UPI, Denver Bur, 57-58; news ed, Powell Tribune, Wyo, 58. Legal Res: Powell, Wyo. Mailing Add: 4307 Selkirk Dr, Fairfax, Va. 22030. (1967)

COOK, KENNETH R. D
R.I. State Rep.
b. Woonsocket, R.I, 4/18/29. Educ: Cumberland schs. Polit. & Govt. Pos: R.I. State Rep, 64- Bus. & Prof. Pos: Shipping clerk. Mil. Serv: Army, 51-53; serv. in Germany. Mem: V.pres, Local 1539, Textile Workers of Am; charter mem. H.B.A; Amvets; hon. mem. Ital. Working Men's Club; mem, Boy Scout Cmt. Mailing Add: 313 Estes St, Woonsocket, R.I. 02895. (1967)

COOK, MARLOW WEBSTER R
U.S. Sen, Ky.
b. Akron, N.Y, 7/27/26; s. Floyd T. Cook and Mary Lee Webster C; m. 11/27/47 to Nancy E. Remmers; c. Christine, Caroline, Nancy, Mary Louise and Marlow Webster, Jr. Educ: Univ. Louisville Col. Arts and Sci, 46-48; Univ. Louisville Sch. Law, LL.B, 50. Polit. & Govt. Pos: Ky. State Rep, 57-61; co. judge, Jefferson Co, 61-69; alternate del, Rep. Nat. Conv, 68; U.S. Sen, Ky, 69- Bus. & Prof. Pos: Attorney at law, Hottell and Stephenson, Louisville, Ky, 52-61. Mil. Serv: Entered as Seaman Recruit, Navy, 44, released as Seaman 1/C, 46, after serv. in Submarine Serv, Atlantic and Pac. Theaters, 45-46. Publ: 'The Challenge of Urbanization,' Am. Co. Govt. Mag, 9/68. Mem: Ky. State and Louisville Bar Asns; Nat. Asn. Co. Off; dir, Neighborhood House, Louisville; chmn. bd. overseers, Ursuline Col; trustee, Univ. Louisville; dir, Louisville Jr. C. of C; Ky. Jr. C. of C; state chmn, Radio Free Europe, 64 & 65; bd. dirs, Bank of Louisville. St. Matthews Jaycee Distinguished Serv. Award, 59; Louisville Jr. C. of C. Man of the Year, 61; Ky. State Jaycee Outstanding Young Man of Ky, 61. Rel: Catholic. Legal Res: Louisville, Ky. Mailing Add: Suite 342, Senate Office Bldg, Washington, D.C. 22202.

COOK, MERCER
b. Washington, D.C, 3/30/03; s. Will Marion Cook and Abbie Mitchell C; m. 8/31/29 to Vashti Smith; c. Mercer and Jacques. Educ: Amherst Col, A.B, 25; Univ. Paris, France, teachers diploma, 26; Brown Univ, M.A, 31; Ph.D, 36; Amherst Col, LL.D, 65; Phi Beta Kappa. Polit. & Govt. Pos: For. rep, Am. Soc. African Culture, 58-60; dir, African Prog. Cong. Cultural Freedom, 60-61; U.S. Ambassador, Niger, 61-64; former U.S. Ambassador, Senegal and Gambia. Bus. & Prof. Pos: Asst. prof, Howard Univ, 27-36 & prof. romantic lang, 45-60; prof. French, Atlanta Univ, 36-43; prof. Eng, Univ, Haiti, 43-45. Publ: Education in Haiti, 48; transl.(Senghor) African Socialism, 59 and (Mâmadou Dia) African Nations and World Solidarity, 61; plus other. Mem: Am. Soc. African Culture; Asn. Study Negro Life and Hist; NAACP; Am. Asn. Teachers French; Acad. Polit. Sci; A.S.C.A.P. Recipient Decoration, Haitian Govt, 45. Rel: Catholic. Mailing Add: 6748 St. Lawrence Ave. S, Chicago, Ill. 60637. (1967)

COOK, NOEL SPEIR R
Md. State Sen.
b. Frostburg, Md, 11/13/05; s. Robert Herman Cook and Minnie Speir C; m. 3/16/35 to Anna Marie Ruddle. Educ: Frostburg State Teachers Col, 22-24; Univ. Md, LL.B. with honors, 30; Phi Kappa Sigma. Polit. & Govt. Pos: City attorney, Lonaconing, Md; city attorney, Frostburg, Md, 64-; Md. State Del, 47-69; Md. State Sen, 69- Mem: Mason (32°); Shrine; Elks; Eagles; Maplehurst Country Club; Tall Cedars of Lebanon. Rel: Lutheran. Legal Res: 77 Ormond St, Frostburg, Md. 21532. Mailing Add: Algonquin Hotel, Cumberland, Md. 21502.

COOK, ORRIN S. R
Mem, Calif. Rep. State Cent. Cmt.
b. San Francisco, Calif, 10/30/24; s. Orrin S. Cook and Yvette Bisset C; m. 2/23/46 to Shirley J. Larson; c. Orrin Douglas, James Stuart and Catherine Elizabeth. Educ: Univ. Calif, Berkeley, A.B, 44; Univ. Calif. Sch. of Med, San Francisco, M.D, 47; Psi Upsilon. Polit. & Govt. Pos: Trustee, Rep. Assocs. of Sacramento, Calif, 63-69; mem, Sacrament Co. Rep. Cent. Cmt, 67-69; mem, Rep. State Cent. Cmt, 67-; chmn, Nelson for Assembly Campaign, 68. Bus. & Prof. Pos: Cert. plastic surgeon, 58- Mil. Serv: Entered as Lt.(jg), Navy, 50, released as Lt, 52, after serv. in U.S. Naval Hosp, Mare Island Camp. Mem: Calif. and Am. Med. Asns; Am. Soc. Plastic and Reconstructive Surgeons; Calif. Soc. Plastic Surgeons; Sacramento Co. Med. Soc; Rotary. Rel: Protestant. Legal Res: 440 Hopkins Rd, Sacramento, Calif. 95825. Mailing Add: 1316 26th, Sacramento, Calif. 95814.

COOK, RICHARD MARTIN D
Dep. Secy. of State, Mich.
b. Greenville, Mich, 6/28/29; s. Martin VanBuren Cook and Elizabeth Rieger C; m. 8/26/50 to Elizabeth Ann Halmo; c. Carol Elizabeth, Richard Joseph and Anne Marie. Educ: Mich. State Univ, 47-48. Polit. & Govt. Pos: Chmn, Ingham Co. Dem. Cmt, Mich, 58-64, exec. bd. mem, 65-; del, Dem. Nat. Conv, 64; Dep. Secy. of State, Mich, 65- Bus. & Prof. Pos: Br. mgr, Mich. Dept. of State, 58-65. Mem: Mich. State Employees Union (exec. bd, 62-64); Am. Soc. for Pub. Admin. Rel: St. Thomas Aquinas Church. Legal Res: 101 Bessemaur St, East Lansing, Mich, 48823. Mailing Add: Room 112, Capitol Bldg, Lansing, Mich. 48918. (1967)

COOK, ROBERT EUGENE R
b. Minneapolis, Minn, 2/13/21; s. George H. Cook and Florence Elizabeth Foote C; m. 9/26/42 to Mary Ann Anderson; c. Diane Jeanine, Robert E, Jr, James Lee and Jaclyn. Educ: Univ. Minn. Inst. Tech, Mil. Sci, 46-49; Adj. Gen. Sch, Carrer Officer Course, grad, 64; Army Engr. Sch. Correspondence, grad, 67. Polit. & Govt. Pos: Secy, Richfield Police Civil Serv. Cmn, Minn, 62-67; campaign chmn, Kirchner Vol. Cmt, 63 & 65; precinct chmn, Richfield Rep. Party, 63-64 and v.chmn, 65-66; Minn. State Rep, Dist. 28B, 67-69. Bus. & Prof. Pos: Dist. mgr, A.O. Smith Corp, 57- Mil. Serv: Pvt, Army, 41, serv. in Africa and Italy; Lt. Comdr. Adj. Gen, 88th Army Res. Command; European Campaign Ribbon with Battle Star; Am. Theater Ribbon; Reserve Medal. Mem: Am. Soc. Heating, Refrig. & Air Conditioning Engrs; Univ. Minn. Alumni Asn; Rotary; Am. Legion; VFW; AF&AM; ROA. Rel: Christian Science. Mailing Add: 7108 Fourth Ave. S, Minneapolis, Minn. 55423.

COOK, RODNEY MIMS R
Ga. State Rep.
b. Atlanta, Ga, 3/23/24; s. James Leslie Cook and Bess Mims C; m. 4/15/50 to Bettijo Hogan; c. Jody, Rodney Mims, Jr. and Laura. Educ: Washington and Lee Univ, B.A, 47; Phi Beta Kappa; Delta Tau Delta. Polit. & Govt. Pos: Mem, Rep. State Cmt, Ga, 61-67; alderman, City of Atlanta, Ga, 61-; Ga. State Rep, 66- Bus. & Prof. Pos: Mem, bd. of trustees, Atlanta Estate Planning Coun, 64-65. Mil. Serv: Entered as A/S, Naval Res, 43, released as Lt, after serv. in Pac; Okinawa Campaign Ribbon. Mem: Pres, Washington & Lee Nat. Alumni Asn, 63-64; Washington & Lee Alumni Bd. of Trustees, Million Dollar Round Table; Am. Legion; Atlanta Civil War Round Table. Charter Life Underwriter. Rel: Methodist. Legal Res: 3495 Valley Rd, N.W, Atlanta, Ga. 30305. Mailing Add: 34 Tenth St, N.E, Atlanta, Ga. 30309.

COOK, SANGER MILLS R
b. Unity, Maine, 9/29/99; s. Jesse E. Cook and Grace Mills C; wid. Educ: Maine Cent. Inst, 4 years; Bowdoin Col, A.B; Harvard Grad. Sch. Educ, 2 years; Delta Kappa Epsilon. Polit. & Govt. Pos: Maine State Rep, 33-37; Maine State Sen, 38-42; del, Rep. Nat. Conv, 52, 64 & 68. Bus. & Prof. Pos: Asst. headmaster, Maine Cent. Inst, Pittsfield, 22-42; owner, Sanger M. Cook Ins. Agency, 42-65. Mil. Serv: Students Army Training Corps, Bowdoin Col, 18. Publ: Pittsfield, on the Sebasticook, Furbush-Roberts, Bangor, Maine, 66. Mem: Maine Teachers Asn; Nat. Teachers Asn; Mason; Am. Legion; Kiwanis. Rel: Protestant. Mailing Add: 110 S. Main St, Pittsfield, Maine 04967.

COOK, WARD H. D
b. Spokane, Wash, 7/5/06; s. George Wiley Cook and Carrie A. Juvinall C; m. 1/1/30 to Marjorie M. Viggers; c. Ward V, Marcia Ann (Mrs. Gartrell) and Linda M.(Mrs. Eddy). Educ: Univ. Ore; Northwest. Col. Law. Polit. &

Govt. Pos: Mem, Sch. Bd, Portland, 42-50; Ore. State Rep, 55-57; Ore. State Sen, 57-67. Bus. & Prof. Pos: Attorney-at-Law, Ore. State Bar Asn, 30-; pres, Ward Cook, Inc, 37- and Ore. Pioneer Savings & Loan Asn, 59- Mem: Mason; Shrine; Grange. Rel: Presbyterian. Legal Res: 4175 S.W. Humphrey Blvd, Portland, Ore. 97221. Mailing Add: 3715 N.E. Klickitat, Portland, Ore. 97212.

COOK, WILLIAM A. R

b. Patrick, S.C, 11/23/25; s. Rev. John Edward Cook (deceased) and Mary Emily Cox C. (deceased); m. 11/8/63 to Wanda A. Edwards; c. William A, Jr. and John Kendrick. Educ: Univ. S.C, A.B, 47, LL.B, 49; Harvard Law Sch, LL.M, 50; mem, Wig and Robe; pres, Omicron Delta Kappa. Polit. & Govt. Pos: Attorney, legis. coun. Gen. Assembly, S.C, 50-53; legis. asst. to U.S. Rep. John J. Riley, 53-62; admin. asst. to U.S. Rep. Albert Watson, 63- Mil. Serv: Entered as Pvt, Army, 44, released as T/Sgt, 46, after serv. in Co. K, 242nd Inf, 42nd Inf. Rainbow Div, ETO, 45-46; Bronze Star; Combat Inf. Badge; Rhineland and Cent. Europe Campaign Ribbons; Maj, Army Res, Judge Adv. Gen. Corps, 47- Mem: Am. Legion; VFW. Rel: Methodist. Legal Res: 213 Academy Way, Columbia, S.C. 29206. Mailing Add: 124 House Office Bldg, Washington, D.C. 20515.

COOK, WILLIAM W. R

b. Beatrice, Nebr, 6/16/06; s. Daniel W. Cook and Sibbie L. Thacker C; m. 5/31/28 to Margaret L. Lawrence; c. Martha E.(Mrs. Robert H. Fricke), Mary E.(Mrs. Jerry D. Schiermeyer) and William W, Jr. Educ: Wentworth Mil. Acad, Lexington, Mo; Univ. Nebr; IBA Grad. Sch. for Sr. Bank Officers, Harvard Univ; Bank PRMA Sch, Northwest. Univ. Polit. & Govt. Pos: Mem, Beatrice Bd. of Educ, Nebr, 18 years and pres, 10 years; past pres, Nebr. Sch. Bd. Asn; past mem, Gage Co. Fair Bd. and Airport Authority; mem, Nebr. Mgt. Anal. Study Group; mem, Nebr. Aeronaut. Cmn, 15 years and chmn, 3 times; mem, State finance cmt, Nebr. Rep. Party; treas, Co. Rep. Cent. Cmt; Mayor, Beatrice, Nebr, 62-66; del, Rep. Nat. Conv, 68; mem, Supreme Court Nominating Cmn, fourth dist, currently serv. second term; mem, Southeast. Nebr. Econ. Develop. Asn, currently, former chmn; v.chmn, and mem. exec. cmt, Nebr. Asn. Commerce and Indust, currently; mem. bd. trustees, Nebr. Coun. on Econ. Educ, currently; mem. tech. serv. adv. cmt, State of Nebr, currently; pres, Bus. Develop. Corp. of Nebr, currently; treas, Nebr. Transportation Inst, currently; treas. and mem. bd. dirs, Beatrice Develop. Corp, currently; mem. adv. cmt, Nebr. Dept. Econ. Develop, currently. Bus. & Prof. Pos: Mgr, Platte Valley Packing Co, Scottsbluff, Nebr, 26-28; loan exam. and farm mgr, Bankers Life Ins. Co. of Nebr, Kansas City, Mo, 28-33; asst. cashier, cashier and exec. v.pres, Beatrice Nat. Bank, Beatrice, Nebr, 33-57, pres, Beatrice Nat. Bank and Trust Co, 57-69 and chmn. bd, chief exec. officer, dir. and trust officer, currently; pres. and mem. bd. dirs, Beatrice State Bank, Pickrell State Bank and Wymore Nat. Bank, currently. Mem: Bd. dirs, Dempster Industs, Inc, Store Kraft Mfg. Co, Mia, Inc. and Lincoln Tel. and Tel. Co; v.chmn. and bd. trustees, John J. Pershing Col; Nebr. Bankers Asn.(past pres. and mem. exec. coun); Bank Pub. Rels. and Mkt. Asn.(past nat. dir); chmn, Nebr. Centennial of Banking; Elks; Mason; Shrine; Jesters; ambassador, Knights of Ak-Sar-Ben; past pres. and dir, Beatrice Rotary Club; Beatrice Country Club (former dir); Jr. C. of C.(charter mem. and past pres, Beatrice Chap. and past nat. dir). First recipient of Outstanding Young Man Award, Beatrice Jr. C. of C; Boss of the Year Award, Beatrice C. of C; Cadwallader Award in Dist. 565, Rotary Int, 64; Univ. Nebr. Builder Award, 66. Rel: Presbyterian. Legal Res: 723 N. Seventh St, Beatrice, Nebr. 68310. Mailing Add: P.O. Box 100, Beatrice, Nebr. 68310.

COOKE, CHARLES MAYNARD, JR. R

Spec. Adv. for Vietnam to the Under Secy. of State

b. Honolulu, Hawaii, 10/19/31; s. Charles Maynard Cooke and Mary Cooper C; m. 2/2/67 to Diane Smith; c. Mary E. and Stephanie M; stepchildren: Kirsten, Scott M. and Mona Lindquist. Educ: U.S. Naval Acad, B.S, 53; Univ. Wash, M.A, 60. Polit. & Govt. Pos: Avionics officer, 45th Bomb Wing, Tucson, Ariz, 54-58; assoc. prof. hist, U.S. Air Force Acad, Colo, 60-65; plans officer, Hq, U.S. Mil. Asst. Command, Vietnam, 66-67; asst. for Vietnam, Off. of Asst. Secy. of Defense, 67-69; spec. adv. for Vietnam to the Under Secy. of State, 69- Mil. Serv: Entered as 2nd Lt, Air Force, 53, released as Maj, 69; Legion of Merit; Bronze Star; Air Force Commendation Medal; Air Force Commendation Ribbon; Repub. of Vietnam Staff Serv. Medal, 1/C. Mem: U.S. Naval Inst. Rel: Episcopal. Legal Res: 3060 Lovall Valley Rd, Sonoma, Calif. 95476. Mailing Add: 5416 Gary Place, Alexandria, Va. 22311.

COOKE, EDWARD FRANCIS D

Mayor, Oakmont, Pa.

b. Boston, Mass, 1/14/23; s. Peter Joseph Cooke and Nora Regan C; m. 7/20/47 to Dorothy Mary Cleary; c. Patricia Anne, Nancy Jean and Mary Elizabeth. Educ: Middlebury Col, A.B, 47; Brown Univ, M.A, 49; Northwest. Univ, Ph.D, 53; Blue Key; Pi Sigma Alpha; Delta Upsilon. Polit. & Govt. Pos: Mem, Pub. Serv. Inst. Bd, Commonwealth of Pa, 60-; chmn, Oakmont Dem. Cmt, Pa, 63-; state co-chmn, Oper. Support, 64; mayor, Oakmont, 66-; treas, Allegheny Co, 68-; exec. dir, Cmt. to Reelect Sen. Clark, 68; del, Dem. Nat. Conv, 68. Bus. & Prof. Pos: From instr. to asst. prof. polit. sci, Knox Col, Ill, 48-55; dir, Citizenship Clearing House for West Pa, 55-62; from asst. prof. to assoc. prof. polit. sci, Univ. Pittsburgh, 55-64, prof, 64-, dir, center for polit, 63- Mil. Serv: Entered as Seaman, Navy, 43, released as Lt.(jg), 46, after serv. in LCI (M) 356, Pac; Silver Star Medal; Navy Unit Citation. Publ: Pennsylvania Politics, Holt, 57; Detailed Analysis of the U.S. Constitution, Littlefield, 58; 'Big City Politics,' In: Practical Politics in the U.S, Allyn and Bacon, 69. Mem: Am. Midwest and Pa. Polit. Sci. Asns; Am. Asn. Pub. Admin; Pa. Hist. Asn; Civic Club Allegheny Co; VFW. Rel: Catholic. Mailing Add: 806 Sixth St, Oakmont, Pa. 15139.

COOKE, FRANK JEROME R

b. Huntington, N.Y, 7/19/21; s. Charles Frank Cooke and Caroline Hillandbrand C; m. 11/7/43 to Carolyn Spear; c. Jeffrey A, Christopher H, Claudia S. and Sarah S. Educ: Rensselaer Polytech. Inst, B.S. in Chem. Eng; Harvard Univ. and Mass. Inst. Tech, postgrad. study in elec. eng. Polit. & Govt. Pos: Mem, City Coun, Norwalk, Conn, 57-61, mayor, Norwalk, 61-67. Bus. & Prof. Pos: Pres. and gen. mgr, Cooke Vacuum Inc, 12 years and engr, Remington Rand, 5 years. Mil. Serv: Entered as Pvt, Marine Corps, 41, released as 1st Lt, 46, after serv. in Pac, 43-45; Marine Corps Res. Mem: Am. Inst. Chem. Eng; Inst. Elec. & Electronics Eng; Amvets; Exchange Club; VFW; K. of C.(4°). Has published vacuum articles. Rel: Catholic. Mailing Add: 15 Channel Rd, South Norwich, Conn. 06854. (1967)

COOKE, ISABELLE (MRS. PATRICK) D

b. Cornwall, Vt, 8/14/00; wid; c. 3 sons, 2 daughters. Educ: Middlebury High Sch. Polit. & Govt. Pos: Vt. State Rep, 59-66, treas, Permanent Legis. Orgn, Vt. State House of Rep, 61. Bus. & Prof. Pos: Retired; formerly farming and housewife. Mem: Home Demonstration Club; pres, Altar Soc; co. chmn, Heart Fund Dr, 61-62; secy, OWLS, 61; v.chmn, State OWLS, 63; mem, Otter Valley Sch. for Retarded Children and Regional Hwy. Coun. Inc. Rel: Catholic. Mailing Add: Bridport, Vt. 05734. (1967)

COOKE, JOHN WARREN D

Va. State Del.

b. Mathews, Va, 2/28/15; m. to Anne Brown Rawn C. Educ: Va. Mil. Inst. Polit. & Govt. Pos: Mem, Va. State Del, 42- Bus. & Prof. Pos: Newspaper publisher, pres, Tidewater Newspapers, Inc; dir, Tidewater Tel. Co. Rel: Episcopal. Mailing Add: Mathews, Va. 23109. (1967)

COOKE, LUCILLE ELLEN R

Chmn, Clear Creek Rep. Cent. Cmt, Colo.

b. Era, Tex, 9/13/98; d. John William Gregory and Louisa Sutton G; wid; c. Edna Earle (Mrs. Elmer Popov). Educ: Col. of Indust. Arts, Denton, Tex, 17-18. Mem: Eastern Star. Rel: Presbyterian. Legal Res: Chicago Creek, Idaho Springs, Colo. 80452. Mailing Add: Box 885, Idaho Springs, Colo. 80452.

COOKE, MARY SWANEY D

Chmn, Donley Co. Dem. Party, Tex.

b. Clarendon, Tex, 7/23/98; d. William Henry Cooke and Halcyon Moore; single. Educ: Clarendon Jr. Col, AA, 18; Univ. Tex, B.A, 24; Alpha Delta Pi. Polit. & Govt. Pos: Committeewoman, Tex. State Dem. Exec. Cmt, 30th Sen. Dist; chmn, Donley Co. Dem. Exec. Cmt; chmn, Donley Co. League of Dem. Women; chmn, Donley Co. Women's Activities, 60-62; chmn, Donley Co. Dem. Party, currently. Bus. & Prof. Pos: Instr, Panhandle Independent Sch, 18, Clarendon Independent Schs, 19-20 and Mary S. Cooke Sch. Dancing, 24-64. Mem: Dir, Clarendon Duplicate Contract Bridge Club affiliated with Am. Contract Bridge League. Rel: Episcopal. Mailing Add: Box 84, Clarendon, Tex. 79226. (1967)

COOKE, WALTER E. D

b. Brooklyn, N.Y, 11/22/09; m. to Lillian Reilly; c. Joanne, Maureen, Deborah. Polit. & Govt. Pos: N.Y. State Assemblyman, 43-44; 64-66; N.Y. State Sen, 54-64; exec. Regular Dem. Orgn, 10th Assembly Dist. Kings Co. Mailing Add: 50 Plaza St, Brooklyn, N.Y. 11238. (1967)

COOKE, WILLIAM LEON D

Chmn, Bertie Co. Dem. Exec. Cmt, N.C.

b. Aulander, N.C, 5/19/25; s. W.A. Cooke and Nina P. C; m. 7/11/53 to Betty Butler; c. Elizabeth L. Educ: Univ. N.C, A.B. and LL.B, 50; Phi Alpha Delta. Polit. & Govt. Pos: Secy, Bertie Libr. Bd, N.C, 53; attorney, Bertie Bd. of Educ; 53-66; chmn, Bertie Co. Dem. Exec. Cmt, currently. Bus. & Prof. Pos: Partner, Pritchett, Cooke & Burch, 50- Mil. Serv: Entered as Aviation Cadet, Navy, 43, released as Ens, 46, after serv. in Pac; Lt.(Ret), Naval Res, 65; Victory Medal; Asiatic-Pac. Theater Ribbon. Mem: Am. and N.C. Bar Asns; Rotary; VFW. Rel: Baptist. Mailing Add: W. Gray St, Windsor, N.C. 27983.

COOLAHAN, JOHN CARROLL D

Md. State Del.

b. Baltimore, Md, 10/29/32; s. John Edward Coolahan and Blanche H. Zimmerman C; m. 4/15/56 to Joanna Helen Sakievich; c. Michael John, William Donald, Kathleen Marie, James Patrick and Joseph Dennis (deceased). Educ: West. Md. Col, A.B. in Econs, 58; Univ. Baltimore, LL.B, 66. Polit. & Govt. Pos: Md. State Del, currently; Dem. Dist. Exec, 62-66; exec. dir, Md. Home Improv. Cmt, State of Md, 62- Mil. Serv: Entered as Pvt, Marine Corps, 51, released as Sgt, 54; Purple Heart; Good Conduct Medal; Korean Area Ribbon. Mem: K. of C; Order of the Alhambra; past pres, Arbutus Social Club; Arbutus Commun. Asn; Patapsco Dem. Club. Rel: Roman Catholic. Mailing Add: 5415 Dolores Ave, Baltimore, Md. 21227. (1967)

COOLEY, FLORENCE H. D

b. Spokane, Wash, 2/21/98; d. Wellington S. De Camp and Sarah Elizabeth Foster D; div; c. Richard B. Educ: Northwest. Col; Kinmen Univ. Polit. & Govt. Pos: Secy, U.S. Rep. Compton White, Idaho, 36-43; admin. asst. to U.S. Rep. James H. Morrison, La, 43-67. Bus. & Prof. Pos: Pub. rels. consult, Law Firm, James H. Morrison, 67-69. Mem: First pres. and life mem. Topside Aviation Club; Cong. Secy. Club. Rel: Episcopal. Legal Res: Seattle, Wash. Mailing Add: 2117 E St. N.W, Washington, D.C. 20037.

COOLEY, HAROLD DUNBAR D

b. Nashville, N.C, 7/26/97; s. Roger A. Pryor Cooley and Hattie Davis C; m. 1923 to Madeline Matilda Strickland; c. Roger A. Bryor Cooley II, Hattie Davis (Mrs. Lawrence). Educ: Law Schs. of the Univ. of N.C. and Yale Univ; Phi Delta Theta; Phi Delta Phi Nat. Law. Polit. & Govt. Pos: U.S. Rep, N.C, 34-66; Mem. of the Exec. Cmt. and the Coun. of Interparliamentary Union and Past Pres. of the Am. Group; Mem, Select Cmt. on Econ. Aid to European Countries (Herter Cmt.) 80th Cong; Pres. Elector in 1932; Mem. and Cong. Adv. to the UNESCO. Bus. & Prof. Pos: Lawyer. Mil. Serv: Naval Aviation Flying Corps, WW I. Mem: Pres, Nash Co. Bar Asn, 33; Nash-Rocky Mount N.C. Bar Asn; N.C. State Bar Asn; Am. Bar Asn; Inter-Am. Bar Asn; Am. Judicature Soc; Jr. Order United Am. Mechs; Elks. Rel: Baptist. Mailing Add: Nashville, N.C. 27856. (1967)

COOLEY, HARRY HALE D

b. Georgia, Vt, 11/13/93; married; c. Two sons, three daughters. Educ: Vt. State Sch. of Agr, 11-13. Polit. & Govt. Pos: Town moderator, Vt; chmn, Town and Co. Dem. Party; town auditor; sch. dir; chmn, Orange Co. Dem. Party; supvr, White River Soil Conserv. Dist, 41-58; Vt. State Rep, 59; Secy. of State, Vt, 64-68. Bus. & Prof. Pos: Pres, White River Dairy Coop, 59-60; farmer; retired agr. teacher. Mem: Randolph Hist. Soc; Randolph Garden

Club; Randolph Town Dem. Cmt; Vt. Chap, SAR. Rel: Congregational. Legal Res: R.F.D. 2, Randolph Center, Vt. 05061. Mailing Add: 148 Main St, Montpelier, Vt. 05602. (1967)

COOLEY, LEWIS WALLACE R
Chmn, Jefferson Co. Rep. Party, Iowa
b. Lucerne, Mo, 12/11/03; s. Jacob Cooley and Mahalla Johnson C; m. 8/2/27 to Carol H. Stokes; c. Glenn F. Educ: Cent. Mo. State Col, B.S. in Educ, 26; Kappa Delta Pi. Polit. & Govt. Pos: Chmn, Jefferson Co. Rep. Party, Iowa, 65-; del, Rep. Nat. Conv, 68. Bus. & Prof. Pos: Ins. salesman, Cooley Ins. Agency, 45- Mem: Nat. Asn. Independent Ins. Agents; Lions (past pres). Rel: Methodist. Mailing Add: 209 E. Fillmore Ave, Fairfield, Iowa 52556.

COOLEY, RALEIGH MINOR D
Mayor, Hillsville, Va.
b. Hillsville, Va, 10/24/23; s. Alva Edison Cooley and Mary Kate McGlothlin C; single. Educ: Col. William and Mary, A.B, 49, B.C.L, 51. Polit. & Govt. Pos: Mayor, Hillsville, Va; del, Dem. Nat. Conv, 68. Mil. Serv: Entered as Seaman 3/C, Navy, 43, released as Qm. 2/C, 46, after serv. in Pac; Philippine Liberation Ribbon with 2 Stars and Asiatic-Pac. Ribbon with 5 Stars; Victory Medal. Mem: Va. and Am. Bar Asns; Lions Int; Mason; Eastern Star; VFW; Am. Legion; Aircraft Owners and Pilots Asn. Rel: Disciples of Christ. Mailing Add: Hillsville, Va. 24343.

COOLEY, REGINALD GARY R
b. Montpelier, Vt, 12/23/34; s. William R. Cooley and Marion Unwin C; m. 12/12/59 to Roslyn Baldwin; c. Randall Gary. Educ: Univ. Vt. night courses. Polit. & Govt. Pos: Former Vt. State Rep, 16th Dist. Bus. & Prof. Pos: V.pres, Cooley Bldg. Corp, Cooley Construct. Co, Cooley Paving Corp, Newburgh Asphalt, Thunder Road Enterprise, Catamount Stadium and Coastal Realty; pres, Airway Realty. Mem: Kiwanis; Shrine; Elks; Assoc. Gen. Contractors of Vt. Rel: Protestant. Legal Res: Orange, Vt. Mailing Add: R.R. 2, Barre, Vt. 05641. (1967)

COOLIDGE, CLYDE ROCHELEAU R
Mayor, Somersworth, N.H.
b. Manchester, N.H, 12/9/38; s. Theodore A. Coolidge (deceased) and Gladys Harris C.(deceased); m. 6/15/62 to Patricia Ann Gagne; c. Catherine Anne, David Matthew and Mary Elizabeth. Educ: Univ. N.H, B.A, 60; Boston Col. Law Sch, J.D, 63; Phi Beta Kappa; Phi Kappa Phi; Pi Gamma Mu; Tau Kappa Alpha; Pi Sigma Alpha; Sigma Beta. Polit. & Govt. Pos: Del, Rep. Nat. Conv, 68; mayor, Somersworth, N.H, 68- Bus. & Prof. Pos: Lectr. taxation, Whittemore Sch. Bus, Univ. N.H, 66-69; attorney, Cooper, Hall & Walker, Rochester, N.H, 66-69; self-employed attorney, Somersworth, 69- Mil. Serv: Entered as 1st Lt, Air Force, 63, released as Capt, 66, after serv. in Air Transport Command and Strategic Air Command, Moody and Pease Air Force Bases, N.H, 63-66. Mem: Am, N.H. and Strafford Co. Bar Asns; Am. Legion. Outstanding Young Man of the Year Award, N.H. Jaycees, 68. Rel: Unitarian. Mailing Add: 2 James Ave, Somersworth, N.H. 03878.

COOLIDGE, GLENN E. R
b. Cripple Creek, Colo, 12/2/02; m. to Margaret Welch. Educ: Calif. Pub. Schs. Polit. & Govt. Pos: Calif. State Assemblyman, 52-66; past pres, S. Calif. Rep. Assembly; del, Rep. Nat. Conv, 56 & 60. Bus. & Prof. Pos: Real estate, construction and investment bus; past pres, S. Calif. Realty Bd; San Lorenzo Valley C. of C; dir, Calif. Real Estate Asn. Mem: Past Dep. Dist. Gov, Lions Int; Elks; Mason; Shrine; Odd Fellows; Commonwealth Club. Mailing Add: Lindsay, Calif. 93247. (1967)

COOMBES, DOROTHY MARGARET R
Secy, Boone Co. Rep. Cent. Cmt, Ill.
b. Belvidere, Ill, 11/23/08; d. John William Balentyne (deceased) and Frances Kamin B; m. 8/24/33 to John Barton Coombes (deceased); c. Colleen (Mrs. Sherman Gray). Educ: Univ. of Wis, 26-30; Delta Zeta; Arden Club; Col. Rep. Polit. & Govt. Pos: Former co-ed, 12th Dist. Rep. Publ, Ill; former mem, 12th Cong. Dist. Rep. Club; mem, Boone Co. Rep. Women's Club, 10 years, past pres. and v.pres, 2 terms; secy, Boone Co. Rep. Cent. Cmt, 66-; mem, Ill. Rep. Cent. Cmt, 66-; mem, Belvidere Rep. Cent. Cmt; mem. and secy, Belvidere Twp. Rep. Cent. Cmt. Bus. & Prof. Pos: Soc. ed, Belvidere Daily Rep. Newspaper, 18 years. Mem: Belvidere Women's Club; Zonta Int.(v.pres); PTA (past pres, Belvidere High Sch. Chap); Sweet Adelines. Rel: Catholic. Mailing Add: 504 S. Main St, Belvidere, Ill. 61008.

COOMBS, WILLIAM ELMER R
Calif. State Sen.
b. Keosauqua, Iowa, 1/17/11; s. Elmer C. Coombs and Myra Moon C; m. 10/20/34 to Katheryn Logan; c. Katheryn Wickham and Ann Siracusa. Educ: Univ. Calif, Los Angeles, B.A. in Econ, 33; Loyola Univ, Los Angeles, J.D, 54; Lambda Chi Alpha. Polit. & Govt. Pos: Mem. planning cmn, Rialto, Calif, 61-62, city councilman, 62-66; mem. adv. bd, San Bernardino Co. Young Rep, 66-68; mem. adv. bd, Calif. Young Am. Freedom, 67-; Calif. State Sen, 20th Dist, 67- Bus. & Prof. Pos: CPA, Los Angeles, 47-51; controller, Twaits-Wittenberg Co, 52-54; overseas bus. mgr, Morrison-Knudsen Int, 54-56; asst. prof, Calif. State Col, Chico, 56-58; treas. and house counsel, Matich Corp, 58-61; sr. partner, Coombs & Friel, attorneys, 62- Publ: Construction Accounting & Financial Management, McGraw-Hill, 58; 'The Farmer Takes a Loss,' Taxes Mag, 53; numerous articles for Mech. Contractor Mag, 65- Mem: Calif. Soc. CPA (pres, citrus belt chap, 65-66); Am. Inst. CPA; Am, Calif, San Bernardino Co. and Los Angeles Co. Bar Asns; Am. Judicature Soc; Rotary Int; C. of C; Regional Econ. Develop. Coun.(pres, 66). Rel: Protestant. Legal Res: 126 E. Morgan St, Rialto, Calif. 92376. Mailing Add: P.O. Box 146, Rialto, Calif. 92376.

COONEY, JOHN L. D
Wash. State Sen.
b. Condon, Ore, 1915; m. to Marguerite C; c. four. Educ: Gonzaga Law Sch. Polit. & Govt. Pos: Wash. State Rep, 2 terms; Wash. State Sen, currently. Bus. & Prof. Pos: Practicing Lawyer. Mem: Elks; Grange; K. of C. Mailing Add: 4403 N. Adams St, Spokane, Wash. 99205.

COONS, MARION M. R
Chmn, Lucas Co. Rep. Cent. Cmt, Iowa
b. Macedonia, Iowa, 4/11/15; s. Lindsey D. Coons and Luella McDowell C; m. 6/23/40 to Margaret Lorrene McReynolds; c. Kenton Richard and Kenneth Lee. Educ: State Univ. Iowa, B.Sc, 38. Polit. & Govt. Pos: Councilman, Lamoni, Iowa, 44-46 and Chariton, Iowa, 52-56; mem. sch. bd, Chariton Commun. Sch. Dist, 62-; chmn, Lucas Co. Rep. Cent. Cmt, 60- Bus. & Prof. Pos: Treas, Hy-Vee Food Stores, Inc, 43-; chmn. bd, Nat. Bank Trust Co, 63- Mem: Pres. Iowa Unit, Nat. Asn. Credit Mgt, 55-56; bd. dirs, Nat. Asn. Credit Mgt, 62-65; Nat. Asn. Acct; Shrine; Mason; Rotary; Chariton Golf & Country Club; Des Moines Club. Rel: Methodist. Legal Res: 607 Ashland Ave, Chariton, Iowa 50049. Mailing Add: 1801 Osceola Ave, Chariton, Iowa 50049.

COOPER, ALDRAGE B, JR. D
City Cmnr, New Brunswick, N.J.
b. New Brunswick, N.J, 9/15/37; s. Aldrage B. Cooper and Ruth Twyman C; m. 8/27/60 to Judith Phyliss Greene; c. Aldrage B, III and Jill E. Educ: Univ. Conn, B.S, 59. Polit. & Govt. Pos: V.pres, Bd. Educ, New Brunswick, N.J, 65-67, city cmnr, 67-; del, Dem. Nat. Conv, 68. Bus. & Prof. Pos: Underwriter, Continental Ins. Co, 59-65; mgr, N.J. Bell Tel. Co, 65-67; personnel mgr, Triangle Conduit and Cable Co, 67-68; asst. dir. pub. affairs, Johnson and Johnson, 68- Mem: F&AM. Law Day Award, 68. Rel: Protestant. Mailing Add: 130 Handy St, New Brunswick, N.J. 08902.

COOPER, ANDREW JAMES, II D
b. Tallassee, Ala, 3/31/20; s. Andrew James Cooper and Margaret Elizabeth Boles C; m. 2/12/44 to Mary Agnes Segrest; c. Anita Ann. Educ: Univ. Ala. Exten. Center. Polit. & Govt. Pos: Ala. State Rep, 62-66. Bus. & Prof. Pos: Banking; v.pres, Ala. Exchange Bank, Tuskegee. Mil. Serv: Served as non-commissioned officer, World War II. Mem: Masons. Engaged in Vet. Affairs Work. Rel: Baptist. Mailing Add: Box 457, Tuskegee, Ala. 36083. (1967)

COOPER, CLINT MARVIN D
Chmn, McPherson Co. Dem. Party, Kans.
b. Beverley, Kans, 9/25/07; s. Charles Robert Cooper (deceased) and Rosa Belle VanCamp C; m. 7/23/30 to Etta Louise Stover; c. Alice Darlene (Mrs. Miles), Gary Lee and Randy Marvin. Educ: Mayview High Sch, Mo. Polit. & Govt. Pos: Treas, McPherson Co. Dem. Party, 56-68 and chmn, 68- Publ: Civil Rights Work, Hutchinson News, Kans. and Church Women United News, Kans. Mem: Oil, Chem. & Atomic Workers (pres, 55-58); organizer and first chmn, McPherson Co. Emergency Aid Group; McPherson Co. Farmer-Labor Coun.(pres. and other off); McPherson Co. and Nat. Farmers Union; Odd Fellows. Rel: Christian Church of N.Am. Mailing Add: 900 W. Woodside St, McPherson, Kans. 67460.

COOPER, DANIEL S. D
Mich. State Rep.
b. Los Angeles, Calif, 3/10/30; m. to Hilda Winshall; c. Eve, Elizabeth, Joanne. Educ: Wayne State Univ, B.A, J.D. Polit. & Govt. Pos: Mich. State Rep, 64- Bus. & Prof. Pos: Attorney. Mil. Serv: Vet. Mem: Detroit Bar Asn; Mich. Bar Asn; Oak Park Youth Guidance Bd; B'nai B'rith. Rel: Hebrew. Mailing Add: 13150 Dartmouth St, Oak Park, Mich. 48067. (1967)

COOPER, DOUGLAS WINSLOW R
b. New York, N.Y, 12/21/42; s. Michael Julian Cooper and Priscilla Taylor C; single. Educ: Cornell Univ, A.B, 64; Pa. State Univ, M.S, 69; Harvard, student, 69-; Delta Sigma Rho. Polit. & Govt. Pos: Del, Rep. Nat. Conv, 68. Bus. & Prof. Pos: Jr. engr, Int. Bus. Machine Corp, Kingston, N.Y, 64; research asst, Center Air Environ. Studies, Pa. State Univ, 66-67. Mil. Serv: Entered as Pvt, Army, 64, released as SP-4, 66, after serv. in Army Biol. Labs, Ft. Detrick, Md, 65-66. Publ: 'Effects of Humidity on Light Scattering by Particulates,' J. Air Pollution Control Asn, 69. Mem: Air Pollution Control Asn. Rel: Protestant. Legal Res: State College, Pa. Mailing Add: Box 152, Rosendale, N.Y. 12472.

COOPER, FRANCES THROCKMORTON R
Mem, Rep. Nat. Cmt.
b. Seattle, Wash, 4/20/12; d. James Sherman Throckmorton and Callie Frances Kanouse T; m. 6/27/45 to Albert L. Cooper; c. James Albert, Carol Ann, George Frederick and Robert Eugene Shanafelt. Educ: Univ. Wash, B.B.A, magna cum laude, 34, Teaching Cert, 35; Phi Beta Kappa; Beta Gamma Sigma; Pi Lambda Theta. Polit. & Govt. Pos: Mem. exec. bd, King Co. Med. Auxiliary, 54-; mem, Wash. Med. Auxiliary, 58-64; mem, Asn. Rep. Women Seattle, 60-64; representative First Cong. Dist, exec. bd, Wash. Rep. Cent. Cmt, 62-64; mem. exec. bd, Wash. Fedn. Rep. Women, 64-; mem, Rep. Nat. Cmt, Wash, 64-; del, Rep. Nat. Conv, 68. Rel: Methodist. Mailing Add: 6822 50th Ave. N.E, Seattle, Wash. 98115. (1967)

COOPER, FRANCIS LOREN R
Chmn, Wilton Rep. Town Cmt, Conn.
b. Dodge Center, Minn, 11/30/19; s. Harold U. Cooper and Grace Miller C; m. 1/27/45 to Shirley Edith Garniss; c. Donald R. and Lynne A.(Mrs. R.D. Lichtermann, II). Educ: Univ. Minn, B.A, 41; Grey Friars; Theta Chi; Sigma Delta Chi. Polit. & Govt. Pos: Mem, Wilton Rep. Town Cmt, Conn, 60-, chmn, 62- Bus. & Prof. Pos: With New York Life since 46, second v.pres, pub. rels. and advert, New York Life Ins. Co, 65-67, v.pres, pub. rels, 67- Mil. Serv: Entered as Pvt, Marine Corps, 41, released as Lt. Col.(Ret), Marine Corps Res, 61; after serv. in First Marine Div, World War II and Second Marine Div, Korean Emergency; Pac. and Am. Theater Ribbons; two Presidential Unit Citations; Victory Medal; Marine Res. Ribbons. Mem: Charter mem, Pub. Rels. Soc. of Am; Life Ins. Advertisers Asn; Mason; Am. Legion. Rel: Congregational. Mailing Add: 28 Powder Horn Hill, Wilton, Conn. 06897.

COOPER, FRANK E. R
b. Seattle, Wash, 11/28/28; s. Frank H. Cooper and Maurgurite Madison C; m. 6/30/51 to Erlene R. Johnson; c. Frank E, Jr. and Dawn R. Educ: Univ. Wash, Pac. Coast Grad. Sch. of Banking, grad; Chi Psi. Polit. & Govt. Pos: Del, Wash. State Conv. and Pierce Co. Conv, 58-68; asst. chmn, Pierce Co. Rep. Party, 60-62, chmn, 63; chmn. finance cmt, Pierce Co. Rep. Cent. Cmt, 62-64, mem, 64-66; Wash. State Rep, 63; dir, Co. Chmn. Nat. Orgn, 64; permanent chmn, Pierce Co. Rep. Conv, 64 & 68; del, Rep. Nat. Conv, 64 & 68; mem, Pierce Co. Rep. Exec. Cmt, 64-66; permanent chmn, Sixth Cong. Dist. Conv, 68; state supvr. banking, Wash, 68- Bus. & Prof. Pos: Pres, Bank of Tacoma. Mil. Serv: Entered as Pvt, Army, 45, released as WOJG, 47. Mem: Dir, Nat.

Asn. of Bank Cmnrs; chmn, West. States Banking Cmnrs; adv. mem, Nat. Consumer Finance Asn; West. Finance Asn; Am. Mgt. Asn; Tacoma C. of C; Tacoma Golf & Country Club; Tacoma Club; past pres, Lions Club; past pres, Univ. Union Club and Young Mens Bus. Club; Legis. Cmt, Wash. Bankers Asn; chmn. bd, Tacoma Jr. Col; dir, Jessie Dslyn Boys Ranch; trustee, Annie Wright Girls Sch; Tacoma Yacht Club; Tacoma Golf and Country Club; Tacoma Club. Rel: Presbyterian. Mailing Add: 4232 N. 38th, Tacoma, Wash. 98407.

COOPER, FRED FERRIS D
b. San Francisco, Calif, 5/12/28; s. Fred F. Cooper and Elizabeth Zandt C; m. 12/25/68 to Virginia Lamanna; c. Jeffrey, Bryan and Kathryn. Educ: Univ. Calif, LL.B, 52. Polit. & Govt. Pos: Del, Alameda Co. Cent. Labor Coun, 49-52; rep, 18th Assembly Dist. Dem. Coun, Calif, 55-57; chmn, Berkeley Caucus, 57; chmn, Alameda Co. Mosk for Attorney Gen. Campaign, 58 & 62; mem, Berkeley Urban Renewal Cmt, 60- and Berkeley Apt. Design Cmt, 62-64; chmn, Dewey for City Coun. Campaign, 63; mem, City-Univ. Liaison Cmt, Calif, 65-; chmn, Alameda Co. Edmund G. Brown for Gov. Calif, 66 and Humphrey-Muskie Campaign, 68. Bus. & Prof. Pos: Trustee, Herrick Mem. Hosp, Berkeley, Calif. and pres, East Bay Rehab. Center, 62-68. Mil. Serv: Entered as Pvt, Army, 52, released as Cpl, 54, after serv. in Heidelberg Area Command, Germany, 53-54; Nat. Serv. Medal; Korean Medal. Mem: Calif. and Alameda Co. Bar Asns; past chmn, Oakland Law Forum; Panel Arbitrator, Am. Arbit. Asn; pres, UN Asn. Alameda Co, 64-65; pres, Alameda Co. Ment. Health Asn, 65-67; Elks; trustee, Voice; past chmn, Oakland Interserv. Club Coun. Rel: Protestant. Legal Res: 345 Laguana Vista Ave, Alameda, Calif. 94501. Mailing Add: Financial Center Bldg, Oakland, Calif. 94612.

COOPER, GLORIA CLAIRE D
Mem, Calif. Dem. State Cent. Cmt.
b. Jamaica, N.Y, 2/22/22; d. Nathan Lebenson and Ruth Baumgarten L; m. 10/10/42 to Albert W. Cooper; c. Ronald Allen and Blair Lee. Educ: Ventura Jr. Col, 6 months. Polit. & Govt. Pos: Mem, Ventura Co. Dem. Cent. Cmt, Calif, 54-56, 69-; secy. women's div, South. Calif. Dem. Orgn, 66-68; mem, Calif. Dem. State Cent. Cmt, 67- Bus. & Prof. Pos: Owner, Sewelson & Cooper Rug and Carpets, 51-69. Rel: Jewish. Mailing Add: 3175 Outrigger Ave, Ventura, Calif. 93003.

COOPER, JAMES LeROY R
Ariz. State Rep.
b. Mesa, Ariz, 12/4/15; s. Orson Prince Cooper and Sybil Cora Newell C; m. to Mildred Adelia Post; James Gary, Gayle (Mrs. Richard H. Bramwell, Morris Post, Conny (Mrs. Laurence N. Johnson), William Newell and Jan. Polit. & Govt. Pos: Ariz. State Rep, 69- Mem: Farm Bur; United Dairymen of Ariz; Maricopa Co. Dairy Herd Improv. Asn; Ariz. Milk, Inc. Hon. State Farmer, Ariz. Future Farmers of Am. Rel: Latter-day Saint. Mailing Add: 1059 S. Stapley Dr, Mesa, Ariz. 85201.

COOPER, JANE ELLEN R
Mem, Calif. Rep. State Cent. Cmt.
b. Los Angeles, Calif, 5/31/20; d. J. Glenn Marks and Floy Pixley M; m. 2/6/42 to John Dean Cooper; c. Christina (Mrs. Charles R. Hastings), Paralee (Mrs. Bruce E. Heath) and Linda Theresa. Educ: Stanford Univ, B.A, 42; Pi Beta Phi. Polit. & Govt. Pos: Founder pres, Bear Valley Rep. Women's Club, Fed, Calif, 64-65; recording secy, San Bernardino Co. Fedn. of Rep. Women, 67-68, 3rd v.pres, 69-; assoc. mem, Calif. Rep. State Cent. Cmt, 67-68, mem, 69-; Mt. Arca campaign chmn. for U.S. Rep. Pettis, Calif, 68. Mem: Corresponding secy, Bear Valley Commun. Hosp. Fund, Inc, 60-; pres, Big Bear Lake Elem. Sch. PTA, 60-62; hon. life mem, Nat. Cong. of Parents and Teachers, 65. Rel: Protestant. Legal Res: 8 Robin Rd, Big Bear Lake, Calif. 92315. Mailing Add: P.O. Box 27, Big Bear Lake, Calif. 92315.

COOPER, JESSE COYT D
Chmn, Moore Co. Dem. Party, Tex.
b. Turkey, Tex, 4/4/13; s. Leo A. Cooper and Texa Edwards C; m. 6/9/35 to Mildred Winona Whiteside; c. Sue Carrollynn (Mrs. Hensley) and Georgia Ann (Mrs. Wright). Educ: Tex. Tech. Univ, 29-33; mgr, La Ventana Year Book, dir, Red Raider. Polit. & Govt. Pos: Sgt. of arms, Dem. Nat. Conv, 52; Gov. appointee, resolution cmn, Tex. State Conv; mem, Cmn. for Higher Educ, 61-66; chmn, Moore Co. Dem. Party, currently. Bus. & Prof. Pos: V.pres, Soil Conserv. Surv, 13 years and pres. for irrigation, 62-; dir, Steering Cmt, 50 years; Study of Water Pollution; dir, Rural Electrification Admin, 12 years. Mil. Serv: Entered as Flight Instr, Air Force, 42, released as Sr. Flight Instr, 45, after serv. in U.S. Mem: Am. Legion; life mem, Khiva Temple; KCCH; dir, N.Plains Research & Develop; mem, Budget and Tax Cmt. Higher Educ. Rel: Presbyterian. Mailing Add: Box 51, Etter Rt, Dumas, Tex. 79029. (1967)

COOPER, JOHN SHERMAN R
U.S. Sen, Ky.
b. Somerset, Pulaski Co, Ky, 8/23/01; s. John Sherman Cooper and Helen Gertrude Tartar C; m. 3/17/55 to Lorraine Rowan Shevlin. Educ: Centre Col, 18-19; Yale Col, A.B, 23; Harvard Law Sch, 23-25; Beta Theta Pi. LL.D, Centre Col, Univ. Ky, Georgetown Col, Berea Col, East. Ky. State Col, Yale Univ. and Univ. Pittsburgh; L.H.D, Lincoln Mem. Univ; D.C.L, Nasson Col, Maine. Polit. & Govt. Pos: Ky. State Rep, 28-30; co. judge, Pulaski Co, 30-38, circuit judge, 45-46; U.S. Sen, Ky, 46-48, 52-54 & 56-, mem, Pub. Works, Rules and Admin. and For. Rels. Cmts, U.S. Senate, mem, Select Cmt. on Standards and Ethics, voting mem, Senate Appropriations Cmt. for pub. works progs. and projs; U.S. Del, Gen. Assembly UN, 49, 50, 51 & 68; adv. to Secy. of State Dean Acheson, NATO Coun. Ministers, London and Brussels, 50; U.S. Ambassador, India and Nepal, 55-56; Cong. adv. to U.S. Del, UNESCO Conf, Paris, 58; mem, President's Cmn. on the Assassination of President John F. Kennedy, 64; Senate adv. to U.S. Del, Treaty Signing Conf. establishing the Asian Develop. Bank, Manila, 65; rapporteur for mil. cmt, NATO Parliamentarians Conf, 66-67. Bus. & Prof. Pos: Mem. law firm, Gardner, Morrison & Rogers, Wash, D.C, 49-51. Mil. Serv: Enlisted as Pvt, Army, 42, released as Capt, 46, after serv. in Third Army, Normandy, France, Luxenbourg, Germany and headed reorgn. German Judicial Syst. of Bavaria; Bronze Star Medal. Mem: Am. and Ky. Bar Asns; bd. trustees, Centre Col; Am. Legion; VFW; Rotary Int. Rep. Recipient of Award for Distinguished Serv. in the Senate for the 88th Cong, Am. Polit. Sci. Asn, 65. Rel: Baptist. Legal Res: Somerset, Ky. 42501. Mailing Add: 125 Old Senate Office Bldg, Washington, D.C. 20510.

COOPER, LEON M. D
Chmn. South. Div, Calif. Dem. State Cent. Cmt.
m; c. Four. Educ: Univ. Calif, Los Angeles, A.B; Harvard Law Sch, LL.B; Univ. South. Calif, LL.M. Polit. & Govt. Pos: Held campaign positions for statewide cand, James Roosevelt, Edmund G. Brown and Richard Richards, Calif, 50-60; legal counsel, Calif. Dem. Coun, 61-65; chmn. research cmt, Richard Richards for Senate, 64; del, Dem. Nat. Conv, 64 & 68; mem. and chmn, Calif. Alcoholic Beverage Controls Appeals Bd, 65-67; chmn, Vol. Orgn. Cmt, Brown for Gov. Campaign, 66; parliamentarian, Calif. Dem. State Cent. Cmt, 66, chmn, elec. reform tax force, 66-68 and chmn. south div, 69-; statewide treas, Kennedy for President Campaign, 68. Bus. & Prof. Pos: Sr. Partner, Cooper, Tepper & Plant, Law Firm, Los Angeles. Legal Res: 2709 Via Alavado, Palos Verdes Estates, Calif. 90274. Mailing Add: 742 S. Hill St, Suite 950, Los Angeles, Calif. 90014.

COOPER, ROLAND D
Ala. State Sen.
b. Robertsdale, Ala, 8/13/13; s. Mr. and Mrs. W. R. Cooper; m. to Stella Handly; c. 3. Polit. & Govt. Pos: Worked with Ala. State Hwy. Dept, 35-39; Mayor, Camden, Ala, 48-54; del, Dem. Nat. Conv, 52; Ala. State Sen, 54- Bus. & Prof. Pos: Service Sta. operator, 37-47; Chrysler-Plymouth dealership, 45-; operator, cattle farm, 50- Mem: Mason; Shrine; Camden Exchange Club. Rel: Baptist. Mailing Add: Camden, Ala. 36726. (1967)

COOPER, SAMUEL V. D
Chmn, Douglas Co. Dem. Cmt, Nebr.
b. Poland, 3/1/22; s. Martin Cooper and Ida Tenenbaum C; m. 11/3/52 to Judith Steinhorn; c. Hollie, Justin, Ronna and Marsha. Educ: Creighton Univ, LL.B, 48. Polit. & Govt. Pos: Mem, Omaha City Charter Conv, Nebr, 56, v.chmn, 65; Douglas Co. Elec. Cmnr, 60 & 61; alternate del, Dem. Nat. Conv, 68; chmn, Douglas Co. Dem. Cmt, currently. Mil. Serv: Entered as Pvt, Army, 43, released as S/Sgt, 46; ETO Ribbon; Philippines Liberation Medal. Mem: Nebr. and Omaha Bar Asns; Cornhuske B'nai B'rith; AF&AM. Rel: Jewish. Legal Res: 4305 N. 56th St, Omaha, Nebr. 68117. Mailing Add: 855 Omaha Nat. Bank Bldg, Omaha, Nebr. 68102. (1967)

COOPER, WALTER CLAUDE D
b. Church Hill, Tenn, 7/26/26; s. Robert Mack Cooper and Martha Frances C; m. 1/4/47 to Margaret Tranbarger; c. Walter Claude, Jr. and James Alan. Educ: Church Hill High Sch. Polit. & Govt. Pos: Mem, Hawkins Co. Court, 60-; city judge, Church Hill Munic. Court, 62-64; del, Dem. Nat. Conv, 64. Bus. & Prof. Pos: Chemist, Eastman Chem. Prod, 66-, Tenn. Eastman Co, 46-66. Mil. Serv: Entered as Seaman, Navy, 43, released as Torpedoman, 46, after serv. in Pac. Area; Submarine Combat Pin; Asiatic-Pac. Theater Ribbon; Philippine Liberation Medal. Mem: Ruritan; Optimists; Scottish Rite Mason (32°); Am. Legion; Submarine Vets; Bay Mt. Country Club. Rel: Methodist. Mailing Add: P.O. Box 22, Church Hill, Tenn. 37642.

COOPER, WILLIAM HURLBERT R
Mem, D.C. Rep. Cent. Cmt.
b. Phila, Pa, 10/19/24; s. Charles M. Cooper (deceased) and Lois Hurlbert C; m. 2/17/51 to Joanne Coffin; c. Charles Morgan B, William Hurlbert, Jr. and Arthur S. Educ: Colgate Univ, Hamilton, N.Y, 42-43; West. Reserve Univ, Cleveland, B.A, 46; George Wash. Univ, M.D, 49; Delta Kappa Epsilon; Nu Sigma Nu. Polit. & Govt. Pos: Founder and chmn, D.C. Polit. Action Cmt, 62-; mem, D.C. Rep. Cent. Cmt, 63 & 68-; alternate del, Rep. Nat. Conv, 68. Bus. & Prof. Pos: Obstetrician-gynecologist, Wash. D.C, 52-; Research projs. done for Wallace Labs, Syntex Labs and Hoffman-LaRoche. Publ: Husband's Guide to Female Menopause, Simon & Schuster, 69; 'The Pill and Figure Changes,' Va. Med. Monthly, 68. Mem: D.C, Kober, Arlington Co. and Pan Am. Med. Socs; Int. Fertility Asn; William Beaumont Med. Soc.(past pres); chmn. commun. health week, Jr. C. of C. D.C, 56; v.pres, Spring Valley-Wesley Heights Citizens Asn. 67-68 and pres, 68-69; Cong. Country Club; George Town Club. Rel: Episcopal. Mailing Add: 5024 Upton St. N.W, Washington, D.C. 20016.

COOPER, WILLIAM VANCE D
b. Graham Co, N.C, 7/19/09; s. Zebulon Vance Cooper and Frankie Ayers C; m. 1950 to Birdie Duvall. Educ: Robbinsville High Sch. Polit. & Govt. Pos: N.C. State Rep, 63-66; city alderman, Robbinsville. Bus. & Prof. Pos: Contractor. Mil. Serv: Shiplifter 2/C, 42-45. Mem: C. of C. Mailing Add: P.O. Box 186, Robbinsville, N.C. 28771. (1967)

COOPERMAN, ARTHUR J. D
N.Y. State Assemblyman
b. New York, N.Y, 12/22/33; s. Herman Cooperman and Rose Hirschfeld C; m. 8/22/59 to Norma Bezrod; c. Seth. Educ: N.Y. Univ. Col, B.A, 55; N.Y. Univ. Sch. of Law, LL.B, 60. Polit. & Govt. Pos: Co. committeeman, 24th Assembly Dist, Queens Co, N.Y, 66-, N.Y. State Assemblyman, 69-; del, Dem. Judicial Conv, Queens Co, 68. Bus. & Prof. Pos: Practising attorney, 61-66; asst. counsel, grievance cmt, Asn. of Bar of City of New York, 67-68; private law practice, currently. Mil. Serv: Entered as 2nd Lt, Army, 55, released as 1st Lt, 57, after serv. in 34th Signal Bn, Seventh Corps, Europe, 56-57. Mem: Asn. of Bar of City of New York; Queens Co. and N.Y. State Bar Asns; Rel: Jewish. Legal Res: 80-22 169th St, Jamaica, N.Y. 11432. Mailing Add: 160-16 Jamaica Ave, Jamaica, N.Y. 11432.

COOPERSMITH, ESTHER LIPSEN D
b. Des Moines, Iowa, 1/18/31; d. Morris Lipsen; m. 11/7/54 to Jack Coopersmith; c. Jonathan, Constance, Jeffrey and Ronald. Educ: Univ. Denver; Univ. Wis. Polit. & Govt. Pos: Nat. cmt, Women Young Dem, Wis, 51-55; exec. secy, Stevenson for Pres. Club, 52; alternate del, Dem. Nat. Conv, 52 & 64, del, 56; polit. worker for Sen. Estes Kefauver, 52-56; mem, Dem. Cent. Cmt, D.C, 56-60; dir, LBJ barbecues for Lynda and Luci, 64; v.chmn, Finance Cmt, Finan for Gov. State of Md; mem, President's Cmn. and President's Cmt. to study sites and plans for visitors facilities and serv. in Wash, D.C; mem, Humphrey Campaign Cmt; co-chmn, $500 Dinner for Humphrey. Bus. & Prof. Pos: Mem, Senate Press Gallery. Mem: Chmn, Civic Opera, Wash, D.C; trustee, St. Mary's Col; Am. Newspaper Women's Club; Women's Cmt, Nat. Symphony; Capital Speaker's Club; Women's Nat. Dem. Club; Arts Adv. Cmt. for Nat. Found. of Arts and Humanities. Chmn. of numerous cmts. for fund raising for U.S. Senators. Rel: Hebrew. Mailing Add: 3219 Park View Rd, Chevy Chase, Md. 20015.

COPADIS, NICHOLAS GEORGE R
b. Manchester, N.H, 6/5/26; s. George D. Copadis and Iphigenia Ghikas C; m. 10/8/50 to Marilyn L. Gosselin; c. George N, Iphigenia D. and Michael G. Educ: Univ. of N.H, B.A, cum laude, 50; Boston Univ. Law Sch, LL.B, 55; Pi Gamma Mu; Scabbard and Blade. Polit. & Govt. Pos: V.chmn, Manchester Rep. City Cmt, N.H, 63-64, city chmn, 64-67. Bus. & Prof. Pos: Attorney, Manchester Fed. Savings and Loan Asn, 55- Mil. Serv: Entered as Pvt, Army, 44, released as Cpl, 46, after serv. in 274th A.F.A. Bn, ETO; re-entered serv. as 2nd Lt, Army, 51, released as 1st Lt, 52, after serv. in 2nd Inf. Div, Korea; ETO Ribbon; Korean Conflict Ribbon; Bronze Star with V device for valor; Combat Inf. Badge; Purple Heart; Presidential Unit Citation. Mem: N.H. Bar Asn; VFW; Am. Legion. Rel: Greek Orthodox. Mailing Add: 451 Milton St, Manchester, N.H. 03103.

COPE, WILLIAM DeLOACH D
b. Hollandale, Miss, 10/12/21; married. Educ: Beta Theta Pi. Polit. & Govt. Pos: Miss. State Rep, 60-69. Bus. & Prof. Pos: Farmer. Mem: Rotary; Farm Bur; VFW (Jr. V.Comdr, 63-64). Rel: Methodist. Mailing Add: Arcola, Miss. 38722. (1967)

COPELAND, DAVID Y, III R
Tenn. State Rep.
b. Tampa, Fla, 1/10/31; s. David Y. Copeland and Lora Kramp C; m. 12/23/50 to Mary Ethel Leamon; c. David Michael and Valerie Anne. Educ: McKenzie Bus. Col, 49. Tenn. State Rep, 68- Bus. & Prof. Pos: Owner, Ace Shade & Awning Co, Chattanooga, Tenn, 53-59; v.pres, Copelands, Inc, 59- Mil. Serv: Entered as Pvt, Army, 51, released as Sgt, 53, after serv. in 71st AAA Gun Bn. Mem: Chattanooga Water Ski Club; Ment. Health Asn. Rel: Baptist. Mailing Add: 8950 Fuller Rd, Chattanooga, Tenn. 37421.

COPELAND, EDWARD JEROME R
Ill. State Rep.
b. Chicago, Ill, 10/29/33; s. Harvey H. Copeland and Lilyan Rubin C; m. 9/2/62 to Ruth Caminer; c. Ellyn. Educ: Carleton Col, B.A, 55; Univ. London, cert, 57; Northwest. Law Sch, J.D, 58. Polit. & Govt. Pos: Claims adjudicator, U.S. Dept. of Health, Educ. and Welfare, 58-60; Ill. State Rep, 10th Dist, currently. Bus. & Prof. Pos: Attorney, self employed, 60- Mem: Am, Ill. and Chicago Bar Asns; Rogers Park and Edgewater Commun. Coun Rel: Jewish. Mailing Add: 6118 N. Sheridan Rd, Chicago, Ill. 60626.

COPELAND, FRED E. (GENE) D
Mo. State Rep.
b. Cooter, Mo, 6/12/32; m. 12/24/52 to Patricia Ann Weber; c. Fred, Lisa Ann, Leslie Ann. Educ: Ark. State Col, Jonesboro, Ark. Polit. & Govt. Pos: Mo. State Rep, 60- Bus. & Prof. Pos: Real estate, ins. and farming; owner, Fred. E. Copeland Agency. Mil. Serv: Navy, 52-56. Mailing Add: 1399 Mill St, New Madrid, Mo. 63869.

COPELAND, LAMMOT duPONT, JR. R
Asst. to State Chmn, Del. State Rep. Cmt.
b. Bridgeport, Conn, 6/4/32; s. Lammot duPont Copeland and Pamela Cunningham C; m. 9/28/58 to Deborah Lovering C; c. Leonore, Lammot duPont, III, Charles Lovering, Carolyn and Alexandra. Educ: Harvard Col, B.A, 54; Phoenix-SK Club. Polit. & Govt. Pos: Mem, San Mateo Co. Rep. Cent. Cmt, Calif, 60-62; mem, Calif. Rep. State Cent. Cmt, 60-62; treas, Young Am. for Freedom, 62-66; mem. tour cmt, Rep. Nat. Cmt, 64; mem, New Castle Co. Rep. Cmt, Del, 65-; treas, Am. Conservative Union, 65; asst. to state chmn, Del. State Rep. Cmt, 68- Bus. & Prof. Pos: Chemist, E.I. duPont de Nemours & Co, Antioch, Calif, 57-59, sales rep, Palo Alto, 60-63 and financial analyst, Wilmington, Del, 64-; publisher, Hollywood Citizen-News, North Hollywood Valley Times and Sunnyvale Standard, Calif, 64- Mil. Serv: Entered as Pvt, Army, 54, released as Sgt, 56, after serv. in 85th Field Artil. Bn, Tenth Inf. Div, Kitzingen, Germany, 55-56. Mem: Am. Chem. Soc. Rel: Episcopal. Legal Res: West of the Rising Sun Lane, Wilmington, Del, 19807. Mailing Add: 2100 DuPont Bldg, Wilmington, Del. 19898.

COPELAND, THOMAS L. R
Wash. State Rep.
b. Pendleton, Ore, 1924; m. to Dol'y C; c. three. Educ: Kemper Mil. Sch; Wash. State Univ; Sigma Nu. Polit. & Govt. Pos: Wash. State Rep, 7th term, speaker pro tem, Wash. House Rep, 67 & 69, Rep. floor leader, 65 session. Bus. & Prof. Pos: Farmer. Mil. Serv: Capt, Army. Mem: Elks; Am. Legion; Farm Bur; Masons; C. of C. Mailing Add: Route 3, Walla Walla, Wash. 99362.

COPELAND, WILLIAM R. D
Mich. State Rep.
b. Washington, Ind, 5/8/09; m. 1936 to Helen Kazmerski. Educ: High Sch. Grad. Polit. & Govt. Pos: Former mem, Wayne Co. Bd. of Supvrs. and City Coun. of Wyandotte; Mich. State Rep, 52- Bus. & Prof. Pos: Rigger. Mem: K. of C. (4°); Eagles (past pres); United Mines Workers (past pres, local 12100); W.Side Polish-Am. Citizens Club; S.End Citizens Club; Pennsalt Club. Rel: Catholic. Mailing Add: 3536 21st St, Wyandotte, Mich. 48192.

COPENHAVER, EVERETT TAYLOR R
State Auditor, Wyo.
b. Kinross, Iowa, 4/22/98; s. Milton Copenhaver and Sarah LeFever C; m. 2/19/30 to Ethel Gertrude Whitman; c. Evalyn Grace (Mrs. Peoples), Ross D. and Constance I.(Mrs. Peetz). Educ: Univ. Nebr, 17-19. Polit. & Govt. Pos: Chmn, Converse Co. Rep. Cent. Cmt, Wyo, 34-36; mem, Wyo. State Legis, 39-42; dep. secy. of state, Wyo, 43-44, asst. state examiner, 45-46, state auditor, 47-54 & 67-, secy. of state, 54-58, state treas, 63-67; treas, Wyo. Rep. State Cent. Cmt, 43-49. Bus. & Prof. Pos: Accountant. Mem: Odd Fellows; Rebekah; Mason; Eastern Star; Shrine; Consistory; KCCH (32°). Rel: Methodist. Legal Res: 404 W. Second Ave, Cheyenne, Wyo. 82001. Mailing Add: Room 116, State Capitol, Cheyenne, Wyo. 82001.

COPPEDGE, CECIL ROBERT R
Chmn, Madison Co. Rep. Cmt, Va.
b. Madison Co, Va, 7/27/99; s. Wesley William Coppedge and Effie Leathers C; single. Educ: Madison Col, 25-27. Polit. & Govt. Pos: Chmn, Madison Co. Rep. Cmt, Va, 26-; mem, Dist. Cong. Rep. Cmt, 26-; v.chmn, Va. State Rep. Cent. Cmt, 48-52. Bus. & Prof. Pos: Fruit grower and mgr, W.W. Coppedge Sons, 40-; gen. farming, 40-; dir, Shen-Valley Meat Packers, 48-; dir, Blue Ridge Fruit Growers, 45- Mem: Madison Co. Farm Bur; Va. State Hort. Soc. Rel: Baptist. Mailing Add: Ethan, Va. 22719.

COPPES, JOHN F. R
Ind. State Rep.
Educ: Purdue and Ind. Univs; Phi Gamma Delta. Polit. & Govt. Pos: Ind. State Rep, 59-; mem, Midwest Coun. of State Govts. Bus. & Prof. Pos: Mfr; pres, Nappanee Sch. Bldg. Corp. Mem: Past pres and past Lt. Gov, Kiwanis; Elks. Rel: Methodist. Mailing Add: 351 E. Walnut St, Napanee, Ind. 46550. (1967)

COPPS, LYMAN WILLIAM R
Chmn, Winnebago Co. Rep. Party, Wis.
b. Marshfield, Wis, 10/2/22; s. Dr. Lyman A. Copps and Stella Murat C; m. 6/12/46 to Charlotte Risch; c. Jane, Marcia and Paul. Educ: Univ. Wis, 40-42; Lawrence Univ, B.S, 47; Psi Upsilon. Polit. & Govt. Pos: Precinct chmn, Neenah Rep. Party, Wis, 55-60, chmn, 60-62; v.chmn, Winnebago Co. Rep. Party, 62-65, chmn, 65- Bus. & Prof. Pos: V.pres. and dir, Nat. Inst. of Locker and Freezer Provisioners, 54-56; chmn. publicity, Nat. Tissue Asn, 60-62. Mil. Serv: Entered as Pvt, Marine Corps Res, released as Lt.(jg), Naval Res, after serv. in Navy, Pac. Mem: Elks; Optimists. Rel: Presbyterian. Mailing Add: 303 11th St, Neenah, Wis. 54956.

CORAY, CARLA WINN R
V.chmn, Hawaii State Rep. Party
b. Smithfield, Utah, 8/25/25; d. William Frank Winn and Lavon Cragun W; m. 8/21/46 to Max S. Coray; c. Craig Winn and Lisa Nalani. Educ: Utah State Univ, B.S; Brigham Young Univ, grad. work; Univ. Hawaii, 66-67; Theta Alpha Phi; Lambda Rho; Alpha Sigma Nu; 12 Outstanding Sr. Class Mems. Fraternity; Spurs; ed, Univ. Yearbook. Polit. & Govt. Pos: Pres, Star Valley League of Rep. Women, Wyo, 56-57; pres, Kona League of Rep. Women, 61-64; W. Hawaii Rep. Rep. State Women's Adv. Coun, 63-64; del, Rep. Nat. Conv, 64; campaign chmn, W.Hawaii Rep, 64; Hawaii State Campaign Chmn, League of Rep. Women; first v.pres, Hawaii State Fedn. of Rep. Women, 67-68; newsletter ed, Oahu League of Rep. Women, 67-68; secy, Hawaii State Rep. Party, 67-68, chmn, 69, v.chmn, 69- Bus. & Prof. Pos: Drama co-chmn, Am. Asn. Univ. Women, 68. Mem: Pres, Southwest Dist. Wyo. Educ. Asn, 57-58, Southwest Dist. Speech Asn, 56-58 and Wyo. Speech Asn, 58; bd. dirs, Rocky Mountain Theater Conf, 55-57; pres, Afton Women's Club, Wyo, 56-57; Am. Educ. Theater Asn; Nat. Children's Theater Conf. Asn; West. Speech Asn; pres, Kona Commun. Theater, 64-65 and resident dir, 64-65; Kona Outdoor Circle; Kona Civic Club; Kona Yacht Club; Maunalua Triangle Commun. Asn, 66-; publicity chmn. and bd. dir, Honolulu Theatre for Youth, 68. Rel: Latter-Day Saint. Mailing Add: 83 Lunalilo Home Rd, Honolulu, Hawaii 96821.

CORBER, ROBERT JACK R
b. Topeka, Kans, 6/29/26; s. Alva Forrest Corber and Katherine Salzer C; m. 7/16/49 to Joan Irene Tennal; c. Janet, Suzanne, Wesley Sean and Robert Jack, II. Educ: Univ. Kans, B.S, in Aero Eng, 46; Washburn Univ, LL.B, cum laude, 50; Univ. Mich, Law Grad. Study, 50-51; Sigma Alpha Epsilon; Phi Alpha Delta. Polit. & Govt. Pos: Chmn, Arlington Co. Rep. Cmt, Va, 60-62; chmn, Tenth Cong. Dist. Rep. Cmt, 62-64; mem, Rep. Nat. Cmt, 64; alternate del, Rep. Nat. Conv, 64; chmn, Va. Rep. State Cent. Cmt, 64-68. Bus. & Prof. Pos: Partner and mem. exec. cmt, Steptoe & Johnson, 51- Mil. Serv: Entered as A/S, Navy, 44, released as Lt.(jg), 47. Publ: Co-auth, Federal Administrative Practice Manual, Jr. Bar Sect, D.C; 'Civil Aeronautics Board,' Admin. Law Rev, Am. Bar Asn, 64;'Interstate Charter Rights for Carriers of Passengers,' ICC Practitioners J, 2/67. Mem: Am. and D.C. Bar Asns; Am. Judicature Soc; Am. Legion; Optimist; C. of C; Int. Club of Wash; Boy Scouts; Oper. Patrick Henry (exec. cmt); State C. of C. Rel: Methodist. Mailing Add: 3701 N. Harrison St, Arlington, Va. 22207.

CORBETT, ALICE CATHERINE D
b. Seattle, Wash, 1929; d. Marshall Richard Reckard and Carolyn Bauer R; m. 1/17/48 to James J. Corbett. Educ: Univ. Ore, B.S, 48; Marylhurst Col, grad. work. Polit. & Govt. Pos: Pres, Multnomah Co. Young Dem, Ore, 54-56; v.chmn, Multnomah Co. Dem. Cent. Cmt, 56-58; credentials chmn, State Dem. Party, 56-58; Ore. State Sen, 59-67; Dem. Nat. Committeewoman, 60-68; del, Dem. Nat. Conv, 68. Bus. & Prof. Pos: Educator, Sch. Dist. 1, Portland, Ore. Publ: 'Retarded Children,' Ore. Dem, 54. Am. Asn. Univ. Women; Multnomah Athletic Club. Rel: Episcopalian. Mailing Add: 2222 N.E. Schuyler, Portland, Ore. 97212.

CORBETT, JAMES NEILSON, JR. D
Mayor, Tucson, Ariz.
b. Los Angeles, Calif. 9/26/24; s. James Neilson Corbett, Sr. and Josephine Roberts C; m. 7/19/47 to Jeanne Ann McQuown; c. Nancye Jeanne, Jamie Colleen, Paula Jo and William James. Educ: Univ. Ariz, 46-48; Kappa Sigma. Polit. & Govt. Pos: Ariz. State Rep, 56-58; city councilman, Tucson, Ariz, 63-67; mayor, Tucson, 67-; del, Dem. Nat. Conv, 68. Mil. Serv: Entered as A/S, Coast Guard, 42, released as Radioman 1st Class, 46, after serving in Southwest Pac, 44-46. Mem: Exec. cmt, League of Ariz. Cities & Towns; Am. Legion; VFW; DAV; Elks; F&AM; Tucson Contract Roofers Asn. Rel: Baptist-Methodist. Legal Res: 3415 E. Fifth St, Tucson, Ariz. 85716. Mailing Add: P.O. Box 5077, Tucson, Ariz. 85703.

CORBETT, JERRY G. D
Ill. State Rep.
b. Hardin, Ill, 1/19/17; s. Barth Corbett and Margaret Fisher C; m. 2/13/55 to Joan Dufner; c. Kelly Ann and J. Dufner. Educ: St. Louis Univ; Univ. Ill. Polit. & Govt. Pos: Precinct committeeman, Hardin, Ill, 60-; mem, Export Adv. Bd. Ill, 62-64; chmn, Calhoun Co. Dem. Cmt, 62-; chmn, Co. Chairmen's Orgn, 20th Dist, 64-67; cand. for reapportionment of Ill, 65; mem, Hwy. Planning Study Cmn. and Hwy. Safety Cmt, 66; mem, Local Govt. Selection Cmn, 67-69; Ill. State Rep, 50th Dist, 68- Bus. & Prof. Pos: Former owner, West. Auto, G.E. Appliance Store, nationwide grocery store and Int. Harvester Dealership, Hardin, Ill; owner, Corbett Farms, 54; owner, Corbett Ford, 56-; pres, Dufner-Corbett Chevrolet-Oldsmobile-Buick, Hermann, Mo, 60- Mil. Serv: Entered as Pvt, Army, 42, released as 1st Lt, 46, after serv. in Hq. Unit of Lord Louis Mountbatten, S.E. Asia Command, 43-46. Mem: Bd. dirs, Hermann Indust. Develop. Corp. and Mo. Auto Dealers Asn, 66; Nat. and Ill. Auto Dealers Asns; pres, Calhoun Co. Indust. Develop. Orgn; Am. Legion; VFW;

Nat. Farmers Orgn; Farm Bur; Feeders Asn. Ill; K. of C; Eagles; treas, Lions; v.pres, Hardin C. of C; Mo. Athletic Club. Played minor league baseball. Rel: Catholic. Mailing Add: French and County Rd, Hardin, Ill. 62047.

CORBETT, JOAN DUFNER D
Chairwoman, Calhoun Co. Dem. Cmt, Ill.
b. St. Louis, Mo, 2/4/28; d. Arthur E. Dufner and Cecelia Higgins D; m. 2/13/55 to Jerry G. Corbett; c. Kelly Ann and J. Dufner. Educ: Miss Hickey's Secretarial Sch, 48; Webster Col, B.S. in biol, 50; St. Louis Univ, B.S. in dietetics, 50. Polit. & Govt. Pos: Chairwoman, Calhoun Co. Dem. Cmt, Ill, 63-; pub. adminstr. and guardian, Calhoun Co. Bus. & Prof. Pos: v.pres, Dufner-Corbett Chevrolet, Oldsmobile, Buick, Hermann, Mo, 60-; mem. adv. bd, Famous-Barr Northwest Plaza, St. Louis, 66- Mem: Webster Col. Alumnae Asn; state dir. and chmn, Calhoun Co. Unit, Am. Cancer Soc, state secy, Ill. Div; pres, Hardin Women's Club; pres, 20th Dist. Bd. and mem. exec. bd. dirs, Ill. Fedn. Women's Clubs; Am. Legion Auxiliary. Organizer and leader, Girl Scouts, 56-59; organizer, job placement for high sch. students, 64-66, candy striper prog. for hosp. and nursing home, 64-66 and summer libr. prog. for children, 65-66; chosen for Webster Col. Alumna Profile. Rel: Catholic. Mailing Add: French and County Rd, Hardin, Ill. 62047.

CORBETT, LAWRENCE E, JR. R
N.Y. State Assemblyman
b. Ft. Edward, N.Y, 5/11/21; s. Lawrence E. Corbett and Mary Hurley C; m. to Joan V. Burns; c. Michael, John, Shiela. Educ: Siena Col, 48; N.Y. Law Sch, 52. Polit. & Govt. Pos: Mem. Town Bd, Ft. Edward, N.Y, 8 years; Justice of the Peace; N.Y. State Assemblyman, 63- Bus. & Prof. Pos; Past pres, dir. Wash. Co. Home for Aged Women, Greenwich. Mil. Serv: Navy, 3 1/2 years; Europe, Pac, Officer, Naval Res, 45-59. Mem: N.Y. State and Am. Bar Asns; v. pres, Wash. Co. Bar Asn; Am. Judicature Soc; Satterlee Hose Vol. Fire Co, Ft. Edward; exec. bd. Mohican Coun. Boy Scouts; K. of C; Lions; Glen Falls Country Club. Rel: Catholic. Mailing Add: 1 Grove St, Ft. Edward, N.Y. 12828.

CORBETT, ORVILLE WILLARD, JR. R
b. Prairie City, Ore, 4/3/28; s. Orville Willard Corbett and Mildred Leland C; m. 10/14/61 to Linda Robinson; c. Robb and Jon Freeman. Educ: Ore. State Univ, B.S, 53; Kappa Psi. Polit. & Govt. Pos: Mem, Ore. Bd. of Pharm, 63; mem, Burns Common Coun, 64-, pres, 65-; chmn, Harney Co. Rep. Cent. Cmt, 64-66; dir, Harney Co. Libr. Bd, 66-; chmn, State Pharmaceutical Polit. Action Cmt, currently. Bus. & Prof. Pos: Pres, Corbett Drug Co, Inc, 63- Mil. Serv: Entered as A/S, Navy, 46, released as Pharmacist Mate 3/C, U.S. Naval Hosp, Mare Island, Calif, 48; Victory Medal. Mem: Mason; Elks; Ore. State Pharmaceutical Asn; U.S. Jr. C. of C;(v.pres, 60-61); Ore. Jr. C. of C.(pres, 59-60); Harney Co. C. of C.(dir, 64-); mem, Ore. Emergency Planning, Health Group, 63- Rel: Episcopal; Vestry St. Andrews Episcopal Church, 63- and Senior Warden, 64- Mailing Add: 406 Broadway, Burns, Ore. 97720. (1967)

CORBETT, ROBERT J. R
U.S. Rep, Pa.
b. Pittsburgh, Pa, 8/25/05; s. Samuel James Corbett and Martha Henderson C; m. to Ruthe McClintock; c. Salley (Mrs. Donald Dunbar). Educ: Allegheny Col, A.B, 27; Univ. Pittsburgh, Wallace Res. Fel. in Hist. and M.A, 29; Phi Alpha Theta; Delta Sigma Rho; Phi Delta Theta. Hon. LL.D, Allegheny Col, 65. Polit. & Govt. Pos: U.S. Rep, 18th Dist, Pa, 38-40 & 44-, dean of Pa. Cong. Del, U.S. House Rep, ranking minority mem, Post Off. & Civil Serv. Cmt, mem, Armed Serv. Cmt, mem, House Rep. Policy Cmt; sheriff Allegheny Co, 41-43; alternate del, Rep. Nat. Conv, 68. Mem: Moose; Elks; Eagles; Kiwanis; Lions. Awarded Distinguished Serv. Cert, Pa. Am. Legion, 67. Rel: Presbyterian. Legal Res: 15 Devon Lane, Pittsburgh, Pa. 15202. Mailing Add: 2467 Rayburn House Office Bldg, Washington, D.C. 20515.

CORBIN, H. OHMER D
Chmn, Grand Isle Co. Dem. Cmt, Vt.
b. Dundee, Mich, 12/9/33; s. William J. Corbin and Marie Jacob C; single. Educ: Dundee High Sch. Polit. & Govt. Pos: Chmn, Grand Isle Co. Dem. Cmt, Vt, 63- Bus. & Prof. Pos: Supt. of Mfg, Thermal Wire of Am, 59- Mil. Serv: Entered as Pvt, Army, 55, released as Pfc, 57. Mem: K. of C; Grand Isle Develop. Corp. Rel: Catholic. Mailing Add: South Hero, Vt. 05486.

CORBIN, LELAND WAYNE R
Mem, Calif. Rep. State Cent. Cmt.
b. Brook, Ind, 9/11/14; s. Zephaniah Franklin Corbin and Sylvania Kemper C; m. 6/26/37 to Catherine Elizabeth Billet; c. David Wayne, Nancy (Mrs. Ransford B. Berry) and Elinor. Educ: Ind. Cent. Col, A.B, 36; Univ. N.Mex, M.A, 50; Univ. South. Calif, 2 summers; Univ. Calif. Exten, San Diego, 2 summers; San Diego State Col, 6 summers; Univ. Ind, Bloomington, 1 year. Polit. & Govt. Pos: Mem, Calif. Rep. Assembly, 64-; mem, Calif. Rep. State Cent. Cmt, 65-; sustaining mem, San Diego Co. Rep. Cent. Cmt, 67- and Rep. Nat. Cmt, 68- Bus. & Prof. Pos: Mem, Calif. State Coun. of Educ, Burlingame, Calif, 67- Mil. Serv: Entered as Ens, Navy Res, 44, released as Lt. (jg), 46, after serv. in Air Support Control Units, Pac. Area, 44-46; Lt, Naval Res.(Ret). Mem: Legis. coun, South. sect, Calif. Teachers Asn, 60-; Nat. Educ. Asn; San Diego Teachers Asn.(bd. dir, 63-68, v.pres, 68-69 and pres, 69-). Rel: Protestant. Mailing Add: 4470 Adair St, San Diego, Calif. 92107.

CORBITT, WILLA WALES D
Chmn, Fremont Co. Dem. Cent. Cmt, Wyo.
b. Cheyenne, Wyo; d. George Lincoln Wales and S. Fay Kelim W; wid; c. Claude Edward and Gilland Wales. Educ: Univ. Colo, B.A; Univ. Wyo, M.A; Kappa Delta Pi; Alpha Chi Omega. Polit. & Govt. Pos: Mayor, Riverton, Wyo, 56-64; Wyo. State Sen, Fremont Co, 64-67; mem, Wyo. Cmn. Status of Women, 66-; chmn, Fremont Co. Dem. Cent. Cmt, 68- Bus. & Prof. Pos: Teacher, High Sch. Mem: Delta Kappa Gamma; Eastern Star; Bus. & Prfnl. Women's Club. Rel: Episcopal. Mailing Add: 108 E. Jefferson, Riverton, Wyo. 82501.

CORCORAN, HOWARD V. R
Mem, Rep. Nat. Finance Cmt, Wash, D.C.
b. Wheeling, W.Va, 9/16/06; s. Harry P. Corcoran and Mary S. Gilligan C; m. 11/3/34 to Margaret M. Sears; c. Mary (Mrs. Richard Pauley), Harriet (Mrs. George Spillers), Margaret (Mrs. Charles Wendy), Howard V, Jr. and John N. Educ: W.Va. Univ, A.B. in Pre-Law, 29; Linsly Tech. Inst, Mech. Eng, 43; Univ. of Pa. Wharton Sch. of Finance, Investment Banking Inst, 3 years; Alpha Sigma Phi; Newman Club. Polit. & Govt. Pos: Chmn, Ohio Co. Rep. Finance Cmt, W.Va, 56-59; v.chmn, W.Va. Rep. State Exec. Cmt, 58-61; chmn, 61-64; chmn, Recruit for 60 Campaign, 60, W.Va. Rep. State Campaign, 60-62 and W.Va. Rep. Finance Cmt, 64-69; mem, W.Va. Rep. State Exec. Cmt, First Sen. Dist, 65-; chmn, Nixon For Pres. Cmt. and Nixon Agnew Cmt, 68; alternate del, Rep. Nat. Conv, 68; mem, Rep. Nat. Finance Cmt, Wash, D.C, 68- Bus. & Prof. Pos: Asst. gen. mgr, Wheeling Steel Corp, 32-52; past pres, Wheeling Hosp; chmn-treas, Corcoran Church Goods Co, W.Va, 52-69; v.pres. and mem. exec. cmt, W.Va. Hosp. Serv; gen. partner and allied mem, A.E. Masten & Co, 60-67. Mil. Serv: ROTC, 33-41. Mem: Investment Bankers of Am; Downtown Wheeling Assoc.(past pres); Bond Club of Pittsburgh; Rotary; K. of C; Knights of St. George; Serra Int; Pittsburgh Club; Ft. Henry Club; Wheeling Country Club; Juniper Club. Recipient of Papal Decoration, Knights of St. Gregory. Rel: Roman Catholic. Legal Res: 6 Brentwood, Crestwood Estates, Wheeling, W.Va. 26003. Mailing Add: P.O. Box 647, Wheeling, W.Va. 26003.

CORCORAN, JAMES PATRICK D
b. Brooklyn, N.Y, 1/5/44; s. Patrick J. Corcoran and Agnes V. Walsh C; single. Educ: Fordham Col, B.A, 65; Columbia Law Sch, J.D, 68; Phi Beta Kappa. Polit. & Govt. Pos: Alternate del, Dem. Nat. Conv, 68; pres, F.D.R, Independent Dem. Club, N.Y, 68- Bus. & Prof. Pos: Teacher, Cathedral High Sch, 68-70; head counsr, Hunts Point Neighborhood Youth Corps, 69. Mem: Am. and N.Y. Civil Liberties Union. Rel: Roman Catholic. Mailing Add: 2754 Grand Concourse, Bronx, N.Y. 10458.

CORCORAN, THOMAS JOSEPH D
Dem. Nat. Committeeman, Kans.
b. Dubuque, Iowa, 11/12/22; s. Clem T. Corcoran and Pauline May Banfield C; m. 9/2/45 to Evelyn Mary Solomon; c. Sister Kathleen, Thomas J, Jr, Patrica and Michael. Educ: Rockhurst Col, Mo; Shrivenham Univ, Eng; Alpha Delta Gamma. Polit. & Govt. Pos: Finance chmn, past state chmn. and treas, Kans. State Dem. Cmt; co-chmn, Kans. Kennedy Campaign Cmt, 60; finance chmn, Kans. Johnson & Humphrey Campaign Cmt, 64; past pres, Young Dem. of Kans; Dem. Nat. Committeeman, Kans, currently. Bus. & Prof. Pos: Mem, bd. dirs, Country Club Bank, Kansas City, Mo, 65-; v.pres, sales and mem, bd. dirs, Aristo Foods, Inc, 66- Mil. Serv: Entered as Pvt, Air Force, 42, released as Pfc, 45; ETO Ribbon with 3 Bronze Stars; Good Conduct Medal. Mem: VFW; K. of C. Rel: Catholic. Mailing Add: 7320 Chelmsford Rd, Topeka, Kans. 66614. (1967)

CORDEL, LAWRENCE A. D
Trustee, Mitchell Co, Kans.
b. Downs, Kans, 7/4/22; s. Matt. J. Cordel and Louise G. Pahls C; m. 10/5/49 to Virginia Ann Arend; c. Diana Lee and Larry James. Educ: St. Benedicts Col, Atchison, 42; St. Benedicts Glee Club; Raven Club. Polit. & Govt. Pos: Treas, Mitchell Co, Carr Creek Twp, 56-62, trustee, 62- Bus. & Prof. Pos: Farmer and stockman, 49; ins. salesman, Blakely Gen. Ins, 65. Mil. Serv: Entered as Pvt, Army, released as Platoon Sgt, 44, after serv. in 20th Armored Div, ETO; Four Campaign Ribbons. Mem: Elks; Am. Legion (Comdr); K. of C.(3° and 4°, comptroller 4°); Farmers Union (dir); Nat. Farmers Union; VFW. Rel: Catholic. Mailing Add: R.F.D, Cawker City, Kans. 67430.

CORDELL, JOSEPH EDWARD R
Chmn, Spalding Co. Rep. Cmt, Ga.
b. N.Y.C, N.Y, 6/10/14; s. John Joseph Cordell and Mary T. Purcell C; m. 3/28/42 to Catharine Imelda Scully; c. Lynn Virginia, Robert Joseph, Joan Barbara and Douglas Robert. Educ: St. John's Univ, B.S; Niagara Univ, M.A; Lamba Chi. Polit. & Govt. Pos: Mem. exec. cmt, Spalding Co. Rep. Party, Ga, 64-66, chmn, Spalding Co. Rep. Cmt, 66- Bus. & Prof. Pos: V.pres. of sales, South. States, Inc, 53-67; pres, Memco Mfg. Inc, Commack, N.Y, 67-; pres. & chmn, Memco Inc, Atlanta, Ga, 67-; chmn. bd, A and A Foundries, Inc, Lindenhurst, N.Y, 68- Mil. Serv: Entered as Ens, Navy, 41, released as Comdr, 46, recalled as Comdr, 53, serv. in Submarine Force, S.W. Pac; Navy Unit Citation; Asiatic-Pac. and Am. Theater Ribbons; Am. Defense Ribbon; Korean Serv. Medal; Submarine Combat Award; Armed Forces Ribbon; Victory Medal; Naval Res. Ribbon. Mem: Inst. Elec. & Electronics Eng; Am. Soc. Mil. Eng; Elks; Moose; Trade Center Club. High Sch. football and basketball and col. basketball. Rel: Roman Catholic. Mailing Add: 914 Mockingbird Lane, Griffin, Ga. 30223.

CORDINER, RALPH JARRON R
b. Walla Walla, Wash, 3/20/00; s. George M. Cordiner and Mary Jarron C; m. 6/24/25 to Gwyneth Annette Lewis; c. Jean (Mrs. Dougherty), Patricia (Mrs. Kiley), Nancy (Mrs. Judge) and Sallianne (Mrs. Lione, Jr). Educ: Whitman Col, B.S; Phi Delta Theta; Delta Sigma Rho. Hon. LL.D, Whitman Col, Union Col. and Stevens Inst. Tech. Polit. & Govt. Pos: Mem, bus. coun, Rep. Nat. Finance Cmt, 52-61 and chmn, 60-61, chmn, Rep. Nat. Finance Cmt, 64; chmn, Defense Adv. Cmt. on Prfnl. and Tech. Co, 56-58. Bus. & Prof. Pos: Chmn. and chief exec. officer, Gen. Elec. Co, 50-63; rancher, Dundee Ranch, Lutz, Fla, 54- Mil. Serv: Naval Officers' Cand. Sch, Bremerton, Wash, 18; Dept. Defense Cert. of Appreciation. Publ: New Frontiers for Professional Managers. Mem: Fel, Am. Acad. Arts and Sci; The Links Club and Univ. Club, N.Y; Cotton Bay Club, Eleuthera; Blind Brook Club, Port Chester, N.Y; Palma Ceia Golf & Country Club, Tampa, Fla. Rel: Presbyterian. Mailing Add: 155 Bayview Dr, Belleair, Clearwater, Fla. 33516.

CORDOVA, JORGE LUIS New Progressive, P.R.
Resident Cmnr, P.R.
b. Manatí, P.R, 4/20/07; m. to Dora Rodríguez; c. Jorge Luis, Jr, Elvira (Mrs. González), Irene (Mrs. Subirá) and Fernando. Educ: Cath. Univ. Am, B.A, 28; Harvard Univ, LL.B, 31. Polit. & Govt. Pos: From judge, Superior Court of P.R. to assoc. justice, Supreme Court of P.R, 40-46; resident cmnr, 69- Bus. & Prof. Pos: Attorney-at-law, San Juan, P.R, 31-40 & 46-68. Mem: P.R. and Fed. Bar Asns. Rel: Roman Catholic. Legal Res: 7 A St, Caparra, Bayamón, P.R. 00619. Mailing Add: 5519 Pollard Rd, Springfield, Bethesda, Md. 20016.

COREY, DEAN ORVILLE R
Iowa State Rep.
b. Morning Sun, Iowa, 8/6/21; s. John Leroy Corey and Maxie Martin C; m. 2/1/42 to Eva Mae Butcher; c. Michael David and Bruce Duane. Educ: Burlington Jr. Col, 1 year; Univ. Calif, Los Angeles, 2 years; S.Dak. Sch. of Mines, 1 semester. Polit. & Govt. Pos: Iowa State Rep, 69- Bus. & Prof. Pos: Elec. contractor, Iowa, 46-50; TV technician, Abbott's, Des Moines, 50-51; electronics instr, Am. Tech. Sch, 51-54; dir. electronics, Am. Tech. Sch. and Col. of Automation, 54-63; owner and dir, Nursing Home, Morning Sun, 63- Mil. Serv: Entered as Pvt, Army, 43, released as Sgt, 46, after serv. in Signal Corps, China-Burma-India, 45-46. Mem: Iowa and Am. Nursing Home Asns; Am. Legion; Lions. Rel: Methodist. Mailing Add: A St, Morning Sun, Iowa 52640.

COREY, WILLIAM WALTER D
b. Manchester, N.H, 10/13/98; married; c. Four. Educ: St. Joseph's High Sch, Manchester. Polit. & Govt. Pos: Del. to Constitutional Conv; former selectman; N.H. State Rep, until 68. Bus. & Prof. Pos: Semi-retired. Mem: Sch. Cmt; Manchester Asn. for Retarded Children; Irish-Am. Club; Lithuanian-Am. Club; E. Manchester Fish & Game Club. Rel: Roman Catholic. Mailing Add: 126 Union St, Manchester, N.H. 03103. (1967)

CORLEY, ROBERT TOWNSEND R
b. Linden, N.J, 7/5/14; m. to Evelyn Baumgardner; c. One daughter. Educ: Pa. State Univ, B.S, M.S; Univ. Nebr; Iowa State Univ, Ph.D. Polit. & Govt. Pos: Lister, Vt; town auditor; sch. dir; Vt. State Rep, 59-66. Bus. & Prof. Pos: Supvr, United Farmers of New Eng, until 48; registered Holstein cattle breeder, 48-; farmer; dairy bacteriologist, 8 years; Vt. State Cols. Bd. of Trustees. Mem: Mt. Vernon Lodge 8, F&AM; Lamoille Grange; Lamoille Co. Farm Bur.(pres). Rel: Protestant. Mailing Add: Wolcott, Vt. 05680. (1967)

CORMAN, JAMES C. D
U.S. Rep, Calif.
b. Galena, Kans, 10/20/20; m. 11/18/67 to Carole Jean Franda; c. Mary Anne and James C, Jr. Educ: Grad. Univ. Calif, Los Angeles, 42 and Univ. South Calif. Law Sch, 48. Polit. & Govt. Pos: Mem, City Coun. Los Angeles, 57-60; U.S. Rep, Calif, 60-, mem. Ways and Means Cmt. and Small Bus. Cmt. Bus. & Prof. Pos: Attorney-at-law, 49-57. Mil. Serv: Entered Marine Corps, 42, serv. in Third Marine Div, World War II at Bougainville, Gaum, Iwo Jima, released 46; reentered, 50 and released, 52; Lt. Col, Marine Corps Res. at present. Mem: Am, Calif, Los Angeles and San Fernando Valley Bar Asns; Elks; Lions; Am. Legion; VFW. Rel: Methodist. Mailing Add: 203 Cannon House Office Bldg, Washington, D.C. 20515.

CORMANEY, PATRICIA K. R
V.Chmn, Young Rep. Nat. Fedn, Region VIII.
b. Cokato, Minn, 8/8/39; d. Conrad F. Katzenmeyer and M. Victoria Ekstrand K.(deceased); m. 2/1/64 to Theodore M. Cormaney. Educ: Univ. Wis, 57-62; Phi Beta; Gamma Phi Beta. Polit. & Govt. Pos: Committeewoman, Wis. Fedn. Young Rep, 61-63 & 65-, nat. committeewoman, 63-65; mem. exec. cmt, Rep. Party Wis, 61-, v.chmn, Second Dist, 63-65; alternate del, Rep. Nat. Conv, 64; v.chmn, Young Rep. Nat. Fedn. Region VIII, 65- Bus. & Prof. Pos: Buyer, Harry S. Manchester, Inc, Madison, 62- Rel: Presbyterian. Mailing Add: 2322 W. Lawn Ave, Madison, Wis. 53711. (1967)

CORMANEY, THEODORE MICHAEL R
b. Buena Vista, Iowa, 7/2/37; s. Melvin Cormaney and Margaret Drackley C; m. 2/1/64 to Patricia Rae Katzenmeyer. Educ: Univ. Wis, 63. Polit. & Govt. Pos: Exec. secy, Wis. Fedn. Young Rep, 63-65; exec. secy, Rep. Assembly Campaign Cmt, 65-; analyst, Wis. State Assembly, 65-67, Rep. caucus pub. rels. dir, 67-; exec. dir, Young Rep. Nat. Fedn, D.C, 67-69; exec. asst. to Congressman William A. Steiger, 69- Mil. Serv: Entered as E-1 Air Force, 57, released as E-3, 60, after serv. in Air Intel. Serv, Alaskan Command. Rel: Episcopal. Legal Res: 2322 W. Lawn Ave, Madison, Wis. 53711. Mailing Add: 1025 Longworth Bldg, Washington, D.C, 20515.

CORNELIUS, STANLEY PRESTON R
Alaska State Rep.
b. Bremerton, Wash, 10/15/41; s. Starling Preston Cornelius and Virginia Sloat C; m. 1/18/64 to Mary Ann Randall. Educ: Wash. State Univ, 59-61; Alaska Methodist Univ, B.A, 64; Univ. N.Mex, J.D, 67; Pi Kappa Alpha. Polit. & Govt. Pos: Pres, Alaska Methodist Univ. Young Reps, 62-63; co-chmn, Stevens for U.S. Senate Cmts, 62 & 68; chmn, Southcent. Alaska Young Reps, 63-64; chmn, Col. & Youth Activities, Alaska Rockefeller for President Orgn, 64; Alaska State Rep, Anchorage Dist, 69- Bus. & Prof. Pos: Attorney, Robison, McCaskey, Strachan & Hoge, Attorneys, Alaska, 67- Mem: Alaska and Anchorage Bar Asns; Laborers Union, Musicians Union, Retail Clerks Union. Rel: Presbyterian. Mailing Add: 1901 Arctic Blvd, Anchorage, Alaska 99503.

CORNETT, HOMER WILSON, JR. D
b. Columbus, Ga, 3/1/23; s. Homer Wilson Cornett and Maud Lee Johns Crane C; m. 9/1/43 to Mary Elizabeth Mathews; c. Mary Booker and David Wilson. Educ: Mid. Ga. Col; Univ. Ala, LL.B; Phi Alpha Delta. Polit. & Govt. Pos: Ala. State Rep, 54-66. Bus. & Prof. Pos: Lawyer, Phenix City, Ala, 50- Mil. Serv: Col. in ROTC Unit; World War II, Lt, Marine Corps Pilot, Marshall Islands. Mem: Am. Legion; past pres, Lions Club. Rel: Baptist. Mailing Add: P.O. Box 88, Phenix City, Ala. 36867.

CORNETT, LEIGHTON M. D
b. Clarksville, Tex, 11/1/16; s. Harvey Marion Cornett and Ada Lillian McGuire C; m. 6/27/42 to Ruth Moore; c. Debra Kay and Guy Wayne. Educ: Paris Jr. Col; Univ. Tex, LL.B. Polit. & Govt. Pos: Del, Dem. Nat. Conv, 64 and 56; first asst. U.S. Attorney's Off, East. Dist. of Tex, Tyler, Tex, 61-63; co. and dist. attorney of Lamar Co, Tex, 52-60; mem, secy. and pres, Bd. of Regents, Paris Jr. Col, 50-60; Lamar Co. Campaign chmn, Kennedy-Johnson Campaign and Sen. Ralph Yarborough, 60; Tex. State Rep, 39-41. Mil. Serv: Entered as Pvt, Army, 41, released as Capt, 46. Mem: Oddfellows; Dist. Gov, 2-X-2, Lions, 59-60; Dep. Judge Advocate, Am. Legion, 50; VFW; Am. and Tex. Trial Lawyers Asn; State Bar of Tex. Rel: Baptist. Legal Res: 904 Pine Bluff St, Paris, Tex. 75460. Mailing Add: Williamson Bldg, 50 N. Main, Paris, Tex. 75460.

CORNING, ERASTUS II D
Mayor, Albany, N.Y.
b. Albany, N.Y, 10/7/09; s. Edwin Corning and Louise Maxwell C; m. 6/23/32 to Elizabeth N. Platt; c. Erastus III and Elizabeth (Mrs. Dudley). Educ: Yale Col, A.B, 32; Phi Beta Kappa; Chi Psi. Polit. & Govt. Pos: N.Y. State Assemblyman, 36; N.Y. State Sen, 37-41; mayor, Albany, N.Y, 42-; del, N.Y. State Constitutional Conv, 67; del, Dem. Nat. Conv, 68. Bus. & Prof. Pos: Pres, Albany Assocs, Inc, 32-; dir, Nat. Commercial Bank, 46-; pres, Ellsworth Builders Supply, 50-, Avrora, Inc, 55 and Union River Lumber Co, 66- Mil. Serv: Entered as Pvt, Army, 44, released as PFC, 45, after serving in 2nd Inf. Div, Europe, 44-45; Combat Inf. Badge. Mem: Am. Legion; VFW. Rel: Episcopal. Mailing Add: 116 S. Lake Ave, Albany, N.Y. 12208.

CORNISH, CHARLES EDWARD R
Asst. Treas, Md. State Rep. Cent. Cmt.
b. Cambridge, Md, 8/11/96; s. James Wesley Cornish and Sophia Stewart C; m. 7/27/20 to Margaretta Miller; c. Geraldine C.(Mrs. Smith) and Lillian C. (Mrs. Green). Educ: Morgan State Col, Hon. D.D.L, 55; Grad. Chapter, Pi Alpha Chapter, Omega Psi Phi. Polit. & Govt. Pos: Councilman, Cambridge, Md, 46-64, pres, city coun, 64-; asst. treas, Md. State Rep. Cent. Cmt, 64-; committeeman, Gov. Cmt. Civilian Defense and Md. Interracial Cmn; bd. mem, Cheltenham Boys' Village; del-at-lg, 2 Rep. Nat. Convs. Bus. & Prof. Pos: Dir, Cambridge-Md. Hosp, 62-65, United Fund of Dorchester, 65 and Wye Inst, 65-66. Mil. Serv: Entered as Pvt, Army, 18, released as Cpl, after serv. in Qm Corps. Mem: Mason (32°); Shrine; Elks; Int. Frontiers of Am; K. of P; C. of C; PTA (Pres, 43-55). Frontiers Int. Serv. Award for outstanding civic and commun. work, 63. Rel: Methodist. Mailing Add: 517 Pine St, Cambridge, Md. 21613. (1967)

CORNWALL, ROBERT DAVID R
Finance Chmn, Klamath Co. Rep. Cent. Cmt, Ore.
b. Syracuse, N.Y, 4/5/26; s. Alfred E. Cornwall, Sr. and Sally Sink C; m. 10/10/53 to Beverly Grace Voogt; c. Robert David and James Patrick. Educ: Pub. Schs, Syracuse and Skaneateles, N.Y. Polit. & Govt. Pos: Pres, 19th Dist. Rep. Assembly, Calif, 60-61; mem, San Francisco Co. Rep. Cent. Cmt, 60-61; mem. bd. of dirs, Calif. Rep. Assembly, 61; co. campaign chmn, Sen. Thomas Kuchel, 62; mem, Calif. State Rep. Cent. Cmt, 65-67, mem, exec. cmt, 67; chmn, Siskiyou Co. Rep. Cent. Cmt, 65-67; chmn, Calif. First Assembly Dist. Cmt, 66-67; area chmn, Calif. Rep. Co. Chmn. Asn, 67; co-chmn, Klamath Co, Ore. Secy of State Campaign, 68; del, Ore. Rep. State Conv, 68; finance chmn, Klamath Co. Rep. Cent. Cmt, 68- Bus. & Prof. Pos: V.pres, Ideas Unlimited, 58-63; sales mgr, Marco Adv, 63- Mil. Serv: Entered as Seaman 3/C, Navy, 44, released as Seaman 1/C, 46, after serv. at Receiving Sta, Philippine Islands; Victory Medal; Am. Theater, Asiatic-Pac. and ETO Medals; Philippine Liberation Ribbon. Mem: Past pres, Mt. Shasta Lions Club; Klamath Falls Lions Club; Elks; Klamath Co. C. of C. Polit. Lectr. to Cols, Schs. and other orgns. Rel: Episcopal. Mailing Add: 929 Pacific Terr, Klamath Falls, Ore. 97601.

CORNWELL, ELMER ECKERT, JR. D
b. Holyoke, Mass, 7/6/24; s. Elmer Eckert Cornwell, Sr. and Eloise Leining C; m. 4/2/49 to Barbara MacMillan; c. Alison and Joan. Educ: Williams Col, A.B, 48; Harvard Univ, A.M, 51, Ph.D, 53; Phi Beta Kappa. Polit. & Govt. Pos: Res. dir, R.I. Constitutional Conv, 65-; alternate del, Dem. Nat. Conv, 64 and 60. Bus. & Prof. Pos: Prof, Polit. Sci, Brown Univ, 65-, assoc. prof, 60-65, asst. prof, 55-60; instr. politics, Princeton Univ, 53-55; instr. polit. sci, Williams Col, 48-49. Mil. Serv: Entered as A/S, Navy Seabees, 43, released as Storekeeper 2/C. Publn: Presidential Leadership of Public Opinion, Ind. Univ. Press, 65. Rel: Congregational. Mailing Add: 26 Elgin St, Providence, R.I. 02906. (1967)

CORR, J. WILLIAM, JR. R
R.I. State Sen.
b. East Greenwich, R.I, 9/4/22; m. to Mary J. Educ: LaSalle Academy, Providence; Univ. R.I, 43. Polit. & Govt. Pos: Mem, East Greenwich Town Coun, R.I, 50-64; R.I. State Sen, 64- Bus. & Prof. Pos: Ins. agent. Mil. Serv: Army, 95th Inf. Div, World War II; Am. Seventh Div, Korean War. Mailing Add: 34 Cypress Court, East Greenwich, R.I. 02818. (1967)

CORR, WILLIAM ERVIN, JR. 'BILL' D
Miss. State Sen.
b. Birmingham, Ala, 2/12/36; married. Polit. & Govt. Pos: Miss. State Sen, currently. Bus. & Prof. Pos: Lawyer. Mem: Kappa Sigma; Omicron Delta Kappa; Phi Alpha Delta; Rotary Int; Lions; Jr. C. of C; Nat. Guard Asn; Panola, Miss. and Am. Bar Asns. Rel: Methodist. Mailing Add: P.O. Box 450, Sardis, Miss. 38666.

CORRIGAN, IONE ELAINE D
b. Oakdale, Calif, 11/8/17; d. Oliver Joseph Muscio and Gilda Pedranti M; m. 6/16/47 to Harold Albert Corrigan; c. Cathy, Rebecca, John and Ann. Educ: San Jose State Col, A.B, 40; Stanford Univ, 46; Stanislaus State Col, reading specialist, 66; Kappa Delta Pi. Polit. & Govt. Pos: Chmn, Oakdale Union High Sch. Bond Elec, 64; co-chmn, Bobby Kennedy Campaign, Stanislaus Co; del, Dem. Nat. Conv, 68. Bus. & Prof. Pos: Elem. sch. teacher, Oakdale, Calif, 40-47; home teacher for the ill or handicapped, 64-66; reading specialist, 66- Publ: 'Helping Parents to Instruct Their Children,' Co. Schs. Supt. Bul, 45. Mem: Am. Asn. Univ. Women; Stanislaus Co. Ment. Health Asn; Int. Reading Asn; Friends of the Libr; Oakdale Dem. Club; Stanislaus Co. Dem. Club. Rel: Catholic. Legal Res: 1274 Magnolia, Oakdale, Calif. 95361.

CORRIGAN, WILLIAM P. D
b. Baltimore, Md, 10/28/12. Educ: Baltimore parochial schs. Polit. & Govt. Pos: Md. State Del, 51-67. Bus. & Prof. Pos: Glass operator. Mem: Chmn, BBBA Local No. 18. Mailing Add: 432 E. Fort Ave, Baltimore, Md. 21230. (1967)

CORRIVEAU, ANTHONY J. R
b. Winthrop, Maine, 9/22/13; married. Educ: Chicago Tech. Col. Polit. & Govt. Pos: Mem, Rochester City Coun, State Apprenticeship Coun. and Governor's Adv. Coun. on Manpower and Training; N.H. State Rep, until 68. Bus. & Prof. Pos: Gen. supt. construction. Mil. Serv: Army, 41-45. Mem: Am. Legion; Elks. Rel: Christian. Mailing Add: 38 Prospect St, Rochester, N.H. 03867. (1967)

CORRIVEAU, PAUL J. R
Mass. State Rep.
b. Worcester, Mass, 7/3/30; Educ: Cole & Trade Sch, Southbridge; Franklin Tech. Inst. Polit. & Govt. Pos: Chmn, Sturbridge Rep. Town Cmt, Mass, and treas, 4 years; Sturbridge Tax Collector, 59-66; Mass. State Rep, 67- Bus. & Prof. Pos: Pratt & Whitney Aircraft Div, United Aircraft Corp, East Hartford, Conn. Mailing Add: Main St, Sturbridge, Mass. 01566.

CORSO, JOSEPH R. D
Justice, Supreme Court of N.Y.
b. Brooklyn, N.Y, 9/11/08; m. to Camilla; c. Mary Lynne and Joanne. Educ: Fordham Univ. Law Sch, 31. Polit. & Govt. Pos: N.Y. State Assemblyman, 48-66; judge, Civil Court, N.Y.C, 67-68; justice, Supreme Court of N.Y, 69- Mem: Past grand Knight of Bushwick Coun. 132, K. of C; Brooklyn and N.Y. State Bar Asns; Cath. Lawyers Guild. Mailing Add: 1579 DeKalb Ave, Brooklyn, N.Y. 11221.

CORSO, PHILIP LOUIS R
Chmn, Chicopee Rep. City Cmt, Mass.
b. Chicopee, Mass, 11/16/42; s. Philip L. Corso (deceased) and Rose A. Giblo C; m. 4/21/61 to Carol Lee Chinnock; c. Corrine and Christine. Educ: Westfield State Col, B.S.E, 64; Univ. Mass, M.A, 70. Polit. & Govt. Pos: Pres, Chicopee Young Rep, Mass, 63-64; co.chmn, Citizens for Nixon-Agnew, 68; chmn, Chicopee Rep. City Cmt, 68- Bus. & Prof. Pos: Soc. studies teacher, Chicopee High Sch, Mass, 64- Mem: Chicopee and Mass. Teachers Asns. Rel: Catholic. Mailing Add: 28 Sunnymeade Ave, Chicopee, Mass. 01020.

CORSON, NEAL CRAIG R
Maine State Rep.
b. Waterville, Maine, 8/24/47; s. Anson George Corson and Eileen Viola Thomas C; single. Educ: Univ. Maine, summer session; Bowdoin Col, 3½ years; Alpha Rho Upsilon. Polit. & Govt. Pos: Chmn, Maine Col. Rep, 67-68; Maine State Rep, 69- Mil. Serv: Army ROTC Cadet. Mailing Add: 9 Houghton St, Madison, Maine 04950.

CORSON, PHILIP LANGDON R
Treas, Rep. State Cmt, Pa.
b. Plymouth Meeting, Pa, 10/31/98; s. Walter Harris Corson and Katherine Irene Langdon C; m. 1/30/30 to Helen Payson. Educ: Haverford Col, B.A, 19. Hon. LL.D, Ursinus Col, 59. Polit. & Govt. Pos: V.chmn, Rep. Finance Cmt, Pa, 58-63; treas, Rep. State Cmt, of Pa, currently. Bus. & Prof. Pos: Pres, G. & W. H. Corson, Inc, Plymouth Meeting, Pa, 33-53, chmn. of the bd, 53-; dir, Hughes Foulkrod Co. and Pa. Mfrs. Asn. Ins. Co; dir. and mem. adv. cmt, Phila. Nat. Bank; mem. bd. of trustees, Germantown Acad. and Ursinus Col. Mil. Serv: Pvt, Army, 18-19. Mem: Merion Cricket Club; Mid-Ocean Club; Pinehurst Country Club; Plymouth Country Club; Racquet Club of Phila; Sunnybrook Golf Club. Phila. Amateur Golf Champion 25-29. Rel: Society of Friends. Mailing Add: Plymouth Meeting, Pa. 19462.

CORY, JAMES KENNETH D
Calif. State Assemblyman
b. Kansas City, Mo, 9/29/37; s. Clifford Cory and Mary Jane White C; m. 4/6/58 to Lucille Ann DesJardins; c. Philip, Janet and David. Educ: Orange Coast Col, 2 years; Univ. South. Calif, 3 years; Univ. Calif, 1 year; Delta Sigma Phi. Polit. & Govt. Pos: Consult. to Educ. Cmt, Calif. State Assembly, 61-63; chief admin. officer, Calif. Legis, 64-65; Calif. State Assemblyman, 69th Dist, 66-; del, Dem. Nat. Conv, 68. Bus. & Prof. Pos: V.pres, Cornet Ins. Counselors, Inc, currently. Mem: Mem, bd. dirs, Easter Seal Soc. Orange Co; mem, bd. dirs, Artificial Kidney Found; Westminster Elks (charter mem); first chmn, Westminster Merit Syst. Cmn. Rel: Protestant. Legal Res: 9051 Vons Dr, Garden Grove, Calif. 92641.. Mailing Add: State Capitol, Room 2167, Sacramento, Calif. 95814.

CORY, RICHARD HENRY D
Tex. State Rep.
b. San Mateo, Calif, 4/7/18; s. Isaac Henry Cory and Minnie Elias C; m. 7/22/44 to Marie Helen Witte; c. Mary Elizabeth and Susan Marie. Educ: San Francisco Jr. Col, B.S, 37; Univ. Calif, B.A, 39; Univ. Calif. Sch. Jurisprudence, Berkeley, J.D, 47; LL.D, Univ. Tex, San Antonio, 69; Phi Alpha Delta. Polit. & Govt. Pos: Judge, Victoria, Tex, 48-53; Tex. State Rep, 43rd Judicial Dist, 55- Bus. & Prof. Pos: Partner, Fly, Cory, Moeller and Stevenson, 63- Mil. Serv: Entered as Pvt, Army, 41, released as M/Sgt, 45, after serv. in Ord. and Inf; Presidential Citation. Mem: Am, Tex, and Victoria Co. Bar Asns; Elks; Kiwanis; Am. Legion; VFW; Farm Bur; YMCA; Audubon Soc; Mid-coastal Sportsmen Club; Tex. Midcoast Water Develop. Asn; Victoria C. of C. Outstanding Young Man Award, Jr. C. of C, 50; Outstanding Legislator in Field of Conserv. for Tex. Award, Tex. Outdoor Writers' Asn, 68; Sr. Citizen's Award, Tex. Rotary Clubs, 69. Rel: Catholic. Legal Res: 2601 Bon Aire, Victoria, Tex. 77901. Mailing Add: American Bank of Commerce Bldg, P.O. Box 3547, Victoria, Tex. 77901.

COSETTI, JOSEPH L. D
b. Youngstown, Ohio, 5/8/29; s. Raymond Cosetti and Mary Theodore C; single. Educ: Ohio State Univ, B.S. and M.B.A; Phi Kappa Sigma. Polit. & Govt. Pos: Del, Pa. Constitutional Conv, 67-68; nominated U.S. Rep, Pa, 68. Mil. Serv: Maj, Army Res. Mem: Am. Mkt. Asn.(v.pres, 67-68); Econ. Club Pittsburgh (treas); Nat. Asn. Bus. Economists; charter mem, Nat. Econ. Club; Pittsburgh Ski Club; bd. dirs, U.S. Amateur Ski Asn; Civic Club of Allegheny Co; West. Pa. Conserv. Rel: Baptist. Mailing Add: 428 Sulgrave Rd, Pittsburgh, Pa. 15211.

COSGROVE, DANIEL PATRICK D
Mem, Dem. State Cent. Cmt, Conn.
b. Branford, Conn, 11/19/17; s. James Cosgrove and Elizabeth O'Brien C; m. 6/3/39 to Alice Brown; c. Daniel T, Mark and Susan Barnes. Educ: Branford High Sch, Conn. Polit. & Govt. Pos: Mem, Dem. Town Cmt, 41-, treas, 46-62; cmnr, Branford Police Cmn, 48-51; minority leader, Branford Representative Town Meeting, 59-63; mem, Dem. State Cent. Cmt, 64-; alternate del, Dem. Nat. Conv, 64, del, 68; del, Dem. State Conv, 64, 66, 68 and Conn. Constitutional Conv, 65; mem, State Revenue Task Force, 69. Bus. & Prof. Pos: Pugilist, New Eng. Area, 36-39; pres, Cosgrove Construction Co. Inc, 40-, Cosgrove Equip. Co. Inc, 55- and Cosgrove Develop. Co. Inc, 66-; mem. exec. cmt, heavy construction div, Conn. Labor Cmn, 2 terms. Mem: K. of C.(4°); Elks; Red Men. Testimonial for dedication and citizenship to the town of Branford & the state of Conn; Elks testimonial for contributionas and efforts to Branford. Rel: Roman Catholic. Legal Res: 99 Todds Hill Rd, Branford, Conn. 06405. Mailing Add: 164 N. Main St, Branford, Conn. 06405.

COSGROVE, JOHN B. D
b. Utica, N.Y, 6/30/30; m. to Nuala Carmody; c. Christina Marie. Educ: Hamilton Col, B.A, 52; Albany Law Sch, 55. Polit. & Govt. Pos: N.Y. State Assemblyman, 64-66; Oneida Co. Charter Cmn; Oneida Co. Code Cmn, 60, 61. Bus. & Prof. Pos: Attorney. Mil. Serv: Army, Counterintelligence Corps Spec. Agert, 55-57. Mem: Holy Name Soc; N.Y. State Bar Asn. Mailing Add: 72 Utica St, Clinton, N.Y. 13323. (1967)

COSSAR, GEORGE PAYNE D
Miss. State Rep.
b. Webb, Miss, 8/26/07; s. John Harper Cossar and Lottie Pattison Thompson C; m. 12/31/33 to Elizabeth Finney; c. George Payne, Jr, John Thompson and Bill Finney. Educ: Univ. of Miss, LL.B, 31; Omicron Delta Kappa; Phi Alpha Delta; Sigma Nu. Polit. & Govt. Pos: Miss. State Rep, 44-48 & 52-; mem. bd, South. Regional Educ. Bd, 58-; mem, nat. exec. cmt, Nat. Conf. of State Legis. Leaders, 62-69; mem. adv. bd, South. Conf. Coun. of State Govts, 66-69. Bus. & Prof. Pos: Lawyer. Mem: State Bldg. Cmn. of State of Miss; Farm Bur; Delta Coun; Mason (32°); Scottish Rite; Shrine; Rotary (pres, Charleston Club, 54, gov, Dist. 680, Rotary Int, 57-68); pres, Ole Miss. Alumni Asn, 50-51. Named to Hall of Fame, Univ. of Miss, 31. Rel: Methodist; teacher of men's Bible class for 25 years. Legal Res: 109 Vine St, Charleston, Miss. 38921. Mailing Add: Cossar Bldg, Charleston, Miss. 38921.

COSTA, CATHERINE AURORA D
b. Brooklyn, N.Y, 3/21/26; d. Salvatore Bravo and Matilde Giamporcaro B; m. 9/7/46 to Joseph F. Costa; c. Nicholas Joseph, Theodore Matthew and Nadine Joan. Educ: Lafayette High Sch, Brooklyn, N.Y, grad. with honor, 43; George Wash. Secretarial Sch, N.Y.C. Polit. & Govt. Pos: Chmn, Local Assistance Bd, Levittown, N.J, 61; committeewoman, Willingboro Dem. Party, 61-, v.chmn, 63, chmn, 63-, v.pres, 64; dep. registr, Willingboro Twp, 61-; welfare dir, Levittown, N.J, 62; stenographer, Willingboro Zoning Bd. Adjustment, 62-66; cmnr, N.J. State Youth Cmn, 64-; corresponding secy, Burlington Co. Dem. Party, 65, v.chmn. exec. bd, 67-68; del. and mem. resolutions and platform cmt, Dem. Nat. Conv, 68; mem, Willingboro Zoning Bd. Adjustment, 69- Bus. & Prof. Pos: Secy, Nat. City Bank N.Y, 43-47; exec. secy, Vincent J. Bravo Inc, Advert. Agency, L.I, N.Y, 47-56; mem. and secy. bd. dirs, Seaford-Mar Marina, Inc, 53-56; fashion show dir. and unit mgr, Sarah Coventy Inc, Md. and N.J, 58-59; soc. news correspondent Burlington Co. Times, Willingboro, N.J, 61; real estate salesman and assoc, John P. McGarvey Real Estate, 65-; notary public, State N.J, 65- Mem: Levittown Libr. Asn.(v.pres, 59, founder, 59); trustee and secy. libr. bd. trustees, Willingboro Munic. Libr; Burlington Co. Women's Club; Willingboro Dem. Club; Women Div. Dem. State Cmt. N.J. Rel: Roman Catholic; First V.pres, Altar and Rosary Soc, Corpus Christi Church, 67-68; Teacher Relig. Pre-Schoolers, 65-67. Mailing Add: 6 Creekview Rd, Willingboro, N.J. 08046.

COSTA, FRANCIS R. D
Chmn, Jamestown Dem. Town Cmt, R.I.
b. Dighton, Mass, 7/27/24; m. to Lily Cabral C. Educ: Pub. Schs. of Somerset, Mass. Polit. & Govt. Pos: R.I. State Sen, 63-66; mem, Dem. State Cmt; chmn, Jamestown Dem. Town Cmt, currently; pres, Portuguese Dem. of R.I; Jamestown Planning Bd; past pres, Jamestown Town Coun; former mem, Jamestown Ferry Cmn. Bus. & Prof. Pos: Owner-operator, Jamestown Golf and Country Club. Mil. Serv: Army, 42-46, ETO. Mem: Am. Legion; VFW; Holy Ghost Soc. Mailing Add: Dewey Lane, Jamestown, R.I. 02835. (1967)

COSTA, MARY MEADE R
Div; c. Five. Polit. & Govt. Pos: State Rep. Party, V.Chmn; State Fedn. of Rep. Women; Rec. Secy, Oahu League of Rep. Women; Del. to Rep. Convs; Windward Fedn. of Rep. Women. Bus. & Prof. Pos: Ed, Rep. News; Realtor. Mem: Capitol Hill Club; Active, Girl Scouts, Red Cross, Nuuanu Elem. Sch. PTA, Commun. Asn, March of Dimes and Easter Seal drives. Mailing Add: 3317 Kaohinani Dr, Honolulu, Hawaii 96817.

COSTA, THOMAS J. R
N.J. State Assemblyman
b. Bronx, N.Y, 6/30/12; s. Joseph Costa and Mary Margarano C; m. 6/19/37 to Alvera Manewal; c. Arlene (Mrs. David Miller and Thomas J, Jr. Educ: New York Univ; John Marshall Law Sch. Polit. & Govt. Pos: Mem. bd. educ, Teaneck, N.J, 9 years, mayor, 4 years; N.J. State Assemblyman, 67- Mem: Teaneck Coun; Teaneck Planning Bd; Rotary (past pres, Teaneck Chap); Teaneck City Club (past pres); Teaneck Little League (past pres. and mgr); Teaneck Athletic Boosters (past pres); TABS Hall of fame; Bergen Co. Sister Elizabeth Kenny Found.(past chmn); treas, Teaneck Vol. Ambulance Corp; dir, Teaneck Commun. Chest; Police Athletic League (past dir); Babe Ruth League (past dir); Elks (charter mem, Teaneck Lodge); charter mem, Teaneck Chap. of Unico, Nat; Town and Gown Soc. of Fairleigh Dickinson Univ; former chmn. Fund Raising Appeals, March of Dimes; Man of the Year Award, Teaneck Chap. of Unico, Nat, 67. Legal Res: 284 Rutland Ave, Teaneck, N.J. 07666. Mailing Add: 691 Cedar Lane, Teaneck, N.J. 07666.

COSTA, WILLIAM THOMAS, JR. D
Committeeman, Vt. Dem. State Cmt.
b. St. Johnsbury, Vt, 6/9/32; s. William Thomas Costa, Sr. and Almina Botazzi C; m. 1/25/64 to Gay Buttura; c. Kelli Gay and Kara Almina. Educ: Norwich Univ, 51-53; Univ. Notre Dame, B.S. cum laude, 56; Sigma Alpha Epsilon. Polit. & Govt. Pos: V.chmn, Caledonia Co. Dem. Cmt, Vt, 61-63; town trustee, St. Johnsbury, 64-67, mem. zoning bd, 64-68; chmn, St. Johnsbury Dem. Cmt, 65-; committeeman, Vt. Dem. State Cmt, 65- Mil. Serv: Entered as 2nd Lt, Army, 56, released as 1st Lt, 58, after serv. in Qm. Corps, Metz, France, ETO, 57-58, Capt, Res, 58- Mem: Vt. Retail Asn.(dir, 68-); Vt. Retail Grocers Asn; Vt. Bowling Asn; K. of C; Rotary Int; Elks; Moose; St. Johnsbury C. of C.(trustee and secy, 59-62); St. Johnsbury Jr. C. of C.(first v.pres, 60-61, pres, 62-63); Vt. Jr. C. of C.(int. state dir, 63-

64); Jr. Chamber Int.(sen). Distinguished Serv. Award, St. Johnsbury Jr. C. of C. Rel: Roman Catholic. Mailing Add: One Woods Dr, St. Johnsbury, Vt. 05819.

COSTANTINI, EDMOND D
b. Wilkes-Barre, Pa, 12/26/32; s. Edmund S. Costantini and Armida Maturi C; m. 8/18/56 to Agnes Hansen; c. Lisa. Educ: N.Y. Univ, B.A, 54; Univ. Conn, M.A, 56; Univ. Calif, Ph.D, 66; Phi Beta Kappa, Pi Sigma Alpha. Polit. & Govt. Pos: Asst. to the North. Calif. campaign mgr, John Kennedy Campaign, 60; asst. campaign mgr, North. Calif, Salinger-for-Sen. Primary Campaign, 64; co. campaign coordinator, Gov. Edmund Brown Campaign, 66; staff secy. for educ, Gov. Calif, 66; pres, Davis Dem. Club, 67-68; mem, Co. Grand Jury, 67-68; mem, Calif. Dem. Adv. Coun, 67-69; co. campaign chmn, Robert Kennedy Campaign, 68; del, Dem. Nat. Conv, 68. Bus. & Prof. Pos: Research analyst pub. affairs, NBC-TV, N.Y, 61-62; research analyst, Inst. Gov. Studies, Univ. Calif, Berkeley, 62 & 64, teaching fel. soc. sci, 62-63; prof. polit. sci, Univ. Calif, Davis, 64- Mil. Serv: Entered as Pvt, Army, 57, released as Sp-4, 63. Publ: Politics and Parties in California, Macmillan, 70; 'Intraparty Attitude Conflict,' 63 and 'Competing Elites within a Political Party,' 69, West. Polit. Quart. Mem: Am. and West. Polit. Sci. Asn; Am. Civil Liberties Union. Falk Fel. Mailing Add: 828 Anderson Rd, Davis, Calif. 95616.

COSTANZA, MARGARET D
V.Chmn, Monroe Co. Dem. Cmt, N.Y.
b. LeRoy, N.Y, 11/28/32; s. Philip Joseph Costanza and Concetta Granata C; single. Educ: East High Sch, 46-50. Polit. & Govt. Pos: Exec. dir, Robert F. Kennedy Sen. Campaign, Rochester, N.Y, 64; v.chmn, Monroe Co. Dem. Cmt, 66-; chmn, N.Y. State Dem. Womens Conf, N.Y. State Dem. Cmt, 68; mem. adv. coun, Small Bus. Admin, 68- Bus. & Prof. Pos: Admin. asst. and exec. secy. to John J. Petrossi, Rochester, N.Y, 54-; mem. adv. cmt, Commun. Savings Bank, Rochester, N.Y, 69- Mem: Dir, Am. Cancer Soc, Rochester, N.Y; mem, Women's Coun. of the Rochester C. of C; secy, Rotary Horse Show Cmt, 65, 66 & 67. Rel: Roman Catholic. Legal Res: 68 Jerold St, Rochester, N.Y. 14609. Mailing Add: 105 Powers Bldg, Rochester, N.Y. 14614.

COSTANZO, NICHOLAS R
V.Chmn, Orange Co. Rep. Cmt, N.Y.
b. Middletown, N.J, 2/8/17; s. Sam Costanzo and Candito Meola C; m. 10/20/46 to Grace Ingrassia; c. Paul and Nicholas, Jr. Educ: Drake Univ, 37-39. Polit. & Govt. Pos: Mem, Middletown Men's Rep. Club, N.Y; sustaining mem, Rep. Nat. Cmt; mem, N.Y. State Gov. Club; chmn, First Ward Rep. Cmt, 61-63; chmn, Middletown Rep. Cmt, 63-67; v.chmn, Orange Co. Rep. Cmt, 67-69; supt, U.S. Assay Off, N.Y.C, 69- Mil. Serv: Entered as Pvt, Army, 42, released as S/Sgt, 46, after serv. in Field Artil, ETO, 44-46. Rel: Catholic. Mailing Add: 132 Wickham Ave, Middletown, N.Y. 10940.

COSTANZO, ROBERT FRANK D
b. Cleveland, Ohio, 3/29/09; s. Joseph Costanzo; m. 4/21/30 to Frances R. Saele; c. Robert, Jr. Educ: Hutchinson Cent. High Sch. Polit. & Govt. Pos: Mem, Erie Co. Dem. State Cmt, N.Y, 43; dep. dir. of water, Buffalo, 58-59, dep. dir. of streets, 59-62; dep. cmnr, N.Y. State Liquor Authority, 59-62; dep. city clerk, Buffalo, 63-65, dep. parks cmnr, 65-; ward chmn, Erie Co. Dem. Cmt; alternate del, Dem. Nat. Conv, 68. Mil. Serv: Entered as Pvt, Army, 43, released as Cpl, 44, after serv. with 1308 Eng. Camp Sutton, N.C. Mem: Past pres. and presently dir, Romulus Club Inc; Remus Club Inc; Local 264, AFL. Rel: Catholic. Mailing Add: 189 Hampshire St, Buffalo, N.Y. 14213.

COSTELLO, DANIEL E. D
b. E. St. Louis, Ill, 12/15/09; m. to Elsie Moore; c. six; five grandchildren. Educ: Pub. and parochial schs. of E. St. Louis. Polit. & Govt. Pos: Ill. State Sen; 3rd four-year term, E. Side Levee and Sanit. Dist. of St. Clair and Madison Cos. Mil. Serv: WWII. Mem: Orgn. Labor, Steamfitters Local 439, 20 years; K. of C; Am. Legion; Ancient Order of Hibernians; E. St. Louis C. of C. Mailing Add: 1528 N. 43rd St, E. St. Louis, Ill. 62204. (1967)

COSTELLO, EDWARD DENIS D
b. Milford, Mass, 6/4/05. Educ: Milford High Sch. Polit. & Gov. Pos: R.I. State Rep, 57-66; former Treas, Woonsocket Dem. City Cmt. Bus. & Prof. Pos: Gage grinder. Mem: Past grand Knight, K. of C, No. 113, Woonsocket. Mailing Add: 216 Farm St, Woonsocket, R.I. 02895. (1967)

COSTELLO, JAMES D
R.I. State Sen.
b. Providence, R.I, 2/25/17; m. to Elena Arute; c. Mary Ann and Deborah. Educ: Chrysler Corp-Master Technician Sch. and Ford Inst, N.Y; Brown Univ, exten. courses in state govt. and admin. Polit. & Govt. Pos: Mem, Lincoln Town Coun, R.I, 6 years; R.I. State Sen, 63- Bus. & Prof. Pos: Automobile Dealer; pres. and treas, Warwick Ford Co. and Jaelco Realty Co. Mem: Past pres, Cumberland-Lincoln Fraternal Order Police; v.pres, R.I. Dealer's Asn; Blackstone Valley Hist. Soc; Warwick Airport Lions Club; Lincoln Civil Defense; Lincoln K. of C. (4°); gov. bd, Pawtucket YMCA; secy. and treas, New Eng. Sports Asn. Mailing Add: Harris Ave, Lincoln, R.I. 02865.

COSTELLO, JOAN D. R
Rep. Committeewoman
b. Chicago, Ill, 10/22/33; d. Arthur C. Zappendorf and Dorothy Bundschuh Z; m. 6/13/53 to Edward J. Costello; c. Michael and Kelly. Educ: Sch. of the Art Inst, Chicago; Chicago Acad. of Fine Arts. Polit. & Govt. Pos: Ed, Young Rep. Newsletter, 60-61; secy, 23rd Ward Woman's Orgn, 61-62; v.pres. and dir, 23rd Ward Regional Rep. Orgn, 62-64; alternate del, Rep. Nat. Conv, 64 & del, 68; Rep. committeewoman, 23rd Ward Regional Rep. Party, 64-; secy, Chicago Committeewomen's Orgn, 66- Bus. & Prof. Pos: Dir, Motorcraft Elec, 60-; columnist, Vondrak Publ, 62- Mem: Nat. League of Am. Penwomen; De Paul Acad. Club; Clearing Women's Club; Clear-Ridge Hosp. Planning Cmt. Rel: Catholic. Mailing Add: 6340 S. Lorel Ave, Chicago, Ill. 60638. (1967)

COSTELLO, TIMOTHY WILLIAM Liberal
Dep. Mayor-City Adminstr, N.Y.C.
b. Brooklyn, N.Y; s. Thomas Costello and Mary Kine C; m. 12/27/41 to Genevieve Sullivan; c. Genevieve (Mrs. William Cusik), Joseph, Mary-Kay, Peter, John and Barbara. Educ: Fordham Univ, B.S, 37, M.A, 39 and Ph.D. in Psychol, 40. Polit. & Govt. Pos: Chmn, N.Y. State Liberal Party, 62-65; Dep. Mayor-City Adminstr, N.Y.C, 66- Bus. & Prof. Pos: Prof. psychol. and mgt, Grad. Sch. of Bus. Admin, N.Y. Univ, 46-66. Mil. Serv: 1st Lt, Army, 43-46. Publ: Abnormal Psychology (w. W. Coville and F.L. Rouke), 60; Psychology in Administration (w. Dr. S. Zalkind), Prentice Hall, 62. Mem: Am. Psychol. Asn; life mem, NAACP; bd. mem, Pride of Judea Children's Serv; bd. of dir, N.Y.C. Coun. on Econ. Educ; bd, Cath. Interracial Coun; prof. adv. bd, Daytop Village; bd. trustees, N.Y.C. Rand Inst; N.Y.C. mem, Bd. of Collective Bargaining; Fordham Univ. Coun; adv. bd, CHOOSE. Rel: Roman Catholic. Legal Res: 75 Landis Ave, Staten Island, N.Y. 10305. Mailing Add: Office of Administration, 250 Broadway, New York, N.Y. 10007.

COSTIKYAN, EDWARD N. D
b. Weehawken, N.J, 9/14/24; s. Mihran N. Costikyan and Berthe Muller C; m. 9/23/50 to Frances Holmgren; c. Gregory John and Emilie Berthe. Educ: Columbia Col, A.B, 47, Law Sch, LL.B, 49. Polit. & Govt. Pos: Leader, Eighth Assembly Dem. Dist, South. N.Y. Co, 55-65; del, Dem. State and Nat. Conv, 56-68; leader, N.Y. Co. Dem. Cmt, 62-64; campaign mgr, N.Y.C. Mayoral Slate, 65. Bus. & Prof. Pos: Partner, Paul, Weiss, Goldberg, Rifkind, Wharton & Garrison, N.Y.C, 60- Publ: Behind Closed Doors: Politics in the Public Interest, Harcourt, 66; 'Who Runs New York City', N.Y. Mag, 68. Mil. Serv: Entered as Pvt, Army, 42, released as 1st Lt, 46, after serv. in 17th Inf. Div, 7th Div, Pac, 45-46; Am. and Pac. Theater Ribbons. Mem: N.Y.C. Bar Asn; various civic and charitable orgns. Rel: Unitarian. Mailing Add: 310 E. 50th St, New York, N.Y. 10022.

COSTIN, CECIL GUERRY, JR. D
Chmn, Gulf Co. Dem. Exec. Cmt, Fla.
b. Port St. Joe, Fla, 10/15/23; s. Cecil Guerry Costin, Sr. and Lola Pridgeon C; m. 12/24/57 to Margaret Mixson; c. Charles Anthony and Margaret Renee. Educ: Univ. Fla, LL.B, 48; Delta Theta Phi; Pi Kappa Phi. Polit. & Govt. Pos: City attorney, Port St. Joe, Fla, 48-67; Fla. State Rep, Gulf Co, 53-63; attorney, Gulf Co. Sch. Bd, 60-; chmn, Gulf Co. Dem. Exec. Cmt, 61-; prosecuting attorney, Gulf Co, 68- Bus. & Prof. Pos: V.pres. and dir, Citizens Fed. Savings & Loan Asn, Port St. Joe, Fla, 58-; pres, St. Joe Natural Gas Co, Inc, 62- Mil. Serv: Entered as Air Cadet, Navy, 43, released as Ens. DL, 46. Mem: Pres, 14th Judicial Circuit Bar Asn, 53; Mason; Morocco Temple Shrine; Kiwanis. Rel: Baptist. Legal Res: 2005 Constitution Dr, Port St. Joe, Fla. 32456. Mailing Add: 221 Reid Ave, Port St. Joe, Fla. 32456.

COSTINE, ROBERT EDWIN R
b. St. Clairsville, Ohio, 5/16/23; s. John Elwood Costine and Jessie Wells Oliver C; m. 6/26/51 to Anna D. Lewis; c. Jane Ann. Educ: Ohio State Univ, 41-42. Polit. & Govt. Pos: Constable, Richland Twp, Ohio, 48-53, trustee, 53-66; precinct committeeman, Rep. Party, 62-65; chmn, Belmont Co. Rep. Exec. Cmt, 64-68. Bus. & Prof. Pos: Transportation supvr. for St. Clairsville Schs, St. Clairsville Richland Pub. Schs, 53-66. Mil. Serv: Pvt, Army, 43, Field Artil. Mem: Belmont Co. Trustees and Clerks Asn.(pres); Ohio State Trustees and Clerks Asn.(dir); Belmont Co. Health Adv. Coun.(pres); Belmont Co. Regional Planning Cmn; Ruritans; Am. Legion; Econ. Opportunity Act. Rel: Methodist. Mailing Add: R.D. 3, St. Clairsville, Ohio 43950. (1967)

COTE, JOSEPH LEO D
N.H. State Rep.
b. Concord, N.H, 9/13/14; s. Joseph A. Cote and Dina Marcotte C; m. Theresa N. Michaud; c. Joseph L, Jr, Linda (Mrs. Paul Bongiovanni), Candace (Mrs. Malcolm McDonald), Donna (Mrs. Larry Banks), Holly J. and Kendall. Educ: Cent. High Sch, grad, 34. Polit. & Govt. Pos: N.H. State Rep, 69- Bus. & Prof. Pos: Commercial pilot and flight instr, 37-65. Mil. Serv: Army Res, 42-43, Pvt; Naval Res, 43-44, A/S. Mem: Ox5 Club. Rel: Catholic. Mailing Add: 659 Hall St, Manchester, N.H. 03104.

CÔTÉ, MARGARET SULLIVAN D
N.H. State Rep.
b. Nashua, N.H, 3/13/98; d. Alfred E. Côté and Margaret Sullivan C; single. Educ: N.H. Univ, B.A, 22; Boston Univ, M.A, 50; Phi Kappa Phi; Alpha Chi Omega. Polit. & Govt. Pos: Mem, Nashua Bd. Educ, N.H, 64-; N.H. State Rep, 69- Bus. & Prof. Pos: Teacher, Nashua High Sch, N.H, 30-63, chmn. mod. lang. dept, 59-63; dir, N.H. Coun. for Better Schs, 63-69; instr. French, Daniel Webster Jr. Col, 68-69. Mem: Am. Asn. Teachers French; Nashua Teachers' Union; Am. Fedn. Teachers (past pres); charter mem, Nashua Commun. Concert Asn.(trustee); charter mem, Nashua Col. Club (past pres); Dem. Womens' Club; Womens' Auxiliary, St. Patrick Parish. Rel: Roman Catholic. Mailing Add: 273 Main St, Nashua, N.H. 03060.

COTHERN, HENRY D. D
Mem, Mo. State Dem. Cmt.
b. Clovis, N.Mex, 2/16/31; s. Thomas D. Cothern and J. Irene Stephens C; div; c. Michael D. and Steven L. Educ: Lamoni High Sch, grad. Polit. & Govt. Pos: Coordinator, East. Jackson Co. Dem. Club, Mo, 61-64; dir. bldg, Jackson Co, 62-63; pres, Jackson Co. Dem. Asn, 64-66; campaign dir, S. and East. Jackson Co. Young Dem, 66-; coordinator, East. Dem. Progress Cmt, 66-; coordinator, Cmt. Co. Progress, 66-; mem, Mo. State Dem. Cmt, 66-; campaign dir, Mo. Young Dem, 67-; del, Dem. Nat. Conv, 68. Bus. & Prof. Pos: Owner and operator of several different types of businesses; bus. consult, currently. Mil. Serv: Entered as Pvt, Marines, 50, released as Pfc, 52, after serv. in First Marines. Mem: Independence Sertoma Breakfast Club (pres, 67-68); Cub Scouts Am.(cub master 60); Boy Scouts (dir, 62); Firemen & Oilers Union. Distinguished Club Pres. Award, Independence Sertoma Club, 67-68. Rel: Reorganized Latter-day Saint. Mailing Add: 1422 Cliff Dr, Lake Lotawana, Mo. 64063.

COTTAM, HOWARD R.
N.Am. Rep, Food and Agr. Orgn. UN
b. St. George, Utah, 7/27/10; s. Heber Cottam and Edith Brooks C; m. 8/30/34 to Katherine Stokes; c. Lillian Meredith. Educ: Brigham Young Univ, A.B, 32; Univ. Wis, Ph.M, 38, Ph.D, 41. Polit. & Govt. Pos: Chief, Prog. Appraisal Div, War Food Admin, 42-44; agr. economist, Paris, 44-46; agr. attache, Rome, 46-47, first secy. and counsel, 47-50, couns. of embassy and

chief food and agr. div, Econ. Coop. Admin. Spec. Mission to Italy, 50-52; assigned to Nat. War Col, Wash, D.C, 52-53; coun. and dep. dir, U.S. Oper. Mission, Int. Coop. Admin, The Hague, 53-56; U.S. Minister and Dir. Oper, Mission, Rio de Janeiro, 56-60; dep. asst. secy. of state, Near East. and S.Asian Affairs, 60-63; U.S. Ambassador to Kuwait, 63-69; N.Am. Rep. Food and Agr. Orgn. UN, 69- Bus. & Prof. Pos: Research asst, fel, teaching asst. and asst. to dean of men, Univ. Wis, 35-39; research asst, Ohio State Univ, 39-40; asst. prof, Pa. State Col, 40-42. Mailing Add: 1325 C St. S.W, Washington, D.C. 20437.

COTTER, WILLIAM R. D
Treas, Conn. State Dem. Cent. Cmt.
b. Hartford, Conn, 7/18/26; s. William W. Cotter and Mary E. O'Loughlin C. Educ: Trinity Col, B.A, 49. Polit. & Govt. Pos: Treas, Hartford Dem. Town Cmt, Conn, 53-60; councilman, Hartford, Conn, 54-55; exec. aide to Gov. A.A. Ribicoff, 55-57; dep. ins. cmnr, 57-64, cmnr, 64-; treas, Conn. State Dem. Cent. Cmt, 62-; del, Dem. Nat. Conv, 64. Mem: K. of C; Exalted Ruler Elks; Wethersfield Country Club. Rel: Roman Catholic. Mailing Add: 247 Fairfield Ave, Hartford, Conn. 06114.

COTTINGHAM, EDWARD BENJAMIN D
S.C. State Rep.
b. Bennettsville, S.C, 6/27/28; s. Vance C. Cottingham and Margaret Waggoman C; m. 6/10/55 to Iris Evans; c. Iris Jean and Edward B, Jr. Educ: Univ. Va, 48-49; Univ. S.C, LL.B, 53; Phi Alpha Delta; Phi Kappa Sigma. Polit. & Govt. Pos: S.C. State Rep, 55-57 & 67-; trustee, Univ. S.C, 60; del, Dem. Nat. Conv, 60. Mil. Serv: Seaman, Navy, 46-48; 1st Lt, Air Force Res, 52. Mem: S.C. and Am. Bar Asns; Mason; VFW; Am. Legion; C. of C; Moose; Rel: Methodist. Legal Res: Lakeshore Dr, Bennettsville, S.C. 29512. Mailing Add: P.O. Box 386, Bennettsville, S.C. 29512.

COTTON, NORRIS R
U.S. Sen, N.H.
b. Warren, N.H, 5/11/00; s. Harry Lang Cotton and Elizabeth Moses C; m. 1927 to Ruth Isaacs C. Educ: Wesleyan Univ; George Wash. Univ. Law Sch. Polit. & Govt. Pos: Former clerk, N.H. State Sen; dist. attorney, Grafton Co, 33-39; justice, Munic. Court of Lebanon, N.H, 39-44; N.H. State Rep, 44-46; U.S. Rep, N.H, 47-54; U.S. Sen, N.H, 54- Bus. & Prof. Pos: Lawyer, firm of Cotton, Tesreau & Stebbins, Lebanon, N.H. Mem: Am, N.H, and Grafton Co. Bar Asns; Lebanon C. of C.(past Pres.); Odd Fellows; Mason; Rotary. Legal Res: 16 Kimball St, Lebanon, N.H. 03766. Mailing Add: U.S. Senate, Washington, D.C. 20510.

COTTON, ROBERT SANFORD D
Mont. State Sen.
B. Glasgow, Mont, 8/27/99; s. Nelson Cotton and Abbie Moses C; m. 7/8/30 to Marie S. Wilson; c. Roberta, Robert, Alleen, Marlene, James and Connie Kaye. Educ: Mont. State Univ. Polit. & Govt. Pos: Mont. State Sen, 43-45 & 51-; Mont. State Rep, 49. Mem: Elks; Mont. Farmers Union; Odd Fellows. Rel: Episcopal. Mailing Add: Box 27, Glasgow, Mont. 59230. (1967)

COTTON, W. DAVIS D
Chmn, Richland Parish Dem. Exec. Cmt, La.
b. Jonesville, La, 2/9/04; s. George Spencer Cotton and Elizabeth Davis C; m. 11/25/27 to Anna Mae Allen; c. Carole, Jean Ann and Stephen Wayne. Educ: La. State Univ. Law Sch, LL.B, 27, J.D, 69. Polit. & Govt. Pos: La. State Sen, 40-44; chmn, Richland Parish Dem. Exec. Cmt, 60- Bus. & Prof. Pos: Pres, First Nat. Bank, Rayville, La, 52- Mil. Serv: Entered as 1st Lt, Army, 42, released as Lt. Col, 46, after serv. in 17th Maj. Post, ETO; Bronze Star; ETO Ribbon with 2 Battle Stars. Mem: Mem. coun, La. Law Inst, 59-; Fel, Am. Bar Found; pres, La. State Bar Asn, 65-66; Mason (32°); pres, La. State Univ. Alumni Fedn, 69-70; Kiwanis, Dist. Gov, 40- and Int. Trustee, 41-42 and 46-48. Rel: Methodist. Legal Res: 219 Julia St, Rayville, La. 71269. Mailing Add: P.O. Box 719, Rayville, La. 71269.

COTTRELL, ARTHUR MAXSON, JR. R
Chmn, Hopkinton Rep. Town Cmt, R.I.
b. Westerly, R.I, 5/8/06; s. Arthur Maxson Cottrell and Virginia Hunkins C; m. 5/8/29 to Violet Harkness Hoegland Tangeman; c. John Trowbridge and Arthur Maxson, III. Educ: Georgetown Univ. Sch. of Foreign Serv, 27-28. Polit. & Govt. Pos: Councilman, Westerly, R.I, 38-39, pres. town coun, 40-45; R.I. State Sen, Westerly, 41-48; R.I. State Rep, 58-60; chmn, Hopkinton Rep. Town Cmt, currently; R.I. State Sen, Hopkinton, 60-68. Bus. & Prof. Pos: Secy, C.B. Cottrell & Sons Co, 31-53. Mil. Serv: Entered as Pfc, 101st Cavalry, N.Y. Nat. Guard, released as B.M. 2/C, after serv. with Coast Guard Temporary Res, 43-45. Mem: YMCA; C. of C; N.Y. Yacht Club; AAONMS; Elks; K. T; Fraternal Order of Police; Watch Hill Yacht Club; F&AM; Westerly Forest 107, TCL; RAM; Soc. of Colonial Wars. Rel: Episcopal. Legal Res: Broad St, Ashaway, R.I. 02804. Mailing Add: Box 37, Westerly, R.I. 02891.

COTTRELL, CORINNE LOUISE R
b. Denver, Colo, 6/30/04; d. Leonard Sanford Anderson and Emma Huober A; m. 6/1/37 to Joseph Frederick Cottrell (deceased). Educ: N. Denver High Sch, grad, 23. Polit. & Govt. Pos: Second dist. capt, Denver Rep. Party, Colo, 53-69; bill clerk, Colo. State Sen, 53- Mem: Denver Rep. Womans Club. Rel: Protestant. Mailing Add: 2238 Julian St, Denver, Colo. 80211.

COTTRELL, GEORGE CAREY D
R.I. State Rep.
b. Newport, R.I, 10/15/36; s. James Joseph Cottrell and Elizabeth Harper C; m. 6/23/55 to Margaret Jane Smith; c. James Joseph, II, George C, Jr, Michael Henry and Patrick Brian. Educ: New England Inst. of Anat. and Mortuary Sci, Boston, Mass, grad, 59. Polit. & Govt. Pos: Newport City Planning Bd. Mem, R.I, 65-68; R.I. State Rep, 97th Dist, 69- Mil. Serv: Entered as Pvt. E-1, Army, 54, released as Sgt. E-5, 58, after serv. in 11th Airborne Div; reentered as Sgt. E-5, 59-62 and serv. in 2nd Armored Div. Mem: Alumni Asn. of New England Inst; K. of C; Newport Men's Dem. Club. Rel: Roman Catholic. Mailing Add: 39 Warner St, Newport, R.I. 02840.

COTTRELL, JOHN BOARDMAN, JR. D
Maine State Rep.
b. Brooklyn, N.Y, 5/15/98; s. John Boardman Cottrell and Julia Randolph C; m. 1/23/26 to Ann Morgan Clark; c. Susan, Nancy and John B, III. Educ: Colgate Univ, B.S, 20; Columbia and Union Theol. Sem, grad. study, 23-25; Am. Col. Life Underwriters, C.L.U, 50; Delta Kappa Epsilon; varsity football-basketball player, Colgate Univ. Polit. & Govt. Pos: Maine State Rep, 63- Bus. & Prof. Pos: Coach, football and basketball, Portland, Maine, 35-49; teacher high sch, Portland, 35-55; underwriter, life ins, 44- Mil. Serv: 18-19. Mem: Mason; Am. Legion. Rel: Congregational. Mailing Add: 36 June St, Portland, Maine 04102. (1967)

COUDERT, FREDERIC REÑE R
b. N.Y.C, 5/7/98; s. Frederic Reñe Coudert and Alice T. Wilmerding C; m. Oct. 1931 to Paula Murray. Educ: Columbia Univ, B.A, 18, LL.B, 22; Kent Scholar, Columbia Univ. Polit. & Govt. Pos: Asst. U.S. Attorney, S. Dist, N.Y, 24-25; chmn, N.Y. Lawyers Cmt. against Jones Act, 29; Rep. cand. for Dist. Attorney, N.Y. Co, 29; N.Y. State Sen, 39-46; mem, Temporary State Cmn. on Govt. Opers, N.Y.C, 59-61; U.S. Rep, N.Y, 80th to 85th Cong. Bus. & Prof. Pos: Lawyer, mem. firm Coudert Bros, 24- Mil. Serv: Army, 17-18; AEF; 1st Lt, 105th Inf, 27th Div; Decorated Chevallier Legion of Honor, France. Mem: Am. and N.Y. State Bar Asns; Asn. of the Bar of the City of N.Y; N.Y. Co. Lawyers Asn; Century, Pilgrim, Raquet and Tennis, Piping Rock, Seawanhaka, Corinthian Yacht and N.Y. Yacht Clubs. Received Univ. medal for distinguished pub. serv. from Columbia, 41. Mailing Add: Pan Am. Bldg, 200 Park Ave, New York, N.Y. 10017.

COUGHLIN, JOHN DENNIS R
N.Dak. State Sen.
b. Scobey, Mont, 2/5/18; s. Richard James Coughlin and Gertrude McMallan C; m. 8/5/42 to Virginia Maureen Hyde; c. Mary Virginia, Jean Ann and John Dennis. Educ: Univ. Notre Dame, 40. Polit. & Govt. Pos: Treas, Ward Co. Rep. Party, N.Dak, 58-; mem, N.Dak. State Bd. Pardons, 59-; N.Dak. State Sen, 67- Bus. & Prof. Pos: Pres, Williston Basin Gas Co, Minot, N.Dak, 54-; dir. and pres, Westland Oil Co, 60-; dir, Union Nat. Bank. Mem: K. of C; Elks; Rotary; Minot Country Club; Minot C. of C.(pres, 59-); Nat. Oil Marketers Asn; bd. dirs, St. Josephs Hosp, John Moses Vet. Hosp, Ryan H.S, N.W. Petroleum Asn, Am. Trucking Asn, N.Dak. Motor Carriers Asn, N.Dak. Stockmens Asn. and Farm Bur. Rel: Catholic. Legal Res: Route 1, Minot, N.Dak. 58701. Mailing Add: P.O. Box 1213, Minot, N.Dak. 58701.

COUGHLIN, R. LAWRENCE, JR. R
U.S. Rep, Pa.
b. Wilkes Barre, Pa, 4/11/29; s. R. Lawrence Coughlin and Evelyn Wich C; m. 9/6/58 to Elizabeth P. S. Worrell; c. Elizabeth S, Lynne W, Sara S. and R. Lawrence, III. Educ: Yale Univ, B.A, 50; Harvard Sch. Bus. Admin, M.B.A, 54; Temple Law Sch, LL.B, 58; St. Anthony Soc. Polit. & Govt. Pos: Pa. State Rep, 65-66; Pa. State Sen, 67-68; U.S. Rep, 13th Dist, Pa, 69- Bus. & Prof. Pos: Plant foreman, Heintz Mfg. Co, Phila, Pa; attorney-at-law and former partner, Saul, Ewing, Remick & Saul, 60-66. Mil. Serv: Entered as 2nd Lt, Marine Corps, 50, released as Capt, 53. Mem: Dir, Rosemont-Villanova Civic Asn; Big Brother Asn; Friendly Sons of St. Patrick; Easter Seal Soc. Outstanding Young Man, Main Line Jr. C. of C, Ardmore, Pa, 65. Rel: Episcopal. Legal Res: 829 Mt. Moro Rd, Villanova, Pa. 19085. Mailing Add: 1726 Longworth Bldg, Washington, D.C. 20515.

COUGHLIN, VIRGINIA MAURINE R
Mem-at-lg, Bd. of Dirs, Nat. Fedn. of Rep. Women, N.Dak.
b. Conception Junction, Mo, 9/21/16; d. Ahi F. Hyde and Elizabeth Simonieg H; m. 8/5/42 to John Dennis Coughlin; c. Mary, Jean and John. Educ: Mont. Univ. Summer Sch, 38; Minot State Col, B.A, 41; Phi Theta; Delta Epsilon Phi; Newman Club. Polit. & Govt. Pos: V.pres, Minot Rep. Women's Club, N.Dak, 59-61, pres, 61-63; pres, N.Dak. Fedn. Rep. Women, 63-65, del, Rep. Nat. Conv, 64; mem-at-lg, bd. dirs, Nat. Fedn. of Rep. Women, N.Dak, 65- Bus. & Prof. Pos: Teacher rural sch, Minot, N.Dak, 35-36, Velva, N.Dak. Pub. Schs, 36-39 and Minot Bus. Col, 41; secy, U.S. Air Force, 42-43. Mem: Minot Art Club; PTA; Our Lady of Grace Confraternity; Farm Bur; N.Dak. Cowbelles; Minot Symphony Asn. Rel: Roman Catholic. Legal Res: Rural, Minot, N.Dak. 58701. Mailing Add: Box 1273, Minot, N.Dak. 58701.

COULSON, ROBERT R
Ill. State Sen.
b. Grayslake, Ill, 5/10/12; c. three. Educ: Dartmouth Col, A.B; Univ. of Chicago, J.D. Polit. & Govt. Pos: Ill. State Rep, 70th, 71st and 72nd Gen. Assemblies; mayor, Waukegan, 49-57; former asst. state's attorney, Lake Co; Ill. State Sen, 62- Mil. Serv: 41-46, counter-intel, OSS agent in China-Burma; Lt. Col, U.S. Inf. Res. Mem: Am. Legion; Shrine; Lake Co. Bar Asn. Mailing Add: 1031 Pacific Ave, Waukegan, Ill. 60085.

COULTER, RAYMOND CURTIS R
Dep. Solicitor, Dept. of the Interior
b. Phila, Pa, 4/8/18; s. Clifton Alison Coulter (deceased) and Elizabeth Mae Hankey C.(deceased); m. 11/22/42 to Ruth Melvina Waldo; c. Linda Alison (Mrs. Andrew Mayo) and Robert Waldo. Educ: Univ. Ore, B.S, 40 and LL.B, 47; Phi Alpha Delta. Polit. & Govt. Pos: Ore. State Rep, 49-51; gen. counsel, League of Ore. Cities, 52-56; regional solicitor, Dept. of the Interior, Portland, Ore, 57-62, asst. solicitor for power, Wash, D.C, 62-66, assoc. solicitor, div. of water resources and procurement, 66-69, dep. solicitor, dept, 69- Bus. & Prof. Pos: Attorney-at-law, Grants Pass, Ore, 47-52 and Eugene, 56-57. Mil. Serv: Entered as Pvt, Army, 42, released as Capt, 46, after serv. in IV Corps Hq. in Italy, Mediterranean Theatre, 44-45. Mem: Ore. State Bar; Fed. Bar of Ore; Ore. State Soc. of Wash, D.C. Rel: Presbyterian. Mailing Add: 3830 N. Oakland St, Arlington, Va. 22207.

COULTER, WILLIAM ALFRED R
b. Palmer, Mass, 6/3/23; s. Alfred Coulter and Jane Henry C; m. 4/19/48 to Constance Elaine Moore; c. Carol Elaine, Susan Mae and James Alfred. Educ: Northeast. Univ, 1 year; Lynchburg Col, 1 year. Polit. & Govt. Pos: Assessor, Palmer, Mass, 16 years, chief assessor, 5 years; mem, Palmer Rep. Town Cmt, 15 years, chmn, 6 years. Bus. & Prof. Pos: Folding paper box salesman, Fed. Paper Bd, 21 years, plant mgr, Palmer Div, 24 years; trustee, Wing Mem. Hosp, 8 years; corporator, Palmer Savings Bank, 5 years. Mil. Serv: Entered as Pvt, Army Air Force, 43, released as Flight Officer, 45, after serv. in 8th Air Force. Mem: Blue Lodge Mason; Scottish Rite, Melha Temple Shriner; Lions; C. of C. Football, Basketball, Softball and Golf. Rel: Protestant. Mailing Add: 77 Squier St, Palmer, Mass. 01069.

COULTRAP, SUSAN ANN R
b. Chicago, Ill; d. Ray Coultrap and Margaret V.H. Slack C; single. Educ: George Wash. Univ, B.A, 53; Phi Beta Kappa; Pi Beta Phi; Pi Gamma Mu. Polit. & Govt. Pos: Secy, Rep. Nat. Cmt, Wash, D.C, 53-54; personal secy. to U.S. Rep. Bentley, 54-55; former secy. and legis. asst. to U.S. Rep. Derwinski, Ill; secy. to v.pres. Richard Nixon, 60. Mem: D.C. Young Rep. Rel: Episcopal. Mailing Add: 4201 Cathedral Ave. N.W, Washington, D.C. 20016. (1967)

COUNCIL, MARY LEE D
b. Seattle, Wash, 5/2/15; d. Walter Wooten and Virginia Scurry C. Educ: Univ. Calif. Polit. & Govt. Pos: Former admin. asst, Sen. Bartlett, Alaska. Received Alaska Press Club Award for weekly Cong. Newsletter. Mailing Add: 2801 Quebec St. N.W, Washington, D.C. 20006.

COUNTERMARSH, ERNEST R. D
b. 12/20/16; married; c. Five. Educ: Amherst Col, Specialized courses. Polit. & Govt. Pos: Former asst. legis. agent, R.R. Brotherhood of Trainmen; former clerk, Lebanon Regional Airport Authority, N.H; former mem, Spec. Cmn. on Non-Resident Taxation; former Ward Moderator; town moderator, 4 terms; chmn, Lebanon Water Cmn, 4 terms; former secy, Lebanon Planning Bd; former city councilor, Lebanon; former Dem. State Committeeman; former chmn, Lebanon Dem. City Cmt; former v.chmn, N.H. State Dem. Party; former chmn, Grafton Co; N.H. State Rep, 45-67; del, Dem. Nat. Conv, 60. Bus. & Prof. Pos: Former water works operator; conductor, B. & M. R.R. Mil. Serv: Marine Corps, World War II. Mem: C. of C; Am. Legion; Elks; Mascoma Club; R.R. Brotherhood of Trainmen; N.H. Munic. Asn; N.H. Water Works Asn; N.E. Water Works Asn; Am. Water Works Asn; N.H. State Aeronautics Cmn. Rel: Catholic. Mailing Add: 5 West St, Lebanon, N.H. 03766. (1967)

COUNTS, THELMA EVELYN D
b. Tom's Creek, Va, 4/9/05; d. Thomas Scott Tate and Kathleen Meade T; m. 6/1/35 to James Palmer Counts; c. twins, Thomas M. and James T. Educ: Radford Col; Univ. Va. Polit. & Govt. Pos: Del, Dem. Nat. Conv, 64 & 68. Mem: Va. Fedn. of Women's Club; first v.pres, Coeburn Women's Club; Wise Co. Dem. Woman's Club; life mem, PTA; Retired Teacher's Asn. Rel: Methodist; active in children's dept, 24-56. Mailing Add: Box 66, Coeburn, Va. 24230. (1967)

COURNOYER, WILFRED W. D
N.H. State Rep.
b. Ashburnham, Mass, 10/4/11; married; c. Three. Educ: Conant High Sch. Polit. & Govt. Pos: N.H. State Rep, 61- Bus. & Prof. Pos: Operates Variety Store. Mil. Serv: Prfnl. Soldier, 36-56; retired, Chief Warrant Officer 2. Mem: K. of C.(3°); ROA; Holy Name Soc; Am. Legion; VFW. Rel: Catholic. Mailing Add: 58 Stratten Rd, Jaffrey, N.H. 03452. (1967)

COURSE, KENNETH W. D
Ill. State Rep.
b. Chicago, Ill; single. Educ: DePaul Univ; C.P.A. coaching, LaSalle Extension Univ; Polit. & Govt. Pos: Ill. State Rep, currently. Bus. & Prof. Pos: Wholesale, retail fuel oil. Mil. Serv: World War II, 101st Airbone Div. Mem: Moose; Lions; Am. Legion; VFW; K. of C. Mailing Add: 3413 W. Armitage Ave, Chicago, Ill. 60647. (1967)

COURTNEY, RICHARD TRAVERS, JR. D
Mem, Worcester Dem. City Cmt, Mass.
b. Worcester, Mass, 8/12/23; s. Richard Travers Courtney and Marguerite L. Dubois C; m. 5/29/48 to Densye M. Tasse; c. Denise (Mrs. Lovendale), Richard T, III, Michael C, Suzette M, Marie Patrice, Mark E, Colleen M, Timothy J, Christopher E, Francis L, Sean J, Peter and Kerry. Educ: Univ. Buffalo, 43; Boston Col. Sch. Bus. Admin, 46-48; Sch. Law, J.D, 50. Polit. & Govt. Pos: Mem, Worcester Dem. City Cmt, Mass, 64-; alternate del, Dem. Nat. Conv, 68. Bus. & Prof. Pos: Judge advocate, U.S. Air Force, Carsell Air Force Base, Ft. Worth, Tex, 51-53; lawyer, Worcester, Mass, 53-; pub. defender, Worcester, 60-63. Mil. Serv: Entered as Pvt, Army Air Force, 43, released as 1st Lt, 45, after serv. in 15th Air Force 750 Bombardment Group, ETO, 44-45; Air Medal with Two Clusters; European Battle Ribbon with Four Stars. Mem: Worcester Co. Bar Asn; Am. Trial Lawyers Asn; Am. Judicial Soc; K. of C; Large Families of Am; Worcester Area Asn. Retarded Children; Dem. Nat. Cmt; Worcester Friends of Pub. Schs; Harmony Club, Worcester. Rel: Catholic. Legal Res: 20 Fourth St, Worcester, Mass. 01608. Mailing Add: 507 Main St, Worcester, Mass. 01608.

COURTNEY, WAYNE NEELY D
Ark. State Rep.
b. Forrest City, Ark, 10/19/35; s. Richard Dale Courtney and Genevieve Melton C; m. 8/27/54 to Gloria Kay Cox; c. Sonya Kay, Linda Susan, Cynthia Lea and Cheryl Ann. Educ: Ark. State Col, 1 year. Polit. & Govt. Pos: Ark. State Rep, Position 2, 69- Mil. Serv: Entered as Pvt, Ark. Nat. Guard, 52, released as Sgt, 59, after serv. in SVC Battery 5 How. Bn. Mem: Farm Bur; Mason; Prod. Credit Asn.(adv. cmt, 64-); Kiwanis (pres, 66-67). Outstanding Young Farmer, Jaycees, 66; Farm Family Year Award, Daily Times Herald, 66. Rel: Baptist. Mailing Add: R.R. 1, Forrest City, Ark. 72335.

COUSSOULE, HECTOR D
N.H. State Rep.
b. Somersworth, N.H, 5/9/16; s. Gregory Coussoule and Rose Triantafilou C; m. 12/14/41 to Zephyra Sideris 'Sally'; c. Marilyn (Mrs. Robert O. Nelson). Educ: Newburyport High Sch, Mass, 4 years. Polit. & Govt. Pos: N.H. State Rep, 63-67 & 69- Bus. & Prof. Pos: Restaurant Owner. Mil. Serv: S/Sgt, 26th Div, 41-45. Mem: Ahepa; Elks; Am. Legion; VFW; Greek-Am. Progressive Asn; Portsmouth Restaurant Asn. Rel: Greek Orthodox. Mailing Add: 250 Hanover St, Portsmouth, N.H. 03801.

COUTERMARSH, GEORGE EARL D
Vt. State Rep.
b. Hartford, Vt, 11/2/11; m. to Catherine Winchell; c. 1 son, 1 daughter. Educ: Hartford High Schs. Polit. & Govt. Pos: Vt. State Rep, 65- Bus. & Prof. Pos: Retired machinist. Mem: W. Windsor Vol. Fire Dept. Mailing Add: RFD 1, Windsor, Vt. 05089. (1967)

COUTRAKON, GEORGE P. R
b. Springfield, Ill, 11/20/06; married; c. George B. Educ: Univ. Ill, LL.B, 31. Polit. & Govt. Pos: Mem, Sangamon Co. Bd. of Supvr, Ill; secy. to Hon. Hugh Green, Speaker, Ill. House Rep, 47; Ill. State Rep, 4 terms; assoc. circuit judge, Seventh Judicial Circuit, Ill, 64- Bus. & Prof. Pos: Lawyer. Mil. Serv: Navy, 42-46, Lt. Mem: Amvets (past comdr); Am. Legion; K. of P; Mason. Rel: Presbyterian. Mailing Add: 1620 Illini Rd, Springfield, Ill. 62704.

COUTTS, FLORA J. R
Vt. State Rep.
b. W. Charleston, Vt, 9/25/97. Educ: Johnson Normal Sch; Boston Univ; Cornell; Pratt Inst; Epsilon Sigma Phi. Polit. & Govt. Pos: Vt. State Sen, 37, 39; mem, State Personnel Bd; state chmn, Interim Cmt. to study Merit Syst, 41; Vt. State Rep, 61- Bus. & Prof. Pos: Teacher, Am. Sch, Pyeng Yang, Korea, 3 years; Boys & Girls 4-H Club agent, Vt. Ext. Serv, Orleans Co, 11 years; exec. secy, Vt. Assoc. for the Crippled, Northeast. Vt. Develop. Asn; asst. state dir, 350th Champlain Anniversary. Mil. Serv: World War II, China-India-Burma Theatre, Club dir, Am. Red Cross. Mem: Charter mem, 251 Club, End-to-Ender, Green Mountain Club; past state pres, Vt. Fedn. Bus. & Prfnl. Women's Clubs and Vt. Order Women Legislators; Newport Women's Club; Eastern Star. Rel: Baptist. Mailing Add: 18 Pleasant St, Newport, Vt. 05855.

COVELESKIE, STANLEY ROBERT D
b. Dickson City, Pa, 11/8/19; s. Frank Coveleskie and Veronica Drobish C; m. 6/14/47 to Margaret Rose Sweder; c. Stanley R. Jr. and Margaret Mary. Educ: Univ. of Scranton, 2 years; Pa. State Univ. Polit. & Govt. Pos: Del, Dem. Nat. Conv, 68; former supvr, U.S. Treas. Dept, Wash, D.C; off. mgr, Assessor's Off, Lackawanna Co, Scranton, Pa, currently. Bus. & Prof. Pos: Dir, First Fed. Savings and Loan Asn, Scranton, Pa, currently; owner and mgr, ins. agency, currently. Mil. Serv: Entered as Pvt, Army, 42, released as Sgt/Maj, 45, after serv. in 80th Inf, ETO, 43-45; ETO Medal with Battle Stars; Two Purple Hearts; Am. Theatre Ribbon; Combat Inf. Badge; Good Conduct and World War II Victory Medals; Letters of Commendation for Bravery and Heroism. Mem: Pulaski Mem. Cmt. of Lackawanna Co. (past pres); Diocesan Coun. of Cath. Men (bd. mem); Cath. Laymen's Retreat League (capt); bd. mem, Lackawanna United Fund; chmn, Midvalley Lackawanna United Fund; Second Ward Dem. Club (charter mem); Pa. State Ins. Club; Life Underwriters Training Coun; K. of C; Lions; C. of C. Rel: Roman Catholic. Mailing Add: 851 Albert St, Dickson City, Pa. 18519.

COVEY, H. DALE D
b. Glen Daniel, W.Va, 4/1/16; s. Fred Covey and Sadie Trump C; m. 4/25/42 to Margaret M. Smith; c. Andrea Margaret, Charles Dale and David William. Educ: Beckley Col. Polit. & Govt. Pos: Former mem, Bd. Educ; W.Va. State Del, 62-66. Bus. & Prof. Pos: Merchant. Mem: Elks; Odd Fellows; Bd. of Dir, Red Cross; Raleigh Co. Develop. Asn; Upper Marsh Fork Watershed Asn. Rel: Christian Church N.Am; Deacon. Mailing Add: Glen Daniel, W.Va. 25844.

COVEY, JOHN KNOX R
b. Coudersport, Pa, 8/25/06; s. James Garfield Covey and Kathyrn Knox C; m. 2/27/30 to Helen Hunt; c. James Hunt and Susan Candace. Educ: Cornell Univ, 28; Lehigh Univ, C.E, 29; Pa. State Univ, 36; Jefferson Med. Col, M.D, 40; Alpha Kappa Kappa. Polit. & Govt. Pos: Pres, Bellefonte Borough Bd. of Health, Pa, 44-50 and Sch. Bd, 47-65; pres, Bellefonte Area Joint Sch. Bd, 53-65 and Joint Sch. Authority, 65-; past pres, Centre Co. Sch. Bd, 60-65; alternate del, Rep. Nat. Conv, 64. Publ: 'Ocular Tumors in a Rural Practice,' Pa. Med. J, 5/46; 'Medical Advice for Counselors,' Chap. on Ophthalmology, Outline for Pa. State Classes, 60; 'Myths and Facts about Eye Care,' Todays Health, 6/62. Mem: Centre Co. Med. Soc.(past pres. and past secy); Kiwanis (past pres, Bellefonte Chap); Pa. Acad. Ophthalmology and Otolaryngology (past pres); bd. mem, Pa. Asn. for Blind, Blair Centre and Centre Co. Tuberc. and Health Soc; Am. Acad. Ophthalmology and Otolaryngology; dipl, Am. Bd. Ophthalmology, 50; Asn. for Research in Ophthalmology; Am. and Pan Am. Med. Asn. and Asn. of Ophthalmology; Pa. Med. Soc; Nittany Country Club; Mason; C. of C. Rel: Presbyterian. Mailing Add: 130 E. Linn St, Bellefonte, Pa. 16823.

COVINGTON, D. D, JR. D
b. Dade City, Fla, 7/22/28; s. DeCarr Dowman Covington and Martha Flowers C; m. 7/13/52 to Joyce Collier; c. DeCarr Dowman, III, Douglas LaMarcus and Martha Kaye. Educ: Univ. Fla, B.A, 50; Sigma Alpha Epsilon. Polit. & Govt. Pos: Chmn, Citrus Adv. Group, Fla, 61-63; mem, Farm Labor Adv. Cmt, Fla. Indust. Cmn, 61-65; Fla. State Sen, 38th Sen. Dist, 62-66, 16th Dist, 66-68; mem, State Aviation Adv, Cmt, 63-65; mem, Fla. Interim Tax Reform Study Cmn. and submts. on educ. financing, munic. and co. funded debt and sales, licenses, use and excise taxes, 65- Bus. & Prof. Pos: Pres. and gen. mgr, Covingtons' Fruit Packing Asn, Inc, Dade City, Fla, 56-; pres, W.Coast Growers Coop, 60-61. Mem: Elks; Mason; Local Cmt. of 100, Gr. Dade City C. of C; Dade City Pirate Boosters; Pasco Co. Farm Bur. Rel: Methodist. Legal Res: Covington Rd, Dade City, Fla. 33525. Mailing Add: P.O. Box 558, Dade City, Fla. 33525. (1967)

COVINGTON, DEAN D
Mem, Exec. Cmt. Seventh Cong. Dist. Dem. Party, Ga.
b. Rome, Ga, 3/14/16; s. Leon Covington and Bobbie Verner C; m. 9/1/39 to Elsie Peace; c. Dean, Jr, William Lee, Robert Culpepper, Richard Peace, Barbara Graham and David Barron. Educ: Univ. Ga, A.B. in polit. sci, Law Sch, LL.B; Sigma Alpha Epsilon; Phi Delta Phi; Blue Key; Scabbard & Blade; Jr. Cabinet; Sigma Delta Kappa. Polit. & Govt. Pos: Asst. solicitor, City Court, Floyd City, Ga, 40-41; mem, bd. registr, Floyd Co, 40-41; Ga. State Rep, 47-52; mem, Gov. Staff, Ga, 49-; former del, Ga. Dem. Conv; del, Dem. Nat. Conv, 64; mem, Exec. Cmt. Seventh Cong. Dist. Dem. Party, Ga, currently. Bus. & Prof. Pos: Officer and mem. bd. dirs, Nat. Home Develop. Co. and Quality Home Builders. Mil. Serv: Entered as Lt, Army, 42, released as Lt. Col, 45, after serv. in 20th Armored Div, ETO; Hon. Res, 65; Bronze Star; ETO Campaign Ribbon. Mem: Am. and Ga. Bar Asns; Am. Jurisprudence Soc; Farm Bur; Kiwanis (pres, Rome Chap, 62, dist. secy, Ga. Dist, 50-51); Am. Legion; VFW; Coosa Country Club; Peachtree Golf Club; officer

and bd. dirs, Boys Club of Am; Defense Conf. Asn.(nat. v.pres, 65); Basketball and Football Referees Asn. Nat. Golf Champion, Kiwanis Int, 50 & 51. Rel: Methodist; Chmn, Bd. of Stewards, First Methodist Church, 64-65. Legal Res: 230 Lakeshore Dr, Rome, Ga. 30161. Mailing Add: 200 Fifth Ave, Dempsey-Covington Bldg, Rome, Ga. 30161.

COVINGTON, HERBERT LOUIS D
Mem, Nev. Dem. Cent. Cmt.
b. Grand Saline, Tex, 10/18/99; s. John Stark Covington and Sally Smoot C; m. 2/26/19 to Elizabeth Smith; c. William S. Educ: Univ. Nev, 2½ years. Polit. & Govt. Pos: Nev. State Assemblyman, 41-46 & 53-54; del, Dem. Nat. Conv, 52, 54 & 63; mem, Nev. Dem. Cent. Cmt. and Washer Co. Cent. Cmt, currently. Bus. & Prof. Pos: Mech. Supvr, South. Pac. Co. R.R, 41-64. Mem: Int. Asn. of Machinists; Am. Rwy. Supvrs. Asn; Lions. Lion of the year, 68-69. Rel: Christian and Missionary Alliance. Mailing Add: 3235 Montecito Dr, Sparks, Nev. 89431.

COWAN, BOYD LYNN R
Chmn, Hopkins Co. Rep. Exec. Cmt, Ky.
b. Sullivan, Ky, 8/22/97; s. Louis Franklin Cowan and Hepsy Mahaley Armstrong C; m. 2/1/33 to Autense Whitfield. Educ: Asbury Col, 1 year; West. Ky. Univ, B.S; Basketball team, West. Ky. Univ, 4 years; Kit Kat Club. Polit. & Govt. Pos: Warrent writer and asst. field clerk, Brooks Tobacco Loose Leaf Floor, U.S. Govt, 55; election cmnr, 58-67; Rep. organizer, 62-; Rep. cand, U.S. Rep, Ky, 63; chmn, Hopkins Co. Rep. Exec. Cmt, 68- Bus. & Prof. Pos: Owner and mgr, coal mine, 35-55; technician, Ky. Artificial Breeders, 55-63 and Hopkins Co. Agr. Stabilization and Conserv. Serv, 20 years. Mil. Serv: Entered as Pvt, Air Force, 17, released as Sgt, 19 after serving in 850th Provisional Aero Squadron Wing. Mem: Chmn, S.Hopkins Ky. Farm Bur. Hon. life mem. and pin, Future Farmers Am; pins and medals for 20 years service as 4-H leader, Farm Bur. Youth. Rel: Christian. Add: R.R. 2, White Plains, Ky. 42464.

COWAN, GEORGE WEBB D
b. Nashville, Tenn, 11/26/08; s. George Robert Cowan and Johnnie Webb C; m. 5/23/39 to Carolyn Pearson; c. Marilyn (Mrs. Howell) and Lynda. Polit. & Govt. Pos: Justice of the peace, Cheatham Co, Tenn, 48-54; secy, Cheatham Co. Dem. Exec. Cmt, 48-62, chmn, 62-68; mayor, Ashland City, 66- Bus. & Prof. Pos: Secy-treas, Ashland City, Industs. Corp, 54-; pres, Cheatham Co. Fair Asn, 56-; pres, Play Ground Inc, 63- Mem: Lions; Farm Bur. Rel: Methodist. Mailing Add: 303 S. Main St, Ashland City, Tenn. 37015. (1967)

COWAN, JIM MAGEE D
b. Lubbock, Tex, 3/25/42; s. Coleman L. Cowan, Sr. and Virginia Magee C; m. 8/8/64 to Barbara M. Gilbert; c. Coleman L, III and Kirstie K. Educ: Tex. Tech. Col, B.A, 64, M.A, 66; Sigma Tau Delta; Kappa Kappa Psi. Polit. & Govt. Pos: Del, Dem. Nat. Conv, 68. Bus. & Prof. Pos: Prof. Eng, Col. of Artesia, 66- Mem: Am. Studies Asn; Mod. Lang. Asn. Rel: Episcopal. Mailing Add: 1202 S. 18th St, Artesia, N.Mex. 88210.

COWAN, ROSA K. D
V.Chmn, Dem. Cent. Cmt, Idaho
b. Vandalia, Mo, 4/13/06; d. Joseph Lee Kellar and Nancy Evelyn Lovelace K; m. 10/3/27 to Charles Columbus Cowan; c. Nancy Lee (Mrs. Malcolm M. MacWilliams), Mary Charlotte (Mrs. George C. Voss) and Robert Gilmore. Educ: Idaho Falls High Sch. Polit. & Govt. Pos: State and precinct committeewoman, Dem. Cent. Cmt, 60-68; alternate del, Dem. Nat. Conv, 68; v.chmn, Dem. Cent. Cmt, Idaho, 68- Bus. & Prof. Pos: Bookkeeper, Clerk and Stenographer, First Security Bank, Idaho Falls, Idaho, 25-41; stenographer-secy, Qm. Corps, Food Procurement, World War II, 42-45; partner, W.E. Anderson Co, Stockton, Calif. & Idaho Falls, 45-48; co-partner, Cowan Co, 48-58. Mem: Toastmistress Club, Idaho Falls; pres, Idaho Falls Women's Golf Asn. Rel: Presbyterian; trustee-secy, 1st Presby. Church, Idaho Falls. Mailing Add: 321 12th St, P.O. Box 1117, Idaho Falls, Idaho 83401.

COWDEN, GEORGE M. D
b. San Antonio, Tex, 12/29/30; s. George Cowden and Frances Coleman C; m. 8/15/52 to Mollie Waldrop; c. George, III, Graves, Gaylynn and Gordon. Educ: Baylor Univ, B.A, 53, LL.B, 59. Polit. & Govt. Pos: Formerly, Tex. State Rep; first asst, Tex. State Attorney Gen. Off, 67-69; chmn, Tex. State Bd. Ins, 68-69. Bus. & Prof. Pos: Gen. counsel and corp. secy, Great Am. Reserve Ins. Co, Dallas. Mil. Serv: Entered as 2nd Lt, Air Force, 54, released as 1st Lt, 56. Rel: Baptist. Mailing Add: 2020 Live Oak St, Dallas, Tex. 75201.

COWDEN, JULIANAN D
b. Midland, Tex, d. Robert Edwin Cowden and Jett Baker C; single. Educ: Hockaday Jr. Col, grad, 41; Univ. of Tex, B.A, 44; Blue Stockings; Zeta Tau Alpha; Touché; pres, Athletic Coun; Student Coun. & House Gov. Coun; Latin Club. Polit. & Govt. Pos: Chmn, Sixth Cong. Dist. Kennedy-Johnson Campaign, Tex, 60; committeewoman, Tex. State Dem. Exec. Cmt, 12th Sen. Dist. and v.chmn, Resolutions Subcmt, 60-68; pres, Johnson Co. Dem. Woman's Club, 60-; chmn, Operation-Support, Sixth Cong. Dist, 62-66; chmn, Sixth Cong. Dist. Johnson-Humphrey Campaign, 64; alternate del, Dem. Nat. Conv, 64; state chmn, Women for Crawford Martin for Attorney Gen, 66; chmn, Del. Cmt. Co. Dem. Conv, 68; del, State Dem. Conv. and mem. cmt. party nomination, 68; del, Dem. Nat. Conv. and mem, Rules & Order of Bus. Cmt, 68; acting chmn, Local Housing Authority Cmt. and mem, Co. Off. Econ. Opportunity, currently. Bus. & Prof. Pos: Instr. and exhibitor, Ft. Worth Art Center, Tex, 64-66; demonstrating craftsman, Salado Craft Show, 67-68 and San Antonio Artist's Jamboree, 67 and Bond's Alley Art Show, 68; mem. bd. and secy, Alvarado State Bank, 69- Mem: Univ. Tex. Ex-Students' Asn; life mem. Hockaday Alumnae Asn; pres, Alvarado Sch. Bd; Nat. Geog. Soc; Ridglea Country Club; hon. mem. Delta Kappa Gamma; bd. trustees, Hockaday Sch; dist. bd, Circle T Girl Scout Coun; sustaining mem, Am. Craft Coun. Exhibit of Jewelry in Southwest. Int. Craft Mus, Santa Fe, N.Mex; exhibit, Int. Folk Art Mus, Santa Fe, 69. Rel: Episcopal. Mailing Add: JAL Ranch, Alvarado, Tex. 76009.

COWDEN, THOMAS K. R
Asst. Secy. of Agr. for Rural Develop. and Conserv, Dept. of Agr.
b. Hickory, Pa, 6/14/08; married; c. Dr. John W. and Jean W. Educ: Ohio State Univ, B.S, 30 and M.S, 31; Cornell Univ, Ph.D, 37. Hon. doctorate, Cornell Univ, 37. Polit. & Govt. Pos: Serv. on many govt. and nat. cmts. for econ. develop. and agr. policy; Asst. Secy. of Agr. for Rural Develop. and Conserv, Dept. of Agr, 69- Bus. & Prof. Pos: Prof. agr. econ, Pa. State Univ, 31-37; Purdue Univ, 37-43; dir. of research, Am. Farm Bur. Fedn, 43-49; head of dept. of agr. econ, Mich. State Univ, 49-54, dean of col. agr. and natural resources, 54-69. Mem: Am. Farm Econ. Asn.(past pres). Legal Res: Mich. Mailing Add: Dept. of Agriculture, 14th St. and Independence Ave. S.W, Washington, D.C. 20250.

COWEN, DAVID CHARLES D
b. Portland, Ore, 6/12/97; m. 4/11/50 to Anna Louise . Educ: Univ. Ore, D.D.S, 18. Polit. & Govt. Pos: Wash. State Sen, 34-66. Rel: Jewish. Mailing Add: 223 S. Coeur D'Alene St, Spokane, Wash. 99204. (1967)

COWEN, EUGENE S. R
Spec. Asst. to the President
b. N.Y.C, 5/2/25; m. 1/29/48 to Phyllis Leatrice Wallach; c. James Sherman and Stephanie Jane. Educ: Syracuse Univ, B.A, 49, M.A, 53; Phi Beta Kappa. Polit. & Govt. Pos: Press secy. to Congresswoman Frances Bolton, Ohio, 53-56; info. specialist, Fed. Flood Indemnity Admin, 56-57 and Off. of the Secy, Dept. of Health, Educ. and Welfare, 57-58; press consult, U.S. Sen. Hugh Scott, Pa, 60-67, admin. asst, 67-69; spec. asst. to the President, 69- Bus. & Prof. Pos: Reporter, Syracuse Herald J, 48-52; v.pres, Standard Pub. Rels, Inc, Wash, D.C, 58-60. Mil. Serv: Entered as Pvt, Army Air Corps, 43, released as Flight Officer, 46, after serv. in Mediterranean Theatre, 44-46; Air Medal. Mem: Nat. Press Club. Rel: Jewish. Mailing Add: 920 Loxford Terr, Silver Spring, Md. 20901.

COWEN, JOE N. D
Chmn, Castro Co. Dem. Exec. Cmt, Tex.
b. Clifton, Tex, 4/26/10; s. John R. Cowen and Florence McFadden C; m. 3/11/39 to Alice Russell Hamilton; c. Joe Hamilton. Educ: Univ. Tex, B.A; Tejas Club; 113-lb. wrestling champion. Polit. & Govt. Pos: Alternate del, Dem. Nat. Conv, 56; exec. committeeman, State Dem. Exec. Cmt, Tex, 56-57; mayor, Dimmitt, Tex, 57-59; chmn, Castro Co. Dem. Exec. Cmt, 58-59 & 66- Mem: Pres, Castro Co. Fair Asn, 49, Castro Co. C. of C, 50, Dimmitt Lions Club, 50, Dimmitt PTA, 51 and Dimmitt Libr. Bd, 52. Rel: Presbyterian; Clerk of the Session, Presbyterian Church, Dimmitt, Tex, 59- Legal Res: 600 Southwest Tenth St, Dimmitt, Tex. 79027. Mailing Add: Drawer 247, Dimmitt, Tex. 79027.

COWGER, WILLIAM OWEN R
U.S. Rep, Ky.
b. Hastings, Nebr, 1/1/22; s. Dr. R.H. Cowger and Catherine Combs C.(both deceased); m. 3/19/45 to Cynthia Thompson; c. Cynthia and David. Educ: Tex. A&M; Carleton Col, B.A; Univ. of Louisville, graduate studies. Polit. & Govt. Pos: Mayor, Louisville, Ky, 61-64; U.S. Rep, Ky, 67-; del, Rep. Nat. Conv, 68. Mil. Serv: Entered as Seaman, Navy, 42, released as Lt.(jg), 46, after serv. in Pac; Am. Defense and Pac. Theater Ribbons; Victory Medal. Mem: Louisville Jr. C. of C.(pres, 53); Louisville Mortgage Bankers Asn. (pres, 54). Rel: Presbyterian. Mailing Add: 2315 Raleigh Lane, Louisville, Ky. 40206. (1967)

COWHERD, COLBY F. D
b. Greensburg, Ky, 12/8/07; s. J. Frank Cowherd and Mabel Tucker C; m. 6/14/34 to Rachel Virginia Skaggs; c. David C. and James C. Educ: Bowling Green Bus. Univ, 1 year. Polit. & Govt. Pos: Dep. co. court clerk, Green Co, Ky, 28-34; court reporter, Green, Taylor, Marion and Wash. Co, 32-46; U.S. Cmnr, 36-; secy, Green Co. Dem. Party, Ky, 25 years, chmn, 61-69. Bus. & Prof. Pos: Owner, ins. agency, 34-59. Mem: Rotary; Greensburg Indust. Fedn. Rel: Baptist. Mailing Add: Box 373, Greensburg, Ky. 42743.

COWHERD, RODERICK GRYMES D
b. Gordonsville, Va, 9/16/87; s. Marcellus Daniel Cowherd and Adeline Rush Harris C; m. 10/14/19 to Elmina Adelaide Walton; c. Marion L.(Mrs. Janney), Alice D.(Mrs. Walker), Mary Jane (Mrs. Cook), Walton Rush and Anne Tyler (Mrs. Handy). Educ: Va. Polytech. Inst. Polit. & Govt. Pos: Mem, Va. State Bd. Agr, 36-61, pres, 61-65; chmn, Orange Co. Dem. Cmt, 36-66; adv, War Draftees, 40-66; chmn, 23rd Sen. Dist. Dem. Cmt, 64-66. Bus. & Prof. Pos: Mgr, Producers Coop, Inc, Gordonsville, Va, 30-; chmn. bd. dirs, Va. National Bank, 58-; past pres, Gordonsville Frozen Foods, Inc. Mem: Va. Bd. Visitors, Va. Polytech Inst. and Radford Col, 61-65; pres, Orange Co. C. of C; Past Master, Waddell Masonic Lodge; past pres, Lions; organizer, Gordonsville Bus. Men's Club; past pres, Orange Co. Poultry Asn; treas, Goshen Baptist Asn. Rel: Baptist. Mailing Add: Box 187, Gordonsville, Va. 22942.

COX, ARCHIBALD D
b. Plainfield, N.J, 5/17/12; s. Archibald Cox and Frances Bruen Perkins C; m. 6/12/37 to Phyllis Ames; c. Sarah, Archibald and Phyllis. Educ: Harvard Univ, B.A, 34, LL.B, 37. Polit. & Govt. Pos: Attorney, Off. Solicitor Gen, U.S. Dept. Justice, 41-43; assoc. solicitor, Dept. Labor, 43-45; chmn, Wage Stabilization Bd, 52; co-chmn, Construction Indust. Stabilization Cmt, 51-52; Solicitor Gen, U.S. Dept. Justice, 61-65. Bus. & Prof. Pos: Attorney, Ropes, Gray, Best, Coolidge & Rugg, Boston, 38-41; lectr. law, Harvard Univ, 45-46, prof, 46-61, Mem. Bd. Overseers, 62-65; Williston Prof. Law, Harvard, Law Sch, 65- Publ: 'Law and National Labor Policy,' 60; 'Cases on Labor Law,' Sixth Ed, 65; 'Civil Rights, The Constitution and the Courts,' 67; 'The Warren Court,' 68. Mem: Am. Bar Asn; Am. Acad. Arts & Sci. Legal Res: Glezen Lane, Wayland, Mass. 01778. Mailing Add: Langdell Hall, Harvard Law Sch, Cambridge, Mass. 02138.

COX, BARBOUR D
Okla. State Rep.
b. Bristow, Okla, 10/29/24; s. Roscoe Cox and Avis Barbour C; single. Educ: Okla. State Univ, B.S, 49; Sigma Alpha Epsilon. Polit. & Govt. Pos: Okla. State Rep, 55- Mil. Serv: Entered as Pvt, Army, 43, released as Pfc, 46, after serving in 14th and 20th Armored Div, ETO, 44-46. Mem: Lincoln Co. Hist. Soc; Mason; Am. Legion; Rotary; C. of C; Lincoln Co. Cattlemen's Asn. Rel: Presbyterian. Mailing Add: 308 W. 8th, Chandler, Okla. 74834.

COX, DAVID M. D
Maine State Rep.
b. Orrington, Maine, 12/21/31; s. Walter M. Cox and Mary Tardiff C; m. 7/10/60 to Janice R. Wheelden; c. Deborah L, David M, II and Daniel M. Educ: Univ. Maine, B.A, 60; Univ. Maine Sch. of Law, J.D, 63; Law Rev. Polit. & Govt. Pos: Mem, Bangor Dem. City Cmt, Maine, 66-; mem. finance and registrn. cmt, Penobscot Co. Dem. Cmt, 68-; Maine State Rep, Bangor, 69- Bus. & Prof. Pos: Partner, Libhart & Cox, Brewer, Maine, 62- Mil. Serv: Pvt, Army, serv. in Ord. Corps, Europe, 52-54; Good Conduct Medal; Am. Defense Medal; Am. Occup. Medal. Mem: Am, Maine and Penobscot Co. Bar Asns; Am. and Maine Trial Lawyers Asns; Elks; Lions Int. Cumberland Co. Bar Asn. Award. Rel: Roman Catholic. Mailing Add: 28 Maple St, Bangor, Maine 04401.

COX, DEAN F D
Chmn, Wayne Co. Dem. Party, Iowa.
b. Corydon, Iowa, 5/13/27; s. John Anderson Cox and Myrtle Annis Dent C; m. 8/13/47 to Willa Jeane Grimes; c. C. Christine (Mrs. Mark C. Bracewell), Joyce Ann and Jeffrey Keene. Educ: Cambria High Sch, Iowa, grad, 45. Polit. & Govt. Pos: Committeeman, Dem. Party, Corydon, Iowa, 65-66; chmn, Wayne Co. Dem. Party, 67- Bus. & Prof. Pos: Owner, Cox's Body Repair, Corydon, 57- Mil. Serv: Entered as A/S, Navy, 45, released as Storekeeper 3rd Class, 46, after serving in Logistic Support Co. 175, Asiatic & Pac. Theatres, 45-46; Sgt. Maj, Army Res, 69- Mem: Am. Legion; 40 et 8; VFW; Baptist Men; past comdr. 5th dist, Am. Legion; Nat. Cmt. on Vet. Preferance, Am. Legion. Rel: Baptist. Mailing Add: 406 S. DeKalb, Corydon, Iowa 50060.

COX, EMIL G. R
Chmn, Dallas Co. Rep. Cent. Cmt, Mo.
b. Urbana, Mo, 9/24/16; s. George Hamilton Cox and Cora Effie Thomas C; m. 12/20/44 to Constance Eleanor Charlotte Hood; c. Conne Mara and Philip Ellis Groombridge. Educ: Urbana Pub. Sch, Mo, 12 years. Polit. & Govt. Pos: Chmn, Dallas Co. Rep. Cent. Cmt, Mo, 68- Bus. & Prof. Pos: Laborer and hobo, 33-41; self employed, farming, trucking and commercial feed retail bus, 41-51; automobile transport driver, Jack Cooper Transport Co, 51-56; self employed, farming and trucking serv, 56-62, retail bldg. materials, 62- Mil. Serv: Entered as Pvt, Army, 41, released as S/Sgt, 45, after serv. in Tenth Sta. Hosp, ETO, 42-45. Mem: AF&AM; Mo. Farmers Asn. Rel: Protestant. Mailing Add: Urbana, Mo. 65767.

COX, ERNEST Y. D
b. Altoona, Kans, 7/17/18; s. Willard Cox and Charlotte Aldridge C; m. 1/18/41 to Elizabeth Brown. Educ: Weber Col, Utah, 48-50. Polit. & Govt. Pos: Admin. Asst, Rep. John E. Moss, D-Calif; Info. Off, Sacramento Co, Calif, 60-61. Bus. & Prof. Pos: Reporter, Sacramento Bee, 51-60; reporter, Salt Lake Tribune, 48-51. Mil. Serv: Army, 40-45. 1967 Legal Res: 9531 Lawnsberry Terr, Silver Spring, Md. No mailing address available. (1967)

COX, FRANK BERNARD D
b. Oklahoma City, Okla, 6/30/25; s. Frank Cox, and Beatrice Elizabeth Hawkins; m. 12/26/48 to Martina Julia Creuzot; c. Kevin Creuzot, Tobi Fae, Kerry Christopher, Kerwin Cedric and Thais Martina. Educ: Fisk Univ, 42-44; Meharry Med. Col, D.D.S, 47; Homer G. Phillips Munic. Hosp, 47-48; Deans List, 42 & 43 & 45-47; Alpha Phi Alpha; Student Christian Asn. Polit. & Govt. Pos: Alternate del, Dem. Nat. Conv, 68; mem. Okla. del. testifying before McGovern Cmt. of Party Reform, 69; mem. steering cmt, Co. Dem. Party on Involvement of Bus. & Prfnl. Men, 69. Mil. Serv: Army, 44, Pfc, serv. in Army Specialized Training Prog, Meharry Med. Col; recalled, 51-52, 1st Lt, serv. in First Calvary Div, Japan. Mem: Meharry Alumni Asn; Okla. City Medephar Soc; Okla. Co, Okla. State and Am. Dent. Soc; Okla. State Med, Dent. and Pharmaceutical Soc.(pres, 64-65); PTA (v.pres, 64, mem. bd. dirs); K. of C.(4°, Faithful Pilot, 63, trustee, 60-61); Christian Family Movement (asst. regional chair couple, 65-66); Corpus Christi Parish Rep. to Okla. Diocese Little Coun; YMCA (corp. bd. mem, boys work cmt, food serv. cmt); YWCA; bd. dirs, Montessori Sch. and Day Care Center; Okla. State Merit Bd. Oral Exam; Citizen Comprehensive Health Surv. Cmt; Citizen's C. of C; NAACP; Oklahomans for Progress; Cath. Inter-racial Coun. (past pres); chmn, Citizens Adv. Cmt. Med. Center Proj, Urban Renewal; Douglass Center Adv. Cmt.(chmn); Eastern Golf Course (bd. dir. and leasee); Urban League Oklahoma City (pres. bd. dirs); Gov. Higher Educ. Adv. Coun; Commun. Coun. Oklahoma City (bd. dirs); Variety Club Health Center (bd. dirs); Serra Club. Rel: Catholic. Legal Res: Route 4, Box 795, Oklahoma City, Okla. 73111. Mailing Add: 1031 N.E. Sixth St, Oklahoma City, Okla. 73117.

COX, FRANK P. D
b. Albany, N.Y, 10/16/93; m. to Etolla L. Barton McCarthy. Educ: Parochial Schs, Albany. Polit. & Govt. Pos: Head of printing, Audit State Comptroller, 13 years; N.Y. State Boxing Cmn. referee; mem, Temporary State Cmn. on Capital City; N.Y. State Assemblyman, until 68. Bus. & Prof. Pos: Former composing room foreman, Argus Co. Mil. Serv: World War I, First Gas Regt, France. Mem: Am. Legion (comdr. Post 960); Elks (Exalted Ruler Albany Lodge); Albany Typographical Union (pres); N.Y. State Typographical Conf; N.Y. State Allied Printing Trades Coun; Int. Typographical Union; Albany Center Fedn. of Labor (v.pres). Rel: Catholic. Mailing Add: 17 Warren St, McKownville, Albany, N.Y. 12202. (1967)

COX, GILBERT W, JR. R
Mass. State Rep.
b. Stoneham, Mass, 2/28/33; s. Gilbert W. Cox and Verna O. Linscott C; m. 6/6/59 to Helen D. Pillsbury; c. Gilbert, David, Carol and Elizabeth. Educ: Northeast. Univ, A.B; Boston Univ. Law Sch, LL.B. Polit. & Govt. Pos: Pres, Needham Young Rep. Club, Mass, 63-64; asst. dist. attorney, 66; chmn, Needham Rep. Town Cmt, 66-69; Mass. State Rep, 69- Bus. & Prof. Pos: Lawyer, 62- Mil. Serv: Ens, Navy, 55-59, Lt. Comdr, Navy Res, 59- Mem: Mass. and Norfolk Co. Bar Asns; pres, Needham Taxpayers Asn, 65-66; dir, Needham YMCA, 64- Mailing Add: 49 Colonial Rd, Needham, Mass. 02192.

COX, GLADYS R
b. Fairview, Kans, 1/10/12; d. Jesse Ernest Van Dalsem and Flora Mitchell V; m. 1933 to C. Kenneth Cox; c. Joy Ann (Mrs. Eddie Brown) and Anita Loyce (Mrs. Ernest Eugene Simmons). Educ: Cent. Bus. Col, Wichita, Kans, grad, 31. Polit. & Govt. Pos: Stenographer, U.S. Sen. Campaign, Kans, 36-37; precinct committeewoman, Sedgwick Co. Rep. Cent. Cmt, 42-, v.chmn, 58-61, ward v.chmn, 68-; steno clerk to Clerk of the Dist. Court, Sedgwick Co, 43-44; steno-clerk to Sedgwick Co. Sheriff, 44-46; temporary steno-clerk to Cmnr. of Elec, Wichita, 47; dep. cmnr. of elec, City of Wichita and Sedgwick Co, 48-57; v.chmn, Kans. Rep. Cmt, 60-61; cmnr. of elec, Sedgwick Co, 61-66; alternate del, Rep. Nat. Conv, 68. Bus. & Prof. Pos: Stenographer, First Baptist Church, 31-33; secy. family bus, Kenco, Inc, Wichita, 67- Mem: Sedgwick Co. Rep. Women; Kans. Fedn. Rep. Women; Nat. Fedn. Rep. Women; R.E.D. Club Bus. & Prfnl. Women; South Wind Chap, Am. Bus. Women's Asn; Prairie Pilot Club Wichita; Pilot Club Int; Eve. Twentieth Century; Campfire Girls; Am. Cancer Soc. Woman of the Year, Am. Bus. Women's Asn, 65-66. Rel: Protestant. Mailing Add: 613 Northcourt, Wichita, Kans. 67204.

COX, GUY JACKSON R
Chmn, Gunnison Co. Rep. Cent. Cmt, Colo.
b. West Vienna, Ill, 10/17/06; s. Jackson Mier Cox and Ollie May Cover C; m. 9/20/30 to Bernice Estelle Smith; c. Garland Don, Zoe Ann (Mrs. C.J. Miller) and Karen Sue (Mrs. Jack Cummins). Educ: Salt City Bus. Col, 1 year. Polit. & Govt. Pos: Secy, Gunnison Co. Rep. Cent. Cmt, Colo, 64-67, chmn, 67- Bus. & Prof. Pos: Sta. agent helper, MoPac R.R, Ordway, Colo, 28-33; city clerk, Ordway, Colo, 33-35; bookkeeper, Zirkle Motor Co, La Junta, 36-38; staff, PowerineOil Co, 38-41; sta. mgr, Continental Air Lines, 42-46; sta. mgr, Monarch Air Lines, Gunnison, 47-49, dist. mgr, Salt Lake City, Utah, 49-51; mgr, C. of C, Gunnison, Colo, 51-55; owner and mgr, Wildwood Motel, 55-62; real estate salesman, Clarke Agency, Gunnison, 62- Mem: Rotary; C. of C. Rel: Protestant; Commun. Church. Mailing Add: P.O. Box 777, Gunnison, Colo. 81230.

COX, HARDIN CHARLES D
Mo. State Rep.
b. Rockport, Mo, 3/4/28; s. Hardin Charles Cox and Frieda Anna Stapel C; m. 1/3/52 to Virginia Ann Heifner; c. Charles Bryan and Mark Hardin. Educ: Univ. Mo, B.A. in Bus, 51; QEBA; Omicron Delta Kappa; Alpha Phi Omega; Sigma Chi. Polit. & Govt. Pos: Mo. State Rep, 65-, chmn, Flood Control and Soil Conserv. Cmt, Mo. House of Rep. Bus. & Prof. Pos: Treas, Farmers Mutual Hail Ins. Co, Columbia, Mo, Farmers Mutual Windstorm Ins. Co, Mo. Farmers Hail Ins. Co. and secy-treas, Farmers Mutual Ins. Co, Rockport, 60- Mil. Serv: Entered as Pvt, Army, 46, released as Cpl, 48, re-entered as Lt, 51, released in 53, after serv. in Army Artil, Korea; Korean Campaign Ribbon with 3 Battle Stars; Victory Medal; Orient Occup. Medal. Mem: Group Millionaire Club Equitable Life, N.Y; AF&AM; Am. Legion; C. of C; Vol. Fireman; pres. coun, Boy Scouts. Univ. Mo. Cotton Bowl team, 45, Gater Bowl team, 48. Rel: Lutheran. Legal Res: 605 Bluff St, Rockport, Mo. 64482. Mailing Add: 300 Main St, Rockport, Mo. 64482.

COX, HAZEL IRENE D
b. Caney, Okla, 5/21/13; d. William Arthur Grimes and Mary Kelley G; m. 6/11/28 to Jesse Marvin Cox; c. Helen Aline (Mrs. Lockwood); grandchildren: Jesse Laverne, Johnny Edward and Jimmy Arthur. Educ: High Sch. Polit. & Govt. Pos: Chmn, 29th Dist. Dem. Cmt. and pres, Riverside Co. Dem. Cmt, 60-62; del, Dem. Nat. Conv, 60 & 64; field rep, Calif. State Assemblyman Sound, 60-64; field secy, 61-63; mem, Calif. Dem. State Cent. Cmt. and chmn, Dem. Women, 38th Dist, 60-68; field secy, Calif. State Assemblyman Tunney, 66-; mem. adv. bd, Calif. Fair Employ. Practice Cmt. and Small Bus. Admin. Bus. & Prof. Pos: Owner, Circle City Florist Shop, 63-66. Mem: Rebekah; Womens Improve. Club; United Fund; Corona Traffic and Survival Bd. Rel: Assembly of God. 1967 Legal Res: Corona, Calif. No mailing address available. (1967)

COX, HERMAN ELMER D
b. Lexington Co, S.C, 4/17/25; s. O. R. Cox (deceased) and Minnie Shumpert C; 2nd m. 6/11/66 to Doris Watson; c. Susan Anne, Karen L. and William E. Educ: George Washington Univ, A.B, 50, LL.B, 51; Phi Delta Phi. Polit. & Govt. Pos: Mem, S.C. State Educ. Finance Cmt, 57-60; secy, Greenville Co. Dem. Exec. Cmt, 64-66. Mil. Serv: Entered as Recruit, Army Air Corps, 43, released as Cpl, 46, after serv. in 1884th Eng. Aviation Bn, Pac. Area. Mem: Nebr. and S.C. State Bar Asns; D.C. and Am. Bar Asns; Am. Legion; Mason; Scottish Rite; Shrine. Rel: Episcopal. Legal Res: 107 Graystone Rd, Greenville, S.C. 29607. Mailing Add: 115 Broadus Ave, Greenville, S.C. 29601.

COX, HERSCHEL W. D
b. Crossville, Tenn, 5/14/18; married; c. 5 boys. Polit. & Govt. Pos: N.H. State Rep, -67; selectman. Bus. & Prof. Pos: Operates grocery store and gas sta. Mil. Serv: Army, 41-45. Mem: VFW; Am. Legion; Masons (32°); Elks; Horseshoe Fish and Game Club; Hillsborough Co. Law Enforcement Asn. Rel: Protestant. Mailing Add: RFD 1, Nashua, N.H. 03060. (1967)

COX, JACK R
b. Breckenridge, Tex, 8/20/21; s. Richard Martin Cox and Louella Cargill C; m. 10/15/42 to Joyce Louise Smyrl; c. Callan Sue (Mrs. Crousen) and Jack, Jr. Educ: Univ. Tex; N.Tex. State Univ, B.S. in Govt, 47. Polit. & Govt. Pos: Tex. State Rep, 47-53; mem, Tex. Cmn. Higher Educ, 54-60; Rep. nominee for Gov, Tex, 62; del, Rep. Nat. Conv, 68. Bus. & Prof. Pos: Asst. to Pres, South. Minerals Corp, Corpus Christi, Tex, 53-56; v.pres, Freedom in Action, Houston, 56-59; partner and v.pres, Pico Drilling Corp, Breckenridge, 60-65; pres, Foty Acres Club, Inc, Austin, 66-; pres, Airline Passengers Asn, Dallas, 69- Mil. Serv: Entered as A/S, Navy, 40, released as Lt. Comdr, 45, after serv. in VP-32, Panama, Hawaiian Sea Frontier. Publ: . . . And the Pursuit of Happiness, Naylor Publ. Co, San Antonio, 62; U.S. Latin American Relations, Assoc. Pres, 62. Mem: Am. Legion. George Wash. Gold Medal of Honor, Valley Forge Freedoms Found, three times; Man and Boy Award, Austin Boys Club; Citizenship Award, Am. Legion. Rel: Protestant. Legal Res: 3815 Hillbrook Dr, Austin, Tex. 78731. Mailing Add: 2500 Guadalupe, Austin, Tex. 78705.

COX, JAMES BURL R
Chmn, Cherokee Co. Rep. Party, Okla.
b. Evansville, Ark, 9/9/96; s. Henry Cox and Annie-Belle Michael C; m. 4/14/28 to Reba West; c. James Michael. Educ: Ark. Tech. Col, 12-15; Okla. State Univ, 16; Northeast. State Col, 22-25. Polit. & Govt. Pos: Postmaster,

Stilwell, Okla, 27-36; chmn, Cherokee Co. Rep. Party, 52-53 & 67-; postmaster, Tahlequah, 55-65. Bus. & Prof. Pos: Sch. teacher, Adair Co, Okla, 16-20; grade sch. prin, Stilwell, 21-27; ins. salesman, Paul Revier Co, Worchester, Mass, 37-41; patrolman, DuPont Co, Pryor, Okla, 42-43; self-employed merchant, Tahlequah, 44-54. Mil. Serv: Entered as Pvt, Army Air Serv, 18, released as Radio Operator, 19, after serv. in Squadron A, Ellington Field, Tex. Mem: Am. Legion (Post Comdr, 33-34); Mason (Worshipful Master, 39-40); Tahlequah C. of C.(pres, 47-48); Nat. Asn. Retired Fed. Employees (pres, 67-68). Rel: Methodist. Mailing Add: 910 Grand Ave, Tahlequah, Okla. 74464.

COX, JAY CARROLL D
Ga. State Sen.
b. Washington, D.C, 5/16/36; s. Marvin Hill Cox and Mary Rountree C; single. Educ: Univ. of Ga, A.B, 59, LL.B, 61; Blue Key; Phi Delta Phi; Sphinx, Sigma Alpha Epsilon. Polit. & Govt. Pos: Ga. State Sen, Dist. 21, 67- Bus. & Prof. Pos: Attorney, Swainsboro, Ga, currently. Mem: State Bar of Georgia. Rel: Baptist. Legal Res: P.O. Box 37, Twin City, Ga. 30471. Mailing Add: P.O. Box 633 Swainsboro, Ga. 30401.

COX, JOHN EDWARD, JR. R
b. San Jose, California, 2/19/44; s. John E. Cox, M.D. and Flora Martens C; m. 8/19/67 to Marianne Schalbert. Educ: Foothill College, 61-63; San Jose State College, BA. in Journalism, 67; Sigma Delta Chi; freshman class pres, 61. Polit. & Govt. Pos: West. regional chmn, Young Am. for Freedom, 63-65, Calif. chmn, 65-66, nat. bd. mem, 63-66; admin. asst. to Calif. State Sen. Clark L. Bradley, 67-69; exec. asst. to U.S. Rep. Barry Goldwater, Jr, Calif, 69- Bus. & Prof. Pos: Newsman, KLIV Radio, San Jose, 65-66 and KXRX Radio, 67-68. Mil. Serv: Pfc, Army Nat. Guard, 66- Mem: Am. Soc. Pub. Admin; Sigma Delta Chi; House Rep. Commun. Asn. Young Am. for Freedom named Outstanding State Orgn, 65, while he was state chmn. Rel: Christian Church. Legal Res: 14755 Oak St, Saratoga, Calif. 95070. Mailing Add: 5112 Elsmere Ave, Bethesda, Md. 20014.

COX, JOHN HENRY D
Ky. State Rep.
b. 1909. Educ: West. State Col. Polit. & Govt. Pos: Ky. State Rep, 40-45 & currently. Bus. & Prof. Pos: Farmer. Mem: Lions (past pres); Odd Fellows (past noble); Hopkins Co. Farm Bur.(past dir); Ky. Farm Bur. Fedn.(state dir); Elks. Rel: Christian. Mailing Add: 54 S. Harrig St, Madisonville, Ky. 42431. (1967)

COX, KENNETH ALLEN D
Cmnr, Fed. Commun. Cmn.
b. Topeka, Kans, 12/7/16; s. Seth Leroy Cox and Jean Sears C; m. 1/1/43 to Nona Beth Fumerton; c. Gregory Allen, Jeffrey Neal and Douglas Randall. Educ: Univ. Wash, B.A, 38, LL.B, 40; Univ. Mich, LL.M, 41; Phi Beta Kappa; Phi Delta Phi; Order of the Coif. Polit. & Govt. Pos: Spec. counsel, TV Inquiry, Senate Commerce Cmt, 56-57 and periodically thereafter; chief, broadcast bur, Fed. Commun. Cmn, 61-63, Cmnr, 63- Bus. & Prof. Pos: Assoc, Little, Palmer, Scott & Slemmons, 49-53, partner, 53-61. Mil. Serv: Entered as Pvt, Army, 43, released as Capt, 46, after serv. in Qm. Sch, 43-45 and Army Intel, The Pentagon, 45-46; re-entered during Korean War, serv. at Ft. Riley, Kans; Army Commendation Ribbon. Publ: 'The Federal Communications Commission's "Fairness Doctrine" with Respect to Broadcast Matter Dealing with Controversial Issues,' The Brief, fall 64; 'The Federal Communications Commission, the Constitution, and Religious Broadcast Programming,' The George Wash. Law Rev, 12/65. Mem: Wash. State & Am. Bar Asns; Cong. Country Club. Rel: Congregational. Legal Res: 2507 29th West, Seattle, Wash. 98199. Mailing Add: 5836 Marbury Rd, Bethesda, Md. 20034.

COX, LAWRENCE MORGAN Independent
Asst. Secy. for Renewal and Housing Assistance, Dept. of Housing and Urban Develop.
b. Norfolk, Va, 3/12/12; m. to Ethel Mae Breeden; c. Lawrence M, Jr. and Mrs. B.S. Merritt. Educ: George Wash. Univ. Polit. & Govt. Pos: Former U.S. Del, Econ. Cmn. for European Int. Conf. on Bldg. Documentation, Geneva and Int. Seminar on Urban Renewal, The Hague; former housing consult, U.S. Housing Cmn. for Germany and Prime Minister of Peru; adv. U.S. Conf. of Mayors and Nat. League of Cities; exec. dir, Redevelop. and Housing Authority, Norfolk, Va, 41-69; Asst. Secy. for Renewal and Housing Assistance, Dept. of Housing and Urban Develop, 69- Bus. & Prof. Pos: Lectr, Grad. Sch. of Ekistics, Athens, Greece, Int. Sch. of Soc. Studies, The Hague, Holland, Univ. Pittsburgh Grad. Sch. of Pub. and Int. Affairs, Univ. Pittsburgh, Univ. Va. Grad. Schs. of Planning and Archit. and Univ. Ill. Mem: Bd. dirs, Nat. Asn. of Housing and Redevelop. Off.(pres, 48 & 49); Am. Soc. of Planning Off.(past pres); Nat. Housing Conf; Urban Land Inst; Nat. Trust for Hist. Preservation; U.S. Renewal Correspondent, Int. Fedn. of Housing and Planning; former cmnr, Norfolk Area Med. Center Authority; bd, Norfolk Gen. Hosp; adv. coun, Va. Wesleyan Col. and Soc. for Preservation of Va. Antiquities. Recipient, Order of Merit, President Prado, Peru, 58. Legal Res: Va. Mailing Add: Dept. of Housing and Urban Development, 451 Seventh St. S.W, Washington, D.C. 20410.

COX, ROBERT EMMETT R
Chmn, Talbot Co. Rep. State Cent. Cmt, Md.
b. Lakewood, Ohio, 2/17/19; s. Christopher P. Cox and Cecel Davidson C; m. 2/15/47 to Mary Louise Collier; c. Christopher, Susan and William. Educ: Princeton, class of 41. Polit. & Govt. Pos: Chmn, Talbot Co. Rep. State Cent. Cmt, Md, 60-; alternate del, Rep. Nat. Conv, 68; mem, Dept. of State Planning Cmn; chmn, First Dist. Rep. Cmt. Mil. Serv: Entered as A/S, Naval Res, 40, released as Lt. Coast Guard, 46, after serv. in N. Atlantic and Southwest Pac. Mem: Elks. Rel: Protestant. Legal Res: St. Michaels, Md. 21663. Mailing Add: Box 759, Easton, Md. 21601.

COX, TOY LOUIS D
S.C. State Rep.
b. Union Bleachery, S.C, 1/22/29; s. Toy Louis Cox and Edith Hawkins C; m. 12/20/58 to Edith Livesay Gardner; c. Robert Gardner, Deborah (Mrs. Gary D. Brannon) and Audrey. Educ: Spartanburg Jr. Col, 51; Wofford Col, 52; Univ. S.C, LL.B, 54. Polit. & Govt. Pos: S.C. State Rep, 67- Bus. & Prof. Pos: Attorney at law, Cox, Thomas & Brooks, Spartanburg, S.C, currently. Mil. Serv: Entered as A/S, Navy, 46, released as EM 3/C, 49, after serv. on U.S.S. Randolph and U.S.S. Kearsage. Mem: Am. and S.C. Trial Lawyers Asns; Spartanburg Co. and S.C. Bar Asns; trustee, Spartanburg Legal Aid Soc, 68-69, Mason (32°). Rel: Presbyterian. Legal Res: Holly Dr, Spartanburg, S.C. 29301. Mailing Add: P.O. Box 1463, Spartanburg, S.C. 29301.

COX, WILLIAM NOEL R
Mo. State Sen.
b. Spokane, Mo, 4/5/11; m. 1933 to Rose Mease; c. William J, Rose Ann and Dwight M. Educ: S.W. Mo. State Col, Springfield. Polit. & Govt. Pos: Mo. State Rep, 4 terms, Minority Caucus Chmn. and Minority Floor Leader, Mo. House of Rep; Mo. State Sen, 52- Bus. & Prof. Pos: Former sch. teacher, 10 years; livestock auction bus, 8 years; owner and operator, livestock farm. Mil. Serv: Citizens Mil. Training Class, Ft. Leavenworth, Kans. Mem: Mason. Rel: Baptist; Deacon. Mailing Add: Ozark, Mo. 65721. (1967)

COYLE, MARTIN ADOLPHUS R
b. Hamilton, Ohio, 3/18/16; s. Caleb Martin Coyle and Talitha Jane Logsdon C; m. 6/22/40 to Lucille Baird; c. Martin A, Jr. and Mary Lou (Mrs. Joseph P. Hughes, Jr). Educ: Miami Univ, A.B, 38; Ohio State Univ. Col. Law, J.D, 47; Commerce Col, Ohio State Univ, and Dayton Univ, spec. studies; Sigma Alpha Epsilon. Polit. & Govt. Pos: Dep. registr. of motor vehicles, Ohio, 39-43, asst. treas, 44-45; chmn, Butler Co. Rep. Exec. Cmt, 48-60, treas, 58-69; Ohio Young Rep. League representative, Rep. Nat. Cmt, 50-51; alternate del, Rep. Nat. Conv, 52 & 64 and del, 56 & 60; mem, Butler Co. Bd. Elecs, 52-64; state chmn, William Saxbe for U.S. Senate Cmt, 54; spec. counsel to Attorney Gen, Ohio, 55-59; secy. to Gov. John W. Brown, 57; speaker, Sch. of Polit. for State Chmn, Wash, 58; mem, Ohio State Rep. Cent. and Exec. Cmts, 58-66; coordinator urban renewal, Hamilton, 60. Bus. & Prof. Pos: Martin A. Coyle Gen. Ins, 37-57; judge and attorney-at-law, 47-; dir, Coyle's, Inc, 57-; pres, treas. and dir, Coyle's Voting Machine Co, 60- Mil. Serv: Pvt, Army, 44. Publ: Precinct Leaders Manual, 54-58. Mem: Ohio Elec. Off. Asn.(past pres); Am, Ohio and Butler Co. Bar Asns; Mason; Elks; Jr. Order of United Am. Mechanics; Columbus Athletic Club; Hamilton City Club. Composer, Taft High Sch. Alma Mater, Hamilton. Rel: Methodist; lay leader, chmn. Pastors Rels. Cmt. and former chmn. bd. trustees, First United Methodist Church, Hamilton. Legal Res: 616 Dick Ave, Hamilton, Ohio 45013. Mailing Add: 830 High St, Hamilton, Ohio 45011.

COYNE, JOHN MARTIN D
Mayor, Brooklyn, Ohio
b. Cleveland, Ohio, 11/11/16; s. Edward Coyne and Katherine C; m. 11/30/41 to Ruth Jean Brophy; c. John M, Jr, Penny Jean (Mrs. James Dixon), Edward and James P. Educ: Ohio Univ, 36-37; LaSalle Exten. Univ. Polit. & Govt. Pos: Treas, Brooklyn Village, Ohio, 40-41 and clerk, 42-47; Mayor, Brooklyn, Ohio 48-; del, Dem. Nat. Conv, 68. Mem: Ohio Mayors Asn; Exec. Bd, Cuyahoga Co. Dem. Party; Cuyahoga Co. Mayors & City Mgrs. Asn.(pres, 58-60 and mem. exec. bd. and former secy); Kiwanis; Evangel. Deaconess Hosp. Bldg. Fund Drive; Boy Scouts; Girl Scouts. Hon. Ambassador, Air Defense. Rel: Catholic. Legal Res: 6620 Glencoe Ave, Brooklyn, Ohio 44144. Mailing Add: 7619 Memphis Ave, Brooklyn, Ohio 44144.

CRABB, DELBERT ELMO R
Chmn, McPherson Co. Rep. Party, Kans.
b. McPherson, Kans, 9/27/16; s. Paul C. Crabb and Louise Molzen C; m. 1/28/37 to Georgana Oelrich; c. Gary Conn. Educ: McPherson Col, 34-36; Univ. Kans, B.S. in Educ, 38, M.S. in Educ, 46; Phi Delta Kappa. Polit. & Govt. Pos: Chmn, McPherson Co. Rep. Party, Kans, 68- Bus. & Prof. Pos: Mem, McPherson City Sch. Bd. of Educ, 49-61 and pres, 3 years. Mil. Serv: Entered as Pvt, Army Air Corps, 42, released as 2nd Lt, 45, after serv. in 64th Combat Cargo Group. 12th Air Force, ETO, 45, Maj, Res, 442nd Mil. Airlift Wing, RG,MO; European Campaign, Po Valley, Appenines, Am. Theatre and S.Am. Ribbons. Publ: Master's Thesis on Guidance, Univ. Kans, 46. Mem: ROA (v.pres, Dept. Kans, 63 & 68); Nat. Asn. Music Merchants; Kans. Music Merchants Asn.(pres, 64); Elks; VFW; comdr, Am. Legion Post 24, 55; Am. Int. Charolais Asn. Rel: Protestant. Mailing Add: 1532 N. Walnut, McPherson, Kans. 67460.

CRABIEL, DAVID B. D
Mayor, Borough of Milltown, N.J.
b. Milltown, N.J, 6/19/30; s. Joseph M. Crabiel and Helen Glock C; m. 2/26/65 to Joyce Creighton; c. Paulette Joy. Educ: Rutgers Univ, 49; Am. Acad. Funeral Serv. in N.Y.C, 55; pres. class, 55; chmn. student coun. Polit. & Govt. Pos: Chmn. civil defense coun, Milltown, N.J, 58-59, borough councilman, 60-67, mayor, 68-; mem, All Am. Coun. Nationality, N.J. State Dem. Cmt, 63-; alternate del, Dem. Nat. Conv, 68. Bus. & Prof. Pos: Pres, Crabiel and Assocs, owners of Crabiel Home for Funerals, Milltown, N.J, Lehrer-Crabiel Funeral Home, Rahway, Gray Funeral Home, Westfield and Gray Mem. Funeral Home, Cranford. Mil. Serv: Entered as Pvt, Army, 51, released as Cpl, 53, after serv. in Alaska. Mem: Middlesex-Somerset Co. Funeral Dirs. Asn. (former secy); Nat. Funeral Dirs. Asn; N.J. Funeral Dirs. Asn; Lions; C. of C; charter mem. Jr. C. of C; Rotary; Elks; Grange; Odd Fellows; Ancient Order of Pluto Lodge 15-$\frac{1}{2}$; Milltown Dem. Club; F&AM; Perth Amboy Forest No. 68 Tall Cedars of Lebanon; YMCA (bd. dirs); Am. Legion; Middlesex Co. Tuberc. and Health League. N.Y. Funeral Dirs. Award. Rel: Methodist; assoc, Baptist church. Mailing Add: 170 N. Main St, Milltown, N.J. 08850.

CRABIEL, J. EDWARD D
N.J. State Sen.
Married to Doris Young; c. Lynda. Educ: Rutgers Univ, B.S, 36. Polit. & Govt. Pos: Mayor, Miltown, N.J, 47-51; alternate del, Dem. Nat. Conv, 48; borough engr, Milltown, 52; mem, State Air Safety Cmn, 54-62; N.J. State Assemblyman, 53-65, asst. majority leader, N.J. Gen. Assembly, 62, majority leader, 63 and minority leader, 64-65; N.J. State Sen, 65-, minority leader, N.J. Gen. Assembly, 68-; mem, N.J. Cmn. Interstate Coop, 60- Bus. & Prof. Pos: V.pres. and dir, Great North Corp, 57-; dir, Edison Bank, Edison, N.J, 66-; pres. and dir, Franklin Contracting Co, F.E. Schroder Inc. and Great North Granule Co, 67-; supervised construct. Oak Island Viaduct, Port Newark; 3 Level Intersection Garden State Pkwy. and N.J. Turnpike, Woodbridge, Trenton Freeway at State St, Trenton Cranford Viaduct and Garden

State Pkwy. Mil. Serv: Lt, Naval Res, serv. in 70th Naval Construct. Bn. Mem: Am. Soc. Civil Engrs; Raritan Valley Soc. Prfnl. Engrs; Rutgers Engr. Soc. Mailing Add: 11 Kearney Dr, Milltown, N.J. 08850.

CRABTREE, GRANVILLE H, JR. R
Fla. State Rep.
b. Chattanooga, Tenn, 11/29/29; s. Granville H. Crabtree and Gladys Wynn C; m. 5/22/56 to Paulette Vitrier; c. Michelle and John G. Educ: Univ. Calif, 53; Mex. City Col, 54; Univ. Mo, B.S, 56; George Wash. Univ, LL.B, 60; Lambda Chi Alpha; Student pres, Pub. & Bus. Admin, Univ. Mo. Polit. & Govt. Pos: Pres, Rep. Party League, Sarasota, Fla, 61; attorney, Sarasota Co. Planning Cmt, 61-62; Fla. State Rep, 119th Dist, 66- Bus. & Prof. Pos: Practicing attorney, 60- Mil. Serv: Entered Officer Cand. Sch, Army, 48, released as Capt, 53, after serv. in numerous units in Europe, Occup. of Germany, Korean War and Occup. of Japan, Res, 53-59; Grad, Officer Cand. Sch, 50; Occup. Germany Medal; Occup. Japan Medal; Korean Serv. Medal with 5 Campaign Stars; Korean Serv. Unit Citation; Commendation Ribbon with Metal Pendant; Airborne Medal. Mem: Am. and Sarasota Co. Bar Asns; Elks; Am. Legion; VFW. Rel: Episcopal. Mailing Add: 4308 Camino Real, Sarasota, Fla. 33581.

CRABTREE, PAUL LEONARD D
b. South Webster, Ohio, 9/1/29; s. Trella R. Crabtree and Margaret Leonard C; m. 11/14/49 to Rita Mae Anderson; c. Margaret V, Jon A, Vyvyanne L, Matthew W. and Carole V. Educ: Rio Grande Col; Marshall Univ; W.Va. State Col, A.B, 66. Polit. & Govt. Pos: Exec. asst. to U.S. Rep. Ken Hechler, 58-61; spec. asst. to Gov. W.Va, 61-65; mem. cmt. on resolutions, W.Va. Young Dem. Clubs, 63, chmn, 64; del, Dem. Nat. Conv, 64 & 68; admin. asst. to Gov. Hulett C. Smith, 65-66, exec. asst, 66-69. Bus. & Prof. Pos: Staff mem, Charleston Gazette, W.Va, 51-57, news ed, 57-58; pres, Paul Crabtree & Assocs, Inc, 69- Mil. Serv: Entered as Pvt, Army, 46, released as Sgt, 47, after serv. in Eighth Army Hq, U.S. Japanese Occup. Forces. Newspaper honors for editorial writing, features and page make-up. Rel: Protestant. Legal Res: 511 McNeill Ave, Point Pleasant, W.Va. 25550. Mailing Add: P.O. Box 106, Point Pleasant, W.Va. 25550.

CRABTREE, PAULETTE R
b. Charleston, W.Va, 4/8/37; d. Herve Paul Vitrieg and Clarice West V; m. 4/22/57 to Granville Hayward Crabtree, Jr; c. Michelle Vivian and John Granville. Educ: Stephens Col, 2 years; George Washington Univ, Sch. of Govt, Washington, D.C; Debate team. Polit. & Govt. Pos: Rep. precinct committeewoman, 15th Precinct, Sarasota Co, Fla, 60-, secy, 5 years, v.chmn, 1 year; del, Rep. Nat. Conv, 68. Bus. & Prof. Pos: Teacher, Soc. Studies, Jr. High, 5 years. Mem: Young Republicans; Sarasota Co. Rep. Women's Club; Sarasota Bay Rep. Women's Club; Venice-Nokomio Rep. Women's Club, Republican Party League; dir, Cancer Soc. of Sarasota; dir, Coun. on Epilepsy; dir, Aslo Theatre Festival Asn. Three awards, Cancer Soc. Rel: Catholic. Mailing Add: 4308 Camino Real, Sarasota, Fla. 33579.

CRADDICK, THOMAS RUSSELL 'TOM' R
Tex. State Rep.
b. Beloit, Wis, 9/19/43; s. Russell Francis Craddick and Beatrice Eleanor Kowalick C; single. Educ: Tex. Tech. Col, B.B.A, 65, M.B.A, 66, study, 66-; Phi Alpha Kappa; Alpha Kappa Psi; Saddle Tramps; Tex. Tech. Finance Asn. Polit. & Govt. Pos: Tex. State Rep, 69- Bus. & Prof. Pos: V.pres. and dir, C.B.C. Inc, Midland, Tex, 67-; v.pres. and dir, Gulf States Enterprises, Inc, 67-; partner, Cowden, Berry, Craddick, 67-; dir, Great West. Sulphur Co, Inc, 69- Mem: Southwest. Finance Asn; Jr. C. of C; Lions; Boys' Club, Midland (dir); Midland Tex. Tech. Col. Ex-Students Asn.(pres). Rel: Catholic. Mailing Add: 1508 W. Missouri, Midland, Tex. 79701.

CRAFT, CECIL I. R
b. Gate, Okla, 5/12/09; m. 10/1/33; c. Cecil I, Jr, John Charles, Thomas Eric and Susan Ann. Educ: Colo. Sch. of Mines; Univ. Okla, Beta Theta Pi. Polit. & Govt. Pos: Nebr. State Sen, 61-66. Bus. & Prof. Pos: Partner, Eng. Firm. Mem: Kiwanis; Am. Legion. Mailing Add: 1512 W. B St, North Platte, Nebr. 69101. (1967)

CRAFT, JERRY DAVID D
Committeeman, Tex. Dem. Exec. Cmt.
b. Jacksboro, Tex, 4/17/37; s. J.D. Craft and Helen Louise Johnson C; m. 11/26/60 to Mary Sue Moore; c. Jay David, Sue Helen and Clint Creighton. Educ: Tex. Tech. Col, B.S, 59; Block & Bridle Club; Sigma Alpha Epsilon. Polit. & Govt. Pos: Del, Dem. State Conv, Tex, 66 & 68 and mem. party officer's cmt, 66; alternate del, Dem. Nat. Conv, 68; committeeman, Tex. Dem. Exec. Cmt, 68 & 69- and chmn. youth affairs subcmt, 69. Bus. & Prof. Pos: Rancher, Tex, Okla. and N.Mex; secy. bd. and part-owner, Bowie Cable TV, Inc. Mem: Tex. Angus Asn; Am. Polled Hereford Asn; Am. Quarter Horse Asn; Tex. and Southwest. Cattle Raiser's Asn; pres, Gr. Jacksboro League; bd. dirs, Jack Co. Water Bd; dir, W.Tex. C. of C; dist. rep, Tex. Tech. Ex-Student Asn; v.pres, Jacksboro C. of C; pres, Jack Co. Young Farmer's Chap. Rel: Methodist; chmn. bd, Jacksboro Methodist Church. Mailing Add: 601 N. Fifth St, Jacksboro, Tex. 76056.

CRAFT, KATHRYN T. D
b. Texarkana, Ark, 2/5/20; d. George Taylor and Nazrene McElroy T; m. 4/23/45 to Seafus William Craft; c. Cheryl Ann and Sandra Eta. Educ: Univ. Ark, M.S, Elem. Educ, 52. Polit. & Govt. Pos: Precinct chmn, D.C. Dem. Cent. Cmt, 64-68, liaison leader, 68-; del, Dem. Nat. Conv, 68. Bus. & Prof. Pos: Teacher, Pine Bluff, Ark. Bd. of Educ, 49-52; teacher, Pittsvania Co. Bd. of Educ, Va, 52-56; teacher, spec. educ, D.C. Bd. of Educ, 56-67; teacher, spec. educ, Prince Georges Co. Bd. of Educ, Md, 67- Mil. Serv: Entered as Pvt, Woman's Army Air Corp, 44, released as Pfc, 45. Mem: Nat. Educ. Asn; Coun. Exceptional Children; Md. State Teachers Asn; Benning Ridge Civic Asn; Bradbury Heights Soil Tillers; 14th Precinct Adv. Coun. Rel: Protestant. Mailing Add: 1100 44th Place S.E, Washington, D.C. 20019.

CRAFT, WILLIAM F. R
Wyo. State Rep.
b. 8/20/26; m. to Ione; c. Nine. Polit. & Govt. Pos: Wyo. State Rep, 4th term; mem, Sch. Bd. Bus. & Prof. Pos: Farmer & Feeder. Mem: Big Horn Co. Sch. Planning Cmn; Am. Legion; Farm Bur; Big Horn Basin Beet Growers Asn. Rel: Catholic. Mailing Add: Box 509, Greybull, Wyo. 82426. (1967)

CRAIG, CARL H. D
b. Olive Branch, Miss, 8/16/05; married. Polit. & Govt. Pos: Miss. State Rep, until 68. Bus. & Prof. Pos: Poultryman; cattleman; feed miller. Mem: C. of C; Cattlemen's Asn; Farm Bur. Rel: Methodist. Mailing Add: Box 404, Brookhaven, Miss. 39601. (1967)

CRAIG, HUBERT MAXTON, JR. R
b. Stanley, N.C, 1/16/31; s. Hubert Maxton Craig and Beulah Rimmer C; m. 8/23/52 to Constance Virginia Rollins; c. Susan Ann, David R, Hubert Maxton, III and Mary Cynthia. Educ: Wake Forest Col, B.S, 52; Delta Sigma Pi; Pi Kappa Alpha. Polit. & Govt. Pos: Treas, Gaston Co. Rep. Party, N.C, 60-64; alternate del, Rep. Nat. Conv, 64 & 68; treas, Tenth Cong. Dist. Rep. Party, 64-65; N.C. State Rep, 67-68. Bus. & Prof. Pos: Pres, Gaston Co. Dyeing Machine Co, 52- and Craig Realty & Develop. Co, 54-; mem. bd. trustees, Gardner-Webb Col, 62-; mem. bd. dirs, Citizens Nat. Bank Gastonia, 64- Mem: Nat. Asn. Mfrs; Nat. Bd. Realtors; Lions Int. Rel: Baptist. Mailing Add: General Wheeler St, Stanley, N.C. 28164.

CRAIG, JAMES DONALD R
Chmn, Brookfield Town Rep. Cmt, Conn.
b. New York, N.Y, 3/6/21; s. Thomas Andrew Craig and Edith Carlson C; m. 1/3/42 to Eleanor Tully; c. Jeffrey T. Educ: Bucknell Univ, B.S, 41; Cap and Dager; Phi Kappa Psi. Polit. & Govt. Pos: Mem, Bethel Town Rep. Cmt, and justice of peace, Conn, 49; chmn, Brookfield Town Rep. Cmt, Conn, 64- Bus. & Prof. Pos: Pres, Hunting Ridge, Inc, 58-62; U.S. Develop. Corp, 60-66, Wooster Co. Inc, 60-66 and White Elephant Corp, 65-66. Mil. Serv: Entered as Pvt, Army Air Force, 41, released as Lt, 44, after serv. in Fifth Air Force, Pac. Theater, 42-43. Mem: Nat. Asn. Home Builders (bd. dirs, 62); Brookfield C. of C.(bd. dirs, 64); maj. gifts chmn, Red Cross, 65-66; Exchange Club; Nat. Coun. of Salesmens Orgns; Navy League; Candlewood Valley Country Club. Rel: Presbyterian. Mailing Add: Stony Hill Rd, Brookfield, Conn. 06804. (1967)

CRAIG, LOUIS G. D
b. Weston, W.Va, 4/29/08; single. Educ: W.Va. Univ, A.B; George Wash. Univ, LL.B; Gamma Eta Gamma; Fi Batar Capper (sic). Polit. & Govt. Pos: W.Va. State Del, 56-66; priority Claimants Chief for War Assets Admin; Selector for Displaced Persons Cmn; Mayor, Weston, W.Va, 61-65. Bus. & Prof. Pos: Lawyer. Mil. Serv: WW II, 66th Inf. Div. Mem: Odd Fellows; Am. Legion; VFW. Rel: Methodist. Mailing Add: Box 775, Weston, W.Va. 26452. (1967)

CRAIG, PAUL E. D
b. Hudson, Iowa, 12/29/20; s. William Craig; m. to Betty Louis Krivohlavy; c. Steven Paul and Cathy Ann. Educ: Univ. of Iowa, 46-47. Polit. Pos: Iowa State Rep-66. Bus. & Prof. Pos: Employee, Northwest Bell Tel. Co, 15 Years. Mil. Serv: WWII, U.S. Navy, 41-45. Mem: Boy Scouts; Am. Legion. Rel: Presbyterian. Mailing Add: 105 Anson Circle, Marshalltown, Iowa 50158. (1967)

CRAIG, ROBERT 'BOB' D
Ill. State Rep.
b. Oakwood, Ill, 10/28/21; married; c. One. Educ: Utterback Bus. Col; Reppert's Sch. of Auctioneering, Decatur, Ind. Polit. & Govt. Pos: Precinct committeeman, Dem. Party, Ill, 46-; secy, Dem. Cent. Cmt, 2 years; twp. supvr, 49, reelected, 53; Ill. State Rep, currently. Bus. & Prof. Pos: Auctioneer; operates grain, dairy, livestock farm. Mailing Add: Indianola, Ill. 61850. (1967)

CRAIG, ROGER E. D
Mich. State Sen.
b. Blairsville, Pa, 4/24/33; married; c. Ryan, Kelly, Carrick and Kimberly. Educ: Wayne State Univ, B.A, J.D. Polit. & Govt. Pos: Past pres, Dearborn Bd. of Educ; mem, State Tenure Cmt; Mich. State Sen, 64- Bus. & Prof. Pos: Attorney. Mem: Am. Civil Liberties Union; Am. for Dem. Action; Mich. Assoc. of Sch. Bd; Am. Trial Lawyers Asn; Mich. State and Dearborn Bar Asns; 16th Dist. Dem. Orgn; 15 Dist. Dem. Orgn; Dem. Clubs of Allen Park, Lincoln Park, Southgate and Taylor. Rel: Protestant. Mailing Add: 7436 Pinehurst, Dearborn, Mich. 41826. (1967)

CRAIG, RUSSELL H. R
Educ: Boston Univ. Polit. & Govt. Pos: Mass. State Rep, until 68; clerk of courts, Dist. Court of Peabody, Mass, currently. Bus. & Prof. Pos: Owner, Craig Realty Corp; Craig Ins. Agency. Mil. Serv: World War II. Mem: Gr. Lynn Real Estate Bd.(pres, secy, treas); Gr. Lynn C. of C.(secy); Am. Red Cross (v.pres. and dir); Lynn Heart Asn; Exec. Cmt. Boy Scouts; dir, Union Hosp; Am. Legion; Elks. Mailing Add: 35 Munroe St, Lynnfield, Mass. 01940.

CRAIG, WILLIAM H. D
Chmn, N.H. Dem. Party
b. Manchester, N.H, 8/26/27; married; c. Four. Educ: St. Anselm's Col; Boston Univ. Polit. & Govt. Pos: Chmn, N.H. Dem. Party, 67-; del, Dem. Nat. Conv, 68. Bus. & Prof. Pos: Attorney-at-law. Mil. Serv: Navy. Rel: Catholic. Mailing Add: 84 Bay St, Manchester, N.H. 03104.

CRAIN, V. RICHARD DFL
b. Lincoln Co, Minn, 1916; married; c. 4. Educ: Ivanhoe Teacher Training Dept. Polit. & Govt. Pos: Minn. State Rep, 64-66. Bus. & Prof. Pos: Grain, livestock farmer; auctioneer; former teacher, 6 years. Mem: Dir, Prod. Credit Asn. of Marshall; Farmers Independent Elevator Co. of Ivanhoe. Mailing Add: Route 1, Hendricks, Minn. 56136. (1967)

CRALEY, N. NEIMAN, JR. D
b. Red Lion, Pa, 11/17/27; s. N. Neiman Craley, Sr. and Alverta Peters C; m. to Ruthe Fortenbaugh; c. Nathaniel, Sally, Stacy and Harry. Educ: Gettysburg Col, B.A, 50; Lambda Chi Alpha. Polit. & Govt. Pos: Asst. Cmnr. for Pub. Affairs, Saipan, 67-; U.S. Rep, 19th Cong.Dist, Pa, 65-67; chmn, York Co. Dem. Cmt, Pa, 62-63. Bus. & Prof. Pos: Pres, Red Lion Furniture Co, 53-65, sales mgr, 50-53. Mem: House Cmt, York YMCA; Izaac Walton League; York Area C. of C; York City Parking Authority; Moose; Gr. Carlisle Area C. of C. Rel: Lutheran. Legal Res: 49 E. Springettsbury Ave, York, Pa. 17403. Mailing Add: P.O. Box 1341, York, Pa. 17405. (1967)

CRAM, OLE ROBERT R
b. Stockton, Kans, 3/22/87; s. James E. Cram and Ida Helen Forrey C; m. 6/30/14 to Elizabeth M. Ringo; c. James J, Ole Robert and Ernest Richard. Educ: Local and McPherson Col, Kans. Polit. & Govt. Pos: Co. surveyor, Cheyenne Co, Kans, 10-12; co. supt. schs, 15-19; Kans. State Rep, 21-23 & 57-67; co. attorney, Cheyenne Co, 32-33 & 35-39. Bus. & Prof. Pos: V.pres, Cheyenne Co. State Bank, St. Francis, Kans, 22-; pres. and attorney for Cheyenne Co. Bldg. & Loan Asn, 28-51. Mem: Kans. Bar; AF&AM; Odd Fellows; Rotary; Local Civil Air Patrol Squadron, 67-, Private Pilot Rating. Rel: Methodist. Mailing Add: 420 E. Spencer, St. Francis, Kans. 67756.

CRAMER, ANN MARIE JOAN D
V.Chmn, Dem. Exec. Cmt, Fla.
b. Buffalo, N.Y, 11/1/25; d. Lawrence Nicholas Bowman and Barbara Herman B; m. 5/30/41 to Hugh Bernard Michael Cramer; c. Ann Marie, Mary Beth, Cathleen Bridget and Twins, Hugh Skiffington and Lawrence Robert. Educ: Rollins Col. Polit. & Govt. Pos: V.chmn, Dem. Exec. Cmt, Fla, 62-; Dem. Precinct committeewoman, Fla, 54-58; state committeewoman, Broward Co, 58-; del, Dem. Nat. Conv, 60, 64 & 68 and mem. Credentials Cmt, 64 and Platform Cmt, 68; v.chmn, Dem. Exec. Cmt, Fla, 62-; asst, Pres. Cmt. Voting Participation and Registration, 63; mem, U.S. Adv. Coun. World's Fair, Toronto, 67. Bus. & Prof. Pos: Real estate broker, 58- Mem: Am. Legion Auxiliary; dir, W.Hollywood C. of C; Women's C. of C. of Hollywood; Gr. Hollywood C. of C; Women of the Moose; past pres, W.Broward Lion's Auxiliary and S.Broward Women's Club; League of Women Voters; v.pres, Cath. Club. Named Fla. Dem. Woman of the Year, Dem. Nat. Cmt, 60. Rel: Catholic; former choir dir, Little Flower and St. Stephens Church. Mailing Add: 6249 S.W. 27th St, West Hollywood, Fla. 33023.

CRAMER, J. ALAN R
Chmn, Wayne Co. Rep. Party, Nebr.
b. Atlantic, Iowa, 7/10/32; s. Mark E. Cramer (deceased) and Margaret Range C; m. 7/28/56 to Diana Fellows; c. Mark Alan. Educ: Wayne State Col, 50; Nebr. Univ, 50-52; State Univ. Iowa, B.A, 55; Sigma Delta Chi; Kappa Alpha Mu; Sigma Alpha Epsilon. Polit. & Govt. Pos: Chmn, City Planning Cmn, Wayne, Nebr, 64-68; pres, bd. gov, N.E. Nebr. Tech. Sch, 67-; chmn, Robert Denney for Cong. Cmt, 68; chmn, Wayne Co. Rep. Party, 68-; trustee, Nebr. State Cols, 69- Bus. & Prof. Pos: Mem. Advisory Cmt, Univ. Nebr. Sch. Journalism, 69. Mil. Serv: Entered as 2nd Lt, Army, 55, released as 1st Lt, 57, after serv. in 1st Inf. Div. Mem: Nebr. Press Advert. Soc.(pres. and dir, 64-68); Aircraft Owners and Pilots Asn; Nebr. Press Asn.(dir, 66-); Air Force Asn; Nat. Newspaper Asn; Elks; Mason. Numerous State and Nat. Press Awards. Rel: Presbyterian. Legal Res: 711 Fairacres Rd, Wayne, Nebr. 68787. Mailing Add: Box 428, Wayne, Nebr. 68787.

CRAMER, WILLIAM C. 'BILL' R
U.S. Rep, Fla.
b. Denver, Colo, 8/4/22; s. Walter B. Cramer and Doreen Emma Walters C; m. to Alice J. Jones; c. William C, Jr, Mark C. and Allyn Walters. Educ: St. Petersburg Jr. Col; Univ. N.C, 46; Harvard Law Sch, LL.B, 48; Class Pres, St. Petersburg Jr. Col; Phi Beta Kappa; Sigma Chi; Phi Alpha Delta. Hon. D. Jurisp, Tampa Univ, 57. Polit. & Govt. Pos: V.chmn, Rep. Conf. Policy Cmt; v.chmn, Rep. Cong. Campaign Cmt; GOP campaign dir, Pinellas Co, Fla, 50; minority leader, Fla. State Legis, 50-52; regional dir, Young Rep. Nat. Fedn, 51-53; chmn, Fla. Col. Electors, 52; v.chmn. Fla. Del, Rep. Nat. Conv, 52-60; co. attorney, Pinellas Co, 53-54; v.chmn, Young Rep. Nat. Fedn, 53-55; U.S. Rep, Fla, 54-, ranking minority mem. cmt. pub. works, U.S. House Rep, currently; Rep. Nat. Committeeman, Fla, 64-; mem. exec. cmt, Rep. Nat. Cmt, currently. Bus. & Prof. Pos: Partner, Law Firm of Ramseur, Bradham, Lyle, Skipper & Cramer, St. Petersburg, Fla, currently. Mil. Serv: Navy, 43-46, Lt.(jg); Citation, Invasion of South. France; Naval Res. Mem: VFW; Am. Legion; Amvets; Elks; Moose; Ahepa; Mason; Shrine; Fed, Am, Mass, Fla. and St. Petersburg Bar Asns. Rel: Methodist. Legal Res: St. Petersburg, Fla. Mailing Add: 6215 Beachway Dr, Falls Church, Va. 22041.

CRAMPTON, RICHARD SNOW R
V.Pres, City Coun, West Hartford, Conn.
b. Hartford, Conn, 6/8/13; s. Edwin Merwin Crampton and Hazel Ann McClunie C; m. 8/18/44 to Barbara Messinger; c. Samuel Richard (deceased), Ann Messinger and Sarah Hosley. Educ: Yale Univ, A.B, 35; Alpha Delta Phi; Book & Snake. Polit. & Govt. Pos: Mem, Second Dist. Rep. Cmt, Conn, 53-; councilman, West Hartford, Conn, 63-67, v.pres, City Coun, 67- Bus. & Prof. Pos: Asst. secy, Conn. Gen. Life Ins. Co, 55- Mil. Serv: Entered as A/S, Coast Guard, 42, released as Lt. Comdr, 48, after serv. in Greenland Patrol, 43-44 and Pac. Theater, 44-45; ETO and Pac. Theater Ribbons; Invasion of Borneo Medal; Tacloban Ribbon; Lt. Comdr, Coast Guard Res.(Ret). Mem: Int. Claim Asn; Yale Club; Thames Yacht Club; Hartford Tennis Club; Red Oak Hill Swimming Club. Rel: Episcopal. Mailing Add: 18 Concord, West Hartford, Conn. 06119.

CRAMTON, LOUIS KAY R
Mem, Rep. Exec. Cmt, Mich.
b. Lapeer, Mich, 12/5/15; s. Louis Convers Cramton and Fame Kay C; m. 4/23/45 to Dorothy Ellen Chapman; c. Margie Kay (Mrs. Louis F. Wojnaroski). Educ: Alma Col, A.B, 38; Tau Kappa Epsilon. Polit. & Govt. Pos: Pres, Lapeer Co. Young Rep, Mich, 39-41; Rep. precinct chmn, 18th Precinct Saginaw; bd. mem, Saginaw Co. Rep. Club; co. del, Rep. State Conv; Rep. precinct del, Lapeer Co. Conv, 39-41, Saginaw Co. Conv, 49-53 and Midland Co. Conv, 53-; treas, Midland Co. Rep. Breakfast Club, 53, pres, 53-64 and mem. exec. bd, 65-; mem, Rep. Exec. Cmt, currently. Mil. Serv: Entered as Pvt, Army, 41, released as Cpl, 45, after serv. in 14th Signal Corps, Aleutians; Pac. Theater Ribbon with 2 Stars; Am. Theater Ribbon. Publ: Columnist, 'This is How I See It.' Mem: Kiwanis; Elks; VFW; Am. Legion; hon. mem. Midland Jr. C. of C; Saginaw Valley Arts Coun; bd. dirs, Mich. Commun. Theatre Asn; bd. dirs, Midland Center of the Arts; finance cmt, Paul Bunyan Coun, Boy Scouts; past pres. and mem. bd, Midland Little Theater Guild; mem. bd. dirs, Midland Co. Rehabilitation Serv. for Handicapped, 68-; past bd. mem. and v.pres, Midland Big Brothers; mem. bd. and past pres, Midland Muscular Dystrophy Asn. Am, Inc. Citizenship Award, Midland Co. Rep. Breakfast Club, 65. Rel: Presbyterian. Mailing Add: 120 Mertz, Midland, Mich. 48640.

CRANDALL, EARLE P. R
Calif. State Assemblyman
b. Rayne, La, 5/31/04; s. Jesse Lawrence Crandall and Lela E. Dodge C; m. 8/25/29 to Margarethe Kroeck; c. Dr. Peter L. and Nancy (Mrs. J. Robert Foster). Educ: Col. of Pacific, A.B, 27, Secondary Credential, 31 and Secondary Admin, 36; Stanford Univ, M.A, 42 and Ed.D, 46; charter mem, Local Field Chap, Phi Delta Kappa. Polit. & Govt. Pos: Calif. State Assemblyman, 25th Dist, 66-; mem, Calif. Rep. State Cent. Cmt, 69- Bus. & Prof. Pos: Teacher, Lodi Union High Sch, 31-36, v.prin, 36-42, prin, 42-46; dir. curriculum, San Jose Unified Sch. Dist, 46-50, supt, 50-66. Mem: Col. Pac. Alumni Asn.(pres); life mem. Nat. Educ. Asn; Bay Area Curriculum Coun. (pres); Am. Asn. Sch. Adminstr; Calif. Teachers Asn.(policies cmn); Calif. Asn. Sch. Adminstr.(bd. gov); Rotary; C. of C; YMCA (bd. dirs); Police Adv. Bd; F&AM; Scottish Rite (32°). Rel: Methodist Episcopal. Legal Res: 1175 Roycott Way, San Jose, Calif. 95125. Mailing Add: 760 N. First St, San Jose, Calif. 95112. (1967)

CRANDALL, ETHEL LEANNA D
W.Va. State Del.
b. Gauley Bridge, W.Va, 4/20/11; d. Willis Oscar Crandall and Mary Robson C; single. Educ: W.Va. Inst. Tech, A.B, 34; W.Va. Univ, summer 34; Phi Mu Gamma. Polit. & Govt. Pos: Treas, Fayette Co. Dem. Exec. Cmt, W.Va, 60-; W.Va. State Del, 62-64 & 66-; mem, Falls Dist. Dem. Woman's Club, 62-; assoc. chmn, Dem. Campaign, Fayette Co, 66. Bus. & Prof. Pos: Teacher, Fayette Co. Schs, W.Va, 34-55; pres. and owner, W. O. Crandall Hardware Co, Gauley Bridge, 55- Mil. Serv: Entered as Pvt, WAAC, 43, released as S/Sgt, 46, after serv. in 12th Mapping and Charting Squadron, 311th Photo Wing, Lowery Field Colo; Victory Medal; Am. Theatre Medal; Good Conduct Medal. Mem: Am. Asn. Univ. Women; W.Va. and Fayette Co. Hist. Socs; former mem, W.Va. Educ. Asn; Order of Women Legislators; Hon. Order of Ky. Colonels; Kanuga Woman's Club; Am. Legion; past matron, Eastern Star, chap. 72, Gauley Bridge; Gauley Garden Club; WAC Vet. Asn; Fayette Co. Ment. Health Asn; Nat. Rehabilition Asn; appointed by W.Va. Univ. Bd. Gov. to Fayette Co. Agr. Serv, 68-; W.Va. Tech. Alumni Asn. Selected as Dem. Woman of the Year, Fifth Dist, W.Va, 63. Rel: Methodist. Mailing Add: Gauley Bridge, W.Va. 25085.

CRANDALL, HORACE CHARLES R
b. North Loup, Nebr, 6/4/96; s. Alpha L. Crandall and Genie Rood C; wid; c. Barbara (Mrs. Lewis). Educ: Univ. Nebr. Col. Agr, B.Sc. in agr, 20; Univ. Wis, grad. work, 6 summers; Univ. Colo, 1 summer; Univ. Nebr, 3 summers; Gamma Sigma Delta; Agr. Club; Dairy Club. Polit. & Govt. Pos: Nebr. State Sen, 46th Dist. 65-66, v.chmn, Agr. Cmt, mem, Educ. Cmt, mem, Labor Cmt. Bus. & Prof. Pos: Mem. of faculty, Univ. Nebr. Sch. Agr, 43 years; asst. supt, 30 years, supt. 2 years, retired, 1963. Mem: Nebr. Educ. Asn; Adminstrs. Asn; Nat. Educ. Asn; Rotary Int, past pres; Curtis Improvement Corp; Wheat Growers Asn; C. of C; Nebr. Alumni Asn; Farm Bur; S.Platt United C. of C. Rel: Methodist. Mailing Add: Curtis, Nebr. 69025.

CRANDALL, VERNIE RAYMOND D
b. Tulsa, Okla, 5/21/15; s. Albert Crandall and Ethel Radford C; m. 10/22/41 to Frances Louise Phillips; c. Stephen G. and Douglas Kent. Educ: Univ. Mo, A.B, 41, LL.B, 48; Delta Theta Phi. Polit. & Govt. Pos: City attorney, Carthage, Mo, 52-60; del, Dem. Nat. Conv, 68. Mil. Serv: Entered as Maj, Army, 41, released 46, after serv. in Ninth Inf. Div, Artil, ETO, 41-45; ETO Medal; Amphibious Landing Medal with Three Stars; Bronze Star; Purple Heart with Cluster of Six Battle Stars. Mem: Mo, Jasper Co. and Fed. Bar Asns; Mason; Shrine; K. of P; Col, Mo. Gov. Staff; A.S.C.L. Rel: Episcopal. Mailing Add: 502 E. Centinnial, Carthage, Mo. 64836.

CRANE, BRUCE R
Mem, Rep. Nat. Cmt.
b. Dalton, Mass, 7/27/09; s. W. Murray Crane and Josephine Boardman C; m. 5/14/32 to Winnie Davis Long; c. 2 daughters, Mrs. William Greene and Mrs. William Mackey. Educ: Yale Univ, 31. Polit. & Govt. Pos: Mem, Mass. Gov. Coun, 53-56; mem, Rep. Nat. Cmt, currently; del, Rep. Nat. Conv, 68. Bus. & Prof. Pos: Pres, Crane and Co, Inc, 51- Rel: Congregational. Mailing Add: 45 Main St, Dalton, Mass. 01226.

CRANE, HENRIETTA PAGE R
V.chmn, Knox Co. Rep. Cmt, Maine
b. Skowhegan, Maine, 1/1/13; d. Blin Williams Page and Edith Nay P; div; c. Kennedy, III, Trudy (Mrs. Housman), Tobey Campbell. Educ: Wellesley Col, B.A, 35; Tau Zeta Epsilon. Polit. & Govt. Pos: V-chmn, Rockport Rep. Party Cmt, Maine, 60-64 and chmn, 64-67; alternate del, Rep. Nat. Conv, 68; co. committeewoman, Rockland Co. Rep. Party Cmt, 68-; v.chmn, Knox Co. Rep. Party Cmt, 68- Bus. & Prof. Pos: Chmn, Maine for Wellesley Col. Develop. Fund, Mass, 52-56; exec. cmt, Gov's Adv. Cmt. on Educ, Maine, 56-61, trustee, Knox Co. Gen. Hosp, 59-; dir, Coastal Ment. Health Asn, 66-; dir, Pinetree Soc. Crippled Children, 67- Mem: Skowhegan Woman's Club (pres, 45-48); Maine chmn. cmt. Skowhegan Sch. Painting & Sculpture, 68- Rel: Congregational. Mailing Add: 30 Shaw Ave, Rockland, Maine 04841.

CRANE, ROBERT DICKSON R
Policy Planner and Syst. Analyst, Dept. of State
b. Cambridge, Mass, 3/26/29; s. John Bever Crane and Catherine Dickson C; m. 3/5/51 to Sigrid Ruedel; c. Marietta, Hanns and Mark. Educ: Northwest. Univ, B.A. summa cum laude, 56; Harvard Law Sch, J.D, 59; Phi Beta Kappa. Polit. & Govt. Pos: Dep. head China Affairs, Defense Research Div, U.S. Air Force, 59-61; chmn. Civil Rights Cmt, Fairfax Co. Rep. Cmt, Va, 64-66; policy planner and syst. analyst, Dept. of State, 69- Bus. & Prof. Pos: Consult, Senate Cmt. on Aeronaut. and Space Sci, U.S. Info. Agency, Dept. of Defense and Bendix Syst. Div, Bendix Corp, 61-69; research prin, Center for Strategic and Int. Studies, Georgetown Univ, 62-66; proj. dir, Hudson Inst, 66-69. Mil. Serv: Entered as Recruit, Army, 50, released as Cpl, 53, after serv. in Eighth Army Hq. Intel. Div, Korea, 52-53; Commendation Ribbon; Unit Citation; Syngman Rhee Commendation Ribbon. Publ: Soviet Military Strategy: A Critical Appraisal, Georgetown Univ, 63; Detente: Cold War Strategies in Transition, Praeger, 65; 'New Directions for American Foreign Policy,' Orbis, summer 69. Mem: Am. Polit. Sci. Asn; Am. Soc. of Int. Law; Mil.

Opers. Research Soc. Research fel, Am. Soc. Int. Law; assoc. fel, Am. Soc. Aeronaut. and Astronaut. Rel: Roman Catholic. Mailing Add: 511 Kramer Dr, Vienna, Va. 22180.

CRANE, ROBERT Q. D
Mass. State Treas. and Receiver Gen.
b. Providence, R.I, 3/21/26; married; c. five. Educ: Boston Col. Sch. Bus. Admin. Polit. & Govt. Pos: Mass. State Rep, 57-64, asst. majority leader, Mass. House of Rep, 2 years and v.chmn, House Cmt. Munic. Finance; Mass. state treas. and receiver gen, 64, 65- Bus. & Prof. Pos: Food broker and sales mgr, 15 years; ins. broker, 8 years. Mil. Serv: Marine Corps. Mem: Am. Legion; K. of C; DAV; VFW; Elks. Mailing Add: 7 Mountview Rd, Wellesley, Mass. 02181.

CRANE, VERBON E. D
Ala. State Rep.
b. Warrior, Ala, 11/13/19; s. James Henry Crane and Nannie Ida Bibb C; m. 10/19/47 to Gladys Parker; c. Susan Carol. Educ: Samford Univ, B.S, 50; Auburn Univ, M.S, 52; Alpha Kappa Psi. Polit. & Govt. Pos: Mem, City Coun, Kimberly, Ala, 51-64, mayor, 66; Ala. State Rep, 67- Bus. & Prof. Pos: Prin, Jefferson Co. Sch. Syst; prin, Snow Rogers Elem. Sch, 48-54; prin, Fultondale Jr. High Sch, 54- Mil. Serv: Entered as Aviation Cadet, Air Force, 42, released as T/Sgt, 45, after serv. in 22nd Statist. Control Unit, China-Burma-India Theater, 43-45; Two Battle Stars; Good Conduct Medal; Bronze Star. Mem: Jr. High Prin. Asn; Ala. and Nat. Educ. Asn; Eagles; Sertoma Club; Am. Legion. Rel: Methodist. Mailing Add: Box 98, Kimberly, Ala. 35091.

CRANGLE, JOSEPH F. D
Exec. Mem, N.Y. State Dem. Cmt.
b. Buffalo, N.Y, 6/12/32; s. Edward J. Crangle and Margarita Anastasia McNutt C; m. to Rita J. Henry; c. Mary Elizabeth, Catherine Ann, Elizabeth Ann, Brigid Marie and Joseph Patrick. Educ: Canisius Col, A.B, 55; Univ. of Buffalo Law Sch, LL.B, 59; Alpha Sigma Nu. Polit. & Govt. Pos: Committeeman, Erie Co. Dem. Cmt, N.Y, 58, ward chmn, 60-65, co. chmn, 65-; exec. asst. to Speaker of N.Y. State Assembly, 66-68; del, Dem. Nat. Conv, 68; exec. asst. and spec. counsel to Minority Leader, N.Y. State Assembly, 69-; exec. mem, N.Y. State Dem. Cmt, currently. Bus. & Prof. Pos: Attorney. Mil. Serv: 2nd Lt, Army, 56; Capt, Army Res, 56- Rel: Roman Catholic. Legal Res: 22 Linden, Buffalo, N.Y. 14214. Mailing Add: 575 Genesee Bldg, Buffalo, N.Y. 14202.

CRANK, MARION HARLAN D
b. Bearden, Ark, 2/18/15; s. Julius Walrath Crank and Mary Hughes C; m. to Mary Pauline Yauger; c. Marianne (Mrs. Neil Maynard), Robert Hughes, Margaret Helen and Elisabeth Jo. Educ: Okla. State Univ. Polit. & Govt. Pos: Ark. State Rep, Little River Co, 50-67, Speaker, Ark. State House of Rep, 63-65; mem, Adv. Cmn. on Intergovt. Rels, 64-67; Dem. nominee, Gov, Ark, 68. Bus. & Prof. Pos: V.pres, Ark. Cement Corp; owner, gen. mercantile bus; chief agr. officer, UN Relief and Rehab. Admin, Hankow, Hupeh Province, China; chief of real property control sect, Farmer Home Admin, Region 8, Dallas, Tex. Mem: Pres, Southwest. Ark. Develop. Coun. and Foreman Indust. Develop. Corp; chmn, Little River Econ. Develop. Coun. and Little River Co. Rural Develop. Authority; dir. S.W. Ark. Water Dist; v.pres, Red. River Valley Asn; past pres, Foreman Rotary Club; mem, Ark. Water Compact Cmn. Rel: Episcopal. Mailing Add: P.O. Box 6, Foreman, Ark. 71836. (1967)

CRANSTON, ALAN MacGREGOR D
U.S. Sen, Calif.
b. Palo Alto, Calif, 6/19/14; s. William MacGregor Cranston and Carol Dixon C; m. 11/6/40 to Geneva McMath; c. Robin MacGregor and Kim MacGregor. Educ: Stanford Univ, B.A, 36; Sigma Nu; Track Team, 35-36. Polit. & Govt. Pos: Chief for. lang. div, Off. War Info, U.S. Govt, 42-44; pres, Calif. Dem. Coun, 53-57; mem. exec. cmt, Dem. State Cent. Cmt, 54-; state controller, Calif. State Govt, 59-67; U.S. Sen, Calif, 69- Bus. & Prof. Pos: For. correspondent, Int. News Serv, 36-38; owner, Cranston Co, 47-50. Mil. Serv: Entered as Pvt, Army, 44, released as Sgt, 45, after serv. in Inf. in U.S. Publ: Mein Kampf (Anti-Hitler version), Noram Co, 39; The Killing of the Peace, Viking & Compass, 45, 60; 'A Million Dollar Loser Looks at Campaigning,' Fortune, 64. Mem: Overseas Press Club; Moose; Elks; pres, United World Federalists, 49-52. Rel: Protestant. Legal Res: Los Angeles, Calif. 36128. Mailing Add: 2102 New Senate Office Bldg, Washington, D.C. 20510.

CRAPO, RAYMOND F. D
b. Phila, Pa, 10/18/34; s. George Swafford Crapo and Helen McNulty C; m. 10/1/57 to Ann Durham; c. Colleen Linne, Valerie Ann and Tara Leigh. Educ: Univ. Va, B.A, 60; Theta Chi; Lambda Pi. Polit. & Govt. Pos: Poll watcher, Cmt. Seventy, 52; committeeman, Tredyffrin Twp. West 3, 63, 64, 66 & 68; chmn, Tredyffrin Twp. Dem. Party, 65-66; zone leader, Zone Four, Chester Co, 65-66 & 67-68; mem. Dem. Nominating Cmt, Chester Co, 64 & 66; chmn, Chester Co. Dem. Conv, 68; alternate del, Dem. Nat. Conv, 68; cand. tax collector, Tredyffrin Twp, 70. Bus. & Prof. Pos: Divisional credit mgr, Straw Bridge & Clothier, Phila, 60-64; credit rep, E.I. du Pont de Nemours, Del, 64-67; asst. to v.pres, Peoples Consumer, Phila, 67- Mil. Serv: Entered as Cpl, Army, 57, released as Cpl, 59, after serv. in Artillery; Four Letters of Commendation; Good Conduct Medal. Mem: Del. Valley Credit Execs. Asn; Va. Club. of Phila; YMCA; PTA. Rel: Episcopal. Mailing Add: 1446 Pennsylvania Ave, Paoli, Pa. 19301.

CRAPO, TERRY LaVELLE R
Majority Leader, Idaho State House of Rep.
b. Idaho Falls, Idaho, 7/2/39; s. George LaVelle Crapo and Melba Olsen C; m. 9/1/58 to Valeria Hatch; c. David John, Christa Ann, Karen Marie and Jennifer Lynn. Educ: Brigham Young Univ, B.A. and M.A, 60; Harvard Univ. Law Sch, LL.B, 63; ed, Harvard Law Rev. Polit. & Govt. Pos: Idaho State Rep, 66-, Majority Leader, Idaho State House of Rep, 68- Bus. & Prof. Pos: Attorney-at-law and partner, Holden, Holden & Kidwell, 63- Mem: Idaho State and Am. Bar Asns; Idaho Farm Bur. Rel: Latter-day Saint. Legal Res: 871 Claireview Lane, Idaho Falls, Idaho 83401. Mailing Add: P.O. Box 129, Idaho Falls, Idaho 83401.

CRAVALHO, ELMER F. D
Mayor, Maui Co, Hawaii
b. 2/19/26; single. Educ: Univ. of Hawaii. Polit. & Govt. Pos: Mem, Hawaii Territorial House, 55-59; Hawaii State Rep. and Speaker, Hawaii State House of Rep, 59-67; Mayor, Maui Co, 67-; del, Dem. Nat. Conv, 68. Bus. & Prof. Pos: Teacher, Dept. of Pub. Instr, Hawaii, 46-54; exec. v.pres. & gen. mgr, Maui Supply Inc; organizer and mgr, Kula Commun. Fed. Credit Union; off. mgr, Companion Ins. Co. Mem: Independent Ranchers of Maui. Mailing Add: Wailuku, Maui, Hawaii 96793.

CRAVEN, JAMES J. JR. D
Mass. State Rep.
b. Boston, Mass; m. to Olivia M. Bartels; c. James Michael, Theresa and Sheila. Educ: Boston Univ. Polit. & Govt. Pos: Mass. State Rep, 49-50 & 57-; secy, Boston Dem. City Cmt, 8 years; mem, Ward 19 Dem. Cmt; del, Dem. Nat. Conv, 68. Mil. Serv: Army, discharged as Capt. Mem: Amvets; DAV; K. of C; dir. of Boy's Club, Inc. of Jamaica Plains. Rel: Catholic; Our Lady of Lourdes Holy Name Soc. Mailing Add: 9 St. John St, Boston, Mass. 02130. (1967)

CRAVEN, KATHERINE PATRICIA D
b. Charlestown, Mass, 10/10/08; d. Henry Kane and Mary Moffett K; m. 6/2/31 to John J. Craven; c. Patricia, Maureen, John, Jr, Sheila, Kathleen, Pauline, Frances X, Brendan, Barbara, Susan and Timothy. Educ: St. Patrick; Bentley Col. Acct. Polit. & Govt. Pos: City councillor, Boston, Mass, 66-67. Bus. & Prof. Pos: Secy, Joseph P. Kennedy Enterprises, 27-31. Mem: Dem. Women on Wheels. Rel: Roman Catholic. Mailing Add: 120 Beacon St, Hyde Park, Boston, Mass. 02136. (1967)

CRAWFORD, ABBOTT LINTON D
Chmn, Habersham Co. Dem. Exec. Cmt, Ga.
b. Hampton, Ga, 4/6/95; s. George Milton Crawford and Corrie Farmer C; m. 2nd time, 10/11/59 to Ernestine Thompson; c. Linton Kimsey, Kathleen C. (Mrs. Tucker) and Anne C. (Mrs. Early). Educ: Boston Col, 1 yr. Polit. & Govt. Pos: Cmnr, Cornelia, Ga, 35-40 & 63-68; mayor, Cornelia, 36-39 & 69-; chmn, Habersham Co. Dem. Exec. Cmt, 46- Bus. & Prof. Pos: Mgr, Cornelia Coca-Cola Bottling Co, 19-63. Mil. Serv: Entered as Pvt, Army, 17, released as 2nd Lt, 19, after serv. in 1st Div, Germany, 18-19; Meuse-Argonne Unit Citation. Mem: Hon. lifetime mem, Ga. Bottlers Asn.(past pres); hon. lifetime mem, Ga. Coca-Cola Bottlers Asn; adv, 4-H Club; Mason (past Master); Am. Legion (past Comdr); Kiwanis (past Lt. Gov. and past dist. treas, Ga. Dist); Ment. Health Soc.(past pres); v.pres, Habersham Co. Cancer Soc. Rel: Baptist. Mailing Add: 820 Wayside St, Cornelia, Ga. 30531.

CRAWFORD, B. HAYDEN R
b. Tulsa, Okla, 6/29/22; s. Burnett Hayden Crawford and Margaret Sara Stevenson C; m. 6/5/46 to Alyn Carolyn McCann C; c. Margaret Louise, Robert Hayden and William Allan. Educ: Univ. Mich, A.B, 44; LL.B, 49; Phi Delta Theta; Phi Delta Phi. Polit. & Govt. Pos: Rep. Cand, U.S. Sen, Okla, 60 & 62; asst. city prosecutor, Tulsa, 51-53, Alternate Munic. Judge, 53-54; U.S. Attorney, N.Dist, Okla, 54-58; spec. asst. to Dep. Attorney Gen, 58-59; Asst. Dep. Attorney Gen, 59-60. Bus. & Prof. Pos: Lawyer, Tulsa, Okla, 49-54, 61- Mil. Serv: Entered as Lt.(jg), Navy, 44, released as Capt, 46. Mem: Am, Okla. and Tulsa Co. Bar Asns. Rel: Presbyterian. Mailing Add: 1414 First National Bldg, Tulsa, Okla. 74103.

CRAWFORD, CAROL FORSYTH R
Mem, Calif. Rep. State Cent. Cmt.
b. Okanogan, Wash, 4/14/11; d. John William Forsyth and Caroline Anderson F; m. 7/31/35 to Hugh Eric Crawford; c. Camilla (Mrs. Hammond). Educ: Univ. Ore, B.S, 32. Polit. & Govt. Pos: Div. chmn, 46th Assembly Dist. Rep. Party, Calif, 52, Westchester co-chmn, 54, Westchester chmn, 56, precinct co-chmn, 58; area chmn, 39th Assembly Dist. Rep. Party, 60, precinct v.chmn, 62, precinct chmn, 64, 66, 68; mem, Calif. Rep. State Cent. Cmt, 66- Bus. & Prof. Pos: Prfnl. soc. worker, R.S.W. State Relief Admin, 34-40; vol. soc. worker, Am. Red Cross, 50-64. Mem: Univ. Women's Club; charter mem, Long Beach Children's Theatre; assoc. mem, Family Serv. (former bd. mem); bd. mem, Camp Fire Girls; Lakewood Long Beach Rep. Women (pres, 61-62); Suburban Rep. Club (secy). Rel: Episcopal. Mailing Add: 4417 Harvey Way, Long Beach, Calif. 90808.

CRAWFORD, CHARLES RAYMOND D
b. Ela, N.C, 7/5/02; s. Gordon L. Crawford and Mary Jane C; m. to Ruby Helen Carr C; c. Robert C, Charles G; grandchildren: five. Educ: West. Carolina Teachers Col, teacher training; Gold Medal, West. Carolina Teachers Col, debating competition. Polit. & Gov. Pos: N.C. State Rep, 57-67. Bus. & Prof. Pos: Feed dealer; Operator, Tourist Court; former teacher, N.C. pub. schs, 2 yrs. Mem: Pres, Ela Gov-Island Commun. Develop. Club, 2 yrs. Rel: Methodist; Lay Leader, Teacher, Men's Bible Class, Supvr. Sunday Sch, 8 years. Mailing Add: Whittier, N.C. 28789. (1967)

CRAWFORD, EDWARD F. R
N.Y. State Assemblyman
b. Oswego, N.Y, 1/1/19; m. to Margaret M. Conlin; c. Michael T, M. Kathryn. Educ: St. Michael's Col, Univ. of Toronto, A.B, Honours, 41; Fordham Univ. Col. of Law, LL.B, 45. Polit. & Govt. Pos: N.Y. State Assemblyman, 56-; Oswego Co. attorney, 5 years. Bus. & Prof. Pos: Lawyer, 45- Mailing Add: 38 E. Bridge St, Oswego, N.Y. 13126. (1967)

CRAWFORD, FLOYD O. R
Rep. State Cent. Committeeman, La.
b. Van Buren, Ark, 10/28/07; s. Edward G. Crawford and Maude Williams C. (both deceased); m. 6/17/30 to Lucille Morris; c. Suzanne (Mrs. Dorris) and Robert Morris. Educ: Alma High Sch, Ark; Int. Correspondence Sch. Polit. & Govt. Pos: Rep. State Cent. Committeeman, La, 64- Bus. & Prof. Pos: Owner, Crawford's Enterprises, 46- Mem: Mason (32°); past Lt. Gov, Kiwanis Int; Pub. Affairs Res. Coun. Rel: Presbyterian; Mailing Add: 440 N. Foster Dr, Baton Rouge, La. 70806.

CRAWFORD, IRVIN COOPER D
b. Bryson City, N.C, 9/1/05; s. Gordon Lee Crawford and Mary Jane Cooper C; m. 8/20/35 to Evelyn Gregory; c. Stephen G. Educ: Duke Univ;

Wake Forest Col. Polit. & Govt. Pos: Chmn, Swain Co. Dem. Exec. Cmt, N.C, 32-40; mem, Swain Co. Bd. Educ, 33-34; mayor, Bryson City, N.C, 35-36; N.C. State Rep, 57-66. Bus. & Prof. Pos: Lawyer. Mem: Elks; Moose. Rel: Methodist. Mailing Add: 10 Hampshire Circle, Asheville, N.C. 28804. (1967)

CRAWFORD, JACK FREDERICK R
b. Malvern, Ark, 5/17/34; s. Earnest Shumpert Crawford and Fenola Winters C; m. 7/6/63 to Elsie Doris Davis; c. Katherine Elizabeth. Educ: San Jose State Col, A.B, 57. Polit. & Govt. Pos: Alternate mem, Calif. Rep. State Cent. Cmt, 65; mem, 47th Assembly Dist. Coordinating Cmt, 66; asst. field dir, United Citizens Nixon-Agnew, 68; spec. asst. to secy, Dept. Housing and Urban Develop, 69; spec. asst. to chmn, Rep. Nat. Cmt, 69- Bus. & Prof. Pos: Employee rels. specialist, Douglas Aircraft, Santa Monica, Calif, 64-66; labor rels. specialist, Lockheed Aircraft, 66-68. Mil. Serv: Entered as 2nd Lt, Army, 57, released as Capt, 63, after serv. in 82nd Airborne Div, ETO, 59-61; Parachutist and Ranger Medals; Distinguished Mil. Grad. Rel: Catholic. Mailing Add: 8908 16th St, Silver Spring, Md. 20910.

CRAWFORD, JAMES FRANCIS D
Ala. State Rep.
b. Abbeville, Ala, 12/1/13; s. Albert Nickolas Crawford and Neaomi Skipper C; married; c. James Francis, Jr. Educ: Henry Co. Pub. Schs. Polit. & Govt. Pos: Mayor, Abbebille, Ala; pres, Ala. League Munic; Ala. State Rep, 63- Bus. & Prof. Pos: Farming, quick freeze and meat processing. Mil. Serv: Army, 43-45. Rel: Baptist. Mailing Add: Abbeville, Ala. 36310.

CRAWFORD, JAMES LAIRD R
Chmn, Hopkins Co, Rep. Party, Tex.
b. Colorado City, Tex, 9/22/08; s. Monroe Turner Crawford and Ida May Adair C; m. 7/11/32 to Anna Louise Ragan; c. Norma Louise (Mrs. Shem Ray, Jr), Margaret (Mrs. Hinton), Ida Sue (Mrs. Putman). Educ: Wesley Col, 1 year; Asbury Col, 1 year; E.Tex. Univ, B.A; North. Ill. Col. Optom, O.D; Tomb & Key. Polit. & Govt. Pos: Del, Rep. Nat. Conv, 40; chmn, Hopkins Co. Rep. Party, Tex, 40- Mem: Rotary (pres, 61-62). 25 years perfect attendance, Rotary. Rel: Church of the Nazarene. Legal Res: 645 Gilmer St, Sulphur Springs, Tex. 75482. Mailing Add: P.O. Box 487, Sulphur Springs, Tex. 75482.

CRAWFORD, OLIVER RAY D
b. Amarillo, Tex, 7/19/25; s. Elizabeth Allston C; m. to Margaret Ann Barker; c. Lynda (Mrs. Joe Bonney), Carolyn Rae and Alan Richard. Educ: Wash. State Col; S. Tex. Sch. Law. Polit. & Govt. Pos: V.pres. and dir, Deep E. Tex. Develop. Asn, 61-69; dir, Jasper Co. Hosp. Dist, 63-69; mem, Tex. Water Coord. Cmt, 63-; alternate del, Dem. Nat. Conv, 64; dir, Tex. Law Enforcement Found, 64-; mem, Tex. Liquor Control Bd, 65-69; dir, Deep E. Tex. Interbasin Navig. Dist, 66. Bus. & Prof. Pos: Div. mgr, Phillips Petroleum Co, 46-52; mgr, Ad Valorem Tax and Fee Land Title Dept, Houston Oil Co, 52-56; gen. mgr, Southwest. Timber Co. and v.pres, Eastex, Inc, 56-; v.pres. and treas, Bleakwood Timber Co, Jasper Timber Co, Newton Timber Co. and San Augustine Timber, 60-; dir, 1st State Bank of Jasper, 64-; v.pres, treas. and dir, Rayburn Country Inc, Rayburn Lodge and Marino Co. and pres, treas. and dir, Rayburn Village Water Co, 65-; pres, East. Tex. Cable TV Inc, subsidiary of Time-Life Broadcast, 67- Mil. Serv: Serv. as Fighter Pilot, Army Air Corps, World War II; 1st Lt, Air Force Res, 45-59. Mem: Pres, South. Forest Research Inst, 63-69, Jasper C. of C, 64 and Jasper Youth Baseball Asn, 65-; dir, Tex. United Fund, Oper. Orphans, Inc. and Am. Pulpwood Asn; counsr, Tex. A&M Univ. Research Found. and Century Coun; dist. chmn, Boy Scouts, 62 and exec. cmt, 66; dir. and exec. cmt, Tex. Forestry Asn. and Tex. Forest Prod. Mfrs. Asn; hon. life mem, Jasper Youth Baseball Asn, Nat. Cong. PTA and Jasper Chap. Future Farmers of Am. Received Hon. Lone Star Degree, Tex. Asn. Future Farmers of Am, 60, Citizenship Award, Jasper C. of C. and Forest Mgt. Award, Nat. Forest Prod. Asn, 65; Named Mr. East Tex, Tyler Co. Dogwood Festival Dirs, 67; Named Man of Month, E.Tex. C. of C. Rel: Presbyterian. Mailing Add: 971 Ogden St, Jasper, Tex. 75951.

CRAWFORD, PATRICIA A. R
Pa. State Rep.
b. Middletown, Pa; d. Patrick F. Farren and Florence Long F; m. 6/14/47 to Robert J. Crawford; c. Janet Louise and John Howard. Educ: Ornstein Sch. Music, Phila, studied voice, 1 year; West Chester State Col, 1 year. Polit. & Govt. Pos: Pres, Valley Forge Coun. of Rep. Women, Pa, 62-64; dir, Pa.Coun. of Rep. Women, 64-69; Pa. State Rep, 69- Mem: Valley Forge Hist. Soc. Rel: Lutheran. Mailing Add: 341 Oakwood Lane, Devon, Pa. 19333.

CRAWFORD, RICHARD ROYCE D
Mem, Calif. Dem. State Cent. Cmt.
b. San Fernando, Calif, 1/26/41; s. Royce W. Crawford and Hildred Eugenia Lewis C; m. 3/3/62 to Maryellen Upshaw; c. Richard Royce, Jr. and Kimberley Kathleen. Educ: Bakersfield Jr. Col, 59-61. Polit. & Govt. Pos: Publicity chmn, Kennedy Campaign San Luis Obispo Co, Calif, 68; Co. chmn, Assemblyman Winfield Shoemaker, San Luis Obispo Co, 68; mem, Calif. Dem. State Cent. Cmt, 68-; mem, San Luis Obispo Co. Dem. Cent. Cmt, 68-; pres, South San Luis Obispo Co. Dem. Club, 69- Bus. & Prof. Pos: Carpenter, San Luis Obispo, 62-65; advert. mgr, South Co. Publ. Co, Arroyo Grande, 66- Publ: 'What in the Hell is R&R,' Calif. Jaycees, 66-67. Mem: Pismo Beach C. of C.(bd. dirs); Arroyo Grande Beautification Cmt; Five Cities Jaycees (bd. dirs); Arroyo Grande C. of C; Grover City Civic Asn; YMCA Indian Guides; Cert. Hunter Safety Instr; Calif. Jaycee Bastard Club; YMCA Century Club; South Co. Dem. Club. Jaycee Key Man Award, 66; Jaycee of the Year, 67, Jaycee Outstanding Dist. Chmn, 67; State Calif. Outstanding Jaycee State Dir, 66-67; Outstanding Dist. Jaycee Chmn, State Calif, 66-67; Outstanding Commun. Serv. Award, Atascadero State Hosp. Jaycees; Outstanding Jaycee Pres, State Calif, 67 & 68; U.S. Jaycees Pres. Award Leadership, 67-68. Rel: Protestant. Mailing Add: 608 Newman Dr, Arroyo Grande, Calif. 93420.

CRAWFORD, RUTH REED R
Mem, Pa. Rep. State Cmt.
b. Phila, Pa, 1/17/03; d. Harry Eviland McCaskey and Margaret Jane Reed M; m. to Dr. James Davidson Crawford (deceased). Educ: Westminster Col, spec. courses, 23. Polit. & Govt. Pos: Mem, Lawrence Co. Rep. Cmt, Pa, 55-59; mem, Pa. Rep. State Cmt, 59-; alternate del, Rep. Nat. Conv, 68. Bus. & Prof. Pos: Off. mgr, Reynolds, Thorne & Summers, New Castle, 22-27. Mem: Bd. trustees, Westminster Col, Pa; Salvation Army (chmn. bd, Lawrence Co. Br); Almira Home Bd.(treas, 25 years); Am. Cancer Soc.(exec. bd); bd. trustees, Clen-Moore United Presby. Church. Rel: United Presbyterian. Mailing Add: 501 N. Mercer St, New Castle, Pa. 16101.

CRAWFORD, VICTOR LAWRENCE D
Md. State Sen.
b. Richmond, Va, 4/19/33; s. Joseph Crawford and Elizabeth Lawrence C; m. 6/15/58 to Clare Wootten; c. Victor Lawrence, Jr. and Charlene Elizabeth. Educ: Univ. Md, B.A, 57; Georgetown Law Center, LL.B, 60; Phi Alpha Delta. Polit. & Govt. Pos: Attorney, Montgomery Elec. Bd, 66; v.pres, East. Montgomery Dem, 66; Md. State Del, 67-69; Md. State Sen, 69- Mem: Md, Am. and Montgomery Bar Asns; Isaac Walton League; VFW. Black Belt, Karate. Rel: Roman Catholic. Mailing Add: 1116 Nora Dr, Silver Spring, Md. 20904.

CREASY, KENNETH BURTON R
Ohio State Rep.
b. Barbourville, Ky, 10/7/32; s. John Samuel Creasy and Pauline Hammons C; m. 1/1/56 to Juddean Lavon Ferguson; c. Kenda Lee and Kathleen Denise. Educ: Ohio Wesleyan Univ, B.A, 55; Grad. study, Ohio State Univ, 55-56. Polit. & Govt. Pos: Rep. councilman, Third Ward, Delaware, Ohio, 55; councilman-at-lg, 57, v.mayor, 57; del, Rep. State Conv, 58-; Ohio State Rep, 18th Dist, 58-, chmn, cmt. pub. welfare, Ohio House Rep; mem, Legis. Serv. Cmn. Cmts. to study pub. welfare admin. and financing in Ohio and juvenile delinquency, mem, Standing Cmts. on Educ, Pub. Welfare, Orgn. State Govt, Govt. Opers, Agr, Taxation, Commerce and Transportation. Bus. & Prof. Pos: High sch. teacher, Del. Willis, Ohio, 56-58 and Olentangy, 61-66. Mem: Young Rep. Club; Ohio and Del. Co. Educ. Asns; hon. mem. Del. Co. Asn. of Twp. Trustees & Clerks; chmn, Rural Div, Del. Co. United Appeals; Kiwanis; C. of C; Law Enforcement Cmt; Cent. Ohio Teachers Asn; Del. Co. Ment. Health Asn. Selected one of two most outstanding first term mems. by Ohio House of Rep, 59; received Distinguished Serv. Award, Del. Jr. C. of C, 62; honored by Del. Co. Coun. Soc. Agencies for outstanding pub. serv. in pub. welfare and ment. health, 66. Rel: Methodist. Mailing Add: 460 W. William St, Delaware, Ohio 43015. (1967)

CRECELIUS, ROBERT ALLEN R
Asst. Treas, Fla. Rep. Exec. Cmt.
b. Gibson Co, Ind, 4/10/27; s. Henry Crecelius and Maude Miley C; m. 11/12/66 to Sylvia Ann Cribb. Educ: Ind. Univ, B.S, 50; Kappa Sigma. Polit. & Govt. Pos: Chmn, Dade Co. Young Rep, Fla, 64-65; mem, Dade Co. Rep. Exec. Cmt, 64-68; 12th dist. v.chmn, Fla. Fedn. Young Rep, 65-67; alternate del, Rep. Nat. Conv, 68; v.chmn, 12th Cong. Dist. Rep. Party, 68-69; asst. treas, Fla. Rep. Exec. Cmt, 69-, Bus. Prof. Pos: Acct. exec, Alexander & Alexander, Inc, 58-67; acct. exec, Hayden, Stone, Inc, 67- Mil. Serv: Entered as A/S, Navy, 45, released as S-4, 46, after serv. in U.S.S. Hornet, Pac. Theatre. Mem: Mason; Elks. Outstanding Young Rep. of Fla, 66. Rel: Presbyterian. Mailing Add: 8420 S.W. 16th St, Miami, Fla. 33155.

CREDLE, LOLA FISH D
V.Chmn, Chesapeake Dem. Town Cmt, Va.
b. Louisville, Ky, 1/3/22; d. Ivan Montez Fish and Ella Noakes F; m. 11/8/40 to Byron Elwood Credle; c. Burnley (Mrs. R.D. Ganus). Educ: Cradock High Sch, dipl, 39; Kee's Bus. Col, 51-52. Polit. & Govt. Pos: Dep. cmnr. revenue, Chesapeake, Va, 53-64; del, Dem. Nat. Conv, 68; v.chmn, Chesapeake Dem. Town Cmt, 68- Mem: Chesapeake C. of C.(woman's div); Portsmouth Gen. Hosp. Auxiliary. Rel: Episcopal. Mailing Add: 1224 Boxwood Dr, Chesapeake, Va. 23323.

CREEDON, RICHARD O. D
Polit. & Govt. Pos: Marion Co. Dep. Prosecutor, 59-61; Ind. State Rep. -66. Bus. & Prof. Pos: Attorney. Mil. Serv: Army Res; Korean War Vet. Mem: Press Club; Am, State, City Bar Asns; Jr. C. of C; Pi Kappa Alpha; Scottish Rite; Shrine. Rel: Episcopal. Mailing Add: 129 E. 50th St, Indianapolis, Ind. 46205. (1967)

CREEDON, ROBERT STANTON, JR. D
Mass. State Rep.
b. Brockton, Mass, 11/13/42; s. Robert Stanton Creedon and Kathryn Connors C; single. Educ: Boston Col, A.B, 64; Boston Col. Law Sch, LL.B, 67. Polit. & Govt. Pos: Mass. State Rep, 69- Mil. Serv: Marines, Pfc. Mem: Boston and Mass. Bar Asns. Rel: Catholic. Mailing Add: 386 Crescent St, Brockton, Mass. 02402.

CREEL, GEORGE R
Dir. of Pub. Affairs, Dept. of Housing and Urban Develop.
b. Birmingham, Ala, 12/26/15; s. George Robert Creel and Olivia Louise Ratchford C; m. 2/25/61 to Louise Geldard Cornish; c. George, Jr. Educ: Auburn Univ, B.S, 37; Command and Gen. Staff Col, 43; Am. Univ, 51; Univ. Wis, M.S, 52; Delta Sigma Phi; Sigma Phi Epsilon. Polit. & Govt. Pos: Dir. pub. affairs, Dept. of Housing and Urban Develop, 69- Mil. Serv: Entered as 2nd Lt, Army, 37, released as Col, 69, after serv. in various high level assignments overseas, ETO, Far East, Wash, D.C. and Continental assignments, 37-69; Legion of Merit; Joint Service and Army Commendation Medals. Publ: Free lance writer, various articles for Christian Sci. Monitor, Milwaukee J. and Army Digest. Mem: Sigma Delta Chi; Asn. of U.S. Army; Nat. Press Clubs of Wash, D.C. and San Francisco; Am. Legion; Army-Navy Club; Army-Navy Country Club. Wilbur Wright Award, Aviation Space Writers Asn, 67. Rel: Protestant. Mailing Add: 8905 Colesbury Place, Fairfax, Va. 22030.

CREER, JOHN PRESTON D
b. N.Y.C, 3/14/33; s. Frank Brockbank Creer and Sara Moyle C; m. 8/28/55 to Jennie Lee Allen; c. Sara Jayne, Catherine Alexandra, John Preston and Frank Moyle. Educ: Univ. Utah, B.S. in banking & finance, 57; George Washington Univ, LL.B, 62; Beta Theta Pi. Polit. & Govt. Pos: Voting dist. chmn, Dem. Party, Utah; del, Dem. Nat. Conv; cong. aid to U.S. Rep. David S. King, 59-62; dep. co. attorney, Salt Lake Co, Utah, 62-63, cmnr, 63-65. Bus. & Prof, Pos: Asst. mgr, Utah-Idaho Sch. Supply Co; mem. law firm, McKay & Burton; attorney-at-law, 66- Mem: Utah State Bar; Salt Lake Co. and Am. Bar Asns; Jaycees; adv. bd, Salvation Army; bd. dirs, Campfire Girls; bd. dirs, Downtown Planning Asn; Univ. Club; Ft. Douglas Golf Club; Salt Lake

Country Club. Hobbies: Skiing, golfing, hunting and tennis. Rel: Latter-day Saint. Legal Res: 1269 Third Ave, Salt Lake City, Utah 84103. Mailing Add: 1010 Kearns Bldg, Salt Lake City, Utah 84111.

CREGO, DORIS IMOGEN R
V.Chmn, Onondaga Co. Rep. Cmt, N.Y.
b. Skaneateles, N.Y, 3/1/14; d. Merton Gilletl and Dora Herrling G; m. 8/25/39 to Ernest A. Crego. Educ: Syracuse Univ, B.A, 37; Pi Beta Phi. Polit. & Govt. Pos: V.chmn, Rep. Town Cmt, Skaneateles, N.Y, 56-63; coordinator, Onondaga Co. Rep. Cmt, N.Y, 63-69, v.chmn, 69- Mem: Onondaga Co. Women's Rep. Club; Van Dyne Hosp. Guild; Commun. Gen. Hosp. Auxiliary; pres, Soc. Skaneateles Bus. Women, 68-69. Rel: Episcopal. Mailing Add: 2 East St, Skaneateles, N.Y. 13152.

CREIGHTON, ROBERT A. R
Chmn, Rawlins Co. Rep. Cent. Cmt, Kans.
b. Colorado Springs, Colo, 1/30/34; s. Alexander E. Creighton and Lila Atkinson C; m. 6/19/60 to Barbara Wilson; c. Alexander and John. Educ: Univ. Kans, B.A, 56, LL.B, 60; Delta Tau Delta; Phi Delta Phi. Polit. & Govt. Pos: Attorney, Rawlins Co, Kans, 61-67; chmn, Rawlins Co. Rep, Cent. Cmt, 66-; chmn, Finance Cmt, 1st Dist, Kans, 69- Bus. & Prof. Pos: Assoc, Forest W. Brown Law Off, 60; partner, Brown & Creighton, Atwood, Kans, 61- Mil. Serv: Army Res, 57-63. Mem; Kans. Bar Asn; Northwest Kans. Bar Asn; Atwood C. of C; Atwood Country Club. Rel: Protestant. Mailing Add: 111 S. Sixth St, Atwood, Kans. 67730.

CREIGHTON, ROBERT EMMETT D
Alderman, Blue Island, Ill.
b. Blue Island, Ill, 5/16/30; s. William Andrew Creighton and Elizabeth M. Reardon C; m. 6/9/56 to Ruth Alice Frasor; c. Paul Anthony, Andrew Richard, James Arthur, Peter Edward and John Francis. Educ: DePaul Univ, Sch. of Commerce, B.Sc, 53, School of Law, 53-55, Graduate Sch, MBA, 58; Beta Alpha Psi; Phi Alpha Delta. Polit. & Govt. Pos: Alderman, Blue Island, Ill, 65-; Dem. nominee, U.S. House Rep, 68. Bus. & Prof. Pos: Prin, Haskins & Sells, Chicago Off, 53-65; v.pres, Solo Cup Company, Chicago, 65-67; mgr, Tax Dept, Glenn Ingram & Company, Chicago, 67- Mil. Serv: Entered as Seaman recruit, Navy, 49, released as FCSN, 50, after serv. in DesRon 4, Atlantic Ocean; FCSN, Inactive Naval Res, 50- Mem: Am. Inst. of Cert. Pub. Accts; Ill. Soc. of Cert. Pub. Accts; Ill. Munic. League. Religion: Roman Catholic. Mailing Add: 2653 Union St, Blue Island, Ill. 60406.

CREIGHTON, TOM D
Tex. State Sen.
b. Mineral Wells, Tex, 2/26/27; s. John Roy Creighton and Flora Boynton C; m. 8/11/50 to Rebecca Sue Sparks; c. Will, Kenneth and Mark. Educ: Univ. Tex, LL.B, 50; Phi Alpha Delta. Polit. & Govt. Pos: Co. attorney, Palo Pinto Co, Tex, 53-60; Tex. State Sen, 22nd Dist, 61- Bus. & Prof. Pos: Attorney, 50- Mil. Serv: Entered as A/S, Naval Res, 45, released as Seaman 1/C. Mem: Lions; local and state Bar Asns; fel, Tex. Bar Found. Rel: Baptist. Legal Res: Route 2, Box 208, Mineral Wells, Tex. 76067. Mailing Add: P.O. Box 546, Mineral Wells, Tex. 76067.

CRENSHAW, THOMAS WILLIAM R
Chmn, Jasper Co. Rep. Party, Tex.
b. Silverton, Tex, 7/3/31; s. Leslie Crenshaw and Opal Brock C; m. 8/14/54 to Norma Dean Petty; c. Kathleen and Leslie Robert. Educ: Univ. Houston, 1 year. Polit. & Govt. Pos: Co. chmn, Jasper Co. Rep. Party, Tex, 67- Bus. & Prof. Pos: Data processing supvr, Tex. Electric Serv. Co, Ft. Worth, Tex, 57-63; head data processing dept, The Visador Co, Jasper, 63- Mil. Serv: Entered as Recruit, Army, 49, released as S/Sgt, 52, after serv. in Fifth Machine Records Unit, Fifth Army Area, 50-52. Publ: 'Data Processing Opens Doors,' Jour. Data Processing, 68; reprinted in NSDJA Jour, 68. Mem: Data Processing Mgt. Asn; Kiwanis. Rel: Church of Christ. Mailing Add: Route 1, Box 22M, Jasper, Tex. 75951.

CRESIMORE, JAMES LEONARD R
Chmn, Fourth Dist. Rep. Party, N.C.
b. Statesville, N.C, 1/24/28; s. Fred Clayton Cresimore and Cleo Edison C; m. 6/3/56 to Mary Josephine Conrad; c. James Conrad, Jennifer Cheryl and Joel Clayton. Educ: High Point Col, B.S. in Bus. Admin, 49. Polit. & Govt. Pos: Del, Rep. Nat. Conv, 64; mem, N.C. Rep. Exec. Cmt, 64-; chmn, Wake Co. Rep. Party, 64-66; mem, N.C. Rep. Cent. Cmt, 66-; chmn, Fourth Dist. Rep. Party, N.C, 66-; mem, Platform Cmt. and del, Rep. Nat. Conv, 68. Bus. & Prof. Pos: Exec. dir, Home Serv. Stores, Inc, High Point, N.C, 49-50; co-founder and secy, Consol. Wholesale Corp, 53-56; owner and operator, Village Super Mkt, 53-56; chmn. bd, Bunker Hill Packing Corp, Bedford, Va, currently; pres, Assoc. Brokers, Inc, N.C, currently. Mil. Serv: Entered as Pvt, Army, 50, released as Sgt. 1/C, 52, after serving in Psychol. Warfare Unit, Dept. Army in U.S, 50-52. Mem: Past pres, Raleigh Food Brokers Asn; past pres, Raleigh Sales and Mkt. Execs. Club; former regional lt. dir, Nat. Food Brokers Asn; Rotary; Mason (32°); Shriner; mem. adv. bd, Salvation Army, Raleigh; int. bd, Sales and Mkt. Exec. Int. Rel: Protestant; Supt. of Sunday Sch, Ridge Road Baptist Church, Raleigh, N.C. Mailing Add: 3720 Williamsborough Court, Raleigh, N.C. 27609.

CRESON, THOMAS KYLE, JR. R
b. Memphis, Tenn, 2/25/31; s. Thomas Kyle Creson and Celeste Walters C; m. 8/1/59 to Jayne Suess; c. Thomas Kyle, III and Barry Franklin. Educ: Wash. & Lee Univ, 49-51; Southwest. Univ, summers 50-52; Univ. Tenn. Med. Sch, M.D, 55; Internship, Residency and Fel, Cook Co. Hosp, Chicago, Ill, 55-59; Sigma Alpha Epsilon; Royal Club; Univ. Club. Polit. & Govt. Pos: V.pres, S.Coast Young Rep, Calif, 59-61; mem, steering cmt, Memphis and Shelby Co. Rep. Party, 65-67; pres, Memphis and Shelby Co. Young Rep. Club, 67-68; chmn, Am. Med. Polit. Action Cmt, 67-; cand, Tenn. State Rep, 68; del, Rep. Nat. Conv, 68; presidential elector, Ninth Dist, 68; mem, Pub. Health Rev. Bd, Memphis and Shelby Co, 68- Bus. & Prof. Pos: Practice of medicine, Memphis, Tenn, 61-; asst. clin. prof. med, Univ. Tenn, 67- Mil. Serv: Entered as Lt, Navy, 59, released as Lt. Comdr, 61, after serv. in Med. Corps, El Toro Marine Hosp. Base, 59-61. Publ: 'Treatment of Duodenal Ulcer,' Am. J. Gastroenterology, 61; 'What to do Before Prescribing a Hematinic,' Consult. J, 66; 'Vagaries of Jaundice,' Memphis & Mid South Med. J, 67. Mem: Am. Med. Asn; Tenn. Med. Asn; fel. Am. Col. Physicians; Physicians & Surgeons J. Club; exec. bd, Boy Scouts; Holly Hills Country Club. Rel: Presbyterian. Mailing Add: 257 S. Belvedere Blvd, Memphis, Tenn. 38104.

CRESSWELL, MILDRED R
b. Bolivar, Mo, 5/31/10; m. to Chester C. Cresswell. Polit. & Govt. Pos: Mem, Gov. Reappointment Cmn; v.chmn, Colo. Rep. Party; secy, Colo. State Fedn. Rep. Women; pres, Denver Women's Rep. Club; secy, Colo. State Sen, 54-66; Colo. State Rep, until 68. Mailing Add: 451 Hudson St, Denver, Colo. 80220. (1967)

CRESSWELL, WILLIAM EPHRAIM D
b. Valley, Miss, 3/30/26; s. Walter Franklin Cresswell and Charlotte Louise Welch C; m. 5/4/46 to Catherine Moore; c. Catherine Rosalie, William Ephraim, Stephen Edward. Educ: Univ. Miss, 43-48, LL.B; Phi Alpha Delta; Sigma Alpha Epsilon. Polit. & Govt. Pos: Admin. Asst. to Sen. Stennis, Miss, 58-; Exec. Asst. to Gov. of Miss, 56-57; asst. attorney gen, Miss, 54-56; Miss. State Rep, 52-54. Bus. & Prof. Pos: Attorney, private law practice, Durant, Miss, 48-54. Mil. Serv: Air Force, 44-45. Mem: Miss. State Bar Asn. Rel: Methodist. Mailing Add: 1208 Westgrove Blvd, Alexandria, Va. 22307. (1967)

CREVELING, WILBUR CURTIS, JR. R
b. Allentown, Pa, 1/15/30; s. Wilbur C. Creveling and Verna C. Race C; m. 5/10/58 to Annabelle B. Roth; c. Curtis C, John J, Robert M. Educ: Muhlenberg Col, A.B, 51; Temple Univ. Sch. of Law, LL.B, 53 and LL.M, 57; Phi Alpha Delta; Dean's List, Temple Law Sch; Case Ed, Temple Law Quarterly. Polit. Pos: Alternate del-at-lg, Rep. Nat. Conv, 64; state chmn, Young Rep. of Pa, 62-64, and nat. committeeman, 60-62; labor chmn, Pa. Rep. Platform Cmt, 62; exec. cmt, Young Rep. Nat. Fedn, 59-61. Govt. Pos: Cmnr, Pa. Workmen's Compensation Bd, 63-; asst. dist. attorney, Lehigh Co, 60-63. Bus. & Prof. Pos: Attorney-at-Law, 53- Mil. Serv: Naval Reserve. Publn: Case ed. and author, various legal articles in Temple Law Quarterly, 51-53. Mem: Lehigh Co. and Pa. Bar Asns; dir, Kiwanis Club; Gen. Legal Counsel, Jr. C. of C, Pa, 58; Gen. Legal Counsel, Pa. Asn. for Retarded Children. U.S. Del, NATO Youth Conf, Bonn, Germany, 63. Rel: United Church of Christ. Legal Res: 944 N. 27th St, Allentown, Pa. 18104. Mailing Add: 523 Linden St, Allentown, Pa. 18101. (1967)

CREW, WILLIAM LUNSFORD D
b. Northamton Co, N.C, 10/29/17; s. James Winfield Crew, Sr. and Texas S. C; m. 11/8/40 to Nancy Horney; c. Nancy A.(Mrs. Butler) and William Lunsford, Jr. Educ: Univ. N.C, A.B, Law Sch, LL.B; Phi Gamma Delta. Polit. & Govt. Pos: N.C. State Sen, 53-63 and Pres. Pro Tem, 61; chmn, N.C. Dem. Exec. Cmt, 63-64. Bus. & Prof. Pos: Mem, N.C. State Bar; trustee, Univ. N.C, 53-69. Mil. Serv: Entered as A/S, Navy, 43, released as Lt.(jg), 46, after serv. in Pac. Area; Presidential Unit Citation. Mem: N.C. and Am. Bar Asns; Am. Legion; VFW; Exchange Club. Rel: Episcopal. Legal Res: Sunset Ave, Roanoke Rapids, N.C. 27870. Mailing Add: Box 160, Roanoke Rapids, N.C. 27870.

CREWS, JOHN J, JR. D
b. Macclenny, Fla, 10/18/21; m. to Paula Williams; c. John J. III, Debra Ann, Bryan Williams. Educ: Fried-Hardeman Col; Univ. of Fla. Polit. & Govt. Pos: Fla. State Rep, 52-66; Co. Prosecuting Attorney; City Attorney for Macclenny and Town of Glen St. Mary. Bus. & Prof. Pos: Attorney. Mil. Serv: U.S.M.C, Aviator. Mem: Masons; Scottish Rite; Lions; Univ. of Fla. Alumni Asn; Am. Legion. Rel: Church of Christ. Mailing Add: P.O. Drawer 525, Macclenny, Fla. 30263. (1967)

CREWS, JOHN ROBERT R
Chmn, Kings Co. Rep. Cmt, N.Y.
b. Brooklyn, N.Y, 7/4/94; s. John Collins Crews and Emma Woolley C; m. 7/25/17 to Florence Marie Specht. Educ: Heffley Inst; hon. LL.D, St. Francis Col, 69. Polit. & Govt. Pos: N.Y. State Assemblyman, 21-22; del, Rep. Nat. Conv, 24-68; chief clerk, Munic. Court, N.Y.C, 26-29, tax cmnr, 29-33, cmnr. elec, 43-66; mem. exec. cmt, N.Y. State Rep. Cmt, 33-; chmn, Kings Co. Rep. Cmt, currently. Bus. & Prof. Pos: Trustee, Hamburg Savings Bank; adv. cmt, Bank of Commerce. Mem: Brooklyn Real Estate Bd; Mason (33°); Shrine; Brooklyn Club; Munic. Club. Rel: Episcopal. Legal Res: 25 Monroe Place, Brooklyn, N.Y. 11201. Mailing Add: 16 Court St, Brooklyn, N.Y. 11201.

CREWS, JULIA L. D
Mem, Admin. Cmt, N.Y. State Dem. Cmt.
b. New York, N.Y, 4/16/00; d. Harris Lesser and Ray Barnett L; m. 9/29/33 to Floyd H. Crews (deceased); c. Dorothy Lilian (Mrs. Hershel Z. Herzberg) and Richard Lawrence. Educ: Barnard Col, B.A, 20; Columbia Univ, M.A. polit. sci, 22; New Sch. for Social Research, 55- Polit. & Govt. Pos: V.chmn, Scarsdale Dem. Cmt, 41-54; pres, Scarsdale Dem. Club, 43-46; 1st v.chmn, Westchester Co. Dem. Cmt, N.Y, 47-67; chmn, White Plains Cmt. on Aging, 52-55; del, Dem. Nat. Conv, 52, 60 & 64, mem, Platform Cmt, 60; Dem. cand, U.S. Rep, 26th Dist, N.Y, 54 & 56; mem, Gov. Cmt. on Aging, N.Y, 54-58; mem, Exec. Coun. Women's Div, N.Y. State Dem. Cmt, 58-, mem. admin. cmt. and adv. coun, 63-; mem, N.Y. State Coun. Crime and Delinquency, 66-; mem, Women's Nat. Dem. Club; bd. dirs, Urban League Westchester; mem, Westchester Nat. Coun. on Crime and Delinquency. Bus. & Prof. Pos: Mem, mgt. and advert. depts, Macy's, N.Y, 22-26; pub. rels. counsel, Gimbel's, N.Y, later with agency and free lance, 26-37; pub. rels. worker for major war serv. orgns, Westchester Co, N.Y, 41-45; lectr. for Am. Christian Palestine Cmn, 56-57; lectr. and forum leader, New Sch. for Soc. Research, 60-; chmn. & mem. exec. cmt, New Sch. Assoc, 65-67. Mem: Dir, Westchester League Women Voters, 40-43; Westchester dir, Am. Asn. Univ. Women, 61-63; trustee, White Plains Commun. Church, 65-68; Social Responsibilities Cmt, 66-; Barnard Col. Alumnae and Columbia Grad. Faculties Alumni; Bus. & Prfnl. Women's Club; Scarsdale Woman's Club; chmn. metrop. dist, Unitarian Universalist Asn. Rel: Unitarian. Mailing Add: 33 Greenwich Ave, New York, N.Y. 10014.

CREWSON, HARRY BERNARR, JR. D
Pres, City Coun, Athens, Ohio
b. Sebring, Ohio, 3/16/13; s. Harry Bernarr Crewson and Laura Shewell C;

m. 8/20/41 to Martha Adeline Walker; c. Karen Randall (Mrs. T. Keith) and John Walker. Educ: Col. Wooster, B.A, 35; Ohio State Univ, M.A, 48, Ph.D. (econ), 53. Polit. & Govt. Pos: Pres, City Coun, Athens, Ohio, 64-; chmn, Exec. Cmt, Athens Co. Dem. Party, 66-68; Dem. cand. for U.S. Rep, Tenth Dist, Ohio, 68; alternate del, Dem. Nat. Conv. and elector, 68. Bus. & Prof. Pos: Prof. econ, Ohio Univ, 49-, chmn. dept, 66-68; vis. prof, Univ. Hawaii, 62. Mil. Serv: Entered as Pvt, Army, 43, released as Tech. 4, 45, after serv. in 386th Artil. Bn, 104th Div, ETO, 44-45; Theatre Awards. Mem: Am. and Midwest Econ. Asns; Am. Asn. Univ. Prof; bd. trustees, Ohio Munic. League, Columbus; Commun. Improv. Corp, Athens; Ohio Univ. Fedn. Teachers; Rotary. Rel: Protestant. Mailing Add: 37 Sunset Dr, Athens, Ohio 45701.

CRICHTON, JACK ALSTON R
Mem, Dallas Co. Rep. Finance Cmt, Tex.
b. Crichton, La, 10/16/16; s. Tom J. Crichton and Mary Boyleston C; m. 12/6/52 to Marilyn Berry; c. Anne and Cathy. Educ: Tex. A&M Univ, B.S, 37, Prfnl. Degree, 52; Mass. Inst. Tech, M.S, 38; South. Methodist Univ, 48; Tau Beta Pi; Sigma Alpha Epsilon; varsity basketball, tennis and cross country, Tex. A&M Univ. Polit. & Govt. Pos: Del, Rep. Nat. Conv, 64; cand. for gov, Tex, 64; mem, Tex. State Rep. Cmt, currently; chmn, Ronald Reagan Luncheon Cmt, Dallas, 67; mem, Dallas Co. Rep. Finance Cmt, 67-; del, Dallas Co. Rep. Conv, 68; del, Tex. State Rep. Conv, 68. Bus. & Prof. Pos: V.pres, DeGolyer & MacNaughton, 46-50 and San Juan Oil Co, 51-53; pres, Oil & Gas Mgt, 53-59, Nafco Oil & Gas, 59-63, Crichton & Co, 63-, Dallas Resources, Inc, 63-, Arabian Shield Develop. Co, 67- and Libya Mercury Petroleum Co, 68-; mem, Am. Petroleum Inst. Del. to Rumania, 63. Mil. Serv: Entered as 1st Lt, Army Air Force, 41, released as Maj, 46, after Serv. in 487th Heavy Bomb Group, ETO, 44-45; Col, Army Res, 46-53, Army Intel. Res, 53-67, Col.(Ret); Bronze Star; Air Medal; ETO Medal with 6 Battle Stars; Pre Pearl Harbor Ribbon; Legion of Merit. Publ: The Dynamic Natural Gas Industry, Univ. Okla, 63; 'Critical Review Estimating Gas Reserves,' Petroleum Tech, 58. Mem: Am. Asn. Petroleum Geologists; Soc. Petroleum Engrs; past nat. pres, Soc. Petroleum Evaluation Engrs; past pres, Dallas Petroleum Engrs; Am. Legion; Mil. Order World Wars; C. of C; nat. pres, Asn. Former Students, Tex. A&M Univ. Nominated for Tex. A&M Athletic Hall of Fame. Rel: Presbyterian, Elder, Preston Hollow Presbyterian Church. Mailing Add: 7436 Kenshire Lane, Dallas, Tex. 75230.

CRIDER, JOHN D
Fla. State Rep.
b. Wichita, Kans, 1/17/33; s. Raymond John Crider and Pearl Wightman C; m. 11/16/68 to Connie Branan; c. Stephen Wightman, Catherine Elizabeth and Julie Lynn. Educ: Univ. Fla. Col. Law, B.A. in Polit. Sci, 55, LL.B. & J.D, 58; Phi Delta Phi; Kappa Alpha Order. Polit. & Govt. Pos: Attorney, Fla. State Beverage Dept, Jacksonville, 61-65; Fla. State Rep, 66- Mem: Am. Bar Asn; bd. gov, Jacksonville Bar Asn, 62; S.Jacksonville Exchange Club (pres, 69); Southside Businessmen's Club of Jacksonville (pres, 65); pres, March of Dimes Drive, 65; chmn, Heart Fund Drive, 66. Rel: Baptist. Legal Res: 2008 Sweetbriar Lane, Jacksonville, Fla. 32207. Mailing Add: 2024 Hendricks Ave, Jacksonville, Fla. 32207.

CRIGLER, BILL J. D
Mo. State Rep.
b. Fayette, Mo, 12/17/27; m. 12/26/48 to Betty Ann George; c. Sue Ann and Danny Joe. Educ: Cent. Methodist Col, B.A, 51. Polit. & Govt. Pos: Clerk, Howard Co, Mo, 55-62; Mo. State Rep, 62- Bus. & Prof. Pos: Auctioneer. Mil. Serv: Army, 46-47. Mem: Masons; Rotary; C. of C. Rel: Christian. Mailing Add: 402 Morrison St, Fayette, Mo. 65248. (1967)

CRIM, BOBBY D. D
b. Kennett, Mo, 12/10/31; m. 1953 to Lila F. Vogel; c. Donald Wayne, Douglas William and David Warren. Educ: Univ. Mich, Flint Exten, B.A. Polit. & Govt. Pos: Mem, Zoning Bd. of Appeals, Davison, Mich, fire cmnr, mayor pro-tem, councilman; Mich. State Rep, 64-66. Bus. & Prof. Pos: Teacher. Mil. Serv: Navy, 4 years. Mem: Lions; Flint Educ. Asn; Mich. Educ. Asn; Am. Fedn. of Teachers; Am. Legion; Davison Area Dem. Club. Received Davison Jr. C. of C. Young Man of the Year Award, 64. Rel: Protestant. Mailing Add: 223 Juniper Dr, Davison, Mich. 48423. (1967)

CRIPPS, GEORGE WASHINGTON R
State Auditor, Del.
b. Norfolk, Va, 1916; m. to Frances Wilson; c. Six. Polit. & Govt. Pos: State auditor, Del, currently. Mil. Serv: 2nd Lt, U.S. Army Officer Cand. Sch, 42; Army Command and Gen. Staff Col; Lt. Col.(Ret); 13 decorations and serv. ribbons. Mem: Am. Cancer Soc; Am. Legion; C. of C; Elks; Nat. Asn. State Auditors, Comptrollers and Treas; Holy Cross Church. Mailing Add: 73 S. Fairfield Dr, Dover, Del. 19901.

CRISCILLIS, WILLIAM LEE, JR. D
b. 1939. Educ: Georgia South. Col; East. State Col. Polit. & Govt. Pos: Ky. State Rep, until 68. Bus. & Prof. Pos: Asst. prin, Cumberland High Sch. Rel: Christian. Mailing Add: Loyall, Ky. 40854. (1967)

CRISP, JACK W. D
Chmn, Meigs Co. Dem. Exec. Cmt, Ohio
b. Omar, W.Va, 9/2/30; s. James Crisp, Sr. and Nell Jarrell C; m. 12/2/47 to Glenna Ruth Ratliff; c. James J, Glen T, Thomas A. and Carlanell. Educ: Massey Tech. Inst, Jacksonville, Fla, grad. in Electronics, 60; Am. Detective Training Sch, Chicago, grad. in Criminal Invest. Polit. & Govt. Pos: Precinct committeeman, Meigs Co. Dem. Exec. Cmt, Ohio, 64, chmn, 68-; press secy, Tenth Dist. Dem. Action Club, 66; chmn, Leading Creek Watershed Asn, 66, mem, currently; pres, Leading Creek Conserv. Dist, 66-; participating mem, Dem. Nat. Cmt, currently. Mem: Aircraft Owners & Pilots Asn; AFL; Odd Fellows; United Mine Workers. Gov. Cmt. Voc. Rehabilitation Cert. Outstanding Serv. by both Local and State Odd Fellows. Rel: Church of Christ; Minister. Mailing Add: Route 1, Langsville, Ohio 45741.

CRISPIN, MARJORIE LAWRENA R
b. Quincy, Mass, 11/19/21; d. Harold Buffum Noyes and Ethel Edna Guild C; m. 6/12/42 to William Donald Crispin; c. Claudia Susan and William Harold. Educ: Higgins Bus. Sch, 2 years; Burdett Bus. Sch, 2 years. Polit. & Govt. Pos: Mem, Braintree Town Meeting, Mass, 9 years; treas, Braintree Housing Authority, 5 years; secy, Rep. Town Cmt, 3 years; dir. registration, Rep. State Cmt, 1 year and area finance chmn, 1 year; second v.pres, Braintree Women's Rep. Club, 2 years; secy, Highland Sch. Bldg. Cmt, 1 year; exec. bd. mem, Better Braintree Cmt. Mem: Pres. bd. dirs, Braintree Visiting Nurse Asn, 3 years; first v.pres, Braintree Philergians, 2 years. Rel: Protestant. Mailing Add: 26 Baker Ave, Braintree, Mass. 02184.

CRIST, HAROLD HOWARD R
b. Scott City, Kans, 5/18/08; s. John Eli Crist and Mattie Shores C; m. 12/23/34 to Alam F. Rodabaugh; c. Nancy (Mrs. Templeton), Robert D. and Richard J. Educ: McPherson Col, B.S, 30; Colo. State Univ, M.S, 39. Polit. & Govt. Pos: Mem, Scott Co. Rep. Cmt, Kans, 42-69, chmn, 48-69; mem, Scott City Rep. Cmt, 42-69 and chmn, 48-69; mem, Kans. State Bd. of Educ, 69- Bus. & Prof. Pos: Coach, Zook High Sch, Kans, 30-31; prin, Roxbury High Sch, 32-40; supt. of schs, Enterprise, 40-42; owner and mgr, Garden Bowl, Garden City, 55-; mgr, Crist Farms, Scott City, 42- Publ: Educational and Financial Inequities of Rural Schools of Kansas, Colo. State Univ. Thesis, 39. Mem: State High Sch. Activities Asn; Kans. State and Nat. Teacher's Asns; Elks; C. of C; Farm Bur. Man of the Year, Farm Bur, 56; Kans. Bankers Award, 58; Master Farmer of Kans, 61. Rel: Church of Brethren; Minister. Mailing Add: 1302 Church, Scott City, Kans. 67871.

CRISTINA, VERNON JOSEPH R
b. San Jose, Calif, 2/28/15; s. Salvador Peter Cristina and Annie Masino C; m. 9/18/38 to Antoinette Sunseri; c. Barry R, Richard A. and Donald V. Educ: Univ. of Santa Clara, grad. Polit. & Govt. Pos: Mem, Santa Clara Co. Rep. Cent. Cmt, Calif, 52-62, chmn, 56-60; mem, Calif. State Rep. Cent. Cmt, 56-66; co. chmn, Reagan for Gov, 66; mem, Calif. Hwy. Cmn, 67-, chmn, 68-69. Bus. & Prof. Pos: Bd. of Gov, State Trucking Asn, 50-58; bd. of dirs. & v.pres, Calif. Warehouseman's Asn, 68-69. Mem: C. of C; Elks; pres, 2nd Dad's Clubs, 52 & 54; Truck Owner's Asn, 55, Traffic Club, 56 and Civic Club, 64. Rel: Catholic. Mailing Add: 777 William E, San Jose, Calif. 95112.

CRISWELL, JOHN D
b. Okla. 1933; single. Educ: Univ. Tulsa. Polit. & Govt. Pos: Press secy, Gov. Edmondson, Okla, 59-63; admin. asst. to U.S. Sen. J. Howard Edmondson, Okla, 63-65; dep. dir, News and Info. Div, 65-66; asst. exec. dir, Cong. Support Prog, Dem. Nat. Cmt, 66-67; treas, Dem. Nat. Cmt, 67-68; dir, Dem. Nat. Conv, 68. Bus. & Prof. Pos: Asst. city ed, The Press; city ed, Phoenix; asst. managing ed, Houston Press; rancher, businessman. Mil. Serv: Army, Korea. Mailing Add: Stigler, Okla. 74462.

CRITTENDEN, EARL M. 'DUKE' R
Chmn, Rep. State Exec. Cmt, Fla.
b. Orange Co, Fla, 8/30/30; s. Charles Franklin Crittenden and Emma Pearl Dodson C; m. 6/22/63 to Helen Joyce Johnson; c. Earl, Jr. Educ: Univ. Fla, B.S, Agr. Econ, 53; Sigma Phi Epsilon. Polit. & Govt. Pos: Mem. and past chmn, Citrus Growers Admin. cmn; mem, Fla. Citrus Cmn; citrus indust. coordinator for gubernatorial campaign, Gov. Claude Kirk; state campaign chmn, Sen. E. J. Gurney; committeeman, Rep. Nat. Cmt. Fla; mem, Rep. State Exec. Cmt, Fla, 69-; mem, Orange Co. Rep. Finance Cmt, currently. Mem: Fla. Citrus Mutual; Elks. Rel: Methodist. Legal Res: 1110 Kasper Dr, Orlando, Fla. 32800. Mailing Add: 3500 S. Conway Rd, Orlando, Fla. 32800.

CRIVELLA, BARBARA ANN R
b. Washington, D.C, 1/6/38; d. Joseph Cavalier Crivella, Sr. and Annette Erdesky C; single. Educ: Notre Dame Acad, Wash, D.C, 4 years. Polit. & Govt. Pos: Exec. secy, U.S. Rep. Albert W. Johnson, Pa, 67- Mem: Rep. Women of Capitol Hill; Cong. Secy. Club. Rel: Catholic. Mailing Add: 8309 Donoghue Dr, New Carrollton, Md. 20784.

CROASDALE, CARL PALMER R
Chmn, Lancaster Co. Rep. Party, Va.
b. Palmer, Va, 8/22/16; s. Thomas Starr Croasdale and Edna Robertson C; m. 10/31/53 to Betty Bartelt; c. Elizabeth P, Edward B. and Carolinda. Educ: Bus. Training. Polit. & Govt. Pos: Secy, Lancaster Co. Rep. Party, Va, 50-65, chmn, 65-; alternate del, Rep. Nat. Conv, 68. Bus. & Prof. Pos: Owner and operator, Hardware and Gen. Merchandise Store, Palmer, 20 yrs; owner and operator, C.P. Croasdale Seafood, Palmer, presently; dealing in oysters primarily as planter & packer. Mil. Serv: Entered as Pvt, Army, 42, released as S/Sgt, in supply, 45, after serv. in 552 Engrs, European Theater-landed, Omaha Beach, Normandy; 5 Battle Campaigns. Mem: Formerly charter mem, Lions. Mailing Add: Palmer, Va. 22533.

CROCKETT, ALBERT STEVENS II R
Conn. State Rep.
b. Greenwich, Conn, 2/16/27; s. Newkirk Crockett and Imogene Lewis C; m. 2/13/60 to Dorothy True Palmer; c. Lisa Jean, Abby Palmer and Gaye Newkirk. Polit. & Govt. Pos: Conn. State Rep, 153rd Dist, 67-; mem, Conn. Transportation Authority, 69- Bus. & Prof. Pos: Agent, Conn. Mutual Life Ins. Co, 54- Mil. Serv: Entered as Seaman, Merchant Marine, 45, released as Ens, 46, after serv. in Atlantic and Pac. Theaters; reentered as Pvt, Army, 50, released as Sgt, 52, after serv. in Greenland and Japan; Atlantic and Pac. Area Bars; Japanese Occup. Ribbon. Mem: Past pres, Old Greenwich Lions. Awarded Silver Beaver, 65, by the Greenwich Council, Inc, Boy Scouts. Rel: Episcopal. Legal Res: 10 Pleasant View Place, Old Greenwich, Conn. 06870. Mailing Add: 16 Arcadia Rd, Old Greenwich, Conn. 06870.

CROCKETT, GLEN M. D
b. Unionville, Mo, 8/27/09; m. 8/10/41 to Melrose Gross; c. Patricia Ann, Glenda Diane, Guy David, Linda Lou, Sandra Sue, George Delmar, Betty Ellen. Educ: Univ. of Mo, Columbia; Nat. Inst. of Dry Cleaners. Polit. & Govt. Pos: Mo. State Rep, 64-66; Kaboka Bd. of Educ, 20 years. Bus. & Prof. Pos: Dry cleaner. Mem: Hiram Lodge 362, Kahoka Chap. 126, Masons, Memphis Commandery 41; Kirksville Coun. 44, R. and S.M. and Ararat Temple of Kans. City. Rel: Presbyterian. Mailing Add: 901 Northwest Ave, Kahoka, Mo. 63445. (1967)

CROCKETT, J. ALLAN
Chief Justice, Utah Supreme Court
b. Smithfield, Utah, 1906; s. John Allan Crockett and Rachel Marette Homer

C; m. 1934 to Eulalia Smith; c. Calvin; one granddaughter. Educ: Univ. Utah, LL.B, 31 and B.A, 46; Order of the Coif. Polit. & Govt. Pos: Asst. attorney, Salt Lake Co, Utah, 33-38; dist. judge, 40-50; supreme court justice, Utah Supreme Court, 51-59 and chief justice, 59- Publ: Initiated writing and publ. of manual for Justices of the Peace and edited and published Jury Instruction Forms for Utah. Mem: bd. dirs, Utah Legal Aid Soc; bd. dirs, Nat. Legal Aid and Defender Asn, 56-; chmn, Regional Traffic Court Conf. of Utah Safety Coun; pres, Regional Safety Conf; Nat. Conf. of Chief Justices (exec. coun, 2 terms); bd. dirs, Utah State Inst. of Fine Arts (past chmn); bd. dirs, Utah Symphony, 43-, pres, 2 years; head March of Dimes for Polio Found, 2 years and chmn. exec. cmt, 2 years; Family Serv. Soc.(bd. dirs. and chmn, 1 term); chmn, Utah Coun. on Family Rels, 67- Mailing Add: State Capitol, Salt Lake City, Utah 84114.

CROFT, JOHN KENDRICK D
Mem, Calif. Dem. State Cent. Cmt.
b. Los Angeles, Calif, 5/7/25; s. John Edward Croft (deceased) and Anna Watson C; div; c. Karen Bettine and Colleen Leta. Educ: Santa Monica City Col, A.A, 47; Stanford Univ, B.A, 49; Calif. Scholarship Fedn. Polit. & Govt. Pos: Finance chmn, Palo Alto-Stanford Dem. Club, Calif, 65-68; del, Calif. Dem. Coun. Co. Coun, 65-69; finance chmn, George Leppert Cong. Campaign, 66; del, Calif. Dem. Coun. Conv, 66-69; alternate del, Dem. Nat. Conv, 68; finance chmn, McCarthy Campaign, 68; finance chmn, Martin Gorfinkel Assembly, 68; mem, Calif. Dem. State Cent. Cmt, 68-; 22nd Assembly Dist, rep, Calif. Dem. Coun, 69- Bus. & Prof. Pos: Regional sales mgr, Life Circulation Co, N.Y, 59-63; salesman, Leisure World, Walnut Creek, Calif, 63-64; admin. asst, Stanford Univ, 64-67, buyer med. purchases, 68; mgr, Buying Serv. Coop, Palo Alto, 69- Mil. Serv: Entered as Pvt, Army Air Corps, 43, released as S/Sgt, 45, after serv. in Eighth Air Force, ETO, 44-45. Mem: Palo Alto-Stanford Dem. Club; NAACP. Mailing Add: 2901 Middlefield Rd, Apt. 9, Palo Alto, Calif. 94306.

CROFT, LELAND CHANCY D
Alaska State Rep.
b. Jennings, La, 8/21/37; s. Leland Reynolds Croft and Dorothy Elizabeth Chancy C; m. 7/8/63 to Anita Toni Ruth Williamson; c. Eric Chancy, Kimberly Geraldine and Lee Conwell. Educ: Univ. Tex, B.A, 59; LL.B, 61; Phi Gamma Delta. Polit. & Govt. Pos: Mem. bd. dirs, Alaska Legal Serv. Corp, 68-69; Alaska State Rep, 69- Bus. & Prof. Pos: Partner, Croft & Bailey. Mil. Serv: Entered as Seaman Recruit, Naval Res, 54, released as A/S, 62. Publ: Revisor, Alaska Law Section, Probate Counsel, 68-69. Mem: Am. Tex, Alaska and Anchorage Bar Asns; Rel: Protestant. Legal Res: 1511 G St, Anchorage, Alaska 99501. Mailing Add: 425 G St, Suite 710, Anchorage, Alaska 99501.

CROFT, SYDNEY FRASER D
b. Georgetown, S.C, 6/26/97; c. Sydney Fraser Croft and Emma Dorcas Boone C; m. 1/19/35 to Elsie Craver; c. Joan (Mrs. Thomas B. Snyder) and Sydney Fraser, Jr. Polit. & Govt. Pos: Dem. precinct chmn, Ward Six, Mecklenburg, N.C, 34-40; mem, State Dem. Exec. Cmt, 34-40; del, Dem. Nat. Conv, 52 and alternate del, 68. Bus. & Prof. Pos: Salesman, Alemite Lubricator Co. Carolinas, Charlotte, 22-24; salesman, Tidewater Oil Co, Atlanta, Ga, 25-30; v.pres, Payne Petroleum Co, 31-32; asst. custodian, U.S. Post Off, 34-40; owner, Janitor Supply Co. Inc, 40-52; pres, Discover Our Nation, Inc, 66- Mil. Serv: Entered as Pvt, Army Signal Corps, 19, released, 19, after serv. in several aero squadrons, St. Mihiel and Aisne Marne Argonne Forest; Personal Citation from Gen. Pershing, 38. Mem: Am. Legion; VFW; DAV; Vet. World War One; Elks; Moose. Rel: Methodist. Mailing Add: Route 4, Box 476, Charlotte, N.C. 28208.

CROLEY, BOYD T. SR. D
b. Memphis, Mo, 3/28/14; m. 3/27/37 to Winifred M. Bertram; c. Sharon Sue and Boyd T. Jr. Educ: Memphis pub. schs. Polit. & Govt. Pos: Mo. State Rep, 64-66. Bus. & Prof. Pos: Businessman; farmer; oil distributing; hatchery, contracting. Mil. Serv: Navy, Seabees, 43-45. Mem: Lions; Am. Legion; VFW; Mason. Rel: First Christian Church. Mailing Add: 321 S. Market St, Memphis, Mo. 63555.

CROMER, ELLA MAE R
b. Bozeman, Mont, 6/19/16; d. Gordon Milton Mandeville and Millie Burtch M; m. 10/10/37 to John William Cromer; c. Edward Gordon, Donald William and Richard Frank. Educ: Mont. State Univ, 35-37. Polit. & Govt. Pos: V.chmn, Gallatin Co. Rep. Party, Mont, 59-62; mem, Bd. of Insts, 63-; budget and finance chmn, Mont. Fedn. of Rep. Women, 64-67; conv. chmn, Mont. Fedn. of Rep. Clubs, 65; del, Rep. State Conv, 68; alternate del, Rep. Nat. Conv, 68. Mem: Trustee, Int. Christian Univ. of Japan, 54-; Mont. Heart Asn. (field rep, 62-63); Mont. Asn. for Mentally Retarded; Mont. Asn. for Mentally Ill; Mont. Tuberc. Asn; Mont. Fedn. of Women's Clubs (pres, 58-60); PEO (pres, Mont. Chap, 60-61, trustee, Record, 61-67); Eastern Star; Daughters of Nile; Butte C. of C; YMCA (bd. mem). Int. Peace Scholarship given to student from Philippines known as Ella Mae Cromer Scholarship, 59. Rel: Presbyterian; First Woman Elder in Butte Church. Mailing Add: 3025 Moulton, Butte, Mont. 59701.

CROMMETT, LEON JAMES D
Maine State Rep.
b. Hersey, Maine, 5/11/01; s. John Fields 'Ted' Crommett and Isabelle 'Bell' Carver C; m. 10/24/52 to Olive Ida Moore. Educ: Patten Academy, grad, 1920. Polit. & Govt. Pos: Mem, Penobscot Co. Dem. Cmt, Maine, 60-68; chmn, Millinocket Town Dem. Cmt, 62-65; Maine State Rep, Millinocket, 63- Bus. & Prof. Pos: Contracting Jobber, Patten, Maine, 20-38; Scaler, U.S. Forest Serv, Keene, N.H, 38; scaler and buyer, Brown Co, Berlin, 38-44; scaler and inspector laborer, Great North. Paper Co, Millinocket, Maine, 44-68. Mem: Mason; Odd Fellows; Rebekahs; Elks; Grange; The Fin and Feather Club; 500 Club; hon. life mem, Int. Brotherhood of Pulp, Sulphite and Paper Mill Workers. Rel: Protestant. Mailing Add: 413 Penobscot Ave, Millinocket, Maine 04462.

CROMWELL, JAMES H. R
b. Chicago, Ill, 8/31/29; s. Ray Risley Cromwell and Mary Carolyn Rennick C; m. 12/30/61 to Molly Ann Cowan; c. James, Jr, Marshall and Mary Kathryn. Educ: Bradley Univ, B.S, 51, post grad study, 55 and 56; Univ. Ill, Ed.M, 54; La Salle Law Sch; Dale Carnegie Leadership Training Course; Sigma Nu; Omicron Delta Kappa; Alpha Delta; Delta Theta Pi. Polit. & Govt. Pos: Former admin. asst. to U.S. Rep. Robert H. Michel; asst. campaign dir, Rep. Nat. Campaign Cmt, 62; pres, Cong. Secy. Club, 63; seminar chmn, Young Rep. Leadership Training Sch, 66. Bus. & Prof. Pos: Exec. dir, Bradley Univ. Nat. Alumni Asn, 54-56; dir. pub. affairs, Gen. Acceptance Corp, Allentown, Pa, 67- Mil. Serv: Entered as Pvt, Army, 51, released as Cpl, 53, after serv. in Gen. Hq, Far East; Korean Serv. Medal; UN Serv. Medal; Cert. of Merit from Adj. Gen, Far East Command. Mem: Mason; Shrine. Research; We Propose A Modern Congress. Rel: Methodist. 1967 Legal Res: Peoria, Ill. No mailing address available. (1967)

CRONIN, A. L. D
b. Chicago, Ill; married; c. Margaret, Ellen. Educ: Loyola Univ. Law Sch, 27. Polit. & Govt. Pos: Ill. State Sen, 54-66; State Rep, 48-50. Bus. & Prof. Pos: Lawyer, Nash, Ahern and McNally. Legal Res: 9546 S. Oakley St, Chicago, Ill. 60643. Mailing Add: 111 W. Washington St, Chicago, Ill. 60602. (1967)

CRONIN, DONALD J. D
b. Huntsville, Ala, 7/1/25; s. Raymond Cronin and Jean Snow C; m. 4/10/57 to Mary Edna Andress; c. Mary Anne. Educ: Univ. Ala, B.S. in Commerce & Bus. Admin, 51, LL.B, 53; Beta Gamma Sigma; Omicron Delta Kappa; pres, Delta Sigma Pi; Phi Eta Sigma; Phi Delta Phi; pres, Alpha Sigma Phi; editor, Corolla; pres. Cotillion Club; pres, Quadrangle; Jasons; Bd. of Publications. Polit. & Govt. Pos: Admin. asst. to U.S. Sen. Lister Hill, Ala, 53-69. Bus. & Prof. Pos: Field rep, Dun & Bradstreet, 50-52; res. asst, Bur. of Bus. Res, Univ. Ala, 50-53, asst. prof, univ, 51-52; mem, Law Firm of Corcoran, Foley, Youngman & Rowe, currently. Mem: Ala. and U.S. Supreme Court Bar Asns; past pres, Asn. of Admin. Assts. of the U.S. Senate; past pres, Univ. of Ala. Alumni Asn. of Washington, D.C. Rel: Episcopal. Legal Res: Montgomery, Ala. Mailing Add: 5406 Blackistone Rd, Westmoreland Hills, Md. 20016.

CRONIN, GEORGE FRANCIS D
Gov. Councillor, Mass. Gov. Coun.
b. Boston, Mass, 11/29/37; s. George F. Cronin and Helen Cummings C; m. 5/12/63 to Mary Louise Rando; c. George F, III, Maribeth and Kerry Marie. Educ: Univ. Notre Dame, B.S, 59; Suffolk Univ, M.B.A, 62; New Eng. Sch. Law, LL.B, 64; hon. H.H.D, Philathea Col, 67. Polit. & Govt. Pos: Mem. adv. cmt, Mass. Coun. Aging, 60-63; mem, Mass. State Dem. Cent. Cmt, 60-64; mem, Dem. Ward & City Cmts, 60-; del, Dem. State Conv, 60-; Gov. Councillor, Mass. Gov. Coun, 63-, mem. pardons and prisons, nominations and vet. affairs cmts. and chmn, finance cmt, 69-; mem, Legis. Cmn. Juvenile Delinquency, 64, Legis. Recess Cmn. on Legis. Reorgn, 64, Gov. Adv. Cmt. Civil Defense and Emergency Planning, 67 and Adv. Cmt. Sci. and Tech, Dept. Commerce, 69. Bus. & Prof. Pos: Practicing attorney, Boston, 64- Mil. Serv: Marine Corps; Distinguished Serv. Award, 69. Publ: Massachusetts Property Tax Problems, Privately Publ, 69. Mem: Mass. Trial Lawyers Asn; Boston and Mass. Bar Asns; U.S. Dist. Court Appeals Bar; Notre Dame Club Boston; Marine Corps League. Rel: Catholic. Mailing Add: 58 Cerdan Ave, Boston, Mass. 02131.

CRONIN, PAUL WILLIAM R
Mass. State Rep.
b. Boston, Mass, 3/14/38; s. William Joseph Cronin and Anna Murphy C; m. 1957 to Kathleen Sears; c. Kevin P. and Kimberley A. Educ: Merrimack Col, 56-58; Boston Univ, B.A, 62; fel, John F. Kennedy Grad. Sch, Govt, Harvard Univ, 68-69, M.P.A, 69; S.B.K. Polit. & Govt. Pos: Mem. and precinct capt, Andover Rep. Town Cmt, Mass, 60-; del, Rep. State Convs, 62, 64 & 66; selectman, Town of Andover, 63-66; admin. asst, Cong. F. Bradford Morse, 63-67; Mass. State Rep, 67-; del, Rep. Nat. Conv, 68. Mem: Mass. Selectmans Asn; Mass. Legis. Asn; Nat. Asn. State Legis; Partners of Alliance; Elks; Hibernians; K. of C; chmn, Mass. Multiple Sclerosis Soc; Bon Secours Hosp. Guild; Men of Merrimack. Outstanding Young Man award, Jaycees; Foreign Policy Asn. Future Leader; Paul Revere Leadership Medal; Young Rep. Outstanding Citizen Award; DAV Distinguished Serv. Award. Rel: Roman Catholic. Mailing Add: 8 Punchard Ave, Andover, Mass. 01810.

CRONIN, ROBERT JOSEPH D
Chmn, Warren Co. Dem. Cmt, N.Y.
b. Glens Falls, N.Y, 6/22/15; s. Bernard Joseph Cronin and Nora Reardon C; single. Educ: Univ. Toronto, B.A, 40; N.Y. State Col. for Teachers, M.A, 50. Polit. & Govt. Pos: Contact officer, Vet. Admin, 46-47; coordinator, Glens Falls Charter Cmn, 60-63; co. supvr, Warren Co, 60-; chmn, Warren Co. Dem. Cmt, 63-; del, Dem. Nat. Conv, 68. Bus. & Prof. Pos: Pvt. bus, 48-59; supvr, N.Y. State Dept. of Highways, 59-60; asst. prof. hist. & govt, Col. St. Rose, 60- Mil. Serv: Entered as Pvt, Army, 42, released as Sgt, 46, after serv. in 804th Mil. Police Co, ETO, 45-46. Mem: Am. Asn. Univ. Prof; N.Y. State Polit. Sci. Asn. Rel: Roman Catholic. Legal Res: 49 Leonard St, Glens Falls, N.Y. 12801. Mailing Add: Box 433, Glens Falls, N.Y. 12801.

CRONSON, ROBERT GRANVILLE R
b. Chicago, Ill, 12/23/24; s. Berthold A. Cronson and Ethel Larson C; m. 4/3/50 to Terese K. Van Wie; c. Karen, Christoper, Keelyn, Morgan and Seth. Educ: Dartmouth Col, A.B. in Econ, 47; Univ. of Chicago Law Sch, J.D, 50; Phi Kappa Psi; Green Key. Polit. & Govt. Pos: Founder and pres, Fourth Ward Young Rep, Chicago, Ill. 51-53; precinct capt, Fourth Ward Rep. Orgn, 51-53; securities cmnr, 53-56; mem, bd. gov, Ill. Young Rep. Orgn, 57-61; asst. secy. of state, Ill, 58-64; v.pres, Sangamon Co. Young Rep, 59-61; mem. screening cmt, Sangamon Co. Rep. Orgn, 63-64; alternate del-at-lg, Rep. Nat. Conv, 64; asst. parliamentarian, Ill. State Rep. Conf, 66; past mem, subcmt. on orgn, Cook Co. Rep. Cent. Cmt; chmn, Ill. Securities Adv. Cmt, 64-; chmn, mgt. adv. cmt, Off. of Secy. of State of Ill, 69- Bus. & Prof. Pos: Salesman, Ideal Dispenser Co, 50-51; lawyer, Daily, Dines, Ross & O'Keefe, 51-53; partner, Law Firm of DeBoice, Greening, Ackerman & Cronson, 57-58; v.pres. & gen. counsel, Ins. City Life Co, 64; v.pres. & secy, Chicago Corp, 65- Mil. Serv: Entered as Pvt, Marine Corps, 42, released as Cpl, 46, after serv. in H & S Co, 26th Marines, Fifth Marine Div; Asiatic Pac. Ribbon; Am. Theater Ribbon; Good Conduct Medal. Mem: Chmn, Midwest Vehicle Proration Compact, 59-61; chmn, Midwest Securities Cmnrs. Asn, 59-64; chmn, state legis. cmt, Cent. States Group, Investment Bankers Asn, 64-66; chmn, Cmt. on Corp. and Securities Law, Ill. State Bar Asn, 64-66; v.chmn, Cmt. on Securities Law, Chicago Bar Asn; Am. Bar Asn; Mason;

Consistory; Shrine. Named Outstanding Young Rep. of Ill, Young Rep. Orgn. of Ill, 61. Rel: Congregational. Mailing Add: Box 171, Route 1, Mundelein, Ill. 60060.

CROOK, ROBERT LACEY D
Miss. State Sen.
b. Bolton, Miss, 4/22/29; s. Walter Barber Crook and Louise Lacey; m. 9/20/53 to Brigita V. Nerings; c. Robert Lacey, II and Hubert William. Educ: Univ. Miss, 52-53; Jackson Sch. Law, LL.B, 65. Polit. & Govt. Pos: Del, Dem. State Conv, Miss, 60 & 64; state dir, Miss. Civil Defense Coun, 60-63; admin. asst. to Gov, Miss, 63; Miss. State Sen, 64- Mil. Serv: Entered as Pvt, Marine Corps, 49, released as Cpl, 52. Mem: Sunflower Co. and Miss. State Bar Asns; Am. Legion; Sons of Confederate Vets; 40 et 8. Rel: Episcopal. Mailing Add: P.O. Box 85, Ruleville, Miss. 38771.

CROOK, THURMAN CHARLES D
b. Miami Co, Ind, 7/18/91; s. Ashford Crook and Sarah Kingery C; m. 4/7/17 to Gladys Martha Stanley; c. Vera Christine. Educ: Valparaiso Univ, B.S. in indust. educ, 30; grad. work, Ind. and Purdue Univs, 30-50. Polit. & Govt. Pos: Ind. State Rep, 39-43; Ind. State Sen, 43-47; mem, Post. Off. and Civil Serv. Cmt, 49-50; former, U.S. Rep, Third Dist, Ind; former, Dem. V.Committeeman. Bus. & Prof. Pos: Teacher and athletic coach, Cass, White, Carroll, Marshall and Miami Co, Ind, 13-20; drafting instr, Cent. High Sch, St. Joseph Co, Ind, 20-48; owner sheep farm, currently; chmn, North. Ind. Crippled Children's Hosp, currently. Publ: Simplified Mechanical Drawing. Mem: Ind. State Teachers Asn; North. Ind. Teachers Fedn; Ind. and Nat. Voc. Asns; Ind. Indust. Educ. Asn; Nat. Educ. Asn; PTA; Ind. Legis. Club; charter mem, South Bend Am. for Dem. Action; hon. mem, Am. Fedn. Teachers. Rel: Baptist. Mailing Add: R.R. 5, Logansport, Ind. 46947.

CROOKER, JOHN H, JR. D
b. Houston, Tex, 10/26/14; s. John H. Crooker and Marguerite Malsch C; m. to Kay Berry; c. Carolyn C. (Mrs. Schwing), John H, III, Linda Ann, Tara and Allison. Educ: Rice Univ, B.A. cum laude, 35; Univ. of Texas, LL.B. summa cum laude, 37; Phi Beta Kappa; Phi Delta Phi; Alpha Tau Omega. Polit. & Govt. Pos: Chmn, Kennedy-Johnson Campaign Cmt, Harris Co. Tex, 60; del, Dem. Nat. Conv, 60 & 64, presidential elector, 60, chmn, regional coordinators, 64; chmn, Civil Aeronaut. Bd, 68-; mem. bd. regents, State Sr. Col, Tex, at present. Bus. & Prof. Pos: Mem, Law Firm of Fulbright, Crooker, Freeman, Bates and Jaworski, 37-67. Mil. Serv: Entered as Ens, Naval Res, 41, released as Lt. Comdr, 45, after serv. on staff, Comdr. 7th Fleet, Southwest Pac. Area, 44-45; Bronze Star Medal; Pac. Theater Ribbon with 2 Battle Stars; Philippines Liberation Ribbon; resigned from Naval Res, 53. Mem: Am. Law Inst; Am. Bar Asn; past chmn. Corp, Banking and Bus. Law Sect, State Bar of Tex; Scottish Rite (32°), Knights Templar; Houston Country Club; River Oaks Country Club; Am. Legion; Rice Univ. Assocs. Rel: Episcopal. Mailing Add: Civil Aeronautics Board, Washington, D.C. 20428.

CROOKS, SAMUEL COULTER D
R.I. State Rep.
b. Belfast, N.Ireland, 11/11/14; nat. citizen; s. James Crooks (deceased) and Margaret Coulter C; m. 9/25/42 to Gwladys Catherine Priestley; c. Bruce Philip, Barry James, Samuel C, Jr. and Brian William. Educ: Brown Univ, A.B, 48. Polit. & Govt. Pos: R.I. State Rep, 69- Bus. & Prof. Pos: Asst. personnel mgr, Collyer Insulated Wire Co, Lincoln, R.I, 48-50, asst. sales mgr, 53-56, plant supt, 56-61, gen. traffic and distributional mgr, 61- Mil. Serv: Entered as Pvt, Army, 42, released as Col, 52, after serv. in Korea 50-52, Army Res. and Nat. Guard, 52-67, (Ret); Commendation Medal; Bronze Star. Mem: Elks; F&AM; VFW; Am. Legion. Rel: Protestant. Mailing Add: 67 Chapel St, Lincoln, R.I. 02865.

CROSBY, JANE A. R
Mem, Calif. Rep. State Cent. Cmt.
b. Pasadena, Calif, 3/31/20; d. Robert Frederick Aldridge and Florence Elizabeth Scott A; m. 8/12/38 to Joseph Marshall Crosby; c. Joseph Scott and William Marshall. Educ: Pasadena City Jr. Col; Woodbury Bus. Col. Polit. & Govt. Pos: Mem. bd, South Pasadena Rep. Women, Federated, Calif, 60-68; assoc. mem, Calif. Rep. State Cent. Cmt, 60-69, mem, 69-; one of many founders, United Rep. Calif, 63, vol. state off. mgr, 66-68; registrn. of voters, Los Angeles Co, 64-69; vol. state off. mgr, Max Rafferty for U.S. Senate Campaign, 68. Mem: South Pasadena Americanism Center (pres. bd). Betsy Ross Award, First Congregational Church of Los Angeles, 62; Woman of the Year, South Pasadena Bus. & Prfnl. Women's Club, 66-67. Rel: Congregational. Mailing Add: 1524 Via del Rey, South Pasadena, Calif. 91030.

CROSBY, JOSEPH MARSHALL R
Mem, Calif. Rep. State Cent. Cmt.
b. Bishop, Calif, 12/7/19; s. Joseph Junius Crosby and Mary Elizabeth Gibson C; m. 8/12/38 to Margaret Jane Aldridge; c. Joseph Scott and William Marshall. Polit. & Govt. Pos: One of many founders, United Rep. Calif, 63, state chmn, 66-68; mem. exec. cmt, Max Rafferty for U.S. Sen. Campaign, 68; del, Rep. Nat. Conv, 68; pub. mem, Bd. State Calif. Dept. Prfnl. and Voc. Standards, 69-; pub. mem, Calif. State Bd. Registrn. for Geologists, 69-; mem, Calif. Rep. State Cent. Cmt, currently; pres, Calif. Rep. Assembly, 54th Assembly Dist. Mil. Serv: 1st Lt, Cadet Army Air Force. Mem: Am. Legion. Rel: Congregational. Mailing Add: 1524 Via del Rey, South Pasadena, Calif. 91030.

CROSE, JACK CURRY D
b. Crane, Mo, 4/15/24; s. W.J.F. Crose and Ina Curry C; m. 7/15/50 to Nadine Stephenson; c. Jana and Megan. Educ: Fresno State Col, A.B, Journalism, 49; McGeorge Col. of Law, Univ. of Pa, J.D, 65. Polit. & Govt. Pos: Legis. asst. to speaker, Calif. State Assembly, 60-66, chief asst. to speaker, 66-69; mem, Kennedy Presidential Del, 68; del, Dem. Nat. Conv, 68. Bus. & Prof. Pos: City hall reporter, McClatchy Newspapers, Modesto, Calif, 50-60; attorney-at-law, 65- Mil. Serv: Entered as Aviation Cadet, Army Air Corps, 43, released as 1st Lt, 46, after serv. in 59th Weather Reconnaissance Squadron, Pac, 45-46. Mem: Calif. and Am. Bar Asns. Rel: Protestant. Mailing Add: 6418 Oakridge Way, Sacramento, Calif. 95831.

CROSIER, DALE THERON D
Iowa State Rep.
b. Delhi Twp, Delaware Co, Iowa, 4/14/03; s. Theron Thatcher Crosier and Densia Guiles C; m. 5/10/30 to A. Marie Finley; c. Dale Finley. Educ: Manchester High Sch, 22. Polit. & Govt. Pos: Iowa State Rep, currently. Bus. & Prof. Pos: Salesman, Armstrong Co, 47- Mem: United Commercial Travelers; Iowa State Hist. Soc; C.R. Traveling Men's Club; Eagles. Rel: Presbyterian. Mailing Add: 1617 Oakland Rd. N.E, Cedar Rapids, Iowa 52402.

CROSKEY, ERMINE MARY D
Pres, Carrol Co. Dem. Women's Fed. Club, Ohio.
b. Amsterdam, Ohio, 6/22/99; d. William Davis Orin and Hester Jane Carson O; m. 6/23/20 to Rae Stanley Croskey, wid. Educ: High Sch. Grad. Polit. & Govt. Pos: Mem, Carroll Co. Bd. Elections, Ohio, 37-41, clerk, 42-45 & 50-54 and chmn, 64-65; mem, Dem. Cent. & Exec. Cmt, 48-65; pres, Carroll Co. Dem. Women's Fed. Club, 54-; del, Dem. State Conv, 62; co-chmn, Dem. Party, 62-63; del, Dem. Nat. Conv, 64; mem, Carroll Co. Bd. Visitors, 68- Bus. & Prof. Pos: Music teacher, 18-21; co-owner, Croskeys Mkt, 24-55. Publ: 'Girl Scouting,' Carroll J, 37-38; 'Current Movies,' Buckeye Messenger, 50-51; 'Poem and Song,' Garden Greetings, 55. Mem: Am. Legion Auxiliary (past pres. Parley, 8 and 40, pres, Tenth Dist, 51-53, dept. commun. serv. chmn, 50-51, historian, 54 and pres, 68-); chmn, March of Dimes Cmt, 41-44; Carroll Co. Bd. Visitors, 39-44; Victory Loan Cmt, 43; chmn, Girl Scout Cmt, 37-44; VFW Auxiliary; Past Noble Grand, Rebekahs; Carrollton Garden Club; Carrollton Book Club (pres, 69). Rel: Presbyterian. Mailing Add: 160 Third St. S.E, Carrollton, Ohio 44615.

CROSS, BILLY JOE D
b. Meridian, Miss; 10/23/31; single. Polit. & Govt. Pos: Miss. State Rep, until 68. Bus. & Prof. Pos: Teacher; coach. Mem: Miss. and Nat. Educ. Asns; Warren Co. Teachers Asn. Rel: Baptist. Mailing Add: 924 Polk St, Vicksburg, Miss. 39180. (1967)

CROSS, DONALD MELVIN D
Miss. State Rep.
b. Meridian, Miss, 8/14/35; s. William Joe Cross and Eula Mae Todd C; m. 6/11/61 to France Lanelle Abernathy; c. Julianne and Donald Joseph. Educ: E. Miss. Jr. Col, 1 year; Meridian Jr. Col, 1 year; Miss. Col, B.S, 57. Polit. & Govt. Pos: Miss. State Rep, 66- Bus. & Prof. Pos: Pres, LeTourneau Vicksburg Fed. Credit Union, 64-66; pres, LeTourneau Activities Asn, 65-67. Mil. Serv: Entered as Pvt, Army, 58, released as Spec. 4, 60, after serv. in Eighth Army Honor Guard, Korea, 59-60. Mem: Jaycees; C. of C; VFW. Rel: Baptist. Mailing Add: 3 Grandview Dr, Vicksburg, Miss. 39180.

CROSS, J. EMORY D
b. Iron City, Ga, 1/26/14; m. to Dorothy Huffman; c. Charles Emory, Gayle and Betty Jean. Educ: Univ. of Fla, B.S.B.A, LL.B, 1945, J.D, 67; Sigma Phi Epsilon; Phi Alpha Delta; Pres, Student Body. Polit. & Govt. Pos: Pres, Young Dem. of Alachua Co; asst. attorney gen, 45-46; co. prosecuting attorney, 48-52; Fla. State Rep, 52-58; Fla. State Sen, 58-68. Bus. & Prof. Pos: Attorney; Bd. of Dir, N. Fla. Eye Bank for Restoring Sight. Mem: Alachua Co. Asn. for Ment. Health; Past Dir, Univ. of Fla. Alumni Coun; Kiwanis; Elks; K. of P; Past Grand Orator, Grand Lodge of F&AM of Fla. Two times awarded Allen Morris Award as mem. of Second Most Effective Legis. Del; One time Most Effective Legis. Del 1961, 1963 Sessions. Rel: Methodist; Bd. of Stewards. Mailing Add: P.O. Box 699, Gainsville, Fla. 32601.

CROSS, JOHN MELVIN D
Committeeman, Dawson Co. Dem. Cent. Cmt, Mont.
b. Alexander, N.Dak, 6/15/18; s. Melvin L. Cross and Olive Iverson C; m. 6/22/43 to C. Louise Jarussi; c. Melvin L, Gregory J, Catherine L, Brian R, Justin M. and Mark A. Educ: Rocky Mt. Col, B.S, 41; Harvard Grad. Sch. Bus. Admin, summer 43. Polit. & Govt. Pos: Chmn, Dawson Co. Dem. Cent. Cmt, 56-60, committeeman, 62-; mem, Mont. Indust. Develop. Adv. Bd, 58-63; coordinator, Kennedy-Johnson Campaign, Dawson Co, 60; mem. adv. cmt, Mont. small Bus. Admin, 62-66; mem, Mont. Bd. Inst, 63-; coordinator Hubert H. Prof. Pos: Research and statist. officer, VA, Ft. Harrison, Mont, 46-51; office mgr, Watson Mfr. Co, Helena, Mont, 51-52; CPA, Cross & Rigg, Glendive, Mont, 52- Mailing Add: P.O. Box 1388, Glendive, Mont. 59330.

CROSS, (WILLIAM) TRAVIS R
b. Salem, Ore, 3/23/27; s. Henry A. Cross and Belvie Gilbert C; m. 10/30/49 to Beverly Jean Briggs; c. Craig, Paul, Jennifer and Sara. Educ: Stanford Univ, A.B. in Polit. Sci, 49; Sigma Delta Chi; Phi Delta Theta; Pi Delta Epsilon. Hon. Doctorate, Willamette Univ, 69. Polit. & Govt. Pos: Asst. to the Chancellor, 50-57; admin. asst. to Secy. of State, Ore, 57-59; coordinator, Hatfield for Gov. Campaign, 58 and Hatfield for Sen. Campaign, 66; asst. to the Gov, Ore, 59-66; participant in presidential campaigns on a loan basis, 60 & 64; adv, Packwood for Sen. Campaign, 68. Bus. & Prof. Pos: Dir, info. and alumni, Willamette Univ, 49-50; pres, Travis Cross & Assoc, Inc, 66-69; v.pres, univ. rels, Univ. of Calif, Berkeley, 69- Mil. Serv: Entered as Seaman 2/C, Navy, 45, serv. in Air Crew Prog. Mem: Am. Legion; Nat. Press Club; Pub. Rels. Soc. of Am; Am. Col. Pub. Rels. Asn; exec. reservist, Off. of Emergency Preparedness. Rel: Congregational. Mailing Add: University of California, 131 University Hall, Berkeley, Calif. 94720.

CROSSLEY, RANDOLPH ALLIN R
Rep. Nat. Committeeman, Hawaii
b. Cupertino, Calif, 7/10/04; s. John P. Crossley and Elizabeth Hall C; m. 7/23/28 to Florence May Pepperdine; c. Meredith C. (Mrs. Jack E. Young). Educ: Univ. Calif, Berkeley, 23-26. Polit. & Govt. Pos: Del. and mem. various cmts, First Constitutional Conv, Hawaii; Hawaii Territorial Rep, 43-45; chmn, Rep. Party, Hawaii 50-52; Hawaii State Sen, 59-64; Rep. cand, Gov. of Hawaii, 66; Rep. Nat. Committeeman, Hawaii, 67-; coordinator, Nixon-Agnew Campaign, 68. Bus. & Prof. Pos: Pres. and exec. officer, Crossley Advert. Co. and Hawaiian Tuna Packers, Ltd, 29-34; pres. & exec. officer, Hawaiian Fruit Packers, Ltd, 34-54; mem, Pub. Utilities Cmn, 45-47; pres. & exec. officer, Crossco, Ltd, Crossley Contracting Co. and Aloha Stamp Co, 54-63; pres. and chief exec. officer, Pac. Savings & Loan Asn, 60-63; chmn. and chief exec. officer, Am. Pac. Life Ins. Co. Ltd, 67-; pres. and chief exec.

officer, Am. Pac. Group, Inc, 67-69; chmn. and dir, Hawaii Corp, 67-69; pres, chief exec. officer and dir, 69- Mem: Trustee, Newcomen Soc. N.Am; Rancheros Visitadores; Oahu Country Club, Honolulu; Pac. Club; Metrop. Club, New York; Bohemian Club, San Francisco; C. of C.(past dir); Rotary (past secy); Community Chest and Salvation Army (past dir). Rel: Protestant. Legal Res: 3073 Noela Dr, Honolulu, Hawaii 96815. Mailing Add: P.O. Box 1061, Honolulu, Hawaii 96808.

CROTHERS, MORRIS KING R
Ore. State Rep.
b. Fort Morgan, Colo, 6/19/06; s. William H. Crothers and Nina Morris C; m. June, 1942 to Eunice Fisher; c. Shirley, Donald and Susan. Educ: Col. Wooster, B.S, 27; West. Reserve, M.D, 31; Phi Beta Kappa; Alpha Omega Alpha; Alpha Kappa Kappa. Polit. & Govt. Pos: Ore. State Rep, 63-64, 65- Bus. & Prof. Pos: Private practice of med, Salem, Ore, 46- Mil. Serv: Lt. Comdr, Naval Med. Corps, 44-46, served in Pac, 44-46; Comdr.(Ret), Naval Med. Corps Res. Mem: Am. Col. of Surgeons; Am. Med. Asn. Rel: Presbyterian. Mailing Add: 1517 Court St, Salem, Ore. 97301.

CROTTY, J. DESMOND D
b. Wagner, S.Dak; s. John M. Crotty and Celestine C; m. 1/17/46 to Margery L. Bartley; c. Daniel, Mary Ellen, Kathleen, Patricia and Maureen. Educ: Cent. Mo. State, 43-44; Creighton Univ, LL.B, 48; Delta Theta Phi. Polit. & Govt. Pos: Spec. agent, Fed. Bur. Invest, 48-52 & 54-65; co. attorney, Pocahontas Co, Iowa, 67-; del, Dem. Nat. Conv, 68. Bus. & Prof. Pos: Attorney, Pocahontas, Iowa, 65- Mil. Serv: Entered as A/S, Navy, 43, released as Lt.(jg), 46, after serv. in U.S. Amphibious Forces, Pac. Theatre, 44-46; 3 Battle Stars, S.Pac. Mem: Am. Legion; VFW; Amvets; Soc. Former Agents of the Fed. Bur. Invest; Kiwanis. Iowa State Championship Debate Team, 42. Rel: Roman Catholic. Mailing Add: 113 Third Ave. S.W, Pocahontas, Iowa 50574.

CROUCH, LEON MEADER R
b. Durham, N.H, 12/11/93; s. Leslie Lincoln Crouch and Amy Bell Meader C; m. 12/27/19 to Mary Mertie Ham; c. Marjorie (Mrs. Robert M. Moore), Barbara (Mrs. Joseph A. Blaise), Leonard and Marilyn (Mrs. William Dresser). Educ: Univ. N.H. Liberal Arts, 17; Kappa Sigma. Polit. & Govt. Pos: Mem, Bd. Selectmen, Durham, N.H, 47-50, secy. bd. and town clerk and tax collector, 50-62; N.H. State Rep, 62-68. Bus. & Prof. Pos: Clerk, R.R. Off, 19-23; off. mgr, Wholesale Wallpaper and Paint Store, 23-46; mgr, Pub. Acct. Off, 44-46; pub. acct, 46- Mil. Serv: Entered as Seaman 2/C, Navy, 17, released as Storekeeper 3/C, 21; Victory Medal. Mem: Mason (32°); Consistory; Shrine; Am. Legion; 40 et 8; Grange. Rel: Protestant. Mailing Add: Bennett Rd, Durham, N.H. 03824.

CROUSE, RUBY ROSE R
Secy-Treas, Chaffee Co. Rep. Cent. Cmt, Colo.
b. Merritt, Ill, 1/16/00; d. Albert John Newman and Nellie Ann Rufus N; wid; c. Albert LeRoy. Educ: Salida High Sch. Polit. & Govt. Pos: Secy-treas, Chaffee Co. Rep. Cent. Cmt, Colo, 54-; Rep. precinct committeewoman, Precinct 15, Chaffee Co, 58-62; secy, 11th Judicial Dist. Rep. Party, 58-69; pres, Chaffee Co. Rep. Women's Club, 66- Rel: Protestant. Mailing Add: Route 1, Box 303, Salida, Colo. 81201.

CROW, DOLORES JEAN R
Corresponding Secy, Idaho State Rep. Women
b. Clovis, N.Mex, 11/14/31; d. Charles D. York and Margaret Gardner Y; m. 10/22/50 to Wayne T. Crow; c. Steven T, Susan D, Kathryn L, David W. and J. Michael. Educ: Henager Stevens Col, 2 years. Polit. & Govt. Pos: Nat. committeewoman, Idaho Young Rep. League, 67-69; del, Rep. Nat. Conv, 68; Rep. precinct committeewoman, Canyon Co, Idaho, 68; dir, Canyon Co. TAR, 69-; corresponding secy, Idaho State Rep. Women, 69- Bus. & Prof. Pos: Secy, Ord. Div, U.S. Army, Ft. Worden, Wash, 50-52; personal secy. to Capt. of Naval ROTC, Univ. Idaho, 52-56; MT/ST programmer, Idaho Legis, 68-69. Mem: Nampa Musettes; Broadmore Country Club; Lincoln PTA. First runner-up, Mrs. Idaho, 65. Rel: Baptist. Mailing Add: 226 Davis Ave, Nampa, Idaho 83651.

CROW, HERSCHAL HILLIAR, JR. D
Okla. State Sen.
b. Olustee, Okla, 3/30/35; s. Herschal Hilliar Crow and Nova Hensley C; m. 6/29/57 to Elizabeth Kay Small; c. David Thomas and Michael Carter. Educ: Okla. State Univ, A.B, 57; Beta Theta Pi. Polit. & Govt. Pos: Okla. State Sen, 68- Mil. Serv: Entered as E-1, Army, 58, Released as E-2, 58. Mem: Okla. Wheat Growers Asn; Mason (32°); Elks. Outstanding Young Farmer, Jackson Co, Okla, 66. Rel: Methodist. Mailing Add: 1906 Sumner Dr, Altus, Okla. 73521.

CROW, JAMES HARRIS, JR. D
b. Decatur, Ala, 10/17/10; s. James Harris Crow and Mary Lou Collier C; m. 6/12/37 to Elizabeth Hand; c. James H, III and Eddie Pat. Educ: Univ. Ala, A.B. and LL.B; Pi Kappa Phi. Polit. & Govt. Pos: Judge, Morgan Co. Court, 40-46; presiding judge, Eighth Judicial Circuit 46-51. Bus. & Prof. Pos: V.pres, Chemstrand Corp, 57-; dir, civic affairs, Southeast Region, Monsanto Co, 63-; dir, Fed. Reserve Bank, Sixth Dist. Mil. Serv: Coast Guard, 42-44. Mem: Dir, Assoc. Industs. of Ala, Ala. Textile Mfg. Asn, Ala. State C. of C. and mem, Adv. Bd, Conserv. of Ala; Mason. Rel: Baptist. Mailing Add: 1912 Country Club Rd, Decatur, Ala. 35601.

CROW, WILLIAM JOSIAH R
b. Uniontown, Pa, 1/22/02; s. Sen. William Evans Crow and Ada Curry C; m. 10/5/23 to Charlotte Elizabeth Sheafer; c. Robert Hustead and Richard Sheafer. Educ: Pa. Mil. Col, Civil Eng, 22; Dickinson Sch. Law, LL.B, 25; Phi Kappa Psi; Corpus Juris. Polit. & Govt. Pos: Probation officer, Fayette Co, Pa, 26-27, asst. dist. attorney, 28-32; mayor, Uniontown, 38-41; U.S. Rep, Fayette Co. and Cumberland Co, Pa, 47-48; admin, Wash. Regional Off, Security and Exchange Cmn, 57-64. Bus. & Prof. Pos: Attorney-at-law, 26-51. Mil. Serv: 2nd Lt, Army Res, 25, retired as Col, 62, active serv. in Ord. Corps, Pac, Ocean Area, 41-46; exec. officer to Ord. Officer, Pac. Ocean Area; Bronze Star; Am. Theater and Pac. Theater Ribbons. Mem: Bd. of Trustees, Pa. Mil. Col, 55-58; Elks; Retired Officers' Asn; U.S. Army Asn; Mason (32°). Rel: Baptist. Mailing Add: 231 N. Hanover St, Carlisle, Pa. 17013.

CROWDER, DALE FARRIS R
Asst. Attorney Gen, Okla.
b. Lehigh, Okla, 12/23/37; s. Leonard Harvey Crowder (deceased) and Fern Farris C; m. 6/2/63 to Phyllis Jean White. Educ: Seminole Jr. Col, Okla, 56-57; Okla. Baptist Univ, B.A, 61; Univ. of Okla, LL.B, 64. Polit. & Govt. Pos: Chmn, Beckham Co. Rep. Party, Okla, 65-67; asst. attorney gen. and chief, criminal div, Okla, 67-; bd. mem, Cent. Okla. Young Rep, 68-; mem, Okla. Co. Rep. Party Cent. Cmt, 69-; dir, Okla. Crime Cmn, 69- Bus. & Prof. Pos: Bd. of Dirs, Elk City C. of C, Okla, 66-67. Mil. Serv: Entered as Pvt, 45th Div, Okla. Nat. Guard, 55, released as S/Sgt, 63. Mem: Am, Okla. and Okla. Co. Bar Asns; pres, Beckham Co. Bar Asn, 65-66; Kiwanis Int; C. of C; All Sports Asn; United Fund. Lettered in Varsity Tennis, Okla. Baptist Univ; Okla. Co. Young Lawyers Asn; Okla. Dist. Attorneys Asn. Rel: Southern Baptist; Deacon. Mailing Add: 4620 N.W. 59th Terrace, Oklahoma City, Okla. 73122.

CROWE, EUGENE BURGESS D
Treas, Ind. State Dem. Cmt.
b. Blue Lick, Ind, 1/5/78; foster parents, Joshua Crowe and Emma Bixler C; wid; one son deceased. Educ: Borden Acad, Borden, Ind, 2 terms. Polit. & Govt. Pos: U.S. Rep, Ninth Dist, Ind, 30-40; del, Dem. Nat. Conv, 68; treas, Ind. State Dem. Cmt, currently. Bus. & Prof. Pos: Retail furniture, until 65; pres, Stone City Nat. Bank; dir. and v.pres, Wabash Valley Asn. Mem: Elks; Ky. Col; Sagamore of the Wabash, Ind. Rel: Methodist. Mailing Add: 1212 14th St, Bedford, Ind. 47421. (1967)

CROWE, MORRILL MARTIN
Councilman, Richmond, Va.
b. St. Louis, Mo, 8/17/01; s. Thomas Crowe and Della S. Meyer C; m. 4/16/38 to Kathryne Skarry. Educ: Wash. Univ, St. Louis, B.S. in Chem. Eng, 23; Pi Kappa Alpha. Polit. & Govt. Pos: Mayor, Richmond, Va, 64-68, councilman, 69- Bus. & Prof. Pos: V.pres, Wm. P. Poythress and Co, Inc, 39- Mem: Kiwanis. Rel: No denominational affiliation. Mailing Add: 3909 Hanover Ave, Richmond, Va. 23221.

CROWE, PHILIP K.
U.S. Ambassador to Norway
b. N.Y.C, 1/7/08; s. Earl Crowe and Kathleen McClellan Higgins C; m. 6/21/37 to Irene Pettus; c. Phillippa, Irene and Mary. Educ: St. Paul's Sch, Concord, N.H, 28; Univ. Va, 32. Polit. & Govt. Pos: Spec. rep, Econ. Coop. Admin, China, 48-49; U.S. Ambassador to Ceylon, 53-56; U.S. Del. to Econ. Cmn. Asia and the Far East Conf. of UN, 54; spec. asst. to Secy. of State, 57-59; U.S. Ambassador to Union of S.Africa, 59-61; U.S. Ambassador to Norway, currently. Bus. & Prof. Pos: Reporter, N.Y. Eve. Post, 33; chief of customers dept, Milmine Bodman, broker, N.Y.C, 34-35; explorer and hunter of big game, French Indo-China, 35-37; dir. travel advert, Life Mag, 37-38; mem. advert. staff, Fortune Mag, 38-41 & 44-48; leader, wildlife mission to Near East, 63, S.Am, 64, Far East, 65 and Mid. East, 66. Mil. Serv: Lt. Col, Army Air Force, 41-44; chief of intel, Off. of Strategic Serv, China-Burma-India Theater; Bronze Star; Order of Yun-Hui, Repub. of China; Officer, French Legion of Honor; Grand Off, Mil. Order of Christ, Portugal, 63. Publ: Sport is Where You Find It, 53; Diversions of a Diplomate in Ceylon, 57; Sporting Journeys, 66. Mem: Trustee, For. Serv. Educ. Found; bd. adv, Sch. of Adv. Int. Studies, Johns Hopkins Univ; bd. dirs, World Wildlife Fund, African Wildlife Leadership Found; fel, Royal Asiatic Soc; Coun. For. Rels; Soc. Colonial Wars; Huguenot Soc; St. Nicholas Soc; former mem, Asn. Squadron A, N.Y. Nat. Guard; Am. Cmt. for Int. Wildlife Protection; Racquet and Tennis Club; Explorers, Brook and Anglers Clubs; Century Asn. Club; Boone and Crocket Club, N.Y.C; Round Table Club, Woodstock, Vt; Harvard Travelers Club, Boston; Hill Club, Ceylon; Metrop. Club, Wash; Flyfishers Club, London; Rand Club, Johannesburg, Union of S.Africa; Chesapeake Bay Yacht Club, Easton, Md; Lokota, Dacor House and Boodles Clubs. Legal Res: Easton, Md. 21601. Mailing Add: U.S. Embassy, Oslo, Norway.

CROWE, ROBERT WILLIAM R
Chmn, Franklin Co. Rep. Cmt, Vt.
b. Sheldon, Vt, 10/16/93; m. to Cora Alice Stephenson; c. Two sons, three daughters. Educ: Burlington Bus. Col, Vt. Polit. & Govt. Pos: Vt. State Rep, 21-23 & 63-66; town auditor, 60-63; chmn, Franklin Co. Rep. Cmt. and Sheldon Town Rep. Cmt, currently. Bus. & Prof. Pos: Former purchasing agent, Standard Packaging Corp. Mem: F&AM; RAM; RSM; K.T; past pres, Sportsman's Club, Inc, Vt. Fedn. of Sportsman's Clubs; Vt. rep, Nat. Wildlife Fedn. York Cross of Honor. Rel: Congregationalist. Mailing Add: Sheldon Springs, Vt. 05485.

CROWELL, LESTER AVANT, JR. R
Chmn, Ninth Cong. Dist. Rep. Cmt, N.C.
b. Lincolnton, N.C, 10/25/04; s. Lester Avant Crowell and Mary Jane Hull C; m. 3/24/32 to Elaine Deal; c. Dr. Gordon C, Marilynn (Mrs. P.L. George), Christine (Mrs. Ralph E. Cochrane, Jr), Virginia Elaine and Ruth Elizabeth. Educ: Univ. of N.C, A.B, 26; Tulane Univ. Sch. of Med, M.D, 30; Phi Chi; Lambda Chi Alpha. Polit. & Govt. Pos: Treas, Lincoln Co. Rep. Exec. Cmt, N.C, 52-56, chmn, 56-64; mem, N.C. Rep. Exec. Cmt, 56-64; chmn, Eighth Cong. Dist. Rep. Cmt, 66-68; alternate del, Rep. Nat. Conv, 60, 64 & 68; chmn, Ninth Cong. Dist. Rep. Cmt, 68- Bus. & Prof. Pos: Internist, Gordon Crowell Mem. Hosp, Lincolnton, N.C, 31-, roentgenologist, 34-; pres, Lincoln Frozen Foods, 44- Publ: 16 scientific medical articles in medical periodicals, 33-56. Mem: Fel, Am. Col. of Physicians; Am. Med. Asn; N.C. State Med. Soc; pres, Lincoln Co. Med. Soc, 59; mem, N.C. State Bd. Med. Exam, 38-44, pres, 44; former mem, Rotary. Cert. internist, Am. Bd. Internal Med, 43. Rel: Methodist. Legal Res: 709 S. Aspen St, Lincolnton, N.C. 28092. Mailing Add: 816 S. Aspen St, Lincolnton, N.C. 28092.

CROWHURST, NORMAN HERBERT R
Spec. Projs. Chmn, Ore. Rep. State Cent. Cmt.
b. London, Eng, 11/3/13; s. Herbert Thomas Crowhurst and Alice Wilson C; m. 7/8/44 to Kathleen Dorothy Chalk; c. Deirdre Michele and Nigel Berwyn. Educ: London Univ, Eng, D.Sc, 35. Polit. & Govt. Pos: V.chmn, Curry Co. Rep. Cent. Cmt, Ore, 66- chmn, 67-68, alternate chmn, 69-; spec. projs. chmn, Ore. Rep. State Cent. Cmt, currently. Bus. & Prof. Pos: Sr. lectr, Goldsmith's Col, Eng, 35-39; chief engr, Tannoy Ltd, Eng, 35-51; design consult. in Eng, 45-53; chief engr, Fairchild Recording, 53-55; design

consult, 55- Publ: Graphical Calculators & Their Design, Hayden, 63; Elements of Electron Physics, Gernsback, 63; Taking the Mysticism from Mathematics, Vantage Press, 68; plus 20 others. Mem: Inst. Elec. & Electronics Eng; Nat. Coun. Teachers Math; Nat. Soc. Prfnl. Eng; Acoustical Soc. of Am; Soc. Motion Picture & TV Eng; Audio Eng. Soc; Rotary; Coun. for Ore. Educ; Found. for Econ. Educ. Rel: Christian. Mailing Add: P.O. Box 651, Gold Beach, Ore. 97444.

CROWLEY, ARTHUR EDWARD, JR. R
Mem, Exec. Cmt, Vt. State Rep. Cmt.
b. Rutland, Vt, 10/18/28; s. Arthur E. Crowley and Mildred Patricia Gilfeather C; m. 7/29/61 to Marcia Colby Smith; c. Robert Arthur, David Stevens and Andrew Coppinger. Educ: Boston Univ. Law Sch. Polit. & Govt. Pos: Dep. Attorney Gen, Vt, 60-61; state's attorney, Rutland Co, 61-65; chmn, Rutland Co. Rep. Cmt, 61-; mem. exec. cmt, Vt. State Rep. Cmt, 61-, chmn, 63-67; city attorney, Rutland, Vt, 65- Mil. Serv: Entered as Pvt, Army, 51, released as 2nd Lt, 63, after serv. in 82nd Airborne Div, U.S. Mem: Vt. and Am. Bar Asns; pres, Vt. Jr. Bar Asn, 63-64; K. of C; Rotary; Am. Legion. Rel: Roman Catholic. Legal Res: 12 Foster Place, Rutland, Vt. 05701. Mailing Add: 27 S. Main St, Rutland, Vt. 05701.

CROWLEY, FRANCIS A. D
b. Proctor, Vt, 5/21/09; m. 1933 to Elma S. Wenner; c. Frances Ann, Paula Marie, Michael David, Timothy Jon. Educ: Manhattan Col, N.Y. City, B.A. Polit. & Govt. Pos: Mich. State Rep, 64-66. Mil. Serv: Army, 4 years. Mem: 1932 Olympic team; Lions Club; Eagles; Am. Legion; K. of C; Midwest Olympic Club. Rel: Catholic. Mailing Add: 7341 Deer Lake Rd, Clarkston, Mich. 48016. (1967)

CROWLEY, FRANK PATRICK R
b. Dallas, Tex, 3/16/24; s. David Martin Crowley and Jennie Loughlin C; m. 4/30/49 to Martha Kirn; c. David, Carol and Michael. Educ: Univ. Notre Dame, B.S. in Commerce, 47. Polit. & Govt. Pos: Admin. asst. to Congressman Bruce Alger, U.S. House Rep, Fifth Cong. Dist, Tex, 55-60; cmnr, Dallas Co, Tex, 61-69; Rep. cand, U.S. House Rep, 13th Dist, 68; alternate del, Rep. Nat. Conv, 68. Bus. & Prof. Pos: Sales, W.C. Nabors Co, Dallas, 49-54; sales assoc, Henry S. Miller Co, Realtors, 69. Mil. Serv: Entered as Seaman, Naval Res, 42, released as Lt, 46, after serv. in Destroyers - Task Force 58/38, S.Pac, 44-45. Rel: Catholic. Mailing Add: 2209 Whitecliff Lane, Richardson, Tex. 75080.

CROWLEY, PAUL F. D
Pa. State Rep.
b. Scranton, Pa, 6/13/34; s. Edward M. Crowley and Alice M. Gunning C; m. 6/20/59 to Mary Louise Nealon; c. Paul, Timothy and Mary Ellen. Educ: Univ. Scranton, B.S, 61. Polit. & Govt. Pos: Pa. State Rep, 69- Bus. & Prof. Pos: Treas, Mark Truck Rental Corp. Mil. Serv: Entered as Recruit, Navy, 52, released as AD 3/C, 56, after serv. in BTU-4. Mem: Nat. Asn. Acct. (v.pres, Northeast Chap, 67-68); Brotherhood Rwy. Clerks (v.pres, local chap, 59-60); Elks; Am. Legion; K. of C. Rel: Roman Catholic. Legal Res: 214 Prospect Ave, Scranton, Pa. 18512. Mailing Add: Capitol Post Office, Harrisburg, Pa. 17101.

CROWLEY, THOMAS M. D
Vt. State Sen.
Polit. & Govt. Pos: Vt. State Sen, 67-; mem, Burlington Traffic Cmn; Chittenden Co. Dem. Comt; Young Dem. Bus. & Prof. Pos: V.Pres, Crowley Ins. Agency, Inc. and Crowley Ins. Agency of Essex, Inc. Mem: Past pres, New England Asn. of Mutual Ins. Agents; past pres. and dir, Burlington Jaycees. Mailing Add: 36 N. Willard St, Burlington, Vt. 05401.

CROWN, ROBERT W. D
Calif. State Assemblyman
b. San Francisco, Calif, 1/23/22; single. Educ: Univ. Calif, B.A; San Francisco Law Sch, J.D. Polit. & Govt. Pos: Assembly Reading Clerk, 51; Calif. State Assemblyman, 56-; del, Dem. Nat. Conv, 68. Bus. & Prof. Pos: Lawyer. Mil. Serv: Army Res, 43-46, 1st Lt. Mem: Lions; Eagles; Elks; Toastmasters; state and co. Bar Asns. Mailing Add: 1111 Jackson St, Room 7018, Oakland, Calif. 94607.

CROWNINSHIELD, HUBERT BROWN R
b. Jamaica, Vt, 11/12/95; s. Stillman T. Crowninshield and Eliza S. Cummings C; single. Polit. & Govt. Pos: Selectman, Winhall, Vt, 32-52; Justice of the Peace, Jamaica, Vt, 32-52 & 55-; Vt. State Rep, 35-37 & 63-65. Mil. Serv: Pfc, Army, Base Hosp. Camp Devers, 18-19. Mem: Mason; Am. Legion. Rel: Protestant. Mailing Add: Box 186, Jamaica, Vt. 05343.

CRUM, WILLIAM BRUCE R
V.Chmn, Frederick Co. Rep. State Cent. Cmt, Md.
b. Sunshine, Md, 6/5/27; s. Bruce Elias Crum and Frances Catherine Howes C; m. 6/22/52 to Barbara Diane Eaves; c. William Bruce, Jr, Barbara Ann, Mark Edward, Susan Marie and Mary Ann. Educ: Walkersville High Sch, 44. Polit. & Govt. Pos: Pres, Frederick Co. Young Rep, Md, 51-53 & 61; v.pres, Md. Fedn. Young Rep, 51-53, dir, 53-55, nat. committeeman, 63-65 and treas, 65-; pres, Frederick Co. Rep. Club, 55; v.chmn, Frederick Co. Rep. State Cent. Cmt, 62-, chmn, 66; del, Young Rep. Nat. Conv. and chmn, State Conv, 63; mem. cmn. to study Md. State Bd. Agr, appt. by Gov. Spiro T. Agnew, 67. Mem: Farm Bur; Grange; Frederick Co. Agr. Soc; Md-Va. Milk Producers Asn; Walkersville Elem. PTA, v.pres, 67-68; Walkersville High Sch. PTA; bd. mgrs, Md-W.Va. Artificial Breeders Coop, Inc. Voted Outstanding Young Rep. of Md, Md. Fedn. of Young Rep, 64. Rel: Methodist. Mailing Add: R.R. 1, Walkersville, Md. 21793.

CRUME, PATRICIA ANN R
b. Wewoka, Okla, 7/26/33; d. Cecil C. Chenoweth and Beatrice Huddleston C; m. 8/25/50 to William Joseph Crume; c. Renée, Ralinda and Raleah. Educ: Claremore High Sch. Polit. Pos: Secy, Okla. State Rep. Cmt, 61-65; v.chmn, Rogers Co. Rep. Party, 62-63 and secy, 58-61; temporary conv. secy, Rep. State Conv, 65 and 64 and del, Okla. State Conv, 65, 64, 63 and 61; mem, Inaugural Ball Cmt. for Okla. 1st Rep. Gov, 62; mem, Gen. Fedn. of Rep. Women. Mem: Pres, Ocieleta Club, 66; pres, Claremont Elem. PTA, 64; TRMS. Winner of 3rd place for oil painting, Co. Art Show and winner of 2nd place for oil and pencil drawing, Co. Fair, 66. Rel: Southern Baptist; nursery coordinator, Youth Cmt. Chmn. and Choir Mem. Mailing Add: 1021 N. Muskogee, Claremore, Okla. 74017. (1967)

CRUMPACKER, SHEPARD J. R
b. South Bend, Ind, 2/13/17; s. Shepard J. Crumpacker and Grace Dauchy C; m. 2/18/50 to Marjorie Patton; c. Richard Owen. Educ: Northwest. Univ, Evanston, Ill, B.S. in Eng, 38; Univ. Mich, Ann Arbor, LL.B, 41. Polit. & Govt. Pos: U.S. Rep, Third Cong. Dist, Ind, 51-56; city attorney, South Bend, Ind, 69- Bus. & Prof. Pos: Assoc, Crumpacker, May, Beamer, Levy & Seares, 46-49, partner, 50; partner, Crumpacker, May, Levy & Seares, 56- Mil. Serv: Entered as Pvt, Army Air Corps, 41, released as 1st Lt, 46, after serv. in Fighter and Bomber Units; Maj, Air Force Res. Mem: Am, Ind. State and St. Joseph Co. Bar Asns; Bar Asn. of the Seventh Fed. Circuit; Am. Judicature Soc; Mason; Elks; Izaac Walton League; Prairie Club of Chicago; Potomac Appalachian Trail Club; Michiana Watersheds, Inc; Farm Bur; Co-op; North. Ind. Hist. Soc; Ind. Hist. Asn; Ind. Pioneers; Rotary. Rel: Presbyterian. Mailing Add: 237 Timber Lane, South Bend, Ind. 46615.

CRUPPER, GORDON R
b. Denver, Colo, 10/7/20; s. John Clayton Crupper and Christine Grace Sutherland C; m. 2/1/43 to Ellen Elizabeth Keen; c. Gordon, Jr, Burton Keen and Jean Elizabeth. Educ: Colo. State Univ, B.S. in Forestry, 42; Yale Univ, 45-46; Forestry Sch. Hon. Fraternity; Scabbard and Blade. Polit. & Govt. Pos: Chmn, Lemhi Co. Rep. Cmt, Idaho, 68. Bus. & Prof. Pos: Mgr. Idaho Div, Intermountain Co. Mil. Serv: Entered as 2nd Lt, Army, 42, released as 1st Lt, 46, after serv. in Field Artil. as Liaison Pilot; Air Medal. Mem: Soc. of Am. Foresters; West. Wood Prod. Asn; Mason; Elks; C. of C; Rotary. Rel: Episcopal. Mailing Add: P.O. Box 1208, Salmon, Idaho 83467.

CRUTCHER, HARRY, III 'BUZZ' D
b. San Antonio, Tex, 6/16/38; s. Maj. Gen. Harry Crutcher, Jr. and Ruth Gibbons C; m. 8/28/65 to Carolyn Joyce Burnett. Educ: Rice Univ, A.B, 60; South. Methodist Univ, LL.B, 63. Polit. & Govt. Pos: Attorney, Dept. Justice, 63 & 64; campaign mgr. for Earle Cabell, U.S. Rep, Tex, 64 & 66, admin. asst, 65-; campaign mgr. for 15 co. Dem. state legislators, 68. Bus. & Prof. Pos: Practicing attorney. Mil. Serv: 1st Lt, Air Force Res, 56. Mem: Tex, Fed. and Am. Bar Asns. Rel: Roman Catholic. Legal Res: 3617 Cragmont, Dallas, Tex. 75205. Mailing Add: 2191 First National Bank Bldg, 1401 Elm St, Dallas, Tex. 75202.

CRUTCHER, JOHN WILLIAM R
b. Ensign, Kans, 12/19/16; s. O.W. Crutcher and Orpha Middleton C; single. Educ: Univ. Kans, A.B, 40. Polit. & Govt. Pos: Kans. State Sen, 53-57; Lt. Gov, State of Kans, 65-69. Bus. & Prof. Pos: Pres, Hutchinson Investment Co, 55- and Countryside West, Inc, 60- Mil. Serv: Entered as A/S, Navy, 41, now Capt. Naval Res. Publ: The Satellite Countries, serial in Wichita Eagle and Beacon, Sept, 65. Mem: Bd. of Gov, Am. Royal, Kansas City, Mo; pres, Red Cross and Jr. C. of C; comdr, Am. Legion; VFW; Mil. Order of World Wars; Mason (32°); Shrine; York Rite, Consistory; Elks; Moose. Rel: Methodist; mem, Off. Bd. Mailing Add: 200 E. 12th, Hutchinson, Kans. 67501.

CRUTCHFIELD, WILLIAM WARD D
b. Chattanooga, Tenn, 12/6/28; s. Thomas Crutchfield and Nel Ward C; m. 6/23/66 to Joan Nunley; c. Candis Ward and Margie Nel. Educ: Univ. Chattanooga; Univ. Tenn; Phi Alpha Delta. Polit. & Govt. Pos: Tenn. State Rep, 57 & 61; Tenn. State Sen, 63 & 65-67. Mil. Serv: Entered as Pvt, Army, 53, released as Pfc, 54. Mem: Chattanooga and Am. Bar Asns; Am. Trial Lawyers Asn; Mason; Sertoma Club of Chattanooga; Elks; Tenn. Valley Dem. Club. Rel: Methodist. Legal Res: 503 Battery Place, Chattanooga, Tenn. 37403. Mailing Add: 509 Cherry St, Chattanooga, Tenn. 37402.

CRUZ, LAURO D
Tex. State Rep.
b. Beaumont, Tex, 5/20/33; s. Manuel Cruz and Margarita Menchaca C; m. 3/5/55 to Alice Clarice Sebesta; c. Christopher Stephens, Camille Elizabeth, Jerry Lauro and Catherine Stannie. Educ: Univ. of Houston, B.S, 61; S.Tex. Col. of Law, 2 years. Polit. & Govt. Pos: Tex. State Rep, 67- Bus. & Prof. Pos: Assoc. dir, Houston Action for Youth, 64-66; dir. of job develop, Crescent Found, 67-68; dir, Southwest Pub. Rels, 68-69. Mil. Serv: Entered as a Pvt, Marines, 50, released as Cpl, 53. Rel: Lutheran. Mailing Add: 7124 Schley St, Houston, Tex. 77017.

CRUZ JIMENEZ, OLGA Popular Dem, P.R.
Rep, P.R. House of Rep.
b. Rio Piedras, P.R, 7/31/33; d. Manuel Cruz Horta and Dolores Jiménez Barredo C; single. Educ: Univ. P.R, B.A. cum laude, 54; Univ. P.R. Sch. of Law, LL.B, 57. Polit. & Govt. Pos: Legal adv, Pub. Works Dept, San Juan, P.R, 57-58 and P.R. Corp. of Housing and Urban Renewal, 58-60; dist. judge, P.R. Justice Dept, 60-62 and spec. dist. attorney, 62-63; Rep, P.R. House of Rep, 68- Mem: P.R. Bar Asn; Am. Judicature Soc; Civic Clubs of Prfnl. and Businesswomen of P.R; Alumni Asn. of Univ. P.R; Club Porcia; Kappa Beta Pi. Award for Achievement, P.R. Bar Asn; First woman lawyer to be elected to P.R. Legis; Award for Polit. Achievement, Exchangetts Club; Award of Achievement, Nu Sigma Beta, San Patricio Chap. Rel: Catholic. Legal Res: Suiza 166, Floral Park, Hato Rey, P.R. 00917. Mailing Add: House of Representatives, Capitol, San Juan, P.R. 00903.

CRUZE, CHESTER T. R
Ohio State Rep.
b. Cincinnati, Ohio, 5/27/38; s. Jack Harvey Cruze and Fay Chryss C; single. Educ: Univ. Cincinnati, B.A, 60, grad. study, 65-67; Salmon P. Chase Col. Law, J.D, 64; Xavier Univ, grad. study, 66-67; Salmon P. Chase Col. Law Deans List Student; Phi Delta Theta; Phi Alpha Delta. Polit. & Govt. Pos: Campaign mgr, Gordon H. Scherer for Ohio State Rep, 64; campaign coordinator, Taft for Senate Cmt, 64; campaign mgr, Frank H. Mayfield for City Coun, 65; conv. chmn, Ohio State Young Rep, 65; v.chmn, Ohio League Young Rep. Club, 65; campaign chmn, Hamilton Co. Rep. Party, 66 & 67; mem, Rep. Nat. Cmt. Campaign Chmn. Conf, 67; chmn, Hamilton Co. Youth for Nixon, 68; mem, Richard M. Nixon Rep. Nat. Conv. Staff, 68; Ohio State Rep, 68th Dist, 69- Bus. & Prof. Pos: Advert. publicity, Am. Laundry Machines, Cin-

cinnati, Ohio, 60-62; mortgage-investment, Union Cent. Life Ins, Co, 62-64, assoc. counsel, 64-65; asst. co. prosecutor, Hamilton Co, Ohio, 65-66; instr. law, Univ. Cincinnati, 67-69; asst. attorney gen, Ohio, 68; attorney, Purcell, Sullivan & Young, currently. Publ: 'Art & Politics,' Mt. Adams Rev, 9/1/67. Mem: Am. Bus. Law Asn; Cincinnati, Ohio and Am. Bar Asns; Nat. Asn. Dist. Attorneys; Nat. Soc. State Legislators; Gr. Cincinnati Jr. C. of C.(pres, 65-67); Univ. Cincinnati Fund Drive, Booster, Cmt. of 100, and 1968 Sesquicentennial Homecoming Cmt; Clifton Town Meeting; Bond Hill Civic Club; Winton Place Civic Club; Torch Club; Cincinnati Club; state govt. affairs chmn, Ohio Jaycees, 66; Kiwanis; Scottish Rite; Shrine; Eagles. Admitted to practice before U.S. Supreme Court, Fed. Dist. Court, Sixth Circuit Court of Appeals, and all Ohio State Courts; Cincinnati's Outstanding Young Man of the Year Award, 64; Key Man Award, Cincinnati Jaycees, 65; Background for Leadership Award, Ohio Jaycees, 66; Jaycee Sound Citizen Award, 66; Gt. Cincinnati C. of C. Award of Appreciation. Legal Res: 880 Lafayette Ave, Cincinnati, Ohio 45220. Mailing Add: 2213 Carew Tower, Cincinnati, Ohio 45202.

CRYAN, JOHN F. D
m. to Mary Carr; c. Six. Educ: W. Side High Sch, Newark, N.J. Polit. & Govt. Pos: N.J. State Assemblyman; Vailsburg Young Dem; Newark Parking Authority; W. Ward Dem. Asn. Mil. Serv: Korean Conflict, 27th Inf. Div, Mem: DAV; Essex Co. Youth & Rehabilitation Cmn; K. of C; Elks; W. Side Mem. Post number 8670. Legal Res: 544 Sanford Ave, Newark, N.J. Mailing Add: Cryans Vailsburg Manor, 88 Halsted, Newark, N.J. 07106. (1967)

CRYER, CLIFFORD EUGENE R
Chmn, Woodford Co. Rep. Cent. Cmt, Ill.
b. Morris, Ill, 10/29/02; s. John Henry Cryer and May Lutzow C; m. 6/1/25 to Carol Ruth Cherry; c. Barbara (Mrs. Bowermaster), Carol J. (Mrs. Tiemann) and Philip E, M.D. Educ: Kirksville Col. of Osteopathy & Surg, D.O, 26. Polit. & Govt. Pos: Secy, Woodford Co. Rep. Cent. Cmt, Ill, 50-58, chmn, currently; coroner, Woodford Co, Ill, 52-64. Mem: Am, Ill. and 4th Dist. Ill. Osteopathic Asns; Am. Osteopathic Soc. of Radiologists; Masonic Lodge 246, Mackey Chap. 130, Couer De Leon Commandery 43, Mohammed Temple Shrine; C. of C; pres, El Paso Kiwanis, 36. Rel: Protestant. Mailing Add: 576 Elmwood Court, El Paso, Ill. 61738.

CSALA, LEA MINER D
b. Wilkes-Barre, Pa, 2/21/30; d. Robert Charles Miner and Elizabeth Chase Carter M; m. 10/17/53 to Gottfried Paul Csala; c. Maria, Martha and Margaret. Educ: Smith Col, B.A, 51. Polit. & Govt. Pos: Del, Dem. Nat. Conv, 68. Mem: League Women Voters, Wilkes-Barre; Wyo. Valley Asn. UN; Nat. Cmt. for Sane Nuclear Policy. Rel: Protestant. Mailing Add: 356 S. River St. Wilkes-Barre, Pa. 18702.

CULBERTSON, STUART A. D
Mem, Pa. State Dem. Cmt.
b. Meadville, Pa, 4/16/96; s. James L. Culbertson and Elizabeth Edmeston C; m. 6/26/64 to Katherine E. Swisher; c. Barbara (Mrs. Royston), Stuart A, Jr. and Mary Beth. Educ: Dickinson Sch. of Law, LL.B, 24. Polit. & Govt. Pos: Chmn, Crawford Co. Dem. Cmt, Pa, 58-66; mem, Pa. State Dem. Cmt, currently. Mem: Crawford Co, Pa. State and Am. Bar Asns; Rotary; Mason; Meadville Round Table; C. of C. Rel: Presbyterian. Legal Res: 703 Walnut St, Meadville, Pa. 16335. Mailing Add: 349 Center St, Meadville, Pa. 16335. (1967)

CULBREATH, JOHN RICHARD D
Fla. State Rep.
b. Tampa, Fla, 6/27/26; s. Hugh Lee Culbreath and Daphne Elizabeth Jackson C; m. 12/26/50 to Barbara Jean Council; c. Sharron Lynne and Candi Elizabeth. Educ: Baylor Sch, Tenn, 44; Univ. Tampa, summers, 47 & 48; Univ. Ga, B.B.A, 49; Kappa Sigma. Polit. & Govt. Pos: Mem, Hernando Co. Dem. Exec. Cmt, Fla, 62-64; chmn, 64-66; Fla. State Rep, Dist. 69, 67- Bus. & Prof. Pos: Mgr, Firestone Stores, St. Petersburg, Fla, 51-52; owner, Bar Bet Farms, Largo, Tampa & Brooksville, 53-; secy-treas, Little Manattee Acres, Inc, Tampa, 55-; pres, Hernando Indust, Inc, Brooksville, 59-; owner, Agr. Consult, 60-; dir, First Nat. Bank, 69- Mil. Serv: Entered as PAC, Army Air Corps, 44, released as Sgt, 46, after serv. in Fifth Air Force, Pac. Theater, 45-46; 1st Lt, Res, Inf; Victory Medal; Good Conduct Medal: Pac. Theater of Opers, Japan Occup, and VJ Medals. Mem: Am-Int. Charolais Asn; Fla. Charolais Asn; Fla. Cattlemen's Asn; Farm Bur; Kiwanis; C. of C; Tampa Yacht and Country Club; Tampa Horse Show Asn; Am. Horse Shows Asn. Fla. Outstanding Young Farmer of the Year, Fla. Jr. C. of C, 60. Rel: Presbyterian. Mailing Add: Route 4, Box 70, Brooksville, Fla. 33512.

CULLAN, DAVID JAMES D
Mem, Nebr. Dem. Coalition Exec. Cmt.
b. Alliance, Nebr, 6/8/40; s. Harry Thomas Cullan and W. Lorene C; single. Educ: Regis Col, B.A, 62; Creighton Univ. Law Sch, J.D, 65; Phi Alpha Delta. Polit. & Govt. Pos: Del, Douglas Co. Dem. Conv. and Nebr. State Dem. Conv, 68; alternate del, Nat. Dem. Conv, 68; campaign coordinator, Douglas Co. Dem. Party, 68; mem, Nebr. Dem. Coalition, Steering Cmt, 68 and Nebr. Dem. Coalition Exec. Cmt, 69-; mem, Second Dist. Dem. Research Cmt, 69. Bus. & Prof. Pos: Legal counsel, Nebr. State Rwy. Cmn, 67-68; attorney-at-law, Foulks, Wall & Wintroub, 68- Mil. Serv: Entered as E-1, Army, 65, released as E-2, 66, after serv. in Army Res. training; E-4, Army Res, 66-69. Mem: Omaha, Nebr. and Am. Bar Asns; Nebr. Asn. of Trial Attorneys; Am. Trial Lawyers Asn; Omaha Barristers Club; Nebr. Motor Carrier Lawyers Asn; Nebr. Transportation Inst. Rel: Catholic. Legal Res: 5056 Grover, Omaha, Nebr. 68108. Mailing Add: 608 Executive Bldg, Omaha, Nebr. 68102.

CULLEN, MIKE D
Calif. State Assemblyman
b. Phillipsburg, Mont, 4/9/27; s. Harold Michael Cullen and Iris Juanita Belden C; m. 9/25/53 to Rita Joyce Beane; c. Lisa Carol, Tamara Shawn Leolani, Erin Natasha and Merritt Christian. Educ: George Washington Univ, A.B, 55; Yale Univ, LL.B, 59. Polit. & Govt. Pos: Calif. State Assemblyman, 67- Mil. Serv: Entered as A/S, Navy, 44, released as Lt, 57, after serv. in Pac. Area, 46-56; Letter of Commendation, Asiatic-Pac. Theater; China Serv. Medal; Navy Occupation Medal; Korean Medal; Viet Nam Medal; Am. Expeditionary Force Medal; Capt, Naval Res, 67. Mem: Nat. Exchange Club; Long Beach C. of C; Am. Bar Asn; Am. Judicature Soc; U.S. Naval Inst; Navy League. Rel: Protestant. Legal Res: 28 La Linda Dr, Long Beach, Calif. 90807. Mailing Add: 444 W. Ocean Blvd, Suite 1044, Long Beach, Calif. 90802.

CULLEN, RITA BEANE D
b. Hamlin, Tex, 11/1/33; d. Gilbert Auther Beane and Hazel Greenslade B; m. 9/25/53 to Michael Cullen; c. Lisa Carol, Tamara Shawn Leolani, Erin Natasha and Merritt Christian. Educ: N.Tex. State, 51-52; George Wash. Univ, B.A. in Elem. Educ, 55; Pi Beta Phi; Phi Sigma Alpha. Polit. & Govt. Pos: Del, Dem. Nat. Conv, 68. Bus. & Prof. Pos: Second grade teacher, Honolulu Sch. Syst, Hawaii, 56; teacher of retarded, Montgomery Co, Md, 57; second and third grade teacher, Branford, Conn, 58, third grade teacher, Glendale, Calif, 59. Mem: Calif. Teachers Asn; PTA; Long Beach Lawyers Wives (past pres); Auxiliary to Long Beach Children's Clin; Yale Law Wives (past pres); Auxiliary to Civic Light Opera; Friends of Long Beach State Col; Lakewood Dem. Club; Speaker's Bur. of United Crusade. Sweetheart of Sigma Chi. Rel: United Methodist. Mailing Add: 28 La Linda Dr, Long Beach, Calif. 90807.

CULLENS, J.R. D
b. Erick, Ga, 7/8/17; s. John Asa Cullens and Gertrude Killebrew C; m. 6/9/40 to Mary Ethel Barfield; c. John Benjamin, Joseph Roy, Mary Ann. Educ: Mid. Ga. Col, 37; Univ. of Ga. Sch. of Law, LL.B, 51, cum laude; Phi Alpha Delta; Phi Kappa Phi; Editor-in-Chief of Ga. Bar Jour, 50-51. Polit. & Govt. Pos: Ga. State Rep, 63-64. Bus. & Prof. Pos: Attorney. Mil. Serv: U.S. Army Inf, WW II. Mem: Lions. Rel: Presbyterian. Mailing Add: Cartersville, Ga. 30120. (1967)

CULLITY, WILLIAM J. D
N.H. State Rep.
b. Manchester, Vt; married. Educ: Manchester Schs. Polit. & Govt. Pos: N.H. State Rep, 59- Bus. & Prof. Pos: Owner, Heating and Appliance bus. Rel: Catholic. Legal Res: N.H. Mailing Add: 338 Laurel St, Manchester, N.H. 03102. (1967)

CULP, CARL LESTER D
Chmn, Armstrong Co. Dem. Party, Pa.
b. Manor Twp, Ford City, Pa, 8/12/22; s. Charles Lawrence Culp and Jessie Heilman C; m. 4/11/47 to Beulah Marie Grafton; c. Bonnie Kay, Robert and Christopher. Educ: Ford City High Sch, Pa, 36-40. Polit. & Govt. Pos: Twp. supvr, Manor Twp, Pa, 53-65, secy-treas, 10 years; mem. planning cmn, Armstrong Co, 59-; secy-treas, Co. Asn. Twp. Officers, 60-65; committeeman, Armstrong Co. Dem. Party, 61-, chmn, 69-; committeeman, Armstrong Co. Agr. Stabilization & Conserv. Serv, currently. Mem: Elks; Lions; co. pres, Pa. Farmers Asn; Pa. Farmers Milk Judging Asn.(secy, 3 years, dir, currently); Agr. Exten. Asn. Rel: Presbyterian. Mailing Add: 2074 Hobson Dr, Ford City, Pa. 16226.

CULPEPPER, RUFUS HORACE D
Chmn, Cullman Co. Dem. Party, Ala.
b. Cullman, Ala, 9/23/22; s. Thomas Perry Culpepper and Nettie Hyatt C; m. 3/10/49 to Rachel Louise Brock; c. Karen, Joe, Kenny, Neal and Tim. Educ: Auburn Univ, B.S. in Agr. Sci, 50. Polit. & Govt. Pos: Mem, Sch. Bd, Cullman, Ala; chmn, Cullman Co. Dem. Party, 66- Mil. Serv: Entered as Pvt, Marines, 42, released as Pfc, 45, after serv. in First Div, S.Pac. Theatre. Mem: Nat. and Ala. Auto Dealers Asn; Chrysler Dealers Coun; VFW; Elks; Am. Legion. Rel: Baptist. Mailing Add: 206 Ninth St, Cullman, Ala. 35055.

CULVER, BARBARA GREEN R
b. Dallas, Tex, 2/9/26; d. Lawrence F. Green (deceased) and Alice Bryson G; m. 8/15/47 to John R. Culver; c. Lawrence L. and J. Bryson. Educ: Tex. Tech. Col, B.A. in Journalism, 47; South. Methodist Univ, LL.B, 51; Theta Sigma Phi; Kappa Beta Pi; DFD. Polit. & Govt. Pos: Judge, Midland Co, Tex. and Juvenile Court Judge, 63-; alternate del, Rep. Nat. Conv, 68. Bus. & Prof. Pos: Private law practice, 51-63. Mem: Tex. State and Midland Co. Bar Asns; State Bar of Tex.(secy. family law sect); Permian Basin Juvenile Coun; Tex. State Juvenile Officers Asn; Nat. Coun. on Crime and Delinquency; C. of C; Midland Altrusa Club; Midland br, Am. Asn. Univ. Women; Bus. and Prfnl. Women of Midland; Commun. Ambassador Bd; Boys Club Adv. Bd; High Sky Girls Ranch Adv. Bd. Rel: Christian Science. Legal Res: 1007 Neely, Midland, Tex. 79701. Mailing Add: County Court House, Midland, Tex. 79701.

CULVER, JOHN CHESTER D
U.S. Rep, Iowa
b. Rochester, Minn, 8/8/32; s. William C. Culver and Mary Miller C; m. to Ann T. Cooper; c. Christina, Rebecca, Catherine and Chester. Educ: Harvard Col, A.B. cum laude, 50-54; Lionel of Jersey Harvard Scholarship to Cambridge Univ, Eng, 54-55; Harvard Law Sch, LL.B, 59-62. Polit. & Govt. Pos: Legis. asst, Sen. Edward M. Kennedy, 62-63; U.S. Rep, Second Dist, Iowa, 65-; del, Dem. Nat. Conv, 68. Bus. & Prof. Pos: Bus. mgr, Culver-Rent-A-Car, 59; attorney-at-law, McGuire, Bernau & Culver, 63-65. Mil. Serv: Marine Corps, 55, released as 1st Lt, 58, after serv. in 1st Marine Div; Capt, Marine Corps Res. Mem: Fed, Iowa and Linn Co. Bar Asns. Rel: Presbyterian. Legal Res: 298 Red Fox Rd. S.E, Cedar Rapids, Iowa 52403. Mailing Add: 107 Cannon Bldg, Washington, D.C. 20515.

CULVER, JOHN LEE D
Ala. State Rep.
b. Marbury, Ala, 11/25/15; s. Tobe Ben Culver and Willie Elizabeth Wells C; m. 6/4/45 to Alma Elizabeth Kirby; c. Janice Elizabeth and Robert Larry. Educ: Univ. Ala. Polit. & Govt. Pos: Ala. State Rep, Dist 18, Tuscaloosa Co, currently. Bus. & Prof. Pos: Cost acct. for U.S. Steel, 10 years; acct. machine and procedure rep, Nat. Cash Register Co, 4 years; comptroller and secy, Dept. Stores, 11 years; owner and operator, Motel, 7 years; owner and operator, Pecan and Cattle Farm, at present. Mil. Serv: Entered as A/S, Naval Res, 44, released as Specialist 2/C, 45, after serv. as Athletic Instr. Mem: Nat. Asn. of Cost Accts; Ala. Cattlemen's Asn; Elks; Am. Legion Post; DAV; Tuscaloosa Cattlemen's Asn; CIO Off. & Tech. Workers 2210, Birmingham. Rel: Methodist. Mailing Add: Route 3, Box 166, Tuscaloosa, Ala. 35401.

CULVERHOUSE, EDGAR ALLEN D
Mem, Va. State Dem. Cmt.
b. Selma, Ala, 9/6/34; s. Allen Culverhouse and Katie Bayne C; m. 10/26/63 to Doris Gilliam. Educ: Richmond Prfnl. Inst; Col. of William & Mary, Norfolk Div. Polit. & Govt. Pos: Pres, Va. Beach Young Dem. Club, Va, 60-64; state pres, Young Dem. Clubs Va, 64-65; spec. asst. to pres, South. Conf. Young Dem. Clubs. Am, 64-65, chmn, 65; mem, Va. State Dem. Cmt, 64-; secy, Va. Beach City Dem. Exec. Cmt, 65. Bus. & Prof. Pos: Dep. cmnr. revenue, Va. Beach, Va, 56-58, spec. tax adminstr, 58-63, dir. personnel, 63- Mem: Pub. Personnel Asn; Fraternal Order of Police (state pres); Mason; Shrine; Nat. Ruritan Club. Rel: Methodist. Legal Res: 1900 Thunderbird Dr, Virginia Beach, Va. 23454. Mailing Add: P.O. Box 162, Virginia Beach, Va. 23458. (1967)

CUMMING, HUGH CLIFFORD D
Mayor, Drummond, Mont.
b. Butte, Mont, 12/21/26; s. Forest Cumming and Mary McDonald C; m. 11/18/47 to Palma McGregor; c. Mary, Mark, Peggy and Toni. Educ: Mont. State Univ, 1 year. Polit. & Govt. Pos: Mont. State Rep, 55-59; Mont. State Sen, Granite Co, 59-67; Mayor, Drummond, Mont, 68- Bus. & Prof. Pos: Shift Boss, Cominco Am, 49- Mil. Serv: Entered as Pvt, Marine Corps, 44, released as Cpl, 46, after serv. in 3rd Marine Div, Pac; Bronze Star, Iwo Jima. Mem: Mason, P.M; Kiwanis; Am. Legion. Rel: Methodist. Mailing Add: Box 426, Drummond, Mont. 59832.

CUMMINGS, FRANK R
b. NYC, 12/11/29; s. Louis Cummings and Florence C. Bonime; m. 7/6/58 to Jill Schwartz; c. Peter Ian and Margaret Anne. Educ: Hobart Col, A.B, 51; Columbia Univ, M.A, 55; Columbia Law Sch, LL.B, 58; Phi Beta Kappa; Tau Kappa Alpha; Articles Ed, Columbia Law Review; Phi Alpha Delta. Polit. & Govt. Pos: Minority counsel, U.S. Senate Cmt. on Labor and Pub. Welfare, Wash, D.C, 65-67; admin. asst. to U.S. Senator Jacob K. Javits, N.Y, 69- Bus. & Prof. Pos: Attorney, Cravath, Swaine & Moore, New York, N.Y, 58-63, Gall, Lane & Powell, Wash, D.C, 63-65 and Poletti Freidin Prashker Feldman & Gartner, New York, N.Y, 67-69. Mil. Serv: Entered as Pvt, Army, 62, released as Cpl, 65, after serv. in U.S. Army, Europe, 62-64. Publ: Miscellaneous articles on labor law, Labor Law J; book rev, 'Psychiatric Justice,' Columbia Law Rev, 66; 'Remarks on Private Pension Plans,' Symp. on Private Pension Plans, Am. Enterprise Inst. of Pub. Policy Res, Wash, D.C. and Proc. of N.Y. Univ. 22nd Annual Inst. on Labor, 69. Mem: Am. Bar Asn; Asn. of the Bar of City of New York (Cmt. on Labor and Social Security); Columbia Univ. Seminar on Labor (former chmn). Mailing Add: 4305 Bradley Lane, Chevy Chase, Md. 20015.

CUMMINGS, JAMES HARVEY D
Tenn. State Rep.
b. Woodbury, Tenn, 11/8/90; s. John Morgan Cummings and Lula Land C; m. 9/6/25 to Hesta Harding McBroom. Educ: Woodbury Acad; Nashville YMCA Law Sch, LL.B; Cumberland Univ, LL.B; Sigma Alpha Epsilon. Polit. & Govt. Pos: Circuit court clerk, Cannon Co, Tenn, 14-22; Tenn. State Sen. and Tenn. State Rep, 29-; Secy. of State, Tenn, 49-53; del, Dem. Nat. Conv, 68. Mem: Elks; Lions Int; K. of P; Farm Fedn. Bur. Rel: Christian. Mailing Add: Court Square, Woodbury, Tenn. 37190. (1967)

CUMMINGS, MINNETTE HUNSIKER R
Maine State Rep.
b. Washington, D.C; d. Harold Whiting Hunsiker and Florence M. Lufkin H; m. 8/1/42 to H. King Cummings; c. Stephen H, Wende (Mrs. Robert A. Richter), Lee L. and Jennifer. Educ: Bennington Col, B.A, 40. Polit. & Govt. Pos: Maine State Rep, 69- Bus. & Prof. Pos: State of Maine Agent, Sch. & Col. Adv. Center, 65- Mem: Newport Woman's Club; trustee, Unity Col; trustee, Newport Pub. Libr; dir, Sch. Admin. Dist. No. 48. Rel: Protestant. Mailing Add: High St, Newport, Maine 04953.

CUNNINGHAM, CLARENCE MARION D
b. Cooper, Tex, 7/24/20; s. Willie Lee Cunningham and Naoni Stokes C; m. 9/16/51 to Janet Ruth Kohl; c. Elizabeth Jane, Daniel Marvin, Steven Charles and Margaret Helen. Educ: Tex. A&M, B.S, 44; Univ. Calif, Berkeley, M.S, 48; Ohio State Univ, Ph.D, 54; Pi Lambda Upsilon, Sigma Xi. Polit. & Govt. Pos: Dem. chmn, Precinct Four, Stillwater, Okla, 60-64 & 69-; secy-treas, Payne Co. Cent. Cmt, 64-67; del, Dem. Nat. Conv, 68. Bus. & Prof. Pos: Instr. chem, Calif. State Polytechnic Col, 48-49; cryogenic engr, Herric L. Johnston Inc, Columbus, Ohio, 52-54; prof. chem, Okla. State Univ, 54- Mil. Serv: Entered as 2nd Lt, Army, 42, released as Maj, 46, after serv. in Anti-Aircraft Artil. C.Z, 42-45; Res, 67-, Col; Am. Theater Medal; World War II Victory Medal; Defense Medal. Publ: Catalytic Conversion of Oil to Parahydrogen, 9/57 and Separation of Orthohydrogen from Parahydrogen by Prefratial Adsorption on Alumina, 9/57, J. Am. Chem. Soc. Mem: Am. Chem. Soc; Am. Phys. Soc; Am. Asn. for Adv. of Sci; Am. Asn. Univ. Prof.(pres, Okla. conf, 64-66); C. of C; Kiwanis. Rel: Society of Friends. Mailing Add: 924 Lakeridge Ave, Stillwater, Okla. 74074.

CUNNINGHAM, GLENN C. R
U.S. Rep, Nebr.
b. Omaha, Nebr, 9/10/12; s. George Cunningham and Emma C; m. July, 1941 to Janis Thelen; c. Glenn, Jr, Judy, Mary, James R, David and Ann Melissa. Educ: Univ. Omaha, B.A, 35. Polit. & Govt. Pos: Mgr, Omaha Safety Coun, Nebr, 42-47; mem, Omaha City Coun. & supt. Dept. Fire Protection and Water Supply, 47-48; mayor, Omaha, 48-54; Nebr. state dir, Savings Bonds Div, U.S. Treas. Dept, 54-56; U.S. Rep, Nebr, 56-; mem, Omaha Bd. Educ. Mem: Exec. secy, Omaha Jr. C. of C, 36-40, mgr, Conv. Bur, 40-41, pres, 45; Legion of Honor, Order of DeMolay, Pi Kappa Alpha; Eagles. Named Outstanding Young Man, Nebr, 46. Rel: Episcopal. Mailing Add: 2447 Rayburn Bldg, Washington, D.C. 20515.

CUNNINGHAM, JOSEPH M, JR. R
Treas, Milton Rep. Town Cmt, Mass.
b. Milton, Mass, 9/20/38; s. Joseph M. Cunningham and Mildred Gallagher C; single. Educ: Colby Col, 57-58; Suffolk Univ, 58-60. Polit. & Govt. Pos: Mem, Milton Town Meeting, Mass, 60-; park cmnr, Milton, 64-66; treas, Milton Rep. Town Cmt, 68- Bus. & Prof. Pos: Stock broker, Hornblower & Weeks-Hemphill, Noyes, 63-69; mgr, Tucker, Anthony & R.L. Day, 69-; asst. treas, Tucker, Anthony Mgt, Co, 69- Mil. Serv: Entered as Pvt, Army, 60, released as Sp-4, 63, after serv. in 508th ASA Group, Eighth Army, Korea, 61-63. Mem: Chmn, Milton United Fund Drive, 65; chmn, S.Area Mass. Bay United Fund, 66; v.chmn, Milton Human Rights Fellowship. Rel: Roman Catholic. Mailing Add: 608 Brush Hill Rd, Milton, Mass. 02186.

CUNNINGHAM, LARRY JACK D
Chmn, Taylor Co. Dem. Exec. Cmt, Tex.
b. McLean, Tex, 10/10/16; s. Russ O. Cunningham and Linnie Craig C; m. 2/1/41 to Geneva Huddleston; c. Beverley, Larry Lyonal and Barry Dean. Educ: Hardin-Simmons Univ, B.S, 40, M.A, 50; Letterman's Club. Polit. & Govt. Pos: Chmn, Taylor Co. Dem. Exec. Cmt, Tex, 68- Bus. & Prof. Pos: Coach football and boxing, Dennison and Childress High Schs, 40-42; coach football, McMurry Col. and Hardin-Simmons Univ, 47-54; real estate oil opers, farming and ranching, racing and raising running horses, 54-69. Mil. Serv: Entered as Ens, Navy, 42, released as Lt, 46, after serv. in S.W. Pac. Theatre; VFW Medal. Rel: Baptist. Legal Res: 760 Mulberry St, Abilene, Tex. 79604. Mailing Add: 1632 Parramore St, Abilene, Tex. 79604.

CUNNINGHAM, MARY ROSALIE D
b. Rulo, Nebr, 4/24/07; d. Stephen W. Cunningham and Susie Plante C; single. Educ: Univ. Kans. Polit. & Govt. Pos: Del, Young Dem. Nat. Conv, 33, 35, 37 & 39; mem, Young Dem. Nat Cmt, 35-40; clerk, State Hwy. Dept, Lincoln, Nebr, 35-41; exam, Gen. Acct. Off, Wash, D.C, 41-46; mem, State Dem. Cmt, 52-56; mem, Dem. Nat. Cmt, 52-60; del, Dem. Nat. Conv, 36, 52, 56, 60, 64 & 68, mem, platform cmt, 56, 60, 64 & 68, mem, site cmt, 56, mem, arrangements cmt, 60. Bus. & Prof. Pos: Land owner and business-woman, at present. Mem: Int. Platform Asn; State Civil War Centennial Cmn; Dist. Judicial Nominating Cmn; Univ. Kans. Alumni Asn. Rel: Roman Catholic. Mailing Add: Rulo, Nebr. 68431.

CUNNINGHAM, MARY VAN ZILE R
b. New York, N.Y, 11/2/87; d. Edward S. Van Zile and Mary Morgan Bulkeley Z; m. 4/29/12 to R. Gerald A. Cunningham, wid; c. Harold (deceased), Mrs. John Nickerson and Richard Poore. Educ: Hartford High Sch; The Gardner Sch, N.Y.C; extension courses, Columbia Univ. Polit. & Govt. Pos: Conn. State Rep. until 67. Rel: Episcopal. Mailing Add: 174 Richmond Hill, New Canaan, Conn. 06840. (1967)

CUNNINGHAM, MATTHEW C. D
R.I. State Rep.
b. Pawtucket, R.I, 12/19/11. Educ: Providence Col; Boston Univ. Law Sch, LL.B, 50. Polit. & Govt. Pos: R.I. State Rep, 55- Bus. & Prof. Pos: Attorney-at-law. Mil. Serv: U.S. Marine Corps (Aviation) World War II. Mem: R.I. Bar Asn; Pawtucket Bar Asn; Pawtucket Coun; K. of C; Holy Name Soc. Rel: Catholic. Mailing Add: 263 Prospect St, Pawtucket, R.I. 02860. (1967)

CUNNINGHAM, NORWOOD R
Wash. State Rep.
b. Sunnyside, Wash, 1916; m. to Florence; c. two sons. Educ: George Fox Col; Post-Grad. work, Univ. of Wash, Univ. of Ore. Polit. & Govt. Pos: Transportation & Maintenance Supvr, Kent Co. Schs, Wash, currently; Wash. State Rep. and chmn, Rep. Caucus, Wash. State House of Rep, currently. Mil. Serv: U.S. Army, World War II. Mem: Rotary; Wash. and Nat. Educ. Asns; Am. Legion; Seattle King Co. Safety Coun. Kenneth Coleman Safety Award. Rel: Presbyterian. Mailing Add: 750 Alvord Ave, Kent, Wash. 98031.

CUNNINGHAM, PATRICK JOSEPH D
Chmn, Exec. Cmt, Bronx Co. Dem. Cmt, N.Y.
b. N.Y.C, 3/12/28; s. Hugh Cunningham and Julia Martyn C; m. 6/30/51 to Mary T. O'Donoghue; c. Stephen Patrick, Philip Edward, Christine, Peterpaul and Patrick Joseph, II. Educ: Fordham Univ, B.S. in Educ, 49; N.Y. Law Sch, LL.B, 56. Polit. & Govt. Pos: Counsel, House Cmt. Fed. Hwys, U.S. House Rep, 63-65; counsel, cmt. labor, N.Y. State Constitutional Conv, 67; alternate del, Dem. Nat. Conv, 68; chmn. exec. cmt, Bronx Co. Dem. Cmt, N.Y, 69- Bus. & Prof. Pos: Pres, Emerald Lawyers Soc. N.Y, 65; arbitrator, Am. Arbit. Asn, 69; mediator, N.Y. State Mediation Bd, 69. Mil. Serv: Entered as Seaman, Navy, 45, released as Boatswain 3/C, 46, after serv. in Pac. and Atlantic; Lt, Res, 49-53. Mem: Bronx Co. Bar Asn; Nat. Dem. Club. Rel: Roman Catholic. Legal Res: 6048 Fieldston Rd, Bronx, N.Y. 10471. Mailing Add: 2488 Grand Concourse, Bronx, N.Y. 10458.

CUNNINGHAM, RAY CREWS R
Iowa State Rep.
b. Conde, S.Dak, 7/14/93; s. Edwin Pierce Cunningham and Isabelle Clark C; m. 5/11/18 to Ethel Hutchinson; c. Glen (deceased), Wayne (deceased), Dorothy (Mrs. Nelson Beverly) and Virginia (Mrs. Gene Gordon). Educ: S.Dak. State Univ, B.S, 17; hon. L.H.D, 64. Polit. & Govt. Pos: Iowa State Rep, Story Co, 57- Bus. & Prof. Pos: Asst. secy, YMCA, Univ. Minn, 19-26; gen. secy, Iowa State Univ, 26-53. Mil. Serv: Entered as Pvt, Army, 18, released as 2nd Lt, 19, after serv. in Spec. Duty Adj. Gen. Dept. Mem: Izaak Walton League; YMCA Retired Secretaries; hon. mem, 4-H Clubs; Cardinal Key. Univ. Centennial Award, presented for distinguished serv. Rel: Presbyterian. Mailing Add: 2218 Storm St, Ames, Iowa 50010.

CUNNINGHAM, REX M. D
b. Iola, Kans, 11/29/07; m. 5/29/31 to Aileen Ann Allen; c. Patricia. Educ: Washburn Col. Polit. & Govt. Pos: Calif. State Assemblyman, 54-66; Bus. & Prof. Pos: Pub. Acct. Mil. Serv: U.S. Army, WWII. Mem: Elks; Kiwanis; Am. Legion; 20-30 Clubs; Am. Soc. Accts; Dem. Cent. Cmt. Mailing Add: Ventura, Calif. 93008. (1967)

CUNNINGHAM, RONALD LEROY R
Mem, Exec. Cmt, Ohio Rep. Finance Cmt.
b. Cambridge, Ohio, 11/10/12; s. Leroy R. Cunningham and Mary Ada Johnston C; m. 6/14/34 to Arlene Elizabeth Peffer; c. Nancy Jane (Mrs. Ramsayer), Ronald Lee and Lawrence B. Educ: McKinley High Sch, Canton, Ohio. Polit. & Govt. Pos: Regional finance chmn, Ohio Rep. Cmt, 63-; mem, exec. cmt, Ohio Rep. Finance Cmt, 64-; del, Rep. Nat. Conv, 68. Bus. & Prof. Pos: Pres, Ohio Ferro-Alloys Corp, 48-; dir, Citizens Savings Asn, 55-; dir, First Nat. Bank, Canton, Ohio, 56- Mem: Mfg. Chem. Asn; Am. Soc. of Metals; Am. Iron and Steel Inst; Duquesne Club, Pittsburgh, Pa; Eldorado

Country Club, Palm Desert, Calif; Congress Lake Country Club, Hartville, Ohio; Canton Club, Canton, Ohio; Bd. Mem, United Fund of Cent. Stark Co, Canton Welfare Bd, Jr. Achievement and Timken Mercy Hosp. Rel: United Church of Christ. Mailing Add: Congress Lake, East Dr, Hartville, Ohio 44632.

CUNNINGHAM, SARAH JANE McQUAIDE R
Parliamentarian, Red Willow Co. Rep. Women's Club, Nebr.
b. Des Moines, Iowa, 2/16/22; d. Paul Harvey Cunningham and Harriet Plummer C; single. Educ: Sterling Col, A.B, 44; Univ. Nebr, LL.B, 59; Kappa Beta Pi. Hon. LL.D, Sterling Col, Kans. Polit. & Govt. Pos: Chmn, Red Willow Co. Rep. Party, Nebr, 54-56; dist chmn, Rep. Women, 60-63; secy, State Rep. Cent. Cmt, 62-64; parliamentarian. Red Willow Co. Rep. Women's Club, 62-; v.chmn, Red Willow Co. Rep. Cent. Cmt, 67-; mem, President's Adv. Coun. on Status of Women, 69- Bus. & Prof. Pos: Teacher; High Sch. & Jr. High, 44-52; owner and mgr, McCook Bus. Serv, 51-56 and Sally's Gift Shop, 53-56; attorney-at-law, Cunningham Law Off, 59- Publ: 'The Proposed Equal Rights Amendment to the United States Constitution,' Women's CPA Jour. and Rep. Women's Newspaper, 60. Mem: Am. and Nebr. Bar Asns; Nat. Asn. of Women Lawyers; Nat. Fedn. of Bus. and Prfnl. Women's Clubs, Inc. (past pres); VFW Auxiliary; Am. Asn. of Univ. Women; DAR; PEO; Eastern Star; v.pres, Int. Fedn. of Bus. and Prfnl. Women's Clubs. Rel: Congregational. Legal Res: 201 Park Ave, McCook, Nebr. 69001. Mailing Add: P.O. Box 983, McCook, Nebr. 69001.

CUNNINGHAM, WILLIAM JOHNSTON, III R
Ill. State Rep.
b. Swanwick, Ill, 10/20/15; s. William Johnston Cunningham II and Frieda Haberman C; m. 6/15/40 to Virginia Irene McElroy; c. Barbara Jean and William J, IV. Educ: Univ. Ill, 37; The Army Adjutant Generals Sch, 42; various ins. trade schs. Polit. & Govt. Pos: City cmnr, Pinckneyville, Ill, 47-51, Mayor, 51-65; v.pres. and mem. bd. of dirs, Ill. Munic. League, 52-60, pres, 60; del, State Nominating Conv, 64; mem, Ill. State Cmns. for Strip Mine Reclamation and Econ. Develop; Ill. State Rep, 64-, mem, Pub. Utilities, R.R. and Aviation, Indust. and Labor Rels. and Munic. Cmts, Ill. House of Rep. Bus. & Prof. Pos: Owner, Cunningham Agency, Ill, 37- Mil. Serv: Entered as Sgt, Army, 41, released as Maj, 46, after serv. in Adj. Gen. Dept, 2nd Army Hq; Victory and Pre-Pearl Harbor Medals; Am. Theater Ribbon; Army Commendation Medal with Oak Leaf Cluster. Mem: AF&AM, Mason (32°); Shrine; Eastern Star; past secy, Eagles; Am. Legion Post 587; past v.pres, C. of C; Elks Country Club; past pres, Pinckneyville Rotary; Vol. Firemens Asn. Rel: Methodist; Trustee, 1st Methodist Church of Pinckneyville. Mailing Add: 804 W. Belle Ave, Pinckneyville, Ill. 62274. (1967)

CUPIT, DANNY EARL D
Chmn, Young Dem. Clubs, Miss.
b. Jackson, Miss, 2/12/45; s. Denon Cupit and Nell Gray C; m. 8/30/69 to Sharon Ruth Miller. Educ: Miss. State Univ, B.S, 67; Univ. Miss. Sch. of Law; Pi Kappa Delta. Polit. & Govt. Pos: Chmn, Miss. State Univ. Young Dem, 65-67; col. v.chmn, Young Dem. Clubs, Miss, 67-69; chmn, Young Mississippians for Kennedy, 68; chmn, Youth for Humphrey-Muskie, 68; del, Dem. Nat. Conv, 68; chmn, Young Dem. Clubs, Miss, 69- Mil. Serv: Entered as E-3, Army Res, 68- Rel: Methodist. Legal Res: 460 Boling St, Jackson, Miss. 39209. Mailing Add: Box 1388, University, Miss. 38677.

CURCIO, SAMUEL A. R
N.J. State Assemblyman
b. Hammonton, N.J, 8/19/19; s. Frank Curcio and Catherine Lucca C; m. 6/28/48 to Lucy C. Ezzi; c. Samuel A, Jr, Susan, James,and Richard. Educ: Glassboro State Col, B.S, 41; Univ. Mich. Law Sch, J.D, 48; Delta Theta Phi. Polit. & Govt. Pos: Mem, Hammonton Bd. Educ, N.J, 50-56, pres, 53-56; munic. attorney, Hammonton, 50-55; coronor, Atlantic Co, 54-56; Munic. Court Judge, Hammonton, 56-61; N.J. State Assemblyman, Atlantic Co, 68- Mil. Serv: Entered as Pvt, Army, 41, released as Maj, 45, after serv. in Air Transport Command, China-Burma-India, 43-45; Air Force Res, Maj. Mem: Atlantic Co, N.J. and U.S. Bar Asns; VFW; Am. Legion. Rel: Catholic. Legal Res: 746 Virginia Ave, Hammonton, N.J. 08037. Mailing Add: 241 Bellevue Ave, Hammonton, N.J. 08037.

CURLEE, CLARENCE LAMAR, SR. D
b. Groesbeck, Tex, 10/23/98; s. Henry Wesley Curlee and Julia Anne Frazier C; m. 11/24/20 to Gladyne Elizabeth Cooper; c. Carrie (Mrs. Neyana), C. Lamar, Jr. and Lynda Lorraine. Educ: Tex. A&M, Bryan, Tex. Polit. & Govt. Pos: Dem. precinct chmn, for years; del. Dem. Nat. Conv, 64. Mil. Serv: Entered as Pvt, Army, 18, released as Sgt. Mem: Pres, Progressive Club; v.chmn. on Hwy. Cmt, C. of C. Hobby, Fishing. Rel: Methodist; Bd. of Stewards; Bd. of Educ; Lay Del. to Tex. Conf. Legal Res: 401 Penn, Van, Tex. 75790. Mailing Add: Box 217, Van, Tex. 75790. (1967)

CURLEY, LUCY A. ALFORD D
V.Chmn, Erie Co. Dem. Cmt, N.Y.
b. Ft. Smith, Ark; d. Lambert M. Alford and Lena Hammer A; m. to Edward P. Curley; c. Lucy L. (Mrs. Paul Teresi), D. Patrick and Michael E. Educ: Univ. Ark. Polit. & Govt. Pos: Mem. exec. cmt, N.Y. State Dem. Coun. and Erie Co. Dem. Cmt, 47-; dep. treas, Buffalo, N.Y, 54-55, city treas, 55-61 & 66-; mem. speakers bur, N.Y. Dem. Gubernatorial Campaign, 54 & 58 and Dem. Sen. Campaign, 64; del, N.Y. State Dem. Conv, 60, 62 & 64, Eighth Judicial Dist. Dem. Conv, 62, 63, 64 & 65 and Dem. Nat. Conv, 64 & 68; v.chmn, Erie Co. Dem. Cmt, chmn, women's div. and co-chmn, Erie Co. Dem. Exec. Cmt, 62- Mem: Dist. chmn, Cancer Crusade, 49; v.chmn, Cath. Charities, Buffalo, 55; Zonta, 55-61; Speakers Bur, United Fund, 60; v.pres, Cathedral Altar Soc; Fedn. of Women's Clubs; Dem. Bus. & Prfnl. Women; Albright-Knox Art Gallery. Rel: Roman Catholic. Legal Res: 1306 Delaware Ave, Buffalo, N.Y. 14209. Mailing Add: City Hall, Buffalo, N.Y. 14202.

CURLIN, WILLIAM P, JR. D
Ky. State Rep.
b. Paducah, Ky, 11/30/33; s. William P. Curlin, Sr. and Margaret Flatt C; m. 8/1/59 to Elizabeth Richardson; c. William P, III, Elizabeth Caroline, Margaret Rowden and Dorothy Richardson. Educ: Univ. Ky, A.B, 58, LL.B, 62; Phi Delta Theta. Pres, Franklin Co. Young Dem, Ky, 65-67; Ky. State Rep, 57th Dist, 68-, v.chmn, revenue and appropriations cmt, Ky. House of Rep, 68- and mem, pub. utilities and transportation cmt, 68-; mem, Dem. Rules Cmn, Ky, 69- Bus. & Prof. Pos: Chmn, Jour. Cmt, Ky. Bar Asn, 63-68. Mil. Serv: Entered as Cpl, U.S. Army, released as Sgt, 57, after serv. in 1st Armored Div, La, 55-57. Mem: Ky. Bar Asn.(chmn, four. cmt, 63-68); Jaycees. Rel: Presbyterian. Mailing Add: 218 Raintree Rd, Frankfort, Ky. 40601.

CURRAN, FRANK E.
Mayor, San Diego, Calif.
b. Cleveland, Ohio, 12/19/13; s. William E. Curran and Anna Hayer C; m. 4/15/36 to Florence McKenney. Educ: San Diego Jr. Col; Balboa Law Sch; San Diego State Col; Univ. Calif. Exten. Polit. & Govt. Pos: Dep. assessor, San Diego Co, Calif, 35-41; supvr. procurement for critical materials, Navy, 40-49; councilman, San Diego, 55-63; v.mayor, 57-58 & 61-62, mayor, 63- Bus. & Prof. Pos: Former laborer, stevedore, co-owner produce market, painter and decorating contractor; storekeeper, Oceanside, Calif, 37-38; secy-mgr, Eagles, San Diego, 49-60 and Shoreline Ins. Co, 60-63. Mem: Gov. Adv. Cmt. on Aviation; spec. rep, Gov. Cmn. of Californias; exec. cmt, Inter-Am. Munic. Orgn; cong. mem, U.S. Conf. of Mayors (commun. rels. cmt); League of Calif. Cities (dir-at-lg, exec. cmt); Nat. League of Cities (v.pres, 69). Legal Res: 4901 Westover Place, San Diego, Calif. 92102. Mailing Add: City Administration Bldg, San Diego, Calif. 92101.

CURRAN, GERALD JOSEPH D
Md. State Del.
b. Baltimore, Md, 3/20/39; s. James W. Curran, Sr. and Sadenia Brown; m. 1/20/57 to Anna Jeanette Brown; c. Kathleen Ann, Gerald Joseph, Jr, John F.X. and Margaret Ann. Educ: Univ. Baltimore, LL.B, 63; Sigma Delta Kappa. Polit. & Govt. Pos: Md. State Del, 67- Bus. & Prof. Pos: Casualty Claims Rep, Firemens Fund Am. Ins. Co, 64-, Continental Ins. Co. and Transit Casualty Ins. Co. Mil. Serv: Entered as Pvt, Md. Nat. Guard, 57, released as Pfc, 60. Mem: Baltimore Claim Men's Asn; K. of C; Holy Name Soc; Friendly Sons of St. Patrick; United 3rd Dist. Dem. Orgn; Ancient Order of Hibernians. Rel: Catholic. Mailing Add: 2831 Montebello Terrace, Baltimore, Md. 21214.

CURRAN, HENRY M. R
b. Pa; m. to Rita Rothmann; c. Three sons, one daughter. Educ: Pace Col. Polit. & Govt. Pos: Mem, Nassau Co. Rep. Cmt, N.Y; dep. sheriff, Nassau Co, chief clerk, Sheriff's Off; town clerk, Oyster Bay, 53-59; N.Y. State Sen, 60-68. Bus. & Prof. Pos: Ins. bus, Corroon, Carroll, Curran & Cooney, Inc. Mil. Serv: Capt, Army, World War II, serv. in Armored Div, ETO; Korean Conflict, 50. Mem: Am. Legion; Holy Name Soc; K. of C; Sagamore Hill Cmt; Theodore Roosevelt Asn. Mailing Add: 66 Melbourne St, Oyster Bay, L.I, N.Y. 11771. (1967)

CURRAN, J. JOSEPH D
City Councilman, Baltimore, Md.
b. Baltimore, Md, 9/5/04; s. James Patrick Curran and Theresa Larkins C; m. 10/8/30 to Catherine Mary Clark; c. J. Joseph, Jr, Margaret, Martin Edward and Robert Walter. Educ: Loyola Col, Md, 23. Polit. & Govt. Pos: Chmn, Dem. State Cent. Cmt, Md, 51-55; v.chmn, United Third Dist. Dem. Orgn, Baltimore, 51-; city councilman, Third Dist, Baltimore, 53-59 & 63-; del, Dem. Nat. Conv, 68. Mem: K. of C; Northwood Asn; Commun. Asn. Govans. Rel: Catholic. Mailing Add: 4222 Kelway Rd, Baltimore, Md. 21218.

CURRAN, J. JOSEPH, JR. D
Md. State Sen.
b. West Palm Beach, Fla, 7/7/31; married. Educ: Univ. of Baltimore; Univ. of Baltimore Law Sch, LL.B, 59. Polit. & Govt. Pos: Mem. Regional Planning Coun, Md; Md. State Del, 59-63; Md. State Sen, 63- Bus. & Prof. Pos: Bd. dirs, Md. Higher Educ. Loan Corp. Mil. Serv: Air Force, 51-55. Mem: Baltimore and Jr. Bar Asns; Friends Sons of St. Patrick. Mailing Add: 1415 Limit Ave, Baltimore, Md. 21212. (1967)

CURRAN, LEIGH RAYMOND R
Iowa State Sen.
b. Cambridge, Ill, 5/28/06; s. John L. Curran and Almeda Nordstrom C; m. 3/10/37 to Dorothy Foster; c. Kaye F.(Mrs. McDonald), Jane A. and Gail L. Educ: Hamilton's Bus. Col; Iowa State Univ, currently. Polit. & Govt. Pos: Precinct committeeman, Rep. Party, Iowa; Iowa State Sen, 60-64 & 68-; Iowa State Rep, 66-68. Bus. & Prof. Pos: Pres, North Iowa Fair, 20 years, dir, currently; chmn, Co. Red Cross, 53; dir, First Nat. Bank, 53-; v.pres, Iowa Beef Producers, 10 years. Mem: Mason; Consistory; Rotary; Shrine; Master Farmer Club of Iowa; Farm Bur; C. of C; YMCA. Master Farmer Award. Rel: Methodist. Mailing Add: Route 3, Mason City, Iowa 50401.

CURRAN, PAUL J. R
b. N.Y.C, 2/21/33; m. to Barbara Ann Frank; c. Five. Educ: Georgetown Univ, A.B; Fordham Law Sch, LL.B. Polit. & Govt. Pos: Former Asst. U.S. Attorney, South. Dist. of N.Y; N.Y. State Assemblyman, 62-66; alternate del, Rep. Nat. Conv, 68. Bus. & Prof. Pos: Attorney, law firm of Kaye, Scholer, Fierman, Hays and Handler. Mil. Serv: Capt, Air Force Res. Mem: Am. and N.Y. State Bar Asns; K. of C; dir, Boys Brotherhood Repub. of N.Y. Mailing Add: 201 E. 21st St, New York, N.Y. 10010. (1967)

CURRAN, RAYMOND JOSEPH D
Maine State Rep.
b. Bangor, Maine, 3/5/98; s. Dennis J. Curran and Ann Varley C; m. 9/2/35 to Mary Veronica Griffith; c. Raymond J, Jr. and Thomas N. Educ: Univ. Maine, B.S; Alpha Tau Omega. Polit. & Govt. Pos: Chmn, Bangor Dem. City Cmt, Maine, 34-36; mem, Maine Dem. State Cmt, 36-38 and 40-42; Maine State Rep, 65- Bus. & Prof. Pos: Rep, Select Pictures, 21-24, Universal Pictures, 24-26 and Metro-Goldwyn-Mayer, 26-62. Mil. Serv: Pvt, Army, 18. Mem: K. of C. (4°); AFL-CIO; Univ. of Maine Alumni Asn. Rel: Roman Catholic. Mailing Add: 188 Maple St, Bangor, Maine 04401.

CURRIE, CLAUDE D
b. Candor, N.C, 12/8/90; s. John C. Currie and Louise McKinnon C. Educ: Univ. of N.C, A.B, LL.B, 26. Polit. & Govt. Pos: N.C. State Sen, 27-29 & 45-68. Bus. & Prof. Pos: Pres, Security Savings & Loan Asn. Mil. Serv: Army Air Corps, Sgt, Pursuit Observer, 17-19. Rel: Presbyterian. Mailing Add: Security Savings and Loan Asn, East Chapel Hill, Durham, N.C. 27705. (1967)

CURRIE, JACK M. R
b. Cando, N.Dak, 3/14/99; married; c. Four. Educ: Iowa State Univ. Polit. & Govt. Pos: N.Dak. State Rep, 51-57 & 61-66. Bus. & Prof. Pos: Farmer. Mem: Am. Legion; Elks. Mailing Add: Cando, N.Dak. 58324. (1967)

CURRIGAN, THOMAS G. D
b. Denver, Colo, 7/8/20; s. Thomas G. Currigan and Mary Fredrica Wheaton C; m. 8/11/42 to Gertrude Curtis; c. Colleen and Thomas G, Jr. Educ: Notre Dame, grad, majored in polit. sci. and educ; Harvard Univ. Polit. & Govt. Pos: Recreation Counselor, City and Co. of Denver, Colo, 49-51; admin. asst. to mayor, 51-54, clerk & recorder, 54-55, auditor, 55-63, mayor, 63-68; alternate del, Dem. Nat. Conv, 68. Bus. & Prof. Pos: Staff v.pres. civil and commun. affairs, Continental Airlines, Los Angeles, Calif, 68- Mil. Serv: Entered as Pvt, Air Corps, 42, released as Capt, 46. Mem: Chmn, Inter-Co. Regional Planning Cmn; Nat. Civil Defense Adv. Coun; Adv. Bd. Nat. League of Cities; Adv. Bd. of U.S. Conf. of Mayors; Nat. Adv. Coun. on Educ. for Health Profession; numerous civic and fraternal orgns. Rel: Catholic. Mailing Add: Continental Airlines, International Airport, Los Angeles, Calif. 90009.

CURRY, HAROLD J. D
b. Phillipsburg, N.J, 6/7/31; s. Harold Joseph Curry and Lucy Kingfield C; m. 6/14/58 to Joanne E. Daly; c. Mary Ellen, Matthew and Robert. Educ: Lafayette Col. and Rutgers Law Sch, grad. Polit. & Govt. Pos: N.J. State Assemblyman, Warren Co, 64-68; del, Constitutional Conv, 66; chmn, Agr, Conserv. & Econ. Develop. Standing Cmt, 66. Bus. & Prof. Pos: Secy, Warren Co. Bar Asn, 60-63. Mil. Serv: Entered as 2nd Lt, Army, 53, released as 1st Lt, 55. Mem: Exalted Ruler, Phillipsburg Elks; bd. of dir, Joseph H. Firth Youth Center; Easton-Phillipsburg Area Human Rels. Cmn; Citizens Adv. Cmt, Phillipsburg; Rotary; K. of C; Holy Name Soc. Rel: Roman Catholic. Legal Res: 303 Irwin St, Phillipsburg, N.J. 08865. Mailing Add: 121-123 S. Main St, Phillipsburg, N.J. 08865. (1967)

CURRY, RICHARD CHARLES R
Dir, Arts and Sci. Div, Rep. Nat. Cmt.
b. Detroit, Mich, 4/18/37; s. Fillmore Smith Curry and Geraldine Grant C; m. 8/30/58 to Susan Helen MacMillan; c. Michael Reid and Peter Evans. Educ: East. Mich. Univ, B.A, 60; Univ. Mich, M.A, 61, Ph.D, 65; Phi Gamma Delta. Polit. & Govt. Pos: City chmn, Williamsburg Rep. Party, Va, 67-69; dir, arts and sci. div, Rep. Nat. Cmt, 69- Bus. & Prof. Pos: Instr. polit. sci, East. Mich. Univ, 63-65; asst. prof. govt, Col. of William & Mary, 65-69, assoc. prof, 69- Mem: South. and Am. Polit. Sci. Asns; Omicron Delta Kappa; Williamsburg Chap, Va. Coun. Human Rels; dir, Williamsburg Area Day Care Center Inc; dir, Housing Opportunities Made Equal Inc; dir, James River Commun. Action Agency. Rel: Presbyterian. Legal Res: 103 Hangman's Lane, Williamsburg, Va. 23185. Mailing Add: 1625 I St. N.W, Washington, D.C. 20006.

CURRY, WILLIAM SEERIGHT R
Wyo. State Rep.
b. Beason, Ill, 1/18/08; s. George A. Curry and Anna Alexandre C; m. 7/23/37 to Peggy Simson; c. Michael M. Educ: Lincoln Col, 26-28; Ill. Wesleyan Univ, A.B, 30; Univ. Wyo, M.A, 39. Polit. & Govt. Pos: Wyo. State Rep, 67- Bus. & Prof. Pos: Teacher and coach, Morrisonville High Sch, Morrisonville, Ill, 31-39; teacher, Natrona Co. High Sch, Casper, Wyo, 39-43; supt. of schs, Midwest Pub. Schs, Midwest, Wyo, 43-46; chmn, Div. of Eng, Casper Col, Wyo. Publ: 'This I Tried and Found Helpful,' Jr. Col. J. Mem: Nat. Coun. Teachers of Eng; AF&AM; Elks; Lions; bd. of dirs, Wyo. Easter Seal Soc. Awarded, Centennial Award for Meritorious Serv. to Educ, by Lincoln Col, 65. Rel: Presbyterian. Mailing Add: 3125 Garden Creek Rd, Casper, Wyo. 82601.

CURTIN, MARGARET MARY D
b. New London, Conn, 9/28/34; d. William Joseph Curtin and Mary Satti C; single. Educ: Williams Mem. Inst, 4 years. Polit. & Govt. Pos: Justice of the Peace, New London, Conn, 55-; secy, treas. and v.pres, Young Dem. of New London, 55-59, first woman pres, 60 & 66; del, Young Dem. State Conv, 57-, nat. Conv. Young Dem, 57-, Probate Conv, 58, Cong. Conv, 60, State Sen. Conv, 62, Dem. State Conv, 64, 66 & 68; mem, Dem. Town Cmt. New London, 60, secy, 64; del. state bd, Young Dem. Conn, 66-, nat. committeewoman, 66-; alternate del, Dem. Nat. Conv, 68; del, UN Youth Coun, Young Dem. Am, 68- Mem: Taxicabs Conn; Am. Ambulance Asn; Ambulance Asn. Conn; Confraternity of Christian Doctrine; Downeyside Inc, Home for Boys, Springfield, Mass; CURSILLO Movement; Model Cities Prog; Hibernians Auxiliary; Lawrence & Mem. Hosp. Auxiliary. Rel: Roman Catholic. Mailing Add: 314 Ocean Ave, New London, Conn. 06320.

CURTIN, WILLARD S. R
b. Trenton, N.J, 11/28/05; s. William Smith Curtin and Edna Grace Mountford C; m. to Geraldine A. Hartman; c. Lawrence B. and Jeffrey H. Educ: Pa. State Univ, A.B, 29; Univ. Pa. Law Sch, LL.B, 32; Sigma Chi. Polit. & Govt. Pos: First asst. dist. attorney, Pa, 38-49; dist. attorney, Bucks Co, 49-54; U.S. Rep, Eighth Dist, Pa, 57-67. Bus. & Prof. Pos: Sr. Partner, Law Firm of Curtin & Heefner, Morrisville, Pa. Mem: Rotary; Elks. Rel: Episcopalian. Mailing Add: 250 N. Pennsylvania Ave, Morrisville, Pa. 19067.

CURTIS, CARL T. R
U.S. Sen, Nebr.
b. Near Minden, Nebr, 3/15/05; m. 6/6/31 to Lois Wylie-Atwater; c. Clara Mae (Mrs. James A. Hopkins) (deceased) and Carl T, Jr. (Tom); grandchild, Denise Hopkins. Educ: Nebr. Wesleyan Univ; Theta Chi; hon. mem, Phi Delta Phi and Pi Kappa Delta. Polit. & Govt. Pos: Co. attorney, Kearney Co, Nebr, 31-35; U.S. Rep, Nebr, 39-55; U.S. Sen, Nebr, 55-; chmn, Nebr. del. and floor mgr. for Sen. Barry M. Goldwater, nominee, Rep. Nat. Conv, 64. Mem: Mason; Odd Fellows; Elks. Rel: Presbyterian Church of U.S.A. Legal Res: Minden, Nebr. 68959. Mailing Add: 6613 31st Place N.W, Washington, D.C. 20015.

CURTIS, DENNIS REX D
State Committeeman, Cassia Co. Dem. Cent. Cmt, Idaho
b. Declo, Idaho, 8/5/37; s. Blaine D. Curtis and Ruth Brower C; m. to Lois Jeanette Sorensen; c. Randy D, Rodney Blaine, Travis Marlin, Denette and Justin Dennis. Educ: Utah State Univ. Polit. & Govt. Pos: Precinct committeeman, Cassia Co. Dem. Cent. Cmt, Idaho, 61-63, state committeeman, 64-65 & 68-; chmn, 65-68. Bus. & Prof. Pos: Mgr, Pella Farms, Ore-Ida Inc, 59-63; mgr, Blaine Curtis and Sons, Registered Herefords, 57-63; instr. agr, Col. South. Idaho, 67-68; gen. mgr, Lost River Ranch, 69- Mem: Campaign chmn, Cassia Co. Chap, March of Dimes, 61-62; chmn, Cassia Co. Chap, Nat. Found. Infantile Paralysis, 63-64; dir, Cassia Co. Urban Rural Rels. Cmt, 65-66; Cassia Co. Cattlemens Asn.(pres, 62-67); Idaho Hereford Asn.(dir, 63-67); Livestock Agr. Exten. Agent (bd. adv, 63-66); Idaho Grassman of the Year (committeeman, 62-66); S.Idaho C. of C.(agr. dir, 67-69); Idaho Jr. Hereford Asn.(dir, 64-68); Burley Jr. C. of C; C. of C; Grange; Am. Hereford Asn; Idaho Cattlemen's Asn; Big D. Roping Club. Idaho State Farmer Award, 55; Hon. Future Farmers Am. Award, 66. Rel: Latter-day Saint. Legal Res: Burley, Idaho 83318. Mailing Add: Lost River Ranch, Route 2, Box 796-B, Klamath Falls, Ore. 97601.

CURTIS, ELIZABETH KENNEDY D
Pres, Conn. Fedn. Dem. Women's Clubs
b. Ossinning, N.Y, 6/15/16; d. John Joseph Kennedy and Agnes Begley K; div; c. Helen Louise and Mary Elizabeth (Mrs. Fishman). Educ: St. Lawrence Univ, 1 year. Polit. & Govt. Pos: Dep. registr. voters, Bridgeport, Conn, 54-; mem. state exec. bd, Conn. Fedn. Dem. Women's Clubs, 55-, first v.pres, 61-65, chmn. campaign activities, 65-67, and pres, 66-; pres, Bridgeport Fedn. Dem. Women, 56-58; pres. and co. organizer, Fairfield Co. Dem. Women's Clubs, 59-61; del, Dem. Nat. Conv, 60 & 68; co-chmn. voter registrn, Dem. State Cent. Cmt, 60-68; mem, Cmt. Revision State Party Rules, 66 & 68-69. Mem: Jr. Guild Bridgeport; Nat. Found-March of Dimes (v.chmn, Fairfield Co. Chap). Received Twenty Year Award from Nat. Found. Rel: Catholic. Mailing Add: 271 Vine St, Bridgeport, Conn. 06604.

CURTIS, HENRY BALDWIN D
City Councilman, New Orleans, La.
b. New Orleans, La, 12/7/95; s. Edward B. Curtis and Hallette S. Baldwin C; m. 12/5/23 to Marguerite B. Grant. Educ: Loyola Univ, A.B, 14, LL.B, 17, Blue Key. Polit. & Govt. Pos: Asst. city attorney, New Orleans, 25-40, city attorney, 46-57, city councilman, 57- Bus. & Prof. Pos: Partner, Curtis & Hall, now Curtis, Foster, Hyde & Mooney, Attorneys, 25- Mil. Serv: Entered as Pvt, Army, 16, released as Col, 46, after serv. in 3rd Army Hq; Bronze Star Medal; North. France, The Rhineland and Cent. Europe Campaign Ribbons. Mem: New Orleans, La. and Am. Bar Asns; La. Law Inst; K. of C; Am. Legion; Rotary; Vet. of World War I; Mil. Order World Wars. Rel: Catholic. Mailing Add: 8142 Panola St, New Orleans, La. 70118.

CURTIS, JACK R
Mo. State Sen.
b. Hartville, Mo, 3/25/12; m. 10/18/39 to Helen Stamate; c. Nancy Ann. Educ: Drury Col, B.A; Univ. of Mo, LL.B. Polit. & Govt. Pos: City attorney, Springfield, Mo, 41-42; proj. attorney, War Relocation Authority, 43-44; Mo. State Sen, 54- Bus. & Prof. Pos: Lawyer. Mil. Serv: Lt, Naval Res, 44-46. Mem: Phi Delta Phi; Sigma Nu; Elks; Am. Legion; Am, Green Co. and Mo. Bar Asns. Rel: Presbyterian. Mailing Add: 1324 E. Loren St, Springfield, Mo. 65804. (1967)

CURTIS, JOHN F. DFL
b. Minneapolis, Minn, 7/19/17; s. Fred E. Eidsvold Curtis and Henrietta Johnson C; m. 4/13/39 to Veronica F. Culhane; c. Loretta Ann and John F, Jr. Educ: Univ. Minn. Polit. & Govt. Pos: Chmn, Statewide Bean Feed and Rally, Minn. Dem-Farmer-Labor Party, 48-66 & 68; del. housing chmn, Minn. Dem-Farmer-Labor Party, 56, 60, 64 & 68; Minn. state housing chmn, State and Nat. Convs. Bus. & Prof. Pos: Bus. agent, Teamsters Union, 38-41; labor rels. rep, Twin City Arsenal, 41-42; dir. orgn, Jewelry Workers, 42-47; dir. orgn, Union 458, AFL-CIO, 47- Mem: Hotel & Restaurant Union Local 458; Eagles; Moose; K. of C; Elks. Rel: Catholic. Mailing Add: 1901 S. Emerson Ave, Minneapolis, Minn. 55403.

CURTIS, KENNETH M. D
Gov, State of Maine
b. Leeds, Maine, 2/8/31; s. Archie M. Curtis (deceased) and Harriet Turner C; m. 11/17/56 to Pauline Brown; c. Susan and Angela. Educ: Maine Maritime Acad, Castine, B.S, 52; Portland Univ. Law Sch, LL.B, 59. Polit. & Govt. Pos: Former asst. to U.S. Rep, James C. Oliver; Legis. Res. Serv, Legal Res, U.S. Libr. of Cong; State coordinator, Area Re-development Admin, Maine, 61-63; Secy. of State, 65-66; Gov, Maine, 67-; del, Dem. Nat. Conv, 68; chmn, New Eng. Gov. Conf, 69-; state co-chmn, New Eng. Regional Cmn; mem. steering cmt, Educ. Cmn. of the States; mem. exec. bd, Nat. Dem. Gov. Conf. Bus. & Prof. Pos: Attorney-at-law. Mil. Serv: Entered as Ens, Navy, 53, released as Lt.(jg), 55, after serv. in Korea; Lt. Comdr, Naval Res, currently. Mem: Amvets; Am. Legion; former pres, South. Maine Chap, Nat. Cystic Fibrosis Research Found; state dir, Nat. Found. March of Dimes, 66-69. Admitted to practice law before U.S. Supreme Court, 65- Rel: Protestant. Legal Res: Augusta, Maine 04330. Mailing Add: State House, Augusta, Maine 04330.

CURTIS, LAURENCE R
b. Boston, Mass, 9/3/93; s. Louis Curtis and Fanny LeLand Richardson C; m. to Helen Schryver. Educ: Harvard, A.B, 16; LL.B, 21; Phi Beta Kappa. Polit. & Govt. Pos: Secy. to Mr. Justice Holmes, 21-22; asst. U.S. Attorney, Boston, 23-30; Boston City Coun, 30-33; Mass. State Rep, 33-36; Mass. State Sen, 36-41; Mass. State Treas, 47-48; U.S. Rep, Mass, 83rd - 87th Cong; Rep. Cand, U.S. Rep, Mass, 68. Bus. & Prof. Pos: Attorney-at-law, Boston, 22- Mil. Serv: Lt, Air Corps, U.S. Naval Res. Force, 17-20; Silver Star Citation; Chevalier of Legion of Honor. Mem: Past Comdr, Mass. Dept. and Past Nat. Sr. Comdr, DAV; Am, Mass, and Boston Bar Asns; Harvard (Boston, NYC), Somerset, Ancient and Honorable Artil. Co. Clubs. Mailing Add: 53 State St, Boston, Mass. 02109.

CURTIS, ROBERT McNOWN D
Chmn, Broward Co. Dem. Exec. Cmt, Fla.
b. Tuscaloosa, Ala, 2/17/19; s. Nathan Stephenson Curtis and Harriet Fisher Wilson C; m. 3/21/44 to Marie Collett; c. Carol (Mrs. Michael E. Zealy), Cay, Robert M, Jr. and Christopher Collett. Educ: Univ. Ala, A.B, 39; Northwest. Univ. Col. Law, 40; Univ. Fla, Col. Law, LL.B, 46; Sigma Chi;

Phi Delta Phi; Tau Kappa Alpha. Polit. & Govt. Pos: Chmn, Broward Co. Dem. Exec. Cmt, Fla, 52-54 & 67-; Dem. committeeman, Precinct 27, Broward Co, 54, Precinct 47, 66; pres, Golden Emblem Club, Ft. Lauderdale, 67- Bus. & Prof. Pos: Past pres, Ft. Lauderdale Youth Center, Inc, Fla, 49; Broward Co. Unit Am. Cancer Soc, 53-55; chmn. bd. cmnrs, North Broward Hosp. Dist, 61-65; chmn, finance sub-cmt, Broward Co, Citizens Cmt. for Qual. Educ, 65-67. Mil. Serv: Entered as 2nd Lt, Army, 41, released as 1st Lt, 44, after serv. in Coast Artil. Anti-Aircraft, Hawaiian Dept, 41-43; Three Ribbons. Mem: Fla. Bar; Am. Bar Asn; Broward Co. Bar Asn.(pres, 66-67); Fla. Acad. Trial Lawyers; Am. Trial Lawyers Asn; F&AM; Elks; SAR; DAV; VFW; Am. Legion; Nova Gold Key; C. of C. Rel: Episcopal. Legal Res: 833 N. Rio Vista Blvd, Ft. Lauderdale, Fla. 33301. Mailing Add: P.O. Drawer 4157, Ft. Lauderdale, Fla. 33304.

CURTIS, SARAH FRANCES R
Conn. State Rep.
b. Roanoke, Va, 2/16/14; d. James Warren Knepp and Sarah Ann Dawson K; div; c. James Robert and Nelson George, Jr. Educ: St. Marys Jr. Col. Polit. & Govt. Pos: Conn. State Rep, 53-58 & 63-, clerk, Interim Cmt, Conn. House of Rep, 55-57, chmn, 58-59 and chmn, House Cmt. Pub. Welfare and Humane Insts, 63-65; clerk, Pub. Personnel, 57; selectman, Newtown, Conn, 59; mem. adv. coun, Ment. Health Planning Proj, 63-65; charter mem, Conn. Hosp. Planning Cmn, 66-69; mem. adv. coun, Bd. of Ment. Health, 66; mem, Conn. Cmn. Intergovt. Coop, 68-69; mem. exec. cmt, Pub. Welfare Interim Cmt, 69. Rel: Episcopal. Mailing Add: Berkshire Rd, Sandy Hook, Conn. 06482.

CURTIS, THOMAS B. R
b. Webster Groves, Mo, 5/14/11; s. Edward Glion Curtis and Isabel Wallace C; m. to Susan Ross Chivvis; c. Elizabeth (Mrs. Thomas Allen), Leland, Allan, Charles and Jonathan. Educ: Dartmouth Col, A.B; Wash. Univ, LL.B; hon. M.A, Dartmouth Col, 51; Alumni Citation, Wash. Univ, 60; hon. LL.D, Westminster Col, Mo, 62. Polit. & Govt. Pos: Mem. bd, St. Louis Co. Elec. Cmnr, Mo, 42; committeeman from Gravois Twp, St. Louis Co. Rep. Cmt, 46-50; mem, Mo. Bd. Law Exam, 48-50; U.S. Rep, Second Dist, Mo, 51-68, ranking Rep, House-Senate Joint Econ. Cmt. and House-Senate Joint Cmt. on Reorgn. of Cong, mem, House-Senate Joint Cmt. on Internal Revenue Taxation, sr. mem, House Cmt. on Ways and Means, mem, U.S. Trade Negotiations Del, Geneva, Switz; nominee for U.S. Sen, Mo, 68. Bus. & Prof. Pos: Attorney at Law, Biggs, Hensley, Curtis and Biggs. Mil. Serv: Entered as Lt.(jg), Navy, 42, released as Lt. Comdr, 45. Publ: 87 Million Jobs, A Dynamic Program to End Unemployment. Mem: St. Louis City, St. Louis Co. and Mo. Bar Asns. Cong. Distinguished Serv. Award, Am. Polit. Sci. Asn, 63; Newel Perry Award, Nat. Fedn. of Blind, 61; Ellis Forshee Award, Mo. Fedn. of Blind, 58; Silver Beaver Award, Boy Scouts. Rel: Unitarian. Legal Res: 462 Florence Ave, Webster Groves, Mo. 63119. Mailing Add: Room 201, 34 N. Brentwood Blvd, Clayton, Mo. 63105. (1967)

CURWOOD, WILLIAM B. D
Treas, Luzerne Co, Pa.
b. Shickshinny, Pa, 11/15/10; s. Ray Curwood and Florence Bredbenner C; m. 6/20/33 to Mary A. Sharretts; c. Sally Rae and William B, Jr. Educ: Wyo. Sem. Polit. & Govt. Pos: Tax collector, Pa, 4 years; Pa. State Rep, 52-67; borough treas, Burgess of Shickshinny, borough councilman; dir, Shickshinny Water Co; trustee, Shickshinny Fire Co; treas, Luzerne Co, currently. Bus. & Prof. Pos: Ins. bus. Mem: F&AM; Eagles; Elks; Rotary. Rel: Methodist. Mailing Add: 51 N. Main St, Shickshinny, Pa. 18655.

CUSANOVICH, LOU R
Calif. State Sen.
b. Los Angeles, Calif, 1912; m. 10/9/37 to Elizabeth McElroy; c. Michael and Gerald. Educ: Southwest. Univ. Polit. & Govt. Pos: Calif. State Assemblyman, 57-66; Calif. State Sen, 67- Bus. & Prof. Pos: Mgr, Lumber Bus; asst. supt. & dir. of activities, McKinley Home for Boys. Mem: Valley Area Welfare Bd; Commun. Chest; Red Cross; Kiwanis; Elks; former mem, San Fernando Valley Welfare Planning Coun; YMCA and Boy Scout work. Mailing Add: 14921 Ventura Blvd, Sherman Oaks, Calif. 91403.

CUSHMAN, EDWARD CHARLES, JR. D
b. Aiken, S.C, 9/21/18; s. Edward C. Cushman, Sr. and Mary Sweringen C; m. 11/15/43 to Ruth Lecil Drummond C; c. Ruth Lecil, Mary Nagel. Educ: Furman Univ, B.A, 39; Univ. of S.C, LL.B, 41; post grad. work, Univ. of S.C. Polit. & Govt. Pos: S.C. State Sen, 61-66; S.C. State Rep, 49-60; U.S. Cmt. East. Dist, S.C. Bus. & Prof. Pos: Lawyer. Mil. Serv: Marine Corps, 42-45; decorated for heroism and meritorious serv; spec. investr, War Frauds, 14th Naval Dist, 46-47. Mem: Masons; Lions; White Shrine of Jerusalem; Am. Legion; Knight Templar. Rel: Baptist. Mailing Add: Box 270, Aiken, S.C. 29801. (1967)

CUSIMANO, FRED D
Mem, Exec. Cmt, Warren Co, Pa.
b. Jamestown, N.Y, 11/11/42; s. Fred John Cusimano and Helen Papa C; m. 6/20/64 to Carol Jean Bosko; c. Fred John, II, Christopher Dean and Mark Anthony. Educ: Jamestown Community Col, 2 years; pres, Student Activities Club. Polit. & Govt. Pos: Mem, Human Rels. Cmn, Jamestown, N.Y, 64-65; mem, Exec. Cmt, Erie Co, Pa, 66-67, mem, Solid Waste Study Cmt, 67; mem, Mayors Cmt. and Mayor's Cmt. Rehabilitation, Erie, 66-67; mem, Exec. Cmt, Warren Co, 67-; v.pres, Warren Co. Young Dem, 68-; mem. chmn, Warren Co. Dem, 68-; del, Dem. Nat. Conv, 68; youth coordinator, West Pa, Citizens for Humphrey, 68. Bus. & Prof. Pos: News dir, WKSN Radio, Jamestown, N.Y, 63-66; day ed, WSEE-TV, Erie, Pa, 66-67; nat. advert. mgr, Whirley Industs, Inc, Warren, Pa, 67- Mil. Serv: Entered as Pvt, Army Res, 60, released as E-4, 68, after serv. in II Corps, Army Corps Engrs. Mem: Sales & Mkt. Exec. Int; Sales & Mkt. Exec. of Erie; Am. Fedn. TV and Radio Announcers; Nat. Asn. Broadcast Engrs. & Technicians. Rel: Roman Catholic. Legal Res: 1413 Pennsylvania Ave. W, Warren, Pa. 16365. Mailing Add: 873 Dawson Rd, Akron, Ohio 44320.

CUSIMANO, FRED J. D
Mem, Chautauqua Co. Dem. Exec. Cmt, N.Y.
b. Jamestown, N.Y, 1/3/19; s. Samuel M. Cusimano and Rose C; m. 7/31/41 to Helen Papa; c. Fred, Jr, Robert and Richard. Educ: Jamestown Commun. Col. Polit. & Govt. Pos: Pres, Jamestown Area Dem. Men's Club, N.Y, 58-60; aide, N.Y. State Dem. Conv, 58, alternate del, 62; mem, Chautauqua Co. Bd. of Supvrs, 60-64; Dem. cand, N.Y. State Sen, 62, N.Y. State Assembly, 65; del, Dem. Nat. Conv, 64; mem, Chautauqua Co. and Jamestown City Dem. Exec. Cmts, N.Y, exec. asst. to co. chmn, Dem. Party; mem, Jamestown City Planning Cmn. Bus. & Prof. Pos: Owner, South Side Sunoco Serv, 52-61; v.pres, Chautauqua Lake Regions, Inc, 60-66; co-ed, Chautauqua Co. Dem. Newspaper, 63-65. Mil. Serv: Entered as Pvt, Army, 41, released as T-4, 45, after serv. in 1843 Serv. Unit, Corps Mil. Police, Europe-Africa-Mid. E. and U.S.A; Am. Defense Serv, Am. Serv, Europe-Africa-Mid. E. Serv. and Good Conduct Medals. Mem: Hon. mem, N.Y. State Election Cmnrs. Asn, 66; C. of C; Better Jamestown Cmt; Dem. Men's Club; Supvrs. Asn. of New York State. Rel: Roman Catholic. Mailing Add: 190 Linwood Ave, Jamestown, N.Y. 14701.

CUSSON, ANNETTE FOREST D
Dem. Nat. Committeewoman, R.I.
b. Providence, R.I; d. Aurele J. Forest and Anna Trottier F; m. 5/4/40 to Horace A. Cusson; c. Paul Ernest. Educ: Exten. courses, Brown Univ. and Bryant Col. Polit. & Govt. Pos: Mem, R.I. Dem. State Speakers Bur, 56 and Platform Cmt, 58; chmn, R.I. Golden Girls for Pres. Kennedy, 60; Dem. Nat. Committeewoman, 60-; mem, Nationalities Div, Dem. Nat Cmt. and Pres. Kennedy's Women's Cmt. on Civil Roghts, 62; R.I. Chmn, Dem. Women's Wash. Conf, 62-64 & 66-; del, Dem. Nat. Conv, 64 & 68, mem, Nat. Dem. Platform Cmt, 64 and mem. and secy, Nat. Cmt. Permanent Orgn, 68; v.chmn, R.I. Humphrey-Muskie Cmt, 68. Bus. & Prof. Pos: Organist and choir dir, St. Paul's Church, Cranston, R.I, 60- Mem: Bd. dirs, R.I. Opera Guild and Int. Inst. R.I; Fedn. Francaise du R.I; Alliance Francaise, R.I; founding mem, R.I. Asn. Retarded Children. Rel: Catholic. Mailing Add: 151 Althea St, Providence, R.I. 02907.

CUSTER, DOROTHY PAULINE R
Mem, Calif. Rep. State Cent. Cmt.
b. Oswego, N.Y, 9/19/16; d. Charles M. Priebe, Sr. and Florence M. Peckham P; m. 5/15/41 to Dr. Edward A. Custer; c. Edward A, Jr, Eric C. and Richard R. Educ: Cent. Islip State Sch. of Nursing, L.I, N.Y, R.N, 39. Polit. & Govt. Pos: Co-chmn, Nixon for Gov. Campaign, Palo Alto, Calif, 62 and Milias for State Assembly, 62 & 64; pres, Palo Alto Rep. Women Fedn, 62-64; chmn, Murphy for Senate Campaign, 64 and Women for Finch Primary Campaign, 66; mem, Calif. Rep. State Cent. Cmt, 64-; educ. chmn, North. Div, Calif. Fedn. of Rep. Women, 65-67 and workshop chmn, 67-68; chmn, Ivy Baker Priest Campaign, Santa Clara Co, 66; women's chmn, Santa Clara Co, Sen. Kuchel primary campaign, 68; chmn, Women for Nixon and Nixon Hq, Palo Alto, 68; mem, Santa Clara Co. Nixon for Pres. Cmt, 68; alternate, Santa Clara Co. Rep. Cent. Cmt, 68-69. Bus. & Prof. Pos: Registered nurse, Bellvue Hosp, N.Y.C, 39-40; private duty nursing, N.Y.C, 40-41; nurse in charge of Red Cross Mobile Blood Bank, Strong Mem. Hosp, Rochester, 41-42; off. nurse, Edward A. Custer, M.D, 44-45. Mem: Palo Alto Art Club (pres, 59); League of Women Voters; Jr. Mus. Soc.(assoc. mem, 67, docent, 68-69). Gen. Efficiency Award, Cent. Islip State Sch. of Nursing, 38. Rel: Protestant. Mailing Add: 1825 Emerson St, Palo Alto, Calif. 94301.

CUTILLO, LOUIS SABINO D
Conn. State Rep.
b. Mansfield, Mass, 9/2/34; s. Louis Nunzio Cutillo and Elizabeth Antosca C; m. 6/30/58 to Robert Doyle; c. Brian, Diane Alane, Judy and Jacqueline. Educ: Univ. Bridgeport. Polit. & Govt. Pos: Constable, Waterbury, Conn, 64-65, mem. town cmt, 66; Conn. State Rep, 88th Dist, 67- Bus. & Prof. Pos: Ins. salesman, Prudential Ins. Co, 60- Mem: Gr. Waterbury Labor Coun; Int. Ins. Workers Union (v.pres, 67-69, pres, Prudential Unit Local 23, 67-69); Eagles; Nat. Life Underwriters. Rel: Roman Catholic. Mailing Add: 22 Birchwood St, Waterbury, Conn. 06708.

CUTLER, DAVID R
b. Boston, Mass, 10/13/22; s. Elliott Carr Cutler and Caroline Pollard Parker C; m. 4/8/61 to Louise Hanson; c. David McRoberts, John Hanson and Caroline Louise. Educ: Harvard Col, A.B, 47; Harvard Bus. Sch, 49; Porcellian Club. Polit. & Govt. Pos: Chmn, Andover Rep. Town Cmt, Mass, 60-68. Bus. & Prof. Pos: Trainee, West. Cartridge Co, 49-50; admin. asst, Raytheon Co, 51-57, plant admin. dept. mgr, 57-59; asst. plant controller, 59-62, div. bus. syst. mgr, 62-66 and bus. syst. consult, 66- Mil. Serv: Entered as Pvt, Army Air Force, 42, released as Sgt, 46; recalled as Cpl, Army, 50, released as Sgt, 51, after serv. in Third Armored Div, Fifth Inf. Div, Am. Theater. Mem: Past campaign chmn, bd. mem. and pres, United Fund of Gr. Lawrence; past exec. cmt. mem, Mass. Red Cross Regional Blood Prog; bd. mem, Family Serv. Asn. of Gr. Lawrence. Rel: Protestant. 1967 Legal Res: Andover, Mass. No mailing address available. (1967)

CUTRELL, FRED LOUIS, SR. D
Chmn, First Cong. Dist. Dem. Party, Wis.
b. LaFayette, Ind, 3/5/98; s. Carrie Coleman Cutrell; m. 1924 to Alma Yehling; c. Alvena (Mrs. Black), Arline (Mrs. Lamb), Eleanor (Mrs. Korakian) Lorna (Mrs. Stoll), Fred, Jr. and Lynn. Educ: High Sch. Polit. & Govt. Pos: Chmn, Racine Co. Dem. Party, Wis, 56-60; alternate del, Dem. Nat. Conv, 60 & 64; v.chmn, First Cong. Dist. Dem. Party, 60-69, chmn, 69- Bus. & Prof. Pos: Mem, bd. dirs, Racine Consumers Coop, 54- and pres, 58- Mil. Serv: Entered as Fireman 3/C, Navy, 17, released as Fireman 1/C, 19, after serv. in ETO. Mem: Eagles; Am. Legion; UAW (pres, Local Union 234, 46-62). Rel: Methodist. Mailing Add: 1900 Arthur Ave, Racine, Wis. 53405.

CUTTING, WENDELL RILEY R
Mem, Calif. Rep. State Cent. Cmt.
b. Hemet, Calif, 8/24/46 to Bert Allen Cutting and Alice Patricia Riley C; single. Educ: Chapman Col, B.A. in Hist. and Govt, 69. Polit. & Govt. Pos: Pres, Hemet-San Jacinto TAR, Calif, 62; pres, Hemet-San Jacinto Young Rep, 65; dir, Riverside Co. Young Rep. Bd, 65, precinct chmn, San Jacinto Rep. Party, 66-; assoc. mem, Calif. Rep. State Cent. Cmt, 67-68, mem, 69-; dep. cong. dist. dir, Calif. Rep. Assembly, 68, mem. polit. strategy and educ. cmts, 68, state dir-at-lg, 68 and cong. dist. dir, 38th Dist, 69-; campaign aide and strategist, Hunter for Cong. Campaign Cmt, 68. Bus. & Prof. Pos: Radio newscaster, KCIN, Victorville, 66. Mem: Am. Polit. Sci. Asn; Am. Hist. Asn; C. of C; Young Am. for Freedom; World Youth Crusade for Freedom. Voice of Democracy Award, VFW. Rel: Methodist. Mailing Add: 23830 Santa Fe, San Jacinto, Calif. 92383.

CUTTINO, JAMES, JR. D
S.C. State Rep.
b. Sumter, S.C, 5/24/24; s. James Cuttino, Sr. and Lucie Quattlebaum Edwards C; m. 4/16/55 to Margaret Lillian Poole; c. Margaret Edwards, Pamela Bradley and James Franklin. Educ: Clemson Col; Univ. N.C; Presbyterian Col. Polit. & Govt. Pos: City Councilman, Sumter, S.C, 60-64; S.C. State Rep, 60-, first v.chmn, Pub. Affairs Cmt, S.C. State House of Rep, currently. Bus. & Prof. Pos: Real Estate, ins; owner and mgr, James Cuttino & Sons. Mil. Serv: Army. Rel: Presbyterian. Legal Res: 45 Mason Croft Dr, Sumter, S.C. 29150. Mailing Add: 112 Broad St, Sumter, S.C. 29150.

CUTTS, ROYAL BARTLETT R
Vt. State Rep.
b. Shelton, Conn, 2/27/10; m. to Caroline Cate; c. One son, two daughters. Educ: Vt. State Sch. of Agr. Polit. & Govt. Pos: Mem, Sch. Bd, Townshend, Vt, auditor, 38-47, town moderator, 43-65 and lister, 45-48; Vt. State Rep, 47-49 & 65- Bus. & Prof. Pos: Ins; tree farm; maple sugar orchard. Mem: Chmn, Asn. to Preserve Vt. Constitutional Govt; Nat, State, Pomona and West River Granges; Townshend Vol. Firemen's Asn; West River Valley Develop. Asn; supvr, Windham Co. Soil Conserv; Vt. Asn. Soil Conserv. Suprv. Rel: Congregational. Mailing Add: Townshend, Vt. 05353. (1967)

CYPERT, JAMES DEAN D
Committeeman, Wash. Co. Dem. Cmt, Ark.
b. Springdale, Ark, 5/24/34; s. Burl Cypert and Opal Sisco C; m. 6/26/56 to Gaye Annette Warren; c. Julie Jan and Jamie Ann. Educ: Univ. Ark, B.S. and B.A, 55, Sch. Law, LL.B, 58; Alpha Kappa Psi; Sigma Nu. Polit. & Govt. Pos: Pres, Wash. Co. Young Dem, Ark, 60; committeeman, Wash. Co. Dem. Cmt, 62-; elec. cmnr, 62-; del, Dem. Nat. Conv, 64. Mil. Serv: Entered as 2nd Lt, Army, 56, released as 1st Lt, 57, after serv. in Artil. training, Ft. Chaffee, Ark. Mem: Kiwanis; chmn, Commun. Fund, 62; pres, Young Lawyers Asn, 65; Exec. Cmt, Ark. Bar Asn, 65; pres, C. of C, 66. Outstanding Young Men of Am; Distinguished Serv. Award, Jaycees, 63. Rel: Methodist. Legal Res: 100 Holcomb St, Springdale, Ark. 72764. Mailing Add: 904 Shipley St, Springdale, Ark. 72764.

CZARNECKI, WALTER R
b. Detroit, Mich, 2/10/14; s. Francis Czarnecki and Agata Wasilewski C; m. 9/1/34 to Katherine Babich; c. Walter Paul, Doris Agata (Mrs. Paul B. Riley) and Mary Ann. Educ: Wayne State Univ, Bus. Admin, 2 yrs. Polit. & Govt. Pos: Precinct del, Rep. Party, Mich, 36-; mem, Mich. State Rep. Cent. Cmt, 50-64; bd. mem, 1st Dist. Rep. Orgn, 44-64; del, Rep. Nat. Conv, 64; mem, Electoral Col, 52; nominee for offices of Detroit City Coun, U.S. Rep. and Mich State Rep. Mem: Polish Nat. Alliance; K. of C; Dom Polski; Wayne Co. Rep. Club; Greater Detroit Home Owner's Coun. Rel: Roman Catholic. Mailing Add: 20142 Riopelle, Detroit, Mich. 48203. (1967)

D

D'ABATE, WILLIAM D
R.I. State Sen.
b. Providence, R.I, 8/11/07; m. to Elizabeth Bond. Educ: Extension Courses, La Salle Inst, Chicago. Polit. & Govt. Pos: Councilman, Providence, R.I, 20 years; former supt. of weights and measures, Providence; mem, Caprio Dem. Club, Seventh Ward Dem. Club, Junction Dem. Club, Sixth Ward Dem. Club and Polit. Action Club; R.I. State Sen, 64-; alternate del, Dem. Nat. Conv, 68. Bus. & Prof. Pos: Salesman. Mem: K. of C; Aurora Club; Bonefro Club; Terrammo Club; Ital-Am. Club. Mailing Add: 173 Sisson St, Providence, R.I. 02911. (1967)

DABROWSKI, EDWARD K.
Sheriff, Bristol Co, Mass.
b. New Bedford, Mass, 3/27/28; s. Feliks Dabrowski and Mary Kolpak D; m. 8/4/56 to Helen P. Gutwinski; c. Jan Edward and Christine Ellen. Educ: Alliance Col, 48-50; Northeast. Univ. Sch. Law, LL.B. with honors, 53; Tau Sigma Pi. Polit. & Govt. Pos: Mem, New Bedford City Coun, Mass, 56-63; asst. dist. attorney, Bristol Co, South. Dist, 61-62; sheriff, Bristol Co, 63-; del, Dem. Nat. Conv, 68. Bus. & Prof. Pos: Mem, Bldg. Authority, S. East. Mass. Univ, 64- Mil. Serv: Entered as A/S, Coast Guard, 45, released as Radioman 3/C, 48, after serv. in various units. Mem: New Bedford, Bristol Co, Mass. and Am. Bar Asns; Eagles; Moose; Elks; Polish Am. Veterans of Mass; Holy Name Soc. Rel: Catholic. Mailing Add: 108 Court St, New Bedford, Mass. 02740.

DADDARIO, EMILIO QUINCY D
U.S. Rep, Conn.
b. Newton Center, Mass, 9/24/18; m. 1940 to Berenice Carbo; c. Edward, Stephen and Richard. Educ: Wesleyan Univ, B.A, 39; Boston Univ. Law Sch, 39-41; Univ. Conn, LL.B, 42. Polit. & Govt. Pos: Mayor, Middletown, Conn, 46-48; judge, Middletown Munic. Court, 48-50; U.S. Rep, Conn, 59-, chmn, Spec. Sub-Cmt. Patents and Sci. Inventions and Sub-Cmt. Sci, Research and Develop, mem, House Cmt. on Sci. and Astronaut, Manned Space Flight Sub-Cmt, currently; del, Dem. Nat. Conv, 68. Bus. & Prof. Pos: Lawyer, 45-50, 52; bd. trustees, Wesleyan Univ. Mil. Serv: Army, 43, Mediterranean Theater; U.S. Legion of Merit, Ital. Medaglia d'Argento Medal; Nat. Guard; Korean Conflict; 43rd Div, Maj, Far East Liaison Group, Korea, Japan. Mem: Conn. and Mass. Bars. Legal Res: Hartford, Conn. Mailing Add: 2524 Que St. N.W, Washington, D.C. 20007.

DADE, GLADYS MAE R
V.Chmn, Reno Co. Rep. Party, Kans.
b. Hutchinson, Kans, 3/6/08; d. Frank Oliver Dean and Zona Guthrie D; m. 7/31/27 to Philip Oliver Dade; c. Philip Eugene. Polit. & Govt. Pos: V.chmn, Reno Co. Rep. Party, Kans, 66-; del, Rep. Nat. Conv, 68. Mem: Altrusa Club of Hutchinson; Farm Bur; South Reno Exten. Homemaker Unit. Rel: Congregational. Mailing Add: R.R. 1, Hutchinson, Kans. 67501.

DAGENHART, EWELL MARTIN R
Chmn, Alexander Co. Rep. Party, N.C.
b. Taylorsville, N.C, 7/12/24; s. Edward Dagenhart and Clara Warren D; m. 11/11/44 to Evelyn Elder; c. Neal Gene and James Lynn. Educ: Correspondence High Sch. Polit. & Govt. Pos: Rep. precinct chmn, 60-66; chmn, Alexander Co. Rep. Party, N.C, 66- Mil. Serv: Entered as Seaman, Navy, 43, released as Seaman 1/C, 45; Asian and European Theater Ribbons. Mem: Chmn, Commun. Develop; leader, 4-H Club; secy, VFW; Am. Legion. Rel: Methodist. Mailing Add: Route 2, Hiddenite, N.C. 28636.

DAGUE, PAUL BARTRAM R
b. Whitford, Pa, 5/19/98; s. William James Dague and Lydia White D; m. 9/15/25 to Mary Virginia Williams. Educ: West Chester State Col, 16-17; Drexel Inst, 19-20. Polit. & Govt. Pos: Prin. asst. supt, Pa. Hwy. Dept, 24-35; chief dep. sheriff, Chester Co, 36-44, sheriff, 44-46; mem, Chester Co. Rep. Cmt, 42-52; U.S. Rep, Ninth Dist, Pa, 47; mem. exec. cmt, Chester Co. Rep. Exec. Cmt, 54-64. Mil. Serv: Entered as Pvt, Marine Corps, 18, released as Pfc, 19; Good Conduct Medal; World War I Victory Medal; Pa. Victory Medal. Mem: Mason; Am. Legion; Marine Corps League; Rotary; Pa. Farmers Asn; C. of C. Rel: United Presbyterian. Legal Res: 106 Uwchlan Ave, Downingtown, Pa. 19335. Mailing Add: P.O. Box 203, Downingtown, Pa. 19335.

DAHL, ALLEN W. R
b. Waldheim, Sask, Can, 4/17/28; s. Henry S. Dahl and Marie Berg D; m. 6/18/54 to Dolores M. Weeks; c. Charles A. and Susan M. Educ: Univ. of Wash, B.S. 51, Med. Sch, M.D, 57. Polit. & Govt. Pos: Rep. precinct committeeman, Snohomish Co, Wash, 65-69; chmn, Snohomish Co. Rep. Party, 66-69; del, Wash. State Rep. Conv, 66 & 68. Bus. & Prof. Pos: Research instr, Univ. of Wash. Med. Sch, 52-63; physician and surgeon, E. Edmond Med. Clinic, Edmonds, Wash, 57- Mil. Serv: Entered as Pvt, Army, 44, released as S/Sgt, 46, after serv. in Inf. Spec. Serv. Unit, Pac, 44-45; Pac. Theatre Ribbon; World War II Victory Medal. Publ: 'Derivatives of Fluorene,' J. Organic Chem, 55; 'Decreased Gastric Activity with Lignin,' Proc. Soc. Exp. Biol. & Med, 57; 'Analysis of Homografts,' Arch. of Path, 60. Mem: Wash. State and King Co. Med. Socs; Am. Med. Asn. Rel: Protestant. Mailing Add: 21810 117th Place W, Edmonds, Wash. 98020.

DAHL, ARDEN D
Chmn, Sixth Dist. Dem. Party, Minn.
b. Cottonwood, Minn, 8/22/13; s. J.B. Dahl and Bertha Anderson D; m. 9/15/33 to Mabel Johnson; c. Robert J. and Janet M. Educ: Cottonwood High Sch. and Cottonwood Bus. Course. Polit. & Govt. Pos: Secy-treas, Lyon Co. Dem. Cmt, Minn, 58-64; third v.chmn, Minn. State Dem. Party, 60, second v.chmn, 62; v.chmn, Sixth Dist. Dem. Party, Minn, 60, chmn, 66-; alternate del, Dem. Nat. Conv, 64, del, 68. Mem: Bd. of Dirs, Tracy C. of C, 62; Kiwanis. Rel: Lutheran. Mailing Add: 249 Elm St, Tracy, Minn. 56175.

DAHL, ARNE R
Cmnr. of Agr, N.Dak.
b. Ringebu, Norway, 5/7/07; s. Martinus Dahl and Gunda Nordrum D; m. 6/1/39 to Helena Krick; c. Philip. Polit. & Govt. Pos: N.Dak. State Rep, 59-65; cmnr. of agr, N.Dak, 65- Mem: K. of C; Kiwanis; Elks. Rel: Catholic. Mailing Add: 1431 N. 15th St, Bismarck, N.Dak. 58501.

DAHL, CURTIS R
Treas, Norton Town Rep. Cmt, Mass.
b. New Haven, Conn, 7/6/20; s. George Dahl and Elizabeth Curtis D; m. 11/15/52 to Mary Huntington Kellogg; c. Julia Curtis and Winthrop Huntington. Educ: Yale Univ, B.A, 41, M.A, 42, Ph.D, 45; Phi Beta Kappa; Elizabethan Club; Berzelius; Chi Delta Theta. Polit. & Govt. Pos: Fence-viewer, Norton, Mass, 64-, mem. town cmt, 65-66 & 68-69; mem, Norton Town Rep. Cmt, 64-, chmn, 64-65, treas, 68- Bus. & Prof. Pos: Prof. Eng, Wheaton Col, Mass, 48-; Fulbright lectr, Univ. Oslo, 65-66. Publ: Robert Montgomery Bird, Twayne Publishers, 63; 'The Victorian Wasteland,' Col. Eng, 55; 'Mr. Smith American Acropolis,' Am. Heritage, 58. Mem: Mod. Lang. Asn; Col. Eng. Asn; Am. Studies Asn; Norton Hist. Soc; Am. Asn. Univ. Prof; Bristol Co. Rep. Club. Guggenheim and Carnegie fels, gen. educ. Rel: Protestant. Legal Res: 189 N. Washington St, Norton, Mass. 02766. Mailing Add: R.F.D. 1, Norton,Mass. 02766.

DAHL, EUGENE RALPH R
N.Dak. State Rep.
b. Gwinner, N.Dak, 8/3/24; s. Ole Joseph Dahl and Anna Stubson D; m. 12/21/47 to Evelyn Mabel Melroe; c. Howard, Laura, Joan and Brian. Educ: N.Dak. State Univ, 2/3 year; Mich. State Univ, 2 1/3 years; N.Dak. Univ, B.S. in Educ. Polit. & Govt. Pos: N.Dak. State Rep, 26th Dist, 66- Bus. & Prof. Pos: Partner, Melroe Mfg. Co, Gwinner, N.Dak, 50-, v.pres, 54- Mil. Serv: Entered as Pvt, Army, 43, released as Cpl, 45, after serv. in 575th Signal Corps, 75th Inf. Div, ETO, 44-45; Good Conduct Medal; Rehabilitation behind lines following occupancy of West Germany. Mem: NAPM; AF&AM; Civic Club; Elks; dir, N.Dak. Blue Cross; v.pres, Minn-Dak. Areawide Comprehensive Health Planning Coun. Rel: Lutheran. Mailing Add: Gwinner, N.Dak. 58040.

DAHL, MATH R
b. Norway; m. to Ragna Madland; c. Arne. Polit. & Govt. Pos: N.Dak. State Rep, 31-37, Speaker of House, N.Dak. House of Rep, 37; former Cmnr. of Agr. and Labor, N.Dak. Mem: Nonpartisan League; Sons of Norway; Odd Fellows; Mason. Rel: Lutheran. Mailing Add: Hazelton, N.Dak. 58544. (1967)

DAHL, OSCAR P. R
S.Dak. State Rep.
b. 4/28/04; married; c. Two daughters. Educ: Agr. Col, 1 year. Polit. & Govt. Pos: Mem, Co. Elec. Bd, S.Dak; mem, Bd. of Civil Defense; co. cmnr, 19 years; mem, Sch. Bd; Twp. Supvr; S.Dak. State Rep, 64- Bus. & Prof. Pos: Farmer; feeder; trucker; connected with bridge construction; real estate rental. Rel: Lutheran; Trustee. Mailing Add: Volga, S.Dak. 57071. (1967)

DAHLBERG, VIRGINIA ISIS R
Chairwoman, Rock Island Co. Rep. Party, Ill.
b. Moline, Ill, 2/22/15; d. John Victor Carlson and Laura Alice Winfree C; m. 4/9/38 to Howard Ernest Dahlberg; c. Nancy (Mrs. Robert H. Cross) and Marvin H. Polit. & Govt. Pos: Chairwoman, Moline City Rep. Party, Ill, 60-62; chairwoman, Rock Island Co. Rep. Party, 62-; alternate del, Rep. Nat.

Conv, 68; Rock Island Co. Chairwoman, Ill. Women for Nixon-Agnew, 68. Bus. & Prof. Pos: Partner, Howard E. Dahlberg and Assoc, 61. Mem: Jr. Serv. League of Moline; Capitol Hill Club, Wash. D.C; Rock Island Co. Hist. Soc; Moline Women's Club; Rep. Women Clubs; YWCA; King's Daughters; Short Hills Country Club. Rel: Congregational. Legal Res: 3226 11th Ave, Moline, Ill. 61265. Mailing Add: Box 116, Moline, Ill. 61265.

DAHLIN, MELBA R. D
Chmn, Isanti Co. Democrat-Farmer-Labor Party, Minn.
b. Emmetsburg, Iowa, 4/9/17; d. Lloyd L. Schaeffer and Hattie Anderson S; m. 12/4/48 to Alvin C. Dahlin; c. Herbert, Angela and Alvin, Jr. Educ: Univ. Minn, 1 year. Polit. & Govt. Pos: Chmn, Isanti Co. Democrat-Farmer-Labor Party, Minn, 50-; alternate del, Dem. Nat. Conv, 68; v.chmn, Third Dist. Democrat-Farmer-Labor Party, chmn; v.chmn, Eighth Dist. Democrat-Farmer-Labor Party. Bus. & Prof. Pos: Mem. staff, Control Data. Mem: VFW Auxiliary; 4-H Club Leader; Sch. Bd.(treas); Co. Nursing Auxiliary; Farmers Union. Rel: Lutheran. Mailing Add: Route 1, Cambridge, Minn. 55008.

DAHLSTROM, ROBERT VICTOR R
Mem. Finance Cmt, Manitowoc Co. Rep. Party, Wis.
b. Conrad, Mont, 3/1/25; s. Victor Oliver Dahlstrom and Jessie Keating D; m. 9/26/52 to Mary Elizabeth Bonnett; c. Rebecca Elizabeth, Timothy Robert and Katie Louise. Educ: Univ. Idaho, B.S. in Chem, 49, M.S. in Agr. Chem, 51; Cornell Univ, Ph.D. in Biochem, 54; Phi Kappa Phi; Sigma Xi; Blue Key; Delta Tau Delta. Polit. & Govt. Pos: Mem. exec. cmt, Manitowoc Co. Rep. Party, Wis, 58-; co. coordinator for Gov. Campaign, 62 & 64, co. chmn, 64-68, mem. finance cmt, 69-; chmn. of co. chairmen, Rep. Party Wis, 66-68, third v.chmn, 66-68, chmn. campaign and cand. cmt, 66-68, chmn. campaign cent. cmt, 68, chmn. state resolutions cmt, 69-; mem. adv. cmt, Dept. of Natural Resources, Wis, 66-; alternate del, Rep. Nat. Conv, 68. Bus. & Prof. Pos: Biochemist, Eli Lilly & Co, Indianapolis, Ind, 54-57; sr. research biochemist, Rahr Malting Co, Manitowoc, Wis, 57-62; v.pres, Rahr Bio-Tech. Labs, 62- Mil. Serv: Entered as Pvt, Army, 43, released as Cpl, 45, after serv. in 517 Parachute Inf. Combat Team, ETO, 44-45; Purple Heart. Publ: 'Influence of Vitamin B_{12} and Antibiotics on Hatchability,' Poultry Sci, 52; 'Relationship of Gibberellic Acid to Enzyme Development,' in: Advances in Chemistry Series, Am. Chem. Soc, 61; 'Physical Factors Affecting Barley Germination,' Cereal Sci. Today, 65. Mem: Am. Inst. Biol. Sci; Am. Soc. Brewing Chemists; Inst. Food Technologists; Soc. Indust. Microbiol; Soc. Plant Physiologists; bd. regents, Univ. Wis, 69-; C. of C. Rel: Presbyterian. Mailing Add: 805 N. 13th St, Manitowoc, Wis. 54220.

DAILEY, HERSCHEL A. R
b. Barnesville, Ohio, 7/23/23; s. Celia Marjorie Taylor D; m. 11/1/56 to Dorothy Evelyn Moore; c. Cynthia Lucille and Leon Austin. Educ: Ohio Univ, B.S.E.E, 50. Polit. & Govt. Pos: Chmn, Yoakum Co. Rep. Party, Tex, 62-69. Bus. & Prof. Pos: Plant engr, Southwest. Pub. Serv. Co, Denver City and Littlefield, Tex, 53- Mil. Serv: Entered as Pvt, Air Force, released as S/Sgt, 45, after serv. in Eighth Air Force, ETO, 44; Distinguished Flying Cross, Air Medal with three Oak Leaf Clusters; Overseas Bar; Europe-Africa-Middle East Serv. Medal with three Bronze Battle Stars; Good Conduct Medal. Mem: VFW. Rel: Methodist. Mailing Add: 313 E. 18th St, Littlefield, Tex. 79339.

DAILEY, MILDRED PARKER D
State Committeewoman, Vt. State Dem. Party
b. North Bennington, Vt, 12/19/03; d. Ernest M. Parker and Minnie E. Colvin P; m. 1/29/23 to William E. Dailey; c. William E, Jr, Elizabeth D.(Mrs. Edma Riley), Patricia D.(Mrs. Deane Cooke) and Donald J. Educ: Troy Bus. Col. Polit. & Govt. Pos: Chmn, Bennington Co. Dem. Women, Vt; state committeewoman, Vt. State Dem. Party, 67- Bus. & Prof. Pos: Treas, William E. Dailey, Inc, 54- Mem: Am. Legion Auxiliary (past nat. v.pres); DAR (secy, Bennington Chap); past state chmn, March of Dimes; Herald Tribune Fresh Air Fund. Rel: Catholic. Legal Res: Elm St, North Bennington, Vt. 05257. Mailing Add: Box 428, North Bennington, Vt. 05257.

DAILEY, ROBERT JR. D
b. 5/27/18; m. March, 1942 to Mary Emanuel D; c. Don, James, Lin, Laura, Patric, Mary Jo. Educ: S.Dak. State Univ, B.S, Naval Aviation Cadet, 35-39. Polit. & Gov. Pos: S.Dak. State Sen, 64-67; mem, Bd. of Regents, Co. Weed Bd. Bus. & Prof. Pos: Dir, Sioux Valley Elec. Coop, 4H Leader, Int. Farm Youth Exchange; Host Parent; Farmer; Cattle Feeder; Commercial Pilot. Mil. Serv: Navy, 41-46; Marine Fighter Pilot, DFC, Air Medal and Purple Heart; served in Air Nat. Guard, 47-48. Mem: Isaak Walton League; Oriental Consistory; past Master, Masonic Lodge No. 11, Flandreau. Rel: Episcopalian; off. in Episcopal Church. Mailing Add: Rural 2, Flandreau, S.Dak. 57028. (1967)

DAILEY, STEVE D
b. Monroeville, Ala, 3/29/37; s. Floyd Searcy Dailey and MaeBelle Sawyer D; m. 2/8/57 to Joyce Crutchfield; c. Mitchell Earl and Philip Sanford. Educ: Samford Univ; Univ. Ala. Polit. & Govt. Pos: Del, Dem. Nat. Conv, 64. Mem: Jr. C. of C; Methodist Bus. Men's Club. Rel: Methodist. 1967 Legal Res: 1519 Third Ave, Tuscaloosa, Ala. 35401. No mailing address available. (1967)

DAILY, FRANK EDWARD, JR. R
Chmn, Comanche Co. Rep. Cent. Cmt, Kans.
b. Ashland, Kans, 4/5/16; s. Frank Edward Daily and Georgia Dale D; m. 11/21/42 to Edith May Railsback; c. Michael Robert and Nicholas Scott. Educ: Washburn Univ, A.B. & LL.B, 40. Polit. & Govt. Pos: Co. attorney, Comanche Co, Kans, 41-42, 46-55 & 59-; clerk, Common Sch. Dist. 1, Coldwater, 49-54; chmn, Comanche Co. Rep. Cent. Cmt, 56- Mil. Serv: Entered as Pvt, Air Force, 42, released as S/Sgt, 45. Mem: Am. Legion; Mason, Wichita Consistory, Midian Shrine; Am, Kans. and Southwest Kans. Bar Asns; Coldwater Country Club; Lions; Coldwater Quarter Back Club. Rel: Methodist. Mailing Add: 311 N. Philadelphia St, Coldwater, Kans. 67029.

DAILY, O.R. 'BUD' D
Wyo. State Rep.
b. Logan, Kans, 11/24/17; s. Otto Pierce Daily and Tessa Mae Clark D; m. 11/7/42 to Iona Bernice Burton; c. Dianne Alice. Educ: Rawlins High Sch, 12 years. Polit. & Govt. Pos: Wyo. State Rep, 61- Bus. & Prof. Pos: Shift supt, Sinclair-Atlantic Richfield, 40- Mil. Serv: Entered as Pvt, Army, 41, released as 1st Sgt, 45, after serv. in 45th Inf. Div, ETO, 43-45; Purple Heart. Mem: Elks; Odd Fellows; VFW; Ansul Firefighters. Rel: Presbyterian. Legal Res: 723 13th St, Rawlins, Wyo. 82301. Mailing Add: Box 1101, Rawlins, Wyo. 82301.

DALE, CLARENCE TAYLOR R
Chmn, Chariton Co. Rep. Cent. Cmt, Mo.
b. Milo, Mo, 12/4/11; s. Charles Beard Dale and Cora Banta D; m. 7/7/35 to Goldie Pearl Johns; c. James L. Educ: Park Col, 29-30; Cent. Bus. Col, 31. Polit. & Govt. Pos: Chmn, Mendon Twp. Bd, Chariton Co, Mo, 52-62, Mendon Twp. committeeman, 54-; v.chmn, Chariton Co. Rep. Cent. Cmt, 60-64, chmn, 64- Bus. & Prof. Pos: Pres, Chariton Co. Farmers Mutual Ins. Co, 54- Mem: Mason. Rel: Methodist. Mailing Add: Mendon, Mo. 64660.

DALE, DON D
b. Guymon, Okla, 6/4/18; s. F. Hiner Dale and Elizabeth Neet D; m. 7/11/47 to Lovina Haffner; c. Deborah Elizabeth and Douglas Don. Educ: Panhandle State Col, 36-38; Mo. Univ, B.J, 41; Okla. Univ, LL.B, 56; TGIF, Mo. Univ; Phi Alpha Delta, Okla. Univ. Polit. & Govt. Pos: Okla. State Rep, Texas Co, Okla, 50-54; chmn, Texas Co. Dem. Party, 66 & 67; assoc. dist. judge, Texas Co, 69- Bus. & Prof. Pos: Mgr, Guymon C. of C, Okla, 48; ed, Guymon Observer, 49-51; mgr, OTK Weather Improv. Asn, formerly; partner, Dale & Dale, Attorneys, Guymon, 56-69. Mil. Serv: Entered as Cadet, Air Force, 41, released as Capt, 46, after serv. in Fifth Pathfinder Squadron, S.Pac. Theatre, 42-43, ETO, 44-45; Distinguished Flying Cross; Purple Heart; Air Medal with 11 Clusters. Mem: Okla. and Am. Bar Asns; Nat. Col. Juvenile Judges; Elks; Kiwanis; Am. Legion; VFW. Rel: Unitarian. Legal Res: 222 N.E. 16th, Guymon, Okla. 73942. Mailing Add: P.O. Box 1403, Guymon, Okla. 73942.

DALE, EDWIN E. R
b. McLeansboro, Ill, 8/9/18; s. S.O. Dale (deceased); m. to Myra Lou Cornwell; c. One son and one daughter. Educ: Univ. Ill. Col. of Dent, D.D.S, 43. Polit. & Govt. Pos: Formerly Ill. State Rep. Mil. Serv: Army, 43-46, ETO, 1 year, dent. surgeon, Ninth Inf. Div. Mem: Am. and Ill. Dent. Asns; past pres, Ill. Dist. Dent. Soc; Moose; Champaign C. of C. First father-son legis. combination in Ill. Mailing Add: 307 Elmwood Rd, Champaign, Ill. 61820. (1967)

DALE, THOMAS JAMES, SR. R
Treas. & Acting Chmn, Salem Rep. Cmt, N.H.
b. Cold Spring, N.Y, 12/2/17; s. Francis Colgate Dale and Imogen Hall James D; m. 5/11/46 to Marie Margaret Mooney; c. Gerald FitzGerald, Thomas James, Jr, David Arthur and Christopher Cullen. Educ: Hamilton Col, 33-34; Wesleyan Univ, 35-37; N.Y. Univ, 37-39; Harvard Univ, 60-62; Northeast. Univ, 65; Psi Upsilon. Polit. & Govt. Pos: V.chmn, Bd. of Adjustment, Salem, N.H, 61-66; del, Rep. State Conv, 64, 66 & 68; dist. del, Rep. Nat. Conv, 64, alternate del-at-lg, 68; treas. & acting chmn, Salem Rep. Cmt, N.H, currently. Bus. & Prof. Pos: Zone mgr, Ford Motor Co, 45-48; v.pres. and works mgr, Durisol Inc, 48-53; production control supvr, Thermo-Form Co, 53-56; mgr. of materials serv, Polaroid Corp, 56-; proprietor, Chippendale Realty, 65- Mil. Serv: Entered as Pvt, Air Force, 42, released as S/Sgt, 45, after serv. in 124th Army Airways Commun. Squadron, China-Burma-India, 43-45; Asiatic-Pac. Theatre Ribbon with 1 Bronze Star; Am. Theatre Ribbon; Good Conduct Medal. Rel: Episcopal. Mailing Add: 17 Lakeview St, Salem, N.H. 03079.

D'ALEMBERTE, TALBOT 'SANDY' D
Fla. State Rep.
b. Tallahassee, Fla, 6/1/33; s. Dan W. D'Alemberte and Eleanor Whitfield D; m. 7/12/68 to Linda Sears. Educ: Univ. of the South, B.A, 55; Rotary Found. fel, Univ. London, 58-59; Univ. Fla, LL.B. with honors, 62; Omicron Delta Kappa; John Marshall Bar Asn; Order of the Coif; Fla. Blue Key; Alpha Tau Omega. Polit. & Govt. Pos: Fla. State Rep, 66- Mil. Serv: Lt, Navy, 55-58. Publ: Comments on Florida's Constitution: Florida Statistics Annotated, West Publ. Co, 69; 'Ombudsman: A Citizen's Grievance Man,' Univ. Fla. Law Review, 6/66; 'Why A Second House?' Nat. Civic Review, 9/66; 'Ombudsman,' Nat. Civic Review, 12/66; 'Journalists under the Axe: Protection of Confidential Sources,' Harvard J. on Legis, 3/69. Mem: Pres, Dade Co. Young Lawyers, 66-67; dir, Dade Co. Bar Asn; The Fla. Bar; Am. Bar Asn; Coun. Int. Visitors; Young Dem. Dade Co; Mental Health Asn. Rel: Episcopal. Legal Res: 7741 S.W. 51st Ave, Miami, Fla. 33143. Mailing Add: 1414 First National Bank Bldg, Miami, Fla. 33133.

D'ALESANDRO, THOMAS, JR. D
b. Baltimore, Md, 8/1/03; s. Thomas D'Alesandro and Mary Annie Foppiano D; m. 9/30/28 to Annunciata M. Lombardi; c. Thomas III, Nicholas, Franklin D. Roosevelt, Nicholas J, Hector, Joseph, Annunciata. Educ: Calvert Bus. Col, Baltimore. Polit. & Govt. Pos: Md. State Del, 26-33; mem, U.S. Conf. of Mayors and chmn, Standing Cmt. on Legis; gen. dep. collector, Internal Revenue, 33-34; mem, Baltimore City Coun, 35-38; U.S. Rep, Md, 76th to 80th Cong; mayor, Baltimore, 47-59; mem, U.S. Renegotiation Bd, 61-69; del, Dem. Nat. Conv, 68. Mem: Holy Name Soc; St. Leo's Confraternity; K. of C; Elks; Eagle; Moose. Rel: Catholic. Mailing Add: 245 Albermarle St, Baltimore, Md. 21202.

D'ALESANDRO, THOMAS J, III D
Mayor, Baltimore, Md.
b. Baltimore, Md, 7/24/29; s. Thomas J. D'Alesandro, Jr. and Nancy Lombardi D; m. 6/8/52 to Margaret Piracci; c. Thomas J, IV, Nicholas, Dominic, Patricia and Gregory. Educ: Loyola Col.(Md), 4 years; Univ. Md, LL.B, 52; hon. LL.D, Mt. St. Mary's Col. Polit. & Govt. Pos: Mem. Bd. of Supvr. of Elec, City of Baltimore, Md, 58-60, pres, 60-62; pres, City Coun, 62-67 and mayor, 67-; del, Dem. Nat. Conv, 68. Bus. & Prof. Pos: Attorney, D'Alesandro and Miliman. Mil. Serv: Army, Judge Adv. Gen. Corps, 3 years. Mem: Bar Asn. Baltimore City; Jr. Bar Asn. Baltimore City; Fed. Bar Asn; U.S. Conf. Mayors; Am. Judicature Asn; Munic. Finance Officers Asn; Md. Plaintiff's Bar Asn; Nat. League of Cities; K. of C; Jr. C. of C; Am. Legion; Civitan Club; Cath. War Vet; Howard Park Civic Asn; Lord Baltimore Lodge; E. Baltimore Boys, Inc; St. Thomas More Soc. Recipient of the John F. Kennedy

Mem. Award, Baltimore Jr. Asn. Commerce. Rel: Catholic. Legal Res: 4308 Greenway, Baltimore, Md. 21218. Mailing Add: Room 230, City Hall, Lexington and Holliday Sts, Baltimore, Md. 21202.

DALEY, ANNE BELISLE D
Mem, Calif. Dem. State Cent. Cmt.
b. Lawrence, Mass, 6/10/07; d. Hector Louis Belisle and Grace Potter B; m. to James Alan Daley (deceased); c. James Alan, Jr, Eliot Alexander, Walter Louis and Eugene Belisle. Educ: Middlebury Col, A.B, 28; Fresno State Col; Univ. Mass. Exten, Boston; Kappa Kappa Gamma. Polit. & Govt. Pos: Mem, Fresno Co. Adv. Cmt, U.S. Wage and Price Controls, Calif, 50-; worker, Dem. Campaigns, 52-; mem, Dem. Cong. Dist. Coun, Fresno, Merced and Madera Counties, Calif, 54-64; secy. and v.pres, Fresno Co. Dem. Women's Club, 55-64; mem. Fresno Co. exec. cmt, Stevenson Campaign, 56, Brown for Gov. Campaign, 62, Zenovich for Calif. State Assembly, 62, Sisk for Cong, until 64, Salinger for U.S. Senate, 64; in charge of issues conf. arrangements, Calif. Dem. Coun, 57, 59 & 60, conv. arrangements secy, 61 and liaison with non-mem. clubs, 69-; secy, Fresno Co. Dem. Coun, 57-62; liaison dir, John F. Kennedy for Pres. and local campaigns, Fresno Co, 60; secy, Fresno Co. Dem. Cent. Cmt, 60-64; mem, Calif. Dem. State Cent. Cmt, 60-, north. div. secy, exec. cmt. women's div, 67-69; coordinator speaker's bur, San Francisco, Salinger for U.S. Senate Campaign, 64; worker, Fresno and North. Calif, Johnson-Humphrey Campaigns, 64; first v.pres. and pres, San Francisco Dem. Women's Forum, 65-68; chmn, San Francisco Vol, Brown Campaign, 66; campaign worker, John Burton for State Sen. Campaign, 67; mem, San Francisco Exec. Cmt. for Robert F. Kennedy Campaign, 68 and Calif. Women's Cmt. for Robert F. Kennedy, 68; secy. pro-tem, San Francisco Co. Dem. Coun, 69- Bus. & Prof. Pos: Secy. sch. textbook advert, Houghton Mifflin, 29-30; secy. advert. dept. and librn, D.C. Heath, Publishers, Boston, Mass, 30-32; pub. rels. and personnel asst, Home Owner's Loan Corp, 33-34; teacher and substitute teacher, High Schs, Fresno Co, Calif, 55-60; secy, United Farm Agency, San Francisco, 68- Mem: Girl Scouts (publicity dir, Wakefield, Mass. Coun, 40-42 and Oakland, Calif. Coun, 43-49); Bay Area Commun. Chest Dr. (from Lt. to Maj, 43-49); den mother and mem. pack cmt, Boy Scouts; PTA (secy, publicity chmn. and v.pres, Montclair Chap, 44-49, secy, Westlake Chap, 48-49, hon. life mem, Fremont Sch. Chap, Fresno, 55-); Am. Asn. Univ. Women (legis. chmn, Fresno Chap, 52-56, mem. state legis. cmt, 54-56); secy. and v.pres, Fresno Co. Women's Civic Coun, 56-62; secy, Fresno Munic. League, 55-57; Women's Archit. Leagues (dir, Calif. Coun, 62-64, pres, San Joaquin Valley League, 63); chmn, Fresno City and Co. Cmt. on Long Range Planning, 62-64; Dem. Women of the Bay Area; mem. steering cmt, San Francisco Coordinating Coun. for Integrated Schs, 65; Assoc. Regional Citizens; C. of C; pub. mem, Calif. Adv. Coun. State Bd. Nursing, Educ. and Nurse Registration, 66-; secy, Serv. Cmt. on Pub. Educ, 69-; San Francisco Dem. Club Charter Rev. Cmt, 69-; Cmt. for Adoption of Revised San Francisco Charter, 69- Swift Poetry Prize, 28; Named N.Calif. Key Woman of the Year, 66. Rel: Catholic. Mailing Add: 1125 Broadway, Apt. 301, San Francisco, Calif. 94109.

DALEY, JOHN J. D
b. Rutland, Vt, 6/21/23; s. John Michael Daley and Bridget Cannon D; m. 6/7/47 to Mary Margaret Creed; c. Mary Patricia, Linda, Judy, Lisa, Suzanne, Nancy, Michael, Sharon, James, Mary Jane and Maureen. Educ: Norwich Univ, B.A, 49; Sigma Phi Epsilon. Polit. & Govt. Pos: Alderman, Rutland, Vt, 57-61, pres, Bd. of Aldermen, 61 and mayor, 61-65; chmn, Rutland City Dem. Party, 61-65; Lt. Gov, Vt, 65-69; del, Dem. Nat. Conv, 68. Bus. & Prof. Pos: Salesman, McKesson, Robbins Drug Co, 49-57. Mil. Serv: Entered as Pvt, Marine Corp, 43, released as Pfc, 46, after serv. in S.Pac. Mem: Am. Legion; VFW; Eagles; Elks; Moose; Kiwanis; K. of C. Rel: Roman Catholic. Mailing Add: 61 Pleasant St, Rutland, Vt. 05701. (1967)

DALEY, KATHERINE FAY R
Mem, Santa Clara Co. Rep. Cent. Cmt, Calif.
b. San Mateo, Calif, 9/9/26; d. John Peter Daley (deceased) and Minerva Bosse D. (deceased); single. Educ: Stanford Univ, A.B, 48; Theta Sigma Phi. Polit. & Govt. Pos: Mem. various campaign cmts; mem. Santa Clara Co. United Rep. Finance Cmt, Calif; founder and pres, Los Altos Young Rep, 52; mem, Palo Alto and Los Altos Chap, Calif. Rep. Assembly, 54-64, secy, Palo Alto chap, 60-62, v.pres, Los Altos chap, 63; mem. steering cmt, U.S. Rep. Charles S. Gubser, 54-; vol. staff mem, Young Rep. Cmt. Arrangement, Rep. Nat. Conv, 56; chmn, Santa Clara Co. Young Rep, 56; regional v.pres, Calif. State Young Rep, 56-57, state conv. chmn, 56, newspaper ed, 57-58 and membership chmn, 58-59; alternate and assoc. mem, Santa Clara Co. Rep. Cent. Cmt, 6 years, mem, 62-, chmn, precinct cmt, 4 years, chmn. pub. rels. cmt, currently; mem. steering cmt, Assemblyman George W. Milias, 62-; mem, Los Altos Rep. Women Federated, 63-; vol. staff mem, pub. rels. off, Rep. Nat. Cmt. for Rep. Nat. Conv, 64; founder and v.pres, Los Altos Chap, Calif. Rep. League, 65, mem, 67-; secy, Stanford Rep. Club, 68-; assoc. mem, Calif. Rep. State Cmt, 4 years, mem, currently; mem. steering cmt. for precinct cmt. and youth activities cmt. Bus. & Prof. Pos: Research writer, Pathfinder News Mag, Wash, D.C; activities ed, Stanford Alumni Asn, 52- Mem: Theta Sigma Phi (past pres, Peninsula Alumnae Chap); Am. Asn. Univ. Women. Rel: Methodist. Legal Res: 201 Cuesta Drive Apt. 8, Los Altos, Calif. 94022. Mailing Add: P. O. Box 387, Los Altos, Calif. 94022.

DALEY, RICHARD J(OSEPH) D
Mayor, Chicago, Ill.
b. Chicago, Ill, 5/15/02; s. Michael Daley and Lillian D; m. 1936 to Eleanor Guilfoyle; c. Patricia (Mrs. William Thompson), Eleanor, Richard, Michael, Mary Carol (Mrs. Vanecho), John and William. Educ: DePaul Univ. Law Sch, LL.B, 33 and St. Vincent DePaul Award, 66. Hon. LL.D, Loyola Univ, 66. Polit. & Govt. Pos: Ill. State Rep, 36-38; Ill. State Sen, 38-46, minority leader, 41-46; dir. revenue, State of Ill, 49, dep. comptroller, Cook Co, Ill, 46-49, clerk, 50-58; chmn, Cook Co. Dem. Party, 53-; mayor, Chicago, Ill, 55-; del, Dem. Nat. Conv, 68. Rel: Roman Catholic. Mailing Add: Room 507, City Hall, Chicago, Ill. 60602.

DALLAS, DeVAN D
Miss. State Rep.
b. Okolona, Miss, 3/4/26; married. Polit. & Govt. Pos: Miss. State Rep, currently. Bus. & Prof. Pos: Automobile and implements dealer. Mem: Tenn. and Miss. Sheriffs and Peace Officers Asn; Am. Legion; VFW; 40 et 8; Pontotoc Boosters Club; Lions; Farm Bur. Rel: Baptist. Mailing Add: 123 W. Oxford St, Pontotoc, Miss. 38863. (1967)

DALTON, GRADY WILLIAM D
Va. State Del.
b. Stuart, Va, 6/19/08; m. to Freya Louise Howell D. Educ: Am. Inst. of Banking. Polit. & Govt. Pos: Mem, Gov. Adv. Bd. on Budget, Va; Va. State Del, 58- Bus. & Prof. Pos: Banker and real estate broker; exec. v.pres, Richlands Nat. Bank, Va. Mil. Serv: Lt. Col, Va. Wing Civil Air Patrol. Mem: Elks; Moose; hon. mem, Gov. Adv. Cmt. on Aviation; past state coun, Jr. O.U.A.M; past Lt. Gov, Kiwanis Int; pres, Richlands C. of C, 63; dir, Va. State C. of C. Mailing Add: 210 Washington St, Richlands, Va. 24641. (1967)

DALTON, HERMAN UDELL R
Chmn, Randolph Co. Rep. Cent. Cmt, Ark.
b. Reyno, Ark, 1/10/29; s. David Lawrence Dalton and Irene Lamb D; m. 10/1/50 to Eula Mae King; c. Sandra Lou, Daniel David and John Elijah. Polit. & Govt. Pos: Chmn, Randolph Co. Rep. Cent. Cmt, Ark, 64- Bus. & Prof. Pos: Dir. of Randolph Children's Home Inc. Rel: Church of Christ. Legal Res: 500 Maple St, Pocahontas, Ark. 72455. Mailing Add: P.O. Box 87, Pocahontas, Ark. 72455.

DALTON, JOHN MONTGOMERY D
b. Vernon Co, Mo, 11/9/00; s. Fred A. Dalton and Ida Jane Poage D; m. 11/22/25 to Geraldine Hall; c. John Hall and Julia Hall. Educ: Univ. Mo, J.D, 23; LL.D, Drury Col, Univ. Mo, Westminster Col. and William Jewel Col; Phi Delta Phi; Phi Gamma Delta. Polit. & Govt. Pos: Legis. counsel, REA Asn, 51-52; city counselor, Kennett, Mo, 44-53; attorney gen, Mo, 52-60; gov, 61-65; mem, Pres. Cmn. Income Maintenance Prog, Wash, D.C, 68-69. Bus. & Prof. Pos: Lawyer, Kennett, Mo, 23-52, Jefferson City, 65-; mem. bd. visitors, Univ. Mo, 49-53; trustee, Westminster Col. and Sch. of the Ozarks; mem. bd. curators, Stephens Col; chmn, Fed. Home Loan Bank, Des Moines, Iowa, 65-68. Mem: Past pres, Nat. Asn. Attorney Gen; past gov, Mo. Lions; Mason. Rel: Presbyterian. Mailing Add: 235 E. High St, Jefferson City, Mo. 65101.

DALTON, JOHN NICHOLS R
Va. State Del.
b. Emporia, Va, 7/11/31; s. Ted Dalton and Mary Turner D; m. 2/18/56 to Edwina Panzer; c. Katherine S, Mary Helen, Ted E. and John N, Jr. Educ: Col. William and Mary, B.A, 53; Univ. Va, LL.B, 57; Omicron Delta Kappa; Sigma Alpha Epsilon. Polit. & Govt. Pos: Chmn, Va. Young Rep. Fedn, 59-61; mem, Rep. State Cent. Cmt, 59-, gen. counsel, Va. Rep. Party, 62-; del, Rep. Nat. Conv, 60, alternate del, 64; chmn, Radford City Rep. Cmt, 62-66; Va. State Del, 66- Bus. & Prof. Pos: Mem, First and Merchants Nat. Bank Adv. Bd, 65- Mil. Serv: Entered as 2nd Lt, Army, 54, released as 1st Lt, 56, after serv. in 547th Armored Field Artil. Bn, Ft. Knox, Ky. Mem: Pres, Radford Rotary, 66; v.pres, Radford Jaycees, 59; Mason; KCCH (32°); Shrine; Am. Legion; Moose; Odd Fellows; Va. Farm Bur. Fedn. Rel: Baptist. Legal Res: 313 Fifth St, Radford, Va. 24141. Mailing Add: P.O. Box 1089, Radford, Va. 24141.

DALTON, REGINALD WALDO R
Second V.Chmn, Durham Co. Rep. Party, N.C.
b. Statesville, N.C, 6/6/18; s. Luther Dalton and Willie Lawrence D; m. 6/20/53 to Theresa Daniels. Educ: Fayetteville State Teachers Col, 47-48; N.C. Col, Durham, B.S. in Commerce, 51; Omega Psi Phi. Polit. & Govt. Pos: Rep. precinct chmn. and judge, Precinct 34, Durham, N.C, 60-64; second v.chmn, Fifth Cong. Dist. Rep. Party 64-66; justice of the peace, Durham Co, 64-66; second v.chmn, Durham Co. Rep. Party, 64-; Rep. cand, N.C. State Rep, 66 & 68; treas, Fourth Cong. Dist. Rep. Party, N.C, 68; alternate del, Rep. Nat. Conv, 68; state chmn. N.C. Caucus, Nat. Coun. of Concerned Afro-Am. Rep, 68-69. Bus. & Prof. Pos: Mgr. filing dept, N.C. Mutual Life Ins. Co, 53-65, supvr. cent. records, 65- Mil. Serv: Entered as Pvt, Army, 44, released as Sgt, 46, after serv. in Co. D, 2804th Engr. Gen. Serv. Bn, Asiatic-Pac. Theatre, 44-46; Asiatic-Pac. Serv. Medal with One Bronze Star; Good Conduct Medal; World War II Victory Medal. Mem: Durham Bus. & Prfnl. Chain; F&AM; AASR; NAACP. Rel: Baptist; faculty mem, Progressive Nat. Baptist, Cong. of Christian Educ; assoc. minister of Mt. Vernon Baptist Church, Durham, N.C. Mailing Add: 108 Barnhill St, Durham, N.C. 27707.

DALY, EDNA M. R
V.Chmn, Monroe Co. Rep. Party, N.Y.
b. Medford, Mass, 1/21/06; d. Warren Leslie Faulkner and Rachel Kennedy F; m. 6/27/36 to Charles Bennett Daly; c. Charles B, II and Edna M.(Mrs. Conley). Educ: Russell Sage Col, B.A, 28. Polit. & Govt. Pos: Pres, 18th Ward Womens Club; pres, Rep. Bus. & Prfnl. Women's Club; state committeewoman, N.Y. Rep. Cmt, 61-67; secy, Monroe Co. Rep. Party, 63-69, v.chmn, 69-; del, Rep. State Conv, 69. Bus. & Prof. Pos: Sci. teacher, Bd. of Educ, Rochester, N.Y, 28-67. Mem: N.Y. State and Rochester Teachers Asns; Sci. Teachers Asn; Nat. Educ. Asn; Eastern Star; Daughters of Nile. Rel: Presbyterian. Mailing Add: 143 Vermont St, Rochester, N.Y. 14609.

DALY, MAVIS GLANDER R
b. Renville, Minn, 5/17/24; d. Paul W. Glander and Clara Schmidt G; m. 4/16/49 to George F. Daly. Educ: Univ. S.Dak, B.A, 45; Phi Beta Kappa; Mortar Bd; ed. of col. newspaper; pres, Asn. Women Students. Polit. & Govt. Pos: Secy, Sen. Harlan Bushfield, 46-48 and Sen. Chan Gurney, 48-50; admin. asst. to U.S. Rep. E.Y. Berry, S.Dak, 50- Mailing Add: 7207 Hawthorne Terr, Hyattsville, Md. 20785.

DALY, MICHAEL JAMES D
Mem, Minn. Dem. State Cent. Cmt.
b. Assumption, Carver Co, Minn, 8/9/04; s. Eugene H. Daly and Elizabeth McCormick D; m. 7/15/33 to Joan R. Martin; c. Mary Joanne (Mrs. Devine), Michael James, Jr, Elizabeth Ellen (Mrs. Hiniker) and Jean Marie. Educ: St. Thomas Col, Minn, B.A. and LL.B. Polit. & Govt. Pos: Secy, Minn. Dem. Party, 38-39; mem, Minn. Dem. State Cent. Cmt. Bus. & Prof. Pos: Attorney-at-law, Scott Co, Minn, 55-66. Mem: Dist, Minn. State and Am. Bar

Asns; state dep, K. of C, 52 & 53; State Cmn. Against Discrimination, 63-68. Rel: Catholic. Legal Res: 217 S. Willow, Belle Plaine, Minn. 56011. Mailing Add: 119 W. Main, Belle Plaine, Minn. 56011. (1967)

DALY, MICHAEL JOHN D
Mass. State Rep.
b. Boston, Mass, 7/18/40; s. Jeremiah C. Daly (deceased) and Bridget O'Mahony D; m. 2/19/66 to Elizabeth A. Buckley. Educ: Boston State Col, B.S. in Educ, 64; Alpha Psi Omega, Rho Beta Chap; Newman Club, pres, Sr. Class. Polit. & Govt. Pos: Del, Mass. Dem. State Conv, 64 & 66; mem, 22nd Ward Dem. Cmt. and Boston City Dem. Cmt, Mass, 64-67; Mass. State Rep, 67-; alternate del, Dem. Nat. Conv, 68. Bus. & Prof. Pos: Teacher, Boston Pub. Sch. Syst, 64-66. Mem: Pres, Boston State Alumni Asn; Allston Civic Asn; Allston-Brighton Citizens' Coun; K. of C. (4°); Gr. Boston Jr. C. of C; Gr. Boston Young Dem. Rel: Roman Catholic. Mailing Add: 8 Eric Rd, Allston, Mass. 02134.

DALY, RICHARD WALKER R
Mass. State Rep.
b. New Bedford, Mass, 3/25/36; s. Walker Webster Daly and Doris Christine Grant D; single. Educ: Harvard Col; Hasty Pudding Club; Harvard Lampoon. Polit. & Govt. Pos: Mem, Wellesley Rep. Town Cmt, 69-; Mass. State Rep, 69- Bus. & Prof. Pos: Polit. ed, Boston Traveler, Mass, 66-67; state house bur. chief, Boston Herald Traveler, 67-68. Mil. Serv: Entered as Pvt, Army, 58, released as T/Sgt, 64, after serv. in Army Res. and Air Force Res, U.S. Mem: Am. Newspaper Guild; Am. Fedn. of TV and Radio Artists; Harvard Club of Boston; Boston Press Club. Rel: Episcopal. Legal Res: 20 Avon Rd, Wellesley, Mass. 02181. Mailing Add: State House, Boston, Mass. 02133.

DAME, WALTER B. R
b. Concord, N.H, 1895; married; c. 1 daughter. Educ: Concord High Sch. Polit. & Govt. Pos: N.H. State Rep, 63-65. Bus. & Prof. Pos: Retired city letter carrier; active in band and orchestra work. Mil. Serv: World War I. Mem: Nat. Asn. Retired Civil Employees; Am. Fedn. Musicians, Local 374; Letter Carriers Asn; Am. Legion. Rel: Roman Catholic. Mailing Add: Box 358, York Beach, Maine 03910.

DAMES, OMER J. D
Mo. State Rep.
b. St. Paul, Mo, 5/8/94; m. 9/1/19 to Madeleine McAtee; c. Isabelle, Agnes, Rita, Angela, Loyola, Laura, Gerald, George and Albert (deceased). Educ: O'Fallon Pub. High Sch. Polit. & Govt. Pos: Mo. State Rep, 58- Bus. & Prof. Pos: Retired rural mail carrier; part-time farming. Mil. Serv: Army Motor Transportation Corps, 18-19. Mem: Am. Legion; K. of C.(4°). Rel: Roman Catholic. Mailing Add: R.F.D. 3, Box 76, O'Fallon, Mo. 63366. (1967)

DAMON, HENRY EUGENE R
Mem, Exec. Cmt, Lauderdale Co. Rep. Party, Miss.
b. Meridian, Miss, 12/20/26; s. Henry Eugene Damon and Em Neville Cochran D; m. 7/22/50 to Wilhelmine Streater Tew; c. Sarah Neville, Wilhelmine Tew and Ann Amelia. Educ: N.Ga. Col, Dahlonega; Univ. of Maine, Orono; Georgia Inst. Tech, B.C.E, 49; Tau Beta Pi, Chi Epsilon, Omicron Delta Kappa; Sigma Alpha Epsilon. Polit. & Govt. Pos: Nominee for mayor, Meridian, Miss, 61 and for Lauderdale Co. Bd. Supvrs, 63; mem. exec. cmt, Lauderdale Co. Rep. Party, 60-; mem, Meridian Munic. Exec. Cmt, 61-65; alternate del, Rep. Nat. Conv, 68. Bus. & Prof. Pos: Asst. City Engr, Meridian, Miss, 49-51; pres. and consult. engr, Meridian Eng, Inc. 53- Mil. Serv: Entered as Pvt, Army, 45, released as Pfc, 46, after serv. in Hq. Third Army, Germany; re-entered as 2nd Lt, Corps Engrs, 51, released as 1st Lt, 53, after serv. in 336th EUD, Hq, Eighth Army, Korea; Capt.(Ret): Army Res; Good Conduct, Am. Theater, World War II Victory, Army of Occupation, UN Command and Korea Commendation Medals. Mem: Am. Soc. Civil Engrs; Nat. and Miss. Soc. Prfnl. Engrs; Am. Water Works Asn; Water Pollution Control Fedn; Consult. Engrs. Coun; Miss. Asn. Land Surveyors; Am. Soc. Planning Officials; Am. Cong. Surveying and Mapping; Rotary; C. of C; dir, Meridian Indust. Found. Mississippi Young Engr. of the Year, 62. Rel: Episcopal. Mailing Add: 3134 38th St, Meridian, Miss. 39301.

DAMRON, WILLIAM ORVILLE R
Mem, Hancock Co. Rep. Cent. Cmt, Ill.
b. Basco, Ill, 10/27/07; s. William Henry Damron and Lucy Agnes Peter D; m. 8/14/41 to Bernice Louise Schilling; c. John Milton, Richard Alan and James David. Educ: Univ. Ill, AB, 29. Polit. & Govt. Pos: Twp. supvr, Bear Creek, Ill, 37-43 & 49-57; pres. bd. trustees, Basco, 46-; mem, Hancock Co. Rep. Cent. Cmt, 35-, chmn, 50-68. Bus. & Prof. Pos: Owner, Damron Radio, 33-; field investr, Ill. Commerce Cmn, 54-61; secy, Wythe Twp. Mutual Fire Ins. Co, 65- Mil. Serv: Entered as A/S, Navy, 43, released as Radio Tech, 2/C, 45, after serv. with Amphibious Forces, Pac. Theatre; Am. Theatre Ribbon; Asiatic-Pac. Ribbon; Victory Medal. Mem: Basco Lodge 618, AF&AM; Ralph Parker Post 682, Am. Legion. Rel: Baptist. Mailing Add: Basco, Ill. 62313.

DAMROW, THOMAS HERMAN D
b. Gage Co, Nebr, 8/24/93; s. Frederick Damrow and Etta Catherine Remmers; m. 2/20/17 to Marie Barbara Magdalena Kechley; c. Ruby (Mrs. Walter Lehmann), Franklin, Rev. Thomas, Jr, Kathryn (Mrs. Harlan Overbeck), Esther (Mrs. Alvin Kispel) and Marjorie (Mrs. Harold Epp). Educ: Beatrice High Sch, Nebr; Northwest. Bus. Col, Beatice, 10-12. Polit. & Govt. Pos: Nebr. State Sen, 63-64. Bus. & Prof. Pos: Chief acct, Swift & Co, Beatrice, Nebr, 13-16; farmer, 17-60; Twp. Bd. Mem, 12 years, Sch. Bd. Mem, 25 years, dir, Farmers Coop. Elevator Co, Beatrice, 41 years, Supvr, Gage Co, 8 years and participated in various other commun. projs. Rel: Lutheran; Treas, St. John's Lutheran Church, 27 years and mem. church coun, 9 years. Mailing Add: R.R. 1A, Beatrice, Nebr. 68310.

DAMSEY, JOAN ROBERTA D
Chmn, 12th Cong. Dist. Dem. Party, Fla.
b. Jamestown, N.Y, 9/12/31; d. Fred V. Landy and Sara Caccamise L; m. 6/11/55 to Lloyd Damsey, M.D; c. Eve, Laurie, Lloyd, Jr. and J. Landy. Educ: Col. of St. Elizabeth, Convent, N.J. and Catholic Univ. Am, B.A. and M.A. Polit. & Govt. Pos: Mem, Dem. State Exec. Cmt. Fla. and adv. cmt, State Dem. Cmt. Fla, 62-; mem. platform and policy cmt. and exec. cmt, platform cmt, Dem. Nat. Conv, 64; chmn, 12th Cong. Dist. Dem. Party, Fla, currently. Bus. & Prof. Pos: Dir. and personnel mgr, Marathon Med. Clin, 57- Mem: Women of the Moose; Elks; Does; Am. Legion Auxiliary; Beta Sigma Phi; Fishermen's Hosp. Auxiliary; San Pablo Altar Soc; dir, Monroe Co. Am. Cancer Soc, Fla; chmn, March of Dimes. Selected by Lyndon B. Johnson to make his nomination by acclamation motion from rostrum at Atlantic City, Dem. Nat. Conv, 64. Rel: Catholic. Mailing Add: 2805 Overseas Highway, Marathon, Fla. 33050.

DANA, DEANE, JR. R
Mem, Calif. Rep. State Cent. Cmt.
b. N.Y.C, 7/9/26; s. Deane Dana and Dorothy L. D; m. 7/14/51 to Doris Weiler; c. Deane, III, Marguerite, Diane W. and Dorothy W. Educ: Stevens Inst. Tech, Hoboken, N.J, M.E, 51; Khoda; Chi Phi. Polit. & Govt. Pos: Pres, Long Beach Suburban Rep. Club, Calif, 62 and Lincoln Rep. Club, 67-69; alternate, 39th Assembly Dist. Rep. Co. Cent. Cmt, 67- and 46th Assembly Dist. Rep. Co. Cent. Cmt, 67-; assoc. mem, Calif. Rep. State Cent. Cmt, 64-67 and mem, 67-; chmn, Nixon for President Cmt, Palos Verdes Peninsula, 68. Bus. & Prof. Pos: Engr. through dist. engr, Pac. Tel. & Tel. Co, Los Angeles, Calif, 51-69. Mil. Serv: Entered as 2nd Lt, Air Force, 51, released as 1st Lt, 53, after serv. in Air Defense Command. Mem: Lincoln Rep. Club; Long Beach Suburban Rep. Club; Peninsula Coun for Youth; area cmnr, Boy Scouts. Rel: Episcopal. Mailing Add: 1633 Espinosa Circle, Palos Verdes Estates, Calif. 90274.

DANAHER, JOHN ANTHONY R
b. Meriden, Conn, 1/9/99; s. Cornelius Joseph Danaher and Ellen Ryan D; m. 2/3/21 to Dorothy King; c. John, Jr, Robert C. and Jeanne (Mrs. Lennhoff), Educ: Yale Col, A.B, 20; Yale Law Sch, 21; Beta Theta Pi; Elihu; Corbey Court. Polit. & Govt. Pos: Asst. U.S. Attorney, Dist. Conn, 22-34; Secy. State, Conn, 33-35; U.S. Sen, Conn, 39-45; U.S. Circuit Judge, D.C. Circuit, 53-69, Sr. Circuit Judge, 69- Mil. Serv: Entered as Pvt, Field Artillery, 17, released as 2nd Lt, 18. Metropolitan Club, Wash, D.C; Sons of Union Veterans of the Civil War. Rel: Roman Catholic. Mailing Add: Groton Long Point, Conn. 06340.

DANCE, JAMES HAROLD, JR. R
Mem, Calif. Rep. State Cent. Cmt.
b. New London, Wis, 8/30/32; s. James H. Dance and Bessie Somers D; single. Educ: Univ. Wis, B.S. Met. Eng, 55; Prog. for Mgt. Develop, Harvard Grad. Sch. Bus, 69; Phi Eta Sigma; Pi Kappa Alpha. Polit. & Govt. Pos: Rep. precinct worker, San Francisco, Calif, 61-65; Rep. precinct chmn, 14th Assembly Dist, 67; v.pres, Alameda Rep. Assembly, 67 & 68, pres, 69-; mem, Calif. Rep. State Cent. Cmt, 69-; mem, Alameda Co. Rep. Cent. Cmt, 69- Bus. & Prof. Pos: Salesman, Kaiser Aluminum & Chem. Corp, Oakland, Calif, 57-61, sr. mkt. analyst, 61-65; mgr, Corp. Invest. Analysis, 66- Mil. Serv: Entered as 2nd Lt, Air Force, 55, released as Capt, 57, after serv. in Research and Develop, Lewis Flight Propulsion Center, NASA, Cleveland, Ohio. Publ: 'Rupture Strength of Several Nickel Base Alloys,' Nat. Adv. Cmt. for Aeronautics, 57. Mem: F&AM. Rel: Methodist. Mailing Add: 428 Coral Reef Rd, Alameda, Calif. 94501.

DANFORTH, JOHN CLAGGETT R
Attorney Gen, Mo.
b. St. Louis, Mo, 9/5/36; s. Donald Danforth and Dorothy Claggett D; m. 9/7/57 to Sally B. Dobson; c. Eleanor, Mary, Dorothy and Johanna. Educ: Princeton, A.B, 58; Yale Univ. Divinity Sch, B.D, 63; Yale Univ. Law Sch, LL.B, 63. Polit. & Govt. Pos: Attorney gen, Mo, 69- Bus. & Prof. Pos: Asst. rector, Church of the Epiphany, N.Y.C, 63-66; attorney, Davis Polk Wardwell Sunderland and Kiendl, 64-66, Bryan, Cave, McPheeters and McRoberts, St. Louis, Mo, 66-68; assoc. rector, Church of St. Michael and St. George, Clayton, Mo, 66-68. Mem: St. Louis Country Club; Jefferson City Country Club. Distinguished Service Award, St. Louis Jaycees, Outstanding Young Man 1968, Mo. Jaycees, 69. Rel: Episcopal. Legal Res: 340 Fox Creek Rd, Jefferson City, Mo. 65101. Mailing Add: Supreme Court Bldg, Jefferson City, Mo. 65101.

DANGERFIELD, CLYDE MOULTRIE D
S.C. State Rep.
b. Oakley, S.C, 2/24/15; s. Obie J. Dangerfield, Sr. and Abbie Locklair D; m. 11/17/46 to Pauline E. Nelson; c. Clyde Jr, Dolores Elizabeth, Shirley Ann, Timothy Nelson and Susan Marie. Educ: Clemson Col, 39-40. Polit. & Govt. Pos: S.C. State Rep, 54- Bus. & Prof. Pos: Owner, Gas and Elec. Appliance Store; pres, Suburban Gas and Appliance Co, Inc. Mil. Serv: S/Sgt, Army, 42-45, serv. in Hq. Inf. Replacement Training Center, Camp Croft, S.C. Mem: Past pres, Exchange Club; Mason; Am. Legion; capt, Vol. Fire Dept, Isle of Palms. Rel: Methodist; Trustee, First Methodist Church, Isle of Palms. Mailing Add: 896 America St, Charleston, S.C. 29403. (1967)

DANIEL, ALICE LEE R
b. Chattanooga, Tenn, 7/21/22; d. Lother C. Spears and Bonnie Tatum S; m. to Woodrow W. Daniel, wid; c. Nanette (Mrs. Hawkins). Educ: Dade Co. High Sch; Edmondson Sch. of Bus. Polit. & Govt. Pos: Chmn, Dade Co. Rep. Party, Ga, 56-68. Bus. & Prof. Pos: V.pres. and secy, Ga. Land Title Agency, Inc, 61- Mem: Nat. Legal Secretaries Asn. Rel: Church of Christ. Mailing Add: Trenton, Ga. 30752. (1967)

DANIEL, C. WELBORN D
Fla. State Sen.
b. Okeechobee, Fla, 6/12/26; c. Lynn Elizabeth and Clay Welborn. Educ: Univ. Fla, LL.B, 50; Phi Kappa Tau; Student Govt. Polit. & Govt. Pos: Prosecuting attorney, Leesburg Munic. Court, Fla; judge, Small Claims Court; Fla. State Rep, 56-62; Fla. State Sen, 64-66 & 68- Bus. & Prof. Pos: Attorney, currently. Mil. Serv: Navy, World War II. Mem: Fla. Jr. C. of C.(past v.pres); Fla. Bar; Am. Bar Asn; Lake Sumter Bar Asn.(past pres); Elks; Moose; Am. Legion; VFW. One of Fla. Five Outstanding Young Men, Fla. Jr. C. of C, 60. Rel: Episcopal. Mailing Add: P.O. Drawer 189, Clermont, Fla. 32711.

DANIEL, CREED ALLEN R
Chmn, Grainger Co. Rep. Exec. Cmt, Tenn.
b. Rutledge, Tenn, 11/22/34; s. William Issac Daniel and Velma Farrar D;

m. 12/22/55 to Muriel Hood; c. Larry Creed. Educ: Carson-Newman Col, A.B; Univ. Tenn. Col. of Law, B.L. & LL.D; Columbian Lit. Soc; Phi Delta Phi. Polit. & Govt. Pos: Chmn, Grainger Co. Rep. Exec. Cmt, Tenn, 58- Mem: Am, Tenn. and Grainger Co. Bar Asns; Tenn. Jr. C. of C; Lions; Clinch View Golf & Country Club. Carson-Newman baseball and basketball teams, 52-56, capt, basketball, 56. Rel: Baptist. Mailing Add: Rutledge, Tenn. 37861.

DANIEL, JOHN HANNAH D
Va. State Del.
b. Charlotte Court House, Va, 3/1/96; m. to Eloise Burney. Educ: Pub. sch, Charlotte Court House, Va. Polit. & Govt. Pos: Chmn, State Soil Conserv. Cmt, Va; chmn, Charlotte Co. Dem. Cmt, currently; Va. State Del, 44- Bus. & Prof. Pos: Farmer, businessman; pres, John H. Daniel Co, Knoxville, Tenn. and Va. Crafts, Inc, Keysville, Va; bd. of trustees, Patrick Henry Found. Inc. Mem: Omicron Delta Kappa; Ruritans; Commonwealth Club; Moose; Va. State C. of C; Mfg. Asn. Inc; Farm Bur. Rel: Presbyterian. Mailing Add: Charlotte Court House, Va. 23923. (1967)

DANIEL, PRICE D
b. Dayton, Tex, 10/10/10; s. Marion Price Daniel and Nannie Partlow D; m. 6/28/40 to Jean Houston Baldwin; c. Price, Jr, Jean (Mrs. Daniel Murph), Houston Lee and John Baldwin. Educ: Baylor Univ, B.A, LL.B. and LL.D; Sigma Delta Chi. Polit. & Govt. Pos: Tex. State Rep, 38-45, speaker, Tex. House of Rep, 43-45; attorney gen, Tex, 47-53; Tex. State Sen, 53-57; Gov, Tex, 57-63; mem, Tex. State Libr. and Hist. Cmn, 64-; del, Dem. Nat. Conv, 68. Bus. & Prof. Pos: Attorney-at-law, 32-43 & 63- Mil. Serv: Entered as Pvt, Army, 43, released as Capt, 45, after serv. in Judge Adv. Dept. and U.S, Pac. Mem: Tex. and Am. Bar Asns; Am. Soc. of Int. Law; Am. Legion; Int. Law Asn; VFW; Rotary Int. Rel: Baptist. Legal Res: Holly Ridge Ranch, Liberty, Tex. 77575. Mailing Add: Brown Bldg, Austin, Tex. 79101. (1967)

DANIEL, PRICE, JR. D
Tex. State Rep.
b. Austin, Tex, 6/8/41; s. Price Daniel and Jean Houston Baldwin D; m. 4/16/66 to Diane Wommack. Educ: Baylor Univ, B.B.A, 63, Law Sch, LL.B, 66; Delta Theta Phi. Polit. & Govt. Pos: Justice of the Peace, Liberty Co, Tex, 66-67; Tex. State Rep, 69- Bus. & Prof. Pos: Partner, Daniel & Morrison, Attorneys-at-law, Liberty, Tex, 66-69. Mem: State Bar of Tex; Tex. Trial Lawyers Asn; Chambers and Liberty Co. Bar Asns; Rotary Int; Jaycees; Liberty Co. Hist. Surv. Cmt. Rel: Methodist. Mailing Add: P.O. Box 1, Liberty, Tex. 77575.

DANIEL, VAN BUREN D
b. Aimwell, Ala, 1/22/00; s. George Daniel and Sarah Mayton D; m. 1922 to Minnie Lee Barr; c. Maline (Mrs. Evans), Maurice Daniel Simision (deceased), Van Buren, Jr, George Ellis. Educ: Aimwell Sch. Polit. & Govt. Pos: Ala. State Rep, 59-66; Marengo Co. Bd. of Revenue, 48-56; supvr, 36-48; Marengo Co. Bd. of Educ, 24-36. Bus. & Prof. Pos: Farmer, forestry, timber bus. Mem: Mason. Rel: Baptist. Mailing Add: Nanafalia, Ala. 36764. (1967)

DANIEL, W. C. 'DAN' D
U.S. Rep, Va.
b. Chatham, Va, 5/12/14; s. Reuben Earl Daniel and Georgia Grant D; m. to Ruby McGregor; c. Jimmie Foxx. Educ: Va. Schs; Dan River Textile Sch. Polit. & Govt. Pos: Civilian Adv. to the Second Army, mem, Reemploy. Rights Cmt, U.S. Dept. of Labor and Selective Serv. adv, formerly; permanent mem, President's People to People Cmt, 57-; Va. State Del, 59-68, mem, Privileges and Elec. Cmt, Cmt. on Educ, Finance Cmt, Militia and Police Cmt. and the Cmt. on Gen. Laws, Va. House of Del; mem, Regional Export Expansion Coun, 65-; U.S. Rep, Fifth Dist, Va, 68-, elected pres, Cong. Freshman Class and mem, Cmt. on Armed Serv, U.S. House of Rep; v.chmn, Richmond Export Coun, currently. Bus. & Prof. Pos: Dir, Vet. Reemploy. Dept. and personnel exec, Dan River Mills, 39-57, asst. to pres, 57-66, asst. to bd. chmn, 66-68. Mil. Serv: Navy, World War II. Mem: Elks; Mason (32°); Shrine; Moose; German Club. of Danville; Kiwanis; past mem, Jr. C. of C. and Exchange Club; bd. vis, U.S. Naval Acad; bd. trustees, Averett Col, Danville; formerly, Va. Adv. Hosp. Coun, bd. mem, Va. Soc. for Crippled Children and Adults, v.chmn, Nat. Affairs Cmt. of The Am. Textile Mfrs. Inst, chmn. bd. dirs, United Fund of Gr. Danville, chmn, Better Roads Cmt, Va. State C. of C, Va. Cmn. on Constitutional Govt. and chmn, Va. Cmn. on Vet. Affairs; State Comdr, Am. Legion, 51, Nat. Comdr, 56; Gov. Cmts. on the Status of Women and Employing of the Handicapped; Va. State Crime Cmn; Dulles Int. Airport Develop. Cmn; Va. Independence Preliminary Cmn; Va. State Symphony Orchestra; Va. Thanksgiving Festival, Inc; chmn, Tobacco Tax Study Cmn; pres, Va. State C. of C; reservist, Bus. and Defense Serv. Admin. of the U.S. Dept. of Commerce; bd. dirs, W. Fred Richardson Security Storage Corp, Va. State C. of C, Va. Soc. for the Prev. of Blindness, Va. Educ. TV, Faith Home of Danville, Patrick Henry Boys Plantation and Security Bank and Trust Co, Danville. Hon. mem, Vet. Asns. in Can, Italy, W.Germany, Belgium, France, Israel and S.Vietnam; Awarded the Star of Ital. Solidarity, First Class, 58; Serv. to Mankind Award, Sertoma Clubs, 58; George Wash. Honor Medal, Freedoms Found, Valley Forge, Pa, 58; Croix du Merite, Repub. of France; hon. mem, Omicron Delta Kappa, Hampden-Sydney Col, 65; Confederacy's Mil. Cross, Va. Div, UDC, 66; Distinguished Virginian Award, Va. Exchange Clubs, 67; First Citizen Award, Hugh T. Williams Post, VFW, 67. Rel: Baptist. Legal Res: Danville, Va. Mailing Add: 1730 Longworth House Office Bldg, Washington, D.C. 20515.

DANIELL, EUGENE S, JR D
b. 1904. Educ: Harvard, S.B, LL.B; Boston Univ, LL.B; Command and Gen. Staff Sch, Ft. Leavenworth, Kans. Polit. & Govt. Pos: Mayor, Franklin, N.H. (3 terms); mem, Franklin Sch. Bd; N.H. State Sen; N.H. Gen. Court Rep; city solicitor, Franklin, N.H; del, Dem. Nat. Conv, 52, 56, 64 & 68. Bus. & Prof. Pos: Lawyer. Mil. Serv: Lt. Col, Army Res, World War II, S.E. Asia, Battery Comdr; two Battle Stars. Mem: Dir, C. of C; Am. Legion (20 years); Rotary (25 years); Boy Scouts; VFW. Rel: Sunday Sch. Teacher. Mailing Add: 10 Franklin St, Franklin, N.H. 03235.

DANIELS, CARY D
Committeeman, Ill. Dem. Cent. Cmt.
b. Marshall, Tex, 3/29/12; s. John Daniels and Bertha Gray D; m. 2/1/38 to Amanda Heretha Chatman. Educ: Wiley Col, 30-32. Polit. & Govt. Pos: Precinct committeeman, Lake Co. Dem. Party, Ill, 50-69; treas, Lake Co. Dem. Cent. Cmt, 60-64; chmn, Human Rels. Cmt. and Fair Housing Bd, North Chicago, 67-69; secy, North Chicago Dem. Munic. Cmt, 69; committeeman, Ill. Dem. Cent. Cmt, 68- Mil. Serv: Entered as Pvt, Army Air Force, 42, released as Pfc, 46, after serv. in 1889th A.E.B, 20th Air Force, Cent. Pac. Theatre, 44-46; Presidential Unit Citation; Good Conduct Medal. Mem: Past Exalted Ruler, Int. Elks; chmn. of bd, Barwell Settlement House, Inc. Rel: Methodist. Mailing Add: 1425 Greenfield, North Chicago, Ill. 60064.

DANIELS, DOMINICK V. D
U.S. Rep, N.J.
b. Jersey City, N.J, 10/18/08; s. John Daniels and Carmela DeStefano D; m. 9/15/35 to Camille Curcio; c. Dolores and Barbara. Educ: Rutgers Univ, LL.B, 30. Polit. & Govt. Pos: V.chmn, Jersey City Civil Rights Cmn, N.J, 52-55; magistrate Jersey City Munic. Court, 52-58; U.S. Rep, N.J, 58-; del, Dem. Nat. Conv, 68. Bus. & Prof. Pos: Sr. mem, Daniels, Colello and Daniels, Jersey City, N.J. Mem: Hudson Co. Bar Asn; Univ. Club Hudson Co; Elks; K. of C.(4°); pres, Jersey City Lions Club, 49-50; pres, Dante Alighieri Soc, Jersey City, Inc, 54-57. Legal Res: 193 Palisade Ave, Jersey City, N.J. 07306. Mailing Add: 403 House Office Bldg, Washington, D.C. 20515.

DANIELS, JACK D
N.Mex. State Rep.
b. Council Bluffs, Iowa, 10/31/23; s. Robert W. Daniels and Adele Davis D; m. 7/6/46 to Elizabeth Donley; c. Dana Adele, Diane Virginia and Robert Guy. Educ: N.Mex. Mil. Inst, 2 years; Univ. N.Mex, 2 semesters; Sigma Chi. Polit. & Govt. Pos: Mem, City Water Bd, Hobbs, N.Mex, 47-68; mem, N.Mex. State Investment Coun, 63-67; chmn, Lea Co. Dem. Party, 66-68; N.Mex. State Rep, currently. Mil. Serv: Entered as Seaman, Naval Res, 43, released as Lt.(jg), 46, after serv. in U.S.S. Walton, Pac. Theatre, 44-46. Mem: Pres, N.Mex. Asn. of Ins. Agents, 53-54 and state nat. dir, 55-59; Million Dollar Round Table; C. of C.(pres, Hobbs Chap, 64-65); Elks; Rotary; AF&AM; pres, N.Mex. Amigos, 67-68. Rel: Episcopal. Legal Res: 623 E. Baja, Hobbs, N.Mex. 88240. Mailing Add: Box 1258, Hobbs, N.Mex. 88240.

DANIELS, JOHN CLIFFORD D
b. Macon, Ga, 4/25/36; s. John Daniels, Sr. and Ludelia Huckaby D; m. 6/30/62 to Madora Beth Bentley; c. Leslie Joy. Educ: Villanova Univ, B.Sc, 60; Alpha Phi Alpha. Polit. & Govt. Pos: Alderman, 19th Ward, Dem. Party, Conn, 60-63, 22nd Ward, 63-65; dep. dir, Cmn. on Equal Opportunities, 65-67; cand. for mayor, New Haven, Conn, 69. Bus. & Prof. Pos: Teacher, West Haven High Sch, Conn, 61-65; proj. dir, Newhallville Area-New Haven Redevelopment Agency, 67-68; proj. dir, Hill Area-New Haven Redevelopment Agency, 68-69; asst. to the pres. on urban affairs, Quinnipiac Col, 69- Mem: Human Rels. Coun; Nat. Conf. of Christians & Jews; mem, cent. mgt. cmt, New Haven YMCA; Urban League; NAACP. Fel. of Trumbull Col, Yale Univ, 63; Named Outstanding Citizen in Am, 68. Rel: Congregational. Mailing Add: 44 Glen Rd, New Haven, Conn. 06511.

DANIELS, JONATHAN WORTH D
b. Raleigh, N.C, 4/26/02; s. Josephus Daniels and Addie Worth Bagley D; m. 9/5/23 to Elizabeth Bridgers, wid. 12/17/29; m. 4/30/32 to Lucy Billing Cathcart; c. Elizabeth Bridgers (Mrs. C.B. Squire), Lucy (Mrs. Thomas P. Inman), Adelaide (Mrs. B.J. Key) and Mary (Mrs. Cleves Daniels Rich). Educ: Univ. of N.C, A.B, 21, M.A, 22; Columbia Law Sch, 22-23; Delta Kappa Epsilon. Hon. degrees, Univ. N.C, Duke, N.C. State and Shaw Univs, Rollins and Elon Cols. Polit. & Govt. Pos: Asst. dir, Off. Civilian Defense, 42; trustee, Vassar Col, 42-48; admin. asst. to the President, 43-45, press secy, 45; U.S. mem, UN sub-cmt. Prev. of Discrimination and Protection of Minorities, 47-53; mem. pub. admin. bd, ECA and Mutual Security Agency, 48-53; Dem. Nat. Committeeman, N.C, 49-52; mem, Fed. Hosp. Coun, 49-53. Bus. & Prof. Pos: Former reporter, Louisville Times, Ky; reporter, Raleigh News and Observer, N.C, Wash. correspondent, 25-28, assoc. ed, 32-33, ed, 33-42, exec. ed, 47 and ed, 48-; mem. ed. staff, Fortune Mag, N.Y, 30-32; contrib. of weekly page, 'A Native at Large' to the Nation, 41-42. Publ: Frontier on the Potomac, 46; The Man of Independence, A Biography of Harry Truman, 50; The End of Innocence, 54; plus others. Mem: Nat. Press Club, Wash, D.C. Rel: Episcopal. Mailing Add: News and Observer, Raleigh, N.C. 27602.

DANIELS, MARVIN KERMIT D
Chmn, Powell Co. Dem. Cent. Cmt, Mont.
b. Deer Lodge, Mont, 11/28/16; s. Joseph E. Daniels and Elma Long D; m. to Judith Elizabeth Wilson; c. Robert C, Margaret J.(Mrs. Altenbrun), Nancy E.(Mrs. Ronald Kelley) and John J. Educ: Mont. State Univ; Univ. of Mont. Law Sch, 46; Phi Delta Phi. Polit. & Govt. Pos: Attorney, Powell Co, Mont, 46-50; Mont. State Rep, 55-61; chmn, Powell Co. Dem. Cent. Cmt, 62- Bus. & Prof. Pos: Attorney-at-law, 53- Mil. Serv: Entered as A/S, Naval Res, 42, released as Lt, 45, re-entered as Lt. Comdr, 52-53; European-Africa and Asiatic-Pac. Theater Ribbons. Mem: Mont. Bar Asn; Mont. Trial Lawyers Asn; Rotary; VFW; Am. Legion; Elks. Rel: Protestant. Mailing Add: 313 Missouri Ave, Deer Lodge, Mont. 59722.

DANIELS, MONCIE LEE, JR. D
b. Manteo, N.C, 11/4/12; s. M.L. Daniels and Belva Lockwood Midgett D; m. 12/19/39 to Muriel S. Green; c. Parmelee (Mrs. Jones) and M.L, III. Educ: Manteo Bus. Col; Univ. N.C. Mgt. Inst, cert. of recognition. Polit. & Govt. Pos: Mem, Town Coun, Manteo, N.C, 48-58; N.C. State Rep, 63-66. Bus. & Prof. Pos: Tug barge operator, Dare Co. Waters for 20 years; partner and mgr, Daniels Oil Co, Manteo, 40- Mem: N.C. Oil Jobbers Asn.(chmn, former dir. and former v.chmn, Consignment Distributors Sect); E. Carolina Oil Heat Inst; Dare Co. Petroleum Industs. Cmt; trustee, Methodist Home for Children, Raleigh, N.C. Rel: Methodist; mem. cmt, Stewardship and Finance, chmn, Bd. of Trustees. Mailing Add: 4 Mother Vineyard Rd, Box 86, Manteo, N.C. 27954. (1967)

DANIELS, ROBERT VINCENT D
Mem, Chittenden Co. Dem. Cmt, Vt.
b. Boston, Mass, 1/4/26; s. Robert Whiting Daniels and Helen Hoyt D; m. 7/2/45 to Alice May Wendell; c. Robert H, Irene L, Helen L. and Thomas L. Educ: Harvard, A.B, 45, M.A, 47, Ph.D, 51. Polit. & Govt. Pos: Mem, Chittenden Co. Dem. Cmt, Vt, 59-; chmn, Policy and Planning Cmt, Vt. Dem.

Party, 62-66; mem. bd. visitors, U.S. Air Force Acad, 65-67; alternate del, Dem. Nat. Conv, 68. Bus. & Prof. Pos: Mem. faculty soc. sci, Bennington Col, Vt, 52-53 & 57-58; asst. prof. Slavic studies, Ind. Univ, Bloomington, 53-55; prof. hist, Univ. Vt. 56-57 & 58-, chmn. dept, 64-; U.S.-Soviet Cultural Exchange Scholar, Univ. Moscow, 66. Mil. Serv: Entered as A/S Naval Res, 44, released as Ens, Supply Corps, 46, after serving on U.S.S. Albany, 45-46. Publ: The Conscience of the Revolution, Harvard, 60; The Nature of Communism, Random, 62; Red October, Scribner, 67. Mem: Am. Asn. Univ. Prof; Am. Hist. Asn; Am. Asn. Advan. Slavic Studies (bd. dirs, 68-70); Vt. Hist. Soc. (trustee). Mailing Add: 195 S. Prospect St, Burlington, Vt. 05401.

DANIELS, RUSSEL O. D
b. Malad, Idaho, 4/7/99; s. Daniel M. Daniels and Catherine Owen D; m. 5/26/25 to La Rue Jorgenson; c. Helen La Rue, Dale Russel and Joseph J. Polit. & Govt. Pos: Bd. mem, Agr. Adjust. Agency, Co. Agr. Bd, Idaho, 34-40; city councilman, Malad City, 47-55; Idaho State Sen, Oneida Co, 58-69. Mem: St. John Cattle Asn.(pres, 40-55); Idaho Cattle Asn; Farmers Union. Rel: Latter-day Saint. Mailing Add: 86 W. 400 North, Malad City, Idaho 83252. (1967)

DANIELSON, GEORGE ELMORE D
Calif. State Sen.
b. Wausa, Nebr, 2/20/15; s. August Danielson and Ida Youngner D; m. to Gladys Ohanian. Educ: Wayne State Teachers Col, 33-35; Univ. of Nebr, B.A, 37, Col. of Law, LL.B, 39; Phi Alpha Delta. Polit. & Govt. Pos: Spec. agent, Fed. Bur. of Invest, 39-44; asst. U.S. Attorney, South. Dist. of Calif, 49-51; mem, Los Angeles Co. Dem. Cent. Cmt, Calif, 60-; mem, Calif. State Dem. Cent. Cmt, 60-, exec. committeeman, 64-66; Calif. State Assemblyman, 63-67, chmn, Majority Caucus, 65-67; mem, Calif. 'Little Hoover' Cmn, 65-67; Calif. State Sen, 67-, chmn, Cmt. on Pub. Utilities and Corp, currently; del, Dem. Nat. Conv, 68. Bus. & Prof. Pos: Lawyer, Danielson, Johnson & Burgard, 48- Mil. Serv: Entered as Ens, Naval Res, 44, released as Lt, 46, after serv. in Amphibious Forces, Pac. Fleet, Pac. Theater, World War II; Pac. Theater, Am. Defense and Victory Medal. Publ: 'Facts and Figures Concerning Executions in California, 1937-1963,' self, 63. Mem: Am. Bar Asn; Soc. of Former Spec. Agents of the Fed. Bur. of Invest; Elks. Legal Res: 1321 Maltman Ave, Los Angeles, Calif. 90026. Mailing Add: State Capitol, Sacramento, Calif. 95814.

DANN, MIMI SEMMES R
b. Memphis, Tenn, 1/1/27; d. Thomas Jenkins Semmes and Elise Humphreys S; m. 7/5/47 to Alexander William Dann, Jr; c. Alexander III, Thomas, Elise and Katherine. Educ: Sweetbriar Col, 1 year; Sarah Lawrence Col, 1 year; Cornell Univ, B.A, 49; Phi Beta Kappa. Polit. & Govt. Pos: Precinct capt. and supvr, Shelby Co. Rep. Party, Tenn, 52-68; chmn, elec. day activities and vol. chmn, Rep. Party Hq, 52-68; women's co-chmn, Dan Kuykendall Campaign; Ike Shop Chmn; alternate del, Rep. Nat. Conv, 68. Mem: Jr. League; Rep. Workshop; Memphis Garden Club; Fedn. of Rep. Women; Art Today; Panel of Am. Women. Rel: Episcopal. Mailing Add: 6246 Green Meadows, Memphis, Tenn. 38117.

DANNEMEYER, WILLIAM EDWIN D
b. Los Angeles, Calif, 9/22/29; s. Henry William Dannemeyer and Charlotte Knapp D; m. 8/27/55 to Evelyn Mae Hoemann; c. Bruce, Kim and Susan. Educ: Valparaiso Univ, B.A. in polit. sci, 50; Univ. Calif. Hastings Col. of Law, LL.B, 52; Rho Lambda Tau. Polit. & Govt. Pos: Dep. dist. attorney, Santa Barbara Co, Calif, 55-57; asst. city attorney, Fullerton, 59-62; Calif. State Assemblyman, 69th Dist, 62-66; cand. for Calif. State Sen, 66. Bus. & Prof. Pos: Partner, Dannemeyer & Lange, Attorneys, Fullerton, 57- Mil. Serv: Entered as Pvt, Army, 52, released as Cpl, 54, after serv. as Spec. Agent, Counter Intel. Corps. Mem: C. of C; Am, Calif. and Orange Co. Bar Asns. Rel: Lutheran. Legal Res: 834 N. Grandview, Fullerton, Calif. 92632. Mailing Add: 1105 E. Commonwealth, Fullerton, Calif. 92631.

DANNER, EDWARD RAY R
Nebr. State Sen.
b. Guthrie, Okla, 2/14/00; m. 7/30/23 to Miller; c. James, Kenneth, Dorothy, Marian, Beverly, Emogene, Laurel, Sharron and Hugh. Educ: Capitol Hill High Sch, Guthrie, Okla, grad. Polit. & Govt. Pos: Nebr. State Sen, 62- Bus. & Prof. Pos: Past field rep. and past v.pres, UPWA. Mem: Mason. Rel: Protestant; Deacon, 20 years. Mailing Add: 2870 Pinkney St, Omaha, Nebr. 68111. (1967)

DANSEY, WILLIAM ELLSWORTH, JR. R
b. Hampton, Va, 1/23/38; s. William Ellsworth Dansey and Ruth Ann Ward D; m. 2/5/69 to Bonnie Lynn Phillips. Educ: Chowan Col, A.A, 60; E.Carolina Univ, B.S, 62. Polit. & Govt. Pos: Pres, Pitt Co. Young Rep, N.C, 64; chmn, Goldwater for Pres. Cmt, 64; campaign mgr, John East for Cong. Cmt, 65 & 66; state finance chmn, Garder for Gov. Cmt, 68; alternate del, Rep. Nat. Conv, 68. Mil. Serv: Entered as Pfc, Army, 56, released as Sgt, 57, after serv. in Artillery. Mem: Greenville Jaycees; Greenville Golf & Country Club; Moose; Exchange Club. Rel: Baptist. Mailing Add: 120 N. Meade, Greenville, N.C. 27834.

DANTON, NICHOLAS WILLIAM D
Maine State Rep.
b. Biddeford, Maine, 12/8/18; s. William Danton and Demetra D; m. 11/19/49 to Frances Mavrides; c. William M. Educ: Portland Jr. Col, 49-50; Portland Univ. Sch. of Law, LL.B, 54. Polit. & Govt. Pos: Mem, Biddeford Dem. City Cmt, Maine, 60-63, York Co. Dem. Cmt, 61-66 and Old Orchard Dem. Town Cmt, 64-66; co-chmn, State Operation Support, 65-66; Maine State Rep, 65- Mil. Serv: Entered as Pvt, Army Air Force, 40, released as M/Sgt, 45, after serv. in Air Transport Command, ETO, 43-45; ETO, S.Pac, N.Am. and Pearl Harbor Ribbons. Mem: Maine Bar Asn; York Co. Bar Asn.(mem. legis. cmt, 65-66); Maine and Nat. Trial Lawyers Asns; VFW; Am. Legion; Amvets; Elks; AF&AM. Rel: Greek Orthodox. Mailing Add: 12 Milliken St, Old Orchard Beach, Maine 04064. (1967)

DAPENA-VIDAL, RAMON ENRIQUE P.R. Union Party
Mem, Dir. Bd, P.R. Union Party
b. Ponce, P.R, 7/9/28; s. Rigoberto P. Dapena-Laguna and Maria Rosa Vidal-Aboy D; m. 2/9/52 to Mildred Joan Guerrero; c. Ramoń E, Rigoberto P. and Rosemarie. Educ: The Citadel, 45-47; Polytech. Inst. of P.R, 47-48. Polit. & Govt. Pos: Pres, Second Precinct Popular Dem. Party, P.R, 63-67; v.pres, Cent. Munic. Cmt, Ponce, 63-67; P.R. State Rep, 26th Precinct, 65-, chmn, Investigating Cmt. on Drug Addiction, 65, chmn, Housing Cmt, 66; mem. founders coun, mem. dir. bd. and coordinator for Ponce and South. P.R, P.R. Union Party, 69- Bus. & Prof. Pos: Pres, Bus. and Ins. Exchange, Inc, P.R, 53-60; gen. agent, Old Repub. Life Ins. Co, 56-64; pres, Dapena and Cia, 60-64; asst. dir, Bohemia Mag, 65; asst. pub. rels, Caribair, 65-66; polit. commentator, Daily Radio Prog, 68- Mil. Serv: Entered as Pvt, Army, 50, released as 1st Lt, 53, after serv. in 65th Inf. Regt, Korea; Bronze Star Medal; Korean Campaign Ribbon; UN Orgn. Medal. Publ: Weekly column in El Dia Newspaper, Ponce, P.R. Mem: Adv, Fedn. of Ins. Orgns, 61-63; P.R. Health Ins. Bd, 61-64; P.R. Ins. Inst. Rel: Christian. Mailing Add: 88 A Street, Buena Vista, Ponce, P.R. 00731.

DARBY, HARRY R
b. Kansas City, Kans, 1/23/95; s. Harry Darby and Florence Isabelle Smith D; m. 12/17/17 to Edith Marie Cubbison; c. Harriet (Mrs. Thomas H. Gibson, Jr), Joan (Mrs. Roy A. Edwards, Jr), Edith Marie (Mrs. Ray Evans) and Marjorie (Mrs. Eugene D. Alford). Educ: Univ. Ill, B.S, 17, M.E, 29. Hon. LL.D, St. Benedict's Col, Westminster Col, Kans. State Univ. and Washburn Univ. Polit. & Govt. Pos: Del, Rep. Nat. Conv, 40-60, chmn, Credentials Cmt, 44, chmn, Kans. Del, 48, 52 & 56, chmn, Ticket Cmt, 56 & 60; mem, Rep. Nat. Cmt. for Kans, 40-64, chmn, Rural Vote Cmt, 41; mem, Exec. Cmt. of 15, 44; U.S. Sen, Kans, 49-50. Bus. & Prof. Pos: With Mo. Boiler Works Co, Kansas City, 11-19; dir. numerous corp; founder and chmn. bd, Leavenworth Steel, Inc. and Darby Rwy. Cars, Inc; with Darby Corp, 20-, now chmn. of bd. and owner. Mil. Serv: Capt, Field Artil, Army, 17-19, AEF. Mem: Dir, Univ. Kans. Research Found; Univ. Ill. Found; exec. cmt, Agr. Hall of Fame; chmn, Eisenhower Presidential Libr. Cmn; trustee and v.pres, Eisenhower Found, Abilene, Kans; trustee, Nat. Cowboy Hall of Fame; Man of the Month Club, Kansas City, Mo; chmn. emer, Am. Royal Livestock and Horse Show; exec. cmt. Kans. Livestock Asn; Kans. Heart Asn; Palomino Horse Exhibitors of Kans; Navy League of U.S. Kans. Registrn. Bd. of Prfnl. Engrs; Am. Soc. Civil Engrs; Am. Soc. Mech. Engrs; Kans. Soc. of Prfnl. Engrs; Am. Hereford Asn; Am. Nat. Livestock Asn; Am. Soc. Agr. Engrs; VFW; Am. Legion; 40 et 8; Mil. Order World Wars; Rotary; Mason (32°); Shrine; Jester; Automobile Club. of Mo; Kansas City, Saddle and Sirloin, River, Terr, Town House, Chicago, Chevy Chase, Capitol Hill, Cherry Hills and Burning Tree Clubs. Rel: Episcopal. Legal Res: 1220 Hoel Pkwy, Kansas City, Kans. 66102. Mailing Add: First St. and Walker Ave, Kansas City, Kans. 66110.

DARBY, HELEN ALMEDA R
Mem, Calif. Rep. State Cent. Cmt.
b. Dresden, Maine, 6/22/98; d. Orrin La Forest Ham and Jennie Blinn H; m. 11/10/22 to Karl Foster Darby; c. Walter O. Educ: Sargent Sch, 16-17. Polit. & Govt. Pos: Pres, S. Bay Federated Rep. Women, Calif, 56-57 and life mem, 60-; Rep. chmn, 46th assembly dist, Calif, 57-64; v.chmn, 46th Assembly Dist. Rep. Cent. Cmt, 60-64; mem, Calif, Rep. State Cent. Cmt, 62-; colonel, Rep. Victory Squad, Redondo Beach, Calif, 66- Mem: Lincoln Rep. Club. Award for Achievement in Precinct Orgn. of Rep. Party, 46th Assembly Dist. Cent. Cmt, 64. Rel: Episcopal. Mailing Add: 421 Ave. G, Apt. D, Redondo Beach, Calif. 90277.

D'ARCY, JAMES ANDREW D
b. Phila, Pa, 4/8/37; s. Anthony Michael D'Arcy and Mary Brennan D; single. Educ: Villanova Univ, B.E.E, 59; Univ. Pa, M.S.E.E, 64; Radio Corp. of Am. Grad. Study Prog, 61-63. Polit. & Govt. Pos: Committeeman, Phila. 64th Ward Dem. Exec. Cmt, Pa, 62-, treas, 66-; alternate del, Dem. Nat. Conv, 68. Bus. & Prof. Pos: Elec. engr, Radio Corp. of Am. Astro Electronics Div, Princeton, N.J, 59-; Registered Prfnl. Engr, State of Pa, 65- Publ: 'Logic and Control System for a Dielectric Tape Camera to be used in a Meteorological Satellite,' Thesis, Univ. Pa, 5/64; 'Logic and Control System for a Panoramic TV Camera,' Third Space Cong, 3/66; 'Photo Dielectric Tape Camera Systems,' Fifth Space Cong, 3/68 and RCA Engr, 12/68 & 1/69. Mem: Engrs. Club of Phila.(pres, Jr. Orgn); Inst. of Elec. and Electronics Engrs; Pa. Soc. of Prfnl. Engrs; Tau Beta Pi; Eta Kappa Nu. Outstanding Jr. Award, Engrs. Club of Phila, 66-67. Rel: Roman Catholic. Mailing Add: 3307 Oakmont Ave, Philadelphia, Pa. 19136.

DARDANELL, EDWARD L. D
b. Penn Hills, Pa, 9/23/23; s. Anthony Dardanell and Domenica Cardone D; m. to Marilyn McGovern. Educ: Univ. of Pittsburgh, A.B. Polit. & Govt. Pos: V.pres, Penn Hills Libr. Bd, Pa; mem, Airport Adv. Cmn; mem. bd. trustees, State's Youth Develop. Centers, 61-63; Pa. State Rep, 64-68. Bus. & Prof. Pos: Newspaper publisher; exec. cmt, Pa. Newspaper Publishers Asn; past dir, Pa. Soc. of Newspaper Ed. Mil. Serv: Army, 1st Lt, platoon leader, Regt. Adj; World War II, served in 4th Inf. Div; served in Korean Conflict, stationed Japan; Army Res. to 53. Mem: Pi Sigma Alpha; Phi Delta Theta; past pres. & dir, Penn Hills C. of C; Oakmont, Verona, Wilkinsburg, Monroeville C. of C; Allegheny Seminar; United Fund chmn. Dist. 2, Cancer Crusade, 61; E. Borough's Coun, Boy Scouts; bd. mem, Better Bus. Bur. Man of the Year Award, Penn Hills, 58; ed. awards in statewide competitions. Mailing Add: 233 Sunset Dr, Pittsburgh, Pa. 15235.

DARDEN, COLGATE WHITEHEAD, JR. D
Mem, State Bd. Educ, Va.
Southampton Co, Va, 2/11/97; s. Colgate W. Darden and Catherine Pretlow D; m. 12/3/27 to Constance S. du Pont; c. Colgate W, III and Irene du Pont (Mrs. Field). Educ: Univ. Va; Columbia Univ; Oxford Univ, England; Phi Beta Kappa; Raven Soc. Polit. & Govt. Pos: Va. State Del, 30-33; U.S. Rep, Va, 33-36 & 39-41; Gov, Va, 42-46; mem, U.S. Del. to UN, 55; mem, Pub. Libr. Bd, Norfolk, 62-; mem, State Bd. Educ, Va, 63- Bus. & Prof. Pos: Dir, DuPont Co, Life Ins. Co. of Va. Newport News Ship and Merchants & Farmers Bank; chancellor, William and Mary Col, 46-47; pres, Univ. Va, 47-59, emer. pres, 59- Mil. Serv: Serv. in Am. Ambulance Serv. with French Army, 16-17; with Naval Aviation, 17 and Marine Corps Aviation, 18, released as 2nd Lt. after serv. in 1st Marine Sq, North. Bombing Group. Rel: Episcopal. Mailing Add: 7438 Flicker Point, Norfolk, Va. 23505.

DARNELL, ALEX WHITEFIELD D
Chmn, Montgomery Co. Dem. Cmt, Tenn.
b. Clarksville, Tenn, 9/9/29; s. Elliott Sinclair Darnell and Mary Anita White-

field D; m. 8/23/52 to Sarah Anne Howser; c. Stanley D, Sarah G. and Thomas W. Educ: Vanderbilt Univ, B.A, 51, Law Sch, LL.B, 54; Alpha Tau Omicron; Phi Delta Phi. Polit. & Govt. Pos: Clerk and master, Chaucery Court, Tenn, 61-; chmn, Montgomery Co. Dem. Cmt, currently. Bus. & Prof. Pos: Attorney-at-law, Clarksville, 56- Mil. Serv: Entered as Pvt, Army, 54, released as Pfc, 56, after serv. in Atomic Security Agency, Europe. Mem: Montgomery Co. and Tenn. Bar Asns; Boy Scouts (past chmn, Cogioba Dist). Rel: Church of Christ. Mailing Add: 110 Madison Terrace, Clarksville, Tenn. 37040.

DARR, RICHARD K D
b. Fremont, Nebr, 5/17/21; s. Glenn Donald Darr and Cathryn Sexson D; div. Educ: Midland Col, A.B, 48; Univ. Nebr, Lincoln, M.A, 52 and Ph.D, 56; Blue Key. Polit. & Govt. Pos: Economist, U.S. Off. Mil. Govt, Germany, 48-49; consult, Nebr. State Tax Cmnr, summer 56; del, Dem. Nat. Conv, 68. Bus. & Prof. Pos: Research asst, Boston and Maine R.R. Hist. Group, Boston, Mass, 53-54; asst. prof. econ, East. Ill. Univ, 55; research asst, Bus. Hist. Found, Great North. R.R, St. Paul, Minn, summers 57 & 58; Ford Found. faculty fel, Mich. State Univ. summer 59; consult. anti-trust legis, Opinion Research Corp, Princeton, N.J, 62. Mil. Serv: Entered as Pvt, Army, 42, released as Sgt, 46, after serv. in 65th Inf. Div, ETO, 44-46; Good Conduct Medal; Am. Theatre Medal and European Theatre Ribbon with two Battle Stars; Combat Inf. Badge. Publ: 'Traveler's Troubles,' N.H. Profiles, 5/58; 'The News Goes to College,' AFL-CIO News, 5/58; 'Full Measure of Devotion; the Ordeal of Private Hugh Sloan, 1864,' Mo. Hist. Rev, 1/66. Mem: Omicron Delta Epsilon; Asn. Evolutionary Econ; Midwest Econ. Asn; Am. Asn. Univ. Prof; Am. Econ. Asn; Lexington Group. Rel: Unitarian. Mailing Add: R.D.1, Box 156, River Falls, Wis. 54022.

DARROW, GEORGE R
b. Osage, Wyo, 8/13/24; s. George Washington Darrow and Marjorie Ord D; m. 7/8/53 to Eileen Doris Riedl; c. Roy Stuart, Karen Josanne, Reed Crandall and John Robin. Educ: Univ. Mich, A.B. in Econ, 45 and B.S. in Geol, 49; Phi Gamma Delta. Polit. & Govt. Pos: Mont. State Rep, 67-68. Bus. & Prof. Pos: Consult. geologist, 59-; pres, Yellowstone-Bighorn Research Asn, 60-62, Buttes Petroleum Corp, 62- and Rocky Mt. Sect, Am. Asn. Petroleum Geologists, 64-65; v.pres, Newmont Resources Corp, 61-; dir, Independent Petroleum Asn. of Am, 67- Mil. Serv: Entered as A/S, Naval Res, 43, released as Ens, 46, after serv. in Pac. Publ: 'Melstone Oil Field,' 51 and 'Gage Field,' 56, Musselshell Co, Mont; 'Oil Exploration History of Central Montana,' Billings Geol. Soc. Guidebook, 56. Mem: Am. Inst. of Prfnl. Geologists; Am. Asn. of Petroleum Geologists; Soc. of Explor. Geophysicists; Soc. of Econ. Paleontologists & Mineralogists; Geol. Soc. of Am; Am. Water Resources Asn; Independent Petroleum Asn. of Am; Am. Arbit. Asn; fel, Am. Geog. Soc; West. Hist. Asn; fel, Am. Asn. for Adv. of Sci; Mont. Geol. Soc; C. of C; Billings Petroleum Club; Mont. Inst. of the Arts; Nat. Wildlife Fedn; Mont. Hist. Soc. Rel: Congregational. Legal Res: 2100 Fairview Place, Billings, Mont. 59102. Mailing Add: 804 Midland Bank Bldg, Billings, Mont. 59101.

DARROW, PETER P. D
Mem, State Dem. Cmt, Mich.
b. Glen Cove, N.Y, 9/12/19; s. Vasili Podorowski Darrow and Michelena D; m. 3/7/45 to Charlotte McMurtrey Noble; c. Duncan Noble and Peter Vasili. Educ: N.Y. Univ, B.S, 42; Univ. Mich. Law Sch, LL.B, 48. Polit. & Govt. Pos: Mem, State and Co. Dem. Cmts, Mich, 46-; chmn, Pittsfield Twp, 48; precinct, ward, city, co. and dist. chmn, Dem. Party, 48-66; pub. adminstr, Washtenaw Co, Mich, 56-66; city chmn, Ann Arbor Dem. Cmt, 57-60; chmn, Wastenaw Co. Dem. Cmt, 60-64; del, Dem. Nat. Conv, 64; chmn, Second Cong. Dist. Dem. Cmt, 64, finance chmn, 65-66, finance chmn, Wes Vivian for Cong. Cmt, Second Cong. Dist; mem. steering cmt, G. Mennen Williams for Sen. Cmt; state prog. chmn, Mich. State Dem. Conv, 66. Bus. & Prof. Pos: Guest lectr, Univ. Mich; secy and mem. bd, Int. Automated Machines, Inc, 64-; organizer and founder, Ann Arbor Commun. Develop, Inc, 65; partner, Mann, Lipnik & Darrow, Attorneys, currently. Mil. Serv: Entered as A/S, Navy, 41, released as Lt.(sg), 45, after serv. in Amphibious Forces, Mediterranean-Europe-Africa; Am. Theater Ribbon; European-African Serv. Ribbon with 11 Battle Stars; Presidential Citation. Mem: Washtenaw Co, Mich. and Am. Bar Asns; Am. Trial Lawyers Asn; Episcopal Soc. for Cultural and Racial Unity; life mem, NAACP; Cong. of Racial Equality; Am. Civil Liberties Union; N.Y. Univ. and Mich. Alumni Asns; Benton Boat Club; ethics cmt, Mich. Bar Asn; comdr, VFW Post 403, 52 and Judge Advocate, 53; chmn, Ann Arbor Am. for Dem. Action and mem. nat. bd. Created first non-profit housing proj. in U.S, 60. Rel: Episcopal; Warden, St. Andrews Episcopal Church; bd. mem, Nat. Episcopal Student Found. Legal Res: 1043 Martin Place, Ann Arbor, Mich. 48104. Mailing Add: 1043 Ann Arbor Trust Bldg, Ann Arbor, Mich. 48108.

DARROW, ROBERT O. R
Chmn, Niobrara Co. Rep. Cent. Cmt, Wyo.
b. Rochester, N.Y, 1/6/33; s. George W. Darrow and Marjorie Ord D; m. 6/15/58 to Beverly Ann Jack; c. Catherine Ann, Diana Lynn and Wendy Sue. Educ: Univ. Colo, 2 years; Univ. Wyoming, B.S, 58; Omicron Delta Kappa; Alpha Zeta; Chi Gamma Iota. Polit. & Govt. Pos: Chmn, Niobrara Co. Rep. Cent. Cmt, Wyo, 66-; chmn, Gov. Adv. Coun. Agr, 68- Mil. Serv: Entered as Pvt, Marines, 55, released as Cpl, 57, after serv. in First Marine Div, Korean Theatre, 56-57. Mem: Gamma Sigma Delta; Mason; Scottish Rite; Am. Nat. Cattlemen's Asn; Wyo. Stock Growers Asn; Am. Legion. Outstanding Civic Leader of America, 67. Mailing Add: Box 5, Lusk, Wyo. 82225.

DARSEY, ELTON A. D
Mem, La. Dem. State Cent. Cmt.
b. Houma, La, 1/26/08; s. Aurestile O. Darsey and Angele Malbrough D; m. 8/14/40 to Clothilde Ostendorf. Educ: Loyola Univ, LL.B, 35; Sigma Nu Phi. Polit. & Govt. Pos: Mem, Terrebonne Parish Dem. Exec. Cmt, La, 40-, chmn, 50-; city attorney, Houma, 46-62; mem, La. Dem. State Cent. Cmt, 64- Mem: Am. Bar Asn; Am. Judicature Soc; La. State Bar Asn; Terrebonne Bar Asn. Legal Res: 125 Cedar St, Houma, La. 70360. Mailing Add: P.O. Box 982, Houma, La. 70361.

DARST, STEPHEN D
b. St. Louis, Mo, 7/19/33; s. James Edward Darst and Katharine Daly D; m. 6/30/63 to Doris J. Gissy; c. Verena Caroline, Elizabeth Standish; Amy Brooke and Doris Jeanne. Educ: St. Louis Univ, B.S, 57. Polit. & Govt. Pos: Former alderman, 25th Ward, St. Louis, Mo; Mo. campaign mgr, McCarthy for Pres. Campaign, 68. Bus. & Prof. Pos: Reporter, St. Louis Globe-Democrat, 58-64; St. Louis Rev, 64- Mil. Serv: Entered as Cadet, Navy, 53, released as Airman, 55. Rel: Roman Catholic. Mailing Add: 22 Washington Terr, St. Louis, Mo. 63112.

DARTLAND, WALTER T. D
b. Detroit, Mich, 1/17/35; s. Walter L. Dartland and Angeline Tkaczyk D; m. 6/3/61 to Florence Anna Marie McNicholas; c. Mark Kevin, Dorothy Marie and Christopher Michael. Educ: Rensselaer Polytech. Inst, B.S.M.E; Univ. Mich, LL.B, Louvain Univ, cert. philos; Pi Tau Sigma; Tau Beta Pi. Polit. & Govt. Pos: Friend of court, 12th Judicial Dist, Mich, 63-; prosecuting attorney, Houghton Co, Mich, 65- Bus. & Prof. Pos: Assoc, Law Firm of Messner & LaBine, Houghton, Mich, 63-65; attorney, Ford Motor Co, Gear and Axle Div. of Timken Co. and Allison Div. of Gen. Motors Corp. Mil. Serv: Entered as 2nd Lt, Marine Corps, 57, released as 1st Lt, 59, after serv. in 3rd Marine Div, Far East. Mem: Soc. of Automotive Engrs; Am. Soc. of Mech. Engrs; Am. Bar Asn; State Bar of Mich; Copper Country Bar Asn; Nat. Asn. of Dist. Attorneys; Mich. Asn. of Prosecuting Attorneys; Mich. Friend of Court Asn; UPCAP-EOA; del, chmn. of Houghton-Baraga-Keeweenaw Commun. Action Agency; pres, Keeweenaw Playhouse Guild; Kiwanis. Rel: Catholic. Legal Res: Star Route, Box 1, Chassell, Mich. 49916. Mailing Add: 416 Sheldon Ave, Houghton, Mich. 49930. (1967)

D'ATTORE, HARRIET J. R
R.I. State Rep.
b. West Warwick, R.I, 11/7/08; m. to Stephen D'Attore, wid. Educ: Schs. of West Warwick. Polit. & Govt. Pos: Mem, Women's Rep. Club, East Greenwich, R.I; R.I. State Rep, 60- Mem: East Greenwich Free Libr; Frenchtown Commun. Club; bd. incorporators, Kent Co. Mem. Hosp; Osteopathic Gen. Hosp. Auxiliary (exec. bd). Mailing Add: 35 Liberty St, East Greenwich, R.I. 02818. (1967)

DAUGHERTY, DAVID BLACK R
W.Va. State Del.
b. Huntington, W.Va, 1/6/36; s. Russell L. Daugherty and Huldah Parrish D; m. 8/17/57 to Mary Lee Walker; c. Elizabeth Parrish, Rebecca Susan and Amy Walker. Educ: Marshall Univ, A.B, 58; W.Va. Univ. Col. of Law, LL.B, 61; Kappa Alpha Order. Polit. & Govt. Pos: W.Va. State Del, 69- Bus. & Prof. Pos: Lawyer, Huntington, W.Va, 61-; divorce cmnr, Cabell Co. Domestic Rels. Court, 68. Mem: Cabell Co. Bar Asn.(mem. law libr. cmt, 65-66, admissions cmt, 66-67); W.Va. Bar Asn; W.Va. State Bar; Elks; Jr. C. of C; YMCA; MEAD (pres). Rel: Presbyterian; Deacon. Legal Res: 1635 Glenway Lane, Huntington, W.Va. 25701. Mailing Add: 737 Fifth Ave, Huntington, W.Va. 25701.

DAUGHERTY, DAVID LEROY R
Secy, Ind. State Senate
b. Bluffton, Ind, 6/18/42; s. Haskiel Leroy Daugherty and Martha Holmes D; m. 9/24/63 to Carolyn Jane Grover; c. Kathy Joan and Jeffrey Leroy. Educ: Ind. Inst. Tech, 2 years; Alpha Omega Tau. Polit. & Govt. Pos: Chmn, Wells Co. Young Rep, Ind, 66; chmn, Wells Co. Rep. Party, 66-; secy, Ind. State Senate, 69- Bus. & Prof. Pos: Sales mgr, Daugherty Equip. Co, Warren, Ind, 64- Mem: Ind. Implement Dealers Asn; Ind. Farm Equip. Asn. Sagamore of the Wabash, 69. Rel: Church of Christ. Mailing Add: Box 202, Liberty Center, Ind. 46766.

DAUGHERTY, JOHN BALCOM R
Chmn, Benzie Co. Rep. Cmt, Mich.
b. Pontiac, Mich, 1/26/32; s. Burton Perry Daugherty and Eloise Marie Le Blanc D; m. 12/2/61 to Gail Florence Anderson; c. John Andrew, Gayle Marie and Matthew James. Educ: Univ. Mich, B.A, 53; Detroit Col. Law, J.D, 58; N.Y. Univ, LL.M, 59; Alpha Tau Omega; Delta Theta Phi. Polit. & Govt. Pos: Prosecuting attorney, Benzie Co, Mich, 63-69; chmn, Benzie Co. Rep. Cmt, 69- Bus. & Prof. Pos: Assoc, Amberg, Law & Fallon, Grand Rapids, Mich, 59-61, Gerald Ford & Philip Buchen, 61; practicing attorney, self employed, Beulah, 61- Mil. Serv: Entered as Pvt, Marines, 53, released as Cpl, 55, after serv. in Second Marine Div. Mem: State Bar Mich; Am. Judicature Soc; Mich. Acad. Sci, Arts & Letters; F&AM (past master); Frankfort Rotary Club (pres); Marine Corps League. Rel: Lutheran. Legal Res: 3072 Warren Rd, Beulah, Mich. 49617. Mailing Add: 263 Benzie Blvd, Beulah, Mich. 49617.

D'AURORA, MINO ROCCO D
W.Va. State Del.
b. Pettorano sul Gizio, Italy, 8/12/09; s. Giovano D'Aurora and Maria De-Stefano D; m. 1/2/61 to Pauline Mary Rhodes; c. Mary Ann, Giovino John, Joseph Anthony, Robert Martin and Paul Michael. Educ: Steubenville Bus. Col; Theta Chi Alpha. Polit. & Govt. Pos: Dep. assessor, Brooke Co, W.Va; mem, Follansbee City Coun, 8 years; W.Va. State Del, 58- Bus. & Prof. Pos: Employee, steel co, 35 years, Ohio Indust. Plant. Mem: Eagles (past Worthy pres); Moose; Sons of Italy; Garibaldi Club; K. of C; Knights of St. Anthony; Knights of St. George; Cedar Lodge; USW; co-chmn, Follansbee Yuletide Cmt. Rel: Catholic. Mailing Add: 937 Jefferson St, Follansbee, W.Va. 26037. (1967)

DAVENNY, ROBERT ALTON R
Rep. Nat. Committeeman, Alaska
b. Edmonds, Wash, 12/16/14; s. Alton Davenny and Olive Meyer D; m. 3/19/55 to Mary Katherine Mendenhall; c. Diane Dee and Robert Alton. Educ: Univ. Wash, 31-34. Polit. & Govt. Pos: Senate dist. Rep. finance chmn, Fairbanks, Alaska, 56-57; state Rep. finance chmn, 58-65; Rep. state chmn, 65-69; Rep. Nat. Committeeman, Alaska, 69- Bus. & Prof. Pos: Pres, Thermo-Engr. Corp, 46-52, R.A. Davenny & Assoc, Inc, 53-, Equip. Leasing Corp, 66- and Insulating & Fiberglass, Inc, 69- Mil. Serv: Entered as Seaman, Navy, 42, released as Metalsmith 1/C, 46, after serv. in ETO and Pac. Theatre. Mem: Elks; Shrine. Rel: Presbyterian. Legal Res: 2414 Susitna Dr, Anchorage, Alaska 99503. Mailing Add: Box 4-2050, Anchorage, Alaska 99503.

DAVENPORT, JOHN EDWIN D
Chmn, Nash Co. Dem. Exec. Cmt, N.C.
b. Nashville, N.C, 4/28/28; s. Louis Ludford Davenport and Bybe Rogers D;

m. 10/10/59 to Mary Elizabeth Pope; c. Mary Elizabeth and Wynn Newman. Educ: Univ. N.C, Chapel Hill, A.B, 48 and LL.B, 51; George Wash. Univ, summer 50; Delta Theta Phi. Polit. & Govt. Pos: Col. organizer, N.C. Young Dem, 54; pres, Nash Co. Young Dem, 55; solicitor, Recorder's Court, Nash Co, 56-57; real property attorney, State of N.C, 57-59; mem, N.C. State Dem. Exec. Cmt, 66; chmn, Nash Co. Dem. Exec. Cmt, 66- Bus. & Prof. Pos: Dist. chancellor, Delta Theta Phi, N.C, 57-; pres, Nashville Indust. Develop. Corp, currently. Mil. Serv: Entered as Pvt, Air Force, 51, released as 1st Lt, 53, after serv. in Hq. Squadron, Parks Air Force Base, 52-53; Air Force Res, Capt.(Ret). Mem: Am. and N.C. Bar Asns; N.C. State Bar; Inc; Nash-Edgecombe Bar Asn.(secy, 54, v.pres, 69, pres, 70); Seventh Judicial Dist. Bar Asn; Am. Legion; AF&AM; N.C. Jr. C. of C.(v.pres); Nashville Jr. C. of C.(pres). Outstanding Young Man of Year, 56. Rel: Methodist. Legal Res: Highway 64 E, Nashville, N.C. 27856. Mailing Add: P.O. Drawer 988, Nashville, N.C. 27856.

DAVENPORT, RAYMOND WILSON, JR. D
b. El Paso, Tex, 7/9/29; s. Raymond Wilson Davenport and Thelma Grace English D; m. 10/5/51 to Marilyn Joan O'Sullivan; c. Raymond, III, W. Michael, Brian P. and Mark G. Educ: Tex. West Col, B.B.A, 51; Univ. N.Mex. Sch. Law, J.D, 67; Delta Sigma Pi; Sigma Alpha Epsilon. Polit. & Govt. Pos: N.Mex. State Rep, 61-69, mem, Cmn. on Intergovt. Coop. and West Interstate Cmt. on Hwy. Policy Probs, N.Mex. House of Rep, 63-69, chmn, Ways and Means Cmt. and v.chmn, Judiciary Cmt, 65-69; mem, Dona Ana Co. Dem. Cent. Cmt, N.Mex, 63-69. Mil. Serv: Entered as Pvt, Marine Corps, 46, released as S/Sgt, 52, after serv. in Marine Aviation Air Traffic Control, U.S; Victory and Nat. Defense Medals. Rel: Catholic. Mailing Add: 1325 Mesilla St, Las Cruces, N.Mex. 88001. (1967)

DAVES, JOEL T. F
b. Atlanta, Ga, 7/14/28; m. to Katherine Paty; c. Joel T. IV, Christian Shannon Paty, B.F. Paty. Educ: Univ. of S, A.B, 1950, Univ. Fla, LL.B, 1953. Polit. & Govt. Pos: Fla. State Rep, 64-66; Palm Beach Co. Solicitor, 59-64. Bus. & Prof. Pos: Attorney. Mil. Serv: U.S.M.C, 53-55; Maj, U.S.M.C.R. Mem: Kiwanis; Am. Legion; Elks. Rel: Episcopalian. Mailing Add: 1302 Chandler Rd, West Palm Beach, Fla. 33406. (1967)

DAVEY, MARY CURTIS R
City Councilman, Los Altos Hills, Calif.
b. Chicago, Ill, 5/29/30; d. Dr. George Curtis and Lucile Atcherson C; m. Jack Proctor Davey, Jr; c. John, III, Kit, and Curt. Educ: Smith Col, B.A, 52. Polit. & Govt. Pos: Mem, Calif. Rep. State Cent. Cmt, 63-; city councilman, Los Altos Hills, Calif, 66- and vice mayor, 67-68; mem, Santa Clara Co. Inter-City Coun. and Mayors Cmt, 66-68; town rep, Asn. of Bay Area Govt, 66- Mem: Pres, Soc. Planning Coun. of Santa Clara Co; pres, Space Sci. Cent. Adv. Cmt, Foothill Col. Dist; bd. mem, Cmt. for Green Foothills, Calif. Rep. League; Jr. League of Palo Alto; NAACP; League of Women Voters; Nature Conservancy; Smith Col. Club; Citizens for Fair Housing; life mem. Sierra Club; Calif. Tomorrow. Citizen of the Year, Philco-Ford Corp, 68. Rel: Protestant. Mailing Add: 12645 La Cresta Dr, Los Altos Hills, Calif. 94022.

DAVEY, PATRICK JAMES D
Chmn, Greeley Co. Dem. Party, Nebr.
b. Greeley, Nebr, 7/12/38; s. Francis Eugene Davey and Mary Louise Clark D; single. Educ: Sacred Heart High Sch, Greeley, Nebr, grad, 56. Polit. & Govt. Pos: Secy, Greeley Co. Dem. Party, Nebr, 67-68, chmn, 68- Mil. Serv: Entered as Seaman Recruit, Navy, 56, released as AG-3, 59, after serv. at Naval Air Sta, Brown Field, 57-59; Good Conduct Medal; Expert Pistol and Expert Rifle Medals. Mem: UPWA; Elks; grand knight, K. of C, 68- Rel: Catholic. Mailing Add: P.O. Box 307, Greeley, Nebr. 68842.

DAVID, THOMAS O. D
Co. Attorney, Blaine, Thomas and Hooker Counties, Nebr.
b. Utica, Nebr, 4/15/30; s. John Wiley David and Veronica Margaret McNiff D; m. 1/10/53 to Marilyn Joyce Christensen; c. Maureen Kay, Teresa Anne, Kathleen Mary, Diana Sue, Janet Marie and Laura Elizabeth. Educ: Univ. Nebr, Lincoln, B.S, 58; Creighton Univ, J.D, 59; Delta Theta Phi. Polit. & Govt. Pos: Chmn, Nebr. State Young Dem, 60-62; chmn, Lincoln Co. Young Dem, 62-63 and Thomas Co. Young Dem, 68-69; co. attorney, Blaines, Thomas and Hooker Counties, 63- Mil. Serv: Entered as Pvt, Marine Corps, 52, released as Cpl, 54, after serv. in Ninth Marines, Far East, 53-54; Unit Citation; UN Ribbon; Korean Ribbon. Mem: Pres, Lincoln Co. Bar Asn, 60-61; Am. Trial Lawyers Asn; Nat. Dist. Attorneys Asn; Elks; VFW; Am. Legion. Rel: Catholic. Mailing Add: Court House, Thedford, Nebr. 69166.

DAVIDOFF, GILBERT D
b. Brooklyn, N.Y, 9/23/34; s. Max Davidowitz and Regina Hudes D; m. 3/23/58 to Sandra Eilender; c. Risë, Alyssa and Elihu. Educ: Yeshiva Col, B.A, 55; Long Island Univ, Brooklyn, 59; New York Univ, to Ph.D, 62-66; founder, Young Dems, Yeshiva Col. Polit. & Govt. Pos: Numerous campaign cmts; alternate del, N.Y. Dem. Conv, 58, 60, 62 & 64 and del, 66; mem, Joint Legis. Cmt. Educ, 66-67; mem, Joint Legis. Cmt. Higher Educ, 67-68; alternate del, Dem. Nat. Conv, 68; educ. adv, Assemblyman Leonard Silverman, 69- Bus. & Prof. Pos: Teacher, soc. studies, New Utrecht High Sch, N.Y, 57-64, dean of boys, 60-64 and coordinator of guid, 64-; teacher, soc. studies, Kamenitzer Mesivta of Boro Park, 63-68, asst. prin, 68-69 and headmaster, 69- Mem: N.Y. Asn. Guid. Counsr; United Fedn. Teachers; Yeshiva Col. Alumni Asn.(pres); founder and past chmn, Boro Park Sunset Park Ment. Health Coun. Citation for contribution to community, Yeshiva Univ; Citation, Boro Park Sunset Park Ment. Health Coun, 69. Rel: Hebrew. Mailing Add: 1444 50th St, Brooklyn, N.Y. 11219.

DAVIDOFF, PAUL D
b. New York, N.Y, 2/28/30; s. Bernard Davidoff and Mildred Cohn D; m. 12/23/64 to Linda Greenberg; c. Susan, Carla and Daniel. Educ: Allegheny Col, A.B, 52; Univ. Pa, M.C.P, 56 and LL.B, 61. Polit. & Govt. Pos: Chmn, Center City Reform Dem, Phila, Pa, 63-64; committeeman, Westchester Co. Dem. Party, N.Y, 67-; Dem. Cand, U.S. House Rep, 68; chmn, Concerned Dem. Larchmont-Mamaroneck, 68- Bus. & Prof. Pos: Town planner, New Canaan, Conn, 56-57; planner, Voorhees, Walker, Smith & Smith, New York, 57-58; assoc. prof. city and regional planning, Univ. Pa, 58-65; prof. and dir, urban planning prog, Hunter Col, 65-; prin, Suburban Action Inst, 69- Publ: 'A Choice Theory of Planning,' 61 and 'Advocacy and Pluralism in Planning,' 65, J. Am. Inst. Planners. Mem: Am. Inst. Planners; Planners for Equal Opportunity (mem. policy cmt). Mailing Add: 18 Forest Park Ave, Larchmont, N.Y. 10538.

DAVIDS, CRAIG E. D
Ariz. State Rep.
b. Charlotte, Mich, 4/7/19; s. Ernest G. Davids and Mary Craig D; m. 4/14/44 to Kathleen Hembroff. Educ: East. Mich. Univ, 38-40; Univ. Mich, A.B, 42, Law Sch, scholarship, 43-45, J.D. with distinction, 45; Pi Kappa Delta; Phi Kappa Phi; Barristers Soc. Polit. & Govt. Pos: Dem. Precinctman, Precinct 23, Pinal Co, Ariz, 66-68; Ariz. State Rep, Dist. 5, Pinal and Gila Co, 68- Publ: 'Equity Clean Hands Doctrine' 10/44 and 'Resulting Trusts and Statute of Frauds,' 12/44, Mich. Law Rev; 'Legal Limitations on Use of Chemical Analysis to Determine Intoxication, Mich. Bar J,' 4/46; plus others. Mem: Mich. Bar. Asn; Mich. Jr. Bar Asn. (chmn, 54-55); Retail Trade Asn, Coolidge, Ariz. (chmn, 65-66); Elks; C. of C. Distinguished Serv. Award, Mich. Jr. Bar Asn, 54-55. Rel: Presbyterian. Legal Res: Phoenix Highway, Coolidge, Ariz. 85228. Mailing Add: P.O. Box 246, Coolidge, Ariz. 85228.

DAVIDSON, CARLTON E. R
Ohio State Rep.
b. Ironton, Ohio, 6/26/08; s. Frank P. Davidson and Rebecca Baker D, both deceased; single. Educ: Tri-State Col. of Eng, B.A. in eng, 31; Univ. Cincinnati, B.S. in educ, 33; Rio Grande Col, 45; Ohio Univ, 60; Marshall Univ, 60-65; Beta Phi Sigma. Polit. & Govt. Pos: Mem, Precinct Rep. Cent. Cmt, Ohio, 32-42; engr. on construct. and survey, Ohio Hwy. Dept, 39-42; cmnr, Lawrence Co, 49-61; Ohio State Rep, 26th Dist, 60-, chmn, Health and Welfare Cmt, Ohio House of Rep, currently. Bus. & Prof. Pos: High sch. teacher and coach, Ohio Pub. Schs, 45-52; sch. adminstr, Lawrence Co. Sch. Dist, 52-60. Mil. Serv: Entered as Pvt, Army, 42, released as Cpl, 45, after serv. in 6th Inf. Div, S.Pac. Theater, 43-45; Capt, Ohio Defense Corps, 57-61; Am. and Asiatic Pac. Theater Campaign Ribbons; Good Conduct and Victory Medals. Mem: Ohio Southeast. Teacher Asn; Ohio State Teachers Asn; pres, Vet. Rep. Club, 47-48; DAV; VFW; Amvets; Am. Legion; 40 et 8; Eagles; Moose; Elks; Grange; United Commercial Travelers; Farm Bur; Tuberc. Asn; F&AM; nat, state and local humane socs. and fish and game asns. Hobbies: Oil Painting, Sculpture and Raising Fancy Chickens. Rel: Protestant. Mailing Add: 1816 Campbell Dr, Ironton, Ohio 45638.

DAVIDSON, CLAYTON C. D
W.Va. State Del.
b. Lexington, W.Va, 6/1/17; s. Elisha E. Davidson and Clara Roberts D; m. 1/11/43 to Edith Lawson; c. Carol Sue, Donetta Gay and Sheila Gayle. Educ: McDowell Co. Pub. Schs. Polit. & Govt. Pos: W.Va. State Del, 62- Bus. & Prof. Pos: Bus driver. Mem: Moose; pres, Trailways Bus Drivers Union, 14 years; Ky. Col. Rel: Christian Church. Mailing Add: 3057 Hughes St, Huntington, W.Va. 25704. (1967)

DAVIDSON, CURTIS VERNON D
Mo. State Rep.
b. Albany, Mo, 12/12/12; s. Charles Edward Davidson and Maude E. Hern D; m. 4/6/35 to Mary Elizabeth Catley; c. Donna Ruth (Mrs. Hutson), Patricia Elizabeth (Mrs. Vaughn) and Mary Kathleen. Educ: Henry Co. Pub. Schs; Mo. Auction Sch, Kansas City, Mo. Polit. & Govt. Pos: Mo. State Rep, 57- Bus. & Prof. Pos: Auctioneer and real estate broker, currently. Mem: Mason; Shrine; Optimists; Elks. Rel: Baptist. Mailing Add: 612 S. Second St, Clinton, Mo. 64735.

DAVIDSON, EVELYN TAYLOR D
b. Hearne, Tex, 5/16/21; d. A. E. Taylor and Annie Grubbs T; m. 11/18/39 to Arthur Rayburn Davidson; c. Lynn. Educ: Hardin Simmons Univ, 1 year; Tex. State Col. for Women, 1 year. Polit. & Govt. Pos: Mem. exec. bd, Colo. and Denver Young Dem, 49-56; nat. committeewoman, Colo. Young Dem, 53-55; precinct committeewoman, Denver, Colo. Dem. Party, 60; v.chmn, Colo. State Dem. Party, 61-65; del. and mem. credentials cmt, Dem. Nat. Conv, 64, del. and mem. rules cmt, 68; chief clerk, Colo. State House of Rep, 65-67; admin. asst. to Lt. Gov, Colo, 67- Bus. & Prof. Pos: Secy, Local 367, Oil Workers Union, 42-48, confidential secy. to pres, Oil, Chemical Workers Union, AFL-CIO, 49-56. Rel: Protestant. Mailing Add: 1840 S. Niagara Way, Denver, Colo. 80222.

DAVIDSON, IRWIN DELMORE D
Justice, Supreme Court of N.Y.
b. N.Y.C, 1/2/06; s. Lafayette Davidson and Tillie Bechstein D; m. 5/31/65 to Marion Doniger; c. James Sylvan and Mark Lewis. Educ: Wash. Sq. Col, B.S, 27; N.Y. Univ. Law Sch, LL.B, 28; Tau Delta Phi. Polit. & Govt. Pos: N.Y. State Assemblyman, 37-48; justice, Court of Spec. Sessions of N.Y, 49-54; U.S. Rep, N.Y, 55-56; justice, Supreme Court of N.Y, 57- Publ: 'The Jury is Still Out,' Harper's, 59. Mem: N.Y. Co. Lawyers' Asn; Asn. of the Bar of the City of N.Y; N.Y. State Bar Asn; Town Club of the City of N.Y; Young Men's Philanthropic League. Rel: Jewish. Legal Res: 785 Fifth Ave, New York, N.Y. 10022. Mailing Add: 100 Centre St, New York, N.Y. 10013.

DAVIDSON, JAMES TREAVER, JR. D
W.Va. State Del.
b. Mullens, W.Va, 12/24/36; s. James Treaver Davidson and Virginia Dunlap D; m. 9/20/61 to Patricia Louise Bateman; c. Jaye Tara. Educ: Concord Col, B.S, 58; Marshall Univ, M.A, 61, Ed.S, 67; Phi Delta Kappa; Phi Alpha Pi. Polit. & Govt. Pos: W.Va. State Del, Wyoming Co, 69- Bus. & Prof. Pos: Teacher, Wyoming Co. Bd. of Educ, 58-64, sec. prin, 64-69. Mem: Wyoming Co. Sec. Prin. Asn.(past pres); W.Va. Educ. Asn; Moose. Rel: Baptist. Mailing Add: 120 Park Ave, Mullens, W.Va. 25882.

DAVIDSON, MURIEL SaRELLS R
b. Niagara Falls, N.Y, 8/6/17; d. John Arnold Wilson and Cordelia Evans W; single. Educ: Niagara Falls High Sch, 4 years. Polit. & Govt. Pos: Committeeman, 13th Ward Rep. Party, 15th Dist, N.Y, currently; mem, 13th Ward Rep. Club, Fedn. of Rep. Women's Clubs and Past Pres. Club of Erie Co; legis. chmn, Metrop. Rep. Women's Club; mem, Masten Dist. Rep. Women's

Club; campaign worker, both Citizens for Eisenhower campaigns, Citizens for Rockefeller, Citizens for Nixon and Citizens for Goldwater, formerly; Rep. cand, N.Y. State Assembly, 65; Rep. cand. for Co. Legislator, 67; alternate del, Rep. Nat. Conv, 68; campaign worker, Citizens for Nixon, 68. Bus. & Prof. Pos: Subscriber serv. rep, Blue Cross of West. N.Y, Inc, 53- Mailing Add: 98 E. Delavan Ave, Buffalo, N.Y. 14208.

DAVIDSON, ROBERT C(AREY) D
b. St. Georges, Del, 5/24/09; s. Robert R. Lee Davidson and Mabel L. Jones D; m. 6/16/34 to Gertrude Winona Bright; c. Shirley Anne (Mrs. Costango), Kenneth Lee and Denise Priscilla (Mrs. White). Educ: Beacom Bus. Col; pres, Red Lion Hundred Dem. Club. Polit. & Govt. Pos: Del. State Sen, 64-66; Del. state rep, 58-64. Bus. & Prof. Pos: Owner-operator, Dairy Queen, 57-; serv. sta. operator, Gulf, 39-57. Mem: Mason. Rel: Presbyterian; Elder. Mailing Add: Box 38, St. Georges, Del. 19733. (1967)

DAVIDSON, W. K. 'KENNY' R
Ill. State Sen.
b. Toledo, Iowa, 6/30/04; m. to Elsie Marie Davis. Educ: Bradley Univ, Peoria, Ill. Polit. & Govt. Pos: Former mem, City Coun, Kewanee, Ill; former Ill. State Rep; Ill. State Sen, 68- Bus. & Prof. Pos: V.pres, Kewanee Fed. Savings and Loan Asn; operator of Davidson's Restaurant, Kewanee, since 31; pres, Ill. State Restaurant Asn, 47, mem. bd. dirs. Mem: Elks; Moline Consistory; Mohammed Shrine. Rel: Presbyterian. Mailing Add: 111½ E. Second St, Kewanee, Ill. 61443.

DAVIDSON, WILLIAM JOHN R
Mem, Rep. State Cmt, Ga.
b. Norfolk, Va, 8/24/28; s. Lloyd Wallace Davidson and Sophia Schaeffer D; m. 6/3/50 to Mary Elizabeth Cox; c. Dale Lee, Toni Leigh, Don Le and Terry L. Educ: Ga. State Col, 65. Polit. & Govt. Pos: Rep. precinct chmn, Smyrna, Ga, 66; mem, Cobb Co. Rep. Cmt, 66- and first v.chmn, 68; mem, Ga. State Rep. Cmt. and Seventh Cong. Dist. Rep. Cmt, 67-; alternate del, Rep. Nat. Conv, 68. Bus. & Prof. Pos: Dept. mgr, Lockheed-Georgia Company, Marietta, 52- Mil. Serv: Entered as A/S, Navy, 46, released as Aviation Photographe 3/C, 48, after serv. in Utility Squadron Four, U.S. Atlantic Fleet, 47-48. Mem: Industry Film Producers Asn; Civitan Int; Moose. Rel: Presbyterian. Mailing Add: 891 Brentwood Dr. S.E, Smyrna, Ga. 30080.

DAVIE, JOHN TURNEY D
Chmn, Fulton Co. Dem. Cmt, Ky.
b. Hickman, Ky, 5/28/11; s. Jones Roper Davie and Faye Saunders D; m. 2/12/41 to Esther Jane Byrd; c. John Wayne and Joyce Lynn. Educ: Sylvan Shade High Sch, 30. Polit. & Govt. Pos: Fulton Co. Sheriff, Ky, 50-54; field agent, Ky. State Alcoholic Dept, State Dept, 56-60; supvr, Fulton Co. Road Dept, 66-68; chmn, Fulton Co. Dem. Cmt, 54- Bus. & Prof. Pos: Farm owner & operator, 30-; agent, Davie Ins. Agency, 62- Mem: Hon. mem, Ky. Sheriff's Asn; C. of C; Ky. Farm Bur; Moose; Hickman Recreational Club. Rel: First Christian Church. Mailing Add: R.R. 4, Hickman, Ky. 42050.

DAVIES, JOHN THOMAS 'JACK' DFL
Minn. State Sen.
b. Harvey, N.Dak, 1/6/32; s. Charles Evan Davies and Marian Healy D; m. to Patricia Ann McAndrews; c. Elizabeth Ann, Ted Elliott and John Thomas, III. Educ: Itasca Jr. Col, A.A, 52; Univ. Minn, B.A, 54, J.D, 60. Polit. & Govt. Pos: Minn. State Sen, 59-; cmnr, Uniform State Laws, 66- Bus. & Prof. Pos: Sports ed, KSTP-TV, 56-57; pvt. law practice, Minneapolis, Minn, 61-65; attorney, Fine, Simon and Schneider, 62-65; registr. and assoc. prof, William Mitchell Col. of Law, 65- Mil. Serv: Entered as Pvt, Army, 54, released as Pfc, 56, after serv. in Army Intel, Japan and Korea. Mem: Hennepin Co. and Minn. Bar Asns. Rel: Unitarian. Mailing Add: 2300 Seabury Ave, Minneapolis, Minn. 55406.

DAVIGNON, RAYMOND LEO D
R.I. State Rep.
b. Central Falls, R.I. 1/23/20; m. to Doris D; c. Dolores (Mrs. Scott Kehoe), Lucille J. and Keith R. Educ: Brown Univ; Tabbutt-Hubbard Bus. Sch, 39. Polit. & Govt. Pos: R.I. State Rep, 54-; v.chmn, State Judiciary Cmt, 68. Bus. & Prof. Pos: Real Estate; Ins; bd. of dirs, Pawtucket Bd. of Realtors; bd. of dirs, Pawtucket C. of C, 68-; mem. credit cmt, Pawtucket Credit Union, currently. Mil. Serv: World War II, Chief Petty Officer, U.S. Navy, 42-45, Atlantic and Pac. Mem: Le Foyer; bd. of corporators, Notre Dame Hosp. and Pawtucket Inst. for Savings; Elks. Rel: Catholic. Mailing Add: 150 Crest Dr, Pawtucket, R.I. 02861.

DAVIS, ANN M. R
Mem, Sixth Cong. Dist. Rep. Exec. Cmt, Tenn.
b. Humphreys Co, Tenn, 4/24/14; d. Andrew J. James and Annie Gray J; m. 4/17/54 to William Claude Davis; c. Glynn K, Wayne L. and Bond Dell Jackson. Educ: High Sch, 31-32. Polit. & Govt. Pos: Mem, Humphreys Co. Rep. Exec. Cmt, Tenn, 55-, secy, 62, chmn, 66-, mem, Co. Elec. Cmn. Humphreys Co, 65-66; campaign mgr, Rep. Campaign for Sen. Howard Baker, Jr, Humpreys, Perry, Lewis and Hickman Co, 66; campaign mgr, President Nixon for Humphreys Co, 60 & 68; U.S. Cmnr, Mid. Dist. Tenn, 68; mem, Sixth Cong. Dist. Rep. Exec. Cmt, 68- Army Navy E Award, 43. Rel: Baptist. Mailing Add: Hurricane Mills, Tenn. 37078.

DAVIS, BETH OLGA R
b. Canaan, Vt, 10/28/09; m. to Crawford E. Davis; c. Two sons, One daughter. Educ: Mt. Notre Dame Convent, Sherbrooke, Que, Can; St. Mary's, Island Pond, bus. course. Polit. & Govt. Pos: Town auditor, East Burke, Vt; treas, East Burke Rep. Town Cmt; chmn, Rep. Ladies Club; Vt. State Rep, 65-67. Bus. & Prof. Pos: Clerk. Mem: Rebekah; United Workers of East Burke Fed. Church; Burke Mt. Club. Rel: Methodist. Mailing Add: East Burke, Vt. 05832. (1967)

DAVIS, C. H. 'CLIFF' R
Wyo. State Rep.
b. Thomas, Okla, 1/31/08; m. to Elma; c. Three. Educ: High Sch. Polit. & Govt. Pos: Co. cmnr, Wyo; mem, High Sch. Bd, 6 years; mem, State Aeronaut. Cmt; Wyo. State Rep, currently. Bus. & Prof. Pos: Rancher and auto dealer. Mem: F.H.A. State Cmt; Elks; Farm Bur; Eagles; Rotary; Odd Fellows; Mason; Shrine; Wyo. Stock Growers Asn. Rel: Presbyterian. Mailing Add: 501 Miller St, Gillette, Wyo. 82716. (1967)

DAVIS, CHARLES E, JR. R
Fla. State Rep.
b. Los Angeles, Calif, 6/18/32; s. Charles E. Davis and Adelaide Plumb D; m. 6/15/57 to Jerry Floyd; c. Laura Elizabeth, Charles Bradford and Mary Catherine. Educ: Stanford Univ, B.A, 55; Univ. South. Calif. Grad. Sch. Bus, 58-61. Polit. & Govt. Pos: Chmn, Indian River Co. Young Rep, Fla, 66-67; Fla. State Rep, 67-; chmn, Brevard, Indian River and Okeechobee counties Legis. Del, 68-69; mem. bd. gov, Nat. Soc. State Legislators, 68-69. Bus. & Prof. Pos: Asst. to the v.pres, Meterology Research, Inc, Altadena, Calif, 59-60; v.pres. and bus. mgr, Bruce L. Baird, Inc, Garden Grove, Calif, 61-63; assoc. and partner Rey Neville, Realtor, Vero Beach, Fla, 64-67; realtor, Charles E. Davis, Jr, 67- Mil. Serv: Entered as Pvt, Army, 55, released as Sp-4, 57, after serv. in Counter Intel. Corps, Mil. Dist. Wash. Mem: Vero Beach Bd. Realtors; Nat. Asn. Real Estate Bds; Fla. Asn. Realtors; Am. Ord. Asn; Int. Oceanographic Found; Nat. Soc. State Legislators; Int. Real Estate Fedn; Nat. Inst. Real Estate Brokers; Riomar Bay Yacht Club; Taxpayers Asn. Indian River Co. Rel: Protestant. Legal Res: 726 Riomar Dr, Vero Beach, Fla. 32960. Mailing Add: P.O. Box 3051, Station 1, Vero Beach, Fla. 32960.

DAVIS, CHARLES J. R
b. Eaton Co, Mich, 12/29/10; married; c. John C. and Julie Caltrider. Educ: Olivet Col, grad; Mich. State Univ, B.S. Polit. & Govt. Pos: Served on first bd. dirs, Ingham Co. Soil Conserv. Dist, Mich; mem, Ingham Co. Bd. of Educ, 12 years; mem, Agr. Stabilization & Conserv. Cmn. of Mich, 4 years; del, Mich. Rep. Constitutional Conv; Mich. State Rep, 62-69. Bus. & Prof. Pos: Past pres, Lansing Dairy Co; v.pres, McDonald Dairy; farmer and businessman. Mem: Am. Dairy Asn. of Mich.(bd. dirs and exec. cmt); past pres, Ingham Co. Farm Bur. Rel: Baptist; Trustee. Mailing Add: Onondaga, Mich. 49264. (1967)

DAVIS, CHARLES RUSSELL D
Chmn, Cass Co. Dem. Exec. Cmt, Tex.
b. Paris, Tex, 2/1/09; s. Henry Bert Davis and Lou Elizabeth Moseley D; m. 2/12/41 to Leita Mary Reeder; c. James Henry and Ernestine Elizabeth (Betsy). Educ: Marshall Coll, A.A, 31; Am. Inst. Banking, Rutgers Univ, 4 years, cert; Dallas Inst. Mortuary Sci, 1 year, licensed mortician. Polit. & Govt. Pos: Chmn, Cass Co. Dem. Exec. Cmt, Tex, 64-; former mayor, Hughes Springs, Tex. Bus. & Prof. Pos: Teller, First Nat. Bank, Marshall, Tex, 32-42; partner, Reeder-Watson-Davis Gen. Merchandise, 46-50; partner and mortician, Reeder-Watson-Davis Funeral Home, 50-67, owner, 68- Mil. Serv: Entered as Pvt, Army Ord. Corps, 42, released as Cpl, 45, after serving in 66th Ord, N. Africa. and ETO, 42-45. Mem: Lions; Cass Co. Cattlemens Asn; E. Tex. Funeral Dirs. Asn. Rel: Methodist. Legal Res: 113 N. Keasler St, Hughes Springs, Tex. 75656. Mailing Add: P.O. Box 488, Hughes Springs, Tex. 75656.

DAVIS, CLARENCE LEONARD D
b. Hayesville, N.C, 10/17/98; s. Oscar Davis and Lillie Sanderson D. (deceased); m. 7/26/26 to Callie Thompson. Educ: 10th Grade High Sch. Polit. & Govt. Pos: Mem, N.C. State Dem. Exec. Cmt, 48-65; chmn, Clay Co. Dem. Exec. Cmt, 34-40. Bus. & Prof. Pos: Mgr, Taxi, 23-65. Rel: Protestant. Mailing Add: P.O. Box 23, Hayesville, N.C. 29804. (1967)

DAVIS, CLETUS ADDISON, JR. D
Tex. State Rep.
b. Houston, Tex, 2/21/30; s. Cletus Addison Davis, Sr. and Bertha Beulah Smith D; m. 8/31/57 to Francis Elizabeth Kolliker; c. Kelley and Kyle Addison. Educ: Allen Mil. Acad. Bryan, Tex, 48-50; Tex. West. Col, 50-53, Geology; S.Tex. Law Sch, LL.B, 62; Sigma Gamma Epsilon; secy, Sr. Class; pres, Lettermen's Club; Phi Alpha Delta. Polit. & Govt. Pos: Tex. State Rep, Harris Co, 67- Bus. & Prof. Pos: Jr. geologist, El Paso Natural Gas Co, Tex, 53-54; dist. sales mgr, Hamilton Mgt. Corp, Houston, 56-57; exploration geologist, Trunkline Gas Co, Lafayette, La, 57-58; dist. sales mgr, Gulf Publ. Co, Houston, Tex, 58-63; asst. dist. attorney, Harris Co. Dist. Attorney's Off, 63-66; partner in gen. law practice, Boswell and O'Toole, 67- Mil. Serv: Entered as 2nd Lt, Army, 54, released as 1st Lt, 56, after serv. in Anti-aircraft and guided missile, U.S, Fort Bliss, Tex, 54-56. Mem: Am, Tex, Houston and Houston Jr. Bar Asns. Chmn, Trial by Jury U.S. Cmt, Award of Merit. Rel: Presbyterian. Legal Res: 14231 Carolcrest, Houston, Tex. 77024. Mailing Add: Suite 806, Central National Bank Bldg, 2100 Travis, Houston, Tex. 77002.

DAVIS, CLIFFORD McKINLEY R
Chmn, Harrison Co. Rep. Exec. Cmt, W.Va.
b. Blandville, W.Va, 12/10/96; s. Linville Bee Davis and Dora Elizabeth Cozad D; m. 12/25/22 to Pearl Morrison. Educ: Salem Col, A.B, 23; W.Va. Univ, M.A, 39; Kappa Delta Pi. Polit. & Govt. Pos: Chmn, Harrison Co. Rep. Exec. Cmt, W.Va, 69- Bus. & Prof. Pos: Teacher hist. and mod. probs, Victory High Sch, Clarksburg, W.Va, 22-35; prin, Carlile Sch, 35-41, Sardis Jr. High Sch. and Grade Sch, 41-42 and Mt. Clare Jr. High Sch. and Grade Sch, 42-65; retired. Mem: W.Va. and Nat. Educ. Asns; adv. coun, DeMolay; AF&AM; RAM; K.T; AAONMS; Ancient Order of the Camel Herders, Past High Priest of Adoniram Chap. 11 and Past Royal Patron of Clarksburg Court 3; Order of the Amaranth; Lions. Rel: Baptist; Deacon, Clarksburg Baptist Church. Legal Res: Davisson Run, Clarksburg, W.Va. 26301. Mailing Add: 650 Empire Bldg, P.O. Box 2066, Clarksburg, W.Va. 26301.

DAVIS, CORNEAL A. D
Ill. State Rep.
b. New Vicksburg, Miss, 8/28/00; s. Dudly D. Davis and Pearl D; m. 12/24/21 to Elma Howell; c. Yvonne (Mrs. Maule). Educ: Tougaloo Col, 17; John Marshall Sch. Law, 48; Moody Bible Inst; Omega Psi Phi. Polit. & Govt. Pos: Ill. State Rep, 41-66 & 69-, chmn, Cmt. on Pub. Aid, Pub. Health and Pub. Welfare, Ill. House of Rep; pres, Second Ward Dem. Orgn, Ill; mem, Ill. Dem. State Cent. Cmt, currently; mem, Bd. of Local Improv, 66- Mil. Serv: Entered as Pvt, Army, 17, released as Cpl, 19, after serv. in Eighth Inf, Ill. Nat. Guard Co. D, Machine Gun Bn, Meuse Argonne Offense, 18. Mem: Mason

(33°); bd. dirs, Wabash YMCA and McKinley Commun. Serv: past Imperial Potentate, Prince Hall Shrines. Rel: Methodist; Asst. Minister. Mailing Add: 3223 S. Calumet Ave, Chicago, Ill. 60616. (1967)

DAVIS, CURTIS LORAN D
Chmn, Elliott Co. Dem. Cmt, Ky.
b. Sandy Hook, Ky, 8/28/10; s. David Davis and Mary Ward D; m. 12/14/29 to Delma Redwine; c. David Roger and Orval Curtis. Educ: Morehead State Univ. Polit. & Govt. Pos: Chmn, Elliott Co. Dem. Cmt, Ky, 60- Bus. & Prof. Pos: Supt, Elliott Co. Bd. Educ, 42-; pres, Davis Contracting Co, Inc, 48- Mil. Serv: Entered as Lt.(jg), Navy, 43, released as Lt, 46, after serv. in S.Pac; Asiatic-Pac. Ribbon. Mem: Pres, East. Ky. Educ. Asn, 48-49; comdr, Am. Legion Post, Sandy Hook; Ky. Educ. Asn; Rotary Int; Mason. Rel: Baptist. Mailing Add: Sandy Hook, Ky. 41171.

DAVIS, DAVID R
b. Bloomington, Ill, 7/29/06; s. David Davis and Edith Melluish D; m. 8/16/41 to Nancy L. Sandstrom; c. Alice M.(Mrs. Cates), David V. and Elizabeth G. Educ: Williams Col, B.A, 28; Univ. S.Dak, LL,B, 31; Theta Chi. Polit. & Govt. Pos: Ill. State Sen, 26th Dist, 53-67, v.chmn, Sch. Probs. Cmn, 53-61, mem, 53-66, mem, Agr, Banks and Savings and Loan Asn, Ins, Judiciary and Reapportionment Cmts. and v.chmn, Rules Cmt, 53-67, mem, Ill. Cmn. on Higher Educ, 54-57, mem, Bd. Aeronaut. Adv, 55-61, chmn, Ill. Cmn. on Intergovt. Coop, 57-67, chmn, Educ. Cmt, Ill. State Sen, 57-67, chmn, Cmt. on Midwest. Agr. Probs, 58-62, mem, Bd. of Gov, Coun. of State Govt, 60-67, chmn. bd. and v.chmn. coun, 63, v.chmn, Midwest. Conf, 64-65, chmn, 66, mem, Interstate Compact for Educ, 66. Bus. & Prof. Pos: Owner and operator of several farms in Cent. Ill; chmn. bd, Nat. Bank of Bloomington, Ill, 65- Mem: Am. and Ill. Bar Asns; pres, McLean Co. Bar Asn, 59; Bloomington Club; Bloomington Country Club; Great Lakes Cruising Club. Rel: Presbyterian. Legal Res: 1114 E. Monroe St, Bloomington, Ill. 61701. Mailing Add: 207 E. Jefferson St, Bloomington, Ill. 61701.

DAVIS, DEANE CHANDLER R
Gov, Vt.
b. East Barre, Vt, 11/7/00; s. Earl Russell Davis and Lois Hillary D; m. 6/14/24 to Corinne Eastman (deceased); c. Deane (deceased), Marian (Mrs. Frank R. Calcagni) and Thomas C; m. 7/5/52 to Marjorie Smith Conzelman. Educ: Boston Univ. Law Sch, LL.B, 22; Delta Theta Phi. Hon. LL.D, Univ. Vt, 57, Middlebury Col, 64 and Boston Univ, 69; Litt.D, Norwich Univ, 63. Polit. & Govt. Pos: Mem. city coun, Barre, Vt, 23-24, city attorney, 24-26 & 28-30; states attorney, Wash. Co, 26-28; Superior Judge, Vt, 31-36; del, Rep. Nat. Conv, 48 and mem. Resolutions Cmt; Gov, Vt, 69- Bus. & Prof. Pos: Attorney-at-law, Barre, Vt, 22-31; partner law firm, Wilson, Carver, Davis & Keyser, 36-40; gen. coun, Nat. Life Ins. Co. Montpelier, Vt, 40-43, v.pres. and gen. counsel, 43-50, pres. and dir, 50-66, chief exec. officer, 66-67, chmn. bd. dirs, 66-68, dir, 68- Publ: Life Insurance and Business Purchase Agreements, 45. Mem: Am. Bar Asn.(Vt. del. and mem. bd. gov); Vt. Bar Asn.(pres. and chmn. bd. of bar exam); Wash. Co. Bar Asn; pres, chmn. and dir. various cmts. and cmns. and conv, Life Ins. Asn. Am; chmn. and dir. various cmts, Inst. Life Ins; Am. Judicature Soc; dir, Mary Fletcher Hosp, Burlington; Vt. Develop. Credit Corp, New Hampshire-Vt. Physicians Serv, New Eng. Power Co, New Eng. Elec. System and Rock of Ages Corp; trustee, Cent. Vt. Med. Center, Inc, Boston Univ, Aldrich Pub. Libr, Bennington Col, New Eng. Kurn Hattin Homes, Inc, Norwich Univ, Vt. State Libr. and Vt. Col; assoc. trustee, Rehab. Center DeGoesbrian Unit, Med. Center Hosp. Vt; mem, Dairy Income Study Cmt; mem. adv. coun, Champlain Col. and Boston Univ. Law Sch; pres, Calvin Coolidge Mem. Found; mem. joint cmt, Practice of Law; dir, Gt. Vt. Asn; mem, Gt. Vt. Asn. Welcome Center Planning Cmt; dir, Vt. Heart Asn, Peoples Nat. Bank, Barre and Union Mutual Fire Ins. Co; chmn, Annual Brotherhood Banquet of Christians and Jews, 42-50; chmn, Cmt. Study Vt. State Govt; curator, Vt. His. Soc; mem. adv. bd. and budget cmt, Barre Unit, Salvation Army; mem. hon. Bd. Overseers, Old Sturbridge Village, Mass; mem. citizens adv. cmt, Univ. Vt. Col. Med; chmn, Cmt. Sch. Bldg. Aid, Vt; pres. and finance chmn, Vt. Arthritis & Rheumatism Found; pres, Vt. C. of C; incorporator, New Eng. Deaconess Hosp, Boston; chmn, Cmt. Selection for Rhodes Scholarships, Vt; Mason (33°); Scottish Rite; F&AM (Past Potentate, Mt. Sinai Temple 3); K. of P; Rotary; Vt. Soc. of Mayflower Descendants; pres, Vt. Morgan Horse Asn; v.pres, Green Mt. Horse Asn; pres, Morgan Horse Club. Man of the Year Award, Ins. Field Publ, 61; Vt. Bankers Asn. Award, 62; Cert. of Merit, SAR. Rel: Methodist. Legal Res: 5 Dyer Ave, Montpelier, Vt. Mailing Add: Office of the Governor, State Capitol, Montpelier, Vt. 05602.

DAVIS, DONALD C. R
b. Newport, Vt, 8/24/96; married: c. Two. Educ: Dartmouth Col, B.S; Boston Univ, grad. study. Polit. & Govt. Pos: Formerly N.H. State Rep; supvr. of checklist, Greenfield, N.H. Bus. & Prof. Pos: Ins. Co. mgr, retired. Mil. Serv: World War I. Mem: Greenfield Coffee Club; Mason. Rel: Protestant. Mailing Add: Olde Francestown Rd, Greenfield, N.H. 03047. (1967)

DAVIS, DONALD D. D
b. Webster Co, Mo, 7/14/18; m. 7/23/38 to Bertha Roberson; c. Donna Reese, Wanda, Jimmy. Educ: Webster Co. Schs. Polit. & Govt. Pos: Mo. State Rep, 62-66; circuit clerk, recorder of deeds, Webster Co, 54-62. Bus. & Prof. Pos: Farming; oil and serv. sta. bus; ins. Mailing Add: RFD 2, Niangua, Mo. 65713. (1967)

DAVIS, DONALD M. D
Pa. State Rep.
b. Fairchance, Pa, 6/6/15; s. Albert Callatin Davis and Bessie Myers D; m. 4/28/36 to Frances Hudock; c. Marlene (Mrs. Joseph Juriga) and Donald L. Educ: Georges Twp. High Sch, 28-32. Polit. & Govt. Pos: Pa. State Rep, 69- Bus. & Prof. Pos: Ins. agent, Metrop. Life, N.Y, 39-51; credit mgr, Cohen Furniture Co, Brownsville, Pa, 51- Mil. Serv: Entered as Pvt, Army, 44, released as 1st. Sgt, 46, after serving in Infantry K-9 Corps. Mem: Optomist Int; Am. Legion. Rel: Lutheran. Mailing Add: R.D. 2, Box 415A, Uniontown, Pa. 15401.

DAVIS, EARL THOMAS R
Ga. State Rep.
b. Toccoa, Ga, 8/24/34; s. Alfred Franklin Davis and Nina Ramey D; m. 6/5/55 to Elaine Richardson; c. Earl T, Jr. and Nina Jane. Educ: Univ. Ga, Atlanta Div, 1 year. Polit. & Govt. Pos: Dir, Ga. Young Rep. 65-66; chmn, Muscogee Co. Young Rep, Ga, 67; Ga. State Rep, Dist. 86, Post 1, 69- Bus. & Prof. Pos: Acct, Tex. Co, Atlanta, Ga; oil well logging engr, Baroid Div, Nat. Lead Co, Houston, Tex, 53-55; gen. salesman, Humble Oil & Ref. Co, Portland, Ore, 55-61; salesman, Standard Oil Co, Ky, 61- Mem: Lions; C. of C; Booster Club. Rel: Baptist. Mailing Add: 2321 Carson Dr, Columbus, Ga. 31906.

DAVIS, ED. N. R
b. Monango, N.Dak, 8/14/02; married; c. 4. Educ: Ellendale State Teachers' Col. Polit. & Govt. Pos: N.Dak. State Rep, 53-63. Mem: Farm Bur; Stockmen's Asn; Greater N.Dak. Asn. Mailing Add: Monango, N.Dak. 58471. (1967)

DAVIS, EDWIN LETTS D
b. Wrightstown, N.J, 5/18/12; s. Edwin Letts Davis and Sara Ridgway D; m. 4/11/37 to Martha Holmes McCoy. Educ: Rider Col, N.J. Polit. & Govt. Pos: Mem, Burlington Co. Dem. Club, N.J; councilman, Borough of Wrightstown, 36-46, assessor, 40-46, Mayor, 46-55; chmn, Pinelands Regional Planning Bd; pres, New Hanover Bd. of Educ; chmn, Burlington Co. Bd. of Taxation; del, Dem. Nat. Conv, 68. Bus. & Prof. Pos: Owner, Edwin L. Davis Agency Ins. and Real Estate, 47-; owner-partner, Edwin L. Davis & Co, Stock Broker, 57-; dir. and treas, Mercer Mutual Ins. Co, Pennington, N.J, currently; dir. of mech, Nat. Bank of Burlington Co, Burlington, currently. Mem: N.J. Asn. of Real Estates Bd; Nat. Asn. of Securities Dealers; Pyramid Lodge 92, F&AM, New Egypt, N.J. Rel: Methodist. Legal Res, 89 Ft. Dix St, Wrightstown, N.J. 08562. Mailing Add: 5 E. Main St, Wrightstown, N.J. 08562.

DAVIS, EMIL L. D
Chmn, Logan Co. Dem. Exec. Cmt, Ohio
b. Jackson Co, Ohio, 9/5/92; s. William McK. Davis and Clara McKinniss D; m. 8/20/33 to Lelia A. Hull; c. Virginia and George R. Shafer. Educ: Lima Cent. High Sch, grad, 11. Polit. & Govt. Pos: U.S. Postmaster, Lakeview, Ohio, 14-21, mem, Village Coun, 44-49, mayor, 50-65; chmn, Logan Co. Dem. Exec. Cmt, 64-; mem, Logan Co. Elec. Bd, 66- Mem: Mason; Scottish Rite. Rel: Protestant. Legal Res: Corner Market and Place, Lakeview, Ohio 43331. Mailing Add: Box 433, Lakeview, Ohio 43331.

DAVIS, FRANK H. R
Treas, Vt.
b. New York, N.Y, 6/13/10; m. to Virginia Hewitt; c. six and four grandchildren. Educ: Night courses, Columbia Univ. and Univ. Vt. Polit. & Govt. Pos: Former chmn. and treas, Burlington, Vt. and former treas, Chittenden Co; mem, Burlington Housing Cmt, 62-, v.chmn, 62-64, chmn, 64-; Vt. State Rep, 67-68, mem. Commerce Cmt, Vt. State House of Rep; Treas, Vt, 69- Bus. & Prof. Pos: With, E.I. Du Pont de Nemours, 29-31; chem, Fuller Rodney, 31-33; Brokerage, Carlisle Jacquelin, 33-42; owner, Self-Serv. Laundry, Vt, 47-55; acct. exec. A.M. Kidder & Co, 55-60, E.I. Du Pont, 60-63 and W.E. Hutton, 63-66. Mil. Serv: Entered as Ens, Coast Guard Res, 42, released as Lt.(sg), 45, after serv. in Atlantic and Pac; commanding officer, Coast Guard Cutter. Mem: Malletts Bay Boat Club; former dir, Lake Champlain Yacht Club. Rel: Congregational; former deacon, Col. St. Congregational Church, pres, 68- Mailing Add: 2 Tower Terr, Burlington, Vt. 05401.

DAVIS, FRANK W. R
Committeeman, Okla. State Rep. Party
b. Ada, Okla, 8/24/36; s. Roscoe Gladstone Davis and Neva Peck D; m. 8/12/61 to Kay Higginbotham; c. David and Paul. Educ: Univ. Ill, 56-57; East Cent. State Col, A.B, 58; Univ. Okla, LL.B, 59; Pi Kappa Delta. Polit. & Govt. Pos: Pres, League of Young Conservatives, East Cent. State Col, 55-56; chmn, Pontotoc Co. Rep. Party, Okla, 57-59; v.pres, Univ. Okla. Young Rep, 59; acting postmaster, Ada, 59-61; co. attorney, Logan Co, 61-65; chmn, Okla. State Rep. Party, Logan Co, 64-69, committeeman, 69- Bus. & Prof. Pos: Attorney-at-Law, 65- Mem: Okla. and Logan Co. Bar Asns; Lions. Rel: Methodist. Mailing Add: 1445 Fogarty, Guthrie, Okla. 73044.

DAVIS, FREDERICK HOWARD D
b. Wrightsville, Johnson Co, Ga, 5/22/15; s. John Thomas Davis and Bessie Brown D; m. to Robena Belcher; c. Martha Kay Roby, Donna Robena, Cherlyn Diana, Frederick Howard, Jr, Scott Gregory, Sharon Ruth and John Thomas. Educ: Pub. schs. of Wrightsville, Ga; studied law; admited Ga. Bar, 41. Polit. & Govt. Pos: Alderman, Wrightsville, Ga, 41; mayor, Brent, Ala, 60; del-at-lg, Dem. Nat. Conv, 60; Chief of Staff, State Militia, 62-66; Ala. State Rep, 63-66. Mil. Serv: Army, Capt, 42-46. Mem: Shrine; Mason; Am. Legion (Past Comdr). Descendant of colonial settlers of Va. Rel: Baptist. Mailing Add: Brent, Ala. 35034.

DAVIS, GEORGE E. R
Mem, N.Mex. Rep. State Cent. Cmt.
b. Tulsa, Okla, 5/2/97; s. Wilson Davis and Nora Tague D; wid. Educ: N. Mex. Normal Univ. Polit. & Govt. Pos: Former Rep. chmn, Precinct 13, N.Mex; mem, N.Mex. Rep. State Cent. Cmt, 52-; chmn, Curry Co. Rep. Party, 62; mem. exec. bd, N.Mex. Rep. Party, 65-66. Bus. & Prof. Pos: Owner and operator, ranching and farming interests, 28- Mil. Serv: Entered as Pvt, Army, 18, released as Disp. Asst, 97th Div. U.S, 19. Mem: Past mem, Am. Legion and Farm Bur. Rel: Methodist. Mailing Add: 2708 Wallace, Clovis, N.Mex. 88101. (1967)

DAVIS, GEORGIA M. D
Ky. State Sen.
b. Springfield, Ky. 10/29/23; d. Ben G. Montgomery and Frances Walker M; div; c. William F. Educ: Louisville Munic. Col, 40-42. Polit. & Govt. Pos: Chmn, Campaign for Cong. Cand, 62; chmn, campaign for Gubernatorial Cand, 64; chmn, 40th Legis. Dist, Jefferson Co. Dem. Exec. Cmt, 64-66; chmn, Blume for Cong. Campaign, 66; app. mem. of Adv. Coun. on Ment. Retardation by Gov. Edward T. Breathitt, Ky, 67-68; del, Dem. Nat. Conv, 68; Ky. State Sen, 68- Bus. & Prof. Pos: Supvr, IBM Data Processing Div, U.S. Census Bur, 59-62; asst. hosp. administr, Louisville, Ky, 66. Mem: South. Christian Leadership Conf; YWCA; Ky. Civil Liberties Union; NAACP; Urban League.

Kennedy-King Meritorious award, Young Dem. Ky, 68; Achievement award, Ky. Cong. Beautician's and Barber's, 68; Annual Achievement Award for first woman and first Negro elected to Ky. Senate, Zion Baptist Church, 68; Cert. of Appreciation, Ky. Sch. Bds. Asn, 68. Rel: Presbyterian. Mailing Add: 733 Cecil Ave, Louisville, Ky. 40211.

DAVIS, GLENN ROBERT R
U.S. Rep. Wis.
b. Mukwonago, Wis, 10/28/14; s. Charles W. Davis and Jennie Wachendorf D; m. 11/29/42 to Dr. Kathryn McFarlane; c. Kathleen, Margaret, Janet, James and Elizabeth. Educ: Wis. State Univ, Platteville, B.Ed, 34, Law Sch, LL.B, 40; Phi Delta Phi; Order of the Coif. Polit. & Govt. Pos: Wis. State Assemblyman, 41-42; U.S. Rep, Wis, 47-57 & 64-; del, Rep. Nat. Conv, 56, 60 & 68. Bus. & Prof. Pos: Attorney-at-law, Waukesha, Wis, 40-42, 45-47 & 57-65; pres. and bd. mem, New Berlin State Bank, 59-65. Mil. Serv: Entered as Ens, Navy, 42, released as Lt.(sg), 45, after serv. aboard U.S.S. Sangamon in Pac. Theater, 43-45; Pac. Campaign Ribbon; 9 Battle Stars; Presidential Unit Citation; Lt.(sg), Naval Res.(Ret), 54. Mem: Pres, Waukesha Co. Bar Asn, 61; bd. mem. and secy, Waukesha C. of C, 58-64; State Bar of Wis; Am. Legion; Elks; Kiwanis; Masonic Orders, including York Rite, Scottish Rite & Shrine. Col. awards in baseball and debate; selected one of Am. Outstanding Young Men by Nat. Jr. C. of C, 48. Rel: United Church of Christ. Legal Res: 3790 S. Center Rd, Waukesha, Wis. 53186. Mailing Add: 2454 Rayburn House Office Bldg, Washington, D.C. 20515.

DAVIS, GORUS LAUREL R
Chmn, Shannon Co. Rep. Cmt, Mo.
b. Shannon Co, Mo, 12/12/93; s. William Preston Davis and Josephine Malone D; m. 12/19/19 to Besse Lemons; c. Wilma (Mrs. Shannon Hartley), Mary Jo (Mrs. Erwin Grant) and Alice Jane (Mrs. Don Layman). Educ: Univ. Mo, Columbia, B.S. in Educ, 25; Alpha Zeta. Polit. & Govt. Pos: Co. Agr. Agent, Mo, 34-40; chmn, Shannon Co. Rep. Cmt, 52- Bus. & Prof. Pos: Voc. Agr. teacher, Elliott, Iowa, 26-27 and Alton, Mo, 32-34; supt. schs, Thomasville, Mo, 27-31; co. agr. exten. agent, Union, Mo, 34-35. Mil. Serv: Entered as Seaman 3/C, Navy, 17, released as Hosp. Apprentice 1/C, 18. Mem: Mo. Teachers Asn; Nat. Educ. Asn; Mason; Am. Legion; Mo. Farmers Asn. Rel: Baptist. Mailing Add: R.F.D. 2, Birch Tree, Mo. 65438.

DAVIS, HAROLD D
Tex. State Rep.
b. Austin, Tex, 3/22/33; s. George Bryan Davis and Inez Turner D; m. 2/6/53 to Frances Cardwell; c. Dwight Cardwell, Cynthia Ann and Harold, Jr. Educ: Baylor Univ, B.M, 55; Tex. Tech. Col, M.E, 62. Polit. & Govt. Pos: Tex. State Rep, Dist. 39, 69- Bus. & Prof. Pos: Owner, Wages-Davis & Co, Austin, Tex, 65-69 and Hay County Implement Co, Kyle, 68-69. Mem: Dir, Boys Club of Am; Million Dollar Round Table; Gideons Int. Bible Soc; Mason (32°); Lions. Rel: Southern Baptist. Legal Res: 413 Honeycomb Ridge, Austin, Tex. 78746. Mailing Add: Capitol Sta, Box 90, Austin, Tex. 79111.

DAVIS, HAYWARD H. D
b. Clewiston, Fla, 8/23/28; m. to Carol Ann Ruttinger; c. Stephen H, Stephanie L, John W. and Michael S. Educ: Univ. Fla, LL.B, 52; Phi Alpha Delta. Polit. & Govt. Pos: Fla. State Sen, 62-66; co. prosecutor, 66- Bus. & Prof. Pos: Attorney. Mil. Serv: U.S. Inf, 46-48, Sgt; 52-53, Lt. Mem: Past pres, Gr. Lake Placid C. of C; past pres, Sebring Jr. C. of C; KX past v.pres, Kiwanis; Elks; Highlands Co. Cattlemen's Asn; Farm Bur; past v.comdr, Am. Legion; VFW; pres, Highlands Bar Asn; Am. Bar Asn. Good Govt. Award, Sebring Jr. C. of C, 63. Rel: Baptist. Mailing Add: Placid Ridge Estates, Lake Placid, Fla. 33852.

DAVIS, ILUS WINIFIELD D
Mayor, Kansas City, Mo.
b. Kans. City, Mo, 4/22/17; s. Dean Davis and Emma Josephine Severs D; m. 11/8/46 to Beatrice Buecking; c. Christopher Dean and Caroline Dalton. Educ: Univ. Kans, A.B, 37; Univ. Mo, LL.B, 39. Polit. & Govt. Pos: Councilman, Kansas City, Mo, 48-55; chmn, Mayor's Cmt. on Munic. Finances, 55-57; mayor, Kansas City, Mo, 63- Bus. & Prof. Pos: With Dietrich, Tyler, Davis, Burrell & Dicus, Kansas City, 39-; chmn. bd, Baltimore Bank; dir, N.Hills Bank; Blue Ridge Bank; bd. dirs, Kansas City Philharmonic Asn; Adv. Cmt, Univ. Kansas City. Mil. Serv: Army, Inf, Maj, 42-46. Mem: Am. Mo.(secy) Bar Asns; Mo. Bar (bd. govs, 56-, pres, 60); Lawyers Asn; pres, Mo. Munic. League, 69- Rel: Christian Church. Mailing Add: 1001 W. 59th Terr, Kansas City, Mo. 64113 or Dwight Bldg, Kansas City, Mo. 64105.

DAVIS, IRA P. D
b. Jacksonville, Fla, 2/16/96; s. Charles C. Davis and Emma Emmerson D; m. 6/30/37 to Louise Stirrup; c. Joyce (Mrs. William C. Oates), Iral (Mrs. David Porter), Ira P, Jr. and Carol (Mrs. Alvin Henley). Educ: Fla. A&M Univ, 15-17; Howard Univ, D.D.S, 29; Alpha Phi Alpha; King of Clubs; Alpha Rho Boule. Polit. & Govt. Pos: Mem, President Johnson's 15-mem. Adv. Cmt. on Older Am, 66-; del. Dem. Nat. Conv, 68. Bus. & Prof. Pos: Intern, Freedman's Hosp, Wash, D.C, 29-30; chmn, bd. trustees, Christian Hosp, 49-60; adv. bd, Bethune Cookman Col, 53; pres, Gr. Miami Urban League, 61-63; mem, Orange Blossom Classic Cmt, 62; dir, Oper. Amigo, Inc, 62. Mil. Serv: Entered as Pfc, Army, 17, released as Pfc, 18, after serv. in Med. Corps, 92nd Div, 17-18. Mem: Bd. mem, Fla. State Med. Dent. and Pharmaceutical Asn; United Negro Col. Fund (past chmn); bd. mem, Counc. Int. Visitors; bd. mem, Am. Red Cross; bd. mem, Welfare Planning Coun. Dade Co; Elks; Mason; Shrine. Citation, Nat. Conf. Christians and Jews; Citation, Bethune Cookman Col. Rel: Episcopal. Legal Res: 3351 Hibiscus St, Miami, Fla. 33133. Mailing Add: 1036 N.W. Second Ave, Miami, Fla. 33136.

DAVIS, ISAAC DABNEY D
Chmn, Green Co. Dem. Cmt, Va.
b. Stanardsville, Va, 4/14/04; s. Dr. Ernest Downer Davis and Corine Stephens D; m. 4/9/55 to Marian Owens; c. Mary Owens and Isaac Garland. Educ: Smithdeal Bus. Col, 1 year; Univ. Richmond, 2 years; DeMolay. Polit. & Govt. Pos: Asst. postmaster, Stanardsville, Va, 34-46; chmn, Greene Co. Dem. Cmt, currently. Bus. & Prof. Pos: Clerk, Nat. Bank & Trust Co, Charlottesville, Va, 21-32; pres, I.D. Davis Ins. Agency, Inc, 21-69; exec. v.pres, Bank of Greene, Inc. Stanardsville, 47-59; v.pres, Va. Nat. Bank, 59-67, dir. and chmn, loan cmt, currently. Mem: Mason (32°); Shrine; Odd Fellows; Elks; Greene Hills Club, Inc. Past master and dist. dep. grand master, Masonic Lodge. Rel: Methodist; Stewart. Mailing Add: P.O. Box 67, Stanardsville, Va. 22973.

DAVIS, JACKSON BEAUREGARD D
La. State Sen.
b. Lecompte, La, 3/27/18; s. Jesse Octo Davis and Litha Pittman D; m. 1/15/44 to Rosemary Slattery; c. Jackson B, Jr, Robert Slattery, Rosemary and Susan Patricia. Educ: La. Col, 32-33; Northwest. State Col, 33-34; La. State Univ, A.B, 36, M.A, 37, LL.B, 40. Polit. & Govt. Pos: La. State Sen, 25th Sen. Dist, 56- Bus. & Prof. Pos: Attorney-at-law, 40- Mil. Serv: Entered as Ens, Navy, 41, released as Lt. Comdr, 46, after serv. in Pac. Theater. Publ: Biography of Confederate General Richard Taylor, La. Hist. Asn, 40. Rel: Baptist. Legal Res: 975 Thora Blvd, Shreveport, La. 71106. Mailing Add: 1605 Slattery Bldg, Shreveport, La. 71101.

DAVIS, JACOB ERASTUS D
b. Beaver, Ohio, 10/31/05; s. George O. Davis and Kathyrn Leist D; m. 9/18/29 to Minnie Eleanor Middleton; c. Jacob Erastus, Eleanor Middleton. Educ: Ohio State Univ, B.A, 27; Harvard, LL.B, 30. Polit. & Govt. Pos: Spec. Asst. Secy. Navy, asst. gen. counsel Navy Dept, 43-44; U.S. Rep, Ohio, 41-43; judge Court of Common Pleas, Pike Co, Ohio, 37-40; Ohio State Rep, 35-37, speaker pro tem, majority floor leader, 36-37; prosecuting attorney, Pike Co, Ohio, 31-35; trustee Ohio State Univ. Bus. & Prof. Pos: V.pres, Kroger Co, Cincinnati, Ohio, 45-; dir, 49-; exec. v.pres, 61; pres, 62. Mem: Cincinnati and Queen City Country Clubs. Mailing Add: 1014 Vine St, Cincinnati, Ohio 45202. (1967)

DAVIS, JAMES ADAIR R
Ky. State Rep.
b. Ashland, Ky, 12/15/41; s. James Harry Davis and Pauline Burton D; m. 7/28/63 to Barbara Calvert; c. Leigh Adair. Educ: Morehead State Univ, B.S, 63; pres, Circle K and Collegiate Knights. Polit. & Govt. Pos: Mem, Grayson Utilities Cmn, Ky, 67-68; Ky. State Rep, 75th Dist, 68- Bus. & Prof. Pos: Owner and mgr, Davis & Davis Distributors, Inc, 63- Mem: South. Coun. State Govt; Ky. Traffic Safety Coord. Cmt; Carter Co. Develop. Asn; Carter Co. Exten Coun; Rotary; Jaycees; C. of C. Outstanding Young Man award, Grayson, Ky, 68. Rel: Christian Church; Deacon. Legal Res: Second St, Grayson, Ky. 41143. Mailing Add: Box 575, Grayson, Ky. 41143.

DAVIS, JAMES CARL D
b. Huntsville, Ala, 3/4/07; s. William Odis Davis and Gertrude Hamlitt D; m. 8/31/26 to Ruth Doyle McCaskille; c. Dorothy Faye (Mrs. Rivers) and Betty Loraine (Mrs. Fort); 5 grandchildren. Educ: Bemis High Sch. Polit. & Govt. Pos: Mem, Madison Co. Court Magistrate, Tenn, 60-66; Tenn. State Rep, Madison Co, 64-67. Bus. & Prof. Pos: Owner and operator, J. Carl Davis Body Works, 45- Mem: Mason (32°); Eastern Star; Scottish Rite; Shrine; K. of P; Elks; Tenn. Law Enforcement Order. Rel: Methodist. Mailing Add: Route 3, Jackson, Tenn. 38301. (1967)

DAVIS, JAMES CURRAN D
b. Franklin, Ga, 5/17/95; s. Thomas Benjamin Davis and Lura Viola Mooty D; m. 12/26/32 to Mary Lou Martin; c. Mary Martin (Mrs. Edward G. Bowen). Educ: Reinhardt Col, 09-10; Emory Col, 10-12; Sigma Alpha Epsilon. Polit. & Govt. Pos: U.S. Rep, Ga, 46-62; del, Dem. Nat. Conv, 52; judge, Superior Courts, Stone Mountain Judicial Circuit, 34-47; attorney, DeKalb Co, 31-34; attorney, Ga. Dept. Indust. Rels, Atlanta, 28-31; Ga. State Rep, DeKalb Co, 24-28. Bus. & Prof. Pos: Gen. law practice, Atlanta, Ga, 19-34; admitted to Ga. Bar, 19; chmn. bd, pub, Atlanta Times, Inc. Mil. Serv: Marine Corps, 17-19. Mem: Masons. Rel: Methodist. Mailing Add: 5401 Memorial Dr, Stone Mountain, Ga. 30083. (1967)

DAVIS, JAMES HORNOR, III D
b. Clarksburg, W.Va, 10/9/28; s. J. Hornor Davis, II and Martha Maxwell D; m. 7/1/50 to Ouida Caldwell; c. James Hornor IV and Lewis Caldwell. Educ: Princeton, A.B; Univ. of Va, LL.B. Polit. & Govt. Pos: W.Va. State Del, 55th Legis; W.Va. State Sen, 62-66, chmn, Citizens Adv. Cmn, W.Va. State Senate. Bus. & Prof. Pos: Lawyer. Mil. Serv: 1st Lt, Air Force, 53-55. Rel: Episcopal. Mailing Add: Kanawha Bank & Trust Bldg, 111 Capital, Charleston, W.Va 25301.

DAVIS, JAMES KEPLER R
b. Tionesta, Pa, 6/12/94; s. James Dale Davis and Nelly Kepler D; m. 6/10/28 to Florida Elizabeth Richard; c. Nancy (Mrs. John C. Jones) and Elizabeth (Mrs. Theodore Raia). Educ: U.S. Naval Acad, B.S, 16. Polit. & Govt. Pos: Pa. State Rep, 50-66. Bus. & Prof. Pos: Ed. and co-publisher, The Forest Rep. and The Marienville Express, 48-50. Mil. Serv: Entered as prfnl. officer, Navy, 12, retired as Rear Adm, 47, after serv. as comdr, of numerous ships and groups of ships and in manufacture of naval guns and ord; Legion of Merit; Commendation Ribbon; Order of Cloud Banner First Class, Chinese Nationalist Repub; Philippine Repub. Commendatory Medal; numerous campaign ribbons. Publ: Weekly column on govt, 'On Soundings,' 48- Mem: U.S. Naval Acad. Alumni Asn; U.S. Naval Inst; Retired Officer's Asn; emer. mem, Pa. Hist. and Mus. Cmn. Rel: Presbyterian. Mailing Add: Elm, Tionesta, Pa. 16353.

DAVIS, JAMES PARKER D
Kans. State Rep.
b. Memphis, Tenn, 7/21/21; s. James Arthur Davis and Chaney Parker D; m. 11/27/47 to Maurita Lois Burnett; c. Je' Parker, Daphne Lynn and Lezlie Duane. Educ: LeMoyne Col, Memphis, Tenn, B.S, 43; Washburn Univ, Topeka, Kans, LL.B, 48; Omega Psi Phi. Polit. & Govt. Pos: First asst. to Wyandotte Co. Attorney, Kans, 51-66; state treas, Young Dem. 52-53; Kans. State Rep, Sixth Dist, 59- Bus. & Prof. Pos: Gen. counsel, Kansas City Embalming & Casket Co, 64-66; mem, Law Firm of Stevens, Jackson, Davis & Haley. Mil. Serv: Entered as Pvt, Army, 43, released as T/5, Chem. Warfare, 46. Mem: Trouveur Club, Inc; Am. Legion; Am, Kans. State, Kansas City and Wyandotte Co. Bar Asns; dir, Catholic Charities; C. of C. Rel: Roman Catholic. Legal Res: 725 Parallel Ave, Kansas City, Kans. 66101. Mailing Add: 1314 N. Fifth St, Douglass State Bank Bldg, Kansas City, Kans. 66101. (1967)

DAVIS, JAMES PRESTON D
b. Mantee, Miss; 4/18/97; married. Polit. & Govt. Pos: Miss. State Sen, 60-69. Bus. & Prof. Pos: Farmer. Mem: Mason; Farm Bur; dir. of Natchez Trace Elec. Power Asn; PTA. Rel: Baptist. Mailing Add: Mantee, Miss. 39751. (1967)

DAVIS, JAMES WOODS D
Va. State Sen.
b. Pedlar Mills, Va, 10/18/13; m. to Corinne Hampton Brown. Educ: Oglethorpe Univ, Atlanta, Ga. Polit. & Govt. Pos: Va. State Del, 62-66; Va. State Sen, 66- Bus. & Prof. Pos: Farmer; real estate broker; secy. and treas, Shout It From the Mountain, Inc. Mem: Ruritan Club, past pres; bd. of supvrs, Amherst Co, 52; Madison Heights Lions Club; Amherst Co. C. of C; bd. of dirs, Lynchburg Gen. Hosp; Sons of Confederate Vets; dir, Piedmont Area Boy Scouts of Am. Coun; Lynchburg Sports Club. Rel: Episcopal; sr. warden and trustee, St. Luke's Episcopal Church. Mailing Add: P.O. Box 188, Monroe Route, Agricola, Va. 24574.

DAVIS, JOHN EDWARD R
Dir. of Civil Defense, Off. of Secy. of Army
b. Minneapolis, Minn, 4/18/13; s. James Ellsworth Davis (deceased) and Helen Wilson D; m. 6/4/38 to Pauline Huntley; c. John Edward, Jr, Richard James and Kathleen Anne. Educ: Univ. N.Dak, B.S, 35; Beta Theta Pi. Polit. & Govt. Pos: Mayor, McClusky, N.Dak, 46-52; N.Dak. State Sen, 52-56; Gov, N.Dak, 56-60; chmn, Rep. Nat. Cmt. N.Dak, 61; Dir. of Civil Defense, Off. of Secy. of Army, 69- Bus. & Prof. Pos: Engaged in farming, ranching and investments, N.Dak; dir, Provident Life Ins. Co, Bismarck, 59-; pres, First Nat. Bank, McClusky, 59- Mil. Serv: Entered as Lt, Army, 41, released as Lt. Col, 45, after serv. in 35th Div, 134th Inf, ETO, 44-45; Silver Star for Valor; Bronze Star; Purple Heart; Combat Infantryman's Badge; Distinguished Unit Citation; Battle Stars for Four Campaigns in ETO. Mem: Mason (33°); Shrine; Elks; Am. Legion (nat. comdr, 67-68); VFW; DAV. Sioux Award for Distinguished Serv. and Outstanding Achievements, Univ. N.Dak. 66. Rel: Lutheran. Legal Res: 216 W. Owens Ave, Bismarck, N.Dak. 58501. Mailing Add: 2000 S. Eads St, Arlington, Va. 22202.

DAVIS, JOHN W. D
U.S. Rep, Ga.
b. Rome, Ga, 9/12/16; s. John Camp Davis and Era DeLay D; m. 2/6/44 to Vivian Hawkins, wid. 2/6/69; c. Katherine DeLay, John W, Jr. and Mary Ellen. Educ: Univ. of Ga, A.B, 37, LL.B, 39. Polit. & Govt. Pos: Former judge, juvenile courts, Catoosa, Dade, Chattanooga and Walker Cos, Ga; solicitor gen, Rome Circuit, Ga, 50-53; judge, Lookout Mt. Judicial Circuit, 55-60; U.S. Rep, Ga, 60-, mem, House Cmt. on Sci. And Astronaut. and House Admin. Cmt. Bus. & Prof. Pos: Practice of law, Rome, Ga, 39-42 and Summerville, 46- Mil. Serv: Entered Army, 42, released 46, after serv. in Counterintel. Corps, S.Am. Mem: Ga. Bar Asn; Lions; Mason; Elks; Am. Legion; VFW. Licensed private pilot. Rel: Presbyterian. Mailing Add: 1728 Longworth Bldg, Washington, D.C. 20515.

DAVIS, JOHN W. D
b. Trenton, N.J, 7/30/18. Educ: Bucknell Univ, B.S, 41; Glassboro State Col; Rutgers; Temple Univ; Kappa Sigma. Polit. & Govt. Pos: Former N.J. State Assemblyman, Majority Leader, N.J. Gen. Assembly, 61, Speaker, 62. Mil. Serv: 2nd Lt, Marine Corps, 3 years, Marine Corps recruiting officer, Salem Co. Mem: Am. Legion; Salem Country Club. Rel: Baptist. Mailing Add: Ft. Mott Rd, R.F.D. 3, Salem, N.J. 08079. (1967)

DAVIS, JOHN WILLIAMS R
Finance Chmn, Buncombe Co. Rep. Party, N.C.
b. Milwaukee, Wis, 6/8/14; s. Price Morgan Davis and Maud Tompkins D; m. 12/28/40 to Evelyn June Thatcher; c. John W, Jr, Elizabeth S, Gwyneth M. and Sara H. Educ: Dartmouth Col, 3 years; Phi Gamma Delta. Polit. & Govt. Pos: Chmn, Monroe Co. Exec. Cmt, Fla, 64-67; finance chmn, Buncombe Co. Rep. Party, N.C. and pres, Buncombe Co. Rep. Club, 68- Bus. & Prof. Pos: Stock clerk and salesman, Shadbolt & Boyd Co, Milwaukee, Wis, 33-40; salesman, Repub. Steel Corp, 40-61; pres, Cay Casa Corp, 63- Mil. Serv: Pvt, Army, 42-45, served with First Spec. Serv. Force, ETO; Asiatic-Pac, Kiska, Aleutian Islands, Italy-Naples-Foggia and Rome-Arno Campaign Ribbons; Prisoner of War in Germany. Mem: Milwaukee Jr. C. of C; Toastmasters (pres, Southernmost Club 2293, 64-65). Rel: Episcopal. Mailing Add: 62 Maney Ave, Asheville, N.C. 28804.

DAVIS, JULIAN MASON, JR. D
Mem, Jefferson Co. Dem. Exec. Cmt, Ala.
b. Birmingham, Ala, 7/30/35; s. Julian Mason Davis and Madeline Harris D; m. 8/12/57 to June Fox; c. Karen Madeline and Julian Mason, III. Educ: Talladega Col, A.B, 56; Univ. Buffalo Sch. Law, LL.B, 59; Alpha Phi Alpha. Polit. & Govt. Pos: Mem, Jefferson Co. Dem. Exec. Cmt, Ala, 66-; del, Dem. Nat. conv, 68; mem, Park and Recreation Bd, Birmingham, Ala, 68- Bus. & Prof. Pos: V.pres. and gen. counsel, Protective Indust. Ins. Co, Birmingham, Ala, 60-; gen. counsel, Nat. Ins. Asn, 62- Mem: Am. and Ala. Bar Asns; Am. Judicature Soc; Mason; Elks; K. of P; NAACP; Operation New Birmingham. Rel: United Church of Christ. Legal Res: 237 11th Ave. S.W, Birmingham, Ala. 35211. Mailing Add: Room 517, 1630 Fourth Ave. N, Birmingham, Ala. 35203.

DAVIS, KENNETH E. R
City Councilman, Charlottesville, Va.
b. Russellville, Ky, 1/2/22; s. Winfrey Davis and Delsie Sillings D; m. 9/29/44 to Eloise Mills; c. Joseph Winfrey. Educ: Mars Hill Col, 41-42; Wake Forest Col, B.S, 47. Polit. & Govt. Pos: Rep. ward chmn, Charlottesville, Va, 65, city chmn, 66-68 and city councilman, 68- Bus. & Prof. Pos: Spec. agent, Prudential Ins. Co, Charlottesville, Va, 55-68; real estate agent, Montague, Miller & Co. Realtors, 68- Mil. Serv: Entered as Seaman, Navy, 42, released as MoMM, 2/C, 45, after serv. in Amphibious, Pac. Theatre; Am. Theatre Ribbon; Asiatic-Pac. Ribbon with 1 star; Philippine Liberation Ribbon; Victory Medal; Good Conduct Medal; Presidential Unit Citation with 1 star. Rel: Baptist. Mailing Add: 2318 Crestmont Ave, Charlottesville, Va. 22901.

DAVIS, KENNETH NEWTON, JR. R
Asst. Secy. of Commerce
b. Greenfield, Mass, 3/26/26; s. Kenneth Newton Davis and Barbara Lufkin D; m. 5/27/50 to Corinne Terry Burge; c. Cynthia Learned, Barbara Beth and Robin Terry. Educ: Mass. Inst. Tech, B.S, 46; Stanford Univ, M.B.A, 49; Kappa Alpha. Polit. & Govt. Pos: Asst. Secy. of Commerce, Dept. of Commerce, 69- Bus. & Prof. Pos: From sales rep. to various managerial pos, Int. Bus. Machines Corp, San Francisco, Calif, 49-64, v.pres. and treas, 64-69. Mil. Serv: Entered as A/S, Naval Res, 43, released as Lt.(jg), 46, after serv. in Atlantic Theatre, 45-46. Mem: Treas. Club; former pres, Financial Exec. Research Found; dir, Financial Exec. Inst; Waccabuc Country Club, N.Y. Rel: Protestant. Legal Res: Stone Hill Rd, Pound Ridge, N.Y. 10576. Mailing Add: Apt. 704 N, Watergate E, 25 W. Virginia Ave. N.W, Washington, D.C. 20037.

DAVIS, LEE MURRAY R
Vt. State Rep.
b. Springfield, Vt, 11/29/03; s. Dan T. Davis and Norah Ellan Annis D; m. 8/3/29 to Winifred Knowles; m. 3/29/64 to Doris Rice; c. James B. Educ: Springfield High Sch, grad, 21. Polit. & Govt. Pos: Selectman, Springfield, Vt, 67-, chmn. bd. selectman, 68-69; Vt. State Rep, 69- Bus. & Prof. Pos: Machine operator, Jones & Lamson Machine Co, 23-26, engr, 26-38, mgr. of eng, 38-68, retired, 68. Mem: Am. Soc. Tool Engrs; Odd Fellows; Elks; Lions Club. Rel: Unitarian Universalist. Mailing Add: 61 Elm St, Springfield, Vt. 05156.

DAVIS, LEON W, JR. D
b. Evansville, Ind, 5/11/27; s. Leon W. Davis, Sr. and Edith Seib D; m. 12/26/53 to Dorothy Charlene Hall; c. Virginia Gail, Jeffrey Hall, Carol Patrice, Leigh Ann and Amy Elizabeth. Educ: Cumberland Univ. Sch. of Law, LL.B, 54; Delta Theta Phi. Polit. & Govt. Pos: Former Tenn. State Rep. Mil. Serv: Entered as A/S, Navy, 45, released as S 1/C, 46, reentered as Pvt, Army, 51, released as Sgt, 53, after serv. in Fifth RCT, Korea. Mem: Am. and Tenn. Bar Asns; Sertoma; St. Judes Men Club. Rel: Roman Catholic. Mailing Add: 3511 Oak Ridge Dr, Chattanooga, Tenn. 37415. (1967)

DAVIS, LEONARD JOHN R
N.Dak. State Rep.
b. Belfield, N.Dak, 1/19/13; s. Harry G. Davis and Matilda Bibow D; m. 6/10/36 to Mildred Ann Owens; c. Con and Penelope. Educ: Dickinson State Col, 33. Polit. & Govt. Pos: Precinct committeeman, N.Dak, 46-60; N.Dak. State Rep, currently. Bus. & Prof. Pos: Pres, Dunn Co. Farm Bur, 47-48, Dunn Mutual Aid Tel. Corp, 50-57, N.Dak. Stockmen's Asn, 58-60 and N.Dak. Beef Coun, 60-61. Mem: Mason; Farm Bur; Farmer's Union; Killdeer Town Criers. Named Man of the Year in Agr, Saddle & Sirloin Club, N.Dak; State Farmer Degree, N.Dak. Future Farmers of Am. Rel: Lutheran. Mailing Add: Killdeer, N.Dak. 58640.

DAVIS, LEWIS WALTER R
b. Pittsburgh, Pa, 8/18/07; s. Adolph Davis and Clara Levenson D; m. 12/21/48 to Selma Goldinger. Educ: Univ. Pittsburgh, Ph.G, 26; Univ. Wash, Exten. Student, 29-30; N.Y. Univ, 43. Polit. & Govt. Pos: Mayor, Tucson, Ariz, 61-67. Bus. & Prof. Pos: Retail pharmacist, 23-28; wholesale drug and mfrs. rep, 28-42; v.pres, Del. River Shipbuilding and Drydock Corp, Phila, Pa, 47-49; pres, and treas, Guild Prod, Newark, 50-51; land developer, realtor, Tucson, Ariz, 52- Mil. Serv: Army, Maj, 42-46. Mem: Mason; Shrine. Mailing Add: 60 Calle Encanto, Tucson, Ariz. 85716.

DAVIS, LOU ANN R
b. Bremen, Ind, 2/26/27; d. Kenneth H. Walter and Hazel E. Robison W; m. 7/2/48 to James R. Davis; c. Kenneth L, Claire L. and Bruce R. Polit. & Govt. Pos: Mem, Calif. Rep. State Cent. Cmt, 67-69; pres, East San Gabriel Valley Rep. Women's Club, Federated, 68. Bus. & Prof. Pos: Legal secy, Hartford Accident & Indemnity Co, 45-50. Mem: West Covina Beautiful. Mailing Add: 1501 E. Vine Ave, West Covina, Calif. 91790.

DAVIS, MARY WRIGHT D
b. Washington, D.C, 12/18/18; d. Calvin Crawford Davis and Irene Douglass D; single. Polit. & Govt. Pos: Staff and admin. pos. with various Mem. of Cong, 39-; admin. asst. to U.S. Rep. Benjamin S. Rosenthal, N.Y, 62- Rel: Roman Catholic. Mailing Add: 3505 Inverness Dr, Chevy Chase, Md. 20015.

DAVIS, MILDRED CHRISTINA D
V.chmn, Henry Co. Dem. Party, Ind.
b. New Castle, Ind, 11/28/21; d. Harry Gilbert Budd and Echo Donica B; m. 5/17/40 to Joseph Dudley Davis; c. Virginia Dee, Joseph Dudley, Jr. and Judith Ann. Educ: New Castle High Sch; New Castle Bus. Col. Polit. & Govt. Pos: V.chmn, Henry Co. Dem. Party, Ind, 60-; mgr, New Castle License Bur, 60- Mem: VFW; Bus. & Prfnl. Women's Club. Rel: Methodist. Mailing Add: R.R. 2, New Castle, Ind. 47362. (1967)

DAVIS, MILFORD NEIL D
Chmn, Gunnison Co. Dem. Cent. Cmt, Colo.
b. Parsons, Kans, 12/21/08; s. Wilson Perry Davis and Estella Pearl Wallace D; m. 12/2/50 to Peggy S. Schalk. Educ: Delta Bus. Col, 2 years. Polit. & Govt. Pos: Chmn, Gunnison Co. Dem. Cent. Cmt, Colo, 69- Mailing Add: 124 E. Virginia, Gunnison, Colo. 81230.

DAVIS, NADA R
Mem, Calif. Rep. State Cent. Cmt.
b. Montpelier, Idaho, 11/20/20; d. Phillip D. Miller and Nada A. Hendricks M; m. 2/17/42 to William Irving Davis; c. Nadette (Mrs. William West), Lynne Irene, Laurie Lee and William Richard. Educ: Santa Monica Jr. Col, 39-41. Polit. & Govt. Pos: Mem, Calif. Rep. State Cent. Cmt, 63-; area chmn, Los Angeles Co. Rep. Fedn, 65, conv. chmn, 67 & 68; pres, GOP Jr, Long Beach, 66. Bus. & Prof. Pos: Part owner, Davis Paint Co, Long Beach, Calif, 49-; real estate broker, Real Estate Store, 69- Mem: Dir, Long Beach Dist. Bd. of Realtors; state dir, Calif. Real Estate Asn; Los Angeles Co. Fedn. of Rep. Women; Fine Arts Affil, Long Beach State Col, Opti Mrs. Club; Ebell Club; Long Beach Dinner Club; Old Ranch Golf Club. Assoc. Realtor of the Year, Long Beach Dist. Bd. of Realtors, 67. Rel: Unity. Mailing Add: 1050 El Mirador Ave, Long Beach, Calif. 90815.

DAVIS, NATHANIEL
U.S. Ambassador to Guatemala
b. Boston, Mass, 4/12/25; s. Harvey Nathaniel Davis and Alice Marian Rohde D; m. 11/24/56 to Elizabeth K. Creese; c. Margaret Morton, Helen Miller, James Creese and Thomas Rohde. Educ: Phillips Exeter Acad, A.B, 42; Brown Univ, A.B, 44; Fletcher Sch. of Law and Diplomacy, M.A, 47, Ph.D, 60; student Russian lang, Columbia Univ, Cornell Univ. and Middlebury Col, 53-54; Phi Beta Kappa. Polit. & Govt. Pos: Entered U.S. For. Serv, 47; v.consul, Florence, Italy, 49-52; second secy, Rome, 52-53 and Moscow, 54-56; Soviet Desk Officer, State Dept, 56-60; first secy, Caracas, Venezuela, 60-62; spec. asst. dir, Peace Corps, 62-63; dep. assoc. dir, 63-65; Ambassador to Bulgaria, 65-66; mem, Security Coun. Staff, 66-68; Ambassador to Guatemala, 68- Bus. & Prof. Pos: Asst. in hist, Tufts Col, 47; lectr. in U.S. Hist, Centro Venezolano-Americano, 61; lectr. Russian and Soviet Hist, Howard Univ, 62- Mil. Serv: Lt.(jg), Naval Res, 44-46. Mem: Bd. dirs, and chmn, Inner City Childrens and Youth Prog, Nat. Capital Area Coun. of Churches, 58-59; Am. For. Serv. Asn.(mem. bd. dir. and v.chmn, 64); Am. Hist. Asn. Recipient, Cinco Aguilas Blancas Alpinism Award, Venezuelan Andean Club, 62. Rel: United Church of Christ. Legal Res: c/o Fife, Colonial House, Castle Pt, Hoboken, N.J. 07030. Mailing Add: U.S. Embassy, Guatemala City, Guatemala.

DAVIS, PAULINE L. D
Calif. State Assemblywoman
b. Verdigre, Nebr, 1/3/17; m. to Lester T. Davis, Sr, wid; c. Karen Joyce (Mrs. Mier), Marlene Kaye (Mrs. Bryan) and John Rodney. Educ: Sacramento Col. Polit. & Govt. Pos: Calif. State Assemblywoman, 52-; mem, Wildlife Conserv. Bd; mem, Ways and Means, Conserv. and Wildlife and Water Cmts. Bus. & Prof. Pos: Dispatcher, West. Pac. R.R, Stockton; former traffic operator, Bell Tel. Co, Omaha. Mem: Eastern Star, Portola; White Shrine of Jerusalem, Beckwourth; Bus. and Prfnl. Women's Club, Yreka; past Pres, Ladies Auxiliary, Brotherhood Locomotive Firemen and Enginemen. Mailing Add: Box 1071, Portola, Calif. 96122.

DAVIS, PERCY TERRY R
Wyo. State Sen.
b. Lisco, Nebr, 10/11/17; s. Percy R. Davis and Mary Herfert D; m. 8/7/43 to Beth Elaine Corliss; c. Terry Eugene, Rebecca Jane (Mrs. Black), Mary Ann, C. Joe and Bob B. Educ: Lisco Nebr. Col. of Mortuary Sci, 46. Polit. & Govt. Pos: Co. coroner, Wyo, 51-67, dep. co. coroner, 67-; Wyo. State Sen, 63-, chmn, Corp. & Polit. Subdiv, Wyo. State Sen, 69- Bus. & Prof. Pos: Secy. and treas, State Bd. Embalming, 65-67. Mil. Serv: Entered as Pvt, Army, 41, released as T-3, 45, after serv. in 134th Inf. Div, European Theatre, 44-45. Mem: Wyo. Peace Officers Asn; Kiwanis; leader, 4-H; past mem. bd, C. of C; Nat. and Wyo. Funeral Dir. Asns; Order of the Golden Rule; Mason; Shrine; Elks; Royal Arch; Am. Legion; VFW; Wyo. Stock Growers Asn. Rel: Episcopal. Mailing Add: 2203 W. Main, Riverton, Wyo. 82501.

DAVIS, PRESTON B. R
Pa. State Sen.
b. West Milton, Pa, 5/19/07; s. Charles W. Davis and Lula M. Becher D; m. to M. Isabelle Lindner; c. Two. Educ: Bucknell Univ, A.B; Univ. Pa. Law Sch, LL.B; Sigma Alpha Epsilon; Phi Delta Phi. Polit. & Govt. Pos: Pres, Susquehanna River Syst. Flood Control Asn, Inc; alternate del, Rep. Nat. Conv, 56, del, 60; Pa. State Sen, 63- Bus. & Prof. Pos: Practicing attorney, Northumberland Co. Courts, Supreme and Superior Courts of Pa; U.S. Dist. Court, Mid. Dist. of Pa. Mem: Am. and Pa. Bar Asns; several Masonic bodies; Elks; Moose. Legal Res: 347 Broadway, Milton, Pa. 17847. Mailing Add: Senate Office Bldg, Harrisburg, Pa. 17105.

DAVIS, RICHARD HALLOCK
b. Jamestown, N.Y, 2/7/13; m. to Harriet Robbins; c. Two daughters. Educ: Princeton Univ, A.B, 35; Harvard Univ, M.B.A, 37. Polit. & Govt. Pos: Career officer, Dept. of State For. Serv, 38-; counsr, Hamburg, 38-39, Tsingtao, 40-42, New Delhi, 42, Chungking, 42-43, Moscow, 43-46, 48-49 and Vienna, 53-55; acting asst. chief, Div. E.European Affairs, 48; officer in charge Soviet Affairs, 50-53; minister-counsr, Moscow, 57-59; dir, Off. Soviet Union Affairs, 59; Sr. Dep, Dep. and Asst. Secy. of State for European Affairs, 59-65; U.S. Ambassador to Rumania, 65-69; State Dept. Adv, Naval War Col, 69- Legal Res: Washington, D.C. Mailing Add: Naval War College, Newport, R.I. 02840.

DAVIS, ROBERT OGDEN R
Pa. State Rep.
b. New Castle, Pa, 7/15/10; s. Thomas Davis and Florence Shearer D; m. 9/17/38 to Jane Elizabeth Wright; c. Sally (Mrs. Pavlovic) and David Wright. Educ: Penn State Univ, A.B, 32; Duquesne Univ. Law Sch, LL.B, 37; Sigma Pi. Polit. & Govt. Pos: Mem, Beaver Sch. Bd, 43-55; Pa. State Rep, 67- Mem: Secy, Beaver Co. Bar Asn, 55-66; Lions Int. Rel: United Presbyterian. Mailing Add: 1350 Second St, Beaver, Pa. 15009.

DAVIS, RUSSELL C. D
Mayor, Jackson, Miss.
b. Rockville, Md, 8/13/22; married. Polit. & Govt. Pos: Miss. State Rep, 60-68; mayor, Jackson, 68- Bus. & Prof. Pos: Gen. Ins. Mem: Sons of Confederate Veterans; Sertoma; C. of C; Independent Ins. Agents; YMCA; Am. Legion; dir, Hinds-Rankin Red Cross; Miss. Econ. Coun. Rel: Methodist. Mailing Add: P.O. Box 2450, Jackson, Miss. 39205.

DAVIS, RUSSELL LEWIS R
Va. State Del.
b. Rocky Mount, Va, 3/8/03; s. Beverly Andrew Davis and Mary (Mollie) Gravely D; m. 10/8/32 to Winifred Cabell Skinell; c. Russell L, Jr, Emily (Mrs. Londos), William G, Julia W. and Katherine R. Educ: Roanoke Col, 20-23; Univ. Va, 24-26; Univ. Va. Law Sch, 2 years; Pi Kappa Phi; Phi Alpha Delta. Polit. & Govt. Pos: Postmaster, Rocky Mount, Va, 26-33; U.S. Cmnr, 35-66; co-chmn, Franklin Co. Rep. Cmt, 40-66; Va. State Del, 66- Mem: Mason; Lions. Rel: Episcopal. Mailing Add: 116 Talioferro S.W, Rocky Mount, Va. 24151.

DAVIS, S. JOSEPH JR. 'JOE' D
b. Leesburg, Ga, 5/19/23; m. to Betty Jane Woodcock; c. Donna Jane, Pamelo Jo and Sheila Joy. Educ: La. Col, 41-42; Stetson Univ, B.A, 52; Stetson Univ. Col. of Law, LL.B, 54; Omicron Delta Kappa; Pi Kappa Alpha; Phi Alpha Delta; pres, Student Bar Asn; Outstanding Law Student of Class; Outstanding ROTC Grad. Polit. & Govt. Pos: Mem, Sanford Zoning and Planning Cmn, Fla; Fla. State Rep, 62-67. Bus. & Prof. Pos: Dir, Sanford Seminole Develop. Co; lawyer, Stenstrom, Davis & McIntosh, 57- Mil. Serv: Navy, 42-48. Mem: Seminole Co. chmn, Citizens for Fla. Future, 63; dir, Seminole Co. C. of C; past v.pres. and dir, Civitans; chmn, Salvation Army Adv. Bd; Seminole Co. Bar Asn.(pres); past pres, Pinecrest Elem. Sch. PTA; Am. and Fla. Bar Asns; Acad. Fla. Trial Lawyers; pres, Henry Shelton Sanford Mem. Libr. and Mus; dir, Sanford Seminole Co. Am. Red Cross. Rel: Baptist; Deacon, Sunday Sch. Teacher and mem, Training Union. Mailing Add: P.O. Drawer 1330, Sanford, Fla. 32771. (1967)

DAVIS, SHELBY CULLOM R
U.S. Ambassador to Switz.
b. Peoria, Ill, 4/1/09; s. George Henry Davis and Julia Mabel Cullom D; m. 1/4/32 to Kathryn Edith Waterman; c. Shelby Moore, Diana and Priscilla Alden (deceased). Educ: Princeton, A.B, 30; Columbia Univ, A.M, 31. Polit. & Govt. Pos: Econ. adv. to Thomas E. Dewey Presidential Campaigns, 40 & 44; chief, for. requirements sect, War Prod. Bd, 42 and div. of statist. and research, Region II, 43; first Dep. Supt. of Ins, N.Y. State, 44-47; U.S. Ambassador to Switz, currently. Bus. & Prof. Pos: Former bus. ed, Current Hist. and Forum Mags; spec. correspondent and assoc. with Columbia Broadcasting Co, Geneva, Switz, 32-34; economist, Investment Corp. of Phila, 34-37; treas, Delaware Fund, Inc, 37-39; mem, N.Y. Stock Exchange, 41-; managing partner, Shelby, Cullom, Davis & Co, 47- Publ: Your Career in Defense, 42; contrib. to several jour. Mem: Chmn, Hist. Alumni Adv. Coun, Princeton; trustee, Col. Retirement Equities Fund; Financial Analysts Soc.(past pres); Gen. Soc. S.R; Soc. Colonial Wars (treas); Mayflower Soc; Knickerbocker, Univ, Ardsley Country, Hartford and Down Town Asn. Clubs; Princeton Club, N.Y; Bar Harbor Club, Maine; Charter Club, Princeton; Everglades Club, Palm Beach, Fla. Legal Res: Broad Oak, Tarrytown, N.Y. Mailing Add: U.S. Embassy, Berne, Switzerland.

DAVIS, STANLEY J. D
Mich. State Rep.
b. Poland, 5/8/08; wid; c. Donald, Barbara (Mrs. John Endres and Gerri (Mrs. Ronald Urbanski). Educ: Univ. of Mich, exten. courses. Polit. & Govt. Pos: Mayor, Grand Rapids, Mich, 4 terms, city cmnr. and former supvr. and chmn, Bd. of Supvr; Mich. State Rep, 64- Bus. & Prof. Pos: Florist, currently. Mem: Elks; Am. Bus. Club; K. of C. Rel: Catholic. Mailing Add: 1336 Leonard St. N.W, Grand Rapids, Mich. 49505. Legal Res: 320 Boltwood N.E, Grand Rapids, Mich. 49505. (1967)

DAVIS, THELMA FAULKNER D
b. Columbus, Ga, 6/20/06; d. John Asa Faulkner and Louise Hill F; m. 3/21/26 to Lewis Herschel Davis; c. Lisa Erline. Educ: Mercer Univ, Macon, Ga, A.B, 53, M.Ed, 59; Univ. Ga, grad. study; Int. Rels. Club. Polit. Pos: Speaker, polit. clinic, Citizenship Cmt, Nat. Educ. Asn, 65; mem, Educators for Johnson and Humphrey, 64-65; speaker, Gov. Conf. on Educ, Ga, 65 and mem, 64-65; Ga. alternate, Nat. Dem. Conv, 64; educ. speaker to Okla. State Legis, 64; del. to Educ. Appropriations Cmt. and Gov, Ga, 60-61; rep, Dist. Dem. Conv, 60. Prof. Pos: Teacher, Pub. Sch. of Ga, 26-31 and 50- Publn: Educational Articles, State Educ. Journals, 64-66 and Ga. Newspapers, 60-66. Mem: Pres, v.pres. and secy, Ga. Educ. Asn, Classroom Teachers Dept, 58-62, pres. and v.pres, 62-65; del, World Conf. of Orgns. of Teaching Profession, Nat. Educ. Asn, Ethiopia, 65, del, Nat. Syndicate of France, Paris, 65; Ga. Fedn. Bus. & Prfnl. Women's Clubs; Am. Asn. of Univ. Women; Delta Kappa Gamma. Rel: Southern Baptist. Mailing Add: 19 Terracedale Court, Griffin, Ga. 30223. (1967)

DAVIS, TRUITT D
City Councilman, Franklin, Ga.
b. Franklin, Ga, 3/7/07; s. Roofus E. Davis and Willie Lee Kirk D; m. 8/17/42 to Onnie Spradlin. Educ: Franklin High Sch, 11 years. Polit. & Govt. Pos: City councilman, Franklin, Ga, 61-; Ga. State Rep, Heard Co, 63, 64 & 65, 33rd Dist, 66; sanitarian, Ga. Agr. Dept, 66-69. Bus. & Prof. Pos: Dry cleaner, Franklin, Ga, 46-69; tree farmer, Heard Co, 46-69; coin operated laundries, Heard Co, 58-69. Mil. Serv: Entered as Pvt, Army, 36, released as Sgt, 45, after serv. in Ninth Div, European Theatre, 42-45. Mem: Ga. Farm Bur; Am. Legion; Mason; Lions. Rel: Methodist. Legal Res: Bridge St, Franklin, Ga. 30217. Mailing Add: Box 153, Franklin, Ga. 30217.

DAVIS, W. LESTER D
Chmn, Harford Co. Dem. State Cent. Cmt, Md.
b. Savage, Md, 6/25/09; s. George Henry Davis and Bertha Shipley D; m. 11/24/38 to Virginia Reamy; c. Marie (Mrs. McCraw), Virginia (Mrs. Ulehla), Leslie (Mrs. Hyatt), W. Lester, II, Debbie Kay, Vickie Lynn and Sheree Gail. Educ: Col, 2 years. Polit. & Govt. Pos: Chmn, Harford Co. Dem. State Cent. Cmt, Md, 16 years; Md. State Del, Harford Co, 58-59. Bus. & Prof. Pos: Pres, Davis Concrete Co, 25 years, pres, Davis Concrete of Del, 25 years; pres, Sparton Concrete Co, Bel Air Concrete Co, Joppa Concrete Co. and Aberdeen Concrete Co, 6 years; first v.pres, First Nat. Bank of North East, 58-; dir, Aberdeen Nat. Bank, Md, 63-; hon. dir, Harford Mem. Hosp, Havre de Grace, 63- Mem: Md. Golf & Country Club; Swan Creek Country Club; Bush River Yacht Club; Moose; Elks. Rel: Methodist. Mailing Add: R.D. 2, Box 35, Aberdeen, Md. 21001.

DAVIS, WALLACE ROBERT D
Committeeman, Calif. Dem. State Cent. Cmt.
b. Orange Co, Calif, 4/21/35; s. Wallace Charles Davis and Margaret Kirker D; m. 7/15/61 to Irmgard Wally Hermann; c. Anja, Mark, Luke, Marisa and Sabrina. Educ: Calif. State Col. at Long Beach, B.A; Univ. of Calif, Los Angeles, J.D; Gemini Club and Woman's Jr. Civic Club Scholarships, 54; Phi Alpha Delta. Polit. & Govt. Pos: Pres, Long Beach Young Dem, Calif, 60, 74th Assembly Dist. Young Dem, 60-61 and LBJ Dem. Club, Orange Co, 64-65; chmn, Orange Co. Viva Johnson Cmt, 64; committeeman, Calif. Dem. State Cent. Cmt, 68- Bus. & Prof. Pos: Assoc. attorney, James E. Walker, Attorney, 64; partner, Walker & Davis Attorneys-at-law, Santa Ana, Calif, 65- Mil. Serv: Entered as Pvt, Army, 56, released as Pfc, 58, after serv. in Spec. Serv, Ft. Ord, Calif; Good Conduct Medal. Mem: Orange Co. Bar Asn; mem. and v.chmn, Orange Co. Bar Cmt. on Fees; C. of C; bd. mem, Disabled Am.

Veterans Charitable Found; Mexican Am. Polit. Asn. Am. Legion Leadership Award, 54. Rel: Roman Catholic. Mailing Add: 9912 Aster Circle, Fountain Valley, Calif. 92708.

DAVIS, WALTER LAMAR R
Ga. State Rep.
b. Atlanta, Ga, 12/27/37; s. Walter Lamar Davis and Charlie Parker D; m. 3/22/58 to Bertha Kate Thompson; c. Terry and Linda. Educ: Ga. State Col, B.B.A, 59. Polit. & Govt. Pos: Ga. State Rep, currently. Bus. & Prof. Pos: Real estate salesman and investor, 62- Mil. Serv: Entered as 2nd Lt, Army, 59, released as 1st Lt, 62; Army Commendation Medal. Rel: Baptist. Mailing Add: 3782 Snapfinger Rd, Lithonia, Ga. 30058. (1967)

DAVIS, WILL DAVID D
Chmn, Tex. Dem. State Exec. Cmt.
b. Houston, Tex, 7/18/29; s. David Davis and Nita Barnett D; m. 12/17/54 to Ann Byargeon; c. Lisa Ann, Mary Lynn and Will David, Jr. Educ: Lamar Col, A.A, 50; Baylor Univ, B.B.A, J.D, cum laude, 54; Omicron Delta Kappa; Phi Alpha Delta; Ed, Baylor Law Review; pres, Baylor Univ. Student Body; v.pres, Am. Law Students Asn; pres, Southwest Conf. Sportsmanship Cmt; Varsity Football. Polit. & Govt. Pos: Asst. Attorney Gen, Tex, 54-57; gen. counsel, Tex. State Bd. of Ins, 57-59; del, Tex. State Dem. Conv, 58-64 and Dem. Nat. Conv, 64 & 68; cong. dist. coordinator, Kennedy-Johnson Campaign, 60 and Johnson-Humphrey Campaign, 64; mem, Tex. Dem. State Exec. Cmt, 62-64, secy, 64-65 and chmn, 65-; mem. and v.chmn, Tex. State Historical Surv. Cmn, 63-; mem, Tex. Elec. Law Study Cmt, 66; chmn, State Dem. Conv, 66 & 68 and Gov. Inaugural Cmt, 67; mem, Austin Independent Sch. Bd. of Trustees, 67-; mem, Tex. Col. and Univ. Syst. Coord. Bd, 68-; presidential Elector, 68; mem, Nat. Dem. Cmt. Conv. Reform and Party Del. Selection, 69. Bus. & Prof. Pos: Partner, Heath & Davis, 59- Mem: Am, Tex. and Local Bar Asns; Fedn. of Ins. Counsel; Jaycees; v.pres. and mem, Bd. of Dirs, Baylor Ex-Students Asn; Headliner's Club; President's Club; Citadel Club. Selected as Outstanding Young Man of Austin, Tex, One of Five Outstanding Young Texans and Outstanding Young Lawyer Tex, 63 and Outstanding Young Men of Am, 65. Rel: Baptist. Legal Res: 2407 Woodmont, Austin, Tex. 78703. Mailing Add: 202 Perry-Brooks Bldg, Austin, Tex. 78701.

DAVIS, WILLIAM ACKELSON D
b. Kirk, Colo, 8/5/03; s. Elias Griffith Davis and Zelma Ackelson D; m. 10/26/26 to Jessie Marian Shaw; c. Jack Presley, William Shaw and Eugene Griffith. Educ: Colo. Univ, 22-24; Phi Gamma Delta. Polit. & Govt. Pos: Nominee, U.S. Rep, Kans, 60; del, Dem. Nat. Conv, 64 and many state and regional conv; chmn, Kans. State Cmt. Farmers Home Admin, U.S. Dept. Agr, 65; chmn, Gov. Cmt. on Sugar Beets, Kans, 65-66; Dem. precinct committeeman; chmn, Sch. Unification Cmt; Sch. Bd; Adv. Cmt, Northwest Kans. Vocational Tech. Sch; Kennedy-Johnson Water Resources Cmt; Goodland Planning Cmn; Citizens Cmt. for Vocational-Tech. Educ; alternate del, Dem. Nat. Conv, 68; mem, Kans. State Banking Bd, 68- Bus. & Prof. Pos: Owner, Davis Implement Co; pres, Wm. A. Davis & Sons Farm Enterprise; director, Esch Lumber Company. Mil. Serv: Pvt, Colo. Nat. Guard, Co. 1, 157th Inf, 22-23. Publ: Numerous articles in Farm and Trade Journals. Mem: Pres, Tri-Co. Beet Growers Asn, 57-66; chmn, Kans-Colo. Beet Asn, 57-66; dir, Mountain State Beet Growers Asn, 63-66; dir, State & Regional Farm and Cattle Asn; pres, Mountain States Hardware & Implement Dealers Asn; finance officer and exec. cmt, Coronado Coun, Boy Scouts; Rotary; Elks; Kans. State C. of C, Agr. Coun; sponsor and leader, 4-H; first sponsor, Am. Legion Baseball Team; Northwest Kans. Free Fair Bd. Recipient of International Award for Outstanding Public Service, Remington-Rand Corp, New Holland Div; Award for Commun. & Industry Pub. Serv, Commercial Credit Co. & Mountain States Asn; Power & Farm Equipment Award, Nat. Farm Equip; Spec. Citation for New Indust. Develop, Kiwanis Int, 68. Rel: Protestant. Legal Res: 1000 East Eighth, Goodland, Kans. 67735. Mailing Add: Box 627, Goodland, Kans. 67735.

DAVIS, WILLIAM BENBOW D
Chmn, Clarendon Co. Dem. Party, S.C.
b. Summerton, S.C, 6/7/20; s. Washington Benbow Davis and Ida Morrison D; m. 6/22/43 to Marjorie Bell; c. Anne, Billy, Becky, Lynn and Bob. Educ: Clemson Col, 1 year; Col. of Charleston, 1 year. Polit. & Govt. Pos: Chmn, Clarendon Co. Welfare Bd, S.C, 61-; chmn, Clarendon Co. Dem. Party, currently. Mil. Serv: Entered as Pvt, Air Force, 41, released as S/Sgt, 45. Mem: State dir, Farm Bur; pres, Sumter, Lee, Clarendon Ginners Asn, 63-65; pres, Lions; comdr, Am. Legion; pres, Jaycees; Mason; Shrine; C. of C; Nat. Cotton Coun; Cotton Producers Inst; Pee Dee Scout Coun. Rel: Baptist. Mailing Add: P.O. Box 371, Summerton, S.C. 29148. (1967)

DAVIS, WILLIAM T. R
Chmn, St. Charles Co. Rep. Cmt, Mo.
b. West Frankford, Ill, 5/4/36; s. W. Floyd Davis and Joan Thornton D; m. June 1962 to Janet M. Wagner; c. Mary Joan and Susan M. Educ: Univ. Ill, B.S. in Eng, 57; Marquette Univ, miscellaneous eng. courses, 62-63. Polit. & Govt. Pos: Treas, St. Charles Co. Rep. Mens Club, Mo, 68; chmn, St. Charles Co. Rep. Cmt, currently. Bus. & Prof. Pos: Engr, A.C. Electronics, Milwaukee, Wis, 57-64; group engr, Conductron-Mo, St. Charles, Mo, currently. Mem: St. Charles Jaycees (bd. dirs). Rel: Methodist. Mailing Add: 1946 Sibley, St. Charles, Mo. 63301.

DAVISON, DENVER N. D
Justice, Supreme Court of Okla.
b. Rich Hill, Mo, 10/9/91; s. Benjamin P. Davison and Lottie Jones D; m. 7/29/17 to Barbara A. Wilhelm. Educ: Univ. Okla, LL.B; Alpha Tau Omega; Phi Delta Phi. Polit. & Govt. Pos: Justice, Supreme Court of Okla, 37- Mil. Serv: Entered as Pfc, Army, 17, released as 2nd Lt, 19. Mem: Mason; Rotary; Elks; K. of P; Am. Legion. Rel: Methodist. Mailing Add: State Capitol Bldg, Oklahoma City, Okla. 73105.

DAVISSON, RUSSELL LEE R
W.Va. State Del.
b. Salem, W.Va, 3/2/22; s. Edwin Roscoe Davisson and Addie Yerkey D; m. 5/12/44 to Mildred Lucille Kemper; c. Andrea Kay (Mrs. John Edward Kenna, IV), Nancy Ann and Daniel Lee. Educ: Salem Col, W.Va, B.S, 44; W.Va. Univ, M.S, 48; Phi Lambda Upsilon; Kappa Alpha Order. Polit. & Govt. Pos: Pres, Jefferson Dist. Rep. Club, St. Albans, W.Va, 52-60; v.pres, Kanawha Co. Young Rep. Club, 54-56; councilman and vice mayor, St. Albans, 61-65; mem, finance cmt, Kanawha Co. Rep. Exec. Cmt, 64, v.chmn, 69-; W.Va. State Del, 67- Bus. & Prof. Pos: Corrosion and materials specialist, Union Carbide Corp, 47- Mil. Serv: Entered as V-7 Student, Navy, 42, released as Lt.(jg), 45, after serv. in Antisubmarine Warfare, Atlantic and Pac. Theaters, 44-45; Atlantic and Pac. Campaign Ribbons; Lt.(jg), Naval Res, 45-55. Publ: A Century with St. Albans, 1863-1963, Harless Printing Co, St. Albans, W.Va, 63. Mem: Nat. Asn. of Corrosion Engrs; Former Jaycee; Am. Legion; W.Va. Wildlife Fedn; Coal River Improv. Asn; Hilawn Swim Club, Inc. Rel: Baptist. Mailing Add: 931 Hughes Dr, St. Albans, W.Va. 25177.

DAVOREN, JOHN FRANCIS XAVIER D
Secy. of the Commonwealth, Mass.
b. Milford, Mass, 7/27/15; s. Thomas F. Davoren (deceased) and Ellen A. Casey D.(deceased); m. 5/1/43 to Eleanor L. Comolli; c. Ellen Ann and Susan Mary. Educ: Col. of the Holy Cross, B.S, 40; Portia Law Sch, LL.B, 63. Hon. D.Sc. Pol, Calvin Coolidge Col; hon. H.H.D, Mass. Col. of Optometry. Polit. & Govt. Pos: Mass. State Rep, Ninth Worcester Dist, 55-67, asst. majority leader, Mass. House of Rep, 61-62, majority leader and acting speaker 63-64, speaker, 65-67; Secy. of the Commonwealth, 67-; del, Dem. Nat. Conv, 68. Bus. & Prof. Pos: Pub. rels. dir, Vet. Admin, Boston, Mass, 46-52 and Off. of Price Stabilization, 52-54. Mil. Serv: Entered as A/S, Navy, 40, released as Lt.(sg), 46, after serv. at Naval Base, San Juan, P.R, Naval Air Sta, Lakehurst, N.J, with GROPAC 8, S.Pac, Naval Beachmaster, Saipan and Tinian and at Naval Base, Saipan; Lt, Naval Res.(Ret); Presidential Unit Citation; ETO and Caribbean Defense Command Ribbons; Pac. Theatre Ribbon with Two Battle Stars. Publ: 'Constitutional Reform: the Continuing Dialogue on the Ways and Means to its Achievement,' Munic. Voice, 2/67. Mem: Nat. Asn. of Secy. of State; Nat. Inst. of Munic. Clerks; Mass. Legislators Asn; dir, Catholic Charitable Bur. of Boston; dir, Portia Law Sch. Alumni; Elks; VFW; Am. Legion; DAV; K. of C; Holy Name Soc; Charitable Irish Soc; State Club of Mass; Knights of Charity; Men of the 200. Cited for Outstanding Interest in and Serv. to Vet—a Nation's Defender, Superior Statesman, Nat. Dept. VFW, 66; hon. mem, Ital-Am. War Vet, Kiwanis, Armenian-Am. Vet, Foggiano Club, Portuguese Club of Milford and Marchegiano Club. Rel: Roman Catholic. Mailing Add: 180 Purchase St, Milford, Mass. 01757.

DAWBARN, HENRY DUNLOP R
Va. State Sen.
b. N.Y.C, 6/14/15; s. Waring Lennox Dawbarn and Alice Carroll Williams D; m. 1/25/69 to Mary Cameron Bufford; c. Henry D, Jr. and Carroll. Educ: Princeton Univ, A.B, 38; Johns Hopkins Univ. Sch. of Eng, 36-46. Polit. & Govt. Pos: Del, Va. Constitutional Conv, 56; city councilman, Waynesboro, 60-64; Va. State Sen, 68- Bus. & Prof. Pos: Pres, Dawbarn Bros, Inc, 50-63 and Dawbarn Div, W.R. Grace & Co, 63-66; chmn. bd, Camac Corp, 68- Mil. Serv: Ens, Naval Res, 45-46, with serv. in Boston Navy Yard. Mem: Chief Execs. Forum. Rel: Episcopal. Legal Res: 855 Fairway Dr, Waynesboro, Va. 22980. Mailing Add: P.O. Box 69, Waynesboro, Va. 22980.

DAWKINS, KIRBY WALLS D
Chmn, Upton Co. Dem. Exec. Cmt, Tex.
b. Baird, Tex, 7/29/13; s. William Henry Dawkins and Clara Elizabeth Walls D; m. 6/19/38 to Lucille Watson; c. Diantha Dee. Educ: Abilene Christian Col, B.S, 35. Polit. & Govt. Pos: Co. precinct chmn, Dem. Party, Tex, 58-60; chmn, Upton Co. Dem. Exec. Cmt, 60-; del, Tex. Dem. State Conv, 64 & 66. Mem: Petroleum Elec. Power Asn.(pres, 64); Lions (pres, zone chmn. and dep. dist. gov); Boy Scouts (30 year vet, mem. coun. exec. bd. and v.pres). Rel: Protestant. Mailing Add: P.O. Box 788, McCamey, Tex. 79752. (1967)

DAWKINS, MAURICE ANDERSON D
Asst. Dir, Off. Econ. Opportunity
b. Chicago, Ill, 1/29/21; s. Anderson M. Dawkins and Marie Von Dickersohn D; m. 5/29/48 to Doris Scott; c. Kimball Maurice and Susan Scott. Educ: Columbia Col, B.A, 43; Union Theol. Sem, M.S, 50, hon. D.D, 64; Alpha Phi Alpha. Polit. & Govt. Pos: V.chmn, N.Y. State Vol. for Stevenson, 52; mem, South. Calif. Campaign Cmt. for Stevenson, 56, for Kennedy, 60; v.chmn, Citizens for Gov. Brown, 58 & 62; mem, Gov. Cmn. Metrop. Area Problems, 59-63 and Mayor's Cmt. Human Rels, Los Angeles, 62-64; mem, South. Calif. Campaign Cmt. for Johnson, 64; mem, Attorney Gen. Adv. Cmt. on Constitutional Rights, Calif, 59-65; state cmnr, Urban Policy, Calif, 59-65; assoc. dir, VISTA, 64-; asst. dir, Off. Econ. Opportunity, 67-; prof. educ, President's Exec. Training Prog, Fed. Exec. Inst, 69- Bus. & Prof. Pos: Assoc. minister and educ. dir, Commun. Church N.Y, 48-54; minister and dir, First Commun. Church Los Angeles, 54-65; founder and first pres, First Commun. Church Home Sr. Citizens, Los Angeles; mem. bd. dirs, Pub. Nat. Bank. Publ: 'Love in Action: A Challenge to the American Negro,' Union Theol. Rev, 44; 'Can Religion Be Democratic,' Thesis, Columbia Univ, 50; 'A Christian Answer,' Calif. Eagle Newspaper, 55. Mem: Am. Acad. Polit. Sci; Am. Psychol. Asn; Mason; Int. Club Wash, D.C; Wash. Athletic Club; Am. Negro Leadership Conf. on Africa; Nat. Urban League; NAACP (pres, Los Angeles Br, v.pres, Southwest area, convention chmn, West Coast, and coast coordinator, March on Wash); founder and chmn, West. Christian Leadership Conf; affiliate, South. Christian Leadership Conf; pres, Int. Coun. Commun. Churches and off. rep, World Coun. Churches. George Washington Carver Award; Urban League Award; Los Angeles Award; Nat. Coun. Negro Women Award. Rel: Council Community Churches. Legal Res: 827 Westchester Place, Los Angeles, Calif. 90005. Mailing Add: Federal Executive Institute, U.S. Civil Service Commission, c/o Thomas Jefferson Inn, Rt. 29 N, Charlottesville, Va. 22903.

DAWSON, BARBARA ANN R
Secy, N.Dak. Rep. Party
b. Washburn, N.Dak, 6/17/27; d. Hans C. Nelson and Irene Haugeberg N; m. 6/23/49 to James R. Dawson; c. Debra Ann, Virginia Lynn, Patricia Sue and Judith Jane. Educ: N.Dak. State Univ, B.S, 49; Sigma Alpha Iota; Alpha Gamma Delta. Polit. & Govt. Pos: Mem. arrangements cmt, Vice President Nixon's Visit to Fargo, N.Dak, 60; campaign off. mgr, Andrews for Gov. Campaign, 62 and mem. steering cmt, Andrews for Cong. Campaign, 63; precinct committeewoman, Cass Co. Rep. Party, 62-; mem, Cass Co. Rep. Exec. Cmt, 63-68; legis. chmn, 21st Dist. Women's Rep. Club, 66; v.chmn, 67; mem,

N.Dak. Rep. State Exec. Cmt, 66-67; mem, N.Dak. Rep. State Cent. Cmt, 66-; secy, N.Dak. Rep. Party, 67-, v.chmn. of publicity cmt, 67-68, chmn, publicity cmt, 69; secy, N.Dak. Rep. State Conv, 68. Mem: Jr. League of Am; PTA. Rel: Presbyterian. Mailing Add: 1749 S. Ninth St, Fargo, N.Dak. 58102.

DAWSON, CARLIN F. D
Polit. & Govt. Pos: Precinct committeeman, Ind. Dem. Party, 6 years; Ind. State Rep, until 66. Bus. & Prof. Pos: Machinist, Delco-Remy Div, Gen. Motors Corp. Mil. Serv: Army. Mem: Am. Legion; Eagles; Local 662, AFL-CIO. Rel: Baptist. Mailing Add: 2324 E. 35th St, Anderson, Ind. 46013. (1967)

DAWSON, DANIEL BOONE R
b. Sissonville, W.Va, 9/12/97; s. David S. Dawson and Lillie Aultz D; wid; c. Anne. Educ: Wash. & Lee Univ, LL.B, 21; Phi Alpha Beta; Omicron Delta Kappa. Polit. & Govt. Pos: Munic. judge, Charleston, W.Va, 31-35, mayor, 35-47; Rep. nominee, Gov, W.Va, 40 & 44; co. attorney, Kanawha Co, 50-54; cmnr. acct, Kanawha Co, 55-; del. and v.chmn, Rep. Nat. Conv, 68. Bus. & Prof. Pos: Attorney-at-law, 47- Mil. Serv: Entered as Pvt, Army, 18, released, 19, after serv. in 220th Engrs. Corps. Mem: Am, W.Va. State and Kanawha Co. Bar Asns; Lions; Elks (Exalted Ruler, Charleston Lodge, 34, Dist. Dep, South. W.Va. Grand Lodge, 51); South. W.Va. Automobile Club (past pres. and present mem. bd. dir). Rel: Baptist. Legal Res: 9 Fern Rd, Charleston, W.Va. 25314. Mailing Add: Box 1405, Charleston, W.Va. 25325.

DAWSON, FRANCES LEDLIE R
Ill. State Rep.
b. Des Moines, Iowa, 12/23/03; d. James Douglas Ledlie and Lydia Sheriff L; m. 6/26/29 to Horace Dawson; c. Mrs. Richard W. Kahlenberg and Mrs. James L. Alkire. Educ: Simpson Col, A.B, 25; Northwest. Univ, M.A, 28; Pi Kappa Delta; Delta Delta Delta. Hon. LL.D, Simpson Col, 68. Polit. & Govt. Pos: Mem, Evanston Plan Cmn, Ill, 45-50; mem, Evanston High Sch. Bd. Educ, 52-57; Ill. State Rep, 57- Bus. & Prof. Pos: Teacher, hist. and civics, Knoxville High Sch, Iowa, 25-27; asst. prof, hist, Simpson Col, 28-29. Mem: Delta Kappa Gamma; Zonta Club of Evanston; Evanston Bus. & Prof. Women's Club; Evanston C. of C; Women's Rep. Club; League of Women Voters; bd. of mgrs, Am. Mid-west chapter, Red Cross, 61-67; mem. bd. of dirs, Nat. Safety Coun, 64-68; Univ. Guild; Lincolnwood Garden Club; Westmoreland Country Club. Received Simpson Col. Alumni Achievement award, 58, and Northwest. Univ. Alumni Merit award, 60. Rel: Presbyterian. Mailing Add: 2609 Lincoln St, Evanston, Ill 60201.

DAWSON, JAMES FRANCIS D
b. New Britain, Conn, 1/12/21; s. James T. Dawson and Agnes Kelly D; m. 11/20/53 to Ann Anthony; c. Christopher James, James Michael and Denise Mary. Educ: Univ. Conn, B.A, 44, LL.B, 50. Polit. & Govt. Pos: Sch. committeeman, New Britain, Conn, 56-58, Mayor, 64-65; agency counsel, New Britain Redevelop. Cmn, 58-61; corp. counsel, Berlin, Conn, 60-64; tax attorney, Conn, 68- Mil. Serv: Entered as Pvt, Army, 42, released as Capt, 46, after serv. in Counter Intel. Corps, ETO; Maj, Army Res; Two Battle Stars. Publ: 'Damages for Wrongful Death', Conn. Bar J, 48; 'The Competent City', J. Housing, 9/67. Mem: Hartford Co. Bar Asn.(pub. cmt, 60-); Conn. Bar Asn; Elks; K. of C; VFW; Lions; Ahepha. Rel: Roman Catholic. Mailing Add: 88 Ten Acre Rd, New Britain, Conn. 06052.

DAWSON, PAUL B. D
b. Rockford, W.Va, 9/22/96; s. C.O. Dawson and Rose V. Batten D; m. 8/4/21 to Mabel Henry; c. Maxiene Linger. Educ: Davis and Elkins Col; Fairmont State Col, A.B; W.Va. Univ, M.A; Sigma Nu. Polit. & Govt. Pos: W.Va. State Del, 64-66. Bus. & Prof. Pos: Teacher; coach, Glenville State Col, 22-26; coach, Fairmont Polar Bears, 28 years; former prin, Miller Jr. High Sch. and Fairmont Jr. High Sch; former pres, Monongahela Valley Athletic Asn, The Big Ten and the State High Sch. Asn; played pro-baseball ten years. Mil. Serv: Naval Res; World War I. Mem: T.B.I; Am. Legion; W.H.S. Coaches Asn. Played football, basketball and baseball for W.Va. Univ. Rel: Methodist. Mailing Add: 526 Benoni Ave, Fairmont, W.Va. 26554. (1967)

DAWSON, TOM HENRY D
Finance chmn, Dem. Party Iowa
b. Fort Dodge, Iowa, 11/20/37; s. Dr. Emerson Blanton Dawson and Pauline Breen D; single. Educ: Univ. Wyo, B.A, 60; Univ. North. Iowa, teaching cert, 66; Sigma Chi. Polit. & Govt. Pos: Pres, Young Dem, Univ. Wyo, 57-60; youth chmn, Campaign for Sen. Gale McGee, U.S. Sen, 58; asst. to youth dir, Youth for Kennedy-Johnson, Wash, D.C, 60; asst. campaign mgr, Dr. E.B. Smith for U.S. Sen, 62 and campaign mgr, 66; finance chmn, Dem. Party Iowa, 67-; del, Dem. Nat. Conv, 68. Bus. & Prof. Pos: Mgr, Dawson Farms, 50- Mil. Serv: Entered as 2nd Lt, Army, 63, released as 1st Lt, 65, after serving in G2 off. of Security, 7th Army, ETO, 63-65; Cert. of Achievement by 7th Army, presented by Gen. Quinn. Mem: Am. Polit. Sci. Asn; Elks; Am. Legion; New Frontier Club of Iowa. Rel: Roman Catholic. Legal Res: 227 S. 12th St, Fort Dodge, Iowa 50501. Mailing Add: 500 Shops Bldg, Des Moines, Iowa 50309.

DAWSON, STEPHEN VANCE R
State Chmn, Co. Chmns. Rep. Orgn, Wis.
b. Greensboro, N.C, 2/14/95; s. George W. Dawson and Lilly Belle Williams D; m. 6/5/17 to Elizabeth Coltrane; c. Mildred Elizabeth (Mrs. George B. Strother). Educ: Elon Col, 2 yrs; Univ. N.C, 1 yr; McClungs Bus. Col. Polit. & Govt. Pos: State chmn, Co. Chmns. Rep. Orgn, Wis; v.chmn, 1st Cong. Dist. Rep. Party and Wis. Rep. State Exec. Cmt; chmn, Walworth Co. Rep. Cmt, 3 yrs. Bus. & Prof. Pos: Sales mgr, South. Br. Armour & Co, 19-25, Barbee-Hayes Co, 26-28 and Tomlinson Furniture Co, 28-31; v.pres, sales and advert, Orange Crush Co, 31-50; pres. and treas, G-S Prod. Lab, Inc. Publ: Articles in nat. antique magazines. Mem: Masonic Lodge 276 AF&AM, Oasis Shrine Temple, Charlotte, N.C; United Commercial Travelers of Am; exec. chmn. bd, Nat. Asn. of Dealers In Antiques Inc; pres, Wis. Antique Dealers Asn. and Kiwanis Club of Whitewater; v.pres, Whitewater Univ. Found. and Southeast. Vacationland Asn; pres, Resort Asn. of Wis; chmn, Wis. State Tourism Coun. Lectr. on Antiques and Art Wares. Rel: Methodist. Mailing Add: 507 W. Main St, Whitewater, Wis, 53190.

DAWSON, WILLIAM L. D
U.S. Rep, Ill.
b. Albany, Ga; m. to Nellie Brown; c. William L, Jr. and Barbara Anne (Mrs. Morgan). Educ: Albany Normal Sch, Ga; Fisk Univ, A.B. magna cum laude; Kent Col. Law, Chicago; Northwest. Univ, LL.B. Polit. & Govt. Pos: State cent. committeeman, First Cong. Dist, Ill, 30-32; alderman of Second Ward, 33-39, Dem. committeeman from Second Ward, 39-; secy, Dem. Cong. Cmt, currently; v.chmn, Dem. Nat. Cmt, currently; v.chmn, Cook Co. Cent.Cmt, currently; U.S. Rep, First Cong. Dist, Ill, 42-, mem, House Cmt. on D.C, 54-, chmn, House Cmt. on Govt. Opers, currently, ranking minority mem, U.S. House of Rep, currently; del, Dem. Nat. Conv, 68. Bus. & Prof. Pos: Attorney. Mil. Serv: Entered Officers' Training Sch, Ft. Des Moines, Iowa, released as 1st Lt. after serv. in 365th Inf, AEF, France, World War I. Legal Res: Chicago, Ill. Mailing Add: 2111 House Office Bldg, Washington, D.C. 20515.

DAY, J. EDWARD D
b. Jacksonville, Ill, 10/11/14; s. James Allmond Day and Frances Wilmot D; m. 7/2/41 to Mary Louise Burgess; c. Geraldine, Mary Louise and James Edward. Educ: Univ. Chicago, A.B, 35; Harvard, LL.B, cum laude, 38; Ill. Col, LL.D; Univ. Nev, LL.D; Phi Kappa Psi; ed, Harvard Law Rev, 36-37. Polit. & Govt. Pos: Legal and legis. asst, Gov. Adlai Stevenson, Ill, 49-50; secy, Ill. Cmn. Intergovt. Coop, 49-53; ins. cmnr. of Ill, 50-53; chmn, Dem. Assocs, Los Angeles, Calif, 58-61; dir, Nat. Capitol Coun, Boy Scouts; v.chmn, Gov. Cmn. Metrop. Area Probs. and mem, Gov. Bus. Adv. Coun, Calif, 50-61; del, Dem. Nat. Conv, 60; Postmaster Gen. U.S, 61-63. Bus. & Prof. Pos: Assoc, Sidley, Austin, Burgess & Harper, 39-41, 45-49; assoc. gen. solicitor, Prudential Ins. Co, 53-56, assoc. gen. counsel, 56, v.pres, West. Opers, Los Angeles, Calif, 57-61; dir, People's Life Ins. Co. and five co. of Zurich Ins. group; bd. fels, Claremont Col, Calif, 58-66; gen. campaign chmn, Los Angeles YMCA, 59; partner, Sidley, Austin, Burgess & Smith, Attorneys, 64- Mil. Serv: Naval Res, Lt, 40-45. Publ: My Appointed Round—929 Days as Postmaster General, Bartholf Street, 46; Humor in Public Speaking, 65. Mem: Nat. Civil Serv. League (pres) 64-67); Nat. Asn. Ins. Cmnrs.(chmn, Midwest zone, 51-53); Am, Fed. and D.C. Bar Asns; chmn, Citizens Conf. on State Legislators; trustee, Meridian House Found; Fed. City, Nat. Press, Int. and Lawyers Clubs. Rel: Methodist. Legal Res: 5804 Brookside Dr, Chevy Chase, Md. 20015. Mailing Add: 1625 Eye St. N.W, Washington, D.C. 20006.

DAY, JACQUELINE R
b. Des Moines, Iowa, 2/17/18; d. Lewis David Armstrong and Mary Jane Reeves A; m. 6/17/38 to Harold Joseph Day; c. Judith Jane (Mrs. Fisher), Timothy Joseph and Anthony Lewis. Educ: East High Sch, Des Moines, Iowa, 33-36; Nat. Honor Soc. Polit. & Govt. Pos: Secy. to chief clerk, Iowa House of Rep, 44-61; secy. to badge cmt, Rep. Nat. Conv, 56, secy. to Iowa del, 60, 64 & 68; secy. to Gov. Norman A. Erbe, 61-62 and Gov. Robert D. Ray, 69-; off. mgr, Rep. State Cent. Cmt, 62-68; mem, fact finding group with U.S. Rep. Fred Schwengel, Iowa and U.S. Rep. William Cowger, Ky, Vietnam, 67. Mil. Serv: Invited to participate in one week of maneuvers, Marines, Camp Pendleton, 68. Publ: 'Vietnam Volunteers,' Cong. Record, 67-68; 'Mom in Vietnam,' Syndicated Newspapers, 67-68. Mem: Iowa Fedn. of Rep. Women; Polk Co. Rep. Women's Club; Marine Corps League; State Little League (dir); Iowa Women's Rep. Club; Navy Mothers' Club; East De Moines Women's Club; Boy Scouts (dir). Lt. Col, Gov. staff; Hon. Marine. Rel: Methodist. Mailing Add: 1414 Royer St, Des Moines, Iowa 50316.

DAY, JAMES MacDONALD R
b. Stamford, Conn, 6/19/30; s. James Day and Catherine Nichols Clark D; m. 9/9/55 to Nancy Carolyn Payne; c. Catherine and James, II. Educ: Piedmont Col, B.A. magna cum laude, 56; Am. Univ, Wash, D.C, LL.B, 59; Delta Theta Phi. Polit. & Govt. Pos: Comptroller and off. mgr, Vol. for Nixon-Lodge, Wash, D.C, 60; dir. admin, Goldwater for Pres. Cmt. and Citizens for Goldwater-Miller, San Francisco, Calif. and Wash, D.C, 63-64; asst. gen. counsel, Young Rep. Nat. Fedn, Wash, D.C, 65-67; civil serv. cmnr, Arlington Co, Va, 66; dir. admin, United Citizens for Nixon, Wash, D.C, 68; chmn, Arlington Co. Rep. Cmt, Va, 68-69; campaign mgr, Echols for Sen, 69. Bus. & Prof. Pos: Mem, Cent. Intel. Agency, Wash, D.C, 56-60; attorney-at-law, 60-69. Mil. Serv: Entered as Pvt, Army, 51, released as Cpl, 53, after serv. in 13th Airborne Rangers and 187th Airborne Recruit, Far East Theatre. Mem: Am. Coun. of Young Polit. Leaders. Rel: Presbyterian. Mailing Add: 2232 N. Madison St, Arlington, Va. 22205.

DAY, JAMES WALTER D
b. Parma, Ohio, 6/5/24; s. George F. Day and Ethel M. Groudle D; m. 6/21/47 to Caroline C. Cismar; c. James W, Jr. Polit. & Govt. Pos: Mem, Zoning Bd. of Appeals, Ohio, 52-54; v.pres, Parma Dem. Club, 54-56; ward leader, Parma, 54-60, councilman, 54-61; mem, Cuyahoga Co. Dem. Exec. Cmt, 55-66; mayor, Parma, 62-67; del, Dem. Nat. Conv, 64; mem, Ohio State Platform Cmt, 64. Bus. & Prof. Pos: Mem. exec. cmt, Regional Planning 58-66; officer, The Higbee Co, v.pres. pub. affairs, currently. Mil. Serv: Entered as Pvt, Army and Army Air Force, 43, released as Navigator, 45. Mem: Cuyahoga Co. Mayors and City Mgrs. Asn, treas, 63-65, v.pres, 65; Ohio Mayors Asn; Seven Co. Transportation Cmt; Am. Legion 213; Elks; St. Charles Club; Parma Slovak Club; hon. mem, Italian Sons and Daughters; Parma Booster Club; Growth Asn; Ad Club; City Club. Rel: Catholic. Mailing Add: 8200 Salisbury Dr, Parma, Ohio 44129.

DAY, JOAN THOMSON R
Mem, Calif. Rep. State Cent. Cmt.
b. Boston, Mass, 9/17/19; d. Stuart Thomson and Dorothy Faunce T; div; c. April (Mrs. Richard Eberle), Susan (Mrs. Bernard Ledieu), Robert W, III and Linda. Educ: Bennington Col, 37-39. Polit. & Govt. Pos: Mem, Calif. Rep. State Cent. Cmt, 67- Rel: Episcopal. Mailing Add: 1440 Westhaven Rd, San Marino, Calif. 91108.

DAY, L. B. D
Ore. State Rep.
b. Omaha, Nebr, 2/22/32; s. L.B. Day Sr. and Neva Grimwood D; m. 2/19/61 to Cynthia Lang; c. Frank E. Educ: Willamette Univ, B.A. in Polit. Sci, 58; Sigma Nu. Polit. & Govt. Pos: Ore. State Rep, currently; chmn, Marion Co. Civil Serv. Cmn, 63-65. Mil. Serv: Entered as Seaman, Navy, 50, released as Qm. 1/C, 55, after serv. in Korean-Far East Theater; Good Conduct, Am. and UN Medals. Mem: Mason; Farmers Union; Cannery Workers Local 670; Family Counselling Serv; Salem Art Asn. Jr. First Citizen, Salem, Ore, 66; One of Ore. Ten Outstanding Young Men, 67; Salem First Citizen, 68. Rel: Presbyterian. Mailing Add: 1391 Warren St. S, Salem, Ore. 97302.

DAY, LAURENCE JAMES D
Wis. State Assemblyman
b. Elderon, Wis, 10/18/13; s. Roy A. Day and Eleanor McPeck D; m. 9/3/35 to Florence M. King; c. Elaine (Mrs. Robert Hanke), Marvel (Mrs. Leonard Adams), Sharon (Mrs. William Wright), Lois (Mrs. Kenneth Karpf), Daniel P, Kenneth L, Warren J, Laurence J, Jr. and Carla A. Educ: Wittenberg High Sch, Wis, grad, 32. Polit. & Govt. Pos: Clerk, Elderon, Wis, 40-; chmn, Marathon Co. Agr. Stabilization & Conserv. Serv, 54-68; Wis. State Assemblyman, 69- Bus. & Prof. Pos: Second v.pres, Consolidated Badger Coop, 48-68. Mem: Elks. Rel: Catholic. Mailing Add: Route 1, Eland, Wis. 54427.

DAY, ROBERT GEORGE R
Ill. State Rep.
b. Peoria, Ill, 11/30/13; s. George Day and Myrtle Entwistle D; m. 4/19/40 to Marthann Judy; c. Susan Wallace, Robert George and Douglas Stephen. Educ: Univ. Ill, B.S, 39. Polit. & Govt. Pos: Mayor, Peoria, Ill, 61-65; Ill. State Rep, 66-, mem, Cmts. on Ins, Munic. and Water Resources, Constitutional Conv, Steering Cmt. and Constitutional Conv. Study Cmn, Ill. House of Rep. Bus. & Prof. Pos: Attorney-at-law, Peoria, Ill, 39- Mil. Serv: Entered as Pvt, Army, 43, released as S/Sgt, 45, after serv. in Field Artil. and Judge Adv. Gen. Corps, ETO, 44-45; Battle Participation Stars, Normandy, North. France and Rhine. Mem: Peoria and Ill. Bar Asns; Admitted to practice before U.S. Supreme Court; Kiwanis; life mem, Ill. Cong. Parents and Teachers. Peoria Jaycees Good Govt. Award; Peoria Izaak Walton League Citation. Rel: Protestant. Legal Res: 2601 North Kingston Dr, Peoria, Ill. 61604. Mailing Add: 1022 Jefferson Bldg, Peoria, Ill. 61602.

DAY, THEODORE D. R
N.Y. State Sen.
b. New York, N.Y, 4/20/17; m. to Frances M. MacPherson; c. Mary (Mrs. Richard Endreney), Richmond and Katharine. Educ: Yale Univ, 40. Polit. & Govt. Pos: Supvr, Covert, N.Y, 49-; N.Y. State Assemblyman, 60-65; N.Y. State Sen, 49th Dist, 65- Bus. & Prof. Pos: Consult. pub. rels, Philip Morris Tobacco Co, 40-41; farmer, 41-43 & 46-64. Mil. Serv: Merchant Marine, 43-46. Mem: F&AM; Grange; Seneca Co. Exten. Serv; Farm Bur; Interlaken Sportsmen's Club. Rel: Reformed Church. Mailing Add: R.D.2, Interlaken, N.Y. 14847.

DAY, WILLIAM S. 'BILL' D
Wash. State Sen.
b. Rockford, Ill, 1923; m. to Norma; c. Five. Educ: Palmer Col. of Chiropractic, Davenport, Iowa. Polit. & Govt. Pos: Former Wash. State Rep. and Speaker, Wash. House of Rep; Wash. State Sen, 69- Bus. & Prof. Pos: Chiropractor. Mil. Serv: Army. Mem: Kiwanis; VFW. Mailing Add: 2721 E. Sprague, Spokane, Wash. 99202.

DEALAMAN, DORIS W. R
First V.Chmn, Somerset Co. Rep. Party, N.J.
b. Hagerstown, Md, 3/1/19; d. Dr. Irvin M. Wertz and Ruth D. Barnhart W; m. 5/3/42 to Laird Wilson Dealaman; c. Frederic J. and Laird Wertz. Educ: Duke Univ, A.B, 40; Columbia Univ, M.S, 43; Phi Beta Kappa. Polit. & Govt. Pos: Munic. chmn, Rep. Party, Bernardsville, N.J, 60-66, borough councilwoman, 64-66; first v.chmn, Somerset Co. Rep. Party, 66-; freeholder, Somerset Co, 67-; mem, N.J. Bd. Pub. Welfare, 68- Bus. & Prof. Pos: Soc. group work, YWCA, Germantown, Pa, 42-45, N.Y.C, 45-48, Jersey City, 48-50 and Plainfield, 50-52. Mem: Voting mem, N.J. Asn. Chosen Freeholders; Nat. Asn. Co. Off.(health and educ. steering cmt); Somerset Co. Coun. Commun. Serv.(v.pres); bd, Somerset Hills YMCA; bd, N.J. Asn. Ment. Health, Inc. Rel: Episcopal. Mailing Add: Round Top Rd, Bernardsville, N.J. 07924.

DEAN, BETTY MANOWN D
Asst. Sgt-at-Arms, W.Va. State Senate
b. Fayette Co, W.Va; d. Rawlston Rector Manown, Sr. and Beulah Mae Dorsey M; m. to James Judy Dean, Sr.(deceased); c. James Judy, Jr, William Allen and Joseph Manown. Educ: Center Col; Greenbrier Col. Polit. & Govt. Pos: Mem, Greenbrier Co. Dem. Exec. Cmt, W.Va, 12 years; asst. doorkeeper, W.Va. State Senate, 2 years, asst. sgt-at-arms, 66-; del, Dem. Nat. Conv, 68. Mem: Eastern Star; Federated Woman's Club. Rel: Methodist. Legal Res: Rupert, W.Va. 25984. Mailing Add: Room 215, State Capitol, Charleston, W.Va. 25305.

DEAN, ERNEST H. D
Utah State Sen.
b. American Fork, Utah, 5/17/14; s. Owen Dean and Amy Dickerson D; m. 12/23/35 to Mildred Glissmeyer; c. Connie Ann (Mrs. Haws), Donna (Mrs. Larsen), Ernest H, Jr. and Millicent (Mrs. D. Pennovich). Educ: Brigham Young Univ, B.S, 37, M.Ed.Admin, 57; Univ. Utah, Ed.D, 68; 4-year Letterman, Track; Phi Delta Kappa. Polit. & Govt. Pos: Utah State Rep, 49-51 & 59-63, Speaker of the House, Utah House of Rep, chmn, Legis. Coun, Majority Leader, Minority Leader and officer, Nat. Legis. Leaders Conf; city judge, American Fork, Utah, 58-59; Utah State Sen, 67-, exec. committeeman, Coun. State Govt, 67-, chmn, Human Resource Cmt, West. Div, 67-69, mem, Fed-State Rels. Cmt, Nat. Legis. Conf, 67-69; alternate del, Dem. Nat. Conv, 68. Bus. & Prof. Pos: Dir. and chmn. bd, Savings and Loan Co; contractor, Dean Construction Co, 61-67; dir, West. Nat. Investment Co, 64-67. Publ: 'Junior College and Vocational Education', Utah Trade Tech. Inst, 66; 'Accreditation of Vocational and Technical Education', State of Utah, 67; 'Factors a Manufacturing Company Consider As They Select Their New Plant Site Locations,' 68; plus 1 other. Mem: Nat. Panel of Consult. on Voc. Educ; Am. Voc. Asn; Utah Educ. Asn; Lions. Rel: Latter-day Saint. Mailing Add: 165 S. Third East, American Fork, Utah 84003.

DEAN, HERSHEL EDWIN D
Secy, Williams Co. Dem. Cent. Cmt, Ohio
b. Center Twp, Williams Co, Ohio, 5/25/04; s. Charles M. Dean and Nora Belle Davis D; m. 7/21/49 to Leona Mae Hicks; c. Doris (Mrs. Goldsberry). Educ: Int. Col, Ft. Wayne, Ind, Gen. Bus, 22-23. Polit. & Govt. Pos: Village letter carrier, U.S. Post Off, Montpelier, Ohio, 24-25, city letter carrier, 25-46, rural letter carrier, 46-64; Dem. precinct committeeman, Montpelier, 65-, mem. city coun. and chmn. street cmt, 66-69; secy, Williams Co. Dem. Cent. Cmt, 66-; mem, Williams Co. Elec. Bd, 66-; mem, Montpelier Planning Cmn, 66-; mem, Williams Co. Regional Planning Cmn, 68- Mil. Serv: Entered as 3/C PO, Navy, 42, released as Mail Man 1/C, 45, after serv. in 53rd Naval Construction Bn, 1st Marine Amphibious Corps, New Caledonia, Guadacanal, Vella La Vella Eniwetok and Guam, 43-45; Naval Unit Citation for first Marine Amphibious Corps; Presidential Unit Citation. Publ: Published newspaper for Williams Co. Conserv. League, 38-42; write hunting and fishing column for Montpelier newspaper, 56- Mem: Nat. Asn. Letter Carriers (secy, Montpelier Br, 25-42, pres, Northwest. Ohio, 31-35); Nat. Asn. Rural Carriers; Ohio State Asn. Letter Carriers (chmn. exec. cmt, 33-35); VFW (comdr, Williams Co. Post 944, 47-49); Am. Legion; DAV; Eagles; Williams Co. Conserv. League (secy, 37-43, 46-49); Ohio Asn. Elec. Officials; Ohio Dem. Party; Nat. Asn. Retired Civil Employees; secy, Montpelier C. of C, 35-37. Rel: Presbyterian. Mailing Add: 207 W. Water St, Montpelier, Ohio 43543.

DEAN, JAMES EDWARD D
Ga. State Rep.
b. Atlanta, Ga, 3/14/44; s. Steve Dean Sr. and Dorothy Cox D; m. 6/12/66 to Vyvyan Ardena Coleman. Educ: San Francisco State Col, summer 62; Clark Col, B.A, 66; Fisk Univ, cert, summer 67; Univ. Ga, cert, fall, 67; Atlanta Univ, M.S.W, 68; Alpha Kappa Delta; Am. Acad. Soc. Sci; Am. Acad. Polit. Sci; Alpha Phi Chap, Alpha Phi Alpha; Eta Lambda Grad. Chap; Coun. on Relig. and Int. Affairs Fel, 68; Atlanta Univ. scholarship, 68-69; Sociol. Research-Multi-Purpose fel, 68-69; Nat. Cmt. on Educ. Affairs fel, 69. Polit. & Govt. Pos: Field rep, On-the-Job Training, Manpower Develop. and Training Act Proj, Atlanta, Ga, 66-67; Ga. State Rep. cand, East Commun. Orgn, 67; mem. bd. dirs, Dekalb Health Bd, 67; mem, Atlanta Commun. Rels. Cmn, City of Atlanta, 68; Ga. State Rep, 76th Dist, Ga. Gen. Assembly, 68- Bus. & Prof. Pos: Cox carpet and cleaning serv. clerk, Magic Carpet, Atlanta, 57-58; rep, Atlanta Daily World, 57-62; mgr. ed. bd, Atlanta Inquirer Inc, 62-65; B.M.C. Realty Co. clerk, B.M.C. Ins, 65-66; counsr. and asst. manpower dir, Econ. Opportunity Atlanta, 65-66; commun. rels. specialist, 68; teacher, Atlanta Bd. of Educ, 66; recreation proj. dir, commun. orgn. consult. and field rep, Atlanta Urban League, 67, dir, New Trust Prog; registrn. worker, Atlanta Citizens Cmt, 68-69. Publ: 'A Study of Community Organization Techniques Utilized By Three Self-Help Projects In Securing Low-Income Involvement, 6/68; author and co-author of numerous Legis. Bills and Resolutions. Mem: Atlanta Soc. Workers Club; Ga. Conf. on Soc. Welfare; Nat. Asn. Soc. Workers, Inc.(rep, State Coun); Nat. Soc. State Legislators; Ga. Sheriffs Asn; Dekalb Cmt. for Respect and Equality; Dekalb Dem. Club; UMCA; Dekalb Youth Coord. Cmt; Atlanta Commun. Rels. Cmn; NAACP; mem, Ga. House of Rep. Educ, Hwy. and Welfare Cmts, Cmt. on Hunger and Malnutrition and Judiciary Matters Subcmt; co-chmn, Metrop. Atlanta Conf. on Hunger and Malnutrition; bd. dirs, Dakalb Co. Unit, Am. Cancer Soc; Ment. Health Adv. Cmt, Dekalb Co; Nat. Cmt. in Support of Pub. Schs; E. Lake Civic League; Young Men on the Go; Men of Clark Club; Atlanta Univ. Alumni Asn; Eastside Commun. Coun. and Urban Leagues. Recognition of Pub. Serv. Achievement Award, Atlanta Inquirer; Sponsored for Elec. Victory as First Black Elec. Official in Dekalb Co. and First Black Suburban Legis. in the World. Rel: Protestant. Mailing Add: 17 E. Lake Dr. N.E, Atlanta, Ga. 30317.

DEAN, JAMES PORTER D
b. Corinth, Miss, 8/26/33; married. Polit. & Govt. Pos: Miss. State Sen, 60-64 & 66-69. Bus. & Prof. Pos: Lawyer. Mem: Am. Legion; Miss. and Am. Bar Asns; Alcorn Co. Hunting and Fishing Club; Kiwanis. Rel: Baptist. Mailing Add: 923 Sixth St, Corinth, Miss. 38834. (1967)

DEAN, JOHN D
Dir. Minorities Div, Dem. Nat. Cmt.
b. Baltimore, Md, 10/17/30; m. to Maryann Franklin; c. Kenneth, Phyllis, Michael and Carole. Educ: Howard Univ, 56-60; Phi Beta Kappa. Polit. & Govt. Pos: For. serv. officer, Am. Embassy, Repub. of Sudan, U.S. Info. Agency, 60-61, for. serv. officer and press attache of Am. Embassy, Liberia and Sierra Leone, 61-62 and desk officer, W.African Affairs, 63; dir, Spec. African Student Progs, African Am. Inst, 63-65; Hq. Commun. Action Progs. desk officer for Mid-Atlantic and Southeast Regional Offices, Off. of Econ. Opportunity, 65-66 and regional adminstr. of Commun. Action Progs, Southeast Region, 66-68; assoc. dir. and mem. local coalition staff, Southeast Region, Urban Coalition, 68-69; dir. minorities div, Dem. Nat. Cmt, 69- Mil. Serv: Air Force, 51-55. Mailing Add: 2600 Virginia Ave. N.W, Washington, D.C. 20037.

DEAN, JOHN BINGHAM 'J.B.' D
b. Denver, Colo, 7/6/23; s. Arthur S. Dean and Mary Omalley D; m. 6/14/48 to Marilyn Stebbins; c. Twins, Mary and Elizabeth, Bingham, Stebbins and Amy. Educ: Univ. Colo, 41-42, 46-49; U.S. Naval Acad, 42; Phi Alpha Delta. Polit. & Govt. Pos: Nominee, U.S. Rep, Nebr, 68. Bus. & Prof. Pos: Co-owner, Stebbins Int. Harvester Co, Gothenburg, Nebr, 58- Mil. Serv: Entered as Pvt, Marines, 43, released as 1st Lt, 46, after serving in Fleet Marine Force, S.Pac. and Alaska. Mem: Am. Legion; Elks; C. of C. Rel: Catholic. Mailing Add: 1615 Lake Ave, Gothenburg, Nebr. 69138.

DEAN, JOHN WESLEY, III R
Assoc. Dep. Attorney Gen, Dept. of Justice
b. Akron, Ohio, 10/14/38; s. John Wesley Dean, Jr. and Sarah Magill D; m. 2/3/61 to Karla Ann Hennings; c. John Wesley, IV. Educ: Colgate Univ, 57-59; Col. Wooster, B.A, 61; Am. Univ. Grad. Sch. of Govt. and Pub. Admin, 61-62; Georgetown Univ. Law Center, LL.B, 65; Phi Sigma Alpha; Sigma Nu. Polit. & Govt. Pos: Chief minority counsel, House Judiciary Cmt, U.S. House of Rep, 66-67; assoc. dir, Nat. Cmn. on Reform of Fed. Criminal Laws, 67-69; assoc. dep. attorney gen, Dept. of Justice, 69- Publ: 'Federalism: Revisited Before and After Reapportionment', D.C. Bar J, 3/65; 'One Man, One Vote—Problems of Judicial Enforcement of Standards of Political Conduct', Okla. Bar Asn. J, 7/65; 'Political Broadcasting—Section 315 of the Communications Act of 1934', Fed. Commun. Bar J, 1/66. Mem: Am. Bar Asn; Sumner Citizens Asn, Md. Mallory Medal; Constitutional Law Award; Law Week Award; Am. Jurisp. Prizes for Excellence in Admin. Law and for Excellence in Legis; Col. Wooster Rep. in Wash. Semester Prog, 60. Rel: Episcopal. Legal Res: Md. Mailing Add: 6013 Overlea Rd, Washington, D.C. 20016.

DEAN, KENNETH LEON D
Mem, Hinds Co. Dem. Cmt, Miss.
b. Rogersville, Tenn, 5/25/35; s. James Charles Deane, Sr. and Bertie Eve

Couch D; m. 5/25/67 to Mary Louise James. Educ: Carson Newman Col, B.A, 59; Colgate-Rochester Divinity Sch, B.D, 65. Polit. & Govt. Pos: Del, Dem. Nat. Conv, 68; mem, Hinds Co. Dem. Cmt, Miss, 69- Bus. & Prof. Pos: Exec. dir, Miss. Coun. Human Rels, 65- Mem: Nat. Asn. Commun. Develop. Rel: Southern Baptist. Mailing Add: 4074 N. State St, Jackson, Miss. 39206.

DEAN, NATHAN D. D
Ga. State Rep.
b. Rockmart, Ga, 5/9/34; s. Thomas James Dean and Ellen Brooke D; m. 9/2/61 to Norma Ann Carpenter. Educ: Shorter Col, B.B.A, 62. Polit. & Govt. Pos: Mem, City Coun, Rockmart, Ga, 60-; Ga. State Rep, 63- Bus. & Prof. Pos: Employee, Lockheed Aircraft Corp. Mil. Serv: Cpl, Army, Research and Eng. Command, 56-58. Mem: Shrine; Jaycees (bd. dirs); Touchdown Club (bd. dirs). Rel: Baptist. Mailing Add: 4009 Third Ave, Rockmart, Ga. 30153. (1967)

DEAN, ROBERT PAYNE D
Md. State Sen.
b. Ridgely, Md, 4/9/09; s. Robert Gary Dean and Maude Jones D; m. 9/7/40 to Miriam Bishop; c. Frances (Mrs. Roschy). Educ: Washington Col, A.B, 31; Blue Key. Polit. & Govt. Pos: Md. State Sen, Queen Annes Co, 55-66, 15th Sen. Dist, 67- Bus. & Prof. Pos: Deck Officer, Merchant Marine, 34-40. Mem: Past pres, Queen Anne's Co. Farm Bur. and Rotary. Rel: Methodist. Mailing Add: Anchor Rest Farm, Centreville, Md. 21617.

DEAN, ROSCOE EMORY, JR. D
Ga. State Sen.
b. Jesup, Ga, 9/2/36; s. Roscoe Emory Dean and Lilly Ellis D; single. Educ: Univ. Ga, B.A. in journalism, 60; John Marshall Univ, J.D, 63; Delta Theta Phi; Theta Chi. Polit. & Govt. Pos: Campaign mgr. for Congresslady Iris Blitch, Ga, 54; mem, Ga. Cong. Dem. Exec. Cmt, 54; state-wide pres, Young Adults for Herman Talmadge for U.S. Sen, 56; Ga. State Sen, Sixth Dist, currently. Bus. & Prof. Pos: Self employed in turpentine, farming, pub. rels. and bus. interests. Mil. Serv: Entered as Basic Trainee, Ga. Air Nat. Guard, 59, released as S/Sgt, 65, after serv. in Inactive Res; Outstanding Grad, Lackland Air Force Base, Tex. Publ: 'Anti-Suicide Centers,' Atlanta J. Newspaper, 65; Ga. Law of Garnishment, John Marshall Univ, 63. Mem: Ga. Peace Officers Asn; Ga. and Wayne Co. Farm Bur; Moose; WOW; Ga. Jaycees. Rel: Baptist. Mailing Add: 612 Cherry St, Jesup, Ga. 31545.

DEAN, RUSSELL J. D
Educ: Butler Univ; Ind. Univ. Sch. of Law; Lambda Chi Alpha; Phi Alpha Delta; Tau Kappa Alpha. Polit. & Govt. Pos: Marion Co. dep. prosecutor, 62; Ind. State Rep, -66. Bus. & Prof. Pos: Attorney. Mem: Brookside Masonic Lodge; Indianapolis Athletic Club; City, State and Nat. Bar Asns. Rel: Methodist; steward, Irvington Methodist Church. Mailing Add: 825 N. Whittier Pl, Indianapolis, Ind. 46219. (1967)

DEAN, THOMAS RICHARD D
Mem, Exec. Cmt, Nebr. Dem. Coalition
b. Scottsbluff, Nebr, 3/14/46; s. Darius Augusta Dean, II and Elizabeth Mae Ellis D; single. Educ: Nebr. West. Col, 64-66; Univ. Nebr, J.D. cand, 66-; Phi Theta Kappa; Delta Theta Pi. Polit. & Govt. Pos: Mem. cent. cmt, Univ. Nebr. Young Dem, 67-68; del, Dem. Nat. Conv, 68; mem. exec. cmt, Nebr. Dem. Coalition, 69- Bus. & Prof. Pos: Pres, Mogul Equities, Inc, 69. Rel: Disciples of Christ. Legal Res: 1114 W. Overland, Scottsbluff, Nebr. 69361. Mailing Add: 1532 N. 24th, Lincoln, Nebr. 68503.

DEAN, WILLIAM DENARD DFL
Chmn, 15th Sen. Dist. New Dem. Coalition, Minn.
b. South Bend, Ind, 7/12/37; s. William Stover Dean and Eleanor Hatcher D; m. 9/17/60 to Patricia Fletcher; c. Jennifer and Colin William. Educ: Carleton Col, B.A, 59; Union Theol. Sem, 59-60; Divinity Sch, Univ. Chicago, M.A, 64 and Ph.D, 67; asst. to Paul Tillich, Divinity Sch, Univ. Chicago, 64-65. Polit. & Govt. Pos: Mem. exec. cmt, Ashland Co. Dem. Party, Wis, 67-68; chmn, Ashland Co. McCarthy for Pres. Cmt, 68; del, Dem. Nat. Conv, 68; chmn, 15th Sen. Dist. New Dem. Coalition, Minn, 69- Bus. & Prof. Pos: Asst. prof. philos. and relig, Northland Col, Ashland, Wis, 66-68; asst. prof. relig, Gustavus Adolphus Col, St. Peter, Minn, 68- Publ: 'Death: A Theological Reappraisal,' Criterion, winter 65; 'Fireflies in a Quagmire,' J. of Relig, 10/68. Mem: Am. Asn. Univ. Prof; Am. Acad. Relig. Research grant, Gustavus Research Fund, 69-70. Rel: Methodist. Mailing Add: 918 S. Washington Ave, St. Peter, Minn. 56082.

DEARBORN, HENRY Independent
b. Lawrence, Mass, 1/30/13; s. Henry Follansby Dearborn and Grace Elizabeth Valpey D; m. 11/16/46 to Maria-Rosa Pareja; c. Pamela M. and Henry Mark. Educ: Dartmouth Col, B.A, 36; Yale Univ. Grad. Sch, M.A, 38; Nat. War Col, 58-59; Kappa Sigma. Polit. & Govt. Pos: V.consul, Am. Consulate, Barranquilla, Colombia, 41-42 and V.Consulate, Manta, Ecuador, 42-44; desk officer for Ecuador, U.S. Dept. of State, Wash, D.C, 44-47, Argentina, 47-52, chief, River Plate Div.(Argentina, Paraguay and Uruguay), 52-54, dep. dir, Off. of S.Am. Affairs, 55; Chief, polit. sect, Am. Embassy, Lima, Peru, 56-58, counselor of embassy, Ciudad Trujillo, Dominican Rep, 59-60, Bogota, Colombia, 61-67, minister-counselor, Mexico, D.F, Mex, 67-; consul gen, Am. Consulate Gen, Ciudad Trujillo, 60-61. Mem: Am. For. Serv. Asn. Rel: Protestant. Legal Res: Morrison Rd, Windham, N.H. 03087. Mailing Add: American Embassy, Mexico, D.F, Mex.

DEARDORFF, JOHN HOWARD R
b. Bendersville, Pa, 10/30/09; s. John Howard Deardorff and Anna Slusser D; m. 6/32 to Mary Emily Dunbar; c. Peggy Ann and John Howard. Educ: High Sch. Polit. & Govt. Pos: City Councilman, Johnstown, Pa, 61-65 & 66-68. Bus. & Prof. Pos: Merchant, 40 years. Mem: Mason; Blue Lodge 538; New Castle Consistory; Jaffa Shrine; Elks; Lions; Advertising Club. Rel: Protestant. Mailing Add: 612 Pine St, Johnstown, Pa. 15902.

DEARDOURFF, JOHN D. R
b. Greenville, Ohio, 3/11/33; s. David J. Deardourff and Ella S. McGreevey D; m. 2/1/58 to Mary Jane McFerran, separated; c. Ann Elizabeth and Katherine McBride. Educ: Wabash Col, B.A, 55; Fletcher Sch. Law and Diplomacy, M.A, 56; Am. Univ. Sch. Int. Serv, 57-59; Blue Key; Phi Delta Theta. Polit. & Govt. Pos: Partner, Campaign Consult. Inc, at present; dir. of res, N.Y. Rep. State Cmt, 65-67; co-dir. of res, John V. Lindsay for Mayor, 65; asst. dir. of res, Rockefeller for Pres, Campaign, 62-64; legis. asst, Rep. Jessica McC. Weis, 38th Dist, N.Y, 59-62; legis. admin. asst, Rep. J. Harry McGregor, 17th Dist, Ohio, 57-59. Mem: Am. Acad. of Polit. and Social Sci; Capitol Hill Club. Rel: Episcopal. Mailing Add: 155 W. 95th St, New York, N.Y. 10025. (1967)

DEATHERAGE, ALICE EUNICE R
V.Chmn, Bent Co. Rep. Party, Colo.
b. Las Animas, Colo, 11/17/37; d. Roy Doig Cooper and Anita Crowe C; m. 11/22/56 to John Miles Deatherage; c. Michael Miles and John Scott. Educ: Colo. State Univ, 56-57. Polit. & Govt. Pos: V.chmn, Bent Co. Rep. Party, Colo, 65- Mem: Inter SeSe; PEO. Rel: Presbyterian. Mailing Add: Route 2, Box 179A, Las Animas, Colo. 81054.

DEATON, CHARLES M. D
Miss. State Rep.
b. Hattiesburg, Miss, 1/19/31; s. Ivan Dean Deaton and Martha Fortenberry D; m. 8/15/51 to Mary Dent Dickerson; c. Beverly Diane and Dara Lane. Educ: Millsaps Col, B.A; Univ. Miss, LL.B; Omicron Delta Kappa; Phi Delta Phi. Polit. & Govt. Pos: Miss. State Rep, 60-, mem. bd. dirs, Miss. Research and Develop. Coun, Miss. House of Rep, 64-, chmn, Leflore Co. Rural Area Develop, 66- Bus. & Prof. Pos: Partner, Law Firm of Brewen, Deaton & Evans, 60-; mem. bd. dirs, Rivers & Harbors Asn, Miss, 62-; secy, Fish & Farms Inc, 66- Mil. Serv: Entered as Seaman, Navy, 51, released as PO 2/C, 54; Nat. Defense Serv, Korean Serv, UN Serv. and Good Conduct Medals. Mem: Miss. and Am. Bar Asns; VFW; Am. Legion; Farm Bur; C. of C; Lions. Received letters in football and basketball, Millsaps Col. Rel: Episcopal. Legal Res: 501 E. Harding, Greenwood, Miss. 38930. Mailing Add: Drawer B, Greenwood, Miss. 38930. (1967)

DeBAISE, PASQUALE JOHN D
Conn. State Rep.
b. Wallingford, Conn, 8/13/26; s. Pasquale DeBaise and Susan DelVechia D; m. 11/22/47 to Florence Ann Carroll; c. John P, Dennis J, Pat J. and Thomas A. Educ: Wallingford Local Schs, 11 years. Polit. & Govt. Pos: Mem, Planning and Zoning Cmt, Wallingford, Conn, 58-66; dist. chmn, Wallingford Dem. Town Cmt, 58-67; Conn. State Rep, 82nd Dist, 67-, clerk, State Develop. Cmt, Conn. House of Rep, 67-69, chmn, Parks and Forest Subcmt. and clerk, Rd. and Bridges Cmt, 67- Mil. Serv: Entered as Seaman, Navy, 44, released as 3/C PO, 46, after serv. in S.Pac. Fleet, Asiatic Theatre, 45-46; Am. Theatre Medal; Victory Medal; Asiatic Pac. Medal; Occupation Medal. Mem: Am. Legion; VFW. Rel: Catholic. Mailing Add: 44 Third St, Wallingford, Conn. 06492.

DEBAR, FRANK RICHARD R
Chmn, Peabody Rep. City Cmt, Mass.
b. Flushing, N.Y, 7/17/30; s. Frank L.E. Debar and Julia Fleming D; m. 5/15/51 to June E. Burgess; c. June Leslie, John Francis and Nancy Jeanne. Educ: East. Nazarene Col, Mass. Polit. & Govt. Pos: Peabody City campaign chmn, Cmt. to Reelect Gov. John Volpe, Mass, 66; mem, Peabody Draft Bd, Planning Bd. and Redevelop. Adv. Cmt, 66-; chmn, Peabody Rep. City Cmt, currently. Bus. & Prof. Pos: Ins. underwriter, John Hancock Ins, 54-; real estate broker and Notary Pub, 66- Mem: Peabody Jaycees (pres, 61-62); Mason, Lynnfield. Rel: Protestant. Mailing Add: 10 Leonard Rd, Peabody, Mass. 01960. (1967)

DEBBINS, WILLIAM R
City Councilman, Mt. Vernon, Iowa
b. Flint, Mich, 3/28/27; s. Joseph Michael Debbins and Nellie Josephine Hyde D; m. 5/30/53 to Solvita Kalnins; c. Paul Alexander and Katherine Kaija. Educ: Cent. Mich. Univ, A.B, 52; Syracuse Univ, M.A, 53, Ph.D, 59. Polit. & Govt. Pos: City councilman, Mt. Vernon, Iowa, 67-; alternate del, Rep. Nat. Conv, 68. Bus. & Prof. Pos: Instr. philos, Syracuse Univ, 56-59; asst. prof, Elmira Col, 59-62; assoc. prof, Cornell Col, 62-65, Erastus Burroughs Soper prof, 65- Mil. Serv: Entered as Aviation Cadet, Army Air Force, 44, released as Sgt, 47, after serv. in European Air Transport Serv, ETO, 46-47. Publ: Constructive Ethics (with T.V. Smith), Prentice-Hall, 61; ed, Essays in Philosophy of History, McGraw-Hill, 66 and Aphorisms of O. Spengler, Henry Regnery, 67. Mem: Am. Asn. Univ. Prof; Mind Asn; Philos. of Sci. Asn; Am. Philos. Asn. Mailing Add: 824 Summit Ave, Mt. Vernon, Iowa 52314.

DeBERARD, FAY F. R
Pres-Pro-Tem, Colo. State Senate
b. Sedgwick, Colo, 3/15/05; s. Fred F. DeBerrard and Myrtle Miller D; m. to Chloe Decker (deceased); m. 5/4/66 to Beverly Burford; c. Fay, Jr, Marilyn (Mrs. Curry) and Robert; five grandchildren. Educ: Colo. Agr. Col, 1 year. Hon. M.A, Rangely Col. Polit. & Govt. Pos: Former co. cmnr, Grand Co, Colo, 7 years; mem, Sch. Bd. and Mid. Park Hosp. Bd, 25 years; Colo. State Sen, 53-, former Majority Leader, 4 years and Pres-Pro-Tem, Colo. State Senate, 68- Bus. & Prof. Pos: Owner and breeder Grand Champion Hereford Cattle. Mem: Nat. Legis. Leaders; Interstate Coop. Adv. Bd, Arapahoe Nat. Forest; adv. coun, Bur. Land Mgt; past pres, Rotary and Colo. Cattlemen's Asn; Colo. chmn, Coun. State Govt; chmn, Interstate Coop; Farm Bur; Denver Art Mus; Botanical Gardens, Denver; Hereford Asn; Craig Golf Club; Grand Lake Golf Club. Award of Merit, Colo. State Univ, 69. Rel: Episcopal. Mailing Add: Box 188, Kremmling, Colo. 80459.

DE BLASI, PASQUALE, SR. R
Chmn, Kings Co. Rep. Cmt, N.Y.
b. Alcamo, Italy, 1/18/10; s. Joseph DE Blasi and Giovanna Impastate D; m. 9/2/34 to Marion Gemco; c. Joseph, Pasquale, Jr. and Frank. Educ: City Col. of N.Y, 3½ years. Polit. & Govt. Pos: Pres, Camarsie Rep. Club, N.Y, 34-38; pres, Camarsie Young Rep. Club, 36-40; del, N.Y. Rep. State Conv, 40-66; chmn, Kings Co. Rep. Cmt, 13th Assembly Dist, N.Y, 56-64, 40th Assembly Dist, 66-; pres, 40th Assembly Dist. Rep. Club, 65-; del, Rep. Nat. Conv, 68. Bus. & Prof. Pos: Acct, 20th Century Fox Film Corp, N.Y.C, 40-64; self-employed acct, 64- Mem: Empire State Asn. of Pub. Acct; Unico; K. of C. Rel: Catholic. Mailing Add: 1021 Remsen Ave, Brooklyn, N.Y. 11236.

DeBLIEUX, JOSEPH DAVIS D
La. State Sen.
b. Columbia, La, 9/12/12; s. Honore Louis DeBlieux, Sr. and Ozet Perot DeB; m. 4/22/46 to Dorothy Mary LePine; c. Paul Louis. Educ: Ouachita Parish Jr. Col, 34; La. State Univ, LL.B, 38; Theta Kappa Phi. Polit. & Govt. Pos: Mem, Dem. State Cent. Cmt, Ouachita Parish, 38-40, E. Baton Rouge Parish, 60-; del, Dem. Nat. Conv, 56, 64 & 68; La. State Sen, 56-60, 64-; chmn, La. State Adv. Cmt, U.S. Cmn. on Civil Rights, 60- Bus. & Prof. Pos: Sr. partner, DeBlieux & Guidry, Attorneys, 59- Mil. Serv: Entered as Pvt, Army, 42, released as S/Sgt, 45, after serv. in Ninth Port Hq, Army Transportation Corps, Middle East Command, Iran, 43-45. Mem: U.S. Supreme Court; Am, La. State and Baton Rouge Bar Asns; bd. dirs, Family Counseling Serv. and Gr. Baton Rouge Ment. Health Asn; Am. Legion; Amvets; Baton Rouge C. of C; Pub. Affairs Research Coun; E. Baton Rouge Lions; K. of C. (3° and 4°); United Commercial Travelers; Serra Club. Made a Knight of St. Gregory by Pope Pius XII, 58. Rel: Catholic. Legal Res: 3755 Churchill Ave, Baton Rouge, La. Mailing Add: Suite 213, 721 Government St, Baton Rouge, La. 70802.

DeBLOIS, ROMEO R. R
N.H. State Rep.
b. Laconia, N.H, 6/6/11; married; c. One daughter. Educ: Laconia Pub. Schs. Polit. & Govt. Pos: N.H. State Rep, currently; Ward Clerk; city councilman; mem, Constitutional Conv. Bus. & Prof. Pos: Realtor. Mil. Serv: Nat. Guard of N.H. Mem: Odd Fellows; Elks. Rel: Protestant. Mailing Add: 132 Lakeside Ave, Weirs Beach, N.H. 03246. (1967)

DeBOLT, EDWARD S. R
Exec. Dir, Rep. State Cent. Cmt, Calif.
b. Sacramento, Calif, 9/17/38; s. Merrill E. Debolt and Frances Schooler D; m. 6/19/60 to Sharron Ann Hoggard; c. Ed, Jr. and Eric. J. Educ: Stockton Col, A.A; San Francisco State, 2 years. Polit. & Govt. Pos: Exec. dir, Rep. Assoc, Stockton, Calif, 63-64 and Sacramento, 64-65; area dir, Rep. State Cent. Cmt. of Calif, 65-66, field dir, 67-68 and exec. dir, 69- Mailing Add: 6605 Gloria Dr, Sacramento, Calif. 95831.

DeBONIS, DANIEL VINCENT, JR. D
Vt. State Rep.
b. Poultney, Vt, 11/2/14; m. to Teresa Daniels; c. Three sons. Educ: Poultney High Sch; Troy, N.Y, High Sch. Polit. & Govt. Pos: Chmn, Town Tax Separation, Poultney, Vt; Vt. State Rep, 65-; alternate del, Dem. Nat. Conv, 68; chmn, Rutland Co. Dem. Party, Vt, 69- Bus. & Prof. Pos: Quarrying; farmer. Mem: Farm Bur; PTA; St. Raphaels Men's Club; Vt. Dairy Asn. Coun. Rel: Catholic. Mailing Add: R.F.D. 1, Poultney, Vt. 05764. (1967)

DeBRUHL, GARRY GLENN D
Va. State Del.
b. Alexander, N.C, 9/14/36; s. Glenn Edward DeBruhl and Virginia West D; m. 11/26/58 to Carol Cooper; c. Mark Reagan, Christopher Dean and Traci Leigh. Educ: Univ. N.C, A.B, 58; Univ. Va, M.A, 63. Polit. & Govt. Pos: Mem, bd. supvr, Patrick Co, Va, 66-68; Va. State Del, 68- Bus. & Prof. Pos: Teacher, Henry Co, Va, 58-63; sales rep, Holt, Rinehart & Winston, Inc, N.Y, 63- Mil. Serv: Entered as Pvt, Army, 60, released as E-4, 61 after serv. in Artillery. Mem: Va. Bookmans Asn; Mason; Rotary; Moose. Rel: Disciples of Christ. Mailing Add: Critz, Va. 24082.

DE BRUYN, WILLIAM EDWARD R
Chmn, Iron Co. Rep. Party, Mich.
b. Norway, Mich, 1/16/22; s. Edward De Bruyn and Edwilda Asselin D; m. 8/17/46 to Florence Lemyra Brown; c. Lemyra, Sidonie, Edwilda, Eduard and Florence. Educ: North. Mich. Univ, 39-42; Marquette Univ, B.A, 47; Tri Mu. Polit. & Govt. Pos: Secy, Iron Co. Rep. Party, Mich, 62-68, chmn, 69- Bus. & Prof. Pos: Teacher, Mather High Sch, Munising, Mich, 46-48; self employed, Fergus Falls, Minn, 48-57; teacher, Bates Twp. Sch, Iron River, Mich, 57-69. Mil. Serv: Entered as Pvt, Air Force, 42, released as S/Sgt, 46, after serv. in 610th Army Air Force Base Unit, Proving Ground Command, Eglin Field, Fla, 43-46. Mem: Mich. Educ. Asn; Nat. Educ. Asn; Iron River Country Club; dist. cmnr, Boy Scouts. Rel: Catholic. Mailing Add: R.R. 1, Iron River, Mich. 49935.

DE BUSK, DAVID LOUIS R
Mem, Ark. Rep. State Exec. Cmt.
b. Heber Springs, Ark, 1/27/34; s. Johnie Jacob De Busk and Ollie Jane Johnson D; m. 9/5/53 to Sue Ward; c. David Louis, Jr. and Sara Denise. Educ: Ark. State Teachers Col, 52-53; Sigma Tau Gamma. Polit. & Govt. Pos: Chmn, Cleburne Co. Rep. Cent. Cmt, Ark, 60-68; mem, Ark. Rep. State Exec. Cmt, 64- Bus. & Prof. Pos: Secy-treas, Red River Feed Co. Mil. Serv: Capt, Army Nat. Guard. Mem: C. of C. Rel: Baptist. Mailing Add: 801 W. Sugar Loaf, Heber Springs, Ark. 72543. (1967)

DE CAUSSIN, EDMUND JOHN, JR. D
Chmn, Seventh Cong. Dist. Dem. Cmt, Mich.
b. Detroit, Mich, 4/13/23; s. Edmund John De Caussin and Dorothy Ardouin D; m. 8/28/48 to Gervaise Anne McCarthy; c. Annette Marie, Joseph Edmund, John Matthew, Maria Teresa, James Patrick, Julia Mary and Paul Martin. Educ: Univ. Detroit, Ph.B, 49; Univ. Mich, M.S.W, 67; French Club (pres); Psychol. Club (pres). Polit. & Govt. Pos: Chmn. bus. cmt, Citizens for Kennedy, 60; del, Dem. Party, Ward 6, Precinct 121, Flint, Mich, 60-64; chmn, Seventh Dist. Conf. Concerned Dem, 67-68; del, Dem. Nat. Conv, 68; del, Dem. Party, Ward 5, Precinct 85, Flint, 68-70; chmn, Mich. Seventh Cong. Dist. Dem. Cmt, 69- Bus. & Prof. Pos: Tech. writer, Ford Motor Co, 50-57; life ins. salesman, N.Y. Life Ins. Co, Detroit, Mich, 57-59; conf. leader, Gen. Motors Inst, 59-60; methods engr, Buick Motor Div, 60-65; dir, Econ. Develop. & Employ. Dept, Urban League of Flint, 65- Mil. Serv: Entered as Pvt, Army Air Corps, 42, released as T/4, after serv. in DEML Hq. and Hq. Detachment O.S.S, ETO, 44-45. Mem: Nat. Asn. Soc. Workers; mem, Christian Family Movement, 51-65, prog. cmt, 57-65. Rel: Catholic. Mailing Add: 1631 Lyon, Flint, Mich. 48503.

DeCELL, HERMAN BRISTER D
Miss. State Sen.
b. Yazoo City, Miss, 9/26/24; s. John Eldridge DeCell and Lucile Brister C; m. 8/11/51 to Harriet Causey; c. Alice, Brister and Causey. Educ: Univ. Miss, B.B.A, 48; Harvard Univ, LL.B, 50; Phi Eta Sigma; Beta Gamma Sigma; Sigma Alpha Epsilon; Lincoln's Inn. Polit. & Govt. Pos: Del, Miss. State Dem. Conv, 60 & 64; mem, State Sovereignty Cmt, Miss, 60-; Miss. State Sen, 20th Dist, 60-; del, Dem. Nat. Conv, 64. Bus. & Prof. Pos: Assoc, Henry & Barbour, 50-57, partner, Henry, Barbour & DeCell, 57- Mil. Serv: Entered as Pvt, Army, 43, released as 1st Lt, 46, after serv. in 108th Engr. Bn, Pac, 45-46; Pac. Theater and Philippine Liberation Medals. Publ: 'Oil and Gas Law,' Miss. Law J, 51; 'Federal Crop Insurance,' Miss. Law J, 56. Mem: Am, Miss. and Yazoo Co. Bar Asns; Lions; Elks; Yazoo Country Club; Am. Legion. Rel: Methodist. Mailing Add: Yazoo City, Miss. 39194.

de CHABERT, ANSETTA D
Dem. Nat. Committeewoman, V.I.
b. Christiansted, St. Croix, V.I, 2/11/08; m. to Ralph de Chabert (deceased); c. Ralph, Austin, Mario, Rita (Mrs. Schuster) and Shirley (Mrs. Highfield). Polit. & Govt. Pos: Mem, Pub. Welfare Bd. and Bd. of Educ, V.I; mem, V.I. Dem. Party, 55-; Dem. Nat. Committeewoman, V.I, 64-; del. and mem. Majority Platform Cmt, Dem. Nat. Cmt, 68; finance chmn, St. Croix Dem. Party. Mem: V.chmn, Red Cross; v.chmn, Welfare; pres, Charles Howard Hosp. Auxiliary; pres, Ment. Health; Bus. & Prfnl. Womens Club; League of Women Voters; Friends of Denmark; Dem. Nat. Womans Club; Buneh Club; Daughters of the King; Child of Mary; den mother; Women of St. John's Church. Mailing Add: P.O. Box 157, Christiansted, St. Croix, V.I. 00820.

DeCHANT, EDWARD WILLIAM D
b. Avon Lake, Ohio, 9/30/88; s. Frank DeChant and Catherin Nesies D; m. 4/26/13 to Florence Mary Buswell; c. Charles, Woodrow (deceased), Philip, Edward and Richard. Educ: Bus. Admin, Commercial Law. Polit. & Govt. Pos: Councilman, Avon Lake, Ohio, 29-35; co. cmnr, 36-41; former Ohio State Rep. Bus. & Prof. Pos: Operating Engr, 41- and farmer. Mem: Eagles; Sertoma; Farm Bur; Operating Engr. Local 18; Moose; K. of C. Rel: Catholic. Mailing Add: 221 Center Rd, Avon Lake, Ohio 44012. (1967)

DeCLUITT, DOUGLAS RONALD R
Mem, Tex. Rep. State Exec. Cmt.
b. Port Arthur, Tex, 2/9/35; s. Samuel Joseph DeCluitt and Margie Chaisson D; m. 6/15/57 to Eleanor Grace Roberts; c. Sherri Lyn. Educ: Tex. A&M Univ, B.S.E.E, 57; Harvard Univ, M.B.A, 62; Phi Kappa Phi; Tau Beta Pi; Eta Kappa Nu; Phi Eta Sigma. Polit. & Govt. Pos: Mem, Tex. Rep. State Exec. Cmt, 66-; chmn, McLennan Co. Rep. Party, 66-68; del, Rep. Nat. Conv, 68. Bus. & Prof. Pos: V.pres. and dir, Gr. Tex. Enterprises, Inc, St. Francis of Birmingham, Inc. and J.M. Wood Found, 64-; v.pres. and dir, Praetorian Corp. and Whitehall Corp, 66- Mil. Serv: Entered as 2nd Lt, Army, 58, released as 1st Lt, 60, after serv. in Air Defense Command; First in class, Officers Basic Course, Ft. Bliss, Tex, Outstanding Lt, 1st Army Air Defense Command, 59. Mem: Rotary. Rel: Unitarian. Mailing Add: 2900 Sanger Ave, Waco, Tex. 76707. (1967)

DeCONCINI, DENNIS D
V.Chmn, Ariz. State Dem. Cmt.
b. Tucson, Ariz, 5/8/37; s. Evo A. DeConcini and Ora Webster D; m. 6/6/59 to Susan Margaret Hurley; c. Denise, Christina and Patrick Evo. Educ: Univ. Ariz, B.A, 59, Law Sch, LL.B, 63; Phi Delta Rho; Phi Delta Theta. Polit. & Govt. Pos: Precinct committeeman, Precinct 53, Pima Co, 58-; mem, Pima Co. Dem. Cent. Cmt, 58-67; mem, Ariz. Dem. State Exec. Cmt, 58-; del, Dem. Nat. Conv, 64; v.chmn, Ariz. State Dem. Cmt, 64-; spec. coun, former Gov. Samuel P. Goddard, Ariz, 65, admin. asst, 65-67. Bus. & Prof. Pos: Legal research, Evo DeConcini, Attorney and real estate and property mgt, Shopping Centers, Inc, 59-63; attorney-at-law, 63-65; partner, DeConcini & McDonald, Attorneys, 68- Mil. Serv: 2nd Lt, Adj. Gen. Corps, Army, 59-60; 15th Control Group, Army Res, 60-64, Judge Adv. Gen. Corps, 64-67, 1st Lt. Mem: Ariz. and Am. Bar Asns; Young Dem. of Tucson; Delta Sigma Rho; Phi Alpha Delta; Nucleus, Tucson Country and Old Pueblo Clubs; Ariz. Pioneer Hist. Soc; chmn. legis. cmt, Tucson Commun. Coun; past mem, St. Vincent De Paul Soc; bd. dirs, Gr. Ariz. Savings & Loan Asn. Rel: Catholic. Legal Res: 243 N. Norton, Tucson, Ariz. 85719. Mailing Add: 510 Valley National Building, Tucson, Ariz. 85701.

DE COSTER, RICHARD J. D
Mo. State Rep.
b. Ewing, Mo, 7/10/21; m. to Jane Herst; c. Richard J, Jules V, Miles, Tommy, Timmy and Patricia Elaine. Educ: St. Louis Univ; Univ. of Mo. Polit. & Govt. Pos: Mo. State Rep, 64-, chmn, Cmt. on Probate and Magistrate Courts, v.chmn, Judiciary Cmt. Bus. & Prof. Pos: Teacher, High Sch, Calif, Mo, 48-51; attorney-at-law. Mil. Serv: Naval Air Corps, World War II. Rel: Catholic. Mailing Add: 815 College St, Canton, Mo. 63435. (1967)

DE COURSEY, JAMES H, JR. D
Lt. Gov, Kans.
b. Kansas City, Kans, 7/7/32; s. James H. De Coursey and Jenny Mathews D; m. 8/16/58 to Joyce Ann Brewer; c. James H, III, Timothy Patrick, Mary Colleen and Theodore Edwin. Educ: Univ. Notre Dame, B.S. in Finance; Univ. Kans. Sch. Law, J.D. Polit. & Govt. Pos: Lt. Gov, Kans, 69- Mil. Serv: Navy, 54-56, Lt.(jg). Rel: Roman Catholic. Legal Res: 6914 W. 52nd Place, Mission, Kans. 66222. Mailing Add: 1600 Plass Ave, Topeka, Kans. 66604.

DEDDEH, WADIE PETER D
Calif. State Assemblyman
b. Bagdad, Iraq, 9/6/20; s. Peter Joseph Deddeh and Hannai Mona D; m. 6/10/51 to Mary-Lynn Drake; c. Peter Charles. Educ: Univ. Bagdad, A.B, 46; Univ. Detroit, M.A, 56. Polit. & Govt. Pos: Calif. State Assemblyman, 67- Bus. & Prof. Pos: Teacher, Arabic lang, Army Lang. Sch, Monterey, Calif, 49-54; teacher, Sweetwater High Sch, National City, 59-62; prof, polit. sci, Southwest. Col, Chula Vista, 62-66. Mem: Calif. Teachers Asn; Nat. Educ. Asn; Calif. Jr. Col. Faculty Asn; K. of C; G I Forum; Calif. Pub. Employees Asn. Rel: Catholic. Legal Res: 1152 Melrose St, Chula Vista, Calif. 92011. Mailing Add: 240 Woodlawn, Suite 8, Chula Vista, Calif. 92010.

DeDOMENICO, PAUL DOMENIC D
Mem, Alameda Co. Dem. Cent. Cmt, Calif.
b. San Francisco, Calif, 12/23/34; s. Paskey DeDomenico and Merrial Reden-

baugh D; m. 5/28/60 to Anita Ludovici; c. Paul and Gina. Educ: Univ. Wash, grad. Polit. & Govt. Pos: Dem. co-chmn. for local cand, 64 & 66; chmn, Golden Assocs; state co-chmn, Businessmen's Cmt. for Sen. Robert Kennedy for Pres, 68; state chmn, Businessmen's Cmt. for Alan Cranson for Sen, 68; del, Dem. Nat. Conv, 68; mem, Alameda Co. Dem. Cent. Cmt, 69- Bus. & Prof. Pos: V.pres, Golden Grain Macaroni Co, currently; pres. and mem. bd. dirs, Ghirardelli Chocolate Co, currently; mem. bd. dirs, Mission Macaroni Co, Seattle, Manteca Bean Co, Manteca, Major Italian Foods Co, Seattle and Buffalo Breeding Asn, Burlingame, currently; adv, Sen. Sub-cmt. Antitrust Monopoly. Mil. Serv: Entered as 2nd Lt, Army, 56, released as 1st Lt, 57; Letter of Commendation. Mem: Commonwealth Club; San Francisco Press Club; Nat. Asn. Advert; San Francisco Advert. Club; San Francisco, San Leandro, Oakland and Fremont C. of C; dir, Alameda Co. Ment. Health Asn, Mira Monte Home, Palo Alto, Ohlone Col. Found, Fremont YMCA Bd. Mgrs. and Alameda Co. Dem. Adv. Cmt; founder and mem, Dads for Better Educ. and Youth-in-Govt; mem. exec. cmt, Boy's Town of Italy and San Francisco Opera League. Rel: Christian. Legal Res: 4581 Faulkner Court, Fremont, Calif. 94536. Mailing Add: 1111 139th Ave, San Leandro, Calif. 94578.

DEEB, RICHARD J. 'DICK' R
Fla. State Sen.
b. Tallahassee, Fla, 9/8/24; s. George J. Deeb and Mary Shaheen D; m. 1/7/50 to Catalina Panayotti; c. Alex, Richard, Teresa and Thomas. Educ: Univ. Notre Dame, B.S.C.E, 47. Polit. & Govt. Pos: Fla. State Rep, 63-64; chmn, St. Petersburg Minimum Housing Standards Bd, formerly; Fla. State Sen, 22nd Dist, currently. Mil. Serv: Entered as Pvt, Army, 44, released as Cpl, 46. Mem: Bd. of Realtors; K. of C; Am. Legion; Exchange Club; Amvets. Rel: Catholic. Mailing Add: 5750 7th Ave, North, St. Petersburg, Fla. 33710.

DEEM, J. FRANK R
W.Va. State Sen.
b. Harrisville, W.Va, 3/20/28; s. F.S. Deem and Lila Matheny D; m. 12/25/46 to Hilda Marie Snyder; c. Deborah Ann, Pamela Ann, Michael Stephen, Patti Carol and Cathy. Educ: Mountain State Bus. Col; Marietta Col, B.S. Polit. & Govt. Pos: W.Va. State Del, 54-62; W.Va. State Sen, 64- Bus. & Prof. Pos: Oil and gas and retail mercantile bus. Mil. Serv: Navy, 45-46. Mem: Alpha Sigma Phi; Pi Epsilon Tau; Ritchie Co. Libr. Bd; Young Rep. Club; PTA. Rel: Protestant. Mailing Add: Second and Sycamore Sts, St. Mary's, W.Va. 26170. (1967)

DEEN, HUGH DORSEY D
b. Alma, Ga, 11/20/15; s. Victor Deen and Allie Pope D; m. 4/17/38 to Ruby Altman. Educ: Alma High Sch, 34. Polit. & Govt. Pos: Ga. State Rep, 61-64; Ga. State Sen, 51-52, 57-58. Bus. & Prof. Pos: Farmer. Mem: Elks; Bacon Co. Farm Bur. Rel: Methodist. Mailing Add: Alma, Ga. 31510.

DEFENBACH, WILL S. R
b. 1926. Educ: Univ. Idaho, B.S, LL.B. Polit. & Govt. Pos: Dep. prosecuting attorney; asst. attorney gen; Idaho State Sen, 67-69; mem. and chmn, Idaho State Industrial Accident Bd, 69- Bus. & Prof. Pos: Attorney-at-law. Mailing Add: 1410 N. 12th St, Boise, Idaho 83702.

DeFRANCES, GUY ROBERT R
Chmn, Meriden Rep. Town Cmt, Conn.
b. New Haven, Conn, 5/13/34; s. Anthony J. DeFrances and Mary Savaresc D; m. 8/17/57 to Elsa Holstebro; c. Guy Robert and William Jeffrey. Educ: Wesleyan Univ, B.A, 56; Univ. Conn, LL.B, 59; Gamma Psi. Polit. & Govt. Pos: Counsel, Meriden Housing Authority, Conn, 61-65; Rep. dist. chmn, Meriden, 63-64; chmn, Meriden Rep. Town Cmt, 64- Mil. Serv: Entered as Pvt, Army, 59, released as S/Sgt, Nat. Guard, 65. Mem: Am. and Conn. Bar Asns; Unison Club, Meriden. Rel: Roman Catholic. Mailing Add: 47 Ox Bow Dr, Meriden, Conn. 06450.

de GAUTIER, FELISA RINCON D
Dem. Nat. Committeewoman, P.R.
m. to Jenaro Gautier. Educ: High sch, dipl; Pharmacy, 1 year. Polit. & Govt. Pos: Mayoress, San Juan, P.R, 46-; mem, Popular Dem. Party; pres, Popular Dem. Cent. Cmt, San Juan; del, Dem. Nat. Conv, 60, 64 & 68; Dem. Nat. Committeewoman, P.R, currently. Contrib. and assessor to Am. Red Cross, YMCA, YWCA and Am. Womans Union. Legal Res: Calle de San Juan, 51, San Juan, P.R. 00902. Mailing Add: Box 1306, San Juan, P.R. 00905.

DEGENHARDT, DARLENE LUCILLE D
Committeewoman, Ill. Dem. Cent. Cmt.
b. Oak Park, Ill, 3/26/29; d. Charles LeRoy Lawson and Clara Anna Case L; m. to Robert Alan Degenhardt; c. Robin Lee (Mrs. Eric D. Rose), Kathleen Michele (Mrs. Bruce Tajak) and Kryselle Alynn (Mrs. Robert Crouch). Educ: York Commun. High Sch, 4 years; Adult Educ. and Mgt. Courses. Polit. & Govt. Pos: Dem. precinct committeewoman, Precinct 21, Milton Twp, 56-; v.chairwoman, Wheaton Dem. Club, 57-58; exec. bd. mem, DuPage Co. Dem. Party, 58-, v.chairwoman, 58-60 and chairwoman, 60-; del, State Dem. Fedn. of Ill, 58-59; exec. secy, 14th Dist. Cong. Campaign, 60; organizer, DuPage Co. Teenagers for Kennedy, 60 and Teens for Johnson, 64; chmn, DuPage Co. Fair Activities, 60-; cand. twp. clerk, Milton Twp, 61; mem, Ill. State Dem. Platform Cmt, 62, 64 & 66; research consult, 39th Dist, Ill. State Sen. Campaign, 66; voter registrn. chmn, 68; committeewoman, Ill. Dem. Cent. Cmt, currently. Bus. & Prof. Pos: Spec. research, Walter Frank Co, 60-61; employ. counsr, State of Ill, 61 and revenue inspector, 61- Rel: Catholic. Mailing Add: 566 Wilshire Ave, Glen Ellyn, Ill. 60137.

DEGENHARDT, MARTIN P. R
Mo. State Rep.
b. Wittenberg, Mo, 1/22/18; m. 11/23/46 to Eleanor Nolle; c. two sons. Educ: Roosevelt High Sch; St. Louis, Mo. Bus. Col; Correspondence Courses in Acct. and Admin. Polit. & Govt. Pos: Mo. State Rep, 52- mem. Constitutional Amendments, Interstate Coop. and Roads & Hwys. Cmt, Mo. House of Rep, 75th Session. Bus. & Prof. Pos: Owner, Woodland Studios, Inc, 46-; acct, Chevrolet Motor Div; instr, Correspondent Sch; acct, Finance Co; operator, 260 Acre Tree Farm. Mil. Serv: Army, 27 Months; served in S.Pac, 17 Months. Mem: Am. Legion; Perry Co. Wildlife Chap; Optimist; C. of C. Rel: Evangelical Lutheran. Mailing Add: RFD 5, Perryville, Mo. 63775.

DEGNAN, JUNE OPPEN D
Mem. finance cmt, Calif. State Dem. Cent. Cmt.
b. New York, N.Y, 6/7/18; d. George August Oppen and Seville Shainwald O; div; c. Aubrey (Mrs. Orly Lindgren). Educ: Sorbonne, Paris; Univ. Calif; Univ. San Francisco. Polit. & Govt. Pos: Mem. finance cmt, Calif. State Dem. Cent. Cmt, 56-; nat. bd. mem, Am. for Dem. Action, D.C, 62-; nat. finance co-chmn, Sen. Eugene McCarthy's Pres. Campaign, 67-68; bd. mem, New Dem. Coalition, 68-69; del, Dem. Nat. Conv, 68. Bus. & Prof. Pos: Publisher, San Francisco Rev, N.Y. and San Francisco, 59-; dir, Norman Thomas Endowment Fund, New Sch. Soc. Research, 68; dir, East West Found, San Francisco, 68; consult, Int. Learning Inst, San Francisco, 69; investor; mem. bd. dirs, Scanlan's Monthly Mag, N.Y. and San Francisco. Mem: Consult, Asn. Lit. Mag; Calif. chmn, Nat. Citizens Cmt. for Broadcasting. Mailing Add: P.O. Box 1036, Ross, Calif. 94957.

deGRAVELLES, CHARLES CAMILLE R
b. Morgan City, La, 6/4/13; m. 9/15/35 to Virginia Wheadon; c. Mary Alix (Mrs. W.P. Begneaud, Jr), Elizabeth Claire (Mrs. Robert A. Cloninger); Virginia Ann (Mrs. Charles W. McBride), and twins Charles Nations and John Wheadon; four grandchildren. Educ: La. State Univ, B.A, 36. Polit. & Govt. Pos: Active in pres. campaigns, 56-68; state dir, La. Rep. Party, 67 and chmn, 68; del, Rep. Nat. Conv, 68; Rep. cand. for various local and dist. off; former committeeman, Rep. Nat. Cmt, La. Bus. & Prof. Pos: Mem. of staff, land dept, oil co, 37-68; teacher of oil and gas law, Univ. of Southwest. La, 55-62; mem. of staff, land dept, Pan Am. Petroleum Co, currently. Mem: Phi Delta Phi; Kappa Alpha Alumni; mem. adv. bd, Salvation Army (past pres). Rel: Episcopal. Legal Res: 409 Azalea St, Lafayette, La. 70501. Mailing Add: Box 51908, Lafayette, La. 70501.

deGRAVELLES, MRS. CHARLES CAMILLE R
Chmn. Educ. and Training, Rep. Party, La.
b. Alexandria, La, 12/4/15; d. Samuel Butler Wheadon and Anna Margery Kilpatrick W; m. 9/14/35 to Charles Camille deGravelles; c. Mary Alix; Elizabeth Claire; Virginia Ann; Charles Nations and John Wheadon (twins). Educ: La. State Univ, B.A, 36; postgrad, Univ. Southwest. La, 60; Kappa Delta. Polit. & Govt. Pos: Mem, Rep. Nat. Cmt, 64-68; chmn. educ. and training, Rep. Party, La, 69- Mem: DAR; Hugenot Soc; La. Colonials; La. Gen. and Hist. Soc. Rel: Episcopal. Mailing Add: 409 Azalea St, Lafayette, La. 70501.

DeGROW, ALVIN JAMES R
Mich. State Sen.
b. Pigeon, Mich, 6/1/26; s. Russell James DeGrow and Vera Harneck D; m. 8/25/46 to Judith Haist; c. Jane, Michael and David. Educ: Alma Col, 1 year. Polit. & Govt. Pos: Mich. State Sen, 69- Mil. Serv: Entered as A/S, Navy, 44, released as Qm. 3/C, 46, after serv. aboard Landing Ship, Tank, Pac. Theatre, 45-46. Mem: Gov, dist. 631, Rotary Int, 64-65; past pres, Pigeon C. of C. Rel: Methodist. Mailing Add: 600 Camelot Lane, Pigeon, Mich. 48755.

DeGUGLIELMO, JOSEPH ARCANGEL D
City Mgr, Cambridge, Mass.
b. Cambridge, Mass, 12/10/08; s. Austin DeGuglielmo and Mary O. Grosso D; m. 9/7/33 to Angela Ferraro; c. Claire (Mrs. Norton). Educ: Harvard Univ, A.B, 29; Boston Univ, LL.B, 33. Polit. & Govt. Pos: Asst. city solicitor, Cambridge, Mass, 37-42, city coun, 47-65, mayor, 52-53 and city mgr, 66-; asst. dist. attorney, Middlesex Co, 58-61; alternate del, Dem. Nat. Conv, 68. Bus. & Prof. Pos: Attorney-at-law, 33- Mem: Nat. pres, Alpha Phi Delta, 40-44, nat. secy, 45-62; pres, Cambridge Bar Asn, 52, Italian Am. Charitable Soc, 56-57 and Middlesex Bar Asn, 67-; Sons of Italy; Amvets; K. of C; Am. Legion; Am. Red Cross. Rel: Roman Catholic. Mailing Add: 34 Mount Vernon St, Cambridge, Mass. 02114. (1967)

DeHART, PEARLE PORTER R
Iowa State Sen.
b. Calhoun Co, Iowa, 1/22/98; s. Rufus Pack DeHart and Nancy McCaully D; m. 6/6/23 to Bernice Isabelle Woodward; c. Robert Pearle. Educ: Calhoun Co. Pub. Sch; Indust. Instr. Training Course, Iowa State Col, 43. Polit. & Govt. Pos: Chief. of party, Materials and Tests Dept, Iowa State Hwy. Cmn, 28-30; inspector, War Ord. Dept. and dep. collector, U.S. Treas. Dept, 41-43; councilman, Ames, Iowa, 50-56 and mayor, 57-65; Iowa State Sen, Story Co, 67-; mem, Gov. Cmn. on State and Local Govt. Bus. & Prof. Pos: Salesman, Vacuum Sales Co, 20-23 and Manhattan Oil Co, 23-26; technician, Maytag Co, 26-28; owner, merchandise bus, 31-41; owner and operator, tax consult. bus, real estate and ins, 44-63. Mem: Dir, Northwest Merchar Users Asn; voter del. to fifth nat. conv. of Am. Munic. Asn; past pres. and former dir, Iowa League of Munic; past pres, Ames Bd. Realtors; Nat. Asn. Realtors; U.S. Conf. of Mayors; C. of C; Lions; Ames Cyclone Club; Ames Golf and Country Club; Elks; Iowa Taxpayers Asn. Received Heaton Award for one who contributed most to Ames Commun, 65; selected one of two Iowa mayors by President Eisenhower, White House dinner for Premier Khruschev and party. Rel: Congregational. Mailing Add: Iowa State Capitol, E. Tenth and Grand Ave, Des Moines, Iowa 50319. (1967)

DE HERRERA, JOE HENRY R
Chief Dep. Sheriff, San Miguel Co, N.Mex.
b. Wagon Mound, N.Mex, 5/19/21; s. Fransisco Antonio De Herrera and Floripa Vigil Duran D; m. 1940 to Esther Armigo; c. Benjamin, Fransisco A, Henrietta Irene, Roma Rosita and Elisa (Mrs. Jose Ignacio). Educ: Ocate High Sch, 3 years. Polit. & Govt. Pos: Chmn, San Miguel Co. Rep. Party, N.Mex, 67-68; chief dep. sheriff, San Miguel Co, 67- Mil. Serv: Pfc, Army, 42-43, serv. in Qm. Corps. Mem: DAV; Fraternal Order Police; San Jose Soc. Rel: Catholic. Mailing Add: General Delivery, Rowe, N.Mex. 87562.

DEIBLER, ADELAIDE PERRINGTON D
Committeewoman, Centre Co. Dem. Cmt, Pa.
b. Armaugh, Pa, 6/13/11; d. Luther Valentine Rhodes and Addie Marston McNitt R; m. 1/1/33 to George Katz, wid; m. 3/28/40 to Ralph S. Deibler; div, 48; c. George David Katz. Educ: Lebanon Bus. Col, Pa, 27-28; St. Joseph's Hosp. Sch. of Nursing, Lancaster, Pa, 31-33. Polit. & Govt. Pos: Pres, State College, Pa. Federated Dem. Women's Club, 50; committeewoman, Centre Co. Dem. Cmt, 52-; alternate del, Dem. Nat. Conv, 64. Bus. & Prof. Pos: Ozalid reproduction, Ord. Res. Lab, Pa. State Univ; registr,

vital statistics, Pa. Dept. of Health, State College, Pa, 56- Mem: Pres, Am. Legion Auxiliary 245, 51 & 59, VFW Auxiliary 321, 60, Mt. Nittany Chap. Am. War Mothers, 61 and 40 et 8 Salon 485, 62; instr, first aid, Am. Red Cross, 60-; Bellefonte Chap. 151, WOTM, Pa; State Women's Bus. and Prfnl. Club. Rel: Episcopal. Mailing Add: 246 S. Fraser St, State College, Pa. 16801. (1967)

DEITZ, WILLIAM THOMAS D
b. Matawan, N.J, 6/13/26; s. Harold Gregory Deitz (deceased) and Vincena Kennedy D; m. 6/10/50 to Mary Elizabeth Creamer; c. Alissa and Randolph. Educ: Rutgers, Litt.B, 53; George Wash. Univ. Sch. of Law, J.D, 68; Phi Beta Kappa, Kappa Tau Alpha. Polit. & Govt. Pos: Admin. asst, U.S. Rep. Frank Thompson, Jr, N.J, 63- Bus. & Prof. Pos: Third and second deck officer, Standard Oil Co, N.J, 46-49; reporter, Asbury Park Press, N.J, 53 & 54, state house correspondent, 54-63. Mil. Serv: Entered as A/S, Navy, 43, released as Qm. 1/C, 46, after serv. in Naval Training Sta, R.I. and U.S.S. LST 656, Atlantic, Mediterranean and Pac. Theatres; Battle Star; Invasion South. France. Mem: Bar of the Dist. of Columbia; N.J. Legis. Correspondents Club. Rel: Roman Catholic. Legal Res: 589 Bellevue Ave, Trenton, N.J. 08618. Mailing Add: 2500 N. Van Dorn St, Alexandria, Va. 22302.

DE JARNATT, ARLIE U. D
Wash. State Rep.
b. Glezen, Ind, 11/13/23, s. Clyde Oscar De Jarnatt and Clara E. Weeks D; m. 9/4/46 to Donna Lee Stoffell; c. Judith Ann, John Douglas, Steven Herrick, Susan Lee and Lisa Jeanne. Educ: Cornell Col, A.B, 48; Colo. State Col, A.M, 51; Portland State Col; Phi Delta Kappa; Delta Phi Rho. Polit. & Govt. Pos: Chmn, Logan Co. Cent. Cmt, Colo, 52-53; pres, Cowlitz Young Dem, 56-57; Wash. State Rep, 61- Bus. & Prof. Pos: Teacher and coach, Sterling High Sch, 48-53, Monticello Jr. High Sch, 53-58 and R.A. Long High Sch, 58- Mil. Serv: Entered as Pvt, Marine Corps, 42, released as Cpl, 46. Mem: Nat. Coun. Soc. Studies, Nat. Educ. Asn; Eagles. Rel: Unitarian. Mailing Add: 1215 23rd Ave, Longview, Wash. 98632.

DeJEAN, HOWARD BENJAMIN, JR. D
La. State Rep.
b. Navarro, Tex, 4/18/24; s. Howard B. DeJean (deceased) and Vita Guilbeau D; m. 2/19/50 to Katherine Carlisle; c. Vita Katherine, Howard Carlisle, Shawn King, Susan Elise, Julie Benedict and William Paul. Educ: La. State Univ, B.S, 50; Law Sch, LL.B, 52; Delta Kappa Epsilon. Polit. & Govt. Pos: Mem, St. Landry Parish. Dem. Exec. Cmt, La, 60-64; mem, La. Dem. State Cent. Cmt, 64-68; chmn, Fifth Supreme Court Dist. Dem. Exec. Cmt, 64-68, chmn, Third Dist. Court of Appeal, Dem. Exec. Cmt, 64-68; La. State Rep, Fifth Rep. Dist, 68-; del, Dem. Nat. Conv, 68. Bus. & Prof. Pos: V.pres. and mem. bd. dirs, St. Landry Loan Co, Inc, Opelousas, La, 53-, St. Landry-Acadia Loan Co, Inc, Rayne, 53-, Welsh Finance Co, Inc, Welsh, 67- and Welsh Furniture Mart, Inc, 67-; pres. and mem. bd. dirs, Bowling Realty Inc, Opelousas, 64- Mil. Serv: Entered as Pvt, Army, 43, released as S/Sgt, 46, after serv. in 544th Signal Serv. Bn, Asiatic Pac. Theatre, 44-46; Good Conduct Medal; Asiatic Pac. Theatre Ribbon; Marksmanship Medal. Mem: St. Landry Parish Bar Asn.(pres, 63-65); La. and Am. Bar Asns; Nat. Asn. Legislators; Elks; Lions; VFW; Am. Legion; St. Landry Parish Cattlemen's Asn; La. Thoroughbred Breeders Asn.(first v.pres. and mem. bd. dirs). Rel: Roman Catholic. Legal Res: 875 Katherine Dr, Opelousas, La. 70570. Mailing Add: P.O. Box 61, Opelousas, La. 70570.

DeJOHN, MARY FRANCES D
Third V.Chmn, Broome Co. Dem. Cmt, N.Y.
b. Susquehanna, Pa, 9/15/25; s. William Canini and Louise Caruso C; m. 9/6/46 to Mario DeJohn Jr; c. Mario III. Educ: High Sch, 4 years. Polit. & Govt. Pos: Actively engaged in all local, state and national elections since 57; Dem. committeewoman, Seventh Ward, Binghamton, N.Y, 58-64; dir, Teen Dems. for Kennedy, 60; dir. women's activities, Julian for Congress Cmt, 60; mem. staff, John Burns Mayoral Campaign, 61; secy, Seventh Ward Dem. Club, 61; secy, Women's Dem. Club Broome Co, 61, mem. bd, dirs, 67, second v.pres, 69-; finance chmn, Maurer for Congress Cmt, 62; dep. city clerk, Binghamton, N.Y, 62-65; third v.chmn, Broome Co. Dem. Cmt, 62-; del, N.Y. State Dem. Conv, 63, founder, Young Dem. Club Broome Co, 65; chmn. Testimonial Dinner for Mayor John J. Burns on his elec. to chmn, N.Y. State Dem. Cmt, 65; secy-treas, Kirkwood Dem. Club; del, N.Y. State Dem. Cmt, 67; coordinator Broome Co. Samuels for Gov. Cmt, 67; committeewoman, Kirkwood Dem. Party, 68. Bus. & Prof. Pos: Mem. staff, Army Ord. Corps and Civil Serv. Cmn, 43-45; mgr, Mario's Floor and Wall Covering Co, Binghamton, N.Y, 54-57, secy. to dir, Urban Renewal, Binghamton, 58-59; secy. to corp. counsel, 60-61; secy, Police Athletic League, 66-67; exec. secy. to gen. mgr, Sheraton Motor Inn, 68-69, indust. sales mgr, 69- Mem: Catholic Daughters Am; Formed Triple-Ettes 62; C. of C.(mem. campaign cmt, 68); St. Mary's Assumption Sodality (past pres. and treas); League of Women Voters; co-founder, Citizens Cmt. Architectural Barriers for Easter Seal Soc. Broome Co; publicity chmn, Easter Seal Soc. Broome Co, 63-; chmn, Am. Italian Heritage Div, All Am. Coun, 64-; mem. nat. cmt, Dante Alighieri Commemorative Stamp Cmt, 65. Rel: Catholic. Mailing Add: R.R. 2, Ostrum Rd, Kirkwood, N.Y. 13795.

DE KOSTER, LUCAS JAMES R
Iowa State Sen.
b. Hull, Iowa, 6/18/18; s. John De Koster and Sarah K. Poppen D; m. 12/30/42 to Dorothea LaVonne Hymans; c. Sarah Kay, Jacqueline Anne, John Gordon, Claire Ellen and Mary Denise. Educ: Iowa State Univ, B.S. in Mech. Eng, 39; Cleveland Marshall Law Sch, LL.B, cum laude, 49; Phi Kappa Phi; Delta Theta Phi. Polit. Pos: Iowa State Sen, 65- Rel: Reformed Church in America. Legal Res: 404 Center St, Hull, Iowa 51239. Mailing Add: 1106 Main St, Hull, Iowa 51239.

DeLaCOUR, JOSEPH L. D
b. 10/27/94; married. Educ: Courses in banking, real estate law, ins. and parliamentary procedure, night sch. Polit. & Govt. Pos: Ill. State Rep, eight terms, Minority Leader, 70th Gen. Assembly; secy, Liquor Control Cmn; former Ill. State Sen. Bus. & Prof. Pos: Civil Serv. Exam, Chicago, Ill. Mil. Serv: World War I Vet. Mem: Am. Legion (past comdr, Sixth Dist. and Cook Co. Coun); Moose; Edgewater Golf Club; bd. of dirs, First Fed. Savings and Loan Asn. of Chicago. Comdr, Chicago's Near North Side Civilian Defense, during World War II, Awarded Silver Medal, U.S. Treas. Dept. for Sale of War Bonds. Mailing Add: 2440 N. Lakeview, Chicago, Ill. 60614. (1967)

DE LA GARZA, ELIGIO 'KIKA' D
U.S. Rep, Tex.
b. Mercedes, Tex, 9/22/27; s. Dario De La Garza and Elisa Villarreal G; m. 5/29/53 to Lucille Alamia; c. Jorge, Michael and Angela. Educ: Edinburg Jr. Col, Tex, 2 years; St. Mary's Univ, LL.B, 52; Delta Theta Phi. Polit. & Govt. Pos: Tex. State Rep, 52-64; U.S. Rep, Tex, 65-; alternate del, Dem. Nat. Conv, 68. Bus. & Prof. Pos: Attorney, mem. of firm of Rankin, Kern, Martinez and De La Garza. Mil. Serv: Seaman 1/C, Navy, 44; 2nd Lt, Army, 50-52. Mem: Mission, McAllen and Rio Grande Valley C. of C; Am. Legion; CWV (past Nat. Judge Advocate); Kiwanis; Int. Good Neighbor Coun; Tex. Legis. Coun; Coun. of State Govt.(Legis. Br); Border Develop. Cmt; League of United Latin Am. Citizens. Rel: Catholic. Legal Res: 1812 Cummings, Mission, Tex. 78572. Mailing Add: House of Representatives, Washington, D.C. 20515.

DELAHANTY, GEORGE EMMETT R
Mem, Rep. State Cent. Cmt, Calif.
b. San Francisco, Calif, 2/3/16; s. George Emmett Delahanty, Sr. and Myrtle May Herlitz D; m. 1/21/43 to Dorothy Ella Steigerwald; c. Kathleen (Mrs. Emanuele) and Richard George. Educ: Am. Inst. Banking, grad, 38. Polit. & Govt. Pos: Mem, Orange Co. Rep. Cent. Cmt, Calif, 64-; mem, Rep. State Cent. Cmt, 64-69; gov, Orange Co. United Rep. Calif, 66-68, state treas, 66-68; mem, Rep. Assocs, 66-69; mem, Calif. Collection Agency Adv. Bd, 67-69, chmn, 69- Bus. & Prof. Pos: Banker, Bank of Am, 35-38 & 46-51 and United Calif. Bank, Los Angeles, 38-42; pres, Transcontinental Credit Serv, Inc, Fullerton, Calif, 51- Mil. Serv: Entered as Pvt, Air Force, 43, released as S/Sgt, 46, after serv. in 25th Bomb Group, 69th Bomb Squadron, Sixth Air Force, 43-44; Victory Medal; Am. Theater Ribbon; Serv. Stripe; Good Conduct Medal. Mem: Calif. Asn. Collectors; Am. Collectors Asn; C. of C; Kiwanis; Elks; Lincoln Club. Outstanding Citizen Award, Fullerton C. of C, 54; Cert. of Merit, Fullerton C. of C, 56-57; Outstanding Citizen Award, Orange Co. Fedn. Commun. Chests, 55; Merit Citation, Assoc. C. of C. Orange Co, 60; Cert. Award, Orange Co. Rep. Cent. Cmt, 66. Rel: Catholic. Legal Res: 2500 Coronado Dr, Fullerton, Calif. 92632. Mailing Add: 213 N. Pomona, Fullerton, Calif. 92632.

de la HOUSSAYE, HARRY LOUIS D
Chmn, St. Martin Parish Dem. Exec. Cmt, La.
b. St. Martinville, La, 2/7/19; s. Ignace C. de la Houssaye and Laura M. Gutekunst H; m. 6/15/46 to Hazel Marie Eastin; c. Harry, Jr. and Richard. Educ: Univ. Southwest. La; U.S. Army Engr. Sch. Polit. & Govt. Pos: Mem, St. Martin Parish Sch. Bd, La, 63-; chmn, St. Martin Parish Dem. Exec. Cmt, 64- Bus. & Prof. Pos: Mgr, Ford Auto Dealership, 48-; owner, Oil Distributing Sta, 51- Mil. Serv: Entered as Pvt, Army, 42, released as Maj, 46, after serv. in Engrs. Corps, S.Pac; Bismarck Archepelago Campaign Ribbon; Philippine Liberation Medal. Mem: Lions; VFW; Cattlemen's Asn. Rel: Catholic. Mailing Add: 118 Theater St, St. Martinville, La. 70582. (1967)

DeLAINE, PHILLIP MORGAN D
Ohio State Rep.
b. Cleveland, Ohio, 1/26/28; s. Charles Jackson DeLaine and Gertrude T. Woolley D; m. 6/14/52 to Shirley L. Gambrell; c. Michele and Phillip, Jr. Educ: Kent State Univ, 48-50; Am. Commons Club. Polit. & Govt. Pos: Patrolman, Cleveland Police Dept, Ohio, 53-67; Ohio State Rep, 69- Bus. & Prof. Pos: Exec. Dir, Police Athletic League, Inc, 63-67; Mil. Serv: Entered as Pvt, Army, 46, released as Pvt, 47, after serv. in 758th Tank Bn; Territorial U.S. Mem: Prog. for Action by Citizens in Educ. Rel: Lutheran. Mailing Add: 18702 Restor Ave, Cleveland, Ohio 44122.

DELANEY, BLANCHE JOHNSON R
V.Chmn, Berlin Rep. Town Cmt, Conn.
b. Kensington, Conn, 8/2/07; d. Charles Fred Johnson and Laura Crane D; m. 11/26/32 to Edward P. Delaney; c. Christine. Educ: Wheaton Col, B.A, 29. Polit. & Govt. Pos: Secy, Berlin High Sch. Bldg. Cmt, Conn, 50-53; mem, Berlin Bd. of Educ, 51-63, secy, 52 & 61-62, chmn, 53 & 55; secy, Fifth Sen. Dist. Cmt, 64-65; chmn, Berlin Rep. Town Cmt, 64-66, secy, 66-68 and v.chmn, 68-; mem, Berlin Bd. of Finance, 65- Mem: Bd. dir, Conn. Asn. Bd. Educ, 51-62, secy, 58-60; mem, Conn. State Coun. on Teacher Educ, 60-63, chmn, 62-63; Berlin Rep. Women's Club, 62-, pres, 63-64; secy, The Constructive Workshop, Inc, New Britain, 64-68, pres, 68-; New Britain-Bristol Ment. Health Coun, 65-; Berlin Individual Home Placement Chmn. for Experiment in Int. Living. Rel: Congregational; Bd. of Trustees, Kensington Congregational Church, 65-67. Mailing Add: 98 Norton Rd, Kensington, Conn. 06037.

DELANEY, CHARLES LAWRENCE D
Vt. State Sen.
b. Swanton, Vt, 11/14/23; m. to Carolyn Strauch; c. 2 sons, 5 daughters. Educ: Miss. State Col. Polit. & Govt. Pos: Vt. State Rep, 59; Vt. State Sen, 61-; secy, Colchester Fire Dist. Two; mem, Colchester Zoning Bd. of Adjust. and Reapportionment Cmn. Bus. & Prof. Pos: Restaurant owner. Mil. Serv: Army Med. Corps, S. Pac. Theatre, World War II, S/Sgt. Mem: Elks; VFW; K. of C.(4°); Burlington Downtown Athletic Club. Rel: Catholic. Mailing Add: R.D. 3, Winooski, Vt. 05404. (1967)

DELANEY, FRANCES I. DFL
Vice Chairwoman, 2nd Cong. Dist. Dem-Farmer-Labor Party, Minn.
b. Pipestone, Minn, 5/21/00; d. Peter Casper Haubrich and Clara Bell Riffel H; wid; c. James B. and Francis D. Educ: High Sch; Bus. Col, Sioux Falls, S.Dak. Polit. & Govt. Pos: Chairwoman, Pipestone Co. Dem-Farmer-Labor Party, 40-66; past chairwoman and secy, Seventh Dist. Dem-Farmer-Labor Party; vice chairwoman, Second Cong. Dist. Dem-Farmer-Labor Party; alternate del, Dem. Nat. Conv, 68. Bus. & Prof. Pos: Former secy. for Co. Treas, Mitchell, S.Dak; teacher; census supvr, Nine Counties, Minn, 50; ins. secy, Nat. Mutual Benefit, Madison, Wis, currently. Mem: Catholic Daughters; Am. Legion Auxiliary; VFW Auxiliary; Dem-Farmer-Labor Women's Club. Rel: Catholic. Mailing Add: 18 Elbon Dr, Pipestone, Minn. 56164. (1967)

DELANEY, JAMES J. D
U.S. Rep, N.Y.
b. N.Y.C, 3/19/01; married; c. Patrick. Polit. & Govt. Pos: Asst. dist. attorney, Queens Co, N.Y, 9 years; U.S. Rep, N.Y, 44-45 & 48- Bus. & Prof. Pos: Lawyer. Legal Res: Long Island City, N.Y. Mailing Add: 1135 16th St, N.W, Washington, D.C. 20035.

DeLANEY, WILLIAM RICHARD D
b. Elmira, N.Y, 9/14/33; s. John J. DeLaney and Elizabeth Sullivan D; single. Educ: Colgate Univ, A.B, 55; Cornell Univ. Law Sch, LL.B, 61; Pi Sigma Alpha; Pi Delta Phi; Phi Kappa Psi. Polit. & Govt. Pos: Judge, Recorder's Court, Elmira, N.Y, 63, 64; secy. and attorney, Munic. Civil Serv. Cmn, Elmira, 65, 66; chmn, Chemung Co. Dem. Party, 66, 67; del, Dem. Nat. Conv, 68; corp. coun, Elmira, 68, 69. Bus. & Prof. Pos: Ins. broker, 58-61; assoc. attorney, Sullivan, Winner and Sullivan, Elmira, N.Y, 61-67; partner and attorney, Winner, Sullivan and DeLaney, 67- Mil. Serv: Entered as 2nd Lt, Air Force, 55, released as 1st Lt, 68, after serv. in Strategic Air Command, Eighth Air Force, 66-68; Capt, Air Force Res; Air Force Commendation Medal. Mem: Chemung Co. Bar Asn; N.Y. State Bar Asn.(munic. law sect.); Asn. of Interstate Commerce Cmn. Practitioners; Trial Lawyers Asn; Am. Arbitration Asn; NAACP; Elks; Jr. Asn. of Commerce; C. of C; Chemung Co. Bd. of Legal Serv, Inc; Elmira Country Club; Elmira City Club; Cold Brook Club. Rel: Catholic. Legal Res: 746 Garden Rd, Elmira, N.Y. 14905. Mailing Add: c/o Winner, Sullivan and DeLaney, 110 Baldwin St, Elmira N.Y. 14901.

DELANO, JOHN LEE R
b. Billings, Mont, 11/10/21; s. John Henry Delano and Helen Lee D; m. Sept. 1951 to Katherine Shallenberger; c. Marcia Lee and Joan Marie. Educ: Univ. Mont, B.A, 47; Alpha Kappa Psi; Phi Delta Theta. Polit. & Govt. Pos: Mont. State Rep, 65-69. Bus. & Prof. Pos: Sales mgr, Mont. Physicians' Serv, 49- Mil. Serv: Entered as Pvt, Army, 41, released as Capt, 46, after serv. in Pac. Theater. Mem: Med. Care Plan Adminstrs; past pres, Helena Kiwanis Club; past pres. and presently secy, Mont. State Trapshooting Asn, Helena Gun Club; Mason; Shrine; Am. Legion; past pres, Univ. Mont. Alumni; past pres, Mont. Jr. C. of C. and Helena Navy League; pres, St. Peter's Hosp, Helena; mem. Boy Scout Coun. Selected as Outstanding Young Man of the Year, Jaycees, 54; State Trapshooting Champion, 60. Rel: Episcopal. Legal Res: 420 S. Wallace, Helena, Mont. 59601. Mailing Add: P.O. Box 1677, Helena, Mont. 59601. (1967)

de la PARTE, LOUIS ANTHONY D
Fla. State Sen.
b. Tampa, Fla, 7/27/29; s. Louis de la Parte and Dulce Santa Cruz P; m 11/23/57 to Helen C. White; c. Louis David and Martha Ann. Educ: Emory Univ, B.A; Univ. of Fla. Law Sch, LL.B; Phi Delta Phi; Eta Sigma Phi; Sigma Alpha Epsilon. Polit. & Govt. Pos: Spec. asst. attorney gen, Fla, 53; asst. co. solicitor, Hillsborough Co, 57-60; asst. state attorney, 13th Judicial Circuit, 60-61; Fla. State Rep, 62-66; Fla. State Sen, 66-; del, Dem. Nat. Conv, 68. Bus. & Prof. Pos: Partner, Hobbs, de la Parte, Gonzalez, Attorneys-at-law, 63- Mil. Serv: Entered as 1st Lt, Air Force, 53, released as Capt, 56, after serv. as Judge Adv. Gen, 12th Air Force, Europe. Mem: Am. and Fla. Bar Asns; Am. and Fla. Trial Lawyers Asns. Most Outstanding First Session Sen, Allen Morris Award, 67; Runnerup for Most Valuable Sen. of 1967 Session, St. Petersburg Times; Legislator of the Year, Fla. Asn. for Retarded Children, 68. Rel: Catholic. Mailing Add: 305 Morgan St, Tampa, Fla. 33602.

DELARODERIE, LAURENCE ALDRICH D
La. State Rep.
b. Baton Rouge, La, 7/23/30; s. Rodolph Audibert Delaroderie, Jr. and Marion L. Walker D; m. 8/13/49 to Juanita Jones; c. Laurence Aldrich, Jr. and Lauren Anita. Educ: La. State Univ, 2 years. Polit. & Govt. Pos: La. State Rep, 34th Dist, 68- Bus. & Prof. Pos: V.pres. traffic, Garig Transfer, Inc, 53-60; v.pres, Modern Rental Serv, Inc, Baton Rouge, La, 56-; off. mgr, John Sexton & Co, Baton Rouge, 59-; v.pres, Garig Warehouse, Inc, Baton Rouge, 60- Mem: La. Motor Transport Asn; Traffic Club Baton Rouge; Nat. Soc. State Legis; Lions; pres, Sertoma Club Baton Rouge; v.pres, Baton Rouge Aircraft Pilots Asn; mem, Aircraft Owners and Pilots Asn; Nat. Pilots Asn; Press Club Baton Rouge, Inc; mem. Sugar Bowl Parade and Pageant Cmt, New Orleans, La; Camelot Club; Exec. Club Baton Rouge. Rel: Baptist. Legal Res: 5745 Berkshire Ave, Baton Rouge, La. 70806. Mailing Add: P.O. Box 11, Baton Rouge, La. 70821.

de la VERGNE, HUGUES JULES, II R
Secy, La. State Rep. Cent. Cmt.
b. New Orleans, La, 2/18/31; s. Charles Edouard de la Vergne and Marcelle Menard V; m. 3/8/66 to Beatrice Blanche Badger D; c. Hugues J, III. Educ: Univ. Notre Dame, 48-49; Tulane Univ, B.A, 53, LL.B, 57; Delta Kappa Epsilon. Polit. & Govt. Pos: Committeeman, Orleans Parish, Wards 12 and 13, 58-; chmn, Young Rep. Fedn. La. Inc, 59-62; del, Rep. Nat. Conv, 60, del. and mem. rules cmt, 64, alternate del, 68; secy, La. State Rep. Cent. Cmt, 63- Bus. & Prof. Pos: Partner, de la Vergne & Meyers, 57-; secy-treas, Bd. of Cmn. of Liberty Place, 59-; v.pres, Mentab, Inc, partner, Lake Properties and partner, Lake Develop. Co, currently. Mil. Serv: Entered as Ens. S.C, Navy, 53, released as Lt.(jg), 55, after serv. in Amphibious Forces, Atlantic Fleet, 54-55. Mem: New Orleans and La. Bar Asn; Statford Club; Pickwick Club; Sons of the Revolution; Soc. of the War of 1812; SAR. Rel: Roman Catholic. Legal Res: 4010 St. Charles Ave, New Orleans, La. 70115. Mailing Add: 1121 Maritime Building, New Orleans, La. 70130.

DeLEO, JAMES ANTHONY D
Committeeman, Wash. State Dem. Party
b. Port Townsend, Wash, 6/26/22; s. Antonio DeLeo and Grace Sofie D; m. 1/23/43 to Dorothy Leadie Sisson; c. Terrance J. and Linda Ann (Mrs. Frank Cassalary). Educ: High sch. grad. Polit. & Govt. Pos: Precinct committeeman, Dem. Party, Wash, 55-; chmn, Jefferson Co. Rep. Party, 56-65; committeeman, Wash. State Dem. Party, 65-; alternate del, Dem. Nat. Conv, 68. Bus. & Prof. Pos: Partner, DeLeo Bros, 47-; partner, Hardee Seafoods, currently. Mil. Serv: Entered as A/S, Coast Guard, 40, released as BM 1/C, 46, after serv. in Pac; Pre-Pearl Harbor, Pac. Theatre, Good Conduct and Asiatic Theatre Medals. Mem: Elks; Am. Legion; Vol. Fire Dept; VFW; C. of C; P.N.G.A; Kiwanis (pres, 55). Man of Year, C. of C, 64. Rel: Catholic. Mailing Add: 1005 Quincy, Port Townsend, Wash. 98368.

DELEZENE, LARRY KEITH R
Chmn, Madison Co. Rep. Party, Mo.
b. Kirksville, Mo, 4/6/33; s. Dr. Edward William Delezene and Marian Beatrice Watson D; m. 5/28/60 to Martha Lou Snider; c. Stephen Craig and Diana Sue. Educ: Southeast Mo. State Col, 51; Univ. of Mo, 52; Gradwohl Sch. of Med. Tech, 57; Kappa Alpha. Polit. & Govt. Pos: Chmn, Madison Co. Rep. Party, Mo, 64- Bus. & Prof. Pos: Pres, Khoury League, Madison Co, Mo, 61-62; co-owner, bowling alley. Mil. Serv: Entered as Airman 3/C, Air Force, 53, released as Airman 2/C, 57, after serv. in Northeast Air Command, N.Atlantic, 55; Good Conduct Medal; Air Force Res, 57-61. Mem: Dist. cmnr, Boy Scouts, 57; 2nd v.pres, Mo. Med. Technologists Soc, 65, 1st v.pres, 66; Am. Soc. Med. Technologists; Am. Med. Technologists; Int. Registry Med. Technologists; Rotary; Jr. C. of C; Masonic Blue Lodge, Miss, Mason (32°); Scottish Rite, Mo; Fredericktown Country Club; Aeronaut. Mechanics Local 837. Bowling, Football and Baseball; Serv. Award, Bd. of Gov, Khoury Asn. of Baseball. Rel: Christian Church; Deacon. Mailing Add: Box 446, Fredericktown, Mo. 63645. (1967)

DELFIN, OSCAR LIBOON D
Sen, Guam Legis.
b. Negros Occ, Philippines, 12/12/24; s. Dionisio B. Delfin and Teodora Liboon D; m. 11/16/49 to Lourdes Jinon Layson; c. Jose Ma, Christian L, Catherene Sussette, Rolando L, Jonathan L. and Robert Anthony L. Educ: Univ. San Agustin, 1 semester; Univ. Cent. Philippines, 1 semester. Polit. & Govt. Pos: Sen, Guam Legis, 67- Bus. & Prof. Pos: Sr. clerk, Luzon Stevedoring Corp, Guam, 47-55; sr. acct, Vinnell Construction Co, 55-56; supply officer, Marianas Stevedoring & Develop. Co. Inc, 56-67, asst. gen. mgr, 67-; pres, Friendly Finance Co, 65-67; pres, Guam Recreation Center, Inc, 63- Mil. Serv: Entered as Pvt, Army, USAFFE, 41, released as Cpl, 45, after serv. in Sixth Mil. Dist, Philippines; Army Res, 45, Cpl. Mem: Philippine Prfnl. of Guam; Pub. Personnel Asn; Comprehensive Health Planning; Philippine Am. Asn. Guam; Panay Negros Asn. of Guam; Kayumanggi Asn. of Guam. Rel: Roman Catholic. Legal Res: Station 18, Agat Village, Agana, Guam 96910. Mailing Add: P.O. Box 373, Agana, Guam 96910.

DEL GIUDICE, ANTHONY SABINO D
R.I. State Rep.
b. Providence, R.I, 2/17/22; s. Dante Del Giudice and Theresa Martellini D; m. 6/11/49 to Alice G. McCormick; c. Stephen J, Peter A, Dante T, Michael F, Anthony E. and Joseph J. Educ: St. Mary's Sem. and Univ, B.A. in Philos, 44; Boston Univ, LL.B, 49; Providence Col, B.A. in Soc. Sci, 67; Delta Theta Phi. Polit. & Govt. Pos: Asst. city solicitor, Providence, R.I, 51-52; sr. trial attorney, tax court, Internal Revenue Serv, Off. of Regional Counsel, Appellate, Wash, D.C, Baltimore, Cincinnati and N.Y.C, 53-60; spec. attorney, legis. drafting, Legis. Counsel's Off, R.I, 61-65; R.I. State Rep, Tenth Dist, 66- Bus. & Prof. Pos: Attorney-at-law, R.I, 49-52 and 61- Mil. Serv: Entered as Pvt, Army, 44, released as Sgt, 46, after serv. in 25th Inf. Div, Pac. Theatre, 45-46. Mem: Elks; Am. Legion; K. of C; Holy Name Soc. Rel: Roman Catholic. Legal Res: 73 Beaufort St, Providence, R.I. 02908. Mailing Add: 187 Academy Ave, Providence, R.I. 02908.

DEL GIUDICE, MICHAEL J. D
b. N.Y.C, 1/15/43; s. Anthony John Del Giudice and Rose Clare Genna G; m. 5/10/63 to Janice Rosemary Hewitt; c. Suzanne and Christopher Jon. Educ: N.Y. Univ. Grad. Sch, 1½ years; City Col. of N.Y, B.B.A; Beta Gamma Sigma; Zeta Epsilon Chi. Polit. & Govt. Pos: Student intern, U.S. Treas. Dept, 63; budget analyst, Nassau Co, N.Y, 65-66; asst. dir. research, Temporary Cmn. to Revise N.Y. State Constitution, 66-67; Dem. cand, U.S. Rep, Fourth Cong. Dist, N.Y, 68; dir. minority staff, ways and means cmt, N.Y. State Assembly, 69- Bus. & Prof. Pos: Govt. consult, assoc, Knight, Gladieux & Smith, Inc, N.Y.C, 67- Mem: Am. Acad. Polit. & Soc. Sci; Am. Soc. Pub. Admin; UN Asns; City Col. Alumni Asn.(bd. dirs); Fedn. Ital-Am. Orgn.(bd. dirs). Rel: Catholic. Mailing Add: 7 Chelsea Dr, Syosset, N.Y. 11791.

DEL JUNCO, TIRSO R
b. Havana, Cuba, 4/20/25; s. Albert del Junco and Violet Mesa d; m. 12/18/54 to Celia Bobadilla; c. Tirso, Jr, Robert, Rose Marie and Maria Elena. Educ: Univ. Havana Med. Sch, M.D, 49; Univ. Pa. Grad. Sch, Surgeon, 55. Polit. & Govt. Pos: State v.pres, Calif. Rep. Assembly, 3 terms, state pres, 68, v.chmn. resolutions cmt, mem. polit. strategy cmt. and mem. fact finding cmt; campaign chmn, Bill Orozco for Cong, 29th Dist, 66 & 68; state chmn, Latin-Am. for Goldwater; chmn, Am. Cmt. to Free Cuba; mem, Calif. State Bd. of Med. Exam, 67-; alternate del, Rep. Nat. Conv, 68; asst. secy, Calif. Rep. State Cent. Cmt, 68-69. Bus. & Prof. Pos: Rotating internship, Hollywood Presby. Hosp, 49-50; resident gen. surg, Queen of Angels Hosp, 51-54; asst. clin. prof. surg, Calif. Col. of Med, currently. Mil. Serv: Capt, Army, 53-57, with serv. as Chief of Surg. and Prfnl. Serv, Camp Hanford Army Hosp, Wash. Mem: United Rep. Fund of Los Angeles Co; Gov. Ball Dinner Cmt, United Rep. of Calif, 67; bd. dirs. and med. dir, Technicolor Corp; bd. trustees, Queen of Angels Clin. and Research Found; chmn, San Gabriel Valley Bus. and Prfnl. Asn; diplomat, Am. Bd. Surg; Inter-Am. Clubs Miami and Los Angeles; Int. Star Class Yacht Racing Asn; Queen of Angels Med. Alumni; Los Angeles Athletic Club; Huntington Harbour Beach Club; fel, Am. Col. Surg. and Am. Col. Angiology; Los Angeles Co. Med. Asn.(mem. legis. cmt); Los Angeles Surg. Soc; Am. Med. Asn; Calif. Med. Asn.(mem. legis. cmt); Pan Am. Med. Asn; Pub. Health League of Calif. Americanism Medal, DAR, 69; Caballero Comendador, Order Santa Brigida de Suecia; Citation for Outstanding Serv, Americanism Educ. League. Rel: Roman Catholic. Legal Res: 1570 San Pasqual, Pasadena, Calif. 91106. Mailing Add: 4924 Sunset Blvd, Los Angeles, Calif. 90027.

DELKER, AUDREY P. R
Secy, Del. Rep. State Cent. Cmt.
b. South Amboy, N.J, 5/3/12; d. Linwood Van Cleaf and Henrietta Seeman V; m. to William A. Piper, wid; m. to John Delker, 7/16/66; c. William A.L. and Paul J. Educ: Coleman's Nat. Bus. Col, Bus. and Secretarial Degree, 29. Polit. & Govt. Pos: Asst. secy, Del. State Sen, 53; secy. to Cmnr, Del. State Alcoholic Beverages Cmn, 53-56; exec. secy. and mgr. Rep. state hq, Del.

Rep. State Cent. Cmt, 56-59, asst. secy, 57-60 and secy, 64-; v.chmn, Brandywine Hundred Rep. Cmt, 59-60; pres, State Bd. of Housing, 60-64. Bus. & Prof. Pos: Secy. to dir. of research, Fabrics and Finishes Dept, E.I. du Pont de Nemours & Co, Wilmington, Del, 59- Mem: Wilderness Soc; Nat. Audubon Soc; YWCA; Am. Red Cross; Active Young Rep. of Wilmington; assoc. mem, Nat. Wildlife Fedn; Du Pont Country Club. Rel: Protestant. Mailing Add: 407 Delaware Ave, Wilmington, Del. 19803. (1967)

DELL, MARIE HACKNEY D
b. Knoxville, Tenn, 4/24/09; d. Chester Ralph Hackney and Nola Anderson H; m. 6/16/34 to Richard Asbury Dell; c. Susan Marie (Mrs. Parker). Educ: Univ. Tenn, B.A, 30; Zeta Tau Alpha; Pan Hellenic; asst. bus. mgr, Orange and White, sch. paper; Spanish Club. Polit. & Govt. Pos: Ward worker, Knoxville, Tenn, 40-46; block chmn, Dem. Party, Va, 64-; alternate Dem. elec. off, Mason Dist, Va, 67-69; del, Fairfax Co. Dem. Conv, 68; alternate del, Dem. Nat. Conv, 68; del. Dem. State Conv, Va, 68. Bus. & Prof. Pos: Elem. sch. teacher, Knoxville, Tenn, 30-34 and Fairfax Co, Va, 54-60; elem. sch. librn, Fairfax Co. Va, 60-64. Mem: Fairfax Educ. Asn; Nat. Educ. Asn; Fairfax Libr. Asn; The Cotillion (pres, 68-69); Lake Barcroft Civic Asn. Rel: Methodist. Mailing Add: 3413 Rusticway Lane, Falls Church, Va. 22044.

DELL, ROBERT ALLEN R
Chmn, Henry Co. Rep. Party, Va.
b. Woodbury, N.J, 9/17/24; s. John Conrad Dell and Mabel Humphries D; m. 3/6/48 to Marilyn Claire Grimmett; c. Justina, Bruce and Donna. Educ: Univ. Pa, B.S, 52; Univ. Richmond, M.S, 62; Pi Kappa Alpha. Polit. & Govt. Pos: Mem. city cmt, Richmond, Va, 61-62; ward committeeman, Rep. Party, Wilmington, Del, 62-64; chmn, Martinsville Rep. Party, Va, 65-; chmn, Henry Co. Rep. Party, 67-; mem, Va. State Rep. Cent. Cmt, 68; alternate del, Rep. Nat. Conv, 68. Bus. & Prof. Pos: Indust. engr, E.I. du Pont de Nemours & Co, Seaford, Del, 52-57, group supvr, Richmond, Va, 58-61, bus. analyst, Wilmington, Del, 62-64, staff asst, Martinsville, Va, 64-66, sect. supvr, 66-68, and area supvr, 68- Mil. Serv: Entered as Pvt, Army Air Force, 42, released as T/Sgt, 45, after serv. in Eighth Air Force, 100th Bomb Group, ETO, 44-45; Good Conduct Medal; Victory Medal; Am. Defense Medal; Air Medal with Four Oak Leaf Clusters; ETO Medal with Four Battle Stars. Mem: Soc. Adv. Mgt; VFW. Rel: Protestant. Legal Res: 914 Corn Tassel Trail, Martinsville, Va. 24112. Mailing Add: Route 4, Box 194-A, Ponderosa Court, Martinsville, Va. 24112.

DELLA, CHARLES A. D
b. Baltimore, Md, 6/5/10; s. Charles Edward Della and Mary Elizabeth Chaney D; m. 4/18/36 to Anna Evelyn Bormuth; c. Charles A, Jr, Nancy Lee and James Edward. Polit. & Govt. Pos: Del, Dem. Nat. Conv, 64. Bus. & Prof. Pos: Officer, Steelworkers Union 2609, 41-50; secy-treas, Md. Indust. Union Coun, 50-57; secy-treas, Md. State and D.C. AFL-CIO, 57-63, pres, 63. Mem: Md. Selective Serv. Field Bd, 60-; Gov. Study Cmt. on Workmen's Compensation Law, 55- and Study Cmt. of Injured Workers Rehab, 60-; Md. Adv. Cmt. of the Atomic Energy Cmn, 66-; bd. of dirs, Md. Heart Asn; Md. Conf. on Soc. Welfare; Anne Arundel Co. Human Rels. Cmt. Rel: Methodist. Legal Res: R.F.D. 3, Box 472, Pasadena, Md. 21122. Mailing Add: 305 W. Monument St, Baltimore, Md. 21201.

DELLA, GEORGE WASHINGTON D
b. Baltimore, Md, 2/9/08; s. George W. Della, Jr, and Ida M. Hill D; m. 6/24/36 to Agnes Helene Mattare; c. George W, IV, Mary E. and Howard R. Educ: Univ. Baltimore, B.B.A. and LL.B. Polit. & Govt. Pos: Md. State Sen, 39-51 & 55-58, pres, Md. State Senate, 51-54 & 59-62; del, Dem. Nat. Conv, 68. Mem: Md, Baltimore City and Am. Bar Asns; Boumi Temple (past potentate, 59); AF&AM (past master, Corinthian Lodge 93, 43); Baltimore Country Club; Annapolis Yacht Club; Merchants Club of Baltimore. Rel: Episcopal. Legal Res: 403 Warren Ave, Baltimore, Md. 21230. Mailing Add: 500 Maryland Trust Bldg, Baltimore, Md. 21202.

DELLA VECCHIA, ARTHUR D
Conn. State Rep.
b. Southington, Conn, 7/25/21; s. Sebastian Della Vecchia and Maria Marcuccio D; m. 9/3/49 to Helen Simone; c. Adele R. and David A. Educ: Univ. Mo, 1 year. Polit. & Govt. Pos: Police cmnr, Southington, Conn, 53-58, selectman, 58-62; Conn. State Rep, 67- Bus. & Prof. Pos: Owner and operator, Della Vecchia Funeral Home, Southington, Conn, 49- Mil. Serv: Entered as Pharmacists Mate 3/C, Navy, 42, released as Pharmacists Mate 1/C, 46, after serv. in U.S.S. Pittsburg, Pac. Theatre, 45-46. Mem: Conn. Asn. of Funeral Dirs; Unico; Moose; Son's of Italy; Lions; Am. Legion; Elks; VFW. Serv. Award, Son's of Italy, 60. Rel: Catholic. Mailing Add: 60 Rourke Ave, Southington, Conn. 06489.

DELLENBACK, JOHN R. R
U.S. Rep, Ore.
b. Chicago, Ill, 11/6/18; s. William H. Dellenback and Margaret Albright D; m. Sept. 48 to Mary Jane Benedict; c. Richard, David and Barbara. Educ: Yale Univ, B.S. in Applied Econ. Sci, 40; Northwest. Univ, 46-49; Univ. Mich. Law Sch, J.D, 49; Phi Beta Kappa; Order of the Coif. Polit. & Govt. Pos: Ore. State Rep, Jackson Co, 61-66, v.chmn, Judicial Coun. and Legis. Tax Study Cmt. and chmn, Constitutional Revision Cmt. and Judiciary Cmt, Ore. House of Rep; U.S. Rep, Ore, 66-, mem, Educ. Labor, Merchant Marine & Fisheries, Cmt, Rep. Policy Cmt. and chmn, Educ. Task Force of House Rep. Conf. Research Cmt, U.S. House of Rep; del, Rep. Nat. Conv, 64 & 68. Bus. & Prof. Pos: Bus. training student, Gen. Elec. Co, 40-42; instr, Bus. Law, Ore. State Col, 49-51; Partner, Van Dyke, Dellenback & DuBay, 51-66. Mil. Serv: Entered as Ens, Navy, 42, released as Lt. Comdr, 46, after serv. aboard U.S.S. Yorktown, Pac; Pac. Ribbon and Two Battle Stars; Presidential Unit Citation. Mem: Bd. trustees, Lewis & Clark Col; Yale Alumni Rep. for Southwest. Ore; Mason; Elks; Phi Alpha Delta. Rel: Presbyterian; Mem. Permanent Judicial Cmn. Gen. Assembly of Cmn. on Ecumenical Mission and Rels, United Presbyterian Church. Mailing Add: Room 1210, U.S. House of Representatives, Washington, D.C. 20515.

DELMONTE, PAUL A. D
Chief Dep. Sheriff, New London Co, Conn.
b. Norwich Conn, 9/4/08; s. Rosario Delmonte and Marcello Longo D; m. 1/3/41 to Katherine Keehan; c. Paula M.(Mrs. Steven Passarello); grandchild, Steven Paul Passarello. Educ: Norwich Bus. Col, 2 years. Polit. & Govt. Pos: Treas, Norwich Dem. Party, Conn, 64; chief dep. sheriff, New London Co, 51-; del, Dem. Nat. Conv, 68. Mem: Nat. Sheriff's Asn; New London Co. Sheriffs Asn.(pres, 64); Elks; Norwich Golf Club; United Italian Soc. Rel: Catholic. Mailing Add: 34 Ward St, Norwich, Conn. 06360.

DELON, RICHARD MARSHALL R
b. Cincinnati, Ohio, 8/28/39; s. Carl B. DeLon and Ivis Hovious D; m. 5/27/67 to Joan Alston Bowser; c. Dana Sue and David Marshall Lyons. Educ: Univ. Cincinnati, B.B.A, 62, M.B.A, 63; Ohio State Univ, 63-66; Deans List, Univ. Cincinnati; grad. marshal, M.B.A. Class; Beta Gamma Sigma; Beta Alpha Psi; Alpha Tau Omega; Alpha Kappa Psi. Polit. & Govt. Pos: Legis. intern, Gen. Assembly, 64-65; orgn. dir, Whalen for Cong. Cmt, 66-67; admin. asst. to U.S. Rep. Charles W. Whalen, Jr, Ohio, 67- Bus. & Prof. Pos: Acct. trainee, Drackett Co, 58-61 and Ben Co, 61-62; grad. asst, Univ. Cincinnati, 62-63; intern, U.S. Treas. Dept, Internal Revenue Serv, 63-64; teaching asst, Ohio State Univ, 63-66. Publ: Co-auth, 'Representation and Reapportionment,' In: Political Studies Number Two, Ohio State Univ, 3/65. Mem: Treas, Cong. Employees Fed. Credit Union. Rel: Protestant. Legal Res: 4058 Vinita Dr, Kettering, Ohio 45429. Mailing Add: 6313 Bardu Ave, Springfield, Va. 22152.

DELONG, R. LUKE R
Ga. State Rep.
b. Augusta, Ga, 9/11/29; s. Otis Clinton Delong, Sr. and Miller Burnett D; m. 2/14/53 to Sara Mae Tanner; c. Darryl, R. Luke Jr. and Regan Delane. Polit. & Govt. Pos: Ga. State Rep, Dist. 80-1, currently. Bus. & Prof. Pos: Pres, DeLong-Waters Publ. Co, currently; gen. mgr, Typesetters Inc, currently. Mil. Serv: Entered as Seaman, Navy, 48, released as Radar Seaman, 52, after serv. in Korea; Good Conduct, Korean Serv, Japanese Occup. and China Serv. Medals; UN Ribbon. Rel: Episcopal. Mailing Add: 2137 Balfour St, Augusta, Ga. 30906.

DE LOTTO, BERT D
Mem, Calif. Dem. State Cent. Cmt.
b. Cleveland, Ohio, 6/21/19; m. to Eileen McDonough D; c. Kevin John and Patricia Eileen. Educ: Fenn Col, Cleveland; Fresno State Col, A.B. Polit. & Govt. Pos: Former mem, Fresno Co. Bd. of Supvrs; mem, Fresno Dem. Asn; v.chmn, Cmt. on Munic. and Co. Govt; Calif. State Assemblyman, 59-62; mem, Calif. Dem. State Cent. Cmt, currently. Bus. & Prof. Pos: Licensed real estate broker; farming interests. Mil. Serv: Naval Res, Lt.(jg). Named Intern in Pub. Affairs, Coro Found. Mailing Add: 2510 Kearney Blvd, Fresno, Calif. 93706.

DELPHEY, CHESTER FRANKLIN D
b. Union Bridge, Md, 10/23/97; s. C. Grant Delphey and Laura C. Hildebrand D; wid; c. Constance V. Educ: Frederick High Sch. Polit. Pos: Wash. Co. Chmn, Dem. State Cent. Cmt, Md, 62-66; mem, Bd. of Co. Cmnrs. of Wash. Co, Md, 50-58 and chmn, 56-58. Bus. Pos: Owner, Delphey's, 25-64. Mil. Serv: Entered as Pvt, Army, 18, released as Pfc, Hq. Co, 33rd Heavy Field Artillery, 18. Mem: Lions; Potomac Fish & Game Club; mem, Bd. of Home for the Aging. Big Game hunter. Rel: Methodist. Mailing Add: 140 N. Potomac St, Hagerstown, Md. 21740. (1967)

DEL RIO, JAMES D
Mich. State Rep.
b. Detroit, Mich, 1/30/24; c. Alan James. Educ: Detroit Inst. of Tech; Univ. of Mich, Detroit Col. of Law. Polit. & Govt. Pos: App. financial consult. to Trade Mission in 62 by Luther H. Hodges, Secy. of Commerce; mem, 15th Cong. Dist. Exec. Bd, 63; Mich. State Rep, 65- Bus. & Prof. Pos: Former teacher, Adult Educ. Dept; mortgage banker, real estate broker and ins. exec; dir. Supreme Life Ins. Co. of Am. Mem: V.pres, Booker T. Washington Bus. Asn, 55; chmn, Job Opportunities Cmt. of the Cotillion Club, 59; chmn, Cadillac Square Dist. Boy Scouts, 63; Small Bus. Admin. Coun; NAACP; Cotillion Estate Bds; Detroit Coun. of Ins. Execs; Builders Asn. of Metrop. Detroit; Detroit Real Estate Brokers Asn. Named Mich. Indust. Ambassador in 61 by Gov. John Swainson; received Theta Gamma Phi Delta Sorority Bus. Award, 38; Businessman of the Year, Booker T. Washington Bus. Asn, 54; Bus. Achievement Award, Mich. Chronicle, 55; Broker of the Year, Detroit Real Estate Brokers, 61. Rel: Trustee, New Bethel Church. Legal Res: Detroit, Mich. Mailing Add: 991 W. Grand Blvd, Detroit, Mich. 48208.

DEL TUFO, GERARDO L. R
N.J. State Sen.
b. Newark, N.J, 11/6/09; s. Gerardo Del Tufo and Carmella Luongo D; m. 12/6/36 to Josephine Ceraso; c. Gerard A. and Ronald J. Polit. & Govt. Pos: Property supvr, N.J. Dept. Pub. Welfare; secy. to Majority Leader, N.J. State Assembly; secy. to State Sen, N.J. State Senate; N.J. State Assemblyman, Trenton; mem, Newark Bd. of Educ; N.J. State Sen, Trenton, 68- Bus. & Prof. Pos: Lawyer. Rel: Catholic. Mailing Add: 510 Highland Ave, Newark, N.J. 07104.

DE LUDE, MARGARET BOWLES R
b. Lynchburg, Va, 11/4/18; married; c. one. Educ: Cazenovia Sem. and Jr. Col; Columbia Univ; Nat. Acad. of Design, N.Y. Polit. & Govt. Pos: N.H. State Rep, 53-57, chmn, House Apportionment Cmt; N.H. State Sen, 57-67, chmn, Sen. Ways and Means Cmt, 63; v.chmn, Sullivan Co. Rep. Cmt. Bus. & Prof. Pos: Dir. women's programming, WTSV-AM-FM, Claremont, currently. Mem: PTA; Grange; trustee trust funds, sch. bd; chmn, N.H. Employ. Servs. Adv. Coun; legis. chmn, Claremont and State BPWC (pres, Claremont Club, 67-69); Sullivan Co. v.chmn, Easter Seal Fund; ranking mem, N.H. Cmn. on Interstate Coop; YMCA West. Dist. chmn, Speakers' Bur; chmn, Southwest. Sch. Bds. Asn, Supvry. Sch. Union 5 and Unity Sch. Bd.(10 year mem); pres, N.H. Order of Women Legislators; chmn, Econ. Growth Survey of N.H. and Sullivan Co. Unit, Cancer Crusade; National Order Women Legislators (Parliamentarian, 68-70). Rel: Protestant. Mailing Add: Star Route, North Charlestown, N.H. 03603.

DELVEAUX, JOSEPH RICHARD D
Chmn, Brown Co. Dem. Party, Wis.
b. Luxemburg, Wis, 9/24/22; s. Joseph R. Delveaux and Adele Nellis D; m. 9/17/49 to Germaine Laverne Degrand; c. Mary Jo, Denise Ann, Joseph Rich-

ard, III and Peter Joseph. Educ: Grammar and sec. schs, Luxemburg, Wis, 10 years. Polit. & Govt. Pos: Co-chmn, Proxmire for Sen. Cmt, Wis, 64; chmn, Brown Co. Dem. Party, 65-; co. chmn, Lucey for Gov. Cmt, 66; dist. chmn, Johnson-Humphrey Cmt, 68. Mil. Serv: Entered as Pvt. and Res. 2nd Lt, Air Force and Civil Air Patrol, 46, released as Cpl, 67, after serv. in Army Air Forces Base Units, Corps Engrs. Mem: Wis. State Fedn. Labor (secy, North. Local Union 213 and secy-treas. Tri-State Dist. Coun); Citizens for Educ. Freedom; K. of C. Rel: Catholic. Mailing Add: 1178 Garland Ave, Green Bay, Wis. 54301.

DeMARCO, RICHARD M. R
b. New York, N.Y, 12/20/37; m. Irmgard Kaspeizer. Educ: N.Y.C. Schs, grad; N.J. Mil. Acad, grad. Polit. & Govt. Pos: Nat. dir. in charge of govt. affairs, U.S. Jaycees, 65-66; Rep. cand, U.S. Rep, Eighth Dist, N.J, 66 & 68. Bus. & Prof. Pos: Pres, I.C.P. Assocs, Inc, currently. Mil. Serv: Paratrooper, Army, 3 years, Capt, Res, currently. Mem: Bd. dirs, Nat. Multiple Sclerosis Soc; Clifton Cmt, United Fund Drive; Mayors Cmt, UN; Welfare League; secy, Nat. Guard Officers Asn; Toastmasters Int; Kiwanis; Optimists; Clifton C. of C; Paterson C. of C; YMCA. Clint Dunagan Mem. Award; lifetime mem, Jr. Chamber Int. Senate. Legal Add: 46 Myrtle Ave, Clifton, N.J. 07013. Mailing Add: 930 Clifton Ave, Clifton, N.J. 07013.

DeMARCUS, WILLIAM HAROLD R
Ky. State Rep.
b. Wilton, Ky, 2/4/13; s. John A. DeMarcus and Dorthy Brock D; m. 10/13/32 to Elizabeth Edwards; c. William Harold, Jr, John Preston, Frank Edwin and David Russell. Educ: Sue Bennett Col, Ky; Univ. Ky. Polit. & Govt. Pos: Councilman, London City Coun, Ky, 34-46; del, Rep. Nat. Conv, 64; Ky. State Rep, 64- Mem: Pres, Stanford Rotary Club, Ky, 60; pres, Stanford C. of C, Ky, 65; Mason; Farm Bureau. Rel: Christian Church. Mailing Add: Route 2, Stanford, Ky. 40484.

DeMASO, HARRY A. R
Mich. State Sen.
b. Battle Creek, Mich, 2/24/21; m. 6/7/47 to Mary Jayne Hocott; c. David, Ray and Thomas Eugene. Educ: Argubright Col; Mich. State Univ. Polit. & Govt. Pos: Supvr, Battle Creek Twp, Mich, 52-65; mem, Calhoun Co. Bd. of Supvrs, 52-65; Mich. State Rep, 56-66; Mich. State Sen, 67-; past pres. and secy-treas, Calhoun Co. Chap, Mich. Twp. Asn; former chmn, Calhoun Co. Planning Cmt, Calhoun Co. Civil Defense Cmt, Battle Creek Area Govt. Coun. and Coord. Coun. on Govt. Prob; exec. dir. and former chmn, Calhoun Co. Safety Cmt; gen. chmn, Mich. State Asn. of Supvrs. Cmt. on the Constitutional Conv; chmn, Commun. Armory Site Cmt; past dir, Battle Creek Twp. Civil Defense and Battle Creek Area Develop. Corp; past pres, Green Arrow Route Asn; mem, Health and Welfare Cmt. of Nat. Asn. of Co. Officials and Mich. Crime and Delinquency Coun. Tech. Cmt. Mil. Serv: Army Air Corps. Mem: Bd. of trustees, Argubright Col; Past Master, Battle Creek Lodge 12, F&AM; past secy-treas, Battle Creek Scottish Rite Club; past asst. scout-master, Troop 23, Springfield Place, Boy Scouts; RAM; Battle Creek Commandery 33; Eastern Star; Mason (32°); Consistory; VFW; Am. Legion; Second Air Div. Asn; Kiwanis; Sportsman's Club; Elks. Enquirer and News George Award for Commun. Serv, 57; Outstanding Serv. Awards, Fraternal Order of Police, Mich, 62; Mich. Probate Judges and Juvenile Offs. Asn, 62 and Keep Mich. Beautiful, Inc, 65; Selected Alumni of the Year, Argubright Col, 62; hon. Legion of Honor, DeMolay, 64. Rel: Methodist. Mailing Add: 40 S. LaVista Blvd, Battle Creek, Mich. 49015.

DEMBLING, PAUL GERALD
Gen. Counsel, NASA
b. Rahway, N.J, 1/11/20; s. Simon Dembling and Fannie Ellenbogen D; m. 11/22/47 to Florence Brotman; c. Ross Wayne, Douglas Evan and Donna Stacy. Educ: Rutgers Univ, B.A, 40, M.A, 42; George Wash. Univ. Law Sch, J.D, 51; Tau Kappa Alpha; Scarlet Barbs. Polit. & Govt. Pos: Mem. staff indust. rels, War Dept, 42-45 and NACA, 46-51; spec. counsel and legal adv, Nat. Adv. Cmt. Aeronaut, 51-58; chmn. bd. contract appeals, NASA, 58-61, asst. gen. counsel, 58-61, v.chmn, inventions & contributions bd, 59-63, asst. admin. legis. affairs, 61-63, dep. gen. counsel, 63-67, gen. counsel, 67- Bus. & Prof. Pos: Grad. asst. and teaching fel, Rutgers Univ, 40-42; prfnl. lectr, George Wash. Univ. Nat. Law Center, 65- Publ: Ed-in-chief, Fed. Bar J, 62-; auth, 'Space Law and the United Nations,' Vol. 32, No. 3, 66 and 'The Evolution of the Outer Space Treaty,' Vol. 33, Nov. 3, 67, J. Air Law and Commerce; 'The Treaty on Rescue and Return of Astronauts and Space Objects,' Col. of William & Mary Law Rev, Vol. 9, No. 3, 68. Mem: Am. and Fed. Bar Asns; Int. Inst. Space Law; Am. Inst. Aeronaut. and Astronaut; Nat. Lawyers Club; v.pres, Merrimack Civic Asn, 56-57; bd. dirs, Merrimack Rec. Asn, 56-59. Army Civilian Meritorious Award; NASA Distinguished Serv. Medal. Legal Res: 6303 Tone Dr, Bethesda, Md. 20034. Mailing Add: 400 Maryland Ave. S.W, Washington, D.C. 20546.

DEMBOSZ, JOSEPH JOHN D
Chmn, Plumas Co. Dem. Cent. Cmt, Calif.
b. Buffalo, N.Y, 12/18/20; s. Edward John Dembosz and Bertha Kajuth D; m. 3/13/45 to Helen Nancy Curren; c. John Edward, Linda Joanne, Timothy James and Stephen Joel. Educ: N.Mex. Highlands Univ, B.A, 49, M.A, 52; Kappa Theta. Polit. & Govt. Pos: Mem, Plumas Co. Dem. Cent. Cmt, 56-, chmn, 60- Bus. & Prof. Pos: Teacher, Plumas Unified Sch. Dist, 50- Mil. Serv: Entered as Seaman, Navy, 42, released as Radioman 2/C, 45, after serv. in S.Pac, 45; Good Conduct Medal. Mem: Calif. and Plumas Co. Teacher's Asns; Nat. Educ. Asn; Elks. Rel: Catholic. Legal Res: 277 Monte Vista, Quincy, Calif. 95971. Mailing Add: P.O. Box 961, Quincy, Calif. 95971.

DEMBOWSKI, JAMES S. D
b. Baltimore, Md, 7/28/16; married. Educ: Baltimore parochial & pub. schs. Polit. & Govt. Pos: Md. State Del, 59-67; Bd. of Govs, 2nd Ward Polish-Am. Dem. Club. Bus. & Prof. Pos: Hotel, tavern operator; longshoreman. Mil. Serv: WW II, U.S.N. Mailing Add: 236 S. Patterson Park Ave, Baltimore, Md. 21231. (1967)

DEMENT, SAM R
Ore. State Sen.
b. Myrtle Point, Ore, 9/23/20; s. Ellis Samuel Dement and Cecile B. Miller D; m. 2/20/43 to Dorothy L. McArthur; c. Diane D.(Mrs. Gary Simon) and Joan L. Educ: Ore. State Univ, B.S. in Agr, 43; Freshman basketball, 1 year; varsity basketball, 3 years; Varsity O; Blue Key; Scabbard and Blade; Withycombe Club; Interfraternity Coun; Sigma Alpha Epsilon (Eminent Archon, 41-42). Polit. & Govt. Pos: Precinct committeeman, Rep. Party, Ore, 62-; Ore. State Sen, 68- Mil. Serv: Entered as 2nd Lt, Army Artil, 43, released as Capt, 46, after serv. in 86th Div, Europe, 45, Philippines, 45-46; Air Medal. Mem: Coos Co. Fair Asn.(pres, 49-61); Coos Co. Livestock Asn.(pres, 50-52); West. Ore. Livestock Asn.(pres, 58-59); Coos Co. Tax Asn.(pres, 67-69); Ore. Cattlemen's Asn.(second v.pres); Ore. Sheep Producers Asn; Curry Co. Livestock Asn; Elks; Lions; Farm Bur. 4-H Serv. Award; Lions Serv. Award. Mailing Add: 724 Seventh St, Myrtle Point, Ore. 97458.

DEMERS, MARY E. D
Mem, Lebanon City Coun, N.H.
b. Boston, Mass, 5/16/16; m. to Edward R. Demers; c. Five. Educ: Lebanon Col; Concord Commercial Col, St. Anselm's Col. Polit. & Govt. Pos: N.H. State Rep, 61-66; clerk, Grafton Co. Del; clerk, Lebanon Co. Del; chmn, Lebanon Dem. City Cmt, 62-65; mem, Lebanon City Coun, 68-; mem, Lebanon Planning Bd, 68- Mem: VFW Auxiliary (past dist. pres); Mascoma Valley Pomona Grange (treas, 23 years); Am. Legion Auxiliary Unit 22 (v.pres); Hartford Emblem Club (past pres); Woman's Relief Corps (Hartford Vt. pres); Lebanon Grange (secy. and past treas); Grange Auxiliary; Lebanon C. of C; Lebanon Cath. Daughters Am.(past grant regent, 5 years). Rel: Catholic. Mailing Add: 68 Mascoma St, Lebanon, N.H. 03766.

DEMERS, RICHARD H. D
Mayor, Chicopee, Mass.
b. Chicopee, Mass, 1/19/28; s. Harry Demers and Josephine Bobala D; m. 9/2/50 to Lauria Piquette; c. Richard F, Lynette C, Robert P, Kenneth E. and Thomas A. Educ: Holyoke Jr. Col; Western New Eng. Col. Polit. & Govt. Pos: Mem. sch. cmt, Chicopee, Mass, 58-59, assessor, 60-65 and Mayor, 66-; del, Dem. Nat. Conv, 68. Bus. & Prof. Pos: Owner, Glenwood Hardware Co, 58- Mil. Serv: Pvt, Marine Corps, 46-47. Mem: Elks; Moose; K. of C. All Western Mass. Football, 45. Rel: Catholic. Mailing Add: 95 Nash St, Willimansett, Mass. 01040.

DeMICHAELS, LaSALLE J. D
b. London, Eng, 10/12/00; married; c. one son, one daughter, four grandchildren. Educ: Pub. High Schs, Milwaukee, Wis. Polit. & Govt. Pos: In Off. of Recorder of Deeds, Cook Co, Ill, 23-57, supt. and chief clerk, 34-57; Ill. State Rep, 62-68. Bus. & Prof. Pos: Admin. Asst. to Comptroller, City of Chicago. Mem: Precinct capt. and pres, 33rd Ward Reg. Dem. Orgn; St. Veronica Holy Name Soc; Moose; Ben Hur Life Asn. Imperial Court; 33rd Div. War Vets; Chicago Police Post; Am. Legion. Mailing Add: 2851 W. Fletcher St, Chicago, Ill. 60618. (1967)

DEMOS, PAUL T. D
b. Provo, Utah, 11/30/22; s. Thomas E. Demos and Mary Dunning D; m. 10/15/44 to Bernice Soulier; c. Brenda, Paula and Tommy. Educ: Univ. N.Mex, B.S, 56, M.A, 58; Georgetown Law Center, LL.B, 65. Polit. & Govt. Pos: Admin. asst, Sen. Joseph M. Montoya, N.Mex, currently. Bus. & Prof. Pos: Attorney-at-law. Mil. Serv: Entered as Seaman, Navy, 42, released as Qm. 1/C, 45, after serv. in Comdr. Submarine Force, Pac. Fleet; reentered as 2nd Lt, Army, 51, released as Capt, 53, after serv. in 717th Antiaircraft Artil. Bn, Germany. Mem: Am. Legion; VFW; DAV; Wash, N.Mex, Am. and Fed. Bar Asns. Mailing Add: 3603 Inverness Dr, Chevy Chase, Md. 20015.

DeMOULIN, CHARLES JOSEPH D
Colo. State Rep.
b. Denver, Colo, 7/6/29; s. Charles Joseph Hookey DeMoulin and Josephine Wareham D; m. 1/12/50 to Patricia Jo Ann Ress; c. Victoria Marie, Michelle Marie, Theresa Ann, Charles Joseph, Jr. and James Arthur. Educ: Local Union 68, Int. Brotherhood of Elec. Workers, 4 years accredited apprenticeship; Denver Univ. Exten. Center; Colorado Univ. Exten. Center. Polit. & Govt. Pos: Dist. Co-capt, Dem. Party, Colo, 62-63, precinct committeeman, 62-66; Colo. State Rep, 65- Bus. & Prof. Pos: Pres. and asst. bus. mgr, Local Union 68, Int. Brotherhood of Elec. Workers, 61-63. Mil. Serv: Entered as Pvt, Marine Corps, 46, released as Pfc, 47. Mem: Local Union 68, Int. Brotherhood of Elec. Workers; Int. Odd Fellows; South Denver Lodge 93, AF&AM, Colo. Consistory, AS&AR; Denver Lodge 86, Elec. Craftsman; Adult Educ. Coun; Denver Dem. Club; Boy Scouts. All City and All State Swimming Letterman. Rel: Episcopal. Mailing Add: 1676 S. Stuart St, Denver, Colo. 80219. (1967)

DEMPSEY, CHESTER E. R
Wis. State Sen.
b. Merton, Waukesha Co, 7/20/96. Educ: Waukesha Co. Schs. Polit. & Govt. Pos: Mem, Waukesha Co. Bd; held various sch. and twp. offices; Wis. State Sen, 34 & 46- Bus. & Prof. Pos: Owner and operator, dairy farm. Mailing Add: Route 1, Hartland, Wis. 53029. (1967)

DEMPSEY, JOHN N. D
Gov. of Conn.
b. Cahir Co, Tipperary, 1/3/15; m. to Mary Frey; c. Rev. Edward, John, Jr, Margaret, Kevin. Educ: St. Anselm's Col, LL.D, 62; Providence Col, LL.D, 63; Univ. of Hartford, LL.D, 63; Fairfield Univ, LL.D; Am. Int. Col, L.H.D. LL.D, Trinity Col, 67 and LL.D, Univ. Bridgeport, 67. Polit. & Govt. Pos: City Councilman, Putnam, Conn, mayor, six terms; Conn. State Rep, 49-53, minority leader, Conn. House of Rep, 53; exec. aide to Gov, 56-58; Lt. Gov, 58-61; mem, Adv. Cmn. on Intergovernmental Rel; Gov. fo Conn, 61-; Nat. Gov. Cmn. on Juvenile Decency; mem, Exec. Cmt, Nat. Gov. Conf; chmn. N.Eng. Gov. Conf, 63-65. Mem: K. of C; Rotary; Elks; Foresters of Am; Putnam Irish-Am. Club. Comdr, Order of Merit, Repub. of Italy. Veritas Award of Providence Col; VFW Award; Americanism Award, Conn. Valley Coun. B'nai B'rith; Americanism Award, Conn. Cath. War Vets; Pro Deo Et Juventute Award, CYO; Adult Americanism Award, Conn. DAR; Silver Beaver Award, Charter Oak Coun, Boy Scouts; St. Jude Man of Year, 66. Mailing Add: 990 Prospect Ave, Hartford, Conn. 06105.

DENBO, SETH THOMAS R
Asst. State Chmn, Ind. Rep. State Cent. Cmt.
b. English, Ind, 4/8/10; s. Robert L. Denbo and Estella Jones D; m. 11/24/28

to Muriel Marie Pavey; c. Ronald Ray, Myrna Yvonne (Mrs. Howard Goldman) and Delma Murdean (Mrs. James Eckerty). Educ: English High Sch, Ind, 26-29. Polit. & Govt. Pos: Chmn, Crawford Co. Rep. Cmt, Ind, 58- and Eighth Cong. Dist. Rep. Party, 62-; campaign coordinator, Ind. Rep. Party, 64; chmn. exec. cmt, Ind. Rep. State Cent. Cmt, 64-, mem. budget and finance cmts, 68-, asst. state chmn, 69- Bus. & Prof. Pos: Mem. bd. dirs, Crawford Co. Coop. Asn, Ind, 44-48; mem. town bd, English, 52-; pres, Kentuckiana Egg & Poultry Asn, 58-62; pres. bd. dirs, Crawford & Dubois Co. REMC, 59-60; dir, Marengo State Bank, 67- Mem: Order of Ky. Col; Sagamore of the Wabash; Columbia Club, Indianapolis; Conserv. Club Crawford Co; Press Club Indianapolis; Corydon and Jasper Country Clubs. Mgr. baseball club, Ind. Kiwanis League; scout for Minn. Twins. Rel: Protestant. Mailing Add: Route 1, English, Ind. 47118.

DENDE, HENRY JOHN D

Mem, Lackawanna Co. Dem. Cmt, Pa.

b. Scranton, Pa, 10/21/18; s. John Dende and Mary Borowski D; m. 1/21/58 to Prospine Kathryn Storace; c. Diane, Henry, John David, Neil Thomas and Christopher S. Educ: Alliance Col, A.A, 38; Univ. Warsaw, Poland, A.A, 39; Univ. Scranton, B.A, 41; Alpha Sigma Nu. Polit. & Govt. Pos: Mem, Scranton Sch. Bd, Pa, 51-; chmn, Polish Div. of Nationalities Sect, Pa. Dem. State Cmt, 54-58; v.pres, Lackawanna Co. Sch. Bd, 61-67; mem, Lackawanna Co. Dem. Cmt, 66-; pres, Lackawanna Co. Voc-Tech. Sch. Bd; chmn. steering cmt, for formation of Community Col. Lackawanna Co; mem. adv. cmt. to Pres, Alliance Col, pres, Scranton Sch. Bd, 69. Bus. & Prof. Pos: Pres, Dende Press, Inc, Scranton, Pa; ed. and co-publ, Polish Am. J, bi-weekly, 4/45- Mil. Serv: Entered as Pvt, Army, 42, released as Sgt, 45; Good Conduct Medal. Mem: Pres, Anthracite Club of Printing House Craftsmen, 60-61; pres, Nat. Alumni Soc, Univ. Scranton, 64-66; Am. Legion; C. of C; Advert. Club; Welfare Coun; Cancer Soc; Heart Soc. and others. Named Printing Man of the Year, 62. Rel: Roman Catholic. Mailing Add: 105 Rhonda Dr, Scranton, Pa. 18505.

DENGLER, CLYDE R. R

Pa. State Sen.

b. Fleetwood, Pa, 5/10/99; s. Elmer D. Dengler and Sallie Reifsnyder D; m. to Pauline V. Waters; c. two. Educ: Univ. Pa, B.S, M.A; Phila. Conservatory, Mus.D; Julliard Grad. Sch; N.Y. Univ. Polit. & Govt. Pos: Pa. State Rep, 56-57; Pa. State Sen, 67- Bus. & Prof. Pos: Teacher, prof. singer. Publ: Read This and Sing, T. Presser Co. Mem: Phi Delta Kappa; Am. Legion; F&AM. Citizenship Award, B'nai B'rith; Outstanding Teacher Award, Valley Forge Freedom Found; Students Army Training Corps, Albright Col, 18. Mailing Add: 551 Netherwood Rd, Upper Darby, Pa. 19082.

DENHAM, MITCHEL BERTRAM D

Ky. State Rep.

b. 1912. Educ: East. Ky. State Col, B.A; Univ. of Louisville Med. Sch, M.D. Polit. & Govt. Pos: Ky. State Rep, 60-; mem, Regional Educ. Bd. Bus. & Prof. Pos: Physician. Mil. Serv: Army, World War II. Mem: Rotary; Am. Legion; VFW; Odd Fellows; K. of P; Ky. State and Am. Med. Asns. Rel: Presbyterian. Mailing Add: 506 Forest Ave, Maysville, Ky. 41056.

DEN HERDER, ELMER HANS R

Iowa State Rep.

b. Sioux Center, Iowa, 8/14/08; s. Gerrit E. Den Herder (deceased) and Jeanette Grotenhuis D.(deceased); m. 6/16/31 to Christine Vreeman; c. James (deceased), Roger, Paul, Phil, Mary (Mrs. Vande Berg), Carol (Mrs. De Ruyter) and 15 Grandchildren. Educ: Orange City Acad; Hope Col; Cosmopolitan. Polit. & Govt. Pos: Iowa State Rep, 67-, Iowa Develop. Cmt, Iowa House of Rep, Iowa Comprehensive Health Planning Coun, Iowa Regional Med. Prog, Iowa Hosp. Adv. Cmn. Bus. & Prof. Pos: Realtor. Mem: C. of C; Farm Bur. Award, Future Farmers of Am; hon. mem, 4-H Girls. Rel: Protestant. Mailing Add: 291 12th St. S.E, Sioux Center, Iowa 51250.

DENIUS, FRANK W. D

b. Athens, Tex, 1/4/25; s. S.F. Denius and Frances Cain D; m. 11/19/49 to Charmaine Hooper; c. Frank Wofford and Charmaine. Educ: Univ. Tex. Polit. & Govt. Pos: Chmn. steering cmt, School Bond Campaign, Tex, 64. Bus. & Prof. Pos: Partner, Lawfirm of Clark, Thomas, Harris, Denius & Winters; dir, South. Union Gas Co, Aztec Oil & Gas Co, Delhi Australian Petrol, Ltd. and Capital Nat. Bank, Austin; secy-treas. and dir, Tex. Capital Corp. Mil. Awards: Silver Star with Two Oak Leaf Clusters; Purple Heart; Presidential Unit Citation; ETO Ribbon with Five Battle Stars. Mem: Travis Co. and Am. Bar Asns; State Bar of Tex; past dir, W. Austin Optimist Club; secy. and dir, Austin Sens; secy. of bd. of trustees and past pres, Headliners Club; chmn, United Fund, Spec. Schs. Div, 60, Pacesetters Div, 61 and Schs. Div, 64; trustee, Austin United Fund; Athens RAM Chap. 55; past pres, Young Men's Bus. League of Austin, Austin Ex-Students' Asn, Univ. of Tex, Longhorn Club of Austin and pres, exec. coun, Ex-Students' Asn, Univ. of Tex; Legis. Constitutional Rev. Cmt. Outstanding Young Man of Austin, Jr. C. of C, 59. Rel: Presbyterian; Elder and past chmn, Bd. Deacons, Westminister Presby. Church. Legal Res: 3703 Meadowbank, Austin, Tex. 78703. Mailing Add: P.O. Box 1148, Austin, Tex. 78767.

DENMAN, DONALD KENNETH R

b. Medford, Ore, 6/13/33; s. Kenneth George Denman and Margaret A. Bolt D; m. 2/7/59 to Sandra Kerr Daley; c. Donna Kaye. Educ: Ore. State Univ, B.S, 55; Willamette Univ, J.D, 62; Phi Delta Theta; Phi Delta Phi. Polit. & Govt. Pos: Chmn, Jackson Co. Planning Cmn, Ore, 63-67; chmn, Jackson Co. Rep. Cent. Cmt, 64-68. Mil. Serv: Entered as 2nd Lt, Air Force, 56, released as 1st Lt, 59, after serv. in Strategic Air Command, U.S; Capt, Air Force Res. Mem: Rotary; Elks. Rel: Presbyterian. Mailing Add: 85 Windsor Ave, Medford, Ore. 97501.

DENMAN, WILLIAM F. D

Iowa State Sen.

b. Des Moines, Iowa, 1925; m. 10/25/63 to Lois M. Clair; c. Bill, Jr, Teresa Ellen, Steven, Mary Jo and Julie Marie. Educ: Univ. of Mo; Drake Univ. Law Sch. Polit. & Govt. Pos: Iowa State Rep, 6 years; Iowa State Sen, currently. Bus. & Prof. Pos: Attorney-at-law. Mem: Toastmasters Int; Am. Legion; Iowa State Bar Asn. Rel: Methodist. Mailing Add: State Capitol, E. Tenth and Grand Ave, Des Moines, Iowa 50319. (1967)

DENNARD, JOE L. D

b. Pineview, Ga, 4/2/04; s. Joseph J. Dennard and Fannie Walker D; m. 8/3/24 to Matibel Turner; c. Mary (Mrs. Lindsey); grandchildren: Mary Stewart Lindsey, Edward Harman Lindsey Jr. and Elizabeth Dennard Lindsey. Educ: Pineview High Sch, 18; Ga-Ala. Bus. Col. Polit. & Govt. Pos: Alderman, Pineview, Ga, 31-32 & 35-36; Mayor, Pineview, 34; mem, Sch. Bd, 36-47, treas, 46-47; chmn, Wilcox Co. Dem. Exec. Cmt, 50-68; Ga. State Rep, 63-64; mem, State Bd. of Registrn. for Dealers in Used Motor Vehicle Parts, Wilcox Co, 67- Bus. & Prof. Pos: Farmer, cattle rancher; with Agr. Commodities Authority, 61-64. Mem: Farm Bur; Lions; WOW. Rel: Baptist. Mailing Add: Pineview, Ga. 31071. (1967)

DENNEY, ROBERT V. R

U.S. Rep, Nebr.

b. Council Bluffs, Iowa, 4/11/16; s. Arthur J. Denney and Helen Weaver D; m. to Ruth C. Conklin; c. Vernon B, David C, Michael R. and Deborah K. Educ: Creighton Univ, Sch. of Law, LL.B. cum laude, 39; Alpha Sigma Nu. Polit. & Govt. Pos: Attorney, Jefferson Co, Nebr, 47-51; attorney, Bd. of Pub. Works, City of Fairbury, 56-66; chmn, Nebr. State Rep. Party, 61-64; Nebr. Rep. for U.S. Sen. Roman L. Hruska, 65; U.S. Rep, Nebr, 67- Mil. Serv: Entered as Pfc, Marine Corps, 42, released as Capt, 46, after serv. in 86th Inf. Co; Lt. Col, Marine Corps Res, 46-60; Bronze Star. Mem: Am. Bar Asn; Am. Col. of Probate Counsel; Mason; Shrine; Lions; C. of C. Rel: Presbyterian. Legal Res: R.F.D. 1, Fairbury, Nebr. 68352. Mailing Add: Box 4, Fairbury, Nebr. 68352.

DENNIS, DAVID WORTH R

U.S. Rep, Ind.

b. Washington, D.C, 6/7/12; s. William Cullen Dennis and Agnes Barker D; m. 12/3/38 to Tresa Justice; c. William C, II and Martha Ellen. Educ: Earlham Col, A.B, 33; Harvard Law Sch, LL.B, 36. Polit. & Govt. Pos: Prosecuting attorney, Wayne Co, Ind, 39-43; Ind. State Rep, Wayne Co, 47-49, Wayne and Union Co, 53-59; U.S. Rep, Tenth Dist, Ind, 69- Bus. & Prof. Pos: Assoc, firm, Rupe, Brown & Reller, Richmond, Ind, 36-39 and Ross, McCord, Ice & Miller, Indianapolis, 43-44; partner, Dennis & Dennis, Richmond, 47-62, Dennis, Dennis & Puckett, 62-67, Dennis, Dennis & Reinke, 67-69 and Dennis, Dennis, Reinke & Vertesch, 69- Mil. Serv: Entered as Pvt, Army, 44, released as 1st Lt, 46, after serv. in Judge Adv. Gen. Div, Southwest Pac, 45-46. Mem: Am, Ind. and Wayne Co. Bar Asns; Am. Trial Lawyers Asn; Nat. Asn. Defense Lawyers Criminal Cases; Am. Soc. Int. Law; Harvard Law Sch. Asn. Rel: Society of Friends. Legal Res: 610 W. Main St, Richmond, Ind. 47374. Mailing Add: 1729 Longworth House Office Bldg, Washington, D.C. 20515.

DENNIS, JAMES LEON D

La. State Rep.

b. Monroe, La, 1/9/36; s. Jenner Leon Dennis and Hope Taylo D; m. 9/7/58 to Camille Smith; c. Stephen James, Gregory Leon, Mark Taylo and John Timothy. Educ: La. Polytech. Inst, B.S. in Bus. Admin, 59; La. State Univ. Law Sch, LL.B, 62. Polit. & Govt. Pos: La. State Rep, Ouachita Parish, 68- Bus. & Prof. Pos: Assoc, Hudson, Potts & Bernstein, Monroe, La, 62-65, partner, 65- Mil. Serv: Entered as Pvt, Army, 55, released as Pfc, 57, after serv. in First Inf. Div, U.S, 56-57. Publ: 'State Involvement in Private Discrimination Under 14th Amendment,' 61, 'Misstatements in Applications for Life Insurance,' 61 and 'Automobiles - Community Mission - Burden of Proof,' 61, La. Law Rev. Mem: Phi Delta Phi; Rotary; C. of C; Boy Scouts; Order of the Coif. Rel: Methodist. Legal Res: 2120 Valencia, Monroe, La. 71201. Mailing Add: P.O. Box 1421, Monroe, La. 71201.

DENNIS, JOHN NEWMAN R

N.J. State Assemblyman

b. East Orange, N.J, 2/25/33; s. Walter N. Dennis and Jean Ames Jones; m. 3/23/57 to Elaine Schermerhorn; c. Suzanne, Pamela and Sandra. Educ: Lehigh Univ, B.S. Bus. Admin, 58; Sigma Nu. Polit. & Govt. Pos: N.J. State Assemblyman, Essex Co. Dist. 11-E, 68- Bus. & Prof. Pos: Sales exec. and mem. bd. of dirs, Annin & Co, Verona, N.J, 59- Mil. Serv: Army, 54-56, with serv. in First Cavalry, Far East, 55-56. Mem: Kiwanis; dir, West Essex Red Cross; dir, Nat. Coun. on Alcoholism; dir, United Fund; dir, Integrity, Inc; hon. mem, Nat. Soc. of Radiologic Technologists. Mailing Add: 55 Hamilton Rd, Verona, N.J. 07044.

DENNIS, MAX HALE R

Ohio State Sen.

b. Dayton, Ohio, 8/9/25; s. Paul B. Dennis and Josephine Hale D; m. Dec, 1943 to Ethel Barrett; c. Jeffrey, Dianne, Jody and Meredith. Educ: Wash. and Lee Univ, A.B, 47, LL.B, 48; Phi Delta Phi. Polit. & Govt. Pos: Asst. Attorney Gen, Ohio, 51; city solicitor, Wilmington, Ohio, 54-55; Ohio State Rep, 55-63; Ohio State Sen, 63-, mem, Criminal Law Study Cmt, Ohio Legis. Serv. Cmn, 66 and Tax Study Cmn, 66. Bus. & Prof. Pos: Attorney-at-law, Wilmington, Ohio, 49- Mem: Clinton Co. and Am. Bar Asns; Mason; Eagles; Rotary. Rel: Church of Christ. Legal Res: 245 N. South St, Wilmington, Ohio 45177. Mailing Add: State Capitol, Columbus, Ohio 43215. (1967)

DENNIS, REMBERT CONEY D

S.C. State Sen.

b. Pinopolis, S.C, 8/27/15; s. Edward J. Dennis and Ella Mae Coney D; m. 10/3/44 to Natalie Brown D; c. six. Educ: Furman Univ, A.B, 36; Georgetown Univ. Law Sch, 36-37; Univ. of S.C, LL.B, 40. Polit. & Govt. Pos: S.C. State Rep, 39-42; S.C. State Sen, 43-; mem, S.C. Dem. State Exec. Cmt, 44; del, Dem. Nat. Conv, 44, 48, 52, 56 & 60. Bus. & Prof. Pos: Lawyer, Dennis and Dennis. Mem: Sigma Alpha Epsilon; Blue Key; Mason (32°); Shrine; Lions; WOW. Rel: Baptist; Bd. of Deacons. Mailing Add: Box 968, Monks Corner, S.C. 29461. (1967)

DENNISON, DAVID SHORT, JR. R

b. Poland, Ohio, 7/29/18; s. David Short Dennison and Cordelia Whitman D; m. 9/7/46 to Margaret Kroehle; c. David Whitman and Jennie. Educ: Williams Col, A.B, 40; West. Reserve Sch. of Law, LL.B, 45; Order of the Coif; Delta Upsilon; Phi Delta Phi. Polit. & Govt. Pos: U.S. Rep, Ohio, 57-58; consult, U.S. Civil Rights Cmt, 59; chmn, Trumbull Co. Rep. Exec. and Cent. Cmts, Ohio, 64-66; mem, Ohio Rep. State Cent. Cmt, formerly; mem, Bd. of Elec, 64-; del, Rep. Nat. Conv, 68. Bus. & Prof. Pos: Trustee, West. Reserve Acad, Hudson; partner, Dennison & Wern, attorneys, 64- Mil. Serv:

Vol. ambulance driver, Am. Field Serv, Libya and N.Africa, 42-43; Africa Star. Mem: Trumbull Co, Ohio State and Fed. Bar Asns; Nat. Lawyers Club; Capitol Hill Club; Elks; Pomona Grange; Buckeye Club. Rel: Episcopal; former Vestryman, Christ Episcopal Church, Warren, Ohio. Legal Res: Route 2, Warren, Ohio 44481. Mailing Add: 813 Union Savings & Trust Bldg, Warren, Ohio 44481.

DENNISON, MARGARET R
Ohio State Rep.
b. Warren, Ohio, 6/14/20; d. Ralph Kroehlo and Marion Gillmer K; m. 9/7/46 to David Dennison; c. Jennie and David Whitman. Educ: Bryn Mawr Col, A.B, 42; grad. work, Kent State Univ, 67-68. Polit. & Govt. Pos: Ohio State Rep, currently. Bus. & Prof. Pos: Ed, Indust. Pub, Peerless Elec. Co, 42-58. Mil. Serv: Am. Red Cross, ETO, 44-46. Mem: Cong. Club; Order of Women Legis; charter mem, Nat. Soc. State Legis.(secy, 67-68); hon. mem, Delta Kappa Gamma. Rel: Episcopal. Mailing Add: R.R. 2, Warren, Ohio 44481.

DENNY, BRADFORD HOUSTON R
Vt. State Rep.
b. Burlington, Vt, 10/12/41; s. Homer Denny and Phoebe Ladd D; m. 4/17/63 to Mary Alice Brown; c. Joseph Justin, Heather Lorraine and Nathan Ladd. Educ: Dartmouth Col, B.A, 64; Alpha Delta Phi. Polit. & Govt. Pos: Vt. State Rep, 69- Bus. & Prof. Pos: Reporter, Rutland Herald, 64-65; news off. mgr. reporter, Times-Argus, 65-67; administr, Union High Sch, Montpelier, 67- Mil. Serv: Entered as Pvt, Marine Corps Res, 60, released as Pfc, 66. Mem: Jaycees. Rel: Episcopal. Mailing Add: 7 Vine St, Northfield, Vt. 05663.

DENNY, JAMES T. D
Chmn, Pettis Co. Dem. Party, Mo.
b. Green Ridge, Mo, 4/28/03; s. Raphael Valentine Denny and Mary Ellen English D; m. 10/28/30 to Mary Vinnie Creegan; c. Patricia Jean (Mrs. Stephen J. Larocca). Educ: Drury Col, 21-24. Polit. & Govt. Pos: Chmn, Pettis Co. Dem. Party, Mo, 68- Mil. Serv: Mo. Nat. Guard, 21-25. Mem: Pres, Cent. Mo. Asn. Life Underwriters, 61 & 62; chmn, Sedalia Chap. Red Cross, 61 & 62; mem, Million Dollar Club, Metrop. Life Ins. Co. N.Y, 62, 63 & 65; pres, Sedalia United Fund, 64 & 65; Pettis Co. Hist. Soc, 64-; Rotary (pres. and organizer, Houston, 53-55); K. of C. (grand knight, 56 & 57); Sedalia Country Club. Rel: Catholic. Mailing Add: 502 E. Fourth, Sedalia, Mo. 65301.

DENO, JOHN WESLEY D
Alderman, Meriden City Coun, Conn.
b. Meriden, Conn, 4/8/12; s. Harold Clayton Deno and Elisabeth Bean D; m. 9/15/32 to Madeline Clare Caturia; c. Magdalen Mary, John Wesley, Jr, Muriel Elisabeth, Marjorie Ann, James Walter and Mary Ellen; 9 Grandchildren. Educ: Meriden Pub. Schs; Lincoln Inst. Polit. & Govt. Pos: Alderman, Meriden City Coun, Conn, currently. Bus. & Prof. Pos: Foreman, New Departure, Gen. Motors Corp, 66. Mil. Serv: Entered as A/S, Navy, 44, released as Pharmacist Mate 3/C. Mem: Eagles; Franco Am; Am. Legion; Franco Am. War Vet; treas, United Vet. Coun. Rel: Catholic. Mailing Add: 170 Miller St, Meriden, Conn. 06450.

DeNOIA, RICHARD JOSEPH D
Pres, Young Dem. Clubs of Conn.
b. Groton, Conn, 2/17/39; s. A. Dominic DeNoia and Bertha Topaz D; m. 4/15/69 to Ann Margaret Galligan. Educ: Providence Col, B.A, 59; Boston Univ, grad. study, 1 year; U.S. Sch. Army Admin, Cert; Editor-in-chief, College Weekly Newspaper; Student Cong; Pyramid Players. Polit. & Govt. Pos: Publicity chmn, Groton Dem. Party, Conn, 62-67; representative, Southeast Conn. Regional Planning Agency, 63-67; secy, Groton Planning Cmn, 63-; pres, Groton Young Dem, 64-; mem, Dem. Town and City Cmts, 65-; exec. bd. chmn, Young Dem. Clubs Conn, 66-68, pres, 68-; pub. info. officer, Nat. Security Seminar, Indust. Col. of the Armed Forces, 67; justice of the peace, Groton, Conn, 67-; alternate del, Dem. Nat. Conv, 68; chmn, Young Citizens for Humphrey-Muskie, Conn, 68; ex officio mem, Conn. Dem. State Cent. Cmt, 68-; mem. rules rev. cmt, Conn. Dem. State Cent. Cmt, 69-; commun. asst. to clerk, Conn. State Senate, 69- Bus. & Prof. Pos: Owner and mgr, R.J. DeNoia Assocs, Groton, Conn, 62-69; chmn, Kennedy Mem. Libr, Groton Dr, 64; ALSAC, Groton-Ledyard, 64; publicity chmn, Am. Cancer Crusade Groton Dr, 64-69; chmn. secy-treas, and dir, Groton C. of C, 66-68; founder and acting chmn, Center City Concerned, Groton, 68-69. Mil. Serv: Entered as Recruit, Army, 60, released as Pfc, 60, after serv. in Personnel Center, Ft. Dix, N.J; Res, 60-66, Pfc; Letter of Commendation. Publ: Weekly column, 'Along the Thames,' Conn. Sunday Herald, 63-65. Mem: Jr. C. of C; Nat. Coun. Cath. Men; Providence Col. Alumni Asn. Copey Best Actor Trophy; Two Citations, Am. Cancer Soc. Rel: Roman Catholic. Mailing Add: 24 Hamilton Ave, Groton, Conn. 06340.

DENOMME, ERNEST FRANCIS R
Chmn, Portsmouth Rep. Town Cmt, R.I.
b. Fiskeville, R.I, 2/2/04; s. Napoleon Joseph Denomme and Melina De Tonnancour D; m. 9/5/38 to Jeanette Nilda Richmond. Educ: Bryant Col, 2 years; Boston Univ, 1 year; Brown Univ. Exten, 3 years. Polit. & Govt. Pos: Mem. welfare bd, Portsmouth, R.I, 30-35, pub. rels. rep, 30-69, moderator, 35-39 chmn. budget cmt, 35-45, mem. zoning and hurricane study, 38-42; chmn, Rep. Gubernatorial Finance, R.I, 50-52; chmn, Eisenhower Local Campaign, 52; mem. Portsmouth Sch. Cmt, 54-58; mem, R.I. Real Estate Cmn, 58-61; secy, Portsmouth Rep. Town Cmt, 60-69, chmn, 64-; chmn, Nixon Local Campaign, 60 & 68; secy, R.I. Legis. Hosp. Cmn, 64-66. Bus. & Prof. Pos: Acct, Pawtuxet Valley Dyeing Co, 21-25; secy. strategy dept, U.S. Naval War Col, 25-26; secy, Wyerhaeuser Timber Co, 26-30, asst. sales mgr, 30-36, sales mgr, 36-62. Publ: 'Romance of the Lumber Industry,' Weyerhaeuser News, 30; 'The Portsmouth Free Library,' R.I. Libr. Asn, 66; 'Stone Bridge and Other Historical Stories,' Sakonnet Times, 68-69. Mem: Newport Eng. Soc; Int. Order Lumbermen; New Eng. Coun. Econ. Develop; K. of C. (4°); Order of Hoo Hoo; C. of C; past pres. and trustee, Portsmouth Free Pub. Libr; R.I. Tuberc. and Health Asn.(v.pres); dir. and exec. cmt. mem, Newport Nat. Bank; corporator, Newport Savings Bank and Trust Co. Medal of St. George, Bishop McVinney; Selective Serv. World War II Medal; Capt. George Bucklin Award, 40 years, Boy Scout; Am. Red Cross Award, 15 years treas. Portsmouth Chap. Rel: Roman Catholic. Mailing Add: 160 Bristol Ferry Rd, Portsmouth, R.I. 02871.

DENSER, JOHN W. R
Chmn, Mineral Co. Rep. Cent. Cmt, Nev.
b. Waukesha, Wis, 2/28/25; s. Clarence Hugh Denser, Sr. and Clara Mae Mider D; m. 1/7/51 to Frances Louise Rogers; c. John Michael and April Susan. Educ: Millsaps Col, B.A, 44; Tulane Sch. of Med, 45-49. Polit. & Govt. Pos: Chmn, Mineral Co. Rep. Cent. Cmt, Nev, 64- Bus. & Prof. Pos: Physician and surgeon, Hawthorne, Nev, 61- Mil. Serv: Entered as Midshipman, Naval Res, 43, released as Ph.M. 2/C, 46, after serv. in Hosp. Corps, U.S. Mem: Lahontan Basin Med. Soc; Nev. State and Am. Med. Asns; pres. elect, Nev. Acad. Gen. Practice; maj, pilot and med. officer, Civil Air Patrol. Rel: Presbyterian. Legal Res: First St. and Bailey Dr, Hawthorne, Nev. 89415. Mailing Add: Box 1366, Hawthorne, Nev. 89415.

DENSFORD, CHARLES FRANCIS R
Chmn, Bandera Co. Rep. Cmt, Tex.
b. Oklahoma City, Okla, 1/26/07; s. James Washington Densford and Pearl May Lutes D; m. 3/12/32 to Cora Esperanza Giano; c. Dolores (Mrs. J.R. Fender), Maj. C.F, Jr, USA, James T, William H, Cora Elena (Mrs. W.C. Watkins) and Daniel D. Educ: U.S. Mil. Acad, B.S, 31. Polit. & Govt. Pos: Chmn, Bandera Co. Rep. Cmt, Tex, 65- Bus. & Prof. Pos: Owner-operator, Densford Ranch, 58-; real estate broker, Densford Realty Co, 62- Mil. Serv: Pvt, Kans. Nat. Guard, 26; Air Force, 31, retired as Col, 59; Air Medal; Am. Defense Serv. Ribbon; Am. Theater Ribbon; Victory Medal; Grado de Comendador Orden de Boyaca, Colombia. Publ: Columnist, 'The Root of the Matter,' Frontier News, 61-, Valdina Clarion, 65-, Independent Am, 65-, Suburban J, 66- Mem: Nat. Rifle Asn; Asn. of Grads, U.S. Mil. Acad; Am. Legion; VFW; Daedalians; Lions Int; San Antonio, Tex. and Nat. Retired Officers Asn; mem, Alamo Area Coun. Govt. Pistol Marksmanship, various nat. records and state and regional championships; Adjutant, U.S. Rifle and Pistol Team, World Shooting Championships, Buenos Aires, 49. Legal Res: Ranch Home, Pipe Creek, Tex. 78063. Mailing Add: Box 174, Pipe Creek, Tex. 78063.

DENT, HARRY SHULER R
Dep. Counsel to the President
b. St. Matthews, S.C, 2/21/30; s. Hampton Nathaniel Dent, Sr. and Sally Prickett D; m. 8/16/51 to Elizabeth Inez Francis; c. Harry S, Jr, Dolly N, Virginia M. and John R. Educ: Presby. Col, B.A, 51; George Wash. Univ, LL.B, 57; Georgetown Univ, LL.M, 59; Blue Key; Phi Alpha Delta; Pi Kappa Alpha. Polit. & Govt. Pos: Admin. asst. to U.S. Sen. Strom Thurmond, S.C, 55-65; state chmn, S.C. Rep. Party, 65-68; del, Rep. Nat. Conv, 68; Dep. Counsel to the President, 69- Bus. & Prof. Pos: Partner, Dent and Kennedy, Attorneys, 65-69. Mil. Serv: Entered as 2nd Lt, Army, 51, released as 1st Lt, after serv. in 24th Inf. Div, Far East Command, 52-53; Maj, Army Res, currently. Rel: Southern Baptist. Legal Res: 4617 Perry Court, Columbia, S.C. 29206. Mailing Add: The White House, 1600 Pennsylvania Ave, Washington, D.C. 20500.

DENT, JAMES WESLEY R
Calif. State Assemblyman
b. Martinez, Calif, 11/16/07; s. James Dent and Susan Potter D; m. 2/7/30 to Frances Jewett Dechman; c. Mrs. John Ruyle, Mrs. Stephen Thomas and James Douglas. Educ: Univ. Calif, A.B, 29, M.A, 36; Columbia and Stanford Univs, grad. study; Phi Beta Kappa; Phi Delta Kappa. Polit. & Govt. Pos: Calif. State Assemblyman, Tenth Dist, Contra Costa Co, 67- Bus. & Prof. Pos: Supt, Campbell Union High Sch. Dist, 44-46; pres, Vallejo Col, 46-48; supt, Mt. Diablo Unified Sch. Dist, Calif, 48-66. Mem: Calif. and Am. Asn. Sch. Adminstrs; Nat. Educ. Asn; Calif. Teachers Asn; Masons; Rotary. Rel: Presbyterian. Legal Res: 1249 Grove Way, Concord, Calif. 94520. Mailing Add: State Capitol Bldg, Sacramento, Calif. 95822.

DENT, JOHN H. D
U.S. Rep, Pa.
b. Johnetta, Pa, 3/10/08; s. Samuel Dent and Genevieve D; m. 4/4/29 to Margaret R; c. Patricia (Mrs. Donald Sharp), John Frederick; grandchildren, John Frederick, Jao Carol, Melissa Ann, Tracy, Susan, Jennifer and Margaret Suzanne. Educ: Great Lakes Naval Aviation Acad; correspondence sch. courses. Polit. & Govt. Pos: Pa. State Rep, 36; Dem. Floor Leader, Pa. State Senate, 17 years, Pa. State Sen, 36-58; U.S. Rep, Pa, 58- Bus. & Prof. Pos: Newspaperman; exec. coal, coke, bldg. and transportation co. Mil. Serv: Marine Air Corps, 24-28. Mem: United Rubber Workers, pres. local 18759, exec. coun, int. coun, 23-27. Student of polits, polit. legis; authority on unemployment, workmen's compensation laws, parliamentary and legis. procedures; written for mag. and labor publ. Legal Res: Jeanette, Pa. 15644. Mailing Add: 2430 House Office Bldg, Wash, D.C. 20515.

DENT, RAYMOND THEODORE R
N.C. State Sen.
b. Asheville, N.C, 12/21/32; s. Raymond Theodore Dent and Mary Hunter Cross D. Educ: Univ. of the South, 52-55; Sigma Alpha Epsilon. Polit. & Govt. Pos: Chmn, Mitchell Co. Rep. Party, N.C, 66; N.C. State Sen, 31st Dist, 67- Bus. & Prof. Pos: Gen. mgr, Diamond Mica Co, 55-60 and pres, 60-66; pres, Hassett Mining Co, 66- Mil. Serv: Entered as Pvt, Army, 53, released as Cpl, 55, after serv. in 54th Qm. Bn, Korean Command; Korean Serv, Good Conduct and UN Serv. Medals; Army Commendation Medal with Medal Pendant. Mem: Am. Inst. Mining Engrs; Soc. Adv. of Mgt; Am. Inst. of Mgt; bd. of trustees, Spruce Pine Commun. Hosp; v.pres, Mitchell Co. United Fund; chmn, Small Bus. Develop. Cmt; dir. and secy-treas, Appalachian Indust. Asn. Rel: Episcopal. Legal Res: 939 New Haw Creek Rd, Asheville, N.C. 28805. Mailing Add: P.O. Box 386, Spruce Pine, N.C. 28777.

DENTON, ASHTON LYLE R
Chmn, Fleming Co. Rep. Exec. Cmt, Ky.
b. Holton, Kans, 10/6/09; s. James Edgar Denton and Della Pierce D; m. 8/12/37 to Maxine Barber; c. James Everett and Glenna Lyle. Educ: Morehead State Univ, A.B, 39, M.A, 53; pres, Morehead State Univ. Alumni Asn, 41-42. Polit. & Govt. Pos: Supvr, Agr. Stabilization & Conserv. Serv, Fleming Co, Ky, 62-63; chmn, Fleming Co. Rep. Exec. Cmt, 64-; admin. asst, State Dept. Ins, 68- Bus. & Prof. Pos: Teacher, Fleming Co. Schs, Ky, 27-33; elem. prin, Hillsboro, Ky, 34-43 & 47-59. Mil. Serv: Entered as Pvt, Army, 43, released as T-4, 46, after serv. in 233rd Army Postal Unit, Asiatic-Pac. Theatre, 44-46; Good Conduct Medal; Battle Star. Mem: Mason; Am. Legion; C. of C; Farm Bur; Ky. Retired Teachers Asn. Rel: Protestant. Mailing Add: P.O. Box 87, Hillsboro, Ky. 41049.

DENTON, HERBERT JACKSON, JR. R
Tenn. State Rep.
b. Kingsport, Tenn, 12/13/41; s. Herbert Jackson Denton, Sr. and Mayme Ellen Campbell D; m. 11/2/66 to Judith Gail Trent; c. Hereward Trent. Educ: Tenn. Tech. Univ, B.S, 64; Nat. Soc. Prfnl. Engrs; Mech. Engrs. Club; Eta Epsilon Sigma; Scabbard and Blade. Polit. & Govt. Pos: Tenn. State Rep, 68-. Bus. & Prof. Pos: Mech. Engr, Tenn. Eastman Co, 64 & 67- Mil. Serv: Entered as 2nd Lt, Army, 65, released as 1st Lt, 67, after serv. in 102 Engr. Co, Construction Support, Dominican Repub. and Vietnam, 65-66, Res, 68-; Parachute Badge; Nat. Defense Serv. Medal; Vietnam Serv. Medal with Bronze Star. Mem: Am. Soc. Mech. Engrs; Mason; K.T; Nat. Rifle Asn; Am. Legion; Moose; Optimist; Farm Bur. Rel: Baptist. Mailing Add: Route 4, Blountville, Tenn. 37617.

DENTON, WINFIELD KIRKPATRICK D
b. Evansville, Ind, 10/28/96; s. George Kirkpatrick Denton and Sara Linda Chick D; m. 12/27/27 to Grace Abernethy; c. Beth (Mrs. Bamberger), Mary and Sara (Mrs. Ong). Educ: DePauw Univ, A.B, 19; Harvard Univ, LL.B, 22; Phi Kappa Psi. Polit. & Govt. Pos: City chmn, Evansville Dem. Party, Ind, 25; co. prosecutor, Vanderburgh Co, 32-36; Ind. State Rep. and Minority Floor Leader, Ind. House of Rep, 36-42; former U.S. Rep, Eighth Dist, Ind. Bus. & Prof. Pos: Attorney-at-law, private practice, 22- Mil. Serv: Entered as Pvt, Army, 17, released as 2nd Lt, 19, after serv. in Second Aviation Instr. Corps, France; reentered as Maj, Army Air Corps, 43, released as Lt. Col, 45, after serv. in Judge Adv. Gen. Dept. in U.S; Pilots Wings; Am. Campaign Medal; World War I and World War II Victory Medals; World War II Medal. Mem: Ind. and Supreme Court Bar Asns; Evansville Bar Asn.(past pres); Mason (32°); Shrine; Elks; Am. Legion; VFW; Vet. of World War I; Amvets. Letters in Football and Basketball; capt, DePauw Basketball Team, 17. Rel: Methodist. Mailing Add: 957 E. Powell Ave, Evansville, Ind. 47713. (1967)

DENTZ, ROBERT JOSEPH D
b. Washington, D.C, 3/11/26; s. Joseph Edwin Dentz and Mary McQuade D; m. 9/15/51 to Marjorie Ann Merylo; c. Barbara Ellen, Susan Eileen and Carol Ann. Educ: George Washington Univ, B.A, 50; Alpha Delta Sigma; Pi Delta Epsilon, Phi Sigma Kappa; past pres, Arts Club. Polit. & Govt. Pos: Md. State Del, 62-66. Bus. & Prof. Pos: Pres, Design Servs, 62-65; exec. v.pres, Compton Jones Assocs, 65-66; pres, Robert J. Dentz, Advert. & Pub. Rels, 66- Mil. Serv: Entered as A/S, Navy, 44, released as Radioman 3/C, 46, after serv. in Am, Asian and European Theaters; Am, Asian and European Ribbons. Mem: Nat. committeeman, Am. Legion and mem. of Post Mortem Club; North West Dem. Club; C. of C; Prince George's Co. Planning Asn; past pres, Carole Highlands Citizen Asn; 4th-6th Precinct Dem. Club; del, Prince George's Civic Fed; Citizens for Decent Literature; Md. Fair Representation Cmt. Rel: Roman Catholic. Mailing Add: 7400 16th Ave, Takoma Park, Md. 20012. (1967)

DePALMA, SAMUEL
Asst. Secy, Bur. of Int. Orgn. Affairs, Dept. of State
Legal Res: Md. Mailing Add: Dept. of State, 2201 C St. N.W, Washington, D.C. 20520.

DE PAOLI, ESTHER ELAYNE R
Chmn, Amador Co. Rep. Cent. Cmt, Calif.
b. San Luis Obispo, Calif, 1/29/20; d. Steve Zegar and Stella Robinson Z; m. 7/15/45 to Angelo J. De Paoli. Educ: Univ. Calif, Los Angeles, A.B, 42; Univ. Calif, Hastings Col. of Law, LL.B, 46, J.D, 68. Polit. & Govt. Pos: Mem, Amador Co. Rep. Cent. Cmt, 58-, v.chmn, 64 and chmn, 65-; pres, Amador Co. Rep. Women Federated, 63 & 64; mem, Calif. Rep. State Cent. Cmt, 65-; pub. mem. adv. bd, Bur. of Electronic Repair Delar Registrn, Dept. of Prfnl. and Voc. Standards, Calif, 67- Mem: Charter mem, Soroptimist Club, Amador Co, dir. dist. IV, Southwest. Region, Soroptimist Fedn. of the Americas Inc, 68-; secy, Amador Co. chap, Am. Red Cross. Legal Res: 126A Rex Ave, Jackson, Calif. 95642. Mailing Add: P.O. Box 875, Jackson, Calif. 95642.

DERGE, DAVID RICHARD R
Research Consult, Rep. Nat. Cmt.
b. Kansas City, Mo, 10/10/28; s. David R. Derge and Blanche Butterfield D; m. 9/4/51 to Elizabeth Anne Greene; c. David and Dorothy. Educ: Univ. Mo, A.B, 50; Northwest. Univ, A.M, 51 and Ph.D, 55; Phi Beta Kappa; Pi Sigma Alpha; Alpha Pi Zeta; Kappa Sigma. Polit. & Govt. Pos: Rep. precinct committeeman, Monroe Co, Ind, 62-66; councilman-at-lg, Bloomington City Coun, 63-67; dir, surv. research, Nixon-Agnew Campaign Cmt, 68; research consult, Rep. Nat. Cmt, 69- Bus. & Prof. Pos: Instr. polit. sci, Univ. Mo, 54-56; prof, Ind. Univ, Bloomington, 56-, assoc. dean, grad. sch, 65-67, assoc. dean faculties, 67-69, exec. v.pres. and dean admin, 69-; pres, Behavioral Research Assocs, 64- Mil. Serv: Entered as Pvt, Army, 46, released as Cpl, 48, after serv. in 21st Ord. Motor Maintenance Co, Army of Occupation, Japan, 47-48; Comdr, Naval Res, 52- Publ: The World of American Politics, Bobbs-Merrill, 68; Institution Building and Rural Development, Ind. Univ, 68; Public Leadership in Indiana, Inst. of Pub. Admin, Ind. Univ, 69. Mem: Am. Polit. Sci. Asn; Midwest Conf. of Polit. Scientists; Soc. for Int. Develop; Midwest Univ. Consortium for Int. Activities, Inc.(dir. and secy). Ulysses G. Weatherly and Brown Derby Awards for Distinguished Teaching, Ind. Univ; Outstanding Young Man of Ind, Ind. Jaycees, 64. Rel: Presbyterian. Legal Res: Woodruff Lane, Bittner Woods, Bloomington, Ind. 47401. Mailing Add: Bryan 200, Indiana University, Bloomington, Ind. 47401.

de RHAM, CASIMIR, JR. R
Chmn. Exec. Cmt, Mass. Rep. State Cmt.
b. N.Y.C, 9/5/24; s. Casimir de Rham and Lucy Patterson de R; m. 6/9/45 to Elizabeth Moran Evarts; c. Elizabeth Morgan, Henry Casimir, Rufus Patterson and Jeremiah Evarts. Educ: Harvard Univ, A.B, 46, LL.B, 49; Fly Club; Hasty Pudding, Ins. of 1770. Polit. & Govt. Pos: Pres, Cambridge Young Rep. Club, 53-54; chmn, Cambridge Rep. City Cmt, 54-58; chmn, Cambridge Rep. Finance Cmt, 58 & 66-68; mem, Mass. Rep. State Cmt, 60-, mem. exec. cmt, 62-65, chmn. exec. cmt, 67-; alternate del, Rep. Nat. Conv, 64 & 68. Bus. & Prof. Pos: Assoc, Palmer & Dodge, 49-51, 52-56, partner, 57- Mil. Serv: Entered as Pvt, Marine Corps, 43, released as 2nd Lt, 46, re-entered as 1st Lt, 51, released as Capt, 52, after serv. in Second Marine Div, Tenth Marine Regt. Publ: 'Joint Returns,' Article, N.Y. Univ. Inst. on Fed. Taxation, 63. Mem: Am, Mass, Boston and Cambridge Bar Asns; Mason, Harvard Lodge AF&AM; Country Club; St. Botolph Club; Marsh Post, Am. Legion; Boys' Clubs of Boston; pres, Mt. Auburn Hosp; chmn. bd, Commonwealth Sch; trustee, St. Mark's Sch; dir, Cambridge Trust Co. Rel: Episcopal. Mailing Add: 47 Lakeview Ave, Cambridge, Mass. 02138.

DERIAN, PATRICIA MURPHY D
Dem. nat. committeewoman, Miss.
b. New York City, N.Y; d. Ronald Thomas Murphy and Ruby Haridman M; m. 3/7/53 to Paul S. Derian, M.D; c. Michael Tabore, Thomas Craig and Renee Brooke. Educ: Palos Verdes Col; Millsaps Col; Univ. Va. Sch. Nursing, grad. Polit. & Govt. Pos: Dem. Nat. Committeewoman, Miss, 68-; mem. bd. dirs, Miss. Coun. Human Rels, Family Serv. Asn, Jackson, Operation Shoestring, Mississippians for Pub. Educ. and Youth Legis. & Govt. Assembly; mem, Uniform Code Enforcement Cmt, Jackson and Neighborhood Recreation Cmt; chmn, Women in Miss. for Humphrey Muskie, 68. Bus. & Prof. Pos: Participant, White House Conf. on Violence, Brandeis Univ, 65 and Conf. to Fulfill These Rights, 66; Lear-Sigler consult, Off. Econ. Opportunity, 66, head start consult, 67; proj. officer, Miss. Action for Progress. Mem: Nat. Cmt. Support of Pub. Schs; DAR; Am. Civil Liberties Union; Acad. Relig. & Ment. Health; Commun. Serv. Coun; Gallery Guild; League of Women Voters. Mailing Add: 2349 Twin Lakes Circle, Jackson, Miss. 39211.

DERIGHTER, JOHN THOMAS D
Mem, Cuyahoga Co. Dem. Exec. Cmt, Ohio
b. England, 8/28/00; s. Samuel Derighter and Mary Blay D; m. 5/20/25 to Susan Williams; c. Alycemae Rose. Educ: Cleveland Col; John Marshall Law Sch. Polit. & Govt. Pos: Dep. sheriff, Cuyahoga Co, Ohio, 24-25; Ohio State Rep, Cuyahoga Co, 35-38 & 41-44; city clerk, Cleveland, 41-42; asst. to Secy. of State, Ohio, 49; Dem. precinct committeeman, Ohio; mem, Cuyahoga Co. Dem. Exec. Cmt. Bus. & Prof. Pos: V.pres. and mgr, Superior Savings & Loan Co, 25-66. Rel: Catholic. Mailing Add: 6900 Sprague Rd, Brecksville, Ohio 44141. (1967)

DERIZOTIS, PARIS C. D
N.Mex. State Rep.
b. Argos, Greece, 3/15/31; s. Christos Derizotis and Vasiliki Blatsou D; m. 6/27/53 to Minnie Esparza; c. Christina, Mona, Paris and Dino. Educ: Col. of Polit. and Econ, Athens, Greece, 2 years. Polit. & Govt. Pos: N.Mex. State Rep, McKinley Co, 69-; v.chmn, McKinley Co. Dem. Party; mem, N.Mex. Dem. State Cent. Cmt. Bus. & Prof. Pos: Restaurant owner, 55- Mem: Odd Fellows; Ahepa. Rel: Greek Orthodox. Mailing Add: 610 Zecca, Gallup, N.Mex. 87301.

DERMODY, JOHN DANIEL D
b. Pleasantville, N.Y, 9/21/09; s. John Joseph Dermody and Catharine Susannah Gallegher D; m. 9/2/38 to Mary Louise Turkal; c. John Paul and Mary Kathleen (Mrs. McGrath). Educ: Fordham Univ, 27-29; Clarkson Tech, B.S, Chem. Eng, 31. Polit. & Govt. Pos: Dem. committeeman, Mt. Pleasant, N.Y, 32-33; del, Dem. Nat. Conv, 68; mem, State Dem. Cmt, Calif, 68-69. Bus. & Prof. Pos: Civil engr, Pub. Works Admin, 33-38; construction engr, Panama Canal Zone, 38-41; projs. mgr, P.J. Walker Co, Calif, 46-58; gen. contractor, J.D. Dermody Co. Inc, Lancaster, 58- Mil. Serv: Entered as Lt.(jg), Navy, Civil Eng. Corps, 41, released as Lt. Comdr, 46, after serv. in 33rd N.C. Regt, Philippines, 44-46; Comdr. Res, 59, Retired. Mem: Soc. Am. Mil. Engrs; Bldg. Indust. Asn.(past chap. pres); Rotary; Elks; K. of C; C. of C. Los Angeles Co. Award of Merit. Rel: Catholic. Mailing Add: 44856 15th St. W, Lancaster, Calif. 93534.

DERMODY, MARY LOUISE D
Mem, Calif. Dem. State Cent. Cmt.
b. Zookspur, Iowa, 6/18/17; d. John Andrew Turkal and Rose Pozega T; m. 9/2/38 to John Daniel Dermody; c. John Paul and Mary Kathleen (Mrs. McGrath). Educ: High sch, grad, 34; Bus. Col, Des Moines, Iowa, 35. Polit. & Govt. Pos: Precinct worker, Presidential Elec, Altadena, Calif, 52 and Lancaster, 56; precinct chmn, Gubernatorial Elec, Lancaster, 58; chmn, precincts, Pres, State and Cong. Elec, 60; chmn, Women for Gov. Brown and mgr, Assembly Cand, 62; mem, Calif. Dem. State Cent. Cmt, 62-; 62nd Assembly campaign mgr, Pierre Salinger and Assembly Cand, 64; co-chmn, Dollars for Democrats, 62nd Assembly Area, 65; Dem. Women's Forum Adv. Cmt, 65-; campaign chmn, Gov. Brown, Antelope Valley, 66; observer, Dem. Nat. Conv, 68; co-chmn, Robert Kennedy Campaign, 68; Dem. cand, Calif. State Assemblyman, 62nd Dist, 68; mem, Dem. Co. Cmt, 68-; chmn. cong. cand, John Van De Kamp, 69. Bus. & Prof. Pos: Acct, Panama Canal Zone, 41; corp. secy, J.D. Dermody Co. Inc, Lancaster, Calif, 58- Mem: Bus. & Prfnl. Women's Club; Women's Div. C. of C; Lancaster Woman's Club; Rotary Anns. Highest Br. Award, Verdugo Heart Asn, 68 & 69; Key Award, Dem. Campaign, 64; Women in Commun. Serv. Outstanding Vol, 67. Rel: Catholic. Mailing Add: 44856 15th St. W, Lancaster, Calif. 93534.

DeROSA, PASQUALE JOSEPH R
Chmn, Derby Rep. Town Cmt, Conn.
b. Derby, Conn; s. Pasquale DeRosa and Josephine Riccio D; m. 8/30/52 to Bernadine Edna Groth; c. Linda Susan, Patricia Ann and David Joseph. Educ: Bridgeport Eng. Inst, 3 years; Univ. Bridgeport, A.S. Polit. & Govt. Pos: Mem, Bd. Apportionment and Taxation, Derby, Conn, 54-64; chmn, Derby Rep. Town Cmt, 68-; Sinking Fund Cmnr, Derby, Conn, 68-69. Bus. & Prof. Pos: Design engr, Farrell Co, Div. of USM, 52- Mem: K. of C. Rel: Catholic. Mailing Add: 106 Olivia St, Derby, Conn. 06418.

DEROUNIAN, STEVEN B. R
Justice, Supreme Court, N.Y.
b. Sofia, Bulgaria, 4/6/18; s. Boghos Derounian and Eliza Aprahamian D; m. 8/20/47 to Emily Ann Kennard; c. Ann Ashby, Steven Blake, Eleanore Kennard. Educ: N.Y. Univ, A.B, 38; Fordham Univ, LL.B, 42; Delta Theta Pi. Polit. & Govt. Pos: Councilman and mem. bd, North Hempstead, N.Y, 48-52; U.S. Rep, N.Y, 83rd-88th Cong. and mem. cmt. Ways and Means, U.S. House of Rep; Justice, Supreme Court, N.Y, 69- Mil. Serv: Capt, Army Inf, 42-46, serv. in 193rd Div; Maj, Res; Purple Heart; Bronze Star with Cluster; Combat Infantrymans Badge. Mem: Am, N.Y. State and Nassau Co. Bar Asns; VFW; Am. Legion; ROA; Mason; Elks; chmn, Cancer Crusade, North Hempstead, 52; Garden City Golf Club. Mailing Add: Supreme Court Chambers, Mineola, N.Y. 15001.

DERR, GRACE WEST D
b. Townsend, Mont, 12/30/07; d. Solamon Ray West and Cynthia Ellen Cole W; m. 8/21/44 to Mark Hanna Derr; wid. Educ: West. Mont. Col. Educ, 24-27; Univ. Chicago, Ph.B, 36. Polit. & Govt. Pos: Secy, Lake Co. Dem. Cent. Cmt, Mont, 58-62, precinct committeewoman, 58-, chmn, 62-67; del, State Dem. Conv, 68. Bus. & Prof. Pos: Teacher, Mont. Pub. Sch, 25-56. Mem: Am. Legion Auxiliary; Past President's Parley. Legal Res: Middle Crow Creek, Ronan, Mont. 59864. Mailing Add: Rt. 1, Box 24, Ronan, Mont. 59864.

DERR, JOHN A. R
b. Frederick Co, Md, 8/2/10; married. Educ: Bridgewater Col, A.B, 34; Univ. of Baltimore Law Sch; Univ. of N.Y. Polit. & Govt. Pos: Md. State Sen, 63-67; Mayor of Frederick, 54-58; Md. State Del, 53-54; Dep. Clerk, Frederick Co. Circuit Court, 36-42. Bus. & Prof. Pos: Roads Const. firm. Mil. Serv: U.S.C.G, 41-45. Mem: Elks; Moose; Amvets. Mailing Add: 604 Rosemont, Frederick, Md. 21701. (1967)

DERRICK, HARLEY SIDNEY D
b. Ontario, Ore, 8/27/34; s. Marve Sidney Derrick and Margaret Willburn D; m. 8/28/58 to Sharon Elaine Cath; c. Michael Sidney, Karen Sue and Kathy Lue. Educ: East. Ore. Col, B.S, 61. Polit. & Govt. Pos: Committeeman, Baker Co. Dem. Party, 64-66, chmn, 66. Bus. & Prof. Pos: High sch. teacher, Pine-Eagle Sch. Dist, Ore, 61- Mil. Serv: Entered as Pvt, Army, 55, released as E-5, 57, after serv. in Group 2, UN Command Hq, Tokyo, 56-57. Mem: Ore, Nat. and Pine-Eagle Educ. Asns; Nat. Coun. for Soc. Sci; Grange; Lions Int. Rel: Protestant. Mailing Add: Box 40, R.R, Halfway, Ore. 97834.

DERRICKSON, VERNON BLADES D
b. Frankford, Del, 4/25/00; s. Joshua Walter Derrickson and Nancy Blades D; m. July, 1930 to Jean Madelyn Riveles; c. Vernon Blades and JoAnn (Mrs. Joseph Rowe Slights, Jr). Educ: Wilmington Conf. Acad; Mercersburg Acad; Duke Univ, A.B, Law Sch; Kappa Alpha; Gamma Eta Gamma. Polit. & Govt. Pos: Aide de camp to Gov, Del, 48-52 & 61-69; mem, Del. Cmn. for the Feeble-Minded, 49-51; mem, Del. Pub. Serv. Cmn, 49-69, chmn, 61-69; chmn, Kent Co. Dem. Cmt, 51-69; mem, Del. Dem. State Cmt. and Policy Cmt, 50-69; cand. for Lt. Gov, Del, 52 & 56; del, Dem. Nat. Conv, 52, 56, 60, 64 & 68; mem, Bldg. Cmn. for State Off. Bldg, 64-69; chmn, Emergency Motor Transport Bd, 65-; cmnr, Del. State Parole Bd, 69- Bus. & Prof. Pos: Pres, V and W Hotel Corp, 38-65; pres, Derrickson Hotels, 40-54, Derrickson, Inc, 54-; v.pres. and dir, Brandywine Raceway, Wilmington, Del, 52-; dir, Farmer's Bank, Del, 55-68. Mem: Chmn, Ocean Hwy. Asn, 55-; pres, Great Lakes Asn. of R.R. and Utilities Cmnrs, 64-65; past pres, Friends of Old Dover; trustee, Wesley Col; dir, Del. State Fair; C. of C.(pres, Dover Chap, 36-37). Certificate for Meritorious Serv. in Football and Varsity D in Swimming, Duke Univ. Rel: Congregational; Trustee, Mem. Bd. Ministries and Mem. Bd. Deacons, Peoples Congregational Church. Mailing Add: 128 Hazel Rd, Dover, Del. 19901.

DERRYBERRY, LARRY DALE D
Okla. State Rep.
b. Altus, Okla, 4/22/39; s. Willis Landrum Derryberry and Willene Faye Woodall D; m. 6/7/63 to Marcia Gale Brazil; c. Darren Bret. Educ: Univ. Okla, B.A, 61, LL.B, 63; Phi Eta Sigma; Phi Delta Phi; Pi Kappa Alpha. Polit. & Govt. Pos: Okla. State Rep, 62-, speaker pro tempore, Okla. House of Rep, 69-70. Bus. & Prof. Pos: Attorney-at-Law, Oden, Oden and Derryberry, 63- Pub: 'Insurance: Rain as Accident Within,' Okla. Law Rev, 5/64. Mem: Jackson Co, Okla, and Am. Bar Asns; Altus Jr. C. of C; Elks. Rel: Methodist. Mailing Add: 620 Vine St, Altus, Okla. 73521.

DERVISHIAN, HAROLD H. D
b. Richmond, Va, 10/20/10; m. to Margaret Elizabeth Adams. Educ: Univ. Richmond, LL.B, 32. Polit. & Govt. Pos: Mem, Richmond City Coun, 52-58; Va. State Del, 58-68. Bus. & Prof. Pos: Lawyer. Mem: Am, Va. and Richmond Bar Asns; Rotary; Exchange Club; W.Richmond Bus. Men's Asn; Downtown Club. Rel: Methodist. Mailing Add: 401 Farm Bureau Bldg, 200 W. Grace St, Richmond, Va. 23220.

DERWINSKI, EDWARD J. R
U.S. Rep, Ill.
b. Chicago, Ill, 9/15/26; s. Casimir Ignatius Derwinski and Sophie Smijewski D; m. 12/26/60 to Patricia Ann VanDerGiessen; c. Maureen and Michael Stephen. Educ: Loyola Univ, Chicago, B.S. in Hist, 51; Alpha Delta Gamma. Polit. & Govt. Pos: Mem, Ill-Ind Bi-State Port Study Cmn, 57-58; Ill. State Rep, 24th Dist, 57-58; U.S. Rep, Fourth Dist, Ill, 59- Bus. & Prof. Pos: Pres, West Pullman Savings and Loan Asn, Chicago, 51- Mil. Serv: Entered as Pvt, Army, 45, released as Technician, 46; Pac. Theater and Japanese Occup. Ribbons; Maj, Army Res. Mem: Kiwanis; Moose; Am. Legion; VFW; Polish Legion of Am. Vets; CWV; Polish Nat. Alliance; K. of C; Polish Roman Catholic Union. Selected by Chicago Jr. Asn. of Commerce and Indust. as one of the Ten Outstanding Young Men in Chicago Metrop. area, 59 & 61. Rel: Roman Catholic. Legal Res: 515 E. 160th Pl, South Holland, Ill. 60473. Mailing Add: 7203 Marine Dr, Alexandria, Va. 22307.

DERZAI, AMY RUTH D
b. Eveleth, Minn, 9/4/04; d. John Derzai and Mary Panyan D; single. Educ: Duluth State Teachers' Col, 2 year dipl, 27; Wash. Univ, summers 32 & 33; Cent. Wash. State Col, B.A, 41, M.A, 54; Honor Student. Polit. & Govt. Pos: Treas, Dem. Journal, Wash, 60-; del, Yakima Co. and Wash. State Dem. Conv, 66; treas, Yakima Co. for McCarthy for Pres, 67-68; del, Dist, Co. and Nat. Dem. Conv, 68. Mem: Yakima, Wash. and Nat. Educ. Asns; Wash. Art Asn; Allied Arts; League of Women Voters. Mailing Add: 7 N. 32nd Ave, Yakima, Wash. 98902.

DeSALVIO, LOUIS F. D
N.Y. State Assemblyman
b. New York, N.Y; m. to Elvira Mongillo; c. John and Maria. Educ: DeWitt Clinton High Sch. Polit. & Govt. Pos: N.Y. State Assemblyman, 40-; dep. collector of internal revenue; mem, John DeSalvio Dem. Club, 2nd Assembly Dist, Manhattan. Mem: Holy Name Soc; N.Y. Soc; Elks; K. of C; Charles Carrol Gen. Assembly; Grand St. Boys Asn; Societa San Gennaro. Rel: Catholic. Mailing Add: 425 W. Broadway, New York, N.Y. 10013. (1967)

DE SANTIS, CARL ROBERT R
Chmn, Warren Co. Rep. Cmt, N.Y.
b. Passaic, N.J, 9/1/26; s. Joseph De Santis and Irene M. Van Hine D.(deceased); m. 1/2/52 to Barbara Wands Ettinger; c. Jonathon M, Carl R. Jr, Joseph B, Holly B. and William A. Educ: Skidmore Col, 3 years. Polit. & Govt. Pos: Town councilman, Lake George, N.Y, 60-64; committeeman, Lake George Rep. Cmt, 60-64, chmn, 62-64; chmn, Warren Co. Rep. Cmt, 64- Bus. & Prof. Pos: Pres. and treas, De Santis Enterprises Inc, Lake George, N.Y, 53-, Northway Restaurant & Catering Co. Inc, Glens Falls, N.Y, 57- and Ontario Restaurants Inc, Oswego, N.Y, 60-; pres, Aviation Rd. Develop. Co. Inc, Glen Falls, N.Y, 67- and Herkimer Restaurants Inc, Herkimer, N.Y, 68-; dir, First Nat. Bank of Glens Falls, 67- Mil. Serv: Entered as Pvt, Army Air Force, 44, released as Sgt, 46, after serv. in Fifth Air Force, Pac. Theater, 46. Mem: Howard Johnson's Nat. Agents Coun.(past chmn); Nat. Restaurant Asn; C. of C; F&AM; Rotary Int.(past pres); Am. Legion; Aircraft Owners and Pilots Asn. Recipient of Howard Johnson Nat. Spotlight Award. Rel: Episcopal. Mailing Add: Hubbell Lane, Lake George, N.Y. 12845.

DESAUTELS, ROBERT JOHN D
Vt. State Rep.
b. Colchester, Vt, 7/16/40; s. Raymond Ernest Desautels and Madeline Mahoney D; m. 9/17/60 to Joyce Elaine Guyette; c. Robert John, Jr, Daniel Christopher, Mary Lyn and Kristin Elaine. Educ: Univ. Vt, B.A, 62; Kappa Sigma; Newman Club. Polit. & Govt. Pos: Mem. zoning bd. adjust, Burlington, Vt, 69-; Vt. State Rep, Dist. 1-7, 69- Bus. & Prof. Pos: From sales to mgr, Swift & Co, New Eng. Area, 62-67; partner, Pizza King, Burlington, 68-; sales rep, Fulton Packing Co, Boston, Mass, 68- Mem: Vt. Restaurant Asn; Elks; Chittenden Co. Fish & Game Club; Jaycees. Rel: Roman Catholic. Mailing Add: 4 Elm Terr, Burlington, Vt. 05401.

DESCHAMBEAULT, FREDERIC D
Treas, York Co. Dem. Cmt, Maine
b. Biddeford, Maine, 5/19/00; s. Frederic Desehambeault and Camille Giguere D; m. M. Antoinette Poisson. Educ: High sch, 2 years. Polit. & Govt. Pos: Mem, Gov. Pub. Safety Co, York Co. and Superior Messenger Court, Maine, 60-; del, Dem. Nat. Conv, 60, 64 & 68; treas, York Co. Dem. Cmt, 63- Bus. & Prof. Pos: Retail grocer, 20-60. Mem: Life mem. Elks; treas, Eagles, 8 years. Rel: Catholic. Mailing Add: 33 Crescent, Biddeford, Maine 04005.

DES CHAMPS, WILLIAM GREEN, JR. D
b. Bishopville, S.C, 8/29/17; s. William Green Des Champs and Etta Hearon D; m. 3/8/44 to Elizabeth N. Davall. Educ: Clemson Col, B.S, 38. Polit. & Govt. Pos: Mem, Bishopville City Coun, S.C, 47-58; Mayor, Bishopville, 58; S.C. State Sen, 63-67. Bus. & Prof. Pos: Shell Oil Jobber; pres, Bishopville Petroleum Co, Inc; co-partner, Des Champs & Webb Ginning and Delinting Plant; owner, Shell Transport Co; dir, The Peoples Bank. Mil. Serv: Army, 47th Field Artil, 41; Hon. Med. Discharge. Mem: Home Fed. Savings Loan Asn; C. of C; bd. of dirs, Clemson Rotary Club; Elks; Am. Legion; pres, S.C. Oil Jobbers Asn, 57-59; Clemson Athletic Coun, 59. Clemson Col. Alumni Distinguished Serv. Award, 62. Rel: Methodist; Off. Bd, Bethlehem Methodist Church, Chmn, 56-58. Mailing Add: Box 302, Bishopville, S.C. 29010. (1967)

DESCHLER, LEWIS
Parliamentarian, U.S. House of Rep.
b. Chillicothe, Ohio, 3/3/05; s. Joseph Anthony Deschler and Lillian Lewis D; m. 1/18/31 to Virginia Cole; c. Lewis, II and Joan Mari (Mrs. William B. Eddy). Educ: Miami Univ, 22-25; George Washington Univ, 25; Nat. Univ, M.P.L, 32 and LL.D, 47; Delta Tau Delta. Polit. & Govt. Pos: Asst. parliamentarian, U.S. House of Rep, 27, parliamentarian, 28- Publ: Ed, House Rules and Manual, 29- Mem: D.C. and Supreme Court Bars; Nat. Portrait Gallery. Asst. secy, Am. Group of Interparliamentary Union Conf, London, 30. Mailing Add: 101 Lucas Lane, Bethesda, Md. 20014.

DESGROSSEILLIERS, EMILE JOSEPH D
b. Manchester, N.H, 8/7/13; married; c. 2 sons. Educ: Cent. High Sch, Manchester, N.H. Polit. & Govt. Pos: N.H. State Rep, -67. Bus. & Prof. Pos: Shoeworker. Mem: Exec. bd, CIO Shoeworkers' Union; Laurier Soc. Club. Rel: Catholic. Mailing Add: 86 Exeter Ave, Manchester, N.H. 03103. (1967)

DeSIMONE, HERBERT FLORIE R
Attorney Gen, R.I.
b. Providence, R.I, 9/5/29; s. Florie DeSimone and Lena Capuano D; m. 11/12/55 to Sally Ann Reynolds; c. Herbert F, Jr, Douglas and Deborah M. Educ: Brown Univ, A.B, 51; Columbia Univ. Sch. Law, LL.B, 54. Polit. & Govt. Pos: Gen. counsel, Dept. Admin, R.I, 59-60, attorney gen, R.I, 67-; del. Rep. Nat. Conv, 68. Bus. & Prof. Pos: Partner, attorney-at-law, DeSimone & DeSimone, 54-67. Mem: R.I. and Am. Bar Asns; Nat. Asn. Attorneys Gen. (exec. cmt, chmn. east. region); Rep. State Cent. Cmt.(exec. cmt); North Providence Rep. Town Cmt; New Eng. Asn. Attorneys Gen.(chmn); Aurora Civil Asn; Brown Club R.I; Columbia Univ. Alumni Asn; K. of C; St. Augustine's Church Holy Name Soc; Elks. Rel: Roman Catholic. Legal Res: 557 Fruit Hill Ave, North Providence, R.I. 02911. Mailing Add: Providence County Courthouse, 250 Benefit St, Providence, R.I. 02903.

DESJARDINS, HELEN D
b. Rollinsford, N.H, 11/23/06; d. Joseph E. Soucey and Lydia LaLiberte S; m. 11/8/26 to Albert J. Desjardins; c. Lydia (Mrs. Richard Mawby), Philip and Leo. Educ: Bus. sch. courses. Polit. & Govt. Pos: Del, N.H. Dem. State Conv; first alternate to N.H. State Sen. J. Ronald Marcotte; alternate del, Dem. Nat. Conv, 68. Mem: Am. Legion. Rel: Catholic. Mailing Add: Rollinsford, N.H. 03869.

DESMARAIS, RAYMOND J. D
b. Winchendon, Mass, 8/4/28; married; c. 3 daughters. Educ: Hesser Bus. Col; Suffolk Univ. Polit. & Govt. Pos: N.H. State Rep, 61-67; Dem. State Committeeman; chmn, Jaffrey Dem. Party; clerk, Jaffrey Dist. Court; treas, Jaffrey Water Works; Civil Defense Dir; Town Clerk; Tax Collector. Mem: L'A. C. A; Holy Name Soc; Jaffrey PTA; pres, Citizen's Scholarship Found. Jaffrey-Rindge; fund chmn, Monadnock Coun. Retarded Children Jaffrey. Rel: Catholic. Mailing Add: 211 Peterborough St, Jaffrey, N.H. 03452.

DESMARAIS, RAYMOND WILFRID R
Chmn, Central Falls Rep. City Cmt, R.I.
b. Central Falls, R.I, 11/12/07; s. Wilfrid Adelard Desmarais and Laura Gerrais D; m. 1/14/29 to Laura Anna Cartier; c. Laura Leona (Mrs. Breault). Educ: Sacred Heart Acad, Central Falls, 4 years; Lincoln Exten. Inst, Correspondent Course, Cleveland, Ohio. Polit. & Govt. Pos: Pres, Central Falls Rep. Club, R.I, 45; founder and pres, Central Fall Good Govt. Club, 46-48; chmn, Central Falls Rep. City Cmt, 67-; mem, Econ. Stabilizing Cmt, State of R.I, 67- Bus. & Prof. Pos: Machinist and toolmaker, Standard Eng. Co, Pawtucket, R.I, 67-; part time ins. agent, Asn. Canado-Am. Manchester, N.H, 67- Mil. Serv: Entered as Pvt, R.I. Militia, 41, released as Pfc, 43, after serv. in Co. M, First Regt. Mem: Int. Asn. Machinists (shop steward, secy. and v.pres); Civic Club Le Foyer Pawtucket (former v.pres); Toastmaster Int.(former treas). Citation, Asn. Canado-Am. for Outstanding Serv. as Secy-Treas, 68. Rel: Roman Catholic. Mailing Add: 78 Tremonth St, Central Falls, R.I. 02863.

DESPOL, JOHN ANTON R
b. San Francisco, Calif, 7/22/13; s. Anton Despol and Bertha Mary Balzer D; m. 12/7/37 to Jeri Kay Steep; c. Christopher Paul and Anthony John. Educ: Los Angeles Jr. Col, 30-31; Univ. South. Calif, 31; Calif. Inst. Tech. Exten, Training within Indust, 40-41; Univ. Calif, Los Angeles Adult Exten, cert, 68. Polit. & Govt. Pos: Pub. mem, Calif. State Defense Coun, 39-41; mem, Los Angeles Co. Dem. Cent. Cmt, 42-44; mem, Tenth Regional War Man Power Cmn, 42-45; panel mem, Tenth Regional War Labor Bd, 42-45; nat. steel panel mem, Nat. War Labor Bd, 44; mem, exec. cmt, Calif. Dem. State Cent. Cmt, 52-56; chmn, 15th Cong. Dist. Dem. Cent. Cmt, 54-56; mem, Calif. Legis. Adv. Cmn. to State Legis, 56-59; del, Dem. Nat. Conv, 48, 52, 56 & 60; mem, Calif. adv. cmt, U.S. Civil Rights Cmn, 58-61; mem, Tech. Adv. Cmt. to Calif. Econ. Develop. Agency, 61-65; mem, Rep. Assocs. of Los Angeles Co, 66-; pub. mem, Calif. Job Training and Placement Coun, 67-68; secy, labor cmt, Calif. Rep. State Cent. Cmt, 67-68; del, Rep. Nat. Conv, 68. Bus. & Prof. Pos: Registered rep, Dempsey-Tegeler & Co, Inc, 68- Publ: California Legislative Analysis and Candidates Questionnaire, 52-54 & 56-58 and Collective Bargaining Strategy, 53, Calif. CIO Coun; California Election Analysis, Calif. Summer Commun. Orgn. and Polit. Educ. Prog, 56. Mem: Am. Asn. of Securities Rep; Nat. Planning Asn; Cmt. for Econ. Develop; retired mem, United Steelworkers of Am.(int. rep, 37-68); secy-treas, polit. action cmt, Calif. CIO, 48-58 and Calif. CIO Coun, 50-58; gen. v.pres, Calif. Labor Fedn, AFL-CIO, 58-60; bd. dir, Town Hall of Calif; bd. dir, Los Angeles World Affairs Coun; Crenshaw Neighbors; YMCA; Los Angeles Cmt. on For. Rels; bd. dirs, Braille Inst. of Am, 62- and Nat. Conf. of Christians and Jews, South. Calif. Region, 61- Cert. for Commun. Leadership. Rel: Protestant. Mailing Add: 5285 Village Green, Los Angeles, Calif. 90016.

DESPOT, GEORGE JOSEPH R
b. Shreveport, La, 1/28/27; s. George Gregory Despot and Katherine Vlahovich; m. 10/31/53 to Pearla Alice Tinsley; c. Susan Alicia and Rebecca Ann. Educ: Univ. Notre Dame, A.B, 47; La. State Univ. Law Sch, LL.B, 50. Polit. & Govt. Pos: Mem, Rep. State Cent. Cmt, La, 63-, asst. to state chmn, 63 & 65-66; mem, Caddo Parish Rep. Exec. Cmt, La, 63-; bd. mem, Rep. State Action Coun, 64-65; Rep. state finance chmn, 67. Bus. & Prof. Pos: Partner, Mecom, Scott and Despot, 54-57; pres, Petroleum Investments, Inc, 59-65. Mil. Serv: Entered as Pvt, Army, 45, released as T-5, 47, after serv. in ETO. Mem: Independent Petroleum Asn. of Am. Rel: Catholic. Mailing Add: 1102 Beck Bldg, Shreveport, La. 71101.

DESSERT, GERALD L. D
Chmn, 14th Cong. Dist. Dem. Party, Mich.
b. Detroit, Mich, 9/28/28; s. J. Leo Dessert and Kathleen Youngblood D; m. 6/20/59 to Regina Harris; Michael L, Patrick E, Kathleen L. and Gerald L, Jr. Educ: Univ. Detroit, B.S, 52; Delta Sigma Pi. Polit. & Govt. Pos: Citizen mem, Detroit Pension Bd, Mich, 64-65; secy, Detroit Water Dept, 65-69; v.chmn, 14th Cong. Dist. Dem. Party, 67-69, chmn, 69-; del, Dem. Nat. Conv, 68; secy, Detroit Fire Dept, 69- Mil. Serv: Entered as Pvt, Army, 46, released as Sgt, 48, after serv. in 516th Signal Serv. Bn, Asian Theatre, 46-48; Victory Medal. Mem: V.pres, DeLaSalle Alumni, 66-69; pres, Church sch. bd, 69- Rel: Roman Catholic. Mailing Add: 11273 Nashville, Detroit, Mich. 48205.

DeSTEFANO, C. GEORGE R
Rep. Nat. Committeeman, R.I.
b. Providence, R.I, 8/2/12; s. Luke D. DeStefano and Amalie Repole D; m. to Janet L. Harrower; c. Richard P, William G. and George O. Polit. & Govt. Pos: Pres, Town Coun, Barrington, R.I, 46-49; R.I. State Rep, 48-54, Dep. Minority Leader, R.I. House of Rep, 51-52; chmn, Barrington Rep. Town Cmt, 51-56; R.I. State Sen, 55-68, Dep. Minority Leader, R.I. State Senate, 58-60, Minority Leader, 60-68, mem, Adv. Cmt. on Legis. Seminars, Eagleton Inst, Rutgers Univ, 65-68, former chmn, R.I. Cmn. on Interstate Coop, mem, Adv. Cmn. on Intergovt. Rels, 65-68, former secy, Joint Legis. Affairs Cmt, former mem, R.I. Legis. Coun; Rep. nat. committeeman, R.I, 68- Bus. & Prof. Pos: Past 1st v.pres, Nat. Conf. of State Legis. Leaders; past 1st v.pres. & chmn. of the bd, Nat. Coun. of State Govts. Mem: Lions; Salvation Army; Am. Red Cross; Bald Mt. Ski Corp, Rangley, Maine; Fraternal Order of Police; Barrington Rod & Reel Club. Rel: Catholic. Mailing Add: 87 Weybosset St, Providence, R.I. 02903. (1967)

DeSTIGTER, MELVIN R
Mich. State Rep.
b. Sioux Center, Iowa, 11/21/28; m. 1950 to Carole Jean Schultze; c. Melanie, Kurt, Kim, Todd and Heidi. Educ: Calvin Col, A.B; Univ. of Mich. Polit. & Govt. Pos: Mich. State Rep, 64- Bus. & Prof. Pos: Sales mgr; teacher. Mil. Serv: Army, Japan, 18 months. Mem: Hudsonville City Cmn, 59-64. Rel: Christian Reformed. Mailing Add: 3487 Hillcrest, Hudsonville, Mich. 49426.

DETERING, GERALD W. R
Ore. State Rep.
m. 1930 to Marie; c. 2 sons, 2 daughters. Educ: Bus. Col; Am. Bus. Mgt. Asn. Polit. & Govt. Pos: Ore. State Rep, 62-; mem, Ore. Coun. Crime and Delinquency. Bus. & Prof. Pos: Pres, Agr. Res. Adv. Coun, Ore. State Univ. Mem: Metro Civic Club; Kiwanis; C. of C.(chmn, Linn Co. Cmt. on State and Nat. Affairs); Grange; Farm Bur. Rel: Christian Church. Mailing Add: Route 1, Box 182, Harrisburg, Ore. 97446. (1967)

DETHMERS, JOHN R. R
Chief Justice, Supreme Court of Mich.
b. Plessis, Iowa, 10/15/03; s. Roy Peter Dethmers and Agnes DeRoos D; m. 4/4/31 to Aleen Elizabeth DeJong; c. John Robert, David Conrad and Marjorie Aleen. Educ: Hope Col; Univ. Mich. Law Sch. LL.B, 27; Pi Kappa Delta; Delta Theta Phi. Polit. & Govt. Pos: Treas, Ottawa Co. Rep. Cmt, Mich, 31-40; Prosecuting Attorney, Ottawa Co, 31-38; v.pres, Mich. Fedn. of Young Rep, 34-38; mem, Mich. Rep. State Cent. Cmt, 36-42, chmn, 42-45; del, Rep. Nat. Conv, 44; Chief Asst. Attorney Gen, Mich, 43-44, Attorney Gen, 45-46; Assoc. Justice, Supreme Court of Mich, 45-56 & 61-66, Chief Justice, 56-61 & 66- Bus. & Prof. Pos: Chmn, State Bar Cmt. on Criminal Jurisp, 37; chmn, Nat. Conf. of Chief Justices, 56-58. Publ: 'Insanity as a Defense,' Young Lawyer, 11/55; 'The Role of the Courts in Tomorrow's America,' U.S. News and World Report, 12/56; 'The First Ten Years of the Conference of Chief Justices,' Am. Bar Asn. J, 1/59. Mem: Am, Mich, Ottawa and Ingham Co. Bar Asns; Am. Judicature Soc.(pres, 56-58); pres, Mich. Prosecuting Attorneys Asn, 37-38; pres, Zeeland Exchange Club, 29; Scribes; pres, Lansing City Club; K. of P; Rotary; Mason. Rel: Presbyterian. Mailing Add: Supreme Court, State Capitol, Lansing, Mich. 48901.

DeTHOMASIS, LOUIS D
Nat. Dir. Finance, Young Dem. Clubs. of Am.
b. Brooklyn, N.Y, 10/6/40; s. Gus DeThomasis and Anna Maggio D; single. Educ: Georgetown Univ, B.S. in For. Serv, 63. Polit. & Govt. Pos: Nat. dir. finance, Young Dem. Clubs. of Am, 66- Bus. & Prof. Pos: Pres, Metro-Graphics, Inc, 63- Mem: Dir, Uptown Jr. C. of C; President's Club. Rel: Roman Catholic. Mailing Add: 536 Central Ave, Bethpage, N.Y. 11714. (1967)

DETJE, ALBERT H. D
b. Hamburg, Germany, 3/14/02; s. Christian Detje and Anna D; m. 6/11/36 to Minna Reese; c. Christian. Educ: Germany, High Sch, Trade Sch; 4 years Night Sch, Chicago. Polit. & Govt. Pos: Trustee, Traer Munic. Utilities, Iowa; mem, Iowa State Aeronaut. Cmt, 55-63; Iowa State Rep, until 66. Bus. & Prof. Pos: In plumbing, sheet metal, heating and ventilation; owner-operator, Serv. Sta; distributor, petroleum, tires, batteries and accessories. Mem: Dir, Traer C. of C; Ground Observer Corps. of Supvr; Int. Flying Farmers; Q.B. Pilot Orgn. Rel: United Church of Christ; Deacon, Trustee. Mailing Add: Traer, Iowa 50675.

DE TOLVE, ANTHONY JOSEPH D
b. Chicago, Ill, 5/26/22; s. Joseph De Tolve and Rose Romano D; m. 11/27/52 to Catherine G. Schieble; div; c. Mark Antony and Maria Elena. Educ: DePaul Univ. Col. Law, LL.B, 46; Delta Theta Phi. Polit. & Govt. Pos: Ill. State Rep, 50-56; Ill. State Sen, 58-65. Mil. Serv: Entered and released as Pvt, 43, after serv. in Field Artil; received dipl. as Cannoneer in Field Artil. for 105 and 155 Howitzers; Marksman Medal. Mem: Chicago Bar Asn; Chicago Law Inst; Delta Theta Phi; AF&AM; Musician's Union in Chicago; Moose; Unico Club of Am; past comdr, Fed. Post, Am. Legion; 40 et 8; Chicago Dearborn Club; Regular Dem. Orgn. of Chicago. Received Award as 'George Jessel' of Ill. Senate in 1965 Session. Rel: Catholic. Legal Res: 1037 Vernon Park, Chicago, Ill. 60607. Mailing Add: Suite 1240, 30 W. Washington St, Chicago, Ill. 60602.

DETWEILER, GERTRUDE HOMAN R
b. Reading, Pa; d. William K. Homan and Ida Susan Printz H; m. to W.H. Detweiler; wid; c. Betty D.(Mrs. Kirk McGregor). Educ: Presby. Hosp, Univ. Pa. Med. Center, 18. Polit. & Govt. Pos: Pres, Jerome Co. Rep. Women's Asn, Idaho, 46; v.pres, Idaho State Rep. Women's Asn, 50, pres, 52-54; del, Rep. Nat. Conv, 56 & 68; Rep. nat. committeewoman, Idaho, 56-60; secy, Nat. Fedn. Rep. Women, 56-60; v.chmn, Idaho Rep. State Cent. Cmt, 58; state committeewoman, Jerome Co. Rep. Party, 60-66. Bus. & Prof. Pos: Head nurse out patients, Twin Falls Hosp, 19. Mem: Idaho State Nursing Asn. (pres, First Dist, 23); Am. Legion Auxiliary (pres, Dept. Idaho, 25-26 and nat. committeewoman, 27, nat. v.pres, 39-40). Rel: Presbyterian; Elder. Mailing Add: Route 1, Box 40 B, Hazelton, Idaho 83335.

DEUKMEJIAN, GEORGE R
Majority Leader, Calif. State Senate
b. Albany, N.Y, 6/6/28; s. C. George Deukmejian and Alice Gairdan D; m. 2/16/57 to Gloria M. Saatjian; c. Leslie Ann, George Krikor and Andrea Diane. Educ: Siena Col, B.A; St. John's Univ. Law Sch, J.D. Polit. & Govt. Pos: Calif. State Assemblyman, 62-66; Calif. State Sen, 67-, majority leader, Calif. State Senate, currently; del, Rep. Nat. Conv, 68. Bus. & Prof. Pos: Attorney-at-law, 52- Mil. Serv: Entered as Pvt, Army, 53, released as Cpl, 55, after serv. in U.S. Army Claims Team, Europe, 55. Mem: Lions; Elks; Navy League; C. of C; Armed Serv. YMCA; Boy Scouts. Rel: Episcopal. Legal Res: 5366 E. Broadway, Long Beach, Calif. 90803. Mailing Add: 555 E. Ocean Blvd, Long Beach, Calif. 90802.

DEUSTER, DONALD EUGENE R
Cong. Rels. Officer, Dept. of Transportation
b. Milwaukee, Wis, 9/26/29; s. Sarto Lewis Deuster and Dorothy M. Sanders D; m. 6/20/53 to Katharine Brigitti Brink; c. Mary Katharine, Ruth Elizabeth, Jane Marguerite and Anne Britta. Educ: Ripon Col, B.A, 52; Univ. Calif, Los Angeles, LL.B, 57; Phi Kappa Pi. Polit. & Govt. Pos: Admin. asst. to U.S. Rep. Robert McClory, Ill, 36-69; pres, Libertyville Young Rep, 59-60; Rep. precinct committeeman, Fourth Precinct, Libertyville Twp, 60-62; educ. chmn, Lake Co. Rep. Cent. Cmt, 61-62; Cong. Rels. Officer, Dept. of Transportation, 69- Bus. & Prof. Pos: Asst. counsel. legal dept, Kemper Ins. Group, Chicago, Ill, 57-62, asst. to chmn. bd, 62-63. Mil. Serv: Entered as 2nd Lt, Army, 52, released as 1st Lt, 54, after serv. in 5th Inf. Training Div, Indiantown Gap Mil. Reservation, Pa and 45th and 24th Inf. Div, Korea. Publ: 'Our National Purpose,' Libertyville Independent-Register, 62; 'Get Into Politics,' Kemper Ins. Mag, 60. Mem: Calif. Bar Asn; Ill. State Bar. Rel: Presbyterian. Legal Res: 62 Sylvan Dr, Sylvan Lake, Mundelein, Ill. 60060. Mailing Add: 610 H St. S.W, Washington, D.C. 20024.

DEUTSCH, BERNARD D
b. Brooklyn, N.Y, 8/25/34; s. Jack Deutsch and Pauline Hagler D; m. 12/25/56 to Sheila Litman; c. Judith Lee, Ira S. and Marc Mitchell. Educ: N.Y. Univ, B.S, acct, 56. Polit. & Govt. Pos: Del-at-lg, Dem. Nat. Conv, 68.

Bus. & Prof. Pos: Investment Banker, Jaffee & Co, N.Y, 67-; adj. prof, L.I. Univ, 68. Mem: N.Y. Univ. Tax Soc; Acct. Asn. N.Y; Mason; B'nai B'rith. Man of Year, Anti Defamation League, B'nai B'rith, United Jewish Appeal and Am. Red Mogen David for Israel. Rel: Hebrew. Mailing Add: 163 Whitman Dr, Brooklyn, N.Y. 11234.

DEUTSCH, PETER R
Dep. State Tax Cmnr, Brooklyn, N.Y.
b. Brooklyn, N.Y, 7/6/06; s. Joshua Deutsch and Rose Lapidus D; m. 12/20/30 to Mae Edelstein; c. Judith and Charles. Educ: St. John's Univ. Sch. of Law, LL.B, 28. Polit. & Govt. Pos: Rep. State Committeeman, 39th Dist, N.Y, 44-69; dep. state tax cmnr, Brooklyn, N.Y, 67- Mem: Am, N.Y. State and Brooklyn Bar Asns; N.Y. Trial Lawyers Asn; K. of P; Gr. N.Y. Civic Asn. Rel: Jewish. Legal Res: 3063 Fulton St, Brooklyn, N.Y. 11208. Mailing Add: 32 Court St, Brooklyn, N.Y. 11201.

DeVANE, MARVIN EUGENE D
b. Ellaville, Ga, 10/27/13; s. Arthur Lee DeVane and Eva Robinson D; m. 8/28/38 to Virginia Laura Durham; c. Carlynn Eugenia, Marvilynn Russell, Vangie Laura, Marvin Eugene,Jr. Educ: Ellaville High Sch, 32. Polit. & Govt. Pos: Ga. State Rep, 63-64. Bus. & Prof. Pos: Wholesale distributor, gas & oil. Mem: Lions. Rel: Methodist. Mailing Add: Ellaville, Ga. 31806. (1967)

DEVANY, CHARLES G. D
b. E. Providence, R.I, 6/7/15. Educ: Providence Col, exten. courses. Polit. & Govt. Pos: R.I. State Sen, 64-66; R.I. State Rep, 63-65; Chmn. of President Johnson's Oper. Support Comm. Bus. & Prof. Pos: Pub. Tel. Mgr. Mem: Citizens League of Johnston; Graniteville Vol. Fire Comp; St. Lawrence Holy Name Soc; Providence C. of C; Chmn, Johnston Small Bus. Div. United Fund; Graniteville PTA; Graniteville Boy Scouts Troop Comm. 1967 Legal Res: 34 Pine Hill Ave, Johnston, R.I. No mailing address available. (1967)

DeVARGAS, HORACE D
N.Mex. State Sen.
b. Ojo Caliente, N. Mex, 7/14/08; s. Moses DeVargas and Margarita Chavez D; m. 12/6/56 to Nathalia Mayowsky; c. Raymond, Debra and Ymelda. Educ: 3 years col. Polit. & Govt. Pos: Co. clerk, Rio Arriba Co, N.Mex, 31-32, sch. supt, 39-42; N.Mex. State Sen, Eighth Sen. Dist, 47-59 & 67-; mem, N.Mex. State Reorgn. Cmn, 49-51; mem, N.Mex. State Bd. Finance, 61-62. Bus. & Prof. Pos: In ins. and invests, 44-; dir, 1st Nat. Bank of Rio Arriba, N.Mex, 53-; v.pres, Southwest Savings & Loan Asn, Santa Fe, 65- Mem: Charter mem, Nat. Legis. Leaders Conf; N.Mex. Asn. of Ins. Agents; immediate past pres, Espanola Lions, 46; Elks. Rel: Catholic. Legal Res: Fairview Lane, Espanola, N.Mex. 87532. Mailing Add: P.O. Box 520, Espanola, N.Mex. 87532.

DEVER, EDWARD JAMES D
Mass. State Rep.
b. Cambridge, Mass, 6/21/36; s. Edward James Dever (deceased) and Dorothy Biggane D; m. 11/21/64 to Patricia Mary Walsh; c. Michelle, Karen and Edward. Educ: Williams Col, B.A, 58; Boston Col. Law Sch, D.J, 61; Phi Gamma Delta; Indust. and Commercial Law Rev; Annual Surv. of Mass. Law. Polit. & Govt. Pos: Mem, Arlington Town Meeting, Mass, 60-61; Mass. State Rep, Sixth Middlesex Dist, 65- Bus. & Prof. Pos: Attorney-at-law, Mass, 61- Mil. Serv: Entered as Airman Basic, Air Nat. Guard, 61, released as Airman 3/C, 65, after serv. in 102nd Tactical Fighter Wing, Berlin Crisis, 61-62. Mem: Cambridge Bar Asn; Elks; K. of C. Award of Appreciation for Commun. Leadership, Arlington Chap, Greater Boston Asn. for Retarded Children; Sr. Citizens Award for Distinguished Serv; Awards for Distinguished Serv. from VFW, Arlington Post 1775 and Am. Legion. Rel: Catholic. Mailing Add: 10 Moccasin Path, Arlington, Mass. 02174.

DEVEREUX, DOROTHY LOUISE R
Hawaii State Rep.
b. Spokane, Wash, 11/8/11; d. John Peter Nelson and Olive Valentine Davis N; m. 9/1/34 to John William Devereux, M.D; c. John William, Jr, Marvin Kingsley, Dorothy Diane (Mrs. Philip Lee Bayles) and Frederick Allen. Educ: Calif. Lutheran Sch. of Nursing, R.N; Univ. Chicago Lying-In Hosp, Post grad. Obstet. Gynec. Nursing. Polit. & Govt. Pos: Hawaii Territorial Rep, 58-59; Hawaii State Rep, 59-; chmn, Adv. Cmt. to Hawaii Div. of Voc. Rehabilitation, 60-64; mem, Nat. Adv. Coun, Voc. Rehabilitation, Dept. of Health, Educ. and Welfare, 62-63; mem, President's Cmt. on Employ. of Handicapped and mem-at-lg, Woman's Cmt, 62-; mem, Precinct Club; del. and mem. platform cmt, Rep. State Conv; mem, Citizen's Adv. Cmt. for Oahu Transportation Study, 64-; mem, Policy Cmt, Hawaii State Voc. Rehabilitation Study, 66- Mem: Calif. Hosp. Nurses' Alumnae Asn; Oahu Dist. Nurses' Asn; Am. and Hawaii Pub. Health Asns. Rel: Congregational. Mailing Add: 2721 Huapala St, Honolulu, Hawaii 96822. (1967)

DEVEREUX, REGINALD S. D
b. Ludlow, Vt, 10/5/09; m. to Rena Tucker; c. 2 sons, 1 daughter. Educ: Black River High Sch; Worchester Trade Sch. Polit. & Govt. Pos: Selectman, Ludlow, Vt, 36-48; town auditor, 48; village auditor, 58-; Vt. State Rep, 63-67. Bus. & Prof. Pos: Painter; paper hanger; hardware merchant. Mil. Serv: Nat. Guard, M/Sgt, 23-28. Mem: Grange. Rel: Baptist. Mailing Add: 196½ Main St, Ludlow, Vt. 05149. (1967)

DEVINE, SAMUEL L. R
U.S. Rep, Ohio
b. South Bend, Ind, 12/21/15; s. John F. Devine, Jr.(deceased) and Kittie M. Leeper D; m. 8/24/40 to Betty M. Galloway; c. Lois, Joyce and Carol. Educ: Colgate Univ, 33-34; Ohio State Univ, 34-37; Univ. Notre Dame, LL.B, cum laude, 40; Sigma Nu; Delta Theta Phi; Varsity O Asn. Polit. & Govt. Pos: Spec. agent, Fed. Bur. of Invest, 40-45; Ohio State Rep, 51-55; prosecuting attorney, Franklin Co, Ohio, 55-58; U.S. Rep, Ohio, 59- Bus. & Prof. Pos: Attorney-at-law, Metcalf, King, Ramey & Devine, 45-48, Hamilton & Kramer Law Off, 48-55. Publ: Various articles, Notre Dame Lawyer, 38-40. Mem: Mason, Scottish Rite and Shrine; Charity Newsies; Ohio Asn. of Football Off; Columbus Country Club. Rel: Methodist. Mailing Add: 195 N. Roosevelt Ave, Columbus, Ohio 43209.

DEVINE, TERENCE D. R
Mem, N.Dak. Rep. Exec. Cmt.
b. Grand Forks, N.Dak, 8/5/37; m. 9/10/60 to Mary Catherine Bowdy; c. Theodore Patrick and Stacey Catherine. Educ: Univ. N.Dak, B.S.B.A, 62, LL.B, 65. Polit. & Govt. Pos: Chmn, 17th Legis. Dist. Rep. Party, N.Dak, 65-; mem, N.Dak. Rep. Exec. Cmt, 67-; state attorney, Nelson Co, 67- Mil. Serv: Entered as Pvt, Army, 56, released as SP-4, 68. Mem: N.Dak. State Bar Asn; Lions; K. of C. Rel: Catholic. Mailing Add: Lakota, N.Dak. 58344.

DEVITT, EUGENE THOMAS R
b. St. Paul, Minn, 11/10/09; s. Thomas P. Devitt and Ethel Maguire D; m. 10/26/40 to Erlys L. Wheeler; c. Thomas P, Patrick D. and Jill. Educ: Univ. N.Dak, LL.B, 36; Order of the Coif; Blue Key. Polit. & Govt. Pos: Trial attorney, Off. of Price Admin, Chicago, Ill, 43-48; committeeman, Hanover Twp. Rep. Cmt, Cook Co, Ill, 62- Bus. & Prof. Pos: Attorney-at-law, Chicago, Ill, 48- Mem: Chicago, Ill. State and Fed. Bar Asns; Catholic Lawyers Guild; Bar Asn. of Seventh Fed. Circuit; Elks; K. of C.(4°). Rel: Catholic. Legal Res: 80 Sherwood Rd, Elgin, Ill. 60120. Mailing Add: 11 S. LaSalle St, Chicago, Ill. 60120.

DEVITT, JAMES C. R
Wis. State Sen.
b. La Crosse, Wis, 10/12/29; m. 10/16/50 to Rita Kosmicki; c. Patricia Ann, Brian James. Educ: Marquette Univ, 47-50. Polit. & Govt. Pos: Pres, Nat. Defense Transportation Asn, 66, state v.pres, 66-69; Wis. State Assemblyman, 66-68; Wis. Rep, Four-State Legis. Cmt. Pollution Lake Mich, 67-69; Wis. State Sen, 69-, Majority Caucus Secy, Wis. State Senate, 69- Bus. & Prof. Pos: Pres, Devitt Cartage Co, Inc, 54-65; chmn. bd. & pres, Devitt Leasing, Inc, 65-68; pres, STC Leasing Corp, 68- Mil. Serv: Army Res. Mem: Am. Legion; Lions; charter inst. rep, Explorer Scout Post 543, 61; pres, Greenfield Jr. C. of C, 62, pres, 64-67; pres, Non-commissioned Officers Adv. Coun, 62; state v.pres, Wis. Jr. C. of C, 62, int. dir, 63; mem. chmn, Asn. U.S. Army, 63; bldg. fund capt, St. Charles Boys Home, 63; dir, United Asn. Retarded Children, 65-68; chmn, March of Dimes, 65; mem, Whitnall Sch. Bd. Planning Cmt, 65-66; pres, Metrop. Jaycees Pres. Coun, 65-66; mem. legis. cmt, Catholic Family Life Movement, 67-69. Non-Commissioned Officers Adv. Coun. Award, 64; One of Five Outstanding Young Men in Wis, 64; Explorer Scout Serv. Award, 64; Distinguished Serv. Award, Greenfield, 65; Outstanding Young Men in Am, 65; Life Mem. Non-Commissioned Officers Coun, U.S. Army Res, 65; Life Mem, Greenfield Jaycees, 68. Mailing Add: 5151 S. Root River Pkwy, Greenfield, Wis. 53228.

DEVLIN, JOHN H. D
b. Pittsburgh, Pa, 8/6/17; m. to Antoinette Giordano. Educ: Duquesne Univ, A.B; Univ. Pittsburgh Law Sch, LL.B; Phi Alpha Delta. Polit. & Govt. Pos: Spec. agent, Fed. Bur. of Invest, 40-57; real estate dep, Sheriff's Off, Allegheny Co, Pa, 47-51; Pa. State Rep, 56-60, mem, Gen. State Authority, State Hwy. and Bridge Authority, State Pub. Sch. Bldg. Authority and Joint Govt. Cmt, Pa. House of Rep; asst. dist. attorney, Allegheny Co, Pa, 56-64; Pa. State Sen, 60-68, Minority Leader, Pa. State Senate, 65-66. Bus. & Prof. Pos: Lawyer, 41- Mem: Variety Club Tent 1; Moose; Elks; St. Thomas More Soc; Eagles; Dapper Dan Club; Allegheny Co. and Pa. Bar Asns; W.Pa. Heart Asn; Lions; I.S.D.A; Knights of Equity; Former Spec. Agents of Fed. Bur. of Invest, Inc. Mailing Add: Bigelow Apt. Hotel, Pittsburgh, Pa. 15219. (1967)

DEVLIN, PHILIP, JR. R
Mem, Fla. Rep. State Exec. Cmt.
b. New Orleans, La, 5/1/16; s. Philip A. Devlin and Frances Moore D; separated; c. Philip F, Cecily Anne, Paul F, Sheila M, Maureen M. and Ellen L. Educ: L.H. Edwards High Sch, Asheville, N.C, grad, 34. Polit. & Govt. Pos: Chmn, Putnam Co. Rep. Exec. Cmt, Fla, 66-; mem, Fla. Rep. State Exec. Cmt, 66- Bus. & Prof. Pos: Formerly engaged in mortgage banking field, Jacksonville, Miami and Pensacola, Fla; asst. mgr, Palatka Abstract & Title Guaranty, Inc, 60- Mil. Serv: Entered as Pvt, Army, 42, released as Chief Warrant Officer, 46, after serv. in Finance Dept, Army Air Forces, Continental U.S; Army Commendation Medal; Am. Theatre Medal. Mem: Am. and Fla. Land Title Asns; Mortgage Banking Asn. of Am; charter mem. and former pres, Palatka Little Theatre; various cmts, Putnam Co. C. of C. Rel: Catholic. Legal Res: 512 S. 15th St, Palatka, Fla. 32077. Mailing Add: P.O. Box 83, Palatka, Fla. 32077.

DEVOE, GOERGE W. R
b. Jersey City, N.J, 1/27/99; s. George W. Devoe and Emma Taft D; m. 4/29/22 to Shirley Spaulding; c. George S. Educ: Pratt Inst, Grad. Polit. & Govt. Pos: Mem, Bridgewater Rep. Town Cmt, at present, chmn, 49-66; v.chmn, Local Bd. 19, Selective Serv, 59-66, chmn, 51-59, chmn, Local Bd. 32, 43-47; chmn, Roxbury Rep. Town Cmt, 33-49. Bus. & Prof. Pos: Pres, Devoe Realty Co, 29- and Litch Co. 4H Found, 53-66. Mil. Award: Selective Serv. Medal. Mem: Grange; Am. Right of Way; Realtors Bd; New Milford Real Estate Bd; Lions; C. of C. Rel: Protestant. Legal Res: Bridgewater, Conn. 06752. Mailing Add: 7 Kent Rd, New Milford, Conn. 06776. (1967)

DeVOURSNEY, MARTIN THOMAS D
Treas, Bergen Co. Dem. Coalition, N.J.
b. Jersey City, N.J, 11/2/20; s. Frederick DeVoursney and Anne Fleming D; m. 7/19/39 to Elizabeth Irene Cargill; c. Elizabeth (Mrs. Caubet), Susan (Mrs. Ganley), Martin, Jr, William and Robin. Educ: Regis High Sch, N.Y, 33-35. Polit. & Govt. Pos: Del, Nat. Dem. Conv, 68; treas, Bergen Co. Dem. Coalition, N.J, 69- Bus. & Prof. Pos: Maintenance mech, Westinghouse Elec. Elevator Co, Jersey City, N.J, 42- Mil. Serv: Entered as Pvt, Army, 44, released as S/Sgt, 46, after serv. in I Co. 21st Inf. Regt, 24th Inf. Div, Southeast Asia; Bronze Star Medal; Two Battle Stars. Mem: IUE, AFL-CIO (pres, Local 486 and chmn. of constitutional cmt, dist. 3); Westinghouse Conf. Bd. (nat. neg. cmt); del, N.J. State AFL-CIO and N.J. State IUE, AFL-CIO Conv; Hudson and Bergen Co. Cent. Labor Coun. Mailing Add: 63 Washington Place, Teaneck, N.J. 07666.

DEVOY, ROBERT D
Mo. State Rep.
b. Brookfield, Mo, 9/3/26; m. 8/11/56 to Clare Reuther; c. Carol, Dennis, Thomas, Ann, Jane and John. Educ: Univ. of Mo; Columbia Univ, A.B, 50, LL.B, 55. Polit. & Govt. Pos: Mo. State Rep, 56- Bus. & Prof. Pos: Lawyer;

prosecuting attorney, Linn Co, 61-64. Mil. Serv: Korean Conflict, 50-52. Rel: Immaculate Conception Church, Brookfield, Mo. Mailing Add: 731 N. Main St, Brookfield, Mo. 64628. (1967)

DEWEES, ELAINE MacDONALD R
Mem, Calif. Rep. State Cent. Cmt.
b. Phila, Pa, 8/5/22; d. William Park MacDonald and Beatrice Boswell M; m. 6/5/48 to Roland Robinson Dewees; c. David William and Scott MacDonald. Educ: Drexel Inst. of Tech, Phila, Pa, 40-42. Polit. & Govt. Pos: Div. chmn, Los Angeles Co. Rep. Precinct Orgn, 58-62; mem, Calif. Rep. State Cent. Cmt, 64-; pres, E.Pasadena-Sierra Madre Fedn. Rep. Women, 65, 66; 20th CD chmn, Los Angeles Co. Bd. Fedn. Rep. Women, 67-68; mem. bd. dirs, Pasadena Rep. Club, Inc, 68-; dep. registrar, Los Angeles Co. Registrar of Voters, 68-; dist. secy, Assemblyman Frank Lanterman, 47th Assembly Dist, 68- Bus. & Prof. Pos: Real estate clerk, Girard Trust Co, Phila, Pa, 42; clerk, Philgas Div, Phillips Petrol. Co, 43-47; clerk, Solgas Div, Sun Oil Co, 47-48. Mem: Nat. Soc. DAR. Rel: Episcopal. Mailing Add: 3657 Ivydale Court, Pasadena, Calif. 91107.

De WETTER, HERMAN PETER D
Mayor, El Paso, Tex.
b. New Rochelle, N.Y, 1/28/20; s. Herman de Wetter and Louise Hurlbutt D; m. 8/7/43 to Margaret Belding; c. Charles Safford, David Brooks and Robert Emerson. Educ: Phillips Exeter Acad, N.H, 39. Polit. & Govt. Pos: Chmn, Civil Serv.Cmn, El Paso, Tex, 64-69, mayor, 69- Bus. & Prof. Pos: Pres, OK Van & Storage Co, Inc, El Paso, Tex, 52-, Las Cruces, N.Mex, 63-, El Paso Terminal Warehouses, Inc, Tex, 64-, El Paso Cartage Co, 64- and Am. Ens. Van Serv, Wilmington, Calif, 64-; mem, adv. bd, Bekins Co, Inc, Los Angeles, 65- Mil. Serv: Entered as Pvt, Army, 42, released as Maj, 45, after serv. in Hq, 51st Ord. Group and G2 Sect. Hq, 1st Army, ETO; Maj, Army Res, 51; ETO Medal; 5 Battle Stars; Bronze Star Medal. Publ: 'The Furniture Warehouseman' and other articles in nat. transportation and warehousing publ. over past eight years. Mem: Southwest Warehouse and Transfer Asn.(pres, 68); Nat. Furniture Warehouseman's Asn; Tex. Transportation Asn; Federacion Internationale Demanaguers Internationaux; Girl Scout Coun.(pres, Rio Grande Chap, 64); Goodwill Industs. of Am.(pres, El Paso Chap, 65); Employers Asn. of El Paso (pres, 65-67); bd, Tex. State Bd. of Mental Health and Retardation, 66-67; El Paso C. of C.(pres, 68); Mental Health Asn. of El Paso; El Paso Indust. Develop. Asn; Asn. of the U.S. Army. Rel: Episcopal; Vestryman, St. Clements Episcopal Church, 67-69. Mailing Add: 908 Blanchard, El Paso, Tex. 79902.

DEWEY, THOMAS EDMUND R
b. Owosso, Mich, 3/24/02; s. George Martin Dewey and Anne Thomas D; m. 6/16/28 to Frances Eileen Hutt; c. Thomas Edmund and John Martin. Educ: Univ. Mich, A.B, 23; Columbia Univ. Law Sch, LL.B, 25; Phi Mu Alpha; Phi Delta Phi. Hon. degrees from many univs. and cols. Polit. & Govt. Pos: Rep. Dist. Capt, N.Y, 26-28; chmn. bd, N.Y. Young Rep. Club, 30-31; chief asst, U.S. Attorney, South. Dist, N.Y, 31-33; U.S. Attorney, 33; spec. asst. to U.S. Attorney Gen, 34-35; spec. prosecutor, Invest. of Organized Crime, N.Y, 35-37; dist. attorney, N.Y. Co, 37-41; Gov, N.Y, 43-54; Rep. nominee for Pres, 44 & 48; del, Rep. Nat. Conv, 52 & 56; mem, Rep. Coord. Cmt, 65-68. Bus. & Prof. Pos: Assoc, Larkin, Rathbone and Perry, Attorneys, 25-27 and McNamara and Seymour, Attorneys, 27-31; attorney-at-law, 34-35 & 42; partner, Dewey, Ballantine, Bushby, Palmer & Wood, Attorneys, 55- Publ: The Case Against the New Deal, Harper & Bros, 40; Journey to the Far Pacific, 52 and Thomas E. Dewey on the Two-Party System, 66, Doubleday. Mem: Am. and N.Y. State Bar Asns; Asn. of Bar, City of New York; N.Y. Co. Lawyers Asn; Coun. For. Rels; Pilgrims; Links, Blindbrook, Recess, Downtown Asn, City Mid Day, Quaker Hill Country, Augusta Nat. and Indian Creek Clubs; Farm Bur; Grange. Awarded Medal for Excellence in recognition of pub. serv, Columbia Univ, 36; Cardinal Newman Dist. Serv. Award, Univ. Ill, 39; plus various other awards. Rel: Episcopal. Legal Res: 141 E. 72nd St, New York, N.Y. 10021. Mailing Add: 140 Broadway, New York, N.Y. 10005.

DeWIND, ADRIAN W(ILLIAM) D
b. Chicago, Ill, 12/1/13; s. Norman DeWind and Ethel Andrews D; m. 6/21/41 to Joan Mosenthal; c. Barbara A. (Mrs. Edward F. Mooney), Adrian W, Jr, Susan V. and John S. Educ: Grinnell Col, B.A, 34; Harvard Law Sch, LL.B, 37. Polit. & Govt. Pos: Mem. staff, U.S. Treasury Dept, 43-45, asst. tax legis. counsel, 45-47, tax legis. counsel, 47-48; chief counsel, subcmt. on admin. of internal revenue laws, Cmt. on Ways and Means, U.S. House of Rep, 51-52; mem, President's Task Force on Tax Policy, 61; chmn, adv. group on city taxation to N.Y.C. Coun. Pres, 66; mem, Cmnr. Internal Revenue's Adv. Group, 66-67; mem, Mayor Lindsay's Adv. Group on N.Y. Constitutional Conv, 67; del, Dem. Nat. Conv, 68. Bus. & Prof. Pos: Lawyer, Sage, Gray, Todd & Sims, N.Y.C, 37-43; partner, Paul, Weiss, Goldberg, Rifkind, Wharton & Garrison, 48- Publ: Articles and reviews in leading tax magazines and law reviews. Mem: Am. Law Inst; Am. Bar Asn.(sect. on taxation); Am. Bar Found. (adv. bd, fed. tax procedure proj); N.Y. Co. Lawyers Asn; Asn. of the Bar of the City of New York; N.Y. State Bar Asn.(chmn, cmt. on tax policy; mem. exec. cmt, tax sect); Fed. Bar Asn. N.Y, N.J. and Conn; Metrop. Club. Legal Res: 37 W. 12th St, New York, N.Y. 10011. Mailing Add: 345 Park Ave, New York, N.Y. 10022.

DeWITT, CLIFFORD M. D
Polit. & Govt. Pos: Dir, Div. of Driver Improv, Ind. Bur. Motor Vehicles, 61-64; Ind. State Rep. until 67, mem, Cities and Towns Cmt, Corp, Lake Co. and Rules Cmts. Bus. & Prof. Pos: Attorney. Mem: Ind. State Bar Asn; Phi Delta Phi; Tau Kappa Alpha. Rel: Methodist. Mailing Add: 609 Union Title Bldg, 155 E. Market St, Indianapolis, Ind. 46204.

DeWITT, JOHN ALLEN D
Chmn, Harrison Co. Dem. Cent. Cmt, Mo.
b. Gilman City, Mo, 2/20/09; s. John William DeWitt and Jennie S. Robertson D; m. 9/19/28 to Amber Gladys Artrip; c. June Ann (Mrs. Marvin Meadows). Educ: Northeast Mo. State Teachers Col, 28; Phi Sigma Epsilon. Polit. & Govt. Pos: Road cmnr, Twp. 1, Mo, 48-60; Dem. committeeman, Sixth Cong. Dist, currently; chmn, Harrison Co. Dem. Cent. Cmt, 64- Bus. & Prof. Pos: Owner of Ins. Agency, Bethany, Mo, 56-; mgr, Bob Broyles & Assocs, 59-64; assoc, Bethany Realty, 64-65; mgr, United Farm Agency, 65-; owner, H & R Block Franchise, 66- Mem: AF&AM, Gilman City; Odd Fellows, Bethany. Mailing Add: Gilman City, Mo. 64642.

DeWITT, LARON WALDO R
Chmn, State Tax Cmn, Ariz.
b. Woodruff, Ariz, 3/28/16; s. Jessie Dilles DeWitt and Maude Jarvis D; m. 1/2/40 to Nancy Mildred Beals; c. Laron Jarvis, Charles Dilles, Mary Darlene (Mrs. Brunkerhoff); Sterling Waldo, Mitchell Jessie and Daniel Elijah. Educ: Gila Jr. Col, Thatcher, Ariz, A.B.A, 39; Block Gila Club. Polit. & Govt. Pos: Ariz. State Rep, 56-64; mem, State Tax Cmn, Ariz, 64-66, chmn, 67- Bus. & Prof. Pos: Construction foreman, Bechtel Construction Co, 41-42; water develop. supt, Phelps Dodge Copper Co, 42-43; farmer and rancher, 43- Mem: Exchange Club; Maricopa Co. Retarded Children's Asn; Farm Bur. Rel: Latter-day Saint; Bishop, 13 years. Legal Res: 1018 W. Eighth St, Mesa, Ariz. 85201. Mailing Add: House Wing, State Capitol, Phoenix, Ariz. 85007.

DEWITTY, THELMA D
b. Beaumont, Tex, 9/13/12; d. Henry Fisher and Esma Randall F; m. 11/2/39 to Hubert Ransom Dewitty; c. Huberta Randi. Educ: Wiley Col, Tex, A.B; Univ. of Wash, Grad. Sch, 3 years; Alpha Kappa Alpha. Polit. & Govt. Pos: V.pres, City Wide Dem. Club, Seattle, Wash, 57-59; trustee, 33rd Dist. Dem. Club, 60-62, v.pres, 62-64 and treas, 65-66; pres, Seattle Dem. Club, 62-64; mem, King Co. Dem. Cent. Cmt, 66-67; del, Dem. Nat. Conv, 68. Mem: Pres. and bd. mem, NAACP, 47-56; chmn. bldgs. and grounds, YWCA, 63-66; pres, Laymen's League of Puget Sound Conv, 63-66; v.pres, John Hay PTA, 64-65; Seattle Teachers Asn.(rep, 64-66, mem. prfnl. rights and responsibilities bd, 66-); leader, Camp Fire Girls, 66-67; Wash. Teacher's Asn; Nat. Educ. Asn; Am. Childhood Educ. Int; Am. Conf. on Educ; Urban League; Jack & Jill, Inc. Named City Wide Dem. Woman of Year, Seattle, 60. Mailing Add: 1101 30th Ave. S, Seattle, Wash. 98144. (1967)

DEXTER, LOUIS MILES R
b. Grand Rapids, Mich, 11/19/01; s. Lucien Adelbert Dexter and Gertrude Zent D; m. 10/1/27 to Alice Catherine Worden; c. Mary Lou and Marjorie Ruth. Educ: Univ. of Mich, A.B, 24. Polit. & Govt. Pos: Chmn, Kent Co. Rep. Finance Cmt, Mich, 62-64; chmn, Fifth Dist. Rep. Finance Cmt, 65-69; treas, State Rep. Finance Cmt, 66-68. Bus. & Prof. Pos: Pres, Dexter Industs, Inc, 32-67; pres, Quality Brass, Inc, 69- Mem: Mason (32°); Shrine; Rotary; Peninsular; Kent Country Club. Rel: Protestant. Mailing Add: 800 Plymouth Rd, S.E, Grand Rapids, Mich. 49506.

DE YOUNG, ROBERT CORNELIUS R
b. Orange City, Iowa, 2/22/24; s. Cornelius De Young and Norma Bosworth D; m. 3/11/44 to Doris Marie Miller; c. Beverly Ann (Mrs. Gorman) and Keith R. Educ: Bryant & Stratton Bus. Inst. Polit. & Govt. Pos: Fla. State Rep, 66-68. Mil. Serv: Entered as Pvt, Air Force, 43, released as S/Sgt, 46, after serv. as Warrant Officer, N.Y. State Nat. Guard and China-Burma-India Theater, 45; China-Burma-India and S. Pac. Theater Ribbons. Mem: Pres, Jaycees, 55, PTA, 57 and North. Palm Beach Co. C. of C, 65; Optimist Int.(past pres, past lt. gov, Distinguished Gov, 56-57); v.pres, North. Palm Beach Co. Bd. of Realtors, 66; F&AM; Elks; Ins. Bd. of the Palm Beaches. Rel: Presbyterian. Legal Res: 754 W. Jasmine Dr, Lake Park, Fla. 33403. Mailing Add: P.O. Box 9995, Riviera Beach, Fla. 33404. (1967)

DIAMOND, ALICE MAE D
Committeewoman, N.J. Dem. State Cmt.
b. Wilmington, Del; d. Harry Francis Atkinson and Bertha Mechem A; m. 12/22/41 to Charles Joseph Diamond. Educ: Penns Grove High Sch, 4 years. Polit. & Govt. Pos: V.pres, Stevenson Dem. Club, 54-58; mem, Salem Co. Dem. Cmt, N.J, 54-69; committeewoman, N.J. Dem. State Cmt, 57-; supvr. of bills, N.J. State Assembly, 59-61; court clerk, Borough of Penns Grove, 59-61; mem, Salem Co. Bd. of Elec, 61-69; alternate del, Dem. Nat. Conv, 68. Mem: Am. Legion Auxiliary; Pennsville Twp. and Quinton Dem. Leagues; Upper Penns Dem. Club. Rel: Catholic. Mailing Add: 44 S. New St, Penns Grove, N.J. 08069.

DIAMOND, LLOYD WEBB R
Mem, Rep. Exec. Cmt, Caddo Parish, La.
b. Shreveport, La, 1/8/37; d. Robert Lee Webb and Jean Guynemer W; m. 5/19/58 to Anthony John Diamond; c. John Webb and Robert Anthony. Educ: Col. of William and Mary, B.A, 59; Theta Alpha Phi. Polit. & Govt. Pos: Pres, Career Women's Rep. Club, 66-67; mem-at-lg, La. Fedn. of Rep. Women, 67-69; precinct orgn. coordinator, Caddo Parish Rep. Polit. Action Coun, 67-69 and ballot security coordinator, 69-; alternate del, Rep. Nat. Conv, 68; secy, Rep. Party of La. Polit. Action Coun, 69-; mem, Rep. Exec. Cmt. of Caddo Parish, La, 69- Bus. & Prof. Pos: Chmn, St. Paul's Episcopal Day Sch, 69- Mem: PTA; Women's Symphony Guild. Rel: Episcopal. Mailing Add: 237 Pierremont Rd, Shreveport, La. 71105.

DIAMOND, TOM D
Chmn, El Paso Co. Dem. Party, Tex.
b. Long Beach, Calif. 3/28/23; s. Thomas M. Diamond and Violet Williams D; m. 1/1/49 to Carolyn Reed Culbertson; c. Jack. Educ: Stanford Univ, B.S. in civil eng, 49; Baylor Univ, LL.B, 57; Theta Chi; Phi Delta Phi. Polit. & Govt. Pos: Engr, Tex. Hwy. Dept, 55-59; admin. asst, El Paso Co, 60-61; chmn, El Paso Co. Dem. Party, 63- Bus. & Prof. Pos: Partner, Diamond & Thorne, Attorneys, 65 and 66. Mil. Serv: Entered as Pvt, Army, 42, released as Capt, 46, after serv. in Asiatic-Pac. Area; Asiatic-Pac. Ribbon with 2 Battle Stars; Philippine Liberation Ribbon with 1 Battle Star; Am. Theater Medal; Good Conduct Medal. Publ: 'New Tools for the Carpenter Case,' Baylor Law Rev, 57. Mem: Nat. Soc. Prfnl. Eng; Tex. Soc. Prfnl. Engrs; State Bar of Tex; Admitted to practice before Supreme Court, U.S; DAV; Mason, Scottish Rite, Shrine; VFW. Rel: Methodist. Mailing Add: 1208 Southwest Nat. Bank Bldg, El Paso, Tex. 79901. (1967)

DIAMONSTEIN, ALAN ARNOLD D
Va. State Del.
b. Newport News, Va, 8/20/31; s. William Diamonstein and Lillian Becker D. Educ: Univ. Va, B.S. in Commerce, 55, LL.B, 58. Polit. & Govt. Pos: Mem, Human Rels. Coun, Newport News, Va; mem, Gov. Coun. for Ment. Retardation; past pres, Hampton Roads Young Dem. Club; pres, Young Dem. Clubs of Va, 68; del, Dem. Nat. Conv, 68; Va. State Del, 68- Bus. & Prof. Pos: Partner, Diamonstein & Drucker, currently. Mil. Serv: Entered Air Force, 50. Rel: Jewish. Legal Res: 7207 River Rd, Newport News, Va. 23607. Mailing Add: P.O. Box 324, Newport News, Va. 23607.

DIAS, FRANCES JEAN R
V.Mayor, Palo Alto, Calif.
b. Manitowac, Wis, 6/15/23; d. Frank Joseph Kracha and Beatrice Rosalie Beale K; m. 9/23/47 to Julius Edward Dias; c. Maryanne, Teresa Frances and Patricia Jean. Educ: Univ. Colo, B.A, 44; Univ. Calif, Berkeley, Gen. Sec. Cred, 47; Delta Sigma Rho; Pi Gamma Mu; Dialectica; Spur; Univ. Colo. Pacemaker, 44; pres, Alpha Omicron Pi, 43-44; Panhellenic Rep, Univ. Colo, debate mgr, cmr. of forensics and War Bond chmn, 43-44. Polit. & Govt. Pos: Mem, Palo Alto Unified Sch. Dist. Bldg. Adv. Cmt, Calif, 53-59; Rep. precinct chmn, Palo Alto, 55; city councilman, Palo Alto, 61-, chmn. planning and procedures cmt, City Coun, 69-, mayor, 66-68 and v.mayor, 69-; mem. or alternate, Santa Clara Co. Trafficways Cmt, 62-65 and mem. Mass. Transit Cmn, 63-65; organizer and mem, Neighbors Abroad, Sister City Orgn, 62-; mem, Cmt. Int. Coop, League Calif. Cities, 62- and Cmt. of Future, 66-; rep, Asn. Bay Area Govt, 62-; mem, Cmt. Int. Coop, Nat. League Cities, 63-; mem, Asn. Bay Area Gov. Cmt. Air Pollution, 65-; mem, Palo Alto City-Sch. Liaison Cmt, 65-; cmnr, Nat. Guard Cmn, Santa Clara Co, 65-66; chmn, Palo Alto Diamond Jubilee, 68-69; bd. dirs, North. Calif. Power Assoc, 68-; founding dir, Town Affiliation Asn. U.S.(one of 9 govt. off). Bus. & Prof. Pos: Asst. librn, Chicago J. Commerce, 43; asst. hist. dept, Univ. Colo, 43-44; teacher, Los Angeles Co. Sch. Syst, 44-45, substitute teacher, Oakland and Berkeley, 47-48; asst. econ, Univ. Calif, 47-49; teacher and discussion leader, Univ. Calif. Exten. Div, 55-58. Mil. Serv: Entered as Pvt, Marine Corps Women's Res, 45, released as Cpl, 46, after serv. in Womens Res. Units at Camp Lejeune and attached to Hq. Co, Hq. Bn. Redistribution Regt, Camp Pendleton, Calif. Publ: Contrib, There Was Light, (in press). Mem: Hon. life mem. Calif. Cong. Parents & Teachers, 60; founder, Palo Alto Sister City Prog, 62; Palo Alto Auxiliary, Stanford Convalescent Hosp; Palo Alto Women's Rep. Club; pres, Jordan Jr. High PTA; parliamentarian, Am. Asn. Univ. Women; past pres, PTA Coun. Palo Alto and Palo Alto Educ. Coun; past trustee Palo Alto Commun. Scholarship Prog; cofounder, Charleston Meadows Homeowners Asn; alumnae pres, Alpha Omicron Pi, San Jose Peninsula Chap, 63. Woman of Achievement Award, B'nai B'rith Palo Alto, 65; Citizen of the Year Award, Palo Alto Real Estate Bd, 68; Alpha Omicron Pi Dist. Alumnae Award, 68. Rel: Catholic. Mailing Add: 766 Garland Dr, Palo Alto, Calif. 94303.

DIBBLE, DANIEL FRANCIS D
Mayor, Holyoke, Mass.
b. Holyoke, Mass, 1/4/26; s. Howard Clark Dibble and Alice Curran D; m. 10/12/45 to Frankie Mae Duty; c. Frances Dean and Daniel, Jr. Educ: Holyoke High Sch. Polit. & Govt. Pos: Alderman, Fifth Ward, Holyoke, Mass, 58-59 and Seventh Ward, 60-61; pres, Holyoke Bd. of Aldermen, 60-61; cmnr, Holyoke Bd. of Pub. Works, 62-63; Mayor, Holyoke, 64- Bus. & Prof. Pos: Incorporator, Mechs. Savings Bank of Holyoke; pres, Tecnifax Employee Credit Union, Tecnifax Employee Coun. Mil. Serv: Entered as Seaman, Navy, 44, released as Seaman 1/C, 46, after serv. in Seaman Guard. Mem: Pres, Mass. League of Cities and Towns; v.pres, Mass. Mayor's Asn; dir, Holyoke Taxpayers Asn. and Holyoke Chap. Am. Red Cross; treas, Holyoke Coun. PTA; Am. Legion (Comdr, Post 260); Jr. C. of C; Civil War Centennial Celebration Cmt; Holyoke High Lettermans Club; Elks; Holyoke Pub. Libr. Asn; Civitan. Rel: Catholic. Mailing Add: 894 Hampshire St, Holyoke, Mass. 01040. (1967)

DiCARLO, DOMINICK L. R
N.Y. State Assemblyman
b. Brooklyn, N.Y, 3/11/28; m. to Esther Hansen; c. four. Educ: St. John's Col, B.A, 50; St. Johns Sch. of Law, 53; N.Y. Univ. Grad. Sch. of Law, LL.M. Polit. & Govt. Pos: Asst. U.S. Attorney, East. Dist, and chief of Organized Crime and Racketeering Sect, N.Y, 59-62; spec. asst. U.S. Attorney, 62; counsel to Minority Leader A.J. Arwleo, N.Y.C. Coun, 62-64; N.Y. State Assemblyman, 64-; 12 Assembly Dist. Regular Rep. Club; Bay Ridge Rep. Club. Bus. & Prof. Pos: Attorney-at-law. Mem: Dyker Heights and Narrows Civic Asn; Men's Asn. of Bay Ridge; Brooklyn Bar Asn; Fed. Bar Asns. of N.Y, N.J. and Conn; N.Y. Dist. Attorney Asn; St. Bernadettes Holy Name Soc; K. of C. Mailing Add: 1345 83rd St, Brooklyn, N.Y. 11228. (1967)

DiCARLO, JOSEPH CARMINE D
Mass. State Sen.
b. Somerville, Mass, 3/21/36; s. Peter DiCarlo, Sr. and Amalia DeMartino C; m. 6/15/58 to Joanne Marie Signore; c. Stephen, Denise and Leanne. Educ: Boston Col, A.B. in polit. sci; Boston Univ, M.E. in educ. admin. Polit. & Govt. Pos: Mass. State Rep, 64-68; Mass. State Sen, 69- Prof. Pos: Sch. teacher, 58-64. Mem: K. of C; Sons of Italy. Rel: Roman Catholic. Mailing Add: 81 Pearl Ave, Revere, Mass. 02151.

DICHTER, DAVID D
Committeeman, N.J. Dem. Party
b. Atlantic City, N.J, 5/7/31; s. Herman Dichter and Jean Mayer D; single. Educ: Ill. Univ, 2 years; Aligarh Univ, India, B.A, 54; Clark Univ, M.A, 60; Birkbeck Col, London Univ, Ph.D, 62. Polit. & Govt. Pos: Br. pub. affairs officer, U.S. Inform. Agency, 57-59; desk officer, Pakistan and Afghanistan, U.S. Peace Corps, 62-63; Dem. cand. for U.S. Rep, Second Cong. Dist, N.J, 68; committeeman, N.J. Dem. Party, 69- Bus. & Prof. Pos: Ed, Youth Leader Mag, Youth for Develop, 68. Mil. Serv: Entered as 2nd Lt, Marines, 55, released as 1st Lt, 57, after serv. in 1st Amphibious Tractor Bn, Third Marine Div, Pac. Theatre; Capt, Marine Corp Res. Publ: Northwest Frontier of West Pakistan, Oxford Univ. Press, 67; Center for Rural Development, Nat. Grange Mag, 67. Nat. Sci. Found. Scholarship; London Univ. Res. Coun. scholarship; Hon. Nat. Track and Field Coach of Thailand. Mailing Add: Ocean Harbour Apts. Q1, Brigantine, N.J. 08203.

DICK, LAWRENCE R
N.Dak. State Rep.
b. Nebr, 8/31/05; married; c. six. Educ: Pub. schs. Polit. & Govt. Pos: N.Dak. State Rep, 53-61 & 69- Bus. & Prof. Pos: Farmer; dir, Farmers State Bank of Lisbon. Mem: Pres, Lutheran Home of the Oakes Circuit. Mailing Add: Englevale, N.Dak. 58028. (1967)

DICKENS, LLOYD EVERTT D
b. Okla, 2/22/02; s. Andrew D. Dickens and Inez G. Newsom D; m. 6/22/36 to Georgie E. Yerby; c. DeLores and Inez E. Educ: Columbia Univ. Polit. & Govt. Pos: Pres, New Era Dem. Club, N.Y. and Dem. leader, 11th Assembly Dist. and Exec. Cmt. mem, 53-64; N.Y. State Assemblyman, 11th Assembly Dist, 59-64; judicial del, state del. and state committeeman; del, Dem. Nat. Conv, past 16 years. Bus. & Prof. Pos: Bd. Dir, Freedom Nat. Bank, 64-; pres, Sure Fire Realty, Inc. and Real Estate and Ins. Broker, 50- Mem: Joppa Lodge 55, Masons; Bd. mem, United Serv. Orgn; NAACP; Urban League; PAL; Shriners; YMCA; Century Club; former pres, Greater N.Y. Realtors Bd. Rel: Presbyterian. Legal Res: 25 W. 123rd St, New York, N.Y. 10037. Mailing Add: 2153 7th Ave, New York, N.Y. 10027. (1967)

DICKERSON, FRANK ARTHUR R
b. Iberia, Mo, 6/3/12; s. Thomas Wesley Dickerson and Annie Hill D; m. 11/14/32 to Grace Thelma Snelling; c. Brenda (Mrs. Norwood Clark, Jr) and Judy (Mrs. Lawson). Educ: Iberia Jr. Col, 2 years. Polit. & Govt. Pos: Treas, Miller Co, Mo, 39-42 and clerk, 43-46; mem, Electorial Col, Eighth Dist, Mo, 44; mem, city coun, Iberia, 48-50; mem, Miller Co. Rep. Cent. Cmt, 50-52; del, Rep. Nat. Conv, 68; treas, Eighth Dist, Nixon-Agnew Campaign Cmt, 68; del. to several State and Dist. Convs. Bus. & Prof. Pos: Exec. v.pres, Bank of Iberia, 47-69. Mem: AF&AM; Lions. Rel: Baptist. Mailing Add: Iberia, Mo. 65486.

DICKERSON, HARVEY D
Attorney Gen. Nev.
b. Ely, Nev, 6/3/05; s. Denver S. Dickerson and Una Reilly D; m. 10/27/38 to Virginia Shephard; c. Carol, Denver Shephard, Valerie and Donald Charles. Educ: Univ. Nev, 30-31; Southeast. Univ. LL.B, 41. Polit. & Govt. Pos: Chief dep. U.S. Marshal, Nev, 33-34; floor secy. to Sen. McCaran, 35-38; jr. tax expert, Civil Aeronaut. Admin, 39; admin. asst, Works Progress Admin, 40; city attorney, Las Vegas, 42-43, Henderson, 53 and North Las Vegas, 56-62; cand, Lt. Gov. Nev, 49; attorney gen, Nev, 54-58 & 62-; U.S. Sen, Nev, 56; gov, Nev, 58; mem. exec. cmt, Dem. Party, 60-61; mem, Gov. Crime Cmn, 69. Mem: Nev. State Bar (dist. gov, 44-49, pres, 54); Am. Bar Asn.(House Del, 55-56); Am. Judicature Soc; Nat. Asn. Attorneys Gen.(exec. cmt, 57 & 69, v.chmn, Habeas Corpus and Bail); chmn, West. Regional Conf. Attorneys Gen, 65; chmn, Pvt. Investr. Licencing Bd, 69; Kiwanis (pres, 48); pres, Las Vegas Shrine Club, 49. Rel: Protestant. Mailing Add: 622 Mary St, Carson City, Nev. 89701.

DICKERSON, THELMA LOUISE D
Chmn, Montgomery Co. Dem. Cent. Cmt, Ind.
b. Crawfordsville, Ind, 10/17/18; d. C. C. Jordan and Mae H. Haycock J; m. 10/1/38 to Philip William Dickerson; c. Barbara (Mrs. Means) and Philip William II. Educ: High Sch. Polit. & Govt. Pos: Secy, Montgomery Co. Dem. Cent. Cmt, Ind, 52-60, v.chmn, 60-63 and chmn, 63-; alternate del, Dem. Nat. Conv, 68. Bus. & Prof. Pos: Secy, Mayor of Crawfordsville, 56-59; clerk, Secy of State, Ind, 60; supvr, license br, Bur. of Motor Vehicles, 61-63 and mgr, 63- Mem: Phi Chi Epsilon; Bus. & Prfnl. Women's Club; various Civic Clubs such as Red Cross and Mental Health. Rel: Presbyterian. Mailing Add: 109 Marshall St, Crawfordsville, Ind. 47933.

DICKERSON, WILFRED LEE D
b. Laurel Creek, W.Va, 9/18/09; s. Wilfred James Dickerson (deceased) and Harriet Etta Boone D.(deceased); m. 11/3/33 to Eunice Elizabeth Turpin Kelly; c. Lillian Elizabeth Kelly (Mrs. Garner), Alice Louise Kelly (Mrs. Simon) and Lacy Alexander Kelly. Educ: W.Va. State Col, 28-30; Kappa Alpha Psi. Polit. & Govt. Pos: Former W.Va. State Del. Mem: UMW, 6613. Rel: True Holiness Temple, Inc; Sr. Bishop. Mailing Add: Bartley, W.Va. 24813. (1967)

DICKEY, BRAD WILFER R
Chmn, Nobles Co. Rep. Party, Minn.
b. Worthington, Minn, 1/14/36; s. Wilfer L. Dickey and Adah Christensen D; m. 9/10/59 to Paula Schildhauer; c. W. Devon. Educ: S.Dak. State Col, 54; Univ. Colo, Pharm, 57. Polit. & Govt. Pos: Nobles Co. chmn, Goldwater for President, 64; v.chmn, Nobles Co. Rep. Party, Minn, 66-68 and chmn, 68- Bus. & Prof. Pos: Pres, Dickey Thrifty Drug Inc, Worthington, Minn, 60-; pres, Worthington Mobile Home Sales Inc, 67- Mem: Nat. Asn. Retail Druggists; Nat. C. of C; Elks; Kiwanis Int. Rel: Episcopal. Mailing Add: 1700 S. Shore Dr, Worthington, Minn. 56187.

DICKEY, CALE R
Publicity Dir, Rep. Party, N.Dak.
b. Wellington, Kans, 3/21/18; s. Willis L. Dickey and Florence Burgess D; m. 3/5/65 to Emma B. Schwinkendorf; c. Dennis W, Gregg E. and Toni Schwinkendorf. Educ: High Sch; Sigma Delta Chi. Polit. & Govt. Pos: Mem, Rep. Party Precinct Cmt, N.Dak, 54-58; publicity dir, Rep. Party, N.Dak, 66- Bus. & Prof. Pos: Assoc. Press reporter; magazine columnist; publisher, weekly newspaper, 48-66. Mil. Serv: Entered as Pvt, Army Air Corps, 41, released as M/Sgt, 45, after serv. in ETO; ETO, Unit Citations, Six Campaign Stars. Mem: Shrine, Scottish Rite, York Rite, KYGCH; Eastern Star; Am. Legion; Lions; Elks; United Commercial Travelers. Rel: Protestant. Mailing Add: 2005 St. Joseph Dr, Bismarck, N.Dak. 58501. (1967)

DICKEY, CHARLES HARDIN, JR. D
Mo. State Rep.
b. Mexico, Mo, 8/7/07; married; c. Betty; grandchild, Kevin Willmering. Polit. & Govt. Pos: Mem, Mexico City Coun, Mo, 50-57, former mayor; Mo. State Rep, 60- Bus. & Prof. Pos: Former auto dealer. Mem: C. of C; Mo. Asn. of Soc. Welfare; Mason, Hebron Lodge 354; Royal Arch Chap. 27, Mexico, Mo; Scottish Rite; St. Louis Consistory, Mollah Temple; St. Louis Little Dixie Shrine Club; Hi 'Twelve Club, past pres; Mexico Lyons Club; Dem. Club. Rel: Presbyterian; Elder, First Presbyterian Church, Mexico, Mo. Mailing Add: P.O. Box 22, Mexico, Mo. 65265. (1967)

DICKEY, DONALD FLOYD R
Chmn, Ripley Co. Rep. Party, Ind.
b. Batesville, Ind, 5/14/27; s. Herschel C. Dickey and Elsie Freeland D; m. 11/27/49 to Cathryn Marie Fries; c. Beverly, John, Glenn, Mary, James, Donald, Jr. and Janine. Educ: Batesville High Sch, grad, 45. Polit. & Govt. Pos: Rep. Precinct committeeman, Ind, 48-; trustee, Laughery Twp, Ripley Co, 66-; vol. dep. sheriff, Ripley Co, 66-; v.pres, Ind. Twp. Trustee Asn, 67-; chmn, Ripley Co. Rep. Party, 68-; supvr. license br, Ninth Cong. Dist, 69- Mil. Serv: Entered as Apprentice, Seabees, 45, released as 2C CM 3/C, 46,

after serving in 1066, 747 Construction Bn. Maintenance Unit, Guam. Mem: VFW; Am. Legion; F&AM; Eagles. Rel: Methodist. Mailing Add: 705 S. Park Ave. Batesville, Ind. 47006.

DICKEY, WILLIAM K, JR. R
Majority Leader, N.J. Gen. Assembly.
b. Phila, Pa, 9/12/20; s. William K. Dickey, Sr. and Catherine Meiklejohn D; single. Educ: Univ. Pa, 4 years; Rutgers Univ. Sch. Law, LL.B. Polit. & Govt. Pos: Municipal court judge, Collingswood, N.J, 53-61; chmn, Munic. Court Cmt, N.J. Supreme Court, 57-60; N.J. State Assemblyman, 63-, Asst. Minority Leader, N.J. Gen. Assembly, 67, Asst. Majority Leader, 68 and Majority Leader, 69-; alternate del, Rep. Nat. Conv, 68. Bus. & Prof. Pos: Attorney-at-law. Mem: Am, N.J. and Camden Co. Bar Asns; Lions; Jaycees (pres, N.J. Jaycees, 52-53). Traffic Court Award for Outstanding Judicial Standards, Am. Bar Asn, 60. Rel: Protestant. Legal Res: 6 Lincoln Ave, Collingswood, N.J. 08108. Mailing Add: 122 Haddon Ave, Collingswood, N.J. 08108.

DICKIE, ALEXANDER, SR. D
b. Johnson Co, Tex, 9/24/94; s. Alexander Dickie and Sarah Jane Lanham D; m. 5/15/21 to Ollie Rambin; c. Dr. Sarah (Mrs. N.L. Gault), Alexander, Jr. and Christine (Mrs. Tom Laney). Educ: Tex. A&M Univ, B.S. in elec. eng, 16, M.S. in rural educ. and psychol, 35; Univ. Tex, Ed.D, 42. Polit. & Govt. Pos: Chmn, Denton Co. Dem. Exec. Cmt, Tex, 64-68. Bus. & Prof. Pos: Supt. schs, Woodson Independent Sch. Dist, 33-37; dep. state supt, Tex. State Dept. Educ, 37-40; registr, N.Tex. State Univ, 40-65; dir. of personnel, Trans-Cold Express, 65- Mil. Serv: Entered as Pvt, Air Corps, 17, released as 1st Lt, 19, after serv. in France; Army Res, 19-30. Mem: Am. and Tex. Asns. of Collegiate Registr. and Admission Officers; Mason; Farmer's Union; Rotary. Rel: Christian. 1967 Legal Res: Denton, Tex. No mailing address available. (1967)

DICKINSON, CLYDE EARL D
b. Modale, Iowa, 11/5/91; s. John Dickinson and Leona Brownrigg D; m. 7/4/17 to Daisy M. Wade; c. Wanda (Mrs. Flynn), Leona (Mrs. Owens) and Arla (Mrs. Fisk). Educ: Soldier High Sch, Iowa. Polit. & Govt. Pos: Postmaster, Soldier, Iowa, 17-22 and rural mail carrier, 22-50. Bus. & Prof. Pos: Newspaper publisher, Soldier Sentinel, 17-44. Mil. Serv: Marines, 18, released as Pfc, with serv. in 330th Field Artil, Quantico, Va. Mem: Rural Carriers Orgn; Dem. of Monora Co; Am. Legion (sr. officer, Soldier Chap); Soldier Relief Cmn. Rel: Christian. Mailing Add: Box 156, Soldier, Iowa 51572.

DICKINSON, DANIEL S, JR. R
b. Binghamton, N.Y, 7/25/17; s. Daniel S. Dickinson and Margaret Egbert D; m. 10/2/45 to Melba Dunn; c. Daniel S, III; Thomas E, John F. and Joan E. Educ: Hamilton Col, 2 yrs; Hartwick Col, B.S; Albany Law Sch, LL.B; Tau Kappa Epsilon; Alpha Delta Omega. Polit. & Govt. Pos: Assemblyman, N.Y. State Legis, 55-65; Judge of Family Court, Broome Co, N.Y, 65- Mil. Serv: Entered as Aviation Cadet, Army Air Corps, 41, released as Capt, 47, after serv. in Pac, European and Am. Theaters; Distinguished Flying Cross; Air Medal; Presidential Unit Citation. Mem: Family Court Judges Asn; Legis. Pilots Asn; Am. Judicature Soc; Am. Legion; Shrine; Hist. Soc. of Broome Co; Am, N.Y. State and Broome Co. Bar Asns. Rel: Methodist. Mailing Add: 1314 Chenango St, Binghamton, N.Y. 13901.

DICKINSON, DONALD WARREN R
Chmn, Henry Co. Rep. Exec. Cmt, Tenn.
b. Lakewood, Ohio, 6/2/29; s. Abraham Becker Dickinson and Carolyn Verhoeff D; m. 4/2/55 to Jane Carolyn Dinkins; c. Carolyn Jane and Donald Warren. Educ: DePauw Univ, B.A, 52; Ind. Univ, M.B.A, 56. Polit. & Govt. Pos: Rep. committeeman, Monmouth Co, N.J, 57-59; chmn, Henry Co. Rep. Exec. Cmt, Tenn, currently. Bus. & Prof. Pos: Mkt. analyst, plastics, Union Carbide Corp, N.Y, 56-62; prod. mgr, Wrisley, Mitchum Co, Paris, Tenn, 62- Mil. Serv: Entered as Pvt, Army, 53, released as Cpl, 55. Mem: Elks; Rotary. Rel: Presbyterian. Mailing Add: 7 Bound Brook Dr, Paris, Tenn. 38242.

DICKINSON, FAIRLEIGH STANTON, JR. R
N.J. State Sen.
b. Rutherford, N.J, 12/9/19; s. Fairleigh Stanton Dickinson and Grace Bancroft Smith D; m. 1946 to Elizabeth Harrington; c. Ann Bancroft and Tracy Harrington. Educ: Williams Col, B.A, 41; Phi Beta Kappa; Delta Upsilon. Polit. & Govt. Pos: Chmn, N.J. Meadowlands Regional Planning Bd, 56; mem, N.J. State Cmn. to Study Meadowland Develop, 62; mem, Nat. Cmn. on Commun. Health Serv, 62; N.J. State Sen, Bergen Co, 68- Bus. & Prof. Pos: Pres, Becton-Dickinson & Co, Rutherford, N.J, 48-, chmn. bd, 68-; chmn. bd, Nat. Commun. Bank, 56-; trustee and treas, Bennington Col, Vt, 58-; dir, Prudential Ins. Co. of Am, Newark, N.J, 67; chmn, bd. trustees, Kent Sch, Conn, 67-; chmn. bd, Fairleigh Dickinson Univ, 68- Mill Serv: Entered as Ens, Coast Guard, 41, released as Lt. Comdr, 45, after serv. aboard U.S.S. Hunter Liggett, N.Atlantic and Solomon Islands; Atlantic and Pac. Theatre Medal with Four Battle Stars; Panamanian Order of Vasco de Balboa Medal. Mem: Am. Found. for Pharmaceutical Educ; Health Info. Found; Pharmaceutical Manufacturers Asn; N.Y. Acad. of Sci; Nat. Soc. of Med. Research; Nat. Cmt. for Soc. Work Educ; Nat. Conf. of Christians and Jews; bd. trustees, N.J. Symphony Orchestra; Urban League for Bergen Co; bd. trustees, Hackensack Hosp; United Fund. Rel: Episcopal. Legal Res: 160 Fairmount Rd, Ridgewood, N.J. 07450. Mailing Add: 205 Union St, Hackensack, N.J. 07601.

DICKINSON, FRED OTIS, JR. D
State Comptroller, Fla.
b. West Palm Beach, Fla, 3/28/22; s. Fred Otis Dickinson, Sr. and Georgia Bell D; m. 1/15/52 to Mildred 'Boots' Goddard; c. Cathy, Danny, Douglas, Dwight and Fred Otis, III. Educ: Univ. Fla, 41-42; John B. Stetson Univ. Sch. Law, LL.B, 48; Pi Kappa Phi; Phi Alpha Delta. Polit. & Govt. Pos: Fla. State Rep, 54; Fla. State Sen, 57-58; mgr, Fla. Dem. Presidential Campaign, 60; spec. counsel, State Dem. Educ. Cmt, 65; state comptroller, Fla, 65-; del, Dem. Nat. Conv, 68. Bus. & Prof. Pos: Law practice, Fisher, Dickinson & Prior, West Palm Beach, 48-65. Mil. Serv: Entered as Pvt, Marines, 42, released as Cpl, 45, after serv. in S.Pac, 42-45; Res, 45-57, 2nd Lt; Citation for Bravery. Mem: Fla. and Am. Bar Asns; N.Am. Securities Cmn; State Banking Cmn; State Mortgage Cmn; Fla. Coun. of 100 (organizer and chmn); Shrine; Kiwanis; VFW; Am. Legion; Elks; DeMolay; YMCA; Fla. Hist. Soc; trustee, Fla. Sheriffs Boy's Ranch; bd. mem, Fla. Children's Home Soc. Outstanding Young Man of the Year, West Palm Beach Jr. C. of C, 56, Fla. Outstanding Young Man, 57; Allen Morris Awards; Outstanding First Term Legislator, Outstanding Fla. Citizen of the Year, 62; Ben C. Williard Award, Stetson Univ. Rel: Methodist, Lay Leader. Legal Res: The Capitol, Tallahassee, Fla. 32304. Mailing Add: 1416 Magnolia Dr, Tallahassee, Fla. 32301.

DICKINSON, JOHN INGRAM R
Chmn, Floyd Co. Rep. Party, Ga.
b. Atlanta, Ga, 7/5/31; s. Ingram Dickinson and Sylvia Blair D; m. 7/10/54 to Sara Longino; c. Jerome Broocks, Mary Ann, Blair Hinton, Roy Stokes and Sylvia Blair. Educ: Amherst Col, B.A, 52; Emory Univ, M.D, 56; Sigma Zi; Chi Phi. Polit. & Govt. Pos: Alternate del, Rep. Nat. Conv, 68; mem, State and Seventh Dist. Rep. Cmt, Ga, 68-; chmn, Floyd Co. Rep. Party, 68- Bus. & Prof. Pos: Private practice gen. surg, 63- Mil. Serv: Entered as Lt, Navy, 61, released as Lt. Comdr, 63, after serv. in Med. Corps, Great Lakes Naval Hosp; presently, Naval Res, Lt. Comdr. Mem: Ga. Surg. Soc; Phi Chi; dipl, Am. Bd. Surg; fel. Am. Col. Surgeons; fel. Southeast. Surg. Cong; Am. Med. Soc; Med. Asn. Ga; mem. state and co. bd. Am. Cancer Soc. Rel: Episcopal; mem. vestry. Mailing Add: 205 Sherwood Rd, Rome, Ga. 30161.

DICKINSON, LEONARD RALPH R
b. Buena Vista, Minn; s. Ralph Herman Dickinson and Addie E. Spellman D; m. 1925 to Agnes Jacobson; c. Richard, Earle, Lois and Muffie. Polit. & Govt. Pos: Chmn, Game and Fish Cmt, Minn, 6 years; del, Rep. Nat. Conv, 3 times; Minn. State Sen, 51-55; Rep. Party officer; former Minn. State Rep. Bus. & Prof. Pos: Pres, Dickinson Lumber Co, Bemidji, Minn. Publ: Three pamphlets on mineral taxation. Mem: Past pres, Bemidji C. of C; Shrine; Elks; Rotary. Prime author of several statewide bills. Rel: Presbyterian; Elder and trustee. Mailing Add: Route 1, Bemidji, Minn. 56601. (1967)

DICKINSON, MERLE EUGENE R
Chmn, McKean Co. Rep. Party, Pa.
b. Norwich Twp, McKean Co, Pa, 10/28/96; s. Charles W. Dickinson and Estella Denison D; m. 11/5/17 to Leora Ness, wid. 10/29/58; c. Louise (Mrs. Allan J. Studholme) and Elsie (Mrs. William A. Murray). Educ: Smethport High Sch, 10 years. Polit. & Govt. Pos: Chief dep. sheriff, McKean Co, Pa, sheriff, 36-40, co. detective, 40-52, registr. of wills, 52- and clerk of orphans' court, 52-; chmn, McKean Co. Rep. Party, Pa, 61- Mil. Serv: Pvt, Machine Gun Co, 116th Inf, Army, 17. Mem: Am. Legion; F&AM; Cent. Dist. Firemen's Asn; Odd Fellows; Sheriffs Asn, Pa; Registr. Wills Asn; Elks. Rel: Episcopal. Mailing Add: 802 Green St, Smethport, Pa. 16749.

DICKINSON, R. DOROTHEA R
b. Brooklyn, N.Y, 7/1/15; d. Martin Richard Dickinson and Marion Haviland D; single. Educ: San Diego State Col, A.B. in Econ, 38; Benjamin Franklin Univ, B.C.S. in Acct, 56; Pi Phi Epsilon; Sigma Phi Omega. Polit. & Govt. Pos: Secy, Mayoralty Campaign, San Francisco and U.S. Navy and Marine Corps Res. Training Center, Los Angeles, 42, House Govt. Oper. Cmt, 54 and to U.S. Rep. Glenard P. Lipscomb, Calif, 65; exec. secy. to U.S. Rep. John E. Henderson, Ohio, 56-60, U.S. Rep. Tom V. Moorehead, Ohio, 61-62, U.S. Rep. Louis C. Wyman, N.H, 63-64 & 67- and to U.S. Rep. Wm. L. Dickinson, Ala, 65-66. Bus. & Prof. Pos: Clerk, San Diego Gas & Elec. Co, Calif, 38-41; secy, Gaylord & Gaylord, Attorneys, Calif, 47-49; secy, Newmyer & Bress, Attorneys, Wash, D.C, 54; secy-off. mgr, Gallan & Kharasch, Attorneys, Wash, D.C, 55-56. Mil. Serv: Entered as A/S, Navy, 42, released, 45, after serv. in Co. 13, Seattle, Wash; reentered 51, released as Lt. Comdr, 54, after serv. in Off. Chief Naval Oper, Wash, D.C; Am. Theater Ribbon; Victory Medal; Korea Serv. and Naval Res. Medals; Lt. Comdr, Res. Mem: Capitol Hill Club, Wash, D.C. Legal Res: 208 Willard Ave, Portsmouth, N.H. 03801. Mailing Add: 4105 Mesa Way, Alexandria, Va. 22312.

DICKINSON, RICHARD KENT D
b. Douglasville, Ga, 7/21/34; s. Walter Harold Dickinson and Sarah Moody D; m. 7/17/54 to Winnona June Hembree; c. Barret Lane and Michael Lee. Educ: John Marshall Univ. Law Sch. Polit. & Govt. Pos: Ga. State Rep, 27th Dist, 65-67. Bus. & Prof. Pos: Ford dealer. Mil. Serv: Entered as Pvt, Army, 55, released as Pfc, 56; Medal of Honor; Good Conduct Medal. Mem: Mason. Hobby, Gun Making. Rel: Protestant. Mailing Add: Route 2, Douglasville, Ga. 30134. (1967)

DICKINSON, VALJEAN L. D
Educ: Omega Psi Phi. Polit. & Govt. Pos: Ind. State Rep, -66; Ind. Gen. Assembly B & P Insts. Cmt; Leg. Apport. Cmt; Pub. Health Comm; Welfare Comm; Mayor's Adv. Comm. for Commun. Improvement; Manpower Training and Redevelop. Comm. Bus. & Prof. Pos: Dir, Sch. for Retarded Children. Mil. Serv: Korean War Vet. Mem: NAACP; Coun. for Retarded Children. Rel: Methodist. Mailing Add: 1417 N. Olive St, South Bend, Ind. 46621. (1967)

DICKINSON, WILLIAM LOUIS R
U.S. Rep, Ala.
b. Opelika, Ala, 6/25/25; s. Henry Kline Dickinson and Bernice Lowe D; m. 9/7/48 to Mary Patterson Stanfield; c. Christopher, Michael, Tara and William L, Jr. Educ: Univ. Ala. Law Sch, LL.B, 50; Sigma Alpha Epsilon. Polit. & Govt. Pos: Judge, Fifth Judicial Circuit, Ala, Lee Co. Juvenile Court and Lee Co. Court of Common Pleas and Opelika City Judge, formerly; U.S. Rep, 65- Mil. Serv: Capt, Air Force Res. Mem: Asst v.pres, South. Rwy. Syst; nat. dir, Ala. Jr. C. of C; comdr, Ala. Jaycees' Rebel Corps; pres, v.pres. and mem. bd, Ala. Ment. Health Asn. and Lee Co. Ment. Health Clin; Gov. Indust. Develop. Cmt. of 100; Elks; Mason. Rel: Methodist. Legal Res: Montgomery, Ala. Mailing Add: 6301 Beachway Dr, Falls Church, Va. 22041.

DICKINSON, WILLIAM STREIT, JR. 'BILL' D
Mem, Calif. Dem. State Cent. Cmt.
b. Fredericksburg, Va, 3/11/19; s. William Streit Dickinson and M. Christine Duval D; m. 4/1/61 to Margaret Hendry; c. Sharon (Mrs. Blankenship) and David R. Danfelt (stepson). Educ: Va. Polytech. Inst, 35-38; U.S. Maritime Officer Cand. Sch, Ens, 44; Univ. Calif, 55-60; Cotillion Club; YMCA; DeMolay. Polit. & Govt. Pos: Co. chmn, Gov. Hwy. Safety Cmt, Norfolk, Va, 50-51; v.chmn, Safety Cmn, Concord, Calif, 57-58; pres, Diablo Dem. Club, 66-;

Dem. nominee for Calif. State Assembly, Tenth Dist, 68; del, Dem. State Conv, 68; presidential elector, Dem. State, 14th Cong. Dist, 68; ex-officio mem, Co. Dem. Cent. Cmt, 68-; mem, Calif. Dem. State Cent. Cmt, 68-; v.pres, Contra Costa Co. Fedn. of Dem. Clubs, 69- Bus. & Prof. Pos: Assembly machinist and inspector, Newport News Shipbuilding & Dry Dock Co, 41-43; prod. control mgr, Garwood Indust, 47-48; dist. sales engr, E.F. Drew & Co, Va. and Calif, 48-54; eng. coordinator, Univ. Calif. Lawrence Radiation Lab, 55-68, sr. tech. assoc, 69- Mil. Serv: Entered as Officer Cand, Maritime Serv, 44, released as Lt, 47, after serv. aboard various maritime vessels, ETO, 44-46; ETO Medal. Mem: Nat. Asn. of Power Engrs.(former state dir); Am. Nuclear Soc; North. Calif. Indust-Educ. Coun; C. of C; Optimist (past pres, Concord Club); life mem, Optimist Int.(past dir); Va. Tech. Alumni (past pres, North. Calif. Chap); v.pres, Boy's Club. of Am; Boy Scouts. Hon. mention, Mt. Rushmore Inscription Contest, Hearst Newspapers. Rel: Baptist. Mailing Add: 4261 Brentwood Circle, Concord, Calif. 94521.

DICKSON, EDITH BRATSCHI R
Mem, Rep. Nat. Cmt.
b. Erin, Tenn, 1/22/10; d. John Wilson Bratschi and Lavella Shelton B; m. 3/25/34 to James Wiley Dickson; c. Bratschi. Educ: Tenn. State Col, 28-29; Austin Peay State Col, 29-30. Polit. & Govt. Pos: Chairwoman, Christian Co. Rep. Party, Ky, 60-68; alternate del, Rep. Nat. Conv, 64; v.pres, Christian Co. Rep. Women's Club, Ky, 65- Mem: Bd. dirs, Christian Co. Red Cross; Rep. Women's Club, Nashville. Rel: Methodist. Mailing Add: Greenfields Farm, Oak Grove, Ky. 42262.

DICKSON, ERNEST C. R
Mem, Rep. Nat. Cmt.
b. Orangeburg, S.C, 3/21/95; s. William L. Dickson and Clarisa Dozier D; m. 6/10/58 to Mabel Terry; c. Vermuta (Mrs. Morris). Educ: S.C. State Col, L.I, 20; Howard Univ. Law Sch, LL.B, 24, LL.M, 26; Tau Delta Sigma. Polit. & Govt. Pos: Mem, D.C. State Rep. Cent. Cmt, 56-; Mem, Lincoln Rep. Club, Wash, D.C, 65-; mem, U.S. Dist. Court and U.S. Court of Appeals, D.C; mem, Rep. Nat. Cmt, currently. Bus. & Prof. Pos: Real estate broker and lawyer, D.C, 25- Mem: Md. and Va. Bar Asns; Supreme Court of U.S; U.S. Court of Claims; Capitol Rep. Club, Wash, D.C; Howard Univ. Alumni Asn; S.C. State Col. Alumni Club; The Pig Skins Club, Wash. D.C. Rel: Presbyterian. Legal Res: 124 47th St. N.E, Washington, D.C. 20019. Mailing Add: 913 U St. N.W, Washington, D.C. 20001.

DICKSON, HAROLD R
Mo. State Rep.
b. Near California, Mo, 6/2/06; m. 9134 to Lorene Gentzsch; c. Robert H. Educ: William Jewell Col, A.B. Polit. & Govt. Pos: Mem. exec. cmt, State Sch. Bd. Asn, Mo, mem. City Bd. Educ, California, and pres. Sch. Bd, formerly; Mo. State Rep, 62- Bus. & Prof. Pos: Coach and teacher, 27-31; inspector, Nat. Battery Co, 31-37; serv. sta operator, 38-62; part-time ins. agent, 17 years. Mem: Charter mem, local Indust. Develop. Cmn; California, Mo. C. of C. Spec. citation for work in interest of pub. libr, Mo. Librn. Asn, 67. Rel: Methodist; mem. Bd. Stewards, chmn, Cmn. of Missions and past pres, Methodist Men. Mailing Add: 400 W. Russell, California, Mo. 65018.

DICKSON, TEMPLE D
Tex. State Rep.
b. Sweetwater, Tex, 10/29/34; s. Temple Dickson II and Mary Heard D; m. 10/25/57 to Katherine Kerbow; c. Allison, Angie, Priscilla and Maria. Educ: Univ. Tex; Am. Univ; Phi Alpha Delta. Polit. & Govt. Pos: Tex. State Rep, 65- Bus. & Prof. Pos: Assoc, Mays, Moore, Dickson & Roberts, Attorneys, 60- Mem: Am. and Nolan Co. Bar Asns; State Bar of Tex. Rel: Methodist. Legal Res: 907 Josephine, Sweetwater, Tex. Mailing Add: Box 638, Sweetwater, Tex. 79556.

DICKSON, WALLACE GORDON D
Va. State Del.
b. Camden, N.J, 8/29/31; married to Mary Jean Ventura. Educ: George Wash. Univ, A.B. and LL.B. Polit. & Govt. Pos: Va. State Del, 66-; mem, Arlington Co. Dem. Cmt. and Arlington Co. Cmt. of 100. Bus. & Prof. Pos: Attorney-at-law. Mil. Serv: S/Sgt, Air Force, B-29 gunner, Strategic Air Command, 51. Mem: Delta Theta Phi. Rel: Unitarian. Mailing Add: 4100 S. 18th St, Arlington, Va. 22204. (1967)

DICUS, HARRY D
b. Columbus, Ga, 11/2/22; s. Harry Dicus and Maude Miller D; m. 8/15/53 to Alice Redmond; c. William Henry, Martha Miller. Educ: Ala. Polytechnic Inst, Auburn, 41-42, 45-46; Emory Univ, LL.B, 48; Pi Kappa Phi; Phi Alpha Delta. Polit. & Govt. Pos: Ga. State Rep, 61-64, 49-50. Bus. & Prof. Pos: Attorney. Mil. Serv: U.S.A.F, WW II, T/Sgt; Air Medal, 3 Oak Leaf Clusters, Distinguished Flying Cross. Rel: Methodist. Mailing Add: Columbus, Ga. 31902. (1967)

DIEHL, NANCY SIMONS R
Mem, Pa. Womens Activities Cmt, Rep. Party.
b. Butler, Pa, 8/23/18; d. Roscoe Simons and Helen Maxwell S; m. 8/17/40 to Gilbert H. Diehl; c. Deborah, Nancy Huston and Eve Ellen. Educ: Grove City Col, A.B; Theta Alpha Phi. Polit. & Govt. Pos: Pres, Greenville Coun. Rep. Women, Pa, 49-51; committeewoman, Rep. Party, 50-56, mem, Pa. Women's Activities Cmt, currently; polit. activities chmn, Northwest Pa. Rep. Coun; pres, Mercer Co. Rep. Coun, 60-62; del, Rep. Nat. Conv, 60; chmn, Mercer Coun. Membership Cmt. Bus. & Prof. Pos: Statistician, U.S. Steel, 40-42; polit. sci. teacher, 42-44. Mem: Mem, bd. trustees, Edinboro State Col; Womans Auxiliary Greenville Hosp; Arabian Horse Asn. of the East. Raising and showing Arabian Horses; Skiing; Riding; Water Skiing. Rel: Presbyterian. Mailing Add: R.D. 1, Greenville, Pa. 16125. (1967)

DIEHL, RALPH E. R
N.Dak. State Rep.
b. Hartley, Iowa, 3/31/05; married; c. Two. Educ: N.Dak. State Univ, B.S. in Agr. Polit. & Govt. Pos: Mem, twp. bd; N.Dak. State Rep, 59-64 & 67- Bus. & Prof. Pos: Farmer; pres, Equity Elevator. Mem: Pres, Nodak Rural Elec; treas, Valley Beet Growers Asn. Recipient of various agr. awards. Mailing Add: Hillsboro, N.Dak. 58045.

DIELSCHNEIDER, WILLIAM NORWOOD R
Ore. State Rep.
b. McMinnville, Ore, 7/25/07; s. William Francis Dielschneider and Winnifred Norwood D; m. 8/30/30 to Edra Anne Seufert; c. Anne (Mrs. Burr N. Boutwell) and James S. Educ: Univ. of Ore, BS, 29; Phi Gamma Delta. Polit. & Govt. Pos: Ore. State Rep, 68- Bus. & Prof. Pos: Dir, Mid Columbia Develop. Corp, 58-68; v.pres, Regional Develop. Coun, 67-69; dir, Interior Elevator Co, 69- Mem: Pac. Northwest Hardware Asn.(pres. & dir, 50-60); C. of C.(pres. and dir, 59-69); Kiwanis (dir, 61-62); Elks; Oregon Cattlemans Asn; Wasco Co. Planning Cmn; Oregon Wheat League; Dalles Country Club; Dalles Yacht Club (past Commodore); Wasco Co. Exten. Adv. Coun, 66-69. Rel: Episcopal; Vestryman, St. Paul Episcopal Church, 66-67. Mailing Add: 1002 Court St, Dalles, Ore. 97058.

DIES, MARTIN, JR. D
Secy. of State, Tex.
b. Greenville, Tex, 12/21/21; s. Martin Dies and Myrtle McAdams D; m. 2/6/46 to Ruth White; c. Martin W, Dianne and David. Educ: Stephen F. Austin State Univ, B.S, 42; South. Methodist Univ. Law Sch, J.D, 48; Barrister; Pi Kappa Alpha. Polit. & Govt. Pos: Tex. State Sen, 59-67, pres. Pro Tempore, Tex. State Sen, 63, mem. nom. and co, cities and towns cmts, mem, finance subcmt, 63 & 65; gov. of Tex, 63; Secy. of State, Tex, 69- Bus. & Prof. Pos: Attorney, Lufkin, Tex, 48- Mil. Serv: Entered as A/S, Navy, 43, released as Lt.(jg), 46, after serv. on U.S.S. Richard W. Suesens in Pac. Theater; Area Combat Ribbons; Presidential Unit Citation. Mem: Tex. Bar Asn; fel, Tex. Bar Found; VFW; AF&AM; Mason. Plaque and rifle, Sportsmen's Asn; Most Distinguished Alumni Award, Stephen F. Austin State Univ, 67; State park at Jasper, Tex. named Martin Dies, Jr. State Park. Rel: Episcopal. Legal Res: 210 House, Lufkin, Tex. 75901. Mailing Add: 1201 Dailey, Austin, Tex. 78711.

DIETZ, LEW D
Mem, Knox Co. Dem. Cmt, Maine
b. Pittsburgh, Pa, 5/22/07; s. Louis Andrew Dietz and Bertha Staiger D; m. 5/31/50 to Denny Sonke. Educ: N.Y. Univ, 3 years. Polit. & Govt. Pos: Mem, Knox Co. Dem. Cmt, Maine, 64-; chmn, Rockport Dem. Town Cmt, 66-; del, Dem. Nat. Conv, 68; mem, Maine Cmn. Arts and Humanities, currently. Bus. & Prof. Pos: Writer. Publ: Pines for the Kings Navy, 55 and the Year of the Big Cat, 69, Little; The Allagash, Holt, 68. Mailing Add: Rockport, Maine 04856.

DI FALCO, ANTHONY G. D
N.Y. State Assemblyman
b. New York, N.Y, 7/14/38; s. S. Samuel Di Falco and Emma Sutera D; div; c. Christina Jean and Anthony Samuel. Educ: Holy Cross Col, Worcester, Mass, B.A. in Econ, 60; N.Y. Law Sch, LL.B, 63; Phi Delta Phi. Polit. & Govt. Pos: Mem, Metrop. Area Study, N.Y. Joint Legis. Cmt, 64; assoc. counsel to Pres-Pro-Tem, N.Y. State Senate, 65 and to Minority Leader, N.Y. State Senate, 66-; N.Y. State Assemblyman, 69- Bus. & Prof. Pos: Counsel, Century Nat. Bank & Trust Co, N.Y.C, chmn. bd. dirs, Italian Cultural Found, Ltd and mem. bd. dirs, Cent. Foundry Co, currently; lectr, Practicing Law Inst, Brooklyn Bar Asn, Rockland Co. Commun. Col, Rockland Co. Bar Asn, Bank Lawyers Conf, Orange Co. Commun. Col. and Orange Co. Bar Asn. Mem: Asn. Bar City of New York; Am. Bar Asn.(mem. local govt, real property, probate and trust law, taxation, housing and urban renewal sects); N.Y. State Bar Asn. (mem. banking, corp. bus. law and munic. law sects); N.Y. Co. Lawyers Asn. (Young Lawyers Cmt); Cath. Lawyers Guild (cmt. on constitutional conv, membership cmt); Columbian Lawyers Asn.(cmt. state legis) Am. Col. Probate Counsel; Consular Law Soc; Nat. Italian-Am. League to Combat Defamation (exec. secy); mem. bd. dirs, Fedn. Italian-Am. Dem. Orgn. N.Y. State, Inc; Columbus Citizens Cmt; Young Men's Div. Albert Einstein Col. Med. Yeshiva Univ.(sponsor and mem. Nat. Legacy and Bequest Cmt); Cmt. for Restoration and Beautification of Peter Stuyvesant, Peter Cooper Farm Area, N.Y.C; N.Y. League for Histadrut; Assoc. Div. Pres. Club, N.Y.(exec. cmt); Elks; K. of C; Police Athletic League; Columbia Civic League; Holy Cross Col. Club N.Y; N.Y. Law Sch. Alumni Asn; Xavier High Sch. Alumni Asn; Holy Cross Col. Alumni Asn; Tiro A' Segno of N.Y., Inc; N.Y. Urban League; Progressive Era Asn; Commun. Planning Bd. Three, N.Y.C; mem. bd. dirs, Legis. Aids and Coun. Asn. N.Y; Stuyvesant Chap. Cancer Care; bd. trustees, Stuyvesant Polyclin. Commun. Humanitarian Award, Stuyvesant Chap. Cancer Care, 68; Rockland Co. Commun. Col. Award, 68; Rockland Co. Bar Asn. Award; Albert Einstein Col. Med, Yeshiva Univ. Award, 66-67; Nat. Jewish Hosp. Distinguished Vol. Serv. Award; Man of the Year Award, Stuyvesant Polyclin, 68. Rel: Catholic. Legal Res: 103 E. Tenth St, New York, N.Y. 10003. Mailing Add: 39 Broadway, New York, N.Y. 10006.

DiFRUSCIA, ANTHONY R. D
Mass. State Rep.
b. Lawrence, Mass, 6/5/40; s. Carmine F. DiFruscia, Sr. and Sebastiana Tine D; m. 6/29/63 to Celeste Ann McDonald; c. Marc Antony and Kara Ann. Educ: Emerson Col, B.A. in Hist. and Speech, 62; New Eng. Law Sch, LL.B, 66; Phi Alpha Tau; Emerson Col. Forensic Soc. Polit. & Govt. Pos: Mass. State Rep, 16th Essex Dist, 67-68 & 69- Bus. & Prof. Pos: Attorney-at-law, Lawrence, 67- Mem: Mass. and Lawrence Bar Asns; Emerson Col. and New Eng. Law Sch. Alumni Asns; Lions Int; Jaycees, v.pres, Jaycees State and Govt. Affairs Cmt; Sons of Italy; K. of C; Elks; Redmen; Young Dem; Arlington Club, Rocca D'Evandro Asn; N.Lawrence Athletic Asn; St. Mary's Holy Name Soc; Augustian Guild of Merrimack Col. Outstanding Young Man of Year, Jaycees; numerous awards for int. and intercollegiate debating; Italian War Vet. Award. Rel: Catholic. Mailing Add: 274 Haverhill St, Lawrence, Mass. 01840.

DIGGS, CHARLES COLES, JR. D
U.S. Rep, Mich.
b. Detroit, Mich, 12/2/22; s. Charles C. Diggs, Sr. (deceased) and Mayme Jones D; m. 3/4/60 to Anna Johnston; c. Charles C, III, Alexis, Denise, Douglas and Carla. Educ: Univ. Mich, 40-42; Fisk Univ, 42-43; Wayne State Univ, 45-46. Hon. Dr, Cent. State Col. and Wilberforce Univ. Polit. & Govt. Pos: Mich. State Sen, 51-54; U.S. Rep, Mich, 54-; del, Dem. Nat. Conv, 56, 60, 64 & 68. Bus. & Prof. Pos: Pres, House of Diggs, Inc, Funeral Homes. Mil. Serv: Entered as Pvt, Army, 43, released as 2nd Lt, 45, after serv. in Tuske-

gee Army Air Field, Ala. Mem: Mich. Select Morticians; Elks; Mason; Am. Legion; Amvets. Rel: Baptist. Legal Res: 1361 Joliet Place, Detroit, Mich. 48207. Mailing Add: 2464 Rayburn Bldg, Washington, D.C. 20515.

DILDAY, JIMMY B. R
b. Dresden, Tenn, 7/8/33; s. Hubert Dilday and Annie Lynn Bowlin D; m. 4/6/57 to Nancy Edith Crawford; c. Marianne and Dwight David. Educ: Dresden High Sch, grad, 52; Gupton Sch. of Mortuary Sci, Mortician, 59. Polit. & Govt. Pos: Chmn, Weakley Co. Rep. Party, Tenn, 66 and treas, 68. Bus. & Prof. Pos: Mortician and mgr, Bowlin Funeral Home, Dresden, Tenn, 59- Mil. Serv: Sgt, Army, 56-58, with serv. in Hq. Detachment, Army Gas Co, Hanford, Wash. Mem: Jaycees (pres, Dresden Chap, 67-68); Rotary (pres, Dresden Club); Elks (chaplin, Dresden Club); Committeeman of the Year, Jaycees, 66-67; Jaycee of the Year, 67-68. Rel: Baptist. Mailing Add: 205 Jones St, Dresden, Tenn. 38225.

DILL, CLARENCE C. D
b. Fredericktown, Ohio, 9/21/84; s. Theodore M. Dill and Amanda M. Kunkul D; m. 5/13/40 to Mabel Aileen Dickson. Educ: Ohio Wesleyan Univ, LL.B; Phi Kappa Psi. Polit. & Govt. Pos: Dep. prosecuting attorney, Spokane Co, Wash, 10-12; secy, Gov. Ernest Lister, 13; U.S. Rep, 15-19; U.S. Sen, 23-25; spec. asst. to Attorney Gen. U.S, 45-52. Publ: Wrote first Radio Law, 27; How Congress Makes Laws, 36; Wrote Radio Law, 36; Communications Act, 1935; Our Government, 1945 Edition; Government of State of Washington, 1945. Mem: Wash. State and Am. Bar Asns; Elks; Moose; Athletic Round Table; C. of C; gov, Int. Platform Asn. Persuaded Franklin D. Roosevelt to start Grand Coulee Dam on Columbia River. Rel: Methodist-Unitarian. Legal Res: 763 Lincoln Bldg, Spokane, Wash. 99201. Mailing Add: 708 Cliff, Spokane, Wash. 99204.

DILL, J. ANTHONY R
Mo. State Rep.
b. St. Louis Co, Mo, 8/31/39; s. Alfred J. Dill and Helene M. Reibestein D; single. Educ: Rockhurst Col, A.B, 61; St. Louis Univ, LL.B, 64; Alpha Sigma Nu; Alpha Phi Omega. Polit. & Govt. Pos: Precinct capt, Gravois Twp. Rep. Orgn, St. Louis Co, Mo, 61-66; alternate del, Mo. State Rep. Conv, 64, del, 68; Mo. State Rep, Dist. 44, 67-; v.pres, Mo. Asn. of Rep, 68- Bus. & Prof. Pos: Lawyer, Stamm, Millar & Neuhoff, St. Louis, Mo. and Millar, Schaefer, White & Ebling, 66- Mil. Serv: S/Sgt, Mo. Nat. Guard, 64- Mem: Phi Delta Phi; Am. and Mo. Bar Asns; Kiwanis. Rel: Roman Catholic. Mailing Add: 8011 Grandvista Ave, Affton, Mo. 63123.

DILL, RICHARD F. 'DICK' D
Ala. State Rep.
b. Birmingham, Ala, 5/13/21; s. R.F. Dill (deceased) and Grace Noe D; m. 5/23/42 to Helen Smith; c. Rebecca J, Rick F, III and Robin E. Educ: Univ. Ala, B.S, Educ, 49; A Club. Polit. & Govt. Pos: Ala. State Rep, 67- Bus. & Prof. Pos: Real estate broker, Dill Realty Co, currently; commercial contractor, GTW Advert. Corp, Birmingham, Ala, currently. Mil. Serv: Entered as Pvt, Army, 43, released as Pfc, 46; European Campaign Decorations and Stars; Purple Heart. Mem: Sertoma East; East End Little League; East Side Commun. Club; Am. Legion; DAV; VFW. All sect. baseball, 48-49 as catcher; football scholarship, 41. Rel: Roebuck Christian; Elder. Mailing Add: 328 Observatory Dr, Birmingham, Ala. 35206.

DILLARD, BENJAMIN HALL, JR. R
Mem, Ga. Rep. State Cmt.
b. Atlanta, Ga, 1/15/37; s. Benjamin Hall Dillard, Sr. and Dorothy Bell D; m. 11/27/60 to Laurie Ann Eidson; c. Benjamin Hall, III and Jonathan Michael. Educ: Univ. Tenn, 55-56; Ga. State Col, 61. Polit. & Govt. Pos: Mem, Fourth Dist. Rep. Exec. Cmt, Ga. and Ga. Rep. State Cmt, 66-; chmn, DeKalb Co. Rep. Party, 66-68; alternate del, Rep. Nat. Conv, 68; admin. asst, Rep. Ben B. Blackburn, Fourth Dist, Ga, 68- Mil. Serv: Seaman, Navy, 55; A.N, Naval Res, 63. Mem: Pres, Metrop. Atlanta Sales Club, 65-66; Glenwood Jr. C. of C; Majestic Acres Civic Club; chmn. adv. cmt, Plantation Manor Home for Children, 61. Jaycee of the Year, 64. Rel: Baptist. Legal Res: 3048 Majestic Circle, Avondale Estates, Ga. 30002. Mailing Add: 141 Trinity Place, Decatur, Ga. 30030.

DILLARD, BENTON OSCAR D
Mayor, Roanoke, Va.
b. Oak Level, Va, 12/23/05; s. Oliver Henry Dillard and Alzie Young D; m. 6/29/29 to Mattie Lee Mullins; c. Richard H. W. Educ: Hargrave Mil. Acad, grad, 25; Roanoke Col, 25-28; Blackstone Col. Law, LL.B, 28-30. Polit. & Govt. Pos: Mem, Roanoke Dem. Exec. Cmt, Va; mem, City Coun, Roanoke, 46-50 & 56-64, mayor, 64- Mil. Serv: Entered as Pvt, Air Force, 42, released as Capt, 46; Lt. Col, Air Force Res, 65; Normandy, North. France, Rhineland and Cent. Europe Campaign Ribbons; Armed Forces Res. Medal with Hour Glass. Mem: Dir, Roanoke Bar Asn, 47; Va. State Bar; Mason (32°); K.T; Shrine; K. of P; Past Grand Master, Va. Odd Fellows; Lions Int; VFW; Am. Legion; ROA; Air Force Asn; U.S. Conf. Mayors; Nat. League Cities; trustee, Roanoke Mem. Hosp; dir, Gr. Roanoke Valley Develop. Found, Inc. and Sister City Cmt, Inc; cmnr, Roanoke Develop. Authority. Rel: Baptist. Legal Res: 1961 Belleville Rd. S.W, Roanoke, Va. 24015. Mailing Add: 610 Colonial-American Bldg, Roanoke, Va. 24011. (1967)

DILLINGHAM, BENJAMIN FRANKLIN, II R
b. Honolulu, 10/14/16; s. Walter Francis Dillingham and Louise Olga Gaylord D; m. 4/26/41 to Frances Andrews; c. Ceseli, Benjamin Franklin III, Gaylord. Educ: Harvard, B.S, 39. Polit. & Govt. Pos: Mem. Rep. Nat. Com. for Hawaii, 63-; cand. for U.S. Sen, 62; U.S. Sen, Hawaii, 48-56; mem. bd. supvrs. City and Co, Hawaii (Honolulu), 46-48. Bus. & Prof. Pos: Dir. B. F. Dillingham Corp, 61-; v.pres, gen. mgr. Oahu Ry. and Land Dir. Better Brands, Ltd; mem. exec. bd, bd. govs. Iolani Sch, 47- Mil. Serv: Army, Maj, 41-45; mem. Air Force Res; decorated Bronze Star. Mem: Am. Legion; VFW; Mil. Order World Wars; Mason (Jester); Clubs: Harvard (N.Y.C.); A.D. (Harvard); chmn. basic gifts devel. fund drive Aloha Coun. Boy Scouts, 64-; campaign chmn, dir. Hawaii Heart Asn, 57; bd. dirs, 58-61; pres, 64-65; area chmn. Harvard Class 39 Fund chmn. Distinguished Serv, Civil Air Patrol; Col. Byrd Leadership Award; Serv. Award, Jr. C. of C, Honolulu. Rel: Episcopalian. Mailing Add: 3227 Diamond Head Rd, Honolulu, Hawaii, 96815 or P.O. Box 3468, Honolulu, Hawaii, 96801. (1967)

DILLON, C(LARENCE) DOUGLAS R
b. Geneva, Switz, 8/21/09; s. Clarence Dillon and Anne McE. Douglas D; m. 3/10/31 to Phyllis C. Ellsworth; c. Phyllis Ellsworth (Mrs. Mark Collins) and Joan Douglas (Princesse Joan of Luxembourg). Educ: Harvard, A.B, 31. Hon. LL.D, N.Y. Univ, 56, Lafayette Col, 57, Univ. Hartford, 58, Columbia Univ, 59, Harvard, 59, Williams Col, 60, Rutgers Univ, 61, Princeton, 61, Univ. Pa, 62, Bradley Univ. and Middlebury Col. Polit. & Govt. Pos: Dir, U.S. and For. Securities Corp, 37-53 and chmn, currently; dir, U.S. Int. Securities Corp, 37-53. Ambassador to France, 53-57; Under Secy of State for Econ. Affairs, 58-59; Under Secy of State, 59-61; Secy. of del, Rep. Nat. Conv, 68. Bus. & Prof. Pos: Mem, Bd. of gov, N.Y. Hosp. and Metrop. Mus; mem, N.Y. Stock Exchange, 31-36; v.pres. and dir, Dillon, Reed and Co, 38-53, chmn. of the bd, 46-53. Mil. Serv: Lt. Comdr, Naval Res, 41-45; Air Medal; Legion of Merit. Mem: Soc. Colonial Wars, N.Y; Racquet and Tennis, Knickerbocker, Links, River and Recess Century Clubs; Pilgrims, N.Y.C. and Metrop, Wash, D.C. Clubs. Legal Res: Far Hills, N.J. 07931. Mailing Add: 767 Fifth Ave, New York, N.Y. 10022.

DILLON, GERALD RICHARD DFL
b. Minneapolis, Minn, 2/23/20; s. Luke Joseph Dillon and Helene Delsing D; m. 7/14/44 to Uva Gilbert; c. Mark, Barbara, Christopher and David. Educ: St. Thomas Col; Univ. Minn, B.A, 42. Polit. & Govt. Pos: Chmn, Fifth Dist, Minn. Dem-Farmer-Labor Party, 55-57 and Hennepin Co. Minn. Dem-Farmer-Labor Party, 66-67. Bus. & Prof. Pos: Pres, Meyers Printing Co, 49-, Dillon Press, 65- Mil. Serv: Entered as Pvt, Army Air Force, 42, released as 1st Lt, 46, after serv. in 20th Air Force, Guam. Publ: 'In The Army They Sing,' Esquire, 43. Mem: Pres, Minn. Planning Asn, 64-65; Minneapolis Citizens League; Foreign Policy Asn; Twin City Printing Indust; pres, North Loop Bus. Asn, 69. Rel: Catholic. Mailing Add: 3 Park Lane, Minneapolis, Minn. 55416.

DILLON, JOHN J. D
b. Indianapolis, Ind, 8/1/26; s. John J. Dillon and Margaret Sweeney D; m. 1/19/57 to Anna Catherine Dean; c. John J, Anne Margaret and Denise M. Educ: Xavier Univ, Cincinnati, Ohio; Ind. Univ. Sch. of Law, LL.B, 52; Pershing Rifle Soc; Sigma Delta Kappa. Polit. & Govt. Pos: 11th Dist. Chmn, Young Dem. of Ind, 50; city attorney, Indianapolis, 56-64; Attorney Gen, Ind, 65-69. Bus. & Prof. Pos: Partner, Dillon & Kelley, Attorneys, 69-; pres, Indianapolis Legal Aid Soc, 69- Mil. Serv: Army Air Force, 44-46; Victory and World War II Serv. Medals; Staff Judge Advocate, Ind. Nat. Guard. Publ: Opinion—Attorney General of Indiana, Attorney General's Office, March 30, 1966. Mem: Lawyers Asn. of Indianapolis; Indianapolis and Am. Bar Asns; Aircraft Owners & Pilots Asn; Indianapolis "500" Festival Assocs; dir, Indianapolis Legal Aid Soc; trustee, Marian Col, Indianapolis and past pres, Marion Col. Assocs; K. of C.(4°). Rel: Roman Catholic. Legal Res: 320 E. Kessler Blvd, Indianapolis, Ind. 46220. Mailing Add: 970 Consolidated Bldg, Indianapolis, Ind. 46204.

DILLON, R(EZON) SAMUEL, JR. D
b. Hancock, Md, 11/27/15; s. R. Samuel Dillon and Martha McAvoy D; m. 10/7/44 to Rebecca Fox Fuller; c. R. Samuel, III, Priscilla McAvoy, Anita Sherwood and David Harvey. Educ: Dartmouth Col, A.B. cum laude, 37; Delta Tau Delta. Polit. & Govt. Pos: Md. State Del, Wash. Co, 63-66, chmn, Educ. Cmt, Md. State House of Del, 63-66, chmn, Wash. Co. Del, 64-66. Bus. & Prof. Pos: Organizer, Hancock Free Libr, 40; v.pres, Wash. Co. Free Libr, 41-54; trustee, Wash. Co. Mus. of Fine Arts, 41-54; secy, Knouse Foods, Inc, 48-60; dir, Hancock Bank, Md, 58-; trustee, Wash. Center for Metrop. Studies, D.C, 60- Mil. Serv: Entered as Ens, Navy, 42, released as Lt, 46, after serv. in Mediterranean and ETO, 43-44 and in Pac, 45. Mem: Md. Hist. Soc; Am. Pomological Soc; pres, Nat. Peach Coun, 60 and Md. State Hort. Soc, 55; Rotary; Am. Legion; VFW; Tonoloway Rod and Gun; Assembly Club; Alsatia; Elks; Touchdown Club. Rel: Episcopal. Mailing Add: Meeting House Rd, Hancock, Md. 21750. (1967)

DILLON, WARREN ADELBERT D
Chmn, Prowers Co. Dem. Cent. Cmt, Colo.
b. Cherokee, Okla, 8/24/02; s. Albert W. Dillon and Etta Bender D; m. 5/23/36 to Ruth Eloise Stein; c. Bert, Donna (Mrs. Thomas) and John S. Educ: Univ. Okla; Okla. State Univ; Cumberland Univ, LL.B, 28; Sigma Delta Kappa; Beta Theta Pi. Hon. J.D, Cumberland Sch. Law, Samford Univ, 69. Polit. & Govt. Pos: Co. attorney, Alfalfa Co, Okla, 28-32; pres, Young Dem. of Alfalfa Co, 29-30; attorney, Okla. Tax Cmn, 32-36; nat. committeeman, Young Dem. of Okla, 34-35; chmn, Alfalfa Co. Dem. Party, formerly; chmn, Prowers Co. Dem. Party, Colo, 50-56; mem, Colo. Dem. State Exec. Cmt, 54-56; mayor, Lamar, 54-58; mem. and v.chmn, Oil and Gas Conserv. Cmn. for Colo, 55-63; chmn, Prowers Co. Dem. Cent. Cmt, 67-; alternate del, Dem. Nat. Conv, 68. Bus. & Prof. Pos: Mem, U.S. Dist. Court of Okla. and U.S. Court of Appeals, U.S. Tenth Circuit, formerly; mem, Regulatory Practices Cmt, Interstate Oil Co. Cmn, 57-62; pres, Lamar Bd. Realtors; mem. legis. cmt. and bd. dirs, Colo. Asn. Real Estate Bds. Mil. Serv: ROTC and Nat. Guard. Mem: Okla. Bar Asn; Mason; Elks; Rotary Int; Farm Bur; Farmer's Union. Rel: Methodist. Legal Res: 906 S. Sixth, Lamar, Colo. 81052. Mailing Add: P.O. Box 1133, Lamar, Colo. 81052.

DILLS, CLAYTON A. D
b. Rosston, Tex, 4/2/08; c. Doris L. (Mrs. Mouser), Richard E. Educ: Pub. Schs, Tex, Ariz, Calif. Polit. & Govt. Pos: Calif. State Assemblyman, 42-62; Chmn, Comm. on Interstate Coop, 57-61; Cmn. on Interstate Coop. & Colo. River Boundary Cmn. Bus. & Prof. Pos: Businessman; Musician. Mem: Masonic Lodge; Lions Club; Elks Club. 1967 Legal Res: 15615 S. Ainsworth St, Gardena, Calif. 90247. No mailing address available. (1967)

DILLS, RALPH C. D
Calif. State Sen.
b. Texas, 1910. Educ: Univ. Calif, Los Angeles; Univ. South. Calif; Loyola Univ. Sch. of Law. Polit. & Govt. Pos: Calif. State Assemblyman, 38-49; munic. judge, 4 terms; mem, Calif. Dem. State Cent. Cmt, currently; Calif. State Sen, 67- Mem: Bd. gov, Nat. Soc. of State Legislators. Mailing Add: 529 W. Eighth St, San Pedro, Calif. 90731.

DiLORENZO, AMATO P. D
b. Providence, R.I, 2/8/22. Educ: Mt. Pleasant High Sch. Polit. & Govt. Pos: R.I. State Rep, 63-66. Bus. & Prof. Pos: Owner and gen. mgr,

DiLorenzo's 1025 Club, Inc. Mil. Serv: Army, mess S/Sgt, 3 years, 3 months. Mailing Add: 132 Ophelia St, Providence, R.I. 02909. (1967)

DiLUGLIO, THOMAS ROSS D
Chmn, Johnston Dem. Town Cmt, R.I.
b. Providence, R.I, 11/25/31; s. Thomas DiLuglio and Elvira J. Rossi D; m. 1/2/52 to Loretta Agnes Migliaccio; c. Thomas A, Mark W, Anthony R, Vera H. and Beth E. Educ: Brown Univ, A.B; Boston Univ. Law Sch, LL.B; Phi Delta Theta. Polit. & Govt. Pos: R.I. State Sen, 60-64; chmn. legis. cmt, Constitutional Conv, 65-; chmn, Johnston Dem. Town Cmt, R.I, currently. Bus. & Prof. Pos: Pres, Exchange Invest. Corp, 64-, Gem Packing Inc, 65- and Cinevision Inc, R.I, 69- Mem: Am. and R.I. Bar Asns; Brown Club of R.I; Classical Varsity Club; bd. dirs, R.I. Opera Guild; bd. dirs, Fed. Hill House; Lions; Metacomet Country Club; Narragansett Village Yacht Club. Rel: Catholic. Legal Res: 934 Hartford Ave, Johnston, R.I. 02919. Mailing Add: 1195 Cranston St, Cranston, R.I. 02920.

DILWORTH, RICHARDSON D
b. Pittsburgh, Pa, 8/29/98; s. Joseph R. Dilworth and Annie Hunter Wood D; m. 8/6/35 to Ann Kaufman Hill; c. Patricia (Mrs. Lees), Anne (Mrs. Hackett, Jr), Deborah (Mrs. Newbold), Marie Hill (Mrs. Townsend), Louis G. Hill, Brockie, Warden and Richardson, Jr. Educ: Yale Univ, 21, Yale Law Sch, 26; Delta Kappa Epsilon; Scroll & Key Soc. Hon. LL.D, Temple Univ, 59, Univ. Pa, 61 and Haverford Col, 69. Polit. & Govt. Pos: Asst. city solicitor, Phila, 27-28, treas, 50-52, Dist. Attorney, 52-55 and mayor, 56-62; Dep. Attorney Gen, Pa, 35-36; chmn, President's Cmt. on Mass Transportation in Boston-Wash. Corridor, 63-; pres, Bd. of Educ, Phila, 65- Bus. & Prof. Pos: Partner, Dilworth, Paxon, Kalish & Green, 38-55 and Dilworth, Paxon, Kalish, Kohn & Dilks, Phila, 62; dir, Lincoln Nat. Bank and Phila. Contributorship. Mil. Serv: Pvt, Marine Corps, 18-19, re-entered as Capt, 42, discharged as Maj, 44; Col, Marine Corps Res.(Ret), 60; Silver Star; Purple Heart; Presidential Unit Citation; Fourragere of Croix de Guerre; Regimental Citation. Mem: Am. Legion; VFW; Racquet Club, Phila; Phila. Club; Racquet & Tennis Club, N.Y.C. Yale Football Team, 20; Yale Crew, 21; Phila. Award, 68. Rel: Episcopal. Mailing Add: 225 E. Washington Square, Philadelphia, Pa. 19106.

DIMMERS, DAVID ALBERT R
Prosecutor, Barry Co, Mich.
b. Hillsdale, Mich, 2/12/37; s. Albert W. Dimmers and Kathleen McFarland D; m. 7/7/63 to Caroline Adair; c. Martha Ann. Educ: Ohio Wesleyan Univ, 55-58; Mich. State Univ, B.S, 60; Wayne State Law Sch, LL.B, 64; Delta Tau Delta. Polit. & Govt. Pos: Prosecutor, Barry Co, Mich, 69- Mem: Barry Co. and Mich. Bar Asns; Mich. Prosecuting Attorneys Asn; Nat. Dist. Attorneys Asn; Kiwanis (bd. of dirs, 67-69); Elks; Hastings C. of C.(bd. dirs, 68); Hastings Youth Coun.(bd. dirs, 69). Rel: Presbyterian; Deacon. Legal Res: 237 E. Lincoln, Hastings, Mich. 49058. Mailing Add: 421 W. State, Hastings, Mich. 49058.

DIMON, JOHN EDWARD R
Chmn, Burlington Co. Rep. Cmt, N.J.
b. Roebling, N.J, 5/14/16; s. George Dimon and Mary Vrabel D; m. 9/6/46 to Virginia Lee Treece; c. Patricia Treece, Mark Vrabel, Blake Arthur, David Jonathan and Mathew. Educ: Villanova Univ; Temple Univ, LL.B, 40. Polit. & Govt. Pos: Guardian Incompetent vet, Burlington Co, N.J, 49-; spec. asst. attorney gen, N.J, 50-52; chmn, Burlington Co. Rep. Cmt, 63-; del, Rep. Nat. Conv, 64 & 68; del. and secy, N.J. Constitutional Conv, 66, secy, continuing cmt, 66-; asst. campaign chmn, Nixon for Pres, N.J, 68; chmn, N.J. Apportionment Cmn, Burlington Co. Bridge Cmn. and N.J. Platform Conv; S. Jersey chmn, Cahill for Gov; N.J. chmn, Nationalities Cmt. Bus. & Prof. Pos: Dir, Roebling Savings & Loan Asn, 52- and Bordentown Banking Co, 54-; free lance and ghost writer; pub. rels. officer for several orgn. Mil. Serv: Entered as Pvt, Army, 40, released as Maj, 46, after serv. as Commanding Officer, Separate Ord. Unit and War Crimes Unit, ETO. Mem: N.J. and Am. Bar Asns; pres, Burlington Co. Bar Asn; pres, Florence Twp. C. of C; comdr, Roebling Am. Legion, 46-48; comdr, Florence Twp. VFW; Elks; K. of C; pres, Trenton Navy League. Rel: Greek Catholic. Legal Res: 200 Blvd, Florence, N.J. 08518. Mailing Add: 200 High St, Mt. Holly, N.J. 08060.

DIMOND, FRANCIS GEORGE D
Chmn, Montgomery Co. Dem. Cmt, N.Y.
b. Fonda, N.Y, 12/30/24; s. Roy C. Dimond and Sara Stevens D; m. 2/8/53 to D. Dorine Oliver; c. Francine M. and Roy S. Educ: Syracuse Univ, B.A, 49. Polit. & Govt. Pos: Justice of Peace, Town of Mohawk, N.Y, 51-60, supvr, 61-69; chmn, Montgomery Co. Dem. Cmt, 62- Bus. & Prof. Pos: Pres, F.G. Dimond, Inc, 49- Mil. Serv: Pvt, Army, 43-45, serv. in Second Inf. Div, ETO, 1944; Purple Heart. Mem: Nat. Remodelers Asn; Am. Legion; Mil. Order Purple Heart; VFW; DAV; Moose. Rel: Catholic. Mailing Add: 1 Park St, Fonda, N.Y. 12068.

DINES, ALLEN D
Colo. State Sen.
b. Denver, Colo, 11/20/21; s. Tyson Dines and Isabel Allen D; m. 8/25/45 to Audrey Kay; c. Sidney and Lucy. Educ: Yale, B.A, 43; Harvard Law Sch, LL.B, 48. Polit. & Govt. Pos: Colo. State Rep, 57-66, speaker, House of Rep, Colo, 65-66; Colo. State Sen, 67- Bus. & Prof. Pos: With U.S. Dept. State and related progs; Attorney-at-law, 54- Mil. Serv: Entered as Ens, Naval Res, 43, released as Lt, 46, after serv. in Caribbean and Pac. Mailing Add: 1350 Logan St, Denver, Colo. 80203.

DINGELL, JOHN D. D
U.S. Rep, Mich.
b. Colorado Springs, Colo, 7/8/26; s. John D. Dingell and Grace Bigler D; m. 6/25/52 to Helen P. Henebry; c. John D, III, Christopher D. and Jeanne Patricia. Educ: Georgetown Univ, B.S. in Chem, 49; Georgetown Univ. Law Sch, J.D, 52; Delta Theta Phi. Polit. & Govt. Pos: Law clerk, U.S. Dist. Judge, 52-53; asst. Wayne Co. Prosecutor, 53-55; U.S. Rep, 16th Dist, Mich, currently; del, Dem. Nat. Conv, 68. Bus. & Prof. Pos: Attorney. Mil. Serv: Entered as Pvt, Army, 44, released as 2nd Lt, 46, after serv. in Panama Canal Zone, Am. Theater. Mem: K. of C; Moose; C. of C; VFW; Am. Legion; Elks. Rel: Catholic. Legal Res: Dearborn, Mich. Mailing Add: 2210 Rayborn Bldg, Washington, D.C. 20515.

DINGER, MARVIN L. D
Mo. State Rep.
b. Ironton, Mo, 9/30/21; m. 4/26/47 to Peggy Ruth McCabe; c. Paula Kaye and Mary Kathryn. Educ: Univ. Mo, Columbia; Wash. Univ, LL.B. Polit. & Govt. Pos: Prosecuting attorney, Iron Co, Mo, 63-64; Mo. State Rep, 64- Bus. & Prof. Pos: Attorney-at-law, 55- Mil. Serv: Army Air Corps, 43-46; Air Force, 47-52. Mem: Lions; VFW; PTA; Mo. Bar Asn; Am. Judicature Soc. Rel: Lutheran. Mailing Add: Route 1, Ironton, Mo. 63650.

DINGWELL, ROBERT E. D
b. Lansing, Mich, 1/13/22; married; c. Sharon, Nancy, Dennis, Vicky, Ricky. Educ: High Sch. grad. Polit. & Govt. Pos: Mich. State Rep, 64-66; precinct del; del. to co, state, nat. Dem. Convs. Bus. & Prof. Pos: Educ. rep, AFL-CIO. Mil. Serv: Fleet Marine serv, S. Pac, China, 44-46. Rel: Methodist. Mailing Add: 305 Isbell, Lansing, Mich. 48910. (1967)

DINI, JOSEPH EDWARD, JR. D
Nev. State Assemblyman
b. Yerington, Nev, 3/28/29; s. Guiseppe Dini and Elvira Castellani D; m. 9/22/49 to Jeanne Marion Demuth; c. Joseph, George, David and Michael. Educ: Univ. Nev, B.A, 51; Phi Sigma Kappa. Polit. & Govt. Pos: Dir, Mason Valley Swimming Pool Dist, Nev, 63-67; mem, Lyon Co. Dem. Cent. Cmt, 66-; Nev. State Assemblyman, 67- Mem: Nev. Gaming Asn, Inc; Lions; Eagles; Nev. Farm Bur; C. of C; Yerington Vol. Fire Dept. Rel: Catholic. Mailing Add: 38 N. Center St, Yerington, Nev. 89447.

DION, ALFRED CHARLES, SR. D
Pres, Putnam City Coun, Conn.
b. Cambridge, Mass, 10/19/18; s. Henry Major Dion and Alice Aggnes Lascend D; m. 1/31/42 to Doris Lucian Perreault; c. Alfred C, James H. and Jane Doris. Polit. & Govt. Pos: Civil defense dir, Putnam, Conn, 54-64; mem, Putnam Town Dem. Cmt, 55-66; alderman, Putnam City Coun, 55-64, pres. and alderman-at-lg, 64-; Conn. State Rep, 59-67. Bus. & Prof. Pos: Auto body shop mgr, George Motors, Worcester, Mass, 46-54; salesman, Zachae Builders, 55-57; foreman, Putnam Herzl Co, 57-62; auto salesman, Mathieu Ford, 62-64; auto salesman, Putnam Sales & Serv, 64-66. Mil. Serv: Entered as Pvt, Army, 42, released as 2nd Lt, 46; 1st Lt, Nat. Guard, 49-51; Am. Theater Ribbon; Victory Medal; Expert Inf. Badge. Mem: Officer's Club of Conn; State Police Asn, Conn; East. Conn. Police Asn; contest dir, Acad. Model Aeronautics; K. of C.(3°); Nocturnal Adoration Soc; Am. Legion; Eastern Conn. Amateur Radio Asn. Auto Race Driver and builder of Midgets, 38-42; Amateur Radio, WIDWX, 56. Rel: Roman Catholic. Mailing Add: 28 Woodstock Ave, Putnam, Conn. 06260. (1967)

Di PAOLO, CARL MICHAEL D
Chmn, Las Animas Co. Dem. Cent. Cmt, Colo.
b. Walsenburg, Colo, 2/22/20; s. Mike Di Paolo and Angelina Guadagnoli D; m. 6/13/48 to Violet Coren. Educ: Trinidad High Sch, Colo, grad, 38. Polit. & Govt. Pos: Chief clerk, Las Animas Co, Colo, 60-; chmn, Las Animas Co. Dem. Cent. Cmt, 68- Mil. Serv: Entered as Pvt, Army, 42, released as S/Sgt, 46, after serv. in 88th Inf. Div, ETO, 43-45; Europe-Africa-Middle East Serv. Medal; Good Conduct Medal. Mem: Cert. Football & Basketball Off. Asn; Int. Asn. Approved Basketball Off; VFW; Izaac Walton League; Goodwill Club. Rel: Catholic. Mailing Add: 411 Colorado Ave, Trinidad, Colo. 81082.

DiPAOLO, ROGER FULVIO D
Chmn, Portage Co. Dem. Exec. Cmt, Ohio
b. Barisciano, Aquilla, Italy, 1/1/25; s. Carlo DiPaolo and Maria D'Alessandro D; m. 8/9/47 to Pauline Martha Siciliano; c. Roger Joseph and Linda Marie. Educ: Kent State Univ, 46-48; Akron Univ. Law Sch, LL.B, 52. Polit. & Govt. Pos: Mem, City Charter Cmt, Kent, Ohio, 63, safety dir, 64, Dem. cent. committeeman, Precinct 2-E, 64-, mem, Charter Rev. Cmt, 69; chmn, Portage Co. Dem. Exec. Cmt, 64-; del, Dem. Nat. Conv, 68. Bus. & Prof. Pos: Deputy sheriff, Portage Co, 50; attorney, Ravenna, Ohio, 52- Mil. Serv: Entered as Pvt, Army, 43, released as T-5, 46, after serv. in 496th Antiaircraft Artillery, Pac. Theatre, 44-46; Pac. Theatre Ribbon with two Battle Stars; World War II Victory Medal. Mem: Am, Ohio & Portage Co. Bar Asns; Chmn. Asn. State of Ohio (treas, 68-); Elks; Am. Legion; VFW; Jr. and Sr. C. of C; Rotary (pres, Ravenna Club, 60-61); Kent Dem. Club. Rel: Roman Catholic. Legal Res: 1147 Norwood, Kent, Ohio 44240. Mailing Add: 221 W. Main St, Ravenna, Ohio 44266.

DiPETRILLO, CARMINE R. R
R.I. State Rep.
b. Providence, R.I, 9/21/27; m. to Norma A. Innocente. Educ: Boston Univ. Col. Bus. Admin, B.S. in bus. admin, 50; Boston Univ. Law Sch, LL.B, 52. Polit. & Govt. Pos: Past pres, Providence Young Rep, R.I; del, Constitutional Conv, 55; mem, Fourth Ward Rep. Cmt. of Providence, 56-59; mem, Ninth Ward Rep. Cmt. of Warwick, 61-; R.I. State Rep, 63- Bus. & Prof. Pos: Attorney-at-Law. Mil. Serv: Army, 46-47. Mem: R.I. Bar Asn; E. Natick Vet. Asn. Mailing Add: 17 Tomahawk Court, Warwick, R.I. 02886. (1967)

DIPPOLD, NORBERT CLEM D
Mem, Mercer Co. Bd. Elec, Ohio
b. St. Henry, Ohio 3/10/11; s. John Dippold and Mary Huelsman D; m. 9/25/37 to Vioma Overman; c. James L, Gerald J, Janice A. and John R. Educ: Columbia Inst, Bus. Admin, 31. Polit. & Govt. Pos: Dep. register, St. Henry, Ohio, 10 years; clerk, Granville Twp, 51-; mem, Mercer Co. Dem. Cent. Cmt, 55- Bus. & Prof. Pos: Supt, Mobil Oil Corp, St. Henry, Ohio, 41- Mem: Knights of St. John. Rel: Catholic. Legal Res: 271 N. Walnut St, St. Henry, Ohio 45883. Mailing Add: 311 W. Main St, St. Henry, Ohio 45883.

DiPRIMA, LAWRENCE D
Ill. State Rep.
b. Chicago, Ill, 6/24/10; married; c. Robert. Educ: Carnegie Inst. Polit. & Govt. Pos: Asst. admin, Ill. Vet. Cmt; 28th Ward Regular Dem. Orgn, 35 years; Ill. State Rep, currently. Mil. Serv: 83rd Inf. Div; Combat Badge; Bronze Star. Mem: Founder, past comdr, Pat Petrone Post Am. Legion; past comdr, Chap. 47, DAV; VFW; Amvets, 83rd Div. Asn; CWV; cmt. chmn, Mayor Daley's Citizens Cmt. for Cleaner Chicago. Softball, bowling league promotor, 30 years. Rel: Catholic. Mailing Add: 624 N. Drake Ave, Chicago, Ill. 60624.

DiPRONIO, LENA D
V.Chairwoman, Seneca Co. Dem. Cmt, N.Y.
b. Seneca Falls, N.Y, 10/4/22; d. Rocco Esposito and Dorotea Lippa E; m. 6/21/41 to Tony DiPronio; c. Grace Marie (Mrs. Cutlip), Dorothy Ann (Mrs. Stuck), John B, Toni Frances and Deborah Jean. Educ: Mynderse Acad, Seneca Falls, N.Y, grad, 40. Polit. & Govt. Pos: Committeewoman, Seneca Co. Dem. Party, N.Y, 63-; elec. cmnr, Seneca Co, 66-; v.chairwoman, Seneca Co. Dem. Cmt, 67-; committeewoman, Town and Village of Waterloo Dem. Cmts, 63-, secy. and treas, 66- Bus. & Prof. Pos: Bookkeeper, Tony DiPronio Plumbing & Heating, Waterloo, N.Y, 52- Mem: Cath. Daughters of Am; Waterloo Sportsmen and Conserv. Club. Auxiliary; Elec. Cmnr. Asn. of the State of N.Y; Civil Serv. Employees Asn, Inc. Rel: Catholic. Mailing Add: 57 N. Seneca St, Waterloo, N.Y. 13165.

DIRCKS, DURWOOD WILLIAM R
Chmn, Scott Co. Rep. Cent. Cmt, Iowa
b. Clarence, Iowa, 2/16/28; s. Arthur Henry Dircks and Edna Dresselhaus D; m. 8/19/50 to Susan Mae Goltman; c. William D, Russell A and David J. Educ: Univ. Iowa, B.A, 50; Drake Univ. Law Sch, J.D, 55; Delta Theta Phi; Theta Xi. Polit. & Govt. Pos: City attorney, Davenport, Iowa, 58-; chmn, Davenport Rep. City Cent. Cmt, 61-; chmn, Scott Co. Rep. Cent. Cmt, 66-; mem, Cmt. to Select Del. to Rep. Nat. Conv, 68. Bus. & Prof. Pos: Attorney-at-law, 55-; sr. partner, Dircks, Berger & Saylor Law Firm, currently. Mil. Serv: Entered as Pvt, Army, serv. in World War II Occup. Army, 45-46 and Korean War, 51-52; Lt. Col, Army Res, currently; World War II Victory Medal; Army of Occup. Japan Medal; Korean War Medal. Mem: Am. and Iowa Bar Asns; ROA; Iowa Munic. Attorneys Asn.(pres, 67-68); Am. Legion; Mason; Shrine; Optimists; Farm Bur; Davenport Plan & Zone Cmn; Iowa-Ill. Bi-State Regional Planning Cmn; Davenport Crime Cmn; Davenport Club; Davenport Country Club; Davenport Police & Fireman's Pension Bd. Rel: Congregational. Mailing Add: 2551 E. Columbia, Davenport, Iowa 52803.

DIRE, MICHAEL D. R
b. Denver, Colo, 4/28/25; c. Two. Educ: Regis Col. Polit. & Govt. Pos: GOP Blockworker. Bus. & Prof. Pos: Businessman, V. Pres, Bonnie Brae Tavern, Inc. Mailing Add: 1060 S. Harrison St, Denver, Colo. 80209. (1967)

DI RIENZO, JOHN LUKE D
b. New Haven, Conn, 5/25/25; s. Angelo Joseph DiRienzo and Marion Pascarella D; m. 9/6/48 to Ann Malin; c. John Luke, Jr. and Angelo Joseph. Educ: Inst. of Applied Sci, grad. Polit. & Govt. Pos: Alderman, New Haven, Conn, 63-; mem, Bldg. Lines Cmt, New Haven, Conn, 61-63. Bus. & Prof. Pos: Pres, John DiRienzo Invests, 62-; chief investigator & v.pres, Montesi Invests. Inc, 59-62. Mil. Serv: Entered as A/S, Navy, 42, released as SK 1/C, after serv. in European & Pac. Theaters, 43-45, 50-52; European Theater, African-Middle-Eastern Theater and Am. Theater Ribbons; World War II Victory, Korean and Good Conduct Medals. Mem: Melibus Club; Shaw Sinon Post, Am. Legion; Umbreto II Club; Int. Police Cong; St. Rose Holy Name Soc. Rel: Catholic. Mailing Add: 31 Saltonstall, New Haven, Conn. 06513. (1967)

DIRLAM, AUBREY WILLIAM R
Majority Leader, Minn. State House of Rep.
b. Pauora, Iowa, 10/20/13; s. Philip E. Dirlam and Hattie Mae Trent D; m. 6/20/42 to Hazelle M. Menz; c. Gordon and Kenneth. Polit. & Govt. Pos: Minn. State Rep, 41-, Majority Leader, Minn. State House of Rep, 63- Bus. & Prof. Pos: Farmer. Rel: Methodist. Mailing Add: Route 1, Redwood Falls, Minn. 56283. (1967)

DISHONGH, HOWARD ALLAN D
Ark. State Rep.
b. Little Rock, Ark, 9/22/31; s. Howard Allen Dishongh and Sarah Crosby D; m. 7/30/65 to Joan Gilbert; c. Sarah Wood. Educ: Tulane Univ, 50-51; Little Rock Univ, 58-60; Univ. Ark. Law Sch, LL.B, 62. Polit. & Govt. Pos: Committeeman, Pulaski Co. Dem. Cmt, Ark, 65-67; Ark. State Rep, 67- Mil. Serv: Entered as Pvt, Marine Corps, 51, released as Cpl, 54, after serv. in Second Bn, First Marine Div, Korea, 51-52. Mem: Am. Trial Lawyers Asn; F&AM; Consistory; Mason (32°); Shrine (past v.pres. & pres, Little Rock Shrine); Royal Order of Jesters. Outstanding Personality of the South, 67; Commun. Leader of Am, 68. Rel: Protestant. Mailing Add: 10 River Ridge Rd, Little Rock, Ark. 72207.

DiSILVESTRO, ANTHONY J. D
b. Phila, Pa, 5/15/04; s. A. Giuseppe DiSilvestro and Mary Califano D'S; m. to Mary Angela Perseo. Educ: Temple Sch. of Law, LL.B; Temple Sch. of Pharm, Ph.G. Polit. & Govt. Pos: Pa. State Sen, 36-67; Pa. State Sen, pres. pro-tem, 61, 62. Bus. & Prof. Pos: Pharmacist-publisher; ed. and publisher Ital-Am. Weekly, LaLibera Parola. Mem: Unione Abuzze, Lodge Iwo Jima 138; Phila. Asn. Retail Druggists; past pres, Temple Univ. Alumni; Pharm. Alumni of Temple Univ. Temple Award, 38. Mailing Add: 1505 S. 15th St, Philadelphia, Pa. 19146. (1967)

DISPONETT, WILLIAM DAVID R
Chmn, Anderson Co. Rep. Party, Ky.
b. Lawrenceburg, Ky, 9/4/35; s. James Disponett and Nora Searcy D; m. 2/9/57 to Brenda Hawkins; c. Lois Ann. Educ: Anderson High Sch, 4 years. Polit. & Govt. Pos: Chmn, Anderson Co. Rep. Party, Ky, 68- Bus. & Prof. Pos: Lab. technician, Kraft Foods, Lawrenceburg, Ky, 55- Rel: Baptist. Mailing Add: 300 Forrest Dr, Lawrenceburg, Ky. 40342.

DISSTON, HARRY R
State Finance Chmn, Rep. Party of Va.
b. Red Bank, N.J, 11/23/99; s. Eugene John Kauffmann and Frances Matilda Disston K; m. 3/26/30 to Valerie Duval, wid. 1/19/50; m. 8/26/60 to Catherine Sitler; c. Robin John Duval and Geoffrey Whitmore. Educ: Amherst Col, A.B, 21; Phi Beta Kappa. Polit. & Govt. Pos: V.chmn. and finance cmt. chmn, Louisa Co. Rep. Cmt, Va, 62-63, chmn, currently; campaign mgr. for Barry Goldwater, Louisa Co. Rep. Cmt, 64; alternate del, Rep. Nat. Conv, 68; chmn, Finance Cmt, mem, Cent. Cmt. and Exec. Cmt, Rep. Party of Va; mem, Nat. Rep. Finance Cmt. and State Budget Cmt. Bus. & Prof. Pos: Exec, N.Y. Tel. Co. and Am. Tel. & Tel. Co, 21-41, mem. exec. adv. staff, Am. Tel. & Tel. Co, 46-60; placement adminstr, Univ. Va. Grad. Sch. Bus. Admin, 66- Mil. Serv: Entered as Pvt, Army, 18, Cent. Officers Training Camp; 2nd Lt. to Capt, Inf. and Cavalry, Army Res; re-entered as Maj, 41, released as Col, 46, after serv. in Cavalry and Gen. Staff Corps; Brig. Gen. (Ret), N.Y. Nat. Guard, 21-57; Legion of Merit; Bronze Star with Oak Leaf Cluster; N.Y. State Distinguished Serv. Medal; Order of Bolivar, Venezuela; Gold Cross, Free Polish Forces; Occup. of Japan, Philippine Liberation, S.W. Pac. and Am. Theaters, Victory and Am. Defense Serv. Medals. Publ: Horse and Rider; Know About Horses; 'Horsemanship and Riding,' Encyclop. Britannica. Mem: Am. Legion; Pilgrims of U.S.; Union Club, N.Y.; Church Club, N.Y.; Keswick Hunt Club, Va; Farmington Country Club; Red Land Club; Jack Jouett Bridle Trails Club; Mil. Order of World Wars; Mil. Order of For. Wars; N.Y. Soc. Mil. and Naval Officers World Wars; judge, Am. and Va. Horse Shows Asn; Torch Club, Va; Cmt. on For. Rels; dir. and mem. exec. cmt, Charlottesville-Albemarle Chap, Am. Red Cross. Rel: Episcopal; Vestry, Grace Episcopal Church, Cismont. Mailing Add: Hidden Hill Farm, Keswick, Va. 22947.

DISTELHORST, MILTON D
b. Des Moines Co, Iowa, 6/24/21; s. Ed Distelhorst and Ann D; m. 1944 to Phyllis Mc Laren; c. Thomas, Christina and David. Educ: Des Moines Co. Schs. Polit. & Govt. Pos: Chmn, Des Moines Co. Bd. of Supvr, Iowa; former Iowa State Rep. Bus. & Prof. Pos: Owner and operator, 320 acre farm, Des Moines Co. Mil. Serv: Army Air Force, 3 years, World War II. Mem: Des Moines Co. Exten. Coun; Iron Workers Local 577; Am. Legion; DAV. Rel: Lutheran. Mailing Add: Route 2, Burlington, Iowa 52601. (1967)

DITMER, WARD NELSON R
Secy, Miami Co. Rep. Cent. and Exec. Cmts, Ohio
b. Covington, Ohio, 12/12/02; s. Ulysses Grant Ditmer and Katherine Anna Sowers D; m. 12/9/22 to Grace Irene Snavely; c. Lt. Col. Robert A. and Clyde Arthur (deceased). Educ: Nat. Security Seminar, Ideal Bus. Sch, Piqua, Ohio; Univ. Dayton Workshops. Polit. & Govt. Pos: City cmnr, Piqua, Ohio, 66-; secy, Miami Co. Rep. Cent. and Exec. Cmts, currently. Bus. & Prof. Pos: Owner-operator, letter shop, 40-67; free lance pub. speaker; asst. to Piqua funeral dir. Mil. Serv: Pvt, Army, 19-20. Mem: Pres, Ohio Rural Letter Carriers Asn, 46-48; Lions (past pres, Piqua Club); C. of C.(former mem. bd. dirs, Piqua Chap); hon. Jaycee; Boy Scouts; chmn. adv. bd, Piqua Salvation Army; mem. bd. and first aid instr, Am. Red Cross; Mason,(mem. chap, coun. and commandery). Outstanding Citizen Award, Jaycees, 67. Rel: United Methodist. Legal Res: 502 E. Greene St, Piqua, Ohio 45356. Mailing Add: P.O. Box 713, Piqua, Ohio 45356.

DiTRAPANO, RUDOLPH LIDANO D
Chmn, State Dem. Exec. Cmt, W.Va.
b. Charleston, W.Va, 7/25/28; s. Luigi DiTrapano and Amelia Filigenzi D; m. 4/27/57 to Martha Caroline Veazey; c. Luisa Caroline, Louis Dante, Lidano Albert and Lia Marta. Educ: Notre Dame Univ, B.S, 50, LL.B, 51. Polit. & Govt. Pos: City attorney, East Bank, W.Va, 58; chmn, State Dem. Exec. Cmt, 68- Mil. Serv: Entered as A/S, Navy, 51, released as Seaman, 53, after serv. in Naval Operating Base. Mem: Am. and Kanawha Co. Bar Asns; Am. and W.Va. Tri-Lawyers Asns; Am. Legion; Serra Club; Rotary; K. of C. Rel: Roman Catholic. Mailing Add: 2604 Kanawha Ave, S.E, Charleston, W.Va. 25304.

DITTLINGER, MICHEAL ADAM, SR. D
Chmn, Allegan Co. Dem. Cmt, Mich.
b. Gobles, Mich, 10/10/09; s. Micheal Adam Dittlinger and Nettie Louise Covert D; m. 10/10/37 to Marion Annabele Bierow; c. Micheal A, Jr. and Josephine Sue (Mrs. Tuffelmire). Educ: Hasting Pub. High Sch, Mich, 2 years; Greer Automotive Sch, 1 year. Polit. & Govt. Pos: Rural sch. bd. dir, Brown Sch, Allegan Co, Mich, 45-52; trustee, Bloomingdale Sch. Bd, 54-55, 62-67 & 68-69; chmn, Allegan Co. Dem. Cmt, Mich, 62- Bus. & Prof. Pos: Steel supt, various construction jobs, 38-69. Mem: Ironworker Local 340; Mason; Mich. Farmers Union. Rel: Methodist. Mailing Add: R.R. 2, Grand Junction, Mich. 49056.

DIVELY, MICHAEL AUGUSTUS R
Mich. State Rep.
b. Cleveland, Ohio, 12/30/38; s. George Samuel Dively and Harriett Grace Seeds D; single. Educ: Williams Col, A.B, 61; Univ. Mich, LL.B, 64; Delta Kappa Epsilon; Phi Alpha Delta. Polit. & Govt. Pos: Peninsula Twp. del, Rep. Party, Mich, 66; del, Rep. State Conv, since 66; secy-treas, Grand Traverse Rep. Exec. Cmt, 66-68; secy, Ninth Cong. Dist. Rep. Cmt, 67-; dir, State TAR, 68-69; spec. adv. youth activities to state chmn, Rep. State Cent. Cmt, 69-; Mich. State Rep, 69- Bus. & Prof. Pos: Partner, Murchie, Calcutt & Brown, Traverse City, Mich, 67- Mem: Am. Bar Asn; State Bar of Mich; Elks; Scottish Rite; Mason; Kiwanis; Shrine. Outstanding Achievement Award, Kiwanis Club, Traverse City; Distinguished Serv. Award, Traverse City Jaycees. Rel: United Church of Christ. Legal Res: 7236 Peninsula Dr, Traverse City, Mich. 49684. Mailing Add: 400 State Bank Bldg, Traverse City, Mich. 49684.

DiVIRGILIO, ALBERT VINCENT D
b. Lynn, Mass, 6/9/42; s. Primo DiVirgilio and Blanche Elizabeth St. Cyr D; m. 10/8/69 to Virginia Sofronas; c. Albert Vincent, II. Educ: Salem State Col, B.S, 64, M.Ed, 66; Suffolk Univ. Law. Sch, 67-68; pres, Beta Chap, Kappa Delta Phi. Polit. & Govt. Pos: Mem, Dem. City Cmt, Lynn, Mass, 64-, treas, Ward One, 68-; nominee, Mass. State Rep, 11th Essex, 68. Bus. & Prof. Pos: Real estate broker and notary pub, Lynn, Mass, 65-; instr. sci, Cobbet Jr. High, 64-66 and biol, Classical High Sch, 66-; owner, Mr. D's Sch. Driving, 69- Mil. Serv: Entered as E-1, Marine Corps Res, 61, released as E-3, 67, after serv. in Second Engr. Co, Lynn, Mass. Mem: V.pres, Lynn Teachers Asn; Bus. Men's Club; YMCA; K. of C; Sons of Italy. Rel: Catholic. Mailing Add: 27 Parker Hill Ave, Lynn, Mass. 01904.

DIX, TIMOTHY VOORHEES R
b. Ravenna, Ohio, 8/14/45; s. Robert Clinton Dix and Helen Westcott D; m. 9/6/69 to Gwen Ellyn Gerland. Educ. Oberlin Col, A.B, 67; student, Univ. Wis. Law Sch, currently; Phi Alpha Delta. Polit. & Govt. Pos: Treas, Ohio League of Col. Young Rep. Clubs, 64-65, v.chmn, 65-66, chmn, 66-67; alternate del-at-lg, Rep. Nat. Conv, 68. Legal Res: Kent, Ohio. Mailing Add: 1923 Sherman Ave, Apt. 4, Madison, Wis. 53704.

DIXON, ALAN JOHN D
Ill. State Sen.
b. Belleville, Ill, 7/7/27; s. William Gerard Dixon and Elsa Tebbenhoff D; m. 1/17/54 to Joan Louise Fox; c. Stephanie Jo, Jeffrey Alan and Elizabeth Jane. Educ: Univ. Ill, B.S, 46; Wash. Univ, LL.B, 49; Delta Upsilon. Polit. & Govt. Pos: Police Magistrate, Belleville, Ill, 49; asst. state attorney, St. Clair Co, 50 and chmn, Judicial Adv. Coun, 3 terms; Ill. State Rep, 49th Dist, 50-62 and chmn, Cmt. Judiciary, Ill. House Rep, two terms; Ill. State Sen, 49th Dist, 63-66; Ill. State Sen, 54th Dist, 68-, Minority Whip, Ill. State Senate, 65-; del, Dem. Nat. Conv, 68. Mil. Serv: Air Cadet, Navy, 45-46. Mem: St. Clair Co, Ill. and Am. Bar Asns; Am. Legion; C. of C; St. Clair Country Club. Rel: Presbyterian. Legal Res: 53 Country Club Place, Belleville, Ill. 62223. Mailing Add: 25 W. Main St, Belleville, Ill. 62221.

DIXON, FRED L. R
Mem, Nat. Rep. Finance Cmt.
b. Pueblo, Colo, 7/18/22; s. Fred L. Dixon and Ella Alacia Crowley D; single. Educ: Pueblo Col, A.A, 42; Univ. Colo, B.S. in bus, 46; Wharton Col, Univ. Pa, Invest. Bankers Inst, grad; nat. secy, Phi Gamma Delta. Polit. & Govt. Pos: Mem, Nat. Rep. Finance Cmt, 57-; treas, Young Rep. Nat. Fedn, 58-59; secy, D.C. Rep. Cmt, 58-68; tour dir, Wm. Miller, V.President Campaign, 64; asst. chmn, Nat. Conv, 60-64; chief page, 56; ticket chmn, Eisenhower and Nat. Dinners, D.C, 60-65; first v.pres, Capitol Hill Club, 64-67; mem. bd. dirs. and treas, Rep. Center, 66-, mem. exec. cmt, 69-; mem, Spec. Nixon-Agnew Finance Cmt, 68; exec. coordinator, Nixon Inaugural and v.chmn. and dir, Gov. Reception, 69. Bus. & Prof. Pos: Chmn, Investments in Am, 61; v.chmn. speaker bur, New York Stock Exchange, 61-64. Mil. Serv: Served as Pvt, Army, 42-45, in Inf. & Army Air Corp. Mem: Lions; CWV; Amvets; Univ. Club; Bond Club. Rel: Catholic. Mailing Add: 2500 Que St. N.W, Washington, D.C. 20007.

DIXON, HARRY DONIVAL D
Ga. State Rep.
b. Waycross, Ga, 3/24/25; s. Hughie Dixon and Mattie Woodard D; m. 8/26/46 to Ruth Starling; c. Harry Donival 'Donnie.' Educ: Wacona High Sch, 42. Polit. & Govt. Pos: Ga. State Rep, 62- Bus. & Prof. Pos: Locomotive Engineman, 46-52; R.R. Engr, 52- Mil. Serv: Maritime Serv, 43-46. Mem: Elks; Brotherhood of Locomotive Firemen and Enginemen. Rel: Baptist. Mailing Add: Waycross, Ga. 31501.

DIXON, ISAIAH, JR. D
Md. State Del.
b. Baltimore, Md, 12/23/22; s. Isaiah Dixon and Evelyn Phillips D; m. 20 years to Miriam Millard; c. Isaiah, III. Educ: Howard Univ, 3 years. Polit. & Govt. Pos: Md. State Del, 67- Bus. & Prof. Pos: Ins. broker and real estate broker. Mem: Realtist; Small Bus. Asn. Rel: Catholic. Mailing Add: 1607 W. North Ave, Baltimore, Md. 21217.

DIXON, MARGARET RICHARDSON D
b. New Orleans, La, 2/27/08; d. Roger Wolcott Richardson and Josephine Pettitt R; m. 7/10/28 to John Muncy Dixon (deceased). Educ: La. State Univ, B.A, 28; Theta Sigma Phi. Polit. & Govt. Pos: Mem. Bd. of Supvrs, La. State Univ, 51-60. Bus. & Prof. Pos: City ed, Morning Advocate, 39-42, polit. reporter and columnist, 42-, asst. managing ed, 42-45, managing ed, 45- Mem: Nat. Fedn. of Press Women; Headliner, Theta Sigma Phi, 60; Woman of Achievement, Nat. Fedn. of Press Women. Rel: Episcopal. Legal Res: Jefferson Hwy, Prairieville, La. Mailing Add: Box 13, Prairieville, La. 70769.

DIXON, PAUL RAND D
Chmn, Fed. Trade Cmn.
b. Nashville, Tenn, 9/29/13; s. James David Dixon and Sarah Munn D; m. 10/11/39 to Dores Busby; c. David Leslie and Paul Randall. Educ: Vanderbilt Univ, A.B, 36; Univ. Fla, LL.B, 38; Phi Delta Phi; Alpha Tau Omega. Polit. & Govt. Pos: Trial attorney, Fed. Trade Cmn, 38-57, chmn, 61-; chief counsel, staff dir. subcmt. antitrust and monopoly, U.S. Sen, 57-61. Bus. & Prof. Pos: Asst. football coach, Univ. Fla, 36-38. Mil. Serv: Naval Res, 42-45. Mem: Vanderbilt Univ. Alumni Asn; Am. Bar Asn; Nat. Lawyers Club; Mason. Rel: Methodist. Legal Res: 5911 Carlton Lane, Glen Mar Park, Washington, D.C. 20016. Mailing Add: Federal Trade Commission, Washington, D.C. 20580.

DIXON, R. EARL R
Fla. State Rep.
b. Bronson, Fla, 3/11/27; s. Joseph Dewey Dixon and Edythe Roberson D; m. 4/11/48 to Louise Wenzel; c. Robert and Carolyn.. Educ: Univ. Fla, B.S.A, 51, grad. work in entomology, 51; Alpha Gamma Rho. Polit. & Govt. Pos: Chmn, Pest Control Cmn. of Fla, 59-62; Fla. State Rep, Dist. 25, 68- Bus. & Prof. Pos: Dir, Jacksonville Nat. Bank, Fla. Mil. Serv: Entered as Tech. 3, Army, 46, released, 48, after serv. in Armored Cavalry and Signal Corps. Mem: Entomological Soc. of Am; Phi Sigma; past dir, Sales & Mkt. Execs. of Jacksonville; past pres. and legis. chmn, Fla. Pest Control Asn; past v.pres, Nat. Pest Control Asn; dir, Downtown Kiwanis Club; St. John's River Yacht Club and Univ. Club; bd. dir, Jacksonville Area C. of C; v.pres, Greater Jacksonville Fair Asn. Rel: Lutheran. Legal Res: 4848 Redbud Lane, Jacksonville, Fla. 32207. Mailing Add: 356 Holland Bldg, Tallahassee, Fla. 32304.

DIXON, WALTER THOMAS, SR. D
City Councilman, Baltimore, Md.
b. Columbia, S.C, 8/13/93; s. William Dixon and Mary Thompson D; m. 12/6/41 to Olivia Pierce; c. Walter T, Jr. Educ: Benedict Col, L.I, 12; Howard Univ, Commercial Dipl, 15; Cent. Col. Chiropractic, D.C, 18; Columbia Univ, B.S, 28, M.A, 32; Am. Sch. of Law, Dipl, 35; Alpha Phi Alpha. Polit. & Govt. Pos: City councilman, Fourth Dist, Baltimore, Md, 55-; mem, Md. Interracial Cmn. and mem, Hosp. Cmt, Baltimore, 60. Bus. & Prof. Pos: Dean, Peters Bus. Sch, 36-66. Mem: Mason (32°); Past Master Corinthian Lodge 18, Shrine; Odd Fellows; Elks. Rel: Episcopal. Mailing Add: 1933 McCulloh St, Baltimore, Md. 21217. (1967)

DIZE, CARLTON YANK R
Md. State Del.
b. Fairmount, Md, 12/6/13; s. James Edward Dize and Arinthia Revell D; m. 5/2/37 to Becky Justice. Educ: Crisfield High Sch. Polit. & Govt. Pos: Mem, State Rep. Cent. Cmt, Md, 46-66; Md. State Sen, 66-67; Md. State Del, 67-; alternate del, Rep. Nat. Conv, 68. Bus. & Prof. Pos: Owner, Chesapeake Motor Sales, Crisfield, Md, 50-67; pres. and owner, Crisfield CATV Inc, 62- Mem: Rotary; Elks; C. of C; Mason; Shrine; Somers Cove Yacht Club; bd. dirs, McCready Mem. Hosp; Salisbury Power Squadron; Crisfield Fire Dept; Somerset Co. Indust. Cmt. Rel: Methodist. Legal Res: Troy Rd, Crisfield, Md. 21817. Mailing Add: P.O. Box 510, Crisfield, Md. 21817.

DMITRICH, MIKE D
Utah State Rep.
b. Murray, Utah, 10/23/36; s. Dan Dmitrich and Mary Milovich D; m. 2/14/58 to Georgia Lorraine Hatsis; c. Stephanie, Michael Anthony and Dana. Educ: Utah State Univ, 1 year; Col. East. Utah, 1 year. Polit. & Govt. Pos: Utah State Rep, Dist. 55, 69- Bus. & Prof. Pos: Off. and credit mgr, Price Trading Co, Utah, 61-63; asst. cashier and asst. mgr, Walker Bank & Trust Co, Price, 64- Mem: Carbon C. of C; Price Elks; F. & A.M. Rel: Greek Orthodox. Mailing Add: 735 N. Sixth East, Price, Utah 84501.

DOANE, J. N. D
b. Clinton, Tenn, 4/15/24; s. William E. Doane and Bertha Cox D; m. 6/7/60 to Juanita Fielden; c. Carol Ann. Educ: New Market High Sch. Polit. & Govt. Pos: Campaign mgr. for Gov. Buford Ellington; mem, Jefferson Co. Planning Cmt, 65-66; Jefferson Co. campaign mgr. for Gov. Frank Clemet, 60, 54 and 52; chmn, Jefferson Co. Dem. Exec. Cmt, 58-60; Co. Hwy. Cmnr, 53-57. Bus. & Prof. Pos: Farmer. Rel: Methodist. Mailing Add: Route 2, New Market, Tenn. 37820. (1967)

DOAR, WILLIAM WALTER, JR. D
S.C. State Rep.
b. Rock Hill, S.C, 3/9/35; s. William Walter Doar and Julia Poag D; m. 8/24/57 to Louise Davis; c. Elizabeth Beckhan and Julia Terrell. Educ: Univ. S.C, B.S, 57, LL.B, 59; Omicron Delta Kappa; Kappa Alpha. Polit. & Govt. Pos: S.C. State Rep, 68- Mil. Serv: Entered as 2nd Lt, Air Force, 59, released as Capt, 62, after serv. in Judge Adv. Gen. Dept. Mem: Am. and S.C. State Asns; Rotary. Rel: Episcopal. Mailing Add: 232 Queen St, Georgetown, S.C. 29440.

DOBBINS, WILLIAM CAMELLUS D
b. Goldville (now Joanna), S.C, 4/11/16; s. William Camellus Dobbins and Cordelia Mathey D; m. 12/7/36 to Helen Blakely D; c. William C. III, James Randolph, Judy. Educ: Clemson Col, 33-36. Polit. & Gov. Pos: S.C. State Rep, 57-60, 61-62. Bus. & Prof. Pos: Businessman. Mem: Mason; Farm Bur-Charter Pres, Lions Club of Joanna. Rel: Epworth Methodist Church; Teacher, Men's Bible Class, 46-48; Bd. of Stewards. Mailing Add: Box 548 Joanna, S.C. 29351. (1967)

DOBBS, OSCAR CLARENCE D
Ala. State Rep.
b. Flatcreek, Ala, 7/11/08; s. John Thomas Dobbs and Mary Ellen Murray D; m. 3/27/26 to Winnie Pearl Quinn; c. Mary Elizabeth (Mrs. Norred). Educ: West Jefferson High Sch, 1 year. Polit. & Govt. Pos: Ala. State Rep, Dist. 13, Walker Co, 67-, mem. conserv. dept, Ala. House of Rep, 67-, mem. transportation and pub. welfare cmts, 67- Bus. & Prof. Pos: Mine foreman, Ala. By-Prod. Corp, 30-40; grocery store owner and mgr, 40-42; flagman, Ala. Great South. Rwy, 42-47; cafe operator and owner, 47- Mem: Mason; WOW; Lions Int; Farm Bur; Ment. Health Asn. Rel: Church of Christ. Legal Res: Linn's Park, Route 2, Cordova, Ala. 35550. Mailing Add: State Capitol, Montgomery, Ala. 36101.

DOBIE, GERTRUDE AGNES R
V.Chmn, Monroe Co. Rep. Cmt, Mich.
b. Wilkes Barre, Pa, 7/10/20; d. Norman A. Getz and Gertrude Loughney G; m. 11/25/38 to Edward Raymond Dobie; c. Patricia (Mrs. Fiore Custode) and Edward R, Jr. Educ: Rocky River, Ohio High Sch, grad, 38. Polit. & Govt. Pos: Former Rep. precinct chmn. and del, Mich; former secy, Monroe Co. Rep. Exec. Cmt; v.chmn, Monroe Co. Rep. Cmt, 66- Bus. & Prof. Pos: Partner, Dobie Co, 47- Mem: Former secy. bd, Am. Red Cross, Monroe Co, Mich, blood prog. chmn, currently. Rel: Methodist; Sunday Sch. secy. and mem, Cmn. of Educ, St. Paul's United Methodist Church, Monroe, Mich. Mailing Add: 3617 Lakeshore Dr, Erie Shores, Monroe, Mich. 48161.

DOBYNS, NORMAN LESTER D
b. Newport News, Va, 1/13/33; s. Lloyd Allen Dobyns and Helen Stokes D; m. 11/29/58 to Yvonne Fox; c. Barbara and Cynthia. Educ: Wash. & Lee Univ, B.A. in journalism, magna cum laude, 54; Wharton Sch. Bus, Univ. Pa; Phi Beta Kappa. Polit. & Govt. Pos: Admin. Asst. to U.S. Rep. Thomas N. Downing, Va, 60- Bus. & Prof. Pos: V.pres, pub. rels, advert. agency, Wash, D.C, 59-60; mem, Pub. Rels. and Advert. Dept, Gen. Elec. Co, 56-59. Mil. Serv: Pub. Rels. Specialist, Army, Off. of Chief of Transportation, 54-56. Mem: Pres, Gr. Springfield Commun. Coun; bd. Springfield YMCA; Fairfax Co. Civic Cultural Center Cmt; del. chmn, Fairfax Co. Fedn. of Civic Asns; alumni rep. to Wash. and Lee Univ. Intercollegiate Athletic Cmt. Rel: Protestant. 1967 Legal Res: Springfield, Va. No mailing address available. (1967)

DOCKING, GEORGE RICHARD D
b. Topeka, Kans, 2/10/31; s. George Docking and Virginia Blackwell D; m. 6/7/52 to Marcia E. Horn; c. G. Gordon, Griffith W, Kent O. and Laura G. Educ: Univ. Kans, B.S. in Bus. Admin, 52, LL.B, 57; Beta Theta Pi; Phi Delta Phi. Polit. & Govt. Pos: Pub. adminstr, Wyandotte Co, Kans, 65-69; del, Dem. Nat. Conv, 68. Bus. & Prof. Pos: Dir. and treas, Kans. Pub. Serv. Co, Lawrence, currently; dir, Highland Park Cemetary Asn, Kansas City, currently; dir, Union State Bank, currently. Mil. Serv: Entered as 2nd Lt, Air Force, 52, released as 1st Lt, 54, after serv. in Tenth Photo Flight, Alaska, 52-54. Mem: Elks; Eagles; Am. Legion; Century Club; C. of C.(dir, Kansas City Br, 65-69). Rel: Protestant. Legal Res: 6901 Garfield Dr, Kansas City, Kans. 66102. Mailing Add: 765 New Brotherhood Bldg, Kansas City, Kans. 66101.

DOCKING, MARSHALL R
b. Manhattan, Kans, 8/2/91; s. Alfred Docking and Anna Marshall D; m. 7/1/48 to Theresa Irene Malone; c. Virginia (Mrs. Bigford), William R, Josephine (Mrs. Jacobson) and Robert M. Educ: Kans. State Univ, 08-09. Polit. Pos: Kans. State Rep, 63-67; state parole officer, Kans, 33-37; sheriff,

Riley Co, Kans, 29-33; clerk of sch. dist. 41, 25-29; trustee, Zeandale Twp, Riley Co, 21-29. Bus. Pos: Serv. Supvr, Am. Dist. Telegraph Co, 37-57; farmer and stockman, until 29. Mem: Mason; Grange. Rel: Presbyterian. Mailing Add: Fall River, Kans. 67047. (1967)

DOCKING, ROBERT BLACKWELL D
Gov. of Kans.
b. Kansas City, Mo, 10/9/25; s. George Docking and Mary Virginia Blackwell D; m. 6/17/50 to Meredith Gear; c. William Russell and Thomas Robert. Educ: Univ. Kans, B.S. with honors, 48; Univ. Wis. Grad. Sch. of Banking, grad; Beta Gamma Sigma; Delta Sigma Pi; Beta Theta Pi. Polit. & Govt. Pos: Chmn, Douglas Co. Dem. Party, Kans, 54-56; v.pres, Kans. Dem. Vet, 57; former treas, Fifth Dist. Dem. Cmt; former mayor and city cmnr, Arkansas City, Kans; Gov. of Kans, 67-; mem, Am. Asn. of Criminology, currently; chmn, Interstate Oil Compact Cmn, currently. Bus. & Prof. Pos: Credit analyst, William Volker Co, 48-50; cashier and asst. trust officer, First Nat. Bank, 50-56; v.pres, Union State Ban, 56-59, pres, 59-; owner, Docking Ins. Agency, currently; asst. treas. and dir, Kans. Pub. Serv. Co, currently. Mil. Serv: Cpl, Army Air Corps, 43-46; 1st Lt, Air Force Res, 46-51. Mem: Pres, Local Govt. Research Corp, Kans. League of Munic, Ark. Basin Develop. Asn. in Kans. and Cowley Co, United Serv. Orgn; past pres, Commun. Chest, United Fund and C. of C; chmn, State of Kans. Small Bus. Admin. Adv. Bd; chmn, Joint City Cmn. of Ark. City and Winfield, 63; Am, Kans. and Cowley Co. Bankers Asns; chap. chmn, Am. Red Cross, 61-62; past comdr, Am. Legion; Kans. Bank Mgt. Cmn; Independent Oil and Gas Asn; Kans. Livestock Asn; Kans. Univ. Alumni Asn; Int. Platform Asn; Am. Asn. for UN, UNESCO; Am. G.I. Forum; Mason, Consistory, Wichita and Commandery, Ark. City, Abdallah Shrine, Kans. City; Elks; Rotary; Eagles; Moose; Cowley Co. Sportsmen's Club. Named Young Man of Year, Kans. State Jr. C. of C, 59. Rel: Presbyterian. Mailing Add: Statehouse, Topeka, Kans. 66612.

DOCKING, VIRGINIA D
b. Columbus, Miss; d. Thomas Grant Blackwell and Annie Strong Duncan B; m. to Gov. George Docking, wid; c. Robert and George Richard. Educ: Wichita State Univ; Univ. Kans, B.S; Gamma Phi Beta. Polit. & Govt. Pos: Del, Dem. Nat. Conv, 68; Publ: Column in 100 Kans. newspapers. Mem: Zonta; hon. mem, Beta Sigma Phi; Int. Platform Asn; Nat. Asn. Am. Pen Women; Kans. Authors Club; Womens Nat. Dem. Club, D.C; Sulgrave Club Wash; Topeka Civic Theatre Bd; Kans. Cultural Arts Adv. Bd; Kans. State Univ. Art Bd. Rel: Protestant. Mailing Add: 1444 Westover Rd, Topeka, Kans. 66604.

DOCTER, CHARLES ALFRED D
Md. State Del.
b. Hamburg, Germany, 8/5/31; s. Alfred J. Docter and Annie Rothschild D; m. 11/23/58 to Marcia Kaplan; c. Will Henry, Michael Warren and Adina Jo. Educ: Kenyon Col, B.A, 53; Univ. Chicago Law Sch, J.D, 56; Tau Kappa Alpha. Polit. & Govt. Pos: Staff asst. to U.S. Sen. Paul H. Douglas, 52; pres, West. Suburban Dem. Club, Montgomery Co, Md, 64-66; v.chmn, Dem. Precinct 6-1, 64-66; Md. State Del, 67- Bus. & Prof. Pos: Trustee in Bankruptcy, Mutual Security Savings & Loan Asn, Inc, 62- Mil. Serv: Entered as Seaman, Navy, 56, released as Lt, 59; Lt, Naval Res. Mem: D.C. Bar Asn; Md. State Bar Asn; B'nai B'rith; Montgomery Co. Civic Fedn; Lions. Rel: Jewish. Mailing Add: 9810 Hillridge Dr, Kensington, Md. 20795.

DODD, FRANK J. D
N.J. State Assemblyman
Educ: Upsala Col; Seton Hall Univ. Polit. & Govt. Pos: Mem, Essex Co. Young Dem, N.J; coordinator for U.S. Rep. J. G. Minish campaigns; N.J. State Assemblyman, currently. Bus. & Prof. Pos: Businessman; pres, Peter J. Dodd Asn. Mil. Serv: Essex Troop, N.J. Nat. Guard. Mem: Orange C. of C; past chmn, Cancer Crusade; Essex Co. Youth and Essex Co. Econ. Rehabilitation Cmn; Elks; Am. Legion; K. of C. Legal Res: Mountain Ave, West Orange, N.J. 07052. Mailing Add: State House, Trenton, N.J. 08625. (1967)

DODD, THOMAS J. D
U.S. Sen, Conn.
b. Norwich, Conn, 5/15/07; m. to Grace Murphy; c. Thomas J. Jr, Carolyn, Jeremy, Martha, Christopher and Nicholas. Educ: Yale Univ. Law Sch, LL.B, 33. Polit. & Govt. Pos: Exec. trial counsel for U. S. at Nurnberg, Germany, 45-46; U.S. Rep, Conn, 52-56; U.S. Sen, Conn, 58-; del, Dem. Nat. Conv, 68. Bus. & Prof. Pos: Attorney. Legal Res: Old Lyme, Conn. 06371. Mailing Add: Senate Office Bldg, Washington, D.C. 20510.

DODD, WILLIAM JOSEPH D
Supt. of Pub. Instr, La.
b. Liberty, Tex, 11/25/09; s. Daniel David Dodd and Virgina Sapp D; m. 8/28/39 to Verone Ford; c. William Ford and L. Bruce. Educ: Northwest. State Col, B.A; La. State Univ, LL.B; Phi Delta Phi; Alpha Phi Gamma. Polit. & Govt. Pos: La. State Rep, 40-48; Lt. Gov, La, 48-52; mem, La. State Dem. Cent. Cmt, 48-56; state comptroller, La, 56-60; mem, La. State Bd. of Educ, 60-64; supt. of pub. instr, La, 64- Bus. & Prof. Pos: Partner, Dodd, Hirsch, Barker, Avant and Wall, 52- Mil. Serv: Entered as Pvt, Army, 42, released as 2nd Lt, 45, after serv. in Third Armored Div, 45; ETO Ribbon. Mem: Am. Legion; VFW; Am. and La. Bar Asns; Mason; Shrine. Prfnl. Baseball, Cotton States League, 30. Rel: Baptist. Legal Res: 4472 Whitehaven, Baton Rouge, La. 70808. Mailing Add: State Capitol, Baton Rouge, La. 70804. (1967)

DODD, WILMA NEVILLE BEARDSLEE D
V.Chmn, Tenn. State Dem. Exec. Cmt.
b. Ridgely, Tenn, 1/2/09; d. Grover Cleveland Beardslee and Charlie Lou Gullette B; m. 7/8/29 to Claude Dodd. Educ: Southwest. at Memphis, 28. Polit. & Govt. Pos: Dir, Lake Co. Civil Defense Tenn, 50-66; dir, Women's Activities, State Off. Civil Defense, 58-59; state rep, Region III Civil Defense, 62-63; pres, Lake Co. Dem. Women's Club, 58-60; chmn, Lake Co. Dem. Women, 58-66; state pres, Fedn. Dem. Women, 60-61, parliamentarian, 65-66; chmn. publicity, State of Tenn. Del, Dem. Nat. Conv, 64, del, secy. Tenn. del. and rep. credentials and rules cmt, 68; mem, Exec. Cmt, W. Tenn. State Travel and Tourist Promotion Coun, 64-; v.chmn, W. Tenn. Opers. Support, 65-66; mem, Adv. Cmt, President's U.S. Civil Defense Coun, 65-66, state rep, 67-69; secy-treas, State Civil Defense Asn, 65-66, pres, 66-69; committeewoman, Eighth Cong. Dist, Tenn. State Dem. Exec. Cmt, currently and v.chmn, 67-; coordinator, Women Eighth Cong. Dist. for Dem. Nominee Ed Jones, 68. Mem: Pres, Lake Co. Bus. & Prfnl. Women's Club; nat. exec. committeewoman and past state pres, Nat. Am. Legion Auxiliary, nat. security chmn, South. Div; Past Worthy Matron and Tenn. chmn, Int. Peace Garden, Eastern Star; Muscular Dystrophy Asn. Am; Nat. Found. Muscular Dystrophy Asn; chmn, Mothers March of Dimes, 16 years. Rel: Presbyterian. Mailing Add: Sans Souci Farms, Ridgely, Tenn. 38080.

DODDS, ROBERT R. D
Iowa State Sen.
b. Burlington, Iowa, 7/27/24; s. Horace Dodds and Florence; m. to Frances; c. Luana Lee, Tami Lynette, Jeffrey, Lisa and Degee. Educ: Burlington Jr. Col. Polit. & Govt. Pos: Iowa State Rep, 3 terms; Iowa State Sen, currently. Bus. & Prof. Pos: Farmer. Mil. Serv: U.S. Army Air Force, World War II, $2\frac{1}{2}$ years. Mem: Farm Bur; Nat. Farmers Orgn; Mason; Shrine; Am. Legion; Zarapath Consistory; Eagles; DAV; Des Moines Co. Livestock Feeder Asn. William Dodds, Grandfather served in 28th, 29th, 32nd, 33rd Sessions, Iowa Gen. Assembly; Bert E. Dodds, Cousin, served in 48th, 49th, 50th, 51st Sessions. Rel: Methodist; Danville Methodist Church. Mailing Add: Danville, Iowa 52623.

DODERER, MINNETTE FRERICHS D
Iowa State Sen.
b. Holland, Iowa, 5/16/23; d. John A. Frerichs and Sophie Sherfield F; m. 8/5/44 to Fred H. Doderer; c. Dennis H.J. and Kay Lynn. Educ: State Col. Iowa; Univ. Iowa, B.A. in Econ, 48; Tau Sigma Delta. Polit. & Govt. Pos: V.Chmn, Johnson Co. Dem. Cent. Cmt, Iowa, 53-58; secy, Iowa Citizen's for Constitutional Conv, 58-60 and v.pres, Iowa Citizens for Fair Representation, 60-62; jury cmnr, Johnson-Iowa Dist. Court, 62-65; Iowa State Rep, Johnson Co, 64-68; mem. coun, State Govt. Midwest. Standing Cmt. on Higher Educ, 65-66; v.pres, Iowa Cmn. on Interstate Coop, 65-67; del, Dem. Nat. Conv, 68; Dem. Nat. Committeewoman, 68-; Iowa State Sen, 69- Mem: Nat. Soc. State Legislators (secy, 65-67); League of Women Voters; UN Asn. of U.S; Nat. Order Women Legislators; dir, Iowa Univ. Sch. Relig, 69- Rel: Methodist. Mailing Add: 2008 Dunlap Court, Iowa City, Iowa 52240.

DODGE, M. EUGENE DFL
Third V.Chmn, Third Cong. Dist. Dem-Farmer-Labor Orgn, Minn.
b. Minneapolis, Minn, 11/1/30; s. Marshall Norum Dodge and Genevieve Coursolle D; m. 9/5/50 to Joan Kedrowske; c. Charles M, Jacqueline M, Sandra A, Michael E, Terese L, Marcelle N. and James F. Educ: Univ. Minn, 1 year. Polit. & Govt. Pos: Secy, Third Cong. Dist. Dem-Farmer-Labor Orgn, Minn, 64-67, third v.chmn, 68-; Dem-Farmer-Labor cand. for Minn. State Sen, 27th Dist, 66; mem, City of Bloomington Libr. Cmt, 66-; chmn, 15th Ward Dem-Farmer-Labor Orgn, 66-67, treas, 68-; alternate del, Dem. Nat. Conv, 68. Bus. & Prof. Pos: Engr. assoc, North. States Power Co, 51- Mil. Serv: Entered as ETSSA, Navy, 51, released as ETSSN, 55, after serv. in 9-115. Mem: Am. Civil Liberties Union; Am. for Dem. Action; United World Federalists; Twin Cities Draft Info. Center; New Dem. Coalition; UN Asn. of Minn. Rel: Secular Christian. Mailing Add: 8532 Thomas Ave. S, Minneapolis, Minn. 55431.

DODGE, ROBERT MAPES R
Del. State Rep.
b. 1917. Educ: Germantown Acad, Phila; Taft Sch, Conn; Cornell Univ, N.Y. Polit. & Govt. Pos: Del. State Rep, 67- Bus. & Prof. Pos: Engr; ins. agent; appliance dealer; boat salesman; teacher; off. mgr. Mil. Serv: Coast Guard Auxiliary. Mem: U.S. Power Squad. Rel: Episcopal. Mailing Add: Canal Zone, Rehoboth Beach, Del. 19971. (1967)

DODSON, CARR GLOVER R
Ga. State Rep.
b. Americus, Ga, 8/29/37; s. William Adolfus Dodson and Mary Crisp Glover D; m. 6/18/60 to Edith Katherine Pilcher. Educ: Univ. Ga, B.B.A, 59 and LL.B, 61; Omicron Delta Kappa; Phi Delta Phi; Sigma Alpha Epsilon. Polit. & Govt. Pos: Ga. State Rep, Dist. 107, 67- Bus. & Prof. Pos: Attorney, Jones, Sparks, Benton & Cork, 64- Mil. Serv: Entered as 2nd Lt, Air Force, 61, released as Capt, 64. Mem: State Bar of Ga; Ga. and Macon Bar Asns; Civic Club of Macon; Idle Hour Country Club. Rel: Methodist. Mailing Add: 3795 Bonita Place, Macon, Ga. 31204. (1967)

DOE, RUSSELL MALLOCH R
b. Berkeley, Calif, 1/8/31; s. Russell A. Doe and Florence Malloch D; m. 11/8/52 to Marilyn Tupper; c. Russell Tupper, Elizabeth Malloch and Catherine Skelly. Educ: Univ. Calif, B.A, 52; Delta Tau Delta. Polit. & Govt. Pos: Dir, Kaweah Delta Water Conserv. Dist, Calif, 66-; secy, Tulare Co. Water Cmn, 69; mem, Calif. Rep. State Cent. Cmt, 68-69. Bus. & Prof. Pos: V.pres, Doeville Ranch, Inc, Visalia, Calif, 61- Mil. Serv: Entered as Seaman, Navy, 53, released as Lt.(jg), 56, after serv. in Tacron One, Korea. Mem: Rotary; Tulare Co. Farm Bur; Elks. Rel: Protestant. Legal Res: 2203 Green Acres Dr, Visalia, Calif. 93277. Mailing Add: P.O. Box 401, Visalia, Calif. 93277.

DOERING, LEE EVERETT R
b. Gaylord, Minn, 2/14/28; s. Edwin John Doering and Alma Rischmiller D; m. 6/14/53 to Joan Marilyn Erickson; c. Pamela Ann and Jill Suzanne. Educ: Gustavus Adolphus Col, B.A; Minneapolis-Minn. Col. of Law, B.S.L; William Mitchell Col. of Law, J.D, cum laude; Delta Theta Phi; Alpha Phi Omega. Polit. & Govt. Pos: Chmn, Lyon Co. Young Rep. League, Minn, 59; chmn, Seventh Dist. Young Rep. League, 60; treas. and finance dir, Lyon Co. Rep. Cmt, 61-63, chmn, 63-65. Mil. Serv: Entered as Pvt, Army, 46, released as Sgt, 47, after serv. in 19th Regt, 24th Div, Japan and Korea. Mem: Pres, Marshall Golf Club, 62, Marshall Shrine Club, 64, Lyon-Lincoln Bar Asn, 65 and Marshall C. of C, 69; Mason, Zuhrah Temple of the Shrine; Fifth Dist. Bar Asn; Minn. State Bar Asn; Farm Bur; Am. Legion; VFW; Isaak Walton League. Rel: Lutheran. Legal Res: 506 Summit, Marshall, Minn. 56258. Mailing Add: 509 W. Main St, Marshall, Minn. 56258.

DOERR, JOHN H. D
b. Buffalo, N.Y, 9/24/21; m. to Jean Twist; c. nine. Educ: Notre Dame Univ, A.B, 42; Fordham Univ. Sch. of Law, LL.B, 49. Polit. & Govt. Pos:

N.Y. State Sen, 64-66; confidential law secy. to Superior Court Justice W. B. Lawless, 8th Judicial Dist, 61-64; chmn. 24th Ward Dem. Cmt; p.pres. 3rd Assembly, Dist. Dem. Club. Bus. & Prof. Pos: Attorney. Mem: Erie Co, N.Y. State and Am. Bar Asns; Leo Knight Movement; Holy Name Soc. of St. Josephs' New Cathedral; Capital Hill Club; Catholic Lawyers Guild. Mailing Add: 164 Lexington Ave, Buffalo, N.Y. 14222. (1967)

DOERR, RAY E. R
Chmn, Rep. Cent. Cmt, Jackson Co, Ill.
b. Elkville, Ill, 9/3/26; s. Clyde Doerr and Ida Easterling D; m. 10/30/44 to Imogene Schimpf; c. Jeffrey Ray. Educ: High Sch. Polit. & Govt. Pos: Mayor, Vergennes, Ill, trustee, 52-60, pres, 60-; Rep. precinct committeeman, Vergennes, 61-; chmn, Rep. Cent. Cmt, Jackson Co, 64-; mem, Ill. Rep. State Cent. Cmt. Bus. & Prof. Pos: Practicing auctioneer; territory mgr, Berry Tractor Co, Inc, 50-57; dist. mgr, Massey Ferguson, Inc, 57-64, sales supvr, 63-64, sales mgr, 64- Mil. Serv: Entered as A/S, Navy, 44, released as R.T. 3, 46, after serv. in Pac; 4 Ribbons and 2 Battle Stars. Mem: Mason, Blue Lodge, Consistory; Farm Bur. Rel: Evangelical United Brethren. Mailing Add: Box 27, Vergennes, Ill. 62994. (1967)

DOERSCHLAG, WALTER A, JR. D
b. Ransom, Kans, 6/5/22; s. Walter Albert Doerschlag and Caroline Johannes D; m. 9/21/46 to Jean Ross; c. James Leonard, John Walter and Gerald Lloyd. Educ: Ft. Hays Kans. State Col, 40-42; Univ. Kans, 42-43; Phi Mu Alpha; Kappa Sigma. Polit. & Govt. Pos: Co. cmnr, Lane Co, Kans, 55-68; chmn, Lane Co. Dem. Party, 64-68. Mil. Serv: Entered as Aviation Cadet, Army Air Force, 42, released as 1st Lt, 46, after serv. in 8th Air Force, ETO, 44-45; Air Medal with 3 Oak Leaf Clusters, Purple Heart, ETO Medal with 3 Battle Stars and Arrowhead; Presidential Unit Citation. Mem: Elks; Am. Legion; VFW. Rel: Methodist. Mailing Add: 2925 Walnut, Hays, Kans. 67601.

DOFFING, GODFREY RAYMOND D
Chmn, Dakota Co. Dem-Farmer-Labor Party, Minn.
b. Tintah, Minn, 8/25/18; s. John P. Doffing and Mary Stump D; m. 11/30/46 to Lorraine Blatz; c. Bernice and Adine. Educ: Hastings Col; Int. Correspondence Sch, 2 year course in labor rels. Polit. & Govt. Pos: V.chmn, Dakota Co. Dem-Farmer-Labor Party, Minn, 62-64, chmn, 64-; mem, City Coun, South St. Paul, 66; alternate del, Dem. Nat. Conv, 68. Bus. & Prof. Pos: Chmn, Bargaining Cmt, Local 167, UPWA, 55-58, pres, 58-63; mem, United Fund Exec. Bd, 59-62; v.pres, First Dist, State AFL-CIO Exec. Bd, 59-64. Mil. Serv: Entered as Pvt, Army, 41, released as S/Sgt, 43, after serv. in 37th Inf. Div, Pac; Purple Heart; Expert Rifleman Medal. Mem: VFW; K. of C. Rel: Catholic. Mailing Add: 144 W. Spruce, South St. Paul, Minn. 55075. (1967)

DOGGETT, ROSWELL CHRISTOPHER D
b. Bolinger, 10/2/28; s. Idrain Doggett and Emmie Louise McCrory D; m. 2/24/50 to Carolyn Patsy Scott; c. Chris, Cym. Educ: Livingston State Col, B.S, 50. Polit. & Govt. Pos: Ala. State Rep, 63-67; chmn, Bd. of Registrs, 2 years. Bus. & Prof. Pos: Owner, mgr. shoe store in Butler. Mil. Serv: Air Force, 51-55. Rel: Methodist. Mailing Add: Butler, Ala. 36904. (1967)

DOHERTY, C.L. 'ROY' R
Pub. Utilities Cmnr, S.Dak.
b. Waterloo, Nebr, 9/19/89; m. Martina Binckly; c. Two sons and four daughters. Educ: Fremont Col, grad. with honors; State Sch. Mines, Rapid City, S.Dak. Polit. & Govt. Pos: City cmnr. and mayor, Rapid City, S.Dak, formerly; S.Dak. Pub. Utilities Cmnr, 36, 40-; pres, Nat. Asn. of R.R. & Pub. Utilities Cmnrs, 53 & 54, mem. exec. cmt, currently. Mem: Dir, C. of C; pres, Retail Merchants Asn. and State Pharmaceutical Asn; dist. gov. Rotary, 57 & 59. Rel: Episcopal. Mailing Add: Public Utilities Commission, Rapid City, S.Dak. 57701.

DOHERTY, EDWARD WILLIAM R
N.Dak. State Sen.
b. Killdeer, N.Dak. 12/16/21; s. I.L. Doherty and Laura Stein D; m. 2/14/47 to Norma Hyland; c. Sharon (Mrs. Richard Olson); Larry and Shelley. Educ: Jamestown Col, B.S, 43. Polit. & Govt. Pos: Mem, 48th Legis. Dist. Rep. State Cent. Cmt. and Rep. Exec. Cmt, 54-57; state Rep. campaign dir, 60; campaign dir, Mark Andrews for Congressman, 63 & 66, on staff, 66; treas, 13th Dist. Rep. Party; Rep. cand. for Gov. N.Dak, 68; N.Dak. State Sen, 13th Legis. Dist, 68- Bus. & Prof. Pos: Ed. and co-publisher, The Killdeer Herald, N.Dak, 46-61; New Rockford Transcript, 61- Mil. Serv: Entered as Midn, Naval Res, 42, released as Lt.(jg), 46, after serv. aboard Destroyers, Pac. Theatre, 44-46; engaged in 7 major campaigns; Philippine Serv. Ribbon with 2 campaign stars. Mem: Sigma Delta Chi; Am. Legion; VFW; Elks; Eagles; K. of C; N.Dak. Stockmen's Asn. Rel: Catholic. Legal Res: 103 N. First St, New Rockford, N.Dak. 58356. Mailing Add: Box 1000, New Rockford, N.Dak. 58356.

DOHERTY, WALTER GERARD R
Press Secy, Mich. Rep. State Cent. Cmt.
b. Cincinnati, Ohio, 9/24/34; s. David Louis Doherty and Mary Bundy D; m. 6/12/65 to Mary Ann Kennett; c. Justin Michael, Ian Patrick and Kathleen Elizabeth. Educ: St. John's Univ, N.Y, B.A, 56; Sigma Rho. Polit. & Govt. Pos: Press Secy, Mich. Rep. State Cent. Cmt, 69- Bus. & Prof. Pos: Gen. ed, NCAA Serv. Bur, N.Y, 56-59; sports info. dir, Univ. Detroit, Mich, 60-63; asst. pub. rels. dir, Detroit Race Course and racing off, Hazel Park Race Course, 63; asst. pub. rels. dir, Arlington Park Race Course, Ill, 64; dir. pub. rels, Sinai Hosp. of Detroit, Mich, 65-69. Mil. Serv: Entered as Pvt, N.Y. Nat. Guard Army Res, 52, released as SP-4, 59, after serv. in 42nd Signal Co, 365th Field Artil. Bn. Rel: Roman Catholic. Mailing Add: 27840 Berkshire, Southfield, Mich. 48075.

DOHMEN, JAMES JOSEPH D
b. Colome, S.Dak, 4/29/25; s. William J. Dohmen and Marie Casey D; single. Educ: Colome High Sch, S.Dak, 4 years. Polit. & Govt. Pos: Tripp Co. chmn, McGovern for Senate, 62 & 68 and Robert Kennedy for Pres, 68; del, Dem. Nat. Conv, 68. Bus. & Prof. Pos: Farmer, 46-56; owner, retail bus, 56-64; owner, Dohmen Real Estate and Ins. Co, Winner, S.Dak, 60- Mil. Serv: Entered Army, 50, released as Pfc, 51, after serv. in Korea; Purple Heart; Good Conduct Medal; Korean Serv. Medal. Mem: VFW; Am. Legion; DAV; Elks; K. of C. All-State-Post Comdr, VFW, 62-63, Outstanding Dist. Comdr, S.Dak, 66-67. Rel: Catholic. Legal Res: 929 E. Fifth, Winner, S.Dak. 57580. Mailing Add: Box 546, Winner, S.Dak. 57580.

DOI, NELSON K. D
b. Pahoa, Hawaii, 1/1/22; m; c. One son and one daughter. Educ: Univ. of Hawaii; Univ. of Minn. Law Sch. Polit. & Govt. Pos: Dep. co. attorney, Hawaii, 49-52, co. attorney, 53; del, State Constitutional Conv, 50 & 68; Territorial Sen, 55-59; Hawaii State Sen, 59-69, pres, Hawaii State Senate, 63-68; first judge, Third Circuit Court, 69- Bus. & Prof. Pos: Attorney-at-law, currently. Mailing Add: 1179 Kahoa Rd, Hilo, Hawaii 96720.

DOLAN, JOHN F. R
Mass. State Rep.
b. 1923; married; c. Two. Polit. & Govt. Pos: Town clerk, Ipswich, Mass; selectman; vet. agent; mem, Ipswich Rep. Town Cmt; mem, Bd. of Trustees, Hillside Sch. for Boys, Marlboro; mem, Conserv. Cmn; Mass. State Rep, 66-, mem, Rep. Adv. Cmt, Mass. State House of Rep. Mem: Am. Legion; VFW; Mass. Audubon Soc; Odd Fellows; Nat. Wildlife Fedn; Nat. Trust for Historic Preservation. Mailing Add: 39 East St, Ipswich, Mass. 01938. (1967)

DOLAN, JOSEPH CHARLES D
b. South Fork, Pa, 3/1/06; s. Samuel J. Dolan and Isabella Kirchner D; m. 12/28/31 to Naomi Ruth Foust; c. Ruth N, Joseph C, Jr. and Mary Anne. Educ: St. Francis Col; Theta Kappa Phi. Polit. & Govt. Pos: Chmn, Cambria Co. Dem. Party, Pa, 40-42; prothonotary, Cambria Co, 48-; del, Dem. Nat. Conv, 68. Bus. & Prof. Pos: Teacher and head of Eng. dept, Gallitzin High Sch, 28-34; basketball coach and comdr, Catholic Civic Clubs Camp, Pine Grove Furnace, Pa, 34-37. Mil. Serv: Entered as Capt, Army, 40, released as Col, 47, after serv. in Middle Pac. Area; Brig. Gen, Pa. Nat. Guard, (Ret). Mem: VFW; Am. Legion; CWV; Elks. Rel: Catholic. Mailing Add: 223 Churchill St, Johnstown, Pa. 19501. (1967)

DOLBASHIAN, EDWARD MARTIN R
Mem, R.I. State Rep. Cent. Cmt.
b. Providence, R.I, 8/28/22; s. Digran Dolbashian and Agavne Kelisian D; m. 6/29/57 to Ann Stanborough Towle; c. Felice Ann and Kenneth Richard. Educ: Brown Univ, A.B, 48; Boston Univ, LL.B, 51. Polit. & Govt. Pos: Chmn, Portsmouth Town Rep. Cmt, R.I, 52-62; mem, R.I. State Rep. Cent. Cmt, 52-, counsel, 54-62; del, R.I. Constitutional Conv, 64. Bus. & Prof. Pos: Partner, Law Firm of Dolbashian & Chappell, 52- Mil. Serv: Entered as Pvt, Army, 42, released as T-5, 45, after serv. in 28th Field Hosp, Aleutians, 43-44, ETO, 44-45; Asiatic Pac. and Am. Theaters and ETO Ribbons. Mem: Brown Clubs of R.I. and Newport Co; Newport Co. and Am. Bar Asns; VFW. Rel: Episcopal. Mailing Add: 600 Boyds Lane, Portsmouth, R.I. 02871. (1967)

DOLE, HOLLIS M. R
Asst. Secy. for Mineral Resources, Dept. of the Interior
b. Paonia, Colo; m. to Ruth Josephine Mitchell; c. Two. Educ: Ore. State Univ, B.S. in Geol, 40, M.S, 42; Univ. Calif, Los Angeles and Univ. Utah, econ. geol. Polit. & Govt. Pos: Mem. staff, Bur. of Mines, Scappoose, Ore, 42 and Geol. Surv, Tucson, Ariz, 46; former Ore. State geologist and dir, Ore. Dept. of Geol. and Minerals Industs; former gen. reporter for Ore, Interstate Oil Compact Cmn; testified before House and Senate Interior Cmts. on hearings regarding gold and chrome probs; Asst. Secy. for Mineral Resources, Dept. of the Interior, 69- Bus. & Prof. Pos: Mem. staff, Bohemia Mines, Cottage Grove, Ore, 34-35 and Am. Trust Co, Palo Alto, Calif, 35-37; former col. instr. geol, Portland and Salt Lake City. Mil. Serv: Entered Navy, 42, released as Lt, 45. Publ: Numerous tech. publ. on mineral resources. Mem: Am. Asn. Petroleum Geologists; Asn. of Am. State Geologists; Ore. Acad. of Sci. Mailing Add: Dept. of the Interior, C St. between 18th & 19th St. N.W, Washington, D.C. 20240.

DOLE, ROBERT J. R
U.S. Sen, Kans.
b. Russell, Kans, 7/22/23; s. Doran R. Dole and Bina D; m. 6/12/48 to Phyllis E. Holden; c. Robin. Educ: Univ. Kans, Lawrence; Washburn Munic. Univ, Topeka, A.B. and LL.B. magna cum laude, 52; Kappa Sigma. Polit. & Govt. Pos: Kans. State Rep, 51-53; co. attorney, Russell Co, 53-61; U.S. Rep, First Cong. Dist, Kans, 60-68; U.S. Sen, Kans, 69-, mem, Agr. and Forestry Cmt, Pub. Works Cmt, Select Cmt. Nutrition and Human Needs and Select Cmt. Small Bus, U.S. Senate. Mil. Serv: Entered as 2nd Lt, Army, 43, released as Capt, 48, after serv. in 10th Mt. Div, Italy; Bronze Star with Oak Leaf Cluster; Combat Inf. Badge; Purple Heart with Oak Leaf Cluster. Mem: Russell Co, Kans. and Am. Bar Asns; pres, Kans. Co. Attorney's Asn, 57; pres, Washburn Alumni Asn; Mason; Shrine; past lt. gov, Kiwanis; C. of C; Am. Legion; VFW; DAV; former chmn, Russell Co. Red Cross; Elks; Boy Scouts; Girl Scouts; 4-H Fair Asn; chmn, Kans. Kiwanis Found. Campaign, 69. Rel: Methodist. Legal Res: Russell, Kans. Mailing Add: U.S. Senate Office Bldg, Washington, D.C. 20510.

DOLEZAL, GEORGE E. R
b. Chicago, Ill, 11/8/19; married; c. five daughters. Educ: DePaul Univ; John Marshall Law Sch. Polit. & Govt. Pos: Past pres, Young Rep. Orgn, Berwyn, Ill; Alderman, First Ward, Berwyn; Ill. State Rep, 4 terms; Mayor, Berwyn, 65-68; assoc. judge, Circuit Court of Cook Co, 68- Bus. & Prof. Pos: Lawyer, Firm of Rathje, Kulp, Sabel, Sullivan. Mil. Serv: 1st Lt, Combat Engrs, infantryman, in S.France and Germany, Seventh Army; Bronze Star. Mem: Chicago and Am. Bar Asns; Am. Legion; Mason (32°); Shrine. Mailing Add: 7010 34th St, Berwyn, Ill. 60402.

DOLL, BERNARD THOMAS R
Chmn, Chippewa Co. Rep. Cmt.
b. Sault Ste Marie, Mich, 12/30/20; s. Edward Doll and Mary Elizabeth Tardiff D; m. 2/10/45 to Elizabeth Donna Ploegstra; c. Nancy Elizabeth (Mrs. Joe Carter), Phyllis Kathryn (Mrs. Loren Jones), Bernard Edward, Teresa Anne, Patrica Jean, Connie Marie and Mary Kay. Educ: Mich. State Univ. grad. course dairy mfg. Polit. & Govt. Pos: Del, Rep. State Cmt; mem. Chippewa Co. Rep. Exec. Cmt; local Rep. del, chmn, Chippewa Co. Rep. Cmt, currently; supvr, Bruce Twp, 59- Bus. & Prof. Pos: Dairy Farmer. Mem: Nat. Milk Prod. Fedn.(nat. dir); State Asn. Supvr. and State Asn. Assessors;

Mich. Milk Prod. Asn.(bd. dirs, 60, dist. dir. and pres); secy, Chippewa Co-Sault Ste Marie Airport Bd; trustee, War Mem. Hosp. Bd; treas, City-Co. Bldg. Authority; Chippewa Co. Planning Cmt; Farm Bur; K. of C.(4°); Munuscong Golf Club. Serv. award as past mem. and chmn, Chippewa Co. Bd. Supvr. Rel: Catholic; Bldg. Cmt; mem. Barbeau Catholic Church. Mailing Add: Route 1, Dafter, Mich. 49724.

DOLLARD, LOUISE FREDERIKKE CHARLOTTE D
b. N.Y.C, 11/23/22; d. Jens Christian Björndal and Martha Bruun B; m. 6/3/45 to Andrew Fulton Dollard; c. Elizabeth Marie. Educ: Hellerupgaard, Copenhagen, Denmark, B.S; Trailblazers; Danish Walking Asn; Ladies Rowing Club, Copenhagen. Polit. & Govt. Pos: Committeewoman, Fairfax Co. Dem. Party, Va, 54-56; legis. asst. to U.S. Rep. Walter S. Baring, Nev, 59- Bus. & Prof. Pos: Researcher, Danish Embassy, Wash, D.C, 43-45; admin-secretarial work, Dept. of State, 45-47; staff researcher, Capital Airlines, 54-59. Mem: League of Women Voters, Fairfax Co, Va; Fairfax Golf and Country Club. Rel: Episcopal. Mailing Add: 3411 Park Hill Place, Fairfax, Va. 22030.

DOLLEY, STEPHAN BLAND, JR. D
b. Gastonia, N.C, 11/16/29; s. Col. S. B. Dolley and Eunice P. D; m. 8/25/54 to Julia B. Page; c. Gladys Frances, Julia Page, Eunice Aurora, Edith Marshall. Educ: Univ. N.C, A.B, 50; Univ. N.C. Law Sch, LL.B, 53. Polit. & Govt. Pos: N.C. State Rep, 59-66; Gastonia Cnty. Young Dems. Bus. & Prof. Pos: Lawyer. Mil. Serv: U.S.A. Res, 50-56. Mem: Gaston Bar Asn; Sigma Phi Epsilon; Delta Theta Phi; past comdr, Am. Legion Post 23; Gastonia Optimist Club; Voiture Locale 1416; La Societe Des 40 Hommes et 8 Chevaux; Eagles. Rel: Methodist. Mailing Add: 101 S. Belvedere St, Gastonia, N.C. 28052. (1967)

DOLLIVER, JAMES I. R
b. Park Ridge, Ill, 8/31/94; s. Robert Henry Dolliver and Mary Elle Barrett D; m. 9/4/28 to Rachel McCreight; c. James M, Arthur M, Margaret E. and Robert H. Educ: Morningside Col, Iowa, A.B, 15; Univ. Chicago, J.D, 21. Polit. & Govt. Pos: Regional Legal Counsel, Int. Coop. Admin, Iran, Iraq, Lebanon, Jordan, Egypt and Lybia; U.S. Rep, Iowa, 45-57. Mil. Serv: Entered as Pvt, Army, 18, released as 2nd Lt, 18. Mem: Iowa Bar Asn; Mason; Am. Legion (Dept. Comdr, Iowa, 37-38); Farm Bur; Rotary. Rel: Methodist. Mailing Add: R.F.D. 3, Spirit Lake, Iowa 51360.

DOLWIG, RICHARD J. R
Calif. State Sen.
b. N. Dak. Educ: Univ. N. Dak; Ohio State Law Sch; Stanford Univ. Law Sch. and Grad. Sch. of Bus. Polit. & Govt. Pos: Calif. State Assemblyman, 47-57; Calif. State Sen, 56- Bus. & Prof. Pos: Attorney-at-law. Mil. Serv: U.S. Army, World War II, 42-46. Mem: Elks; Eagles; Commonwealth Club; Am. Legion; Amvet; San Mateo Co. Bar Asn.(past pres). Mailing Add: 181 Second Ave, San Mateo, Calif. 94401.

DOMINICK, D. CLINTON, III R
N.Y. State Sen.
b. Newburgh, N.Y, 6/14/18; s. DeWitt C. Dominick; m. to Nancy Ragan; c. Three sons and two daughters. Educ: Va. Mil. Inst; Columbia Univ. Law Sch. Polit. & Govt. Pos: Mem, Orange Co. Rep. Cmt, N.Y; mem, N.Y. Rep. State Cmt; N.Y. State Assemblyman, 55-58; N.Y. State Sen, 58- Bus. & Prof. Pos: Lawyer, Dominick & Fogarty; bd. of dirs, Highland Nat. Bank of Newburgh. Mil. Serv: Army, Lt. Col, 5½ years, Ninth Army, Europe; Honor Grad. Army Command and Gen. Staff Col, Ft. Leavenworth, Kans, 57; N.Y. Nat. Guard; Col, Army Res. Mem: Past pres, Newburgh Kiwanis; Am. Legion; VFW; F&AM; past pres, Newburgh City Bar Asn; Orange Co. and N.Y. State Bar Asns. Rel: Methodist; Trustee. Mailing Add: Sloane Rd, R.D. 1, Newburgh, N.Y. 12550. (1967)

DOMINICK, PETER HOYT R
U.S. Sen, Colo.
b. Stamford, Conn, 7/7/15; s. Gayer G. Dominick (deceased) and Eleanor Hoyt D.(deceased); m. 7/12/40 to Nancy Parks; c. Peter, Jr, Sandy, Michael and Lynne. Educ: Yale Univ, B.A, 37, Law Sch, LL.B, 40; Phi Delta Phi; Fence Club; Scroll and Keys. Polit. & Govt. Pos: Colo. State Rep, 57-61; U.S. Rep, Colo, 61-63; U.S. Sen, Colo, 63-; del, Rep. Nat. Conv, 68. Bus. & Prof. Pos: Partner, Holland & Hart, Denver, Colo, 47-61. Mil. Serv: Entered as Cadet, Army-Air Corps, 42, released as Capt, 45, after serv. in Training and Transport Command and China-Burma-India Theatre; Air Medal with Cluster; Distinguished Flying Cross; Col, Air Force Res, 61- Mem: Am, Colo, Denver and Arapahoe Co. Bar Asns; C. of C; VFW. Rel: Episcopal. Legal Res: 5050 E. Quincy, Englewood, Colo. 80110. Mailing Add: Old Senate Office Bldg, Washington, D.C. 20510.

DOMINICK, RICHARD FAHEY D
Ala. State Sen.
b. Birmingham, Ala, 10/26/27; s. Richard Bascom Dominick and Nell Fahey D; m. 4/26/58 to Charlotte Lane; c. Richard Lane and Dirksen Lane. Educ: Univ. Ala, B.S, 50; Birmingham Sch. Law, LL.B, 57; Kappa Alpha Order. Polit. & Govt. Pos: Ala. State Rep, 62-66; Ala. State Sen, 67- Mil. Serv: Entered as Seaman 3/C, Navy, released as Seaman 1/C. Mem: Am, Ala. and Birmingham Bar Asns. Rel: Methodist. Mailing Add: 927 Brown Marx Bldg, Birmingham, Ala. 35203. (1967)

DOMITROVICH, FRANK ANTHONY D
b. Ontonagon, Mich, 10/8/26; s. Frank S. Domitrovich and Mary Strebenac D; m. 10/23/48 to Mary Jane Amich; c. Carl M, Dorothy A, John A, Cathy H, Thomas M. and Gerald F. Educ: Mich. State Col, 47. Polit. & Govt. Pos: Supvr, Ontonagon Twp, Mich, 55-58; mem. and pres, Ontonagon Twp. Sch. Bd, 57-65; juvenile officer, Ontonagon Co, 59-65; chmn, Ontonagon Co. Dem. Cmt, 66-69; v.pres, Gogebic-Ontonagon Intermediate Sch. Dist, 67- Bus. & Prof. Pos: Secy-treas, Dick Wagner Ins. Agency, Inc, Ontonagon, Mich, 65-69. Mil. Serv: Entered as Pvt, Army, 44, released as S/Sgt, 46, after serv. in Third Army, ETO, 45-46. Mem: Upper Peninsula Ins. Agents Asn; VFW; Lions; K. of C. Rel: Catholic. Legal Res: Route 2, Ontonagon, Mich. 49953. Mailing Add: 234 River St, Ontonagon, Mich. 49953.

DOMONOSKE, MERTON ELZWICK R
b. Berkeley, Calif, 1/11/23; s. Arthur Boquer Domonoske and Gladys Eloise Boydstun D; m. 8/19/50 to Nadine Marie Hursh. Educ: Univ. Nev, B.S, 47; State Col. Wash, grad. work; Scabbard and Blade; Sigma Rho Delta. Polit. & Govt. Pos: Finance chmn, Churchill Co. Rep. Cent. Cmt, Nev, 58-60, chmn, 62-67; councilman, Fallon, 60-, mayor pro tem, 63-; mem, Nev. State Rep. Cent. Cmt, 62-; mem, Nev. State Legis. Cmt, 62-; dir, Nev. Munic. Asn, 63- Bus. & Prof. Pos: Co. supvr, Farmers Home Admin, Dept. of Agr, 48-52; ins. agent and real estate broker, E.H. Hursh Gen. Ins, 52-60; corp. secy, E.H. Hursh, Inc, 60- Mil. Serv: Entered as Pvt, Army, 42, released as 1st Lt, 46, after serv. in 165th Inf, 27th Div, Pac; Asiatic Pac. Medal, Bronze Star; Am. Campaign Medal; Victory Medal; Army of Occup. Medal; Combat Inf. Badge. Mem: North. Nev. Independent Ins. Agents Asn; Am. Legion; VFW; Rotary; Elks; F&AM; Shrine; RAM; RSM; C. of C. Rel: Protestant. Mailing Add: 376 W. Williams Ave, Fallon, Nev. 89406. (1967).

DONAHEY, GERTRUDE WALTON D
b. Goshen, Ohio, 8/4/08; d. George Sebastian Walton and Mary Ann Thomas W; m. 4/12/30 to John W. Donahey (deceased); c. John William, Jr. Educ: Bus. Col. Polit. & Govt. Pos: Oper. support chmn, Ohio Dem. Party, 63-, mem-at-lg, State Platform Cmt, 64 & 68; field aide in Cent. and South. Ohio for U.S. Sen. Stephen M. Young, Ohio, 63-69, staff asst, 69-; del, Dem. Nat. Conv, 64, del-at-lg. and mem. Platform and Resolutions Cmt, 68. Bus. & Prof. Pos: Private secretarial work until 30; vol. work for commun. orgn, Ohio, 30- Mem: Secy, mem. exec. cmt. and state bd. mem, Ohio Ment. Health Asn. Rel: Episcopal. Mailing Add: 2838 Sherwood Rd, Columbus, Ohio 43209.

DONAHUE, JOSEPH PATRICK D
b. Waterbury, Conn, 4/11/17; s. Patrick Donahue and Mary Margaret Mulhall D; m. 6/6/40 to Teresa G. Sweeney; c. Patricia Ann, Jill Mary, Joseph Patrick. Polit. & Govt. Pos: Admin. asst, U.S. Rep. John Stephen Monagan, Conn, at present and to Rep. Smith, Conn, 38-41; former dep. judge, Naugatuck Court. Bus. & Prof. Pos: Reporter, A.P, Wash. and N. Haven, 41-43; Ed, Naugatuck News, 43-61. Mil. Serv: T/Sgt, 1st Marine Div, S. Pac; Bronze Star. Mem: Elks; Marine Corps League; Nat. Press Club; VFW. Legal Res: Naugatuck, Conn. Mailing Add: 1201 Longworth House Office Bldg, Washington, D.C. 20515. (1967)

DONAHUE, R. PATRICK D
b. Detroit, Mich, 12/3/31; s. Thomas J. Donahue and Agnes Lappin D; m. 10/19/63 to Barbara Muldoon; c. R. Patrick, Jr, Kathleen Anne and Daniel Joseph. Educ: Univ. Mich, A.B. in Econ. and LL.B, 57; Delta Theta Phi. Polit. and Govt. Pos: Chmn, 14th Cong. Dist. Dem. Party, Mich, 67-68; del, Dem. Nat. Conv, 68; traffic court referee, Detroit, Mich, 68- Bus. & Prof. Pos: Practicing attorney, Detroit, Mich, 57-68. Mil. Serv: Capt, Air Force Res, currently. Mem: Detroit and Mich. Bar Asns. Rel: Roman Catholic. Mailing Add: 4645 Haverhill, Detroit, Mich. 48224.

DONAHUE, RICHARD KING D
b. Lowell, Mass, 7/20/27; s. Joseph Paul Donahue and Dorothy Riordan D; m. 9/19/53 to Nancy Lawson; c. Gail, Timothy, Michael, Nancy, Richard, Jr, Daniel, Stephen, Christopher and Tara. Educ: Dartmouth, A.B, 48; Boston Univ. Sch. of Law, LL.B, 51. Polit. & Govt. Pos: Expert consult. to Postmaster Gen, 64-; v.chmn, Mass. Dem. State Cmt, 56-64; asst. to President John F. Kennedy, 60-63; dept. dir. of orgn, Dem. Nat. Cmt, 60; mem, Lowell Sch. Cmt, 52-56. Bus. & Prof. Pos: Partner, Donahue & Donahue, 51-66. Mil. Serv: A/S, Navy, 45, released as Seaman 1/C, 46. Rel: Catholic. Legal Res: 52 Belmont Ave, Lowell, Mass. 01852. Mailing Add: 21 George St, Lowell, Mass. 01852. (1967)

DONALD, ANN CARBERRY R
Chmn, Sweet Grass Co. Rep. Cent. Cmt, Mont.
b. Dayton, Ohio, 6/6/19; d. Robert Black Carberry and Margaret Oliver C; m. 6/6/46 to William Henderson Donald; c. Eleanor Louisa and William Henderson, III. Educ: St. Mary's Sch, New York; Katharine Gibbs Sch. Polit. & Govt. Pos: Chmn, Sweet Grass Co. Rep. Cent. Cmt, Mont, 62- Rel: Episcopal. Mailing Add: Melville, Mont. 59055.

DONALD, ROBERT HICKS, II D
Miss. State Rep.
b. Quitman, Miss, 9/7/25; s. Robert Hicks Donald and Mae Alice Martin D; m. 1/1/49 to Julia Sue Patton; c. Kathy Sue, Betty N, Mae Alice, Robert H, III and James Patton. Educ: Miss. State Univ, 3½ years; Sigma Alpha Epsilon; Scabbard and Blade. Polit. & Govt. Pos: Alderman, Quitman, Miss, 65-67; Miss. State Rep, 36th Dist, 68- Bus. & Prof. Pos: Mgr, Quitman Motor Co, Miss, 51-66; owner, Donald Construction, 66-69; ins. agent, State Farm Ins, 67- Mil. Serv: Entered as Pvt, Air Force, 43, released as Cpl, 46, after serv. in 489th Bomb Group, U.S.A, 45-46. Mem: Am. Legion. Rel: Methodist. Legal Res: 203 S. Jackson Ave, Quitman, Miss. 39355. Mailing Add: P.O. Box 183, Quitman, Miss. 39355.

DONALDSON, CHARLES RUSSELL Non-Partisan
Assoc. Justice, Supreme Court of Idaho
b. Helena, Mont, 2/2/19; s. Charles M. Donaldson and Mabel King D; m. 4/1/44 to Jeanne Coleman; c. Karen Elliott, Holly, Jean, Laurel, Sarah and Charles. Educ: Willamette Univ, 37-38; Univ. Idaho, B.A. and LL.B, 48; Delta Tau Delta; Phi Alpha Delta. Polit. & Govt. Pos: Idaho State Rep, Ada Co, 55-57; Dist. judge, Ada, Elmore, Boise and Valley Co, 64-68; assoc. justice, Supreme Court Idaho, 69- Bus. & Prof. Pos: Private practice law, Boise, 48-64. Mil. Serv: Entered as Pvt, Army, 42, released as Capt, 45, after serv. in Signal Intel, Italy, 44-45. Rel: Methodist. Mailing Add: 621 Highland View Dr, Boise, Idaho 83702.

DONALDSON, JOHN WEBER R
Ind. State Rep.
b. Lebanon, Ind, 10/13/26; s. Fred Raymond Donaldson and Esther Ann Coombs D; m. 11/22/53 to Sara Jane Rudolph; c. Carmen Jane, Cathy Ann and John Bradford. Educ: U.S. Naval Acad, 45-48; DePauw Univ, A.B, 51; Ind. Univ. Sch. Law, J.D, 54; Delta Theta Phi; Beta Theta Pi. Polit. & Govt. Pos: Co. chmn, Young Rep, Ind, 54-56; Ind. State Rep, 56-58 & 60-; mem, Ind. Judicial Study Cmn, 65-; city attorney, Lebanon, 66-68. Mil. Serv: Entered as A/S, Navy, 44, released as Midshipman 1/C, 49; Am. Theatre and Victory Medals. Mem: Boone Co. Bar Asn.(pres, 58-65); Ind. and Am. Bar Asns; past pres, Kiwanis; past dir, Jaycees; past pres, Co. United Fund; dir, Red

Cross and Cancer Soc; Elks; Am. Legion; DAV; C. of C; Lebanon Armory Bd. Distinguished Serv. Award, Outstanding Commun. Serv, Lebanon Jaycees, 57. Rel: Presbyterian; Choir Mem, Ordained Elder and Deacon. Mailing Add: 2101 Elizaville Rd, Lebanon, Ind. 46052.

DONALDSON, LEE A, JR. R
Pa. State Rep.
b. Etha, Pa, 8/11/25; s. Lee A. Donaldson and Mildred Whitehill D; m. to Katherine Marner; c. Three. Educ: Allegheny Col, A.B; Univ. Pitts. Sch. of Law, LL.B. Polit. & Govt. Pos: Pa. State Rep, 54-; del, Rep. Nat. Conv, 68. Bus. & Prof. Pos: Practicing attorney before U.S. Dist. Court, Pittsburgh, Appellate Courts of Pa. and Allegheny Co. Courts. Mil. Serv: Army, overseas. Mem: Allegheny Co. Bar Asn; Phi Gamma Delta; Etna Sportsmen's Club; Past Exalted Ruler, Elks; Am. Legion. Mailing Add: 2648 Miller Dr, Allison Park, Pa. 15101. (1967)

DONEGAN, GEORGE J. R
Mo. State Rep.
b. St. Louis, Mo, 5/23/23; s. Samuel Patrick Donegan and Anna Catherine Cunningham D; m. 1/15/43 to Elizabeth Sheppard; c. George, Jr, Elizabeth Ann, Cecilia, Michael, Kathleen, Mary Darby, Patrick, Laura, Timothy, Sean and Charles. Educ: Drury Col, B.A. cum laude in econ, 47; Georgetown Univ. Sch. Law, J.D, 50; Phi Delta Phi; Sigma Nu. Polit. & Govt. Pos: Asst. dist. counsel, Off. Price Stabilization, D.C, 51-52; trial attorney, criminal div, Justice Dept, 52-54; Asst. U.S. Attorney, D.C, 54-56; chmn, Publicity Cmt, Greene Co. Rep. Party, Mo, 58; co-chmn, Nixon Rally, Springfield, 60 and chmn, 68; chmn, Goldwater Rally, 64; Mo. State Rep, 143rd Dist, 67-; mem, Election Law Study Cmn of Mo; cmnr, Greene Co. Welfare Off; chmn, Springfield Housing Authority. Bus. & Prof. Pos: Partner, Miller, Fairman, Sanford, Carr & Lowther, 56-65; pvt. law practice, currently. Mil. Serv: Entered as Pvt, Army, 43, released as Cpl, 46, after serv. in Air Force, Army Specialized Training Prog. and Army Hq, Ft. Devens, Mass. Mem: Mo. and Am. Bar Asns; Greene Co. Bar Asn.(pres, 61); K. of C.(state advocate, 60-62); dir. and past pres, United Fund of Springfield & Greene Co, 64; dir, Community Youth Center, Springfield Boys' Club, adv. bd, Mercy Villa and Southwest Mo. Ecumenical Center. Rel: Roman Catholic. Legal Res: 1471 E. Meadowmere, Springfield, Mo. 65804. Mailing Add: 1714-18 E. Meadowmere, Springfield, Mo. 65804.

DONELSON, LEWIS R, III R
Mem, Tenn. State Rep. Exec. Cmt.
b. Memphis, Tenn, 10/9/17; s. Lewis R. Donelson, Jr. and Katherine Campbell D; m. 2/3/45 to Janice Ost; c. Janice, Lewis R, IV and Loring. Educ: Southwestern at Memphis, B.A, 38; Georgetown Univ, LL.B, 41; Omicron Delta Kappa. Polit. & Govt. Pos: State chmn, Citizens for Eisenhower, Tenn, 56; pres, Shelby Co. Rep. Asn, 62-64; del, Rep. Nat. Conv, 64 & 68; mem, Tenn. State Rep. Exec. Cmt, currently; councilman, Memphis, Tenn, 69- Bus. & Prof. Pos: Attorney, Civil Aeronauts. Bd, 41-42; law clerk, U.S. Circuit Judge, 43-44; private practice of law, 44-45; partner, Snowden, Davis, McCloy and Donelson, 45-54, Donelson and Adams, 54-65 and Heiskell, Donelson, Adams, Williams & Wall, 64- Mem: Am, Tenn, Memphis and Shelby Co. Bar Asns; Sigma Alpha Epsilon; past pres, Shelby United Neighbors; past pres, Traveler's Aid Soc. of Memphis. Rel: Presbyterian; Elder, Idlewild Presbyterian Church. Legal Res: 134 E. Cherry Dr, Memphis, Tenn. 38117. Mailing Add: 2020 First National Bank Bldg, Memphis, Tenn. 38103.

DONIELSON, ALLEN LEE R
b. Maquoketa, Iowa, 5/22/27; s. Paul L. Donielson and Trula D; m. 12/21/52 to Susan Janan Waughtal; c. Erik and Christopher. Educ: Univ. Iowa; Drake Univ, LL.B, grad. study in econ; Phi Alpha Delta. Polit. & Govt. Pos: Campaign dir, Schroeder for Iowa State Rep, 52 and Abels for Attorney Gen, 60; civil serv. cmnr, West Des Moines, Iowa, 62; precinct committeeman, 64; Iowa campaign dir, Rockefeller for Pres, 64; chmn, Polk Co. Rep. Party, 65-69; del, Rep. Nat. Conv, 68; U.S. Dist. Attorney, South. Dist, Iowa, 69- Bus. & Prof. Pos: Assoc, Smedal & Maurer, Ames, Iowa, 52-54; mgr. admin. serv, Preferred Risk Ins. Co, Des Moines, 54-66; partner, Baird, Donielson & Karn, Attorneys, 66- Mil. Serv: Entered as A/S, Navy, 45, released as Pharmacist 3/C, 46. Publ: 'Disbarment in Iowa,' Drake Law Rev, 52; 'Night Shift in an Office,' The Office, 58; 'Printing Comprehensively,' Best's Ins, 60. Mem: West Des Moines Develop. Bd. Dirs; pres, Inter-Racial Coun; YMCA; Admin. Mgr. Soc. Rel: Presbyterian; Elder. Mailing Add: 1233 17th, West Des Moines, Iowa 50265.

DONLEY, OWEN JOSEPH D
b. Elk Point, S.Dak, 2/24/24; s. Owen C. Donley and Mabel C. Donnelly D; m. 5/1/54 to Carole Scott; c. Patricia, Scott, Shannon and twins, Kerry and Kelly. Educ: Notre Dame Univ, A.B, cum laude, 48; Univ. S.Dak, LL.B, 51. Polit. & Govt. Pos: Admin. asst. to U.S. Sen. George S. McGovern, S.Dak, 63- Bus. & Prof. Pos: Attorney-at-Law, 51-63; co. attorney, Union Co, S.Dak, 54-58. Mil. Serv: Entered as Pvt, Army, 43, released as Cpl, 45, after serv. in Signal Corps; China-Burma-India Campaign Ribbon with 2 Battle Stars. Mem: Am. Bar Asn; S.Dak. State Bar; K. of C; Notre Dame Alumni Asn. Rel: Roman Catholic. Legal Res: Elk Point, S.Dak. 57025. Mailing Add: 1400 Kingston Ave, Alexandria, Va. 22302.

DONLEY, RUSS R
Wyo. State Rep.
b. Salt Lake City, Utah, 2/3/39; s. R. Lee Donley and Leona Sherwood D; m. 6/4/60 to Karen Kocherhans; c. Tammera, Tonya and Christina. Educ: Univ. Wyo, B.S.C.E. with honors, 61; Univ. Fla, M.S.E; Phi Epsilon Phi; Omicron Delta Kappa; Sigma Tau; Iron Skull; Sigma Nu. Polit. & Govt. Pos: Chmn, Young Rep. Club, Thermopolis, Wyo, 62-64; Rep. precinct committeeman, Thermopolis, 63-65 and Powell, 66-68; chmn, State Young Rep. Club, Wyo, 66-68; Wyo. State Rep, 69- Bus. & Prof. Pos: Prin, West. Engrs-Architects, Inc, 62-69. Mem: Wyo. Asn. Consult. Engrs. & Surveyors; Consult. Eng. Coun; Wyo. Soc. Prfnl. Engrs; Wyo. Eng. Soc; Toastmasters. Rel: Methodist. Legal Res: 1140 Ivy Lane, Casper, Wyo. 82601. Mailing Add: 2111 E. Second, Casper, Wyo. 82601.

DONLON, JOHN JOSEPH D
Mem, Colo. Dem. State Cent. Cmt.
b. Colo, 1/10/31; s. John Andrew Donlon and Kathleen M. Neer; m. 11/12/49 to Joan Ann Stoddard; c. Deborah Ann, Lori M, Mark J. and Brad A. Educ: High Sch. Polit. & Govt. Pos: Colo. State Sen, 65-67; mem, Colo. Dem. State Cent. Cmt, currently. Bus. & Prof. Pos: Bus. mgr, Local Union 113, IBEW, 57-67; v.pres, Bldg. Trades Coun, 65-; v.pres, Colo. Labor Coun, South. Colo, 66- Mil. Serv: Entered as Pvt, Air Force, 51, released as Airman 1/C, 56, after serv. in 3200 Electronics. Special Recognition as an Outstanding Citizen. Rel: Catholic. Legal Res: 2434 Zane Place, Colorado Springs, Colo. 80909. Mailing Add: 414 W. Pikes Peak Ave, Colorado Springs, Colo. 80903. (1967)

DONNELL, FORREST C. R
b. Quitman, Mo, 8/20/84; s. John Cary Donnell and Barbara Waggoner D; m. 1/29/13 to Hilda Hays; c. Ruth and John Lanier. Educ: Univ. of Mo, A.B, 04, LL.B, 07; Phi Beta Kappa; Kappa Sigma; Phi Delta Phi; Order of the Coif. Hon. LL.D, Westminster Col, 41 and Univ. of Mo, 60. Polit. & Govt. Pos: Pres, Asn. of Young Rep. of Mo, 16; Gov. Mo, 41-45; U.S. Sen, Mo, 45-51. Bus. & Prof. Pos: With Selden P. Spencer, 07-11; lawyer, Spencer & Donnell, 11-25, Spencer, Donnell & McDonald, 25-28, Holland, Lashly & Donnell, 28-33 and Donnell and McDonald, 33-41; attorney-at-law, St. Louis, 51-56; lawyer and mem. firm Donnell, Schoenbeck and Donnell, 56- Mem: Chmn. bd, Downtown YMCA, 32-35; past chmn, St. Louis World Court Cmn; Am, Mo. and St. Louis Bar Asns; Am. Law Inst; Asn. of Bar, N.Y.C; Mason (33°), Past Grand Master, Grand Lodge of Mo; Scottish Rite (dep. for Mo, 37-39); Noonday;chmn. bd. of mgr, Mo. Sch. for the Blind, 31-34; pres, Mo. Sunday Sch. Coun. of Relig. Educ, 29-31; pres, St. Louis City Evangelization Union of M.E. Church, 30-34; Mo. Acad. Squires. Rel: Methodist. Legal Res: 245 Union Blvd, St. Louis, Mo. 63108. Mailing Add: 611 Olive St, St. Louis, Mo. 63101. (1967)

DONNELL, JOHN DICKSON R
Mem, Santa Fe Co. Rep. Cent. Cmt, N.Mex.
b. Santa Fe, N.Mex, 8/26/25; s. Dee H. Donnell and Elda Dickson D; m. 1/1/49 to Jimmie N. Gryder; c. Jack, Nancy, William and Catherine. Educ: Univ. N.Mex, J.D, 51; Pi Kappa Alpha. Polit. & Govt. Pos: Mem; Santa Fe Co. Rep. Cent. Cmt, N.Mex, 62-; del, Rep. Nat. Conv, 64; mem, N.Mex. State Rep. Cent. Cmt, 65; cand, Attorney Gen, 66, spec. asst, Attorney Gen, 67- Mil. Serv: Entered as Pvt, Marine Corps, 43, released as Cpl, 46, after serv. in G Co, 2nd Bn, 24th Marine Corps, Pac. Area; Asiatic-Pac. Ribbon with 3 Battle Stars; Good Conduct Medal; Purple Heart. Mem: Am, N.Mex. and Santa Fe Co. Bar Asns; Santa Fe Vol. Fire Dept. Rel: Episcopal. Legal Res: 428 Camino de Los Animas, Santa Fe, N.Mex. 87501. Mailing Add: 209 E. Marcy, Santa Fe, N.Mex. 87501.

DONNELLEY, DIXON D
Spec. Asst. for Pub. Affairs to Secy. of Treas.
b. Forest Hills, N.Y, 7/29/15; s. Patrick John Donnelley and Katherine Marie Dixon D; m. 3/27/43 to Lucia Tarquinio de Sousa; c. Leigh Patricia. Educ: Columbia, 34-37. Polit. & Govt. Pos: Reporter, N.Y. Daily News, 36-37; city ed, Havana Post, Cuba, 37-40; asst. city ed, Wash. Daily News, 41-42; news ed, Off. Coordinator of Inter-Am. Affairs, 42; press attache, Am. Embassy, Mexico City, 46-47, asst. pub. affairs officer, Santiago, Chile, 47-48 and press attache, Buenos Aires, Argentina, 48-50; info. officer, Am. Rep. Area, State Dept, 50; ed, Pub. Vision News Mag, Rio de Janeiro, Brazil, 50-52; mem. pub. rels. staff, Creole Petroleum Corp, 54-55; ed. dir, Cmn. on Juvenile Delinquency, U.S. Senate, 55; pub. rels. dir, Kefauver Presidential Campaign, 55-56; consult. info, Pres. Cmt. Scientists and Engrs, 56-58; spec. asst. to Under Secy. of State, 58-61; spec. asst. for pub. affairs to Secy. of Treas, 61-66 & 69-; Asst. Secy. of State for Pub. Affairs, 66-69. Mil. Serv: Army Air Force, 42-46. Mem: For. Serv. Asn; Nat. Press Club, Wash; Overseas Press Club, New York. Establishing and operating a small newspaper, 46. Mailing Add: 4100 Cathedral Ave. N.W, Washington, D.C. 20016.

DONNELLON, EDWARD JAMES D
V.Chmn, Hamilton Co. Dem. Cent. Cmt, Ohio
b. Cincinnati, Ohio, 3/22/24; s. Andrew Joseph Donnellon and Loretta Kroger D; m. 11/25/48 to Mary Margaret Nolan; c. Thomas Edward, Terrance Michael, Stephen James and Daniel John. Educ: St. Vincent's Col, 43-44; Univ. Cincinnati, 46-47; Chase Col. Law, LL.B and J.D, 51; v.chancellor, Kappa Psi Delta. Polit. & Govt. Pos: Solicitor, Deer Park, Ohio, 61-66; referee, Juvenile Court, Hamilton Co, 61-66, Domestic Rels, 65-68; exec. dir, Hamilton Co. Dem. Party, 64-66; v.chmn, Hamilton Co. Dem. Cent. Cmt, 65-; alternate del, Dem. Nat. Conv, 68; solicitor, Golf Manor, Ohio, 69- Bus. & Prof. Pos: Attorney-at-law, Cincinnati, Ohio, 51-; treas, Cincinnati Claims Asn, 60, mem, bd. dir, 61-62, pres, 63; legal adv, Americana Ins. Adjusting, 69- Mil. Serv: Entered as Pvt, Air Force, 43, released as Sgt, 46, after serv. in 495th Bomb Squadron, 344th Bomb Group, ETO, 45; Air Medal with Two Oak Leaf Clusters. Mem: Negligence, Domestic Rels, Workmens Compensation and Judiciary and Legal Reform Cmts, Cincinnati Bar Asn; Cincinnati Claims Asn; bd. dir, Moeller High Sch, 67-69; bd. dir, Bishop Fenwick Coun. 2927, K. of C, 67-69. Rel: Catholic. Legal Res: 7584 Trailwind Dr, Cincinnati, Ohio 45242. Mailing Add: 8005 Plainfield Rd, Cincinnati, Ohio 45236.

DONNELLY, HELENE ROSALYN R
b. Dover, N.H, 8/23/03; d. Frank Charles Stone and Mary R. Casey S; wid; c. Two. Educ: Lawrence and Newton, Mass. Polit. & Govt. Pos: Mem, Dover Third Ward Dem. Cmt; publicity chmn, Strafford Co. Dem. Women; chmn, Strafford Co. Dem. Women's Disaster Prog. to Help Flood Victims and Dover Dem. Women's Cmt; v.chmn, State Dem. Women's Orgn; mem. exec. bd, Dover Citizen's for Fair Taxes; N.H. State Rep, formerly; secy. and treas, Ward II Dem. Cmt, 68- Bus. & Prof. Pos: Housewife. Mem: Publicity bd, Dover Swimming Pool Cmt; treas. and founder, Granite State Milk Consumers League; dir, N.H. Heart Asn; Dover United Appeal; chmn, Dover Pollution Cleanup Prog; chmn, Petition for Return of Prayer to Dover Schs; Am. Heart Asn. Co-sponsor, Amendment for Prayer in Schs, 65. Rel: Catholic. Mailing Add: 13 Durrell St, Dover, N.H. 03820.

DONNELLY, HUGH P. D
b. Nebr. Polit. & Govt. Pos: Calif. State Sen, 42-66; Calif. State Assemblyman, 34-43, Speaker pro tem, 39. Bus. & Prof. Pos: Ins. broker. Mem: Hon. Rotarian; Past Master, Turlock Grange; Past Master, Stanislaus Co. Pomona Grange. Mailing Add: 953 Sierra Dr, Turlock, Calif. 95350. (1967)

DONNELLY, THOMAS J. D
b. Locust Gap, Pa, 9/6/99; s. Eugene Donnelly and Catherine O'Neill D; m. to Evelyn A. Armstrong; c. one. Educ: High sch. Polit. & Govt. Pos: Inheritance tax appraiser, 32-38; revenue agent, Warren State Hosp, Pa; mem, Draft Bd. 1, Northumberland Co, 40-47; price aid, Off. Price Admin, 42-45, solid fuel analyst, 51-53; treas, Northumberland and Wallen Co. Dem. Party; committeeman, Sixth Ward, Wallen, Pa; Pa. State Rep, 64-67; Cmnr, Warren Co, 67- Bus. & Prof. Pos: Merchant. Mem: Elks; K. of C; Holy Name Soc. Rel: Catholic. Mailing Add: 707 Madison Ave, Warren, Pa. 16365.

DONNEWALD, JAMES H. D
Ill. State Sen.
b. Carlyle, Ill, 1/29/25; m. to Ruth Evelyn; c. Eric John, Craig James and Jill Yvonne. Educ: St. Louis Univ, 42-44, Lincoln Col. of Law, 49. Polit. & Govt. Pos: Committeeman, Precinct 1, Dem. Party, Carlyle, Ill, 48-50; supvr, Carlyle Twp, 49-51; Ill. State Rep, 2 terms; Ill. State Sen, 66-; alternate del, Dem. Nat. Conv, 68. Bus. & Prof. Pos: Attorney-at-Law, currently. Mil. Serv: Korean Vet. Mem: Lions; Elks; Moose; K. of C. Rel: Catholic. Mailing Add: 340 N. 11th St, Breese, Ill. 62230. (1967)

DONNO, ALDO DAVID R
b. Terni, Italy, 11/18/11; s. David Donno and Antonia Amadio D; m. 9/7/40 to Josephine Franz; c. David, Richard and Dianne. Educ: Univ. Kans, 30-32; Hofstra Univ, 41-43. Polit. & Govt. Pos: Mem. and chmn, Huntington Zoning Bd. Appeals, N.Y, 58-64; zone leader, Suffolk Co. Rep. Cmt, 59-69; N.Y. State del, Suffolk Co. Rep. Cmt, 62 & 66; mem, Huntington Planning Bd, 67-; del. Rep. Nat. Conv, 68- Bus. Prof. Pos: Varying tech. supvry. and managerial pos, Grumman Aerospace Corp, Bethpage, 41-, spec. test equip. bus. mgr, currently. Mem: Am. Soc. Mfg. and Tool Engrs; Am. Welding Soc; Am. Soc. Aeronaut. and Astronaut. Engrs. Citation for Extraordinary Commun. Serv, Am. Soc. Mfg. and Tool Engrs, 58. Rel: Catholic. Mailing Add: 70 Straight Path, Dix Hills, N.Y. 11746.

DONO, BOBBIE T. D
b. New York, N.Y, 6/7/39; d. James V. Dono and Virginia M. D, single. Educ: Univ. N.C, B.A, 61; Sigma Delta Pi; staff of yearbook and daily newspaper; Carolina Symposium; State Student Legis; Air Force ROTC Angel; Orientation Counselor to New Students, plus others. Bus. & Prof. Pos: Teacher, Benjamin Franklin High Sch, 61-62; Appointments Secy. to U.S. Sen. Harrison Williams, Jr, N.J, 62- Mem: Young Dem, Wash, D.C. Rel: Episcopal. Legal Res: 765 Salem St, Teaneck, N.J. 07666. Mailing Add: 2718 Devonshire Place N.W, Washington, D.C. 20008.

DONOGHUE, MARION P. D
m. to Myron D. Donoghue; c. Three. Educ: Burdett Col. Polit. & Govt. Pos: Dem. Town Comm; del, Dem. State Conv, 64; del, Campaign Conf. for Dem. Women, Wash, D.C; v.pres, N.E. Region Dem. Women; pres, Gr. Boston Dem. Women on Wheels. Mem: Pres, Jr. Riverside Club; v.pres, Ladies' Cath. Benevolent Asn; charter organizer, E. Saugus Improv. Asn; v.pres, Saugus Gen. Hosp. Aux; pres, Armitage PTA; United Fund; Cancer Fund; Heart Fund. Rel: Catholic. Mailing Add: 172 Essex St, Saugus, Mass. 01906. (1967)

DONOGHUE, PATRICK JOSEPH D
b. Holyoke, Mass, 7/29/24; s. Patrick F. Donoghue and Alice C.D. Educ: Georgetown Univ, B.S. Polit. & Govt. Pos: Admin. asst. to U.S. Rep. Boland, Mass, currently. Bus. & Prof. Pos: News reporter, Providence, R.I, 47-50; news reporter, Springfield Daily News, Mass, 51-55. Mil. Serv: Navy, Radarman 3/C, svc. antisubmarine and convoy duty, Atlantic Theater, and radar-picket destroyer, U.S.S. Higbee (DD-806), Third, Fifth Fleets, Pac. Legal Res: Springfield, Mass. Mailing Add: 215 C St. S.E, Washington, D.C. 20003. (1967)

DONOHUE, DEWEY C. D
b. Columbia City, Wash, 1897; m. to Marguerite; c. Five. Educ: Bus. Col. Polit. & Govt. Pos: Wash. State Rep, 6 terms; Wash. State Sen, 2 terms. Bus. & Prof. Pos: Farmer. Mem: Elks; Eagles; Mason. Mailing Add: 506 E. Richmond, Dayton, Wash. 99328. (1967)

DONOHUE, HAROLD D. D
U.S. Rep, Mass.
b. Worcester, Mass, 6/18/01; single. Educ: Northeast. Univ. of Law. Polit. & Govt. Pos: With Worcester City Govt, Mass; U.S. Rep, Mass, 46-; del, Dem. Nat. Conv, 68. Bus. & Prof. Pos: Lawyer. Mil. Serv: Lt. Comdr, Navy. Mem: Mass. Bar Asn. Legal Res: 82 Forest St, Worcester, Mass. 01609. Mailing Add: House Office Bldg, Washington, D.C. 20515.

DONOHUE, HUBERT FRANCIS D
Wash. State Sen.
b. Dayton, Wash, 9/24/21; s. Dewey C. Donohue and Marguerite Hopkins D; m. 3/8/44 to Evelyn Barclay; c. Randall, Timothy, Ryan and Kelly. Educ: Wash. State Univ, 3 years; Phi Sigma Kappa. Polit. & Govt. Pos: Mem, Columbia Co. Planning Cmn, Wash, 62-69; Wash. State Sen, 69- Bus. & Prof. Pos: Farmer, 20 years. Mil. Serv: Entered as Aviation Cadet, Air Force, 42, released as Capt, 45, after serv. in 323rd Bomber Squadron, Eighth Air Force, ETO, 43-45; Lt. Col, Air Force Res, currently; Air Medal with 4 clusters; ETO Medal; 3 Battle Stars; Am. Theater Medal. Mem: Toastmaster Int; Elks; Eagles; Farm Bur; Wheat Asn; Kiwanis; C. of C. Rel: Protestant. Mailing Add: Route 2, Box 13, Dayton, Wash. 99328.

DONOLOW, BENJAMIN R. D
Pa. State Sen.
b. Philadelphia, Pa; s. Israel Donolow and Tillie D; married; c. One daughter and one son. Educ: Temple Univ; Temple Law Sch. Polit. & Govt. Pos: Mem, Enforcement Div, Off. of Price Admin; solicitor, Recorder of Deeds, Phila. Co, Pa; mem, Phila. Dem. Cmt, 48-; Pa. State Sen, 54- Bus. & Prof. Pos: Lawyer; Supreme and Superior Courts of Pa; Courts of Phila. Co. Mil. Serv: Army. Mem: Phi Alpha; Am. Legion. Mailing Add: 1804 Rittenhouse Sq, Philadelphia, Pa. 19103. (1967)

DONOVAN, EILEEN ROBERTA
U.S. Ambassador to Barbados and Spec. Rep. to W.I. Assoc. States
b. Boston, Mass, 4/13/15; d. William Francis Donovan and Mary Barry D; single. Educ: Girls Latin Sch, Boston, grad, 32; Boston Teachers Col, B.S. in Educ, 36 and M.Ed, 37; Sch. Mil. Govt, Univ. Va; Civil Affairs Training Sch, Univ. Mich, 44-45; Harvard, For. Serv. Inst. fel, 56 and M.P.A, 57. Polit. & Govt. Pos: Career officer, U.S. For. Serv, 48-; second secy. and v.consul, Off. of U.S. Polit. Adv, Tokyo, Japan, 48-49; mem. staff, Bur. of Far East. Affairs, Japan-Korea Pub. Affairs, 49-52; State Dept. mem, Educ. Exchange Surv. Mission to Japan, summer 49; second secy. and consul, Am. Embassy, Manila, Philippines, 52-54; consul, U.S. Consulate Gen, Milan, Italy, 54-56; chief of South. Europe br, Bur. of Intel. and Research, 57-59; sr. seminar in for. policy, State Dept, 59; prin. officer, Am. Consul-Gen, Barbados, 60-62; U.S. consul gen, Barbados and the Windward and Leeward Islands, W.I, 62-65; asst. dir, Off. of Caribbean Affairs, 65-69; U.S. Ambassador to Barbados & spec. rep. to W.I. Assoc. States, 69- Bus. & Prof. Pos: Teacher hist, pub. schs, Boston, 38-43. Mil. Serv: Entered as Pvt, WAC, 43, released as Capt, 46; civilian adv, Japanese women's and secondary educ. to Supreme Comdr. Allied Powers, Tokyo, 46-48. Mailing Add: U.S. Embassy, Bridgetown, Barbados.

DONOVAN, JAMES HUBERT R
N.Y. State Sen.
b. Holland Patent, N.Y, 11/12/23; s. Francis John Donovan and Lena Hurley D; m. Sept. 1947 to Esther Moretti; c. Gary, James, Karen, Jerome, Michael, Barry and Kim. Educ: Whitesboro Cent. High Sch, 4 years. Polit. & Govt. Pos: Town councilman, New Hartford, N.Y, 62 & 63, town supvr, 64 & 65; N.Y. State Sen, 44th Dist, 66- Bus. & Prof. Pos: Pres. and specialty contractor, J.H. Donovan & Sons, Inc, 49- Mil. Serv: Entered as Pvt, Marines, 42, released as Sgt, 45, after serv. in Marine Aviation, Pac. Theatre, 43, 44 & 45; Pac. Combat Ribbon with one star; Good Conduct Medal. Mem: Oneida Co. Farm Bur, N.Y; Am. Legion, Chadwicks; past pres, Chadwicks Sch. Bd; K. of C, Utica Coun; VFW, Clinton; ex-officio dir, Christian Appalachian Proj, Lancaster, Ky. Rel: Roman Catholic. Legal Res: 9409 Elm St, Chadwicks, N.Y. 13319. Mailing Add: 3895 Oneida St, Washington Mills, N.Y. 13479.

DONOVAN, JOHN FRANCIS, JR. D
b. Chelsea, Mass, 8/21/31; s. John Francis Donovan and Agnes Crowley D; m. 10/26/57 to Marguerite Walsh; c. Jane Martha, John F, III, Catherine Cuddy and Maryann Crowley. Educ: Holy Cross Col; Boston Col. Law Sch, B.S, 57, LL.B. Polit. & Govt. Pos: Mem, Chelsea Dem. Cmt, Mass; Mass. State Rep, 63-68. Bus. & Prof. Pos: Attorney, Donovan, Sullivan and Donovan, Chelsea, Mass, 65- and Dever, Dever, Donovan, Dwyer & Monahan, Boston, 65-; exec. v.pres, Boston Red Sox, 68- Mem: K. of C; YMHA-YWHA; Sagamore Club. Rel: Roman Catholic. Mailing Add: 409 Broadway, Chelsea, Mass. 02150.

DONOVAN, JOSEPH L. DFL
Secy. of State, Minn.
b. Champion, Mich, 6/16/93; m. Mary Noldin; c. 1 daughter. Educ: St. Ambrose High Sch, Ironwood, Mich. Polit. & Govt. Pos: Various pos. with Fed. Govt. including: Indust. analyst, Nat. Prod. Authority, dist. mgr, U.S. Dept. Field Serv, supvr, Bur. Census, dist. mgr, Duluth Off. Smaller War Prod. Corp. and indust. spec, War Prod. Bd, 42-45; Secy. State, Minn, 54-; del, Dem. Nat. Conv, 68. Bus. & Prof. Pos: Sales promotion, Private Industry, 25 years. Mem: Exec. Coun. Cmn. Am. Asn. Motor Vehicles Admin, past pres, Region III; past pres, Nat. Asn. Secy. State. Outstanding Citizenship Award, Am. Heritage Found, 61; Serv. Recognition Award, Minn. Safety Coun, 62. Mailing Add: 2085 Eleanor Ave, St. Paul, Minn. 55116.

DONOVAN, MARGARET WALSH D
b. Champaign Co, Ill, 1904; d. Michael F. Walsh and Anna Carey W; wid; c. Alice, Margaret Clare, Annamary (Mrs. John Feeney) and Bernard T, Jr. Educ: Univ. Ill, A.B, 27; Debate Team. Polit. & Govt. Pos: Chairwoman, Macon Co. Dem. Women's Orgn, Ill, 60-66; del, Dem. Nat. Conv, 64 & 68. Bus. & Prof. Pos: Teacher soc. sci, Commun. High Sch, 27-35. Mem: Macon Co. Farm Bur; Macon Co. Homemakers Exten. Asn; Diocesan Coun, Catholic Womens' Bd. Rel: Catholic. Mailing Add: Cerro Gordo, Ill. 61818. (1967)

DONOVAN, RICHARD J.
b. New Rochelle, N.Y, 26; m. 50 to Peggy D; c. Roxie and Libby. Educ: San Diego State Col; Univ. San Diego Law Sch, LL.B. Polit. & Govt. Pos: Mem, Nat. City Police Dept, Calif, 50-56; mem, Marshal's Off, S.Bay Judicial Dist, 56-57; clerk, S.Bay Munic. Court, 57-62; Calif. State Assemblyman, 77th Dist, 63-66, v.chmn, Transportation and Commerce Cmt. and mem, Criminal Procedure, Govt. Orgn, Revenue and Taxation, Legis. Rep, Joint Budget, Joint Legis. and Gen. Adv. Cmts, 63-66; munic. court judge, San Diego, Calif, 66- Mil. Serv: Navy, 43-47, Africa, Italy and France; Lt.(jg), Naval Res.(Ret). Mem: Calif. Bar; Nat. City and Chula Vista Kiwanis Clubs; K. of P; Chula Vista Elks; SAR; VFW; Am. Legion; Traffic Safety Coun; San Diego Bd. Vol. of Am; Nat. City C. of C; Am. Cancer Soc; United Team; PTA. Rel: Congregational. Mailing Add: Courthouse, 220 W. Broadway, San Diego, Calif. 92101.

DONOVAN, THEODORE MARTIN R
Chmn, Bristol Rep. Party, Conn.
b. Bristol, Conn, 12/3/32; s. Joseph M. Donovan and Anna E. Dickert D; m. 11/24/56 to Diane M. Gombar; c. Michael, Beth, Susan and Sheila. Educ: Georgetown Univ, B.S, 54, J.D. and LL.B, 59. Polit. & Govt. Pos: Chmn, Bristol Rep. Party, Conn, 68- Mil. Serv: Entered as 2nd Lt, Air Force, 55, released as 1st Lt, 57, after serv. in ATC, 55-57. Mem: Conn, Hartford Co. and Am. Bar Asns. Rel: Catholic. Mailing Add: 125 Haviland St, Bristol, Conn. 06010.

DOOCY, FRED J. D
b. Hartford, Conn, 5/5/13; m. June 42 to Mary O'Keeke; c. Virginia, Eileen, Fred, Catherine, Paul. Educ: Am. Inst. Banking; grad. Sch. of Banking; Rutgers Univ. Polit. & Govt. Pos: Conn. State Sen, 58-67; past pres. pro-tem Conn. State Sen; S. Windsor Bd. of Educ; town treas. Bus. & Prof. Pos: V. pres. E. Hartford Nat. Bank and Trust Co, 59-; secy, 50-59; Hartford Nat. Bank asst. treas, 45-50; head bookkeeper, teller, 31-42. Mil. Serv: Air Force, 42-45. Mem: Am. Legion; E. Hartford Rotary Club; past pres. E. Hartford C. of C. S. Windsor Lion's Club Citizen of Year Award, 63. Mailing Add: 2093 Ellington Rd, Wapping, Conn. 06087. (1967)

DOOLEY, ALBERT JOHN D
b. Chapin, Lexington Co, S.C, 6/10/30; s. Oscar Lee Dooley and Velma O. Cannon D; m. 6/15/51 to Connie E. Spoon D. Educ: Univ. of S.C, B.S, 51, LL.B, 54. Polit. & Gov. Pos: S.C. State Rep, 58-66. Bus. & Prof. Pos: Lawyer. Mem: Lions; Merchants Asn; WOW Chap. No. 273; Phi Alpha Delta; Mason; Lexington C. of C. Inst. of Mil. Subj. Rel: St. Davids Lutheran Church of W. Columbia. Mailing Add: Box 518, Lexington, S.C. 29072. (1967)

DOOLEY, EDWIN BENEDICT R
b. Brooklyn, N.Y, 4/13/05; s. Joseph Augustus Dooley and Isabelle Delaney D; m. Sept 1955 to Anita M. Gillies (deceased); m. 1/9/64 to Margaret Sheefel; c. Edwin Benedict. Educ: Dartmouth, A.B, 27; Fordham Univ, LL.B, 30. Polit. & Govt. Pos: Mayor, Mamaroneck, N.Y, 50-56; mem, N.Y. State Cmt. of Nat. Capitol Sesquicentennial Commemoration, 51; U.S. Rep, 57-62. Bus. & Prof. Pos: Feature writer, N.Y. Sun, 27-38; v.pres, Don Spencer Co, Advert. Agency, 38-42; dir. pub. rels, Gen. Foods Corp, 42-46; assoc, Inst. Pub. Rels, 46-48. Mem: Pub. rels. cmt, Boy Scouts, 48-50; exec. dir, N.Y. div, Am. Cancer Soc, 48-50; Dartmouth Club (pres, Westchester, 53-54; Touchdown Club (chmn, 45-46); Orienta Beach Club; Univ. Club, Mamaroneck; Rep. Club, D.C; N.Y. Athletic Club; dir, Commun. Chest. Mailing Add: 810 Oakwood Rd, Mamaroneck, N.Y. 10543.

DOOLEY, JOHN F. D
b. Crossville, Tenn, 8/13/26; s. Brooks Leslie Dooley, Sr. and Virginia Katherine Forgy D; m. 11/14/65 to Earla Marie King; c. George C, Michael L. and John T. Educ: Cumberland Co. High Sch, Crossville, Tenn. Polit. & Govt. Pos: Cmnr, Dept. Pub. Utilities, Crossville, Tenn, 59-60, mayor, 65-66, cmnr, Police and Fire Dept, 69-, cmnr, Sanit. and Recreation Dept, 70-; Tenn. State Rep, 65-66. Owner-mgr, Dooley's Food Town Super Mkt, 54-69; mem. bd. dirs, Bi-Rite Food Stores, Inc, Nashville, Tenn, 67-68. Mil. Serv: Air Force, 53. Mem: Chmn. Cumberland Co, Am. Red Cross, 54-55; chmn, Boy's Club of Cumberland Co, 66-67; Am. Legion Crossville; Vol. Fire Dept; Auxiliary Police Dept. Sr. Div. Model Airplane Contest Flying Glider Nat. Record Holder, 50-51; Outstanding Young Man of The Year, Jr. C. of C, 60. Rel: Church of Christ. Legal Res: McLary Lane at Dooley St, Crossville, Tenn. 38555. Mailing Add: 512 W. Fourth St, Crossville, Tenn. 38555.

DOOLIN, DENNIS JAMES D
Dep. Asst. Secy. of Defense for E.Asian and Pac. Affairs
b. Omaha, Nebr, 10/28/33; s. Russell James Doolin and Sarah Pickard D; m. 1/29/56 to Maryann Lund; c. Maureen Elizabeth, David Hamer and Sarah Ellen. Educ: Univ. San Francisco, B.S. summa cum laude, 58; Stanford Univ, M.A, 60, Ph.D, 64. Polit. & Govt. Pos: Sr. analyst, Asian Affairs, U.S. Cent. Intel. Agency, 67-69; Dep. Asst. Secy. of Defense for E.Asian and Pac. Affairs, Dept. of Defense, 69- Bus. & Prof. Pos: Research curator, E.Asian Collections, Hoover Inst, Stanford Univ, 64-67. Mil. Serv: Entered as Seaman Recruit, Navy, 50, released as QMQ 2/C, 54, after serv. in U.S.S. Albuquerque and U.S.S. Laws, Pac. Fleet; Korea Medal; UN Medal; China Serv. Medal; Japan Occup. Medal; Nat. Defense Medal. Publ: Communist China: The Politics of Student Opposition, 64, Territorial Claims in the Sino-Soviet Conflict, 65 and The Chinese People's Republic, 66, Hoover Inst. Mem: Am. Polit. Sci. Asn; Asn. for Asian Studies. Woodrow Wilson fel; Ford For. Area fel. Rel: Catholic. Legal Res: 6602 Jerry Place, McLean, Va. 22101. Mailing Add: Office of the Assistant Secretary of Defense, International Security Affairs, Pentagon, Washington, D.C. 20301.

DOOLIN, DON D
Chmn, Kern Co. Dem. Cent. Cmt, Calif.
b. Trenton, Mo, 5/29/14; s. Henry Crooks Doolin and Cusa Keith D; m. 1/24/36 to Juanita Dockery; c. Gary Donald and Diana Kay. Educ: Trenton Jr. Col, A.A, 35; Univ. Mo, Columbia, B.S, 37; Univ. Calif, Berkeley, Sec. Teachers Credential, Sec. Admin. Credential and M.A; Sigma Alpha. Polit. & Govt. Pos: V.pres, Bakersfield Dem. Club, Calif, 55-57 and pres, 57-59; city councilman, Bakersfield, 55-67 and v.mayor, 57-63; Kern Co. campaign mgr, Lt. Gov. Glen Anderson, 58-66; chmn, Kern Co. Dem. Cent. Cmt, 68-; mem, Calif. Dem. State Cent. Cmt, 68- Bus. & Prof. Pos: Prin, Tennant High Sch, Calif, 40 and Butte High Sch, Dorris, Calif, 42-43; coach and dean of boys, Yreka High Sch, 40-42; counsr. and teacher, San Francisco Jr. Col, 46-47; coach and counsr, St. Joseph Jr. Col, Mo, 47-48; teacher, high sch, Bakersfield, Calif, 48-, coach, 48-51; vet. day chmn, Bakersfield, 52- Mil. Serv: Entered as Ens, Navy, 43, released as Lt, 46, after serv. in U.S. Pac. Fleet, Pac. Theatre; Navy Res, 46-64, Comdr; Am. Theatre, Invasion of Philippines, Okinawa Invasion and Good Conduct Medals. Publ: Changing Emphasis in Grading in Physical Education, 40. Mem: Nat. Educ. Asn; Kern Co. Teachers Asn; Bakersfield Teachers Club; Bakersfield, Calif. and Nat. Asns. for Retarded Children; Kern Co. Ment. Health Asn; ROA; Bakersfield Dem. Club; Am. Legion; Civitan Club; Order of Redman; Am. Red Cross. Meritorious Serv. Awards, Am. Legion, 62, 63 & 67; State of Calif. Citation for Vet. Serv, 66; Five Year Centennial Cmt. Award, Kern Co. Bd. of Supvr; Award for Outstanding Serv. Rendered, Kern, Inyo and Mono Counties Cent. Labor Coun; Plaque for Outstanding Serv. Rendered, Bakersfield, Calif; Spec. Serv. Rendered Award, Bakersfield Dem; Outstanding Citizen Award, KAFY Radio; Helping Hand Award, Retarded Children Asn. Rel: Congregational. Mailing Add: 805 Hogan Way, Kern City, Calif. 93309.

DOORLEY, JOSEPH ALOYSIUS, JR. D
Mayor, Providence, R.I.
b. Providence, R.I, 10/12/30; s. Joseph A. Doorley and Nora Cannon D; m. 6/13/53 to Claire Walsh; c. Joseph, III, Michael, Brian, Dennis, Carleen and Patricia. Educ: Notre Dame Univ, A.B, 53; Boston Col. Law Sch, LL.B, 58. Polit. & Govt. Pos: Research technician, R.I. Develop, Coun, 55; mem, Young Dem, R.I, 55-; admin. asst. to Gov. of R.I, 56-58, legis. counsel, 61-62; state chmn, Kennedy for President Cmt, 60; city councilman, Providence, R.I, 63-65, mayor, 65-; mem, Dem. City Cmt, 65; nat. Dem. committeeman, 66-; del, Dem. Nat. Conv, 68. Bus. & Prof. Pos: Attorney-at-law. Mem: Am. and R.I. Bar Asns; K. of C; Ancient Order of Hibernians. Rel: Roman Catholic. Mailing Add: 97 Hilltop Ave, Providence, R.I. 02908.

DOOTSON, JACK D
b. Pasadena, Calif, 1914; single. Educ: George Wash. Univ. Law Sch; Univ. of Wash, Sch. of Econ. & Bus; George Wash. Univ. Columbian Col; Purdue Univ; Mexico City Col. Polit. & Govt. Pos: Wash. State Rep, 4 terms to 1966. Bus. & Prof. Pos: Engr, Great North. Rwy. Mil. Serv: Lt. Comdr, U.S. Navy; Aviator. Mailing Add: 3601 Rockefeller Ave, Everett, Wash. 98201. (1967)

DORAN, HILARY BRUMLEY, JR. D
Tex. State Rep.
b. Del Rio, Tex, 8/16/36; s. Hilary Brumley Doran and Emma Jane Glover D; m. 10/4/58 to Diane Scrutchin; c. H. B. 'Trey,' III, David Lee and Gregory Lance. Educ: Southwest Tex. State Col, B.A, 58; Univ. of Tex. Sch. of Law, LL.B, 65; Pi Gamma Mu; Pi Sigma Chi; Delta Theta Phi; student body pres, Southwest Tex. State Col. Polit. & Govt. Pos: City and utilities bd. attorney, Del Rio, Tex, 66; Tex. State Rep, 65th dist, 67- Mil. Serv: Entered as 2nd Lt, Air Force, 58, released as 1st Lt, 62, after serv. in 921st Air Police Squadron, Pac. Air Command, 59-62; Capt, Air Force Res, 69-; Marksmanship Ribbon; Longevity Ribbon; Outstanding Unit Ribbon. Mem: State Bar of Tex; Border Bar Asn; Val Verde Co. Bar Asn.(v.pres, 67); C. of C.(dir, Del Rio Chap, 67); chmn, Val Verde Co. Cancer Crusade, 66; F&AM; VFW; life mem. Tex. Execs. Asn. Toastmasters Achievement Award. Rel: Protestant. Legal Res: 2 Edna St, Del Rio, Tex. 78840. Mailing Add: P.O. Box 1485, Del Rio, Tex. 78840.

DORBECKER, DORIS L. R
Ind. State Rep.
b. Faribault Co, Minn, 6/21/19; d. Terrence O. Phipps and Agnes M. McCullough P; m. 1/19/46 to Orville E. Dorbecker; c. Robert E. and Jeneil A. Polit. & Govt. Pos: Ind. State Rep, 68- Mil. Serv: W.A.V.E, World War II. Mem: PTA (pres, Perry Twp. Coun, 66 and past pres, Marion Co. Coun); Library Bd.(former secy, Marion Co. Bd); secy, Ind. Cent. Little League; Boy Scout Den Mother. Rel: Protestant. Mailing Add: 409 Mellowood Dr, Indianapolis, Ind. 46217.

DORE, FRED H. D
Wash. State Sen.
b. Seattle, Wash, 1925; m. to Mary; c. Four. Educ: Seattle Univ; Georgetown For. Serv. Sch; Georgetown Law Sch. Polit. & Govt. Pos: Wash. State Rep, 7 terms; Wash. State Sen, currently. Bus. & Prof. Pos: Lawyer. Mem: Eagles; Elks. Mailing Add: 1424 Washington Bldg, Seattle, Wash. 98101. (1967)

DOREN, JOSEPH C. D
b. Plainfield, N.J. Educ: Albright Col; Rutgers Univ. Law Sch. Polit. & Govt. Pos: Former acting magistrate, Borough of Dunellen, N.J; former attorney, S. Plainfield Sewerage Authority and Borough of S. Plainfield; pres. and legal adv, Middlesex Co. Young Dem. Club; regional v.pres, N.J. Young Dem. Club; twp. attorney, Piscataway; former N.J. State Assemblyman. Bus. & Prof. Pos: Consult. at-law; attorney for Dunellen-Middlesex Police Benevolent Asn. and S. Plainfield Police Benevolent Asn. Mil. Serv: Army. Mem: Elks. Mailing Add: 621 N. Washington Ave, Dunellen, N.J. 08812.

DORF, PAUL AARON D
b. Baltimore, Md, 6/29/26; s. Herman J. Dorf, M.D. and Ada Levinson D; m. 6/1/52 to Rhona Lynn Pollack; c. Jayme, James and Cynthia. Educ: Univ. Md, 46-48; George Wash. Law Sch, 49; Univ. Md. Law Sch, LL.B, 51; Nu Beta Epsilon; Sigma Alpha Mu. Polit. & Govt. Pos: Asst. city solicitor, Baltimore, 54-60; chief judge traffic court, 59-60; Md. State Sen, 61-68, chmn, Vet. and Civil Defense Cmt, v.chmn, Joint Cmt. on Invest. and mem, Finance, Chesapeake Bay and Tributaries, Educ, Juvenile Probs. and Motor Vehicles Cmts, Md. State Senate; del, Dem. Nat. Conv, 68; judge, Supreme Bench, Baltimore, 68- Bus. & Prof. Pos: Partner, Dorf, Pollack & Cahn, Md, 60-68. Mil. Serv: Entered as Seaman 1/C, Navy, 44, released as Naval Cadet, 46. Mem: Real Estate Bd. Gr. Baltimore; Advert. Club Baltimore; Variety Clubs Int; Md. Law Enforcement Officer's Asn; Md. Crime Invest. Cmt; Moose; Safety First Club Md; Trial Magistrates Asn. Md; Standing Cmt. on Unlawful Employ, Baltimore City Bar Asn; Md. State and Am. Bar Asns; NACCA Bar Asn; Am. Trial Lawyers Asn; Mason; Yedz Grotto; Md. Vet. Asn; Optimists; bd. mem, Beth Tfiloh Synagogue; Brotherhood, Greenspring Valley Synagogue and Beth Jacob Synagogue; B'nai B'rith; Independent Order Brith Sholom; Jewish War Vet; Am. Legion; Baltimore Asn. Commerce; Metrop. Civic Asn. Admitted to practice law before U.S. Dist. Court, Court of Appeals and Supreme Court; Outstanding Man of Year Award, Nu Beta Law Fraternity. Rel: Jewish. Legal Res: 2506 Shelleydale Dr, Baltimore, Md. 21209. Mailing Add: Court House, Baltimore, Md. 21202.

DORGAN, BYRON LESLIE D
Tax Cmnr, N.Dak.
b. Dickinson, N.Dak, 5/14/42; s. Emmett Patrick Dorgan and Dorothy Bach D; m. 8/21/63 to Janet Faye Nordstrom; c. Scott Michael. Educ: Univ. Denver, M.B.A, 66; Univ. N.Dak, B.S.B.A, 64; Sigma Alpha Epsilon. Polit. & Govt. Pos: Dep. Tax Cmnr, N.Dak, 67-69, Tax Cmnr, 69- Bus. & Prof. Pos: Financial specialist, Martin/Marietta Corp, Denver, Colo, 66-67. Mem: Am. Mgt. Asn; Nat. Asn. Tax Adminstr; Elks; Farmers Union; Jeffersonian Club. Rel: Lutheran. Mailing Add: 2040 N. Second St, Bismarck, N.Dak. 58501.

DORMAN, ARTHUR D
Md. State Del.
b. N.Y.C, 10/21/26; married. Educ: Geo. Wash. Univ; Pa. Col. of Optom, O.D, 53; Beta Sigma Kappa. Polit. & Govt. Pos: Mem, Vansville Dist. Dem. Club; mem, N.W. Dem. Club; mem, Co. Coun. of Dem. Clubs; pres, Langley Park Dem. Club; Md. State Del, 65- Bus. & Prof. Pos: Optometrist. Mil. Serv: Army, 45-47. Mem: Beth Torah Congregation; Beltsville Citizens Asn; bd. of dirs, Prince George's Co. Boys' Club; past pres, bd. of dirs, Kiwanis; past pres, Cent. Md. Optom. Soc; Nat. Capital Optom. Asn; Md. Optom. Asn; Vision Care Serv; Beltsville Swimming Club. Mailing Add: 11107 Montgomery Rd, Beltsville, Md. 20705. (1967)

DORMAN, HENRY D
Wis. State Sen.
b. Racine, Wis, 9/24/16; s. Zachary Dorman and Eva Nosalevitch D; m. 5/28/49 to Jean Phillips; c. Robin, Wendy, Lynne and Heidi. Educ: Univ. Wis, Ph.B. in Am. Insts, 39, Law Sch, J.D, 47; Tau Epsilon Rho. Polit. & Govt. Pos: Secy, Dem. Party of Racine Co, Wis, 7 years; Racine Co. supvr, 2 years; mem, Racine Co. Bd, 56-58; secy, Mayor's Cmt. on Human Rights, 5 years;

Wis. State Sen, 21st Dist, 65-, mem. Sen. Pub. Welfare Cmt, 65 and Joint Cmt. on Finance and Joint Cmt. on Rev, Repeals and Uniform Laws, 65, mem, Legis. Coun. Local Govt. Cmt, 65-67; mem. task force on local govt. finance and orgn, Gov. Cmt. on Law Enforcement; Wis. legis. rep, Nat. Conf. on Law Enforcement and Crime Control, 67. Mil. Serv: Entered as Pvt, Army Air Force, 42, released as 1st Lt, 45, after serv. in Army Airways Commun. Syst, U.S. Mem: Racine Co. and Wis. State Bar Asns; Nat. Soc. State Legislators (mem. bd. dirs); B'nai B'rith; Church Bd. of Dirs; Jaycees. Rel: Jewish. Mailing Add: 422 16th St, Racine, Wis. 53403.

DORMINY, ARTHUR B. C, JR. D
Ga. State Rep.
b. Ben Hill Co, Ga, 4/20/15; s. A.B.C. Dorminy and Martha Fletcher D; m. 10/18/36 to Emma Myrtle Mitchell; c. Arthur B.C, III. Educ: Fitzgerald High Sch, 32. Polit. & Govt. Pos: Ga. State Rep, 57- Bus. & Prof. Pos: Farmer; pulpwood bus. Rel: Baptist. Mailing Add: 701 W. Central Ave, Fitzgerald, Ga. 31750. (1967)

DORN, FRANCIS EDWIN R
Referee, Supreme Court, N.Y.
b. Brooklyn, N.Y, 4/18/11; s. Jacob J. Dorn and Adelaide Leman D; m. 5/2/43 to Dorothy E. McGann; c. Thomas, Therese, Karen Patricia, Steven and Vincent. Educ: Fordham Col, A.B, 32; Fordham Law Sch, LL.B, 35. Polit. & Govt. Pos: N.Y. State Assemblyman, 40-42; asst. attorney gen, N.Y, 45-50; referee, Supreme Court, N.Y, 50-; U.S. Rep, N.Y, 52-60. Mil. Serv: Entered as Lt.(jg), Navy, 42, released as Lt. Comdr, 45, Comdr, Naval Res. Publ: 'Samuel Chester Reid,' Am. Legion Mag, 2/58. Mem: Eagles; Elks; Am. Legion; VFW. Rel: Roman Catholic. Legal Res: 17 Prospect Park W, Brooklyn, N.Y. 11215. Mailing Add: 32 Court St, Brooklyn, N.Y. 11201.

DORN, ROBERT ALAN D
Chmn, Clark Co. Dem. Party, Wis.
b. Neillsville, Wis, 5/26/45; s. Lowell E. Dorn and Mildred M. Olson D; div; c. Marc Daniel and Michelle Marie. Educ: Col. St. Thomas, 2 years. Polit. & Govt. Pos: Chmn, Clark Co. Dem. Party, Wis, 66- Bus. & Prof. Pos: Secy-treas, Dorn Furniture, Inc, Abbotsford, Wis; pres, Northwest Credit, Inc; secy-treas, Abbotsford Enterprises. Mem: Lions; Abbotsford Investment Club; C. of C; Jaycees. Rel: Catholic. Mailing Add: P.O. Box 98, Abbotsford, Wis. 54405.

DORN, WILLIAM JENNINGS BRYAN D
U.S. Rep, S.C.
b. Greenwood Co, S.C, 4/14/16; s. T.E. Dorn, Sr. and Pearl Griffith D; m. 12/8/49 to Millie Johnson; c. Briana Pearl, Olivia Byrd, Debbie Gail, William Jennings Bryan, Jr. and Johnson Griffith. Educ: Hon. LL.B, Lander Col, 65. Polit. & Govt. Pos: S.C. State Rep, 39-40; S.C. State Sen, 41-43; U.S. Rep, Third Dist, S.C, 47-49 & 51-, former secy, S.C. Cong. Del, U.S. House of Rep, mem, Dem. Steering Cmt. and House Pub. Works Cmt, secy, House Textile Cmt, v.chmn, House Vet. Affairs Cmt. and chmn, Compensation Subcmt. Bus. & Prof. Pos: Cattleman and tree farmer. Mil. Serv: Entered Army Air Force, 43, released as Cpl, 46. Selected Outstanding Young Man of Year in S.C. by Jr. C. of C, 48. Rel: Baptist. Legal Res: Route 1, Greenwood, S.C. 29646. Mailing Add: 2256 Rayburn House Office Bldg, Washington, D.C. 20515.

DORRINGTON, GEORGE JORDAN D
b. Dubuque, Iowa, 8/27/18; s. Arthur Jordan Dorrington and Sarah Ellen Jordan D; m. 1/30/43 to Ruth Ann Baum; c. Arthur Jordan, Deborah Ann and Kevin Douglas. Educ: Loras Col, Dubuque; Drama Club; Speech Club; Varsity Athletics; Tennis Champion. Polit. & Govt. Pos: Asst. coordinator, Kennedy for Pres, 60-62; asst. coordinator, John Schmidhauser for Cong, 64-66; coordinator, John Culver for Cong, 64-66; mem, Platform Cmt, State Dem. Conv, 64 & 66; precinct chmn, 66; former mem, Iowa State Dem. Cent. Cmt. Bus. & Prof. Pos: Broadcast bus, 27 years; regional Sales mgr, WMT TV, currently. Mem: Rotary (bd. mem); past pres, Regis Club; Elmcrest Gold and Country Club; Holy Name Soc; C. of C; charter mem, Jr. C. of C, Dubuque & Decorah and past officer. Rel: Catholic. Mailing Add: 2399 Blake Blvd. S.E, Cedar Rapids, Iowa 52403.

DORRIS, JOHN L. D
Chmn, Luzerne Co. Dem. Cmt, Pa.
b. Shenandoah, Pa, 11/15/97; s. Dennis Dorris and Mary Henrietta Brennan D; m. 6/30/24 to Sarah Veronica Dunlap; c. Kathleen (Mrs. Reese), John Raymond and Mary Alice (Mrs. Brokenshire). Educ: Bucknell Univ, Pre-Med, 16-19; Temple Univ, M.D, 23; Sigma Chi; Omega Epsilon Phi. Polit. & Govt. Pos: Police surgeon, Phila, Pa, 25-28; committeeman, Nanticoke Dem. City Cmt, 40-42; chmn, Fourth Legis Dist. Luzerne Co. Dem. Party, 42-48; chmn, Pa. Workmen's Compensation Bd, 54-61 and cmnr, Pub. Utility Cmn, 61-; mem, Pa. Dem. Exec. Cmt, 56-; del-at-lg, Dem. Nat. Conv, 59 and del, 62; mem, Nanticoke Redevelop. Authority, 66-; chmn, Luzerne Co. Dem. Cmt, currently. Bus. & Prof. Pos: Consult, Nanticoke State Hosp. and Vet. Admin. Hosp, 35-; chief staff, Mercy Hosp, Wilkes-Barre, Pa, 35-; mem. bd, Wyo. Nat. Bank, 64- Mil. Serv: Pvt, Army Med. Corps, 18. Mem: Fel, Am. Col. Surgeons; Int. Col. Surgeons; Am. Legion. Rel: Roman Catholic. Mailing Add: 41 W. Broad St, Nanticoke, Pa. 18634.

DORSEY, MAY FLORENCE R
Mem, Calif. Rep. State Cent. Cmt.
b. Union, Ore, 9/15/21; d. George Foster Steele and Ida Pearl Upton S; m. 12/13/66 to Peter Joseph Dorsey; c. Barbara (Mrs. Joe E. Leming) and Maria (Mrs. Mike H. Gamez). Educ: Wichita State Univ, 4 years. Polit. & Govt. Pos: Ward chmn. and precinct committeewoman, Wichita Rep. Party, Kans, 56-66; tech. officer, Census Bur, 60; mem. staff, Internal Revenue Serv, 61-62; nominee, Kans. State Rep, Wichita, 66; campaign mgr, 68th Assembly Dist. cand, Calif, 68; mem, 68th Assembly Dist. Rep. Cent. Cmt, 68 & 69; alternate mem, Los Angeles Co. Rep. Cent. Cmt, 68 & 69; pres, Gateway Rep. Womens Club Federated, 68 & 69; mem, San Pedro and Wilmington Rep. Precinct Orgn, 68-69; mem, Calif. Rep. State Cent. Cmt, 68- Bus. & Prof. Pos: Rep, Am. Mfg. Co. of Tex, Kans, 53-60, oil field equip. rep, 62-66. Mem: Am. Bus. Womens Asn. Rel: Christian Church of N.Am. Mailing Add: 1113 N. Fries, Wilmington, Calif. 90744.

DORSEY, ROBERT SCHULT D
Mem, Mo. State Dem. Cmt.
b. Caruthersville, Mo, 12/26/17; s. William Henry Dorsey and Edna Ann Schult D; m. 6/12/42 to Lulagene Johnson; c. Bobbiegene, Barbara Ann and William Johnson. Educ: Mo. Sch. of Mines, B.S. in Chem. Eng, 42. Polit. & Govt. Pos: Mayor, City of Brookfield, Mo, 54-56; chmn, Linn Co. Dem. Cmt, 56-66; chmn, Mo. Sixth Cong. Dist. Dem. Cmt, 61-66; mem, Mo. State Dem. Cmt, 66- Bus. & Prof. Pos: Owner, Gen. Ins. Agency, 45-56; cashier, Security State Bank, 56-58, pres, 58- Mil. Serv: Entered as Flying Cadet, Air Force, 41, released as 1st Lt, 45, after serv. as Multiengine Pilot, Training Command. Mem: Lions; Am. Legion; K. of C. (3°); Eagles; Elks; Col, Gov. Staff. Rel: Roman Catholic. Legal Res: 921 N. Main, Brookfield, Mo. 64628. Mailing Add: 216 N. Main, Brookfield, Mo. 64628.

DORWIN, JACK CROSBY R
b. Minneapolis, Minn; 12/23/26; s. Harvey C. Dorwin and Alice S. Larson D; m. 8/9/59 to Margot Ann Fisher; c. David Bailey and Paul Andrew. Educ: Univ. South. Calif, B.S.M.E, 52. Polit. & Govt. Pos: Chmn, Citizens-By-Choice, Santa Clara, Calif, 66; mem, Santa Clara Co. Rep. Cent. Cmt, 66-69; chmn, 24th Assembly Dist. Registrn, 67; cand. Calif. State Assemblyman, 24th Dist, 68; mem, Calif. State Rep. Cent. Cmt, 68-69. Bus. & Prof. Pos: Sr. design engr. and mgr, Lockheed Missiles & Space Co, Sunnyvale, Calif, 52-68; mgr. work authority control, Ingalls Shipbuilding Co, 69. Mil. Serv: Entered as Pvt, Army, 44, released as Capt, 47, after serv. in 562nd Bt. Maintenance Bn, Second Eng. Brigade, Pac. Theatre, 45-46; Bronze Star; Purple Heart; Combat Inf. Badge. Mem: Am. Asn. for Adv. of Sci; Inst. of Elec. and Electronics Engrs; F&AM; pres, Seacliffe Homeowners Asn. Rel: Protestant. Mailing Add: 109 Seacliffe Dr, Gautier, Miss. 39553.

DOSEK, EDWIN FRANCIS D
Mem, All Am. Coun, Dem. Nat. Cmt.
b. Ulysses, Nebr, 10/9/20; s. Edward A. Dosek and Philomene Kabourek D; m. 10/27/45 to Betty Rees Scott; c. J. Richard, Kathryn Ann, E. Scott and Teresa Rees. Educ: Univ. Nebr, B.S, 42; Creighton Univ. Col. of Law, LL.B, 48; Delta Theta Phi; Delta Sigma Rho; Delta Tau Delta. Polit. & Govt. Pos: Pres, Young Dem. of Lancaster Co, Nebr, 49-50; del, Lancaster Co. Dem. Conv, 52-54, Nebr. State Dem. Conv, 54; mem, Mayors Cmt. on Youth Crime Prev, 54-59; del, Dem. Nat. Conv, 60 & 64; mem, All Am. Coun, Dem. Nat. Cmt, 64- Bus. & Prof. Pos: Attorney-at-law, 49- Mil. Serv: Entered as Pvt, Army, 42, released as Capt, 46, after serv. in Army Transportation Corps, Asiatic-Pac. Theater, 42-43; Am. and Asiatic Pac. Theater Medals; Victory Medal; Army Commendation, Good Conduct and Reserve Medals; Lt. Col, Army Res. Mem: Lincoln, Lancaster Co, Nebr. State and Am. Bar Asns; Nat. Parole and Probation Asn; Delta Sigma Rho; Am. Legion; K. of C; Lions; Elks; dir, Am. Heart Asn, 60-62; Nebr. Heart Asn; nat. v.pres, Jr. C. of C, 53-54. Rel: Roman Catholic. Mailing Add: 1725 Skyline Dr, Lincoln, Nebr. 68506.

DOSLAND, WILLIAM BUEHLER R
Minn. State Sen.
b. Chicago, Ill, 11/10/27; s. Goodwin Leroy Dosland and Beatrice Buehler D; m. 9/15/56 to Donna M. Mathisen; c. David William and Susan Elizabeth. Educ: Concordia Col, Moorhead, Minn, B.A, 49; Univ. Minn. Col. of Law, LL.B, 54; Mem. Ed. Bd, Minn. Law Rev; Delta Theta Phi. Polit. & Govt. Pos: Minn. State Sen, 59- Bus. & Prof. Pos: Partner, Dosland, Dosland & Nordhougen, Attorneys, 54- Mil. Serv: Entered as A/S, Navy, 45, released as Aviation Cadet, 47; recalled as Ens, Naval Res, 51, released as Lt.(jg), 53, after serv. with 6th Fleet, Mediterranean; Comdr, Navy, 66. Mem: VFW; Am. Legion. Rel: Lutheran. Mailing Add: 929 S. 21st Ave, Moorhead, Minn. 56560.

DOTSON, BOBBY JOE R
Chmn, Wise Co. Rep. Party, Va.
b. Pound, Va, 9/3/31; s. Edward S. Dotson and Pearl Beverly D; m. 12/27/57 to Nancy Carol Collins; c. Lisa Ellen and Elizabeth Carol. Educ: Emory and Henry Col, B.A, 54; Univ. Va, M.Ed, 63; Phi Delta Kappa. Polit. & Govt. Pos: Chmn, Wise Co. Rep. Party, Va, 68-; admin. asst, U.S. Rep. William C. Wampler, Va, 69. Bus. & Prof. Pos: High sch. teacher and coach, Coeburn, Va, 54-60 and prin, 61-68; supt, Norton City Schs, 69- Mem: Wise Co, Lonesome Pine, Dist. 'O,' Va. and Nat. Prin. Asns; Va. High Sch. League; Wise Co, Va. and Nat. Educ. Asns; Mason; Highland Country Club. Named to Outstanding Men of the South, 66. Rel: Protestant. Legal Res: Center St, Coeburn, Va. 24230. Mailing Add: 109 11th St, Norton, Va. 24273.

DOTSON, WILLIAM FRANCIS D
Chmn, Lyon Co. Dem. Cent. Cmt, Kans.
b. San Antonio, Tex, 11/6/15; s. William Harrison Dotson and Carrie Adel Strittmatter D; m. 12/20/35 to Dorothy Lea Bruner; c. Mary (Mrs. Marchetti), William David, Jane (Mrs. Clabattari) and Denise Lea. Educ: Bethel Col, 2 years. Polit. & Govt. Pos: Chmn, Lyon Co. Dem. Cent. Cmt, Kans, currently. Bus. & Prof. Pos: Locomotive engr, Santa Fe RR. Mem: Brotherhood Locomotive Firemen and Enginemen; C. of C; United Transportation Union. Rel: Congregational. Mailing Add: 1324 Washington, Emporia, Kans. 66801.

DOTSON, WILLIAM SHAKESPEARE D
b. Cave City, Ky, 9/29/12; s. Samuel L. Dotson and Pearl Overstreet D; m. 6/4/32 to Alice Duncan. Educ: Ky. State Col, B.S, 36; Omega Psi Phi; Esquire Soc. Club. Polit. & Govt. Pos: Adv. to the Gov. of Ky, 63-; del, Dem. Nat. Conv, 64; state mem, Dem. Club of Ky. Bus. & Prof. Pos: Dist. mgr, Supreme Life Ins. Co, 61- Mem: NAACP (state treas, Ky. State Conf, 46-); Ky. State Col. Nat. Alumni Asn.(past pres); mem. bd, Gen. Agents and Mgrs. Conf. of Ky, 65-; Bluegrass Asn. for Mentally Retarded Children (v.pres, 66-); Mason (32°); F&AM; commissioned a Ky. Col. by the Gov. of Ky, 65- Rel: Baptist. Mailing Add: 432 E. Fifth St, Lexington, Ky. 40508.

DOTY, RUSSELL LEIGH, JR. D
b. Great Falls, Mont, 6/7/42; s. Russell Leigh Doty, Sr. and Eleanor Caroline Peters D; m. 12/23/67 to Janet Rae Maurer. Educ: Wash. State Univ, B.A. in polit. sci, 65; Mont. State Univ; Univ.Mont; Univ. Ore, 68-69; Alpha Kappa Lambda. Polit. & Govt. Pos: Intern, Nat. Center for Educ. in Polit, 64; postal clerk and carrier, U.S. Post Off. Dept, 66; Mont. State Rep, 67-68; alternate del, Dem. Nat. Conv, 68; precinct committeeman, Cascade Co, Mont,

68- Bus. & Prof. Pos: Campaign aid to Congressman John Melcher, 66; teacher soc. studies, Meadow Hill Sch, Missoula, 69- Mil. Serv: Marine Corps, 66. Mem: Am. Polit. Sci. Asn; West. Govt. Research Asn. Rel: Methodist. Legal Res: 220 18th St. S, Great Falls, Mont. 59401. Mailing Add: 541 E. Beckwith, Missoula, Mont. 59801.

DOUBLE, BARBARA TURNER D
Mem. Exec. Cmt, Calif. Dem. State Cent. Cmt.
b. Miami, Fla, 12/3/26; d. Ernest Cecil Turner and Lilian Darracott T; m. 12/6/48 to Harry McCallister Double; c. Addison Turner. Educ: Pasadena Playhouse Sch. of the Theatre, 2 years plus grad. work. Polit. & Govt. Pos: Mem, Calif. Dem. State Cent. Cmt, 56-58, 62-63, 66-67 & 68-, mem. exec. cmt, 68-; pres, Hollywood Hills Dem. Club, 58-59; polit. action chmn, Calif. Dem. Coun, 59 & 60, secy, 60-63; alternate del, Dem. Nat. Conv, 60. Bus. & Prof. Pos: Corp. secy, Double Elec, Inc, 64- Mem: League of Women Voters; Pasadena-Foothill Urban League (bd. gov). Rel: Episcopal. Mailing Add: 1455 Ontario Ave, Pasadena, Calif. 91103.

DOUD, J. PHIL D
Chmn, Montgomery Co. Dem. Cmt, Pa.
b. Norristown, Pa, 7/12/12; s. J. Phil Doud and Theresa Quinn D; m. 8/1/35 to Eleanor Bolger; c. Stephen, J. Phil, III, Mary Theresa and Dennis. Educ: Wharton Sch; Univ. Pa. Polit. & Govt. Pos: Mem, Pa. Dem. State Cmt, 52-53 and Pa. Dem. Policy Cmt, 54-55 & 60-; v.chmn, Montgomery Co. Dem. Cmt, Pa, 54-60, chmn, 60-; mem, Pa. Electoral Col, 60, 64 & 68. Bus. & Prof. Pos: Pres. and bus. mgr, Int. Brotherhood of Boilermakers, 43-61; dir, Dept. of Auditor Gen, 61- Mem: K. of C; Alhambra; Gen. Wash. Country Club. Rel: Roman Catholic. Legal Res: 1671 Peachtree Lane, Norristown, Pa. 19401. Mailing Add: 325 Swede St, Norristown, Pa. 19401.

DOUGHERTY, DANIEL D. D
Ill. State Sen.
b. Chicago, Ill, 4/26/06; married; c. two sons, one daughter. Educ: Bowen High Sch; courses in blast furnaces and power plant eng. Polit. & Govt. Pos: Secy, Tenth Ward Dem. Orgn, Ill; Ill. State Sen, currently. Bus. & Prof. Pos: Chief dep. clerk, Co. court of Cook Co. Mem: K. of C; (4°); pub. rep, Am. Red Cross; Ahepi; Boy Scout Activities; 50 Fund Raising Drives. Mailing Add: 1957 E. 93rd St, Chicago, Ill. 60617.

DOUGHERTY, ELEANOR MARY D
b. Green Bay, Wis, 5/23/86; d. James Dougherty and Josephine McLean D; single. Educ: Valley City, N.Dak. Teachers Col, 08; Moorhead, Minn. Teachers Col, 20; Univ. Minn, B.A, 22; Columbia Univ, M.A, 26; Col. of Great Falls, Hon. Ph.D, 62; nat. platform, Delta Kappa Gamma. Polit. & Govt. Pos: Former Mont. State Rep, Cascade Co. Bus. & Prof. Pos: Teacher civics, Minneapolis, Minn, 2 years; teacher, training dept, high sch, 20-36; prin, high sch, 36-40; prof. polit. sci. and hist, Col. of Great Falls, 40- Mem: Am. Polit. Sci. Asn; Mont. Sci. Asn. Recipient of three nat. awards. Rel: Catholic. Mailing Add: 517 Third Ave. N, Great Falls, Mont. 59401.

DOUGHERTY, ESTHER HAWLEY R
b. Arrowsic, Maine, 7/6/20; d. Norman Hinckley Drummond and Emma Toothaker; m. to Warren F. Hawley, Jr, wid; m. to John F. Dougherty, M.D. Educ: Univ. Maine, B.A, 41; Delta Delta Delta. Polit. & Govt. Pos: Exec. bd, Maine Fedn. Rep. Women, 58-66; mem, Maine Rep. State Cmt, 60-62, v.chmn, 62-68; mem, Maine State Retirement Bd, 60-67; chmn, Maine State Personnel Bd, 60-69; del, Rep. Nat. Conv, 64 & 68. Bus. & Prof. Pos: Speech supvr, Pine Tree Soc, 48-60; commercial mgr, WJTO Radio, Bath, Maine, 60-67. Rel: Episcopal. Mailing Add: 42 Summer St, Bath, Maine 04530.

DOUGHERTY, JEAN MARIE CORDINER R
b. Seattle, Wash, 6/10/27; d. Ralph Jarron Cordiner and Gwyneth Lewis C; m. 6/24/49 to John Ward Dougherty; c. Sharon Cordiner, Diane Jean, Jonathan Maynard, Ralph Cordiner, Leslie Ann, Janet Lee, Joseph Wardle and Ward Lewis. Educ: Northwest. Univ, B.S, 49; Univ. S.Fla, 67-69; Gamma Phi Beta. Polit. & Govt. Pos: V.chmn, Conn. Fedn. Rep. Women, 64-65; finance chmn, Hillsborough Co. Women's Rep. Club, Fla, 67-68, recording secy, 68-69, treas, 69-; del, Rep. Nat. Conv, 68; mem, Hillsborough Co. Charter Cmn, 69- Mem: Easter Seal Guild; GOPers; Hillborough Co. Rep. Club; Krewe of Venus; Quail Hollow Country Club. Rel: Presbyterian. Mailing Add: Van Dyke Rd, Route 2, Box 1212, Lutz, Fla. 33549.

DOUGHERTY, MARY B. R
Secy, San Juan Co. Rep. Cent. Cmt, Colo.
b. Smyrna, N.Y, 3/5/13; d. Fred L. Boos and Gertrude Miles B; m. 8/20/38 to James E. Dougherty. Educ: High Sch, Norwich, N.Y, grad, 29. Polit. & Govt. Pos: Secy, San Juan Co. Rep. Cent. Cmt, Colo, 62- Mem: Secy, Silverton C. of C; Club 20. Rel: Protestant. Mailing Add: 1846 Green St, Silverton, Colo. 81433.

DOUGHERTY, TOM D
Iowa State Rep.
b. Eddyville, Route 1, Monroe Co, Iowa, 2/2/10; s. John H. Dougherty and Jennie D; m. 10/29/55 to Lucille Mottet; c. Theresa Anne. Educ: St. Patrick's High Sch, 28. Polit. & Govt. Pos: Iowa State Rep, currently. Bus. & Prof. Pos: Farmer. Mem: K. of C.(4°), McMullen Assembly, Past Grand Knight; Eagles; agr. v.chmn, Albia C. of C; ex officio dir, Iowa Farm Bur; dir. and state pres, Iowa Rural Young Peoples Assembly. State Level Land Plowing Champion, 50; Co. Contour Plowing Champion 3 years; Participant in 2 Nat. Plowing Matches and Wheatland and Big Rock Matches in Ill; Judge, Co, State, Dist. Matches; Conservation Award, 53; 4-H Emerald Clover Award for 25 years of 4-H Leadership. Rel: Catholic. Mailing Add: 202 Sixth Ave. E, Albia, Iowa 52531. (1967)

DOUGHERTY, WILLIAM JOSEPH D
Dem. Nat. Committeeman, S.Dak.
b. Sioux Falls, S.Dak, 4/6/32; s. Wm. J. Dougherty and Alice Walsh D; m. 12/19/53 to Louise Hulsabus; c. Patrick, Jennifer and Timothy. Educ: S.Dak. State Univ, B.S, 54. Polit. & Govt. Pos: Pres, S.Dak. Young Dem, 59; chmn, Kennedy for President, 60; del, Dem. State Conv, 60, 62, 64, 66 & 68; cand, S.Dak. State Sen, 62; chmn, Herseth for Gov, 62; treas, Minnehaha Co. State Cent. Cmt, 66-68; cand, S.Dak. State Rep, 68; chmn, Kennedy for President, 68; chmn. S.Dak. del, Dem. Nat. Conv, 68; nat. chmn, McGovern for President, 68; Dem. nat. committeeman, S.Dak, 68- Bus. & Prof. Pos: Pres. and gen. mgr, Adams-Dougherty Livestock, 61-; pres, Sioux Falls Livestock Exchange, 63; pres, Sioux Falls Livestock Found, 64; bd. dir, River Mkt, 65. Mem: K. of C; Elks; chmn, S.Dak. Multiple Sclerosis Soc; S.Dak. Livestock Feeders Asn. Rel: Catholic. Mailing Add: 2901 S. Fourth St, Sioux Falls, S.Dak. 57105.

DOUGHTY, ESTHER S. R
b. Wis. Educ: Horicon High Sch. Polit. & Govt. Pos: Wis. State Assemblywoman, 62-68. Bus. & Prof. Pos: Ins. and real estate agent. Mailing Add: 211 N. Hubbard St, Horicon, Wis. 53032. (1967)

DOUGHTY, WARREN BROWE D
Mem, Mich. Dem. State Cent. Cmt.
b. Detroit, Mich, 5/20/21; s. Lloyd William Doughty and Bertha L. Browe D; m. 1/11/47 to Thelma Jean Wiltz; c. Brent Walker, Gregory Lloyd and Sandra Jean (Mrs. Alexander Mann). Educ: Wayne State Univ, B.A. and M.A; plus additional grad. work. Polit. & Govt. Pos: Dem. precinct del, Trenton, Mich, 62-; mem, Mich. Dem. State Cent. Cmt, 65-, by-laws cmt, 67-; alternate del, Dem. Nat. Conv, 68; mem, Haber Cmn. on Polit. Reform, 69-; mem, Wayne Co. Dem. Cmt, currently; mem, 16th Cong. Dist. Dem. Party and mem, exec. bd, currently; mem, Wayne Co. Dem. Finance Cmt, currently; mem, bd. dir, Trenton Dem. Club, currently. Bus. & Prof. Pos: Teacher and sr. adv, Detroit Bd. of Educ, Mich, 49-69. Mil. Serv: Entered as Pvt, Army, 42, released as T/Sgt, 46, after serv. in 12th Armored Div, ETO, 43-46; Purple Heart; ETO Medal with Three Battle Stars. Mem: Nat. Coun. of Soc. Studies; Detroit Fedn. of Teachers; Mason; Knights Templar; DAV; Detroit Schoolmens Club; Quiet Birdman; Goodfellows. Rel: Protestant. Mailing Add: 1847 Edsel Dr, Trenton, Mich. 48183.

DOUGLAS, C. THOMAS 'TOM' D
Miss. State Sen.
b. Dentville, Miss, 1/13/12; married. Polit. & Govt. Pos: Miss. State Rep, 40-44; Miss. State Sen, 60- Bus. & Prof. Pos: Partner, Hercules Tire & Rubber Co. Mem: C. of C; Farm Bur; Citizens Coun; Hazlehurst Booster Club; Nat. Tire Dealers Retreaders Asn. Rel: Christian. Mailing Add: Box 431, 226-A, N. Exten, Hazlehurst, Miss. 39083. (1967)

DOUGLAS, EMILY TAFT D
b. Chicago, Ill, d. Lorado Taft and Ada Bartlett T; m. to Paul H. Douglas; c. Jean Taft. Educ: Univ. Chicago, B.A, 20. Polit. & Govt. Pos: Ill. State Rep-at-lg, 45-46; adv. to Am. del, UNESCO, Paris, 50. Publ: Appleseed Farm, Abingdon-Cokesbury, 48; Remember the Ladies: The Story of Great Women who Helped Shape America, G.P. Putnam's Son, 66. Rel: Unitarian; moderator, Am. Unitarian Asn, 59-60, v.pres, 61. Mailing Add: 2909 Davenport St. N.W, Washington, D.C. 20008.

DOUGLAS, GUY D
Doorkeeper, W.Va. State Senate
b. Bigbend, W.Va, 7/26/95; s. Eldred Douglas and Eliza Walker D; m. 3/25/17 to Goldie Amick, wid; c. Six daughters. Educ: Pub. Schs. of W.Va. Polit. & Govt. Pos: Doorkeeper, Fayette Co. Court, 36-48, court pres, 6 years; doorkeeper, W.Va. State Senate, 49- Bus. & Prof. Pos: Farmer, sch. teacher. Mem: Mason; Scottish Rite; Shrine. Rel: Methodist. Mailing Add: Lookout, Fayette Co, W.Va. 25868. (1967)

DOUGLAS, JOHN WOOLMAN D
b. Philadelphia, Pa, 8/15/21; s. Paul Howard Douglas and Dorothy Sybil Wolff D; m. 7/14/45 to Mary Evans St. John; c. Katherine St. John, Peter Roderick. Educ: Princeton, B.A, 43; Yale, LL.B, 48; Oxford Univ, Eng, Rhodes Scholar and D.Phil, 50. Polit. & Govt. Pos: Law clerk to U.S. Supreme Court Justice Burton, 51-52; asst. attorney gen, Civil Div, Dept. of Justice, 63-66. Bus. & Prof. Pos: Lawyer, Covington & Burling, Wash, D.C, 50-51 & 52-58, partner, 58-63 & 66- Mil. Serv: Naval Res, 43-46. Mem: Am. Bar Asn. Rel: Presbyterian. Mailing Add: 5700 Kirkside Dr, Chevy Chase, Md. 20015. (1967)

DOUGLAS, LEWIS W. D
b. Bisbee, Ariz, 7/2/94; s. James Stuart Douglas and Josephine Leah Williams D; m. 6/19/21 to Peggy Zinsser; c. James Stuart, Lewis W. and Sharman. Educ: Amherst Col, B.A, 16; Mass. Inst. Tech, 16-17; Amherst Col. and Harvard Univ. hon. LL.D, 33; hon. LL.D. from Queens Col, Princeton, Brown, N.Y. and Wesleyan Univs, 38, Univ. Ariz, 40, Leeds, Eng, 48, Univ. Bristol, St. Andrews and London, 49, Edinburgh, Birmingham and Glasgow, 50, Univ. Calif, McGill Univ, Columbia and Dalhousie, 51; D.C.L, Oxford, Eng, 48. Polit. & Govt. Pos: Ariz. State Rep, 23-25; U.S. Rep, Ariz, 27-33; dir. of Budget, 33-34; Dep. War Shipping Adminstr, 42-45; spec. adv. to Gen. Clay, German Control Coun, 45; U.S. Ambassador to Gt. Brit, 47-50. Bus. & Prof. Pos: Instr, Amherst Col, 20, emer. trustee; mining and gen. bus, Ariz, 21-; v.pres. and dir, Am. Cyanamid Co, 34-38; prin. and vice chancellor, McGill Univ, Montreal, 38-39; pres, Mutual Life Ins. Co. of N.Y, 40-47, chmn. bd, 47-59, chmn. exec. cmt. of bd. dirs. and dir, 59-; hon. chmn. bd. dirs, South. Ariz. Bank & Trust Co. and Douglas Investment Co; dir, Tech. Studies, Inc, West. Bancorp, Gen. Motors Corp, Int. Nickel Co, Newmont Mining Corp. and Union Corp. Ltd. Mil. Serv: 1st Lt, Army, World War I, serv. in Field Artil, AEF, France; citation from Gen. Pershing; decorated Croix de Guerre (Belgium); Grand Croix de la Legion d'Honneur (France); Grand Croix de l'Order de la Couronne (Belgium); hon. Knight Grand Cross Order Brit. Empire. Mem: Chmn, Nat. Policy Bd; pres. and chmn, Am. Assembly; Alfred P. Sloan Found; Rockefeller Found; Am. Mus. Natural Hist; pres. and trustee, Acad. Polit. Sci; nat. chmn, Am. Shakespeare Festival Theatre; hon. pres, Nat. Soc. for Prev. of Blindness; adv. bd, Mem. Hosp; Eng. Speaking Union; v.pres, Nat. Inst. Soc. Sci; Am. Philos. Soc. Rel: Episcopal. Mailing Add: Sonoita, Ariz. 85637.

DOUGLAS, PAUL H. D
b. Salem, Mass, 3/26/82; m. to Emily Taft; c. Helen (Mrs. Paul Klein), John, Dorothea (Mrs. Robert John), Paul and Jean (Mrs. Ned Bandler). Educ: Bowdoin Col, A.B; Columbia Univ, Ph.D, 21. Polit. & Govt. Pos: Alderman, Fifth Ward, Chicago City Coun, 39-42; adv. to President Roosevelt on N.Y. Soc. Security Probs; U.S. Sen, Ill, 48-66; chmn, Nat. Cmn. on Urban Probs,

67-68; del, Dem. Nat. Conv, 68. Bus. & Prof. Pos: Prof, dept. econ, Univ. Chicago, 20-48. Mil. Serv: Entered as Pvt, Marine Corps, 42, released as Lt. Col, 46, after serv. in 1st Marine Div, Peleliu and Okinawa; wounded in Peleliu; awarded Bronze Star. Publ: The Theory of Wages; Real Wages in the United States; Social Security in the United States. Mem: Pres, Am. Econ. Asn, 47. Drafted 1st Ill. Old Age Pension Act; helped draft Ill. Unemploy. Ins. Law; helped revise Fed. Soc. Security Act, 39. Legal Res: Chicago, Ill. Mailing Add: 2909 Davenport St, Washington, D.C. 20008.

DOUGLAS, WILLIAM ORVILLE D
Assoc. Justice, U.S. Supreme Court
b. Maine, Minn, 10/16/98; s. William Douglas and Julia Bickford Fiske D; m. 1966 to Kathleen Heffernan; c. Mildred Riddle (Mrs. Norman T. Read) and William Orville. Educ: Whitman Col, Wash, B.A, 20; Columbia Univ, LL.B, 25; Beta Theta Pi; Phi Alpha Delta; Delta Sigma Rho; Phi Beta Kappa. Hon. LL.D, Whitman Col, 38, Wesleyan Univ, 40, Wash. and Jefferson Col, 42, William and Mary Col, 43, Nat. Univ, 49, New Sch. for Soc. Research, 52, Univ. Toledo, 56, Dalhousie Univ, 58 and Colby Col, 61. Polit. & Govt. Pos: Bankruptcy studies, Yale Inst. Human Rels. and Dept. of Commerce, 29-32; secy, cmt. on bus. fed. courts, Nat. Cmn. on Law Observance and Enforcement, 30-32; dir. protective cmt. studies, Securities & Exchange Cmn, 34-39; assoc. justice, U.S. Supreme Court, 39- Bus. & Prof. Pos: Attorney-at-law, N.Y.C, 25-27; mem. faculty, Columbia Univ, 25-28, Yale, 28-34. Mil. Serv: Pvt, Army, 18. Publ: Democracy's Manifesto, 62; The Anatomy of Liberty, 63; Mr. Lincoln and the Negroes, 63. Mem: Royal George Soc, London; Mason; Yale Club; Himalayan Club, Delhi, India; Univ. Club, Wash; Overseas Press Club. Rel: Presbyterian. Legal Res: Gooseprairie, Wash. 98929. Mailing Add: U.S. Supreme Court, Washington, D.C. 20543.

DOUGLASS, CALVIN ALBERT D
Md. State Del.
b. Baltimore, Md, 9/1/09; s. George Henry Douglass and Florence Butler D; m. 2/14/69 to Dorthy Lewis; c. Calvin, Jr. and Mercedes (Mrs. Rankins). Educ: Shaw Univ, B.S, 28; Univ. Md, College Park, LL.B; Phi Beta Sigma. Polit. & Govt. Pos: Asst. city solicitor, Baltimore, Md, 48-59; magistrate, West. Police Sta, 59-61; Md. State Del, Fourth Dist, 66- Mem: Urban League; Trenton Dem. Club; NAACP; Fourth Dist. Dem. Orgn. Rel: Presbyterian. Legal Res: 2910 Auchentoroly Terr, Baltimore, Md. 21217. Mailing Add: 1531 Pennsylvania Ave, Baltimore, Md. 21217.

DOUGLASS, GUS R. D
Cmnr. of Agr, W.Va.
b. Mason Co, W.Va, 2/22/27; s. Gus R. Douglass and Fanny Elizabeth D; m. 10/23/47 to Anna Lee Roush; c. Mary Lee, Stephen Ruben, Thomas Oscar and Cynthia Sue. Educ: Pub. schs. Polit. & Govt. Pos: Mem. bd. dirs, Pub. Land Corp. and Agr. Hall of Fame, Kans; chmn. agr. adv. cmt, Educ. Develop. Conf, Glenville State Col; supvr, West. Soil Conserv. Dist, 10 years; chmn, Geol. Surv. Cmn, Econ. Opportunity Cmn. and State Soil Conserv. Cmt; mem, W.Va. Manpower, Tech. and Training Cmn. and Air Pollution Control Cmn; mem. bd, Pub. Works; asst. cmnr. of agr, W.Va, 57-64, cmnr. of agr, 64- Mem: Mason; dir. and secy, Mason Co. Farm Bur; past chmn, Mason Co. Agr. Stabilization Cmt; Farmers Home Admin; Future Farmers of Am, state pres. and v.pres, nat. pres; State Fair. W.Va. State Farmer Award. Rel: Baptist. Mailing Add: Point Pleasant, W.Va. 25550.

DOUGLASS, ROBERT LEE D
City Councilman, Baltimore, Md.
b. Winnsboro, S.C, 6/23/28; s. John Douglass and Jannie Bell Stevenson D; m. 10/25/47 to Bernice Viola Sales; c. Beverly Eileen, Ronald Keith, Eric Lee and Loren Robert. Educ: Morgan State Col, B.S. in Math, 53; Johns Hopkins Univ, B.S. in Elec. Eng, 62. Polit. & Govt. Pos: City councilman, Baltimore, Md, 67-; del, Dem. Nat. Conv, 68. Bus. & Prof. Pos: Teacher, Baltimore City Pub. Schs, 55-62 & 64-65; design engr, Bendix Corp, 62-64; instr. electronics, eve. div, Commun. Col. Baltimore, 62-67; lectr. math, Morgan State Col, 62-67; systs. engr, Int. Bus. Machines Corp, 65-68, pres. and co-founder, Baltimore Electronics Assocs, Inc, 68- Mil. Serv: Entered as 2nd Lt, Army, 53, released as 1st Lt, 55, after serv. in 61st AAA Bn, Third Armored Div, U.S, 54-55; Nat. Serv. Medal. Mem: Inst. Elec. and Electronics Engrs. Rel: African Methodist Episcopal. Legal Res: 2110 Homewood Ave, Baltimore, Md. 21218. Mailing Add: 2313 Homewood Ave, Baltimore, Md. 21218.

DOUMAR, ROBERT GEORGE R
Chmn, Norfolk Rep. Party, Va.
b. Norfolk, Va, 2/17/30; s. George Joseph Doumar and Margot Meshaka D; m. 4/28/62 to Dorothy Mundy; c. Robert G, Jr. and Charles C. Educ: Univ. Va, B.A, 51, LL.B, 53; Raven Soc; Order of Coif; Delta Upsilon; Phi Delta Phi. Polit. & Govt. Pos: Chmn, Norfolk Rep. Party, Va, 60-62 & 66-; mem, Va. Rep. State Cent. Cmt, 66-68; del, Rep. Nat. Conv, 68. Bus. & Prof. Pos: Sr. partner, Doumar, Pinus, Anderson & Knight, 58- Mil. Serv: Entered as 2nd Lt, Army, 53, released as 1st Lt, 55, after serv. in Transportation Mil. Roadway Serv, Korea, Far East Command, 54-55; Res, Maj. Mem: Am, Fed. and Va. Bar Asns; K. of C; Elks; Optimist; Am. Legion. Rel: Roman Catholic. Legal Res: 1400 Armistead Bridge Rd, Norfolk, Va. 23507. Legal Res: 1350 Virginia National Bank Bldg, Norfolk, Va. 23510.

DOUTHIT, JACKSON SHERROD D
b. Rockwall, Tex, 7/19/12; s. William Lee Douthit and Anna Elizabeth Jackson D; m. 6/21/41 to Mary Evelyn Herridge; c. Mary Lee and Collin Jackson. Educ: Angelo State Col. Polit. & Govt. Pos: Justice of the Peace, Irion Co, Tex, 38-44; chmn, Sterling Co. Dem. Exec. Cmt, 47-69; dir. of Upper Colo. River Authority, 60-69. Bus. & Prof. Pos: Publisher, Mertzon Star, 37-44, Sterling City News-Record, 44-66. Rel: Methodist. Mailing Add: Box 608, Sterling City, Tex. 76951.

DOUTHITT, FRANKLIN JOSEPH D
b. Wichita Falls, Tex, 2/18/37; s. Ambrose Christian Douthitt and Elizabeth Imhoff Donnell D; m. 5/27/61 to Sandra Hamilton. Educ: Midwest. Univ, 57-58; Tex. Tech. Col, B.B.A, 60; Univ. Tex. Sch. Law, LL.B, 67; Pi Kappa Alpha. Polit. & Govt. Pos: Chmn, Clay Co. Dem. Exec. Cmt, Tex, 64-69; Co. and Dist. Attorney, Clay Co, 69- Bus. & Prof. Pos: Partner and former mgr. in A.C. Douthitt Ranch, Henrietta, Tex. Mil. Serv: Entered as Pvt, Army Nat. Guard, 60, released as Sgt, 66, after serv, 49th Armored Div, Ft. Polk, La; Sgt. E-5. Mem: V.pres, Clay Co. Farm Bur, Tex. Rel: Episcopal. Legal Res: Route 1, Henrietta, Texas. 76365. Mailing Add: 111 S. Main St, Henrietta, Tex. 76365.

DOW, ARTHUR L. D
N.Mex. State Rep.
b. Picacho, N.Mex, 11/7/26; s. Eugene Charles Dow and Jennie Peppin D; m. 4/6/50 to Mary A. Cross; c. Jennie Carolyn and Mary Reon. Educ: U.S. Armed Forces Inst, Col. Exten; Univ. of N.Mex, bus. admin. Polit. & Govt. Pos: Precinct div. chmn, Dem. Party, N.Mex, 59-62; mem, Co. Dem. Cent. Cmt, 62-64; N.Mex. State Rep, 65-; del, Dem. Nat. Conv, 68. Bus. & Prof. Pos: V.pres, N.Mex. State Fedn, AFL-CIO, 57-62, pres, Barber Local 501, 61 and pres, Co. Cent. Labor Coun, 63-64. Mil. Serv: Fireman 1/C, Navy, 44-46, serv. in Amphibious Pac, 46; Am. Theatre Ribbon; Asiatic-Pac. Ribbon with Four Battle Stars; Victory Medal. Mem: VFW; DAV; Barber Union, AFL-CIO; Civitan Int; C. of C. Rel: Baptist. Mailing Add: 3718 Candelaria Rd. N.E, Albuquerque, N.Mex. 87110.

DOW, JOHN GOODCHILD D
b. New York, N.Y, 5/6/05; s. Joy Wheeler Dow and Elizabeth Goodchild D; m. 10/18/30 to Harriet; c. Thomas G, Timothy T, Diantha E. (Mrs. Walter B. Schull) and A. Sophia. Educ: Harvard Col, A.B, 27; Columbia Univ, M.A, 37. Polit. & Govt. Pos: Chmn, Orangetown Dem. Cmt, N.Y, 57-62; chmn, Grand View Zoning Bd. of Appeals, 64-65; U.S. Rep, 27th Dist, N.Y, 65-68; del, Dem. Nat. Conv, 68; staff aide to group of U.S. Rep, 69- Bus. & Prof. Pos: Asst. mgr. systs. and procedures, ACF Industs, Inc, N.Y.C, 54-65. Rel: Episcopal; Mem, Int. Peace Adv. Cmt, Episcopal Church, 65-68. Mailing Add: 195 River Rd, Grand View, N.Y. 10960.

DOWD, JOSEPH D
N.Y. State Assemblyman
b. Brooklyn, N.Y. Educ: N.Y. Univ, B.S; St. Johns Univ. Sch. of Law, LL.B. Polit. & Govt. Pos: Asst. corp. counsel, N.Y.C; N.Y. State Assemblyman, 60- Bus. & Prof. Pos: Lawyer. Mil. Serv: Marine Corps. Mailing Add: 220 Congress St, Brooklyn, N.Y. 11201. (1967)

DOWD, PHOEBE MARY D
State Committeewoman, Mass. Dem. Party
b. West Springfield, Mass. 3/3/24; d. Ralph Joseph Ferrentino and Margaret Liquori F; m. 9/21/46 to Donald Joseph Dowd; c. Deborah Ann. Educ: Cathedral High Sch, Springfield, Mass, grad, 41. Polit. & Govt. Pos: State Committeewoman, Mass. Dem. Party, Hampden-Berkshire Co, 64-; del, Dem. Nat. Conv. and mem. credentials cmt, 68. Mem: Ramapogue Women's Club (pres, 64-65); Holy Child Guild (dir. aid, 65-); Holy Rosary Soc.(treas, 60-64); Springfield Country Club. Rel: Catholic. Mailing Add: 69 Hale St, West Springfield, Mass. 01089.

DOWD, THOMAS FRANCIS, JR. R
Conn. State Sen.
b. Newton, Mass, 5/4/30; s. Thomas Francis Dowd and Kathleen Macbeth D; m. 3/13/54 to Carol Cray; c. Terry Lynne, Thomas James and Glenn William. Educ: Rutgers Univ, B.S, 53; Scabbard and Blade; Chi Psi. Polit. & Govt. Pos: Conn. State Rep. 64-69, asst. minority leader, Conn. House of Rep, 67-69; Conn. State Sen. and asst. minority leader, Conn. State Senate, 69- Bus. & Prof. Pos: Employee rels. trainee, Gen. Elec. Co, 56-60, specialist, pub. affairs, 60-66, mgr. pub. affairs, 66- Mil. Serv: Entered as 2nd Lt, Army, 54, released as 1st Lt, 56, after serv. in 69th Inf. Div. Mailing Add: 71 Arden Rd, Trumbull, Conn. 06611.

DOWDS, JAMES ALEXANDER R
Mem, Exec. Cmt, Rep. State Cmt, Mass.
b. Holyoke, Mass, 7/11/43; s. James Patrick Dowds and Martha Paterson D; single. Educ: Harvard Univ, A.B, 69. Polit. & Govt. Pos: Coordinator for E.L. Richardson for Lt. Gov. Campaign, Mass, 64; del, Rep. State Conv, 67; mem, Rep. State Cmt, 68, mem, exec. cmt, 69- Bus. & Prof. Pos: Banker, New Eng. Merchants Nat. Bank, Boston, Mass, 69- Mil. Serv: Entered as E-1, Army, 61, released as E-4, 68, after serv. in Mass. Army Nat. Guard. Mem: Eagle Scout; scoutmaster, Boy Scout Troop 437. Coach, Holyoke Boys Club. Rel: Roman Catholic. Mailing Add: 31 Charpentier Blvd, Chicopee, Mass. 01013.

DOWDY, JOHN D
U.S. Rep, Tex.
b. 2/11/12; m. to Johnnie Deana 'J.D' Riley; c. Carol Sue (Mrs. Forrest Earle Roberts, Jr) and John 'Skip' Jr. Polit. & Govt. Pos: Dist. attorney, Third Judicial Dist, Tex, 44-52; U.S. Rep, Tex, 52- Bus. & Prof. Pos: Lawyer, licensed to practice, 40. Legal Res: Athens, Tex. Mailing Add: 2301 House Office Bldg, Washington, D.C. 20515.

DOWDY, LEWIS CARNEGIE D
b. Eastover, S.C, 9/1/17; s. William Wallace Dowdy and Alice Shivar D; m. 6/26/43 to Elizabeth Smith; c. Lewis C, Jr, Lemuel and Elizabeth. Educ: Allen Univ, A.B, 43; Ind. State Col, M.A, 49; Ind. Univ, Bloomington, Ed.D, 65; Alpha Phi Alpha; Greensboro Men's Club; Conversation Club. Polit. & Govt. Pos: Del, Dem. Nat. Conv, 68. Bus. & Prof. Pos: Pres, N.C. Col. and Univ. Publ: 'Seven Principles Underlying Academic Planning,' Improving Col. and Univ. Teaching, summer 62; 'Creating an Atmosphere Conducive to Learning,' Negro Educ. Rev, 1/63; 'The Vital Role of a Modern College,' Vital Speeches of the Day, 65. Mem: Nat. Educ. Asn; N.C. Teachers Asn; Nat. Conf. Prof. Educ. Admin; exec. cmt, Nat. Asn. Land-Grant Col. and State Univ; bd. dirs, Greensboro C. of C; bd. dirs, Greensboro United fund; Greensboro Commun. Coun. and Human Rel. Cmt; adv. cmt. nursing educ. and commun. col. adv. coun, N.C. Bd. Educ; N.C. Film Bd; N.C. State Teacher Educ. Eval. Cmt; N.C. Coun. Human Rels; cmt. educ. prog, Piedmont Univ. Center, N.C; Greensboro Libr. Planning Cmt; Greensboro Neighbor Coun; Cmn. Study Pub. Schs. N.C; tech. action cmt, U.S. Dept. Agr; Educ. Cmn. States; Atomic Energy Adv. Cmt; Gov. Coord. Coun. Aging; cmt. educ. policy, Am. Coun. Educ; Greensboro Commun. Fel; YMCA. Outstanding Alumnus Award, Ind. State Univ; Citizen Greensboro Award, Greensboro C. of C. Rel: Baptist. Legal Res: 900 Bluford St, Greensboro, N.C. 27411. Mailing Add: North Carolina Agricultural and Technical State University, Greensboro, N.C. 27411.

DOWELL, BENNIE C. D
b. Lusby, Md, 10/27/00; married. Educ: Calvert Co. pub. schs. Polit. & Govt. Pos: Md. State Del, 55-67. Bus. & Prof. Pos: Seafood dealer. Mem: Masons; Shrine; Lions; YMCA; Calvert Co. Hist. Soc; Solomons Island Yacht Club. Rel: Methodist. Mailing Add: Lusby, Md, 20657. (1967)

DOWELL, RICHARD A. D
Chmn, Kiowa Co. Dem. Party
b. Wellsford, Kans, 9/16/69; s. Frank E. Dowell and Eva Thomas D; m. 5/17/41 to Shirley Faye Asher; c. John Michael, James Phillip, Mary Ann (Mrs. Cukjati) and Peggy Jane. Educ: Wichita State Univ, A.B, 40; v.pres, Pi Sigma Alpha. Polit. & Govt. Pos: Dem. precinct committeeman, Brenham Twp, Kans, 50-69; chmn, Kiowa Co. Dem. Party, 59- Bus. & Prof. Pos: Mem, bd. trustees, Haviland Farmers Coop, Kans, 50-65; mem, Kans. State Highway Adv. Cmt, 64-66. Mem: Farmer's Union; Nat. Farmer's Orgn; Rotary. Rel: Methodist. Mailing Add: R.F.D. 1, Haviland, Kans. 67059.

DOWLING, EDWARD C. D
Mayor, Hammond, Ind.
b. Morocco, Ind, 11/5/00; s. John E. Dowling and Margaret Meadows D; m. 9/27/23 to Opal M. Hendryx; c. James, William, Robert, Edward, Theresa and Margaret (deceased). Educ: Pub. Schs. Polit. & Govt. Pos: Supt, Water Works, Hammond, Ind, 36-48 and Wicker Park, 49-50; registrn. officer and co. comnr, Lake Co, 51-55; mayor, Hammond, 55-; precinct committeeman and city chmn, Dem. Party; del, Dem. Nat. Conv, 56 & 60. Bus. & Prof. Pos: Machinist apprentice, 19-23; locomotive machinist, Ind. Harbor Belt R.R, 25-35. Mem: Lions; Eagles; Elks; K. of C; Moose; Exchange Club. Legal Res: 2727 163rd Place, Hammond, Ind. 46323. Mailing Add: 5925 Calumet Ave, Hammond, Ind. 46320.

DOWLING, JOHN ROBERT R
42nd Dist. Committeeman, Ill. Rep. Cmt.
b. Woodson, Ill, 8/20/33; s. John W. Dowling and Hattie Mae Cooper D; m. 1/28/55 to Reta Ann Miller; c. Michael John and David Harris. Educ: East. Ill. Univ, B.S. Ed, 55; Univ. Ill, 62-64; Ill. State Univ, M.S. Ed, 68; Tau Kappa Epsilon. Polit. & Govt. Pos: Secy, v.pres, pres, Iroquois Co. Young Rep, 60-68; 42nd dist. committeeman, Ill. Rep. Cmt, 68- Bus. & Prof. Pos: Teacher-coach, Armstrong High Sch, Ill, 55-59, Crescent-Iroquois High Sch, 59-63 and Watseka Commun. High Sch, 63-69. Mil. Serv: Entered as Pvt, Army Res, 52, released as Sp. 3, 60, after serv. in Hq. 338th Inf. Regt. Publ: History of Iroquois County, Iroquois Co, 68. Mem: Nat. Coun. for Soc. Studies; Nat. Coun. for Geographic Educ; Ill. and Nat. Educ. Asns; Lions (dir, Watseka Club). Rel: Presbyterian. Mailing Add: 315 S. Third St, Watseka, Ill. 60970.

DOWLING, YOUNG DANIEL R
Chmn, Geneva Co. Rep. Party, Ala.
b. Hartford, Ala, 8/31/22; s. Elder Leon Dowling and Lela Stewart D; m. 1/28/40 to Katherine Peters; c. Daniel F, Terry S. and Jean (Mrs. Sammons). Polit. & Govt. Pos: Chmn, Geneva Co. Rep. Party, Ala, 66-; mem. Ala. State Rep. Exec. Cmt, currently. Bus. & Prof. Pos: Owner-mgr, Dowling Lumber Co, 55. Mem: Mason; Bus. & Prfnl. Men's Orgn. Rel: Protestant. Mailing Add: 500 Seventh Ave, Hartford, Ala. 36344.

DOWNES, JOHN P. D
Ill. State Rep.
c. Two daughters. Educ: Chicago Schs. Polit. & Govt. Pos: Mem, 19th Ward Reg. Dem. Orgn; Ill. State Rep, 70th Assembly, currently. Mem: Elks; Moose; dist. dep, K. of C; treas, St. Ethelreda Holy Name Soc. Mailing Add: 8831 S. Paulina St, Chicago, Ill. 60620. (1967)

DOWNING, FRANK O. D
b. Savannah, Ga, 4/24/21; s. Robert Francis Downing, Jr. and Julia Sullivan D; m. 2/16/47 to Cornelia Love; c. Caren Love, Frank Oliver, Jr. Educ: Benedictine Mil. Sch, 41; Woodrow Wilson Col. of Law, LL.B, 49. Polit. & Govt. Pos: Attorney, 51-. Mil. Serv: USN, WW II, 41-45; five Battle Stars. Mem: Past Pres, Eagles, Am. Legion, 40 et 8, VFW, K. of C; Sertoma-Elks. Rel: Catholic. Mailing Add: Savannah, Ga. 31202. (1967)

DOWNING, MAURICE ALBERT D
Ala. State Rep.
b. N.Y.C, 10/14/15; s. Patrick Maurice Downing and Rose Etta Casey D; m. 12/7/42 to Helen Frances Rallis; c. Helen P, Maurice A. Jr, Cecilia Marie, John Anthony and Mary Margaret. Educ: McGill Inst; Univ. Ala, LL.B, 50. Polit. & Govt. Pos: Former border patrolman, Emigration & Naturalization Serv; Ala. State Rep, 63- Bus. & Prof. Pos: Lawyer; prfnl. musician; policeman. Mil. Serv: World War II, Lt. Mem: VFW; Elks; Am. Legion; K. of C. Rel: Catholic. Mailing Add: 920 Dauphin St, Mobile, Ala. 36604.

DOWNING, MAURICE J. D
N.H. State Rep.
b. Marysville, N.B, Can, 8/18/98; married; c. One. Educ: Ft. Fairfield, Maine High Sch; New Eng. Jewelers Inst. Polit. & Govt. Pos: Town auditor; sch. moderator; overseer check list; selectman; N.H. State Rep, 34- Bus. & Prof. Pos: Retail jeweler, retired; ins. broker. Mil. Serv: World War I. Mem: Am. Legion; K. of C; Moose; Rotary; DAV. Rel: Catholic. Mailing Add: Unity Rd, P.O. Box 538, Newport, N.H. 03773. (1967)

DOWNING, NEIL FREDERICK D
Mem, Mich. Dem. State Cent. Cmt.
b. Atlanta, Mich, 1/27/10; s. Lewis Andrew Downing and Maude Manier D; m. to Jeanette Bernice Kenville; c. Robert L, Neil F, Jr. and Frederick A. Educ: Atlanta High Sch, Mich. Polit. & Govt. Pos: Village pres, Makinaw City, Mich, 54-64; sch. bd. trustee, Makinaw City, 67-; mem, Mackinaw Island Park Cmn, 59-62; mem, Upper Great Lakes Adv. Cmn, 68-; mem, Mich. Dem. State Cent. Cmt, currently. Mem: Mason; Lions. Rel: Protestant. Mailing Add: 1352 Valley Dr, Mackinaw City, Mich. 49701.

DOWNING, T. MAC R
b. Macomb, Ill, 1891; m. to Margaret Scripps D; c. Toliver Scripps. Educ: U. of Ill; U. of Mich; Phi Delta Theta; Phi Delta Phi. Polit. & Gov. Pos: Ill. State Sen, 36-64; Ill. State Rep, 59th Gen. Assembly. Bus. & Prof. Pos: Lawyer; farming interests. Mem: Mich. and Ill. Bar Asn, 15-; Masons; Elks; Am. Legion. Mailing Add: Macomb, Ill. 61455. (1967)

DOWNING, THOMAS N. D
U.S. Rep, Va.
b. Newport News, Va, 2/1/19; s. Dr. Samuel Downing (deceased) and Mrs. Joseph Phillips; m. to Virginia Dickerson Martin; c. Susan Nelms and Samuel Dickerson Martin. Educ: Va. Mil. Inst, B.S; Univ. Va, LL.B. Polit. & Govt. Pos: U.S. Rep, Va, 58- Bus. & Prof. Pos: Attorney, Downing & Andrews. Mil. Serv: Army, World War II, combat troop comdr, Mechanized Cavalry, Third Army; Silver Star. Mem: Newport News Bar Asn.(past pres); Hampton, Va. State and Am. Bar Asns; bd. of visitors, Merchant Marine Acad; Am. Legion; VFW; Lions. Rel: Episcopal; Trustee, St. Stephen Episcopal Church, Newport News, Va. Legal Res: William Clairborn Bldg, Hampton, Va. 23369. Mailing Add: 2000 Connecticut Ave, Washington, D.C. 20008.

DOWNING, WILLIAM S. D
Chmn, Clay Co. Dem. Cent. Cmt, Ind.
b. Brazil, Ind, 3/12/15; s. William R. Downing and Josephine Howard D; m. 9/5/42 to Margaret R. Coltharp; c. Margaret L.(Mrs. Pugh), Elizabeth L. (Mrs. McVey) and Sandra Kay. Educ: High Sch, grad, 33. Polit. & Govt. Pos: Del, Dem. State Conv, 52, 54, 56, 58 & 60; sheriff, Clay Co, Ind, 54-62; chmn, Clay Co. Dem. Cent. Cmt, 56-; del, Dem. Nat. Conv, 60. Bus. & Prof. Pos: Ed. and publisher, Ind. Sheriffs' Asn. Off. Publ, 64- Mem: Ind. Sheriffs' Asn. (pres, 59, chmn. exec. cmt, 60, chmn. bd. trustees, 63-); F&AM; Scottish Rite; C. of C; Ind. Farm Bur. Ind. Sheriff of the Year Award, 61. Rel: Protestant. Mailing Add: 918 S. Walnut St, Brazil, Ind. 47834.

DOWNS, ARTHUR WALTER R
V.Pres, Md. Fedn. Young Rep.
b. Baltimore, Md, 9/1/38; s. Louis J. Downs and Margaret Walter D; m. 6/13/64 to Jane Frith. Educ: Baltimore Jr. Col, 56-58; Loyola Col, Baltimore, 63; Univ. Md, College Park, 65. Polit. & Govt. Pos: Rep. cand, U.S. Rep, Md, 68; v.pres, Md Fedn. Young Rep, 69-; pres, Baltimore Co. Young Rep. Club, 69; dir, Eng. Consul Independent Rep. Asn, 69. Bus. & Prof. Pos: Instr, Commercial Radio Inst, Baltimore, 60-61; eng. aide, Westinghouse Corp, 62-63; eng. writer, Tech. Serv. Corp, Glen Burnie, Md, 63-65; eng. writer, Bendix Corp/NASA, 65-66; eng. writer, Volt Tech. Corp/NASA, 66-67; consult, Franklin Corp, Phila, Pa, 67; sr. egn. writer, Tate Tech. Serv. Corp, Glen Burnie, 68- Mem: Inst. Elec. & Electronics Engr; Am. Ordnance Asn; Wynnewood Commun. Asn; Prince Georges Co. Young Rep. Asn; Baltimore Co. Young Rep. Club; Alexander Hamilton Rep. Club; Young Am. for Freedom; Nat. Rifle Asn; Eng. Consul Independent Rep. Asn. Rel: Catholic. Mailing Add: 1811 Palo Circle, Baltimore, Md. 21227.

DOWNS, CRAWFORD HUGH D
b. Effie, La, 10/1/11; s. Uriah Thomas Downs and Callie McCann D; m. 9/30/33 to Melba Alice Daigre; c. Ellarene Daigre (Mrs. Karl Eikel Harvey), James Crawford and Alice Ann (Mrs. Herman Allen Stuart). Educ: La. Col, Pineville, B.A, 32; La. State Univ, M.S, 33, LL.B, 46; Phi Kappa Phi; Omicron Delta Kappa; Phi Beta Kappa; Order of the Coif. Polit. & Govt. Pos: La. State Rep, 44-48; La. State Sen, 48-52 & 56-60, floor leader, La. State Senate, 56-60; del. and mem, Credentials Cmt, Dem. Nat. Conv, 64; chmn, La. State Dem. Cent. Cmt, 64-68; admin. asst. to Gov. John J. McKeithen, La, 65- Bus. & Prof. Pos: Teacher and football coach, Glenmora High Sch, La, 33-39; attorney-at-law, Peterman, Gravel and Downs, 46-48, Gravel and Downs, 48-55 and Downs and Gremillion, 55- Mil. Serv: Lt.(jg), Navy, 45. Publ: 'Comments, Statutory Injunction Against Gambling Nuisance in Louisiana,' 5/45 and 'The Effect of Discharges in Bankruptcy on Torts Judgments with Respect to Keeping of Animals,' 12/45, La. Law Rev. Mem: La. Bar Asn; bd. dirs, C. of C, Alexandria, La, 60-; Cattleman's Asn; Lions; Elks; Mason. Rel: Baptist. Legal Res: 3006 Elliott, Alexandria, La. 71303. Mailing Add: P.O. Box 1643, Baton Rouge, La. 70150. (1967)

DOWNS, EDWARD LARSON D
Chmn, Cape Co. Dem. Cmt, Mo.
b. Charleston, Mo, 11/30/20; s. Jesse E. Downs and Betty Rogers; m. 6/3/50 to Juanita Schumacher; c. Edward L, Jr. Educ: Westminster Col, Fulton, Mo, A.B, 42; Mo. Univ. Law Sch, J.D, 48; Delta Tau Delta. Polit. & Govt. Pos: City attorney, Cape Girardeau, Mo, 52; asst. attorney gen, Cape Co, 52 & 64-68; chmn, Cape Co. Dem. Cmt, 66-; del, Dem. Nat. Conv, 68. Bus. & Prof. Pos: Sr. partner, Downs & Johnson, 60- Mil. Serv: Entered as Pvt, Army, 42, released as 2nd Lt, 46, after serv. in Signal Corps, S.Atlantic, 43-44; Good Conduct Medal; Spec. Serv. Award Overseas. Mem: Am. and Mo. Bar Asns; Cape Co. Bar Asn.(pres, 64); Mason; Optimist; Elks. Rel: Methodist. Mailing Add: 1331 W. Cape Rock Dr, Cape Girardeau, Mo. 63701.

DOWNS, JOHN E. D
Mo. State Sen.
b. Joseph, Mo, 5/12/17. Educ: Univ. of Mo, LL.B. Polit. & Govt. Pos: Prosecuting attorney, Buchanan Co, Mo; group attorney, Securities and Exchange Cmn, Wash, D.C; asst. city counselor, St. Joseph, Mo; Mo. State Rep, 56-60, chmn, Cmt. on Correctional Inst, Mo. State House of Rep, v.chmn, Conserv, Parks; Mo. State Sen, 60-, chmn, Judiciary Cmt, Mo. State Senate, currently; del, Dem. Nat. Conv, 68. Bus. & Prof. Pos: Attorney, sr. partner, Downs & Pierce. Mil. Serv: Marine Corps; fighter pilot, Southwest Pac. Rel: Catholic. Mailing Add: 304 Corby Bldg, St. Joseph, Mo. 64500.

DOWSE, DUANE ARLO D
b. Kempton, Ill, 3/16/10; s. George V. Dowse and Elizabeth Sutton D; m. 3/31/34 to Estelle M. Cloos. Educ: Univ. Wis, 1 year; Sigma Chi. Polit. & Govt. Pos: Investr, Ill. State Labor Dept, 48-53; hwy. supvr, PW & B, 61-69; del, Dem. Nat. Conv, 68; license investr. for secy. of state, 69- Bus. & Prof. Pos: Farmer, 32-50; real estate broker, 50-69; bowling alley proprietor, 52-58; owner, breeder and trainer of thoroughbred race horses, 56-69. Mem: Mason (32°); Elks; Farmer's Union; Shrine. Rel: Protestant. Mailing Add: R.R, Kempton, Ill. 60946.

DOYLE, CLARENCE O'DELL D
Sgt. at Arms, S.C. State Senate
b. West Columbia, S.C, 2/8/97; s. John K. Doyle and Maggie Douglas D; m.

12/5/22 to Meta Holt. Educ: St. Johns High Sch, Darlington, S.C. Polit. & Govt. Pos: Sgt. at Arms, S.C. State Senate, 54- Mil. Serv: 105th Ammunition Train, 30th Div, 17-19. Mailing Add: 3300 Duncan St, Columbia, S.C. 29205. (1967)

DOYLE, DONALD VINCENT D
Iowa State Rep.
b. Sioux City, Iowa, 1/13/25; s. William E. Doyle and Nelsine E. Sparby D; m. 8/9/63 to Janet E. Holtz; c. Dawn Renee. Educ: Colo. Agr. & Mech. Col; Univ. Nebr; Morningside Col, B.S, 51; Univ. S.Dak. Law Sch, LL.B, 53; Iowa State Univ. Cert. for Radiological Defense and Radiological Monitor Instr; Delta Theta Phi and Scholarship Key. Polit. & Govt. Pos: Iowa State Rep, Woodbury Co, 57-60, 65-67 & 68- Bus. & Prof. Pos: Lawyer, 53- Mil. Serv: Entered as Pvt, Army Air Corps, released as Cpl, 46, after serv. in India; China-Burma-India and N.Am. Ribbons. Mem: State comdr. Iowa, China-Burma-India Vet. Asn. and past nat. and past state judge advocate of Nat. China-Burma-India Vet. Asn. Photog. and Radio Commun; in charge of Civil Defense Mobile Commun. for Sioux City and Woodbury Co. for 2 years; radiological defense officer in Civil Defense for State of Iowa. Legal Res: 1701 Isabella St, Sioux City, Iowa 51103. Mailing Add: 224 Insurance Exchange Bldg, Sioux City, Iowa 51101.

DOYLE, JOHN AUGUSTINE D
Mem, Calif. Dem. State Cent. Cmt.
b. Dublin, Ireland, 8/29/26; s. Richard Doyle and Roseanna Murray D; m. 9/3/49 to Harriette Elizabeth Montague; c. Eileen, Mary, John, Kevin, Brigid, Sheila and Michael. Educ: St. Mary's Col, B.S. in Econ, 50; Univ. San Francisco Law Sch, J.D, 56; Phi Alpha Delta. Polit. & Govt. Pos: Mem, Alameda Co. Dem. Cent. Cmt,Calif, 64-66, v.chmn, 66-68;admin. asst. to Congressman, George P. Miller, 66-; mem, Calif. State Dem. Cent. Cmt, 68- Bus. & Prof. Pos: Attorney-at-law, 57- Mil. Serv: Army Air Corp, 45-47. Mem: Alameda Co, East Oakland and South. Alameda Co. Bar Asns; State Bar Calif; Am. Legion. Rel: Roman Catholic. Mailing Add: 15341 Inverness St, San Leandro, Calif. 94579.

DOYLE, MARJORIE POOR R
V.Chmn, Arlington Rep. Town Cmt, Vt.
b. Arlington, Vt, 5/9/18; d. Raymond John Poor and Florence Hurd P; m. 9/22/45 to Edward J. Doyle; c. John, Kathryn, Jo Ann, Kevin and Mark. Educ: Middlebury Col, B.S, 40. Polit. & Govt. Pos: Vt. State Rep, 65-66; secy, Bennington Co. Rep. Cmt, Vt, 66; mem, Gov. Adv. Cmt. on Ment. Retardation, 66-68; mem, Comprehensive Health Planning Cmt, 67-; v.chmn, Arlington Rep. Town Cmt, 68-; sch. bd. mem, Arlington Sch. Dist, 69. Bus. & Prof. Pos: Sec. sch. teacher, 40-46. Mem: Arlington PTA (past pres); Red Cross Blood Bank (former dir); Arlington Commun. Pub. Health Nursing Serv.(past pres); dir, Bennington Friends of Retarded Children; pres. and mem. adv. coun, Vt. Asn. of Retarded Children. Rel: Catholic. Mailing Add: Main, Arlington, Vt. 05250.

DOYLE, NORMAN, JR. D
N.J. State Assemblyman
b. Kearny, N.J, 3/31/39; s. Norman A. Doyle, Sr. and Muriel A. Carey D; single. Educ: Seton Hall Univ, A.B, 60; N.Y. Univ. Law Sch, LL.B, 63; Cross & Crescent. Polit. & Govt. Pos: Asst. prosecutor, Hudson Co, N.J, 64; N.J. State Assemblyman, 68- Bus. & Prof. Pos: Private law practice. Mil. Serv: Entered as 1st Lt, Army, 65, released as Capt, 68, after serv. in Vietnam, 67-68; Capt. Res, 68-69, Capt; Vietnamese Serv. Medal; Bronze Star. Mem: Hudson Co, N.J. and Am. Bar Asns. Rel: Roman Catholic. Mailing Add: 280 Maple St, Kearny, N.J. 07032.

DOYLE, ROY H. D
Chmn, Fannin Co. Dem. Exec. Cmt, Tex.
b. Cooper, Tex, 3/30/07; s. William H. Doyle and Mary Eva Kyle D; m. 10/2/32 to Mattie Cunningham; c. Billy Roy and Jimmy Lynn. Polit. & Govt. Pos: Dem. precinct officer, Tex, 36-40; weight inspector, State Dept. of Agr, 41-42; dep. sheriff, 42-44; chmn, Fannin Co. Dem. Exec. Cmt, 64- Bus. & Prof. Pos: Salesman, Hunts Dept. Store, Bonham, Tex, 45. Mem: Kiwanis (pres, 69). Rel: Baptist; Deacon; Sunday sch. teacher. Mailing Add: 209 S. 14th, Honey Grove, Tex. 75446.

DOYLE, STANLEY MORTON Non-Partisan
Assoc. Justice, Mont. Supreme Court
b. Revere, Minn, 2/4/98; s. Francis Patrick Doyle; m. 8/15/45 to Aileen Davison Doyle. Educ: St. Thomas Col, St. Paul; Drake Univ, LL.B, 22; Delta Theta Phi; Sigma Alpha Epsilon. Polit. & Govt. Pos: Assoc. Justice, Mont. Supreme Court, 61- Mil. Serv: Entered as Flying Cadet, Army Air Corps, 17, released as Lt. Pilot, 19. Mem: Past pres, Mont. Bar Asn, 60-61; Am. and West. Mont. Bar Asns; Order of Daedalians; Shrine; Commandery; Elks; Am. Legion; DAV; Nat. Comdr, 40 et 8, 25-26. Distinguished Alumni Award, Drake Univ, 62. Rel: Protestant. Legal Res: Box 930, Polson, Mont. 59860. Mailing Add: Capital Bldg, Helena, Mont. 59601. (1967)

DOYLE, WILLIAM THOMPSON R
Vt. State Sen.
b. N.Y.C, 5/8/26; s. Edward Thompson Doyle and Irene Wagner D; m. 8/21/56 to Olene May Ottaway; c. Kelly Irene, Keith Bryan and Lee William. Educ: Princeton Univ, B.A, 49; Columbia Univ. Teachers Col, 54-60, M.A. and Ed.D; Cannon Club, Princeton Univ. Polit. & Govt. Pos: Mem, sch. bd, Montpelier, Vt, 64-68, chmn, 67-68; mem, Wage Labor Bd, Vt, 66-69, chmn, 68-69; mem, Union Dist. High Sch. Bd, 67-68; Vt. State Sen, 69- Bus. & Prof. Pos: Teacher, Lawrenceville Sch, N.J, 49-50 and Montclair Acad, 55-58; dir, educ. resources proj, Johnson State Col, Vt, 58-60, assoc. prof. soc. sci, 60-69. Publ: Unified School Districts in Vermont, Vt. State Dept. Educ, 68. Mem: Am. Hist. Asn; Am. Polit. Sci. Asn; Vt. Educ. Asn; Vt. Farm Bur; Green Mt. Club. Distinction of Merit, Vt. Coun. Soc. Studies, 68; Outstanding Serv. Award, Montpelier Sch. Bd, 68. Rel: Congregational. Mailing Add: Murray Rd, Montpelier, Vt. 05602.

DRABINOWICZ, ALICE ROSE THERESA D
N.H. State Rep.
b. Nashua, N.H, 11/4/23; d. Raymond Harvey LaValley and Alice Enright L; m. 7/2/49 to Stanley Frank Drabinowicz; c. John Michael. Educ: Gen. Educ. Develop. Dipl. of high sch. equivalency, Manchester, N.H, 58. Polit. & Govt. Pos: Secy, Nashua Dem. Women's Club, N.H, 63; pres, 65-67; selectman, Ward 4, 67-; N.H. State Rep, Dist. 17, 67-; mem, N.H. and Nat. Orgn. of Women Legislators, 67-; mem, Forty-three Club, N.H. Gen. Court, 67- Bus. & Prof. Pos: Head inspector, Nashua Textile Coop, 54 & 55; credit clerk, Montgomery Ward, Nashua, N.H, 56-57. Mem: VFW Auxiliary; DAV Auxiliary; League of Women Voters; Nat. Coun. of World Affairs. Received several citations from the DAV Auxiliary and the Nat. VFW and Auxiliary. Rel: Catholic. Mailing Add: 56 Temple St, Nashua, N.H. 03060.

DRACH, GEORGE E. R..
b. Springfield, Ill, 8/25/06; c. three. Educ: U. of Ill, LL.B. Polit. & Gov. Pos: Ill. State Sen, -66; Asst. majority leader, Ill. State Sen. Bus. & Prof. Pos: Attorney; partner, Drach's Restaurant. Mil. Serv: W.W. II, U.S. Navy. Mem: Sangamon City Bar Asn, past pres; Ill, Am. Bar Asn. Outstanding Sen. of 68th, 69th Assemblies by Legis. Corresp. Asn. Mailing Add: 1824 Noble Ave, Springfield, Ill. 62706. (1967)

DRAHEIM, WILLIAM A. R
Wis. State Sen.
b. Neenah, Wis, 12/15/98. Educ: Lawrence Col. Polit. & Govt. Pos: Mem, Co. Bd; Wis. State Sen, 50- Bus. & Prof. Pos: Former mill worker, statistician-acct, prod. planner and sporting goods dealer; retired. Mil. Serv: World War I and World War II; after 40 years in Nat. Guard and Army, retired as Col. Mailing Add: 913 Hewitt St, Neenah, Wis. 54956. (1967)

DRAJEM, IRENE THERESA D
V.Chmn. Womens Div, Erie Co. Dem. Cmt, N.Y.
b. Dillonvale, Ohio, 11/23/20; d. Felix Golebiewski and Agnes Andrzejewski G; m. 8/25/36 to Victor A. J. Drajem; c. Victor A, Jr. and Robert A. Educ: Villa Maria Acad, N.Y, 4 years; Bryant & Stratton Bus. Sch, N.Y, 4 years. Polit. & Govt. Pos: Committeewoman, N.Y. State Rep. Party, 48-58; organizer and pres, Gr. Buffalo Dem. Women's Club, 55-69; mem, N.Y. State Dept. Commerce, 57-61; mem, Buffalo Bd. Commun. Rels, 61-63; mem, Battle of Lake Erie Sesquecentennial Celebration Cmt, 62; alternate del, Dem. State Conv, 62; del, State Judicial Conv, 64; alternate del, Dem. Nat. Conv, 68. Bus. & Prof. Pos: Off. mgr, Polish Am. Trading Co, 39-49; off. mgr, Peoples Clothing Co, 49- Mem: Am. Heart Asn.(dir); Polish Union Am; Polish Roman Cath. Union Am.(secy, 25 years); Villa Maria Alumnae Asn; Pulaski Day Cmt. Awards from March of Dimes, Police Athletic League, Red Cross, Cath. Charities and Heart Fund; Mothers Day Award, Am. Pol. Eagel Paper, Kiwanis Club, Buffalo. Rel: Roman Catholic. Mailing Add: 35 Gerald Place, Buffalo, N.Y. 14215.

DRAKE, ARTHUR MILES R
N.H. State Rep.
b. Copiague, N.Y, 12/18/15; s. Joseph Miles Drake and Eva Baldwin D; m. 1/10/42 to Margaret Elaine Ellis; c. Miles Ellis. Educ: N.Y. State Merchant Marine Acad. Polit. & Govt. Pos: Chmn, Lancaster Rep. Cmt, N.H, 53-61; N.H. State Sen, 61-65, chmn, State Legis. Coun, 63-65; co-chmn, Coos Co. Rep. Cmt, N.H, 65-68; N.H. State Rep, 67-, mem, House Appropriations Cmt, 67-, chmn, House Rules Cmt. and Joint House-Senate Rules Cmt, 69- Bus. & Prof. Pos: Owner and operator, Drake's Store, 46-; asst. fire chief, Lancaster Fire Dept, 55-65, chief, 65- Mil. Serv: Entered as Ens, Navy, 41, released as Lt. Comdr, 45, after serv. in Asiatic-Pac. Area; Am. Defense and Asiatic-Pac. Ribbons. Mem: Pres, Lancaster C. of C, 56-58; Kiwanis; White Mountains Region Asn. Rel: Protestant. Mailing Add: Stevens Terrace Ext, Lancaster, N.H. 03584.

DRAKE, JAMES ELLSWORTH D
b. Garden City, Kans, 11/11/32; s. Robert James and Helen Lucille Young D; m. 6/17/55 to Nancy Sherwood; c. Jennifer, Leslie and Robert. Educ: Northwest. Univ, B.S. and M.S.J; Univ. Tenn. Polit. & Govt. Pos: Admin. asst, U.S. Rep. Richard Fulton, Tenn, currently. Mil. Serv: Army, Sgt. E-5; Good Conduct Medal. Mem: Jr. C. of C; Sigma Delta Chi (charter mem, v.pres); Mason; Davidson Co. Young Dem. Legal Res: 1104 Clifton Lane, Nashville, Tenn. 37204. Mailing Add: 4426 Q St. N.W, Washington, D.C. 20007.

DRAKE, JOAN EDITH D
Committeewoman, Vt. Dem. Cmt.
b. Claremont, N.H, 7/22/32; d. Charles A. Tarro and Katherine Dumont T; m. 8/28/54 to David A. Drake, Sr; c. David A, Jr. and Phillip C. Educ: Bowling Green State Univ, 1 year. Polit. & Govt. Pos: Mem, Springfield Dem. Town Cmt, Vt, 59-61, secy, 61-65 and chmn, 65-68; mem, Windsor Co. Dem. Cmt, 63-68; pres, Springfield Dem. Women's Club, 64-66; justice of the peace, Springfield, Vt, 66; mem. staff, legis. coun, Vt. House Rep, 67; secy, Montpelier Dem. City Cmt, 67-; mem, Wash. Co. Dem. Cmt, 67-; mem. off. staff, Vt. State Senate, 68 & 69; secy, Vt. Dem. State Chmn, 68; del, Dem. Nat. Conv, 68; publicity chmn, Vt. Fedn. Dem. Women Clubs, 68-69; committeewoman, Vt. Dem. Cmt, 69-; first v.pres, Wash-Orange Co. Dem. Women's Club, 69- Bus. & Prof. Pos: Secy. to v.pres. and secy, Nat. Life Ins. Co, Montpelier, Vt, 69- Mem: Vt. Fedn. Dem. Women's Clubs; Wash-Orange Co. Dem. Women's Club; Montpelier Theatre Guild. Rel: Unitarian Universalist. Mailing Add: 10 Lague Dr, R.D. 2, Montpelier, Vt. 05602.

DRAKE, RICHARD FRANCIS R
Iowa State Rep.
b. Muscatine, Iowa, 9/28/27; s. Frank Drake and Gladys Young D; m. 6/29/50 to Shirley Jean Henke; c. Cheryll Dee and Ricky Lee. Educ: Iowa State Univ; U.S. Naval Acad, grad, 50; Sigma Chi; Navy Crew Team. Polit. & Govt. Pos: Chmn, Young Rep. Orgn, Iowa, 54-56; admin. asst, Muscatine Co. Rep. Cmt, 56-58, chmn, 58-66; First Dist. chmn, Rep. State Cent. Cmt, 66-; Iowa State Rep, Muscatine Louisa Dist, 69- Bus. & Prof. Pos: Gen. farm operator and mgr, 54- Mil. Serv: Entered as Midn, Navy, 46, released as Lt. Comdr, 54, after duty in over 50 countries; Capt. of Minesweeper, U.S.S. Crow; Naval Res.(Ret); Victory Medal; Am. Defense and China Theater Ribbons; Korean Serv. Ribbon with 2 stars; UN Korean Serv. Medal; Korean Presidential Unit Citation. Mem: AF&AM; Scottish Rite Shrine (32°); Elks; Eastern Star; Iowa Farm Bur; VFW; Am. Legion. Rel: Lutheran. Mailing Add: 420 Parkington Dr, Muscatine, Iowa 52761.

DRAKE, ROBERT BERT D
Chmn, Stephens Co. Dem. Cmt, Tex.
b. Breckenridge, Tex, 7/13/36; s. Jack Drake and Peggy Eaton D; m. 4/7/61 to Virginia Mae Singleton; c. Dina Anjanette and Robert Jack. Educ: Tex. Tech, 1 year; Tex. Christian Univ, $1\frac{1}{2}$ years. Polit. & Govt. Pos: Chmn, Stephens Co. Dem. Cmt, Tex, 68- Mem: Jaycees. Rel: Baptist. Mailing Add: Route 1, Box 324, Breckenridge, Tex. 76024.

DRAKE, RONALD L. D
Educ: Ind. State Col, B.S, M.A; Ind. Univ. Law Sch, LL.B. Polit. & Govt. Pos: Ind. State Rep, 63-66. Bus. & Prof. Pos: Attorney. Rel: Primitive Baptist. Mailing Add: R.R. 2, Farmersburg, Ind. 47850.

DRAKE, TOM D
Ala. State Rep.
b. Falkville, Ala, 12/5/30; m. to Christine McCoy; c. One daughter. Educ: Univ. of Chattanooga; Univ. of Ala. Polit. & Govt. Pos: Ala. State Rep, 63- Bus. & Prof. Pos: Lawyer. Mil. Serv: Army, World War II. Mem: Elks. Rel: Baptist. Mailing Add: Route 5, Cullman, Ala. 35055. (1967)

DRAKE, WILTON RODWELL D
b. Macon, N.C, 8/23/19; s. Francis Marvin Drake, Sr. and Ida Rodwell D; m. 11/3/44 to Margery L. Rice; c. Wilton R. Jr, Charles Edward, Frances Jean. Educ: Warren Co. Pub. Schs; Ins. Insts. Polit. & Govt. Pos: N.C. State Rep, 63-66; mayor, Macon, N.C, 50-64; Del. Dem. Nat. Conv, 52; Better Sch. and Rds. Inc, dir; N.C. Cmt. of 100; N.C. Citizens Cmt. for Better Schs. Bus. & Prof. Pos: Gen. Ins. Mem: Carolinas Asn. of Mutual Ins. Agents; Travelers Protective Asn. of Am; Warrenton Lions. Rel: Macon Methodist Church, chmn. Offic. Bd, 58-62; lay leader, 50-; Assoc. lay leader Raleigh Dist. N.C. Conf. Mailing Add: Macon, N.C. 27551. (1967)

DRANE, DAVIS CLARK R
Mem, Calif. Rep. State Cent. Cmt.
b. Columbia, Mo, 8/27/21; s. J.C. Drane and Mary Dinkle D; m. Feb. 1945 to Mildred Janssen; c. Mary Margaret (Mrs. Matza) and Susan. Educ: Univ. Calif, Los Angeles Sch. Exten; Valley Jr. Col. Polit. & Govt. Pos: Cmnr. bd. of zoning appeal, Los Angeles, Calif; cmnr. water appeals bd, Los Angeles Co; mem, Calif. Rep. State Cent. Cmt, currently. Bus. & Prof. Pos: Owner, Clark Drane Ins. Agency. Mil. Serv: Entered as Seaman, Navy, 43, released as PO, 46, after serv. in S.Pac. Theatre; various medals. Mem: Ins. Asn; Am. Legion (past comdr); Lions; Mason; Scottish Rite; PTA; C. of C.(past pres); YMCA (past pres); liaison cmt, Univ. of Redlands. Rel: Baptist. Mailing Add: 6914 Grenoble St, Tujunga, Calif. 91042.

DRAPER, DANIEL DAVID, II D
Chmn, Delaware Co. Dem. Party, Okla.
b. Elk Point, S.Dak, 6/26/11; s. Jesse Sylvester Draper and Bertha Sawtelle D; m. 7/3/37 to Elva Anderson; c. Shirley (Mrs. Don Gard), Kay (Mrs. William E. Miller) and Daniel D, Jr. Educ: Northeast. State Col, 37; Okla. State Univ, 49; Univ. Ark, 50-54. Polit. & Govt. Pos: Okla. State Rep, Cherokee Co, 38-42; chmn, McIntosh Co. Dem. Party, Okla, 46-54; chmn, Delaware Co. Dem. Party, 65-; mayor, Colcord, Okla, 69- Bus. & Prof. Pos: Pres, Cherokee Co. Educ. Asn, 37; pres, McIntosh Co. Educ. Asn, 48; chmn, sch. adminstr, Northeast. Dist. Okla, 56; supt, Colcord Pub. Schs, 53-; pres, Delaware Co. Educ. Asn, 61. Publ: 'The Draper Family History,' and 'The Carpender Family Hist, Delaware Co. J, 63. Mem: Okla. and Nat. Educ. Asns; Colcord C. of C.(pres, 67-); Mason. Rel: Methodist. Legal Res: W. Blocker St, Colcord, Okla. 74338. Mailing Add: Box 128, Colcord, Okla. 74338.

DRAPER, WILLIAM HENRY, III R
Mem, San Mateo Co. Rep. Finance Cmt, Calif.
b. White Plains, N.Y, 1/1/28; s. William Henry Draper, Jr. and Katharine Baum D; m. to Phyllis Culbertson; c. Rebecca Starr, Polly Carey and Timothy Cook. Educ: Yale Univ, B.A; Harvard Grad. Sch. Bus, M.B.A; Torch Honor Soc. Polit. & Govt. Pos: Campaign chmn, Lee Kaiser for Sen, Calif, 64; assoc. mem, Calif. Rep. State Cent. Cmt, 64-66; mem, San Mateo Co. Rep. Finance Cmt, 64-; mem, Calif. Rep. League, 64-; campaign chmn, Lt. Gov. Robert Finch, 66; San Mateo Co. Chmn, Nixon for Pres, 68. Bus. & Prof. Pos: Sales rep, Inland Steel Co, Chicago, Ill, 54-59; assoc, Draper, Gaither & Anderson, Palo Alto, Calif, 59-62; pres, Draper & Johnson Investment Co, 62-65; pres, Sutter Hill Capital Co, 65- Mil. Serv: 1st Lt, Army, serv. in 25th Inf. Div, 52; Combat Infantryman's Badge; Meritorious Combat Serv. Ribbon with Medal Pendant; Airborne Infantryman's Badge. Mem: West. Asn. Small Bus. Investment Co.(pres, 67-68); Rotary; Civic Interest League, Atherton; Calif. Tomorrow. Rel: Presbyterian. Legal Res: 126 Isabella Ave, Atherton, Calif. 94025. Mailing Add: 2600 El Camino Real, Suite 500, Palo Alto, Calif. 94306.

DRAWBAUGH, ROBERT WAYNE D
Chmn, Franklin Co. Dem. Cmt, Pa.
b. Chambersburg, Pa, 10/24/33; s. Lewis B. Drawbaugh Sr. and Lillian M. Kohler D; single. Educ: Shippensburg State Col. Polit. & Govt. Pos: Auditor, Greene Twp, Franklin Co, Pa, 59-65; pres, Chambersburg Area Dem. Club, 59-61; state committeeman, Pa. Dem. Cmt, 60-64; chmn, Franklin Co. Dem. Cmt, 65-; admin. asst. State Treas. Dept, 66-; del, Dem. Nat. Conv, 68. Bus. & Prof. Pos: Construction engr, Pa. Dept. of Hwy, Harrisburg, 55-60, asst. supt. of hwy, 60-62 and supt. of hwy, 63; asst. supt. of construction, E.D. Plummer & Sons, Chambersburg, Pa, 63; supt. of construction, H.B. Reasner Contractor, 63-66; Publ: Franklin Co. Dem. Cmt. Report, Franklin Co. Dem. Cmt. 65-; 'The Franklin County Democrat Report,' Garnet Thrush Printing; 'Public Form,' Pub. Opinion, 65-68. Mem: Am. Soc. Hwy. Engrs; Mason; Shrine; Elks. Rel: Lutheran. Mailing Add: 262 W. Main St, Fayetteville, Pa. 17222.

DREBENSTEDT, FRANCES SAMS D
Secy, Marion Co. Dem. Cent. Cmt, Mo.
b. Marion Co, Mo, 4/23/09; d. Jacob Burditt Sams and Anna Maria Frances Leake S; m. 12/4/41 to William E. Drebenstedt. Educ: Culver-Stockton Col; Hannibal-LaGrange Col; Kirksville State Teachers Col; Univ. Mo. Polit. & Govt. Pos: Caseworker, Marion Co. Welfare Dept, Mo, 41-45; dep. circuit clerk, Hannibal Court of Common Pleas, 46-55; v.chmn, Ninth Cong. Dist. Dem. Cmt; secy, Marion Co. Dem. Cent. Cmt, 48-; del, Dem. Nat. Conv, 64. Bus. & Prof. Pos: Elem. teacher, Hannibal Pub. Sch, 55- Mem: Nat. Educ. Asn; Mo. State Teachers Asn; Hannibal Commun. Teachers Asn; Am. Asn. of Univ. Women; Marion Co. Dem. Club; Marion Co. Womens Dem. Club; Young Dem. Club of Marion Co; Mo. Historical Soc; Bus. & Prfnl. Womens Club; Women of the Moose. Rel: Baptist. Mailing Add: Star Route, Philadelphia, Mo. 63463. (1967)

DREILING, NORBERT R. D
Chmn, Ellis Co. Dem. Cent. Cmt, Kans.
b. Gorham, Kans, 4/7/25; s. Richard A. Dreiling and Millie Eichman D; m. 8/18/48 to Donna Jean Myerly; c. Jan Margaret, Mark Myerly, Curtis Richard and Kathy Jean. Educ: Fort Hays Kans. State Col, B.A, 46; Washburn Law Sch, LL.B, 49. Polit. & Govt. Pos: Pres, Kans. Collegiate Dem, 48; co. attorney, Ellis Co, Kans, 51-55; precinct committeeman, 51-; chmn, Ellis Co. Dem. Cent. Cmt, 57-; chmn, Sixth Cong. Dem. Cmt. and mem, Kans. Dem. State Exec. Cmt, 58-62; campaign chmn, Elmo Mahoney Sixth Dist. Cong. Race, 58; original Kennedy organizer in Kans. before 1960 presidential campaign; del, Dem. Nat. Conv, 60, 64 & 68; co-chmn, Operation Support, Johnson Presidential Campaign, Kans. Bus. & Prof. Pos: Attorney-at-law, Hays, Kans, 49- Mem: Ellis Co. Bar Asn.(past pres); Kans. and Am. Bar Asns; Am. and Kans. Trial Lawyers Asn; Elks; Kiwanis (past pres, Hays Club, past Lt. Gov, Kans. Div. 9 and del, Int. Conv, 57); Phi Alpha Delta; St. Joseph's Mil. Acad. Alumni Asn.(past pres); Fort Hays State Col. Alumni Asn; Fort Hays State Col. Endowment Asn.(bd. trustees); K. of C.(4°). Legal Res: 2900 Willow St, Hays,Kans. 67601. Mailing Add: P.O. Box 579, Hays, Kans. 67601.

DRENNEN, ALAN TRAVIS, JR. D
Mem, Birmingham City Coun, Ala.
b. Birmingham, Ala, 4/29/25; s. Alan T. Drennen and Mary Habood Alexander D; m. 4/22/50 to Rachel Rebecca Kracke; c. Mary Alexander, Virginia Elise and Alan T, III. Educ: Univ. Ala, A.B. Polit. & Govt. Pos: Mem, Birmingham City Coun, Ala, 63-; del, Dem. Nat. Conv, 68. Bus. & Prof. Pos: Agent, ins. sales, Penn Mutual Life, 49-60; gen. agent, Protective Life, 60- Mil. Serv: Entered as Pvt, Army, 43, released as Sgt, 46, after serv. in Pac. Rel: Presbyterian. Mailing Add: 3600 Douglas Rd, Birmingham, Ala. 35213. (1967)

DRESSLER, JAMES R. D
b. Millerburg, Pa, 9/18/32; m. to Florence C. Losco; c. Donna Marie, Terese Diane, James Ronald, Jr, Ronald Anthony and Carol Jean. Educ: Univ. of Fla, A.B, 53, LL.B, 56; Pi Kappa Alpha; Tau Kappa Alpha; Phi Alpha Delta; Debate Team; Student Coun. Polit. & Govt. Pos: Fla. State Rep, 63; Fla. State Sen, 64-66. Bus. & Prof. Pos: Attorney. Mil. Serv: Naval Air Res. Mem: Kiwanis. Rel: Catholic. 1967 Legal Res: Cocoa, Fla. No mailing address available. (1967)

DREW, EDWIN HARRIS D
Justice, Supreme Court, Fla.
b. Fargo, Ga, 10/28/03; s. William Thomas Drew and Florence Idella Edwards D; m. 6/10/27 to Edith Mae Turner; c. Melanie Mae (Mrs. Mitchell). Educ: Stetson Univ, LL.B, 23; Phi Alpha Delta; Delta Sigma Phi. Hon. LL.D, Stetson Univ, 56. Polit. & Govt. Pos: Town attorney, Palm Beach, Fla, 23-52; mem, Bd. Pilot Cmnrs, West Palm Beach, 40-51; attorney, Jupiter Inlet Dist, Jupiter, 40-52; attorney, Everglades Drainage Dist, West Palm Beach, 50-52; mem, Game and Freshwater Fish Cmn, Tallahassee, 51-52; justice, Supreme Court Fla, 52-, chief justice, 55-56 & 64-65. Publ: Numerous articles in Fla. Bar J. Mem: Mason; Demolay (Chevalier Legion Honor); Gold Key; Jury Freedoms Found. Award for Outstanding Contribution in Law Workmens Compensation; Ben C. Willard Award, Stetson Univ. Rel: Episcopal. Mailing Add: 2922 N. Monroe, Tallahassee, Fla. 32301.

DREW, HAROLD FRANKLIN R
N.H. State Rep.
b. Haverhill, Mass, 6/17/98; s. Kibby N. Drew and Margaret Connelly D; m. 12/28/25 to Dorothy Connelly. Educ: Middlebury Col, B.S, 18; Harvard Univ. Grad. Sch. of Educ, Ed.M, 28. Polit. & Govt. Pos: Supvr. of check list, Ward Five, Keene, N.H, 67-, N.H. State Rep, 69- Bus. & Prof. Pos: Prin, Canaan High Sch, N.H, 19; teacher and coach, Mansfield High Sch, Mass, 19-20, Lyons High Sch, Kans, 20-22 and Watertown High Sch, Mass, 22-24; coach, submaster and prin, Keene High Sch, N.H, 24-64; retired. Mil. Serv: Pvt, Army, serv. in Students Army Training Corps, Middlebury Col, 18. Mem: Nat. Retired Teacher's Asn; Am. Legion; SAR; Mason; Nat. Coun. on Crime and Delinquency. Rel: Protestant. Mailing Add: 71 Ridgewood Ave, Keene, N.H. 03431.

DREW, LIONEL EDWARD, JR. D
b. Savannah, Ga, 9/13/20; s. Lionel Edward Drew and Patience Barrow D; m. 7/3/58 to Julie B. Olmstead; c. Mary Martha, Julie Beckett and George T. Olmstead, III. Educ: Univ. Ga. Sch. of Law, LL.B. Polit. & Govt. Pos: Town attorney, Vernonburg, Ga, 63-; former Ga. State Rep. Mil. Serv: Entered as Aviation Cadet, Army Air Corps, 42, released as 1st Lt, 45, after serv. in ETO; Air Medal and 2 Oak Leaf Clusters. Mem: Ga. and Fed. Bar Asns; Savannah Bar Asn.(mem, Vol. Defenders Cmt, 64-65, chmn, Legis. Cmt, 66); Am. Legion; Soc. of Colonial Wars. Rel: Episcopal. Mailing Add: 5513 Woodland Dr, Savannah, Ga. 31406. (1967)

DREW, RAYMOND PATRICK D
Chmn, Franklin Co. Dem. Party, Iowa
b. Decorah, Iowa, 12/18/30; s. Raymond Patrick Drew, Sr. and Theresa Carolan D; m. 6/6/59 to Lois Elaine Foltz; c. James Michael, Thomas Leo and Ann Marie. Educ: Iowa State Univ, B.A, 59, J.D, 60. Polit. & Govt. Pos: Chmn, Franklin Co. Dem. Party, Iowa, 62- Mil. Serv: Entered as Pvt, Marine Corps, 51, released as Cpl, 53. Rel: Catholic. Mailing Add: 303 Second S.E, Hampton, Iowa 50441. (1967)

DREW, ROBERT B. R
N.H. State Rep.
b. Middleton, N.H, 7/25/04; married; c. one son, two daughters. Educ: Middleton Union Pub. Sch. Polit. & Govt. Pos: Chief of police; dep. sheriff; motor vehicle examiner; N.H. State Rep, 59- Bus. & Prof. Pos: Cattle dealer. Rel: Protestant. Mailing Add: S. Main St, Farmington, N.H. 03835.

DREXEL, DAVID ANTHONY R
b. N.Y.C, N.Y, 9/26/27; s. John R. Drexel, Jr. and Jane Barbour D; m. 7/27/48 to Joan Gripenberg; c. Carole, George, Tina, Catherine, Angela and Francisca. Educ: Ga. Inst. Tech. Polit. & Govt. Pos: Chmn, Moore Co. Rep. Party, N.C, 66-67; cand. for N.C. State Sen, 68. Bus. & Prof. Pos: Owner and operator, Sandhill Sail Supply Co. Mil. Serv: Entered as A/S, Naval-Air Force Training Prog, 45, released as Cadet, 47. Mem: Americans for Constitutional Action; Am. Conserv. Union; YMCA; life mem, Nat. Rifle Asn; bd. dirs, Outward Bound; coun. cmnr, Boy Scouts; Country Club of N.C. Outstanding Young Man of Year Award, Southern Pines J.C. Rel: Catholic. Mailing Add: Box 1221, Southern Pines, N.C. 28387.

DREXLER, JOHN M. R
Educ: Bus. Col. Polit. & Govt. Pos: Minn. State Legis, 39-45. Bus. & Prof. Pos: Justice of Peace at-large, St. Paul, Minn; real estate broker. Mem: Past pres. St. Paul Restaurant Asn. Mailing Add: 1602 Selby Ave, St. Paul, Minn. 55104. (1967)

DRIEHAUS, DONALD D
b. Cincinnati, Ohio, 4/12/33; s. Leo A. Driehaus and Julia Normile D; m. 4/27/57 to Clare Ann Linneman; c. Donald G, Dianne M, Denise M, Cathy, Steven G. and Joseph G. Educ: Xavier Univ, Cincinnati, Ohio, B.S. in Polit. Sci, 55; Pi Alpha Phi. Polit. & Govt. Pos: Dem. cand, U.S. Rep, Ohio, 68. Mil. Serv: Entered as 2nd Lt, Army, 55, released as Capt, 64, after serv. in Fifth Howitzer Bn, 28th Artil. Rel: Roman Catholic. Mailing Add: 5425 Romilda Dr, Cincinnati, Ohio 45238.

DRIGGS, DON WALLACE D
Mem, Washoe Co. Dem. Cent. Cmt, Nev.
b. Phoenix, Ariz, 9/26/24; s. Golden Kenneth Driggs and Maude Macdonald D; div; c. Deborah Eileen, Pamela Elaine and Christopher Golden. Educ: Brigham Young Univ, B.S, 50; Harvard Univ, M.A, 55, Ph.D, 56. Polit. & Govt. Pos: Del, Nev. Dem. State Conv, 60, 66 & 68; del, Dem. Nat. Conv, 68; mem, Washoe Co. Dem. Cent. Cmt, 68- Bus. & Prof. Pos: Instr. and prof. polit. sci, Univ. Nev, 56-61; chmn. div. soc. sci, Stanislaus State Col, 61-63, asst. to pres, 64-65; assoc. prof. polit. sci, Univ. Nev, 65-68, prof. and chmn. dept, 68- Mil. Serv: Entered as Aviation Cadet, Air Force, 43, released as 1st Lt, 46, after serv. in Fifth Air Force, Pac. Theatre; re-entered Air Force, 51-52; Lt. Col, Air Force Res, 69; Seven Battle Stars; Air Medal. Publ: Constitution of State of Nevada: A Commentary, Univ. Nev. Press, 61; 'The President as Chief Educator on Foreign Affairs', West. Polit. Quart, 12/58; 'Nevada Politics', chap in Western Politics, Univ. Utah Press, 61. Mem: West. Polit. Sci. Asn.(secy-treas, 66-69); Am. Polit. Sci. Asn. Speaker of faculty, Stanislaus State Col, 62-63; chmn, faculty senate, Univ. Nev, 68-69. Mailing Add: 945 Joshua Dr, Reno, Nev. 89502.

DRIGOTAS, FRANK MARTIN D
Maine State Rep.
b. Auburn, Maine, 11/25/09; s. Martin Drigotas and Caroline Stelmok D; first wife deceased, 8/58; remarried, 11/20/65 to Lauretta Jones; c. Frank M, Jr, Carolyn (Mrs. Thomas) and Martin D. Polit. & Govt. Pos: V.chmn, Auburn Dem. Cmt, 61, chmn, 63-64 & 66-67; mem, Androscogin Co. Dem. Cmt, 63-67; Maine State Rep, currently. Bus. & Prof. Pos: Owner, Frank's Store for Men, 39-61, now semiretired. Mem: Past Exalted Ruler, Lewiston, Maine Lodge, Elks, 43-49; dir, Lewiston-Auburn C. of C, 46-59. Rel: Catholic. Mailing Add: 402 Court St, Auburn, Maine 04210. (1967)

DRISCOLL, JOHN THOMAS D
b. Medford, Mass, 10/26/25; s. William Jeremiah Driscoll and Mary Mahoney D; m. 6/23/51 to Jean M. Francis; c. John T, Jr, William J, James F, Jean Marie, Paul J, Maureen F. and Robert E. Educ: Boston Col. Arts & Sci, B.S, 49; Sr. Class Pres, 49. Polit. & Govt. Pos: Mass. State Rep, Boston, 55-60; treas. and receiver gen, Commonwealth of Mass, 60-64; chmn, Mass. Turnpike Authority, 64-; ex-officio, Gov. Adv. Coun. Transportation Metrop. Area Planning Coun; del, Dem. Nat. Conv, 68; asst. assessor, Boston, currently. Bus. & Prof. Pos: Driscoll Construct. Co, Boston, Mass; owner, Driscoll Insur. Mil. Serv: Entered as A/S, Navy, 44, released as Signalman, 3/C, 46; after. serv. in Am. Theatre; World War II Victory Medal; Am. Theatre Medal. Mem: Mass. Assessors Asn; Int. Bridge, Tunnel & Turnpike Asn.(v.pres); N.Eng. Rd. Builders Asn; Am. Rd. Builders Asn; Engrs. Club; Gr. Boston C. of C; Boston Rotary; Am. Legion; DAV; K. of C; Holy Name Soc; Boston Col. Alumni Asn; Mass. Legis. Asn; Boston Eng. High Sch. Alumni Asn; dir, Mass. Bay United Fund; dir, Mass. Safety Coun; trustee, St. Elizabeth's Hosp, Brighton, Mass. One of Ten Outstanding Young Men of Gr. Boston, Jr. C. of C, 61. Rel: Roman Catholic. Mailing Add: 50 Clearwater Dr, Dorchester, Mass. 02126.

DRISCOLL, KATHLEEN VIRGINIA D
Secy, Iowa Co. Dem. Cent. Cmt, Iowa
b. Williamsburg, Iowa, 2/19/24; d. William Henry Clear and Mary A. Jones C; m. 8/30/45 to John V. Driscoll, Jr; c. Charles Elliott and Erle Gerard. Educ: Parnell Consoll. Sch, Iowa, grad, 42; Cedar Falls summer course, correspondence courses and Williamsburg Sch. night courses, 60-68. Polit. & Govt. Pos: Secy, Iowa Co. Dem. Cent. Cmt, 64-, fund-raising chmn, 64-68; v.chmn, Iowa Co. Dem. Women's Club, 64, pres, 68; Dem. Precinct committeewoman, Troy Twp, 64; hon. secy, Nat. Del. and del, Dem. Nat. Conv, 68. Bus. & Prof. Pos: Secy, Iowa Co. Am. Automobile Asn, 42-46; partner and secy, Walridge Farms, 56-69. Mem: Dir, Federated State Scholarship Bd; co.chmn, Am. Cancer Soc; dir, Davenport Diocesan Coun. of Cath. Women; treas, Davenport Forester Asn; chmn, VFW Auxiliary; pres, Nat. Coun. of Foresters Court 832 and Hawkeye Angus Auxiliary; Farm Bus. Asn; Nat. Farmers Orgn; Farm Bur; Marcia Federated Club; St. Mary's Alter & Rosary; Sport Hill Country Club; Co. Hist. Soc; Nat. Soc. of Cath. Foresters; Better Schs. Citizen Cmt. Conserv. Citation; Scholarship Awards; Del. to Nat. Events, Cath. Church Fraternal. Rel: Catholic. Mailing Add: R.R. 3, Williamsburg, Iowa 52361.

DRISCOLL, RICHARD MICHAEL D
Chmn, Russell Co. Dem. Party, Kans.
b. Dorrance, Kans, 5/9/19; s. James J. Driscoll and Elizabeth Miller D; m. Colette M. Driscoll (deceased); c. Tim J, Jerry E, II and Kelly Patrick. Educ: Univ. Kans, 37-41; Washburn Munic. Univ. Sch. Law, 41-43; Univ. Kans. Lettermans Club; Phi Delta Theta. Polit. & Govt. Pos: Co. attorney, Russell Co, Kans, 46-48; city attorney, Luray, 46-; chmn, Russell Co. Dem. Party, 50-; judge, Munic. Court, Russell, 54-68; state hwy. cmnr, Third Div, 58-62; mem, Kans. Econ. Develop. Cmn, 69- Bus. & Prof. Pos: Pres, Kim Oil Co, Inc, 54-; dir, Peoples State Bank, Luray, Kans, 58-; dir, Kans. Homestead Rehabilitation Corp, and Kans. Emergency Relief Corp, 67- Mil. Serv: Entered as Paymaster Sgt, Marines, 43, released as Cpl, 46, after serv. in 1st Bn, 1st Marine Div, Pac. Theatre, 43-45. Mem: Am, Kans, Northwest Kans. and Russell Co. Bar Asns; Am. Legion; VFW; Elks; K. of C. Rel: Catholic. Legal Res: 308 Wisconsin, Russell, Kans. 67665. Mailing Add: 726½ Main, Russell, Kans. 67665.

DRISTLE, RONALD LEE, SR. D
b. Syracuse, N.Y, 7/9/29; s. Edwin Ernest Dristle and Carolyn Van Derpool D; m. 4/13/69 to Ulla Olsson; c. Carolyn, Edwin, II, Ronald, Jr. and Elizabeth. Educ: Univ. Tampa, B.S. in Hist. & Polit. Sci; Colo. State Col, M.A; Phi Delta Kappa; Pi Kappa Phi. Polit. & Govt. Pos: Supvr, Fla. Beverage Dept, 53-54; charter pres, N.W. Colo. Young Dem, 58-61; secy, Moffat Co. Dem. Cent. Cmt, Colo, 61-65, chmn, 65-66; mem, Colo. State Dem. Cent. Cmt, 65-66. Bus. & Prof. Pos: Chmn. soc. studies, Jr. High, Craig, Colo, 57-66; secy-treas, Morrison Creek Land & Livestock Co, 59-60; v.pres, N.W. Colo. Pipe & Storage Co, Craig, Colo, 62-64; sch. adminstr. Sch. Dist. 67, Lake Forest, Ill, 66- Mil. Serv: Entered as Pvt, Marine Corps, 46, released as Sgt, 50, after serv. in Inf; China Serv. Medal; World War II Victory Medal; Navy Occup. Medal; Good Conduct Medal. Mem: Mason, El Jebel Shrine, Denver, Colo. Consistory, Fel. Lodge 265; Am. Personnel & Guid. Asn; Nat. Educ. Asn. Coach, boxing and football; Int. award, State of Colo. Hunters' Safety Curriculum. Rel: Episcopal. Mailing Add: 1056 Greentree, Deerfield, Ill. 60015.

DRIVER, MARJORIE M. R
V.Chmn, Livingston Co. Rep. Party, Mich.
b. Maple City, Mich, 8/30/19; d. Henry W. Cork and Bertha E. Salisbury C; m. 3/11/42 to Louis B. Driver; c. Jo Ann (Mrs. La Pree). Educ: Rochester High Sch, Commercial, grad, 36. Polit. & Govt. Pos: Prog. chmn, Green Oak Rep. Club, Mich, 65-69, treas, 67 & 68; secy, Livingston Co. Rep. Exec. Cmt, 67-68; v.chmn, Livingston Co. Rep. Party, 69-; precinct del, Green Oak Twp. Rep. Party, dep. clerk, 67- Mem: Farm Bur. Rel: Methodist. Mailing Add: 9235 Silverside Dr, South Lyon, Mich. 48178.

DRIVER, RICHARD JOHN D
Mayor, Franklin Twp, N.J.
b. Brooklyn, N.Y, 6/22/37; s. Dr. Daniel Milton Driver and Julia M. Dreyer D; m. 12/31/57 to Margarete K.M. Schumacher; c. Deana M. Educ: Rutgers Univ, B.A, 63, M.A, 65, 66; Pi Sigma Alpha. Polit. & Govt. Pos: Councilman, Franklin Twp. Dem. Party, Somerset Co, N.J, 67-; del, Dem. Nat. Conv, 68; chmn. Somerset Co. Del, N.J. New Dem. Coalition Conv, 69; mem, N.J. New Dem. Coalition State Steering Cmt, 69; mayor, Franklin Twp, N.J. Bus. & Prof. Pos: Research asst, Rutgers Univ, 63-64, teaching asst, 64-65, research fel, 66- Mil. Serv: Entered as Airman, Air Force, 54, released as S/Sgt, 60. Publ: "Now That You've Been Elected,' Proc. 1967 Munic. Orientation Conf, Bur. Govt. Research, Rutgers Univ, 68; 'The United State Supreme Court and the Chronic Drunkenness Offender, Quart. J. Studies on Alcohol, 69. Mem: Am. Polit. Sci. Asn; N.Am. Asn. Alcoholism Prog. Rel: Protestant. Mailing Add: Box 405 E, R.D. 3, Somerset, N.J. 08873.

DRIVER, ROBERT FARR D
b. Ogden, Utah, 7/25/08; s. George William Driver and Mary Louena Farr D; m. 4/6/35 to Fredricka Beulah Brown; c. Robert James, George Fredrick, Sandra Louise (Mrs. Milton Gordon) and Mary Lynn (Mrs. Patrick Fix). Educ: San Diego High Sch, grad, 27; Pi Delta Kappa. Polit. & Govt. Pos: Pres, Young Dem, San Diego, Calif, 32-35; Dem. nominee for Calif. State Assemblyman, 80th Assembly Dist, 44 & 57; chmn, Calif. Dem. State Cent. Cmt, 46-48; chmn, Red Cross Fund Dr, 48; mem, San Diego Co. Grand Jury, 53; pres, Commun. Welfare Coun, 54-55; mem, Calif. Horse Racing Bd, 60-64, pres; del, Dem. Nat. Conv, 68. Bus. & Prof. Pos: Pres, Robert F. Driver Co, 46-69. Mil. Serv: Asst. field dir, Am. Red Cross, 45, with serv. in 82nd Seabee Bn, Okinawa. Mem: Calif. Ins. Brokers Asn; San Diego Ins. Agents Asn.(pres, 35-36); Nat. Surety Bond Producers Asn; Lions (pres, Hillcrest Club, 36); Univ. Club, San Diego; Mason. Spec. Award, Commun. Welfare Coun. Rel: Latter-day Saint. Legal Res: 2938 Ocean Front, Del Mar, Calif. 92014. Mailing Add: 400 Cedar St, San Diego, Calif. 92101.

DRIVER, WILLIAM JOSEPH D
b. Rochester, N.Y, 5/9/18; s. John J. Driver and Bridget Anna Farrell D; m. 8/18/47 to Marian R. McKay; c. William Joseph, Jr. and Kellie McKay. Educ: Univ. Niagara, B.B.A. cum laude, 41; George Wash. Univ, LL.B, 52, M.A. in Pub. Admin, 65. Polit. & Govt. Pos: Dir. Compensation and Pension Serv, Vet. Admin, Wash, D.C, 56-59, Chief Benefits dir, 59-61, Dep. Adminstr. Vet. Affairs, 61-64 and Adminstr. Vet. Affairs, 64-69; mem, President's Coun. on Aging, Cmt. on Employ. of Physically Handicapped and Cmt. on Equal Opportunity in Housing, 65-69. Bus. & Prof. Pos: Pres-elect, Mfg. Chemists Asn, 69, pres, 69- Mil. Serv: Lt. Col, Army, 41-45 and 51-53; Letion of Merit; Bronze Star; Order of Brit. Empire; Croix de Guerre, France. Mem: D.C. Bar. Meritorious Serv. Medal, Vet. Admin, 57, Exceptional Serv. Medal, 60; Career Serv. Award, Nat. Civil Serv. League, 64; Achievement Award, Soc. for Adv. of Mgt, 65. Legal Res: 215 W. Columbia St, Falls Church, Va. 22046. Mailing Add: 1825 Connecticut Ave. N.W, Washington, D.C. 20009.

DROMS, FRED WILLIAM, JR. R
N.Y. State Assemblyman
b. Rexford, N.Y, 10/20/17; s. Fred William Droms and Cora Belle Johnson D; m. 1/16/42 to Judith Elizabeth Grell; c. Carolyn Marie (Mrs. Arnold) and Linda Louise (Mrs. Platel). Educ: Univ. Ala; Theta Chi. Polit. & Govt. Pos: Supvr, Clifton Park, Saratoga Co, N.Y, 62-67; N.Y. State Assemblyman, 67- Bus. & Prof. Pos: Owner and mgr, Droms Tractor Co, Rexford, N.Y, 54- Mem: F&AM; Saratoga Co. Farm Bur; AFL-CIO; Rotary; Schenectadt Yacht Club; Elks; Am. Legion. Mailing Add: R.F.D. 2, Rexford, N.Y. 12148.

DROZ, CHARLES CLINTON R
S.Dak. State Rep.
b. Miller, S.Dak; s. Leslie Gordon Droz and Lola Irene Taylor D; m. 6/21/48

to Fern Elizabeth Matre; c. Marilyn Mae, Catherine Irene, Eric Charles, Kent Leslie, Marcia Gay and Janelle Marie. Educ: S.Dak. State Univ, 47-48. Polit. & Govt. Pos: Chmn, Hand Co. Young Rep. Orgn, 58-62; S.Dak. State Rep, 57-, speaker, S.Dak. House of Rep, 65-66, speaker pro tem, 63-64, mem, Exec. Bd. Legis. Res. Coun, 61-62, 65- Mil. Serv: Entered as Pvt, Army Signal Corp, 45, released as Pfc, 46, Pac. Theater Ribbon. Mem: Mason; Grange; Am. Legion; Wall Lake Sportsman Club. Rel: Presbyterian. Mailing Add: R4 Box 59, Miller, S.Dak. 57362.

DRUM, DAVID GEORGE R
b. Rushville, Ind, 3/7/23; s. Jay Gould Drum and Francis Frazee D; m. 12/29/47 to Dorothy May Gates; c. Jeri Lynn, David Charles and Daniel William. Educ: Univ. Mont, B.A. in bus, 46; Sigma Chi. Polit. & Govt. Pos: Mont. State Rep, 67-68. Bus. & Prof. Pos: V.pres, Y.V. Fertilizer Corp, 54-66; pres, T-Bone Feeders, Inc, 60-66; pres, Kampgrounds of Am, Inc, 62-66. Mil. Serv: Entered as Pvt, Marine Corps, 43, released as Capt, after serv. in Okinawa, S.Pac, World War II, 1st Marine Div. and Korean Conflict, 3rd Marine Div; Purple Heart; Unit Citations. Mem: Rotary; Am. Legion; Elks; Farm Bur. Rel: Congregational. Mailing Add: 3112 Radcliff Dr, Billings, Mont. 59103. (1967)

DRUMM, WILLARD C. R
b. Niverville, N.Y, Oct, 97; m. to Eva Peplinski; c. Patricia (Mrs. Clyde R. Lewis), Robert W. and Dr. Richard H. Educ: Rensselaer. Polit. & Govt. Pos: N.Y. State Assemblyman, 46-66; Columbia Co. Rep. Cmt, 34 years. Bus. & Prof. Pos: Farmer; dairy cattle breeder; coop. milk mkt. orgn. Rel: Methodist. Mailing Add: Niverville, N.Y. 12130. (1967)

DRUMMET, J. DUDLEY D
Secy, Whiteside Co. Dem. Cent. Cmt, Ill.
b. Prophetstown, Ill, 6/23/29; s. John William Drummet and Margaret Deering Dudley D; m. 11/6/58 to Lois Anne Egert; c. John Daniel, James David and Carol Ann. Educ: Staunton Mil. Acad, grad, 47; Northwest. Univ, 47-49. Polit. & Govt. Pos: Secy, Whiteside Co. Young Dem, Ill, 59-61; Dem. precinct committeeman, Prophetstown, 59-, mayor, 65-; secy, Whiteside Co. Dem. Cent. Cmt, 66- Bus. & Prof. Pos: Pres, Ace Store 116 Inc, Prophetstown, Ill, 58-; chmn, Bus. Promotion Cmt. Prophetstown, 58-65, mem, 65-; secy, Whiteside Co. Nat. Farmers Orgn, 60-62; mem, Rock River Valley Develop. Cmn, N.West, Ill, 67- Mem: Nat. Hardware Retailers Asn; Rock River Valley Develop. Cmn; Prophetstown Booster Club; Nat. Farmers Orgn; Prophet Hills Golf Club. Rel: Congregational. Mailing Add: 309 W. Second St, Prophetstown, Ill. 61277.

DRUMMOND, ADDISON PEAIRS D
Chmn, Holmes Co. Dem. Exec. Cmt, Fla.
b. New Concord, Ohio, 2/8/07; s. Addison Cephus Drummond and Estelle Peairs D; m. 8/8/43 to Marguerite Phillips. Educ: Univ. Ala, LL.B, 32; Delta Sigma Pi; Scabbard and Blade; Delta Tau Delta. Polit. & Govt. Pos: Co. attorney, Holmes Co, Fla, 35-; sch. bd. attorney, Holmes Co. and city attorney, Bonifay, Fla, over 20 years; Fla. State Rep, 37-40 & 59-60; Fla. State Sen, 40-44; chmn, Holmes Co. Dem. Exec. Cmt, Fla, currently. Bus. & Prof. Pos: V.pres, The Bank of Bonifay, Fla, 33-49, pres, 49-53; pres, The Independent Bankers Asn, 42-44. Mil. Serv: Entered as 1st Lt, Army, 42, released as Lt. Col, 46, after serv. in Judge Adv. Corps, Mil. Justice, Pac. Area, 44-45, Col, Res, 46-54; Pac. Theatre, Victory, Philippine Liberation and Army Commendation Medals. Mem: Am, Fla. and Circuit Bar Asns; Mason; Shrine; Elks; dept. comdr, Am. Legion, Fla, 52-53; past nat. chmn, Internal Affairs Cmn, For. Rels. Cmn. and Nat. Security Cmn. Civilian aide to Secy. of Army for Fla, 61- Rel: Episcopal. Legal Res: 302 N. Oklahoma St, Bonifay, Fla. 32425. Mailing Add: P.O. Box 157, Bonifay, Fla. 32425.

DRUMMOND, GREG NEAL R
Cmnr, Seminole Co. Bd. Cmnrs, Fla.
b. Phila, Pa, 10/27/30; s. Oliver Drummond and Alice Biskup D; m. 4/20/53 to Johanna Garrett; c. Douglas G, Geoffrey N. and Christopher F. Educ: Valley Forge Mil. Acad. Jr. Col, Wayne, Pa, A.A, 53. Polit. & Govt. Pos: Publicity chmn, Orange Co. Rep. Exec. Cmt, Fla, 59-60; mem, Seminole Co. Gov. Adv. Bd, 68; chmn, Seminole Co. Rep. Exec. Cmt, 68-69; cmnr, Seminole Co. Bd. Cmnrs, 69- Bus. & Prof. Pos: Instr, Orange Co. Adult Exten. Serv, 68. Mil. Serv: ROTC, Cert. of Completion, Army, 53. Mem: Orlando Asn. Independent Insurors; Jr. C. of C; 4-H Leader, Orange Co; Boy Scout Adv. Coun. Rel: Protestant. Mailing Add: P.O. Box 381, Alberta St, Allamonte Springs, Fla. 32701.

DRUMMOND, JOHN D
S.C. State Sen.
b. Greenwood, S.C, 9/29/19; s. James William Drummond and Fannie Smith D; m. 6/12/47 to Holly Self. Educ: Aviation Cadet Training Sch, 43. Polit. & Govt. Pos: S.C. State Rep, 64-66, past chmn, Cmt. Pub. Works, S.C. State House of Rep; S.C. State Sen, 66- Bus. & Prof. Pos: Gulf Oil Distributor; pres, Drummond Oil Co; pres, Greenwood Petroleum Co; bd. of trustees, Brewer Hosp; bd. trustees, Baptist Col. at Charleston, S.C, 68- Mil. Serv: 262nd CA, 39-41; Air Force, 43-47, Fighter Pilot, Capt. 405th Fighter Bomber Group, Eng, France and Germany, 44-45; Distinguished Flying Cross; 2 Purple Hearts; 9 Air Medals; 3 Battle Stars; Presidential Citation. Mem: Bldg. cmt, Brewer Hosp, 58; pres, PTA, 57; pres, Lions; Worshipful Master, Eureka Lodge 48; Mason (32°); Shrine; Comdr, Am. Legion; v.pres, C. of C; chmn, Greenwood-Laurens Co. Tuberc. Asn. Christmas Seals. Young Man of Year, 60. Rel: Baptist; Chmn, Forward Prog; Chmn, Plans Cmt; Supt, Sunday Sch; Bd. of Deacons. Mailing Add: Box 748, Greenwood, S.C. 29646.

DRYFOOS, GEORGE ELLIS D
Committeeman, Westchester Co. Dem. Cmt, N.Y.
b. N.Y.C, 6/16/19; s. Walter Dryfoos and Lucy Feibleman D; m. 9/11/49 to Joy Abby Gidding; c. Paul René. Educ: Columbia Univ, 37-39. Polit. & Govt. Pos: Committeeman, Westchester Co. Dem. Cmt, N.Y, 55-65 & 69-; village trustee, Hastings-on-the Hudson, 58-60; co-chmn, Westchester Concerned Dem, 67-69; alternate del, Dem. Nat. Conv, 68. Bus. & Prof. Pos: Sales engr, Picker X-Ray, N.Y, 45-60; v.pres. and sales mgr, L. Gidding & Co, 61- Mil. Serv: Entered as Pvt, Army, 39, released as 1st Lt, 43, after serv. in Army Med. Unit, ETO, 40-43. Rel: Jewish. Mailing Add: 20 Circle Dr, Hastings on Hudson, N.Y. 10706.

DUARTE, JOHN GOMES D
b. Wailuku, Maui, 7/10/96; s. Feliciano Gomes Duarte and Jacinta Silva Novita D; m. 9/22/18 to Adelaide H. Sylva; c. Adelaide C. (Mrs. Rowland). Educ: St. Anthony Boys Sch, Wailuku, Maui. Polit. & Govt. Pos: Hawaii State Sen, 3rd Sen. Dist, 65-66; Hawaii State Rep, 63-64; Sen, Territory of Hawaii, 48-59. Bus. & Prof. Pos: Gen. supt, Printing & Newspaper Plant, Maui News, Maui, for 20 yrs; owner and mgr, Valley Isle Chronicle, 20 yrs; owner and mgr, Haleakala Hotel, 20 yrs; 1st boxing promoter, County of Maui; 28-36. Mil. Serv: Army Nat. Guard, 14-17. Mem: Holy Name Soc; Foresters; Young Men's Inst. Rel: Catholic. Mailing Add: P.O. Box 442, Wailuku, Maui, Hawaii 96793. (1967)

DUBBELDE, HERMAN HENRY R
Chmn, Delta Co. Rep. Cmt, Mich.
b. Prairietown, Ill, 8/8/21; s. Herman Dubbelde and Hattie Reinhardt D; m. 3/12/47 to Ruth Sinks; c. Denise and Marybeth. Educ: Dartmouth Col, 43-44; Univ. Ill, Champaign, Mkt. Mgt, 47. Polit. & Govt. Pos: Mem, Exec. Bd, 16th Congressional Dist. Rep. Party, Mich, 64-66; precinct del, 64-66; pres, Dearborn Rep. Club, 66-; campaign coordinator, Sen. Griffin, 66; chmn, Delta Co. Rep. Cmt, 69- Bus. & Prof. Pos: Dept. Mgr, Sears Roebuck, Detroit, Mich. Mil. Serv: Entered as A/S, Navy, 42, released as SF 3/C, 45, after serv. in Pacific. Mem: Class v.pres, North. Mich. Sch. of Banking; Rotary Club; C. of C. Rel: Presbyterian. Mailing Add: 1907 Park Ave, Escanaba, Mich. 49829.

DUBBIN, MURRAY H. D
Fla. State Rep.
b. Miami, Fla, 8/1/29; m. to Helene Faye Shonbrun; c. Clifford B, Samuel J, David C. and Eric S. Educ: Univ. of Fla, B.A, 49, LL.B, 51; Tau Epsilon Phi; Phi Alpha Delta; Fa. Players; John Marshall Bar Asn. Polit. & Govt. Pos: Group chmn, Dist. 7, Dem. Party, Fla; Dem. exec. committeeman, 54-58; spec. asst. attorney gen, 62; Fla. State Rep, 63-, chmn, Legis. Coun. Cmt. on Commerce, Fla. State House of Rep, 68-69, chmn, House Interim and Standing Cmt. on Constitutional Revision, 68-69. Bus. & Prof. Pos: Lawyer. Mem: Elks; PTA; Hemophilia Research Orgn, Inc; Dade and Fla. Bar Asns; dir, South Dade Coun, Inc; Miami-Dade C. of C; Young Dem. Club of Dade Co; Dem. Club of Miami Beach. Nominated for the St. Petersburg Times award, Most Valuable Member of the House for the 1967 Session; Alumni Heart Serv. Award, Tau Epsilon Phi at Univ. of Fla, 68. Rel: Jewish. Mailing Add: 6015 S.W. 64th Place, South Miami, Fla. 33143.

DUBIN, LEONARD R. D
Orgn. Chmn, Los Angeles Co. Dem. Cent. Cmt, Calif.
b. Milwaukee, Wis, 10/15/37; s. David Dubin and Rose Chudnof D; m. Loretta Concoff; c. Lindsey. Educ: Univ. Wis, B.S, 60; Univ. Wis. Law Sch, J.D, 62. Polit. & Govt. Pos: Mem, Los Angeles Co. Dem. Cent. Cmt, Calif, 66-, orgn. chmn, 68-; mem, Calif. State Dem. Cent. Cmt, 68- Bus. & Prof. Pos: Attorney-at-law and partner, Wolf & Dubin, Beverly Hills, Calif, currently. Mem: Calif. and Wis. Bar Asns; Am. Trial Lawyers Asn; Optimist Club. Mailing Add: 7107 Mammoth Ave, Van Nuys, Calif. 91405.

DUBIN, MARTIN DAVID D
Chmn, DeKalb Co. Dem. Party, Ill.
b. N.Y.C, 8/7/31; s. Harry Dubin and Rose Nenner D; m. 6/18/53 to Eileen Latterman; c. Aaron Stuart and Deborah Lynn. Educ: City Col. New York, B.A. with honors, 52; Columbia Univ, 52-53; Ind. Univ, Bloomington, M.A, 55, Ph.D, 60; Pi Sigma Alpha; Phi Alpha Theta; Alpha Phi Omega. Polit. & Govt. Pos: Chmn, DeKalb Co. Dem. Party, Ill, 68- Bus. & Prof. Pos: Teaching assoc. and lectr, Ind. Univ. Calumet Center, 56-59; from asst. to assoc. prof, Roosevelt Univ, 59-65; assoc. prof, North. Ill. Univ, 65- Mem: Am. Polit. Sci. Asn; Midwest Conf. Polit. Scientists; Am. Asn. Univ. Prof; Cmt. on Ill. Govt; Am. Fedn. TV and Radio Artists; B'nai B'rith. Rel: Jewish. Mailing Add: 1627 Schifly Lane, DeKalb, Ill. 60115.

DUBINO, HELEN MARY R
b. Greenfield, Mass, 7/18/26; d. John Dubino and Carrie Kucher D; single. Polit. & Govt. Pos: Staff asst. to House Cmt. on Interstate and Foreign Commerce and Exec. Secy. to U.S. Rep, William L. Springer, 64-; admin. asst. to U.S. Rep, John B. Bennett, 60-64; confidential asst, Dep. Admin. Financial Assistance Prog, Small Bus. Admin, 59-60; admin. asst. to U.S. Rep, Hubert Scudder, 57-59; off. mgr, U.S. Rep. Florence Dwyer, 57; res. asst, U.S. Sen. Thomas Kuchel, 56; secy, U.S. Rep. John W. Heselton, 50-56. Rel: Catholic. Legal Res: 8 Laurel St, Greenfield, Mass. Mailing Add: 803 Independence Ave, S.E, Washington, D.C. 20003. (1967)

DUBINSKY, DAVID Liberal
b. Brest-Litovsk, Poland, 2/22/92; s. Zallel Dubinsky and Shaine Wishingrad D; m. 1915 to Emma Goldberg; c. Jeanette. Educ: Schs. in Poland; evening schs, N.Y.C. Polit. & Govt. Pos: One of founders, Am. Labor Party, N.Y. State, 36; Am. Labor Party and Dem. Party presidential elector, 36; mem, War Dept. Bd, 41; mem. bd. dirs, Nat. War Fund; mem, bd. dirs, Joint Distribution Cmt; mem. bd. dirs, Am. Overseas Aid-UN Appeal for Children; mem, Trade Union Adv. Cmt. on Int. Labor Affairs, U.S. Dept. of Labor; founder and v.chmn, Liberal Party, N.Y. State, 44; mem. bd. dirs, Wilkie Mem, 45; mem, Spec. Cmt. on Labor Standards and Soc. Security; AFL consult, UN Econ. and Soc. Coun, 46; mem. bd. dirs, F.D. Roosevelt Mem. Fund; founder, Am. for Dem. Action, 47. Bus. & Prof. Pos: Joined Local 10, ILGWU, 11, mgr-secy, 21-29, v.pres, 22-29, gen. secy. treas, 29-32, pres, 32-65; v.pres, exec. coun, AFL, 34-36 & 45; AFL rep, Gov. Body Int. Labor Off, Geneva, Switz, 35; mem, Conf. on Workers Educ. called by IFTU, London, 36; mem, Conf. Int. Clothing Workers Fedn, 36; mem, Wage and Hour Ladies Apparel Indust. Cmn, 38-41; mem, Spec. Wage and Hour P.R. Cmn, 40; v.chmn, Am. Labor Conf. on Int. Affairs; labor rep, Nat. Coat and Suit Indust. Rev. Recovery Bd, 42; AFL rep, Mgt. and Labor Conf, 45; mem. bd. dirs, Gr. N.Y. Fund; v.pres, AFL-CIO. Mem: Exec. cmt, Citizen's Cmt. to Support the Marshall Plan; exec. cmt, Workers Educ. Bur; Gr. N.Y. for United Negro Col. Fund, 48; Nat. Sponsors Cmt. of Am. Heart Asn. Legal Res: 201 W. 16th St, New York, N.Y. 10011. Mailing Add: 1710 Broadway, New York, N.Y. 10019. (1967)

DU BOIS, B. F. 'PAT' DFL
b. Sauk Centre, Minn, 1915; m; c. two daughters. Educ: Harvard Univ. Sch. of Bus. Admin, bank seminar course grad. Polit. & Govt. Pos: Minn. State

Rep, 62-69. Bus. & Prof. Pos: Banker; pres. First State Bank of Sauk Centre. Mil. Serv: Navy, 43-46. Mailing Add: 300 5th St, Sauk Centre, Minn. 56378.

DU BOIS, RADFORD EUGENE, JR. D
b. Cleveland, Miss; 3/5/27; married. Polit. & Govt. Pos: Miss. State Rep, 60-68. Bus. & Prof. Pos: Businessman. Mem: Shrine; Mason; Nat. Guard Asn; VFW; Am. Legion; C. of C; Citizens Coun. Rel: Presbyterian. Mailing Add: Yazoo City, Miss. 39194. (1967)

DUBORD, RICHARD JOSEPH D
Mem. Dem. Nat. Cmt, Cmn. on Rules
b. Waterville, Maine, 11/17/21; s. F. Harold Dubord and Blanche L. Letourneau D; m. 9/2/43 to Evelyn Parnell; c. Stephen F, William P. and Susan P. Educ: Holy Cross Col, B.S, 43; Boston Univ, LL.B, 48; Delta Epsilon Sigma; Phi Delta Phi. Polit. & Govt. Pos: Mayor, Waterville, Maine, 52-56; committeeman, Dem. State Cmt, 55-56; del. and mem. credentials cmts, Dem. Nat. Conv, 56, 60, 64 & 68; nat. committeeman, Maine Dem. Party, 56-68; attorney gen, State of Maine, 65-66; dep. coordinator, Muskie Campaign Staff, 69; mem. Dem. Nat. Cmt, Cmn. on Rules, 69- Bus. & Prof. Pos; Partner, Dubord & Dubord, 48-63, Marden, Dubord, Bernier & Chandler, 63- Mil. Serv: Entered as Pvt, Air Force, 42, released as Capt, 46, after serv. in 14th Air Force, China Theatre; Asiatic Pac. Theatre Ribbon, 2 Battle Stars; Asiatic Defense Theatre Ribbon. Mem: Waterville, Kennebec Co, Maine State & Am. Bar Asns; Maine Medico-Legal Soc; Am. Legion; K. of C; Kiwanis; trustee, Thayer Hosp; corporator, Waterville Savings Bank; dir, Kennebec Fed. Savings & Loan Asn. Rel: Catholic. Legal Res: 145 Silver St, Waterville, Maine 04901. Mailing Add: 44 Elm, Waterville, Maine 04901.

DUBUQUE, CHESTER R. D
b. North Hero, Vt, 6/30/08; m. to Lorraine Sarvic; c. One son and one daughter. Educ: Burlington High Sch. Polit. & Govt. Pos: Selectman; town lister, 60-; Vt. State Rep, 65-66. Bus. & Prof. Pos: Carpenter. Mem: Alburg Grange; K. of C; North Hero Fire Dept. Rel: Catholic. Mailing Add: North Hero, Vt. 05474. (1967)

DUBUQUE, LOUIS THEODORE R
Chmn, Moore Co. Rep. Party, Tex.
b. Amarillo, Tex, 10/29/40; s. Louis Clifford Dubuque and Josphine Crabtree D; m. 3/19/66 to Phylis Ann Brandon. Educ: Tex. Tech. Col, B.B.A, 62; Baylor Univ, LL.B, 66; Phi Alpha Delta. Polit. & Govt. Pos: Chmn, Moore Co. Rep. Party, Tex, 68- Mem: 69th Judicial Dist. Bar Orgn.(v.pres, 68-69); State Bar Asn. Tex. Rel: Baptist. Mailing Add: 117 Carson, Dumas, Tex. 79029.

DUCHARME, RAYMOND R. D
b. Manchester, N.H, 7/2/27; married; c. Three. Educ: Local Schs. Polit. & Govt. Pos: N.H. State Rep, -67. Bus. & Prof. Pos: Stereotyper; Manchester Union Leader. Mem: Pinardville Club; Lions Int; I.S. & E.U. of N. Am. Rel: Catholic. Mailing Add: 17 Duclos St, Goffstown, N.H. 03045. (1967)

DUCKER, JOHN LACKNER R
Fla. State Sen.
b. Ft. Thomas, Ky, 9/3/22; s. Stuart Reilly Ducker and Margaret Lackner D; single. Educ: Yale Univ, B.A, 44, Law Sch, LL.B, 50, Univ. Iowa, 43; Univ. Nebr, 44; Phi Beta Kappa. Polit. & Govt. Pos: Mem, Orange Co. Rep. Exec. Cmt, Fla; Fla. State Rep, 60-68; Fla. State Sen, 68- Bus. & Prof. Pos: Practice of law. Mil. Serv: Entered as Pvt, Army-Air Corps, 43, released as 2nd Lt, 46, after serv. in Army Signal Corps, U.S. Mem: Fla. and Orange Co. Bar Asns; Am. Legion; Nat. Rifle Asn. Am; Univ. Club of Winter Park; Orlando Area C. of C; Fla. Educ. Asn; Orange Co. Sportsmen's Asn; Past Exalted Ruler, Elks; Optimist. Rel: Episcopal. Legal Res: 2810 W. Fairbanks Ave, Winter Park, Fla. 32789. Mailing Add: 205 E. Jackson St, Orlando, Fla. 32801.

DUCKWORTH, WILLIAM HENRY R
b. 1887. Polit. & Govt. Pos: N.Mex. State Sen, -66; Lt. Gov; tax cmnr. Bus. & Prof. Pos: Retired druggist; bd. of regents, Portales; secy-treas. Bd. of Pharm. Mem: Mason; Elk; Rotary Club. Rel: Christian. Mailing Add: 310 Main St, Clovis, N.Mex. 88101. (1967)

DUCKWORTH, WILLIAM HENRY D
Chief Justice, Supreme Court, Ga.
b. Blairsville, Ga, 10/21/94; s. John F. Duckworth and Nablet D; m. 7/2/22 to Willibel Pilcher; c. Mary, Dorothy and William Henry, Jr. Educ: Young Harris Col; Phi Chi. Polit. & Govt. Pos: Ga. State Sen, 31-32; city attorney, Cairo, 33-34; Asst. Attorney Gen, Ga, 37-38; Justice, Supreme Court, Ga, 38-48, Chief Justice, 48- Mil. Serv: Seaman, Naval Res, 18. Mem: Mason; Elks; Odd Fellows; Woodmen; Kiwanis; Scot Lake Country Club; Capital City Club; Piedmont Club. Rel: Baptist. Legal Res: Decatur, Ga. Mailing Add: 514 Judicial Bldg, Atlanta, Ga. 30334. (1967)

DUCOMMUN, CHARLES EMIL R
Mem, Rep. State Cent. Cmt, Calif.
b. Los Angeles, Calif, 4/27/13; s. Emil Constant Ducommun and Bescelia Shemwell D; m. 6/15/49 to Palmer Gross; c. Robert Constant and Electra Bradford. Educ: Stanford Univ, A.B, Econ, 35; Harvard Univ, M.B.A, cum laude, Bus. Admin, 42; Delta Kappa Epsilon. Polit. & Govt. Pos: Mem. budget and expenditures cmt, Los Angeles Co. Rep. Cent. Cmt, 48-58; v.chmn. finance, Nixon Sen. Campaign, 50; chmn, Los Angeles Co. Eisenhower-Nixon Campaign, 52; mem, Rep. Nat. Finance Cmt, 53-54; chmn. finance cmt, Rep. State Cent. Cmt, 53-54; mem, Rep. State Cent. Cmt, 53-56 & 64-; v.chmn, Eisenhower-Nixon Campaign, 56; chmn. task force evaluate impact sci. and tech, Rep. Cmt. Prog. and Progress, 59; v.chmn, Nixon Pres. Cmt, 60; del, Rep. Nat. Conv, 60 & 68. Bus. & Prof. Pos: Dir, Ducommun Inc, 38 and pres 50-; trustee, Rep. Assocs, 50-63; dir, Pac. Tel. and Tel. Co, 57-, Security Pac. Nat. Bank, 59- and Lockheed Aircraft Corp, 61-; adv. dir, Invest. Co. Am, 61- Mil. Serv: Entered as Ens, Navy, 42, serv. as aide to Chief Staff, U.S. Fleet; Lt, Res, 44-46. Rel: Episcopal. Legal Res: 237 Strada Corta, Los Angeles, Calif. 90024. Mailing Add: 612 S. Flower St, Suite 460, Los Angeles, Calif. 90017.

DUDA, RICHARD JOSEPH D
Conn. State Rep.
b. Jewett City, Conn, 1/20/35; m. to Barbara A. Perkins; c. Mary Beth. Educ: Univ. Conn, B.A, 57; Georgetown Univ. Law Sch, J.D, 60. Polit. & Govt. Pos: Conn. State Rep, 58th Dist, 63- Mailing Add: 11 Faust St, Jewett City, Conn. 06351.

DUDA, WALTER R
Ill. State Sen.
b. Chicago, Ill, 8/10/11; s. Frank Duda and Rozalia Stojek D; m. 10/16/43 to Lilyan Dywan; c. Deanna, Amy, Walter and Rosemary. Educ: DePaul Univ, Ph.B, 41; Loyola Univ, M.A.S, 51; Pi Gamma Mu. Polit. & Govt. Pos: Probation officer, Family Court of Cook Co, Ill, 41-51, U.S. Probation Court, 44-45; v.pres, 45th Ward, Rep. Party, Ill, 61-66, exec. secy, 66-67; Ill. State Sen, 67- Bus. & Prof. Pos: Sch. counsr, Niles Twp. High Sch, Ill, 51-55; teacher, Dist. 68, Skokie, 55-66. Mem: Nat. and Ill. Educ. Asns; NASA; Polish Roman Cath. Union; Polish Nat. Alliance. Rel: Roman Catholic. Mailing Add: 5334 W. Sunnyside, Chicago, Ill. 60630.

DUDLEY, EDWARD RICHARD D. D
Justice, N.Y. Supreme Court
b. South Boston, Va, 3/11/11; s. Edward R. Dudley and Nellie Johnson D; m. 1/31/42 to Rae Elizabeth Olley; c. Edward, Richard and Dudley. Educ: Johnson C. Smith Univ, B.S, 32; St. John's Univ. Law Sch, LL.B, 41; Alpha Phi Alpha. Polit. & Govt. Pos: Asst. attorney gen, N.Y, 42-43; coun. to Gov. V.I, 45-47; U.S. Ambassador, Liberia, 48-53; judge, Domestic Rels. Court, 55-61; boro pres, Manhattan, N.Y, 61-64; chmn, N.Y. Co. Dem. Cmt, 63-65; justice, N.Y. Supreme Court, 65- Mem: Nat. Bar Asn. Rel: Presbyterian. Mailing Add: 549 W. 123rd St, New York, N.Y. 10027. (1967)

DUDLEY, GUILFORD, JR. R
U.S. Ambassador to Denmark
b. Nashville, Tenn, 6/23/07; s. Guilford Dudley and Anne Dallas D; m. to Jane Anderson; c. Guilford, Robert Lusk and Trevania Dallas. Educ: Loomis Inst, Peabody Col; Vanderbilt Univ. A.B, 29. Polit. & Govt. Pos: U.S. Ambassador to Denmark, currently; former chmn, Tenn. Rep. Finance Cmt; mem, Rep. Nat. Finance Cmt. Bus. & Prof. Pos: Pres. and dir, Life & Casualty Ins. Co, Radio Sta. WLAC, WLAC-TV and Casualty Ins. Co. of Tenn; chmn. and dir, World-Wide Life Assurance Co, Ltd, London; dir, Life Ins. Investors, Inc, Third Nat. Bank, Nashville, Bank of Palm Beach & Trust, Vehicle & Gen. Ins. Co, London. Mem: Bd. dirs, Cumberland Col, Vanderbilt Univ, Ensworth Sch, Tenn. Bot. Gardens and Fine Arts Center, Jr. Achievement, YMCA, United Givers Fund and South. States Indust. Coun; Nat. Planning Asn; Nat. Steeplechasing and Hunt; Midwest Hunt Racing Asn; Phi Delta Theta; Turf and Field Club; Cumberland, Hillsboro Hounds Hunt, Belle Meade Country, Everglades, Bath and Tennis, Coral Beach and Lost Tree Clubs; River Club, N.Y.C; Nashville City Club, Cumberland; Palm Bay Club, Miami, Fla; Seminole Golf Club, Palm Beach, Fla. Rel: Episcopal. Legal Res: Harding Place at Hillsboro Rd, Nashville, Tenn. 37215. Mailing Add: U.S. Embassy, Copenhagen, Denmark.

DUDLEY, L. LELAND R
b. Auburn, N.Y, 1/20/95; m. to Virginia Bartlett; c. One son and one daughter. Educ: Harvard Col, B.S, 21; Harvard Sch. of Educ, M.Ed, D.Ed, 27. Polit. & Govt. Pos: Town auditor; Vt. State Rep, 65-66. Bus. & Prof. Pos: Retired supt. of Schs. Mil. Serv: Army, 36th Inf, 19. Mem: Odd Fellows; Rotary Club of Ludlow; Vt. Weavers Guild. Rel: Congregational. Mailing Add: Belmont, Vt. 05730. (1967)

DUDLEY, TILFORD ELI D
b. Charleston, Ill, 4/21/07; s. Dr. Gerry Brown Dudley and Esther Shoot D; m. 8/28/37 to Martha Fairchild Ward; c. Donica Ward, Gerrie Ward and Martha Fairchild. Educ: Wesleyan Univ, Ph.B, 28; Harvard Univ. Law Sch, LL.B, 31; Delta Sigma Rho. Polit. & Govt. Pos: Chief legal sect, Land Prog, Fed. Emergency Relief Admin, 34-35; chief land sect, Suburban Resettlement Admin, 35-37; chief land acquisition, Nat. Park Serv, 36-37; trial exam, Nat. Labor Rels. Bd, 37-42; principle mediation officer, Nat. War Labor Bd, 42-43, regional dir, Disputes, 43-44; del, Dem. Nat. Conv, 48, 52 & 60; alternate mem, Dem. Nat. Cmt, 48-; mem, D.C. Dem. Cent. Cmt, 48-, treas, 61-64, v.chmn, 64-67, chmn, 67-68; chmn, Citizens Coun. of D.C. Govt, 62-67. Bus. & Prof. Pos: Partner, Law firm of Mighell, Gunsul, Allan & Latham, Aurora, Ill, 31-34; asst. to Sidney Hillman, chmn. of CIO-PAC, 45-46; asst. dir, Cmt. on Polit. Action, CIO, 46-55, asst. dir, Cmt. on Polit. Educ, 55-58; dir, Speakers Bur, AFL-CIO, 58- Publ: The Harvard Legal Aid Bureau: Its History and Purposes, 31; Digest of Decisions of the National Labor Relations Board, 40. Mem: Gen. bd, Div. of Christian Life & Work, Nat. Coun. of Churches, 54 & 64, exec. bd, 54-65, exec. bd, Div. of Christian Life & Mission, 65-; Am. for Dem. Action; NAACP; Urban League; YMCA; Harvard Club of D.C. Rel: Methodist and United Church of Christ. Legal Res: 2942 Macomb St. N.W, Washington, D.C. 20008. Mailing Add: 815 16th St. N.W, Washington, D.C. 20006.

DUDLEY, WILLIAM McGARVEY 'BILL' D
Va. State Del.
b. Bluefield, Va, 12/24/21; m. to Elizabeth Leininger. Educ: Univ. Va, B.S. in Educ. Polit. & Govt. Pos: Va. State Del, 66-, mem, House Educ. Cmt. and House Finance Cmt, Va. House of Del, currently. Bus. & Prof. Pos: Ins. Mil. Serv: Lt, Army Air Corps. Mem: Prfnl. Football Hall of Fame; Lynchburg Estate Planning Coun; Lynchburg Scholastic Football League; Million Dollar Round Table; metrop. Transporation Study Cmn; Gov. Cmt. for Youth; bd. mem, Bank of Cent. Va, Roanoke Buckskins Pro-Football Team and YMCA; Lynchburg C. of C; Va. State C. of C; chmn, Va. Athletic Cmn, Life Underwriters Asn. Rel: Presbyterian; Deacon, First Presbyterian Church. Mailing Add: P.O. Box 23, Lynchburg, Va. 24505.

DUEHOLM, HARVEY L. D
Wis. State Assemblyman
b. Bone Lake, Wis, 1/29/10. Educ: Luck High Sch. Polit. & Govt. Pos: Commun. committeeman, Agr. Conserv. Serv, 38-53; town chmn, 45-59; chmn, Co. Bd, 57-59; Wis. State Assemblyman, 58- Bus. & Prof. Pos: Dairy farmer; mem. various coop. exec. bds. Mailing Add: Route 2, Luck, Wis. 54853.

DUENSING, GEORGE, JR. R
b. Concordia, Mo, 7/22/00; m. 10/18/22 to Minerva Blanke; c. JoAnn, Norma Jane (Mrs. R.H. Hohenstein); grandchildren Robert P, John R, David H, Mary Elizabeth, Marth Ann Hohenstein. Educ: Concordia Pub. Schs. Polit. & Govt. Pos: Mo. State Rep, 54-66. Bus. & Prof. Pos: Pres. Cent. Mo. Retail Lumber Dealers Asn, 46. Mem: Concordia Lodge 464; Masons. Rel: Evangelical and Reformed Church. Mailing Add: 902 Main St, Concordia, Mo. 64020. (1967)

DUERK, JAMES ALLEN R
b. Defiance, Ohio, 7/13/30; s. Karl Duerk and Alice Bybee D; m. 6/9/51 to Dolores M. Hempstock; c. Karla Annette, Kathryn Jeanne and Kristin Elizabeth. Educ: Centre Col. Ky; Bowling Green State Univ; Sigma Chi. Polit. & Govt. Pos: Press asst, Congressman Oliver P. Bolton, Ohio, 64; pub. rels. dir, Campaign of Congressman Clarence J. Brown, Jr, 65; dir. pub. rels, Ohio Rep. State Hq, 65-69; asst. to Gov. James A. Rhodes, Ohio, 69- Bus. & Prof. Pos: Sports ed, Sentinel-Tribune, Bowling Green, Ohio, 51-52; reporter and columnist, Crescent-News, Defiance, 52-55; pub. rels. rep, Columbia Gas of Ohio, Inc, 55-63. Publ: Publisher and ed, Ohio Republican News, 65-69. Rel: Lutheran. Legal Res: 393 Franklin Court, Worthington, Ohio 43085. Mailing Add: Statehouse, Columbus, Ohio 43215.

DUFF, JAMES H. R
b. Mansfield, Carnegie, Pa, 1/21/83; s. Joseph Miller Duff and Margaret Morgan D; m. 10/26/09 to Jean Taylor. Educ: Princeton, A.B, 04; Univ. of Pa. Law Sch, 04-06; Univ. of Pittsburgh, LL.B, 07. Hon. LL.D, Duquesne Univ, Albright Col, Pa. Mil. Col, Lafayette Col, Franklin and Marshall Col, Wash. and Jefferson Col, Univ. of Pa, Temple Univ, St. Francis Col, Geneva Col, Lincoln Univ, Villanova Col, Jefferson Med. Col, Elizabethtown Col, Lebanon Valley Col, Drexel Inst, Lehigh Univ, Rollins Col. and Univ. of Pittsburgh; D.C.L, Hahnemann Med. Col. and Hosp; Litt.D, Wayneburg Col; D.Sc, Phila. Col. of Osteopathy. Polit. & Govt. Pos: Nat. elector, Pa, 12; del, Rep. Nat. Conv, 32, 36, 40, 48 & 52; Attorney Gen, Pa, 43-47, Gov, Pa, 47-51; U.S. Sen, Pa, 50-57. Bus. & Prof. Pos: Law practice, 07-43; partner, Duff, Scott & Smith, Pittsburgh, Pa; pres, Va. Manor Co; mem. law firm, Davies, Richberg, Tydings, Landa & Duff, Wash, D.C, currently. Mem: Life trustee, Carnegie Libr, Carnegie, Pa; Allegheny Co. Bar Asn; Mason; Elks; Rotary. Legal Res: R.D. 4, Linglestown, Pa. 17105. Mailing Add: 1000 Vermont Ave. N.W, Washington, D.C. 20005.

DUFF, JOHN BERNARD D
Committeeman, Essex Co. Dem. Party, N.J.
b. Orange, N.J, 7/1/31; s. John B. Duff and Mary Cunningham D; m. 10/8/55 to Helen Mezzanotti; c. Michael, Maureen, Patricia, John and Robert. Educ: Fordham Col, B.S, 53; Seton Hall Univ, M.A, 58; Columbia Univ, Ph.D, 64. Polit. & Govt. Pos: Del, N.J. State Constitutional Conv, 66; committeeman, Essex Co. Dem. Party, 67-; Dem. cand. for cong, 12th Cong. Dist, 68; v.chmn, bd. trustees, Essex Co. Col, 66- Bus. & Prof. Pos: Sales rep, Remington-Rand Corp, Newark, N.J, 55-57, dist. mgr, Jersey City, 57-60; instr, Seton Hall Univ, 60-63, asst. prof, 63-66, assoc. prof, 66-69, prof, 69-. Mil. Serv: Entered as Pvt, Army, 53, released as Pfc, 55, after serv. in 74th Regt. Combat Team, Ft. Devens, Mass, 53-55; Nat. Defense Medal; Good Conduct Medal. Publ: American Political Philosophy, Monarch Press, 65; co-auth, The Immigrants' Influence on Wilson's Peace Policies, Univ. Ky. Press, 67; auth, The Irish in the United States, Wadsworth Publ, 69. Mem: Am. Hist. Asn; Orgn. of Am. Historians; Am. Asn. Univ. Prof; Immigration Hist. Research Group; K. of C; Phi Alpha Theta. Rel: Catholic. Mailing Add: 8 Laurel Ave, Livingston, N.J. 07032.

DUFFECK, FRANK GUSTAV R
b. Toledo, Ohio, 5/16/14; s. Frank William Duffeck and Norma Leser D; m. 7/1/44 to Joy Louise Paulson; c. Kaaren Marie and Christie Sue. Educ: Toledo Univ, B.A, 35. Polit. & Govt. Pos: Dist. leader, Pierce Co. Rep. Cent. Cmt, Wash, 64-65, precinct committeeman, 64-66 and chmn, 65-66; Housing Improv. Rep, Tacoma, 67- Bus. & Prof. Pos: Pres, Elec. Power Maintenance Co, 45-59, B&M Distributing Co, 59-64 and Frank Duffek & Assocs, 64- Mil. Serv: Entered as 2nd Lt, Army, 41, released as Major, 45, Ord. Dept, U.S; Am. Defense and Army Commendation Ribbons. Mem: Elks; Rotary; Optimist Club; Navy League of U.S. Rel: Lutheran. Mailing Add: 5106 Harbor View Dr, Tacoma, Wash. 98422.

DUFFEY, JOSEPH D. D
Nat. Chmn, Am. for Dem. Action
b. Huntington, W.Va, 7/1/32; s. Joseph I. Duffey and Ruth Wilson D; m. 8/24/52 to Patricia Fortney; c. Michael Robert and David King. Educ: Marshall Univ, A.B, 54; Andover Newton Theol. Sch, B.D, 57; Yale Univ, S.T.M, 63; Hartford Sem. Found, Ph.D, 69; Omicron Delta Kappa; Rockefeller Found. doctoral fel, 64-65. Polit. & Govt. Pos: Chmn, Conn. Campaign for Eugene McCarthy, 68; mem, Dem. State Platform Cmt, 68; del, Dem. Nat. Conv, 68; chmn, Caucus of Conn. Dem, currently; nat. chmn, Am. for Dem. Action, currently. Bus. & Prof. Pos: Dir, Center for Urban Studies, Hartford, Conn, 67- Publ: 'The Supreme Court Decision Regarding Church and State,' United Church Herald, 63; 'The Liberals Plight,' Christianity and Crisis, 11/67. Rel: United Church of Christ. Mailing Add: 175 Ridgefield St, Hartford, Conn. 06112.

DUFFIELD, JOHN RICHARD D
Chmn, Dem. Party, Ariz.
b. Elizabeth, N.J, 5/17/30; s. Stuart Duffield and Mary Horning D; m. 6/15/55 to Mary Rose Carroll; c. Christopher, John, Jennifer and Marjorie. Educ: Williams Col, B.A, 52; Yale Law Sch, LL.B, 57; Phi Beta Kappa, Order of the Coif; Phi Gamma Delta. Polit. & Govt. Pos: Chmn, Pima Co. Dem. Cent. Cmt, Ariz, 64-66; chmn, Dem. Party, Ariz, 66- Bus. & Prof. Pos: Partner, Spaid, Fish, Briney & Duffield, Lawyers, 63- Mil. Serv: Entered as 2nd Lt, Air Force, 52, released as 1st Lt, 54. Mem: Am, Pima Co. and Ariz. Bar Asns. Rel: Episcopal. Legal Res: 4125 Camino Encerrado, Tucson, Ariz. 85716. Mailing Add: 711 Transamerica Bldg, Tucson, Ariz. 85701.

DUFFY, F. RYAN D
b. Fond du Lac, Wis, 6/23/88; s. Francis Fee Duffy and Hattie E. Ryan D; m. 1/26/18 to Louise Haydon; c. Mrs. Ann L, Judge F. Ryan, Jr, Dr. Haydon R. and Rev. James H. Educ: Univ. Wis, B.A, 10, B.B.L, 12, LL.D, 52; De Paul Univ, LL.D, 55; Delta Sigma Rho. Polit. & Govt. Pos: U.S. Sen, Wis, 33-39; U.S. Dist. Judge, 39-49; U.S. Circuit Judge, 49-; chief judge, U.S. Court of Appeals, Seventh Circuit, 54-59. Mil. Serv: Entered Army, 17, released as Maj, 19, after serv. in Motor Transport Corps, AEF. Mem: Pres, Milwaukee Legal Aid Asn, 10 years; state comdr, Am. Legion, 22-23, nat. vice comdr, 23-24; Milwaukee Athletic Club; Milwaukee Club. Alumni of the Year Award, Univ. Wis. Law Sch, 68. Rel: Roman Catholic. Legal Res: 3107 N. Hackett Ave, Milwaukee, Wis. 53211. Mailing Add: 718 Federal Bldg, Milwaukee, Wis. 53202.

DUFFY, FRANCIS PATRICK R
Chmn, Prospect Rep. Town Cmt, Conn.
b. Waterbury, Conn, 9/20/22; s. Michael Duffy and Mary Emmett D; m. 9/20/47 to Frances Mary Jodoin; c. Susan, Emmett, Kathleen and Patricia. Educ: Wilby High Sch, Waterbury Conn, 4 years. Polit. & Govt. Pos: Chmn, Prospect Charter Cmn, Conn, 66-67; chmn, Prospect Rep. Town Cmt, 66-; justice of the peace, 69- Mil. Serv: Entered as A/S, Navy, 42, released as Yeoman 1/C, 46, after serv. in Naval Air Sta, Sitha, Alaska, N.Pa, 42-45. Mem: Waterbury Stereotypers Union. Rel: Roman Catholic. Mailing Add: 60 Beach Dr, Prospect, Conn. 06712.

DUFFY, GORDON W. R
Calif. State Assemblyman
b. Hanford, Calif, 4/24/24; s. Carl Henry Duffy and Fannie Andersen D; m. 4/11/58 to JoAnn Mary Hein; c. Brian Edwin, Mark Carl, Eric Nathaniel, Sean Christian and Nancy Jean. Educ: Univ. Calif, Berkeley, A.B, 44, B.S, 48; Kappa Sigma. Polit. & Govt. Pos: Mem. and chmn, Hanford Planning Cmn, Calif, 52-55; mem, Hanford Elem. Sch. Bd, 55-61; v.mayor, Hanford, 62-64 and mayor, 64; Calif. State Assemblyman, 65-, chmn, Assembly Cmt. on Health and Welfare, 69- Bus. & Prof. Pos: Optometrist, 58- Mil. Serv: Entered as A/S, Navy, 44, released as Lt.(jg), 46, after serv. in S.Pac. and Philippine Theaters. Mem: Calif. Optom. Asn; fel. Am. Acad. of Optom; fel. Am. Sch. Health Asn; hon. life mem, Calif. PTA; VFW; Moose; Farm Bur; Am. Legion; Lions; Mason; Navy League. Selected 'Man of the Year,' Univ. Calif. Optom. Alumni Asn, 68. Rel: Presbyterian; Elder, First Presby. Church. Legal Res: 805 Laura Lane, Hanford, Calif. 93230. Mailing Add: Room 202, 208 N. Douty St, Hanford, Calif. 93230.

DUFFY, J. HOWARD D
R.I. State Rep.
b. East Providence, R.I, 1/4/06; m. to Mary S. Educ: Bryant Col; Brown Univ, ext. courses; Univ. R.I. Polit. & Govt. Pos: Mem, 24th Dist. Dem. Cmt; labor rep, Minimum Wage Bd, 53; R.I. State Rep, 61-; mem, Providence & House Steering Cmt. Bus. & Prof. Pos: Bus. agent, Hotel & Restaurant Serv. Employees & Bartenders Union 285. Mem: Legis. Cmt. of State Coun, CIO. Mailing Add: 171 Reynolds Ave, Providence, R.I. 02905. (1967)

DUFFY, JAMES EVAN R
b. White Plains, N.Y, 7/1/32; s. James Evan Duffy and Pearl Kath D: m. to Carol Letitia Brugh; c. Jacquelyn Carol and James Evan, III. Educ: Clemson Univ, 50-54; Phi Chi Eta; bus. mgr, Sr. Platoon, Clemson Univ; Pershing Rifles; Scabbard and Blade. Polit. & Govt. Pos: Mem, Speakers Bur, S.C. Rep. Party, 60; del, Co. Rep. Conv, S.C, 61, 62, 64, 66 & 68; Rep. state committeeman, Anderson Co, 61-65; del, S.C. State Rep. Conv, 62, 64, 66 & 68; chmn, Steering Cmt, 64 & 68, v.chmn, Steering Cmt. and chmn, Agenda and Order of Bus. Cmt, 66; del, 13-State Regional Rep. Conv, 63; Third Dist. Ballot Security Officer, S.C, 63; chmn, Third Dist. Rep. Party, 63-65; mem, S.C. State Rep. Finance Cmt, 63-68; mem, S.C. State Rep. Cent. Adv. Cmt, 63-68; Presidential Elector, 64; del. and mem, Credentials Cmt, Rep. Nat. Conv, 64; State Ballot Security Chmn, 64, 66 & 68; state finance chmn, S.C. Rep. Party, 65-66; mem, Nat. Rep. Finance Cmt, 65-66; mem, S.C. State Personnel Cmt, 65-66; v.chmn, S.C. State Rep. Finance Campaign Cmt, 66-68; co. committeeman, Arcadia Precinct, Richland Co, 66; mem, Richland Co. Rep. Adv. Cmt, 66; secy, Second Cong. Dist. Rep. Cmt, 66; chmn, Second Cong. Dist. Rep. Party, 66-68; pres, Mission Precinct Club, Greenville Co. Rep. Party; orgn. dir, S.C. State Rep. Party, 68; chmn, Ravenel for Gov, S.C, 69-70. Bus. & Prof. Pos: Personnel dir, Orr-Lyons Mills, 57-59; asst. dir, qual. control, Cent. Mfg. Div, M. Lowenstein & Sons, 59-65; asst. to gen. mgr, Pac. Columbia Mills, 65-66, tech. supt, 66-68; syst. analyst, United Merchants & Mfrs, Greenville, S.C, 68- Mil. Serv: Entered as 2nd Lt, Army, 55, released as 1st Lt, 57. Mem: Chmn, Clemson Univ. Liaison Cmt, Area 9; Textile Qual. Control Asn; past secy, Anderson Co. Personnel Club; class agent, Clemson Univ. Alumni Asn; past pres, Anderson Commun. Concert Asn; past co-chmn, United Fund Drive; past bd. mem, Greater Anderson Commun. Chest; chmn, Civil Rights and For. Affairs Cmt, Columbia C. of C; chmn, Merrifield Park Commun. Action Cmt. Rel: Episcopal; past Jr. Warden, Vestryman, Bible Teacher, Treas. and Lay Reader, currently. Legal Res: 105 Seabury Dr, Greenville, S.C. 29607. Mailing Add: Box 2148, Greenville, S.C. 29602.

DUFFY, JOHN L. D
b. Dubuque, Iowa, 5/22/99; m. 1922 to Antoinette M. Freisinger; c. Thomas M, Shiela and Roger. Educ: Loras Col; Iowa State Univ; Univ. of Notre Dame, LL.B. Polit. & Govt. Pos: Former Iowa State Rep. Bus. & Prof. Pos: Lawyer. Mem: Am. Legion; Cath. Order of Foresters; Iowa Bar Asn. Rel: Catholic. Mailing Add: 220 Bryant St, Dubuque, Iowa 52001. (1967)

DUFFY, JOHN PATRICK D
b. Green Bay, Wis, 5/16/21; s. John Joseph Duffy and Stella Golden D; m. 10/13/51 to Kathleen Maloney; c. Dennis, Eileen, Patrick, Brian, Molly, Kathleen, Timothy and Matthew. Educ: Univ. Wis, B. A. and LL.D; Phi Delta Phi. Polit. & Govt. Pos: Chmn, Brown Co. Dem. Party, Wis, 50-53; del, Dem. Nat. Conv, 52, 56, 60, 64, 68; v.chmn, Eighth Dist. Dem. Party, Wis, 56. Rel: Catholic. Mailing Add: 503 N. Platten St, Green Bay, Wis. 54303.

DUFFY, MARTIN J, JR. D
b. 1910. Educ: Univ. of Louisville Law Sch, LL.B. Polit. & Govt. Pos: Ky. State Sen, 52-68, Dem. Caucus Chmn, 64. Rel: Catholic. Mailing Add: 2555 Woodbourne Ave, Louisville, Ky. 40205. (1967)

DUFFY, STEPHEN FRANCIS D
b. Ridgway, Ill, 10/19/06; s. John Duffy and Hannah Doherty D; m. 1/30/40 to Mary Pauline Lowe; c. Kenneth Wayne, Martin James, Stephen Lowe and

David Keith. Polit. Pos: Chmn, Gallatin Co. Dem. Cmt, Ill, 54-66, precinct committeeman, 37-66; mem, Ill. Commerce Cmn, 61-; Inheritance Tax Investr, 59-61; game warden, Dept. of Conserv, 49-53. Govt. Pos: New Haven Twp.Supvr, 59-63; New Haven Twp.Road Cmnr, 39-47; city treas, New Haven, 34-38; dep. sheriff, 29-35. Bus. Pos: Farmer, 26- Mem: K. of C; bd. mem, Gallatin Co. Farm Bur. Rel: Catholic. Mailing Add: P.O. Box 136, New Haven, Ill. 62867. (1967)

DUFFY, THOMAS A. D
b. Queens Co, N.Y; m. to Helen M. Fisher; c. three. Educ: Fordham Univ. Sch. of Law. Polit. & Govt. Pos: N.Y. State Sen, 56-66; N.Y. State Assemblyman, 48-56; Jackson Heights Regular Dem. Club, Inc. Bus. & Prof. Pos: Lawyer. Mem: Past pres. Queens Borough Rotary; Queens Co. and N.Y. State Bar Asn; C. of C Borough of Queens; Queensboro Lodge Elks 878; K. of C; Holy Name Soc. of St. Joan of Arc. Mailing Add: 33-32 75th St, Jackson Heights, N.Y. 11372. (1967)

DUGAN, PAUL FLEMING D
Mem, Calif. Dem. State Cent. Cmt.
b. Orange, N.J, 10/29/00; s. Daniel A. Dugan and Anna C. Davis D; m. 10/7/32 to Mary C. Workman; c. Ann Elizabeth (Mrs. A. N. Hurteau), David Paul, Mary Deborah (Mrs. Louie) and Daniel William. Educ: U.S. Naval Acad, Annapolis, Md, B.S, 23, postgraduate sch, 29-30; Harvard Univ, M.S, 31; U.S. Naval War Col, diploma, 41; San Diego State Col, M.A, 56; Phi Alpha Theta. Polit. & Govt. Pos: Campaign chmn, Assemblyman James R. Mills, San Diego, Calif, 62 & 64; mem, San Diego Co. Dem. Cent. Cmt, Calif, 63-69; Calif. State chmn, Sr. Citizens for Pat Brown, 66; campaign chmn, Sen. James R. Mills, 66; Dem. registrn. chmn, San Diego Co, 66 & 68; mem, Gov. Adv. Cmt. Vet, 66; mem, Econ. Stabilization Task Force, 66-68; South. Calif. chmn, Sr. Citizens for Humphrey, 68; mem, Calif. Dem. State Cent. Cmt, currently. Bus. & Prof. Pos: Teacher math. and sci, Rosary High Sch, San Diego, 52-54; Bishop's Sch, La Jolla, 54-59 and St. Augustine High Sch, San Diego, 59-67. Mil. Serv: Entered as Midn, Navy, 19, Ret. as Rear Admiral, 50, after serv. in various units and commands, Atlantic, Pac. fleets and U.S. Shore Commands, 23-50; Legion Merit (Combat V); Bronze Star (Combat V); Two Navy Unit Commendations (Combat); China Serv, Am. Defense, Nicaraguan Campaign, World War II Victory and Philippine Campaign Liberation Medals; Pac. Campaign Medal with Seven Battle Stars. Publ: 'Historic Documents,' trans. and illustrated, 37-38 and translator, 'First Typhoon Recorded in Guam,' 4/38, Guam Recorder; various book reviews, U.S. Naval Inst, 47-49 & 54. Mem: U.S. Naval Inst; Gr. San Diego Math. Coun, Calif. Math. Coun; San Diego Hist. Soc; Nat. Coun. Math. Teachers; U.S. Naval Acad. Alumni Asn; Harvard Alumni Asn; Nat. Coun. Sr. Citizens (nat. adv. cmt); K. of C.(dir. publicity, state coun, 69-); House Pac. Rels.(past pres, 62 & 63); Citizens Interracial Cmt; Am. Legion; World Affairs Coun; UN Asn.(v.pres, San Diego Chap, 67-); Fine Arts Asn; Old Globe Theatre. House of Pac. Rels. Plaque, 62-63; Key to City of San Diego, 62; Achievement Award, Off. Emergency Planning, Exec. Off. President. Rel: Roman Catholic. Mailing Add: 3759 Grim Ave, San Diego, Calif. 92104.

DUGAN, ROBERT JOSEPH R
Ward Six Chmn, Springfield Rep. City Cmt, Mass.
b. Quincy, Mass, 5/27/37; s. Mrs. Berandine Kiley D; m. to Kathleen Marie Varrieur; c. Elizabeth Ann and Gerard Frederick. Educ: Mass. State Teachers Col, Boston, 3 years; Am. Int. Col, currently. Polit. & Govt. Pos: Ward Six Chmn, Springfield Rep. City Cmt, Mass, 68- Mil. Serv: Entered as A/S, Navy, 56, released as FT-3, 60, after serv. in Sea Duty, 3 years, 1 month; Good Conduct Medal. Mem: DAV. Rel: Catholic. Mailing Add: 38 Wilmont St, Springfield, Mass. 01108.

DUGDALE, ROBERT EARL R
Ore. State Rep.
b. Toledo, Ohio, 2/11/17; s. Ralph E. Dugdale and Ethel Vivian Roberts D; m. 1/12/61 to Marie C. Pederson; c. Robert Danford. Educ: Ohio State Univ; Ohio North. Univ; Univ. Colo; Sigma Chi. Polit. & Govt. Pos: Ore. State Rep, 69- Bus. & Prof. Pos: Builder and property investments, 10 years. Rel: Methodist. Mailing Add: 2616 N.W. 81st Place, Portland, Ore. 97229.

DUGGAN, FITZHUGH LEE, JR. D
b. Houston, Tex, 8/14/31; s. F. L. Duggan, Sr. and Kathleen Rucker D; m. 4/16/60 to Annette Wicker; c. Linda Annette. Educ: Rice Inst, Houston, Tex, B.A, 52; Univ. Tex. Sch. Law, Austin, LL.B, 55; Phi Alpha Delta; Delta Tau Delta. Polit. Pos: Tex. State Rep, Harris Co, Dist. 24, Pos. 2, 64-66; asst. dist. attorney, Harris Co, Tex, 59-61. Bus. & Prof. Pos: Instr, S. Tex. Col. Law, 60-62. Mil. Serv: Entered as Pvt, Army, 55, released as Sgt, 57. Mem: Houston, Tex. and Am. Bar Asns. Rel: Methodist. Legal Res: 5755 Wigton, Houston, Tex. 77035. Mailing Add: 1406 Fannin Bank Bldg, Houston, Tex. 77025. (1967)

DUGGAN, ROBERT WARD R
b. Pittsburgh, Pa, 1/27/26; s. Frank L. Duggan and Blanche Kane D. Educ: Univ. Pa; Univ. Pittsburgh, B.S, 49, LL.B, 51; Delta Kappa Epsilon; Phi Delta Phi. Polit. & Govt. Pos: Mem. bd. of dirs, Allegheny Co. Rep, Pa, 52-57; chmn, E. End Young Rep, 53-55; asst. dist. attorney, Allegheny Co, 53-55 and dist. attorney, 64-; del, Rep. Nat. Conv, 64 & 68. Bus. & Prof. Pos: Partner, Grier, Duggan, Hampsey & Ludwig, Pa; mem, exec. bd. of dirs, Mercy Hosp, Pittsburgh and Pittsburgh Playhouse. Mil. Serv: Aviation Cadet, Army Air Corps, 44-45. Mem: Exec. cmt, Pa. Dist. Attorney's Asn; Nat. Dist. Attorney's Asn; Am. Legion; Nat. Crime Cmn. (bd. mem); Pa. Crime Cmn. (adv. cmt). Rel: Catholic. Legal Res: 4609 Bayard St, Pittsburgh, Pa. 15213. Mailing Add: 301 Court House, Pittsburgh, Pa. 15219.

DUGGER, JAMES ALLISON D
Chmn, Watauga Co. Dem. Exec. Cmt, N.C.
b. Vilas, N.C, 3/26/28; s. John Gray Dugger and Ruth Combs D; m. 10/25/51 to Lucille H. Winebarger; c. Diane K. and Deborah C. Educ: Johns Hopkins Univ. Polit. & Govt. Pos: Registr. and judge of elec, N.C, 61-64; pres, Watauga Co. Young Dem. Club, 62-63; mem, Watauga Co. Dem. Exec. Cmt, 62-63, chmn, 64- Bus. & Prof. Pos: Engr, N.C. State Hwy. Cmn, 50-62, asst. research engr, 62- Mil. Serv: Entered as Hosp. Corpsman 2/C, Navy, 46, released as Pharmacist Mate 3/C, 48. Mem: Grange; Young Dem. Clubs of Am. Rel: Baptist. Mailing Add: Route 1, Box 1, Boone, N.C. 28607.

DUGGER, JOHN FRANK R
Tenn. State Sen.
b. Atheus, Ga, 1/7/23; s. George Frederick Dugger and Rena Hyder D; m. 12/11/49 to Peggy Barkley; c. Brenda, Rebecca and John Frank, Jr. Educ: The Citadel, 40-42; Univ. Tenn, LL.B, 45-48; Phi Alpha Delta; Order of the Coif. Polit. & Govt. Pos: Asst. U.S. attorney, 53-60; Tenn. State Sen, 63- Mil. Serv: Entered as Cadet, Air Force, 42, released as 1st Lt, 45, after serv. in 384th Bomb Group, 8th Air Force; Distinguished Flying Cross; Air Medal with three Oak Leaf Clusters; European Theater Ribbon. Mem: Tenn. Bar Asn; Am. Legion; VFW; Shrine. Rel: Methodist. Mailing Add: 209 E. Main St, Morristown, Tenn. 37814.

DUGUID, ROBERT LEE R
Mem, Calif. State Rep. Cent. Cmt.
b. Humboldt, Ariz, 7/28/17; s. William Duguid and Lola Carey D; m. 3/26/39 to Zell Frances Lanyon; c. Charles William and James Francis. Educ: Clarkdale High Sch, Ariz, grad, 37. Polit. & Govt. Pos: Pres, Employee Mgt. Coun, China Lake, Calif; v.mayor and city councilman, Ridgecrest; mem, Calif. State Rep. Cent. Cmt, 69- Bus. & Prof. Pos: Dist. mgr, Farmers Ins. Group, 57-65; pres, Desert Ins. Agency, Ridgecrest, Calif, 65- Mem: Mason; Kiwanis; Elks; Shrine; Ridgecrest C. of C.(pres, 67 & 69). Rel: Protestant. Mailing Add: 330 Lenore St, Ridgecrest, Calif. 93555.

DUIS, HERBERT J. R
Nebr. State Sen.
b. Gothenburg, Nebr, 4/26/16; s. John H. Duis and Anna Schram D; m. 3/2/44 to MaryJane Trusdale; c. John Robert and Mary Elizabeth. Educ: Gothenburg Pub. Schs, 12 years. Polit. & Govt. Pos: Nebr. State Sen, 39th legis. dist, 51-54 & 69- Bus. & Prof. Pos: Pres, Duis & Co, Nebr, 33- Mil. Serv: Entered as Pvt, Signal Corps, Army, 41, released as M/Sgt, 45, after serving in 3145th Signal Base Group, Pac. Theater, 44-45. Mem: AF&AM; Kiwanis. Rel: Presbyterian. Mailing Add: 1013 Lake Ave, Gothenburg, Nebr. 69138.

DUISBERG, LUELLA ANNABELLE D
b. Danube, Minn, 7/31/12; d. John Frederick Kottke and Alvina L. Struder K; m. 12/18/46 to Dr. Peter Caspar Duisberg; c. twins, Larry Warner and Gerald Timothy. Educ: St. Cloud Teachers Col, 2 year standard, cum laude, 36; Univ. Minn, B.S, cum laude, 45; Univ. Pa, 46. Polit. & Govt. Pos: Faculty adv. and dir, Student Christian Asn. in rescue of 2 displaced person students from European Displaced Person Camps, 48-49; chmn, Race-Rels. United Church Women for desegregation of El Paso, Tex, 62; leader of dr. and first pres, El Paso Chap. UN, 63-64; blockleader, Dem. Party, El Paso, 62-64; alternate del, Dem. Nat. Conv, 68. Mem: C.Z. Regional Dem. Party; dir, Pan Amigos Intercultural Dance Club; Inter Am. Geodetic Serv. Wives Club. Rel: Protestant. Mailing Add: Box 709, Curundu, C.Z.

DUKE, ANGIER BIDDLE D
b. N.Y.C, 11/30/15; married. Educ: Yale Univ, 34-37. Polit. & Govt. Pos: Second secy, Buenos Aires, 49-51; spec. asst. to U.S. Ambassador to Spain, 51-52; U.S. Ambassador to El Salvador, 52-53; chmn, N.Y. Dem. State Conv. Cmt, 54 and Nationalities and Intergroup Rels. Cmt, N.Y. Dem. State Cmt, 60; chief of protocol, Dept. of State, 61-65; U.S. Ambassador to Spain, 65-68 and Denmark, 68-69. Bus. & Prof. Pos: Pres, Int. Rescue Cmn, Refugee Resettlement Agency, 55-60. Mil. Serv: Maj, Army Air Force, 41-46. Mailing Add: 8 S. Eaton Place, London, S.W.1, Eng.

DUKERT, JOSEPH MICHAEL R
b. Baltimore, Md, 9/19/29; s. Andrew Joseph Dukert and Margaret Przybyl D; m. 4/14/52 to Virginia Linthicum (deceased); m. 5/19/68 to Betty Cole. Educ: Univ. Notre Dame, B.A. magna cum laude, 51; Georgetown Univ, grad. study Int. Rels, 51-52; Hopkins Sch. Adv. Int. Studies, Bologna, Italy, 55-56; Johns Hopkins Univ, grad. study, Int. Rels, 56-57: Wranglers; German Club. Polit. & Govt. Pos: Del, Rep. Nat. Conv, 60 & 68, alternate del, 64, v.chmn. of Md. del, 68; v.chmn, Rep. State Cent. Cmt. of Md, 62-66, chmn, 66-69; mem, Baltimore City Jail Bd, 63-68; founder and pres, Second Dist. Citizen Action Orgn, 65-66. Bus. & Prof. Pos: Dir. pub. rels, Research Inst. adv. Studies, 62-65; free lance consult, mkt. & indust. commun, 65- Mil. Serv: Entered as 2nd Lt, Army Air Force, 51, released as 1st Lt, 53, after serv. in 13th Air Force, Philippines. Publ: Atompower, 61 and This is Antarctica, Coward McCann, 65. Mem: Nat. Assoc. Sci. Writers; Aerospace Writers Asn; Antarctican Soc; charter mem, Atomic Indust. Forum's Cmt. Pub. Understanding; bd. mem, Criminal Justice Cmn; bd. mem, Citizens Planning & Housing Asn; bd. mem, Am-Israel Soc; Capitol Hill Club; bd. mem, Baltimore Civic Opera Co; Baltimore Mus. Art. Exec. producer, Power for Continent 7 (voted best indust. sales film of the year at the Rome Film Festival) and Atoms for Space (voted outstanding TV news released film, 1962). Rel: Roman Catholic. Legal Res: Crestview, Md. Mailing Add: 4709 Crescent St, Washington, D.C. 20016.

DUKES, ELISHA D
b. Frankford, Del, 2/28/13; s. Elisha Franklin Dukes and Roxie McCabe D; m. to Mae McCabe. Polit. & Govt. Pos: V.chmn, Del. Dem. Cmt, until 63; Secy. of State, Del, 61-68. Bus. & Prof. Pos: Exec, Auto Supply Co. Mil. Serv: Joined Merchant Marines, 35. Mem: Mason; Shrine. Mailing Add: Church St, Selbyville, Del. 19975. (1967)

DULANY, WILLIAM BEVARD D
b. Sykesville, Md, 9/4/27; s. William W. Dulany and Helen Bevard D; m. 8/16/52 to Anna Winifred Spencer; c. W. Bryant, T. Patrick and Anne French. Educ: West. Md. Col, A.B, 50; Univ. Mich. Law Sch, 50-51; Univ. Md. Law Sch, LL.B, 53; Phi Alpha Delta. Polit. & Govt. Pos: Chmn, Kennedy for Pres, Carroll Co. Md, 62; pres, Carroll Co. Dem.Club, 63-65; Md. State Del, 63-66, mem, Regional Planning Coun, 64-66; del, Md. Constitutional Conv, 67-68; cmnr, Md. Cmn. on Human Rels, 69- Bus. & Prof. Pos: Pres, Carroll Co. Bar Asn, 65-66. Mil. Serv: Entered as A/S, Navy, 45, released as AER. M 2/C, 48. Mem: Carroll Co, Md. and Am. Bar Asns; v.pres, Heart Asn. of Md. Rel: Episcopal; Vestryman and Mem. Regional Cmn. for Diocese. Mailing Add: 123 E. Main St, Westminster, Md. 21157.

DULLEA, EDWARD J, JR. D
s. Edward J. Dullea, Sr,(deceased) and Eliz. Walsh D; m. to Marie Splaine; c. Kathleen, Edward, Eileen, Michael, Anne Marie. Educ: Boston Univ, B.S;

attend. Suffolk Univ. Law Sch. Polit. & Govt. Pos: Peabody Sch. Cmt. Bus. & Prof. Pos: Businessman. Mil. Serv: Korean War, Air Force. Mailing Add: 59 Gardner St, Peabody, Mass. 01960. (1967)

DULSKI, THADDEUS J. D-L
U.S. Rep, N.Y.
b. Buffalo, N.Y, 9/27/15; married; c. Five. Educ: Canisius Col; Univ. Buffalo. Polit. & Govt. Pos: With Bur. of Internal Revenue, Treas. Dept, 40-47; spec. agent, Price Stabilization Admin, 51-53; Walden Dist. Councilman, 53; mem, Finance Coun. Cmt, chmn, Taxation Coun. Cmt. and Wage Classification Cmt; councilman-at-lg, Buffalo, N.Y, 57; U.S. Rep, N.Y, 58- Bus. & Prof. Pos: Acct, tax consult, 47. Mil. Serv: World War II. Legal Res: Buffalo, N.Y. Mailing Add: 205 Cannon House Office Bldg, Washington, D.C. 20515.

DUMAS, J. STEWART D
b. Bennington, Vt, 9/23/19; m. to Marie Pellierin; c. one son and one daughter. Educ: Ithaca Col; New Eng. Conservatory of Music, B.S. in Music. Polit. & Govt. Pos: Chmn, Danby Sch. Bd; chmn. and former secy, Motor Vehicle Racing Cmn; Vt. State Rep, 62-65. Bus. & Prof. Pos: Snack bar operator; musician (arranger); with Vt. Marble Co. Mem: Am. Fedn. of Musicians; Arranger's Guild; United Stone Workers Union; Elks; K. of C; Eagles. Rel: Catholic. Mailing Add: R.F.D, Danby, Vt. 05739.

DUMAS, WILLIAM LAWRENCE, JR. D
b. Talladega, Ala, 10/12/08; s. William Lawrence Dumas and Mary Hicks D; m. 12/4/40 to Donald (sic) Berry; c. Aleta McDonald, Lawrence, III, William Berry and John Hicks. Educ: Davidson Col, A.B. summa cum laude; Harvard Univ, LL.B; George Wash. Univ, LL.M; Georgetown Univ, J.D; Phi Beta Kappa; Omicron Delta Kappa; Phi Gamma Delta. Polit. & Govt. Pos: Ala. State Rep, 47-55; Ala. State Sen, 59-66; mem, Ala. Legis. Coun, 47-66, chmn, 54-55 & 65-66. Bus. & Prof. Pos: Lawyer. Mem: Am, Ala. and Birmingham Bar Asns; Mason; AAONMS (Potentate, 67); Eagles; Birmingham Exchange Club (past pres). Rel: Methodist. Mailing Add: 1414 Brown Marx Bldg, Birmingham, Ala. 35203.

DUMAS, WOODROW WILSON D
Mayor, Baton Rouge, La.
b. Opelousas, La, 12/9/16; s. J.E. Dumas and Margaret A. Jernigan D; m. 1/18/40 to Carol E. Epperson; c. Diane and Woodrow Huntley. Educ: East Baton Rouge Parish Schs. Polit. & Govt. Pos: Mayor-Pres, Baton Rouge and Parish of East Baton Rouge, La, 64-; Gr. Baton Rouge Port Cmn, chmn, secy. and v.pres, Fed. Projs. Cmt; mem, Nat. Adv. Cmt. for Hwy. Beautification; mem, Nat. Adv. Cmt. for Youth Opportunity; v.pres. at large, La. Munic. Asn, 67-; mem, City-Parish Coun, 12 years; past pres, La. Police Jury Asn; pres, sixth Cong. Dist. Police Jury Asn, 3 years; former mem, Dem. State Cent. Cmt, La; former mem, La. Air Control Cmn. Mil. Serv: Navy, 11 years, grad. of U.S. Submarine Sch, New London, Conn, with submarine forces in S.Pac, World War II; Korean War. Mem: Nat. Asn. of Counties, pres, 65; chmn, Baton Rouge Symphony Fund-raising Cmt, 66; Am. Legion; VFW; Eagles; United Commercial Travelers; Elks; Moose; Independent Workers Union at Humble Oil and Refining Co, Baton Rouge, 21 years. Named Outstanding Police Juror, La, 63 and Outstanding Police Juror of sixth Dist. Rel: Methodist, former mem, Bd. of Stewards, Baker Methodist Church. Legal Res: Route 1, Box 3, Baker, La. 70714. Mailing Add: Room 208, Municipal Bldg, Baton Rouge, La. 70801.

DUMBAULD, PETER THEODORE D
Pa. State Rep.
b. Somerset, Pa, 11/14/09; s. James M. Dumbauld and Eva Weigle D; m. 11/28/34 to Mildred Rodger. Educ: Calif. State Col, Pa, 26-30; Pa. State Univ, 31-32. Polit. & Govt. Pos: Pa. State Rep, 65-; mem, Pa. Constitutional Conv, 67-68; del, Dem. Nat. Conv, 68. Bus. & Prof. Pos: Sch. teacher, 32-42; adminstr, Pa. Tire Co, 43-45; owner, Dumbauld's Tire Serv, Somerset, Pa, 45- Mil. Serv: Entered as Pvt, Army, 42, released as Officer Cand, Sect. II, 43. Mem: Pa. Motor Truck Asn; Nat. Asn. of Independent Tire Dealers; Am. Trucking Asn; Nat. Tire Dealers and Retreaders Asn; past dist. gov, Rotary Int; Somerset Co. Develop. Coun; bd. of dirs, Somerset C. of C; past mem, Munic. Authority of Somerset; past pres, Somerset Co. Soc. for Crippled Children and Adults; past mem, Bd. of Gov, Somerset Country Club. Pres, Pa. Asn. of State Col. Trustees. Rel: Christian Church. Legal Res: 344 High St, Somerset, Pa. 15501. Mailing Add: P.O. Box 148, Somerset, Pa. 15501.

DUMM, LUCILLE R
b. Circleville, Ohio, 10/3/13; d. Leroy H. Dumm and Lillie Martin D; single. Educ: Circleville High Sch, Ohio, 4 years. Polit. & Govt. Pos: Pres, GOP Booster Club, 43-69; secy-treas, Pickaway Co. Rep. Cent. and Exec. Cmts, Ohio, 52-69; mem, Pickaway Co. Bd. of Elec, 62- Mem: Pickaway Co. Women's Rep. Club; Pickaway Co. Hist. Soc. Rel: Protestant. Mailing Add: 340 Walnut St, Circleville, Ohio 43113.

DUMONT, DONALD ALBERT
Chief of Dept. of State's For. Affairs Research Coun. Staff
b. Boston, Mass, 12/6/11; s. Joseph Dumont and Emma Hayward D; m. 1945 to Marie Paris; c. Patrick, Philippe and Cedric E. Educ: Oberlin Col, 30-31; Trinity Col, B.S, 34, A.M, 39; grad. student int. rels, Yale Univ, 38-39; master hist. and sci, Brent Sch, Baguio, Philippines, 35-37; Sigma Nu. Polit. & Govt. Pos: U.S. For. Serv, 40-; consul, Tunis, Istanbul and Stuttgart; formerly v.consul, Dakar and Rabat; assigned to Dept. State, 54-57, adv. U.S. del, UN Gen. Assembly, 55, consul gen, Dakar, Senegal, 58-62, U.S. Minister to Kingdom of Burundi, 62, U.S. Ambassador, 63-66, vis. prof. and State Dept. dipl-in-res, Univ. Tenn, 66-67, chief of Dept. State's For. Affairs Research Coun. Staff, 67- Bus. & Prof. Pos: Instr. Eng, Trinity Col, 37-39. Recipient Superior Serv. award, Dept. of State, 59; author of numerous articles. Legal Res: 1661 Crescent Place, N.W, Washington, D.C. 20009. Mailing Add: Foreign Affairs Research Council, Dept. of State, Washington, D.C. 20525.

DUMONT, WAYNE, JR. R
N.J. State Sen.
b. Paterson, N.J, 6/25/14; s. Wayne Dumont and Sallie I. Hunt D; m. 9/19/38 to Helen S. Williamson; c. Wayne Hunt. Educ: Lafayette Col; Univ. of Pa. Law Sch. Hon. D.Litt, Glassboro State Col, 64. Polit. & Govt. Pos: Mem, N.J. Rep. State Cmt, 48-52; N.J. State Sen, 52-65 & 69-; mem, N.J. State Tax Policy Cmt, 54-65 and chmn, 64-65; dist. del, Rep. Nat. Conv, 60; Rep. nominee for Gov, N.J, 65. Bus. & Prof. Pos: Practicing attorney, Phillipsburg, N.J, 41- Mil. Serv: Entered as Pvt, Army, 43, released as 1st Lt, 46, after serv. in Pac; Maj, N.J. Army Nat. Guard; dir of instr, N.J. Mil. Acad, Sea Girt; G-5, 50th Armored Div, Hq, E. Orange, at present. Mem: Dir. and seal sale chmn, Warren Co. Health Asn, 47-; trustee, Lafayette Co. Alumni Asn, 54-60 and Warren Hosp, 55-; Elks; K. of P; Moose; Mason (32°); Am. Legion; VFW; Phillipsburg Exchange Club; N.J. Farm Bur; N.J. State Bar Asn. Award for Distinguished Serv. to Educ, N.J. Educ. Asn. 54 and Warren Co. Educ. Asn. 63: Meritorious Serv. Cert, N.J. Dept, VFW, 54; Phillipsburg Outstanding Citizen Award, B.J. Donovan Post 203, Am. Legion, 56; Man of Year Award, Phillipsburg C. of C, 62; Award for Outstanding Serv. to Warren Co. Agr, Warren Co. Bd. of Agr, 63; Shield Plaque for Outstanding Achievements in Cause of Civil Serv, 64 and Honored for Distinguished Serv. to N.J. Agr, 64, N.J. Farm Bur. Rel: Presbyterian. Legal Res: 701 Hillcrest Blvd, Phillipsburg, N.J. 08865. Mailing Add: 97 S. Main St, Phillipsburg, N.J. 08865. (1967)

DUNAWAY, CHARLES CLIFFORD D
b. Montgomery, W.Va, 4/5/16; s. Frank Lionel Dunaway, Sr. and Lucille Hardy D; m. 4/9/39 to Freeda Harper; c. Suzzanne. Educ: Pub. schs, Malden, W.Va. and Granville, Ohio. Polit. & Govt. Pos: W.Va. State Del, 64-66. Bus. & Prof. Pos: Machinist. Mem: York Rite; Scottish Rite; KCCH; Shrine; Jesters Royal Order of Scotland; grand treas. of Grand Lodge of Masons of W.Va; Hon. Legion of Honor; DeMolay; Du Pont 25 Year Club; Meadowbrook Recreation Club. Rel: Baptist. Mailing Add: 704½ Red Oak St, Charleston, W.Va. 25302.

DUNBAR, CHARLES EDWARD, III R
b. New Orleans, La, 4/19/26; s. Charles Edward Dunbar, Jr. and Ethelyn Legendre D; m. 7/23/59 to Marguerite Stephanie Dinkins; c. Ladd Dinkins, Charles E, IV, Ethelyn Legendre and George Bauer. Educ: Univ. Nebr, 46; Tulane Univ, B.A, 49, LL.B, 51; Phi Beta Kappa; Delta Kappa Epsilon; Phi Delta Phi. Polit. & Govt. Pos: V.chmn, Eisenhower for Pres. Legal Cmt, New Orleans, La, 52; mem, New Orleans steering cmt, Charlton Lyons, Rep. Cand. for Gov. Campaign, 64; founding dir, La. Draft Goldwater Cmt, 64; del, Rep. Nat. Conv, 68; finance chmn, Rep. Party City New Orleans, La, 68- Bus. & Prof. Pos: Admitted to Bar, 51; practiced law, New Orleans, 51-; partner, law firm, Phelps, Dunbar, Marks, Claverie & Sims, 55- Mil. Serv: Entered as A/S, Navy, 44, released as Seaman 1/C, 46, after serv. aboard LCS(L) 86 in Pac. Theatre, Okinawa, 44-45. Mem: Am, La. State and New Orleans Bar Asns; Maritime Law Asn. of U.S.(cmt. of admissions, 67-69); Asn. Average Adjusters; La. Civil Serv. League (bd, 60-, v.chmn, 64-); charter mem, Info. Coun. Americas (bd, 64-68); C. of C; Propeller Club U.S; Am. Legion; Boston, La. and Stratford Clubs. Rel: Roman Catholic. Mailing Add: 411 Fairway Dr, New Orleans, La. 70124.

DUNBAR, DUKE R
Attorney Gen, Colo.
Educ: Univ. Mich, LL.B. Polit. & Govt. Pos: Mem, Nat. Cmt. on Uniform Traffic Laws and Ord; former Asst. City Attorney, City and Co. of Denver, Colo; former First Asst. Attorney Gen, Colo, former Dep. Attorney Gen, Attorney Gen, currently. Bus. & Prof. Pos: Attorney. Mailing Add: c/o State Capitol, Denver, Colo. 80203.

DUNBAR, FRANK HAYDEN D
Chmn, Hancock Co. Dem. Cmt, Maine
b. Penobscot, Maine, 2/24/07; s. Frank Wardwell Dunbar and Laura Wardwell D; m. 6/26/27 to Kathleen Leach; c. Betty (Mrs. Thurston), Frank Manley and Donna (Mrs. Putman). Educ: Pub. Schs, Penobscot, Maine. Polit. & Govt. Pos: Pres, Local 1357, Int. Longshoremen's Asn, Bucksport, Maine, pres, Local 1058, IBEW, Rockland, acting int. rep, Int. Longshoremen's Asn; pres. pulp & sulphite, Local 88, Bucksport Exec. Bd. mem, Maine Fed. Labor Coun; first v.pres, Maine Dist. Coun. Paper Mill Workers; chmn, Hancock Co. Dem. Cmt, currently. Bus. & Prof. Pos: Treas, Penobscot Bay Local 88; Engr, St. Regis Paper Co, Bucksport, Maine. Coach and mgr, Bucksport Baseball Team, 48-52. Rel: Methodist. Mailing Add: 34 School St, Bucksport, Maine 04417.

DUNBAR, HOWARD RAYMOND R
Tenn. State Sen.
b. Limestone, Tenn, 3/11/38; s. Thomas Moody Dunbar and Edith Woolsey D; m. 6/12/59 to Peg M. Wharter; c. Cynthia Dawn and William Warren. Educ: Univ. Tenn, B.S, 57, LL.B, 59, J.D, 61; Phi Sigma Kappa; Phi Delta Phi. Polit. & Govt. Pos: Tenn. State Sen, 68- Mem: Bd. dirs, Wash. Col. Acad. Alumni, 67-71; Wash. Co. Bar Asn.(treas, 68-69); Tenn. Bar Asn; Am. Trial Lawyers Asn; Elks; Moose; Nat. Rifle Asn; Jaycees (pres, Johnson City Club, 68-69); Young Rep. Key Man of Year, Jaycees, nominee for Outstanding Young Man of Year, 68. Rel: Presbyterian. Legal Res: 1612 Woodland Ave, Johnson City, Tenn. 37601. Mailing Add: P.O. Box 337, Johnson City, Tenn. 37601.

DUNCAN, ANDREW CLAUDE R
b. Butler, Tenn, 7/26/90; s. James Harrison Duncan and Margaret Dugger D; m. 12/21/13 to Fannie Smith Fritts; c. James Hoyle, Sarrah Margaret, Andrew Claude, Jr, Betty Ruth. Educ: Pub. Schs. of Knox Co, Tenn. Polit. & Govt. Pos: Ga. State Rep, 61-66. Bus. & Prof. Pos: Minister; steel metal and structural steel layout (retired). Mem: Mason; Eastern Star. Rel: Church of Christ. Mailing Add: McCaysville, Ga. 30555. (1967)

DUNCAN, DAVID L. D
Treas, Utah State Dem. Party
b. Greenup Co, Ky, 6/13/33; s. Charles Edward Duncan and Grace Raynor D; m. 6/8/56 to Leah H. Stuart; c. Charles, Ruth and David. Educ: Stevens Henager Bus. Col, A.C.S, 64. Polit. & Govt. Pos: Dep. treas, Weber Co, Utah, 58-62, chief dep. treas, 62-65, treas, 65-; treas, Weber Co. Young Dem, 62-65; del, Co. and State Dem. Conv, 62-; dist. chmn, Weber Co. Dem. Party, 65-; treas, Utah State Dem. Party, 65-; mem, Utah State Welfare Bd, 67-; del, Dem. Nat. Conv, 68. Bus. & Prof. Pos: Pres. and Dir, Ogden Munic. Employees Credit Union, 66- Mil. Serv: Entered as Airman, Air Force, 52, released as Airman 1/C, 56, after serv. in Tactical Air Command; Korean, Nat. Defense and UN Serv. Medals; Good Conduct Medal. Mem: Utah State

Asn. of Co. Off; Nat. Asn. of Co. Off; Nat. Asn. of Treas. and Finance Off; Lions. Rel: Baptist. Legal Res: 1062 Hudson St, Ogden, Utah 84404. Mailing Add: Municipal Bldg, Ogden, Utah 84401.

DUNCAN, JASON CHARLIE D
S.C. State Rep.
b. Lyman, S.C, 6/27/29; s. William Jason Duncan and Arry Nodine D; m. 6/6/53 to Patricia Miller; c. Kimber Lee and Jason Charlie, Jr. Educ: Wofford Col, A.B, 51; Univ. S.C. and Furman Univ, grad. work in psychol. Polit. & Govt. Pos: S.C. State Rep, Spartanburg Co, 69- Bus. & Prof. Pos: Teacher, Blue Ridge High Sch, Greenville, 51-59; teacher, Palmetto High Sch, Anderson, 59-60; asst. prin. and dir. guid, Boiling Spring High Sch, Spartanburg, 60-66. Mem: WOW; Ruritan; Sertoma; Spartanburg Co. Livestock Producers (dir); Boy Scouts (committeeman, Troop 271); Mason; Shrine. Most Inspiring Teacher Award, Chapman High Sch, 68-69. Rel: Methodist. Mailing Add: Route 1, Lyman, S.C. 29365.

DUNCAN, JOHN BONNER D
b. Springfield, Ky, 2/6/10; s. Samuel E. Duncan and Lena Bell Jordan D; m. 7/2/38 to Edith L. West (deceased); remarried 8/14/69 to B. Dolores Berry; c. John Bonner and Joan West. Educ: Howard Univ, A.B, 34, Grad. Sch. Philos. scholarship, 33-35, Grad. Sch. of Law, 35-38; Terrell Law Sch, LL.B, 38. Polit. & Govt. Pos: Trustee, Barney Neighborhood House; with Dept. Interior, 34-41; attorney, Off. of Price Admin, 43-46; expediter, U.S. Off. Housing, 47-49; sr. attorney, Housing and Home Finance Agency, 49-52; recorder of deeds, D.C, 52-61; cmnr, D.C, 61-67; Asst. Secy. Interior, 67-68. Bus. & Prof. Pos: Attorney, Bituminous Coal Cmn, 42-43. Publ: New Dimension Bidding in Contract Bridge, 63. Mem: V.pres, Nat. Capital area, Nat. Coun. of Churches; sponsor, Club of Am. Nations; bd. dirs, Nat. Capital area, United Givers Fund; bd. dirs, and chmn, Personnel Cmt, Nat. Capital area Big Bros. Received Afro-Am. Newspaper Award, 50; Citation from Pittsburgh-Courier, 51; Annual Award, D.C. Fed. Civic Asn, 52 & 62; Citation from Chicago Defender, 55; Wash. Urban League Award, 59; Brotherhood Award, Nat. Conf. Christians and Jews, 61; Awards for Commun. Serv. from Am. Legion, 62, Nat. Asn. of Colored Women's Clubs, 62 and Nat. Capital area Coun. of Churches, 62. Rel: African Methodist Episcopal Zion Church. Mailing Add: Watergate Apartments, Apt. 708-N, 2500 Virginia Ave. N.W, Washington, D.C. 20037.

DUNCAN, JOHN JAMES R
U.S. Rep, Tenn.
b. Scott Co, Tenn; m. to Lois Swisher; c. Beverly, James, Joe and Becky. Polit. & Govt. Pos: Asst. Attorney Gen, Tenn, 47-56; dir, Legal Dept, Knoxville, 56-59; Mayor, Knoxville, 59-64; U.S. Rep, Tenn, 64-; del, Rep. Nat. Conv, 68. Bus. & Prof. Pos: Pres, Knox Fed. Savings & Loan Asn; dir, World Heritage Life Ins. Co. Mil. Serv: Army, 42-45. Mem: Am. Tenn. and Knoxville Bar Asns; Am. Legion (State Comdr, 54); pres, Knoxville Prfnl. Baseball Club, 56-64; dir, Knoxville Baseball Club; v.pres. and past pres, S.Atlantic Baseball League. Good Govt. Award, Jaycees; Nat. Conf. of Christians and Jews Annual Citizenship Award, 63; Annual City Salesman Award. Rel: Presbyterian: Elder, Eastminister Presbyterian Church, Knoxville, Tenn. Legal Res: Tenn. Mailing Add: 3803 Cameron Mills Rd, Alexandria, Va. 22305.

DUNCAN, JOSEPH ELVIN (EBB) D
b. Douglasville, Ga, 2/18/09; s. John Raymond Duncan and Pearl Perkins D; m. to Antionette Talmadge Tyus; c. Richard Allen, Joseph Elvin, Jr. Educ: Young Harris Col, 28. Polit. & Govt. Pos: Ga. State Rep, 49-66. Bus. & Prof. Pos: Theatre owner; Dir. and Gen. Agent for United Am. Life Ins. Co; Dir, W. Ga. Nat. Bank. Mem: Masons; Rotary; W.O.W; Dir, C. of C; Variety Club; Sunset Hills Country Club; Jr. C. of C; Carroll Serv. Coun. Rel: Methodist; Bd. of Stewards, First Methodist Church, Carrollton. Mailing Add: Carrollton, Ga. 30117. (1967)

DUNCAN, NORMAN E. D
b. Tulsa, Okla, 6/15/33; s. Louis J. Duncan and Camilla Norman D; m. 9/4/52 to Betty Lou Rushing; c. Norman E, II, Steven Bruce, Diana Leigh and Scott Kieth. Educ: Univ. Okla, 52-54. Polit. & Govt. Pos: Admin. Asst. to U.S. Rep. Graham Purcell, 13th Dist, Tex, 62-69; mem, Inaugural Cmt, 65. Bus. & Prof. Pos: Dir. news and pub. affairs, KFDX-TV, Wichita Falls, Tex, 54-59 & 60-62; news ed, KOTV-TV, Tulsa, Okla, 59-60; state legis. rep, J.C. Penny Co, Inc. Mem: Sigma Delta Chi; pres, Wichita Falls Tex. Press Club; Press Club of Dallas, Maskat Shrine; Burro Club. of Wash, D.C; former mem, Radio & TV News Dir. Asn. and Nat. Press Photographers Asn. Rel: Baptist. Mailing Add: 606 S. Cottonwood, Richardson, Tex. 75080.

DUNCAN, OLIVER O. R
b. 1901. Polit. & Govt. Pos: Ky. State Rep, 54-56; Ky. State Sen, 56-68. Bus. & Prof. Pos: Merchant; farmer. Mem: Mason; Shrine; Kiwanis. Rel: Baptist. Mailing Add: Whitley City, Ky. 42653. (1967)

DUNCAN, RICHARD MELOAN D
b. Platte Co, Mo, 11/10/89; s. Richard Franklin Duncan and Margaret Meloan D; m. 6/4/13 to Glenna Davenport; c. Richard D. Educ: Christian Bros. Col, 09. Polit. & Govt. Pos: City counsr, St. Joseph, Mo, 27-30; U.S. Rep, Mo, 33-43; U.S. Sr. Dist. Judge, E. and W. Dist. of Mo, 43- Mem: Am, Mo. and Kansas City Bar Asns; life mem, St. Joseph Lodge 40, Elks; Eagles Lodge 49; Carriage Club; hon. mem, Univ. Mo, Kansas City, Law Sch. Alumni, Bench and Robe and Cooley Chap, Phi Delta Phi; Acad. of Squires. Rel: Presbyterian. Legal Res: 1217 W. 59th, Kansas Ctiy, Mo. 64113. Mailing Add: U.S. Court House, Kansas City, Mo. 64106.

DUNCAN, ROBERT BLACKFORD D
b. Normal, Ill, 12/4/20; s. Eugene Frank Duncan and Katheryn K. Blackford D; m. to Marijane Dill; c. Nancy Jane, Robert Angus, David Bruce, James Douglas, Laurie Ann, Bonnie Dee and Jeannie Elizabeth. Educ: Ill. Wesleyan Univ, B.A; Univ. Mich. Law Sch, LL.B. Polit. & Govt. Pos: Ore. State Rep, 56-58, Speaker, Ore. State Legis, 58-62; U.S. Rep, Fourth Dist, Ore, 62-67; mem, Adv. Cmn. on Intergovt. Rels; cong. adv, World Food Conf, Food & Agr. Orgn, 63; Dem. nominee for U.S. Sen, Ore, 66. Bus. & Prof. Pos: Attorney; counsel to Lindsay, Nahstoll, Hart, Dafoe & Krause, 66- Mil. Serv: Entered as Aviation Cadet, Navy, 42, released as Lt.(jg), 45, after serv. in Atlantic & Pac. Theaters, but stateside duty; Comdr, Naval Res. Rel: Methodist. Legal Res: Route 1, Box 803-A, Gresham, Ore. 97230. Mailing Add: Ninth Floor, Loyalty Bldg, Portland, Ore. 97204.

DUNCAN, RUSSELL R
b. Calvin, N.Dak, 8/5/10; s. Merritt Smith Duncan and Margaret Higgins D; m. 6/15/34 to Anna Marie Mohagen; c. Marvin Russell, Marilynn Marie and David Roger. Educ: N.Dak. State Univ, short course in politics, econs. & agr. Polit. Pos: N.Dak. State Rep, 64-66; chmn, Finance Cmt, Dist. Rep. Party, 62-64, precinct committeeman, 54-64 and twp. supvr, 39-44. Govt. Pos: Testified before Senate Agr. Cmt. on sponsoring new farm legis, 62, 60 and 59; traveled to 20 foreign countries on People to People Good Will Tours sponsored by U.S. Dept. of Agr. Publn: What I saw Behind the Iron Curtain, Pierce Printers, 12/64. Mem: Pres, N.Dak. Seed Trade Asn, 61; Northern Seedmens Asn; N.Dak. Grain Dealers Asn; dir. Red River Valley Fair Asn; Youth Cmt, Exchange Club; Govt. Affairs Cmt, C. of C; Farm Bur; Farm Mgrs. Asn; former mem, leader and scholarship donor, 4-H. Numerous placings on grain at Int. Grain & Livestock Show at Chicago; recipient, Ford Motor Co. Award for top wheat production record in U.S. Rel: Lutheran; Nat. Bd. of Admin, Asn. of Free Lutheran Churches. Mailing Add: 1534 Third St. N, Fargo, N.Dak. 58102. (1967)

DUNCAN, VERNON FRED R
Chmn, Franklin Co. Rep. Cent. Cmt, Nebr.
b. Bloomington, Nebr, 6/28/42; s. Eldon Fred Duncan and Maxine Podewitz D; m. 6/27/64 to Karen Joan Stratman; c. James. Educ: Kearney State Col, B.A, 63; Univ. Nebr. Col. Law, J.D, 66; Pi Kappa Delta; Delta Theta Phi; Theta Xi. Polit. & Govt. Pos: Co. attorney, Franklin Co, Nebr, 67-69; chmn, Franklin Co. Rep. Cent. Cmt, 68- Bus. & Prof. Pos: Partner, Long & Duncan, Attorneys, 66-69. Mem: Nebr. State and Am. Bar Asns; U.S. Jaycees; Lions Club; C. of C. Am. Jurisp. prize in Natural Resources Law; Am. Jurisp. prize in Commercial Law. Rel: Methodist. Mailing Add: 707 14th Ave, Franklin, Nebr. 68939.

DUNCAN, WILLIAM GRAHAM, IV R
Chmn. Exec. Cmt, Christian Co. Rep. Cmt, Ky.
b. Hopkinsville, Ky, 12/9/35; s. William Graham Duncan, III and Elizabeth Fort D; m. 8/6/56 to Mary Alice Major; c. William Graham, V, Rives Major and Andrea Louise. Educ: Purdue Univ, B.S. in agr, 57; Pershing Rifles; Scabbard and Blade; pres, Alpha Zeta; Ceres; Arnold Air Soc. Polit. & Govt. Pos: Chmn. Exec. Cmt, Christian Co. Rep. Cmt, Ky, 66-; chmn, Tri-Co. Rep. Campaign Cmt; Christian Co. campaign chmn. for John Sherman Cooper; co-chmn, 1st Cong. Dist. campaign for John Sherman Cooper. Bus. & Prof. Pos: Mgr, Duncan Farms, currently. Mil. Serv: Entered as 2nd Lt, Air Force, 58, released as 1st Lt, 61, after serv. in 603rd ACW Squadron, Germany. Mem: Farm Bur; charter mem, Pennyroyal Farm Anal. Group; Rotary; Athenaeum Soc. Rel: Presbyterian; Ordained Elder. Mailing Add: Route 1, Hopkinsville, Ky. 42240. (1967)

DUNFEY, ROBERT JOHN D
Mem, Dem. Finance Cmt, Maine
b. Lowell, Mass, 2/9/28; s. LeRoy William Dunfey and Catherine Agnes Manning D; m. 9/16/50 to Shirley Mae Corey; c. Robert J, Jr, Roy, Eileen, Brian and Maryanne. Educ: Keith Acad, Lowell, Mass. Polit. & Govt. Pos: Advance work, John F. Kennedy Campaign, 60; campaign mgr, Curtis for Gov, 66; mem, Maine Recreation Authority, 66-; mgr, Robert F. Kennedy Campaign, Maine, 68; campaigned for Robert F. Kennedy in Ore, Calif. and S.Dak. Primaries, 68; state chmn, Businessmen for Humphrey-Muskie, Maine, 68; del, Dem. Nat. Conv, 68, set up and organized Draft Ted Campaign Hq, 68; mem, Maine Cmn. on Party Structure and Del. Selection, 69; mem, Dem. Finance Cmt, 69- Bus. & Prof. Pos: Treas, dir. and dir, corporate develop, Dunfey Family Hotels and Motor Inns of New Eng, 40-, treas, Dunfey Family Affiliated Corp, currently; dir, Maine Fidelity Life Ins. Co, 65-; mem, Greater Boston Real Estate Bd, 69- Mem: Dir, Wash. Cmt, Nat. Asn. of Realtors, 58-61; pres, N.H. Asn. of Realtors, 60 and Portsmouth Asn. of Realtors, 61; dir, New Eng. Innkeepers Asn, 65-; Cumberland Club; K. of C; United Commercial Travelers; dir, Greater Portland C. of C, 65-68. Maine Hotel Man of the Year, 65. Rel: Catholic. Legal Res: 26 Oakhurst Rd, Cape Elizabeth, Maine 04107. Mailing Add: 157 High St, Portland, Maine 04101.

DUNFEY, WILLIAM LEO D
b. Lowell, Mass, 10/10/25; s. Leroy William Dunfey and Catherine Manning D; m. 6/14/56 to Ruth Elaine Thomas; c. Julie Ann. Educ: Miami Univ, B.A, 48; Univ. N.H, M.A, 50. Polit. & Govt. Pos: Del, Dem. Nat. Conv, 52; cmnr, N.H. Libr, 54-59; chmn, N.H. Stevenson for Pres. Cmt, 56; regional rep, Dem. Nat. Cmt, New Eng, N.Y. State, N.J, Del, 58-60; Kennedy Campaign Coordinator, N.Y. State, New Eng, 60; former mem, Dem. Nat. Cmt, N.H; Johnson Campaign Coordinator, N.Y. State and New Eng, 64; mem, Site Cmt, Dem. Nat. Conv, 64; former chmn, N.H. State Dem. Cmt. Bus. & Prof. Pos: Office mgr, Dunfey Assocs, Hampton, N.H, 50-; Dunfey Corp, Hampton, N.H, 56-; supvr, mgt. training progs; owner, operator, Lamie's Tavern and Motor Inn, Hampton; Eastland Motor Hotel, Portland, Maine; Wayfarer Motor Inn; Carpenter Motor Hotel, Manchester, N.H. Mil. Serv: Marine Corps Res, 43-46. Mem: Nat. Asn. Real Estate Bd; Am. Hotel and Restaurant Asn. Legal Res: 43 Moulton Rd, Hampton, N.H. 03842. Mailing Add: 490 Lafayette Rd, Hampton, N.H. 03842. (1967)

DUNGAN, RALPH ANTHONY
b. Phila, Pa, 4/22/23; m. to Mary Theresa Rowley; c. Six; Educ: St. Joseph's Col, B.S, 50; Princeton Univ, M.P.A, 52. Polit. & Govt. Pos: With Bur. of the Budget, 51-56; legis. asst. to Sen. J.F. Kennedy, 56-57; staff mem, Senate Cmt. on Labor and Pub. Welfare, 57-60; spec. asst. to the President, 61-64; U.S. Ambassador to Chile, 64-69. Mil. Serv: Lt.(jg), Navy, 42-45. Legal Res: Princeton, N.J. Mailing Add: c/o U.S. Dept. of State Foreign Service, Washington, D.C. 20521. (1967)

DUNHAM, MARSHALL J. D
b. Franklin, Vt, 9/21/91; m. to Louise Messier; c. One son and one daughter. Educ: Franklin High Sch, 07. Polit. & Govt. Pos: Selectman, 30-33; Vt. State Rep, 33; sch. dir, 33-36; auditor, 39-46; moderator, 41-; lister, 47-; asst. judge, Franklin Co, 55-56; Vt. State Sen, 57-68. Bus. & Prof. Pos:

Formerly farmer, 40 years; dir, Nat. Farm Coop, Inc; retired. Mem: Farm Bur; Past Master, Sheldon Grange 510; Franklin Co. A.C.P. Cmt; Milk Control Bd. Rel: Catholic. Mailing Add: Franklin, Vt. 05457. (1967)

DUNLAP, CARTER WESLEY 'PAT' R
Mem, Calif. State Rep. Cent. Cmt.
b. Licking, Mo, 8/29/14; s. Edward Franklin David Dunlap and Ethel Mitchell D; m. 11/30/49 to Barbara Jeanne Albertson; c. Natilee Ann and Carter Wesley, Jr. Educ: Univ. of the Pac, A.B, 40; Harvard Grad. Sch. Bus, 40-41; Rho Lambda Phi. Polit. & Govt. Pos: Mem. and del, Calif. Rep. Assembly, 64-69; co. chmn, Reagan for Gov, 66; mem, San Joaquin Rep. Cent. Cmt, 67-68, chmn, 69-; assoc. mem, Calif. Rep. State Cent. Cmt, 67-68, mem, 68-; chmn, Nixon for Pres, 68; v.chmn, Kuechle for Sen. Primary Campaign, 68; alternate del, Rep. Nat. Conv, 68. Bus. & Prof. Pos: Pres. and chmn, Dunlap Electronics, Inc, 46- Mil. Serv: Entered as Ens, Navy, 42, released as Lt, 46, after serv. in Comdr. S.Pac. and Comdr, Serv. Squadron, S.Pac, 43-45; Lt, Naval Res; Commendation Ribbon. Mem: Nat. Electronic Distributors Asn; Electronic Indust. Show Corp; Rotary; Tennis Club; Yosemite Club. Rel: Protestant. Mailing Add: 1460 W. Alpine St, Stockton, Calif. 95204.

DUNLAP, FRED EVERETT R
Chmn, Linn Co. Rep. Party, Kans.
b. Carlyle, Kans, 10/21/03; s. A.M. Dunlap and Sadie Jones D; m. 8/12/32 to Ermalea Hart; c. Lynn (Mrs. E.D. Marshall) and Wallace H. Educ: Kans. State Univ, 2 years; Col. Osteop. Med. & Surg, 4 years, D.O; Delta Tau Delta. Polit. & Govt. Pos: Chmn, Linn Co. Rep. Party, Kans, 44-; presidential elector, 48; del, Rep. Nat. Conv, 52; secy-treas, Cong. Dist. Rep. Party, Kans, 52-56, chmn, 60-64. Mem: Rotary Int; Mason (33°); Shrine. Rel: Presbyterian. Mailing Add: Pleasanton, Kans. 66075.

DUNLAP, JOHN FOSTER D
Calif. State Assemblyman
s. Harry Crum Dunlap and Amy Louise Coombs D; m. 7/13/46 to Janet Louise Jack; c. Jill Bonner, David Anderson, Peter Trask and Jane Hamilton. Educ: Univ. Calif, B.A, 46; Univ. Calif, Hastings Col. of Law, LL.B, 49; Zeta Psi. Polit. & Govt. Pos: Dept. city attorney, City of Napa, Calif, 50; sch. dist. trustee, Mt. George Union Sch. Dist, 50-61; mem, Napa Co. Dem. Cent. Cmt, 56-66, chmn, 60-64; dir, Calif. Dem. Coun, 60-64; dep. dist. attorney, Napa Co, 61; mem, Calif. Dem. Cent. Cmt. and Calif. State Dem. Cent. Cmt. Exec. Bd, 62-66; chmn, Napa Co. Ment. Health Serv. Adv. Bd, 64-66; Calif. State Assemblyman, Fifth Dist, 67-, v.chmn, Agr. Cmt, mem, Cmt. on Educ, Transportation Cmt. and Joint Cmt. on Regional Bay Area Orgn, currently. Mil. Serv: Entered as Pvt, Army Air Corps, 42, released as Sgt, 46, after serv. at Training Schs. and as a combat gunnery instr. at Muroc Army Air Base. Mem: Pres, Napa Co. Bar Asn, 59 and 60; Calif. State Bar Asn; Am. Legion; Napa Grange; Sons of Italy; Lions; Sierra Club. Legal Res: 2087 Third Ave. N, Napa, Calif. 94558. Mailing Add: 1110 First St, Napa, Calif. 94558.

DUNLAP, ROBERT R. Non-Partisan
b. 1921; m; c. 5. Educ: Univ. of Minn. Law Sch, LL.B, 41. Polit. & Govt. Pos: Minn. State Sen, -66. Bus. & Prof. Pos: Lawyer. Mil. Serv: WWII, overseas. Mailing Add: 350 W. 4th, Plainview, Minn. 55964. (1967)

DUNLAP, WESLEY TAYLOR R
Mem, N.C. Rep. State Exec. Cmt.
b. Stokes Co, N.C, 4/20/20; s. William Taylor Dunlap and Mollie Sapp D; m. 1/29/44 to Margie Carroll; c. Wesley Carroll and William Durwood. Educ: Coyne Elec. Sch, Chicago, Ill, grad. Polit. & Govt. Pos: Pres, young Rep, N.C, 52-58; chmn, Stokes Co. Rep. Exec. Cmt, 58-62 & 64-66; mem, N.C. Rep. State Exec. Cmt, 58-; alternate del, Rep. Nat. Conv, 64; cand. for sheriff, 66. Bus. & Prof. Pos: Serv. mgr, Montgomery Wards, Daytona Beach, Fla, 44-45; owner-mgr, West. Auto Assocs. Store, 50-66. Mem: Mason (3°); Traffic Dept, Walnut Dove Vol. Fire Dept, 4 years. Rel: Baptist. Mailing Add: P.O. Box 222, Walnut Cove, N.C. 27052.

DUNMIRE, GEORGE Q. R
Chmn, Dunklin Co. Rep. Cent. Cmt, Mo.
b. Kennett, Mo, 2/6/15; s. John H. Dunmire and Maggie Quertermous D; m. 10/18/69 to Gordyne McLendon; c. Martha Anne (Mrs. John Perry White) and Susan H. Educ: Southeast Mo. State Col, A.B, 35; Univ. Tenn. Col. Med, M.D, 40. Polit. & Govt. Pos: Chmn, Dunklin Co. Rep. Cent. Cmt, Mo, 64- Mil. Serv: Entered as 1st Lt, Army, 42, released as Capt, 46, after serv. in Med. Corps, 42-46. Mem: Dunklin Co. Med. Soc; Mo. and Am. Med. Asns; Am. Acad. Gen. Practice; Scottish Rite; Am. Legion; VFW; Mason (32°); Shrine; Moolah. Rel: Disciples of Christ. Mailing Add: 504 S. Baker Dr, Kennett, Mo. 63857.

DUNMIRE, JOE R. R
S.Dak. State Rep.
b. Clark Co, Iowa, 7/12/02; m. to Ruth Breeding; c. Georgia and Carol. Educ: Yankton Col, B.A; Univs. of Iowa, Colo. and Calif. Polit. & Govt. Pos: S.Dak. State Rep, 52-, mem, Legis. Research Coun, 63. Bus. & Prof. Pos: Former athletic coach; recreational dir, Homestake Mining Co. Mem: Mason; Shrine; past pres. and Lt. Gov, Kiwanis. Rel: Presbyterian. Mailing Add: 705 Glendale Dr, Lead, S.Dak. 57754. (1967)

DUNN, AUBREY L. D
N.Mex. State Sen.
b. 1928. Educ: N.Mex. West. Univ, 3 years. Polit. & Govt. Pos: N.Mex. State Sen, currently. Bus. & Prof. Pos: Newspaper bus. mgr. Mil. Serv: Navy. Mem: Am. Legion; C. of C; Lions. Rel: Protestant. Mailing Add: Alamogordo, N.Mex. 88310. (1967)

DUNN, BARBARA BAXTER R
Conn. State Rep.
b. Danbury, Conn, 10/24/26; d. William Charles Baxter and Dorthea Oestmann B; m. 7/3/48 to William Coburn Dunn; c. Joanne, Kimberly and James Scott. Educ: Univ. Conn, B.A, 48; Delta Zeta. Polit. & Govt. Pos: Mem, East Hartford Rep. Town Cmt, Conn, 52-, treas, 59, secy, 60; mem, Charter Revision Cmn, 62; councilman, East Hartford Town Coun, 63-67; mem, Cmn. on Necessity & Feasibility of Metrop. Govt, Gen. Assembly, 65-67; mem. personnel bd, East Hartford Ord. Cmt, 66-67; Conn. State Rep, 67- Mem: Bd. dirs, Univ. of Conn. Alumni Coun, secy, Alumni Asn; League of Women Voters; Glenbrooke Club; Podunk Mill Club; pres, Greater Hartford Panhellenic Asn. Rel: Episcopal. Mailing Add: 1203 Silver Lane, East Hartford, Conn. 06118.

DUNN, CHARLES WYTHE R
b. Bloomington, Ill, 10/8/40; s. Charles W. Dunn and Teresa Goodrich D; m. 11/25/67 to Carol V. Nelson. Educ: Ill. State Univ, B.S, 62; Fla. State Univ, M.S, 63; Ph.D, 65; Pi Sigma Alpha, Phi Alpha Theta, Pi Gamma Mu, Pi Kappa Delta; Nat. Defense Educ. Act fel, 62-65. Polit. & Govt. Pos: Spec. asst. to Gov. D.J. Evans, Washington, 65-66; spec. asst. to U.S. Rep. Leslie Arends, Wash, D.C, 66-68; dep. dir, Rep. Planning and Research Cmt. U.S. House of Rep, Washington, D.C, 68; admin. asst, U.S. Sen, Charles Goodell, N.Y, 68- Publ: 'White Papers on Washington State Government' Rep. State Cent. Cmt. of Wash. State; 'Castro and the New York Times: An Image in Transition,' Modern Age, 67; 'Committee Staff Manual on Legislative Procedure in the U.S. House of Rep,' House Rep. Policy Cmt, 67. Post-Doctoral Faculty Fellow, Nat. Cmt. for Educ. in Polit. Rel: Protestant. Mailing Add: 150 Duddington Place S.E, Washington, D.C. 20003.

DUNN, FREDERICK H. D
Mayor, Jamestown, N.Y.
b. Jamestown, N.Y, 12/6/00; s. Francis Dunn and Maude Benson D; m. to Annette Hoge; c. Annette (Mrs. Johnson), Terence Castle Weaver, Fredrica, Prudence (Mrs. Jones) and Frederick H, Jr. Educ: Mt. St. Marys, Md. Polit. & Govt. Pos: Elec. cmnr, Chautauqua Co, N.Y, 31; dep. collector, Internal Revenue, U.S. Treas, 35-63; mayor, Jamestown, N.Y, 64- Mem: Rotary; Moose; SAR. Rel: Roman Catholic. Mailing Add: 341 E. Fifth St, Jamestown, N.Y. 14701. (1967)

DUNN, GERALD RAYMOND D
b. Saginaw, Mich, 12/20/34; s. Roy F. Dunn and Mae Bouchard D; m. Aug, 1957 to Patricia Ann Luptowski; c. Leslie J, Terrance P, Carolyn L. and Stephen R. Educ: Cent. Mich. Univ, B.S. in Polit. Sci, 59; Univ. Mich, grad. study. Polit. & Govt. Pos: Chmn, Young Dem. of Genesee Co, Mich, 61-63; v.chmn, Young Dem, Mich, 62; orgn. chmn, Genesee Co. Dem. Cmt, 63-64; Mich. State Sen. and chmn, Senate Educ. Cmt, 65-68; del, Dem. Nat. Conv, 68; mem. bd. regents, Univ. Mich, 68-; exec. secy, Metrop. Asn. for Improved Sch. Legis, 69- Mil. Serv: Entered as Pvt, Army, 54, released as Sp-4, 57, after serv. in U.S. Commanders Off, Berlin, Germany. Rel: Roman Catholic. Mailing Add: 1011 Coutant, Flushing, Mich. 48433.

DUNN, HARRY H. R
b. Abbyville, Kans, 9/20/99; s. Francis Marion Dunn and Cora Crow D; m. 6/25/32 to Florence Tieperman; c. Mary and John Galbreath. Educ: Southwest. Col, A.B, 23; Univ. Chicago, J.D, 28; Pi Kappa Delta. Polit. & Govt. Pos: Co. attorney, Kans, 42-46; Kans. State Rep, 49-52; mem, Cmt. on Uniform State Laws, 52-53; chmn, Dole Cong. Cmt, 62; del, Rep. Nat. Conv, 64. Bus. & Prof. Pos: Dir, Cent. State Bank, 52-; partner, Martindell, Carey, Hunter & Dunn, 59- Mem: Am. and Kans. State Bar Asns; Kans. Hist. Soc; Ky. Hist. Soc, 48-56; Kiwanis; Mason (32°); Elks. Helms Found. Award; Finalist, Amateur Athletic Union Basketball, 21-22. Rel: Methodist. Mailing Add: 303 W. 19th, Hutchinson, Kans. 67501.

DUNN, JAMES RANDALL R
Mem, Rep. State Cent. Cmt, Calif.
b. Los Angeles, Calif, 7/26/37; s. William Edward Dunn, Jr. and Bernice Theresa Kuhfus; single. Educ: Stanford Univ, B.S, 59, Law Sch, LL.B, 62; Alpha Kappa Lambda; Phi Delta Phi. Polit. & Govt. Pos: Legal adv. and compliance officer, off. civil rights, Dept. Health, Educ. & Welfare, Wash, D.C, 66-67; assoc. mem, Rep. State Cent. Cmt, Calif, 67-68 and mem, 68-; dep. dist. attorney, Los Angeles Co, 67-69; ex officio mem, 65th Assembly Dist. Cent. Cmt, 68-; ex officio mem. and secy, 31st Cong. Dist. Cent. Cmt, 68-; ex officio mem, Los Angeles Co. Cent. Cmt, 68-; Rep. nominee, U.S. House Rep, 68; del, Calif. State Conv, 69. Bus. & Prof. Pos: Attorney, Kadison & Quinn, Los Angeles, 63-66; spec. counsel, Calif. State Bar Cmt. on Ethics & Discipline, 65; spec. hearing exam, Calif. State Bar Disciplinary Bd, 69-; attorney, private practice, 69- Mil. Serv: Entered as Airman, Air Nat. Guard, 62, released as Sgt, 69, after serv. in 146th ATW, Van Nuys, Calif. & 231 Mobile Commun. Squadron, Wash, D.C; Honor Grad, Admin. Specialist Sch, 320th Tech. Sch, Amarillo AFB, Tex; Commendation Ribbon, Calif. Air Nat. Guard. Publ: 'Title VI, The Guidelines and School Desegregation in the South,' Univ. Va. Law Rev, 1/67. Mem: Los Angeles Co. Bar Asn.(chmn, prfnl. rels. subcmt. and commun. rels. cmt); Calif. State Bar Asn; Asn. Dep. Dist. Attorneys; charter mem, Los Angeles Co. Mus. Art; Town Hall; Los Angeles World Affairs Coun. Rel: Protestant. Mailing Add: 223 W. Queen St, No. 14, Inglewood, Calif. 90301.

DUNN, LUCY M. D
Mem, Calif. Dem. State Cent. Cmt.
b. Cuero, Tex, Aug. 24, 19; d. Anthony H. McNary and Ella Johnson M; m. 1/27/44 to Vestel T. Dunn; c. Darlene E. Educ: Metrop. Col. Bus, Los Angeles, Calif, 45-46; Univ. Calif. Los Angeles, Exten, 46-47. Polit. & Govt. Pos: Dep. registr. voters, Los Angeles, Co, Calif, 61-; pres, Athens Women's Dem. Club, 62-69; mem, Calif. Dem. State Cent. Cmt, 62-; assembly dist. representative, 55th Assembly Dist. Coun, 65-67; secy, Negro Polit. Action Asn. Calif, 65-68; mem, Dem. South Calif, 69- Bus. & Prof. Pos: Elem. sch. secy, Los Angeles City Sch. Dist, 45-61; real estate salesman, Angel City Realty Co, 58-63; real estate broker-owner, L.M. Dunn Realty, 63-69; secy-dir, Los Angeles Area Econ. Develop. Agency, 63-69; secy-dir, Skills Training & Employ. Inc, 66-68; dir, El Segundo Develop. Corp, 68-69. Mem: Eastern Star; Prince Hall Rite of Adoption; Heroines of Jerico; Watts-Compton Improv. Asn; NAACP; Los Angeles Sch. Employees Union. Eastern Star's Mother of Year, 60; PTA Serv. Pin; Girl Scouts Adult Vol. Five Year Pin; numerous certificates of appreciation from Mothers March of Dimes, Congressman Augustus F. Hawkins, Assemblymen Leon Ralph and Bill Greene, Los Angeles Co. Labor Cmt, and Calif. Assembly Resolution, 68. Rel: Presbyterian. Mailing Add: 12219 S. Central Ave, Los Angeles, Calif. 90059.

DUNN, MABEL ELAINE D
b. Paola, Kans, 6/24/02; d. Charles Louis Werner and Nellie J. Saffell; m. 9/1/44 to Ewell Ernest Dunn; c. William Jack Massey and Charles Louis Massey. Educ: Cent. High Sch, Ft. Worth, Tex, 16-18. Polit. & Govt. Pos: Secy, Adams Co. Dem. Club, Colo, 54-57, exec. bd. mem, 54-69; secy, Second Cong. Dem. Cent. Cmt, 61-69; additional mem, Colo. Dem. State Cent. Cmt, 63-69; secy, Colo. Fedn. Jane Jefferson Dem. Clubs, 64, treas, 65-66, v.pres, 67-68. Bus. & Prof. Pos: Confidential secy. to pres, Oil, Chem. & Atomic Workers Int. Union, AFL-CIO, 42-68. Rel: Methodist. Mailing Add: 9260 Lillian Lane, Thornton, Colo. 80229.

DUNN, MARTY HOYLE R
b. Portales, N.Mex, 6/16/35; s. Walter Talmadge Dunn and Sylvia Lorena Kinsey D; m. 8/8/53 to Donna Faye Edwards; c. Timothy Hoyle and Susan Leanne. Educ: East. N.Mex. Univ. Polit. & Govt. Pos: Chmn, Roosevelt Co. Rep. Party, N.Mex, 65 & 67. Bus. & Prof. Pos: Owner and mgr, Tam Dunn Motor Co, 59- Mil. Serv: Entered as Pvt, Army, 57, released as Specialist, 59, after serv. in Seventh Cavalry Regt, First Cavalry Div, Korea, 58-59; 1st Lt, Army Res; Capt, N.Mex. Nat. Guard. Mem: Jaycees (v.pres, 63). Rel: Methodist. Mailing Add: Route 1, Box 292, Portales, N.Mex. 88130.

DUNN, ROBERT G. Conservative
Minn. State Rep.
married; 5 children. Educ: Amherst Col, 48. Polit. & Govt. Pos: Chmn, Mille Lacs Co. Rep. Cmt, Minn; Minn. State Rep, 64- Bus. & Prof. Pos: Lumber dealer; bldg. contractor. Mil. Serv: Marine Corps, 42-46, 50-52. Mem: Chmn, Princeton Planning Cmn; Mille Lacs Co. Red Cross; C. of C. (past. pres, Princeton Chap). Mailing Add: 503 Eighth Ave. S, Princeton, Minn. 55371.

DUNNE, ISABELLE MARY D
Chmn, Wayne Co. Dem. Cmt, Pa.
b. Honesdale, Pa, 9/20/01; d. Thomas J. Canivan and Catherine Ryan C; wid; c. Margaret C.(Mrs. Himpele), Patricia (Mrs. O'Neill), Rita D.(Mrs. Soete), Ann Marie (Mrs. Bursis) and Thomas F.(deceased). Educ: Pa. State Col. Polit. & Govt. Pos: Mem, Wayne Co. Dem. Cmt, Pa, 32-, secy, 32-44 & 46-63, chmn, 63-; co. auditor, Wayne Co, 44; dep. collector of Internal Revenue, Internal Revenue Serv, 44-46; regional dir, Pa. Fedn. Dem. Women, Harrisburg, 58-62 & 64-; appraiser, Inheritance Tax Div, Co. of Pa, Harrisburg, 59 & 62; alternate del-at-lg, Dem. Nat. Conv, 60, del-at-lg, 64; pres, Wayne Co. Dem. Women's Club, 61-66. Bus. & Prof. Pos: Acct. and tax consult, 46- Mem: Secy, Wayne Co. Prfnl. Women, 61-62; Cath. Daughters of Am, Court St. Martin; North. Wayne Dem. Club. Rel: Roman Catholic. Mailing Add: 415 15th St, Honesdale, Pa. 18431.

DUNNE, MARTHA LUCILLE R
Mem: Bernalillo Co. Rep. Cent. Cmt, N.Mex.
b. St. Joseph, Mo, 11/27/20; d. Samuel Elbert Hill and Nettie Mae Denny H; m. 6/2/42 to Edward Earle Dunne; c. Jacqueline Ann and April Jean. Educ: High sch, St. Louis, Mo, grad, 37; Epsilon Sigma Alpha. Polit. & Govt. Pos: Pres, S.E. Fedn. Rep. Women, N.Mex, 65-66; Rep. precinct chmn, Precinct 17, Albuquerque, 66-; treas, Bernalillo Co. Fedn. Rep. Women, 66-68, pres, 69-; alternate del, Rep. Nat. Conv, 68; mem, Bernalillo Co. Rep. Cent. Cmt, N.Mex, 68- Bus. & Prof. Pos: Treas, West. Chuck Wagon, Inc, Albuquerque, N.Mex, 56- Mem: Mobile Indust. Caterers Asn; N.Mex. Mobile Food Serv. Asn; N.Mex. Bus. & Mfg. Asn; C. of C; Bernalillo Co. Sheriff's Posse. Rel: Protestant. Mailing Add: 1312 Girard S.E, Albuquerque, N.Mex. 87106.

DUNNELL, MILDRED HAZEL R
Chmn, 12th Dist. Rep. Party, Mich.
b. Wampum, Pa, 5/15/11; d. George H. Evans and Anna Ault E; wid; c. Nancy Mae (Mrs. Morehouse). Polit. & Govt. Pos: Womens finance chmn, Macomb Co. Rep. Party, Mich, 58-62; del, Rep. State and Co. Conv, 58-69; alternate del-at-lg, Rep. Nat. Conv, 60; chmn, Macomb Co. Rep. Party, 67-; chmn, 12th Dist. Rep. Party, 69- Bus. & Prof. Pos: Pres, Bristol Corp, Detroit, 40-69; secy, Wayne Leasing, Detroit, 67- Mem: Detroit Tooling Asn; Detroit C. of C; Nat. Tool & Die Mfg. Asn; Zonta Club of Detroit. Rel: Protestant. Mailing Add: 34304 Jefferson, Mt. Clemens, Mich. 48043.

DUNPHY, ROBERT G. D
Sgt-at-Arms, U.S. Senate
b. 9/1/20; m. to Theresa P; c. five. Polit. & Govt. Pos: Sgt-at-Arms, U.S. Senate, 66- Legal Res: Westerly, R.I. 02891. Mailing Add: Williamsburg Rd, Davidsonville, Md. 21035.

DUNTON, GEORGE ALBERT D
b. North Leeds, Maine, 8/2/13; s. Percy Edwin Dunton and Mable Edna Pratt D; m. 6/13/36 to Nathalie Caldwell; c. Bruce Albert, Roberta May (Mrs. Lenord DiPiano), Marlene Edna and Darryl Elden. Educ: Leavitte Inst, Turnerm, Maine, 4 years. Polit. & Govt. Pos: Chmn, Housing Authority, Rahway, N.J, 58-61; alternate del, Dem. Nat. Conv, 68. Bus. & Prof. Pos: Pres, Union Co. Indust. Coun, CIO, Linden, N.J, 54-58; pres, Dist. 8 Coun, Oil Chem. and Atomic Workers Int. Union, Newark, 60-64, int. rep, Denver, Colo, 64-69. Mil. Serv: Entered as Pvt, Army, 31, released as Pfc, 34, after serv. in 55th Coast Artil, Honolulu, Hawaii. Mem: F&AM. Rel: Protestant. Legal Res: Devon St, Forked River, N.J. 08731. Mailing Add: P.O. Box 336, Forked River, N.J. 08731.

DUNTON, HAROLD HARTLEY R
Finance Chmn, Clearwater Co. Rep. Party, Minn.
b. Buffalo, Minn, 10/1/96; s. Arthur Mayo Dunton and Kate Norton D; single. Educ: Crookston Minn. Sch. Agr, grad. Polit. & Govt. Pos: Chmn, Clearwater Co. Rep. Party, Minn, 65-68, finance chmn, currently. Bus. & Prof. Pos: Secy, Clearwater Co. Farm Bur, 32-62, pres, 62-68, secy, currently; bd. mem, Bagley Coop. Creamery, 18 years; pres, Bagley Coop Elevator, 10 years. Mailing Add: Route 2, Bagley, Minn. 56621.

DUNTON, KEITH H. D
Iowa State Rep.
b. Poseshiek Co, near Deep River, Iowa, 3/20/15; s. Le Roy Dunton and Sarah Faye D; m. 3/7/37 to Ethel Cowan; c. Cynthia Kay. Educ: Thornburg High Sch, 32. Polit. & Govt. Pos: Chmn, Keokuk Co. Sch. Bd, Iowa, 10 years; Iowa State Rep, currently. Bus. & Prof. Pos: Farming; livestock; former hardware and implement merchant. Mem: Nat. Cmt. for Support of Pub. Schs; Mason; Eastern Star; Consistory; Shrine; Elks; Lions; Izaak Walton League; charter mem, Flying Farmers; Farm Bur. Rel: Methodist; Lay Leader, Thornburg; Lay Leader, Keokuk Co. Mailing Add: Thornburg, Iowa 50255. (1967)

DUPLANTIER, ADRIAN GUY D
La. State Sen.
b. New Orleans, La, 3/5/29; s. Frederick Robert Duplantier and Amelie Rivet D; m. 7/15/51 to Sally Thomas; c. Adrian, Jr, David, Thomas, Jeanne, Louise and John. Educ: Loyola Univ, New Orleans, LL.B, cum laude, 49; Alpha Sigma Nu. Polit. & Govt. Pos: First Asst. Dist. Attorney, New Orleans, La, 54-56; La. State Sen, 60-; del, Dem. Nat. Conv, 68. Bus. & Prof. Pos: Attorney-at-law, 49- Publ: Various articles in Loyola and Tulane Law Reviews, 49-64. Mem: Mem. exec. cmt, New Orleans Bar Asn; formerly mem. Bd. of Govs, La. State Bar Asn; mem. coun, La. State Law Inst; La. Judicial Coun; K. of C. Rel: Roman Catholic. Legal Res: 5601 Charlotte Dr, New Orleans, La. 70122. Mailing Add: P.O. Box 19797, New Orleans, La. 70119.

DUPONT, THOMAS E. D
Conn. State Sen.
b. Fall River, Mass, 4/30/35; s. Michael W. Dupont and Gertrude Murphy D; m. 9/12/59 to Patricia F. Urban; c. Thomas E, Jr, Michael L. and Wesley Educ: Providence Col, A.B. in Polit. Sci, 57; Boston Col. Law Sch, LL.B, 61; Dean's List, Boston Col; Boston Col. Moot Court Prog; mem. staffs, Boston Col. Law Rev. and Surv. Mass. Law; Cadet Officers' Honor Club, Providence Col; Fall River Club. Polit. & Govt. Pos: Law clerk to U.S. Dist. Court Judge, T. Emmet Clarie, Hartford, Conn, 61-62; mem, Borough Zoning Bd. Appeals, Danielson, Conn, 62-64; pub. defender, 11th Circuit Court, 65-68; Conn. State Sen, 29th Dist, 69- Bus. & Prof. Pos: Assoc, Attorney Basil T. Tsakonas, Danielson, Conn, 62-65; partner, Law Firm of Dupont & Scheibeler, 65- Mil. Serv: Inf. Officer, Army, 58-59; Capt, Army Res. Mem: Windham Co. Bar Asn.(secy. & treas); Am. Bar Asn; Conn. Bar Asn; Killingly Mem. Sch. Parent Teachers Community Asn.(pres); Dyer Manor Fire Dist.(dir); K. of C; Elks (judge advocate Danielson Lodge); United Commercial Travelers. Am. Jurisprudence Prize. Rel: Catholic. Legal Res: Black Rock Ave, Danielson, Conn. 06239. Mailing Add: 23 Academy St, Danielson, Conn. 06239.

DUPPER, ERVIN E. R
b. Campbell Co, S.Dak; 1/8/23; m. 8/31/52; c. Sally, Ross and Lois. Educ: Univ. Ore, B.A, 48; Univ. S.Dak, LL.B, 51; Delta Theta Phi; Lambda Chi Alpha. Polit. & Govt. Pos: Walworth Co. States Attorney, S.Dak, 55-56; S.Dak. State Sen, 64-68. Bus. & Prof. Pos: Lawyer; abstractor. Mem: Past pres, S.Dak. Title Asn; Rotary; dir, Mobridge C. of C; secy-treas, Abstractors Bd. of Exam; Bridge City Boat Club; Oahe Sportsman Club. Rel: Congregational; trustee, United Congregational Church. Mailing Add: Mobridge, S.Dak. 57601.

DUPREE, FRANKLIN TAYLOR, JR. R
Chmn, Wake Co. Rep. Party, N.C.
b. Angier, N.C, 10/8/13; s. Franklin T. Dupree, Sr. and Elizabeth Wells D; m. 12/30/39 to Rosalyn Adcock; c. Elizabeth Rosalyn (Mrs. J.C. Proctor) and Nancy Alice (Mrs. Philip R. Miller, Jr). Educ: Univ. N.C, A.B, 33, LL.B, 36. Polit. & Govt. Pos: Mem, Wake Co. Bd. Elec, N.C, 62-68; chmn, Wake Co. Rep. Party, 67- Bus. & Prof. Pos: Partner, law firm, Dupree, Weaver, Horton, Cockman & Alvis, 52- Mil. Serv: Entered as Ens, Navy, 43, released as Lt, 46, after serv. in Amphibious Forces, European and Asian Theaters, 43-45. Mem: Wake Co, N.C. and Am. Bar Asns; Am. Judicature Soc; Int. Asn. Ins. Counsel; Lions; Elks. Rel: Baptist. Legal Res: 713 Westwood Dr, Raleigh, N.C. 27607. Mailing Add: P.O. Box 17623, Raleigh, N.C. 27609.

DUPREE, JAMES A. D
b. Detroit, Mich, 8/31/33; s. Silas Dupree and Virginia Corrigan D; married 4/21/62 to Shirley Rae Holmes; c. James Anthony, Jr. Educ: Univ. Fla, B.A. Polit. & Govt. Pos: Aide to U.S. Rep. Boyle, 59-60 and U.S. Rep. Finnegan, 61-65; admin. asst. to U.S. Rep. Ronan, Ill, 65-69. Mem: Sigma Chi. Legal Res: Chicago, Ill. Mailing Address: 127 E St. S.E, Washington, D.C. 20003. (1967)

DURAN, EFRAIN A. D
Co. Cmnr, Starr Co, Tex.
b. Santa Elena, Tex, 3/24/20; s. Eulalio Duran and Juliana Hinojosa D; m. 3/25/43 to Dina Ponce; c. Maria Dina, Santiago H, Maria Christina, Efrain A, II, Noel Ruben, George X. and Eduardo C. Educ: Tex. A&I Univ, 1 year. Polit. & Govt. Pos: Tax assessor and collector, Starr Co, Tex, 49-54, co. cmnr, 55-; del, Dem. Nat. Conv, 68. Mil. Serv: 1st Sgt, Army, 39-45, serv. in 91st Inf. Div, ETO, 43-45; Purple Heart with Oak Leaf Cluster; Bronze Medal. Mem: K. of C; Am. Legion; VFW; DAV. Rel: Catholic. Mailing Add: 311 Lee St, Rio Grande City, Tex. 78582.

DURAN, JUNE CLARK R
Mem, Calif. Rep. State Cent. Cmt.
b. Los Angeles, Calif, 6/10/19; d. Willis Winfield Clark and Ethel May King C; m. 4/26/40 to Frank Michael Duran; c. Timothy Clark and Patricia Ellen. Educ: Santa Monica City Col, 35-37; Univ. Calif, Los Angeles, 37-39; Univ. South. Calif, B.A, 49; Univ. Calif, Berkeley, 53; Polit. & Govt. Pos: Pres, Hollywood Rep. Women's Club, Los Angeles, Calif, 58-60; v.pres, Monterey Bay Rep. Women's Club, 62-65; mem, Calif. Rep. State Cent. Cmt, 62-, mem, Monterey Co. Rep. Cent. Cmt, 63-; mem. bd. dirs, Seventh Dist. Agr. Asn, 68- Bus. & Prof. Pos: Dir. opers, Calif. Test Bur, Los Angeles, 55-59, admin. v.pres, 59-65; secy-treas, Clark Develop. Co, Monterey, 60-65; asst. v.pres, CTB Div, McGraw-Hill Book Co, 65- Mem: Soc. Adv. Mgt; Am. Personnel and Guid. Asn; Calif. Educ. Research Asn; Grange; Monterey Hist. and Art Asn. Rel: Protestant. Mailing Add: 6 Cielo Vista Place, Monterey, Calif. 93940.

DURANT, PHIL S. R
Chmn, South Cent. Dist. Nine Rep. Party, Alaska
b. St. Charles, Ill, 2/15/98; s. Harvey L. Durant and Esther Borg D; m.

5/16/46 to Mildred H. Sallows; c. Phil, Jr, John and stepdaughters, Ruth (Mrs. Chester Brown) and Charlotte (Mrs. Charles Simon). Educ: Univ. Ill, B.S, 23; Nat. Journalistic Soc; Chi Phi. Polit. & Govt. Pos: Chmn, South Cent. Dist. Nine Rep. Party, Alaska, 68-; councilman, utility dist. mem. and chmn, Seward Harbor Cmn. Bus. & Prof. Pos: Mgr. and owner, Wheaton Illinoian, Newspaper, 23-39. Mil. Serv: Entered as Pfc, Army, 17, released as Cpl, 19, after serv. in 42nd Engrs, AEF, 17-19. Mem: Mason; Elks; Am. Legion. Rel: Lutheran. Legal Res: 517 Sixth Ave, Seward, Alaska 99664. Mailing Add: Box 737, Seward, Alaska 99664.

DURFEE, CHARLES HERMAN R
Kans. State Rep.
b. Franklin Grove, Ill, 3/28/00; s. Franklin Charles Durfee and Virgie Caroline Reigle D; m. 6/27/23 to Gertrude Geraldine Key; c. Dale Burton and Dorothy Grace. Educ: Sch. Eng. Polit. & Govt. Pos: Councilman, Dighton, Kans, 46-47; mem. planning cmt, Ness City, Kans, 54-66, mayor, 67-; Kans. State Rep, 57-60 & 63- Bus. & Prof. Pos: Owner and mgr, Durfee Implement Co, 45-64. Mil. Serv: Entered as Pvt, Army, 17, released as Sgt, 19, after serv. in 66th Field Artil. Brigade, AEF; Defensive Sector-Ainse-Marne-Champlin-Ainse-St. Michiel and Meuse-Argonne Campaign Ribbons. Mem: Elks; Mason; Odd Fellows; VFW; Am. Legion. Rel: Methodist. Legal Res: 322 Court St, Ness City, Kans. 67560. Mailing Add: Box 416, Ness City, Kans. 67560.

DURFEE, RAYMOND M. R
R.I. State Rep.
b. Cranston, R.I, 4/25/22; m. to Elizabeth G. Educ: Brown Univ, 44. Polit. & Govt. Pos: R.I. State Rep, 63- Bus. & Prof. Pos: Mgr. and treas, Durfee Hardware, Inc. Mil. Serv: Entered as Ens, Navy, 42, released as Lt.(jg), 46, after serv. as asst. to Pac. Fleet Disbursing Officer; Lt.(sg), Naval Res, Jacksonville Naval Air Sta, Fla, 51-52. Mailing Add: 29 Glenmere Dr, Cranston, R.I. 02920.

DURHAM, RICHARD C. D
Chmn, P.R. Dem. Party
Mailing Add: Banco de Ponce Bldg, Suite 713, Ponce de Leon Ave, Santurce, P.R. 00907.

DURKAN, MARTIN JAMES D
Wash. State Sen.
b. Great Falls, Mont, 6/30/23; s. Martin James Durkan and Jen O'Neill D; m. 1951 to Lorraine Noonan; c. Kathleen, Martin James, III, Ryan, Jenny, Matthew, Timothy and Meagan. Educ: Univ. Wash. Law Sch, LL.B, 53. Polit. & Govt. Pos: Legal counsel to speaker, Wash. House of Rep, 55, Wash. State Rep, 56-57; Wash. State Sen, 58-, chmn, Legis. Budget Cmt, Wash. State Legis, 60-64, Munic. Cmt, 64-68, Revenue and Taxation Cmt, 65 and Ways and Means Cmt, 67-69. Bus. & Prof. Pos: Attorney. Mil. Serv: Enlisted in Marines and transferred to Navy, World War II, released as Ens, after serv. in Atlantic, Mediterranean and Pac. Theatres. Mem: Seattle-King Co. and Am. Bar Asns; DAV; Am. Legion; VFW; Eagles; Moose; K. of C; life mem, Young Men's Dem. Club. Legal Res: 4049 W. Lake Sammish Blvd, South Issaquah, Wash. 98027. Mailing Add: 404 Olympic National Life Bldg, Seattle, Wash. 98104.

DURLAND, WILLIAM R. D
Va. State Del.
b. New York, N.Y, 3/28/31; m. to Leona Maryann Semenas. Educ: Bucknell Univ, B.A; Georgetown Law Sch, LL.B. Polit. & Govt. Pos: Treas, Tenth Dist. Cong. Campaign, Va, 62; mem, Hwy. and Transportation Cmn; del, Fairfax Co. Fedn. of Civil Asns; chmn, Mason Dist. Dem. Party; adv. co-ordinator, Johnson-Humphrey campaign staff, 64; Va. State Del, 66-; del, Dem. Nat. Conv, 68. Bus. & Prof. Pos: Attorney-at-law. Mil. Serv: Army, commendation discharge, 57. Publ: 'Defamation and the Clergy,' Law Rev. Digest, 2/59. Mem: Am. Bar Asn; v.chmn, Int. Judicial Coop. Cmt; past pres, Springfield Civic Asn; pres, Nat. Polit. Sci. Hon, 53. Received 1966 Civitan Legis. Award; Va. Asn. for Retarded Children Award for Legislation, 68 & 69. Rel: Catholic. Mailing Add: 4705 Briar Patch Lane, Fairfax, Va. 22030.

DURNING, LAWRENCE WARREN R
Chmn, Tenth Cong. Dist. Rep. Party, Wis.
b. Waupun, Wis, 12/19/34; s. George Warren Durning and Eleanor Gulczynski D; m. 10/28/61 to Katherine Valley McIntyre; c. W(arren) McIntyre and Hugh Anthony. Educ: Univ. Wis, Madison, B.A, 61, J.D, 63; Phi Alpha Delta. Polit. & Govt. Pos: V.chmn, Gov. Cmn. Human Rights, Youth and Young Adult Bds, Wis, 53-55; chmn, Dodge Co. Young Rep, 58-62; chmn, Univ. Wis. Young Rep, 59-60; chmn, Tenth Cong. Dist. Young Rep, 63-65; chmn, Oneida Co. Rep. Cmt, 65-66; chmn, Tenth Cong. Dist. Rep. Party, 67-; del, Rep. Nat. Conv, 68; dist. attorney, Eau Claire Co, Wis, 69- Bus. & Prof. Pos: Attorney, Wis, 63-69. Mil. Serv: Entered as Pvt, Army, 55, released as Cpl, 58. Mem: State Bar of Wis; Am. and Eau Claire Co. Bar Asns; Am. Judicature Soc; Wis. Dist. Attorney Asn; YMCA. Rel: Protestant. Legal Res: 415 Third Ave, Eau Claire, Wis. 54701. Mailing Add: Courthouse, Eau Claire, Wis. 54701.

DURNO, EDWIN RUSSELL R
b. Albany, Ore, 1/26/99; s. John P. Durno and Clara Estell Waddell D; m. 2/10/29 to Evelyn Baker; c. Anne (Mrs. Richard Hensley), Janet (Mrs. Brian Stringer) and Kaye (Mrs. Ronald Louis). Educ: Univ. Ore, B.S; Harvard Med. Sch, M.D, cum laude; Mass. Gen. Hosp, Surg. Training; Phi Delta Theta; Nu Sigma Nu. Polit. & Govt. Pos: Mem, State Bd. of Med. Exam, Ore, 47-59; Ore. State Sen, 59-60, mem, Ways & Means Cmt, Fiscal Cmt. and Taxation Cmt, 59-60; alternate del, Rep. Nat. Conv, 60, del, 64; U.S. Rep, Ore, 61-63, mem, Interior Cmt, 61-63. Mil. Serv: Sgt, Army, 18, reentered serv. as Capt, Army, 42, released as Maj, 45, after serv. in First Auxiliary Corps, ETO; Purple Heart; 3 Campaign Ribbons. Mem: Co, State and Nat. Med. Socs; Am. Col. of Surgeons; Mason; Scottish Rite; Shrine. All-Am. basketball, Univ. Ore, 21. Rel: Protestant. Mailing Add: 2512 E. Main St, Medford, Ore. 97501.

DURRETT, CHADD LANIER, SR. D
b. Griffin, Ark, 2/12/11; s. Everett Edward Durrett and Dixie May Williams D; m. 1/30/31 to Faye Irma Turbeville; c. Chadd L, Jr. and Martha Elizabeth. Educ: El Dorado Jr. Col; Miss McKays Secretarial Col. Polit. & Govt. Pos: Ark. State Rep, Union Co, 53-68, former chmn, Oil and Gas Cmt, Ark. State House of Rep; del, Dem. Nat. Conv, 64. Bus. & Prof. Pos: Div. landman, Murphy Oil Corp, Ark, 45-53, staff landman, El Dorado, 53-62, with Govt. Affairs-Pub. Rels. Dept, 62-66. Mil. Serv: Entered as Pvt, Army, 42, released as T/Sgt, 45, after serv. in 9th Armored Div, ETO; POW, Muhlberg, Germany, 44-45; Purple Heart; Good Conduct Medal; Europe-Africa-Middle East Serv. Medal. Mem: Union Co. Bar Asn; Nat. Legis. Leaders Cmt, Mid-Continent Oil & Gas Asn; Mason (32°); Shrine; Kiwanis; comdr, Am. Legion, 46; 40 et 8; Farm Bur. Rel: Baptist. Legal Res: Pine Acres Farm, Strong, Ark. 71765. Mailing Add: Murphy Bldg, El Dorado, Ark. 71730. (1967)

DURRETT, JAMES MELTON, SR. D
b. Walters, Okla, 3/6/13; s. Charles Albert Durrett and Cora Missouri Ellen Sanders D; m. 6/2/34 to Dorothy Miller Rainwater; c. James M, Jr. and Leonora Sue (Mrs. Bobroff). Educ: Fed. Bur. Invest. Nat. Acad, grad, 40. Polit. & Govt. Pos: Co. cmnr, San Juan Co, N.Mex, 65-67; chmn, San Juan Co. Tenth Dem. Precinct, 67- Bus. & Prof. Pos: Owner-mgr, Serv. Sta, Tucumcari, N.Mex, 34-35, police officer, 36; N.Mex. state police officer, 37-38; chief of police, Tucumcari, 38-41; spec. agent, Fed. Bur. Invest, 42-63; real estate salesman, 67- Mem: AF&AM; Shrine; Elks. Rel: Church of Christ. Mailing Add: Route 1, Box C-4, Aztec, N.Mex. 87410.

DURYEA, PERRY BELMONT, JR. R
Speaker, N.Y. State Assembly
b. East Hampton, N.Y, 10/18/21; s. Perry Belmont Duryea and Jane Stewart D; m. 4/4/44 to Elizabeth Ann Weed; c. Lynn and Perry B, III. Educ: Colgate Univ, B.A; Delta Upsilon. Hon. LL.D, Adelphi Suffolk Col. and Southampton Col. Polit. & Govt. Pos: Mem, Suffolk Co. and N.Y. State Rep. Cmts. and Montauk Fire Dept; pres, bd. trustees, Montauk Pub. Schs, 54-60; N.Y. State Assemblyman, 61-, minority leader, N.Y. State Assembly, 66-68 and speaker, 69-; del, Rep. Nat. Conv, 68; pres, L.I. State Park Cmn, Bethpage Park Authority and Jones Beach State Pkwy. Authority, currently. Bus. & Prof. Pos: Pres, Montauk Airstrip Inc. and Perry B. Duryea & Son; treas, Sea and Sky Portel Inc. Mil. Serv: Entered as Ens, Navy, 42, released as Lt, 45, after serv. in Naval Air Transport, Pac. Theater; Atlantic, Pac. and Philippine Campaign Ribbons. Mem: C. of C; Lions; Am. Legion; VFW; Suffolk Co. Rep. Club; bd. overseers, Adelphi Suffolk Col; dir, Suffolk Co. Div, Am. Cancer Soc. Hobby: Aviation. Rel: Presbyterian. Mailing Add: Old Montauk Hwy, Montauk, N.Y. 11954.

DUSATKO, ALAN A. D
Chmn, Colfax Co. Dem. Cmt, Nebr.
b. Clarkson, Nebr, 10/30/03; s. Anthony Dusatko and Anna Maresh D; m. 1/28/42 to Ann K. Pedersen; c. Alan Anthony and Patricia Ann. Educ: Nebr. Univ, 3 years; Creighton Univ. Law Sch, 3 years; Alpha Sigma Nu. Polit. & Govt. Pos: Chmn, Colfax Co. Dem. Cmt, Nebr, currently. Bus. & Prof. Pos: Attorney-at-law, self employed, 43- Mem: Lions; Commercial Club; Tangier Shrine; Nat. Farmers Orgn; chmn, Nebr. Tuberc. Asn; v.chmn, Boy Scout Coun. Rel: Presbyterian. Mailing Add: Clarkson, Nebr. 68629.

DUSCI, JOSEPH VINCENT D
b. Wheeling, W.Va, 8/16/20; s. Gasper Vincent Dusci and Bertha LaCava D; m. 12/12/58 to Lois Connor Edge; c. Dawn're and Mark Joseph. Educ: Brooklyn Col, 2 years. Polit. & Govt. Pos: Mem, Gov. Fed. Housing Admin. Adv. Housing Cmn, 61-62; W.Va. State Rep, 64-66; cand. for State Sen, 66; Co. cmnr, Ohio Co, W.Va, 69-; pres, Co. Commissioners, 69- Bus. & Prof. Pos: Owner, Dusci Construction Co, 58-; pres, Bank of Wheeling, 66-67 and Elm Grove Elec. Co, 67-; v.pres, B & W Distributing Co, 67-; pres, Dusci Realty Co. Mil. Serv: Entered Marine Corps, 41, released 45, after serv. in Pac. Theater. Mem: W.Va. Realtors Asn; Fed. Home Bldg. Asn; W.Va. Home Bldg. Asn.(founder and past pres); Wheeling Asn. of Home Bldg.(past pres); Ment. Health Bd. of North. W.Va.(pres); W.Va. Bankers Asn; VFW; Eagles; Civitan Int; Farm Bur; Vol. Fire Dept. of West Liberty, Italian Am. Club; dir, Ohio Valley Ironmen Football Team. Jaycees Man of the Month; Co-pilot, Pilot Int; Civic Affairs Award, Civitan Int, 67; Award for Improv. of City Landmark, 68; Award for Ment. Health Work, Jr. Women of W.Va; Ky. Col. Rel: Catholic. Legal Res: Mark One Acres, R.D. 1, Bethany, W.Va. 26032. Mailing Add: Windmill, Grandview St, Wheeling, W.Va. 26003.

DUTREMBLE, RICHARD DONALD D
Sheriff, York Co, Maine
b. Biddeford, Maine, 10/1/31; s. Honore Dutremble (deceased) and Rose Anna Binette D; m. 2/22/54 to Anne Marie Seymoor; c. Pamela, Judith, Richard H, Kenneth and David. Educ: St. Louis High Sch, Biddeford, grad. Polit. & Govt. Pos: Sheriff, York Co, Maine, 63-; chmn, Biddeford City Dem. Cmt, 67; del, Dem. Nat. Conv, 68. Mil. Serv: Entered as Pvt, Army, 55, released as Cpl, 57, after serv. in South. European Task Force, Hq. Italy, 56-57. Mem: Elks; K. of C; Eagles; Amvets. Rel: Catholic. Mailing Add: 3 Greenwood Ave, Biddeford, Maine 04005.

DUTT, GEORGE FREDERICK R
Chmn, Seneca Co. Rep. Cent. Cmt, Ohio
b. Tiffin, Ohio, 6/4/31; s. Roller E. Dutt and Jennie Arthur D; m. 6/9/56 to Janet Kathryn Funk; c. Laurence L. and Laura L. Educ: Heidelberg Col, B.A, 53; Bowling Green State Univ, M.Ed, 57, Sp.Ed, 67; Nu Sigma Alpha. Polit. & Govt. Pos: Committeeman, Tiffin Rep. Party, Ohio, 62-; pres, Tiffin City Coun, 66-68; chmn, Seneca Co. Rep. Cent. Cmt, 68- Bus. & Prof. Pos: Teacher, Tiffin Pub. Schs, 54-57, prin, 57- Mem: Dept. Elem. Prin; Nat. and Ohio Educ. Asns; Elks; Rotary Int; Mason; Shrine. Outstanding Young Man of Year, Jr. C. of C, 67. Rel: Methodist. Mailing Add: 90 Northview Dr, Tiffin, Ohio 44883.

DUTTON, FREDERICK G. D
b. Julesburg, Colo, 6/16/23; s. Dr. F. G. Dutton and Lucy Elizabeth Parker D; m. 6/26/46 to June Klingborg; c. Christopher, Lisa and Eve. Educ: Univ. Calif, B.A, 46; Stanford Law Sch, LL.B, 48; Delta Tau Delta. Polit. & Govt. Pos: Chmn, Stevenson-Kefauver Presidential Campaign, South. Calif, 56; chief asst. attorney gen, Calif, 57-58; state dir, Brown for Gov. Campaign, 58; exec. secy. to Gov. of Calif, 59-60; dep. nat. chmn, Citizens for Kennedy and Johnson, 60; spec. asst. to President John F. Kennedy and secy. to the Cabinet, 61-62; Asst. Secy. of State, U.S. Dept. of State, 62-64; Regent, Univ.

Calif, 62-; dir. research and planning, Presidential Campaign, Dem. Nat. Cmt, 64 and dir. platform cmt; personal campaign asst. to Robert F. Kennedy, Presidential Primaries, 1968. Bus. & Prof. Pos: Assoc, Wilson, Kirkbridge, Wilson & Harzeeld, 49-50; chief asst. gen. counsel, South. Counties Gas Co. of Calif, 52-56; organizing dir, John F. Kennedy Mem. Libr. Oral Hist. Proj, 63-65; partner, Dutton, Gwirtzman & Zumas, Attorneys, D.C, 64-; exec. dir, Robert F. Kennedy Mem. Found, 68- Mil. Serv: Entered as Pvt, Army, 42, released 45, after serv. in Inf, Europe, and German Prisoner of War; also serv. as 1st Lt, 51-52, Judge Adv. Gen. Corps, Japan and Korean Conflict; Bronze Star; Combat Inf. Badge; Purple Heart; 3 Battle Stars. Publ: American Politics in the 1970's, McGraw-Hill, 69. Rel: Episcopal. Mailing Add: 1225 19th St. N.W, Washington, D.C. 20036.

DUTTON, JUDSON DUNLAP R
Chmn, Morgan Co. Rep. Party, Ind.
b. Martinsville, Ind, 11/13/08; s. Harry Freeman Dutton and Hazel Dunlap D; m. 2/27/32 to Nina Pauline Hayes; c. Carolyn Hayes. Educ: Wabash Col, A.B, 30; Beta Theta Pi. Polit. & Govt. Pos: Rep. precinct committeeman, Ind, 36-48; city councilman, Martinsville, 40-43; chmn, Morgan Co. Rep. Party, 46-; clerk and treas, Martinsville, 62- Bus. & Prof. Pos: Mgr, Artesian Laundry, 34-62. Mem: Kiwanis; Mason; Scottish Rite; past exalted ruler, Elks; Moose. Rel: Presbyterian. Legal Res: 410 S. Jefferson St, Martinsville, Ind. 46151. Mailing Add: P.O. Box 407, City Hall, Martinsville, Ind. 46151.

DUVAL, CLAUDE BERWICK D
La. State Sen.
b. Houma, La, 10/24/14; s. Stanwood R. Duval and Mamie Richardson D; m. 4/6/38 to Betty Bowman; c. Dorothy. Educ: La. State Univ, Baton Rouge, 1 year; Tulane Univ. Col. Law, LL.B; Pi Kappa Alpha. Polit. & Govt. Pos: La. State Sen, 15th Sen. Dist, 63- Bus. & Prof. Pos: Attorney, Houma, 37-; mem. bd. dirs, Citizens Nat. Bank & Trust Co. of Houma, Pelican Lake Oyster & Packing Co, Inc, Duval, Whitney Stevenson, Inc. and Casing & Well Serv, Inc; sr. partner, Duval, Arceneaus & Lewis; Attorneys-at-law. Mil. Serv: Entered as Pfc, Marines, 42, released as Capt, 45, after serv. in Co. K, Third Bn, 23rd Marines, Fourth Marine Div, four Pac. Theater land operations, 42-45, Res, 44-55, Lt. Col.(Ret); Bronze Star and Am. Defense Medals; Purple Heart Medal, Iwo Jima; Letter of Commendation; two Presidential Unit Citations; Asiatic Pac. Ribbon with Four Stars. Am. Judicature Soc; Am. Bar Asn; La. State Bar Asn.(formulary and law reform cmts, cmt. on prfnl. econ. and off. mgt, former mem. cmt. on pub. rels. and house of del. cmt. on rev. of appellate jurisdiction in La); Terrebone Bar Asn.(pres, twice); La. Supreme Court (cmt. on jury instrs); Am. Legion (past state Comdr); La. State C. of C.(past pres); VFW; Pub. Affairs Research Coun. of La; Coun. for a Better La; Elks; Mason; Houma-Terrebonne Golf Club; Houma Country Club; Plimsoll Club; Petroleum Club of Morgan City; Camelot Club; Press Club of Baton Rouge. Outstanding Young Man Award, Jr. C. of C, 47. Rel: Episcopal. Legal Res: 18 Country Club Dr, Houma, La. 70360. Mailing Add: 311 Goode St, Houma, La. 70360.

DuVAL, CLIVE L, II D
Va. State Del.
b. N.Y.C, 6/20/12; m. to Susan Holdrege Bontecou. Educ: Yale Univ, B.A, LL.B; Phi Beta Kappa; ed, Yale Law J. Polit. & Govt. Pos: Va. State Del, 66- Bus. & Prof. Pos: Lawyer. Mil. Serv: Lt. Comdr, Naval Res, 42-46. Mem: Yale Club of Wash; Nat. Press Club of Wash; Chevy Chase Club. Rel: Presbyterian. Mailing Add: 1214 Buchanan St, McLean, Va. 22101.

DUVALL, C. HAYES D
b. Anne Arundel Co, Md, 4/5/07; married. Educ: Anne Arundel Co. schs. Polit. & Govt. Pos: Md. State Del, 63-67. Bus. & Prof. Pos: Paving contractor. Mem: past pres, Eastport Civic Asn; Kiwanis; Md. Sch. Bus. Asn; Anne Arundel Sch. Bus. Asn. Mailing Add: 525 Horn Pt. Dr, Annapolis, Md, 21403. (1967)

DUVALL, LESLIE R
Ind. State Sen.
b. Indianapolis, Ind, 2/23/24; s. John L. Duvall and Maud E. Buser D; m. 8/11/45 to Carolyn S. Coxen; c. John Allen and David Blanton. Educ: Butler Univ, A.B, 48; Ind. Univ, LL.B, 49; Sigma Delta Kappa; Sigma Chi. Polit. & Govt. Pos: Chmn, 11th Dist. Young Rep, Ind, 54; probate cmnr, Marion Co. Probate Court, 55-56; chmn, Ind. State Young Rep, 57-58; attorney exam, Ind. Pub. Serv. Cmn, 57-58, cmnr, 58-60; committeeman, Rep. Precinct, 58-; chmn, Ind. Draft Goldwater Cmt, 63, Ind. Goldwater for Pres. Cmt, 64 and Ind. Citizens for Goldwater Cmt, 64; Ind. State Sen, currently. Mil. Serv: Pvt, Army, 43, 1st Lt, Judge Adv. Gen. Corps, 55. Mem: Sigma Delta Kappa (nat. pres, 58); Indianapolis Bar Asn.(mem. bd. of dirs, 57); Am. Legion. Rel: Presbyterian. Mailing Add: 731 Nottingham Court, Indianapolis, Ind. 46240.

DUXBURY, LLOYD L, JR. Conservative
Minn. State Rep.
b. Caledonia, Minn, 2/1/22; married; c. Two. Educ: Phillips Exeter Acad; Harvard Col; Harvard Law Sch. Polit. & Govt. Pos: Minn. State Rep, 51-, Conservative Floor Leader, Minn. State House of Rep, 59 & 61, Speaker, 63, 65, 67 & 69. Legal Res: 274 S. Kingston, Caledonia, Minn. 55921. Mailing Add: 2000 L St. N.W, Washington, D.C. 20036.

DVORAK, CHARLES VINCENT D
Chmn, Dist. 36 Dem. Orgn, N.Dak.
b. Dickinson, N.Dak, 10/4/17; s. Vincent Dvorak and Mary Kovash D; m. 10/23/39; c. Edith (Mrs. Ludwig Meduna), Robert, Richard, Susan and Sandra. Educ: Grade and 2 years Correspondence Sch. Polit. & Govt. Pos: Co. Chmn, Dem. Party, N.Dak, 58-68; co. cmnr, N.Dak, 61-68; chmn, Dist. 36 Dem. Orgn. N.Dak, 68- Bus. & Prof. Pos: Dir, Farmers Union Oil, Killdeer, N.Dak, 55-; dir, Dunn Co. Farmers Union, 61-; dir, Consolidated Telephone & Cooperative, Dickinson, 64- Mem: Elks; Eagles; K. of C; U.S. & State Farmers Unions. Community Leader of America, 68. Rel: Catholic. Mailing Add: Manning, N.Dak. 58642.

DWIGHT, MARIA BURGEE R
b. Holyoke, Mass, 12/23/34; d. Henry V. Burgee and Marcelle Melun B; m. 9/25/54 to William Dwight, Jr; c. William Henry, Leslie Rathbun, Vallé Elizabeth, Timothy Monk and Ryan Hamilton. Educ: Bryn Mawr Col, 52-54. Polit. & Govt. Pos: Committeewoman, State Rep. Cmt, 64-68; cmnr, Dept. Pub. Welfare, Holyoke, 65-68; del, Rep. Nat. Conv, 68; dir. and chmn, Munic. Nursing Home, 68-69; cmnr. adv. bd, Mass. Dept. Pub. Welfare, 68- Mem: Jr. League Holyoke (pres, 64-66); dir, Vis. Nurse Asn; chmn, Urban Ministry; Asn. Improv. Minorities; Community and Regional Opportunity Prog, Off. Econ. Opportunity. Young Woman of the Year Award, 62. Mailing Add: 30 Cleveland St, Holyoke, Mass. 01040.

DWINELL, LANE R
b. 11/14/06; m. to Elizabeth. Educ: Dartmouth Col, A.B; Amos Tuck Sch, M.C.S; Theta Delta Chi. Hon. degrees, Suffolk Univ, D.C.S, Dartmouth Col, M.A, Univ. N.H, LL.D. and New Eng. Col, D.C.L. Polit. & Govt. Pos: Mem, State Bd. Educ, N.H, speaker, N.H. House Rep. and pres, N.H. Senate, formerly; del, Dem. Nat. Conv, 52, 56 & 68; Gov, N.H, 55-58; Asst. Secy. of State, 59-60. Bus. & Prof. Pos: Pres, Carter & Churchill Co, Inc, 36-66; pres, Nat. Bank of Lebanon, 60-67, chmn. bd, 67-; asst. adminstr, Agency for Int. Develop, 69- Mem: Theta Delta Chi; SAR; Rotary Int; Moose; Grange. Rel: Congregational. Mailing Add: 94 Bank St, Lebanon, N.H. 03766.

DWORAK, JAMES JOSEPH
b. Omaha, Nebr, 9/4/25; s. Ad. J. Dworak and Anna Swoboda D; m. 6/3/46 to Audrey Hendrickson; c. Paula, Andrew, Michaela, Claudia and Allen. Educ: Creighton Univ, pre-med. student, 46-47; San Francisco Col. Mortuary Sci, 48. Polit. & Govt. Pos: Mem, Omaha City Coun, Nebr, 57-61; former Mayor, Omaha; mem. adv. bd, U.S. Conf. Mayors. Bus. & Prof. Pos: Dworak Mortuary, Omaha, 48-; bd. dirs. Joslyn Lib. Arts Soc. Mil. Serv: Army Air Force, 45-47. Mem: Am, Nebr. and Omaha Funeral Dirs. Asns; Am. Legion; 40 et 8; Czech. Civic Alliance; K. of C; Elks; Te Deum Int. Rel: Catholic. Mailing Add: 6223 S. 36th Ave, Omaha, Nebr. 68107. (1967)

DWORKIN, MARTIN DFL
Mem, Ramsey Co. Dem-Farmer-Labor State Cent. Cmt, Minn.
b. New York, N.Y, 12/3/27; s. Hyman Bernard Dworkin and Pauline Herstein D; m. 2/2/57 to Nomi Rees Buda; c. Jessica and Hanna. Educ: Ind. Univ, B.A, 51; Univ. Tex, Ph.D, 55. Polit. & Govt. Pos: Mem, State Steering Cmt, Minn. New Dem. Coalition; alternate del, Dem. Nat. Conv, 68; mem, Ramsey Co. Dem-Farmer-Labor State Cent. Cmt, Minn, 68- Bus. & Prof. Pos: Res. fel, Univ. Calif, Berkeley, 55-57; from asst. prof. to assoc. prof, Ind. Univ, Indianapolis, 57-62; from assoc. prof. to prof, Univ. Minn, Minneapolis, 62- Mil. Serv: Entered as Pvt, Army, 46, released as Sgt, 48, after serving in 1st Cavalry Div, Japan, 46-48; World War II Medal. Mem: Chmn. gen. div, Am. Soc. Microbiol; Brit. Soc. Gen. Microbiol; Soc. Develop. Biol. Career develop. award, Nat. Insts. Health. Mailing Add: 2123 W. Hoyt Ave, St. Paul, Minn. 55108.

DWYER, CLAIRE BUCKLEY D
Mem, Mass. Dem. State Cmt.
b. Somerville, Mass, 5/9/30; d. Hugh E. Buckley and Grace M. Fyffe B; m. 2/23/48 to James J. Dwyer; c. James J, II. Educ: Col. Polit. & Govt. Pos: Mem, Mass. Dem. State Cmt, Seventh Middlesex Dist, 64-; exec. secy, Humphrey Campaign, 68; del, Dem. Nat. Conv, 68; mem, Mass. Electoral Col, 68; clerk, Middlesex Co. Court, currently. Mem: DAV Auxiliary; Dem. Women on Wheels; Fedn. Dem. Women, Mass; Mass. State and Co. Employees Asn. Rel: Catholic. Mailing Add: 16 Frederick Dr, Woburn, Mass. 01801.

DWYER, FLORENCE P. R
U.S. Rep, N.J.
b. Reading, Pa; m. to M. Joseph Dwyer; c. one son. Polit. & Govt. Pos: Mem, N.J. Legis, 49-56; U.S. Rep, N.J, 56-; mem, U.S. Adv. Cmn. on Intergovt. Rels, 59- Mem: Former state legis. chmn, N.J. Fedn. of Bus. & Prfnl. Women's Clubs. Legal Res: Elizabeth, N.J. Mailing Add: Congressional Hotel, Washington, D.C. 20003.

DWYER, FRANCIS GERARD R
Mem, Exec. Cmt, Rep. State Cent. Cmt, R.I.
b. Newport, R.I, 11/3/22; s. James William Dwyer and Margaret Walsh D; single. Educ: Georgetown Univ, B.A, 47. Polit. & Govt. Pos: R.I. State Rep, 55-59; mem, exec. cmt, Rep. State Cent. Cmt, 56-; Rep. Cand. for Lt. Gov, 58; chmn, R.I. Turnpike and Bridge Authority, 60-; del, Rep. Nat. Conv, 68. Bus. & Prof. Pos: Secy-treas, G.J.S. White, Inc, Newport, R.I, 55-; dir, Newport Savings Bank, 66-; dir, Newport Elec. Corp, 67-; pres, Newport Co. C. of C, 69. Mil. Serv: Entered as Pvt, Marines, 42, released as Capt, 52, after serving in Fourth and Sixth Marine Div, Pac. Theatre, 43-46; Am. Defense, Pac. Theatre and China Serv. Ribbons. Mem: VFW; Am. Legion; Rotary. Newport Co. Man of the Year Award, 66. Rel: Roman Catholic. Legal Res: 513 Paradise Ave, Middletown, R.I. 02840. Mailing Add: 37 Bellevue Ave, Newport, R.I. 02840.

DWYER, R. BUDD R
Pa. State Rep.
b. St. Charles, Mo, 11/21/39; s. Robert M. Dwyer and Alice Mary Budd D; m. 8/23/63 to Joanne M. Grappy; c. Robert Ross and Dyan Danuta. Educ: Thiel Col, 57-58; Allegheny Col, B.A. in Econ, 61, M.A. in Educ, 63; Theta Chi. Polit. & Govt. Pos: Pa. State Rep, 65- Bus. & Prof. Pos: Asst. alumni secy, Allegheny Col, 67- Jaycee-Outstanding Young Man, 64-65; YMCA-Serv. to Youth Award, 66; Commun. Leader of Am, 67 & 68. Rel: Baptist. Mailing Add: 616 Center St, Meadville, Pa. 16335.

DWYER, ROBERT A. R
b. Chicago, Ill, 3/23/26; s. John E. Dwyer and Selina Higgins Dwyer; m. 6/10/48 to Patricia Marian McGuire; c. Robert A, Jr. and Maura Elizabeth. Educ: Loyola Univ, Ill, 2 years. Polit. & Govt. Pos: Leader, Young People's Sect, Dewey for President Orgn, Ill, 48; mem, 43rd Ward Young Rep. Orgn, 48; helped form the Ill. Citizens for Eisenhower Cmt, 52; v.chmn, Ill. Citizens for Eisenhower-Nixon Campaign and chmn, Youth for Eisenhower-Nixon, 56; cand. for Cong, 13th Cong. Dist, Ill, 62; chmn, Citizen's Adv. Bd. to Sheriff of Cook Co, 63-66; nat. vol. chmn. for Vice Presidential cand. William E. Miller, 64; cand. for State Treas, Ill, 66, Lt. Gov, Ill, 68; alternate del, Rep. Nat. Conv, 68; regional dir, Small Bus. Admin, U.S. Govt, 69- Bus. & Prof. Pos: V.pres, Alexander & Alexander, Inc, Chicago, 48-66; pres,

Robert A. Dwyer Enterprises, Inc, 66-; dir, Civic Center Bank of Chicago, 68, LaSalle Street Capital Corp, 68. Mil. Serv: Entered as Pfc, Army Air Force, 44, released as Cpl, 46, after serv. in Squadron A, 244th Army Air Force; Am. Campaign Medal; Victory Medal; World War II Medal; Good Conduct Medal. Mem: North Shore Country Club; Bob O'Link Golf Club; Mich. Shores Club; Mid-Am. Club; Attic Club; co-founder, past v.pres, and dir, Brain Research Foundation; dir, Catholic Charities, Inc. Rel: Catholic. Mailing Add: 884 Higginson Lane, Winnetka, Ill. 60093.

DWYER, ROBERT EUGENE D
Chmn, Second Cong. Dist. Dem. Cmt, Mich.
b. Waukegan, Ill, 6/14/35; s. Donal James Dwyer and Carol Barnes D; m. 6/23/56 to Marilyn Alma James; c. Linda Marilyn. Educ: Wayne State Univ, 55-59. Polit. & Govt. Pos: Chmn, Mich. Jaycees Constitutional Conv. Dr, 59; chmn, Plymouth Dem. Club, Mich, 61; investr, Mich. Racing Cmn, 61-62; secy, Second Dist, Wayne Co. Dem. Party Orgn, 64, chmn, 65-69, v.chmn, 69-; chmn, Plymouth Commun. Schs. Bd. of Canvassers, 67-; alternate del, Dem. Nat. Conv, 68; trustee, Wayne Co. Dem. Cmt, Mich, 69-; chmn, Second Cong. Dist. Dem. Cmt, Mich, 69- Mem: Mich. Br. Mgr. Asn; charter mem, Kiwanis of Colonial Plymouth; Cert. of Merit, Mich. Dem. Party; Cert. of Appreciation, Plymouth Dem. Club; Jaycee of the Month Award. Rel: Unitarian. Mailing Add: 1274 Penniman Ave, Plymouth, Mich. 48170.

DWYER, RONALD F. D
b. Wellington, Kans, 12/14/32; s. Mat F. Dwyer and Sibyl G. Fletcher D; m. 5/5/57 to Mable June Lee; c. Bret, Bart, Rhonda and Charles. Educ: Tex. A&M Univ, 50-51; Okla. Univ, 51-53; Wichita State Univ, B.A, 58. Polit. & Govt. Pos: Dem. precinct committeeman, Sumner Co, Kans, 60-64; chmn. cent. cmt, Sumner Co. Deml Party, 64-68. dir, State Property Valuation Dept, 67- Mil. Serv: Entered as Pvt. E-2, Army, 53, released as Pfc, 55, after serv. in Spec. Serv, Kans. Mem: Int. Asn. of Assessing Officers; C. of C. Various athletic awards. Rel: Christian Church of N.Am. Mailing Add: 3739 Sena Dr, Topeka, Kans. 66604.

DWYER, THEODORE JOHN R
Chmn, Jackson Co. Bd. Cmnrs, Mich.
b. Jackson, Mich, 11/26/26; s. William A. Dwyer and Mildred Jennings D; m. 6/17/50 to Anne Marie Bakken; c. Elizabeth, Martha Mary and Laura Jean. Educ: Jackson Commun. Col, 46-48; Univ. Mich, 48-49; Cent. Mich. Univ, 50-51. Polit. & Govt. Pos: Supvr, Liberty Twp, Jackson Co, Mich, 61-68; del, Rep. Nat. Conv, 68; chmn, Jackson Co. Bd. of Cmnr, Mich, 68- Bus. & Prof. Pos: Ins. salesman, John Dobben Agency, 61-69. Mil. Serv: Entered as Pvt, Air Force, 43, released as Cpl, 45, after serv. in Am. Theatre. Mem: Am. Legion; Jackson Co. Fair Bd; chmn, Jackson-Hillsdale Commun. Ment. Health Serv. Bd. Rel: Roman Catholic. Mailing Add: 6211 Springbrook Rd, Horton, Mich. 49246.

DWYER, WILLIAM FRANCIS R
b. Rochester, N.Y, 3/30/35; s. Leo Francis Dwyer and Laura Mayfield Costello D; m. 4/16/55 to Eleanor Moffett Clark; c. Elizabeth Clark and Geoffrey Cooke. Educ: Princeton Univ; Univ. Rochester; Delta Kappa Epsilon. Polit. & Govt. Pos: Campaign mgr, Rep. Cmt, Rochester, N.Y, 61-62; chmn, Monroe Co. Rep. Forum, 62-63; admin. asst. to U.S. Rep. Frank Horton, N.Y, 63-67; adv, Rep. Cmt, Rochester, 67- Bus. & Prof. Pos: Staff announcer, WGVA, Geneva, N.Y, 54-55; mem. news staff, WBBF, Rochester, 55-56 and WHAM, Rochester, 56-61; v.pres. and dir, Astro Agency, 61-62; v.pres. pub. affairs, Darcy Assocs, Inc, 67- Mem: Am. Fedn. of TV and Radio Artists; Assoc. Industs. of N.Y. State; Gov. Club; C. of C; Genesee Valley Club. Accredited mem. of Pub. Rels. Soc. of Am. Rel: Episcopal. Legal Res: 253 Dorchester Rd, Rochester, N.Y. 14610. Mailing Add: 760 Security Tower, Rochester, N.Y. 14604.

DWYER, WINIFRED BRENNAN R
b. Missoula, Mont, 8/21/04; d. William R. Brennan (deceased) and Donna Marie MacDonald (deceased); m. 8/28/31 to Thomas Leo Dwyer, M.D; c. Mariwyn, Donna Marie and Richard Michael. Educ: Univ. Mont, B.A, 26; Ill. Training Sch. Nurses, Univ. Chicago, Cert. Diatetics, 27; Mortar Board; Delta Delta Delta. Polit. & Govt. Pos: Dir, Training Projs. for Women, Nat. Youth Admin, 38-40; state dir, Maid Training Projs. for Mo, WPA, 40-41; del. and alternate del. to Dist. and State Rep. Women's Club numerous times, pres, Mexico Rep. Women's Club, Mo, 52; Rep. cand, State Rep. from Audrain Co, 62; del, Rep. State Conv, Ninth Dist, 64; alternate del, Rep. Nat. Conv, 64; state co-chmn, Constitution Party of Mo, 65- Bus. & Prof. Pos: Asst. prof, home econ, Univ. Mont, 27-28; dir, dept. home econ, Am. Meat Inst, Chicago, 28-30; asst. prof. and dir. of dormitories, Mo. State Teachers Col, 31-32. Mem: Am. Asn. Univ. Women; Audrain Co. Med. Soc. Woman's Auxiliary. Rel: Catholic. Mailing Add: 301 N. Cole St, Mexico, Mo. 65265.

DYAL, KEN W. D
Married; c. Kynra Gay (Mrs. Gordon Lyman), Karen Rae, Timothy and Terence. Polit. & Govt. Pos: U.S. Rep, 33rd Cong. Dist, Calif, 64-67, mem, House Pub. Works Cmt; mem. adv. bd, State Feather River Proj. Asn. and cmts; campaign mgr. for U.S. Rep. Harry R. Sheppard; former mem. bd. dirs, San Bernardino Co. Supplemental Water Asn; postmaster, San Bernardino, 47-54; chmn, Mayor's Adv. Planning Cmt; secy, Co. Bd. Supvrs. Bus. Pos: Trustee, Patton State Hosp; secy-mgr. and treas, Nat. Orange Show, 60-64, pres, 39th Show, former mem. bd. dirs, former chmn, Govt. Exhibits Div. and Entertainment of Guests Cmt, aide, Citrus Inst. and Co. Bd. Trade, events; mem. bd. dirs, Los Angeles Airways, Inc, 58-64. Mil. Serv: Lt. Comdr, Naval Res, 42-46. Mem: Kiwanis; Retired Postmasters Asn; Am. Legion; hon. mem. bd. dirs, Goodwill Indust. San Bernardino and Riverside Co; former secy, Real Estate Bd; chmn, Mil. Affairs Cmt, San Bernardino C. of C, 4 yrs. and past chmn, Water Cmt; past pres, Inter-Serv. Club Coun. and Postmaster's Asn; campaign chmn. and later pres, Commun. Chest; pres, Covered Wagon Days; past co. chmn, Am. Cancer Soc. Fund Drive. DAR Annual Citizen Award; Bd. of Trade Award for Meritorious Serv. to Co; Citizen of Month Award, Exchange Club. Rel: Latter-day Saint. Mailing Add: 6907 Dwight Way, San Bernardino, Calif. 92404. (1967)

DYAR, ROSWELL E. R
Maine State Rep.
b. Strong, Maine, 6/19/31; s. Colin Dyar and Orra Welch D; m. 10/5/51 to Ethel Haley; c. Walter, Thomas, Colin and Scott. Educ: Becker Col, A.S, 51; Phi Theta Pi. Polit. & Govt. Pos: Mem, Co. Rep. Cmt, Maine, 64-; del, Young Rep. Conv, 65 and del. and mem. platform cmt, 67; chmn, Maine Fedn. Young Rep, 66-67; mem, Second Cong. Dist. Rep. Cmt, 68-69; Maine State Rep, 69- Bus. & Prof. Pos: Mgr, J.J. Newberry Co, 51-62; pres, Dyar's Northland Trading Center, Strong, 63- Mil. Serv: Entered as Sgt, Army Res, 55, released as Sgt, 57, after serv. in First Armored Div, Tex. and La. Mem: C. of C; Young Rep; Scottish and York Rites; Grange; Exten. Serv; Businessmen's Club; past master, AF&AM; high priest chap, Royal Arch Mason; past pres. and zone chmn, Lions Int; potentates ambassador, Shrine. Rel: Protestant. Mailing Add: Strong, Maine 04983.

DYBVIG, CLARENCE ADOLPH R
S.Dak. State Rep.
b. Colton, S.Dak, 6/3/19; s. Henry N. Dybvig and Agnes Sundal D; m. 6/15/41 to Ethel Sagmoe; c. Ronald Gene, Richard Allen and Trudy Ann. Educ: St. Olaf Col, 1 year; S.Dak. State Univ, 1 year. Polit. & Govt. Pos: Twp. supvr, Dell Rapids Twp, S.Dak, 51-69; S.Dak. State Rep, Minnehaha Co, 69- Bus. & Prof. Pos: Pres, Baltic Coop. Bldg. Supply, 59-66. Mem: S.Dak. Farm Bur; S.Dak. Crop Improv. Asn.(pres, 59-67); secy, Baltic Farmers Elevator Asn, 68-69. Master Pork Producer Award. Rel: Lutheran. Mailing Add: Route 1, Baltic, S.Dak. 57003.

DYBWAD, JEAN I. R
b. Larimore, N.Dak, 7/14/30; d. Jens Peter Mortensen and Lillie C. Rasmussen M; m. 7/24/48 to Alton O. Dybwad; c. David Bruce, Kaaron Llie and Phillip Stephen. Educ: Various univ. exten courses; Glacier Col, courses in creative writing and polit. sci, summer 66. Polit. & Govt. Pos: Mem, bd. of dirs, Flathead Co. Rep. Women, Mont, 62-63, legis. chmn, 64-; mem, Mont. State Rep. Cent. Cmt; v.chmn, Flathead Co. Rep. Cent. Cmt, 63-64, chmn, 64-68. Mem: Lutheran Women's Mission League; VFW; Toastmistress (Speak Off Dist. winner, 2 consecutive years). Rel: Lutheran; Missouri Synod. Mailing Add: 583 Second Ave. W.N, Kalispell, Mont. 59901. (1967)

DYE, GEORGE W. R
Educ: Ind. Univ. Sch. of Bus. Polit. & Govt. Pos: Ind. State Sen, 63-66, mem, agr, co. and twp, elec, finance, labor, pub. health and roads cmts. Bus. & Prof. Pos: Farmer. Mem: South. Ind, Inc; Mason; Eastern Star (past Grand Patron, 58-59); Scottish Rite; Murat Shrine; Lions. Rel: Methodist. Mailing Add: R.R. 3, Shoals, Ind. 47581.

DYE, ROBERT FLOYD R
Mont. State Rep.
b. Roundup, Mont, 10/30/21; s. Floyd L. Dye and Francis Hall D; m. 2/12/47 to Mary Katherine E. Reif; c. Gregory Kent. Educ: Local schs, grad, 39. Polit. & Govt. Pos: Mont. State Rep, 65-, chmn, Capitol Bldg. Cmt, Mont. House of Rep, 67-69, chmn, Mont. Hwy. Ushers Conf, 68-69, chmn, Hwy. Cmt, 69 and mem, Hwy. Interim Cmt, 69- Bus. & Prof. Pos: Rep. for Pontiac, Oldsmobile and GMC Truck Dealers in dealer coun. meetings with factory rep, past 10 years. Mil. Serv: Entered as Pvt, Army, 40, released as T/Sgt, 45, after serv. in 41st Inf. Div, Pac. Theatre, 42-45; Purple Heart with Cluster; Distinguished unit Citation; Combat Inf. Badge; Pac. and Am. Theatre Ribbons. Mem: Pres, 41st Nat. Inf. Div. Asn, 66; Am. Legion; Elks; Mason; Shrine; C. of C,(mem. bd. of dirs, Bozeman Chap, 58). Rel: Episcopal. Mailing Add: 610 S. Willson, Bozeman, Mont. 59715.

DYELL, MARY LAVERNE R
Secy, 1st Cong. Dist. Women's Rep. Club, Mich.
b. Chicago, Ill, 1/2/23; d. Arthur Crowley Fenton (deceased) and Mollie Frederich F.(deceased); m. 11/1/47 to Donald David Dyell; c. Jeffrey Donald, Jennifer Diane and Jonathon Douglas. Educ: Lawrence Col, B.A, 44; Pi Beta Phi. Polit. & Govt. Pos: Precinct del, 60-64; secy-treas, Stockmeyer for Secy. of State Cmt, 62; secy, 13th Cong. Dist. Rep. Cmt, 62-64; alternate del, Rep. Nat. Conv, 64; campaign dir, First Cong. Dist. Milliken for Lt. Gov. Cmt, 64; secy, First Cong. Dist. Women's Rep. Club, 65-; asst. secy, Wayne Co. Rep. Educ. Coun, Mich, 66- Bus. & Prof. Pos: Secy, Russell Elec. Co, Chicago, Ill, 44-47; secy, Atkinson & Jones Construction Co, Okinawa, 47; secy, Gen. Motors Corp, 48-49; secy, Tri-Co. Realty, Inc, 54-63; secy, Campbell-Ewald, Detroit, Mich, 63- Mem: Mem, Light Guard Womens Auxiliary, Detroit, 56-60, pres, 59-60 and treas, 56-58; Cub Scout Den Mother, Detroit, 59; Women's Club, Lewistown, Mont, 49-52; chmn, World Affairs Cmt, 49-51 and pres, 51-52; pres, Jayceens, Lewistown, Mont, 50-52. Rel: Presbyterian. Mailing Add: 440 W. Robinwood Ave, Detroit, Mich. 48203. (1967)

DYER, DONALD J. R
Chmn, Rep. Town Cmt, Townsend, Mass.
b. Greenfield, Mass, 8/16/34; s. Charles H. Dyer, Sr. and Valentine R. Papillon D; single. Educ: Nichols Jr. Col, Dudley, Mass, A.B.A, 54. Polit. & Govt. Pos: Chmn, Volpe for Gov. Cmt, Mass, 60, 62 & 64; mem, Planning Bd. and Zoning Adv. Cmt, Townsend, Mass, 60-65, chmn. and finance chmn, Rep. Town Cmt, 62-, mem, Bd. Assessors, 65-, chmn, Bd. Water Comnrs, 67- and mem, Bd. Selectmen, 69-; del, Mass. Rep. State Conv, 62 & 64. Bus. & Prof. Pos: Eng. dept. head, Sprague & Carleton Co, Milford, N.H, 58-62; mgr, Merrivale Mfg. Inc, Nashua, 62-68; off. and personnel mgr, United-Alcon Inc, Townsend, Mass, 68- Mil. Serv: Entered as Pvt, Army, 57, released as Specialist, 59. Rel: Roman Catholic. Mailing Add: 8 Bow St, Box 441, Townsend, Mass. 01469.

DYER, LOUISE SEEBURGER R
b. Des Moines, Iowa, 10/7/19; d. Vernon Raymond Seeburger and Merze Marvin S; m. 9/19/45 to Robert Wayne Dyer; c. Ray, George, Charles and Susan. Educ: Univ. Iowa, B.Sc, 41; Beta Gamma Sigma; Mortar Bd; Pi Gamma Mu; Kappa Alpha Theta. Polit. & Govt. Pos: Mem, bd. of educ, San Diego Unified Sch. Dist, Calif, 65-68, pres, 68-69. Bus. & Prof. Pos: Del, Coun. of Big Cities, Nat. Sch. Bds. Asn, 67-; mem. del. assembly, Calif. Sch. Bds. Asn, 67-, mem. sch. personnel cmt, 69- Mem: Am. Asn. Univ. Women; Women's Div, San Diego Co. Chap, Freedoms Found. at Valley Forge; hon. alumni, Univ. Calif, San Diego; San Diego Hist. Soc; spec. gifts cmt, San Diego Pub. Libr; Women's Auxiliary, San Diego Symphony. Named San Diego Woman of Valour, 66. Rel: Lutheran. Mailing Add: 3412 Browning St, San Diego, Calif. 92106.

DYER, MARGARET LOUISE R
Mem, Md. Rep. State Cent. Cmt.
b. Baltimore, Md, 5/15/14; d. Walter Parker (deceased) and Sadie Conquest P; m. 9/17/30 to Martin Dyer; c. Martin Appell and Alma Mae (Mrs. Lawson). Educ: Course on polit. behavior, Morgan State Col, 64-65. Polit. & Govt. Pos: Clerk, Baltimore Bd. Supvrs. Elec, Md, 66-69; ward exec, 19th Rep. Dist. Party, 66; del, Rep. Nat. Conv, 68; mem, Baltimore Rep. Cmt. and Md. Rep. State Cent. Cmt, currently. Mem: Elks; Eastern Star (officer); NAACP (secy. exec. bd. Baltimore Br); Rep. Women's Club Baltimore; Urban League Baltimore Br. Trophy for outstanding work done during voter registrn. drive, NAACP, 57; Plaque for participation in voter educ-registrn. drive, Afro-Am. News Papers, 64. Rel: Baptist. Mailing Add: 1742 E. Oliver St, Baltimore, Md. 21213.

DYER, MRS. ROBERT C. 'GIDDY' R
Ill. State Rep.
b. Atlanta, Ga, 5/28/19; d. Edward Jones Erwin and Mary Louisa Browne E; m. 10/12/40 to Robert Campbell Dyer; c. C. Robert C. and Wynn. Educ: Agnes Scott Col, A.B, 38. Polit. & Govt. Pos: Pres, Western Springs League Women Voters, Ill, 55-56; pres, Du Page Co. Rep. Workshops, 57-58; Legis. chmn, PTA Coun, Hinsdale, 58; state bd. mem, Ill. Rep. Workshops, 58-60; nat. bd. mem, Nat. Coun. Rep. Workshops, 60-61; Rep. precinct committeeman, 62-69; asst. supvr, Downers Grove Twp, 61-68; mem, Du Page Co. Bd. Supvrs, 61-68; Ill. State Rep, 38th Dist, 68- Mailing Add: 441 E. Third St, Hinsdale, Ill. 60521.

DYER, ROSS WATKINS D
Chief Justice, Tenn. Supreme Court
b. Halls, Tenn, 3/10/11; s. Clarence Watkins Dyer and Zona Smith D; m. 11/1/38 to Agnes Rebecca Moss; c. Thomas Ross. Educ: Univ. of Tenn, 29-30; Cumberland Univ, 30-31; YMCA Law Sch, LL.B, 37; Phi Delta Phi. Polit. & Govt. Pos: Mayor, Halls, Tenn, 46-48; mem, Limited Tenn. Constitutional Conv, 53; Tenn. State Sen, 57-59; exec. asst. to Gov. of Tenn, 59-61; assoc. justice, Tenn. Supreme Court, 61-69, Chief Justice, 69- Mil. Serv: Entered as Pvt, Army, 43, released as 1st Lt, 46, after serv. in Third Army, ETO, 44-46. Mem: Mason; Am. Legion. Rel: Methodist. Mailing Add: Halls, Tenn. 38040.

DYKEMAN, CALVIN CARROLL R
R.I. State Sen.
b. New Orleans, La, 9/22/25; s. Valentine Fitzgerald Dykeman and Mary Elmena Tresky D; m. 5/23/46 to Eleanor Frances Pavao; c. Eileen Mary and Thomas Calvin and Christopher Carl. Educ: Univ. Calif, 1 year; Univ. R.I, 2 years. Polit. & Govt. Pos: Third Ward committeeman, East Providence Rep. City Cmt, 66-; R.I. State Sen, 43rd Dist, 67- Bus. & Prof. Pos: Pres, Dykeman Elec. Co, E. Providence, R,I, 49- Mil. Serv: Entered as Able Seaman, Navy, 43, released as Electrician Mate 1/C, 46, after serv. in U.S.S. Putnan, S.Pac. Theatre, 44-45; Asiatic Pac. Theatre Medal with 3 Bronze Stars; Am. Area Medal; World War II Victory Medal. Mem: R.I. Elec. Contractors Asn.(pres, 56-60); Elks; Am. Legion; C. of C; R.I. Col. Asn. Rel: Catholic. Mailing Add: 50 Plymouth Rd, East Providence, R.I. 02914.

DYKES, WINGATE D
Chmn, Sumter Co. Dem. Exec. Cmt, Ga.
b. Americus, Ga, 12/3/15; s. William W. Dykes and Agnes Hawkins D; m. 5/10/69 to Mary Burke; c. Frances (Mrs. Carnes); Marsha (Mrs. Nelson) and Sara Lynn. Educ: Lumpkin Law Sch, Univ. Ga, LL.B, 38; Phi Delta Theta. Polit. & Govt. Pos: Chmn, Sumter Co. Dem. Exec. Cmt, Ga, 48-; cmnr, Franklin Roosevelt Warm Springs Mem. Cmn, 50-; solicitor gen, Southwest. Judicial Circuit, 51-52; del, Dem. Nat. Conv, 56; v.chmn, Ga. Ports Authority, 56-60; secy, Third Dist. Dem. Cong. Cmt, 64-; mayor protem, Sumter Co, Ga. Bus. & Prof. Pos: Attorney, Dykes & Dykes, 38-; pres, Bainbridge TV Cable, Ga, 67- Mil. Serv: Entered as 1st Lt, Air Force, 43, released as 2nd Lt, 45, after serv. in Tactical Center. Mem: Charter mem, World Peace Through Law Center; Ga. Gar Asn.(bd. gov, 11 years); Am. Judicature Soc; Am. Bar Asn.(house del, 4 years); fel, Int. Acad. Law & Sci; Rotary (pres); Americus Country Club; Shrine; Ponte Vedra Country Club Fla; Doublegate Country Club, Ga; Atlanta Athletic Club; East Lake Country Club; Lanier Yacht Club; Americus Sumter Co. C. of C.(pres). Rel: Methodist. Mailing Add: 925 11th Ave, Albany, Ga. 31705.

DYMALLY, MERVYN M. D
Calif. State Sen.
b. Trinidad, W.I, 5/12/26; s. Hamid Dymally and Andreid Richardson D; m. to Alice Gueno; c. Mark and Lynn. Educ: Calif. State Col. Los Angeles, B.A, 54; Sacramento State Col, M.A, 69; Kappa Alpha Psi. Polit. & Govt. Pos: V.chmn, Youth for Kennedy, 60; state treas, Calif. Fedn. of Young Dem, 60-61; mem, Dem. State Cent. Cmt, Calif, 62-; Calif. State Assemblyman, 53rd Dist, 63-66, chmn, Assembly Cmt. on Indust. Rels, 65-66; Calif. State Sen, 29th Dist, 67-, chmn, Senate Cmt. on Soc. Welfare, 68; del, Dem. Nat. Conv, 68. Bus. & Prof. Pos: Fel, Metrop. Appl. Research Center, 67-; co-chmn, Nat. Conf. of Black Elec. Off, 67-; pres, Urban Affairs Inst, 67-; lectr. polit. sci, Univ. Calif, Davis, 69-; lectr. govt. and educ, Claremont Cols, 69- Publ: 'Civil Rights and the War in Viet Nam,' Urban West, 10/67; 'Power, Politics and Black People,' Breakthrough, 3/69; ed, 'Black Politician,' 6/69. Mem: Am. Acad. of Polit. & Soc. Sci; Calif. Adv. Cmt. to U.S. Civil Rights Cmn; Nat. Soc. of State Legislators; Nat. Cmt. Against Discrimination in Housing; NAACP; Urban League; PTA; Mason; Elks. Am. specialist to U.S. Dept. of State, E. and Cent. Africa, 64, Caribbean and Guyana, 65. Rel: Episcopal. Legal Res: 217 W. First St, Los Angeles, Calif. 90012. Mailing Add: State Capitol, Sacramento, Calif. 95814.

DYSON, JOHN STUART D
b. Washington, D.C, 3/7/43; s. Charles H. Dyson and Margaret MacGregor D; single. Educ: Cornell Univ, B.S, 65; Woodrow Wilson Sch. Pub. & Int. Affairs, M.P.A, 67; Phi Eta Sigma; Phi Kappa Phi; Alpha Delta Phi. Polit. & Govt. Pos: Legis. asst. to J.Y. Resnick, N.Y, 66-68; campaign mgr, Robert Fouhy, Dutchess Co. Exec. Cand, 67; cand, U.S. House Rep, 28th Cong. Dist, 68; chmn. rural affairs task force, adv. coun. commun. and pub. affairs, N.Y. State Dem. Cmt, 69. Bus. & Prof. Pos: V.pres, The Dyson Found, 66-; publisher, Millbrook Round Table, 68-; pres, Dymer Commun, Millbrook, 68- Mil. Serv: Entered as 2nd Lt, Army Intel. Corps, 68- Publ: Our Historic Hudson, James B. Adler, 68. Mem: Wilderness Soc; Nat. Trust for Hist. Preservation; local and co. hist. socs; Am. Acad. Polit. Sci; Adv. Coun, Wash. Planning Bd; Mid-Hudson Pattern for Progress; Asn. Am. Indian Affairs; Progress in Poughkeepsie; NAACP. Rel: Presbyterian. Mailing Add: Spring Hill Farm, Millbrook, N.Y. 12545.

DZENDZEL, RAYMOND D. D
Mich. State Sen.
b. Port Clinton, Ohio, 7/29/21; s. John Dzendzel and Georgianna D; m. 1947 to Eleanor Borland; c. Sandra Kaye, Judith Ann, Cheryl Lynn and Lee Ann. Educ: Detroit Inst. of Tech, B.A, 51. Polit. & Govt. Pos: Mem, 17th Dist. Dem. Club, Mich; Mich. State Rep, 54-56; Mich. State Sen, 58-, Minority Leader, 62, 67 & 68, Majority Leader, 64-66, asst. Minority Leader, 69-, chmn, Legis. Coun, 69- Bus. & Prof. Pos: Bus. rep, Carpenter's Local 982. Mil. Serv: Coast Guard, 42-46. Mem: Mason; VFW; Wolverine Post 171; AFL Local 982; Shrine; Redford Lions Club; past pres. Brightmoore Commun. Center; Detroit Commandery 1, K. T; Moose. Rel: Episcopal. Mailing Add: 18501 Shiawassee, Detroit, Mich. 48219.

DZIALO, RAYMOND JOHN D
Conn. State Rep.
b. Middletown, Conn, 7/24/31; s. John Joseph Dzialo and Adela Berdysz D; m. 6/17/61 to Irene Biernacki. Educ: Quinnipiac Col, B.S, 57. Polit. & Govt. Pos: Conn. State Rep, Middletown, 58-; admin. asst. to U.S. Rep. Frank Kowalski, 59-61; pres, Pulaski Dem. Club, 59-; mem, Middletown Dem. Town Cmt, 60-; admin. asst. to mayor, Middletown, 65- Bus. & Prof. Pos: Owner, Dzialo Ins. Agency, Conn, 62- Mil. Serv: Entered as Pvt, Army, 52, released as 2nd Lt, 54; Capt, 169th Inf, Army Res, currently; Good Conduct and Korean Serv. Medals; UN Serv. Ribbon. Mem: Am. Legion; VFW; Polish Falcons of Am; Eagles; Lions. Distinguished Serv. Award, Middletown Jaycees, 64. Rel: Catholic. Mailing Add: Lisa Lane, Middletown, Conn. 06457. (1967)

DZIVI, RICHARD D
Mont. State Sen.
b. Kalispell, Mont, 2/19/36; s. Joseph Dzivi and Margaret Lawless D; m. 8/27/53 to Beverly Nelson; c. Pamela, Kathryn and Bartly. Educ: Univ. Mont, B.S, 59, LL.B, 60. Polit. & Govt. Pos: Del, Mont. Dem. State Conv. and Dem. Nat. Conv, 64; co-chmn, Renne for Gov. Club, Mont, 64; precinct committeeman, Dem. Party, 64-; mem, Mont. State Rules Cmt, 65-67; Mont. State Sen, 67- Bus. & Prof. Pos: Assoc, Church, Harris, Johnson & Williams, 60-62; partner, Dzivi & Conklin, 62- Mem: Mont. and Cascade Co. Bar Asns; Am. and Mont. Trial Lawyers Asn; Int. Union of Operating Engrs; dir, N.Mont. Chap, Arthritis Found. All-Am. scholastic football team and hon. mention, 55. Rel: Presbyterian. Mailing Add: 2008 Fifth St, N.W, Great Falls, Mont. 59401.

E

EADS, EDNA C. R
Mo. State Rep.
b. Farmington, Mo, 8/8/13; d. Alfred Montgomery Burch and Minnie Dietzler B; m. 4/11/34 to Charles Paul Eads; c. Ronald Wayne, James David and Robert Eugene. Educ: Elvins High Sch; St. Louis Bus. Col. Polit. & Govt. Pos: Committeewoman and secy, Perry Twp. Rep. Cmt, 48-54; secy, Eighth Cong. Dist. Rep. Cmt, 50-54, Tenth Cong. Dist. Rep. Cmt, 62-; postmaster, Bonne Terre, 54-58; secy, Mo. State Rep. Cmt, 66-; Mo. State Rep, 66- Bus. & Prof. Pos: Real estate, 49- Mem: Bus. and Prfnl. Women's Club; Co. Heart Fund; Ment. Health; Cancer Soc; pres, Bonne Terre Centennial Corp. Rel: Congregational. Mailing Add: 112 Pine St, Bonne Terre, Mo. 63628.

EADS, FELIX 'BUCK' D
Chmn, Adair Co. Dem. Party, Okla.
b. Stilwell, Okla, 2/20/11; s. Fred Lewis Eads and Penelope Ross E; m. 9/24/32 to Jewell Worley; c. Patsy Lynn (Mrs. W. Neil Morton) and James Louis. Educ: Northeast. State Col, M.A, 58. Polit. & Govt. Pos: Chmn, Adair Co. Dem. Party, 60-; del, Dem. Nat. Conv, 68. Bus. & Prof. Pos: Prin, Bell Sch, Stilwell, 33- Mem: Okla. Educ. Asn. Rel: Baptist. Legal Res: Route 1, Stilwell, Okla. 74960. Mailing Add: Box 602, Stilwell, Okla. 74960.

EAGAN, JAMES JOSEPH
Mayor, Florissant, Mo.
b. St. Louis, Mo, 3/4/26; s. Patrick Eagan and Marguerite Franey E; m. 1/31/48 to Frances May Regan; c. Kathleen, J. Regan, Kevin, Margaret, Patrick, Michael, Mary Frances and Timothy. Educ: St. Louis Univ, LL.B, 54. Polit. & Govt. Pos: Trustee, Woodson Terr, Mo, 54-55; prosecuting attorney, Florissant, 54-58, city attorney, 57-58 and mayor, 63-; village attorney, Hazelwood, 57-58; Judge, St. Louis,Co, 58-63. Mil. Serv: Yeoman 2/C, Navy, 44-46. Rel: Catholic. Mailing Add: 1620 Jodphur, Florissant, Mo. 63033.

EAGER, HENRY L. D
b. Harlan, Ky, 1/6/04; s. George A. Eager and Lizzie Howard E; m. 7/21/24 to Mary Jane Armstrong; c. Murph H; two granddaughters. Educ: N.Mex. Mil. Inst; Los Angeles Bus. Col. Govt. & Polit. Pos: N.Mex. State Sen, 36-38, 44-56 and 64-67; N.Mex. State Corp. Cmnr, 38-44; v.chmn, N.Mex. Econ. Develop. Cmn, 49-53. Bus. & Prof. Pos: Chmn. bd, Game Protective Asn, 64- and Quay Co. Bd. on Poverty Prog, 65-; v.pres, N.Mex. Realtors Asn, 66- Mem: Elks; N.Mex. Real Estate Asn; Cattle Growers Asn. N.Mex; C. of C; Nat. Asn. of Real Estate Bds; Tucumcari Country Club; Revelers. Basketball, football, boxing, state recognition. Rel: Methodist. Legal Res: 1923 S. Third St, Tucumcari, N.Mex. 88401. Mailing Add: Box 762, Tucumcari, N.Mex. 88401.

EAGLE, HAROLD BENTLEY R
Mayor, Hinton, W.Va.
b. Hinton, W.Va, 7/22/14; s. Edward Calvin Eagle and Mary Baker E; m. 1/25/40 to Doris Ethel Loomis; c. Harold Bradley. Educ: W.Va. Univ, A.B, and LL.B; Sigma Phi Epsilon. Polit. & Govt. Pos: W.Va. State Del, 46-48; Mayor, Hinton, 53-61 & 65-; alternate del, Rep. Nat. Conv, 68. Bus. & Prof. Pos: Pres, Summers Co. Bar Asn, 62-65. Mil. Serv: Entered as 1st Lt, Army, 41, released as Lt. Col, 52, after serv. in 8th Army, Korea; Col. Army Res, 61-66; Am, Japanese and Korean Theater Ribbons; Bronze Star;

Combat Inf. Badge; S.Korean and Am. Presidential Unit Citations. Mem: Past comdr, Am. Legion Post 6; Past Exalted Ruler, Elks Lodge 821; past pres, Kiwanis Club of Hinton; VFW; Moose. Mailing Add: City Hall, Hinton, W.Va. 25951.

EAGLES, ALOHA TAYLOR R
N.Dak. State Rep.
b. Duluth, Minn, 11/8/16; d. Edward R. Browne and Belle Taylor B; m. 8/9/39 to Donald Emmitt Eagles; c. Donald Taylor and Keehn Emmitt. Educ: Univ. Minn, 34-35; Hibbing Jr. Col, grad, 36; Va. Jr. Col, 36-37. Polit. & Govt. Pos: Secy. exec. cmt, S.E. Region Commun. Action Prog, N.Dak, 65-69; N.Dak. State Rep, 66- Mem: Local pres. and dir. local and state bd, League of Women Voters; Shrine Auxiliary; Ment. Health Auxiliary; Voc. Rehabilitation Auxiliary; secy, Fargo Moorhead Symphony; Bd. of Church Women United; PEO; Round Table. Rel: Presbyterian. Mailing Add: 1745 S. Eighth, Fargo, N.Dak. 58102.

EAGLES, JOSEPH ELLIOTT D
N.C. State Rep.
b. Crisp, N.C, 1/6/10; s. Benjamin F. Eagles, Sr. and Susan R. Pitt E; m. 1/1/35 to Mary Scott McLean; c. Joseph E, Jr. and Jacqueline (Mrs. Rand). Educ: Augusta Mil. Acad, Ft. Defiance, Va, 28-29; Duke Univ, 29-30. Polit. & Govt. Pos: Mem, S.Edgecombe Sch. Cmt, 18 years; mem. speakers bur, Gov. Traffic Safety Coun; N.C. State Rep, 61-; Edgecombe Co. Draft Bd. Bus. & Prof. Pos: Merchant and farmer; mem, bd. of dir, Edgecombe Bank & Trust Co, Tarboro, N.C; bd. of dir, Merchants & Farmers Bank, Macclesfield, N.C; v.pres. and mem, bd. of dir, Edgecombe Mutual Fire Ins. Asn; bd. of dir, Halifax Co. Mutual Fire Ins. Co. Mem: Crisp Ruritan Club; Farm Bur; pres, Tarboro Rotary Club, 40-41; Nat. Coun. Jr. United Am. Mech; bd. of trustees, Edgecombe Mem. Libr; bd. of trustees, Chowan Col; bd. of trustees, Baptist Home for the Aged, Hamilton, N.C; exec. bd. of E.Carolina Coun, 56-58; exec. bd, region 6, Boy Scouts. Awarded Silver Compass, E.Carolina Coun, Boy Scouts, 53; Silver Beaver, 52; Order of Arrow, 51. Rel: Baptist; Eagles Baptist Missionary Church; bd. of deacons, 54-65, chmn, 55-62; chmn. bd. of trustees, 54-64; supt, Sunday Sch, 55-60; former moderator, S.Roanoke Baptist Asn. Mailing Add: Crisp Rural Station, Macclesfield, N.C. 27852. (1967)

EAGLETON, RICHARD ERNEST D
b. Peoria, Ill, 6/29/30; s. William Lester Eagleton and Mary Louise Chandler E; m. 1/31/53 to Elizabeth Louise Waterman; c. David Pierce and Margaret Waters. Educ: Yale Univ, B.A, 52; Univ. Ill, LL.B, 58. Polit. & Govt. Pos: Asst. U.S. Attorney, Ill, 61-63; Dem. Cand. Circuit Judge, Ill, 63; U.S. Attorney, Ill, 65-69. Bus. & Prof. Pos: Lawyer; dir, S. Side Trust and Savings Bank; bd. dirs, Peoria Ment. Health Clin, 59-65; proj. dir, spec. proj. on crime prevention and control, Am. Bar Asn, 69- Mil. Serv: Naval Res, 52-55. Mem: Am, Ill. and Peoria Co. Bar Asns; Phi Gamma Delta, Phi Delta Phi; Mason. Rel: Baptist. Legal Res: 1610 W. Moss Ave, Peoria, Ill. 61606. Mailing Add: American Bar Center, 1155 60th St, Chicago, Ill. 60637.

EAGLETON, THOMAS F. D
U.S. Sen, Mo.
b. St. Louis, Mo, 9/4/29; s. Mark D. Eagleton and Zitta Swanson E; m. 1/21/56 to Barbara Ann Smith; c. Terence and Christin. Educ: Amherst Col, A.B; Harvard Law Sch, LL.B. Hon. J.D, Suffolk Univ, Boston, 58. Polit. & Govt. Pos: Circuit attorney, St. Louis, Mo, 56; Attorney Gen, Mo, 60, Lt. Gov, 64-68; U.S. Sen, Mo, 69- Mil. Serv: Navy, 48-49. Mem: Pres, Mo. Prosecuting Attorneys Asn; mem. bd. dir, Nat. Dist. Attorneys Asn; elected mem. bd. dir, Nat. Asn. of Attorney Gen, 63. Furtherance of Justice Award from Nat. Dist. Attorneys Asn, 57; Civil Liberties Award, St. Louis Civil Liberties Cmt, 60; Distinguished Serv. Award, St. Louis Jr. C. of C, 61; Distinguished Serv. Award, Clayton Jr. C. of C, 62; Civic Award, Alpha Kappa Psi of St. Louis Univ. Sch. of Commerce and Finance; recognized by Life Mag. as One of Top 100 Young Leaders in the U.S; nominated by St. Louis Jr. C. of C. as One of the Country's Ten Outstanding Young Men; Bicentennial Award of Pub. Serv, St. Louis Bar Asn, 64. Mailing Add: Senate Office Bldg, Wash, D.C. 20510.

EAKINS, ARNOLD GEORGE R
b. Lyndon Sta, Wis, 10/18/13; s. Irwin Truell Eakins and Mary Gunderman E; m. 4/21/43 to Genevieve Annette Mohns; c. John T. and twins, Richard R. and Douglas B. Educ: Marquette Univ, Pre-Dent, 30-32. Polit. & Govt. Pos: Rwy. Mail Serv, 46; city alderman, New Lisbon, Wis, 57-59; Rep. precinct chmn, 59-63; chmn, Juneau Co. Rep. Orgn, Wis, 63-69. Bus. & Prof. Pos: Gen. mgr, Eakins Garage, 35-42; owner, Eakins' Motors, 47- Mil. Serv: Entered as Pvt, Army, 42, released as Maj, 52, Res. Unit Comdr, 46-50, Aberdeen Proving Ground Sch, 50-52. Mem: Mason; Consistory; Shrine. Rel: Protestant. Legal Res: 516 W. Liberty St, New Lisbon, Wis. 53950. Mailing Add: 405 State St, New Lisbon, Wis. 53950.

EARDLEY, JAMES GARFIELD R
First V.Chmn, Mahoning Co. Rep. Cent. and Exec. Cmts, Ohio
b. Kittanning, Pa, 11/12/92; s. Samuel Lawrence Eardley and Dillie Margaret Snyder E; m. 7/19/22 to Ruth Miriam Hall; c. Charlotte Hall. Educ: Mt. Union Col, 09-10. Polit. & Govt. Pos: Village treas, Sebring, Ohio, 16-20, village clerk, 22-26; mem, Mohaning Co. Rep. Exec. Cmt, 30-; first v.chmn, Mahoning Co. Rep. Cent. and Exec. Cmts, 35-; chmn, Mohoning Co. Bd. of Elec, 40-44; del, Rep. Nat. Conv, 56, 60 & 64; mem, State Platform Cmt, 60 & 62. Bus. & Prof. Pos: V.pres. and dir, Midland-Buckeye Fed. Savings and Loan Asn, 28-; pres. and trustee, Grandview Cemetery Asn, 35-; trustee, Citizens Hosp. Asn, Alliance, Ohio, 50-; pres. and dir, Alliance Auto Club, 50-; dir, Alliance First Nat. Bank, 51- Mil. Serv: Entered as Pvt, Army, 17, released as 2nd Lt, 19, after serv. in 158th Depot Brigade and Second Inf. Replacement Regt. Mem: Mason; Am. Legion. Rel: Methodist. Mailing Add: 1425 Glenking Lane, Alliance, Ohio 44601.

EARLE, LEWIS SAMUEL R
Fla. State Rep.
b. Gibbstown, N.J, 8/22/33; s. Lewis Reade Earle and Alice Freas Richie E; m. 5/24/52 to Marilyn Jean Moore; c. Eric Dwight and Lewis Reade. Educ: St. Petersburg Jr. Col, Fla, A.A, 53; Univ. Fla, 53-54; Emory Univ, D.D.S, 58; Omicron Kappa Upsilon; Psi Omega. Polit. & Govt. Pos: Mem, Orange Co. Rep. Exec. Cmt, Fla, 62-, finance chmn, 66-67; bd. mem, Orange Co. Econ. Opportunity, Inc, 67-69; Fla. State Rep, 43rd Dist, Orange and Seminole Co, 68- Bus. & Prof. Pos: Lab. aide, Fed. Bur. Invest, 51-52; partner, Earle Elec. Co, 53-58; lab. research asst, Emory Univ, 56-58; self employed dentist, 61- Mil. Serv: Entered as Ens, Naval Res, 58, released as Lt, 61, after serv. in Fleet Air Serv. Squadron 51 and Sanford Naval Air Sta, Fla, Comdr, Naval Res, 61-69; Award of Merit, Mil. Order of The World Wars. Mem: Orange Co. Dent. Soc; Fla. and Am. Dent. Asns; Int. Asn. for Dent. Research; Am. Asn. for Adv. Sci; Rotary; C. of C; Audubon Soc; Young Rep; Mason; Reserve Officers Asn. Univ. Scholarship Awards; Award of Excellence, Am. Security Coun. Rel: Methodist. Legal Res: 630 S. Lake Sybelia Dr, Maitland, Fla. 32751. Mailing Add: 255 N. Lakemont Ave, Winter Park, Fla. 32789.

EARLE, RALPH LOUIS, SR. R
Conn. State Rep.
b. Columbus, Ohio, 8/21/23; s. William Jones Earle and Elizabeth Lutes E; m. 1/19/50 to Polly Content Mansfield; c. Peter Mansfield, Pamela Roberts, Christopher John and Ralph Louis, Jr. Polit. & Govt. Pos: Mem, Park Cmn, North Haven, Conn, 57, Cmn. Revise Elec. Laws, 61, North Haven Rep. Town Cmt, 63, Finance Adv. Cmt, 65, Rep. Party Platform Cmt, 68 and Gov. Econ. Cabinet, 69; Conn. State Rep, 99th Dist, 58-, asst. minority leader, Conn. House of Rep, 69- Mil. Serv: Entered as Pvt, Army, 43, released, 45, after serv. in ETO, 43-45. Mem: Trustee, Conn. Educ. TV; dir, New Haven Br, Am. Red Cross; Rotary; North Haven Grange; North Haven Hist. Soc. Rel: Episcopal. Mailing Add: 101 Mansfield Rd, North Haven, Conn. 06473.

EARLEY, ROBERT EMMETT D
Mem, N.H. State Dem. Cmt.
b. Nashua, N.H, 7/3/96; s. John M. Earley and Nellie Harrington E; m. 6/21/38 to Evelyn C. Blankenberg; c. Robert E, Jr. and Eleanor B.(Mrs. McGinn). Educ: Harvard Col; Boston Univ, LL.B, 24; pres, Boston Univ. grad. class of 24. Polit. & Govt. Pos: N.H. State Rep, 20-21; chmn, Dem. City Cmt, Nashua, 23; solicitor, Nashua, 28-32; del, Dem. Nat. Conv, 32, 44, 48 & 62 and chmn, 44; attorney, Fed. Home Loan Asn, 36; chmn, N.H. State Dem. Cmt, 40-44, mem, currently. Bus. & Prof. Pos: Mem, N.H. Judicial Coun. and New Eng. Law Inst, 47- Mil. Serv: Seaman, Navy, 17-21. Mem: Pres, N.H. Bar Asn, 52-53; Am. Bar Asn; Elks; comdr, Am. Legion, James E. Coffey Post 3, 26; Nashua Country Club. Rel: Roman Catholic. Mailing Add: 5 Lincoln Ave, Nashua, N.H. 03060.

EARLEY, ROBERT GRAY R
b. Enumclaw, Wash, 3/26/21; s. Roy Thomas Earley and Flora P. Gray E; m. 3/1/42 to Barbara Jeanne Kramer; c. Steven R. (deceased), Shannon Fisher and Eileen Hemstreet. Educ: Stadium High Sch, Tacoma, Wash. Polit. & Govt. Pos: Wash. State Rep, 61-64; committeeman, Rep. State Cmt, Wash, 63-65; chmn, Wash. Horse Racing Cmn, 65-; pres, Tacoma Port Cmn, 67-; alternate del, Rep. Nat. Conv, 68. Bus. & Prof. Pos: Partner, Roy T. Earley Co, 47-58; pres, Earley Equip. Co, 54-68; pres, Earley Construction Co, 58- Mil. Serv: Entered as CM 2/C, Navy Res, 42, released as CM 1/C, 45, after serving in 21st Naval Construction Bn, Pac. Theatre, 42-45. Rel: Episcopal. Mailing Add: 4908 Harbor View Dr, Tacoma, Wash. 98422.

EARLY, JACK JONES R
b. Corbin, Ky, 4/12/25; s. Joseph Maynor Early and Lela May Jones E; m. 6/1/52 to Nancye Whaley; c. Lela, Judith and Laura. Educ: Union Col, B.A, 48; Univ. Ky, M.A, 53, Ed.D, 56; Lexington Theol. Sem, B.D, 56; Sigma Phi Epsilon. Polit. & Govt. Pos: V.pres, Young Rep. Clubs of Ky, 49-50; v.pres, Lincoln Rep. Club, 50-51; mem, speakers bur, Eisenhower-Nixon Campaign, 52; Ky. State Rep, 52-54, asst. minority leader, Ky. House of Rep; del, Rep. Nat. Conv, 68; chmn, S.Dak. United Citizens for Nixon Campaign, 68. Bus. & Prof. Pos: Methodist minister, Ky. and Tenn, 42-52; teacher Eng. and speech, Hindman High Sch, Ky, 48-51; dean of men, Hindman Settlement Sch, 48-51; assoc. minister and dir. educ, Park Methodist Church, Lexington, 52-54; interim minister, 56; asst. to the pres, dean of faculty and prof. educ. and psychol, Athens Col, 54-55; religious news commentator, WLAP, Lexington, Ky, 55-56; instr, grad. sch, Univ. Ky, summer, 56; v.pres, dean and prof. educ. and psychol, Iowa Wesleyan Col, 56-58; pres, Dakota Wesleyan Univ, 58-69; pres, Pfeiffer Col, 69- Publ: Luther as Educator; Religious Practices in the Public Schools in Selected Communities in Kentucky. Mem: Past pres, Upper Ky. River Educ. Asn; past v.pres, classroom teachers and rep, planning bd, Ky. Educ. Asn; Nat. Educ. Asn; Asn. of Higher Educ; legis. cmn. and chmn, cmt. on pub. rels, S.Dak. Educ. Asn; Asn. for Student Teaching; pres, S.Dak. Found. of Pvt. Cols, 60-62; pres, S.Dak. Asn. of Cols. and Univs, 62-64; Mason (32°), grand orator, Grand Lodge of S.Dak, 63-64; instnl. rep, Boy Scouts (chmn, Ree Dist, 63-64); del, Gen. Conf. of the Methodist Church, Pittsburgh, Pa, 64; del, N.Cent. Jurisdictional Conf, Cleveland, Ohio, 64; pres, S.Dak. Asn. of Church-Related Cols, 65-; cmnr, N.Cent. Asn. of Cols. and Secondary Schs. Cmn. on Cols. and Univs, 66-; former chaplain, Ky. Mt. Club; Univ. Ky. and Union Col. Alumni Asns; Mitchell C. of C.(former mem, bd. dir. and v.pres); Rotary, fel. cmt, Rotary Found; YMCA (bd. dir); S.Dak. Conf, Methodist Church; Jr. C. of C.(former mem, bd. dir. and v.pres); Hon. Order of Ky. Col; rep, Upper Midwest Research and Develop. Coun; Int. Platform Asn; Eng-Speaking Union; Pi Kappa Delta; Phi Delta Kappa; Kappa Delta Pi; Alpha Psi Omega; Pi Tau Chi; Theta Phi; Kappa Phi Kappa; Blue Key; Phi Kappa Phi; Sigma Tau Delta; bd, William L. Phillips Scholarships, Sigma Phi Epsilon; bd, Scottish Rite Fel. Cmt. Hon. Citizen of S.Dak; Citation for Distinguished Leadership in the Field of Educ, VFW, Ky, 50; South. Scholar, recipient of South. Fel. Fund Grant, 55-56; Spoke Award for Outstanding Commun. Serv, Mitchell Jr. C. of C, 59, Distinguished Serv. Award as the Young Man of the Year, 60; S.Dak. Distinguished Serv. Award for the Outstanding Young Man, S.Dak. Jr. C. of C, 60; O'Tucks Award for the Outstanding Former Kentuckian, 63; elected to the Univ. Ky. Hall of Fame by the Univ. Ky. Alumni Asn, 64; elected as an hon. Fel. of Wroxton Col, Eng. Rel: United Methodist. Mailing Add: Pfeiffer College, Misenheimer, N.C. 28109.

EARMAN, DON E. R
Va. State Del.
b. Harrisonburg, Va, 6/19/33; s. Carpenter B. Earman and Margaret Martz E; m. 9/11/55 to D. Jean Bowman; c. Don E, Jr, D. William, Daniel C, Debora A. and D. Kimberly. Educ: Col. William & Mary, A.B, 55; Univ. Va, LL.B, 57; Delta Theta Phi. Polit. & Govt. Pos: Del, Va. Rep. State Conv, 57, 61 & 65; chmn, Harrisonburg Rep. Cmt, 58-62; U.S. Cmnr, West. Dist. Va,

60-64; chmn, Rockingham Co. Rep. Cmt, 62-64; del, Rep. Nat. Conv, 64 & 68, mem. platform cmt, 68; Va. State Del, 65- Mem: Pres, Harrisonburg-Rockingham Co. Bar Asn, 65; Va. State Bar; Va. and Am. Trial Lawyers Asn; Am. Bar Asn; Harrisonburg Jaycees; Lions; Elks; Moose. Rel: Evangelical United Brethren. Legal Res: Rt. 1, Harrisonburg, Va. 22801. Mailing Add: 66 S. Court Square, Harrisonburg, Va. 22801.

EARNHARDT, WILEY J. P, JR. D
b. Elizabeth City, N.C, 8/27/31; s. Wiley J. P. Earnhardt and Carolina Virginia Miller E; m. 6/22/63 to Judy LaRue Horne. Educ: Duke Univ, B.A, 53, LL.B, 60; Beta Omega Sigma; Sophomore Hon. Soc; Sigma Chi. Polit. & Govt. Pos: Solicitor, Recorder's Court, Chowan Co, N.C, 62-65; N.C. State Rep, 65-67. Bus. & Prof. Pos: Secy-treas, First Dist. Bar Asn, 65-66. Mil. Serv: Entered as Ens, Navy, 53, released as Lt.(jg), 56; Comdr, Naval Res, 67; Navy Occup. Medal; Am. Defense Serv. Medal. Mem: Am. and N.C. Bar Asns; N.C. State Bar; Rotary Int; C. of C; Am. Legion. Rel: Episcopal. Legal Res: 107 Blount St, Edenton, N.C. 27932. Mailing Add: P.O. Box 445, Edenton, N.C. 27932.

EARNHART, MILT D
Ark. State Sen.
b. St. Louis, Mo, 4/1/18; s. Charles Stanley Earnhart and Anna Sullivan E; m. 6/19/43 to Mary Elizabeth Robben; c. Anne Cecile, Thomas P. and David M. Educ: High Sch. and Domestic and Serv. Schs. Polit. & Govt. Pos: Ark. State Rep, 59-66; Ark. State Sen, Fourth Sen. Dist, 66- Bus. & Prof. Pos: Sales mgr, Encyclop. Britannica, Cincinnati, Ohio, 49-50; v.pres, Armbruster & Co, Inc, 50- Mil. Serv: Entered as Pvt, Army, 42, released as Sgt, 45, after serv. in 3137 Sig. Mtr. Message Co, ETO; ETO, Battle of Bulge, Germany Campaign Ribbons; plus others. Mem: Lions; Am. Legion; VFW; K. of C; Elks; C. of C; Explorers; Boys Club; Quarterback Club. TV news personality, KFSA-TV Channel 5, Ft. Smith, Ark, 53- Rel: Catholic. Mailing Add: 2319 S. Greenwood Ave, Ft. Smith, Ark. 72901.

EARTHMAN, JIM R
Tex. State Rep.
b. Houston, Tex, 9/21/34; s. James Bradshaw Earthman and Blanche Bastien E; m. 11/24/56 to Dorothy Monroe; c. James B, IV, Dorothy Ann and William J. Educ: Univ. Tex, Austin, B.B.A, 56; Chi Phi. Polit. & Govt. Pos: Tex. State Rep, 69- Bus. & Prof. Pos: Pres, Resthaven Mem. Park, 69; v.pres, Earthman's Inc. and Mission Life Ins. Co, 69- Mem: C. of C; Jaycees; life mem, Houston Rodeo Asn; Sons of Confederate Veterans. Rel: Catholic. Mailing Add: 5936 Deerwood, Houston, Tex. 77027.

EASLEY, MACK D
N.Mex. State Sen.
b. Akins, Okla, 10/14/16; s. John Robert Easley and Mary Ellen Duggins E; m. 11/17/39 to Loyce Anna Rogers; c. June Elizabeth (Mrs. James T. Hudson, Jr.) and Roger. Educ: Northeast. State Col, 35-39; Univ. Okla, LL.B, 47; Order of the Coif; Sigma Tau Gamma. Polit. & Govt. Pos: Pres, League of Young Dem, Univ. Okla, 46-47; asst. dist. attorney, Lea Co, N.Mex, 49-50; N.Mex. State Rep, Lea Co, 51-52 & 55-62, speaker, N.Mex. House Rep, 59-60; chmn, Lea Co. Dem. Cent. Cmt, 56-64; chmn, Legis. Coun, 59; chmn, Dem. State Conv, 60; Lt. Gov, N.Mex, 63-66; N.Mex. State Sen, 67-, majority whip, N.Mex. State Senate, 69- Mil. Serv: Entered as Pvt, Army Air Corps, 41, released as S/Sgt, 46, after serv. in Cryptography Sch. and Army Airways Commun. Syst, Alaska and the Aleutian Islands. Mem: Lea Co. Bar Asn. (pres, 50); N.Mex. and Am. Bar Asns; Nat. Conf. Lt. Govs.(exec. cmt, 64-66); Nat. Coun. Better Schs; Am. Legion; VFW; Lions. Rel: Presbyterian. Mailing Add: 523 E. Yucca Dr, Hobbs, N.Mex. 88240.

EASLEY, MORRIS EWELL, SR. D
Chmn. of St. Helena Parish Dem. Cmt, La.
b. Easleyville, La, 4/3/01; s. Franklin Monroe Easley and Nancy Polene Bridges E; m. 8/14/25 to Lillie Mae Alford, div; c. Morris, Jr. Polit. & Govt. Pos: Chmn. of St. Helena Parish Dem. Cmt, La, 33- Bus. & Prof. Pos: Owner, Gen. Store, 28- Rel: Methodist. Mailing Add: Route 2, Box 243, Greensburg, La. 70441. (1967)

EAST, JOHN PORTER R
b. Springfield, Ill, 5/5/31; s. Laurence John East and Virginia Porter E; m. 9/26/53 to Priscilla Sherk; c. Kathryn P. and Martha Ellen. Educ: Earlham Col, B.A, 53; Univ. Ill, Urbana, LL.B, 59; Univ. Fla, M.A, 61, Ph.D, 64; Phi Beta Kappa; Pi Sigma Alpha. Polit. & Govt. Pos: Del, Rep. Nat. Conv, 68. Bus. & Prof. Pos: Assoc. prof, polit. sci, E. Carolina Univ, 64- Mil. Serv: Entered as Pvt, Marine Corps, 53, released as 1st Lt, 55. Publ: Council-Manager Government, Univ. N.C, 65; 'Pragmatism & Behavioralism,' West. Polit. Quart, 12/68; 'Containment: the Military Imperative,' The New Guard, 2/69. Mem: Am. Polit. Sci. Asn; South. Polit. Sci. Asn; Am. Hist. Asn; Fla. Bar Asn. Rel: Protestant. Mailing Add: 212 Longmeadow Rd, Greenville, N.C. 27834.

EAST, VIC R
Mont. State Rep.
b. London, Eng, 10/11/05; s. P.V. East and Fanny Snashall E; m. 7/19/32 to Violet Jean Vick; c. Gary V. and Myrna M. Educ: Billings Polytech. Inst. Polit. & Govt. Pos: Mont. State Rep, Rosebud Co, 63-, chmn, labor and compensation cmt, 67- Bus. & Prof. Pos: Pres, East. Solar Gas, 63- Mem: Mason; Shrine; Lions; Elks; Odd Fellows. Rel: Episcopal. Mailing Add: 210 N. Seventh, Forsyth, Mont. 59327.

EASTHAM, JOHN P. R
N.Mex. State Sen.
b. Methuen, Mass, 2/7/28; s. James Saville Eastham and Marcia Hill E; m. 3/17/53 to Hester Fuller; c. William Sterling Parsons, Clarissa, Miranda Saville, Sebastian John Doolittle and Nicholas Paul Eliot. Educ: Princeton Univ, A.B, 49; Harvard Univ, LL.B, 52; Phi Beta Kappa. Polit. & Govt. Pos: N.Mex. State Rep, 57-58, N.Mex. State Sen, 67- Bus. & Prof. Pos: Assoc, Ropes & Gray, 52-54; assoc, Rodey, Dickason, Sloan, Akin & Robb, 54-58, partner, 58- Rel: Protestant. Legal Res: 1441 Columbia Dr. N.E, Albuquerque, N.Mex. 87106. Mailing Add: P.O. Box 2034, Albuquerque, N.Mex. 87103.

EASTHAM, THOMAS GRANVILLE D
Chmn, Falls Church Dem. Town Cmt, Va.
b. Flint Hill, Va, 5/16/17; s. Franklin Dabney Eastham and Mary Pullen E; m. 11/30/63 to Margaret Lougene Harty; c. Thomas Harty. Educ: South. Col, 1 year. Polit. & Govt. Pos: City councilman, Falls Church, Va, 63-69; chmn, Falls Church Dem. Town Cmt, 67- Bus. & Prof. Pos: Pres, Falls Church Jewelers Inc, Va, 47-; dir, Guaranty Bank & Trust, Fairfax, 64- Mil. Serv: Entered as Pvt, Air Force, 42, released as T/Sgt, 45, after serv. in 312th Bomb Group, New Guinea, Southwest Pac, 63-65. Mem: Am. Legion; Kiwanis. Rel: Methodist. Mailing Add: 408 Park Ave, Falls Church, Va. 22046.

EASTLAND, ANNE STACY D
b. Austin, Tex, 5/23/22; d. William Gillespie Stacy and Agnes Lincoln Doran S; m. 9/7/45 to Seaborn Eastland, Jr; c. Seaborn Stacy; Nancy Anne and Richard Gillespie. Educ: Mills Col, 39-40; Univ. Tex, Austin, B.J, 43; Kappa Kappa Gamma; Orange Jackets. Polit. & Govt. Pos: Del, Co. and State Dem. Conv, Tex, 62-68; secy, Tex. State Dem. Exec. Cmt, 64, v.chmn, 66-68; del, Dem. Nat. Conv, 68. Bus. & Prof. Pos: Part owner of private girls' camp, Camp Mystic, Hunt, Tex, 42-; salesman and continuity writer, Radio Sta. KTBC, Austin, 43-45. Mem: Jr. League; River Oaks Garden Club; Forest Club Women's Asn.(past pres); pres, Women's Auxiliary of Houston Bar Asn; Kappa Kappa Gamma Alumnae Asn; Tex. Ex Asn; PTA. Rel: Episcopal. Mailing Add: 255 Pine Hollow Lane, Houston, Tex. 77027.

EASTLAND, JAMES OLIVER D
U.S. Sen, Miss.
b. Doddsville, Miss, 11/28/04; s. Woods Caperton Eastland and Alma Austin E; m. 7/6/32 to Elizabeth Coleman; c. Nell, Ann, Sue and Woods Eugene. Educ: Univ. Miss, 22-24; Vanderbilt Univ, 25-26; Univ. Ala, 26-27. Polit. & Govt. Pos: Miss. State Rep, 28-32; U.S. Sen, Miss, 41- Bus. & Prof. Pos: Attorney and farmer. Rel: Methodist. Legal Res: Doddsville, Miss. 38736. Mailing Add: 2241 New Senate Office Bldg, Washington, D.C. 20510. (1967)

EASTMAN, EDWIN WINTER R
N.H. State Rep.
b. Exeter, N.H, 6/18/94; married. Educ: Phillips Exeter Acad, Kimball Union Acad. Polit. & Govt. Pos: N.H. State Rep, 53-; Constitutional Conv, 56-64. Bus. & Prof. Pos: Retired mfrs. rep; trustee, trust funds; trustee, Exeter Cemetery; trustee, Exeter Hosp; trustee, Gilman Park & Robinson Fund, Exeter; trustee, Kensington, N.H. Libr. Mil. Serv: 189 Aero Squadron, WWI. Mem: N.H. Soc. Colonial Wars, N.H. Hist. Soc; Sons of Am. Revolution; Exeter Hist. Soc; Knight Templar. Rel: Congregationalist. Mailing Add: 76 Court St, Exeter, N.H. 03833. (1967)

EASTMAN, IRVING WILLARD R
b. St. Johnsbury, Vt, 5/23/96; m. to Christine Webster; c. 2 sons. Educ: St. Johnsbury Acad; Middlebury Col. Polit. & Govt. Pos: Holds several town offices; officer, number of co. and state orgns; Vt. State Rep, 55-61; Vt. State Sen, 63-66. Bus. & Prof. Pos: Retired; former admin. officer, Am. Tel. and Tel. Mil. Serv: Navy, World War I. Mem: Masons; Am. Legion; SAR; Chi Psi; Shrine. Rel: Congregational. Mailing Add: Whiting,Vt. 05778.

EASTMAN, LILLIAN M. R
b. Williamstown, Mass, 2/22/96; m. to William H. Eastman. Educ: Sanderson Acad, Ashfield, Mass. Polit. & Govt. Pos: Vt. State Rep, 65-66. Bus. & Prof. Pos: Housewife. Mem: Grange; Farm Bur; PTA. Rel: Protestant. Mailing Add: P.O. Box 46, Topsham, Vt. 05076. (1967)

EASTWOOD, JAMES RANDOLPH D
b. Keeling, Va, 6/19/20; m. to Pauline E. Cox. Educ: Dan River High Sch; Farm Vet. Training, 4 years. Polit. & Govt. Pos: Va. State Del, 66-69. Bus. & Prof. Pos: Ins. agent and farmer. Mil. Serv: Coast Guard, 42-47. Mem: Mason; Sertoma Club; Young Farmers and Life Underwriter's Asn; PTA. Rel: Baptist. Mailing Add: Route 1, Keeling, Va. 24566. (1967)

EATHERLY, JAMES EDWARD R
b. Johnston City, Ill, 12/27/30; s. Curtis Virgil Eatherly and Nathalie Dominguez E; m. 4/30/52 to Rita Joy Richey; c. Deborah Joy and April Elaine. Educ: South. Ill. Univ, B.S, 59, grad. work, 1 year. Polit. & Govt. Pos: Ill. State Rep, 58th Dist, 67-69; active on local level as election worker and judge. Mil. Serv: Entered as Pvt, Army, 51, released as Cpl, 53, after serv. in 101st Air Borne Inf. and First Guided Missile Group, Korea. Mem: Ill. Educ. Asn; Am. Farm Bur; Am. Legion. Rel: Baptist. Mailing Add: R.F.D 1, Galatia, Ill. 62935. (1967)

EATON, ANNE KINDER D
Mem, Summit Co. Dem. Exec. Cmt, Ohio
b. Cleveland, Ohio, 6/29/22; d. Walter Tupper Kinder and Evelyn Ewing Leader K; m. 12/20/57 to Cyrus Stephen Eaton; c. Mrs. Alfred E. Heller. Educ: Vassar Col, 44; hon. L.H.D, Wilberforce Univ, 59. Polit. & Govt. Pos: Del-at-lg, Dem. Nat. Conv, 60 & 64; mem, Summit Co. Dem. Exec. Cmt, Ohio and Ohio Adv. Cmt, currently. Bus. & Prof. Pos: Teacher and leader, dept. of continuing educ, Cleveland Col, 54-57. Publ: 'Observations: Trip to Soviet Union and Pugwash Conference at Vienna,' Series, Cleveland Press, 9/58; 'Women in Geneva,' Bul. Atomic Scientists, 9/62; 'Observations: European Tour—France, Czechoslovakia, Hungary, Soviet Union,' Series, Cleveland Plain Dealer, 5/5-22/65. Mem: Women's Bd, Univ. Chicago; Women's Asn. of Cleveland Col; trustee, UN Asn. of Cleveland; Jr. League; Garden Club; Cleveland Vassar Club; Rainbow Hosp. Corp; Pugwash Park Cmn, N.S. Speaker on polit, civic and social responsibilities and int. rels. Rel: Presbyterian. Mailing Add: Acadia Farms, P.O. Box 405, Northfield, Ohio 44067.

EATON, JONATHAN CHASE, JR. D
Chmn, Fifth Dist. Dem. Party, N.Dak.
b. Fargo, N.Dak, 2/26/27; s. Jonathan Chase Eaton, Sr. and Ellen Miller E; m. 2/28/50 to Betty Marie Arndt; c. Elizabeth and Mary. Educ: Northwest. Univ, B.S, 49; Stanford Univ. Law Sch, LL.B, 52. Polit. & Govt. Pos: Precinct committeeman, Dem. Party, N.Dak, 54; mem, N.Dak. Dem. State Exec. Cmt, 60-66; del, Dem. Nat. Conv, 68; chmn, Fifth Cong. Dist. Dem. Party, N.Dak, currently. Bus. & Prof. Pos: Partner, Funke & Eaton, Attorneys, currently. Mil. Serv: Seaman 1/C, Navy, 45-46. Rel: Episcopal. Mailing Add: Box 1697, Minot, N.Dak. 58701.

EATON, JOSEPH MARCH R
N.H. State Rep.
b. Salisbury, Mass, 12/1/01; s. Stephen J. Eaton and Ellen C. Merrill E; m. 6/28/30 to Mildred P. Pehrson; c. Joseph M, Jr, Nancy W.(Mrs. Whitelaw) and Pauline M.(Mrs. Attridge). Educ: Boston Univ, B.B.A, 26. Polit. & Govt. Pos: Chmn, Registrn. of Voters, Fairhaven, Mass, 30-42; Fed. investr, Travel Status, 42-47; N.H. State Rep, 61-, chmn, Cmt. on Appropriations and Adv. Budget Cmt, N.H. House of Rep, 65-, chmn, Joint House and Senate Fiscal Cmt, 65-, mem, Legis. Serv. Cmt, 65- and Coord. Cmt, 69- Mailing Add: 11 Walnut St, Hillsboro, N.H. 03244.

EATON, WENDELL HOME R
Vt. State Rep.
b. South Royalton, Vt, 1/18/99; m. to Norma P. Clifford; c. Two sons, one daughter. Educ: Pub. schs, South Royalton, Vt. Polit. & Govt. Pos: Vt. State Rep, 65-; former town auditor, town agent and justice of the peace, South Royalton, Vt. Bus. & Prof. Pos: Owner, mgr, lumber bus. Mem: Mason. Rel: Protestant. Mailing Add: South Royalton, Vt. 05063. (1967)

EATROS, ALEXANDER MICHAEL D
b. Marshall, Minn, 4/9/22; s. James Eatros Sr. and Marguerite Hutchinson E; m. to Pearl Ann Klein; c. Michael, Kathryn and Thomas. Educ: Univ. of Minn, 2 years. Polit. & Govt. Pos: Chmn, Lyon Co. Dem. Party, Minn, 65-68. Bus. & Prof. Pos: Restaurant owner, Marshall, Minn, 45-69. Mil. Serv: Entered as Pvt, Army, 43, released as T-5, 45, after serv. in 174 Gen. Hosp, ETO, 44-45. Mem: Am. Legion; VFW. Mailing Add: 702 S. Bend, Marshall, Minn. 56258.

EAVES, JOHN M. D
b. Kilgore, Tex, 11/21/38; s. J.W. Eaves and Ermalea Kindrick E; m. 9/28/63 to Mary Ann Craig; c. John Craig. Educ: Univ. N.Mex, 56-60; Sigma Alpha Epsilon. Polit. & Govt. Pos: Former N.Mex. State Rep, First Dist, Bernalillo Co. Bus. & Prof. Pos: V.pres, Jeffries-Eaves, Inc, 60- Mil. Serv: Entered as Pvt, Army Nat. Guard, Air Guard, N.Mex, 57, released as S/Sgt, Air Nat. Guard, 63, after serv. in 150th Fighter Group, N.Mex. Mem: Mason; Lions; Aircraft Owners & Pilots Asn. Rel: Episcopal. Mailing Add: 2308 Dietz Place N.W, Albuquerque, N.Mex. 87107. (1967)

EBERLE, ED J. D
Chmn, Kay Co. Dem. Party, Okla.
b. Wheeling, W.Va, s. Ed J. Eberle and Blanche O. Riddle E; m. 4/2/53 to Eva Lee Jarman; c. Susan Lynn, Brent Allen and Lee Ann. Polit. & Govt. Pos: Chmn, Kay Co. Dem. Party, Okla, 64-; precinct elec. chmn, Ponca City, 64-; Justice of the Peace. Bus. & Prof. Pos: Employed by Refinery Lab, Cities Serv. Oil Co, Ponca City, Okla. Mil. Serv: S/Sgt, Air Force, serv. in China-Burma-India. Mem: Tulsa Shrine, Akdar Temple; Hon. mem. in Young Dem. Club; AF&AM; Scottish Rite; Rel: Methodist. Mailing Add: 2025 John St, Ponca City, Okla. 74601.

EBERLE, HAROLD FREDERICK, JR. R
b. Los Angeles, Calif, 5/14/25; s. Harold Frederick Eberle and Sarah Martha Woodbury E; c. Mark and Karen. Educ: Woodbury Col, B.B.A, 48; Sacramento State Col, B.A, 54; Cong. Staff Fel, Am. Polit. Sci. Asn, 65-66. Polit. & Govt. Pos: Assoc. mem, Calif. State Rep. Cent. Cmt. and pres, Oakland Young Rep, 54-55; for. serv. officer, Dept. State, 55-61; admin. asst. to U.S. Rep. Robert J. Corbett, 61- Bus. & Prof. Pos: Acct. exec, Dean Witter & Co, Oakland, Calif, 54-55. Mil. Serv: Entered as Aviation Cadet, Army Air Corps, 43, released as 2nd Lt, 45, after serv. in 305th Bomb Group, 336th Bomb Squadron, Eighth Air Force, Eng, recalled 48, released as Capt, 53, after serv. in Japan and Berlin Airlift; Air Medal with 2 Oak Leaf Clusters; ETO Ribbon with 2 Battle Stars; Good Conduct Medal; Am. Theater Ribbon; Occup. Ribbon for Japan and Germany. Mem: Retail Clerks Union, AFL; chmn. steering cmt, Bull Elephants. Legal Res: 2101A 38th Ave, Oakland, Calif. Mailing Add: 6040 Richmond Hwy. 114, Alexandria, Va. 22303.

EBERLE, ROBERT DEAN R
b. St. Joseph, Mo, 11/19/34; s. Adolph H. Eberle and Emma Reinert E; m. 6/16/57 to Kay Faulkner; c. Susan Kathleen, Daniel Karl and Jill Marie. Educ: St. Joseph Commun. Col, A.S, 54; Univ. Mo. Sch. of Mines and Metallurgy, Rolla, B.S.M.E, 57; Univ. Ala, M.S, Eng, 60; Univ. Wash, 61-62; Pi Tau Sigma. Polit. & Govt. Pos: Precinct leader, Rep. Party, Seattle, Wash, 60-62; state treas, Goldwater For President Cmt, Wash, 63-64, West. Wash. Chmn, 64; Wash. State Rep, 62-64, v.chmn, State Govt. Cmt; state treas, Wash. Young Rep. Fedn, 65-67, state pres, 67-69, chmn. leadership training sch, 69; King Co. Freeholder, 67-68; Rep. cand, U.S. House Rep, Seventh Dist, 68. Bus. & Prof. Pos: Instr. mech. engr, Univ. Ala, 59-60; machine designer, Gulf States Paper Co, 59-60; Res. Engr, Boeing Co, Wash, 60-; Mil. Serv: Entered as Pvt, Army Res, 57, released as Pfc, 58; First Honors, Fire Direction Control Sch, Ft. Chaffee, Ark. Mem: Seattle Prfnl. Engrs. Asn.(v.chmn, transportation cmt); Nat. Rifle Asn; Gr. Bellevue C. of C.(rd. & bridges and rapid transit cmts); Lake Wash. Good Rds. Asn.(action cmt); YMCA (youth in govt. cmt). Rep. Serv. Award, 34th Legis. Dist. Wash. State; Outstanding Young Man of Am, 69. Rel: Lutheran. Mailing Add: 3229 74th S.E, Mercer Island, Wash. 98040.

EBERSPACHER, EDWARD CHRISTIAN D
b. Shelby Co, Ill, 12/18/08; s. Edward C. Eberspacher and Rose E. Rau E; m. 6/27/47 to Josephine Frawley Yantis; c. Chris, Jo Ann and David. Educ: Univ. Ill, B.A, 30, LL.B, 37; Phi Delta Phi; Kappa Delta Rho. Polit. & Govt. Pos: State's attorney, Shelby Co, Ill, 40-42 & 48-52; Ill. State Rep, 54-60; Ill. State Sen, 60-64, Dem. Whip, Ill. State Senate, 63-65; judge, appellate court, Ill, 64- Bus. & Prof. Pos: Practicing attorney, 37-65. Mil. Serv: Entered as Lt.(jg), Naval Res, 42, released as Comdr, 47, after serv. in Mediterranean and European Theatres; Secy. of Navy Commendation Medal; Crown of Italy; European-African Medal with 3 Stars; Am. Theater Ribbon. Mem: Ill. State Bar Asn; Mason (32°), Shrine; VFW; Am. Legion. Rel: Protestant. Legal Res: 219 N. Washington St, Shelbyville, Ill. 62565. Mailing Add: 244 E. Main St, Shelbyville, Ill. 62565.

ECHOLS, M. PATTON, JR. R
Va. State Sen.
b. Honolulu, Hawaii, 10/1/25; s. Marion Patton Echols and Nancy McArthur E; m. 11/10/56 to Susanne Stokes; c. R. Carter, M. Patton, III, T. Tucker and S. Campbell. Educ: Va. Mil. Inst, B.S. in civil eng, 45; Univ. Del. Sch. Chem. Eng, grad. student, 54; George Wash. Univ, J.D, 58; George Wash. Univ. Law Rev. Registered Prfnl. Engr, Va. Polit. & Govt. Pos: Mem, Dept. Commerce, Exec. Res, 55-63; cand, Va. State Legis, 63; v.chmn, Arlington Co. Rep. Cmt, 63-64, chmn, 64-66; mem. campaign cmt, Joel T. Broyhill for Cong, 64, 66 & 68; mem, Va. Rep. State Cent. Cmt, 66-; Va. State Sen, Ninth Dist, 69- Bus. & Prof. Pos: Instr. and trainee, York Corp, York, Pa, 45-47, appln. engr, Atlanta, Ga, 47-50, br. mgr, Wilmington, Del, 53-55, asst. to v.pres. corp, D.C, 55-58; assoc, Ball & McCarthy, Attorneys, Arlington, Va, 58-62; attorney-at-law, Arlington, 62- Mil. Serv: Entered as Recruit, Army, 50, released as Lt, 53, after serv. in 928th Engr. Aviation Group, 52-53; Major, Army Res, 65- Publ: 'Air Conditioning Hospitals,' Hosp. Mgt, 57. Mem: Am. Soc. Prfnl. Engrs; Am. Soc. Civil Engrs; Am. Soc. Refrigerating Engrs; Am. Soc. Heating, Ventilating and Air Conditioning Engrs; Soc. Am. Mil. Engrs; Bar of Va, D.C, and various U.S. Courts; Arlington Co. and Va. State Bar Asns; Va. Trial Lawyers Asn; del, Arlington Civic Fedn, 66-; Arlington Co. Equalization of Real Estate Assessments Bd, 67-; legis. cmt, North. Va. Ment. Health Asn; charter mem. and former v.pres, Morning Optimist Club, Arlington; former dir, v.pres. and secy, Jr. C. of C; pres, Ft. Myer Heights Civic Asn, Arlington; Arlingtonians for Preservation of the Palisades Pkwy; Arlington C. of C; Citizens Asn; Arlington Cmt. of 100; former mem, Nat. Press Club and Army-Navy Club; life mem, Amateur Trapshooting Asn; former Boy Scout Dist. Committeeman. Rel: Episcopal; Vestryman, St. Andrews Episcopal Church, Arlington, 67- Legal Res: 2529 23rd Rd. N, Arlington, Va. 22207. Mailing Add: 2060 14th St. N, Arlington, Va. 22201.

ECHOLS, TALMAGE B. D
b. Franklin Co, Ga, 10/31/07; s. Morton M. Echols and Sallie Bruce E; m. 10/10/29 to Louise Dean; c. Edwin C, Gerald T. Educ: Cornelia High Sch, 25; Atlanta Bus. Col, 27. Polit. & Govt. Pos: Ga. State Rep, 57-66. Bus. & Prof. Pos: Merchant. Mem: Lion. Rel: Methodist. Mailing Add: Thomaston, Ga. 30286. (1967)

ECHTMAN, IRWIN M. D
Mem, Nassau Co. Dem. Cmt, N.Y.
b. New York, N.Y, 6/21/37; s. Harry Echtman and Celia Manas E; m. 6/3/61 to Leila Goldberg; c. Steven Jay, Barry Theodore and Elyse Debra. Educ, Hunter Col, B.A, Yale Law Sch, LL.B; A.P.O. Polit. & Govt. Pos: Del, Dem. Nat. Conv, 68; mem, Nassau Co. Dem. Cmt, N.Y, 68- Bus. & Prof. Pos: Partner, Easton & Echtman, N.Y, 67- Legal Res: 30 Bluebird Dr, Roslyn Heights, N.Y. 11577. Mailing Add: 6 E. 39th St, New York, N.Y. 10016.

ECKARD, HAYES WOODROW D
Chmn, Juniata Co. Dem. Party, Pa.
b. Blairs Mills, Pa, 11/16/16; s. Shelburn Wesley Eckard and Rose A. Kauffman E; m. 10/31/42 to Nan E. Lytle; c. Hayes W, Jr. Educ: Juniata Col, 34-36. Polit. & Govt. Pos: Auditor, Milford Twp, Juniata Co, Pa, 42-48 and Justice of Peace, 42-; chmn, Juniata Co. Dem. Party, 65- Bus. & Prof. Pos: Bookkeeper and salesman, W.H. Manbeck & Co, Mifflin, Pa, 45-54; lumber salesman, Lewistown Lumber & Supply Co, 54-57; salesman and acct, Switzer Chevrolet Co, Mifflintown, 57-60; acct. and off. mgr, Riverside Oil Co, 60- Mem: Am. Radio Relay League; Perry-Juniata Petroleum Asn; Mil. Amateur Radio Syst; Mifflin Fire Co; Juniata Co. Sportsmen Asn; Union Co. Sportsmen Club; Juniata Valley Amateur Radio Club; past dir, Civil Defense. Rel: Presbyterian; treas, Westminster-United Presby. Church. Mailing Add: Box 35, Mifflin, Pa. 17058.

ECKELMANN, LOUIS CHARLES, JR. R
Chmn, Carter Co. Rep. Cmt, Mo.
b. Cape Girardeau, Mo, 6/16/20; s. Louis Charles Eckelmann, Sr. and Edna Auchter E; m. 7/6/44 to Marilyn McClintock; c. Louis Charles, III, David C, Gary L. and Dixie L. Educ: Southeast Mo. State Col, 38-39; Webster Lit. Soc. Polit. & Govt. Pos: Pub. adminstr, Carter Co, Mo, 64-68; chmn, Carter Co. Rep. Cmt, 69- Bus. & Prof. Pos: Co. rep, Gooch Milling & Elevator Co, Lincoln, Nebr, 45-56; owner, Lou Eckelmann Gen. Ins, Van Buren, Mo, 56- Mil. Serv: Entered as A/S, Navy, 40, released as Aviation Machinist 1/C, 45, after serv. in Aviation Corps, S.Pac. Theater, 42-45; Distinguished Flying Cross; Presidential Group Citation. Mem: Rotary (pres, 66-67); C. of C.(pres, Van Buren Chap, 68-69). Rel: Methodist. Mailing Add: Box 338, Van Buren, Mo. 63965.

ECKENSBERGER, WILLIAM H, JR. D
Pa. State Rep.
b. Cementon, Pa, 4/29/28; s. William H. Eckensberger and Hilda Rebecca Gruver E; m. to Louise A. Wolbach; c. Gail Patricia, Jill Louise and William Henry, III. Educ: Muhlenberg Col, B.A; George Washington Univ. Law Sch, LL.B; Phi Alpha Delta. Polit. & Govt. Pos: Pa. State Rep, 64-; justice of the peace. Bus. & Prof. Pos: Attorney-at-law. Mil. Serv: Army, 50-52. Mem: Lehigh Co. Bar Asn; Whitehall Twp. C. of C; Whitehall Exchange Club. Mailing Add: 839 Fairmont Ave, Whitehall, Pa. 18052.

ECKER, PEDER KALOIDES D
Chmn, S.Dak. Dem. Party
b. Sioux City, Iowa, 10/21/29; s. Peder K. Ecker, Sr. and Amalia Kaloides E; m. 3/18/51 to Dorothy Severson; c. Diane, Debra, Dorothy, Dawn and Donna. Educ: Univ. S.Dak, A.B, 54 and LL.B, 55; Phi Delta Phi; Alpha Tau Omega. Polit. & Govt. Pos: Chmn, Lawyers for John F. Kennedy, 60; chmn, Minnehaha Co. Young Dem, S.Dak, 60-61; Minnehaha Co. Committeeman, Dem. State Cent. Cmt, 60-62; nat. committeeman, S.Dak. Young Dem, 62; state chmn, Young Citizens for Johnson-Humphrey, 64; chmn, Minnehaha Co. Dem. Party, 66 & 68; chmn, Minnehaha Co. Dem. for Robert F. Kennedy, 68; del. and mem. rules cmt. and McGovern for Pres. Cmt, Dem. Nat. Conv, 68; chmn, S.Dak. Dem. Party, 68- Bus. & Prof. Pos: Bd. mem. and pres, S.Dak. Young Lawyers, 64-65; mem. bd. comnrs, State Bar S.Dak, 65-68. Mil. Serv: Army, 48-49, serv. in 2nd Inf. Div; Judge Adv. Gen. Corps, Army Res, 62-68, Capt. Mem: Minnehaha Co, Nebr. and Am. Bar Asns; S.Dak. Bar Asn. (mem. legal aid cmt); S.Dak. and Am. Trial Lawyers Asns; Multiple Sclerosis Soc. (past S.Dak. chmn); Minnehaha Co. March of Dimes (past v.chmn, two terms); Noon Toastmasters and Dale Carnegie Class (past pres); Eagles (past pres, Sioux Falls); Elks; Mason; Kiwanis (dir, Downtown Club); dir, Sioux Falls

Civic Fine Arts Asn; bd. mem, Salvation Army; pres, Sioux Falls Park Bd, 63- Rel: Lutheran. Legal Res: 721 E. 21st St, Sioux Falls, S.Dak. 57105. Mailing Add: 131 N. Main Ave, Sioux Falls, S.Dak. 57102.

ECKES, J. KENNETH D
Secy, Dunn Co. Dem. Party, N.Dak.
b. Wahpeton, N.Dak, 11/9/90; s. W.F. Eckes and Magsaline Pahl E; m. 7/17/39 to Martha Worth; c. Kaye (Mrs. Hoffert) and Ron Worden. Educ: State Sch. of Sci, 2 years; Dickinson State Col, 1 quarter; Univ. N.Dak, LL.B, Sigma Alpha Epsilon. Polit. & Govt. Pos: States attorney; munic. judge; mem, first N.Dak. State Parole Bd; chmn, first two war loan drives, Dunn Co, N.Dak; mem, State Bar Exec. Cmt; co.chmn, Infantile Paralysis, 25 years; secy, Dunn Co. Dem. Party and mem, Dunn Co. Dem. Exec. Cmt, currently; mem, N.Dak. State Dem. Exec. Cmt, 6 years; chmn. of del, Dem. Nat. Conv, 56 and del, 60; a founder, Kennedy Mem, state hq, Bismarck, N.Dak; former pres, Sixth Judicial Dist. Bar Asn. Bus. & Prof. Pos: Dir. in several corp. Mem: N.Dak. State Bar Asn; K. of C; Elks; Farmers Union. Medal for Selective Serv. Work. Rel: Catholic. Mailing Add: Killdeer, N.Dak. 58640.

ECKHARDT, ROBERT CHRISTIAN D
U.S. Rep, Tex.
b. Austin, Tex, 7/16/13; s. Joseph Carl Augustus Eckhardt and Norma Wurzbach E; m. 3/8/62 to Nadine Cannon; c. Orissa, Rosalind, Sarah, Sidney, Shelby and William. Educ: Univ. Tex, B.A, 35, LL.B, 39; Sigma Chi; Alpha Nu Chap. Polit. & Govt. Pos: Southwest. Rep, Coordinator on Inter-Am. Affairs, 44-46; Tex. State Rep, 58-66; U.S. Rep, Eighth Dist, 67- Bus. & Prof. Pos: Attorney-at-law, 46- Mil. Serv: Pfc, Army, 42-44, serv. as Primary Flying Sch. Instr, 42-44. Rel: Presbyterian. Legal Res: Route 6, Box 596-A, Houston, Tex. 77016. Mailing Add: Longworth House Office Bldg, Washington, D.C. 20515.

ECKHART, HENRY WORLEY D
Chmn, Speakers Bur, Ohio Dem. Party
b. Columbus, Ohio, 11/12/32; s. Jay Vincent Eckhart and Alice Worley E; m. 3/23/63 to Claudine Lalli; c. Anne Elizabeth. Educ: Ohio State Univ, B.S. in B.A, 54; Univ. Mich, J.D, 58; Kappa Sigma; Phi Delta Phi. Polit. & Govt. Pos: Cent. committeeman, and mem. exec. cmt, Franklin Co. Dem. Party, Ohio, 67-: alternate del-at-lg, Dem. Nat. Conv, 68; chmn, Speakers Bur, Ohio Dem. Party, 68- Bus. & Prof. Pos: Attorney-at-law, 58-68; field counsel, Fed. Nat. Mortgage Asn, 67-69. Mem: Columbus and Am. Bar Asns; Jr. C. of C; Univ. Mich. Club of Columbus (pres); Kappa Sigma Alumni Asn. (treas); Dem. Lawyers Club.(treas). Mailing Add: 1850 Upper Chelsea Rd, Upper Arlington, Ohio 43221.

ECKSTEIN, OTTO D
b. Ulm, Germany, 8/1/27; s. Hugo Eckstein (deceased) and Hedwig Pressburger E; m. 6/27/54 to Harriett M. Mirkin; c. Warren, Felicia and June Beth. Educ: Princeton Univ, A.B, 51, hon. LL.D, 66; Harvard Univ, A.M, 52, Ph.D, 55; Phi Beta Kappa. Polit. & Govt. Pos: Tech. dir, study of employ, growth and price levels, Joint Econ. Cmt, U.S. Cong, 59-60; mem, Coun. Econ. Adv, Exec. Off. of President, 64-66. Bus. & Prof. Pos: Mem. faculty, Harvard Univ, 55-63, prof. econ, 63- Mil. Serv: Entered as Pvt, Army, 46, released as T/4, 48, after serv. in Signal Corps, Japan. Publs: Books on econ. policy, pub. finance, water resource develop; articles on employ, wages, prices, productivity, taxation, budgets. Rel: Jewish. Legal Res: 24 Barberry Rd, Lexington, Mass. 02173. Mailing Add: Dept. of Economics, Harvard University, Littauer Center, Cambridge, Mass. 02138.

ECONOMY, GEORGE P. D
Chmn, Carbon Co. Dem. Party, Wyo.
b. Andravida Ellis, Greece, 12/5/97; s. Dr. Panayes Economopulos and Polyxeni Skizas E; single. Educ: Varvakion Lykeion Col, Athens, Greece, 4 years. Polit. & Govt. Pos: Chmn, Carbon Co. Dem. Party, Wyo, 41- Bus. & Prof. Pos: Cafe owner, 28-64. Mem: Inst. Intercontinental Studies; K. of P; Greek-Am. Progressive Asn; Moose; Eagles. Spec. letter from President Johnson for serv. to Dem. Party; Loyal Serv. plaque, Dem. Women's Club of Carbon Co; Gold Pin for 40 years serv, Dem. of Carbon Co. Rel: Hellenic Orthodox. Legal Res: 102 E. Cedar, Rawlins, Wyo. 82301. Mailing Add: P.O. Box 718, Rawlins, Wyo. 82301.

EDDINS, ANGUS N. R
b. Stanardsville, Va, 9/10/24; s. James Angus Eddins and Mary Buckner E; m. 12/18/48 to Ramona O. Hood; c. James Angus, William Nelson and Addison Hood. Educ: Monroe High Sch. Polit. & Govt. Pos: V.chmn, Bd. of Supvrs, Greene Co, Va, 63-; chmn, Greene Co. Rep. Party, 64-69. Bus. & Prof. Pos: Farmer and ins. agent. Mil. Serv: Entered as Pvt, Army, 45, released as Pfc, after serv. in European Theater, 46. Mem: Greene Co. Planning Cmn; Am. Legion; Fraternal Order Fire Fighters; Piedmont Stella No. 50; Odd Fellows; PTA; pres, Stanardsville Vol. Fire Co; bd. dirs, R.A. Greene Co. Youth Center; Madison Livestock Mkt; chmn, Local Adv. Bd, South. States Adv. Bd. Rel: Baptist; Bd. of Deacons, Stanardsville Baptist Church. Mailing Add: Route 1, Box 190, Stanardsville, Va. 22973. (1967)

EDDINS, EDWARD OSWELL D
b. Demopolis, Ala, 7/27/04; s. John William Virgil Eddins and Martha Seale E; m. 6/7/31 to Anne Goode Eskridge; c. Martha Anne (Mrs. Kelly) and Edward Oswell, Jr. Educ: Pub. Schs, Demopolis, Ala. Polit. & Govt. Pos: Chmn, Demopolis Planning Bd, Ala, 2 years; mem, Demopolis City Coun, 40-44; Ala. State Rep, 43; tax assessor, Marengo Co, 43-49; Ala. State Sen, 50-66; chmn. and mem, Demopolis Sch. Bd, 5 years; mem, Ala. Bldg. Cmt, 4 years; chmn, Civil War Centennial Cmt, Lackey-Edwards Educ. Study Cmt. and Educ. Cmn; mem, Task Force Two, Financial Sub-Cmt; v.chmn. interim cmt, Ad Valorem Tax Cmn; mem, Oil and Gas Bd, 65-71; mem. adv. coun, State Small Bus. Admin; Ala. Rep, Interstate Oil Compact Cmn. Bus. & Prof. Pos: Sales rep, W.R. Willett Lumber Co, Louisville, Ky; owner and operator, Eddins Dist. Co. and Eddins Realty Co, past 38 years; dir, Watkins Banking Co, Faunsdale; consult. pub. affairs, Gulf States Paper Corp, Tuscaloosa. Mil. Serv: Marines. Mem: C. of C. (pres, 43-47); Demopolis Country Club (organizer and former dir); dir, Warrior-Tombigbee Develop. Asn. Rel: Baptist. Legal Res: 408 N. Commissioner St, Demopolis, Ala. 36732. Mailing Add: 1326 Highway 80 E, Demopolis, Ala. 36732.

EDDY, FRANK VINCENT R
Chmn, Newington Rep. Town Cmt, Conn.
b. New Britain, Conn, 8/15/22; s. Vincent Luce Eddy and Charlotte M. Rowley E; m. 7/19/46 to Esther Kathleen Mangone; Joshua Frank, Norah Esther. Educ: Moody's Bus. Sch, 45; Univ. Conn, Dairy Mfg, 47. Polit. & Govt. Pos: Mem, Newington Rep. Town Cmt, Conn, 49-, chmn, 67-; selectman, Newington, Conn, 62- Bus. & Prof. Pos: Owner, Eddy Dairy, 51-65; v.pres, Red Rock Develop. Corp, 62-; secy, Mowhawk Farms Inc, 66-68; dir. local bd, New Britain Bank & Trust Co, 67-; pre., F.V. Eddy Inc, Car Rental, 68- Mil. Serv: Entered as Pvt, Army, 42, released as Pfc, 45, after serv. in 102nd Inf. Div, ETO, 44-45; Expert Combat Infantry Badge; Purple Heart; Bronze Star. Mem: Am. Legion; Mason; Kiwanis; Conn. Farm Bur; DAV. Rel: Congregational. Mailing Add: 200 Church St, Newington, Conn. 06111.

EDDY, JAMES ROLLINS R
b. Canton, Conn, 2/23/31; s. George William Eddy and Anne Rollins E; m. 10/16/54 to Marlene Smith; c. Deborah Ann and J. Carlton. Educ: Duke Univ, A.B, 53; Univ. Miami, LL.B, 59; Delta Theta Phi. Polit. & Govt. Pos: Fla. State Rep, 63-68; asst. city attorney, Lighthouse Point, Fla, 64-69, asst. city judge and prosecutor, 64-; prosecutor, Margate and Pompano Beach, 65-66; pres, N.Broward Rep. Club, 69- Bus. & Prof. Pos: Partner, Alexas and Eddy, 62-64; partner, Eddy & Byrne, 65-66; James R. Eddy, Attorney-at-law, 66- Mil. Serv: Entered as 2nd Lt, Air Force, 54, released as 1st Lt, 55, after serv. in Third Bomb Wing, Tactical Air Command, Far East Theatre; Capt, Air Force Res. Mem: Am, Fla, Broward Co. and N.Broward Bar Asns; Nat. Asn. State Legis; Equipé Rapidé Sports Car Club; Shrine; Gt. Pampano Beach C. of C; Walton League. Rel: Episcopal. Legal Res: 4411 N.E. 30th Ave, Lighthouse Point, Fla. 33064. Mailing Add: 3650 N. Federal Hwy, Lighthouse Point, Fla. 33064.

EDDY, VERA LOUISE R
V.Chmn, Wyoming Co. Rep. Cmt, N.Y.
b. Castile, N.Y, 9/20/21; d. Harry Charles Jenison and Ethel Clum J; m. 1/31/48 to Hugh Owen Eddy; c. Owen Elmer, Darryl Charles and Nancy Elaine. Educ: Sch. Commerce, Rochester, 1 year. Polit. & Govt. Pos: Secy. and treas, Castile Town Rep. Cmt, N.Y, 58-; corresponding secy, Wyoming Co. Women's Rep. Club, 64-; v.chmn, Wyoming Co. Rep. Cmt, 64- Mem: Am. Legion Auxiliary; Castile Hist. Soc; Nat. Campers & Hikers Asn. Rel: Methodist. Legal Res: 20 Beechwood Ave, Castile, N.Y. 14427.

EDELMAN, EDMUND DOUGLAS D
City Councilman, Los Angeles, Calif.
b. Los Angeles, Calif, 9/27/30; s. Nathan Edelman and Buddie Rothman E; married. Educ: Univ. Calif, Los Angeles, B.A, 54, Sch. of Law, LL.B, 58; Phi Beta Kappa; pres, Phi Sigma Alpha. Polit. & Govt. Pos: Arbitrator, Fed. Mediation and Conciliation List; dep. legis. counsel, Calif. State Legis, 61-62; counsr, subcmt. on educ. and labor, U.S. House of Rep, 62-63; spec. asst. to gen. counsel, Nat. Labor Rels. Bd, 63-64; councilman, Fifth Dist, Los Angeles City Coun, 65-, chmn. revenue and taxation cmt; mem. steering cmt. and chmn. revenue and taxation cmt, Los Angeles Co. Div, League of Calif. Cities; pres, Beverly Hills Young Dem. Bus. & Prof. Pos: Law clerk to U.S. Dist. Court judge, 58-60; attorney, 58-; teacher, Fairfax Eve. High Sch, 59-61; lectr, inst. indust. rels, Univ. Calif, Los Angeles, 63. Mil. Serv: Entered as Yeoman Seaman, Navy, 51, realeased as Yeoman 3/C, 52. Mem: Jewish War Vets; Town Hall; B'nai B'rith; Anti-Defamation League (mem. regional adv. bd). Rel: Jewish. Legal Res: 118 S. Wetherly Dr, Los Angeles, Calif. 90048. Mailing Add: Room 336, City Hall, Los Angeles, Calif. 90012.

EDENFIELD, BERRY AVANT D
b. Statesboro, Ga, 8/2/34; s. Perry Edenfield and Vera Berry E; m. to Melvis Bryant. Educ: Univ. Ga, B.B.A. and LL.B; Phi Alpha Delta; Blue Key. Polit. & Govt. Pos: Former Ga. State Sen, Fourth Sen. Dist. Mem: Former pres, Statesboro Jaycees and Tenth Region Jaycees; Kiwanis. Rel: Baptist. Legal Res: 221 South Edgegood Dr, Statesboro, Ga. 30458. Mailing Add: P.O. Box 129, Statesboro, Ga. 30458. (1967)

EDENS, CHARLES JOSEPH R
b. Elizabethton, Tenn. 1/22/30; s. Charles J. Edens, Sr. and Ludia Hodge E; m. 11/21/51 to Betty Joan Jordan; c. Charles J, III, Elizabeth Jill and Steven James. Educ: East Tenn. State Univ, B.S. in bus. admin. Polit. & Govt. Pos: Cong. chmn, Carter Co, 65-; Tenn. State Rep, Carter Co, 65-67; mem, Carter Co. Rep. Exec. Cmt, charter mem, Nat. State Legis. Asn. Bus. & Prof. Pos: Dir, Outdoor Amusement Bus. Asn, 66-; pres, C & E Amusement Co. Inc, 63-; pres, Edens Enterprises Inc, 60-; Pres, Carter-Johnson-Unicol-County Human Develop. Corp. Mil. Serv: Entered as Pvt, Air Force, 50, released as Sgt, Hq. & Hq. Squadron, 3700 Air Base Group, 51. Mem: Am. Legion; Elks; Lions; dir, Carter Co. C. of C. Four year Letterman Basketball, East Tenn. State Univ. Rel: Christian. Mailing Add: Rt. 6, Elizabethton, Tenn. 37643. (1967)

EDENS, HENRY CURTIS D
b. Hebron Commun, 7/1/93; s. Henry Thomas and Alice Spears Edens; m. 12/15/20 to Nellie Spicer Moore; c. 1 son, 3 daughters. Educ: Bailey Mil. Inst, 12-14. Polit. & Govt. Pos: S.C. State Rep, 51-58; 63-67; mem. Co. Forestry Bd; Co. Bd. of Cmnrs, 8 years; pres. Co. Farm Bur, 2 years. Bus. & Prof. Pos: Dir, Va-Carolina Peanut Asn. Mil. Serv: Hq. Co, 323 Reg. 81st Div, 17-18. Mem: Sumter Carnegie Libr. Bd. Mailing Add: Dalzell, S.C, 29040. (1967)

EDENS, J. DRAKE, JR. R
V.Chmn, Rep. Nat. Cmt.
b. Columbia, S.C, 5/13/25; s. J. Drake Edens, Sr. and May Youmans E; m. 5/28/46 to Ferrell McCracken; c. Jenny and Robert M. Educ: Univ. S.C, B.S. in bus. admin, 49; Eta Mu Pi. Polit. & Govt. Pos: State exec. committeeman, Richland Co. Rep. Party, S.C, 62-63; state chmn, S.C. Rep. Party, 63-65; del, Rep. Nat. Conv, 64 & 68, chmn. S.C. del, 64; chmn, S.C. Presidential Campaign for Sen. Barry Goldwater, 64; campaign chmn. for re-election of U.S. Rep. Albert W. Watson, 65; Rep. Nat. Committeeman, v.chmn, Rep. Nat. Cmt, mem. exec. cmt. and Nat. Rep. Coord. Cmt, 65-; mem, Nixon for President Nat. Adv. Cmt. and Nat. Finance Cmt. and State Finance Chmn. for S.C, Nixon Campaign, 68. Bus. & Prof. Pos: V.pres, Edens Food Stores, Inc, 49-

55; pres. and gen. mgr, Edens-Turbeville Gen. Ins. Agency, 56-64; self-employed, securities, real estate investments, farming and timber mgt, 64- Mil. Serv: Entered as Pvt, Marine Corps, 43, released as Cpl, 46, after serv. in Sixth Marine Div. and various other units with duty in Pac. Theatre, 44-45. Mem: Nat. Alliance of Businessmen, the appointment being made by President Nixon, 69; Gr. Columbia and S.C. State C. of C; Columbia Commun. Rels. Coun, Inc; First V.Pres. Alston Wilkes Prisoner Aid Soc; trustee, S.C. Arthritis Found; Cmt. of One Hundred, Emory Theol. Sem, Emory Univ; Univ. S.C. Acad. and Athletic Scholarship Found, Educ. Found. and Alumni Asn; Nat. Wildlife Fedn; Wateree Gun Club; S.C. Farm Bur; Mason; Forest Lake and Spring Valley Country Clubs; Palmetto Club; Columbia YMCA (former mem. bd. dirs). Rel: Methodist. Mailing Add: 905 Arbutus Dr, Columbia, S.C. 29205.

EDGAR, JOSEPH T. R
Secy. of State, Maine
b. Jersey City, N.J, 4/1/10; s. Joseph A. Edgar and Alice C. Tappen E; m. 1939 to Margaret Sanford; c. Margaret. Educ: Princeton Univ, A.B, 32; Univ. Pa. Law Sch, 2 years. Polit. & Govt. Pos: Mem. town coun, Bar Harbor, Maine, 48-49; Maine State Rep, 55-60, speaker, Maine House of Rep, 57-60; Maine State Sen, 61; Dep. Secy. of State, 61-65, Secy. of State, 67- Bus. & Prof. Pos: Retailer, Clothing Store, Bar Harbor. Mem: Bar Harbor C. of C. (pres, 50-52). Rel: Protestant. Legal Res: 31 Ridgeway Dr, Hallowell Post Office, Maine 04347. Mailing Add: State House, Augusta, Maine 04330.

EDGAR, THOMAS C. D
W.Va. State Del.
b. Hillsboro, W.Va, 4/18/15; s. George P. and Laura Callison E; m. 6/14/42 to Betsy Jordan; c. George Thomas and Martha Irene. Educ: W.Va. Univ. Polit. & Govt. Pos: W.Va. State Del, 60- Bus. & Prof. Pos: Farmer. Mil. Serv: Army, 41-47; Comdr, Gun Co. Tank Destroyer Bn, Europe, 45-47. Mem: Am. Legion. Rel: Presbyterian. Mailing Add: Hillsboro, W.Va. 24946.

EDGINGTON, FLOYD P, SR. R
Iowa State Rep.
b. Poweshiek Co, Iowa, 2/4/99; m. 1920 to Mildred Best; c. Margaret (Mrs. Mateer) and Floyd, Jr. Polit. & Govt. Pos: Iowa State Rep, currently; pres, Co. Fair Bd; past mem, Sch. Bd; mem, Farm Security Admin. Bus. & Prof. Pos: Live stock farming and prod. of hybrid seed corn. Mem: Mason; Odd Fellows; Prod. Mkt. Asn; CRUSADE Chmn; Franklin Co. Cancer Soc. Rel: Methodist. Mailing Add: 412 Maple St, Sheffield, Iowa 50475. (1967)

EDINGTON, PATRICIA GENTRY D
b. Mobile, Ala, 3/17/38; d. Curtis A. Gentry, Jr. and Mildred Delchamps G; m. 6/2/62 to Robert Sherard Edington; c. Sherard Caffey. Educ: Auburn Univ, B.S, 60. Polit. & Govt. Pos: Del. and mem, Credentials Cmt, Dem. Nat. Conv, 68. Mem: Pres, Mobile Historic Develop. Cmn; Jaycettes; Historic Mobile Preservation Soc; various other Historic Preservation Groups. Distinguished Young Woman of Mobile, 67; Arthritis Foundation's Distinguished Serv. Award. Rel: Presbyterian. Mailing Add: 307 Conti St, Mobile, Ala. 36602.

EDINGTON, ROBERT SHERARD D
Ala. State Rep.
b. Mobile, Ala, 11/18/29; s. David Henry Edington and Laura Cornelia Owen E; m. 6/2/62 to Patricia Adrienne Gentry; c. Sherard Caffey. Educ: Univ. Mil. Sch. in Mobile; Southwest. Univ, B.A; Univ. Ala. Sch. of Law, grad. Polit. & Govt. Pos: Ala. State Rep, 63-; del, Dem. Nat. Conv, 68. Bus. & Prof. Pos: Partner, Caffey, Gallalee and Edington, Attorneys. Mil. Serv: Aviation Intel. Officer with the U.S. 7th Fleet, Korea. Consul-ad-honoram of Guatemala, Mobile, Ala, 59- Rel: Presbyterian. Mailing Add: 50 St. Emanuel St, Mobile, Ala. 36602.

EDLIN, IRA D
b. Belle Fourche, S.Dak, 9/10/29; s. Ira Edlin and Lois Turner E; m. 9/19/66 to Mary Lou on the Tree. Educ: Black Hills State Col, B.S. Polit. & Govt. Pos: Chmn, Butte Co. Dem. Cent. Cmt, S.Dak, 63-69; mem, State Dem. Party Adv. Cmt, 64- Mem: Mason (32°); Shrine; Elks. Rel: Episcopal. Mailing Add: Box 363, Belle Fourche, S.Dak. 57717. (1967)

EDMONDS, CHARLES MYERS 'BUD' R
Colo. State Rep.
b. Topeka, Kans, 3/11/22; s. Leslie Earl Edmonds and Mary Myers E; m. 9/8/49 to Madelyn J. Barrett; c. Karen Leslie and Raymond Charles. Educ: Colo. Col, 51; Delta Tau. Polit. & Govt. Pos: Mem, Manitou Springs City Coun, Colo, 51-52; secy. and pres, Sch. Dist. 14, 57-69; Colo. State Rep, 22nd Dist, 67- Bus. & Prof. Pos: Owner and chief engr, Research Assocs, Manitou Springs, Colo, 43- and Radio Sta. KCMS, 53- Publ: 'Small Audio Console,' 55 and 'Micro-Midget Remote Broadcast Amplifier,' 59, Audio Engr. Sch. Bell Award, Colo, 65. Rel: Episcopal. Legal Res: 105 Trestle Trail, Manitou Springs, Colo. 80829. Mailing Add: Box 592, Manitou Springs, Colo. 80829.

EDMONDS, EDWIN BENTON R
b. Russell Co, Ky, 9/17/19; s. Benjiman Harrison Edmonds and Nettie G. McGahan E; m. 10/5/42 to Hazel Sullivan; c. Jimmie Lee and Jerry Dale. Educ: Russell Co. High Sch. Polit. & Govt. Pos: Chmn, Russell Co. Rep. Cmt, Ky, 63-69. Mem: State v.pres, Ky. Nat. Farmers Orgn; pres, Russell Co. Feeder Pig Asn; Master Conservationist. Rel: Baptist. Mailing Add: Russell Springs, Ky. 42642. (1967)

EDMONDSON, BETTY LAVERN R
Dir, Fourth Cong. Dist, Wash. Fedn. Rep. Women
b. Camarillo, Calif, 2/23/24; d. Dr. Charles Allen Laws and Zina Shumway L; m. 6/28/43 to Merwin Paul Edmondson; c. George Henry, Kelley Allen and Brian Paul. Educ: Univ. Wash; Alpha Chap. Chi Omega. Polit. & Govt. Pos: Bd. mem. pub. rels. and chmn. mem. cmt, Wash. Fedn. Rep. Women, 59-65, v.chmn, Yakima Co. Rep. Cent. Cmt, 60-64, state committeewoman, 64-69; precinct committeewoman, Yakima Co. Rep. Party, 60-; del. and panel mem. pub. rels, Biennial Meeting, Nat. Fedn. Rep. Women, Phoenix, 63 and del, Wash, D.C, 67; alternate del-at-lg, Rep. Nat. Conv, 64; secy, Wash. State Rep. Cent. Cmt, 66-69; arrangements chmn, Rep. State Conv, 66- and mem. rules and orders cmt, 68; mem, Gov. Task Force Cmt, 66-; chmn. rules and order cmt, Yakima Co. Rep. Conv, 68; arrangement chmn, Wash. Fedn. Rep. Women Conv, 68; treas, Yakima Co. Citizens Cmt. Nixon-Agnew, 68; agency participation coordinator, cabinet mem, Yakima Co. United Good Neighbor Campaign, 68 & 69; commun. chmn, Wash. State Fedn. Women's Clubs, 68-70 and chmn, State Conv. Prog, 69; dir, Fourth Cong. dist, Wash. Fedn. Rep. Women, 68- Bus. & Prof. Pos: Secy, Douglas Aircraft Co, Los Angeles, 43; bookkeeper and typist, Fairway Finance, Yakima, 44-46; Cascade TV Homemaker, KIMA-TV, Yakima, KLEW-TV, Lewiston, Idaho and KEPR-TV, Tri-Cities, 56-58; field rep, McCall's Mag, 58-68; commentator, style shows, People's Store and Serv. Orgns, 58- Publ: 'Manual on Public Relations,' adopted and published by Nat. Fedn. of Rep. Women, 61. Mem: Bd. mem, YWCA, 62-68; Moose Auxiliary; Agenda Club; pres, Woman's Fed. Club, 66-68; city chmn, Yakima March of Dimes, 63; State & Dist. Wool Growers Auxiliary style show commentator; Yakima C. of C; Steering Cmt. Juvenile Delinquency, 64-65; Alma Graham Hosp. Guild. Rel: Latter-day Saint; Dir. of Drama & Speech, Mutual Improv. Asn, 58-68. Mailing Add: 624 S. 34th Ave, Yakima, Wash. 98902.

EDMONDSON, ED D
U.S. Rep, Okla.
b. Muskogee, Okla, 4/7/19; s. Edmond Augustus Edmondson and Esther Pullen E; m. 3/5/44 to June Maureen Pilley; c. James Edmond, William, John, June and Brian. Educ: Univ. Okla, A.B, 40; Georgetown Univ. Law Sch, LL.B, 47; Phi Beta Kappa; Phi Delta Phi; Delta Sigma Rho; Phi Gamma Delta. Polit. & Govt. Pos: FBI, 40-43; attorney-at-law, Muskogee, Okla, 47-49; Muskogee Co. attorney, 49-53; U.S. Rep, Okla, 53- Bus. & Prof. Pos: Newspaperman, Muskogee Daily, Okla; United Press, 36-38; Wash. correspondent, Muskogee Phoenix, Sapulpa Herald, Holdenville News and Daily Ardmoreite, 46-47; admitted to D.C. and Okla. Bars, 47; assoc, J. Howard Edmondson, 48. Mil. Serv: U.S. Navy, 43-46. Mem: Am. Legion; VFW; Am. and Okla. Bar Asns; Mason; Elks; Kiwanis. Legal Res: P.O. Box 11, Muskogee, Okla. 74401. Mailing Add: 2402 Rayburn House Office Bldg, Washington, D.C. 20515.

EDMONDSON, JAMES HOWARD D
b. Muskogee, Okla, 9/27/25; s. Edmond Augustus Edmondson and Esther Pullen E; m. to Jeanette Bartleson; c. James Howard, Jeanne, Patricia Lynn. Educ: Univ. of Okla, LL.B, 48; Phi Gamma Delta. Polit. & Govt. Pos: U.S. Sen, Okla, 63-65, Sen. com. on aero and space sci, agr. and forestry; Gov. of Okla, 59-63; co. attorney, Tulsa Co, 54-58; chief prosecutor's office, Tulsa Co. Attorney, 53. Bus. & Prof. Pos: Lawyer, private practice Muskogee, Okla, 48-53; counsel to firm Fellers, Snider, Baggett and McLane, Okla. City, Okla. Mem: Am. Legion; 40 et 8; Okla. Bar Asn; Air Force Asn; Univ. of Okla. Alumni Asn; Mason; Rotary. Named one of ten Outstanding Young Men of Nation, 59; named to Okla. Hall of Fame. Rel: Presbyterian. Mailing Add: Edmond, Okla. 73034. (1967)

EDWARDS, ATTICUS FITZGERALD D
Chmn, Wichita Co. Dem. Exec. Cmt, Tex.
b. Waxahachie, Tex, 5/4/90; s. Henry Batte Edwards and Mary Strickland E; m. 10/6/25 to Louise Wright. Educ: Ft. Worth Polytech. Col, 08-12; Trinity Univ, 14-16; Univ. Tex, B.A, 20; South. Methodist Univ. fel, 21-23 and 23; Univ. Calif. at Los Angeles, summer, 26; Univ. Colo, summer, 27; Phi Kappa Gamma. Polit. & Govt. Pos: Precinct chmn, Dem. Party, 38-64; secy, Wichita Co. Dem. Exec. Cmt, Tex, 60-64, chmn, 64-; admin. asst. to Maurice Doke, Tex. Legislator, 63; alternate del, Dem. Nat. Conv, 68. Mil. Serv: Home Guard in World War II. Mem: Mo. Valley Col. Teachers Asn; pres, Wichita Falls City Teachers Asn, 31-32, Col. Classroom Teachers Asn, 48-49 and Retired Teachers Asn, 62-64; Mason; Knife and Fork Club; past pres, Rotary Club of Southwest. Wichita Falls. Rel: Methodist; mem. off. bd. and Sunday Sch. teacher. Mailing Add: 2160 Ave. H, Wichita Falls, Tex. 76309.

EDWARDS, CHOICE R
Ind. State Rep.
b. Indianapolis, Ind, 1/20/42; s. Elroy Alfred Edwards and Josephine Rasdall E; m. 6/6/64 to Judy Denise Waller; c. Kelli Denise and Kerry Douglas. Educ: Ind. Univ, 2 years; Cent. State Univ, Ohio, 1 year. Polit. & Govt. Pos: Ind. State Rep, 68- Bus. & Prof. Pos: V.pres, Davidson-Hardy Assoc. Advertising & Pub. Rels, 67-68; commercial mgr, Ind. Bell Tel. Co, currently. Mem: Nat. Asn. of Mkt. Developers; Marion Co. Young Rep; Bell Men's Club; Indianapolis Jr. C. of C; Nat. Bus. League; Nat. Soc. of State Legislators; Marion Co. Ment. Health Asn. Rel: Methodist. Mailing Add: 4610 E. 34th, Indianapolis, Ind. 46218.

EDWARDS, DEIGHTON OCTAVIUS, JR. R
Committeeman, N.Y. Rep. Party
b. Jamaica, N.Y, 6/17/36; s. Deighton O. Edwards, Sr. and Marion Wilson E; m. 12/13/55 to Gail Pricilla Robinson; c. Marc Deighton and Derek Wilfred. Educ: N.Y.C. Commun. Col. Polit. & Govt. Pos: Chmn, bd. gov, John V. Lindsay Young Rep, N.Y, 64-68; committeeman, N.Y. Rep. Party, 65-; alternate del, Rep. Nat. Conv, 68; bd. mem, Creedmoor State Mental Hosp, Queens Co, 68- Bus. & Prof. Pos: Clerical asst, Off. of the Messrs Rockefeller, 54-55; asst. to off. mgr, Ibec. Housing Corp, 55-59; asst. off. mgr, Off. of Gov. Nelson Rockefeller, 59-67; pres, Promon Assocs, Inc, 63-66; v.pres, Aroco Import & Exports, Inc, 64-69; asst. mgr, Franklin Nat. Bank, 67- Mem: Bd, Soc. for Prevention of Cruelty to Children; Queens Hearing Aid Asn; St. Peter Claver; Jamaica Commun. Corp; Jamaica Commun. Develop. Coun. Corp; human resources coun, Jamaica C. of C; L.I. Sailing Asn; Rainbow Yacht Club. Named Man of the Year by the 26th Assembly Dist. Regular Rep. Asns. Rel: Episcopal. Mailing Add: 138-20 175th St, Springfield Gardens, N.Y. 11434.

EDWARDS, DON D
U.S. Rep, Calif.
b. San Jose, Calif; m. Clyda; c. Leonard Perry II, Thomas Charles, Samuel Dyer, Bruce Haven and William Don. Educ: Stanford Law Sch, 36-38; Stanford Univ. Polit. & Govt. Pos: U.S. Rep, Calif, 62-; del, Dem. Nat. Conv, 68. Bus. & Prof. Pos: Spec. Agent, Fed. Bur. Invest, 40-41; pres, Valley Title Co. Mil. Serv: Navy, 42-45. Legal Res: 40 N. First St, San Jose, Calif. 25113. Mailing Add: 9201 Fox Meadow Lane, Potomac, Md. 20854.

EDWARDS, DOROTHY BEATRICE R
R.I. State Rep.
b. Fall River, Mass, 3/22/24; d. George Albert Jackson and Esther Holland J;

m. 11/17/44 to Edwin B. Edwards, Jr; c. E. Branford, III, Gary Charles and twins, Debbi Suzanne and Cindy Joanne. Educ: Rogers High Sch, Newport, R.I, grad. Polit. & Govt. Pos: Mem, Portsmouth Rep. Town Cmt, R.I, 62-; mem, R.I. Rep. State Cent. Cmt, 66-; R.I. State Rep, Dist. 94, 67-; legis. chmn, R.I. Fedn. of Rep. Women, Providence, 68-69. Bus. & Prof. Pos: Telephone operator, New Eng. Telephone, Newport, R.I, 41-42 and U.S. Navy Dept, 42-45. Mem: Portsmouth Rep. Women's Club. Rel: Episcopal. Mailing Add: 25 Cove St, Portsmouth, R.I. 02871.

EDWARDS, E. NEEL, JR. D
b. Cairo, Ga, 12/10/39; s. Edwin Neel Edwards and Ruby Sorgee E; m. 6/27/59 to Joyce Calmes; c. Susan E, Timothy H. and Jennifer L. Educ: La. State Univ, 56-57; La. Col, B.A, 61. Polit. & Govt. Pos: Admin. asst. to U.S. Rep. John R. Rarick, La, 67- Mem: Press Club; La. Govt. Asn; U.S. Naval Inst; Men's Garden Club; Jefferson Hist. Soc; La. Col. Alumni Asn. Rel: Baptist. Legal Res: 1355 Ashbourne Ave, Baton Rouge, La. 70815. Mailing Add: 1525 Longworth Bldg, Washington, D.C. 20515.

EDWARDS, EDWIN W. D
U.S. Rep, La.
b. Marksville, La, 8/7/27; s. Clarence W. Edwards and Agnes Brouillette E; m. 1949 to Elaine Schwartzenburg; c. Anna Laure (Mrs. Richard Hensgens), Victoria Elaine, Stephen Randolph and David Edwin. Educ: La. State Univ, LL.D, 1949. Polit. & Govt. Pos: Mem. city coun, Crowley, La, 54-62; La. State Sen, 64-65; U.S. Rep, 65- Bus. & Prof. Pos: Sr. partner, Edwards & Edwards Law Firm. Mil. Serv: Navy Air Corps, 44. Mem: Lions (past pres); Int. Rice Festival (past pres); Greater Crowley C. of C; Am. Legion (past adjutant). Rel: Catholic. Legal Res: Crowley, La. 70526. Mailing Add: U.S. House of Representatives, Washington, D.C. 20515.

EDWARDS, ELLERTON H. R
b. Hyde Park, Mass, 4/13/00; married; c. Four. Educ: Pub. schs. Polit. & Govt. Pos: Del, N.H. Constitutional Conv, 56; N.H. State Rep, 57-69; former dir, Monadnock Region Asn; former selectman, town auditor and mem. Park Cmn. Bus. & Prof. Pos: Gen. contractor. Mil. Serv: World War I. Mem: Am. Legion; PTA; Odd Fellows. Rel: Protestant. Mailing Add: N.Main St, Antrim, N.H. 03440. (1967)

EDWARDS, ELLSWORTH JAMES R
Chmn, Wyandotte Co. Rep. Party, Kans.
b. Mount Carmel, Pa, 9/18/08; s. John Edwards and Anna Eliza Jeanette Carmitchel E; m. 3/28/33 to Rosa Mae Maxwell; c. Judith Kay (Mrs. Charles O. Whitcraft). Educ: Univ. Kans, 30-34. Polit. & Govt. Pos: Investigator, Wyandotte Co. Sheriff's Off, Kans, 34-41; detective, Kansas City Police Dept, 41-43; sheriff, Wyandotte Co, 43-47 & 51-55, co. clerk, 47-48, marshal, city court, 48-50; supt. of sewers and st, St. Dept, 55-61; traffic engr, Kansas City, 61-; chmn, Wyandotte Co. Rep. Party, currently. Mem: Mo. Valley Sect, Inst. of Traffic Engrs; past pres. and life mem, Kans. Peace Officer Asn; life mem, Optimist Club; life mem, Shrine; Kansas City Area C. of C. Cong. Forum. Award in Gallantry, VFW, 35; Nat. Safety Coun. Class A City's First Place Award in Traffic Eng, 61, 62, 63 & 64; State of Kans. First Place Award in Traffic Eng, 61, 62, 63 & 64, Second Place, 66. Rel: Protestant. Legal Res: 4700 Wood Ave, Kansas City, Kans. 66102. Mailing Add: 803 N. Sixth St, Room 403, Kansas City, Kans. 66101.

EDWARDS, ELTON D
N.C. State Sen.
b. Wayne Co, N.C, 8/14/23; s. Charles Henry Edwards and Lillie Thornton E; m. 3/27/54 to Jessie Macon Sapp; c. Elton Thornton, Jr. and Ruth Macon. Educ: Univ. N.C, A.B, 43, LL.B, 48; Phi Alpha Delta. Polit. & Govt. Pos: Mem, State Bd. Juvenile Correction, N.C, 55-65; N.C. State Rep, 64-68; N.C. State Sen, 68- Bus. & Prof. Pos: Partner, Moseley, Edwards & Greeson, 54- Mil. Serv: Pvt, Army, 43-45; Maj. Air Force Res, currently. Mem: Am, N.C. and Greensboro Bar Asns; Am. Judicature Soc; Mason (32°); Oasis Shrine; Kiwanis; Jaycees (pres, Greensboro Jaycees, 53-54). Rel: Presbyterian; Elder, First Presbyterian Church. Legal Res: 309 N. Tremont Dr, Greensboro, N.C. 27403. Mailing Add: P.O. Box 118, Greensboro, N.C. 27402.

EDWARDS, G. KENT R
Attorney Gen, Alaska
b. Ogden, Utah, 10/3/39; s. George Edwards and Ruth Engelke E; m. 6/9/64 to Barbara Lee Day; c. Scott and Stacey. Educ: Occidental Col, A.B, 61; Univ. Calif, Berkeley, J.D, 64; Sigma Alpha Epsilon. Polit. & Govt. Pos: Legis. counsel, Alaska Legis. Coun, 64-66; dep. attorney gen, Alaska, 67-68, attorney gen, 68- Bus. & Prof. Pos: Partner, Stevens, Savage, Holland, Erwin & Edwards, 66-67; cmnr, Nat. Conf. Cmnr. Uniform State Laws, 68- Mem: Am, Alaska and Juneau Bar Asns; State Bar of Calif. Rel: Episcopal. Mailing Add: P.O. Box 287, Juneau, Alaska 99801.

EDWARDS, GEORGE D
b. Dallas, Tex, 8/6/14; s. George Clifton Edwards and Octavia Nichols E; m. 4/10/39 to Margaret McConnell; c. George Clifton III and James McConnell. Educ: South. Methodist Univ, B.A, 33; Harvard Univ, M.A, 34; Detroit Col. Law, J.D, 39; Phi Beta Kappa; Kappa Sigma. Polit. & Govt. Pos: Chmn. cmt. on admin. of criminal law, U.S. Judicial Conf; mem, Nat. Cmn. for Reform of Fed. Criminal Laws; dir, Mich. Welfare League; mem, Nat. Adv. Coun. Judges, Nat. Coun. on Crime and Delinquency and Detroit Coun. For. Rels; dir. and secy, Detroit Housing Cmn, 40-41; mem, Detroit Common Coun, 41-49, pres, 45-49; chmn, 13th Cong. Dist. Dem. Party, 50-51; probate judge in charge Wayne Co. Juvenile Court, 51-54; circuit judge, Wayne Co, 54-56; justice, Supreme Court, Mich, 56-62; dep. judge admin. tribunal, Int. Labor Orgn, 61-63, police cmnr, Detroit, 62-63; judge, U.S. Court Appeals, Sixth Circuit, 63- Bus. & Prof. Pos: Rep, UAW-CIO, 37, dir, 38-39; attorney, Edwards & Bohn, 46-50; attorney, Rothe, Marston, Edwards & Bohn, 50-51. Mil. Serv: Entered as Pvt, Army, 43, released as Lt, 46, after Serv. in Inf. Publ: A Councilman Reports to the People, 42; The Juvenile Court After 50 Years, 52; Meeting the Challenge of a Juvenile Code, 53, plus others. Mem: Mich. Bar; Am, Mich. and Detroit Bar Asns; Inst. Judicial Admin; chmn, Southeast Mich. Cancer Crusade, 50-51; VFW; Am. Legion; Mason. Award for Commun. Work for Soc. Progress, Workmen's Circle, 49; Award for Commun. Work for Civil Rights, St. Cyprian's Episcopal Church, 50; Americanism Award, Jewish War Vet, 53; Award for Outstanding Achievement in Juvenile Rehabilitation, VFW, 53; St. Peter's Medal for Outstanding Serv. in Youth, St. Peter's Episcopal Church, Detroit, 56. Rel: Episcopal. Legal Res: 19925 Briarcliff, Detroit, Mich. 48221. Mailing Add: U.S. Court of Appeals, 722 Federal Bldg, Detroit, Mich. 48226.

EDWARDS, GEORGE H. D
Mich. State Rep.
b. Brunswick, Ga, 2/13/11; married; c. Harry, Verne, Robert, Pamela. Educ: Morehouse Col, Atlanta, Ga, A.B. in bus. admin. & acct; grad. study at Atlanta Univ. and N.Y. Univ. Polit. & Govt. Pos: Mich. State Rep, 54-; precinct del. and dist. exec. bd. mem. Bus. & Prof. Pos: Bus. adminstr. Mem: Metropolitan Lodge 962, Elks. Rel: Episcopalian. Mailing Add: 87 Woodland, Detroit, Mich, 48202. (1967)

EDWARDS, HORACE HALL D
City Mgr, Richmond, Va.
b. Isle of Wight, Va, 8/21/02; s. Samuel Edwards and Helen Hope Hall E; m. 12/22/27 to Mary Olive Lynch; c. Mary Ann (Mrs. Johnson Clinton Moss, Jr.), Horace Hall and Helen (deceased). Educ: Univ. Richmond, LL.B, 26; Phi Kappa Sigma; Delta Theta Phi; Tau Kappa Alpha; Omicron Delta Kappa. Polit. & Govt. Pos: Va. State Del, 34-38; campaign mgr, Roosevelt Campaign, 36; mem, Gov. Cmn. Nat. Tax Conf, Detroit, 38; city attorney, Richmond, Va, 38-46; gen. dir, Roosevelt Campaigns, 40 & 44; mem, Cmn. to Study State Taxation and Cmn. to Study Annexation, Va. Adv. Legis. Coun, 42; mem, Cmn. to Study Tax Laws Rev, 44; chmn, Legis. Cmn. Va. Munic. League, 40-48; chmn, State Dem. Cmt, 40-48; mayor, Richmond, Va, 46-48; chmn, Planning Cmn. and mem. Cmn. Study Rev. Alcoholic Beverage Control Laws, Richmond, 53; city mgr, Richmond, Va, 54- Bus. & Prof. Pos: Mem. firm, Edwards and Davenport, Richmond, Va, 32-38 and Edwards, Rogers & Cudlipp, 48-53. Mem: Nat. Inst. Munic. Law Officers (pres, 43); Am, Va. Bar Asns; Int. City Mgrs. Asn.(pres. Va. Sect, 58-59, v.pres, dir, 62-63); Newcomen Soc. of N.Am; Mason; Rotary; Commonwealth Club. Rel: Baptist. Legal Res: 1406 Palmyra Ave, Richmond, Va. 23227. Mailing Add: City Hall, Richmond, Va. 23219. (1967)

EDWARDS, JACK R
U.S. Rep, Ala.
b. Birmingham, Ala, 9/20/28; s. William J. Edwards, Jr. and Sue Fuhrman E; m. 1/30/54 to Jolane Vander Sys; c. Susan Lane and Richard Arnold. Educ: U.S. Naval Sch, Acad. & Col, 47-48; Univ. Ala, B.S, 52, Sch. Law, LL.B, 54; pres, Kappa Alpha Fraternity, 51-53 and Univ. Ala. Student body, 52-53; Omicron Delta Kappa. Polit. & Govt. Pos: U.S. Rep, Ala, 64- Bus. & Prof. Pos: Attorney at-law, Mobile, Ala, 54-58; legal counsel, Gulf, Mobile & Ohio R.R, Mobile, 58-64. Mil. Serv: Marine Corps, 46-48, 50-51. Mem: Pres, Mobile Jr. C. of C, 61-62. Chosen Outstanding Local Pres. of Ala. Jr. C. of C, 61-62 and one of Outstanding Young Men of Am. by U.S. Jr. C. of C, 64. Rel: Presbyterian. Legal Res: 1910 Hunter Ave, Mobile, Ala. 36606. Mailing Add: 137 House Office Building, Washington, D.C. 20515.

EDWARDS, JOHN ALBERT R
Idaho State Rep.
b. Washington, D.C, 4/14/19; s. John W. Edwards and Irene Woodyatt E; m. 7/18/42 to Mary Portia Johnson; c. Jonathan P, Hugh W, Joyce I, Mark A, Owen L. and Allan T. Educ: George Wash. Univ, A.B, 40, M.D, 43; Phi Chi; Beaumont Soc; Smith-Reed-Russell Soc. Polit. & Govt. Pos: Physician, Adams Co, Idaho, 49-66; trustee, Sch. Dist. 13, 50-; Idaho State Rep, Adams Co, 64-66, Dist. 9-A, 68- Bus. & Prof. Pos: Mem, Council Sch. Bd, Idaho, 54-66; sr. aviation medical exam, Fed. Aviation Agency, 65- Mil. Serv: Entered as 1st Lt, Army Med. Corps, 44, released as Capt, 46, after serv. in 92nd Field Hosp. and Mil. Govt, Pac-Asiatic Theatre, 44-46; Pac-Asiatic, Philippine Liberation and Japan Occup. Medals; Sr. Surgeon, U.S. Pub. Health Serv. Res, 63- Mem: Am. and Idaho Med. Asns; Southwest Idaho Dist. Med. Soc; Am. Acad. Gen. Practice; Aerospace Med. Asn; C. of C.(pres, 62); Southwest Idaho Water Develop. Asn; Am. Legion; VFW; Grange; Council Flying Club (pres, 64-). Mailing Add: Box 3, Council, Idaho 83612.

EDWARDS, JOSEPH ROBERT R
Chmn, Nemaha Co. Rep. Cent. Cmt, Nebr.
b. Auburn, Nebr, 6/9/32; s. Charles Harold Edwards and Pearl Moody E; m. 6/13/54 to Paula Jean Scharman; c. Kathleen Sue, Beth Yvonne and David Charles. Educ: Univ. Nebr, B.S. in Agr, 54; Block and Bridle Club; Farm House. Polit. & Govt. Pos: Finance chmn, Nemaha Co. Rep. Cent. Cmt, Nebr, 62, chmn, 64-; dist. chmn, More Prog, 66. Mil. Serv: Entered as 2nd Lt, Army, 54, released as 1st Lt, 56, after serv. in 134th Inf, Nat. Guard; Capt, Army Res, 61. Mem: Mason; Elks; Farm Bur; Am. Legion. Rel: Methodist. Mailing Add: 116 N. 12th St, Room 1100, Lincoln, Nebr. 68508. (1967)

EDWARDS, JULIAN WARD D
Ga. State Rep.
b. Howard, Ga, 2/28/30; s. Julian Willis Edwards and Lillian Brown E; m. 6/15/56 to Billie Salmon; c. Hallie Ward. Educ: Gordon Mil. Col; Univ. Ga; John Gupton Sch. of Mortuary, Nashville, Tenn. Polit. & Govt. Pos: Aide to Lt. Gov. of Ga, 58-62; liaison officer, State Hwy. Dept, 63-64; Ga. State Rep, currently. Bus. & Prof. Pos: Mortician, Edwards Funeral Home, Butler, Ga. Mil. Serv: Entered as Pvt, released as S/Sgt, after serv. in Northeast. Air Command, 52-54. Mem: VFW; Elks; Kiwanis. Rel: Methodist. Legal Res: Garward Circle, Butler, Ga. 31006. Mailing Add: P.O. Box 427, Butler, Ga. 31006.

EDWARDS, LAWRENCE KIRKLAND, JR. D
b. Irvine, Fla, 6/22/17; s. Lawrence Kirkland Edwards and Inez Mathews E; m. 9/27/40 to Marjorie Griggs; c. Lawrence Kirkland, III, Martha Jane (Mrs. Davis), Elizabeth Ann and John Martin. Educ: Univ. Fla, Col. Agr, B.S.A, 39; Blue Key; Phi Delta Theta. Hon. LL.D, Atlanta Law Sch, 63. Polit. & Govt. Pos: Chmn, Marion Co. Dem. Exec. Cmt, Fla, 43; postmaster, Irvine, 45-50; Fla. State Sen, 14th Dist, 54-69, chmn, Appropriations, Finance and Taxation, Educ, Natural Resources Cmts. and chmn, Legis. Coun, Fla. House of Rep. Bus. & Prof. Pos: Pres, Irvine Crate & Basket Co, Irvine, Fla. and First Marion Bank, Ocala; livestock and timber farmer. Mem: Kiwanis; past state pres, Univ. Fla. Alumni Asn; Mason; Shrine; Elks; Moose; Farm Bur; WOW. Cert. of Meritorious Serv, Stetson Univ, 58. Rel: Baptist; Mem, Exec. Cmt, South. Baptist Conv, 6 years. Mailing Add: Irvine, Fla. 32653. (1967)

EDWARDS, LEE MARK R
b. Harlan, Iowa, 11/4/30; s. Leslie L. Edwards and Evelyn Vinding E; m. 3/25/51 to Ruth Johnson; c. Sandra, Linda and Roger. Educ: Iowa State Col, 2 years. Polit. & Govt. Pos: Chmn, Harrison Co. Rep. Party, Iowa, 64-69; precinct chmn, Morgan Twp. Rep. Party. Mem: Masonic York Rite Bodies, Abu Bekr Shrine; Lt. Gov, Kiwanis. Rel: Methodist. Mailing Add: Box 287, Mondamin, Iowa 51557. (1967)

EDWARDS, LEVERETT
Chmn, Nat. Mediation Bd.
b. Cordell, Okla, 1/21/02; s. Thomas Allison Edwards and Rose Catherine Leverett E; m. 11/5/29 to Louise Replogle; c. Jamie Louise and Katherine Allison. Educ: Univ. Okla, LL.B, 26; Phi Delta Phi; Phi Delta Theta. Polit. & Govt. Pos: Attorney gen, Okla, 26-27; chmn, Rwy. Emergency Bds. under Rwy. Labor Act, 46-49; mem, Indust. Cmn, Okla, 49-50; mem, Nat. Mediation Bd, Wash, D.C, 50-52, chmn, 52-; mem, Indust. Adv. Cmt. on Aviation Mobilization and Civil Aeronaut. Bd. Mem: Am, Okla. and Co. Bar Asns; Am. Law Inst; Nat. Acad. Arbitrators. Legal Res: 5300 Westbard Ave, Washington, D.C. 20016. Mailing Add: 1230 16th St. N.W, Washington, D.C. 20036. (1967)

EDWARDS, MARGARET MARY D
Committeewoman, N.J. State Dem. Orgn.
b. Fall River, Mass, 12/28/37; d. Leo A. Fournier and Eileen V. Skehan F; m. 8/18/56 to George C. Edwards; c. Candy and Glenn. Educ: Emerson Col, 1 year. Polit. & Govt. Pos: Committeewoman, Ocean Co. Dem. Orgn, N.J, 63-69, v.chmn, 66-69, chmn, 69; alternate del, Dem. Nat. Conv, 68; mem, Ocean Co. Bd. Elec, 68, secy-cmnr, 69-; mem. cmn. on youth involvement, N.J. State Dem. Orgn, 68, mem. cmn. on registrn, 69, committeewoman, 69- Mem: N.J. State Asn. Elec. Bd; PTA; Holbrook Little League Auxiliary; Jackson Dem. Club; Ocean Co. Dem. Women's Orgn; N.J. State Dem. Women's Orgn; Jackson Commun. Players; Jackson Civic Asn. Rel: Catholic. Mailing Add: 13 Oregon Ave, Jackson, N.J. 08527.

EDWARDS, NELSON JACK D
Mem. Steering Cmt, Mich. State Dem. Party
b. Montgomery, Ala, 8/3/17; s. Garfield Edwards and Annie Chapel E; m. 1937 to Laura Logan; c. Lorraine and Nelson, Jr. Educ: Completed 11th grade. Polit. & Govt. Pos: Del, Dem. Nat. Conv, 68; mem. steering cmt, Mich. State Dem. Party, currently; mem. steering cmt, Wayne Co. Dem. Party, currently; mem. adv. cmt. voc. educ, U.S. Dept. Health, Educ. and Welfare and U.S. Dept. Labor; mem, Mich. Civil Rights Cmn. on Cmt. Affirmative Action in Construction Indust; mem, Dem. State Cent. Cmt, Mich; mem, Wayne Co. Civil Serv. Cmn; consult. panel for voc. personnel develop. progs, U.S. Dept. Labor. Bus. & Prof. Pos: Laborer and local union officer, Dodge Main Plant, Chrysler Corp, 37-42; laborer and local union officer, Lincoln Plant, Ford Motor Co, 42-48; int. rep. Region 1A-Staff, Int. Union, UAW, 48-62, exec. bd. mem-at-lg, 62- Mem: Am. Civil Liberties Union; Mich. State Apprenticeship Progs; Mich. Partners of the Alliance; NAACP (second v.pres, Detroit Br); Nat. Safety Coun; Bd. United Found; Citizens Crusade Against Poverty; Citizens Adv. Cmt. on Equal Educ. Opportunities; Commun. Action Neighbors; Cmn. for City of Detroit's Coord. Coun. on Human Rels; Gen. Adv. Cmt. on Voc-Tech. Educ, Detroit Pub. Schs; Ad Hoc Cmt. Citizens Concerned with Equal Educ. Opportunities. Rel: Baptist. Legal Res: 17224 Wildemere St, Detroit, Mich. 48221. Mailing Add: International Union, United Automobile Workers of America, 8000 E. Jefferson, Detroit, Mich. 48214.

EDWARDS, RICHARD GUY R
Councilman, Co. of Hawaii.
b. Elkhart, Ind, 4/13/29; s. Joseph Oliver Edwards and Helen E. Baker E; div; c. Cynthia Ann. Educ: Trinity Univ, 50-51; Ind. Univ, B.A, 52; Georgetown Univ, 53-55; Acacia. Polit. & Govt. Pos: State conv. credentials chmn, Rep. Party, Hawaii, 65, first dist. chmn, 65-66, mem. state cent. cmt, 65-66; chmn. co. platform cmt, 66, chmn. co. rules cmt, 67 and mem. co. exec. cmt, 67-68; cand, Hawaii State Constitutional Conv, 68; del, Rep. Nat. Conv, 68; mem. nat. cmt. permanent orgn, Rep. Party, 68; councilman, Co. of Hawaii, 69- Bus. & Prof. Pos: Analyst, U.S. Govt, 54-60; resident mgr, Hawaii Subdiv, 62-68; broker and realtor, Hawaii-Hilo Realty, 67-69. Mil. Serv: Air Force, 48-52. Mem: Nat. Soc. Photogrammetry; Mason (32°); Volcano Isle Develop. Asn; Shriner; C. of C; Lions; Puna Young Farmers. Rel: Protestant. Mailing Add: SR Box C-10, Keaau, Hawaii 96749.

EDWARDS, TOM D
R.I. State Rep.
b. Etowah, Tenn, 9/5/08; m. to Lillian R. Polit. & Govt. Pos: R.I. State Rep, 63-; Dir, Newport Civilian Defense. Bus. & Prof. Pos: Bookkeeper. Mailing Add: 17 Cummings Rd, Newport, R.I. 02842. (1967)

EDWARDS, TOM W, JR. D
S.C. State Rep.
b. Nashville, Tenn, 11/11/29; s. Tom W. Edwards, Sr. and Mary Hill E; m. 3/7/64 to Dorothy Ballew; c. Anita Dawn. Educ: Presby. Col, 3 years; Univ. Denver, 1 year; Sigma Nu; Block P Club. Polit. & Govt. Pos: S.C. State Rep, Spartanburg Co, 67-, mem, Ways and Means Cmt, S.C. House of Rep, 68- Bus. & Prof. Pos: Sales Mgr, Crawford Door Co, 60-69. Mil. Serv: Entered Navy, 51, released as Adv. Navigator 1/C, 55, after serv. in Comdr. Air Force, Pac. Fleet, San Diego, Calif. Mem: Prfnl. Sales Engrs. Asn; South. Conf. Football Off. Asn; Carolina Intercollegiate Football Off. Asn; Sertoma; adv. bd, Boy Scouts; Jaycees; bd. dir, Nat. Co. Found; chmn, March of Dimes, 61; alumni adv, Sigma Nu, Wofford Col; panelist, Keep Am. Beautiful, Inc, 69. Rel: Methodist. Legal Res: 504 Perrin Dr, Spartanburg, S.C. 29302. Mailing Add: Box 1911, Spartanburg, S.C. 29301.

EDWARDS, W. RUSSELL, JR. D
Maine State Rep.
b. Falmouth Foreside, Maine, 11/14/33; s. W. Russell Edwards and Doris Jackson E; m. 2/6/58 to Shirley Sewell; c. Kimberley Joy, W. Russell, III, Loraine Mae and Terrence John. Educ: Univ. Maine. Polit. & Govt. Pos: Maine State Rep, 65- Mil. Serv: Air Force. Mem: Eagles; Jr. C. of C. Rel: Protestant. Mailing Add: 7 Bryant St, Portland, Maine 04103.

EDWARDS, WALTER MALCOLM D
b. Kinston, Ala, 4/5/09; s. Leroy Mansfield Edwards and Charlotte Morgan E; m. 12/8/30 to Amelia A. Thompson; c. Malcolm Lamar, Doris Marie (Mrs. Gene Jackson). Educ: Santa Rosa (Fla) Pub. Schs. Polit. & Govt. Pos: Ala. State Rep, 55-59, 63-67; chmn, E. Brewton Water Works Bd. Bus. & Prof. Pos: Bus, 25 years. Mem: Woodmen of the World. Rel: Baptist. Mailing Add: E. Brewton, Ala. 36426. (1967)

EDWARDS, WILLIAM CHARLES R
Chmn, Bon Homme Co. Rep. Cmt, S.Dak.
b. Kansas City, Mo, 1/27/05; s. Ernest Smith Edwards and Eleanor Hoefner E; m. 11/24/32 to Myrtle O. Thompson; c. Ernest T. Educ: Iowa State Univ, B.S, 30; Kappa Sigma. Polit. & Govt. Pos: Chmn, Bon Homme Co. Rep. Cmt, S.Dak, 61-; mem. sch. bd, Tyndall, 53-56, councilman, 61-68 and mayor, 68- Bus. & Prof. Pos: Adminstr, St. Michaels Hosp, Tyndall, S.Dak, currently. Mem: S.Dak. Dairy Asn; Farmers Union; Mason; Rotary; C. of C. Rel: Methodist. Mailing Add: Box 53, Tyndall, S.Dak. 57066.

EDWARDS, WILLIAM DEARA
b. EcLectic, Ala, 7/7/16; s. Oscar Parker Edwards and Annie Chapman E; m. 5/26/39 to Virginia Spencer; c. Spencer Chapman, William Parker. Educ: Auburn Univ, B.A. Polit. & Govt. Pos: Ala. State Rep, 62-66. Bus. & Prof. Pos: Cattle bus, 58-; farm implement bus, 37-58. Mem: Mason. Rel: Methodist. Mailing Add: Ft. Deposit, Ala. 36032. (1967)

EFIRD, HOYLE TIMOTHY D
b. Stanly Co, N.C, 7/11/06; s. Henry P. Efird and Sallie Braswell E; m. Jan. 31 to Dora M. Ham; c. Tom David. Educ: Elon Col, B.S, Bus. Admin, 29; Inst. of Govt, Univ. of N.C, 48. Polit. & Govt. Pos: N.C. State Rep, 61-66; sheriff, Gaston Co, 44-54; past pres, Gaston Co. Young Dem. Club; N.C. Sheriffs' Asn. Bus. & Prof. Pos: Pres, Gastonia United Oil Co, Inc; Distributors Coun, Am. Oil Co; bd. of dirs, N.C. Oil Jobbers Asn. (pres, 64). Mil. Serv: Hq. Co, Nat. Guard, Albemarle, N.C, 21-23. Mem: Mason; Elks; Shriner; Eagles; Gaston Country Club. Rel: Presbyterian. Mailing Add: 1215 Oakwood Ave, Gastonia, N.C. 28052. (1967)

EGAN, MICHAEL JOSEPH R
Ga. State Rep.
b. Savannah, Ga, 8/8/26; s. Michael Joseph Egan and Elise Robider E; m. 4/14/51 to Donna Jean Cole; c. Moria, Michael, Donna, Cole, Roby and John. Educ: Yale Univ, A.B, 50; Harvard Law Sch, LL.B, 55. Polit. & Govt. Pos: Ga. State Rep, 66-; del, Rep. Nat. Conv, 68. Bus. & Prof. Pos: Assoc, Sutherland, Asbill & Brennan, 55-61, partner, 61- Mil. Serv: Entered as Pvt, Army, 45, released as 2nd Lt, 47; recalled to active duty, 50, released as 1st Lt, 52, after serv. in Pac. Theater with 86th Inf. Div, 46 and in Korea with 2nd Inf. Div, 9th Inf. Regt, 51-52. Publ: Problems of Federal Taxation of Estates-Gifts-Trusts, Am. Law Inst. and Am. Bar Asn, 66. Mem: Am. and Atlanta Bar Asns; State Bar of Ga; Atlanta Lawyers Club; Piedmont Driving Club; Commerce Club. Rel: Roman Catholic. Legal Res: 97 Brighton Rd. N.E, Atlanta, Ga. 30309. Mailing Add: First National Bank Building, Atlanta, Ga. 30303.

EGAN, RENA ADELE R
b. New York, N.Y, 9/14/23; d. Dr. Reginald B. Weiler and Effie May Russell W; m. 7/25/40 to Walter Steve Egan; c. B. Steve and J. Susan. Educ: Pueblo Jr. Col, A.A; Colo. Col, B.S; St. Francis Hosp, Colo. Springs, Registry of Med. Technologist. Polit. & Govt. Pos: Admin. asst. to co. chmn, Colo, 64-68; voting machine instr, Pueblo, Colo, 66-68 and educ. chmn, 69-; mem, Rep. State Cent. Cmt, 67-69; del, Rep. Nat. Conv, 68. Bus. & Prof. Pos: Head hematology technologist, lab, St. Francis Hosp, 59-62; head technologist, lab, Alamosa Commun. Hosp, 62-63 and Parkview Episcopal Hosp, 63-67; head technologist, lab. mgr, Marsh Path. Labs, 67-69. Publ: Five articles in, Colorado Medical Technologist on Hematology. Mem: Pueblo Soc. Med. Technologists (past pres, and secy); Colo. Soc. Med. Technolgists (pres, 67-68 and legis. chmn); Am. Soc. Med. Technologists; Am. Soc. Clin. Pathologists; chmn. Yellow Rose Ball cancer fund, Beta Sigma Phi; pres, Am. Bus. Women's Asn. Rocky Mt. Chap; major, Easter Seal Drive, 69; chmn, Ment. Health Bell Ringers Drive, 69; Bd. Commun. Youth Found. Inc. Woman of the Year, Am. Bus. Women's Asn. Rocky Mt. Chap. Rel: Episcopal. Legal Res: Route 1, Box 28, Beulah, Colo. 81020. Mailing Add: 2520 Seventh Ave, Pueblo, Colo. 81003.

EGAN, WILLIAM ALLEN D
b. Valdez, Alaska, 10/8/14; s. William Edward Egan and Cora Allen E; m. 11/16/40 to Neva McKittrick; c. Dennis William. Educ: Valdez High Sch, grad, 32; Alaska Methodist Univ, LL.D. Polit. & Govt. Pos: First gov, Alaska, 59-67; Alaska Tenn. Plan Senator in Statehood effort, Wash, D.C, 57-58; pres, Alaska Constitutional Conv, 55-56; Alaska State Sen, 53-55; speaker, Alaska House of Rep, 51; Alaska State Rep, 41-51; mayor, Valdez, 46, city councilman, 41-45 and 37-38. Bus. & Prof. Pos: Owner, Valdez Supply, Valdez, Alaska, 46-; chmn, Western Governors' Conf, 61. Mil. Serv: Entered as Pvt, Army, 43, released as Sgt, 46. Mem: Pioneers of Alaska; VFW; Am. Legion; pres, C. of C, 48; Elks; Eagles; Rotary; Moose; Lions Int; OX5 Club. Pilot, private flying. Rel: Catholic. Mailing Add: Box 445, Anchorage, Alaska 99501. (1967)

EGBERT, RICHARD ALEXANDER D
b. Tetonia, Idaho, 8/23/06; s. Hyrum S. Egbert and Annie McGhie E; m. 5/11/32 to Alta Phillips; c. LaRae (Mrs. Merrill Wilson) and Richard Phillips. Educ: Ricks Col. Polit. & Govt. Pos: Idaho State Rep, 41-48 & 60-62, asst. minority leader, Idaho House of Rep, 47-48; Idaho State Sen, 63-69, asst. minority leader, Idaho State Senate, 63-66. Bus. & Prof. Pos: Owner and mgr, livestock ranch. Mem: Former chmn, Teton Dist. and former mem. bd, Teton Peaks Coun, Boy Scouts; adv. coun, Targhee Nat. Forest; adv. bd, Bur. of Land Mgt; pres, Targhee Woolgrowers Asn. Rel: Latter-day Saint. Mailing Add: Tetonia, Idaho 83452.

EGEBERG, ROGER O. D
Asst. Secy. Health and Sci. Affairs, Dept. of Health, Educ. and Welfare
b. Chicago, Ill, 11/13/03; m. to Margaret McEchron Chahoon; c. Dagny (Mrs. William Hancock), Sarah (Mrs. Robert Beauchamp), Roger Olaf and Karen

(Mrs. Richard Warner). Educ: Cornell Univ, B.A, 25; Northwest. Univ, M.D, 29. Polit. & Govt. Pos: Chmn, Gov. Cmt. for Study of Med. Care and Health, Calif, 59-60; Asst. Secy. of Health and Sci. Affairs, Dept. of Health, Educ. and Welfare, 69- Bus. & Prof. Pos: Intern, Wesley Hosp, Chicago, Ill; resident, Univ. Hosp, Ann Arbor, Mich; private practice int. med, Cleveland, Ohio, 32-42; chief of med. serv, Vet. Admin. Hosp, Los Angeles, Calif, 46-56; med. dir, Los Angeles Co. Hosp, 56-58; staff mem, Los Angeles Co. Gen. Hosp. and Rancho Amigos Hosp, Downey; prof. med, Univ. Calif, Los Angeles, 48-64 and Col. Med. Evangelists, 56-64; prof. med, Univ. South. Calif, 56-69, dean sch. of med, 64-69. Mil. Serv: Entered as Maj, Med. Corps, Army, 42, released as Col, 46, after serv. as personal physician and aide-de-camp to Gen. Douglas MacArthur, 44-45; Bronze Star; Legion of Merit; St. Olaf's Medal, Norway. Publ: 'Regional Medical Programs,' Calif. Med, 1/68; 'Balance Between Medical Education and Medical Service in Medical Schools,' J. Am. Med. Asn, 5/68; 'Discussion of Group Practice in the Education of Medical Students,' J. N.Y. Acad. of Med, 11/68; plus others. Mem: Nat. Adv. Cancer Coun; spec. med. adv. group, Vet. Admin; Calif. Bd. of Pub. Health; chmn, Calif. Cmn. on Regional Med. Progs; dipl, Am. Bd. Internal Med; fel. Am. Col. Physicians; Am, Calif. and Los Angeles Co. Med. Asns; Am. Clin. and Climatological Asn; Calif. Soc. of Internal Med; Alpha Omega Alpha; Phi Kappa Phi. Legal Res: 6918 Oporto Dr, Los Angeles, Calif. 90028. Mailing Add: Dept. of Health, Education and Welfare, 330 Independence Ave. S.W, Washington, D.C. 20201.

EGERMAN, HOWARD DOUGLAS D
b. San Francisco, Calif, 8/2/46; s. Alvin Prince Egerman and Enid Yampol E; single. Educ: Univ. Calif, Davis, B.A, 68; Univ. Calif, Riverside, 68-; Pi Sigma Alpha; Young Dem; Hillel; Cal Aggie Newspaper. Polit. & Govt. Pos: Treas, Yolo Co, Young Citizens for Johnson-Humphrey, Calif, 64; chmn, Youth for Brown and Anderson Youth Corps, Davis, 66; pres, Davis Young Dem, 66-68; dep. regional dir, Calif. Fedn. Young Dem, 67-68; publicity chmn, Yolo Co. Citizens for Beilenson Senate, 68; chmn, Davis Students for Kennedy, 68; del, Dem. Nat. Conv, 68. Mem: Am. Polit. Sci. Asn; Am. Civil Liberties Union. Rel: Jewish. Legal Res: 556 Bradley Ave, San Jose, Calif. 95128. Mailing Add: 640 Linden St, No. 764, Riverside, Calif. 92507.

EGGERS, JEAN ETHALEN R
V.Chmn, Minnehaha Co. Rep. Cent. Cmt, S.Dak.
b. Sioux Falls, S.Dak, 4/19/28; d. Russell Glenn Bachtell and Ethalen Johnson B; m. 3/2/46 to Curtis Ordell Eggers; c. Sandra Dean (Mrs. Sorum), Kathleen, Lanette, Timothy and Michael. Educ: Wash. High Sch, Sioux Falls, S.Dak, 4 years. Polit. & Govt. Pos: Rep. precinct committeewoman, Mapleton Twp, S.Dak, 52-; v.chmn, Minnehaha Co. Rep. Cent. Cmt, 60- Mem: Pres, Renner Luthern Church womans group; v.pres, Dist. 1, Am. Legion Auxiliary. Rel: Lutheran. Mailing Add: Renner, S.Dak, 57055.

EGGERS, PAUL WALTER R
Gen. Counsel, U.S. Treasury Dept.
b. Seymour, Ind, 4/20/19; s. Ernest H. Eggers and Ottillie Carre E; m. 12/29/46 to Frances May Kramer; c. Steven Paul. Educ: Valparaiso Univ, B.A, 41; Univ. Tex, Austin, LL.B, 48. Polit. & Govt. Pos: Past chmn, Cmt. on Rules and Procedures, Tex. Rep. Party; chmn, Wichita Co. Rep. Party, 66-68; Rep. cand. for Gov, 68; del, Rep. Nat. Conv, 68; gen. counsel, U.S. Treasury Dept, currently; chmn, Rep. Task Force, Revenue and Fiscal Policy Cmt, 66-68. Bus. and Prof. Pos: Attorney-at-law, 48-52; Law Firm of Eggers, Sherrill, Pace and Rogers, Wichita Falls, Tex, 53-69; dir, City Nat. Bank, 67-69. Mil. Serv: Pvt, Air Corps, 41, Maj, 46. Mem: Chmn, taxation sect, State Bar of Tex, 68-69, dir, real estate and probate sect; Am. and Fed. Bar Asns; Am. Judicature Soc. Sports Illustrated Silver Anniversary All Am. Award, 66; Outstanding Layman of Year, Episcopal Diocese of Dallas, 68. Rel: Episcopal. Legal Res: 2513 Amherst Drive, Wichita Falls, Tex. 76308. Mailing Add: 3220 Klingle Road, N.W, Washington, D.C. 20008.

EGGERT, FRED W. D
b. Bronx, N.Y; m. to Doris T. Higgins; c. six. Educ: Fordham Col; Fordham Sch. of Law; N.Y. Univ. Sch. of Law. Polit. & Govt. Pos: N.Y. State Assemblyman, 54-65; asst. dist. attorney Bronx Co, 3 years; N.Bronx Dem. Club. Bus. & Prof. Pos: Lawyer, Eggert and Higgins, N.Y. Mil. Serv: World War II, Capt, Europe, 2 years. Mem: N.Y. State, Bronx Co. Bar Asn; VFW; K. of C; dir. Bronx Regional Nat. Conf. Christians and Jews; Rotary Club of Bronx. Mailing Add: 4742 White Plains Ave, Bronx, N.Y. 10466.

EGGLE, DORIS E. R
Chmn, Osceola Co. Rep. Party, Mich.
b. Adrian, Mich, 3/14/23; m. 12/12/44 to Robert J. Eggle; c. Robert J, Jr, David J, Randall L. and Marsha A. Polit. & Govt. Pos: Chmn, Osceola Co. Rep. Party, Mich, 3 years; pres, Osceola Co. Rep. Women, 5 years. Bus. & Prof. Pos: Homemaker. Mem: Farm Bur. Rel: Baptist. Mailing Add: Route 2, Tustin, Mich. 49688.

EHLERS, THOMAS MARTIN R
Area Chmn, Sixth Cong. Dist. Rep. Party, Minn.
b. Worthington, Minn, 2/6/37; s. Martin Andrew Ehlers and Genevieve Ellen Rust E; m. 4/12/64 to Sandra Joan McCartney; c. Joseph Martin and Genevieve Elizabeth. Educ: Am. Univ, 57; Hamline Univ, B.A, 59; N.Y. Univ, M.S.R, 60; Pi Gamma Mu; Pi Kappa Delta; Eta Mu Pi; Tau Kappa Epsilon. Polit. & Govt. Pos: Chmn, Redwood Co. Rep. Party, Minn, 65-67; mem, Rep. State Cent. Cmt, Minn, 65-; area chmn, Sixth Cong. Dist. Rep. Party, 67- Bus. & Prof. Pos: Exec. trainee, Abraham and Straus, Minneapolis, Minn, 59 and Daytons, 60; buyer, Ehlers, Inc, 61-63, v.pres. and merchandise mgr, 64- Rel: Episcopal. Mailing Add: 521 E. Third St, Redwood Falls, Minn. 56283.

EHRLICH, ELEANOR EWING D
Secy-Treas, Niskayuna Dem. Town Cmt, N.Y.
b. Pontiac, Ill, 1/18/18; d. William McCord Ewing and Sarah Lovelock E; m. 7/7/45 to Richard Ehrlich; c. Paul Ewing and Joan Ewing. Educ: Univ. Ill, Urbana, B.A, 41, M.A, 43; Cornell Univ, 46-47; Phi Beta Kappa; Pi Mu Epsilon; Presbyterian Hall. Polit. & Govt. Pos: Committeeman, Niskayuna Dem. Party, N.Y, 66-; alternate del, Dem. Nat. Conv, 68; Dem-Liberal Cand, N.Y. State Assembly, 68; secy-treas, Nishayuna Dem. Town Cmt, N.Y, 68- Bus. & Prof. Pos: Math. instr, Pratt-Whitney Aircraft, East Hartford, Conn, 43-44; mathematician, theoretical physics div, Manhattan Proj, Los Alamos, N.Mex, 44-45. Mem: Adv, Newcomer's Club; Knolls Atomic Power Lab; Cornell Women's Club (secy-treas); Am. Asn. Univ. Women. War Dept. Appreciation Serv. Award. Rel: Presbyterian. Mailing Add: 2125 Lynn Plaza, Schenectady, N.Y. 12309.

EHRLICHMAN, JOHN DANIEL R
Counsel to the President
b. Tacoma, Wash, 3/20/25; s. Rudolph I. Ehrlichman and Lillian Danielson E; m. 8/21/49 to Jeanne Fisher; c. Peter, Jan, Tom, Jody and Robert. Educ: Univ. Calif, Los Angeles, A.B, 48; Stanford Univ, LL.B; Phi Eta Sigma; Kappa Sigma. Polit. & Govt. Pos: Counsel to the President, 69- Bus. & Prof. Pos: Partner, Hullin, Ehrlichman, Roberts & Hodge, 52-68. Mil. Serv: Entered as Aviation Cadet, Army Air Corps, 43, released as 1st Lt, 45, after serv. in Eighth Air Force, ETO, 43-45; Air Medal with Clusters; Distinguished Flying Cross. Mem: Am, Calif. and State of Wash. Bar Asns. Rel: Christian Science. Legal Res: 330 Chesapeake Dr, Great Falls, Va. 22066. Mailing Add: The White House, Washington, D.C. 20500.

EICHER, BOB HENRY R
b. Louisville, Ky, 1923. Educ: Northwest. Univ. Radio Eng. Sch, Fed. Eng. License. Polit. & Govt. Pos: Former Ky. State Rep. Bus. & Prof. Pos: Spec. Events Dir, Newsman, WKLO Radio. Mil. Serv: Army Air Force, World War II. Mem: Am. Legion; pres, Methodist Men's Club. Am. Legion Spec. Award for Heroism (DuPont Explosion Work). Rel: Methodist. Mailing Add: 1369 S. First St, Louisville, Ky. 40208. (1967)

EICHHORN, JANICE E. D
b. St. Louis, Mo; d. W. Herschel Eichhorn and Bernice Saphian E; single. Educ: Wash. Univ. and Univ. Ill, Urbana. Polit. & Govt. Pos: Pres, S.W. Young Dem. Club D.C, 67; precinct chmn, D.C. Dem. Party, 67 and Ward chmn, 67-68; alternate del, Dem. Nat. Conv, 68; dep. admin. asst. to U.S. Sen. Gaylord Nelson, Wis, 69- Mem: S.W. Community House, Inc.(secy, bd. dirs, 68-); S.W. Neighborhood Assembly (secy, 67, ed, Southwester, 68); bd. dirs, Gr. Wash. Americans for Dem. Action, 69- Women's Doer Award, D.C. Dem. Women's Club, 67. Mailing Add: 529 A Fourth St. S.E, Washington, D.C. 20003.

EICHHORN, VON ARDEN D
Chmn, Wells Co. Dem. Party, Ind.
b. Bluffton, Ind, 5/4/06; s. Charles R. Eichhorn and Harriet Jane Brickley E; m. 7/31/26 to Myrtle A. Fairchild; c. Mary Jane (Mrs. Wheeler), Gloria (Mrs. Buckner) and Thomas. Educ: Union High Sch. Polit. & Govt. Pos: Ind. State Sen, 39-67; chmn, Wells Co. Dem. Party, 64-, dist. treas, Dem. Party chmn. of many cmns. Mem: K. of P; Speakers Bur. Rel: Lutheran. Mailing Add: Box 127, Uniondale, Ind. 46791.

EIDSON, WANDA CARROLL R
b. Weldon, Tex, 8/15/22; d. Ira Lee Carroll and Wera Keeling C; m. 3/17/44 to Jack L. Eidson; c. Jack, Jr, Mark, Scott, Carroll and Jon. Educ: Tex. State Col. for Women, B.S. in Music, 43; Univ. Tex, M.A. in Music, 45; Mary Eleanor Breckenridge Club; Mod. Choir. Polit. & Govt. Pos: V.chmn, Parker Co. Rep. Party, Tex, 62-64, chmn, 64-69; alternate del, Rep. Nat. Conv, 64. Bus. & Prof. Pos: Choir dir. and soloist, Presbyterian Church Choir, Weatherford, Tex, 50- Mem: Cecilian Music Club; Nat. Duplicate Bridge Asn; Tex. life mem, PTA; mem. cmt, Girl Scouts, 55-65; den mother, Boy Scouts, 60-65; Rep. Womens Club; Ft. Worth Woman's Club; Ridglea Country Club, Ft. Worth; Live Oak Country Club, Weatherford. Rel: Presbyterian. Mailing Add: 607 W. Columbia, Weatherford, Tex. 76086. (1967)

EIGENBROD, WILBUR F. D
b. Mountain Top, Pa, 1/31/15; s. Mr. and Mrs. W. H. Eigenbrod; m. to Ethel T. Fairchild; c. Kenneth Lee Jr, Mrs. David Parks. Educ: Pa. State Univ. Sch. of Exten. Polit. & Govt. Pos: Health and safety mgt. asst, U.S. Dept. Interior Bur. Mines, 67-; dir, W.Va. Dept. of Mines, 63-67 and safety engr, 61-63. Bus. & Prof. Pos: Safety dir, New River and Pocahontas Consol. Coal Co. Mines in W.Va. and Ky, safety inspector for same co. Mem: Young Dem. Club of W.Va; Mason (32°). Rel: Methodist. Mailing Add: 1241 Woodland Dr, Charleston, W.Va. 25302. (1967)

EILBERG, JOSHUA D
U.S. Rep, Pa.
b. Phila, Pa, 2/12/21; s. David B. Eilberg (deceased) and Miriam Jaspan E; m. 1/2/44 to Gladys Greenberg; c. William H. and Amy B. Educ: Wharton Sch, Univ. Pa, B.S; Temple Univ. Law Sch, J.D. Polit. & Govt. Pos: Asst. dist. attorney, Phila, Pa, 52-54; Pa. State Rep, 54-66, mem. exec. bd, Gen. State Authority, exec. bd, Joint State Govt. Cmn, Interstate Coop. Cmn, Pa. House of Rep, 54-64 and Minority Whip and Majority Leader, 64-66; del, Dem. Nat. Conv, 60, 64 & 68; U.S. Rep, Pa, 67-, mem. Judiciary cmt. and subcmt, Immigration and Nationality, U.S. House of Rep. Mil. Serv: Entered as Ens, Navy, 41, released as Lt.(sg), 45, after serv. in Fleet Air Wing One, Pac. Area; Pac. Theater Ribbon. Mem: Am. Bar Asn; first v.pres, Phila. chap, Fed. Bar Asn; Am. Judicature Soc; nat. panel arbitrators, Am. Arbit. Asn; chmn, Frontier Dist, Boy Scouts; trustee, Col. Podiatry Phila; bd. mem, Phila. Geriatric Center; bd. mem, Cruiser Olympia Asn; hon. pres, Northeast Ment. Health Clinic Phila; VFW; Am. Legion; Jewish War Vets; DAV; Mason; B'nai B'rith. Rel: Jewish; Trustee, Congregation Beth Emeth. Legal Res: 1522 Longshore Ave, Philadelphia, Pa. 19149. Mailing Add: 1130 Longworth House Office Bldg, Washington, D.C. 20515.

EILERT, DAVID DeWITT D
Chmn, Pike Co. Dem. Cent. Cmt, Ind.
b. Stendal, Ind, 8/21/06; s. William H. Eilert and Rosina C. Egbert E; m. 6/16/40 to Edna L. Wellemeyer; c. Donald E. and Lois Jean. Educ: Oakland City Col, 2 year cert; Am. Inst. of Banking, course in Pub. Rels. Polit. & Govt. Pos: Chmn, Pike Co. Dem. Cent. Cmt, Ind, 52-; secy, Eighth Dist. Dem. Party, 62- Bus. & Prof. Pos: Sch. teacher, 25-54, coach, 4 years; recreation supvr, Works Progress Admin, five co. in South. Ind, 39-42; asst. cashier, Holland Nat. Bank, 54-62, cashier, 64-; cashier, First Nat. Bank, Spurgeon, 62-64. Mem: Past pres, Quad-Co. Bankers Asn; past dir, local Kiwanis Club; Originator and first pres, local Methodist Men's Orgn. Rel: Methodist; Off. Bd. Mem, 20 years. Mailing Add: Stendal, Ind. 47585.

EILTS, HERMANN FREDERICK
U.S. Ambassador to Saudi Arabia
b. Germany, 3/23/22; s. Friedrich Alex Eilts and Meta Dorothea Prüser E; nat, 1930; m. 6/12/48 to Helen Josephine Brew; c. Conrad Marshall and Frederick Lowell. Educ: Ursinus Col, B.A, 42, LL.D, 60; Johns Hopkins Univ. Sch. Adv. Int. Studies, M.A, 47. Polit. & Govt. Pos: Career officer, U.S. Dept. of State For. Serv, 47-; mem. staff, Am. Embassy, Tehran, 47-48 and Jidda, 48-50, v.consul and consul, Aden, 51-53; second secy, Baghdad, 54-56; officer-in-charge, Baghdad Pact and SEATO Affairs, 57-60 and Arabian Peninsular Affairs, 60-61; with Nat.War Col, 61-62; first secy, London, 62-64; dep. chief of mission and counselor, Tripoli, 64-65; U.S. Ambassador to Saudi Arabia, 65- Mil. Serv: 1st Lt, Army, 42-45. Arthur S. Flemming Award for Govt. Serv, 58. Legal Res: Scranton, Pa. Mailing Add: American Embassy, APO New York 09697.

EINARSON, F. M. R
b. Mountain, Dak. Territory, 7/11/88; married; c. Three. Educ: Bus. Col. Polit. & Govt. Pos: N.Dak. State Rep, 47-61; co. cmnr; sch. and twp. bds. Bus. & Prof. Pos: Retired farmer. Mailing Add: Mountain, N.Dak. 58262.

EINHAUS, LYLE L. R
Chmn, Spokane Co. Rep. Party, Wash.
b. Hampton, Iowa, 6/6/23; s. Edward R. Einhaus and Amanda E; m. 3/17/50 to Jean L; c. Mark and Brad. Educ: Univ. N.Dak, B.S. Polit. & Govt. Pos: Chmn, Spokane Co. Rep. Party, Wash, 66- Rel: Lutheran. Mailing Add: 2027 E. 37th, Spokane, Wash. 99203.

EISENBERG, RONALD AARON R
b. Cleveland, Ohio, 5/3/42; s. Saul Eisenberg and Evelyn Tomarkin E; m. 10/10/65 to Frances Rafelson. Educ: Colgate Univ, 60-62; West. Reserve Univ, A.B. in Eng, 64; Ohio State Univ, M.A. in Radio-TV, 67; George Wash. Univ. Col. Law, currently; Tau Kappa Epsilon. Polit. & Govt. Pos: Press secy, Taft for Cong. Cmt, 66; press secy, U.S. Rep. Robert Taft, Jr, 67-68, admin. asst. and press. secy, 68- Bus. & Prof. Pos: News ed-announcer, WCOL Radio, Columbus, Ohio, 65 and WTVN Radio, 65-66; spec. correspondent, Radio and TV, Dem. and Rep. Nat. Conv, Taft Broadcasting Co, 68. Publ: 'Vehicles of Communication Employed by Robert Taft, Jr, Candidate for Congress, 1966 Congressional Elections,' Master's Thesis, Ohio State Univ, 67. Legal Res: 2348 Vista Place, Cincinnati, Ohio 45208. Mailing Add: 430 M St. S.W, Washington, D.C. 20024.

EISENHOWER, JOHN SHELDON DOUD R
U.S. Ambassador to Belgium
b. Denver, Colo, 8/3/22; s. Dwight David Eisenhower and Mamie Geneva Doud E; m. 6/10/47 to Barbara Jean Thompson; c. Dwight David, II, Barbara Anne (Mrs. Fernando Echavarria-Uribe), Susan Elaine and Mary Jean. Educ: U.S. Mil. Acad, grad, 44; Columbia Univ, M.A. in Eng. and Comp. Lit, 50. Polit. & Govt. Pos: Asst. staff secy, White House, 58-61; U.S. Ambassador to Belgium, 69- Mil. Serv: Entered as 2nd Lt, Army, 44, released as Lt. Col, 63, after serv. in Inf. Div, Europe and Korea, 52-53; Col, Army Res, 69; Legion of Merit; Bronze Star; Army Commendation Ribbon; Combat Inf. Badge. Publ: The Bitter Woods, G. P. Putnam's Sons, 69. Rel: Presbyterian. Legal Res: 111 White Horse Rd, Phoenixville, Pa. 19460. Mailing Add: American Embassy, APO New York 09667.

EISENHOWER, MILTON STOVER R
b. Abilene, Kans, 9/15/99; s. David Jacob Eisenhower and Ida Stover E; m. 10/12/27 to Helen Elsie Eakin, wid; c. Milton Stover and Ruth Eakin. Educ: Kans. State Univ, B.S, 24; Pi Kappa Phi; Sigma Alpha Epsilon; Alpha Zeta. Hon. degrees from 31 cols. and univs. Polit. & Govt. Pos: Am. v.consul, Edinburgh, Scotland, 24-26; Asst. to Secy. of Agr, 26-28; dir. info, Dept. of Agr, 28-41; mem. various govt. cmns, 40-; dir, War Relocation Authority, 42; assoc. dir, Off. of War Info, 42-43; mem, Famine Emergency Relief Cmt, 46; mem. exec. bd, UNESCO, 46, chmn, U.S. Nat. Cmn. for UNESCO, 46-48 and del, UNESCO Conf, 46, 47, 48 & 49; trustee, Nat. Cmt. Econ. Develop, 47-51; chmn, Gen. Awards Jury, 50; mem, President's Cmt. on Govt. Orgn, 53-60; spec. ambassador and personal rep. of President, Latin Am. Affairs, 53 & 57-60. Bus. & Prof. Pos: Dir, Freedoms Found. Inc, 51-, Geisinger Mem. Hosp, 52- and Fund for Adult Educ, 53-61; chmn, Am. Korean Found, 52-53; dir, B&O R.R, C&O R.R, Commercial Credit Co; F.A.S. Int; Chicago Bd. Trade; I.S.I. Growth Fund; pres, Kans. State Univ, 43-50, Pa. State Univ, 50-56 and Johns Hopkins Univ, 56-57, emer. pres, 67-; chmn, President's Cmn. Causes and Prevention of Violence; mem. bd. visitors, U.S. Naval Acad, 58-61; pub. gov, N.Y. Stock Exchange, 62-65. Publ: The Wine is Bitter, 63; numerous fed. leaflets. Mem: Fel. Am. Acad. Arts and Sci; Kans. Acad. Sci. Received several awards from for. govt. Rel: Episcopal. Mailing Add: 4545 N. Charles St, Baltimore, Md. 21210.

EISENMAN, JANE MORLEY R
b. Detroit, Mich, 2/18/22; d. Howard Peter Morley and Zelma Hinz M; m. 3/19/45 to Walter Eisenman; c. Jean, Judith and John. Educ: Ward-Belmont Jr. Col. for Women; Univ. of Mich. Polit. & Govt. Pos: Del, Dist, Co. and State Rep. Conv, 60-66; pres, Minn. Fedn. Rep. Women, 63-65, mem. exec. cmt, 65-67; alternate del, Rep. Nat. Conv, 64; mem, Minn. Rep. State Platform Cmt, 64-68; v.chairwoman, Eighth Cong. Dist. Rep. Party, Minn. and chairwoman, 63rd Legis. Dist. Rep. Party, 65-67; del-at-lg, Gov. Adv. Bd. on Handicapped, Gifted and Exceptional Children, 69- Mil. Serv: Entered as Ens, Waves, 44, released as Lt.(jg), 46, after serv. in Commun, D.C. Mem: Med. Auxiliary; Legis. chmn, Minn. State Med. Auxiliary; Am. Asn. Univ. Women; League of Women Voters; bd. of dirs. of Arch. Rel: Lutheran. Mailing Add: 2527 Seventh Ave. E, Hibbing, Minn. 55746.

EISENSTADT, THOMAS STEPHEN D
High Sheriff, Suffolk Co, Mass.
b. Boston, Mass, 5/21/36; s. Benjamin Eisenstadt and Mary Ellen Husher E; m. 2/6/65 to Linda Ann Morgan; c. Kristin Victoria. Educ: Boston Univ. Col. of Lib. Arts, A.B, 58; Boston Univ. Sch. of Law, LL.B, 61. Polit. & Govt. Pos: Mem, Boston Sch. Cmt, Mass, 62-, past treas. and chmn; del-at-lg, Dem. Nat. Conv, 68; High Sheriff, Suffolk Co, Mass, 69- Bus. & Prof. Pos: Lawyer, 61-69. Mem: Boston and Mass. Bar Asns; Mass. Asn. of Sch. Cmts; Nat. Coun. for Pub. Schs; Nat. Sheriff's Asn; chmn, City of Boston Week-Day Relig. Educ. Cmt; trustee, City of Boston Teachers' Retirement Fund; bd. dirs, Eng. High Alumni Asn; K. of C.(4°); bd. mgr, Dorchester YMCA; Am. Legion (assoc. mem, William G. Walsh Post); Dorchester Civic Club; bd. dirs, Dorchester Little League, Nat. Conf. on Christians and Jews and Action for Boston Commun. Develop; pub. educ. cmt, Nat. Cancer Soc, Mass; educ. chmn, Nat. Cancer Crusade; legis. cmt, Nat. Sch. Bd. Asn; dir. Great Cities Prog. for Sch. Improv; Nat. Coun. for Support of Pub. Schs. Jr. B'nai B'rith Cert. for Outstanding Contributions to Educ, 60; Pub. Serv. Award, Mass. Young Dem, 62; Jr. C. of C. Award for One of Ten Outstanding Men, 64; Outstanding Young Man in Am, 65. Rel: Roman Catholic. Mailing Add: 30 Avon St, Jamaica Plain, Mass. 02130.

EIVERS, GEORGE R
Ore. State Sen.
b. 12/3/14; m. to Ruth; c. Five sons, four daughters. Educ: Northwest. Col. of Law, LL.B. Polit. & Govt. Pos: Former mem, Clackamas Co. Welfare Cmn, Ore; campaign chmn. for Secy. of State Howell Appling, Jr, 60; Ore. State Sen, 66- Bus. & Prof. Pos: Small business man. Mem: Clackamas Co. Farm Bur; N.Clackamas C. of C; K. of C; Elks; Am. Legion. Mailing Add: 12345 Stanley Ave, Milwaukie, Ore. 97222.

ELAM, CLARENCE RICHARD R
Mem, Rep. City Cmt, Boston, Mass.
b. Cambridge, Mass, 10/3/23; s. Robert Harry Elam and Blanche D. Lee E; m. 11/4/56 to June Olive Range; c. Lovie Regina, Brenda Lee and C. Richard. Educ: Boston Univ, B.S. in Bus. Admin, 44, M.A. in Bus. Educ, 48; Suffolk Univ, LL.B, 65; Hayden Scholar; Omega Psi Phi. Polit. & Govt. Pos: Mem, Selective Serv. Bd, Durham, N.C, 48-49; exec. secy, Gov. Herter and counc. asst. to Dir, Boston Civil Defense, 50-52; mem, Rep. City Cmt, Boston, 50-; asst. sgt-at-arms, Rep. Nat. Conv, 56, del, 64 & 68; mem, U.S. Adv. Cmt. Civil Rights Mass, 54-56; chmn. Licensing Bd, Boston, 56-; mem, Edward W. Brooke for Attorney Gen. Cmt, 62 & 64 and for U.S. Sen, 66. Bus. & Prof. Pos: Instr, Commercial Sci, N.C. Col, Durham, 47-49; secy. to v.pres, Vets. Sales Co, Quincy, 49-50; dir, Commonwealth Nat. Bank, Boston, 64-; Attorney-at-Law; chmn. bd, Spring-Matic Indust, Inc, Springfield, 69- Mil. Serv: Entered as Pvt, Army, 43, released as M/Sgt, 45; Bronze Star; Good Conduct and Victory Medals; European-African-Middle East, Asiatic-Pac. and Philippine Liberation Ribbons; Air Offensive Europe, Rome-Arno, North. and South. France and North Appennines-Rhineland-Po Valley Campaign Ribbons. Mem: Mass. and Boston Bar Asns; Elks; Middlesex Rep. Club; Rep. Club Mass; Amvets; life mem. NAACP. Rel: Congregational. Mailing Add: 340 Walnut Ave, Boston, Mass. 02119.

ELAM, CLAYTON PAUL D
b. Houston, Tex, 3/22/20; s. Claude Pete Elam and Amanda Gladbach E; m. 9/2/50 to Pearl Hopper; c. Clayton P, Jr. and Tammy Anne. Educ: Univ. Tenn, extension div, 2 years. Polit. & Govt. Pos: Agent, Shelby Co. Right of Way, Tenn, 66-; Tenn. State Sen, 67-69. Mil. Serv: Entered as Pvt, Army, 40, released as Warrant Officer, after serv. in 221st C.I.D, Asiatic-Pac; 12 Medals. Mem: Shelby Co. Emergency coord, Am. Radio Relay League; v.pres, Optimist Club; pres, Mid-South Amateur Radio Asn; pres, Mid-South Ultra-High-Frequency Club; VFW. Rel: Catholic. Mailing Add: 1447 Merrycrest Dr, Memphis, Tenn. 38111.

ELBRICK, C. BURKE
U.S. Ambassador to Brazil
b. Louisville, Ky, 3/25/08; s. Charles J. Elbrick and Lillian Burke E; m. 7/27/32 to Elvira Lindsay Johnson; c. Alfred Johnson and Valerie Burke. Educ: William Col, B.A, 29; Phi Delta Theta. Hon. LL.D, Hartwick Col. Polit. & Govt. Pos: Vice-consul, Panama, 31-32 and Southampton, Eng, 32-34; 3rd secy, Port-au-Prince, Haiti, 34-37, Warsaw, Poland, 37-38, Praha, 38-39, Warsaw, Poland, 39, Bucharest, 39, Warsaw (Angers, France), 39-40 and Madrid, Spain, 40; vice-consul, Lisbon, Portugal, 40-41, 3rd secy, 41, 2nd secy, 41-43; 2nd secy, Tangier, 43-44; 2nd secy, Div. of African Affairs, Dept. of State, 44-45; 1st secy, Warsaw, Poland, 45; asst. chief, Div. East. European Affairs, Dept. of State, 46-48; student, Nat. War Col, 48-49; counsr, Havana, 49-51; counsr, N.Atlantic Coun. Del, London 51 and Paris, 52-53; Dep. Asst. Secy. of State, 53-56; Asst. Secy. of State, 57-58; U.S. Ambassador to Portugal, 59-63; U.S. Ambassador to Yugoslavia, 64-69; U.S. Ambassador to Brazil, 69- Mem: Metrop. and Chevy Chase Clubs. Legal Res: 2137 R St. N.W, Washington, D.C. 20008. Mailing Add: American Embassy, Rio de Janeiro, Brazil, APO New York 09676.

ELDER, CHARLES D
b. Purcell, Okla, 2/23/33; s. Arthur Revere Elder and Helen Gold E; m. 8/31/57 to Beverly Beck; c. Charles, II and Todd Hester. Educ: Univ. Okla, B.A. in polit. sci, 55, LL.B, 58; Delta Sigma Rho; Phi Eta Sigma; Phi Alpha Delta. Polit. & Govt. Pos: Secy-treas, Okla. League of Young Dem, 52-55; del, Dem. Nat. Conv, mem. Platform Cmt. and exec. cmt. of the Platform Cmt, 64; asst. to chmn. of the State Dem. Cent. Cmt, Okla, 64- Mem: Am. and Okla. Bar Asns; Tenth Circuit Judicial Conf; pres, Purcell Rotary Club, 65-66. Rel: Episcopal. Mailing Add: P.O. Box 667, Purcell, Okla. 73080.

ELDER, DAVID MAYNE D
b. Watkinsville, Ga, 9/10/18; s. David M. Elder and Ola Edwards E; m. 2/19/49 to June Carol Anthony. Educ: Univ. of Ga, B.S.Agr.E, 40. Polit. & Govt. Pos: Councilman, Watkinsville, Ga, 49-58; Ga. State Rep, 55-59; admin. asst. to U.S. Rep. Robert G. Stephens, Jr, Ga, 62- Bus. & Prof. Pos: Coordinator and off. mgr, Dept. of Vet. Serv, Ga, 47-61. Mil. Serv: Entered as Ens, Naval Res, 41, released as Lt. Comdr, 42, after serv. in European and Pac. Theatres, 41-46; Coast Guard Res, Comdr. Mem: Elks; Am. Legion; VFW. Rel: Protestant. Legal Res: P.O. Box 7, Watkinsville, Ga. 30677. Mailing Add: Apt. 836, Dominion Towers, 1201.S. Court House Rd, Arlington, Va. 22204.

ELDER, HAYES D
b. Ketchikan, Alaska, 1938; m. to Sylvia E. Educ: U. of Wash, Magna Cum Laude in Polit. Sci; U. of Wash. Law Sch; Phi Beta Kappa. Polit. & Gov. Pos: Wash. State Rep, 64-66. Bus. & Prof. Pos: Attorney. Mailing Add: 3250 Calif, S.W, Seattle, Wash. 98116. (1967)

ELDER, JAMES BRYAN D
Tenn. State Rep.
b. Decatur, Tenn, 7/7/26; s. David Scott Elder and Leola Melton E; m.

1/21/47 to Sammie Joyce Blount; c. Susan Jeannine and Sarah Joyce. Educ: Meigs Co. Schs, grad, 44. Polit. & Govt. Pos: Tenn. State Rep, 64-66 & 68-; cmnr, Educ. of States, 69-; mem, Educ. Cmt, 69-; mem, Gen. Welfare Cmt, 69- Bus. & Prof. Pos: Pres, Rhea Co. Limestone Co, 57-69, Rhea Redi-Mix, 65-69, Rhea Assoc, 65-69, Rhea Properties, 67-69 and Ideal Construction Co, 69- Mil. Serv: Entered as Pvt, Army, 44, released as Sgt, 47, after serv. in 444th Inf. Mem: Rotary; C. of C; Mason. Commun. Leader of Am; Tenn. FFA Honorary Chap. Farmer. Rel: Protestant. Legal Res: Salem Rd, Dayton, Tenn. 37321. Mailing Add: P.O. Box 168, Dayton, Tenn. 37321.

ELDER, WILLIAM J. D
Chmn, Switzerland Co. Dem. Cent. Cmt, Ind.
b. Bear Branch, Ind, 2/15/27; s. William J. Elder, Sr. and Maude Holbert E; m. 3/25/67 to Emma B. Liggett; c. Marilyn Ramseyer, Deborah Elder, Betty Grant and Gerry Furnish. Educ: Dillsboro High Sch, Ind, 4 years. Polit. & Govt. Pos: Trustee, Craig Twp. Dem. Party, Ind, 62-; chmn, Switzerland Co. Dem. Cent. Cmt, 63- Mil. Serv: Entered as Pvt, Army, 46, released as Pfc, 47, after serv. in 107 Gen. Hosp. Mem: F&AM. Rel: Protestant. Mailing Add: Route 3, Vevay, Ind. 47043.

ELDRIDGE, DON D. R
Speaker of the House, Wash. House of Rep.
b. Mt. Vernon, Wash, 12/26/19; s. Raymond L. Eldridge and Blanche Thorpe E; m. 9/15/45 to Harriett Clow; c. Raymond E, Jean M, Sally A. and Jon D. Educ: West. Wash. State Col, B.A. in educ, 44; Phi Delta Theta; Alpha Phi Omega. Polit. & Govt. Pos: Past field adv, Small Bus. Admin, 10 years; past mem. bd. trustee, West. Wash. State Col, 10 years, chmn. bd, 57-59; Wash. State Rep, 53-, mem. interim cmt. on educ, Wash. House Rep, 59-63, v.chmn, 59-60, mem. Wash. State Legis. Coun, 57-58 & 65-, chmn, 67- and Speaker of the House, currently; mem, Wash-Ore. Boundary Cmn, 55-56. Bus. & Prof. Pos: Mem. exec. cmt, Wash. Retail Coun, 62-64; mem. bd. dirs, Asn. of Wash. Indust, 64-; owner, Eldridge's Stationery Store. Mil. Serv: Army Air Corps, 43, Pvt. Mem: Skagit Develop. Asn.(pres, 58); U.S. Jr. C. of C.(past v.pres); Mt. Vernon Jr. C. of C.(past pres); Wash. State Jr. C. of C. (past pres), Mt. Vernon C. of C.(past mem. bd. dirs); Rotary (past pres, Mt. Vernon Club); Nat. Coun.(past v.chmn. and mem. region II exec. cmt); Boy Scouts (past pres. Mt. Baker Coun); YMCA (past mem. bd. dirs, Mt. Vernon). Distinguished Serv. Award Jr. C. of C, 47; Silver Beaver, Boy Scouts, 60, Silver Antelope, 62. Rel: Episcopal. Legal Res: 1535 Kincaid St, Mt. Vernon, Wash. 98273. Mailing Add: 510 First St, Mt. Vernon, Wash. 98273.

ELESER, GOLDA EASLEY R
Mem, La. State Rep. Cent. Cmt.
b. Magnolia, Miss, 11/10/27; d. Augusta Easley and Gladys Johnson E; m. 1/23/46 to Louis Peter Eleser, Jr; c. Glynn Barry, Ronald Wayne, Pamela Jean, Cynthia Ann and Deborah Lynn. Educ: Southeast. La. Col, Hammond, 2 years. Polit. & Govt. Pos: Co-chmn, Nixon Campaign, Hammond, La, 60; chmn, Tangipahoa Parish Rep. Exec. Cmt, 60-69; mem, La. State Rep. Cent. Cmt. and Sixth Dist. Rep. Polit. Action Coun, 64-; chmn, Goldwater Hq, Tangipahoa Parish and Lyons Campaign, 64; del, Rep. Nat. Conv, 64; sponsor, Young Rep. Camp Meet, 65. Mem: League of Women Voters; former historian, area B pres, pres, v.pres. and del. to state conv, Am. Legion Auxiliary; Clio Sportsman League; Hammond High & Hammond Jr. High PTA; Hammond High Boosters Club; Sixth Dist. Rep. Club; Tangipahoa Parish Rep. Club; area chmn, Heart Fund Drive, 61-63; den mother, Cub Scouts, 59-60; pres, VFW Auxiliary Post 2885, 57-58. Recipient of Farm Bur. 'Freedom Award,' for promoting the causes of Am. Patriotism, 63. Rel: Catholic. Legal Res: 129 Florence Dr, Hammond, La. 70401. Mailing Add: P.O. Box 7, Hammond, La. 70401. (1967)

ELFERS, EARL H. D
b. Bassett, Wis, 5/26/13. Educ: Chandler Sch. of Auctioneering; grad. as licensed auctioneer; Spenderian Col, Milwaukee. Polit. & Govt. Pos: Wis. State Assemblyman, 62-66; town chmn, 6th term; mem. of Kenosha Co. Bd; 10 years sch. bd. dir; mem. of Farm Bur. Bus. & Prof. Pos: Auctioneer and real estate broker; also in boat-bait-tackle and food serv. bus; farmed 1,200 acres until 58. Mailing Add: Box 86, Trevor, Wis.53179. (1967)

ELFSTROM, ROBERT LEWIS R
Ore. State Sen.
b. Concordia, Kans, 8/30/04; s. Evar V. Elfstrom and Anna Johnston E; m. 12/16/28 to Hulda Roth; c. Robert Lewis, Jr. and Patricia (Mrs. William Johnson). Educ: Kans. State Agr. Col, 23-24. Polit. & Govt. Pos: Pres, League of Ore. Cities, 47-48; mayor, Salem, Ore, 46-50; chmn, Liquor Control Cmn, 51-52; Ore. State Rep, 53-62, Minority Leader, Ore. State House of Rep, 59; del, Rep. Nat. Conv, 56, 60 and 64; Ore. State Sen, Marion Co, 62-, chmn, Cmt. on Hwys, Ore. State Senate. Bus. & Prof. Pos: Pres, Continental Enterprises, Inc, 64-; chmn. bd, Commercial Bank; trustee, Willamette Univ. Mem: Multnomah Athletic Club; Arlington Club; Illahe Country Club; Mason (32°); Shrine; past pres, Rotary. Rel: Presbyterian. Legal Res: 325 13th St. N.E, Salem, Ore. 97301. Mailing Add: P.O. Box 470, Salem, Ore. 97308.

ELGIN, GEORGE KENNETH R
Chmn, Karnes Co. Rep. Party, Tex.
b. Hannibal, Mo, 7/21/21; s. George Elgin and Leta Virginia Wright E; m. 7/5/44 to Charlotte Lucille Person; c. Joan. Polit. & Govt. Pos: Chmn, Karnes Co. Rep. Party, Tex, 64- Bus. & Prof. Pos: Dept. tax collector-assessor, Karnes Co, Tex, 56-59; mgr, Karnes Co. Abstract Co, 59- Mil. Serv: Entered as Cadet, Naval Air Force, 42, released as Ens, 44; Army, 45-46, with serv. in Asiatic-Pac. Theatre; Am Theatre Ribbon; Asiatic-Pac. Ribbon; Victory Medal. Mem: C. of C; VFW; Tex. Land Title Asn. Rel: Protestant. Legal Res: 110 N. Panna Maria Ave, Karnes City, Tex. 78118. Mailing Add: 502 E. Broadway, Karnes City, Tex. 78118.

ELIASON, AL BURTON D
b. Stoughton, Wis, 7/16/23; s. Alfred Eliason and Ruby Berry E; m. 11/16/52 to Marie E. Wiese; c. Christen Marie. Educ: Milton Col, B.S, 48; Garrett Theol. Sem, Northwest. Univ, B.D, 52; Pi Kappa Delta. Polit. & Govt. Pos: Del, Wis. Rep. Conv, 41-42, 46-47 & 50-51; pub. mem, family law cmt, Wis. Legis. Coun, 57-59 and youthful drinking and driving study cmt, 61-63; registered lobbyist, Wis. Legis, 59-66; del, Wis. Dem. Conv, since 61, chmn, registrn. cmt, 62; chmn. prog. cmt, Sheboygan Co. unit, Wis. Dem. Party, 62-63 and mem. exec. cmt, Fond du Lac Co. unit, 66-68; alternate del, Dem. Nat. Conv, 68. Bus. & Prof. Pos: Mem, E.Wis. Annual Conf. Methodist bd. missions, 54-63, mem. bd. ministerial training and qualifications and chmn. resolutions cmt, 58-61; pres, Milwaukee Subdist, Methodist Ministers, 59-60; chmn. soc. action cmt, Fond du Lac Area Ministers Asn, 63-65. Mil. Serv: Entered as Pvt, Army Air Force, 43, released as Pfc, 45, after serv. in ETO, 43-45; Four Battle Stars. Publ: On the Pastoral Prayer in Protestant Churches (in press). Mem: Mason; VFW. One of 12 sr. preachers, voted by 360 classmates, Garrett Theol. Sem, 51. Rel: United Methodist. Mailing Add: 3100 S. Stigler Rd, New Berlin, Wis. 53151.

ELIASSEN, HERB O. R
Chmn, Okanogan Co. Rep. Cent. Cmt, Wash.
b. Colgan, N.Dak, 9/2/15; s. Peter Eliassen and Thea Wold E; m. Sept, 1940 to Cecile; c. Robin, Thea and Gary. Polit. & Govt. Pos: Chmn, Okanogan Co. Rep. Cent. Cmt, Wash, 68- Mil. Serv: Entered in Navy, 45, released, 46, after serv. in Fleet Ship Salvage, Pac. Theatre. Mem: Americanism chmn, Am. Legion; Okanogan and Nat. C. of C; Toastmasters. Rel: Presbyterian; Deacon. Legal Res: 446 S. Fir, Omak, Wash. 98840. Mailing Add: 338 S. Second, Box 822, Okanogan, Wash. 98840.

ELICKER, CHARLES WILLIAM R
Wash. State Sen.
b. Pittsburgh, Pa, 1/11/26 ; c. Charles William Elicker and Marjorie L. MacArthur E; div; c. Charles W, Drew M, Barton A. and Jessica K. Educ: Univ. Wash, B.A, 44, J.D, 49; Univ. Mich, LL.M, 50; Phi Beta Kappa; Order of the Coif; Delta Tau Delta. Polit. & Govt. Pos: Mem, Bainbridge Island Sch. Bd, Wash, 60-65; Wash. State Rep, Tenth Dist, 67-69, Wash. State Sen, 69- Mil. Serv: Entered as A/S, Navy, 42, released as Lt.(jg), 45, after serv. in Pac. Theatre, 43-45; Naval Res.(Ret), 65; Navy Commendation Medal. Mem: Wash. State Bar Asn; Pres, Wash. State Health Facilities Asn; Am. Legion; Rotary. Rel: Congregational. Mailing Add: 344 Wyatt Way, Winslow, Wash. 98110.

ELIOT, THOMAS HOPKINSON D
b. Cambridge, Mass, 6/14/07; s. Samuel Atkins Eliot and Frances Stone Hopkinson E; m. 10/10/36 to Lois A. Jameson; c. Samuel Atkins and Nancy. Educ: Harvard, A.B, 28, LL.B, 32; Emmanuel Col, Cambridge, Eng, 28-29. Hon. LL.D, Drury Col; L.H.D, Hobart and William Smith Col. Polit. & Govt. Pos: Asst. solicitor, U.S. Dept. Labor, 33-35; counsel, Pres. Cmn. Econ. Security, 34-35; gen. counsel, Soc. Security Bd, 35-38; regional dir, Wage and Hour Div, U.S. Dept. Labor, 39-40; U.S. Rep, Mass, 41-43; spec. asst. to ambassador and Head of Brit, Div, London Off. War Info, 43; with Nat. War Labor Bd, 43-44 and Off. Strategic Serv, 44; chief counsel, div. power, Dept. of Interior, 44-45; exec. dir, Spec. Cmn. on Structure of State Govt, 50-52; v.chmn, U.S. Adv. Cmn. Intergovt. Rels, 64-67. Bus. & Prof. Pos: Assoc, Kenefick, Cooke, Mitchell, Bass & Letchworth, Buffalo, 32-33; lectr. govt, Harvard, 37-38 & 48-51 and mem. bd. overseers; partner, Foley, Hoag & Eliot, 45-52; prof. and chmn. dept. polit. sci, Wash. Univ, 52-61, prof, constitutional law, law sch, 58-62, dean, col. liberal arts, 61-62, chancellor, 62-; vis. prof, Princeton, 58-59. Publ: American Government Problems for Analysis, 59; Governing America, 60; co-auth, State Politics and the Public Schools, 63 plus one other. Mem: N.Eng. chmn, United Negro Col. Fund, 46-48; trustee, Monticello Col, 58-60; Am. Civil Liberties Union; Am. Polit. Sci. Asn; Am. Acad. of Arts and Sci. Rel: Unitarian. Mailing Add: 6420 Forsyth Blvd, Clayton, Mo. 63105.

ELISH, PETER D
Co. Controller, Washington Co, Pa.
b. Poplar Bluff, Mo, 6/23/14; s. Anton Elish and Mary Junzio E; m. 8/20/53 to Agnes Jeanne Ducar; c. Peter Mark. Educ: Univ. Pittsburgh, 45-53. Polit. & Govt. Pos: Councilman, Canonsburg, Pa, 40-42; Pa. State Rep, 45-47; co. treas, Washington Co, Pa, 48-52, co. controller, 54-; del, Dem. Nat. Conv, 68. Bus. & Prof. Pos: Pres, Washington Co. Fed. Credit Union, 57- Mil. Serv: Pvt, Army, 41-42, serv. in Ord. Corps. Mem: Pres, Alexander Coop. Asn, Strabane, Pa, 67-; secy, Am. Investors Mutual Soc, Canonsburg, 67-; nat. v.pres, Slovene Nat. Benefit Soc, Chicago, Ill, 66- Rel: Christian. Mailing Add: 503 Bluff Ave, Canonsburg, Pa, 15317.

ELKIN, RICHARD R
Pub. Serv. Cmnr, N.Dak.
b. Richardton, N.Dak, 10/28/32; s. Alfred Elkin and Olinda E; m. 6/15/54 to Agnes Mae Sattler; c. Jay Dee, Corby, Beth and Beverly. Educ: Dickinson State Col. Polit. & Govt. Pos: N.Dak. State Rep, 62-66; co. chmn, Stark Co. Rep. Party, 63-66; Pub. Serv. Cmnr, N.Dak, 66- Mem: Lions Int; Elks; Farm Bur; N.Dak. Stockmens Asn. Rel: Catholic. Mailing Add: 1230 E. Highland Acres Rd, Bismarck, N.Dak. 58501.

ELL, LEON J. R
b. Poland, 5/17/96; s. Peltiel M. Ell and Zepora Jacobi E; m. 5/24/31 to Alyce D. Katz; c. Sandra (Mrs. Joel Dalkin). Educ: Northwest. Univ. Law Sch, LL.B, 20. Polit. & Govt. Pos: State Rep. Chmn. for Minorities, Fla, 52-60; del, Rep. Nat. Conv, 56 & 68; mem, White House Conf. on Refugees, 56-; U.S. Rep, Intergovt. Cmt. on European Migration, Geneva, 58-; mem, U.S. Refugees Cmt, 60- Bus. & Prof. Pos: Attorney-at-law, Chicago, Ill, 20-43; investment consult, 43- Mil. Serv: Army, World War I. Publ: Events That Shaped History; columnist for Miami Times; writer on hist, polit, soc. and relig. topics for Miami Beach Sun and Jewish Floridian. Mem: Bd, Gr. Miami Jewish Fedn, 50-; bd. dirs, Union of Am. Hebrew Congregations, 58-60; trustee, Hebrew Union Col, 58-60; United Fund; Ment. Health Inst; pres. coun, Jewish Nat. Fund of Gr. Miami, 60-; exec. cmt, Jewish Nat. Fund, 61- and bd. dirs, 62. Rel: Jewish; Past Pres, Temple Beth Sholom. Legal Res: 16 Island Ave, Belle Isle, Miami Beach, Fla. 33139. Mailing Add: 1451 N. Bayshore Dr, Miami, Fla. 33132.

ELLENBOGEN, HENRY D
b. Vienna, Austria, 4/3/00; s. Samson Ellenbogen and Rose Franzos E; m. 12/18/27 to Rae Savage; c. Naomi and Judith. Educ: Royal-Imperial Univ. Vienna, Austria, 18-21; Duquesne Univ, A.B, 23, LL.B, 24 and LL.D. Polit.

& Govt. Pos: U.S. Rep, Pa, 32-38; judge, Court of Common Pleas, Allegheny Co, 38-, president judge, 63- Publ: 'Report of the Sub-Committee on Judicial Administration of the Pennsylvania Bar Association regarding Administrator for the Courts in Pennsylvania,' Pa. Bar Asn, 59; 'Automation in the Courts,' Am. Bar Asn. J, 7/64; 'The English Courts as Seen by an American Judge,' Pa. Bar Asn. Quart, 3/67. Mem: Fel, Int. Acad. Law and Sci; Am, Pa. and Allegheny Co. Bar Asns; Am. Judicature Soc; Pa. Conf. State Trial Judges; Urban League of Pittsburgh; YMCA; Westmoreland Country Club. Mailing Add: 705 City-County Building, Pittsburgh, Pa. 15219.

ELLENDER, ALLEN JOSEPH D
U.S. Sen, La.
b. Montegut, La, 9/24/90; m. to Helen Calhoun Donnelly, wid; c. Allen J, Jr. Educ: St. Aloysius Col; Tulane Univ. of La, M.A. and LL.B. Polit. & Govt. Pos: City attorney, Houma, La, 13-15; dist. attorney, Terrebonne Parish, 15-16; del, La. Constitutional Conv, 21; La. State Rep, 24-36, floor leader, La. House Rep, 28-32, speaker, 32-36; U.S. Sen, La, 37-; Dem. Nat. Committeeman, 39-40. Bus. & Prof. Pos: Lawyer; farmer. Mil. Serv: World War I. Legal Res: Houma, La. Mailing Add: 3900 Connecticut Ave. N.W, Washington, D.C. 20008.

ELLER, ARMENA MORSE R
Mem, Calif. Rep. State Cent. Cmt.
b. Santa Ana, Calif; d. Thomas Oliver Morse and Leila Dawes M; m. 1917 to Dr. Willard H. Eller; c. Willard Morse. Educ: Univ. of Calif, Berkeley, B.S, 17; Univ. of Hawaii, 32-33 & 48. Polit. & Govt. Pos: Mem, Rep. Women's Club of Honolulu, 48-58; tel. chmn, 14th Rep. Precinct Club, Honolulu, 50-54, secy, 54-56; del, State Rep. Conv, Honolulu, 50, 52, 54 & 56; co-dir, Rep. Sch. of Polit, Manoa Sch, 52; v.pres, Oroville Area Rep. Women's Club, Calif, 58, pres, 58-60, bul. ed, Area News, 58-; mem, Butte Co. Rep. Cent. Cmt, Calif, 60-62, 64-66 & 68-, chmn, Oroville Dist, 66-68; mem, Calif. Rep. State Cent. Cmt, 62-64 & 68-; del, Calif. Rep. Asn. Conv, Disneyland, 62, Fresno, 64. Bus. & Prof. Pos: Sci. illustrator, Univ. of Calif. Berkeley, 25-28 and Pineapple Research Inst, Honolulu, 28-29, illustrator, 37-38; archit. designer, Lake Bldg. Corp, 28-35; art instr, Cent. and Stevenson Schs, Honolulu, 35-36; designer for Gump's, Roosevelt High Sch, Honolulu, 40-56, head of art dept, 40-46 & 48-57. Publ: Illustrator, Kinetic Theories of Gases, Leonard Loeb, McGraw-Hill, 28; Star Over the Pacific, Grove Day and Carl Stroven, 56. Rel: Protestant. Mailing Add: 17 Adelaide Way, Oroville, Calif. 95965.

ELLETT, ALBERT HAYDEN
Justice, Supreme Court of Utah
b. Huntsville, Ala, 2/4/98; s. Isaac William Ellett and Martha Catherine Green E; m. 8/20/24 to Florence Rowe; c. Kenneth William, Walter Rowe and Jeanne (Mrs. Clifford Parks). Educ: Univ. Utah, B.A, Blackstone Col. Law, LL.B, 30; Phi Kappa Phi; Phi Beta Kappa; Order of the Coif. Polit. & Govt. Pos: Co. dep. attorney, Salt Lake City, Utah, 33-34; city judge, Salt Lake City, 34-40; dist. court judge, Utah, 41-66; justice, Supreme Court of Utah, 67- Bus. & Prof. Pos: Sch. teacher, Tex, 16-18 & 19-20, Utah, 20-21 & 22-23, La, 21-22. Mil. Serv: Pvt, ROTC, East Tex. State Normal Col, 18. Mem: Salt Lake Co. Bar Asn; Utah State Bar; Am. Judicature Soc. Rel: Latter-day Saint. Legal Res: 3910 Luetta Dr, Salt Lake City, Utah 84117. Mailing Add: 332 State Capitol, Salt Lake City, Utah 84114.

ELLINGSON, BERTRUM EDWIN D
S.Dak. State Rep.
b. Rosholt, S.Dak, 4/17/21; s. Bert Ellingson and Esther Stanley E; m. 5/15/43 to Nilda Renfroe; c. Robert, Faye Marie and Linda Sue. Polit. & Govt. Pos: S.Dak. State Rep, 69- Mil. Serv: Entered as Pvt, Air Force, 41, released as Lt. Col, 63, after serv. in various overseas and stateside units; Silver Star; Distinguished Flying Cross with Two Oak Leaf Clusters; Air Medal with Six Oak Leaf Clusters; Army Commendation Medal. Mem: Am. Legion; VFW. Rel: Lutheran. Mailing Add: Sisseton, S.Dak. 57262.

ELLINGSON, HERMAN E. R
Chmn, Big Stone Co. Rep. Cent. Cmt, Minn.
b. Oldham, S.Dak, 2/6/18; s. Peter Ellingson and Nora Anderson E; m. 12/4/49 to Alice I. Bjella; c. Gary, Patricia, David, James, Susan and John. Polit. & Govt. Pos: Mayor, Odessa, Minn, 58-; mem, Gov. Cmt. on Small Bus, 61; Recount Team, Minn. Gov. Elec, 62; chmn, Big Stone Co. Rep. Cent. Cmt, 59- Bus. & Prof. Pos: Owner, Herman Ellingson & Sons, 48- Mil. Serv: Entered as Pvt, Army, 43, released as Capt, Air Force, 46, after serv. in 425th Bomber Squadron, 99th Bomb Group, 15th Air Force, ETO, 45-46; Victory, Am. Campaign and European African Middle East. Campaign Medals. Mem: Past comdr, Am. Legion Post 520; VFW; former co. chmn, Farm Bur; past comdr, Am. Legion Co. Coun; past chmn, Gr. Minn. Improve. Asn. Rel: Lutheran. Mailing Add: Box 68, Odessa, Minn. 56276.

ELLINGTON, EARL BUFORD D
Gov, Tenn.
b. Holmes Co, Miss, 6/27/07; s. Abner E. Ellington and Cora Grantham E; m. 12/20/29 to Catherine Cheek; c. John Earl and Anna Belle (Mrs. Timothy Wagner). Educ: Millsaps Col, 25-29; hon. Alpha Zeta, Alpha Gamma Rho and Delta Kappa. Polit. & Govt. Pos: Tenn. State Rep, 49-51; cmnr, Dept. Agr, Tenn, 53-58; gov, Tenn, 59-63 & 67-; chmn, South. Regional Educ. Bd, 61; mem. exec. cmt, Nat. Gov. Conf, 61-62; chmn, South. Gov. Conv, 61-62; dir, Off. Emergency Planning, 65-66; chmn, Nat. Gov. Conf, 68-; pres, Coun. State Govt, 68- Bus. & Prof. Pos: Mgr, Tenn. Farm Bur. Ins. Serv, 49-51; v.pres, L & N R.R, 63-65. Mem: Bd. trustees, Univ. Tenn, Rust Col. and George Peabody Col; bd. dirs, Millsaps Col. Alumni Asn; Bill Wilkerson Speech & Hearing Center; chmn, Cordell Hull Found; Farm Bur; Mason (33°); Shrine; hon. mem, Nat. Coun. Boy Scouts. Rel: Methodist. Legal Res: Curtiswood Lane, Nashville, Tenn. 37204. Mailing Add: State Capitol, Nashville, Tenn. 37219.

ELLIOTT, ALFRED JAMES D
b. Guinda, Calif, 6/1/95; s. Ishmeal James Elliott and Mary Jane Harrison E; wid; c. I.J. and Esther (Mrs. Vancil). Educ: Calif. Pub. Schs. Polit. & Govt. Pos: Secy-mgr, Tulare Co. Fair, Calif, 29-65; chmn, Tulare Co. Bd. Supvrs, 33-37; U.S. Rep, Tenth Dist, Calif, 37-49. Bus. & Prof. Pos: Practical farmer and livestock raiser. Mem: Tulare Co. Farm Bur. Rel: Methodist. Legal Res: 615 E. Bardsley Ave, Tulare, Calif. 93274. Mailing Add: P.O. Box 134, Tulare, Calif. 93274.

ELLIOTT, CARL D
Mem. Tech. Adv. Bd, U.S. Dept. Commerce
b. Vina, Ala, 12/20/13; s. George W. Elliott and Lenora Massey E; m. 6/3/40 to Jane Hamilton; c. Carl, Jr, Martha Owen, John Hamilton and Lenora Jane. Educ: Univ. Ala, A.B, 33, LL.B, 36; Omicron Delta Kappa; Philomathic Literary Soc; Jasons; Phi Alpha Delta; pres, Student Body, 35-36. Hon. LL.D, Tufts Univ, 65. Polit. & Govt. Pos: Mem, Franklin Co. Dem. Exec. Cmt, Ala, 36; U.S. Cmnr, 38-39; recorder, City Court of Jasper, 39-42 & 44-46; secy, Walker Co. Dem. Exec. Cmt, 42; mem, State Dem. Exec. Cmt, 42-50; city attorney, Jasper, Ala, 45-46; U.S. Rep, Ala, 49-65, mem. vet. affairs cmt, U.S. House Rep, 49-51, cmt. on educ. and labor, 51-60, cmt. on house admin, 56-60 and rules cmt, 61-65, chmn. select cmt. on govt. res, 63-65; mem, President's Cmn. on Librs, 66-68; mem. tech. adv. bd, U.S. Dept. Commerce, 68- Bus. & Prof. Pos: Attorney, Elliott & Naftalin, Wash, D.C. and Elliott, Elliott, O'Rear & Robinson, Jasper, Ala. Mil. Serv: Entered as Pvt, Army, 42, released as 1st Lt, 44, after serv. in Inf. Mem: Lions; Mason; Odd Fellows; Am. Legion; life mem, DAV; bd. of lay govs, St. Bernard Col, Cullman, Ala; Ala. Hist. Asn. Rel: Methodist. Mailing Add: 1700 Birmingham Ave, Jasper, Ala. 35501.

ELLIOTT, DAISY D
Mich. State Rep.
b. Filbert, W.Va; c. Three. Educ: Detroit Inst. of Commerce, grad; Wayne State Univ; Univ. Detroit. Polit. & Govt. Pos: Mich. State Rep, 62-; former del. to Constitutional Conv; alternate del, Dem. Nat. Conv, 68. Mem: Lady Camile Temple of Elks; Nat. Jr. League; Progressive Civic Arts Club; Trade Union Leadership Coun; YWCA; Hist. Soc. of Mich; Eta Phi Beta; Sigma Amis; MDELCA; NAACP; League of Women Voters; Mich. Fedn. Dem. Club. Rel: Peoples Commun. Church. Mailing Add: 2220 Oakman, Detroit, Mich. 48238. (1967)

ELLIOTT, EDWARD EMERSON D
b. 1911; m. 1952 to Carol Milman E. Educ: Woodbury Col; Calif. Univ. Exten. Serv. Polit. & Govt. Pos: Calif. State Assemblyman, 47-69. Mil. Serv: Army, Pac-Asiatic Theatre, 2 years. Mem: Am. Legion; VFW; Commun. Serv. Orgn. Mailing Add: 1171 N. Miller Ave, Los Angeles, Calif. 90063. (1967)

ELLIOTT, F. DUNLAP D
Secy, Garrard Co. Dem. Cmt, Ky.
b. Bryantsville, Ky, 5/19/11; s. Dr. William Micajah Elliott and Margaret Snoddy Cochran E; m. 4/17/37 to Martha Gober West; c. Margaret West and Martha Gober. Educ: Univ. Ky, 31-33; Kappa Alpha. Polit. & Govt. Pos: City clerk, Lancaster, Ky, 35-41, councilman, 46-58, mayor, 58-66; chmn, Combs for Gov. Cmt, Garrard Co, 59 and Breathitt for Gov. Cmt, 63; del, Ky. State Dem. Conv, 60 & 64; del, Dem. Nat. Conv, 64; secy, Garrard Co. Dem. Cmt, 64-; dir, Motor Vehicle Inspection, Dept. Pub. Safety, Frankfort, Ky, 66-68. Bus. & Prof. Pos: Dir, Nat. Bank Lancaster, Ky, 48-; registered rep, Levenson, Preston & Sturgill, Investment Securities, 68- Mem: Past pres, Lancaster Kiwanis Club; past secy, Lancaster Rotary Club. Rel: Disciples of Christ. Mailing Add: 321 Maple Ave, Lancaster, Ky. 40444.

ELLIOTT, FRANK, JR. R
Chmn, Hart Co. Rep. Party, Ky.
b. Bonnieville, Ky, 4/19/20; s. Frank Elliott and Birdie Hatfield E; m. 2/14/46 to Mary Stella Carter; c. Demetra (Mrs. Lester M. Bradway), Regina (Mrs. Fredrich W. Hodges), Belinda (Mrs. Gary Walters) and Micheal R. Educ: Bonnieville Grade Sch, grad, 34. Polit. & Govt. Pos: Campaign chmn, Hart Co, Ky, 63; Chmn, Hart Co. Rep. Party, 68- Bus. & Prof. Pos: Retail merchant. Mil. Serv: Entered as Pvt, Army, 42, released as T-5, 43, after serv. in 25th Engr. Bn. Mem: Mason; Farm Bur; Optimist Club. Rel: Protestant. Mailing Add: Bonnieville, Ky. 42713.

ELLIOTT, GUY D
N.C. State Rep.
b. Surry, N.C, 5/10/95; s. John Thomas Elliott and Mary Elizabeth Thomas E; m. 6/30/20 to Gertrude Bowling Jones; c. Mary Elizabeth (Mrs. Best) and Guy, Jr. Educ: Indust. Christian Col, 08-12; Univ. N.C. Law Sch, 15-17. Polit. & Govt. Pos: Mem. bd. trustees, Kinston Grade Sch. Dist, N.C, 10 years and mem. welfare bd, Lenoir Co, 5 years, formerly; judge, Recorders Court, 20-28; assoc. with Hon. J.A. Powers, Solicitor of Sixth Judicial Dist; attorney, Lenoir Co, 33-37; mayor, Kinston, 45-63; N.C. State Rep, Lenoir Co, 65- Bus. & Prof. Pos: Attorney-at-law, Kinston, 19- Mem: Lenoir Co, N.C. and Am. Bar Asns; Eighth Dist. and N.C. State Bars; AF&AM; RAM; K.T; AAONMS; Shrine; past pres, Kinston Kiwanis; Lt. Gov, Seventh Div, Carolinas Dist, Kiwanis Int; Farm Bur; past pres. and life mem. bd. dirs, Kinston C. of C; Commercial Law League of Am; pres, N.C. Christian Missionary Conv. and State Baraca Philathea Union Conv; chmn. bd. of mgrs, N.C. Christian Missionary Soc. Rel: Christian Church; Past Deacon and Elder, Gordon St. Christian Church. Legal Res: 105 E. Vernon Ave, Kinston, N.C. 28501. Mailing Add: P.O. Box 974, Kinston, N.C. 28501.

ELLIOTT, HUMPHREY TAYLOR R
Chmn, Casey Co. Rep. Party, Ky.
b. Gilpin, Ky, 3/12/33; s. Green Lee Elliott and Manilla Taylor; single. Educ: East. Ky. State Col, B.S, 59, M.A, 61. Polit. & Govt. Pos: Chmn, Casey Co. Rep. Party, Ky, 64- Mil. Serv: Entered as Airman, Air Force, 52, released as S/Sgt, 56, after serv. in Fla, Japan, Formosa and Ga. Mem: Mason; Kiwanis; Farm Bur; Am. Legion. Rel: Christian. Mailing Add: Box 113, Liberty, Ky. 42539. (1967)

ELLIOTT, JACK MARK R
Chmn, Ringgold Co. Rep. Cent. Cmt, Iowa
b. Mount Ayr, Iowa 9/25/27; s. Mark Elliott and Ilah Spencer E; m. 11/22/45 to Mildred Ellen Dixon; c. Craig, Richard, Kirk and Karen. Educ: Mount Ayr High Sch, grad, 45. Polit. & Govt. Pos: Chmn, Ringgold Co. Rep. Cent. Cmt, Iowa, 60-; pres, Mount Ayr Commun. Sch. Bd, 64- Mem: Mason; Eastern Star; Lions; Farm Bur. Iowa Master Swine Producer, 67. Rel: Methodist. Mailing Add: R.R. 2, Mount Ayr, Iowa 50854.

ELLIOTT, JAMES ALTON D
Ariz. State Sen.
b. Blandville, Ky, 9/30/04; s. Ernest E. Elliott and Atha Swindle E; m.

6/10/31 to Ruth Katheryn Donohoe; c. Ruth (Mrs. Ralph Aldridge), Martha and Veronica (Mrs. Thomas E. Price). Educ: Riverside Jr. Col, 26-28; North. Ariz. Univ, B.A, 30; Univ. Ariz, M.A, 41; Sigma Alpha. Polit. & Govt. Pos: Ariz. State Rep, Dist. 2, 45-46, 49-50 & 61-68; mem, Ariz. State Retirement Bd, 55-60; Ariz. State Sen, Dist. 2, 69- Bus. & Prof. Pos: Teacher, McNary, Ariz, 30-33; elem. teacher, Douglas, 34-41, high sch. teacher, 41-47, elem. sch. prin, 47- Nat. Educ. Asn; Douglas Educ. Asn.(pres, 46-47); Ariz. Educ. Asn.(pres, 57-58); Phi Delta Kappa; K. of C.(4°); Elks. Douglas High Sch. Yearbook 'Copper Kettle' dedicated to him, 47; life mem, Nat. Educ. Asn, 56; received sterling silver State Seal paper weight token from Ariz. State Univ, 57. Rel: Catholic. Mailing Add: 1450 13th St, Douglas, Ariz. 85607.

ELLIOTT, JAMES SEWELL R
b. Augusta, Ga, 12/20/22; s. Lester Franklyn Elliott and Frances Sewell E; m. 6/25/47 to Mary Jones Grace; c. James, Jr, Lester Franklyn, II, Walter Grace, Randolph Squire and Robert Bruce. Educ: The Citadel, B.S. in Bus; U.S. Mil. Acad, B.S. in Eng; Walter F. George Sch. of Law, Mercer Univ, Macon, Ga, LL.B; Gridiron Secret Soc. of the Univ. of Ga. Polit. & Govt. Pos: Ga. State Rep, 107th Dist, 66-67. Mil. Serv: Army, 46-50; Maj, Ga. Nat. Guard, 48-58. Mem: Am, Macon and Ga. Bar Asns; Elks; v.pres. & dir, Kiwanis; Am. Legion; Idle Hour Country Club; past chmn, Commun. Planning Coun. of Macon and Bibb Co; past trustee, United Givers Fund; YMCA; v.pres. exec. bd, Cent. Ga. Coun. Boy Scouts. Rel: Christ Episcopal; mem. Vestry. Legal Res: 480 Pierce Ave, Macon, Ga. 31204. Mailing Add: Suite 506 American Federal Bldg, Macon, Ga. 31201.

ELLIOTT, JOHN D. R
b. Keyesport, Ill, 12/12/27; s. James Edward Elliott and Minnie Apple E; m. 2/1/47 to Betty Lou Gambill; c. Bobby Lee, Susan Lynn, Terry Sue, Tina Marie and Claudia Jean Ann. Educ: Carlyle C.C, Unit 1, 12 years. Polit. & Govt. Pos: Secy, Clinton and Bond Co. Rep. Cmt, 1 year and precinct committeeman, 8 years; justice of the peace, Keyesport, Ill, 4 years and twp. supvr, 60- Bus. & Prof. Pos: Farmer, 25 years. Mem: Farm Bur; Nat. Farmers Orgn; Boy Scouts. Rel: Methodist. Mailing Add: R.R, Box 12, Keyesport, Ill. 62253.

ELLIOTT, MARIE SPIVEY D
b. Columbus Co, N.C, 9/6/13; d. Duckry Spivey and Hattie Gore S; m. 12/21/29 to Norman Elliott, wid; c. Ethel Frances (Mrs. Paul Smith) and Evelyn Anne (Mrs. J.D. Young). Educ: Elizabeth City Prog. of Practical Nursing, LPN, 63. Polit. & Govt. Pos: Assoc. chmn, Dem. precinct, Perquimans Co, N.C, 65; secy, Perquimans Co. Dem. Exec. Cmt, 65 and chmn, 65-68. Bus. & Prof. Pos: Pvt. duty nurse, Albemarle Hosp, Elizabeth City, N.C, 63; off. nurse, Dr. Peters & West, 63-67; pub. health nurse, Dist. Health Dept, 68- Mem: N.C. Pub. Health Asn; Hertford Bus. and Prfnl. Women's Club. Rel: Baptist; Teacher of adult women's Sunday Sch. Class. Mailing Add: 510 Pennsylvania Ave, Hertford, N.C. 27944.

ELLIOTT, ROBERT AMOS R
Ore. State Rep.
b. Portland, Ore, 11/13/16; s. Harry Clayton Elliott and Beatrice Janet Parsons E; m. 10/9/43; c. John Douglas and Robin Leigh. Educ: Univ. Ore, B.S, 40; Phi Delta Theta. Polit. & Govt. Pos: State chmn, Ore. State Young Rep, 46; del-at-lg, Rep. Nat. Conv, 48, 52 & 56; chmn, Multnomah Co. Rep. Cent. Cmt, 48-50 & 61-62; chmn, State Rep. Cent. Cmt, 50-52; state campaign chmn, Tom McCall for Gov, 66; Ore. State Rep, 67- Mil. Serv: Entered as Pvt, Army, 41, released as Capt, 46, after serv. in 104th Div, ETO; Lt. Col, Army Res, 46-58; Bronze Star; Armed Forces Res, Occup, Am. Campaign, Europe-Africa-Mid. East, Cent. Rhineland and Victory Medals; Combat and Expert Infantryman Badges. Mem: Lions Int. Rel: Episcopal; former key layman, Episcopal Diocese of Ore. Mailing Add: 11036 N.E. Everett St, Portland, Ore. 97220. (1967)

ELLIOTT, ROSS LILES D
b. Breckenridge, Tex, 1/7/16; s. Ross Elliott and Katie Mattie Liles E; m. 4/17/41 to Frances Russell; c. Janice Ann (Mrs. Vice), Linda Gay (Mrs. Ledbetter), Mary Frances and Ross Liles, Jr. Educ: John Tarleton Jr. Col, 35; Univ. Tex, B.B.A. & LL.B, 40; Delta Tau Delta. Polit. & Govt. Pos: Co. attorney, Stephens Co, Tex, 41-42 & 47-48, census dir, 50; chmn, Stephens Co. Dem. Cmt, 56-68. Bus. & Prof. Pos: Sr. Partner, Elliott, Bevill & Clark, Attorneys, Breckenridge, currently. Mil. Serv: Entered as Aviation Cadet, Air Force, 42, released as 1st Lt, after serv. as Base Intel. Officer, Air Force, Hammer Field, 46. Mem: Am. and Tex. Bar Asns; Breckenridge Country Club. Rel: Methodist. Legal Res: 200 N. Harding Ave, Breckenridge, Tex. 76024. Mailing Add: P.O. Box 29, Breckenridge, Tex. 76024.

ELLIOTT, THOMAS EDWARD D
Treas, Richland Co, S.C.
b. Columbia, S.C, 8/2/29; s. David Onslow Elliott and Nora Stevens E; m. 9/5/48 to Gertrude Agnes Bultman; c. Robert Cone, Thomas Edward, Jr, Stevens Bultman and Lyon Lambert. Polit. & Govt. Pos: S.C. State Rep, 58-61; treas, Richland Co, S.C, 61-; alternate del, Dem. Nat. Conv, 64, del, 68. Bus. & Prof. Pos: Owner, Elliott's on Devine, retail food and produce store, 55-61. Mem: Elks; S.C. Food Retailers Asn.(treas, 60-62); del, Nat. Food Retailers Conv, 60. Rel: Christian Church of N.Am. Mailing Add: Route 1, Box 7, Eastover, S.C. 29044.

ELLIOTT, TYRON CLIFFORD R
V.Chmn, Second Cong. Dist. Rep. Party, Ga.
b. Cordele, Ga, 10/27/42; s. Seniamon Byron Elliott and Bertie Williams E; m. 6/13/65 to Pinky Marilyn Gill; c. Clifford Douglas. Educ: Mercer Univ, A.B, 64, LL.B, 66; Blue Key; Sigma Nu; Phi Delta Phi. Polit. & Govt. Pos: Chmn, Tift Co. Rep. Party, Ga, 68-; v.chmn, Second Cong. Dist. Rep. Party, 68- Bus. & Prof. Pos: Assoc, Law Firm of Reinhardt, Ireland, Whitley & Sims, 66- Mem: Exchange Club. Rel: Baptist. Mailing Add: 1003 Prince Ave, Tifton, Ga. 31794.

ELLIOTT, WALTER CARLTON D
b. Gladys, Va, 2/1/03; s. Andrew W. Elliott and Nannie Fletcher Daniel E; m. 11/30/30 to Margaret Elizabeth Jenks; c. Fred Carlton, Nancy Jane (Mrs. Ketron) and Margaret Ann. Educ: Univ. Richmond, B.S, 25; Med. Col. Va, M.D, 28. Polit. & Govt. Pos: Va. State Del, 52-66. Bus. & Prof. Pos: Staff and chief of surg, Lebanon Gen. Hosp, Va, 30-; med. dir, Clinchfield Coal Co, 42- Mem: Am. Med. Asn; Va. Med. Soc.(v.pres, 56); Russell Co. and Southwest Va. Med. Socs; Va. Acad. Gen. Practice; Mason; Shrine; Lions (pres, 51); Russell Co. C. of C. Rel: Baptist; Past Deacon. Legal Add: Lebanon, Va. 24266. Mailing Add: Lebanon Gen. Hosp, Lebanon, Va. 24266.

ELLIOTT, WILFRED MARION D
b. Abilene, Kans, 10/22/07; s. Walter J. Elliott and Mabel E. Heller E; m. 6/8/30 to Elizabeth Mills; c. Barbara (Mrs. Bryon E. Taylor), Mary (Mrs. Carl L. Wettig) and Elizabeth Ann. Educ: Holcomb High Sch, Kans, dipl, 22-26. Polit. & Govt. Pos: Chmn, high sch. bd, White City, Kans, 50-62; cand, Kans. State Rep, 4 times; chmn, Morris Co. Dem. Cent. Cmt, 67-69. Bus. & Prof. Pos: Owner and operator, cattle ranch, White City, Kans, 41-; fieldman, Council Grove Prod. Credit Asn, 56-66; v.pres, Salina Prod. Credit Asn, 66- Mem: Chmn, Morris Co. Farm Bur, 48-50; Kans. Farm Bur. Membership Cmt, 46-47; chmn. tax cmt, Kans. Farmers Union, 67-; Elks; Lions. Rel: Methodist. Legal Res: Route 2, White City, Kans. 66872. Mailing Add: 1436 Pawnee, Salina, Kans. 67401.

ELLIS, ALBERT JOSEPH D
N.C. State Sen.
b. New Bern, N.C, 6/6/13; s. Joseph Ellis and Mary Rachide E; m. 10/14/40 to Marie Hargett; c. Patricia (Mrs. Richard D. Hedrick), Mary H, Susan H, Elizabeth H. and Albert Charles. Educ: Univ. N.C, B.S. in commerce, 35; Univ. N.C. Law Sch, LL.B, 38. Polit. & Govt. Pos: Nat. committeeman, Young Dem. Club, 43; co. attorney, Onslow Co, 52-62; del, Dem. Nat. Conv, 56 & 64; chmn, Onslow Co. Dem. Exec. Cmt, 58-62 and Third Cong. Dist. Dem. Cmt, 60-62; chmn, Onslow Co. Jacksonville Airport Cmn, 61-; N.C. State Sen, Sixth Sen. Dist, currently; mem, Legis. Research Cmn, 67-69, N.C. Constitutional Study Cmn, 68 and Legis. Serv. Cmn, 69- Bus. & Prof. Pos: Pres, Jacksonville United Serv. Orgn, 42-; mem, Nat. United Serv. Orgn, 56-; trustee, Fayetteville State Col, 58-68; chmn, Univ. N.C. Law Found, 66-67; trustee, Univ. N.C, 68- Mil. Serv: Entered as Pvt, Army, 44, released as Lt, 45, after serv. in Judge Adv. Gen. Dept. Mem: Am, N.C. and Onslow Co. Bar Asns; Fourth Dist. Judicial Bar Asn.(pres, 56); Judicature Soc; pres, Univ. N.C. Law Alumni Asn, 63; Kiwanis; Elks; K. of C; Moose; Am. Legion; 40 et 8; Navy League; Jacksonville C. of C; Jacksonville Country Club. Rel: Catholic. Legal Res: 105 Keller Court, Jacksonville, N.C. 28540. Mailing Add: Drawer AE, Jacksonville, N.C. 28540.

ELLIS, CHARLES EDWARD R
Chmn, Hays Co. Rep. Party, Tex.
b. Greenville, Miss, 1/30/36; s. John T. Ellis and Allene Voss E; m. 8/25/56 to Nancy Ann Hanks; c. Janet Lynn and Julie Ann. Educ: Southwest Tex. State Univ, 2 years. Polit. & Govt. Pos: Precinct chmn, Rep. Party, Tex, 67; chmn, Hays Co. Rep. Party, 68- Bus. & Prof. Pos: Supvr, Tex. Womens Univ, 60-63; lead operator, Tex. Instruments, Dallas, 63-66; programmer, Southwest Tex. State Univ, 66- Mil. Serv: Tex. Air Nat. Guard Res, 54-62. Rel: Methodist. Mailing Add: Route 1, Box 184, San Marcos, Tex. 78666.

ELLIS, CLYDE T. D
b. Garfield, Ark, 12/21/08; s. Cecil Oscar Ellis and Minerva Jane Taylor E; m. 9/23/66 to Camille Waldron Fitzhugh; c. Patricia Suzanne (Mrs. Marti) and Mary Lynn (Mrs. Duty). Educ: Univ. Ark, B.S. in Bus. Admin. Polit. & Govt. Pos: Mem, Nat. Water Cmn, 68-; U.S. Rep, 39-43; Ark. State Sen, 35-39; Ark. State Rep, 33-35. Mil. Serv: Entered as Lt.(jg), Naval Res, 43, released as Lt, 45, after serv. in North Atlantic Command. Publ: A Giant Step, Random House, 66. Mem: Cosmos Club; Author's Guild; Congressional Country Club. Legal Res: 5317 Kenwood Ave, Chevy Chase, Md. 20015. Mailing Add: 818 18th N.W, Washington, D.C. 20006.

ELLIS, DEAN D. R
V.Chmn, Clark Co. Rep. Party, Wash.
b. Creighton, Nebr, 10/16/28; s. C.G. Ellis and Ethel Andersen E; m. 9/15/51 to Mary L. Martin; c. David W. and Daniel G. Educ: Wash. State Col, B.S. in Agr, 48-52. Polit. & Govt. Pos: Co. supvr, Farmers Home Admin, Wash, 52-56; mem, Rep. Cent. Cmt; campaign chmn, Sam Jones for Wash. State Rep, 64; v.chmn, Clark Co. Rep. Party, Wash, currently. Bus. & Prof. Pos: Asst. cashier, First Nat. Bank, Montesano, Wash, 58-59; asst. br. mgr, First Ind. Bank, 59-65, br. mgr, 66- Mil. Serv: Entered as Pvt, Army, 46, released as Technician, 48, after serv. in Sixth Inf. Div, Army of Occup, Korea, 47. Mem: Wash. Bankers Asn; Wash. State Univ. Alumni Asn; PTA; C. of C; Little League. Mailing Add: 9601 N.W. 24th Ave, Vancouver, Wash. 98665. (1967)

ELLIS, EDWARD DALE D
Treas, Venango Co. Dem. Party, Pa.
b. Franklin, Pa, 4/19/14; s. Edward Luke Ellis and Mazie Mitchell E; m. 2/24/46 to Antionette Marie Leta; c. Edward Dale, Frank Thomas, James Paul, Mary Helen and William Lewis. Educ: Int. Commercial Sch, Scranton, Pa; Univ. Ky; home study in architecture and law. Polit. & Govt. Pos: Treas, Venango Co. Dem. Cmt, Pa, 65- and on exec. cmt; founding mem, Citizens for Humphrey, 68; del, Dem. Nat. Conv, 68. Bus. & Prof. Pos: Consult. Engr, 56-; dealer, Walker/Parkensburg Steel Bldgs, Div. of Textron, 68-; dealer, Lyco Sewage Treatment Plants, 68- Mil. Serv: Entered as Pvt, Army, 43, released as 2nd Lt, 45, after serv. in 12th Army Group, ETO; 1st Lt, Res, 45-54; ETO and Good Conduct Medals; Five Battle Stars. Mem: Pres, Venango Co. ROA; past v.cmdr, Catholic War Vets; Am. Legion. Rel: Catholic. Mailing Add: 411 15th St, Franklin, Pa. 16323.

ELLIS, FRANK BURTON D
b. Covington, La, 2/10/07; s. Harvey Eugene Ellis and Margaret Whiteside E; m. 11/18/65 to Marjorie Lou Wheatley; c. Lilian Emerson (Mrs. Stewart McClendon), Stephen Grima and Frank B, Jr. Educ: Univ. Va, 24-26; La. State Univ, LL.B, 28; Zeta Psi. Polit. Pos: Sr. U.S. Judge, Eastern Dist. of La, 65- and U.S. Dist. Judge, 62-65; del, Dem. Nat. Conv, 56 and 52; Dem. nat. committeeman, La, 52-54; La. State Sen. and Pres. Pro Tempore, 40-44. Govt. Pos: Nat. dir, Off. Emergency Planning and mem, Nat. Sec. Coun, 61; spec. asst, Attorney Gen. of La. Bus. & Prof. Pos: Attorney, Ellis, Lancaster & King; gen. counsel, Greater New Orleans Expressway. Mem: Admitted to La. Bar, 30; former v.pres, Aviation Bd; Int, Am, La. and New Orleans Bar Asns; C. of C; La. State Univ. Found; Boston Club of New Orleans; New Orleans Country Club; South. Yacht Club; Athletic Club; Petrol.

Club; Young Men's Bus. Club; Covington Country Club; Reading Room; York Country Club; Bal Harbour Club; Racquet Club; Canyon Country Club. Legal Res: New Orleans, La. Mailing Add: 2233 Camino Real, Palm Springs, Calif. 92262. (1967)

ELLIS, FRANK C. D
b. Lithium, Mo, 12/11/13; m. 10/3/37 to Jewel Bollinger; c. Gregory, Pamela, Anthony and Patrick. Educ: High Sch, Sedgewickville, Mo. Polit. & Govt. Pos: Mo. State Rep, 62-69; former mem, Co. Health Unit, Fed. Housing Admin. Bus. & Prof. Pos: Farmer. Mem: Odd Fellows; bd. mem, Black River Elec. Coop; Sedgewickville Sch. Bd; Active in civic and co. orgns. Rel: Methodist. Mailing Add: Sedgewickville, Mo. 63781. (1967)

ELLIS, G. RICHARD R
b. Kokomo, Ind, 9/22/19; s. Ernest E. Ellis and Marie Shenk E; m. 12/25/41 to Jane F. Owen; c. Cartwright and Melissa Winfield. Educ: Ind. Univ, B.S. in bus admin, 47 and LL.B, 47; Phi Delta Phi; Phi Kappa Psi. Govt. Pos: Mem, Ind. State Off. Bldg. Cmn, 58-61; Ind. State Sen, Howard and Miami Cos, 50-54. Mil. Serv: Entered as Pvt, Air Force, 42, released as Capt, 45. Mem: Mem, Bd. of Mgrs, Ind. State Bar Asn, 60-62; pres, Howard Co. Bar Asn, 59; Am. Bar. Asn; fel, Am. Col. Trial Lawyers; Am. Judicature Soc; pres, C. of C, 55; Ind. State C. of C; pres, Kiwanis, 52; Elks; VFW; Am. Legion; hon. mem, Am. Fedn. Musicians, Local 141; Kokomo Country Club; Columbia Club; Ind. Soc. of Chicago. Rel: Congregational. Legal Res: 1425 Kingston Rd, Kokomo, Ind. 46901. Mailing Add: 421 W. Sycamore, Kokomo, Ind. 46901.

ELLIS, GALEN LANE D
b. Newton, W.Va, 7/27/29; s. Lee Ellis and Nannie Nester E; m. 5/13/55 to Evelyn Elswick; c. Galen Lane, Jr. and June Ann. Polit. & Govt. Pos: Mem, Clay Co. Bd. Educ, W.Va, 62-64; W.Va. State Del, 67-69. Mil. Serv: Entered as Pvt, Army Nat. Guard, 48, released as Sgt. 1/C, 57, after serv. in Co. D, 150th Inf, Spencer, W.Va. Mem: BRT; Odd Fellows; Lions. Rel: Baptist. Mailing Add: Box 348, Clay, W.Va. 25043. (1967)

ELLIS, JOHN HAGOOD R
Chmn, Lowndes Co. Rep. Party, Ala.
b. Ft. Deposit, Ala, 12/15/28; s. Hense Reynolds Ellis and Ellen Hagood E; m. 8/22/54 to Rose Herlong; c. Eric Herlong, Joana Salley, Hense Reynolds, II and Clara Rose. Educ: Univ. Ala, B.S, 50. Polit. & Govt. Pos: Chmn, Lowndes Co. Rep. Party, Ala, 62-; mem, Lowndes Co. Soil Conserv. Dist, 64-; mem, Ala. Forestry Coun, 65- Mil. Serv: Entered as Pvt, Army, 50, released as M/Sgt, 52, after serv. in 28th Inf. Div, Germany, 51-52. Mem: Farm Bur; Lowndes Cattlemen's Asn; Forest Farmers Asn; Mason; Civitan Club. Rel: Baptist. Mailing Add: Drawer L, Ft. Deposit, Ala. 36032. (1967)

ELLIS, MORRISS WREN D
Ga. State Rep.
b. Soddy, Tenn, 9/19/15; s. Edwin Wren Ellis and Nellie Morriss E; m. 2/14/50 to Anna McKinney; c. Cindy Anne (Mrs. Lynnah) and Jeni Wren. Educ: Auburn Univ, 2½ years; Sigma Alpha Epsilon. Polit. & Govt. Pos: Ga. State Rep, 69- Bus. & Prof. Pos: Dist. sales mgr, Delta Air Lines, 46-50; pres. and gen. mgr, Asphalt Camiens, Inc, 50-; v.pres. and gen. mgr, Coastal Mack Sales, Inc, 55-; pres, Transport Leasing Corp, 56- Mil. Serv: Entered as Pvt, Army, 41, released as Capt, 45, after serv. in 703rd Tank Destroyer Bn. Third Armored Div, ETO First Army, 43-45; Am. Theater and ETO Ribbons with 2 battle stars. Mem: Rotary; VFW; Am. Legion. Rel: Presbyterian. Mailing Add: 312 Gordonston Ave, Savannah, Ga. 31404.

ELLIS, ROBERT LAWSON, JR. D
Ala. State Rep.
b. Birmingham, Ala, 3/27/22; s. Robert Lawson Ellis, Sr. and Evelyn Donahoo E; m. 1/7/43 to Mary Florence Thomas; c. Don Wayne, Mary Gail and Sherry Ellen. Educ: Auburn Univ; Univ. Ala, mech. eng. Polit. & Govt. Pos: Mem, Jefferson Co. Bd. Educ, Ala, 60-66; mem, Birmingham-Jefferson Co. Regional Planning Cmt, 64-; Ala. State Rep, 14th Dist, 67- Bus. & Prof. Pos: Draftsman, U.S. Steel, T.C.I. Div, 45-48 and James A. Evans, 48-50; engr. and planning engr, S.Nat. Gas Co, 50-66. Mil. Serv: Entered as Pvt, Air Force, 42, released as Sgt, 45, after serv. in Training Command. Mem: Am. Soc. of Heating and Refrig. Engrs; Nat. and Ala. Sch. Bd. Asns; Int. Counsr, Lions; Silver Beaver, Boy Scouts; Am. Legion; West. Sections Best Citizen Asn, Inc. Personally organized 20 Lions' Clubs in Ala. Rel: Methodist. Mailing Add: Route 1, Box 509, Poplar Lane, Adamsville, Ala. 35005.

ELLIS, S. THOMAS D
b. Atlanta, Ga, 7/10/21; s. John M. Ellis and Rosa Crowell E; m. 6/2/46 to Ann Branan; c. Thomas Anthony, Ann Elaine, Mary Lynn. Educ: Crichton Bus. Col; Atlanta Law Sch, LL.B, 50. Polit. & Govt. Pos: Ga. State Sen, 63-64; Ga. State Rep, 57-60; City Coun. of McDonough, 51-52. Bus. & Prof. Pos: Attorney. Mil. Serv: U.S.A.F, WW II, 41-45. Mailing Add: McDonough, Ga. 30253. (1967)

ELLIS, VERNA JEANNE R
V.Chmn, Clayton Co. Rep. Party, Iowa
b. Cedar Falls, Iowa, 2/15/26; d. Hans C. Smith and Edna Nielsen S; m. 9/27/46 to Lynn Milford Ellis; c. Sherilyn Kay (Mrs. Ronald Foster) and Stephen Ross. Educ: Univ. North. Iowa, B.S, 58; Upper Iowa Col, summer 68; Univ. Womens League Bd; Univ. Sr. Counsr; Sigma Sigma Sigma; Womens Athletic Asn; Womens Phys. Educ. Club. Polit. & Govt. Pos: Committeewoman, Black Hawk Co. Rep. Party, Iowa, 58-60; campaign activities chmn, Black Hawk Co. Rep. Women, 60-64; secy, Clayton Co. Rep. Women, 65-66; chmn. and adv, Clayton Co. TAR, 65-67; v.chmn, Clayton Co. Rep. Party, 67-; chmn, Clayton Co. Women for Nixon-Agnew, 68- Mem: Mem. bd. and camp chmn, Conestoga Coun. Girl Scouts, 56-60; mem. bd, Sartori Mem. Hosp. Auxiliary, Cedar Falls, Iowa, 59-64; mem. bd. and adv, Teenagers Recreation Asn, 60-64; pres, Florana Flower Club, 63-64; Am. Asn. Univ. Women; Am. Asn. Health, Phys. Educ. & Recreation; Nat. Iowa State and Starmont Educ. Asns; Univ. North. Iowa Alumni Asn; Nat. Fedn. Womens Clubs; Nat. Fedn, Second Dist. Iowa and Clayton Co. Rep. Women; Am. Legion Auxiliary; Am. Lutheran Church Women; Backbone Golf and Country Club; Amvets Auxiliary. Pins for serv, Black Hawk Co. Rep. Party, Iowa. Rel: Lutheran. Mailing Add: 306 Prairie Ave, Strawberry Point, Iowa 52076.

ELLISON, CHARLES E, JR. DFL
Chmn, Grant Co. Minn. Dem-Farmer-Labor Party
b. Elbow Lake, Minn, 2/13/07; s. Charles E. Ellison, Sr. and Roxy Stillman E; m. 9/23/31 to Evalyn D. Larson; c. C. Eugene and Barbara R. Educ: Univ. Minn. Polit. & Govt. Pos: Town clerk, Delaware Twp, Minn, 29-38; mem. sch. bd, Dist. 39, 42-48; supvr. town bd, Elbow Lake, 50-; del, all Co, Dist. and State Dem-Farmer-Labor Conv, 54-; secy, Grant Co. Minn. Dem-Farmer-Labor Party, 54-66, chmn, 66-; mem. exec. cmt, Seventh Cong. Dist, 58-64; dist. chmn, Dem-Farmer-Labor Cmt. for Kennedy, 60; mem, Farmers Home Admin. Co. Cmt, 60-; del, Dem. Nat. Conv, 64. Mem: Farmers Union; Nat. Farmers; Odd Fellows. Rel: Lutheran. Mailing Add: R.R. 1, Elbow Lake, Minn. 56531.

ELLISON, O. ERNEST, JR. 'ERNIE'
Fla. State Auditor
b. Panama City, Fla, 9/16/23; m. to Evelyn M. Whitney; c. Sharon Alice and Ernest W. Educ: Fla. State Univ, B.S, 52; Alpha Kappa Psi; Beta Alpha Psi. Polit. & Govt. Pos: With State Auditing Dept, Fla, 53-59, asst. state auditor, 59-63, state auditor, 63- Bus. & Prof. Pos: Price Waterhouse & Co, N.Y.C, 52; CPA, 57- Mil. Serv: Army, 42-46. Mem: Kiwanis. Rel: Episcopal. Mailing Add: Room 415, Carlton Bldg, Tallahassee, Fla. 32304. (1967)

ELLSASSER, EDWARD CHARLES, JR. D
b. Mishawaka, Ind, 8/6/14; s. Edward Charles Ellsasser, Sr. and Katherine Decker E; m. 6/26/36 to Ruth Arline Grandstaff; c. James Curtis, Robert Charles and Ruth Ann. Educ: High Sch, 4 years. Polit. & Govt. Pos: Cmnr, Ind. State Aeronaut. Cmn, 61-; del, Dem. Nat. Conv, 68. Bus. & Prof. Pos: Dir, First Nat. Bank of Mishawaka, Ind, currently; pres, Sun Realty Corp, currently. Mem: Mich. Pure Milk Dealers Asn; Diamond Lake Yacht Club, Cassopolis, Mich; Morris Park Country Club, South Bend, Ind. Rel: Catholic. Mailing Add: 409 Edgewater Dr, Mishawaka, Ind. 46544.

ELLSWORTH, BARBARA LANGE R
V.Chmn, Dubuque Co. Rep. Cent. Cmt, Iowa
b. Dubuque, Iowa, 5/17/20; d. Harvey Malcolm Lange and Geraldine Dennis L; m. 4/26/41 to Theodore Richards Ellsworth; c. Ann, Mareth, Theodore Richards, Jr, Sarah and Katharine. Educ: Smith Col, 38-40; Smith Col. Alumnae Asn. Polit. & Govt. Pos: Govt. clerk, Off. Price Admin, 42-44; precinct committeewoman, Rep. Party, Iowa, 60-; v.chmn, Dubuque Co. Rep. Cent. Cmt, 62-; del, Rep. Nat. Conv, 64. Bus. & Prof. Pos: Clerk, Cook's Travel Agency, Chicago, Ill, 41-42. Mem: Pres. bd, Mt. Pleasant Home; Dubuque Golf and Country Club. Three time winner Women's Golf Championship of Dubuque Golf and Country Club. Rel: Episcopal; Vestrywoman, St. John's Episcopal Church. Mailing Add: 1492 Locust St, Dubuque, Iowa 52001.

ELLSWORTH, ROBERT F. R
U.S. Ambassador to NATO
b. Lawrence, Kans, 6/11/26; m. to Vivian Sies; c. Robert William and Ann Elizabeth. Educ: Univ. Kans, B.S; Univ. Mich, J.D; Beta Theta Pi; Phi Delta Phi. Polit. & Govt. Pos: Legal asst. to v.chmn. maritime affairs, Fed. Maritime Bd, U.S. Dept. of Commerce; U.S. Rep, Kans, 61-66; asst. to President and U.S. Ambassador to NATO, 69- Bus. & Prof. Pos: Attorney-at-law, 49-; admitted to practice law in the highest State Courts of Mass, Kans. and D.C, U.S. Patent Off, U.S. Treas. Dept, U.S. Dist. Court and U.S. Supreme Court; mem. faculty, Univ. Kans. Sch. of Bus, 56-57. Mil. Serv: Lt. Comdr, Navy Res, active duty in World War II and Korean Conflict. Mem: Am. Legion; VFW; Optimist Club. Legal Res: Lawrence, Kans. 66044. Mailing Add: 36 Ave. du Vert Chasseur, Brussels 18, Belgium.

ELLSWORTH, W. FISHER R
Idaho State Sen.
b. Lewisville, Idaho, 4/9/05; s. Frank Blair Ellsworth and Minnie Jane Fisher E; m. 6/22/27 to Carmen Rich; c. Gary Rich. Educ: Univ. Idaho, B.S. in Bus, 28; Blue Key; Scabbard and Blade; Beta Theta Pi. Polit. & Govt. Pos: Gen. chmn, Bonneville Co. Rep. Cent. Cmt, Idaho, 50; mem-dir, Idaho State Highway Bd, 50-53; Idaho State Sen, Dist. 30, 68- Bus. & Prof. Pos: Pres. and gen. mgr, Ellsworth-Dodge Co, Idaho Falls, Idaho, 45-65; retired. Mil. Serv: Entered as Lt.(jg), Naval Res, 42, released as Lt.(sg), 45, after serv. in Armed Guard, Aleutian and S.Pac, 43-45. Mem: Rotary Int; Elks. Rel: Latter-day Saint. Mailing Add: 2800 Fieldstream Lane, Idaho Falls, Idaho 83401.

ELMAN, PHILIP
Cmnr, Fed. Trade Cmn.
b. Paterson, N.J, 3/14/18; m. 12/21/47 to Ella M. Shalit; c. Joseph, Peter and Anthony. Educ: City Col. New York, A.B, 36; Harvard, LL.B, 39; Phi Beta Kappa. Polit. & Govt. Pos: Law clerk to Mr. Justice Frankfurter, 41-43; asst. to the Solicitor Gen, Dept. of Justice, 44-61; cmnr, Fed. Trade Cmn, 61- Contrib. to various legal publ. Recipient, Rockefeller Pub. Serv. Award, 67. Mailing Add: 6719 Brigadoon Dr, Bethesda, Md. 20034.

ELMORE, CLARENCE C. D
Cmnr, Alcohol Beverage Control, W.Va.
b. Princeton, W.Va, 9/17/10; s. W.B. Elmore; m. 3/4/31 to Mary Louise White; c. Alma Christine, Connie Sue, Clarence C, Jr; Three grandchildren. Educ: Pub. schs, Mercer Co, W.Va. Polit. & Govt. Pos: Constable, East River Dist, W.Va, 33-36; dep. sheriff, Mercer Co, 37-40, sheriff, 49-52; justice of the peace, East River Dist, Mercer Co, 41-44; doorkeeper of the W.Va. State Senate, 53; gen. field supvr, Liquor Control Cmn, 53-55, cmnr, 61-; cmnr, Mercer Co. Court. Bus. & Prof. Pos: Ins. and automobile bus, 56-58. Mil. Serv: Navy, 45-46. Mem: Elk; Moose; Modern Woodman. Rel: First Christian Church. Mailing Add: Princeton, W.Va. 24740. (1967)

ELMORE, DOROTHY D
b. Montgomery Co, Ind, 11/29/05; m. to Eston Elmore; c. Two sons; four grandchildren. Polit. & Govt. Pos: V.Chmn, Montgomery Co. Dem. Party, Ind, 48-53; v.chmn, Sixth Dist. Dem. Party, 53-64; presidential elector, Ind, 64; Dem. Nat. Committeewoman, Ind, 64-69; del, Dem. Nat. Conv, 68. Mem: Red Cross Nurses' Aid Corps; Eastern Star. Rel: Baptist. Mailing Add: 118 S. Vine St, Crawfordsville, Ind. 47933. (1967)

ELROD, A. DON D
Nebr. State Sen.
b. Loup City, Nebr, 5/8/25; s. Lawrence Ray Elrod and Adelia Minnie Bichel E; m. 6/8/47 to Helen Dorothy Niemoth; c. Mary Jo and James Alan. Polit. & Govt. Pos: Secy-treas, Grand Island Fedn. Labor and Cmt. on Polit. Educ, AFL-CIO, Nebr, 57-; chmn, Hall Co. Dem. Cent. Cmt, 62-64; exec. bd. mem, Nebr. State AFL-CIO, 63-; Nebr. Dem. State Cent. Committeeman, 35th Dist, 64-; pres, Typographical Union 31, 65-; Nebr. State Sen, 66- Mil. Serv: Entered as A/S, Navy Seabees, 43, released as Ship Serviceman 3/C, 46; Am. Theater Medal; Asiatic Pac. Medal with Two Battle Stars; Victory Medal. Mem: Am. Legion; VFW; YMCA; Eagles. Rel: Lutheran. Legal Res: 2327 N. Sheridan, Grand Island, Nebr. 68801. Mailing Add: P.O. Box 17, Grand Island, Nebr. 68801.

ELROD, IRMA PETSCH D
Chmn, Kimball Co. Dem. Party, Nebr.
b. Pleasant Dale, Nebr, 7/5/16; d. Albert Roy Petsch and Milada Mary P; m. 5/19/37 to Leslie Delphia Elrod; c. Douglas Roy and Delwyn Loy. Educ: Doane Col, 1 year; Univ. Nebr. correspondence sch, 12 hours; Lincoln Sch. Commerce, Nebr, 1 summer. Polit. & Govt. Pos: Secy, Kimball Co. Dem. Party, 58-66, chmn, 66- Bus. & Prof. Pos: Teacher, Sch. Dist. 19, Seward Co, Nebr, 35-36, Dist. 7, 36-37, Dist. 76, 38-40 and Dist. 95, 41-42; Petsch & Elrod Farm Equipment, Kimball, Nebr, 42-59. Mem: Pythian Sisters, Plains Temple, No. 40; Farm Bur; Federated Women's Garden Clubs; Exten. Club; life mem. Woman's Soc. Christian Serv. and PTA; Farmers and World Affairs; Farm Land Industs; commun. counsr for Head Start. Outstanding Farmer; Outstanding Homemaker; Alumnae award for serv. in 4-H. Rel: Methodist; lay-leader to Methodist Conf. Legal Res: 409 N. Chestnut, Kimball, Nebr. 69145. Mailing Add: North Star Route, Box 1, Kimball, Nebr. 69145.

ELROD, RICHARD JAY D
Ill. State Rep.
b. Chicago, Ill, 2/17/34; s. Arthur X. Elrod and Della Glasser E; m. 6/18/55 to Marilyn Arline Mann; c. Steven Michael and Audrey Marlene. Educ: Northwest. Univ, B.A, 55, Law Sch, J.D, 58; Phi Epsilon Pi; Phi Alpha Delta. Polit. & Govt. Pos: Asst. corp. counsel, Chicago, Ill, 58-, chief city prosecutor, 65-; chmn, Young Dem. Cook Co, 61-62; del, State Representative Nominating Conv, 64; Ill. State Rep, 13th Rep. Dist, 69- Mem: Chicago and Ill. Bar Asns; Decalogue Soc. Lawyers; Am. Judicature Soc; Nat. Soc. State Legis; Amvets; Mason; B'nai B'rith. Awards received from, Chicago Police Dept, Amvets, Jewish War Vet, Young Dem. Cook Co, Jewish United Fund and Anti-Defamation League. Rel: Jewish. Mailing Add: 6122 N. Sacramento Ave, Chicago, Ill. 60645.

ELROD, ROBERT HARDING R
b. Henryville, Ind, 3/15/26; s. Stephen Bruce Elrod and Mildred Bartholomew E; m. 9/7/51 to Jean McAllister; c. Deborah Ann and Thomas Edward. Educ: Purdue Univ, B.S, 51; Sigma Delta Chi; Delta Tau Delta. Polit. & Govt. Pos: Treas, Orange Co. Rep. Exec. Cmt, 61-62, chmn, 62-63; Fla. State Rep, 63-66; Fla. State Sen, 66-68; mgr. govt. affairs, Orlando Area C. of C, 69- Bus. & Prof. Pos: Dir, Air Groves, Inc, Winter Garden, 54-, Space Groves, Inc, 55- and Roper Growers Coop, 68- Mil. Serv: Army Air Corps, 44-45, Cadet. Mem: Orlando Downtown Lions Club (dir); C. of C; Orange Co. Sportsmens Asn; Univ. Club Orlando; West Orange Country Club. Good Govt. Award, Winter Garden Jaycees, 69. Rel: Episcopal. Legal Res: 1000 Second Ave, Windermere, Fla. 32786. Mailing Add: P.O. Box 106, Windermere, Fla. 32786.

ELSESSER, BETTY R
V.Chmn, Huron Co. Rep. Party, Mich.
b. Bad Axe, Mich, 11/16/26; m. 6/25/49 to John O. Elsesser; c. John, James and Mark. Educ: Cent. Mich. Univ, B.S. Polit. & Govt. Pos: V.chmn, Huron Co. Rep. Party, Mich. and Huron Co. Rep. Women, currently. Bus. & Prof. Pos: Teacher hist, Lakers Jr. High, Mich. Mem: Past pres, Womens Civic Club; Eastern Star; VFW Auxiliary; PTA; Women's Soc. for Christian Serv. Rel: Methodist; Bd. mem, Elkton United Methodist Church; Sr. High Methodist Young Folks and Sunday Sch. Adv. Mailing Add: 225 N. Main St, Elkton, Mich. 48731.

ELSON, ROY LANE D
b. Elrama, Pa, 10/1/30; s. LeeRoy Elson and Pearl Edie E; m. 3/9/57 to G. Minor Boring; Roy Lane and Jean Edie. Educ: Univ. Ariz, B.A, 52; Wash. Col. of Law, 58; Phi Gamma Delta. Polit. & Govt. Pos: Asst. secy. to U.S. Sen. Carl Hayden, Ariz, 52-53, secy, 57-60, admin. asst, 60-64 & 65-69; cand. for U.S. Sen, Ariz, 64 & 68. Mil. Serv: Entered as 2nd Lt, Air Force, 53, released as 1st Lt, 55, after serv. in 781st Troop Carrier Squadron, ETO. Publ: 'CAP: Where do We Stand,' Tucson Daily Citizen, 8/63. Mem: Nat. Capital Dem. Club; Phoenix Jr. C. of C; Univ. Ariz. Alumni Asn; Ariz. State Soc. Rel: Presbyterian. Legal Res: Tucson, Ariz. Mailing Add: 1811 Edgehill Dr, Alexandria, Va. 22307. (1967)

ELSTON, DOROTHY ANDREWS R
Treas. of the United States
b. Wilkes-Barre, Pa, 3/22/17; d. Reginald Hastings Andrews and Mabel Aston A; m. 9/30/36 to Russell Ransom Elston, div. 1960. Polit. & Govt. Pos: Trustee, Kruse Sch, 54-57; pres, Del. State Fedn. Rep. Women, 54, v.pres. bldg. fund, presently; mem. bd. dirs, Nat. Fedn. Rep. Women, 54-, mem. exec. cmt, 56- and pres, 63-68; state adv, Farmer's Home Admin, 56-59; del, Rep. Nat. Conv, 56 & 60, alternate del, 68, mem. rules cmt, 56, speaker, 64; mem. platform cmt, Del. State Rep. Conv, 56 & 58; mem, TAR Adv. Cmt, Young Rep. Nat. Fedn. and founder, STARS, Sub Teen Age Rep; past pres, New Castle Co. Rep. Women's Club; Rep. committeewoman, Odessa Voting Dis; mem. state cent. cmt. and second dist. cmt; mem. adv. bd, N.Y. World's Fair, 64-65; del, White House Conf. on Int. Coop, 65; Treas. of U.S, 69- Bus. & Prof. Pos: Mem. legal dept, DuPont Co, Wilmington, Del, owner and operator, 183 acre nursery farm, McDonough, 46- Mem: Chmn. for conserv. and past regent, Elizabeth Cook Chap, DAR, past chmn. good citizens cmt. and past chmn. for conserv, State Soc, past v.chmn. for conserv, Nat. Soc; past legis. chmn, chaplain, lectr. and pub. rels. chmn, Cent. Grange 61; state lectr, Mid. Atlantic Grange Lectr. Asn, 4 years, state health chmn, 2 years and pres, 2 years; former second v.pres, Odessa Women's Club; Am. Newspaper Women's Club; Am. Newspaper Women's Club; Capitol Hill Club. Named 1 of 12 Outstanding Polit. Women in Country, League of Women Voters, 64; Women of Achievement for Year, Del. State Fedn. Women's Clubs, 66. Rel: Methodist; Steward, Trustee, chmn, Pastoral Rels. Cmt. and chmn, Wills and Legacies, St. Paul's Methodist Church of Odessa. Legal Res: Dae-Brake Farm, R.D.2, Middletown, Del. 19709. Mailing Add: 2112 Treasury Bldg, Washington, D.C. 20220.

ELTSE, RALPH ROSCOE R
b. Oskaloosa, Iowa, 9/13/85; s. John J. Eltse and Jennie Sarah West E; m. 10/30/51 to Ruth Williams. Educ: Haverford Col, B.A, 10; Pa. State Univ, M.A, 10; Univ. Calif. Boalt Sch. of Law, 12-14. Polit. & Govt. Pos: Mem, Calif. State Cent. Cmt, 33-36; U.S. Rep. Seventh Dist, Calif, 33-34; mem, Naval Affairs Cmt, Coinage Weights and Measures; chmn, City of Berkeley Transportation Cmt, 24-26. Bus. & Prof. Pos: Partner, Clark, Nichols & Eltse, 15-42. Mem: Calif. and Alameda Co. Bar Asns; past pres, Berkeley C. of C. and Berkeley Commun. Chest; dir. and treas, Berkeley YMCA, intermittently; organizer and treas, League Supreme Court Independence, 36-37; life mem, Univ. Calif. Alumni; Elks; City Commons Club. Rel: Presbyterian; pres, First Presbyterian Church Found. Mailing Add: 1440 Walnut St, Berkeley, Calif. 94709. (1967)

ELVERS, ADOLPH WALTER D
Iowa State Sen.
b. Elkader, Iowa, 8/4/11; s. Adolph J. Elvers and Mary Dittmer E; m. 11/26/34 to Lola Alma Hanson. Educ: Elkader High Sch, grad, 29. Polit. & Govt. Pos: Clerk, Cox Creek Twp, Iowa, 46-52; Dem. Chmn, Clayton Co, 54-60; Iowa State Sen, Ollamakee and Clayton Co, 61- Bus. & Prof. Pos: Life long farmer; ins. license, Mutual Serv, eight years, and Des Moines Casualty, ten years. Dir, Cent. Dairy Coop, 44-; pres, Iowa Dairy Products Asn, 48-; pres, Elkader Coop. Co, 49-; dir, Nat. Milk Producers Fedn, 59-, mem. exec. cmt, 64-; Civil Defense Dir, Clayton Co, 69- Mem: Farm Bur; Masons; Rotary; Lions. Commun. Leader Award; 68; Dairy Shrine Club, 68. Rel: United Church of Christ. Mailing Add: R.R, Elkader, Iowa 52043.

ELVEY, HARRY M. R
b. McConnellsburg, Pa, 12/22/10; s. George Boyd Elvey and Hester Stevens E; m. to Alma Nelson Kendall; c. two. Educ: Ogontz Col. of Civil Defense. Polit. & Govt. Pos: Pa. State Rep, 60-67; former Civil Defense dir. of Fulton Co; Rep. committeeman and Co. chmn; served on borough coun. 10 years; co. treas, 48-52; clerk to Co. Cmnrs, 44-48. Bus. & Prof. Pos: Pres, McConnellsburg Vol. Fire Co. 10 years. Mil. Serv: Army, 6th Field Artil, Battery D, Ft. Hoyle, Md, C.M.T.C. Mem: Glee Club; Lit. Soc; Chambersburg Local 616 Carpenters and Joiners of Am; Odd Fellows; Nat. Rifle Asn; Pa. Farmers Asn; charter mem, Fulton Co. Sportsmens League; former Sunday Sch. supt; mgr, M.H.S. baseball team; Red Cross First-Aid instr. Rel: Trustee of McConnellsburg United Presbyterian Church. Mailing Add: 218 E. North St, McConnellsburg, Pa. 17233. (1967)

ELWARD, PAUL FRANCIS D
Ill. State Rep.
b. Chicago, Ill, 4/19/26; s. Joseph F. Elward and Daisiann Lenert E; m. 9/26/53 to Eileen McGuiness; c. Joseph, William, John, Thomas and Patrick. Educ: Loyola Univ, Ill, A.B. with honors, 47; Delta Theta Phi; Alpha Sigma Nu; Blue Key. Polit. & Govt. Pos: Precinct capt, 49th Ward Dem. Orgn, Ill, 55-; Ill. State Rep, 57-, majority whip, House of Rep, Ill, 65-67, chmn, Exec. Mansion Cmn, 66-, mem, Ill. Budgetary Cmn, 67-; secy, Judicial Adv. Coun. of Ill, 61-67; del, Dem. Nat. Conv, 68. Bus. & Prof. Pos: Dir, Evanston Bus Co, Ill, 65- Mil. Serv: Entered as A/S, Navy, 44, released as Seaman 1/C, 46. Mem: City Club, Chicago Cath. Interracial Coun; Rogers Park Commun. Coun; pres. coun, Mundelein Col; Irish Fel. Club. Rel: Catholic. Mailing Add: 1532 W. Chase Ave, Chicago, Ill. 60626.

ELWOOD, CLELL D. R
S.Dak. State Sen.
b. 8/9/24; m. 5/20/45 to Beverly J. Rasband; c. Mitchel, Robert and Debra. Educ: Col. of Idaho. Polit. & Govt. Pos: S.Dak. State Rep, 63-66; S.Dak. State Sen, 67-; dir. state planning, 67- Bus. & Prof. Pos: Former tel. co. owner; ins. bus. Mil. Serv: Air Force, World War II. Mem: Masons; Rotary; C. of C.(past dir); Am. Legion Serv. Off. Rel: Protestant. Mailing Add: 505 N. Jackson, Pierre, S.Dak. 57501.

ELY, HERBERT LEONARD D
Chief Counsel, Ariz. Dem. State Party
b. Brooklyn, N.Y, 11/13/33; s. Jacob Ely and Edith Marcus E; m. 12/17/55 to Elaine J. Goldberg; c. Daymon, Zane and Elise. Educ: Lebanon Valley Col, B.A, 55; Univ. Pa. Law Sch, LL.D, 57. Polit. & Govt. Pos: Mem, Ariz. State Dem. Exec. Cmt, 64-68; chief counsel and parliamentarian, Ariz. Dem. State Party, 65-; counsel, Maricopa Co. Dem. Cent. Cmt, Ariz, 66-68; del, Dem. Nat. Conv. and mem. platform cmt, 68; co-chmn, Humphrey Campaign, Phoenix, Ariz, 68. Bus. & Prof. Pos: Attorney-at-law, Gorey & Ely, Phoenix, Ariz, currently. Mem: Am, Ariz. and Maricopa Co. Bar Asns; Am. and Ariz. Trial Lawyers Asn; pres, Phoenix Trial Lawyers Asn, 66-67; Am. Arbit. Asn; Am. Civil Liberties Union; Ariz. Civil Liberties Union (former counsel); former counsel, Local NAACP. Nat. Honor Soc; Grad. Honors from Univ. Pa. Law Sch, 69. Rel: Jewish. Mailing Add: 6745 N. Central, Phoenix, Ariz. 85012.

ELY, JOHN M. D
b. Cedar Rapids, Iowa, 1919; m. 1942 to Polly Ward; c. John M. III, Martha M, Nathaniel W. Educ: Princeton Univ, 1941. Polit. Pos: Iowa State Sen, 64-66; Iowa State Rep, 2 Terms. Bus. & Prof. Pos: Ingredients Buyer, Quaker Oats Co; World War II, Served in Merchant Marine As Purser For United Fruit Co. Mem: Bd. Mbr. of Cedar Rapids Visiting Nurse Asso; Linn Co. Mental Health Asso. Rel: Unitarian. Mailing Add: 203 23rd. St, N.E, Cedar Rapids, Iowa. 52402. (1967)

ELY, WILLIAM MARVIN R
b. New London, Conn, 7/22/32; s. Julian Griffin Ely, M.D. and May Richardson E; single. Educ: Univ. N.H. Thompson Sch. Agr, grad, 56; Univ. N.B. Canadian Studies Prog, 64; Univ. Md, B.A. in govt. and polit, 64, M.A. in Int. Rels. and Comp. Govt, 67; Pi Sigma Alpha. Polit. & Govt. Pos: Campaign

asst. for Horace Seely-Brown, Jr, Conn, 60; campaign mgr. for Joseph H. Goldberg, Rep. cand. for Cong, Second Dist, Conn, 66; chmn, Lyme Town Rep. Cmt, Conn, 66-69; research asst. to U.S. Rep. H.W. Pollock, Alaska, 67-69. Bus. & Prof. Pos: Research asst, Univ. Md, 64-67. Mil. Serv: Entered as Pfc, Army, 54, released as Sgt, 55 after serv. in Third Inf. Div, Korea, 54 and First Cavalry Div, Japan, 55. Mem: Am. and Can. Polit. Sci. Asns; Can. Hist. Soc. Rel: Congregational. Mailing Add: R.F.D. 2, Old Lyme, Conn. 06371. (1967)

EMANUEL, JOSEPH D
Chmn, Ashland Co. Dem. Party, Ohio
b. N.Y.C, 4/22/12; s. Giacinto Emanuel and Frances Dettore E; m. 9/7/40 to Margaret Dorothy Thomas; c. Joseph Evan, Jr. and Margaret. Educ: Cleveland Col, 50; Kent State Univ, 58. Polit. & Govt. Pos: Mayor, Mifflin, Ohio, 56-; chmn, Ashland Co. Dem. Party, 64- Bus. & Prof. Pos: Factory personnel dir. and employ. mgr, Cleveland Chain Mfg. Co, 35-53. Mem: Mason (32°); Lions; Elks; Eagles; Eastern Star. Rel: Protestant. Mailing Add: R.D. 4, Box 364, Ashland-Mifflin, Ohio 44805.

EMANUEL, MEYER M, JR. D
Md. State Sen.
b. Washington, D.C, 4/4/19; s. Meyer Emanuel, Sr. and Julia Cohen E; m. 12/8/40 to Selma Ruskin; c. Judith (Mrs. Sheehan), Roberta and Jonathan. Educ: City Col. Of N.Y, B.B.A, 40. Polit. & Govt. Pos: Md. State Del, 63-66; Md. State Sen, 67- Bus. & Prof. Pos: CPA, 47- Mil. Serv: Entered as Pvt, Army Corps of Engrs, 42, released as Chief Warrant Officer, 46, after serv. in Continental U.S; Meritorius Serv. Award. Mem: Am. and D.C. Insts. of CPA's; Md. Fiscal Officer's Asn; City Col. of N.Y. Alumni Asn. Rel: Jewish. Mailing Add: 1401 K St. N.W, Washington, D.C. 20005.

EMERSON, GALO PUTNAM, JR. R
b. Peabody, Mass, 11/19/32; s. Galo Putnam Emerson and Joanne Bresnahan; m. 2/12/55 to Sally Ann Goldsmith; c. Kim Elizabeth, Wendy Ellen, Eric Bruce and Nathan Putnam. Educ: Merrimack Col, A.B.A. Polit. & Govt. Pos: Former chmn, Danvers Rep. Town Cmt, Mass; mem, Gov. Adv. Cmt. on Vacation Travel, 65- Bus. & Prof. Pos: Past pres, Essex Co. Tourist Coun, Mass, and New Eng. Retail Confectioners Asn. Mil. Serv: Entered as Seaman, Navy, 52, released as Personnelman 2/C, 56, after serv. in Sixth Fleet, European Occupation, Am. Defense and Good Conduct Medals. Rel: Protestant. Mailing Add: 431 Maple St, Danvers, Mass. 01923.

EMERSON, JUNIUS M. D
Pa. State Rep.
b. Anderson, S.C, 6/23/26; s. Hasker Butler Emerson and Beatrice Bell E; m. to Martha J. Lee; c. Three. Educ: LaSalle Col. Polit. & Govt. Pos: Dem. Committeeman, 28th Ward, 11 years, Ward Secy, 2 years, Ward Chmn, 1 year; inheritance tax clerk, Bd. of Rev. of Taxes, 54-64; Pa. State Rep, 64- Bus. & Prof. Pos: Real estate salesman. Mil. Serv: Army, 82nd Airborne Div, 4 years. Mem: N. Cent. Businessmen's Asn; Mason; NAACP; YMCA; Boy Scouts; Strawberry Mansion Civic Asn. Mailing Add: 2603 N. Corlies St, Philadelphia, Pa. 19132.

EMERSON, N. WILLIAM R
b. St. Louis, Mo, 1/1/38; s. Norvell Preston Emerson and Marie Reinemer E; m. 6/25/60 to Evelyn Fairbanks Zwahl; c. Elizabeth and Abigail. Educ: Westminster Col, Mo, B.A, 59; Univ. Baltimore, LL.B, 64; Pi Delta Epsilon; Phi Gamma Delta. Polit. & Govt. Pos: Prog. dir, Youth for Nixon-Lodge, 60; asst. to U.S. Rep. Robert F. Ellsworth, Md, 61-65; admin. asst. to U.S. Rep. Charles McC. Mathias, Jr, 65-69, spec. asst. to U.S. Sen. Charles McC. Mathias, Jr, 69- Mil. Serv: 1st Lt, Air Force Res, 63- Rel: Episcopal. Mailing Add: 8762 Preston Place, Chevy Chase, Md. 20015.

EMERSON, RALPH WALDO D
b. Greeneville, Tenn, 10/14/32; s. John Williams Emerson and Dorothy Moore E; m. to Claudia Nicks; c. Reagan Katheryn and J. Thomas. Educ: E.Tenn. State Univ, B.S, 57; Cumberland Univ, LL.B, 58; Phi Sigma Kappa; Delta Theta Phi. Polit. & Govt. Pos: Senate bill clerk, Tenn. Gen. Assembly, 61; delinquent tax attorney, Tenn, 58-60, property serv. attorney, 61-62 and property adminstr, 63-64; mem, Tenn. Indust. Research Adv. Cmt, 64; chmn, Tenn. State Tech. Serv. Adv. Coun, 65; co-chmn, Trade Cmt. for Tenn-U.S. State-Mex. Rels. Prog, 65; mem, Tenn. Resource Mgt. Plan, Pres. Off. Emergency Planning; dir, Staff Div. Indust. Develop, Tenn, 64-67; admin. asst. to U.S. Rep. Ray Blanton, 67-68. Bus. & Prof. Pos: Pres, Diversified Franchises, Inc, 68- Mil. Serv: Entered as Apprentice, Navy, 52, released as TE3, 54; Maj, Tenn. Army Nat. Guard, at present. Mem: Am, Tenn. and Nashville Bar Asns; Nat. Guard Asn. U.S; Asn. of Alumni of Judge Adv. Gen. Sch; exec. cmt, Asn. State Planning and Develop. Agencies, 66; chmn. indust. develop, Tenn. Jaycees, 65; chmn, Am. Heart Asn. Campaign, 66. Rel: Presbyterian. Legal Res: Nashville, Tenn. Mailing Add: 8603 Cushman Place, Alexandria, Va. 22308.

EMERSON, ROLLO E. R
Twp. Committeeman, Dickinson Co. Rep. Cent. Cmt, Iowa
b. Lake Park, Iowa, 7/13/17; s. Justin William Emerson and Ida E. Henderson E; single. Polit. & Govt. Pos: Mem, Dickinson Co. Rep. Cent. Cmt, Iowa, 48-55, twp. committeeman, 63-; alternate del-at-lg, Rep. Nat. Conv, 64. Mil. Serv: Pvt, Army, 41; Lt. Col, Army Res, 52-; Bronze Star; Korean Serv, Am. Defense, Asiatic-Pac. and Philippines Serv. Ribbons; Unit Citation. Mem: Am. Legion. Rel: Methodist. Mailing Add: Lake Park, Iowa 51347.

EMERSON, WILLIAM O. R
b. Lancaster, N.H, 8/30/83; s. Charles H. Emerson and Fennie Morse E; m. to Maud Cushman; c. Two. Polit. & Govt. Pos: N.H. State Rep, 13-39, 41-43, 51-53, 59-61 and 65-67; tax cmnr. and tobacco tax inspector; former town clerk for 51 years; sch. moderator and treas; del, Constitutional Conv, 38, 56, 60 and 64. Bus. & Prof. Pos: Dir, Whitefield Savings Bank and Trust Co. Mem: Mason; Grange, secy; Eastern Star. Rel: Congregational. Mailing Add: R.F.D. 2, Whitefield, N.H. 03598.

EMERY, EUGENE MARSHALL D
Maine State Rep.
b. Poland, Maine, 1/31/24; s. Marshall Fields Emery and Ruth Elizabeth Hunt E; m. 5/27/67 to Ida Frenchette Lemieux Pepin; c. Arthur R. Lemieux. Educ: Int. Correspondence Schs, 57-61; Machine Tools. Polit. & Govt. Pos: City councilman, 67-69; mem, Auburn City Dem. Cmt, Maine, 68- and Androscoggin Co. Dem. Cmt, 69-; Maine State Rep, 69-, mem, Pub. Utilities Cmt, Maine House of Rep, 69- Bus. & Prof. Pos: Tool specialist, Bath Iron Works, 64- Mil. Serv: Entered as A/S, Navy, 43, released as Machinist Mate, 46, reentered, 51, released as Machinist Mate 2/C, 52, after serv. in SeaBees, ETO, Atlantic Theatre, Pac-Asiatic-Japanese Occupation for 49 months; Citation from Commandant Adm. Towers, Atlantic Fleet; Combat Stars. Mem: United Shipbuilding and Marine Workers of Am-AFL-CIO. Rel: Methodist. Mailing Add: 20 Towle Ave, Auburn, Maine 04210.

EMERY, JAMES LOUIS R
N.Y. State Assemblyman
b. Lakeville, N.Y, 7/22/31; s. James B. Emery and Ruth Wamser E; m. 2/15/57 to Elsie McPhail; c. James L, Jr. and Jon Scott. Educ: Univ. Cincinnati, B.B.A, 53. Polit. & Govt. Pos: Sheriff, Livingston Co, N.Y, 60-63; N.Y. State Assemblyman, 64-, dep. majority leader, N.Y. State Assembly, 64-69. Mil. Serv: Entered as 2nd Lt, Air Force, 53, released as Lt, 55, after serv. in 22nd Dist OSI; Res, Maj. Mem: Genesee Valley Real Estate Bd; Livingston Co. Exten. Serv; N.Y. State Sheriffs Asn; Am. Legion; Boy Scouts (exec. bd, Genesee Coun); Lakeville Fire Dept; Rotary (past pres); Livingston Co. Asn. Town Hwy. Supts; Am. Red Cross (past chmn, Lakeville Br). Mailing Add: 5477 Lakeville Rd, Genesco, N.Y. 14454.

EMERY, MICHAEL C. D
b. Berkeley, Calif, 4/16/40; s. William Edwin Emery, Jr. and Mary McNevin E; m. 4/27/63 to Suzanne H. Steiner; c. Maria Therese, Andrea Christine and Shannon C. Educ: St. Mary's Col, Minn, 58-60; Univ. Minn, B.A, 62; M.A, 64, Ph.D, 68; Kappa Tau Alpha; Pi Delta Epsilon; Sigma Delta Chi. Polit. & Govt. Pos: Pub. rels. dir, Walworth Co. McCarthy for Pres, Wis, 68; co. liaison, Maiers for Cong, First Cong. Dist, 68; del, Wis. Dem. State Conv, 68; alternate del, Dem. Nat. Conv, 68; San Fernando Valley organizer, Kennedy Dem, Los Angeles, Calif, 68 and Bradley for Mayor, 69. Bus. & Prof. Pos: Reporter, United Press Int, Minneapolis, 61-64, major league baseball writer, 64 season; pub. info. writer, Wis. State Univ, Whitewater, 64-66, journalism instr, 64-66 & 68; from instr. to asst. prof. journalism, San Fernando Valley State Col, 68- Mil. Serv: Entered as Pvt, Army, 62, released as 1st Lt, 68, after serv. in 360th Psychol. Opers. Bn, St. Paul, Minn, 1st Lt, Army Res. Officer's Sch, Madison, Wis; Fourth in Class, Army Info. Sch, Ft. Slocum, N.Y, 62; Citation for Spec. Psychol. Opers. Proj, Ft. Devens, Mass, 64. Publ: 'Minnesota Vikings,' Sporting News, 8/61; 'The Munich Crisis Broadcasts,' Journalism Quart, autumn 65; America's Front Page News, 3-M Co. and Vis-Com, Inc; Moon Men Slide Series 69. Mem: Sigma Delta Chi (adv, San Fernando Valley State Col. Chap); Asn. for Educ. in Journalism. Rel: Roman Catholic. Mailing Add: 10101 Amestoy, Northridge, Calif. 91324.

EMETT, ROBERT LYNN R
Mem. Exec. Cmt, United Rep. Finance Cmt, Los Angeles Co, Calif.
b. Oxnard, Calif, 8/9/27; s. Edward Llewellyn Emett and Isabel Vaughan E; c. Michael Scott, Sherry Lynn, Robert Charles, Lindy Louise and James Stewart. Educ: Clarmont Men's Col, B.A, 50; Mem, Claremont Men's Col. Affiliates Bd. and pres, Alumni Asn, 63-64; dir, Calif. Cong. Recognition Proj. Polit. & Govt. Pos: State chmn, Budget and Finance Cmt, Young Rep, 56-57; mem. exec. cmt, Calif. Goldwater Adv. Cmt, 63; mem, Calif. State Rep. Finance Cmt, 64-; mem. exec. cmt. and budget and expenditures cmt, Los Angeles Co. United Rep. Finance Cmt, 64- Bus. & Prof. Pos: Dir, Emett & Chandler, 60-, v.pres, 61-63, pres, 63-68; pres, Pinehurst Financial Inc, 68. Naval Res, S.Pac, 45-46; 1st Lt, Air Force Res, 51-59. Mem: Young Presidents' Orgn; dir, Los Angeles Co. Heart Asn. and John Tracy Clin; Rotary; Am. Legion. Rel: Presbyterian. Mailing Add: 2999 W. Sixth St, Los Angeles, Calif. 90005.

EMMONS, ROME AUGUSTUS, JR. R
Secy, Miss. Rep. Party
b. Meridian, Miss, 9/12/29; s. Rome Augustus Emmons, Sr. and Nita Flynt E; m. 6/12/54 to Cola Catherine O'Neal; c. Peggy O'Neal, Rome Augustus, III and Jane Wilson. Educ: Univ. Miss, Oxford, B.B.A, 50; Delta Sigma Pi; Kappa Alpha Order. Polit. & Govt. Pos: Mem. exec. cmt, Forrest Co. Rep. Cmt, Miss, 60-64, v.chmn, 68-; mem. exec. cmt, Miss. State Rep. Party, 64-68, secy, 68- Bus. & Prof. Pos: Pres, Phoenix Laundry, Hattiesburg, Miss, 60. Mil. Serv: Entered as Airman, Air Force, 50, released as Airman 1/C, 52, after serv. in 108th Fighter Bomber Wing, U.S, 50-52. Mem: Nat. Inst. of Drycleaning; Am. Inst. of Laundering; Hattiesburg Exchange Club. Rel: Methodist. Mailing Add: 120 Mandalay Dr, Hattiesburg, Miss. 39401.

EMORY, SAMUEL THOMAS, JR. R
Chmn, Fredericksburg City Rep. Cmt, Va.
b. Durham, N.C, 6/22/33; s. Dr. Samuel Thomas Emory and Mary Dortch E; m. 7/12/59 to Sylvia Callaway; c. Samuel Thomas III and Greer Callaway. Educ: Univ. N.C, Chapel Hill, A.B, 54, M.A, 58; Univ. Md, Ph.D, 64; Phi Eta Sigma; Kappa Sigma. Polit. & Govt. Pos: Mem, Fredericksburg Planning Cmn, Va, 61-, secy, 62-64, chmn, 64-; city campaign mgr, Lynwood Holton for Gov, 65, James Ould for Sen, 65, Lawreance Trailor for Sen, 65, William L. Scott for Cong, 66 & 68 and Richard Nixon for Pres, 68; chmn, Fredericksburg City Rep. Cmt, 65- presidential elector, Electoral Col, 68; mem, Bd. Historic Bldg, 68. Bus. & Prof. Pos: Instr, Mary Wash. Col, 59, asst. prof, 60-65, assoc. prof, 65-68, prof, 68-, chmn. dept. geog. and geol, 60-; owner The Little Shop, 65- Mil. Serv: Army Res, until 64; Cpl. Publ: 'Regional Variation in the Lower Shenandoah Valley,' Southeast. Geographer, 64; 'Geology, Soils and Crops in the North Carolina, Piedmont,' Virginia, J. Sci, 1/64. Mem: Am. Asn. Geographers (mem. steering cmt, S.E. Div); Am. Geog. Soc; Va. Geog. Soc.(ed, Va. Geographer); Va. Educ. Asn; Va. Acad. Sci; Sigma Xi. Rel: Episcopal. Mailing Add: 608 Hawke St, Fredericksburg, Va. 22401.

EMRICH, MARVIN EARL R
Wyo. State Rep.
b. Hillsdale, Mich, 12/6/32; s. Earl F. Emrich and Ellen L. Wrench E; m. 7/6/68 to Maureen A. Burke. Educ: Northwest Nazarene Col, Nampa, Idaho, B.A, 55; Univ. Wyo, M.Ed, 62; Ind. Univ, Bloomington, Post Grad, summers 67 & 69; Sigma Lambda Alpha. Polit. & Govt. Pos: Wyo. State Rep, Natrona Co, 67-, mem, Wyo. Youth Coun, 69- Bus. & Prof. Pos: Bus. Teacher, Burlington

High Sch, Wyo, 58-60; bus. and soc. studies teacher, E. Jr. High, Casper, 60-67; dir. audiovisual serv, Casper-Midwest Schs, 67- Mil. Serv: Entered as E-1, Army, 55, released as Sgt. in Res, 58, after serv. in Hq. Co, Armed Forces Radio and TV Serv. Alaskan Command and Res. Unit, Alaskan Command, 55-57; Good Conduct Medal. Mem: Nat. Educ. Asn; Wyo. Educ, Asn. (pres, currently); Casper-Midwest Classroom Teachers Asn.(former pres); Natrona Co. Young Rep. Club (past pres). Outstanding Young Man of the Year Award, Casper Jaycees, 68. Rel: Nazarene. Mailing Add: 1932 S. Mitchell, Casper, Wyo. 82601.

EMSHWILLER, THOMAS C. D
Chmn, Fountain Co. Dem. Cent. Cmt, Ind.
b. Montpelier, Ind, 5/14/14; s. Fred Owen Emshwiller and Elma Inez Craven E; m. 9/1/39 to Jean Hammond; c. Jon A, Mary Joan and Jane Kay (Mrs. Moore). Educ: Univ. Wis, 1 year; Delta Chi. Polit. & Govt. Pos: V.pres, Wells Co. Young Dem, Mich, 36-38; city councilman, Covington, 52-60; treas, Troy Township Dem, 56-; secy-treas, Ferguson Dem. Club, 56-; chmn, Fountain Co. Dem. Cent. Cmt, 66- Bus. & Prof. Pos: V.pres, Covington Swimming Pool Inc, 56-59. Mem: Danvill Personnel Asn; F&AM (past secy); Eastern Star (past Worthy Patron); Covington Band Parents (past pres); Covington C. of C.(secy, 59-63). Rel: Methodist. Mailing Add: 808 Third St, Covington, Ind. 47932.

ENEBO, STANLEY A.
b. Hennepin Co, Minn, 1926; m. to Lois; c. Nancy, Stanley. Educ: Univ. of Minn. Polit. & Govt. Pos: Minn. State Rep, 58-66; Bus. & Prof. Pos: Electrician. Mil. Serv: Vet. WWII; awarded Bronze Star Medal for bravery. Mem: Local 292, Int. Brotherhood of Elec. Workers; Eagles; Sons of Norway. Rel: Lutheran; Sunday Sch. teacher at Holy Trinity Lutheran Church. Mailing Add: 3304 E. 25th St, Minneapolis, Minn. 55406. (1967)

ENEGUESS, DANIEL FRANCIS R
Exec. Cmt. Mem, Peterborough Rep. Town Cmt, N.H.
b. Steubenville, Ohio, 10/24/22; s. Daniel Francis Eneguess and Mary M. E; m. 7/29/50 to Ann Cavanaugh; c. David M, Daniel F, III, Katharine Ann and John M. Educ: Boston Col, A.B, Econ, 47. Polit. & Govt. Pos: Finance chmn, Hillsboro Co. Rep. Cmt, N.H, 62-66; exec. cmt. mem, Peterborough Rep. Town Cmt, 64-; del, N.H. State Rep. Conv, 66; alternate del, Rep. Nat. Conv, 68. Bus. & Prof. Pos: Owner, Eneguess Publ. Co; owner, Daniel F. Eneguess Assocs. Mil. Serv: Entered as Pvt, Marine Corps, 43, released as 1st Lt, 47, after serv. in Third Marine Div, Pac, 44-46; Am. and Pac. Theater Ribbons. Mem: Rotary; Am. Legion; N.H. Vacation Travel Coun; Conn. River Watershed Coun; Swiftwater Girl Scout Coun; Daniel Webster Boy Scouts Coun. Rel: Catholic. Mailing Add: Old Dublin Rd, Peterborough, N.H. 03458.

ENGEBRETSON, GARY DUANE R
Chmn, Winneshiek Co. Rep. Cent. Cmt, Iowa
b. Cresco, Iowa, 6/24/37; s. Henry Tuttle Engebretson and Edna Thompson E; m. 5/31/54 to Margaret Frances Brown; c. G. Allan, Janet Lee, David Mark and Margie Sue. Polit. & Govt. Pos: Pres, Winneshiek Co. Young Rep, 63-64; organizational chmn, Winneshiek Co. Rep. Cent. Cmt, Iowa, 64-65, chmn, 66- Mem: Elks. Rel: Protestant. Mailing Add: R.R. 2, Blue Ridge Stables, Decorah, Iowa 52101.

ENGEL, AUSTIN GEORGE, JR. D
Mem, N.Dak. State Dem. Cmt.
b. Little Falls, Minn, 8/9/28; s. Austin George Engel and Eugenia Donahue E; m. 8/11/50 to Mary Berwick Roessel; c. David James, Michael Robert, Peter Clarke, Paul Monteath and Steven Johnstone. Educ: Macalester Col, B.A, 50; Yale Divinity Sch, B.D, 54; Univ. Mich, Summer, 60. Polit. & Govt. Pos: Mem. campaign cmt, N.Dak. Dem. Non-Partisan League, 62; regional dir, 64; mem, Mountrail Co. Dem. Non-Partisan League Exec. Cmt, 62-66; del, Dem. Nat. Conv. and mem, Credential Cmt, 64; precinct committeeman, Burleigh Co, 66-; mem, Burleigh Co. Dem. Exec. Cmt, 66-; chmn, Burleigh Co. Dem. Party, 68-; mem, N.Dak. State Dem. Cmt, 68-; mem, N.Dak. State Dem. Finance Cmt, 68- Bus. & Prof. Pos: Pastor, United Church of Christ, New Town, N.Dak, 54-61; spec. worker, Indian Work in N.Dak, United Church of Christ, 61-65, adminstr, 65-67; exec. dir, N.Dak. Indian Affairs Cmn, 65-; mem. bd. dirs, Charles L. Hall Youth Serv, 65-; secy, United Tribes of N.Dak. Develop. Corp, 68- Publ: 'On the Move at Ft. Berthold,' Children's Religion, 2/62. Mem: Bd. Dirs, N.Dak. Conf. United Church of Christ, chmn, 62. Rel: United Church of Christ. Mailing Add: 1324 N. Second St, Bismarck, N.Dak. 58501.

ENGEL, DAVID CHAPIN R
Mem. Bd. Appeals, Kensington, N.H.
b. New York, N.Y, 10/6/31; s. Robert Albert Engel and Mabel Gretchen Eshbaugh E; m. 6/8/54 to Joan Talbot; c. Karen Chapin, Kathleen Christy, Julie Talbot, Peter Otis and Rebecca Eaton. Educ: St. Lawrence Univ, B.A, 54; N.Y. Univ, LL.B, 56; Sigma Chi; Student Union; Student Gov. Rep. Polit. & Govt. Pos: Attorney, N.H. Attorney Gen. Off, 56-58; pres, Kensington Rep. Club, 60-62; state campaign v.chmn, Perkins Bass for U.S. Sen, 62; del-at-lg, Rep. Nat. Conv, 64; mem, Rockingham Co. Rep. Exec. Cmt. and Rep. Co. Finance Chmn, 65-; mem. bd. appeals, Kensington, 65-; del, Rep. State Conv, 66 & 68. Bus. & Prof. Pos: Secy, Rockingham Co. Bar Asn, 61; chmn, N.H. Bar Asn. Legis. Cmt, N.H. Bar Asn, 68-69. Mem: Am. N.H. and Rockingham Co. Bar Asns; Am. Trial Lawyers Asn; arbitrator, Am. Arbit. Asn; Rockingham Co. Rep. Club; Boy Scouts; Soc. for Preserv. and Encouragement of Barbershop Quartet Singing in Am, Inc. Eagle Scout with Four Palms. Rel: Congregational. Legal Res: Drinkwater Rd, Kensington, N.H. Mailing Add: R.F.D. 2, Exeter, N.H. 03833.

ENGEL, IRVING M. D
b. Birmingham, Ala, 10/19/91; s. Michael P. Engel and Sophie Kronenberg E; m. 1/14/26 to Katharine I. Asher (deceased); c. Susan (Mrs. Levy). Educ: Yale, LL.B. cum laude, 13. Hon. D.Litt, Dropsie Col. of Hebrew Learning, 58; L.H.D, Hebrew Union Col-Jewish Inst. Relig, 58; LL.D, L.I. Univ, 64. Polit. & Govt. Pos: Mem. and co-chmn. policy cmt; Citizens Cmt. on Displaced Persons, 47-50; mem. bd. gov, Real Estate Bd, N.Y, 48-51; mem, Nat. Cmt. on Segregation in Nations Capital, 49; cand. for cong, Dem. and Liberal Parties, N.Y, 50; mem, President's Cmt. on Govt. Contract Compliance, 51-53; mem, President's Spec. Mission, Inauguration Pres. Remun, Panama, 52; alternate del, Dem. Nat. Conv, 52, alternate del-at-lg, 56; mem, State Cmt. on Pub. Employee Security, 54; co-chmn. gov. bd, Consultative Coun. Jewish Orgn, 54-59; chmn, Civil Rights Cmt, Dem. State Adv. Cmt; del, Ger-Am. Conf. East-West Tensions, 59, 61 & 62; chmn. exec. cmt, N.Y. Cmt. for Dem. Voters, 59-61; mem, For. Policy Subcmt, Nat. Adv. Coun, Dem. Nat. Cmt, 59-61; chmn, Polit. & Planning Cmt, N.Y. Citizens for Kennedy and Johnson, 60. Bus. & Prof. Pos: Lectr. real estate and taxation, Practicing Law Inst. of Am. Bar Asn. attorney-at-law, Birmingham, Ala, 13-24, N.Y.C, 24-; Title Ins. Adv. Cmt, Title Guarantee Co, 48-; mem. bd. dir, N.Y. Higher Educ. Assistance Corp, 65-67; sr. partner, Engel, Judge & Miller. Mil. Serv: 319 F.A, A.E.F, Lt, 12-19; decorated Grand Officier Order Nicham Ifikhar, Tunisian Legion Honor, 54; Chevalier of the French Legion of Honor, 58. Publ: 'Income Taxes and Real Estate'. Mem: First pres, Ala. Jr. C. of C, 20-21; Coun. For. Rels; Yale Law Sch. Asn. (v.pres, dir); Nat. Citizens Cmt. on Commun. Rels; Univ. and Yale City Clubs; pres, Educ. Found. for Jewish Girls, 45-50, now hon. chmn. bd; hon. pres, Am-Jewish Cmt, 54-59; Am. Cmt. for Israel's Tenth Anniversary Celebration (v.chmn. policy cmt, 58). Rel: Jewish. Legal Res: 24 Central Park S, New York, N.Y. 10019. Mailing Add: 52 Vanderbilt Ave, New York, N.Y. 10017.

ENGEL, JOHN A. D
b. Avon, S.Dak, 8/27/09; s. Joseph Engel and Elizabeth Rueb E; m. 6/30/39 to Thelma Mitchell; c. Patricia D.(Mrs. Odens), Mary J. and Jan A. Educ: Univ. S.Dak, LL.B, 38; Delta Theta Phi. Polit. & Govt. Pos: City attorney, Avon, S.Dak, 46-58, mayor, 58-64; chmn, Bon Homme Co. Dem. Party, 50-58, finance chmn, 58-65; chmn, State Highway Cmn, 59-61; chmn, S.Dak. Dem. Party, 62-64; Committeeman, S.Dak. State Dem. Cent. Cmt, Bon Homme Co, 62-; mem, Platform Cmt, Nat. Dem. Party, 64; chmn, S.Dak. Del, Dem. Nat. Conv, 64; former S.Dak. State Rep. Bus. & Prof. Pos: Attorney-at-law, 40- Mil. Serv: Pvt, Army, 43; entered as Lt.(jg), Navy, 43, released as Lt. Comdr, 45, after serv. in ETO and Am, Asiatic-Pac. and N.African Theaters; Lt, Naval Res,(Ret); ETO, Am, Asiatic-Pac. and African Campaign Ribbons. Mem: State Bar of S.Dak; Am. Bar Asn; Am. Legion; VFW; Lions. Rel: Presbyterian. Mailing Add: Avon, S.Dak. 57315.

ENGEL, MYLAN ROBERT D
Ala. State Sen.
b. Summerdale, Ala, 7/24/23; s. Edward John Engel and Sophia Christina Goetz; m. 4/17/47 to Erika Maria Hofer; c. Carla Maria, Mylan Robert, Jr. Educ: Univ. Ala, B.S, 52, LL.B, 53. Polit. & Govt. Pos: Former Ala. State Rep; Ala. State Sen, 67- Bus. & Prof. Pos: Lawyer. Mil. Serv: Army, World War II. Rel: Lutheran. Mailing Add: Drawer 1045, Mobile, Ala. 36601.

ENGELBRECHT, ARTHUR DFL
b. Alexandria, Minn, 1918; m. to Agnes; c. Jerry and Jeanne. Educ: Pub. schs. Polit. & Govt. Pos: Minn. State Rep, 64-69; chmn, town bd. of supvrs. Bus. & Prof. Pos: Farmer. Mem: Past Master, Masonic Lodge; v.pres, Douglas Agr. Asn; 4-H adult leader. Cited as top Minn. Farmer-Sportsman, 64. Mailing Add: Route 4, Alexandria, Minn. 56308. (1967)

ENGELBRECHT, MARLENE VIVIAN R
V.Chairwoman, Hand Co. Rep. Cmt, S.Dak.
b. St. Lawrence, S.Dak, 10/27/24; d. Henry George Rettmer and Alta Keyser R; m. 7/31/48 to Myrl Arthur Engelbrecht; c. Mark Arthur and Marilee Kim. Educ: S.Dak. State Univ, B.S, 46; Sigma Lambda Sigma; Theta Sigma Phi. Polit. & Govt. Pos: V.Chairwoman, Hand Co. Rep. Cmt, S.Dak, 66- Bus. & Prof. Pos: Assoc. ed, S.Dak. Exten. Ed. Staff, Brookings, 46; advert. mgr, Herberger's Dept. Store, Watertown, 46-48; case worker, Douglas Co. Welfare Off, Alexandria, Minn, 48; rural sch. teacher, Hand Co, Miller, S.Dak, 3 terms, teacher's aide, 2 terms. Mem: Am. Legion Auxiliary; Exten. Club; 4-H Club Leader. Rel: Methodist. Mailing Add: R.R. 1, Zell, S.Dak. 57483.

ENGEN, GERALD B(OB) R
Wyo. State Rep.
b. Laramie, Wyo, 6/11/22; s. Ernest J. Engen and Olga Bothen E; m. 7/16/50 to Rose Y. Arant; c. Gary, Paul, Juanita and Robin. Educ: Univ. Wyo, B.S, 49; 53. Polit. & Govt. Pos: V.chmn, Albany Co. Rep. Cent. Cmt, Wyo, 61-65 and chmn, 65-69; Wyo. State Rep, 69- Bus. & Prof. Pos: Rancher, Centennial, Wyo, 53-63; orgn. dir, Wyo. Farm Bur. Fedn, 60-64; retail merchant, Laramie, 64-; real estate salesman, 65- Mil. Serv: Entered as Pvt, Army Air Force, 42, released as Pfc, 46, after serv. in Eighth Air Force, ETO, 44-46. Mem: Am. Legion (past Post Comdr); VFW; Mason; Elks; Farm Bur; Turtles. Rel: Lutheran. Mailing Add: 1930 Custer, Laramie, Wyo. 82070.

ENGLAND, JACK R
b. Mt. Vernon, Wash, 1927; m. to Sharon; c. two. Educ: Univ. of Wash, B.A, LL.B. Polit. & Govt. Pos: Wash. State Sen, second session to 1966; Wash. State Rep, one term. Bus. & Prof. Pos: Attorney. Mil. Serv: Army Air Corps, World War II. Mem: Delta Chi; Delta Theta Phi; Lions; Elks; Mason. Mailing Add: 1624 Wash. Bldg, Seattle, Wash. 98101.

ENGLANDER, SOPHIA D
Committeewoman, Fla. Dem. Party
b. Atlanta, Ga, 7/24/24; d. Joseph Tendrich and Bessie Miller T; m. 3/14/43 to Judge Malvin Englander; c. Nicki Yverne (Mrs. Mel Grossman), Donna Lynn, Patti Lu, Tobi Sue, Marla Chanelle and Joseph Robert. Educ: Univ. Miami, 2 years. Polit. & Govt. Pos: Dist. committeewoman, Dade Co. Opers. Support Chmn, Fla; alternate del, Dem. Nat. Conv, 60 & 68, del, 64; v.chmn, Third Cong. Dist. Dem. Party; co-chmn, Oper. Clean Sweep; Dade Co. 4 for 64 Chmn; fifth dist. chmn, Kennedy-Johnson Campaign; v.chmn, 11th Cong. Dist. Dem. Party; chmn, Miami Beach Div. Dem. Exec. Cmt; chmn, Adlai Stevenson Mem. Fund Dinner; state chmn, Fla. Dollars for Dem. Drive, 66; committeewoman, Fla. Dem. Party, currently; original mem, Fla. Consumers Coun, 68, reappointed, 68-70; originator of Cabinet Level Secy. of Youth Affairs Bill introduced by U.S. Rep. Claude Pepper into U.S. House Rep, 69. Mem: Am. Legion Auxiliary; Jewish War Vet. Auxiliary; Eastern Star; Anna Miller Circle; Hadassah; B'nai B'rith; Carih; Adlai Stevenson and Dade Co. Dem. Women's Clubs; PTA; Hebrew Acad; Miami Beach Chmn, Police Appreciation and Recruitment Week, Apr. 28 to May 4, 69. Elected Dem. Mother of the Year, 66; Nominated Dem. Woman-Doer For Dade Co, Fla, 68-69. Rel: Jewish. Mailing Add: 4620 Pinetree Dr, Miami Beach, Fla. 33140.

ENGLE, WILLIAM D
Chmn, Perry Co. Dem. Party, Ky.
b. 1920. Educ: Ky. Wesleyan Col; Cincinnati Col. of Embalming. Polit. & Govt. Pos: City cmnr, Hazard, Ky, 49-50; Ky. State Rep, 52-54; Ky. State Sen, 63-66; chmn, Perry Co. Dem. Party, 69- Bus. & Prof. Pos: Mortician. Mil. Serv: World War II. Mem: Am. Legion; Mason; Shrine; C. of C; former pres. State Funeral Dirs. Asn. of Ky; pres. Hazard Lions Club; v.comdr, VFW. Rel: Baptist. Mailing Add: Hazard, Ky. 41701. (1967)

ENGLEHART, HARRY A, JR. D
Pa. State Rep.
s. Harry A. Englehart and Esther Davis E; m. to Mercedes Parsons; c. Four. Educ: U.S. Naval Acad; Yale Law Sch; holds B.S. and LL.B. Polit. & Govt. Pos: Pa. State Rep, 64- Bus. & Prof. Pos: Attorney-at-law. Mil. Serv: Navy, Lt.(jg), World War II; Pac. Theater; Korean War. Mem: Dir, U.S. Nat. Bank, Johnstown, Pa; Cambria Co. Bar Asn; Elks; Eagles; Moose; Am. Legion; VFW; K. of C. Mailing Add: 317 N. Phaney St, Ebensburg, Pa. 15931.

ENGLERT, KENNETH EDWARD R
Chmn, Chaffee Co. Rep. Party, Colo.
b. Lodge Pole, Nebr, 2/28/11; s. Frank Englert and Lois Lough E; m. 3/31/41 to Lorene Baker; c. Kendra (Mrs. Earl Bowers), Steven and Holly. Educ: Lodge Pole and Sunol High Schs, Nebr. Polit. & Govt. Pos: Committeeman, Colorado Springs Rep. Cmt, 50-65; chmn, Chaffee Co. Rep. Party, 66- Bus. & Prof. Pos: Owner, restaurant and lounge, Colorado Springs, Colo, 38-42 and package liquors, 46-65; raising buffalo, Salida, Colo, currently. Mil. Serv: Entered as A/S, Navy, 42, released as Gunner 2/C, 45, after serv. in Armed Guard, S.Pac. Theatre, 42-45. Publ: Raids by Reynolds, 56 and Milling All Around, 60, Westerners Band Books; Oliver Perry Wiggings, Filter Press, 68. Mem: Colo. State Hist. Soc; Colo. Archaeol. Soc; Hist. Soc. of the Pikes Peak Region; Elks; past comdr, Colorado Springs DAV. Rel: Methodist. Mailing Add: Garfield Route, Salida, Colo. 81201.

ENGLERT, LORENE BAKER R
b. Colorado Springs, Colo, 9/30/15; d. Scott Winfield Baker and Helen S. Richel B; m. 3/31/41 to Kenneth Edward Englert; c. Kendra, Steven W. and Holly W. Educ: Univ. Mex, 36; Randolph-Macon Woman's Col, B.A, 37; Colo. Col, M.A, 40; Calif. Inst. Tech, 42. Polit. & Govt. Pos: V.chmn, El Paso Rep. Party, Colo, 60-62; v.chmn, Third Cong. Dist, 62-64; del, Rep. Nat. Conv, 64. Publ: Articles on History. Rel: Protestant. Mailing Add: Old Poncha Rd, Salida, Colo. 81201.

ENGLISH, ELEANOR JEAN D
Chmn, Shoshone Co. Dem. Party, Idaho
b. Wallace, Idaho, 6/16/21; d. Sam Hammer and Ellen Ottem H; div; c. William P. Educ: Univ, Idaho, 39-40. Polit. & Govt. Pos: Dem. precinct committeeman, Shoshone Co. Cent. Cmt, Idaho, 65-68; chmn, Shoshone Co. Dem. Party, 68- Bus. & Prof. Pos: Secy, Am. Smelting & Refining Co, 49- Rel: Lutheran. Mailing Add: Idaho Bldg, Wallace, Idaho 83873.

ENGLISH, JOHN C. R
b. Wink, Tex, 8/8/32; s. Lester F. English and Lucille Redfern E; m. 7/30/51 to Bennie C. Stephenson; c. Janet Kay and Robert Wayne. Educ: Sul Ross State Col. Polit. & Govt. Pos: Chmn, Winkler Co. Rep. Party, Tex, 65-68. Mil. Serv: Entered as Pvt, Army, 52, released as S/Sgt, 54. Rel: Methodist. Mailing Add: Box 926, Artesia, N.Mex. 88210.

ENGLISH, JOHN FRANCIS D
Dem. Nat. Committeeman, N.Y.
b. Brooklyn, N.Y, 4/21/26; s. Thomas English and Anne Daley E; m. 11/17/51 to Dolores Hofler; c. Danette. Educ: Iona Col, B.A, 52; Fordham Law Sch, 55; Hofstra Univ. Citizens Cmt. Polit. & Govt. Pos: Committeeman, Franklin Square Dem. Orgn, N.Y, 47; secy, Nassau Co. Dem. Cmt, 53, chmn, 58-; Dem. Zone Leader, Franklin Square, 54; leader and state committeeman, First Assembly Dist, Nassau Co, 55; town leader, Hempstead, N.Y, 56; law secy. to Hon. Mario Pittoni, 56-58; cmnr, Bd. Elecs, 61-64; Dem. Nat. Committeeman, N.Y, 68- Bus. & Prof. Pos: Attorney-at-law, English, Cianciulli & Reisman, 61- Mil. Serv: Entered as Sailor, Navy, 43, released as Qm. 3/C, 47; Navy Unit Citation with Four Battle Stars; Philippine Liberation Medal. Mem: Nassau Co. Bar Asn; Legal Aid Soc. Nassau Co; Friends of Mercy Hosp; dir, L.I. Chap, Nat. Conf. Christians and Jews; adv. bd, United Cerebral Palsy Asn, L.I; dir, Boys' Town of Italy; Emerald Asn. L.I; VFW. Recipient of L.I. Daily Press Distinguished Serv. Award, for bringing a strong 2-party system to Nassau Co, 63. Rel: Catholic. Legal Res: Split Rock Rd, Syosset, L.I, N.Y. 11791. Mailing Add: 240 Mineola Blvd, Mineola, N.Y. 11501.

ENGLISH, RICHARD MATTHEW D
b. Buffalo, N.Y, 7/22/28; s. Matthew D. English and Marion C. Osborne E; m. 9/6/52 to Anna M. Kinney; c. Mary Regina and Richard T. Educ: Univ. Buffalo, Pre-Law, 49-51; Univ. Buffalo Sch. Law, LL.B, 53; Sigma Alpha Nu. Polit. & Govt. Pos: Chmn, Brown for Gov. and Engle for Sen, Lynwood, Calif, 58; pres, Lynwood Dem. Club, 58-60; city councilman, 58-61; dir, League of Calif. Cities, 58-61; 18th, 19th, 23rd and 24th Cong. Dist. field rep, Citizens for Kennedy, 60; mem, Los Angeles Co. Dem. Cent. Cmt, 61 & 69; Dem. nominee for Calif. State Assemblyman, 52nd Assembly Dist, 66; mem, Calif. Dem. State Cent. Cmt, 66-68; state chmn, Dem. Vol. of Calif, 67-69; del, Dem. Nat. Conv, 68. Mil. Serv: Entered as Pvt, Army, 46, released as Pfc, 47, after serv. in First Cavalry Div, Pac. Theatre. Mem: Am, Los Angeles Co, Criminal Courts and Southeast Bar Asns; Calif. State and N.Y. State Bars; Am. Trial Lawyers Asn; Nat. Asn. of Defense Lawyers; VFW; Elks, Huntington Park; Moose, Compton; Amvets, Compton; AFL-CIO Local 518. Distinguished Service Award, 58; Lynwood's Most Outstanding Young Man. Rel: Catholic. Legal Res: 11132 Pine St, Lynwood, Calif. 90262. Mailing Add: 11301 Long Beach Blvd, Lynwood, Calif. 90262.

ENGLISH, ROBERT R
N.H. State Sen.
b. Cambridge, Mass, 9/18/03; s. Walter C. English and Anna E. Durfer E; m. 3/16/57 to Dorothee Knapp; c. Ann Durfor (Mrs. Anthony Anable) and Joseph Grew. Educ: Univ. Dijon, France, dipl, 25; Harvard, A.B, 26. Polit. & Govt. Pos: N.H. State Rep, 49-55; N.H. State Sen, 55-; del, Rep. Nat. Conv, 56 & 60, alternate del, 64; past v.chmn, Hillsborough Rep. Cmt; supvr, Town Adv. Cmn; moderator, Sch. Dist. Bus. & Prof. Pos: Writer, lectr; pres, Monadnock Commun. Col. Mil. Serv: with For. Serv. Mem: Rotary; Mason; Grange; bd, Amos Fortune Forum; Nat. Defense Exec. Res, Wash; U.S. Nat. Cmn. UNESCO. Rel: Protestant. Mailing Add: Hancock, N.H. 03449.

ENGLUND, MERRILL WAYNE D
s. Elbert M. Englund and Leona Hazel Bussard E; m. 3/3/46 to Geraldine Mildred Lando; c. Eric, Gretchen and Karl. Educ: Univ. Nebr, B.S. Polit. & Govt. Pos: Exec. Asst, U.S. Rep. Metcalf, 53-60; admin. asst, Staff of Sen. Metcalf, 61-; instr. on admin. opers. for cong. asst, Grad. Sch, U.S. Dept. Agr, 67- Mil. Serv: Navy, Lt. Comdr, Patrol Bombing Squadron 102, Naval Air Transport Serv, Pac. Mem: Sigma Delta Chi; Innocents, sr. men's hon; Kappa Sigma; Montgomery Co. Oratorio Soc; Am. Newspaper Guild. Rel: Unitarian. Mailing Add: 11703 College View Dr, Silver Spring, Md. 20902.

ENGSTROM, ARNELL R
b. Traverse City, Mich, 6/6/97; m. 1919 to Mareda Heiges; c. Louis and Richard. Educ: High Sch. Grad. Polit. & Govt. Pos: City cmnr, mem. and pres, bd. of educ. and mem, bd. of supvrs, Traverse City, Mich, formerly; Mich. State Rep, 40-68. Bus. & Prof. Pos: Co-owner of ins. agency; dir, Traverse City State Bank. Mem: Secy, Traverse City Indust. Fund and one of its incorporators; dir, Northwest. Mich. Fair Assoc; Mason; Elks; Kiwanis. One of the incorporators of Northwestern Mich. Col, served as trustee for many years. Rel: Congregational. Mailing Add: 540 W. 8th St, Traverse City, Mich. 49684.

ENGSTROM, ELTON E. R
Alaska State Sen.
b. Juneau, Alaska, 2/26/35; s. Elton E. Engstrom (deceased) and Thelma Wait E.(deceased); m. 2/16/63 to Sally Grey Hudson; c. Cathy and Elton. Educ: Univ. Ore, B.A, 58; Harvard Law Sch, LL.B, 60. Polit. & Govt. Pos: Alaska State Rep, 65-66; Alaska State Sen, 67- Mil. Serv: Entered as 2nd Lt, Army, 61, released as 1st Lt, 63. Mailing Add: Box 723, Juneau, Alaska 99801.

ENGWALL, CARL A, JR. R
N.Mex. State Rep.
b. Kansas City, Mo, 12/25/26; s. Carl August Engwall and Beula Hazaleus E; m. 8/21/49 to Ruth Aileen Brown; c. Steven Carl, Larry Glen and Nelson Thomas. Educ: Univ. Kans, B.S, 51. Polit. & Govt. Pos: N.Mex. State Rep, 67- Bus. & Prof. Pos: From geologist to staff geologist, Gulf Oil Corp, Ft. Worth, Tex, 51-53, regional geologist, Midland, Tex, 53-60 and Roswell, N.Mex, 60-62; consult. geol. engr, 62-69. Mil. Serv: Entered as Seaman 2/C, Navy, 44, released as ARM 3/C, 46, after serv. in Training Schs, Flying Duty and Shore Patrol; Naval Res, 46-69, Lt. Comdr. Mem: Am. Asn. Petroleum Geologists; Cert. Petroleum Geologist, Roswell; Geol. Soc; Am. Legion (past comdr). Rel: Presbyterian. Mailing Add: 601 Barnett, Roswell, N.Mex. 88201.

ENNA, IRVING R
Chmn, Ore. Rep. State Cent. Cmt.
b. N.Y.C, 7/26/14; m. 8/12/37 to Margaret; c. Carol and twins, David and Ronald. Educ: Franklin High Sch, Portland, Ore, grad, 32. Polit. & Govt. Pos: Chmn, Hatfield Cmts, Multnomah Co, Ore, 56 & 58 and Multnomah Co. Rep. Cent. Cmt, 64-67; chmn, Ore. Rep. State Cent. Cmt, 67-; alternate del, Rep. Nat. Conv, 68. Bus. & Prof. Pos: Life ins. underwirter with Standard Ins, 52- Mem: Pres, Portland and Ore. Life Ins. Underwriters Asns. Life mem, Million Dollar Roundtable, Standard Ins. Co; Ins. Man of the Year for Ore, 59 & 61; Portland Jr. First Citizen, 49. Legal Res: 6224 S.E. 31st Ave, Portland, Ore. 97002. Mailing Add: Standard Insurance, 1029 S.W. Columbia, Portland, Ore. 97201.

ENOCH, DONALD K. R
Mayor, Wichita, Kans.
b. Neosho, Mo, 6/22/16; s. William Kirk Enoch and Breta McCune E; m. 12/1/46 to Margery Ellen Trively; c. Rolland, Craig, Mark and Dawn. Educ: Friends Univ, Wichita, 33-34; Wichita Univ, A.B, 37; Northwest. Univ, Evanston, M.A. magna cum laude, 40; Nat. Honor Soc; Blue Key; Kappa Delta Pi; Phi Upsilon Sigma; pres, Alumni Asn. Polit. & Govt. Pos: Secy, Young Rep. Club, 37; mem, Wichita Planning Cmn, Kans, 51-59, v.pres, 58-59; mem, Wichita Traffic Cmn, 58-59 and City Cmn, 67-, pres, City Cmn, 68-69; mayor, Wichita, 69-, chmn, S.Cent. Kans. Regional Coun. of Gov, mem. bd. dirs, Kans. League of Munic. and chmn, Finance & Tax Cmn, 69- Bus. & Prof. Pos: Pres, Wichita Brush & Chem. Co, 47-, Sanit. Counsr. 59- and Sanit. Res. Asn, 65-66. Mil. Serv: Entered as Aviation Cadet, Army Air Corps, 41, released as Capt, 45, after serv. in West. Flying Training Command, U.S, 42-45. Publ: Articles in various trade mag. Mem: Kiwanis. Distinguished Serv. Award, Jr. C. of C, 49. Rel: Methodist. Mailing Add: 158 N. Roosevelt, Wichita, Kans. 67208.

ENSIGN, W. SCOTT D
b. Battle Creek, Mich, 1/28/09; married; c. Natalie Louise (Mrs. Cunningham, Thomas D, Deborah A. Educ: Grad. Hillsdale Col, B.S; Ferris State Col, B.C; Delta Sigma Phi. Polit. & Govt. Pos: Mich. State Rep, 64-66. Bus. & Prof. Pos: Printer and publisher. Mem: Chmn, Battle Creek Civil Serv. Cmn, 63-64; bd. of dirs, Battle Creek Area United Fund, 54-64; bd. of dirs, Calhoun Co. Tuberc. Asn, 62; chmn, Commun. Adv. Cmt. under Fed. Manpower Develop. and Training Act; chmn, Battle Creek Skills Pool; pres, Battle Creek Fedn. of Labor, 56-62; v.pres, AFL-CIO Calhoun Co. Coun, 62-64; Commun. Health Servs. Comm; Calhoun Co. Legal Aid Soc; Comm. of 100 for four co. area for study of youth problems and high sch. drop-outs; Metrop. Airport Study Comm, 61; Optimist Int; F&AM; RAM; Knights Templar; YMCA; Fraternal Order of Police (assoc. mem); Int. Asn. of Firefighters (hon. mem); Int. Typographical Union; C. of C; Mich. Press Asn. Rel: Episcopal. Mailing Add: 245 Calhoun St, Battle Creek, Mich. 49017. (1967)

ENSIGN, WILLIAM JAMES D
Mayor, Toledo, Ohio
b. Cleveland, Ohio, 6/21/24; s. Harmon Oliver Ensign and Isabella T. McKay E; m. 11/18/50 to Joan Marie Kennedy; c. Maria Therese, Kimberly Anne, Christopher William, Joel Francis, Madonna Maureen and Thomas Shannon. Educ: East. Ill. State Col, 46-48; Univ. Notre Dame, A.B, 50, A.M, 51; Sigma Tau Gamma. Polit. & Govt. Pos: Caseworker and juvenile parole officer,

South Bend, Ind, 50-51; probation officer, Lucas Co, Ohio, 51-60; exec. secy, Ohio Pardon and Parole Cmn, 60-63; welfare dir, Lucas Co, 63-67; mayor, Toledo, 67- Bus. & Prof. Pos: Purchasing agent, Broadhead-Garrett Co, Cleveland, 41-42; part time instr. sociol, Mary Manse Col, 53-60 & 63-67. Mil. Serv: Entered as Pvt, Marines, 42, released as Sgt, 46, after serv. in 3rd Marine Div. and 3rd Amphibious Corps, U.S, S.Pac. and Asiatic Theatres, 42-46; Good Conduct Medal; Am. Theatre Ribbon; Pac. Theatre Ribbon; Presidential Unit Citation; Occup. of China Ribbon. Mem: U.S. Conf. Mayors; Nat. League Cities; Lucas Co. Dem. Cmt; Am. Legion; DAV; Old Newsboys Goodfellow Asn. Rel: Roman Catholic. Mailing Add: 1707 Potomac Dr, Toledo, Ohio 43607.

EPSTEIN, HARVEY A. D
Md. State Del.
b. Baltimore, Md, 4/12/37; m. Educ: Univ. Baltimore; Univ. Baltimore Law Sch, LL.B, 59; Nu Beta Epsilon. Polit. & Govt. Pos: Mem. Young Dem, Md; law clerk to city solicitor, 57-60; Md. State Del, 63- Bus. & Prof. Pos: Bd. of dir, Baltimore Area Coun. on Alcoholism. Mem: Am. & Baltimore City Bar Asns; Menorah Lodge 771, B'nai B'rith; Am. Arbit. Asn.(chmn. cmt. on invests, mem. cmn. on Inter-govt. Coop). Admitted to Md. Bar, 59. Mailing Add: 601 Maryland Trust Building, Baltimore, Md. 21202.

EPSTEIN, RUBIN D
b. Boston, Mass, 10/10/07; s. William Epstein and Ida Glass E; m. 12/23/30 to Ethel Kadetsky; c. Dorothy Ann (Mrs. Herbert Carver) and Marjorie Jane (Mrs. C. Gerard Drucker). Educ: Boston English High Sch, 21-25. Polit. & Govt. Pos: Alternate del, Dem. Nat. Conv, 60 & 64, del-at-lg, 68. Bus. & Prof. Pos: V.pres, Am. Finance Corp, Boston, Mass, 34-37; pres, Atlantic Corp, Boston, 37-57 and City Bank & Trust Co, Boston, 57- Mem: Pres, Brookline Hosp; mem. finance cmt, Mass. Asn. for Ment. Health; trustee, Nat. Jewish Hosp. and Research Center; v.pres, New Eng. Sinai Hosp; chmn. pres. coun, Boston Col; nat. v.chmn. of fels, Brandeis Univ; C. of C; mem. exec. cmt, Nat. Commercial Finance Conf; Mass. Rep. to Small Bus. Admin. Nat. Adv. Coun; mem. exec. bd, Gr. Boston Chap, Am. Jewish Cmt; dir, Boston Chap, Am. Technion Soc; mem. exec. cmt, Assoc. Synagogues of Mass; bd. mem, B'nai B'rith Anti-Defamation League; adv. bd. mem, B'nai B'rith Amos Lodge; trustee, B'nai B'rith Realty Lodge; dir, Brookline-Brighton-Newton Zionist Dist; trustee and treas. businessmen's coun, Combined Jewish Philanthropies; treas, Histadrut-Cardinal Cushing Hosp. in Galilee; hon. dir, K. of P; dir, Maimonides Sch; v.pres. and life trustee, Temple Emanuel of Newton; mem. exec. cmt, Mass. Cmt. Cath, Protestants and Jews; past chmn, Brookline Cancer Fund; past gen. chmn, Brookline Heart Fund; past asst. chmn, Red Cross; mem. exec. bd. and chmn. annual $100 Dinner, Nat. Found. March of Dimes; dir, Kiddie Kamp Corp; chmn, Youth Educ. Assistance Inc; past pres. and treas. class of 25, English High Sch. Alumni Asn; Pine Brook Country Club; Newton Squash and Tennis Club; AF&AM. Rel: Jewish; v.pres, Temple Emanuel, Newton, Mass. Mailing Add: 174 Laurel Rd, Chestnut Hill, Mass. 02167.

EPSTEIN, SEYMOUR FRANCIS D
Mass. State Rep.
b. Providence, R.I, 11/7/19; s. Louis Epstein and Jennie Fine (deceased); m. 11/23/44 to Pearl Fine; c. Marlene Enid. Educ: Boston Eng. High Sch, grad, 38; Bridgton Acad, Maine, 39. Polit. & Govt. Pos: Treas, Dem. Ward Cmt, Mass, 60-64, mem, 68-72; mem, Boston City Dem. Cmt, 60-64 & 68-72; Mass. State Rep, Tenth Suffolk Dist, 69-70. Bus. & Prof. Pos: Ins. exam, Commonwealth of Mass, Div. of Ins, 56-68. Mem: Temple Beth Hillel Brotherhood (past pres); King Solomon Humanitarian Found. for Crippled Children (v.pres); King Solomon Lodge, K. of P.(officer); Gr. Boston Lions Club (chmn, annual Christmas Dinner for the blind, first v.pres); past chmn, Heart Fund; Zerubbabel Lodge, AF&AM; Mason; Dorchester Civic Club; Dorchester Free Loan Asn; dir, Lord Beaconsfield Credit Union; co-organizer and officer, Mattapan Little League; New Eng. Asn. Baseball Umpires. Former semi pro and prfnl. pitcher. Rel: Hebrew. Mailing Add: 654 Walk Hill St, Mattapan, Mass. 02126.

EPTON, KATHRYN D
b. Idaho; m. to Dr. John W. Epton; c. Five. Educ: Gonzaga, M.A. Polit. & Govt. Pos: Wash. State Rep, 57-63 & 65-67. Bus. & Prof. Pos: Teacher; adminstr, Parents' Coop. Soc. for the Handicapped. Mailing Add: 7 N. Walnut Rd, Spokane, Wash. 99206.

ERB, LILLIAN EDGAR R
Conn. State Rep.
b. Stonington, Conn, 7/28/22; d. Edward Matthew and Lillian Ellis M; m. 1/28/43 to David Charles Erb; c. David Lawrence, Dana Louise and Gregory Barron. Educ: East. State Col, Conn, 65-66; Univ. Conn, 67-68. Polit. & Govt. Pos: Justice of the peace, Groten, Conn, 54-58 & 62-64; mem, Rep. Town Cmt, Groten, 54-, v.chmn, 54-58; Conn. State Rep, 62-; dir. and secy, Conn. Student Loan Found, 66-; first v.pres, Conn. Order Women Legis, 69- Bus. & Prof. Pos: Owner-mgr, Erb Cleaners & Laundry, Noank, Conn, 47-60 and Erb Apts, 52- Mem: Prfnl. & Bus. Women's Club; Toastmasters; Nat. Asn. Women Legis; Conn. Order Women Legis; Women's Rep. Club; New London Co. Women's Rep. Club; charter mem. Noank Hist. Soc; bd. dirs, Child and Family Serv, Inc, Conn. Rel: Catholic. Mailing Add: 51 Front St, Noank, Conn. 06340.

ERBE, NORMAN ARTHUR R
Boone, Iowa, 10/25/19; s. Otto L. Erbe and Louise Festner E; m. 9/27/42 to Jacqueline D. Doran; c. DeElda, Jennifer and Kevin. Educ: Univ. Iowa, B.A, 46; J.D, 47. Polit. & Govt. Pos: Chmn, Boone Co. Rep. Cent. Cmt, 52-57; spec. asst. attorney gen, Iowa Hwy. Cmn, 55-57; attorney gen, Iowa, 57-61, Gov, 61-63. Bus. & Prof. Pos: Exec. dir, Nat. Paraplegia Found. Mil. Serv: Army, Co-Comdr. Inf, 41-42; Air Force Pilot, 43-45; Maj, Iowa Nat. Guard, 47, Col.(Ret); Distinguished Flying Cross; Air Medal with Clusters. Publ: Iowa Highway Road and Street Laws, 56; Iowa Drainage Laws, 57. Mem: Chmn, E.Boone Co. Chap, Am. Red Cross, 49-50; past pres, Boone C. of C; Am, Iowa and Boone Co. Bar Asns; Am. Judicature Soc; Lutheran Laymens League; past pres, Boone Golf and Country Club; Lions. Rel: Lutheran. Legal Res: 509 S. Story St, Boone, Iowa 50036. Mailing Add: 450 E. Park St, Arlington Heights, Ill. 60005.

ERDAHL, ARLEN INGOLF R
Minn. State Rep.
b. Blue Earth, Minn, 2/27/31; s. Christian A. Erdahl and Inga Fosness E; m. 7/18/58 to Ellen Marie Syrdal; c. Rolf, Eric, John, Lars and Laura. Educ: St. Olaf Col, B.A, 53; Harvard Univ, M.P.A, 66; Toastmaster's Club. Polit. & Govt. Pos: Del, State and Dist. Rep. Conv, 63-64; Minn. State Rep, 63-, chmn, Minn. House Labor Cmt, Minn. House of Rep; chmn, Dist. Young Rep. Coun, 64; chmn, Twp. Rep. Party, 64-65; cong. fel. with U.S. Rep. Gerald R. Ford and U.S. Sen. Mark Hatfield, 67-68. Bus. & Prof. Pos: Farm owner, mgr. and operator. Mil. Serv: Entered as Pvt, Army, 54, released as Specialist, 56, after serv. in Spec. Category Army with Air Force in Japan, 54-56. Mem: St. Olaf Col. Alumni Letterman's Club; Farm Bur; St. Olaf Co. Alumni Assoc. Freedoms Found. Award, 56; Distinguished Serv. Award, Blue Earth Jr. C. of C, 64; One of Ten Outstanding Young Men of Minn, 64; Bush Found. Leadership Fel, 65. Rel: Lutheran, Mem. Church Coun, Dell Lutheran church. Legal Res: R.R. 2, Blue Earth, Minn. 56013. Mailing Add: State Capitol, St. Paul, Minn. 55101.

ERDMANN, MARIAN SANDS R
b. Devon, Mont, 1/16/12; d. Carl Holcomb Sands and Clara Brathovde S; m. 7/8/38 to Charles Edgar Erdmann; c. Carolyn (Mrs. H. Peers Brewer), Charles, II and Betty. Educ: Mont. State Univ, 30-31; Delta Delta Delta. Polit. & Govt. Pos: V.chmn, Cascade Co. Rep. Cmt, Mont, 56-57; pres, Cascade Co. Rep. Women's Club, 58-59; del, White House Conf. on Children and Youth, 60; state and precinct committeewoman, Rep. Party, 60-61; alderman, Great Falls City Coun, Ward 4, 61; mayor, Great Falls, 63-67; Mont. del, Health Conf, San Francisco, 65; mem, Libr. Bd, Park Bd, City-Co. Convalescent Hosp. Bd. and City-Co. Health Bd; former sponsor, Col. Young Rep. Bus. & Prof. Pos: Employee, govt. depts, Wash, D.C, 32-38. Mem: Bd. mem, YWCA, 54-56; organizer, Cosmos Club, 50; Civil Defense Cmn; worker, Cub Scouts and Camp Fire, 52-54; Braille writer, Red Cross; C. of C; Mont. Club; Great Falls Symphony; Pub. Works Asn; Sons of Norway; Travel Club; Meadow Lark Country Club. Outstanding Rep. Americanism Award, Cascade Young Rep. Club, 63; Mont. Woman of Year Award, State Bus. & Prfnl. Women's Club, 64. Rel: Lutheran. Legal Res: 2118 Fourth Ave. N, Great Falls, Mont. 59401. Mailing Add: Civic Center Bldg, P.O. Box 1609, Great Falls, Mont. 59401. (1967)

ERICKSON, CARL WENDELL R
Chmn, Pipestone Co. Rep. Cent. Cmt, Minn.
b. Dedham, Mass, 9/30/20; s. John Albert Erickson and Alice E; m. 3/10/50 to Ruth Elizabeth Paulson; c. Paul, Mark, John and Mitchell. Educ: Univ. Tampa, 49-51; Univ. Mo, B.S. in Journalism, 53. Polit. & Govt. Pos: Chmn, Pipestone Co. Rep. Cent. Cmt, Minn, 66- Bus. & Prof. Pos: Publisher, Seneca News Dispatch, 53-57, Bonne Terre Register, 57-64, Pipestone Co. Star, 65-, Jasper J, 65- and Farm & Mkt. News, 67- Mil. Serv: Entered as Pfc, Army, 38, released as Sgt, 45, after serv. in 211th Coast Artil, N.S, 40-45; U.S. Theater Ribbon; Good Conduct Medal. Mem: Minn. Press Asn; C. of C; Am. Legion. Pipestone Jaycees News Award. Rel: Episcopal. Mailing Add: 301 Third Ave. S.E, Pipestone, Minn. 56164.

ERICKSON, LARRY DUANE D
Chmn, N.Dak. Dem. Non-Partisan League Exec. Cmt.
b. Minot, N.Dak, 8/6/30; s. Lawrence Erickson and Nellie Miller; m. 7/6/52 to Claryce Irene Thompson; c. Susan, Vicky, Julie and Jon. Educ: Minot State Col, B.S. Polit. & Govt. Pos: Pres, N.Dak. Young Dem, 58; secy, N.Dak. Dem. Party, 62-; N.Dak. State Rep, 64-66; chmn, N.Dak. Dem. Non-Partisan League Exec. Cmt, 68- Bus. & Prof. Pos: Dir, First West. State Bank, Minot, N.Dak, 64- Mil. Serv: Entered as Recruit, Army, 50, released as Pfc, 52, after serv. in 47th Inf. Div. Mem: Moose; Elks; Farmers Union; N.Dak. Water Users Asn. Rel: Lutheran. Mailing Add: R.R. 3, Minot, N.Dak. 58701. (1967)

ERICKSON, LEIF D
Mem. Nat. Committeeman, Mont.
b. Cashton, Wis, 7/29/06; s. Oluf Erickson and Dora B. Swanson E; m. 12/29/32 to Huberta B. Brown; c. Katherine (Mrs. David Mitchell), Leif Barton and Elizabeth Ruth. Educ: Univ. N.Dak, 25-26; Univ. Chicago, Ph.B, J.D. Polit. & Govt. Pos: Co. attorney, Richland Co, 26-37; assoc. justice, Mont. Supreme Court, 38-46; Dem. Nominee for Gov, Mont, 44 and for U.S. Sen, 46; mem. presidential emergency bd, Rwy. Labor Bd, 45-52; mem. platform drafting cmt, Dem. Nat. Conv, 52, 56 & 60, del, 68; chmn, Mont. Dem. Party, 56-57; Dem. Nat. Committeeman, 62- Bus. & Prof. Pos: Attorney-at-law, Helena, Mont. Mem: Chmn, Helena Commun. Chest, 58; Am, Mont, and Lewis and Clark Bar Asns; past pres, Mont. Club. Mailing Add: 347 N. Last Chance Gulch, Helena, Mont. 59601.

ERICKSON, LEROY R
m. to Lila Moxness. Polit. & Govt. Pos: N.Dak. State Rep, 67-69. Bus. & Prof. Pos: Farmer. Mailing Add: DeLamere, N.Dak. 58022. (1967)

ERICKSON, NELLIE D
b. Glendon, Iowa, 2/9/00; d. Grant Miller and Edith Morton M; m. 1/14/23 to Lawrence Erickson; c. Jeanne, June, Larry and Bonnie. Educ: Minot State Teachers Col, summer sessions, 3 years. Polit. & Govt. Pos: Worker, Dem. Party, 21-; dist. chairwoman, N.Dak. Dem. Non-Partisan League Women, 61-63; prog. chmn, N.Dak. Dem. Non-Partisan League Women's Club, 61-; del, Dem. Nat. Conv, 64. Bus. & Prof. Pos: Sch. teacher, 17-23; farm wife, Diamond T Ranch, N.Dak, 23- Publ: The Minot Farmers Union Oil Co, 53; Eddie Mem: Farmers Union; League of Women Voters; PTA; Minot League Women Voters Club (chmn); Kennedy Mem. Center Hist. Arch. Rel: Presbyterian. Mailing Add: Route 3, Minot, N.Dak. 58701.

ERICKSON, ORBIN A. R
Chmn, 16th Dist. Rep. Party, N.Dak.
b. Hoople, N.Dak, 10/28/17; s. Gustav Erickson and Molly Gjevre E; m. 8/27/47 to Mary Jane Gillespie; c. Molly Ann and Richard. Educ: N.Dak. State Univ, 3 years; Kappa Sigma Chi. Polit. & Govt. Pos: Chmn, 16th Dist. Rep. Party, N.Dak, 67- Mil. Serv: Entered as Pvt, Air Force, 42, released as Sgt, 45, after serv. in 311th Fighter Bomber Group, China-Burma-India, 43-45. Mem: Mason; Am. Legion; Farm Bur. Rel: Lutheran. Legal Res: Dundee Twp, Hoople, N.Dak. 58243. Mailing Add: R.R. 1, Hoople, N.Dak, 58243.

ERICKSON, WAYNE CURTIS R
b. Brainard, Minn, 8/27/37; s. Alfred Leonard Erickson and A. Oveidia Anderson E; m. 6/8/57 to Mary Ann Knutson; c. Jeffrey Lang, Craig James, Wayne Curtis, Jr. and Kristin Melissa. Educ: Univ. Wash, B.A; Univ. South. Calif, Los Angeles, Sch. of Mkt; Knights; Sigma Nu. Polit. & Govt. Pos: Former chmn, Kitsap Co. Rep. Cent. Cmt, Minn. Mem: Kiwanis; C. of C; Knife and Fork Club; Univ. South. Calif. and Univ. Puget Sound Alumni Asns. Rel: Lutheran. Mailing Add: 1332 East Hope St, Bremerton, Wash. 98310. (1967)

ERICKSON, WENDELL O. Conservative
Minn. State Rep.
b. Isanti Co, 1925; married; c. Four. Educ: Univ. Minn, B.S. Polit. & Govt. Pos: Minn. State Rep, 64- Bus. & Prof. Pos: Teacher. Mil. Serv: Army, Pac. Theatre. Mem: Past chmn. and treas, Minn. Voc. Agr. Inst. Asn; chmn, Southwest. Div-MEA-Agr. Section, 63; Am. Legion; Rock Co. Fair Bd. Rel: Lutheran; past chmn, Trinity Lutheran Church. Mailing Add: Hills, Minn. 56138. (1967)

ERICKSON, WILLIAM A. D
N.Dak. State Rep.
b. Lostwood, N.Dak, 2/19/10; s. Anton E. Erickson and Anna C. Thompson E; m. 11/1/28 to Gladys Morene Fish; c. Delmar, Carole (Mrs. Roger Davick), Phyllis (Mrs. Elmer Lewis) and Bonnie (Mrs. Colin Loudahl). Educ: High Sch. Polit. & Govt. Pos: N.Dak. State Rep, 63- Bus. & Prof. Pos: Chmn, Mountrail Elec. Coop, Inc, Stanley, 48-; v.chmn, Farmers Union Oil Co, Powers Lake, N.Dak, 54- Mem: Lions. Rel: Lutheran. Mailing Add: 414 Fourth St. S.E, Stanley, N.Dak. 58740.

ERICKSTAD, RALPH JOHN R
Assoc. Justice, N.Dak. Supreme Court
b. Starkweather, N.Dak, 8/15/22; s. John T. Erickstad and Anna Myklebust E; m. to Lois Katharine Jacobson; c. John Albert and Mark Anders. Educ: Univ. N.Dak, 3 years; Univ. Minn, B.Sc.L. & LL.B. Polit. & Govt. Pos: Munic. Judge, Devils Lake, N.Dak; state's Attorney, Ramsey Co; N.Dak. State Sen, Ramsey Co, 57-62, Asst. Majority Floor Leader, N.Dak. State Senate, 59-61; Assoc. Justice, Supreme Court, N.Dak, 63- Mil. Serv: Entered as Pvt, Air Corps, 43, released as Sgt, 45, after serv. in Eighth Air Force, ETO. Mem: Am, Bar Asn; State Bar Asn. N.Dak; Nat. Judicature Soc; Am. Legion; VFW; Boy Scouts; Mo. Valley Family YMCA; Kiwanis. Rel: Lutheran. Legal Res: 1266 W. Highland Acres Rd, Bismarck, N.Dak. 58501. Mailing Add: North Dakota Supreme Court, Bismarck, N.Dak. 58501.

ERIKSEN, LU DEAN D
V.Chmn, Idaho State Dem. Cent. Cmt.
b. Downey, Idaho, 10/12/19; d. S. Albert Christensen and Phoebe M. Bowman C; m. 1/13/40 to Warren Eriksen; c. Tim, Stephan and Kevin. Educ: Univ. Idaho, South. Br. Polit. & Govt. Pos: Pres, Bannock Co. Dem. Women's Club, Idaho, 58-60; precinct committeewoman, Bannock Co. Dem. Cent. Cmt, 57-64, v.chmn, 58-60 and state committeewoman, 60-62; secy, Idaho Fifth Dist. Citizens for Kennedy Cmt, 60-63; v.chmn, Idaho State Dem. Cent. Cmt, 60-; alternate del, Dem. Nat. Conv, 68. Bus. & Prof. Pos: Soc. worker, Bannock Co. Welfare Dept, 67-69, Bannock Co. Commun. Center, 69- Mem: Bd, Bannock Mem. Hosp, 56-60; asst. chmn, Jr. Div. Co. Fair Bd, 59-60; co. chmn, Am. Heart Asn, 60-62. Individual Award, Young Women's Mutual Improv. Asn. Gen. Bd, 59. Rel: Latter-day Saint; mem. stake bd, Young Women Mutual Improv. Asn, 58-64. Mailing Add: 127 Charles Place, Pocatello, Idaho 83201.

ERKERT, ROGER WILLIAM R
Treas, Winnebago Co. Rep. Cent. Cmt, Ill.
b. Peoria, Ill, 8/28/31; s. William Christian Erkert and Mary Hanna Sommer E; m. 8/25/56 to Joan Elizabeth Matthews; c. Matthews Sommer, Elizabeth Lyn and John Graham. Educ: Northwest. Univ, Sch. of Bus, B.S, 53; Phi Kappa Psi. Polit. & Govt. Pos: Mem, Young Rep, Rockford, Ill, 58; precinct committeeman, Rockford, 62; Rep. Rep. Committeeman, 66; secy, Winnebago Co. Rep. Cent. Cmt, 64, treas, 66-; clerk, treas. and mem. bd. trustees, Rockford Sanitary Dist, 66; mem, exec. cmt, Winnebago United Rep. Fund, 66; Co. campaign chmn. for John Altorfer Gubernatorial Primary, 68. Bus. & Prof. Pos: Customer serv. mgr, Nat. Lock Co. Div. Keystone Consolidated Industries, 57-60, dir. materials, 60-64, asst. to pres, 64-68 and v.pres, fastener sales, 68- Mil. Serv: Entered as Officer Cand, Navy, 53, released as Lt.(jg), 57, after serv. in Com. Serv. Ron. 3, 53-55; Combat Info. Center Officer, U.S.S. Lake Champlain, 55-57. Mem: Rotary; C. of C; Rockford Country Club; Univ. Club of Rockford. Rel: Congregational. Mailing Add: White Oak Ave, Rockford, Ill. 61111.

ERLANDER, ROSE DFL
Mem, Minn. Dem-Farmer-Labor State Cent. Cmt.
Polit. & Govt. Pos: Chmn, Tenth Ward Dem-Farmer-Labor Club, 60-66; Mem, Minn. Dem-Farmer-Labor State Cent. Cmt, 64-66; mem, Minn. Dem-Farmer-Labor State Sustaining Fund, currently. Bus. & Prof. Pos: V.pres, Gibson-Erlander Inc, advert. agency; advert. mgr, Telex, Inc, 43-52; acct. exec, Wm. L. Baxter Advert, 52-56. Mem: League of Women Voters (unit chmn, 46-50); Campfire Girls (publicity cmt, 64-66); Women's Advert. Club Minn, 52-60; Twin City Int. Prog. Soc. Workers and Youth Leaders (publicity chmn). Mailing Add: 2867 James Ave. S, Minneapolis, Minn. 55408.

ERLANDSEN, EINAR E. D
b. Escanaba, Mich, 4/27/08; m. to Rose M. McMahon; c. Leon. Educ: local schs. Polit. & Govt. Pos: Mich. State Rep, 48-68. Bus. & Prof. Pos: Serv. bus; former paper maker. Mem: Local 209, Paper Makers. Rel: Lutheran. Mailing Add: 1014 N. 16th St, Escanaba, Mich. 49829.

ERLENBORN, JOHN NEAL R
U.S. Rep, Ill.
b. Chicago, Ill, 2/8/27; s. John H. Erlenborn and Veronica M. Moran E; m. 5/10/52 to Dorothy C. Fisher; c. Debra Lynn, Paul Nelson and David John. Educ: Univ. Notre Dame, 44; Ind. State Teachers Col, 44-45; Univ. Ill, 45-46; Loyola Univ. Chicago Sch. Law, LL.B, 49; Elmhurst Col, LL.D, 68. Polit. & Govt. Pos: Asst. states attorney, DuPage Co, Ill, 50-52; pres, Elmhurst Young Rep, Ill, 54; Ill. State Rep, 56-64; U.S. Rep, Ill, 65- Bus. & Prof. Pos: Lawyer, Joseph Sam Perry, Wheaton, Ill, 49-50; partner, Erlenborn and Bauer, 52-63; partner, Erlenborn, Bauer and Hotte, 63- Mil. Serv: Naval Res, 44-46. Mem: DuPage Co. and Ill. Bar Asns; past officer, Elmhurst Am. Legion; Lions; past mem. bd. dir, Elmhurst C. of C. Rel: Roman Catholic. Legal Res: 445 Emery Lane, Elmhurst, Ill. 60126. Mailing Add: 8960 Colesbury Pl, Fairfax, Va. 22030.

ERLEWINE, DALE Independent
b. Perkins Co, Nebr, 8/8/00; s. Chas A. Erlewine and Ida M. Moore E; m. 6/28/52 to Ruth L. May Knutson; c. Larry Dale, Harry Gale and Keith R. Polit. & Govt. Pos: Nebr. State Sen, 59-64. Bus. & Prof. Pos: Farmer. Mem: Farmers Coop. Bds; Perkins Co. Farm Bur. Bd; Nebr. Farm Bur. Bd. (v.pres); Nebr. Rural Elec. Authority (pres); dir, Nebr. Wheatgrowers Asn; adv. staff, U.S. Dept. Agr; Midwest Elec. Mem. Asn, Rural Elec. Authority (pres); Tri-State Generation and Transmission Asn.(v.pres); Perkins Co. Red Cross (chmn); dir, Ogallala Commun. Hosp; Elks; charter mem, Lions. Good Neighbor Award, Ak-sar-ben. Rel: Congregational. Mailing Add: RFD, Grant, Nebr. 69140.

ERNST, MORRIS LEOPOLD D
b. Uniontown, Ala, 8/23/88; s. Carl Ernst and Sarah Bernheim E; m. 3/1/23 to Margaret Samuels; c. Constance, Roger and Joan. Educ: Williams Col, A.B, 09; N Y. Law Sch, LL.B, 12; hon. mem, Phi Beta Kappa; Phi Gamma Delta; Gargoyle Soc; hon. mem, Gamma Chap, Alpha Kappa Delta. Hon. J D, Nasson Col, 63; D.H.L, Lincoln Univ, 64. Polit. & Govt. Pos: Mem, N.Y. State Banking Bd. since inception, by app. Gov. Roosevelt and Gov. Lehman, 33-45; app. by President to adv. bd. for the Post Off, confirmed by Senate; app. by President Truman to Truman's Civil Rights Cmn; served as arbitor for Mayor La Guardia in taxicab strike, 34; drafted legis. for Gov. Lehman on ins. and banking matters; mem, Pa. Anthracite Coal Cmn; mission to V.I, 35; personal rep. to President Roosevelt during war on various missions to Eng; spec. consult, War Prod. Bd; counsel to N.Y. State Legis. Cmt. for Hard of Hearing; spec. asst. to attorney gen. in elec. fraud matters; govt. mission, Germany, 46. Bus. & Prof. Pos: Mfr. shirts, 09-11; mfr. retail furniture, 11-15; attorney, Law Firm, Greenbaum, Wolff & Ernest, N.Y.C, 15-; spec. counsel, Am. Newspaper Guild; counsel, Dramatist Guild and Authors League of Am; lectr, clubs and cols; weekly column, The Villager. Publ: Discovery by Chance (with Mary Batten), Funk & Wagnalls, 68; Black on Tripple-Cross-tricks (with Eleanora B. Black), Bantam Press 68; Back and Forth (with Malcolm A. Hoffman), Peter Pauper Press, 69; plus 24 others; contrib, mag. and encyclop. Mem: N.Y.C. Bar Asn; Co. Lawyers Asn; Savile Club, Eng; City Club (past trustee); Williams Club, N.Y; N Y. Players Club; PEN; Am. Polit. Sci. Asn; N.Y. Univ. Faculty Club; hon. mem, Soc. Anthropology, Sociol. and Research. French Decoration, Order of the French Legion of Honor; Honored by N.Y.C. Bar Asn, 60. Legal Res: 2 Fifth Ave, New York, N.Y. 10011. Mailing Add: 437 Madison Ave, New York, N.Y. 10022.

ERRECA, ROBERT CRONWELL D
Chmn, Merced Co. Dem. Cent. Cmt, Calif.
b. Los Banos, Calif, 2/2/36; s. John Erreca and Ida May Cronwell E; m. 6/16/63 to Marie Accardo. Educ: St. Mary's Col, Moraga, Calif, B.S, 57; Int. Rels. Club. Polit. & Govt. Pos: Dir, Merced Co. Fair, Calif, 62-, pres, 67-68; mem, exec. cmt, Calif. Dem. State Cent. Cmt, 66-; chmn, Merced Co. Dem. Cent. Cmt, 66- Mem: Sportsmen's Club; 20-30 Club; bd. dir, Los Banos Commun. Chest. Rel. Catholic. Mailing Add: 139 North Santa Rosa, Los Banos, Calif. 93635.

ERRICO, CHESTER L. D
Chmn, Hunterdon Co. Dem. Cmt, N.J.
s. Leon M. Errico and Olimpia Lauritano E; m. 3/4/43 to Virginia Schermerhorn; c. Chester L. Jr, Marie, Peter and Kimberly-Ann. Educ: High Sch. grad; exten. courses. Polit. & Govt. Pos: Mayor, Borough of Stockton, N.J, 50-; chmn, Hunterdon Co. Dem. Cmt, N.J, 55-; del, Dem. Nat. Conv, 60, 64 & 68; mem. and former chmn, Del. River Joint Toll Bridge Cmn, 62-; freeholder, Hunterdon Co, 64. Bus. & Prof. Pos: Owner, Errico's Quality Market and Errico's Esso Servicenter; trustee, Hunterdon Med. Cent, Flemington, N.J. Mem: Kiwanis; Moose; K. of C; Doylestown Country Club. Rel: Roman Catholic. Mailing Add: Bridge St, Stockton, N.J. 08559.

ERTOLA, JOHN ANDREW D
b. San Francisco, 11/4/26; s. Charles Alfred Ertola and Marie Valentine Ferro E; m. 11/6/49 to Shirley Jean Clark; c. Chadwick Clark and Jill Marie. Educ: Stanford Univ, 51; Univ. San Francisco Law Sch, 54; Alpha Pi; Sigma Chi. Polit. & Govt. Pos: Mem, San Francisco Co. Dem. Cent. Cmt, 58-62, State of Calif. Vets. Bd, 59-61 and bd. supvrs, City and Co. of San Francisco, 64-; pres, San Francisco Bd. Supvrs, 68 & 69; del, Dem. Nat. Conv, 68. Bus. & Prof. Pos: Partner, Law firm of Scampini, Mortara & Ertola, 54- Mil. Serv: Entered as Pvt, Army, 45, released as Cpl, 47, after serv. in Mil. Police. Mem: F&AM; San Francisco Easter Seal Soc. for Crippled Children & Adults; San Francisco, Calif. and Am. Bar Asns; Am. Legion. Rel: Christian Church N.Am. Legal Res: 219 32nd Ave, San Francisco, Calif. 94121. Mailing Add: 300 Montgomery St, San Francisco, Calif. 94104.

ERVIN, SAM J, JR. D
U.S. Sen, N.C.
b. Morganton, N.C, 9/27/96; m. 6/18/24 to Margaret Bruce Bell; c. Sam J, Mrs. Gerald M. Hansler and Mrs. Hallett S. Ward. Educ: Univ. of N.C, A.B, 17; Harvard Law Sch, LL.B, 22. Hon. LL.D, Univ. N.C, 51; LL.D, West. Carolina Col, 55; D.P.A, Suffolk Univ, 57. Polit. & Govt. Pos: N.C. State Rep, 23, 25 & 31; chmn, Burke Co. Dem. Exec. Cmt, 24; trustee, Morganton Graded Schs, 27-30; mem, N.C. State Dem. Exec. Cmt, 30-37; trustee, Univ. N.C, 32-35, 45-46 and Davidson Col, 48-58; judge, Burke Co. Criminal Court, 35-37; judge, N.C. Superior Court, 37-43; mem, N.C. State Bd. of Law Exam, 44-46; U.S. Rep, N.C, 46-47; chmn, N.C. Cmn. for Improv. of the Admin. of Justice, 47-49; assoc. justice, N.C. Supreme Court, 48-54; U.S. Sen, N.C, 54-; del, Dem. Nat. Conv, 56, 60, 64 & 68. Bus. & Prof. Pos: Lawyer. Mil. Serv: World War I, First Div, France; Nat. Guard; Awarded French Fourragere; Purple Heart with Oak Leaf Clusters; Silver Star; Distinguished Serv. Cross. Mem: Dir, First Nat. Bank of Morganton; Am. and N.C. Bar Asns; Am. Judicature Soc; N.C. State Bar; Farm Bur; Grange; Morganton C. of C; Newcomen Soc; Wildlife Asn; Am. Legion; DAV; Legion of Valor; Soc. of First Div; VFW; Vets of the First World War; Royal Arch Mason; Royal and Select Masters; Scottish Rite Mason (33°); Hon. Legion of DeMolay; Shrine; Ahepa; Dokies;

Jr. Order; K. of P; Moose; Am. Hist. Asn; Burke Co. Hist. Soc; N.C. Soc. for the Preservation of Antiquities; N.C. Folklore Soc; N.C. Lit. and Hist. Asn; Roanoke Island Hist. Asn; Soc. of the Cincinnati; State Gov, Soc. of Mayflower Descendants; SAR; S.C. Hist. Soc; South. Hist. Asn; Polit. Sci. Asn; W. N.C. Hist. Asn; Morganton Kiwanis; Gen. Alumni Asn. of N.C.U. Morganton's Man of the Year, 54; cited by N.C. Dept. of Am Legion, SAR and UDC; Grand Orator, Grand Lodge of Masons of N.C, 63; Awarded Cross of Mil. Serv, UDC; Good Citizenship Medal, SAR; Distinguished Citizenship Cert, N.C. Citizens Asn; Patriotic Serv. Medal, Am. Coalition of Patriotic Soc. Rel: Presbyterian; Elder, Morganton Presby. Church. Legal Res: Morganton, N.C. Mailing Add: 337 Old Senate Office Bldg, Washington, D.C. 20510.

ERWAY, JULIAN B. D
b. Groton, N.Y, 3/17/99; m. 1928 to Genevieve Ryan (deceased 9/6/62). Educ: Albany Law Sch, LL.B, 24. Polit. & Govt. Pos: N.Y. State Sen, 42-44 & 57-69; dist. attorney, Albany Co, 45-53. Bus. & Prof. Pos: Lawyer, Townor & Erway, Albany, N.Y. Mil. Serv: Marine Corps, Parris Island, S.C; Portsmouth, Va; Quantico, Va; replacement 81st Machine Gun Bn, Sixth Regt. Mem: Ft. Orange Club; Ft. Orange Post Am. Legion; Marine Corps League. Admitted to Bar, June 1925. Mailing Add: 37 Morris St, Albany, N.Y. 12208. (1967)

ERWIN, FRANK CRAIG, JR. D
Mem, Dem. Nat. Cmt.
b. Waxahachie, Tex, 1/25/20; s. Frank Craig Erwin and Margaret Edwards E; married to June Carr; c. Frank Craig. Educ: Univ. of Tex, 48; Kappa Sigma; Phi Beta Kappa; Phi Eta Sigma; Phi Sigma Alpha; Phi Delta Phi. Polit. & Govt. Pos: V.chmn, Citizens Cmn, Tex, drafted new city charter for Austin, 52; chmn, Travis Co. Dem. Conv, 62; past chmn. and past secy, Tex. Dem. State Exec. Cmt; del. and v.chmn. Tex. del, Dem. Nat. Conv, 64, del, 68; mem, Dem. Nat. Cmt, currently. Bus. & Prof. Pos: Partner, firm of Brown, Sparks & Erwin, Austin, Tex; v.chmn. bd. of regents, Univ. of Tex. Mil. Serv: Naval Res, 41-46; PTO. Mem: Am. Bar Asn; Travis Co. Bar Asn.(past pres, chmn. bd. of dirs); State Bar of Tex; Int. Asn. of Ins. Attorneys; Defense Research Inst; Tex. Asn. Defense Counsels; Univ. of Tex. Ex-Students Asn.(past pres. of Travis Co, life mem); hon. mem, T. Asn; founder, Longhorn Club. Rel: Episcopal. Legal Res: 2307 Woodlawn Blvd, Austin, Tex. 78703. Mailing Add: Brown Bldg, Austin, Tex. 78701. (1967)

ERWIN, JAMES SHREWSBURY R
Attorney Gen, Maine
b. New York, N.Y, 11/27/20; s. James Robinson Erwin and Elizabeth Mathilda Davidson E; m. 5/31/47 to Charlotte Anne Ruprecht; c. Charlotte Elizabeth, Sarah Anne, James Robinson and Martha Jane. Educ: Dartmouth Col, A.B, 42; Columbia Univ. Law Sch, LL.B, 49; Alpha Delta Phi; Sphinx. Polit. & Govt. Pos: Trustee, York Sch. Dist, Maine, 51-62; chmn, York Co. Rep. Cmt, 54-58; mem, State Rep. Cmt, 58-64; Maine State Sen, 61-62; Maine State Rep, 65-66; Attorney Gen, Maine, 66- Bus. & Prof. Pos: Partner, Sewall, Strater, Erwin & Winton, 53-66; dir, Portsmouth Trust Co, Portsmouth, N.H, 60-66. Mil. Serv: Entered as Pvt, Army, 42, released as 2nd Lt, 45, after serv. in Sixth Port Hq, European-African-Middle East Theater; Campaign Ribbon with Four Stars; European-African-Middle East. Theater Ribbon. Mem: Am. and York Co. Bar Asns; Maine State Bar Asn.(pres, 67-68); Am. Judicature Soc; Mason, Shrine; Am. Legion; VFW; Dartmouth Seacoast Club; Agamenticus Yacht Club; Portland Club; York Golf and Tennis Club. Rel: Protestant. Legal Res: 107 York St, York, Maine 03909. Mailing Add: York, Maine 03909.

ERWIN, WILLIAM WALTER R
b. Plymouth, Ind, 9/28/25; s. Lewis Erwin and Eleanor Fribley E; m. 6/12/48 to June Bramlet; c. Hope Ellen, Lewis, II and James William. Educ: Univ. Ill, B.S, 49; Scabbard and Blade; Beta Theta Pi. Polit. & Govt. Pos: Chmn, Ind. Young Rep. 52-56; mem, Nat. Young Rep. Exec. Cmt, 54-56; mem, Rep. Cmt. on Prog. and Progress, 55; farm rep. for Eisenhower, 56 and for Nixon, 60; mem, Conserv. Study Cmt. for Dept. of Agr, 58; chmn, Ind. Adv. Cmt, U.S. Civil Rights Cmn, 60-62; pres, Cmt. on Commun. Rels, 62; Ind. State Sen, 65-69; Rep. nominee for U.S. Rep, Ind, 68. Bus. & Prof. Pos: Mem, Field Crops Adv. Cmt, Am. Farm Bur. Fedn, 60-; mem. bd, Found-for Am. Agr, 62-; pres. and gen. mgr, Triple E Farm, Inc. Mil. Serv: Entered as Pvt, Air Force, 44, released as Cadet, 45, commisioned 2nd Lt, 48. Mem: Am. Legion; Am. Soc. of Farm Mgrs. and Rural Appraisers; Mason; Lions; Purdue Farm Policy Study Group (chmn, 69). Rel: Methodist. Mailing Add: Box 195, Etna Green, Ind. 46524.

ESAU, GILBERT D. Conservative
Minn. State Rep.
b. Mt. Lake, Minn, 1919; m; c. 4. Educ: Mt. Lake pub. schs. Polit. & Govt. Pos: Councilman, Mt. Lake, Minn, 54-63; Minn. State Rep, 62- Bus. & Prof. Pos: Automobile garage owner. Mil. Serv: Army, 41-45, ETO and Asiatic Theatre. Mailing Add: Mt. Lake, Minn. 56159.

ESCH, MARVIN L. R
U.S. Rep, Mich.
b. Flinton, Pa, 8/4/27; s. Paul J. Esch and Susan M. Gill E; m. 6/17/50 to Olga Jurich; c. Emily, Leo and Thomas. Educ: Univ. Mich, A.B, 50, M.A, 51, Ph.D, 57. Polit. & Govt. Pos: Mich. State Rep, 65-66; U.S. Rep, Mich, 67-, mem, Educ. & Labor Cmt, Rep. Research Cmt. and chmn, Social Security & Human Needs Task Force, U.S. House of Rep. Bus. & Prof. Pos: Assoc. prof. speech, Wayne State Univ, 55-64; lectr, Univ. Mich-Wayne State Univ. Inst. Labor & Indust. Rels, 55-64. Publ: 'The Need for Reform,' Republican Papers, Anchor Bks, 68. Rel: Presbyterian. Legal Res: 1821 Covington, Ann Arbor, Mich. 48103. Mailing Add: 501 Cannon Bldg, Washington, D.C. 20515.

ESCOBEDO, JOSEPH HERMAN D
b. Trinidad, Colo, 7/18/33; s. Herman Q. Escobedo and Dora Rivera E; m. 5/27/54 to Martha Belle Cordova; c. Joseph Herman, Jr. and Jo-Ann. Educ: Cent. High Sch, Cheyenne, Wyo, grad, 51. Polit. & Govt. Pos: Dem. Precinct committeeman, Cheyenne, Wyo, 60-68; del, Wyo. State Dem. Conv, 68; alternate del, Dem. Nat. Conv, 68. Bus. & Prof. Pos: Carman, Union Pac. R.R, Cheyenne, Wyo, over 16 years. Mem: BRCA; St. Joseph's Cath. Men's Club. Rel: Catholic. Mailing Add: 347 Stinson, Cheyenne, Wyo. 82001.

ESELY, WILLIAM JOSEPH R
Mem, Mo. State Rep. Cmt.
b. Stewartsville, Mo, 2/29/32; s. Roy H. Esely and Josephine Grimes E; m. 8/23/58 to Glenda Carol Greis. Educ: Univ. Mo, A.B. in Polit. Sci, 54 and LL.B, 59; Phi Delta Phi; Law Rev. Polit. & Govt. Pos: City attorney, Gilman City and New Hampton, Mo; city attorney, Bethany, 62-; alternate del, Rep. Nat. Conv, 64, del, 68 and mem. Platform Cmt, 68; mem. and secy, Sen. Reapportionment Cmn, 65; prosecuting attorney, Harrison Co, 60-; co-chmn, Harrison Co. Rep. Cmt, 64-; mem, Mo. State Rep. Cmt, 66-, mem. budget cmt, 68- Bus. & Prof. Pos: Practicing attorney, 59-; owner and pres, Harrison Co. Abstract Co, Inc, 65-; farming interests; mem. bd. dirs, Calhoun Mfg. Co, 68- and Rep. Clipper, 69- Mil. Serv: Entered as Airman 3/C, Air Force, 54, released as Lt, 56, after serv. in Training Command. Mem: Am, Mo, Circuit and Co. Bar Asns; Mason (32°); Shrine; Odd Fellows; Jr. C. of C; C. of C; Farm Bur; Rotary; Alumni Asn, Univ. Mo; Bethany Country Club. Rel: Methodist. Legal Res: 518 S. 15th, Bethany, Mo. 64424. Mailing Add: Box 410, Bethany, Mo. 64424.

ESEROMA, LIGOLIGO KURESA R
V.Speaker, Am. Samoa House Rep.
b. Fitiuta, Am. Samoa, 10/5/28; s. Paopao Eseroma and Vasalealofi Mikaio Moliga E; m. 12/4/57 to Saini Muamua Utu; c. Jean Susan, Esther Maopu, Janet Sinasaumane, Faafetai L, Colleen Lauli'i, Diego Faresa, Dean Rusk and Thomas Stafford Eliu. Educ: Frederic Barstow Found. High Sch, Am. Samoa, grad, 49. Polit. & Govt. Pos: Asst. chief immigration officer, Govt. Am. Samoa, 65-69, chief weights and measures inspector, 69-; secy, Fitiuta Youth Orgn, Am. Samoa, 66-67, v.pres, 67-; Rep, Am. Samoa House Rep, 67-, V.Speaker of House, 69- Mil. Serv: Entered as Seaman Recruit, Navy, 54, released as PO 2/C, 64, after serv. in U.S.S. Inglesol, Pac. Fleet, 63-64; Nat. Defense Serv. Medal; Two Navy Good Conduct Medals. Publ: '40 Consecutive Days of the Legislature of American Samoa,' Samoa Times, 5/69. Mem: VFW; Fleet Reserve Asn.(secy, 67-). Rel: Congregational Christian; Secy, Samoan Congregational Christian Church. Legal Res: Fitiuta, Manua, American Samoa 96920. Mailing Add: P.O. Box 654, Pago Pago, Nu'uuli, Tutuila, American Samoa 96920.

ESHBACK, J. RUSSELL R
Pa. State Rep.
b. Bushkill, Pa, 4/28/98; m. to Irene Reynolds. Educ: Pa. State Col, B.S; Columbia Univ, M.A. Polit. & Govt. Pos: Pa. State Rep, 58-; past co. treas, prothonotary, register and recorder, and co. cmnr. Bus. & Prof. Pos: Farmer, former teacher. Mailing Add: Bushkill, Pa. 18324. (1967)

ESHLEMAN, EDWIN D. R
U.S. Rep, Pa.
b. Lancaster Co, Pa, 12/4/20; s. Reeder L. Eshleman and Mary B. E. (deceased); m. to Kathryn E. Dambach; c. E. Bruce and R. Lee. Educ: Franklin and Marshall Col, B.S. in polit. sci; U.S. Coast Guard Acad, Res. Officer Training Course; Temple Univ, grad. study in polit. sci. Polit. & Govt. Pos: Dir, Bur. Co. Audits, Dept. Auditor Gen, Pa, 49-53; mem. bd. dirs, Young Rep. Lancaster Co, 50-53 & 55-57, pres, 51, 52 & 54; exec. asst, State Treas. Dept, 53-55; Pa. State Rep, 54-66, chmn, House Educ. Cmt, Pa. House Rep, 63-64, majority whip, 64 and minority whip, 65-66; v.chmn, Pa. Higher Educ. Assistance Agency, 64-; U.S. Rep, Pa, currently. Bus. & Prof. Pos: Pub. sch. teacher, 45-49. Mil. Serv: Entered as Lt, Coast Guard Res, 42, released 54, after 38 months active duty, 18 months overseas; commendations for conduct-in-action at Salerno, Anzio and Normandy. Mem: Am. Legion; Lancaster Co. Sportsmen Asn; F&AM; Elks; Acad. Polit. Sci, Columbia Univ; Lancaster Co. Hist. Soc; Pa. Soc, N.Y. Distinguished Serv. Award as Outstanding Young Man of Year, Lancaster Jr. C. of C, 56. Rel: Lutheran. Mailing Add: 2173 W. Ridge Dr, Lancaster, Pa. 17603.

ESPOSITO, FRANCIS JAMES D
Vt. State Rep.
b. Lebanon Springs, N.Y, 12/30/13; s. Ralph Esposito and Stella Marie E.(deceased); m. 9/15/45 to Eileen Joy Warner; c. Francis J, Jr. and Michael J. Educ: Mt. St. Joseph's Acad, Rutland, Vt, 4 years. Polit. & Govt. Pos: Mem, Rutland City Dem. Cmt, 61-; mem, Rutland Co. Dem. Cmt, 65-; Vt. State Rep, 66-; chmn, Rutland del, Vt. Dem. Conv, 68; state chmn, Vt. Dem. Party, 68- Bus. & Prof. Pos: Trainman, Rutland Rwy. Corp, 40-62, conductor, 50-62, gen. chmn, Rutland Rwy. Corp, BRT, 52-62; self-employed, real estate and ins, 61- Mil. Serv: Entered as Pvt, Army Air Force, 42, released as Warrant Officer, 45, after serving in Pac. Theatre, 42-45. Mem: Mt. St. Joseph Athletic Bd.(past pres); K. of C.(4° and past Grand Knight); Am. Legion; Kiwanis Int.(first v.pres, Rutland Club); BRT Lodge 704. Rel: Catholic. Mailing Add: 104 South St, Rutland, Vt. 05701.

ESPOSITO, MICHAEL P. D
N.J. State Assemblyman
b. Jersey City, N.J, 1/22/13; s. John Esposito and Marianna Delisa E; m. 2/15/36 to Theresa Orrico; c. Marianne (Mrs. Costello). Educ: Bucknell Univ, 4 years; Alpha Phi Delta. Polit. & Govt. Pos: Mem. and dir, Jersey City Bd. of Educ, 65-68; N.J. State Assemblyman, 68- Bus. & Prof. Pos: Pres, John Esposito & Sons Inc, Hardware Co, 47- Mem: Friendly Merchants Businessmens Asn.(former pres); Columbus Triangle Bus. and Prfnl. Mens Asn.(pres); Holy Rosary Holy Name Soc.(former pres); Paul Revere Boys' Club (former chmn. bd); Boys' Club of Am. Recipient of Outstanding Am. Award, 59; Medallion Award, Boys' Club of Am, 61. Rel: Catholic. Legal Res: 366 Second St, Jersey City, N.J. 07302. Mailing Add: 275 Newark Ave, Jersey City, N.J. 07302.

ESSER, HAROLD JOSEPH R
Mo. State Rep.
b. Boonville, Mo, 2/11/23; s. John Lawrence Esser and Elizabeth Fischer E; m. 12/26/53 to Lorraine Joan Anderson; c. David Anderson. Educ: St. Benedict's Col, 40-41; Univ. Mo, Columbia, 46-48; Kappa Alpha. Polit. & Govt. Pos: Mo. State Rep, 69- Mil. Serv: Entered as Pvt, Army, 43, released as Cpl, 46, after serv. in Med. Corps, Europe and Asia. Mem: Pres, S. Kans. City Kiwanis Club, 64. Rel: Catholic. Mailing Add: 3 West Glen Arbor Rd, Kansas City, Mo. 64114.

ESSEX, THOMAS L. 'TOM' D
Polit. & Govt. Pos: Ind. State Rep, -66; mem, Twp. Adv. Bd. Bus. & Prof. Pos: V.pres, Saps Bakery, Inc. Mil. Serv: Navy. Mem: Adv. Coun, Small Bus. Admin; adv. bd, LaRue Carter Hosp; v.pres, Columbus Arts Guild; Am. Legion C. of C; Ind. Mfrs. Asn. Rel: Methodist, bd. of trustees. Mailing Add: R.R. 4, Columbus, Ind. 47201. (1967)

ESTES, KATE REED D
b. Trenton, Tex, 6/28/17; d. Charles Burgher Reed and Frances Lucile Morrow R; div. Educ: Tex. Women's Univ; E.Tex. State Univ, B.S. and M.S; grad. study, N.Tex. State Univ. and Univ. Tex; Mu Phi Epsilon; Delta Kappa Gamma. Polit. & Govt. Pos: Chmn. Women's Activities and Fannin Co. Campaign Chmn, Ray Roberts for Cong, 61; admin. asst. to Sen. Ray Roberts, 61 and to Sen. Ralph Hall, 63-65; del, Dem. Nat. Conv, 64; chmn. Fannin Co. Del. to State Dem. Conv, 64, v.chmn, 66; Fannin Co. Campaign Chmn, Crawford Martin for Attorney Gen. of Tex, 66; chmn, local precinct conv, 68; secy, Fannin Co. Conv, 68; Fannin Co. Del. to Tex. State Dem. Conv, 68. Bus. & Prof. Pos: Teacher, 38-44; elem. supvr. of schs, Fannin Co, Tex, 44-58 & 65-66; elem. educ. consult, Harcourt, Brace World Book Co, 58-59; elem. consult, Educ. Resources Corp. Asn, 66-67; admin. serv. consult, Educ. Serv. Center-Region, 67- Mem: Nat. Educ. Asn; Tex. State Teachers Asn; Asn. of Supvrs. and Curriculum Develop; Am. Asn. of Univ. Women; Fannon Co. Dem. Women's Club; Nat. Fedn. of Musicians Union; Int. Platform Asn. Prfnl. musician; mem, Tex. State Textbook Cmt, 57. Rel: Methodist. Mailing Add: Box 245, Trenton, Tex. 75490.

ETCHART, MARK S. R
b. Glasgow, Mont, 8/31/23; s. John Etchart and Catherine Urquilux E; m. 5/11/49 to Delores Stroble; c. Colette, Brian, Diane and Denise. Educ: St. Thomas Col, St. Paul, Minn, 40-41; Carroll Col, Helena, Mont, 41-42; Mont. State Univ, B.S. in Animal Indust, 51; Alpha Zeta; Lambda Chi Alpha. Polit. & Govt. Pos: Mont. State Rep, Valley Co, 61-65, mem. legis. coun, Mont. State House of Rep, 63-65; Mont. State Rep, Dist. 5B, 67-69. Bus. & Prof. Pos: Partner, Etchart Ranch, 43-66; dir, Buggy Creek State Grazing Dist, 64-66; pres, Glasgow Irrigation Dist, 66. Mil. Serv: Entered as A/S, Navy, 45, released as AMM 3/C, 46, after serv. in Fleet Air Wing 14, Hq. Squadron 14-1, San Diego, Calif. Mem: Mont. Pilots Asn; Farm Bur; Am. Legion; Elks; K. of C; C. of C; Valley Develop. Coun; Nat. Reclamation Asn; Mont. Stockgrowers Asn; Mont. Woolgrowers Asn. Airplane pilot with instr, instrument ratings and commercial license; Aircraft and Powerplant Mech. License. Rel: Catholic. Legal Res: 514 Sixth Ave. N, Glasgow, Mont. 59230. Mailing Add: Box 229, Glasgow, Mont. 59230.

ETHERIDGE, JACK PAUL D
b. Atlanta, Ga, 3/16/27; s. Judge Anton Lee Etheridge and Jessie Brown E; m. 2/2/52 to Ursula Mararetha Schlatter; c. Jack P, Mary E and Margaret A. Educ: Davidson Col, B.S; Emory Univ. Law Sch, LL.B; Beta Theta Pi. Polit. & Govt. Pos: Ga. State Rep, 63-66; judge, Superior Court, Atlanta, 66- Bus. & Prof. Pos: Attorney, 56-; trustee, Davidson Col, currently. Mil. Serv: Naval Res, World War II; Merchant Marine, Cadet Corps, Pac. and Far East Theaters, 45-46; Army Infantry, 1st Lt, Korean War, 50-52; Aide de Camp to Brig. Gen. Theo. Wessells & Brig. Gen. Harry Sherman. Mem: Jr. C. of C; Atlanta Bar Asn.(pres, 62). Young Man of the Year in Professions, Atlanta Jr. C. of C, 61. Rel: Presbyterian. Mailing Add: Superior Court of the Atlanta Judicial Court, Atlanta, Ga. 30303.

ETHEREDGE, ROBERT FOSTER D
b. Birmingham, Ala, 7/14/20; s. Joel Hilliard Etheredge and Nell Ora Cain E; m. 8/28/48 to Joanna Carson; c. Robert Foster, Nell Carson and Nancy Boyd. Educ: Univ. Ala, B.A, 46, LL.B, 49; Nat. Interfraternity Coun; Omicron Delta Kappa; dist. pres, Pi Kappa Alpha, 61-62. Polit. & Govt. Pos: Ala. State Rep, 63-66. Mil. Serv: ETO, discharged as 1st Lt; received battlefield cmn; 5 Bronze Battle Stars. Mem: Am, Ala. and Birmingham Bar Asns; Am. Judicature Soc; dir, Ala. Defense Lawyers Asn; Ala. Law Inst; Am. Legion; VFW; dir, Ala. and Jefferson Co. Soc. Crippled Children and Adults; Birmingham Country Club; Adv. Cmt, Family Court; Elks; Eagles; Rotary. Rel: Methodist. Mailing Add: 800 First National Bldg, Birmingham, Ala. 35203.

ETHERTON, TRUDY SLABY R
Auditor, Ind.
b. South Bend, Ind, 6/6/42; d. Frank A. Slaby and Alice E. Michalec S; m. 2/7/67 to William M. Etherton. Educ: Ind. Univ, Bloomington; Butler Univ, B.S, 64, spec. Grad. student, currently; Delta Gamma; Panhellenic. Polit. & Govt. Pos: V.pres, Butler Univ. Young Rep, 62, pres, 63-64; region co-chmn, Col. Young Rep, 63; del, Rep. Nat. Conv, 64; dir, Young Rep, South Bend, Ind, 65, v.pres, 66; auditor, Ind, 68- Bus. & Prof. Pos: Teacher Penn-Harris-Madison School Corp, 64-68; dep. Registrn. officer, St. Joseph County, Ind. Mem: Ind. State Teachers Asn; Nat. Educ. Asn; Nat. Asn. Soc. Studies Teachers; Notre Dame Faculty Club; Butler Univ. Alumni Asn; Delta Gamma Alumni; Elks Auxiliary; Polish Nat. Alliance; Indianapolis Press Club; South Bend Press Club; State Assembly Women's Club; Our Lady of the Lake Sem. Asn. Rel: Catholic. Legal Res: 23721 S.R. No. 2, South Bend, Ind. 46619. Mailing Add: State House, 200 W. Washington, Indianapolis, Ind. 46204.

ETHRIDGE, WILLIAM NATHANIEL, JR. D
b. Columbus, Miss, 8/3/12; s. W.N. Ethridge and Laura Mae Ramage E; m. 12/14/46 to Lura Clark; c. William N, IV, David F, Paul R, Ruby Milbourn, and Thomas C. Educ: Univ. Miss, B.A, 34, LL.B, 37; Univ. South. Calif, LL.M, 40; Univ. Chicago, grad. res, 41; Omicron Delta Kappa; Phi Delta Phi; Sigma Alpha Epsilon. Polit. & Govt. Pos: Assoc. justice, Supreme Court, Miss, 50-65, presiding justice, 65-66, chief justice, 66- Bus. & Prof. Pos: Attorney, Ethridge and Ethridge, Oxford, Miss, 37-42; attorney, Wells, Wells, Newman & Thomas, Jackson, 44-48; prof. Univ. Miss. Sch. Law, 48-50. Mem: Am. Law Inst, Am. Bar Asn; Miss. State Bar; Am. Judicature Soc; Inst. Judicial Admin. Rel: Presbyterian. Legal Res: 1013 S. 11th St, Oxford, Miss. 38655. Mailing Add: 554 Woodson Court, Jackson, Miss. 39206.

ETZELL, GEORGE FERDINAND R
Mem, Rep. Nat. Cmt, Minn.
b. Clarissa, Minn, 2/1/09; s. George Adolph Etzell and Ida Hammer E; m. 10/4/34 to Ione Margaret Koch; c. Peter, Gretchen, Paul, Mary and Martha. Polit. & Govt. Pos: Mem, Minn. Rep. Nat. Cmt; village clerk, Clarissa, Minn, 30-34; mem, Young Rep. League, Sixth Cong. Dist. Rep. Orgn, 36-38; Printer, State of Minn, 39-43; chmn, Sixth Cong. Dist. Rep. Orgn, 46-51; spec. adv, Gov. C. Elmer Anderson, 51-52; v.chmn, Rep. Nat. Conv. Rules Cmt, 56, chmn, 60 & 64; mem, Rep. Nat. Cmt, 52- Bus. & Prof. Pos: Pres, Etzell Publ, Inc, 63-; ed. and publisher, The Clarissa Independent, 39- Publ: Author of children's stories, articles, etc. published in about 100 mag. since 1930. Mem: Nat. Ed. Asn; Minn. Newspaper Asn; charter mem, Minn. Press Club; Minneapolis Athletic Club; K. of C; Farm Bur; Clarissa Commercial Club (pres, 4 years); Clarissa Sch. Bd. (mem, 19 years, chmn, currently); Sigma Delta Chi. Rel: Roman Catholic. Mailing Add: Clarissa, Minn. 56440.

EUBANKS, RAYMOND CONVERSE, JR. D
b. Spartanburg, S.C, 12/18/33; s. Raymond C. Eubanks and Sarah Louise Brown E; m. 4/17/65 to Frances Carolyn West; c. Raymond C, III. Educ: Wofford Col, A.B, 56; Univ. S.C, LL.B, 59; pres, Freshman Class, 52-53; Kappa Alpha Order; Phi Delta Phi. Polit. & Govt. Pos: Mem, staff of late U.S. Sen. Olin D. Johnston, S.C, 59; asst. gen. counsel to Trading with the Enemy Act Subcmt, U.S. Sen. Judiciary Cmt, 59-60; secy, Young Dem. of Spartanburg Co, 64-65; S.C. State Rep, 64-68; v.chmn, Fourth Cong. Dist, Young Dem, 65-; mem. study cmt, S.C. Truth in Lending Law Cmt, currently. Bus. & Prof. Pos: Attorney, Brown and Eubanks, Spartanburg, S.C, 63-68; attorney, Cauthen & Eubanks, 68- Mil. Serv: Entered as 1st Lt, Air Force, 60, released as Capt, 63, after serv. as Asst. Staff, Judge Adv, Moody Air Force Base, Ga; Capt, Air Force Res, 63- Mem: Am, S.C. and Spartanburg Co. Bar Asn; Am. Judicature Soc; Mason (32°); Shrine; WOW; K. of P; Optimists Int. Rel: Presbyterian. Legal Res: 233 Holly Dr, Spartanburg, S.C. 29301. Mailing Add: P.O. Box 22, Spartanburg, S.C. 29301.

EULER, JACK RICHARD R
Kans. State Rep.
b. Wathena, Kans, 4/1/29; s. Everett Euler and Gladys Wiegant E; m. 4/30/58 to Rose Marie Doane; c. Jennifer Lynn, Jack Richard, II and Joel Randall. Educ: Washburn Univ. and Law Sch, A.B, LL.B, 53; Delta Theta Phi. Polit. & Govt. Pos: Co. attorney, Doniphan Co, Kans, 57-63; city councilman, Wathena, 61-63 and mem, Bd. of Educ, 63-65; Kans. State Rep, 52nd Dist, 64-; mem, Gov. Cmt. on Crime and Law Enforcement, 65-67 and Kans. Judicial Coun, 65-; Bus. & Prof. Pos: V.pres, Farmers Lumber & Supply Co, Inc, Wathena, Kans, 66-; secy-treas, St. Joseph Toyota Motors, Inc, St. Joseph, Mo, 68- Mil. Serv: Fifth Army, Ft. Chaffee, Ark, 54-56. Mem: Doniphan Co, Northeast Kans. and Am. Bar Asns; chmn, Prospective Legis. Cmt, Kans. Bar Asn, 68-; Am. Trial Lawyers Asn; Eastern Star; Mason; Scottish Rite; Shrine; Elks; Am. Legion. Rel: Protestant. Mailing Add: 606 N. Sixth, Wathena, Kans. 66090.

EULISS, JACK MANNING D
N.C. State Rep.
b. Burlington, N.C, 8/27/21; s. Cyrus M. Euliss and Myrtle Cooper E; m. 2/25/43 to Ione Cheek; c. Jack Manning, Jr, Ann Cheek, William McAdoo. Educ: Wake Forest Col, 42. Polit. & Govt. Pos: Mayor-pro-tem, Burlington, N.C, 59-61, mem. city coun, 59-62; N.C. State Rep, 63- Bus. & Prof. Pos: Trustee, Campbell Col, 63-; mgr, Alamance Motors, Inc. Mil. Serv: Army Air Force, 42-45. Mem: Past master, Bula Lodge 409, AF&AM; Burlington Chap. DeMolay, Legion of Honor, 57; past pres, Kiwanis, 54; Lt. Gov, Carolinas Kiwanis, 57; trustee, N.C. Baptist Children's Homes, 54-58. Jaycee Young Man of the Year, 53; Alamance Co. Citizen of the Year, 58. Rel: Baptist; former Sunday sch. supt. and teacher, deacon. Mailing Add: Lake Dr. E, P.O. Box 913, Burlington, N.C. 27215.

EURE, THAD D
Secy. of State, N.C.
b. Gates Co, N.C, 11/15/99; s. Tazewell A. Eure and Armecia Langstun E; m. 11/15/24 to Minta Banks; c. Thad Jr. and Mrs. J. Norman Black. Educ: Univ. N.C, 19; Univ. Law Sch, 22; Elon Col, LL.D, 58. Polit. & Govt. Pos: Chmn. bd. trustees, Elon Col; mayor, Winton, N.C, 23-28; co. attorney, Hertford Co, 23-31; N.C. State Rep, 29; prin. clerk, N.C. House of Reps, 31-36; escheats agent, Univ. N.C, 33-36; Secy. State, N.C, 36-; keynote speaker, Dem. State Conv, 50 and permanent chmn, 62. Bus. & Prof. Pos: Attorney-at-law. Mem: Pres, Ahoski Kiwanis, 27; Theta Chi Jr. Order; Grand Lodge Chair Officer, Elks, 56; Am. Legion; 40 et 8; pres, Nat. Asn. Secy. State, 42, dean, 61; T.P.A. Rel: Congregational. Legal Res: Winton, N.C. 27986. Mailing Add: State Capitol, Raleigh, N.C. 27602.

EURICH, EDWARD RICHARDSON R
Vt. State Rep.
b. Warren, Vt, 5/24/16; m. to Alleen N. Doods; c. Five. Educ: Burlington Bus. Col. Polit. & Govt. Pos: Former sch. dir, 2 terms; selectman, Waitsfield, Vt, 56-; Vt. State Rep, 65- Bus. & Prof. Pos: Farmer. Mem: Wash. Co. Farm Bur; Vt. Farm. Bur.(mem. bd. trustees); bd. trustees, Farm Show; Eastern Star; F&AM; Vt. Consistory SPRS (32°). Rel: Congregational. Mailing Add: Waitsfield, Vt. 05673. (1967)

EUSTIS, WARREN PENHALL DFL
Finance and Personnel Chmn, Minn. State Dem-Farmer-Labor Exec. Cmt.
b. Fairmont, Minn, 11/30/27; s. Irving Nelson Eustis and Florence Penhall E; div; c. Lillian, Paul and Lee. Educ: Carleton Col, B.A, 50; Univ. Chicago, J.D, 53; Univ. Ark, M.A, 56; Phi Alpha Theta; Delta Upsilon. Polit. & Govt. Pos: Del, Minn. Coun. of Churches, 57-; city trial counsel, Rochester, Minn, 57-; chmn, First Cong. Dist. Dem-Farmer-Labor Party, 59-65; cmnr, Rochester Charter Cmn, 61-; finance and personnel chmn, Minn. State Dem-Farmer-Labor Exec. Cmt, 63-; Cmnr. Higher Educ, Minn, 65-; pres, Rochester Coun. of Churches, 65-; spec. counsel, Upper Midwest Res. & Develop. Coun, 69- Mil. Serv: Entered as Pvt, Army, 54, released from Detached Duty, Sci. and Prfnl. Corps, 56. Publ: Trial Procedures for Police, City of Rochester, 60. Mem: Olmstead Co. Bar Asn.(v.pres, 65-); Minn. Trial Lawyers Asn.(bd. gov, 64-); Orgn. Am. Historians; Am. and Minn. Bar Asns; Am. Trial Lawyers Asn; Am. Judicature Soc. Rel: United Church of Christ. Mailing Add: 1606 Mount Curve Ave, Minneapolis, Minn. 55403.

EUZZINO, ANDREW A. D
b. New York City, N.Y; c. two. Educ: DePaul U, LL.B, 28. Polit. & Gov. Pos: Ill. State Rep, 63rd-73rd Gen. Assemblies; asst. Attorney Gen, 37-41. Mem: Ill. State Bar Asn; Am. Judicature Soc. Mailing Add: 905 S. Western, Chicago, Ill. 60612. (1967)

EVANS, ALBERT HENRY, JR. D
Chmn, Choctaw Co. Dem. Exec. Cmt, Ala.
b. Bolinger, La, 7/1/13; s. Albert Henry Evans and Omer Purcell E; m. 6/21/38 to Josephine Dansby; c. Ann (Mrs. Harry Horner Bates), William Albert, James Dansby and Marcita. Educ: Livingston State Col; Univ. Ala; Alpha Kappa Psi. Polit. & Govt. Pos: Chmn, Choctaw Co. Cmn, Ala, 20 years; mem, Ala. Dem. State Exec. Cmt, 50-; chmn, Choctaw Co. Dem. Exec. Cmt, currently; former Ala. State Sen. Bus. & Prof. Pos: Bank cashier, Choctaw Bank, Butler, Ala. Mil. Serv: Army. Mem: Mason; Shrine. Rel: Methodist. Mailing Add: Butler, Ala. 36904. (1967)

EVANS, ARTHUR HAYDEN R
Chmn, Sierra Co. Rep. Cent. Cmt, N.Mex.
b. Phoenix, Ariz, 10/18/22; s. A.A. Evans and Mildred E. Hayden E; m. 4/9/43 to Wanda Ruth Giblin; c. Hayden Lee, April Lynn and Mikel Ray. Polit. & Govt. Pos: Chmn, Sierra Co. Rep. Cent. Cmt, N.Mex, 66-; mem, N.Mex. Rep. Cent. Cmt, 66- Bus. & Prof. Pos: Cattle foreman, Tovrea Land & Cattle Co, Phoenix, Ariz, 53-58; ranch mgr, Ladder Ranch Co. Inc, Roswell, N.Mex, 58-60 and ranch mgr, Lincoln Co. Livestock Co, Ladder Ranch Div, 60- Mil. Serv: Entered as A/S, Navy, 44, released as S.O.M.3/C, 46. Mem: N.Mex. Cattlegrowers Asn.(forest cmt); N.Mex. Farm & Livestock Bur.(Sierra Co. pres). Rel: Protestant. Mailing Add: P.O. Box 792, Truth or Consequences, N.Mex. 87901.

EVANS, BUFORD D
Chmn, Lawrence Co. Dem. Exec. Cmt, Tenn.
b. Lawrence Co, Tenn, 11/30/24; s. Martin C. Evans and Effie Newton E.(deceased); m. 2/1/47 to Geraldine Chapman; c. Terry, Martha, Mack Alan, Sarah, Roger Joe and James David. Educ: Loretto High Sch, Tenn. Polit. & Govt. Pos: Tenn. State Rep, 58-62; chmn, Lawrence Co. Dem. Exec. Cmt, 60- Bus. & Prof. Pos: Owner, Buford Evans Realty & Auction Co, 21 years; pres, Nashville Auction Sch, currently. Mil. Serv: Entered as Pvt, Army, 44, released as S/Sgt, 47, after serv. in Co. H, 85th Mt. Inf. Regt, 10th Mt. Div, Italy, 44-45; Purple Heart. Mem: Tenn. and Nat. Auctioneers Asns; Am. Legion; VFW (state comdr, 54-55). Rel: Church of Christ. Mailing Add: 235 Pulaski St, Lawrenceburg, Tenn. 38464.

EVANS, C.E. 'CHUCK'
Wash. State Rep.
b. 1932; m. to Valene; c. Shirley, Kent, Dennis and Chrie. Educ: Cent. Wash. State Col, B.A. in Sci, 57, M.A. in Sch. Admin, 63; Wash. State Univ, post-grad. study, 66. Polit. & Govt. Pos: Supt, Benton Co. Schs, Wash, 63-68; Wash. State Rep, 69- Bus. & Prof. Pos: Science and math teacher, Kennewick Sch. Dist, 57-63; summers commercial photographer, farmer, gen. laborer, Hanford Proj. and mgr. camera sporting goods dept. Mem: Wash. State Co. Superintendents' Asn.(mem. legis. and budget cmt, 65, secy. state asn, 66, v.pres, 67, pres, 68); S.E. Wash. Co. Superintendents' Asn.(secy, 63-66, chmn, 63-67); Wash. Educ. Asn. (Bldg. rep, local unit, 61-63); Nat. Educ. Asn; Nat. Rural Educ. Asn; Am. Asn. Sch. Adminstr; PTA (v.pres. and secy. treas); Phi Delta Kappa; Boy Scouts (explorer adv. and asst. scout master, 64-68, mem. coun. bd, Blue Mt. Coun. S.E. Wash. and N.E. Ore, 66-68, v.pres, Blue Mt. Coun, 67-68, finance chmn, Ben-Franklin Dist, 66-67, World Jamboree Selection and Host Cmt. chmn, 67, coun. chmn, staff mem. and instr, Seventh Nat. Jamboree, 68); Kiwanis (pres, Columbia Club, 64-67); Mid-Columbia Sci. Fair Asn.(past pres); finance chmn. educ. div, United Crusade, 66-67; chmn. educ. and city govt. div, U.S. Savings Bond Dr, 68; Am. Legion. Mailing Add: 1926 W. Third Ave, Kennewick Wash. 99336.

EVANS, CHARLES BORDOE, JR. R
b. Elko, Nev, 9/6/26; s. Charles Bordoe Evans and Nelle Wilkinson E; m. 10/6/51 to Mary Ellen O'Connor (deceased); c. Susan Mary, Ann Bordoe, Sally Kathleen and Patricia Maureen. Educ: Stanford Univ, B.A, 49; Hastings Col. of the Law, LL.B, 52; Bus. mgr, Hastings Law J. Polit. & Govt. Pos: Mem. adv. bd, Nev. Small Bus. Admin, 61-66; mem. bd, Nev. Agr. Dist. Four, 65-; former chmn, Elko Co. Rep. Cent. Cmt. Bus. & Prof. Pos: Attorney-at-Law, 53- Mil. Serv: Pvt, Air Force, 45. Mem: Elko Co, Nev. and Am. Bar Asns; Am. Col. of Probate Counsel; Am. Trial Lawyers Asn; Rotary; Elks; C. of C. Rel: Episcopal. Legal Res: 189 Court St, Elko, Nev. 89801. Mailing Add: P.O. Box 511, Elko, Nev. 89801. (1967)

EVANS, DANIEL JACKSON R
Gov. of Wash.
b. Seattle, Wash, 10/16/25; s. Daniel Lester Evans and Irma Ida E; m. 6/6/59 to Nancy Ann Bell; c. Daniel Jackson, Mark Lawrence and Bruce McKay. Educ: Univ. Wash, B.S, 48, M.S, 49; Hon. LL.D, Whitworth Col, 66, Seattle Pac. Col, 67, St. Martin's Col, 68, Linfield Col, 69 and Whitman Col, 69; hon. Dr. Eng, Worcester Polytech. Inst, 69. Polit. & Govt. Pos: Wash. State Rep, 56-64, Rep. Floor Leader, Wash. State House of Rep, 61-65; mem. Seattle-King Co. Safety Coun, 60-64; permanent chmn, Wash. Rep. Conv, 62; Gov. of Wash, 64-; chmn. campaign cmt, Nat. Rep. Gov, 65-66, mem. policy cmt, 67-68; mem. exec. bd, Nat. Gov. Conf, 66-67, chmn, Constitutional Rev. Cmt, 66-68; and chmn. cmt. exec. mgt. and fiscal affairs, 69; mem. steering cmt, Educ. Cmn. States, 67-68; mem, Nat. Rep. Coord. Cmt, 67-68; keynote speaker, Rep. Nat. Conv, 68; chmn, West. Gov. Conf, 68-69; del, Rep. Nat. Conv, 68; mem, Nixon's Critical Issues Adv. Cmt. Campaign, 68; mem. exec. cmt, Rep. Gov. Asn, 69; mem, Rep. Gov. Adv. Bd. to the President, 69. Bus. & Prof. Pos: Mem. struct. design team, City of Seattle, 49-51; asst. mgr, Mt-Pac. Assoc. Gen. Contractors, 53-59; partner, Gray & Evans struct. and civil engrs, 59-65. Mil. Serv: Naval Res, 43-46, 51-53, Lt. Mem: Boy Scouts (exec. bd. chief, Seattle Coun, 56-64); Wash. Heart Asn.(pres, 63); Wash. Mem. Struct. Engrs. Asn; Wash. Soc. Prfnl. Engrs; Urban Coalition (steering cmt, 69-). Key Man Award, Seattle Jr. C. of C, 55; Outstanding Freshman Legislator, Wash. House Rep, 57; Human Rights Award, Pac. Northwest Chap, Nat. Asn. Intergroup Rels. Officials, 67; Scales of Justice Award, Nat. Coun. Crime and Delinquency, 68; Silver Beaver Award, Boy Scouts; Award for Serv. to the Profession, Consult. Engrs. Coun, 69. Rel: Congregational. Mailing Add: State Capitol, Olympia, Wash. 98501.

EVANS, DAVID R. R
Chmn, Napa Co. Dem. Cent. Cmt, Calif.
b. Dayton, Ohio, 4/28/32; s. Albert R. Evans and Virginia Moran E; m. 6/14/58 to Nancy Greenhoe; c. Lisa, Katherine, Amy and Laura. Educ: Univ. Dayton, A.B, 54; Univ. Mich, 57-58; Miami Univ, M.A.T, 60; Phi Alpha Theta. Polit. & Govt. Pos: Mem, Napa Co. Dem. Cent. Cmt, Calif, 61-62, chmn, 69-; mem, Calif. State Dem. Cent. Cmt, 62-63 and mem. exec. cmt, 68-; admin. asst, Calif. State Assembly, 67-68. Bus. & Prof. Pos: Teacher, Napa Pub. Schs, 59-65, Napa Jr. Col, 65- Mil. Serv: Entered as Pvt, E-1, Army, 54, released as Cpl, 56, after serv. in Third Armored Div, Ft. Knox, Ky. Mem: Calif. Teachers Asn; Asn. Teachers Calif. Jr. Col. Mailing Add: 4048 Escuela Dr, Napa, Calif. 94558.

EVANS, DAVID VERNON D
b. Holdrege, Nebr, 12/9/41; s. Charles Vernon Evans and Mildred Frost E; single. Educ: Grinnell Col, B.A, 64; Eagleton Inst, Rutgers Univ, M.A, 65; Pa. State Univ, 66-67; Pi Sigma Alpha; Young Dem. Polit. & Govt. Pos: Campaign secy, Whelan for Cong, Nebr. 60; Adams Co. Youth Chmn, Kennedy for Pres, 60; campaign asst, Nebraskans for Morrison, 62; coordinator, Downing for Attorney Gen, 64; del, Dem. State Conv, 64; spec. asst, Gov. Frank Morrison, 65-66; secy, Dem. State Adv. Coun. on Educ, 67-68, chmn, 69-; State Chmn, McCarthy for Pres, 68; del, Dem. Nat. Conv, 68; research analyst, Gov. Frank Licht, R.I, 69- Bus. & Prof. Pos: Instr. polit. sci, Wayne State Col, 67-68; v.pres, Harney Advert, Lincoln, Nebr, 68-69. Mem: Am. Polit. Sci. Asn; Am. Asn. Univ. Prof; Am. Civil Liberties Union; Coun. for Livable World. Rel: Presbyterian. Mailing Add: 83 Medway St, Providence, R.I. 02906.

EVANS, EARL WESLEY R
Chmn, Ballard Co. Rep. Cmt, Ky.
b. Barlow, Ky, 8/17/06; s. John Wesley Evans and Carrie Lancaster E; m. 2/21/36 to Lawanda Williamson; c. Ellen (Mrs. Phillip Noth) and John E. Educ: Georgetown Col, 1 year; Bowling Green Col. Commerce, B.S, 26. Polit. & Govt. Pos: Mayor, Barlow, Ky, 40-44; chmn, Ballard Co. Rep. Cmt, Ky, 48- Bus. & Prof. Pos: Elec. cmnr, Ballard Co, 40-44; dir, Citizens State Bank, 60- Mem: Barlow Lions Club (treas, 50-54); C. of C; Ballard Co. Country Club (dir, 67-); Axe Lake Hunting & Fishing Club. Rel: Baptist; Treas, Barlow First Baptist Church, 40-, Deacon, 44- Mailing Add: Barlow, Ky. 42024.

EVANS, EDWARD T, JR. R
Md. State Del.
b. Frostburg, Md, 10/15/28; married. Educ: Allegany Co. pub. schs. Polit. & Govt. Pos: Md. State Del, 64-; Allegany Co. Rep. State Cent. Cmt. Bus. & Prof. Pos: Emp, Baltimore & Ohio R.R. Mil. Serv: U.S. Army Sig. Corps. Mem: S. Cumberland Bus. & Civic Asn; Mason; Shrine; Tall Cedars of Lebanon. Mailing Add: 1315 Kentucky Ave, Cumberland, Md. 21503. (1967)

EVANS, ERNESTINE DURAN D
Secy. of State, N.Mex.
b. Alamosa, Colo, 9/5/17; d. Gilberto Evans Duran and Maria G. Martinez D; m. 4/3/39 to Alcadio Griego; m. second time 6/24/45 to Seth L. Evans; c. Stanley G. Educ: Highlands Univ, 36-40. Polit. & Govt. Pos: N.Mex. State Rep, 40-42; secy, N.Mex. Hwy. Dept, 42-43; admin. secy. to Gov. of N.Mex, 59-60 & 63-66; off. mgr, Legis. Coun, 61-62; Secy. of State, N.Mex, 66- Bus. & Prof. Pos: Teacher, elem. sch, N.Mex, 36-40; adminstr, Bruns Gen. Hosp, 43-45; head royalty div, N.Mex. Land Off, 45-52; off. mgr, Bd. Educ. Finance, Santa Fe, 53-58. Mem: Defense Adv. Cmt. on Women in Serv, 66- Legal Res: 413 Calle de la Paz, Santa Fe, N.Mex. 87501. Mailing Add: State Capitol, Santa Fe, N.Mex. 87501.

EVANS, FOSTER D
b. Salt Lake City, Utah, 1/16/15; s. George F. Evans (deceased) and Susannah Lake Hull E.(deceased); m. to Cerda Donovan; c. one daughter, Mrs. Nancy Borofsky and one granddaughter, Nadine Borofsky. Educ: Brigham Young Univ, B.S, 36; Univ. Chicago, Ph.D, 41; Sigma Xi; Sigma Chi. Polit. & Govt. Pos: Mem, N.Mex. State Dem. Cent. Cmt, 62-66; N.Mex. State Rep, 63-66; chmn, Gov. Exec. Cmt. Ment. Health Planning, 63-67; mem, State Judicial Syst. Study Cmt, 65-66; mem, State Constitutional Rev. Cmn, 65-66. Bus. & Prof. Pos: Instr. physics, Univ. Wis, 40-41; asst. prof, Univ. Colo, 41-46; theoret. physics div, Los Alamos Sci. Lab, 46- Publ: Technical articles in Physical Review, Journal of Fluid Mechanics and American Journal of Physics. Mem: Am. Phys. Soc; Am. Asn. Physics Teachers; AAAS. Award for Outstanding Contributions in the Promotion of Human Rights from UN, 65. Legal Res: 196 Paseo Penasco, Los Alamos, N.Mex. 87544. Mailing Add: P.O. Box 1663, Los Alamos, N.Mex. 87544.

EVANS, FRANK EDWARD D
U.S. Rep, Colo.
b. Pueblo, Colo, 9/6/23; s. Frank Edward Evans (deceased) and Mildred Hoag E; m. 4/5/52 to Eleanor Trefz; c. Peter, Susan, Frances and Charles. Educ: Pomona Col, Calif, 41-43; Denver Univ, B.A. and LL.B, 46-49. Polit. & Govt. Pos: Colo. State Rep, 61-65; U.S. Rep, Third Cong. Dist, Colo, 65- Bus. & Prof. Pos: Chmn. of bd, Ark. Valley Bank, Pueblo, Colo, 53- Mil. Serv: Entered as Cadet, Naval Res, 43, released as Ens, 46. Mem: Am, Colo. and Pueblo Co. Bar Asns. Rel: Presbyterian. Legal Res: Pueblo, Colo. Mailing Add: 4935 Quebec St. N.W, Washington, D.C. 20016.

EVANS, HAZEL ATKINSON D
Dem. Nat. Committeewoman
b. Atlanta, Ga, 8/16/31; d. Alex Pierce Robert and Hazel Thomas R; div; 2nd m. 11/30/68 to Robert Winfield Evans; c. W. Reed Talley, Jr. and Alex R. Talley. Educ: Wash. Sem, Atlanta, Ga, 45-49; Marjorie Webster Jr. Col, Wash, D.C, 49-51; Beta Sigma Phi. Polit. & Govt. Pos: Pres, Manatee Co. Dem. Woman's Club, Fla, 57-60; v.chmn, Manatee Co. Dem. Exec. Cmt, 62-64; state secy, Young Dem. Clubs of Fla, 62-63 and state v.pres, 63-64; del, Dem. Nat. Conv, 64 & 68, mem. credentials cmt, 68; state Dem. committeewoman, Pinellas Co, Fla; Dem. Nat. Committeewoman, Fla, 68- Mem: State adv. on women's activities, Nat. Found. of March of Dimes, 57-61; bd. of dirs, Fla. Heart Asn, 62-67; Fla. Ment. Health Asn, 63-64 and Pinellas Co. United Fund, 67-; pres, Suncoast Heart Asn, 65-66 and chmn. of bd, 66-67. U.S. Sen. George Smathers Award, 62, Franklin D. Roosevelt Award, 63 and President's Awards, 63 & 64, Young Dem. Clubs of Fla; Am. Heart Asn. Meritorious Serv. Awards, 60, 64 & 66. Rel: Baptist. Mailing Add: 1146 41st Ave. N.E, St. Petersburg, Fla. 33703.

EVANS, HENRY NELSON R
b. Dummerston, Vt, 4/22/04; m. to Olive L. Gray; c. Two. Educ: Dummerston pub. schs. Polit. & Govt. Pos: Former road cmnr, Vt; selectman, Putney, Vt, 57 and former moderator; Vt. State Rep, 61-69. Bus. & Prof. Pos: Farmer; carpenter. Mil. Serv: Nat. Guard, 20-32. Mem: Grange; trustee, Farm Bur; PTA; master, Subordinate Grange; master, Windham Co. Pomona Grange; dist. dep, Vt. State Grange; v.pres, Windham Co. Farm Bur; Windham Co. Ext. Serv. Adv. Comm. Rel: Congregational. Mailing Add: RFD. 2, Putney, Vt. 05346. (1967)

EVANS, HOWARD B. D
Chmn, Crane Co. Dem. Party, Tex.
b. Roscoe, Tex, 4/7/14; s. Henry D. Evans and Vera Buford E; m. 5/22/38 to Dorothy Coe; c. Jerald Coe. Educ: Kress High Sch, Tex, 29-33. Polit. & Govt. Pos: Precinct chmn, Tex. Dem. Party, 52-58; chmn, Crane Co. Dem. Party, 58- Mem: Baseball cmnr, Crane Co; pres. and organizer, Crane Co. Little League; pres. and mem. bd, Crane Mem. Hosp; mem. bd. dirs. summer youth prog, Lions. Howard Evans Day proclaimed in 1968 for 20 years outstanding serv. to Crane Co. Little League, with trophy. Rel: Methodist; mem. bd. dirs. Legal Res: 609 23rd St, Crane, Tex. 79731. Mailing Add: P.O. Box 583, Crane, Tex. 79731.

EVANS, HOWARD DAVID D
Chmn, Appanoose Co. Dem. Cent. Cmt, Iowa
b. Mystic, Iowa, 8/24/91; s. Lee Edgar Evans and Minnie Haines E; m. 2/25/14 to Jessie Lee Long; c. Byron Long, Enid (Mrs. Jack Beattie) and Claud Richard. Educ: Mystic High Sch, 11. Polit. & Govt. Pos: Clerk Dist. Court, Centerville, Iowa, 32-40; chmn, Appanoose Co. Dem. Cent. Cmt, 59- Bus. & Prof. Pos: Farmer and livestock shipper, Mystic, 14-28; auto and machinery dealer, Centerville, -51; owner, real estate agency, 51- Mem: Elks; Mason; Rotary Int. Rel: Methodist. Mailing Add: Country Club Rd, Centerville, Iowa 52544.

EVANS, HUBERT CAROL D
Chmn, Gladwin Co. Dem. Cmt, Mich.
b. Beaverton, Mich, 12/25/21; s. A.C.P. Evans and Edna E. Walke; m. 10/12/46 to Delaine A. Boske; c. Mark Brian. Educ: Univ. Mich, 56; Mich. State Univ, 57; Cent. Mich. Univ, 58. Polit. & Govt. Pos: Councilman, Gladwin, Mich, 61; cand. for State Senate to fill vacancy, 28th Sen. Dist. and Constitutional Conv, 28th Sen. Dist, 61; chmn, Gladwin Co. Dem. Cmt, 61-; cand, U.S. House Rep, Tenth Dist, 62, 64 & 66; treas, Tenth Cong. Dist. Dem. Cmt, 67-; alternate del, Dem. Nat. Conv, 68; mayor pro-tem and mem. police cmt, Gladwin, 69. Mil. Serv: Entered as Pvt, Army, 42, released as Pfc, 45, after serv. in 49th Combat Engr, European-African-Mid.East. Theatres, 43-45; Good Conduct Medal; Am. Theatre Serv. Medal; European, African, Mid. East. Theatre Medals with Five Bronze Stars. Mem: United Mine Workers of Am.(mem. bargaining cmt, Local 12075, Dist. 50, 68); Mich. Munic. League. Rel: Lutheran. Mailing Add: 529 N. Antler, Gladwin, Mich. 48624.

EVANS, JAMES LARKIN D
Mem, Calif. Dem. State Cent. Cmt.
b. Mallakaoff, Tex, 8/10/21; s. Frank Lewis Evans and Clyde Kennedy E; m. 11/29/68 to Arlene Ann Palczyk; c. Janice Louise, Larry Ray Joyce and James L, Jr. Educ: Mallakaoff High Sch, Tex, grad, 36. Polit. & Govt. Pos: Campaign chmn. of various Dem. cand, 56-64; chmn, Co. Dem. Cent. Cmt, Calif, 58-60; mem. civil and constitutional rights cmt, Attorney Gen. Cmn, 59-62; mem. and dir, 28th Agr. Dist. Asn, 59-63; sgt. at arms, Calif. Dem. Del, 60; mem, San Bernardino City Civil Serv. Cmn, 60-62; mem, Calif. Dem. State Cent. Cmt, 68- Bus. & Prof. Pos: Locomotive fireman and engr, San Bernardino, 44-64; coach, mgr. and founder, East Baseline Little League, 53-57; Calif. state legis. dir, United Transportation Union, Sacramento, 64- Mem: mem. bd. of dirs, Arrowhead United Fund, 58-62, chmn, budget cmt, 60-61 and labor cmt, 62; Mason; Elks; Roofers Local; Teamsters; Operating Engrs. Local; BRT; Brotherhood of Locomotive Firemen and Enginemen. Rel: Protestant. Legal Res: 3905 Valencia, San Bernardino, Calif. 92404. Mailing Add: 1127 11th St, Room 521, Sacramento, Calif. 95814.

EVANS, JAMES WELDON R
Chmn, Terry Co. Rep. Party, Tex.
b. Post, Tex, 2/14/26; s. Charles Cranfil Evans; m. 7/28/50 to Janelle Jo Turner. Educ: Tex. Tech. Col, B.B.A, 50; Tech. Mgt. Asn; Saddle Tramps. Polit. & Govt. Pos: Chmn, Terry Co. Rep. Party, Tex, 60-; alternate del, Rep. Nat. Conv, 68. Bus. & Prof. Pos: With Pan Am. Petroleum Corp, 50- Mil. Serv: Entered as Pvt, Marines, 43, released as Cpl, 45, after serv. in 3rd Marine Div, Pac. Theater; Maj, 9827th Air Res. Squadron, Air Force Res, at present; Asiatic-Pac. Ribbon with Two Stars; Naval Unit Citation; Presidential Unit Citation; Victory, Am. Theater and Air Force Res. Ribbons. Mem: Pres, Pan Am. Employees Asn; Am. Legion; Brownfield Optimist Club; Tex. Tech. Alumni Asn; Farm Bur; Boys Club; bd. mem, Boy Scout Troop Cmt. Rel: Baptist. Legal Res: 1204 E. Warren, Brownfield, Tex. 79316. Mailing Add: P.O. Box 3, Brownfield, Tex. 79316.

EVANS, JEFF W. D
b. Lyman, Miss; 10/20/15; married. Polit. & Govt. Pos: Former Miss. State Rep. Bus. & Prof. Pos: Real estate broker. Mem: Moose; VFW. Rel: Methodist. Mailing Add: 420 Champlin St, Handsboro, Gulfport, Miss. 39501. (1967)

EVANS, JOHN F. R
Chmn, Champaign Co. Rep. Exec. Cmt, Ohio
b. Mechanicsburg, Ohio, 7/3/18; s. Earl E. Evans (deceased) and Florence France E.(deceased); m. 7/1/41 to Ruth Iloh Rasmussen; c. Jane E, Margaret A. and John E. Educ: Ohio State Univ, 37-38. Polit. & Govt. Pos: Pres, Mechanicsburg Bd. Educ, Ohio, 51-55; exec. secy, Ohio Rep. Farm Div, 54-; v.chmn, Champaign Co. Rep. Exec. Cmt, 57-59, chmn, 59-; mem, Ohio expositions Cmn, 64-; mem, Champaign Co. Elec. Bd, 66- Mem: Ohio Shorthorns Breeders Asn.(bd. dirs, 50-66, pres, 59, v.pres, 66-); Ohio Jr. C. of C. (v.pres, 49-50); U.S. Jr. C. of C.(chmn, 51-52); Urbana Area C. of C.(bd. dirs 69-). Mailing Add: RFD 2, Mechanicsburg, Ohio 43044.

EVANS, JOHN MARION R
b. Sumter, S.C, 1/15/22; s. John Lynwood Evans and Mildred Boone E; m. 9/12/42 to Elizabeth Dingle; c. John Dickey, Ingrid Elaine and Henry Pitts. Educ: Presby. Col, Clinton, S.C. Polit. & Govt. Pos: Mem, Sumter Co. Planning Cmn, Va, 61-62, secy, 62-63 and chmn, 63-64; v.chmn, Cmn. for Higher Educ, 65-; Sumter Co. Rep. Campaign Dir; adv. to Cent. Adv. Cmt; former mem, S.C. State Rep. Cmt; exec. dir, S.C. Rep. Party, 67-68; exec. asst. to Sen. Strom Thurmond, S.C, 69- Bus. & Prof. Pos: Pres, John Evans Sales Co, 52-56; pres, Evans Realty Co, 56- and Broad Street Realty Co, 64- Mil. Serv: Entered as Pvt, Air Force, 42, released as S/Sgt, 45, after serv. with 1st Air Force. Mem: Mason; Shrine; Jester; former bd. mem, Kiwanis Int; Am. Legion; State & Nat. Asn. of Real Estate Bds; past pres, Co. Bd. of Realtors; past mem. bd. of dirs, Am. Red Cross for Sumter Co; past v.pres. and mem. of adv. bd, Sumter Chap. Salvation Army. Rel: Methodist. Mailing Add: 8512 Canterberry Dr, Annandale, Va. 20003.

EVANS, LEE EARL R
Maine State Rep.
b. Monson, Maine, 1/14/05; s. John Bernard Evans and Maude Johnson E; m. 7/15/29 to Avis Eleanor Pease. Educ: Baypath, Springfield, Mass, 1 year. Polit. & Govt. Pos: Selectman, Freedom, Maine, 7 years; Maine State Rep, 63- Mem: Rotary; Odd Fellows; Mason (32°); Shrine; Grange (6°). Rel: Congregational. Mailing Add: Route 1, Freedom, Maine 04941.

EVANS, MARTHA WRIGHT D
N.C. State Sen.
b. Philadelphia, Pa; d. William John Wright and Martha Hemphill W; m. to Charles H. Evans. Educ: Boston Univ, B.S; Columbia Univ; La Fayette Col, 57; Sch. for Advanced Int. Studies, John Hopkins Univ; Duke Univ, 60; St. Louis Univ, 61; Am. Christian Palestine Cmt. fel. for study in Middle East, 56; Nat. Manpower Cmn. grant to attend seminar at Arden House, Columbia Univ, 58; Japan Soc. & Asian Found. scholarship, Duke Univ, 58; Carnegie Found. scholarship grant for study at World Affairs Center, N.Y.C, 59. Polit. & Govt. Pos: Designated by U.S. Conf. of Mayors as first woman del. to Int. Union of Local Authorities in Rome, Italy, 55; mem. U.S. Army Adv. Cmt; mem, Charlotte City Coun, N.C, 55 & 57; N.C. State Rep, 63-65; N.C. State Sen, 65- Mem: Am. Asn. of Univ. Women; Am. Cancer Soc; N.C. Coun. Women's Civic Orgns; Mecklenburg Co. Tuberc. & Health Asn; Nat. Conf. of Christians & Jews; League of Women Voters; United Appeal Chmn, Residential Div, 60; leader, coordinator, troop consultant, Girl Scouts; hon. mem, Hadassah. Charlotte's First Woman of the Year, Pi Phi Chap. Omega Psi Phi Fraternity, 61; Acknowledgment award by Session of the Myers Park Presby. Church. Rel: Presbyterian; Orphanage Rep, Pastor's Aide, Teacher, Circle Chmn, Myers Park Presbyterian Church. Mailing Add: 2441 Hassel Place, Charlotte, N.C. 28209.

EVANS, MELVIN H. R
Gov, Virgin Islands
b. V.I, 1917; m. to Phyllis Anderson; c. Four. Educ: Howard Univ, grad. magna cum laude, 40; Howard Univ. Col. Med, M.D, 44; Univ. Calif, Berkeley, Sch. Pub. Health, M.P.H, 67. Polit. & Govt. Pos: Asst. chief munic. physician, St. Croix, V.I, 50-51, chief munic. physician, 51-54; asst. cmnr. of health, V.I, 51-54, cmnr. of health, 59-67; dir. of health serv, St. Croix, 54-56 & 57-59; Gov, V.I, 69- Bus. & Prof. Pos: Intern, Harlem Hosp, N.Y.C, 44-45; physician in charge, Frederiksted Mem. Hosp, St. Croix, 45-48 & 50-; U.S. Pub. Health Serv. sr. asst. surgeon stationed as teaching fel. in med, Howard Univ, 48-50; fel. cardiol, Johns Hopkins Hosp, Md, 56-57; private practice, St. Croix, 67- Mailing Add: The Capitol, Charlotte Amalie, V.I. 00801.

EVANS, NANCY WHITTEMORE D
b. Boston, Mass, 5/5/90; d. James F. Sheldon and Marion Whittemore S; m. 12/11/44 to Brig. Gen. E.A. Evans; c. Nancy (Mrs. Maury) and Bruce Edwards. Educ: George Wash. Univ; Univ. Miami. Polit. & Govt. Pos: Mem, War Dept, Mil. Intel, C.Z, 41-42; mem. staff, Off. Censorship, Miami, Fla. 42-43 & D.C, 43-45; vol. worker, Dem. Campaigns, Fla, 52; chmn, Women's Div, Dade Co. Vol. for Stevenson, 55-56; co-chmn, Women's Div, Dade Co. Dem. Campaigns, 56; alternate del, Dem. Nat. Conv, 56 & 64 and del, 60; organizer, Dem. Women's Club Dade Co, 57, pres, 57-58; v.pres, Fourth Cong. Dist, Dem. Women's Club, Fla, 57-60, pres, 58-60, parliamentarian, 60-68; Dem. exec. committeewoman, Dist. 35, Dade Co, 58; organizer, Dollars for Dem, Dade Co, 58; co-chmn, Jefferson-Jackson Day Dinner, Miami, 58; mem, White House Bi-Partisan Conf. and chmn, regional conf, For. Aspects of U.S. Nat. Security, 58; organizer, Dem. Women's Club South Dade, 59; mem, Nat. Dem. Women's Campaign Conf, D.C, 58, 62 & 66; mem, Defense Adv. Cmt. on Women in Serv, 65-; asst. chmn, Women's Div, Johnson Campaign for Fla; co-chmn, Women's Div, Kennedy-Johnson Campaign for Fla. Bus. & Prof. Pos: Assoc. mem, Kendall-Perrine Bd. Realtors. Mem: Am. Artists Prfnl. League (past pres, 67); Florence Crittenden Homes Asn; Women's Div, Miami-Dade Co. C. of C; Mil. Affairs Cmt, Fla. C. of C, 66; United Fund Worker, Dade Co; ROA (past pres, ladies) Miami City Beautification Cmt, 59-63; Miami Fine Arts Cmn, 58; Calif. State Soc, D.C.(v.pres, 48-50); Red Cross (bd. dirs, Dade Co. Chap); Variety Children's Hosp (womens cmt). Rel: Episcopal. Mailing Add: 13291 Old Cutler Rd, Miami, Fla. 33156.

EVANS, RAYMOND T. R
b. 8/13/28; m. to Gwendolyn; c. Gail, Sharon, Raymond, Jr. and Carol. Educ: Howard High Sch. Polit. & Govt. Pos: Del. State Rep, 67-69; pres, Price Run Commun. Coun; del, Rep. Nat. Conv, 68. Bus. & Prof. Pos: Mgr, package store-bar; Wilmington Camera Shop. Mem: Kingswood Men's Club; treas, Usher Union of Wilmington; v.pres, Howard High Sch. Athletic Boosters; chmn, S.Price Run Serv. Center. Rel: Methodist; secy, Usher Bd, Mt. Carmel Methodist Church, Wilmington, Del. Mailing Add: 2107 N. Locust St, Wilmington, Del. 18802. (1967)

EVANS, WILLIAM DENT, JR. D
Mem, Fairmont City Firemen's Civil Serv. Cmn, W.Va.
b. Fairmont, W.Va, 7/6/07; s. William Dent Evans and Ora Kinsey; single. Educ: Fairmont State Col, 24-25; W.Va. Univ, 27-30; Sigma Delta Chi; Mountain. Polit. & Govt. Pos: Pub. rels. consult, Nat. Bituminous Coal Cmn, Wash, D.C, 36-37; mem, Mayor's Adv. Cmt, Fairmont, W.Va, 47-50; alternate del, Dem. Nat. Conv, 52, 56, 64 and del, 68; mem, Fairmont City Firemen's Civil Serv. Cmn. and Pricketts Fort State Park Cmn, currently. Bus. & Prof. Pos; With newspapers in Morgantown, Clarksburg, Martinsburg and Wheeling, W.Va, since starting as reporter on, Fairmont Times, 23; mgr. ed. and sports ed, Fairmont Times, 47-59, ed, 59- Mem: United Press Int. Eds. Asn; Foot-

ball Writers of Am; U.S. Basketball Writers Asn; South. Conf. Sports Writers Asn, W.Va. Sports Writers Asn; Elks; Moose; Charleston Press Club; Touchdown Club; Montmarte Club; Gr. Fairmont Develop. Asn. Rel: Presbyterian. Legal Res: 509 Fairmont Ave, Fairmont, W.Va. 26555. Mailing Add: The Times, Fairmont, W.Va. 26555.

EVANS, WILLIAM THOMAS D
Speaker-Pro-Tem, Md. House of Del.
b. Newton Falls, Ohio, 2/14/25; s. William David Evans and Florence Greggs E; m. 10/9/43 to Mary Smith; c. William Robert, James Carroll and Thomas Lee. Educ: Univ. Baltimore, LL.B, 52; Phi Beta Gamma. Polit. & Govt. Pos: Magistrate, Baltimore Co, Md, 60-62, mem, Planning Bd, 62-63; Md. State Del, 65-, coun. to Ways and Means Cmt, Md. House of Del, 65-67, Speaker-Pro-Tem, 67- Bus. & Prof. Pos: Lawyer, 52- Mil. Serv: Entered as Pvt, Army Air Force, 43, released as 1st Lt, 46, after serv. in Pac. Theatre, 45-46. Mem: Md. State and Baltimore Co. Bar Asns; Mason; Moose; VFW. Rel: Protestant. Mailing Add: 7824 St. Gregory Dr, Dundalk, Md. 21222.

EVARTS, KATHARINE AVERY R
b. Oyster Bay, N.Y, 10/29/98; d. Edwin Denison Morgan and Elizabeth Moran M; m. to Jeremiah Maxwell Evarts, div; c. Mary (Mrs. Steele), Maxwell, Katharine (Mrs. Albert W. Merck), Elizabeth (Mrs. Casimir de Rham, Jr) and Jasper Morgan. Educ: Merchants & Bankers Bus. Sch, N.Y.C; Radcliffe Col, studies hist. Polit. & Govt. Pos: Former mem, Kent Park and Recreation Cmn; Conn. State Rep, Kent, 59-67; former mem. and v.chmn, Kent Town Planning Cmn, and chmn, 61; pres, Litchfield Co. Rep. Women's Asn, 62-63; mem, Kent Town Rep. Cmt, currently, v.chmn, 66-69; chmn, 50th Anniversary Fund Drive, State of Conn. Child Welfare Asn, currently, bd. dirs, several years. Mem: Grange; Litchfield Co. Farm Bur.(bd. dirs, 65-66); League of Women Voters until 65, pres, Kent League, 56-59; trustee, Housatonic Psychiat. Asn. Rel: Congregational; Mem, Bd. Deacons, 1st Congregational Church, Kent, currently. Mailing Add: Cobble Rd, Kent, Conn. 06757.

EVE, ARTHUR O. D
N.Y. State Assemblyman
b. N.Y.C, 3/23/33; s. Arthur B. Eve and Beatrice Clark E; m. 6/3/56 to Lee Constance Bowles; c. Arthur, Jr. and Leecia R. Educ: W.Va. State Col, 50-53; Erie Co. Tech. Inst, 57; Canisius Col, evening sch, 62-63. Polit. & Govt. Pos: Founder and v.pres, Masten Dist. Young Dem, N.Y, 58; committeeman, 13th Ward Dem. Cmt, 60-, v.chmn, 60-62 and chmn, 62-; N.Y. State Assemblyman, 143rd Dist, 67- Bus. & Prof. Pos: Engr, City of Buffalo Civil Serv, 59-; ed. and pres, Buffalo Challenger News Weekly, 62- Mil. Serv: Entered as Pvt, Army Signal Corps, 53, released as Cpl, 55, after serv. in Germany. Mem: Amvets; NAACP; Urban League; United Auto Workers. Basketball: All city and state, Miami, Fla, 48; All CIAA, West Va. State Col, 52; All army, Germany, 54. Rel: Episcopal; Vestryman. Mailing Add: 14 Celtic Place, Buffalo, N.Y. 14208. (1967)

EVENSEN, ROBERT EDWARD R
b. Gardner, Mass, 10/27/23; s. Ernest Andrew Evensen and Lora W. E; m. 5/30/47 to Violette Beaumier; c. Candace and Sonya. Educ: Boston Univ, 41; Sigma Alpha Epsilon. Polit. & Govt. Pos: Former Ga. State Rep. Bus. & Prof. Pos: Gen. ins. agent; mem, Million Dollar Round Table, 65. Mil. Serv: Entered as Pvt, Army, 43, released as Pfc, 46, after serv. in Eighth Armored Div, ETO. Mem: Mason; Shrine Mounted Patrol; Leaders Asn. Rookie of the Year, New Eng. Life Ins, 65. Rel: Unitarian. Mailing Add: 10 Blueberry Hill Rd, Wilbraham, Mass. 01095.

EVENSON, MARVIN ARNOLD DFL
Chmn, Seventh Cong. Dist. Dem-Farmer-Labor Party, Minn.
b. Rutland, N.Dak, 9/9/12; s. Edwin S. Evenson and Hannah Johnson E; m. 3/17/38 to Donna Joan Erickson; c. Edwin Kent, Karen Joyce (Mrs. Gast), Susan Mary (Mrs. Henry) and Pamela Mae. Educ: Ellendale Normal and Indust. Sch, N.Dak, Teacher's Cert, 32; Interstate Bus. Col, Fargo, 34. Polit. & Govt. Pos: Mem. and local officer, Sargent Co. Young Dem, N.Dak, 33-34; mem, exec. cmt, Sargent Co. Dem. Party, 34-38; mem, Yellowstone Co. Dem. Party, Mont, 41-45; mem, Dakota Co. Dem-Farmer-Labor Party, Minn, 46-48; finance dir, Ninth Dist. Dem-Farmer-Labor Party, 50-56, chmn, 56-58; del, Dem. Nat. Conv, 60 & 68; v.chmn, Seventh Cong. Dist. Dem-Farmer-Labor Party, Minn, 62-68, chmn, 68- Bus. & Prof. Pos: Sch. teacher, Sargent Co, N.Dak, 32-34; off. and yard clerk, West Fargo Stockyards Co, 36-40; off. mgr, Billings Pub. Stockyards, Mont, 40-45; br. mgr, Farmers Union Livestock Asn, 45, gen. mgr, S. St. Paul, Minn, 46-48; sales rep, various co, N.Dak. and Minn, 48- Mem: Mason (past master, Moorhead Lodge); Eastern Star (past patron, Moorhead Chap). Rel: Lutheran. Mailing Add: 914 S. 17th St, Moorhead, Minn. 56560.

EVERETT, ANNABELLE SMITH 'BELLE' D
Dem. Nat. Committeewoman, Del.
b. Marydel, Md, 10/15/98; d. Frank S. Smith and Mary E. Bickling S; m. 11/4/16 to Levi L. Everett, Jr; c. Franklin L. and T. Marvel. Polit. & Govt. Pos: State treas, Del, 59-67; Dem. nat. committeewoman, currently; v.chmn, Kent Co. Dem. Party, 18 years, state v.chmn. and mem. state cmt, 8 years; organizer and pres, Kent Co. Women's Dem. Club, 7 years; mem. bd, State Dept. Welfare, 10 years; del, Dem. Nat. Conv, 68. Bus. & Prof. Pos: Former bd. mem, Childrens Bur, Del. Mem: Past mem, Cancer Crusade. Rel: Methodist; mem. bd. and treas, Kenton Methodist Church. Mailing Add: Kenton, Del. 19977. (1967)

EVERETT, DONN JAMES R
Kans. State Rep.
b. Emporia, Kans, 4/29/29; s. Harry Willard Everett and Nelle Batchelor E; m. 6/29/56 to Fredrica Voiland; c. Brinton, Bradford, Brooke, Brian and Brock. Educ: Col. Emporia, 47-49; Univ. Kans, A.B, 51; Kans. Univ, LL.B, 56; Sigma Alpha Epsilon. Polit. & Govt. Pos: Asst. city attorney, Manhattan, Kans, 58-63, city cmnr, 68-69; co. attorney, Riley Co, 64-68; Kans. State Rep, 69- Mil. Serv: Entered as Pvt, Marines, 51, released as 1st Lt, 53, after serv. in First Marine Div, Korea, 52-53; Marine Corps Res; Bronze Star; Combat V Medal. Mem: Am. Travelers Asn; Judicature Soc; Am. and Kans. Bar Asns; Elks; Am. Legion; VFW; pres, Manhattan C. of C, 68. Distinguished Service Award, City of Manhattan, 63. Rel: Episcopal. Legal Res: 1730 Fairview, Manhattan, Kans. 66502. Mailing Add: P.O. Box 816, Manhattan, Kans. 66502.

EVERETT, NATHAN CLARK, SR. D
Miss. State Rep.
b. Newton, Co, Miss; 12/2/00; married. Polit. & Govt. Pos: Miss. State Rep, 44-48 & 68-; former chancery clerk. Bus. & Prof. Pos: Hardware bus. Mem: Odd Fellows; Rebekah; Elks; Rotary. Rel: Baptist. Mailing Add: 812 Griffin St, Moss Point, Jackson Co, Miss. 39563.

EVERETT, RAYMOND LEO 'RAY' R
Ariz. State Rep.
b. Clarksdale, Miss, 8/3/38; s. Welborn Leo Everett and Dorothy Mackey E; m. 12/22/68 to Jan Margaret Hyde. Educ: Miss. Col. and Univ. Miss, 1 year; Ariz. State Univ, B.A, 64, M.A, 66; grad. study, Ariz. State Univ, North. Ariz. Univ, Univ. St. Andrews and Cambridge Univ; Young Rep; Ariz. State Univ. Forum. Polit. & Govt. Pos: Campaign mgr, Sam Steiger for Cong. Cmt, 64; state co-chmn, Youth for Goldwater, 64; state chmn, Col. Young Rep. of Ariz, 64-65; precinct committeeman, Rep. Party of Ariz, 64-66 & 68-; chmn, Yavapai Young Rep. League, 65-66; nat. committeeman, Ariz. Young Rep. League, 66; Ariz. State Rep, 69- Bus. & Prof. Pos: Comput. programmer, U.S. Army, Ft. Devens, Mass, 59-61; IBM machine operator, Maricopa Co. Data Processing Center, Phoenix, Ariz, 61-63; govt. teacher, Prescott High Sch, Ariz, 64-; area secy, Am. Inst. for Foreign Study, Greenwich, Conn, 68-69. Mil. Serv: Entered as Pvt, Army, 59, released Sp-4, 61, after serv. in Army Security Agency; 2 Good Conduct Medals; Sharpshooter. Publ: Rhodesia: A New Prospect in Africa, Craigney, 68; Arizona Constitution and Government, privately publ, 68. Mem: Am. Polit. Sci. Asn; Nat. Asn. Soc. Stud; AF&AM. Outstanding Col. Young Rep. Man of Year, 65; Young Rep. Col. Chmn. Award; DECA Free Enterprize Award; Community Leader Award. Rel: Southern Baptist. Mailing Add: P.O. Box 1089, Prescott, Ariz. 86301.

EVERETT, REYNOLDS MELVILLE R
Asst. Attorney Gen, Henry Co, Ill.
b. Atkinson, Ill, 8/1/07; s. Melville M. Everett and Maude Reynolds E; m. 10/23/35 to Annette Young; c. Reynolds M, Jr. Educ: Knox Col, 24-26; Univ. Ill, LL.B, 26-29; Delta Sigma Rho; Zeta Psi; Gamma Eta Gamma. Polit. & Govt. Pos: States attorney, Henry Co, Ill, 44-52; asst. attorney gen, Ill, 53-60 & 69-; chmn, Henry Co. Rep. Party, Ill, 56- Bus. & Prof. Pos: Mem. bd. gov, Ill. State Bar Asn, 60-63. Mem: AF&AM; Elks; Consistory; Shrine; Odd Fellows. Rel: Congregational. Legal Res: 412 N.W. Fourth St, Galva, Ill. 61434. Mailing Add: Yocum Bank Bldg, Galva, Ill. 61434.

EVERHART, ELMER REECE R
b. Lexington, N.C, 11/1/00; s. Riley Everhart and Mary McCrary E; m. 11/24/26 to Ella Mae Sink; c. Doris (Mrs. Gaines Whitley), Ann (Mrs. Reid Clodfelter) and Pat (Mrs. Melvin Palmer). Educ: Catawba Col, 17-19. Polit. & Govt. Pos: Coop. weather observer, U.S. Weather Bur, 41-66; asst. clerk, Davidson Co. Superior Court, N.C, 46-57, clerk, 57-58 & 66-; crew leader, Census Bur, 59, supply clerk, 60; chmn, Davidson Co. Rep. Exec. Cmt, 64-68. Bus. & Prof. Pos: Farmer, 20-; prin, Arnold High Sch, 20-21; rental mgr, Realty Bond Co, 35-36. Mem: Grange; Civitan; Rotary. Rel: United Church of Christ. Mailing Add: Route 8, Lexington, N.C. 27292.

EVERLY, J. DONALD R
b. Kingwood, W.Va, 11/28/10; s. J. Ami Everly and Lillie Wolfe E; m. 9/14/31 to Glendolyn Morey; c. Mary Elizabeth (Mrs. John A. Hull) and John Donald, Jr. Educ: W.Va. Univ, 1½ years; Lewis Hotel Training Sch, grad; Phi Delta Theta. Polit. & Govt. Pos: Mem. and pres, Preston Co. Bd. of Educ, W.Va, 46-66; del, Rep. Nat. Conv, 68; mem, Gov. Task Force for State, Regional and Local Planning, currently. Bus. & Prof. Pos: Mgr. and owner, The Inn Hotel, 30-47; clerk, supt, gen. mgr. and v.pres, W.Va. North. R.R. Co, 42-; pres, Bowyer and Everly, Inc, 47-64; secy-treas, Kingwood Farm and Garden Store, 60- Mil. Serv: Entered as Pvt, W.Va. Nat. Guard, 27, released as Sgt, 41, after serv. in 201st Inf; Nat. Guard Bur. Guardsman Award. Mem: Bd. dirs, Am. Short Line R.R. Asn; pres, Kingwood Area C. of C; pres, Preston Co. Planning Cmn; chmn, Preston Co. Bd. of Health; mem. bd. dirs, Preston Bus. Develop. Corp; Eagles (past state pres). Pres. Award and Distinguished Serv. Award, W.Va. Sch. Bd. Asn. Rel: Methodist Episcopal. Mailing Add: 203 Morgantown St, Kingwood, W.Va. 26537.

EVERROAD, JOHN R
Lt. Gov. of Nebr.
b. Columbus, Ind, 1/13/13; m. 11/6/36 to Ruby Baker; c. John E, Jr. Educ: Franklin Col. Polit. & Govt. Pos: Lt. Gov. of Nebr, 66-; del, Rep. Nat. Conv, 68. Bus. & Prof. Pos: Pres, Cummins Mid-West Co, Inc. and Cummins S.Dak, Inc; chmn. of the bd, Everroad Supply Co, Inc. and E & R, Inc; farm owner; pres, Omaha Safety Coun, Omaha, Nebr, 68-69; trustee, John F. Kennedy Col, Wahoo, 69- Mem: Past pres, Nebr. Safety Coun. and Nebr. Motor Carriers Asn; past chmn, Omaha Subcmt. of Omaha C. of C. Pub. Highways Cmt. and Inter-City Cmt; past dir, Happy Hollow Country Club; allied mem, Assoc. Gen. Contractors of Am; dir, State C. of C; v.pres, Am. Trucking Asn. from Nebr; Pub. Affairs Cmt. and Legis. Cmt, Omaha C. of C; Downtown Rotary; Nat. Oil Field Mfg. Assoc. Del. Soc. Rel: First Christian Church. Legal Res: 9214 Farnam St, Omaha, Nebr. Mailing Add: 5555 Center St, Omaha, Nebr. 68105.

EVERS, CHARLES D
Dem. Nat. Committeeman, Miss.
Mailing Add: Fayette, Miss. 39069.

EVERSON, RONALD ALBIN R
Minn. State Rep.
b. Brainerd, Minn, 7/8/30; s. Albin Everson and Naomi Landstrom E; m. 6/22/52 to Jerrie Lee Phillips; c. Robbin Lee, Sharon Kay, Scott Phillips, Nancy Sue and Paul Ronald. Educ: Univ. Minn, B.B.A, 51; Delta Sigma Pi. Polit. & Govt. Pos: Minn. State Rep, 54th Dist, 61- Bus. & Prof. Pos: V.pres. and treas, Goetz-Everson Motors, 51-; secy-treas, Gem Rentals, Minn, 62- Mil. Serv: Entered as E-1, Army, 52, released as E-4, 54, after serv. in

503rd Mil. Police Bn, Ft. Bragg, N.C. Mem: Lions; Am. Legion; C. of C; Jr. C. of C; AF&AM. Rel: Congregational. Mailing Add: 224 Madison Ave. S.W, Wadena, Minn. 56482. (1967)

EVINS, JOE LANDON D
U.S. Rep, Tenn.
b. Smithville, Tenn, 10/24/10; s. James Edgar Evins and Myrtie Goodson E; m. 6/7/35 to Ann Smartt; c. Joanna (Mrs. Carnahan), Jane Fancher and Mary Adelaide. Educ: Vanderbilt Univ; Cumberland Univ. Law Sch; George Wash. Univ. Post Grad. Sch; Phi Kappa Sigma; Phi Delta Phi. Polit. & Govt. Pos: Past. chmn, DeKalb Co. Dem. Exec. Cmt; mem. legal staff and asst. secy, Fed. Trade Cmn, 35-41; del, Dem. Nat. Conv, 48, 52, 56, 58, 60, 64 & 68; U.S. Rep, Fourth Dist, Tenn, 47-, chmn. subcmt. independent offices, U.S. House Rep, subcmt. housing and urban develop. appropriations and house small bus. cmt, mem. subcmt. pub. works appropriations and mem. cmt. appropriations. Bus. & Prof. Pos: Pres, First Nat. Bank, Smithville, Tenn, 54-65, chmn. bd, 65- Mil. Serv: Entered as 1st Lt, Army, 42, released as Maj, 46, after serv. in Judge Adv. Gen. Corps, ETO; Cross of Mil. Serv. Publ: Understanding Congress, Clarkson Porter, 62. Mem: Tenn. and Am. Bar Asns; Am. Legion; VFW; Mason; Army and Navy Club; Lions; trustee, Cumberland Col. and David Lipscomb Col, currently. Rel: Church of Christ. Legal Res: 300 E. Main St, Smithville, Tenn. 37166. Mailing Add: 2300 Rayburn Bldg, Washington, D.C. 20515.

EWELL, MILTON WATKINS, JR. D
b. Dyersburg, Tenn, 1/4/35; s. Milton Watkins Ewell, Sr. and Winnie Orr E; m. 12/6/58 to Nancy Jean McMillan; c. Diana Lynn, Michael Watkins and Anna Elizabeth. Educ: Univ. Tenn, B.S. in Bus. Admin, 56; LL.B, 58; Phi Delta Phi Omicron Delta Kappa. Polit. & Govt. Pos: Tenn. State Rep, 62-66; Tenn. State Sen, 27th Dist, 66-68. Bus. & Prof. Pos: Mem, bd. dirs, First Fed. Savings & Loan Asn. of Dyersburg and city attorney, Dyersburg, currently Mem: Mason; Moose; Rotary; Dyersburg-Dyer Co. C. of C; Dyer Co. Unit of Am. Cancer Soc. Rel: Methodist. Legal Res: 1011 Troy Ave, Dyersburg, Tenn. 38024. Mailing Add: P.O. Box 763, Dyersburg, Tenn. 38024.

EWELL, RAYMOND WHITNEY D
Ill. State Rep.
b. Chicago, Ill, 12/29/28; s. Whitney Ewell and Severine Ray E; m. 9/19/53 to Joyce Marie Haywood; c. David Raymond and Marc Whitney. Educ: Univ. Ill, B.A, 49, M.A, 51; Univ. Chicago, J.D, 54. Polit. & Govt. Pos: Adv, 17th Ward Young Dem, Ill, 64-; Ill. State Rep, 29th Dist, 67- Bus. & Prof. Pos: Teacher, Chicago Bd. of Educ, 49-57; attorney-at-law, Dixon, Ewell, Graham & McCormick, 56- Mil. Serv: Pfc, Army, 54-55. Rel: Episcopal. Mailing Add: 52 W. 78th St, Chicago, Ill. 60620. (1967)

EWING, BAYARD R
Mem, R.I. Rep. State Cent. Cmt.
b. Sorrento, Mo, 8/19/16; s. Thomas Ewing and Anna Cochran E; m. 9/2/39 to Harriet M. Kelley; c. Linda L.(Mrs. R.T. Leeson), Gillian C.(Mrs. M.W. Ehrich), Bayard C, Gifford P. and Harriet K. Educ: Yale, A.B, 38; Harvard, LL.B, 41. Polit. & Govt. Pos: Mem, Rep. State Control Cmt, R.I, 48-; del, Rep. Nat. Conv, 48-; mem, R.I. Pub. Expenditures Coun; R.I. State Rep, 50-52; cand. U.S. Sen, 52 & 58; Rep. Nat. Committeeman, R.I, 55-68. Bus. & Prof. Pos: Partner, Graham, Reid, Ewing & Stapleton, Providence, 49-; dir, Boston & Providence R.R. Co; Title Guarantee Co. of R.I; dir, Providence Inst. Savings; trustee, Providence Lying-In-Hosp; R.I. Sch. of Design. Mem: Am, R.I. Bar Asns; Mason (32°); trustee and v.pres, United Commun. Funds and Couns. of Am; trustee, United Fund of R.I, 61-; trustee, Boy's Club. Rel: Episcopal. Legal Res: 1220 Ives Rd, East Greenwich, R.I. 02818. Mailing Add: 15 Westminster St, Providence, R.I. 02903.

EWING, EDWIN C. R
b. Coraopolis, 11/26/02; s. E.J. Ewing and Etta Clark E; m. to Esma Eakin; c. Two. Educ: Petroleum Sch, Cincinnati, Ohio. Polit. & Govt. Pos: Pa. State Rep, 39-40 & 43-64; Pa. State Sen, 64-67. Bus. & Prof. Pos: Sales engr; dir, Lincoln Bank and Trust Co. Mem: Delta Sigma Pi; Mason; Shrine; 103rd Med. Unit, Coraopolis. Mailing Add: 35 Lebanon Hills Dr, Mt. Lebanon, Pittsburgh, Pa. 15228. (1967)

EWING, M. JEAN R
State Committeewoman, Fla. Rep. Party
b. Parkdale, Ark, 5/11/25; d. Burl J. White, Sr. and Annie Carol Mitchell W; m. 8/16/47 to William James Ewing; c. Dana (Mrs. David A. Samball) and Leesa Jan. Educ: Univ. Fla, B.A.E, 63 and M.Ed, 65; Phi Kappa Phi; Pi Lambda Theta (secy, v.pres. and pres, Univ. Fla. Chap). Polit. & Govt. Pos: Co-founder, Alachua Co. Young Rep. Club, Fla, 65; ballot security officer, Alachua Co, Fla, 66 & 67; campaign coordinator, Rep. Precinct Committeemen and Committeewomen, 66 and Rep. Cand. to State Supreme Court and Dist. II for Richard Nixon, 68; state committeewoman, Fla. Rep. Party, 66-; coordinator tel. solicitation, Senate and House Races, 67; secy. Fla. Del, Rep. Nat. Conv, 68; mem, State Jr. Col. Coun, 68- Bus. & Prof. Pos: Secy, U.S. Govt, Lambert Air Force Base, 45-46, Judge Adv. Gen. Off, 46-47; Cleveland Welfare Fedn, 47-48 and Florator, Inc, 48-50; instr, St. Johns River Jr. Col, 65-67; soc. studies coordinator, Mebane High Sch, Alachua Co, Fla, 68- Mem: Mod. Lang. Asn; Nat. Coun. of Teachers of Eng; Fla. Col. Eng. Asn; Int. Reading Asn; Nat. Coun. for Soc. Studies; Nat. Coun. for Geog. Educ; Higher Educ. Facilities Action Cmt; Phi Kappa Phi (jour. correspondent, Gainsville Chap); life mem, Pi Lambda Theta; Friends of the Libr; League of Women Voters. Rel: Protestant. Mailing Add: 3527 N.W. Tenth Ave, Gainsville, Fla. 32601.

EWING, SAMUEL EVANS R
b. Bryn Mawr, Pa, 7/27/06; s. Samuel Evans Ewing and Fanny Badger Neff E; m. 3/22/47 to Harriet Corning (deceased); c. Samuel E, Jr, Steven Neff and stepsons, Wharton, III, Edwin C. and Peter Sinkler; second marriage, 7/23/66 to Mary Alice Johnston. Educ: Princeton Univ, A.B, 27; Univ. Pa, LL.B, 30. Polit. & Govt. Pos: V.chmn, Young Rep. of Pa, 38-41; cmnr, Lower Merion Twp, Pa, 40-42 & 48-52, v.pres. bd. cmnr, 52-56 and pres. bd. cmnr, 56-60; del-at-lg, Rep. Nat. Conv, 56 & del, 64; chmn, Southeast. Pa. Citizens for Scranton-Van Zandt, 62; chmn, Rep. Finance Cmt. Pa, 55-57, mem, 55-67. Bus. & Prof. Pos: Assoc. and partner, Saul, Ewing, Remick & Saul, Phila, 30-47; counsel, eng. prod. dept, RCA Victor Div, 47-48, gen. attorney, mfg. & serv. div, Radio Corp. Am, 48-60, staff v.pres. and gen. attorney, 60-67; v.pres, Wash, D.C, 67-, mem, Fed. City Coun, Wash, D.C, 68-, exec. cmt, 69-; mem. bus. admin. adv. cmt, Wash. Tech. Inst, 69- Mil. Serv: Entered as Pvt, Army, 41, released as Maj, 45, after serv. in 12th Army Group Hq, ETO, 44-45; 5 Campaign Stars; Bronze Star Medal. Mem: Phila, Pa, Fed, Am. and Fed. Commun. Bar Asns; Juristic Soc; Lawyers Club. Phila; Nat. Lawyers Club; bd. trustees, Temple Univ. Mem, U.S. Olympic Field Hockey Team, 32 & 36. Rel: Presbyterian. Legal Res: 4125 52nd St. N.W, Washington, D.C. 20016. Mailing Add: 1725 K St. N.W, Washington, D.C. 20006.

EXLER, JOHN J. D
Recorder of Deeds, Allegheny Co, Pa.
b. Pittsburgh, Pa, 3/29/17; s. John E. Exler and Elizabeth McConnell E; m. 5/3/44 to Ruth Haberman; c. Ellen, Janice and John. Educ: High Sch. Polit. & Govt. Pos: Recorder of Deeds, Allegheny Co, Pa, 47-; del, Dem. Nat. Conv, 68. Mil. Serv: Army, 42-46. Mem: K. of C; K. of E; VFW; Am. Legion; DAV. Rel: Roman Catholic. Legal Res: 10 Mt. Hope St, Pittsburgh, Pa. 15223. Mailing Add: County Office Bldg, Pittsburgh, Pa. 15219.

EXON, J. JAMES D
Dem. Nat. Committeeman, Nebr.
b. Geddes, S.Dak, 8/9/21; s. John J. Exon and Luella Johns E; m. 8/18/43 to Patricia A. Pros; c. Stephen James, Pamela Ann and Candace Lee. Educ: Univ. Omaha, 39-41. Polit. & Govt. Pos: Active on state cmts. for Lt. Gov. Sorensen, 54, U.S. Rep. Callan, 54 and Gov. Brooks, 57; state campaign mgr, Morrison for Gov. Cmt, 59; del, Dem. Nat. Conv, 64; state coordinator, Johnson-Humphrey Campaign, 64; chmn, Nebr. Jefferson-Jackson Day Dinner, 65; mem. exec. cmt, Nebr. Dem. State Dem. Party, 64-; v.chmn, Nebr. State Dem. Cent. Cmt, 64-68; Dem. Nat. Committeeman, Nebr, 68- Bus. & Prof. Pos: Br. mgr, Universal Finance Corp, 46-54; pres, Exon's Inc, 54- Mil. Serv: Entered as Pvt, Army Signal Corps, 42, released as M/Sgt, 45, after serv. in New Guinea, Philippines and Japan, 43-45; Southwest Pac. and Philippine Campaign Ribbons; M/Sgt, Army Res. until 49. Mem: Lincoln C. of C; Nat. Off. Prod. Dealers Asn; Mason (32°); Shrine; Elks; past pres, Lincoln Optimist Club; past Lt. Gov, Dist. 10, Optimist Int; Am. Legion; Hillcrest Country Club. Rel: Episcopal. Legal Res: 1615 Brent Blvd, Lincoln, Nebr. 68506. Mailing Add: 23rd and O St, Lincoln, Nebr. 68510.

EYERLY, GEORGE BROWN R
b. Canton, Ill, 3/20/17; s. William H. Eyerly, Jr. and Ruth Brown E; m. 5/3/47 to Margery Boyd; c. Alison, Elaine and Annette. Educ: Univ. Ill, B.S. in ceramic eng, 40; Univ. Wash, M.S. in mineral eng, 41; Tau Beta Pi; Keramos. Polit. & Govt. Pos: Mem, Hot Spring Co. Elec. Cmn, Ark, 64-67, chmn, 67-; chmn, Hot Spring Co. Rep. Party, 64-67; mem, Ark. Gov. Task Adv. Cmt, 66-67; mem, Ark. Geol. Cmn, 67. Bus. & Prof. Pos: Chief tech. sect. research div, U.S. Atomic Energy Cmn, Oak Ridge and Manhattan Proj, 46-47; asst. prof, Univ. Wash, 47-48; chief ceramic sect, Argonne Nat. Lab, 48-52; proj. engr, Allen Bradley Co, 52-55; secy, chief engr. and mem. bd, Malvern Brick & Tile Co, 55-67; sr. engr, D.H. Steward Mfg. Co, 67- Mil. Serv: Entered as 2nd Lt, Army, 41, released as Maj, 47, after serv. with Manhattan Proj. Mem: Am. Chem. Soc; Am. Soc. for Metals; Am. Asn. for the Adv. of Sci; Am. Ceramic Soc; chmn, Cent. Ark. Develop. Coun, 65-67. Rel: Methodist. Mailing Add: 185 Woodcliff Circle, Signal Mountain, Tenn. 37377.

EZZARD, CLARENCE GRAY D
Ga. State Rep.
b. Atlanta, Ga. 4/16/05; s. Dock S. Ezzard and Rena Alexander E; m. 6/17/30 to Etta Mae Green; c. Clarence G, Jr, Merian T, Myrtle V, Joel G. and Wesley P. Polit. & Govt. Pos: Ga. State Rep, 69- Bus. & Prof. Pos: Letter carrier, U.S. Post Off, Atlanta, 29-68. Rel: Episcopal. Mailing Add: 245 Atlanta Ave. S.E, Atlanta, Ga. 30315.

F

FAAMAUSILI, SUIAUNOA TALO R
Rep, Am. Samoa House of Rep.
b. Masefau, Am. Samoa, 6/20/31; s. Liusa Talo Faamausili and Aifili Suiaunoa F; m. 5/27/54 to Masae Tupuola; c. Tulua, Avaoali'i, Mapuitiga, Tauma'oe, Donald, Poseta, Lupelele, Taulagi and Talimalo. Polit. & Govt. Pos: Rep, Am. Samoa House of Rep, currently; chief clerk, Off. Samoan Affairs, currently. Rel: Congregational. Mailing Add: Masefau Village, American Samoa 96920.

FABER, HERMAN E. R
Chmn, Butler Co. Rep. Cmt, Iowa
b. Butler Co, Iowa, 10/14/14; s. Fred H. Faber and Martha Molhoeck F; m. 2/12/38 to Jennie Reints; c. Sharon (Mrs. Crosser) and David. Polit. & Govt. Pos: Chmn, Third Dist, Gross for Cong. Campaign, Iowa, 66; chmn, Butler Co. Rep. Cmt, 66-; del, Rep. Nat. Conv, 68. Bus. & Prof. Pos: Ins. agent, Parkersburg, Iowa, 20 years; partner, Faber's Ins. Agency, Inc, at present. Mem: Past pres. and past nat. dir, Iowa Asn. of Ins. Agents; C. of C; Rotary; pres, Butler Co. Fair; Co. Conserv. Bd; Farm Bur. Rel: Baptist. Mailing Add: 509 Fourth St, Parkersburg, Iowa 50665.

FABRIZI, JOHN H. D
Chmn, Ontario Co. Dem. Cmt, N.Y.
b. Phelps, N.Y, 6/7/14; s. Angelo Fabrizi and Mary Ornato F; m. to Margaret Cassidy, wid. Educ: Clifton Springs High Sch, 30-32. Polit. & Govt. Pos: Chmn, Ontario Co. Dem. Cmt, N.Y, 57-; mem. exec. cmt, N.Y. State Dem. Cmt, 62-; del, Dem. Nat. Conv, 64 & 68; chmn, Upstate Dem. Rural Cmt, N.Y, 66- Bus. & Prof. Pos: Pres, Retail Restaurant Asn, 53. Mem: Pres, Rotary, Clifton Springs, 56-57; pres, Clifton Springs Co. Club, 59-63; K. of C.(4°); Elks; C. of C. Rel: Roman Catholic. Mailing Add: R.D. 2, Clifton Springs, N.Y. 14432.

FABRIZIO, JOHN ARTHUR R
Conn. State Rep.
b. Norwalk, Conn, 11/17/23; s. John Joseph Fabrizio and Mary Elizabeth Perrella F; m. 8/4/62 to Dr. Tuula Irja Jokinen; c. John Arne and Robert Arthur. Educ: N.Y. Univ. Sch. Commerce, B.S, 46; N.Y. Law Sch, LL.B, 60;

NYU Mgt. and Hon. Clubs; Phi Thea Phi. Polit. & Govt. Pos: Mem, Norwalk Zoning Bd. of Appeals, Conn, 62-; mem, Norwalk Rep. Ward A. Cmt, 65-; mem, Norwalk Rep. Town Cmt, 68-; Conn. State Rep, 69- Bus. & Prof. Pos: Owner and operator, Norwalk Auto Transit Co. and Fabrizio Bus. Co, 62- Mem: Long Shore Country Club. Rel: Roman Catholic. Mailing Add: 15 Highwood Ave, Norwalk, Conn. 06850.

FACE, ALBERT R. R
Chmn, Yuma Co. Rep. Cent. Cmt, Ariz.
b. Aberdeen, S.Dak, 3/31/19; s. Ray James Face and Elsie Sloan F; m. 1/31/42 to Ellenore Ambur; c. Carol (Mrs. Clark) and Ray Jay. Educ: S.Dak. State Col, B.C, 41; Colo. State Col, 45; Alpha Zeta; Agr. Club; Col. 4-H. Polit. & Govt. Pos: Dist. 4-H leader, S.Dak. Agr. Exten. Serv, 43-45; co. 4-H exten. agent, Yuma Co, Ariz, 45-49, co. agr. exten. agent, 49-55; pres, Yuma Co. Citizens for Goldwater, 64; chmn, Laguna Precinct Rep. Party, 67-69; treas. and campaign chmn, Goldwater for U.S. Sen, Yuma Co, 68; committeeman, Gov. Williams Adv. Cmt, 68-69; chmn, Yuma Co. Rep. Cent. Cmt, 68- Bus. & Prof. Pos: Cattle supt, Bruce Church, Inc, Yuma, 55-, ranch mgr, 59- Mil. Serv: Entered as 2nt Lt, Army, 41, released as 1st Lt, 43, after serv. in Transportation Corps, Caribbean Theater, 42-43. Mem: Int. Brangus Breeders Asn; Ariz. Cattle Feeders; Ariz. Cattle Growers; Rotary; Farm Bur. Yuma Co. Man of the Year, 52. Rel: Lutheran, Mo. Synod. Mailing Add: Route 3, Box 310-A, Yuma, Ariz. 85364.

FADDIS, CHARLES I. D
b. Loudonville, Ohio, 6/13/90; s. Samuel Cranz Faddis and Edna Moredock F; m. 12/1/17 to Jane Morris; c. William George, James Ely, Edna Gertrude and Laura Lucille. Educ: Pa. State Col, A.B, 15; Gen. Staff & Command Sch, U.S. Army, Ft. Leavenworth, Kans, 30. Polit. & Govt. Pos: U.S. Rep, Pa. and mem, House Cmt. on Mil. Affairs, 33-42. Bus. & Prof. Pos: Gen. contractor, Mainly of Rds. and Bridges; Broker in and Operator of Oil, Gas, Coal and Timber Properties. Mil. Serv: Entered as Capt, Army, 17, released as Lt. Col, 20, after serv. in 47th Inf. and 4th Ammunition Train, 4th Div, France and Germany; re-entered as Col, 42-46, in N.Africa, Italy, France and Germany; Campaign Bars for serv. in all major offensives in Europe and Africa during both World Wars; 2 Purple Hearts; 2 Bronze Stars; Silver Star from Gen. Pershing. Publ: 'Why The Farmer Is Loosing Out,' Pa. Farmer Shorthorn World, 5/55 and 10/55; 'The Right To Work;' 7/57 and 'Palaces For Protectors,' 9/57, The Freeman. Mem: Elks; Am. Legion; VFW; SAR. Mailing Add: 355 Park Ave, Waynesburg, Pa. 15370.

FADELEY, EDWARD NORMAN D
Ore. State Sen.
b. Williamsville, Mo, 12/13/29; s. Robert Sylvester Fadeley and Nelle Norman F; m. 6/11/53 to Nancie Newell Peacocke; c. Charles Norman and Shira Nannette. Educ: Univ. Mo, A.B, 51; Univ. Ore, J.D, 57; Order of the Coif; Alpha Pi Zeta; Phi Alpha Delta; Varsity debater; ed, Ore. Law Review. Polit. & Govt. Pos: Precinct committeeman, Dem. Party, Eugene, Ore, 56-, area chmn, 58-64; Ore. State Rep, Lane Co, 61-63; Ore. State Sen, Lane Co, 63-, chmn, Disclosure of Influences on Govt. Cmt, 64-66 and mem, 5-man State Steering Cmn, Cmt. to Repeal the Death Penalty, Ore. State Senate; permanent chmn, Dem. State Platform Conv, 64-66; chmn, Dem. Party Ore, 67-68; del, Dem. Nat. Conv, 68; Dem. nominee for U.S. Rep, Ore, 68. Bus. & Prof.Pos: Secy-treas, Ore. Research Inst, Inc, 60-; chmn, Uniform Laws Cmt, Ore. State Bar, 63-65; presiding chmn, State Conv, Ore. State Bar. Mil. Serv: Entered as Midn, Navy, 47, released as Lt.(jg), 54, after serv. in Mediterranean, Atlantic and Caribbean, 52-53; European Occup. and Nat. Defense Ribbons; Lt, Naval Res, 66. Publ: 'Clean Hands in Oregon,' Ore. Law Rev, 57-58. Mem: Am. Acad. of Polit. & Soc. Sci; Am. Bar Asn.(mem, Sections on Family, Criminal & Pub. Utility Law); Ore. State Bar (mem, Family Law Cmt); Am. Judicature Soc; participant in three Northwest Assemblies on Cong, Courts, Legis, Am. Assembly Prog; Elks; Moose; C. of C; Am. Civil Liberties Union; Metrop. Civic Club; bd.mem, Lane Co. Coun. on Alcoholism; pres, Lane Co. Asn. for Retarded Children, 66-69. All conf. tackle, conf. championship team, Grant City, Mo, 46; nominated Distinguished Jr. Citizen, Eugene, 63 & 64. Rel: Methodist. Mailing Add: 260 Sunset Dr, Eugene, Ore. 97401.

FADELEY, NANCIE PEACOCKE D
b. St. Louis, Mo, 7/11/30; d. Charles Sidney Peacocke and Nannette Wood P; m. 6/11/53 to Edward Norman Fadeley; c. Charles Norman and Shira Nanette. Educ: Cent. Methodist Col, B.A, 52; Duke Univ, 52-53; Univ. Ore, 55-69. Polit. & Govt. Pos: Various pos. in Dem. Party Orgn, Lane Co, Ore; alternate del, Dem. Nat. Conv, 68; secy. to Ore. State Sen. Ed Fadeley, currently. Bus. & Prof. Pos: Former sch. teacher; free-lance writer, currently. Publ: 'The Wizardy of Os,' Emerald Empire Mag, 1/68. Rel: Methodist. Mailing Add: 260 Sunset Dr, Eugene, Ore. 97403.

FADEM, JERROLD ALAN D
Mem, Los Angeles Co. Dem. Cent. Cmt, Calif.
b. St. Louis, Mo, 1/19/26; s. Samuel H. Fadem and Betsy Sparks F; m. 6/17/51 to Joyce Abrams; c. Cheryl Marlene and Judith Allison. Educ: Wash. Univ, 43-44; Univ. Calif, Los Angeles, B.S. in Econ, 47; Loyola Univ, J.D, 53; Zeta Beta Tau. Polit. & Govt. Pos: Spec. consult, State Lands Cmn, 64-65; mem, Calif. Dem. State Cent. Cmt, 64-66; consult. airport noise, Cmt. on Transportation, Calif. State Assembly, 68-69; mem, Los Angeles Co. Dem. Cent. Cmt, 68-; oral examiner, Los Angeles City Civil Serv. Dept, 69. Bus. & Prof. Pos: Partner, Fadem & Kanner, 53- Mil. Serv: Entered as Pvt, Army, 44, released as S/Sgt, 46, after serv. in Hq. Sect, Fourth Army. Publ: Ed. and co-auth, Condemnation Practice Handbook, Continuing Education of the Bar of Calif, 62; auth, Negative Argument on Proposition D, November Election, 68. Mem: Calif. State Bar.(cmt. condemnation law and procedure); Los Angeles Co. Bar Asn.(cmt. on condemnation law); Mason (32°); Scottish Rite; Justice Lodge, B'nai B'rith; Town Hall. Rel: Jewish. Mailing Add: 427 S. McCadden Place, Los Angeles, Calif. 90005.

FADEM, JOYCE A. D
Mem, Calif. Dem. State Cent. Cmt.
b. Los Angeles, Calif, 2/25/32; d. Arthur J. Abrams and Regina Goodman A; m. 6/17/51 to Jerrold A. Fadem; c. Cheryl Marlene and Judith Allison. Educ: Univ. Calif, Los Angeles, B.A. in polit. sci, 52, Gen. Secondary Teaching Credential, 53 and M.A, 61; Phi Beta Kappa; Pi Lambda Theta; Pi Gamma Mu; Pi Sigma Alpha; Alpha Epsilon Phi. Polit. & Govt. Pos: Coordinator vol. serv, Dem. Nat. Conv, 60; mem, Calif. Dem. State Cent. Cmt, 60-64 & 66-; secy, Calif. Dem. Coun, 63-67; alternate del, Dem. Nat. Conv, 64 & 68; mem, Los Angeles Co. Cent. Cmt, 66-; coordinator, Educators for Alan Cranston, 1968 Sen. Elec. Bus. & Prof. Pos: Proj. writer, sch. educ, Univ. Calif, Los Angeles, 60-61, lectr, educ. exten, 63-65; instr, Los Angeles City Col, 62-; consult, Calif. State Dept. Educ, 64-66; mem. faculty, Immaculate Heart Col, Los Angeles, 67- Publ: Bill of Rights: A Source Book for Teachers, Calif. State Dept. Educ, 66; 'Making Freedom Real,' Calif. Teachers Asn. Jour, 1/65; We Teach Freedom, Constitutional Rights Found, Los Angeles, 65. Mem: Chmn, Jr. Col. Cmt, Calif. Teachers Asn, 68-; chmn, Acad. Freedom Cmt, Nat. Coun. for Soc. Studies, Nat. Educ. Asn, 65, 68-69; dir-at-lg, South Calif. Soc. Sci. Asn, 64-; chmn, Teachers Adv. Cmt, Constitutional Rights Found, 62-64, mem, 64-; Calif. Coun. Soc. Studies: Am. Fedn. of Teachers. Rel: Jewish. Mailing Add: 427 S. McCadden Place, Los Angeles, Calif. 90005.

FADEM, ROBERT STANLEY R
b. St. Louis, Mo, 12/9/23; s. Leonard Fadem and Lillian Belle Kirlander F; m. 5/27/49 to Mary Goss Oliphant; c. Pamela Oliphant, Kathleen Joy, Robert Stanley, Jr. and Blair Washburn. Educ: Wash. Univ. Sch. Med, M.D, 47; N.Y. Univ. Postgrad. Sch. Med, 50-52. Polit. & Govt. Pos: Mem, Finance Cmt. for Bob Wilson, San Diego, Calif, 66 and 68; mem, Calif. Rep. State Cent. Cmt, 67-69; mem, finance cmt, Nixon's The One, San Diego, 68; mem, Gov. Reagan's Calif. Correctional Task Force, 69; mem, Rep. Assocs, San Diego Co, Calif. Mil. Serv: Pfc, Army, 43-47; Lt.(jg), Navy, 47-48. Publ: Numerous articles in med. jour. Mem: San Diego and Calif. Med. Socs; Am. Med. Asn; Soc. Nuclear Med; Salvation Army (chmn. adv. bd, San Diego Chap, 68-69); adv, Girls Club of San Diego, 69. Rel: Episcopal. Legal Res: 2441 Presidio Dr, San Diego, Calif. 92103. Mailing Add: 233 A St, San Diego, Calif. 92101.

FAGAN, JAMES W. D
b. Casper, Wyo, 7/13/27; s. Thomas M. Fagan and Josephine Warner F; m. 9/17/50 to Lita Kaan; c. Curtis Page, Patrick Lance, Thomas Mathew and Nora Lynn. Educ: Univ. Wyo, B.A. and B.S.L, 53, LL.B, 55; Sigma Alpha Epsilon. Polit. & Govt. Pos: Dem. Precinct committeeman, Natrona Co, Wyo, 59-68; Wyo. rep, U.S. Sen. Gale McGee, 59-69; mem. exec. bd, Wyo. Young Dem, 62; bus. mgr. and organizer, The Spokesman, 63-; mem. finance cmt, Wyo. Dem. Party, 66; del, Dem. Nat. Conv, 68. Legal Res: 123 S. Kimball, Casper, Wyo. 82601. Mailing Add: 142 N. Center, Casper, Wyo. 82601

FAGAN, LAWRENCE JAMES R
Mem, Rep. Town Cmt, Berlin, Conn.
b. New Britain, Conn, 12/24/30; s. Edward Joseph Fagan and Margaret Fitzsimmons F; m. 10/5/63 to Mary Ann Milewski; c. John A. and Christopher J. Educ: Fairfield Univ, B.S, 53; Boston Col. Law Sch, LL.B, 56. Polit. & Govt. Pos: Mem, Bd. Finance, Marlborough, Conn, 62-66; Conn. State Rep, 63-67; mem, Rep. Town Cmt, Berlin, Conn, 69- Mil. Serv: 1st Lt, Air Force, 57, serv. in Judge Adv. Gen. Dept. Mem: Am, Conn. and Hartford Co. Bar Asns; Am. Trial Lawyers Asn; Blackledge Country Club. Rel: Roman Catholic. Mailing Add: 79 Butternut Lane, Kensington, Conn. 06037.

FAGAN, MICHAEL ROBERT D
City Councilman, San Bernardino, Calif.
b. Seattle, Wash, 4/25/37; s. Charles H. Fagan and Edith S. Underwood F; m. 6/12/60 to Sally Elaine Cherniss; c. Judi Lynn, Jill Ann and Joyce Marie. Educ: Bellarmine Col; Long Beach State Col; Univ. South Calif. Polit. & Govt. Pos: Mem, Big Co. Dem. Club and Uptown Dem. Club, San Bernardino, Calif; city councilman, Second Ward, San Bernardino, 65- Bus. & Prof. Pos: Br. mgr, Swim Art Club, 56-60; sr. zoning enforcement officer, San Bernardino Co, Calif, 60-66; land use planner and zoning consult, 66- Mil. Serv: Pfc, Marine Corps Res. Mem: Nat. Prfnl. Geog; Am. Inst. of Planners; Am. Soc. of Planning Off; Regional Econ. Develop. Coun; Eagles; Argonauts; March of Dimes; YMCA; Calif. Roadside Coun; Wilsonian Club; Am. Fedn. of State,Co. & Munic. Employees; C. of C. Rel: Catholic. Legal Res: 2349 Newport Ave, San Bernardino, Calif. 92404. Mailing Add: P.O. Box 3264, San Bernardino, Calif. 92404. (1967)

FAGAN, THOMAS JOHN R
b. Covington, Ky, 4/8/21; s. Thomas Matthias Fagan and Nora Bolan F; m. 1/3/44 to Elizabeth Elgin Brooks. Educ: Marquette Univ, B.S. in bus. admin, 48; Beta Gamma Sigma; Alpha Sigma Nu. Polit. & Govt. Pos: Former chmn, Monroe Co. Rep. Cmt, Miss. Bus. & Prof. Pos: Sales mgr, DeKoven Mfg. Co, 55-58; purchasing agent, Walker Mfg. Co, 58- Mil. Serv: Entered as Aviation Cadet, Army Air Force, 42, released as T/Sgt, 45, after serv. in Eighth Air Force, 447th Bomb Group, ETO, 44-45; DFS, Air Medal with Five Clusters; Five Major Battles in ETO Campaign. Publ: Articles on purchasing and sales in various trade jour. Mem: Am. Legion; Exchange Club; K. of C; Aberdeen Golf and Country Club. Rel: Catholic. 1967 Legal Res: Aberdeen, Miss. No mailing address available. (1967)

FAGAN, THOMAS LEO D
City Councilman, Pittsburgh, Pa.
b. Homestead, Pa, 3/31/17; s. Patrick T. Fagan and Ida Bernarding F; m. 8/16/41 to Mary Wilma Cuddayre; c. Nora (Mrs. John DelPaine), Thomas Jr. and Janie. Educ: South Hills High Sch, grad, 36. Polit. & Govt. Pos: Del, Nat. Dem. Conv, 68 and Pa. Constitutional Conv, 68; city councilman, Pittsburgh, Pa, 68- Bus. & Prof. Pos: Truck driver, May Sterns, 36; v.pres, Teamsters Local 249, 47, pres, 47-; trustee, West. Pa. Motor Carriers and Teamsters Pension and Welfare Funds. Mil. Serv: Entered as Pvt, Army, 42, released as Platoon and T/Sgt, 45, after serv. in Anti-Aircraft Div, 63rd and 36th Inf, Heavy Weapons, ETO; Bronze Star. Mem: VFW; Am. Legion; K. of C; Knights of Equity; hon. pres, Southcrest Lodge, Ital. Sons and Daughters; trustee, Commun. Col. of Allegheny Co; adv. bd, Holy Family Inst; Gr. Pittsburgh Labor Adv. Coun; Better Traffic Cmt. of Pittsburgh. Israel Bonds Labor Award. Rel: Catholic. Legal Res: 111 Roswin Dr, Pittsburgh, Pa. 15226. Mailing Add: 4701 Butler St, Pittsburgh, Pa. 15201.

FAGG, HARRISON GROVER R
Mont. State Rep.
b. Billings, Mont, 10/27/31; s. Mearl Leonard Fagg and Frances Soule F; m. 8/28/52 to Darlene Rae Bohling; c. Sherril Soule, Russel Charles and Grantland Mearl. Educ: Mont. State Univ, 1 year; Univ. Ore, B.S. in Archit; Sigma Chi. Polit. & Govt. Pos: Mont. State Rep, Dist. Nine, Yellowstone Co,

69- Bus. & Prof. Pos: Proj. designer, Orr Pickering & Assocs, 56-58; proj. designer, Nordquist & Sundell, 58-59; owner, archit. firm, Harrison Fagg & Assocs, 59- Mil. Serv: Entered as 2nd Lt, Air Force, 54, released as 1st Lt, 56, after serv. as an Air Installations Engr, Larson Air Force Base, Moses Lake, Wash. Mem: Mont. State Am. Inst. Architects; Am. Inst. Architects; Licensed Architect in Mont, Idaho, N. and S.Dak; Nat. Coun. Architects Registrn. Bd; Shrine; Air Craft Owners & Pilots Asn; AF&AM; Rep. Club. of Yellowstone Co; Kiwanis; Elks; Sigma Chi; Billings Jaycees (pres, 64); Mont. Jaycees (pres. and nat. dir, 65); U.S. Jaycees (nat. v.pres, 66); Jr. Chamber Int.(sen). Outstanding Young Man of Billings, Mont, 58; Outstanding Young Man of Mont, 59. Rel: Presbyterian. Legal Res: 1414 Mystic Dr, Billings, Mont. 59101. Mailing Add: 3210 Third Ave. N, Billings, Mont. 59101.

FAHY, CHARLES D
b. Rome, Ga, 8/27/92; s. Thomas Fahy and Sarah Jonas F; m. 6/26/29 to Mary Agnes Lane; c. Charles (Dom Thomas Fahy, O.S.B.), Anne Marie (Mrs. Rourke Sheehan), Sarah Agnes (Sister Charles Mary, S.N.D.) and Mary Agnes (Mrs. John C. Johnson). Educ: Univ. Notre Dame, 10-11; Georgetown Univ, LL.B, 14, LL.D, 42. Polit. & Govt. Pos: App. first asst. solicitor, Dept. of Interior, 33; app. mem. of Petroleum Bd, 33; chmn, Petroleum Admin. Bd, 34-35; app. gen. counsel, Nat. Labor Rels. Bd, 35; app. asst. solicitor gen. of U.S, 40; mem, President's Naval and Air Base Cmn. to London, 41; solicitor gen. of U.S, 41-45; adv. to Am. Del, San Francisco Conf, 45; legal adv. and dir, U.S. Legal Div. Mil. Govt, Germany 45-46; app. legal adv, Dept. of State, 46; U.S. mem. legal cmt, Gen. Assembly, UN, N.Y, 46, alternate rep. to Gen. Assembly, UN, 47 & 49; chmn, President's Cmt. on Equality of Treatment and Opportunities in Armed Forces, 48 and Personnel Rev. Security Bd, Atomic Energy Cmn, 49; app. judge, U.S. Court of Appeals for D.C, 49. Bus. & Prof. Pos: Admitted to D.C. Bar, 14; practical law, Wash, 14-24, Santa Fe, N.Mex. 24-33; attorney-at-law, D.C, 47-49. Mil. Serv: Naval Res, 17-19; naval aviation; Navy Cross; Medal of Merit. Publ: Contrib. of articles to many publ. Mem: Am, D.C. and N.Mex. Bar Asns; Cath. Asn. for Int. Peace (pres, 49). Robert S. Abbott Mem. Award to President's Cmn, 51; Russwurm Award, 51; John Carroll Award, Georgetown Univ. Rel: Catholic. Mailing Add: 5504 Chevy Chase Pkwy. N.W, Washington, D.C. 20008. (1967)

FAIR, FAY E. D
b. Sparta, Ill, 1/24/03; s. Charles Edward Fair and Sadie Snider F; m. 6/7/41 to Ida Elizabeth Rice; c. Frank Edward, Elizabeth Rhae, Charles R. and Don R. Polit. & Govt. Pos: Mem, Rationing Bd, Chester, Ill, 40-42; mem, Judicial Cmn, Iowa; chmn, Iowa State Rural Am. for Johnson-Humphrey, 64; del, Dem. Nat. Conv, 64 & 68; mem, Gov. Hughes Hon. Col. Staff, 67. Bus. & Prof. Pos: With Ill. Commerce Cmn, 33-41; mgr, East. Iowa Light & Power Corp, 42- Bus. & Prof. Pos: Mgr, East. Iowa Light & Power Corp, 42-; with Ill. Commerce Cmn, Ill, 33-41. Mem: Zone chmn, Lions Int, Ill, 40; Mason (32°), Shriner; The New Frontier Club; Farm Bur. Third Place Winner in Nat. Mgrs. Competition, Rural Electrification Admin. Rel: Methodist. Mailing Add: 1010 East St, Wilton Junction, Iowa. 52778.

FAIR, MICHAEL EDWARD R
b. Birmingham, Ala, 12/11/42; s. Roland Eugene Fair, Sr. and Viola Parrish F; m. 12/28/63 to Serena Emily Zuckerman; c. Michael E, II. Educ: Univ. Okla, 63-66. Polit. & Govt. Pos: Okla. State Rep, Dist. 91, 67-68. Mil. Serv: Entered as Pvt. E-1, Army, 61, released as Pfc. E-3, 63, after serv. in 4th Cavalry Regt, 1st Cavalry Div, UN Forces, Korea, 62-63. Mem: Capitol Hill Real Estate Bd. Rel: Presbyterian. Mailing Add: 2333 S.W. 46, Oklahoma City, Okla. 73159.

FAIR, NORMAN G. D
b. Bellows Falls, Vt, 3/5/10; m. to Sigrid Moller; c. 1 son, 3 daughters. Educ: Bellows Falls High Sch. Polit. & Govt. Pos: Vt. State Rep, 65-67. Bus. & Prof. Pos: Builder; land developer. Mem: Home Builders Asn; Health Dept. Asn. Mailing Add: Box 12, Bondville, Vt. 05340. (1967)

FAIRBANKS, CLYDE GERRISH D
b. Webster, N.H, 4/13/98; married; c. Five daughters. Educ: Boscawen and Penacook Schs. Polit. & Govt. Pos: Constitutional Conv; former mem, sch. bd, water cmn, pub. welfare; former selectman; retired supvr; N.H. State Rep, 63-67; mem, N.H. Passenger Tramway Safety Bd. Mem: Odd Fellows; Elks. Rel: Protestant. Mailing Add: High St, Boscawen, N.H. 03303.

FAIRBANKS, MADGE H. R
Rep. Nat. Committeewoman, Utah
b. Washington, D.C; m. 11/21/47 to Bryce J. Fairbanks; c. Bryce J, II, Jeffrey M, Jerald R, Jan L. and James A. Educ: St. Joseph's High Sch, Manchester, N.H, 43; Margaret Pillsbury Sch. of Nursing, R.N, 47. Polit. & Govt. Pos: State v.chmn, Young Rep, 57-59, Salt Lake Co. v.chmn, Utah, 65-67; mem. state bd, Rep. Women's Fedn, 59-61; del, Rep. Nat. Conv, 60, alternate del, 64; Rep. Nat. Committeewoman, Utah, 67- Bus. & Prof. Pos: Nurse, 47-49. Mem: UN Asn. of U.S, bd. dirs, 56-62 and chmn, UN High Sch. Model Assembly, 59-62; League of Women Voters; Salt Lake Med. Auxiliary, chmn, Ment. Health Cmn, 62-64; Commun. Action Prog; Citizens Adv. Cmt. to Salt Lake Co. Cmn; den mother, Boy Scouts, 50-60. Rel: Latter-day Saint. Mailing Add: 2757 St. Mary's Way, Salt Lake City, Utah 84108.

FAIRCHILD, ALFRED CHARLES D
Mem, Mich. Dem. State Cent. Cmt.
b. Ludington, Mich, 11/19/19; s. Alfred E. Fairchild and Blanche Bowhall F; m. 11/29/47 to Virginia D. Campbell; c. Mark. Educ: Muskegon Commun. Col. Polit. & Govt. Pos: V.chmn, Muskegon Co. Dem. Party, Mich, 60-61, treas, 61-65; chmn, 65-66; mem, Bd. of Rev, Muskegon Twp, 60-62; mem, Mich. Dem. State Cent. Cmt, Ninth Dist, 68- Bus. & Prof. Pos: Motor tester, Continental Motors, Muskegon, Mich, 41-61 & 66-; mgr, Muskegon Br, Mich. Dept. of State, 61-66; mem, Mich. State Conserv. Citizens Cmn. on Deer, 66- Mil. Serv: Entered as Pvt, Army, 42, released as S/Sgt, 46, after serv. with 121st Gen. Hosp. Unit, ETO. Mem: Eagles; Mason; Local 113 of AFL-CIO. Mailing Add: 893 Center St, Muskegon, Mich. 49442.

FAIRCHILD, RUTH D
Mem. Exec. Cmt, S.Dak. Dem. Party
b. Pierre, S.Dak, 5/19/18; s. Mervin Curtis Sherwood and Fleta May Weeks S; m. 9/4/38 to Wayne Leo Fairchild; c. Kent Leo, Bruce Wayne and Marsha May (Mrs. Billy Ray Sumpter). Educ: Philip High Sch, Grad, 37, Valedictorian; Aberdeene Bus. Col, 37-38. Polit. & Govt. Pos: Chmn, Haakon Co. Dem. Party, S.Dak, 64-68; mem. exec. cmt, S.Dak. Dem. Party, 68- Mem: Haakon Co. Chmn, Farmers Union. Rel: Presbyterian. Mailing Add: Star Route, Philip, S.Dak. 57567.

FAIRCLOTH, EARL D
Attorney Gen, Fla.
b. Chiefland, Fla, 9/24/20; s. Joseph William Faircloth and Emma Hogan F; m. 6/5/45 to Wilma Smith; c. Amy Lynn and David Earl. Educ: Univ. Fla, B.A, LL.B; pres, Student Body, 49-50; Fla. Blue Key; Hall of Fame; Nat. and South. Oratorical Championships; South. After-Dinner Championships; Nat. Declamation Championship; Delta Theta Phi; Tau Kappa Alpha. Polit. & Govt. Pos: Organized Fla. Cmt. for Fair Apportionment, 59; Fla. State Rep, 62-64; Attorney Gen, Fla, 64- Bus. & Prof. Pos: Attorney-at-law. Mil. Serv: Interpreter, Army Engrs, Cent, S.Am, 44-45. Mem: Moose; Am. Legion; VFW; WOW. Most Outstanding First Termer, Fla. Staff, House of Rep, 63. Rel: Baptist. Mailing Add: State Capitol, Tallahassee, Fla. 32304.

FALCEY, ROBERT M. D
Asst. Secy. of State, N.J.
b. Trenton, N.J, 6/15/13; s. Edward J. Falcey and Sara Marie Bird F; m. 4/9/47 to Kathryn Borne; c. Robert M, Jr. Educ: Cathedral High Sch, 4 years. Polit. & Govt. Pos: Campaign coordinator, Mercer Co. Dem. Party, N.J, 49-61, campaign registrn. coordinator, 51-63; Asst. Secy. of State, 54- Bus. & Prof. Pos: Prin. clerk, supreme and superior court, 39-54. Mil. Serv: Pvt, Army, 41-43, serv. in 112th Field Artil, U.S. Rel: Catholic. Mailing Add: 18 Woodside Ave, Trenton, N.J. 08618.

FALCIGNO, PAUL ANTHONY D
b. New Haven, Conn, 11/21/30; s. Pasquale Vincent Falcigno and Teresa Del Preto F; single. Educ: Quinnipiac Col, B.S. in bus. admin, 54; Univ. Pa, Wharton Sch. Finance and Commerce, M.B.A, 58; Phi Theta Kappa; Kappa Delta Mu. Polit. & Govt. Pos: Alderman, New Haven, Conn, 64-; chmn, Cmt. on Urban Develop. Bd. of Alderman, 66- and Cmt. on Streets and Squares, 65; mem, Charter Rev. Cmn. on Educ, 65-, and Charter Rev. Cmn. on Redistricting, 66- Bus. & Prof. Pos: Prof, Quinnipiac Col, 58-, chmn. dept. mkt, 69-, pres, Col. Senate, 69-70; consult, Paul A. Falcigno & Assocs, 60- Mil. Serv: Entered as Pvt, Army, 54, released as Pvt. 1/C, 56, after serv. as Instr, Specialist Training Regiment, Unit Supply Sch, Ft. Dix, N.J, 54-56; Nat. Defense and Good Conduct Medals. Publ: 'The Place of the Furniture Mart in the Furniture,' 58; several articles in prep. Mem: Am. Mkt. Asn; Am. Statistical Asn; New Haven Conoly Hist. Soc; Am. Asn. Univ. Profs; Soc. for Advancement of Mgt; Quinnipiac Col. Alumni Asn; Faculty Club of Quinnipiac Col; Wooster Square Commun. Coun; K. of C; Quinnipiac Coun, Boy Scouts; Conn. Golf Asn; Riverview Country Club. Rel: Roman Catholic. Mailing Add: 31 Lyon St, New Haven, Conn. 06511.

FALCONE, ERNANI CARLO D
Chmn, Del. Co. Dem. Cmt, Pa.
b. Upper Darby, Pa, 7/16/28; s. Nicholas Falcone and Julia Di Georgio F; m. 4/13/52 to Rachel Bateman Rogers; c. Julia C, Ernani C. and Claude D. Educ: Princeton Univ, B.A, 50; Univ. Pa, M.A, 55. Polit. & Govt. Pos: Worker, Haverford Twp. Dem. Cmn, Pa, 55-57; committeeman, Marple Twp. Dem. Assoc, 57-64; cmnr, Marple Twp, 63-65; chmn, Del. Co. Dem. Cmt, 64-; del, Dem. Nat. Conv, 68. Bus. & Prof. Pos: Instr, soc. sci, Swarthmore High Sch, 57- Mil. Serv: Entered as Pvt, Army, 51, released as 2nd Lt, 55, after service in Eng. Depot, Kaiserslautern Germany, ETO, 55; Maj, Res. Mem: Res. Officers Asn; Nat. Educ. Asn. Rel: Roman Catholic. Mailing Add: 430 Portland Dr, Broomall, Pa. 19008.

FALLIN, JAMES HOLDER D
b. Louisville, Ky, 9/13/45; s. James Taylor Fallin and Frances Irene Holder F; m. 7/28/68 to Sharon Faye Simmons; c. Angela Lynn. Educ: Brescia Col, B.S, 67; Delta Phi Omega; Midwest Model UN. Polit. & Govt. Pos: Pres, Brescia Col. Young Dem, Ky, 64-66; admin. asst. to Wendall Ford for Lt. Gov, 67; chmn, Ky. Del, Young Dem. of Am. Conv, 67; committeeman, Ky. Young Dem, 68; admin. asst. state youth chmn, Katherine Peden for U.S. Sen, 68; alternate del, Dem. Nat. Conv, 68. Mil. Serv: 2nd Lt, Army Res, currently; Direct Cmn. into the Army Res. as a Civil Affairs Officer. Chosen by the Young Dem. of Am. as one of five Young Dem. to lead Pledge of Allegiance before the Dem. Nat. Conv, Chicago, Ill, 68. Rel: Roman Catholic. Legal Res: P.O. Box 201, Lewisport, Ky. 42351. Mailing Add: 3217 Kemmons Dr, Apt. 2, Louisville, Ky. 40218.

FALLON, GEORGE H. D
U.S. Rep, Md.
b. Baltimore, Md, 7/24/02; s. Lawrence Fallon Sr. and Mary Dempsey F; m. 1929 to Willa Thomas; c. Mary Joyce. Educ: Calvert Bus. Col; John Hopkins Univ. Polit. & Govt. Pos: Chmn, Md. Dem. State Cent. Cmt, 38; Baltimore City councilman, 39-44; U.S. Rep, Md, 44-; del, Dem. Nat. Conv, 68. Legal Res: 3806 Hadley Square E, Baltimore, Md. 21218. Mailing Add: U.S. House of Representatives, Washington, D.C. 20515. (1967)

FALLON, JOHN J. D
b. Baltimore, Md, 2/2/24; married. Educ: Baltimore parochial, pub. schs. Polit. & Govt. Pos: Md. State Del, 63-67; Anne Arundel Dem. Coun; Lake Shore Dem. Club Inc; Anne Arundel Co. Recreation Commis. Bus. & Prof. Pos: Clerk, Baltimore & Ohio R.R. Co. Mil. Serv: WW II, U.S.N. Mem: Past pres, Brotherhood of Railway & Steamship Clerks Union, Local 511; K. of C; Am. Legion; VFW. Mailing Add: 4 Park Dr, Pasadena, Md. 21124. (1967)

FALLS, ARTHUR JOSEPH R
Asst. State Treas, Ill.
b. Astoria, N.Y, 8/27/26; s. Joseph Francis Falls (deceased) and Estelle C. Branigan F; m. 8/18/51 to Nancy Ann Stribling; c. Robert Arthur, Betsy Ann and Joseph Stribling. Educ: Fla. South. Col, B.S. in Journalism, 52; Lambda Chi Alpha. Polit. & Govt. Pos: Asst. state safety coordinator, Ill, 55-59; downstate dir, United Rep. Fund, Ill, 59-64; Rep. precinct committeeman, 61-; alternate del, Rep. Nat. Conv, 64; chmn, Cass Co. Rep. Cent. Cmt, 64-69; asst. state treas, Ill, 64- Bus. & Prof. Pos: Dir. student financial aid,

Univ. Ill, Chicago Circle, 67- Mil. Serv: Entered as A/S, Navy, 44, released as Seaman 1/C, 46. Mem: Pres, Lions Int, Ashland, 66; Elks; Am. Legion; Lions. Rel: Roman Catholic. Mailing Add: 1008 Fairview, Lombard, Ill. 60148.

FALLS, ROBERT ZEMRI D
N.C. State Rep.
b. Cleveland Co, N.C, 4/15/12; s. Alfred Falls and Lula Crowder F; m. 11/20/35 to Jennie Blanton. Educ: Gardner-Webb Jr. Col. Polit. & Govt. Pos: N.C. State Rep, 63- Bus. & Prof. Pos: Farmer. Mem: Rotary; Shelby C. of C; Cleveland Co. Agr. Cmt. Rel: Baptist; Deacon, 53, Westview Baptist Church, Shelby, N.C. Mailing Add: 1308 Wesson Rd, Shelby, N.C. 28150. (1967)

FANNIN, HOMER WINDELL R
Chmn, Elliott Co. Rep. Party, Ky.
b. Isonville, Ky, 9/15/12; s. Roy B. Fannin and Lona Kazee F; m. 8/30/34 to Verna Hutchinson; c. Dorsa (Mrs. Carson Hay), Homer, Jr, Roy W. and Cary A. Educ: Berea Col, Ky, 2 years. Polit. & Govt. Pos: Chmn, Elliott Co. Rep. Party, Ky, 68- Bus. & Prof. Pos: Trucking bus, 34-40; construction, 40-50 & 62-; oil producer, 50-62. Mem: Plumbers & Steam Fitters Union 248, Ashland, Ky. Rel: Protestant. Mailing Add: R.R. 2, Box 10, Isonville, Kay. 41149.

FANNIN, PAUL JONES R
U.S. Sen, Ariz.
b. Ashland, Ky, 1/29/07; s. Thomas Newton Fannin and Katherine Davis F; m. 5/6/34 to Elma Addington; c. Tom, Bill, Bob and Linda; five grandchildren. Educ: Univ. Ariz; Stanford Univ, B.A, 30; Kappa Sigma. Polit. & Govt. Pos: Gov, Ariz, 59-64; chmn, West. Gov. Conf, 63; mem. exec. cmt, Nat. Gov. Conf, 3 terms, chmn, Cmt. on Roads and Hwy. Safety; mem, Pres. Civil Defense Adv. Coun, 63-65; U.S. Sen, Ariz, 64- Bus. & Prof. Pos: V.pres, Fannin's Gas & Equip. Co, 32-56, pres, 56-58; pres, Fannin's Serv. & Supply, 45- Mem: Nat. Coun, Boy Scouts; Elks; Moose; Rotary; pres, Maricopa Co. Better Bus. Bur, 48-49; past chmn, Indust. Develop. Cmt, Phoenix C. of C. Rel: Methodist. Legal Res: Phoenix, Ariz. Mailing Add: 140 Senate Office Bldg, Washington, D.C. 20510.

FANNING, JOHN PATTON D
W.Va. State Sen.
b. Iaeger, W.Va, 8/14/34; s. James Patton Fanning and Gertrude Neal F; m. 2/4/56 to Marianna Young; c. Brenda Jean, Deborah Ann and John William. Educ: Davis & Elkins Col, degree, 55; Cincinnati Col. Embalming, degree, 59; Alpha Sigma Phi; Phi Sigma Eta. Polit. & Govt. Pos: Mayor, Iaeger, W.Va, 64-66; W.Va. State Sen, Sixth Dist, 68- Bus. & Prof. Pos: Mgr, Fanning Funeral Home, 59- Mem: Rotary (pres, 69-); AF&AM. Rel: Methodist. Mailing Add: Box 68, Iaeger, W.Va. 24844.

FANTASIA, MARY D
Dem. Nat. Committeewoman, Mass.
b. Arlington, Mass; m. to Anthony; c. Patricia M.(Mrs. James Stewart), Kevin Paul and Joanne Mary. Educ: Bryant Stratton Bus. Sch. Polit. & Govt. Pos: Precinct worker, every election; head of women's div. and v.chmn, Mass. Dem. State Cmt; chmn, Middlesex Co. Dem. Party, currently; del, five Mass. State Dem. Conv; Dem. State Committeewoman, Mass, 57-; Presidential Elector, 60 & 64; Dem. Nat. Committeewoman, Mass, 62-; del, Dem. Nat. Conv, 64 & 68; mem, Somerville Dem. Ward and City Cmt. Bus. & Prof. Pos: Liaison officer between the State and Fed. Govt. for the Mass. Dept. of Commerce and Develop, 64-66; exec. secy. to Mayor of Somerville, 66- Mem: Hon. pres, Mass. Women on Wheels; PTA (former pres. and secy); bd. dirs, Somerville Cath. Charities and Mass. Bay United Fund; Somerville Hosp. Ladies Cmt; League of Cath. Women. Rel: Roman Catholic. Mailing Add: 181 Hudson St, Somerville, Mass. 02144.

FANTASIA, NICK D
W.Va. State Del.
b. Kingmont, W.Va, 1/3/23; s. Louis Fantasia and Rose DiGiacama F; m. 6/18/49 to Carmella Simonetti; c. Georgeanna, Rosemary, Nicolena, Gina, Annette and Nick Louis. Educ: Fairmont State Col, B.A, 49; W.Va. Univ, M.A, 53. Polit. & Govt. Pos: W.Va. State Del, 54-58 & 64- Bus. & Prof. Pos: V.pres, gen. mgr, WTCS Radio Sta, Fairmont; prin, teacher, Marion Co. Schs, 16 years. Mil. Serv: Army, 3 years serv. Mem: Moose; Am. Legion; VFW; Eagles; Classroom Teachers Asn; life mem, Nat. Educ. Asn; pres, Izaac Walton League; former pres, Elem. Prin. Asn; former pres, W.Va. State Sportscasters Asn; former pres, Local Union 4006; pres, Christopher Columbus Lodge; Holy Name Soc. Rel: Catholic. Mailing Add: Box 64, Kingmont, W.Va. 26578. (1967)

FARBER, EARL CLARENCE R
Chmn, Hamilton Co. Rep. Cmt, N.Y.
b. Norway, N.Y, 6/19/02; s. Henry C. Farber and Rosilda Grassel F; m. 10/17/31 to Elizabeth Nancy Butler; c. Gene Earl. Educ: Herkimer High Sch. Polit. & Govt. Pos: Supvr, Town of Morehouse, N.Y, 36-43; co. clerk, Hamilton Co, N.Y, 43-; v.chmn, Hamilton Co. Rep. Cmt, 44-63, chmn, 45 & 63-; Rep. committeeman, Town of Morehouse, 45-; trustee, Sch. Dist. Three, 52- Bus. & Prof. Pos: Agent, Travelers Ins. Co, 29-; agent, Am. Surety Co, Transamerica Ins. Co, 36- Mem: F&AM; Mohawk Valley Consistory; Ziyara Shrine; Herkimer Lodge, Elks. Rel: Baptist. Mailing Add: Town of Morehouse, Hoffmeister, N.Y. 13353.

FARBSTEIN, LEONARD D
U.S. Rep, N.Y.
b. New York, N.Y; s. Louis Farbstein and Yetta Schlanger F; m. to Blossom Langer; c. Louis J. Educ: City Col. of N.Y; N.Y. Univ. Law Sch, LL.B. Polit. & Govt. Pos: N.Y. State Assemblyman; U.S. Rep, N.Y, 56- Mil. Serv: Coast Guard Res, World War II. Mem: Am. Judicature Soc; N.Y. Co. Lawyers Asn; Am. & N.Y. Bar Asns; Asn. of Bar of N.Y.C; K. of P; B'nai B'rith; C. of C; Lower East Side Dem. Asn. Legal Res: 500-A Grand St, New York, N.Y. 10002. Mailing Add: Rm. 2455, Rayburn House Bldg, Washington, D.C. 20515.

FARENGA, FELIX ANTHONY D
b. New York, N.Y, 11/3/20; s. Salvatore A. Farenga and Emma Caruso F; m. 2/27/43 to Irene Dorothy O'Keefe; c. Barbara (Mrs. Salice) and Salvatore A, II. Educ: Fordham Univ, B.S. Polit. & Govt. Pos: Alternate del, Dem. Nat. Conv, 68. Bus. & Prof. Pos: Pres, Farenga Bros. Inc, 45- Mil. Serv: Entered as Pvt, Marines, 43, released as S/Sgt, 46, after serv. in Radio Intel. Corps, Pac, 43-46; Unit Citation, Okinawa; Japanese Intercept Operator Medal; Pac. Theatre Medal; Good Conduct Medal. Mem: Metropolitan Funeral Dirs. Asn.(pres); Motor Hearse & Car Owners Asn.(v.pres); N.Y. Athletic Club; pres, Columbus ESEA Alliance; Am. Legion; Amvets; Siwanoy Dem. Club. Testimonial Dinner, 68. Rel: Roman Catholic. Legal Res: 2429 Morgan Ave, Bronx, N.Y. 10469. Mailing Add: 204 E. 116th St, New York, N.Y. 10029.

FARENTHOLD, FRANCES TARLTON D
Tex. State Rep.
b. Corpus Christi, Tex, 10/2/26; d. Benjamin Dudley Tarlton and Catherine Bluntzer T; m. 10/6/50 to George E. Farenthold; c. Dudley Tarlton, George E, Jr, Emilie, James Dougherty and Vincent Bluntzer (deceased). Educ: Vassar Col, A.B, 46; Univ. Tex. Law Sch, LL.B, 49; woman's hon. legal soc. Polit. & Govt. Pos: Munic. app. mem, Human Rels. Cmt, Tex, 63-68; mem, Tex. Adv. Cmt. to U.S. Cmn. on Civil Rights, 68-; Tex. State Rep, Dist. 45, Place 1, 69- Mem: Tex. and Am. Bar Asns. Rel: Roman Catholic. Add: 625 S. Upper Broadway, Corpus Christi, Tex. 78401.

FARGARSON, ROBERT MELVYN D
b. Aransas Pass, Tex, 2/23/32; s. Melvin Lavone Fargarson and Bobbie Inez Lawrence F; m. 7/25/53 to Jonetta Lovett; c. Kim, Dabney and Robert M, Jr. Educ: South. Methodist Univ; Cumberland Univ. Sch. Law; 'M' Asn; Sigma Alpha Epsilon; Delta Theta Phi. Polit. & Govt. Pos: Law clerk to U.S. Dist. Judge, 56-58; Tenn. State Rep, 63-67. Mil. Serv: Entered as Pvt, Marine Corps, 51, released as Sgt, 55, after serv. in Marine Air Wing; Nat. Defense, Korean Theatre and U.N. Serv. Medals. Mem: Pres, Tenn. Young Lawyers, 66-67; bd. gov, Tenn. Bar Asn, 66; pres, Memphis and Shelby Co. Jr. Bar, 63-64; Acad. Law and Sci; Am. Legion; Colonial Country Club; Summit Club; Young Dem. Easter Seal Soc; W.Tenn. Cerebral Palsy Coun; Tenn. Defense Lawyers Asn; Mason; Club La Rhonde; Intergovt. Coop. Hobby: Golf. Rel: Episcopal. Legal Res: 4510 Normandy Rd, Memphis, Tenn. 38117. Mailing Add: 724 Lincoln American Tower, Memphis, Tenn. 38103.

FARGHER, LAWRENCE LeROY R
Mem, Calif. Rep. State Cent. Cmt.
b. Helena, Mont, 9/16/32; s. Lawrence Arthur Fargher and Maude Lauson F; m. 5/16/53 to Camille Marie Augusta; c. Larry Lee, Leighton Lynn, Lauson Layne, Lindel Lee and Laure Lynne. Educ: Univ. Omaha, B.S. in eng, 54; Univ. Santa Clara, M.B.A, 65. Polit. & Govt. Pos: Dir, Santa Clara Co. Sanitation Dist. 4, Calif, 63-; councilman and mayor, Santa Clara, 64-65, mayor pro tem, 69; cand, U.S. House of Rep, Ninth Cong. Dist, Calif, 68; mem, Gov. Cmt. on Hiring the Handicapped, 68-; mem, Calif. and Santa Clara Co. Rep. Cent. Cmts, currently. Bus. & Prof. Pos: Engr, Boeing Airplane Co, 58; eng. writer, Westinghouse Elec. Corp, 58-62; head systs. eng, United Tech. Center, 62- Mil. Serv: Entered as 2nd Lt, Air Force, 54, released as 1st Lt, 58, after serv. in 9th Bomb Sq, 7th Bomb Wing, Heavy Strategic Air Command, 55-58. Mem: Calif. and Nat. Socs. of Prfnl. Engrs; past pres. and founder, Darvon Civic Club of Calif. Wrestling, Nebr. Rel: Catholic. Legal Res: 1755 Shamrock Ave, Santa Clara, Calif. 95051. Mailing Add: City Hall, 1500 Warburton Ave, Santa Clara, Calif. 95051.

FARIES, McINTYRE R
b. Wei Hsien, Shantung Province, China, 4/17/96; s. William Reid Faries and Priscilla Ellen Chittick F; m. 10/7/22 to Margaret Lois Shorten, wid; m. 12/3/65 to Geraldyne Brewer Bergh; c. Barbara Lois (Mrs. Kenneth J. Simpson) and Marjorie Ann (Mrs. John William Gaines). Educ: Occidental Col, A.B, 20; Univ. South. Calif, 19-22; Southwest. Univ. Los Angeles, J.D, 26; Phi Beta Kappa; Olive Crown; Phi Delta Phi; Phi Gamma Delta; Econ. Club; Blackstonian. Polit. & Govt. Pos: Del. and mem. exec. cmt, Rep. Nat. Conv, 36, del, 40, 44, 48 & 52; v.chmn, Calif. Rep. State Cent. Cmt, 38; pres, Calif. Rep. Assembly, 38; chmn, Rep. Campaign Cmt. South Calif, 40 & 42, mem. exec. cmt, 50; chmn, Sen. William F. Knowland Campaign, 46 & 52; mem, Rep. Nat. Cmt, 47-53, mem. exec. cmt. and v.chmn, 48-53; mem. exec. cmt, Calif. Campaigns, Gen. Dwight D. Eisenhower, 52, Richard M. Nixon for Congressman, Sen. and V.President, Thomas F. Kuchel for Senate, twice and Earl Warren for Gov, three times; judge, Superior Court, Calif, 53-69, pretrial div, 60, presiding judge, criminal div, 61-64 and appellate dept, 65. Bus. & Prof. Pos: Pres. and mem. exec. cmt, El Pueblo de Los Angeles, Inc, Calif, 53-68. Mil. Serv: Entered as Seaman 2/C, Navy, 17, released as Ens, Naval Res, 19, after serv. in Pac, 17-19; Naval Res, 19-20, Ret. Mem: Co-chmn, Los Amigos del Pueblo; pres, Los Angeles City Birthday Celebration, 66; pres, El Pueblo de Los Angeles State Hist. Monument Cmn, 66-67; mem, Calif. State Park and Recreation Cmn, 68-69; mem, Calif. Bicentennial Cmn, 69; Am. Law Inst; U.S, Calif. and L.A. Co. Bar Asns; Calif. Water Asn.(past pres); Sixth Dist. Agr. Asn.(pres); Am. Acad. Polit. & Soc. Sci; Judicature Soc; Calif. Club; Lincoln Club; San Marino City Club; Oneonta Club (past pres); Hwa Pei Benevolent Asn. South. Calif; patron, Pasadena Tournament of Roses; Los Angeles World Affairs Coun; San Marino Lodge; San Marino Post; Hist. Soc. South Calif; Acacia Club; Mason. Rel: Presbyterian. Mailing Add: 400 S. Burnside, Apt, 5-C, Los Angeles, Calif. 90036.

FARKAS, DANIEL JOHN D
Committeeman, Calif. Dem. State Cent. Cmt.
b. Hazel Park, Mich, 9/26/39; s. John Farkas and Julia Fanchal Marshall F; m. 4/6/68 to Jilleene Marie Peacha. Educ: Whittier Col, In-Resident Scholarship, 66-68, A.B, 68; Univ. South. Calif, Herman fel, 68-; Most Outstanding Polit. Sci. Student, Whittier Col, 67; Pi Sigma Alpha. Polit. & Govt. Pos: Campaign Mgr, 43rd Assembly Dist, Calif, 68; committeeman, Calif. Dem. State Cent. Cmt, 68- Bus. & Prof. Pos: Microwave Technician, Pac. Tel. & Tel, Los Angeles, Calif, 57-65; admin asst, Latin-American Studies, Univ. South. Calif, 68. Mil. Serv: Entered Airman Recruit Naval Air Res, 62, released Aviation Electrician 2/C, 68, after serv. in Jet Attack Squadron 776, Los Alamitos, Calif. Mem: Order of Repeatermen and Testboardman; IBEW, AFL-CIO (Steward). Rel: Protestant. Mailing Add: 4334 Winchester Ave, Los Angeles, Calif. 90032.

FARLEY, FRANK S. R
N.J. State Sen.
b. Atlantic City, N.J, 12/5/01; m. to Marie 'Honey' Feyl. Educ: Univ. Pa; Georgetown Univ. Law Sch, LL.B, 25; Delta Kappa Epsilon. Polit. & Govt. Pos: N.J. State Assemblyman, 37-40; acting Gov. for Gov. Edge and Gov. Hughes, N.J, 3 times; N.J. State Sen, 40-, Majority Leader, N.J. State Sen, 45, pres, 62 and pres. pro tem, 63-65; del, Rep. Nat. Conv, 44-64 & 68; chmn, Atlantic Co. Rep. Party, N.J, 68- Bus. & Prof. Pos: Lawyer. Mem: Atlantic Co. Bar Asn.(past pres); Crippled Childrens Cmn. of N.J; Rep. Co. Chmn. Asn. of N.J.(pres); bd. gov, Georgetown Univ. Mailing Add: State Capitol, Trenton, N.J. 08625. (1967)

FARLEY, GUY O, JR. D
Va. State Del.
b. Staunton, Va, 9/6/32; married. Educ: Hampden-Sydney Col, B.S; Univ. Va, LL.B. Polit. & Govt. Pos: Va. State Del, 64- Bus. & Prof. Pos: Lawyer. Mem: Fairfax Co. Jr. C. of C.(past pres); PTA (past pres); Fairfax Co. C. of C; Fairfax Co, Va. State and Am. Bar Asns; Va. Commonwealth's Attorneys Asn; Va. Trial Lawyers Asn; Nat. Asn. of Commonwealth's Attorneys. Rel: Presbyterian. Mailing Add: 1616 Chimney House Rd, Reston, Va. 22070.

FARLEY, JAMES A. D
b. Grassy Point, N.Y, 5/30/88; s. James Farley and Ellen Goldrick F; m. to Elizabeth A. Finnegan (deceased); c. Elizabeth (Mrs. Glenn D. Montgomery), Ann (Mrs. Edward J. Hickey, III) and James A. Educ: Packard Commercial Sch, N.Y.C, 06. Hon. D.C.L, Univ. of South, 33, Lincoln Mem. Univ, 35, St. Ambrose Col, 41, and Villanova Col, 42; LL.D, Canisius Col, Manhattan Col, John Marshall Col. of Law, 34, Niagara Univ, 35, Hendrix Col, 39, Oglethorpe Univ, 40, Seattle Univ, 50, Ithaca Col, Loras Col, St. Anselm's Col, 51, St. Joseph's Col, 55 and L.I. Univ, 57; D.C.S, N.Y. Univ, 50 and Suffolk Univ, 56; citation, Univ. of Fla, 50; D.S.S, Duquesne Univ, 53. Polit. & Govt. Pos: Town clerk, Stony Point, N.Y, 12/19; port warden, Port of N.Y, 18-19; chmn, Rockland Co. Dem. Cmt, 19-29; supvr, Rockland Co, 20-23; past v.pres, Nat. Dem. Club, N.Y.C; N.Y. State Assemblyman, 23; mem, N.Y. State Athletic Cmn, 23-33 and chmn, 25-33; del, Dem. Nat. Conv, 24, 28, 32, 36, 40, 44, 48 & 68; secy, N.Y. Dem. State Cmt, 28-30 and chmn, 30-44; chmn, Dem. Nat. Cmt, 32-40; Postmaster Gen. of U.S, 33-40; mem, Cmn. on Orgn. Exec. Br. of Govt, 53 and N.Y. State Banking Bd, 55- Bus. & Prof. Pos: Bookkeeper, Merlin Heilholtz Paper Co, N.Y.C, 06; sales mgr, Universal Gypsum Co, 26; organizer, James A. Farley & Co, 26, merged with five other bldg. materials firms to form Gen. Builders Supply Corp, 26, pres. and dir, 29-33 & 49; dir, Coca Cola Co, dir, Campania Embotelladora Coca-Cola, S. A, pres. and dir, Coca-Cola Int, chmn. bd. and dir, Coca-Cola Co. of Can, Ltd, chmn. of bd, Coca-Cola Export Corp, 40. Publ: Behind the Ballots, 38; Jim Farley's Story, 48. Mem: Pan-Am. Soc, Inc; N.Y. State Hist. Asn; Am. Soc. of Polit. and Soc. Sci; Am. Acad. Polit. & Soc. Sci; Albany Soc. N.Y; Latin Am. Sect, N.Y. Bd. of Trade; Mex. C. of C. of U.S; Cuban C. of C; Friendly Sons of St. Patrick; Ancient Order of Hibernians; Eagles; Elks; Red Men; K. of C; Sales Execs, Circumnavigators, Export Mgrs. of N.Y. and N.Y. Athletic Clubs; Nat. Press Club. Order Francisco de Mirando, Venezuela; Capt. Robert Dollar Mem. Award; Freedoms Found. Award, 53; Cardinal Newman Award, 56; Am. Irish Hist. Soc. Award, 56; Cross of Isabel la Catolica, Spain. Rel: Catholic. Mailing Add: 301 Park Ave, New York, N.Y. 10022. (1967)

FARLEY, JAMES WALLACE D
Lee Twp. Committeeman, Platte Co. Dem. Cent. Cmt, Mo.
b. Kansas City, Mo, 7/31/28; s. Wallace J. Farley and Idabelle Vanlandingham F; m. 8/20/50 to Marcella Lee Whittaker; c. Emma Susan, James Wallace, Jr. and John Walter. Educ: Univ. Mo, Columbia, B.S. in Bus. Admin, 49, LL.B, 52; Phi Alpha Delta.. Polit. & Govt. Pos: Lee Twp. committeeman, Platte Co. Dem. Cent. Cmt, Mo, 50-, chmn, 60-68; mem. and secy, Platte Co. Planning Cmt, 52-54; treas, Mo. Young Dem. Clubs, 54-55, pres, 55-56; Mo. State Rep, 56; del, Dem. Nat. Conv, 56 & 68; mem, Mo. State Dem. Cmt, 60-68; mem, Sixth Cong. Dist. Dem. Cmt, Mo, 60-68; co-chmn, Mo. Sen. Redistricting Cmt, 61. Bus. & Prof. Pos: Mem, Kansas City Metrop. Planning Cmn, 68- Mem: Exec. secy, Northwest Water Asn; pres, Platte Co. Bar Asn, 65; Mason; RAM; coun, K.T; Shrine; dir, Platte Valley Baseball League; Farley Athletic Asn; Leavenworth Country Club. Rel: Disciples of Christ; Deacon, First Christian Church, Platte City, Mo. Mailing Add: Box 33, Farley, Mo. 64028.

FARLEY, REX JAY R
b. Bridgeport, Conn, 5/16/23; s. William Henry Farley and Marie Gardner F; m. 10/20/56 to Mary Evelyn Hughes; c. Craig, Kevin and Mark. Educ: U.S. Merchant Marine Acad, 42-43; Syracuse Univ, 52-54; Ariz. State Univ, B.S. in Mgt, 62. Polit. & Govt. Pos: Ariz. State Rep, 67-69. Bus. & Prof. Pos: Supvr, claims dept, Ariz. Employ. Security Cmn, 56-62, programmer and systs. analyst, 62-64; asst. mgr. data processing, Ariz. State Univ, 64-67. Mil. Serv: Entered as Pvt, Army, 49, released as Cpl, 51, after serv. in Co. F, 32nd Inf, 7th Inf. Div, Korea, 50-51. Rel: Catholic. Mailing Add: 3120 W. Stella Lane, Phoenix, Ariz. 85017.

FARLEY, THOMAS T. D
Minority Leader, Colo. House of Rep.
b. Pueblo, Colo, 11/10/34; s. John B. Farley and Mary Tancred F; m. 5/14/60 to Kathleen Murphy; c. John Baron, Kelly Kathleen, Michael Murphy and Anne Michele. Educ: Univ. of Santa Clara, B.S, 56; Univ. Colo, LL.B, 59. Polit. & Govt. Pos: Dep. dist. attorney, Pueblo Co, Colo, 60-62; nat. committeeman, Young Dem. of Colo, 62-66; Colo. State Rep, 67-, minority leader, Colo. House of Rep, 67- Mil. Serv: Army. Mem: Pueblo, Colo. and Am. Bar Asns; Downtown Adv. Asn.(pres, 65-66); Asn. of U.S. Army Pueblo Chap; Coun. Cath. Mem; Rotary; Elks; K. of C. Rel: Catholic. Mailing Add: 117 E. Orman Ave, Pueblo, Colo. 81005.

FARMER, EARL RAYMOND R
b. Milfay, Okla, 3/15/10; s. Leanord Raymond Farmer and Dollie Cooper F; m. 10/3/32 to Mildred E. Gibson; c. Harold Dane, Raymond Leon, Willa Dean and Barbara Jean. Educ: Cameron Jr. Col. Polit. & Govt. Pos: Chmn, Creek Co. Rep. Party, Okla, 65-67; dist. committeeman, Rep. Party, 63-65 and precinct chmn, 56-64. Bus. & Prof. Pos: Dist. sales mgr, Fluid Packed Pump, 55-, store mgr, 50-55, field salesman, 45-50 and pump repairman, 43-45; unit operator, Mobil Oil Corp, 35-43. Mem: Mason,Lodge 468; Elks; Deepfork watershed mem. All-State basketball and baseball player. Rel: First Christian Church. Mailing Add: Route 1, Box 65, Drumright, Okla. 74030. (1967)

FARMER, JAMES Liberal, N.Y.
Asst. Secy, Dept. Health, Educ. and Welfare
b. Marshall, Tex, 1/12/20; s. James Leonard Farmer and Pearl Marion Houston F; m. 5/21/49 to Lula A. Peterson; c. Tami and Abbey. Educ: Wiley Col, B.S, 38; Howard Univ, B.D, 41. Hon. H.H.D, Morgan State Col, 64; LL.D, Muhlenberg Col. Polit. & Govt. Pos: Founder, Cong. of Racial Equality, 42, nat. chmn, 42-44 & 50, nat. dir, 61-66, leader, Freedom Ride, 61; race rels. secy, Fel. of Reconciliation, 44-45; organizer, Upholsterers' Int. Union of N.Am, 45-47; lectr. race and labor probs, 48-50; student field secy, League for Indust. Democracy, 50-54; int. rep, State, Co. and Munic. Employees Union, 54-59; v.chmn, Liberal Party of N.Y. Co, 54-61; prog. dir, NAACP, 59-61; mem. nat. exec. bd, Am. Cmt. on Africa, 59-64; sponsor, Am. Negro Leadership Conf. on Africa; chmn, Coun. of United Civil Rights Leadership, 63-; head, Center for Commun. Action Educ, 66-; asst. secy, Dept. Health, Educ. and Welfare, 69- Publ: Freedom—When?, 65. Mem: Bd. dirs, League for Indust. Democracy; Am. Civil Liberties Union; Am. for Dem. Action. Am. Friendship Club Award, 61; Omega Psi Phi Award, 61, 63; Amvets Commun. Award, 62; John Dewey Award, League for Indust. Democracy, 62. Legal Res: 165 Park Row, New York, N.Y. 10038. Mailing Add: Dept. of Health, Education and Welfare, Washington, D.C. 20201.

FARMER, LEON, JR. D
Ga. State Rep.
b. Athens, Ga. 5/23/37; s. Leon Farmer and Eloise Harmon F; m. 4/26/58 to Marilyn Wade; c. Terri Leigh, Lisa René, Joni Denise and Leon, III. Educ: Univ. Ga, B.B.A, 64; Univ. Ga. Sch. Law, J.D, 67; pres, Law Sch. Class; Chi Phi; Phi Alpha Delta. Polit. & Govt. Pos: Commandant, Ga. Marine Corps, 67-; Ga. State Rep, 67-, mem, Criminal Code Study Cmt, Ga. House of Rep, 67, Pub. Defender Study Cmt, 67-68, chmn, Spec. Study Cmt. on Univ. Syst. of Ga, 67-68, mem, Spec. Judiciary Cmt, Code Rev. Subcmt, Univ. Syst. of Ga. Cmt, chmn, Long Range Prog. Subcmt. and mem, Welfare Cmt, Juvenile Matters Subcmt, 67-, mem, Corp. Code Study Cmt, 68 and mem, Cent. Computerized Criminal Records Syst. Study Cmt, 68-69; del. and temporary floor chmn, regular Ga. del, Dem. Nat. Conv, 68. Bus. & Prof. Pos: Attorney-at-law, Athens, Ga, 66- Mil. Serv: Entered as Pvt, Marine Corps, 57, released as Cpl, 59, after serv. in Second Bn, Second Marines, Second Marine Div, F.M.F, Lebanon, 58; Decorated for Serv. in Lebanon Landing, 58. Mem: State Bar of Ga; Athens Bar Asn; Jaycees; Elks; Moose; Am. Legion; Amvets; DAV; VFW; Young Dem. YMCA Heavyweight Boxing Champion; All Mid-South Football Player; Selected as Outstanding Young Man of Am, 67; Commended by Ga. House of Rep. on three separate occasions for outstanding contributions. Rel: Baptist. Mailing Add: 1000 Old Creek Rd, Athens, Ga. 30601.

FARMER, LYLE T. DFL
b. Mankato, Minn, 1921; m. to Ellen; c. David, Kathleen, John. Educ: Mankato State Col, B.S; Univ. of Minn, M.A. Polit. & Govt. Pos: Minn. State Rep, 62-66. Bus. & Prof. Pos: Former high sch. teacher. Mil. Serv: Army, 43-46. Mem: Secy-Treas, St. Paul Teachers' Retirement Fund Asn. Mailing Add: 755 E. Montana Ave, St. Paul, Minn. 55106. (1967)

FARMER, MALCOLM, JR. R
b. Phoenixville, Penn, 12/1/11; s. Malcolm Farmer and Alice Savory McKey F; m. 10/17/36 to Louise Russell; c. Malcolm III, Peter R, Louis R. and R. Tenney. Educ: Yale Univ, B.A, 34; Delta Kappa Epsilon. Polit. & Govt. Pos: Chmn, Rep. Finance Cmt, R.I, 52-54; treas, United Rep. Fund, R.I, 57-60, chmn, 66-69. Bus. & Prof. Pos: V.pres, G. H. Walker & Co, Inc, 60- Mil. Serv: Entered as Lt.(jg), Navy, 42, released as Lt. Comdr, 46, after serv. in Air Combat Intel. Torpedo Squadron 89, Pac, 44-45; ETO; Am. & Pac. Ribbons. Mem: Hope Club; Agawam Hunt; Yale Club, N.Y.C. Rel: Episcopal. Mailing Add: 168 Bowen St, Providence, R.I. 02906.

FARMER, MERLE L. D
Chmn, Yavapai Co. Dem. Cent. Cmt, Ariz.
b. Tularosa, N.Mex, 10/23/06; d. Arthur L. Douglass and Blanche Rachael Parker D; m. to Paul R. Farmer, div. Educ: High Sch, Tularosa, N.Mex, grad, 23; Bus. Col, Albuquerque, N.Mex, grad, 24. Polit. & Govt. Pos: Sr. clerk, Yavapai Co. Welfare Bd, Ariz, 35-53, mem. adv. bd, 68-; precinct committeeman, Yavapai Co, Prescott, 15 years; postmaster, Legis. Post Off, Ariz. State Legis, Phoenix, 60-64; pres, Ariz. Fedn. Dem. Women's Clubs, 62-63; chmn, Yavapai Co. Dem. Cent. Cmt, 62-; supt, Ariz. Pioneer Home, Prescott, 65-67; del, Dem. Nat. Conv, 68. Bus. & Prof. Pos: Owner, Holsum Bread Agency, Prescott, Ariz, 50-57. Mem: Am. Cancer Soc.(pres. and serv. chmn, Ariz. Div, Yavapai Co, Prescott, many years, bd. dirs. for State, Phoenix, currently); charter mem, Soroptimist; Am. Legion Auxiliary; Bus. & Prfnl. Women's Club (pres, Prescott Club, 43-44); VFW Auxiliary. Received 25 Year Pin as Vol, Am. Cancer Soc. Rel: Methodist. Legal Res: 607 Country Club, Prescott, Ariz. 86301. Mailing Add: P.O. Box 189, Prescott, Ariz. 86301.

FARMER, THOMAS LAURENCE D
b. Berlin, Germany, 7/26/23; s. Laurence Farmer and Else Dienemann F; m. 9/8/51 to Elizabeth Fairchild Becker; c. Daniel Fairchild, Sarah Bennett and Elspeth Lanham. Educ: Harvard, B.A, 43; LL.B, 50; Brasenose Col, Oxford Univ, B.A. in Jurisprudence, 48, M.A, 50; Lincoln's Inn Soc. Polit. & Govt. Pos: Chmn. adv. bd, Nat. Capitol Transportation Agency, 61-64; gen. counsel, Agency Int. Develop, 64-68. Bus. & Prof. Pos: Clerk to Judge Manley O. Hudson, Int. Law Cmn. of Gen. Assembly UN, Geneva, Switz, 50; assoc, Simpson, Thacher & Bartlett, N.Y.C, 54-57, Wash, 58-64; partner, Kominers, Fort, Schlefer, Farmer & Boyer, 68- Mil. Serv: Entered as Pvt, Army, 43, released as Sgt, 46, after serv. in Mil. Intel. Res. Sect, War Dept. Gen. Staff, 44-46. Mem: D.C, N.Y, Am, Fed. Bar Asns; Am. Soc. Int. Law; trustee, United Planning Orgn; trustee, Lincoln Univ; vis. cmt, Harvard, 59-65; Grey's Inn Soc; Metrop. and Fed, City Clubs, D.C; Harvard Law Sch. Asn, D.C. (pres); chmn. adv. cmt, Cmt. World Justice and Peace, Conf. Roman Catholic Bishops; exec. cmt. and trustee, Overseas Develop. Coun; chmn, Int. Develop. Adv. Panel, C. of C. U.S; Harvard Club N.Y; Nat. Capital Dem. Club. Rel: Episcopal. Legal Res: 3456 Macomb St. N.W, Washington, D.C. 20016. Mailing Add: 529 Tower Bldg, 1401 K St. N.W, Washington, D.C. 20005.

FARNHAM, RODERICK EWEN R
Maine State Rep.
b. Brownville Junction, Maine, 1/23/10; s. Willard Farnham and Marian Morrison; m. 8/20/38 to Margaret Davis; c. Patricia A.(Mrs. Russell), Alden, R. Ewen, M. Jane (Mrs. Rabeni) and Barbara M.(Mrs. Briggs). Educ: Colby Col, B.S, 31; Lambda Chi Alpha. Hon. M.A, Colby Col. Polit. & Govt. Pos: Mem, adv. coun, Maine State Employ. Serv, 52-68; Maine State Rep, 69- Bus. & Prof. Pos: With Great North. Paper Co, 43-, admin. asst. to v.pres, currently. Mem: Am. Soc. Personnel Adminstr.(former pres, Maine Chap); Mason; Kiwanis; Sch. Bd; former trustee, Colby Col. Rel: Protestant. Legal Res: Sunset Ave, Hampden, Maine 04444. Mailing Add: M.R.C, Box 17, Bangor, Maine 04401.

FARNSLEY, CHARLES ROWLAND PEASLEE D
b. Louisville, Ky, 3/28/07; s. Burrel Hopson Farnsley and Anna May Peaslee F; m. 2/27/37 to Nancy Hall Carter; c. Mrs. Robert Bird, Jr, Mrs. Ronald Gascoyne, Douglass Charles Ellerbe, Alexander, IV and Burrel Charles. Educ: Univ. Louisville, LL.B, 30, A.B, 42; Delta Upsilon; Omicron Delta Kappa. Hon. LL.D, Univ. Louisville, 50, Wesleyan Univ, 59. Polit. & Govt. Pos: Ky. State Rep, 36-40; mayor, Louisville, 48-54; U.S. Rep, Third Dist, Ky, 64-66. Bus. & Prof. Pos: Law practice, 30-48 & 54-64; mem. bd. trustees, Louisville Free Pub. Libr, 43-48; trustee, Univ. Louisville, 46-48, secy. bd. trustees, 47-48, mem. bd. overseers, 47-58; curator, Transylvania Univ, 47-58; pres, Lost Cause Press Co, currently. Publ: 'Sources of Democracy,' Govt. News, 6/50. Mem: Am, Jefferson Co. and Ky. Bar Asns; Sons of Confederate Vet.(comdr, Andrew Broadus Pos, 361); Louisville Philharmonic Soc.(dir, 47-48); Soc. Colonial Wars; Masons; Pendennis, Wynn Stay, Filson, Harmony Landing, Century and Grolier Clubs. Rel: Episcopal. Mailing Add: The Dartmouth, Apt. 11B, 1416 Willow Ave, Louisville, Ky. 40204.

FARNSWORTH, JAMES S. R
Mich. State Rep.
b. Paw Paw, Mich, 6/29/07; married; c. Stanley and Diane (Mrs. Barry Crown). Polit. & Govt. Pos: Former finance chmn, Allegan Co. Rep. Cmt, Mich; mayor, Otsego; mem, Allegan City Bd. of Rev, 8 years; mem, Allegan Co. Bd. of Supvrs, 7 years; del, Constitutional Conv, 61-62; Mich. State Rep, 62- Bus. & Prof. Pos: Automobile dealer, 30- Mem: Elks; Rotary; Farm Bur; bd. of dir, Kalamazoo Child Guidance Clinic. Rel: Protestant. Mailing Add: Gun River Dr, Plainwell, Mich. 49080. (1967)

FARNUM, BILLIE SUNDAY D
b. Saginaw, Mich, 4/11/16; m. to Maxine DeCoe; c. Eugene, Norman, Ronald, five grandchildren. Polit. & Govt. Pos: U.S. Rep, Mich, 64-66; Auditor-Gen, Mich, 61-64; dep. state chmn, Mich. Dem. Party, 60-61; dep. secy. of state, Mich. 57-60; asst. secy. of state, Mich, 55; admin. aide, former Sen. Blair Moody, 52-54; cmnr, Mich. State Fair. Bus. & Prof. Pos: Pontiac Motor Co, 36; UAW-CIO posts from steward to int. rep. Mem: Masons; Shrine; Elks; Eagles; Boy Scouts; PTA; Civilian Conserv. Corps; consult. and adv. to civic bodies, bds, cmns. Rel: Congregational. Mailing Add: Drayton Plains, Mich. 48020. (1967)

FARR, CASWELL JAMES R
Wash. State Rep.
b. Garfield, Wash, 9/4/21; s. Ted H. Farr and Grace Krous F; m. 8/24/46 to Marlys Kropf; c. Craig and Marya. Educ: Wash. State Univ, 39-41; Univ. Wash, Seattle, B.S. in chem, 50, B.S. in pub. health, 51, D.D.S, 55; Psi Omega. Polit. & Govt. Pos: Wash. State Rep, 42nd Dist, 67- Mil. Serv: Entered as Pvt, Army, 42, released as 1st Lt, 46, after serv. in 66th and 83rd Inf. Div, ETO, 44-45; 1st Lt, Army Res, until 52; Five Campaign Stars; Combat Inf. Medal. Mem: Am. and Wash State Dental Asns; Mt. Baker Dental Soc; Assoc. Gold Foil Study Club; Mason; C. of C; Mental Health Clinic; Pub. Assistance Adv. Bd. Photography. Rel: Methodist. Legal Res: Suite H-25, 800 C St, Bellingham, Wash. 98225. Mailing Add: 1800 C St, Bellingham, Wash. 98225.

FARR, FRED S. D
b. Piedmont, Calif; m. 1938 to Janet Haskins F; c. Sam, Francesca, Nancy. Educ: Univ. of Calif, A.B, 32; Boalt Hall, LL.B, 35. Polit. & Govt. Pos: Calif. State Sen, 55-66; Del, Dem. Nat. Conv, 59; Del, White House Conf. on Children and Youth, 59; War Shipping Admin. Labor Rel. Rep, Port of N.Y, 43; Admin. Asst, U.S. Maritime Cmn, 42; Cmnr, Nat. Conf. on Uniform State Laws; Calif. Pub. Libr. Cmn. Bus. & Prof. Pos: Lawyer, Indust. Rel. Consult, Puerto Rico, 45. Mem: Am, State, and Monterey Co. Bar Asns; Rotary; Commonwealth Club; Monterey Hist. and Art Asn; past Pres, Monterey Co. Citizens Planning Asn; Tuberc. and Health Asn. Mailing Add: Box 3305, Carmel, Calif. 93921. (1967)

FARR, GEORGE A. D
b. New York, N.Y, 2/21/24; s. George Farr and Ruth Townley F; m. 2/22/45 to Patricia Dunlap Sorlie; c. Patricia, Bruce and Scott. Educ: Rutgers Univ, 42-43; Concordia Col, B.A, 49; Univ. Minn, summers 49-54. Polit. & Govt. Pos: Secy, Moorhead Dem-Farmer-Labor Party, Minn, 55-56; finance chmn, Ninth Dist. Dem-Farmer-Labor Party, 56-57; exec. secy, Minn. Dem-Farmer-Labor Party, 57-58, chmn, 61-68; exec. secy. to Lt. Gov, Minn, 58-59, Gov. Freeman, 59-60; alternate del, Dem. Nat. Conv, 68. Bus. & Prof. Pos: Prin. and teacher, Comstock High Sch, 49-54; coordinator, dept. phys. educ, Concordia Col, 54-57. Mil. Serv: Entered as Pvt, Army Air Force, 43, released as 1st Lt, 47. Rel: Congregational. Mailing Add: 8125 Abbott Ave. S, Bloomington, Minn. 55431. (1967)

FARR, WILLIAM S, JR. R
Chmn, Kent Co. Rep. Party, Mich.
b. N.Y.C, 3/10/35; m. 6/14/57 to Kay C. Cougill; c. Gregory William, Sheryl Lynn and Cynthia Kay. Educ: Wash. Univ, A.B; Univ. Mich, LL.B. Polit. & Govt. Pos: Chmn, Mich. Teachers Tenure Cmn. and Kent Co. Rep. Party, currently. Bus. & Prof. Pos: Attorney-at-law, Mem: Media chmn, Kent Co. United Fund Dr, 68; bd. dirs, Grand Rapids Area Coun. of Churches. Rel: Presbyterian; Elder and former Deacon, Eastminster Presby. Church. Legal Res: 2102 Griggs S.E, Grand Rapids, Mich. 49502. Mailing Add: 430 Federal Square Bldg, Grand Rapids, Mich. 49502.

FARRAR, FRANK L. R
Gov, S.Dak.
b. Britton, S.Dak, 4/2/29; m. to Patricia Henley; c. Jeanne M, Sally A, Mary S, Robert J. and Ann M. Educ: Univ. of S.Dak, B.S, 51, LL.B, 53; pres. Univ. Student Asn, Inter-Fraternity Coun, Alpha Tau Omega; Phi Delta Phi. Polit. & Govt. Pos: Fed. internal revenue agent, judge and states attorney, Marshall Co, S.Dak; former chmn, Marshall Co. Young Rep; former mem, sch. bd; chmn, Marshall Co. Sr. Rep; asst. sgt. of arms, Rep. Nat. Conv, 60; pres, S.Dak. States Attorneys Asn, 61; Attorney Gen, S.Dak, 62-69, Gov, 69- Bus. & Prof. Pos: Attorney-at-law. Mil. Serv: Korean Vet; Capt, Army Res.(Ret). Mem: Boy Scouts; Lions; Elks; Mason; Shrine; Odd Fellows; bd, Northeast S.Dak. Ment. Health Asn; S.Dak, Ind, Wash. and Am. Bar Asns; Marshall Co. Mentally Retarded Chap; Sportsmen's Club; U.S. Army Officers Asn; Jaycees; vol. chmn, S.Dak. March of Dimes; finance chmn, S.Dak. Ment. Health Asn; v.pres, Nat. Attorney Gen. Asn. Citizenship Award, Jaycees; S.Dak. Young Rep. Man of the Year, 63. Rel: Presbyterian; Adult Sunday Sch. teacher and former deacon, Presbyterian Church. Mailing Add: State Capitol, Pierre, S.Dak. 57501.

FARRAR, REGINALD WARREN, JR. R
Mem, La. State Rep. Cent. Cmt.
b. El Dorado, Ark, 8/2/22; s. Reginald Warren Farrar, Sr. and Katherine Grigsby F; m. 8/6/49 to Ann Mills; c. Gail, Katherine and Cynthia. Educ: La. Polytech. Inst, B.A, 43; La. State Univ, J.D, 48; Alpha Lamba Tau; Gamma Eta Gamma. Polit. & Govt. Pos: U.S. cmnr, West. Dist. La, 54-; chmn. personnel cmt, Lake Charles, La, 56-59; dep. dir, DeLesseps S. Morrison Campaign Gov, 59; chmn, Lake Charles Munic. Fire & Police Civil Serv. Bd, 67-; del. Rep. Nat. Conv, 68; mem, La. State Rep. Cent. Cmt, 68- Bus. & Prof. Pos: Partner, Hall, Raggio, Farrar & Barnett, Attorneys, 50- Mil. Serv: Entered as A/S, Coast Guard, 43, released as Sig.M 3/C, 46, after serv. in Atlantic and Pac. Theatres, 43-46. Mem: La. Defense Counsel Asn.(pres. elect); Defense Res. Inst; Int. Asn. Ins. Counsel; La. State Bar Asn.(bd. gov); Southwest La. Bar Asn.(pres); Rotary; Am. Legion. Rel: Episcopal. Legal Res: 2220 Barbe Court, Lake Charles, La. 70601. Mailing Add: P.O. Box 820, Lake Charles, La. 70601.

FARRELL, GEORGE JOSEPH, JR. R
N.Y. State Assemblyman
b. Brooklyn, N.Y, 9/27/30; s. George J. Farrell (deceased) and Mae Travers F; m. 1/26/57 to Patricia Carney; c. Kathleen, Joseph, Kevin and Elizabeth. Educ: Fordham Col, A.B, 52; Brooklyn Law Sch, J.D, 57. Polit. & Govt. Pos: Mem. zoning bd. of appeals, Village of Floral Park, N.Y, 60-63, trustee, 63 and mayor, 63-65; N.Y. State Assemblyman, 16th Assembly Dist, 66-, chmn, Joint Legis. Cmt. on Towns & Villages, N.Y. State Legis, 69; alternate del, Rep. Nat. Conv, 68; mem, Rep. Exec. Cmt, 68-; v.chmn, Nassau Co. Rep. Party, 68- Mil. Serv: Entered as Pvt, Army, 52, released 54, after serv. in 25th Inf. Div, 53-54. Mem: Bar Asn. of Nassau Co; Trial Lawyers Sect, Nassau & Suffolk Bar Asn; Am. Bar Asn; Elks; Lions; Am. Legion. 1968 Friendship Award, Nat. Info. Bur. for Jewish Life. Rel: Roman Catholic. Legal Res: 116 Carnation Ave, Floral Park, N.Y. 11001. Mailing Add: 114 Old Country Rd, Mineola, N.Y. 11501.

FARRINGTON, CHARLES EDWARD D
Freeholder, Mercer Co, N.J.
b. N.Y.C, 5/17/14; m. to Estelle Hepburn. Educ: Sch. Indust. Arts, Rider Col; Rutgers Univ. Law Sch. Polit. & Govt. Pos: Mem. exec. bd. and pres. 2 terms, W. Mercer Dem. Club; State Assemblyman, N.J. 58-68; v.chmn, bd. of trustees, Trenton State Col, 68-; freeholder, Mercer Co, 69- Bus. & Prof. Pos: Played clarinet and saxophone, Orchestra on Ile de France and Pan. Am; secy. and acct; laborer in steel indust; attorney-at-law. Mil. Serv: PO 1/C, Coast Guard; security work; parachute exp. work. Mem: Trenton Musical Asn; AFM, AFL-CIO, chmn. exec. cmt, Local 62, 52-; first pres, Hopewell Twp. Babe Ruth League; past v.pres, Trenton Toastmasters; treas, Princeton Bar Asn; Am. Legion, baseball cmt. and judge advocate, Pennington Post 413; Delaware Valley United Fund; Mercer Co. and N.J. State Bar Asns; Mercer Co. Legal Aid Soc; treas, Mercer Co. Health Asn. and Princeton Red Cross; treas. and founder, Mercer Symphonic Develop. Orchestra. Mailing Add: 82 Overbrook Dr, Princeton, N.J. 08540.

FARRINGTON, ELIZABETH PRUETT R
Dir, Off. of Territories, Dept. of Interior
b. Tokyo, Japan, 5/30/98; d. Robert Lee Pruett and Josephine Baugh P; m. 5/17/20 to Joseph Rider Farrington, wid, June, 1954; c. Beverly (Mrs. Hugh F. Richardson) and John. Educ: Univ. Wis, B.A, 18; Theta Sigma Phi; Alpha Omicron Pi. Polit. & Govt. Pos: Prog. chmn, League of Rep. Women, D.C, 45-46, pres, 47-48; nat. chmn. pub. rels, Nat. Fedn. Rep. Women, 47-49, pres, 49-53; U.S. Rep, Hawaii, 54-57; del, Hawaii State Rep. Conv, 54-66; del, Rep. Nat. Conv, 56; mem, Hawaii State Cmn, N.Y. World's Fair and Hawaii rep, Nat. Bd. Dirs, 64 & 65; dir, Off. of Territories, Dept. of Interior, 69- Bus. & Prof. Pos: Reporter, Wis State. J, Madison, 18-20; Wash. D.C. Cong. correspondent and columnist, Lee Syndicate Newspapers, 20-23; founder, Wash. Press Serv, 23; art and music critic for Honolulu papers, 27-36; originator and ed, Wash. Newsletter, 45-54; pres. and chmn. bd. dirs, Honolulu Star Bul, Ltd. and subsidiary corps, Star Bul, Commercial Printing Co, Hilo Tribune-Herald, KGMB Radio and TV and Honolulu Lithography Co, 57-61. Mem: Pan-Pac. Union; pres, Cong. Club 45; 1925 F St. Club; Capitol Hill Club; Am. Asn. Univ. Women; Bus. & Prfnl. Women's Club; Am. Newspaper Women's Club; Am. Nat. Publishers Asn; Assoc. Press; Am. Penwomen's Club; researcher pub. rels. and exec. dir, Honolulu Art Soc, 27-36; pub. rels. and publ. dir, YWCA Hosp. and Soc. Serv. Asn, 27-36. Named one of Ten Most Powerful Women in Politics in Nation, McCall's Mag, 51; Named one of Twelve Outstanding Women in Nation in Any Field of Endeavor, Gen. Fedn. Women's Clubs, D.C, 52; Outstanding Grad. in Field of Journalism, Univ. Wis. Col. Journalism, 55; selected to debate, N.Y. Herald Tribune Forum, 48. Rel: Disciples of Christ. Legal Res: 3180 Pacific Heights Rd, Honolulu, Hawaii 96813. Mailing Add: Office of Territories, Dept. of Interior, Washington, D.C. 20240.

FARRINGTON, WARREN ARTHUR R
b. Danville, Vt, 3/25/95; m. to Mildred Tellier; c. 1 stepson, 2 stepdaughters. Educ: Danville High Sch. Polit. & Govt. Pos: Mem, Co. Bd. Rd. Cmn, Vt, mem, Selective Serv. Bd, former mem, Co. Tax Appeal Bd, Selectman,

31-48, Rd. Cmnr, 34-38, Moderator, 48-58 and Lister, 53-54; Vt. State Rep, 51-57 & 59-67. Bus. & Prof. Pos: Retired farmer; state park caretaker. Mil. Serv: Pvt, Army Inf, 18-19. Mem: Am. Legion; Peacham Men's Club. Rel: Congregational. Mailing Add: East Peacham, Vt. 05862. (1967)

FARRIS, NORMAN EDWIN R
Ky. State Sen.
b. Ware, Ky, 4/11/21; s. William Earnest Farris (deceased) and Sina Frances Hodge F.(deceased); m. 6/17/44 to Melba Ray Deweese; c. Frances Ann (Mrs. Jerry Ray Girdler) and Mark Edwin. Educ: Ky. Sch. of Mortuary Sci, grad, 48. Polit. & Govt. Pos: Coroner, Pulaski Co, Ky, 62-68; Ky. State Sen, 15th Dist, 68-, minority whip, 68. Bus. & Prof. Pos: Mgr-partner, Farris-Morris-Hislope Funeral Home, Science Hill, Ky, 57- Mil. Serv: Entered as Pvt, Air Force, 42, released as Sgt, 45, after serv. in 1043rd Guard Squadron and Aviation Cadet Center, San Antonio, Tex. and prisoner of war guard, Ft. Meade, Md. Mem: Past pres, Southeast. Funeral Dir. Asn; Somerset, Ky. Gideon Camp; Kiwanis; F&AM (past master, No. 225, Science Hill); Mason (32°); Shrine. Rel: Methodist. Mailing Add: Science Hill, Ky. 42553.

FASCELL, DANTE B. D
U.S. Rep, Fla.
b. Bridgehampton, N.Y, 3/9/17; m. to Jeanne-Marie Pelot; c. Sandra Jeanne, Toni and Dante Jon. Educ: Univ. of Miami, LL.B, 38; Kappa Sigma. Polit. & Govt. Pos: Pres, Dade Co. Young Dem. Club, Fla, 47-48; legal attache, State Legis. Del. from Dade Co, 47-50; Fla. State Rep, 50-53; U.S. Rep, Fla, 54-, mem, House Cmt. on For. Affairs and chmn, Subcmt. on Inter-Am. Affairs, mem, House Cmt. on Govt. Opers. and chmn, Subcmt. on Legal and Monetary Affairs; alternate del, Dam. Nat. Conv, 68. Bus. & Prof. Pos: Mem, Law firm of Turner, Hendrick, Fascell, Guilford, Goldstein and McDonald. Mil. Serv: With Fla. Nat. Guard, 41, 2nd Lt, 42, released as Capt, 46, after serv. in African, Sicilian and Italian Campaigns. Mem: Iron Arrow Soc; pres, Italian-Am. Club, 47-48; Lions; Coral Gables, Dade Co, Fla, Am. and Fed. Bar Asns; Am. Legion; Mil. Order of World Wars. Selected as 1 of 5 outstanding Men in State, Fla. Jr. C. of C, 51. Legal Add: Miami, Fla. Mailing Add: U.S. House of Representatives, 2160 Rayburn House Office Bldg, Washington, D.C. 20515

FASI, FRANK FRANCIS D
Mayor, Honolulu, Hawaii
b. East Hartford, Conn, 8/27/20; s. Carmelo Fasi and Josephine Lupo F; m. 5/25/58 to Joyce Miyeko Kono; c. Toni Anne, Kathleen Helen, Carl Frederick, Francesca Maria, Paul Francis, Charles Francis, Frank Francis, II, Gina Marisa, David Francis, Gioia Melissa and Salvatore Francis. Educ: Trinity Col, B.S; Sigma Nu. Polit. & Govt. Pos: Dem. precinct pres. and secy, Hawaii Dem. State Cent. Cmt, 50; Dem. Nat. Committeeman, Hawaii, 52-56; Hawaii State Sen, 59; councilman-at-lg, Honolulu, 65-69, mayor, 69- Bus. & Prof. Pos: Owner, Frank F. Fasi Supply Co, 47-66. Mil. Serv: Entered as Pfc, Marine Corps, 42, released as Capt, 46, after serv. in Pac. Area, 42-46. Mem: Ex-Rotary; pres, Kalihi Bus. Asn, 54; dep.comdr, VFW, 50; Am. Legion; Boy Scouts. Photography; Football-Basketball, Trinity Col, 38-42. Rel: Catholic. Mailing Add: 2054 Makiki St, Honolulu, Hawaii 96822.

FASSLER, JOSEPH LEO D
Chmn, Fremont Co. Dem. Party, Colo.
b. Spead, Mo, 10/15/97; s. Joseph John Fassler and Annie Bell Erheardt F; m. 9/15/25 to Frances Konty; c. Helen (Mrs. Holden), Paul, John, James, Edward and David. Polit. & Govt. Pos: Mem, City Coun, Canon City, Colo, 37-47 & 57-61; chmn, Fremont Co. Dem. Party, 50-61 & 67- Bus. & Prof. Pos: Owner, Fassler Builders, 24- Mil. Serv: Entered as Pvt, Army, 17, released as Pfc, 19, after serv. in 129 M.G. Bn, AEF, 18-19. Mem: K. of C; Carpenters Union; VFW; Am. Legion; Elks; Boy Scouts. Silver Beaver Award. Rel: Catholic. Legal Res: 718 Allison Ave, Canon City, Colo. 81212. Mailing Add: Box 182, Canon City, Colo. 81212.

FATZER, HAROLD R. R
Justice, Kans. Supreme Court
b. Fellsburg, Kans, 8/3/10; s. John R. Fatzer (deceased) and Rella Shannon F.(deceased); m. 1936 to Frances Josephine Schwaup; c. John Richard. Educ: Kans. State Univ, 2 years; Washburn Col. Law Sch, LL.B; Dean's Honor Roll; Tau Delta Phi; Kappa Sigma. Polit. & Govt. Pos: Co. attorney, Edwards Co, Kans, 34-41; chief counsel, State Bd. Welfare, 41-43; Asst. Attorney Gen, Kans, 43 & 45-49, Attorney Gen, 49-56; Justice, Kans. Supreme Court, 56- Bus. & Prof. Pos: Mem, Appellate Judges Seminar, N.Y. Univ, 59; mem. bd. trustees, Washburn Col, 67. Mil. Serv: Entered as Pvt, Army, 43, released as Sgt, 45, after serv. in FARTC, Ft. Sill, Okla; Good Conduct Medal. Mem: Kans. and Am. Bar Asns; Kans. Co. Attorneys Asn.(pres, 39-40); Nat. Asn. Attorneys Gen.(pres, 52-53); Am. Judicature Soc; Inst. Judicial Admin; Delta Theta Phi; Washburn Alumni Asn.(pres, 66); Mason; Shrine; Jester; Am. Legion; 40 et 8; Amvets; DAV. Distinguished Serv. Award, Washburn Univ, 64 and Washburn Law Sch. Asn, 67; Hon. Asst. Attorney Gen, State of Ga; Adm, The Great Navy of the State of Nebr. Rel: Protestant. Legal Res: Kinsley, Kans. Mailing Add: 1415 Ward Pkwy, Topeka, Kans. 66604.

FAUBUS, ORVAL EUGENE D
b. Combs, Ark, 1/7/10; s. John Samuel Faubus and Addie Joslin F; m. 11/21/31 to Alta Mozell Haskins; c. Farrell Eugene; m. 3/21/69 to Elizabeth Drake Thompson; stepchildren: Kim and Ricci Westmoreland. Educ: Huntsville Vocational Sch, grad, 34; Exten. course, Univ. Ark; Lone Scouts; Boy Scouts; Future Farmers of Am. Polit. & Govt. Pos: Circuit clerk and recorder, Madison Co, Ark, 38-42; acting and permanent postmaster, Huntsville, 46-54; hwy. cmnr, dir. and admin. asst. to Gov, 49-53; Gov, Ark, 55-67. Bus. & Prof. Pos: Sch. teacher, 28-38; ed-publisher, Madison Co. Record, Huntsville, Ark, 46-69; ed-publisher, The Spectator, Ozark, Ark, 68-69; pres, Dogpatch, U.S.A. Recreational Enterprises, 69- Mil. Serv: Entered as Pvt, Army, 42, released as Maj, 46, after serv. in 35th Inf. Div, ETO; Maj. (Ret), Army Res; Combat Inf. Badge; Bronze Star; Six Battle Stars. Mem: Pres, Combs 4-H Club, 27; Huntsville Lions, secy-treas, N.W. Ark. Lions, 35-36; Madison Co. Dir, Ozark Playground Asn, 40; pres, Madison Co. C. of C, 53-54; Am. Legion; VFW; Mason (32°); v.chmn, South Gov. Conf, 60-61, chmn, 62-63; exec. cmt, Nat. Gov. Conf, 60; exec. cmt, 35th Inf. Div. Asn. and pres, 54-55; Sons of Confederate Vet; Alpha Kappa Lambda. Am. Legion Man of Year, 57; One of the Ten Men in the World Most Admired by Americans, 58; Munic. Man of Year, 65; Conservationist of Year, 66. Rel: Baptist. Legal Res: Skyline Terr, Harrison, Ark. 72601. Mailing Add: Dogpatch, USA, Dogpatch, Ark. 72648.

FAULK, LAWRENCE JOHN R
Wash. State Sen.
b. Tacoma, Wash, 6/20/36; s. Theodore E. Faulk and Katherine Strojan F; m. 5/22/65 to Mary Grace Ellsperman; c. Jennifer Mary and John Lawrence. Educ: Seattle Univ, B.A, 61. Polit. & Govt. Pos: Asst. precinct committeeman, Rep. Party, Wash, 60-62; Wash. State Sen, 67- Bus. & Prof. Pos: Staff asst, Boeing Co, 61- Mil. Serv: Entered as Pvt, Army, 54, released as Spec. 4, 57. Mem: Elks; Wash. Athletic Club; exec. bd, Design for Progress; adv. bd, Pub. Assistance; Pierce Co-Tacoma Libr. Coun. Rel: Roman Catholic. Mailing Add: 3410 N. Ferdinand, Tacoma, Wash. 98407.

FAULK, ROLAND R. D
b. Troy, Ala, 1/1/00; s. Timothy S. Faulk and Ada E. Roland F; m. 7/10/28 to Ann Miller. Educ: Univ. of Ala, 19-20. Polit. & Govt. Pos: Ala. State Rep, 47-66; Samson city councilman. Bus. & Prof. Pos: Mercantile bus. Mem: Shriner. Mailing Add: Samson, Ala. 36477. (1967)

FAULKNER, ELLEN R
b. Keene, N.H, 8/31/90; single. Educ: Bryn Mawr Col, A.B, M.A. Polit. & Govt. Pos: N.H. State Rep, 57-67; dir, N.H. Soc. Welfare Coun; dir, N.H. Coun. on For. Affairs; del, Constitutional Conv, 65. Bus. & Prof. Pos: Former prin, Milton Acad. Girl's Sch, Milton, Mass. Mem: Keene League of Women Voters; Farm Bur; Headmistresses Asn. of the East. Rel: Protestant. Mailing Add: W. Surry Rd, Keene, N.H. 03431. (1967)

FAULKNER, JAMES EUGENE R
Chmn, San Jacinto Co. Rep. Cmt, Tex.
b. Concord, Tex, 12/17/10; s. George B. Faulkner and Carry D. Lacy F; m. 6/28/58 to Hildegard Phillipine Stodner Klemm; c. James Jefferson, Charlotte (Mrs. Pugh), Frederick Eugene 'Fritz,' Barbara (Mrs. Dunaway), Elizabeth Ann and Jodie Ann (Mrs. Winn). Educ: Tyler Commercial Col, Tex; Stephen F. Austin State Col; South Tex. Col. of Law; La Salle Univ. Law Sch, Ill. Polit. & Govt. Pos: Attorney and naturalization exam, U.S. Dept. of Justice, San Antonio, Tex, 42-44; co. attorney, San Jacinto Co, 47-48 and census dir, 60; chmn, San Jacinto Co. Rep. Cmt, 48-; co. campaign mgr. for Eisenhower, Nixon, Goldwater, Bush and Tower; del, Rep. State Convs, 50-; appeals attorney, Selective Serv, Coldspring, 64-; city attorney, Shepherd, 67- Mil. Serv: Pvt, Nat. Guard, Tex, 27-29. Mem: State Bar of Tex; Coldspring, Tex, Bar; Dist. and Co. Attorney's Asn, 47-48; Clinton Lodge 23, AF&AM of Tex; Houston Consistory, Scottish Rite, Valley of Houston, Orient of Tex; Arabia Temple, AAONMS of Houston; Trinity Valley Shrine Club, Coldsprings, Tex; pres, San Jacinto Co. Lions Club; Woodman of the World; PTA; former local pres, Red Cross. Forward on county and district high school Champions, Concord, Tex, 26 & 27. Rel: Methodist; Dir, Methodist Church, Coldspring. Legal Res: Suite 101-102, Faulkner Bldg, Coldspring, Tex. 77331.

FAULKNER, ROBERT WESLEY R
b. Malvern, Ark, 2/4/38; s. James Hershel Faulkner and Helen Parker Hensley F; m. May, 1958 to Linda Jane Duke; c. Paul, Angela and Kelli. Educ: Ouachita Baptist Univ, B.A. in bus. admin, 60; Univ. Ark. Sch. Law, LL.B, 66. Polit. & Govt. Pos: Mem, exec. bd, Young Rep. League, Ark, 63- and chmn, 63-65; mem, exec. bd, Ark. State Rep. Cmt, 63-65; hq. mgr, Rockefeller for Gov. Campaign, 64; mem, steering cmt, Permanent Voter Registrn. Cmt, Amendment 54, 64. Mil. Serv: Entered as 2nd Lt, Army, 61, released 62, after serv. in 23rd and 2nd Inf. Divs; Distinguished Mil. Grad. of Ouachita Baptist Univ. Mem: Pres, Malvern Kiwanis; chmn, Hot Spring Co. Dist. Boy Scouts; Ark. and Am. Bar Asns. Rel: Baptist. Legal Res: 1023 Toler St, Malvern, Ark. 72104. Mailing Add: 115 E. Second, Malvern, Ark. 72104. (1967)

FAUSSET, H. W. D
b. Henry Co, Ill, 2/11/10; m. to Florella; c. two. Educ: High Sch. Polit. & Govt Pos: Wyo. State Rep, -1966; Mem, Worland Bd. of Educ, 3rd term; Bd. Mem, Bluff Irrigation Dist. Bus. & Prof. Pos: Businessman and Rancher. Mem: Wyo. Dir, Upper Mo. Water Users Asn; Bd. Chmn, Upper Bluff Irrigation Dist. Mailing Add: Route 2, Worland, Wyo. 82401. (1967)

FAUST, WILLIAM PAUL D
Mich. State Sen.
b. Bucyrus, Ohio, 3/29/29; s. Paul Joseph Faust and Teresa Johnson F; single. Educ: Univ. Ind, 48-49; Univ. Mich, A.B, 52; East. Mich. Univ, 55-56. Polit. & Govt. Pos: Trustee, Nankin Twp, Mich, 60-63, supvr, 63-65; chmn, Nankin Twp. Planning Cmn, 65-66; Mich. State Sen, 13th Dist, 67- Bus. & Prof. Pos: Managing Ed, Wayne Eagle, Wayne, Mich, 60-62. Mem: C. of C; Civitan Club. Rel: Roman Catholic. Mailing Add: 35215 Cady, Westland, Mich. 48185. (1967)

FAWELL, HARRIS W. R
Ill. State Sen.
b. West Chicago, Ill, 3/25/29; s. Walter R. Fawell and Mildred Nelson F; m. 8/9/52 to Ruth Johnson; c. Richard, Jane and John. Educ: N.Cent. Col, Naperville, 47-51; Chicago-Kent Col. Law, LL.B, 52. Polit. & Govt. Pos: Past pres, Naperville Young Rep, Ill; asst. state attorney, DuPage Co, 53-57; Ill. State Sen, 63-, chmn, Welfare Cmn, Ill. State Senate; del, Rep. Nat. Conv, 68. Bus. & Prof. Pos: Mem. law firm, Fawell and Larson, 52-67; Fawell, Larson & Jervis, 67- Mem: DuPage Co, Ill. and Am. Bar Asns; Am. Trial Lawyers Asn; past pres, W.Chicago Jaycees; mem. bd, YMCA; Kiwanis; pres, DuPage Co. Family Serv. Asn, 46-60. Outstanding Freshman State Sen, 73rd Gen. Assembly, Newsman Awards, Best Freshman State Sen, Ill. Polit. Reporter; John Howard Asn. Award, 67; Best Legislator Award, Independent Voters Ill, 67; Ill. Distinguished Serv. Award, Ill. Welfare Asn, 67. Rel: Methodist; past pres. bd. trustees, First Methodist Church, Naperville. Mailing Add: 444 S. Sleight St, Naperville, Ill. 60540.

FAXON, JACK D
Mich. State Rep.
b. Detroit, Mich, 6/9/36. Educ: Wayne State Univ, B.S, M.Ed; Univ. Mich,

M.A, Hist. Polit. & Govt. Pos: Mich. State Rep, currently. Bus. & Prof. Pos: Teacher of Am. govt. and hist, Southwest. High Sch, formerly. Mem: NAACP; Mich. Regional Adv. Bd, Anti-Defamation League of B'nai B'rith; bd. dirs, Am. Civil Liberties Union of Mich. and Theol. Inst. of Episcopal Diocese of Mich; Mich. Hist. Soc; Bagley Commun. Coun. Mailing Add: 17594 Kentucky, Detroit, Mich. 48221.

FAY, ALBERT BEL R
b. New Orleans, 2/26/13; s. Charles Spencer Fay and Marie Dorothy Bel F; m. 2/3/35 to Homoiselle Haden; c. Katherine (Mrs. Chester S. Sadler, Jr.); Marion (Mrs. Peder Monsen); Albert Bel. Educ: Yale, B.S, 36; Delta Psi. Polit. & Govt. Pos: Mem, Rep. Nat. Cmt, Tex, 60-69; del, Rep. Nat. Conv, 68. Bus. & Prof. Pos: Exec. v.pres. and dir, Lacassane Co, Lake Charles, La; founder and v.pres, Eagle Lake Rice Dryer, Tex; co-founder, v.pres. and dir, Bel Oil Corp, Lake Charles, La; partner, Quatre Parish Co, Lake Charles; founder and dir, Lake Arthur Rice Drier, La; founder and dir, Seabrook Shipyard, Tex; bd. trustees, Mus. of Natural Hist, Houston; Alumni Bd, Yale Univ. Mil. Serv: Naval Res, Lt.(sg). Mem: Am. Brahman Breeders Asn.(dir, 52-); St. Anthony, Yale Univ, Cruising of Am. N.Y.C, Seawanhaka Corinthian Yacht Oyster Bay, L.I, Houston Country, Tejas, Bayou, Yale of Southeast. Tex, Petroleum, Galveston Artillery, and Tex. Corinthian Yacht Clubs; Galveston Bay Cruising Asn. Legal Res: 99 N. Post Oak Lane, Houston, Tex. 77024. Mailing Add: 1801 Dallas Ave, Houston, Tex. 77003.

FAY, JOHN J, JR. D
N.J. State Assemblyman
b. Elizabeth, N.J, 6/8/27; s. John Logan Fay and Ann Mulcahy F; m. 5/26/51 to Elizabeth Stankunas. Educ: Seton Hall Univ, B.A, 58, M.A, 60. Polit. & Govt. Pos: Councilman, Woodbridge Twp, N.J, 62-64; freeholder, Middlesex Co, 64-67; N.J. State Assemblyman, Middlesex Co, 67- Bus. & Prof. Pos: Stillman's helper, Esso Standard Oil, Bayway, N.J, 49-58; high sch. teacher, Linden High Sch, 58- Mil. Serv: Entered as A/S, Navy, 44, released as Seaman 1/C, 46, after serv. in Underwater Demolition; Victory Medal. Mem: Am. Fedn. of Teachers; K. of C. B'nai B'rith Citizenship Award; Eagleton fel. grant. Rel: Roman Catholic. Mailing Add: 115 Amherst Ave, Colonia, N.J. 07067.

FAY, THOMAS FREDERIC D
R.I. State Rep.
b. Central Falls, R.I, 10/13/40; s. Joseph A. Fay and Ethel Lupton F; m. 6/12/65 to Paulette R. Demers; c. Kelly Ann and Thomas Joseph. Educ: Providence Col, A.B, 62; Boston Univ. Law Sch, LL.B, 65. Polit. & Govt. Pos: Mem, Dem. Cmt, Lincoln, R.I, 63-66; R.I. State Rep, 72nd Dist, 69- Bus. & Prof. Pos: Partner, Oster, Espo, and Fay, 69-; legal counsel, Pawtucket Jr. C. of C, 69- Mem: R.I. and Pawtucket Bar Asns; Trial Lawyers Asn; Am. Judicature Soc; Jr. C. of C; Lions. Rel: Roman Catholic. Legal Res: 103 Clay St, Central Falls, R.I. 02863. Mailing Add: 936 Smithfield Ave, Lincoln, R.I. 02905.

FEARS, WILLIAM EARL D
Va. State Sen.
b. Jonesboro, Ark, 9/28/21; s. Arthur Earl Fears and Mary Catherine Scarry F; m. 6/24/44 to Betty Belle DeCormis; c. Barbara Anderson and Richard Bradford. Educ: Yale Univ, B.E, 42; Univ. Cincinnati, LL.B. and J.D, 48; Phi Delta Phi. Polit. & Govt. Pos: Commonwealth's attorney, Accomack Co, Va, 55-59; Va. State Sen, First Dist, 68- Bus. & Prof. Pos: V.pres, Avemco Ins. Co, Bethesda, Md, 64-66. Mil. Serv: Entered as Aviation Cadet, Army Air Corps, 43, released as 1st Lt, 46, after serv. in 92nd Bombardier Group, Eng, Eighth Air Force, ETO, 45-46; Maj. Army Res, currently; Occup. Europe Medal with 3 Battle Stars; Va. Serv. Medal; ETO and Am. Theater Medals; Presidential Unit Citation. Mem: Norfolk-Portsmouth, Accomack-Northampton and Am. Bar Asns; Am. Trial Lawyers Asn; Shrine; Mason (32°); Elks; Moose; Red Men. Rel: Baptist. Legal Res: Box 38, Accomac, Va. 23301. Mailing Add: Box 247, Accomac, Va. 23301.

FEATHERSTONE, HAROLD G. D
Fla. State Rep.
b. Miami, Fla. Educ: Univ. of Miami Law Sch. Polit. & Govt. Pos: Fla. State Rep, 67- Bus. & Prof. Pos: Attorney. Mem: Am. Bar Asn; Govt. Res. Coun. of Miami-Dade C. of C. Mailing Add: 700 E. Eighth Court, Hialeah, Fla. 33010. (1967)

FECTEAU, WILLIAM C, JR. D
R.I. State Sen.
b. Coventry, R.I, 1/15/18; m. Gladys M. Educ: Coventry High Sch. Polit. & Govt. Pos: Mem, Coventry Town Coun, R.I, 8 years, pres, 5 years; R.I. State Sen, 59-; chmn, Coventry Town Dem. Cmt, R.I, 61- Bus. & Prof. Pos: Ins. broker. Mil. Serv: Chief PO, Navy, 3 years, Pac. Theatre. Mailing Add: 956 Tiogue Ave, Coventry, R.I. 02816. (1967)

FEDA, GERALD C. R
Mont. State Rep.
b. Carlos, Minn, 6/7/26; s. John L. Feda and Jennie Brazzell F; m. 6/10/50 to Audrey L. Wingo; c. Valerie Jo, Daniel Charles, Janice Ellen, and Donna Jean. Educ: High sch, grad. Polit. & Govt. Pos: Mont. State Rep, Dist. 5B, 69- Bus. & Prof. Pos: Owner and partner, Glasgow Ins. & Realty, Inc, 59- Mil. Serv: Entered Merchant Marines, 44, released as Refer Engr, 47. Mem: Brotherhood of Locomotive Engrs; Lions, C. of C. Rel: Catholic. Mailing Add: 907 Fifth Ave. N, Glasgow, Mont. 59230.

FEDERER, ESTELLE ANASTATIA D
Mem. Exec. Bd, Sheboygan Co. Dem. Party, Wis.
b. Rossiter, Pa, 4/4/15; d. John Moskewich and Mary Rinkavich M; m. 1/25/35 to Robert W. Federer; c. Patricia (Mrs. Donnel Lee Hanson) and Susanne (Mrs. James E. Kuhn). Educ: Sheboygan Cent. High Sch, grad, 33; Sheboygan Tech. Sch. Adult Educ. Polit. & Govt. Pos: Treas, Sch. Bd, Wis; chmn, Women's Cmt, Dem. Party of Wis; secy. and chmn, Dem. Party, Wis; mem. exec. bd, Sixth Cong. Dist. Dem. Party; mem, exec. bd, Sheboygan Co. Dem. Party, 69- Mem: League of Women Voters; Red Cross; March of Dimes; Univ. Wis. Exten. Homemaker Coun; Cath. Daughters Am. Cert. or pins for Serv. from Dem. Nat. Cmt, Red Cross, March of Dimes, Univ. Wis. Exten. Homemaker Coun. and Cath. Daughters Am. Rel: Catholic. Mailing Add: 622 Maine, Adell, Wis. 53001.

FEDERICI, ANTHONY NICHOLAS D
Chmn, Columbia Co. Dem. Cent. Cmt, Ore.
b. St. Helens, Ore, 3/21/37; s. Nicholas Anthony Federici and Rose Albrizio F; m. 7/10/65 to Nancy Alice Weeks. Educ: Univ. Ore, Eugene; Chi Psi. Polit. & Govt. Pos: Precinct committeeman, Dem. Party, Ore, 65-66; chmn, Columbia Co. Dem. Cent. Cmt, 66- Bus. & Prof. Pos: Teacher sci, Salem Pub. Schs, Ore, 63-65; owner, Tony's Shoes, St. Helens, 65- Mil. Serv: Entered as Pvt, Army, 60, released as Specialist 4/C, 62, after serv. in Ft. Leonard Wood, Mo. Mem: Lions Int. Rel: Roman Catholic. Legal Res: 254 S. 14th St, St. Helens, Ore. 97051. Mailing Add: 2021 Columbia Blvd, St. Helens, Ore. 97051.

FEE, FRANK H. D
b. Ft. Pierce, Fla, 6/6/13; s. Fred Fee; m. to Katherine Gross; c. Judy, Frank H. III and Mary Kate. Educ: Univ. Fla, LL.B, 1935; Pi Kappa Alpha; Phi Delta Phi. Polit. & Govt. Pos: Munic. judge, Ft. Pierce, Fla, 43-46, City Cmnr, 46-52 and mayor, 49-52; Fla. State Rep, 52-53 & 62-67. Bus. & Prof. Pos: Attorney. Mil. Serv: Navy, Amphibious, Pac. Mem: Elks; Moose; VFW; C. of C; past pres, St. Lucie Bar Asn; Fla. and Am. Bar Asns; Am. Judicature Soc. Rel: Methodist, Trustee, Bd; Lay Leader. Mailing Add: P.O. Box 1000, Ft. Pierce, Fla. 33450. (1967)

FEEHAN, THOMAS R
Chmn, Will Co. Rep. Cent. Cmt, Ill.
b. Joliet, Ill, 3/1/26; s. Leo M. Feehan and Zita Broderick F; m. 11/22/53 to Beverly Long; c. Colleen, Kathleen, Thomas, Brian and Kevin. Educ: Loyola Univ, B.S, 49, J.D, 53. Polit. & Govt. Pos: Chmn, Will Co. Rep. Cent. Cmt, Ill, 64-; dir, Ill. State Toll Hwy. Authority, 69. Mil. Serv: Navy, 44-46. Mem: Ill. State and Am. Bar Asns; Am. Trial Lawyers Asn; dir, United Crusade, Will Co, Ill; dir, George W. Buck Boys Club, Joliet; dir, Joliet Region C. of C; Kiwanis; Elks. Rel: Catholic. Mailing Add: 409 W. Bevan Dr, Joliet, Ill. 60435.

FEELEY, FRANCIS B. D
Chmn, Waterbury Town Dem. Cmt, Conn.
b. Waterbury, Conn, 3/16/19; s. Francis E. Feeley and Agnes O'Hara F; m. 9/2/44 to Arlene Chatfield; c. Francis B, Jr, Kathleen, Robert and Arlene. Educ: Col. of Holy Cross, A.B; Univ. of Conn, LL.B. Polit. & Govt. Pos: Chmn, Waterbury Town Dem. Cmt, Conn, 64-; alternate del, Dem. Nat. Conv, 68. Bus. & Prof. Pos: Partner, Law Firm of Feeley, Elliott & Nichols, 47-; dir, Buell Industs, Inc, 61- Mil. Serv: Aviation Cadet, Air Force, 42-44. Mem: Waterbury, Conn. and Am. Bar Asns; Elks (Past Exalted Ruler and past pres); Waterbury Area Rehabilitation Center. Rel: Roman Catholic. Legal Res: 120 Columbia Blvd, Waterbury, Conn. 06702. Mailing Add: 59 Central Ave, Waterbury, Conn. 06702. (1967)

FEENEY, JOSEPH FRANCIS D
b. Boston, Mass, 5/26/18; s. Michael Feeney and Mary Joyce F; m. June, 1952 to Joan Carroll; c. Joan, Maryjoyce, John McC. and Joseph F, Jr. Educ: George Wash. Univ; Boston Univ. Sch. Law; Phi Delta Phi; Newman Club. Polit. & Govt. Pos: Secy. to U.S. Rep. John W. McCormack, 40-48 & 53-60; asst. U.S. Attorney, Dept. Justice, 52-53; legis. clerk, U.S. House of Rep, 54-60; asst. dist. attorney, Suffolk Co, Mass, 55-58; justice, Munic. Court, S.Boston Dist, Mass, 58-; del, Dem. Nat. Conv, 64; chmn, Sch. Cmn, Sch. Bldgs. Dept, Boston, 64-66. Bus. & Prof. Pos: Partner, Feeney and Malone, 52-66. Mil. Serv: Entered as Enlisted Man, Navy, 42, released as Lt, 46, after serv. in Pac; Asiatic-Pac. Campaign Ribbon; Am. Theater Ribbon with 5 Battle Stars; Philippine Campaign Award; Good Conduct Medal; Commendation Award. Mem: Mass. and D.C. Bars; pres, Spec. Justices Asn, Mass, 66; Am, Mass. and Boston Bar Asns; Am. Trial Lawyers Asn; DAV; VFW; Am. Legion; K. of C; Navy League; past pres, S.Boston Citizens Asn. Selected as One of Ten Oustanding Young Men of Gr. Boston, Jr. C. of C, 52. Rel: Roman Catholic. Legal Res: 116 Grampian Way, Boston, Mass. 02125. Mailing Add: Law Offices Feeney and Malone, 131 State St, Boston, Mass. 02109.

FEENEY, RICHARD EDWARD D
b. Minneapolis, Minn, 4/29/38; s. William Arthur Feeney and Charlotte Bernadette Glynn F; m. 1/4/69 to Anne Kathleen Kelly. Educ: Portland State Univ, B.A, 62; Theta Delta Phi; Editor, Portland State Univ. Newspaper, The Vanguard. Polit. & Govt. Pos: Chmn, Young Citizens for Kennedy-Johnson, Ore. Kennedy Campaign, 60; research intern to U.S. Rep. Edith Green, Ore, 60-61, press and staff asst, 66-67, admin. asst, 67-; exec. secy, Dem. Campaign Kickoff Dinner, Ore. Dem. Party, 66; press asst. to U.S. Sen. Robert Kennedy Campaign, Portland, Ore, 68; alternate del, Dem. Nat. Conv, 68. Bus. & Prof. Pos: Polit. Reporter, Portland Daily Reporter, Ore, 63-64; Eng. Instr, Middle East Tech. Univ, Ankara, Turkey, 64-65; Ed. Asst, Pulse, Daily Digest of Turkish Press, 64-65. Mil. Serv: Entered as Pvt, Army, 61, released as Sp-4, 62, after serv. in 226 Mil. Intel. Detachment; grad, U.S. Army Intelligence Sch; grad. in Turkish, U.S. Army Language Sch, Monterey. Mem: 1620 Club; City Club of Portland, Ore; Past mem. and del. to Central Labor Coun. from Portland Local, Am. Newspaper Guild. Latham Award and Viking Award, Portland State Univ, 60, Middle E. Center for Arab Studies Award, 61. Rel: Roman Catholic. Legal Res: Beaverton, Ore. Mailing Add: 2441 Rayburn Bldg, House of Rep, Wash. D.C. 20515.

FEGGANS, EDWARD LELAND R
Chmn, D.C. Rep. Cmt.
b. Atlantic City, N.J, 3/5/19; s. Edward L. Feggans and Ethel McIntyre F; m. 2/25/50 to Ozra Kimus Young; c. James E. Kearney and Helen A. Thombani. Educ: Howard Univ; Suffolk Univ; La Salle Exten. Univ, Law, 1 year. Polit. & Govt. Pos: Mem, D.C. Rep. Cmt, 62-, chmn, 68-; precinct coordinator, Rockefeller for President, 63; mem, Ed Brooke for U.S. Sen. Cmt, 66. Bus. & Prof. Pos: Asst. sales mgr, Kaplan & Crawford, 53-57; sales mgr, Fuller Prod. Co, 57-64; bus. consult, Small Bus. Develop. Center, Wash, D.C, 64-66, asst. dir, Small Bus. Guid. & Develop, 66-; secy, Nat. Bus. League and first v.pres, D.C. C. of C, 69- Mil. Serv: Entered as Pvt, Army, 41, released as Technician, 45, after serv. in 449th Army Serv. Force Band; Good Conduct, Am. Defense Serv. and Victory Medals; Am. Theater Campaign Ribbon. Publ: 'Business Talk,' Wash. Afro American, 68. Mem: Life mem, Local 161-710 AFM D.C. Fedn. of Musicians; secy, Uptown Progress Cmt; bd. mem, Neptune Yacht Club. Received Man of the Year Award, Neptune

Yacht Club; cert. instr, Bus. Leadership Motivational Training, Sterling Inst. Rel: Episcopal; Licensed layreader, Episcopal Church. Mailing Add: 2504 South Dakota Ave. N.E, Washington, D.C. 20018.

FEHRENBACH, EDWIN JOSEPH R

b. Brooklyn, N.Y, 3/19/19; s. Henry Q. Fehrenbach and Margaret Costello F; m. 2/11/42 to Lillian Ruth Schinkel; c. Diane and Regina. Educ: Hofstra Univ, B.A, 55; Nat. Debate Soc. Polit. Pos: Mem, N.Y. State Thruway Authority; N.Y. State Assemblyman, 59-65; rep. leader, Bethpage, L.I, N.Y, 54-59; dep. supvr, Town Oyster Bay, 54-58. Bus. & Prof. Pos: V.pres, Hempstead Bank, 58- Mil. Serv: Entered as Pvt, Army, 41, released as 1st Sgt, 45. Publn: 'Finance of Public Education,' Massapequa Post, 61. Mem: K. of C; Am. Legion. Rel: Catholic. Mailing Add: 14 Manchester Dr, Bethpage, N.Y. 11714.

FEIGHAN, MICHAEL A. D

U.S. Rep, Ohio

b. Lakewood, Ohio; m. 6/21/30 to Florence J. Mathews; c. William M. and Fleur M. Educ: Princeton Univ, A.B, 27; Harvard Univ, LL.B, 31; Princeton Elm Club. Polit. & Govt. Pos: Ohio State Rep, 37-40, Dem. leader, Ohio House Rep, 39-40; U.S. Rep, 20th Dist, Ohio, 43- Mem: K. of C; Cleveland Citizens League; Hiberians; Burning Tree Club; Cong. Country Club; City Tavern Asn. Rel: Roman Catholic. Legal Res: 219 Superior Ave. W, Cleveland, Ohio 44101. Mailing Add: 2204 Rayburn House Office Bldg, Washington, D.C. 20515.

FEIGHAN, WILLIAM MATHEWS D

b. Cleveland, Ohio, 4/14/39; s. Michael A. Feighan and Florence Mathews F; single. Educ: Georgetown Univ; N.Y. Univ; N.Y. Univ. Grad. Sch. Polit. & Govt. Pos: Ohio State Rep, 61-67; admin. asst. to U.S. Rep. Michael Feighan, Ohio, currently. Bus. & Prof. Pos: Management. Mem: Univ. Club, Cleveland; Athletic Club Columbus; Ohio Press Club Ohio; City Club Cleveland; Jr. C. of C; Cong. Country Club. Outstanding First Term Legislator, Legis. Digest and Rev, Columbus, Ohio, 61. Rel: Catholic. Legal Res: 219 Superior W, Cleveland, Ohio 44101. Mailing Add: 2204 Rayburn Bldg, Washington, D.C. 20515.

FEIL, PAUL ARNOLD R

Chmn, Luna Co. Rep. Cent. Cmt, N.Mex.

b. Albuquerque, N.Mex, 10/22/22; s. Paul Julius Feil and Erna Bertha Schulze F; m. 7/2/49 to Alma Ruth Barr; c. Paul Alan, Nancy Ruth, David Arnold and Anita Louise. Educ: Univ. N.Mex, B.S, 44; Baylor Univ, M.D, 48; Phi Sigma. Polit. & Govt. Pos: Chmn, Luna Co. Rep. Cent. Cmt, N.Mex, 65- Bus. & Prof. Pos: Mem. city coun, Deming, N.Mex, 58-62; mem. sch. bd, 59-65, secy, 61-63 and pres, 63-65. Mil. Serv: Entered as A/S V-12, Navy, 41, released as Lt.(jg), 50. Mem: Luna Co. and N.Mex. Med. Socs; Am. Med. Asn; Am. Acad. Gen. Practice (secy, N.Mex. chap, 58-59, dir, 62-64, v.pres, 64-65, pres, 65-66); Lions; Luna Co. Farm Bur. Rel: Methodist. Legal Res: 719 W. Ash St, Deming, N.Mex. 88030. Mailing Add: P.O. Box 670, Deming, N.Mex. 88030.

FEILD, KAY CAROL R

Committeewoman, Ark. State Rep. Cmt.

b. Somerset, Pa, 2/9/38; d. Earl William Barclay and Velma Ankney B; m. 4/30/60 to Theophilus A. Feild, III, M.D; c. Katherine Bolling, Elizabeth Barclay, Anne Gardner and Janie Duckett. Educ: Johns Hopkins Hosp. Sch. of Nursing, R.N, 60. Polit. & Govt. Pos: Secy, Sebastian Co. Rep. Women, 65-66, v.chmn, 66-67; chmn, Sebastian Co. Rep. Cmt, 66-68, secy, 68-; committeewoman, Ark. State Rep. Cmt, 66-; alternate del, Rep. Nat. Conv, 68. Bus. & Prof. Pos: Staff nurse, Henry Ford Hosp, Detroit, Mich, 60-61. Mem: Johns Hopkins Hosp. Nurses Alumnae Asn; St. Edward Mercy Hosp. Auxiliary; Sparks Mem. Hosp. Womens Bd; Sebastian Co. Mental Health Asn; Sebastian Co. Med. Auxiliary; League of Women Voters; Jr. League of Ft. Smith, Inc; DAR. Rel: Episcopal. Mailing Add: 5601 Duncan Rd, Ft. Smith, Ark. 72901.

FEIN, ARNOLD L. D

b. Boston, Mass, 4/22/10; s. Jacob Fein and Annie L. Kanter F; m. 10/4/45 to Margaret L. Roach. Educ: N.Y. Univ, B.S, 31, Law Sch, J.D, 33. Polit. & Govt. Pos: Spec. counsel, U.S. Sen. Crime Invest. Cmn, 51; div. and appellate counsel, Off. Price Stabilization, 51; counsel, Pres. N.Y.C. Coun, 52-53; del. and committeeman, Dem. State and Local Conv, 54-64; mem. hearing bd, U.S. Coast Guard, 54-; mem. and pres, E.Midtown Reform Dem. Club, 59; v.chmn, N.Y. Cmt. for Dem. Voters, 60-61, chmn, 61-65; asst. campaign mgr, Wagner for Mayor, N.Y.C, 61; mem, Mayor's Cmt. Judiciary, N.Y.C, 61; del, Dem. Nat. Conv, 64; judge, Civil Court, N.Y.C, 65-69; justice, Supreme Court, State of N.Y, 69- Bus. & Prof. Pos: Lawyer, private practice, 34-65; mem. nat. panel of arbitrators, Am. Arbit. Asn, 46-66; lectr. and instr, N.Y. Univ. Grad. Sch. Pub. Admin, 55-64. Mil. Serv: Entered as Pvt, Army, 42, released as Maj, 46, after serv. in War Crimes Invest. Dept, GHQ AFPAC, Asiatic Pac, Hq. and OSS, 45-46; Army Commendation Ribbon, twice; Am. and Asiatic Pac. Campaign Medals; World War II Victory Medal; Distinguished Unit Badge; Lt. Col, Judge Adv. Gen. Corps, Army Res, 53. Mem: Am. and N.Y.C. Bar Asns; N.Y. Co. Lawyers Asn; N.Y. Univ. Law Rev. Alumni Asn; Am. Vets. Cmt; NAACP; Am. Civil Liberties Union; Am. for Dem. Action. Res: Jewish. Mailing Add: 601 E. 20th St, New York, N.Y. 10010.

FEINSTEIN, OTTO D

b. Vienna, Austria, 5/18/30; s. Abraham Feinstein and Bella Silber F; m. 12/6/61 to Nicolette Margaret Cecelia Carey. Educ: Univ. Chicago, B.A, 50, Ph.D, 65; Grad. Inst. Int. Studies, Univ. Geneva, Licenciate, 53. Polit. & Govt. Pos: Precinct del, 13th Dist. Dem. Orgn, Mich, 64-, v.chmn. and mem. exec. bd, 66-69; mem. resolutions cmt, Mich. Dem. Party, 65-69, mem. polit. reform cmt, 69 and cand. for chmn, 69; del, Dem. State Conv, 65, 66, 67, 68 & 69; mem. Cmt. of 99 on Co. Home Rule, Wayne Co, 67-68; alternate del, Dem. Nat. Conv, 68; exec. secy. and chmn, McCarthy for President Campaign, 68. Bus. & Prof. Pos: Asst. Prof, Monteith Col, Wayne State Univ, 60-64, assoc. prof, 64- Mil. Serv: Entered as Pvt, Army, 53, released as Pfc, 55; Good Conduct medal. Publ: Two Worlds of Change, Anchor Press, 65; 'Scholars Look at U.S. Foreign Policy,' Bul. Atomic Scientist, 59-60. Mem: Am. and Int. Polit. Sci. Asns; Nat. Planning Asn; Latin Am. Studies Asn; Int. Studies Asn; Am. Acad. Polit. & Soc. Sci; Am. Civil Liberties Union; Am. Fedn. Teachers; Urban Alliance; Council Indust. Conversion. Mailing Add: 667 W. Hancock, Apt. 206, Detroit, Mich. 48201.

FEKETY, JOHN J. D

N.J. State Assemblyman

b. Bayonne, N.J, 8/15/27; m. to Dorothy E. Yaczko; c. Karen, Beth and John J. Educ: St. Peter's Col. Polit. & Govt. Pos: Mem, Bayonne Zoning Bd. of Adjust, N.J, 62-65; N.J. State Assemblyman, currently. Bus. & Prof. Pos: Employee, N.J. Bell Tel. Co, staff supvr, Hudson Div. Plant. Mil. Serv: Navy, Pac. Theatre. Mem: CWV (Comdr, Msgr. A. L. Adzima Post 621 and Hudson Co. Chap); Am. Legion; Amvets; past Grand Marshall, Bayonne Mem. Day Cmt; past pres, Cath. Tel. Employees of Hudson Co; K. of C; Star of Sea Coun. 371; Order of Alhambra El Jarrow Caravan 154; Holy Name Soc. Rel: Catholic. Legal Res: 567 Ave. E, Bayonne, N.J. 07002. Mailing Add: State House, Trenton, N.J. 08625.

FELDMAN, GEORGE JOSEPH

b. Boston, Mass, 11/6/04; m. to Marion Schulman; c. two. Educ: Boston Univ, LL.B, 25. Polit. & Govt. Pos: Dir. and chief counsel, U.S. House Select Cmt. on Astronaut. and Outer Space, 58; mem, U.S. del. to 14th UN Gen. Assembly, 59; consult. to legal adv, Dept. of State, 59-60; mem, U.S. del. to Second UN Conf. on Law of Sea, 60; mem, U.S. NATO Citizens Cmt, 61-62; chmn, Finance Cmt, U.S. Cmt. for Refugees, 62-65; U.S. Ambassador to Malta, 65-69. Bus. & Prof. Pos: Attorney, private practice, 25-42 & 48-65; dir, Mastan Co, N.Y.C, Columbia Mills, Syracuse; one of original incorporators of Commun. Satellite Corp, Wash, D.C. Mil. Serv: Army Air Force, 42-45. Publ: Author, numerous books and articles on bus. law and space. Mailing Add: c/o U.S. Dept. of State, Washington, D.C. 20520.

FELDMAN, GERALD SAUNDERS D

b. Brooklyn, N.Y, 1/8/26; s. Meyer Feldman and Ethel Greenberg F; m. 8/27/44 to Elinore Coren; c. Jeffrey Mark, Clifford Irwin, Barbara Lynn and Allan Dennis. Educ: Hunter Col, N.Y, 1 year; Mass. Col. of Optom, Dr. Optom; Pi Omicron Sigma. Polit. & Govt. Pos: Cand, N.J. State Assemblyman, 65; chmn, Sussex Co. Dem. Party, 67-68; del, Dem. Nat. Conv, 68; founding mem, Citizens for Humphrey, 68. Bus. & Prof. Pos: Optometrist, Newton, N.J; pres, Dover Hearing Aid Ctr. Inc, Newton and Dover; mem. bd. mgrs, Glen Gardner Sanatorium for Chest Diseases. Mil. Serv: Entered as Pvt, Army, 44, released as 1st Sgt, 46, after serving in 76th Inf. Div. and 4th Armored Div, ETO, 44-46. Mem: Nat. Eye Research Found; Am. and N.J. Optom. Asns; VFW; Mason; Elks; Am. Legion; B'nai B'rith; Kiwanis; Shrine; crusade chmn, Sussex Co. Cancer Soc; pres, Newton Dem. Club. Rel: Judaic. Mailing Add: 4 Dogwood Dr, Newton, N.J. 07860.

FELDMAN, HENRY LEE D

b. Warrensburg, Mo, 5/15/03; s. Henry Feldman and Mary O'Brian F; m. 10/24/42 to Mary Louzann Hayes McKimstray; stepsons: Jerry D. and Jackie Z. Polit. & Govt. Pos: Chmn, Putnam Co. Dem. Party, Mo, 46-67; mem, Mo. Dem. State Cmt, 58-64. Mem: Lions Int.(counsr); Elks. Rel: Catholic. Mailing Add: 109 S. 16th, Unionville, Mo. 63565. (1967)

FELDMAN, JUSTIN N. D

Spec. Counsel, N.Y. State Dem. Cmt.

b. N.Y.C, 5/25/19; s. Hyman Feldman and Jennie Zolitarov F; m. 4/11/47 to Janet Cutting; c. Geoffrey C, Diane T. and Jane T. Educ: Columbia Univ, A.B, 40; Columbia Univ. Sch. Law, LL.B, 42. Polit. & Govt. Pos: Attorney, Nat. Prod. Authority, 51-52; admin. asst, U.S. Cong, 52-55; dir. N.Y. Off, N.Y. State Dept. Commerce, 56; spec. hearing officer, U.S. Dept. Justice, 61-68; consult, U.S. Dept. Commerce, 62-64; counsel, N.Y. Co. Dem. Cmt, 62-64; spec. counsel, N.Y. State Dem. Cmt, 62-; del, Dem. Nat. Conv, 64, 68; mem. & borough pres. Manhattan, Community Planning Bd, 66- Bus. & Prof. Pos: Mem. labor arbit. panel, Am. Arbit. Asn, 47-; mem, arbit. panel, N.Y. State Mediation Bd, 56-; partner, Landis, Feldman, Reilly & Akers, 58-64 and Poletti, Freidin, Prashker, Feldman & Gartner, 64-; mem, mediation & fact-finding panel, N.Y. State Pub. Employees Rel. Bd, 67-; dir, N.Y. Sugar Indust, Inc, 68-; dir, Bishop Industs, Inc, 69. Mil. Serv: Entered As Pvt, Army Air Force, 43, released as 1st Lt, 46, after serving in Judge Adv. Gen. Dept. Publ: 'How Tammany Holds Power', Nat. Munic. Rev, 49. Mem: Am. and N.Y. State Bar Asns; Asn. Bar City of New York; bd. dir, Mobilization for Youth Legal Serv. Corp; N.Y. Urban Coalition; lawyers div. exec. cmt, Fedn. Jewish Philanthropies; cmn. law & soc. action, Am. Jewish Cong; bd. dir, Columbia Law Sch. Alumni Asn. Legal Res: 410 W. 24th St, New York, N.Y. 10011. Mailing Add: 777 Third Ave, New York, N.Y. 10017.

FELDMAN, MARTIN L. C. R

Gen. counsel, Rep. Party, La.

b. St. Louis, Mo, 1/28/34; s. Joseph Feldman and Zelma Bosse F; m. 11/26/58 to Melanie Pulitzer; c. Jennifer and Martin, Jr. Educ: Tulane Univ, B.A, 55, LL.B, 57; Order of the Coif; Tulane Law Rev; Sigma Alpha Mu. Polit. & Govt. Pos: Pres, New Orleans Young Rep. Club, 59-60; dist. mgr, Nixon-Lodge Campaign, 60; v.chmn. and gen. counsel, La. Young Rep. Fedn, 61; v.chmn, Orleans Parish Rep. Exec. Cmt, 62-67; election day chmn, Goldwater-Miller Campaign, 64; gen. counsel, Rep. Party, La, 65-; mem, Orleans Parish Election Reforms Coun, 66-68; finance chmn, Rep. Party, New Orleans, 67; parliamentarian, La. Rep. State Cent. Cmt, 67-; chmn. spec. events, Nixon-Agnew Campaign, 68; del-at-lg, Rep. Nat. Conv, 68. Bus. & Prof. Pos: Partner, Bronfin, Heller, Feldman & Steinberg, New Orleans, dir. & v.pres, Wembley Inc, secy, Textile Reality Corp, secy, 1st Chestnut St. Corp. and secy, Advance Planning Consult, Inc, currently. Mil. Serv: Entered as Pvt, Army, 57, released as Pfc, 57, after serving in Adj. Gen. Corps; Capt, Army Res, 57-69. Publ: 'Relationship Between Principles of Copyright and Unfair Competition,' Copyright Law Symp, 57; 'Employee-Management Committees and the Labor-Management Relations Act of 1947,' Tulane Law Rev, 60; 'Trafficking in Net Operating Loss Corporations-Revisited,' La. Bar J, 68. Mem: Am, La. and Mo. Bar Asns; New Orleans Estate Planning Coun; Int. House, New Orleans; Lakewood Country Club. Nat. winner, Nathan Burkan Mem. Copyright Law Competition, 57; Lemann-Stern Leadership award, New Orleans Jewish Welfare Fedn, 60. Rel: Jewish. Mailing Add: 1121 Leontine, New Orleans, La. 70115.

FELDMAN, MATTHEW D

b. 1920; m. to Muriel Gunsberg; c. Beth Ellen, Rachel and Daniel. Educ: Univ. N.C; Panzer Col. of Phys. Educ. Polit. & Govt. Pos: Former mayor, Teaneck, N.J; former N.J. State Sen. Bus. & Prof. Pos: V.pres, Fedway Assocs, Jersey City. Mil. Serv: Capt, Army Air Corps, 5 years; Awarded

Citation for Skilled Training of Bombardiers, Cadets and Parachutists by Comdr, 8th A.F. Mem: Am. Legion; Jewish War Vet.(past Comdr, Dept. N.J); v.pres, Hebrew Home & Hosp. of N.J; adv. bd, Sch. of Nursing, Holy Name Hosp. Brotherhood Award, Bergen Co. Chap, Nat. Conf. of Christians and Jews, 63. Mailing Add: 138 Vandelinda Ave, Teaneck, N.J. 07666. (1967)

FELDMAN, MYER D
b. Philadelphia, Pa, 6/22/17; s. Israel Feldman and Bella Kurland F; m. 10/26/41 to Silva Moskovitz; c. Jane Margaret and James Alan. Educ: Girard Col, Phila, 22-31; Wharton Sch, Univ. Pa, B.S, 35, fel, 38-39, LL.B, 38. Polit. & Govt. Pos: Spec. counsel, exec. asst. to chmn, Securities Exchange Cmn, 46-54; counsel, Banking & Currency Cmn, U.S. Senate, 55-57; legis. asst. to Sen. John F. Kennedy, 58-61; dep. spec. counsel to Presidents Kennedy and Johnson, 61-64; counsel to President Johnson, 64-65; del, Dem. Nat. Conv, 68. Bus. & Prof. Pos: Attorney-at-law, Phila, 39-42; lectr. law, Univ. Pa, 41-42; prof, Am. Univ, 55-56; pres, Radio Assocs, Inc, 59; partner, Key Sta, 60; bd. overseers, Virgin Islands Univ, 62-; trustee, Eleanor Roosevelt Mem. Found, 63- and United Jewish Appeal; bd. dirs, Weitzman Inst, 63-; partner, Ginsburg & Feldman, Wash, D.C, 65-; dir, Flying Tiger Line, Inc, Flame of Hope, Inc, Imperial-Am. Corp. and Royal Resources Corp; chmn. bd, Speer Publ, Capital Gazette and Bay Publ. Publ: Standard Pennsylvania Practice, 4 Vols, 58; plus articles. Mil. Serv: Army Air Force, 42-46. Mem: Pres, Tau Epsilon Rho, 38; pres, Univ. Pa. Alumni Law Asn, Wash, 52-58. Mailing Add: 1700 Pennsylvania Ave, Suite 300, Washington, D.C. 20006.

FELGER, FOSTER F. D
b. Davenport, Iowa, 5/10/08; s. Charles Felger and Lura F; m. 1932 to Siri Peterson; c. Richard and Mrs. Thomas Ewoldt; three grandchildren. Educ: Central High Sch, 1926. Polit. & Govt. Pos: Fed. Investr, World War II; Iowa State Rep, until 67; investr, Iowa Dept. Agr, until 68; chief dep. auditor, Slott Co, currently. Bus. & Prof. Pos: Operated following bus. in Davenport, Kahl Bldg. Cigar Store, Steak House, Cedar St. Inn, Hi-De-Ho Tavern and Instnl. Foods, formerly; real estate broker. Mem: Moose; Mason (32°), Philbrook Lodge; AF&AM Zarepath Consistory; Kaaba Temple; Kaaba Shrine Club. Mailing Add: 1818 W. 37th St, Davenport, Iowa 52806.

FELKNOR, JOE HILL R
Chmn, Jefferson Co. Rep. Exec. Cmt, Tenn.
b. Livingston, Tenn, 9/13/25; s. Adrian E. Felknor and Nelle Zirkle F; m. 6/24/60 to Priscilla Donahoo; c. George Zirkle and Priscilla Anne. Educ: Univ. Tenn, Knoxville, J.D, 50; Pi Kappa Alpha; Phi Alpha Delta. Polit. & Govt. Pos: Chmn, Jefferson Co. Rep. Exec. Cmt, Tenn, 66- Bus. & Prof. Pos: Attorney-at-law, Dandridge, Tenn, 50- Mil. Serv: Entered as Pvt, Army, 43, released as S/Sgt, 46, after serving in 45th Infantry Div, ETO, 44-46; Purple Heart Medal; Good Conduct Medal. Mem: Jefferson Co. and Tenn. Bar Asn: Mason; Lions Int; VFW. Rel: Methodist. Mailing Add: P.O. Box 117, Dandridge, Tenn. 37725.

FELL, GEORGE HENRY R
Secy, Lucas Co. Rep. Exec. Cmt, Ohio
b. Toledo, Ohio, 9/28/08; s. George Nicholas Fell and Anna McDonald F; div; c. George N, Madelyn L, Richard A, James F, Charles F. and John E. Educ: St. John's Col, Toledo, Ohio, A.B, 30; Harvard Law Sch, LL.B, 33. Polit. & Govt. Pos: First asst, Legal Sect. Bank Liquidation, Toledo, Ohio, 39-42; Rep. precinct committeeman, Toledo, 42-; secy, Lucas Co. Rep. Exec. Cmt, Ohio, 43-; Asst. Attorney General, Ohio, 51-57; mem, Toledo Regional Bd. Rev, Workmen's Compensation Law, 57-59, attorney examiner and original hearing officer, 59. Mem: Am. Ohio and Lucas Co. Bar Asns; Toledo Bar Asn.(treas, 45-50); K. of C; The Toledo Club; North Cape Yacht Club. Rel: Roman Catholic. Legal Res: 2444 Scottwood Ave, Toledo, Ohio 43620. Mailing Add: 730 National Bank Bldg, Toledo, Ohio 43604.

FELLER, MILDRED MANLEY D
State Dem. Exec. Committeewoman, Fla.
b. Maryville, Mo, 4/5/00; d. Winfield O. Manley and Mary Agnes Vance M; 1st m. 4/14/20 and 2nd m. 11/10/55 to P. LeRoy Feller; c. Virginia (Mrs. V. Croudall Miller), Kathleen Lenore (Mrs. Aeurtis Padgette), Ralph W. and Keith I. Taylor. Educ: S.Dak. State Teachers Col, B.S. Polit. & Govt. Pos: Chmn, Bd. Pub. Instr, 36-40, mem, 36-60, v.chmn, 50-60; State Dem. Exec. Committeewoman, 42-; v.chmn, Sixth Cong. Dist. Dem. Party, 44-; mem, Co. Dem. Exec. Cmt, Hendry Co, 44-; mem, State Dem. Adv. Cmt, 46-66; del-at-lg, Dem. Nat. Conv, 48, 56 & 64, alternate del, 68; mem, Fla. Constitutional Rev. Cmt, 52; mem, Fla. Electoral Col, 56. Bus. & Prof. Pos: Sch. teacher, S.Dak, 19-21. Mem: Eastern Star; DAR; La Belle Woman's Club; charter mem, Hendry Co. Farm Bur; pres, PTA, 5 years; chmn, Cancer Soc, 2 years and dist. dir, 3 years; C. of C; State Cattlemens Asn. Selected Most Prominent Woman of Hendry Co, Bus. & Prfnl. Women's Club, 52. Rel: Methodist. Legal Res: State Rd. 830A, La Belle, Fla. 33935. Mailing Add: P.O. Box 637, La Belle, Fla. 33935.

FELLERS, VERA LESLEY R
Secy, Kit Carson Co. Rep. Party, Colo.
b. Des Moine, N.Mex, 2/5/33; d. George Lee Lesley and Helen Agnes Milliken L; m. 11/23/51 to Lloyd Lester Fellers; c. Leslie Jay, Charlotte Joan, Donald Lee and Carol Anne. Educ: High sch. grad, 51. Polit. & Govt. Pos: Secy, Kit Carson Co. Rep. Party, Colo, 69- Mem: Am. Legion Auxiliary; Gingham Girls Home Exten. Unit; Colo. Fedn. of Rep. Women, Farm Bureau. Rel: Protestant. Mailing Add: Route 1, Flagler, Colo. 80815.

FELLONI, JULIO D
b. Watertown, Mass; m. to Lilyan Norian. Educ: Mass. Col. of Pharmacy. Polit. & Govt. Pos: Chmn, Watertown Bd. of Health, 62-; assoc. mem, Dem. Town Cmt. Bus. & Prof. Pos: Chief Pharmacist, Cambridge City Hosp. Mil. Serv: Purple Heart, WWII. Mem: Founder, past Comdr, Amvets, Post 14; Boy Scouts. Misc: Past sponsor, Towners Softball Team. Mailing Add: 43 Fairfield St, Watertown, Mass. 02172. (1967)

FELLOWS, DOUGLAS MERRITT R
b. Everett, Mass, 2/23/10; s. James Albert Franklin Fellows and Elizabeth Merritt F; m. 10/29/32 to Catherine Mary Fontaine; c. Varney Douglas and Lura Fontaine (Mrs. Butt). Educ: Univ. Hartford, B.A. and M.Ed; Alpha Delta Psi. Polit. & Govt. Pos: Mem. bd. educ, Hebron, Conn, 56-57; mem, Land Evaluation Cmt, Hebron, 58; Conn. State Rep, 61-67; mem, Constitutional Conv, Conn, 65; chmn, Bd. Tax Rev, Hebron, 68- Bus. & Prof. Pos: Mgr. and photo engraver, Artcraft Photo-Engraving Co, 36-38, graphic expert, 43-45; ed. and writer, Hartford Courant, 38-45; mgr. and vet. adv, Hartford Sch. Music, 45-52; admin. dir, Univ. Hartford, Ward Tech. Inst, 62-69, consult. for tech. educ, Univ. Hartford, 69- Publ: 'This is Your America' and 'A Small Town Votes,' The Hartford Courant. Mem: Am. Society Polit. & Soc. Sci; Am. Asn. for Adv. of Sci; Am. Tech. Ed. Soc; Am. Soc. Eng. Ed; Nat. Ed. Asn; Conn. Personnel & Guidance Asn; Am. Ordnance Asn; Am. Air Force Asn; Garden Writers Asn. of Am; Am. Hort. Soc; Conn. Hort. Soc; Cape Coral Press Club; Conn. R.R. Hist. Asn. Mailing Add: Mill Stream Rd, Amston, Conn. 06231.

FELS, MARGARET KATHERINE R
Dir, Pa. Coun. Rep. Women
b. Erie, Pa, 4/29/27; d. Charles Porter McGeary, Sr. and Chelsie Schenck M; m. 10/8/49 to Raymond Lee Fels; c. Bryan Lee and Brett Garey. Educ: Grove City Col, 45-47; Chatham Col, B.A, 49. Polit. & Govt. Pos: Pres, Erie Coun. Rep. Women, Pa, 61-63; Erie Co. chmn, Women's Polit. Activities, 62-63; mem, Exec. Cmt, Erie Co. Rep. Party, 62-64; N.W. Regional chmn. membership, Pa. Coun. Rep. Women, 62, state chmn. membership, 63-65, state chmn. prog, 65-67, dir, 65-; mem, Resolutions Cmt, Pa. Coun. Rep. Women Conv, 63; pres, Erie Co. Fedn. Rep. Women's Coun, 63-64; alternate del, Rep. Nat. Conv, 64; dir, Fairview Coun. Rep. Women, 66-68; del. for Pa, Nat. Fedn. Rep. Women Conv, 67- Bus. & Prof. Pos: Teacher, Erie Bus. Center, 49-53 and Behrend Center of Pa. State Univ, 50-51; curriculum coordinator, Erie Bus. Center, 67- Mem: Past v.pres, YWCA, bd. of dirs; past bd. mem, Ment. Health Asn. Pa; PEO; Am. Asn. Univ. Women; pres, Jaycee Wives, Erie Jaycees, 58-59; del, Nat. United Presby. Women's Meeting, Purdue Univ, 67; charter mem, Corpe Diem Soc, Mercyhurst Col, 65. Delivered Party-to-People Forum Report to Gen. Eisenhower, 64; Honorarium, Cmn. on Ecumenical Mission Rels, 65; Name enshrined, Rep. Mem. in Nat. Mus. at Gettysburg Battlefield, 69. Rel: Presbyterian; Deacon, United Presbyterian Church of the Covenant. Mailing Add: Manchester Rd, Fairview, Pa. 16415.

FELTON, DANIEL HENRY, JR. D
Chmn, Lee Co. Dem. Cent. Cmt, Ark.
b. Felton, Ark, 7/1/20; s. Daniel Henry Felton and Felecia Curtis F; m. 10/8/44 to Counts McCollum; c. Daniel Henry, III, Martha Counts and Richard Trent. Educ: Univ. Ariz, 39-41. Polit. & Govt. Pos: Chmn, Lee Co. Elec. Cmt, Ark, 54-; chmn, Lee Co. Dem. Cent. Cmt, 54-; mem, Ark. State Dem. Cmt, 62-; mem, Ark. State Cmn. Coord. Higher Educ. Finance, 62- Bus. & Prof. Pos: Dir, First Nat. Bank, Marianna, Ark, 53-; dir, Forrest City Cotton Oil Co, 64-; owner, Dan Felton Jr. Farms; operating partner, Dan Felton & Co; owner, Felton Angus Farms. Mem: Farm Bur; dir, Ark. Agr. Coun; dir, Ark-Mo. Ginners Asn; dir, Ark. Angus Asn; Am. Angus Asn; dir, Marianna Country Club; Oakwood Club, Inc; Rivermont Club, Memphis. Rel: Methodist. Mailing Add: P.O. Box 555, Marianna, Ark. 72360.

FELTON, JULE WIMBERLY, JR. D
Ga. State Rep.
b. Macon, Ga, 7/22/32; s. Jule Wimberly Felton and Mary Julia Sasnett F; m. 5/15/65 to Kate Hudmon Gillis; c. Mary Katherine, Laura Borden and Jule Wimberly, III. Educ: Emory Univ, 1 year; Univ. Ga, A.B, 54, LL.B. cum laude, 55; Phi Delta Theta; Phi Delta Phi (pres); Sphinx; Gridiron Soc.(pres); Student Coun. Polit. & Govt. Pos: Ga. State Rep, 69- Bus. & Prof. Pos: Partner, Law Firm, Honsell, Post, Brondon & Dorsey, Atlanta, 57-65. Mil. Serv: Judge Adv. Gen. Corps, Army, 55-56, 1st Lt. Mem: Am. and Atlanta Bar Asns; Am. Judicature Soc; State Bar of Ga; Lawyers Club of Atlanta; Am. Trial Lawyers Asn; Asn. of R.R. Trial Lawyers; Lions; Buckheart Fifth Club. Rel: Methodist. Mailing Add: 2580 Woodward Way, N.W, Atlanta, Ga. 30305.

FELTON, KATHERINE LOFGREN D
b. Denver, Colo, 4/30/20; d. A.E. Lofgren and Loretto Mattingly L; m. 1/25/47 to John Richard Felton; c. James Lofgren and Joyce Adele. Educ: Simpson Col, B.A, 44; Pi Gamma Mu; Representative Woman. Polit. & Govt. Pos: Campaign mgr. Adlai Stevenson, Eastern Kern Co, Calif, 56 and Ralph Richardson, 62; chmn, UN Day, Nebr, 64; campaign worker, Eugene McCarthy, 68; alternate del, Dem. Nat. Conv, 68; campaign worker, City Coun. Cand. and Sch. Bd, currently. Bus. & Prof. Pos: Teacher, elem. sch, China Lake, Calif, 57-62, remedial teacher, Nebr. Penal Complex, 64-65; remedial teacher, Lincoln Job Corps, 65-68; teacher, Adams Pub. Sch, 68-69; teacher, Lincoln Adult Basic Educ. Prog, 69- Mem: NAACP; Am. for Dem. Action; Am. Civil Liberties Union; Indian Wells Valley Dem. Club, Calif.(pres, 61-62). Rel: Unitarian. Mailing Add: 3481 Anaheim, Lincoln, Nebr. 68506.

FENA, JACK DFL
b. Hibbing, Minn, 1923; m. to Kathleen Kaim; c. Lynn, James, Susan, Sally, Peter, Margaret, Christopher, Batholomew, Mary Ann and Andrew. Educ: Notre Dame Univ. Polit. & Govt. Pos: Minn. State Rep, 59-68. Bus. & Prof. Pos: Attorney, Firm of Fena and Mathias. Mil. Serv: World War II vet. Mailing Add: 2530 Third Ave. W, Hibbing, Minn. 55746. (1967)

FENDLER, OSCAR D
Committeeman, Mississippi Co. Dem. Cent. Cmt, Ark.
b. Blytheville, Ark, 3/22/09; s. Alfred Fendler and Rae Sattler F; m. 10/26/46 to Patricia Shane; c. Frances Shane and stepson Tilden P. Wright, III. Educ: Univ. Ark, B.A, 30; Harvard Law Sch, LL.B, 33. Polit. & Govt. Pos: Committeeman, Mississippi Co. Dem. Cent. Cmt, Ark, 47-; spec. trial judge, Circuit Court, Mississippi Co. Ark, 52; del, Dem. Nat. Conv, 68; spec. assoc. justice, Ark. Supreme Court, currently. Bus. & Prof. Pos: Attorney-at-law, Blytheville, Ark, currently. Mil. Serv: Entered as Lt.(jg), Naval Res, 41, released as Comdr, 46, after serv. in Continental U.S, Southwest Pac, China and Philippines; Res, 46-, Comdr. Publ: 'Uniform Limited Partnership Act,' 56 and 'Arkansas Judicial System at the Crossroads,' 63, Ark. Law Rev; 'The Legal Profession and the Anti-Poverty Program,' N.H. Bar J, 66. Mem: Blytheville Bar Asn; Ark. Bar Asn.(pres, 62-63); Am. Bar Asn.(chmn. sect. gen. practice, 66-67, mem. standing cmt. educ. about communism, 67-70); Am. Judicature Soc; Am. Col. Probate Counsel; Scribes; Ark. Judicial Coun; fel. Am. Bar Found; dir, Ark. Law Rev; Nat. Conf. Bar Pres.(exec.

coun, 63-65); state adv. coun, Small Bus. Admin; State Adv. Coun. Pub. Elem. and Sec. Educ. Rel: Jewish. Legal Res: 1062 W. Hearn St, Blytheville, Ark. 72315. Mailing Add: P.O. Box 548, Blytheville, Ark. 72315.

FENDLEY, FURMAN LESTER D
S.C. State Rep.
b. Oconee Co, S.C, 5/16/18; s. Robert E. Fendley and Essie Rholetter F; m. 9/3/43 to Sue Whitney. Educ: Oconee Schs. Polit. & Govt. Pos: S.C. State Rep, currently. Bus. & Prof. Pos: Dairy farmer, currently. Mil. Serv: Navy, 42. Mem: Pres, Farm Bur; Am. Legion. Rel: Baptist; Chmn, Bd. of Deacons, Hebron Baptist Church, Union, S.C. Mailing Add: R.F.D. 3, Union, S.C. 29379. (1967)

FENN, DAN HUNTINGTON, JR. D
b. Boston, Mass, 3/27/23; s. The Rev. Dan Huntington Fenn and Anna Yens F; div; c. Peter H, Ann H, David E. and Thomas O. Educ: Harvard Col, A.B, 44; Harvard Univ. Grad Sch. of Arts and Sci; Phi Beta Kappa; Polit. & Govt. Pos: Del, Mass. State Dem. Conv, 54, 56, 58 & 60; chmn, Dem. Town Cmt, Lexington, 56-61; secy, Lexington, Mass. Sch. Cmt, 58-61; alternate del, Dem. Nat. Conv, 60; spec. asst. to U.S. Sen. Benjamin A. Smith, Mass, 61; staff asst. to the President, 61-63; cmnr, U.S. Tariff Cmn, 63-67, v.chmn, 64-65. Bus. & Prof. Pos: Asst. dean of freshmen, Harvard Col, 46-49; exec. dir, World Affairs Coun. Boston, 49-54; mem. faculty, Harvard Bus. Sch, 55-61, lectr, 69-, asst. ed, Harvard Bus. Rev, 55-61; pres, Center Bus-Govt. Rels, 67-; prof. lectr, Am. Univ, 67-69. Mil. Serv: Entered as Pvt, Army Air Force, 43, released as Warrant Officer (jg), 45, after serv. in 767th Bomb Sq, 461st Bomb Group, Italy, 44-45. Publ: Ed, Seven-volume series on management, McGraw-Hill, 55-61; Cases in Business and Government, (w. Donald Gruenwald and Robert Katz), Prentice Hall, 66; 'The Would-be Lobbyist,' Harvard Bus. Rev, 66. Mem: Am. Soc. for Pub. Admin; Harvard Bus. Sch. Club, D.C.(bd. dirs); Montgomery Co. Oratorio Soc.(pres); Nat. Capital Area Civil Liberties Union (bd. dirs). Decorated by Govt. of Morocco, 52. Rel: Unitarian. Mailing Add: 4008 Everett St, Kensington, Md. 20795.

FENN, HENRY FORSTER 'HANK' D
Ariz. State Rep.
b. Mesa, Ariz, 1/5/25; s. Alvah Fenn and Carmen Forster F; m. 1/23/45 to Mae Dean Kennedy; c. Linda Kaye (Mrs. Alfred Leon Talley). Educ: Benson High Sch. Polit. & Govt. Pos: Ariz. State Rep, Dist. Two, 69- Bus. & Prof. Pos: Miner, Phelps Dodge Mining, Bisbee, Ariz; Owner, Sand & Gravel Trucking, Benson, Ariz; Construction worker, El Paso Natural Gas Co, Scoffield, Utah and The Dalles Dam, The Dalles, Ore; Owner, Produce Trucking, Farmington, N.Mex; Owner, Hank's Coffee Shop, Benson, Ariz, 15 years. Mil. Serv: Navy, 42. Publ: 'The Cowboy Baker' Western Livestock J; 'Manor Man and Owner' Tucson Citizen, Feb. 62. Rel: Latter-day Saint. Legal Res: Pomerene Rd, Benson, Ariz. 85602. Mailing Add: Drawer H, Benson, Ariz. 85602.

FENNELL, MELVIN R
Mem, Rep. Town Cmt, Fairfield, Conn.
b. New York, N.Y, 6/24/12; s. Herman Fennell and Minnie Sanders F; m. 5/17/42 to Estelle Murov; c. Gary Ritchie. Educ: Yale Col, B.A, 32; Harvard Law Sch, LL.B, 35. Polit. & Govt. Pos: Clerk, Fairfield Town Court, Conn, 50; mem, Fairfield Rep. Town Meeting, 47-61; Conn. State Rep, 61-67; mem, Rep. Town Cmt, Fairfield, 62- Bus. & Prof. Pos: Lectr, Univ. Bridgeport, 40-42 & 65-66. Mil. Serv: Entered as Pvt, Army, 44, released as T/4, 45, after serv. in Army Signal Corps. Mem: Conn. and Bridgeport Bar Asns; Citizens Sch. Study Coun; Red Cross; Lions; Am. Legion; Stratfield Vol. Fire Dept. 3; Fairfield Boat Owners; Yale Club. Rel: Hebrew. Mailing Add: 91 Lockwood Rd, Fairfield, Conn. 06430.

FENNER, BERTINE LORRAINE D
Chmn, MacKinac Co. Dem. Party, Mich.
b. Thompson, Mich, 8/10/15; d. Edward John Miller and Ida M; m. 2/22/41 to Milford Sherman Fenner; c. Richard Lloyd. Educ: High Sch. Polit. & Govt. Pos: Mem, Dem. Nat. Cmt; v.chmn, MacKinac Co. Dem. Party, Mich, 56, chmn, 58-; mem, MacKinac Co. Planning Cmt, 65. Mem: Am. Legion Auxiliary; Moose. Mailing Add: Route 2, St. Ignace, Mich. 49781. (1967)

FENRICH, ANDREW T. D
Pa. State Rep.
b. Pittsburgh, Pa, 2/20/14; m. to Mary Pattonrick; c. Arlene, Phyllis, Karen and Sandra. Polit. & Govt. Pos: Former secy. to Mayor of Pittsburgh, Pa; exec. dir, Allegheny Co. Dem. Orgn; Pa. State Rep, 49-54 & 62- Mem: Past pres, Local 296, Paper Box Workers Union; past comdr, Am. Legion; Amvets; VFW; Elks; Moose; Eagles. Mailing Add: 2014 Veronica St, Pittsburgh, Pa. 15212. (1967)

FENSTER, LEO D
Mem, Calif. Dem. State Cmt.
b. New York, N.Y, 5/20/22; s. Morris Fenster and Bessie Geffner F; m. 5/6/45 to Maryann Weinstein; c. Alan, Stephen and Michael. Educ: Santa Monica City Col, A.A, 42; Univ. Calif, Los Angeles, 42; Univ. South. Calif. Law Sch, 45-46; Southwest. Univ. Law Sch, LL.B, 50. Polit. & Govt. Pos: V.chmn, 16th Cong. Dem. Coun, Los Angeles, Calif, 56; Dem. nominee, Calif. State Assembly, 60th Dist, 64, 66 & 68, chmn, 60th Assembly Dist. Dem. Coun, Los Angeles, 67; mem, Calif. Dem. State Cmt, 64- Bus. & Prof. Pos: Attorney, Los Angeles, 51-69. Mil. Serv: Entered as Air Cadet, Army Air Force, 43, released as 1st Lt, 45, after serv. in 9th Air Force, ETO, 44-45; Purple Heart; Air Medal with 12 Oak Leaf Clusters. Mem: State Bar of Calif; Santa Monica Bar Asn; C. of C; B'nai B'rith; Optimist. Rel: Jewish. Mailing Add: 961 Bluegrass Way, Los Angeles, Calif. 90049.

FENTON, ISABELLE B. R
Chmn, Delaware Co. Rep. Cmt, N.Y.
b. New Rochelle, N.Y, 5/13/22; d. Bertram Ormand Bentley and Louise McCumber B; m. 1/25/44 to Donald McLean Fenton; c. Andrea (Mrs. William J. Campbell), John Donald and James Thomas. Educ: State Univ. Col. at Oneonta, N.Y, B.Ed, 43, 27 hours of grad. work; Arethusa Sorority; Glee Club. Polit. & Govt. Pos: Committeewoman, Middletown, Delaware Co, N.Y, 51-69; secy, Rep. Town Cmt. of Middletown, 56-68; v.chmn, Delaware Co. Rep. Cmt, 59-69, chmn, 69- Bus. & Prof. Pos: Teacher, Bayport Sch, Long Island, N.Y, 43-45, Margaretville Cent. Sch, 49-52 & 58- Mem: Margaretville and N.Y. State Teachers Asns; Eastern Star; Middletown Women's Rep. Club; Women's Soc. of Presby. Church; Margaretville Mem. Hosp. Auxiliary; Parent Teachers Group; Delaware Co. Women's Rep. Club. Rel: Presbyterian. Mailing Add: Mountain Ave, Margaretville, N.Y. 12455.

FENTON, LAWRENCE LYMAN R
Chmn, Crowley Co. Rep. Cent. Cmt, Colo.
b. Rocky Ford, Colo, 6/2/26; s. Ward Caldwell Fenton and Charlotte Burgess F; m. 3/27/55 to Reta Hollister; c. Hollis Sue. Educ: Univ. Colo, B.A, 49, J.D, 52. Polit. & Govt. Pos: State chmn, Colo. Young Rep. League, 56-58; co. attorney, Crowley Co, 57-; chmn, Crowley Co. Rep. Cent. Cmt, 58- Mil. Serv: Entered as Pvt, Army, 44, released as S/Sgt, 46, after serv. in Qm. Corps, Japan, 45-46. Mem: Colo. Bar Asn. Rel: Protestant. Legal Res: 608 Idaho, Ordway, Colo. 81063. Mailing Add: P.O. Box 26, Ordway, Colo. 81063.

FENTRESS, GEORGE H. R
Colo. State Rep.
b. Nashville, Tenn, 9/13/20; s. H.G. Fentress and Daisy Murkin F; m. 3/31/44 to Madeline I. McPherson; c. David L, Marilyn K. and Kenneth P. Educ: Colo. Sch. of Mines, Geol. Eng. Degree, 49; Beta Theta Pi. Polit. & Govt. Pos: Colo. State Rep, Jefferson Co, 65-, mem, Water, Water Pollution, State Affairs, Natural Resources, Health Welfare and Insts, Educ. Beyond High Sch, Orgn. of State Govt, Joint Budget and Appropriations Cmts. Bus. & Prof. Pos: Clerk and draftsman, Lion Oil Co, 38-43, trainee and surveyer, geophys. dept, 49-50, subsurface geologist, 50-52, dist. geologist, 52-56; mgr. explor. and prod, Baumgartner Oil Co, 56-59 and Exeter Drilling Co, 59-62; independent consult. geol. engr, 62- Mil. Serv: 2nd Lt, Army Air Force, 44-46, served as Navigator. Publ: 'Little Beaver Field, Colorado, A Stratigraphic, Structural and Sedimentation Problem,' Am. Asn. Petrol. Geologists Bul, 2/55; 'The Denver Basin,' Kans. Geol. Soc. Field Conf. Guidebook, 9/58; 'Denver Basin of Colorado,' Petroleum and Natural Gas Sect, Mineral Resources of Colo, First Sequel, Colo. Mineral Resources Bd, 60. Mem: Rocky Mt. Asn. Geologists, chmn. field trip cmt, summer 55 and co-chmn, fall 55, chmn. res. cmt, 58, first v.pres, 60; chmn. field trip cmt, Am. Asn. Petroleum Geologists, 58-61; dist. rep, Am. Asn. Petroleum Geologists; Soc. Petroleum Engrs; Am. Geol. Inst; Am. Inst. Prfnl. Geologists; Registered Prfnl. Engr, Colo, pres. Jefferson chap, Prfnl. Engrs, 69-70; Soc. Independent Prfnl. Earth Scientists; Asn. Eng. Geologists; dir, East Jefferson C. of C; co-chmn, Bus. Educ. Day Cmt, 64; treas. and pres, Wheat Ridge Jr. High PTA, 64-66; Indust. for Jefferson Co; Jefferson Co. Govt. Asn. Rel: Episcopal; Vestry, Calvary Church, Golden, 54-56; chmn. bldg. fund, St. James Church, Wheat Ridge, 65. Mailing Add: 2935 Webster St, Lakewood, Colo. 80215.

FENTRESS, LEO FREEDOM D
Chmn, Floyd Co. Dem. Party, Ind.
b. Grayson Co. Ky, 5/11/18; s. Ferd Fentress and Lydia Cannon F; m. 6/25/38 to Taletha Litsey; c. Michael Timothy and David Warren. Educ: Short Creek High Sch, 4 years. Polit. & Govt. Pos: Chmn, Floyd Co. Dem. Party, Ind, 64-; precinct committeeman, currently. Bus. & Prof. Pos: Former field rep, Dept. Revenue, Ind; asst. foreman, Olin Mathesion Chem. Corp, 69-. Mem: Mason; Red Men; Odd Fellows. Rel: United Methodist. Mailing Add: 464 Luther Rd, New Albany, Ind. 47150.

FERENCY, ZOLTON A. D
b. Detroit, Mich, 6/30/22; s. John Ferency and Mary Jankovics F; m. 6/14/47 to Ellen Jane Dwyer; c. Michael John and Mark Dwyer. Educ: Mich. State Univ, B.A, 46; Detroit Col. Law, J.D, 52; Wayne State Univ. Grad. Law Sch, Labor Law, 52-55. Polit. & Govt. Pos: Personnel technician, Detroit, Mich, 46-48; relocation dir, Detroit Slum Clearance Prog, 48-53; v.chmn, 14th Dist. Dem. Orgn, 56-62; cmnr, Liquor Control Cmn, 57-58; dir, Workmen's Compensation Dept, 58-60; exec. secy. to Gov. Mich, 61-62; chmn, Mich. State Dem. Cent. Cmt, 63-68; del, Dem. Nat. Conv, 68. Bus. & Prof. Pos: Lectr, State Bar Inst, Upper Peninsula, Inst. on Continuing Legal Educ, and NACCA Law Inst; lawyer, Ferency, Sweeney and Markus, Detroit, 53-55, Marston, Ganos and Ferency, 60-61 and Hardy, Starr and Ferency, Lansing, 66- Mil. Serv: Entered as Pvt, Army, 42, released as M/Sgt, 45, after serv. in 42nd Inf. Div. and 18th Airborne Corps, Mil. Intel. Serv, ETO, 44-45; ETO Ribbon with 3 Battle Stars. Publ: Workmens Compensation Practices, Inst. on Continuing Legal Educ, Revised 64. Mem: State Bar of Mich.(Labor Law Sect. and Workmens Compensation Sect); Hungarian-Am. Dem. Club; Local 212 UAW, AFL-CIO; NAACP; CWV; bd. dirs, Polish-Hungarian Fedn; VFW. Rel: Catholic. Legal Res: 120 Maplewood, East Lansing, Mich. 48910. Mailing Add: 900 W. Michigan, Lansing, Mich. 48915. (1967)

FERGUSON, BRUCE STUART D
b. Union, Ky, 3/21/29; s. Walter Ferguson and Shirley Rice F; m. 8/11/51 to Elizabeth Reynolds; c. Carol, Martha, Stuart, Miriam and Philip. Educ: Univ. Ky, 49-50; Thomas More Col, B.A, 65; Pi Kappa Alpha. Polit. & Govt. Pos: Co. judge, Boone Co, Ky, 63-; del, Dem. Nat. Conv, 68. Mem: Jr. C. of C; Farm Bur; Mason. Man of the Year, Jr. C. of C. Rel: Presbyterian. Mailing Add: Union, Ky. 41091.

FERGUSON, C. VAUGHN, JR.
b. Schenectady, N.Y, 1/12/15; s. Charles Vaughn Ferguson and Harriet Esther Rankin F. Educ: Harvard Univ, A.B, 37, grad. study, 37-38. Polit. & Govt. Pos: Vice consul, Winnipeg, Dept. State 40-41, Tehran, 41-46 and Bucharest, 46-48, consul, 48-49, officer-in-charge, Iranian Affairs, 49-52, consul gen, Naval War Col, 52-53, Dakar, 53-55, counsr. of legation, Tangier, 55-56, consul gen, 55-57, dir, Off. Mid. and S. African Affairs, 57-60, Off. W.African Affairs, 60-62, U.S. Ambassador to Malagasy Repub, 62-69. Mem: Univ. Club, Wash, D.C. 1967 Legal Res: Washington, D.C. No mailing address available. (1967)

FERGUSON, CHARLES WRIGHT, JR R
N.H. State Rep.
b. Quincy, Mass, 3/7/27; married; c. seven. Educ: Univ. Ala, B.A; Boston Univ. Law Sch, LL.B. Polit. & Govt. Pos: Mem, Cmt. on Serv. for Older Persons, N.H. Soc. Welfare Coun; chmn, Milford Sch. Bd; N.H. State Rep,

63- Bus. & Prof. Pos: Owner, grocery store, nursing home. Mil. Serv: Army, released 47, serv. in Korea, 10 months. Mem: Past pres, Lions; past pres, N.H. Nursing Home Asn. Rel: Congregational. Mailing Add: 3 Cherry St, Milford, N.H. 03055. (1967)

FERGUSON, CLARENCE CLYDE, JR. R
Spec. Coordinator for Nigerian Relief, Dept. of State
b. Wilmington, N.C, 11/4/24; s. Clarence Clyde Ferguson, Jr. and Georgeva Owens F; wid; c. Claire, Hope and Eve. Educ: Wilberforce Univ, 42-43; Ohio State Univ, A.B. cum laude, 48; Harvard Law Sch, LL.B. cum laude, 51; Phi Beta Kappa; Alpha Phi Alpha. Polit. & Govt. Pos: Gen. counsel, Civil Rights Cmn, 62-63; spec. legal adv, U.S. Mission to the UN, Dept. of State, 63; asst. U.S. attorney, Dept. of Justice, 54-55; Spec. Coordinator for Nigerian Relief, Dept. of State, 69- Bus. & Prof. Pos: Teaching fel. and teaching asst, Harvard Univ, 50-52; law firm assoc, Baltimore, Paulson & Canudo, 52-54; asst. gen. counsel and chmn, Cmt. on Invest. of Harness Racing, State of N.Y, 53-54; prof, Rutgers Univ. Law Sch, 55-63 & 69; dean, Howard Univ. Law Sch, 63-69. Mil. Serv: Army, 42-46; ETO and Pac. Theatre of Opers. Decorated Bronze Star. Publ: Desegregation and the Law: The Meaning and Effect of the School Segregation Cases (with A.P. Blaustein), 60; Enforcement and Collection of Judgments and Liens, 61; Secured Transactions, Article IX Uniform Commercial Code in New Jersey, 61. Mem: Am, Fed. and Nat. Bar Asns; Harvard Law Sch. Alumni. Numerous honors and awards. Rel: Presbyterian. Mailing Add: 1601 Kalmia Rd. N.W, Washington, D.C. 20012.

FERGUSON, CLIFFORD LINDEL R
Chmn, Haakon Co. Rep. Party, S.Dak.
b. Rural Haakon Co, S.Dak, 1/1/11; s. Messer Alexander Ferguson and Sueie Hall F; m. 9/5/43 to Retta Mae Lancaster; c. Beverly Joan and Linda Sue Ferguson and Larry Paul Blake. Educ: S.Dak. State Univ, Civil Eng, 34, Blue Key. Polit. & Govt. Pos: Chmn, Haakon Co. Sch. Bd, S.Dak, 56-; chmn, Haakon Co. Rep. Party, 58-; pres, State Fair Bd, 63-66; mem, S.Dak. Bldg. Authority, 68- Mem: Mason; Elks; Oriental Consistory; Shrine. Rel: Presbyterian. Mailing Add: Philip, S.Dak. 57567.

FERGUSON, DOROTHY MAUDE R
Secy, Amador Co. Rep. Cent. Cmt, Calif.
b. Cherry Co, Nebr, 5/31/95; d. Hugh Bovill and Charlotte Emily Robinson B; m. 4/22/19 to James Ross Ferguson. Educ: Univ. Idaho, 10-12. Polit. & Govt. Pos: Secy. and fund drive chmn, Amador Co. Rep. Cent. Cmt, Calif, 46-; dep. registrar, Amador Co, 50-; charter mem, Rep. Women Federated Amador Co, 61-; mem, Calif. State Rep. Finance Cmt, 65-; mem, Calif. State Rep. Cent. Cmt, 67- Bus. & Prof. Pos: Censor, Calif. Youth Authority, Preston Sch. Indust, Ione, Calif, 50-64. Mem: Charter mem. VFW Auxiliary; v.chmn, Amador Co. Chap. Am. Red Cross, 67-69 (fund drive chmn, 48-57 & 69). Eleven citations from Am. Red Cross; plaque, State Rep. Cmt, 66 & 67; plaque for State Quota Fund Drive, 68. Rel: Episcopal. Mailing Add: Route 1, Box 9A, Sutter Creek, Calif. 95685.

FERGUSON, GEORGE ROBERT, JR. D
Miss State Rep.
b. Learned, Miss 8/13/33; s. George Roberts Ferguson (deceased) and Eugenia Williams F; m. 7/5/59 to Martha Gillespie; c. Martha Elizabeth and George Robert, III. Educ: Hinds Jr. Coll, Raymond, Miss, 1 year; Miss. State Univ, B.S, 55; Jackson Sch. Law, LL.B, 65; Blue Key; Pi Delta Epsilon; Sigma Delta Kappa; Pi Kappa Alpha; Delta Sigma Pi. Polit. & Govt. Pos: Miss. State Rep, Hinds Co, 68- Bus. & Prof. Pos: Rep, Procter & Gamble Co, 58-60; dir. advert. and pub. rels, Standard Life Ins. Co, Jackson, Miss, 60-64; v.pres, L.E. Davis and Assocs, 64-65; attorney-at-law, Raymond, 65-; owner and publisher, Miss. Valley Stockman Farmer, 65- Mil. Serv: Entered as Pvt. E-1, Army, 56, released as Pfc, 58, after serv. in 23rd Antiaircraft Artillery Bn, U.S. and Germany. Mem: Miss. and Hinds Co. Bar Asns; Greater Jackson Advert.Club; Indust. Ed. Asn. of Miss.(past pres); Scottish Rite; Mason; Shrine; Lions; Moose; Farm Bur. Named to Outstanding Young Men of Am, 68. Rel: Presbyterian; Elder, Presby. Church, Raymond. Mailing Add: P.O. Drawer 89, Raymond, Miss. 39154.

FERGUSON, GLENN W.
b. Syracuse, N.Y, 1/28/29; s. Forrest E. Ferguson and Mabel Walker F; m. to Patricia Lou Head; c. Bruce Walker, Sherry Lynn and Scott Sherwood. Educ: Cornell Univ, B.A, 50, M.B.A, 51; Georgetown Univ, 51-52; Univ. Santo Tomas, Philippines, 52-53; George Wash. Univ. Law Sch, 53-55; Univ. Chicago Law Sch, 55-56; Univ. Pittsburgh, J.D, 57. Polit. & Govt. Pos: Consult, Int. Coop. Admin, Pakistan, 59; Peace Corps rep, Bangkok, 61-63, assoc. dir, 63-64; dir, VISTA, 64-66; U.S. Ambassador to Kenya, 66-69. Bus. & Prof. Pos: Asst. secy-treas. and asst. ed, Am. Judicature Soc, 55-56; admin. asst. to chancellor and asst. dean grad. sch, Pub. & Int. Affairs, Univ. Pittsburgh, 56-60; mgt. consult, McKinsey & Co, Wash, D.C, 60-61; chancellor, L.I. Univ, 69- Mil. Serv: Entered as 2nd Lt, Air Force, 51, released as 1st Lt, 53, after serv. in 13th Air Force, Korea and Philippines, 52-53. Publ: Various pub. admin. and comparative govt. articles for prfnl. journals. Mem: Fed. Bar Asn; Am. Polit. Sci. Asn. Coun. on For. Rels. Arthur Flemming Award, 68. Mailing Add: 187 Post Rd, Old Westbury, N.Y. 11568.

FERGUSON, HOMER R
b. Harrison City, Pa, 2/25/89; s. Samuel Ferguson and Margaret Bush F; m. 6/20/13 to Myrtle Jones; c. Amy (Mrs. Charles R. Beltz). Educ: Univ. Pittsburgh, 10-11; Univ. Mich, LL.B, 13; Sigma Delta Kappa. Hon. LL.D, Univ. Mich, 51; hon. degrees, Detroit Col. Law, Kalamazoo Col. and Muhlenberg Col. Polit. & Govt. Pos: Mem, Second Hoover Cmn; spec. attorney for Dept. of Defense; judge, Circuit Court, Wayne Co, 29-41; U.S. Ambassador to Philippines, 55-56; assoc. judge, U.S. Court of Mil. Appeals, 56- Bus. & Prof. Pos: Attorney, private practice, 13-29. Mem: Am. and Detroit Bar Asns; Wash. Inst. of Foreign Affairs; Inst. of Fiscal & Polit. Educ; Metrop. Club, Washington, D.C. Rel: Presbyterian. Legal Res: 5054 Millwood Lane N.W, Washington, D.C. 20016. Mailing Add: U.S. Court of Military Appeals, Washington, D.C. 20442.

FERGUSON, JO O. R
Chmn, Pawnee Co. Rep. Party, Okla.
b. Willow Springs, Mo, 6/29/89; s. David S. Ferguson and Martha Isabel Young F; m. 1920 to Anna Stogsdill; c. David Jo, Dolores Ann (Mrs. Frank Hooper) and Larry Ross. Educ: Willow Springs High Sch, Mo, 3 years; Univ. Mo. Law Sch, 1 year. Polit. & Govt. Pos: Mem, City Coun, Pawnee, Okla, 22-24; Okla. State Sen, Tenth Dist, 24-32; Rep. nominee for Cong, 36, Lt. Gov, 42 and Gov, 50; del, Rep. Nat. Conv, 40 & 52; chmn, Pawnee Co. Rep. Party, Okla, 61- Bus. & Prof. Pos: Ed-publisher, Pawnee Courier-Dispatch, Okla, 22-30, Cleveland Am, 34-62 and Pawnee Chief, 41-52. Mil. Serv: Entered Army, 17, released as 1st Lt, 19, after serv. in 140th U.S. Inf, European Theatre, 18-19; Combat and Serv. Badges. Mem: Okla. Press Asn; Mason; Am. Legion; VFW. Rel: Protestant. Mailing Add: 1111 Denver Rd, Pawnee, Okla, 74058.

FERGUSON, JOEL IRVING D
Mayor Pro-Tem, Lansing, Mich.
b. Lansing, Mich, 11/14/38; s. Rollin Ferguson and Josephine Jeffries F; m. 5/12/63 to Erma Townsley; c. Barry, Dori, David and Jenifer. Educ: Mich. State Univ, B.A. in Ed, 65. Polit. & Govt. Pos: Mem, Ingham Co. Bd. of Supvr, Mich, 67-69; mem, Lansing City Coun, 67-; del, Dem. Nat. Conv, 68; Mayor Pro-Tem, Lansing, 67- Mil. Serv: Entered as Pvt, Marines, 56, released as Pfc, 58, after serv. in T-3-7. Mem: Urban League; NAACP. Rel: Methodist. Mailing Add: 3412 Sandhurst, Lansing, Mich. 48910.

FERGUSON, LAWRENCE W. D
Chmn, Yellow Medicine Co. Democrat-Farmer-Labor Party, Minn.
b. Canby, Minn, 4/23/15; s. Ole Ferguson and Jule Hanson F; m. 2/10/45 to Erma Dodge. Educ: Canby High Sch. Polit. & Govt. Pos: Dem. chmn, Precinct Two, Canby, Minn, 56-60; v.chmn, Yellow Medicine Co. Democrat-Farmer-Labor Party, 60-65, chmn, 65- Bus. & Prof. Pos: Farmer. Mem: Odd Fellows; Farmers Union. Rel: Lutheran. Mailing Add: R.R. 3, Canby, Minn. 56220.

FERGUSON, LESLIE GUY R
Okla. State Rep.
b. Bucklin, Mo, 3/8/94; s. John Thomas Ferguson and Mabel Ellen Brandow F; m. 5/24/22 to Fairy Fay Bird (deceased); c. Theodore R, Robert L. and Joan (Mrs. Walter R. Fuller). Educ: Cent. State Col, Okla, B.A, 24; Univ. Tulsa, M.A, 52; Univ. Okla, 1 year; Kappa Delta Pi; Red Red Rose Club for Men Teachers. Polit. & Govt. Pos: Okla. State Rep, Dist. 79, 64- Bus. & Prof. Pos: Teacher, Drumright, Okla, 17-18, Skiatook, 18-19; supt. schs, Avant Pub. Schs, 19-22, Marshall Pub. Schs, 22-23; teacher math, El Reno, 23-24, Tulsa Pub. Schs, 24-47; Tulsa Co. Supt. Schs, 47-59. Mil. Serv: A/S, Navy, 18; Inactive Naval Res, until 24. Mem: Life mem. Okla. Educ. Asn; life mem. Okla. Teachers Retirement Syst; life mem, Okla. PTA; Mason (32°); Shrine; Am. Legion. Rel: Christian Church N.Am. Mailing Add: 2419 S. Knoxville Ave, Tulsa, Okla. 74114.

FERGUSON, ROBERT EARL D
N.Mex. State Sen.
Polit. & Govt. Pos: N.Mex. State Sen, currently. Bus. & Prof. Pos: Real estate and ins. Mil. Serv: Army Air Corps, 3 years. Mem: Am. Legion; C. of C; United Fund; Elks; Mason; Shriners; Kiwanis. Rel: Methodist. Mailing Add: P.O. Box 609, Artesia, N.Mex. 88210. (1967)

FERGUSON, RODGER O. R
b. Freeport, Ill, 9/13/25; s. Leonard Ferguson and Mildred F; m. 8/17/46 to Margaret Antrim; c. Wendy, Kim and Candis. Educ: Hamilton Col, B.A; Delta Upsilon. Polit. & Govt. Pos: City Councilman, Monrovia, Calif, 52- and Mayor, 58-67. Mil. Serv: Entered as Seaman, Navy, 46, released as Lt. (jg). Mem: Rotary; Elks; Am. Legion; VFW; Town Hall. Rel: Presbyterian. Mailing Add: 505 N. Magnolia, Monrovia, Calif. 91016.

FERGUSON, ROSETTA D
Mich. State Rep.
b. Florence, Miss, 7/1/20; d. Gabriel Sexton and Earnie S; c. Four. Educ: Detroit Inst. of Tech. Polit. & Govt. Pos: Mem, Mich. Dem. State Cent. Cmt, First Dist; Mich. State Rep, 64- Bus. & Prof. Pos: Gen. mgr. staff, real estate firm. Mem: Den Mother, Cub Scouts; Gray Lady, Red Cross; PTA; NAACP; Women's Pub. Affairs Cmt. of 1,000, Inc; Trade Union Leadership Coun; Wayne Co. Dem. rep, Human Rels. Coun. on Civil Rights. Rel: Baptist. Mailing Add: 2676 Arndt, Detroit, Mich. 48207.

FERGUSON, STEPHEN LUTHER R
Ind. State Rep.
b. Indianapolis, Ind, 1/3/41; s. Luther Short Ferguson and Arline Middleton F; m. 7/21/62 to Jean Byrd; c. Elizabeth, Matthew and Amy Mayfield. Educ: Wabash Col, A.B, 63; Ind. Univ, J.D, 66; Phi Delta Phi; Order of Coif; Kappa Sigma. Polit. & Govt. Pos: Ind. State Rep, Brown, Lawrence and Monroe Cos, currently. Bus. & Prof. Pos: Attorney-at-law, Ferguson, Berry, Ferguson & Bridges, 66-; mgr, Ferguson Herefords, Inc. Mem: Monroe Co. and Ind. Bar Asns; Ind. Cattlemen's Asn. Rel: Episcopal. Legal Res: 410 Park Ridge Rd, Bloomington, Ind. 47401. Mailing Add: 121½ W. Kirkwood Ave, Bloomington, Ind. 47401.

FERGUSON, THOMAS EDWARD D
b. Lancaster, Ohio, 11/6/28; s. Joseph T. Ferguson and Clara Kost F; m. 6/10/52 to Helen Kreitzer; c. Janet, David, Douglas, Ruth and Ted. Educ: Ohio State Univ, B.A. in bus. admin, 50; Tau Kappa Epsilon. Polit. & Govt. Pos: Auditor, Ohio, 51-52; asst. state treas, Ohio, 59-63; Dem. Cand. for treas, Ohio, 62 and for auditor, 66; dir. Cincinnati Office, U.S. Dept. Commerce, 67- Bus. & Prof. Pos: Sales, Allstate Ins. Co, 54-55; acct. rep, Royal-McBee Corp, 55-57; supvr. cost acct, Ford Motor Co, 57-59; mgr. data processing, The Ohio Co, 63- Mil. Serv: Entered as Seaman Recruit, Naval Res, 63; Korean Serv. Medal. Mem: Res. Officers Asn; Elks; Shamrock Club; Nat. Kidney Found; Leukemia Soc; World Trade Club; Rotary. Rel: Catholic. Mailing Add: 8817 Tulipwood Center, Cincinnati, Ohio 45242.

FERGUSON, VERLE MARION D
b. Rushsylvania, Ohio, 9/21/10; s. Arley W. Ferguson and Elva Frey F; m. 7/14/33 to Betty Phyllis Coons; c. B. Marilyn (Mrs. Eichenlaub) and V. Leo. Polit. Pos: Chmn, Logan Co. Dem. Cent. Cmt, Ohio, 65-66, mem, exec. cmt, until 66; precinct committeeman, Dem. Party, 62-66. Mem: Elks; past pres, Lions, Old Monarch Award, Lions Int; Ins. Asn. Achievements: Cert. for study and written exam. in theory of piloting and small

boat handling; cert. for 3 yr. training prog, Nat. Coun, Boy Scouts; Cert. of Merit for completing pub. rels. prog, N.Y.C. R.R, 47. Rel: Christian Church. Mailing Add: 423 Woodland Dr, Bellefontaine, Ohio 43311. (1967)

FERLAND, ROLAND O. D
Mem. Exec. Cmt, Dem. State Cmt, R.I.
b. Pawtucket, R.I, 9/6/28; s. Alphage Ferland and Roseanna Martel F; m. 11/24/49 to Arline Mary Leonard; c. Roland James and Roger Joseph. Educ: Providence Col, 46-47; Univ. Rhode Island, 47-48. Polit. & Govt. Pos: Mem. exec. cmt, Dem. State Cmt, R.I, 65-; alternate del, Dem. Nat. Conv, 68. Bus. & Prof. Pos: Corporator, Pawtucket Inst. for Savings. Mil. Serv: Entered as Pvt, Army, 46, released as S/Sgt, 48, after serv. in 32nd Inf. Div, 24th Army Corps, Asia, 46-48. Mem: Home Builders Asn. R.I.(past pres); Nat. Asn. Home Builders (v.pres); Pawtucket Real Estate Exchange; Pawtucket Indust. Develop. Cmn.(chmn); Pawtucket/Blackstone Valley C. of C.(bd. dirs); Woonsocket C. of C; Pawtucket Mem. Hosp.(bd. trustees). Rel: Catholic. Legal Res: 2 Naushon Court, Pawtucket, R.I. 02861. Mailing Add: 180 Armistice Blvd, Pawtucket, R.I. 02860.

FERMAN, ALLAN S. D
b. New York, N.Y, 8/11/41; s. Louis Ferman and Sarah Rudnitzsky F; single. Educ: City Col, N.Y, B.A, 62; N.Y. Univ, LL.B, 65; Pick and Shovel; Lock and Key. Polit. & Govt. Pos: Chmn, N.Y. State Students for Johnson-Humphrey-Kennedy, 64; northeast. conf. chmn, Col. Young Dem. Clubs Am, 64-65; mem. exec. cmt, Village Independent Dem, 64-68; pres, N.Y. State Young Dem, 67-69, nat. committeeman, 69-; alternate del, Dem. Nat. Conv, 68; mem. youth participation cmt, N.Y. State Dem. Cmt, 69- Bus. & Prof. Pos: Dir, Welsh Corp, Longview, Wash, 66-; attorney, Stone & Webster Mgt. Consult, Inc, 67- Mem: Asn. Bar City New York. Rel: Jewish. Mailing Add: 88 Charles St, New York, N.Y. 10014.

FERN, BENJAMIN R.
b. N.J, 5/18/21; m. Ruth Roberts; c. Marion Victoria and Nancy Catherine. Educ: Queens Col, N.Y, A.B, 42; George Wash. Univ. Law Sch, J.D, 57. Polit. & Govt. Pos: Chief counsel, Select Cmt. on Standards and Conduct, U.S. Senate, Wash, D.C, 65- Mil. Serv: Entered as A/S, Navy, 42, released as Capt, 65. Mem: Am. and Fed. Bar Asns. Legal Res: 925 Woburn Court, McLean, Va. 22101. Mailing Add: Select Cmt. on Standards and Conduct, U.S. Senate, Washington, D.C. 20510.

FERNALD, JULIA GREGG 'JUDY' R
V.Chmn, Montclair Co. Rep. Cmt, N.J.
b. Washington, D.C. 11/5/27; d. Morris Gregg and Julia Mae Clark G; m. 5/19/57 to David G. Fernald; c. David G, Jr, Julia Dana and John Gregg. Educ: Syracuse Univ, B.A, 49; Eta Pi Upsilon; Alpha Epsilon Rho; Zeta Phi Eta; Theta Sigma Phi; Chi Omega. Polit. & Govt. Pos: Mem. exec. cmt, N.Y.C. Youth for Eisenhower, 52, v.chmn, Speaker's Bur, N.Y. Citizens for Eisenhower-Nixon, 56; pres, Young Women's Rep. Club, N.Y, 54-56; recording secy, N.Y. Fedn. Rep. Women, 55-57; chmn, Young Rep. Del, NATO Study Trip, 59; co-chmn, Young Rep. Nat. Fedn, 59-61; secy, Nat. Goldwater for Pres. Cmt, 63, co-chmn, N.J. Goldwater for Pres. Cmt, 64; alternate del, Rep. Nat. Conv, 64; v.chmn, Montclair Co. Rep. Cmt, N.J, currently; membership chmn, N.J. Fedn. of Rep. Women, currently. Bus. & Prof. Pos: Acct. supvr, Eugene Gilbert & Co, 54-57; asst. advert. mgr, Mosler Safe Co, 57-60. Mem: Pres, Women's Club of Upper Montclair; Docent, Montclair Art Mus; Jr. League of Montclair. Rel: Congregational. Mailing Add: 102 Lorraine Ave, Upper Montclair, N.J. 07043. (1967)

FERNANDEZ, JOACHIM OCTAVE D
b. New Orleans, La, 8/14/96; s. Octave Gonzales Fernandez and Mary Benson F; 2nd m. 11/30/56 to Josephine Jessie Franek; c. Florau J, Joachim Octave, Jr, Mercedes and June Rose. Educ: Sophie Wright High Sch. Polit. & Govt. Pos: Head, Income Tax Sect, State of La, 51-63; collector, Internal Revenue, Dist. of La, 43-46; U.S. Rep, La, 31-41; La. State Sen, 28-30; La. State Rep, 24-28; mem, Constitutional Conv, La, 21. Mil. Serv: Lt. Comdr, Naval Res, 41-43; Victory Medal. Mem: Am. Legion. Rel: Catholic. Mailing Add: 3110 Derby Place, New Orleans, La. 70119. (1967)

FERNICOLA, NICHOLAS D
b. Newark, N.J, 8/10/03; m. to Marie Florin; c. Two; six grandchildren. Educ: Syracuse Univ, B.A. and LL.B, 29. Polit. & Govt. Pos: Confidential aide to Supt. of Educ, Newark, N.J; secy, Dept. of Pub. Safety, Newark; judge, Third Criminal Court, 48; co. counsel, Essex Co, 59; former N.J. State Sen. Bus. & Prof. Pos: Attorney-at-law. Mem: Nat. Asn. Co. Attorneys; Essex Co. Bar Asn; Syracuse Univ. Alumni Asn; United Appeals. Mailing Add: 744 Broad, Newark, N.J. 07102. (1967)

FERRALL, GRACE LOIS D
Chmn, Shawano Co. Dem. Club, Wis.
b. Weyerhauser, Wis, 6/29/13; d. Michael J. Ellison and Pauline Goodness E; m. 7/21/35 to Russell Brown Ferrall; c. R. Michael and Ellison W. Educ: Sch. of Cosmetology, 32-33; Wis. State Col, Stevens Point, 59-60. Polit. & Govt. Pos: Secy, Shawano Co. Dem. Club, Wis, 60-64, chmn, 64- Mem: Fel. Poets, Wis; Past Matron, Eastern Star; Bus. and Prfnl. Woman's Club; past pres. & past secy, Gresham Woman's Club; Co. Dist. and State Adv. Conf. for Youth; Ment. Health Cmt, Shawano Co. Rel: Methodist. Mailing Add: Rock & Rill Box 53, Gresham, Wis. 54128.

FERRALL, RUSSELL BROWN D
Statutory Secy, Shawano Co. Dem. Club, Wis.
b. Omaha, Nebr, 2/28/06; s. Charles Russell Ferrall and Lillian Barr F; m. 7/21/35 to Grace Lois Ellison; c. R. Michael and Ellison W. Educ: Univ. Minn, 24-28; Wis. State Col, Stevens Point, 59-60. Polit. & Govt. Pos: Secy-treas, Shawano Co. Dem. Club, Wis, 47-60, statutory secy, 66- Mem: Wis. Fel. of Poets (pres, 68-); Nat. Fedn. State Poetry Socs.(2nd v.pres, 69-); Wis. Regional Writers Asn; Racontours; Mason; F&AM; past secy, Lions; Transportation-Commun. Employees Union, AFL-CIO. Rel: Methodist. Mailing Add: Rock & Rill, Box 53, Gresham, Wis. 54128.

FERRALL, WILLIAM J. D
N.Y. State Sen.
b. Brooklyn, N.Y; m. to Kathleen T. Delaney; c. three. Educ: Fordham Col; Fordham Law Sch. Polit. & Govt. Pos: N.Y. State Sen, 64-; asst. corp. counsel, sr. trial counsel, Kings Co. Superior Court, N.Y.C. Law Dept; hearing rep. on workmens compensation claims, Dept. of Labor; clerk to Justice J.V. Coin, R.J. Broeck, Munic. Court of N.Y. Mil. Serv: Coast Guard, 42-46, chief war off. Mem: Cathedral Club of Brooklyn; Friendly Sons of St. Patrick; Police Athletic League; Am. Red Cross; CWV. Mailing Add: 423 Ninth St, Brooklyn, N.Y. 11215. (1967)

FERRAN, GILBERT HIPOLITO R
V.Chmn, N.Mex. State Rep. Party
b. Santa Fe, N.Mex, 9/18/29; s. Isidore Hipolito Ferran and Flossie Cortez F; m. 9/3/55 to Grace Noemi Archuleta; c. Naomi Grace, Yvette Maria, Gilbert Gregory, Michelle Denise, Regina Louise and Andrew Michael. Educ: N.Mex. State Univ, B.S. in Zool, 58; Phi Kappa Tau. Polit. & Govt. Pos: Chmn, Rio Arriba Co. Young Rep, 66; v.chmn, N.Mex. State Rep. Party, 68 & 69-; secy, Rio Arriba Co. Rep. Cent. Cmt, 68-69; precinct chmn, Rio Arriba Co. Rep. Party, San Pedro, 68-69. Bus. & Prof. Pos: Staff mem, Los Alamos Sci. Lab, 48- Mil. Serv: Entered as Pvt, E-1, Army, 51, released as Pfc, 52, after serv. in 45th Inf. Div, Field Command, Far East, 52-53. Publ: Co-auth, A study of Two Stage Air Samplers Designed to Simulate The Upper and Lower Respiratory Tract, 60; Size-Selective Sampling of Plutonium and Uranium Aersols, 64. Mem: Am. Indust. Hygiene Asn; Rocky Mt. Am. Indust. Hygiene Asn; Rocky Mt. Farmers Union. Rel: Catholic. Mailing Add: Route 1, Box 392, Española, N.Mex. 87532.

FERRARI, DANTE LOUIS D
Mem, Richmond Co. Dem. Exec. Cmt, N.Y.
b. N.Y.C, 2/14/15; s. Joseph Ferrari and Theresa Alduini F; m. 4/23/39 to Rose Riggi; c. Theresa A.(Mrs. Fausak), Sister Mary St. Diane and Diane L. (Mrs. Ciofoletti). Educ: Curtis High Sch, 4 years. Polit. & Govt. Pos: Chief clerk, Surrogates Court, N.Y, 62-; zone leader, Dem. Party, N.Y, 62-; mem, Richmond Co. Dem. Exec. Cmt, 62-; cand, N.Y. Constitutional Conv, 66; alternate del, Dem. Nat. Conv, 68. Bus. & Prof. Pos: Secy-treas, Elco Shipyards, 43-48; ins. broker, 48-58. Mem: Am. Cancer Soc.(crusade chmn, chmn. bd. dirs); Cerebral Palsy (v.chmn); Guide Serv. Blind (chmn); bd. dirs, Silver Lake Day Care Center; K. of C.(4°). Man of the Year Award, Am. Cancer Soc; 68; Good Scouting Award, Boy Scouts, 67 & 68; Rel: Catholic. Mailing Add: 416 Cromwell Ave, Staten Island, N.Y. 10305.

FERRARO, ANTHONY MICHAEL D
R.I. State Rep.
b. Everett, Mass, 10/18/35; s. Michael Ferraro and Mary Capone F; m. 9/2/61 to Sheila Mae Murphy; c. Aileen Marie, Anthony M, Jr. and Christopher Alan. Educ: Providence Col, A.B; Suffolk Univ. Law Sch, 1 year; Royal Inst. Chem, I.T.E. and Ed.M; Year Book Staff; Ship and Scales Club; Providence and Cranston Club; St. Thomas More Club; soc. chmn, Student Coun. Polit. & Govt. Pos: Chmn, State Correspondence Schs, R.I, 67; mem, State Cmt. to Study Open Dumping, 67; v.chmn, Cmt. to Study State Scholarships, 67; v.chmn, State Dept. of Health, Educ. and Welfare, 69; mem, state cmt, Motor Vehicle Code, 69; mem, State Cmt. to Study Exec. Sch. Year, 69; R.I. State Rep, Dist. 25, 69- Mil. Serv: Entered as Airman Basic, Air Force, 59, released as A/2C, 60, after serv. in Air Nat. Guard; Cert. of Merit; Supply Sch. Award; Honors Award. Publ: 'Commission Study on Correspondence Schools, 1/69. Mem: Warwick and Cranston PTA; R.I. Personnel and Guid. Serv. Cmt. to Study Recreation in West. Cranston; Cmt. to Study Blockhouse Parents; R.I. Educ. Asn; Warwick Teachers Union; Commun. Caucus; YMCA; Jewish Commun. Center; Fifth Ward Dem. Club; Dem. Mens Club of Cranston; W.End Dem. Club; committeeman, Boy Scouts; pres, Stoney Brook Civic Asn, 65-67, chmn. bd, 67-68. Rel: Catholic. Mailing Add: 86 Stone Dr, Cranston, R.I. 02920.

FERRE, LUIS A. R
Gov, P.R.
b. Ponce, P.R, 2/17/04; s. Antonio Ferré and Mary Aguayo F; m. 5/30/31 to Lorencita Ramirez de Arellano; c. Antonio Luis and Rosario (Mrs. de Trigo). Educ: Mass. Inst. of Tech, B.S. and M.S; LL.D, Springfield Col; hon. D.C.L, Catholic Univ. P.R; hon. L.H.D, Inter-Am. Univ. P.R. and Pace Col. Polit. & Govt. Pos: Mem, P.R. Constitutional Conv, 50-51; P.R. State Rep, 52-56; cand. for Gov, P.R, 56, 60 & 64; mem, U.S.-P.R. Status Cmn, 64-66; Rep. nat. committee committeeman, P.R; Gov, P.R, 69- Bus. & Prof. Pos: Co-chmn. & dir, P.R. Cement Co. Inc; exec. v.pres. & dir, Puerto Rico Iron Works, Inc; pres. & dir, P.R. Glass Corp; v.chmn, Maule Industs, Inc; mem, Corp, Mass. Inst. of Tech. Publ: 'Industrial Democracy,' 'The American Citizenship.' Mem: Am. Soc. Mech. Engrs; Pres, Fedn. YMCA P.R; Past Exalted Ruler, Elks. Rel: Roman Catholic. Mailing Add: La Fortaleza, San Juan, P.R. 00936.

FERRELL, DONALD FORREST R
Okla. State Sen.
b. Oklahoma City, Okla, 1/6/29; s. Forrest Shae Ferrell and Theresa Cooper F; m. 8/29/53 to Sally May Bourne; c. Susan Jane and Cynthia. Educ: Okla. State Univ, B.A. in Journalism, 53; Sigma Delta Chi; Kappa Sigma. Polit. & Govt. Pos: Former mem, Airport Cmn, Chandler, Okla; info. staff officer, Off. Gov, Okla, 65-67; Rep. state committeeman, Lincoln Co, 65-; Okla. State Sen, 18th Dist, 66- Bus. & Prof. Pos: Managing ed, Muskogee Co. News, 53; news ed, Henryetta Daily Free Lance, 53-54; asst. personnel dir, Okla. Publ. Co, 54-62; ed. and publisher, Lincoln Co. News, Chandler, 62- and The Meeker Herald, 64- Mil. Serv: Entered as Pvt, Army Air Force, 46, released as Sgt, 49, after serv. in 4th Tactical Reconnaissance Squadron, Panama and Panama Canal Zone, 47-49; World War II Victory Medal; Lt. Col, Air Nat. Guard, 54- Mem: Okla. Press Asn; Okla. Farm Bur; Lions. Rel: Presbyterian. Legal Res: Route 3, Chandler, Okla. 74834. Mailing Add: Box 248, Chandler, Okla. 74834.

FERRELL, F. DOUGLAS D
b. Tex, 2/21/15; s. Robert S. Ferrell; m. 6/10/45 to Esther Mae Nash; c. Frederick D, Jr, Sheridan R. and Stephanie Camille. Educ: Bishop Col, Dallas, Tex; Los Angeles Theological Seminary; Interdenominational Ministerial Alliance. Polit. & Govt. Pos: Calif. State Assemblyman, 63-67. Bus. & Prof. Pos: Ordained Baptist Minister; pres, Ferrell Enterprise Casket Co, 68-; bd. mem, Falco Auto Leasing, 69; bd. mem, Kedren Commun. Ment. Health Center, 69. Mem: YMCA; Mason; NAACP; Urban League. Rel: Baptist. Mailing Add: 816 E. 116th Place, Los Angeles, Calif. 90059.

FERRON, ALBERT J. R
b. Woonsocket, R.I, 3/26/15; married; c. three. Educ: Woonsocket Schs. Polit. & Govt. Pos: Former N.H. State Rep. Bus. & Prof. Pos: Retail merchant. Mem: Pres, Lions; K. of C; C. of C. Rel: Catholic. Mailing Add: Newfields Rd, Exeter, N.H. 03833. (1967)

FERRY, MILES YEOMAN 'CAP' R
Utah State Sen.
b. Brigham City, Utah, 9/22/32; s. John Yeoman Ferry, Jr. and Alda Cheney F; m. 5/19/52 to Suzanne Call; c. John Yeoman, Suzanne, Jane and Benjamin Call. Educ: Utah State Univ, B.S, 54; Phi Kappa Phi; Pi Kappa Alpha. Polit. & Govt. Pos: Chmn, Corinee Rep. Voting Dist, Utah, 62-64; chmn, Lawrence J. Burton for U.S. Rep. Campaign, 62-66; del, Rep. State Conv, 62, 64 & 66; Utah State Rep, 65-66; Utah State Sen, 67- Mem: Utah Farm Bur.(dir, Fedn, 64); pres, South Box Elder Farm Bur, 64; chmn, Agr. Stabilization & Conserv. Dist, 64; Brigham City Jaycees; Corinne PTA; Nat. Golden Spike Asn. Selected as One of Ten Outstanding Nat. Dirs, U.S. Jr. C. of C, 62; one of Three Outstanding Young Men, Utah, 62. Rel: Latter-day Saint. Mailing Add: Box 70, Corinne, Utah 84307.

FERST, JEANNE ROLFE R
b. Chicago, Ill, 9/6/18; d. Mark A. Rolfe and Rose Kominsky R; m. 6/12/40 to Robert H. Ferst; c. Suzanne F.(Mrs. Nelson Neiman) and Robin. Educ: Univ. Chicago, 36-38. Polit. & Govt. Pos: Co-chmn, Nixon Rally, Fulton Co, Ga, 60; Rep. precinct chmn, 60; mem, Fulton Co. Rep. Exec. Cmt, 60-68; del. co. and state conv, 60-; v.chmn, Ga. Rep. State Finance Cmt, 61-66; co-chmn, finance cmt, O'Callaghan for Cong, Atlanta, 62; co-chmn, Circle R and Cmt. of 100, Fulton Co, 62-64; asst. treas, Fulton Co. Rep. Party, 64-68; chmn, Calloway for Gov. Rally, 66; chmn, Dirksen Dinner, Atlanta, 67 and Nixon Dinner, 68; alternate del, Rep. Nat. Conv, 68; adv. and mem, U.S. Del. to the Eighth Gov. Coun. of the UN Develop. Prog, Geneva, Switz, June-July, 69. Mem: Atlanta Symphony Mem. Guild; officer, High Mus. Mem. Guild; bd, Multiple Sclerosis Soc; Atlanta Munic. Theatre Women's Guild; Atlanta Ballet Guild; Atlanta Opera Guild; Nat. Rep. Womens Club, N.Y.C; Ga. Fedn. Rep. Women. Rel: Jewish. Mailing Add: 3585 Woodhaven Rd. N.W, Atlanta, Ga. 30305.

FERTIG, HAROLD D
Mem, Nassau Co. Dem. Policy Cmt, N.Y.
b. New York, N.Y, 12/27/21; s. Abraham Fertig and Rae Spatz F; m. 10/11/47 to Harriet L. Gorman; c. Joyce Marilyn, Roberta Jeanne and Steven Howard. Educ: City Col. New York, B.B.A, 42; Fordham Univ, LL.B, 46. Polit. & Govt. Pos: Zone leader, Syosset South Dem. Party, N.Y, 59-64; del, Dem. State Conv, 62; law secy. to Justice Joseph Liff, N.Y. Supreme Court, 63-; alternate del, Dem. Nat. Conv, 64; assembly dist. leader and town leader, Oyster Bay, 64-; N.Y. State Dem. committeeman, 64-; mem, Nassau. Co. Dem. Policy Cmt, currently; Judge, Fourth Dist. Court, Nassau Co, 69- Bus. & Prof. Pos: Acct, various CPA firms, 42-48; partner, Fertig & Sommerfield, CPA, 48-62; individual practitioner, Harold Fertig, Attorney, 48-62. Publ: 'N.Y.C. Excise Taxes—Administrative Procedures in Connection with Audits, Protests and Refunds,' The N.Y. Certified Pub. Acct, 11/56. Mem: Am, N.Y. State, N.Y. Co. and Nassau Bar Asns; N.Y. State Soc. of CPA; Fordham Law Sch. Alumni; Masons; B'nai B'rith; chmn, North Shore Chap, March of Dimes; Citizens Adv. Cmn. on Adult Educ. Cent. Sch. Dist. Two; pres, Syosset Jericho Dem. Club. Rel: Jewish. Mailing Add: 28 Lincrest St, Syosset, N.Y. 11701.

FERTIG, RALPH DAVID D
b. Chicago, Ill, 2/24/30; s. August Joseph Fertig and Lottie Berg F; m. 9/24/67 to Marjorie Hays Bamberger; c. Karen and Jill Bamberger and Jack August, David Ralph and Katherine Fertig. Educ: Roosevelt Univ, 47-48 & 50-51; Univ. Chicago, B.A, 50, 52-54; Columbia Univ, M.A. in Sociol, 52; Student Govt, Nat. Student Asn. Polit. & Govt. Pos: Nat. bd. mem, Am. for Dem. Action, dep. chmn, Wash. Chap, 69; del, Dem. Nat. Conv, 68. Bus. & Prof. Pos: Exec. dir, Wash. Welfare Asn, Southeast Neighborhood House, 62-67; proj. dir, New Careers Training Prog, Georgetown Univ, 67-68; consult, Off. Econ. Opportunity, 68; consult, A.L. Nellum and Assocs, 68; exec. dir, Metrop. Wash. Planning & Housing Asn, 68- Publ: 'Men and Work,' Anthologist, 66. Mem: Gr. Wash. Chap, Nat. Asn. Soc. Workers (pres, 65-67); co-founder Southeast Neighbors D.C; co-founder Chatham-Avalon Park Commun. Coun. Chicago; Neighbors Inc, D.C; Hyde-Kenwood Commun. Conf, Chicago; Jewish Commun. Coun.(urban affairs subcmt). Legal Res: 3749 Oliver St. N.W, Washington, D.C. 20015. Mailing Add: 1225 K St. N.W, Washington, D.C. 20005.

FESTGE, OTTO D
b. Cross Plains, Wis, 1/1/21; s. Otto William Festge and Ernestine Wille F; m. 9/4/42 to Evelyn Dybdahl; c. Michael, Susan and Cynthia. Educ: Univ. Wis; Phi Mu Alpha. Polit. & Govt. Pos: Assessor, Cross Plains, Wis, 46-52; clerk, Dane Co, Wis, 52-65; mem. exec. bd, Dane Co. Dem. Party, Wis; mayor, Madison, 65-69. Bus. & Prof. Pos: Teacher, Black Earth Pub. Schs, Wis, 48-52. Mem: Wis. Co. Clerks Asn; Wis. League of Munic; Nat. League of Cities; U.S. Conf. of Mayors; Lions Int; Nat. Farmers Union. Rel: Lutheran. Legal Res: 4310 Herrick Lane, Madison, Wis. 53711. Mailing Add: Room 403, 210 Monona Ave, Madison, Wis. 53709.

FETNER, AUEY EMORY R
Mem, Ala. State Rep. Exec. Cmt.
b. Malone, Ala, 11/24/21; s. Walter Dewey Fetner and Dovie Daniel F; m. 1/9/42 to Wilma Ann Moncus; c. Aaron D, James E, Karen Ann, David W. and Brian T. Educ: Wadley High Sch, grad. Polit. & Govt. Pos: City councilman, Gardendale, Ala, 55-56, mem. city zoning bd, 58-; vol. for Nixon, Jefferson Co, 59, precinct chmn, Rep. Party, Jefferson Co, 62-64, regional precinct coordinator, 64-67, precinct dir, 67-68, cand. recruitment chmn, Ala, 68-; mem, Ala. State Rep. Exec. Cmt, 65-; alternate del, Rep. Nat. Conv, 68. Mil. Serv: Entered as Pvt, Army Air Corps, 43, released as Pfc, 45, after serv. in 410th Bomb Group, Ninth Air Force, ETO, 44-45; Good Conduct Medal; Silver Star; Bronze Star; Presidential Unit Citation with Oak Leaf Cluster. Mem: Mason; Civitan; C. of C. Gardendale Citizen of the Year, 65. Rel: Methodist. Mailing Add: Route 3, Brookwood Estates, Gardendale, Ala. 35071.

FETRIDGE, WILLIAM HARRISON R
Pres, United Rep. Fund of Ill.
b. Chicago, Ill, 8/2/09; s. Matthew Fetridge and Clara Hall F; m. 6/27/41 to Bonnie Jean Clark; c. Blakely (Mrs. Harvey H. Bundy, III) and Clark. Educ: Northwest. Univ, B.S, 29; Beta Theta Pi; Deru; Sargent Scholar. Hon. LL.D, Cent. Mich. Univ, 54. Polit. & Govt. Pos: Founder and first pres, Evanston Young Rep. Club, Ill; mem, bd. gov, United Rep. Fund of Ill, 47-, v.pres, 60-67, pres, 67-; campaign mgr, Merriam for Mayor, 55; alternate del, Rep. Nat. Conv, 56, del, 68; chmn, Midwest Volunteers for Nixon-Lodge, 60; chmn, Nixon Recount Cmt, 60; mem, Rep. Nat. Finance Cmt, 66- Bus. & Prof. Pos: V.pres, Popular Mech. Mag, 45-53, exec. v.pres, 53-59; v.pres, Diamond T Motor Truck Co, 59-61, exec. v.pres, 61-65; pres, Dartnell Corp, 65- Mil. Serv: Entered as Lt, Naval Res, 42, released as Lt. Comdr. after serv. in Am. and European Theatre, 42-45. Publ: The Navy Reader, Bobbs-Merrill, 43; Republican Precinct Workers Manual, 46 and Am. Political Almanac, 52, Capitol House. Mem: Nat. v.pres, Boy Scouts; past pres. and mem, bd. trustees, Latin Sch. of Chicago; trustee, Lake Forest Col; Chicago Club; Union League; Saddle and Cycle Casino; C. of C. Silver Buffalo, Silver Antelope and Silver Beaver, Boy Scouts. Rel: Episcopal. Legal Res: 2430 Lake View Ave, Chicago, Ill. 60614. Mailing Add: 4660 N. Ravenswood, Chicago, Ill. 60640.

FETTEROLF, CAROLYN BAUER R
Pres, Royersford Coun. Rep. Women, Pa.
b. Bryn Mawr, Pa, 3/1/30; d. Paul Conrad Bauer and Cora Rohm B; m. 4/15/50 to John Stanford Fetterolf, Jr; c. Jeri Lynn, John, III and Jeffrey Paul. Polit. & Govt. Pos: V.chmn, Montgomery Co. Primary Campaign Cmt, Pa, 63; del, Rep. Nat. Conv, 64; pres, Royersford Coun. Rep. Women, Pa, currently. Rel: Church of Christ. Mailing Add: 750 Spruce St, Royersford, Pa. 19468. (1967)

FETTINGER, GEORGE EDGAR D
N.Mex. State Rep.
b. 1929. Educ: Hobart Col, B.B.A; Univ. N.Mex, LL.B. Polit. & Govt. Pos: N.Mex. State Rep, currently, Majority Floor Leader, N.Mex. House of Rep, 69-; alternate del, Dem. Nat. Conv, 68. Bus. & Prof. Pos: Attorney-at-law. Mil. Serv: Fighter Pilot, Air Force, 4 years, Res, 7 years. Mem: C. of C; Boy Scouts; Lions; Elks. Rel: Presbyterian. Mailing Add: Drawer M, Alamogordo, N.Mex. 88310.

FEUER, MORTIMER D
b. New York, N.Y, 11/25/09; s. William Feuer and Gussie Goldenberg F; m. 7/29/37 to Louise Gottschall; c. Richard Dennis and Thomas Nelson. Educ: City Col. New York, B.S, 28; Columbia Univ. Law Sch, J.D, 31; ed, Columbia Law Rev, 29-31. Polit. & Govt. Pos: First v.pres, Amsterdam Dem. Club, N.Y, 58-61, v.chmn. bd. gov, 59-61; del-at-lg, Dem. Nat. Conv, 60, alternate del-at-lg, 64; v.chmn, Dinner Cmt, N.Y. Co. Dem. Cmt, 63, 64 & 66; co. committeeman, many years; cmnr, N.Y. State Cmn. to Commemorate the War of 1812 and the Composition of the Star Spangled Banner, 64- Bus. & Prof. Pos: Partner, Hays, Feuer, Porter & Spanier, 39-; lectr. corp. law, Practicing Law Inst, 54 & 58; dir, Condec Corp, 55-; dir, Varifab, Inc, Old Greenwich, Conn, 67-; pres. and dir, Dextra Baldwin McGonagle Found, N.Y.C, 68- Publ: 'The Patent Monopoly and the Anti-Trust Laws,' Columbia Law Rev, 38; Personal Liabilities of Corporate Officers and Directors, 61 and Handbook for Corporate Directors, 65, Prentice-Hall; 'The Legal Liabilities of Executives,' Dun's Rev, 2 parts, 5-6/67; plus various other articles in legal periodicals. Mem: N.Y. Co. Lawyers Asn; corp. law cmt, N.Y.C. Bar Asn; N.Y. State Bar Asn; West Side Dem. Club; City Col. New York Alumni Asn; Columbia Law Sch. Alumni Asn. Rel: Jewish. Mailing Add: 445 Park Ave, New York, N.Y. 10022.

FEW, MARY REAMEY THOMAS R
b. Martinsville, Va, 7/12/85; d. Lyne Starling Thomas and Elizabeth Sheffield T; m. 8/17/11 to William Preston Few, first pres. of Duke Univ, wid; c. William, Lyne Starling, Kendrick Sheffield, Randolph Reamey and Preston Yancey (deceased). Educ: Duke Univ, A.B, magna cum laude, 06; Columbia Univ, A.M, 07; Kappa Delta; hon. mem, Am. Women Vol. Serv. Polit. & Govt. Pos: Rep. Nat. Committeewoman, N.C. and mem, Rep. Nat. Exec. Cmt, 42-56; del-at-lg. and mem. platform cmt, Rep. Nat. Conv, 48 & 52; app. mem. of the Assay Cmn, 53. Bus. & Prof. Pos: Secy, Lakewood Shopping Center, Durham, N.C, 59-; pres, Kendrick Estates Investment Corp. and Randolph Estates, 60-; secy. sub-div, Preston Woods, 68- Mem: Am. Asn. Univ. Women; DAR; Colonial Dames of Am; Huguenot Soc; Magna Charta Dames. Named Mother of the Year, Durham, N.C, 52. Rel: Methodist. Mailing Add: 208 N. Buchanan Blvd, Durham, N.C. 27701.

FEWELL, SAMUEL BRUCE, JR. D
S.C. State Rep.
b. Rock Hill, S.C, 7/8/39; s. Dr. Samuel B. Fewell and Rebecca Reed F; m. 5/21/66 to Kerrina Cramer; c. Karen Sloan and Samuel B, III. Educ: Univ. of S.C, B.S, 61 and LL.B, 65; Sigma Chi; Block 'C' Club; Phi Delta Phi. Polit. & Govt. Pos: S.C. State Rep, currently. Mem: Jr. C. of C; Moose; Elks. Pro football, Chicago and Montreal. Rel: Presbyterian. Mailing Add: Box 929, Rock Hill, S.C. 29730.

FIA, TOFU T. Am. Samoa Party
Rep, Am. Samoa House of Rep.
b. Am. Samoa, 7/31/31; s. Soliai Fia and Talaetele F. Soliai F; m. 9/8/56 to Ilaisa T. Pola; c. Samoa T, Tofu T, Jr, To'atautali T, Meleane T, Faipule T. and Alaisea T. Educ: Cannon's Sch. Bus, Honolulu, Hawaii, 67; Legis. Procedures, State Capitol, Honolulu, 69; Clickity-Sixty-Club. Polit. & Govt. Pos: Clerk typist, Customs Dept, Govt. of Am. Samoa, 54-55, payroll clerk, Budget and Finance Dept, 56-58, supvr. payroll sect, 59-62, asst. hosp. adminstr, Med. Serv. Dept, 63-65, chief revenue div, Admin. Serv. Dept, 66-, and police reserve officer, Police Dept, 68-; Rep, Am. Samoa House Rep, 12th Dist, 65- Bus. & Prof. Pos: Shareholder, Am. Samoa Develop. Corp, 65-; chief acct, Yellow Line Transportation Serv, 66- Rel: Methodist. Legal Res: Nu'uuli, Pago Pago, American Samoa 96920. Mailing Add: P.O. Box 222, Pago Pago, American Samoa 96920.

FICHTER, JOSEPH WILLIAM D
b. Aberdeen, Ohio, 7/12/94; s. Andrew Fichter and Sarah Hiett F; m. 6/2/17 to Orveda Beckett; c. Jean (Mrs. Warner H. Shugert), Robert B,

Richard H. and J. Hal. Educ: Miami Univ, A.B, 15; Univ. Cincinnati, grad. study, 35-36; Phi Beta Kappa; Tau Kappa Alpha; Phi Kappa Tau. Polit. & Govt. Pos: Del-at-lg, Dem. Nat. Conv, 40, 64 & 68; mem, Nat. Adv. Bd. to U.S. Surgeon Gen. under the Hosp. Survey and Construction Act, 47-51; agr. consult. and price analyst, Econ. Stabilization Admin, 51. Bus. & Prof. Pos: Prin, Hanover Twp. High Sch, Butler Co, Ohio, 15-21; teacher Eng, Hamilton High Sch, Ohio, 21-23; supt, Butler Co. Schs, Ohio, 23-31; asst. state dir. educ, Ohio, 31-35; mem. faculty, Miami Univ, 36-58. Publ: Diamond Jubilee History of Ohio State Grange, 47 and Handbook for Grange Leaders, 50, Ohio State Grange; columnist, 'The Lay of the Land,' weekly newspapers, 53- Mem: Ohio Div. Nat. Farmers Union (chmn, 53-); Ohio State Grange (lectr, 26-42 and master, 42-50); chaplain, Nat. Grange, 45-47; bd. trustee, Nat. Planning Asn, 45-; Mason (32°); dist. gov, Rotary Int, 39-40; chmn, Rural Sect. Nat. Health Assembly in 40's; mem, Nat. Cmn. on Chronic Illness; mem, Cmn. Econ. Life, Nat. Coun. Churches, 45-, consult, World Coun. Churches Assembly, 54, mem. cmn. econ. life, Nat. Coun. Churches, 45-67. Rel: Methodist. Mailing Add: 28 E. Vine St, Oxford, Ohio 45056.

FICKLE, WILLIAM D
Mo. State Rep.
b. Parkville, Mo, 9/3/04; m. 1939 to Elvarea Dick; c. William Dick. Educ: Park Col. Acad. and Bus. Col. Polit. & Govt. Pos: Mo. State Rep, 61- Bus. & Prof. Pos: Contractor, 40 years; pres, William Fickle Construction Co, Parkville Grain and Feed Co. and Mid Continent Asphalt Co. Mem: Mason; Scottish Rite; Shrine; Optimist Club; Rotary; DeMolay (trustee). Rel: Presbyterian. Mailing Add: 7406 Tomahawk, Parkville, Mo. 64151.

FIDLER, WALTHER BALDERSON D
Va. State Del.
b. Sharps, Va, 4/18/23; m. to Martha Spencer. Educ: Randolph-Macon Col, A.B, 44; Univ. Richmond Law Sch, LL.B, 49. Polit. & Govt. Pos: Chmn, North. Neck Regional Planning and Econ. Develop. Cmn; mem, Atlantic State Marine Fisheries Cmn; mem. adv. coun, Needs of Handicapped Children; mem, Richmond Co. Dem. Cmt; Va. State Del, 60- Bus. & Prof. Pos: Lawyer and oysterman. Mil. Serv: Lt.(jg), Navy, 43-46. Mem: North. Neck, Va. and Am. Bar Asns; Phi Delta Theta; Omicron Delta Kappa; past pres, Ruritans; VFW; Farm Bur; Commonwealth Club. Rel: Presbyterian. Mailing Add: Sharps, Va. 22548.

FIEDLER, BETTY MAE R
b. Cleveland, Ohio, 3/3/25; d. Maurice Glenroy Miles and Grace Hodgson M; m. 7/2/44 to Edwin Gustav Fiedler, Jr; c. Edwin, III, Eric and William. Educ: Hahnemann Sch. of Nursing, Phila, 2 years. Polit. & Govt. Pos: Committeewoman and secy. exec. cmt, Lancaster Co. Rep. Cmt, Pa, 62-64, precinct orgn. chmn, 69-; Rep. registrn. chmn, Lancaster Co, 64; pres, Lancaster Co. Women's Rep. Club, 65-66; mem, Cong. Campaign Cmt, 66 & 68; TAR coordinator, Pa. Coun. Rep. Women, 67-; alternate del, Rep. Nat. Conv, 68. Mem: Lancaster Gen. Hosp. Auxiliary; Child Devel. Center Auxiliary; Iris Club; Presby. Women (hon. mem. cmn. ecumenical mission and rels). Rel: Presbyterian. Mailing Add: 1515 Country Club Dr, Lancaster, Pa. 17601.

FIEDLER, WALTER R D
Dir. Insts, N.Dak.
b. Burt, N.Dak, 12/25/13; s. Richard Fiedler and Christian Schmautz F; m. 9/29/40 to Norma Osmon. Educ: Pub. Schs, Hettinger Co, N.Dak. Polit. & Govt. Pos: N.Dak. State Sen, 55-61; dir. labs, N.Dak, 65-68; dir. insts, 69- Bus. & Prof. Pos: Rancher. Mem: Stockmen's Asn; Hereford Asn; Farmers Union; Elks. Rel: Presbyterian. Legal Res: Ryder, N.Dak. 58779. Mailing Add: State Capitol, Bismarck, N.Dak. 58501.

FIELD, ANDREW ROBERT R
Chmn, Washington Co. Rep. Cmt, Vt.
b. Cleveland, Ohio, 12/22/26; s. George Howard Field and Louise Hamm F; m. 9/13/47 to Juanita Virginia Baird; c. Nora, Sarah, Elizabeth and Emily. Educ: West. Reserve Univ, B.B.A, 50; Cleveland Marshall Law Sch, LL.B. cum laude, 58; Delta Theta Phi. Polit. & Govt. Pos: Chmn, Washington Co. Rep. Cmt, Vt, 67- Bus. & Prof. Pos: Asst. mgr, Bond Dept, Otis & Co, Cleveland, Ohio, 47-52; investment security salesman, Singer, Deane & Scribner, 52-53; asst. dist. supvr, Nat. Life Ins. Co, Cleveland, Ohio, 53-58, counsel, Montpelier, Vt, 58- Mil. Serv: Entered as Pvt, Army, 45, released as Pfc, 47, after serv. in Mil. Police, Third Army, Germany, 45-47. Mem: Vt, Washington Co, Ohio and Am. Bar Asns; Am. Land Title Asn; K. of C; Elks. Delta Theta Phi Scholarship Key. Rel: Roman Catholic. Mailing Add: Spring Hollow Lane, Montpelier, Vt. 05602.

FIELD, DONALD WILLIAM R
Mem, City Adv. Coun, San Leandro, Calif.
b. Portland, Ore, 3/21/20; s. Leslie William Field and Clara Lutes F; m. 1/2/44 to Beverly Eileen Hacker; c. Jeffery B. and Gregory C. Educ: Willamette Univ, 42-43; Calif. Podiatry Col, D.P.M, 49; Theta Upsilon Tau. Polit. & Govt. Pos: V.chmn, San Leandro Unit, Calif. Rep. Assembly, 60; pres, Alameda Co. Rep. Coord. Coun, 61-62; chmn, Bay Area Co. Goldwater for Pres. Clubs, 63-64; del, United Rep. of Calif, 63-64; mem, Alameda Co. Rep. Cent. Cmt, 63-65; co-chmn, Alameda Co, Goldwater-Miller Campaign, 64; del, Rep. Nat. Conv, 64; mem. finance cmt, Alameda Co. for Ivy Baker Priest and for Ronald Reagan, 66; San Leandro chmn, Richard M. Nixon for Pres. Campaign, 68; finance chmn, Max Rafferty for U.S. Sen, 68; mem, San Leandro Adv. Coun, 69- Bus. & Prof. Pos: Mem, Hosp. Cmt, Calif. Podiatry Asn, 63-64; chief, Podiatry Serv, Levine Gen. Hosp, Hayward, 64-66. Mil. Serv: Entered as Pvt, Army, 43, released as S/Sgt, 46, after serv. in Enlisted Res. Corps, QM; Good Conduct Medal; ETO Ribbon; Battle Star for Invasion France. Publ: 'Podiatry,' N.Y. Podiatry J, 56; 'Dignity-Stature-Recognition,' Calif. Podiatry Asn. Newsletter, 56. Mem: Pres, Alameda-Contra Costa Podiatry Soc, 62-63; Calif. Podiatry Asn; Am. Podiatry Asn; Am. Asn. Hosp. Podiatrists; assoc. mem, Am. Col. Foot Surgeons; pres, San Leandro Kiwanis, 60; v.comdr, Am. Legion Post 117, San Leandro, 59; hon. mem, Boys Club of Am; Cub Scouts of Am; mem. bd. dirs, San Leandro C. of C, 67-68; pres, Bay-O-Vista Home Owners Asn, 68-69; app. to Calif. State Podiatry Exam. Cmt, 68-; chmn. registrn, Nat. Fedn. of Podiatry Bd, 69. Outstanding Citizen, San Leandro Optimist Clubs, 55; San Leandro Kiwanis Club's Outstanding Citizen, 53; Outstanding Young Man of the Year Award, San Leandro Jr. C. of C, 54. Leader in Int. Campaign to change name of profession from Chiropody to Podiatry, 55-59. Rel: Catholic. Mailing Add: 1446 Daily Dr, San Leandro, Calif. 94577.

FIELD, FREDERICK GORHAM, JR. R
N.Y. State Assemblyman
b. Albany, N.Y, 4/13/32; s. Frederick G. Field, Sr. and Elizabeth A. Loucks F; m. 2/14/49 to Patricia Bak; c. Frederick John, Linda Patrice, Jeffery Donald, Ronald David and Kimberly Ann. Educ: Rensselaer Polytech. Inst, 58-59. Polit. & Govt. Pos: Councilman, Town of Colonie, N.Y, 60-67, Rep. committeeman, 60-; N.Y. State Assemblyman, 103rd Dist, Albany Co, 69- Bus. & Prof. Pos: Indust. engr, Allegheny Ludlum Steel Corp, Watervliet, N.Y, 50-63, indust. eng. supvr, 63- Mem: Soc. for Adv. Mgt; Am. Inst. Indust. Eng; F&AM; Rotary (pres, Latham Club); bd. dirs, Health Serv. of Rensselaer Area; Int. Narcotic Enforcement Officers Asn; Vol. Fireman of Colonie; pres, Colonie Youth Recreation Centers, Inc. Rel: Dutch Reformed. Mailing Add: 16 E. Newton Rd, Newtonville, N.Y. 12128.

FIELD, JAMES ARTHUR R
b. Ferrisburg, Vt, 4/10/41; m. to Daisy Mae Tracy; c. one son. Educ: Vergennes Union High Sch. Polit. & Govt. Pos: Vt. State Rep, 63-66. Bus. & Prof. Pos: Mechanic; ins. agent. Mem: Grange; F&AM. Rel: Methodist. 1967 Legal Res: Ferrisburg, Vt. No mailing address available. (1967)

FIELD, JOHN D
b. Dallas, Tex, 9/30/22; s. Joe Y. Field and Rose Cockrell F; m. 5/12/51 to Beverly Jane Kinard; c. Joel Y, Thomas Knight and John Auther. Educ: Tex. Tech. Col; South. Methodist Univ. Polit. & Govt. Pos: Former Tex. State Rep. Bus. & Prof. Pos: Real Estate Invest. Mil. Serv: Air Corps, 4 years as Aviation Cadet. Rel: Baptist. Mailing Add: 3612 Euclid St, Dallas, Tex. 75205. (1967)

FIELD, JOHN A, III R
Secy, First Cong. Dist. Rep. Cmt, Va.
b. Charleston, W.Va, 3/6/38; s. John A. Field, Jr. and Elizabeth Goode F; m. 3/16/59 to Patricia Marie Netzer; c. John A, IV, Robert Scott and Gary Arthur. Educ: Hampden-Sydney Col, 56-57; Ohio Univ, 60; Univ. Va, LL.B, 63; Lambda Chi Alpha. Polit. & Govt. Pos: Cand, Va. State Del, 67; v.chmn, Virginia Beach City Rep. Cmt, Va, 67, chmn, 68-; treas, Nixon-Agnew Campaign Cmt, 68; del, Va. Rep. State Conv, 68 & 69; mem. and secy, First Cong. Dist. Rep. Cmt, Va, 68- Mem: Am. Judicature Soc; Am, Va. State and Norfolk-Portsmouth Bar Asns; Jaycees. Rel: Protestant. Mailing Add: 3841 Thalia Dr, Virginia Beach, Va. 23452.

FIELD, LEON B. D
Okla. State Sen.
b. San Augustine, Tex, 9/21/02; s. Jerry R. Field and Katherine Horn F; m. 5/26/26 to Velma L. Heady; c. Albert Ray and Larry Lee. Educ: Hills Bus. Col, Okla; Panhandle A&M Col. Polit. & Govt. Pos: Mem, Okla. State Bd. of Agr; mem, Texhoma Sch. Bd, 42-50; Okla. State Rep, 46-50; Okla. State Sen, 50-, Majority Floor Leader, Okla. State Senate, 61 & 65. Mem: Okla. Ins. Agents Asn; Rotary Int; C. of C; Masonic Lodge 382, Guthrie Consistory Orient of Okla; India Shrine Temple, Okla. City; Eastern Star. Rel: Methodist. Legal Res: 510 N. Second, Texhoma, Okla. 73949. Mailing Add: Box 307, Texhoma, Okla. 73949. (1967)

FIELD, PETER D
Chmn, Weston Co. Dem. Party, Wyo.
b. Fuerth, Germany, 3/23/26; s. Else Borchardt; m. 8/26/50 to Margaret Elizabeth Farnham; c. Christopher B. and Lisa A. Educ: Univ. Calif, Berkeley, A.B, 50. Polit. & Govt. Pos: Alternate del, Dem. Nat. Conv, 68; chmn, Weston Co. Dem. Party, Wyo, 68- Mil. Serv: Entered as Pvt, Army, 44, released as Cpl, 46, after serv. in 502nd Parachute Regt, 101st Airborne Div, ETO, 44-46. Mem: Mason; Lions. Rel: Unitarian. Mailing Add: Box 684, Newcastle, Wyo. 82701.

FIELD, RUTH D
b. New York, N.Y, 5/5/07; d. Robert Field and Betty Metcalf Pruyn F; m. 1/15/36 to Marshall Field; c. Henry Ogden (deceased), Robert Lansing Phipps, Phyllis (Count Louis de Flers) and Fiona (Mrs. David E. Rust). Educ: Brearly Sch; hon. L.H.D, Hofstra Col, 61. Polit. & Govt. Pos: Hon. trustee, Sarah Lawrence Col; trustee, Eleanor Roosevelt Mem. Found. Bus. & Prof. Pos: Dir, The Field Found. Inc, N.Y.C, 40-, chmn. bd, 66- Mem: Adv. cmt, Dalton Schs; v.pres, Citizens Cmt. for Children of N.Y.C. Mailing Add: 100 E. 85th St, New York, N.Y. 10028.

FIELD, SHIRLEY A. R
b. Ft. Wayne, Ind, 2/27/23; d. Abraham Field and Clara Riddner F; single. Educ: Stephens Col, 40-41; Univ. Mich, A.B, 43; Yale Sch. Law, LL.B, 46. Polit. & Govt. Pos: Ore. State Rep, 57-61 & 63-65; del, Rep. Nat. Conv, 60 & 68 and mem. Platform Cmt, 64 & 68; mem, Big City Polit. Cmt, Rep. Nat. Cmt, 61; hon. life mem, Ore. Young Rep. Fedn. Bus. & Prof. Pos: Attorney-at-law, Ore. Publ: Various articles on Australia and New Zealand, Oregonian-Forum, 66. Stephens Alumnae Recognition, 60. Legal Res: 7525 S.W. Kelly, Portland, Ore. 97219. Mailing Add: 603 Corbett Bldg, Portland, Ore. 97204.

FIELDING, ELIZABETH MAY R
b. New London, Conn, 5/16/17; d. Frederick James Fielding and Elizabeth Martin F; single. Educ: Conn. Col. for Women, B.A, 38; Am. Univ. Sch. Pub. Affairs, M.A. in pub. admin, 44; Phi Beta Kappa. Polit. & Govt. Pos: Postmaster, Substation One, New London, Conn, 36-38; spec. agent, Census Bur, 38-39; personnel clerk, Labor Dept, 39, govt. economist and personnel asst, 41-42; sci. asst, Nat. Insts. Health, 39-40; campaign and research writer, Rep. Nat. Cmt, 40 & 42-48, acting dir. research, 44, asst. dir. research, 48-53 and assoc. dir. research, 54-57; speech writer and consult. to several U.S. Congressmen, 48-54; legis. asst. to U.S. Sen. Wiley, Wis, 53-54; pub. rels. dir, Nat. Fedn. Rep. Women, 61-68; dir. spec. activities, women's div, United Citizens for Nixon-Agnew, 68; finance coordinator, 69 Inaugural Cmt, 68-69; spec. and confidential asst. to Asst. Postmaster Gen, 68- Bus. & Prof. Pos: Staff Writer, Nat. Asn. of Elec. Co, Wash, D.C, 57-60. Publ: Ed, The Republican Clubwoman, Nat. Fedn. Rep. Women, 61-68; author, numerous Rep. Party publ, campaign manuals and study papers including, A History of the Republican Party, 1854-1948. Mem: D.C. League Rep. Women; Rock Creek

Rep. Women's Club; Am. Newspaper Women's Club Wash; Am. Polit. Sci. Asn; Am. Soc. for Pub. Admin; Am. Asn. for Adv. Sci; Am. Acad. Polit. and Soc. Sci; Am. Mgt. Asn; Columbia Hist. Soc; Antique Automobile Club Am; Capitol Hill Club. Hon. citizen of several U.S. cities; Outstanding Serv. Award, Nat. Fedn. Rep. Women Pres, 63 & 67. Rel: Methodist. Legal Res: 3 D.C. Village Lane S.W, Washington, D.C. 20032. Mailing Add: Room 5402, U.S. Post Office Dept, 12th and Pennsylvania Ave, N.W, Washington, D.C. 20260.

FIELDS, FRANK PADDISON R

b. Morresville, N.C, 4/5/26; s. Frank Van Duzer Fields and Isabelle Paddison F; m. to Ann Moore; c. Thomas Eric, Frank Paddison and Wendy Anne. Educ: Catawba Col, A.B, 51; Appalachian State Teachers Col. Grad Sch, 54. Polit. & Govt. Pos: V.chmn, Iredell Co. Rep. Club, N.C, 62-64; pres, South Iredell Co. Rep. Club, 62-66; del, Rep. Nat. Conv, 64; chmn, Lake Norman Marine Cmn, 69-; mem, Mayor's Civil Action Cmt, 69- Bus. & Prof. Pos: Supvr, Burlington Ind. Inc, 52-60; chemist, I.C.I. Organics, Inc, 60- Mil. Serv: Entered as A/S, Navy, 43, released as Hosp. Corpsman 1/C, 45, after serv. in ETO and Pac. Theater, 43-45; Am. Theater Ribbon; World War II Victory Medal; European-African-Middle East. Theater Ribbon; Asiatic-Pac. Theater Ribbon; Navy Occup. Medal; 2 Bronze Stars. Publ: 'Level Dyeing of Basic Dyes on Acrylic Fibers,' Knitted Outerwear Times, 3/67. Mem: Am. Asn. Textile Chemists and Colorists (mem. sectional cmt); 40 et 8 (state cmdr. of N.C, 58 and nat. v.comdr, 60); Am. Legion; Kiwanis; Moose; Mason; Scottish Rite (14°). Rel: Methodist. Mailing Add: 133 Heritage Place, Mooresville, N.C. 28115.

FIELDS, RICHARD EARL D

b. Charleston, S.C, 10/1/20; s. John Fields and Mary Cook F; m. 2/4/50 to Myrtle Thelma Evans; c. Mary Diane and Richard Earl, Jr. Educ: W.Va. State Col, 40-44; Howard Univ, 44-47; Alpha Phi Alpha. Polit. & Govt. Pos: Mem, Bd. Parks and Playgrounds, Charleston, S.C, assoc. munic. judge, currently; del, City, Co, State and Nat. Dem. Conv, 68. Bus. & Prof. Pos: Mem. bd. trustees, Claflin Univ, 56-; mem. bd. dirs, United Fund, 62-67, Charleston Co. Family Serv, 62- and McClennan Banks Hosp, 62- Mem: Am, Nat, S.C. and Charleston Co. Bar Asns; F&AM; Alpha Phi Alpha; Charleston Co. and S.C. Dem. Party. Civic Award for Lawyers; Outstanding Civic Award, Omega Psi Phi, Outstanding Citizen Award for Lawyers. Rel: Methodist; Mem, gen. bd. of Soc. Christian Concern, United Methodist Church. Legal Res: 1734 Heritage Park Rd, Charleston, S.C. 29407. Mailing Add: 65 Spring St, Charleston, S.C. 29403.

FIELDS, ROBERT CRUMP D

Chmn, Greene Co. Dem. Cmt, Mo.

b. Lebanon, Mo, 10/12/34; s. Robert Crump Fields, Sr. and Frances Reynolds F; m. 6/7/57 to Sallie Sue Sawyer; c. Lee S. and Leslie L. Educ: Univ. Mo, A.B, 56, J.D, 58; Phi Eta Sigma; Delta Sigma Rho; Pi Sigma Alpha; Omicron Delta Kappa; Epsilon Beta Eta; Beta Theta Pi. Polit. & Govt. Pos: Cmt. mem, Greene Co. Dem. Cmt, Mo, 64-, chmn, 66-; del, Dem. Nat. Conv, 68; corp. counsel, Off. of Secy. of State, 69- Mil. Serv: Entered as 2nd Lt, Army, 58, released as 1st Lt, 61, after serv. in Judge Adv. Gen. Corps. USAAD CEN, Ft. Bliss, Tex; Capt. Res. Mem: AF&AM; Scottish Rite; Shrine. Rel: Disciples of Christ. Mailing Add: 4470 Valley Rd, Springfield, Mo. 65804.

FIENBERG, GEORGE MITCHELL D

b. New York, N.Y, 8/26/10; s. Harry Fienberg and Anna Goldman F; m. 9/5/36 to Nesbith Perelman; c. Rosalind (Mrs. Kaplan). Educ: Univ. Vt; Albany Law Sch. Polit. & Govt. Pos: Municipal judge, Bennington, Vt, 63-; chmn, Bennington Co. Dem. Party, 59-61 and secy, 55-59; chmn, Bennington Town Dem. Party, 59-61 and mem, Town Cmt, 52-66; mem, Bennington Co. Dem. Cmt, 55-66; chmn, Gov. Hoff Inaugural Dinner, 63. Mem: Pres, 64-65, Bennington Co. Bar Asn; Vt. Bar Asn; Am. Bar Asn; dir, 42-44, Bennington C. of C; Bennington Club; Mason, Shrine; Elks; Mt. Anthony Country Club. Rel: Jewish. Legal Res: Convent Ave, Bennington, Vt. 05201. Mailing Add: 469 Main St, Bennington, Vt. 05201. (1967)

FIKE, ED R

Lt. Gov, Nev.

b. Hopkins, Mo; married. Educ: Westminster Col; Cornell Univ. Polit. & Govt. Pos: Former local and state pres, Young Rep; Nev. State Assemblyman, 3 sessions; Lt. Gov, Nev, 67-; alternate del, Rep. Nat. Conv, 68. Mil. Serv: Marine Corps, S. Pac, World War II; Korea. Mem: Lions (past dir); exec. bd, Boulder Dam Area Coun, Boy Scouts; Shrine (past mem, bd. of dirs); Student-Aid Found; founders bd, Boys Club; Las Vegas Jr. C. of C.(past pres; bd, C. of C; Elks, Kerak Temple; F&AM; Nat. Conf. Christians and Jews. Mailing Add: Box 1957, Las Vegas, Nev. 89101.

FIKE, STANLEY REDFIELD D

b. Warrensburg, Mo, 6/7/13; s. Lyman Walter Fike and Bethana Redfield F; M. 7/10/35 to Mildred Curry; c. Margaret (Mrs. Anthony Gray), Bethana (Mrs. John Cartland, Jr.) and Joann Dorace. Educ: Kans. City Jr. Col, 30-31. Polit. & Govt. Pos: Mem, Kansas City, Mo. Bd. Educ, 52; admin. asst. to U.S. Sen. Stuart Symington, Mo, 53-; exec. dir, Symington for President Campaign, 60. Bus. & Prof. Pos: Gen. mgr. and ed, Inter-City Press, Inc, Mo, 30-53; pres, Lee's Summit J, 49-65; v.pres, Jackson Co. Times, Inc, 52-53. Mem: Hon. mem. Univ. Mo. Sch. Journalism Alumni Asn; Sigma Delta Chi; Mo. Press Asn.(past pres); N.W. Mo. Press Asn.(past pres); bd. dirs, Kansas City Area Coun, Boy Scouts; founder and first pres, Jackson Co. Commun. Chest; organizer, Jackson Co. YMCA; Inter-City Kiwanis (past pres); Mo-Kans-Ark. Dist, Kiwanis (past Lt. Gov). Academy of Mo. Squires, 67. Rel: Reorganized Latter-day Saint. Legal Res: 610 N. Delaware, Independence, Mo. 64050. Mailing Add: 229 Senate Office Bldg, Washington, D.C. 20510.

FILES, WALLACE LEE R

W.Va. State Del.

b. Martinsburg, W.Va, 2/19/26; s. Lloyd T. Files (deceased) and Mary E. Cross F. (deceased); m. 1/13/47 to Bernice B. Fitzwater; c. Beatrice A. Educ: Hargestown Barber Sch, 49-50; Wheeling Barber Sch, 50. Polit. & Govt. Pos: W.Va. State Del, 67- Bus. & Prof. Pos: owner, Barber Shop, 50- Mil. Serv: Entered as Pvt, Army, 44, released as Pfc, 46; Purple Heart; Bronze Star; 5 Battle Stars; Good Conduct Medal; Victory Ribbon. Mem: Moose; Elks; Am. Legion Post 14; VFW; DAV (comdr, chap. 8, 68 & 69). Rel: Evangelical United Brethren. Mailing Add: 1109 Circle Dr, Martinsburg, W.Va. 25401.

FILL, LEON D

b. Stolin, Poland, 5/17/14; U.S. citizen; s. Norman Fill and Mary Kowal F; m. 3/20/43 to Clothilde Lanuette; c. Carole and Norman. Educ: Wayne Univ, 34-36; Wis. Univ, 36-37; Laval Med. Sch, B.S, B.M. and M.D, 42. Polit. & Govt. Pos: V.pres, State Bd. Educ, Mich; finance chmn, Swainson for Gov. Cmt, 60; finance dir, Mich. State Dem. Cent. Cmt, 60-62; del, Dem. Nat. Conv, 64; treas, Neil Staebler for Gov, Mich, 64. Bus. & Prof. Pos: Pres, Columbia Med. Hosp; chmn, Lakeside Med. Center, 50-; mem. adv. coun, Tuberc. Sanit, 60-62; mem. legal cmt, Mich. State Med. Soc, 65- Mil. Serv: Entered as Lt, Med. Corps, Army, 42, retired as Capt, 46, after serv. in ETO, 43-46; Purple Heart; Bronze Star; Inf. Med. Badge; ETO Medal with 3 Amphibious Invasion Clusters; plus others. Mem: Col. Obstet. & Gynec; Am. Med. Asn; Mason (32°); VFW; Econ. Club; Bd. of Commerce, B'nai B'rith; DAV; Crisis Club of Detroit; Mich. United Cons. Club. Rel: Hebrew. Legal Res: 8776 Nadine, Huntington Woods, Mich. 48070. Mailing Add: 2310 Cass, Detroit, Mich. 48201.

FILLBACH, GEORGE WILSON R

S.Dak. State Sen.

b. Cobb, Wis, 4/6/03; s. Charles Adam Fillbach and Kathryn Kosherak F; m. 12/22/26 to Kathryn Mabel Smith; c. Marrelyce (Mrs. David Seaman) and Carolyn (Mrs. Stanley Tanner). Educ: High sch, 1 year. Polit. & Govt. Pos: City councilman, Faulkton, S.Dak, 35-63, fire chief, 40-65, mayor, 57-64; S.Dak. State Rep, 57-65; S.Dak. State Sen, 65- Bus. & Prof. Pos: Owner, Faulkton Motor, 33- Mem: Elks; Odd Fellows; Shrine; Mason; pres, S.Dak. Auto Dealers. Benjamin Franklin Award. Mailing Add: St. Johns, Faulkton, S.Dak. 57438.

FILLMORE, LILLIAN GARNET R

V.chmn, Lawrence Co. Rep. Party, S.Dak.

b. Redfield, S.Dak, 4/3/01; d. Charles William Waterfall and Maud Connor W; m. 9/26/22 to William Orlo Fillmore; c. LaEtta (Mrs. Heltibridle), Lineal (Mrs. Falk), Billie June (Mrs. Bradshaw), Sarah (Mrs. Buittner) and Charles William. Educ: Redfield High Sch, S.Dak, grad, 18; MacPhail Sch. Music, Minneapolis, Minn, 21. Polit. & Govt. Pos: V.chmn, Lawrence Co. Rep. Party, S.Dak, 58-; committeewoman, Rep. State Cent. Cmt, 60-66. Bus. & Prof. Pos: Secy, Fillmore & Co, Inc, Spearfish, S.Dak, 51-, Am. Mining & Smelting, Inc, 52-, Caldak Metallurgical, Inc, 59- and Beardsley & Fillmore, Inc, 67- Mem: Eastern Star (Past Matron); Rebekah (past state assembly pres); Spearfish Federated Women's Club (past local and dist. pres); dir, Community Concert Asn. Rel: Methodist. Legal Res: 344 Fifth St, Spearfish, S.Dak. 57783 Mailing Add: Box 328, Spearfish, S.Dak. 57783.

FILO, JULES D

b. Czech, 1909; married. Educ: High sch, 2 years study abroad. Polit. & Govt. Pos: Pa. State Rep, 48-68; co. treas. off; dep. coroner, Allegheny Co. Morgue, 24 years; v.pres, Young Dem. Clubs of Pa. and Allegheny Co; pres, Young Dems, 33rd Cong. Dist. Bus. & Prof. Pos: Fitter stockman; expediter, elec. mfg. co, 7 years. Mem: W. Mifflin Vol. Fire Dept. Rel: Lutheran. Mailing Add: 4109 Greenspring Ave, West Mifflin, Pa. 15122. (1967)

FILSON, GENE H. D

b. Bartlett, Kans, 4/28/15; s. Harve Filson and Jessie Thornton F; m. 8/5/39 to Evelyn Anderson; c. James William and Eva Jean. Educ: Northwest. State Col, 3 years; Wrangler Club. Polit. & Govt. Pos: Dem. precinct chmn, Woods Co, Okla, 59-61; chmn, Woods Co. Dem. Cent. Cmt, 61-69. Mem: Pres, Alva C. of C, 55; charter mem, Alva Lions Club (pres, 60); parade chmn, Alva Homecoming Cmt, 63-68; grand patriarch, Grand Encampment of Okla, 60-61; treas, Cherokee Strip Orgn, 63-69; worshipful master, Alva Masonic Lodge, 69-, Mason (32°); Odd Fellows; Alva Encampment; Buffalo Patriarchs Militant; Elks; Scottish Rite. Award for serv. rendered in Boy Scouts. Rel: Christian. Legal Res: 1016 Second St, Alva, Okla. 73717. Mailing Add: Box 258, Alva, Okla. 73717.

FINA, EUNYCE ALOYS R

V.Chmn, Cong. Dist. Rep. Cmt, Mich.

b. Kittanning, Pa, 9/26/39; d. Carl William Johnson and Anna R. Fry J; m. to Kenneth Michael Fina; c. Lynda and Carole Ann. Educ: Henry Ford Commun. Col, 2 years. Polit. & Govt. Pos: Del, Rep. State Conv, Mich, 62-69; Rep. Precinct Del, Dearborn, 62-; asst. campaign mgr, Sen. N. Lorraine Beebe, 66; statutory mem, 16th Cong. Dist. Rep. Cmt, 66-67, secy, 67-68 and v.chmn, 69-; vol. coordinator, Nixon Hq, 68; alternate del, Rep. Nat. Conv, 68. Mem: W. Dearborn Rep. Club. Rel: Roman Catholic. Mailing Add: 23331 Oak Ave, Dearborn, Mich. 48128.

FINAN, THOMAS B. D

Assoc. Justice, Supreme Court, Md.

b. Cumberland, Md, 6/30/14; m. 1941 to Isabel Jean North; c. Two. Educ: Georgetown Univ, B.A, 36; Univ. Md. Sch. of Law, LL.B, 39. Polit. & Govt. Pos: Chmn, Allegany Co. Dem. Cent. Cmt, Md, 54-59; del, Dem. Nat. Conv, 56 & 60; chmn, Md. Dem. State Cent. Cmt, 59; Secy. of State, Md, 59-61 and Attorney Gen, 61-65; Judge, Md. Court of Appeals, 66-69; Assoc. Justice, Supreme Court, Md, 69- Bus. & Prof. Pos: Officer, bus. firms. Mil. Serv: Capt, Army, 41-45, serv. in ETO; Prisoner of War; Legion of Merit; Maj, Army Res. Mailing Add: 532 Washington St, Cumberland, Md. 21502. (1967)

FINCH, HEBER, JR. D

Okla. State Rep,

b. Dresden, Tenn, 11/15/16; s. Heber Finch and Bertha C. Templeton F; m. 10/11/43 to Waldean Autry; c. Dwayla Dean and Lillian. Educ: Univ. Okla, B.A, 37, LL.B, 39; Phi Delta Phi. Polit. & Govt. Pos: Okla. State Rep, 54- Mil. Serv: Entered as Pvt, Army, 41, released as T/Sgt, 45, after serv. in Counter Intel. Corps, ETO, 44-45. Mem: Okla. Bar Asn; C. of C; DAV; VFW; Am. Legion. Rel: Methodist. Legal Res: 1225 S. Adams, Sapulpa, Okla. 74066. Mailing Add: 230 Security Bldg, Sapulpa, Okla. 74066.

FINCH, HUGH EDSEL D

S.C. State Rep.

b. Moore, S.C, 6/21/28; s. Robert L. Finch, Sr. and Rosa Wyatt F; m. 9/5/53 to Geraldine Delores Green; c. Deborah and Susan. Educ: Wofford Col, A.B, 52. Polit. & Govt. Pos: S.C. State Rep, 57- Bus. & Prof. Pos: Newspaper reporter, Spartanburg Herald J, 52-54; high sch. teacher, 55-56; owner-operator, Finch Agency, 56-; with Reeves Bros Acct, 57. Mem: Spartanburg

Asn. Fire & Casualty Ins. Agents; S.C. Asn. Ins. Agents; past pres, Ruritan; Lions; Jr. C. of C; PTA; Mason; Shrine. Rel: Methodist. Mailing Add: 1111 Greenville Hwy, Spartanburg, S.C. 29303.

FINCH, ROBERT HUTCHISON R
Secy. of Health, Educ. and Welfare
b. Tempe, Ariz, 10/9/25; s. Robert L. Finch and Gladys Hutchison F; m. 2/14/46 to Carol Crothers; c. Maureen, Kevin, Priscilla and Cathleen. Educ: Occidental Col, B.A. in Polit. Sci, 46; Univ. South. Calif, J.D, 51; Kappa Sigma; Phi Alpha Delta. Hon. LL.D, Occidental Col, Lincoln Univ, Univ. Calif, Los Angeles and Univ. South. Calif. Polit. & Govt. Pos: Exec. secy, U.S. Rep. Poulson, Calif, 47-48; del, Rep. Nat. Conv, 48, 56 & 68; ed, Nat. Young Rep. Newspaper, 48; Rep. nominee for U.S. Rep, 52 & 54; chmn, Los Angeles Co. Rep. Cent. Cmt, 56-58; trustee, Rep. Assocs. of Los Angeles, 58-66, chmn. exec. cmt, 64-65; admin. asst. to V.Pres. Richard Nixon, 58-60; mgr, Richard Nixon's Presidential Campaign, 60; state-wide dir, George Murphy's Sen. Campaign, 64; Lt. Gov, Calif, 66-69; former pres, Calif. State Senate, chmn, Calif. Job Training and Placement Coun, Interagency Coun. for Ocean Resources, Bicentennial Celebration Cmn, Cmn. of the Californias and Electronic Data Processing Policy Cmt, mem. exec. cmt, Inter-govt. Coun. on Urban Growth, mem, State Lands Cmn, Cmn. on Interstate Coop, Adv. Panel-Teaching of the Bill of Rights, Toll Bridge Authority, Gov. Cabinet and Gov. Coun, 66-69; mem. exec. cmt, Nat. Conf. Lt. Gov, 67; Secy. of Health, Educ. and Welfare, 69-, mem, Cabinet Cmts, Vol. Action and Environ. Qual. Cmts. and Urban Affairs Coun. and chmn, President's Coun. on Aging and Cmt. on Retardation, Interdept. Cmt. on Children and Youth, Air Qual. Adv. Bd. and Fed. Radiation Coun, currently. Bus. & Prof. Pos: Instr. and trustee, Palos Verdes Col, Calif, 52-56; partner, Finch, Bell, Duitsman & Margulis, 53-69; organizer and pres, Palos Verdes Fed. Savings & Loan, 56-58; chmn. bd, Marine Fed. Savings & Loan Asn, 58-59. Mil. Serv: Marine Corps, 43-45, recalled in 51 and released as 1st Lt, 53, after serv. in Korean Theatre. Publ: The New Conservative Liberal Manifesto, Viewpoint Books, 68. Mem: Legion Lex; Calif, Los Angeles Athletic, Commonwealth and Jonathan Clubs; Town Hall; former mem. bd. dirs, Centinela Valley YMCA; Cmt. of YMCA Youth Govt; Los Angeles Dist. Attorney's Adv. Cmt; adv. bd, CORO Found; Little League Mgr, 62-65; regent, Univ. Calif; trustee, Calif. State Cols. and Occidental Col; adv. bd, Palos Verdes Col. and Marymount Col, Calif. Rel: Presbyterian. Legal Res: Pasadena, Calif. Mailing Add: 330 Independence Ave, Washington, D.C. 20201.

FINCHER, DICK D
Fla. State Sen.
b. Rochester, N.Y, 9/27/27; s. Harry West Fincher and Lucille C. Schmitz F; m. 1/19/57 to Gloria De Haven; c. Harry West and Faith Frances. Educ: Cornell Univ, B.A, 49; Phi Delta Theta. Polit. & Govt. Pos: Fla. State Rep, 63-65; Fla. State Sen, 67-; del, Dem. Nat. Conv, 68. Bus. & Prof. Pos: Pres, Fincher Motors, Inc, 52- Mil. Serv: 2nd Lt, Army, 53-54. Mem: Orange Bowl Cmt; Indian Creek Country Club; La Gorce Country Club; former pres, Miami Automobile Dealers Asn; Brain Trust Cmt. of Hire the Handicapped; Citizens Bd, Univ. of Miami; chmn, Heart Asn. of Greater Miami. Rel: Catholic. Legal Res: 1800 W. 24th St, Sunset Island 3, Miami Beach, Fla. 33140. Mailing Add: 1740 N.E. Second Ave, Miami, Fla. 33132.

FINCHER, JACK CHAMBERS, SR. D
Ga. State Sen.
b. Canton, Ga, 11/22/15; s. William Wesley Fincher, Sr. and Mary Chambers F; m. 9/5/36 to Katherine Elena Wink; c. Jack C. Jr, John Herman and William Wesley, III. Educ: Reinhardt Col, 33-34; Ga. Tech, 36-37; South. Col. of Pharm, B.S, 52; Kappa Psi. Polit. & Govt. Pos: Mem, Cherokee Co. Sch. Bd, Ga, 57-63; mem, Canton City Sch. Bd, 57-63; mayor, Canton, 57-63; mem, Canton City Coun, 57-63; Ga. State Sen, 62- Bus. & Prof. Pos: Druggist, 35- Mil. Serv: Sgt. T3, Army, 43-46. Mem: Mason; chmn. bd. of trustees, Canton Womans Club; bd. dirs, Cherokee Co. Indust. Develop. Corp, 60-61; pres, Canton Retail Merchants Asn, 59; pres, Canton Little League Baseball, 59; chmn, Cherokee Pickens Dist. Boy Scouts, 62. Rel: Methodist. Mailing Add: Canton, Ga. 30114. (1967)

FINCHUM, FRANK DEWAYNE R
Chmn, Orange Co. Rep. Party, Tex.
b. Port Arthur, Tex, 5/18/32; s. Frank Edward Finchum and Jessie Lorraine Hunt F; m. 8/17/55 to Nancy Jo Benfield; c. Tab Damon, Frank Dewayne, Jr. and Barbara Nan. Educ: Univ. Tex, Austin, B.B.A; Int. Correspondence Sch, Pulp and Paper Making Degree; Scabbard and Blade; Col. Independents. Polit. & Govt. Pos: Rep. precinct chmn, Orange, Tex, 67-68, finance chmn, 68; chmn, Orange Co. Rep. Party, 68- Bus. & Prof. Pos: Prod. supvr, Equitable Bag Co, Inc, Orange, Tex, 55-58, safety dir, 58-60, dir. personnel and safety, 60-62, prod. mgr, 62- Mil. Serv: 2nd Lt, Army, 67, serv. in Res. Officers Prog, Ft. Lee, Va, 6 months; Capt, Army Res, 54-62. Mem: Second v.pres, bd. dirs, United Fund; bd. dirs, C. of C; pres, bd. dirs, Sunset Grove Country Club. Rel: Methodist. Mailing Add: 1809 Decker, Orange, Tex. 77630.

FINDLEY, PAUL R
U.S. Rep, Ill.
b. Jacksonville, Ill, 1921; m; c. Craig and Diane. Educ: Ill. Col, B.A; Phi Beta Kappa. D.H.L, Lindenwood Col. Polit. & Govt. Pos: U.S. Rep, 20th Dist, Ill, currently, mem. for. affairs and govt. opers, U.S. House Rep, currently. Bus. & Prof. Pos: Pres. and publisher, Pike Press, Inc, Pittsfield, Ill. Mil. Serv: Navy, World War II, served as Supply Corps Officer, Seabees, Guam invasion and Japanese occupation. Publ: Federal Farm Fable, Arlington House. Mem: Am. Legion; VFW; Navy League; Lions; bd. trustees, Ill. Col; bd. dirs, Lincoln Group of D.C. and Fedn. Union, Inc. Rel: Congregational. Legal Res: 306 S. Jackson St, Pittsfield, Ill. 62363. Mailing Add: 7207 Normandy Lane, Falls Church, Va. 22042.

FINE, MORRIS HELLER R
b. Norfolk, Va, 10/13/30; s. Louis B. Fine and Minnie Snyder F; single. Educ: Univ. Va, B.A, 53, LL.B, 54; Phi Epsilon Pi. Polit. & Govt. Pos: City treas, Norfolk, Va, 64-68; alternate del, Rep. Nat. Conv, 68. Mil. Serv: Entered as OCSA, Navy, 54, released as Lt.(jg), 58, after serv. at Corpus Christi, Tex, Res, 58-, Lt. Comdr. Mem: Am. and Va. State Bar Asns; Am. and Va. Trial Lawyers Asns; AF&AM; Shrine; Tidewater Anglers Club; C. of C; Exchange Club. Rel: Jewish. Legal Res: 1601 Runnymede Rd, Norfolk, Va. 23515. Mailing Add: Law Bldg, 147 Granby St, Norfolk, Va. 23510.

FINEMAN, HERBERT D
Pa. State Rep.
b. Phila, Pa, 7/4/20; s. Joseph Fineman and Esther Best F; m. to Frances Brownstein; c. two. Educ: Temple Univ, B.S; Temple Sch. of Law, LL.B; Hon. LL.D, Sch. Osteopathic Med, 68. Polit. & Govt. Pos: Secy. and mem. exec. bd, Gen. State Authority; exec. bd, Joint State Govt. Cmn. Commonwealth Pa; mem, Pa. Hwy, and Bridge Authority; mem, Pa. Pub. Sch. Bldg. Authority; mem, Pa. Higher Educ. Assistance Agency; investigator, illegal use of wire tapping in Pa; Pa. State Rep, 54-, majority whip, Pa. House Rep, 65-66, minority floor leader, 67-68, speaker of the house, 69-; chmn, Joint State Govt. Cmn. Task Force on Proc. Against Juveniles, Eminent Domain and Rev. of Penal Code; leader, 52nd Ward Dem. Exec. Cmt; mem, Dem. Party Speakers Bur; del, Dem. Nat. Conv, 68. Bus. & Prof. Pos: Practicing attorney 46-; partner, Fineman and Fineman. Mem: Pa. Co. and Appellate Courts; Fed. Courts for East. Dist. Pa; Pa. State Bar Asn; Brandeis Law Soc; Lawyers' Club Phila; Phila. Trial Lawyers Asn; Phila. Bar Asn.(cmt. civil legis. and civil liberties); Phila. Fel. Cmn; B'nai B'rith; Gamma Lodge; past zone chmn, United Commun. Campaign Drive; Nat. Pop Warner Conf; chmn. annual maintenance campaign, Down Town Home for Aged; Circus Saints and Sinners Club of Am; YMCA; Variety Club; bd. dirs, Col. Podiatric Med; bd. dirs, Child Guid. Center; trustee, Phila. Col. Podiatry; Nat. Conf. State Legis. Leaders (exec. bd). Mailing Add: 2291 Bryn Mawr Ave, Philadelphia, Pa. 19131.

FINGER, HAROLD BEN
Asst. Secy. for Research and Tech, Dept. of Housing and Urban Develop.
b. N.Y.C, 2/18/24; s. Ben Finger and Anna Perelmutter F; m. 6/11/49 to Arlene Karsch; c. Barbara Lynn, Elyse Sue and Sandra Ruth. Educ: City Col. N.Y, B.S. in Mech. Eng, 44; Case Inst. Tech, M.S. in Aeronaut. Eng, 50. Polit. & Govt. Pos: Aeronaut. research scientist, Lewis Research Center, Nat. Adv. Cmt. for Aeronaut, Cleveland, Ohio, 44-52, head, axial flow compressor sect, 52-54, assoc. chief, compressor research br, 54-58, head, nuclear radiation shielding group and nuclear rocket design analysis group, 58; chief, nuclear propulsion, NASA, 58-60, asst. dir, nuclear applications, 60-61, dir, nuclear syst, 61-64, dir, space power and nuclear syst, 64-67, assoc. adminstr. for orgn. and mgt, 67-69; mgr, Space Nuclear Propulsion Off, 60-67; dir, space nuclear syst. div, Atomic Energy Cmn, 65-67; Asst. Secy. for Research and Tech, Dept. of Housing and Urban Develop, 69- Publ: Numerous tech. reports and papers. Mem: Am. Inst. of Aeronaut. and Astronaut. Co-winner, Manley Mem. Award for the best paper on aeronaut, Soc. Automotive Engrs, 57; Outstanding Leadership Medal, NASA, 66; James H. Wyld Propulsion Award, Am. Inst. for Aeronaut. and Astronaut, 68. Mailing Add: 6908 Millwood Rd, Bethesda, Md. 20034.

FINGER, SEYMOUR MAXWELL
Ambassador and Sr. Adv. to Permanent Rep. to UN, U.S. Mission to UN
b. N.Y, 4/30/15; s. Samuel Finger and Bella Spiegel F; m. 4/5/56 to Helen Kotcher; c. Mark. Educ: Ohio Univ, B.S, 35; Univ. Cincinnati, 42; Littauer Sch. Pub. Affairs, Harvard Univ, 53-54; Phi Beta Kappa; Kappa Delta Pi. Polit. & Govt. Pos: Second secy, Am. Embassy, Paris, France, 49-51; mem. staff, Econ. Defense Off, Rome, Italy, 54-55; first secy, Am. Embassy Vientiane, Laos, 55-59; second secy. and econ. officer, Am. Legation, Budapest, Hungary, 51-53; ambassador and sr. adv. to permanent rep. to UN, U.S. Mission to UN, 56- Mil. Serv: Entered as Pvt, Army, 43, released as S/Sgt, 45, after serv. in ETO. Mem: Coun. on For. Rels. Cert. of Merit, Ohio Univ. Alumni Asn, 67. Mailing Add: 476 Morris Ave, Rockville Center, N.Y. 11570.

FINK, EARL BARTON D
Chmn, Mifflin Co. Dem. Cmt, Pa.
b. Granville, Pa, 7/7/19; s. Earl Truman Fink and Jessie Barton F; m. 11/10/45 to Betty Jane Moist; c. Earl Barton, Jr. and Todd Patrick. Polit. & Govt. Pos: Sch. dir, Granville Twp. Sch. Dist, Pa, 50-54; tax collector, Granville Twp, 54-; registrn. chmn, Mifflin Co. Dem. Cmt, 60-64, chmn, 64- Bus. & Prof. Pos: Owner, Grocery Store, Granville, Pa, 45-55. Mem: F&AM; Shrine; Consistory; Jaffa Temple; United Commercial Travelers; Methodist Men's Club; Elks; Mifflin Co. Dem. Club. Rel: Protestant. Mailing Add: Box 41, Granville, Pa. 17029. (1967)

FINK, ERIC FRANK R
Mo. State Rep.
b. Jefferson Co, Mo, 5/19/37; s. Arthur C. Fink, Sr. and Maude J. Dohack F; m. 7/19/58 to Charlotte M. Poe; c. Eric F, Jr, Todd Alan and Laurie Ann. Educ: Univ. Mo, Columbia, 1 year; Wash. Univ, night sch, 1 year. Polit. & Govt. Pos: Mo. State Rep, 67- Bus. & Prof. Pos: Mem. bd. dirs, Rockwood Commun. Hosp, 68-; pres, Circulus, Inc, 69- Mil. Serv: Entered as Pvt, Army, 56, released as Spec. 4, 59, after serv. in Transportation, Korea, 57-58. Mem: AF&AM. St. Louis Suburban Teachers Award, 68; Commun. Leaders Award. Rel: Methodist. Mailing Add: 1325 Froesel, Ellisville, Mo. 63011.

FINK, RALPH WILLIAM R
b. Milwaukee, Wis, 2/9/17; s. Edward J. Fink and Mary Hoye F; m. 6/14/41 to Evelyn Ronan; c. Edward J, William R, Virginia M, Mary Beth, Thomas A, Daniel R. and David M. Educ: Marquette Univ, Ph.B, 38, J.D, 40; Sigma Nu Phi. Polit. & Govt. Pos: Dist. attorney, Richland Co, Wis, 65-; chmn, Richland Co. Rep. Orgn, 69- Bus. & Prof. Pos: V.pres. finance dept, Spincraft Inc, Milwaukee, Wis, 60-64, Mem: Wis. State Bar Asn; Richland Co. Bar Asn.(pres); C. of C. Rel: Catholic. Mailing Add: 325 S. Sheldon, Richland Center, Wis. 53581.

FINK, THOMAS A. D
Mem, Monroe Co. Dem. Cmt, N.Y.
b. Albany, N.Y, 10/15/34, s. Arthur C. Fink and Anna May Richolson F; m. 8/24/58 to Janet E. Katz; c. Barbara L, Karen L. and Robert A. Educ: Cornell Univ, B.A, 57, Law Sch, LL.B, 59; Beta Sigma Rho. Polit. & Govt. Pos: Mem, Monroe Co. Dem. Cmt, N.Y, 60-; mem. exec. cmt, Brighton Dem. Town Cmt, 63-69; pres, Brighton Dem. Club, 66-68; del, Dem. Nat. Conv, 68; mem. exec. cmt, Monroe Co. Coalition for Dem. Action, 68-69. Bus. & Prof. Pos: Partner, Houghton, Pappas & Fink Attorneys, 63-; lectr, grad. sch. bus, Univ. Rochester, 65-67. Publ: 'The Law and Problems of Water Pollution,' Sci. and Citizen, 3/67; 'Water Pollution—Changes in the Law,' Rochester Cmt. Sci. Info. Bul, 68. Mem: N.Y. State, Monroe Co. and Fed. Bar Asns; Am.

Asn. Trial Lawyers; Rochester Cmt. Sci. Info.(past pres); pres, Tempeo Develop; Rochester Club. Times Union Salute. Rel: Jewish. Mailing Add: 186 Clovercrest Dr, Rochester, N.Y. 14618.

FINKEL, ROBERT S. D
b. Pittsburgh, Pa, 3/25/18; s. William Lloyd Finkel and Esther Rosenthal F; m. 1946 to Jane Kramer; c. Theresa and Pamela. Educ: Carnegie Inst. Tech, B.A, 40; Alpha Epsilon Rho; Beta Sigma Rho. Polit. & Govt. Pos: Alternate del, Dem. Nat. Conv, 68; Hollywood laison, Off. Econ. Opportunity; produced shows for Robert Kennedy Campaign, 68. Bus. & Prof. Pos: TV producer, Nat. Broadcasting Co, 59-69. Mil. Serv: Entered as Pvt, Army, 40, released as Lt, 45, after serv. in 181st Signal Repair Co, China-Burma-India Theatre, 42-45; Unit Merit Award; China Campaign Ribbon with one Battle Star; India Burma Campaign ribbon with one Battle Star. Mem: TV Acad. Arts and Sci; Mason; Variety Club; Am. Fedn. Musicians; Am. Fedn. TV and Radio Actors; Actors Equity; pres, Producers Guild of Am; bd. dirs, Dirs. Guild Am; pres, W. Coast Drama Clan, Carnegie Mellon Univ; adv. bd, TV, radio-film dept, Stephens Col. Peabody Award; 3 Emmy Awards. Rel: Jewish. Mailing Add: 1215 Lexington Rd, Beverly Hills, Calif. 90210.

FINKELSTEIN, JERRY D
Chmn. Finance Cmt, N.Y. State Dem. Cmt.
b. New York, N.Y, 1/26/16; s. Albert A. Finkelstein and Ethel Kaufman F; m. 3/20/42 to Shirley Marks; c. Andrew Jay and James Arthur. Educ: N.Y. Univ; N.Y. Law Sch, LL.B, 38. Polit. & Govt. Pos: Research dir, N.Y. State Senate, 38-41; mem. aviation cmt. pub. schs, N.Y. State Bd. Regents, 41; mem. official cmt. extension civil serv, N.Y. State Legis, 41; campaign mgr, Mayoralty Campaign, N.Y.C, 49; chmn. planning cmt, City Planning Cmn, N.Y.C, 50-51; chmn. finance cmt, N.Y. State Dem. Cmt, currently; del, Dem. Nat. Conv, 68. Bus. & Prof. Pos: Mem. of staff spec. prosecutor Thomas E. Dewey, 35-36; reporter, civil serv. ed, N.Y. Mirror, 37-39; founder, Pub. Civil Serv. Leader, N.Y, 39-; dir, Struthers Scientific and Int. Corp; chmn. bd. and chmn. exec. cmt, Struthers Wells Corp; publ, N.Y. Law J, 64-; chmn. bd, Struthers Capital Corp, ABC Industries, and Sci. and Govt. Publs, Inc; pres. and chmn. bd, N.Y. Law Pub. Co; dir, Commercial Bank N.Am, N.Y.C. Mil. Serv: Coast Guard Res, 43-45. Mem: Trustee, N.Y. Law Sch; bd. overseers, Jewish Theol. Sem. of Am; chmn. fine arts gifts cmt, Nat. Cult. Center; mem. exec. coun, Southampton Col, L.I. Univ; mem. pres. coun, Grad. Sch. Pub. Admin, N.Y. Univ; mem. bd. visitors, U.S. Mil. Acad, 69; Am. Jewish Cmt; Soc. Silurians; Newspaper Reporters Asn; founder, Albert Einstein Col. of Med; Nat. Dem. Club; Overseas Press Club; Advert. Club. Scroll for Outstanding Efforts Civic Betterment, Cmt. of 1000, 51; Recipient Knickerbocker Award for Outstanding City Planning, 51; Decorated Knight, Order of Merit, Italy, 58. Legal Res: 812 Park Ave, New York, N.Y. 10021. Mailing Add: 630 Fifth Ave, New York, N.Y. 10020.

FINLEY, JOSEPH CALDWELL R
N.Y. State Assemblyman
b. Marion, N.Y, 5/31/16; s. Fremont Finley and L. Blanche Rich F; m. 9/14/46 to Lorraine Blanchard; c. Gary L. and Lee B. Educ: Newark Collegiate Center, 34-35. Polit. & Govt. Pos: Committeeman, Dist. One, Rep. Party, N.Y, 44-64; mem. bd. educ, Walworth Union Free Sch, 45-49; town supvr, Walworth, 51-55; co. clerk, Wayne Co, 56-60; chmn, Wayne Co. Rep. Party, 57-64; N.Y. State Assemblyman, 129th Assembly Dist, 61- Bus. & Prof. Pos: Co-owner, Newark Stationery, Newark, N.Y, 63- Mem: Pres, Wayne Co. Hist. Soc, 65; F&AM; Farm Bur; N.Y. State Asn. of Co. Clerks; C. of C; N.Y. State Coun. of Retail Merchants; N.Y. State Agr. Asn. Rel: Methodist. Mailing Add: 38 Sherburne Rd, Walworth, N.Y. 14568.

FINLEY, MORGAN M. D
b. Chicago, Ill, 8/31/25; m. to Betty Burke; c. James and Patrick. Educ: DePaul Univ. Polit. & Govt. Pos: Secy, 11th Ward Regular Dem. Orgn, Ill, 16 years; former Ill. State Sen; alternate del, Dem. Nat. Conv, 68. Bus. & Prof. Pos: Real estate and ins. Mil. Serv: Navy. Mem: VFW; Am. Legion; Moose; K. of C; founder and pres, Bridgeport Little Major League; pres, Bridgeport C. of C; mem, Chicago Real Estate Bd; trustee, Cent. Mfg. Dist. Club. Mailing Add: 3530 S. Halsted St, Chicago, Ill. 60609. (1967)

FINLINSON, FRED LYMAN R
Mem, Utah State Rep. Cent. Cmt.
b. Oak City, Utah, 9/30/06; s. Joseph Trimble Finlinson and Edith Elzina Lyman F; m. 6/13/39 to Luella Wheeler; c. Fred Wheeler, David Wheeler and Judith. Educ: Univ. Utah, LL.B, 35; Delta Phi Kappa. Polit. & Govt. Pos: Pres, Salt Lake Co. Young Rep. Club, Utah, 40; del, Rep. Nat. Conv, 40 & 64, alternate del, 48 & 68; West. Regional dir. and mem. exec. cmt, Young Rep. Nat. Cmt, 46-49; admin. asst. to U.S. Sen. Arthur V. Watkins, 48; arrangement chmn, Nat. Young Rep. Conv, 49; chmn, Utah Cmt. for Taft for President, 52, chmn, Utah Cmt. for Goldwater, 64; secy, Utah State Rep. Cent. Cmt, 58-63, legal counsel, 63-65 and mem, 65-; mem, Utah State Rep. Exec. Cmt, 65- Bus. & Prof. Pos: Mem, Law Firm of Riter, Cowan, Finlinson & Daines, 45-66, sr. mem, 66-; dir, Surety Life Ins, 59-, Murray State Bank, 60- Mem: Utah State Bar Asn.(cmnr, 42-43, exam. bd, 59-66); Salt Lake Co. Bar Asn.(pres, 48-49); Univ. Club of Salt Lake City; Lions. Rel: Latter-day Saint. Legal Res: 776 E. Vine St, Salt Lake City, Utah 84107. Mailing Add: Kearns Bldg, Salt Lake City, Utah 84101. (1967)

FINMAN, SUSAN F. D
Chmn, Dane Co. Dem. Party, Wis.
b. Berlin, Germany, 12/11/28; d. Benar Heifetz and Olga Band H; m. 1/2/50 to Ted Finman; c. Rona and Terry. Educ: Univ. Chicago, B.A, 50. Polit. & Govt. Pos: Precinct committeewoman, Albuquerque Dem. Party, N.Mex, 60-62; mem. exec. cmt, Dane Co. Dem. Party, Wis, 65, secy, 66-67 and chmn, 69-; exec. secy, Kastenmeier for Cong. Campaign, 66; del, Dem. Nat. Conv, 68. Bus. & Prof. Pos: Research asst, Univ. Wis, 66-69. Rel: Jewish. Mailing Add: 1 S. Rock Rd, Madison, Wis. 53705.

FINMAN, TED D
b. San Francisco, Calif, 2/10/31; s. Samuel Finman and Dora Weinberg F; m. 1/2/50 to Susan F. Heifetz; c. Rona and Terry. Educ: Univ. Chicago, A.B, 50; Stanford Univ, LL.B, 54; Order of the Coif. Polit. & Govt. Pos: Precinct committeeman, Albuquerque Dem. Party, N.Mex, 60-61; mem. exec. cmt, Dane Co. Dem. Party, Wis, 65 & 66; state treas, McCarthy for Pres, Campaign, 68; del, Dem. Nat. Conv, 68. Bus. & Prof. Pos: Asst. prof. law, Univ. N.Mex, 59-62; assoc. prof. law, Rutgers Univ, 62-63; assoc. prof. law, Univ. Wis, Madison, 63-66, prof. law, 66- Publ: The Lawyers in Modern Society (w. V. Countryman), Little, 66; 'The Request for Admissions in Federal Civil Procedure,' Yale Law J, 62; 'Civil Litigation and Professional Responsibility,' Coun. Educ. Prfnl. Responsibility, 66. Mem: Calif. State Bar Asn; Am. Asn. Univ. Prof. Rel: Jewish. Mailing Add: 1 S. Rock Rd, Madison, Wis. 53705.

FINN, JOHN RODERICK D
Chmn, Franklin Co. Dem. Cmt, Vt.
b. St. Albans, Vt, 10/9/23; s. James Grover Finn and Marieanne Limoges F; m. 12/27/49 to Elmerine Bove, separated; c. Michael John. Educ: Norwich Univ, B.A. in Eng, 48; Dean's List; pres, Theta Chi; Commencement Week Chmn; pres, Intrafraternity Coun; v.pres, Skull & Swords; v.pres, NUVA; Marshall, Theta Chi; Glee Club; Newman Club; chmn, Homecoming Week. Polit. & Govt. Pos: Party organizer and trailer operator, Vt. Dem. Campaign, 54, party organizer, 56; sheriff, Franklin Co, Vt, 56-; chmn, St. Albans City Dem. Cmt. and campaign mgr, St. Albans and Franklin Co, 60-65; advance man, Hoff for Gov. Campaign, 66; former v.chmn, Franklin Co. Dem. Cmt, chmn, currently; alternate del, Dem. Nat. Conv, 68. Bus. & Prof. Pos: Pres, Franklin Co. Develop. Asn, Inc, 62-; chmn, Champlain Valley Off. Econ. Opportunity, Inc, 64- Mil. Serv: Entered as Pvt, Army, 43, released as Sgt, 45, after serv. in Mil. Police and Armored Inf; ETO Ribbon with 3 battle stars; Purple Heart; Good Conduct Ribbon. Mem: Dir, Vt. State Sheriff's Asn, 57-, pres, 57-59; dir, Nat. Sheriffs Asn, 57-58; Am. Legion; 40 et 8; VFW; Past Exalted Ruler, Elks; Moose; Eagles; K. of C; bd. mem, Vt. Youth Opportunity Center, Burlington. Singing scholarship, Univ. of Vt, 42; Hon. mention, All-State Football, 41. Rel: Roman Catholic. Mailing Add: 30 Lincoln Ave, St. Albans, Vt. 05478. (1967)

FINNEGAN, EDWARD R. D
b. Chicago, Ill, 6/5/05; s. Patrick Finnegan and Margaret Rowen F; m. 9/14/35 to Katherine Coyle; c. Sarah (Mrs. L.A. Harrs), Moira, Kathleen. Educ: DePauw Univ, LL.B, 30. Polit. & Govt. Pos: Circuit Court Judge of Cook Co, 65- Bus. & Prof. Pos: Lawyer, 31-; asst. corp. counsel, 56-57; asst. states attorney, 45-57. Mem: Am, Ill, Chicago Bar Asns; Elks; K. of C; Nat. Cap. Dem. Club; Lake Shore Club; Dairymens Country Club. Rel: Catholic. Mailing Add: 1360 N. Sandburg Terr, Chicago, Ill. 60610. (1967)

FINNELL, CHARLES ADKINS D
Tex. State Rep.
b. Wichita Falls, Tex, 9/16/43; s. Leslie Burrow Finnell and Mary Frances Adkins F; m. 8/31/68 to Merrill Shields. Educ: Univ. Tex, Austin, B.A, 65; Phi Kappa Tau; Interfraternity Coun. Polit. & Govt. Pos: Tex. State Rep, Dist. 61, 67- Mem: Archer Co. C. of C; life mem, Univ. Tex. Alumni Asn. Rel: United Methodist. Mailing Add: Box 468, Holliday, Tex. 76366.

FINNEY, FLORENCE D. R
Conn. State Sen.
b. L.I. City, N.Y, 1903; married. Polit. & Govt. Pos: Conn. State Rep, 49-55; Conn. State Sen, 55- Bus. & Prof. Pos: Businesswoman. Mailing Add: 59 River Rd, Cos Cob, Conn. 06807.

FINNEY, JERVIS SPENCER R
Md. State Sen.
b. Baltimore, Md, 9/22/31; s. George Gross Finney and Josephine Stewart F; single. Educ: Princeton Univ, A.B, 53; Harvard Law Sch, LL.B, 58. Polit. & Govt. Pos: Mem, Baltimore Co. Coun, Md, 62-66 and Regional Planning Coun, 63-66; Md. State Sen, currently. Mil. Serv: Entered as Pvt, Army Paratroops, 53, released as Cpl, 55, after serv. in 11th Airborne Div. Mem: Am. and Md. Bar Asns; bd. dirs, Citizens Planning and Housing Asn. and Md. Div, Multiple Sclerosis Soc; Baltimore co. chmn, Am. Cancer Soc. Crusade, 66; Jaycees; Baltimore Co. Admin, Keep Md. Beautiful. Rel: Presbyterian. Legal Res: Stevenson, Md. 21153. Mailing Add: 1600 Maryland National Bank Bldg, Baltimore, Md. 21202.

FINNIE, HUBERT NOEL D
Miss. State Rep.
b. Panola Co, Miss, 6/13/00; married. Polit. & Govt. Pos: Mem, Citizens Coun, Miss; mem, Bd. of Supvr, 40-48; Miss. State Rep, 56-60 & 68- Bus. & Prof. Pos: Cattle and cotton farmer; teacher; merchant. Mem: Lions; Batesville C. of C; Farm Bur; Miss. Cattlemens Asn; trustee, Eleemosynary Insts. Rel: Baptist. Mailing Add: Courtland, Miss. 38620. (1967)

FINO, PAUL A. R
b. New York, N.Y, 12/15/13; s. Isidoro Fino and Lucia Patané F; m. 1/22/39 to Esther C. Liquori; c. Lucille (Mrs. Dimuro) and Paul A, Jr. Educ: St. John's Univ, 33-35, Sch. of Law, LL.B, 37. Polit. & Govt. Pos: Asst. Attorney Gen, N.Y, 43-44; N.Y. State Sen, 45-50; Civil Serv. Cmnr, N.Y.C, 50-52; U.S. Rep, N.Y, 53-68; mem-at-large, N.Y. State Rep. Cmt. and chmn, Bronx Co. Rep. Cmt, 61-68; del, Rep. Nat. Conv, 68; Fed. Judge, 68- Bus. & Prof. Pos: Mem, Law Firm, Paley, Levy & Fino, N.Y.C, 53- Publ: My Fight for a National Lottery, 60. Mem: Am, Fed. and Bronx Co. Bar Asns; Paul A. Fino Rep. Club; Elks; Grand Street Boys; Royal Arcanum; Columbus Alliance; Sons of Italy. Rel: Catholic. Mailing Add: 1518 Fielding St, Bronx, N.Y. 10069. (1967)

FIOCCA, CLAUDE MICHAEL D
Ohio State Rep.
b. Akron, Ohio, 7/16/31; s. Joseph Anthony Fiocca and Anna Marie D'Amico F; m. 11/20/65 to Marjorie Anne Liptak. Educ: Kent State Univ, A.B, 55; Cleveland-Marshall Law Sch, LL.B, 59; Ohio North. Univ; Delta Theta Phi. Polit. & Govt. Pos: Asst. law dir, Akron, Ohio, 61-64; Ohio State Rep, 95th Dist, 67- Mil. Serv: Entered as Pvt, Marine Corps, 51, released as Cpl, 53. Mem: Akron, Ohio and Am. Bar Asns; Univ. Club, Akron, Ohio. Akron Golf Championship. Rel: Roman Catholic. Legal Res: 1114 Linden Ave, Akron, Ohio 44310. Mailing Add: State Capitol, Columbus, Ohio 43215. (1967)

FIRESTONE, GEORGE D
Fla. State Rep.
b. New York, N.Y, 5/13/31; s. Benjamin Firestone and Sally Gollon F; m. 8/24/52 to Helene A. Eiserman. Polit. & Govt. Pos: Econ. Adv. Bd, Miami,

Fla, 60-62; chmn, Dade Co. Personnel Adv. Bd, 62-64; Fla. State Rep, 67- Mil. Serv: Entered as Pvt, Army, 48, released as Sgt 1/C, 52, after serv. in 519th Field Artil. Bn, ETO, 49-52. Mem: Past pres, Miami Jr. C. of C. and Northwest Miami Property Owners Asn; past v.pres, Dade Co. Coun. of Civic Orgns; past dir, Greater Miami Accident & Health Underwriters Asn; Kiwanis; South. Dade Dem. Club; Dade C. of C; Dade Young Dem; trustee, Miami Jaycee Capital Improv. Fund; Miami Progress Club. Rel: Jewish. Mailing Add: 2424 S. Dixie Highway, Miami, Fla. 33133.

FIRLEY, CARL FRANKLIN D
b. Riverside, Ill, 9/22/33; s. Carl F. Firley Sr. and Marthanna Johnson F; m. 11/19/66 to Sirkka Sinikka Hohtari; c. Sinikka Susan and Aulikki Angela (deceased). Educ: Lyons Twp. Jr. Col, 51-52; Ill. State Univ, B.S. in Educ, 57; Univ. Ill, grad work in Commun, 57-61. Polit. & Govt. Pos: Cand, U.S. Rep, 22nd Cong. Dist, Ill, 68. Bus. & Prof. Pos: Civics teacher, Edison Jr. High Sch, Champaign, Ill, 61-64; Fulbright grantee, Helsinki, Finland, 64-65; Am. Finnish loan grant, Tampere, 65-66; asst. dean of men, Univ. Ill, Champaign, 66-67, asst. dean of student progs. and serv. 67-69; dir. of housing, North. Mich. Univ, 69- Mil. Serv: Entered as Pvt, E-2, Army, 54, released as Pfc, 56, after serving in Fifth Div, Germany; Good Conduct Medal. Mem: Nat. Asn. Stud. Personnel Adminstr; Nat. Educ. Asn. Rel: Methodist. Mailing Add: 13 E. Nicolet Blvd, Marquette, Mich. 49855.

FISCHER, DONALD FREDERICK R
Chmn, Venanago Co. Rep. Cmt, Pa.
b. Oil City, Pa, 8/15/27; s. William F. Fischer and Susie Fox F; m. 9/7/57 to Elaine Winger; c. Curtis Lee, Tracey Lynn and Donald Christian. Educ: Franklin Bus. Sch; LaSalle Univ. Polit. & Govt. Pos: V.chmn, Venanago Co. Young Rep, Pa, 59-61, chmn, 61-63; chmn, Venanago Co. Rep. Cmt, 68-; co. prothonotary, Venanago Co, 68-; clerk courts, 68- Mil. Serv: Entered as Pvt, Army, 45, released as T-5, 47, after serv. in Ord. Corps, Pac. Theatre, 46-47. Mem: Lions. Rel: Lutheran. Mailing Add: 1135 Allegheny Ave, Oil City, Pa. 16301.

FISCHER, EDWARD MICKAEL D
Pres, Third Ward Dem. Cmt, N.Y.
b. Albany, N.Y, 11/26/04; s. Louis B. Fischer and Amie Brown F; m. 4/13/26 to Florence Barbra Maikowski; c. Joseph Edward and Helen Florence. Polit. & Govt. Pos: Mem, Third Ward Dem. Cmt, N.Y, 58-, pres, 63-; mem, Anti Poverty Cmn, 66-; alternate del, Dem. Nat. Conv, 68. Bus. & Prof. Pos: Foreman, Tobin Packing Co, Albany, N.Y. Mem: Holy Name Soc; mgr, Leading Semi Baseball Clubs. Rel: Roman Catholic. Mailing Add: 595 Warren St, Albany, N.Y. 12208. (1967)

FISCHER, GLENNON JOHN R
Chmn, Ste. Genevieve Co. Rep. Party, Mo.
b. Ste. Genevieve, Mo, 11/8/27; s. Charles Ludwig Fischer and Philamena Fritch F; m. 5/8/54 to Mary Magdalen Klein; c. Constance, Paulette, Lisa, Mary, Edward, Geraldine, Joseph, John and Rita. Educ: River Aux Vases Grade Sch, 8 years. Polit. & Govt. Pos: Chmn, Ste. Genevieve Co. Rep. Party, Mo, 68-; mem. sch. bd, Ste. Genevieve Dist. R-11, 69- Mil. Serv: Pvt, Army, 46, serv. in Antiaircraft, re-entered as Pvt, 50, released as Sgt, 52, after serv. in Combat Engrs. Mem: United Glass and Ceramic Workers of N.Am; AFL-CIO-CLC; Am. Legion. Rel: Catholic. Mailing Add: Star Route 1, Ste. Genevieve, Mo. 63670.

FISCHER, HAROLD O. R
Iowa State Rep.
b. Wellsburg, Iowa, 8/4/17; m. 7/30/42 to Jean Arthur; c. James, Nancy and Mary. Educ: Am. Inst. of Bus. Polit. & Govt. Pos: Iowa State Rep, currently. Bus. & Prof. Pos: Acct, Look Mag, Hardware Store Operator and salesman, A.Y. McDonald Mfg. Co, formerly; Ins. and Real Estate Broker, 52- Mil. Serv: Entered as Pvt, Army, 41, released as Capt, 45, after serv. in ETO. Mem: Am. Legion; Amvets; 40 et 8. Rel: Lutheran. Mailing Add: Wellsburg, Iowa 50680.

FISCHER, ROGER M. D
Chmn, Erie Co. Dem. Party, Pa.
b. Erie, Pa, 6/28/34; s. Sebastian Fischer and Josephine Daubler F; m. 6/13/59 to Gloria Ann Deegan; c. Julie M, Eric A. and Joan M. Educ: Pa. State Univ, B.A, 55; Univ. Pittsburgh Sch. Law, J.D, 58. Polit. & Govt. Pos: Legal aid attorney, Erie Co, Pa, 62 & 63, register of wills, 64-; mem, Young Dem. Pa, 64; del, Dem. Nat. Conv, 64 & 68; mem, Dem. State Policy Cmt, 68; chmn, Erie Co. Dem. Party, 68- Mil. Serv: Entered as Pvt, Army, 58, released as Cpl, 60, after serv. in First Army, Ft. Dix, N.J, 58-60. Mem: Phi Alpha Delta; Erie Co, Pa. and Am. Bar Asns; Am. Judicature Soc; Am. for Dem. Action; Am. Civil Liberties Union (state rep). Rel: Roman Catholic. Legal Res: 353 E. 41st St, Erie, Pa. 16504. Mailing Add: 332 E. Sixth St, Erie, Pa. 16507.

FISCHER, ROGER RAYMOND R
Pa. State Rep.
b. Washington, Pa, 6/1/41; s. Raymond Luther Fischer and Louise Gartley F; single. Educ: Washington & Jefferson Col, B.A, 63; Carnegie Inst. Tech, grad. work in nuclear eng; Delta Epsilon; Lambda Chi Alpha; Letterman's Club. Polit. & Govt. Pos: Sch. dir, Wash. Sch. Bd, Pa, 65-; mem, legis. coun. Pa. Sch. Bds. Asn, 66-67; Pa. State Rep, 66-, chmn, organized crime cmt, Pa. Crime Cmn. Region V Planning Coun. and mem, Joint State Govt. Task Force to Investigate State Prisons, Pa. State House of Rep. Bus. & Prof. Pos: Research engr, Jones & Laughlin Research, 66-67. Mil. Serv: Entered as Airman Basic, Air Force, released as 2nd Lt, 66, after Officers Training Sch; 2nd Lt, Air Force Res, 66- Mem: Am. Inst. Physics; Am. Nuclear Soc; U.S. Steel Workers Local 1141; bd. dirs, City Mission; bd. dirs, Wash. Co. Soc. Crippled Children and Adults; ROA; Washington & Jefferson Alumni Asn; Am. Legion; Jr. C. of C; YMCA. Red Cross Water Safety Instructor. Rel: Lutheran. Legal Res: 525 Duncan Ave, Washington, Pa. 15301. Mailing Add: Box 195, State House of Representatives, Harrisburg, Pa. 17101.

FISCHER, THELMA THOMAS R
Committeewoman, Fla. Rep. State Exec. Cmt.
b. Bellefonte, Pa, 7/5/15; d. Robert Leslie Thomas and Mary Miller T; m. 4/30/37 to Charles Robert Fischer; c. Linda L.(Mrs. J.L. Alderman), Rodney S, Karen J. and Barbara A. Educ: Bellefonte High Sch, Pa; Pierce Bus. Col, Phila, Pa. Polit. & Govt. Pos: Pres, Clearwater Women's Rep. Club, Fla, 55-56; del, Rep. Nat. Conv, 56, 60 & 64, mem, Rules Cmt, 64; state committeewoman for Pinellas Co. and v.chmn, Eighth Cong. Dist, Fla. Rep. State Exec. Cmt, 58-; pres, Fla. Fedn. of Rep. Women, 61-63; v.chmn, Pinellas Co. Rep. Exec. Cmt, 65- Bus. & Prof. Pos: Registered salesman, Fla. Real Estate Cmn, 52-; secy-treas, S.C. Land Co, Inc, 60-; mem, Clearwater-Largo Bd. of Realtors, 63-; treas, Curlew Homes, Inc, 66- Mem: Clearwater Woman's Club; Clearwater League of Women Voters; PTA. Rel: Methodist. Mailing Add: 112 Palmetto Lane, Largo, Fla. 33540.

FISCHER, VICTOR D
b. 5/5/24; s. Louie Fischer and Bertha F; m. to Gloria R; c. Ann, Greg and Joe. Educ: Univ. Wis, B.A, 46; Mass. Inst. Tech, M.C.P, 50; Harvard Univ, 61-62; Alpha Kappa Delta; Littaeur fel. Polit. & Govt. Pos: Town planner, Peterborough, N.H, 49; town planner, U.S. Dept. Interior, Alaska, 50-51; planning dir, City of Anchorage, 52-55; exec. dir, League of Alaskan cities, 52-56; del, Alaska Constitutional Conv, 55-56; Alaska State Rep, 57-58; asst. dir, Alaska State Housing Authority, Anchorage, 57-61; asst. admin, U.S. Housing & Home Finance Agency, Dept. Housing & Urban Develop, Wash, D.C, 62-66; del, Dem. Nat. Conv, 68. Bus. & Prof. Pos: Planning and develop. consult, local govt, State of Alaska, Off. Econ. Opportunity, commun. action agencies and various other orgn, 55-; prof. polit. sci. and dir. inst. soc, econ. and govt. research, Univ. Alaska, 66- Mil. Serv: Served, 42-46. Publ: Miscellaneous govt. and prfnl. publ. Mem: Am. Inst. Planners; Am. Soc. Planning Officials; Am. Soc. Pub. Admin; Am. Polit. Sci. Asn; Am. Asn. Adv. Sci. (pres, Alaska div); Am. Civil Liberties Union. Legal Res: 715 Chandalar Dr, College, Alaska 99701. Mailing Add: P.O. Box 5537, College, Alaska 99701.

FISCHER, W. CASPER Conservative
Minn. State Rep.
b. Marshall, Minn, 1929. Educ: Lynd, Minn. pub. schs. Polit. & Govt. Pos: Minn. State Rep, 62-; supvr, Lynd Twp. Bd. Bus. & Prof. Pos: Farmer, beef cattle feeder. Mailing Add: Route 2, Marshall, Minn. 56258. (1967)

FISCHER, WILLIAM RAYMOND D
Chmn, Wallingford Dem. Town Cmt, Conn.
b. Bound Brook, N.J. 8/31/26; s. Harold Clifford Fischer (deceased) and Florence Gatto F; m. 5/3/52 to Anna Mae Francolino; c. William Raymond, Jr, David Thomas, Marianne, Diana and Harold Clifford, II. Educ: Lyman Hall High Sch, 4 years. Polit. & Govt. Pos: Mem, Wallingford Dem. Town Cmt, Conn, 55-, chmn. exec. bd, 60, chmn, 64-; treas, West Side Dem. Club, 57; chmn, Bd. Assessors, Wallingford, 59. Bus. & Prof. Pos: Barber, Ralph Roudi's Barber Shop, 41-61; owner, Fischer's Barber Shop, 61- Mil. Serv: Entered as Pvt, Army, 44, released as T-4, 46, after serv. in Vienna Area Command Hq. Co, ETO, 45-46; Army Occup. Medal; Europe-Africa-Middle East Campaign Medal; World War II Victory Medal; Good Conduct Medal. Mem: Am. Legion; Holy Name Soc.(past pres); Commun. Leader Award, 67. Rel: Catholic; Trustee, Holy Trinity Church. Mailing Add: 31 Sunrise Circle, Wallingford, Conn. 06492.

FISH, HAMILTON, JR. R
U.S. Rep, N.Y.
b. Washington, D.C, 6/3/26; m. to Julia Mackenzie; c. Hamilton, III, Alexa, Nicholas S. and Peter L. Educ: Harvard, A.B, 49; N.Y. Univ. Sch. Law, LL.B, 57; John F. Kennedy Sch. Pub. Admin. Polit. & Govt. Pos: V.consul, Ireland, U.S. For. Serv; attorney, N.Y. Assembly Judiciary Cmt; dir, Civil Defense and former bd. mem. cmt. for econ. opportunity, Dutchess Co; U.S. Rep, N.Y, 68- Mil. Serv: Naval Res, 44-46. Mem: N.Y. State and Dutchess Co. Bar Asns; exec. cmt, Dutchess Co. Coun, Boy Scouts; bd. mgrs, Holiday Hills YMCA; agent, Harvard Class of 47; F&AM; Elks; Am. Legion; VFW; Dutchess, Ulster and Greene Co. Hist. Soc. Rel: Episcopal; mem. bd. of missions, Episcopal Diocese of N.Y. Legal Res: Millbrook, N.Y. 12545. Mailing Add: 1230 Longworth House Office Bldg, Washington, D.C. 20515.

FISH, ODY J. R
Rep. Nat. Committeeman, Wis.
b. Sauk Centre, Minn, 6/16/25. Polit. & Govt. Pos: Rep. Nat. Committeeman, Wis, state chmn. Wis. Rep. Party and chmn, Midwest and Nat. Rep. State Chmn. Asns, currently; del, Rep. Nat. Conv, 68. Bus. & Prof. Pos: Pres, Pal-O-Pak Insulation Co, Inc, Hartland, Wis. and Woodland Mfg. Co; v.pres, Pal-O-Pak Mfg. Co, Ltd, Whitby, Ont. Mem: Rotary; Lions; Milwaukee Athletic Club; Waukesha YMCA. Legal Res: 323 Main St, Pewaukee, Wis. 53072. Mailing Add: 135 Cottonwood Ave, Hartland, Wis. 53029.

FISHBONE, WILLIAM M. R
Chmn, Bozrah Rep. Town Cmt, Conn.
b. Norwich, Conn, 6/20/25; s. Isadore Fishbone and Annie Zeigman F; m. 11/21/48 to Adele Dembrow; c. Neil, Marc, Eric, Cheryl and Anida. Educ: Norwich Free Acad; New York Tech. Inst, N.J. Polit. & Govt. Pos: Prosecutor, Bozrah Town Court, Conn, 55-61; Conn. State Rep, 61-63; Justice of the Peace, Fitchville, Conn, 65-67; chmn, Fitchville Rep. Town Cmt, 66-68; chmn, Bozrah Rep. Town Cmt, 68- Bus. & Prof. Pos: Owner and operator, Storm Master of Norwich Home Improv, 57-65; gen. mgr, Norwich Auto Sales, 65- Mil. Serv: Entered as Seaman, Coast Guard, 43, released as PO 1/C, 45; 2 Bronze Stars; Am. Theater, European Theater, Mediterranean Theater and Mid. East Theater Ribbons; Unit Citation. Rel: Jewish. Mailing Add: R.F.D. 1, Main St, Fitchville, Conn. 06334. (1967)

FISHER, ARNOLD R. R
Chmn, Madison Co. Rep. Cmt, N.Y.
b. Hamilton, N.Y, 10/31/23; s. Seymour A. Fisher and Flora Faulkner F.(deceased); m. 7/12/50 to Winona Brower; c. Daphne and Denise. Educ: Cornell Univ. Polit. & Govt. Pos: Former chmn, Sixth Judicial Dist. Young Rep. Clubs, N.Y; former pres, Madison Co. Young Rep. Club; mem, Madison Co. Rep. Cmt, 50-, chmn, 61-; Cmnr. of Jurors, Madison Co, 57-, Clerk, 58- Mem: Hamilton Cent. Sch. Adv. Cmt, 57; former exec. dir, Commun. Mem. Hosp. Jamboree; Commun. Hosp. Adv. Cmt. bd. dirs, State Univ. at Morrisville and N.Y. State Fair; former v.pres, N.Y. Cmnr. Jurors Asn; former pres, N.Y. Asn. Co. Clerks; chmn. bd. cmt. for new Madison Co. Farm & Home Center; dir, Madison Co. Farm & Home Coun; Madison Co. Farm Bur; 15-man state cmt. on reorgn. of Exten. Serv. in N.Y; Madison Co. 4-H Beef

Cattle Commodity Cmt; Elks; Hamilton Lodge F&AM; former secy. bd. dirs, Madison Co. Exten. Serv; past chmn. and mem. exec. cmt, Madison Co. 4-H; past chmn, Madison Co. Farm & Home Show; former mem. bd. dirs, Madison Co. Fair. Awarded N.Y. State 4-H Alumni Award in 59 and Dept. of State Distinguished Serv. Award, 65. Legal Res: Lebanon St, Hamilton, N.Y. 13346. Mailing Add: Box 57, Hamilton, N.Y. 13346.

FISHER, AUDREY HORN R
Mem. Exec. Cmt, Calif. Rep. State Cent. Cmt.
b. Waynesfield, Ohio; m. 7/13/29 to Robert Bradley Fisher. Educ: Henry Ford Hosp. Sch. Nursing, grad; Sch. Neuropsychiat. Nursing, Dibble Army Hosp, Calif. Polit. & Govt. Pos: Mem, Los Altos Rep. Women Federated, Calif, 17 years, pres, 54-55; mem. Santa Clara Co. Rep. Cent. Cmt, 55-65, treas, 2 years, v.chmn, 3½ years, chmn. precinct orgn, acting chmn, 60; mem, United Rep. Finance Cmt. Santa Clara Co, 5 years; mem. bd. dirs, Calif. Fedn. Rep. Women, 9 years, v.pres, 59-60 & 66-67, gen. chmn, biennial conv, 61 & 67, parlimentarian North. Div, 7 years; mem, Calif. Rep. State Cent. Cmt, 54-, mem. precinct cmt, mem. platform cmt, auth, Preamble to 58 and 60 State Rep. Platforms, mem. exec. cmt, currently; alternate del, Rep. Nat. Conv, 60; Rep. cand, Calif. State Assembly, 22nd Dist, 62; campaign coordinator, Co. Cent. Cmt, 62; mem. city coun, Los Altos, Calif, 64-, mayor protem, 66, mayor, 67-68; state chmn. women's activities, Spencer Williams for Attorney Gen, 66; del, Nat. Rep. Women's Conf, five times; del, Nat. Fedn. Rep. Women's Conv, 4 times; observer, legis. session and legis. cmt. hearings; mem, State Health Planning Coun; chmn, Environ. Health Cmt. Comprehensive Health Planning; mem. citizens cmt. to form El Camino Hosp. Dist; Los Altos precinct chmn, Hosp. Bond Elec. Bus. & Prof. Pos: Registered nurse, private duty, gen. hosp. and doctor's off, Mich, Ohio and Calif; secy-treas, West. Sales Co, 38- Mil. Serv: Army Nurse Corps, 45, 2nd Lt, Res, 46-49. Mem: Charter and life mem, El Camino Hosp. Auxiliary (auxiliary bd. dirs, 3 years); Quota Club Los Altos; League of Women Voters; Los Altos Chap. United Fund (bd. dirs. and allocations cmt); Am. Legion. Legal Res: 120 Hawthorne Ave, Los Altos, Calif, 94022. Mailing Add: P.O. Box 415, Los Altos, Calif. 94022.

FISHER, C. RAYMOND R
Iowa State Rep.
b. Grand Junction, Iowa, 7/13/07; m. 1929 to Eunice Rinker; c. Roger and Tom; seven grandchildren. Educ: Grand Junction High Sch. Polit. & Govt. Pos: Mem, Co. Youth Found. Bd, Iowa; mem, Soil Conserv. Serv; mem, Farm Home Admin; mem, Co. 4-H Cmt; mem, Gov. Cmn. on State and Local Govt; mem, Grand Junction Planning and Zoning Bd; Iowa State Rep, currently. Bus. & Prof. Pos: Farmer. Mem: Pres, Iowa Master Farmer Club; Farm Bur; Farm Bus. Mgt. Asn; Lions; Mason; Scottish Rite; Shrine. Master Farmer Award, 56. Rel: Presbyterian; Elder. Legal Res: 12th and Herron St, Grand Junction, Iowa 50107. Mailing Add: State Capitol, E. Tenth and Grand Ave, Des Moines, Iowa 50319. (1967)

FISHER, ED LAMONT D
b. Glen Richey, Pa, 9/26/16; both parents deceased; m. to Alberta G. Fye, wid. Educ: Wayne Univ, 2 years. Polit. & Govt. Pos: Precinct chmn, First Ward, Curwensville, Pa, 53-63; mem, Clearfield Co. Patronage Cmt, 58-62; chmn, Clearfield Co. Dem. Cmt, 63-68. Bus. & Prof. Pos: Owner, Fisher Restaurant, Curwensville, Pa. Mil. Serv: Entered as Pvt, Army Air Corps, 42, released as Sgt. Maj, 45, after serv. in 305th Air Base, China-Burma-India, 42-45. Mem: Charter mem. and past pres, Lions; VFW; Am. Legion; past comdr, Odd Fellows; Elks. Rel: Methodist. Legal Res: 502 Filbert St, Curwensville, Pa. 16833. Mailing Add: P.O. Box 205, Curwensville, Pa. 16833.

FISHER, ETHEL VIRGINIA R
Chmn, Clay Co. Rep. Cent. Cmt, Ind.
b. Brazil, Ind; d. William H. Hill and Emma Maria Young H; m. to Raymond C. Fisher, wid; c. Phyllis (Mrs. Melvin Francis). Educ: High Sch. and Bus. Col grad. Polit. & Govt. Pos: V.precinct committeeman, Rep. Cent. Cmt, Ind, 45-50; pres, Women's Rep. Club, 50-60; v.chmn, Clay Co. Rep. Cent. Cmt, 60-68, chmn, 68-; mgr, Brazil License Br. 17, Brazil, Clay Co, currently. Bus. & Prof. Pos: Buyer, Ideal Ladies' Dept. Store, Clay City, Ind, 56- Mem: Clay Co. Women's Rep. Club; Harrison Twp. Women's Rep. Club; Eastern Star; Women's Study Club Clay City; Women's Bus. Club Clay City; Brazilian Toastmistress Club of Brazil, Ind; Clay Co. Tuberc. Asn.(pres); Ind. State Bd. Tuberc. Asn; Clay Co. Ment. Health Asn.(bd. mem); Rel: Methodist; Organist, Teacher. Mailing Add: 604 Main St, Clay City, Ind. 47841.

FISHER, GEORGE L. R
Educ: Ind. Univ, B.S, M.S. Polit. & Govt. Pos: Ind. State Rep, 57-66. Bus. & Prof. Pos: Ins. salesman; farm operator; high sch. teacher, athletic coach, 26 years. Mem: Elks; Moose; Masons; Knights Templar; Shrine. West. Conf. wrestling champion, 25. Rel: Methodist. Mailing Add: R.R. 2, Leesburg, Ind. 46538. (1967)

FISHER, GERMAINE EDWARD D
b. New Derry, Pa, 8/6/13; s. John Edward Fisher and Mary Louise Ransil F; m. 1/8/37 to Adeline Canale; c. Joan (Mrs. Edward Mullin) and Edward. Educ: Pleasantville High Sch, N.J, grad, 30. Polit. & Govt. Pos: Head clerk, Dept. Pub. Works, Atlantic City, N.J, 61-68, supt. of streets, 68-; chmn, Atlantic Co. Bd. of Elec, 65-; alternate del, Dem. Nat. Conv, 68. Mem: Am. Pub. Works Asn; N.J. State Asn. of Co. Bd. of Elec; K. of C; Fourth Ward Regular Men's Dem. Club (secy, 8 years, v.pres, 4 years). Knight of the Year, 66; Award for Best K. of C. News Bul. in State, 5 consecutive years. Rel: Catholic. Mailing Add: 30 N. Montgomery Ave, Atlantic City, N.J. 08401.

FISHER, HUGO MARK D
b. San Diego, Calif, 1921; m. to Lucia Sloane F; c. Anne Marie and Girard. Educ: San Diego State Col; Balboa Univ, LL.B. Polit. & Govt. Pos: Mem, Calif. Dem. Coun; mem. exec. bd, Calif. Dem. State Cent. Cmt; mem, White House Conf. on Aging and Gov. Cmt. on Med. Aid and Care; del, Dem. Nat. Conv, 52 & 56; Calif. State Sen, 58-66; adminstr, Resources Agency, Calif, 63-66; Judge of Superior Court, 66- Bus. & Prof. Pos: Attorney-at-law. Mem: San Diego, Calif. and Am. Bar Asns; Am. Judicature Soc; Cabrillo Hist. Asn; San Diego Hist. Soc; Univ. Club, San Diego. Mailing Add: Courthouse, 220 W. Broadway, San Diego, Calif. 92101.

FISHER, JOEL MARSHALL R
Asst. to the Dep. Counsel to the President
b. Chicago, Ill, 6/24/35; s. Dr. Dan Fisher and Nell Kolvin F; single. Educ: Univ. South. Calif, A.B, 55; Univ. Calif, Berkeley, LL.B, 61, M.A, 62; Claremont Grad. Sch. and Univ. Center, Ph.D, 68; Pi Sigma Alpha; Blue Key; Delta Phi Epsilon; Phi Beta Kappa; Blackstonian; Phi Alpha Delta. Polit. & Govt. Pos: Pres, Trojan Young Rep, Univ. South. Calif, 57; mem. bd. dirs, Calif. Young Rep, 58 & 60-62; campaign dir, Rep. Cong. Campaigns, 60 & 66; pres, Calif. Young Rep. Col. Fedn, 61; fieldman, First and 12th Cong. Dists, 62; regional campaign dir, Keating for Senate Cmt, 64; orgn. dir. and acting exec. dir, Rep. Citizens Cmt. of U.S, 64-65; chmn, arts and sci, Calif. Rep. State Cent. Cmt, 68; dir, arts and sci. div, Rep. Nat. Cmt, 68-69; Asst. to the Dep. Counsel to the President, 69- Bus. & Prof. Pos: Dir. pub. rels, World Peace Through Law, Rhyne & Rhyne, 65; asst. prof. polit, Calif. State Col, Fullerton, 66- Mil. Serv: Entered as 2nd Lt, Army, 54, released as 1st Lt, 57, after serv. in Army Intel, Europe, 56-57. Publ: Citizens for X, Rep. Citizens Cmt, 64; 'Out of Power: GOP in America,' Swinton J, United Kingdom, fall 65; 'Political Public Relations: The Magic Makers?,' Reason, spring 66. Mem: Am. and West. Polit. Sci. Asns; Am. Soc. Int. Law; Am. Asn. for Adv. Slavic Studies; Town Hall Los Angeles; Commonwealth Club Calif; Asn. U.S. Army; South. Calif. Center for Educ. in Pub. Affairs, Inc; Chesapeake Found; Richard Ports Cong. Intern Fund; Spokane Club; George Town Club, Inc. Noble Found. grantee, Falk Fel, Am. Polit; Rep. Nat. Conv. Faculty Fel; Am. Polit. Sci. Asn. Cmt. Fel. Rel: Episcopal. Legal Res: 3410 N. Glenrose Ave, Altadena, Calif. 91001. Mailing Add: Apt. 905 S, 1600 S. Eads St, Arlington, Va. 22022.

FISHER, JOHN BROOKINS R
b. Ridgefield Park, N.J, 12/15/17; s. Henry C. Fisher and Jennie Mann F; m. 1940 to Frances Wilder; c. Marilyn (Mrs. J. B. Boynton). Educ: Harvard Univ, A.B, cum laude, 41; Phi Beta Kappa. Polit. & Govt. Pos: Admin. asst. to U.S. Sen. Saltonstall, Mass, 50-56, dir. reelection campaign, 54; former staff consult, Joint Sen. and House Rep. Conf, former counsel, Rep. Leadership of Cong, staff consult. to Joint Sen-House Rep. Leadership, 69- Bus. & Prof. Pos: Staff mem, Security-First Nat. Bank of Los Angeles, 34-37; teacher, 45-47; mgt. consult, Wash, D.C, 56-64; v.pres, Nat. Shawmut Bank of Boston. Mil. Serv: 1st Lt, Navy, 42-45; Order of Generosity, 1/C, Iran. Publ: Author of dramatic radio series, 'Great Fires of History' and 'Listen to This.' Mem: Dir. fund raising, Am. Unitarian Asn, 47-50; Abraham Lincoln Sesquicentennial Cmt; trustee, 4th Int. Cong. Persian Art and Archaeol; trustee, Mt. Holyoke Col, Pine Manor Jr. Col, Dana Hall Sch. and Ten Acre Country Day Sch; adv. coun, Suffolk Univ. Sch. of Bus. Admin; rep. of Mass. Metrop. Club to Algonquin Col, Union Col. and Harvard Univ. Mailing Add: 430 M St. S.W, Washington, D.C. 20024. (1967)

FISHER, JOHN J. R
Fla. State Sen.
b. Punxutawney, Pa, 9/17/23; s. Frederick W. Fisher and Edna Skelton F; m. to Marjorie Evans; c. Ellen, Jr, Margaret Nancy, John Jacob, III, Frederick Emil Novak, Prudence, Sara Ann, Elizabeth and Kurt Winslow Marshall. Educ: Princeton Univ, M.D, 57; Univ. Pittsburgh, M.D, 58. Polit. & Govt. Pos: Fla. State Sen, 67- Mil. Serv: Naval Air Corps, 42-43. Mem: Duval Co. Med. Soc; Am. Med. Asn; Fla. Obstetric-Gynecologic Soc; Am. Soc. for Study of Sterility; Am. Col. of Obstetricians and Gynecologists; Jacksonville Ob-Gyn Soc. Rel: Episcopal. Legal Res: 2359 Seminole Rd, Atlantic Beach, Fla. 32233. Mailing Add: Box 12, Atlantic Beach, Fla. 32233.

FISHER, JOSEPH LYMAN Independent
b. Pawtucket, R.I, 1/11/14; s. Howard C. Fisher and Caroline Nash F; m. to Margaret W. Educ: Bowdoin Col, B.S. in Econ, 35; Harvard Univ, Ph.D. (econ), 47; George Wash. Univ, M.A. in Educ, 51; hon. D.Sc, Bowdoin Col, 65, LL.D, Allegheny Col, 66; Phi Beta Kappa. Polit. & Govt. Pos: Pres. and mem. bd. of dirs, Metrop. Wash. Conf. Govt; mem, bd. trustees, United Planning Orgn, Wash; mem, Arlington Co. Bd, 63-, chmn, 65; chmn, Arlington Planning Cmn. Bus. & Prof. Pos: Pres, Resources for the Future, Inc; exec. officer, Coun. Econ. Advisers; planning technician, Nat. Resources Planning Bd. Mil. Serv: Entered Army, 43, released as T/Sgt, 46, after serv. in Pac. Publ: Resources in America's Future, Johns Hopkins Press, 63; World Prospects for Natural Resources, 64. Mem: Am. Econ. Asn; Am. Soc. for Pub. Admin; dir, Am. Forestry Asn. Rel: Unitarian; moderator and chmn. bd, Unitarian-Universalist Asn. Legal Res: 2608 24th St, North, Arlington, Va. 22207. Mailing Add: 1755 Massachusetts Ave. N.W, Washington, D.C. 20036.

FISHER, JOSEPHINE D
b. Baltimore, Md, 6/2/00; single. Educ: Bryn Mawr Col, A.B, 22, Ph.D, 32. Polit. & Govt. Pos: Retired research analyst, Nat. Security Agency; Vt. State Rep, 65-67. Mem: Strafford Hist. Soc; S. Strafford Ladies Aid; Justin Smith Morrill Found. Rel: Episcopal. Mailing Add: S. Strafford, Vt. 05072. (1967)

FISHER, LEE ELLIOTT R
Treas, S.Cent. Dist. Rep. Party, Alaska
b. Spokane, Wash, 5/6/27; s. Gail T. Fisher and Mildred Lee F; m. 7/20/56 to Phyllis Harrington; c. Scott Richard, Rodrick Gail, Todd Elliott and Lora Diane. Educ: Kinman Bus. Univ, B.C.S, 49. Polit. & Govt. Pos: Mem, Hickel for Gov. Action Cmt, Alaska, 66-67; treas, S.Cent. Dist. Rep. Party, 67-; alternate del, Rep. Nat. Conv, 68. Bus. & Prof. Pos: Owner, Lee E. Fisher, CPA, 64- Mil. Serv: Entered as A/S, Navy Air Corps, 44, released as Aviation Radioman 3/C, 46 after serv. in PBM Mariner Squadrons, Atlantic Seaboard and Caribbean, 45-46. Mem: Alaska State Soc. of CPA; Kiwanis (chmn, Pac. Northwest Dist, 63); Elks; Moose. IDY Award, Kinman Bus. Univ, 47; Outstanding State Chmn. Award, Wash. State Jaycees, 53; Fish Award for 17 pound 6 ounce Rainbow Trout, Sports Afield and Field and Stream Trophy (1968 State Record). Rel: Episcopal; Licensed lay minister and treas, All Saint's Church, Anchorage. Mailing Add: 2609 Spenard Rd, Anchorage, Alaska 99503.

FISHER, LEO FRANK DFL
V.Chmn, Steele Co. Dem-Farmer-Labor Party, Minn.
b. Owatonna, Minn, 3/5/17; s. Henry Leo Fisher and Elizabeth Renchin F; single. Polit. & Govt. Pos: Precinct chmn, Dem-Farmer-Labor Party, Minn, 57-; del, Minn. Dem. State Conv, 57; del, Minn. Dem. State Cent. Cmt, 63;

v.chmn, Steele Co. Dem-Farmer-Labor Party, Minn, 65-; del, Dem. Nat. Conv, 68. Mil. Serv: Entered as Pvt, Army, 42, released as Pfc, 45, after serv. in 576 Ambulance Bn, ETO, 44-45; Seven Major Campaign Ribbons. Mem: VFW; Am. Legion; Int. Brotherhood of Carpenters and Joiners Am. Rel: Catholic. Mailing Add: 317 N. Elm St, Owatonna, Minn. 55060.

FISHER, M. BYRON R
Utah State Rep.
b. Honolulu, Hawaii, 12/5/36; s. Milton B. Fisher and Louise Larsen F; m. 6/9/60 to Joan Peterson; c. Debra Joan, Michael Byron and Janae. Educ: Brigham Young Univ, B.A, 61; George Wash. Univ, J.D, 64. Polit. & Govt. Pos: Utah State Rep, 67-; mem, Utah Legis. Coun, 69- Mem: Salt Lake Co. and Am. Bar Asns; Utah State Bar; Brigham Young Univ. Cougar Club; Kiwanis. Rel: Latter-day Saint. Mailing Add: 1264 E. 3700 S, Salt Lake City, Utah 84106.

FISHER, NORRIS D
Chmn, Real Co. Dem. Cmt, Tex.
b. Barksdale, Tex, 12/29/25; s. Jack Emesly Fisher and Mabel Belle Howard F; m. 6/6/47 to JoAnn Brice; c. Clinton Norris and Lisa Lynette. Educ: High Sch. Polit. & Govt. Pos: Chmn, Real Co. Dem. Cmt, Tex, 60- Bus. & Prof. Pos: Mgr, Local Grocery Store, 48-54; owner, Leakey Drug Store, 54- Mil. Serv: Entered as A/S, Navy, 44, released as Coxswain, 46, after serv. in Amphibious Forces in S. Pac; Saipan and Guam Invasion Ribbons. Mem: Pres, Leakey Sch. Bd. Trustees, 8 years; mem. bd, Frio Canyon C. of C. Rel: Protestant. Mailing Add: P.O. Box 255, Leakey, Tex. 78873. (1967)

FISHER, O. CLARK D
U.S. Rep, Tex.
b. Junction, Tex, 11/22/03; s. Jobe B. Fisher and Rhoda Clark F; m. 9/12/27 to Marian DeWalsh; c. Rhoda. Educ: Univ. Tex; Baylor Univ, LL.B, 29. Polit. & Govt. Pos: Co. Attorney, Tom Green Co, Tex, 31-35; Tex. State Rep, 35-37; Dist. Attorney, 51st Judicial Dist, Tex, 37-43; U.S. Rep, Tex, 42- Bus. & Prof. Pos: Attorney. Publ: It Occurred in Kimble, 37. Mem: Mason; K. of P; Eastern Star; Rotary. Legal Res: San Angelo, Tex. 76901. Mailing Add: U.S. House Office Bldg, Washington, D.C. 20515. (1967)

FISHER, PRISCILLA MARY EVELYNN R
Mem, Calif. Rep. State Cent. Cmt.
b. Detroit, Mich, 7/29/18; s. H. William Grane and Mary Evelynn Christian G; m. 8/26/50 to Lloyd Bennington Fisher; c. Charles James, Jonathan Edward and Lawrence William. Educ: Pasadena Jr. Col, A.A; Sawyer Univ. of Commerce, 1 year. Polit. & Govt. Pos: First v.pres, Highland Park Rep. Women, 65 & 66, pres, 67 & 68, parliamentarian, 69; 29th Cong. dist. chmn, Los Angeles Fedn. of Rep. Women, 69-; mem, Calif. Rep. State Cent. Cmt, 69- Mil. Serv: Entered as Pvt, WAC, 43, released as S/Sgt, 46, after serv. in Sta. Hosp, Ft. Des Moines, Iowa, Seventh Serv. Command; WAAC Serv, Good Conduct, Am. Campaign and World War II Victory Medals. Publ: Bul. for three orgn. Mem: Am. Legion Press Asn; Am. Legion; Women's Past Comdr. Club of Calif; 20/4 Echelon No. 1, Nat. Honor Soc. of Women Legionnaires; Am. Legion Auxiliary; Nat. Cong. of Parents and Teachers. Serv. Award Plaque for Publicity and Membership Chairmanships, Blade & Edge Club of Pasadena; Medals of Merit, Bronze Membership for Post Comdr. and Gold for Dist. Child Welfare Chairmanship, Dept. of Calif. Am. Legion. Rel: Protestant. Mailing Add: 862 Elyria Dr, Los Angeles, Calif. 90065.

FISHER, RALPH E. R
Ohio State Rep.
b. Wooster, Ohio, 12/10/02; s. George A. Fisher and Katharine H. Rockey F; m. 9/5/31 to Deltha Shook; c. John R. and Elizabeth K. (Mrs. John T. Miller). Educ: Ohio State Univ, B.Sc. Commerce, 26; Kappa Kappa Psi; Delta Sigma Phi. Polit. & Govt. Pos: Councilman-at-lg, 34-40; mayor, Wooster, Ohio, 40-48; Ohio State Rep, 49- Bus. & Prof. Pos: Owner, Fisher Monuments; dir. & v.pres, Wayne Savings & Loan Co, 42-; dir, Fiedelity Nat. Life Ins. Co. Mem: Mason (32°); Grand Lodge of Ohio F&Am (dist. dep. Grand Master); Lions; Ohio Farm Bur; Odd Fellows. Rel: Methodist. Mailing Add: 1558 Bellevue Dr, Wooster, Ohio 44691.

FISHER, RICHARD ASHLEY D
b. Covington, Tenn, 5/4/38; s. Ferd Rodgers Fisher, Jr. (deceased) and Jeanette Foust F; m. 3/31/61 to Karen Parker; c. Ralph Kevin and Kerri Frances. Educ: Southwest. Col, 56-58; Univ. Tenn, 58-60, LL.B, 61, J.D, 63; Kappa Alpha Order; Phi Delta Phi. Polit. & Govt. Pos: Co-chmn, Univ. Tenn. Youth for Kennedy-Johnson, 59; del, Tenn. Constitutional Conv, 65; chmn, Bradley Co. Dem. Party, 67-68; Hon. Col. aide-de-camp, Gov. Buford Ellington, 67-69; alternate del-at-lg, Dem. Nat. Conv, 68. Mem: Bradley Co, Tenn. and Am. Bar Asns; Tenn. and Am. Trial Lawyers Asns; Lions; Elks. Rel: Methodist. Legal Res: 2322 Georgetown Pike N.W, Cleveland, Tenn. 37311. Mailing Add: P.O. Box 1351, Cleveland, Tenn. 37311.

FISHER, WILFRED JOSEPH D
Mayor, Barre, Vt.
b. Barre, Vt, 10/2/19; s. Ernest Fisher and Amelia Therrienne F; m. 8/3/41 to Evelyn Gochey; c. Pamela (Mrs. Robert Parro), David, Steven, Michele and Debra. Educ: Spaulding High Sch, 4 years. Polit. & Govt. Pos: V.chmn, Barre Dem. Party, Vt; committeeman, Washington Co. Dem. Party; alderman, Barre, Vt, 3 years, mem. recreation bd, 14 years and mayor, 68-; mem, Vt. Dem. State Cmt. Bus. & Prof. Pos: Mem. staff, Granite Mem. Mfr, 46- Mil. Serv: Army, 44-46, S/Sgt, with serv. in Engr. Heavy Shop Co, ETO. Mem: Elks; Kiwanis; Am. Legion; VFW; Can. Club; Youth Sports Asn; C. of C. Rel: Catholic. Mailing Add: 12 Edgewood Ave, Barre, Vt. 05641.

FISHMAN, ALVIN D
State Chmn, New Dem. Coalition of Mich.
b. Los Angeles, Calif, 11/18/27; s. Harry C. Fishman and Bertha Berkenfeld F; m. 3/23/51 to Margaret Radulovich; c. Marcia and Daniel. Educ: N.Y. Univ, 1 year; Univ. Mich, 2 years; Wayne State Univ, B.S. Polit. & Govt. Pos: Precinct del, Detroit Dem. Party, Mich, 55-; v.chmn, Mich. Conf. of Concerned Dem, 65-67; state chmn, New Dem. Coalition of Mich, 67-; alternate del, Dem. Nat. Conv, 68; v.chmn, First Dist. Dem. Party Orgn, currently. Mailing Add: 18995 Warrington, Detroit, Mich. 48221.

FISHMAN, SAMUEL WILLIAM D
b. Vergennes, Vt, 4/15/13; m. to Betty Seder; c. Two. Educ: Univ. of Vt; Boston Univ. Law Sch. Polit. & Govt. Pos: Judge, Addison Munic. Court, Vt, 14 years; alderman, Vergennes, 6 years; Vt. State Rep, 57-63; Vt. State Sen, 63-66; del, Dem. Nat. Conv, 68. Bus. & Prof. Pos: Lawyer; trustee, Univ. of Vt. and DeGoesbriand Mem. Hosp. Mem: V.pres, Vt. Asn. for the Crippled; past pres, Vt. Munic. Judges Asn; past pres, Vergennes Rotary; F&AM; Scottish Rite; Mason (32°); past pres, Elbon Shrine Club. Mailing Add: 60 Green St, Vergennes, Vt. 05491. (1967)

FITE, RANKIN D
Speaker, Ala. House of Reps.
b. Montgomery, Ala, 9/1/16; s. Ernest Baxter Fite and Minnie Pierce F; m. 7/5/41 to Ruby Morris; c. Ernest Adams. Educ: Starke Univ; Univ. of Ala, LL.B, 39. Polit. & Govt. Pos: Ala. State Sen, 47-51; Ala. State Rep, 51-, speaker, Ala. House of Rep, 55-59, 67-, speaker pro tempore, 63-67. Bus. & Prof. Pos: Attorney, Fite and Fite. Mil. Serv: U.S. Army, 41-46, released as 1st Lt. Mem: Civitan Club. Rel: Methodist. Mailing Add: Box 157, Hamilton, Ala. 35570.

FITTERER, B.P. D
Chmn, Lebanon Co. Dem. Party, Pa.
b. Lebanon, Pa, 4/20/22; s. Paul A. Fitterer and Mary J. F; div; c. Judith Ann and Dennis James. Educ: Lebanon Valley Coll, 2 years; Palmer Col. Chiropractic. Polit. & Govt. Pos: Mem. exec. cmt, Lebanon Co. Dem. Party, Pa, 60-, chmn, 65- Mil. Serv: Entered Army, 42, released 45, after serving in ETO; Bronze Star. Mem: Elks; Mason; Am. Legion. Rel: Protestant. Legal Res: 114 E. Maple St, Palmyra, Pa. 17078. Mailing Add: 112 E. Maple St, Palmyra, Pa. 17078.

FITZGERALD, ELAINE ELIZABETH D
b. Barron Co, Wis, 10/3/29; d. Gerald FitzGerald and Lora Fay Cornwall F; single. Educ: Ind. Cent. Col, 47-50; Univ. Wis, LL.B, 53; Asn. Law Sch. Women. Polit. Pos: V.Chmn, 3rd Dist, Wis, 65-66; alternate del, Dem. Nat. Conv, 64. Govt. Pos: Dist. Attorney, Richland Co, Wis, 59-62. Bus. & Prof. Pos: Secy, Richland Co. Bar Asn, 59-60. Rel: Evangelical. Legal Res: Village of Boaz, Wis. 53581. Mailing Add: R. 1, Richland Center, Wis. 53581. (1967)

FITZGERALD, GEORGE S. D
Mich. State Sen.
b. Troy, N.Y, 12/26/01; married; c. William B. Educ: Holy Cross Col, Worcester, Mass, B.A; Univ. Detroit, LL.B; Gamma Eta Gamma. Polit. & Govt. Pos: Dem. Nat. Committeeman; former mem, Mich. Soc. Welfare Cmt; Asst. Prosecuting Attorney, Wayne Co, Mich; Asst. U.S. Dist. Attorney; legal adv, U.S. Customs; Mich. State Sen, 64- Bus. & Prof. Pos: Lawyer; former instr, Univ. Detroit Law Sch. Mem: Del, Coun. of Soc.Agencies and Am. Asn. of Soc. Workers; Detroit, Mich, Am. and Fed. Bar Asns; Am. Judicature Soc; Detroit Yacht Club; N.Y. Athletic Club; Mich. Aeronaut. and Space Club; K. of C; Elks; Holy Cross Varsity Club; Nat. Law Club; Detroit Press Club; Bayview Yacht Club; C. of C; Knights of Equity; Nat. Welfare and Pension Fund Conf. Rel: Roman Catholic. Mailing Add: 1334 Buckingham, Grosse Pointe, Mich. 48230. (1967)

FITZGERALD, JOHN J. D
m. to Margaret Fenton; c. Sheila Ellen, John Jr, Maureen Ann (Mrs. Miguel Hnatow). Polit. & Govt. Pos: Former Mass. State Rep, 65-66. Mil. Serv: WWII, Korean vet; Commanding off, Marine Corps, VTU 1-18. Mem: Liberty Legion, Post 430; Van Horn Parents Asn; Home City K. of C; Holy Name Soc. of Sacred Heart Church; Laymen's Retreat League; Sportsmen's Club; Holy Cross Alumni and Varsity Clubs of Springfield. Rel: Catholic. Mailing Add: 16 Cornwall St, Springfield, Mass. 01104. (1967)

FITZGERALD, JOHN JAMES D
b. Holyoke, Mass, 10/9/41; s. George Michael Fitzgerald and Bridget Patricia Buckley; single. Educ: Univ. Mass, Amherst, B.A. in Polit. Sci, 63; Univ. Mass, Amherst Grad. Sch, currently; Young Dem. Polit. & Govt. Pos: Campaign worker and organizer, Dem. party; del, Dem. Nat. Conv, 68. Mil. Serv: Entered as Pvt. E-1, Army, 64, released as Capt O-3, 68, after serv. in Fourth Bn, Ninth Inf, 25th Inf. Div, S.Vietnam, 66; Bronze Star for Valor; Purple Heart; Nat. Defense Medal; Republic of Vietnam Defense Medal. Mem: Am. Civil Liberties Union; Mass. PAX; Citizens for Participation Politics; Am. for Dem. Action; New England and N.E. Polit. Sci. Asns; Amherst Valley Peace Cent; New Eng. Polit. Sci. Asn; Am. Polit. Sci. Asn; ROA. Mailing Add: 40 Gates St, Holyoke, Mass. 01040.

FITZGERALD, PATRICK F. D
b. Wakefield, Mass, 22. Educ: Boston Univ. Polit. & Govt. Pos: Mem, Town Meeting. Bus. & Prof. Pos: Real Estate; ins. broker. Mem: Past exalted ruler, trustee, Quincy Elks. Mailing Add: 47 Winter St, Braintree, Mass. 02184. (1967)

FITZGERALD, PAULINE McNAMARA D
b. Boston, Mass, 6/29/19; d. Joseph Leo McNamara and Marguerite Coleman M; m. 10/20/45 to Edward Joseph Fitzgerald; c. Rosemary and Joan Elizabeth. Educ: Trinity Col, Wash, D.C, A.B, 40; T Pin Award. Polit. & Govt. Pos: Dir. womens activities, teas and receptions for John F. Kennedy Senate Campaign, 52 and receptions for John F. Kennedy, Wis. and W.Va. Primaries, 60; scheduled activities of women in Kennedy family throughout country, John F. Kennedy Presidential Campaign, 60; scheduled activities of women in Kennedy family and organized receptions, Robert F. Kennedy Senate Campaign, N.Y, 64 and Robert F. Kennedy Presidential Campaign, Ind. and Calif, 68; del, Dem. Nat. Conv, 68. Bus. & Prof. Pos: Mem, Nat. Adv. Coun. Health Research Resources, 63-64 and Nat. Adv. Coun. Health Research Facilities, 64-68; mem, Pres. Adv. Bd, Emmanuel Col, Boston, Mass, 66-, dir. of pub. info, 67- Rel: Roman Catholic. Mailing Add: 38 Barbara Rd, Needham, Mass. 02192.

FITZGERALD, ROBERT CLAYTON D
Va. State Sen.
b. Alexandria, Va. 9/22/21; s. M.D. Fitzgerald and Margaret L. DeMasters F; 2nd m. 4/12/69 to Nancy Jean Reiff; c. Sandra Leigh and Cheryl Coleen.

Educ: Univ. Va. B.A, and LL.B. Polit. & Govt. Pos: Co. Court Judge, Fairfax Co, Va, 51-55; commonwealth's attorney, 55-63; Va. State Sen, 64-; mem, Dulles Int. Airport Develop. Cmn, 68 and Va. Airport Authority, 69, Va. State Senate. Bus. & Prof. Pos: Lawyer. Mil. Serv: Entered as Pvt, Marine Corps, 42, released as Capt, 46, after serv. in Second Marine Div, Pac, 43-45; Capt, Res, 46-57; Presidential Unit Citation. Mem: Fairfax Co. and Va. Bar Asns; Lions; Delta Theta Phi. Rel: Baptist. Mailing Add: Suite 510, The Mosby, 10560 Main St, Fairfax, Va. 22030.

FITZGERALD, WILLIAM B. D
Mich. State Rep.
b. Troy, N.Y, 2/3/14; married; c. William B, Jr. and Timothy E. Educ: Univ. Detroit; Detroit Col. of Law; completed the Wayne State Univ. Exec. Develop. Course sponsored by Detroit Civil Serv. Cmn; Delta Theta Phi. Polit. & Govt. Pos: Mich. State Rep, 64-; precinct del. Bus. & Prof. Pos: Licensed real estate salesman; former legal investr, Detroit Dept. of St. Rwy. Mem: Hon. mem, Nat. Rwy. Hist. Soc; Local 214, AFSCME AFL-CIO. Rel: Catholic. Mailing Add: 5550 Courville, Detroit, Mich. 48224. (1967)

FITZPATRICK, DUROSS R
b. Macon, Ga, 10/19/34; s. Mark William Fitzpatrick and Jane Duross F; m. 3/17/63 to Beverly Jean O'Connor. Educ: Univ. of the S, 53-54; Univ. Ga, B.S. in Forestry, 61 and LL.B, 66; Sigma Alpha Epsilon. Polit. & Govt. Pos: Gen. counsel, Bleckley Co. Rep. Party, Ga, 69; legal aide to minority leader, Ga. House of Rep, 69- Bus. & Prof. Pos: Assoc. attorney, J. Sewell Elliott, Attorney-at-Law, Macon, Ga, 66-67; attorney-at-law, Cochran, 67- Mil. Serv: Entered as Pvt, Marines, 54, released as Sgt, 57, after serv. in Marine Transport Squadron 252, U.S. Mem: State Bar of Ga; Am. Bar Asn; Rotary. Rel: Episcopal. Legal Res: R.F.D. 1, Jeffersonville, Ga. 31044. Mailing Add: P.O. Box 43, Cochran, Ga. 31014.

FITZPATRICK, JEROME M. D
b. Pittsford, Vt, 9/8/93; married; c. 3 sons, 4 daughters. Educ: Univ. Vt. Polit. & Govt. Pos: Town auditor, Pittsford, Vt; Vt. State Rep, 57-59 & 63-67. Bus. & Prof. Pos: Sch. adminstr, retired. Mil. Serv: Air Force, 18-19. Rel: Catholic. Mailing Add: Pittsford, Vt. 05763. (1967)

FITZPATRICK, JOHN J. D
b. St. Louis, Mo, 3/20/10; m. 1939 to Oliva Perez; c. Margaret, Katherine, John, Thomas. Educ: Holy Redeemer High Sch; spec. courses in govt. cost acct. at Wayne State Univ. Polit. & Govt. Pos: Mich. State Rep, 48-66. Bus: Acct. Mem: K. of Equity; Gaelic League; Irish Am. Club; Old Corktown Club; 15th Cong. Dist. Club. Rel: Catholic. Mailing Add: 5844 Baker, Detroit, Mich. 48209. (1967)

FITZPATRICK, MARJORIE GRACE 'MARGEE' R
Rep. Nat. Committeewoman, Alaska
b. St. John, N.B, Can, 2/16/18; d. Archie Albin and Margaret Tiplady A; m. 12/13/47 to Dr. James Joseph Fitzpatrick; c. Jeanne K. (Mrs. Bishop). Educ: Kings Co. Hosp. Sch. of Nursing, Brooklyn, N.Y, R.N, 39. Polit. & Govt. Pos: Precinct committeewoman, Alaska Rep. Party, 61-, dist. committeewoman, 63-68; del, Rep. Nat. Conv, 68; Rep. nat. committeewoman, Alaska, 68-; mem, Cmn. on the Status of Women, 68- Bus. & Prof. Pos: Registered nurse, Kings Co. Hosp, Brooklyn, N.Y, 39-41, St. Alphonsus Hosp, Boise, Idaho, 47-52 and various physicians' off, 52-57. Mil. Serv: Entered as 2nd Lt, Army, 41, released as 1st Lt, 46, after serv. in Army Nurse Corps, 204th Gen. Hosp, Pac. Theatre, 42-45. Mem: Alaska and Anchorage Med. Auxiliaries; Nat. Asn. of Parliamentarians. Rel: Episcopal. Legal Res: 2407 Cottonwood, Anchorage, Alaska 99504. Mailing Add: Box 1712, Anchorage, Alaska 99501.

FITZPATRICK, MARK WILLIAM R
Chmn, Twiggs Co. Rep. Party, Ga.
b. Twiggs Co, Ga, 12/12/89; s. William Hart Fitzpatrick and Thulia Massey F; m. 6/22/33 to Jane Lippincott Duross, wid; c. Duross, Jane Lippincott (Mrs. Turner), Loxley Childs and Barry Kelly. Educ: Gordon Inst; Univ. Ga, B.S.C.E, cum laude; Sr. Round Table; Gridiron Iron Secret Soc; Sigma Chi. Polit. & Govt. Pos: Research engr. and asst. div. engr, Ga. Hwy. Dept, 34-46; tax cmnr, Twiggs Co, 49-60; Ga. State Sen, 61-62; chmn, Twiggs Co. Rep. Party, 64- Bus. & Prof. Pos: Civil engr, South. Rwy, 13-18; gen. mgr. of saw mill and bookkeeper for farm, I. & M.W. Fitzpatrick, 19-34. Mil. Serv: Entered as Acting 1st Sgt, Army, 18, released as 1st Sgt, 19, after serv. with 20th Engrs, France; Citation for Exceptionally Meritorious and Conspicuous Servs. at Cambrai, France. Mem: Am. Legion; Ga. Farm Bur; Idle Hour Golf and Country Club, Macon, Ga. Rel: Baptist. Mailing Add: Tarversville, Jeffersonville, Ga. 31044.

FITZPATRICK, ROSALYN M. R
Mem, Calif. Rep. State Cent. Cmt.
b. Marshfield, Wis, 4/19/11; d. Antone J. Meidl and Mary C. Streveler M; m. to Edward J. Fitzpatrick, wid; c. Karalyn (Mrs. James D. Belcher). Educ: San Mateo Col, 33-34. Polit. & Govt. Pos: Mem, Pajaro Valley Fedn. of Rep. Women, Watsonville, Calif, 58-; mem, Calif. Rep. State Cent. Cmt, 58-; co. chmn. for Calif. State Assemblyman Alan G. Patte, Monterey Co, Calif, for Calif. Sen. George Murphy, 64 and for Robert E. Finch for Lt. Gov, 66. Bus. & Prof. Pos: Secy. to Henry J. Mello, chmn, Bd. of Supvr, Santa Cruz Co, Calif, 63-69. Outstanding citizen award, Pajaro Valley Fedn. of Rep. Women. Rel: Catholic. Legal Res: 21 Secondo Way, Watsonville, Calif. 95076. Mailing Add: P.O. Box 47, Watsonville, Calif. 95076.

FITZSIMONS, RICHARD W. Conservative
Minn. State Rep.
b. Argyle, Minn, 1/19/22; m. to Janice; c. Mark Patrick and Lori Anne. Polit. & Govt. Pos: Minn. State Rep, 52- Bus. & Prof. Pos: Grain farmer. Mailing Add: R.D. 1, Argyle, Minn. 56713. (1967)

FIX, GEORGE ARTHUR D
Chmn, Yuma Co. Dem. Cent. Cmt, Colo.
b. Wray, Colo, 11/28/25; s. George Fix and Julia Shivley F; m. 11/2/47 to Betty Jeanne Reed (deceased) and 6/12/59 to Cleora Louvetta Welp; c. Vikki Lorraine, Douglas Lane, Margaret Grace, Amy Collen, Curtis Dale, Dixie Lynette, James Albert, Nancy Elaine and Janette Lynn Witte. Educ: Colo. A&M Col, 47. Polit. & Govt. Pos: Dem. Committeeman, McGee Precinct, Colo, 53-58; capt, cmnr. dist. two, 55-59; treas, Yuma Co, 59-; mem, exec. cmt, Yuma Co. Dem. Cent. Cmt, 60-66 and chmn, 69-; pres, Yuma Co. Young Dem, 66. Mil. Serv: Entered as Pvt, Army Air Corps, 43, released as S/Sgt, 46, after serving in 19th Air Force 21st Bomber Command, Pac. Theater, 45-46; Good Conduct Medal; Am. Serv. Medal, Asiatic Pac. Serv. Medal; Victory Medal; Presidential Unit Citation with Oak Leaf Cluster; Aerial Gunnar Badge. Mem: Colo. Asn. of Co. Treasurers (mem. legis. cmt, 63-68, pres, 66-67); Am. Title Asn; Colo. Land Title Asn; Lions; Am. Legion; VFW; Lutheran Laymen's League. Rel: Lutheran. Mailing Add: 1030 W. Seventh St, Wray, Colo. 80758.

FIX, JACOB JOHN R
Chmn, Faulk Co. Rep. Cmt, S.Dak.
b. Onaka, S.Dak, 11/24/11; s. Jacob Fix and Catherine Gisi F; m. 10/18/38 to Rose Mary Deis; c. Roger, Larry, Cyril, Cynthia and Sylvan. Polit. & Govt. Pos: Chmn, Faulk Co. Rep. Cmt, S.Dak, 65- Bus. & Prof. Pos: Agent, Standard Oil Co, 41-43; grain elevator operator, 44-59; farmer and livestock feeder. Mil. Serv: Pvt, Army, 43. Mem: Foresters; K. of C; Am. Legion. Rel: Catholic. Mailing Add: Onaka, S.Dak. 57466. (1967)

FLACK, HAROLD E. R
b. Plymouth, Pa, 12/30/99; s. Rev. Dr. Ebenezer Flack and Sarah Hutcheson F; m. to Elizabeth Dissinger; c. Charles. Educ: Scranton High Sch. Polit. & Govt. Pos: Pa. State Sen, 54-67; Pa. State Rep, 42-54. Bus. & Prof. Pos: Gen. ins. agent; bd. of dirs, Wyo. Valley Hosp. Mem: Past pres, Kiwanis; C. of C; Masons; Elks; Moose; Odd Fellows; Westmoreland Club. Mailing Add: Room 209, 15 S. Franklin St, Wilkes-Barre, Pa. 18701. (1967)

FLADAGER, MILTON WALLACE R
Chmn, Daniels Co. Cent. Cmt, Mont.
b. Scobey, Mont, 9/26/18; s. Wilhelm Paul Fladager and Marie Lavanger F; m. 6/29/45 to Lois Loraine Lowthian; c. Loren Stanley, Brian Milton, Warren Irwin, Wallace Archie, Kathleen Georgetta, Willard Keven and Armand Lee. Educ: Peerless High Sch. Polit. & Govt. Pos: Dep. assessor, Daniels Co, Mont, 45-46; Crop Ins. Adjuster, Fed. Crop Ins. Corp, 46-55; mem, Agr. Soil Conserv. Cmt, Daniels Co, 53; Mont. State Rep, Daniels Co, 59-60; mem, State Land Use Cmt, 61-64; chmn, Daniels Co. Rep. Cent. Cmt, Mont, 62-; State Committeeman, Mont. Rep. Party, 69- Mil. Serv: Entered as Cadet, Air Force, 42, released as Cpl, 44 after serv. as Radio Operator in 9th Air Force. Mem: Chmn, N.E. Mont. Div, Designing Educ. for Future Cmt; chmn, Bd. of Educ, 48-56; Am. Legion; Farm Bur; Farmers Union; Mason; AF&AM. Rel: Lutheran. Mailing Add: Peerless, Mont. 59253.

FLADMO, EINER MARTIN D
b. Terry, Mont, 6/28/21; s. Jacob Fladmo and Ragnhild Rusten F; m. 7/15/42 to Mildred Maxine Biehl; c. Robert Duane. Educ: Billings Polytech; LaSalle Exten. Univ. Polit. & Govt. Pos: Secy-treas, Richland Co. Dem. Cent. Cmt, Mont, 58-60, former chmn. Bus. & Prof. Pos: Gen. clerk, North. Pac. Rwy. Co, 42, cashier, 47. Mem: Moose. Rel: Lutheran. Mailing Add: 417 Third St. S.E, Sidney, Mont. 59270. (1967)

FLAGG, MORGAN D
Chmn, Monterey Co. Dem. Cent. Cmt, Calif.
b. Oakland, Calif, 3/13/26; s. A.J. Flagg and Mabel Yeagel F; m. 12/2/50 to Claire E. Barker; c. Lawrence, Brian Edward, James Morgan, John Patrich, Janine Alane, Lori Ruth, Kerri Louise and Mary Claire. Educ: Fremont High Sch, Oakland, Calif, 40-43. Polit. & Govt. Pos: File clerk, Calif. State Senate, 47, 48 & 49; alternate del, Dem. Nat. Conv, 64; mem, Cmn. on Housing & Commun. Develop, State of Calif, 65, 66 & 67; chmn, Monterey Co. Dem. Cent. Cmt, 68- Bus. & Prof. Pos: Del, Home Builders Conf. of Calif, 64 & 65. Mil. Serv: Cadet, Army Air Corp, 44-45, serv. in O.L.T. Prog, Continental U.S. Mem: Commonwealth Club of San Francisco; Elks; Olympic Club. Rel: Christian. Legal Res: 1450 Manor Rd, Monterey, Calif. 93940. Mailing Add: P.O. Box 145, Pacific Grove, Calif. 93950.

FLAHERTY, CHARLES FRANCIS, JR. D
Mass. State Rep.
b. Boston, Mass, 10/13/38; s. Charles Francis Flaherty and Anna Coughlin F; m. 11/3/62 to Evelyn Ann Walsh; c. Charles Thomas, Timothy Richard, Maureen and Daniel Paul. Educ: Boston Col, B.S. in B.A, 60; Boston Col, Grad. Sch. of Arts and Sci, polit. sci, 67-68. Polit. & Govt. Pos: Mass. State Rep, 67- Bus. & Prof. Pos: Asst. dir. univ. research, Boston Col, 65- Mil. Serv: Entered as Ens, Navy, 60, released as Lt, 65, after serv. in USS Bearss (DD-654), Atlantic Fleet, 60-65; Lt, Naval Res, 65-; Naval and Armed Forces Expeditionary Medal; Nat. Defense Medal. Publ: 'ASW-Are We Missing the Boat?' U.S. Naval Inst. Proc, 2/66; 'Toward a Uniform State Building Code in Massachusetts,' The Bldg. Inspector, 6/67; 'Adopt a Tot-Lot,' Mag. of Cambridge, 7/68. Mem: Am. Acad. Polit. and Soc. Sci; Acad. Polit. Sci; Am. Polit. Sci Asn; Am. Soc. Pub. Admin; Nat. Coun. Univ. Research Adminstrs; Amvets; Am. Legion; VFW; K. of C; Holy Name Soc; Jr. C. of C. Freedoms Found. Award, 64 & 65. Rel: Catholic. Mailing Add: 14 Woodbridge St, Cambridge, Mass. 02140.

FLAHERTY, DANIEL T. D
Chmn, Third Cong. Dist, Dem. Party, Wis.
b. West Bend, Wis, 7/22/23; s. Raymond J. Flaherty and Hildegard Michels F; m. 5/29/47 to Lorraine J. Lousier; c. Daniel F, Maureen B, Ellen E. and Catherine J. Educ: Dartmouth Col, 43-44; Univ. of Wis, LL.B, 49. Polit. & Govt. Pos: V.chmn, La Crosse Co. Dem. Party, Wis, 58-62, mem, exec. cmt, 58-; mem, Gov. Cmt. on Constitution and Rev, 62-65; chmn, Third Cong. Dist, Dem. Party, 63-; mem, admin. cmt, Dem. Party, Wis, 63- Bus. & Prof. Pos: Partner, Johns Pappas & Flaherty Attorneys, 49- Mil. Serv: Entered as A/S, Naval Res, 43, released as Lt.(jg), 46, after serv. in Amphibian Forces, Pac. Theater. Mem: Am. Bar Asn; State Bar of Wis; La Crosse Co. Bar Asn; Am. Judicature Soc; K. of C; Elks; Gr. La Crosse C. of C; Kiwanis. Rel: Catholic. Legal Res: 1925 King St, La Crosse, Wis. 54601. Mailing Add: 616 Exchange Bldg, La Crosse, Wis. 54601. (1967)

FLAHERTY, DAVID THOMAS R
N.C. State Sen.
b. Boston, Mass, 12/9/28; s. Thomas Patrick Flaherty and Mabel Seely F; m. 12/7/52 to Nancy Ann Hamill; c. David T. Jr, Stephen Francis, Deborah Ann,

Jon Earl and Robert Emmett. Educ: Burdett Col; Boston Univ, B.S.B.A; Alpha Kappa Psi. Polit. & Govt. Pos: Former state chmn, nat. committeeman, nat. co-chmn. for campaigns, state v.chmn. and co-chmn N.C. Young Rep; precinct chmn. and co-chmn. Broyhill for Cong. Cmt; del, N. Atlantic Treaty Orgn, Youth Conf, Bonn, Germany, 63; N.C. State Sen, 68- Bus. & Prof. Pos: Advert. mgr, Broyhill Furniture Indust. Mil. Serv: Entered as Pvt, Army, 49, released as Sgt, 52, after serv. in Inf. Mem: Former dist. scout chmn, cubmaster and v.chmn. orgn and exten, Boy Scout Am; founder and first pres, Bunny Maynard Midget Football League; Optimist; little league baseball coach, past comdr, DAV. N.C. Outstanding Young Rep, 64; Scouter of the Year, 68; Silver Beaver in Scouting, 69; pres. Dist. Award, Boy Scouts Am, 69. Rel: Methodist. Mailing Add: 803 Hospital Ave, Lenoir, N.C. 28645.

FLAHERTY, LEO BERNARD, JR. D
Chmn, Vernon Dem. Party, Conn.
b. Rockville, Conn, 5/25/23; s. Leo B. Flaherty and Eileen Murphy F; m. 3/2/46 to Regina McMahon; c. Paul, Eileen, Timothy and Robert. Educ: Univ. of Conn, mech. eng, 49, law, 56; Pi Tau Sigma. Polit. & Govt. Pos: Pres, Young Dem. Club of Vernon, Conn, 47; v.pres, Young Dem. Club of Am, 48, state exec. chmn, 49-51, mem, Nat. Cmt, 51-53; tax collector, Rockville, 50; mem. bd. of educ, Vernon, 53-59; mayor, Rockville, 59-65; mem, Conn. State Bd. Educ, chmn, Vernon Dem. Party and Conn. Presidential Electors Col, currently. Bus. & Prof. Pos: Treas, Tolland Co. Bar Asn, 63-64, pres, 64-65; partner, Flaherty & Burke, currently. Mil. Serv: Pvt, Army, 42; U.S. Naval Acad, 43. Mem: Am, Conn, Hartford Co. and Tolland Co. Bar Asns; Nat. Hon. Eng. Soc. Rel: Catholic. Mailing Add: 6 Earl St, Rockville, Conn. 06066.

FLAHERTY, MICHAEL FRANCIS D
Mass. State Rep.
b. Boston, Mass, 9/6/36; s. John James Flaherty and Mary Joyce F; m. 11/25/61 to Margaret Joanne McGlone; c. Margaret J. and Michael F, Jr. Educ: Boston Col, A.B; Portia Law Sch, LL.B; Ballermine Speakers Club. Polit. & Govt. Pos: Mass. State Rep. 67-, asst. majority leader, Mass. House of Rep, 69-; del, Dem. Nat. Conv, 68; mem, Ward Seven Dem. Cmt, South Boston-Dorchester, 68- Bus. & Prof. Pos: Acct. clerk, Boston Edison Co, Mass, 60-63; ins. claim adjuster, Travelers Ins. Co, 63-67. Mil. Serv: Entered as Seaman Recruit, Navy, 54, released as PN-2, 57, after serv. on U.S.S. Northampton, 55-57; Nat. Defense and Good Conduct Medals; selected as Honor Man by fellow recruits while in basic training. Mem: Mass. State Legis. Asn; K. of C; South Boston Residents Group; South Boston Citizens Asn; Dorchester-Dudley Civic Coun. Past gen. chmn, St. Patrick's Day Celebration; South Boston Outstanding Citizen's Award, 62 Club, 69. Rel: Catholic. Mailing Add: 182 O'Callaghan Way, South Boston, Mass. 02127.

FLAHERTY, VIRGINIA CHATFIELD R
b. Tacoma, Wash, 9/20/21; d. William Russell Chatfield and Luella Troughton C; m. 5/10/47 to Terrence Floyd Flaherty; c. Flavia V. and Teresa C. Polit. & Govt. Pos: Co-chmn, Skagit Co. Young Rep, Wash, 60; v.chmn, Skagit Co. Rep. Cent. Cmt, 64-66, chmn, 66; pres, Sedro-Woolley-Burlington Women's Rep. Club, 67, 68, 69; v.chmn, Second Cong. Club, 67-68; Rep. precinct committeewoman, 69, precinct area chmn, 69. Mem: Fedn. Women's Rep. Clubs; Wash. State Fair Cmnr; Wash. Fair Asn. Dir. Rel: Episcopal. Mailing Add: Route 2, Box 163, Mt. Vernon, Wash. 98273.

FLAKNE, GARY W. R
Minn. State Rep.
b. Minneapolis, Minn, 1934; married; c. Brian, Ross, Keith and Mark. Educ: Univ. of Minn, B.S.L; William Mitchell Col. of Law, J.D. Polit. & Govt. Pos: Counsel, State Sen. Judiciary Cmt, Minn, 61; Minn. State Rep, 62-; alternate del, Rep. Nat. Conv, 68. Bus. & Prof. Pos: Attorney-at-law; instr. bus. law, Metrop. Jr. Col, Minneapolis. Mil. Serv: Capt, Minn. Army Nat. Guard. Mem: Co, State and Am. Bar Asns; Am. Judicature Soc; AF&AM; Shrine. Rel: Lutheran. Mailing Add: 4901 11th Ave. S, Minneapolis, Minn. 55417.

FLANAGAN, ROBERT KELLEHER D
W.Va. State Del.
b. Logan, W.Va, 11/15/23; s. Robert K. Flanagan, Sr. and Kathryn Judy F; m. 10/23/49 to Janis Pinson; c. Cathy, Kelly, Bruce and Kevin. Educ: Univ. Cincinnati, B.S. in pharm, 52; Sigma Chi. Polit. & Govt. Pos: W.Va. State Del, currently. Bus. & Prof. Pos: Owner, Flanagan's Pharmacy, Kenova, W.Va, 48-; co-owner, Wayne Pharmacy, 64-; pres, South. W.Va. Pharmaceutical Asn. and treas, W.Va. Pharmaceutical Asn, 66-67. Mil. Serv: Entered as Pvt, Army Air Corps, 42, released as Lt. Navigator, 45, after serv. as Instr. Mem: Nat. Asn. Retail Druggist Medicare and Welfare Cmt; Elks 313; Am. Legion; charter mem, Isaac Walton League; 1st pres. and founder of Ceredo-Kenova Jr. C. of C. Rel: Catholic. Mailing Add: 916 B. St, Ceredo, W.Va. 25507.

FLANAGAN, RUTH WALLACE D
V.Chmn, Windsor Locks Dem. Town Cmt, Conn.
b. Windsor Locks, Conn, 12/29/16; d. George M. Wallace (deceased) and Sarah Fitzpatrick W.(deceased); m. 9/5/38 to James Joseph Flanagan; c. Maryellen (Mrs. Robert A. Andersen) and Faith. Educ: High Sch. Polit. & Govt. Pos: Conn. State Rep. and mem, Pub. Health and Safety Cmt, 59-67, clerk, Elec. Cmt, Conn. Gen. Assembly, 63-65; mem, Windsor Locks Dem. Town Cmt, 64-66, v.chmn, 66-; mem, Selectmens Adv. Bd, Windsor Locks, 64-67; v.chmn, Housing Cmn. of Windsor Locks. Mem: Pres, Jeffersonian Club, 65-66; past pres, Windsor Locks Coun. Cath. Women; Saint Mary's Parish Club, v.chmn, St. Mary's Parish Coun. Rel: Roman Catholic. Mailing Add: 2 James St, Windsor Locks, Conn. 06096.

FLANAGAN, SID R
Wash. State Rep.
b. Bellingham, Wash, 1909; m. to Vyvien F; c. Three. Educ: Univ. of Wash. Polit. & Govt. Pos: Wash. State Rep, currently. Bus. & Prof. Pos: Farmer, cattleman. Mem: Elks; Moose. Mailing Add: Route 1, Box 205, Quincy, Wash. 98848. (1967)

FLANDERS, RALPH EDWARD R
b. Barnet, Vt, 9/28/80; s. Albert W. Flanders and Mary L. Gilfillan F; m. 11/1/11 to Helen E. Hartness; c. Helen Elizabeth (Mrs. Ballard), Anna H. (Mrs. Balivet, deceased) and James Hartness. Educ: Hon. M.A, Dartmouth Col, 32, LL.D, 51; hon. M.E, Stevens Inst. Tech, 32; hon. D.Sc, Middlebury Col, 34, Rose Polytech. Inst, 35, Univ. Vt, 35, Norwich Univ, 39 and Northwest. Univ, 40; LL.D, Harvard Univ, 50; hon. degrees from Polytech. Inst. Brooklyn, 34, Northwest. Univ, 42, Clarkson Inst. Tech, 49, Marlboro Col, 49, Univ. R.I, 51, Allegheny Col, 53 and Rollins Col, 54; Tau Beta Pi; Phi Beta Kappa. Polit. & Govt. Pos: Bus. Adv. and planning coun, U.S. Dept. Commerce, 33; mem, Indust. Adv. Bd, Nat. Recovery Admin, bd, Subsistence Homestead Admin. and Off. Prod. Mgt, 41; trustee and chmn. research cmt, Cmt. Econ. Develop. and pres, New Eng. Coun, 41-42; mem, Econ. Stabilization Bd, 42-44; Combined Prod. and Resources Bd, 43; U.S. Sen, Vt, 46-58. Bus. & Prof. Pos: Machinist apprentice and draftsman, Providence and Woonsocket, 97-01; designer, Int. Paper Box Mach. Co, Nashua, N.H, 03; assoc. ed, Mach, N.Y, 05-10; engr, Fellows Gear Shaper Co, 10; dir. and mgr, Jones & Lamson Mach. Co, 12, pres, 33-46; mem, Nat. Screw Thread Cmn, 20-24; dir, Soc. Sci. Coun, 32-36; pres, Bryant Chucking Grinder Co, 34-36; mem. adv. coun, Nat. Life Ins. Co; pres, Fed. Reserve Bank Boston, 44-46; pres, Am. Research & Develop. Corp, 46, hon. dir, currently; Godkin lectr, Harvard, 49. Publ: Platform for America, 36; The American Century, 50; Letter to a Generation, 56; Senator from Vermont, 60. Mem: Bd. Am. Standards Asn; v.pres, Am. Engr. Coun; pres, Am. Soc. Mech. Engrs, 34; past pres, Nat. Machine Tool Builders; Acad. Polit. & Soc. Sci; Am. Econ. Asn; Engr. Club, N.Y.C; Union Club, Boston; Cosmos Club, Wash. Worcester-Warner Medal, 38. Rel: Congregational. Mailing Add: Box 479, Springfield, Vt. 05156.

FLANIGAN, ROBERT M. R
Chmn, Colo. Rep. Party
b. 9/25/30; m. 3/6/54 to Joan; c. Ned, Stan, Chris, Aimee and Kevin. Polit. & Govt. Pos: Chmn, Summit Co. Rep. Party, Colo, 65-69; chmn, Cong. Dist. Rep. Party, 67-69; chmn, Colo. Rep. Party, 68- Bus. & Prof. Pos: Rancher. Rel: Roman Catholic. Legal Res: Lazy Shamrock Ranch, Kremmling, Colo. Mailing Add: 1901 E. 47th Ave, Denver Colo. 80216.

FLANNERY, JAMES JOSEPH D
Ohio State Rep.
b. Cleveland, Ohio, 10/31/38; s. Joseph Eugene Flannery and Margaret Hurrel F; m. 9/5/59 to Judith Haluscsak; c. James P, Kelly Ann, Michele, Daniel J, Mary Lou, Bryan E. and Judi L. Educ: Univ. Notre Dame, B.B.A, 60; capt, Notre Dame Bowling Team, 59-60. Polit. & Govt. Pos: Ohio State Rep, Dist. 48, 67-; mem, Cuyahoga Co. Dem. Exec. Cmt, 67- Bus. & Prof. Pos: Staff acct, Touche, Ross, Bailey & Smart, 60-64; sr. acct, CPA, Keister, Cerio & Radice, 64-66; partner, CPA, Cerio & Flannery, 66 and Maurer, Boecker & Cerio, 66- Publ: CPA and Politics, Ohio CPA, Winter 68. Mem: Am. Inst. of CPA's; Cleveland, Ohio Soc. of CPA's; bd. of dirs, Notre Dame-Cleveland Alumni Orgn. and St. Colman's Fed. Credit Union; K. of C; Citizens League; West Side Civic Coun. Selected to participate in Eagleton Inst. of Politics, 6/69. Rel: Roman Catholic. Mailing Add: 6907 Lawn Ave, Cleveland, Ohio 44102.

FLATH, DON EDGAR R
Chmn, Wayne Co. Rep. Cent. Cmt, Ohio
b. Wadsworth, Ohio, 8/28/22; s. Leonard Flath and Theresa Garbett F; m. 7/17/48 to Barbara Ann Timmerman; c. Richard C, Ian Douglas and Penelope Ruth. Educ: Wittenberg Univ, A.B, 47; William McKinley Law Sch, LL.B. magna cum laude, 52; Dean's List for Scholarship; Phi Kappa Psi; Delta Theta Phi. Polit. & Govt. Pos: Solicitor, Dalton Village, Ohio, 58-; Rep. precinct committeeman, 58-; v.chmn. exec. cmt. and chmn, Wayne Co. Rep. Cent. Cmt, 62-; mem, State Bd. Educ, 65. Bus. & Prof. Pos: Adjuster, Travelers Ins. Co, 51-54; asst. to pres, Erie Ins. Exchange, 54-56; Attorney-at-law, 56- Mil. Serv: Entered as Pvt, Air Force, 43, released as Aviation Cadet, 46, after serv. in Med. Dept, 2nd Air Force, U.S. Mem: Trustee, Wayne Co. Lib; Mason; Scottish Rite; Shrine; past pres, Rotary. Edward Hardie Roche Nat. Award, Ins. Knowledge. Rel: Lutheran. Mailing Add: 130 W. Main St, Dalton, Ohio 44618.

FLATT, JOSEPH B. R
Iowa State Sen.
b. Des Moines, Iowa, 12/24/21; m. May 1944 to Dorothy Rothwell; c. Joseph Jr, Kevin, Christine and Sharon. Educ: Drake Univ. Polit. & Govt. Pos: Chmn, Iowa Civil War Centennial Cmn; Iowa State Rep, 59-60; Iowa State Sen, 61- Bus. & Prof. Pos: Operator, Flatt's Clothing Stores. Mil. Serv: Army, 41-45; Battlefield Cmn, N.Africa, 43; Brig. Gen, Iowa Nat. Guard. Mem: Past pres, Winterset C. of C; past comdr, Sons Union Vets; Lions; Am. Legion. Rel: Baptist. Mailing Add: 722 W. Court St, Winterset, Iowa 50273.

FLAVIN, RAY M. D
b. Litchville, N.Dak, 8/25/12; married; c. Raymond, Joan, Lyn Judy, Julye. Educ: Assessing studied in short courses. Polit. & Govt. Pos: Mich. State Rep, 64-66; Genesee Co. Bd. of Supvrs. and the Genesee Co. Planning Cmn. Bus. & Prof. Pos: Former trustee and supvr, Flint Twp. Mem: Swartz Creek Lodge 458, F. & A.M; Bay City Ancient Accepted Scottish Rite; Elf Khurafeh Shrine; Mich. Twp. Asn; Mich. Supvrs. Asn. Rel: Church of God. Mailing Add: 2089 S. Elms Rd, Swartz Creek, Mich. 48473. (1967)

FLAX, ALEXANDER HENRY
b. Brooklyn, N.Y, 1/18/21; s. David Flax and Etta Schenker F; m. 8/25/51 to Ida Leane Warren; c. Laurel Elizabeth. Educ: N.Y. Univ, B.A, 40; Univ. of Buffalo, Ph.D, 58; Sigma Xi. Polit. & Govt. Pos: Mem, NACA, 52-54; mem, adv. cmt, NASA, 58-62; chief scientist, Air Force, 59-61; asst. secy. for research and develop, Dept. of Air Force, 63-68. Bus. & Prof. Pos: With Curtis Wright Corp, 40-44, Piasecki Helicopter Corp, 44-46 and Cornell Aeronaut. Lab, 46-63. Mem: Fel. Am. Inst. Aeronaut. and Astronaut; Cosmos Club, Wash, D.C. Lawrence Sperry Award, 49; Wright Bros. lectr, 59. Mailing Add: 4355 Klingle St. N.W, Washington, D.C. 20016. (1967)

FLEECE, WILLIAM HAROLD R
Fla. State Rep.
b. Pontiac, Mich, 10/1/35; s. Moses Harris Fleece and Jeanette Stein F; m. 12/25/61 to Ellen Lisbeth Richman; c. Jonathan Marc and David Michael. Educ: Ind. State Univ, 54 & 57; Ohio State Univ, B.S. in Psychol, 57; Stetson Col. Law, 59 & 60; Ind. Univ. Sch. Law, Bloomington, J.D, 61; Zeta Beta Tau.

Polit. & Govt. Pos: Fla. State Rep, 66-, v.chmn. ad valorem taxation cmt, Fla. House of Rep, mem. pub. health and welfare cmt, mem. pub. sch. educ. cmt. Bus. & Prof. Pos: Attorney-at-law, McCutcheon, Fleece & Kennedy, 62-69, Werly & Fleece, 69- Publ: 'Medical and Legal Justifications for Autopsy, Should They be Extended,' Ind. Med. Asn. J, 6/61. Mem: Bar of the Supreme Court of U.S; Bar of U.S. Court of Appeals, Fifth Dist; Bar of U.S. Dist. Court; Am, Fla. and St. Petersburg Bar Asns; Pinellas Co. Adv. and Coord. Cmt. on Ment. Retardation; Bath Club, Redington Beach; Mason; Breakfast Optimist Club of St. Petersburg; Young Rep. Club; St. Petersburg Rep. Club; B'nai B'rith. Keyhole Award, Dixie Publ. News, Fla. State Capitol, 67 Regular Session; Spoke Award, St. Petersburg Jr. C. of C. Rel: Jewish. Legal Res: 7872 Causeway Blvd. N, St. Petersburg, Fla. 33707. Mailing Add: P.O. Box 13209, 6641 Central Ave, St. Petersburg, Fla. 33733.

FLEETWOOD, THIRVIN DOW D
Mem, Calif. Dem. State Cent. Cmt.
b. Henryetta, Okla, 10/4/22; s. Sanford Cal Fleetwood and Willie Mae Pendergrass F; m. 1/8/44 to Norma Lasters; c. Sharron (Mrs. Paul Noland), Karen (Mrs. Robert Gilson) and Ronald Gene. Educ: St. Louis Univ, 46; Long Beach City Col, Tech. Dipl, 50; Harbor Jr. Col, 65-66. Polit. & Govt. Pos: Planning cmnr, Torrance City Hall, Calif, 54-62; mem, Los Angeles Co. Dem. Cent. Cmt, 56-66; mem, Inter City Hwy. Cmt, S.Bay, Los Angeles Co, 59-62; mem, Calif. Dem. State Cent. Cmt, 66-; spec. asst. to Calif. State Assemblyman Le Townsend, 67th Assembly Dist, 68- Bus. & Prof. Pos: Utility worker, South. Calif. Gas Co, 48-; financial secy, Local 132, Utility Workers, AFL-CIO, 52-56, chief steward, 58-60, v.pres, 60-61 and area chmn. southwest div, 62-64. Mil. Serv: Entered as A/S, Coast Guard, 42, released as BM 3/C, 45, after serv. in Southwest Pac. Theatre, 44-45; Am. Defense Medal; Pac. Theatre Medal; Good Conduct Medal; Bronze Star. Mem: Third v.pres, North Torrance Lions; chmn. Club 67, Gardena, Calif. Dem. Party; chmn, 67th Assembly Dist. Dem. Coun. Resolution from Calif. State Assembly. Rel: Baptist. Mailing Add: 3637 W. 182nd St, Torrance, Calif. 90504.

FLEGEL, ALBERT GORDON D
Ore. State Sen.
b. Portland, Ore, 5/14/06; s. Austin Finck Flegel and Dora Dawley F; m. 4/8/39 to Margaret Louise Maroney; c. Alice Anne (Mrs. Baker). Educ: Willamette Univ, 24-25; Univ. Ore, 25-27; Beta Theta Pi. Polit. & Govt. Pos: Mayor, Roseburg, Ore, 46-52; mem, Bur. Land Mgt. Adv. Bd, 52-; Ore. State Rep, Douglas Co, 57-60; Ore. State Sen, 61- Bus. & Prof. Pos: Dir, Ore. Trucking Asn. and Ore. Draymen and Warehousemen's Asn, 57- Mil. Serv: Entered as Pvt, Army, 43, released as S/Sgt, 45, after serv. in 261st Field Artil. Bn, 401st Field Artil. Group, ETO; Rhine and ETO Ribbons. Mem: Am. Legion; VFW; Mason; Shrine; Elks; Kiwanis; dir, Ore. Hist. Soc, 68-74. Rel: Episcopal. Legal Res: 1376 S.E. Lane Ave, Roseburg, Ore. 97470. Mailing Add: P.O. Box 1065, Roseburg, Ore. 97470.

FLEMING, GEORGE GAINS R
Treas, N.J. State Rep. Cmt.
b. Jacksonville, Fla, 2/5/12; s. Frank Fleming and Georgiana Hopkins F; m. 12/24/44 to Katherine Louise Biot; c. LaVerne Estella. Educ: Bordentown Mil. Acad; Life Ins. Mgt. Inst; Life Underwriters Training Coun, L.U.T.C. Polit. & Govt. Pos: Mem, Gov. Bipartisan Coun, N.J; chmn, Pub. Assistance Div, Bd. Pub. Welfare, D.C; state cmnr, N.J. Educ. Facility Authority; treas, N.J. State Rep. Cmt, 65- Bus. & Prof. Pos: Assoc, Progressive Life Ins. Co, 30 Years, regional v.pres, 63-66, sr. v.pres, 66- Publ: Dollars Down the Drain. Mem: Life Ins. Officers Mgt. Asn; Wash, D.C. NAACP; bd. dirs. and exec. cmt, Boy Scouts of Monmouth Co, N.J; former mem. bd. dirs, Urban League; former secy. and bd. mem, Nat. Conf. of Christians & Jews, D.C; former v.pres, Big Bros. Exec. Cmt. Winner, Afro-Am. Outstanding Citizen Award, Wash, D.C, 54; United Givers Found. Oscar Awards. Rel: Protestant. Mailing Add: 355 Broad St, Red Bank, N.J. 07701. (1967)

FLEMING, GEORGE H. R
b. Seward, Nebr, 10/17/00; m. 4/4/23 to Sylvia Phelps; c. Glen G. and Phillip E. Educ: Rural Schs. Polit. & Govt. Pos: Co. cmnr; Nebr. State Sen, 61-68. Bus. & Prof. Pos: Businessman; farmer; rancher. Mem: Past pres, Nebr. Asn. of Co. Officers; Elks; Kiwanis; C. of C; Nebr. Alumni Asn; Nebr. Stock Growers Asn; bd, Nebr. Welfare Asn; Mason; Shrine. Rel: Lutheran. Mailing Add: 1145 14th Ave, Sidney, Nebr. 69162. (1967)

FLEMING, JAMES G. R
Mich. State Sen.
b. Jackson, Mich, 11/5/29; s. James Francis Fleming and Bernadine L. Switzer F; m. 11/9/57 to Shanna B. Fransted; c. Amy Theresa, Kelly Ann and James Brian. Educ: Jackson Commun. Col, A.A, 50; Univ. Detroit Sch. Law, LL.B, 54; Scholarship Key, Delta Theta Phi, 53; Hosmer Senate, Univ. of Detroit Sch. of Law. Polit. & Govt. Pos: Attorney, Hanover and Concord, Mich; city cmnr, Jackson, Mich, 56-57; circuit court cmnr, Jackson Co, 55-58, chief asst. prosecutor, 58-60, prosecuting attorney, 60-66; mem, Jackson Co. Rep. Exec. Cmt, 60-66; Mich. State Sen, 19th Dist, 67-, chmn, State Senate Hwy. Cmt. and mem, Senate Judiciary, Labor Cmt. and Cmt. on Cmts. Bus. & Prof. Pos: Attorney-at-Law, 54-; dir, Jackson Credit Exchange, 62-66; dir. and secy, Power Transmission Co, Inc, 65-66. Mem: Jackson Co, Mich. and Am. Bar Asns; Nat. Dist. Attorney's Asn; Am. and Mich. Trial Lawyers Asn; South. Mich. Law Enforcement Asn; dir, Mich. Prosecuting Attorney's Asn, 60- and pres, 65-66; Country Club of Jackson, Mich. Rel: Catholic. Legal Res: 2507 Horton Rd, Jackson, Mich. 49201. Mailing Add: 204½ S. Jackson St, Jackson, Mich. 49201.

FLEMING, JOHN GRANT D
Chmn, Woodbury Dem. Cmt, Conn.
b. North Tarrytown, N.Y, 7/7/14; s. Robert Wilson Fleming and Elizabeth Grant F; m. 10/22/39 to Marlice J. Buner; c. Deryl Marlice. Educ: N.Y. Univ, B.S. in elec. eng, 36; Brooklyn Polytech. Inst, grad. work, 37; N.Y. Univ. and Trinity Col, Conn, 48; Tau Beta Pi; Iota Alpha; chmn. student sect, Am. Inst. Elec. Engrs. N.Y. Area Cols. Polit. & Govt. Pos: Mem, Gov. Fact Finding Cmt. in Educ, 48-50; chmn, Woodbury Dem. Cmt, Conn, 52-57 & 60-; pres, Small Town Dem, 53-57; mem, Dem. Party Rules Cmt, 56 & 69; chmn, Fifth Cong. Conv, 56, Sixth Cong. Conv, 64 and 68. Bus. & Prof. Pos: Develop. engr, Cambridge Instrument Co, Ossining, N.Y, 36-45; mgr. product planning, Bristol Co, Waterbury, 45-57; mgr, new bus. planning, Int. Bus. Machines Corp, Conn, 57- Publ: 'Man Runs a Power Plant,' Pa. Elec. Assocs. Conf, 52; 'Human Engineering in Power Plant Instrumentation,' Proc. Instrument Soc. Am, 53. Mem: Inst. Elec. & Electronics Engrs; Am. Computing Machine Inst; Lions; Nat. Soc. Corporate Planning; N.Y. Univ. Club; Wash. Club. Outstanding Eng. Achievement Citation, N.Y. Univ, 55. Rel: United Church of Christ. Mailing Add: Cowles Rd, Woodbury, Conn. 06798.

FLEMING, NEIL WAYNE D
b. Hamilton, N.Dak, 4/22/43; s. Charlie F. Fleming and Nina Geiger F; m. 8/13/66 to Charlotte Conner; c. James Conner. Educ: Univ. N.Dak, Ph.B, 65, J.D, 68; Delta Tau Delta; Phi Alpha Delta. Polit. & Govt. Pos: Pres, Univ. N.Dak. Young Dem, 63-65; v.pres, N.Dak. Young Dem, 65-66, secy-treas, 66-67 & 68; Dem. precinct committeeman, Grand Forks, N.Dak, 66-68; del, Dem. Nat. Conv, 68. Bus. & Prof. Pos: Asst. states attorney, Pembina Co, N.Dak, 68. Mil. Serv: 1st Lt, Army, 68- Publ: 'House Bill 628, An Analysis of North Dakota's Anti Corporation Farming Law,' Univ. N.Dak. Law Rev, 1/68. Mem: N.Dak. and Am. Bar Asns. Numerous scholarships; selected as N.Dak. Outstanding Young Dem, 67. Rel: Catholic. Mailing Add: R.R. I, Hamilton, N.Dak. 58238.

FLEMING, RICHARD LEO D
Chmn, Webster Co. Dem. Cent. Cmt, Iowa
b. St. Paul, Minn, 7/22/12; s. Richard Leo Fleming and Delia Agnes Foley F; m. 12/27/65 to Corinne Marion Hastings; c. Phyllis. Educ: S.Dak. State Col, 1 year. Polit. & Govt. Pos: Chmn, Webster Co. Dem. Cent. Cmt, Iowa, 66-; alternate del, Dem. Nat. Conv, 68. Bus. & Prof. Pos: Various positions with Southern R.R. in Des Moines leading to terminal supt, Ft. Dodge, 39-69; salesman, Lincoln Life and Casualty, Ft. Dodge, 69- Mem: Moose (fel. degree); Elks; Brotherhood of Rwy. and Airline Clerks; assoc. mem. Am. Legion Country Club. Rel: Catholic. Mailing Add: 1751 14th St, Ft. Dodge, Iowa 50501.

FLEMING, RICHARD THORPE R
b. Melrose, Mass, 2/7/32; s. Herbert Paul Fleming and Sally Thorpe F; single. Educ: Dartmouth Col, A.B, 53; Amos Tuck Sch. Bus. Admin, Dartmouth Col, M.B.A, 58. Polit. & Govt. Pos: Research dir, F. Bradford Morse for Cong. Cmt, Mass, 60; research dir, Mass. Rep. State Cmt, 61-64, admin. asst. to chmn, 62, exec. secy, 63; schedules dir, Elliot L. Richardson for Lt. Gov. Cmt, Mass, 64; legis. asst. to Lt. Gov, Commonwealth of Mass, 65-66; assoc. research dir, Rep. Nat. Cmt, 66-67; exec. dir, Rep. Gov. Asn, 67-69. Bus. & Prof. Pos: Mkt. trainee, Gen. Elec. Co, 58-59, sales rep, 59-61; sr. admin. analyst, ABT Assocs, Inc, 69- Mil. Serv: Entered as Officer Cand. A/S, Navy, 53, released as Lt.(jg), 57, after serv. in U.S.S. Hale and U.S.S. Brister, Combat Info. Center Officers Sch, Atlantic Theatre, Naval Air Tech. Training. Mem: U.S. Naval Inst; Rep. Club of Mass: Ripon Soc. Rel: Episcopal. Legal Res: 49 Mt. Vernon St, Boston, Mass. 02108. Mailing Add: 55 Wheeler St, Cambridge, Mass. 02138.

FLEMING, ROBERT D. R
Pa. State Sen.
b. Sharpsburg, Pa, 3/8/03; s. Robert H. Fleming and Daisy Doty F; m. to Jean Varner; c. Jean Frances. Educ: Univ. of Pittsburgh, B.S. Polit. & Govt. Pos: Pa. State Rep, 38-50; Pa. State Sen, 50-; mem, Port Authority, Allegheny Co, 58-; mem, Pa. Constitutional Rev. Cmn, 59; del, Rep. Nat. Conv, 60, alternate del, 68. Bus. & Prof. Pos: Ins, real estate broker. Mem: Kiwanis; Mason; Elks; Sportsmen's Club. Mailing Add: 405 Freeport Rd, Pittsburgh, Pa. 15215. (1967)

FLEMING, WILLIAM M, JR. D
b. Winston-Salem, N.C, 10/20/24; s. William M. Fleming and Effie Lee Neville F; m. 8/14/65 to Marilyn B. Neehan. Educ: Univ. of Ga; Lumkin Law Sch. Polit. & Govt. Pos: Ga. State Rep, 59-68. Mil. Serv: Air Force, 43-46. Mailing Add: 3 Johnson Bldg, Augusta, Ga. 30902. (1967)

FLEMING, WILMOT E. R
Pa. State Sen.
b. Phila, Pa, 12/20/16; s. Wilmot Fleming and Lillie F. Bains F; m. to Pauline Barnard; c. Jeffrey. Educ: Univ. of Pa, 4 year scholarship and B.S. Polit. & Govt. Pos: Mem, Jenkintown Bd. of Sch. Dirs, 9 years, pres, 6 years; Pa. State Rep, 62-64; Pa. State Sen, 64- Bus. & Prof. Pos: Regional bd. dirs, Indust. Valley Bank and Trust Co. Mem: Past pres, Rotary; trustee, Beaver Col; former bd. mem, YMCA; trustee, Wharton Sch. Alumni Asn; zone chmn, United Fund. Outstanding Jr. Award, Phila. Engrs. Club. Rel: Presbyterian; Former trustee and elder, Grace Presby. Church. Mailing Add: 306 Wyncote Rd, Jenkintown, Pa. 19046.

FLEMMING, ARTHUR SHERWOOD R
b. Kingston, N.Y, 6/12/05; s. Harry H. Flemming and Harriet Sherwood F; m. 12/14/34 to Bernice Virginia Moler; c. Elizabeth Anne (Mrs. George Speese), Susan Harriet (Mrs. John Parker), Harry Sherwood and twins, Arthur Henry and Thomas Madison. Educ: Ohio Wesleyan Univ, A.B, 27; Am. Univ, A.M, 28; George Wash. Univ, LL.B, 33; Alpha Sigma Phi; Delta Sigma Rho; Omicron Delta Kappa. Hon. degrees from 40 insts. in the U.S. Polit. & Govt. Pos: Mem, U.S. Civil Serv. Cmn, 39-48; chief labor supply, Labor Div, Off. of Prod. Mgt, 41-42; chmn, Adv. Cmt. on Personnel Mgt, Atomic Energy Cmn, 43-53; men., Adv. Coun, Retraining and Reemploy. Admin, Dept. Labor, 44-47; mem, Cmn. on Orgn. Exec. Br. of Govt, 47-49 & 53-55; mem, Int. Civil Serv. Adv. Bd, 50-64; Secy. of Health, Educ. and Welfare, 58-61; mem, Nat. Adv. Cmt, Peace Corps, 61- Bus. & Prof. Pos: Instr. govt. and debate coach, Am. Univ, 27-30, dir, Sch. Pub. Affairs, 34-39, exec. officer, 38-39; ed. staff, U.S. Daily, 30-34; ed, Uncle Sam's Diary, weekly current events newspaper for high sch. students, 32-35; pres, Ohio Wesleyan Univ, 48-53 & 57-58; v.pres, Nat. Coun. Churches of Christ in Am, 50-54 & 64-66, pres, 66-69; trustee, T. Roosevelt Mem. Asn; pres, Univ. Ore, 61-68; pres, Macalester Col, 68- Mem: Ore. Coun. Churches (pres, 64-). Awarded travelling fel, Wash. Br, Eng-Speaking Union, 28; Medal of Freedom, 57; Alexander Meiklejohn Acad. Freedom Award, 62. Rel: Methodist. Mailing Add: Office of the President, Macalester College, St. Paul, Minn. 55101.

FLEMMING, HARRY S. R
Spec. Asst. to the President
b. Washington, D.C, 9/15/40; s. Arthur S. Flemming and Bernice Moler F.

Educ: Ohio State Univ; Am. Univ; Phi Gamma Delta. Polit. & Govt. Pos: V.chmn, Tenth Dist. Rep. Cmt, Va, 66-68; spec. asst. to the chmn, Rep. Nat. Cmt, 68; co-chmn, Nixon for President, Va, 68; alternate del, Rep. Nat. Conv, 68; city councilman, Alexandria, Va, 68-69; Spec. Asst. to the President, 69- Bus. & Prof. Pos: V.pres, Madigan Electronic Corp, 66-68; secy-treas, J. Newspapers, Inc, 68-69; pres, North. Va. Commun, Inc, 68- Mailing Add: P.O. Box 1355, Alexandria, Va. 22313.

FLETCHER, ARTHUR ALLEN R
Asst. Secy. for Wage and Labor Standards, Dept. of Labor
b. Phoenix, Ariz, 12/22/24; s. Andrew A. Fletcher and Edna Miller F; m. 5/5/65 to Bernyce Ayesha Hasson; c. Phyliss, Sylvia, Arthur, Jr, Paul and Phillip. Educ: Washburn Univ, B.A, 50; Kans. State Univ, 53-54; San Francisco State Col, 64-65. Polit. & Govt. Pos: V.chmn, Kans. Rep. State Cmt, 54-56; v.chmn, Schawnee Young Rep, Calif, 56-57; chmn, adv. cmt. on civil rights, Calif. Rep. Assembly, 62-64; committeeman, Alameda Co. Rep. Cent. Cmt, 62-65; Rep. cand, City Coun, Pasco, Wash, 67; Rep. cand. for Lt. Gov, Wash, 68; city councilman, Pasco, 68-69; Asst. Secy. for Wage and Labor Standards, Dept. of Labor, 69- Mil. Serv: Army, 43-45. Mem: Kans. and Calif. Teachers Asns; Northwest Asn. of Personnel Officers; Am. Legion; NAACP. Nat. Freedom Found. Award, 68. Legal Res: 628 North Beech Ave, Pasco, Wash. 99301. Mailing Add: 874 Azalea Dr, Rockville, Md. 20850.

FLETCHER, CHARLES KIMBALL R
b. San Diego, Calif, 12/15/02; s. Ed Fletcher and Mary Catherine Batchelder F; m. 11/27/26 to Jeannette Toberman; c. Charles K, Jr; Peter T. and Dale (Mrs. Lingenfelder). Educ: Stanford Univ; Pembroke Col, Oxford Univ; Phi Delta Theta. Polit. & Govt. Pos: U.S. Rep, Calif, 46-48; del, Rep. Nat. Conv, 68. Bus. & Prof. Pos: Chmn. of bd, Home Fed. Savings & Loan, San Diego, Calif, 34- and Pioneer Savings & Loan, Hawaii, 63- Mil. Serv: Lt, Navy, 3 years. Rel: Congregational. Mailing Add: 2940 Ocean Front, Del Mar, Calif. 92014. (1967)

FLETCHER, HENRY ARNOLD D
b. Parkdale, Ark, 7/29/33; s. Arnold Vester Fletcher and Jimmie Lee Almond F; m. 6/2/52 to Ethelene Twilley; c. Henry, Jr, David Ronald, Glenda Diane and Brenda Carol. Educ: Int. Bible Col, 49-51. Polit. Pos: Tex. State Rep. until 67. Mem: Mason; Odd Fellows; Lions. Rel: United Pentecostal. Mailing Add: 730 Bois Darc, Lockhart, Tex. 78644. (1967)

FLETCHER, JAMES WILLIAM D
Chmn, Rappahannock Co. Dem. Cmt, Va.
b. Sperryville, Va, 10/19/18; s. William Meade Fletcher and Martha Ball Buckner F; m. 10/21/39 to Mildred Miller Thornton; c. Mildred Buckner, Catherine Mead (Mrs. Littleton), Louise Miller, James William, III and Martha Stuart Thornton. Educ: Univ. Richmond, B.S, 37; T.C. Williams Sch. Law, Univ. Richmond, LL.B, 40; Phi Kappa Sigma; McNeil Law Soc. Polit. & Govt. Pos: Chmn, Rappahannock Co. Dem. Cmt, Va, 40's-; mem, Seventh Cong. Dist. Dem. Cmt, 40's-, chmn, 40's-68; mem, Cmn. Study Reorganization of State Govt; attorney mem, Va. State Bd. Acct; mem, Va. Cmn. Study Pub. Educ, 50's-60's; mem. bd. visitors, Va. Sch. for Deaf and Blind, 63-; chmn, Va. State Bd. Elec, 64- Mem: Va. State and Am. Bar Asns; Rotary (past pres, Rappahannock Club). Rel: Episcopal. Mailing Add: Sperryville, Va. 22740.

FLETCHER, KATHLEEN R
Mem, Official Bd, Kans. Fedn. Rep. Women
b. Wichita, Kans, 2/14/20; d. A. Warren Keating and Gladys Drake K; m. 8/2/46 to Fred Franklin Fletcher; c. Susan Kathleen and Julie Ann. Educ: Univ. Wichita, A.B. in educ, 41; Colo. Col, grad. study, 58. Polit. & Govt. Pos: V.chmn, Ford Co. Rep. Cmt, Kans, 56-; v.chmn, First and Fifth Cong. Dist. Cmt, 58-62; v.chmn, Kans. Rep. State Cmt, 62-64; del, Rep. Nat. Conv, 64; mem. and chmn, Sub-Cmt. on Health and Commun, Gov. Cmn. on Status of Women, 65-; mem, Official Bd, Kans. Fedn. Rep. Women, 65- Bus. & Prof. Pos: Teacher, Bucklin High Sch, Kans, 41-50 & 66- and Ford High Sch, 55-59. Mem: Nat. Educ. Asn; Ford Co. and Kans. State Teachers Asns; PEO; Eastern Star; 2 Local Fedn. Women's Clubs. Rel: Presbyterian. Mailing Add: Box 235, Bucklin, Kans. 67834. (1967)

FLETCHER, PETER B. R
Chmn, Second Cong. Dist. Rep. Cmt, Mich.
b. Ypsilanti, Mich, 2/29/32; s. Foster L. Fletcher and Mary E. Schneider F; single. Educ: Univ. Mich, A.B. in polit. sci, 54; Phi Beta Kappa; Phi Kappa Phi; Phi Eta Sigma; Pi Sigma Alpha; Univ. Mich. Young Rep. and Bot. Club. Polit. & Govt. Pos: Dir, Peoples Commun. Hosp. Authority, Mich, 58-66; treas, Ypsilanti City Rep. Cmt, 60-62, mem, 62-64; chmn, Romney for Gov, Washtenaw Co, 64 & 66; chmn, Washtenaw Co. Rep. Cmt, 64-66; chmn, Second Cong. Dist. Rep. Cmt, currently; del, Rep. Nat. Conv, 68. Bus. & Prof. Pos: Sales analyst, Frigidaire Div, Gen. Motors Corp, 54-57; comptroller, Credit Bur. of Ypsilanti, 57-; dir, First of Wayne Corp, 64-; dir, Nat. Bank of Ypsilanti, 64- Mem: Presidents Club, Univ. of Mich; Rotary; Jr. C. of C; life mem, Mich. Alumni Asn. Outstanding Young Man of the Year Award, Ypsilanti Area, 60. Rel: Methodist; Chmn. of the Off. Bd, First Methodist Church, Ypsilanti. Legal Res: 302 S. Huron St, Ypsilanti, Mich. 48197. Mailing Add: P.O. Box 407, Ypsilanti, Mich. 48197. (1967)

FLETCHER, THOMAS WILLIAM D
Dep. Mayor-Commissioner, District of Columbia
b. Portland, Ore, 3/1/24; s. Irving Archibald Fletcher and Florence Ada Cooper F; m. 12/27/45 to Margerie Frances Muller; c. Thomas Franklin, Heidi Ann and Dean Thurston. Educ: Army Specialized Training Prog. in Pre-Med, Stanford Univ, 43-45 and Univ. Nebr, 45-46; Univ. Calif, Berkeley, B.A, 51. Polit. & Govt. Pos: Asst. to City Mgr, San Leandro, Calif, 51-52; city adminstr, Davis, 52-55; asst. to City Mgr, San Diego, 55-61, city mgr, 61-66; dep. asst. secy, Housing Assistance Admin, Dept. of Housing and Urban Develop, 67; dep Mayor-Commissioner, District of Columbia, 67- Bus. & Prof. Pos: Pres, Foodmaker Franchise Corp, San Diego, Calif, 66-67. Mil. Serv: Entered as Pvt, Army, 43, released as Pfc, 46, after serv. in Army Specialized Training Program, U.S. Theatre. Publ: 'Innovation and Change: A City's Management on the Move,' Institute for Local Self Govt; 'Organizing Cities to Cope with Change,' Annual Proceedings, Nat. League of Cities, 66; 'Decision Making in Government,' Engineering Management. Mem: Nat. Acad. of Pub. Admin; Western Governmental Research Asn; League of Calif. Cities; Int. City Mgrs. Asn; Nat. Munic. League; Pub. Official Adv. Coun. Off. of Econ. Opportunity; Bd. Gov, Local Inst. for Self Govt; Boy Scouts; Young Men's Christian Asn. Rel: Episcopal. Legal Res: 3001 Veazey Terr. N.W, Washington, D.C. 20008. Mailing Add: District Bldg, 14th & E St. N.W, Washington, D.C. 20004.

FLETCHER, VIRGIL T. D
Ark. State Sen.
b. Benton, Ark, 12/1/16; s. John T. Fletcher and Lula Ballard F; m. 4/12/41 to Eda S. Kruse; c. John Karl, William Ferral and Mark Edward. Polit.& Govt. Pos: Ark. State Rep, 54-62; Ark. State Sen, 62- Bus. & Prof. Pos: Owner, Real Estate and Ins. Bus. Mem: Lions; Mason (32°); Shrine. Rel: Baptist. Mailing Add: P.O. Box 604, Benton, Ark. 72015.

FLETCHER, VIRGINIA CAROL D
b. Norton, Va, 11/17/44; d. Ada Fugate F; single. Educ: J.I. Burton High Sch. Polit. & Govt. Pos: Exec. secy, U.S. Rep. Dan Rostenkowski, Ill, 63- Rel: Methodist. Mailing Add: 123 Sixth St. N.E, Washington, D.C. 20002.

FLETCHER, W. FRED D
b. Colonial Heights, Va, 8/13/28; s. James Kilby Fletcher and Mary Estelle Wharton F; m. 6/12/54 to Catherine Elaine Wade; c. Karen Elaine and Barbara Suzanne. Educ: Wash. Bible Col, 52-55; Am. Univ, B.A, 60, M.A, 64. Polit. & Govt. Pos: Admin. asst, U.S. Rep. W.M. Abbitt, Va, 52- Bus. & Prof. Pos: Reporter and assoc. ed, The Progress-Index, 47-52. Distinguished Serv. Award, Petersburg Jr. C. of C, 52; Jaycee Key Award, 52. Rel: Baptist. Legal Res: 823 W. Washington St, Petersburg, Va. 23803. Mailing Add: 3701 Lyons Lane, Alexandria, Va. 22302.

FLINN, MONROE LAWRENCE D
Supvr, St. Clair Co, Ill.
b. Batesville, Ark, 12/17/17; s. Monroe Jesse Flinn and Rue Hanks F; m. 12/1/40 to Freda Florence Tullock; c. Donald L, Carol (Mrs. Samuel Millatti) and Debra S. Educ: High sch. grad. Polit. & Govt. Pos: Supvr, St. Clair Co, Ill, 61-; del, Dem. Nat. Conv, 68. Bus. & Prof. Pos: Gen. yardmaster, Granite City Steel Co, Ill, 56-; chmn. bd. trustees, Cahokia Pub. Water Dist, 67- Mem: Moose; Mason; Scottish Rite; Shrine. Rel: United Church of Christ. Mailing Add: 2746 Camp Jackson Rd, Cahokia, Ill. 62206.

FLINT, PHILIP SHERIDAN R
City Councilman, Palo Alto, Calif.
b. Vallejo, Calif, 10/28/23; s. Philip Sheridan Flint and Marguerite Snyder F; m. 7/27/57 to Nancy Spence Fraser; c. Louise Marie and David Fraser. Educ: Harvard Univ, B.S. in chem; Fuller Theological Sem; Phi Beta Kappa. Polit. & Govt. Pos: Chmn, Citizens Cmt. for Pub. Transportation of Santa Clara Co, Calif, 61-64; city councilman, Palo Alto, 63- Bus. & Prof. Pos: Sr. mem, tech. staff, Fairchild Semiconductor, 58-64 and Molectro Corp, 64; consult. and physicist, semiconductor indust, 64- Mil. Serv: Entered as Cadet Officer, Navy, 43, released as Lt.(jg), 46, after serv. in Pac. Mem: Electrochem. Soc; Conserv. Cmt, Sierra Club, 60-62 and treas, Loma Prieta Chap, 62-63; Wilderness Soc; Nature Friends. Various scientific articles on semiconductor fabrication techniques, presented at the Electrochem. Soc. meetings. Rel: Episcopal. Mailing Add: 2256 Santa Ana St, Palo Alto, Calif. 94303. (1967)

FLITNER, HOWARD E. R
Wyo. State Sen.
b. Noble, Okla, 4/5/01; m. to Maureen; c. Four. Educ: Univ. of Kans, B.A. Polit. & Govt. Pos: Mem, Shell Creek Sch. Bd, Wyo, 14 years; Wyo. State Rep, 6 terms; Wyo. State Sen, currently. Bus. & Prof. Pos: Rancher. Mem: Wyo. Stock Growers; pres, Wyo. Wool Growers; Farm Bur; Lions. Rel: Catholic. Mailing Add: Diamond Trail Ranch, Greybull, Wyo. 82426. (1967)

FLOOD, DANIEL J. D
U.S. Rep, Pa.
b. Hazleton, Pa, 11/26/03; m. 9/24/49 to Catherine H. Swank. Educ: Syracuse Univ, A.B, M.A; Harvard Law Sch; Dickinson Sch. of Law, LL.B, 29, hon. LL.D. Polit. & Govt. Pos: Secy, Dem. Soc, Pa; counsel for Pa. Liquor Control Bd, 35-39; dep. attorney gen; exec. asst. to State Treas, 41-44; dir, Bur. of Pub. Assistance Disbursements, State Treas; U.S. Rep, Pa, 44-46, 48-52 & 54- Bus. & Prof. Pos: Spec. master R.R. Reorganization, U.S. Circuit Court; bd. trustees, Col. Misericordia; bd. dirs, Kingston Nat. Bank; attorney-at-law, 30-; attorney, Home Owner's Loan Corp, 34-35. Mil. Serv: Chmn, Marine Corps Vol. Res. Cmt. Mem: Luzerne Co, Pa. and Am. Bar Asns; pres, Wilkes-Barre C. of C; bd. of dirs, Wyo. Valley Motor Club; bd. of dirs, Cath. Charities; bd. of trustees and bd. of gov, Welfare Fedn; mem. bar, D.C. and U.S. Supreme Courts; v.chmn, spec. cmt. to investigate Katyn Massacre, murder of Polish officers by Russians. Mailing Add: The Congressional Hotel, Washington, D.C. 20003.

FLORA, HELEN ELIZABETH D
V.Chmn, Monroe Co. Dem. Party, Ind.
b. Moran, Ind, 10/27/11; d. Lewis Walter White and Maude Clare Suver W; m. 9/15/31 to Tom L. Flora; c. Suzanne (Mrs. Evins) and Bonnie Jo (Mrs. Rechter). Educ: Cutler High Sch. Polit. & Govt. Pos: Dem. precinct committeewoman or v.committeeman, Bloomington, Ind, 48-; del, State Dem. Conv, 58-68; mem. publicity cmt, Nat. Dem. Women's Conv, 60; pres, Women's Dem. Club, 3 years and treas, 2 years; secy, Monroe Co. Dem. Party, 62-63, v.chmn, 63-66 & 68- Bus. & Prof. Pos:Bookkeeper, water off, Bloomington, Ind, 58-63; secy, State Rev. Off, 63; mgr, Monroe Co. License Br, Bur. Motor Vehicles, 64- Mem: Girl Scout leader and cookie chmn, 10 years; Eastern Star, Star Point, 2 years. Worked in United Fund, Cancer, Heart and other civic drives; group leader for several years and secy-treas of Women's Div. for 2 years, First Christian Church; Am. Bus. Women's Asn. Rel: Christian Church. Mailing Add: 409 W. Second, Bloomington, Ind. 47401.

FLORENCE, BRIAN RICH D
Utah State Rep.
b. Ogden, Utah, 8/16/41; s. L.H. Florence and Goldie Brian F; m. 3/13/64 to LeAnna Read; c. Trent Brian. Educ: Weber State Col, B.S, 65; Univ. Utah, J.D, 68. Polit. & Govt. Pos: Pres, Young Dem. of Weber Co, Utah, 65-67;

secy, Weber Co. Dem. Party, 66-68; Utah State Rep, 69- Bus. & Prof. Pos: Instr. police sci, Weber State Col, 68-69; attorney-at-law. Mil. Serv: Airman 2/C, Air Force Res, 59-66. Mem: Utah State and Weber Co. Bar Asns; Utah Educ. Asn; NAACP; Am. Civil Liberties Union. Rel: Latter-day Saint. Mailing Add: 516 Eccles Bldg, Ogden, Utah 84401.

FLORES, ALFRED SAN NICOLAS D
Sen, Guam Legis.
b. Inarajan, Guam, 6/20/16; s. Jose Duenas Flores and Rafaela Lujan San Nicolas F; m. 2/18/39 to Esther Paulino Duenas; c. Lucille (Mrs. Robert Berzoy), Mae and Fred. Educ: Attended Guam Inst. Polit. & Govt. Pos: Assemblyman, Guam Assembly, 49-50; mem. Bd. of Educ, Govt. of Guam, 52-56; treas, Popular Party of Guam, 56-57; Sen, Guam Legis, 57-64 & 67-; chmn, Selective Serv. Bd, currently. Bus. & Prof. Pos: Poultry and cattle rancher, 58-; real estate broker, 58-; owner, retail-gen. store, 39- Mem: Farmers Coop; Civic Improv. Club; Food Defense Coun. Cert. for Active Membership in Selective Serv. Rel: Roman Catholic. Legal Res: Inarajan Village, Agana, Guam 96910. Mailing Add: P.O. Box 991, Agana, Guam 96910.

FLORES, ANGEL A. R
b. Zapata, Tex, 9/24/20; s. Adalberto Flores and Josefa San-Miguel F; m. 1/4/48 to Salome Judith; c. Sandra M. and David A. Educ: Massey Bus. Col, Houston. Polit. & Govt. Pos: Mem, exec. cmt, Zapata Co. Rep. Party, Tex, 60-64, former chmn. Bus. & Prof. Pos: Motel owner and operator; field off. mgr, Olsen Eng. Corp, 57-65, asst. supt, 65- Mil. Serv: Entered as A/S, Navy, 40, released as Chief Pharmacist's Mate, 46, after serv. in Submarine Serv, Southwest Pac, 41-46; Submarine Combat Pin; Pre Pearl Harbor, Pac. and Am. Theater Ribbons; Good Conduct Medal. Mem: Am. Legion (Comdr, Post 486, 47-53); VFW; Submarine Vet. World War II. Rel: Catholic. Mailing Add: P.O. Box 448, Zapata, Tex. 78076. (1967)

FLORES, ARTURO FRANCISCO D
Mayor, Eagle Pass, Tex.
b. Eagle Pass, Tex, 9/20/28; s. Arturo Flores and Margaret Streigler F; m. 1/31/50 to Martha Henderson; c. Deborah Kay and Arturo Francisco, Jr. Educ: Sul Ross State Col, B.B.A, 50; Tex. A&M Col, 45-48. Polit. & Govt. Pos: Trustee, Eagle Pass Independent Sch. Dist, Tex, 59-61, pres, Bd. of Trustees, 62; del, Tex. State Dem. Conv, 62, 64 & 66; mayor, Eagle Pass, Tex, 66-; del, Dem. Nat. Conv, 68. Bus. & Prof. Pos: Secy-treas, Arturo Flores Trading Corp, 58-; pres, Am-Tube Co, 59-64; gen. mgr, Arturo Flores Forwarding, 59-; dir, First Nat. Bank, Eagle Pass, 66-; pres, Hallmark Aviation, 67- Mil. Serv: Entered as Pvt, Marine Corps, 52, released as Cpl, 64, after serv. in 11th Marines, First Marine Div, Korea, 53-54; Korean Theatre Ribbon with One Battle Star on Combat Medal. Mem: C. of C.(past dir); Concho Valley Boy Scout Coun.(exec. bd. mem); S.Tex. Regional Export Expansion Coun; Rotary (past pres); United Fund (advance gifts chmn). App. by Gov. to Criminal Justice Coun, Tex. Rel: Catholic. Legal Res: 576 Ceylon St, Eagle Pass, Tex. 78852. Mailing Add: P.O. Box 707, Eagle Pass, Tex. 78852.

FLOURNOY, CAROLYN CLAY R
V.Chmn. Cuddo Parish, Rep. Exec. Cmt, La.
b. Pine Bluff, Ark, 7/1/24; d. Paul Eugene Clay and Ruth Elmer C; m. 5/14/47 to Camp Rogers Flournoy; c. Clay McAfee, John Craig, Kathryn and Charles Rogers. Educ: Centenary Col, B.S, 45; Northwest. Univ, M.A, 47; Chi Omega; Maroon Jacket; Cencoe. Polit. & Govt. Pos: Rep. cand, Sch. Bd, La, 66; v.chmn, Polit. Action Cmt, 67; alternate del, Rep. Nat. Conv, 68; v.chmn, Cuddo Parish Rep. Exec. Cmt, 68- Bus. & Prof. Pos: Copywriter, Bozell & Jacobs Agency; Shreveport, 47-48; asst. prof, Centenary Col, 51-54, alumni and public rels. dir, 54-56; feature writer Woman's Page, Shreveport Times, 68- Mem: La. Press Women's Asn; Shreveport Jr. League; Woman's Dept. Club; Shreveport Country Club; Cotillion Club; Royal Club; YWCA (mem. bd); Goodwill Industries(mem. bd); Chi Omega Alumnae; Am. Contract Bridge League. Rel: Episcopal. Mailing Add: 818 Erie, Shreveport, La. 71106.

FLOURNOY, HOUSTON IRVINE R
Calif. State Controller
b. New York, N.Y, 10/7/29; s. William Raymond Flournoy and Helen Horner F; m. 7/11/54 to Marjorie Elsie Westerkamp; c. David Houston and Jean Douglas. Educ: Cornell Univ, B.A, 50; Princeton Univ, M.A, 52, Ph.D, 56; Pi Sigma Alpha; Lamba Chi Alpha. Polit. & Govt. Pos: Research asst, Div. Law Rev. and Legis. Info, N.J. Legis, 54-55; legis. asst. to U.S. Sen. H. Alexander Smith, N.J, 55-57; Calif. State Assemblyman, 61-66, secy, Assembly Rep. Caucus, 61-62; mem, Los Angeles Co. Rep. Cent. Cmt. and Calif. Rep. State Cent. Cmt, 61-69, chmn, Div. Arts and Sci. and Platform and Principles Cmt, 63; del, Rep. Nat. Conv, 68; Calif. State Controller, currently. Bus. & Prof. Pos: Assoc. prof. govt, Pomona Col. and Claremont Grad. Sch, 57-67. Mil. Serv: Entered as 2nd Lt, Air Force, 52, released as 1st Lt, 54, after serv. in 474th Fighter Bomber Group, Korea, 53-54; Maj, Calif. Air Nat. Guard, at present; Korean Theater and Am. Defense Ribbons; UN Serv. Medal. Publ: Legislative Bodies in California, Dickinson Publ. Co, 66; 'The Role of the California Republican Delegation' in Inside Politics: The National Conventions, 1960, ed. by Paul Tillett, Oceana, 62. Mem: West. and Am. Polit. Sci. Asns. Rel: Congregational. Mailing Add: State Capitol, Sacramento, Calif. 98515.

FLOURNOY, ROBERT EDWARD, JR. D
Chmn, Cobb Co. Dem. Exec. Cmt, Ga.
b. Atlanta, Ga, 9/30/30; s. Robert Edward Flournoy, Sr. and Myrtis Hitchcock F; m. 12/29/51 to Elaray Palm Griggers; c. Robert E. II, Matthew C, Claudia G. and Natalie R. Educ: Emory Univ, B.A, 51; Univ. Ga, LL.B, 52; Kappa Alpha; Omicron Delta Kappa; Phi Delta Phi; Pi Sigma Alpha; Demosthenian Lit. Soc. Polit. & Govt. Pos: Asst. attorney gen, Ga; Ga. State Rep, 63-64; chmn, Cobb Co. Dem. Exec. Cmt, currently. Bus. & Prof. Pos: Law clerk, Judge Ralph H. Pharr, 53; assoc. law practice, Dunaway & Embry, 54-56; attorney and partner, Reed, Flournoy and Tate, 57- Mil. Serv: Air Force, Judge Adv. Gen. Dept, 52-53, 1st Lt; Capt, Air Force Res. Publ: Various prfnl. articles and case notes, Ga. Bar Jour. Mem: Mason; Scottish Rite; Shrine; Kiwanis; Marietta Citizens Adv. Cmt. Rel: Southern Baptist. Mailing Add: Blair Bldg, Marietta, Ga. 30060. (1967)

FLOWERS, RICHMOND McDAVID D
b. Dothan, Ala, 11/11/18; s. John Jefferson Flowers and Ila McDavid F; m. 4/18/46 to Mary Kathrine Russell; c. Mary Russell, Jefferson Hampton and Richmond M, Jr. Educ: Auburn Univ, B.S, 39; Univ. Ala, LL.B, 48; Blue Key; Phi Delta Phi; Sigma Alpha Epsilon. Polit. & Govt. Pos: Attorney Gen, State of Ala, 63-67; Ala. State Sen, 55-59. Mil. Serv: Entered as Pvt, Army, 42, released as Capt, 46, after serv. in Gen. Hq, Pac, 45-46. Publns: 'Southern Plain Talk,' Look Magazine, April 17, 65; 'Citizenship and Respect for Law,' Univ. Tenn. Law Review, Spring, 66. Mem: VFW; Am. Legion; Rotary; Elks; Masons. Rel: Methodist. Mailing Add: 3501 Lansdown Dr, Montgomery, Ala. 36111. (1967)

FLOWERS, WALTER WINKLER, JR. D
U.S. Rep, Ala.
b. Greenville, Ala, 4/12/33; s. Walter Winkler Flowers, Sr. and Ruth Swaim F; m. to Margaret Pringle; c. Vivian, Walter W, III and Victor. Educ: Univ. Ala, A.B, 55; Univ. London, Eng, LL.B, 57; Phi Beta Kappa; Omicron Delta Kappa; Jasons Soc; Phi Delta Phi; Sigma Alpha Epsilon; pres, Student Govt. Asn, Univ. Ala. Polit. & Govt. Pos: Former mem. and chmn, Tuscaloosa City Civil Serv. Bd, Ala; U.S. Rep, Ala, 69- Mil. Serv: Res. officer, Mil. Intel, Army, 55, released as Lt, 59. Mem: Local, Ala. State, Miss. State and Am. Bar Asns; Black Warrior Coun, Boy Scouts; YMCA; former pres, Tuscaloosa Co. Red Cross and Tuberc. Asn; former pres, Tuscaloosa Co. Ment. Health Asn; Rotary; United Fund. Rel: Episcopal. Legal Res: 273 Woodland Hills, Tuscaloosa, Ala. 35401. Mailing Add: 1314 Longworth House Office Bldg, Washington, D.C. 20515.

FLOY, DELBERT WILLIAM D
b. Thornton, Iowa, 2/28/27; s. Christian C. Floy and Anna F; m. 9/8/51 to Mary Madden; c. Christopher, Stephanie and Regina. Educ: Thornton Pub. Schs. Polit. & Govt. Pos: Iowa State Sen. until 66; postmaster, Thornton, 67- Bus. & Prof. Pos: Former fertilizer dealer; securities salesman and farmer. Mil. Serv: Air Force, 45-46. Mem: Farmers Union. Rel: Catholic. Mailing Add: Thornton, Iowa 50479.

FLOYD, ERVIN RICHARD R
Chmn, Jasper Co. Rep. Party, S.C.
b. Tillman, S.C, 3/29/34; s. Clarence Wilson Floyd (deceased) and Flossie Ivey F; m. 12/10/55 to Shirley Ann Jones; c. Ervin R, Jr. and Clarence Mitchell. Educ: Ridgeland High Sch. Polit. & Govt. Pos: Finance chmn, Goldwater for Pres. Campaign, S.C, 64; chmn, First Cong. Dist. Voter Registrn, S.C. Rep. Party, 65; chmn, Jasper Co. Rep. Party, S.C, 65-; cand, U.S. House of Rep, 66. Bus. & Prof. Pos: Sales rep, Coastal Paper Co, 59- Mil. Serv: BM-3, Navy, 57-59; Naval Res, 6 yrs. Mem: Bd. of dirs, Ridgeland Jaycees, 64, v. pres, 65 and state dir, 66; Civitan Club; Jasper Co. C. of C; Am. Lodge 98, AFM. Organized the first Rep. Party in the hist. of Jasper Co, 65; received following awards from Jaycees: Spoke, Spark Plug, Speak-up Jaycee; selected Outstanding Young Man of the Year in Jasper Co, 64. Rel: Baptist. Mailing Add: P.O. Box 602, Ridgeland, S.C. 29936.

FLOYD, JAKE CARLSON R
b. Jena, La, 1/14/19; s. William Benjamin Floyd and Ethel Simmons F; m. 2/10/52 to Mary Lois Calcote; c. James Edwin and Vicki Lynne. Educ: Tyler Commercial Col, Tex; Southwest. Diesel Eng. Sch, Houston, Tex. Polit. & Govt. Pos: Former chmn, Bowie Co. Rep. Party, Tex. Bus. & Prof. Pos: Mgr, Lindsey & Newsom, Ins. Adjusters, 46- Mil. Serv: Entered as Pvt, Army, 41, released as 1st Lt, 46, after serv. in 193rd Ord. Depot Co, Southwest Pac. Area; Asiatic-Pac. Campaign Medal with Bronze Star; Am. Campaign Medal. Mem: Okla. Claim Men Asn; Ark. Adjusters Asn; Tex. and Nat. Asns. Independent Ins. Adjusters; Am. Legion; VFW; Kiwanis. Rel: Baptist. Legal Res: 3002 Meadows Dr, Texarkana, Tex. 75501. Mailing Add: P.O. Box 1375, Texarkana, Tex. 75501. (1967)

FLOYD, JAMES H. D
Ga. State Rep.
b. Trion, Ga, 2/4/20; s. John H. Floyd and Lessie Parris F; m. 1/29/43 to Doris R. Smallwood; c. Nancy Jim, Susan Myra and James Henson, Jr. Educ: Trion Ga. High Sch, grad; Middle Ga. Jr. Col. Polit. & Govt. Pos: Ga. State Rep, 53- Bus. & Prof. Pos: Salesman. Mil. Serv: Air Force, Maj, 41-46. Mem: Mason; past state comdr, VFW of Ga; Am. Legion; past pres, Seventh Dist. Legis. Asn. Rel: Baptist. Mailing Add: 11 Sunset Lane, Trion, Ga. 30753. (1967)

FLOYD, MAYNARD D
City Councilman, Wilmington, Ohio
b. Wilmington, Ohio, 10/31/01; s. William H. Floyd and Mary A. Morris F; m. 12/4/36 to Mary Frances Tharp; c. Lucy (Mrs. R. Lee Brooks), Stanley E, Phillip J. and Phyllis K. Educ: Wilmington High Sch, Ohio, 4 years. Polit. & Govt. Pos: Chmn, Clinton Co. Dem. Exec. Cmt, Ohio; city councilman, Wilmington, Ohio, 57- Bus. & Prof. Pos: Br. mgr, Abbott Linen, 50-68. Mem: Laundry and Linen Supply Union; Eagles (state pres, 63-64 and grand v.pres, currently); VFW. Rel: Protestant. Legal Res: 761 Douglas St, Wilmington, Ohio 45177. Mailing Add: Box 202, Wilmington, Ohio 45177.

FLOYD, NOAH EUGENE D
W.Va. State Sen.
b. Chattaroy, W.Va, 6/10/17; s. William Troy Floyd, Sr. and Lillie Adair F; m. 1/25/37 to Thelma Farley; c. Janith Sue (deceased), Patricia Jane (Mrs. D.E. Staker) and Alana Jean (Mrs. Thomas J. Mearns). Educ: Glenville State Col, A.B, 48; Marshall Univ, M.A, 54. Polit. & Govt. Pos: W.Va. State Del, 54-62; W.Va. State Sen, Sixth Dist, 56-; chmn, Mingo Co. Dem. Exec. Cmt, 63- Bus. & Prof. Pos: Prin. and asst. supt. schs, Mingo Co, W.Va, 54-62; dist. mgr. and consult, Charles E. Merrill Publ. Co, 62- Mil. Serv: Pvt, Army, 43. Mem: W.Va. and Ky. Bookmens Asn; past pres, Mingo Co. Prin. Asn; Int. Platform Cmt; Moose; Kiwanis. Rel: Baptist. Mailing Add: 210 Oak, Williamson, W.Va. 25661.

FLOYD, PAUL D
b. 5/4/29. Educ: Tulane Univ, B.A; Univ. Houston Law Sch, LL.B. Polit. & Govt. Pos: Asst. state attorney gen, Tex, 59-61; Tex. State Rep, 61-68. Bus. & Prof. Pos: Attorney-at-law. Mil. Serv: Korean War Vet. Tex. Rehab. Asn. Legislator of the Year Award. Mailing Add: 2406 Bluewater Lane, Houston, Tex. 77018. (1967)

FLOYD, SIDNEY THOMAS D
S.C. State Rep.
b. Horry Co, S.C, 8/25/29; s. William Cater Floyd and Ruth Smith F; m. 6/4/56 to Alice Anne Skinner; c. Frances Mozell, Patricia Ann, Anita Ruth and William Thomas. Educ: Univ. S.C, 47-50; Univ. S.C. Law Sch, LL.B, 56; Pi Kappa Phi; Alpha Delta Phi. Polit. & Govt. Pos: City Judge, Conway, S.C, 59-64; U.S. Cmnr, 64-67; S.C. State Rep, 69- Mil. Serv: Pvt, Qm. Corps, Army, ETO, 51-53. Mem: S.C. State and Horry Co. Bar Asns; C. of C; pres, Jaycees 58. Rel: Baptist. Mailing Add: 1115 Third Ave, Conway, S.C. 29526.

FLURY, JOSEPH EDWARD D
b. Cleveland, Ohio, 5/12/10; s. Jacob E. Flury and Genevieve Foy F; m. 6/16/34 to Helen Anna Konkoy; c. Paul J, Irene L, Robert J. and Barbara E. Educ: Cleveland Col, West. Reserve Univ, B.Sc, 34. Polit. & Govt. Pos: Councilman, Oak Harbor, Ohio, 48-52, mayor, 52-60; secy, Ottawa Co. Dem. Cent. Cmt, 50-52, chmn, Dem. Exec. Cmt, 52-66. Bus. & Prof. Pos: Chemist, Standard Brands, Inc, 28-34; chemist and prod. mgr, J. Weller Co, 34-66. Publ: 'Reducing Costs in Food Production,' Food Industs, 48. Mem: K. of C; C. of C. Rel: Roman Catholic. Mailing Add: 216 Oak St, Oak Harbor, Ohio 43449.

FLYNN, ANN DOLORES R
Monmouth Co. State Committeewoman
b. Asbury Park, N.J, 10/17/12; d. John De Sarno and Carmel Vacchiano D; m. 10/18/46 to John Doyle Flynn; c. Angela T. and Ellen E. Educ: Beans Bus. Col, Asbury Park. Polit. & Govt. Pos: Exec. secy, Monmouth Co. Rep. Cmt, N.J, 35-53; dist. elec. bd. mem, Asbury Park, 55-60; finance chmn, State Fedn. Rep. Women, 62, pres, 67-; pres, Monmouth Co. Affiliated Women Rep. Clubs, 63-64; del, Rep. Nat. Conv, 64 & 68; secy. and v.chmn, State Asn. of N.J.; v.pres, N.J. State Rep. Fedn. Women; v.chmn, Monmouth Co. Rep. Exec. Cmt, currently; asst. campaign mgr, N.J. State for Nixon Campaign, 68; Monmouth Co. State Committeewoman, 69- Bus. & Prof. Pos: Secy. Bur. Health and Publ. Dept, Asbury Park, N.J, 36-38, registrar Vital Statistics, 38-50 and mem. Welfare Cmt. Mem: Chmn, Red Cross Drive; area capt, Commun. Chest; chmn, Muscular Dystrophy Drive; secy, PTA, Mt. Carmel Sch; v.pres, PTA, St. Rose High Sch; secy, Opera Guild of Monmouth Co; pres, Bus. & Prfnl. Women, Shore Area, 61-62; pres, Women's Columbian League of Monmouth Co, 53-56; pres, Princess Maria Jose Lodge of Asbury Park, 39-40; officer, Cmnrs. of Orphanage Home, Nutley. Rel: Catholic. Mailing Add: 133 Norwood Ave, Deal, N.J. 07723.

FLYNN, DAVID L. D
Mass. State Rep.
b. 2/5/33; s. Thomas J. Flynn and Edith Yeaton F; m. 9/17/54 to Jean S. Denton; Thomas Michael and Daniel Patrick. Educ: Bridgewater State Col, B.S. in Educ, 58; Mass. Inst. Tech, grad. work in Am. Govt. and Physics, 59; Bache & Co, Middletown, N.J, adv. study in Stocks, Bonds & Investment Procedure, 61; Am. Mgt. Asn. Sch, 69; Alpha Upsilon. Polit. & Govt. Pos: Park Cmnr, Bridgewater, Mass, 56-59; mem, Bd. Selectment, Assessors and Overseers of Welfare, 64-67, chmn, 67; mem, Great and Gen. Court, Mass, 64-; chmn, Indust. Develop. Corp, Bridgewater, 66-68, mem, currently; town moderator, Bridgewater, 69-; Mass. State Rep, currently. Bus. & Prof. Pos: Mem, bd. dir, Bridgewater Coop. Bank, Mass. and corporator, Bridgewater Savings Bank, currently. Mil. Serv: Navy Med. Dept, 51-54. Mem: Bd. dir, Bridgewater Vet, Inc, 61-67, clerk, 65-66; Kiwanis Club, Bridgewater, Mass; Mitchell Mem. Club, Middleboro; Am. Legion. Distinguished serv. award, Jaycees, 69. Rel: Catholic. Legal Res: 317 Water St, Bridgewater, Mass. 02324. Mailing Add: P.O. Box 33, Bridgewater, Mass. 02324.

FLYNN, G. ELMER D
Mont. State Sen.
b. Missoula, Mont, 1/2/19; s. John J. Flynn and Mary Helterline F; m. 1/21/39 to Mary A. Ahern; c. Marifrances (Mrs. Edward K. Courtney) and Colleen Carol. Educ: Missoula Schs, 12 years. Polit. & Govt. Pos: Mont. State Rep, 63-67; Mont. State Sen, 67- Bus. & Prof. Pos: Mem, Hellgate Sch. Bd, 10 years; dir, Hellgate Valley Irrigation Co, 17 years. Mem: Moose; Eagles; K. of C. Rel: Catholic. Mailing Add: Mullan Rd, Missoula, Mont. 59801.

FLYNN, GERALD THOMAS D
b. Racine, Wis, 10/7/10; s. John Joseph Flynn and Margaret Williams F; m. 8/3/38 to Mary Cecilia McAvoy; c. Ellen, Dennis, Gerald, Jr. and Agnes. Educ: Marquette Univ. Law Sch, J.D, 33; Delta Theta Phi. Polit. & Govt. Pos: Wis. State Sen, 21st Dist, 50-54; U.S. Rep, First Dist, Wis, 59-61. Bus. & Prof. Pos: Attorney-at-law, 33- Mem: Elks; Eagles. Rel: Catholic. Legal Res: 3065 Ruby Ave, Racine, Wis. 53403. Mailing Add: 310 Fifth St, Racine, Wis. 53402.

FLYNN, JAMES JAY, JR. D
Mayor, Perth Amboy, N.J.
b. Perth Amboy, N.J, 6/4/10; s. James J. Flynn and Mary Rodecker F; m. 11/14/36 to Estelle Wodzinski; c. Dr. James J, III, Dennis S. and Brendan J. Educ: Renouard Sch. Mortuary Sci, 30-31. Polit. & Govt. Pos: Coroner, Middlesex Co, N.J, 38-41 & 45-48; del, Dem. Nat. Conv, 56, 60, 64 & 68; mayor, Perth Amboy, 50- Bus. & Prof. Pos: Pres, Flynn and Son Funeral Homes, 33-66; dir, Perth Amboy Nat. Bank. Mem: Nat. and N.J. Funeral Dirs. Asns; U.S. Conf. of Mayors; Elks; Moose; Eagles; Hibernians; K. of C; Royal Arcanium; Am. Fedn. of Musicians; Lions; Navy League; Exempt Firemens Asn. Boating, sport participation. Rel: Roman Catholic. Legal Res: 157 High St, Perth Amboy, N.J. 08861. Mailing Add: 424 East Ave, Perth Amboy, N.J. 08861. (1967)

FLYNN, JOHN E. R
N.Y. State Sen.
married; c. four daughters. Educ: N.Y. Univ; Columbia Univ. Polit. & Govt. Pos: Mayor, Yonkers, N.Y, 61-66; N.Y. State Sen, 67- Bus. & Prof. Pos: Partner, V.Pres, Blakeley & Tobin, Inc, Oil Distributors. Mem: Past Pres, Jr. C. of C; Catholic Youth Orgn; United Givers Fund. Distinguished Serv. Award, N.Y. State Jr. C. of C; B'nai B'rith Brotherhood Award, 64. Rel: Catholic. Mailing Add: 15 Huron Rd, Yonkers, N.Y. 10710.

FLYNN, JOHN JAMES D
b. Ottawa, Ill, 8/28/94; s. James J. Flynn and Josephine Rassitoi F; m. 4/14/17 to Nellie V. Cole. Polit. & Govt. Pos: Justice of peace, Dayton Twp, Ill, 27-61 and assessor, 61-; committeeman, Wedron Dem. Cmt, Ill, 34-; rep. committeeman, Ill. Dem. Cmt, 66- Bus. & Prof. Pos: Agent, Continental Ins, Wedron, Ill, 32- Mem: Elks; Am. Red Cross. Rel: Catholic. Mailing Add: P.O. Box 56, Wedron, Ill. 60557.

FLYNN, ROBERT DOUGLAS R
Ky. State Sen.
b. Lexington, Ky, 7/25/27; s. Clarence Melvin Flynn and Delina Brandenburg F; m. 8/3/46 to Ella Ritchey Crowe; c. Robert Douglas, Jr, Melanie Dee and Bradley Clark. Educ: Univ. Dayton, 4 years. Polit. & Govt. Pos: Ky. State Sen, 68- Mil. Serv: Entered as Pvt, Army, 46, released as 2/5, 47, after serv. as admin. clerk, Army Grounds Force Serv, Ft. Bragg, 46-47. Mem: All sports asns. in dist. Rel: Baptist. Mailing Add: 428 McKenna Court, Lexington, Ky. 40505.

FLYNT, JOHN J, JR. D
U.S. Rep, Ga.
b. Griffin, Ga, 11/8/14; s. John J. Flynt, Sr. and Susan Banks F; m. 2/7/42 to Patricia Bradley; c. Susan Banks, John James III and Crisp Bradley. Educ: Univ. of Ga, A.B, 36; Geo. Wash. Univ. Law Sch, LL.B, 40; Sigma Alpha Epsilon; Phi Delta Phi. Polit. & Govt. Pos: Former asst. U.S. attorney, North. Dist. Ga; Ga. State Rep, 47-48; solicitor gen, Griffin Judicial Circuit, 49-54; U.S. Rep, Ga, 54- Bus. & Prof. Pos: Attorney-at-law. Mil. Serv: Army, 41-45; grad, Command & Gen. Staff Sch. and Air Corps Adv. Flying Sch, Brooks Field, Tex; Col, Army Res; Bronze Star Medal. Mem: Past pres, Solicitors Gen. Asn. of Ga; past pres, Ga. Bar Asn; Griffin Circuit and Am. Bar Asns; Mason; Shrine; Am. Legion; VFW; Kiwanis; WOW; Elks. Admitted to practice before all courts. Rel: Methodist; Chmn, Bd. of Stewards. Legal Res: Griffin, Ga. Mailing Add: 2335 Rayburn House Office Bldg, Washington, D.C. 20515. (1967)

FLYNT, WALES THORNTON D
b. Sharon, Ga, 11/26/97; s. James Wesley Flynt and Mamie Meadows F; m. to Ruth Chew; c. Kathlyn Mitchell (Mrs. Augustus Barksdale); grandchildren: Wales Flynt Barksdale, Augustus Randolph Barksdale, III, Kathleen Mitchell Barksdale, Brett Barksdale. Educ: Sharon High Sch. Polit. & Govt. Pos: Ga. State Rep, 51-66. Bus. & Prof. Pos: Flynt Lumber Co; V.pres, Union Point Bank. Rel: Methodist. Mailing Add: Crawfordville, Ga. 30631. (1967)

FOERSTER, ALVIN E, JR. R
b. Rosenberg, Tex, 12/4/35; s. Alvin E. Foerster and Esther Jamieson F; m. 11/21/59 to Tommy Sue Morehead. Educ: Tex. A&M Univ, B.B.A, 58. Polit. & Govt. Pos: Precinct chmn, Rep. Party, Tex, 60-64; former chmn, Ft. Bend Co. Rep. Exec. Cmt. Bus. & Prof. Pos: Co-owner and mgr, Foerster Ins. Agency, 58-; chmn, Rosenberg Tax Cmn, 64-66. Mil. Serv: 2nd Lt, Army 59; 1st Lt, Res, 59-66. Mem: Pres, Rosenberg Lions Club; officer and dir, Rosenberg C. of C. Rel: Methodist. Legal Res: 1802 Klauke, Rosenberg, Tex. 77471. Mailing Add: Box 471, Rosenberg, Tex. 77471. (1967)

FOERSTER, THOMAS JOSEPH D
Co. Cmnr, Allegheny Co, Pa.
b. Pittsburgh, Pa, 4/17/28; s. J. Edward Foerster and Eleanor Heyl F; single. Educ: Slippery Rock State Col, 45-47; Univ. Pittsburgh, B.S, 50. Polit. & Govt. Pos: Admin. asst, Pittsburgh City Coun, Pa, 55-57; staff mem, Civil Serv. Cmn, Pittsburgh, 57-59; admin. asst, Pittsburgh, 59-; Pa. State Rep, 58-68, v.chmn, State Govt. Cmt, Pa. State House of Rep, 61-62, chmn, Fisheries Cmt, 65-66 and Spec. Clean Streams Cmt, 66; co. cmnr, Allegheny Co, 67-; del, Dem. Nat. Conv, 68. Mem: Water Pollution Control Asn. of Pa; Moose; Eagles; Lions; Perry Athletic Asn; K. of C. Varsity Football, Slippery Rock State Col. Rel: Catholic. Mailing Add: 3714 Ruggles St, Pittsburgh, Pa. 15214.

FOGG, EDNA D. R
b. Gorham, Maine; married; c. Two. Educ: Gorham Normal Sch. Polit. & Govt. Pos: N.H. State Rep, 63-67; former mem, Milan Sch. Bd. Bus. & Prof. Pos: Housewife; former teacher. Mem: Grange. Rel: Methodist. Mailing Add: RFD 1, Berlin, N.H. 03570. (1967)

FOGG, LORIN RUSSELL R
Idaho State Rep.
b. Salem, Idaho, 8/21/09; s. Charles H. Fogg and Merilla Judy F; m. 9/4/39 to Neta May Browning; c. Gary, Reed, Marc, Barbara (Mrs. Lynn Bidstrup), Karen (Mrs. Dennis Chase) and Leon Howe. Educ: Col. of Idaho, 28-31; Univ. Idaho, South. Br, B.S. in Pharm, 33; Phi Delta Ki. Polit. & Govt. Pos: Idaho State Rep, Bonnevill Co, 55-59, Dist. 30, 68- Bus. & Prof. Pos: Pharmacist, Ford Drug, Pocatello, Idaho, 33-38; pharmacist and mgr. Moore Drug, 38-42; pharmacist and pres, Fogg Drug Co, Idaho Falls, 42- Mem: Idaho State Pharm. Asn; Kiwanis; C. of C. Rel: Latter-day Saint. Legal Res: 135-12th Idaho Falls, Idaho 83401. Mailing Add: Fogg Drug Co, 401 Park, Idaho Falls, Idaho 84301.

FOGLEMAN, JOHN ALBERT D
Assoc. Justice, Ark. Supreme Court
b. Memphis, Tenn, 11/5/11; s. John Franklin Fogleman and Julia McAdams F; m. 10/24/33 to Annis Adell Appleby; c. John Albert, Jr, Annis Adell (Mrs. Henry M. Rector) and Mary Barton (Mrs. Charles L. Williams, Jr). Educ: Univ. of Ark, 27-31; Univ. of Memphis Law Sch, LL.B, 34; Sigma Chi; Alpha Chi Sigma; Delta Theta Phi; Scabbard and Blade. Polit. & Govt. Pos: Dep. Circuit Court Clerk, Crittenden Co, Ark, 33-34; chmn, Crittenden Co. Dem. Cent. Cmt, 37-44; secy, Bd. Elec. Cmnrs, 37-44; dep. prosecuting attorney, Crittenden Co, 46-57; chmn, Ark. Judiciary Cmn, 63-65; mem. Ark. Constitutional Rev. Study Cmn, 67; assoc. justice, Ark. Supreme Court, 67- Bus. & Prof. Pos: Private practice, Marion, Ark, 34-44; partner, Hale & Fogleman, West Memphis, Ark, 44-66. Mil. Serv: Entered as Pvt, Army, 44, released as 1st Lt, 46, after serv. in Judge Adv. Gen. Dept, West. Pac, 45-46. Mem: State Bd. Bar Exam; Ark. Bar Asn.(past pres); Crittenden Co. Bar Asn.(past pres); Am. Bar Asn; Am. Judicature Soc; fel. Am. Col. Trial Lawyers; Rotary; Mason;

Am. Legion; VFW. Man of Year, West Memphis, Ark, 61. Rel: Methodist. Legal Res: Cherry St, Marion, Ark. 72364. Mailing Add: Justice Bldg, State Capitol, Little Rock, Ark. 72201.

FOGLIETTA, THOMAS M. R
City Councilman, Phila, Pa.
b. Phila, Pa, 12/3/28; s. Michael Foglietta and Rose F; single. Educ: St. Joseph's Col, B.S. in polit. sci, 49; Temple Univ. Sch. Law, LL.B, 52; Univ. Pa, Fels. Inst. State and Local Govt, 58 and 62. Hon. L.H.D, Phila. Col. Podiatry, 69. Polit. & Govt. Pos: First v.pres, Young Rep. Club Phila, Pa, 54-; city councilman, Phila, 55-, minority floor leader, city coun, 59-; del, Rep. Nat. Conv, 56, alternate del, 66; mem, Mayor's Freedom Week Cmt, 62; mem, Adv. Cmt. to Supt. Pub. Schs. on Integration and Inter-Group Activities. Bus. & Prof. Pos: Attorney-at-law, Phila, Pa, 53- Mem: Phila. and Am. Bar Asns; Justinian Soc. Phila; bd. dirs, Grant Cmt, Temple Univ. Alumni Asn; Loyal Legion; Temple Law Sch. Alumni Asn; Libr. Bldg. Fund Cmt, Temple Univ. Law Sch; St. Thomas Moore Soc; v.chmn, Easter Seal Drive, Phila. Soc. for Crippled Children and Adults; 61-66; dir, S.Phila. Br, Am. Red Cross; sponsor, S.Phila. Sandlot Sport Activities; chmn, South. Div, United Fund Drive; bd. trustees, St. Luke's and Children's Med. Center; Cmt. to Build James C. Giuffre Clin. for Aged; bd. dirs, Phila. Col. Podiatry; Citizens' Cmt. for Commun. Col; Sons of Italy; Men of Malvern; bd. trustees, Theatre of the Living Arts, Phila. and Am. Col. of Monaco, Monte-Carlo. Rel: Roman Catholic. Legal Res: 708 Clymer St, Philadelphia, Pa. 19147. Mailing Add: 592 City Hall, Philadelphia, Pa. 19151.

FOLCARELLI, GIOVANNI D
b. Providence, R.I, 5/30/26; m. to Jane Walsh. Educ: Boston Col, B.S, 1950; Boston Univ, LL.B, 52; Univ. R.I, M.P.A, 67; Pi Sigma Alpha. Polit. & Govt. Pos: Mem, Central Falls Dem. Club, R.I; mem, Young Dem. of R.I, 47-60; mem, R.I. Dem. State Cmt, 50-56; chmn, Scituate Dem. Town Cmt, 56; del, Dem. Nat. Conv, 60 & 64; mem, R.I. Narcotics Cmn, Rights of Way Cmn. and Emergency Milk Control Bd; admin. aide, Sen. Green, 56-60; spec. counsel to Attorney Gen, 61-64; Lt. Gov, R.I, 64-66. Bus. & Prof. Pos: Attorney-at-law. Mem: DAV; past v.pres, United Vets. Coun; W. Warwick Post Number 2, Am. Legion; K. of C; Providence Lodge of Elks; Boston Col. Club; Brown Club; Urban League; NAACP; Nat. Civic League; Am. Soc. for Pub. Admin; corp. mem, Providence Lying-In Hosp; Pocasset Casino Club; State Employees Local 904, AFL-CIO; Nat. Honor Soc. for Polit. Scientists; Kelley-Gazzero Post, VFW. Mailing Add: Chopmist Hill Rd, Scituate, R.I. 02857.

FOLEY, ALLEN RICHARD R
Vt. State Rep.
b. Framingham, Mass, 11/11/98; single. Educ: Dartmouth Col, A.B, 20; Univ. of Wis, M.A, 24; Harvard Univ. Polit. & Govt. Pos: Moderator, Norwich, Vt, 57-; chmn, Norwich Town Rep. Cmt, 64; Vt. State Rep, 65- Bus. & Prof. Pos: Former prof. hist, Dartmouth Col; trustee, Thetford Acad. Mil. Serv: Pvt, Army, 18. Mem: Hanover Rotary; Am. Legion; N.H. and Norwich Hist. Socs; Miss. Valley and Am. Hist. Asns; Vt. Civil War Centennial Cmt; trustee, Vt. Hist. Soc. Rel: Congregational. Mailing Add: McKenna Rd, Norwich, Vt. 05048. (1967)

FOLEY, CHARLES W. D
b. Concord, Mo, 12/7/94; m. 10/2/30 to Bertha Cooper. Educ: Rubicam Commercial Col. of St. Louis. Polit. & Govt. Pos: With Police Force, Tulsa, Okla, 3 years; Mo. State Rep, 50-68. Bus. & Prof. Pos: Elec. inspector, Pemiscot-Dunklin Elec. Coop, 10 years; electrician for musical comedies. Mil. Serv: Sgt. Maj, Army, World War I; elec. inspector, Navy, World War II, 9 months. Mem: Am. Legion; 40 et 8; Chef De Gare Passe, Voiture 156. Rel: Methodist. Mailing Add: North Park, Hayti, Mo. 63851. (1967)

FOLEY, EILEEN D
N.H. State Sen.
b. Portsmouth, N.H, 2/23/18; m; c. Three. Educ: Syracuse Univ, B.A; Univ. N.H; Beta Sigma Phi. Polit. & Govt. Pos: V.chmn, State Dem. Cmt, N.H; former v.chmn, Rockingham Co. Dem. Orgn; city clerk, Portsmouth, 5 years; secy, Portsmouth Dem. City Cmn, former chmn; mem, Portsmouth Sch. Bd, Second term; N.H. State Sen, 65-; mayor, Portsmouth, currently. Bus. & Prof. Pos: Dir, Portsmouth Rehabilitation Center; spec. serv. work, Navy. Mil. Serv: Women's Army Corp, 44-45. Mem: Frank Booma Post 6; Adult Coun, CYO; Portsmouth Col. Women's Club; K. of C. Auxiliary; St. Thomas Aquinas Mother's Guild; Immaculate Conception Alter Soc; Nat. Defense Adv. Cmt. on Women in Serv. Jaycees Distinguished Serv. Award, 68; Women Doer's Award in the field of politics, Nat. Dem. Women's Div; Rose of Honor Award, League of Women Voters. Rel: Catholic. Mailing Add: 39 Sunset Rd, Portsmouth, N.H. 03801.

FOLEY, EUGENE PATRICK D
b. Wabasha, Minn, 11/22/28; s. John Robert Foley (deceased) and Ellen Monica Brennan F.(deceased); m. 6/19/54 to Frances Mary Dillon; c. Anne Doris, Robert Dillon, Margaret Mary and Paul Hubert. Educ: St. Thomas Col, B.A, 52; Inst. European Studies, 52; Univ. Minn. Law Sch, LL.B, 55. Polit. & Govt. Pos: Legal counsel, U.S. Senate Small Bus. Cmt, 59-61; dep. asst. secy. of commerce, Bus. and Defense Serv. Admin, 61-62, adminstr, 62; dep. to Secy. of Commerce, Dept. of Commerce, 61-63; adminstr, Small Bus. Admin, 63-65; Asst. Secy. of Commerce and dir. of econ. develop, Dept. of Commerce, 65-68. Mil. Serv: Entered as Pvt, Army, 46, released as Cpl, 48. Publ: 'The Negro Businessman: In Search of a Tradition,' Daedalus, Winter, 66. Mem: Fed. Bar Asn; Philos. Soc. of Wash. D.C, VFW. Rel: Roman Catholic. Legal Res: 853 Lincoln Ave, St. Paul, Minn. 55105. Mailing Add: 9508 Burning Tree Rd, Bethesda, Md. 20034. (1967)

FOLEY, FRANK W. D
Wash. State Sen.
b. Spokane, Wash, 1913; m. to Betty. Educ: Wash. State Univ, B.A; Gonzaga Univ, LL.B. Polit. & Govt. Pos: Wash. State Sen, 57- Bus. & Prof. Pos: Attorney-at-law. Mil. Serv: Lt. Col, Army. Mem: Am. Legion; Elks. Mailing Add: 3924 Wayna Vista Dr, Vancouver, Wash. 98661. (1967)

FOLEY, JOHN FIELD R
Chmn, Santa Clara Co. Rep. Cent Cmt, Calif.
b. Tulsa, Okla, 8/6/31; s. Lyndon Lyman Foley and Margaret Cray F; m. 6/28/69 to Shirley L. Brancato. Educ: Univ. of Mich, 49-51; Stanford Univ, A.B, 53, LL.B, 56; Chi Phi. Polit. & Govt. Pos: Mem, Santa Clara Co. Rep. Cent. Cmt, Calif, 62-, chmn, 69- Mem: Santa Clara Co. and Am. Bar Asns; State Bar of Calif; Barristers Club of Santa Clara Co.(pres, 63); San Jose Stanford Club (pres, 64); Univ. Club of San Jose. Rel: Episcopal. Mailing Add: 18441 Hernandez Lane, Monte Sereno, Calif. 95030.

FOLEY, JOHN WELDEN R
b. Racine, Wis, 7/31/29; s. Jerome J. Foley and Rose I. Welden F; m. to Karolyn A. Smith; c. Elizabeth K. and Stephenie A. Educ: Marquette Univ, Ph.B, LL.B. and J.D; Delta Theta Phi. Polit. & Govt. Pos: Chmn, Racine Co. Rep. Party, Wis, 67-69. Mem: Am. and Wis. Bar Asns. Rel: Catholic. Legal Res: 3310 N. Main St, Racine, Wis. 53402. Mailing Add: 835 Wisconsin Ave, Racine, Wis. 53403.

FOLEY, THOMAS STEPHEN D
U.S. Rep, Wash.
b. Spokane, Wash, 3/6/29; s. Ralph E. Foley and Helen F. Educ: Univ. of Wash, B.A, 51, LL.B, 57. Polit. & Govt. Pos: Dep. prosecuting attorney, Spokane Co, Wash, 58; asst. attorney gen, Wash, 60; asst. chief clerk, Spec. Counsel, U.S. Senate Cmt. on Interior and Insular Affairs, 61-63; U.S. Rep, Wash, 64-; del, Dem. Nat. Conv, 68. Bus. & Prof. Pos: Mem, Law firm of Higgins & Foley, 57-; instr. constitutional law, Gonzaga Univ. Law Sch. Legal Res: 1228 29th Ave, Spokane, Wash. 99202. Mailing Add: 325 Cannon House Office Bldg, Washington, D.C. 20515.

FOLGER, FRED, JR. D
N.C. State Sen.
b. Mount Airy, N.C, 6/14/26; s. Fred Folger and Mary Mills Fawcett F; m. 3/24/51 to Elizabeth Cornelia Murray; c. Mary Mills Murray and Barbara Elizabeth. Educ: Duke Univ, A.B, 49, LL.B, 52; Kappa Alpha. Polit. & Govt. Pos: Co. attorney, Surry Co, N.C, 59-68 and chmn, Surry Co. Dem. Exec. Cmt, 65-68; N.C. State Sen, 69- Bus. & Prof. Pos: Dir, The First Nat. Bank, 59- Mil. Serv: Enlisted in Navy, 44, released as Aviation Radioman 2/C, 46. Mem: Am, N.C. and N.C. State Bar Asns; 17th Judicial Dist. Bar Asn. (pres, 68-69); Elks; Rotary. Rel: Methodist. Legal Res: 1015 N. Main St, Mount Airy, N.C. 27030. Mailing Add: P.O. Box 428, Mount Airy, N.C. 27030.

FOLGER, JOHN CLIFFORD R
b. Sheldon, Iowa, 5/28/96; s. Homer Folger and Emma Funston F; m. 11/2/29 to Kathrine Dulin; c. John Dulin and Lee Merritt. Educ: State Col. Wash, B.S, 17, M.S, 18. Polit. & Govt. Pos: Chmn, Rep. Nat. Finance Cmt, 55-57 & 60-61; Am. Ambassador to Belgium, 57-59. Bus. & Prof. Pos: Chmn. Bd, Folger, Nolan, Fleming & Co, Inc; dir, Int. Bus. Machines Corp, Hiram Walker-Gooderham & Worts, Ltd, Ont, Hilton Hotels Int, World Banking Corp. Limited, Nassau and Va. Indust, Inc. Mem: Former mem. bd. govs, N.Y. Stock Exchange; pres, Investment Bankers Asn, 43-45; chmn. D.C. chap, Am. Red Cross, 42, now hon. chmn, Wash. Cathedral chap, 1925 F. Street, Metrop, Chevy Chase, Alfalfa, Washington, D.C, The Brook, Pilgrims, Down Town Asn, New York, Lyford Cay, Nassau, Everglades, Bath and Tennis and Palm Beach Clubs. Rel: Episcopal. Legal Res: 2991 Woodland Dr. N.W, Washington, D.C. 20008. Mailing Add: 725 15th St. N.W, Washington, D.C. 20005.

FOLGER, THOMAS LEWELLYN 'JACK' D
b. Mt. Airy, N.C, 2/2/26; s. Alonzo Dillard Folger and Gertrude Reece F; m. 11/20/54 to Suzanne Robinson; c. Suzanne Winston. Educ: Northwest. Univ, Cmn. in Navy, 44; Univ. N.C, Chapel Hill, A.B, 48; Kappa Sigma; Carolina Polit. Union. Polit. & Govt. Pos: Pres, Surry Co. Young Dem, N.C, 50-51; del, Young Dem. Co. Conv, 51, 54 & 56; v.pres, Gaston Co. Young Dem, 54-55; Dem. v.chmn, Mt. Airy Precinct, 61, chmn, 62, 63 & 64; Surry Co. co-chmn, Moore for Gov. 64 and campaign mgr, Taylor for Lt. Gov, 68; trustee, Surry Community Col. and North. Surry Hosp. Found, 68; alternate del, Dem. Nat. Conv, 68. Bus. & Prof. Pos: Nat. Bank exam, Eighth Fed. Reserve Bank, 49-50; teacher-coach, Franklin High Sch, N.C, 50-54; sales rep, Carolina Container Co, 54-60; asst. prod. mgr, Qual. Mills, 60-64; asst. sales mgr, Spencer's Inc, 64- Mil. Serv: Entered as A/S, Navy, 43, released as Lt.(jg), 46, after serving on USS LCI Flotilla, U.S. Seventh Amphibious Fleet, S.Pac. Theatre, 44-46; S.Pac. Ribbon with two Stars; Philippine Liberation Ribbon with one Star; Presidential Unit Citation, Victory Medal. Mem: Am. Apparel Mfrs. Asn; Underwear Inst; Eagles; Elks; Rotary; VFW. Total Develop. Award, Gov. of N.C. Rel: Presbyterian. Mailing Add: 232 Grace St, Mt. Airy, N.C. 27030.

FOLK, DANIEL PAUL, II D
b. Wauchula, Fla, 8/28/27; s. William R. Folk and Pauline Wells F; m. 5/13/49 to Betty Mayer; c. Cheryl, Paul, Bill and Sarah. Educ: Clemson Col, 44-47; Newberry Col. Polit. & Govt. Pos: Mem, Co. Develop. Bd, S.C; chmn, Co. Youth Welfare Cmt, 61-62; chmn, Co. Nat. Found, 61-63; S.C. State Rep, 61-68. Bus. & Prof. Pos: Life underwriter, Equitable Life Assurance Soc. Mem: Farm Bur; Mason; Lions; Nat. Asn. of Life Underwriters; chmn, Co. March of Dimes, 59; past pres, Co. Girl Scout Coun; pres, Jaycees, 59-60; past state chmn, Civic Improv. of S.C. Rel: Mem, Bd. of Deacons, Chmn, 59-60, past pres, Men of the Church, Sunday Sch. teacher and supt. of Sabbath Schs, Newberry ARP Church. Mailing Add: 1220 Summer St, Newberry, S.C. 29108. (1967)

FOLKS, JAMES N. R
Mich. State Rep.
b. Hanover, Mich, 10/19/97; m. 11/5/19 to Jennie Strait; c. Esther, Lloyd, Richard, Philip and Beverly. Educ: Mich. State Univ, grad. Polit. & Govt. Pos: Former mem, Jackson Co. Tax Allocation Bd, Mich; chmn, Jackson Co. Ways and Means Cmt, 4 years; supvr, Spring Arbor Twp, 30-58; Mich. State Rep, 55- Bus. & Prof. Pos: Farmer. Mil. Serv: World War I. Mem: Former pres, Beth Moser Ment. Health Clin. Adv. Bd; v.chmn, Jackson Co. Soil Conserv. Dist; Concord Lions Club; Mason; Farm Bur; Spring Arbor Kiwanis Club. Rel: Protestant. Mailing Add: 6810 Moscow Rd, Horton, Mich. 49246. (1967)

FOLLETT, MURIEL R
Secy, Vt. Rep. State Cmt.
b. East Jamaica, Vt; m. to Robert C. Follett; c. Robert, Jr. and Jean (Mrs. Harold Willard). Educ: Leland & Gray Sem, Townshend, Vt, grad; Univ. Vt.

Polit. & Govt. Pos: Mem, Weathersfield Town Cmt, Vt; worked for State of Vt. on War Hist. Cmn, 44; mem. and secy, Springfield Town Planning Cmn, 53-62; secy, Windsor Co. Rep. Cmt; second v.pres, Vt. Fedn. Rep. Women, 67-69; secy, Vt. Rep. State Cmt, currently; mem, State Bd. Ment. Health, 69- Bus. & Prof. Pos: Elem. sch. teacher; farmer, 42- Publ: Auth, New England Years; A Drop in the Bucket; Springfield, The Machine Tool Town, Vt. Anthology. Mem: Hist. Soc; Assoc. Country Women of the World (Vt. rep, Triennial Conf, London, 39, del, Edinburgh, Scotland, 59 and Vt. rep, conf, East Lansing, Mich); Grange; Exten. Homemakers' Clubs; Weathersfield Citizens' Asn. Rel: Ascutney Union Church. Mailing Add: Ascutney, Vt. 05030.

FOLMER, LOUIS H. R

b. Biggsville, Ill, 4/15/04; m. to Elizabeth Butler; c. John and Richard. Educ: Cortland Normal Sch; Syracuse Univ. Col. of Law. Polit. & Govt. Pos: Dist. attorney, Cortland Co, N.Y, 35-41; N.Y. State Assemblyman, 50-68. Bus. & Prof. Pos: Partner, Folmer, Fenstermacher & Yesawich, Attorneys, currently. Mem: Cortland Co, N.Y. State and Am. Bar Asns; Cortland Lodge 470, F&AM; Elks. Mailing Add: 86 S. Main, Homer, N.Y. 13077.

FOLSOM, MARION BAYARD R

b. McRae, Ga, 11/23/93; s. William B. Folsom and Margaret Jane McRae F; m. 11/19/18 to Mary Davenport; c. Jane McRae (deceased), Marion Bayard and Frances. Educ: Univ. Ga, A.B, 12; Harvard, M.B.A, 14. Hon. LL.D, Univ. Rochester, 45, Hobart & William Smith Cols, 51, Syracuse Univ. and Tufts Univ, 55, Brown Univ, 57, Swarthmore Col, 57 and Hamilton Col, 62; D.C.S, N.Y. Univ, 50; D.C.L, Rollins Col, 57; D.P.S, Springfield Col, 62; D.Sc, Albany Med. Col, 66; Phi Beta Kappa; Sigma Nu. Polit. & Govt. Pos: Mem, Pres. Adv. Coun. Econ. Security, 34-35; employer del. from U.S. to Int. Labor Conf, Geneva, 36; mem, N.Y. State Adv. Coun. Unemploy. Ins, 35-50; mem, Fed. Adv. Coun. Soc. Security, 37-38; div. exec, Nat. Adv. Defense Cmn, 40-41; mem, Regional War Manpower Cmn, 42-45; staff dir, U.S. House of Rep. Spec. Cmn. Postwar Econ. Policy and Planning, 43-46; v.chmn, Pres. Adv. Cmn. Merchant Marine, 47-48; mem, Soc. Security Adv. Coun, U.S. Sen. Finance Cmn, 48; chmn. bd. trustees, Cmn. Econ. Develop, 50-52; Under Secy, Dept. of Treas, 53-55; Secy, Dept. Health, Educ. and Welfare, 55-58; mem, Fed. Hosp. Coun. and Fed. Adv. Coun. Soc. Security Financing; pres, Cmn. Heart Disease, Cancer and Stroke; chmn, Gov. Cmt. Hosp. Costs; v.chmn. bd. trustees, Cmt. Econ. Develop, 60-; chmn, adv. cmn, U.S. Pub. Health Serv, 61-62; chmn, Nat. Cmn. Commun. Health Serv, 62-; mem, Spec. Cmt. Social Sci, 68-69. Bus. & Prof. Pos: With Eastman Kodak, 14, treas, 35-53 and dir, 47-53 & 58-; trustee, Rochester Savings Bank, 31-49 & 58-; pres, Rochester Coun. Soc. Agencies, 34-36; pres, Eastman Savings & Loan Asn, 47-52; bd. overseers, Harvard Col, 51-57; bd. dirs, Brookings Inst; trustee, Univ. Rochester; bd. dirs, Nat. Bur. Econ. Research and Monroe Commun. Col, Rochester. Mil. Serv: Entered as 1st Lt, Army, 17, released as Capt, 19 after serv. in Officers Training Camp and Qm. Corps, overseas. Mem: Am. Statist. Asn; Acad. Arts and Sci; Am. Econ. Asn; hon. life mem. Nat. Educ. Asn; dir, Rochester Commun. Chest; Rochester C. of C.(past pres); N.Y. State Hosp. Rev. and Planning Coun, 65-; Univ. Club; Rochester Country Club; Genesee Valley Club; Pundit Club, Rochester; Harvard Club, N.Y.C; Metrop. Club, Wash, D.C. Albert Einstein Medal for Citizenship, 58. Rel: Presbyterian. Legal Res: 106 Oak Lane, Rochester, N.Y. 14610. Mailing Add: 343 State St, Rochester, N.Y. 14650.

FOLTZ, ANDY R

Del. State Sen.

b. 1926. Educ: Wesley Jr. Col; LaSalle Col. Polit. & Govt. Pos: Chmn, Kent Co. Rep. Cmt, Del, formerly; Del. State Sen, 67- Bus. & Prof. Pos: Dir, West-Dover Develop. Corp. and Indust. Develop. Cmn; pres, Int. Underwriters Ins. Co, currently. Mem: Past pres, Hartly Lions Club and Hartly Fire Co. Mailing Add: 804 Monroe Terrace, Dover, Del. 19901.

FOLZ, RICHARD E. R

Lt. Gov, Ind.

b. Evansville, Ind, 1/14/22; s. Frank J. Folz, Sr. and Mary Metzger F; single. Educ: Georgetown Univ; Ind. Univ, Bloomington. Polit. & Govt. Pos: Eighth Dist. chmn, Young Rep, Ind; treas, Ind. Rep. State Cmt, 68; Lt. Gov, Ind, 69- Bus. & Prof. Pos: Treas, F.J. Folz Co, Inc, Evansville, Ind, 46-69. Mil. Serv: Entered as Aviation Cadet, Navy, 42, released as Lt.(jg), 46. Legal Res: 723 S.E. Riverside Dr, Evansville, Ind. 47712. Mailing Add: 1901 Summit House, Indianapolis, Ind. 46204.

FONG, HIRAM LEONG R

U.S. Sen, Hawaii

b. Honolulu, Hawaii, 10/1/07; s. Lum Fong and Chai-Ha Shee Lum F; m. 6/25/38 to Ellyn Lo; c. Hiram Leong, Jr, Rodney, Merie Ellen and Marvin Allan. Educ: Univ. Hawaii, B.A, 30; Harvard Law Sch, LL.B, 35; Phi Beta Kappa. Hon. LL.D, Univ. Hawaii, 53, Tufts Univ, 60, Lafayette Col, 60; hon. L.H.D, L.I. Univ, 68. Polit. & Govt. Pos: Clerk, supply dept, Navy Shipyard, Pearl Harbor, 24-27; chief clerk, Suburban Water Syst, 30-32; dep. attorney, City and Co. of Honolulu, Hawaii, 35-38; Hawaii State Rep, 38-54, v.speaker, Hawaii House of Rep, 44-48, speaker, 48-54; v.pres, Hawaii State Constitutional Conv, 50; del, Rep. Nat. Conv, 52-68, Favorite Son nominee for President, 64 & 68; U.S. Sen, Hawaii, 59-, mem, Post off. and Civil Serv, Appropriations and Judiciary Cmts. and Spec. Cmt. on Aging U.S. Senate; mem, Rep. Policy Cmt; U.S. Del, 150th Anniversary Celebration of Argentine Independence, 60; mem, U.S. Del, Can-U.S. Interparliamentary Conv, 61 & 65; U.S. Observer, Commonwealth Parliamentary Asn. Meeting, Wellington, N.Z, 65; Off. U.S. Del, 55th Interparliamentary Union Conv, Tehran, Iran, 66. Bus. & Prof. Pos: Operator, banana farm and fish pond; chmn. bd, Hwy. Construction Co, Ltd; pres, Ocean View Cemetery, Ltd; founder, pres. and chmn. bd, Finance Factors, Grand Pac. Life Ins, Finance Realty, Finance Home Builders, Finance Investment, Finance Factors Found. and Market City; founder, Cosmopolitan Law Firm, Fong, Miho, Choy and Robinson, Honolulu, Hawaii. Mil. Serv: Entered as 1st Lt, Army Air Corps, 42, released as Major, 44, after serv. as Judge Adv, Seventh Fighter Command, Seventh Air Force; Col. (Ret), Air Force Res. Mem: Kau-Tom Post, Am. Legion; post 1540, VFW; Kalihi Commun. Improv. Club; Army, Navy and Civilian Young Men's Christian Assns; Downtown Improv. Club; PTA; Lions; Boy Scouts; Chinese Am. Club; Warriors of Pac; Commercial Assocs; Univ. Hawaii Alumni Asn; Harvard Club of Hawaii; Chinese Civic Club; C. of C; Chinese C. of C. Elector for Hall of Fame; Outstanding Nat. Award, Nat. Conf. Christians and Jews, 60; Citation for Meritorious Serv, Nat. Asn. Retired Civil Employees, 63. Rel: Congregational. Legal Res: 1102 Alewa Dr, Honolulu, Hawaii 96817. Mailing Add: 9 Highboro Court, Bethesda, Md. 20034.

FONG, MARCH K. D

Calif. State Assemblyman

b. Oakdale, Calif, d. Yuen Kong and Shiu Shee K; c. Matthew Kipling and Marsha Suyin. Educ: Univ. Calif, Berkeley, B.S; Mills Col, M.Ed, Stanford Univ, Ed.D, 54; post grad. study, Columbia Univ. and Calif. State Col, Hayward; Delta Kappa Gamma. Polit. & Govt. Pos: Mem, Alameda Co. Bd. Educ, Calif, 56-, pres, 61-62, legis. advocate, 63; co-chmn, Richards for Senate Campaign, Alameda Co, 62; women's chmn, Petris for Assembly Campaign, 62 & 64; dir, Key Women for Kennedy, 63 and Key Women for Alameda Co, 64; dir. and v.pres, Eighth Cong. Dist. Dem. Coun, 63; mem, Calif. Dem. State Cent. Cmt, 63-65; mem, Gov. Adv. Cmn. Compensatory Educ, 63-; spec. consult, Bur. Intergroup Rels, Calif. State Dept. Educ; mem. exec. cmt, 47 Million Dollar Bond Campaign, Peralta Jr. Col; mem, Oakland Econ. Develop. Coun, 64-; mem, Alameda Co. Elected Off. Cmt, Johnson for Pres, 64; women's v.chmn, North. Calif. Johnson for Pres. Campaign, 64; Calif. State Assemblyman, 15th Dist, 67-, v.chmn, Legis Cmt. Revenue and Taxation and mem, Cmt. Educ. and Cmt. Pub. Utilities and Commerce, Calif. State Assembly; del, Dem. Nat. Conv, 68. Bus. & Prof. Pos: Educ, and legis. consult, Sausalito Pub. Schs, Santa Clara Co, Calif; lectr. health educ, Mills Col, Oakland; supv. dent. health educ, Alameda Co. Schs; dent. hygienist, Oakland Pub. Schs; chmn, div. dent. hyg, Univ. Calif. Med. Center, San Francisco. Mil. Serv: Dent. Hygienist, World War II, Presidio, San Francisco. Mem: Pres, Am. Dent. Hygienists' Asn, 56-57; Alameda Co. Sch. Bds. Asn, second v.pres, 63, first v.pres, 64 and pres, 65; Calif. Sch. Bds. Asn; study panel, Prfnl. Standards Cmn, Calif. Teachers Asn, 65; N.Calif. State Dent. Hygienists Asn; Oakland League of Women Voters; area rep. in educ, Am. Asn. Univ. Women; Calif. Teachers Asn; pres, Chabot Dem. Club; bd. dir, Oakland YWCA, 65; judge, Mayor's Cmt. on Excellence of Youth; Oakland Econ. Develop. Coun; Citizens Cmt. on Housing; charter pres. and hon. life mem, Howard Elem. Sch. PTA; budget panel, Bay Area United Fund; charter pres, Chinese Young Ladies Soc. of Oakland; v.chmn, Adv. Cmt. for Youth Study Centers & Ford Found. Interagency Proj, 62-63. Recipient, Annual Award for Outstanding Achievement, Eastbay Intercultural Fel, 59. Rel: Unitarian. Mailing Add: State Capitol, Sacramento, Calif. 95814.

FONNER, PAUL E. 'DOC' R

Chmn, Piatt Co. Rep. Cmt, Ill.

b. Newman, Ill, 3/28/96; s. Charles Fonner and Dora Gertrude Cameron F; m. 8/16/20 to Millie Holier; c. Carmin (Mrs. Robert W. Huisinga). Educ: High Sch, Newman, Ill, 2 years. Polit. & Govt. Pos: Rep. committeeman, Twp, Ill, 30-69; chmn, Piatt Co. Rep. Cmt, 40-; mem, Ill. Rep. State Cent. Cmt, 46-52. Bus. & Prof. Pos: In mercantile bus, DeLand, Ill, 16-45; dir. and v.pres, DeLand State Bank, 45- Mil. Serv: Sgt, Army, 17-19, with serv. in Coast Artil, overseas, 18-19. Mem: Am. Legion; AF&AM; Shrine; Farm Bur. Rel: Protestant. Mailing Add: DeLand, Ill. 61839.

FONNESBECK, VERDUN FRANCE D

b. Howell, Utah, 8/7/17; s. Christian Fonnesbeck and Maria Jorgensen F; m. 1/16/41 to Leone Nelson; c. Arnold Bruce, Vicki F.(Mrs. Lauritzen), Gregory, Kristi and Karla. Educ: Logan High Sch, Utah, grad, 36. Polit. & Govt. Pos: Dist. chmn, Howell City Dem. Party, Utah, 57-59, Sixth Dist. Dem. Party, Brigham City, 59-61 and 11th Dist. Dem. Party, 62-64; chmn, Box Elder Co. Dem. Party, 67-69; mem, Utah State Dem. Cent. Cmt, 67-69; mem, Utah State Patronage Cmt, 67-69; mem, Utah State Dem. Platform Cmt, 68. Bus. & Prof. Pos: Prod. supvr, Thiokol Chem, 58-67. Mil. Serv: Pvt, Nat. Guard, 36-38, serv. in Battery C, Logan, Utah. Mem: Brigham City Golf & Country Club (bd. dirs, 66-68). Rel: Latter-day Saint. Mailing Add: 660 S. Fourth East, Brigham City, Utah 84302.

FONTAINE, GERARD LOUIS R

b. Roxton, Can, 12/1/15; m. to Rose Lanoue; c. One son and three daughters. Educ: Derby Schs. Polit. & Govt. Pos: Lister, 7 years; Justice of the Peace, 8 years; chmn, Bd. of Civil Authority, 2 terms; Vt. State Rep, 65-68. Bus. & Prof. Pos: Farmer. Mem: Orleans Co. Red Cross. Rel: Catholic. Mailing Add: Box 46, Newport Center, Vt. 05857. (1967)

FONTAINE, PAUL AURAY D

R.I. State Sen.

b. Woonsocket, R.I, 7/4/40; s. Auray H. Fontaine and Angelina Daignault F; m. 7/13/63 to Louise Fontaine; c. Marc, Lyse, Monique and Nicole. Educ: Assumption Col, A.B, 60; Boston Univ. Sch. Law, LL.B, 63. Polit. & Govt. Pos: R.I. State Rep, 65-66; chmn, Woonsocket Citizens Adv. Bd, 66; chmn, Soc. Progress Action Corps, Antipoverty Orgn, 66-67; R.I. State Sen, Dist. 32, 67-; v.chmn, R.I. Senate Dem. Steering Cmt, 69. Bus. & Prof. Pos: Assoc, Law Firm of Keefer & Kirby, 63-; regional pres, Artisans Ins. Co, 68-69. Mem: R.I. Bar Asn; dir, Club Marquette; dir, Club Richelieu. Rel: Catholic. Legal Res: 189 Annette Ave, Woonsocket, R.I. 02895. Mailing Add: 52 Hamlet Ave, Woonsocket, R.I. 02895.

FONTANA, JOHN COLUMBUS D

b. Cleveland, Ohio, 1/21/07; s. Attilio Fontana and Amelia Buonamici F; m. 10/19/34 to Mary Morrow III; c. Jeanine (Mrs. Fairand) and Mary B. (Mrs. Lorms). Educ: Univ. Notre Dame, A.B, 28; West. Res. Univ. Law Sch, LL.B, 30. Polit. & Govt. Pos: Asst. Attorney Gen, Ohio, 37-39; admin. asst. to U.S. Sen. Stephen M. Young, Ohio, 59-66; del, Dem. Nat. Conv, 68. Bus. & Prof. Pos: Private practice of law, Fontana Ward & Kaps, Attorneys, 39- Rel: Roman Catholic. Legal Res: 2703 Henthorn Rd, Upper Arlington, Ohio 43221. Mailing Add: 50 W. Broad St, Columbus, Ohio 43215. (1967)

FONTANA, RAYMOND JOSEPH. R

Gov. Coun, State of Mass.

b. Springfield, Mass, 6/19/23; s. Dante Albert Fontana and Mary Gallini F; m. 10/12/50 to Maria Meola; c. Diama, Dante, John and Raymond, Jr. Educ: Dartmouth Col, B.A, 44; Northeast. Univ. Sch. Law, LL.B, 49; C.P.C.U, Am. Inst. Property & Liability Underwriters, 64; Kappa Sigma. Polit. & Govt. Pos: Mem, Longmeadow Rep. Town Cmt, Mass, 61-; coordinator for Gov. John A. Volpe, West. Mass, 61-66; Gov. coun, West. Mass, 67-; del, Rep. Nat. Conv, 68. Bus. & Prof. Pos: Pres, R.J. Fontana Ins. Agency Inc, Springfield,

Mass, 54-; attorney, 64-; dir, Union Fed. Savings Bank, 68- Mil. Serv: Entered as A/S, Navy, 43, released as Lt, 46, after serv. in Amphibious commands, Pac. Theatre, 44-46; Japanese Occup, Philippine Liberation, European Atlantic Theatre Opers and Pac. Theatre Opers. ribbons; Korean War Medal. Mem: Am. Legion; Elks; Unico Nat; Dartmouth Alumni Club. Rel: Catholic. Legal Res: 47 Normandy Rd, Longmeadow, Mass. 01106. Mailing Add: 95 State St, Springfield, Mass. 01103.

FOOR, PERCY G. R
Pa. State Rep.
b. Everett, Pa, 4/12/13; s. Albert F. Foor and Jennie C. F; m. to Marjorie Gephart; c. Two sons. Educ: Everett High Sch. Polit. & Govt. Pos: Pres, Everett South. Joint Sch. Dist, Pa, 12 years, past state moderator and mem, State Trustees; justice of the peace, 56-60; Pa. State Rep, 60- Bus. & Prof. Pos: Realtor, currently. Mem: Past master, Everett F&AM; Harrisburg Consistory; Lions; Nat. Asn. Real Estate Bds; Jaffa Temple AAONMS; past pres, Everett Vol. Fire Co. Mailing Add: 139 W. Main St, Everett, Pa. 15537.

FOOTE, ELLSWORTH BISHOP R
Mem, North Branford Rep. Town Cmt, Conn.
b. North Branford, Conn, 1/12/98; s. Frank Foote and Ellen Bishop F; m. 1/1/25 to Ruth Magill; c. Robert M, Richard B, Roberta (Mrs. Koontz) and Anne Marie (Mrs. Floyd). Educ: Yale Bus. Col, 16; Georgetown Univ. Law Sch, LL.B, 23. Polit. & Govt. Pos: U.S. Rep, Third Dist, Conn, 47-48; asst. legis. cmnr, Conn. Gen. Assembly, 53; mem, North Branford Rep. Town Cmt, currently. Bus. & Prof. Pos: Practicing attorney before all Courts in Conn, 24- and before U.S. Supreme Court, 29-; attorney, North Branford, 24-46 & 49-63; spec. asst. to the U.S. Attorney Gen, Wash, D.C, 25-26; chmn, Bd. of Finance, North Branford, 34-46 & 49-63; judge of probate, North Branford, 38-46; attorney, New Haven Co, 42-46 & 49-60; acting judge of probate, New Haven, 44-45; secy. and dir, Bank and Trust Co. of North Branford, 61. Mil. Serv: Capt, Gov. Foot Guard, former mem. of Troop A Cavalry, Conn. Nat. Guard. Mem: Am, Conn. and New Haven Co. Bar Asns; New Haven Choral Club; Totoket Grange P. of H; hon. mem, Exchange Club. Rel: Congregational. Legal Res: Twin Lake Rd, North Branford, Conn. 06471. Mailing Add: 265 Church St, P.O. Box 54, New Haven, Conn. 06501. (1967)

FOOTE, KATHLEEN ACKERSON R
b. Lincoln, Nebr, 9/24/26; d. Dr. Clifton Walter Ackerson and Harriet Wooster Smith A; m. 8/28/48 to Frank Osler Foote; c. Kathleen Louise, Karen Jo, John Francis and James Stanley. Educ: Stanford Univ, B.A. in soc. sci, 48; Univ. Nebr, M.A. in educ, psychol, 64, grad. work in hist, 64-66. Polit. & Govt. Pos: Dist. IV adult sponsor, Gov. Cmt. on Youth; del, White House Conf. on Educ, 55; Nebr. State Sen, 31st Dist, 55-59. Bus. & Prof. Pos: Research librn, Curtis Publ. Co, Phila, Pa, 46-47; asst, press and exten. div, Univ. Nebr, 47-48. Mem: Del, Nat. Order of Women Legislators, 57; Nebr. del, Cmt. Intergovt. Coop, Coun. of State Govts, 57-58; Am. Asn. of Univ. Women; Minden Woman's Club; Farm Bur. Rel: Presbyterian. Legal Res: R.R. 1, Axtell, Nebr. 68924. Mailing Add: 1709 L, Lincoln, Nebr. 68508.

FOOTE, MARGIE ELLEN D
Nev. State Assemblyman
b. Reno, Nev, 12/23/29; d. Harry Stephen Foote and Marie Alice Williams F; single. Educ: Cottey Jr. Col, A.A, 49; Univ. Nev, B.A, 51; Delta Delta Delta. Polit. & Govt. Pos: Alternate del, Dem. Nat. Conv, 64; v.chmn, Washoe Co. Dem. Cent. Cmt, Nev, 64-66; Nev. State Assemblyman, 67- Bus. & Prof. Pos: Owner and operator, children's apparel shop, 55- Mem: PEO; Eastern Star; Daughters of the Nile. Rel: American Baptist. Mailing Add: 5585 Wedekind Rd, Sparks, Nev. 89431.

FOOTE, RALPH ALBERT R
b. Proctor, Vt, 1/22/23; s. Ralph Abram Foote and Sylvia Pastene F; m. to Nancy Lee Dickey; c. Ralph Anthony, Peter Vinton, Charles Brian, Richard Pastene and Kristen Cory. Educ: Amherst Col, B.A, 43; Union Univ. Albany Law Sch, LL.B, 49; Sphinx, Amherst Col; Delta Kappa Epsilon. Polit. Pos: Chmn, Exec. Cmt, Vt. State Rep. Cmt, 60-63; chmn, Addison Co. Rep. Cmt, 56-60. Govt. Pos: Lt. Gov. Vt, 61-65; Vt. State Rep, 57-61. Bus. & Prof. Pos: Dir, Cooperative Fire Ins. Asn. Vt, 59- Mil. Serv: Entered as Pfc, Marine Corps, 43, released as Capt, 52, after serv. in 3rd Corps Artil, Pac. Theater, 43-46 and 50-52; Okinawa Campaign Ribbon; Pacific Theater Ribbon. Mem: Pres, Addison Co. Bar Asn, 65-; bd. mgrs, Vt. Bar Asn, 66-; Am. Bar Asn; Am. Legion; VFW; Elks; Grange; Mason; Moose; Italian-Am. Club. Rel: Congregational. Mailing Add: 5 Blinn Lane, Middlebury, Vt. 05753. (1967)

FORAN, JOHN FRANCIS D
Calif. State Assemblyman
b. San Francisco, Calif, 7/11/30; s. James Edward Foran and Kathleen Egan F; m. 6/28/58 to Costanza G. Ilacqua; c. David John, Mary Carmel and Thomas Edward. Educ: Univ. San Francisco, B.S, 56; Univ. San Francisco Law Sch, LL.B, 59. Polit. & Govt. Pos: Calif. State Assemblyman, 63-, chmn, Transportation Cmt, Calif. State Gen. Assembly. Mil. Serv: Entered as Pvt, Army, 51, released as Cpl, 54, after serv. in 32nd Inf. Regt, 7th Div, Korea; Purple Heart; Combat Infantrymans Badge; Korean Campaign Medal; UN Medal. Mem: Calif. and San Francisco Bar Asns; Calif. Lawyers Asn; Lawyers Club of San Francisco; DAV; VFW; Ancient Order Hibernians; Sons of Italy. Rel: Catholic. Mailing Add: 350 McAllister St, San Francisco, Calif. 94102.

FORAND, AIMÉ J. D
b. Fall River, Mass, 5/23/95; s. Francois Xavier Forand and Méli Luce Ruest F; m. 11/16/31 to Gertrude B. Bedard. Educ: Columbia Univ. Polit. & Govt. Pos: U.S. Rep, R.I, 41-60 and 37-38; chief dir, Soldiers Relief and Commandant, R.I. Soldiers Home, 35-36; secy. to U.S. Rep, Francis B. Condon, 30-35 and to U.S. Rep. Jeremiah E. O'Connell, 29-30; R.I. State Rep, 23-27. Bus. & Prof. Pos: Reporter and off. mgr, Providence News-Tribune, R.I, 22-27. Mil. Serv: Entered as Pvt, Army, 18, released as Sgt. 1/C, 19, after serv. in 461st Motor Transport Co, France; AEF Ribbon; Victory Medal. Mem: Elks; VFW; Am.Legion; K. of C. (4°). Rel: Catholic. Mailing Add: 1600 Sabal Palm Dr, Boca Raton, Fla. 33432.

FORBES, EUREKA BERNICE R
Hawaii State Sen.
b. Fort Worth, Tex, 10/17/04; d. Ambrose Eugene Ryan and Gladys Bates R; m. 6/3/32 to Frederick Blatchford Forbes; c. Doris Leone, David William and Kathleen (Mrs. Russell F. Coover). Educ: Univ. Calif. Los Angeles, Teacher's Certificate, 24; Univ. Hawaii, B.A, 33, M.A, 38; grad. work in govt. and admin; former pres, Theta Chap, Delta Kappa Gamma; Alpha Phi; Prytannean Soc. Polit. & Govt. Pos: Mem, Adult Adv. Coun, Dept. of Pub. Educ, 50-56; teacher, Honolulu Pub. Schs, 51-59; del, Hawaii Territorial Rep. Conv, 52-; mem, Territorial Cmn. on Children and Youth, 53-59; mem, City and Co. Honolulu Charter Cmn, 55-58; secy, Oahu Co. Rep. Cmt, 57-61; Hawaii State Rep, 59-67; alternate del, Rep. Nat. Conv, 64 & 68; corresponding secy, Hawaii State League of Rep. Women, 66-67; Hawaii State Sen, 67- Bus. & Prof. Pos: Music instr, Univ. Hawaii, 37-40; adminstr. and owner, Pokii Kindergarten and Nursery Sch, 37-41; teacher, Kamehameha Schs, 42-43; counsellor and prof, govt, polit. sci. and hist, Jackson Col, Honolulu, 62-65; semi-weekly Radio Commentary Program, 62-; part owner dress shop, My House, 64-; pres, bd. trustees, Hawaii Pac. Col, Honolulu, 65, mem, 65- Publ: Life and work of Cochran Forbes, Univ. Hawaii, 38. Mem: Acad. Polit. Sci; v.pres, Hawaii Cong. Parents and Teachers, 49-51; Nat. Coun, Am. Parents Cmt; Hawaii State Rep, Nat. Cmt. for Support of Pub. Schs; adv, Oahu Youth Coun; bd. dirs, Goodwill Industs, Honolulu; speaker, Nat. Conv, 61; pres, Hawaii State Div, Am. Asn. Univ. Women, 62-66; legis. chmn, Bus. and Prfnl. Women's Club, del, Spec. Conv. on Econ; League of Women Voters; Honolulu Art Acad; Women's Symphony Soc; Univ. Hawaii Alumni Asn.(2nd v.pres, 64-65, 1st v.pres, 65, pres, 66-69); Nat. League Am. Pen Women. Rel: Protestant. Mailing Add: 3697 Woodlawn Dr, Honolulu, Hawaii 96822.

FORBES, ROXIE A. R
N.H. State Rep.
b. Gilsum, N.H, 6/27/94. d. Ben E. Guillow and Nellie J. Mason G; m. 10/2/33 to Roy E. Forbes. Educ: Kimball Union Acad, 4 years valedictorian, Silver Cup, Latin and Math Award; Tiffin Bus. Sch. Polit. & Govt. Pos: Former overseer of the poor, sch. auditor, town auditor and sch. bd. mem; past chmn, Marlow Woman's Div, Rep. Party; N.H. State Rep, 45-49 & 59, 63, 65, 67 & 69-; del, Constitutional Conv, 48-64. Bus. & Prof. Pos: Private secy. Mem: Eastern Star; White Shrine; Women's Club; Bus. & Prfnl. Woman's Club; past v.pres, Manchester Beagle Club; past secy. and treas, Marlow Hill Beagle Club; Vt. Beagle Club; Northampton Club; Ashuelot, Excelsior and Pomona State Granges; past treas, Marlow Old Home Day Asn; secy. treas, Supvry. Union, 60; 43 Club; O.W.L. Rel: Protestant. Mailing Add: Marlow Hill, Marlow, N.H. 03456.

FORBES, WILLIAM ALFRED D
b. Winterville, N.C, 8/13/14; s. W.A. Forbes and Norma McGlohon F; m. 8/9/36 to Theraldine Henry; c. W.A, III. Educ: E. Carolina Col, 31-32. Polit. & Govt. Pos: Mem, Bd. of Educ, 6 years; N.C. State Rep, 63-68. Bus. & Prof. Pos: Farmer; grain dealer; tobacconist. Mem: Redmen; Moose; past pres, Kiwanis, 61; Ruritan Club; bd, Pitt Co. Cancer Soc. Rel: Missionary Baptist. Mailing Add: Box 94, Winterville, N.C. 28590. (1967)

FORD, CHARLES REED R
Okla. State Rep.
b. Tulsa, Okla, 8/2/31; s. Juell Reed Ford and Marzee Lane F; m. 4/26/51 to Patricia Ann Ojers; c. Christopher Reed, Roger Howard, Karin Rebecca and Robyn Ann. Educ: Okla. State Univ, 49-51; Alpha Sigma Eta. Polit. & Govt. Pos: Trustee, Tulsa Exposition and Fair Corp, 55-67; v.chmn, Tulsa Metrop. Area Planning Cmn, 60-65; past officer, Tulsa Co. Young Rep; Okla. State Rep, Dist. 80, 67-, minority whip, currently. Bus. & Prof. Pos: Engr, aide, Corps of Engrs, 51-53; designer, Sunray-DX, 53-55; asst. mkt. engr, Tidewater Oil Co, 55-58; developer; archit. designer. Mil. Serv: Naval Res, 48-53. Mem: Tulsa, Okla. and U.S. Homebuilders Asns; Tulsa Jr. C. of C; (Okla. Pres, 59-60, U.S. V.pres, 60-61 and Int. V.pres, 63). Selected Outstanding Young Man, Okla, 60. Rel: Protestant. Legal Res: 3421 E. 63rd St, Tulsa, Okla. 74135. Mailing Add: 4100 E. 51st St, Tulsa, Okla. 74135.

FORD, GERALD R. R
Minority Leader, U.S. House of Rep.
b. Omaha, Neb, 7/14/13; m. to Elizabeth Bloomer; c. Michael Gerald, John Gardner, Steven Meigs and Susan Elizabeth. Educ: Univ. of Mich, B.A, 35; Yale Univ. Law Sch, LL.B, 41. Hon. LL.D, Mich State Univ, Albion Col, Aquinas Col. and Spring Arbor Col, 65. Polit. & Govt. Pos: U.S. Rep, Mich, 48-, Minority Leader, U.S. House of Rep, 65- Bus. & Prof. Pos: Attorney. Mil. Serv: Navy, 42-46. Recipient Grand Rapids Jaycees Distinguished Serv. Award, 47; U.S. Jaycee Distinguished Serv. Award, 49; Distinguished Cong. Serv. Award, Am. Polit. Sci. Asn, 61; George Washington Award, Am. Good Govt. Soc, 66. Legal Res: 425 Cherry St. S.E, Grand Rapids, Mich. 49502. Mailing Add: 514 Crown View Dr, Alexandria, Va. 22314.

FORD, JOE T. D
Ark. State Sen.
b. Conway, Ark, 6/24/37; s. A.W. Ford and Ruby Watson F; m. 8/9/59 to Jo Ellen Wilbourn; c. Alison and Scott. Educ: Ark. State Univ; Univ. Ark, B.S. B.A; Alpha Kappa Psi; Blue Key; Pi Kappa Alpha. Polit. & Govt. Pos: Ark. State Sen, 18th Dist, Pulaski and Lonoke Co, 67- Bus. & Prof. Pos: V.pres-treas, Allied Tel. Co, Little Rock, Ark, 59-, Allied Tel. Co, of Ark, Inc, Allied Tel. Co. of Okla, Inc, Allied Utilities Corp, Triangle Tel. Co, Swan Lake Tel. Co, Stover Tel. Co. and Madison Tel. Co, currently; pres, Mart, Inc, currently. Mil. Serv: Capt. and Unit Comdr, Ark. Nat. Guard, 62-67. Mem: Fifty for the Future. Rel: Baptist. Legal Res: 321 Colonial Court, Little Rock, Ark. 72205. Mailing Add: P.O. Box 2177, Little Rock, Ark. 72203.

FORD, JOHN OBERTON D
Mem, Ohio Dem. State Exec. Cmt.
b. Dunglen, Ohio, 2/1/17; s. Johnson S. Ford and Rosezella Dixon F; m. 11/27/47 to Dorothy Louise Johnston; c. Deborah Darlene and Don Oberton. Educ: Allegheny Tech. Inst, Pittsburgh, Pa, 2 years; W.Liberty State Col, 67- Polit. & Govt. Pos: City councilman, Wintersville, Ohio, 64-, mayor, 67, Dem. precinct committeeman, 67-; mem, Jefferson Co. Dem. Exec. Cmt, 67-; pres, Jefferson Co. Commun. Action Coun, Steubenville, 69; mem, Ohio Dem. State Exec. Cmt, 69- Bus. & Prof. Pos: Mem, bd. dir, Home Finders Realty Co, 50- and Steubenville City Rescue Mission, Ohio, 68- Mil. Serv: Entered as Pvt, Air Force, 42, released as Sgt, 45, after serv. in 1564th Army Air Force

Base Unit, European-Africa-Middle East. Theater; Europe-Africa-Middle East. Theater Medal with Three Bronze Stars; Good Conduct Medal. Mem: Mason; Lions; v.pres, Jefferson Co. Regional Planning Cmn; Brooke-Hancock-Jefferson Co. Metrop. Planning Cmn; bd. dirs, Upper Ohio Valley Dapper Dan Club; cmt. chmn, Wintersville Troop 12, Boy Scouts. Rel: Protestant. Mailing Add: 104 Orchard St, Wintersville, Ohio 43952.

FORD, LEWIS FRANKLIN R
b. Salem, Ore, 9/25/29; s. Bert T. Ford and Margaret Griffith F; m. 9/5/52 to Prudence Craig; c. Bert T, Katharine and Melissa. Educ: Univ. Ore, B.S. in psychol; Willamette Col. Law. Polit. & Govt. Pos: Orgn. chmn, Lincoln Co. Rep. Cent. Cmt, Ore, 60-63, chmn, 63-67; chmn, Taft-Nelscott-Delaice Water Dist, Ore, 60-65; Delake Lincoln Co. chmn, Nixon for Ore. Primary campaign. Bus. & Prof. Pos: Owner-mgr, Coast Burner Oil Co, 57-67; pres, Oceanlake Land & Cattle Co, 59-; secy-treas, Int. Distributors, Inc, 65-; v.pres, Siletz Fishermans Wharf, 66. Rel: Catholic. Legal Res: 3327 S. Anchor, Nelscott, Ore. Mailing Add: Box 2065, Taft, Ore. 97367.

FORD, LINWOOD FRED R
b. Guildhall, Vt, 9/5/10; single. Educ: Elec. sch, Bridgeport, Conn. Polit. & Govt. Pos: Town auditor, 20 years; Justice of the Peace, 20 years; Vt. State Rep, 37-41 & 61-66; Road Cmnr, 60- Bus. & Prof. Pos: Self-employed. Mil. Serv: Coast Artil, 42-45. Mem: Mason. Rel: Methodist. Mailing Add: Guildhall, Vt. 05905. (1967)

FORD, ORON RUSSELL R
Chmn, Gibson Co. Rep. Party, Tenn.
b. Tarrant City, Ala, 10/2/20; s. George Elbert Ford and Minnie Chaffin F; m. 2/1/41 to Sybil Marie Phillips; c. Patricia (Mrs. Conrad) and Orrin Russell. Educ: Univ. Ala; Howard Col, Ala, grad; Beta Gamma Sigma. Polit. & Govt. Pos: Agent, Internal Revenue Serv, 48-50 & 52-59, supvr, field audit group, 59-60; area dir, Nashville Bur. Labor-Mgt. Reports, 60-61; chmn, Gibson Co. Rep. Party, Tenn, currently. Bus. & Prof. Pos: Acct, Wayne Knitting Mills, 61- Mil. Serv: Entered as Aviation Cadet, Army Air Corps, 42, released as 1st Lt, 45, after serv. in 5th Air Force, Asiatic-Pac; re-entered as 1st Lt, Air Force, 50, released as 1st Lt, 52, after serv. in Strategic Air Command; Air Medal; Asiatic-Pac. Ribbon. Mem: Am. Legion; Toastmasters Int. Rel: Baptist. Mailing Add: 640 Hillside Dr, Humboldt, Tenn. 38343. (1967)

FORD, ROBERT C. D
Chmn, Howard Co. Dem. Cmt, Ind.
b. Crothersville, Ind, 12/2/19; s. Irvin Ford and Nellie F; m. 6/29/41 to Betty L. Young; c. Dixie Lee, Constance, Penelope and Robert C, II. Educ: High Sch, grad. Polit. & Govt. Pos: State farm chmn, Kennedy for President Cmt, Ind, 60; chmn, Howard Co. Dem. Cmt, 62-; Dem. nominee for U.S. Rep, Ind, 68. Bus. & Prof. Pos: Mgr, Cross Transit Corp, Kokomo, Ind, 51-54; mgr, Downtown License Bur, 63-65; farmer. Mem: Elks; Howard Co. Farmers Union; K. of C; Travelers Protective Asn, Kokomo. Rel: Catholic. Mailing Add: 3910 W. Jefferson Rd, Kokomo, Ind. 46901.

FORD, SEABURY H. R
Chmn, Portage Co. Rep. Exec. Cmt, Ohio
b. Burton, Ohio, 9/26/02; s. Carl Boughton Ford and Elizabeth Hurd F; m. 12/22/41 to Helen Paar Jherrick. Educ: West. Reserve Univ, 6 years; Sigma Delta Chi; Alpha Delta Phi. Polit. & Govt. Pos: Precinct committeeman, Aurora Rep. Party, Ohio, 36-58; councilman, Aurora, 41-44, law dir, 66-69; committeeman, Ohio Rep. State Cent. Cmt, 43-48; prosecuting attorney, Portage Co, 45-53; chmn, Portage Co. Rep. Exec. Cmt, 68- Bus. & Prof. Pos: Pres, Portage Co. Title Co, currently; pres, First Portage Corp, currently; dir, First Nat. Bank & Trust Co, Ravenna, currently. Mem: Portage Co. Bar Asn.(pres, 50); Fel. Ohio State Bar; Akron and Cleveland Bar Asns; Am. Judicature Soc; Elks; F&AM; Kiwanis; Am. Red Cross (chap. chmn). Rel: Protestant. Legal Res: 12 W. Garfield Rd, Aurora, Ohio 44202. Mailing Add: 200 W. Main St, Ravenna, Ohio 44266.

FORD, TEDROE JAY, JR. R
Chmn, Upshur Co. Rep. Exec. Cmt, Tex.
b. Port Arthur, Tex, 5/6/28; s. Tedroe Jay Ford, Sr. and Ada Malone F; m. 8/2/52 to Margaret Cecile Fenley; c. Tedroe Jay, III, Mary Jane, William Fenley and Jenifer Cecile. Educ: Univ. Tex, Austin, B.A, 50; Baylor Univ. Col. Med, M.D, 55; St. Mary's Law Sch, 58 & 59; Phi Chi; Theta Xi; Phi Delta Phi. Polit. & Govt. Pos: Chmn, Upshur Co. Rep. Exec. Cmt, 63-; alternate del, Rep. Nat. Conv, 68. Bus. & Prof. Pos: Physician and surgeon, Ragland Clin, Gilmer, Tex, 49- Mil. Serv: Entered as Capt, Army, 47, released as Capt, 49, after serv. in Army Med. Serv. Sch, Brooks Med. Center, Ft. Sam Houston, 47-49. Mem: Tex. and Am. Med. Asns; Am. Soc. Abdominal Surgeons; Rotary. Rel: Baptist. Mailing Add: 1307 Frost St, Gilmer, Tex. 75644.

FORD, THOMAS G, SR. R
Mich. State Rep.
b. Grand Rapids, Mich, 7/15/18; married; c. Thomas G, Jr. and Julie G. Educ: Univ. of Mich, grad; Delta Kappa Epsilon. Polit. & Govt. Pos: East Grand Rapids City Cmnr, Mich, 50-58; mem, Kent Co. Bd. of Supvr, 58-64; Mich. State Rep, 64- Mil. Serv: Pre-Pearl Harbor, Am-European-Pac. Theatres; Capt, Naval Res. Mem: Big Ten football official, 53-62; Am. Legion, Furniture City Post 258, Malta Lodge 465; DeWitt Clinton Consistory; Saladin Temple Shrine; Naval Res. Asn; Naval Hist. Soc; Am. Mgt. Asn; Univ. Mich. Alumni Asn; Grand Rapids Army-Navy Club. Rel: Episcopal. Mailing Add: 900 Pinecrest S.E, Grand Rapids, Mich. 49506.

FORD, WENDELL H. D
Lt. Gov, Ky.
b. 1924. Educ: Univ. Ky; Md. Sch. Ins. Polit. & Govt. Pos: V.chmn, Ky. Turnpike Authority; mem, Ky. State Property and Bldg. Cmn. and Ky. Coun. Educ; chmn, Ky. Legis. Research Cmn; pres, Ky. State Senate; mem, President's Coun. Youth Fitness; chief asst. to Gov, Ky, 59-61; former Ky. State Sen; del, Dem. Nat. Conv, 68; chmn, Davies Co. Dem. Cmt, 69-; Lt. Gov, Ky, 69- Bus. & Prof. Pos: Ins. Mil. Serv: Vet, World War II. Mem: Second Army Adv. Cmt, Am. Legion; Nat. Coun. Relig. in Am. Life; Owensboro Jaycees (past dir, v.pres. and pres); State Jaycees (past dir, treas, v.pres, and pres); Nat. Jaycees (past v.pres. and pres). Outstanding Young Man, Owensboro, 54 and Ky, 55. Rel: Baptist. Legal Res: Owensboro, Ky. 42301. Mailing Add: State Capitol Bldg, Frankfort, Ky. 40601.

FORD, WILLIAM DAVID D
U.S. Rep, Mich.
b. Detroit, Mich, 8/6/27; c. William D, Jr, Margaret and John. Educ: Wayne Univ; Univ. Denver, B.S, LL.B; Phi Delta Phi. Polit. & Govt. Pos: Precinct del, Dem. Party and v.chmn. and chmn, Taylor Twp. Dem. Club, Mich, formerly; justice of the peace, Taylor Twp, 55-57, attorney, 57-64; city attorney, Melvindale, 57-59; mem. exec. bd, 16th Dist. Dem. Orgn, 59-64, corresponding secy, 60-62; del, Constitutional Conv, 61-62; Mich. State Sen, 62-64; U.S. Rep, Mich, 64-; del, Dem. Nat. Conv, 68. Bus. & Prof. Pos: Attorney-at-law, 54- Mil. Serv: Navy, 44-46; Air Force Res, 50-58, discharged as 1st Lt.(legal officer). Mem: Taylor Twp. Businessmen's Asn; Am, Mich. and Downriver Bar Asns; Nat. Inst. of Munic. Law Officers; Rotary. Distinguished Serv. Award, Jr. C. of C, 62. Legal Res: Taylor, Mich. 48180. Mailing Add: 125 House Office Building, Washington, D.C. 20515.

FORDHAM, DELBERT ARTHUR D
Chmn, Wash. Co. Dem. Exec. Cmt, Ohio
b. Marietta, Ohio, 9/13/14; s. Harlan A. Fordham and Irene Hawkins F; m. 6/13/37 to Winifred Irene Kraft; c. William D, Robert A. and Delbert Arthur, Jr. Educ: Marietta Col, A.B; Lambda Chi Alpha. Polit. & Govt. Pos: Mem, Traffic Cmn, Marietta, Ohio, 66-67; mem, Planning Cmn, Wash. Co, 68-69; mem, Ohio Dem. State Exec. Cmt, 69; chmn, Wash. Co. Dem. Exec. Cmt, currently. Bus. & Prof. Pos: Partner and co-owner, Fordham & Fordham Ins. Agency, 38-69. Mem: Independent Ins. Agents Asn; Marietta Advert. Club. Rel: Presbyterian. Legal Res: 224 Franklin St, Marietta, Ohio 45750. Mailing Add: P.O. Box 622, Marietta, Ohio 45750.

FORE, SAM O, JR. D
Mem, Tex. State Dem. Exec. Cmt.
b. Cuero, Tex, 5/3/91; s. Sam L. Fore and Letitia Chenault F; m. 7/27/11 to Elma Teas; c. Marion (Mrs. W.C. Keach) and Evelyn (Mrs. Robert F. Spruce). Educ: Floresville High Sch. Polit. & Govt. Pos: Mem, Tex. State Dem. Exec. Cmt, 64-; del, Dem. Nat. Conv. Bus. & Prof. Pos: Owner and publisher, The Floresville Chronicle-Journal, Tex, 50 years; co-owner and publisher, Robstown Record, currently. Mem: Past pres, Tex. Press Asn; past pres, South Tex. Press Asn; life mem, Tex. Press; Lions; Mason (32°); Shrine; Wilson Co. Farm Bur; exec. bd, South Tex. C. of C; Beaver Scout. Rel: Methodist. Legal Res: 1607 S. Second St, Floresville, Tex. 78114. Mailing Add: P.O. Box 815, Floresville, Tex. 78114. (1967)

FORELL, ORA E. R
Treas, Lyman Co. S.Dak.
b. Chester, Nebr, 12/28/88; s. Adolph Carl Forell and Catherine Daley F; m. 12/25/12 to Julia Woodward; c. Caryl (Mrs. David Rearick), Melba (Mrs. Wayne Quinn), Kenneth, Ardith (Mrs. William S. Moore) and Darlene (Mrs. Robert Iosty). Educ: Hubbell High Sch, grad. Polit. & Govt. Pos: Auditor, Lyman Co, S.Dak, 49-52, treas, 69-; chmn, Lyman Co. Rep. Party, 62-68. Bus. & Prof. Pos: Farmer and rancher, 18-49; treas, Lower Brule Sch, 28-48; pres, Hill Tel. Co, 30-34; owner, Ins. agency, 56-68. Mem: Mason. Award, State Orgn. Co. Officers Orgn. Rel: Methodist. Mailing Add: Kennebec, S.Dak. 57544.

FOREMAN, ED R
U.S. Rep, N.Mex.
b. Portales, N.Mex, 12/22/33; s. Edgar F. Foreman, Sr. and Lillian Childdress F; m. 8/26/55 to Barbara Southard; c. Kirk and Rebecca. Educ: N.Mex. State Univ, B.S. in civil eng, 55; Sigma Tau. Polit. & Govt. Pos: U.S. Rep, 16th Dist, Tex, 63-64 and mem, House Armed Serv. Cmt; chmn, N.Mex. Rep. Cong. Campaign Cmt, formerly; U.S. Rep, Second Dist, N.Mex, 69- Bus. & Prof. Pos: Pres, Valley Transit Mix, Foreman Oil, Inc. and Atlas Land Co, 65- Mil. Serv: Entered Corps Engrs, Navy, 56, released, 62, after 6 months active duty and $5\frac{1}{2}$ years Res; Capt, Air Force Res, 66. Mem: Am. Soc. Civil Engrs; Am. Petrol. Inst; N.Mex. Ready-Mix Concrete & Sand & Gravel Asn; Rotary; C. of C; Mason, Shrine; Jester. Outstanding Young Man of Odessa, 60; 1 of 5 Outstanding Young Men in Tex. 62; 1 of 10 Outstanding Young Men of Am, U.S. Jr. C. of C, 64. Rel: Methodist. Legal Res: 2245 Thomas Dr, Las Cruces, N.Mex. 88001. Mailing Add: 1721 House Office Building, Washington, D.C. 20515.

FOREMAN, EUGENE HARLEY R
Mem-at-Lg, Cleveland Co. Rep. Exec. Cmt, Okla.
b. Guyman, Okla; s. Frank B. Foreman and Myrtle Baker F; m. 2/25/45 to Cora R. Lampe; c. Billy Allen, Stanley La Chance (stepson), Rae Christensen (stepdaughter) and Joan Kuepker (stepdaughter). Educ: Panhandle A&M Col, B.A, 35, B.S, 36; Okla. A&M Col, 36-37. Polit. & Govt. Pos: Precinct 12 chmn, Cleveland Co. Rep. Party, Okla, 65-67, co. chmn, 67-69; mem, Cleveland Co. Rep. Cmt, 65-69; cand. develop. chmn, Cleveland Co. Rep. Exec. Cmt, 66-67, mem-at-lg, 69-; mem, Okla. Rep. State Cmt, 67-69. Mil. Serv: Entered as PO 2/C, Naval Res, 42, released as Lt.(jg), 46, after serv. in many units, U.S; Lt. Comdr.(Ret), Naval Res, 64; one commendation. Mem: Okla. and Nat. Realtors Asns; Lions. Named Honorary Am. Farmer by Future Farmers of Am. Rel: Baptist. Mailing Add: 1423 Oakwood Dr, Norman, Okla. 73069.

FOREMAN, FRED WILSON D
Chmn, Palo Pinto Co. Dem. Party, Tex.
b. Strawn, Tex, 3/12/13; s. Grover Cleveland Foreman and Jimmie Knight F; m. 2/8/47 to Juanita Howard; c. Vicki Lynn. Polit. & Govt. Pos: Sheriff, Palo Pinto Co, Tex, 47-61; chmn, Palo Pinto Co. Dem. Party, 62- Bus. & Prof. Pos: Agent, Sinclair Ref. Co, 59- Mil. Serv: Entered as Pvt, Army, 41, released as Warrant Officer, 45; ETO Ribbon with Three Battle Stars; Bronze Star; German Occup. Ribbon. Mem: Am. Legion; Palo Pinto Co. Sheriff's Posse; Palo Pinto Livestock Asn; Lions. Rel: Methodist. Mailing Add: 2205 N.W. Fourth Ave, Mineral Wells, Tex. 76067.

FORESTER, WILLIAM DAVIS R
b. Harlan, Ky, 9/6/13; s. Jerimiah Grant Forester and Jane Hall F; m. 12/23/33 to Elizabeth Spillman; c. Karl Spillman and Jane Whitney. Educ: East. State Col, A.B; East. Ky. Univ, M.A. Polit. & Govt. Pos: Pres, Young Rep, 8 years; city councilman, Harlan, Ky, 6 years; former chmn. and secy, Harlan Co. Rep. Exec. Cmt. Mem: Charter mem, Harlan Lions Club; Kiwanis; United Commercial Travelers. Rel: Baptist. Mailing Add: Marse Dr, Harlan, Ky. 40831. (1967)

FORKER, PAUL C. D
Committeeman, Ill. Dem. Cent. Cmt.
b. Olmsted, Ill, 6/30/22; s. Charles H. Forker and Lizzetta Dagner F; m. 10/5/46 to Ann Decker. Educ: Lincoln Park High Sch, Mich, grad, 40. Polit. & Govt. Pos: Precinct committeeman, Olmsted, Ill, 57-65; v.chmn, Pulaski Co. Dem. Party, 60-65; committeeman, Ill. Dem. Cent. Cmt, 65- Mil. Serv: Entered as Apprentice, Coast Guard, 42, released as FF 3/C, 46, after serv. in Am. Theatre. Mem: Am. Legion; Lions. Rel: Protestant. Mailing Add: Box 30, R.R. 1, Olmsted, Ill. 62970.

FORKNER, RICHARD E. R
N.Dak. State Sen.
b. Langdon, N.Dak, 5/29/09; s. Mark Isaac Forkner and Jeanette Ethel Braithwaite F; m. 2/14/35 to Joyce May Rasmusson; c. Richard Earl, Mark Otto and Susan Claire. Educ: Dacotah Bus. Col, Fargo, N.Dak, 30. Polit. & Govt. Pos: N.Dak. State Sen, Tenth Dist, 62-, mem, Transportation Cmt, 62-, v.chmn, 65-67, chmn, 69-, mem, State and Fed. Govt. Cmt, 62-, mem, Indust, Bus. and Labor Cmt, 62-, v.chmn, 63, 65 & 67, chmn, Legis. Coun. Interim Transportation Cmt, 69-, N.Dak. State Sen. and mem. transportation cmt, Midwest Coun. of State Govt, 69- Bus. & Prof. Pos: Co-owner and co-publisher, Cavalier Co. Rep, 35-69. Mil. Serv: Platoon Sgt, Army, 26-29, serv. in Citizens Mil. Training Camp, Ft. Snelling, Minneapolis, Minn, 26, 27 & 29 and Ft. Lincoln, Bismarck, N.Dak, 28; Army Enlistees Res, 29-39. Mem: Chmn, transportation cmt, Langdon C. of C, 35-; secy, Cavalier Co. Fair Asn, 37-60, mem, bd. dir, 60-62; treas, U.S. Durum Show, 42-63, dir, 63-65; dir, Tri-State Harness Horse Asn, 45-60; v.pres, five-co. Hwy. 1 Asn, 48; secy-treas, Langdon Commercial Club, 49, pres, 51; pres, Langdon City Fire Dept, 49-52; Knight Comdr. of the Court of Honor, Scottish Rite, 50-; secy, N.Dak. Asn. of Fairs, 51-56; pres, N.Dak. Fair Mgr. Asn, 56-57; dir, Cavalier Co. Mem. Hosp. Asn, 68-; AF&AM; Masonic Holding Corp; Int. Pembelier Dam Dmt. Awarded life membership, Langdon City Fire Dept, 52; Hon. Chap. Farmer Degree, local chap, Future Farmers of Am, 54; Good Citizen Award, Langdon K. of C, 66; Outstanding Citizen Award, Langdon City Jaycees, 68. Rel: United Methodist; treas. of the bd, Methodist Church, 38-39, mem, bd. trustees, 46-47, mem, bd. stewards, 40- Mailing Add: 1005 Sixth St, Langdon, N.Dak. 58249.

FORNOS, WERNER H. D
Md. State Del.
b. Leipzig, Germany, 11/5/33; s. Jamie Fornos and Lilly E. Warmbold F; m. 6/24/61 to Margaret Lynn Sampson; c. Werner H, Jr, Elizabeth Ann and Jamie Martin. Educ: Univ. Md, B.S. in govt. and politics, 65; Sigma Delta Chi. Polit. & Govt. Pos: Pub. information officer, Ft. George G. Meade, Md, 58-60; dir of info, Army, Rocket & Guided Missile Agency, Huntsville, Ala, 60-62; pub. affairs officer, President's Missile Sites Labor Cmn, 62-63; chief of spec. activities, Off. of Secy. of Labor, 63-65; dep. asst. manpower adminstr, U.S. Dept. of Labor, 65-66; del, Md. Constitutional Conv, 68; Md. State Del, currently. Bus. & Prof. Pos: Ed. apprentice, Boston Post Publ. Co, 50-54; Pan Am. World Airways, currently. Mil. Serv: Entered as Pvt, Army, 54, released as Sgt, 58, after serv. in Germany; Army Commendation Medal; Nat. Defense Serv. Medal; Good Conduct Medal. Mem: Nat. Press Club; Press Club of Anne Arundel Co; bd. dirs, Univ. Md. Alumni Asn; pres, Univ. Col. Chap, Univ. Md. Alumni; Young Dem. of Anne Arundel Co; Ruritan; bd, South States Farm Coops; bd, Commun. Chest of Anne Arundel Co. Gold Award, United Appeal of Baltimore for Serv, 58-60; chmn, 1966 Non-Partisan Voter Registrn. Dr; Young Man of the Year for Md, Jaycees, 68. Rel: Methodist. Mailing Add: Hilltop Farm, Davidsonville, Md. 21035.

FORREST, ERIN GEORGE D
b. Alturas, Calif, 1/12/20; s. George Forrest and Rosie Baker F; m. 2/10/52 to Stella Shoemaker; c. Poco Erin. Educ: Riverside Jr. Col, 2 years. Polit. & Govt. Pos: Mem, numerous local and state cmts, particularly in the fields of wildlife, conservation, Indian affairs and econ. develop, 46-; chmn, Modoc Co. Dem. Cent. Cmt, Calif, 62-69; mem, Calif. State Dem. Cent. Cmt, 62-69; admin. aide to Assemblywoman Pauline L. Davis, 66-69. Bus. & Prof. Pos: Mgr, tribal opers, XL Indian Reservation, 46-69; state inheritance tax appraiser, Calif, 61-66. Mil. Serv: Entered as Pvt, Army, 43, released as Pfc, 45, after serv. in 202nd Gen. Hosp, ETO, 44-45. Publ: Co-auth, American Indian Statement of Purpose, Univ. Chicago, 61; auth, numerous ed. concerning Am. Indians. Mem: Calif. State Inheritance Tax Appraisers Asn; Calif-Ore. Interstate Deer Herd Cmn; State Adv. Cmn. on Indian Affairs; Gov. Interstate Indian Coun; first pres, Calif. Intertribal Coun; Kiwanis; Modoc Co. Farm Bur. Named Outstanding Am. Indian from the West by the Am. Indian Chicago Conf, 61; received Coveted Rural Serv. Award from Sargent Shriver, Off. Econ. Opportunity, 68. Rel: Protestant. Mailing Add: Box 763, Alturas, Calif. 96101.

FORREST, LEONARD WILLIS, JR. D
R.I. State Representative
b. Providence, R.I, 4/18/31; s. Leonard W. Forrest and Lucy Duffy F; m. 10/13/56 to Carol A. Turbitt; c. Leonard W, III, Kathleen Ann, Maryellen, Eileen Louise and Thomas Joseph. Polit. & Govt. Pos: R.I. State Rep, 30th Dist, 69- Rel: Catholic. Mailing Add: 31 Moorland Ave, Cranston, R.I. 02905.

FORRESTER, E. STEWART R
b. Wicomico Church, Northumberland Co, Va, 2/6/31; s. Eugene M. Forrester and Amy Stewart F; single. Educ: Richmond Prof. Inst. of the Col. of William and Mary, B.S, 58; George Wash. Univ, grad. study. Polit. & Govt. Pos: Campaign mgr, Lawrence Traylor for U.S. Sen, Va; v.chmn, Eighth Dist, Rep. Party; cand. for Rep. nomination, U.S. Rep, Va, 66. Bus. & Prof. Pos: Prog. designer, Spec. Juvenile Delinquency Study, Wash, D.C; owner-operator, small bus; teacher, Dist. Pub. Schs; teacher, Va. Pub. Schs; dir, United Planning Orgn, Wicomico Church, Northumberland Co, Va; dir, Job Crops Screening Center for Metrop. Wash, D.C; mem, Manpower Admin, Middle-Atlantic Region, Dept. of Labor, currently. Mil. Serv: Air Force, 51-55. Mem: Va. Retail Merchants Asn; Va. Jr. C. of C; Lions; Va. Educ. Asn; Nat. Educ. Asn; D.C. Educ. Asn; Va. Rep. Party; Northumberland Co. Rep. Party; Nat. Cmt. for Children and Youth; Wash. Urban League. Rel: Episcopal. Mailing Add: 1110 Portner Rd, Alexandria, Va. 22314.

FORRESTER, M. M. 'DUKE' R
b. Emerson, Iowa, 1/3/83; s. George Forrester and Harriett C. Jenkins F; wid; c. Barbara (Mrs. Sliger) and Jay W. Educ: Hastings Col, 07. Polit. & Govt. Pos: Past mem, sch. bds and twp. bds; Nebr. State Sen, 61-65. Bus. & Prof. Pos: Worked on newspaper and taught sch, formerly; Owner and operator, cattle ranch, Custer Co, Nebr, 07- Traveled in more than sixty countries. Rel: Presbyterian. Mailing Add: Anselmo, Nebr. 68813.

FORSETH, DONALD E. Conservative
Minn. State Rep.
b. 1931. Educ: St. Olaf Col, 49-50; St. Cloud State Col, B.S, 57. Polit. & Govt. Pos: Secy, Madelia C. of C; exec. v.pres, Crystal C. of C; Minn. State Rep, 67- Bus. & Prof. Pos: Teacher, Madelia Pub. Schs, 57-61; salesman, Prudential Ins. Co, 61-62. Mil. Serv: Marines, 2 years. Mem: Crystal Interagency Youth Coun; Jaycees; pres, Pi Omega Pi; pres, Madelia Educ. Asn. Mailing Add: 5839 Jersey Ave. N, Crystal, Minn. 55428. (1967)

FORSGREN, F. LESLIE R
b. McGregor, N.Dak, 8/13/21; s. Evald Forsgren and Caroline Ryan F; m. 8/8/48 to Joy Ann Mullis; c. Caroline June and Frank Mullis. Educ: Univ. of N.Dak, LL.B, 45; Phi Delta Phi; Sigma Nu. Polit. & Govt. Pos: States Attorney, Divide Co, N.Dak, 51-55; chmn, Divide Co. Rep. Party, 64-68; attorney, Farm House Admin, Crosbey, 69- Mil. Serv: Entered as Pvt, Marine Corps, 45, released as Pfc, 46, after serv. in Marine Carrison Forces, S. Pac. Mem: Lawyer Pilot Bar Asn.(nat. v.pres, 59-61); N.Dak. State and Am. Bar Asns; N.Dak. Vet. Serv. Officer's Asn; Elks; Mason; Am. Legion (state v.comdr, N.Dak); 40 et 8; Moose; Kiwanis Int. Rel: Lutheran. Mailing Add: 707 S.W. First St, Crosby, N.Dak. 58730.

FORSGREN, RICHARD ARVIL D
b. Brigham City, Utah, 7/22/23; s. R.P. Forsgren and Clarice Wright F; m. 6/7/44 to Clayta Christensen; c. Richard Earl, Terri Lynn and Barbara Ann. Educ: Univ. Utah; W.Tex. State Univ. Polit. & Govt. Pos: Wyo. State Rep, 63-67; v.pres, Gov. Wyo. Youth Coun; mem, Gov. Employ. the Handicapped Cmt. Mil. Serv: Entered as Cadet, Air Force, 43, released as Capt, 47, after serv. in Eighth Air Force. Mem: V.pres, Wyo. Health Asn. and Wyo. Tuberc. and Respiratory Disease Asn; nat. dir, State Ment. Health Asn; chmn, Wyo. Girl Scouts; Elks (Past Exalted Ruler); Exchange Club (dist. gov, trustee and past pres); Eagles; Am. Legion; DAV; C. of C; dir, Southwest Wyo. Commun. Col. Distinguished Serv. Award, Jaycees. Rel: Latter-day Saint. Mailing Add: 1115 McKinley Ave, Rock Springs, Wyo. 82901.

FORSYTH, DON D
Committeeman, State Dem. Cent. Cmt, Ill.
b. Mt. Vernon, Ill, 2/7/08; s. William Thorne Forsyth and Lucie Dewey F; m. 6/15/32 to Claire Kelly; c. William D, Jr. and Mary Lucinda (Mrs. Gebben). Educ: Univ. Ill, B.S, 29; Phi Eta Sigma; Beta Theta Pi. Polit. & Govt. Pos: Gen. supvr, auto dept, Off. of Ill. Secy. of State, 33-43; mem, Ill. Vet. Cmn, 48-52; campaign mgr, Dem. Cand. for Gov, 52; organizer, Down State Ill. Citizens for Kennedy-Johnson, 60; mem, Ill. Ins. Adv. Cmn. under Gov. Kerner, 61-69; committeeman, State Dem. Cent. Cmt, 20th Dist, 63- Bus. & Prof. Pos: Pres, Forsyth Ins. Agency Inc, 46-; dir, Town & Country Bank, Springfield, Ill, 62-; dir, Liberty Investment, 64-; dir, Land of Lincoln Abstract Co, 66- Mil. Serv: Entered as Lt.(jg), Navy, 43, released as Lt, 45, after serv. in Transportation Br, Wash, D.C, 43-45. Mem: Amvets; Navy League. Rel: Protestant. Mailing Add: 1923 Wiggins Ave, Springfield, Ill. 62704.

FORSYTH, WILLIAM FRANK D
b. Andrews, N.C, 7/21/15; s. William Thomas Forsyth and Xena Bristol F; m. 1938 to Ruth Lail; c. William Frank Jr. and Robert Ashley. Educ: Emory and Henry Col; exec. prog, Univ. of N.C; N.C. Bankers Conf, Univ. of N.C, 4 summers; Rutgers Univ. Sch. of Banking. Polit. & Govt. Pos: Past chmn, Cherokee Co. Dem. Exec. Cmt. and Cherokee Co. Infantile Paralysis Cmt, N.C; chmn, Elec. Power Syst, Murphy; chmn, bd. of trustees, Carnegia Libr, Murphy, 40-54; chmn, Group Ten, N.C. Bankers Asn, 58; N.C. State Sen, 59-66; del, Dem. Nat. Conv, 68. Bus. & Prof. Pos: Pres, Citizens Bank & Trust Co. of Murphy, Andrews, Hayesville, Robbinsville, Sylva, Cashiers, Cullowhee and Franklin. Publ: A Banker Looks at the Forests of Western North Carolina. Mem: Past pres, Lions; Mason; Shrine. Rel: Methodist; Trustee, Men's Bible Class, First Methodist Church, Murphy. Mailing Add: Murphy, N.C. 28906.

FORSYTHE, EDWIN B. R
N.J. State Sen.
b. Westtown, Pa, 1/17/16; s. Albert H. Forsythe and Emily Matlack F; m. 8/24/40 to Mary McKnight; c. Susan. Educ: Westtown Sch. grad, 33. Polit. & Govt. Pos: Secy, Bd. of Adjust, Moorestown, N.J, 48-52, mem, Bd. of Health, 53-62, Mayor, 57-62, chmn, Planning Bd, 62-63; committeeman, Moorestown Twp. Rep. Party, 53-62; bd. mem, N.J. State League of Munic, 58-62; N.J. State Sen, 64-; del, Rep. Nat. Conv, 68. Bus. & Prof. Pos: Gen. mgr, Locust Lane Farm Dairy, 33-60, secy-treas, 60-; pres, S. Jersey Milk Dealers Asn, 58-61 and N.J. Milk Indust. Asn, 60-62. Mem: Pres. and mem. bd. of dirs, Burlington Co. YMCA. Rel: Society of Friends. Legal Res: 265 W. Second St, Moorestown, N.J. 08057. Mailing Add: P.O. Box 128, Moorestown, N.J. 08057.

FORSYTHE, JOHN EDWARD R
Chmn, Montgomery Co. Rep. Exec. Cmt, Miss.
b. Memphis, Tenn, 3/19/37; s. Arthur Harold Forsythe and Elizabeth Ann Ingram F; m. 3/1/68 to Eleanor Elizabeth Salveson; c. Elizabeth Ann. Educ: Univ. Miss, 5 years; Kappa Alpha. Polit. & Govt. Pos: Chmn, Montgomery Co. Rep. Exec. Cmt, Miss, 64- Bus. & Prof. Pos: Owner, Walker Ins. Agency, 65- Mil. Serv: Sgt, Air Nat. Guard Res, 60-69; Am. Spirit of Honor Medal. Mem: Miss. Mutual Ins. Agents Asn; v.pres, Winona Rotary Club. Rel: Methodist. Mailing Add: 604 Summit St, Winona, Miss. 38967.

FORSYTHE, ROBERT AMES R
Mem, Minn. State Rep. Cent. Cmt.
b. Menomonie, Wis, 10/22/21; s. Robert Alvin Forsythe and Elvera Hovlid F; m. 7/18/42 to Mary MacCornack; c. Robert Ames, Mary Pauline, Jean Louise, Ann Maureen and Joan Carol. Educ: Univ. Cambridge, Eng, 46-47; St. Olaf Col, B.A, 47; Univ. Minn, LL.B, 49; Blue Key; Pi Kappa Delta; Phi Delta Phi. Polit. & Govt. Pos: State chmn, Minn. Rep. Fedn. Col. Rep. Clubs, 47-48; nat. committeeman, Minn. Young Rep. League, 51-53; chief counsel, U.S. Senate

Small Bus. Cmt, 53-55; admin. asst. to U.S. Sen. Edward J. Thye, 55-59; cong. liaison officer, Dept. Health, Educ, and Welfare, 59, asst. secy, 59-61; chmn, Minn. State Rep. Cent. Cmt, 61-65, mem, currently; cmnr, President Kennedy's Voter Registrn. and Participation Cmn, 63; nat. voter registration chmn, Rep. Nat. Cmt, 64; mem, Minn. State Rep. Exec. Cmt; alternate del, Rep. Nat. Conv, 68. Bus. & Prof. Pos: Lawyer, Cant, Haverstock, Beardsley, Gray and Plant until 68; partner, Cant, Haverstock, Gray, Plant and Mooty, 68- Mil. Serv: Entered as Pvt, Air Force, 42, released as Capt, 46, after serv. in Ninth Air Defense Command, ETO; Bronze Star. Mem: Hennepin Co. and Minn. Bar Asns; Minneapolis C. of C; Citizens League of Gr. Minneapolis; bd. dirs, St. Olaf Col. Alumni Asn; bd. advs, Concordia Col. Lang. Camps, Moorhead, Minn; bd. regents, Augustana Col, Sioux Falls. Rel: Lutheran; mem. bd. trustees, Bethlehem Lutheran Church, Minneapolis. Mailing Add: 4605 Edina Blvd, Edina, Minn. 55424.

FORTAS, ABE D
b. Memphis, Tenn, 6/19/10; s. William Fortas and Ray Berson F; m. 7/9/35 to Carolyn Eugenia Agger. Educ: Southwest. Col, Memphis, A.B, 30; Yale, LL.B, 33; Omicron Delta Kappa; Order of the Coif. Polit. & Govt. Pos: Dir. div. power, Dept. Interior, 31-42, Under Secy. of the Interior, 42-46; asst. chief legal div, Agr. Adjust. Admin, 33-34; asst. dir. corporate reorgn. study, Securities Exchange Cmn, 34-37, consult, 37-38 and asst. dir. pub. utilities div, 38-39; gen. counsel, Pub. Works Admin, 39-40 and Bituminous Coal Div, 39-41; acting gen. counsel, Nat. Power Policy Cmn, 41; mem. bd. legal exams, Civil Serv. Cmn, 41-43; mem, Pres. Cmn. to Study Changes in Organic Law of Puerto Rico, 43; adv. to U.S. Del, UN, San Francisco, 45 and London, 46; Assoc. Justice, U.S. Supreme Court, 65-69. Bus. & Prof. Pos: Asst. prof, Yale, 33-37, vis. prof, 46-47; dir, Festival Casals, Inc; trustee, Carnegie Hall. Mailing Add: 3210 R St. N.W, Washington, D.C. 20007.

FORTIER, DONALD LOUIS D
La. State Rep.
b. New Orleans, La, 10/27/22; s. Almicar Ernest Fortier and Claire Charbonnet F; m. 10/12/47 to Audrey Raymontine Rabe; c. Donald Louis, Jr, David Paul, Dawn Frances and Deanne Cecile. Educ: Tulane Univ, B.Ed, 49. Polit. & Govt. Pos: La. State Rep, 64-; mem, South Regional Educ. Bd, 65-67. Bus. & Prof. Pos: Teacher and coach, Terrebonne Parish, 49-52 and Orleans Parish Sch, 53- Mil. Serv: Entered as Seaman, Navy, 42, released as AFC 3/C, Air Force, 46, after serv. in Asiatic-Pac; Asiatic Pac, Am. Theater, Victory and Good Conduct Medals. Mem: La. Teachers Asn; Am. Legion; VFW; YMBC; Lions; Nat. Soc. State Legis. Letter Football, Tulane Univ, 46, 47 & 48. Rel: Catholic. Mailing Add: 7110 Foch Rd, New Orleans, La. 70126. (1967)

FORTIER, GUY JOSEPH
N.H. State Rep.
b. Livermore Falls, Maine, 1/13/93; s. Patrick Fortier and Eva Lofrance F; wid; c. Dr. Milton and Dr. Norman. Polit. & Govt. Pos: Mem, Berlin City Coun, N.H, 46-56, mayor, 56-58; N.H. State Rep, currently. Bus. & Prof. Pos: Real estate, 20-60; owner, restaurant, 32-35; owner, Cocala Bottling Co, 35-38. Mem: Club Joliette; Milfield Sporting Club; AFL. Rel: Catholic. Mailing Add: 49 Mt. Forist St, Berlin, N.H. 03570. (1967)

FORTIER, MALCOLM JOHN D
Maine State Rep.
b. Skowhegan, Maine, 4/9/14; s. Wilfred H. Fortier and Mary Boufford F; m. 9/18/37 to Yvette M. Bolduc; c. Wayne A, Donna E.(Mrs. Urbach), Pierre B, Renee M.(Mrs. Joseph Jabar), John M, Linda Ann and David E. Polit. & Govt. Pos: Councilman, Waterville, Maine, 40-41, alderman, 40-42 and mayor, 66 & 67, mem, Zoning Bd. and Bd. of Assessment Rev; Maine State Rep, 65- Bus. & Prof. Pos: Food Broker, 38-61; local agent, State Farm Ins. Co, 61-69. Mem: Lions; Hwy. Beautification Cmt. Rel: Catholic. Mailing Add: 4 Oakdale St, Waterville, Maine 04901.

FORTIN, JOHN O. D
N.H. State Rep.
b. Greenville, N.H, 5/15/05; s. Frank Fortin and Josephine Bourgault F; m. to Mary J. Beausoleil (deceased). Educ: Steven Bus. Col, Fitchburg, Mass. Polit. & Govt. Pos: N.H. State Rep, 53- Bus. & Prof. Pos: Owner, ins. and real estate co. Mem: Amherst Country Club. Rel: Catholic. Mailing Add: Main St, Greenville, N.H. 03048.

FORTINBERRY, TOXEY THOMAS R
Chmn, Yalobusha Co. Rep. Party, Miss.
b. Tylertown, Miss, 5/15/08; s. Thomas Calvin Fortinberry and Irene Magee F; m. 12/11/37 to Martha Reeves Costen; c. Sylvia L, Merle I, Martha C, Toxie Ann, Sabrian S.G, Marjorie E, Thomas A, Luther W. and Mary Lu. Educ: Holmes Jr. Col, 31; Southwest. Col, 33; Univ. Tenn, cert. in real estate, 55; Reperts Sch. Auctioneering, 58; pres, Freshman Class; bus. mgr, Weekly Paper; Glee Club. Polit. & Govt. Pos: Chmn, Yalobusha Co. Rep. Party, Miss, 63- Bus. & Prof. Pos: Park dir, Memphis, Tenn, 33-34; salesman, Nat. Life Ins. Co, 34-40; real estate broker, builder and auctioneer, 41-66. Mem: Mason (32°), Shrine, Shrine Chanters; Rotary; Kiwanis; Lions; Int. Traders Club; State and Nat. Realtors Asns; State and Nat. Auctioneers Asns. Awarded Football Scholarship to Holmes Jr. Col. and Southwest. Col. Rel: Baptist; Deacon and Sunday Sch. Teacher. Legal Res: 555 Markette, Water Valley, Miss. 38965. Mailing Add: Box 70, Water Valley, Miss. 38965.

FORTSON, BEN W, JR. D
Secy. of State, Ga.
b. Tignall, Ga, 12/19/04; s. Benjamin Wynn Fortson and Lillie Wellborn F; m. 5/15/26 to Mary Cade; c. Ann McNeill (Mrs. George Mandus). Educ: Starks Univ, 20-23; Ga. Inst. Tech, 23-24; hon. mem, Alpha Kappa Psi, Pi Sigma Alpha. Hon. DD.L, John Marshall Law Sch. Polit. & Govt. Pos: Ga. State Sen, 50th Dist, 39-42; Ga. State Rep, Wilkes Co, 42-44; secy. of State, Ga, 46- Bus. & Prof. Pos: Asst. cashier, Atlanta and Citizens Nat. Bank, Wash, 24-26, Atlanta and Lowry Nat. Bank, Trust Co. Ga. and Wash. Loan & Banking Co, Ga, 26-29. Mem: Pres, Bd, Nat. Asn. of Secy. of State, 54; Mason; Moose; Kiwanis; Gridiron Club; past pres, Ga. Soc. for Crippled Children and Adults. Speaking and Essay Medals; Military Medal, Starks Univ. Sch; mem, boxing team, Light Heavyweight Champion, Ga. Tech. Rel: Methodist. Legal Res: Tignall Rd, Washington, Ga. Mailing Add: 214 State Capitol, Atlanta, Ga. 30334.

FORTSON, ELEANOR ANN D
Committeewoman, Wash. State Dem. Party
b. Renton, Wash, 3/7/04; d. Peter Dullahant and Emma Pothecary D; m. 1/2/25 to William Felton Fortson; c. Barbara (Mrs. Donald Wise), George Peter and Stephen Michael. Educ: Cent. Wash. Col. Educ, Elem. Teacher Cert, 25; West. Wash. Col. Educ, B.A. in Educ, 56, M.A. in Educ, 60; Honor Roll, 2 years; pres. Sr. Class, Cent. Wash. Col. Educ; Herodetean. Polit. & Govt. Pos: Pres, Camano Island Dem. Party, Wash, 54-67, secy, 67-68; secy, Second Dist. Dem. Coun, 58-; chmn, Co. Cmt. to Elect. Dem. Gubernatorial, Wash. State Rep. and U.S. Rep. Nominees, 66 & 68; committeewoman, Wash. State Dem. Party, 66-; del, Dem. Nat. Conv, 68; del, many Co. and State Dem. Conv. Bus. & Prof. Pos: Elem. teacher, Kennydale, Wash, Sch. Dist, 22-24, Bur. Indian Affairs, Shungnak, Noorvik, Alaska, 25-28, Deering, 31-36, Snohomish Co, 45-46 and Stanwood, Wash, 51-59, elem. prin, 60- Mem: Delta Kappa Gamma Int. Soc; Wash. State Elem. Prin. Orgn; Nat. Educ. Asn.(del. nat. conv, 60); Wash. Educ. Asn.(legis. state cmt, del. state conv, 3 terms); Camano Island Educ. Asn.(pres, 2 terms); Wash. State Grange;(state intern cmt. educ, master and lectr. exec. bd); Rebekah. Rel: Protestant. Mailing Add: Route 4, Box 1043, Camano Island, Wash. 98292.

FOSHEE, KATHERINE ALMIRA R
Chmn, Creek Co. Rep. Party, Okla.
b. Garber, Okla, 11/24/26; d. Richard Oril Hill and Myrtle Jane Ernst H; m. 10/22/63 to Roy Edmond Foshee; c. Richard Allen Hughes; grandchildren, Deborah Kay and Kimberly Michelle. Educ: Hughes Beauty Acad, Tulsa, Okla, 58. Polit. & Govt. Pos: Precinct chmn, Allen Precinct, Creek Co. Rep. Party, Okla, 57-65; precinct elec. judge, 64-; v.chmn, Creek Co. Rep. Party, 67-68, chmn, 68- Bus. & Prof. Pos: Ticket cashier, Criterion Theatre, Sapulpa, 45-46; waitress, Liberty Cafe, 46-47, Loraine Hotel Coffee Shop, 47-49 and West. Chicken House, 49-53; waitress and cafe owner; Park Inn Cafe, 54; glass tester, Liberty Glass Lab, 55-58; Beauty shop owner and operator, 59- Mem: Am. Legion Auxiliary; Nat. Fedn. Rep. Women; Dorcas Kelly Chap. Rep. Women's Club Creek Co. Rep. Women of the Year, Dorcas Kelly Chap. Rep. Women's Club Creek Co. Rel: Protestant. Mailing Add: Route 1, Box 58A, Sapulpa, Okla. 74066.

FOSNESS, IRENE D
V.Chmn, Marshall Co. Dem. Cent. Cmt, Iowa
b. Hendricks, Minn, 4/10/06; d. John A. Waugh and Hulda Benz W; m. 5/9/31 to Paul M. Fosness. Educ: Minn. State Col, B.S, 45; Univ. Iowa, M.A, 52; Kappa Delta Pi; Pi Lambda Theta; Blackfriars; YWCA; Atheneum Literary; Kappa Phi; Wesley Players; Commun. Theater; radio broadcasts. Polit. & Govt. Pos: Mem, Frontier Club, 62-69; chmn, Marshall Co. Citizens for Johnson Cmt, 64; mem, Marshall Co. Citizens for Hughes Cmt, 64 & 66-68; del, Dem. Nat. Conv, 64 & 68; del, Dem. Women's Conv, Wash, D.C, 64 & 66; mem, Cent. Iowa Econ. Develop, Inc, 64 & 66; secy, Marshall Co. Dem. Women's Club, 64-66, pres, 66-69; secy, Marshall Co. Dem. Cent. Cmt, 65-68, v.chmn, 68-; co-ordinator, Sen. Harold Hughes and Frazenburg for Gov. Campaigns, Marshall Co, 68; chmn, Iowa State Fair Sch. Exhibit, 67-68 & 69. Bus. & Prof. Pos: Teacher, Eng. and speech, Foley High Sch, Minn, 44-45, Conrad High Sch, Iowa, 45-48 and St. Anthony High Sch, 48-49; elem. prin, St. Anthony, Iowa, 49-56; teacher, Eng. and speech, L-D-F Commun. Sch, LaGrand, Iowa, 56-66; news correspondent, Times-Rep, Marshalltown; dir. summer plays, Piney Woods Sch, Piney Woods, Minn, 67-68 & 69. Publ: An Arithmetic Study, 50; and Geography Class Takes Air Trip, 65, Midland Schs; Poems in a Brochure of Iowa Poetry Day Asn. Mem: Iowa State and Marshall Co. Educ. Asns; L-D-F Commun. Sch. Local Asn; Teacher Educ. and Prfnl. Standards Cmn. (chmn, local, co. and dist, mem, state cmn); Nat. and Iowa Classroom Teachers; sponsor, Future Teachers Club; Iowa Sponsors of Future Teacher Clubs (pres, 58-59); Iowa State Educ. Asn. Fel. Cmt.(chmn, 65-66); del, Nat. Educ. Asn. Conv, 63-66; Am. Asn. Univ. Women (pres, Marshalltown Br, 64-66); Cent. Iowa Art Asn.(pres, v.pres. and mem. bd); City Fedn. Women's Clubs (mem. bd); Hist. Soc. Marshall Co.(mem. bd); State Hist. Soc. Iowa; Marshalltown Citizens for Decent Literature. Sponsor of three orphans in foreign countries. Rel: Methodist: Pres, Wesleyan Serv. Guild and Sunday Sch. Teacher, 10 Years, First Methodist Church, Marshalltown. Mailing Add: 201 N. Second Ave, Marshalltown, Iowa 50158.

FOSS, JOSEPH JACOB R
b. Sioux Falls, S.Dak, 4/17/15; s. Frank Foss (deceased) and Mary F. (deceased); m. 1942 to Donna Wild Hall; c. Mrs. Richard Bittner, Harry Dean Hall, Mrs. Robert King, Mrs. John Finke and Frank. Educ: Sioux Falls Col; Augustana Col; Univ. S.Dak, B.S, 40; Sigma Alpha Epsilon. Polit. & Govt. Pos: S.Dak. State Rep, 48-50 & 51-53; Gov. State of S.Dak, 54-58. Bus. & Prof. Pos: Pres, Joe Foss, Inc; owner-operator, C. Lazy U Guest Ranch, Granby, Colo; v.pres, Raven Indust, 59; Pres, Foss-Halmi, Inc; cmnr, Am. Football League, 60-66. Mil. Serv: Maj, Marine Corps, World War II, Col, Air Force, Korea; Distinguished Flying Cross; Cong. Medal of Honor; Brig. Gen. and Chief of Staff, S.Dak. Air National Guard, currently. Mem: Air Force Asn.(chmn. bd, past pres); Air Force Acad.(bd. dirs); Nat. Soc. Crippled Children & Adults (past. pres, bd. trustees); Aeronautics Cmt.(v.pres); Am. Legion; Nat. Defense Coun. Am. Legion; U.S. Nat. Guard Asn.(exec. bd); Boy Scouts (bd. dirs. Roosevelt Coun); bd. dirs, Valley of the Sun Sch. Ment. Retarded Children; Tex. Am. Oil Co.(bd. dirs); Imperial Am. Resources Funds (bd. dirs); Int. Energy Co.(bd. dirs); Raven Indust.(bd. dirs); Phoenix Air Mus. (bd. dirs); bd. dirs, Gov. Cmt. Alaska Bus. Coun. Rel: Methodist. Mailing Add: 5922 East Cheney Rd, Scottsdale, Ariz. 85251.

FOSSEEN, NEAL RANDOLPH Independent
b. Yakima, Wash; s. Arthur Benjamin Fosseen and Florence Neal F; m. 9/26/36 to Helen Witherspoon; c. Neal Randolph, Jr. and William Roger. Educ: Univ. Wash, B.A, 29; Alpha Kappa Psi; Beta Theta Pi. Hon. LL.D, Whitworth Col. Polit. & Govt. Pos: Mayor, Spokane, Wash, 60-67, emer. mayor, 68- Bus. & Prof. Pos: V.pres and dir, Wash. Bancshares, Inc, Spokane, dir, Old Nat. Bank, dir, Utah-Idaho Sugar Co, Salt Lake City, dir, Day Mines Inc, Wallace, Idaho and dir, Securities-Intermountain, Inc, Portland, Ore, currently. Mil. Serv: Marine Corps, 42-45, First Marine Air Wing; Col, Marine Corps Res; S. Pac. Campaign Ribbon with Solomon's and

Upper Solomon's Campaign Stars. Mem: Hon. mem, Int. Rotary; life mem, Elks; perpetual mem, Mil. Order of World Wars. Hon. citizen, Nishinomiya, Japan. Mailing Add: W. 1002 Riverside, Spokane, Wash. 99201.

FOSSUM, CHESTER R
b. Maxbass, N.Dak, 7/9/28; married; c. 4. Educ: Minot State Teachers Col. Polit. & Govt. Pos: N.Dak. State Rep, 59-61, 66; mem, local township and sch. bds. Bus. & Prof. Pos: Livestock and grain farmer. Mailing Add: Maxbass, N.Dak. 58760. (1967)

FOSTER, ALBERT JAMES D
Miss. State Sen.
b. Atmore, Ala, 9/17/07; married. Polit. & Govt. Pos: Miss. State Sen, currently; trustee, Monroe Co. Hosp. Bus. & Prof. Pos: Farmer-merchant; dir, Monroe Banking and Trust Co. Mem: Mason. Rel: Baptist. Mailing Add: R.F.D. 2, Aberdeen, Miss. 39730. (1967)

FOSTER, BEN R
Kans. State Sen.
b. Hutchinson, Kans, 3/31/26; s. True E. Foster and Leta Brady F; m. 10/29/55 to Lucinda Stevens. Educ: Kans. Univ, A.B, 48, LL.B, 51; Phi Delta Phi; Kappa Sigma. Polit. & Govt. Pos: Judge, Court of Common Pleas, 59; Kans. State Rep, 65-69; munic. judge, Wichita, 67-69; Kans. State Sen, 69-. Mil. Serv: Cadet, Navy, 44-46; entered as 2nd Lt, Air Force, 51, released as 1st Lt, 52, after serv. in Thule, Greenland; Lt. Col, Air Force Res, 52-65; Am. Theater and Korean Serv. Ribbons; Victory Medal. Mem: Wichita and Kans. Bar Asns; Am. Legion. Rel: Episcopal. Legal Res: 600 Longford Lane, Wichita, Kans. 67206. Mailing Add: 808 Brown Building, Wichita, Kans. 67202.

FOSTER, BERTHA M. R
b. Underhill, Vt, 4/6/16; m. to Maurice Foster. Educ: Univ. of Vt. Polit. & Govt. Pos: Mem, Vt. Educ. Asn. and Co. Asn; town del. to state conv; mem, Nat. Fedn. Rep. Women; Vt. State Rep, 65-66. Bus. & Prof. Pos: Elem. teacher. Mem: PTA; Ladies Aid. Rel: Exec. Bd, Westford Federated Church. Mailing Add: Star Route, Essex Junction, Vt. 05452. (1967)

FOSTER, CLAUDE W. R
N.H. State Rep.
b. 11/22/95; married; c. Two. Educ: Haverhill. Polit. & Govt. Pos: City councilman, Lakeport, N.H, 2 terms; other ward offs; N.H. State Rep, currently. Mil. Serv: World War I. Mem: Mason. Rel: Protestant. Mailing Add: 82 Franklin St, Lakeport, N.H. 03246. (1967)

FOSTER, CLIFTON N(EAL) R
b. Benedict, Nebr, 2/27/34; m. 8/24/62 to Marilyn Jensen; c. John Wesley, Matthew Jay and Natalie Anne. Educ: Nebr. Wesleyan Univ, A.B, 57; Mo. Sch. of Mines, 58; Oak Ridge Inst. of Nuclear Studies, 59; Univ. Nebr, M.Ed, 62 and Ed.D, 65; Theta Chi; Phi Delta Kappa. Polit. & Govt. Pos: Nebr. State Sen, 62-65. Bus. & Prof. Pos: Lectr, former teacher. Mil. Serv: Entered Army, 53, released as Sgt, 55, after serv. in 57th FA Bn, Korea, 54-55. Mem: Elks. Rel: Methodist. Mailing Add: R.R. 4, Charleston, Ill. 61920.

FOSTER, DORIS VESA R
Secy, Buncombe Co. Rep. Exec. Cmt, N.C.
b. Houston, Tex, 7/7/25; d. Max Carl Mennike and Mary Russell M; m. 11/2/46 to Eugene Philip Foster; c. Cheryl Kit and Philip Eugene. Educ: Univ. Houston, 1 year. Polit. & govt. Pos: Pres, Buncombe Co. Rep. Womens Club, 63-65; gen. chmn, Buncombe Co. Rep. Campaign Hq, 64; del, Nat. Fedn. Rep. Women, Louisville, Ky, 64 & N.C. del-at-large, Wash, D.C, 67; prog. chmn, N.C. Fedn. Rep. Women, 64-65, v.pres, 66 & 67; precinct chmn, Biltmore Precinct Rep. Party, 66 & 68; secy, Buncombe Co. Rep. Exec. Cmt, 66-; 11th cong. dist. co-chmn, Jim Gardner for Gov. Campaign, 68; N.C. chmn, Retired Citizens for Nixon, 68; del. and mem. credentials cmt, Rep. Nat. Conv, 68; campaign coordinator for seven Rep. cand. for Asheville City Coun, 69. Bus. & Prof. Pos: Receptionist, Shell Oil-Shell Chem. Co, 44-51; owner-mgr, Hilltop Mobilehome Park for Retired Persons, 52- Mem: Asheville Mobilehome Asn.(secy, 60); Green Thumb Garden Club (pres, 62); Biltmore Estate Home Exten. Club (pres, 62); Newton Sch. PTA (pres, 68-69 and secy. to Citizens Cmt. for Better Schs, 69-); Rep. Club (soc. chmn, 69); Christians Womens Club. Rel: Baptist; Active in Sunday Sch. Adult Class and mem. Church Social Cmt, Asheville First Baptist Church. Mailing Add: 932 Hendersonville Rd, Asheville, N.C. 28803.

FOSTER, ELEANOR CORINNE R
Ward Chmn, Lowell Rep. City Cmt, Mass.
b. Lowell, Mass, 5/12/19; d. Wilbrod Lagasse and Donia Lequin L; div; m. 2/19/52 to Lyndwood D. Foster, Jr; c. Patricia Ann (Mrs. Leo Stromvall), Roland Larry, Jr. and Kenneth R. Hughes and Gertrude D, Frederick A, Linda D. and John J. Foster. Educ: Lowell High Sch, dipl, 38. Polit. & Govt. Pos: Publicity chmn, Gr. Lowell Rep. Women, Mass, 64-66, mem. bd, 66-68; ward chmn, Lowell Rep. City Cmt, 67- Mem: Gr. Lowell Rep. Womens Club; Asn. Educ. Franco-Am; Mothers and Wives of War Vet; Merrimack Valley Goodwill Industs; Middlesex Womens Club. Rel: Catholic. Mailing Add: 186 Tenth St, Lowell, Mass. 01850.

FOSTER, FRANK D
b. 1901. Educ: West. N.Mex. Univ, B.S; Highlands Univ. Polit. & Govt. Pos: Co. supt. of schs, N.Mex, 37-41; mem, State Game Cmn, 56-58; N.Mex. State Rep, 61-68. Bus. & Prof. Pos: Teacher; farmer. Mem: AF&AM; Farm Bur; N.M.E.A; life mem, Nat. Rifle Asn. Rel: Baptist. Mailing Add: Box 983, Clovis, N.Mex. 88101. (1967)

FOSTER, FRED W. D
b. 1912. Educ: West. N.Mex. Univ, A.B. and M.S. Polit. & Govt. Pos: Chmn, Co. Libr. Bd, N.Mex; former co. sch. supt; N.Mex. State Rep, 55-68. Bus. & Prof. Pos: Sch. prin; rancher. Mem: Mason; Scottish Rite. Rel: Protestant. Mailing Add: Mangus Route, Silver City, N.Mex. 88061. (1967)

FOSTER, HOWARD ALBERT R
Vt. State Sen.
b. Middlebury, Vt, 1/20/02; m. to Beatrice Kirby; c. Three daughters. Educ: Middlebury Schs. Polit. & Govt. Pos: Mem, Salisbury Sch. Bd, Vt, 49-61; mem, Middlebury Union High Sch. Bd, 56-; Vt. State Rep, 65-66; Vt. State Sen, 67- Bus. & Prof. Pos: Farmer; dir, Middlebury Fed. Land Bank; pres, Middlebury Coop. Credit Union; dir, Commun. Light & Power Co; dir, NEMPA. Mem: Past pres, Farm Bur; Addison Co. dir, Vt. Sugar Makers' Asn. Rel: Methodist; Lay leader, Middlebury Methodist Church. Mailing Add: Salisbury, Vt. 05443. (1967)

FOSTER, LaMAR, SR. D
b. Ill, 4/4/98; m. 1920 to Mary Thomason; c. Five. Educ: James Milliken Univ. Polit. & Govt. Pos: Mayor and pres. commun. sch. bd, West Branch, Iowa, formerly; Iowa State Rep. until 66 and speaker, Iowa House of Rep. Bus. & Prof. Pos: Sch. teacher and prin; farmer. Mem: Mason; Consistory; S.A.T.C, James Milliken, Decatur, Ill. Rel: Methodist. Mailing Add: 223 N. Fifth St, West Branch, Iowa 52358. (1967)

FOSTER, ROLAND RAYMOND R
b. Claremont, N.H, 5/1/21; m. to Mavis; c. Two daughters. Educ: W. Springfield High Sch. Polit. & Govt. Pos: Trustee, Wash. Elec. Coop, Inc; selectman, 52-; Vt. State Rep, 61-63 & 65-66. Bus. & Prof. Pos: Carpenter; contractor. Mil. Serv: Air Force, 42-45, Sgt. Mem: Mason; F&AM. Rel: Methodist. Mailing Add: R.F.D, Moretown, Vt. 05660. (1967)

FOSTER, ROY GUYLUS, JR. R
Chmn, Jefferson Co. Rep.Cmt, Ga.
b. North Wilkesboro, N.C, 10/9/26; s. Roy Guylus Foster and Lula Lee Stokes F; m. 3/30/46 to Parkie Leigh Camp; c. Roy G, III, Terri Leigh, William Hayes and Parkie Camp. Educ: Univ. Ga; U.S. Mil. Acad; Kappa Alpha. Polit. & Govt. Pos: Nat. treas, Nat. Fedn. Young Rep, 55-57; chmn, South. Coun. Young Rep, 57-59; councilman, Wadley, Ga, 57-64; mem, Jefferson Co. Bd. of Educ, 62-64; Ga. State Sen, 21st Dist, 65-66; chmn, Jefferson Co. Rep. Cmt, 68- Bus. & Prof. Pos: Pres, Savannah Terminals, Inc, Ga. and R.G. Foster & Co, Wadley, Ga, 62- Mil. Serv: Entered as Pvt, Army, 46, released as Cpl, 48, after serv. in Army Occupation, Germany. Mem: Am. Legion; Mason; PTA; Farm Bur; Lions. Rel: Methodist. Mailing Add: Dalmatian Plantation, Wadley, Ga. 30477. (1967)

FOSTER, WILLIAM CHAPMAN
b. Westfield, N.J, 4/27/97; s. Jed S. Foster and Anna Louise Chapman F; m. 5/9/25 to Beulah Robinson; c. Seymour Robinson. Educ: Mass. Inst. Tech, 18. Hon. LL.D, Syracuse Univ, 57, Bowdoin Col. and Rutgers Univ, 68; hon. D.Pub.Serv, George Wash. Univ, 63; hon. D.H.L, Kenyon Col, 68. Polit. & Govt. Pos: Consult, War Prod. Bd, 41; spec. rep, Under Secy. War on Procurement for Army Air Force, World War II; dir. purchases, Div. Army Serv. Forces; Under Secy of Commerce, 46-48; dep. spec. rep, Marshall Plan, Econ. Coop. Admin, Europe, 48-49, dep. adminstr, 49-50, adminstr, 50-51; Dep. Secy. of Defense, 51-53; co-chmn, Security Resources Panel, 57; with Nat. Planning Cmn, 60-61; dir, U.S. Arms Control and Disarmament Agency, 61-69. Bus. & Prof. Pos: Officer and dir, Pressed and Welded Steel Prod. Co, Inc, 22-46; pres, Mfg. Chemists Asn, Inc, 53-55; exec. v.pres. and dir, Olin Mathieson, 55-58; dir, v.pres. and sr. adv, Olin Mathieson Chem. Corp, 58-61; chmn. bd. and pres, United Nuclear Corp, 61. Mil. Serv: Army, World War I; U.S. Medal of Merit; Commendations for Civilian Serv, War Dept, Dept. of Defense, World War II. Mem: Univ. Club; Links Club, N.Y.C; Metrop. and Chevy Chase Clubs, Wash, D.C. Distinguished Honor Award, Arms Control and Disarmament Agency, 69. Mailing Add: 3304 R St. N.W, Washington, D.C. 20007.

FOSTER, WILLIAM EDWARD R
b. Laramie, Wyo, 2/24/31; s. Edward Horatio Foster and Beaulah Cook F; m. 12/29/51 to Margaret Florence Evans; c. Ann Therese, Elizabeth Marie, William Edward, Laura Ellen, Timothy Evans and Peter Ryan. Educ: Univ. Wyo, LL.B. cum laude, 55; Omicron Delta Kappa; Sigma Chi. Polit. & Govt. Pos: Pres, Wyo. Young Rep, 52-53; secy-treas, Mesa Co. Rep. Party, Colo, 58-60; precinct committeeman, 62-64; Colo. State Rep, 64-66. Bus. & Prof. Pos: Attorney and partner, Foster & Farina, 56-; dir, Best Plastic Container Corp, 62-; v.pres. and dir, Dixson, Inc, 63- and Mesa Sanitary Supply Co, 64-; dir, Powderhorn Ski Corp, 65-; v.pres. and dir, Thermo Dynamics Corp, Shawnee Mission, Kans, 68-; pres. and dir, CBW Builders Inc, Grand Junction, Colo, 69-; v.pres. and dir, D.E.A. Prod, Inc, Tempe, Ariz, 69- Mil. Serv: Entered as Pvt, Army, 50, released as Cpl, 51, after serv. in 141st Tank Bn. Mem: Wyo, Colo. and Am. Bar Asns; K. of C; Farm Bur; Lions; Am. Legion. Selected Outstanding Young Man, Mesa Co. and One of 3 Outstanding Young Men, Colo, 66, Jr. C. of C. Rel: Catholic. Mailing Add: 1701 Orchard Ave, Grand Junction, Colo. 81501.

FOUNTAIN, L. H. D
U.S. Rep, N.C.
b. Leggett, N.C, 4/23/13; s. Lawrence H. Fountain and Sallie Barnes F; m. 5/14/42 to Christine Dail; c. Nancy Dail. Educ: Univ. of N.C, A.B, 34, LL.B, 36; Wiley P. Mangum Oratorical Medal; Mary D. Wright Debate Medal; pres, Univ. N.C. Philantropic Lit. Soc. Polit. & Govt. Pos: Reading clerk, N.C. State Senate, 36-41; pres, Edgecombe Young Dem. Club, 40; east. organizer Young Dem. Clubs N.C, 41; N.C. Sen, 47-52; U.S. Rep, N.C. Second Dist, 53-, past chmn. exec. cmt, Second Dist, chmn. intergovernmental rels. subcommittee, House Govt. Opers. Cmn, chmn. Near E. Subcommittee, House For. Affairs Cmt; U.S. Del, UN Gen. Assembly, 67. Bus. & Prof. Pos: Attorney-at-Law; officer, Coastal Plains Broadcasting Co, radio sta. WCPS, Tarboro, N.C, 49-69, v.pres, 69- Mil. Serv: Entered as Pvt, Army, 42, released as Maj, 46, after serv. in Inf. and Judge Adv. Gen. Office; Lt. Col, Army Res. Mem: Mem. bd. trustees, St. Andrews Presby. Col, Laurinburg, N.C; exec. cmt, E.Carolina Coun. Boy Scouts; Elks; Kiwanis (pres, Zarboro, N.C. Kiwanis and Lt. Gov. sixth N.C. Div. of Carolinas Dist, Kiwanis Int); Edgecombe Co. and N.C. Bar Asns; Farm Bur; Grange; Am. Legion. Distinguished Serv. Award, Man of the Year, Tarboro Jr. C. of C, 48. Rel: Presbyterian; Elder. Legal Res: 1102 Panola St, Tarboro, N.C. 27886. Mailing Add: 2400 Rayburn House Office Bldg, Washington, D.C. 20515.

FOURMY, JAMES C, SR. R
b. Houston, Tex, 7/13/24; s. Sewall Myer and Emily Kohli M; m. 6/23/51 to Mary Louise Moore; c. Emily and James C, Jr. Educ: Univ. Tex, B.B.A, 50; Sigma Chi. Polit. & Govt. Pos: Del, Rep. State Conv, Tex, 64, 66 & 68;

chmn, spec. forces ballot security, Harris Co. Rep. Party, 64-, precinct chmn, 64-, chmn, Vacancy Cmt, 65 & 67-70, chmn, 15th Sen. Dist. Exec. Cmt, 68, permanent chmn, 15th Sen. Dist. Conv, 68; del, Rep. Nat. Conv, 68. Bus. & Prof. Pos: Asst. treas. & credit mgr, Straus-Frank Co, San Antonio, Tex, 53-61; v.pres. & br. mgr, Dittmar & Co, Inc, Houston, 62- Mil. Serv: Entered as Pvt, Army Air Corps, 42, released as 2nd Lt, 45, after serv. in 15th Air Force-Italy, European Theatre; Air Medal; Presidential Unit Citation. Rel: Episcopal. Mailing Add: 9015 Marlive Lane, Houston, Tex. 77025.

FOUSE, CLARA MAE R

b. Tilton, Ga, 4/21/21; d. Robert Lee Jones and Ollie Lucy Bishop J.(both deceased); m. 11/10/41 to Clarence Duncan Fouse, Sr; c. Reverend Clarence Duncan, Jr. Educ: Grad, DeKalb Co. High Sch, Ft. Payne, Ala; completed courses, Lindsey Hopkins Voc. Sch, real estate, 57, Miami Bd. of Realtors Sch. of Appraisal and Univ. Mortgage-Broker Course, Miami Sr. High Sch. Polit. & Govt. Pos: Precinct and dist. committeewoman, Dade Co. Rep. Exec. Cmt, Fla, 49-66; charter mem, Young Rep. Club of Miami, 50; life mem, Rep. Club of Dade Co, 54; first v.pres, Rep. Women's Club of Coral Gables, Fla, 60, pres, 63; alternate del, Rep. Nat. Conv, 60, del. and mem. Credentials Cmt, 64; mem, Publicity Cmt, Fla. Fedn. Rep. Women; Fla. del-at-lg, Nat. Fedn. Rep. Women, Phoenix, Ariz, 62; mem, Rep. Nat. Adv. Cmt, Fla, 66; mem, Steering Cmt. and Fla. Publicity Chmn, 15th Annual Women's Conf, Little Rock, Ark, 67; hq. chmn, Dade Co. Gurney for Senate Cmt. and pres. of club to elect Nixon-Agnew for President and V.President, 68. Bus. & Prof. Pos: Real estate broker and realtor, 57- Mem: Coconut Grove Woman's Club; Miami Bd. Realtors; Miami-Dade Co. C. of C; Miami Tourist and Conv. Bur; Better Bus. Bur. of S.Fla; Better Govt. Asn; past sr. counselor, United Commercial Travelers of Am. Ladies Auxiliary 386, Grand Sentinel, Ga-Fla. Grand Auxiliary, 68-69; United Fund; Heart Fund; March of Dimes; Cancer Fund; Builders of Women and Retarded Children and World Missions; Arkansas Travelers. Listed in Commun. Leaders of Am. and Two Thousand Women of Achievement, 69. Rel: Presbyterian; Leadership and resources chmn. and one of four prog. chmn, Women of Shenandoah Presby. Church. Mailing Add: 2401 S.W. 13th St, Miami, Fla. 33145.

FOWLE, ELEANOR CRANSTON D

b. Palo Alto, Calif; d. William MacGregor Cranston and Carol Dixon C; m. to John Miller Fowle; c. Michael and Linda (Mrs. Burke). Educ: Stanford Univ, 2 years; Alpha Phi. Polit. & Govt. Pos: Chmn, Santa Clara Co. Key Women for President Johnson, 64; Tenth Cong. Dist. Co-Chmn, 64-65; mem. exec. and steering cmts, Calif. State Dem. Cent. Cmt, 64-; mem. North. Calif. Exec. Cmn, West State Conf, 65; women's chmn, North. Calif. Dem. State Cent. Cmt, 66-68; mem. exec. cmt, Gov. Brown's Campaign, 66; mem. exec. cmt, Alan Cranston's Campaign for U.S. Sen, 68. Mem: Former bd. mem, North. Santa Clara Co. Commun. Coun; League of Women Voters; UN Asn; former 1st v.pres, Family Serv. Asn, Los Altos and Palo Alto; Nat. Exec. Coun, United World Federalists. Rel: Congregational. Mailing Add: 27060 Old Trace Rd, Los Altos Hills, Calif. 94022.

FOWLER, HAMMOND D

Cmnr, Tenn. Pub. Serv. Cmn.
b. Rockwood, Tenn, 4/6/01; s. Hammond Fowler, Sr. and Zoe Leland F; m. 4/26/52 to Netha McCorkle. Educ: Univ. Tenn; Maryville Col; Cumberland Univ. Law Sch, LL.B; Lambda Chi Alpha. Polit. & Govt. Pos: Mem, Roane Co. Dem. Exec. Cmt, Tenn, 22-; city attorney, Rockwood, Tenn, 33-53; Tenn. State Sen, 34-36; chief counsel, Employ. Security Dept, Tenn, 39-47; cmnr, Tenn. Pub. Serv. Cmn, 48-, chmn, 51-54, 59-60 & 65-66. Bus. & Prof. Pos: Pres, Times Printing Co, Rockwood, Tenn, 22-42; dir, Rockwood Fed. Savings & Loan Asn, 34-, v.pres, 46- Mil. Serv: Pvt, Army, 41, entered Naval Res. as Lt, 42, released as Lt. Comdr, 45; Comdr, Naval Res, 45-63; Am. Defense Serv, Am. Theater and Victory and Naval Res. Medals. Mem: K. of P; Am, Tenn. and Roane Co. Bar Asns; Civitan Club; Hon. mem, Rotary Club; Am. Legion; VFW; Mil. Order of World Wars; SAR; Soc. of Colonial Wars; Rockwood Golf and Country Club. Rel: Presbyterian. Legal Res: 421 S. Douglas Ave, Rockwood, Tenn. 37854. Mailing Add: Tennessee Public Service Commission, Cordell Hull Bldg, Nashville, Tenn. 37219.

FOWLER, HENRY HAMILL D

b. Roanoke, Va, 9/5/08; s. Mack Johnson Fowler and Bertha Browning F; m. 10/19/38 to Trudye Pamela Hathcote; c. Mrs. Roy C. Smith IV and Mrs. Susan F. Gallagher. Educ: Roanoke Col, A.B, 29; Yale Univ, LL.B, 32, J.S.D, 33; Pi Kappa Phi; Phi Delta Phi; Tau Kappa Alpha. Polit. & Govt. Pos: Counsel, Tenn. Valley Authority, 34-38, asst. gen. counsel, 39; spec. asst. to U.S. Attorney Gen. as chief counsel, subcmt. of Sen. Cmt. on Educ. and Labor, 39-40; asst. gen. counsel, Off. of Prod. Mgt, 41 and War Prod. Bd, 42-44; econ. adv. U.S. Mission Econ. Affairs, 44; spec. asst. to Adminstr, For. Econ. Admin, 45; dep. adminstr, Nat. Prod. Authority, 51, adminstr, 52; dir, Off. of Defense Mobilization and adminstr, Defense Prod. Admin, 52-53; under secy. of treas, U.S. Dept. of Treas, 61-64, Secy. of Treas, 65-68. Bus. & Prof. Pos: Partner, Fowler, Leva, Hawes & Symington, 46-51, 53-61 & 64-65; investment banker; partner, Goldman, Sachs & Co, 69- Mem: Trustee, Funds Diocese of Va; bd. trustees, Roanoke Col; Nat. Cmn. on Money and Credit; Nat. Coun. on Foreign Relations; Yale Law Sch. Asn, N.Y; Recess and Pinnacle Clubs; Links Club, Wash; Nat. Capital Dem. Club; Metrop. Club. Rel: Episcopal. Mailing Add: 209 S. Fairfax St, Alexandria, Va. 22314.

FOWLER, HENRY J. D

Md. State Del.
b. Mechanicsville, Md, 8/5/09. Educ: Charlotte Hall Mil. Acad; Newspaper Inst. of Am. Polit. & Govt. Pos: Md. State Del, 51-55, 59-62 & 63-; Md. State Sen, 62-63. Bus. & Prof. Pos: Secy, Gas Co; farmer. Mil. Serv: Army, 42-45. Mem: Bd. of dirs, St. Mary's Hist. Soc; Red Cross; UGF; Farm Bur; St. Mary's Co. Fair Bd; Mechanicsville Vol. Fire Dept; dir, Md. Jousting Asn; Mechanicsville Lions; K. of C. Mailing Add: Mechanicsville, Md. 20659.

FOWLER, HUGH CHARLES R

Colo. State Sen.
b. Chicago, Ill, 5/21/26; s. Frank Parker Fowler and Dorothy Hinckley F; m. 7/7/49 to Shirley Sprague; c. Laurie Lynn and Hugh Charles, Jr. Educ: Univ. Wis, 1 year; Univ. Colo, B.S. in Bus, 48; Phi Kappa Tau. Polit. & Govt. Pos: Various app. jobs, Arapahoe Co. Rep. Cent. Cmt, Colo, 56-66, secy, 66-68; Colo. State Sen, 21st Dist, 69- Bus. & Prof. Pos: Sales and gen. mgt. in mfg and publ, 48-58; acct. exec, advert. agencies in Denver, 58-64; owner, Fowler & More Advert. Agency, Englewood, Colo, 64-69. Mil. Serv: Entered as A/S, Naval Res, 43, retired as Lt, 58, after serv. in S.Pac; recalled in 51 for Korean duty on U.S.S. Bremerton, 51-52. Mem: Mason; Shrine; Scoutmaster. Rel: Presbyterian; Elder. Mailing Add: 5399 S. Clarkson St, Littleton, Colo. 80120.

FOWLER, JAMES DARWIN R

Chmn, Emanuel Co. Rep. Party, Ga.
b. Toombsboro, Ga, 11/10/27; s. H.G. Fowler and Emma Lee Brantley F; m. 8/30/47 to Sue Johnson Allen; c. E. Joanne and James D. Educ: Swainsboro High Sch, grad, 45. Polit. & Govt. Pos: Chmn, Emanuel Co. Rep. Party, Ga, currently; mem, First Dist. Rep. Cmt, currently; mem, Ga. State Rep. Cent. Cmt, currently. Bus. & Prof. Pos: Home builder, currently. Mil. Serv: Entered as Seaman, Navy, 45, released as Seaman 1/C, 48, after serv. in Atlantic Fleet. Mem: VFW; Moose. Rel: Episcopal. Legal Res: Allen Dr, Swainsboro, Ga. 30401. Mailing Add: P.O. Box 438, Swainsboro, Ga. 30401.

FOWLER, JAMES FAULKNER R

Mem, Clark Co. Rep. Cent. Cmt, Wash.
b. Mabton, Wash, 7/31/19; s. James Goodman Fowler and Mildred Faulkner F; m. 1/20/50 to Georgia Fay; c. Kerry (Mrs. Fox). Educ: Wash. State Univ; Sigma Delta Chi. Polit. & Govt. Pos: Precinct committeeman, Rep. Party, Wash, 61-; mem, Clark Co. Rep. Cent. Cmt, 62-; mem, Clark Co. Rep. Exec. Cmt, 64-; chmn, Rep. Cand. Selection Cmt, 64- Mil. Serv: Entered as Pvt, Air Corps, 41, released as Capt, 44, after serv. in 340 Bomb Group, African Theater; Pre-Pearl Harbor, ETO and African Campaign Ribbons. Mem: Pub. Rels. Soc. of Am.(bd. of dirs, 62-, treas, 63-64, v.pres, 67); chmn, Vancouver Parks and Recreation Cmn; cmt. chmn, C. of C; v.pres, Vancouver YMCA; dir, Kiwanis. Rel: Methodist. Legal Res: 116 N. Garrison Rd, Vancouver, Wash. 98661. Mailing Add: 303 E. 16th St, Vancouver, Wash. 98661. (1967)

FOWLER, LEONARD D

Chmn, Loup Co. Dem. Party, Nebr.
b. Arcadia, Nebr, 9/15/05; s. Morris Fowler and Laura Ellen Middaugh F; m. 6/28/25 to Faye Erna Jensen; c. Darlene and Gilbert. Polit. & Govt. Pos: Chmn, Loup Co. Dem. Party, Nebr, 64- Bus. & Prof. Pos: Farmer-rancher. Rel: Protestant. Mailing Add: Taylor, Nebr. 68879. (1967)

FOWLER, LESLIE R. R

Colo. State Sen.
b. 1924; m. to Jane; c. Three. Educ: Univ. Colo, B.S, 48. Polit. & Govt. Pos: Precinct capt. and committeeman, Rep. party, Colo; mem, Boulder City Coun, 56-62; Colo. State Rep, 67-69; Colo. State Sen, 69- Mil. Serv: Navy, 43-46. Mem: Bd. of dirs, Jr. Achievement; former pres, Boulder United Fund. Coach, Univ. of Colo. Golf team. Rel: Methodist. Mailing Add: 2280 Bluebell Ave, Boulder, Colo. 80302.

FOWLER, MARILYN LEE D

b. Bertrand, Nebr, 12/26/25; d. Chas. R. Larson and Dorothy Strickler L; m. 1/7/45 to Gene Fowler; c. Thomas, Melinda, Richard, Daniel and Felecia. Educ: Hastings Col; Theta Psi Beta. Polit. & Govt. Pos: Committeewoman, Young Dem. of Nebr, 58-62; mem, Nebr. Dem. State Cent. Cmt, 64-66; chmn, Gosper Co. Dem. Party, 64-68. Mem: Womans Club; Jane Jefferson Clubs; Hosp. Auxiliary. Eleanor Roosevelt Mem. Award, Young Dems. of Nebr. Rel: Catholic. Mailing Add: R.R. 2, Box 114, Lexington, Nebr. 68850. (1967)

FOWLER, R. LYNN R

Chmn, Third Cong. Dist. Rep. Cmt, Mich.
b. Eaton Rapids, Mich, 5/27/23; s. Rice C. Fowler and Gladys I. Scott F; m. 9/11/48 to Kathleen M. Mikesell; c. Mindy A, Rice T. and Dort E. Educ: Mich. State Univ, 1 year; U.S. Naval Acad, B.S, 45. Polit. & Govt. Pos: Held various co. Rep. orgn. off, Eaton Co, Mich, 58-64; city councilman, Charlotte, 60-66; mem, Third Cong. Dist. Rep. Cmt, 64-66, chmn, 66- Bus. & Prof. Pos: Owner, Fowler's Inc, Chevrolet-Oldsmobile, Charlotte, 51- Mil. Serv: Entered as Ens, Navy, 45, released as Lt.(jg), 47, after serv. on U.S.S. North Carolina, BB-55 and U.S.S. Manchester, CL-83, Pac. and Mediterranean Theatre, Lt, Res, 51-53, serv. on USS Black, DD-666 and USS Zellars, DD-777 as Gunnery Officer. Mem: Rotary: C. of C; Charlotte Country Club; Mason. Rel: Congregational. Legal Res: 1182 E. Clinton Trail, Charlotte, Mich. 48813. Mailing Add: 125 E. Lawrence Ave, Charlotte, Mich. 48813.

FOWLER, RAYMOND WILLIAM 'BILL' D

V.Chmn, Cherokee Co. Dem. Cmt, Kans.
b. Arcadia, Kans, 6/8/22; s. James Thomas Fowler and Ada M. Davenport F; m. 2/28/43 to Wadean Davis; c. Joseph William. Educ: Ft. Scott Jr. Col, 2 years. Polit. & Govt. Pos: V.chmn, Cherokee Co. Dem. Cmt, Kans, 66-; mem, Kans. Mined Land Bd. and Kans. Export Coun, 68-; cmnr, Kans. Forestry Fish and Game Cmn, 68- Bus. & Prof. Pos: Pres, Citizens Bank of Weir, Kans, 51- and Home State Bank, Arcadia, 60-; dir, Weir Grain & Supply, 67- Mil. Serv: Sp. D, Coast Guard, 42-45. Mem: Mason; Scottish Rite; Shrine; Commandery; Elks; Eagles; Am. Legion; 40 et 8. Rel: Protestant. Legal Res: R.R. 1, Weir, Kans. 66781. Mailing Add: c/o Citizens Bank of Weir, Weir, Kans. 66781.

FOWLES, OLIVE GRACE R

Mem, Calif. Rep. State Cent. Cmt.
b. Chicago, Ill, 9/15/00; d. Benjamin John Caldbeck and Sarah Ann McArthur C; m. 7/11/21 to Frank H. Fowles, Jr; c. Frank H, III. Educ: Columbia Univ, Exten. courses, 23-24. Polit. & Govt. Pos: Pres, Solano Co. Coun. Rep. Women, Federated, Calif, 49-51; mem, Calif. Rep. State Cent. Cmt, 56-; chmn, pub. rels. cmt, Calif. Fedn. of Rep. Women, N. Div, 58-66; v.chmn, Solano Co. Rep. Cent. Cmt, 58-60 and treas, 60-69; mem, Cong. Dist. Cand. Selection Cmt; coordinator, Solano Co. Nixon for Pres. Cmt, 60 and mem, 68; chmn, Solano Co. Women for Murphy Cmt, 64. Bus. & Prof. Pos: Radio commentator, Radio KGYW, Vallejo, Calif, 50-56; pub. rels. dir, N. Bay United Crusade, 56-58 and Irwin Mem. Blood Bank, San Francisco, 62-66; pub. rels. consult, Pub. Rels. Projs, Vallejo, 58-60; organizational secy, Solano Co. Taxpayers Asn, 60-62; fund develop. and pub. rels. dir, Vallejo Gen. Hosp, 66- Publ: Extensive by-line articles, Vallejo Times Herald, 56-; Press releases,

Metrop. Press, San Francisco and other area newspapers, 62- Mem: Nat. Asn. for Hosp. Develop; Soroptimist Club of Vallejo; C. of C; Solano Co. Hist. Soc. Rel: Presbyterian. Mailing Add: 1338 Louisiana St, Vallejo, Calif. 94590.

FOX, ABIJAH UPSON R
Conn. State Rep.
b. Brooklyn, N.Y, 1/20/05; s. Abijah Charles Fox and Helen Manlove Shawhan F; m. 11/26/35 to Isabel Place Sullivan; c. Abijah Shawhan, Jarvis Powell and Suzanne Angevine. Educ: Rutgers Col, Litt.B. cum laude, 26; Beta Theta Pi. Polit. & Govt. Pos: Dep. dir. for. funds control, U.S. Treas. Dept, Wash, D.C, 41-44, dir, Off. Surplus Property, 45, dep. dir. finance div, Mil. Govt, Frankfurt, Germany, 45-46; mem, Greenwich Pre. Town Cmt, Conn, 57-, seventh dist. leader, 64-68; mem, Greenwich Representative Town Meeting, 60-65; mem, Conn. Rep. Finance Cmt. and Conn. Rep. Budget Cmt, 64-68; mem, Greenwich Bd. of Estimate and Taxation, 65-68; chmn, Greenwich Rep. Finance Cmt, 68-; Conn. State Rep, 152nd Assembly Dist, 69- Bus. & Prof. Pos: Exec, Nat. City Bank of N.Y, Tokyo, Japan, 27-34; partner, Swau, Culbertson & Fritz, Shanghai, Hong Kong, and Manila, 34-41; chmn, Mathieson Alkali Works, N.Y.C, 46-48; v.pres. and dir, Am. Thread Co, 48-59; v.pres, Hayden, Stone, Inc, 59- Mem: Am. Arbit. Asn; Belle Haven Club; Indian Harbor Yacht Club, Greenwich; Union League Club, N.Y; Navy League; Boy Scouts; C. of C; Commun. Chest; Commun. Coun; Greenwich Taxpayers Asn; Bepam Rep. Club; Greater Greenwich Rep. Club. Silver Beaver, Greenwich Boy Scouts Coun. Rel: Episcopal. Mailing Add: 200 North St, Greenwich, Conn. 06830.

FOX, ARTHUR H. R
N.H. State Rep.
b. Acton, Maine, 8/7/96; married; c. Two sons. Educ: Bates Col. Polit. & Govt. Pos: N.H. State Rep, currently. Bus. & Prof. Pos: Pres, W.M. Lord Co, Inc, Union, N.H. Mil. Serv: Army, World War I; Coast Guard Res, World War II. Mem: Past master, Mason; past patron, Eastern Star; past pres, Lions. Rel: Congregational. Mailing Add: Union, N.H. 03887. (1967)

FOX, DAVID, JR. D
b. Huntington, W.Va, 2/19/21; s. David Fox and Blanche Goodman F; m. 7/27/45 to Charlotte Glazier; c. Ellen E, David, III and Stephen G. Educ: Marshall Col, 2 years. Polit. & Govt. Pos: City councilman, Huntington, W.Va, 56-58; chmn, Kennedy for Pres. Campaign, Cabell Co, 60; del, Dem. Nat. Conv, 64; mem, Cabell Co. Dem. Exec. Cmt, W.Va, 64-68; Cabell Co. Assessor, 68- Bus. & Prof. Pos: Pres, Branchland Pipe & Supply Co, 65; v.pres, David Fox Oil Co, 65. Mil. Serv: Entered as Cadet, Army Air Force, 43, released as 1st Lt, 45, after serv. in 332nd Bomb Squadron, 12th Air Force, ETO, 44-45; 2 Presidential Citations; Purple Heart; Air Medal with 6 Oak Leaf Clusters. Mem: Past pres, Huntington Jr. C. of C; past state v.pres, W.Va. Jr. C. of C; bd. dirs, Huntington C. of C; Rotary; Elks; Guyan Golf and Country Club. Rel: Presbyterian. Legal Res: 331 Ninth Ave, Huntington, W.Va. 25709. Mailing Add: Box 486, Huntington, W.Va. 25709.

FOX, DONALD WILLIAM R
Pa. State Rep.
b. Hillsville, Pa, 5/28/22; s. William R. Fox and Lulu Robison F; m. 5/11/44 to Anne Boliver; c. Margaret Anne and John William. Educ: Westminster Col, A.B, 44; Tau Kappa Alpha; Pi Delta Epsilon; Alpha Sigma Phi. Polit. & Govt. Pos: Pa. State Rep, 57- Bus. & Prof. Pos: Partner, Fox's Dairy, 46- Mil. Serv: Entered as A/S, Naval Res, 43, released as Lt.(jg), 46, after serv. in Amphibious Forces, Pac. Mem: Am. Legion; Rotary, Grange. Rel: United Presbyterian. Mailing Add: R.R. 2, Enon Valley, Pa. 16120.

FOX, HARRY M. R
b. New Castle, Pa, 4/29/24; s. Homer F. Fox and Thelma Whitfield F.(deceased); m. 10/12/57 to Pauline Baculik; c. Suzanne M. and Patricia A. Polit. & Govt. Pos: Secy. to U.S. Rep. John P. Saylor, Pa, 49- Bus. & Prof. Pos: Secy, Valley Novelty Co, 41-42; teller, Armstrong Co. Trust Co, 42-43; secy, Pittsburgh Plate Glass Co, 46-49. Mil. Serv: Entered as A/S, Navy, 43, released as Yeoman 1/C, 46, after serv. in Pac. Theater, 43-46; Am. Theater Ribbon; Asiatic-Pac. Theater Ribbon with 2 Stars. Mem: Am. Legion; VFW; Eagles; Jednota. Rel: Catholic. Legal Res: 1136 Sixth Ave, Ford City, Pa. 16226. Mailing Add: 5306 Blacksnake Dr, Washington, D.C. 20031.

FOX, HEISEL MARION R
b. Cairo, W.Va, 3/3/06; s. Elwood Ezra Fox and Lena Hopkins F; m. 11/22/30 to Virginia Lee Bryan. Educ: W.Va. Univ, 57-58. Polit. & Govt. Pos: Cpl, W.Va. Dept. of Pub. Safety, 25-34; Mayor, Worthington, W.Va, 45-; Lincoln Dist. committeeman, Lincoln Dist. Rep. Party, 51-66; chmn, Marion Co. Rep. Exec. Cmt, 65-68. Bus. & Prof. Pos: Supt. of motor transportation, Consolidation Coal Co, 34-61; pres, W.Va. Infra-Red Equip. & Supply Co, 60-66; secy-treas, Fairmont Tire Shop, Inc, 61-66. Mem: W.Va. Alumni Asn; dir, Am. Red Cross, 11 years and Tuberc. Asn, 7 years; allotment cmt, United Fund Marion Co; past pres. and past zone chmn, Worthington Lions; Mining Electro-Mech. Maintenance Asn; North. W.Va. Coal Mining Inst; W.Va. Hist. Asn; Marion Co. Hist. Soc; SAR; Green Hills Country Clubs, Inc; St. Johns Lodge, Lodge of Perfection, Wheeling Consistory. Rel: Christian; Treas-trustee, Worthington Christian Church. Mailing Add: 258 Main St, Worthington, W.Va. 26591.

FOX, J. LEWIS D
b. New York, N.Y, 8/6/09; m. to Ruth L. Schumer; c. David, Jeffrey, Janet (Mrs. Sidle). Educ: N.Y. Univ; Brooklyn Law Sch, LL.B. Polit & Govt. Pos: N.Y. State Assemblyman, 48-66; confid. asst. to Spec. Asst. Dist. Attorney H. C. Todd, 32; 5th Ward Young Men's Dem. Club. Bus. & Prof. Pos: Lawyer, Koss and Fox. Mem: Hon. pres. Gustave-Hartman YM-YWHA; past pres. Rockaway Lawyer's Club; hon. pres. Edgeman Civic Asn; Queens Co. Bar Asn; Fedn. of Queens Lawyers; dir, C. of C. of Rockaways; past chancellor Rockaway Beach Lodge K. of P; adv. bd. Rockaway Beach Hosp; dir. of counsel to Hebrew Inst. of Long Island. Mailing Add: 1179 Beach 9th St, Far Rockaway, N.Y. 11691. (1967)

FOX, J. RONALD
Asst. Secy. of the Army
b. Binghamton, N.Y, 12/11/29; s. John C. Fox and C. Frances Lilly F; m. 6/25/68 to Dorris A. Campbell. Educ: LeMoyne Col, B.S. in Physics, 51; Harvard Univ, M.B.A, 59, M.A, 67 and Ph.D, 68; Alpha Sigma Nu. Polit. & Govt. Pos: Dep. asst. secy. of the Air Force, 63-65; Asst. Secy. of the Army, 69- Bus. & Prof. Pos: V.pres. and gen. mgr, Mgt. Syst. Corp, 60-63; assoc. prof, Harvard Univ, 65-69. Mil. Serv: Entered as Ens, Navy, 53, released as Lt, 57, after serv. in Armed Forces Spec. Weapons Proj, U.S, Far East and Europe. Publ: Defense and Aerospace Glossary for Project Management, Hawthorne Publ, 69; 'Research and Development Cost Planning and Control,' Armed Forces Comptroller, 64; 'Pert Cost,' Aerospace Mgt, 65. Mem: Pres, Armed Forces Mgt. Asn, 69. Air Force Exceptional Civilian Serv. Award. Legal Res: Boxford, Mass. Mailing Add: 6801 Benjamin St, McLean, Va. 22101.

FOX, RUSSELL LAMBERT D
b. Jackson, Miss, 7/11/09; married. Polit. & Govt. Pos: Miss. State Rep, 36-65; state bd. of dirs, Farm Bur; state bd. of dirs, CDC. Bus. & Prof. Pos: Farmer; livestock breeder. Mem: Masons; Lions; Sigma Chi. Rel: Presbyterian. Mailing Add: Pattison, Miss. 39144. (1967)

FRALEY, VANCE LEVOY R
Committeeman, Ill. Rep. Cent. Cmt.
b. Taylorville, Ill, 5/11/34; s. Everett Leonel Fraley and Ethel Lipe F; m. 8/13/67 to Mary Kate Reeder; c. Karen and Leneé. Educ: Univ. Ill, B.S, 56, J.D, 58; Sigma Phi Epsilon; Phi Delta Phi. Polit. & Govt. Pos: Corresponding secy, Christian Co. Young Rep, Ill, 64-65; del, Ill. Rep. Conv, 64 & 66; fund raising dinner chmn, Christian Co. Rep. Party, 66, 67 & 68; 52nd dist. committeeman, Ill. Rep. Cent. Cmt, 66- Bus. & Prof. Pos: Partner, Tipsword & Fraley, Taylorville, Ill, 61-67 and Coale, Taylor, Tipsword & Fraley, 67- Mil. Serv: 1st Lt, Army 58-61, with serv. in Judge Adv. Gen. Coprs, Judge Advocates Off, Ft. Eustis, Va, 59-61; Capt, Res, 61-66. Mem: Ill. State, Christian Co. and Am. Bar Asns; Kiwanis (v.pres, 67 & 68, pres, 69). Rel: Methodist. Mailing Add: 728 Kenton Blvd, Taylorville, Ill. 62568.

FRAME, RICHARD C. R
Pa. State Sen.
b. Franklin, Pa, 7/16/26; s. Thomas C. Frame and Martha Crawford F; m. to Josephine German; c. Three. Educ: Yale Univ, A.B; Univ. of Va. Law Sch, LL.B. Polit. & Govt. Pos: Mem, Rep. State Exec. Cmt, Pa; chmn, Venango Co. Reps; Pa. State Sen, 62- Bus. & Prof. Pos: Attorney; dir Exchange Bank and Trust Co. and other corps. Mil. Serv: Army, Sgt. Publ: Rep. Campaign Manual. Mem: Am. Bar Asn; Venango Co. Bar; Supreme and Superior Courts of Pa; U.S. Dist. Court; W. Dist. of Pa; dir, Venango Co. Indust. Develop. Corp; past pres, Franklin Area C. of C. Mailing Add: 1335 Liberty St, Franklin, Pa. 16323.

FRANCE, ALFRED E. Conservative
Minn. State Rep.
b. Pa, 1927; m; c. Three. Educ: Univ. of Minn, B.A. Polit. & Govt. Pos: Former admin. asst. to Govs. Youngdahl and C. Elmer Anderson; Minn. State Rep, 62- Bus. & Prof. Pos: Pub. rels. dir, Duluth firm. Mil. Serv: Army, 45-47. Mailing Add: 2107 Vermilion Rd, Duluth, Minn. 55803. (1967)

FRANCE, MARK L. D
b. Huntington, Ind, 6/23/08; s. Harvey H.P. France and Mertie M. Neff F; m. 6/14/34 to Mary Helen McNarney; c. Michael H, Stephen C, Joseph M, Sarah A.(Mrs. Donald Zurbuch) and Kathleen A. Educ: Manchester Col, 24-26; Ind. Univ. Exten. Polit. & Govt. Pos: Pres, Wabash Co. Young Dem, Ind, 32-34; field supvr, Ind. Dept. of Revenue, 33-40, regional supvr, 67-69, mgr, Indianapolis Dist, 69, training and info. adminstr, dept, currently; treas, Fifth Dist. Young Dem, 34-35; pres, Fourth Dist. Young Dem, 36-39; dep. collector, Internal Revenue Serv, 40-42; off supvr. and bd. mgr, Off. of Price Admin, 42-45; precinct committeeman, Dem. Party, 59-61; dist. chmn, Allen Co. Dem. Cent. Cmt, 61-64; mem, Tax Adjust. Bd, Allen Co, 59-63; State Auditor, Ind, 64-66. Bus. & Prof. Pos: Pub. acct, 45-68; dir. from Ind, Nat. Soc. Pub. Acct, 59-60; pres, Ind. Soc. Pub. Acct, 60-62. Mem: Nat. Soc. Auditors and Comptrollers; Elks; K. of C.(4°). Rel: Catholic. Legal Res: 4922-C Hawthorn Terr, Indianapolis, Ind. 46220. Mailing Add: 100 N. Senate Ave, Room 203, Indianapolis, Ind. 46204.

FRANCIS, E. LEE R
Lt. Gov, N.Mex.
b. Seboyeta, N.Mex, 3/16/13; s. Narciso Francis and Filomena Michael F; m. 12/11/33 to Ethel Gotlieb; c. Carol Lee (Mrs. Sanchez), Kathleen Ann (Mrs. Swanquist), Paula Marie (Mrs. Brown), E. Lee, III and John Cecil. Educ: St. Mary's High Sch, 1 year; Albuquerque High Sch, 1 year. Polit. & Govt. Pos: Chmn, Valencia Co. Rep. Party, N.Mex; cmnr, State Fair Cmn; mem, Valencia Co. Rep. Cent. Cmt; Lt. Gov, N.Mex, 67-; mem. exec. cmt, Nat. Lt. Gov. Conf, 68-69, v.chmn, West. Region, 69- Bus. & Prof. Pos: Dealer, Int. Harvester, 41-; agent, Continental Oil Co, West. Valencia Co, 45; distributor, B.F. Goodrich Tires; pres, Francis Oil & Tire Co. and Owner, Cubero Trading Co, currently. Mem: Cattle Growers Asn; Wool Growers Asn; Farm Bur; K. of C.(4°); Eagles; life mem. Rotary; Lions (past pres. and charter mem) Grants C. of C. Rel: Roman Catholic. Legal Res: P.O. Box 67, Cubero, N.Mex. 87014. Mailing Add: State Capitol Bldg, Santa Fe, N.Mex. 87501.

FRANCIS, LOUIS PATRICK R
b. Oakland, Calif, 5/24/23; m. 12/23/44 to Alice Corcoran F; c. Patrick, Michesle, Janice, Mark. Educ: U.S. Merchant Marine Acad; San Francisco Law Sch, LL.B. Polit. & Gov. Pos: Calif. State Assemblyman, 56-62; mem, Rep. State Cent. Cmt, 56; mem, San Mateo Co. Rep. Cent. Cmt, 54; past Pres, San Mateo Young Rep; past V.Pres, State Young Rep. Bus. & Prof. Pos: Attorney. Mil. Serv: Navy, Lt, Res. Mem: Elks; Am. Legion; VFW; Military Order of World Wars; Am. Judicature Soc; Calif, San Mateo Co. Bar Asns; NSGW; Lafayette Club; K. of C; St. Matthew's Men's Guild; Druids; Family Serv. Agency; Peninsula Symphony Asn; past Dir, Boys' Club, San Mateo; past Pres, San Mateo Commun. Asn; former Dir, Red Cross; San Mateo Co. Develop. Asn; former Asst, Dist. Cmt, Boy Scouts. 1967 Legal Res: San Mateo, Calif. No mailing address available. (1967)

FRANCIS, PETER DAVID D
Wash. State Rep.
b. Seattle, Wash, 10/28/34; s. Jack Albert Francis and Alice Scudder F; m.

5/30/59 to Elva Green; c. Thomas Michael and Daniel Green. Educ: Stanford Univ, B.A, Polit. Sci, 56; Stanford Law Sch, J.D, 61; Kappa Sigma; Phi Delta Phi. Polit. & Govt. Pos: Dem. precinct committeeman, 92nd Precinct, Wash, 67-; Wash. State Rep, 32nd Dist, 69- Bus. & Prof. Pos: Law Clerk, Wash. State Supreme Court, Olympia, 61-62; instr, Univ. Wash. Law Sch, Seattle, 62-63; attorney-at-law, 63-; partner, Francis & Ackerman, 69- Mil. Serv: Entered as 2nd Lt, Marine Corps, 56, released as 1st Lt, 59; Capt, 61-68. Mem: Am, Wash. and Seattle Bar Asns; Trial Lawyers Asn; Greenlake C. of C.(pres); Lions; Elks; YMCA. Rel: Presbyterian; Elder. Legal Res: 4324 Dayton Ave. N, Seattle, Wash. 98103. Mailing Add: 7300 E. Greenlake Dr. N, Seattle, Wash. 98115.

FRANCIS, ROBERT ELLSWORTH R
Chmn, Durham Rep. Town Cmt, Conn.
b. Middletown, Conn, 1/19/16; s. Frank Jay Francis and Maude LeCompte F; m. 8/19/67 to Kathryn Gene Gilbert; c. Dorothy (Mrs. Kulak), Linda (Mrs. Estelle), Robert W. and Bonnie L. (Mrs. Slonina) and Robert T, Kathryn C, Sandra G. and Terri G. Raney. Educ: Wesleyan Univ, 1 year. Polit. & Govt. Pos: Registr. voters, Durham Rep. Party, Conn, 37-60; dep. sheriff, Middlesex Co, 50-56; chmn, Durham Rep. Town Cmt, 58-; fire chief, Durham Vol. Fire Dept, 59-64; Conn. State Rep, 61-67; fire marshall, Durham, 62- Bus. & Prof. Pos: Owner, Durham Tool & Die Co, 58- Publ: 'Punch & Die,' Diemaking, Diecutting Mag, 3/68, 6/68 and 9/68. Mem: AF&AM; Shrine; Exchange Club; K. of P; Durham Ambulance Corps; Durham Vol. Fire Co. Mr. Republican, Durham, 68. Rel: Congregational. Mailing Add: Maple Ave, Durham, Conn. 06422.

FRANCIS, WILMER J. D
Chmn, Shelby Co. Dem. Cent. Cmt, Ohio
b. Russia, Ohio, 4/24/04; s. Felix Francis and Anna F; m. 8/27/27 to Cora; c. Norma Jean, Carolyn Ann, Lawrence F, Linda L. and Judith S. Educ: Russia Schs, Ohio. Polit. & Govt. Pos: Chmn, Shelby Co. Dem. Cent. Cmt, Ohio, 68- Bus. & Prof. Pos: Partner-owner, Francis Bros. Chevrolet Dealer, 33- Mem: K. of C; dir, Shelby Co. Motor Club; dir, Shelby Co. Tuberc. & Health Asn; mem. bd, Wilson Mem. Hosp. Rel: Roman Catholic. Mailing Add: P.O. Box 97, Russia, Ohio 45363.

FRANCISCO, JAMES LEE D
Kans. State Rep.
b. Lamar, Colo, 10/10/37; s. James Rufus Francisco and Wilma G. White F; m. 10/18/58 to Sharon Lynn Maddux; c. James D, Brenda L, Debra M. and Jerald L. Educ: Wichita State Univ; Friends Univ. Polit. & Govt. Pos: Committeeman, Dem. Party, Kans; Kans. State Rep, 69th Dist, currently; del, Dem. Nat. Conv, 68. Mil. Serv: Entered as Pvt, Marine Corps, 57, released as Pfc, 60. Mem: Am. Legion; Int. Asn. of Machinists; Kans. State Fedn. of Labor; Kans. State Coun. of Machinists; Lions. Rel: Methodist. Mailing Add: 309 S. Central, Mulvane, Kans. 67110. (1967)

FRANCO, HELEN MORRIE D
Vt. State Rep.
b. Barre Town, Vt, 5/3/28; d. Alfred Joseph Morrie and Anna Ryan M; m. 9/16/50 to John Lewis Franco; c. Karen Ann and John Lewis, Jr. Educ: Becker Col, Mass, A.S, 48; Beta Chi Sigma. Polit. & Govt. Pos: Mem, Barre Dem. Town Cmt, Vt. and Wash. Co. Dem. Cmt; Vt. State Sen, 65; secy. to Secy. of State, Vt, 66; Vt. State Rep, currently. Mem: Catholic Daughters of Am; Parent-Teachers' Club; Woman's Club; Parent's Club; Vt. Grange; Vt. Farm Bur; Elks; Order of Women Legislators; Canadian Club. Rel: Roman Catholic. Mailing Add: Rd. 1, Barre Town, Vt. 05641. (1967)

FRANCOIS, TERRY ARTHUR D
Mem, Calif. Dem. State Cent. Cmt.
b. New Orleans, La, 8/28/21; s. Terry A. Francois and Leona Keller F; m. 11/1/47 to Marion Claire Leblanc; c. Wade Adrian, Gary Anthony, Brian Andrew, Eric Alfred and Carol Ann. Educ: Xavier Univ, B.A, 40; Atlanta Univ, M.A, 42; Hastings Col. of Law, Univ. Calif. San Francisco, LL.B, 49; Alpha Phi Alpha. Polit. & Govt. Pos: Mem, San Francisco Fair Employ. Practices Cmn, Calif, 57-59; mem, San Francisco Interim Human Rights Cmt, 63-64; mem, San Francisco Bd. Supvr, 64-; mem, Calif. Ment. Retardation Adv. Bd, 66-; mem, Dem. Co. Cmt, 67-; mem, Calif. Dem. State Cent. Cmt, 68-; chmn, Regional Criminal Justice Adv. Bd, 69- Bus. & Prof. Pos: Attorney at law, San Francisco, Calif, 50- Mil. Serv: Entered as Pvt, Marines, 42, released as Platoon Sgt, 45, after serv. in 51st Defense Bn, S.Pac. Theater, 44-45. Mem: State Bar of Calif; San Francisco Bar Asn; San Francisco Lawyers Club; Charles Houston Law Club; pres, San Francisco Br, NAACP, 59-62; former mem. bd. dirs, San Francisco Urban League, Coun. for Civic Unity, North. Calif. Serv. League. Served as Acting Mayor of San Francisco on several occasions during Mayor's absence. Rel: Catholic. Legal Res: 20 Taraval St, San Francisco, Calif. 94116. Mailing Add: 497 Fulton St, San Francisco, Calif. 94102.

FRANDOLIG, CHARLES A. D
b. Rockport, Tex, 8/22/24; s. Frank Matthew Frandolig and May Cecilia Morrell F; m. 11/28/53 to Joan Grossman; c. Charles Christopher. Educ: Univ. Tex, journalism, 50; Sigma Delta Chi. Polit. & Govt. Pos: Asst. to U.S. Rep. Bob Casey, 22nd Dist, Tex, 59- Bus. & Prof. Pos: Reporter, Galveston News, Tex, 50 and United Press Asn. and WOAI and WOAI-TV, 51; asst. city ed. and polit. reporter, Houston Chronicle, 53-59. Mil. Serv: Entered as Pvt, Army Air Force, released as Sgt, after serv. in 354th Fighter Sq, ETO; Presidential Unit Citation and Cluster; ETO Campaign Ribbon with 6 Battle Stars; ETO Victory and Good Conduct Medals. Mem: Houston and Nat. Press Clubs. Sigma Delta Chi award for distinguished reporting. Rel: Catholic. Legal Res: 4431 Sanford Dr, Houston, Tex. 77035. Mailing Add: 4605 46th St. N.W, Washington, D.C. 20016.

FRANDSEN, ALLEN JOHN R
b. Clarion, Utah, 8/27/19; s. Peter Lafayette Frandsen and Ida Larsen F; m. 3/30/42 to Evelyn Mackay; c. Joan (Mrs. Gardner), Ronald M, Rita (Mrs. Gardner), Russell M, Tracy M. and Kelly M. Educ: Snow Col, 1 year. Polit. & Govt. Pos: Cmt. mem, Sanpete Co. Farmers Home Admin, Utah, 52-55, chmn, 54-55; del, Sanpete Co. Rep. Party, 63-64, chmn, 65-69; del, Utah Rep. Party, 63-64, mem, cent. cmt, 65-69; committeeman, Agr. Stabilization and Conserv. Serv, 69- Bus. & Prof. Pos: Pres, Mayfield Irrigation Co, 59-64. Mil. Serv: Entered as Pvt, Army, 40, released as Cpl, 43, after serv. in 115th Army Engr. Corps, U.S, 41-43. Mem: Gunnison Valley Jaycees; Lions; S.Cent. Knife and Fork; Am. Legion; Utah State Farm Bur; Utah Cattlemen's Asn; pres, Utah State Young Farmers Asn, 48-49; v.pres, Sanpete Co. Farm Bur, 49-53, pres, 53-65. Outstanding Utah State Young Farmer. Rel: Latter-day Saint. Mailing Add: Centerfield, Utah 84622.

FRANDSEN, VIGO BISHOP R
Chmn, Mohave Co. Rep. Cent. Cmt, Ariz.
b. Fresno, Calif, 3/7/17; s. Thorvald Frandsen and Carrie Jepsen F; m. 6/9/59 to Donna Abbey; c. Patricia (Mrs. Sunderland), Rodger Gary, Dennis, Penny O'Day (Mrs. Hubert), and Debbie O'Day (Mrs. Johnson). Educ: Otis Art Inst, Los Angeles, 38. Polit. & Govt. Pos: Precinct committeeman, Mohave Co. Rep. Party, Ariz; chmn, Mohave Co. Rep. Cent. Cmt, 68- Mem: Elks; Rotary. Mailing Add: P.O. Box 792, Bullhead City, Ariz. 86430.

FRANK, BARBARA D
b. Sheridan, Wyo; m. to Jack Frank; c. Five. Polit. & Govt. Pos: Former Colo. State Rep. Bus. & Prof. Pos: Housewife. Mailing Add: 893 S. Gilpin St, Denver, Colo. 80209. (1967)

FRANK, GERALD WENDEL R
b. Portland, Ore, 9/21/23; s. Aaron M. Frank (deceased) and Ruth Rosenfeld F. (deceased); single. Educ: Stanford Univ, 41-42; Loyola Univ. of Los Angeles, 43-44; Cambridge Univ, B.A, 48, M.A, 53. Polit. & Govt. Pos: Mem, Gov. Adv. Cmt, Econ. Develop. Cmn, State of Ore, 57-, chmn, 8 years; gen. chmn, Gov. Mark Hatfield for U.S. Sen. Cmt, Ore, 66, spec. asst. to U.S. Sen. Mark Hatfield, Ore, 67-; del-at-lg, Rep. Nat. Conv, 68. Bus. & Prof. Pos: V.pres, and store mgr, Meier & Frank Co, Portland and Salem, Ore, 48-65. Mil. Serv: Entered as Pvt, Army, 43, released as Sgt, 46, after serv. in 89th Inf. Div, ETO, 44-46. Mem: Chmn, Ore. Symphony Soc-Ford Found. Matching Funds Campaign; pres, Salem Area C. of C, 65-67; pres, Marion-Polk Co. United Good Neighbors, 65-67; organizing trustee, Ore. Grad. Center for Study and Research; mem. bd. gov. and trustee, Willamette Univ; chmn, ZOOMSI Auction for Ore. Mus. of Sci. and Indust. and Portland Zoo, 61; gen. chmn, Citizens' Conf. leading to All-Am. City Award for Salem, 59; pres, Cascade Area Coun, Boy Scouts, 59-61, mem, Region XI Exec. Cmt. and mem-at-lg, Nat. Coun; dir, Jr. Achievement-Columbia Empire, Inc; dir, Portland Rose Festival Asn; trustee, Salem YWCA; mem. adv. bd, Sunshine Div, Portland Police Reserves, Salem League of Women Voters and Salem Salvation Army; mem. lay bd, St. Vincent Hosp, Portland; trustee, Pac. Int. Livestock Expos, Inc, Portland; Rotary; Am. Legion; Elks. Award for Exemplary Achievement in Serv. to Youth, Jr. Achievement of Portland, 54; Named Portland Vol. of Week, 4/15/55; Named Salem's Jr. First Citizen of 57; U.S. Jr. C. of C. Distinguished Serv. Award as one of three outstanding young men of Ore, 57; OMSI Award for contribution to growth of Northwest Sci. Educ, Ore. Mus. of Sci. and Indust, 61; Pac. Northwest Serv. to Mankind Award, Sertoma, 67; Named State of Ore. Outstanding Salesman of 61; Silver Beaver Award, Boy Scouts, 63; Named Admiral, Astoria Regatta, 64; Named Salem First Citizen of 64. Legal Res: 3250 Crestview Dr, Salem, Ore. 97302. Mailing Add: Standard Insurance Bldg, Salem, Ore. 97301.

FRANK, HELEN JOYCE D
Committeewoman, S.Dak. Dem. State Cent. Cmt.
b. Manchester, S.Dak, 3/3/32; d. Elmer O. Grotta and Lottie Beachler G; m. 6/18/50 to Stanley Richard Frank; c. Blair Stanley, Rhonda Lee and Brenda Kay. Educ: Wash. High Sch, Sioux Falls, grad. Polit. & Govt. Pos: Dem. precinct committeewoman, Minnehaha Co, S.Dak, 65-69; committeewoman, S.Dak. Dem. State Cent. Cmt, 66-; del, Dem. Nat. Conv, 68. Mem: AFL-CIO Auxiliary (pres, Sioux Falls Coun, past secy-treas, S.Dak. State Coun); Eastern Star; United Commercial Travelers. Woman Doer of the Year, Minnehaha Co. Dem. Party, 67. Rel: Methodist. Mailing Add: 827 S. Euclid Ave, Sioux Falls, S.Dak. 57104.

FRANK, JAY FREDERICK R
Co. Attorney, Iredell Co, N.C.
b. Mt. Holly, N.J, 6/7/35; s. Frederick Carl Frank and Alice Donovan F.(deceased); m. 9/5/59 to Martha Patricia Lackey. Educ: Univ. Pa, A.B, 57; Univ. Pa. Sch. of Law, LL.B, 60; Psi Upsilon; Phi Kappa Beta; Sphinx Sr. Soc; Jesters. Polit. & Govt. Pos: Secy, Iredell Co. Rep. Party, N.C, 62-66; co. attorney, Iredell Co, 66-; del, Rep. Nat. Conv, 68. Mem: Am, N.C, 22nd Judicial Dist. and Iredell Co. Bar Asns; Am. Judicature Soc; N.C. Acad. Trial Lawyers; exec. cmt. trustees, Mitchell Col, Statesville, N.C; Statesville Jr. C. of C; Statesville Country Club; Elks; Am. Red. Cross Adv. Bd. Outstanding Young Man, 57, Statesville, N.C; United Fund Campaign Award, 65. Rel: Catholic. Legal Res: 636 West End Ave, Statesville, N.C. 28677. Mailing Add: P.O. Box 1594, Statesville, N.C. 28677.

FRANK, JOHN PAUL D
b. Appleton, Wis, 11/10/17; s. Julius Paul Frank and Beatrice Ullman F; m. 5/11/44 to Lorraine Weiss; c. John Peter, Gretchen, Karen, Andrew and Nancy Jo. Educ: Univ. Wis, B.A, 38, M.A, 40, LL.B, 40; Yale Univ, J.S.D, 46. Polit. & Govt. Pos: Law clerk to Justice Black, 42-term; asst. to Secy. Interior, 43-44; asst. to Attorney Gen, 44-45; Dem. precinct committeeman, Arcadia Precinct, Phoenix, Ariz, 56-; counsel, Ariz. State Dem. Party, 62-65; del, Dem. Nat. Conv, 68. Bus. & Prof. Pos: Asst. prof. law, Ind. Univ, 46-49; assoc. prof. law, Yale Univ, 49-54; attorney, Lewis Roca Beauchamp & Linton, 54- Publ: The Warren Court, 64 and American Law: The Case for Radical Reform, 69, Macmillan; Justice Daniel Dissenting, Harvard Univ, 64. Mem: Judicial Coun. of U.S.(adv. cmt. on civil procedures); Am. Law Inst; Phoenix Fine Arts Asn.(bd. dirs); Phoenix Urban League; Phoenix Legal Aid Soc. Legal Res: 5829 E. Arcadia Lane, Phoenix, Ariz. 85018. Mailing Add: 114 W. Adams, Phoenix, Ariz. 85003.

FRANK, MURRAY D
b. New York, N.Y, 5/10/08; s. Paul Frank and Pauline Waxman F; m. 4/7/35 to Frieda Itzkowitz; c. Paul Allen, David Elliott and Judith Sharon. Educ: N.Y. Univ, 31-33; George Wash. Univ, B.A, 36; Am. Univ, M.A, 37. Polit. & Govt. Pos: Asst. econ. analyst, Dept. of Commerce, 41-43; econ. analyst, U.S. For. Econ. Admin, 43-45; consult. to U.S. Rep. Sol Bloom, chmn, House For. Affairs Cmt, 47-49; admin. asst. to A.J. Multer, N.Y, 49-51, Louis

B. Heller, N.Y, 51-55, Victor L. Anfuso, N.Y, 55-63 and U.S. Rep. William L. St. Onge, Conn, 63- Bus. & Prof. Pos: Free lance newspaper correspondent, papers in N.Y, London, Argentina and Israel, 45-58; contrib, periodicals in the U.S. and abroad, 45-63; dir, religious radio program, Voice of Israel, Wash, 58-61. Publ: Industrialization of Latin America, W. Lloyd Hughlett, 46; This is B'nai B'rith, Book of Facts, 47, revised 49. Mem: Am. Hist. Soc; Am. Acad. for Polit. and Soc. Sci; nat. dir. of info, B'nai B'rith, 45-47. Rel: Jewish. Mailing Add: 11724 Auth Lane, Silver Spring, Md. 20902.

FRANK, SAMUEL W. D
Pa. State Rep.
b. Wilkes-Barre, Pa, 5/30/04; s. Abe Frank and Fannie Tuck F; m. to Ida Fischman; c. Three. Educ: Allentown Schs. Polit. & Govt. Pos: State committeeman, Rep. Party, Pa, 52-53; spec. consult, President's Cmt. on Juvenile Delinquency and Youth Crime; Pa. State Rep, 54, 58 & 64- Bus. & Prof. Pos: Bus. consult. Mem: Police Athletic League; secy, treas, Lehigh Valley Showman's Asn; secy-treas, Lehigh Valley Old Time Boxers Asn; Hall of Fame; pres, Allentown Recreation Comm; bd. mem, Coun. of Youth; mem, Nat. Recreation Cmt. Mailing Add: 428 N. Albright Ave, Allentown, Pa. 18104. (1967)

FRANKEL, CHARLES D
b. N.Y.C, 12/13/17; s. Abraham Philip Frankel and Estelle Edith Cohen F; m. 8/17/41 to Helen Beatrice Lehman; c. Susan and Carl. Educ: Columbia Col, N.Y.C, A.B. with honors, 37 and Columbia Univ, Ph.D, 46; Cornell Univ, 37-38; Phi Beta Kappa. Hon. LL.D, Mercer Univ, 68. Polit. & Govt. Pos: Asst. secy. of State, Wash, D.C, 65-67. Bus. & Prof. Pos: Faculty mem, Columbia Univ, 39-, prof. philos, 56-; host, TV Prog, World of Ideas, 59; chief consult. ed, Current Mag, 60-65; planning dir, Vassar Inst. Adv. of Col. and Univ. Teaching, Vassar Col, 68-69; ed-at-lg, Saturday Rev, N.Y.C, 68- Mil. Serv: Lt.(sg), Naval Res, 42-46. Publ: Neglected Aspect of Foreign Affairs, 66; Education and the Barricades, W.W. Norton, 68; High on Foggy Bottom, Harper & Row, 69; plus others. Mem: Pres. bd. trustees, Rockland Co. Day Sch, 59-64, chmn. bd. trustees, 64-65; co-chmn, Nat. Assembly for Teaching Principles of Bill of Rights, 62-64; Am. Philos. Asn; Am. Asn. Univ. Prof; Authors League of Am; Coun. on For. Rels; Century Asn. Club, N.Y.C; P.E.N. Club; Cmn. on Acad. Affairs, Am. Coun. on Educ. Woodbridge Prize Philos, Columbia Univ, 47; Fulbright Research Prof, Univ. Paris, 53-54; Guggenheim Fel, 53-54; Carnegie Corp. Reflective Year Fel, 59-60. Legal Res: 317 Phillips Hill Rd, New City, N.Y. 10956. Mailing Add: 340 E. 51st St, New York, N.Y. 10022.

FRANKEN, JOHN H. D
Chmn, Carroll Co. Dem. Cent. Cmt, Mo.
b. Norborne, Mo, 1/14/15; s. Joseph H. Franken and Anna Barkley F; m. 7/19/52 to Priscilla Tatro; c. John C. and Dennis T. Educ: Northwest Mo. State Col, 33-35; Univ. of Mo, 35-36. Polit. & Govt. Pos: Mayor, Norborne, Mo, 50-56; chmn, Carroll Co. Dem. Cent. Cmt, currently; del, Dem. Nat. Conv, 68. Bus. & Prof. Pos: Mo. Bar Asn, 40- Mil. Serv: Entered as Aviation Cadet, Army Air Corps, 41, released as 1st Lt, 45, after serv. in Training Command. Mem: K. of C. Rel: Catholic. Mailing Add: Norborne, Mo. 64668. (1967)

FRANKLIN, CECIL DeWAYNE D
b. Cincinnati, Ohio, 4/3/36; s. Gordon Cecil Franklin and Inez Jones F; m. 10/8/59 to Jerry Jean Flake; c. Kimberley Reane and Rory Jean. Educ: Roger Bacon High Sch, Cincinnati, Ohio, grad, 53; N.Tex. State Univ, 58-59. Polit. & Govt. Pos: Committeeman, Dem. Party, Denver, Colo, 66-67, dist. capt, 67-; mem. exec. bd, Young Dem. of Colo, 67-68; del, Dem. Nat. Conv, 68. Mil. Serv: Entered as Airman Basic, Air Force, 54, released as Airman 1/C, 58, after serv. in Air Traffic Control, Continental U.S; Good Conduct Medal. Mem: Amalgamated Transit Union, Local 1001, Denver. Rel: Episcopal. Mailing Add: 10984 W. Exposition Place, Denver, Colo. 80228.

FRANKLIN, LAWRENCE ELLIOT R
b. Guilford, Vt, 5/11/24; s. Warren Bartlett Franklin and Jennie Scranton F; m. 11/9/46 to Pauline Jefts; c. Lawrence E, Jr. Polit. & Govt. Pos: Overseer of poor, Guilford, Vt, 59-; Vt. State Rep, 61-67, Majority Leader, Vt. House of Rep, 66-67, chmn, Agr. Cmt, 63-65; Justice of Peace, Guilford, 64-, mem, Legis. Coun, 65-67. Bus. & Prof. Pos: Owner, Dairy farm. Mil. Serv: Entered as Pvt, Marine Corps, 42, released as S/Sgt, 48, after serv. in 9th Aircraft Wing; Am. Theater Ribbon; Good Conduct and Victory Medals. Mem: Dir, Greater Vt. Asn; trustee, Windham Co. Farm Bureau and Camp Waubanong, 4-H; past treas, Vt. State 4-H Found, pres, Barttleboro local NEMPA; Grange (7°). Rel: Methodist. Mailing Add: R.F.D. 3, Guilford, Vt. 05301. (1967)

FRANKLIN, MELVIN MADISON D
b. Tula, Miss, 12/16/96; married. Polit. & Govt. Pos: Miss. State Rep, 56-60; former Miss. State Sen. Bus. & Prof. Pos: Merchant; farmer. Mem: Am. Legion; Farm Bur; Cattlemen's Asn. Rel: Methodist. Mailing Add: P.O. Box 282, Oxford, Miss. 38655. (1967)

FRANKS, VAUDRY LEE D
Chmn, Franklin Co. Dem. Exec. Cmt, Ala.
b. Guin, Ala, 3/27/21; s. Willie O. Franks and Mertie Stowe F; m. 3/16/40 to Vaudine Pickens; c. Jerry L. and Larry J. Educ: Glen Allen High Sch, Ala, 12 years; col. bus. course, $1\frac{1}{2}$ years. Polit. & Govt. Pos: Chmn, Franklin Co. Dem. Exec. Cmt, Ala, 60-; co. Dem. campaign mgr, 60- Bus. & Prof. Pos: Merchant, Russelville, Ala, 56-61; agent, Metropolitan Life Ins. Co, 64- Mil. Serv: Entered as Pvt, Army, 44, released as Cpl, 46, after serv. in 82nd Air Borne Div, Berlin Occupation, Europe, 45; Good Conduct Medal; Unit Presidential Citation; French & Belgian Unit Awards; European Medal. Mem: Civitan; VFW; Am. Legion. Hon. Lt. Col, Gov. Lurleen B. Wallace's Staff, Ala. Rel: Baptist. Mailing Add: P.O. Box 69, Russelville, Ala. 35653.

FRANTZ, ALBERT EDWARD, JR. D
b. Dallas, Tex, 12/4/23; s. Albert Edward Frantz and Julia Lee Caston F; m. 7/10/48 to Peggie June Frost; c. Susan, Larry David, William Edward, Donald Eugene, John Robert and James. Educ: Blackstone Sch. of Law, LL.B, 59, J.D, 60. Polit. & Govt. Pos: Ariz. State Rep, 62-66. Bus. & Prof. Pos: Pres, Frantz Realty Co, 62- Mil. Serv: Entered as Pvt, Air Force, 43, released as Capt, 61, after serv. in ETO; Air Force Commendation Medal. Rel: Methodist. Mailing Add: 3129 W. Pierson, Phoenix, Ariz. 85017.

FRANTZ, ALBERT THIBAUT D
b. Denver, Colo, 12/9/03; s. Eugene Frantz and Emma Frank F; m. 6/25/29 to Dorothy Delia Spry; c. Eugene A, Robert H. and Collette Diane. Educ: Regis Col, 24-25; Univ. Notre Dame, LL.B, 29; hon. mem, Phi Alpha Delta. Polit. & Govt. Pos: Judge, Second Judicial Dist. Court, 52-56; justice, Colo. Supreme Court, 57-68. Publ: 'Colorado Appellate Courts - The First Hundred Years,' 139 Colo. XI, 59 and Dicta, 3 & 4/59; 'The Law Mirrors History' in Essays in Legal History in Honor of Felix Frankfurter, Bobbs-Merrill, 66. Mem: Am, Colo. and Denver Bar Asns; Denver Exchange Club; Elks; Denver Urban League; Multiple Sclerosis Soc. of Colo; K. of C. Rel: Catholic. Mailing Add: 949 S. Josephine St, Denver, Colo. 80209. (1967)

FRANTZ, MOULTON LEWIS CHARLES R
Chmn, Lehigh Co. Rep. Cmt, Pa.
b. Allentown, Pa, 8/12/04; s. Stephen C. Frantz and Katie Lentz F; m. 7/6/27 to Dorothy M. Braden; c. Moulton L.C, Jr. Polit. & Govt. Pos: Bur. of Indentification, Allentown Police Dept, Pa, 35-36; tax clerk, Lehigh Co, 36-40, chief dep. sheriff, 40-48; minor judiciary, Allentown, 48-51; clerk, Quarter Sessions, Lehigh Co, 51-61; legis. chmn, Pa. Elected Co. Officials, 58-66; pres, Prothonotary and Clerk's of Courts Asn. of Pa, 60-61; mem, Pa. State Rep-Exec. Cmt, 60-; asst. to U.S. Rep. Willard S. Curtin, Eighth Cong. Dist; chmn, Lehigh Co. Rep. Cmt, currently. Bus. & Prof. Pos: Photographer and head, Photographic Dept, Allentown Call-Chronicle Newspaper, 22-35. Mem: Mason; Elks; Am. Bus. Club. Rel: Church of Christ. Mailing Add: 118 N. Ninth St, Allentown, Pa. 18102.

FRANZ, W. J. Conservative
Minn. State Sen.
b. Mt. Lake, Minn, 1907; married. Educ: Univ. of Minn. Col. of Bus. Admin. Polit. & Govt. Pos: Village clerk, Mt. Lake, Minn. 37-41; co. cmnr, Cottonwood Co, 41-55; Minn. State Sen, 54- Bus. & Prof. Pos: Owner and operator, gen. store. Outstanding Serv. Award for Indust. and Serv. in Govt, Minn. Food Retailers Asn, 57. Mailing Add: 255 Tenth St, Mount Lake, Minn. 56159. (1967)

FRANZEN, RICHARD S. D
b. Bloomington, Ind, 5/31/28; s. G.F. Franzen and Florence Buker F; m. 9/24/55 to Edith Eskola; c. Carl, David B. and Lisa. Educ: Yale, B.A. Polit. & Govt. Pos: Admin. asst. to U.S. Rep. Jacobs, Ind, 65-68. Bus. & Prof. Pos: Salesman, R.R. Donnelly and Sons, Chicago, 53-57; reporter, Terre Haute Star, Ind, 57-59 and Indianapolis News, 59-65. Mil. Serv: Army, Korea, 51-53, Pvt. to Sgt. Mem: Butler-Tarkington Neighborhood Asn. Rel: Unitarian. Mailing Add: 2405 Daphne Lane, Alexandria, Va. 22306. (1967)

FRANZENBURG, PAUL D
b. Conrad, Iowa, 11/18/16; s. Paul Franzenburg and Bertha Beck F; m. 1940 to Barbara Stewart; c. Ross, Stephen and Christine. Educ: Pierson Consolidated Sch, Woodbury Co. Polit. & Govt. Pos: State Treas, Iowa, 64-68; v.chmn, Iowa Develop. Cmn; mem, Gov. Cmn. on State and Local Govt; mem, Conrad Bd. of Educ: Dem. cand, Gov, Iowa, 68. Bus. & Prof. Pos: Owner, Franzenburg Provision Co, Family Meat Processing Enterprise, 38-; sch. band organizer, teacher and conductor. Mem: Past pres, Iowa Refrigerated Locker Asn. and Nat. Locker Inst; Inst. of Food Technologists; Lions; Am. Legion. Founder, James Van Allen Scholarship Fund. Rel: Methodist. Mailing Add: Conrad, Iowa 50621. (1967)

FRANZI, EMIL ANTHONY R
Mem, Calif. State Rep. Cent. Cmt.
b. Boston, Mass, 7/4/38; s. Emilio Anthony Franzi and Jean Ratazzi F; m. 4/23/65 to Kathleen Anne Pylant; c. Carroll Angela. Educ: Univ. Ariz, B.A. in Hist, 61; Phi Kappa Psi (pres. twice). Polit. & Govt. Pos: Mem, Pima Co. Rep. Cent. Cmt, Ariz, 62-67; mem, Ariz. State Rep. Cent. Cmt, 62-64 & 66-67; field rep, Calif. State Sen. H.L. Richardson, 19th Dist, 69; mem, Calif. State Rep. Cent. Cmt, 69-; pres, Los Angeles Co. Young Rep, Calif, 69- Bus. & Prof. Pos: Salesman, Occidental Life & Mutual of N.Y, Tucson, Ariz, 63-65; dept. mgr, Montgomery Ward, Tucson, Ariz. and Rosemead, Calif, 65-67; soc. worker, Los Angeles Co, 67-69. Mil. Serv: Entered as E-1, Ariz. Air Nat. Guard, 61, released as S/Sgt, 67, after serv. in 162nd Fighter Group, (AD), Tucson. Rel: Presbyterian. Mailing Add: 3500 Hillhaven, West Covina, Calif. 91790.

FRAPPIER, J. H. R
Mo. State Rep.
b. Milwaukee, Wis, 8/8/31; s. Francis S. Frappier and Dorothy Ihrig A; m. 9/11/55 to Marian Joyce Pridgen; c. Bettina Jo, Michelle Rae and Lisa René. Educ: Ind. Univ, B.S, 57, M.B.A, 58. Polit. & Govt. Pos: Councilman, Florissant, Mo, 63 & 65; Mo. State Rep, 24th Dist, 67- Bus. & Prof. Pos: Methods Coordinator, Laclede Gas Co, 66. Mil. Serv: Entered as Pvt, Marine Corps, 51, released as Sgt, 53, after serv. in Korea, 52-53; Presidential Unit Citation; UN Medal; Korean Medal with Two Stars Rel: Christian. Mailing Add: 2335 Hummingbird, Florissant, Mo. 63033.

FRASCELLA, THOMAS A. D
b. 11/28/22; s. Daniel Frascella and Catherine McMullen F; m. to Mary Reilly; c. Thomas Jr, Michael, Daniel, Mary, Joseph, David, Theresa, Helen. Educ: Trenton Cath. Boys High Sch. Polit. & Govt. Pos: Pa. State Rep, 54-67; 37th Ward Dem. Comm; former mem, Dem. State Comm. Mil. Serv: Army, Inf· wounded twice, ETO. Mem: United Steelworkers of Am. Local 5398; Am. Legion. 1967 Legal Res: Philadelphia, Pa. No mailing address available. (1967)

FRASER, DONALD MacKAY DFL
U.S. Rep, Minn.
b. Minneapolis, Minn, 2/20/24; m. to Arvonne Skelton; c. Six (one deceased). Educ: Univ. Minn, B.A. cum laude, 44, LL.B, 48, Naval ROTC. Polit. & Govt. Pos: Democrat-Farmer-Labor Activities, 47-; Minn. State Sen, 54-62; chmn, Minn. Citizens for Kennedy, 60; secy, Minn. Del. to Dem. Nat.

Conv, 60, del, 68; U.S. Rep, Minn, 62-; participation mem, Anglo-Am. Parliamentary Conf. on Africa, 64-; v.chmn, Cmn. on Dem. Selection of Presidential Nominees, 68. Bus. & Prof. Pos: Partner, Law Firm of Lindquist, Fraser & Magnuson, 54-62. Mil. Serv: Navy, radar officer, Pac. Theatre, World War II. Mem: Bd, Minn. Law Alumni Asn; Minneapolis For. Policy Asn.(past pres); Minneapolis Citizens' League (former secy. and v.chmn); Minneapolis Citizens' Cmt. on Pub. Educ.(former v.chmn); bd, Legal Aid Soc. Legal Res: Minneapolis, Minn. Mailing Add: 1253 Fourth St. S.W, Washington, D.C. 20024.

FRASER, DONALD ROSS R
Ohio State Rep.
b. Toledo, Ohio, 5/21/27; s. Malcolm Wicks Fraser and Elizabeth Ross F; m. 8/16/52 to Caroline Pilliod; c. Donald Ross, Jr. and Marguerite Ann. Educ: Univ. Toledo, B.S, 52; George Wash. Univ, J.D, 54; Phi Kappa Psi. Polit. & Govt. Pos: Ohio State Rep, 69- Bus. & Prof. Pos: Partner, Law Firm of Wilson & Fraser, Toledo, Ohio, currently; owner, Fabrics, Unlimited, currently; pres, Springbrook Construction Co, currently. Mil. Serv: Entered as Pvt, Army, 44, released as Sgt, 46, after serv. in Corps of Engrs, Mediterranean Theatre of Opers, 44-46; Good Conduct Medal; Mediterranean Theatre of Opers. Medal; Army of Occup. Medal. Mem: Am. and Toledo Bar Asns; Am. Patent Law Asn; Nat. Soc. State Legislators; Univ. Club, Wash, D.C; Kenwood Golf and Country Club; Inverness Club, Toledo, Ohio; Rotary. Rel: Presbyterian. Legal Res: 4719 Springbrook, Toledo, Ohio 43615. Mailing Add: 504 Libbey-Owens-Ford Bldg, Toledo, Ohio 43624.

FRASER, EDWIN G. D
Secy, Fla. State Senate
b. Newberry, Fla, 12/30/14; m. to Jessie Thelma Walters; c. Sandra June and Gary Kent. Polit. & Govt. Pos: Fla. State Rep, 36-40; Fla. State Sen, 44-, Secy, Fla. State Senate, 63- Bus. & Prof. Pos: Nurseryman. Mem: Mason; Shrine; Moose; Lions; Fla. and South. Nursery Asns. Rel: Methodist; former Sunday Sch. Supt. Mailing Add: The Capitol, Tallahassee, Fla. 32304. (1967)

FRASER, KEITH R
Polit. & Govt. Pos: Ind. State Sen, 55-58; 63-66; Jay Co. prosecuting attorney 49-54. Bus. & Prof. Pos: Lawyer. Mil. Serv: Army. Mem: Am. Legion; Masons; Elks; various bar asns. Rel: Presbyterian. Mailing Add: P.O. Box 14, Portland, Ind. 47371. (1967)

FRASER, MARIE FLORENCE D
Chmn, Sweetgrass Co. Dem. Party, Mont.
b. Osakis, Minn, 2/13/14; d. Walter Lyle Bayers and Lena Trimble B; m. 4/3/33 to Sidney W. Fraser; c. William S, Marilyn J.(Mrs. Iversen) and Janet K. Educ: West. Mont. Col, 31-32. Polit. & Govt. Pos: Precinct committeewoman, Dem. Party, Mont, 54-; Dem. state committeewoman, Sweetgrass Co, 60-; del, Dem. Nat. Conv, 64; pres, Sweetgrass Co. Dem. Women's Club, Mont, 64-66; chmn, Sweetgrass Co. Dem. Party, currently. Bus. & Prof. Pos: Teacher, 32-33 & 57-58; substitute teacher, intermittently. Mem: Civil Defense, 2 years; Leader, 4-H, 10 years; Bridger Creek Federated Club; Kent Community Home Dem. Club; T-Bone Cowbelles; Mont. Hereford Asn. Auxiliary. Rel: Congregational; Sunday Sch. Teacher, 3 years. Mailing Add: Reed Point, Mont. 59069. (1967)

FRASER, THOMAS JEFFERSON D
Mem, Scotts Bluff Co. Dem. Cmt, Nebr.
b. Bonne Terre, Mo, 12/23/32; s. John M. Fraser and Velma M. Highley F; m. 9/8/59 to Virginia Helen Reves; c. Thomas L, Theodore P, Laurel Elizabeth and Paul Jon (deceased). Educ: Flat River Jr. Col, A.A, 52; Cent. Col, Mo, B.A, 54; Perkins Sem, South. Methodist Univ, B.D, 57; Jr. Col. Scholastic Hon; Church Scholarships. Polit. & Govt. Pos: Mem, Knox Co. Dem. Cmt, Nebr, 64; mem, State Dem. Cmt, 68; alternate del, Dem. Nat. Conv, 68; mem, Scotts Bluff Co. Dem. Cmt, 68- Bus. & Prof. Pos: United Methodist minister, Genoa, Nebr, 57-61, Norfolk, 61-64, Bloomfield, 64-67, Gering, 67-69 and Wauneta, 69-; conducted youth summer camping progs, 6 summers. Mem: Nebr. Conf. Mem, United Methodist Church; Am. Friends Serv. Cmt; Lions; Optimists; Rotary; Cosmopolitan Club; C. of C. Mo. Boys State Award, 49; Danforth Award, 50. Rel: United Methodist. Legal Res: c/o T.C. Reeves, R.F.D. 1, Central City Nebr. 68826. Mailing Add: Box 398, Wauneta, Nebr. 69045.

FRASER, WALTER SAMUEL D
b. Georgetown, S.C, 4/29/17; s. Thomas Pettigru Fraser and Eunice Lillian Moultrie F; single. Educ: Claflin Col, A.B, 40; Am. Acad. of Mortuary Research and Allied Sci, N.Y.C, M.S, 47; Nat. Embalmers Fraternity; Societé des Beaux Arts; Omega Psi Phi; Oxford Club; King and Queen Club. Polit. & Govt. Pos: Del, city Dem. conv, S.C, 49, co. Dem. conv, 50- and state Dem. conv, 68; precinct 1 leader, Georgetown Co. Dem. Orgn, 57-; alternate del, Dem. Nat. Conv, 68. Bus. & Prof. Pos: Mortician and owner, Fraser Funeral Home, Georgetown, S.C, 49-; teacher, Rosemary High Sch, Andrews, 50-51; real estate appraiser, Georgetown, 59- Mil. Serv: Entered as Pvt, Army, 40, released as 1st Sgt, 45, after serv. in 369th Anti-Aircraft Artil, Pac. Theatre, 41-45; Good Conduct Medal; Am. Defense Medal; Asiatic Pac. Medal; Instr. Dipl. in Chem. Warfare; Instr. Dipl, Hawaiian's Mines and Incendiary Sch. Mem: S.C, Sixth Dist. and Nat. Funeral Dirs. Asns; Mason (32°); Elks; Am. Legion; City Bd. Health; City Zoning and Planning Cmn; Pee Dee Area for Co. Develop; Coastal Region Planning Cmn; trustee, Allen Univ. Rel: African Methodist Episcopal; Trustee, Bethel African Methodist Episcopal Church. Mailing Add: 202 Wood St, Georgetown, S.C. 29440.

FRASER, WILLARD E. Independent
Mayor, Billings, Mont.
b. Gardner, Kans, 1/26/09; s. John Brown Fraser and Sadie Irene Gay F; m. to Marjorie Frost (deceased); c. Robin (Mrs. David Beecher Hudnut). Educ: Univ. Colo, B.A, 32. Polit. & Govt. Pos: Mayor, Billings, Mont, third term. Mil. Serv: Sgt, Army, serv. in Eighth Inf. Div, ETO, 42-45. Mem: Elks; Mason; Shrine. Rel: Congregational. Legal Res: 118 S. 38th St, Billings, Mont. 59101. Mailing Add: City Hall, Billings, Mont. 59101.

FRASER, WILLIAM CHARLES R
Mem, Nebr. Rep. State Cent. Cmt.
b. Walnut, Iowa, 6/20/87; s. William E. Fraser and Dora Burton F; m. 9/27/09 to Mabel Gray; c. Dorothy (Mrs. Samuel), Mary (Mrs. Nicholson), Robert G. and Barbara (Mrs. Martin). Educ: Creighton Univ, LL.B, 08. Polit. & Govt. Pos: Mem, Post War Planning Cmn; treas, Nebr. Rep. State Cmt, 36-46; mem, Nebr. Rep. State Cent. Cmt. and Finance and Budget Cmt, 36-; chmn, Rep. Founders Day, 55; del, Rep. Nat. Conv, 60 & 64; Presidential Elector from Nebr, 68. Bus. & Prof. Pos: Mem. bd. dirs, Musser-Mosler Cattle Co. and Fawn Lake Ranch Co, 35 years. Mil. Serv: World War I; mem, U.S. Navy State Selection Cmt. and Air Corps Civilian Cmt, World War II. Mem: Regional chmn, Nebr. Adv. Defense Cmt, 41-46; Nebr. Develop. Cmt, 41-45; bd. dirs, Omaha C. of C, 36-46, pres, 40-41; Nebr. State Capitol Bldg. Cmn, 12 years; Nebr. State Bd. of Bar Exam, 5 years; pres, Omaha Commun. Chest, 30-31 and Omaha Bar Asn, 24-25; bd. dirs, Boy Scouts, many years; mem. Adv. bd, St. Catherine's Hosp, 60-; Nebr. State Chmn, United Serv. Orgn, 43-47; Omaha, Nebr. State and Am. Bar Asns; Air Force Asn; Asn. of the U.S. Army; Century Club; Creighton Univ; Boys Clubs of Omaha; Omaha Urban League; Nat. Parks Asn; Nat. Wildlife Fedn; Fel. of Am. Bar Asn; Nat. Conf. of Christians and Jews; Grand Knight, K. of C, 17-18; Omaha Club; Omaha Athletic Club; Nebr. State and Nat. Reclamation Asns; Plaza Club; state chmn, Liberty Bond Drive. Rel: Catholic. Legal Res: 3630 Burt St, Omaha, Nebr. 68131. Mailing Add: 510 Electric Bldg, Omaha, Nebr. 68102.

FRASSINELLI, ATTILIO D
Lt. Gov, Conn.
b. Stafford, Conn, 8/7/08; s. John D. Frassinelli and Josephine Dell'Agnese F; m. to Mildred M. McLagan; c. Gordon, David, Claire (Mrs. Wilmer West), Nancy (Mrs. Richard Bilyak) and Virginia (Mrs. Richard Pisciotta). Educ: Metrop. Schs. of Acct, Boston; LaSalle Univ. Polit. & Govt. Pos: Mem. sch. bd, Conn, 40-48; chmn. town cmt, 44-48; Conn. State Rep, 46-50; selectman, 47-59; Cmnr. of Food and Drugs, 55-59; Cmnr. of Consumer Protection, 59-66; Lt. Gov, Conn, 66-; mem, Civil Defense Adv. Coun. and chmn, Exec. Cmt. on Human Rights and Opportunities, 67-; mem, Viet Nam Bonus Appeals Bd. and Inter-govt. Coop. Cmn, 68- Bus. & Prof. Pos: Ins. and Real Estate Broker. Mem: Pres, Rotary; K. of C; Cent. Atlantic States Asn. Italian Execs. William Paca Award. Mailing Add: 1 Grant Ave, Stafford Springs, Conn. 06076.

FRAZER, D. R. D
W.Va. State Del.
b. Tioga, W.Va, 11/22/21; s. James H. Frazer and Loretta P. Cummins F; m. 6/28/52 to Lota G. Carnifax. Educ: Morris Harvey Col, Charleston, W.Va. Polit. & Govt. Pos: W.Va. State Del, 57- Mil. Serv: Served as Seaman 2/C, Navy, Korean War, 52-53 and as Maj, Marine Corps Res, World War II in Pac. Mem: Lions; Mason; Moose; VFW; Am. Legion. Rel: Methodist. Legal Res: 14 Park Place, Richwood, W.Va. 26261. Mailing Add: Box 149, Richwood, W.Va. 26261.

FRAZER, ROBERT NUNN R
s. Dr. T. Atchison Frazer; m. to Dorothy Tucker; c. William Roberts and Bohn Atchison. Polit. & Govt. Pos: Chmn, Crittenden Co. Rep. Party, Ky, 56-60 and del. to last 2 conv. Bus. & Prof. Pos: Pres, Ky. Fluorspar Co, 22-66. Rel: Methodist. Legal Res: Clark Street, Marion, Ky. 42064. Mailing Add: P.O. Box 431, Marion, Ky. 42064.

FRAZIER, BERT LEE R
Chmn, Lee Co. Rep. Cmt, Miss.
b. Burem, Tenn, 11/13/26; s. Dana Frazier and Mattie Mitchell F; m. 4/4/53 to Joan Price; c. Margaret Ann and William Dana. Educ: E. Tenn. State Univ, B.S. in mkt, 51; grad. study, Univ. Tenn and Univ. Miss. Polit. & Govt. Pos: Mem, Lee Co. Rep. Exec. Cmt, Miss, 62-63; chmn, Lee Co. Rep. Cmt, currently; alternate del, Rep. Nat. Conv, 68. Bus. & Prof. Pos: Lab. staff and time keeper, Eastman Kodak, 47 & 51-52; ins. adjuster, Commercial Credit Corp, 52-54 and Gen. Adjustment Bur, 54-57; claims mgr, Hartford Fire Ins. Co. Group, 57-59; owner, One Hour Martinizing Drycleaning and Robo Car Wash, presently. Mil. Serv: Entered as Pvt, Army, 45, released as Pfc, 47, after serv. in Aviation Engrs, Philippines. Mem: Blue Goose Int; bd. dirs, Tupelo Merchant's Cmt. and Miss. Laundry and Cleaning Asn; chmn, Tupelo Laundry and Cleaning Asn; Am. Legion; VFW; Flying Club; Aircraft Owners and Pilots Asn; Nat. Inst. of Drycleaning; Am. Inst. of Laundering; off. and past mem, Jaycees. Rel: Baptist. Legal Res: 123 Enoch Ave, Tupelo, Miss. 38801. Mailing Add: P.O. Box 721, Tupelo, Miss. 38801.

FRAZIER, ELVA BRINDLEY D
b. Hartselle, Ala; d. Thaddeous Bunyan Brindley and Martha Louisa Woods B; m. 8/25/35 to Edwin M. Frazier. Educ: Univ. Ala, B.S. in educ, 27, M.A, 30; Univ. Chicago, 34; Delta Kappa Gamma; Delta Kappa Pi. Polit. & Govt. Pos: Alternate del, 40, 52, 56 and 60, del, 64 & 68; mem, Steering Cmt, Ala, 60-64; co-chmn, Morgan Co. Dem. Party, 60-64, chmn. bd. 62-64; chmn. prog. cmt, Study of Am. Govt. Politics. Bus. & Prof. Pos: Teacher, elem. grades, several years; elem. educ. supvr, Marengo Co, Ala, 29-34, DeKalb Co, 34-39 and Morgan Co, 39-42; owner, Frazier Machinery & Supply Co, Decatur. Mem: DAR; Bus. & Prfnl. Women's Club; Eastern Star; Am. Asn. Univ. Women; Women's C. of C. Rel: Methodist. Legal Res: 850 Jackson St, S.E, Decatur, Ala. 35601. Mailing Add: P.O. Box 429, Decatur, Ala. 35601.

FRAZIER, JAMES BERIAH, JR. D
b. Chattanooga, Tenn, 6/23/90; s. James Beriah Frazier and Louise Douglas Kieth F; m. 3/30/39 to Elizabeth Hope; c. Elizabeth Hope. Educ: Univ. of Va; Chattanooga Col, LL.B, 14. Polit. & Govt. Pos: U.S. Attorney, East. Dist, Tenn, 33, 37 & 41-48; U.S. Rep, Tenn, 49-62. Bus. & Prof. Pos: Lawyer with firm Frazier and Frazier. Mil. Serv: Maj, World War I. Rel: Methodist. Mailing Add: 211 Glenwood Dr, Chattanooga, Tenn. 37404.

FRAZIER, LINCOLN B. R
Chmn, 11th Cong. Dist. Rep. Party, Mich.
b. Aurora, Ill, 9/20/05; s. Lincoln B. Frazier and Bertha Plumb F; m. 6/15/39 to Anne Maxwell Reynolds; c. Julia, Peter W. and Lincoln B, Jr. Educ: Univ, Wis, B.S, 27; Delta Kappa Epsilon. Polit. & Govt. Pos: Finance chmn, Marquette Co. Rep. Party, Mich, 58-68; chmn, 11th Cong. Dist. Rep. Party, 69- Bus. & Prof. Pos: Pres, Campbell Supply Co, 40- Mil. Serv: Entered as Lt, Navy, 42, released as Lt. Comdr, 46, after serv. as Inspector of Naval Material, U.S.A. Mem: C. of C. Rel: Protestant. Mailing Add: 460 E. Ridge St, Marquette, Mich. 49855.

FRAZIER, ROBERT E. D
b. Braintree, Mass, 23. Educ: Franklin Tech. Inst; Avon Consol. Schs. Polit. & Govt. Pos: Selectman, Braintree; mem, town meeting, 14 yrs; Bd. of Health; Bd. of Pub. Welfare. Bus. & Prof. Pos: master plumber. Mem: K. of C; Holy Name Soc; Norfolk Co. Selectmens Asn; Am. Legion. Mailing Add: 347 Pearl St, Braintree, Mass. 02184. (1967)

FRAZIER, WILLIAM GOULD R
Ind. State Sen.
b. Albany, Ind, 11/8/36; s. Francis Arron Frazier and Dorothy Alice Shellenbarger; m. 1/8/56 to Joan Ellen Cassel; c. Joan Annette and Susan Carol. Polit. & Govt. Pos: Ind. State Sen, 68- Bus. & Prof. Pos: Pres, Bill Frazier Mobile Homes, Inc, 62- Mil. Serv: Entered as Pvt. E-2, Army, 55, released as Sgt. E-6, 57, after serv. as Sr. Parachutist, Hq & Hq Co. 325 ABN. Inf. Regt, 82nd ABN. Div, Ft. Bragg, N.C. Mem: Mason; YMCA; Exchange Club; Ind. Mobile Home Asn; Ind. Young Rep. Fedn; Muncie Del. Co. C. of C; Aircraft Owners and Pilots Asn. Rel: Methodist. Legal Res: RR 3, Box 159, Muncie, Ind. 47302. Mailing Add: RR 1, Albany, Ind. 47320.

FRAZZINI, MARY R
Nev. State Assemblyman
b. Oakland, Calif, d. Hugh Cort Cameron and Johanna Vollmar C; m. 11/11/39 to Carson Frazzini; c. Carson Cameron. Educ: Glendale City Col, Calif, 2 years; Glendale Bus. Col, 8 months. Polit. & Govt. Pos: Clerk, Co. Sch. Bd, 40-44; mem, Co. Rep. Cent. Cmt, 57-; mem, Nev. Rep. Cent. Cmt, 61-; del, Rep. Nat. Conv, 64; Nev. State Assemblyman, 64-; v.chmn, Gov. Cmn. Status Woman, 67- Bus. & Prof. Pos: Owner, food concession, 62- Mem: Reno Bus. and Prfnl. Women's Club; Nev. Fedn. Bus. and Prfnl. Women's Club; Rep. Women's Club, Reno (pres, 57-59); Nev. Fedn. Rep. Women (pres, 61-65); Garden Club; Twentieth Century Club; Delta Kappa Gamma, Int. Soc. for Women Teachers (hon. mem. and chmn. state bd). Mailing Add: 1630 Van Ness Ave, Reno, Nev. 89503.

FREAR, JOSEPH ALLEN, JR. D
b. Rising Sun, Del, 3/7/03; s. Joseph Frear and Clara Lowber F; m. 2/11/33 to Esther Viola Schauer; c. Fred, Clara, Louise. Educ: Univ. of Del, B.S, 24; Sigma Nu. Polit. & Govt. Pos: Mem. Securities and Exchange Cmn, 61-63; U.S. Sen, Del, 49-61; state cmnr, Del. State Hosp, 46-48, Old Age Welfare, 37-48, State Col, 36-41. Bus. & Prof. Pos: V.Pres, Wilmington Trust Co, Dover, Del; agriculturist, 22-; dir, chmn. bd, 46-48, Fed. Land Bank, Baltimore; dir. Farmer's Bank, Dover, and Baltimore Trust Co, Camden, Del; past pres. Kent Gen. Hosp. Mil. Serv: WWI and WWII; Lt. Col, Officer Res. Corps, WWII. Mem: C. of C; Am. Legion; Am. Hosp. Asn; Del. State Farm Bur; Mason; K. T; Shriner; Dover Rotary; Del. Motor Club; Maple Dale Country Club. Mailing Add: 622 S. State St, Dover, Del. 19901. (1967)

FREAS, HOWARD GEORGE
Mem. Interstate Commerce Cmn.
b. Fogelsville, Pa, 7/13/00; s. Oscar Wilson Edmond Freas and Katie Jemina George F; m. 7/3/24 to Adelaide Trygstad; c. Howard George (deceased), Ann, Jean and William. Educ: Allentown Bus. Col, 16; Mercersburg Acad, 21; Univ. Nev, 21-22; Univ. of Calif, 22; LaSalle Univ, 34-36. Polit. & Govt. Pos: Consult, U.S. Maritime Cmn; asst. rate expert, Calif. State Pub. Utilities Cmn, 28-33, exam, 33-35, rate expert, 35-53; mem, Interstate Commerce Cmn, 53-, chmn, 58. Bus. & Prof. Pos: Teacher, land and air transportation, Stanford Univ, 42-45. Mil. Serv: Merchant Marine, 21-22, Mines Expert. Mem: U.S. Nat. Cmn; Pan Am. Rwy. Cong. Asn; Mason. Legal Res: Oakland, Calif. Mailing Add: Interstate Commerce Commission, Washington, D.C. 20025. (1967)

FREBURG, CHARLES RAYMOND R
b. Walnut Grove, Ill, 1/16/12; s. Ernest Victor Freburg and Laura Beatrice Raymond F; m. 6/17/39 to Mary Josephine Snell; c. Lindsay Mark. Educ: Eureka Col, A.B. Polit. & Govt. Pos: Admin. asst. to U.S. Rep. Fred Schwengel, Iowa, 55-64; admin. asst. to U.S. Rep. Chester L. Mize, Kans, 64- Bus. & Prof. Pos: Sch. teacher, Prairie City, Ill, 35-38; prog. dir, WOC, WOC-TV, Davenport, Iowa, 38-53; asst. to pres, KWWL-TV, Waterloo, 53-54; radio-TV dir, Sperry-Boom, Inc, Davenport, 54-55. Mil. Serv: Army, Sgt, Inf, 43-46; Inf. Replacement Training Cent, Camp Roberts, Calif. Mem: Tau Kappa Epsilon. Mailing Add: 2000 Stirrup Lane, Alexandria, Va. 22308.

FREDA, ALDO D
R.I. State Rep.
b. Providence, R.I, 7/18/21. Educ: Cent. High Sch; courses in Life Ins. Off. Mgt. Polit. & Govt. Pos: Past chmn, 12th Rep. Dist. Cmt, R.I; R.I. State Rep, Dist. 14, 61-, Dep. Majority Leader, R.I. State House of Rep, 69-; mem, 14th Rep. Dist. Cmt, currently. Bus. & Prof. Pos: Dist. off. supvr, John Hancock Life Ins. Co. Mil. Serv: Sgt, Air Force, 42-46, Chief Clerk, Radar Sect. Rel: Past Pres, Holy Name Soc, Our Lady of Mt. Carmel Church, Providence, R.I. Mailing Add: 115 Vinton St, Providence, R.I. 02909.

FREDA, CARMINE R
Chmn, Rockland Co. Rep. Party, N.Y.
b. Manhattan, N.Y, 5/4/01; s. Louis Alfonse Freda and Sophia Mellucio F; m. 7/1/37 to Hazel Loretta Burnie; c. William C. and Louis J. Educ: First Inst. Podiatry; L.I. Col, D.P, 21; Fordham Univ, 22. Polit. & Govt. Pos: Village trustee, Grand View on the Hudson, N.Y, 48-56; sch. bd. trustee, Cent. Sch. Dist. 1, 48-66; mayor, Grand View Nyack, 55-66; mem, Adv. cmt, Hudson River Valley Scenic Cmn, 64-; chmn, Rockland Co. Rep. Party, 66-; alternate del, Rep. Nat. Conv, 68; mem, med. adv. cmt, N.Y. State Dept. of Soc. Serv, 68-; cmnr, N.Y. State Cmn. on Pure Waters, 69. Mil. Serv: Lt, Coast Guard Auxiliary, 41-42; entered as Lt, Navy, 42, released as Comdr, 47, after serv. in Naval Aviation as officer in charge of aviation training, Corpus Christi, Tex. and U.S. Marine Corps Air Sta, Cherry Point, N.C, 42-43; Comdr.(Ret), Naval Res, 47-62; Pearl Harbor Medal; Am. Theatre Medal; 10 Year and 20 Year Good Conduct Medals; Presidential Commendation Medal with Pendant; plus others. Publ: Articles and booklet. Mem: Chmn, Asn. Am. Foot Specialists; polit. action cmt, Affiliated Podiatrists of N.Y; U.S. Naval Aviation Asn; Floyd Bennett Field Naval Aviation Commandery; Naval Order of the U.S; many officers clubs; U.S. Power Squadrons; former comdr, Brooklyn Power Squadron; Retired Officers Asn. Rel: Catholic. Mailing Add: 85 River Rd, Grand View on the Hudson, Nyack, N.Y. 10960.

FREDERICK, CAROLYN ESSIG R
S.C. State Rep.
b. Atlanta, Ga; d. Philip Martin Essig and Lillian Margaret Hall E; m. 10/1/33 to Holmes Walter Frederick; c. Lynn (Mrs. John Grant Williamson) and Rosa Margaret (Mrs. Glen Smith). Educ: Agnes Scott Col, A.B, 28. Polit. & Govt. Pos: S.C. State Rep, Greenville Co, 66- Bus. & Prof. Pos: Pub. rels. consult, 54-; mgr, Greenville Symphony Orchestra, 54-, mem. bd, currently; pub. rels. dir, YWCA Develop. Prog, 58-64; newspaper writer, formerly; dir. advert. and sales prom, Burdine's, Miami, Fla, formerly. Mem: Nat. League Am. Pen Women; Am. Asn. Univ. Women (S.C. State Bd, mass media cmt, pres, S.C. Div, 59-61, past pres, Ithaca, N.Y. and Greenville, S.C. Br); asst. dir, Gr. Greenville Commun. Chest Coun, 50-53; YWCA; Greenville Woman's Club; White House Conf. Children and Youth (co. steering cmt); Converse Col. Master Arts in Teaching Prog.(adv. cmt, 61-66); exec. dir, Arts Festival of Greenville, 63-65. Outstanding Woman in Commun. Serv, Greenville Piedmont Award, 63; Career Woman of the Year, Zonta, 67. Rel: Presbyterian. Mailing Add: 326 Chick Springs Rd, Greenville, S.C. 29609.

FREDERICK, MELVIN LYLE R
First V.chmn, First Dist. Rep. Party, Minn.
b. West Concord, Minn, 11/24/29; s. Elmer J. Frederick and Martha E. Pagel F; m. 6/3/56 to Donna M. Christopherson; c. Mitchell Scott, Debra Leigh and Michael Alan. Educ: West Concord High Sch, Minn, 4 years. Polit. & Govt. Pos: Rep. precinct chmn, West Concord, Minn, 61-67; v.chmn, Dodge Co. Rep. Cmt, 65-67, chmn, 67-69; first v.chmn, First Dist. Rep. Party, 69- Mil. Serv: Entered as Pvt, Army Nat. Guard, 48, released as M/Sgt, 52, after serv. in Co. E, 19th Inf. Regt, 24th Div, Korea, Far East Command, 51-52; Japan Occup. and UN Medals; lo/s Bar; Combat Infantrymans Badge; Korean Serv. Medal with One Bronze Serv. Star. Mem: Minn. Food Retailers Asn; West Concord Businessmens Asn.(pres, 62 and treas, 64-69); Mason; Am. Legion; Lions Int. Rel: United Methodist. Mailing Add: 414 Clyde St, West Concord, Minn. 55985.

FREDERICK, WILLIAM L. R
Del. State Rep.
b. 1935. Polit. & Govt. Pos: Del. State Rep, 67-, chmn, House Health and Welfare Cmt, Del. House Rep; mem, Gov. Task Force for Exec. Reorgn. Bus. & Prof. Pos: Wilmington Trust Co; secy-treas, Joseph Frederick & Sons, Inc, State Line Machine Corp, Two-Twenty-Two Bldg. Inc. and Pen-Del. Equip. Corp. Mem: Pres, Full Gospel Businessmen's Fellowship Int; Gideons Int; Lions; Coun. State Govt. Mailing Add: 2400 W. Parris Dr, Cedarcrest, Wilmington, Del. 19808.

FREDERICKSON, LYLE L. R
Chmn, Third Dist. Rep. Party, N.Dak.
b. Rural Norma, N.Dak, 11/30/05; s. Harry Frederickson and Pauline Tredt F; m. 12/8/29 to Margaret Marie Carstens. Educ: Kenmare High Sch, grad; 1 year col. Polit. & Govt. Pos: Precinct 3 committeeman, Third Dist. Rep. Party, N.Dak, 61-, chmn, 67- Bus. & Prof. Pos: Independent food store merchant, 30-57; farmer, 38- Mem: Lions; Farm Bur. Membership Awards. Rel: Lutheran. Mailing Add: 204 N.W. Sixth St, Kenmare, N.Dak. 58746.

FREDLUND, RAY R
Mem, State Rep. Cent. Cmt, La.
b. Valley Stream, N.Y, 7/31/25; s. Nils Victor Fredlund and Alice Mason F; m. 3/2/47 to Lorene Hilda Jesse; c. Loren Raymond, Alice Marie, Susan Lee, Glen George and Taffie Ruth. Educ: Rensselaer Polytech. Inst. B.Ch.E, 50. Polit. & Govt. Pos: Mem, Rep. State Cent. Cmt, La, 66-; chmn, Parish Polit. Action Coun, Iberville Parish, 67-68, v.chmn, 69 and chmn, parish exec. cmt, 67-; alternate del, Rep. Nat. Conv, 68. Bus. & Prof. Pos: Chem. engr, Austin Co, Tex, 50; proj. leader, Dow Chem. Co, Tex, 51-56, plant supt, Plaquemine, La, 57-67 and mgr, plant tech. serv, 67- Mil. Serv: Entered as Pvt, Army Air Force, 43, released as 2nd Lt, 45, after serv. in 487th Bomb Group, 8th Air Force, ETO, 45. Mem: Am. Inst. Chem. Engrs; Registered Prof. Engr, La; Elks. Rel: Methodist. Legal Res: 204 Pecan Tree Lane, Plaquemine, La. 70764.

FREDRIKSEN, ARNOLD LOUIS DFL
b. Goodhue, Minn, 6/29/98; s. Frederik Paul Frederiksen and Theresia F; m. 6/29/29 to Inga Lund; c. Arnold Lund. Educ: Concordia Col, Moorhead, Minn, B.A; N.Dak. State Univ, grad. study work, 1 yr. Polit. & Govt. Pos: Chmn, Dodge Co. Dem. Cmt, 53-66 and secy, 43-52; mem, Minn. Dem-Farmer-Labor Cent. Cmt, 52-66; Endorsed cong. cand, 1st Dist, and del, Nat. Dem. Conv, 56; Endorsed cand. for State Sen, 54; Elected presidential elector 36, but resigned; secy, 9th Cong. Dist. Dem. Cmt, 30-34 and Clay Co. Dem. Cmt, 24-34. Bus. & Prof. Pos: Mayor, Hayfield, Minn, 59-66, chmn, Bd. of Educ, 47-56; chmn, Dodge Co. Cmt. of Reorgn. of Sch, 47-53; dist. supvr. of educ. for the WPA, 35-42; supt. of schs, Dilworth, 23-34; mem, Legis. Assembly, Minn. High Sch. League, 30-33. Mil. Serv: Pvt, Army, 18. Mem: Concordia Col. Alumni Asn; former mem, Minn. Educ. Asn; Eagles; Mason; Lions; C. of C; comdr, Am. Legion; Hayfield, 43-44 and Dilworth, 33-34, Americanism chmn, Dist 1, 39-46; Am. Asn. of Retired Persons; chmn, Dodge Co. Asn. of Retired Persons; Farmers Union; Farm Bur. Rel: Lutheran. Mailing Add: 701 First Ave S, Hayfield, Minn. 55940. (1967)

FREE, EDWIN WHITMORE R
Vt. State Rep.
b. Brooklyn, N.Y, 2/12/00; m. to Antoninette Louis; c. One son; two daughters. Educ: Manual Training High Sch, Brooklyn; spec. Naval schs. Polit. & Govt. Pos: Sch. dir, Vt, 62-; mem, Spec. Records Cmt, Middlesex; Vt. State Rep, 65- Bus. & Prof. Pos: Former staff supvr, Metrop. Life Ins. Co. Mil. Serv: Chief Warrant Officer, Navy, World War I and World War II, Navy Res, 45-60. Mem: Mason; Eastern Star; Am. Legion; City Club of Montpelier. Rel: Baptist. Mailing Add: Star Route, Montpelier, Vt. 05602. (1967)

FREED, ELAINE EILERS D
b. Hinton, Iowa, 1/14/34; d. Fred Eilers and Frieda Borchers E; m. 6/20/53 to Douglas Freed; c. David and Casey. Educ: Univ. Minn, B.A, 58. Polit. & Govt. Pos: Mem, Colo. Dem. Cent. Cmt, 61-65; mem, El Paso Co. Exec. Cmt, 61-65; co-chmn, Frank Evans Cong. Cmt, 64; del, Dem. Nat. Conv. and mem.

platform cmt, 68. Bus. & Prof. Pos: Teacher, elem. sch, Colo, 58-60; teacher, nursery sch, 67-68. Outstanding Young Women, Am, 68. Mailing Add: 2111 N. Tejon, Colorado Springs, Colo. 80907.

FREED, MELVYN NORRIS D
b. Kansas City, Mo, 4/30/37; s. Carl Freed and Betty Wachtel F; single. Educ: Univ. Mo, Kansas City, B.A, 59; South. Ill. Univ, M.S.E, 62, Ph.D, 65; Phi Kappa Phi; Omicron Delta Kappa; Kappa Delta Pi; Phi Delta Kappa; Alpha Epsilon Pi. Polit. & Govt. Pos: Admin. asst. to U.S. Rep. Bill Alexander, Ark, 69. Bus. & Prof. Pos: Research asst, South. Ill. Univ, 62-65, vis. asst. prof, summer 68; dir. instnl. research, Ark. State Univ, 65-; research specialist, S.Cent. Region Educ. Lab, 66. Publ: 'Why Your College Should Study Itself and How to Go About It,' Col. & Univ. Bus, 6/64; 'The Regional Education Laboratories: Bane or Benefit,' Sch. & Soc, 12/9/67; 'The Responsibilities of Being Educated,' Phi Kappa Phi J, winter 68. Mem: Am. Asn. Higher Educ: Asn. Instnl. Research; Ark. Educ. Research and Develop. Coun.(pres); Jr. C. of C. Outstanding Young Man of Am, 67. Mailing Add: 1400 Judy St, Apt. 209, Jonesboro, Ark. 72401.

FREEDBERG, JOHN MICHAEL R
Chmn, Ward 11 Rep. Cmt, Jamaica Plain, Mass.
b. Boston, Mass, 6/6/40; s. Dr. Harry Freedberg and Ruth Mugglebee F; single. Educ: Phillips Acad, Andover, 55-58; Princeton Univ, A.B, 62; Harvard Law Sch, LL.B, 65. Polit. & Govt. Pos: Chmn, Volpe Campaign, Salem, Mass, 66; chmn, John Sears Campaign, Jamaica Plain, 67, Jamaica Plain, 68; chmn, Ward 11 Rep. Cmt, Jamaica Plain, 68- Bus. & Prof. Pos: Treas, Jampac Fed. Credit Union, 69- Mem: Harvard Law Sch. Asn; West Roxbury Civic League; Essex Co. Club; Suffolk Co. Rep. Club; hon. mem, Boston Police Dept. Rel: Jewish. Legal Res: 43 Beech Glen Rd, Roxbury, Mass. 02179. Mailing Add: 606 Centre St, Jamaica Plain, Mass. 02130.

FREEDMAN, CLAIRE FRIEDMAN R
b. Bainbridge, Ga, 2/15/15; d. Lester August Friedman and Bertha M. Nussbaum F; m. 12/21/37 to Dr. Louis Murray Freedman; c. Benton Edward, Murray Allen and Donald Stewart. Educ: Univ. Ala, B.S. in Home Econ. Polit. & Govt. Pos: Secy, First Dist. of Ga. Rep. Party, 62-64, vice chairwoman, 64-65; pres, Chatham Co. Rep. Club, 65-66; secy, Chatham Co. Rep. Party, 65-66, vice chairwoman, 66-67; asst. secy, Rep. Party of Ga, 66-67; secy, Savannah-Chatham Co. Bd. of Tax Assessors, 67- Mem: Bd. of dirs, Savannah Chap, Am. Red Cross; bd. of dirs, United Commun. Serv. Rel: Jewish. Mailing Add: 140 E. 44th St, Savannah, Ga. 31405.

FREEDMAN, FRANK HARLAN R
Mayor, Springfield, Mass.
b. Springfield, Mass, 12/15/24; s. Alvin Samuel Freedman and Ida Rosenberg F; m. 7/26/53 to Eleanor Edith Labinger; c. Joan Robin, Wendy Beth and Barry Alan. Educ: Springfield Col; Trinity Col; Boston Univ. Sch. of Law, LL.B. and LL.M; Tau Epsilon Rho. Polit. & Govt. Pos: City Coun, Sixth Ward, Springfield, Mass, 60 & 61, city coun-at-lg, 62-67, mayor, 68-; mem, Ward and City Rep. Party and v.chmn, City Rep. Party, 63; Asst. Attorney Gen, Mass, 63-67; del, Rep. Nat. Conv, 64 & 68 and 3 Mass. Rep. State Conv; mem, State Indust. Finance Bd, 68-69 and Adv. Cmt. on Commun. Affairs, 69- Bus. & Prof. Pos: Mem, Lewis Marshall Club on legal jurisp, 50-, pres, 63. Mil. Serv: Entered as A/S, Navy, 43, released as Ens, 46. Mem: Hampden Co. Bar Asn; B'nai B'rith; Forest Park Zool. Soc; chmn, Muscular Dystrophy co. drive, 62. Rel: Jewish. Legal Res: 9 Normandy Rd, Springfield, Mass. 01106. Mailing Add: Administration Bldg, 36 Court St, Springfield, Mass. 01103.

FREEH, EDWIN JAMES, JR. D
b. Beacon, N.Y, 10/18/30; s. Edwin J. Freeh and Myrtle Pearce F; m. 9/30/55 to Janet M. Gray; c. Carol, Connie and Laura. Educ: Detroit Bus. Col, B.C.S; Univ. Chicago. Polit. & Govt. Pos: Acct, Dearborn Heights, Mich, 56-61; trustee, Bd. Educ, 60-61; city clerk and treas, Garden City, Mich, 61-64, formerly mayor. Bus. & Prof. Pos: Pres, Employees Credit Union, 59-61; v.pres, Westland Advert, 64-66; mgr, Garling Real Estate, currently. Mil. Serv: Entered as Pvt, Marine Corps, 51, released as Sgt, 54, after serv. in Tank Corps, Korea, 51-52; Expert Rifle, Pistol and Good Conduct Ribbons. Mem: Pres, Goodfellows, 59, Civic Asn, 59 and Little League, 58; bd. of dirs, Salvation Army; VFW; Mason; Shrine; Am. Legion; Big Brothers of Am; 1st Marine Div. Asn; Civic Group; Moose; Dem. Club; Lions; Jaycees. Distinguished Serv. Award, 59-62; voted one of five Outstanding Young Men of Mich, 64. Rel: First Methodist. Mailing Add: 14695 Bradner, Plymouth, Mich. 48170.

FREEMAN, BRIAN A. R
b. Erie, Pa, 10/30/40; s. A. Austin Freeman and Ellen Green F; m. 7/6/68 to Mabel Anna Gilbert. Educ: Oberlin Col, A.B, 62; Ohio State Univ, J.D, 65; Phi Delta Phi. Polit. & Govt. Pos: Chmn, Jr. Rep. of Erie Co, Pa, 56-57; chmn, Youth for Nixon, Lorain Co, Ohio, 60; secy, Ohio League Col. Rep, 60-61, exec. dir, 61-62, chmn, 62-63; asst. to chmn, Ohio League Young Rep, 63-64, campaign dir, 64-65, exec. secy, 65-66, co-chmn, 66-67, chmn, 67-68; youth coordinator, Ohio Citizens for Goldwater, 64; asst. attorney gen, Ohio, 66-67; alternate del-at-lg, Rep. Nat. Conv, 68. Bus. & Prof. Pos: Asst. prof, Franklin Law Sch. of Capital Univ, Columbus, Ohio, 67- Mil. Serv: Entered as 1st Lt, Air Force, 67, released as Capt, 69, after serv. in 121st Tactical Fighter Group and 840th Combat Support Group, Lockbourne Air Force Base, Ohio, 68-69; Capt, Air Nat. Guard. Mem: Columbus, Ohio and Am. Bar Asns. Rel: Protestant. Mailing Add: 2395 Berwick Blvd, Columbus, Ohio 43209.

FREEMAN, BRUCE N. R
Mass. State Rep.
b. Watertown, Mass, 3/4/21; s. Forrest Ervin Freeman and Ethel V. Noyes F; m. 4/28/45 to Daphne Grace Russell; c. Bruce R, Gary R, Deborah A. and Dale H. Educ: Newton High Sch, Mass, grad, 39. Polit. & Govt. Pos: Mem, Rep. Town Cmt, Chelmsford, Mass, 61-; pres, Chelmsford Rep. Club, 65-66; Mass. State Rep, 32nd Middlesex Dist, 69- Bus. & Prof. Pos: Salesman, Liggett & Myers Tobacco Co, 46-50; div. sales mgr, 50-58; ins. agent, Prudential Ins. Co. Am, 58- Mil. Serv: Entered as Pvt, Army, 42, released as T-4, 46, after serv. in 96th Machine Unit, Adj. Gen. Dept, European and Pac. Theatres, 42-46; Good Conduct Medal; European African Mid. East. Theatre Campaign Ribbon; Asiatic Pac. Theatre Ribbon; Am. Theatre Campaign Ribbon; Philippine Liberation Ribbon; Victory Medal; Meritorious Award. Mem: Life Underwriters Asn; Millionaire Club, Prudential Ins. Co; charter mem, Prudential Ins. Co. Acad. of Honor; Mason; Am. Legion; VFW; Chelmsford Conserv. Cmn; Hist. Soc; pres. & treas, Fairbanks Family of Am, Inc; Mass. Legislators Asn; Secy. Northeast Chap, Mass. Heart Asn; v.pres. Greater Lowell Coun, Boy Scouts. Pres. Citation, Prudential Ins. Co. Rel: Protestant. Legal Res: 7 Kenwood St, Chelmsford, Mass. 01824. Mailing Add: State House, Boston, Mass. 02133.

FREEMAN, DENNIS L. R
Iowa State Rep.
b. Paton, Iowa, 3/2/39; s. Lester M. Freeman and Leona Fredrickson F; m. 6/10/62 to Mary Louise Hawkinson; c. Mark D, Sara L, Cary D. and Maret S. Educ: Gustavus Adolphus Col, B.S, 61. Polit. & Govt. Pos: Iowa State Rep, 69- Mil. Serv: Navy. Mem: Kiwanis; Jaycees; Elks. Rel: Lutheran. Legal Res: 622 Iowa St, Storm Lake, Iowa 50588. Mailing Add: State House of Representatives, Des Moines, Iowa 50139.

FREEMAN, EDWIN D
Ky. State Sen.
b. Mercer Co, Ky, 12/10/21; s. James Wheeler Freeman and Dora Alice Robinson F; m. 11/21/40 to Elsie Kirkland; c. Ann Harriett. Polit. & Govt. Pos: Ky. State Rep, 56-57 & 62-63; chmn, Mercer Co. Dem. Party, Ky, 65-; judge, Mercer Co, 66-68; del, Dem. Nat. Conv, 68; Ky. State Sen, 69- Bus. & Prof. Pos: Chmn, bd. of dirs, West. Pioneer Life Ins. Co; mem, bd. of dirs, Mercer Co. Nat. Bank and Mercer Savings & Loan; bd. of trustees, South. Col, Louisville, Ky. Mem: Mason; Shrine; Scottish Rite; Farm Bur; Nat. Auctioneers Asn. Rel: Baptist. Mailing Add: 505 Beaumont Ave, Harrodsburg, Ky. 40330.

FREEMAN, FRANKIE MUSE
b. Danville, Va; d. William B. Muse and Maud B. Smith M; m. to Shelby T. Freeman; c. Shelbe Patricia. Educ: Hampton Inst, 33-36; Howard Univ, LL.B, 47; Delta Sigma Theta. Polit. & Govt. Pos: Assoc. gen. counsel, St. Louis Housing and Land Clearance Authorities, 56-; asst. attorney gen, Mo, 55-56; mem, Cmn. Civil Rights. Prof. Pos: Lawyer; instr. bus. law, Sampson Col, 47-48. Mem: Am. Bar Asn; Lawyers Asn. St. Louis; Nat. Asn. Housing and Redevelopment Officials; Nat. Housing Conf; NAACP; Nat. Coun. Negro Women; treas, YWCA of St. Louis, 57- Named outstanding citizen, Mound City Press Club, 53; woman of achievement, Nat. Council Negro Women, 56. Rel: Baptist. Legal Res: 1209 N. Grand Blvd, St. Louis, Mo. 63100. Mailing Add: 2031 Olive St, St. Louis, Mo. 63103. (1967)

FREEMAN, FULTON
b. Pasadena, Calif, 5/7/15; m. to Phyllis Eaton; c. three. Educ: Pomona Col, A.B, 37; Princeton Univ, 37-38; Lingnan Univ, Canton, China, 34-35; Univ. of Calif, spec. study, 42. Polit. & Govt. Pos: Career officer, U.S. Dept. of State, 39-; v.consul, Mexico City, 39-40; 3rd secy, Peiping, 40-42 and Chunking, 43-45; v.consul, Peiping, 45-46, consul, 46-48; asst. chief, Div. of Chinese Affairs, 48-49; acting dep. dir, Off. of Chinese Affairs, 49-50; Nat. War Col, 50-51; 1st secy, Rome, 51-55; polit. adv, Supreme Allied Comdr. Atlantic, 55-58; counsel, Brussels, 58-61; U.S. Ambassador, Colombia, 61-64; former U.S. Ambassador to Mex. Legal Res: Route 3, Box 267B, Carmel, Calif. 93921. Mailing Add: c/o Dept. of State, Washington, D.C. 20520. (1967)

FREEMAN, KENNETH DONALD D
Co-Chmn, Eighth Dist. Dem. Party, Calif.
b. Oakland, Calif, 12/8/12; s. Herbert R. Freeman and Florence F. Carr F; m. 12/8/36 to Amelia H. Tyler; c. Shirley A, Kenneth M, Donald T. and Lionel W. Educ: Lincoln Law Sch, Oakland, Calif, 3 years; Merritt Bus. Sch, Oakland, 3 years; U.S. Treas. Dept. acct. courses. Polit. & Govt. Pos: Mem, Gov. Adv. Cmt. on Children and Youth, Calif, 64-65; mem, Calif. Dem. State Cent. Cmt, 6 years; treas, Eighth Cong. Dist. Dem. Coun. of Dem. Clubs, 1 year, pres, 2 years; pres, Eighth Cong. Dist. Dem. Club, currently; co-chmn, Eighth Dist. Dem. Party, 64- Bus. & Prof. Pos: Dep. collector, Internal Revenue Serv, 42-51; pub. acct, 52- Mem: Bd. dir, East Bay Chap, Calif. Soc. of Pub. Acct; K. of C.(4°); Alameda Co. Insts. Cmn; Diocese Soc. Justice Cmn; Bay Area Coun. of Soc. Planning; Alameda Co. Cmt. for Prevention of Juvenile Delinquency; chmn, supvry. cmt, NAACP Credit Union. Rel: Catholic. Mailing Add: 1452 70th Ave, Oakland, Calif. 94621.

FREEMAN, LeROY HOMER D
b. Los Angeles, Calif; s. LeRoy Homer Freeman (deceased) and Ella Binyon F.(deceased); m. 12/23/43 to Mary Elouise Prichard; c. Jeri, Victoria (Mrs. Evans), Martin and Lee. Educ: Ill. Col. of Optometry, D.O. Polit. & Govt. Pos: Chmn, Whatcom Co. Dem. Cent. Cmt, Wash, 61-66; former Dem. State Committeeman, Wash; Dem. committeeman, Precinct 1, Van Wyck, currently. Mil. Serv: Entered as Pvt, Army, 44, released as S/Sgt, 45, after serv. in 34th Field Hosp, Philippine Islands and S.Pac. Mem: Legal and legis. cmt, C. of C, chmn, 65-66; Wash. State Optom. Bd, 61-66; Wash. Optom. Asn; Elks. Rel: Catholic. Legal Res: 2196 Bayview, Bellingham, Wash. 98225. Mailing Add: 1328 Cornwall Ave, Bellingham, Wash. 98225.

FREEMAN, ORVILLE LOTHROP D
b. Minneapolis, Minn, 5/9/18; s. Orville E. Freeman; m. 5/2/42 to Jane Charlotte Shields; c. Constance Jane and Michael Orville. Educ: Univ. Minn, B.A, 40, LL.B, 46; Phi Beta Kappa; Delta Theta Phi; Iron Wedge; M Club; Alpha Zeta. Hon. LL.D, Univ. Seoul, St. Joseph's Col, Fairleigh Dickinson Univ, and Am. Univ. Polit. & Govt. Pos: Chmn, Civil Serv. Cmn, Minneapolis, Minn, 46-49; state chmn, Dem-Farmer-Labor Party, 48-50; Gov, Minn, 56-60; Secy. of Agr, 61-69; del, Dem. Nat. Conv, 68. Bus. & Prof. Pos: Law partner, Larson, Loevinger, Lindquist, Freeman and Fraser, 47-54; pres, EDP Tech. Int, Inc, currently. Mil. Serv: Entered as Pfc, Marine Corps, 42, released as Capt, 45, after serv. in Ninth Regt, Third Div, Pac; Col, Marine Corps Res; Purple Heart; Pac. Campaign Ribbon. Mem: Minn. Bar Asn; pres, Minn. Asn. of Plaintiffs Attorneys; Am. Legion; VFW; DAV; Am. Vet. Cmt; Marine Corps League; Isaac Walton League; mem. bd. trustees, Nat. Recreational and Parks Asn. Rel: Lutheran; former deacon, Ebenzer Lutheran Church; mem. exec. cmt, Lutheran Church in Am. Legal Res: Minneapolis, Minn. Mailing Add: 2805 Daniel Rd, Chevy Chase, Md. 20015.

FREEMAN, WAYNE W. D
b. Graves Co, Ky, 12/25/12; s. Otha Niley Freeman and Lula Mae Fundaugh F; m. 6/17/44 to Jennie Drury Chancellor. Educ: Murray State Univ, B.S, 36; Jefferson Sch. Law, LL.B, 48; Univ. Louisville Law Sch, LL.B, 51; pres, Murray Col. Young Dem. Club and Int. Rels. Club, Murray State Univ, 36. Polit. & Govt. Pos: Ky. State Rep, Graves Co, 40-44; dep. collector, U.S. Internal Revenue Serv, Louisville, Ky, 43-47; field investr, Ky. Pub. Serv. Cmn, 48-56; Ky. State Sen, 52-60; R.R. Cmnr, 1st Ky. R.R. Dist, 56-67; del, Dem. Nat. Conv, 60 & 68. Bus. & Prof. Pos: Attorney-at-law, Ky, 44- Mem: Past pres, Graves Co. Bar Asn; Ky. State and 1st Judicial Dist. Bar Asns; Mason; Symsonia, Lowes, Melber and Boaz Civic Clubs; hon. mem, Graves Co. Young Dem. Club, 66. Rel: Baptist. Mailing Add: 800 Brand St, Mayfield, Ky. 42066.

FREIBERG, LOUIS K. R
b. 10/13/25; married; c. Kevin. Educ: S.Dak. Sch. of Agr, 42; Creighton Univ, LL.B, 52. Polit. & Govt. Pos: Chmn, Pennington Co. Rep. Party, 56 & 58; secy-treas, S.Dak. Cement Cmn, 58-59; precinct committeeman, 6 years; chmn, Pennington Co. Mundt for Sen. Club, 60; S.Dak. State Rep, 63-67. Bus. & Prof. Pos: Partner, law firm, Rapid City. Mil. Serv: Army Air Corps, WW II, Navigator; discharged as 1st Lt, 46. Mem: K. of C; Elks; Am. Legion; S.Dak. and Am. Bar Asns; secy-treas, S.Dak. Reclamation Asn, 52-54. Rel: Catholic. Mailing Add: Box 2003, Rapid City, S.Dak. 57701.

FREISE, HERBERT H. R
b. Palatine, Ill, 1917; married to Vera; c. Three. Educ: Valparaiso Univ, A.B. and LL.B. Polit. & Govt. Pos: Former Wash. State Sen. Bus. & Prof. Pos: Lawyer. Mil. Serv: Navy. Mailing Add: 200 Jones Bldg, Walla Walla, Wash. 99362. (1967)

FREITAS, EDWARD WARREN D
Mem, Calif. Dem. State Cent. Cmt.
b. San Jose, Calif, 11/17/21; s. John Andrew Freitas and Margaret Fereirra F; m. 9/5/42 to Velma June Riessen; c. Tye Edward (deceased), Diane Lee (Mrs. Rooney) and Timothy Warren. Educ: U.S. Armed Forces Inst, B.S. Mil. Sci; Golden Gate Col. Law, 1 year. Polit. & Govt. Pos: Mem, Calif. Dem. State Cent. Cmt, 62-63 & 66-; pres, Calabazas Dem. Club, 66; nominee, Calif. State Sen, 14th Dist, Santa Clara and Alameda Counties, 66; mem, Santa Clara Co. Dem. Cent. Cmt, 66- Bus. & Prof. Pos: Pres, Ampco Paving Co, 64- Mil. Serv: Entered as Pvt, Army, 39, released as Capt, 60, after serv. in 3rd Div, Korea, 50-51 and as commanding officer, Hosp. Detail, Ft. Ord, Calif, 56-59; Bronze Star. Mem: Calif. Native Sons; Golden Gate Col. Law Alumni Asn. Rel: Catholic. Mailing Add: Route 2, Box 652, Morgan Hill, Calif. 95037.

FRELINGHUYSEN, PETER H.B. R
U.S. Rep, N.J.
b. N.Y.C, 1/17/16; s. Peter H.B. Frelinghuysen, Sr.(deceased) and Adaline Havemeyer F.(deceased); m. 9/7/40 to Beatrice S. Procter; c. Peter, Beatrice, Rodney, Adaline and Frederick. Educ: Princeton Univ, B.A, magna cum laude in hist, 38; Yale Law Sch, LL.B, 41. Polit. & Govt. Pos: Staff mem, Hoover Cmn. For. Affairs Task Force, 48; U.S. Rep, Fifth Dist, N.J, 53-, mem, House For. Affairs and Rep. Policy Cmts. and former mem, House Educ. and Labor Cmt; del, UN 20th Gen. Assembly, 65; U.S. Cong. Del, NATO Parliamentarians' Conf; mem. Rep. Truth Squad, 64 & 68; mem, Rep. Platform Cmt, 64 & 68; del, Rep. Nat. Conv, 64 & 68; Cong. adv, 18 Nation Disarmament Conf, 67, 68 & 69. Bus. & Prof. Pos: Mgr. family bus; with law firm of Simpson, Thacher and Bartlett, 41-42; dir, Metrop. Mus. Art, N.Y; trustee, Kennedy Cultural Center; mgr, Howard Savings Inst, Newark, N.J; dir, Trust Co. Nat. Bank, Morristown, N.J; dir, North Jersey Conserv. Found. Mil. Serv: Entered Navy, 42, released as Lt, 45, after serv. in Naval Intel, Off. Chief Naval Opers. Mem: Am. Bible Soc.(v.pres); trustee, Morristown Mem. Hosp. Rel: Episcopal; Former Vestryman, St. Peter's Episcopal Church. Legal Res: Sand Spring Lane, Morristown, N.J. 07960. Mailing Add: Room 2162, Rayburn House Office Bldg, Washington, D.C. 20515.

FRENCH, ELEANOR CLARK D
b. Phila, Pa, 6/29/08; d. Herbert Lincoln Clark and Elizabeth Conway Bent C; m. 2/3/50 to John French; stepchildren, John, III, Roberts W. and Mary (Mrs. Corbet.) Educ: Sorbonne Univ; Harvard Univ; Columbia Univ. Polit. & Govt. Pos: Cand. for N.Y. State Sen, 56; v.chmn, N.Y. State Dem. Cmt, 57-60; chmn, Women for Kennedy, 60; chmn, Vol, Wagner Campaign, 61; mem, City Cmn. on Human Rights, N.Y.C, 61-69; city cmnr, UN, 62-66; Dem. and Liberal cand. for U.S. Rep, 17th Cong. Dist, N.Y, 64; del, Dem. Nat. Conv, 64 & 68. Bus. & Prof. Pos: Teacher and Supvr, Elemen. Sch, 32-43; Off. Inter-Am. Affairs, 43-46; assoc. dir, France Unitarian Serv. Cmt, 46, 47-; women's ed, N.Y. Times, 49-55. Publ: 'Women in Politics,' N.Y. Times Mag, 56. Mem: Bd. mem, Foreign Policy Asn; nat. bd, Am. for Dem. Action; adv. cmt, N.Y. Urban League. Rel: Unitarian. Mailing Add: 144 E. 38th St, New York, N.Y. 10016.

FRENCH, GEORGE A.
b. Conn, 1901; married; c. two. Educ: Univ. Minn. Polit. & Govt. Pos: Minn. State Rep, 41-66. Bus. & Prof. Pos: Attorney. Mailing Add: 5140 Pa. Ave. S, Minneapolis, Minn. 55426. (1967)

FRENCH, JIM R
Mem. Exec. Cmt, Kans. State Rep. Cmt.
b. St. John, Kans, 11/16/17; s. William James French and Hattie Halley F; m. 12/28/37 to Lavone Luella Hoagland; c. Kathryn Jane, Constance Rae and William James, III. Educ: Washburn Univ, 35-37; Alpha Delta. Polit. & Govt. Pos: Contact rep, Vet. Admin, 46-49; mem, Seward Co. Bd. Educ, Kans, 55-63, pres, 5 years; precinct committeeman, Ward Six, Liberal, Kans, 56-; secy-treas, Seward Co. Rep. Cent. Cmt, 58-60, chmn, 60-; crew chief, Census Bur, 60; area chmn, First Dist. Rep. Cmn, 62-65; mem. exec. cmt, Kans. State Rep. Cmt, 65-; chmn, First Cong. Dist. Cmt, 65-; del. and mem. Cmt. on Resolutions, Rep. Nat. Conv, 68. Mil. Serv: Entered as Pvt, Air Force, 43, released as M/Sgt, 45, after serv. in Eighth Air Force, 452nd Heavy Bombardment Group, ETO, 54; Distinguished Flying Cross; Air Stars; Presidential Unit Citation. Mem: Elks; Masons; Rotary; Am. Legion; Farm Bur; Rep. Assocs. of Southwest Kans. Rel: Methodist. Legal Res: 926 N. Carlton Dr, Liberal, Kans. 67901. Mailing Add: P.O. Box 1427, Liberal, Kans. 67901.

FRENCH, ROBERT BRYANT, JR. R
Mem, Ala. State Rep. Exec. Cmt.
b. Howell, Tenn, 9/16/33; s. Robert B. French, Sr. and Nina Sibley F; m. 9/22/55 to Celeste I. Mongiello; c. Michelle. Educ: Univ. Ala. Sch. Commerce and Bus. Admin, B.S, Law Sch, LL.B. Polit. & Govt. Pos: Dir. of orgn, Tuscaloosa Co. Rep. Party, Ala, 62-63; co-chmn, Tuscaloosa Young Rep. Club, 62-63; state chmn, Ala. Young Rep. Fedn, 63-65; mem, Ala. State Rep. Exec. Cmt, 63-; del, Rep. Nat. Conv, 64 & 68; precinct chmn, Beat Nine, Ft. Payne, 66-; mem, DeKalb Co. Rep. Exec. Cmt, 66-; v.chmn, Ala. Rep. Party, 69- Mil. Serv: Enlisted Air Force, 53, released as Sgt, 57, after serv. in East. Air Defense Force; Good Conduct Medal. Mem: Assoc. Indust. Ala, 59-63; Ala. Bar Asn, 63-66; DeKalb Co. Bar Asn.(secy-treas, 65-66, pres, 68-69); West Ala. Personnel Asn.(secy-treas, 60-63); Indust. Rels. Conf. Ala. (planning cmt, 62); Ala. Mt. Lakes Asn.(bd. dirs); DeKalb Co. Tourist Asn. (pres). Selected One of Outstanding Young Men of Am, Nat. Jr. C. of C, 65; One of Ten Outstanding Young Rep. State Chairmen, 65; Man of the Year, Ft. Payne, 68; One of Four Outstanding Young Men of Ala, 68; nominated Ten Outstanding Young Men of Am, 68. Rel: Baptist. Legal Res: Scenic Hwy, Ft. Payne, Ala. 35967. Mailing Add: P.O. Box 596, Ft. Payne, Ala. 35967.

FRENETTE, HENRY N, JR. R
Chmn, Brockton Rep. City Cmt, Mass.
b. Holyoke, Mass, 6/11/33; s. Henry N. Frenette, Sr. and Estelle Turcotte F; m. 10/16/54 to Janet E. Hultman; c. David P. and John H. Educ: Univ. Mass; Boston Univ. Law Sch; Boston Univ. Grad. Law Sch; v.pres. & treas, Boston Univ. Law Sch. Class of 59. Polit. & Govt. Pos: Asst. city solicitor, Brockton, Mass, 64-; chmn, Brockton Rep. City Cmt, 65- Bus. & Prof. Pos: Practicing attorney-at-law, Keith, Reed & Wheatley, 60- Mil. Serv: Entered as Pvt, Army, 54, released as Specialist 2/C, 56, after serv. in 82nd Airborne Div, Korea; Various Unit Citations; Commendation Ribbon. Publ: Author of miscellaneous articles on the law of taxation. Mem: Plymouth Co. and Mass. Bar Asns; City Solicitors' Asn; secy, YMCA; officer, Brockton Symphony Orchestra; pres, Brockton Hosp. Bldg. Fund; chmn, Brockton Area Cmt. for Progress; Thorny Lea Golf Club. High Sch. & Col. Athletics. Rel: Catholic. Mailing Add: 436 W. Elm St, Brockton, Mass. 02401.

FRENTZ, ROY R
Co. Chmn, Rep. Party, Minn.
b. Mankato, Minn, 3/20/15. Educ: Northwestern Univ, B.S, 36. Polit. & Govt. Pos: Mem, Minn. Rep. State Cent. Cmt, 61-67; co. chmn, Rep. Party, Minn, 61- Mailing Add: 520 Van Brunt St, Mankato, Minn. 56001.

FRENZEL, WILLIAM ELDRIDGE R
Minn. State Rep.
b. St. Paul, Minn, 7/31/28; s. Paul William Frenzel and Paula Schlegel F; m. 6/9/51 to Ruth Purdy; c. Deborah Anne, Pamela Ruth and Melissa Lee. Educ: Dartmouth Col, B.A, 50, M.B.A, 51; Sigma Nu. Polit. & Govt. Pos: Minn. State Rep, 30th Dist, 63-; transportation dir, Hennepin Co. Civil Defense, Minn. and mem. exec. reserves, Off. of Emergency Transportation, Dept. of Commerce, 65- Bus. & Prof. Pos: Employee, Minneapolis Terminal Warehouse Co, 54-57, mgr, 57-60, pres. and dir, 60- Mil. Serv: Entered as Ens, Naval Res, 51, released as Lt.(jg), 54, after serv. in Amphibious Forces, Korea; Lt.(Ret), Naval Res. Mem: Past pres, Upper Miss. Waterway Asn, Minn. N.W. Warehouseman's Asn. and Minneapolis Transfermen's Asn; dir, Miss. Valley Asn. and Camden-Northwest. State Bank; adv. cmt, Nat. Rivers and Harbors Cong; adv. coun, Minn. Dept. of Employ. Security; exec. cmt, Am. Warehousemen's Asn; Am. Legion; C. of C; Citizen's League. Selected as One of Outstanding Young Men of Am, U.S. Jr. C. of C, 64; citation for work in Civil Defense, Minneapolis, 63. Mailing Add: 233 Janalyn Circle, Minneapolis, Minn. 55416.

FRERICHS, DONALD L. R
b. 1931. Educ: Mankato State Col, B.A. Polit. & Govt. Pos: Rep. cand, Minn. State Rep, 66; co. chmn, Rep. Party, Minn; alternate del, Rep. Nat. Conv, 68. Bus. & Prof. Pos: Owner, mgr, Frerich's Hardware, Miracle Mile; off. mgr, hardware mgr. and furniture mgr, Rickbeils, Inc, Worthington. Mem: Bd. of dirs, Salvation Army and Olmsted Co. Businessmen's Asn; Nat. Retail Hardware Asn; Minn. Retail Hardware Asn. Mailing Add: 1802 Merrihills Dr, Rochester, Minn. 55901. (1967)

FREW, MYRON H. D
b. Bradshaw, Nebr, 10/26/96; m. 11/10/44 to Dorothy Williams; c. Joanne (Mrs. Allan Ledbetter) and Erlaine. Educ: Univ. of Calif, Davis, creamery sch. course; Univ. of S. Calif. Polit. & Govt. Pos: With sales tax div, State Bd. Equalization, Calif, 10 years; postmaster, Dinuba, Calif, 52; State Assemblyman, 57-65. Bus. & Prof. Pos: Merchant, clothing bus, 44-59; creamery bus. Mil. Serv: Army, 22 months. Mem: Elks; Am. Legion; VFW; C. of C; Merchants Asn; Eastern Star. Mailing Add: 359 N. L St, Dinuba, Calif. 93618.

FREY, LOUIS, JR. R
U.S. Rep, Fla.
b. Rutherford, N.J, 1/11/34; s. Louis Frey and Mildred Engel F; m. Marcia Turner; c. Four. Educ: Colgate Univ, B.A. cum laude, 55; Univ. Mich. Law Sch, J.D. with honors, 61; asst. ed, Univ. Mich. Law Rev; Order of the Coif. Polit. & Govt. Pos: Asst. co. solicitor, Orlando, Fla, 61-63; acting gen. counsel, Fla. State Turnpike Authority, 66-67; former mem, Fla. Rep. State Exec. Cmt; former treas, Fla. State Rep. Party; former chmn, Fla. Fedn. Young Rep; U.S. Rep, Fla, 68- Bus. & Prof. Pos: Attorney-at-law, Orlando, Fla, 61-63; assoc. and partner, Gurney, Skolfield & Frey, Winter Park, 63-67; partner, Mateer, Frey, Young & Harbert, Orlando, 67. Mil. Serv: Entered Navy, 55, released as Lt.(jg), 58, after serv. in Naval Aviation; Lt. Comdr (Ret), Naval Res. Mem: Orange Co, Fla. and Am. Bar Asns; Phi Gamma Delta; Phi Delta Phi; dir, Winter Park Youth Center and Am. Cancer Soc, Orange Co; assoc. bd, Fla. Symphony. Legal Res: Winter Park, Fla. 32789. Mailing Add: 1315 Longworth House Office Bldg, Washington, D.C. 20515.

FREY, TOM J. R
Iowa State Sen.
b. 1902; m. Educ: Waterloo Bus. Col. Polit. & Govt. Pos: Iowa State Rep, 51-59; Iowa State Sen, 69- Bus. & Prof. Pos: Newspaper publ. Mil. Serv: Navy, 42-45. Mailing Add: Neola, Iowa 51559.

FRICK, ARTHUR H, SR. Conservative
Minn. State Rep.
b. Belleville, Ill, 1895; m. c. four; 10 grandchildren, 4 great grandchildren. Educ: Univ. Ill, B.S. in Agr. Polit. & Govt. Pos: Past pres, Minn. Asn. of Co. Agr. Agents; dir, Grand Rapids Sch. Bd, 59-63; Minn. State Rep, Dist. 58B, Itasca Co, 62-, v.chmn, game and fish cmt, mem, elec. and reapportionment, forestry and pub. domain, gen. legis. and vet. affairs, hwy, univs. and cols, claims and pub. instr. cmts. Bus. & Prof. Pos: Retired co. agr. agent. Mem: Lions (past pres). Superior Serv. Award, U.S. Dept. Agr; Distinguished Serv. Award, Nat. Asn. of Co. Agr. Agents. Mailing Add: 812 N.W. Seventh Ave, Grand Rapids, Minn. 55744.

FRICK, JOHN J. D
Ind. State Sen.
Polit. & Govt. Pos: Former Ind. State Rep; Ind. State Sen, currently; chmn, Mayor's Traffic Cmt; mem, TV Licensing Bd. Bus. & Prof. Pos: Owner, two electrical stores. Mil. Serv: Air Force. Mem: Credit Bur. Bd; dir, Better Bus. Bur; bd. chmn, TV Dealers of St. Joseph Co, Retail Merchants of St. Joseph Co. and Miami Bus. and Prfnl. Asn. Rel: Protestant. Mailing Add: 1901 Miami St, South Bend, Ind. 46613.

FRIDAY, ELMER OTTO, JR. D
Fla. State Sen.
b. Bartow, Fla, 2/23/24; s. Elmer Otto Friday and Mayo Yates F; m. 6/15/47 to Betty Jo Guthrie; c. Eugenia Lee, Jo Ellen, Richard Otto and Mitchel Ann. Educ: La. Polytech. Inst, 2 years; Univ. of Okla, 1 year; Univ. of Fla, LL.B, 49; Delta Theta Phi; Kappa Sigma. Polit. & Govt. Pos: Mem, Constitution Adv. Cmn, Fla, 55-57; judge, Lee Co, 57-61; mem, Fla. Judicial Coun, 59-61; Fla. State Sen, 24th Dist, 62-; mem, Fla. Juvenile Delinquency Cmn, 65-66; mem, Fla. Constitution Revision Cmn, 66; mem, exec. cmt, Nat. Legis. Conf, 66-; mem, exec. cmt, Coun. State Govt, 68-; mem, exec. cmt, South. Regional Conf, 68- Mil. Serv: Entered as A/S, Naval Res, 42 released as Aviation Machinist's Mate, 46. Mem: Real Property and Probate Sect, Am. Bar Asn; Fla. Trial Lawyers; Asn. of State Govt; secy, Fla. Juvenile Judge's Asn, 60; v.pres, Fla. Co. Judge's Asn, 60-61; pres, Jr. Bar Sect, Fla. Bar Asn, 54-55; Bd. of Gov, The Fla. Bar, 55; exec. secy, Lawyers' Title Guaranty Fund, 50-55; Mason; Shrine Audubon; Fla. Educ. Asn; Methodist Men; Optimists; Am. Legion. Rel: Methodist. Legal Res: 8733 Beacon Villas, Ft. Myers, Fla. 33901. Mailing Add: Drawer 1000, Ft. Myers, Fla. 33904.

FRIEDEL, SAMUEL NATHANIEL D
U.S. Rep, Md.
b. Washington, D.C, 4/18/98; s. Philip Friedel and Rose Franklin F; m. 3/8/39 to Regina B. Johnson. Educ: Pub. Schs, Baltimore. Polit. & Govt. Pos: Md. State Del, 34-38; mem, Baltimore City Coun, 39, 43 & 51; U.S. Rep, Md, 53-, chmn, House Admin. Cmt, Joint Cmt. on the Libr, Transportation and Aeronautics Subcmt. of House Interstate and For. Commerce Cmt. and v.chmn, Joint Cmt. on Printing, U.S. House of Rep, currently; del, Dem. Nat. Conv, 68. Mem: Wash. Improv. Asn; Elks; Am. Israel Soc; Sports Boosters; Safety First Club of Md; Md. Law Enforcement Officers Asn. Legal Res: 2201 South Rd, Baltimore, Md. 21209. Mailing Add: 2110 Rayburn House Office Bldg, Washington, D.C. 20515.

FRIEDEN, ERMA ROSE D
V.Chmn, Barber Co. Dem. Cent. Cmt, Kans.
b. Haselton, Kans, 4/22/07; d. Jonathan Franklin Albright and Rose Starks A; m. 6/18/27 to Clarence H. Frieden; c. Sheryll (Mrs. Ingram), John C. and Harold A. Educ: Kiowa High Sch, 4 years. Polit. & Govt. Pos: V.chmn, Barber Co. Dem. Cent. Cmt, Kans, 68- Mem: Eastern Star. Rel: United Church of Christ. Mailing Add: Hardtner, Kans. 67057.

FRIEDERSDORF, MAX LEE R
b. Grammer, Ind, 7/7/29; s. John Lewis Friedersdorf and Lola Frances Fox F; m. 10/17/53 to Priscilla Marion Jones; c. Kristine Lee and Fritz John. Educ: Franklin Col, A.B, 52; Butler Univ; Am. Univ, M.A, 69. Polit. & Govt. Pos: Admin. asst. to Rep. Richard L. Roudebush, Ind, 61- Mem: Sigma Delta Chi; Am. Polit. Sci. Asn; Cong. Secy. Club. Rel: Protestant. Legal Res: R.R. 3, Franklin, Ind. 46131. Mailing Add: 7708 Manor House Dr, Fairfax Station, Va. 22039.

FRIEDHEIM, JERRY WARDEN R
Dep. Asst. Secy. of Defense for Pub. Affairs
b. Joplin, Mo, 10/7/34; s. Volmer Havens Friedheim and Billie Warden F; m. 10/17/56 to Shirley Margarette Beavers; c. Daniel, Cynthia and Thomas. Educ: Univ. Mo, B.J, 56, A.M, 62; Indust. Col. of Armed Forces, 68; Omicron Delta Kappa; Kappa Tau Alpha. Polit. & Govt. Pos: Asst. to U.S. Rep. Hall, Mo, 62; asst. to U.S. Sen. Tower, Tex, 63-69; Dep. Asst. Secy. of Defense for Pub. Affairs, 69- Bus. & Prof. Pos: Reporter and ed, Neosho Daily News, Mo, Joplin Globe and Columbia Missourian, 58-61; instr, Univ. Mo, 61-62. Mil. Serv: Entered as 2nd Lt, Army, 56, released as 1st Lt. 58, after serv. in Second and Tenth Inf. Div, Europe; Capt, Army Res, 58-69. Publ: 'Where Are the Voters,' Nat. Press, Inc, 68. Mem: Sigma Delta Chi; Am. Polit. Sci. Asn. Award for Distinguished Reporting of Pub. Affairs, Am. Polit. Sci. Asn, 61, cong. fel. Rel: Protestant. Mailing Add: 3412 Old Dominion Blvd, Alexandria, Va. 22305.

FRIEDLAND, DAVID J. D
N.J. State Assemblyman
b. Jersey City, N.J, 12/20/57; s. Jacob Friedland. Educ: Tufts Univ; Rutgers Law Sch; Tau Epsilon Phi. Polit. & Govt. Pos: N.J. State Assemblyman, currently; counsel to Mayor Whelan's Labor Adv. Cmt, Jersey City. Bus. & Prof. Pos: Attorney-at-law. Mem: Elks; Nat. Honor Forensic Soc; Am. Judicature Soc; Citizens Civic League of Hudson Co. Mailing Add: 591 Summit Ave, Jersey City, N.J. 07306. (1967)

FRIEDLER, CARL LOBE D
Md. State Sen.
b. Baltimore, Md, 9/19/34; s. Ellis Friedler and Rose Sapperstein F; m. to Harriette Lee Solomon; c. Ellen and Marci. Educ: Univ, Md, B.A, 54; Univ. Md. Sch. of Law, LL.B, 57. Polit. & Govt. Pos: Former nat. committeeman, Young Dem. Clubs of Md; asst. city solicitor, Baltimore, 61-64; mem, Gov. Adv. Coun. on Hosp. Construction, 65-; Md. State Sen, Fifth Dist, 66-; del, Dem. Nat. Conv, 68. Bus. & Prof. Pos: Mem, bd. dir, Talmudical Acad. of Baltimore, Md, currently. Mil. Serv: Army Res, 55-62. Mem: Md. State Bar Asn; Mason; Yetz Grotto; Jr. C. of C; Golden Eagle Sq. and Compass Club; bd. dir, Safety First Club; bd. dir, Morris Kasoff Lodge; past grand master, Independent Order of Brith Shalom. Rel: Jewish. Legal Res: 6302 Fordham Rd, Baltimore, Md. 21215. Mailing Add: 412 Equitable Bldg, Baltimore, Md. 21202.

FRIEDMAN, BENJAMIN A. D
Mayor, Taunton, Mass.
b. Taunton, Mass, 4/12/15; s. James Friedman and Rose Kalans F; single. Educ: Suffolk Law Sch, J.D, 38. Polit. & Govt. Pos: Master, Chancery court, Mass, 40-55; mem, munic. coun, Taunton, 61-62; mem, Mass. Dem. Exec. Cmt, 63-68; mayor, Taunton, 63-; U.S. Mayors' rep, Geneva World Conf, Peace in Law, 67; del, Dem. Nat. Conv, 68. Bus. & Prof. Pos: Dir. of two banks. Mil. Serv: Air Force, World War II. Publ: Contrib. to numerous articles on fed, state and munic. probs. and their solutions. Mem: Mass, Am, Bristol Co. and Taunton Bar Asns; Elks; Am. Legion; Eagles; Rotary. Mailing Add: 49 Davenport St, Taunton, Mass. 02780.

FRIEDMAN, BETH HOLLAND D
b. New York, N.Y; d. Samson Hollander and Florence Leibman H; m. 8/28/53 to Louis L. Friedman; c. Ellen Lynn and Cathy Jayne. Educ: Hunter Col; Long Island Univ. Polit. & Govt. Pos: Del, Dem. State Convs, 56, 60, 62 & 66; alternate del, Dem. Nat. Conv, 60 & 64. Bus. & Prof. Pos: Radio commentator, Sta. WABC; actress, TV, Moving Pictures and Stage. Mem: Troupers; Actors Equity; Am. Fedn. TV and Radio Artists; Screen Actors Guild; Kings Co. Dem. Club. Rel: Jewish. Mailing Add: 2166 80th St, Brooklyn, New York 11214.

FRIEDMAN, DON R
Colo. State Rep.
b. Denver, Colo, 3/21/30; married; c. three. Polit. & Govt. Pos: Colo. State Rep, currently, chmn, Finance Cmt; mem, Gov. Local Affairs Study Cmn; mem. bd, Hemophilia Found. Bus. & Prof. Pos: Mem. staff, Bd. of Denver Educ. Sr. Citizens, Inc. Mem: Past pres, Denver Lodge 171, B'nai B'rith. Mailing Add: 3206 S. St. Paul St, Denver, Colo. 80210.

FRIEDMAN, EDWARD DAVID D
Consult, Cmn. on Rules, Dem. Nat. Conv.
b. Chicago, Ill, 5/2/12; s. Jacob Friedman and Bessie Levison F; m. 11/1/47 to Mary Louise Melia; c. Michael John, Daniel Shay, Maryel and Elizabeth Anne. Educ: Univ. Chicago, A.B. with honors, 35, James Nelson Raymond fel, 37; Univ. Chicago Law Sch, J.D. cum laude, 37; Order of the Coif; assoc. ed, Univ. Chicago Law Rev, 36-37; Order of the Wig and Robe. Polit. & Govt. Pos: Mem, gen. counsel's staff, Securities and Exchange Cmn, 39-43; chief counsel, Off. of Price Admin, 42-43; spec. asst. to solicitor, Dept. of Labor, 43-48, spec. asst. for. farm labor prog, Secy. of Labor, 65, dep. solicitor, Dept. of Labor, 65-69, acting solicitor, 69; exec. asst. to assoc. gen. counsel, div. of law, Nat. Labor Rels. Bd, 48-57, chief law officer, Fifth Regional Off, 57-59, asst. gen. counsel, Nat. Labor Rels. Bd, 59-60; mem, Garrett Park. Town Coun, Md, 54-58; labor counsel to U.S. Sen. John F. Kennedy, Mass, 60-61; mayor, Garrett Park, Md, 60-66; labor counsel to U.S. Sen. Wayne Morse, Ore, 61-65; labor counsel, U.S. Senate Labor and Pub. Welfare Cmt. and counsel, subcmts. on labor, manpower and railway retirement, 61-65; counsel, majority and minority floor mgrs. for U.S. Sen. Clark, Pa. and Case, N.J, Civil Rights Bill, 64; U.S. del, Orgn. for Econ. Coop. and Develop, Paris, France, 68; consult, cmn. on rules, Dem. Nat. Conv, currently. Bus. & Prof. Pos: Assoc, Rosenberg, Toomin & Stein, Chicago, Ill, 38-39; partner, Bernstein, Alper, Schoene & Friedman, Wash, D.C. 69- Publ: Racial Problems in Labor Relations: The Civil Rights Act, N.Y. Univ, Eighteenth Annual Conf. on Labor, 66; various law rev. articles, Univ. Chicago Law Rev. Mem: Am. and Fed. Bar Asns. Legal Res: 10702 Weymouth St, Garrett Park, Md. 20766. Mailing Add: 818 18th St. N.W, Washington, D.C. 20006.

FRIEDMAN, FRANCES R
Mem, Calif. State Rep. Cent. Cmt.
b. Brooklyn, N.Y, 6/28/27; d. Charles Nadell and Mollie Steinberg N; m. 5/18/46 to Al K. Friedman; c. Ellyn Jo, Steven Louis and Jeffrey Alan. Educ: Los Angeles City Col, 44-46. Polit. & Govt. Pos: Chmn, United Rep. Party, Calif, 63-64, chmn. 43rd Assembly Dist, 63-66; alternate del, Rep. Nat. Conv, 64; alternate mem, Los Angeles Rep. Co. Cent. Cmt, 64-67; mem, Calif. State Rep. Cent. Cmt, 64-, sect-area precinct chmn, 68-69. Bus. & Prof. Pos: Corp. secy, Cadillac Furniture Industs, 50; mem, Govt. Affairs Cmn, Calif. Mfrs. Assoc, 66. Mem: Los Angeles Co. Dist. Attorneys Adv. Cmt; PTA Pres, John Marshall High Sch, Los Angeles; Dir. and Charter Mem, Couples Club of Temple Israel, Hollywood. Rel: Jewish. Mailing Add: 2307 Inverness Ave, Los Angeles, Calif. 90027.

FRIEDMAN, IRVING D
b. 2/3/13; married. Educ: Baltimore Pub. Schs. Polit. & Govt. Pos: Md. State House of Dels, 65-67; 5th Dist. Dem. Club; Woodland Dem. Club; Admin. secy. to Mayors Grady and Goodman; secy. to Congressman Friedel. Bus. & Prof. Pos: Ins. broker. Mailing Add: 5973 West. Run Dr, Baltimore, Md. 21209. (1967)

FRIEDMAN, JIMMY ELIZABETH D
Mem, Dem. Cent. Cmt, La.
b. Bastrop, La, 10/16/12; d. James Higginbotham and Edna McElwee H; m. 6/19/35 to Sylvan N. Friedman; c. Samuel James. Educ: Northwestern State Col. Polit. & Govt. Pos: Mem, Dem. Cent. Cmt, La, 64- Bus. & Prof. Pos: Sch. teacher. Mem: Natchitoches Serv. League; Natchitoches Hist. Asn. Rel: Jewish. Mailing Add: Natchez, La. 71456.

FRIEDMAN, SOL J. D
Md. State Del.
b. Baltimore, Md, 3/20/19; married. Educ: Univ. of Baltimore, LL.B, 45. Polit. & Govt. Pos: Md. State Del, 55-; mem, Gov. Cmn. to Study Workmen's Compensation Laws; unit chief, enforcement sect, Off. of Price Admin. Mem: Am. Bar Asn; Jr. Bar Asn. of Baltimore City; Nat. Asn. of Claimants Compensation Attorneys; K. of P; Elks; Mason; Shrine; B'nai B'rith. Mailing Add: 115 Equitable Bldg, Baltimore, Md. 21202. (1967)

FRIEDMAN, SYLVAN N. D
La. State Sen.
b. Natchez, La, 5/19/08; s. Samuel Friedman; m. 6/19/33 to Elizabeth Higgenbothem; c. Sam. Educ: Tulane Univ, 24; Soule Bus. Col, 25. Polit. & Govt. Pos: Mem, Natchitoches Parish Police Jury, La, 32-44, pres, 36-44; La. State Rep, 44-52; La. State Sen, 52-, pres. pro tem, La. State Senate, 62-64. Bus. & Prof. Pos: Dir, Peoples Bank & Trust, Natchitoches, La, Progressive Mutual Bldg. & Loan and Valley Farmers Coop, currently. Mem: Elks; La. Cattlemens Asn.(pres, 48); v.pres, Am. Nat. Cattlemens Asn; Farm Bur; past pres, Lovely La. Tourism Asn; Mason; Shrine. Rel: Jewish. Mailing Add: Box 165, Natchez, La. 71456.

FRIEND, HARLAN DILLMAN D
Chmn, Liberty Co. Dem. Exec. Cmt, Tex.
b. Flora, Ill, 1/20/24; s. Harlan Downs Friend and Erba Dillman F; m. 9/21/52 to Dorothy Helen Weil; c. Shelley Anne, Harlan Jefferson and Shannon Lea. Educ: Baylor Univ, B.B.A, 49, LL.B, 56; Sigma Delta Chi; Delta Sigma Pi; Phi Delta Phi. Polit. & Govt. Pos: Del, Tex. Dem. State Conv, 56 & 66, Dem. Nat. Conv, 64; chmn, Planning and Zoning Cmn, Liberty, Tex, 58-62; City Attorney, Dayton, 60-; chmn, Liberty Co. Dem. Exec. Cmt, 60- Mil. Serv: Entered as Seaman, Navy, 42-46, serv. in S.Pac. Theater, 45-46; Asiatic Theater Ribbon; Good Conduct Medal. Publ: 'Tex Talks,' a polit. column, Waco Record, 47-48. Mem: Chambers-Liberty Co. Bar Asn, secy, 58, v.pres, 59 and pres, 60-61; State Bar of Tex; Tex. Trial Lawyers Asn; Am. Bar Asn; Mason; Elks; VFW; Am. Legion; Doberman Pinscher Club of Am. Rel: Unitarian. Legal Res: 110 Linden Lane, Liberty, Tex. 77575. Mailing Add: P.O. Box 151, Liberty, Tex. 77575.

FRIEND, HAZEL IRENE R
Mem, Calif. Rep. State Cent. Cmt.
b. Ray, Kans, 9/25/06; d. William Orvel Frazer and Mary Rice F; m. 8/21/29 to Cecil William Friend, wid; c. Mary Love (Mrs. Frederic P. Burnside) and Delores Darlene (Mrs. Herbert W. Speck). Educ: Southwest. Col, 24-25; Kans. State Teachers Col, Teachers Cert, 25; Kans. Teachers Normal, Co. Cert, 2 years; Delta Kappa Chi. Polit. & Govt. Pos: Asst. postmaster, Rolla, Kans, 25; mem, Calif. Rep. State Cent. Cmt, 67- Bus. & Prof. Pos: Piano teacher, private lessons, Rolla, Kans, 25-30 and teacher, Rolla Grade Sch, 26-30; manage own property, Bellflower, Calif. and Morton & Stevens Co, Kans. and Fla, 65-69. Mem: Bellflower Coun. of Rep. Women, Federated; Women's Club of Bellflower; PEO; sustaining mem, Rep. Party Nat. Hq; YMCA (century Club Mem, Los Cerritos Chap); S.W. Kans. Royalty Asn; patron mem, Cerritos Col. Commun. Serv; C. of C.(assoc. mem, Bellflower Chap); PTA. Plaque, Los Cerritos YMCA Century Club; Several cert. for vol. work in philanthropic orgn. such as Red Cross and Heart Found. Rel: Presbyterian. Mailing Add: 16910 S. Bixby Ave, Bellflower, Calif. 90706.

FRIEND, KELSEY E. D
Secy, Pike Co. Dem. Exec. Cmt, Ky.
b. Pikeville, Ky, 3/18/22; s. J.P. Friend and Clarrissa Mullins F; m. 8/11/45 to Margaret Jones Earp; c. Kelsey E, Jr, Joe Jett and Clarrissa Mauree. Educ: Pikeville Col, Teacher's Cert, 42; Univ. Ky. Law Sch, LL.B, 49; Duke Univ, LL.M, 50. Polit. & Govt. Pos: Master cmnr, 35th Judicial Dist, Pike Co, Ky, 50-52, commonwealth attorney, 58-63; co. attorney, Pike Co, 54-57; chmn, Pike Co. Dem. Exec. Cmt, 64-67, secy, 68- Bus. & Prof. Pos: Attorney-at-law, 49- Mil. Serv: Entered as Pvt, Army, 42, released as 1st Lt, 46, after serv. in Co. E, 357th Regt, 90th Inf. Div, ETO, 44-45; Maj, Army Res; Inf. Combat Badge; Purple Heart; Bronze Star Medal and First Oak Leaf Cluster; Victory Medal; ETO Medal with 3 Battle Stars. Mem: Ky. State Bar Asn; Mason; Noble, Mystic Shrine, El Hasa Temple, Ashland, Ky. Rel: Methodist. Legal Res: Route 1, Pikeville, Ky. 41501. Mailing Add: Box 771, Pikeville, Ky. 41501.

FRIES, DAVID JOHN Socialist
State Chmn, Socialist Party of Wis.
b. Racine, Wis, 3/9/30; s. John Andrew Fries, Jr. and Katherine M. Steketee F; m. 1/23/55 to Roberta Gail Krieger; c. John Andrew, III and Robert David Anthony. Educ: Univ. Wis, B.A, 52 and Law Sch, LL.B, 57. Polit. & Govt. Pos: Young Dem. rep, Dem. Party Admin. Cmt, Wis, 55-56 and mem-at-lg, 63-65; chmn, Jefferson Co. Dem. Party, 61 & 62; state chmn, Am. for Dem. Action, 65 & 66; v.chmn, Second Dist. Dem. Party, 65-69; city attorney, Watertown, Wis, 65-69; chmn, Jefferson Co. McCarthy for Pres. Cmt, 68; del, Dem. Nat. Conv, 68; alternate mem, Socialist Party Nat. Cmt, 68-; state chmn, Socialist Party of Wis, 68- Bus. & Prof. Pos: Attorney-at-law, Watertown, Wis, 59- Mem: State Bar of Wis; Commercial Law League of Am; Milwaukee Bar Asn; Jefferson Co. Asn. for Retarded Children (legis. chmn); prog. and polit. action chmn, Watertown Human Rels. Coun; Jefferson Co. Ment. Health Asn.(dir). Rel: Unitarian-Universalist. Mailing Add: 322 Riviera Lane, Watertown, Wis. 53094.

FRINK, BETTYE JEAN D
b. Crossville, Ala, 2/19/33; d. Lester Love Haynes and Edna Leora McMillian H; m. 7/7/51 to William David Frink; c. Victor Farrell, William D, Jr, Bettye Lynn and Leigh Ellen. Educ: High Sch; Bus. Col; Beta Club. Polit. & Govt. Pos: State auditor, Ala, 63-67, Secy. of State, 59-63; del, Dem. Nat. Conv, 60. Bus. & Prof. Pos: Chmn, Healing Arts Bd. of Ala, 60-63; v.pres, Jefferson Radio Corp, 58-61. Mem: League of Women Voters; Pilot Club; Bus. & Prfnl. Women's Club. Rel: Protestant. Mailing Add: Route 1, Odenville, Ala. 35120.

FRINK, GARY R. D
b. Pontiac, Mich, 1/22/33; s. Wayne C. Frink (deceased) and Helen Snyder F; m. 3/25/55 to Sherry Lou Rood; c. Christopher Rood and Geoffrey Richard. Educ: Mich. State Univ, 51-54; Univ. Americas, Mexico City, B.A, 55; Univ. Mich. Law Sch, LL.B, 63; Lambda Chi Alpha. Polit. & Govt. Pos: Legal asst, Off. Gen. Counsel, Dept. Commerce, 63-64; legis. asst, U.S. Rep. Weston E. Vivian, Mich, 65-66; spec. counsel, Task Force on Environ. Health, Dept. Health, Educ. and Welfare, 66-67; staff dir. and counsel, postal facilities and modernization subcmt, Post Off. and Civil Serv. Cmt, U.S. House of Rep, 67-68; Dem. cand, U.S. Rep, 19th Dist, Mich, 68. Bus. & Prof. Pos: Attorney-at-law, Elliott & Naftalin, 68- Mem: Mich, Fed. and Inter-Am. Bar Asns. Rel: Protestant. Legal Res: 115 LeGrande, Pontiac, Mich. 48058. Mailing Add: Suite 300, 1510 H St. N.W, Washington, D.C. 20005.

FRISBY, ROBERT W. R
b. Casper, Wyo, 9/23/20; s. J.E. Frisby and Bessie Snyder F; m. 4/14/43 to Peggy Holm; c. Robert E, Donald R. and Gloria J. Educ: Univ. Wyo, 38-41. Polit. & Govt. Pos: Co. assessor, Park Co, Wyo, 55-60; precinct committeeman, Park Co. Rep. Party, 60-64; co. chmn, Park Co. Rep. Cent. Cmt, 64-66; Rep. State Committeeman, Park Co, 66-68. Bus. & Prof. Pos: V.pres, First State Bank, Cody, Wyo, 60- Mil. Serv: Entered as Pvt, Air Force, 42, released as Capt, 46, after serv. in Air Transport Command, China-Burma-India, 45; India-Burma Campaign Ribbon. Mem: Exec. coun, Wyo. Bankers Asn; secy, bd. of trustees, Northwest Commun. Col; AF&AM; Rotary; Am. Legion. Rel: Methodist. Mailing Add: 2007 Newton Ave, Cody, Wyo. 82414.

FRITTER, LINDBERGH ALEXANDER R
Chmn, Stafford Co. Rep. Party, Va.
b. Stafford Co, Va, 5/25/28; s. Thomas Alexander Fritter and Grace Bell Randall F; m. 12/23/49 to Edna Catherine DeShields; c. Elizebeth (Mrs. Daniel Burton), Wendy Marie and Patricia Ann. Educ: Stafford High Sch, Va, 3 years. Polit. & Govt. Pos: Chmn, Stafford Co. Rep. Party, Va, 64- Mem: Moose. Rel: Methodist. Mailing Add: Route 3, Box 541, Stafford, Va. 22554.

FRITZ, ABNER MARVIN D
Mem, Calif. Dem. State Cent. Cmt.
b. New York, N.Y, 6/7/27; s. William Fritz and Minnie Silverman F; m. 7/30/61 to Sylvia Ann Labovitch; c. Marilyn E, Barbara J, William J, Claire R. and Susan C. Educ: San Jose State Col, A.B, 48; Santa Clara Univ, J.D, 62; Alpha Phi Omega. Polit. & Govt. Pos: Pres, Whittier Jefferson-Jackson Club, Calif, 58; del, Dem. Nat. Conv, 68; mem, Orange Co. Dem. Cent. Cmt, Calif, 68-; mem, Calif. Dem. State Cent. Cmt, 68-; chmn, Orange Co. Dem. Fedn, Calif, currently; pres, La Habra Dem. Club, currently. Bus. & Prof. Pos: Mem, Pac. Southwest Regional Adv. Bd, Anti-Defamation League, 69. Mil. Serv: Entered as Seaman, Navy, 44, released 46, after serv. on USS PC 576, Am. and European Theatres. Mem: Whittier Bar Asn.(treas, 68, secy, 69); Am, Calif. and Southeast Bar Asns; Whittier B'nai B'rith (pres, 65); Mason; Elks. Rel: Jewish. Legal Res: 9141 Gordon Ave, La Habra, Calif. 90631. Mailing Add: 12507 E. Philadelphia St, Whittier, Calif. 90601.

FRITZ, GEORGE H. R
Chmn, Barber Co. Rep. Cmt, Kans.
b. Lake City, Kans, 12/31/19; s. George Louis Fritz and Eliza Lane F; m. 8/16/42 to Dorothy A. Kimball; c. Janis Louise and Randy. Educ: Kans. State Univ, grad, 46; Farm House. Polit. & Govt. Pos: Mem. sch. bd, Brookville, Kans, 58-66; precinct committeeman, Brookville Rep. Party, 60-66; chmn, Barber Co. Rep. Cmt, 68- Bus. & Prof. Pos: Co. agr. agent, Hodgeman Co, Kans, 46-48; ranch mgr, CK Ranch, Brookville, 57-66; rancher, Lake City, 66- Mil. Serv: Entered as Pvt, Army, 42, released as T-4, 46, after serv. in Med. Corps, ETO, 44-46; Good Conduct Medal. Mem: Mason; Kans. Hereford Asn.(past pres); Am. Royal Bd. Gov; Kans. Livestock Asn.(resident-elect); Barber Co. Cattlemen's Asn.(secy-treas). Diamond Award, Kans. Livestock Asn, 57. Rel: Methodist. Mailing Add: Star Route, Box 9, Lake City, Kans. 67071.

FRITZSCHE, LEALAND CARL R
b. Glen Mary, Tenn, 7/25/06; s. Max Fritzsche and Emma Molyneux F; m. 4/30/30 to Nora Margared Grasham; c. Flora M.(Mrs. Don Barber). Educ: Rockwood High Sch; grad, 24. Polit. & Govt. Pos: Co. chmn, Rep. Party, Tenn, 51-56; alternate del, Rep. Nat. Conv, 56 and 64. Bus. & Prof. Pos: Merchant. Mem: Past v.pres, C. of C; Nat. Farmers Orgn; pres, past dir, Tenn. Walking Horse Breeders Asn. Rel: Presbyterian; Mem, Bd. Deacons. Mailing Add: 602 E. Lane St, Shelbyville, Tenn. 37160.

FRIZZELL, KENT R
Attorney Gen, Kans.
b. Wichita, Kans, 2/11/29; s. Elton Sanderson Frizzell (deceased) and Irma A. Hays F; m. 11/26/55 to Shirley Elaine Piatt; c. Gregory, Damon, Kirsten, Angela and Blaine. Educ: Friends Univ, B.A, 53; Washburn Univ. Law Sch, LL.B, 55; Phi Alpha Delta; Phi Kappa Psi. Polit. & Govt. Pos: Precinct committeeman, Co. Rep. Cent. Cmt, Kans, 51-66; pres, Wichita Bd. Educ, 59-65; mem, State Munic. Acct. Bd, 60-65; Kans. State Sen, 25th Sen. Dist, 65-69; Attorney Gen, Kans, 69- Bus. & Prof. Pos: Private law off, 55-63; partner, McCarter, Frizzell & Wettig, 63-68. Mil. Serv: Entered as Cpl, Marine Corps, 48, released as Sgt, 50. Mem: Am. Bar Asn; Am. Legion. Am. Legion Nat. Oratorical Contest winner and Methodist Church Nat. Pub. Speaking Contest winner, 47. Rel: Methodist. Legal Res: 8937 N.W. Rochester Rd, Topeka, Kans. 66617. Mailing Add: State Capitol, Topeka, Kans. 66612.

FRIZZELL, MARTHA McDANOLDS R
N.H. State Rep.
b. Branchville, N.J, 11/18/02; d. George A. McDanolds and Kate E. Roe M; m. 6/9/27 to Theodore J. Frizzell; c. Katherine (Mrs. Edwin E. Blaisdell), Theodora (Mrs. Gordon Duke Duncan), Elizabeth (Mrs. Allyn M. Bascom), Robert T. and James A; 15 grandchildren. Educ: Univ. N.H, B.S, 24; Columbia Univ. Polit. & Govt. Pos: Libr. trustee, Charlestown, N.H, over 25 years; N.H. State Rep, 51-; del, Constitutional Conv, 56 & 64; women's chmn, Rep. Party, Sullivan Co, 56-58; mem, New Eng. Bd. of Higher Educ, 57-64, exec. cmt, 60-64; chmn, Sullivan Co. Del, 59 & 63, clerk, 61. Publ: Second History of Charlestown, N.H. 55; History of Walpole. Mem: Farm Bur; Grange; pres, Women's Club; pres, N.H. OWLS, 63; pres, N.H. Libr. Trustee Asn, 62. Univ. N.H. Citation for Commun. Serv. Rel: Congregational; Trustee, N.H. Congregational Christian Conf. Mailing Add: Charlestown, N.H. 03603.

FRIZZELLE, DR. NOLAN R
b. Los Angeles, Calif, 10/16/21; s. Charles Henry Frizzelle and Marie Nolan F; m. 12/22/43 to Mary Lewis; c. Roger Scott, David Nolan, Diane and Robert Lewis. Educ: Stanford Univ; Univ. Calif, Berkeley; Univ. Calif, Los Angeles; Los Angeles Col. Optometry. Polit. & Govt. Pos: Cong. dist. dir, Calif. Rep. Assembly, 61-64, pres, 64-65; alternate to v.chmn, Calif. Del, Rep. Nat. Conv, 64; mem, Calif. Rep. State Cent. Cmt, 64-68. Mil. Serv: Entered as Pvt, Marine Corps, 43, released as 1st Lt, 46, after serv. in Pac. Theatre, 45-46. Mem: Orange Co, Calif. and Am. Optometric Asns. pres, Newport-Balboa Rotary Club, 60-61. Rel: Protestant. Legal Res: 412 E. 21st St, Newport Beach, Calif. 92660. Mailing Add: 833 Dover Dr, Newport Beach, Calif. 92660.

FROEHLICH, HAROLD VERNON R
Wis. State Assemblyman and Speaker, Wis. State Assembly
b. Appleton, Wis, 5/12/32; s. Vernon W. Froehlich (deceased) and Lillian Wohlfeil; single. Educ: Univ. of Wis, B.B.A, 59, Law Sch, LL.B, 62; Phi Kappa Phi. Polit. & Govt. Pos: Co-chmn. and treas, Outagamie Co. Young Rep, Wis, 56-57; dist. chmn, Wis. Fedn. Young Rep, 58, state treas, 59; precinct committeeman, Outagamie Co. Rep. Party, 56-62; chmn, Outagamie Co. Statutory Cmt, 58-62; Wis. State Assemblyman, 63-, chmn, Wis. Assembly Rep. Caucus, Wis. State Assembly, 65-67 and Speaker, 67- Bus. & Prof. Pos: Staff acct, Reuschlein & Storteon, CPA, 61; partner, Froehlich & Jensen, attorneys-at-law and Bollenbeck, Patterson, Froehlich, Jansen & Wylie, 64- Mil. Serv: Entered as A/S, Navy, 51, released as Aviation Electronics Technician 1/C, 55, after serv. in 30th Antisubmarine Squadron, European Occupation, 52-55; European Occupation and Good Conduct Medals. Mem: Cmt. on Legis, Wis. Soc. CPA, 63-66; chmn, Legis. Cmt, Northern Chap. of CPA, 66; Am. Inst. Cert. Pub. Accts; Am, Wis. and Outgamie Co. Bar Asns; Am. Asn. of Attorney-Cert. Pub. Accts; Am. Legion; VFW; Optimists. One of Wis. Five Outstanding Young Men, Wis. Jaycees, 67. Rel: Lutheran. Legal Res: 421 W. Sixth St, Appleton, Wis. 54911. Mailing Add: 322 E. College Ave, Appleton, Wis. 54911.

FROEHLKE, ROBERT FREDERICK R
Asst. Secy. of Defense for Admin.
b. Neenah, Wis, 10/15/22; s. Herbert O. Froehlke and Lillian P. Porath F; m. 11/9/46 to Nancy Jane Barnes; c. Bruce, Jane, Ann and Scott. Educ: Univ. Wis. Law Sch, Madison, LL.B, 49; Order of the Coif. Polit. & Govt. Pos: Asst. Secy. of Defense for Admin, 69- Bus. & Prof. Pos: Assoc. lawyer, McDonald & MacDonald, Madison, Wis, 49-50; prof, Univ. Wis. Law Sch, 50-51; legal adv, Sentry Ins. Co, 51-59, v.pres, sales, 67-68; exec. v.pres, Sentry Life Ins. Co, 59-67; resident v.pres, Sentry Ins, Boston, Mass, 68-69. Mil. Serv: Entered as Pvt, Army, 43, released as Capt, 46, after serv. in Inf, ETO, Mem: Am. and Wis. Bar Asns. Rel: Presbyterian. Mailing Add: 5440 Jordan Rd. N.W, Washington, D.C. 20016.

FROELICH, JACOB HENRY, JR. D
Chmn, Guilford Co. Dem. Exec. Cmt, N.C.
b. High Point, N.C, 9/29/30; s. Jacob Henry Froelich and Elizabeth Gaskins F; m. 6/20/53 to Mary Strickland; c. Mary Elizabeth, Jacob Henry, III and Samuel Blair. Educ: Woodberry Forest Sch, grad, 48; Univ. N.C, Chapel Hill, B.S, M.B.A; Scabbard and Blade; Beta Theta Pi; Alpha Phi Omega; Gorgon's Head Lodge. Polit. & Govt. Pos: Mem, city coun, High Point, N.C, 60-62; chmn, High Point Twp. Dem. Exec. Cmt, 62-68; chmn, Guilford Co. Dem. Exec. Cmt, 67-; v.chmn, N.C. Stadium Authority, 67-; del, Dem. Nat. Conv, 68. Bus. & Prof. Pos: Pres, Jake Froelich Veneers Inc, N.C, 64-69; v.pres, Froelich Co, 67-69; trustee, Univ. N.C, 67-; pres, Ply Prod. Inc, S.C, 68-69. Mil. Serv: Entered as 2nd Lt, Air Force, 54, released as 1st Lt, 56, after serv. in 1239th Air & Airways Commun. Squadron, Chaumont, France, 54-56. Mem: Rotary; Emerywood Country Club; String and Splinter Club; Young Man of the Year, High Point, N.C, 60. Rel: Episcopal. Legal Res: 606 Parkway, High Point, N.C. 27262. Mailing Add: Box 588, High Point, N.C. 27261.

FROHNMAYER, DAVID BRADEN R
Asst. to Secy, U.S. Dept. Health, Educ. and Welfare
b. Medford, Ore, 7/9/40; s. Otto J. Frohnmayer and Marabel Fisher Braden F; single. Educ: Harvard Col, A.B, magna cum laude, 62; Oxford Univ, B.A, 64; Univ. Calif. Berkeley, Sch. Law, J.D, 67; Phi Beta Kappa; Order of Coif; bd. ed, Calif. Law Rev, 65-67; grad. class speaker, 67. Polit. & Govt. Pos: Assoc. mem. and gen. counsel, San Francisco Co. Rep. Cent. Cmt, 68-69; mem, Calif. Rep. State Cent. Cmt, 68-69; asst. to the secy, U.S. Dept. Health, Educ. and Welfare, 69- Bus. & Prof. Pos: Law clerk, Frohnmayer, Lowry & Deatherage, Ore, 65; law clerk, Pillsbury, Madison & Sutro, Calif, 66 and assoc, 67-; consult, Adv. Cmt. Probate Law Rev, State of Ore, 66-69. Publ: 'The University and the Public: the Right of Access by Non-Students to Public University Property,' Calif. Law Rev, 66; 'The Left at Oxford,' Oxford Tory, 64. Mem: Am. and San Francisco Bar Asns; State Bar Calif; Barrister's Club San Francisco; Harvard Club San Francisco. Rhodes Scholar; Detur Prize, Harvard Col. Rel: Presbyterian. Mailing Add: Dept. Health, Education and Welfare, Room 5717, 300 Independence Ave. S.W, Washington, D.C. 20201.

FROMMELT, ANDREW G. D
Iowa State Sen.
b. Dubuque Co, Iowa, 10/18/21; m; c. one son and one daughter. Polit. & Govt. Pos: Iowa State Rep, 55th-57th Gen. Assemblies; Iowa State Sen, 58-, Minority Floor Leader, 59th, 60th and 63rd Gen. Assemblies, Majority Leader, 61st and 62nd Gen. Assemblies. Bus. & Prof. Pos: Ins. rep; real estate broker. Rel: Catholic. Mailing Add: Route 3, Box 269, Dubuque, Iowa 52001.

FROSCH, ROBERT ALAN
Asst. Secy. of the Navy for Research and Develop.
b. Bronx, N.Y, 5/22/28; s. Herman Louis Frosch and Rose Bernfeld F; m. 12/22/57 to Jessica Rachel Denerstein; c. Elizabeth Ann and Margery Ellen. Educ: Columbia Col, A.B, 47; Columbia Univ, A.M, 49, Ph.D, 52; Zeta Beta Tau; Phi Beta Kappa; Sigma Xi. Polit. & Govt. Pos: Dir, nuclear test detection, Adv. Research Projs. Agency, Dept. Defense, Wash, D.C, 63-65, dep. dir, 65-66, Asst. Secy. of the Navy for Research and Develop, 66- Bus. & Prof. Pos: Teacher, Pupin Physics Lab, Columbia Univ, 50-51; scientist, Hudson Labs, N.Y, 51-54, assoc. dir, 54-56 and dir, 56-63. Publ: Numerous scientific and technical articles. Mem: Vis. Cmt. Earth Sci, Mass. Inst. Tech; fel. Am. Asn. Adv. Sci; fel. Inst. Elec. and Electronics Engr; Am. Phys. Soc; Am. Geophys. Union; Seismological Soc. Am; Soc. Explor. Geophysicists; Marine Tech. Soc; Acoustical Soc. Am; Cosmos Club. Arthur S. Flemming Award, 66. Rel: Jewish. Mailing Add: 10105 Hurst St, Bethesda, Md. 20014.

FROST, DAVID GRIFFITH R
Ore. State Rep.
b. Cloquet, Minn, 8/14/35; s. O.W. Frost and Agnes Williams F; m. 6/10/56 to Barbara Mitchell; c. Griffith D, Kristin B, Katherine A. and Thomas M. Educ: Willamette Univ, B.A, 57; Willamette Univ. Col. of Law, LL.B, 60; Beta Theta Pi. Polit. & Govt. Pos: Ore. State Rep, Wash. Co, 67- Bus. & Prof. Pos: Attorney-at-law, Hillsboro, Ore, 60- Mem: Ore. and Am. Bar Asns; Am. Trial Lawyers Asn. Rel: Presbyterian. Legal Res: 1845 300 Ave. N.W, Hillsboro, Ore. 97123. Mailing Add: P.O. Box 438, Hillsboro, Ore. 97123.

FROST, FRANK LESLIE R
b. Crescent, Iowa, 7/12/98; s. Alexander Frost and Caroline Omeak F; m. 9/1/26 to Hazel Isabel Fugate; c. Carol Jean (Mrs. Chapman) and Jack Allan. Educ: Univ. Omaha. Polit. & Govt. Pos: Dir, Metrop. Utilities Dist, 41-, chmn. of bd, several times; past precinct chmn, past ward chmn, past mem, Douglas Co. Rep. Cent. Cmt. and Nebr. State Rep. Cent. Cmt. Mem: Am, Nebr. and Omaha Bar Asns; past Master, Masonic Blue Lodge; Scottish Rite; Mason (32°); K.T. York Rite Masons; past Potentate, Tangier Temple Shrine; past Worthy Patron, Eastern Star; past pres, Downtown Optimist Club; past pres, Allied Bus. Counsellors; past big chief, Tribe of Yessir, Omaha C. of C; past chmn. adv. bd, DeMolay; active in Order of Rainbow for Girls; Sq. and Compass Club; mem. bd. of dirs. and past pres, Travelers Protective Asn; Omaha Post; YMCA; Odd Fellows. Rel: Christian Church; mem. Off. Bd. and Trustee, First Christian Church, Omaha. Legal Res: 2381 S. 87th St, Omaha, Nebr. 68124. Mailing Add: 700 Keeline Bldg, Omaha, Nebr. 68102.

FROST, JACK WESLEY R
Chmn, Johnson Co. Rep. Cent. Cmt, Kans.
b. Kansas City, Mo, 3/14/33; s. Earl W. Frost and Esther Houston F; m. 12/27/54 to Doris Sites; c. Leigh C, Laura J, Lizabeth A. and John L. Educ: Univ. Kans, B.A. in Elec. Eng, 55; Sigma Tau; Phi Delta Theta. Polit. & Govt. Pos; Co. campaign mgr, Gov. William Avery, Kans, 64; committeeman, Johnson Co. Rep. Cent. Cmt, 65-, chmn, 67-; campaign mgr, Congressman Larry Winn, Third Dist, 66; city councilman, Prairie Village, 67- Bus. & Prof. Pos: V.pres, Nationwide, Inc, Chicago, Ill, 63-; pres, Hardin & Stockton Co, Kansas City, 64-; pres, Century Mortgage Corp, Prairie Village, 65-; chmn, Kans. Real Estate Cmn, 66-; dir, Ranchmart State Bank, Overland Park, 67-; v.pres, Lawyers Title Co. Kansas City, Olathe, 68- Mil. Serv: Entered as 2nd Lt, Air Force, 55, released as 1st Lt, 57, after serv. in 1885 AACS, Far East Command, Tokyo, 55-57, Res, 57-63. Mem: Nat. Asn. Real Estate Bd; Real Estate Bd. Kansas City, Mo; Real Estate Bd. Johnson Co, Kans; Cosmopolitan Club. Rel: Presbyterian. Mailing Add: 4401 W. 94th, Prairie Village, Kans. 66207.

FROST, JAMES L. 'JACK' R
Recorder, Brown Co, Ohio
b. Georgetown, Ohio, 3/14/06; s. Willie A. Frost and Mary J. Snider F; m. 10/5/40 to Florence Payne; c. Carol Ann and James L, Jr. Educ: Millers Bus. Col, 25-26; Univ. Cincinnati, 31-32. Polit. & Govt. Pos: Treas, Brown Co, Ohio, 45-61, recorder, 69-; Ohio State Rep, Brown Co, 61-67; state exam. of co. off, Bur. of Inspection and Supv. of Pub. Off; cand. for Co. Auditor. Bus. & Prof. Pos: Jack Frost's Ins. Agency, 35-; banker, Bank of Russellville, Ohio, 38- Mil. Serv: Entered as Pvt, Army, 42, released as Cpl, 43; Sharp Shooters Medal. Mem: DAV; Am. Legion; C. of C; Farm Bur; Farmers Union; State Grange. Rel: Church elder for 20 years. Mailing Add: 410 S. Main St, Georgetown, Ohio 45121.

FROST, NORMA W. R
Pres, Conn. Fed. of Rep. Women's Clubs
b. Miami Co, Ohio, 8/26/27; d. Fred J. Webster and Hazel Jones W; m. 9/6/47 to John E. Frost; c. Marcia, Lynn and James. Educ: Otterbein Col, $1\frac{1}{2}$ years; Tau Epsilon Mu. Polit. & Govt. Pos: Mem, Fairfield Rep. Town Cmt, Conn, 63-70, 9th dist. leader, 64-66, voter registrn. chmn, 65-66 and v.chmn, 66-70; state affairs chmn, Fairfield Co. Rep. Women's Asn, 64-66; first v.pres, Fairfield Rep. Women's Club, 66-68, pres, 69-; state affairs chmn, 4th Cong. Dist. Rep. Women's Asn, 66-69; mem, Fairfield Co. Rep. Orgn. and 4th Cong. Dist, Rep. Orgn, 66-70; alternate del, from 4th Cong. Dist, Rep. Nat. Conv, 68; first v.pres, Conn. Fedn. of Rep. Women's Clubs, 69- Bus. & Prof. Pos: Asst. med. lab. technician, Miami Valley Hosp, Dayton, Ohio, 47 and Miami Univ, 47-48; blood bank technician, St. Vincent's Hosp, Bridgeport, Conn, 63. Mem: Former officer, League of Women Voters; PTA; Fairfield Oratorio Soc. Rel: Protestant; mem, First Church of Christ choir. Mailing Add: 182 Hillcrest Rd, Fairfield, Conn. 06430.

FROST, ROBERT HOCKADAY D
Mo. State Rep.
b. Plattsburg, Mo, 8/4/99; s. Robert Carter Frost and Elizabeth Hockaday F; m. 7/16/21 to May L. Ray; c. Betty F.(Mrs. Walters), Robert H, Jr, Shirley A.(Mrs. Stoll) and Lewis F. Educ: Mo. Univ, 18-20; Kappa Sigma. Polit. & Govt. Pos: Prosecuting attorney, Clinton Co, Mo, 43-52; Mo. State Rep, 55-, chmn, Judiciary Cmt, Mo. House of Rep. Mil. Serv: Pvt, Army, 18. Mem: Chmn, Co. and Judicial Dist. Bar Asns; Mason; Shrine; Am. Legion; Farm Bur. Rel: Christian Church. Mailing Add: 101 Frost St, Plattsburgh Mo. 64477. (1967)

FROST, RUSSELL HASTINGS D
Secy, Hardin Co. Dem. Cent. and Exec. Cmts, Ohio
b. Kenton, Ohio, 10/5/38; s. Arthur Albert Frost and Betty Jail Hastings F; m. 9/3/61 to Marilee Mae Vance. Educ: Kenton High Sch, grad, 56. Polit. & Govt. Pos: Secy, Hardin Co. Dem. Cent. and Exec. Cmts, Ohio, 68-; Dem. nominee, councilman, Third Ward, Kenton, 69; sustaining mem, Ohio Dem. Party, 69-; mem, Hardin Co. Dem. Club, 69- Bus. & Prof. Pos: Fire fighter, Kenton Fire Dept, Ohio, 61-65; shoe salesman, Mason Shoe Co. Chippewa Falls, Wis, 68- Mil. Serv: Entered as Pvt, Army, 57, released as Pfc, 60, after serv. in 319th ASA Bn, Helmstedt, Germany, 58-60. Mem: UAW (trustee, Local 1437, 68-); Allied Indust. Workers Union (steward, chief steward, pres, Local 310, 66-68); Mem. Park Golf Club; Ohio Hardin Co. Automobile Club; Boy Scouts (asst. scoutmaster, Troup 125, 63-65). Little League (coach, Dodgers Club, 67-68). Rel: Methodist. Mailing Add: $209\frac{1}{2}$ W. Carrol St, Kenton, Ohio 43326.

FROST, THOMAS NEWTON D
Va. State Del.
b. Marshall, Va, 4/5/05; m. to Frances Hundley F. Educ: Va. Episcopal Sch. Polit. & Govt. Pos: Va. State Del, 52- Bus. & Prof. Pos: Automobile dealer; dir, Fauquier Nat. Bank. Mem: Rotary. Rel: Episcopal. Mailing Add: Warrenton, Va. 22186. (1967)

FRUGE, JACK C. D
Chmn, Evangeline Parish Dem. Exec. Cmt, La.
b. Mamou, La, 2/27/23; s. J. Cleveland Frugé and Georgianna Tate F.(deceased); m. 7/27/46 to Carmen LaFleur; c. Jack C, Jr, Christopher B. and Margaret Ann. Educ: Springhill Col, 40-41; Southwest. La. Inst, summer, 42; Loyola Univ, LL.B, 48. Polit. & Govt. Pos: Chmn, Evangeline Parish Dem. Exec. Cmt, La, 49-; chmn, La. Dem. State Cent. Cmt, 52-56; La. State Sen, 17th Dist, 56-68; mem, State Bd. Educ, Second Pub. Serv. Cmt. Dist, 62-68. Mil. Serv: Entered as Pvt, Army, 42, released as T/Sgt, 45, after serv. in Signal Corps, China-Burma-India Theater, 43-45; Am. Theater Campaign Medal; Asiatic-Pac. Campaign Medal with 3 Bronze Stars; Good Conduct Medal; Distinguished Unit Badge; Meritorious Unit Award; Victory Medal. Mem: Past pres, 13th Judicial Dist. Bar Asn, 59; La. and Am. Bar Asns; La. Law Inst. Farm Bur; K. of C; WOW; Am. Legion; VFW; C. of C; Evangeline Area and Evangeline Dist. Boy Scout Coun; Rotary. Rel: Catholic. Legal Res: 705 Hi-School Dr, Ville Platte, La. 70586. Mailing Add: 131 Court St, Ville Platte, La. 70586.

FRUITS, KATHERINE D
Married. Educ: Butler Univ, A.B; Delta Theta Tau. Polit. & Govt. Pos: Treas, 21st Ward Dem. Club and Marion Co. Dem. Women's Clubs, Ind; precinct committeeman, Dem. Party, ward v.chmn; relief investr, Gov. Unemploy. Relief Cmn; Ind. State Rep, 65-66. Mil. Serv: Chief Investr, Provost Marshal's Off. Mem: Women for Better Govt; Fedn. of Women's Clubs. Rel: Catholic. Mailing Add: 5801 Kingsley Dr, Indianapolis, Ind. 46220.

FRY, HOWARD M. R
Chmn, Rep. Finance Cmt. of Berks Co, Pa.
b. Reading, Pa, 2/7/31; s. Samuel R. Fry and Margaret Thun F; m. to Nancy L. Nickerson; c. Victoria Lee, Allison Brooks, Julia Nickerson and Howard Morton, III. Educ: Yale Univ, B.A, 53; Harvard Law Sch, LL.B, 57. Polit. & Govt. Pos: Del, Rep. Nat. Conv, 68; chmn, Rep. Finance Cmt. Berks Co, Pa, currently. Legal Res: 1156 Old Mill Rd, Wyomissing, Pa. 19610. Mailing Add: P.O. Box 679, Reading, Pa. 19603.

FRY, LESLIE McGEE R
Mem, Nev. Rep. State Cent. Cmt.
b. Louisiana, Mo, 3/13/13; s. Octa McGee Fry and Sallie Wilcoxen F; m. 5/2/36 to Jean Sauer; c. Leslie Mack, Maralyne (Mrs. Mallott), Sally (Mrs. Woycichowsky), Robert James and Stanley Preston. Educ: Univ. Mo, pre-law, 30-35; Univ. Louisville, LL.B, 40; Kappa Alpha. Polit. & Govt. Pos: Chmn, Washoe Co. Rep. Party, Nev, 56-58 & 64-66; mem, Nev. Rep. State Cent. Cmt, 56-; alternate del, Rep. Nat. Conv, 58 & 68. Bus. & Prof. Pos: Attorney, Reno, Nev, 39- Mil. Serv: Entered as 1st Lt, Army, 41, released as Maj, 46, after serv. in 37th Div. Field Artil, Pac. Theater, 42-45, Res, 45-66, Lt. Col. (Ret); Bronze Star. Mem: Am, Nev. and Washoe Co. Bars; Future Farmers Am.(nat. pres); Lions; Boy Scouts; VFW (nat. comdr-in-chief). Silver Beaver and Order of Antelope, Boy Scouts. Rel: Presbyterian. Legal Res: 991 Whitaker Dr, Reno, Nev. 89503. Mailing Add: 105 N. Sierra St, Reno, Nev. 89501.

FRYE, HENRY E. D
N.C. State Rep.
b. Ellerbe, N.C, 8/1/32; s. Walter A. Frye (deceased) and Pearl A. Motley F; m. 8/25/56 to Shirley Taylor; c. Henry Eric and Harlan Elbert. Educ: A&T State Univ, B.S, 53; Syracuse Univ. Law Sch, summer 58; Univ. N.C, Chapel Hill, J.D, 59; Alpha Kappa Mu; Beta Kappa Chi; Kappa Alpha Psi. Polit. & Govt. Pos: Asst. U.S. dist. attorney, U.S. Dept. of Justice, 63-65; N.C. State Rep, 69- Bus. & Prof. Pos: Prof, N.C. Col. Law Sch, 65-67; partner, Frye and Johnson, Attorneys, 68- Mil. Serv: Entered as 2nd Lt, Air Force, 53, released as 1st Lt, 55, after serv. in Eighth Fighter Bomber Wing, Korean Theatre, 54; Capt, Air Force Res, currently. Mem: Am, Nat, Fed, N.C. and Greensboro Bar Asns; Southeast. Lawyers Asn; v.pres, Greensboro Commun. Fel; C. of C; v.chmn, East. Dist, Boy Scouts; bd. dir, Jr. Achievement; bd. dir, N.C. Coun. on Human Rels; v.pres, Greensboro Legal Aid Found. First Negro State Representative in N.C. since 1899. Rel: Baptist. Mailing Add: 1920 Drexmore Ave, Greensboro, N.C. 27406.

FRYE, KIETH DUANE D
b. Chester, Nebr, 1/13/28; s. Clarence Henry Frye and Lulla Pressnall F; m. 11/24/48 to Norma Beth Johnson; c. Chris Douglas and Carla Beth. Educ: Byron High Sch, Nebr, $1\frac{1}{2}$ years. Mailing Add: Chester, Nebr. 68327.

FRYE, WILLIAM, III D
b. Pensacola, Fla, 4/20/29; s. John William Frye, Jr. and Louise Bennett F; m. 12/26/52 to Renée Lintz. Educ: Univ. Fla. Col. Law, LL.B, 57, J.D, 68; Fla. Blue Keys; Phi Alpha Delta; Sigma Phi Epsilon; Univ. Hall of Fame. Polit. & Govt. Pos: Asst. co. solicitor, Escambia Co, Fla, 59-60; pres, Escambia Co. Young Dem. Club, 59-61; state attorney, Fla, 61-66; dir, Escambia Co. Johnson Campaign, 64; del, Dem. Nat. Conv, 64; pres, Young Dem. Clubs of Fla, 64-65; circuit judge, First Judicial Circuit, Fla, 66- Mil. Serv: Entered as Pvt, Air Force, 48, released as S/Sgt, 52, after serv. in Korean Theater; Presidential Unit and S.Korean Presidential Unit Citations; Korean Campaign Ribbon with Five Stars; UN Ribbon; Good Conduct Medal. Mem: Pres, W.Fla. Coun. on Crime & Delinquency, 66-68; state treas, Fla. Prosecuting Attorneys Asn, 64-66; Am. and Fla. Bar Asns; Nat. Dist. Attorneys Asn; Soc. of the Bar, 1st Judicial Circuit; Fla. Coun. on Crime & Delinquency; Fla. Peace Officers Asn; Pensacola Jaycees; Elks; Pensacola Civitan Club; Fla. Chap. Arthritis Found, Fla. Alumni Asn. Elected as one of Fla. Five Outstanding Young Men, 65 and Young man of the Year of Escambia Co, Fla, 64. Rel: Methodist. Legal Res: Beard Lane, Shalimar, Fla. 32579. Mailing Add: Okaloosa Island Authority Bldg, Ft. Walton Beach, Fla. 32548.

FRYER, LESTER K. D
Pa. State Rep.
b. Colebrookdale Twp, Pa; s. William B. Fryer and Edna Hoffman F; m. to Mary Ellen Wolfe; c. Charles E. Educ: Army Finance Sch, Ft. Harrison. Polit. & Govt. Pos: Pres, Boyertown Dem. Club; chmn. bldg. cmt, Boyertown Area Schs; sch. dir, Colebrookdale Twp, 54-57; pres. of bd. and sch. dir. Boyertown Borough, 58-63; Pa. State Rep, 62- Bus. & Prof. Pos: Beverage distributor. Mil. Serv: Army, S/Sgt, 42-45; 8th Inf. Div, Normandy, N.France, Rhineland, Cent. Europe Campaigns. Mem: Past Condr, VFW; chmn, Boyertown Chap, Am. Red Cross; v.chmn, Boyertown Area United Fund; past pres, Boyertown Businessman's Asn. Mailing Add: 402 E. Third St, Boyertown, Pa. 19512.

FRYMIRE, RICHARD L. D
b. 1931. Educ: Centre Col, A.B; Univ. Ky, LL.B. Polit. & Govt. Pos: Ky. State Rep, 62-65; Ky. State Sen, 66-69, Majority Leader, Ky. State Senate, 68-69. Bus. & Prof. Pos: Attorney-at-law. Mil. Serv: Lt. Col, Marine Corps; Ky. Air Nat. Guard. Rel: Methodist. Legal Res: Madisonville, Ky. 42431. Mailing Add: Box 442, Moore, Morrow & Frymire, Madisonville, Ky. 42431.

FUDRO, STANLEY J. DFL
Minn. State Rep.
b. Minneapolis, Minn, 1918; m. to Ramona; c. Beth; Angelle; Lisa. Educ: St. Thomas Col; Univ. of Minn. Polit. & Govt. Pos: Minn. State Rep, 57- Bus. & Prof. Pos: Union bus. agent. Mil. Serv: Vet, World War II. Mem: Boys' dir, Northeast Neighborhood House; boxing coach, Margaret Barry Settlement House; Commun. Chest, Heart Fund; Mothers March on Polio Drives; Golden Gloves Boxing Cmt; Corker Club; 49 Centennial Club; Northeast Boosters Club. Mailing Add: 2322 Second St. N.E, Minneapolis, Minn. 55418. (1967)

FUGATE, JAMES BOYD D
Va. State Del.
b. Clinchport, Va, 11/2/20; m. to Margaret Eller F. Educ: Va. Polytech. Inst; King Col, Tenn. Polit. & Govt. Pos: Va. State Del, 60- Bus. & Prof. Pos: Livestock dealer, farmer and newspaper publisher. Mil. Serv: World War II. Mem: Am. Legion. Rel: Methodist. Mailing Add: Box 656, Gate City, Va. 24251.

FUGAZZI, FRED E. D
City Cmnr, Lexington, Ky.
b. Lexington, Ky, 2/26/15; s. Fred Fugazzi and Irene Joyce F; m. 6/4/38 to Betty Bruce Nunn; c. Betty Bruce (Mrs. Douglas Frisbie), Fred E, Jr. and Joyce Ann. Educ: Univ, Ky, A.B. in Econ, 37; Alpha Tau Omega; Newman Soc. Polit. & Govt. Pos: City cmnr. and mayor pro tem, Lexington, Ky, 50-52, mayor, 52-56 & 64-68, city cmnr, 68-; del, Dem. Nat. Conv, 68. Bus. & Prof. Pos: Pres, Paymaster Loans, Inc, Lexington, Ky, 47-; owner-partner, Mid State Distributing Co, 55- Mil. Serv: Entered as Ens, Signal Corps, Naval Res, 43, released as Lt, 46, after serv. in U.S.S. Charger, Atlantic Theatre; Lt.(Ret), Naval Res. Mem: Ky. Munic. League (pres); Ky. Consumer Finance Asn.(pres); mem. adv. bd, U.S. Conf. of Mayors; C. of C; Lexington Country Club; K. of C.(State Dep. and Grand Knight); Am. Legion; Navy League; Lexington Yacht Club (Comdr). Rel: Roman Catholic. Mailing Add: 274 S. Hanover Ave, Lexington, Ky. 40502.

FUGINA, PETER X. DFL
m. to Virginia Britt; c. Britt. Educ: Hamline Univ, B.S; Univ. of Minn; Univ. of Washington; Stanford Univ; Purdue Univ; Princetown Univ. Polit. & Govt. Pos: Minn. State Rep, 55-66, Minn. Adv. Cmt. on Compact for Educ; del, Va. Cent. Labor Union; dir, Iron Range Rehabilitation Center. Bus. & Prof. Pos: Pub. sch. instr; ins. and real estate; bd. mem, Range Ment. Health Center. Mil. Serv: Navy, Amphibious Forces, S.Pac. Mil. Govt. in Japan, Korea. Mem: Va. Kiwanis; K. of C; Elks; Moose; VFW; Am. Legion; Am. Fed. of Teachers; NEA; Am. Personnel & Guidance Asn. Mailing Add: 5 Merritt Dr, Virginia, Minn. 55792. (1967)

FUHR, JOHN D. R
Colo. State Rep.
b. Aledo, Ill, 9/9/28; married; c. Three. Educ: Colo. State Univ, Vet. degree. Polit. & Govt. Pos: Colo. State Rep, 66- Bus. & Prof. Pos: Vet, owner of Aurora Animal Hosp. and Broadview Kennels. Mem: State legis. chmn, Colo. Vet. Med. Soc; past pres, Aurora C. of C; Rotary; Shrine. Aurora Distinguished Serv. Award for Commun. Serv, 64. Mailing Add: 11075 E. Colfax Ave, Aurora, Colo. 80010. (1967)

FUKUSHIMA, YASUTAKA R
b. Honolulu, Hawaii, 6/3/16; s. Mutsuo Fukushima and Koyo Shimura F; m. 3/31/43 to Helen Kawano; c. Everett Alan, Susan Naomi and Howard Mutsuo. Educ: Univ. of Hawaii, B.A, 37; Harvard Law Sch, LL.B, 40. Polit. & Govt. Pos: Asst. pub. prosecutor, City and Co. of Honolulu, Hawaii, 46-47; del, Constitutional Conv, 50; mem, House of Rep, Territory of Hawaii, 50-59; Hawaii State Sen, 59-66; judge, First Circuit Court, Honolulu, 67- Mil. Serv: Entered Army, 43, released 45, after serv. in 100th Inf. Bn, ETO, 43-44 and War Crimes Cmn, Manila and Tokyo, 45. Mem: Bar Asn. of Hawaii; Am. Bar Asn. Rel: Congregational. Mailing Add: 2386 E. Manoa Rd, Honolulu, Hawaii 96822.

FULBRIGHT, JAMES WILLIAM D
U.S. Sen, Ark.
b. Sumner, Mo, 4/9/05; s. Jay Fulbright and Roberta Waugh F; m. 6/15/32 to Elizabeth Kremer Williams; c. Elizabeth (Mrs. John Winnacker) and Roberta (Mrs. Thaddeus Foote). Educ: Univ. Ark, B.A, 25; Oxford Univ, Pembroke, Rhodes Scholar, B.A, 28 and M.A, 31; George Wash. Univ. Law Sch, LL.B. with distinction, 34; Sigma Chi. Hon. Doctorate, Oxford Univ, 53. Polit. & Govt. Pos: Spec. attorney, Anti-Trust Div, Dept. of Justice, 34-35; U.S. Rep, Ark, 43-44, mem, For. Affairs Cmt, U.S. House of Rep; U.S. Sen, Ark, 45-, chmn, Cmt. on For. Rels, mem. Finance Cmt. and Joint Econ. Cmt. and chmn, Banking and Currency Cmt, 55-59; U.S. del. to UN Gen. Assembly, 54. Bus. & Prof. Pos: Lectr. law, George Wash. Univ, 35-36; instr. law, Univ. Ark, 36-39, pres, 39-41. Publ: Prospects for the West, Harvard Univ. Press, 63; Old Myths and New Realities, 64 and Arrogance of Power, 66, Random House. Rel: Disciples of Christ. Legal Res: Fayetteville, Ark. 72701. Mailing Add: Senate Office Building, Washington, D.C. 20510.

FULFORD, ED D
b. Dawson, Ga, 7/22/20; s. Stephen David Fulford and Rushie Miller F; m. 8/10/39 to Donna Lee Newton; c. Ed T, Jr, Donna Gail. Educ: Dawson High Sch. Polit. & Govt. Pos: Ga. State Rep, 63-66. Bus. & Prof. Pos: Merchant, West. Auto Store. Mil. Serv: WW II, 42-45, ETO, Sgt; enlisted Ga. Nat. Guard, 11/47-; V.pres, Nat. Guard Asn. of Ga, 61-62. Mem: W.O.W; Mason; Shrine;

VFW; Am. Legion; Rotarian; Chmn, Merchants Asn, Terrell Co, 57-58, 60-61; Dir, Terrell Co. C. of C, 62. Rel: Baptist. Mailing Add: Dawson, Ga. 31742. (1967)

FULFORD, WILLIAM EDMOND D
Fla. State Rep.
b. Orlando, Fla, 7/9/23; s. Jesse Curtis Fulford and Effie Hansel F; m. 6/22/43 to Mary Ramsey; c. Danny, Mickey, Pat and Jeff. Educ: Univ. Fla, 41. Polit. & Govt. Pos: Fla. State Rep, 66- Bus. & Prof. Pos: Pres, Fulford Van & Storage Co, Inc, Orlando, Fla, 48- Mil. Serv: Entered as Aviation Cadet, Army Air Corps, 42, released as 1st Lt, 45, after serv. in 26th Fighter Squadron, 14th Air Force, China-Burma-India Theatre, 43-44; Air Medal; Distinguished Flying Cross. Mem: Past pres. and hon. life mem, Orange Co. Sportsmen's Asn; past pres, Fifty Dist. Sportsmen's Asn; past dir, Fla. Wildlife Fedn; C. of C; Farm Bur; Seminole Co. Sportsmen's Asn. Rel: Protestant. Legal Res: 3221 Alamo Dr, Orlando, Fla. 32805. Mailing Add: P.O. Box 1226, Orlando, Fla. 32801.

FULKS, PAUL MOODY D
b. Paris, Tex, 10/3/03; s. James Aubrey Fulks and Eva Jane Jackson F; m. 3/8/24 to Oza Nicholson; c. Paul M, Jr. Educ: High Sch. and Col. exten. courses; Sigma Delta Chi. Polit. & Govt. Pos: Chmn, Tex. Aeronauts Cmn, 58-66, mem, 66-; mem, Tex. State Dem. Exec. Cmt, 62-68. Bus. & Prof. Pos: Co-owner and publisher, Lamar Co. Echo, Paris, Tex, 22-25; sales mgr, Liner Newspaper Syndicate, Chicago, 26-30; pres, Tex. Tag & Specialty Co, Wolfe City, Tex, 31- Mem: Tex. Press Asn.(pres, 48-49); North and East Tex. Press Asn.(pres, 46-47); charter mem, Nat. Pilots Asn.(dir, 54-55); Tex. Private Flyers Asn.(pres, 50-51); Am. Soc. Am. Arms Collectors. Winchester Firearms Collector; many nat. awards for best hist. collection in nation. Rel: Methodist. Legal Res: 103 Santa Fe St, Wolfe City, Tex. 75496. Mailing Add: Drawer D, Wolfe City, Tex. 75496.

FULLE, FLOYD THEODORE R
Chmn. Exec. Cmt, Cook Co. Rep. Cent. Cmt, Ill.
b. Chicago, Ill, 2/15/21; s. Fred A. Fulle and Bernice Rasch F; m. to Patricia Lowry; c. Ricky, Talbert and Michael. Educ: Knox Col, A.B, 42; Phi Delta Theta. Polit. & Govt. Pos: Asst. precinct capt, precinct capt. and twp. co-ordinator, Maine Twp. Regular Rep. Orgn, 49-61, chmn. twp. Rep. reorgn. cmt, 61, committeeman, 63-; co. cmnr, Cook Co, 64-; treas, Suburban Committeemen's Asn, 64-; chmn. audit and budget cmt, Cook Co. Rep. Cent. Cmt, 64-, chmn, exec. cmt, 66-; del, Rep. Nat. Conv, 68. Bus. & Prof. Pos: Founder and publisher, Suburban Progress; owner, Rosemont Publ; co-owner, Des Plaines Travel Agency. Mil. Serv: Entered as 2nd Lt, Army, 42, released as Maj, 47, after serv. in 379th Transportation Corps and 248th TRK Bn, Mediterranean, European and Philippine Theaters, 42-45, Lt. Col, Res; Bronze Star. Mem: Cook Co. Suburban Publishers Asn.(pres, 58); Ill. Press Asn; Sigma Delta Chi; Chicago Press Club; Headline Club; Ill. Nat. Guard (pres, 228th Inf. Officers Asn, 33rd Div, 51); pres, U.S. Army Res. Officer's Res. Training Session, Ft. Benning, Ga, 58-60; Lions (pres, Edison Park Club, 49-50); Mason; Shrine; Am. Legion; VFW; Boy Scouts (dir, Northwest Suburban Coun); YWCA (mem. adv. bd. and past dir, Northwest Suburban Branch). Best Ed. Award, Ill. Press Asn, 55; Am. Legion Americanism Award for Ed, 58; Outstanding Serv. Award, Jr. C. of C, 60; Ill. Award for Prom Traffic Safety, 65; Knox Col. Alumni Achievement Award, 66. Rel: Protestant. Mailing Add: 666 Laurel Ave, Des Plaines, Ill. 60016.

FULLER, CHARLES EUGENE, JR. D
Chmn, Chambers Co. Dem. Exec. Cmt, Ala.
b. LaFayette, Ala, 7/26/09; s. Charles Eugene Fuller, Sr. and Daisy Schuessler F; m. 9/20/34 to Mary Faye Riser; c. Frieda (Mrs. Gibbons), Charles Eugene, III, Mary Faye, Cecelia, Roseanne and William Riser. Educ: Univ. Ala, B.A, 31; Auburn Univ, 32; Phi Gamma Delta. Polit. & Govt. Pos: Dep. solicitor, Chambers Co, Ala, 37-38 & 50-56; mem, Interstate Commerce Cmn, 40; chmn, Chambers Co. Dem. Exec. Cmt, 42-; mem, Ala. Dem. State Exec. Cmt; mem, League of State Dem. Exec. Cmts. of the Co. Dem. Cmts. of Ala. Bus. & Prof. Pos: Attorney-at-law, LaFayette, Ala, 31- Mem: State of Ala. Bar Asn; charter mem, LaFayette Rotary Club. Rel: Methodist. Legal Res: 308 S. LaFayette St, LaFayette, Ala. 36862. Mailing Add: Court House, LaFayette, Ala. 36862.

FULLER, DENNIS L. D
b. Medical Springs, Ore, 8/4/22; s. James Fuller and Edna B. Turner F; m. 5/4/46 to H. Betty Tanner; c. James D, Richard T, Christopher C, Keri E. and Katrina Jo. Educ: Baker Bus. Col, 46. Polit. & Govt. Pos: Clerk, Baker Co, Ore, 60-; chmn, Baker Co. Dem. Cent. Cmt, 62-66. Mil. Serv: Entered as Pvt, Army, 42, released as Tech 4/C, 46, 231st Gen. Hosp, Japan; ETO and Asiatic Pac. Theater Campaign Ribbons; Philippine Liberation Medal; Sgt. Major E-9, Ore. Nat. Guard, 47-66. Mem: Past comdr, Post 3048, VFW; Lions; PTA. Rel: Latter-day Saint. Mailing Add: 2580 17th Baker, Ore. 97814.

FULLER, DON EDGAR R
Chmn, Ross Co. Rep. Cent. Cmt, Ohio
b. Columbus, Ohio, 8/9/28; s. Francis Edgar Fuller and Irene Hagerson F; m. 11/24/53 to Virginia Rose Ashmore; c. John, Leslee, Ralph, Donna, Ginger, Frank and Christie. Educ: Ohio State Univ, B.A, 50; Franklin Univ, J.D, 54; Beta Theta Pi; Phi Delta Phi. Polit. & Govt. Pos: Rep. cent. committeeman, Ross Co, Ohio, 62-; secy, Ross Co. Rep. Exec. Cmt, 62-68; asst. city solicitor, Chillicothe, 65-67, city solicitor, 68-; chmn, Ross Co. Rep. Cent. Cmt, 66- Bus. & Prof. Pos: Attorney-at-law, Chillicothe, Ohio, 54- Mem: Lions (past pres, Chillicothe Eve. Club); Am, Ohio State and Ross Co. Bar Asns; bd. dirs, Ross Co. YMCA. Rel: Presbyterian; Bd. Deacons, First Presby. Church. Mailing Add: 173 Sharon Rd, Chillicothe, Ohio 45601.

FULLER, FRANKLIN APOLLOS R
Mem, Suffield Rep. Town Cmt, Conn.
b. Suffield, Conn, 6/27/21; s. Henry Fuller and Hattie Johnson F; m. 10/1/44 to Gloria Marion. Educ: Univ. Conn, B.A, 43; Theta Xi. Polit. & Govt. Pos: Mem, Suffield Rep. Town Cmt, 48-; mem, Suffield Civic Center Bldg. Cmt, 62; mem, State Legis. Cmt. Study Dredging of Conn. River, 63-65; Conn. State Rep, 63-67. Mem: Conn. Independent Ins. Agents Asn; Mutual Ins. Agents Asn; Suffield Rotary (past pres); AF&AM; Mason (32°); Eastern Star; Grange. Rel: Second Baptist Church. Mailing Add: 1189 Mapleton Ave, Suffield, Conn. 06078.

FULLER, FRED ARCHIE, JR. D
S.C. State Rep.
b. Laurens, S.C, 3/6/20; s. Fred A. Fuller and Mary Reid F; m. 4/27/46 to Anne Campbell F; c. Preist, Fred III, Jane and Anne. Educ: The Citadel, B.S, 43. Polit. & Govt. Pos: S.C. State Rep, 59- Bus. & Prof. Pos: Pres. and treas, Fred A. Fuller Appliances, Inc, Greenville. Mil. Serv: 1st Lt, Air Force, 42-45. Mem: Rotary; Mason; Elks. Rel: Baptist. Mailing Add: Box 76, Greenville, S.C. 29602. (1967)

FULLER, JOSEPH C. D
b. Lakeland, Fla, 2/15/22; s. Robert Barnwell Fuller and Mabel Cardwell F; m. 11/23/49 to Audrey McClelland; c. Joseph C, Jr, George Barnwell, John Douglas and Audrey Naomi. Educ: Univ. of the South, Tenn, B.A, 44; Univ. Fla, B.S.A, 48; Kappa Alpha; Order of Gownsmen; Green Ribbon Soc; German Club. Polit. & Govt. Pos: Admin. Asst. to Speaker, Fla. House of Rep; formerly Admin. Asst. to State Chmn, Fla; exec. dir, S.W. Fla. Water Mgt. Dist, 62; admin. dir, Fla. Citrus Cmn, 57-58; admin. asst. to mem. of Cong, 54-57. Mil. Serv: Entered as Pvt, Army, 44, released as 1st Lt, 46, after serv. in Mil. Intel, Asiatic-Pac. Area, also serv. during Korean War; Capt.(Ret), Army Res. Mem: Am. Legion; Elks; Fla. Sheriffs Asn; Kiwanis. Rel: Episcopal. 1967 Legal Res: 5000 18th Ave. W, Bradenton, Fla. 33505. No mailing address available. (1967)

FULLER, LOREN WILLIAM R
b. Warren, Vt, 6/23/90; m. to Gertrude Kingsbury. Educ: Warren Graded Sch. Polit. & Govt. Pos: Former town fire warden, Warren, Vt, overseer of the poor, 15 years, selectman, 12 years and town lister, 6 years; Vt. State Rep, 63-67. Bus. & Prof. Pos: Farmer; blacksmith. Mem: Grange. Rel: Congregational. Mailing Add: Warren, Vt. 05674. (1967)

FULLER, RALPH C. R
Chmn, Luce Co. Rep. Cmt, Mich.
b. Newberry, Mich, 2/7/15; s. Edward R. Fuller and Clara Miller F; m. 4/12/42 to Marjorie McMahon; c. Melissa C, Jane E. and Virginia G. Educ: Mich. State Univ, 36-40. Polit. & Govt. Pos: Clerk, McMillan Twp. Bd, Mich, 41-42 & 47-65; v.chmn, Luce Co. Rep. Cmt, Mich, 50-51, chmn, 52-; mem, Mich. Tourist Coun, 64- Bus. & Prof. Pos: Pres, Newberry Indust. Develop. Corp, 60- Mil. Serv: Entered as Pvt, Air Force, 43, released as Sgt, 46, after serv. in Air Transport Command, ETO, 45; Good Conduct Medal; ETO and Am. Theater Ribbons. Mem: F&AM; Shrine; Elks; Odd Fellows; Am. Legion; VFW; Newberry Golf Club; C. of C. Rel: Presbyterian. Mailing Add: 205 W. Truman Ave, Newberry, Mich. 49868.

FULLER, ROBERT TURNER R
Mem. Exec. Cmt, Seekonk Rep. Town Cmt, Mass.
b. Pawtucket, R.I, 8/6/32; s. John Richard Fuller and Alice Kirkham F; m. 4/21/56 to Marjorie Ruth Drummond; c. Robert Charles, Steven John and Deborah Jean. Educ: Univ. R.I, 50-52; Bryant Col, B.S. in acct, 58. Polit. & Govt. Pos: V.chmn, Seekonk Rep. Town Cmt, Mass, 63-64, chmn, 64-65 and mem. exec. cmt, 65-; area coordinator, Volpe for Gov. Cmt, 64; mem, Seekonk Elem. Sch. Bldg. Cmt, 65- Bus. & Prof. Pos: Cost acct. and mgr. of data processing, Cumberland Eng. Co, Inc, Providence, R.I, 59-66; asst. gen. mgr, Greenhaugh Mills Inc, Pawtucket, 66- Mil. Serv: Entered as Seaman, Coast Guard, 52, released as Yeoman 2/C, 56. Mem: Nat. Asn. of Accts; F&AM, E.L. Freeman Lodge; adv, DeMolay; YMCA; Seekonk Scholarship Fund. Rel: Protestant. Mailing Add: 450 Cole St, Seekonk, Mass. 02771. (1967)

FULLER, VINCENT CEFALU R
Chmn, Hall Co. Rep. Party, Ga.
b. Atlanta, Ga, 10/19/12; s. John Lambert Fuller and Annie Shaw F; m. 1/15/38 to Emily Parker Burns; c. Vincent Garth and Melissa (Mrs. Michael Bel Welborn). Educ: Univ. of Ga, Gainesville Exten, 1 year. Polit. & Govt. Pos: Petition chmn, Jack Prince Cong. Campaign, Ga, 64; Hall Co. Del. to Ninth Dist. Rep. Conv, 66 & 68, State Rep. Conv, Macon, 66 and Atlanta, 68; ninth dist. finance chmn, Howard H. Callaway Gubernatorial Campaign, 66; Rep. precinct chmn, Flowery Branch, 66-68; secy. and mem. exec. cmt, Ninth Dist. Rep. Party, 66-68; precinct del, Hall Co. Rep. Conv, 66 & 68; chmn, Hall Co. Rep. Party, 66- Bus. & Prof. Pos: Various pos. to utility foreman, Lago Oil & Transport Co. Ltd, Aruba, Netherland Antilles, 31-42, various supvry. pos. to supt, gen. serv. dept, 43-63; parent bottler's rep, The Coca Cola Bottling Co, Atlanta and Dallas, 42-43; partner, Harte Develop. Co. and Frances Blankenship Realty, Atlanta, 64-65; plant supt, Chattahoochee Furniture Co, Flowery Branch, 67-68; sales rep, Develo Corp, Atlanta, 69- Mem: Kiwanis. Rel: United Methodist. Legal Res: Blue Waters Dr, Paradise Point, Flowery Branch, Ga. 30542. Mailing Add: Route 1, Box 201, Flowery Branch, Ga. 30542.

FULLER, WAYNE CLYDE R
b. Starksboro, Vt, 7/26/93; m. to Bertha Alger; c. One son and two daughters. Educ: Bristol High Sch. Polit. & Govt. Pos: Chmn, Bristol Rep. Town Cmt; Justice of the Peace, 5 years; constable and tax collector, 12 years; overseer of the poor, 4 years; selectman, 6 years; Vt. State Rep, 51-53 & 65-67. Bus. & Prof. Pos: Farmer; ins. agent. Mem: Trustee, Lincoln Cemetery Asn; Walter S. Burnham Found. Fund; F&AM; Farm Bur; Grange; Lincoln Vol. Fire Dept. Rel: Baptist. Mailing Add: R.F.D. 1, Bristol, Vt. 05443. (1967)

FULLER, WAYNE P. D
Chmn, Canyon Co. Dem. Cent. Cmt, Idaho
b. Twin Falls, Idaho, 8/19/32; s. Wesley M. Fuller and Elsa Rosenbaum F; m. 8/31/54 to Margaret Denison Cathcart; c. Douglas, Leslie, Neal, Hilary and Stuart. Educ: Stanford Univ, B.A, 54, LL.B, 57; Phi Beta Kappa; Los Arcos Club; Alpha Phi Omega; Phi Alpha Delta; Stanford Polit. Union. Polit. & Govt. Pos: Dep. prosecuting attorney, Canyon Co, Idaho, 59-60; precinct committeeman, Caldwell Dem. Party, 62-66; finance chmn, Canyon Co. Dem. Cent. Cmt, 64-65, chmn, 66-; state finance chmn, Idaho Dem. Party, 65-66. **Bus.**

& Prof. Pos: Partner, Brauner & Fuller, Attorneys, Caldwell, 59-66; partner, Brauner, Fuller & Doolittle, 66- Mil. Serv: Entered as Pvt, Army Res, 55, released as Capt, 66, after serv. in Judge Adv. Gen. Detachment, Sixth Army, U.S, 59-66. Publ: 'Defining a Liberal,' Caldwell News Tribune, 11/66; 'A Review of Legal Insurance,' Advocate, 2/69. Mem: Am, Idaho and Third Dist. Bar Asns; Canyon Co. Lawyer's Club; Lions; Elks; C. of C; dist. coun, Boy Scouts Am. Rel: Presbyterian. Legal Res: 1910 Ray Ave, Caldwell, Idaho 83605. Mailing Add: P.O. Box 130, Caldwell, Idaho 83605.

FULLERTON, BERT R
b. Correctionville, Iowa, 10/11/02; s. Alex.H. Fullerton and Elsie Bower F; wid; c. Mary (Mrs. Gary Meyers) and Rev. Dean Fullerton. Polit. & Govt. Pos: Dir, Bd. of Educ, Correctionville, Iowa, 32-40; twp. clerk, 32-54; Rep. precinct committeeman, 34-40; mem, City Coun, 40; bd. mem, Woodbury Co. Selective Serv, 40-48; Iowa State Rep, 67-69. Bus. & Prof. Pos: Dir, Farmers Coop. Elevator, 44-52. Mem: Pres, Co. Farm Bur, 50-51; Mason; Eastern Star; Scottish Rite; Shrine; West. Iowa Experimental Farm Asn. W.G. Shelly Agr. Achievement Award. Rel: Methodist. Mailing Add: Correctionville, Iowa 51016. (1967)

FULLMER, DONALD K. R
State Committeeman, Wash. Rep. Party
b. Rockyford, Colo, 4/11/15; s. Clinton G. Fullmer and Florence Kitchen F; m. 6/5/34 to Ardyth N. Creesy; c. Robert E, Maxine (Mrs. Duffield) and Phyllis (Mrs. Danielson). Educ: Am. Col. Life Underwriters, C.L.U, 67. Polit. & Govt. Pos: Chmn, Group Harbor Co. Rep. Party, Wash, 64-68, precinct committeeman, 64-69, state committeeman, Wash. Rep. Party, 69- Bus. & Prof. Pos: Life underwriter, N.Y. Life, 54- Mil. Serv: Entered as Pfc, Army, 45, released as Pfc, 45, after serv. in Ground Forces. Mem: Twin Harbor Life Underwriters Asn; Wash. State Asn. Life Underwriters (pres); Kiwanis; Mason. Rel: Methodist. Mailing Add: P.O. Box 611, Montesano, Wash. 98563.

FULLMER, WAYNE J. D
b. New Virginia, Iowa, 1/2/16; s. Glenn B. Fullmer and Leila Jane F; m. 12/27/38 to Ruby Rhoades; c. Bruce K. Educ: Newton Comun. High Sch. Polit. Pos: Iowa State Rep, 66; Del, Last Four Dem. State Convs; Former Mayor and City Councilman; Mem, Future Planning and Zoning Cmn. Bus. & Prof. Pos: Merchant. Rel: Lutheran. Mailing Add: 118 Oakwood Dr, Newton, Iowa 50208. (1967)

FULMER, EUGENE M. R
Pa. State Rep.
b. Ephrata Twp, Pa, 11/17/17; s. H.W. Fulmer and Elizabeth F. Educ: Pa. State Univ, B.S; Gould Acad; Northeast. Inst. for Commercial and Trade Asn. Execs, Yale Univ. Polit. & Govt. Pos: Pa. State Rep, 58- Bus. & Prof. Pos: Part-time instr, Pa. State Univ, 52-55; pub. rels. counsel. Mil. Serv: Army, Inf. Mem: Exec. secy, State College Area C. of C, 51-58; exec. v.pres, Pa. Home Builders Asn; Pa. State Alumni Club of Centre Co; Am. Legion; 40 et 8; F&AM; Consistory; Mason; Moose; Amvets; past pres, Pa. Rural Youth Asn. Outstanding Independent Man Award, Pa. State Club, 48. Mailing Add: 221 S. Barnard St, State College, Pa. 16801. (1967)

FULTON, JAMES G. R
U.S. Rep, Pa.
b. Allegheny Co, Pa, 3/1/03; s. James Ernest Fulton and Emilie Fetterman F; single. Educ: Pa. State Univ, A.B, 24; Harvard Law Sch, LL.B, 27; Carnegie Inst. Tech, 28-29; Phi Delta Theta. Polit. & Govt. Pos: Pa. State Sen, 45th Dist, 39-40; solicitor, Dormont Borough, 42; U.S. Rep, 27th Dist, Pa, 45-, mem, Sci. and Astronautics and For. Affairs Cmts, chmn, Subcmts. for Europe and to Investigate Displaced Persons; U.S. del, UN Gen. Assembly, 59; del, Rep. Nat. Conv, 68. Bus. & Prof. Pos: Banking attorney, Alter, Wright & Barron, 28-42; owner, Mt. Lebanon News, Boro News, News Progress, Chartiers Valley Times Progress, News Tribune & Dormont News, Allegheny Co, Pa. Mil. Serv: Entered as Lt, Navy, 42, released, 44, after serv. in Pac. Combat Area; Capt, Naval Res. Publ: Co-Author, Definitive Study on International Trade Orgn. Mem: Am, Pa. and Allegheny Co. Bar Asns; Allegheny Co. Bd. of Law Exams, 34-42; bd. dirs, Pittsburgh Playhouse and Pittsburgh Opera Bd; VFW; Am. Legion; Harvard Yale Princeton; Lions; Elks; Eagles; Moose; Duquesne Club; Civic Club Allegheny Co; St. Clair Country Club; Chartiers Country Club. Decorated by Repub. of Italy, 56. Rel: United Presbyterian. Legal Res: 2850 Espy Ave, Pittsburgh, Pa. 15216. Mailing Add: U.S. House Office Bldg, Washington, D.C. 20515. (1967)

FULTON, RICHARD HARMON D
U.S. Rep, Tenn.
b. Nashville, Tenn, 1/27/27; s. Lyle Houston Fulton and Labina Plummer F; m. to Jewel Simpson; c. Richard, Michael, Barry, Donna and Linda. Educ: Univ. Tenn. Polit. & Govt. Pos: Tenn. State Sen, 59; U.S. Rep, Tenn, 63-, mem, House Ways and Means Cmt, U.S. House of Rep, currently; del, Dem. Nat. Conv, 68. Bus. & Prof. Pos: Real estate broker. Mil. Serv: Seaman 1/C, Navy, 45-46. Mem: Mason (32°); Shrine; Civitan; Sertoma; Am. Legion; VFW; Methodist Laymen's Club; pres, bd. dirs, Cerebral Palsy, Tenn. Rel: Methodist. Legal Res: 911 Preston Dr, Nashville, Tenn. 37206. Mailing Add: 401 House Office Bldg, Washington, D.C. 20515.

FULTON, ROBERT D. D
Dem. Nat. Committeeman, Iowa
b. Waterloo, Iowa, 5/13/29; s. Lester Charles Fulton and Fern Ryan F; m. 9/10/55 to Rachel Breault; c. Susan, Mary, Jack and James. Educ: State Univ. Iowa, B.S.C, 52 and J.D, 58; Phi Delta Phi. Polit. & Govt. Pos: Iowa State Rep, 58-60; Iowa State Sen, 62-64; Lt. Gov, State of Iowa, 64-68; del, Dem. Nat. Conv, 68; Dem. Nat. Committeeman, Iowa, 68- Bus. & Prof. Pos: Attorney, State Legal Aid, 59-61. Mil. Serv: Entered as Pvt, Air Force, 53, released as Cpl, 55. Mem: Iowa State and Black Hawk Co. Bar Asns; Amvets; Am. Legion; C. of C. Legal Res: 616 Lafayette St, Waterloo, Iowa 50702. Mailing Add: 2753 Fairlane, Waterloo, Iowa 50702.

FULTON, WILLIAM McKINNEY R
N.C. State Rep.
b. Kewanee, Ill, 9/20/00; s. Wilson C. Fulton and Elizabeth M. McKinney F; m. 8/27/59 to Mary Atkins; c. William M, Jr, Joan F.(Mrs. White) and Sarah F.(Mrs. Trebbe). Educ: Knox Col, B.S, 22; State Univ. Iowa, M.A, 30, J.D, 36; Delta Sigma Rho. Polit. & Govt. Pos: N.C. State Rep, 69- Bus. & Prof. Pos: Attorney-at-law, Monmouth, Ill, 36-55. Rel: Episcopal. Mailing Add: 207 Myrtle St, Morganton, N.C. 28655.

FULWILER, TOBY EDWARD D
b. Milwaukee, Wis, 12/6/42; s. Harold E. Fulwiler and Mary Wood F; m. 6/14/66 to Laura Seaman. Educ: Univ. Wis, B.S, 65, M.S, 66 and Ph.D. cand. Polit. & Govt. Pos: Alternate del, Dem. Nat. Conv, 68. Bus. & Prof. Pos: Instr, Wis. State Univ. Stevens Point, 67-69. Mailing Add: Route 2, Box 84, Stevens Point, Wis. 54481.

FUNDERBURK, KENNETH LeROY R
Chmn, Russell Co. Rep. Party, Ala.
b. Phenix City, Ala, 9/13/36; s. Lemuel LeRoy Funderburk and Ruth Duke F; m. 10/5/58 to Judy Barbee; c. Rebecca Lee, Kimberly Ann and Eric Barbee. Educ: Howard Col, A.B, 57; Miss. State Univ, 57-58; Univ. Ala, LL.B, 65; Trident; Bench and Bar; Lambda Chi Alpha; Kappa Pi; Mu Alpha Chi; Sigma Delta Kappa. Polit. & Govt. Pos: Chmn, Russell Co. Rep. Party, Ala, 66- Bus. & Prof. Pos: Credit mgr, Cobb Hosp, 58; rep, Canned Meat Div, Armour & Co, 58-60; partner, Phillips & Funderburk, Law Off, 65- Mil. Serv: Entered as E-1, Army Res, 58, released, 58, recalled, 61 and released as E-3, 62, after serv. in Med. C. and as a Chaplain Asst. Mem: Ala. Bar Asn; Russell Co. Bar; Lions; Jr. C. of C. Rel: Baptist. Legal Res: 3303 Fifth Ave, Phenix City, Ala. 36867. Mailing Add: P.O. Box 1025, Phenix City, Ala. 36867.

FUNK, ALBERT GAIL R
b. Sterling, Utah, 2/18/25; s. Charles Buckley Funk and Emily Sigrid Johnson F; m. 8/15/63 to Arla Wangsgard; c. Christine. Educ: Brigham Young Univ, B.S; Univ. Utah, Ph.D; Sigma Xi. Polit. & Govt. Pos: Alternate del, Rep. Nat. Conv, 64; del, Rep. State Conv, 64 & 66. Bus. & Prof. Pos: Chemist, Thiokol Chem, 58-59; asst. prof, Univ. Utah, 59-64; research scientist, Ireco Chem, Salt Lake City Utah, 64- Mil. Serv: Entered as Pvt, Army, 45, released as Technician 5/C, 47, after serv. in 7th Army, Seoul, Korea; Army of Occup. and World War II Victory Medals. Publ: 'Chemical Factors in External Detonation-Generated Plasmas,' Third ONR Symposium on Detonation, Princeton Univ, 9/60; 'Strain Electrometry and Corrosion. IV. Film Properties and Strain Potential,' J.Electrochem. Soc, 2/59; 'Strain Electrometry and Corrosion. I. General Consideration on Interfacial Electrical Transients,' Proc. of the Nat. Acad. of Sciences, 43: 421, 1957; plus 2 others. Rel: Latter-day Saint. Mailing Add: 1035 East Third South, Salt Lake City, Utah 84102.

FUNK, ARTHUR JOSEPH D
Ga. State Rep.
b. Savannah, Ga, 6/14/98; s. John Sebastion Funk and Jane Wilson F; single. Educ: Savannah High Sch; attended summer schs. Johns Hopkins Univ; Columbia Univ; Univ. of Ga. Polit. & Govt. Pos: Ga. State Rep, 61- Bus. & Prof. Pos: Teacher and prin. Mil. Serv: Coast Guard Res, Lt, training officer, 42-45. Mailing Add: Grimball Point Rd, Savannah, Ga. 31406. (1967)

FUNKE, DIANE TREW R
Mem, Kern Co. Rep. Cent. Cmt, Wash.
b. Coalinga, Calif, 12/10/38; d. James Lewis Trew and Dorothy Harris T; m. 2/8/59 to William Henry Funke, Jr; c. Sharon Renée and William Henry, III. Educ: The Principia Col, Jr. Col. degree, 58. Polit. & Govt. Pos: Mem, Calif. Rep. State Cent. Cmt; area chmn, Bill Ketchum, Bob Mathias and Max Rafferty; mem, Kern Co. Rep. Cent. Cmt, Wash, currently. Mem: PEO. Rel: Christian Science. Mailing Add: 1934 Ninth Ave, Kennewick, Wash. 99336.

FUNKHOUSER, DONALD KAGEY R
Va. State Del.
b. Edinburg, Va, 8/19/33; s. Silas Alvin Funkhouser and Sarah Louise Kagey F; m. 12/7/57 to Betty Jean Dovel; c. Tzena Lynn; Alvin T. and Tracey Elliot. Educ: Bridgewater Col, B.A, 53. Polit. & Govt. Pos: Va. State Del, 50th Del. Dist, 66- Bus. & Prof. Pos: Mgr, Radio Sta. WSIG, Mt. Jackson, Va, 61- Mil. Serv: Entered as Airman Basic, Air Force, 53, released as Airman 1/C, 57, after serv. in Air Training Command, U.S. Mem: Rotary; C. of C; Farm Bur. Rel: Lutheran. Mailing Add: Route 1, Mt. Jackson, Va. 22842.

FUNKHOUSER, RICHARD
U.S. Ambassador to Gabon
b. Trenton, N.J, 9/10/17; s. Edgar Bright Funkhouser and Evelyn Hayes F; m. 3/4/44 to Phyllis Parkin; c. Phillip (deceased), Bruce Bedford and Blaine. Educ: Princeton Univ, B.A. summa cum laude, 39; Nat. War Col, grad, 54. Polit. & Govt. Pos: Joined For. Serv, 45; assigned Am. Embassies, Paris, Bern, Brussels and Luxembourg, 45-47; officer-in-charge, Iraq, Syria and Lebanon Affairs, Dept. of State, 50-52; polit. officer, dep. chief of mission and chargé d'affaires, Am. Legation, Bucharest, Rumania, 54-55; chief, polit. and econ. sect, Am. Embassy, Damascus, Syria, 56-58; spec. asst. to Asst. Secy. of State, 59-60; counselor, econ. affairs, Am. Embassy, Moscow, U.S.S.R, 61-64; counselor, polit. affairs, Paris, France, 65-69; U.S. Ambassador to Gabon, 69- Bus. & Prof. Pos: Consult, Bethlehem Steel Co, 39, Shell Union Oil Co, 39 and Standard Oil Co, Venezuela, 40-42. Mil. Serv: Entered Air Force, 43, released as 1st Lt, 45; Distinguished Flying Cross with three Oak Leaf Clusters; Air Medal with four Oak Leaf Clusters. Mem: Phi Beta Kappa; Princeton Club, Wash. and N.Y; Racing, Automobile Club, Paris. Rel: Presbyterian. Legal Res: 3319 N St. N.W, Washington, D.C. 20007. Mailing Add: Embassy, Libreville, Gabon.

FUQUA, DON D
U.S. Rep, Fla.
b. Jacksonville, Fla, 8/20/33; s. J.D. Fuqua and Lucille Langford F; m. to Doris Akidakis; c. Laura and John Eric. Educ: Univ. Fla, 51-53, B.S, 57; Alpha Gamma Rho; Gamma Sigma Delta. Polit. & Govt. Pos: Fla. State Rep, 58-62; U.S. Rep, Fla, 62- Bus. & Prof. Pos: Dairy and gen. farm operator, currently. Mil. Serv: Sgt, Army Med. Corps, 53-55. Mem: Am. Legion; Elks; Jaycees; WOW; bd. trustees, Fla. Sheriffs Boys Ranch; Mason; Shriner. Named One of Five Outstanding Young Men, Fla. Jr. C. of C, 63. Rel: Presbyterian. Legal Res: Altha, Fla. Mailing Add: Room 434, Cannon Bldg, Washington, D.C. 20515.

FUQUA, J. B. D
b. Prince Edward Co, Va, 6/26/18; m. 2/10/45 to Dorothy Chapman; c. Rex and Alan. Educ: Pub. Schs. of Va. Polit. & Govt. Pos: Ga. State Rep. and chmn, House Banking Cmt, 58-62; chmn, Ga. State Dem. Exec. Cmt, 62-66; Ga. State Sen. and chmn, Senate Banking Cmt, 63-64; mem, Ga. State Adv. Coun. and Ga. Sci. and Tech. Cmn. Bus. & Prof. Pos: Pres, Fuqua Nat, Inc, 49-; chmn. bd. and chief exec. officer, Fuqua Industs, Inc, 65- Mem: Ga. Asn. Broadcasters; Young Pres. Orgn.(former v.pres); pres, Augusta C. of C, 62; pres, Augusta Exchange Club, 49; Augusta Aviation Cmn; former mem, Univ. Hosp. Authority; Chief Execs. Forum, Inc; bd. dir, Atlanta C. of C; bd. visitors, Berry Col; active in various orgns. such as United Fund. Boss of the Year, Augusta Jaycees, 59; Named Ga. Broadcaster-Citizen of the Year, Ga. Asn. Broadcasters, 62. Rel: Presbyterian. Legal Res: 3574 Tuxedo Rd. N.W, Atlanta, Ga. 30305. Mailing Add: 3800 First National Bank Tower, Atlanta, Ga. 30303.

FURCOLO, FOSTER D
b. New Haven, Conn, 7/29/11; s. Dr. Charles L. Furcolo and Alberta Foster F; m. to Kay Foran; c. Charles Mark, David, Foster, Jr, Hope and Richard. Educ: Yale Col, A.B, 33, Law Sch, LL.B, 36; Yale Labor Mgt. Center, Cert, 47. Various hon. degrees including LL.D, L.H.D. and Dr. Admin. from several cols. and univs. Polit. & Govt. Pos: U.S. Rep, Second Dist, Mass, 48-52; Treas. & Receiver Gen. of Mass, 52-54; Gov. of Mass, 57-61. Mil. Serv: Navy, 42-46. Publ: Let George Do It, Harcourt-Brace, 58; 'The Story of Katyn,' Challenge Press, 66. Mem: Hampden Co. Barristers, Mass.(former pres); Mass. Bar Asn.(former mem. bd. gov); Hampden Co. Bar Asn. (former mem. exec. cmt.). Rel: Catholic. Mailing Add: 558 Beacon St, Newton Center, Mass. 02159.

FURLONG, FRANK J. D
Chmn, Luce Co. Dem. Cmt, Mich.
b. Sault Ste. Marie, Mich, 9/3/28; s. Francis Patrick Furlong and Margaret K. Jordan F; m. 8/5/61 to Jane C. Turner; c. Frank T, Patrick M, Kate M. and Courtney A. Educ: St. Norbert Col, B.Sc. in Hist. and Econ; Varsity Club; Collegiate Players. Polit. & Govt. Pos: Chmn. Luce Co. Dem. Cmt, Mich, 62-; mem, Mich. State Adv. Coun, Small Bus. Admin, 66-67. Bus. & Prof. Pos: Mem, Luce Co. Planning Cmn, 63-64; mem, St. Gregory Sch. Bd, 65- Mil. Serv: Entered as Ens, Naval Res, 51, released as Lt, 55, after serv. afloat several commands in the Atlantic and Far East Theatres, 51-55, Lt. Comdr, Naval Res, Retired; Presidential Unit Citation. Mem: Am. Legion; Elks; U.S. Naval Acad. Found; K. of C; Luce Co. C. of C.(pres, 63). Rel: Catholic. Mailing Add: 306 W. Harrie St, Newberry, Mich. 49868.

FURNESS, BETTY (MRS. LESLIE MIDGLEY) D
b. N.Y.C, 1/3/16; d. George Choate Furness and Florence Sturtevant F; m. 11/26/37 to John Waldo Green, div; m. 1/3/45 to Hugh B. Ernst (deceased); m. 8/15/67 to Leslie Midgley; c. Barbara Sturtevant. Educ: Brearly Sch, N.Y.C; Bennett Sch, Millbrook, N.Y. Polit. & Govt. Pos: Spec. asst. to President of U.S. for Consumer Affairs, 67-69. Bus. & Prof. Pos: Actress, TV personality; appeared in movies, Magnificent Obsession and Swing Time and stage plays, Golden Boy, My Sister Eileen and Doughgirls; gave Westinghouse TV commercials, 49-60; appeared in TV shows, Success Story, 51, Penthouse Party, 51, Meet Betty Furness, 53 and At Your Beck and Call, 61. Mem: Acad. of TV Arts and Sci, N.Y.(pres); Am. Acad. Dramatic Arts. 1967 Legal Res: New York, N.Y. No mailing address available. (1967)

FURR, DOROTHY PRESSER R
Secy, N.C. State Rep. Party
b. Milwaukee, Wis, 8/9/29; d. Erwin Joseph Presser and Erna Splavec P. Polit. & Govt. Pos: Treas, v.pres. and cmt. chmn, Mecklenburg Young Rep, N.C, 49-63; asst. secy, N.C. State Rep. Party, 53-66, secy, 66-; exec. secy, N.C. Young Rep, 53-54, mem. exec. cmt, 53-66, Nat. Committeewoman, 55-57; mem, Mecklenburg Co. Rep. Exec. Cmt, 53-, asst. v.chmn, Precinct Orgn, 62-66; asst. secy, Nat. Young Rep. Fedn, 59-61; alternate del-at-lg, Rep. Nat. Conv, 60 & 64; chmn, State Plan of Orgn. Cmt, 60, 62, 64, 66 & 68; organizing pres, Mecklenburg Co. Evening Rep. Women's Club, 62; mem, Charlotte-Mecklenburg Young Rep, currently; Presidential elector, 68. Bus. & Prof. Pos: Prod. mgr, E.J. Presser & Co, Advert. Agency. Mem: Int. Platform Asn; Charlotte Toastmistress Club. Mailing Add: P.O. Box 4286, Charlotte, N.C. 28204.

FURRA, LEON D
Elector, State of Calif. Dem. Party
b. Russia, 8/12/14; s. Passer M. Furra and Lena Schlian F; m. 1/19/47 to Leah Doris Rosenstein; c. Ralph A. and Dana S. Polit. & Govt. Pos: Finance chmn. for Rep. Ronald Brooks Cameron, 62-66; mem. State Finance Cmt, 62-66, finance chmn, 25th Cong. Dist. for President Johnson, 64; mem, State Dem. Cent. Cmt, 64-66; elector, State of Calif. Dem. Party, 64- Bus. & Prof. Pos: Pres, Ralph Enterprises Inc, 49-66; pres, Dana Invest. Co. Inc, 53-66; mem. adv. bd, Inland Bank, 64-66. Mil. Serv: Entered as Pvt, Air Force 41, released as T/Sgt, 45, after service in East. Flying Training Command. Mem: Elks; Masons (32°); Shriners; C. of C; Past Pres. Eastland Chapter, City of Hope. Calif. State Assembly Resolution 89 for outstanding service to community, 63. Rel: Jewish. Mailing Add: 150 N. Clark Dr, Beverly Hills, Calif. 90211.

FURY, ROBERT FLOYD R
Secy-treas, Dolores Co. Rep. Cent. Cmt, Colo.
b. Cortez, Colo, 4/2/46; s. Frank Fury and Mary Schovance F; single. Educ: Ft. Lewis Col, 1 year. Polit. & Govt. Pos: Secy-treas, Dolores Co. Rep. Cent. Cmt, Colo, 69- Bus. & Prof. Pos: Farmer, South Dove Creek. Mem: Commun. committeeman, Dolores Co. Agr. Stabilization & Conserv. Star Chap. Farmer Award, Dolores Co. Future Farmers of Am, 64; Bus Drivers Safety Award, 69. Rel: Catholic. Mailing Add: Box 314, Dove Creek, Colo. 81324.

FUTCH, SIDNEY R
City Cmnr, Adel, Ga.
b. Adel, Ga, 12/3/39; s. Loy A. Futch and Lillie Purvis F; m. 2/21/59 to Scottie Johnson; c. Sidney Andrew and Christopher Scott. Educ: Valdosta State Col. Polit. & Govt. Pos: Chmn, Cook Co. Rep. Party, Ga, 64-65; City Cmnr, Adel, currently. Bus. & Prof. Pos: Procurement mgr, Del-Cook Timber Co; secy-treas, Cook Co. Ins. Agency. Mem: Dir, Georgia-Florida Pulpwood Dealers Asn; Ga. Forestry Asn; Southern Pulpwood Conservation Asn; Jaycees; United Fund; Farm Bur. Rel: Methodist. 1967 Legal Res: Adel, Ga. No mailing address available. (1967)

FUTRELL, ASHLEY BROWN D
b. Rich Sq, N.C, 10/27/11; s. James Thomas Futrell and Addie Brown F; m. 11/25/49 to Rachel Fox; c. Ashley Jr. Educ: Duke Univ, B.A, 33; Sigma Delta Chi. Polit. & Govt. Pos: Wash. City Bd. of Educ, N.C, 56-; N.C. Court Reform Cmn, 58-59; N.C. Seashore Cmn, 62-; N.C. State Sen, 63-65. Bus. & Prof. Pos: Athletic coach, Wilson High Sch, Atlantic Christian Col, 36; former tobacco buyer, Imperial Tobacco Co; former sch. teacher; ed. and publisher, Wash. Daily News, Wash, N.C. Mil. Serv: Sgt, Army, 42-44. Mem: Past pres, E.N.C. Press Asn; past pres, N.C. Press Asn; South. Newspaper Asn; Am. Legion; VFW; Moose; Rotary; Mason; Shrine; pres, Men's Club, 56; Official Bd, 50-; lay leader; Sunday Sch. teacher; vice-chmn, N.C. Conf. Bd. of Lay Activities; N.C. Conf. Bd. of Pub. Info, Lay Speaker. Misc: Commun. Serv. Awards, 57, 62; Best Eds, 56, 59; Best Features, 60, N.C. Press Asn. Rel: Methodist; chmn, Official Bd, First United Methodist Church. Mailing Add: 1206 Summit Ave, Washington, N.C. 03280.

G

GAAR, NORMAN EDWARD R
Kans. State Sen.
b. Kansas City, Mo, 9/29/29; s. William Edward Gaar and Lola McKain G; m. 8/1/53 to Joanne Rupert; c. Anne Elizabeth, James Rupert, William Edward and John Lawrence. Educ: Baker Univ, 47-49; Univ. Mich, A.B, 55, Law Sch, J.D, 56; Delta Theta Phi; Kappa Sigma. Polit. & Govt. Pos: Munic. judge, Westwood, Kans, 59-63, Mayor, 63-65; Kans. State Sen, 65- Mil. Serv: Entered as Aviation Midshipman, Navy, 49, released as Lt.(jg), 53, after serv. in 111th Fighter Squadron Task Force 77, Seventh Fleet, Korea, 51-52; Japanese Occup. and UN Serv. Medals; Korean Theater Ribbon with 2 Battle Stars; Korean Presidential Unit Citation; Navy Unit Citation; 2 Air Medals; Letter of Commendation for Valor with Combat Distinguishing Device; Naval Res. Ribbon. Mem: Kansas City and Am. Bar Asns; Kansas City Lawyers Asn.(v.pres. jr. bar sect, 62); Mo, Kans. and U.S. Supreme Court Bars; Am. Judicature Soc; Optimists Int. Amateur Radio WØDEZ; commercial pilot license. Rel: Presbyterian. Mailing Add: 2340 W. 51st, Westwood, Kans. 66205.

GABRESKI, MAX PAUL D
b. Oil City, Pa, 9/12/25; s. Stanley Gabryszewski and Josephine Woloszczak G; m. 8/19/50 to Eileen Schossler; c. Paul, James, Karen, Bridget, Brian, John Francis, Blase and Ralph. Educ: Univ. Notre Dame, Ph.B, 50, LL.B, 51. Polit. & Govt. Pos: Chmn, Venango Co. Dem. Cmt, Pa, 62-67; v.pres. bd. trustees, Edinboro State Col, 66- Bus. & Prof. Pos: Solicitor, Oil City Gen. Authority, Oil City, Pa, 62-66; solicitor, Venango Fed. Savings & Loan Asn, Franklin, 64-66. Mil. Serv: Entered as Seaman, Navy, 43, released as Yeoman 1/C, 46, after serv. in Asiatic-Pac. Theater of War. Mem: Elks; Eagles; VFW; K. of C; bd. dirs. and pres, Venango-Clarion Tuberc. and Health Soc; former mem. bd. dirs, Venango Co. Indust. Develop. Corp. Rel: Roman Catholic. Legal Res: 1305 Grandview Rd, Oil City, Pa. 16301. Mailing Add: 1 Main St, Oil City, Pa. 16301.

GABRIEL, ARTHUR WILFRED R
Kans. State Rep.
b. Eudora, Kans, 5/13/10; s. Samuel J. Gabriel and Sophia Brown G; m. 6/4/37 to Alberta Bell Rohe; c. Belva (Mrs. James Kobler) and Arlen Arthur. Educ: High sch, Eudora, Kans, 24-28. Polit. & Govt. Pos: Mem. sch. bd, DeSoto, Kans, 38-42, mem. city coun, 39-42; Kans. State Rep, 67- Bus. & Prof. Pos: Pres, DeSoto State Bank, DeSoto, Kans, currently; dir, Centennial State Bank, Mission, 60- and Lenexa State Bank, 68-; mem. adv. group, Kans. Bankers Asn. Mil. Serv: Entered as Pvt, Army, 42, released as Sgt, 45, after serv. in 103rd Inf. Div, ETO, 44-45; Bronze Star. Mem: Pres, Johnson Co. Bankers Asn, 47; Taxation and Finance Coun, Kans. C. of C; Lions; Mason (32°); Scottish Rite; VFW; Am. Legion; dir, Johnson Co. Health, Welfare and Recreation Coun. Rel: Methodist. Legal Res: Third and Kickapoo, DeSoto, Kans. 66018. Mailing Add: Box 495, DeSoto, Kans. 66018.

GABRIELSON, GUY GEORGE R
b. Sioux Rapids, Iowa, 5/22/91; s. Frank August Gabrielson and Ida Jansen G; m. 2/5/18 to Cora M. Speer; c. Guy George; Nancy G. (Mrs. Owens). Educ: Univ. of Iowa, B.A, 14; Harvard Univ, LL.B, 17; Upsala Col, LL.D. (hon), 32. Polit. & Govt. Pos: Chmn, Rep. Nat. Cmn, 49-52; mem, N.J. House of Assembly, 26-30, Speaker 29, majority leader, 28; Rep. Nat. committeeman for N.J. Bus. & Prof. Pos: Attorney, private practice, N.J, 19-; practice N.Y.C, 31-; chmn, dir. Nicolet Industs, Inc; dir, Somerset Hills Nat. Bank; trustee, Drew Univ; trustee, Colby Col. Mem: N.J. Bar Asn; N.Y. Co. Lawyers Asn; Am. Legion; SAR; N.Y. Union League; Downtown Asn; N.J. Essex Club; Nat. Press Club. Rel: Methodist. Mailing Add: Bernardsville, N.J. 07924.

GABY, DANIEL M. D
State Chmn, New Dem. Coalition of N.J.
b. Scranton, Pa, 11/22/33; s. Simon Gaby and Frieda Golnick G; m. 9/12/56 to Patricia Ann Venokur; c. Lisa Ann, Suzanne Karen, Keith Lael and Vanessa Jane. Educ: Rutgers Univ, B.S, 57. Polit. & Govt. Pos: Pres, John F. Kennedy Dem. Club, Bridgewater Twp, N.J, 65; campaign mgr, Meredith for State Senate, Somerset and Hunterdon Co, 65 and Jefferson for Cong, Fifth Dist, 66; advert. adv, N.J. Dem. State Cmt, 67; co-chmn, McCarthy pledged conv. del. from N.J, 68; del, Dem. Nat. Conv, 68; state chmn, New Dem. Coalition of N.J, 69- Bus. & Prof. Pos: V.pres. and creative dir, Keyes, Martin & Co, 57- Mil. Serv: Entered as Pvt, Army Res, 57, released as SP-3C, 57, after serv. in Anti-Aircraft Artil, U.S. Publ: A Marriage of Convenience, Bantam Books, 53. Mem: Asn. of Indust. Advertisers; NAACP; Nat. Cmt. for Sane Nuclear Policy. Rel: Jewish. Mailing Add: P.O. Box 75, Millstone, N.J. 08849.

GABY, GENE PAUL D
Chmn, Greene Co. Dem. Exec. Cmt, Tenn.
b. Greene Co, Tenn, 9/15/42; s. Martin V. Gaby and Ruby Long G; m. 10/21/67 to Kay Shannon. Educ: Tusculum Col, 3 years; Univ. Tenn. Col.

Law, J.D, 66; Phi Alpha Delta. Polit. & Govt. Pos: Chmn, Greene Co. Dem. Exec. Cmt, Tenn, 66- Bus. & Prof. Pos: Attorney, Greeneville, Tenn, 66- Mil. Serv: SP-4, Tenn. Army Nat. Guard, 66- Mem: Elks; Tenn. Farm Bur. Am. Jurisp. Equity Award, Univ. Tenn. Col. Law, 66. Rel: Church of Brethren. Mailing Add: Route 9, Love St, Greeneville, Tenn. 37743.

GACKLE, WILLIAM FREDERICK R
N.Dak. State Rep.
b. Kulm, N.Dak, 12/7/27; s. Otto Gackle and Alice Higdem G; m. 8/20/50 to Marilyn Bernice Goehner; c. Frederick, David, Mary Alice and Jonathan. Educ: San Angelo Jr. Col, 48-49. Polit. & Govt. Pos: N.Dak. State Rep, 63- Mil. Serv: Entered as Pvt, Army Air Force, 46, released as Sgt, 49, after serv. in Training Command; M/Sgt, N.Dak. Nat. Guard, 54-60. Mem: Elks; Lions. Rel: Protestant. Mailing Add: Kulm, N.Dak. 58456.

GAFFNEY, BETTY JANE D
Dem. Nat. Committeewoman, Ohio
b. Toledo, Ohio 4/17/28; d. John J. Gaffney and Helen Quinn G; single. Educ: Ursuline Acad, grad; St. Louis Univ; Mary Manse Col, grad. Polit. & Govt. Pos: Col. coordinator, Young Students for Truman; exec. asst. to Frazier Reams, Jr, titular head, Ohio Dem. Party; chmn. press and publicity, Federated Dem. Women's Clubs of Ohio; del, Ohio Young Dem; state cent. committeewoman, Ninth Cong. Dist; mem. and v. chmn, Lucas Co. Dem. Exec. Cmt; Dem. committeewoman, Precinct 10-M; mem, Lucas Co. Dem. Policy Cmt; nat. committeewoman, Ohio Young Dem, 62-66; nat. chmn, Young Women Activities, Young Dem. Clubs Am, 62-66; Field rep, Dem. Nat. Cmt. on Block Worker Prog, Ohio, Ind. and Wis, 64; state coordinator, Reams for Gov. Campaign, 66; del, Dem. Nat. Conv, 68; Dem. Nat. Committeewoman, 68-; co-chmn, Nat. Registration Drive; mem. credentials cmt, Dem. Nat. Cmt, 69- Bus. & Prof. Pos: Pub. affairs and promotion dir, WCWA, Radio, Toledo. Mem: League of Women Voters, co-dir, You the Voter Prog; bd. mem, Toledo Coun. World Affairs; Cath. Interracial Coun; Women's Advert. Club Toledo; dept. commun, Cath. Conf. Ohio; Zonta Club Int; Nat. Broadcasters Asn; Ohio Asn. Broadcasters; Am. Women Radio and TV; Commun. and World Serv. Asn. Rel: Catholic. Mailing Add: 2848 Rockwood Place, Toledo, Ohio 43610.

GAFFNEY, EDWARD McGLYNN D
b. N.J; m. 1926 to Mary Catherine Wright; c. Sister Eleanor Marie (Notre Dame); Matthew Thomas, Peter Joseph, Edward McGlynn, Jr, Margaret Mary, Helena Regina (deceased). Educ: St. John's Col, N.Y. Polit. & Govt. Pos: Calif. State Assemblyman, 54-66; Supvr, 5th Cong. Dist; 16th Decennial Census; past pres, 24th Dist. Dems. Club, Inc. Mil. Serv: U.S. Army Transport Serv. Mem: Commonwealth Club, Civic League of Improv. Clubs; Cent. Coun. of Civic Clubs; S.F. Ins. Brokers' Ech; N.A.A.C.P; South of Mkt. Boys, Inc; St. Francis Assembly, K. of C; Elks; Hibernians; Eureka Valley Prom. Asn. Mailing Add: 3977 17th St, San Francisco, Calif. 94117. (1967)

GAFFNEY, J. BRIAN R
Conn. State Rep.
b. New Britain, Conn, 3/25/33; s. Cyril F. Gaffney and Helen M. Downes Sullivan G; m. 9/26/59 to Mary Lou Blinn; c. Mary Alicia, Laura Anne, Kateri Ellen, Cyril F. and John Brian, Jr. Educ: Univ. Notre Dame, B.A, 55; Fordham Sch. Law, LL.B, 58; Irish Club; Conn. Club. Polit. & Govt. Pos: Mem, Coun, New Britain, Seventh Dist, Conn, 62-64; Alderman-at-lg, 64-65; chmn, New Britain Rep. Town Cmt, 65-; asst. corp. counsel, City of New Britain, 66-68; Conn. State Rep, 29th Dist, 67- Bus. & Prof. Pos: Clerk of Superior Court, 60-62. Mil. Serv: Pvt, Army, 59; Army Res, 3 years. Mem: New Britain, Hartford Co. and Conn. Bar Asns; Lions. Rel: Roman Catholic. Legal Res: 36 Westwood Dr, New Britain, Conn. 06052. Mailing Add: 30 Bank St, New Britain, Conn. 06051.

GAFFNEY, WILLIAM L. D
N.H. State Rep.
b. Claremont, N.H, 7/7/96. Educ: Stevens High Sch, Claremont, N.H. Polit. & Govt. Pos: Assessor, N.H, 47, 59 & 60; ballot clerk; N.H. State Rep, 59- Bus. & Prof. Pos: Retired. Mil. Serv: World War I. Mem: K. of C. Rel: Catholic. Mailing Add: 24 School St, Claremont, N.H. 03743. (1967)

GAGAN, MICHAEL STEPHEN D
b. Albuquerque, N.Mex, 12/29/42; s. John Alexander Gagan and Catherine Elizabeth Johnson G; single. Educ: Monterey Inst. of For. Studies, 63-64; Univ. Calif, Davis, B.A, 66, M.A, 68; del, Univ. Calif. Grad. Acad, 66-68; pres, Grad. Asn. of Polit. Sci. Students, 66-68; Nat. Defense Educ. Act. Doctoral fel, 66-69; pres, Pi Sigma Alpha, 67-68. Polit. & Govt. Pos: Pres, Monterey Peninsula Young Dem, Calif, 60-61; pres, Commun. Dem. Club, 64-65; del, Calif. Dem. Coun, 64-69; mem, Calif. State Dem. Cent. Cmt, 64-69; admin. asst. to Calif. State Assemblywoman March F. Kong, 67-; asst. to secy, Calif. Del, Dem. Nat. Conv, 68. Bus. & Prof. Pos: Research asst, Inst. Govt. Affairs, Univ. Calif, Davis, 67-68, assoc. in Polit. Sci, 68-69. Publ: 'A Heretic's View of the Theology of Science,' 69; 'The Politics of Scientific Expertise,' 69. Mem: Am. Polit. Sci. Asn; Am. Acad. Polit. and Soc. Sci; Am. Soc. Pub. Admin; Acad. Polit. Sci; Aircraft Owners and Pilots Asn; Pilots Int. Asn; Am. Civil Liberties Union; IBT, AFL-CIO. Mailing Add: 228 B St, Davis, Calif. 95616.

GAGE, A. STUART R
b. Grafton, N.H, 10/21/94; s. Fred Gage and Laura E. Bucklin G; m. to Hannah E. Caswell; c. four. Polit. & Govt. Pos: Former moderator, trustee trust funds and sch. bd. mem; N.H. State Rep, 61-67. Bus. & Prof. Pos: Real Estate. Mem: Grange; Clifton Davis Men's Club. Rel: Protestant. Mailing Add: Grafton, N.H. 03240.

GAGE, EDWARD AUGUSTUS R
N.H. State Rep.
b. Haverhill, Mass, 4/29/19; s. Carl Webster Gage and Janette Wells Mitchell G; m. 7/10/54 to Margaret Bailey Clark; Carl Webster, II, Edward Anthony, Thomas Underwood and Susan Chase. Educ: Dartmouth Col, 37-39; Univ. Va, B.A, 41; Law Sch, LL.B, 48; Zeta Psi. Polit. & Govt. Pos: Treas, Eastchester Rep. Town Cmt, N.Y, 49-62; Rep. Committeeman, 20th Elec. Dist, Bronxville, 50-62; chmn, Bronxville Village Rep. Cmt, 60-62; v.chmn, Exeter Rep. Club, N.H, 63-64; v.chmn, Rockingham Co. Rep. Cmt, 65-66, finance chmn, 66-67; N.H. State Rep, 16th Dist, Rockingham Co, 69- Bus. & Prof. Pos: Asst. secy. and asst. treas, Allegheny Power Syst, Inc, N.Y, 55-62; West Penn Power Co, Greensburg, Pa, 57-62 and Monongahela Power Co, Fairmont, W.Va, 58-62. Mil. Serv: Entered as Seaman 2/C, Naval Res, 41, released as Lt, 46, after serv. as a Naval Aviator, Aviation Training Command and Pac. Theater, 41-46, Res, Lt. Comdr.(Ret). Mem: Va, N.H. and Am. Bar Asns; Asn. of the Bar of the City of N.Y; Rockingham Co. Bar Asn.(secy, 67-69); Lions Int; Mason; Am. Legion. Rel: Protestant; Vestryman, Christ Church of Exeter. Mailing Add: 12 Lincoln St, Exeter, N.H. 03833.

GAGE, FRED KELTON 'KELLY' R
Minn. State Sen.
b. Minneapolis, Minn, 6/20/25; s. Fred Kelton Gage and Vivian L. Johnson G; m. 6/12/49 to Audrie Anne White; c. Deborah Lee, Penelope Jane, Fred Kelton, III, Amy Lynn and Lawrence. Educ: Univ. Minn, B.S.L, 48 and LL.B, 50; Order of the Coif; Phi Delta Phi; Delta Upsilon. Polit. & Govt. Pos: V.chmn, Sch. Bd, 56-66; mem, Minn. State Col. Bd, 60-64; Minn. State Sen, 11th Dist, 67- Bus. & Prof. Pos: Partner, Blethen, Ogle, Gage & Krause, Law Firm, 55- Mil. Serv: Entered as A/S, Naval Res, 43, released as Yeoman 2/C, 46. Mem: Minn. Law Rev; Minn. and Am. Bar Asns; Kiwanis; Am. Legion. Rel: Protestant. Mailing Add: 141 S. Skyline Dr, Mankato, Minn. 56001.

GAGE, JOHN BURDETTE D
b. Long Beach, Calif, 10/9/42; s. James Robert Gage and Harriett Doris Burdette G; single. Educ: Univ. Calif, Berkeley, 60-68; Univ. Paris, 62-63; Harvard Univ. Grad. Sch. Bus. Admin, 68-69. Polit. & Govt. Pos: Mem, Commun. for New Polit, later, Peace and Freedom Party, Calif, 66-68; co-chmn, Berkeley-Alameda Co. Kennedy Campaign, Calif, 68; del, Dem. Nat. Conv, 68. Bus. & Prof. Pos: Dir, Commun. Projs. Off, Univ. Calif, Berkeley, 66-68; staff asst, Robert F. Kennedy Mem, Wash. D.C, 69. Mil. Serv: E-1, Army, 65-; E-3, Air Force Res, 69- All-Am, Swimming, 63 & 64; Student Commun. Award, Univ. Calif, Berkeley, Alumni Asn, 68. Mailing Add: 67 Beacon By, Newport Beach, Calif. 92662.

GAGE, WILLIAM McCUTCHEON R
b. Green Bay, Wis, 5/18/14; s. Harry Bidwell Gage and Nathalie Keyes G; m. 1947 to Helen Douglas; c. Kathryn K, Anne D, William M, Jr. and Christina W. Educ: Univ. Wis, 34-35. Polit. & Govt. Pos: Admin. Asst. to U.S. Rep. John W. Byrnes, Wis. Mil. Serv: Entered as Pvt, Army, 41, released as Capt, Field Artillery, 46, after serv. in 32nd Div, Australia, New Guinea, Netherlands, East Indies, Philippines and Japan, 42-45; Bronze Star; Asiatic-Pac. Ribbon with 3 Battle Stars and 1 Arrowhead; Philippine Liberation Ribbon with 2 Stars. Mailing Add: 4001 Garrison St. N.W, Washington, D.C. 20016. (1967)

GAGNON, REBECCA A. D
N.H. State Rep.
b. Berlin, N.H, 11/11/94; wid; c. Five. Educ: St. Regis Acad. Polit. & Govt. Pos: Mem, Women's Dem. Club, N.H; del, Constitutional Conv, 38, 48, 56 & 64; N.H. State Rep, 39- Mem: Am. Legion Auxiliary; Women's Relief Corps Auxiliary; Club Raquetteurs Joliette; Costumes & Soc. Rel: Catholic. Mailing Add: 412 Goebel St, Berlin, N.H. 03570. (1967)

GAILEY, JOHN R, JR. D
b. York, Pa, 9/1/26; s. John R. Gailey and Jean Bossert G; m. to Deborah E. Belfield; c. Three. Educ: Notre Dame Univ; Haverford Col, B.A; Yale Law Sch, LL.B. Polit. & Govt. Pos: Pas State Rep, 56-68. Bus. & Prof. Pos: Attorney. Mil. Serv: Navy. Admitted to York Co, Pa. Supreme Court and U.S. Supreme Court Bars. Mailing Add: 401 Roosevelt Ave, York, Pa. 17404. (1967)

GAILLARD, JOHN PALMER, JR. D
Mayor, Charleston, S.C.
b. Charleston, S.C, 4/4/20; s. John Palmer Gaillard and Eleanor Ball Lucas G; m. 7/15/44 to Lucy Huguenin Foster; c. John Palmer, III, William Foster and Thomas Huguenin. Polit. & Govt. Pos: Alderman, Charleston, S.C, 51-59, mayor, 59-; pres, Munic. Asn. S.C, 64-65. Mil. Serv: Entered as Seaman 1/C, Navy, 41, released as Lt, 45. Mem: Elks; Carolina Yacht Club; Hibernian; C. of C; St. Andrews Soc; Charleston Club. Good Neighbor Award, Navy Times, 61. Mailing Add: 77 Montagu St, Charleston, S.C. 29401.

GAIN, KENNETH JAY D
Mem, Alaska Dem. State Cent. Cmt.
b. Belleville, Ill, 8/21/41; s. Henry George Gain and Grace Kesler G; m. 9/8/61 to JoAnne Frances Wilbanks; c. Kelly Elizabeth and Kristine Annette. Educ: Univ. Alaska, 2 years. Polit. & Govt. Pos: Dist. chmn, Young Dem. Cent. Dist. Cmt, Alaska, 62-63, mem, 62-64; chmn, Young Dem. State Conv, 64 & 66; alternate del, Dem. Nat. Conv, 68; mem, Alaska Dem. State Cent. Cmt, 68- Bus. & Prof. Pos: Salesman, Glenn Willacy Realty, Fairbanks, 62-63; appraiser, Sch. Dist. Assessor, 63-64; appraiser, State Hwy. Dept, 64; urban renewal mgr, Alaska State Housing Authority, 64-67; area rep, Fed. Housing Admin, 67-68; appraiser and consult, Ken Gain Assocs, 68-69, Gain & King, Appraisers, currently. Mem: Gr. Fairbank Real Estate Bd; assoc. mem. Soc. Real Estate Appraisers; cand. for mem, Am. Inst. Real Estate Appraisers; C. of C; Golden Heart Toastmasters; Jaycees. Second place winner, State of Alaska Toastmasters Speech Contest, 67; Outstanding Freshman Cadet, ROTC, Univ. Alaska. Rel: Methodist. Legal Res: 1527 Noble St, Fairbanks, Alaska 99701. Mailing Add: Box 406, Fairbanks, Alaska 99701.

GAINER, CARL E. D
W.Va. State Sen.
b. Montrose, W.Va; s. Marvin J. Gainer and Pearle Poling G; m. 5/23/48 to Clarise Smith; c. Frewen, Carl, Jr. and Grace Ann. Educ: Alderson-Broaddus Col, B.A; Duke Univ, grad. work. Polit. & Govt. Pos: W.Va. State Sen, 58-; del, Dem. Nat. Conv, 64 & 68. Bus. & Prof. Pos: Oil co. distributor; former sch. prin. in Barbour Co. Mil. Serv: Naval Res, Commanding Officer of U.S.S. LSM 556. Mem: Shrine; Elks; Moose; Rotary; Am. Legion; VFW; former pres, Cent. W.Va. Develop. Asn. Rel: Methodist. Mailing Add: Riverside Addition, Richwood, W.Va. 26261.

GAINER, DENZIL LEE D
State Auditor, W.Va.
b. Mt. Zion, W.Va, 9/12/13; s. Lee Gainer and Laura Elliot G; m. 3/9/35

to Lucille Reading; c. Phillip Lee, Kenneth Lee and Karen Reading. Educ: LaSalle Exten. Univ; Morris Harvey Col, 46-48. Polit. & Govt. Pos: Asst. dir. of budget, W.Va, 41-47, dir. of budget, 47-57, asst. legis. auditor, 57-60, state auditor, 61- Mil. Serv: Entered as Pvt, Marine Corps, 44, released as Cpl, 46, after serv. in Am. Theater. Mem: Ambassador, Morris Harvey Col; United Fund Bd; Mason (32°); Shrine; Moose; Civitan Club. 75th Anniversary Hon. Award, Morris Harvey Col. Rel: Methodist. Mailing Add: 3633 N. Crede Dr, Charleston, W.Va. 25302.

GAINES, CLARENCE LLEWELLYN D
City Councilman, Cleveland, Ohio
b. Dallas, Tex, 3/9/16; s. Clarence E. Gaines and Ella Walker Gaines Vesha; m. 6/13/42 to Pearl Jones; c. Pearl Carol, Delaney (Mrs. Hairston), Clarence Llewellyn and George Leo. Educ: Wiley Col; West. Reserve Univ, grad; Cleveland Marshall Law Sch, grad. Polit. & Govt. Pos: Dir, Health and Welfare, Cleveland, Ohio, 63-; city councilman, Cleveland, 63- Bus. & Prof. Pos: Attorney-at-law, Gaines, Smith & Assocs, 56- Mil. Serv: Entered as Pvt, Army, 41, released as 1st Lt, 46, after serv. in 555 Paratrooper Unit. Mem: Glenville Area Commun. Coun; NAACP; Area Coun. Asn; Postal Alliance; Cory Recreation Center; Boy Scouts; Cent. Planning Bd; Cmt. on Juvenile Delinquency; Fair Housing Cmt; Glenville Rehabilitation Bd. Rel: Methodist. Mailing Add: 9909 Westchester, Cleveland, Ohio 44108 (1967)

GAINEY, DANIEL CHARLES R
b. Winona, Minn, 11/28/97; s. Daniel Gainey and Ella Towey G; m. May, 1962 to Elaine L. Frock; c. Daniel J. Educ: Hamline Univ, A.B, 21; Delta Sigma Phi; Tau Kappa Epsilon. Hon. D.B.A, Hamline Univ, 48. Polit. & Govt. Pos: Del, Rep. Nat. Conv, 48, 52, 56 & 60, alternate del, 64; mgr, Stassen Hq, D.C, 52; Nat. finance chmn, Goldwater Pre-Conv. Campaign; Nat. treas, Rep. Party; mem, Nat. Finance Cmt, Cmt. on Prog. and Progress and Rep. Surv. Cmt; mem, President's Cmt. on Govt. Contracts. Bus. & Prof. Pos: Rancher, Ariz. and Calif; athletic coach and teacher pub. schs, Hancock, Minn, 21-22; with Jostens, Inc. since 22, chmn. bd, 33-68, chmn. bd. emer, 68- Mil. Serv: Pvt, Army, 18. Mem: Dir, Nat. Asn. of Mfrs; pres. and dir, Educ. Jewelry Mfrs. Asn; dir, Jewelers Vigilance Cmt, Inc; v.chmn, Minn. War Relief, World War II; State of Minn. Selective Serv. Bd, World War II; Am. Legion; C. of C; Izaak Walton League; Pres, Arabian Horse Club Registry of Am. Inc. Arabian Horse Breeder. Legal Res: Route 2, Owatonna, Minn. 55060. Mailing Add: c/o Jostens, Inc, Owatonna, Minn. 55060.

GAIOTTI, ANDREW JOHN Independent-D
b. Danby, Vt, 10/6/07; m. to Berenice Dawson; c. One son and two daughters. Educ: Pub. schs, Danby, Vt. Polit. & Govt. Pos: Lister, Vt; selectman; constable, 16 years; Mt. Tabor tax collector; Vt. State Rep, 49-51, 59-61 & 65-67. Bus. & Prof. Pos: Retired machinist, Fellows Gear Shaper. Rel: Catholic. Mailing Add: P.O. Box 57, Danby, Vt. 05739.

GALAZAN, JEANNE K. D
b. Lincoln, Nebr, 9/5/12; d. Morris Kaplan and Dora Rosenfeld K; m. 12/20/36 to Michael M. Galazan; c. Gene and Lynn. Educ: Crane Col, Chicago; Chicago Musical Col; Layton Sch. Art, Univ. Wis, Milwaukee. Polit. & Govt. Pos: Mem. chmn, Concerned Women for McCarthy, 68; del. and mem. rules cmt, Dem. Nat. Conv, 68. Mem: Milwaukee Music Teachers Asn. Mailing Add: 4636 N. Morris Blvd, Milwaukee, Wis. 53211.

GALBRAITH, MRS. CARL B.(MARY JANE MOORE) D
b. Fayette City, Pa; d. George Henry Moore and Irene Vaughan M; m. 2/14/41 to Carl Galbraith. Educ: Private study in adv. bus. work and court reporting. Polit. & Govt. Pos: Shorthand reporter for spec. session, W.Va. Legis, 32, secy. to Speaker, W.Va. House of Del, regular session, 33 and spec. session, 34; secy. to bd. of rev.(appeal bd), W.Va. Dept. Unemploy. Compensation, Charleston and shorthand reporter, 38-41; del, Young Dem. Nat. Conv, Louisville, Ky, 41; mem. bd, Ohio Co. Dem. Women's Club, 44-48; v.pres, Ohio Co. Young Dem. Club, 44-48; Dem. Nat. Committeewoman, W.Va, 44-52; mem, North. Dist. W.Va. Dem. Steering Cmt, 64. Bus. & Prof. Pos: Secy. to agency dir, N.Y. Life Ins. Co, 34-38; trustee, Ohio Co. Pub. Libr. Mem: Oglebay Inst, W.Va; Ohio Co. Bar Auxiliary (dir, 53-, pres, 56-57); W. Va. Libr. Asn; Upper Ohio Valley Hort. Soc.(pres, 52-); dir, Wheeling Garden Center, 54-; Upper Ohio Hort Soc.(pres, 62-63); pres, Garden Center, 60-61; bd. dirs, Coun. Retarded Children, 58-61; Nat. Coun. State Garden Clubs; Old Trails Dist. Garden Clubs (dir); Wheeling Symphony Auxiliary; Little Theater; Wheeling Civic Clubs Asn.(dir, 56); Women's Club; W.Va. and Cloverleaf Garden Club; Wheeling Country Club; Thursday Music Club; exec. cmt, Upper Ohio Valley United Fund, 68-69. Jaycee Citizen of the Month for effort in upgrading W.Va. libraries, Nov, 67. Mailing Add: Hubbard Lane, Wheeling, W.Va. 26003.

GALBRAITH, FRANCIS J.
U.S. Ambassador to Indonesia.
b. Timber Lake, S.Dak, 12/9/13; m. to Martha Townsley Fisher; c. Susan, Kathleen and Kelly Francis. Educ: Col. of Puget Sound, B.A, 39; Univ. Wash, B.A, 40, Yale Univ, 48-49. Polit. & Govt. Pos: Career officer, U.S. Dept. of State For. Serv, 46-, v.consul, Hamburg, Germany, 46-48, Batavia, 49-50, Djakarta, 50-51; officer in charge, Indonesian and Pac. Island affairs, 51-55, U.S. consul, Medan, Indonesia, 55-56, Air War Col, 57-58, London, Eng, 58-62, dep. chief of mission to Djakarta, 62-65, For. Serv. inspector, 66, U.S. Ambassador to Singapore, 66-69 and Indonesia, 69- Mil. Serv: Capt, Army, 41-46, serv. in Artil, W.New Guinea. Legal Res: Sisseton, S.Dak. Mailing Add: U.S. Embassy, Djakarta, Indonesia.

GALBRAITH, J. KENNETH D
b. Iona Station, Ont, Can, 10/15/08; s. William Archibald Galbraith and Catherine Kendall G; m. 9/17/37 to Catherine Atwater; c. Alan, Peter and James. Educ: Univ. Toronto, B.S, 31; Univ. Calif, M.S, 33 and Ph.D, 34; Cambridge Univ, 37-38. Hon. LL.D, Bard Col, 58, Miami Univ, 59, Univ. Mass, Brandeis Univ. and Univ. Toronto, 63, Univ. Guelph and Univ. Saskatchewan, 65. Polit. & Govt. Pos: Econ. adv, Nat. Defense Adv. Cmn, 40-41; asst. admin, Price Div, Off. Price Admin, 41-42, dep. admin, Off. of Price Admin, 42-43; dir, U.S. Strategic Bombing Surv, 45; dir, Off. of Econ. Security Policy, State Dept, 46; U.S. Ambassador, India, 61-63; nat. chmn, Am. for Dem. Action, 67-69. Bus. & Prof. Pos: Economist; Soc. Sci. Research Coun. fel, 37-38; instr. and tutor, Harvard Univ, 34-49, lectr, 48-49, prof. econ, 49-, Paul H. Warburg Prof. econ, 59-61 & 63-; asst. prof. econ, Princeton Univ, 39-42; mem. bd. ed, Fortune Mag, 43-48. Publ: The New Industrial State, 67; The Triumph, 68; Indian Painting: The Scene Themes and Legends, 68; The Affluent Society, Rev. Ed, 69; plus others. Mem: Trustee, 20th Century Fund; fel, Am. Acad. Arts and Sci; Am. Econ. Asn; Am. Farm Econ. Asn; Century Club; Saturday Club, Boston. Medal of Freedom, Am. Farm Econ. Asn, 46. Mailing Add: 207 Litauer Center, Harvard University, Cambridge, Mass. 02138.

GALBRAITH, JAMES RONALD R
Dir. Pub. Rels, Rep. Gov. Asn.
b. Crystal Falls, Mich, 3/18/36; s. Edwin Galbraith and Lillian Robichaud G; m. 6/23/62 to Mary Redington; c. Richard Lee, Timothy Scott and John Redington. Educ: Pasadena City Col, 53-55; Univ. South. Calif, 55-56; Calif. State, Los Angeles, 56-60; Omicron Mu Delta; Beta Phi Gamma; Pi Kappa Delta. Polit. & Govt. Pos: Asst, U.S. Rep. E.W. Hiestand, 60-62; asst. dir. pub. rels, Nat. Rep. Cong. Cmt, 64-69; dir. pub. rels, Rep. Gov. Asn, 69- Bus. & Prof. Pos: Columnist and asst. news ed, Pasadena Independent Star-News, 55-60; broadcaster, Three Star Extra, NBC Radio, 62-64; managing ed, Wash. World Mag, 62-64. Mem: Capitol Hill Club; Nat. Press Club; Bull Elephants Club; K. of C; Toastmasters Int. Hon. grad, Pasadena City Col, 55; Outstanding Toastmaster of the Year Award, Capitol Hill Toastmasters Club, 69; first place winner of club, area and div. serious speech competition, Toastmasters Int, 69; nat. and west. states oratory championships during col. Rel: Roman Catholic. Mailing Add: 5007 Roslyn Rd, Annandale, Va. 22003.

GALBRAITH, JOHN ALLEN R
Ohio State Rep.
b. Toledo, Ohio, 8/23/23; s. Evan G. Galbraith and Nina Allen G; m. 3/25/50 to Cynthia Finn; c. John Michael, Geoffrey, Cynthia and Tenley. Educ: Univ. Mich, LL.B, 49; Phi Delta Phi; Chi Psi. Polit. & Govt. Pos: Pres, Young Rep. Lucas Co, Ohio, 63-65; asst. attorney gen, Ohio, 63-67; Ohio State Rep, 67- Bus. & Prof. Pos: Legal dept, Electric Auto Lite, 49-56; gen. mgr, Community Sanitation, 56-62; pres, Maumee Construction Co, 63- Mil. Serv: Entered as A/S, Navy, 42, released as Lt. Comdr, 53, after serv. in World War II; Lt. Comdr, Naval Res, 66; Am, European and Pac. Theater Campaign Ribbons; Philippine Victory Medal; Naval Res. Medal; Victory Medal; Korean Serv. Medal; China Serv. Medal; Philippines Commendation Medal. Mem: Rotary; Toledo Zoo, Orchestra and Museum. Mailing Add: 602 Pierce St, Maumee, Ohio 43537.

GALBRAITH, WILLIAM EUGENE R
Dep. Under Secy. of Agr. for Cong. Rels, Dept. of Agr.
b. Beemer, Nebr, 1/22/26; m. to Gwen Jean Taylor; c. Claudia Jean and William Deane. Educ: Univ. Nebr, degree in Agr. Exten. and Tech. Sci. Polit. & Govt. Pos: Dep. adminstr. for state and co. opers, Agr. Stabilization and Conserv. Serv, 69; Dep. Under Secy. of Agr. for Cong. Rels, Dept. of Agr, 69- Bus. & Prof. Pos: Instr. agr, West Point High Sch, Nebr. and farm mgr. and operator. 49-60; livestock feeder, farm owner and operator, 60- Mil. Serv: Navy, World War II. Mem: Dir, Commun. Develop. Corp, Beemer; Am. Legion (past nat. comdr); chmn, Nebr. Centennial Cmn; co-chmn, Gov. Conf. on Educ; Nebr. Swine Producers Orgn.(first pres, 64); dir, Nebr. Youth Coun; 4-H Club Leader; Nebr. Livestock Feeders Asn. Two Awards for Outstanding Contrib. to Educ. as a Layman, Nebr. State Educ. Asn, 65. Legal Res: Nebr. Mailing Add: Dept. of Agriculture, 14th St. and Independence Ave. S.W, Washington, D.C. 20250.

GALBREATH, CHARLES D
b. Goodlettsville, Tenn, 1/12/25; s. John Caldwell Calhoun Galbreath and Nell Moncreif G; m. 6/9/50 to Joyce Brown; c. Charles, Sarah Nell and Michael. Educ: Cumberland Univ, LL.B, 47; Cumberland Law Sch, Samford Univ, J.D, 69. Polit. & Govt. Pos: Tenn. State Rep, Davidson Co, 61-66; pub. defender, Davidson Co, 62-64; judge, Tenn. Court of Criminal Appeals, 68- Mil. Serv: Entered as Pvt, Marine Corps, 41, released as Pfc, 45. Mem: Am. Bar Asn; Am. Judicature Soc. Mailing Add: 410 Supreme Court Bldg, Nashville, Tenn. 37219.

GALEA'I, TALIMANU O. T. D
Rep, Am. Samoa House of Rep.
b. Leone, Am. Samoa, 5/18/33; s. Apelu Galea'i, Sr. and Lina Schmidt G; m. 9/26/59 to Suataute Mativa; c. Edwin L, Florida S, Lina A, Douglas O.T, Bismarck N. and Ja Cinta S. Educ: Los Angeles City Col, 56; Seattle Pac. Col, 56-58. Polit. & Govt. Pos: Chmn, Ed. House, 59-60; Rep, Am. Samoa House Rep, currently, chmn. of educ, 69- Bus. & Prof. Pos: Sales clerk, Max Haleck, 52; messenger, Honolulu Dent. Supply, 52; advert. layout man, Tradewell Stores, Inc, 59-64; mgr, Book Shop, 66- Mil. Serv: Entered as Pvt, Marines, 52, released as Cpl, 55, after serv. in Marine Barracks, Yokuska, Japan, First Marine Div; Good Conduct and Korean War Medals. Mem: Dem. Party, Am. Samoa; Marist Bros. Old Boys Asn. Rel: Protestant. Legal Res: Leone, Pago Pago, American Samoa 96920. Mailing Add: P.O. Box 578, Pago Pago, American Samoa 96920.

GALETICH, LOUIS ROBERT D
Chmn, Carroll Co. Dem. Cent. Cmt, Iowa.
b. Highbridge, Iowa, 1/21/29; s. John Galetich and Katherine Sabel G; m. 8/17/57 to Elizabeth Jean Leiting; c. Elizabeth Ann. Educ: St. Ambrose Col, B.A. in polit. sci, 52; Future Teachers of Am. Polit. & Govt. Pos: Precinct committeeman, Carrol Co. Dem. Cent. Cmt, Iowa, 60, chmn, 62-68 and treas, 68-; mem, State Judicial Nominating Cmn, 63; adv. mem, City Planning Cmn, Carroll, 64; Seventh Dist. committeeman, Iowa State Dem. Cent. Cmt, 64-; city councilman, Carroll, 67-; del, Dem. Nat. Conv, 68. Mem: Iowa State Educ. Asn; Am. Polit. Sci. Asn; Young Dems; K. of C; Elks; Kiwanis. Coached Clinton St. Mary's, State Basketball Champions, 53 & Davenport Diocesan Champions, 54 and Carroll Kuemper High Sch, Sioux City Diocesan Champions, 60 and 61. Rel: Roman Catholic. Mailing Add: 410 S. Elm, Carroll, Iowa 51401.

GALIBER, JOSEPH LIONEL D
N.Y. State Sen.
b. N.Y.C, 10/26/24; s. Joseph F. Galiber and Ethel Bowser G; m. 11/28/46 to Emma Evangeline Shade; c. Pamela Susan and Ruby Dianne. Educ: City Col.

N.Y, B.S, 50; N.Y. Law Sch, LL.B, 62. Polit. & Govt. Pos: Del. and asst. majority leader, N.Y. State Constitution Conv, 67; chmn, Bronx Co. Dem. Cmt, N.Y; N.Y. State Sen, 69- Bus. & Prof. Pos: Attorney-at-law, 65- Mil. Serv: Entered as Pvt, Army, 43, released as S/Sgt, 45, after serv. in 4010 Qm. Truck Co, ETO, 43-45; European-African-Mid. East. Serv. Medal; Good Conduct Medal; World War II Victory Medal. Mem: Bronx Bar Asn; N.Y. Trial Lawyers; NAACP. Rel: Presbyterian. Mailing Add: 595 E. 167 St, New York, N.Y. 10456.

GALICICH, MARGUERITE PARKER R
V.Chmn, Sweetwater Co. Rep. Party, Wyo.
b. Rock Springs, Wyo, 11/17/18; d. Harry G. Parker and Marguerite Travis P; m. 6/29/41 to Albert G. Galicich; c. Marguerite (Mrs. Terry L. Cummings). Educ: Univ. Colo, 36-38 & 41; Woman's Club. Polit. & Govt. Pos: Rep. precinct committeewoman, Sweetwater Co, Wyo, 64-68; state committeewoman, Sweetwater Co. Rep. Party, 66-68, v.chairwoman, 68-; alternate del, Rep. Nat. Conv, 68. Bus. & Prof. Pos: Elem. pub. grade sch. teacher, Rock Springs, 38-42; co-owner and buyer, Marguerite's Fine Gifts and Jewelry, 43- Rel: Christian. Mailing Add: 734 D St, Rock Springs, Wyo. 82901.

GALIFIANAKIS, NICK D
U.S. Rep, N.C.
b. Durham, N.C, 7/22/28; s. Mike Galifianakis (deceased) and Sophia Kastrinakis G; m. 4/5/63 to Louise Cheatham Ruggles; c. Stephenie, Katherine and Jon Mark. Educ: Duke Univ, A.B, 51, Law Sch, LL.B, 53; Delta Theta Phi. Polit. & Govt. Pos: N.C. State Rep. Durham Co, 61-65, chmn, Judiciary and Ment. Insts. Cmts, and v.chmn, Appropriations, Finance and Educ. Cmts, N.C. Gen. Assembly; U.S. Rep, Fourth Dist, N.C, 66-, mem, Banking and Currency Cmt. and Subcmts. on Domestic Finance, Bank Supv. and Int. Trade, U.S. House of Rep. Bus. & Prof. Pos: Partner, Upchurch and Galifianakis; asst. prof. bus. law, Duke Univ, 60-67. Mil. Serv: Marine Corps, 53-56, Maj, Marine Corps Res, Commanding Officer, 41st Rifle Co, 60-63; Lt. Col, Civil Air Patrol. Mem: Am. N.C, Durham Co. and 15th Judicial Dist. Bar Asns; Am. Hellenic Educ. Progressive Asn; bd. dirs, N.C. Bd. Sci. and Tech, Durham Co. Ment. Health Asn, Am. Cancer Soc, United Fund, Cerebral Palsy Fund and other charitable orgns; mem. bd. adv, Association International des Etudiants en Sciences Economiques et Commerciales; Jaycees; Kiwanis; Young Dem. Club. Outstanding Young Man of the Year, N.C. Jr. C. of C, 63; Distinguished Serv. Award, Durham Jaycees; named among Outstanding Young Men in Am, 64. Rel: Greek Orthodox; Trustee, St. Barbara's Church, Durham. Legal Res: Durham, N.C. Mailing Add: 513 Cannon House Office Bldg, Washington, D.C. 20510.

GALINET, PETER C. D
b. Hancock, Mich. 10/14/01; s. Peter Galinet and Lucy Carutti G; m. 2/14/48 to Georgia E. Schmidt; c. William, Peter F, Herbert R, Lucille (Mrs. La Chance) and Betty (Mrs. Hutson). Educ: High Sch. grad, 17; Bus. Col, 18-20. Polit. & Govt. Pos: Chmn, St. Joseph Co. Dem. Party, Mich, 65-66, City Dem. Party, 46-50 and 34-42. Bus. & Prof. Pos: Dir, Three Rivers Savings & Loan Co, Three Rivers, Mich, 60-; Real Estate broker and appraiser, 58-; Remodelling contractor and appraiser, 51-58; Restaurant owner, 46-51; asst. prod. mgr, Fairbanks Morse Co, 28-37. Mil. Serv: Entered as Sgt, Army, 42, released as M/Sgt, 45, after serv. in Allied Military Govt, ETO, 42-45; Unit Citation, 3 Combat Stars. Mem: Soc. of Real Estate Appraisers; chmn, Salvation Army, local unit, 15 years; life mem, Elks; charter mem, Eagles; life mem, Disabled Am. Vets. and past comdr, Chap. 56, Three Rivers, Mich; Am. Legion; VFW; Moose; Fraternal Order of Police; hon. mem, Boys Town, Nebr. Hobbies: Fishing and hunting. Rel: Lutheran. Mailing Add: 213 Portage Ave, Three Rivers, Mich. 49093. (1967)

GALLAGHER, CHRISTINE SHIRLEY D
b. Walstonburg, N.C, 2/19/21; d. George Clayton Shirley and Lena Shackelford S; m. to Karl Eugene Gallagher, Jr.(deceased). Educ: King's Bus. Col, Raleigh, N.C, dipl. Polit. & Govt. Pos: Secy. to State Dir, Agr. Stabilization & Conserv. Serv, U.S. Dept. Agr, Raleigh, N.C, 39-50 & 52-53; exec. secy. to U.S. Rep. Harold D. Cooley, 53-59; chief clerk, Agr. Cmt, U.S. House of Rep, 59- Rel: Baptist. Legal Res: Walstonburg, N.C. 27888. Mailing Add: 2500 Q St. N.W, Washington, D.C. 20007.

GALLAGHER, CORNELIUS E. D
U.S. Rep, N.J.
b. Bayonne, N.J, 3/2/21; s. Cornelius E. Gallagher and Ann Murphy G; m. 10/22/43 to Claire Richter; c. Diane, Christine, Patrice and Bridget. Educ: John Marshall Law Sch, LL.B. cum laude, 48. Polit. & Govt. Pos: Organizer and first pres, Hudson Co. Young Dem, N.J, 49; del, Dem. Nat. Conv, 52, 56, 60, 64 & 68; mem, Hudson Co. Dem. Exec. Cmt, 50-; freeholder, Hudson Co, 53-55; cmnr, N.J. State Turnpike Authority, 55-57, v.chmn, 57-61; U.S. Rep, 13th Dist, N.J, 59-, mem, for. affairs cmt, U.S. House of Rep, 59-, chmn, int. orgns. and movements subcmt, mem, Govt. Opers. Cmt, 62- Bus. & Prof. Pos: Prof. mil. sci. and tactics, Rutgers Univ, 46-47; attorney-at-law, 49- Mil. Serv: Entered as Enlisted Res, Army, 41, released as Capt, 46, after serv. in 80th Div, 318th Inf; re-entered for 1 year in Korean War; Army Res, until 52; Two Bronze Stars; Three Purple Hearts; Presidential Citation; Commendation Ribbon; Combat Inf. Badge; Three Battle Stars. Mem: Chmn, Spec. Subcmt. on Invasion of Privacy, Am. Bar Asn; Hudson Co. and N.J. Bar Asns; chmn, U.S.-Can. Inter-Parliamentary Group; U.S. Del. to the Disarmament; cong. adv, Standing Cmt. on the Peaceful Uses of the Seabed; Woodrow Wilson Mem. Cmn; chmn. fund-raising drives, Bayonne Red Cross, Commun. Chest, PAL and YMCA; organizer, N.J. Heart Fund; K. of C; Am. Legion; DAV; Elks. Award, Nat. Coun. of Christians and Jews, 60. Rel: Catholic. Legal Res: 102 W. Fifth St, Bayonne, N.J. 07002. Mailing Add: 235 Cannon House Office Bldg, Washington, D.C. 20515.

GALLAGHER, FRANCIS XAVIER D
b. Baltimore, Md, 2/25/28; s. Frank Augustine Gallagher and Ellen Doyle G; m. 6/9/51 to Mary Inez Kelly; c. Mary Ellen, Francis X, John Joseph, Patrick Edward and James Lawrence. Educ: Loyola Col.(Md), A.B, 49; Johns Hopkins Univ, M.A, 51; Univ. Md, LL.B, 52; hon. LL.D, Mt. St. Mary's Col, 68; Tau Kappa Alpha; Alpha Sigma Nu. Polit. & Govt. Pos: Asst. city solicitor, Baltimore, Md, 53-57; Md. State del, 59-61; people's counsel, Md, 61-63; del, Md. Constitutional Conv, 67-68 and chmn. legis. cmt, 67-68; del, Dem. Nat. Conv, 64 & 68 and v.chmn. Md. del, 64; chmn, Johnson for Pres, Md, 64; chmn, Kennedy for Pres, Md, 68. Bus. & Prof. Pos: Partner, Tydings, Rosenberg and Gallagher, 51-68; partner, Gallagher, Evelius and Finnerty, 68- Knight, St. Gregory, 63. Rel: Roman Catholic. Legal Res: 5408 Purlington Way, Baltimore, Md. 21212. Mailing Add: 1100 One Charles Center, Baltimore, Md. 21201.

GALLAGHER, HAROLD MILTON R
Chmn, Richmond Co. Rep. Party, Va.
b. Warsaw, Va, 7/4/06; s. John Edward Gallagher and Rosa Belle Mothershead G; m. 4/8/33 to Katherine Louise Beauchamp; c. Sarah Louise. Educ: Warsaw High Sch, 12-22. Polit. & Govt. Pos: Chmn, Richmond Co. Rep. Party, Va, 35-; mem, Va. Rep. State Cent. Cmt, 50-60; city councilman, Warsaw, 56-60. Bus. & Prof. Pos: Construction rep, H.M. Gallagher Co, 25-, real estate appraiser, 46-, state cert. auctioneer, 62-; Ins. underwriter, Rappahannock Gen. Ins. Agency, Warsaw, 60- Mil. Serv: Entered as CPO, Navy, 43, released as CPO, 44, after serv. in Seabees, Pac. Theater, 43-44. Mem: Rappahannock Baptist Asn.(moderator, 60-62); bd. trustees, Va. Baptist Children's Home, 60-; Eastern Star (Patron, Emily B. Chinn Chap, 50 & 55); Mason (Master, Warsaw Bauman Lodge, 55). Rel: Baptist; Trustee, Warsaw Baptist Church, 45- Mailing Add: 118 Hamilton Blvd, Warsaw, Va. 22572.

GALLAGHER, JAMES AUGUSTINE D
b. Newport, R.I, 5/21/09; s. Anthony F. Gallagher and Margaret Mary Dougherty G.(both deceased); m. to Marion Louise Dowd; c. Margaret Ann (Mrs. Robert D. Grenier) and James A, Jr. Educ: De LaSalle Acad, 4 years; Newport Bus. Col, 4 years. Polit. & Govt. Pos: Chmn. Dem. Cmt, Jamestown, R.I, 5 years, moderator, 2 terms and mem. town coun, 8 years; mem, R.I. Constitutional Conv; R.I. State Rep, 61-66. Bus. & Prof. Pos: Salesman, J.T. O'Connell, Inc, Kelleher Paint Supply Co, $3\frac{1}{2}$ years and Don Geyer Buick, 60-69; supvr, R.I. Registry of Motor Vehicles, 69- Mil. Serv: Entered as Storekeeper, Naval Construction Bn; released after serv. $3\frac{1}{2}$ years in S.Pac. Theatre. Mem: Past pres. and past treas, Jamestown Lions; Am. Legion. Rel: Roman Catholic. Mailing Add: 31 Clinton Ave, Jamestown, R.I. 02835.

GALLAGHER, JAMES J. A. D
Pa. State Rep.
b. Philadelphia, Pa, 9/19/27; m. 1948 to Lavinia E. Sismore; c. James, Sharon Ann, Shiela Ann and Kathleen Marie. Educ: U.S. Marine Corps Inst; St. Joseph's Col. Indust. Rels. Sch. Polit. & Govt. Pos: Past chmn, Bristol Twp. Sch. Dist. Authority, Pa, 6 years; first treas. and trustee, Bucks Co. Free Libr. 58-; mem, State Libr. Adv. Coun. on Develop, 61-62; Pa. State Rep, 59-, chmn, Higher Educ. Cmt. and mem, Elec. and Apportionment, Pub. Utilities, Hwy, Munic. Corp, Hwy. Safety, Commun. Col, Dem. Policy Cmts, Joint State Govt. Cmn. Task Force Cmts. and Cmt. on Intermediate Units, State Bd. Educ. and chmn, House Educ. Cmt, Pa. State House of Rep; alternate del, Dem. Nat. Conv, 68. Bus. & Prof. Pos: Owner, Gallagher Tour Serv, Pa. Mil. Serv: Marine Corps, 45-46. Mem: Marine Corps League; past secy-treas, Cmt. on Polit. Educ, Bucks Co. AFL-CIO, hon. chief steward, Local 282, Transport Workers Union Am. and past pres, 8 yrs. Mailing Add: 26 Flower Lane, Levittown, Pa. 19055.

GALLAGHER, JAMES V. D
b. Carroll, Iowa, 2/18/33; s. Vincent Gallagher and Benita G; m. 9/29/55 to Carlene Spaen; c. Michael, Daniel, John and Steven. Educ: State Col. Iowa. Polit. & Govt. Pos: Former Iowa State Rep. Bus. & Prof. Pos: Bell Tel. Co, 14 years. Mil. Serv: Army, Korean War, 2 years. Mem: K. of C; CWA; Am. Legion; Isaak Walton League. Rel: Catholic; St. Edwards Catholic Church. Mailing Add: 2528 Orchard St, Waterloo, Iowa 50702. (1967)

GALLAGHER, JOHN T. R
N.Y. State Assemblyman
b. N.Y.C, 1/25/30; s. John T. Gallagher and Julia Callahan G; m. 7/6/57 to Mary T. Macario; c. John T, Tracy Ann, Christopher James, Mary Kathleen and Daniel Joseph. Educ: St. Johns Univ, B.B.A, 51, Law Sch, J.D, 56. Polit. & Govt. Pos: N.Y. State Assemblyman, 66- Mil. Serv: Entered as Pvt, Army, 51, released as Spec. Agent, 53, after serv. in CIC, Europe, 52-53. Rel: Catholic. Legal Res: 49-14 217th St, Bayside, N.Y. 11364. Mailing Add: 136-21 Roosevelt Ave, Flushing, N.Y. 11354.

GALLAGHER, MARY CECELIA D
Chmn, Lawrence Co. Dem. Cent. Cmt, Ohio
b. Pine Grove, Ohio, 11/11/98; d. Cornelius Gallagher, M.D. and Elizabeth F. Goldcamp G; single. Polit. & Govt. Pos: Chmn, Lawrence Co. Bd. of Elections, Ohio, 46-; secy, Dem. State Cent. and Exec. Cmts, 48-68; chmn, Lawrence Co. Dem. Cent. Cmt, 68- Bus. & Prof. Pos: Owner, Mary C. Gallagher, Ins. Rel: Catholic. Mailing Add: 1705 S. 3rd St, Ironton, Ohio 45638.

GALLAGHER, MICHAEL J. D
b. Indianapolis, Ind, 1911; m. to Dorothy G. Educ: Bus. Col. Polit. & Gov. Pos: Wash. State Sen, until 66; Wash. State Rep, ex. 43-44, ex. 49-50. Bus. & Prof. Pos: Real estate. Mailing Add: 8045 Burke Ave. N, Seattle, Wash. 98103. (1967)

GALLAGHER, P. J. 'JIM' D
Wash. State Rep.
b. Taylor, Wash, 1915; m. to Mabel; c. Six. Educ: Wash. State Univ. Polit. & Govt. Pos: Wash. State Rep, currently. Bus. & Prof. Pos: Owner-operator, service station, 22 years. Mem: K. of C; Eagles. Mailing Add: 125 S. 72nd St, Tacoma, Wash. 98408. (1967)

GALLAGHER, S. RENFREW D
Vt. State Rep.
b. Craftsbury, Vt, 9/10/89; wid; c. One son and one daughter. Educ: Craftsbury Acad; Albany Bus. Col. Polit. & Govt. Pos: Vt. State Rep, 25 & 63-; side judge, Franklin Co, 60 & 61. Bus. & Prof. Pos: Farmer and livestock dealer. Mem K. of C; Vt. Cattlemen's Asn. Rel: Catholic. Mailing Add: R.F.D. 1, St. Albans, Vt. 05478. (1967)

GALLAGHER, WILLIAM C. D
Educ: N.Mex. A&M; Colo. A&M. Polit. & Govt. Pos: N.Mex. State Sen, -66; Co. Cmnr, 4 years; Dem. Co. Chmn, 4 years. Bus. & Prof. Pos: Rancher.

Mil. Serv: Air Force, Bomber Squadron II AF, radar navigator, air-sea rescue, 4 years. Mem: Am. Legion; Marnick Club; TV Assoc. Club. Rel: Catholic. Mailing Add: Eagle Nest, N.Mex. 87718. (1967)

GALLAGHER, WILLIAM F. D
b. Fall River, Mass, 1/15/07; m. to Antoinette E. Educ: B.M.C. Durfee High Sch, Fall River, Mass. Polit. & Govt. Pos: R.I. State Rep, 61-66. Bus. & Prof. Pos: Dental technician. Mailing Add: 3 Narragansett Heights, Portsmouth, R.I. 02871. (1967)

GALLAHAN, RUSSELL WAYNE D
Chmn, Miami Co. Dem. Party, Ind.
b. Mexico, Ind, 11/17/20; s. Floyd Nathan Gallahan and Isa Leora Fishburn G; m. 10/10/50 to Gertrude Stanton; c. Dawn. Educ: Mexico High Sch, Ind, 4 years. Polit. & Govt. Pos: Del, Dem. Nat. Conv, 68; chmn, Miami Co. Dem. Party, Ind, 68- Mil. Serv: Entered as Pvt, Air Force, 42, released as Pvt, 46, after serv. in A.S.C.S, Caribbean. Mem: Elks; Am. Legion; Mason; Scottish Rite; Shrine. Rel: Church of the Brethren. Legal Res: Mexico, Ind. 46958. Mailing Add: 8 E. Second St, Peru, Ind. 46970.

GALLAHER, JOHN K. D
Mem, N.C. State Dem. Exec. Cmt.
b. Mexico, Mo, 9/12/24; s. James William Gallaher and Iona Melvina Smith G; m. 5/20/50 to Christine Gray; c. John K, Jr, Christine L, David N, Thomas G. and James. Educ: Univ. Mo; Univ. Wis. Polit. & Govt. Pos: Local precinct chmn, Dem. Party, N.C, 60-61; bd. mem, Winston-Salem, Forsyth Co. Planning and Zoning Bd, 61; chmn, Forsyth Co. Dem. Exec. Cmt, 61-65; mem, N.C. State Dem. Exec. Cmt, 62-; del. and mem, Credentials and Appeals Cmt, Dem. Nat. Conv, 64; mem. from 21st Dist, State Dem. Judicial Dist. Exec. Cmt, 64-66; mem. from 23rd Dist, State Dem. Sen. Exec. Cmt, 64-66; chmn, N.C. Real Estate Licensing Bd, 64-66; mem, Platform and Resolutions Cmt, N.C. Dem. Conv, 66. Bus. & Prof. Pos: Pres, Gallaher Realty Co, N.C, 57-; pres, Winston Develop. Co, 60- Mem: Nat. Asn. of Real Estate Bds; past dir, Twin City Mens Club; Old Town Club; Legis. Cmt, C. of C; N.C. Realtors Legis. Cmt. and Speakers Bur; past dir, Lions. Rel: Presbyterian. Legal Res: 1056 Kent Rd, Winston-Salem, N.C. 27107. Mailing Add: Box 3082, Winston-Salem, N.C. 27602.

GALLAND, MARION GIBBS D
Va. State Del.
b. Montvale, N.J, 11/18/13; d. Edwin Gibbs and Anne Crawford G; m. 11/11/38 to George Freeman Galland; c. Anne Freeman and George Freeman, Jr. Educ: Vassar Col, 30-33; Barnard Col, B.A, 34. Polit. & Govt. Pos: V.chmn, Alexandria Dem. Cmt, Va, 59-63; v.chmn, Tenth Cong. Dist, Va. Dem. Cmt, 60-64; mem, Va. State Dem. Cent. Cmt, 60-68; Va. State Del, 64- Bus. & Prof. Pos: Legal Secy, Chadbourne, Wallace, Parke & Whiteside, 34-37, Baldwin, Todd & Young, N.Y.C, 37-41 and expenditures cmt, U.S. House of Rep, 48. Mem: League of Women Voters; Am. Asn. of Univ. Women; Bus. & Prfnl. Women's Club; Zonta; PTA; bd. mem, Alexandria Ment. Hygiene Clinic and Alexandria Commun. Health Center; Va. Asn. Ment. Health; Sr. Citizens Employ. Serv. Alexandria. Rel: Episcopal. Mailing Add: 1403 Bishop Lane, Alexandria, Va. 22302.

GALLATIN, ALBERT HAROLD R
b. Denver, Colo, 2/13/22; s. Albert B. Gallatin and Elise Reeves G; c. Bruce Paul. Educ: Univ. Denver, 51-54. Polit. & Govt. Pos: Admin, asst. to Sanit. Engr, Denver, Colo, 51-59; motor vehicle dir, Denver, 59-63; dep. auditor, City and Co. of Denver, 63-64; admin. asst. to U.S. Sen. Gordon Allott, 64-67. Bus. & Prof. Pos: Partner, United Plastic Prod. Co, 43-46. Mil. Serv: Entered as Pvt, Air Force, 42, released as Pfc, 43. Mem: Mason; Am. Soc. of Publ. Admin; Nat. Off. Mgr. Asn; Int. Exec. Serv. Corps; Int. City Mgr. Asn. Black Belt Judo; Jiu Jitsu; Brown Belt Karate. Rel: Christian Science. Mailing Add: 2525 S. Dahlia St, Denver, Colo. 80222.

GALLEHER, JOHN D
Va. State Sen.
b. Leesburg, Va, 1/28/98; m. to Louise Falligant. Educ: Va. Mil. Inst; Univ. Va. Law Sch, LL.B. Polit. & Govt. Pos: Organizer, Young Dem. Clubs of Va; former mem, Va. Dem. State Cent. Cmt, 33 years; former chmn, Eighth Cong. Dist. Dem. Cmt; former mem, Va. State Bd. Accountancy; former dir, Nat. Coun; former commonwealth attorney, Loudoun Co; Va. State Sen, 66- Bus. & Prof. Pos: Lawyer; newspaper publisher; businessman. Mil. Serv: World War I. Mem: Am. Legion; Mason; Lions. Rel: Episcopal; Former Vestryman, Trinity Episcopal Church. Mailing Add: P.O. Box 190, Manassas, Va. 22110.

GALLEN, JAMES J. R
Pa. State Rep.
b. Reading, Pa, 8/15/28; s. A. Joseph Gallen and Anna V. Strain G; m. to Sara C. Boyle; c. Five boys and three girls. Educ: Villanova Univ, B.S. Polit. & Govt. Pos: Mem, Young Rep. Club, Pa; Pa. State Rep, 64- Bus. & Prof. Pos: Ins. agent. Mil. Serv: Army, Korean War. Mem: Clubmaster; chmn, Berks Co. Cmt. Problems Older Workers; Am. Legion; Shillington Keystone Fire Co. Mailing Add: 302 Hendel St, Shillington, Pa. 19607. (1967)

GALLEN, THOMAS M. D
Fla. State Rep.
b. Tampa, Fla, 12/28/32; s. Thomas M. Gallen and Mary Ellen Satterfield G; m. to Linda C. Pruitt; c. Thomas M, Jr. Educ: Univ. Tampa, 50-52; Fla. State Univ, 55-57; Univ. Fla. Col. Law, LL.B, 60; Dean's List, Fla. State Univ; Phi Delta Phi; Phi Delta Theta; John Marshall Bar Asn. Polit. & Govt. Pos: Fla. State Rep, Manatee Co, currently. Mil. Serv: Entered as Pvt, Army, 52, released as Sgt, 55, after serv. in 10th Spec. Forces Airborn, ETO. Mem: Manatee Co. Bar Asn.(treas, 64); Fla. Bar; Am. Bar Asn; Fla. Acad. of Trial Lawyers; Univ. Fla. and Fla. State Univ. Alumni Asns; past v.pres, Bradenton Jaycees; v.pres. and dir, Manatee Players; past chmn, Speakers Bur; March of Dimes; Toastmasters; crewman, DeSoto Celebration, 2 years; K. of C; Am. Legion; VFW. Key Man Award, Bradenton Jaycees. Rel: Catholic. Legal Res: 5506 Ninth Ave. Drive W, Bradenton, Fla. 33505. Mailing Add: 701 11th St. W, Bradenton, Fla. 33505. (1967)

GALLI, AMERICO JOHN D
Vt. State Rep.
b. Crenna, Italy, 4/12/03; s. Giovanni Galli and Luigia Marelli G; m. 4/17/26 to Lina Eva Calcagni; c. Elizabeth G. Calcagni and Alelia M. Educ: Spaulding High Sch, Barre, Vt, 4 years. Polit. & Govt. Pos: Sch. cmnr, Barre, Vt, 42-65; chmn, Barre City Sch. Cmnr, 5 years; justice of the peace and mem. bd. of civil authority, Barre, Vt, 61-65; Vt. State Rep, Dist. 7-4, 67- Bus. & Prof. Pos: Apprentice, journeyman, plant foreman and owner, granite bus, 23-67. Mem: Granite Cutters Int. Asn; F&AM; MWA (local secy, 50). Rel: Methodist. Mailing Add: 97 Berlin St, Barre, Vt. 05641.

GALLION, MacDONALD D
Attorney Gen. of Ala.
b. Montgomery, Ala, 4/5/13; s. Dr. Thomas Travis Gallion; m; c. Two. Educ: Univ. Ala, LL.B, 37. Polit. & Govt. Pos: Asst. Attorney Gen, Ala, 45-57, Attorney Gen, 58-62 & 67-; spec. counsel for state in Phenix City Cleanup, 54; del, Dem. Nat. Conv, 60; Presidential elector, 68. Bus. & Prof. Pos: Lawyer, Gallion & Hare, 37-43, 50-55 & 63-67. Mil. Serv: Marine Corps, 1st Lt. Mem: Nat. Attorney Gen. Asn.(mem. exec. bd); chmn, South. Attorneys Gen. Conf; Mont, Ala. and Am. Bar Asns; former Asn. Ed. of Ala. Lawyer, Off. State Bar; Nat. Asn. Prosecuting Attorneys; Am. Judicature Soc; Ala. Sheriffs and Peace Officers Asn; WOW (mem. bd. dirs); Am. Legion; VFW; Sons of Conf. Vet; Elks; Moose; Mason. Rel: Presbyterian. Mailing Add: State Capitol, Montgomery, Ala. 36104.

GALOTTI, EDWARD FRANCIS D
Mass. State Rep.
b. Everett, Mass, 5/11/25; s. Rocco C. Galotti and Gertrude Blay G; m. 10/8/55 to Carol Crocker; c. Kathleen M. and Edward F, Jr. Educ: Boston Col, B.S, B.A, 49; Nat. Students Asn. Polit. & Govt. Pos: Mem, Belmont Dem. Town Cmt, Mass, 65-; town meeting mem, Belmont, 66-, selectman, 67- and munic. light cmnr, 67-; Mass. State Rep, 69- Bus. & Prof. Pos: Pres, Ambassador Aluminum Prod, Inc, 54-; proprietor, Edward F. Galotti Realty, 65- Mem: Middlesex Co. Selectmen's Asn; Nat. Asn. Acct; Munic. Elec. Asn. of Mass; The 100 Club; Elks; Sons of Italy; K. of C; Belmont Town Club; Belmont Civic Asn; Am. Legion; Foresters; Italian Workingmen's Asn. Rel: Roman Catholic. Mailing Add: 80 Clark St, Belmont, Mass. 02178.

GALPERIN, SIMON HIRSCH, JR. D
W.Va. State Del.
b. Charleston, W.Va, 8/5/31; s. Simon Hirsch Galperin and Fan Lavenstein G; m. 6/18/58 to Rose Marie Rogers; c. Stephen Hirsch and Gregory Lee. Educ: Wash and Lee Univ, B.S. in commerce, 53; Alpha Kappa Psi; Zeta Beta Tau. Polit. & Govt. Pos: Committeeman, Kanawha Co. Dem. Exec. Cmt, W.Va, 64-65; W.Va. State Del, Kanawha Co, 67- Bus. & Prof. Pos: Pres, Galperin Music Co, 63-; treas, Creative Arts Festival of W.Va. Mil. Serv: Entered as Ens, Navy, 53, released as Lt.(jg), 56; Lt, Naval Res, currently. Mem: Pres, Nat. Asn. of Young Music Merchants, 64-65; bd. of dirs, Nat. Asn. of Music Merchants, 65-67; Pi Tau Pi; Rotary; treas, Pub. Affairs Conf. of W.Va; Isaac Walton League (treas, Mountain State chap); bd. of trustees, B'nai B'rith. Rel: Jewish. Mailing Add: 111 Hickory Rd, Charleston, W.Va. 25314.

GALVIN, JOHN RAYMOND D
R.I. State Rep.
b. Pawtucket, R.I, 2/5/16; s. Patrick J. Galvin and Annie V. Elwood G; m. 5/30/40 to Catherine Doris Fogarty; c. Barry John and Brian David. Educ: Pawtucket High Sch, 4 years. Polit. & Govt. Pos: Dem. ward committeeman, Pawtucket Second Dist, R.I, 38-69; R.I. State Rep, 81st Dist, 67- Mem: Painter & Decorating Contractors of Am; K. of C; Elks; committeeman, Boys Scouts. Rel: Catholic. Mailing Add: 78 Warwick Rd, Pawtucket, R.I. 02861.

GALYEAN, ROY HORTON D
b. Bentonville, Ark, 7/8/15; s. Wilmer Elmo Galyean and Hattie Geneva Patton G; m. 12/21/35 to Emma Vernita Woods; c. Edward Roy. Educ: High Sch, Benton Co, Ark. Polit. & Govt. Pos: Ark. State Rep, 59-66. Bus. & Prof. Pos: Minister of the Gospel, Baptist Church, 48- Rel: Baptist. Mailing Add: R.R. 3, Bentonville, Ark. 72712.

GAMACHE, WILLIBERT D
b. Manchester, N.H, 5/20/88; married; c. eight; 34 grandchildren. Educ: St. Raphael Sch. Polit. & Govt. Pos: N.H. State Rep, 29-55; 61-63; -67; selectman. Bus. & Prof. Pos: Retired contractor and builder. Mem: Sachem of the Improved Order of Redmen; past pres, St. Francis of Assisi Holy Name Soc; Grange; Citizens Soc. Club; Laurier Club; Goffs Falls Civic Club. Rel: Catholic. Mailing Add: 2083 Goffs Falls Rd, Manchester, N.H. 03103. (1967)

GAMBILL, BRUCE WARREN R
Chmn, Osage Co. Rep. Party, Okla.
b. Carlsbad, N.Mex, 11/22/30; s. Oren Bain Gambill and Wilma Ally G; m. 6/4/52 to Patricia Hill; c. Bruce David, Dan Alan and Linda Michelle. Educ: Univ. Okla, B.S, 52, LL.B, 57; Scabbard and Blade; Lambda Chi Alpha. Polit. & Govt. Pos: Pres, Tulsa Co. Young Rep, Okla, 59, Tulsa Co. Rep. Exec. Cmt, 59-61 and Osage Co. Rep. Exec. Cmt, 63-64; chmn, Osage Co. Rep. Party, 64-, state committeeman, 69- Bus. & Prof. Pos: Asst. co. attorney, Wash. Co, 57-; indust. rels. mgr, Sinclair Oil & Gas, Tulsa, 58-63; partner, McCoy, Kelly & Gambill Law Firm, 63-64; partner, Kelly, & Gambill Law Firm, 64- Mil. Serv: Entered as 2nd Lt, Army, 52, released as 1st Lt, 54, after serv. in Seventh Inf. Div, Korea, 52-54; Korean Campaign Medal; Battle Ribbons. Mem: Okla. Bar Asn; Mason; Rotary; Am. Legion; C. of C; Boy Scouts; Osage Co. Bar Asn.(pres); Co. Bar Pres.(pres). Rel: Episcopal. Legal Res: R.R. 1, Pawhuska, Okla. 74056. Mailing Add: P.O. Box 321, Pawhuska, Okla. 74056.

GAMBILL, WALTER RAY R
1st V.Chmn, Rep. Party, Va.
b. Fredericksburg, Va, 7/12/22; s. Charles Joseph Gambill and Eva G; m. 9/26/42 to Jean; c. Walter R, Jr, Kenneth B, Steven Lee and Donna Jean. Educ: Richmond College, Univ. of Richmond, B.A, 42, T.C. Williams Sch. of Law, LL.B, 49; Univ. of Mich. Law Sch. Polit. & Govt. Pos: 1st v.chmn, Rep. Party, Va, 61- Bus. & Prof. Pos: Lawyer, 49- Mil. Serv: Entered as Pvt, Army Air Force, 42, released as Sgt, 45, after serv. in Tenth Weather Squad-

ron, China-India-Burma Theater. Mem: Mason; Am, Va. State and Richmond Bar Asns. Rel: Episcopal. Legal Res: 2401 Sunnybrook Rd, Richmond, Va. 23239. Mailing Add: 536 Granite Ave, Richmond, Va. 23226. (1967)

GAMBLE, MICHAEL P. D
Ohio State Rep.
b. 1907; married; c. Seven. Polit. & Govt. Pos: Councilman-at-lg, Canton, Ohio, 2 terms and councilman, 2 terms; Ohio State Rep, 67- Bus. & Prof. Pos: Salesman. Mailing Add: 2618 Clyde Place, Canton, Ohio 44706.

GAMBLE, WALKER RUBIN D
b. Bingham, Ill, 9/6/07; s. Charles W. Gamble and Iva Mayfield G; m. 12/15/33 to Anna M. McMahon; c. Teresa (Mrs. Dennis Macey). Educ: Fillmore High Sch, Grad, 29. Polit. & Govt. Pos: Committeeman, Lisle Dem. Town Cmt, Ill, 62-; del, Dem. Nat. Conv, 68. Bus. & Prof. Pos: Sales mgr, McIntosh & Co, Real Estate, 46-63; owner, Walker Gamble Agency, 63- Mil. Serv: Entered as Seaman, Navy, 43, released as Storekeeper II, 45, after serv. in Asiatic Pac; Asiatic Pac. Ribbon. Mem: VFW (past comdr); Lisle Lions Club (past pres); Lisle C. of C.(past pres); Dupage Bd. Realtors. Rel: Protestant. Mailing Add: 5136 Main St, Box D, Lisle, Ill. 60532.

GAMMAL, ALBERT ABRAHAM, JR. R
b. Lynn, Mass, 12/31/28; s. Albert A. Gammal and Jenny Shaker G; m. 12/4/55 to Margaret Ann Romley; c. Candith Ann, Sandra Ann, Gayle Ann and Joseph Albert. Educ: Clark Univ, B.B.A, 52; Suffolk Univ, LL.B, 66; Delta Sigma; Clark Univ. Players Soc. Polit. & Govt. Pos: Pres, Young Rep. Club, Worcester, Mass, 52-54; del, Mass. Rep. State Conv, 56-68; chmn, Mass. Coun. Young Rep. Clubs, 58-59; Rep. Jr. Nat. Committeeman, 60-61; chmn, Worcester Rep. Ward Cmt, 60-62; state rep, Mass. Gen. Court, 61-68; admin. asst, U.S. Sen. E.W. Brooke, 67-; del, Rep. Nat. Conv. 68. Bus. & Prof. Pos: Treas-dir, Gammal Chem. Co. Inc, 53-62; trustee, Gardner State Hosp, 54-69; attorney, 67- Mil. Serv: Entered as Pvt, Army, 46, released as Pfc, 48, after serving in 17th Inf, 1st Bn, 24th Corp, Far East, Korea, 46-47; Inf. Reserves, 48-50; Cpl, Air Force Reserves, 50-52. Mem: Mass. Bar Asn; Nat. Soc. State Legislators; Mass. Legislators Asn; Mason (32°); Shrine; Worcester Art Mus; Am. Legion; New Eng. Aquarium Soc. Outstanding Young Man award, Gr. Worcester Jr. C. of C; Serv. award and Red Triangle award, YMCA. Rel: Greek Orthodox. Mailing Add: 73 Sagamore Rd, Worcester, Mass. 01609.

GAMSER, HOWARD GRAHAM D
Counsel, Cmn. on Rules, Dem. Nat. Cmt.
b. N.Y.C, 9/24/19; s. Gustave Gamser and Rose Harris G; m. 10/5/52 to Doris P. Gold; c. Matthew Simon and Diona Marion. Educ: City Col. New York, B.S.S, 40; Columbia Univ, M.A, 41; N.Y. Univ, LL.B, 52; Phi Beta Kappa. Polit. & Govt. Pos: With Nat. Labor Rels. Bd, 46-52 and Wage Stabilization Bd, 52-53; chief counsel, Cmt. on Educ. and Labor Rels, U.S. House of Rep, 61-63; mem, Nat. Mediation Bd, 64-67, chmn, 67-69; counsel, cmn. on rules, Dem. Nat. Cmt, 69- Bus. & Prof. Pos: Attorney and arbitrator, N.Y.C, 52-61; partner, Boleroff, Olonoff & Scharf, 52-; lectr. labor law, Columbia Univ, 57-61; adj. prof. labor law, Georgetown Univ, 64-; counsel, Dutton, Gwertzman, Zumas & Wise, 69- Mil. Serv: Capt, Army, 41-46. Publ: Articles in various legal and econ. periodicals. Mem: Indust. and Labor Rels. Asn; Am. Econ. Asn; N.Y, D.C. and Fed. Bar Asns. Legal Res: 44 W. Tenth St, New York, N.Y. 10011. Mailing Add: Suite 702, 1225 19th St. N.W, Washington, D.C. 20036.

GANDY, EDYTHE EVELYN D
State Treas, Miss.
b. Hattiesburg, Miss, 9/4/22; d. Kearney C. Gandy and Abbie Whigham; single. Educ: Univ. of South. Miss, 39-41; Univ. Miss, J.D, 44. Polit. & Govt. Pos: Miss. State Rep, Forrest Co, 48-52; attorney, Miss. State Dept. Pub. Welfare, 52-58; Asst. Attorney Gen, Miss, 59; state treas, Miss, 60-64 & 68-; Cmnr. Pub. Welfare, Miss, 64-68. Bus. & Prof. Pos: State pres, Miss. Fedn. Bus. & Prfnl. Women's Clubs, 53-54; bd. dirs, Miss. Cong. PTA, 64-67; bd. dirs, Miss. Hosp. and Med. Serv, 67-; chmn, Pub. Employees' Retirement Syst. Miss, 68-69; chmn, Bd. Savings and Loan Asns, Miss, currently. Mem: Miss. State Bar Asn; Nat. Asn. Women Acct; Am. Pub. Welfare Asn; Miss. Bus. & Prfnl. Women's Club; Jackson, Miss. Altrusa Club; Miss. Econ. Coun; Miss. Women's Cabinet Pub. Affairs; Official Miss. Women's Club. First women in Miss. to be elected to statewide constitutional office. Rel: Baptist. Legal Res: Route 1, Hattiesburg, Miss. 39401. Mailing Add: 727 Arlington St, Jackson, Miss. 39202.

GANGLE, RUTH ALICE D
b. Waldport, Ore, 2/3/17; d. James Joseph Wolfe and Ruth Stone W; m. 2/18/38 to Lawrence Christian Gangle; c. Lawrence Christian, Printice James, Eugene Martin, Alice Marie, Stephen Robert, Rose Marta, Darice Lucille and George Hillary. Educ: Ore. State Col, 35-37; Univ. Ore, B.A, 41; Kappa Kappa Alpha. Polit. & Govt. Pos: Co-coord, Kennedy Campaign Off, Sacramento Co, Calif, 68; del. Dem. Nat. Conv, 68; precinct chmn, Humphrey Hq, Sacramento, 68. Rel: Roman Catholic. Mailing Add: 1005 San Ramon Way, Sacramento, Calif. 95825.

GANN, DONALD L. R
Mo. State Rep.
b. Sparta, Mo, 6/16/40; m. 9/21/62 to Joyce Kehr. Educ: Southwest Mo. State Col, B.S. in educ. Polit. & Govt. Pos: Mo. State Rep, 64-; mem, Christian Co. Young Rep. Club. Bus. & Prof. Pos: Pub. sch. teacher. Rel: Baptist. Mailing Add: 706 N. Tenth St, Ozark, Mo. 65721. (1967)

GANNETT, ANN COLE R
Mass. State Rep.
b. Brookline, Mass, 11/7/16; d. Benjamin Edwards Cole and Ann Sheafe C; m. 4/18/36 to Thomas B. Gannett, wid; c. Thomas B, Jr, Ann G.(Mrs. Hurlbut), Benjamin H, Deborah G.(Mrs. Brooks) and Peter C. Educ: Abbot Acad, cum laude, 33; Vassar Coll,33-35. Polit. & Govt. Pos: Chmn, Wayland Rep. Town Cmt, 49-52, mem, 46-; trustee, State Hosp, 50-56; mem, Gov. Herter Adv. Cmt, 52-54; mem, Mass. Rep. Finance Cmt, 52-60; mem, Mass. Rep. State Cmt, 52-67; mem, Civil Defense Cmn, 60-; del, Rep. Nat. Conv, 64; Mass. State Rep, 69- Rel: Roman Catholic. Mailing Add: 85 Old Connecticut Path, Wayland, Mass. 01778.

GANNON, WILLIAM J. D
Minority Leader, Iowa State House of Rep.
b. Mingo, Iowa, 7/9/37; s. Lio Gannon and Teresa; single. Educ: College, three years. Polit. & Govt. Pos: Iowa State Rep. and Minority Leader, Iowa State House of Rep, currently; del, Dem. Nat. Conv, 68. Bus. & Prof. Pos: Grain and livestock farming, 57- Mem: Elks; Farmers Union; Nat. Farmers Orgn. Rel: Choir Dir, Sacred Heart Church of Valeria. Mailing Add: Route 1, Mingo, Iowa 50168.

GANT, CHARLES GREEN D
Mem, Orange Co. Dem. Cent. Cmt, Calif.
b. Nashville, Tenn, 9/24/16; s. Charles Green Gant and Elizabeth Bell G; m. 2/14/41 to Margaret Weidner G; c. Michael Sebastian. Educ: Antioch Col, B.A, 42; Am. Univ, 46-50. Polit. & Govt. Pos: Dir, Calif. Dem. Coun, 63-65; v.pres, South. Calif. Dem. Coun, 64-65; mem, Orange Co. Dem. Cent. Cmt, 64- Bus. & Prof. Pos: Controller, Nat. Sci. Found, 51-53 and dir. of spec. studies, 53-54; bus. mgr, Res. Labs, Lockheed Aircraft Corp, 54-56; contracts mgr, Aeronutronic Div, Ford Motor Co, 56-62 and mgr. reentry progs, 59-62; dir. Newport Beach Opers, Space and Reentry Div, Philco Corp, 62- Mil. Serv: Ohio Nat. Guard, 37-39; entered as Ens, Navy, 43, released as Lt, 46, after serv. in Supply Corps, Pac, 43-46; Am. and Pac. Theater Ribbons. Mem: Am. Ord. Asn; Air Force Asn; Army Asn; Am. Inst. of Aeronaut. and Astronaut; dir, Santa Ana Commun. Chest. Rel: Protestant. Mailing Add: 1101 Tropic Lane, Santa Ana, Calif. 92705. (1967)

GANT, JOSEPH ERWIN, JR. D
N.Mex. State Sen.
b. Alamance Co, N.C, 2/4/12; s. Joseph Erwin Gant and Mary Gilmer Banner G; m. 2/11/38 to Opal Martin; c. Joseph Erwin, III and Mary Martin. Educ: Univ. N.C, B.S. chem, 34; Alpha Tau Omega. Polit. & Govt. Pos: Chmn, Eddy Co. Dem. Party, N.Mex, 48-; pub. mem, N.Mex. State Invest. Coun, 59-60; chmn, Eddy Co. Bd. Cmnr, 67-68; N.Mex. State Sen, Dist. 22, 68- Bus. & Prof. Pos: Chemist, U.S. Borax & Chem. Co, 34-67. Mem: Am. Chem. Soc; N.Mex. Asn. Co; Elks. Rel: Episcopal. Legal Res: 602 Riverside Dr, Carlsbad, N.Mex. 88220. Mailing Add: P.O. Box 909, Carlsbad, N.Mex. 88220.

GARAAS, JOHN O. D
b. Wheelock, N.Dak, 9/1/22; married; c. Four. Educ: St. Olaf Col; Univ. N.Dak. Polit. & Govt. Pos: N.Dak. State Sen, 57-61; state chmn, Dem. Party, N.Dak, 60-61; U.S. Dist. Attorney, N.Dak, 61-68. Bus. & Prof. Pos: Attorney-at-Law, Fargo, currently. Mil. Serv: World War II. Mailing Add: 2623 S. 12th St, Fargo, N.Dak. 58102.

GARABEDIAN, ADRIA W. D
b. Carson City, Nev, 2/1/15; d. Isaac Fernando Wiseman and Edna Sullivan W; m. 5/9/42 to Armenog Garabedian; c. Michael Nigo and Bonnie. Educ: Univ. Calif, Berkeley, A.B, 37; Tulane Sch. Soc. Work, 40-41; Pi Phi Delta. Polit. & Govt. Pos: Pres, Dem. Women's Forum, San Francisco, Calif, 68- Bus. & Prof. Pos: Ed-mgr, The Haight-Ashbury Record, currently. Mem: Dem. Women's Forum of San Francisco; Women's Int. League for Peace and Freedom; Bd, Haight-Ashbury Neighborhood Coun. Mailing Add: 191 Delmar St, San Francisco, Calif. 94117.

GARABEDIAN, JOHN MICHEL R
b. Fresno, Calif, 2/28/09; s. Michel Garabedian and Emma Tanchodian G; m. 8/10/29 to Bertha Minnasian. Educ: High Sch, 4 years. Polit. & Govt. Pos: Mem, State Bd. Agr, Calif, currently. Legal Res: 3104 Huntington Blvd, Fresno, Calif. 93702. Mailing Add: P.O. Box 788, Fresno, Calif. 93712.

GARBARINO, JOHN ALFRED R
Justice,Supreme Court, N.Y.
b. New York, N.Y, 11/18/18; s. John Garbarino and Adelaide Ghilina G; m. 4/5/45 to Helen Marie Lawlor. Educ: St. Peters Col, N.J, B.S, 39; Fordham Univ. Sch. Soc. Serv, M.A, 41; St. John's Univ. Sch. Law, LL.B, 52. Polit. & Govt. Pos: Admin. asst. to U.S. Rep. John H. Ray, N.Y, 53-62; cand, Dist. Attorney, Richmond Co, N.Y, 59; chmn, Richmond Rep. Co. Cmt, 62-68; del, Rep. Nat. Conv, 64 & 68; Justice, N.Y. Supreme Court, Second Judicial Dist, 69- Bus. & Prof. Pos: Dir. voc. and educ. counseling serv, Halloran Gen. Hosp, Staten Island, N.Y, 46-47; chmn. rehab. bd, Vet. Admin. Regional Off, Brooklyn, 47-50; med. social worker, U.S. Pub. Health Serv. Hosp, Staten Island, 50-52; attorney-at-law, 52-; pres, Providence Estates Inc, 55-64; and Wil Gar Realty Corp, 55- Mil. Serv: Entered as Pvt, Army, 41, released as Capt, 46, after serv. in Signal Corps, Alaskan Command, 43-45. Mem: New York State Bar Asn; dir, Richmond Co. Bar Asn; Am. Asn. of Soc. Workers. Rel: Roman Catholic. Legal Res: 586 Ocean Terr, Staten Island, N.Y. 10301. Mailing Add: 350 St. Marks Place, Staten Island, N.Y. 10301.

GARBETT, RICHARD WALKER R
Dir. Commun, Rep. Nat. Cmt.
b. Gary, Ind, 8/18/26; s. Roy Arthur Garbett and Evelyn Walker G; m. 6/11/55 to Mary Elizabeth Welford; c. Barbara Lee, Margaret Elizabeth, Richard Welford and Mary Hannah. Educ: Yale Univ, B.A, 49; Yale Polit. Union. Polit. & Govt. Pos: Pub. rels. dir, Yale Young Rep. Club, 49-50; nat. committeeman, Active Young Rep. of Del, Inc, 49-53; pub. rels. adv. cmt, N.J. Rep. Cmt, 61-62; pres, Florham Park Rep. Club, 61; munic. Rep. chmn, Florham Park, 62; dist. chmn, Morris Co. Rep. Cmt, 63-64, mem. exec. cmt, 63-67; pub. rels. dir, U.S. Rep. Peter Frelinghuysen, N.J, 62 & 64 and campaign mgr, 66; v.chmn, N.J. Nixon Now Cmt, 68; nat. field advert. dir, Nixon-Agnew Campaign Cmt, 68; dir. commun, Rep. Nat. Cmt, 69- Bus. & Prof. Pos: Mkt. exec, Vick Chem. Co. N.Y.C. and Manila, P.I, 50-57; acct. exec, Compton Advert. Inc, N.Y.C, 57-59; prod. mkt. mgr, Thomas J. Lipton, Inc, Englewood Cliffs, N.J, 59-62; v.pres. and acct. supv, Kenyon and Eckhardt, Inc, N.Y.C, 62-69. Mil. Serv: Entered as A/S, Navy, 44, released as Radioman 2/C, 46, after serv. in U.S.S. LCI 682, Asiatic-Pac. Theater, ADCOMPHISFOR PAC-Guam, 45-46; Ens, Naval Res, 46-55; Victory Medal; Am. Theater and Pac. Theater Medals. Mem: Export Mgrs. Club. N.Y; Yale Club N.Y.C; Capitol Hill Club, Wash, D.C. Rel: Protestant. Mailing Add: 11116 Luxmanor Rd, Rockville, Md. 20852.

GARBOSE, DORIS RHODA R
State Committeewoman, Mass. Rep. State Cmt.
b. Bridgeport, Conn, 3/11/24; d. David Lewis Lesser and Betty Lessler; m.

8/19/45 to Judge William Garbose; c. Daniel Marvin, James Lesser, David Lewis and Susan Beth. Educ: Univ. Mich, Ann Arbor, B.A, 45; Zeta Phi Eta; Sigma Delta Tau. Polit. & Govt. Pos: State committeewoman, Mass. Rep. State Cmt, 60-; mem, Athol Town Rep. Cmt, Mass, 60-, v.chmn, 62-66; alternate del, Rep. Nat. Conv, 68. Bus. & Prof. Pos: Dir. and clerk, Keystone Nursing Home, Inc, Leominster, Mass, 60-67, adminstr. and dir, 67-, Franklin Nursing Home, Inc, Greenfield, 64-; dir, Gardner Manor Nursing Home, Gardner, 65- Mem: Quota Club; Am. Col. of Nursing Home Adminstrs; Hadassah. Rel: Jewish. Mailing Add: 1192 Main St, Athol, Mass. 01331.

GARCIA, JOSEPH ALBERT R
Finance Chmn, San Benito Co. Rep. Cent. Cmt, Calif.
b. Hollister, Calif, 10/12/02; s. Jose Silveira Garcia and Mary Rose G; m. 6/24/44 to Cecelia Ann Dicklich; c. Vernon Joseph. Educ: San Benito Co. Jr. Col, 2 years. Polit. & Govt. Pos: Mem, San Benito Co. Rep. Cent. Cmt, Calif, 63- and chmn. finance cmt, 65-; mem, Rep. State Cent. Cmt, Calif, 64- Bus. & Prof. Pos: Secy, acct. and gen. mgr, Waldo Rohnert Co, Hollister, Calif, 27-46; dealer in livestock, furs and sporting goods, Joseph A. Garcia & Son, 46- Mil. Serv: Entered as Pfc, Nat. Guard, Calif, 42, released as 1st Sgt, 46, after serv. in Rifle Co. Mem: Elks; F&AM; Eastern Star; K.T; AAONMS; I.D.E.S; San Benito Co. Farm Bur; San Benito Co. Cattlemen's Asn; Assoc. Farmers of San Benito Co; life mem, Nat. Rifle Asn; Am. Forestry Asn; Fur Takers of Am; Nat. Trappers Asn; San Benito Co. Alumni Asn; San Benito Co. Saddle Horse Asn; Nat. Geog. Soc; Assoc. Farmers of Calif. Rel: Catholic. Mailing Add: 3761 Fairview Rd, Hollister, Calif. 95023.

GARCIA, JOSEPH ALEXANDER, JR. D
Tex. State Rep.
b. Brownsville, Tex, 9/26/36; s. Joseph Alexander Garcia, Sr. and Bertha Champion G; m. 11/25/61 to Sue Ann Barr; c. J. Alex, III, Felicia Anne and Sandra Sue. Educ: Tex. A&I Univ, B.S, 60; Aggie Club; Newman Club. Polit. & Govt. Pos: Tex. State Rep, 46th Dist, Place 3, 68- Bus. & Prof. Pos: Ranch mgr, Santa Berta Ranch, 60- Mem: Educ. cmt, Bi-Nat. Planning Cmn; Gov. Cmt. of 500; Order of Alhambra; Farm Bur; Lower Rio Grande Valley C. of C. Rel: Catholic. Legal Res: 800 S. Ninth, Raymondville, Tex. 78580. Mailing Add: P.O. Box 573, Raymondville, Tex. 78580.

GARCIA, ROBERT D
N.Y. State Sen.
b. Bronx, N.Y, 1/9/33; s. Rafael Garcia and Rosa Rodrigues G; m. 5/2/59 to Anita Theresa Medina; c. Rosalind, Robert and Kenneth. Educ: R.C.A. Inst, E.E, 57; Commun. Col. N.Y, 1 year; City Col. N.Y, B.A. Polit. & Govt. Pos: Cong. asst. to Congressman James H. Scheuer, 21st Cong. Dist, 65-66; N.Y. State Assemblyman, 83rd and 77th Assembly Dist, 66-67; N.Y. State Sen, 29th Sen. Dist, 67- Bus. & Prof. Pos: Pres. and owner, Bruckner Volkswagen, 2 years. Mil. Serv: Entered as Pvt, Army, 50, released as Sgt, 53, after serv. in Third Inf. Div, Korea, 51-52; Korean Serv. Ribbons; Korean Combat Ribbon; 2 Bronze Stars; Good Conduct Medal. Mem: Adlai Stevenson Club; P.R. Vet. Asn; P.R. Nat. Asn. for Civil Rights; NAACP. Rel: Protestant. Legal Res: 563 Cauldwell Ave, Bronx, N.Y. 10455. Mailing Add: 221 St.Annis Ave, Bronx, N.Y. 10454.

GARCIA, SANTIAGO D
Sen, V.I. Legis.
b. Vieques, P.R, 7/25/23; s. Emilio Garcia and Natividad Cruz G; m. 6/17/51 to Aida Perez; c. Jose Luis, Migdalia, Santiago, Jr, William, Luis Epifanio and Nereida. Educ: Vieques High Sch, P.R, 4 years. Polit. & Govt. Pos: Sen, V.I. Legis, 67- Bus. & Prof. Pos: Mgr, private enterprises, 46-67. Mil. Serv: Army, 43-45, Cpl, serv. in 521st Inf. and Qm, Pac, 45-46; Good Conduct Medal. Rel: Roman Catholic. Legal Res: 132 Golden Rock, Christiansted, St. Croix, V.I. 00820. Mailing Add: P.O. Box 726, Christiansted, St. Croix, V.I. 00820.

GARCIA, ZARAGOZA D, JR. D
Chmn, Jim Wells Co. Dem. Party, Tex.
b. Ben Bolt, Tex, 11/3/25; s. Zaragoza Garcia and Concepcion Gonzales de G; single. Educ: Ben Bolt High Sch, grad, 43. Polit. & Govt. Pos: Chmn, Jim Wells Co. Dem. Party, Tex, 65- Mil. Serv: Entered as Pvt, Army, 44, released as Sgt, 46, after serv. in 9th Inf. Div, ETO, 44-46; three battle stars, Inf. Combat Badge; Presidential Citation; Good Conduct Medal. Rel: Catholic. Mailing Add: Route 1, Box 108, Alice, Tex. 78332.

GARCIA-MENDEZ, MIGUEL A. R
Pres, Directory Cmt. of the Statehood Rep. Party, P.R.
b. Aguadilla, P.R, 11/17/02; s. Juan Bautista García-Figueroa and Carmen Méndez-Elías G; m. 6/25/26 to Fredeswinda Ramírez de Arellano-Bártoli; c. Ileana (Mrs. Carr) and Fredeswinda (Mrs. Frontera). Educ: Univ. P.R, LL.B, 22; Princeton, Diploma on Constitutional Law; pres, Grad. Class of 1922; Res. Officers Training Corps. Polit. & Govt. Pos: Judge, Munic. Court of San Germán, P.R, 23; Rep, P.R. House of Rep, 32-33, Floor Leader, 33; mem, Rep. Party of P.R. Minority Constitutional Conv, 51-52; Sen-at-lg. and Floor Leader, P.R. Legis. Assembly, 52; mem, U.S-P.R. Cmn. on the Status of P.R; pres. directory cmt. and state chmn, Statehood Rep. Party, P.R, 52-; del, Rep. Nat. Conv, 68. Bus. & Prof. Pos: Pres, Mayaguez Ins. Serv, Inc, 43; pres, West. Fed. Savings & Loan Asn. Cent. Igualdad, Inc, Super-A Fertilizer Works, Inc. and Mayaguez Motors Corp, currently. Publ: Puerto Rico—The Link of the Americas, Cartas al Pueblo del Presidente del Partido Estadista, Political and Parliamentarian Speeches. Mem: Lawyers' Col. of P.R; Am. Bar Asn; Asn. of the U.S. Army; Ateneo de P.R; Sociedad de Periodistas, YMCA; Lions; hon. pres, Casa de España; Presbyterian Hosp; Asn. of Sugar Producers of P.R; Casino de Mayaguez; Shooting & Rifle Club; Pro-Arte Musical; Casino de San Germán, P.R. Rel: Catholic. Legal Res: Cerro de Las Mesas, Mayaguez, P.R. Mailing Add: P.O. Box 599, Cerro Las Mesas, Mayaguez, P.R. 00709. (1967)

GARCIA-TANON, JOSE D
b. Santurce, P.R, 8/15/34; s. Pedro Garcia-Hoyo and Genoveva Tañón G; m. 9/30/61 to Ana Luz Rodriguez; c. Jose Armando. Educ: Univ. of P.R, B.A. in humanities. Polit. & Govt. Pos: Rep, P.R. House of Rep, 64-68; mem, San Juan Cent. Cmt, Popular Dem. Party, P.R. Mem: Pres, Local Union 1768, Am. Fedn. State, Co. and Munic. Employees. Rel: Catholic. Mailing Add: J-O Coin Villa Andalucia, Rio Piedras, San Juan, P.R. 00928. (1967)

GARDELLA, HAZEL LUCILLE R
b. Ruth, Nev, 12/20/15; d. Charles Henry Smith and Mabel Draper S; m. 4/7/40 to Louie Andrew Gardella; c. L. Gene, Bruce R. and Kent A. Educ: White Pine High Sch, grad, 35; Excelsis Sch. Cosmetology, 38. Polit. & Govt. Pos: Charter mem, Lyon Co. Rep. Women's Club, Nev, 52; mem, Rep. Women's Club Reno, 55; v.chairwoman, Washoe Co. Rep. Cent. Cmt, 64-66; del, Rep. Co. and State Conv, 64, 66 & 68; v.pres, Nev. Fedn. Rep. Women, 65, pres, 67-69; staff mem, Gov. Paul Laxalt's Campaign, 66; mem, Nev. Employ. Coun, 67; chmn, employ. cmt, Gov. Cmn. Status Women, 67; staff mem, Lt. Gov. Fike for Sen. Campaign, 68; del. and platform cmt. rep, Rep. Nat. Conv, 68. Bus. & Prof. Pos: Mgr. and operator, beauty salon, 39-42; mkt. research interviewer, Reno, 55-63; crew leader, U.S. Census Bur, 60; hairdresser, Morturary, Reno, currently. Mem: Cross and Crescent Club; Prospector Hill Property Owner's Asn.(treas); bd. mem, YWCA; life mem, PTA. Rel: Episcopal. Mailing Add: 135 Boxer Dr, Reno, Nev. 89502.

GARDINER, SHERRY BIGGERS R
b. Toledo, Ohio, 12/30/18; d. John David Biggers and Mary Kelsey B; m. 10/22/41 to Sprague H. Gardiner, M.D; c. John Biggers, William Sprague, Thomas Kelsey and Ann Sherret. Educ: Vassar Col, A.B, 40. Polit. & Govt. Pos: Del, Rep. State Conv, Ind, 54, 60, 62 & 68; precinct committeeman, Marion Co, Rep. Party, 60-, vol. chmn, 64, vice ward chmn, 66-, assoc. vol. chmn, 66 & 67 and vol. worker at Rep. hq, 66-; area capt, Rep. Action Cmt, Marion Co, 66; alternate del, Rep. Nat. Conv, 68; mem, Campaign Coordinating Cmt, Marion Co, Ind, 68; mem, Ind. Inaugural Cmt, Marion Co, Ind. and Wash, D.C, 68-69; spec. asst. to chmn, Marion Co. Rep. Cent. Cmt, Ind, 68- Mem: Junior League of Indianapolis; Marion Co. Rep. Workshop; Day Nursery Assoc. of Indianapolis; League of Women Voters; Suemma Coleman Home (Bd. mem); Meridian Hills Country Club; Marion Co. Med. Auxiliary. Rel: Protestant. Mailing Add: 330 West 62nd St, Indianapolis, Ind. 46260.

GARDNER, GEORGE DEXTER D
Ind. State Rep.
b. Vincennes, Ind, 3/17/32; s. Dexter Carl Gardner and Hellen Tracy G; m. 6/8/52 to Virginia Johnson; c. Jan Ruth and David Dexter. Educ: Ind. Col. Mortuary Sci, 1 year; pres. of class. Polit. & Govt. Pos: Co. coroner, Knox Co, Ind, 57-60 & 60-64; Ind. State Rep, Knox Co, 69- Mil. Serv: Entered as Pvt, Army, 52, released as Cpl, 54, after serv. in 398th Graves Registrn. Qm. Mem: Pres, Ceretery Bd. Regents, Vincennes, Ind, 60-69; pres, Ind. State Coroners Asn, 61; nat. membership chmn, Nat. Selected Morticians, 68; Elks; Mason; York Rite; Scottish Rite; Shrine; Harmony Soc; Moose; Eagles; Am. Legion; Rotary. Distinguished Serv. Award. Rel: Methodist. Mailing Add: 1425 McDowell Rd, Vincennes, Ind. 47591.

GARDNER, GEORGE W. R
b. Scituate, R.I, 2/22/99. Educ: U. of R.I, Exten. Polit. & Govt. Pos: R.I. State Rep, 61-66; Scituate Town Coun, 16 yrs. Bus. & Prof. Pos: Retired; former asst. Treas, Congdon & Carpenter Co. Mem: former Pres, Treas, Hope and Jackson Fire Co; Hope Assoc; Lodge of Masons; Scituate Police Asn. Rel: Hope Methodist Church. Mailing Add: Hope, R.I. 02831. (1967)

GARDNER, J. HORACE R
Ill. State Rep.
b. Cairo, Ill; m. to Edith Foster. Educ: Public high schs. Polit. & Govt. Pos: Alternate del, Rep. Nat. Conv, 36; Ill. State Rep, 48-; Rep. ward committeeman, 48-; mem, Ill. State Rep. Cent. Cmt, 68- Bus. & Prof. Pos: Pub. rels. Mailing Add: 6014 S. Indiana Ave, Chicago, Ill. 60637. (1967)

GARDNER, JAMES CARSON R
b. Rocky Mount, N.C, 4/18/33; s. James C. Gardner and Sue T. G; m. 10/5/57 to Marie Tyler; c. Beth, Terry and Christopher. Educ: N.C. State Univ, 53-56. Polit. & Govt. Pos: N.C. Cong. cand, 64; chmn, N.C. State Rep. Party, 65; U.S. Rep, N.C, 67-68; del, Rep. Nat. Conv, 68; cand. for Gov. of N.C, 68. Bus. & Prof. Pos: V.pres, Gardner Dairy Prod, 56-61; exec. v.pres, Hardee's Food Systems, Inc, 62-66; pres. and chmn. of bd, Quick Food Syst, Inc, 68; pres, Gardner Properties, 68; pres, and chmn. of bd, South. Sports Corp, 69. Mil. Serv: Entered as Pvt, Army, 54, released as Pfc, 56, after serv. in Signal Corps. Publ: A Time to Speak, 68. Mem: Elks; Am. Legion; Morning Optimist; United Commun. Serv. Young Man of the Year award, Rocky Mount Jr. C. of C, 67. Mailing Add: 3404 Hawthorne Rd, Rocky Mount, N.C. 27801.

GARDNER, JAY D. R
Mem, State Rep. Exec. Cmt, Ga.
b. Camilla, Ga, 9/23/29; s. Bernard Clay Gardner and Annie Williams G; m. 6/19/51 to Ruth Carleen Gaulden; c. James Robert, Jay D, Jr. and Katherine. Educ: Emory Univ; Univ. Ga, B.B.A, 51, LL.B, 56; Chi Phi; Phi Beta Kappa. Polit. & Govt. Pos: Chmn, Chatham Co. Rep. Cmt, Ga, 66-67, counsel and mem, currently; former Ga. State Sen; mem, State Rep. Exec. Cmt, currently. Bus. & Prof. Pos: Partner, Adams, Adams, Brennan and Gardner, 59- Mil. Serv: Entered as 2nd Lt, Air Force, 51, released as 1st Lt, 53, after serv. in 20th Fighter Bomber Wing, ETO; Maj, Air Force Res, Admin. Officer, 9899th Air Res. Squadron, currently. Mem: Am. and Ga. Bar Asns; Rep. Club, First Cong. Dist. of Ga.(mem. bd. dirs); F&AM; Optimist (past Lt. Gov). Rel: Episcopal. Legal Res: 616 E. 50th St, Savannah, Ga. 31405. Mailing Add: P.O. Box 1208, Savannah, Ga. 31402.

GARDNER, JOHN PICKENS D
b. Darlington, S.C, 7/18/23; s. Charles E. Gardner and Elizabeth Peden G; m. to Lucylee Arthur G; c. Harriet, John Jr. Educ: Wofford Col; Univ. of S.C, LL.B, 48. Polit. & Gov. Pos: S.C. State Rep, 59-66. Bus. & Prof. Pos: Lawyer. Mil. Serv: Air Force, Aerial Gunner, 410th Bomb Group, 9th AF, 65 Combat missions, 43-45. Mem: Mason; VFW; Cub Scout master; Co, State and Am. Bar Asns. Rel: First Baptist Church of Darlington. Mailing Add: Darlington, S.C. 29532. (1967)

GARDNER, JOHN WILLIAM R
b. Los Angeles, Calif, 10/8/12; s. William Gardner and Marie Flora G; m. 8/14/34 to Aida Marroquin; c. Stephanie (Mrs. Philip Trimble) and Francesca (Mrs. John R. Reese). Educ: Stanford Univ, A.B, 35, A.M, 36; Univ. Calif, Ph.D, 38, LL.D, 59. Hon. degrees from various cols. and univs. Polit. & Govt. Pos: Head Latin-Am. Sect, For. Broadcast Intel. Serv, Fed. Commun.

Cmn, 42-43; mem. bd. mgr, State Charities Aid Asn, 50-54; chmn, Soc. Sci. Panel Sci. Adv. Bd, U.S. Air Force, 51-55; chmn, U.S. Adv. Cmn. Int. Educ. and Cultural Affairs, 62-64; mem. and chmn, White House House Conf. on Educ, 65; mem, Coun. on For. Affairs; secy, Health, Educ. and Welfare, 65-68; chmn, Urban Coalition, 68- Bus. & Prof. Pos: Asst. psychol. teacher, Univ. Calif, 36-38; instr, Conn. Col, 38-40; asst. prof. psychol, Mt. Holyoke Col, 40-42; staff mem, Carnegie Corp, N.Y, 46-47, esec-assoc, 47-49, v.pres, 49-55 and pres, 55-; pres, Carnegie Found, 55-; trustee, N.Y. Sch. Soc. Work, 49-55; mem, Adv. Cmt. Soc. Sci, Nat. Sci. Found, 59-62; Trustee, Metrop. Mus. of Art, 60-63; dir, Woodrow Wilson Found, 60-63 and Boys' Clubs of Am, 61-64. Mil. Serv: Capt, Marine Corps, 43-46, with serv. in Off. Strategic Serv, Mediterranean and ETO, 44-45; Air Force Exceptional Serv. Award, 56; Presidential Medal of Freedom, 64. Publ: Author, Excellence; Self Renewal; No Easy Victories; ed, To Turn the Tide. Mem: Am. Psychol. Asn; Am. Asn. for Adv. Sci.(dir); N.Y. Acad. Sci; Royal Soc. Arts (Benjamin Franklin fel); Pilgrims U.S; Century Asn, Coffee House, Stanford (N.Y.C), Cosmos (Wash, D.C) and Dutch Treat Clubs. Mailing Add: 5325 Kenwood Ave, Chevy Chase, Md. 20015.

GARDNER, LLOYD H. R
Mem, Exec. Bd, Wash. State Rep. Cent. Cmt.
b. La Junta, Colo, 6/28/20; s. Chester J. Gardner and Annie Halberg G; m. 9/11/50 to Lucille Bischof; c. Susan, Barbara, Nancy, Jeanne, Patricia and George. Educ: Univ. Colo, B.S. in mech. eng, 42; Tau Beta Pi; Sigma Tau; Pi Tau Sigma. Polit. & Govt. Pos: Training chmn, Neighbor-to-Neighbor chmn, area chmn. and precinct committeeman, King Co. Rep. Party, Wash, 62-64; chmn, 30th Legis. Dist. Rep. Party, 63-; alternate del, Rep. Nat. Conv, 64; mem. exec. bd, Wash. State Rep. Cent. Cmt, 64- Bus. & Prof. Pos: Research engr, Boeing Airplane Co, 42-53, eng. supvr, 53- Mem: Am. Soc. Mech. Engrs. Mailing Add: 30210 56th S, Auburn, Wash. 98002. (1967)

GARDNER, REECE B. R
Mem, Lenoir Co. Rep. Exec. Cmt, N.C.
b. Bennettsville, S.C, 9/27/32; s. John Tilghman Gardner and Amy Lee Shaw G; m. 11/5/60 to Emma V; c. Jessica and Reece B, Jr. Educ: Clemson Col, 2 years; Univ. S.C, 2 years; Pi Kappa Alpha. Polit. & Govt. Pos: State chmn, Am. for Independent Action, N.C, 64-65; Second Dist. Rep. cand. for U.S. Cong, 66, First Dist. cand, 68; v.chmn, Second Dist. Young Rep, 67; aide to President Nixon, 69; mem, Lenoir Co. Rep. Exec. Cmt, 69- Bus. & Prof. Pos: V.pres. & treas, Fred C. Gardner Co, Inc, 64-; bd. dirs, Lenoir Plumbing & Heating Co, Inc, 68- Mil. Serv: Entered as Seaman, Navy, 51, released as PN-1, 55, after serv. in Mediterranean Theatre, 53-54; Award for outstanding leadership, Naval Air Sta, Pensacola, Fla. Publ: 'For Love of Country,' Hallmark Mag, 6/56. Mem: Am. Legion; Local and Nat. C. of C. Rel: Baptist. Legal Res: 2506 Hodges Rd, Kinston, N.C. 28501. Mailing Add: P.O. Box 1536, Kinston, N.C. 28501.

GARDNER, VAN H. R
N.H. State Rep.
b. Bethlehem, N.H, 1/17/00; married; c. One daughter. Educ: Schs. of Bethlehem and Littleton. Polit. & Govt. Pos: Police chief, N.H, 19 years; N.H. State Rep, 49-51, 53-55, 65-67 & 69- Bus. & Prof. Pos: New Eng. Elec. Syst, retired 65. Mil. Serv: Civilian recruiting officer, Army, World War II. Mem: Odd Fellows; Eagles; Elks; life mem, N.H. Police Chiefs Asn. Rel: Methodist. Mailing Add: 85 Pleasant St, Littleton, N.H. 03561.

GARFF, KEN D. R
Rep. Nat. Committeeman, Utah
b. Draper, Utah, 7/17/05; s. Royal B. Garff and Rachael Day G; m. 1931 to Marjorie Heiner; c. Gary, Robert and Janie. Educ: Univ. Utah, grad. Polit. & Govt. Pos: Mem, local, state and nat. campaigns; dist. chmn, Rep. Party, Utah, 60-64; Rep. nat. committeeman, Utah, 64- Bus. & Prof. Pos: Owner, Ken Garff Co; pres, Ken Garff Trailer Sales and Aetna Trailer Sales; part owner, Deseret Livestock Co; dir, First Security Bank, 60- Mem: Dir, YMCA, 62-; exec. dir, Boy Scouts, 63-; co-chmn, United Fund, 64; dir, Country Club; Alta Club; Hunting Club; New State Duck Club; Univ. of Utah Boosters. Rel: Latter-day Saint. Mailing Add: 2720 St. Mary's Way, Salt Lake City, Utah 84108.

GARFIELD, JOHN CLEMENT D
Chmn. Task Force on Party Reform, New Dem. Coalition
b. Ames, Iowa, 8/13/30; s. Hon. Theodore G. Garfield and Carolyn Crosby G; div; c. John David and Holly Melissa. Educ: Iowa State Univ, B.S, 51; Harvard Univ, 53-54; Univ. Iowa, M.A, 57 and Ph.D, 63; Psi Chi; Phi Kappa Psi. Polit. & Govt. Pos: Mem. and former finance chmn, Johnson Co. Dem. Cent. Cmt, Iowa; del, Iowa Dem. State Conv, 60, 62, 64, 66 & 68; mem. exec. cmt, Citizens for Harold E. Hughes for Gov, 64; local chmn, Johnson Co. E.B. Smith for Sen, 66; del, Dem. Nat. Conv, 68; Iowa Campaign Dir, Eugene McCarthy, 68; chmn. task force on party reform, New Dem. Coalition, 68- Bus. & Prof. Pos: Dir. psychol. serv, State Serv. for Crippled Children, Univ. Iowa, 59-66 and asst. dir, 66; clin. psychologist, Iowa City, 67-; lectr. psychol, Univ. Iowa, 67- Mem: Iowa, Midwest and Am. Psychol. Asns; Am. Orthopsychiat. Asn; Soc. for the Psychol. Study of Soc. Issues; Sigma Xi; Iowa Dem. Conf; Iowa and Am. Civil Liberties Union. Rel: Unitarian. Legal Res: 2405 Towncrest Lane, Iowa City, Iowa 52240. Mailing Add: P.O. Box 403, Iowa City, Iowa 52240.

GARFIELD, THEODORE GREENLIEF R
Chief Justice, Supreme Court of Iowa
b. Humboldt, Iowa, 11/12/94; s. George Selwyn Garfield and Mary Ellen White G; m. 6/30/24 to Carolyn Crosby; c. Theodore Greenlief, Jr, David C, John C. and Carol (Mrs. Thomas L. Carson). Educ: State Univ. of Iowa, B.A, 15, LL.B, 17; Phi Beta Kappa; Delta Sigma Rho; Order of the Coif; Phi Kappa Psi; Phi Delta Phi. Polit. & Govt. Pos: Judge, 11th Judicial Dist, Iowa, 27-40; Chief Justice, Supreme Court of Iowa, 41-; chmn, Nat. Conf. of Chief Justices, 65-66. Mil. Serv: Entered as Cadet, Army, 17, released as 1st Lt, 18, after serv. in Field Artil. Mem: Iowa State and Am. Bar Asns; Iowa Law Sch. Found.(chmn, bd. of trustees, 52-); Iowa Am. Judicature Soc. (dir); Univ. of Iowa Alumni Asn.(pres, 48-51); trustee, Ames Pub. Libr, 26-68. Rel: Unitarian. Mailing Add: 1109 Ridgewood Ave, Ames, Iowa 50010.

GARIBALDI, PETER PAUL R
N.J. State Assemblyman
b. New Brunswick, N.J, 9/12/31; s. Petro Garibaldi and Katherine Richuisa G; m. 8/24/56 to Lynne Margaret Wright; c. Peter, Valerie, Rhonda, David, Authur and Michael. Educ: Rutgers Univ, 1 year; Riders Col, B.S, 55. Polit. & Govt. Pos: Committeeman, Rep. Party, Monroe Twp, N.J, 63-66; mem, Monroe Twp. Planning Bd, 65; chmn, Recreation Cmt. and Pub. Bldg. and Grounds Dept, 66; pres, Monroe Rep. Orgn, 66; N.J. State Assemblyman, Dist. 7A, 68-, chmn, Ways and Means Cmt, N.J. State Assembly, 68, v.chmn, Labor Rels. Cmt, 69 and mem, Fed. and Inst. Rels. Cmt, 69. Bus. & Prof. Pos: Pub. Acct, 56-; auditor, Bricklayers, Masons and Plasters Union, 57-59; enrolled to practice for Internal Revenue, 66- Mil. Serv: Entered as Aviation Cadet, Air Force, 49, released as 1st Lt, 54, after serv. in 624th Bomber Squadron, Korea, 52-53. Mem: Italian Exec. Am.(dir. bd. gov); Am. Italian Descent; Nat. Soc. Pub. Acct; N.J. Asn. Pub. Acct; Bricklayers, Masons and Plasters Union; charter mem. S.River Water Shed Asn; Monroe-Jamesburg Jaycees. Rel: Catholic. Legal Res: R.D. 1, Half Acre Rd, Cranbury, N.J. 08512. Mailing Add: 25 Forsgate Dr, Jamesburg, N.J. 08813.

GARINGER, ELMER HENRY D
b. Mt. Vernon, Mo, 7/13/91; s. John A. Garinger and Catherine Julia Moore G; m. 1920 to Katherine Thomas, deceased 1968. Educ: Univ. Mo, B.A, 16; Teachers Col, Columbia, M.A, 21; Ph.D, 35. Polit. & Govt. Pos: Supt, Charlotte-Mecklenburg Schs, N.C, retired 62; N.C. State Rep, 63-66. Bus. & Prof. Pos: Peabody Col, 21; Univ. N.C, 24-32 & 36; Univ. Mo, 35; Clark Univ, 38 & 40; vis. prof, Appalachian State Teachers Col, summers, 62-67. Mil. Serv: Sgt, Tenth Div, 17. Publ: Administration of Discipline in the High School, Columbia, 35; co-auth, Administrative Practices in Large High Schools, Am. Book Co; 'The North Carolina Program of School Support,' Dept. Sec. Sch. Prin, Minn, 33. Mem: Bd. dirs, Bank of Charlotte; Am. Asn. Adv. Sci; Nat. Soc. Study of Educ; Phi Delta Kappa; Omicron Delta Kappa; bd. dirs, NEA, 37-43; bd. dirs, NCEA, 37-43; State Dept. adv. cmt, Educ. TV; libr. bd. city-co, 49-62; bd. health, city-co, 49-62; bd. dirs, Charlotte Rehab. Hosp; chmn, bd. gov, Gov. Sch. of N.C. Distinguished Serv. Award, Am. Asn. Sch. Adminstrs, 62; Distinguished Serv. Award, Charlotte Rotary Club, 62. Rel: Methodist; Mem, bd. of stewards, 46-49. Mailing Add: 2625 Briarcliff Place, Charlotte, N.C. 28207.

GARLAND, PETER A. R
married; c. four. Educ: Bowdoin Col, Maine. Polit. & Govt. Pos: U.S. Rep, Maine, 61-62; mayor, Saco, Maine, 4 terms. Bus. & Prof. Pos: Owner and operator, Merrymeeting Farms; officer and dir. Garland Mfg. Co and Snocraft Co. for 17 years. Mil. Serv: Air Force, 42-46. Mailing Add: Merrymeeting Bay, Topsham, Maine. 04086. (1967)

GARLAND, RAY LUCIAN R
Va. State Del.
b. Roanoke, Va, 5/20/34; s. Walter Burnham Garland and Minnie Allen G; single. Educ: Roanoke Col, B.A; Univ. Va, Charlottesville, M.A; Univ. London, Eng, summers; Jefferson Soc. Polit. & Govt. Pos: Va. State Del, 68- Bus. & Prof. Pos: Asst. mgr, Garland Drug Co, 49-60; teacher, Roanoke Col, 60-68. Mem: Moose; United Commercial Travellers. Rel: Methodist. Mailing Add: 3752 Sunrise Ave. N.W, Roanoke, Va. 24012.

GARLAND, THOMAS JACK R
Tenn. State Sen.
b. Kingsport, Tenn, 6/16/34; s. Jack Warren Garland and Martha Potter G; m. to Helen Patricia Kitchens; c. Deborah Ann, Thomas, Jr. and Lisa Carol. Educ: E. Tenn. State Univ; Pi Kappa Alpha. Polit. & Govt. Pos: Chmn, Col. Young Rep. Club, Tenn, 58; pres, Greene Co. Young Rep. Club, 63-64; Tenn. State Sen, currently. Bus. & Prof. Pos: Gen. mgr, Chapman Exterminating Co, Inc, 60- Mil. Serv: Entered as Pvt, Air Force, 52, released as Airman 1/C, 56, after serv. in ETO; Nat. Defense and Good Conduct Medals. Mem: Exchange; Elks; VFW; Am. Legion; Mason. Rel: Cumberland Presbyterian. Legal Res: 203 Doak Dr, Greeneville, Tenn. 37743. Mailing Add: Box 187, Greeneville, Tenn. 37743.

GARLEY, GILBERT MANUEL, JR. D
b. Bernalillo, N.Mex, 7/23/38; s. Gilbert M. Garley, Sr. and Emma Tenorio G; m. 5/9/59 to Theresa Chavez; c. Tony Charles and Lloyd Matthew. Educ: Univ. of N.Mex, 1 year. Polit. & Govt. Pos: Chief dep. clerk, Sandoval Co, N.Mex, 60-61 and treas, 62-65; mem, Bd. of Educ, Bernalillo, N.Mex, 65-67; chmn, Sandoval Co. Dem. Party, 66-68. Bus. & Prof. Pos: Accountant, Bernalillo Pub. Sch, 67- Mem: Rotary; Bernalillo Develop. Club; Bernalillo Christmas Club. Rel: Catholic. Mailing Add: 523 Placitas, Bernalillo, N.Mex. 87004.

GARMATZ, EDWARD A. D
U.S. Rep, Md.
b. Baltimore, Md, 2/7/03; m. to Ruth Burchard. Educ: Polytech. Inst. Polit. & Govt. Pos: Mem, Md. State Racing Cmn, 3 years; Police magistrate, 44-47; U.S. Rep, Md, 47-; del, Dem. Nat. Conv, 68. Bus. & Prof. Pos: Elec. bus. Legal Res: 1112 Federal Office Bldg, Baltimore, Md. 21201. Mailing Add: 2187 Rayburn House Office Bldg, Washington, D.C. 20515.

GARNER, CYRUS ROBY, SR. R
b. Jackson Creek, N.C, 12/15/06; s. William Roby Garner and Asenath Spencer G; m. 12/26/37 to Ora Mae Wright; c. Cyrus Roby, Jr. and Mrs. W. R. Tyler. Educ: Teachers Training Sch, Asheboro, N.C. 26. Polit. & Govt. Pos: N.C. State Rep, 61-68. Bus. & Prof. Pos: Co-owner, Piedmont Baseball Camp; merchant. Mem: Kiwanis; Modern Woodmen of the World; United Travelers of Am; Boy Scout Inst. Rep; Red Cross; Am. Legion Ball Club; United Fund. Rel: Methodist; Supt, Sunday Sch, 52-56; Chmn, Cmn. on Educ. Mailing Add: 509 E. Salisbury St, Asheboro, N.C. 27203. (1967)

GARNER, DALE B. R
Polit. & Govt. Pos: Idaho State Rep, 60-66. Bus. & Prof. Pos: Businessman. Mem: Boy Scouts (scoutmaster and chmn, Minidoka Scouting Dist); adv, Parks & Recreation Cmt; adv, Co. Youth Coord. Cmt. Recipient Jr. C. of C. Distinguished Serv. Award. Mailing Add: 223 Fifth, Rupert, Idaho 83350. (1967)

GARNER, DAVID BROWN D
b. Kansas City, Mo, 6/11/36; s. David Bowman Garner and Myrtle Iva Revis G; m. 12/26/62 to Patricia Lynn Thomas; c. Christophor Thomas, John Bowman and Robert Davis. Educ: Denver Univ, B.A, 65. Polit. & Govt. Pos: Del, Dem. Nat. Conv, 68; cand, U.S. House Rep, Second Dist, S.Dak, 68; exec. dir, S.Dak. Dem. Party, 68 & 69; chmn, Black Hills Civil Rights Cmt, Rapid City, 69. Bus. & Prof. Pos: Territory mgr, Johnson and Johnson, Houston, Tex, 69- Mil. Serv: Entered as SR, Navy, 54, released as SO 3, 60, after serv. in Destroyers, Asia, Africa, Europe, Australia, 55-60. Rel: Methodist; Mem. Bd. Christian Soc. Concerns, 69. Mailing Add: 10218 Woodwind, Houston, Tex. 77025.

GARNER, HARL A. D
b. Winston, Mo, 12/8/95; m. 8/16/62 to Mildred P. Edwards; c. Jo Ann (Mrs. Stoner), Mary Virginia (Mrs. Croy), Buford W, John F. Educ: Daviess Co. Pub. Schs. Polit. & Govt. Pos: Mo. State Rep, 58, 60, 64-66; collector of revenue, Daviess Co; Daviess Co. Dem. Cmt, chmn. Bus. & Prof. Pos: Farmer; real estate; ins. Mem: Masons; Odd Fellows. Rel: Methodist. Mailing Add: Winston, Mo. 64689. (1967)

GARNER, JOHN BROMLEY D
Exec. Secy, Madison Co. Dem. Exec. Cmt, Miss.
b. Chicago, Ill, 7/21/37; s. Orrin O.B. Garner and Lillian Bromley G; m. 8/19/61 to Margrit Schmid; c. Stephen Mark and Evelyn Silvia. Educ: Carleton Col, B.A, 59; Univ. Ill, Urbana, M.S, 62; Brown Univ, 64-65. Polit. & Govt. Pos: Mem, Miss. State Dem. Nominating Cmt, 68; mem, Madison Co. Dem. Conv. and Fourth Cong. Dist. Dem. Conv, Miss, 68; del, Dem. Nat. Conv, 68; exec. secy, Madison Co. Dem. Exec. Cmt, Miss, 68- Bus. & Prof. Pos: Assoc. prof. physics, Tougaloo Col, 62- Mem: Am. Asn. Physics Teachers; Miss. Acad. Sci; Coun. for a Livable World, Am. Civil Liberties Union. Rel: Methodist. Mailing Add: Tougaloo College, Tougaloo, Miss. 39174.

GARNER, MARIE G. D
Chmn, Centre Co. Dem. Cmt, Pa.
b. South Fork, Pa, 3/6/24; d. Joseph R. Grillo and Mary Forest G; m. 6/28/47 to John A. Garner; c. Evelyn A, Margaret Jeanne and twins John A. and M. Judy. Educ: Pa. State Univ. Exten, voc, 3 years. Polit. & Govt. Pos: Chmn, Calling Cmt. for J.F. Kennedy, 59; Dem. committeewoman, South Precinct, State Col, Pa, 56-69; treas, Federated Dem. Women's Club, 60-66, adv, currently; chmn, Jane's For Joe, 62 and 4 For 64 Nat. Cmt, 64; v.chmn, Centre Co. Dem. Cmt, 64-66, chmn, 66-; chmn, 47th Sen. Dist. Constitutional Nominating Conv, 67; del-at-lg, Pa. Dem. State Cent. Cmt, 68; del, Dem. Nat. Conv, 68. Bus. & Prof. Pos: Lectr. on Aeronaut. for Army Air Force Air Power Show, Museum of Sci. and Indust, Rockefeller Center, N.Y, 44-45; instr, Pa. State Sch. of Aeronaut, Harrisburg and Olmsted Field, Pa, 44-46; mgr, Family Jewelry Store, Bellefonte, Pa, 46-48. Mil. Serv: Citation from Gen. Clark and Gen. Aronald for outstanding performance as a civilian instr. with the Army Air Force. Named One of Ten Outstanding Women in Pa. by J.F. Kennedy, 62; Elected as the Outstanding Co. Chmn. in Pa. by State Teen Dem, 68. Rel: Catholic. Mailing Add: 1214 Old Boalsburg Rd, State Col, Pa. 16801.

GARNER, MARY TEXAS D
b. Scottsboro, Ala, 10/3/28; d. Frank Paul Hurt and Allie Snodgrass H; m. 11/3/56 to William Emmett Garner; c. Mary Texas. Educ: George Wash. Univ, A.B, 49 and LL.B, 52; Phi Mu; Kappa Beta Pi. Govt. Pos: State treas, State of Ala, 64-67, state auditor, 60-64, secy. of state, 56-60, asst. attorney gen, 55-56. Bus. & Prof. Pos: Practicing attorney, 52-55. Mem: Ala. State Bar Asn; Bus. & Prfnl. Women's Club; Eastern Star. Rel: Presbyterian. Mailing Add: 2446 LeRuth Ave, Montgomery, Ala. 36106. (1967)

GARNER, THOMAS FRANKLIN, SR. D
Tenn. State Rep.
b. Trimble, Tenn, 8/10/15; s. Jesse B. Garner and Lela Todd G; m. 12/29/38 to Mary Williamson; c. Thomas Franklin, Jr, Alice Ann, Sara Irene and Mary Emily. Educ: Trimble High Sch; Col. of Mortuary Sci. Polit. & Govt. Pos: Alderman, Ripley, Tenn, 16 yrs; Tenn. State Rep, currently. Bus. & Prof. Pos: Mem. Tenn. State Bd, Funeral Dirs. & Embalmers, 64- Mem: Mason; Shrine. Rel: Baptist. Legal Res: 524 Jefferson, Ripley, Tenn. 38063. Mailing Add: Box 473, Ripley, Tenn. 38063.

GARNHAM, HAROLD P. D
b. Rochester, N.Y, 3/11/13; m. to Madeline; c. two daughters and one son. Educ: Rochester Sch. of Commerce; Cornell Univ. Polit. & Govt. Pos: Mem, Webster Dem. Club; Dem. Co. Committeeman; supvr, Webster, 54-63; mem, Monroe Co. Bd. Supvr, 54-63, minority leader, 62-63; N.Y. State Assemblyman, 65. Bus. & Prof. Pos: Mgr, dairy, until 37, supt, 37-46, owner, 46-56; dir, Rochester Eye Bank; land developer; real estate broker, 67- Mem: Lions; W. Webster Vol. Fire Dept; C. of C; Grange. Rel: Methodist. Mailing Add: 762 Valley View Pkwy, Webster, N.Y. 14580.

GARNSEY, JAMES F. D
Chmn, Herkimer Co. Dem. Cmt, N.Y.
b. Utica, N.Y, 5/6/31; s. Silas W. Garnsey and Anna Murphy G; m. 9/20/52 to Dorothy Elizabeth Loopman; c. Margaret, Susan, James, Thomas and Robert. Educ: Utica Col, 3 years. Polit. & Govt. Pos: Pres, Ilion Dem. Club, N.Y, 60-62; chmn, German Flatts Dem. Cmt, 62-68 and Herkimer Co. Dem. Cmt, 68- Bus. & Prof. Pos: Commun. serviceman, N.Y. Tel. Co, 53-69. Mil. Serv: Entered as A/S, Navy, 49, released as PO 2/C, 53, after serv. in Fleet Air Serv. 118 and Helicopter Anti-Submarine 4, Pac. Theatre. Mem: Commun. Workers of Am; Elks. Rel: Catholic. Mailing Add: 21 Gordon Place, Ilion, N.Y. 13357.

GARNSEY, WILLIAM SMITH R
Colo. State Sen.
b. Billings, Mont, 11/5/11; s. William Smith Garnsey and Agnes Sprague Wood G; m. 6/27/36 to Louisa Boulton Herrick; c. Louisa (Mrs. Samuel Waldron Lambert, III), William Herrick and Anson Herrick. Educ: Yale Col, B.A, 33; Skull and Bones Honor Soc; Alpha Delta Phi. Polit. & Govt. Pos: Mem, sch. bd, Dist. Six, Greeley, Colo, 49-55; Colo. State Sen, Dist. Eight, Weld Co, 67-; mem. adv. cmt, Cmn. Higher Educ, 67-; mem, Gov. Fiscal Study Cmt, 68-69; mem, Legis. Coun. Study Cmt. Govt. Employee Negotiations, 69. Bus. & Prof. Pos: Property mgr, Van Schaack & Co, Denver, Colo, 34-37; mgr. mortgage loan dept, Capitol Life Ins. Co, Denver, 37-47; partner, Garnsey & Wheeler Co, Greeley, 47-58, pres, 58-; v.pres, Garnsey & Wheeler Rebuilders Inc, 51- Mil. Serv: Entered as Lt.(jg), Naval Res, 42, released as Lt. Comdr, 45, after serv. in Naval Training Sch, Hq. Squadron 9-1, Altantic Fleet. Mem: Past pres. and dir, Colo. Automobile Dealers Asn; Elks; Am. Legion; VFW; Greeley C. of C.(past pres); Colo. State C. of C.(past pres). Rel: Episcopal. Legal Res: 1926 23rd Ave, Greeley, Colo. 80631. Mailing Add: P.O. Box D, Greeley, Colo. 80631.

GARRAHY, J. JOSEPH D
Lt. Gov, R.I.
b. Providence, R.I, 11/26/30; m. to Margherite Di Pietro. Educ: La Salle Acad, 48; Univ. of R.I; Univ. of Buffalo. Polit. & Govt. Pos: Mem, Cmt. to Study Juvenile Delinquency; mem, Cmt. to Study Drug Addiction; treas, Young Dem. of R.I, 62-63; R.I. State Sen, 63-69; del, Dem. Nat. Conv, 68; Lt. Gov, R.I, 69- Bus. & Prof. Pos: Sales rep. Mil. Serv: Air Force. Mem: Advocate, Dillon Coun, K. of C; Holy Name Soc, Blessed Sacrament Parish; Hibernians; Shamrock Soc. of N. Providence. Rel: Catholic. Legal Res: 45 Biltmore Ave, Providence, R.I. 02903. Mailing Add: State Capitol Bldg, Providence, R.I. 02903. (1967)

GARREN, DON HARVEY R
N.C. State Rep.
b. Henderson Co, N.C, 12/16/33; s. Harvey Horace Garren and Edith Fair McKillop G; single. Educ: Univ. of N.C, B.A, 56; Wake Forest Col, LL.B, 63. Polit. & Govt. Pos: N.C. State Rep, 65-, Minority Leader, N.C. State House of Rep, 67- Bus. & Prof. Pos: Lawyer. Mil. Serv: U.S. Navy, Lt, 56-60. Mem: Henderson Co. and N.C. Bar Asns; Sigma Phi Epsilon; Phi Alpha Delta. Mailing Add: 414 N. Church St, Hendersonville, N.C. 28739.

GARRETT, AVERY D
Wash. State Rep.
b. Georgia, 1916; m. to Edna May G; c. One son, three daughters. Educ: High Sch. Polit. & Govt. Pos: City councilman, Renton, Wash, and Wash. State Rep, currently. Bus. & Prof. Pos: Sheet metal worker. Mem: Masonic Lodge; Royal Arch Masons. Mailing Add: Langston Rd, Renton, Wash. 98055.

GARRETT, CHARLES G. D
S.C. State Sen.
b. Fountain Inn, S.C, 11/9/18; s. C. G. Garrett and Lucy Pullen G; m. 7/9/45 to Martha Inez Jones; c. Lucy, Sally and Glenn. Educ: Furman Univ, B.A, 41. Polit. & Govt. Pos: Former mayor, Fountain Inn, S.C; S.C. State Rep, 49-68; S.C. State Sen, currently. Bus. & Prof. Pos: Textiles; dir, Fed. Savings & Loan Asn. Mem: Rotary. Man of the Year, Fountain Inn, S.C. Rel: Presbyterian. Mailing Add: Box 535, Fountain Inn, S.C. 29644.

GARRETT, CLYDE DAVIS R
Mem, D.C. Rep. State Cmt.
b. Washington, D.C, 10/25/87; s. John Pfouts Garrett and Emma Caywood G; m. 9/13/41 to Belle Hoagland; c. Marshall Jones. Educ: George Wash. Univ, LL.B, 10; Theta Delta Chi. Polit. & Govt. Pos: Rep. Nat. Committeeman, 48-60; mem, D.C. Rep. State Cmt, currently. Bus. & Prof. Pos: Gen. counsel, Equitable Life Ins. Co, 44-68, v.pres, 61-68; legal consult, 68- Mem: D.C. Bar, 11-; Am. and D.C. Bar Asns; Am. Judicature Soc; Lawyers Club of Wash. D.C; Capitol Hill and Univ. Clubs; Columbia and Farmington Country Clubs; Temple-Noyes Masonic Lodge (32°); Almas Temple Shrine; Scottish Rite; Wash. Metrop. Bd. of Trade. Rel: Episcopal. Legal Res: 3300 Rittenhouse St. N.W, Washington, D.C. 20015. Mailing Add: 3900 Wisconsin Ave. N.W, Washington, D.C. 20016.

GARRETT, ERNEST G, JR. D
b. Richmond, Va, 4/15/23; both parents deceased; m. 8/25/50 to Lois A. McClanahan; c. Carol, Kathryn and John. Educ: Richmond Col; T.C. Williams Sch. of Law; McNiel Law Soc. Polit. & Govt. Pos: Mem, Henrico Co. Dem. Cmt, Va, 53-, chmn, 63-66 and v.chmn, 62-63. Prof. Pos: Partner, May, Garrett, Miller and Newman, Attorneys, 50- Mil. Serv: Entered as Aviation Cadet, Air Force, 42, released as Capt, 45, after serv. in ETO. Mem: Va. Bar; Am, Va. and Richmond Bar Asns; Ruritans; Lions. Rel: Baptist. Mailing Add: Cedar Brooke Lane, Richmond, Va. 23229. (1967)

GARRETT, HOWARD M. D
Mo. State Rep.
b. Albany, Ala, 6/16/18; s. J. Ben Garrett; m. 11/12/39 to Bessie C. Morris; c. Carla Jean, William Joseph and David Wayne. Educ: DeSoto, Mo, Pub. Schs. Polit. & Govt. Pos: Mo. State Rep, 62- Bus. & Prof. Pos: Wholesale and retail sales of gasoline, oil and tires. Mil. Serv: Army, ETO, 44-46; Combat Inf. Badge; Bronze Star. Mem: Mason; Scottish Rite; VFW. Rel: Deacon, Fairview Christian Church. Mailing Add: 1540 Westvale, Festus, Mo. 63028. (1967)

GARRETT, JAMES NEAL, JR. D
b. Detroit, Mich, 3/13/22; s. James N. Garrett, Sr. and Willa Belle Whitehead G; m. 12/30/49 to Ethel Louise Weston; c. Eric V, Marc H, Glenn N, Alan C. and Janine. Educ: Wayne State Univ, A.B, 58. Polit. & Govt. Pos: Del, Dem. Nat. Conv, 68; Dem. cand, Detroit Common Coun, Mich, 69. Mil. Serv: Entered as Pre-Aviation Cadet, Air Force, 44, released as Pvt, 45, after serv. in Am. Theatre; Am. Theatre Ribbon; Good Conduct Medal; Victory Medal. Mem: Cotillion Club; Northwest. High Sch. Study Cmt; Fitzgerald Commun. Coun; Lib. Conf; 17th Cong. Dist. Dem. Party; Urban Alliance; St. Peter's Home for Boys; Human Rights Day Recognition Cmt; Coord. Coun. on Human Rels. Cotillion of the Year Award; CKLW-Radio Citizen of the Day. Rel: Protestant. Mailing Add: 16580 Ohio, Detroit, Mich. 48221.

GARRETT, JAMES PAUL D
Chmn, Greer Co. Dem. Cent. Cmt, Okla.
b. Mangum Okla, 1/5/22; s. Wilkins B. Garrett and Willie Margaret Latimer G; m. 8/21/43 to Nedra Lee Wilson; c. Stephen Paul, Linda Jane and Susan Lee. Educ: Southwest. State Col, Okla, 39-41; Okla. Univ, B.S. in bus. admin. 43, and LL.B, 48; Pi Kappa Alpha. Polit. & Govt. Pos: Asst. co. attorney, Carter Co, Okla, 49-50; asst. attorney gen, Okla, 51-58; mem, Pardon and

Parole Bd, 59-63; chmn, Greer Co. Dem. Cent. Cmt, 64-; mem. bd. educ, Mangum, 65-66. Mil. Serv: Entered as Seaman, Naval Res, 42, released as Lt.(jg), 46, after serv in European, Am. & Pac. Theaters; ETO, Am. Theater and Pac. Theater Ribbons; Philippine Liberation and Victory Medals; Battle Stars. Mem: Okla. Bar Asn; Am. Trial Lawyers Asn; past pres, Uptown Toastmasters Club, Okla. City, Mangum Rotary Club and Mangum C. of C; Rotary Int; Am. Legion; VFW; Mangum & Greer Co. C. of C; Mason; Elks; Toastmasters. Rel: Baptist. Legal Res: 321 S. Robinson, Mangum, Okla. 73554. Mailing Add: Box 603, Mangum, Okla. 73554.

GARRETT, LOYAL CLAYTON D
Chmn, Davis Co. Dem. Cent. Cmt, Iowa
b. Ottumwa, Iowa, 7/6/14; s. John Wesley Garrett and Amanda Ellen Jones G; m. 6/25/32 to Hazel Belle Dearborn; c. Richard Lee and Willamae (Mrs. Heckethorn). Educ: Eldon High Sch, Iowa, 4 years. Polit. & Govt. Pos: Precinct committeeman, Bloomfield Dem. Party, Iowa, 65-66; chmn, Davis Co. Dem. Cent. Cmt, 66- Bus. & Prof. Pos: Tester and researcher, John Deere Ottumwa Works, Iowa, 37-56; owner and mgr, Buick-Pontiac, Bloomfield, 56-61; owner small farming oper, 61-69; salesman, Ernest Chevrolet, 65-67. Mem: Iowa New Car Dealers Asn; Bloomfield C. of C; United Auto Workers; Davis Co. New Car Dealers Asn; Isaac Walton League; Bloomfield Country Club. Knudsen Award, Pontiac Motor Div; Cert. for Chevrolet Truck Sales. Rel: Christian Church of N.Am. Mailing Add: R.R. 3, Bloomfield, Iowa 52537.

GARRETT, TOM D
Ky. State Sen.
b. 1921. Educ: Univ. Ky. Col. of Law, LL.B. Polit. & Govt. Pos: Ky. State Sen, 62-64 & 69- Bus. & Prof. Pos: Attorney. Mil. Serv: Army Air Force. Mem: Paducah Exchange Club. Rel: Baptist. Mailing Add: 700 Hillgate, Paducah, Ky. 42002. (1967)

GARRETT, WALTER EUGENE D
Ala. State Rep.
b. Uriah, Ala, 12/3/28; s. William Walter Garrett and Ardis Lilly Lancaster G; m. 6/4/53 to Mary Jane Watson; c. William Caswell, Ardis Eugenia, Leura Jane, Ida Amanda and Walter Eugene, Jr. Educ: Univ. Ala, B.S. and LL.B; Phi Kappa Sigma; Delta Sigma Pi; Phi Alpha Delta. Polit. & Govt. Pos: Ala. State Rep, 34th Legis. Dist, 67- Mem: Farm Bur; Ala. Cattlemen's Asn; Blacksher Lodge. Rel: Methodist. Mailing Add: Box 6, Uriah, Ala. 36480.

GARRIGAN, EDGAR L, JR. R
b. Akron, Ohio, 3/11/25; s. Edgar L. Garrigan and Edna K. Hess G; m. 2/1/47 to Charlotte F. Kelley; c. Edgar L, III, Maureen E, Charlotte A, Brian W. and Hugh T. Educ: Univ. Akron, B.S. in bus. admin, 49; Phi Delta Theta. Polit. Pos: Ohio State Sen, 35th Dist, 63-67. Bus. & Prof. Pos: Sales mgr, Tower Agencies, Inc, 62-; pres, Garrigan Ins. Agency, Inc, 52-63. Mil. Serv: Entered as Pvt, Marine Corps, 43, released as Sgt, 45, after serv. in 4th Div. and 5th Corps, Marshalls, Saipan, Tinian and Iwo Jima; Bronze Star; Purple Heart; Presidential Unit Citation. Mem: Ohio Legis Serv. Cmn; Am. Legion; VFW; Kiwanis; Hibernians; Izaak Walton League of Am; Am. Rifle Asn. Rel: Roman Catholic. Mailing Add: 1950 Garland Ave, Akron, Ohio 44313. (1967)

GARRIGUES, GEORGE LOUIS R
Chmn, Inyo Co. Rep. Cmt, Calif.
b. Bishop, Calif, 7/25/26; s. Louis Garrigues and Mildred Yaney G; m. 7/15/50 to Barbara Robinson; c. Sally E, William R, Patricia A. and John L. Educ: Stanford Univ, B.A, 50; El Tigre Eating Club. Polit. & Govt. Pos: Mem, Inyo Co. Rep. Cent. Cmt, Calif, 60-; mem, Bishop Elem. Sch. Bd, 65-69, pres, 68; mem, Calif. Rep. State Cent. Cmt, 67-; chmn, Inyo Co. Rep. Cmt, 69- Bus. & Prof. Pos: Self employed, Pinon Book Store, Bishop, Calif, 58-; dir, Inyo-Mono Nat. Bank, Bishop, 64- Mil. Serv: Entered as Seaman, Navy, 44, released as RM 3/C, 46, after serv. in Asian Theatre, 45-46. Mem: Rotary; C. of C. Rel: Episcopal. Mailing Add: 666 Sycamore Dr, Bishop, Calif. 93514.

GARRIGUS, CHARLES B. D
b. Benton, Ill, 6/13/14; m. 12/28/36 to Fern Marie Fetters G; c. Marmarie, Charles, Jr, Richmond, Karis, Rose Ann. Educ: Univ. of Ill, B.A, M.A. Polit. & Gov. Pos: Calif. State Assemblyman, 58-66. Bus. & Prof. Pos: Instr, philos, hist, lit, Eng, Reedley Col, Calif. Speaker, educ, civil, polit. forums. Mailing Add: 18588 E. Adams, Reedley, Calif. 93654. (1967)

GARRIGUS, FOREST ORA, JR. R
Chmn, Deschutes Co. Rep. Cent. Cmt, Ore.
b. Forest Grove, Ore, 6/12/30; s. Forest Ora Garrigus and Leatha Sohren G; m. 8/17/50 to Patsy Ruth Wasson; c. Forest O, III and John P. Educ: Univ. Ore, 49-50; Linfield Col, B.S, 55; Pi Gamma Mu; Pi Kappa Gamma; Delta Upsilon. Polit. & Govt. Pos: Chmn, Deschutes Co. Rep. Cent. Cmt, Ore, 69- Mil. Serv: Entered as Seaman, Navy, 48, released as Radarman 2, 52, after serving in USS Bairoko, CVE-115, Pac. Theatre, 50-52; Korean Service Medal; Presidential Unit Citation. Mem: Elks; Mason; Shrine; Bend Jaycees. Senator, Jr. Chamber-Inter. Rel: Protestant. Legal Res: 147 Reed Market Rd, Bend, Ore. 97701. Mailing Add: P.O. Box 1170, Bend, Ore. 97701.

GARRISON, DENZIL DOSS R
Minority Leader, Okla. State Senate
b. Norman, Okla, 11/20/26; s. Joseph Don Garrison, Sr. and Nita Ellen Smith G; m. 4/3/54 to Barbara Lee Hopper; c. Charles Alfred, Ellen Marie, Kathryn Ann, Elizabeth Lee and Martha Amanda. Educ: Univ. of Okla, LL.B, 53; Phi Alpha Delta; Beta Theta Pi. Polit. & Govt. Pos: Attorney, Washington Co, Okla, 55-56; Okla. State Rep, 57-59, minority leader, Okla. House of Rep, 59-61; Okla. State Sen, 61-63, asst. minority leader Okla. State Senate, 63-65, minority leader, 65- Mil. Serv: Entered as Pvt, Army, 45, released as Capt, 52, after serv. in Field Artil, ETO and Korean Conflict; Maj, Army Res. Mem: Washington Co. Bar Asn.(pres, 63-64); Okla. Bar Asn.(mem, Civil Procedure Cmt, 67-); Am. Bar Asn; Mason; Elks. Named Outstanding Young Oklahoman, Okla. Jaycees, 60. Rel: Church of Christ. Legal Res: 929 S. Cherokee, Bartlesville, Okla. 74003. Mailing Add: P.O. Box 1217, Bartlesville, Okla. 74003.

GARRISON, FRANK SHERIDAN R
Chmn, Boone Co. Rep. Party, Ark.
b. Harrison, Ark, 7/22/34; s. Ben F. Garrison and Pauline Terry G; m. 12/20/53 to Jo Ann English; c. Daniel Albert, David Terry, Thomas Robert and William Paul. Educ: Univ. Ark, B.S,B.A, with honors, 55. Polit. & Govt. Pos: Chmn, Boone Co. Rep. Party, Ark, 68- Bus. & Prof. Pos: Treas, Garrison Motor Freight, Inc, Ark, 55-66 and pres, 66- Mem: Beta Gamma Sigma; various trucking organizations; Rotary; Elks; C. of C. Rel: Presbyterian. Legal Res: Hwy. 43 W, Harrison, Ark. 72601. Mailing Add: P.O. Box 969, Harrison, Ark. 72601.

GARRISON, THOMAS EDMOND D
S.C. State Sen.
b. Anderson, Welcome Comm, S.C, 1/21/22; s. Thomas Edmond Garrison and Nettie C. McPhail G; m. 5/10/55 to Juanita Bartlett; c. Carol Gaye, Thomas Edmond, III, James Bartlett, Anitia Lee. Educ: Clemson, B.S, 42; hon. State Farmer Degree of F.F.A, Clemson, 55. Polit. & Govt. Pos: S.C. State Rep, 59-66; S.C. State Sen, currently. Bus. & Prof. Pos: Teacher, Vet. Agr. Class, Boys' High Sch, Anderson, S.C, 46-53; dairy farmer, agr. teacher, 54-58. Mil. Serv: Air Force, pilot, 42-45; 69th Medium Bombardment Squadron, 13th Air Force S.Pac, 65 missions; Air Medal with 5 Oak Leaf Clusters. Mem: Former bd. chmn, Anderson Soil Conserv. Dist. Supvrs; former pres. S.C. Asn. Soil Conserv. Supvrs; former dir. Co. Fair Asn; former pres. and dir, Co. Farm Bur; former pres. S.C. Young Farmers Asn; former chmn. Co. Tuberc. Christmas Seal Sale; former dir. Am. Dairy Asn. of S.C; Hejaz Shrine. Selected Outstanding Young Farmer of the Year, Anderson Jaycees, 57. Rel: Baptist; Deacon, Welcome Baptist Church; Teacher, Men's Bible Class. Mailing Add: Clemson Hwy, R.F.D, 2, Anderson, S.C. 29621. (1967)

GARRISON, WILLIAM L. R
b. Kenosha, Wis, 6/21/11; s. Monroe T. Garrison and Mary Elizabeth Loy G; m. 1/2/37 to Eleanor Dorothea Wolter; c. William Monroe and Rita Ann. Educ: Univ. Wis, 30-32. Polit. & Govt. Pos: City councilman, Baraboo, Wis, 48-54; membership chmn, Sauk Co. Rep. Orgn, 63, finance chmn, 64, chmn, 65-67; Third Dist. Chmn, Wis. Citizens for Goldwater Cmt, 64. Bus. & Prof. Pos: Mgr, Garrison Outdoor Advert, 37-56, owner, 56-62; owner, Mid-State Outdoor Advert. Co, 41-56; owner and pres, Wis. Outdoor Displays, Inc, 56-61. Mil. Serv: Entered as Pvt, Army, 43, released as Pfc, 45. Mem: Elks; Mason; Shrine; Baraboo Country Club; Kiwanis. Mailing Add: 1515 Elizabeth St, Baraboo, Wis. 53913.

GARTEN, MEREDITH 'PETE' R
Mem, Mo. State Rep. Cmt.
b. Ottawa Co, Okla, 11/24/97; s. William Garten and Maud Ellen Meador G; m. 12/30/26 to Alice Winifred Amery; c. Gretchen (Mrs. James Tatum) and Beth (Mrs. Forest Brown). Educ: Col. of Emporia, Kans, B.A; Univs. Kans. and Mo, grad. study; Sigma Delta Chi; Pi Kappa Delta. Polit. & Govt. Pos: Del, Mo. Constitutional Conv, 43-44; Mo. State Rep, 46-48; Mo. State Sen, 48-52; mem, Mo. State Senate Reapportionment Cmn, 59; chmn, Lawrence Co. Rep. Cmt, Mo; mem, Mo. State Rep. Cmt, 66- Bus. & Prof. Pos: Pres, Mo. Press Asn, 46 and Ozark Press Asn; pres, Mo. Rep. Editorial Asn, 47. Mem: Mason; Shrine; Kiwanis (Lt. Gov, Div. 10, Mo-Ark. Dist); plus others. Rel: Congregational. Mailing Add: 314 Elm St, Pierce City, Mo. 65723.

GARTLAND, JAMES WESLEY FRANCIS D
b. New Haven, Conn, 12/8/11; s. Hugh J. Gartland and Mary Agnes Doheny G; m. 7/23/43 to Florence Blake; c. James Francis, Patricia Louise, Michael Sheridan. Educ: Catholic Univ, A.B; Cornell Grad. Sch; Hartford Col. of Law, LL.B, Phi Beta Kappa (Catholic Univ.). Polit. Pos. and Govt. Pos: Admin. asst, Sen. Thomas J. Dodd, Conn; former chmn, Dem. Town Comm, E. Haven; judge, Munic. Court, E. Haven, Conn, 55-59; pres. of Claims Mgrs. Asn, E. Haven, 51-52; city prosecutor, E. Haven, 49-51. Mem: Elks, exalted ruler, 50- Legal Res: New Haven, Conn. Mailing Add: 6014 Berkshire Dr, Camp Springs, Md. 20023. (1967)

GARTLAND, ROBERT J. D
b. Carthage, S.Dak, 6/26/05; s. James Gartland and Mary Dailey G; single. Educ: Wash. Univ, D.D.S, 32; Xi Psi Phi. Polit. & Govt. Pos: Chmn, Minnehaha Co. Dem. Party, S.Dak, 61-67. Bus. & Prof. Pos: Pres, S.Dak. Dental Examiners, 60-65. Mil. Serv: Entered as 1st Lt, Army, 43, released as Major, 46; 3 Campaign Ribbons; Bronze Star. Mem: Pres, 2nd Dist. Dental Soc, 50 and Marquette Toastmasters, 55; Elks; Am. Legion; K. of C.(4°); Bridge. Rel: Catholic. Mailing Add: 2000 W. 13th St, Sioux Falls, S.Dak. 57104. (1967)

GARTNER, DAVID G. D
b. Des Moines, Iowa, 9/27/35; s. Carl D. Gartner and Mary M. Gay G; m. 10/15/65 to Suzanne U. Schmidt. Educ: State Univ. Iowa, B.A, 59. Polit. & Govt. Pos: Mem. staff, U.S. Rep. Carter, Iowa, 59, U.S. Rep. Harold Johnson, Calif, 60-61; asst. to Vice President Hubert Humphrey, 61-68. Bus. & Prof. Pos: Reporter, correspondent, Des Moines Register, 56-59. Mil. Serv: Navy. Mem: Nat. Capitol. Dem. Club. Rel: Roman Catholic. Mailing Add: 3420 N. George Mason Dr, Arlington, Va. 22207. (1967)

GARTNER, FRED CHRISTIAN R
b. Phila, Pa, 4/14/96; s. Fred Gartner and Anna Marie Staudenmayer G; m. 10/26/21 to Margaret Schnaebels; c. Peggy (Mrs. McKee) and Carole. Educ: Brown Col. Preparatory Sch; Temple Univ. Law Sch. Polit. & Govt. Pos: Committeeman, 61st Ward, Phila, Pa, 66-; U.S. Rep, Pa, 39-40; Pa. Gen. Assembly, 33 and 34; Civil Serv. Cmnr, Phila, 28-32. Bus. & Prof. Pos: Chmn. of the Bd, Hol-Gar Mfg. Corp, Primos, Pa, 41-66. Mil. Serv: Yeoman 1/C, Navy and Lt. Comdr, Naval Supply Corps, 41; World War I Ribbon. Mem: Phila. Bar Asn; Lawyers' Club of Phila; Mason; Penn Athletic Club; Seaview Country Club; Phila. Rifle Club; plus others. Rel: Lutheran. Mailing Add: 6601 N. Third St, Philadelphia, Pa. 19126. (1967)

GARTON, ROBERT DEAN R
b. Chariton, Iowa, 8/18/33; s. Dr. J. Glenn Garton and Irene Wright G; m. 6/17/55 to Barbara Arlene Hicks; c. Bradford Glenn and Brenda Arlene. Educ: Iowa State Univ, B.S, 55; Sch. Indust. and Labor Rels, Cornell Univ, M.S, 59; Beta Theta Pi. Polit. & Govt. Pos: Chmn, Young Rep. Club Bartholomew Co, Ind, 64-65; mem. bd. dirs, Nat. Rep. Workshops, 65-67; mem. state and nat. exec. cmt, Young Rep. Club, 66-67; Rep. cand, U.S. Rep, Ninth Dist, Ind, 68; charter mem. and secy, Coun. Independent Action, Gov. Cmt, 69- Bus. & Prof. Pos: Temporary field organizer, Dist. 50, United Mine

Workers, summer 57; indust. rels. trainee, Proctor & Gamble, Cincinnati, Ohio, 59; col. recruiting adminstr, Cummins Engine Co, Inc, Columbus, Ind, 59-61; owner, Robert D. Garton Assocs, 61- Mil. Serv: Entered as 2nd Lt, Marine Corps, 55, released as 1st Lt, 57, after serv. as a Spec. Serv. Officer and Provost Marshall, Supply Schs, Camp Lejeune, N.C, 55-57, Res, 57-63; Outstanding Marine Grad, Iowa State Univ. Publ: Author of articles in N.Y. State Labor Report, 59, Personnel Administration, 60 and Jour. Col. Placement, 61. Mem: Nat. Mgt. Asn.(lectr); fel, Ind. Mgt. Insts; Rotary Int; Columbia Club; Harrison Lake Country Club; Toastmasters; Southwest Bartholomew Water Coun. Winner, Toastmasters Int. Speech Contest, 62; Winner, Ind. Jaycee Speak-up Contest, 62; Hon. Citizen, State of Iowa; One of Five selected to initiate Hon. Masters Prog. at Iowa State Univ, 64; Distinguished Serv. Award, Columbus Jr. C. of C, 68; named One of Ind. Five Outstanding Young Men, Ind. Jr. C. of C, 68. Rel: Methodist. Legal Res: R.R. 7, Wood Lake, Columbus, Ind. 47201. Mailing Add: 405½ Washington St, Columbus, Ind. 47201.

GARVEY, JAMES SUTHERLAND R
State Committeeman, Tex. Rep. Party
b. Colby, Kans, 12/30/22; s. Ray Hugh Garvey and Olive White G; m. 11/30/47 to Shirley Fox; c. Janet Lee, Carol Jo and Richard Fox. Educ: Wichita State Univ, B.A, 47; Beta Theta Pi. Polit. & Govt. Pos: State committeeman, Tenth Dist, Tex. Rep. Party, currently; del, Rep. Nat. Conv, 68. Bus. & Prof. Pos: Pres, Jim Garvey Ranches, Inc, Garvey Ranch Mgt, Inc. and J.C.R. Investments, Inc; managing partner, Garvey Farms Mgt. Co; pres, Garvey Elevators, Inc; mem, Chicago Bd. of Trade and Kansas City Bd. of Trade; dir. and v.pres, Garvey Exploration, Ltd; dir, Ft. Worth & Denver R.R; dir; Graham Magnetics Inc. and Ft. Worth Nat. Bank; pres, Venture Co, Inc; dir, Bangor Punta Corp; chmn. of bd. and dir, Petroleum, Inc; dir, Garvey, Inc; v.pres, Garvey Tex. Found, Inc; mem, Garvey Found. Mil. Serv: Reserve Corp, 42; Armored Force, 43-46. Mem: Trustee, Tex. 4-H Found; dir, Wichita State Univ. Alumni Asn, Tex. Christian Univ. Research Found, Ft. Worth Country Day Sch, Van Cliburn Quadrennial Found, Ft. Worth Metrop. YMCA, Ft. Worth C. of C, Southwest Exposition and Fat Stock Show and Southwest Motor Club AAA; Am. Legion; VFW; Rivercrest Country Club; Shady Oaks Country Club; Ft. Worth Club; dir, Downtown Rotary; Exchange Club of Ft. Worth; Mason; Shrine; Longhorn Coun, Boy Scouts. Mailing Add: P.O. Box 1688, Ft. Worth, Tex. 76101.

GARVIN, WILLIAM HENRY D
Chmn, Butler Co. Dem. Cent. Cmt, Ohio
b. Middletown, Ohio, 9/6/31; s. William Henry Garvin and Minnie Johnston G; m. 12/26/60 to Cleo Angelina Garofalos; c. Anna and Marian. Educ: Miami Univ, B.A. math, 58, M.A. polit. sci. cum laude, 69. Polit. & Govt. Pos: Chmn, Butler Co. Dem. Cent. Cmt, Ohio, 67- Bus. & Prof. Pos: Programmer, Int. Bus. Machines Corp, Bethesda, Md, 62-; programmer, Armco Steel, Middletown, Ohio, 64; teacher algebra and computer programming, Fenwick High Sch, Middletown, 66-69; teacher Russian, Miami Univ, 69. Mil. Serv: Entered as Pvt, Air Force, 51, released as Airman 1/C, 51, after serv. in Air Training Command, 51-55. Mem: Am. Hellenic and Educ. Soc. Rel: Roman Catholic. Mailing Add: 3109 Poinciana Rd, Middletown, Ohio 45042.

GARY, ARCHIE THOMAS D
Ga. State Rep.
b. Atlanta, Ga, 10/11/23; s. William Homer Gary and Gussie Berta Seagraves G; m. 7/1/50 to Carolyn Thelma Gay; c. Bart and Ross. Educ: Atlanta Law Sch. Polit. & Govt. Pos: Mayor, Riverdale, Ga, 62-63; Ga. State Rep, 65- Bus. & Prof. Pos: Pres, Co-op Commun. Co, Inc, 58-, Blue & Gray Cabs, 58-, Courtesy Cabs, 62- and Carriage Caps, 65-; secy-treas, Residential Develop. Corp, 63- and Realty Assocs, Atlanta, Ga, 65- Mil. Serv: Entered as Pvt, Army, 43, released as T/Sgt, 46, after serv. in 1st Army. Mem: Moose; Atlanta Conv. Bur; Atlanta C. of C; Clayton Co. C. of C. Collector of Civil War Relics. Rel: Methodist. Mailing Add: 626 Valley Hill Rd, Riverdale, Ga. 30274.

GARY, J. VAUGHAN D
b. Richmond, Va, 2/25/92; s. T. Jack Gary and Mary Harris Vaughan G; m. 11/23/18 to Eunice Croswell; c. Carolyn (Mrs. Laurence V. Hugo) and J. Vaughan. Educ: Univ. Richmond, B.A, 12, LL.B, 15; Sigma Phi Epsilon; Delta Theta Phi; Phi Beta Kappa; Omicron Delta Kappa. Hon. LL.D, Univ. Richmond, 54. Polit. & Govt. Pos: Asst. counsel, Va. Tax Bd, 16-18, counsel and exec. asst, 19-24; claims exam, Va. Indust. Cmn, 19; Va. State Del, 26-33; dir, State Dem. Speakers Bur, Presidential Campaigns, 36 & 44; chmn, Va. Post War Employ. Cmt, 43-45; chmn, Mayor's Cmt, Richmond Juvenile and Domestic Rels. Court; U.S. Rep, Va, 45-64; del, Dem. Nat. Conv, 68. Bus. & Prof. Pos: Pres, Richmond Stadium, Va; secy, Nat. Agr. Adv. Cmt, 18; secy, Nat. Cmt. on Inheritance Taxation, 25-26; teacher, Blackstone Acad. for Boys, Blackstone, Va. Mil. Serv: Army. Mem: Bd. Trustees, Univ. Richmond and Fork Union Mil. Acad, Va. World War II Hist. Cmn; War Bond Cmt, 41-43; bd. dirs, Va. Coop. Educ. Asn; past pres, Va. State C. of C; past pres, Va. Tuberc. Asn; past pres, Richmond Bar Asn; past chmn. exec. cmt, Va. Bar Asn; Am. Bar Asn; Am. Legion; Mason (33°); Shrine. Distinguished Serv. Award, U.S. Treas. Dept, 64. Rel: Baptist. Mailing Add: 10 S. Tenth St, Richmond, Va. 23219.

GARY, RAYMOND D. D
b. Madill, Okla, 1/21/08; s. D.R. Gary and Winnie Edith Romans G; m. 9/1/29 to Emma Mae Purser; c. Raymond Jerdy and Mona Mae (Mrs. Waymire). Educ: Southeast. State Col, Okla. Polit. & Govt. Pos: Co. supt. of schs, Marshall Co, Okla, 32-36; Okla. State Sen, 41-54 and pres. Pro Tem, Okla. State Senate, 53-54; Gov. of Okla, 55-59. Bus. & Prof. Pos: Pres, Sooner Oil Co, 45-; mem. bd. dirs, Kansas City South. R.R, 59-, Kansas City South. Ind. R.R, 62- and La. & Ark. R.R; pres, Gary Industs, Inc. and Gary Cattle Co, 64-; dir, Southwest Baptist Theol. Sem, 64- Mem: Rotary; pres, Marshall Co. Indust. Found; Okla. Farmers Union. Rel: Southern Baptist. Mailing Add: Box 40, Madill, Okla. 73446.

GASDIA, FRANK ROBERT R
b. Newark, N.J, 8/26/19; s. Frederick J. Gasdia and Bertha Jackson G; m. 3/1/44 to Elenore Lucille Cairns; c. Brian Frank. Educ: Southwest. Univ, Law Degree, 51. Polit. & Govt. Pos: Trustee, Los Angeles Co. Law Libr, Calif, 67-68; cmnr, Hosp. Authority Cmn, Downey, 69; mem, Calif. Rep. State Cent. Cmt, 69. Bus. & Prof. Pos: Ins. broker, Huntington Park, Calif, 46-47; attorney-at-law, Downey, 52-; arbitrator, Am. Arbit. Asn, 63- Mil. Serv: Entered as Pvt, Army, 40, released as 1st Lt, 45, after serv. in Inf, Field Artil, Mil. Police and Antiaircraft Artil, U.S. and European Theatres. Mem: Calif, Los Angeles Co. and Southeast Dist. Bar Asns; Lions; Mason. Rel: Protestant. Mailing Add: 7705 Irwingrove Dr, Downey, Calif. 90241.

GASQUE, J. RALPH D
S.C. State Sen.
b. near Mullins, S.C, 5/16/13; s. Cordie A. Gasque and Jennie Price G. Educ: Nat. Univ. Law Sch, LL.B, 41; LL.M, 42. Polit. & Govt. Pos: U.S. claims exam, U.S. Govt. Gen. Acct. Off; spec. agent, U.S. Internal Revenue Serv; chief, Mil. Personnel Sect, Provost Marshall Gen. Sch; prin. custodian officer, D.C. Penal Inst; S.C. State Rep, 45-48; S.C. State Sen, 49-52, 56-62 & 64-; del, Dem. Nat. Conv, 60 & 68. Mem: WOW; Mason; Eastern Star; Sigma Delta Kappa; Shrine. Mailing Add: Box 127, Marion, S.C. 29571. (1967)

GASSER, ROBERT ALAN D
b. Trenton, N.J, 11/9/37; s. Robert Davis Gasser (deceased) and Mildred Gunning G.(deceased); m. 4/5/64 to Marilyn T. Vanecek; c. Robert Christian and Jennifer Lynn. Educ: Rutgers Univ, B.A, 59; Hong Kong Univ, Cert. Attendance, 61; Columbia Univ. Law Sch, LL.B, 63; N.J. State Scholarship; Food Fair Grant; Columbia Univ. Grant; Rotary Found fel, 60-66. Polit. & Govt. Pos: Dem. cand, U.S. House Rep, 68; asst. pub. defender, Ocean Co, N.J. Bus. & Prof. Pos: Attorney, Joseph A. Citta, Esquires, 64; partner, Citta, Gasser & Carluccio, Esquires, 65-69; instr, police sci, Ocean Co. Col, 68-69. Mil. Serv: Entered as Pvt, Army Res, 63, released as Sgt, 69, after serv. in N.J. Nat. Guard, Off. Cand. Sch, Sea Girt, N.J. Mem: Bd. dirs, Legal Serv. Inc; N.J. and Ocean Co. Bar Asns; Rotary; C. of C.(bd. dirs); Big Bros; Am. Cancer Soc.(bd. dirs, N.J. Div); Tom River Country Club. Rel: Episcopal. Legal Res: 21 Cedar Dr, Toms River, N.J. 08753. Mailing Add: 248 Washington St, Toms River, N.J. 08753.

GAST, ROY ANDREW R
b. Detroit, Mich, 3/30/25; s. Roy Hatcher Gast and Ena Kantola G; m. to Grace West Kent; c. Jeanne, Stuart, Thomas. Educ: Mich. State Univ, B.S; University of Md. (Zurich, Switz.). Polit. & Govt. Pos: Exec. secy, Rep. William S. Broomfield. Mil. Serv: Army, T-4 Sgt; serv. with 1263 Engr. Combat Bn, Reconnaissance Section; ETO, Rhine, Germany. Mem: Sigma Delta Chi. Legal Res: Berkley, Mich. 48072. Mailing Add: 3611 Spruell Dr, Silver Spring, Md. 20902. (1967)

GASTL, EUGENE FRANCIS D
b. Shawnee, Kans, 4/28/32; s. Bert Joseph Gastl and Bessie Bell G; m. 6/7/59 to Deanna J. Cordon; c. Philip E, Catherine L. and David Bruce. Educ: Kansas City Jr. Col, 50-52; Univ. Kans, 52-56, A.B. and LL.B; Delta Theta Phi. Polit. & Govt. Pos: Committeeman, Johnson Co. Dem. Cent. Cmt, Kans, 56-; Kans. State Rep, 11th Dist, 61-65; Kans. State Sen, 14th Dist, Johnson Co, 65-69. Mil. Serv: Entered as Pvt, Army, 56, released as Specialist 3/C, 58. Mem: Am, Kans. and Johnson Co. Bar Asns; C. of C; Univ. Kans. Alumni Asn; Optimists (dir, Shawnee, Kans. Club, 64-65). Rel: Methodist. Mailing Add: 6117 Ballentine, Shawnee, Kans. 66203.

GATER, DAVID WINFIELD R
Mem, Calif. Rep. State Cent. Cmt.
b. Council Bluffs, Iowa, 2/6/33; s. Roy Winfield Gater and Leona Bays G; m. 6/1/58 to Eva Bertine Hollingsworth; c. Elizabeth Anne, Roy David, Michael David, Susan Annette and Catherine Anne. Educ: Iowa State Univ, 54-55; Simpson Col, B.A. in Math. and Physics, 59. Polit. & Govt. Pos: Campaign mgr, 34th Cong. Dist, Orange Co, Calif, 65-66; area chmn, Orange Co. Rep. Precinct Orgn, 66; assoc. mem, Calif. Rep. State Cent. Cmt, 67-69, mem, 69-; assoc. mem, Orange Co. Rep. Cent. Cmt, 67-; mem, Orange Co. Steering Cmt, Nixon and Rafferty Campaigns, 68; chmn, Orange Co. Coord. Rep. Assembly, 68-69; chmn, Orange Co. Rep. Speakers Bur, 69-; 34th Cong. Dist. dir, Orange Co. Rep. Party, 69- Bus. & Prof. Pos: Mem, tech. Staff, Hughes Aircraft Co, Fullerton, Calif, 61- Mil. Serv: Entered as Pvt, Army, 50, released as Sgt. E-5, 54, after serv. in 45th Anti-aircraft Artil. Brigade, Army Anti-aircraft Command; Korean War Serv. Medal; Good Conduct Medal. Publ: Permanent Precinct Operation, privately publ, 65; Grassroots Campaign Mechanics, Starter Publ, 69; 'The Pieces of the Party,' Orange Co. Observer, 69. Rel: Protestant. Mailing Add: 437 N. La Reina St, Anaheim, Calif. 92801.

GATES, ROBERT DAVID D
b. Auburn, N.Y, 10/2/23; s. Arthur A. Gates and Regina Martin G; m. 10/12/45 to Regina Murphy; c. Margaret (Mrs. Kline), Alecia (Mrs. Lewis), Mary Lisbeth, David Robert, Barbara Masyln, Arthur Jerome and Richard Charles. Educ: Syracuse Univ, B.S, 47, M.S, 48, Ed.D, 54; Epsilon Rho Tau; Phi Delta Kappa; Rho Alpha Chi. Polit. & Govt. Pos: Coordinator spec. educ, Hillsborough Co. Schs, 49-50; coordinator state fed. rels, State of Fla, 50-66; Dem. cand, U.S. House Rep, 68; consult, U.S. Off. Educ, Wash, D.C, 68- Bus. & Prof. Pos: Dir. educ. opers, Philco Ford Corp, Phila, Pa, 66-68; dir. research, Edinboro State Col, Pa, 68- Mil. Serv: Entered as Pvt, Army Air Force, 41, released as Capt, 45, after serv. in Pac, 43-45; Distinguished Flying Cross; Air Medal; Bronze Star; Good Conduct and Theatre Medals; Presidential Unit Citation. Publ: The Florida Story, Rose Printing, 54; Electronic Education, Univ. Press, 61; Educational Technical Digest, Philco Ford, 68. Mem: Nat. Educ. Asn; Coun. Exceptional Children; Am. Asn. Sch. Admin; Asn. Educ. Data Systs; K. of C; Elks; Int. Christian Leadership; Int. Asn. of Torch Clubs. Recipient of U.S. Supreme Court's Citation for Amicus Curiae Breif, 54; State of Fla. Instnl. Develop. Citation, 54; Nat. Retarded Children Asn. Prfnl. Citation, 54; Nat. United Cerebral Palsy Prfnl. Citation, 56; Cape Canaveral Area Develop. Citation, 58; Gov. Conf. on Educ. Citation, Tampa, Fla, 66; Fla. State Dept. of Educ. Meritorious Serv. Citation, Tallahassee, 66; Bd. of Cmnr. of State Insts. Conf. of Dirs. Spec. Citation, Tallahassee, 66; Aid to Asn. of Educ. Data Syst. Honor Award, Detroit, Mich, 67; Laureate Citation, Epsilon Pi Tau, Buffalo, N.Y, 69; Distinguished Serv. Award, CEDS, Seattle, Wash, 69. Rel: Catholic. Legal Res: Hilltop Rd, Edinboro, Pa. 16412. Mailing Add: P.O. Box 81, Edinboro, Pa. 16412.

GATES, ROBERT E. R
Chmn, Fourth Dist. Rep. Party, Ind.
b. Columbia City, Ind, 11/19/20; s. Ralph F. Gates and Helene Edwards G;

m. 6/9/48 to Harriett K. Brown; c. Marjorie B, Anne E. and Mary Ellen. Educ: Ind. Univ, B.S, 42, J.D, 48; Phi Eta Sigma; Sigma Alpha Epsilon; Phi Delta Phi. Polit. & Govt. Pos: Chmn, Whitley Co. Rep. Party, Ind, 59-; chmn, Fourth Dist. Rep. Party, 61-; Rep. cand. gov, 64; del, Rep. Nat. Conv, 68. Mil. Serv: Entered as Ens, Navy, 42, released as Lt, 46, after serv. in U.S.S. N.Mex, Pac. Theatre, 43-45; Eight Battle Stars. Mem: Ind. and Am. Bar Asns; Whitley Co. Bar Asn.(secy, 51-53, pres, 69); Elks; Eagles; Moose; Am. Legion; VFW; Rotary; Columbia Club; Ind. Soc. Chicago; Mason; Scottish Rite; Shrine. Rel: Presbyterian. Legal Res: 701 W. Park Dr, Columbia City, Ind. 46725. Mailing Add: Gates, Gates & McNagny, Columbia City, Ind. 46725.

GATES, THOMAS S. R

b. Germantown, Pa, 4/10/06; s. Thomas Sovereign Gates and Marie Rogers G; m. 9/29/28 to Millicent Anne Brengle; c. Millicent Anne, Patricia S, Thomas S. (deceased) and Katharine Curtin. Educ: Univ. of Pa, A.B, 28; Phi Beta Kappa. Hon. LL.D, Univ. of Pa, Yale Univ, Columbia Univ. and Univ. of Toledo. Polit. & Govt. Pos: Under Secy of Navy, 53-57; Secy. of Navy, 57-59; Dep. Secy of Defense, 59; Secy. of Defense, 59-61. Bus. & Prof. Pos: Assoc, Drexel & Co, Phila, Pa, 28, partner, 40-53; dir, Gen. Elec. Co, Scott Paper Co, Campbell Soup Co, Ins. Co. N.Am, Smith Kline & French Lab. and Cities Serv. Co; life trustee, Univ. of Pa; chmn, exec. cmt, Morgan Guaranty Trust Co, 61-62, pres. and dir, 62-65, chmn. of bd. and chief exec. off, 65-68, chmn. of exec. cmt, 68- Mil. Serv: Lt. Comdr, Naval Res, 42-45, served overseas. Mem: Acad. Polit. Sci; Coun. For. Rels; Navy League; Colonial Soc. of Pa; Phila. Racquet, Gulph Mill Golf, Chevy Chase, Metrop. Links Clubs; Econ. Club (N.Y.C.). Legal Res: Mill Race Farm, Devon, Pa. 19333. Mailing Add: 23 Wall St, New York, N.Y. 10015.

GATHINGS, EZEKIEL CANDLER D

b. Prairie, Miss, 11/10/03; s. Melville Williamson Gathings and Virgie Eva Garner G; m. 4/10/39 to Tolise Kirkpatrick; c. Tolise Kirkpatrick and Joseph Royston. Educ: Univ. Ala, 23-26; Univ. Ark, LL.B, 29; Blue Key; Phi Alpha Delta; Pi Kappa Alpha. Polit. & Govt. Pos: Former mem. zoning cmn, West. Memphis, Ark. and Crittenden Co. Bd. Elec. Cmnrs; Ark. State Sen, 35-39; U.S. Rep, Ark, 39-69. Mem: Mason (32°); Shrine; Eastern Star. Rel: Baptist. Legal Res: 421 W. Barton, West Memphis, Ark. 72301. Mailing Add: Holiday Plaza Mall, West Memphis, Ark. 72301.

GAUCHER, CLIFFORD O. D

b. Marlboro, Mass, 3/28/17; s. Ovila P. Gaucher and Della Morin G; m. 7/2/38 to Janette Vivian Denoncourt; c. Robert Clifford and Paul Gerard. Educ: Assumption Col, Worcester, Mass. Polit. & Govt. Pos: Admin. asst. to Rep. Philbin, 43- Bus. & Prof. Pos: Ed, Maynard Mass. Enterprise, 42; advert. mgr, Southbridge Mass. Press, 40-41; wire copy chief, Fitchburg Mass. Star, 39; asst. to city ed, Worcester Mass. Post, 37-38. Legal Res: Marlboro, Mass. Mailing Add: 241 1 32nd St, S.E, Washington, D.C. 20020. (1967)

GAUD, WILLIAM S

b. New York, N.Y, 8/9/07; s. Wm. S. Gaud and Isabel Cleland Williams G; m. 6/1/35 to Eleanor Mason Smith; c. Anne Timothy. Educ: Yale Univ, B.A, 29, LL.B, 31. Polit. & Govt. Pos: Spec. asst. to Secy. of War, 45-46; asst. adminstr. for Near E. of South. Asia, Agency for Int. Develop, 61-64, dep. adminstr, 64-66, dir, 66-69. Bus. & Prof. Pos: Instr, Yale Law Sch, 31-33; attorney-at-law, 33-35; asst. corp. counsel, N.Y.C, 35-41; law firm, Carter, Ledyard & Milburn, 46-61; consult, Int. Bank for Reconstruction and Develop, 69- Mil. Serv: Army, Col, 42-45; 2 years China, Burma, India; Legion of Merit with Oak Leaf Cluster; Order of Brit. Empire. Mailing Add: 4926 Rockwood Pkwy. N.W, Washington, D.C. 20016.

GAUDETTE, DONALD ROGER D

Mass. State Rep.

b. Acushnet, Mass, 12/16/26; s. Charles Ovide Gaudette, Sr. and Aurore M.R. Gregoire G; m. 5/31/48 to Theresa Annete Castonguay; c. Janice Marie, Donald R, Jr, Rachel J. and Robert C. Educ: New Bedford Voc. High Sch, 4 years. Polit. & Govt. Pos: City coun, New Bedford; Mass, 62-67 and city coun. pres, 65; Mass. State Rep, Boston, 67- Mem: Eagles; K. of C.(4°); Cath. Order of Foresters; Mass. Legislators Asn. Rel: Catholic. Legal Res: 1125 Pequot St, New Bedford, Mass. 02745. Mailing Add: State House, Boston, Mass. 02133.

GAUDIN, EDWARD CLARK R

b. New Roads, La, 12/26/31; s. Alton F. Gaudin and Vida Swindler G; m. 2/7/59 to Marianne Hurst; c. Allison, Dana and Todd. Educ: La. State Univ, B.S, 52, J.D, 58; Sigma Nu. Polit. & Govt. Pos: La. State Rep, East Baton Rouge Parish, 67-68; alternate del, Rep. Nat. Conv, 68; chmn. polit. action coun, East Baton Rouge Rep. Party, 69- Bus. & Prof. Pos: Partner, Smith & Gaudin, Attorneys, 61- Mil. Serv: Entered as 2nd Lt, Army, 52, released as 1st Lt, 54, after serv. in 196th Field Artillery Bn; Korean Theatre, 53-54; Res, Judge Adv. Gen. Crops, 54-68, Maj. Mem: La. State and Baton Rouge Bar Asns; Kiwanis; K. of C; Alhambra; East Baton Rouge Rep. Party; Pelican Pioneers (pres, 68-69). Rel: Roman Catholic. Mailing Add: 3165 Murphy Dr, Baton Rouge, La. 70809.

GAUDINEER, LEE H. D

Iowa State Sen.

b. Des Moines, Iowa; married; c. Four. Educ: Grinnell, B.A; Univ. Mo, LL.M; Drake Univ. Sch. Law, J.D. Polit. & Govt. Pos: Mem. staff, Legis. Research Bur, Iowa; asst. city attorney; asst. co. attorney; former Iowa State Rep; Iowa State Sen, 67- Bus. & Prof. Pos: Lawyer. Mil. Serv: Parachutist, Korean War, 3 years. Mailing Add: 1248 39th St, Des Moines, Iowa 50311.

GAUDREAU, LORENZO J. D

Maine State Rep.

b. Brunswick, Maine, 9/5/23; s. Clarence Gaudreau and Cedea Longtin G; m. 8/8/42 to Rolande E. Pelletier; c. Therese, Diane, Lorraine and Marc. Educ: Brunswick High Sch, grad. Polit. & Govt. Pos: Mem, Zoning Bd, Lewiston, Maine, 53-58 and mem, Lewiston Fire Cmn, 58-63; Maine State Rep, 65- Bus. & Prof. Pos: Owner, grocery store, 45-61 and restaurant, 61- Mil. Serv: Entered as A/S, Navy, 45, released as 2/C PO, after serv. in Pac; Atlantic and Pac. Campaign Ribbons. Mem: Am. Legion; Le Montagnard Social Club. Rel: Catholic. Mailing Add: 289 Pleasant St, Lewiston, Maine 04240. (1967)

GAUGH, JAMES H. D

b. Menominee, Mich, 6/21/40; s. George J. Gaugh and Alice Peterson G; single. Educ: North. Mich. Col. Polit. & Govt. Pos: Former v.pres, Menominee Co. Dem. Club, Mich; alternate del, Dem. Nat. Conv, 64; alderman, Sixth Ward, Menominee, 65-69. Bus. & Prof. Pos: Engr. supvr, Kargard Co, Wis, 61-64, mgr. sales, Order Dept, 64-68. Mem: Elks; Fun-O-Rama Corp; Scandinavian Day Cmt; St. Patrick's Day Cmt; Menominee Co. Dem. Club. Rel: Protestant. Mailing Add: 2801 13th St, Menominee, Mich. 49858.

GAUKLER, GEORGE D

Treas, N.Dak. Dem. Non-Partisan League

b. Lidgerwood, N.Dak, 8/22/36; single. Educ: Valley City State Col, N.Dak, B.S. in Math, 62; pres, Student Asn, 61-62; viking pilot, Col. Leadership, 2 years; Kappa Delta Pi. Polit. & Govt. Pos: Former pres, Valley City State Col. Young Dem; state pres, N.Dak. Young Dem, 61-62; mem. state exec. cmt, N.Dak. Dem. Non-Partisan League, 61-69; chmn, Great Plains Conf. Young Dem. Am, 62-64; state treas, N.Dak. Dem. Non-Partisan League Sr. Party, 63- Bus. & Prof. Pos: V.chmn, Valley City Develop. Corp, N.Dak; chmn, N.Dak. Real Estate Cmn; pres, N.Dak. Bd. Realtors; pres, Jamestown and Valley City Bd. Realtors. Mem: Valley City Jaycees (past pres); Valley City Amvets (past adj); K. of C; Toastmasters; Eagles; Elks; C. of C; Col. Viking Century Club; Valley City State Col. Alumni Asn; chmn, Barnes Co. March of Dimes, 64-69. N.Dak. Govt. Affairs State Award, 67; Distinguished Serv. Award, 68. Rel: Usher and lector, St. Catherines Church, Valley City, N.Dak. Mailing Add: 1348 Sixth Ave. N.E, Valley City, N.Dak. 58072.

GAUL, DEWIE J. D

b. Earling, Iowa, 9/18/28; s. John A. Gaul and Odelia Schnuettgen G; m. 10/27/56 to Mavis Georgia Cwach; c. Jacqueline, Sandra, Thomas, Robert, Randal and Laurie. Educ: Loras Col, A.B, 50; Georgetown Univ, LL.B, 55. Polit. & Govt. Pos: Justice of the Peace, Westphalia Twp, Shelby Co, Iowa, 50-52; committeeman, 16th Precinct, Sioux City, 60-; chmn, Woodbury Co. Dem. Cent. Cmt, 62-66; alternate del, Dem. Nat. Conv, 68. Bus. & Prof. Pos: Lawyer, Sifford, Wadden and Davis. Mil. Serv: Entered as Seaman, Navy, 49, released as YNT-3, 53, after serv. on U.S.S. Tarawa, 52-53. Mem: Am, Iowa State and Sioux City Bar Asns; Asn. of Ins. Attorneys; K. of C. Rel: Catholic. Legal Res: 1906 Iowa St, Sioux City, Iowa 51104. Mailing Add: 750 Orpheum Electric Bldg, Sioux City, Iowa 51101.

GAULT, SUE NELLE R

b. Gainesville, Mo, 6/18/20; m. 8/12/39 to Henry Gault; wid; c. James Mark, Edward Dean, Joe Gary. Educ: Gainesville, Mo. Pub. Schs. Polit. & Govt. Pos: Mo. State Rep, 64-66; dep. to Ozark Co. Sheriff; asst. Ozark Co. Assessor; secy, Welfare Office. Bus. & Prof. Pos: Ins. saleslady, Mid-West Fire and Casualty Co; owner-operator, restaurant, Gainesville. Mem: Rebekah Lodge; Exten. Club. First woman ever elected Rep. from Ozark Co. Rel: First Christian Church. Mailing Add: Gainesville, Mo. 65655. (1967)

GAULTIER, GERALD DOUGLAS R

Chmn, Kalkaska Co. Rep. Cmt, Mich.

b. South Boardman, Mich, 4/11/34; s. P. Vere Gaultier and Eleanor Johnson G; m. 10/15/54 to Elaine Marie Brockway; c. Douglas, Shaleen, Toni and Melanie. Educ: Mich. Col. of Mining & Technology, 1 year; Ind. Technical Col, ½ year; Northwestern Col, ½ year; Col. Newspaper Cartoon Editor "Lode," Mich. Col. Mining & Tech. Polit. & Govt. Pos: Treas, Bd. Educ, South Boardman, Mich, 58-59, secy, 67-; mem, Kalkaska Co. Rep. Exec. Cmt; chmn, Kalkaska Co. Rep. Cmt, 68-, treas, 68. Bus. & Prof. Pos: Owner, Boardman Valley Construction Co. 65- Mil. Serv: Entered as Airman, Air Force, 54, released as Staff Sgt, 58, after serv. in 98th Bomb Wing 818th Air Div. Strategic Air Command, 54-58; S/Sgt, Res, 58-; National Defense Service Medal; Good Conduct Medal; "Outstanding Crew Chief for 98th Bombardment Wing." Mem: Nat. Rifle Asn. Am; Nat. Honor Soc. Rel: Methodist. Mailing Add: Mill St, S. Boardman, Mich. 49680

GAUTHIER, LAURENCE WILLIAM R

Vt. State Rep.

b. Barre, Vt, 11/25/01; s. Charles Laurence Gauthier and Carrie Taft G; m. 10/24/45 to Jessie Ewen; c. Charlene Carol. Educ: Bay Path Inst, Springfield, Mass, 1 year. Polit. & Govt. Pos: Alderman, Montelier, Vt, 36-38 & 48-50; Vt. State Rep, Dist. 9-3, 69- Bus. & Prof. Pos: From field agent, income tax div. to chief of property taxes, Vt. Dept. of Taxes, 33-67; fee appraiser, real estate broker and Registered Pub. Acct, currently. Mil. Serv: Entered Vt. State Guard, 42, released as Capt, 45, after serv. in Co. H. and Bn. Hq. Publ: Vermont Handbook for Listers, 58 and co-author, Vermont Timberland Appraisal Guide, 60, Vt. Dept. of Taxes. Mem: Secy-treas, Vt. Asn. of Listers and Assessors; Mason; Shrine. Catherine Pardee Award, Northeast. Regional Asn. of Assessing Officers, 68. Rel: Congregational. Mailing Add: 11 Derby Dr, Montpelier, Vt. 05602.

GAUTHIER, RICHARD HUGH D

b. New Orleans, La, 3/18/33; s. Joseph F. Gauthier and Amelie Lucas G; m. 8/8/64 to Melanie Odinet; c. Christine and Richard H, Jr. Educ: Notre Dame Univ, 50-52; La. State Univ. Law Sch, LL.B, 56; Gamma Eta Gamma. Polit. & Govt. Pos: Chmn, St. Bernard Parish Libr. Bd, La, 58-60; mem, La. State Cent. Dem. Cmt, St. Bernard Parish, 63-; secy-treas, St. Bernard Parish Police Jury, 64-66; judge, 25th Judicial Dist. Court, 66- Mil. Serv: Pvt, Army, 56-58; Capt, Standby Res, currently; Commendation Ribbon with Medal Pendant. Mem: Am. and La. State Bar Asns; Am. Judicature Soc; Notre Dame Alumni Asn; La. State Univ. Alumni Asn; C. of C; Jaycees. Rel: Roman Catholic. Legal Res: 900 Le Beau, Arabi, La. 70032. Mailing Add: St. Bernard Court House, Chalmette, La. 70034.

GAUTIER, AUGUSTO R. D

Mem, P.R. Dem. Party Cmt.

b. Santurce, P.R, 9/5/32; s. Aurelio R. Gautier and Carmen Luisa Mayoral G; m. 10/16/55 to Carmen Margarita Lloveras; c. Augusto, Carmen Margarita, Carlos and Luis. Educ: Rensselaer Polytech. Inst, B.Arch, 55; Tau Beta Pi; Sigma Xi; Scarab; Am. Inst. Architects Sch. Medal; Pi Kappa Phi; Phi Eta Mu. Polit. & Govt. Pos: Mem, P.R. Dem. Party Cmt, 63-; mem, Bd. of Exam. of Engrs, Architects & Surveyors of P.R, 63-, pres, 65-67; alternate del, Dem. Nat. Conv, 64, del, 68; del, Popular Dem. Party of P.R. Conv, 64 & 68; mem. munic. cent. cmt, Popular Dem. Party of P.R, 64-

Mil. Serv: Entered as 2nd Lt, Army, 55, released as 1st Lt, 57, after serv. in 84th Bn, Conarc; Maj, Mil. Intel, Army Res, 69. Mem: Engrs, Architects & Surveyors Asn. of P.R; Inst. of Architects of P.R.(pres, 64-65); Am. Inst. of Architects; pres, Pan-Am. Fedn. of Architects Asn, 68-; mem. cmt. on int. reciprocity, Nat. Coun. Archit. Registr. Bd; hon. mem, Colombian Soc. of Architects, Inst. of Architects of Brazil and Mex. Soc. of Architects; Lions; Casino de P.R. Rel: Catholic. Legal Res: DA 4, F.P. Hastings St, Garden Hills, Bayamon, P.R. 00619. Mailing Add: Box 11591, Santurce, P.R. 00910.

GAUTIER, ERNEST WILLIAM D
b. Dunedon, Fla, 3/12/10; s. Elias Bryan Gautier and Charolette Williams G; m. 4/5/42 to Anne Berge Sams; c. Patricia B. and Priscilla S. Educ: St. Petersburg Jr. Col, L.I, 29; John P. Stetson Univ, LL.B, 32; Univ. Fla. post-grad, 32; Phi Alpha Delta; Pi Kappa Phi. Polit. & Govt. Pos: Mem, Bd. of Pub. Instr, Volusia Co, Fla, 40-41; Fla. State Sen, 28th Dist, 50-66. Bus. & Prof. Pos: Dir, Bank of New Smyrna, 63 and Halifax Nat. Bank, Port Orange, Fla, 64. Mil. Serv: Entered as 2nd Lt, Army Air Force, 41, released as Col, 46, after serv. in ETO; Col, Air Force Res, 45; Bronze Star; Am. Defense Medal; ETO Ribbon with 3 Battle Stars; German Occup. Medal. Mem: Volusia Co, Fla. and Am. Bar Asns; Rotary; Yacht Club; Elks; Mason; Shrine. Rel: Episcopal. Legal Res; 1200 Magnolia St, New Smyrna Beach, Fla. 32069. Mailing Add: P.O. Box 128, New Smyrna Beach, Fla. 32069.

GAUTIER, REDMOND BUNN, JR. D
b. Miami, Fla, 4/3/09; s. Redmond Bunn Gautier and Ida Miller G; m. 11/19/37 to Frances Roe; c. Gary Bunn and Vicki Frances. Educ: Wash. and Lee Univ; Sigma Alpha Epsilon. Polit. & Govt. Pos: Fla. State Rep, 43-47; Fla. State Sen, 13th Dist, 49-55; mem, State Improvement Cmn, Fla, 56-57. Bus. & Prof. Pos: Dir, Gr. Miami Fed. Savings and Loan Asn, 54-; mem, Orange Bowl Cmt, 59-; trustee and mem. exec. bd, Univ. Miami, 62-; dir, Merchants Bank of Miami, 65- Mil. Serv: Entered as Lt, Naval-Air Force, 43, released as Lt.(sg), 46. Mem: Life mem, Hon. Adv. Coun, Miami Young Dem; hon. life mem, Univ. Miami Law Sch. Alumni Asn; Kiwanis; Am. Legion; Riviera Country Club; Miami Club. Rel: Methodist. Legal Res: The Island House, 1 Ocean Lane Dr, Miami, Fla. 33149. Mailing Add: 200 S.E. First St, Miami, Fla. 33131.

GAVAN, HENRY F. D
N.J. State Assemblyman
b. Elizabeth, N.J, 2/21/23; m. to Geraldine; c. Nancy, Maureen and Henry. Educ: Seton Hall Univ, B.S, 54. Polit. & Govt. Pos: Mem, State Adv. Cmt. Sewage Disposal N.J; pres, Ninth Ward Dem. Club; mem, Ninth and Tenth Ward Dem. Clubs; trustee, Linden City Dem. Club; health officer, Linden; N.J. State Assemblyman, currently. Bus. & Prof. Pos: Health officer; bd. of mgrs, John E. Runnells Hosp. for Chest Diseases and Chronically Ill, Berkeley Heights. Mil. Serv: Army, 43-46. Mem: Seton Hall Alumni Asn; Am. Legion; Moose; N.J. Health Officers Asn.(pres, 63-64). Mailing Add: 2109 Orchard Terr, Linden, N.J. 07036.

GAVIN, JAMES ALOYSIUS D
b. Paterson, N.J, 12/10/28; s. John Aloysius Gavin and Gertrude Furrey G; m. 5/2/64 to Sarah Christine Lane; c. James A, Jr, William J, John A. and Beth Ann. Educ: Fordham Univ, B.S; Wharton Sch. of Finance and Commerce, M.B.A. Polit. & Govt. Pos: Second v.pres, Cong. Secy. Club, 66 & 67, first v.pres, 69, pres-elect, currently; admin. asst, U.S. Rep. Charles S. Joelson, N.J, currently. Bus. & Prof. Pos: Purchasing trainee, Ford Motor Co, 56-57; regional sales mgr, St. Regis Paper Co, 58-60. Mil. Serv: Entered as Pvt, Marine Corps, 52, released as Capt, 55, after serv. in H Co, Third Bn, Fourth MAR. Mem: Am. Legion. Rel: Roman Catholic. Legal Res: 420 19th Ave, Paterson, N.J. 07524. Mailing Add: 9721 Indian Princess Dr, Ft. Foote, Md. 20022.

GAY, CHARLES HENRY R
N.H. State Rep.
b. Boston, Mass, 3/18/07. Educ: Mass. Nautical Sch; Bay State Sch. of Navigation and Adv. Astron. Polit. & Govt. Pos: N.H. State Rep, 51 & 55-; v.chmn, Rockingham Co. Del. Bus. & Prof. Pos: Mem. of staff, U.S. Coast Guard, U.S. Pub. Health Serv. and U.S. Army Engrs, 23 years. Mil. Serv: Army, Corps of Engrs, World War II, Capt. Mem: F&AM; Mt. Sinai Chap, St. George Commandery; Mason (32°); Valley of Nashua; All Shrine Clubs in N.H, Maine and Mass; officer, Bektash Temple, AAONMS; ROA; past comdr, Derry VFW; Amvets; DAV; Am. Legion. Mailing Add: Drawer 89, Derry, N.H. 03038. (1967)

GAY, CLAY R
b. Sizerock, Ky, 4/20/23; s. John Gay and Ibbie Hensley G; m. 1/6/66 to Barbara Horne; c. Donna Jo and Debbie. Educ: East. Ky. Univ, B.S, 49, M.A, 51, summers for counsr, 57 & 60-63; Univ. Louisville Col. of Law Evening Div, 58; Utah State Univ. Summer Sch. for Math. Teachers, 65; Ohio Univ. Summer Sch. for Guid. Counsr, Ed.S, 68. Polit. & Govt. Pos: Pres, Leslie Co. Young Rep. Club, 56-57; Ky. State Rep, 56-58; Ky. State Sen. and minority whip, Ky. State Senate, 64-68. Bus. & Prof. Pos: Prin, Blue Diamond Elem. Sch, Perry Co. Bd. of Educ, Hazard, Ky, 49-50; surveillance inspector, Blue Grass Ord. Depot, Richmond, 51-52; teacher of math. and govt, Leslie Co. High Sch, Hyden, 52-, guid. counsr. dir, 65-; prin, Harrison Elem. Sch, Harrison Co. Bd. of Educ, Cinthiana, 56-57; teacher of math, City Sch, Hamilton, Ohio, 60-63. Mil. Serv: Sgt. 1/C, Gen. Pattons 3rd Army, serv. in Inf, 76th Div, ETO, 44-45; Sgt. 1/C, Army Res, 55-63; Combat Inf. Badge; Purple Heart; Bronze Star with V; World War II Victory, ETO, Good Conduct and Am. Campaign Medals. Mem: Ky. Personnel and Guid. Asn; Ky. and Nat. Educ. Asns; Leslie Co. Teachers Asn; Voc. Guid. and Personnel Asn; Mason; Am. Legion; VFW; nat. hon. mem, Fraternal Order of Police; Leslie Co. Fish and Game Club; past pres, Jaycees. Ky. Col. Rel: Protestant. Mailing Add: Box 43, Hyden, Ky. 41749.

GAY, JAMES HOYT R
Chmn, Chambers Co. Rep. Cmt, Ala.
b. Lanett, Ala, 6/1/02; s. Henry Mitchell Gay and Mattie J. Autrey M; m. 9/7/21 to Maude Avery; c. Gwendolyn (Mrs. Rowe Staples), Ernestine (Mrs. Jesse Shaddix) and Betty (Mrs. Heard). Educ: Lanett High Sch. Polit. & Govt. Pos: Secy, Chambers Co. Rep. Cmt, Ala, 27-62, chmn, 62-; alternate del, Rep. Nat. Conv, 56 & 68; mem, Ala. Rep. State Exec. Cmt, 63. Bus. & Prof. Pos: Shipping clerk, cotton dept, Lanett Mill Div, West Point-Pepperell, Inc, 20-26, mgr. cotton dept, 26-55, supvr. cotton & waste dept, 55-65, retired. Mem: Moose; WOW; Valley Hexagon Club; bus. mgr, Valley Baseball Club; secy, Ga-Ala. League. Silver Beaver Award, Boy Scouts. Rel: Methodist. Legal Res: 409 S. Eighth Ave, Lanett, Ala. 36863. Mailing Add: P.O. Box 271, Lanett, Ala. 36863.

GAY, LIZZIE REED R
b. Kingston, La, 1/25/01; d. Randall Hunter Walker and Dafhny Thomas W; m. 10/20/67 to Rev. John H. Gay. Polit. & Govt. Pos: Alternate del, Rep. Nat. Conv, 68; mem, Caddo Rep. Action Coun. Orgn, La, 69- Composer of song 'Forward' dedicated to Rep. Party. Mailing Add: 1334 Marshall St, Shreveport, La. 71101.

GAY, OLIN DOW R
Vt. State Sen.
b. Tunbridge, Vt, 8/16/86; m. to Bernice Butterfield; c. One son; two daughters. Educ: Lowell Tech. Inst. Hon. degree, Middlebury Col, 35. Polit. & Govt. Pos: Former moderator and sch. dir; Vt. State Rep, 53-57, mem, Bd. of State Bldgs. and Legis. Cmt. on Reapportionment; Vt. State Sen, 57- Bus. & Prof. Pos: Retired woolen mfg. Rel: Protestant. Mailing Add: 198 Summer St, Springfield, Vt. 05156.

GAYDOS, JOSEPH MATTHEW D
U.S. Rep, Pa.
b. Braddock, Pa, 7/3/26; s. John Gaydos and Helen Magella G; m. 11/26/55 to Alice Ann Gray; c. Joseph, Jr, Kelly, Kathleen, Coleen and Tammy. Educ: Duquesne Univ, 46-48; Notre Dame Univ, LL.B, 51. Polit. & Govt. Pos: Asst. attorney gen, Commonwealth, Pa, 3 years; asst. solicitor, Allegheny Co, 13 years; Pa. State Sen, 45th Dist, 1 term; U.S. Rep, Pa, 20th Dist, 68- Bus. & Prof. Pos: Attorney at law. Mil. Serv: Entered as Seaman 2/C, Navy, 44, released as S/M-3/C, 46, after serv. in Naval Res. Amphibious Forces, S.Pac, Philippines and Far East, 44-46; Two Battle Stars. Mem: Allegheny Co. and Pa. Bar Asns; all vet. orgn. Man of the Year Award, Allegheny Co. Chap. CWV. Rel: Catholic. Legal Res: 3000 Valley Ridge Rd, McKeesport, Pa. 15132. Mailing Add: U.S. House of Representatives, Washington, D.C. 20515.

GAYLORD, CLAYTON RUSSELL R
b. Rockford, Ill, 1/18/19; s. Robert M. Gaylord and Mildred Ingersoll G; m. 12/20/68 to Joan Ryan; c. Jeannette (Mrs. Charles B. Lorch), Holly (Mrs. Bernard W. Windox), March Ingersoll, Russell Gartz and step-daughter, Andrea Marion Zulfer. Educ: Princeton Univ, A.B, 41; Tiger Inn, Princeton Univ. Polit. & Govt. Pos: Chmn, Winnebago United Rep. Fund, Ill, 58-, mem, Downstate Fund Cmt, United Rep. Fund, 67; alternate del, Rep. Nat. Conv, 68; mem, Gov. Ogilvie's Adv. Coun, Ill, 69; mem, Ill. Rep. Finance Coord. Cmt, 69. Mil. Serv: Entered as Pvt, Army Air Force, 41, released as Capt, 46, after serv. in Third Air Force, U.S. and Air Training Command, Burma China Theater, 45-46. Mem: Rockford Mem. Hosp.(pres, 55, bd. trustees, 55-); Keith Country Day Sch.(bd. trustees, 57-, chmn, 57-61); Ill. Nat. Bank & Trust Co.(bd. dirs); Rockford C. of C.(adv. cmt); Inland Lake Yachting Asn.(bd. dirs, 67-); Lake Geneva Country Club; Rockford Country Club. Rel: Episcopal. Mailing Add: 2310 Spring Creek Rd, Rockford, Ill. 61107.

GAYLORD, E. FRANCES R
Ind. State Rep.
b. Lafayette, Ind, 5/8/08; d. Oliver M. Henderson and Rebecca Edwards H. (both deceased); m. to George C. Gaylord, wid; c. G. Robert and Lynn D. Educ: DePauw Univ. Polit. & Govt. Pos: Mgr, Auto License Br, Tippecanoe Co, Ind, 54-61; v.chmn, Tippecanoe Co. Rep. Cent. Cmt, 54-66; prin. clerk, Ind. State House of Rep, 61-65; mem, Rep. Women's Club, Tippecanoe Co; Ind. State Rep, Tippecanoe Co, 67- Bus. & Prof. Pos: Off. mgr. and exec. secy, Dean of Women, Purdue Univ, 65-66; mem. pub. rels. staff, commercial dept, Lafayette Nat. Bank, 67- Mem: Am. Legion Auxiliary; Elks Ladies; Bus. & Prfnl. Women's Club; Purdue Women's Club; YWCA; Home Hosp. Asn; Home Hosp. Auxiliary; Lafayette and Indianapolis Symphony; Nat. Soc. of State Legislators. Rel: Methodist. Mailing Add: 469 Vine St, West Lafayette, Ind, 47906.

GAYLORD, MARY FLETCHER R
b. Detroit, Mich, 6/2/15; d. Harold Fletcher Wardwell (deceased) and Helen Russel W; m. to Charles Gaylord; c. Edith (Mrs. Harrison), Gretchen (Mrs. Bering), Henry, III and Helen (Mrs. Evans, deceased). Educ: Bennington Col, B.S, 36; Simmons Sch. Soc. Work, M.A, 43. Polit. & Govt. Pos: Precinct committeewoman, Denver Co. Cent. Cmt, 48-52, dist. capt, 50-54; mem, Denver Commun. Rels. Cmn, 48-62; treas, Colo. Fedn. Rep. Women, 52-54; state finance v.chmn, Colo. Rep. State Cent. Cmt, 54-56; Rep. Nat. Committeewoman, Colo, 56-68; mem, Denver Libr. Cmn, 59-65. Mem: Bd, Winter Park Recreational Asn, 50-; treas, Colo. Ment. Health Asn, 62-64; treas. and bd. mem, Vis. Nurse Asn, 50-62; trustee, Bennington Col, 52-58; bd, League of Women Voters, 46-50; Denver Art Mus, Symphony Soc. and Libr. Found. Rel: Episcopal. Mailing Add: 410 Marion St, Denver, Colo. 80218.

GAYNER, JOHN M. III R
b. Salem, N.J, 1/10/31; s. Edward J. Gayner III; Emma Fox G; m. 9/4/54 to Dorothy Nowell. Educ: Princeton Univ, B.A, 52; Univ. Ga, LL.B, 56; Phi Beta Kappa; Phi Kappa Phi; Omicron Delta Kappa; Gridiron Soc; Blue Key; Princeton Tower Club; Phi Alpha Delta. Polit. & Govt. Pos: Ga. State Sen, 63-66. Bus. & Prof. Pos: Attorney, Bennet, Gilbert, Gilbert & Whittle, Brunswick, Ga, 57-; attorney, Athens, Ga, 56-57; asst. prof. of law, Univ. Ga, 56-57. Mil. Serv: 52-53, Sampson Air Force Base and Keesler Air Force Base, A3/c; Lakeland Air Force Base, officer cand; 2nd Lt, Slocum, N.Y. Capt, Air Force Res. Mem: Bd. of govs, Brunswick Country Club, 58-61; exec. coun, Younger Lawyers Sect, Ga. Bar Asn, 59-; Glynn-Brunswick Mem. Hosp. Authority, 61-; Rotary. Written and edited, 'Summary of Laws Affecting Social Govt', 56; Agency-Ga. Encyclopedia of Law, 59; ed, Brunswick Rotarygram. Rel: Presbyterian. Mailing Add: Brunswick, Ga. 31520. (1967)

GAYRON, T. HAROLD D
Mass. State Rep.
b. Lynn, Mass; m. to Mary Garneau; c. Frances and Patricia. Educ: New Eng. Inst. of Anat. Polit. & Govt. Pos: Dem. mem, Ward Coun, Mass, 58-66; Mass.

State Rep, 66- Bus. & Prof. Pos: G.E. River Works; owner-operator, T. Harold Gayron Funeral Home. Mem: IUE-CIO (former shop steward, Local 201). Mailing Add: 19 Hood St, Lynn, Mass. 01905. (1967)

GEANAKOS, GEORGE J. R
b. 1928. Polit. & Govt. Pos: Sch. Cmt, Chmn; Precinct Club, Inc; Essex Club, Rep. Bus. & Prof. Pos: self employed grocer. Mem: Am. Legion; Mass. Sch. Comm. Asn. Mailing Add: 1 Burleigh Ave, Ipswich, Mass. 01938. (1967)

GEARTY, EDWARD JOSEPH DFL
Minn. State Rep.
b. Minneapolis, Minn, 3/17/23; s. John Edward Gearty and Elletta Newton G; m. 8/7/65 to Lorraine Margaret Breher. Educ: Col. of St. Thomas, B.A, 52; Georgetown Univ. Law Sch, LL.B, 55. Polit. & Govt. Pos: Park cmnr, Minneapolis Park Bd, 59; Minn. State Rep, 63- Bus. & Prof. Pos: Attorney, Minneapolis Park Bd, 63. Mil. Serv: Entered as A/S, Navy, 42, released as AMM 3/C, 48. Rel: Catholic. Legal Res: 3810 Xerxes Ave. N, Minneapolis, Minn. 55412. Mailing Add: 1100 W. Broadway, Minneapolis, Minn. 55411.

GEBHARDT, RICHARD G. D
Mem, Colo. Dem. State Cent. Cmt.
b. Denver, Colo, 5/18/31; married; c. Three. Polit. & Govt. Pos: Off, Boulder Dem. Party, Colo; former Colo. State Rep; del, Dem. Nat. Conv, 68; mem, Colo. Dem. State Cent. Cmt, 69- Bus. & Prof. Pos: Ins. agent. Mem: Jaycees. Distinguished Serv. Award, Boulder Jaycees; One of Three State Awards. Mailing Add: 875 Circle Dr, Boulder, Colo. 80302. (1967)

GEDDES, JOHN ARRINGTON R
Chmn. Commun. Cmt, San Diego Co. Rep. Cent. Cmt, Calif.
b. Berkeley, Calif, 2/8/22; s. William D. Geddes and Mabel Arrington G; m. 6/29/47 to Alice E. Price; c. John W, Lynn M. and James A. Educ: Univ. Calif, Los Angeles; Univ. Wis; San Diego State Col, B.A, 55; Long Beach State Col, M.A, 57; San Diego State Col, Calif. Pupil Personnel Credential, 64; Univ. Calif, Los Angeles, 59-63; U.S. Int. Univ, Ph.D, 68; Phi Delta Kappa. Polit. & Govt. Pos: Mem, Rep. campaign cmts. for state and nat. cand, Calif, 57-68; chmn. legis. affairs cmt, La Jolla Town Coun, 60-61; mem, Rep. Advocates, 62; chmn. commun. cmt, San Diego Co. Rep. Cent. Cmt, 62-; ed, San Diego Rep, 63-69; mem, Calif. Rep. Assembly, 63-64; mem, Calif. Rep. State Cent. Cmt, 69. Bus. & Prof. Pos: Teacher, counsr. and acting v.prin, Midway Adult High Sch, San Diego, Calif, 59-63; counsr, teacher and curriculum designer, San Diego City Col, 63-67; counsr. and assoc. dean of student affairs and placement, Univ. Calif, San Diego, 67-69. Mil. Serv: Entered as Aviation Cadet, Navy, 42, released as Lt, 54, after serv. on Naval Aviation Squadrons Staffs and on ships, Pac. Theater, World War II and Korean War, 44-45, 50-51; Asiatic Pac. Theater Ribbon with One Battle Star; Korean Theater Ribbon with Six Battle Stars; Confidential Letter of Commendation Cin Clant for proposing an ASW tactic, 52. Publ: Techniques of Study, a Curriculum Guide, San Diego City Schs, 66; Vocational Guidance Papers, Univ. Calif, San Diego, 68-69; 'What's Wrong on Campus,' San Diego Union and Seminar, 11/68-69; plus 1 other. Mem: Am. and Calif. Educ. Research Asns; Am. Personnel & Guid. Asn; Lamplighters Club of La Jolla. Golden Apple Teacher of the Week Award, local TV station, 63; Eagle Scout. Rel: Christian Church. Mailing Add: 5522 Rutgers Rd, La Jolla, Calif. 92037.

GEDDES, KENNETH WHITEHILL R
Chmn, El Paso Co. Rep. Cmt, Colo.
b. Boone, Iowa, 1/5/23; s. Kenneth William Geddes and Margaret Whitehill G; m. 1/6/44 to Helen Hatcher; c. Brian Nelson, Ann Lurette and William Kenneth. Educ: Colo. Col, 40-43; Univ. Colo, LL.B, 48; Order of the Coif; Kappa Sigma; Phi Delta Phi. Polit. & Govt. Pos: Chmn, El Paso Co. Rep. Cent. Cmt, Colo, 69- Mil. Serv: Entered as Pvt, Army, 43, released as T-5, 45, after serv. in Transportation Corps, S.Pac. Theatre, 44-45. Rel: Episcopal. Legal Res: 1536 Wood Ave, Colorado Springs, Colo. 80907. Mailing Add: Box 2137, 513 Mining Exchange Bldg, Colorado Springs, Colo. 80901.

GEE, BILL F. R
Chmn, Marshall Co. Rep. Cmt, Ind.
b. Elnora, Ind, 3/23/34; s. William McKinley Gee and Callie Bales G; m. 12/30/56 to Mary Lynn Johnson; c. Elizabeth Bales. Educ: Vanderbilt Univ, B.A, 56; Alpha Tau Omega. Polit. & Govt. Pos: Mem, Daviess Co. Young Rep, Ind, 58-62, Marshall Co. Young Rep, 62-; chmn, Marshall Co. Rep. Cmt, 66-; mgr, Marshall Co. Auto License Bur, 69- Bus. & Prof. Pos: Mgr. for Ind, Harper & Row, Publishers, 62-; pres, Ind. Prfnl. Bookmen of Am, 67-68. Mil. Serv: Entered as 2nd Lt, Marines, 56, released as 1st Lt, 58. Mem: Elks; Mason; Scottish Rite; Kiwanis. Rel: Methodist. Mailing Add: 222 E. Shalley Dr, Plymouth, Ind. 46563.

GEE, HARVEY F. R
Wis. State Assemblyman
b. Wisconsin Rapids, Wis, 2/29/08. Educ: Rollins Col, B.A, 32. Polit. & Govt. Pos: Mem, Co. Bd, Wis, 38-60; athletic field and park cmnr, Wisconsin Rapids, 47-; Wis. State Assemblyman, 60- Bus. & Prof. Pos: Land developer. Mil. Serv: Army. Mem: Am. Legion; state organizer, Nat. Infantile Paralysis Found. Mailing Add: 170 14th Ave, South Wisconsin Rapids, Wis. 54494. (1967)

GEE, ROBERT S. D
b. Oklahoma City, Okla, 2/24/32; s. Robert L. Gee and Vernice Doughty G; m. 8/23/53 to Nancy Ann Neil; c. Robert Neil, Catherine Ann, Elizabeth Ruth and James Kenneth. Educ: Muskogee Jr. Col, A.A, 51; Univ. Okla, A.B, 53, LL.B, 55; Phi Delta Phi; Phi Theta Kappa; Okla. Law Rev. Polit. & Govt. Pos: Pres, The Young Dem, Univ. Okla. Chap, 52-53; asst. co. attorney, Ottawa Co, Okla, 55-59, co. attorney, 60-64; Okla. State Sen, 65-68. Bus. & Prof. Pos: Partner, law firm, Wallace & Owens, 65- Mem: Ottawa Co, Okla. and Am. Bar Asns; Lions; Jaycees; C. of C. Rel: Presbyterian. Mailing Add: 421 G N.W, Miami, Okla. 74354.

GEER, PETER ZACK, JR. D
b. Colquitt, Ga, 8/24/28; s. Peter Zack Geer and Juanita Rawlings G; c. Carol. Educ: Middle Ga. Col; Oglethorpe Univ; Mercer Univ, A.B. and LL.B, 51; SAE; Delta Theta Phi. Received freshman scholarship award of law sch. Mercer Univ; received scholarship award Walter F. George Sch. of Law, cum laude; Student Annual Add. to Ga. Bar Asn, 51. Polit. & Govt. Pos: Lt. Gov, 63-67; exec. secy, Gov. S. Ernest Vandiver, 59-61, resigned; Miller Co. attorney; Ga. State Rep, 53-54; chmn. Home Rule Sub-Cmt, Constitutional Rev. Cmn, 63-64. Mem: Moose; Elk; Gridiron Club; chmn. Civil War Centennial Cmn. Listed Who's Who in Am; One of five 'Outstanding Young Men of the Year, 63'. Rel: Methodist. Mailing Add: Route 2, Box 436 G, Albany, Ga. 31701. (1967)

GEERLINGS, EDGAR ALLEN R
Mich. State Rep.
b. Zeeland, Mich, 4/24/37; s. Alvin R. Geerlings and Dorothy Otting G; m. 6/13/59 to Mary Jane Watterworth. Educ: Cent. Mich. Univ, B.S, 59 and M.A, 61; Delta Sigma Phi. Polit. & Govt. Pos: Mich. State Rep, 97th Dist, 67- Mem: Mich. Educ. Asn; legis. chmn, Muskegon Co. Educ. Asn, 65-67; Mich. Coun. Teachers of Math; Mich. High Sch. Athletic Asn; UAW Local 480. Rel: Reformed Church of America. Mailing Add: 850 Fennwood Circle E, Muskegon, Mich. 49445.

GEERNAERT, GERALD L. R
Mem, Calif. Rep. State Cent. Cmt.
b. Berkeley, Calif, 11/29/29; s. Theodore Geernaert and Thelma Borgen G; c. Linda Marrie, Gerald, Jr, Carla Ray, Richard Warren and David Michel. Educ: City Col. San Francisco, A.A; Univ. Calif. Dent. Col, D.D.S; Kenney Univ. Law Sch, 1 year; Psi Omega. Polit. & Govt. Pos: Mem, Calif. Rep. State Cent. Cmt, 69- Bus. & Prof. Pos: Dentist, 58- Mil. Serv: Seaman, Navy, 48-49, serv. aboard U.S.S. S.M. Moore; Naval Res. Officer Cand. Sch, 50. Mem: Contra Costa, Calif. and Am. Dent. Socs; Operating Engrs. Union; Lions; United Rep. of Calif; C. of C; Rep. Alliance. Rel: Protestant. Mailing Add: 3790 A Happy Valley Rd, Lafayette, Calif. 94549.

GEESEY, EUGENE RONALD R
Pa. State Rep.
b. Dallastown, Pa, 12/1/31; s. Luther Elwood Geesey and Rose Jennings G; m. 5/15/54 to Joanne Elizabeth Tarbert; c. Cynthia, David, Ann, Beth, Sue and Joe. Educ: Lebanon Valley Col, B.S. in Econ, 56. Polit. & Govt. Pos: Auditor, Fairview Twp, Pa, 65-69; Pa. State Rep, 92nd Dist, 69- Bus. & Prof. Pos: Pres, Central Pa. Ins. Asn, 66. Mil. Serv: Entered as Pvt, Army, 51, released as Cpl, 53. Mem: Lions. Rel: Protestant. Mailing Add: Box 141, R.D. 1, New Cumberland, Pa. 17070.

GEFKE, CAROLINE LAWRENCE R
Pres, Racine Co. Fedn. of Rep. Women, Wis.
b. Milwaukee, Wis, 11/18/33; d. Larry Lawrence and Caroline McGrath L; m. 6/25/55 to Henry J. Gefke; c. Brian and David. Educ: Northwest. Univ; Univ. Wis, grad. study in Psychol. Polit. & Govt. Pos: V.chmn, Racine Co. Rep. Party, Wis, 60-; v.chmn, First Dist. Rep. Party, 63-65; mem, Wis. Rep. State Exec. Cmt; alternate del, Rep. Nat. Conv, 64; pres, Racine Co. Fedn. Rep. Women, currently. Bus. & Prof. Pos: Milwaukee TV work, 54-60; teacher civics and hist, 55-59. Mem: AAUW; bd. of dirs, Racine Urban League; Civic Music Asn; Lauback Literacy Coun; Am. Red Cross; Lawyers Wives Asn. Mailing Add: 5318 Valley Trail, Racine, Wis. 53402. (1967)

GEFREH, ADAM R
b. Linton, N.Dak, 12/21/18; married; c. 2. Educ: Cath. Univ, Wash, D.C. Polit. & Govt. Pos: N.Dak. State Sen, 59-61; N.Dak. State Rep, 53-59. Bus. & Prof. Pos: Lawyer. Mailing Add: Linton, N.Dak. 58552. (1967)

GEHMAN, EARL W. R
Chmn, Fairfax City Rep. Cmt, Va.
b. Churchtown, Pa, 6/1/17; s. Isaac H. Gehman and Cathryne Weaver G; m. 9/5/42 to Helen J. Johnson; c. Stacey E, Linda (Mrs. Daniel Stegall), Raymond K, Cathrine R. and Helen J. Educ: York Jr. Col, 55-56; George Wash. Univ, 57-59. Polit. & Govt. Pos: Chmn, Fairfax City Rep. Cmt, Va, 68- Bus. & Prof. Pos: Electronic engr, Melpar, Falls Church, Va, 57-59; sr. electronic engr, Scope Inc, 59-67; proj. engr, Vega Precision Labs, Vienna, 67- Mil. Serv: Entered as Pvt, Army, 41, released as S/Sgt, 45, after serv. in 12th Inf, Fourth Div, ETO, 44-45; Bronze Star with Oak Leaf Cluster. Rel: Presbyterian. Mailing Add: 3912 Estel Rd, Fairfax, Va. 22030.

GEHRES, HELEN L. D
b. Decatur, Ind, 2/20/21; d. Rufus Samuel Roop and Bessie Ogg R; m. 2/14/53 to Walter Arnold Gehres. Educ: Decatur High Sch, grad, 39. Polit. & Govt. Pos: Dep. clerk bd. elec, Van Wert Co, Ohio, 2 years; pres, Van Wert Co. Woman's Dem. Club, 2 years; precinct elec. off, Third Precinct, Van Wert, 59- Bus. & Prof. Pos: Secy, 20 years. Mem: Van Wert Co. Woman's Dem. Club; Federated Van Wert Woman's Club; Alpha Delta Omega; Lady Elks. Rel: United Methodist. Mailing Add: 1026 Elm St, Van Wert, Ohio 45891.

GEHRES, LESLIE EDWARD R
Mem, Calif. Rep. State Exec. Cmt.
b. Newark, N.Y, 9/23/98; s. Charles Peter Gehres and Phoebe Ann Thomas G; m. 6/16/23 to Rhoda Elizabeth Cooley Rumsey; c. Leslie Virginia (Mrs. Girard). Educ: Numerous U.S. Navy schs. and courses, 17-45; U.S. Naval War Col. Polit. & Govt. Pos: Rep. cand. for Cong, 50; chmn, Wilson for Cong, 52, 54 & 56; chmn, Knowland for Gov, 58; co-chmn, Nixon for President, 60; chmn, Nixon for Gov, San Diego Co, 62; mem, Calif. Rep. State Cent. and Exec. Cmts, 62-; chmn, San Diego Co. Rep. Cent. Cmt, 62-; pres, Calif. Asn. Rep. Co. Cent. Cmt. Chmn, 69- Bus. & Prof. Pos: V.pres, Constitutional Found. of San Diego, 51-53; personnel dir, Ryan Aeronaut. Co, 53-61; gen. mgr, Nat. Marine Terminal, Inc, 61-, v.pres, 63-; pres, Yellow Cab Co, San Francisco and Alameda Co, 62-63; corp. dir. indust. rels, Westgate-Calif. Corp, 63- Mil. Serv: Entered as Boatswains' Mate 2/C, Naval Militia N.Y, mobilized into active serv, Navy, 17, released as Rear Adm, 49, after serv. in all oceans, all theaters, World Wars I and II, comdr. all naval aviation forces in N.Pac, 41-43; World War I and II Victory Medals; Am. Defense, Am. Campaign, Asiatic-Pac. Campaign, Philippine Liberation and Navy Air Medals; Navy Cross; 2 Legion of Merit Awards with Combat V; Distinguished Flying Cross; Purple Heart. Mem: Indust. Security Soc. U.S.(pres, San Diego Chap, 56); San Diego Urban League; San Diego Hist. Soc; C. of C; pres, Jr. Achievement San Diego, 63-64; Kiwanis (pres, San Diego Club, 55); Am. Legion; Mil.

Order World Wars; Legion of Valor; Retired Officers' Asn; Navy League; Propeller Club, Port of San Diego. Leader, U.S. Navy Fighter-plane acrobatic team, forerunner of Blue Angels, 29-30; Seven George Washington Gold Honor Medals for pub. address, Freedoms Found. at Valley Forge; John Henry Towers Mem. Award for contrib. to naval aviation, Aviation Commandery, Naval Order of U.S, 69. Rel: Protestant. Mailing Add: 8001 Vista Dr, LaMesa, Calif. 92041.

GEHRES, WALTER ARNOLD D
Secy, Van Wert Co. Dem. Cent. Cmt, Ohio
b. Wren, Ohio, 4/20/20; s. Walter Gehres and Lorena Giessler G; m. 2/14/53 to Helen L. Roop. Educ: Wren High Sch, Ohio, grad, 38. Polit. & Govt. Pos: Dem. precinct committeeman, Van Wert Co, Ohio, 55-; secy, Van Wert Co. Dem. Cent. Cmt, 68- Bus. & Prof. Pos: Traveling speciality salesman, 5 years; dept. mgr, Montgomery Wards, Van Wert, 54- Mem: Elks; Van Wert Co. Men's Dem. Club. Rel: Methodist. Mailing Add: 1026 Elm St, Van Wert, Ohio 45891.

GEHRETT, VIRGINIA DALTON R
Committeewoman, Powell Co. Rep. Cent. Cmt, Mont.
b. Mansfield, Wash, 10/20/19; d. Stanley Charles Dalton and Anna Graybeal D; m. 8/10/46 to Joseph Owen Gehrett; c. Virginia Anne, Joseph Owen, Jr. and George Dalton. Educ: Univ. of Wash, 1 year, Univ. of Va, ½ year; Wilson Teachers Col, B.S, 41; George Wash. Univ, LL.B. and J.D, 46. Polit. & Govt. Pos: Chmn, Powell Co. Rep. Women's Club, Mont, 64-66; chmn, Powell Co. Rep. Cent. Cmt, 66-68, committeewoman, 68-; chmn, nominating cmt, Rep. State Cent. Cmt, 67. Bus. & Prof. Pos: Teacher, Wash, D.C. Pub. Schs, 42-44; Co-publisher and co-ed, The Silver State Post, 63- Mem: PEO; Mont. Women's Club. Rel: Presbyterian. Mailing Add: 830 Missouri, Deer Lodge, Mont. 59722.

GEHRIG, JAMES JOSEPH D
b. Milwaukee, Wis, 11/7/21; s. Joseph Phillip Gehrig and Theresa Neuser G; m. 8/11/49 to Susan Helen Kleinz; c. James Joseph, Jr, Teresa Sue, Leigh Michelle, Renee Lorraine, William Lee, Benjamin Phillip, Helen Kleinz and Paul Neuser. Educ: Colo. State Univ, 43-44; Univ. Wis, B.S, 49; Univ. Wis. Grad. Sch, 50; Univ. Del, 51-53; Univ. Calif, Los Angeles, 55-59; Pi Mu Epsilon. Polit. & Govt. Pos: Legis. asst, then spec. asst. to Sen. Stuart Symington, U.S. Senate, 61-65; staff dir, Senate Cmt. on Aeronaut. and Space Sci, Wash, D.C, 65- Bus. & Prof. Pos: Chief, artil. effectiveness group, weapons systs. lab, Ballistic Research Lab, Aberdeen, Md, 50-54; chief. strategic systs. group, systs. anal, Northrop Corp, Hawthorne, Calif, 54-61. Mil. Serv: Entered as Pvt, Army, 43, released as 1st Lt, 46, after serv. in 24th Inf. Div, Philippines and Japan, 44-46; Asiatic Pac. Campaign Medal; Combat Infantryman's Badge; Bronze Star Medal for Valor. Mem: Opers. Research Soc; Am. Asn. Math; Am. Asn. Adv. Sci; Am. Inst. Aeronaut. and Astronaut. Rel: Roman Catholic. Mailing Add: 1118 Gatewood Dr, Alexandria, Va. 22307.

GEHRMANN, BERNARD EUGENE R
b. Mellen, Wis, 11/6/20; s. Bernard J. Gehrmann and Mary Miller G; m. 9/24/47 to Mary Rose Jellish; c. Kevin, Richard, Lynn, Bernard and Denise. Educ: Wis. State Univ, B.S, 42. Polit. & Govt. Pos: Councilman, Ashland, Wis, 60-65, pres. coun, 61-65; Supvr, Ashland Co, 60-68; Wis. State Assemblyman, Ashland-Bayfield-Iron, 64-68; Secy, State Hwy. Cmn, 69- Mil. Serv: Entered as Pvt, Marine Corps, 41, released as Capt, 45, after serv. in 3rd Amphibious Corps, Pac. Theatre; Letter of Commendation. Mem: Elks; VFW; Am. Legion. Rel: Catholic. Legal Res: 801 Prentice Ave, Ashland, Wis. 54806. Mailing Add: 7106 Donna Dr, Middleton, Wis. 53562.

GEIB, G. HARRIET R
Del-at-Large, Minn. Rep. State Exec. Cmt.
b. Moorhead, Minn, 8/3/13; d. Olaf Jenson Hagen and Moselle Edna Weld H; m. 9/23/39 to Marvin Jacob Geib; c. Peter Jacob. Educ: Moorhead State Col, Minn, 31-32; Concordia Col, 32-33 & 34-35; Univ. Minn, 33-34 & 35-38; Gamma Phi Beta. Polit. & Govt. Pos: Rep. precinct secy, Moorhead, Minn, 52-56; v.chairwoman, Clay Co. Rep. Party, 58-61, chairwoman, 61-63; appointee, Minn. Rep. State Exec. Cmt, 64, del-at-lg, 69-; alternate del, Rep. Nat. Conv, 64, del, 68; chairwoman, Seventh Cong. Dist. Rep. Party, Minn, 65-69. Bus. & Prof. Pos: Med. technologist, Fargo Clin, N.Dak, 38-39 & 42. Mem: Registry of Med. Technologists, Am. Soc. of Med. Pathologists; PEO; Fargo-Moorhead Symphony Bd; YWCA; Am. Field Servs; St. Ansgar and St. Lukes Hosp. Auxiliaries; First Dist, N.Dak. and Clay Co. Med. Auxiliaries; Sigma Alpha Iota (Patroness); Am. Legion Auxiliary; Fine Arts Club; Fedn. Rep. Women; Red River Art Center; Friends of the Libr. Rel: Protestant. Mailing Add: 1219 Fourth Ave. S, Moorhead, Minn. 56560.

GEIER, ROBERT ALBERT R
b. Pittsburgh, Pa, 8/28/12; s. Bernard Adam Geier and Laurelda Helbling G; m. 4/13/42 to Phyllis May White; c. Robert W, Corry Leland and Kelly James. Educ: Univ. Pittsburgh, 31-33 & 37; Santa Ana and Orange Coast Cols, 40's; Am. Univ, 54. Polit. & Govt. Pos: Aeronaut. inspector, Civil Aeronaut. Admin, 43-46; admin. asst. to Congressman James B. Utt, 53-57 & 67-, field rep, 58-63; Rep. nominee, U.S. Cong, 34th Dist, Calif, 62 & 64. Bus. & Prof. Pos: Owner, garage and serv. sta, Avalon, Pittsburgh, Pa, 34-35; plant supt, Citrus Juice & Flavor, Santa Ana, Calif, 35-39; chief pilot and instr, Martin Sch. Aviation, 40-43, mgr. and chief pilot, 46-50; owner, pub. rels. agency, Santa Ana, 50-52, Santa Ana and Orange, 58-66. Mil. Serv: Sgt, ROTC. Publ: Various aviation articles in West. Aviation and other periodicals, 40's; Weekly column, Sky-Bobbing, Santa Ana Register, 46-66. Mem: C. of C; Rotary; Elks; Optimist; Pilot orgns. Rel: Catholic. Legal Res: 528-B W. Hampshire, Anaheim, Calif. 92805. Mailing Add: 6234 Kilmer Court, Falls Church, Va. 22044.

GEIS, ELLEN FLORENCE R
Mem, Calif. Rep. State Cent. Cmt.
b. San Francisco, Calif, 4/29/16; d. Alfred James Whittaker and Florence Mary Smith W; m. 2/10/37 to Harry George Geis; c. Gary Wayne and Douglas Neal. Educ: College of Marin; Marian Madsen, School of Business, Oakland; Burrough's Calculating-Machines School, San Francisco. Polit. & Govt. Pos: Chmn, San Leandro Rep. Hq, Calif, 64 & 66; pres, Chabot Rep. Women's Club, Federated, 65-66; mem, Calif. Rep. State Cent. Cmt, 65-; chmn, Women of Alameda Co. for Spencer William, Attorney Gen, Calif, 66; coordinator, for Assemblyman Ray Moser, 14th Assembly Dist, 66 & 68; mem, Alameda Co. Rep. Cent. Cmt, 69- Mem: Eastern Star; Alta Mira Women's Club; Calif. Fedn. and Nat. Fedn. Women's Clubs; Estudillo Homeowners Asn.(pres, 68-69); Assoc. Homeowners San Leandro. Rel: Protestant. Mailing Add: 834 Cary Dr, San Leandro, Calif. 94577.

GEISLER, JERRY HUBERT R
Va. State Del.
b. Big Stone Gap, Va, 7/6/34; m. to Betty Lou Coyle. Educ: Emory and Henry Col, B.A; T.C. Williams Sch. of Law, LL.B. Polit. & Govt. Pos: Chmn, Carroll Co. Rep. Cmt, Va, formerly; Va. State Del, 66- Bus. & Prof. Pos: Attorney. Mem: Past pres, v.pres. and local dir, Hillsville Jaycees; past pres, Izaak Walton League. Rel: Methodist. Mailing Add: Box 516, Hillsville, Va. 24343.

GEISLER, MARGARET S. D
Mem, Calif. Dem. State Cent. Cmt.
b. N.Y.C, 10/30/18; d. Sydney B. Simms and Sonia R. Levine S; m. 6/15/41 to Dr. Murray A. Geisler; c. Gary Evan and Lauren Sonia. Educ: Univ. Wis, B.S, 38; Columbia Univ. Teachers Col, M.A, 39. Polit. & Govt. Pos: Del, 60th Assembly Dist. Dem. Coun, Santa Monica, Calif, 59-69; del, 28th Cong. Dist. Dem. Coun, 60-69, pres, 68-69; membership chmn. and bd. mem, Canyon Dem. Club, 60-69, pres, 64-65; rep. from 60th Assembly Dist. to Los Angeles Co. Dem. Cent. Cmt, 64-69; chmn, Dollars-for-Dem. Drive, 60th Assembly Dist, 65-68, Los Angeles Co, 69; mem, Calif. Dem. State Cent. Cmt, 68- Bus. & Prof. Pos: Writer for Small Bus. Admin, Wash, D.C, 52-54; teacher, Los Angeles City Schs, 60-69. Publ: 'Analyzing Your Government Contract,' 53, 'Sound Pricing Policies for Government Contractors,' and 'Sound Cost Accounting For Small Businessmen,' 54, Small Bus. Admin, U.S. Govt. Mem: League of Women Voters. Rel: Jewish. Mailing Add: 1353 Beckwith Ave, Los Angeles, Calif. 90049.

GEITTMANN, IDA MAE D
b. Sesser, Ill, 9/3/23; d. Louie Jones and Carmen Bishop J. Educ: South. Ill. Univ, B.S. in educ, 44 and M.S. in educ, 52; Ill. State Normal Univ, grad. work, 45; Pi Kappa Delta; Sphinx for Outstanding Leadership; received speech Medals; Pi Kappa Sigma. Polit. & Govt. Pos: Supt. of children and youth activities, Ill. State Fair, 50-52; capt, 75th precinct, Springfield, 52; chmn, Beltrami Co. Dem-Farmer-Labor Party, Minn, 57-61; adv, Beltrami Co. Young Dem, 58-60; mem, Minn. Dem-Farmer-Labor State Cent. Cmt. and chairwoman, Seventh Dist. Dem-Farmer-Labor Party, 58-65; civil defense dir, Beltrami Co. and Bemidji, 60-62; mem. nominating cmt, Minn. State Dem-Farmer-Labor Conv, 60; cmt. mem, State Bd. of Prominent Women for Sen. Eugene McCarthy, 64; del, Dem. Nat. Conv, 64. Bus. & Prof. Pos: Dept. mgr, Peers Store, 41-44; personnel interviewer, U.S. Cartridge Co, 43; dean of girls and teaching supvr, Rochester High Sch, 48-53; radio announcer, WCVS, Springfield, Ill, 50-52; camp dir, YWCA, 51-53; dean of girls, drama coach and instr, Christopher High Sch, 53-55; dean of girls and dir. of guid, Sesser High Sch, 55-57; asst. dean of students and dir. of housing, Bemidji State Col, Minn, 57-69; partner, Lee's Secretarial Serv, 61-66; gen. agent, Planned Future Life Ins. Co, 66-; asst. to v.pres. for admin, Bemidji State Col, 69-; v.pres. pub. rels, Sudan Holding Corp, Minneapolis, 69-; sales consult, Horizon Land Corp, Tucson, Ariz, 69- Publ: Health Bibliography, State of Ill, 46. Mem: Am. Personnel and Guid. Asn; Nat. Dean of Women Asn; Am. Asn. Univ. Women; Minn. Dean of Women's Asn; North. Minn. Counsr. Asn; Bus. and Prfnl. Women. Rel: Methodist. Mailing Add: Birchmont Rd, Bemidji, Minn. 56601.

GEKAS, GEORGE WILLIAM R
Pa. State Rep.
b. Harrisburg, Pa, 4/14/30; s. William Gekas and Mary Touloumes G; single. Educ: Dickinson Col, A.B, 52, Dickinson Sch. of Law, LL.B, 58; Sigma Alpha Epsilon. Polit. & Govt. Pos: Asst. Dist. Attorney, Dauphin Co, Pa, 60-66; Pa. State Rep, 67- Mil. Serv: Entered as Pvt, Army, 53, released as Cpl, 55, after serv. in Inf, Caribbean Theater, 54-55. Mem: Dauphin Co. and Pa. Bar Asns; v.pres, Coun. of Churches of Greater Harrisburg; dir, Police Athletic League; Dauphin Co. Hist. Soc; YMCA; Moose; Elks; Ahepa. Rel: Greek Orthodox. Legal Res: 411 Radnor St, Harrisburg, Pa. 17110. Mailing Add: 227 N. Second St, Harrisburg, Pa. 17101.

GELBER, LOUISE CARP D
Mem. Exec. Cmt, Dem. State Cent. Cmt.
b. Detroit, Mich, 10/24/21; d. Jacob Carp and Gusta Schneider C; m. 7/10/43 to Milton Gelber; c. Jack, Bruce and Julie. Educ: Los Angeles City Col, 1 year; Univ. Mich, 1 year; Univ. Calif, Los Angeles, 1 year; Univ. Calif, Berkeley, B.A. and J.D, 44. Polit. & Govt. Pos: Dem. nominee for Calif. State Sen, 19th Dist, 68; asst. treas, Los Angeles Co. Dem. Cmt, Calif, 68, mem, 68-; mem. exec. cmt. and co-chmn, 24th Cong. Dist, Calif. Dem. State Cent. Cmt, 68- Bus. & Prof. Pos: Attorney-at-law, Gelber and Gelber, Attorneys, El Monte, Calif, 45-; legis. advocate, Calif. Bus. and Prfnl. Women's Clubs, 59. Publ: 'Joint Tenancy and Safe Deposit Boxes', 43 and 'Property Settlement Agreements', 43, Calif. Bar J; 'Equal Rights Amendment California Analysis', Calif. Bus. and Prfnl. Women's Clubs, 59. Mem: Am, Calif, Los Angeles Co. and Pomona Valley Bar Asns; Arcadia C. of C; Tournament of Roses Asn; PTA; Eastern Star; League of Women Voters; Am. Red Cross; Commun. Chest; United Way; Cub Scouts; Girl Scouts; South. Calif. Women Lawyers (treas, 46-48); Am. Asn. of Univ. Women; chmn, Speakers' Bur, El Monte C. of C, 68; Int. Platform Asn; El Monte Bus. and Prfnl. Women's Club; Iota Tau Tau. Co-Woman of Year Award, El Monte Bus. and Prfnl. Women's Club, 60; Award of Honor, El Monte-South El Monte C. of C, 68; Dictionary of Int. Biography Cert. of Merit, 68. Rel: Christian Science. Mailing Add: 1225 Rancho Rd, Arcadia, Calif. 91006.

GELFAND, EUGENE D
Pa. State Rep.
b. Philadelphia, Pa, 6/17/19; s. Israel Gelfand and Yetta Schaeffer G; m. to Elsie Snyder. Educ: Temple Univ, B.S; Temple Univ. Law Sch, LL.B, second honor man Law Sch. grad. class. Polit. & Govt. Pos: Mem, Joint State Cmt. Higher Educ, Pa; mem, Joint State Gov. Cmt. Juvenile Delinquency; mem, Dem. Exec. Cmt; Pa. State Rep, 54- Bus. & Prof. Pos: Attorney, 50- Mil. Serv: Intel. Off, Pac. Theater, 42-45, Capt; former Capt, Air Force Res. Mem: Lafayette Lodge; F&AM; Geo. Wash. Lodge of Perfection; Jewish War

Vet; Am. Jewish Cong; v.pres, Del. Co. Coun, Am. Jewish Cong; Nat. Gov. Coun. of AJC; Phila. Bar; Tau Epsilon Rho; Phila. Trial Lawyers Asn. Rel: Jewish. Mailing Add: 5600 Ogontz Ave, Philadelphia, Pa. 19141. (1967)

GELLER, MICHAEL D
b. Brooklyn, 15. Educ: Roxbury High Sch; Boston Cent. Eve. Sch. Polit. & Govt. Pos: Dem. Town Cmt. Bus. & Prof. Pos: Owner, Milton Flower Shop; Former Exec. Secy, Milton C. of C. Mem: United Fund; Milton Hosp. Dr; Boy Scout work. Mailing Add: 583 Blue Hills Pkwy, Milton, Mass. 02189. (1967)

GELT, JEANETTE R
N.H. State Rep.
b. Newburyport, Mass, 8/21/16; d. Joseph Lebman and Agnes Goldsmith L; m. 11/25/37 to George Gelt; c. Sylvia and Gloria. Educ: Newburyport High Sch. Polit. & Govt. Pos: N.H. State Rep, 64- Mem: Rep. Women's Club; Garden Club; Women's Club; Visiting Nurses Asn; Hadassah. Rel: Jewish. Mailing Add: 21 Martin Ave, Salem, N.H. 03079.

GENCARELLI, FRANCIS A. R
R.I. State Sen.
b. Westerly, R.I, 6/30/30; s. Cosmo D. Gencarelli and Minnie Terrenoya G; m. 5/30/53 to Jayne F. Bradshaw; c. David, Ann, Lisa and Francesca. Educ: Univ. R.I, B.S, 53; Sigma Alpha Epsilon. Polit. & Govt. Pos: Councilman, Westerly, R.I, 62-66; R.I. State Sen, 66- Bus. & Prof. Pos: mem. staff, Gen. Dynamics Corp, Groton, Conn, 57-63; P.L. Monroe & Son Inc, Cranston, R.I, 63- Mil. Serv: Entered as 2nd Lt, Army, 53, released as 1st Lt, 56, after serv. in Qm. Corps, Ft. Lee, Va. Mem: Lions; Elks; Navy League; Italo-Am. Club; Church News Club. Rel: Catholic. Mailing Add: 51 Elm St, Westerly, R.I. 02891.

GENDRON, JOSEPH SAUL D
R.I. State Sen.
b. Pawtucket, R.I, 1/24/38; s. Henry Leonard Gendron and Elizabeth Hughes G; m. 5/31/65 to Nancy Kelly; c. Patricia, Martha, Anne Elizabeth and Joseph S, III. Educ: Georgetown Univ, B.S. in Biol, 59; Univ. R.I, B.S. in Chem, 61; Suffolk Univ. Law Sch, J.D, 69. Polit. & Govt. Pos: R.I. State Sen, 67- Mil. Serv: Sp-5, Army Res, 61-67. Mem: R.I. Pharmaceut. Soc. Rel: Roman Catholic. Mailing Add: 101 Glenmeadow Dr, Pawtucket, R.I. 02861.

GENETTE, SIDNEY WILSON, JR. D
b. Memphis, Tenn, 3/10/28; s. Sidney Wilson Genette and Lucy Orgill G; m. 9/14/53 to Carolyn Jane McSpadden; c. Albert Sidney, Carolyn Jane, Lucy Orgill and Madeline. Educ: Duke Univ, A.B, 51; Harvard Bus. Sch, M.B.A, 54: Phi Delta Theta. Polit. & Govt. Pos: Admin. Asst. to U.S. Rep. George W. Grider, 65-67. Bus. & Prof. Pos: Pres, Security Title Co. Inc, 67- Mil. Serv: Pvt, Marine Corps, 46-48. Rel: Episcopal. Mailing Add: 1489 Goodbar Ave, Memphis, Tenn. 38104.

GENGLER, JOHN F. D
b. Slope Co, N.Dak, 1/6/16; married; c. Thirteen. Educ: Dickinson Schs. Polit. & Govt. Pos: N.Dak. State Rep, 61-66. Bus. & Prof. Pos: Brakeman, N.Pac. RR. Mailing Add: 835 E. Second St, Dickinson, N.Dak. 58601. (1967)

GENOVESI, DONALD S. R
Conn. State Rep.
b. Manchester, Conn, 1/10/32; s. Louis M. Genovesi and Josephine Pagani G; m. 6/14/58; c. Diane, Maryann and Lynn Marie. Educ: Univ. Conn, B.A, 54. Polit. & Govt. Pos: Conn. State Rep, 67- Bus. & Prof. Pos: Pres, Aldo Pagani Ins. Agency, Inc. Mil. Serv: Entered as 2nd Lt, Army, 55, released as 1st Lt, 57, after serving in Ord. Corps. Mem: Manchester Asn. of Independent Ins. Agents (pres); K. of C; Rotary. Rel: Roman Catholic. Legal Res: 71 Strickland St, Manchester, Conn. 06040.

GENOVESI, VINCENT ARTHUR R
b. Manchester, Conn, 12/26/27; s. Louis M. Genovesi and Josephine Pagani G; m. 10/15/55 to Josephine H. Martin; c. Mark, John, Paul, Peter and Gina. Educ: Bryant Col, B.S. in bus. admin, 51; Tau Epsilon. Polit. & Govt. Pos: Dist. leader, Manchester, Conn; pres, Young Rep. Club; dir. and leader, Eighth Utilities Dist, Manchester; mem, Manchester Zoning Bd; selectman, Manchester, 64-66; Conn. State Rep, 18th Dist, 67-69. Mil. Serv: Entered as Pvt, Army, 46, released as Sgt, 47. Mem: Elks; K. of C; Army and Navy Club; Holy Name Soc. Coach of Little League Football. Rel: Catholic. Mailing Add: 30 Baldwin Rd, Manchester, Conn. 06044. (1967)

GENTILE, JAMES D
Chmn, Middlebury Town Dem. Cmt, Conn.
b. Waterbury, Conn, 1/12/31; s. Fred Gentile and Josephine De Santo G; m. 6/10/50 to Jeanne Molnar; c. Gary and Kris. Educ: Wilcox Tech. Sch, grad, 53. Polit. & Govt. Pos: Mem, Middlebury Town Dem. Cmt, Conn, 58-, chmn, 62-; campaign coordinator for U.S. Rep. Bernard Grabowski, 64; mem, Conn. Dem. State Cent. Cmt, 65; mem, Conn. State Planning and Zoning Cmt, 66. Bus. & Prof. Pos: Mem, exec. bd, United Rubber, Cork, Linoleum and Plastic Workers of Am, 62-; mem, Naugatuck Valley Labor Coun, 63-65. Mem: Lions; Middlebury Vol. Fire Dept; Local Union 45; Waterbury Adequate Wiring Asn. Rel: Protestant. Mailing Add: Bronson Dr, Middlebury, Conn. 06762. (1967)

GENTRY, HERSCHEL A, SR. R
b. Forest, Ind, 4/4/98; s. James D. Gentry and Rosa A. Irwin G; m. 2/4/20 to Mabel A. Hedge; c. Herschel A, Jr. Educ: Pittsboro High Sch. Polit. & Govt. Pos: Rep. precinct committeeman, Middle Twp, Ind, 32-66; alternate del, Rep. Nat. Conv, 64. Bus. & Prof. Pos: Dir, Independent Milk Producers Asn, 59-64 and Miami Valley Milk Producer's Asn, 65- Mil. Serv: Pvt, Army, 18-19. Mem: Lions Club; Optimist Club; Am. Legion; Vet. of World War I. Rel: Disciples of Christ. Mailing Add: Pittsboro, Ind. 46167.

GENTRY, JAMES WORTH D
N.C. State Rep.
b. King, N.C, 8/4/08; s. I.G. Gentry and Mary Kreeger G; m. 6/16/34 to Marguerite Precilla Slate; c. Two. Educ: Draughans Bus. Col, 29. Polit. & Govt. Pos: Chmn, Sch. Bd, N.C. 10 years; co. cmnr, 56-57; former N.C. State Sen; N.C. State Rep, 69- Bus. & Prof. Pos: Farmer; cattle raiser; fertilizer dealer. Mem: Chmn, finance cmt. and mem. bd. dirs, Stokes-Reynolds Mem. Hosp, 54-64; Mason; charter mem, Kings Lions, past pres; past pres, Stokes Co. United Fund; Stokes Co. Ind. Cmt, N.W. Develop. Asn. Citizen of the Year, Lions Club Award, 58. Rel: Methodist; Steward, 52-64. Mailing Add: King, N.C. 27021. (1967)

GENTRY, RICHARD HAYDEN R
Mem, Fairfax Co. Rep. Cmt, Va.
b. Dodge City, Kans, 11/16/33; s. Richard B. Gentry and Estella A. Hayden G; m. to Jean Blair; c. Jennifer Lorien. Educ: Occidental Col, B.A; Am. Univ, M.A. Polit. & Govt. Pos: Mem, Fairfax Co. Rep. Cmt, Va, 60-; Justice of Peace, Fairfax Co, 63-67; treas, North. Va. Presidential Campaign Cmts, 64 & 68; mgr, Lt. Gov. Campaign, Va, 65; pres, Old Dominion Rep. Club, 65-66; treas, Va. Rep. State Finance Cmt, 65-69; cand, Va. State Senate, 67. Bus. & Prof. Pos: Pub. rels. consult, campaign mgr, advisor and free lance writer. Mil. Serv: Army Security Agency, 53-56, Korea, 53-54. Mem: Acad. Polit. Sci; Am. Asn. Pub. Opinion Research; Am. Polit. Sci. Asn; Pi Sigma Alpha; Capitol Hill Club; Mail Advert. Club of Wash. Rel: Presbyterian. Mailing Add: 6151 Tompkins Dr, McLean, Va. 22101.

GEOFFROY, FULDA EMILE D
R.I. State Rep.
b. West Warwick, R.I, 8/21/11; s. Henri Geoffroy and Alma Archambault G; m. 11/18/44 to Madeline E. McCabe. Educ: Providence Col, Ph.B, 32; Boston Univ. Law Sch, LL.B, 35. Polit. & Govt. Pos: Judge, Probate Court, West Warwick, R.I, 36-42, town clerk, 42-46, mem, Town Coun, 58-62; del, R.I. Constitutional Conv, 64-; R.I. State Rep, 67- Bus. & Prof. Pos: Title exam, Title Guarantee Co. of R.I, 46- Mem: Elks. Rel: Catholic. Mailing Add: 46 West St, West Warwick, R.I. 02893.

GEOGHEGAN, JAMES FRANCIS D
b. McNair, Miss, 8/17/27; married. Polit. & Govt. Pos: Miss. State Rep, 60-68; mem, Miss. State Dem. Exec. Cmt, 60- Bus. & Prof. Pos: Cattleman; ins. Mem: Mason; Shrine; Kiwanis. Rel: Methodist. Mailing Add: Box 236, Fayette, Miss. 39069. (1967)

GEORGE, HARRY W. R
b. Lehr, N.Dak, 4/23/03; married. Educ: Dak. Bus. Col; Ellendale Teachers Col. Polit. & Govt. Pos: N.Dak. State Sen, 57-61; N.Dak. State Rep, 53-55. Bus. & Prof. Pos: Banker; rancher. Mem: N.Dak. Stockmen's Asn; Masonic Lodge; Shrine; Lions. Mailing Add: Steele, N.Dak. 58482. (1967)

GEORGE, JESSE TAYLOR D
b. Meadow, Tex, 12/7/40; s. G.L. George and Lois Grissom G; single. Educ: Sul Ross State Col, B.S, 63; Univ. Tex. Sch. Law; Alpha Chi; Kappa Delta Phi; pres, Tex. Intercollegiate Press Asn; Student Educ. Asn; pres, Sul Ross Student Asn; Rodeo Club. Polit. & Govt. Pos: Del, Dem. Nat. Conv, Young Citizens for Johnson, 64; pres, Terry Co. Young Dem, Tex, 64-65; Tex. State Rep, 64-68; exec. committeeman, Tex. Young Dem, 65; area coordinator, Crawford Martin Campaign for Tex. Attorney Gen, 66. Bus. & Prof. Pos: Admin. asst, Tex. Tech. Col, Lubbock, 64-65; instr, S.Plains Col, Levelland, 65; mgr, Morton Area C. of C, 65- Mem: Tex. Law Enforcement and Youth Develop. Found; nat. dir, U.S. Jaycees; state dir, Tex. Jaycees; Lions; S.Plains Agr. Club; chmn, Cochran Co. Area Youth Conf. on Crime; sponsor, Five Co. Area Youth Conf. on Crime. Rel: Presbyterian. 1967 Legal Res: Brownfield, Tex. No mailing address available. (1967)

GEORGE, JOHN HENDRIX R
Idaho State Rep.
b. Salisbury, N.C, 11/7/26; s. Jerome Milton George, Sr. and Bessie Hendrix G; m. 5/12/56 to Patricia Francis Somsen; c. Marshall Allen, Stephanie Helen and John Hendrix, Jr. Educ: Univ. N.C, Chapel Hill, A.B. in Eng; Lambda Chi Alpha. Polit. & Govt. Pos: Rep. precinct committeeman, Lincoln Co, Idaho, 65-66; chmn, Lincoln Co. Rep. Cent. Cmt, 66-67; Idaho State Rep, 67- Bus. & Prof. Pos: Publisher, Lincoln Co. J, Idaho, 62-69 and Wendell Irrigationist, 63-69. Mil. Serv: Entered as A/S, Navy, 44, released as S 1/C (qm), 66, after serv. in Port Dir. Div, Kwajalein, Marshall Islands, Pac. Theater, 43-44. Mem: Idaho and Nat. Press Asns; Rotary; Kiwanis; Lions. Rel: Baptist. Legal Res: 403 E. Third, Shoshone, Idaho 83352. Mailing Add: P.O. Box 584, Shoshone, Idaho 83352.

GEORGE, LOURENE W. R
Pa. State Rep.
b. Harrisburg, Pa, 7/1/13; d. Lloyd M. Walker and Romaine Senseman; wid. Educ: Germantown Dispensary and Hosp. Sch. of Nursing; Germantown Dispensary and Hosp. Sch. of Anesthesia, Cert. Registered Nurse-Anesthetist degree. Polit. & Govt. Pos: Bd. mem, Cumberland City Fed. Rep. Women, Pa; past pres, Carlisle Co. Rep. Women; past chmn, Cumberland City Rep. Orgn, 58-60; Pa. State Rep, 62- Bus. & Prof. Pos: Nurse-anesthetist. Mem: Am. Asn. Nurse-Anesthetists (former trustee); Pa. Asn. Nurse-Anesthetists (past pres); Mid. Atlantic Assembly of Nurse-Anesthetists (past secy-treas. and bd. mem); Cumberland City and Tri-City Asns. Retarded Children; Cumberland City Med. Soc. Health and Trust Fund; C. of C; Eastern Star; Am. Legion Auxiliary. Rel: Presbyterian. Mailing Add: 114 S. West St, Carlisle, Pa. 17013.

GEORGE, NEWELL A. D
b. Kansas City, Mo, 9/24/04; s. Adolphus K. George and Ida Scobee G; m. 4/16/34 to Jean M. Hannan. Educ: George Wash. Univ, LL.B, 34, LL.M, and M.P.L, 35; Delta Theta Phi. Polit. & Govt. Pos: Pres, Wyandotte Co. Young Dem, 32; pres, Kans. Dem. Club, Wash, D.C, 35 & 36; attorney, Reconstruction Finance Corp, Wash, D.C, 35-37; regional attorney, Fed. Security Agency, 37-52; regional counsel, War Manpower Cmn, 42-43; first asst. to Wyandotte Co. Attorney, 53-58; U.S. Rep, Kans, 59-60; del, Dem. Nat. Conv, 60; U.S. Attorney, Kans, 61-68. Bus. & Prof. Pos: Practicing antitrust and probate law, currently. Publ: Contrib. to Kans. Law Rev. Mem: Wyandotte Co, Kans. State, Am. and Fed. Bar Asns; Am. Judicature Soc; Int. Platform Asn; Am. Acad. of Polit. and Soc. Sci; Optimists; Terrace Club; C. of C; High Twelve; Mason; Shrine. Knute Rockne Club Award, Law Enforcement Man of the Year, 66. Rel: Presbyterian. Mailing Add: 1831 New Jersey Ave, Kansas City, Kans. 66102.

GEORGE, RALPH WEIR R
Chmn, Hill Co. Rep. Party, Tex.
b. Milford, Tex, 8/26/32; s. Van Theodore George, Sr. and Mayna Sybol Weir G; m. 11/4/61 to Charlsie Sue Terry; c. Teresa Sue, Jerry Van and Terry Van. Educ: Tex. A&M Col, D.V.M, 55; Phi Zeta; Phi Kappa Phi. Polit. & Govt. Pos: Chmn, Hill Co. Rep. Party, Tex, 64- Mil. Serv: Entered as 1st Lt, Air Force, 55, released as Capt, 57, after serv. in Air Force Vet. Med. Corps. Mem: Am. and Tex. Vet. Med. Asns; Rotary; Jaycees; Farm Bur. Rel: Methodist. Legal Res: 1411 Old Brandon Rd, Hillsboro, Tex. 76645. Mailing Add: Box 293, Hillsboro, Tex. 76645.

GEORGE, RAYMOND DAVID D
Chmn, 60th Legis. Dist. Dem. Cmt, R.I.
b. Woonsockt, R.I, 1/17/17; s. Wilbur George and Agnes Sawyer G; m. 6/12/37 to Margaret E. Guthrie; c. Carol (Mrs. Robitaille) and Scott J. Educ: Burrillville High Sch; Ins. Sch; Labor Exten. Courses. Polit. & Govt. Pos: Asst. chief clerk, R.I. Dept. Pub. Health, 36-42; chief clerk, Men's Reformatory, 42-44; record clerk, Attorney Gen. Off, 65-; mem, 27th Sen. Dist. Dem. Cmt, 66-; chmn, Burrillville Dem. Town Cmt, 66-; chmn, 60th Legis. Dist. Dem. Cmt, 66- Bus. & Prof. Pos: Self employed, Construct. Co, 25 years. Mem: Past Grand Knight, Pascoag Coun. K. of C. 383. Rel: Catholic. Legal Res: Reservoir Rd, Pascoag, R.I. 02859. Mailing Add: Box 105, Pascoag, R.I. 02859. (1967)

GEORGE, SAMUEL R
b. New Castle, Pa, 11/26/22; s. Tony George and Alice Solomon G; m. 6/13/51 to Mary Nell Rhodes; c. Lisa and Samuel Rhodes. Educ: Westminster Col, B.A, 50; Univ. Zurich, Switz, 48-49; Univ. Pittsburgh, M.L, 53; Phi Alpha Theta; Delta Phi Alpha; Alpha Sigma Phi. Polit. & Govt. Pos: Alternate del, Rep. Nat. Conv, 68. Mil. Serv: Entered as Pvt, Army, 43, released as Pfc, 45, after serv. in 54th Field Hosp, ETO, 44-45; S/Sgt, Army Res, Mil. Intel, 529 Misp, Germany, 50. Rel: Protestant. Mailing Add: 3002 N. Mercer St. Extension, New Castle, Pa. 16101.

GERARD, SUMNER, JR. R
b. Melville, N.Y, 7/15/16; s. Sumner Gerard and Helen Coster G; m. 7/7/43 to Louise Grosvenor, div; m. Sept, 1968 to Teresa Dabrowska; c. Jenny, Molly (Mrs. Wheelock), Helen, Ann and Sumner III. Educ: Trinity Col, Cambridge, B.A. & M.A, 37; Univ. Wis, post-grad. work. Polit. & Govt. Pos: Asst. to dir, Wis. State Dept. Commerce, 38-39; secy. to Rep. minority, N.Y. City Coun, 39; asst. to administr, Bur. Export Control, Wash, D.C, 40-41; Rep. precinct, co. and state committeeman, 50-54; Mont. State Rep, 55-60, Minority Leader, Mont. State House of Rep, 59; alternate del, Rep. Nat. Conv, 56, del, 60, polit. secy. to Gov. Aronson, conv, 56 & 60; chmn, Rep. State Finance Cmt, 58-60; chmn, Platform Cmt, Rep. State Conv, 62; asst. campaign dir, Nat. Rep. Cong. Cmt, 62-64; dep. dir. tech. serv. orgn, Rep. Nat. Cmt, 64; Mont. State Sen, Madison Co, 62-66, Minority Leader, Mont. State Senate, 65-66. Bus. & Prof. Pos: Asst. to dir. int. div, Radio Corp. Am, N.Y, 45-46; v.pres. and dir, Aeon Int. Corp, 46-48; ranching, oil and land develop, Mont, 48-69; pres. and dir, Aeon Realty Co, exec. v.pres. and dir, Immer Realty Corp, treas. & dir, Shelter Island Farms, Inc, dir, Financial Gen. Corp, Wash, D.C, pres. & dir, Ennis Co, Mont, pres. and dir, Newmont Resources Corp. and dir, Cardinal Petrol. Corp, Billings, currently. Mil. Serv: Entered as Pvt, Army Air Force, 41, released as Capt, Marine Corps. Res, 45 after serv. in Army, Navy and Marine Corps, N.African and China-Burma-India Theaters, 3 years; Army Commendation; Order of British Empire. Mem: Bd. trustees, Mont. State Hist. Soc, 55-63; adv. cmt, Sch. Bus. Admin, Mont. State Univ, 59-67, pres, Friends of the Libr, 61-67 and Adv. Coun. of Fifty, 64-67; agr. adv. cmt, Upper Midwest Research & Develop. Coun, 60-68; Mont. Arts Coun, 65-68; Knickerbocker Club, N.Y; Racquet & Tennis Club, N.Y; Bar Harbor Yacht Club, Maine; Shelter Island Yacht Club, N.Y; Mashomack Fish & Game Preserve, N.Y; Mill Reef Club, Antiqua, W.I; Mont. Club; VFW; Aircraft Owners & Pilots Asn; Mont. Pilots Asn; Marine Corps ROA; Navy League; Nat. Cattleman's Asn; hon. life mem. Nat. Geog. Soc. Rel: Episcopal. Legal Res: 61 Hodge Rd, Princeton, N.J. 08540. Mailing Add: 1350 Ave. of Americas, New York, N.Y. 10019.

GERAUD, LAWRENCE J. R
married; c. One daughter. Educ: Univ. of Wyo. Polit. & Govt. Pos: Mem, Sch. Bd, Wyo; former Wyo. State Rep. Bus. & Prof. Pos: Farming and sheep raising. Mailing Add: 210 N. Ninth St, Riverton, Wyo. 82501. (1967)

GERBER, CALVIN OTTO D
b. Wausau, Wis, 6/4/37; s. Otto Robert Gerber and Nova Mae Lehman G; m. 6/18/60 to Carol Mary Hernke; c. John Calvin, Gregory Paul and Michael Robert. Educ: Heidelberg Col, A.B, 59; United Theol. Sem. of Twin Cities, B.D, 62; Vanderbilt Univ, S.T.M, 67; Case West. Res. Univ, 68-; Eta Sigma Phi; Nu Sigma Alpha; grad. fel, Case West. Res. Univ. Polit. & Govt. Pos: Exec. secy, Sheboygan Co. McCarthy for Pres, 68; alternate del, Dem. Nat. Conv, 68. Mem: Nat. Asn. Col. and Univ. Chaplains. Rel: United Church of Christ. Legal Res: Route 3, Plymouth, Wis. 53073. Mailing Add: Apt. 17, 4480 Granada Blvd, Cleveland, Ohio 44128.

GERBER, MORRIS D
b. Philadelphia, Pa, 11/29/08; s. Samuel Gerber and Frances Needleman G; m. 10/15/33 to Frances Cohen; c. A. Richard and David S. Educ: Univ. Pa, B.S. in Econ, 29, LL.B, 32. Polit. & Govt. Pos: Committeeman, Dem. Party, 34-56; dep. Attorney Gen, Pa, 35-39; del, Dem. Nat. Conv, 52, alternate del, 64, del-at-lg, 68; finance chmn, Montgomery Co. Dem. Cmt, 52-57 & 60-62; dist. chmn, Montgomery Co. Dem. Exec. Cmt, Pa, 54-57 & 60-62; chmn. bd. trustees, Norristown State Hosp, 55-63; judge, Court Common Pleas, 57-60; bd. mem, West Norriton Twp. Sch. Authority, 60-65; Chief Counsel. to Auditor Gen, Pa, 61-65 and to State Treas, 65-69; mem, Pa. Bd. Finance and Revenue, 61-63; mem. bd. claims, Pa, 61-69; cmnr, Del. River Junction Toll Bridge Cmn, 61-69. Bus. & Prof. Pos: Partner, Law Firm of Wisler, Pearlstine, Talone & Gerber, 45-57 & 61-; pres. and mem. bd, Schuylkill Valley Lines, Inc, 60-; mem. bd. dirs, Hart Labs, 63- Mem: Am, Pa. and Phila. Bar Asns; Montgomery Co. Bar Asn.(dir, 46-49); Brandies Soc. Phila; Am. Judicature Soc; Int. Bridge, Tunnel and Turnpike Asn; Pa. Soc. of N.Y; Nat. Coun, Am. Jewish Cmt; Nat. Coun, Jewish Joint Distribution Cmt; B'nai B'rith. Rel: Jewish. Legal Res: 2615 DeKalb Pike, Norristown, Pa. 19401. Mailing Add: 515 Swede St, Norristown, Pa. 19401.

GERBER, SAMUEL ROBERT D
V.Chmn, Ohio Dem. State Exec. Cmt.
b. Hagerstown, Md, 8/22/98; s. Judah Hyman Gerber and Bessie Nachenson G; div; c. Roberta Lee. Educ: Valparaiso Univ, 17-18; Cincinnati E. Med. Col, M.D, 22; Cleveland Marshall Law Sch, LL.B, 49. Hon. L.H.D, Ohio Col. of Podiatry, 60; hon. LL.D, Cleveland Marshall Law Sch, 61. Polit. & Govt. Pos: Mem, Cuyahoga Co. Dem. Exec. Cmt, Ohio, 36-, secy, 67-; coroner, Cuyahoga Co, 37-; del, Dem. Nat. Conv, 56, 60, 64 & 68; mem, Ohio State Dem. Cent. Cmt, 68; v.chmn, Ohio State Dem. Exec. Cmt, 68-; secy, Cuyahoga Co. Dem. Cent. Cmt, 68-; Dem. precinct committeeman, ward 19, Cleveland, 68- Bus. & Prof. Pos: Physician-in-charge, Warrensville Correction Farms, Dept. Pub. Health & Welfare, Cleveland, Ohio, 25-27; acting chief physician for med. serv-parochial schs, Div. Child Hygiene, Dept. of Health, Cleveland, 27-33; physician-in-charge, med. aid for unattached person, Co, State and Fed. Relief Admin, 33-37; assoc. in legal med, Dept. of Pathology, Sch. of Med, Case West. Reserve Univ, 53-68, asst. clin. prof. in legal med, 68-; co-founder and co-dir, The Law-Med. Center, Case West. Reserve Univ. and Cuyahoga Co, 53- Publ: 'Practical Use of Biochemical Tests for Alcohol,' Am. Bar Asn. J, 5/61; 'The Physician's Relations with the Medicolegal Officer,' in The Environment of Medical Practice, Yearbook Med, 63; 'Causation in Death after Trauma with Preexisting Cardiac Disease,' Cleveland Marshall Law Rev, 9/66. Mem: Am. and Ohio State Med. Asns; Acad. of Med. of Cleveland; Am, Ohio State, Cuyahoga Co. and Cleveland Bar Asns; Int. Asn. Coroners and Med. Exam. (Nat. Asn. Coroners, pres, 37-38, secy-treas, 43-68); secy, Ohio State Coroners Asn, 39-; Am. Acad. Forensic Sci.(pres, 61-62, secy-treas, 65-69, secy-treas. emer, 69-); Cmt. on Test. for Intoxication, Nat. Safety Coun, 37-40, Cmt. on Uniform Traffic Accident Statistics, 37-, Cmt. on Definitions of Home Accidents, 58-, Cmt. on Alcohol and Drugs, 60-; v.pres. in charge of statistical and research, Gr. Cleveland Safety Coun, 40-64, chmn, Green Cross Campaign, 60-63, chmn, Blueprint for Life, 61-62, pres, 64-65; Cuyahoga Co. Charter Cmts.(elected mem, 48-50 & 58-59); Metrop. Study Cmn, 57-59; trustee, Suburban Hosp; Subcmt. on Med. Cortication of Death in Medicolegal Cases, U.S. Dept. Health, Educ. & Welfare, 56-60, Study Group on Medicolegal Certification of Death, 60-; U.S. Dept. Commerce Nat. Adv. Cmt. Flammable Fabrics, 68-; ASSR; Shrine; Cleveland Grays; Clevelander Club. Rel: Reformed Judaism. Legal Res: 11424 Cedar Glen Parkway, Cleveland, Ohio 44106. Mailing Add: 2121 Adelbert Rd, Cleveland, Ohio 44106.

GERDES, GEORGE C. R
b. Alliance, Nebr, 9/28/98; m. 10/11/23 to Minnie Spetman, wid; c. Gene and Gladys (Mrs. Fairhead). Educ: Nebr. Sch. of Agr. Polit. & Govt. Pos: Nebr. State Sen, 59-69. Bus. & Prof. Pos: Rancher and farmer. Mil. Serv: World War I Vet. Mem: Former chmn. and current pres, Nebr. Wheat Growers Asn; Co. Cmn, Agr. Stabilization & Conserv. Cmt. & Triple A; REA Bd; Rural Phone Lines; v.pres, Nat. Wheat Growers Asn; adv. bd, Nebr. Stock Growers Asn; Elks; Eagles; Am. Legion. Mailing Add: Marple Route, Alliance, Nebr. 69301. (1967)

GERENA, VICTOR M. R
Exec. Secy, Statehood Rep. Party, P.R.
b. Quebradillas, P.R, 11/14/35; s. Victor Gerena and Gloria Cancel G; single. Educ: Univ. P.R, currently. Polit. & Govt. Pos: Exec. secy, P.R. Rep. Party, 63-68, del, 66; exec. secy, Statehood Rep. Party, 66-; asst. Minority Leader, P.R. Senate, 67-68; alternate del, Rep. Nat. Conv, 68. Bus. & Prof. Pos: Inside salesman, Honeywell, Inc, 57-62; mem, claim dept, Lykes Lines, Inc, 63. Mem: Asn. Univ. Student for Statehood; Action for Statehood; Young Rep. Club; Asn. U.S. Army. Award, DAR, 53; Three medals and one dipl, Asn. of the Hist. Mus; Dipl, Univ. Student for Statehood. Legal Res: Calle 9-E35, Sierra Berdecia, Guaynabo, P.R. 00657. Mailing Add: P.O. Box 285, San Juan, P.R. 00902.

GERHART, H. L. R
Nebr. State Sen.
b. Newman Grove, Nebr, 12/17/97; m. 9/6/27 to Dorothy Hallgren: c. Harold L, Jr. and Mary E.(Mrs. Peterson). Educ: Univ. of Nebr. Polit. & Govt. Pos: Pres. bd. of educ. and mayor, Newman Grove, Nebr, formerly; Nebr. State Sen, 61- Bus. & Prof. Pos: Pres, Newman Grove First Nat. Bank. Mem: Mason; Scottish Rite Lodge; Odd Fellows. Mailing Add: Newman Grove, Nebr. 68759.

GERHART, JOHN DONALD D
Chmn, Tippecanoe Co. Dem. Cent. Cmt, Ind.
b. Battle Ground, Ind, 7/4/34; s. Charles M. Gerhart and Gladys Hobaugh G; m. 9/18/55 to Shirley I. Brummett; c. Randall Lee and Michelle Ann. Educ: Purdue Univ, B.S. in Pharm. Polit. & Govt. Pos: Precinct committeeman, Dem. Party, Ind, 58-; chmn, Tippecanoe Co. Dem. Cent. Cmt, 63-; chmn, Battle Ground Town Bd, 60-64; del, Dem. Nat. Conv, 68. Mil. Serv: Entered as Pvt, Nat. Guard, 52, released as 2nd Lt, 58, after serv. in 113 Med. Bn. Mem: Ind. Pharmaceut. Asn.(legis. cmt, 65); Am. Pharmaceut. Asn. Rel: Methodist. Mailing Add: Box 303, Battle Ground, Ind. 47920. (1967)

GERKE, HAROLD EDWARD D
Mont. State Rep.
b. Cherokee, Iowa, 5/1/12; s. William H. Gerke and Hannah Bredahl G; m. 12/30/30 to Vera E. Adamson; c. Harold Dean. Educ: Globe Bus. Col. Polit. & Govt. Pos: Alderman, Billings, Mont, 59-61, Mayor, 61-62; Mont. State Rep, 65- Bus. & Prof. Pos: Pres. and gen. mgr, Midland Propane Co, 46-55; pres, Petrolan Supply Co, 55-63; secy-treas, Am. Galloway Asn, 63- Mem: L.P. Gas Asn; AF&AM. Rel: Lutheran. Mailing Add: 202 Mountain View, Billings, Mont. 59101.

GERKEN, JOHN RAYMOND, JR. R
Chmn, Huron Co. Rep. Cent. Cmt, Ohio
b. Norwalk, Ohio, 8/7/26; s. John Raymond Gerken and Elizabeth Helen Cole G; m. 2/14/48 to Norma Eileen Bachman; c. James Ethan and Ann Elizabeth. Educ: Colgate Univ, A.B, 47; Delta Kappa Epsilon. Polit. & Govt. Pos: Pres, Norwalk Rep. Club, Ohio, 63; secy, Huron Co. Rep. Cent. Cmt, 64-66, chmn, 66-; alternate del, Rep. Nat. Conv, 68; mem, Ohio Rep. Cent. Cmt, 68- Bus. & Prof. Pos: Pres, Norwalk Furniture Corp, 50-66. Mil. Serv: Entered as Seaman, Naval Air Force, 44, released as Aviation Cadet, 45, Rel: Episcopal. Mailing Add: R.D. 2, Norwalk, Ohio 44857. (1967)

GERLING, GORDON DOUGLAS D
b. Morton, Minn, 9/3/21; s. Roy Edward Gerling and Harriett Bishop G; m. 8/20/44 to Bette Joy Knight; c. Michael Gordon, Scott Douglas, Terri Lynn and Janene Adele. Educ: Univ. Minn; Dunwoody Inst. Polit. & Govt. Pos: Minn. State Rep, 53rd Dist, Morrison Co, 57-65; legis. rep, Rural Power Coop. Asn, 68- Bus. & Prof. Pos: Ins. agent. Mil. Serv: Entered as Pvt, Army Air Force, 42, released as M/Sgt, 46, after serv. in 404th Bomber Squadron, Pac. Theater. Mem: Conserv. Orgn; Am. Legion; VFW. Mailing Add: Route 1, Little Falls, Minn. 56345.

GERMAN, CHARLES GRADY D
Chmn, Fannin Co. Dem. Exec. Cmt, Ga.
b. Blue Ridge, Ga, 12/30/97; s. Jervis German and Orvy Orton G; m. 3/2/20 to Alice Velma Green; c. Ray and Violet (Mrs. Cantrell). Educ: Alsobrook Acad; Univ. Ga; Gridiron Secret Soc. Polit. & Govt. Pos: Chmn, Fannin Co. Kennedy for President Cmt, Ga, 60; lt. col, Staff Gov. Carl Sanders; chmn, Fannin Co. Dem. Exec. Cmt, currently. Bus. & Prof. Pos: Self-employed, timber business, 18-62. Mem: F&AM; RAM; Shrine. Rel: Church of Christ. Mailing Add: P.O. Box 25, Blue Ridge, Ga. 30513.

GERMINO, DONALD OWEN R
Chmn, Merced Co. Rep. Cent. Cmt, Calif.
b. Los Banos, Calif, 10/1/39; s. D. Oliver Germino and Helen King G; m. 8/18/62 to Sheila Marren; c. Michelle Lynn. Educ: Univ. South. Calif, A.B, 61; Univ. Calif, Berkeley, Law Sch, LL.B, 61, J.D, 64; Sigma Chi. Polit. & Govt. Pos: Mem, Calif. Young Rep, 59-66; del, Calif. State Rep. Cent. Cmt, 67-69; v.chmn, Merced Co. Rep. Cent. Cmt, 67-68, chmn, 69- Mem: Am, Calif. and Merced Co. Bar Asns; Lions (pres, Los Banos Club, 69-70); Commun. Chest (pres, 67-); Sportsman's Asn. Outstanding Serv. awards, Los Banos Commun. Chest and Yosemite Area Coun, Boy Scouts, 65. Rel: Roman Catholic. Legal Res: 1614 Sixth St, Los Banos, Calif. 93635. Mailing Add: P.O. Box 591, Los Banos, Calif. 93635.

GERSHMAN, LOUIS D
Treas. 18th Dist. Dem. Non-Partisan League Exec. Cmt, N.Dak.
b. Grand Forks, N.Dak, Jan. 21; s. Sam Gershman and Sarah Chuckman G; m. 11/9/47 to Sue Striker; c. Marilyn, Bruce, Neil, Nancy, Debra and Sandra. Educ: Grand Forks Central High School, grad. Polit. & Govt. Pos: Dem. Non-Partisan League nominee, N.Dak. State Sen, Seventh Legis. Dist, 64; finance chmn, Grand Forks Co. Dem. Non-Partisan League Orgn, 64-66; finance chmn, 18th Dist. Dem. Non-Partisan League Cmt, 66-; Dem. committeeman, First Precinct First Ward, 18th Legis. Dist, N.Dak, 66-; treas, 18th Dist. Dem. Non-Partisan League Exec. Cmt, 66-; mem. legis. adv. coun, State N.Dak. Dem. Non-Partisan League, 66-; del, Dem. Nat. Conv, 68. Bus. & Prof. Pos: Pres, Gershman Enterprises; secy-treas, Gershman Real Estate; owner, Northland Packing; secy-treas, Grand Forks Airmotive Inc. Mil. Serv: Entered as Pvt, Army, 41, released as S/Sgt, 45, after serv. in Combat Engrs, Europe-Africa-Middle East; Unit Citation, Invasion of Normandy and Omaha Beach. Mem: N.Dak. State Aeronaut. Cmn; N.Dak. Small Bus. Adv. Coun; DAV (N.Dak. Comdr, 59-60, Tenth Dist. committeeman); Elks; Am. Legion; Eagles; VFW. Rel: Jewish; Past Pres, B'Nai Israel Synagogue, Grand Forks, N.Dak. Mailing Add: 423 Reeves Dr, Grand Forks, N.Dak. 58201.

GERVASINI, WILLIAM VICTOR R
b. Torrington, Conn, 10/18/39; s. Orlando Peter Gervasini and Josephine Pagani G; single. Educ: Dean Jr. Col, Franklin, Mass, A.A, 61; Univ. Denver, 63-64. Polit. & Govt. Pos: Blockworker and vol, Col. Young Rep. Nixon for Pres. Campaign, 60; task force coordinator, Goldwater for Pres. Campaign, 64; dist. 11 lt, Rep. Party, 65; del, Denver Co. Rep. Conv, 66 & 68, sgt-at-arms, 68; del, Colo. State Rep. Conv, 66 & 68; worked with Col. Rep. and TAR, Pearson For U.S. Rep. Campaign, 66; bd. dirs, Denver Young Rep. League, 67, pres, 68-; campaign mgr, Albert Moore for City Coun, Denver, 67; participant, Denver Co. Rep. Orgn. Nat. Campaign Mgt. Seminar, Univ. Okla, 67; alternate del, Rep. Nat. Conv, 68; attended Young Rep. Leadership Training Sch, Wash, D.C, 69; bd. dirs, Young Rep. League Colo, 69. Mem: Nat. Employ. Asn; Colo. Private Employ. Agency Asn; Denver C. of C; Denver Jr. C. of C; YMCA. Outstanding Young Man of Am. Rel: Roman Catholic. Mailing Add: 800 Emerson 204, Denver, Colo. 80216.

GESSERT, HARRY L. R
b. Elkhart Lake, Wis. Educ: Plymouth Bus. Col, 2 years. Polit. & Govt. Pos: Justice of the peace, Elkhart Lake, Wis, 55; mem, Co. Bd, 59; mem, Gov. Reynold's Budget Tour; Wis. State Assemblyman, 60-68. Bus. & Prof. Pos: Operator, restaurant and retail store. Mem: Elkhart Lake Serv. Club; C. of C. Mailing Add: 222 Lake St, Elkhart Lake, Wis. 53020. (1967)

GETCHELL, EARLE DUNCAN R
Mem, Mobile Co. Rep. Exec. Cmt, Ala.
b. Medford, Mass, 12/15/16; s. George Elmer Getchell and Anne Marie Robertson G; m. 4/17/44 to Jean Elder Thompson; c. Earle Duncan, Jr. and Anne (Mrs. Riviere). Educ: Royal Can. Air Force and U.S. Army Air Corps Schs. Polit. & Govt. Pos: Dir, Aircraft Div. For. Liquidation Cmn, Latin Am. and Caribbean Div, 46-47; mem, Mobile Co. Rep. Exec. Cmt, 66-67 & 68-; alternate del, Rep. Nat. Conv, 68- Bus. & Prof. Pos: Exec. v.pres, Mobile Glass Co, Inc, Mobile, Ala, 58-64, pres, 64- Mil. Serv: Aircrew trainee, Royal Can. Air Force, 46; Capt, Army Air Corps, 46. Mem: Construction Indust. Asn, Mobile (v.pres); Rotary. Rel: Methodist. Mailing Add: 323 Bromley Place, Mobile, Ala. 36606.

GETSCHER, EDWIN CLARKE R
b. Lincoln, Nebr, 1/16/38; s. Edwin August Getscher and Ione Earhart G; single. Educ: State Univ. Iowa, B.A, 60, LL.B, 63; Delta Theta Phi. Polit. & Govt. Pos: Chmn, Fremont Co. Rep. Party, Iowa, 65-68. Bus. & Prof. Pos: Partner, Getscher & Getscher, 63-66. Mil. Serv: 2nd Lt, Nebr. Army Nat. Guard, 63. Mem: Fremont Co, Southwest Iowa and Iowa State Bar Asns; AF&AM; Odd Fellows; Eagles; Elks; Kiwanis Int; C. of C. Rel: Methodist. Legal Res: 4 Skyline Dr, Hamburg, Iowa 51640. Mailing Add: 209 East St, Hamburg, Iowa 51640. (1967)

GETTEL, GERHARD F. R
Chmn, Midland Co. Rep. Cmt, Mich.
b. Owendale, Mich, 3/9/15; s. John W. Gettel (deceased) and Catherine Schnepp G; m. 9/13/47 to Ruhh M. Berkenstock. Educ: Mich. State Col, B.S; Cornell Univ, M.S; Mich. State Univ, Ph.D; 4H Club; Dairy Club; Jr. Farm Bur; Walther League. Polit. & Govt. Pos: Rep. precinct leader, Midland, Mich, 58; ward chmn, Rep. Party, Midland, 58-62; mem, Rep. Co. Cmt. and Exec. Cmt, 62-66; pres, Midland Co. GOP Breakfast Club, 68; chmn, Midland Co. Rep. Cmt, 68- Mil. Serv: Entered as Pvt, Army, 42, released as Pfc, 46, after serv. in Mil. Govt, ETO, 44-46; Rifleman Medal; Good Conduct Medal; ETO Medal with four stars. Publ: 'Your School District,' Nations Schs, 51; several minor articles. Mem: Instr. and instr. trainer, Am. Red Cross First Aid, 57-; pres, Midland Co. Canvassing Bd, Mich, 60-; first aid counsellor, Boy Scouts, Midland, 60-; Midland Asn. Life Agents (pres, 65 and nat. committeeman currently); pres, St. Johns Lutheran Church, 65; mem, United Conservation Clubs, Mich, 65-; mem, People to People, Midland, 65-; mem, Midland Estate Planning Coun, 66-; dir, Mich. Dist, Lutheran Church, 66-; Lutheran Acad. of Scholarship; citizenship chair, Midland Co. Farm Bur, currently. Citation form Red Cross, Kiwanis Club, Lyons Club and C.L.U, 67. Rel: Lutheran. Mailing Add: 2309 Burlington Dr, Midland, Mich. 49640.

GETTO, VIRGIL M. R
Nev. State Assemblyman
b. Fallon, Nev, 6/19/24; s. Andrew Getto and Desolina Longo G; m. 12/14/47 to Barbara Mason; c. Virgil (Mike), Andrea, David M. and Marlea. Educ: Churchill Co. High Sch, grad. Polit. & Govt. Pos: Mem, Cmt. Future Water Needs Nev, 67-; Nev. State Assemblyman, 69-, chmn. agr. cmt, Nev. State Assembly, 69-, chmn, Subcmt. Pub. Employ. Practices, 69-, mem, Interim Legis. Cmt. Studying Hwy. Safety and Motor Vehicle Laws, 69-, alternate, Legis. Cmn, 69-; v.pres, Citizen Adv. Cmt, Col. Agr, Univ. Nev. Mem: Am. Dairy Asn; Agr. Stabilization & Conserv.(bd. dirs); Rotary; C. of C.(mem. bd, Churchill Co); Churchill Co. Econ. Develop. Bd; Future Farmers Am.(Nat. officer, 46). Rel: Catholic. Mailing Add: 1400 Lovelock Hwy, Fallon, Nev. 89406.

GETTYS, THOMAS SMITHWICK D
U.S. Rep, S.C.
b. Rock Hill, S.C, 6/19/12; s. John E. Gettys and Maud Martin G; m. 12/9/47 to Mary Phillips White; c. Julia Martin, Sara Elizabeth. Educ: Clemson; Erskine Col, B.A, 33; Duke Univ, Winthrop Col, grad. work. Polit. & Govt. Pos: Rock Hill postmaster, 51-54, secy. to Congressman James P. Richards, 7 years; U.S. Rep, S.C, 64- Bus. & Prof. Pos: Teacher and coach, Rock Hill High Sch; prin, Cent. Sch; law practice, 54- Mil. Serv: Navy, Pac. Theater. Mem: York Co. and Am. Bar Asns; Am. Legion; VFW; Elks; C. of C.(past pres, Rock Hill Chap); Rotary (past pres); YMCA (past pres. bd); past chmn, United Fund Champaign; past chmn. bd. trustees, Rock Hill Sch. Dist. Rel: Presbyterian; former deacon and elder, Associate Reformed Presbyterian Church of Rock Hill. Legal Res: Rock Hill, S.C. Mailing Add: 331 Cannon House Office Bldg, Washington, D.C. 20515.

GETZWILLER, POLLY D
Ariz. State Rep.
b. Luna, N.Mex, 3/8/24; d. William T. Johnson and Grace Ross Birdwell J; m. 6/13/54 to Marion H. Getzwiller; c. Billie Lou, William Albert and Marion Joe. Polit. & Govt. Pos: Ariz. State Rep, currently; del, Dem. Nat. Conv, 68. Mem: Bus. & Prfnl. Women's Club; Dem. Women; Woman's Club; Nat. Platform Asn; Colo. River Water Asn; Ariz. Cotton Growers; Farm Bur. Rel: Presbyterian. Mailing Add: Box 127, Casa Grande, Ariz. 85222.

GEYERMAN, PETER THOMAS D
Treas, Pennington Co. Dem. Cmt, S.Dak.
b. Huron, S.Dak, 10/7/31; s. Peter Rudolph Geyerman and Ella Forking G; m. 2/4/53 to Frances Darlene Scott; c. Clay Scott. Educ: Univ. Minn. Polit. & Govt. Pos: Pres, Pennington Co. Young Dem, S.Dak, 58-60 & 61-64; Dem. precinct committeeman, 58-66; treas, Pennington Co. Dem. Cmt, 66- Mil. Serv: Entered as Airman Recruit, Navy, 51, released as PO 2/C, 55, after serv. in Patrol Squad 46, Philippines. Mem: Pres, Downtown Improvement Asn, 63-64; mem. bd, Retail Cmt, Rapid City C. of C, 58-66; Lions; Elks. Rel: Protestant. Mailing Add: P.O. Box 1910, Rapid City, S.Dak. 57701. (1967)

GFALL, TOM KARL D
b. Plum City, Wis, 6/9/11; s. George Gfall and Mathilda Spiss G; m. 5/5/34 to Caurita Wright; c. Patricia Ann (Mrs. Jack Hei), Nancy Lu (Mrs. Robert Hulverson) and Thomas G. Educ: Pub. schs, 12 years. Polit. & Govt. Pos: Acting postmaster, Plum City, Wis, 61-; chmn, Pierce Co. Dem. Party, Wis, 68. Bus. & Prof. Pos: Tavern owner, 34-59; fireman, Plum City Fire Dept, 34-69; store owner, 60; order clerk, Bauer Built Inc, Durand, Wis. Mem: Pierce Co. Conserv. Cong, 44-67, chmn, two years. Rel: Catholic. Mailing Add: Plum City, Wis. 54761.

GHERINI, PIER A. R
Finance Chmn, Santa Barbara Co. Rep. Party, Calif.
b. San Francisco, Calif, 11/5/12; s. Ambrose Gherini and Maria Rossi G; m. 8/2/41 to Margaret; c. Pier, Jr, Elena, John and Thomas. Educ: Univ. Calif, Berkeley and Law Sch; Phi Delta Phi. Polit. & Govt. Pos: Police judge, Santa Barbara, Calif, 46-51; mem, Calif. State Rep. Finance Cmt, 65-66; chmn, Bd. Freeholders, Santa Barbara, 66; Finance Chmn, Santa Barbara Co. Rep. Party, Calif, 66-; chmn, Calif. Fair Employ. Practices Cmn, 67- Bus. & Prof. Pos: Attorney at law, Santa Barbara. Mil. Serv: Entered as 1st Lt, Air Force, 41, released as Col, Air Force Res. Mem: Calif. and Am. Bar Asns; Santa Barbara Co. Bar Asn.(past pres); Psi Upsilon; Univ. Club, Santa Barbara. Rel: Catholic. Legal Res: 1807 Mira Vista, Santa Barbara, Calif. 93103. Mailing Add: 1114 State St, Room 230, Santa Barbara, Calif. 93104.

GHIZ, LUTHER HARVEY D
W.Va. State Del.
b. Logan, W.Va, 3/23/06; s. Harvey Ghiz and Ady Klele G; m. 1/9/37 to Ruby Thompson; c. Luther H, Jr. and Jack T. Educ: Marshall Univ, B.A; Sigma Phi Epsilon. Polit. & Govt. Pos: Mem, Logan City Coun. and chmn, Logan Dem. Exec. Cmt, formerly; W.Va. State Del, 60- Bus. & Prof. Pos: Oil and gas serv. sta, parking lot. Mil. Serv: Navy, Gunnery Officer. Mem: Rotary; Elks; VFW; past comdr, Am. Legion; Va. Sr. Golf Asn; W.Va. State C. of C; Logan City. C. of C; Logan Bus. Men's Asn. Rel: Baptist. Mailing Add: Box 1168, Logan, W.Va. 25601.

GHOLSON, ISSAC WILLIAM D
Chmn, Stonewall Co. Dem. Party, Tex.
b. Aspermont, Tex, 2/14/12; s. James Monroe Gholson and Lila Elizabeth Hart G; m. 8/6/60 to Jenora Kathlyn Davis; c. Bobby Roe, William Alec, Carolyn Louise (Mrs. Albright) and James W. Educ: High sch, Aspermont, Tex. Polit. & Govt. Pos: Chmn, Stonewall Co. Dem. Party, Tex, 42- Bus. & Prof. Pos: Rancher, currently. Mem: Farm Bur; Odd Fellows. Rel: Baptist. Mailing Add: Route 1, Box 16, Aspermont, Tex. 79502.

GHOLSON, JEROME BUSLER D
Committeeman, Ill. Dem. Cent. Cmt.
b. Eldorado, Ill, 4/30/35; s. Elmo Gholson and Abbie Busler G; m. 11/23/62 to Beulah Frances Fowler. Educ: South. Ill. Univ, B.S. in Bus. Admin, 58; Ky. Sch. of Embalming, 60; MEA Ky. Sch. of Embalming Award. Polit. & Govt. Pos: Dep. coroner, Hamilton Co, Ill, 64-; committeeman, Ill. Dem. Cent. Cmt, 66- Bus. & Prof. Pos: Funeral dir, Gholson Funeral Home, McLeansboro, Ill, 57-; dir, Off. of Econ. Opportunity, Wabash Area, 66-. Mil. Serv: Pvt, Army Res, 58, released as Pfc, 64, after serv. in Berlin Crisis, 61-62. Mem: C. of C; Kiwanis; Elks; Odd Fellows; Jaycees (pres, Hamilton Co. Chap, 68). Rel: Baptist. Mailing Add: 107 W. Randolph, McLeansboro, Ill. 62859.

GIADONE, WILLIAM BIAGIO R
Chmn, Fitchburg Rep. City Cmt, Mass.
b. Italy, 10/9/09; s. Salvatore Giadone and Domica Guinta G; m. 6/27/32 to Beuna Baldarelli; c. Dorothy, Barbara (Mrs. Gerald Gallent) and Sandra (Mrs. William D. Leger). Educ: Several short courses in Merchandising, Advert, and Financing. Polit. & Govt. Pos: Coordinator, Gov, Volpe, 62-; chmn, Fitchburg Rep. City Cmt, 68- Bus. & Prof. Pos: Pres, Giadone's Furniture Co, 32-69. Mem: Arm of Retail Merchants; Retailers Mkt. Guild; Nat. Retail Furniture Asn; Sons of Italy; Rotary; Fitchburg C. of C.(pres, 65-66). Man of the Year Award, Sons of Italy, 65; Devoted Serv. Award, Fitchburg C. of C, 66. Rel: Catholic. Legal Res: 475 Water St, Fitchburg, Mass. 01420. Mailing Add: 325 Water St, Fitchburg, Mass. 01420.

GIAIMO, ROBERT N. D
U.S. Rep, Conn.
b. New Haven, Conn, 10/15/19; s. Rosario Giaimo and Rose Scarpulla G; m. 5/17/45 to Marion Schuenemann; c. Barbara Lee. Educ: Fordham Col, A.B, 41; Univ. Conn. Law Sch, LL.B, 43. Polit. & Govt. Pos: Mem, Bd. of Educ, North Haven, Conn, 49-55 and Bd. of Finance, 52-55; third selectman, North Haven, 55-57; chmn, Conn. Personnel Appeals Bd, 55-58; U.S. Rep, Third Dist, Conn, 59-, mem, Appropriations Cmt, U.S. House of Rep, currently; alternate del, Dem. Nat. Conv, 68. Bus. & Prof. Pos: Lawyer, New Haven, 46-; assoc, Sachs, Sachs, Giaimo & Sachs, currently. Mil. Serv: Entered Army, 43, released as 1st Lt, 46; Capt, Judge Adv. Gen. Corps, Army Res. Admitted to Conn. Bar, 46. Rel: Roman Catholic. Legal Res: 23 Marlen Dr, North Haven, Conn. Mailing Add: Room 2338, Rayburn House Office Bldg, U.S. House of Representatives, Washington, D.C. 20515.

GIANGIACOMO, ANTHONY D
R.I. State Rep.
b. Providence, R.I, 9/19/26; s. Dionino Giangiacomo and Josephine Pronda G; single. Educ: Johnston & Wales Bus. Col, Acct. dipl, 50; Life Ins. Mkt. Inst, Purdue, Univ, dipl, 56. Polit. & Govt. Pos: Del, R.I. Constitutional Conv, 64-68; R.I. State Rep, 12th Dist, Providence, 67-, mem. Finance Cmt, East. Regional Cmt. on Policy Probs. and Transportation, 67-, Cmt. to Study Regionalization of State and Local Serv, 68- and chmn, Pub. Rights of Way Cmn, 69-, R.I. House of Rep. Bus. & Prof. Pos: Licensed pub. acct. and ins. agent and broker, 55- Mil. Serv: Entered as Pvt. Army, 44, released as Cpl, 46, after serv. in Inf, Pac. Theatre, 45-46. Mem: Nat. Soc. of Pub. Acct; past comdr, Dept. of R.I, Ital-Am. War Vet; Am. Legion; VFW; St. Vincent dePaul Soc; Our Lady of Peace Retreat League. Rel: Catholic. Mailing Add: 24 Melissa St, Providence, R.I. 02909.

GIANNINI, ANTHONY ALBERT D
Chmn, R.I. Dem. Party
b. Providence, R.I, 7/17/22; s. Anthony Giannini and Elvira Izzi G; m. 11/12/51 to Eleanor Antonette Ruggerio; c. Anthony A, Jr, William T, Stephen M. and Judith M. Educ: Boston Col, LL.B. Polit. & Govt. Pos: Legal counsel, Div. Pub. Utilities, R.I, 57-59; exec. secy, Gov. John A. Notte, Jr, 61-62; exec. committeeman, R.I. Dem. Party, 65-68, chmn, 68- Mil. Serv: Entered as Pvt, Army Air Force, 42, released as Sgt, 45. Mem: R.I. Bar Asn.(exec. committeeman, 64-66); Am. Bar Asn; K. of C; Lions; Serra Int. Rel: Catholic. Mailing Add: 39 Sheffield Ave, Providence, R.I. 02911.

GIANNOTTI, VIRGINIA LYTLE D
b. Overton, Nev, 2/27/20; d. John A. Lytle (deceased) and Mary Virginia Perkins L; m. 3/13/40 to Edwin N. Giannotti. Educ: Latter-day Saints Bus. Col, Salt Lake City, Utah, Bus. Admin, 38, Hanagar Bus. Col, Bus. Admin, 39; Univ. Nev, Polit. Sci, Creative Writing and Spec. Classes. Polit. & Govt. Pos: Secy, Nev. State Hwy. Dept, 40-43; secy, U.S. Govt. Camp Williston and Las Vegas Army Air Base, 43-47; secy, Washoe Co. Dem. Women's Club, 65 & 69-, pres, 66 & 67; mem,Washoe Co. Dem. Cent. Cmt, 65-68; mem, Nev. Dem. State Cent. Cmt, 65-68; del, Dem. Nat. Conv, 68; Dem. nat committeewoman, Nev, 68-69. Mem: Washoe Co. Legal Secy; VFW Auxiliary (state hosp. dir, 48-69, pres. Nev. State Chap, 55-56, mem. Nat. Coun, Nev, Calif. and Ore, 57-58, pres, Nat. Coun. Club and West. States Conf, 59, nat. historian, nat. cancer dir. and nat. asst. hosp. dir, 59-64); Washoe Co. Dem. Women; Moapa Valley High Alumni Asn; Sons of Italy (secy, Reno Lodge); R.R. Conductors Auxiliary (secy); Reno Vet. Hosp. Vol. Serv. Cmt.(chmn, Christian activities, 20 years, chmn. pub. rels, currently). Rel: Latter-day Saint. Mailing Add: 1295 Gordon Ave, Reno, Nev. 89502.

GIBB, ARTHUR R
Vt. State Rep.
b. Brooklyn, N.Y, 4/16/08; s. Henry Elmer Gibb and Grace Dwight G; m. 6/28/32 to Barbara Lowrie Gibb; c. John Dwight, Arthur, Jr, Lowrie, Barbara Grace and Henry F. Educ: Yale Univ, A.B, 30. Polit. & Govt. Pos: Chmn, Weybridge Civil Defense Cmn. and Weybridge Zoning Bd. of Adjustment, Vt; chmn, Rep. City Cmt. and mem, Rep. State Cmn; lister, 53-59; town agent, 63-; Vt. State Rep, 63-, v.chmn, Cmt. on Ways and Means, Vt. State House of Rep, 65 & 69, chmn, Cmt. on Natural Resources, 66, 67 & 69; chmn, Legis Coun. Tax Study, 67 & 68 and Cmt. on Equal Opportunity, 68, v.chmn, Legis. Coun, 68 & 69; chmn, Gov. Cmn. on Environ. Control, 69. Bus. & Prof. Pos: Farming, Angus cattle breeder; estate trustee; banking and investment counsel. Mil. Serv: Entered as Lt, Naval Res, 42, released as Comdr, 45, after serving in U.S.S. Lexington, Pac. Theater, 43-45; Capt. (Ret), Naval Res; Bronze Star with Combat V; Presidential Unit Citation; Pac. Area Ribbon with ten Battle Stars. Mem: Nat. Pilots Asn; Farm Bur; pres, Porter Hosp; chmn, Vt. State YMCA. Rel: Congregational. Legal Res: Weybridge, Vt. Mailing Add: Box 42, Route 1, Middlebury, Vt. 05753.

GIBB, LAURENCE V. R
b. Sewickley, Pa, 3/19/99; s. Samuel Gibb and Jennie Stoker. Educ: Pittsburgh Sch. of Acct; Duquesne Univ. Polit. & Govt. Pos: Pa. State Rep, 54-67; Mayor, Sewickley, Pa, 57-; Justice of Peace, Sewickley, 36 yrs; Rep. Chmn. Sewickley, 30-; Rep. State Comm, 48-56; Tax Collector; Spec. Investr. Allegheny Co. D.A, 52-56. Bus. & Prof. Pos: Real estate and ins. Mil. Serv: WW I, Pvt, Battery B, 107th Field Artil, 28th Div; WW II, Capt, U.S.A.F, 42-45. Mem: Past Comdr, Sewickley Valley Post No. 4, Am. Legion; 107th Field Artil. Vets. Asn; Sewickley Valley Bd. of Trade. Mailing Add: 606 Centennial Ave, Sewickley, Pa. 15143. (1967)

GIBBLE, HAROLD McKINSTRY D
Committeeman, Lancaster Co. Dem. Party, Pa.
b. Lancaster, Pa, 7/25/02; s. Harry Kauffman Gibble and Maude Apple McKinstry G; m. 1/20/24 to Kathryn Minerva Enck; c. Harold M, Jr.(deceased), Harry Nelson, Thomas Burton and Susan Diane (Mrs. John W. Wolf). Educ: Franklin & Marshall Col, B.A, 23; LaSalle Exten. Univ, cert, 25; Alexander Hamilton Inst, cert, 27; Wharton Sch. Finance, cert, 29. Polit. & Govt. Pos: Secy, Lancaster Co. Dem. Cmt, Pa, 30-36; pres, Lancaster Co. Fedn. of Dem. Clubs, 32-37; committeeman, Lancaster Co. Dem. Party, 32-44 & 60-; mem, Dem. Nat. Cmt, 33-35; field agent, Bur. of Animal Indust, 34-37; mem, Pa. Dem. State Cent. Cmt, 36-40; asst. dir. bur. of sch. audits, Dept. of the Auditor Gen, 61-; del, Dem. Nat. Conv, 68. Bus. & Prof. Pos: Tax consult. and pub. acct, 20- Mem: Nat. Asn. Pub. Acct; Nat. Asn. Acct; Pa. Soc. Pub. Acct; Elks; K. of M; Odd Fellows; Lancaster Automobile Club; Lancaster Leiderkranz; Fraternal Order of Police; Sixth Ward Citizens Asn; Mfgs. Asn. of Traffic Club; Fed. Postal Employees Asn. Rel: United Church of Christ. Legal Res: 420 Lancaster Ave, Lancaster, Pa. 17604. Mailing Add: P.O. Box 1002, Lancaster, Pa. 17604.

GIBBONS, BOYD H, III R
Dep. Under Secy, Dept. of the Interior
Mailing Add: C St. between 18th & 19th St. N.W, Washington, D.C. 20240.

GIBBONS, DELMAR DALE Prohibition Party
b. Decatur, Ill, 9/8/12; s. Cecil Gibbons and Verna L. Mowry G; m. 7/27/31 to Dorothy E. Scott; c. Delmar E, Mary Ellen, David L. and Karen E. Educ: Lincoln Chiropractic Col, D.C. and Ph.C, 37; Spring Arbor Col, 54; Nat. Col. Chiropractic, post-grad. work, 62-63. Polit. & Govt. Pos: State chmn, Mich. Prohibition Cmt, 57-63; exec. nat. chmn, Prohibition Party, 63-67. Bus. & Prof. Pos: Ed. or managing ed, Mich. Statesman, 44-62; off. ed, Sunday Sch. J, 54-55; ed, Nat. Statesman, 63- Mem: Am. Chiropractic Asn; past chmn, x-ray and research cmt, Mich. State Chiropractic Asn; chmn, Eastside Improv. Asn, 65-66; bd. dirs, Kalamazoo Youth for Christ, 62-63. Raised prizewinning parakeets, 52-55; Won 146 trophies in 15 shows, 63. Rel: Methodist; Ordained Lay Preacher and Lay Del. Gen. Confs. of Church, 55, 60 and 64; Free Methodist Church. Mailing Add: 1520 E. Main St, Kalamazoo, Mich. 49001.

GIBBONS, HARRY J. D
Chmn, Cape May Co. Dem. Orgn, N.J.
b. Phila, Pa, 9/11/22; s. Jeffrey F. Gibbons and Anne M. Fossett G; m. 4/4/45 to Anne M. Marsh; c. John J, Anne Marie (Mrs. Edward Elliot), Catherine, Jeffrey, Harry, Terese, Regina, Edward, Joseph, Paul and Patricia. Educ: LaSalle Col, B.S, 48; Franklin and Marshall Col, 63; Villanova Univ, 64. Polit. & Govt. Pos: Munic. leader, Cape May, N.J, 60-69; co. treas, Cape May Co. Dem. Orgn, N.J, 61-63, chmn, 68- Bus. & Prof. Pos: Prof. acct, LaSalle Col, eve. div, 51-; math. teacher, Wildwood Cath. High Sch, Wildwood, 57-64; controller, Cape May-Lewes Ferry, 64-69. Mil. Serv: Entered as Aviation Cadet, Army Air Force, 42, released as 1st Lt, 45, after serv. in Seventh Air Force, Cent. Pac, 44-45; Distinguished Flying Cross; Air Medal and Six Clusters; Three Battle Stars; Victory Medal; Am. Theater and Pac. Theater Medals. Publ: Pity the Poor Entrepeneur, St. Joseph's Col, 62. Mem: Am. Acct. Asn; Cross Keys; bd. dirs, LaSalle Col. Alumni (past pres); Cape May Little League past pres); Holy Name Soc.(past pres). Outstanding Serv, LaSalle Col. Alumni, 58. Rel: Roman Catholic. Mailing Add: 1325 New York Ave, Cape May, N.J. 08204.

GIBBONS, SAM M. D
U.S. Rep, Fla.
b. Tampa, Fla, 1/20/20; s. Gunby Gibbons and Jessie Kirk Cralle G; m. to Martha Hanley; c. Clifford, Mark and Timothy. Educ: Univ. of Fla, LL.B; Blue Key; Univ. Hall of Fame; Alpha Tau Omega. Polit. & Govt. Pos: Fla. State Rep, 52-58; Fla. State Sen, 58-62; U.S. Rep, Fla, 62-; del, Dem. Nat. Conv, 68. Bus. & Prof. Pos: Law firm, Gibbons, Tucker, McEwen, Smith, Cofer & Taub, 47- Mil. Serv: Army, 501st Parachute Inf, 101st Airborne Div, in initial assault landing, D-Day, Europe, in Bastogne oper, released as Maj; Bronze Star. Mem: Am. and Fla. Bar Asns; former dir, Tampa and Hillsborough Co. Bar Asn; first pres, Univ. of S. Fla. Found. Tampa's Outstanding Young Man of the Year, 54; C. of C. Pres. Award, One of Ten Top State Legislators in both House and Senate. Rel: Presbyterian; Deacon, First Presbyterian Church of Tampa. Legal Res: 940 S. Sterling Ave, Tampa, Fla. 33609. Mailing Add: 430 Cannon House Office Bldg, Washington, D.C. 20515.

GIBBS, FRANKLIN PHILIP, JR. R
S. Dak. State Sen.
b. Oakland, Calif, 7/17/25; s. Franklin Philip Gibbs and Mabel Meders G; m. 2/7/47 to Jeannette Rysdorp; c. Jeffrey, Andrea, Patricia and Barbara. Educ: San Francisco City Col, A.A, 46; Univ. Calif; Hastings Col. Law; Univ. S.Dak. Law Sch, LL.B, 51; Phi Alpha Delta. Polit. & Govt. Pos: Dep. States Attorney, Minnehaha Co, S.Dak, 53-54 & 59-60, States Attorney, 55-58; S.Dak.

State Rep, 61-66; S.Dak. State Sen, 67-, chmn, Legis. Research Coun, 69- Bus. & Prof. Pos: Attorney and assoc, Jones & Matthews, 52-53; attorney, Barnes & Gibbs, 53-58; attorney and partner, Simons, Gibbs & Feyder, 58- Mil. Serv: Entered as Pvt, Air Force, 43, released as 2nd Lt, 46; Capt, Air Force Res. Mem: Am, Fed. and Minnehaha Co. Bar Asns; State Bar of S.Dak; Am. Trial Lawyers Asn; Am. Judicature Soc; AF&AM; Consistory; Shrine; Elks; Am. Legion; High Twelve Club; DeMolay Chapter Advisor, leader, Hi Y Club, 10 yrs. Rel: Presbyterian. Mailing Add: 912 Edward Dr, Sioux Falls, S.Dak. 57103.

GIBBS, HENRY LAWRENCE, JR. D
La. State Rep.
b. Monroe, La, 3/7/19; s. Henry L. Gibbs (deceased) and Annie Kelly G; m. 5/3/41 to Bobbie Regenia Hibbard (deceased); c. Henry Lawrence, III, Kenneth Lane, Bobby Keith and Gary Dean. Polit. & Govt. Pos: La. State Rep, 56-, chmn, House Educ. Cmt, La. House Rep, currently; mem, La. Dem. State Cent. Cmt, 60-68. Mil. Serv: Entered as Pvt, Army, 44, released as Sgt, 45, after serv. in 28th Inf. Div, ETO; ETO Medal with two Battle Stars; Good Conduct Medal; Presidential Unit Citation. Mem: Mason; Consistory; Shrine; Am. Legion. Rel: Methodist. Mailing Add: 3718 Grammont St, Monroe, La. 71201.

GIBBS, JOHN ALLEN R
Chmn, 18th Cong. Dist. Rep. Cmt, Mich.
b. Springfield, Mass, 3/31/32; s. Orville E. Gibbs and Catherine Leppleman G; m. 8/20/56 to Constance Suzanne McCort. Educ: Ohio State Univ, 50-52; Gen. Motors Inst. Co-operative course, A.B, 56; Beta Theta Pi. Polit. & Govt. Pos: Precinct del, Rep. Party, Birmingham, Mich, 56-58; chmn, Oakland Co. Young Rep, 57-58; exec. secy, Oakland Co. Rep. Cmt, 57-61; exec. asst. to Rep. State Chmn. Mich, 61-63; mem. campaign adv. cmt, Gov. Romney, 62; statewide campaign dir, state elec, 62-63; adv, Gov. Cmn. Status Women, 63-64; chmn, 18th Cong. Dist. Rep. Cmt, 67-; mem, Gov. William Milliken's Action Cmt, 68- Publ: 'Dynamics of Organization-Blueprint for Republican Victory,' Rep. State Cent. Cmt, 63; 'Civic and Community Affairs Programs-a New Management Imperative,' Mgt. Personnel Quart, Univ. Mich. Grad. Sch. Bus. Admin, 63. Mem: Sales Promotion Exec. Asn.(Detroit Chap); Econ. Club Detroit. Rel: Episcopal. Mailing Add: 2755 Somerset Blvd, Troy, Mich. 48084.

GIBBS, JUNE NESBITT R
Rep. Nat. Committeewoman, R.I.
b. Newton, Mass, 6/13/22; d. Samuel F. Nesbitt and Lulu H. Glazier N; m. 12/8/45 to Donald T. Gibbs; c. Elizabeth. Educ: Wellesley Col, B.A, 43; Boston Univ, M.A, 47. Polit. & Govt. Pos: V.chmn, Rep. State Cent. Cmt, R.I, 60-69; del, Rep. Nat. Conv, 68; Rep. Nat. Committeewoman, R.I, 69- Mil. Serv: Entered as Midn, Navy, 43, released as Lt.(jg), 46. Rel: Congregational. Mailing Add: 163 Riverview Ave, Middletown, R.I. 02840.

GIBLIN, JOHN JOSEPH D
b. County Roscommon, Ireland, 2/14/09; s. John Giblin and Elizabeth Callalley G; m. Aug, 1940 to Theresa Moran; c. Eileen (Mrs. Coyne), John Joseph, Thomas P, Vincent J. and Mary C. Educ: Irish Nat. Schs; night sch, West Side High Sch, Newark; Newark Prep. Sch; Newark Voc. Sch. Polit. & Govt. Pos: Freeholder, Essex Co, N.J, 54-57; mem, Newark Charter Cmn; clerk, Essex Co. Jury Cmn, 59-61; mem, Essex Co. Right of Way Cmn, 61-66; N.J. State Sen, Essex,Co, 66-68; del, Dem. Nat. Conv, 68. Bus. & Prof. Pos: Stationary engr, Prudential Ins. Co, 29-43; stationary engr, Newark Bd. Educ, 43-48; bus. mgr, Local 68, Int. Union Operating Engrs, 48- Mem: Pres, Independent Irish Soc, Inc; Exec. Coun, N.J. State AFL-CIO; del, Essex Trades Coun, Essex Co. Bldg. & Construct. Trades Coun. and Cent. Labor Unions of Hudson and Passaic Co; K. of C; Elks. Rel: Roman Catholic. Mailing Add: 12 Rosney Terr, West Orange, N.J. 07052. (1967)

GIBNEY, ROBERT EMMET R
Mem, Calif. Rep. State Cent. Cmt.
b. Pittsburgh, Pa, 9/10/15; s. Christopher Arthur Gibney and Anna Haggerty G; m. 8/14/46 to Dorothy May Gasselman; c. Linda Anne, Robert Emmet, Nancy Jean, Mary Susan, William David and Kathleen Louise. Educ: Univ. Pittsburgh, B.S, 37; Phi Kappa Theta; Newman Club. Polit. & Govt. Pos: Mem, Eisenhower, Nixon and Goldwater for Pres. Cmts; mem, Reagan Finance Cmt, Calif; mem, United Rep. Finance Cmt, Los Angeles Co; capt, 80th Precinct, 23rd Cong. Dist; mem, Calif. Rep. State Cent. Cmt, 69- Bus. & Prof. Pos: Owner and mgr, Robert E. Gibney Assocs, Mfgs. Rep, Los Angeles, 48- Mil. Serv: Entered as 2nd Lt, Army, 42, released as Maj, 46, after serv. in several units including Hq, Am, European and Asiatic Theatres, 44-46; Lt. Col, Army Res, 46-69; 2 Battle Stars, Ardennes, Rhineland; 2 Commendations from 2 Maj. Gen; Citation, President's Interdepartmental Cmt. Mem: Los Angeles Athletic Club; Boy Scouts; Am. Legion; Am. Legion Luncheon Club; Mil. Order World Wars; trustee, Americanism Educ. League. Citation for Outstanding Serv. to Americanism Educ. League, 69. Rel: Roman Catholic. Legal Res: 10446 Downey Ave, Downey, Calif. 90241. Mailing Add: P.O. Box 1102, Downey, Calif. 90240.

GIBSON, ANDREW E. R
Maritime Adminstr, Maritime Admin, Dept. of Commerce
b. N.Y.C, 2/19/22; s. Andrew Gibson and Louisa Ann Tozer G; m. to Jane Louise Mork; c. Janet P, Andrew K, John S, Alexander S. and Ann C. Educ: Mass. Maritime Acad, 42; Brown Univ, B.A. cum laude, 51; N.Y. Univ, M.B.A, 59. Polit. & Govt. Pos: Maritime Adminstr, Maritime Admin, Dept. of Commerce, 69- Bus. & Prof. Pos: Former capt, U.S. Lines ocean freighter; asst. dept. mgr, Firestone Latex Prod. Co, 46-48; asst. to treas, Grace Line, Inc, N.Y.C, 53-54, cargo mgr, 54-57, terminal mgr, 57-62, asst. v.pres, 62-64, v.pres. of terminal opers, 64-65, sr. v.pres. of opers, 65-67; v.pres, Diebold Group, 67-69. Mil. Serv: Entered as Lt, Navy, 51-53, Asst. Controller, Budget, Mil. Sea Transportation Serv. Mailing Add: 11900 Old Bridge Rd, Rockville, Md. 20852.

GIBSON, BEN J, JR. R
Mem, Exec. Cmt, Polk Co. Rep. Cent. Cmt, Iowa
b. Des Moines, Iowa, 3/18/22; s. Ben J. Gibson and Anna Ralston G; m. 9/9/42 to Katherine Chase; c. Ben J, III, Megan Elizabeth, Chase Fredrick, Wendell Stewart and Brian Charles. Educ: Univ. Va, B.A, 47, Grad. Sch, grad. work in Am. Hist, 47; Sigma Nu. Polit. & Govt. Pos: Rep. cand. for Cong, Fifth Dist, Iowa, 64; chmn, Resolutions Cmt, Polk Co. Rep. Orgn, 66; mem, Platform Cmt, State Rep. Orgn, 66; campaign mgr, Polk Co. Rep. Cand, 66; mem, exec. cmt, Polk Co. Rep. Cent. Cmt, 66- Bus. & Prof. Pos: Pres, Gibson Co, Inc. and The Book Store, Inc, Des Moines. Mil. Serv: Entered as Pfc, Marine Corps, 42, released as 1st Lt, 46, after serv. in Inf, 46. Mem: Exec. secy, Midland Booksellers Asn, Des Moines; treas, bd. of dirs, Des Moines Health Center; mem, Des Moines C. of C. Rel: Presbyterian. Mailing Add: 4137 Greenwood Dr, Des Moines, Iowa 50312.

GIBSON, CATHARINE R
b. Sullivan, Ind, 9/29/07; d. C. Edward Coffman and Alice MacDonald C; m. 10/11/24 to Peter Gibson; c. Isabel (Mrs. Douglas W. Taylor). Educ: Wicker Sch. Fine Arts, Detroit, 27-30. Polit. & Govt. Pos: Pres, Rep. Women's Fedn, Mich, 48-53; del, Rep. Nat. Conv, Chicago, 52 and San Francisco, 56; first v.pres, Nat. Fedn. Rep. Women, 52-56; v.chmn, Rep. Cent. Cmt, Mich, 53-57; chmn, Rep. v.chmn. Coun, Midwest & Rocky Mt. States, 54-57; pres, Nat. Fedn. Rep. Women, 57-60, mem. exec. cmt, 61-63; Presidential appointee, Assay Cmn, 58. Mem: DAR; Eastern Star; Order of Rainbow for Girls; Bus. & Prfnl. Women's Clubs. Rel: Presbyterian. Mailing Add: Woodland Beach, Monroe, Mich. 48161.

GIBSON, CHARLES EDWARD, JR. R
b. St. Johnsbury, Vt, 12/20/25; s. Charles Edward Gibson and Elizabeth Fulton Garvin G; single. Educ: Univ. Mich, A.B, 49, Law Sch, 52. Polit. & Govt. Pos: States attorney, Caledonia Co, Vt, 55-60; judge, Caledonia Munic. Court, 60-61; Dep. Attorney Gen, Vt, 61-63, Attorney Gen, 63-65; past mem, State Small Claims Cmn, Interstate Corp. Cmn, and St. Johnsburg Rep. Cmt; mem, Bd. Bar Exams, Vt, 66- Bus. & Prof. Pos: With, Waterman and Downs, St. Johnsbury, Vt, 63-64; partner, Paterson, Gibson, Noble & Brownell, Montpelier, currently. Mem: Vt. and Am. Bar Asns; Am. Judicature Soc; Vt. and Am. Trial Lawyers Asn; former chmn, Vt. Jr. Bar Conf; Rotary; St. Johnsbury Jr. C. of C.(past pres. and dir). Outstanding Young Man of the Year, St. Johnsbury, Vt, 61. Rel: Presbyterian. Mailing Add: 242 Elm St, Montpelier, Vt. 05602.

GIBSON, CHARLES MacDONALD D
b. Charleston, S.C, 8/16/32; s. Charles E. Gibson and Helen Woodcock G; m. 9/11/54 to Elizabeth Carter; c. Four. Educ: Univ. Va, B.A, 54; Univ. S.C, LL.B, 59. Polit. & Govt. Pos: Mem, Co. Elec. Cmt, formerly; S.C. State Rep, 61-66; S.C. State Sen, 67-68. Bus. & Prof. Pos: Lawyer. Mil. Serv: Army, Lt, Transportation Corps, 159th Boat Bn, 54-56. Mem: West Charleston Sertoma Club; former ed, S.C. Law Quart; Wig and Robe; Phi Delta Phi. Mailing Add: Box 1018, Charleston, S.C. 29402.

GIBSON, DONALD BANCROFT D
Mem, Hampton Dem. Exec. Cmt, Va.
b. Hampton, Va, 1/19/28; s. Stuart Mather Gibson and Elizabeth Rowe Souder G; single. Educ: King Col, 47-49; Univ. Richmond, 49-52; Theta Chi. Polit. & Govt. Pos: Dep. clerk, Circuit Court, Va, 59-; del, Dem. State Conv, 60, 64 & 68; secy, Hampton Roads Young Dem. Club, 62-63, v.pres, 63-64 and pres, 64-66; del, Dem. Nat. Conv, 64; dep. clerk, Court of Law and Chancery, 64-; mem, Hampton Dem. Exec. Cmt, Va, 69- Bus. & Prof. Pos: Asst. underwriter, N.Am. Assurance Soc, 55-58; Ins. agent, Home Beneficial Life Ins. Co, 58-59. Mil. Serv: Entered as Recruit, Coast Guard, 52, released as SN, 54; Nat. Defense Serv. Medal; Coast Guard Res, 54-60. Mem: Elks; Peninsula Exchange Club. Rel: Presbyterian. Legal Res: 329 Hampton Roads Ave, Hampton, Va. 23361. Mailing Add: Clerks Office, Circuit Court, Hampton, Va. 23369.

GIBSON, D(ONALD) JACK R
Rep. Nat. Committeeman, S.Dak.
b. Spearfish, S.Dak, 11/14/23; s. George L. Gibson and Irene Adams G; m. 2/8/44 to Donna Rae Searls; c. Claudia Lea and David John. Educ: S.Dak. State Univ, 41-43; Okla. State Univ. Army Specialized Training Prog, 44-45; Columbia Univ. Sch. Bus. and Transportation Mgt. Sch, 59; Harvard Bus. Sch, mgt, 68. Polit. & Govt. Pos: Mem, Sioux Falls Independent Bd. of Educ, S.Dak, 63-68; chmn, S.Dak. Citizens for Goldwater-Miller, 64; chmn, Karl Mundt for Sen, 65 & 66; chmn, S.Dak. Nixon for Pres. Cmt, 68; del. and secy-treas, S.Dak. Del, Rep. Nat. Conv, 68; chmn, Nixon-Agnew, S.Dak, 68; Rep. Nat. Committeeman, 68- Bus. & Prof. Pos: Pharm. apprentice, Blue Drug Co, Spearfish, S.Dak, summers 41-42; from various job assignments to opers. mgr, Wilson Truck Syst, Sioux Falls, 46-51; pres, Midwest Coast Transport, Inc, 51- Mil. Serv: Entered as Pvt, Army, 43, released as T/Sgt, 46, after serv. in 409th Inf, ETO, 44-46; Combat Inf. Badge; Purple Heart. Mem: Dir. and mem. exec. cmt, Am. Trucking Asn; dir, Common Carrier Conf, Irregular Route; dir, S.Dak. Motor Carrier Asn, pres, 65-67; S.Dak. Producers, Bus. and Indust; Nat. and S.Dak. Hwy. Users Conf; dir, Karl E. Mundt Hist. and Educ. Found; trustee, Am. Good Govt. Soc; dir, Sioux Falls Rotary Club; Gr. S.Dak. Asn; Young Pres. Orgn; Nat. Defense Exec. Reserve; Elks; Am. Legion; Sioux Falls Consistory; Shrine. Sioux Falls Citizen of the Week. Rel: Episcopal. Legal Res: 904 E. 35th St, Sioux Falls, S.Dak. 57105. Mailing Add: P.O. Box 1233, Sioux Falls, S.Dak. 57101.

GIBSON, ERNEST WILLIAM R
b. Brattleboro, Vt, 3/6/01; s. Ernest Willard Gibson and Grace Fullerton Hadley G; m. 1/61 to Ann H. Haag; c. Ernest William, Grace, Robert Hadley and David Alan. Educ: Norwich Univ, A.B, 23; George Washington Law Sch, 24-27; Phi Delta Phi; Theta Chi. Polit. & Govt. Pos: Fed. Dist. Judge for Dist. of Vt, 50-; Gov. of Vt, 47, 48, resigned to become judge; R.R. Tax Cmn. of Vt, 39-40; U.S. Sen, Vt, app. to Sen. on death of father; secy. Vt. State Sen, 33-40, asst. secy, 31-33; States' attorney of Windham Co, Vt, 28, 30; mathematician Coast and Geodetic Surv, 24-27. Bus. & Prof. Pos: Lawyer, sr. partner Gibson, Gibson & Crispe; teacher and track coach N.Y. Mil. Acad, N.Y, 23-24. Mil. Serv: Army, Col, G.S.C, War Dept; served overseas with combat div; Silver Star; Legion of Merit; Purple Heart; War Dept. Citation Medals. Mem: Past nat. chmn. Com. to Defend Am. by Aiding the Allies; Vt. Bar Asn; Mason; Odd Fellow; Elk; Eagle. Rel: Episcopalian. Mailing Add: Fed. Court Bldg, Brattleboro, Vt. 05301. (1967)

GIBSON, JAMES ISAAC D
Nev. State Sen.
b. Golden, Colo, 3/22/25; s. Fred Daniel Gibson and May Emma Borsberry G; m. 6/23/47 to Audrey June Brinley; c. James Brinley, David Scott, Robin

Lee, Terry Lynn, Cynthia Rae and Holly Jo. Educ: Univ. Kans, 43-44; Univ. Colo, 44; U.S. Nacal Acad, B.S, 47; Rensselaer Polytech. Inst, B.C.E, 48, M.C.E, 50; Sigma Xi. Polit. & Govt. Pos: Trustee, Henderson Sch. Dist, Nev, 54-56; Nev. State Assemblyman, 58-66; mem, Interim Finance Cmt, 60-, chmn, 66; mem, Legis. Cmn, 62-, chmn, 65 & 67; mem. adv. bd, Bur. Land Mgt, Nev. and Desert Research Inst, Univ. Nev, 60-; Nev. State Sen, First Dist, 67-; v.pres, West. Conf, Coun. State Govt, 68, pres, 69. Bus. & Prof. Pos: Asst. chief engr, West. Electro Chem. Co, 53-54, chief engr, 54-55; plant engr, Am. Potash & Cehm. Corp, 55-61, adv. engr, 58-61; chief engr, Pac. Eng. & Prod, 61-66, exec. v.pres, 66- Mil. Serv: Entered as A/S, Navy, 43, released as Lt, 53, after serv. in 104th Construction Bn, Provost Marshall, Port Hueneme, Staff, Pub. Works Off, Potomac River Naval Command; Am. Theater and Korean Campaign Ribbons. Mem: Nat. and Nev. Soc. Prfnl. Engrs; Soc. of Mil. Engrs; Registered Prfnl. Engr; Soc. Plant Engrs, Nev. and Ariz; Am. Legion Post 40; v.pres, Boulder Dam Area Coun, Boy Scouts, 66-. Silver Beaver Award, Boy Scouts, 69. Rel: Latter-day Saint; Stake Pres, Lake Mead Stake. Mailing Add: 117 Beech, Henderson, Nev. 89015.

GIBSON, JAMES OLIVER D

b. Atlanta, Ga, 4/1/34; s. Calvin Harrison Gibson, Sr. and Julia G; m. 7/18/64 to Kathryn DeFrantz; c. Julia Louise. Educ: Duquesne Univ, B.A, 56; Atlanta Univ, 59-60; Temple Univ, 60-61; Sigma Tau Delta; Alpha Psi Omega. Polit. & Govt. Pos: Consult, White House Conf. on Civil Rights, 65-66; consult, U.S. Civil Serv. Cmn, 66-68; mem, President's Nat. Adv. Cmn. on Rural Poverty, 67-68; consult, U.S. Bur. Census, U.S. Dept. Health, Educ. and Welfare and U.S. Dept. Housing and Urban Develop, 67-69; del, Dem. Nat. Conv, 68; consult, U.S. Dept. Agr, 68-69; mem, Nat. Capital Planning Cmn, 68- Bus. & Prof. Pos: Reporter and columnist, The Atlanta Inquirer, Atlanta, Ga, 60-61; prog. dir, Flanner House, Indianapolis, Ind, 63-64; dir. neighborhood develop. prog, United Planning Orgn, Wash, D.C, 64-66; exec. assoc, Potomac Inst, 66- Mil. Serv: Entered as E-1, Army, 56, released as E-5, 59, after serv. in 11th Armored Cavalry Regt, ETO, West Germany, 57-59. Publ: 'Rural Poverty: Challenge to An Urban Society,' Am. Voc. J, 11/68; 'Black Art,' The Wash. Post STYLE, 1/69; 'Ghetto Economic Development,' Civil Rights Quart, summer 69. Mem: Nat. Asn. Intergroup Rels. Off; Urban Am; Nat. Asn. Commun. Develop; life mem, NAACP (exec. secy, Atlanta, Ga. Chap, 61-63); Wash. Planning and Housing Asn; New Sch. of Afro-Am. Thought; Am. Dem. Action; Am. Civil Liberties Union. Unheralded Citizen of the Year, Atlanta YMCA, 62. Mailing Add: 3462 Macomb St. N.W, Washington, D.C. 20016.

GIBSON, JARRETT DEMPSEY D

W.Va. State Del.

b. Dunbar, W.Va, 2/21/27; s. George W. Gibson and Susie Pribble G; m. 10/23/47 to Maxine Jewel Hager; c. Tami Ann. Educ: Morris Harvey Col, 45-46. Polit. & Govt. Pos: Committeeman, W.Va. Dem. Party, 69-; W.Va. State Del, 69- Bus. & Prf. Pos: Owner, Gibson's Furniture Co. Inc, Nitro, W.Va, 56-61 and St. Albans, W.Va, 61-69. Mil. Serv: Air Force, 51-55, 56, S/Sgt, with serv. in Air Defense Command, Colorado Springs, Colo. Mem: C. of C. (pres, St. Albans Chap, state dir, W.Va. Chap); Lions; Elks; Am. Legion. Named Businessman of the Year. Rel: Baptist. Legal Res: 924 Helene St, St. Albans, W.Va. 25177. Mailing Add: 2412 Kanawha Terr, St. Albans, W.Va. 25177.

GIBSON, JOHN S. D

Councilman, Los Angeles, Calif.

b. Geneseo, Kans, 8/11/02; s. John Samuel Gibson and Flora Dix G; m. 1/16/21 to Mina Workman; c. Marlyn (Mrs. Buehler) and Dixie (Mrs. Blackwelder); ten grandchildren. Educ: Kans. Univ, ½year; Am. Inst. of Banking of Los Angeles and Calif. Real Estate Asn. Polit. & Govt. Pos: City police judge, Geneseo, Kans, mayor, 23; councilman, 15th Dist, Los Angeles, Calif, 51-, pres, 53-61; chmn, City Coun. Planning Cmt. Bus. & Prof. Pos: Assoc. with George M. Bronaugh, gen. contractor, San Pedro, 34-41; gen. contractor, 41- Mem: Pres, Calif-Israel C. of C, 54-60, hon. pres; former first v.pres. of mayor's and councilmen's dept, League of Calif. Cities; v.pres, Calif. State Jr. C. of C, 36-37; Town Hall; Mason; Shrine; Elks; Commandery; KT; Tenth Dist. PTA; v.pres, Pac. Southwest Youth for Christ in Los Angeles; Christian Bus. Men's Asn. Founder, first Boys' Club in Calif, 35. Rel: Baptist; Bd. of Deacons, First Baptist Church, San Pedro. Legal Res: 1604 Sunnyside Terr, San Pedro, Calif. 90732. Mailing Add: 317 City Hall, Los Angeles, Calif. 90012. (1967)

GIBSON, JOSEPH RICHARD D

b. Poca, W.Va, 1/2/30; s. Robert Lawrence Gibson and Fern Shank G; m. 3/25/51 to Rosalie Kind; c. Angela Lynn, Alice Dorence, Karen Danele, Joseph Richard, Jr. and Jeffery Dwayne. Educ: Charleston Sch. of Commerce; Int. Acct. Soc, extended studies. Polit. & Govt. Pos: Pres, Putnam Co. Young Dem. Club, councilman, Bancroft; W.Va. State Del, 64-66. Bus. & Prof. Pos: Merchant and chem. worker. Mil. Serv: Korean War. Mem: UMW. Rel: Church of God Mission. Mailing Add: Route 1, Bancroft, W.Va. 25011. (1967)

GIBSON, L. P. 'PETE' D

b. Bainbridge, Ga, 11/1/22; m. to Jimmie O'Quinn; c. Margaret Gretchen, Harriette Elizabeth, Paul Harper and Robin Arlene. Educ: Univ. of Fla, A.A, 42; Fla. State Univ, B.S, 53; Sigma Nu. Polit. & Govt. Pos: Fla. State Sen, 62-68; asst. civil defense dir, Taylor Co, Fla. Bus. & Prof. Pos: Timberlands mgr; Fla. Bd. of Forestry; dir, Fla. Sheriff's Boy's Ranch; Tr. Tri Co. Elec. Co-op.(past pres). Mil. Serv: Naval Res. Mem: Mason; Shrine (past pres); Eastern Star (past worthy patron); Am. Legion (past dist. cmdr); 40 et 8; Elks; Rotary; Moose; WOW (past cmdr). One of five Oustanding Young Men, Fla. Jr. C. of C, 57. Rel: Methodist. 1967 Legal Res: Perry, Fla. No mailing address available. (1967)

GIBSON, ROBERT EDWARD D

Va. State Del.

b. Norfolk Co, Va, 5/15/18; m. to Margaret Elizabeth McHorney. Educ: Hampden-Sydney Col; Univ. Richmond, LL.B. Polit. & Govt. Pos: Asst. trial justice, South Norfolk, Va, 47; town attorney, Portlock, 48-50; commonwealth's attorney, South Norfolk, 51-56; Va. State Del, 62- Bus. & Prof. Pos: Lawyer. Mem: Va. State Bar Asn; Chesapeake Better Bus. Club; Delta Theta Phi; former pres, South Norfolk Jr. C. of C; Nat. Asn. Housing and Redevelop. Off; Harbor Club. Rel: Christian Church. Mailing Add: Box 5025, Chesapeake, Va. 23324.

GIBSON, ROBERT GLENN D

b. Flat River, Mo, 9/8/27; s. Glenn H. Gibson and Viola Amos G; m. 9/1/50 to Martha Evelyn Helton; c. Marsha and Randy. Polit. & Govt. Pos: Chmn. and cmnr, Granite City Housing Authority, Ill, 56-61; chmn, Granite City Dem. Cent. Cmt, 58-62; v.chmn, Madison Co. Dem. Cent. Cmt, 58-62; del, White House Conf. on Children, 60; pres, Young Dem, Ill, 60-62; treas, Young Dem. Am, 61-63; cmnr, Ill. Pub. Aid Cmn, 63-; del, Dem. Nat. Conv, 64 & 68. Bus. & Prof. Pos: Secy-treas, Ill. State AFL-CIO, 63- Mil. Serv: Entered as A/S, Coast Guard, 45, released as Seaman 1/C, 46; Am. and S.Pac. Theater Ribbons. Mem: Am. Pub. Health Asn; Nat. Coun. on the Aging; Nat. Coun. Sr. Citizens; USW; VFW; Elks; state pres, USO; bd. of dirs, Mid Am. Chap, Red Cross. Rel: Presbyterian. Legal Res: 1507 W. Touhy, Chicago, Ill. 60626. Mailing Add: 300 N. State, Chicago, Ill. 60610.

GIBSON, THEODORE MORTON R

Chmn, Burke Co. Rep. Party, N.Dak.

b. Great Falls, Mont, 1/14/16; s. Nathan Gibson and Wilma Grubb G; m. 8/1/41 to Alvera Nancy Enget; c. Theadonna (Mrs. Johnson), Jeraldine Ann, Nathan Theodore and Vaughn Ellis. Polit. & Govt. Pos: Mem, Burke Co. Sch. Bd, N.Dak, 51-54; mayor, Powers Lake, 56-64; mem, Burke Co. Water and Flood Control Bd, 58-66; chmn, Burke Co. Rep. Party, currently. Bus. & Prof. Pos: Employee, N.Am. Aviation, 41; sales agent, Standard Oil Co, 45- Mil. Serv: Entered as Pvt, Army Air Force, 42, released as Cpl, 45, after serv. in Fourth Dep. Rep. Squadron, Fifth Air Force, S.W. Pac. Theater; Good Conduct and Asiatic-Pac. Serv. Medals; Philippine Liberation Medal with one Bronze Serv. Star. Mem: Am. Legion; pres, Commun. Club, 53-56; Farm Bur. Rel: Baptist. Mailing Add: Powers Lake, N.Dak. 58773. (1967)

GIBSON, TYREE JIM D

b. Memphis, Tenn, 10/16/21; s. James Gibson and Minnie Moore G; m. 4/18/60 to Letral Adams; c. Debra, Chere, Christopher and Gregory. Educ: Ford Motor Co. Sch, salesman course, 65-66; Dale Carnegie sales course, currently. Polit. & Govt. Pos: Co. committeeman, 53rd Dem. Assembly Dist, Calif, 60-; campaign mgr, Lt. Gov. Glen Anderson, 64; spec. asst. to Sen. Mervin Diamond, 65; spec. asst. to Calif. State Assemblyman Bill Greene, 68- Bus. & Prof. Pos: Employee, Gen. Motors, South Gate, 52-60; owner meat mkt, Santa Barbara, Calif, 60-63; salesman, O'Connor Lincoln & Mercury, 65- Mil. Serv: Pfc, Army, 41-45 serv. in 93rd Inf. Div, Pac; Res, 45-60; five battle stars. Mem: Pres, Wall St. Dem. Club. Rel: Baptist. Mailing Add: 4106 S. Wall St, Los Angeles, Calif. 90011.

GIBSON, WILLIAM L. R

Fla. State Rep.

b. 10/3/06, Huntington, W.Va; m. Ocie A. Mossburg; c. Patricia (Mrs. E. Stallings), William L, Jr, Karl B. and Gregory T. Educ: Univ. Md; George Wash. Univ. Polit. & Govt. Pos: Fla. State Rep, 45th Dist, 67- Bus. & Prof. Pos: Security supvr, Avco Missile Div, Cape Kennedy, 3 years. Mil. Serv: Col, Air Force, World War II, Col.(Ret), 62; Air Force Commendation Medal with two Oak Leaf Clusters; Am. Campaign Medal; European-African-Mid. East. Campaign Medal; Asiatic-Pac. Campaign Medal; World War II Victory Medal; Medal for Humane Action; Nat. Defense Serv. Medal and Air Force Serv. Award with three Bronze Oak Leaf Clusters. Mem: Mason; Seminole Sojourners; Leaf Soc; ROA; Air Force Asn; Retired Citizens Asn; Fla. Fedn. of Sr. Clubs; Cent. Fla. Traffic Club; Orlando Area C. of C; past v.pres. and state secy, W.Va. Jr. C. of C; past pres, YMCA Y's Men Club and Tri-State Nat. Aeronaut. Asn. One of Nation's First Transportation Brokers; Licensed by Atomic Energy Cmn. as Radiation Control Officer; Fed. Aviation Agency Commercial Pilot License. Rel: Methodist. Mailing Add: 1432 Knollwood Circle, Orlando, Fla. 32804.

GIEBLER, RICHARD OWEN R

Chmn, Franklin Co. Rep. Cent. Cmt, Mo.

b. Washington, Mo, 1/22/38; s. John Thomas Giebler and Hilda Marie Gilgrease G; m. 8/25/62 to Barbara Ann Block; c. Karen Marie and Denise Louise. Educ: Wash. Univ, 59; Southeast Mo. State Col, B.S, 62; Southwest Mo. State Col, 66; Sigma Phi Epsilon. Polit. & Govt. Pos: Twp. committeeman, Franklin Co. Rep. Cent. Cmt, Mo, 62-, treas, 66-68, chmn, 68-; pres, BOLES-Calvey Rep. Club, 65-66. Bus. & Prof. Pos: Teacher, Rockwood High Schs, 62-67; sr. salesman, Addison Wesley Publ, 67- Mil. Serv: Entered as Pvt, Army, 56, released as Sgt, 59, after serv. in Armor. Mem: Mo. State Teachers Asn; Zeta Chap, Prfnl. Bookmen of Am; Pac. Jaycees; Mo. Jaycees; U.S. Jaycees; Mo. and Franklin Co. Hist. Socs. Mailing Add: R.R. 2, Pacific, Mo. 63069.

GIERAU, PAUL WILLIAM, III D

Chmn, Keya Paha Co. Dem. Party, Nebr.

b. Milboro, S.Dak, 6/4/30; s. Paul W. Gierau and Byrle Manifold G; m. 6/5/52 to Arlene Joyce Clark; c. Pamela Sue, Valissa Lynn and Teri Ann. Educ: Chadron State Col, 1 year; Thespians. Polit. & Govt. Pos: Chmn, Keya Paha Co. Dem. Party, Nebr, 60- Bus. & Prof. Pos: Auctioneer; master of ceremonies for numerous announcing P.A. Systs. Mil. Serv: Entered as A/S, Navy, 48, released as Seaman, 49. Mem: Educ. Corp.(co. pres); Tri-Co. Exten. Bd.(pres); Elks; Local and Nat. Hereford Orgns; Nebr. Stockgrowers Asn. Rel: Methodist. Mailing Add: Springview, Nebr. 68778.

GIERSDORF, J. ROBERT D

b. Thompson Falls, Mont, 2/24/35; s. Joseph Robert Giersdorf and Genevieve Nicolas G; m. 6/24/69 to Lorraine V. Heinle; c. Deborah Gay and David Alan. Educ: Univ. Ore, 52-54; Skull and Dagger; Sigma Chi. Polit. & Govt. Pos: Alaska State Rep, v.chmn, State Affairs Cmt. and Mem, Commerce and Labor Cmts, Alaska House of Rep, 59-60; mem, Alaska Legis. Coun, 59-60; del, Dist. and State Conv; dist. committeeman, precinct chmn. and v.chmn, Cent. Dist. Cmt, Dem. Party; del, Dem. Nat. Conv, 60, alternate del, 64 & 68. Bus. & Prof. Pos: Transportation agent, Northwest Orient Airlines, 55-56; sta. mgr, North. Consolidated Airlines, 56-59; dist. sales mgr, Alaska Airlines, Inc, 59-62, asst. v.pres. and gen. sales mgr, 62-63, v.pres. traffic and sales, 63- Mem: Dir, Alaska Travel Promotion Asn, pres, 60-63, v.pres.

and v.pres. in charge of advert; bd. gov, Seattle Tourist and Conv. Bur. and West. Am. Conv. and Travel Inst; Lions; Fairbanks Jr. C. of C; Sen, Jr. Chamber Int; Dem. Club, Fairbanks; finance chmn, Highline Dist. Coun, Boy Scouts. Rel: Protestant. Mailing Add: 12852 S.E. 265th, Kent, Wash. 98031.

GIESEN, ARTHUR ROSSA, JR. 'PETE' R
Va. State Del.
b. Radford, Va, 8/8/32; m. to Dorothy Ann Hopkins. Educ: Yale, B.A, 54; Harvard Grad. Sch. Bus. Admin, M.B.A, 56. Polit. & Govt. Pos: Mem, Va. Rep. State Cent. Cmt; Va. State Del, 64-; Rep. nominee, U.S. Rep, Va, 68. Bus. & Prof. Pos: Pres. and treas, Augusta Steel Corp. Mem: Bd. trustees, Marion Col; Staunton Chap, Va. Asn. Ment. Health; Staunton Cmt, United Negro Col. Fund. Rel: Lutheran; Church Coun; chmn, Christian Educ. Cmt. Mailing Add: 891 Preston Dr, Scranton, Va. 24401. (1967)

GIESEY, WALTER W. D
b. Utica, N.Y, 3/20/24; s. Wilfrid Marcellus Giesey and Genevieve Turner G; single. Educ: Univ. Pittsburgh, 2 years. Polit. & Govt. Pos: Pub. rels. secy, Mayor's Off, Pittsburgh, Pa, 50-54, exec. secy, 54-59; secy. admin. and exec. secy, Gov. Off, Pa, 59-63; staff dir, President's Cmt. on Equal Opportunity in Housing, Wash, D.C, 63-68; exec. asst. to chmn, Dem. Nat. Cmt, 68; alternate del, Dem. Nat. Conv, 68. Bus. & Prof. Pos: Assoc. ed, Pittsburgh Bul-Index, 45-49; consult, various orgn, 69- Mil. Serv: Entered as Aviation Cadet, Army Air Force, 42, released as 2nd Lt, 45, after serv. in Continental U.S, 42-45. Mailing Add: 3808 Fulton St. N.W, Washington, D.C. 20007.

GIESICK, GARY RONALD R
Mont. State Rep.
b. Billings, Mont, 4/9/41; s. Elmer Giesick and Wilma Roe G; m. 3/22/68 to Linda Reichenbach; c. Tamra. Educ: Rocky Mt. Col, 3 years; Univ. of Mont, 1 year; Rho Alpha Rho. Polit. & Govt. Pos: Pres, Yellowstone Co. Young Rep, Mont, 65-66; Mont. State Rep, Dist. Nine, 66- Bus. & Prof. Pos: Self-employed farmer and livestock feeder. Mem: Mont. Farm Bur. Fedn; AF&AM; Scottish Rite. Int. Farm Youth Exchange Del. to N.Z, 63-64. Rel: Protestant. Mailing Add: Route 4 Central, Billings, Mont. 59102.

GIETZEN, WILLIAM NICHOLAS D
Mem, N.Dak. Dem. Non-Partisan League Legis. Coun.
b. Morton Co, N.Dak, 11/1/92; s. Peter Joseph Gietzen and Elizabeth Simon G; m. 6/29/19 to Anna Lou Hartman; c. Mary Ann (Mrs. Evenson), William Frederic, Robert Paul and Betty Lou (Mrs. Remmick). Educ: Assumption Abbey, Richardton, N.Dak, prep sch, 08-09. Polit. & Govt. Pos: Clerk of sch, N.Dak, 22-23; sch. dir, 23-28; twp. supvr, 28-40, chmn. bd, 31-40; precinct committeeman, N.Dak. Dem. Non-Partisan League, 28-58; chmn. bd, 48-60, city alderman, 48-66; mem, N.Dak. Dem. Non-Partisan League Co. Cmt, 58-66; N.Dak. State Rep, 61-66; mem, Policy, Population, Subdiv. and Urban Affairs Cmts, N.Dak. Non-Partisan League Legis. Coun, 64- Bus. & Prof. Pos: Owner and operator, Livestock and grain farm, 16-61; owner and mgr, City Milk Supply, 37-44; owner, restaurant, 45-54; cmn. agent, Greyhound Bus Lines, 45-59; temporary adminstr, nursing home, 69. Mem: Hon. mem, K. of C; N.Dak. Farmers Union. Rel: Roman Catholic. Legal Res: 302 Ash Ave. W, Glen Ullin, N.Dak. 58631. Mailing Add: Box 95, Glen Ullin, N.Dak. 58631.

GIFFEY, DONALD FRANCIS D
N.Dak. State Rep.
b. Minot, N.Dak, 10/4/20; s. Ernest Giffey, Sr. and Marvelle Larson G; m. 2/27/44 to Avis Thompson; c. Nancy Carol (Mrs. John Renhowe) and Donald C. Educ: Makoti High Sch. Polit. & Govt. Pos: N.Dak. State Rep, 61-, Majority Floor Leader, N.Dak. State House of Rep, 65, Asst. Minority Leader, 67. Bus. & Prof. Pos: Owner, grain farm; mem, bd. of dirs, Garrison Farmers Union Elevator. Rel: Lutheran. Mailing Add: Roseglen, N.Dak. 58775.

GIFFORD, WILLIAM LEO R
b. Weston, Conn, 8/30/30; s. Rolland Wyckoff Gifford and Margaret Mary Clifford G; m. 10/27/56 to Marion Frances Miletti; c. Margaret Rose, William Leo, Jr. and David Wyckoff. Educ: Fordham Univ, A.B, 52; Univ. Conn. Sch. Law, 52-55. Polit. & Govt. Pos: Spec. Asst. to Secy. Labor for Legis. Affairs, 69- Bus. & Prof. Pos: Reporter, various newspapers. Mem: Nat. Press Club. Rel: Roman Catholic. Legal Res: 43 Walnut St, Jamestown, N.Y. 14701. Mailing Add: 1106 Neal Dr, Alexandria, Va. 22308.

GIGERICH, WILLIAM EDWARD D
b. Indianapolis, Ind, 9/10/44; s. Lawrence A. Gigerich and Eva Faye Vestal G; m. 6/19/65 to Carolyn Sue Vasil; c. Lawrence Edward. Educ: Cathedral High Sch, Indianapolis, Ind. Polit. & Govt. Pos: Dem. precinct committeeman, Indianapolis, Ind, 66-; campaign asst, Ind. State Dem. Cmt, 68; asst. to Marion Co. Chmn, 68; campaign asst, Robert Kennedy Campaign, Ind, Ore. & N.Y, 68; del, Dem. Nat. Conv, 68; spec. asst. to congressman, Andrew Jacobs, 11th dist, Ind, 69- Bus. & Prof. Pos: Data processing supvr, Merchants Bank, Indianapolis, 62-68; bus. mgr, WTLC Radio, 68- Mem: Young Dem; E.Side Dem. Club; Rel: Catholic. Mailing Add: 3630 Watson Rd, Indianapolis, Ind. 46205.

GIGUERE, NOEL A. D
b. Woonsocket, R.I, 12/25/05. Educ: Sacred Heart Sch. Polit. & Gov. Pos: R.I. State Rep, 55-66; City Coun, 52. Bus. & Prof. Pos: Owner, cleansing plant. Mem: Gen. Stephan Moglar Assembly; Mod. Woodmen of Am; K. of C. Coun No. 113, 4th degree. Mailing Add: 342 Paradis Ave, Woonsocket, R.I. 02895. (1967)

GILBERT, ANDREW JACKSON D
b. Sun, La, 7/29/07; s. Andrew Jackson Gilbert and Nannie Mai Barbee G; m. 11/7/32 to Helen Grace Hawkins; c. Andrew Jackson, III and Nancy Ann. Educ: Univ. Ariz, B.S. in civil eng, 29; Tau Beta Pi; Theta Tau; Phi Kappa Phi. Polit. Pos: Speaker, Ariz. House of Rep, 65-66. Bus. & Prof. Pos: Pres, Gilbert Construct. Co, 46- Mil. Serv: Entered as Lt.(jg), Navy, 42, released as Lt, 46, after serv. in Civil Eng. Corps, S.Pac, 44-45; Iwo Jima Campaign Ribbons; Lt.(Ret), Naval Res, 55. Mem: Am. Inst. Mining Engrs; Masons; Am. Legion; Kiwanis; Elks. Rel: Protestant. Mailing Add: 204 Vista, Warren, Ariz. 85642. (1967)

GILBERT, J. C. D
La. State Sen.
b. Gilbert, La, 3/6/22; s. Jess C. Gilbert and Fannie Adams G; m. 7/10/46 to Barbara Jane Peck; c. Barbara (Mrs. Enright) and Jess, Jr. Educ: Northeast Jr. Col, 2 years; La. State Univ, Baton Rouge, ½ year; La. State Univ, Chambers, 1 year. Polit. & Govt. Pos: Police juror, Catahoula Parish, La, 56-60; La. State Sen, 60- Bus. & Prof. Pos: Farmer. Mil. Serv: Entered as Pvt, Army Air Force, 42, released as Sgt. Maj, 46, after serv. in Eighth Air Force, ETO (Eng. and Africa), 43-45. Mem: Am. Legion; Farm Bur; Cattlemens Asn; Mason; Shrine. Rel: Methodist. Mailing Add: Sicily Island, La. 71368.

GILBERT, JACOB H. D
U.S. Rep, N.Y.
b. Bronx, N.Y, 6/17/20; m. June 1949 to Irma Steuer; c. Miriam Sharon, Sandra and Samuel Stephen. Educ: St. John's Col; St. John's Law Sch, LL.B, 43. Polit. & Govt. Pos: Asst. corp. counsel, N.Y.C, 49-50; N.Y. State Assemblyman, 51-54; N.Y. State Sen, 55-60; U.S. Rep, N.Y, 60-, mem, Cmt. on Ways and Means, U.S. House of Rep. Bus. & Prof. Pos: Attorney, Foley, Hickey, Gilbert and Currie, N.Y.C. Mem: Bronx Co. Bar Asn; Fed. Bar Asn. of N.Y, N.J. and Conn; N.Y. Trial Lawyer's Asn; Nat. Dem. Club; Bronx River YM-YWHA; AFL-CIO; Adv. Bd. of Commun. Centre P.S.65; South Bronx Commun. Coun; NAACP, Bronx Chap, N.Y; Bronx C. of C; B'nai B'rith; Am. Jewish Cong; Bronx Boys Club; Bronx Lions Club. Rel: Jewish. Legal Res: 1160 Evergreen Ave, Bronx, N.Y. Mailing Add: 2429 Rayburn House Office Bldg. N.W, Washington, D.C. 20515.

GILBERT, JOHN G. R
Ill. State Sen.
b. Carbondale, Ill, 2/4/12; s. John P. Gilbert and Dora Gray G; m. 6/17/39 to Helen Dollins; c. Pamela, Gail and Phil. Educ: South. Ill. Univ, B.Ed, 33; Univ. Ill, LL.B, 38. Polit. & Govt. Pos: Spec. agent, Fed. Bur. Invest, 42-44; states attorney, Jackson Co, Ill, 48-56; Ill. State Sen, 56th Dist, 60- Mil. Serv: Entered as Lt.(jg), Naval Res, 44, released as Lt, 46. Mem: Jackson Co. and Ill. State Bar Asns; Ill. Asn. of Professions; Elks; Eagles; C. of C; Am. Legion; United Cerebral Palsy Asn. Rel: Methodist. Legal Res: 513 W. Walnut, Carbondale, Ill. 62901. Mailing Add: P.O. Box 1054, Carbondale, Ill. 62901.

GILBERT, LELA S. R
b. Goessel, Kans; married; c. one daughter. Educ: Law degree, bachelor's and master's degrees in polit. sci; presently completing work for Ph.D. Polit. & Govt. Pos: Colo. State Rep, 57-63. Bus. & Prof. Pos: Attorney; taught polit. sci, Univ. Colo, 1 semester; taught bus. law, Metrop. State Col, Denver, 68-69. Mailing Add: 1165 S. Dale Court, Denver, Colo. 80219.

GILBERT, ROBERT BACON, JR. D
b. Greenville, Ga, 9/27/05; s. Dr. Robert Bacon Gilbert and Marilu Irvin G. Educ: Mercer Univ, 29-31; Cumberland Univ, LL.B, 33; Blue Key; Sigma Delta Kappa; Lambda Chi Alpha; Cauldron; bus. mgr, Col. Annual; M Club; mgr, football team. Polit. & Govt. Pos: Mem, Ga. State Dem. Exec. Cmt, 44-46 & 63-66; mem, Co. Dem. Exec. Cmt, 46-66; del, Dem. Nat. Conv, 48, 52 & 64, alternate del, 68; mem, Gov. Staff, 63-66; mem, Ga. Dem. Cmt. of One Hundred, 65-66; mem, President Club; mem, Fulton Co. Dem. 500 Club. Bus. & Prof. Pos: Owner, Greenville Cotton Warehouses, 46-66; dir, Kennesaw Life & Accident Ins. Co, 58-66; dir, Atlanta Int. Raceway, 60-64; dir, Ga. Cotton Warehouse & Compress Asn, 60-66; dir, Md. Nat. Ins. Co, 63-66. Mem: Atlanta Athletic Club; C. of C; Commerce Club; Farm Bur; Cherokee Town and Country Club; Elks. Rel: Baptist. Mailing Add: Box 236, Greenville, Ga. 30222.

GILBERT, SYLVIO JOSEPH R
b. Augusta, Maine, 7/1/14; s. Augustin Joseph Gilbert (deceased) and Anna Gilbert G.(deceased); m. 10/7/40 to Jacqueline Pelletier; c. Anne Marie (Mrs. Hans Peter Bernau) and Jeanne Marie (Mrs. Walter MacFarland). Educ: St. Augustine Elem. Sch, 8 years; spec. night courses. Polit. & Govt. Pos: With Fed. Construction Prog, Augusta, Maine, 32-34; retail and wholesale dept, State Liquor Cmn, 34-37; mem, Bd. of Registrn, 46-48; mayor, Augusta, Maine, 59-69, tax assessor, 69-; Maine State Sen, Kennebec Co, 61-62, chmn, Pub. Utilities Cmt, Maine State Senate, 61-62. Bus. & Prof. Pos: Garage and automobile dealership, Augusta, Maine, 38-62; broker, Nat. Distillers Prod. Co, 63-69; played, managed, coached and scouted baseball, 31-67. Mem: Elks; Calumet Club (former pres); Order of Eagles; Maine Munic. Asn.(former pres. and dir); K. of C.(4°); Am. Munic. Cong.(various cmts). Assoc. Press and United Press Int. Award; Radio and TV Award for Outstanding Story for Legis. Document SP 1188, 61; Am. Legion Award for Outstanding Work with Youth, 61; B'nai B'rith Award, 61; Calumet Club Award for Outstanding Commun. Work, 61; City of Augusta Award for Outstanding Performance, 68; new elem. sch. in Augusta named the Sylvio J. Gilbert Sch, 69. Rel: Catholic. Legal Res: 82 Western Ave, Augusta, Maine 04330. Mailing Add: Box 150, Augusta, Maine 04330.

GILBERT, THOMAS MARTIN D
b. Elkmont, Ala; s. Van Buren Gilbert and Mary McWilliams G; single. Educ: Athens Col, A.B, 49; Am. Univ, grad. work. Polit. & Govt. Pos: Admin. asst, U.S. Rep. Armistead Selden, 53-69 and U.S. Rep. George Andrews, Ala, 69- Mil. Serv: Entered as Seaman, Navy, 45, released as PO, 46. Rel: Episcopal. Legal Res: Greensboro, Ala. Mailing Add: Apt. 1122, 2000 S. Eads St, Arlington, Va. 22202.

GILBERT, WILLIAM LEWIS D
b. Pelham, N.Y, 4/22/15; s. Lewis Gilbert and Betty Stewart G; m. 8/19/40 to Margaret Ruth Holmes; c. Joann (Mrs. R. von Sternberg) and Virginia L. (Mrs. Kirk Robertson). Educ: N.Y. Univ, B.S. cum laude in Indust. Eng. and Bus. Admin; Mass. Inst. Tech, grad. study; Delta Mu Delta. Polit. & Govt. Pos: Affiliate mem, Calif. State Dem. Cent. Cmt; mem, Dist. Attorney's Adv. Coun. and various local and fed. govt. cmts. and cmns, including War Labor Bd, 41-; del. and alternate del, Dem. Nat. Conv, 60 & 64; secy, Los Angeles Co. Dem. Cent. Cmt, Calif, 61-64. Bus. & Prof. Pos: Officer and rep, various nat. and local unions, 36-50; field rep, Nat. AFL-CIO, 50-63, dir, Los Angeles-Orange Co. Orgn. Cmt, 63-68 and asst. regional dir. for Calif, Ariz. and Nev, 68- Mil. Serv: Entered as Pvt, Army Air Corps, 44,

released as Sgt, 46, after serv. with Aviation Engrs; Good Conduct Medal. Publ: Various articles in labor and polit. publ, Mem: IAMAW; United Furniture Workers; Religion and Labor Coun; NAACP; Urban League Emergency Cmn. to Aid Farm Workers; Dem. Vol. Cmt; Dem. Assocs. and other Dem. groups; Indust. Rels. Res. Asn.(pres, South. Calif. Chap, currently); Am. Legion. Rel: Protestant. Mailing Add: 2016 Strand, Manhattan Beach, Calif. 90266.

GILCHRIST, JAMES ROBERT D
b. Athens, Ala, 8/31/27; s. Claude B. Gilchrist and Mary Emily Bush G; m. 6/9/55 to Margaret Sample; c. Margaret Ruth, Helen Jennette. Educ: Univ. of Ala, B.A, 52; LL.B, 55. Polit. & Govt. Pos: Ala. State Sen, 63-66; Ala. State Rep, 55-63. Bus. & Prof. Pos: Lawyer. Mil. Serv: Navy, 46-48. Mem: Kiwanis; Delta Chi; Pi Alpha Delta; Am. Legion; Ala. Bar Asn. Rel: Methodist. Mailing Add: P.O. 312, Decatur, Ala. 35601. (1967)

GILCHRIST, LAWRENCE BARNT R
Chmn, Franklin Co. Rep. Cent. Cmt, Iowa
b. Denison, Iowa, 8/13/32; s. L. V. Gilchrist and Genevieve Barnt G; m. 5/19/56 to Wilda Jean Williams; c. Lawrence Wesley, Margaret Ann, Julie Diane and Elizabeth Jean. Educ: Coe Col, B.A, 54; Iowa Univ. Law Sch, J.D, 60; Phi Alpha Delta; Alpha Sigma Phi. Polit. & Govt. Pos: Co. attorney, Franklin Co, Iowa, 63-67; chmn, Franklin Co. Rep. Cent. Cmt, 66- Mil. Serv: Entered as 2nd Lt, Air Force, 55, released as 1st Lt, 58; Capt, Air Force Res, 62. Mem: Iowa State and Franklin Co. Bar Asns; Res. Officers Asn; pres, Hampton Jaycees, 65-66; v.chmn, North Iowa Red Cross, 63-66; v.pres, Hampton C. of C, 63; VFW; Farm Bur; Forum Club. Rel: Methodist; mem. bd, NIACC Found, 68- Mailing Add: Route 3, Hampton, Iowa 50441.

GILDEA, AUSTIN CORNELIUS D
b. Elkhart, Ind, 9/7/06; s. Augustine R. Gildea and Mary McCurry G; m. 11/22/36 to Margueritte Clair; c. John R. and Kathleen (Mrs. Swanton). Educ: Univ. Notre Dame, LL.B, 30. Polit. & Govt. Pos: Justice of the Peace, Concord Twp, Ind, 30-33; pres, Jefferson Club, Elkhart Co, 30-34; local counsel, Home Owners Loan Corp, 34-41; Elkhart city attorney, 41-51; del, Dem. State Conv, 32-64; del, Dem. Nat. Conv, 68. Mem: Am. and Ind. State Bar Asns; Elkhart Co. Bar Asn.(pres, 65); Elkhart City Bar Asn.(pres, 57); pres, Elkhart Co. Soc. Crippled Children and Adults; former pres, Elkhart Symphony Soc; former pres, Elkhart Concert Club, currently, dir. Rel: Roman Catholic. Mailing Add: 5 St. Joseph Manor, Elkhart, Ind. 46514.

GILE, ROBERT HALL R
N.H. State Rep.
b. Providence, R.I, 11/26/33; s. Alonzo Robertson Gile and Inza Winona Hall G; m. July, 1960 to Charlotte Alice Pillion; c. John Pillion. Educ: Dartmouth Col, A.B, 56; Georgetown Univ, 59-60; Delta Sigma Rho; Delta Upsilon Undergrad. Coun; pres, Forensic Union; chmn, Dartmouth Col. Conf. on Polit. Affairs. Polit. & Govt. Pos: Staff mem, N.H. Interim Cmn. on Educ, 62-63; chmn, Hopkinton Town Rep. Cmt, 66-; N.H. State Rep, 67- Bus. & Prof. Pos: Gen. mgr, Gile's Dairy, 63- Mil. Serv: Entered as Ens, Navy, 56, released as Lt, 62, After Serv. in U.S.S. Frank E. Evans, 56-58, Aide to the Commandant, Potomac River Naval Command, 56-61 and U.S.S. Dewey, 61-62; China Serv. Medal; Nat. Defense Serv. Medal; Lt. Comdr, Res, currently. Mem: Trustee, Future Farmers of Am; dir, N.H. Coun. Better Schs; N.H. Milk Dealer's Asn.(pres); C. of C. (pres. Franklin Br); chmn, State Conf. Educ; Rotary; Elks. Rel: Protestant. Legal Res: 1 Checkerberry Lane, Hopkinton, N.H. 03301. Mailing Add: Route 1, Concord, N.H. 03301.

GILES, JACK D
Ala. State Sen.
b. Marion Junction, Ala, 11/21/15; s. Thomas Hendricks Giles and Ora Edens G; m. Marjorie Brown; c. Phyllis Marjorie, Jack, Jr, Judith Elizabeth, Thomas William and Mary Grace. Educ: Snead Col, 2 years; Auburn Univ, 1 year; Univ. Ala, LL.B, 48; Omicron Delta Kappa; Phi Alpha Delta. Polit. & Govt. Pos: Past mem, Madison Co. Dem. Exec. Cmt, Ala; past recorder, Huntsville; past register in Chancery, Madison Co; past mem, Huntsville Planning Cmn; past mem, Huntsville Construction Industs. Appeal Bd; past mem, Huntsville Planning Cmn; past mem, Huntsville Construction Industs. Appeal Bd; past mem, Huntsville City Traffic Study Cmt; past city attorney, Huntsville, 4 years; dir, Ala. Indust. Rels, 63-64; past mem, Gov. Cmt. Status of Women; Dem. presidential elector, 64; past mem, President's Appalachian Regional Cmn; past mem, President's Cmn. for Study of Traffic Courts; v.chmn, Ala. State Sovereignty Cmn, currently; v.chmn, State Ala. Space Sci. Cmn, currently; mem. bd. dirs, Huntsville Indust. Expansion Cmt, currently; Ala. State Sen, Third Dist, currently, v.chmn. municipalities and munic. orgn, local legis. one, judiciary, finance and taxation, educ, agr, milt. and rev. of the journal cmts, Ala. State Sen, currently. Bus. & Prof. Pos: Attorney-at-law, Huntsville. Mil. Serv: Entered Engrs. Corps, released as Capt, after serv. in Aleutian Islands, China-Burma-India Theater, World War II; Lt. Col, Ala. Nat. Guard, 33-; Purple Heart; Am. Defense Medal with Clasp; Am. Theater Campaign Medal; Pac. Asiatic Medal with Four Battle Stars; Victory Medal; Presidential Unit Citation. Mem: Huntsville-Madison Co. Bar Asn. (past pres); bd. trustees, Troy Univ; Ala. Arts Coun; Army Adv. Coun. for Third Army; Rotary; Am. Legion; VFW; DAV. Outstanding Alumnus, Snead Col, 64. Rel: Presbyterian; Deacon, Trustee and past Young Adult Sunday Sch. Class Teacher, Huntsville Cent. Presby. Church. Legal Res: 5832 Criner Rd, Huntsville, Ala. 35802. Mailing Add: 401 Franklin St, Huntsville, Ala. 35802.

GILES, LEON MANSFIELD R
Mem, Calif. Rep. State Cent. Cmt.
b. Savannah, Ga, 10/29/01; s. Phillip Giles and Ruth Price G; div; c. William L. Educ: La Salle Univ, Acct; Phi Beta Sigma. Polit. & Govt. Pos: Mem, Los Angeles Co. and Calif. Rep. State Cent. Cmts, 48-; asst. secy, Calif, Rep. Assembly, 49; cand. for Cong, 26th Dist, Calif, 54 and presidential elector, 56; Rep. nominee, Calif. State Assembly, 62nd Dist, 60. Bus. & Prof. Pos: Field auditor, Atlanta Life Ins. Co, 23-30; home off. mgr. Afro-Am. Life Ins. Co, 30-36; pub. acct, 36-69; retired. Publ: Republican Party and The Negro, 52. Mem: Elks (past pres, Pac. States Asn); Master Mason; RAM; K.T; Shrine (32°); K. of P; C. of C.(past pres, Los Angeles Eastside C. of C); founder, Calif. Mil. Affairs Cmt. Civil Defense Policeman; O.P.A. Selective Serv. Adv. Bd. Scrolls from Presidents Roosevelt and Truman and Gov. Earl Warren. Rel: Episcopal. Mailing Add: 670 E. 36th St, Los Angeles, Calif. 90011.

GILFEATHER, PATRICK JAMES D
Mont. State Sen.
b. Deer Lodge, Mont, 3/28/08; s. Thomas J. Gilfeather and Cora M. Sandidge G; m. 8/7/37 to Margaret L. Raitt; c. G. Grant, Frank L, and Glen P. Educ: Intermountain Union Col, B.A, 30; Univ. Mont. Law Sch, LL.B, 33. Polit. & Govt. Pos: Attorney, Petroleum Co, Mont, 34-36; v.chmn, Cascade Co. Dem. Cent. Cmt, 40-51, chmn, 51-52; asst. attorney gen, State of Mont, 43-45; city attorney, Great Falls, Mont, 50-52; mem, Mont. Legis. Coun, 59-60; Mont. State Rep, 59-60 & 65-67; Mont. State Sen, 67- Mil. Serv: Entered as A/S, Navy, 45, released as Seaman 1/C, 46. Mem: Permanent panelist legal seminars, Nat. Rural Elec. Coop. Asn, 65-; Cascade Co. Bar. Asn.(pres, 49); Elks; Civitans; Am. Legion; Mont. Farmers Union. Rel: Episcopal. Mailing Add: 2816 Fourth Ave. S, Great Falls, Mont. 59401.

GILGOUR, JOHN HENRY R
Committeeman, Caldwell Co. Rep. Cent. Cmt, Mo.
b. Breckenridge, Mo, 4/18/38; s. Clyde Gilgour and Louetta Stout G; m. 8/29/58 to Judith Carol Neiman; c. Mitchell, David, Steven and Richard. Educ: Breckenridge High Sch. Polit. & Govt. Pos: Chmn, Caldwell Co. Rep. Cent. Cmt, Mo, 64-66, committeeman, currently; mem, Coun, Breckenridge, Mo, currently; committeeman, Breckenridge Twp. Rep. Cmt, currently. Mem: V.pres, Lions, currently; pres, Rotary, 62-64; Mason; Mo. Press Asn. Rel: Methodist. Mailing Add: Box 176, Breckenridge, Mo. 64625. (1967)

GILHOOLEY, JOHN JOSEPH R
b. Brooklyn, N.Y, 10/9/21; s. Francis Girard Gilhooley and Ann Flynn G; m. 9/17/49 to Josephine Ann Bergin; c. John J. Jr, Paul Girard, Mark Francis, Thad Phillip, David Martin and James Mitchell. Educ: St. John's Univ, N.Y, B.B.A, 42; Harvard Univ, 42-43; Cornell Univ, LL.B, 49. Polit. & Govt. Pos: Asst. Secy. Labor, U.S. Dept. of Labor, 57-60; cmnr, N.Y. Transit Authority, 62-68; del, Rep. Nat. Conv, 68. Bus. & Prof. Pos: Assoc. and partner, Parr, Doherty, Polk & Sargent, 49-53, 61-62; chmn, Urban Industs. Inc, N.Y, currently. Mil. Serv: Entered as Ens, Naval Res: 43, released as Lt. (sg), 46, after serv. in U.S.S. Tex, N.Atlantic, European, S.Pac. and Japanese Theaters, 43-45; N.Atlantic, European, S.Pac. and Japanese Theater Ribbons; Five Combat Stars; Commendation Medal from Adm. Chester Nimitz, Okinawa and Iwo Jima. Publ: 'Weary Erie,' Cornell Law Rev, spring 49; numerous articles and speeches printed, 53-68. Mem: N.Y.C. and Am. Bar Asns. Awards from various nat. and local civic orgn. Rel: Roman Catholic. Mailing Add: 35 Prospect Park W, Brooklyn, N.Y. 11215.

GILKEY, ROBERT C. D
Mem, Hawaii State Dem. Cent.Cmt.
b. Oakland, Calif, 2/17/28; s. Errol C. Gilkey and Katharine Carlton G; m. to Conchita Ortiz; c. John Henry, Maria Cristina, Maria Victoria, Philip Michael, Daniel Francis, Joseph Errol and Vincent Anthony. Educ: Univ. Santa Clara, B.S, 52. Polit. & Govt. Pos: Secy, Oahu Co. Dem. Cmt, 59-60; mem, Hawaii State Dem. Cent. Cmt, 60-, v.chmn, 62-68; state campaign coord. for President Lyndon B. Johnson, 64. Bus. & Prof. Pos: Personnel dir, St. Francis Hosp, Honolulu, Hawaii, 57-67; dep. dir, Hawaii State Dep. Labor & Indust. Rels, 67- Mem: Diocesan Bd. Educ, 68-, v.chmn, 69- Rel: Roman Catholic. Mailing Add: 1325 Palolo Ave, Honolulu, Hawaii. 96816.

GILL, ALASTAIR D. R
b. New Orleans, La, 9/13/21; s. Thomas A. Gill and Margaret Parker G; m. 2/13/54 to Betty Jane Miller; c. Denise, Cindy, Joan and George. Educ: Tex. Christian Univ, B.A, 48. Polit. & Govt. Pos: Area Coordinator, Harris Co. Rep. Party, Tex, 63-65, precinct chmn. and exec. committeeman, 60-63; alternate del, 22nd Cong. Dist, Tex, Rep. Nat. Conv, 64. Mil. Serv: Entered as A/S, Navy, 43, released as Radioman 2/C, after serv. in Pac. Area, 46; Pac. Theater Ribbon; Unit Citation; Lingayan Gulf Operation Ribbon. Mem: AF&AM; Mason (32°), Shrine. Rel: Disciples of Christ. Mailing Add: 127 Sunset Dr, Pittsburgh, Pa. 15237. (1967)

GILL, BETTY D
Pres, W.Va. Fedn. Dem. Women
b. Farmington, W.Va, 1/10/21; d. William Wayne Bainbridge and Nelle Jones B; m. 9/27/50 to Joseph Max Gill. Educ: Marion Co. High Sch, Farmington, W.Va, grad, 37; W.Va. Bus. Col, secy, 38. Polit. & Govt. Pos: Prog. chmn, Marion Co. Dem. Women's Club, W.Va, 60-63; 1st dist. dir, W.Va. Fedn. Dem. Women, 63-67, pres, 68-; del, Dem. Nat. Conv, 68. Bus. & Prof; Pos: Mgr, Cent. Small Loan Exchange, Fairmont, W.Va, 53- Mem: Quota Club of Fairmont (secy. & publicity, 64-65, 2nd v.pres, 69-); YWCA (secy, 56-58, 1st v.pres, 59-60); Women of the Moose; Homemaker's Club of the Exten. Serv; pres, Sorores Club, 54-58. Rel: Church of Christ. Mailing Add: 1150 Avalon Rd, Fairmont, W.Va. 26554.

GILL, EDWIN MAURICE D
N.C. State Treas.
b. Laurinburg, N.C; s. Thomas Jeffries Gill and Mamie North G. Educ: Trinity Col, 22-24; Duke Univ, LL.D, 59; hon. mem, Omicron Delta Kappa, hon. mem, Beta Gamma Sigma, Univ. N.C, 63. Polit. & Govt. Pos: N.C. State Rep, 29-31; private secy, Gov. Gardner, N.C, 31-33; mem, Cmn. of Paroles, 33-42, and Cmn. Revenue, 42-49; collector and dir, Internal Revenue, Greensboro, 50-53; N.C. State Treas, 53- Bus. & Prof. Pos: Law firm, Gibson and Gill, 24-31; law firm, Gardner, Morrison & Rogers, 49-50. Mem: Am. Parole Asn.(former pres); SE. State Probation and Parole Asn.(former pres); Am. Prison Asn.(former dir); Nat. Tax Asn.(former exec. cmt); State Banking Cmn.(chmn); Local Gov. Cmt.(chmn, dir); Tax Rev. Bd. (chmn); Teachers & State Employees' Retirement Syst.(chmn, invest. officer, and bd. trustees); State Bd. Educ: Sinking Fund Cmt; Nat. Asn. Tax Administr.(former exec. cmt); Law Enforcement Officers (bd. cmnrs); Benefit and Retirement Fund; Local Govt. Employees' Retirement Fund (invest. officer and bd. trustees); N.C. State Art Mus.(bd. trustees); Am. Legion; Sigma Nu Phi. Rel: Methodist. Mailing Add: State Capitol, Raleigh, N.C. 27602.

GILL, JAMES MAXWELL D
Chmn, Placer Co. Dem. Cent. Cmt, Calif.
b. Los Angeles, Calif, 7/14/25; s. Frederick Maxwell Gill and Caroline Burnett G; m. 6/15/58 to Catherine Mae Church; c. Mary Catherine and James Patrick. Educ: San Jose State Col, B.A; Sacramento State Col, M.A. Polit. & Govt. Pos: Chmn, Placer Co. Dem. Cent. Cmt, Calif, 63-; co-chmn, Second Cong. Dist, 66- Bus. & Prof. Pos: Head, bus. educ. dept, Roseville Union High Sch, 60- Mil. Serv: Entered as A/S, Naval Res, 43, released as Rdm 3/C, 45, after serv. in Pac. Theater; Asiatic-Pac. and Am. Theaters Ribbon. Mem: Bd. of dirs, North. Sect, Calif. Teachers Asn; Roseville Rotary Club; Elks. Rel: Roman Catholic. Mailing Add: 214 Bonny Knoll Rd, Roseville, Calif. 95678.

GILL, JOHN WORDEN R
Mem, D.C. Rep. Cent. Cmt.
b. Washington, D.C, 11/17/22; s. Theodore Nicholas Gill and Juliet Parris G; m. 4/22/50 to Elene Forman Essary; c. Margaret Elene, Theodore Nicholas, IV John Worden, Jr. and Laura Essary. Educ: Univ. Va, 1 year; George Wash. Univ, 3 years. Polit. & Govt. Pos: Mem, D.C. Rep. Cent. Cmt, 64-, chmn, transportation cmt, 69; Rep. chmn, Precinct 28, Wash, D.C, 68-69; pres, Spring Valley West. Heights Citizens Asn, 69. Mil. Serv: Entered as Pvt, Army Air Corps, 42, released as S/Sgt, 45, after serv. in 99 Bomb Group, ETO, Foggia Italy, 43-44; ETO Ribbon; Air Medal with Nine Oak Leaf Clusters Presidential Unit Citation. Mem: Wash. Bd. Realtors (chmn. transportation cmt, 66-, bd. trustees, 67-); City Tavern Asn; Chevy Chase Club. Rel: Episcopal. Mailing Add: 4907 Tilden St. N.W, Washington, D.C. 20016.

GILL, KATHLEEN O'CONNOR D
b. Salamanca, N.Y, 8/19/20; d. Bernard L. O'Connor and Bertha Van Fleet O; m. 11/12/38; div; c. Dennis Larry. Educ: N.Y. Secretarial Sch, 42. Polit. Pos: Chmn, Genesse Co. Dem. Party, N.Y, 63-65, v.chmn, 63. Mem: St. Jeromes Hosp. Guild; pres, Bus. & Prfnl. Women's Club, 65-66, v.pres, 64-65 and finance chmn, 62-63; Cancer Crusade chmn, Cancer Soc, 64-65; YWCA; Genesee Co. Women's Club. Rel: Baptist. Mailing Add: 6 Walker Place, Batavia, N.Y. 14020. (1967)

GILL, THOMAS P. D
Lt. Gov. of Hawaii
b. Honolulu, Hawaii, 4/21/22; married; c. five sons and one daughter. Educ: Univ. Hawaii; Univ. Calif. Law Sch. Polit. & Govt. Pos: Campaign chmn, Oahu Co. Dem. Party, 52 & 54, chmn, 54-58; Senate attorney, 55; admin. asst. to Speaker House, Hawaii House Rep, 57-58; Hawaii State Rep, 58-62, majority floor leader, Hawaii House Rep, 59-62; del, Dem. Nat. Conv, 60 & 64; U.S. Rep, Hawaii, 62-64; Lt. Gov. of Hawaii, 66- Bus. & Prof. Pos: Attorney; dir, Hawaii Off. of Econ. Opportunity, 65-66. Mil. Serv: Hawaii Territorial Guard and 24th Inf. Div; Bronze Star; Purple Heart. Legal Res: 4104 Roundtop Dr, Honolulu, Hawaii 96822. Mailing Add: State Capitol, Honolulu, Hawaii 96813.

GILL, WILLIAM ALEXANDER, JR. D
La. State Rep.
b. McComb, Miss, 9/1/11; s. William Alexander Gill, Sr. and Helen Virginia Cotrell G; m. 2/20/38 to Rosella Bacot; c. Rosella Lorice (Mrs. Say). Educ: La. State Univ; La. Col, B.A; Vandercook Col, M.A. Polit. & Govt. Pos: La. State Rep, 66-67 & 68- Bus. & Prof. Pos: Sch. teacher; Educ. consult. Mem: Rotary; La. Teachers Asn; Lions; Am. Fedn. Teachers. Mailing Add: 6220 Cameron Blvd, New Orleans, La. 70122.

GILLASPEY, CLARENCE JAMES D
b. Gunnison, Colo, 3/18/03; s. William Albert Gillaspey and Ada M. Sales G; m. 4/20/46 to Evelyn Martha Worthington. Educ: Western State Col. of Colo, Univ. of Ill. and Calif. Univ, Civil Engr. and Mech. Engr, 5 yrs; Sigma Phi Epsilon; Kappa Delta Mu. Polit. & Govt. Pos: Colo. State Rep, 65-67; supt. of maintance and construct, Corp. of Army Engrs, 9th Serv. Command, 42-44; appraiser, 9th Dist, Fed. Land Bank, Wichita, Kans, 33-35. Bus. & Prof. Pos: Gen. Mining, 23-; legis. consult, Mining Asn. of Colo; mfrs. agent, sales promotion; gen. legis. consult, Colo. Legis; gen. contractor, 45-48. Rel: Latter-day Saint. Mailing Add: 1710 Norwood Ave, Pueblo, Colo. 81001. (1967)

GILLEN, ARTHUR F. R
V.Chmn, Minn. Rep. Party
b. South St. Paul, Minn, 10/10/19; s. Leonard P. Gillen and Cecelia Koppy G; m. 4/28/45 to Louise R. Powers; c. Robert, Theodore, Anne Marie, Peter, Janice and Mary. Educ: Univ. Minn, B.S.L. and D.J; Gamma Eta Gamma. Polit. & Govt. Pos: Minn. State Rep, 42-50; Minn. State Sen, 50-58; dist. v.chmn, Minn. First Dist. Rep. Party, 65-66; v.chmn, Minn. Rep. Party, 66- Bus. & Prof. Pos: Attorney, 43- Minn. and Am. Bar Asns; C. of C; Jr. C. of C; Kiwanis; Boy Scouts (exec. bd); K. of C. Distinguished Serv. Award, Jr. C. of C, 48; Man of Year, South St. Paul, 50. Rel: Catholic. Legal Res: 24 Manitou Island, White Bear Lake, Minn. 55110. Mailing Add: Drovers Bank Bldg, South St. Paul, Minn. 55075.

GILLEN, JAMES BLAKE D
b. Blooming Grove, Tex, 9/20/22; s. Drew Gillen and Bertha Thompson G; m. 2/6/44 to Doris Underwood; c. Gay, James Blake, Jr. and Mary Nell. Educ: Tex. A&M, 40 and 41. Polit. & Govt. Pos: Co-chmn, 14th Cong. Dist, Johnson for Senate and Kennedy-Johnson Campaigns, Tex, 60; asst. chmn, Connally for Gov, 62, state orgn. chmn, 64; state orgn. chmn, Johnson-Humphrey Campaign, 64. Mem: Karem Shrine, Waco; Dallas Consistory; Kiwanis; Corpus Christi C. of C; YMCA. Rel: Baptist. Legal Res: 4003 Edgefield Court, Austin, Tex. 78731. Mailing Add: P.O. Box 1043, Austin, Tex. 79167.

GILLENWATERS, EDGAR MARTIN R
b. Klamath Falls, Ore, 3/16/32; s. Theodore Roosevelt Gillenwaters and M. Elizabeth Ramsby G; m. 4/24/55 to Jane Anne Haas; c. Carey Elizabeth, Theodore Martin and Gretchen Anne. Educ: Univ. Colo; Mexico City Col; Mesa Col, Colo; Alpha Tau Omega. Polit. & Govt. Pos: Former admin. asst. to U.S. Rep. Bob Wilson, Calif; chmn, Nat. Rep. Cong. Cmt, 63-66; spec. asst. to Gov. Reagan as Calif. Dep. Dir. of Finance, Wash, D.C, 66-68; asst. to Gov. Reagan for White House & Cong. Liaison, Sacramento, 69- Bus. & Prof. Pos: Asst. mgr, Jalisco Airlines, Mex, 53-54; gen. mgr, Edgemont Mining and Uranium Corp. and Uranium Eng. Corp, 54-58; staff asst. to bd. dirs, Giant Resources, Inc; staff asst. and corp. sales rep, Rohr Aircraft Corp, 58-60; acct. exec, Barnes-Chase Co, 60-62. Mil. Serv: Army Inf, 51-53, serv. as Forward Observer, 224th Regt. Combat Team, Korea. Rel: Episcopal. Mailing Add: 4801 Kipling Dr, Carmichael, Calif. 95608.

GILLESPIE, CHARLES B, JR. R
b. Claremore, Okla, 8/28/25; s. Charles B. Gillespie and Sallie Long G; m. 4/5/46 to Earnestine Williamson; c. Barbara and Deborah. Educ: Okla. Baptist Univ, 46-47; Okla. Univ, B.S. in Geol, 49; Sigma Alpha Epsilon. Polit. & Govt. Pos: Rep. precinct chmn, Tex, 60-62; chmn, Midland Co. Rep. Party, 62-69. Bus. & Prof. Pos: Geologist, Major Oil Co, 49-57; consulting geologist, 57-62; independent oil operator, Tex, 62- Mil. Serv: Entered as Aviation Cadet, Army Air Force, 43, released as Cpl, 46. Mem: Am. Asn. Petroleum Geologists; W. Tex. Geol. Soc; Kiwanis. Rel: South. Baptist. Legal Res: 3000 Lockheed, Midland, Tex. 79701. Mailing Add: Box 1179, Midland, Tex. 79701. (1967)

GILLESPIE, CHESTER KARL R
Mem, Ohio State Rep. Cent. and Exec. Cmts.
b. Home City, Ohio 4/4/97; s. Warren Gillespie and Lulu Trail G; m. 9/27/24 to Dorothy Thomas. Educ: Baldwin Wallace Col, LL.B, 20; Kappa Alpha Psi. Hon. LL.D, Wilberforce Univ, 33. Polit. & Govt. Pos: Asst. law dir, Cleveland, Ohio, 22; Ohio State Rep, Cuyahoga Co, 33-34, 39-40 & 43-44; del, Rep. Nat. Conv, 48 & 68, asst. sgt-at-arms, 52, alternate del, 64; mem, Cuyahoga Co. Rep. Cent. and Exec. Cmts; rep. 21st Dist, Ohio State Bd. Educ; rep. 20th Cong. Dist, Ohio State Rep. Cent. and Exec. Cmts. Mil. Serv: Entered as Pvt, Army, 18, released as Sgt. Maj, 18. Mem: Exec. cmt, Cleveland Bar Asn, 45; Citizens League of Cleveland; Cleveland City Club; Am. Legion. Rel: Protestant. Legal Res: 934 Herrick Rd, Cleveland, Ohio 44108. Mailing Add: 33 Public Square, Cleveland, Ohio 44113.

GILLESPIE, ROBERT GILL
Presiding Justice, Supreme Court of Miss.
b. Madison, Ala, 9/17/03; s. Philander M. Gillespie and Flora Gill G; m. 6/30/30 to Margaret Griffith; c. Robert Gill and Virgil Griffith. Educ: Huntsville Jr. Col, 23-24; Univ. Ala, 24-26; Delta Tau Delta. Polit. & Govt. Pos: Spec. agent, Fed. Bur. of Invest, 34-35; chancellor, Second Chancery Court of Miss, 39; presiding justice, Supreme Court of Miss, 54- Bus. & Prof. Pos: Attorney, Bailey & Gillespie, 39-43, Gillespie & Minniece, 45-48 and Gillespie, Huff & Williams, 48-54. Publ: 'Some Animadversions on Land Line Cases,' Miss. Law J, 3/62; 'The Matter of Perspective,' Tenn. Bar J, 2/65. Mem: Bd. dirs, Southwest. Col. at Memphis, 52-60; Am. Judicature Soc; awards jury, Freedoms Found; Miss. and Am. Bar Asns. Rel: Presbyterian. Legal Res: 432 Dunbar St, Jackson, Miss. 39216. Mailing Add: 204 New Capitol Bldg, Jackson, Miss. 39205.

GILLESPIE, WILLIAM MILLER D
Fla. State Rep.
b. Daytona Beach, Fla, 4/19/28; s. James U. Gillespie and Hazel Moore G; m. 9/5/58 to Sally M. Igo. Educ: Univ. Fla, A.A, 51; Fla. State Univ, B.S, 52; Stetson Univ. Col. Law, J.D, 56; Pi Kappa Phi; Phi Alpha Delta. Polit. & Govt. Pos: Asst. city attorney, New Smyrna Beach, Fla, 58-59, munic. judge, 64-67; city attorney, Oak Hill, 64-; Fla. State Rep, 37th Dist, Volusia Co, 66- Mil. Serv: Entered as Pvt, Army, 46, released as Tec/5, 48, after serv. in First Calvary Div, Army of Occup, Japan, 47-48. Mem: Am. Bar Asn; Fla. Bar; Volusia Co. Bar Asn.(pres, 68-69); Am. Trial Lawyers Asn; state dir, Stetson Lawyers Asn, St. Petersburg, Fla, 66-68; Am. Legion; VFW; Moose; Elks; Mason; Kiwanis. Good Govt. Award, New Smyrna Beach Jaycees, 67; Ray Starr Award, 67 Session Fla. Legis. Rel: Episcopal. Legal Res: 610 N. Peninsular Ave, New Smyrna Beach, Fla. 32069. Mailing Add: P.O. Box 580, New Smyrna Beach, Fla. 32069.

GILLETTE, GUY MARK D
b. Cherokee, Iowa, 2/3/79; s. Mark D. Gillette and Mary Hull G; m. 6/17/07 to Rose Freeman, wid, 1/6/56; c. Mark Freeman. Educ: Drake Univ, LL.B, 00. Hon. LL.D, Drake Univ. and Ambrose Univ. Polit. & Govt. Pos: Co. attorney, Cherokee Co, Iowa, 07-09; city attorney, Cherokee, 11; Iowa State Sen, 12-16; U.S. Rep, Iowa, 32-36; U.S. Sen, Iowa, 36-44 & 48-54; chmn, U.S. Surplus Property Bd, 45; chief counsel, Senate Cmt. on Judiciary Subcmts, U.S. Senate, 56 & 64. Mil. Serv: Sgt, Inf, Spanish American War, 98; Capt, Inf, World War I. Mem: Pres, Am. League for Free Palestine, 44-46; Past Master, Masonic Blue Lodge; Past Grand Marshall, Iowa Masons; Past Chancellor and Comdr, K. of P; State Comdr, United Spanish War Vet; Am. Legion; VFW; Rotary. Rel: Presbyterian. Mailing Add: 111 N. 11th St, Cherokee, Iowa 51012.

GILLETTE, HELEN D. D
Pa. State Rep.
b. Pittsburgh, Pa; d. Louis Frederick and Georgia E. Mohn F; m. to Michael J. Gillette; c. Michael J, Jr, Georgia A. (Mrs. Nixon) and Rebecca Rae. Educ Univ. Pittsburgh, 2 years. Polit. & Govt. Pos: Pa. State Rep, 31st Dist, 66- Bus. & Prof. Pos: Ins. agent and acct, 47- Mem: Nat. Order Women Legislators; Cath. Daughters Am; Bus. & Prfnl. Women; Women's Club Allegheny Valley. Rel: Catholic. Mailing Add: 1917 Freeport Rd, Natrona Heights, Pa. 15065.

GILLETTE, HENRY E. D
b. Bradford, Pa, 7/3/05; s. Angelo Gillette and Angelina DeRisi G; m. 4/30/38 to Emily V. Lodico. Educ: St. Bonaventure Univ, 24-26; Columbia Univ, A.B, 28; Harvard Univ, LL.B, 32. Polit. & Govt. Pos: Del, N.Y. Dem. Conv, 50-62; Judge City Court, Rochester, N.Y, 51-55; alternate del, Dem. Nat. Conv, 52-60, del, 64; counsel, N.Y. Dept. Agr, 56-58; campaign chmn, Monroe Co. Dem. Cmt, 57-63, v.chmn, 61-64 and former committeeman; city councilman, Rochester, 59-, mayor, 62-63; former mem. adv. coun, N.Y. State Dem. Cmt. Bus. & Prof. Pos: Lawyer, self employed, 33- Mem: N.Y. State and Rochester Bar Asns; C. of C; Bus. Men's Asn. of Rochester; Prfnl. Men's Asn. of Rochester; Ridgemont Golf Club; Rochester Mem. Art Gallery; Rochester Civic Music Asn; Harvard, Columbia and St. Bonaventure Clubs of Rochester. Rel: Catholic. Legal Res: 550 Seneca Pkwy, Rochester, N.Y. 14613. Mailing Add: 19 West Main St, Rochester, N.Y. 14614. (1967)

GILLETTE, ROY ROBERT D
b. Fostoria, Iowa, 11/18/35; s. Roy U. Gillette and Ruth Bounds G; m. 2/4/55 to Sharlene Furman; c. Thomas Scott, Lynne Marie, Robert Mathew, William Jon and Suzanne, foster children Mary Anne and Robert Green. Educ: Univ. Nebr, 53-55; Iowa State Univ, B.S, 58; Phi Kappa Phi; Gamma Sigma Delta. Polit. & Govt. Pos: Mem, Midwest. Region Econ. Develop. Cmt, Interstate Coop. Cmt, 65-; Iowa State Rep, 65-67; real estate officer, U.S. Post Off. Dept, currently. Bus. & Prof. Pos: Owner, Gillette Real Estate, 61-; dir, Iowa Cent. Investment Corp, 63 and Univ. Center Apt. and Red Rib Inc, 64- Judge for Big 8 Gymnastics Competition, also Nat. Asn. Intercollegiate Athletics and other collegiate asns. Rel: Methodist. Mailing Add: 1209 Lee, Ames, Iowa 50010.

GILLETTE, W. R. (RILEY) D
b. Dickinson Co, Iowa, 3/19/24; s. Lester S. Gillette and Cecilia Murray G; m. 1949 to Doris Morningstar; c. Corinne, Michael and Charles. Educ: Iowa State Univ. Polit. & Govt. Pos: Iowa State Rep, 66. Bus. & Prof. Pos: Grain and Livestock Farmer. Mil. Serv: Korean War and World War II Vet, Served in overseas area. Mem: bd. dirs, Iowa State Farm Safety Cmn; Iowa State Crop Improv. Asn; Farm Flock Asn.(former v.pres); Farm Bur; K. of C. (past dist. dep); Am. Legion. Master Lamb Producer, 61; qualified livestock judge. Rel: Catholic. Mailing Add: Route 2, Spencer, Iowa 51301.

GILLIAM, GODFREY CLINE D
Miss. State Rep.
b. Millport, Ala, 11/17/16; married. Polit. & Govt. Pos: Miss. State Rep, 56-64 & 68- Bus. & Prof. Pos: Merchant; farmer. Mem: Mason; WOW; Am. Legion; VFW; Farm Bur; Miss. Cattlemen's Asn. Rel: Methodist. Mailing Add: Route 3, Columbus, Miss. 39701. (1967)

GILLIAM, JEAN MARIE D
Chmn, Gilliam Co. Dem. Cent. Cmt, Ore.
b. Syracuse, N.Y, 6/14/23; d. Charles Martin Cline and Faye Marie Crego C; m. 4/19/47 to Louis Leonard Gilliam; c. Cheryl Jean, Richard Louis, Mary Jane and Juliann. Educ: Powelson Bus. Inst, Syracuse, N.Y, 1 year. Polit. & Govt. Pos: Chmn, Gilliam Co. Dem. Cent. Cmt, Ore, 64- Bus. & Prof. Pos: Secy, Syracuse and Rome Air Bases, 43-47; ed, Condon Globe-Times, Ore, 65-; correspondent, East-Oregonian, Pendleton, 65- and Assoc. Press, 66- Publ: Articles in the Condon Globe-Times, East-Oregonian and Assoc. Press. Mem: Ore. Press Women's Club; PTA; Altar Soc. Rel: Roman Catholic. Legal Res: 414 E. Well St, Condon, Ore. 97823. Mailing Add: Box 106, Condon, Ore. 97823.

GILLIES, FREDERICK MONTAGUE R
b. Chicago, Ill, 12/9/95; s. William Gillies and Blanche Browne G; m. 1/8/38 to Blanche Wilder. Educ: Cornell Univ, 14-17; Alpha Delta Phi. Polit. & Govt. Pos: Rep. committeeman, 22nd Ward, Chicago, Ill, 40-44; chmn, Rep. State Finance Cmt, 61-69 and mem. various cmts. Bus. & Prof. Pos: Supvr. to works mgr, Inland Steel Co, 22-50; v.pres. to chmn. of bd, Acme Steel Co, 50-61. Mil. Serv: Entered as CPO, Navy, 17, released as Ens, 19, after serv. in Naval Air Force. Mem: Univ. Club of Chicago; Flossmoor Country Club, Chicago; Chickaming Country Club, Lakeside, Mich. Rel: Christian Scientist. Mailing Add: 1308 Dartmouth Rd, Flossmoor, Ill. 60422. (1967)

GILLIGAN, JOHN JOYCE D
b. Cincinnati, Ohio, 3/22/21; s. Harry J. Gilligan and Blanche Joyce G; m. 6/28/45 to Mary Kathryn Dixon; c. Donald, Kathleen, John and Ellen. Educ: Univ. Notre Dame, B.A, 43; Univ. Cincinnati, M.A, 47. Polit. & Govt. Pos: Mem, Cincinnati City Coun, Ohio, 53-67; U.S. Rep, Ohio, 64-66; Dem. nominee for U.S. Sen, 68; del-at-lg, Dem. Nat. Conv, 68. Bus. & Prof. Pos: Instr, Xavier Univ, 48-53; partner, Sauter-Gilligan & Assocs, Ins, 68- Mil. Serv: Entered as Midn, Navy, 42, released as Lt, 45, after serv. in Atlantic, Mediterranean and Pac. Theaters; 3 Area Campaign Ribbons; 5 Battle Stars; 2 Naval Unit Citations; Silver Star for gallantry in action. Mem: Fel, John F. Kennedy Inst. of Polit, Harvard Univ, 69; fel, Adlai Stevenson Inst. of Int. Studies, Univ. of Chicago, 69. Rel: Catholic. Mailing Add: 1875 William Howard Taft Rd, Cincinnati, Ohio 45206.

GILLIGAN, JULIE D
b. Lynn, Mass, 8/5/11; d. Peter G. Petros and Julia Pappas P; m. 7/3/37 to James Edward Gilligan; c. James Paul, Paul Edward and Emily. Educ: Burdett Bus. Col. Polit. & Govt. Pos: Secy, Lynn City Dem. Cmt, 56-60; Mass. State Rep, 61-69. Mailing Add: 96 Lafayette Park, Lynn, Mass. 01902. (1967)

GILLILAND, ROY J. R
b. Jackson Co, Ohio, 4/25/27; s. Roy Delbert Gilliland and Mable Stephenson G; m. 12/19/51 to Karleene Mullen; c. Kyle R, Arla L. and Bret J. Educ: Ohio State Univ, B.S. in bus. admin, 50, LL.B, 52, J.D, 67; Delta Theta Phi. Polit. & Govt. Pos: Munic. solicitor, Coalton, Ohio, 56-67; prosecuting attorney, Jackson Co, 57-63; Ohio State Rep, Jackson Co, 63-67; judge, Common Pleas Court, 67- Bus. & Prof. Pos: Secy, Wellston Assocs, Inc, 59-; secy, Jackson Co. Bar, 60 and pres, 63. Mil. Serv: A/S, Navy, 45 released as Seaman 1/C, 46 after serv. in Pac. Theater; Lt. Comdr, Naval Res, 51-; Asiatic Pac, Am. Theater and World War II Ribbons; U.S. Naval Res. Medal. Mem: Am, Ohio State and Jackson Co, Bar Asns; Mason; Lions; Grange; Am. Legion; Farm Bur; C. of C; Eagles; United Commercial Travelers. Rel: Methodist. Mailing Add: 347 S. Pennsylvania Ave, Wellston, Ohio 45692.

GILLILLAND, WHITNEY R
Mem, Civil Aeronaut. Bd.
b. Glenwood, Iowa, 1/13/04; s. Shirley Gillilland and Elsie Moulton G; m. 2/19/26 to Virginia Wegmann; c. William S. and Thomas M. Educ: Iowa State Univ, 21-22; Univ. Nebr, 23-26; Phi Alpha Delta. Polit. & Govt. Pos: Judge, Iowa Dist. Court, 38-41; mem, Iowa Rep. State Party, 47-50; chmn, Iowa Del, Rep. Nat. Conv, 48; mem, Rep. Nat. Strategy Cmt. and chmn. Rep. Exec. Cmt, 49-50; asst. orgn. dir, Rep. Nat. Cmt, 52; asst. to Secy. Agr, Wash, D.C, 53; mem, War Claims Cmn, 53-54; chmn, For. Claims Settlement Cmn, 54-59; mem, Civil Aeronaut. Bd, 59- Bus. & Profl Pos: Attorney, Iowa, 28-52. Publ: Several articles in various legal publ. Mem: Pres, Fed. Bar Asn, 59-60; house of del, Am. Bar Asn, 62-63; pres, Wash. For. Law Soc, 65-66; Iowa State Bar Asn; Inter-Am. Bar Asn; Mason. Rel: Congregational. Mailing Add: 4150 N. 41st St, Arlington, Va. 22207.

GILLIS, CARL L, JR. R
b. Adrian, Ga, 8/29/17; s. Carl L. Gillis, Sr. and Vina Lou Rowland G; m. 2/7/53 to Iris Mackey; c. Gwenda, Carl, III and Gayla. Educ: Univ. Ga, 3 years. Polit. & Govt. Pos: Mayor, Adrian, Ga, 50-58; del, Rep. Nat. Conv, 68. Bus. & Prof. Pos: Pres, Builtwell Homes, 59-62; pres, Adrian Housing Corp, 63- Mem: Lions; Elks; Ga. Farm Bur; Exchange Club. Rel: Methodist. Mailing Add: Box 246, Adrian, Ga. 31002.

GILLIS, HUGH MARION D
Ga. State Sen.
b. Soperton, Ga, 9/6/18; s. Jim L. Gillis, Sr. and Annie Lois Walker G; m. 1948 to Jean; c. Hugh, Jr, Donald Walker and Jean Marie. Educ: Ga. Mil. Col, 36; Univ. Ga, B.S, 39; Sigma Alpha Epsilon. Polit. & Govt. Pos: Chmn, Treutlen Co. Hosp. Authority, Ga; Ga. State Rep, 41-43 & 49-52; Ga. State Sen, 57-58 & 63-, Pres. Pro Tempore, Ga. State Senate, currently. Bus. & Prof. Pos: Farmer; Naval Stores; John Deere dealer. Mem: Livestock Asn. (pres); Farmers Coop; Farm Bur.(pres, Treutlen Co. Chap). Rel: Baptist; trustee, Baptist Church. Mailing Add: Soperton, Ga. 30457.

GILLIS, JEAN W. R
Chmn, Crook Co. Rep. Cent. Cmt, Ore.
b. DeSmet, Idaho, 1/11/14; d. Winfield Howard Williamson and Helene MacKay W; wid; m. 7/30/65 to James Phillips Gillis; c. Anne W. Benedict. Educ: St. Nicholas Sch, Wash, grad, 32. Polit. & Govt. Pos: Precinct committeewoman, Crook Co. Rep. Cent. Cmt, Ore, 45-, v.chmn, 56-60, chmn, 60- Mem: Crook Co. Tuberc. and Health Asn.(exec. secy, 49-65); Ore. Tuberc. and Health Asn; Eagles Auxiliary; Bus. & Prfnl. Women; Rotana (former pres. and former ed, Rotanan); Crook Co. Youth Coun; Pioneer Mem. Hosp. Auxiliary; Pink Ladies. 25 year Serv. Pin, Ore. Tuberc. and Health Asn. Rel: Episcopal; former secy. Vestry, former treas, Guild and former secy. Dist. Church Women. Mailing Add: 271 S. Elm, Prineville, Ore. 97754.

GILLMAN, MICHAEL J. R
Chmn, Tenth Cong. Dist. Rep. Orgn. Mich.
b. Bay City, Mich, 6/6/39; s. Robert E. Gillman and Betty Jane Lindebaum G; m. 1/27/62 to Betty J. Gradowski; c. Michael A, Steven Scott, Jason Robert, Andrew B. and Christian Alan. Educ: Univ. Mich, B.A, 61; Druids Honorary; Zeta Psi. Polit. & Govt. Pos: Mem, Rep. State Cent. Cmt. Mich, 67-69; mem, Bay Co. Bd. Supvrs, 67-; chmn, Tenth Cong. Dist. Rep. Orgn. of Mich, 69- Bus. & Prof. Pos: Claims rep, northeast Mich, Ins. Co. of N. Am, 63-66; workmen's compensation coordinator, Dow Chem. Co, Midland, Mich, 66- Mil. Serv: Pfc, Mich. Nat. Guard, 56-60. Mem: Jr. Chamber of Commerce; C. of C; K. of C. Bernie Swanson Mem. Award as Outstanding Sports Writer in the Big Ten Cols, Minneapolis Tribune, 61; Bay City Jaycee Sound Citizen Award, 66. Rel: Roman Catholic. Mailing Add: 1812 Fifth Ave, Bay City, Mich. 48706.

GILLMOR, GARY GEORGE D
Mayor, Santa Clara, Calif.
b. San Francisco, Calif, 8/3/36; s. George Gillmor and Rose Dias G; m. 9/7/57 to Dorothy June Navarro, wid; c. Michelle, Lisa, David and René. Educ: Univ. of Santa Clara, B.A; San Jose State Col, teaching fel. and M.A; Noel Coward Scholarship; Block Soc. Polit. & Govt. Pos: City councilman, Santa Clara, Calif, 65-69, Mayor, 69- Bus. & Prof. Pos: Teacher, Buchser High Sch, 60-66 and West Valley Col, 66. Mil. Serv: 2nd Lt, Army, 59, Army Res, currently. Mem: Calif. Teachers Orgn; Elks; K. of C. Rel: Catholic. Mailing Add: 3531 Earl Dr, Santa Clara, Calif. 95051.

GILLMOR, PAUL EUGENE R
Ohio State Sen.
b. Tiffin, Ohio, 2/1/39; s. Paul Marshall Gillmor and Lucy Fry G; m. 8/4/62 to Brenda Luckey; c. Linda Dianne and Julie Ellen. Educ: Ohio Wesleyan Univ, B.A, 61; Univ. Mich. Law Sch, J.D, 64; Pi Sigma Alpha; Sigma Alpha Epsilon; Phi Delta Phi; Phi Delta Sigma. Polit. & Govt. Pos: Ohio State Sen, 12th Dist, 67- Bus. & Prof. Pos: Attorney-at-law, 64-65. Mil. Serv: Capt, Air Force; served in 314th Combat Support Group, Tactical Air Command. Mem: Am. and Ohio State Bar Asns. Rel: Lutheran. Mailing Add: P.O. Box 705, Tiffin, Ohio 44883.

GILLOCK, EDGAR HARDIN 'ED' D
Tenn. State Sen.
b. Savannah, Tenn, 7/30/28; s. Edgar Cherry Gillock and Ruth Hardin G; m. 7/3/48 to Joan Frederickson; c. Debra Ruth (Mrs. Burks), Lee Hardin, Vicky Denise, Laura Elizabeth, Lorri June and Robert Neils. Educ: Memphis State Univ, B S. M.A. & LL.B, Kappa Alpha, National Forensic Club, National History Club. Polit. & Govt. Pos: Tenn. State Rep, 63-66; asst. city attorney, Memphis, Tenn, 64-66; Tenn. State Sen, 69-; mem, Coun. State Govt, Tenn, currently. Bus. & Prof. Pos: Attorney, Irwin, Owens, Gillock and Colton, 60- Mil. Serv: Army, 51, Pfc, serv. in 196th Field Artil. Mem: Shelby Co. and Tenn. Bar Asns; Am, Tenn. and Shelby Co. Trial Lawyers Asns; Nat. Soc. State Legislators; Scottish Rite; Nat. Dem. Party; East Frayser Civic Club; Exchange Club. Rel: Baptist. Mailing Add: 2563 Capewood, Memphis, Tenn. 38127.

GILMAN, BENJAMIN A. R
N.Y. State Assemblyman
b. Poughkeepsie, N.Y, 12/6/22; s. Harry Gilman and Esther G; m. 10/19/52 to Jane Prizant; c. Jonathan, Harrison, David, Susan and Ellen. Educ: Univ. of Pa, Wharton Sch, B.S, 46; N.Y. Law Sch, LL.B, 50; Phi Sigma Delta. Polit. & Govt. Pos: Asst. state attorney gen, N.Y, 53-55; attorney, N.Y. State Temporary Cmn. on the Courts, 56-57; N.Y. State Assemblyman, 95th Dist, 67-; mem, J.L.C. on Real Property Tax Exemptions, 69; mem, Southeast. Water Cmn, 69. Bus. & Prof. Pos: Gilman and Gilman, 55- Mil. Serv: S/Sgt, Air Force, 43-45; D.F.C. and Air Medal. Mem: Past Co. Comdr, VFW; chmn, Little League; v.pres, Orange Co. Health Asn; adv. cmt, N.Y. State START Center; former nat. committeeman, N.Y. State Young Rep; Am, N.Y. State and Orange Co. Bar Asns; N.Y. Trial Lawyers; Elks. Rel: Hebrew. Legal Res: 10 Coolidge Court, Middletown, N.Y. 10940. Mailing Add: P.O. Box 443, Middletown, N.Y. 10940.

GILMAN, GEORGE R
N.H. State Sen.
b. Cambridge, Mass, 7/23/25; s. George Phillips Brooks Gilman and Karen E.

Theller G; m. 9/10/49 to Polly Harris; c. Shelley, Steven, Timothy and Jean. Educ: Univ. N.H, B.A, 50. Polit. & Govt. Pos: Staff, U.S. Senate Armed Serv. Investigating Cmt, 50-51; exec. asst, U.S. Sen. Styles Bridges, N.H, 51-55; N.H. State Rep, 57-61, Majority Leader, N.H. House of Rep, 59-61; N.H. State Sen, Fourth Dist, 69- Bus. & Prof. Pos: Treas, G.F. Mooney & Son, 56- Mil. Serv: Entered as Seaman, Navy, 43, released as PO 2/C, 46, after serv. in Submarine Serv, Pac. Theater; Army Res, 1st Lt.(Ret). Mem: Trustee, Univ. N.H. Mailing Add: R.F.D, Farmington, N.H. 03835.

GILMAN, GORDON ST. JOHN R
b. Wallingford, Conn, 12/21/33; s. Wilfred Gordon Gilman and Veronica M. St. Jean G; single. Educ: Univ. Vt, B.A, 57; Univ. Detroit Law Sch, LL.B, 63; Sigma Phi Epsilon; Gamma Eta Gamma; Univ. Vt. Student Court; Univ. Detroit Moot Court Bd. Dirs. Polit. & Govt. Pos: Precinct del, St. Clair Shores, Rep. Party, Mich, 64-69; treas, Macomb Co. Rep. Exec. Cmt, 66-69; treas, 12th Cong. Dist. Rep. Cmt. and mem. exec. cmt, 66-69; del, Rep. Nat. Conv, 68; U.S. Attorney, Dept. Justice, 69- Bus. & Prof. Pos: Technical revenue officer, Internal Revenue Serv, Detroit, Mich, 57-59, estate tax examiner, 60-64; tax attorney, Gen. Motors Corp, 64-69. Mil. Serv: Entered as Recruit, Army, 58, released as S/P 4, 60, after serv. in USAG 1362, First Army, Ft. Totton, Flushing, N.Y; Commendation Award. Mem: Am. and Mich. Bar Asns; Young Rep; First Soc. of Detroit; Five O'Clock Forum; Grosse Point Commun. Chorus. Superior Performance Award, Int. Revenue Serv. Rel: Catholic. Mailing Add: A-811 1400 S. Joyce St, Arlington, Va. 22202.

GILMAN, WIGGIN S. D
N.H. State Rep.
b. 9/11/91; married; c. Two. Educ: New Hampton Sch. Polit. & Govt. Pos: N.H. State Rep, 29-31 & 59-; former mayor, Franklin, 5 years; coun. mem, Franklin, 6 years; co. comm, 51-52; tax assessor, 4 years; former mem. sch. bd. and water bd. Bus. & Prof. Pos: Retired. Mem: Dir, Franklin Develop; Odd Fellows; Webster Encampment; Aras Sanctorum. Rel: Congregational. Mailing Add: 24 W. Bow St, Franklin, N.H. 03235. (1967)

GILMORE, EDDIE HUBERT D
Ala. State Sen.
b. Gilmore, Ala, 6/12/26; s. Eddie Henry Gilmore and Grovie Elizabeth Franklin G; m. 12/21/46 to Elizabeth Jackson; c. Randall, Joanne, Lea, Julie and Elizabeth. Educ: Birmingham-South Col. Polit. & Govt. Pos: Former Street Supt, Bessemer, Ala; Ala. State Rep, 62-66; Ala. State Sen, 67- Bus. & Prof. Pos: Contracting, 46-51 & 55- Mil. Serv: Maj, Ala. Nat. Guard; Army, World War II and Korea. Mem: Mason; Shrine. Rel: Methodist. Mailing Add: Box 546, Bessemer, Ala. 35020. (1967)

GILMORE, JAMES STANLEY, JR. R
b. Kalamazoo, Mich, 6/14/26; s. James Stanley Gilmore, Sr. and Ruth McNair G; m. 5/21/49 to Diana Holdenreide Fell; c. Bethany, Sydney, James S, III, Elizabeth and Ruthie. Educ: Culver Mil. Acad; West. Mich. Univ; Kalamazoo Col, 45. Polit. & Govt. Pos: Mem. adn past chmn, Mich. Water Resources Cmn; mayor, Kalamazoo, Mich, 59-61; former mem, Kalamazoo Co. Bd. of Supvr; chmn, Congressman Garry Brown Polit. Campaign; past pres, Kalamazoo Co. Young Rep; past chmn, Kalamazoo City Rep. Exec. Cmt; chmn. exec. cmt, Rep. 100 and One Cmt; del, Rep. Nat. Conv, 68. Bus. & Prof. Pos: Dir, v.pres, secy. and treas, Gilmore Bros. Dept. Store, Inc, 47-58; owner and pres, Jim Gilmore Enterprises, currently; sponsor, Gilmore Broadcasting Spec-Gordon Johncock Racing Team; v. pres. and dir, Holiday Inn-Continental Corp, Mich; dir. and mem. trust cmt, First Nat. Bank & Trust Co, Kalamazoo, mem, Holding Co. Cmt; trust cmt, Dalton Estate; dir, Mich. Carton Co, Battle Creek; dir. and asst. secy, Fabri-Kal Plastics Corp, Kalamazoo; bd. mem, Shakespeare Co. Mil. Serv: Army Air Force, World War II, ETO. Mem: Wolverine Charitable Found.(pres); Bronson Methodist Hosp.(bd. trustees and bldg. cmt); Kalamazoo Co. Red Cross (former chmn. and bd. dirs); Kalamazoo Col.(former mem. bd. trustees and finance cmt, mem. adv. group for Center of Urban Studies and Commun. Serv); West. Mich. Univ.(mem. pres. adv. cmt); Kalamazoo Nature Center (v.chmn. and bd. trustees); Vietnam Fund Raising Campaign (former chmn. local group); Loan Improv. Fund Today Found.(bd. trustees); Family Serv. Center of Kalamazoo (life mem, bd. dirs); Constance Brown Hearing and Speech Center (bd. dirs); Nazareth Col.(lay mem, chmn. bd. trustees); Martin Luther King Mem. Fund Bd.(founder and bd. mem); Douglass Commun. Asn, Kalamazoo (bd. mem); N.Cent. Airlines (presidential adv); Mich. Bd. Dirs, Radio Free Europe; Boys' Club of Am.(assoc. dir); March of Dimes (life mem); Greater Mich. Develop. Found.(trustee); Mich. Alvin Bentley Charitable Found.(bd. trustees); Hosp. Research and Educ. Reserve (bd. dirs); Ducks Unlimited (nat. sponsor); Mich. C. of C. Law and Order Cmt; Kalamazoo Co. Retail C. of C. Cmt; Mich. Retail Dry Goods Asn.(bd. dirs); Mich. Econ. Develop.(exec. mem); Mich. Coun. on Fair Employ. Practices; Nat. Asn. of Mfrs.(indust. mem); Nazareth Col. Capital Improv. Bldg. Campaign (chmn); Kalamazoo Co. Commun. Chest-Red Feather Campaign (chmn); Kalamazoo Co. Muscular Dystrophy Fund Drive (chmn, 2 years); Kalamazoo Co. C. of C.(pres, bd. dirs, 5 years); Israel Bond Drive, Kalamazoo, Kent and Calhoun Counties (joint chmn, financial chmn. and acting yearly as master of ceremonies); Episcopal Diocese of West. Mich.(bd. trustees); Episcopal Diocese Cathedral Drive (chmn); Park Club, Kalamazoo; Kalamazoo Country Club; Gull Lake Country Club, Richland; Mid-Am. Club, Chicago, Ill; Otsego Ski Club, Gaylord, Mich; Capitol Hill Club, Wash, D.C. Young Man of the Year for Kalamazoo Co, 60; One of Mich. Five Outstanding Young Men of the Year, Nat. Jr. C. of C, 60; past participant and group speaker on Greater Kalamazoo Downtown Mall before Nat. Retail Dry Goods Asn, N.Y.C. and Time-life Retail Seminar, Bretton Woods, Conn; Selected by State Dept. when Mayor of Kalamazoo to meet in Israel for conf. purposes; Selected by Radio Free Europe to rep. U.S. in Germany; Annual Serv. to Mankind Award, Sertoma. Rel: Episcopal. Mailing Add: 1550 Long Rd, Kalamazoo, Mich. 49001.

GILMORE, SIBYL IRENE D
Chmn, Borden Co. Dem. Exec. Cmt, Tex.
b. Clyde, Tex, 9/28/18; d. Ewell Stanley Lewis and Kattie Owens L; m. 12/7/35 to Joe Clayton Gilmore; c. Nelda Jo (Mrs. Colvin). Educ: Vincent High Sch, 4 years. Polit. & Govt. Pos: Chmn, Borden Co. Dem. Exec. Cmt, Tex, 66- Mem: Borden Co. Homemakers Club; Borden Co. Hist. Surv. Cmt. Rel: Church of Christ. Mailing Add: Box 42, Gail, Tex. 79738.

GILMORE, THOMAS ODELL D
b. Julian, N.C, 11/15/36; s. Glenn Gordon Gilmore, Sr. and Mary Elizabeth Harris G; m. 8/16/58 to Betty Lou Shoffner; c. Thomas Odell, Jr. and Dwayne Gordon. Educ: Am. Landscape Sch, 57; N.C. State Univ, B.S. in horticulture, 59; Blue Key; Alpha Zeta; Pi Alpha Xi; Farm House Fraternities; Horticulture Club; Apollo Club; Agr. Ed. Staff; Agr. Club; Sen, Student Govt, Inter Fraternity Coun; v.pres, Sr. Class; elected permanent class pres, Class of 59. Polit. & Govt. Pos: Mem, various state cmts, Young Dem. Clubs, N.C, 57-66, state pres, 64, state organizer, 60-62, state pres, 64; pres. and treas, N.C. State Col. Young Dem. Club, 58-59; asst. state mgr, Gov. Terry Sanford's Young Voters Prog, 60; mem, State Bd. Agr, N.C, 61-; mem, Greensboro Young Dem. Club; secy-treas, Local Dem. Precinct, 62-63; mem. exec. cmt, Young Dem. Club, Guilford Co, 63; mem, State Voting Cmn, 64; del, Dem. Nat. Conv, 64, alternate del, 68. Bus. & Prof. Pos: V.pres, Gilmore Plant and Bulb Co, Inc, 59-; mem. adv. coun. sch. agr, N.C. State Univ, 60-63 & 68- Mem: N.C. Asn. Nurserymen (former mem. bd. dirs. and chmn. legis. cmt, chmn. hwy. beautification cmt, pres, 68-, chmn. bd, 69-); Am. Asn. Nurserymen (Mem. Nat. hwy. beautification cmt, chmn, hwy. cmt, 69-); Rotary; Forest Oaks Country Club.(bd. gov, 68-); dir, Dr. Clyde M. Gilmore Mem. Park, Inc; Wolfpack Club, N.C. State Univ; Alumni Asn, N.C. State Univ. Most Outstanding Collegiate Young Dem. in N.C. and One of Top Three Collegiate Young Dem. in Nation, 58; One of Top Ten Young Dem. in N.C, 62; N.C. Most Outstanding Young Dem, 68; Guilford Co. Most Outstanding Young Farmer, 68. Rel: Methodist. Mailing Add: Julian, N.C. 27283.

GILMORE, VOIT D
b. Winston-Salem, N.C, 10/13/18; s. John M. Gilmore and Helen H. Hensel B; m. 1/21/45 to Kathryn Kendrick; c. Kathryn, Peter, Geraldine, David and Susan. Educ: Univ. of N.C, A.B. in Journalism & Polit. Sci, 39; Nat. Inst. of Pub. Affairs, Wash, D.C, grad, 40; Phi Beta Kappa; Chi Psi. Polit. & Govt. Pos: Mayor and councilman, Southern Pines, N.C, 53-57; mem, Bd. of Conserv. & Develop, N.C, 57-61; dir, U.S. Travel Serv, 61-64; N.C. State Sen, 64-68; chmn, N.C. Cmn. Educ. and Employ. Women, 67-; cand. for U.S. Rep, Eighth Dist, 68. Bus. & Prof. Pos: Pres, Storey Corp, 50- and Holly Corp, 56- Mil. Serv: Entered as Ens, Navy, 42, released as Lt.(jg), 46, after serv. in Naval Air Transport Serv, S.Atlantic, Pac. and Asian Theatres; Pac. Theater Ribbon. Publ: Articles in various mag. concerning Arctic and Antarctic explor. performed between 1958 and 1964. Mem: Explorers Club, N.Y.C; Bohemian Club, San Francisco. Rel: Presbyterian. Mailing Add: 700 E. Indiana Ave, Southern Pines, N.C. 28387.

GILPIN, R. WAYNE R
b. Baltimore, Md, 8/19/39; s. Douglas K. Gilpin and Carolyn Booker G; single. Educ: Baltimore Jr. Col, 60; Univ. Md, 61-63; Life Underwriters Col, L.U.T.C, 66; Baltimore Asn. for Adv. of Scrabble. Polit. & Govt. Pos: Del, Rep. Nat. Conv, 64; del, Rep. Nat. Young Rep. Conv, 65; v.pres, Spartan Rep. Club, Md, 65; ward exec. Md. State Rep. Cent. Cmt, 65-69; former pres, Baltimore City Young Rep. Bus. & Prof. Pos: Agents adv. coun, Aetna Ins. Co, 65; exec. asst. to v.pres, Chesapeake Life Ins. Co, 66. Mil. Serv: Entered as E-1, Army, released as E-5, after serv. in Army Intel, U.S; Expert on M-1 and M-1 Carbine; E-5 Inactive Res. Publ: States Rights Sham, Baltimore Sun, 5/64. Mem: Life Underwriters Hon. Coun; Baltimore Life Underwriters Speakers Bur. Letters in col. and high sch, tennis and football. Rel: Lutheran. Mailing Add: 6738 E. Pratt St, Baltimore, Md. 21224. (1967)

GIMER, RICHARD HARL R
b. Eagle Grove, Iowa, 3/24/40; s. Thomas Woodrow Gimer and Marie L. Klein G; m. 5/26/62 to Millicent Ann Stutzman; c. Melissa Ann and Jennifer Lynn. Educ: Iowa State Univ, B.S, 62; George Wash. Univ. Sch. Law, J.D. with honors, 65; pres. student body, Iowa State Univ, 61-62; Order of the Coif; Cardinal Key; Gamma Gamma; Acacia; Delta Theta Phi. Polit. & Govt. Pos: Zone leader, Polk Co. Rep. Party, 65-66; admin. asst, U.S. Rep. William J. Scherle, Iowa, 67-69; mem, Citizens for Holton Coord. Cmt, Va, 69. Bus. & Prof. Pos: Attorney, Howrey, Simon, Baker & Murchison, D.C, currently. Mem: Am, Fed, D.C, Iowa State and Polk Co. Bar Asns; Nat. Lawyers Club; Cong. Secy. Club; Bull Elephants. Rel: Presbyterian. Legal Res: 6420 Wainfleet Court, Springfield, Va. 22152. Mailing Add: 1707 H St. N.W, Washington, D.C. 20006.

GINN, RONALD B. D
b. Morgan, Ga, 5/31/34; s. Elijah Mathis Ginn and Annie Laura Bryan B; m. 4/8/56 to Gloria Ann Averitt; c. Lauren Kacy, Julie and Ronald Bryan, Jr. Educ: Abraham Baldwin Agr. Col, 51-53; Ga. South. Col, B.S, 53-56. Polit. & Govt. Pos: Former admin. asst. to U.S. Rep. Hagen, Ga; admin. asst. to U.S. Sen. Talmadge, Ga, currently. Bus. & Prof. Pos: Teacher, Coffee Co. High Sch, Douglas, Ga, 56-57; asst. mgr, pub. rels, Planters EMC, Millen. Mem: Jr. C. of C; Ga. Farm Bur. Legal Res: Millen, Ga. Mailing Add: 5419 Charlottesville Rd, Springfield, Va. 22151. (1967)

GINN, ROSEMARY LUCAS R
Rep. Nat. Committeewoman, Mo.
b. Columbia, Mo, 8/28/12; d. Reuben E. Lucas and Mary Bewick L; m. 6/21/34 to Milton Stanley Ginn; c. Nancy Bewick and Sally Reuben. Educ: Univ. Mo, B.A, 33, grad. work, 33-34; Phi Beta Kappa; Alpha Kappa Delta; Delta Sigma Rho; Alpha Phi Zeta; Delta Delta Delta. Polit. & Govt. Pos: Mem, Mo. Rep. Speakers Bur, 36-54; pres, Lawrence Co. Women's Rep. Club, 37-39; dist. v.pres, Mo. Young Rep. Clubs, 48; pres, Boone Co. Women's Rep. Club, 48-49; del, Co, Dist. and State Rep. Conv, 48-56; permanent secy, Mo. Rep. Conv, 56; mem, Columbia Bd. Health, 56-59; alternate del-at-lg, Rep. Nat. Conv, 56, del, 68; pres, Fedn. Rep. Women's Clubs of Mo, 59-61; Rep. Nat. Committeewoman, Mo, 60- Bus. & Prof. Pos: Dir, Mo. Stores Co, Columbia, Mo, 39-; adv, Columbia Coun. Clubs, 56-58; trustee, Nat. Mortar Bd. Found, 56-; bd. dirs, Boone Co. Hosp. Auxiliary Friends of Arrow Rock. Mem: Budget Cmt, United Fund Campaign, 55-57, dir, 57-59; Asn. Col. Honor Socs.(rep, Mortar Bd, 49-57, exec. coun, 53, pres, 55-57, rep, nat. conf. on fraternities and sororities, 56); Mortar Bd.(secy. dir, 35-45, nat. dir. expansion, 45-48, nat. pres, 48-55); Nat. Asn. Women Deans and Counsr; Am. Legion Auxiliary (counsr, Mo. Girls, 56-); League Women Voters; Kings Daus; Hawkeye Beagle Orchid Soc; Tuesday Club, Columbia; Columbia Country Club; Women's City Club, Berkeley, Calif. Rel: Baptist. Mailing Add: 303 W. Boulevard S, Columbia, Mo. 65201. (1967)

GINSBERG, MARTIN R
N.Y. State Assemblyman
b. Brooklyn, N.Y, 6/7/30; s. William Ginsberg and Ethel Orenstein G; m. 12/25/48 to Joan Kraus; c. Wendy and Susan. Educ: St. Johns Univ, 48-49; St. Johns Law Sch, J.D. cum laude, 52; Philamonic Coun; Phi Delta Phi; Law Rev; Phi Chi Pi. Polit. & Govt. Pos: Pres, Plainview Rep. Club, L.I, N.Y, 63; first v.pres, Coun. Rep. Club Pres, Oyster Bay, 63-64; mem. adv. bd, Joint Legis. Cmt. Family & Matrimonial Law, 63-65; N.Y. State Assemblyman, Nassau Co, 66- Bus. & Prof. Pos: Managing attorney legal dept, Great Am. Ins. Co, 52-55; sr. partner, Lebkuecher, D'Auria and Ginsberg, 55-64; sr. partner, Ginsberg, Strugats & Fertig, 64- Publ: 'Agency—Adverse Interest,' 50 and 'Jus Terti' Under Common Law and N.I.L,' 51, St. Johns Law Rev. Mem: Am, N.Y. State, Nassau Co, Queens Co. and Kings Co. Bar Asns; S.Nassau Lawyers Group; N.Y. State Asn. Plaintiffs' Trial Lawyers; Trial Lawyers Asn. Jewish Nat. Found; Am. Judicature Soc; Plainview C. of C.(pres, 65-66, mem. bd. dirs, legal coun); chmn, Plainview-Old Bethpage Common Market Cmt; Kiwanis (mem. bd. dirs. and chmn. laws cmt); Plainview Rep. Club (past pres); Oyster Bay Coun. Rep. Club Pres. (first v.pres); Nassau Co. Chmn, Cerebral Palsy Fund Raising Campaign, 68; Elks; K. of P; hon. mem. Ancient Order Hibernians; Plainview Jewish Center (mem. laws cmt). Nassau Co. Acad. Phys. Therapy Award; Mid-Island Hebrew Day Sch. Award; Heart Fund Award; Nassau Co. Cancer Soc. Award; Boy Scouts Award; Plainview Rep. Club Award; Outstanding Legis. Serv. Award, Home Improv. Indust; Fedn. Handicapped Award; March of Dimes Award; Plainview C. of C. Award; Kiwanian of the Year Award, 64; Outstanding Citizen of the Year Award, Nat. Columbus Day Cmt. U.S; Man of the Year Award, Cancer Care Inc; Outstanding Legislator for Humanitarian Serv. Award, Nassau Co. Brain Injured Asn; hon. Citizen Award, Father Flanagan's Boy's Town; Humanitarian of the Year Award, Anti-Defamation League, B'nai B'rith; Nassau Co. Cerebral Palsy Found. Award; Muriel Goodman Coun. Waldemar Cancer Research Found. Award; Outstanding Legislator in N.Y. State Assembly, Nat. Inform. Bur. for Jewish Law 68. Rel: Hebrew. Mailing Add: 30 Roxton Rd, Plainview, L.I, N.Y. 11803.

GIOFFRE, ANTHONY B. R
N.Y. State Sen.
b. Port Chester, N.Y, 10/10/07; s. Bruno Gioffre and Anna Messina G; m. 9/17/33 to Louise M. Giorno; c. Bruno J, Anthony B, Jr, Anna (Mrs. DeCarlo) and Donald B. Educ: Syracuse Univ, B.S, 29; Brooklyn Law Sch, L.O.B. and J.D. Polit. & Govt. Pos: Treas, Village of Port Chester, N.Y, 44-54, Mayor, 54-56; state tax attorney, N.Y, 59; N.Y. State Assemblyman, 60-65; N.Y. State Sen, 35th Sen. Dist, 66- Bus. & Prof. Pos: CPA and attorney-at-law, 37- Mem: N.Y. State Soc. CPA; Westchester Co. and Port Chester Bar Asns; N.Y. State Trial Lawyers Asn; mem. and former chmn. and treas, Don Bosco Bd. of Dirs; pres, Scilla Commun. Hosp. Fund, Inc; Italian Hist. Soc. of Am; Lions; Eagles; Port Chester Yacht Club; adv. cmt, Salvation Army; K. of C; Order Sons of Italy; Port Chester Sports Club; Cariddi Italian-Am. Soc. Club. Knight Order of Star of Italian Solidarity. Rel: Catholic. Legal Res: 61 Betsy Brown Rd, Port Chester, N.Y. 10573. Mailing Add: 220 Westchester Ave, Port Chester, N.Y. 10573.

GIOMI, JOHN FRANK D
b. Yerington, Nev, 3/6/17; s. Frank J. Giomi and Cherubina Benetti G; m. to Jere Dorman Patten; c. Joseph A. and John C. Educ: Univ. Nev, grad, 41. Polit. & Govt. Pos: Nev. State Assemblyman, 53-65; mem, Lyon Co. Draft Bd, 53-69. Bus. & Prof. Pos: Mgr, Giomi Bros. Farm Mach. Co, 46-69; retired. Mil. Serv: Entered as Pvt, Army, 42, released as T/Sgt, 45, after serv. in 78th Inf. Div, ETO; Bronze Star; Purple Heart; Combat Inf. Badge; European Campaign Ribbon. Mem: Rotary; VFW; Farm Bur. Rel: Catholic. Mailing Add: Topaz Lake, via Gardnerville, Nev. 89410.

GIORDANO, DOMINIC THOMAS D
b. Meriden, Conn, 1/1/18; s. James V. Giordano and Joesephine Figliole G; m. 7/13/39 to Nadine Desire Briggs; c. Sandra Dale (Mrs. Clifton Russell), Sherrill Lee (Mrs. Millard Hayden), Roxanne Leslie (Mrs. Charles Hansen), Mark Prentis, Bridgett Sue (Mrs. Gerald Bray), Marcia Irene, Cynthia Rae, Justin Jeffry and Dominic T. II. Educ: Pequod Sch. Bus, Conn, 2 years; Northeast. Univ, admin. 6 months. Polit. & Govt. Pos: Chmn, Sangerville Town Dem. Party, Maine, 64 & 69; secy, Piscataquis Co. Dem. Party, 64-69; chmn. cmt. on aging of Maine, 67-; del, Dem. Nat. and Maine State Conv, 68; Justice of the Peace, Sangerville, Maine 68- Bus. & Prof. Pos: Sr. adminstr, Giordano Enterprises, Sangerville, 58-; adminstr, St. Dominic's Nursing Home, Dexter, 60- Mil. Serv: Entered as Pvt, Air Force, 46, released as Sgt, 52; after serving in Med. and Training units, Far East Theater, 47-52; Merit Badge; Good Conduct Medal. Mem: Maine Asn. Nursing Homes; Am. Col. Nursing Home Adminstr; Am. Legion, Sangerville; Grange; Jr. C. of C, Dexter. Rel: Catholic. Legal Res: Silvers Mills Rd, Sangerville, Maine 04779. Mailing Add: 266 Maine St, Dexter, Maine 04930.

GIORGI, E. J. 'ZEKE' D
Ill. State Rep.
b. Rockford, Ill, 9/5/21; s. Gabriele Giorgi and Louise DiMarco G; m. 11/29/43 to Josephine Buttacavoli; c. Barbara, Beverly and Betty. Educ: Washington & Lee Univ. Polit. & Govt. Pos: Dep. assessor, Rockford Twp, Ill, 46-50, alderman, Fifth Ward City Coun, 55-; Ill. State Rep, 64-, mem, Appropriations, Indust. and Labor and Traffic and Hwy. Safety Cmts, Ill. House Rep; mem, Cmn. Ment. Health and Cmn. to Study Not for Profit Corp. Legis; mem. adv. coun, Reference Bur. Bus. & Prof. Pos: Stove mfg, Roper Inc, 46; sales rep, Midwest Dist. Co, 56-66; bd. chmn, N.I.S.C.O. Corp. Mil. Serv: Entered as Pvt, Army, 42, released as Sgt, 46, after serv. in Co. C, 742 Tank Bn, Continental Limits, 40 months; Good Conduct and Victory Medals; Am. Theater Ribbon. Mem: Am. Munic. Asn, Wash, D.C; Robert Carlson Am. Legion Post; IBEW 196, steward; St. Anthonys Sr. Holy Name; St. Ambrose Mutual Benefit; Order Sons of Italy. Rel: Catholic. Mailing Add: 1024 Blake St, Rockford, Ill. 61102.

GIPSON, THOMAS ZACHARIAH D
b. Baton Rouge, La, 10/2/23; married. Polit. & Govt. Pos: Former Miss. State Rep. Bus. & Prof. Pos: Pharmacist. Mem: Miss. State Pharm. Asn; Miss. Cattlemen's Asn; Marion Co. Hist. Soc; Farm Bur; Mason; C. of C; Gideons Int; VFW; Citizens Coun. Rel: Baptist. Mailing Add: Route 4, Box 90, Columbia, Miss. 39429. (1967)

GISH, DAVID HILTON R
b. Lincoln, Nebr, 2/2/34; s. Harold Stanley Gish and Blossom Virginia Hilton G; m. 6/2/56 to Beverley Ann Becton; c. David Hilton, Jr. and Lisa Gail Becton. Educ: South. Methodist Univ; Sigma Alpha Epsilon. Polit. & Govt. Pos: Precinct chmn, Hunt Co. Tex, 61-; del, Tex. Rep. State Conv, 62-68; alternate del, Rep. Nat. Conv, 64. Bus. & Prof. Pos: Design engr, Ling-Temco-Vought, Inc, 56- Mem: Cadillac LaSalle Club; Horseless Carriage Club of Am; asst. scoutmaster, Boy Scouts. Rel: Episcopal. Mailing Add: 2504 Beverley Dr, Greenville, Tex. 75401.

GISS, HAROLD C. D
Ariz. State Sen.
b. Minneapolis, Minn, 2/5/06; s. David Giss and Katherine Edna Glazer G; m. 2/21/37 to Goldie Pearl Stool; c. Maurice M, Kenneth A. and Gerald D. Educ: Southwest. Univ. Law, Los Angeles, less than 1 year; Lambda Delta Beta. Polit. & Govt. Pos: Ariz. State Rep, 49-50; Ariz. State Sen, 51-, Majority Leader, Ariz. State Senate, 55-66, Minority Leader, 67- Bus. & Prof. Pos: Real estate and indust. consult. Mem: Elks; Eagles; hon. mem. Yuma Chap, State Future Farmers of Am. Man of the Year, Yuma, 57. Rel: Jewish. Legal Res: 501 Eighth Ave, Yuma, Ariz. 85364. Mailing Add: P.O. Box 1351, Yuma, Ariz. 85364.

GISSBERG, WILLIAM A. D
Wash. State Sen.
b. Everett, Wash, 1922; m. to Helen; c. Five. Educ: Univ. Wash. Polit. & Govt. Pos: Wash. State Sen, 52-, Pres-Pro-Tem, Wash. State Senate. Bus. & Prof. Pos: Attorney. Mem: Moose; Elks; Swedish W.A.C. Mailing Add: 10928 Maple Lane, Lake Stevens, Wash. 98258.

GITTINS, HARRY RAYMOND R
b. Neola, Iowa, 8/10/10; s. Ray W. Gittins and Eva Lena Johnson G; m. 10/1/40 to Ramona Peterson; c. Harriet, Patricia, Robert, Rodney and Roger. Educ: Univ. Nebr, A.B, 35; Univ. South. Calif, M.S, 40. Polit. & Govt. Pos: Dir, Pottawattamie Co. Inst. Affairs, Iowa, 54-67; Iowa State Rep, 61-64 & 67-69. Bus. & Prof. Pos: Sch. teacher and supt, Iowa and Calif, 35-40 & 41-54; farm owner and mgr, 46- Mem: Farm Bur; Kiwanis. Rel: Lutheran. Mailing Add: 238 Sylvan Dr, Council Bluffs, Iowa 51501. (1967)

GIVAN, RICHARD MARTIN R
Judge, Ind. Supreme Court
b. Indianapolis, Ind, 6/7/21; s. Clinton Hodell Givan and Glee Bowen G; m. 2/28/45 to Pauline Marie Haggart; c. Madalyn (Mrs. Larry Hesson), Sandra, Patricia and Elizabeth. Educ: Ind. Univ, LL.B, 51; Sigma Delta Kappa. Polit. & Govt. Pos: Dep. pub. defender of Ind, 52-54; dep. attorney gen, Ind, 54-65; dep. prosecuting attorney, Marion Co, 65-67; Ind. State Rep, 67-68; Judge, Ind. Supreme Court, 69- Bus. & Prof. Pos: Partner, Givan & Givan Law Firm, 52-59, Bowen, Myers, Northam & Givan, 59-69. Mil. Serv: Entered as Pvt, Army Air Corps, 42, released as 2nd Lt, 45, after serv. in 95th Div, Troop Carrier Command, Air Transport Command, S.Atlantic Theatre. Mem: Indianapolis and Ind. Bar Asns; Ind. Trial Lawyers Asn; Ind. Judges Asn; Lions Int; Rep. Vet. Marion Co; Ind. Arabian Horse Club; Indianapolis Press Club; Ind. Soc. of Chicago; Newcomen Soc. N.Am. Rel: Society of Friends. Mailing Add: R.R. 2, Box 376, Indianapolis, Ind. 46231.

GIVEN, D. P. 'SHERIFF' D
b. Upperglade, W.Va, 5/6/17; s. of H.F. Given and Susan R. Paugh G; m. 9/6/46 to Hazel Cochran; c. Donna Jane. Educ: Glenville State Teachers Col. Polit. & Govt. Pos: Webster Co. Court, 46-52; W.Va. State Del, 58-66. Bus. & Prof. Pos: Contractor, real estate dealer. Mil. Serv: Air Force, World War II, five years. Mem: Moose; Am. Legion; VFW. Rel: Presbyterian. Mailing Add: Webster Springs, W.Va. 26288. (1967)

GIVENS, DAVID D. D
b. Jackson, Tenn, 7/11/11; s. David Charles Givens and Irene Doyle G; m. 5/11/39 to Hazel Hamil; c. Emily and David D, Jr. Educ: Memphis State Univ, B.S, 40, M.A, 53; Kappa Sigma. Polit. & Govt. Pos: Chmn, Fayette Co. Dem. Cmt, Tenn, 49-51; mem. exec. cmt, South. Regional Educ. Bd, Somerville, Tenn, 60-; secy, Tenn. Legis. Coun, 63-69; chmn, Fayette Co. Libr. Bd, 64-; chmn, South. Conf. Coun. State Govt, 65-; mem. exec. cmt, Coun. State Govt; Former Tenn. State Rep. and Majority Floor Leader, Tenn. State House of Rep. Mem: Nat. Educ. Asn; Col, Staff of Governors Buford Elling and Frank Clement; Mason; Farm Bur. Rel: Presbyterian. Mailing Add: 424 N. Main, Somerville, Tenn. 38068. (1967)

GIVHAN, WALTER COATS D
Ala. State Sen.
b. Perry Co, Ala, 5/7/02; s. Walter Pope Givhan and Betty Coats G; m. 1961 to Mrs. Frank James; c. Walter Houston, Samuel Pope. Educ: N.Ga. Col, B.S, 21. Polit. & Govt. Pos: Ala. State Rep, 30 & 42-50; mem, State Sovereignty Cmt; Ala. State Sen, 54- Bus. & Prof. Pos: Planter; chmn, Farmers Mkt. Authority; dir, Planters and Merchants Bank, Uniontown. Mem: State bd. dirs, Ala. State Farm Bur. Fedn; Ala. Farm Bur.(secy-treas); C. of C.(bd. dirs, Selma and Dallas City); bd, dirs, S.Farm Bur. Life Ins. Co; Kiwanis; Mason; Sigma Nu. Rel: Methodist. Mailing Add: Safford, Ala. 36773.

GJESDAL, LARS B, JR. R
Chmn, Aurora Co. Rep. Party, S.Dak.
b. Plankinton S.Dak, 12/18/26; s. Lars B. Gjesdal and Inga M. Hoysted G; single. Polit. & Govt. Pos: Chmn, Aurora Co. Rep. Party, S.Dak, 58-; S.Dak. State Sen, 60-62. Mem: Farm Bur. Rel: Lutheran. Mailing Add: Plankinton, S.Dak. 57368.

GLACKIN, PAUL LOUIS D
Mem, Md. State Dem. Cent. Cmt.
b. Delta, Pa, 12/17/23; s. Charles A. Glackin and Mahala McCallister G; m. 4/8/51 to Dorothy Marvin; c. Susan L. Educ: Univ. Baltimore, 5 years. Polit. & Govt. Pos: Mem, Md. State Dem. Cent. Cmt, 54-; mem, Harford Co. Planning and Zoning, 58-62; mem, Harford Co. Study Cmn, 67-; appraiser, Orphans Court, Harford Co, Co. Cmnr, Dept. Pub. Works and Parks and Recreation Cmn; del, Dem. Nat. Conv, 68. Bus. & Prof. Pos: Pres, Paul L. Glackin, Inc, 62-, Dublin Manor, Inc, 62- and Glackin Umbarger Inc, 62-; dir, Commercial and Saving Bank, 68- Mil. Serv: Served in Merchant Marine.

Mem: Nat. Inst. Real Estate Brokers; Nat. Asn. Realtors; Md. Asn. Realtors; Harford Co. Bd. Realtors (dir, 59-, pres, 69-); Md. Home Builders; K. of C; Elks; Dublin Grange; Pomona Grange; Holy Name Soc; Md. Golf and Country Club; Water Gap Country Club; Young Dem; Belair Fire Dept; Belair and Baltimore C. of C. Rel: Roman Catholic; lay corporator, St. Mary's Church, Pyhesville, Md. Mailing Add: Chesnut St, Cardiff, Md. 21024.

GLADDEN, ROBERT E.
Asst. Secy. of N.J. State Sen.
b. 1922; m. to Grace; c. Robert, Jeffrey, Stephen, Eileen, Michael and Norman. Educ: Rutgers Law Sch, 52. Polit. & Govt. Pos: Asst. to Speaker, N.J. State Assembly,58-60; asst. secy, N.J. State Senate, 61- Bus. & Prof. Pos: Attorney; Ross & Gladden; bd. of treas. Rutgers Univ; teacher part-time Camden Rutgers Law Sch. and exten. div. Rutgers Univ, Camden. Mil. Serv: World War II, OSS, Eng, France, Italy, Egypt, India. Mem: Past pres. Camden Rutgers Varsity Club; Lions; Am. Legion; past chancellor, Rutgers Law Sch. Alumni Asn. Mailing Add: 420 Mansfield Ave, Haddonfield, N.J. 08033. (1967)

GLADDER, CARLTON ARTHUR R
Wash. State Rep.
b. Atwater, Minn, 6/29/09; s. Edwin Ellsworth Gladder and Pauline Swanson G; m. 6/29/40 to Jeanne Adele Wade; c. Gail Anne, Kip Alan and Edwin Ellsworth, II. Educ: Drake Univ, A.B, 33; Omicron Delta Kappa; Sigma Alpha Epsilon. Polit. & Govt. Pos: Wash. State Rep, 67- Bus. & Prof. Pos: Pres, Spokane Life Underwriters, Inc, 53-54. Mil. Serv: Glider Pilot, Air Force Res, 42-43. Publ: Articles for trade journals. Mem: Past pres, Spokane Gyro Club; past dist. gov, Gyro Int, Dist. VIII, 61-62. Rel: Protestant. Mailing Add: 501 Fidelity Bldg, Spokane, Wash. 99201. (1967)

GLADDING, HARRY TILDEN, JR. R
Chmn, Essex Co. Rep. Cmt, Va.
b. Richmond, Va, 8/24/36; s. Harry Tilden Gladding and Elsie Schmidt G; m. 3/31/56 to Ann Montgomery; c. Roy M, Allison and Harry T, III. Educ: Hargrave Mil. Acad. Polit. & Govt. Pos: Chmn, Essex Co. Rep. Cmt, Va, 64- Bus. & Prof. Pos: Employee, Va. Farm Bur. Mutual Ins. Co, 58; employee, Daingerfield Ins. Agency, 60-63, owner, 63- Mil. Serv: Entered as Pvt, Army Res, 54, released as Sgt, 62. Mem: Tappahannock C. of C; chief, Tappahannock Vol. Fire Dept; Lions. Rel: Baptist. Mailing Add: 637 Cradle Ave, Tappahannock, Va. 22560. (1967)

GLADSON, CHARLES L. R
Mem, Calif. Rep. State Cent. Cmt.
b. Glendale, Calif, 1/25/34; s. Virgil H. Gladson and Marjorie Brewer G; m. 7/7/57 to Elizabeth Jane Morgan; c. Linda Jayne, Karen Elizabeth, Marcia Ann and Stephen Robert. Educ: San Jose State Col, A.B, 57; Univ. Calif. Hastings Col. of Law, J.D, 63; Phi Delta Phi; Kappa Alpha. Polit. & Govt. Pos: Co. campaign v.chmn, San Bernardino Co. Gov. Ronald Reagan, 66; campaign chmn, West. San Bernardino Co. Lt. Gov. Robert Finch, 66 and Congressman, Jerry Pettis, 33rd Dist, 66 & 68; mem, Calif. Rep. State Cent. Cmt, currently. Bus. & Prof. Pos: Partner, Covington & Crowe, Law Firm, 65- Mil. Serv: Entered as Ens, Naval Res, 57, released as Lt, 60, after serv. in Naval Commun. Sta, Pearl Harbor, Hawaii; Lt, Res, 60-; Letter of Commendation. Publ: 'Securities Regulation,' Hastings Law J, 58. Mem: Am. and Calif. Bar Asns; Am. Judicature Soc; Kiwanis Int.(dir, (Upland, Calif); Ontario, Calif. C. of C.(dir). Rel: Protestant. Legal Res: 7940 Red Hill Country Club Dr, Cucamonga, Calif. 91730. Mailing Add: 1047 W. Sixth St, Ontario, Calif. 91761.

GLADSTEIN, NANCY ROBIN D
b. San Francisco, Calif, 12/1/41; d. Richard Gladstein and Caroline Decker G; div. Educ: San Francisco State Col, B.A, 64; Col. Notre Dame, Calif, 64-69; Univ. Calif, 67-69; Am. Asn. Univ. Women; Kappa Alpha Theta. Polit. & Govt. Pos: Mem, George Romney Favorite Son Demonstration Cmt, Rep. Nat. Conv, 64; educators cmt, No on Proposition 9, 68; proposition 1-A cmt, Calif. Constitutional Rev, 68; mem, women's cmt. and Kennedy Girl, Robert F. Kennedy campaign, 68; founding mem. and dir, Kennedy Action Corps of Calif, 68; alternate del, Dem. Nat. Conv, 68. Bus. & Prof. Pos: Med. secy, Univ. Calif. Med. Center, 61-64; teacher, San Bruno Park Schs, Calif, 64- Mem: Nat. and San Bruno Educ. Asns; Calif. and San Mateo Co. Teachers Asns; San Francisco Symphony Found; San Francisco Mus. Art; Tri-City Concert Asn; League of Women Voters; Assoc. Dem. Club, North. Calif; Porsche Club of Am. Rel: Unitarian. Legal Res: 2323 Lake St, San Francisco, Calif. 94114. Mailing Add: c/o Winslow, 320 N. La Peer Ave, Beverly Hills, Calif. 90211.

GLADSTONE, BERNARD C. D
R.I. State Rep.
b. Fall River, Mass, 8/3/23; m. to Harriet. Educ: Brown Univ, B.A, 47; Univ. Va. Law Sch, LL.B, 50. Polit. & Govt. Pos: R.I. State Rep, 61-, mem, Third Ward Dem. Cmt. Bus. & Prof. Pos: Attorney. Mem: V.pres, Summitt Ave. PTA; safety chmn, R.I. Cong. of PTA; pres, E.Side Neighborhood Coun. Rel: Past Pres. Temple Beth Sholom. Mailing Add: 134 Woodbine St, Providence, R.I. 02906. (1967)

GLADSTONE, LOUIS I. D
Comptroller, Conn.
b. Bridgeport, Conn, 1927; m. to Jean Rockey; c. Maren, Cassy, Jason. Educ: Univ. Bridgeport; Univ. Conn; N.Y. Univ. Law Sch, LL.B, 52. Polit. & Govt. Pos: Former treas. and membership secy, Bridgeport Young Dem; mem, Bridgeport Common Coun, 55-59, minority leader, 55, pres, 57; Conn. State Sen, 58-67, Majority Leader, Conn. State Senate, 61-67; mem. platform cmt, Dem. State Conv, 60-66; comptroller, Conn, 67-; del, Dem. Nat. Conv, 68. Mil. Serv: Navy, 45-46 on board the carrier, Franklin D. Roosevelt. Mem: Bridgeport and Conn. Bar Asns; Loyalty Lodge; Jewish Commun. Center; Coun. Key Club. Mailing Add: 171 Golden Hill St, Bridgeport, Conn. 06604.

GLADSTONE, WILLIAM D
Chmn, 17th Dist. Dem. Orgn, Mich.
b. Detroit, Mich, 6/21/25; s. Irving Gladstone and Ida Rabinowitz G; m. 6/21/50 to Hannah Levin; c. Deborah Ann and Judith Ellen. Educ: Wayne State Univ, 43-50; Sigma Alpha Mu. Polit. & Govt. Pos: Precinct del. and bd. mem, 17th Cong. Dist, Mich, 64-66, chmn, 17th Dist. Dem. Orgn, 67-; del, Dem. Nat. Conv, 68. Bus. & Prof. Pos: Retailer, 50-54; merchandise mgr, Crown Furniture Co, Detroit, 54-60; retailer, Gladstone's Inc, Wayne, 61- Mem: B'nai B'rith; NAACP; Am. Civil Liberties Union; Nat. Asn. Small Bus; Two-Ten Assocs. Rel: Jewish. Mailing Add: 20287 Greenview, Detroit, Mich. 48219.

GLADWELL, BEATRICE HOWARD R
Committeewoman, Pocahontas Co. Rep. Exec. Cmt, W.Va.
b. Buckeye, W.Va, 7/31/14; d. Judson Luke Howard and Jennie Aurora Barker H; m. 8/16/41 to Carl Harry Gladwell; c. twins, Sharla Howard and Carla Howard (Mrs. James C. Totten). Educ: Davis and Elkins Col, A.B, 57; Delta Kappa Gamma. Polit. & Govt. Pos: Committeewoman, Pocahontas Co. Rep. Exec. Cmt, W.Va, 56- Publ: Poems in Co. Papers, 41-42; 'Adult Education in Pocahontas Co,' W.Va. Sch. J, 8/67. Mem: W.Va. Classroom Teachers Asn; W.Va. and Nat. Educ. Asns; Delta Kappa Gamma (pres, 63); Am. Legion Auxiliary (charter mem, Pocahontas Co, pres, 49); Eastern Star (Worthy Matron); Pocahontas Co. Teachers (pres, 64-65); Pocahontas Co. Farm Women's Asn. All Star Orgn, W.Va. 4-H Alumni Woman. Rel: Presbyterian. Mailing Add: Buckeye, W.Va. 24924.

GLAESCHER, KENNITH PARKER D
Chmn, Henry Co. Dem. Cent. Cmt, Ind.
b. Mt. Summit, Ind, 10/29/02; s. William J. Glaescher and Odessa L. Rader G; m. 11/22/25 to Martha Lucille Washington. Educ: Miss. State Univ, 23-27; Ball State Univ, 45-46. Polit. & Govt. Pos: Dep. collector, Internal Revenue, Ind, 42-47; town clerk-treas, Mt. Summit, 50-55; trustee, Prairie Twp, Henry Co, 55-62; chmn, Henry Co. Dem. Cent. Cmt, 65- Bus. & Prof. Pos: Agent, Standard Oil Co. of Ky, Columbus, Miss, 28-35; with Chrysler Corp, New Castle, Ind, 35-41; partner, Reece & Glaescher Ins. Agency, Mt. Summit, 50-65; retired. Mem: Mason; Scottish Rite; York Rite; Shrine; Optimist. Rel: Protestant. Legal Res: Willard St, Mt. Summit, Ind. 47361. Mailing Add: P.O. Box 206, Mt. Summit, Ind. 47361.

GLANTON, WILLIE STEVENSON D
m. to Luther T. Glanton, Jr; c. Luther T. Glanton, III. Educ: Tenn. A. & I, B.S; Robert H. Terrell Law Sch, LL.B. Polit. & Govt. Pos: Iowa State Rep -66; Asst. Polk Co. Attorney; Polk Cty. Women's Dem. Club; Polk Cty. Women's Activities, Dem. Club; past committeewoman, John F. Kennedy Dem. Club. Bus. & Prof. Pos: Attorney. Mem: Bd, Willkie House, Inc; Polk Cty. Soc. For Crippled Children; Town and Country YWCA; Libr. Adv. Bd; former bd, Urban Renewal for City of Des Moines; participant, Know Your Neighbor panel; Des Moines Bd. Int. Educ; Delta Sigma Theta; Links, Inc; Jack and Jill, Inc; Co, State, and Nat. Bar Asns. Sent to Africa and S.E. Asia by U.S. State Dept. cultural exchange program for 4 1/2 months, 1962. Mailing Add: 818 15th St, Des Moines, Iowa 50314. (1967)

GLASER, NORMAN DALE D
Nev. State Assemblyman
b. Elko, Nev, 4/4/21; s. Clarence Webster Glaser and Margaret Layer G; m. 8/7/43 to Nelda Marie Lancaster; c. Steven, Sharon and Brent. Educ: Okla. State Univ, B.S. in Agr. Eng. Polit. & Govt. Pos: Mem, Elko Co. Sch. Bd, 54-60; Nev. State Assemblyman, currently, Speaker-Pro-Tem, Nev. State Assembly, 61-66; mem, Elko Co. Dem. Cent. Cmt, Nev, currently. Mil. Serv: Entered as Ens, Navy, 44, released as Lt.(jg), 46, after serv. in Pac; Pac. Theater and Leyte Gulf Ribbons. Mem: Pres, Nev. Farm Bur, 62-65; dir, Elko C. of C, 55-57; Toastmasters; VFW; Farm Bur; Nev. Cattle Asn. Outstanding Young Farmer, Nev, 55. Rel: Presbyterian. Mailing Add: Halleck, Nev. 89824.

GLASGOW, LESLIE L. R
Asst. Secy. for Fish and Wildlife, Parks and Marine Resources, Dept. of the Interior
b. Jay Co, Ind, 1914. Educ: Purdue Univ, B.S. in Wildlife and Forestry; Univ. Maine, M.S. in Wildlife; Tex. A&M Univ, Ph.D. in Wildlife Mgt. Polit. & Govt. Pos: Asst. Secy. for Fish and Wildlife, Parks and Marine Resources, Dept. of the Interior and U.S. Cmnr, Int. Cmn. for Northwest Atlantic Fisheries, Dept. of State, 69- Bus. & Prof. Pos: Formerly waterfowl biologist, Ind. Conserv. Dept; prof. wildlife mgt, La. State Univ. and res. in wildlife wetlands mgt, Agr. Exp. Sta, 18 years; dir, La. Wildlife & Fisheries Cmn, 66-69. Recipient of Gov. Award, La. Wildlife Fedn, 67. Legal Res: La. Mailing Add: Dept. of the Interior, Washington, D.C. 20240.

GLASPEY, M. E. D
N.Dak. State Rep.
b. Minnesota, 1901; married; c. Three. Educ: Pub. Schs. Polit. & Govt. Pos: N.Dak. State Rep, currently. Bus. & Prof. Pos: Farmer, auctioneer. Mem: Farmers Union; Lions. Rel: Lutheran. Mailing Add: Lignite, N.Dak. 58752. (1967)

GLASS, FOLSOM LaMONT D
b. Greenville, Ala, 12/22/92; s. Ross Callen Glass and Rebecca Adriana Tillery G; m. 11/14/17 to Lillie Belle Kern; c. Elaine (Mrs. E.N. Clark); Foretta (Mrs. N.P. Clark). Educ: Garland schs. Polit. & Govt. Pos: Ala. State Rep, 59-66. Bus. & Prof. Pos: Merchant; tel. operator, L&N RR. Mem: Masonic Lodge; W.O.W. Rel: Presbyterian. Mailing Add: Greenville, Ala. 36037. (1967)

GLASS, THOMAS REAKIRT D
b. Lynchburg, Va, 5/13/28; s. Carter Glass, Jr. and Ria Binford Thomas G; m. 9/29/51 to Julia Marguerite Thomason; c. Julia Eastham, Mary Byrd, Laura Binford and Blair Thomas. Educ: Va. Mil. Inst, 46-47; Wash. and Lee Univ, B.A. in journalism, 49; Sigma Delta Chi; Phi Delta Theta. Polit. & Govt. Pos: Va. State Del, 58-66; v.chmn, Lynchburg Dem. Cmt, Va, 60-62; mem, State Cmn. on Educ, 60-62 and State Cmn. on Boating, 62-64; chmn, Jefferson Jackson Day Dinner for the State of Va, 64; mem, State Study Cmn. on Tourism, 64-66; v.chmn, Va. State Bd. for Community Cols, 66-68; mem, Va. State Hwy. Cmn, 69-; active in gubernatorial campaigns. Bus. & Prof. Pos: Co-publisher, v.pres. and exec. editor, Lynchburg News, Inc. and Lynchburg Daily Advance, Inc; v.pres, Carter Glass and Sons, Inc; bd. mem, Fidelity Nat. Bank, Lynchburg, 56- Mil. Serv: Entered as Pvt, Air Force, 50, released as 1st Lt, 53, after serv. in U.S. and Korea; Korean Campaign Ribbon. Mem: Elks; Odd Fellows; Lions; Shrine; Scottish Rite; Mason; Lynchburg Naval Adv.

Bd; Boonsboro Country Club; Commonwealth Club, Richmond; C. of C.(pres, Lynchburg Chap, 60-61). Outstanding Young Man of Lynchburg, Jr. C. of C, 56; Outstanding Young Men of Am, 65. Rel: Episcopal. Legal Res: 3130 Landon St, Lynchburg, Va. 24503. Mailing Add: Lynchburg News, Inc, Lynchburg, Va. 24505.

GLASSMIRE, DANIEL F. D
Chmn, Potter Co. Dem. Cmt, Pa.
b. Coudersport, Pa, 8/27/13; s. Daniel F. Glassmire and Jeanette Schuhmacher G; m. 4/29/39 to Beatrice Lignian; c. Daniel F. Educ: Coudersport High Sch. Polit. & Govt. Pos: Chmn, Potter Co. Dem. Cmt, Pa, currently. Mem: F&AM 785, Niagara Falls, N.Y, Coudersport Consistory; Elks 508, Deadwood, S.Dak; Galeton Moose. Rel: Protestant. Mailing Add: R.R. 3, Coudersport, Pa. 16915. (1967)

GLAVIN, JAMES HENRY, III D
Chmn, Saratoga Co. Dem. Cmt, N.Y.
b. Albany, N.Y, 10/6/31; s. James Henry Glavin, Jr. and Elizabeth Gibbons G; m. 6/1/63 to A. Rita Chandellier. Educ: Villanova Univ, A.B, 53; Albany Law Sch, LL.B, 56; mem, ed. bd, col. newspaper, Villanovan and literary quarterly, Lynx. Polit. & Govt. Pos: Committeeman and mem. exec. cmt, Saratoga Co. Dem. Cmt, N.Y, 61-, chmn, 64-; attorney, Water Cmn, Waterford, 61-, mem, Planning Cmn, 62-; area campaign coordinator, N.Y. State Dem. Cmt, 65. Bus. & Prof. Pos: Mem, Nat. Panel of Arbitrators, Am. Arbit. Asn, 65- Mil. Serv: 1st Lt, 839th Air Div, Staff Judge Adv. Off, Tactical Air Command, 57-60; Capt, Air Force Res, 60-; Air Force Outstanding Unit Award. Mem: Am. Trial Lawyers Asn; Am, N.Y. State, Albany Co. and Saratoga Co. Bar Asns; Fed. Bar Asn; Motor Carrier Lawyers Asn; Interstate Commerce Practitioners Asn; N.Y. State Asn. of Trial Lawyers; K. of C.(4°); v.pres, Lions, Waterford, N.Y; Mohawk Golf Club, Schenectady, N.Y; Univ. Club, Albany; Air Force Asn. Rel: Roman Catholic. Legal Res: 69 Second St, Waterford, N.Y. 12188. Mailing Add: P.O. Box 40, Waterford, N.Y. 12188. (1967)

GLAVIN, WILLIAM FRANCIS R
N.H. State Rep.
b. Wenham, Mass, 4/19/97; s. Timothy Francis Glavin and Mary Louise Cummings G; m. 10/2/29 to Ruth Ellen Jenkins; c. Mabel E. (Mrs. Stickney), Jean Elaine (Mrs. Leavitt), Ann (Mrs. Grobe) and Geraldine May (Mrs. Decker). Educ: Mass. Agr. Col, B.S, 20; Univ. N.H, M.E, 42; Sigma Phi Epsilon. Polit. & Govt. Pos: N.H. State Rep, 69- Bus. & Prof. Pos: Tree surgeon, F.J. Bartlett Tree Expert Co, Stamford, Conn, 22-23; teacher voc. agr, Simonds Free High Sch, Werner, N.H, 25-42; supvr, Farm Security Admin, 42; supvr. food prod. prog, N.H. Dept. Educ, 42-44; counsr. voc. rehabilitation, State Dept. Educ, 44-65. Mil. Serv: Entered as Pvt, Marine Corps, 18, released as Sgt, 19, after serv. as Bayonet instr. and Gas. Bomb Sch. Mem: Nat. Rehabilitation Asn; Mason; Am. Legion. Three Serv. Awards, Am. Legion. Rel: Congregational. Mailing Add: 44 Stone St, Concord, N.H. 03301.

GLEASON, CLYDE K. R
b. Lincoln, Ill, 5/16/07; s. Lewis Gleason and Inez Etterlien G; m. 3/17/62 to Helen Olson; c. Harold. Educ: Lincoln High Sch, 4 years. Polit. & Govt. Pos: Sch. bd. mem, Dist. 102, Ill, 37-49; treas, Westmont, Ill, 41-45; exam, Dept. Financial Inst, 55-59; supvr, Downers Grove Twp, 59- Bus. & Prof. Pos: Owner, retail food bus, 25-55. Mem: Lions; Kiwanis; Elks. Rel: Congregational. Mailing Add: 11 Indian Dr, Clarendon Hills, Ill. 60514.

GLEASON, LEONARD J. R
b. Chicago, Ill, 2/26/06; s. William J. Gleason and Hedwig Breitensteen G; m. 6/21/41 to Dorothy A. Dailey; c. Philip and Harriet. Educ: Univ. Pittsburgh. Polit. & Govt. Pos: Former chmn, Rusk Co. Rep. Cmt, Wis. Bus. & Prof. Pos: Acct, Great Lakes Mill Corp, 56- Mem: Boy Scout Leader. Rel: Roman Catholic. Mailing Add: Route 3, Ladysmith, Wis. 54848.

GLEASON, MARTIN JOHN D
b. Joliet, Ill, 1/8/31; s. Martin Patrick Gleason and Margaret Dougherty G; m. 12/29/58 to Marjorie Collette Hempel; c. Lisa Mary and Cara Maureen. Educ: Univ. Notre Dame, B.A, 55; Univ. Chicago Grad. Div, 57. Polit. & Govt. Pos: Pres, Col. Young Dem, 52; presidential elector, Dem. Party, 52; committeeman, 14th Cong. Dist. State Dem. Cent. Cmt, 62-69; del, Dem. Nat. Conv, 64. Bus. & Prof. Pos: V.pres, Gleason Equipment Inc, 57- Mil. Serv: Entered as Pvt, Army, 55, released as Pfc, 56, after service in Signal Corps, Korea. Rel: Roman Catholic. Mailing Add: 600 Cornelia St, Joliet, Ill. 60435. (1967)

GLEASON, ROBERT A. R
Chmn, Cambria Co. Rep. Party, Pa.
b. Philipsburg, Pa, 1/16/09; s. Gus M. Gleason and Helen Rumberger G; m. to Thelma Kremer; c. Robert A, Jr, Christopher K. and Pamela J. Educ: St. Francis Col, B.A, 32; Sigma Chi. Polit. & Govt. Pos: Alderman, Johnstown, Pa, 34-40; chmn, Cambria Co. Rep. Party, 49-; councilman, Westmont Borough, 56-60. Bus. & Prof. Pos: Pres, Gleason Agency, 32- Mil. Serv: Pfc, Air Force, 43-44, serv. in Supply Unit, U.S. Mem: Bd. adv, St. Francis Col; Moose; Am. Legion; 40 et 8. Rel: Roman Catholic; Mem. Bd, Our Mother of Sorrows Church. Legal Res: 543 Elknod Lane, Westmont Borough, Pa. 15905. Mailing Add: 504 Swank Bldg, Johnstown, Pa. 15901.

GLEASON, THEODORE MICHAEL D
b. Blairsburg, Iowa, 4/4/04; m. six children. Educ: State Col. of Iowa. Polit. Pos: Iowa State Rep, 66; Gilmore City Town Coun. Bus. & Prof. Pos: Farm Owner-Operator; Owner-Operator, Movie Theater; Lumber Yard Worker; Rural Sch. Teacher. Rel: Catholic. Mailing Add: Gilmore City, Iowa 50541. (1967)

GLEICH, RUDY J. D
Finance Chmn, Beadle Co. Dem. Party, S.Dak.
b. Ravinia, S.Dak, 11/10/19; s. Rudolph Gleich and Anna Brodsky G; m. 10/3/42 to Betty Kuk; c. Mavis Wochnick, Maryln, Keith, Dale, Craige and Harvey. Educ: Notre Dame Jr. Col, S.Dak, 1 year. Polit. & Govt. Pos: Dem. Precinct Committeeman, ward six, Huron, S.Dak, 64-; chmn, Robert F. Kennedy Campaign, Beadle, Hand, & Sanborn Co, 68; del, Dem. Nat. Conv, 68; finance chmn, Beadle Co. Dem. Party, 69- Mem: Brotherhood of Railway Clerks; Elks. Rel: Presbyterian. Mailing Add: 975 Ohio Ave, S.W, Huron, S.Dak. 57350.

GLEIM, IRA KENNY D
b. Mt. Holly Springs, Pa, 12/15/09; s. Ira Clarence Gleim and Lue Klepp G; m. 1/31/31 to Dorothy Sidsinger; c. Doris S. Polit. & Govt. Pos: Mem, Cumberland Co. Dem. Cmt, Pa, 32-66, treas, 66-69; pres, Borough Coun, Mt. Holly Springs, Pa, 48-52, treas, 50-58; chmn, S.Dist. Cumberland Co. Dem. Party, 60-66; alternate del, Dem. Nat. Conv, 64. Bus. & Prof. Pos: Foreman, Peter J. Schweitzer Div, Kimberly Clark Corp, 42-66. Mem: Eagles; White Circle Lodge; Mt. Holly Fish and Game Asn; Mt. Holly Springs Dem. Club; Mt. Holly Springs Fire Co. Rel: Methodist. Mailing Add: 202 Chestnut St, Mt. Holly Springs, Pa. 17065.

GLENN, DOROTHY NORMAN D
b. Bladenboro, N.C, 2/25/14; d. Dr. John Standing Norman and Estelle Sikes N; m. 11/29/41 to Charles Arthur Glenn, M.D; c. John Lucius. Educ: Lenoir-Rhyne Col, A.B; Univ. N.C, C.M; Woman's Med. Col, M.D, 38; Chi Omega; Gaston Co. Debutante Club. Polit. & Govt. Pos: Former mem. adv. cmt, N.C. State Young Dem. Club; secy, Gaston Co. Young Dem. Club, 47-55, mem. exec. cmt. and pres, 64-66; first v.chmn. and acting chmn, Gaston Co. Dem. Party, 60-64; del, Dem. Nat. Conv, 64. Bus. & Prof. Pos: Chmn, Nursing Serv. Cmt, Med. Found. N.C, 59-; mem. exec. cmt. and trustee, N.C. Orthopedic Hosp, 61-; trustee, Univ. N.C, 63-; mem. visiting cmt. med. alumni, Univ. N.C. Med. Sch, 65-; organizer, first maternal and infants clin. in Gaston Co. Mem: Fel. Am. Col. Surgeons and Am. Col. Obstetrics and Gynecology; Am. Med. Asn; N.C. State Med. Soc; former pres. and secy, Gaston Co. Med. Soc; dir, United Fund, 3 terms, Cancer Soc. and Heart Asn; Am. Legion Auxiliary; VFW Auxiliary. Selected Tenth Cong. Dist. Dem. Woman of Year, 64. Rel: Episcopal. Legal Res: 1319 Park Lane, Gastonia, N.C. 28052. Mailing Add: Box 1492, Gastonia, N.C. 28052. (1967)

GLENN, FRED ANDREW D
Chmn. Co. Cmnrs, Adams Co, Idaho
b. Fruitvale, Idaho, 5/10/12; s. John E. Glenn and Mary E. Robertson G; m. 4/10/35 to Amy Grace Fisk; c. Nelma Grace (Mrs. George Green), Maxine Joice (Mrs. Paul Nichols) and Tommy Fred. Educ: Spec. course in voc. agr. Polit. & Govt. Pos: Mem, Adams Co. Sch. Bd, Idaho, 42-59; mem, Cemetery Dist, 58-68; co. chmn, Fed. Housing Admin. and Agr. Stabilization & Conserv. Serv. Cmt, Council, Idaho, 60-63; Idaho State Sen, 63-68, mem, Transportation, Defense, Educ, Agr, Livestock and Fish & Game Cmts, Idaho State Senate; chmn. co. cmnrs, Adams, Co, 69- Mem: Secy-treas, Fruitvale Cattle Asn, 35-66; Forest Adv. Bd, Nat. Cattle Asn, Payette, 44-60; X Club; Grange; C. of C. Rel: Protestant. Mailing Add: Fruitvale, Idaho 83620.

GLENN, GENE W. D
Iowa State Sen.
b. Wapello Co, Iowa, 11/13/28. Educ: State Univ. Iowa, B.A, 50; Int. Grad. Sch, Univ. Stockholm, Sweden, 55; George Washington Univ. Law Sch, LL.B, 60. Polit. & Govt. Pos: For. Affairs Asst. to U.S. Rep. Frances P. Bolton, 56-61; former Iowa State Rep; Iowa State Sen, 67- Bus. & Prof. Pos: Attorney. Mil. Serv: Army, Korea, 3 years. Mem: United Packinghouse Workers of Am; Omicron Delta Kappa. U.S. del, nat. student YMCA World Conf. of Christian Youth, Oslo, Norway, 47. Rel: Christian Church. Legal Res: Route 7, Ottumwa, Iowa 52501. Mailing Add: State Capitol, E. Tenth & Grand Ave, Des Moines, Iowa 50319. (1967)

GLENN, JOHN HERSCHEL, JR. D
b. Cambridge, Ohio, 7/18/21; s. John Herschel Glenn and Clara Sproat G; m. Apr. 43 to Anna Margaret Castor; c. Carolyn Ann and John David. Educ: Muskingum Col, 39; Univ. Iowa, naval aviation cadet, 42; Naval Air Training Center, Corpus Christi, Tex. grad. flight sch, 43; Navy Test Pilot Training Sch, Md, 54. Hon. D.Sc, Muskingum Col, 61. Polit. & Govt. Pos: Proj. officer, fighter design br, Navy Bur. Eero, Wash, D.C, 56-59; astronaut, Proj. Mercury, Manned Space-Craft Center, NASA, 59-64, pilot, Mercury Atlas 6, orbital space flight launched from Cape Kennedy, Fla, 62. Bus. & Prof. Pos: V.pres. of corporate develop. and dir, Royal Crown Cola Co, currently. Mil. Serv: Entered as 2nd Lt, Marine Corps, 43, released as Lt. Col, 57, after serv. in Fourth Marine Aircraft Wing, Marshall Islands Campaign, 44, Ninth Aircraft Wing, 45-46, First Marine Aircraft Wing, N. China Patrol and Guam, 47-48, flight instr. adv. flight training, Corpus Christi, 49-51, asst. G-2/G-3 Amphibious Warfare Sch, Quantico, Va, 51, Marine Fighter Squadron 311, exchange pilot 25th Fighter Squadron, Air Force, Korea, 53 and non-stop supersonic transcontinental flight, 57; five D.F.C; 18 Air Medals; Astronaut Medal, Marine Corps; Navy Unit Commendation; Korean Presidential Unit Citation. Publ: Co-auth, We Seven, 62. Mem: Soc. Exp. Test Pilots; hon. mem, Int. Acad. of Astronaut. Distinguished Merit Award, Muskingum Col; Medal of Honor, N.Y.C. Rel: Presbyterian. Legal Res: 186 Friendship Dr, New Concord, Ohio 43762. Mailing Add: 203 Sleepy Hollow Court, Seabrook, Tex. 77586.

GLENN, ROBERT EASTWOOD R
Chmn, Roanoke City Rep. Cmt, Va.
b. Catlettsburg, Ky, 12/24/29; s. Albert Sydney Glenn and Pauline Elizabeth Eastwood G; m. 3/16/56 to Clydenne Reinhard; c. Pauline E. and Robert E, Jr. Educ: Wash. & Lee Univ, B.S, 51, LL.B, 53; Beta Gamma Sigma; Phi Delta Phi; Alpha Kappa Psi; Pi Kappa Phi. Polit. & Govt. Pos: Pres, Roanoke City Young Rep, Va, 60; Chmn, Roanoke City Rep. Cmt, 68- Bus. & Prof. Pos: Assoc, Eggleston & Holton, Attorneys, Roanoke, 57-59, partner, Eggleston, Holton & Glenn, 60-62; partner, Eggleston, Holton, Butler & Glenn, 62- Mil. Serv: 1st Lt, Air Force, 53-57, Maj, Res, currently. Mem: Roanoke, Va. State and Am. Bar Asns; Newcomen Soc; Kiwanis; Roanoke Valley Kiwanis (pres, 67). Rel: Roman Catholic. Legal Res: 2659 Nottingham Rd, S.E, Roanoke, Va, 24014. Mailing Add: P. O. Box 2887, Roanoke, Va. 24001.

GLEWWE, ROLLIN BERT R
Minn. State Sen.
b. St. Paul, Minn, 5/2/33; s. Rueben B. Glewwe and Ethel Marie Hymers G; m. 6/20/53 to Joan Adele Brossoit; c. Rae Marie, Lou Ann Elizabeth, Scott Rollin, Barbara Joan and Kelton Edward. Educ: Univ. Minn, 51-53 & 67. Polit. & Govt. Pos: Mem, South St. Paul Charter Cmn, Minn, 64-66; Minn.

State Sen, 12th Dist, 67- Bus. & Prof. Pos: Prod. mgr. pub. rels, Glewwe Food Mkts, 53- Mem: Pres, United Fund of South St. Paul; past pres, C. of C; past pres, Jr. C. of C; past pres, 'S' Club; pres, South St. Paul Develop. Corp; dir, North. Dakota Co. Develop. Corp; AFL-CIO Food Handlers Local 380. Outstanding Young Man of Year, Jr. C. of C, 62; Outstanding Man of Year, City Newspapers, 65. Rel: Baptist. Mailing Add: 138 W. MacArthur St, South St. Paul, Minn. 55075.

GLIEDMAN, HOWARD BENJAMIN R
b. New York, N.Y, 6/21/13; s. Morris Gliedman and Mollie Lipsitz G; m. 10/24/37 to Rae Konowitch; c. Anthony Bruce and Kenneth Richard. Educ: Univ. Pa, A.B, 33; Columbia Univ. Sch. Law, LL.B, 36; Phi Epsilon Pi. Polit. & Govt. Pos: Former counsel, N.Y. State Asn. Young Rep. Clubs; asst. dist. attorney, Kings Co, 45; alternate del, Rep. Nat. Conv, 54, del, 60 & 64; chief criminal div, U.S. Attorney's Off, N.Y, 55-57; spec. asst. to Attorney Gen. U.S, 57-58; asst. campaign mgr, Kenneth Keating for U.S. Sen, 58; mem. exec. cmt, Kings Co. Rep. Party, 61-69; 45th Assembly Dist. committeeman, N.Y. State Rep. Cmt, 61-69. Bus. & Prof. Pos: Attorney-at-Law, N.Y.C, 38- Mem: Brooklyn Bar Asn; N.Y. Co. Lawyers Asn; Kings Co. Criminal Bar Asn; Fed. Bar Asn; Fed. Bar Asn. for N.Y, New Jersey and Conn; Elks; past comdr, K. of P; Grand Lodge, Free Sons of Israel and past pres, Jonothan Lodge, Kings Hwy. C. of C; Univ. Pa. Alumni Asn; Columbia Law Sch. Alumni Asn; East Midwood Jewish Center; Plandome Country Club; Mega-Caristi VFW Mem. Asn; N.Y. State Dist. Attorneys Asn; B'nai B'rith. Rel: Jewish. Legal Res: 1202 E. 23rd St, Brooklyn, N.Y. 11210. Mailing Add: 29 Broadway, New York, N.Y. 10006. (1967)

GLINSKI, FRANK J. D
N.Y. State Sen.
b. Buffalo, N.Y; m. to Veronica Schultz; c. Two. Educ: Masten Park High Sch, Buffalo. Polit. & Govt. Pos: Former mem, Fifth Assembly Dist. Dem. Club, N.Y; mem. bd. supvrs, Erie Co, 4 terms; supvr, Tenth Ward, 36-43; councilman-at-lg, Buffalo, 49-53; exec. secy. bldg. div, Buffalo, 54-58; Pres-Pro-Tem, Common Coun, 58; N.Y. State Sen, 58-; del, Dem. Nat. Conv. 68. Bus. & Prof. Pos: Salesman. Mil. Serv: World War II, serv. in First and Third Armies, Europe. Mem: Prfnl. & Businessmen's Asn, Inc; St. Lukes Holy Name Soc; Capitol Hill Club of Erie Co; Leonard Post 625, VFW; Amvets; Crusade for Freedom Post 209; A. Plewacki Post 799, Am. Legion; Past Comdrs. Club Erie Co, Am. Legion; 15th War & Civic Commun. Asn, Inc. Mailing Add: 1913 Bailey Ave, Buffalo, N.Y. 14211. (1967)

GLOTFELTY, MARTHA IMOGENE R
b. Hoyes, Md, 8/31/08; d. Nathan Hamill Casteel and Sadie Ellen DeWitt C; m. 2/11/31 to Kermit Shoup Glotfelty; c. Donald Richard, Hamill Josephus and Kenneth Irving. Educ: Summer courses at Waynesburg Col, Pa, 29 and Calif. State Col, Pa, 30. Polit. & Govt. Pos: Former Md. State Del, Garrett Co; pres, Garrett Co. Rep. Women's Club, 58-63. Mem: Life mem. PTO; Farm Bur; Nat. Order of Women Legislators. Rel: Lutheran. Mailing Add: Accident, Md. 21520. (1967)

GLOVER, DONALD HAIR D
b. Port Arthur, Tex, 1/9/18; s. William Carl Glover and Geneva Hair G; m. 12/18/43 to Helen Dunlap Barfield; stepson, Sam C. Barfield. Educ: Rice Univ, Houston, Tex, 41; student conductor, Thomas Jefferson High Sch. Band, 34-36; Rice Univ. Band, Solo Trumpet, 37-38; Polit. & Govt. Pos: Mem. 15 man co. campaign for Humphrey-Muskie, 68. Pres, Brazos Co. Water Control & Improv. Dist, 64-; chmn, Precinct 46, Jefferson Co. Dem. Exec. Cmt, 63-66; chmn, South Jefferson Co. Dem. Campaign, Johnson and Humphrey, 64; del, Dem. Nat. Conv, 64; committeeman, Tex. State Dem. Exec. Cmt, 4th Sen. Dist, 62-64; pres, Jefferson Co. Dem. Club, 58-62; chmn, South Jefferson Co. Dem. Campaign, Kennedy and Johnson, 60; pres, Jefferson Co. Young Dem. Club, 52-54. Bus. & Prof. Pos: Spec. analytical tester, Atlantic Richfield, 42-66; teller, Merchants Nat. Bank, 40-41. Mil. Serv: Played Solo Trumpet, 11th Engrs. Band Sect, Tex. Nat. Guard, 37-41. Mem: Charter mem, Evening Lions Club; pres, Port Arthur Unit, Tex. T.B. Asn, 64-65 and bd. mem, 56-66; Local 4-23 OCAW AFL-CIO Negotiating Cmt, 51-53, chmn, 51-52 and v.pres, Local 4-23, 49-51; YMCA. Rel: First Baptist Church, Port Arthur. Mailing Add: 4311 Big Bend, Port Arthur, Tex. 77640.

GLOVER, KERMIT P. D
b. Mokane, Mo, 8/3/20; m. 1/20/53 to Vivien Bozarth; c. Brent, Marge, Betsy, Debbie, Jeffrey. Educ: Univ. of Mo. Polit. & Govt. Pos: Mo. State Rep, 64-66. Bus. & Prof. Pos: Clothing merchant, 45- Mil. Serv: Mo. Nat. Guard, 40-46. Mem: VFW; Am. Legion; AF&AM. Rel: Christian Church. Mailing Add: 1304 4th St, Boonville, Mo. 65233. (1967)

GLOVSKY, C. HENRY R
b. Salem, Mass, 3/26/18; s. Abraham Glovsky and Ruth Slotnick G; m. 10/2/41 to Natalie E. Tarlow; c. John E, Mark B. and Alan M. Educ: London Sch. of Econ. and Polit. Sci, 37-38; Dartmouth Col, A.B, 39; Harvard Law Sch, LL.B, 42. Polit. & Govt. Pos: Del, Rep. Nat. Conv, 64; adv, U.S. Del, Coun. of Intergovt. Cmt. for European Migration, 55-56; consultant to Asst. Secy. of State in Refugee Affairs, 56; Mass. State Sen, 54-56; Mass. State Rep, 51-53. Bus. & Prof. Pos: Dir, Bay Bank and Trust Co, 55- Mil. Serv: Entered as Pvt, Army, 42, released as Capt, 46, after serv. in India-Burma Theater. Mem: Rotary; Essex Co. Rep. Club; Mass, Essex Co. and Salem Bar Asns. One of Ten Outstanding Young Men of Gr. Boston, 53. Rel: Hebrew. Legal Res: 23 Ober St, Beverly, Mass. 01915. Mailing Add: 8 Washington St, Beverly, Mass. 01915.

GLUBA, WILLIAM EVAN D
Exec. Secy, Davenport City Dem. Cent. Cmt, Iowa
b. Davenport, Iowa, 10/7/42; William Lee Gluba and Ellen Conboy G; m. 8/28/65 to Patricia Ann Keefe. Educ: St. Ambrose Col, B.A, 64; Univ. Iowa, Grad. Work, 64- Polit. & Govt. Pos: Active in President Kennedy's Campaign, 60; pres, St. Ambrose Col. Young Dem, 62; secy, Young Dem. Clubs, Iowa, 62, nat. committeeman, 63-64, pres, 64-65; voter registrn. and orgn. dir, Scott Co. Dem. Cent. Cmt, 64, exec. secy, 65; exec. secy, Davenport City Dem. Cent. Cmt; Dem. precinct committeeman, Iowa, 66- Mem: Univ. Iowa Polit. Sci. Grad. Club; Univ. Iowa Young Dem; Young Dem. Clubs Am; St. Ambrose Col. Alumni Asn; Davenport Catholic Interracial Coun. Outstanding Young Dem, Iowa, 64. Rel: Catholic. Mailing Add: 328 W. 12th St, Davenport, Iowa 52803. (1967)

GLUCK, JOSEPH D
s. J.M. Gluck and Freda Kehl G; m. to Bertha Weiner. Polit. & Govt. Pos: Former Dem. Nat. Committeeman from Wash; presidential elector, Wash, 49, hon. v.chmn, Nat. Conv, 52, 56 & 60; finance chmn, King Co. Dem. Cmt. Bus. & Prof. Pos: Diamond importer, 23- Mem: Young Men's Dem. Club; Mason; B'nai B'rith; Zionist Orgn. Am. Rel: Jewish. Mailing Add: 615 Bellvue E, Seattle, Wash. 98102. (1967)

GLUSAC, MICHAEL M. Non-partisan
b. Highland Park, Mich, 7/28/30; s. Mitchell Glusac and Violet Kovacevich (deceased); m. 6/22/57 to Adele Marie Lindgren; c. Earl John, Elaine Marie and Emily Mildred. Educ: Wayne State Univ, B.A. in Eng, 53, Law Sch, J.D, 56; Omicron Delta Kappa; Wayne Law Rev. ed. staff. Polit. & Govt. Pos: Councilman, Highland Park, Mich, 63-65, Mayor, 65-68, pres, City Coun, 68-; mem, Wayne Co. Bd. of Supvr, 66-68; mem. exec. cmt, S.E. Mich. Coun. of Govts, 67-; mem. bd. trustees, Mich. Munic. League, 68- Bus. & Prof. Pos: Attorney, 57- Mem: Am. Judicature Soc; Am. and Mich. Bar Asns; Highland Park Bar Asn. (past pres); dir, Highland Park Boys Club. Distinguished Serv. Award, Highland Park Jaycees, 63. Rel: Protestant. Legal Res: 84 Puritan, Highland Park, Mich. 48203. Mailing Add: 13700 Woodward, Highland Park, Mich. 48203.

GOADY, CHARLES WILLIAM R
b. Rutherford, N.J; s. Charles Amos Goady and Miriam Washington G; m. 8/29/48 to Marion Marie Crews; c. Ronald C, Robert A. and Soon Anne. Educ: L.I. Univ, B.S. in Acct, 49; N.Y. Univ. Grad. Sch. Pub. Admin, 50; Ind. Univ. Grad. Sch. Bus. Admin, Cert. Savings and Loan, 63. Polit. & Govt. Pos: Cmnr, Oakland Civil Serv, Oakland, Calif, 64-69; sch. bd. dir, Oakland, 69- Mil. Serv: Entered as Pvt, Army Air Force, 42, released as Sgt, 45, after serv. in Signal Corps, Mediterranean Theatre. Mem: Oakland C. of C. (dir). Rel: Baptist. Mailing Add: 1032 Ardmore Ave, Oakland, Calif. 94610.

GOCKEL, GLADYS R
Mem, Okla. Rep. State Exec. Cmt.
b. Tulsa, Okla, 2/25/26; d. Ralph M. Darnell and Dencie Stebbins D; m. 7/29/50 to Ashford R. Gockel; c. Tad and Dencie. Educ: Univ. Okla, 43-45; Univ. Colo, B.A, 47; Kappa Alpha Theta. Polit. & Govt. Pos: Rep. block worker and Rep. precinct chmn, Okla, 61; organizer, Nichols Hills Rep. Women's Club, 61, v.pres, 69-; Rep. area chmn. and Rep. ward co-chmn, 62; mem, Henry Bellmon's Campaign and Sooners for Crawford, 62; v.chmn, Oklahoma Co. Rep. Party, 63-66; mem, Young Rep, 63-66; registr-at-lg, Rep. Party, 63-66; fifth dist. v.pres, State Fedn. of Rep. Women, 64; mem, Bud Brigadeer and Goldwater Girl, 64; chmn, GOP fair booth, Okla. State Fair, 65; ed, GO Party Line, 65 & 69-; committeewoman, Fifth Dist. Rep. Cmt, 66; helped set up and organize Vondel Smith's hq, 66; dep. registr, Rep. Party, 66 & 69-; participant, Campaign Mgt. Sem, Norman, 67; in charge of arrangements, George Murphy Dinner, 67; committeewoman, Okla. Rep. State Cmt, 67-69; mem, Okla. City Rep. Women and Nichols Hills Rep. Women, 68; del, Rep. Nat. Conv, 68; sponsor, Okla. Co. TAR, 69-; historian, Okla. Fedn. of Rep. Women, 69-; mem, Okla. Rep. State Exec. Cmt, 69- Mem: Jr. League. Rel: Presbyterian Church in the U.S. Mailing Add: 1208 Glenwood, Oklahoma City, Okla. 73116.

GODDARD, ALPHEUS JOHN, JR. R
Mem, Stephenson Co. Rep. Finance Cmt.
b. Sycamore, Ill, 6/19/02; s. Alpheus John Goddard and Abby Rogers G; m. Jane Dillon, div; c. Alpheus John, III and Paul D. Educ: Amherst Col, A.B, 25; Delta Sigma Rho; Psi Upsilon; Cotillion Club; Scarab. Polit. & Govt. Pos: Del, various state and judicial Rep. Convs; mem, Freeport Planning Cmn, Ill, 62-65; del, Rep. Nat. Conv, 64; mem, Stephenson Co. Rep. Finance Cmt, currently. Bus. & Prof. Pos: Sales mgr, Stover Mfg. Co, 25-26; div. mgr, Armstrong Cork Co, 26-50; secy. and dir, Northwest. Steel & Wire Co, 50-58; self employed invest. mgt, 58- Mem: Mason; Consistory; Shrine; Elks; Union League Club, Chicago; Univ. Club, Chicago; Freeport Country Club. Rel: Episcopal. Legal Res: 1706 W. Harrison St, Freeport, Ill. 61032. Mailing Add: P.O. Box 37, Freeport, Ill. 61032.

GODDARD, DON REUBEN R
Ohio State Rep.
b. Cutler, Ohio, 12/12/98; s. Frank E. Goddard and Elizabeth Hull G; m. 12/20/22 to Josephine Kinney; c. Eleanor, Mary Ruth, Janet and Patricia. Educ: Ohio Univ, B.S. in Educ, 25; Theta Chi. Polit. & Govt. Pos: Clerk, Wesley Twp, Ohio, 30-64; mem, Bank Adv. Bd, Ohio, 57-60 & 63-65; Ohio State Rep, 29th Dist, 65- Bus. & Prof. Pos: Mem. and past pres, Washington Co. Fair Bd, 31-64 and Washington Co. Bd. of Educ, 37-63. Mil. Serv: Pvt, Army, 18. Mem: Mason (32°); Eastern Star; White Shrine; Grange; Vet. Orgn. Rel: Methodist. Mailing Add: Bartlett, Ohio 45713.

GODDARD, RALPH E. D
b. Kans. City, Mo, 12/4/10; m. 6/14/36 to Lorraine Lane; c. Ralph Lane. Educ: Braymer, Mo. high Sch. Polit. & Govt. Pos: Pres, Braymer Bd. of Educ, Mo, 5 years; committeeman, Davis Twp, Caldwell Co, 2 terms; mem, Braymer City Coun, 2 terms; Mo. State Rep, 64-66; E.S. Technician Mo. Div. of Employment Security, St. Joseph, 67-68, Chillicothe, 68-69. Bus. & Prof. Pos: Retail grocery bus, 36-54; specialty advert. jobber, 55-62; radio news announcer, 6 years; Mo. Farmers Ins. Agent, 7 years; collector, Mo. Power and Light Co, 7 years. Mem: Lodge 135, F&AM, Shrine; Eastern Star. Rel: First Christian Church. Mailing Add: Box 415, Braymer, Mo. 64624.

GODDARD, SAMUEL PEARSON, JR. D
b. Clayton, Mo, 8/8/19; s. Samuel Pearson Goddard and Florence Denham G; m. 7/1/44 to Julia Hatch; c. Samuel Pearson, III, Pascal Hatch and William Denham. Educ: Harvard, A.B, 41; Univ. Ariz, LL.B, 49; Phi Alpha Delta; Kirkland House, Harvard. Polit. & Govt. Pos: State chmn, Dem. Party, Ariz, 60-62; Gov, Ariz, 65-67; del, Dem. Nat. Conv, 68; Dem. cand, Gov, Ariz, 68. Bus. & Prof. Pos: Lawyer, Terry & Wright, 50-58, Goddard, Gin, Hanshaw & Gianas, Tucson, Ariz, 58-68 and Goddard, Sophy & L'Ecuyer, Phoenix and Tucson, 68- Mil. Serv: Entered as Pvt, Army Air Corps, 41,

released as Maj, 46; European, Pac. and Am. Theater Ribbons; Victory Medal; Am. Defense Serv. Ribbon; Col, Air Force Res. Mem: Am, Ariz. and Pima Co. Bar Asns; Air Force Asn; Res. Officers' Asn; Am. Legion; Old Pueblo Club; Rotary Club of Tucson; Harvard Varsity Club; Ariz. Acad; trustee, Nat. Rowing Found; Harvard Varsity Crew, 40-41; pres, United Commun. Campaign, Tucson, 60-62 and West. Conf. of United Commun. Funds and Couns. of Am, 61-63; bd. of dirs, United Commun. Funds and Couns. of Am, 63-68; bd, Associated Harvard Alumni, 68- Rel: Unitarian. Mailing Add: 4813 Calle Jabeli, Tucson, Ariz. 85711.

GODDARD, VOLTA F. R

b. Maryville, Tenn, 2/15/91; s. Nathan Goddard and Dorcas Morton G; m. June, 1920 to Ruth Lassfolk; c. Ruth Elizabeth and Barbara Jean. Educ: Maryville Col, B.A, 13 and Ph.D. of Pedagogy, 53; Univ. Mich, M.A, 28. Polit. & Govt. Pos: Mem. bd. control, Tenn. Sec. Athletic Asn, 35-37; mem. bd. trustees, Tenn. Teachers Retirement Syst, 45-57; exec. secy, Tenn. Pub. Sch. Officers Asn, 46-57; Tenn. State Rep, 61-67. Bus. & Prof. Pos: Supt. schs, Chassell, Mich, 13-16 and Crosby, N.Dak, 16-24; instr, summer sch, State Col, Minot, N.Dak, 18-23; supt. schs, Aloca, Tenn, 24-57; instr, Maryville Col, Tenn, 57-59. Publ: 'Objectives of Secondary Education,' Tenn. Educ. Surv, 35; 'Curriculum Adjustment,' Am. Asn. Sch. Admin, 50; 'Cutting Dimes of Save Dollars,' Progressive Farmer, plus 1 other. Mem: Tenn. and Nat. Educ. Asns; Am. Asn. Sch. Adminstr; Farm Bur; Tenn. Livestock Asn; Rotary. Rel: Methodist. Mailing Add: Route 7, Maryville, Tenn. 37801.

GODFREY, JAMES E. D

Mo. State Rep.

b. Litchfield, Ill, 11/9/22; m. 5/15/54 to Ellen Rose Higgins; c. Timothy Sean, Dennis Michael, James Edward Jr. and Kathleen. Educ: Univ. Notre Dame, B.A, 43, LL.B, 48. Polit. & Govt. Pos: Mo. State Rep, 60-, Speaker, Mo. House of Rep, 67-; del, Dem. Nat. Conv, 68. Bus. & Prof. Pos: Law practice; trial lawyer, Transit Casualty Co. Mil. Serv: Army Inf, 3 years; Naval Cmn, retired Navy. Mem: St. Louis, Am. and Mo. Bar Asns; Lawyers' Asn; K. of C; Am. Legion. Rel: Catholic. Mailing Add: 6227 Devonshire Ave, St. Louis, Mo. 63109.

GODLEY, G. McMURTRIE

U.S. Ambassador to Laos

b. N.Y.C, 8/23/17; m. 3/26/66 to Elizabeth McCray; c. George McMurtrie, Jr. and Nicholas Franchot. Educ: Yale Univ, A.B, 39; Univ. Chicago. Hon. LL.D, Hartwick Col, Oneonta, N.Y. Polit. & Govt. Pos: Career officer, U.S. Dept. of State For. Serv, 41-; v.consul, Marseille, 41; third secy, Bern, 41-46; second secy, Brussels, 46-48; first secy, Paris, 52-55; counsr, Cambodia, 55-57; Sr. Seminar in For. Policy, For. Serv. Inst, 60-61; counsr, Congo, 61-62; dir, Off. of Cent. African Affairs, 62-64; U.S. Ambassador to the Congo, 64-66; For. Serv. Inspector, 67; Dep. Asst. Secy, E.Asian Affairs, 68; U.S. Ambassador to Laos, 69- Mil. Serv: Ens, Naval Res, 39-41; Marine Corps, 45-46. Rel: Protestant. Legal Res: Morris, N.Y. 13808. Mailing Add: American Embassy, APO San Francisco 96352.

GODLEY, GENE EDWIN D

b. Houston, Tex, 10/6/39; s. Thomas Edwin Godley and Jewel Drain G; m. 9/19/64 to Lisbeth Kamborian. Educ: South. Methodist Univ, Dallas, B.A, 60; Univ. Chicago Law Sch, J.D, 63. Polit. & Govt. Pos: Counsel, Vet. Subcmt, U.S. Senate Labor and Pub. Welfare Cmt, 64, labor subcmt, 67; press and research asst. to U.S. Sen. Ralph Yarborough, 65, legis. asst, 68 and admin. asst, 69- Bus. & Prof. Pos: Consult, Booz, Allen & Hamilton, Wash, D.C, 66. Mil. Serv: Pvt, Army Res, 64, Capt, Res. Mem: Phi Delta Phi; Tex. Bar Asn; Am. Bar Asn. Legal Res: 2927 Garapan, Dallas, Tex. 75224. Mailing Add: 712 Sixth St. S.W, Washington, D.C. 20024.

GODSEY, ANDREW EMMETT D

Chmn, Cumberland Co. Dem. Cmt, Va.

b. Cumberland, Va, 7/6/05; s. Andrew Emmett Godsey and Mary Courtney Foster G; m. 3/12/26 to Eloise Brightwell Blanton, wid. Educ: Cumberland High Sch, grad, 22; LaSalle Correspondence Sch, sponsored by Standard Oil Co, 1 year. Polit. & Govt. Pos: Pres, Young Dem. Club, 39-45; chmn, Cumberland Co. Dem. Cmt, Va, 45-; campaign mgr. gov. elec. for Mills Godwin, Albertis Harrison, Tom Stanley and Lindsay Almond and Watkins M. Abbitt for Congressman, A. Willis Robertson, Harry F. Byrd Sr. and Harry F. Byrd Jr. for U.S. Sen, 50- Bus. & Prof. Pos: Salesman, Standard Oil Co, N.J, 25-50, retired; farming and real estate. Mem: Mason (32°); Master of Lodge, chmn. various cmts); Scottish Rite; Shrine; Puritan Club; Moose; Kiwanis; Travelers Protective Asn. Rel: Baptist. Mailing Add: Cumberland, Va. 23040.

GODWIN, CHARLES EDWARD D

S.C. State Rep.

b. Lake City, S.C, 11/23/37; s. Samuel Louie Godwin, Sr. and Roylee Parnell G; m. 8/21/59 to Patricia Webster; c. Patricia Kim, Charles Edward, Jr. and Tara Webster. Educ: Wofford Col, A.B, 60; Palmetto Mil. Academy, Lexington, S.C, 61-62; Univ. S.C. Law Sch, J.D, 67; Phi Delta Phi. Polit. & Govt. Pos: S.C. State Rep, Florence Co, 68- Mil. Serv: Entered as Pvt. E-1, Army, 60, released 1st Lt, 66, after serv. in Army, 6 months active duty, S.C. Nat. Guard, 2½ years and Army Res. Mem: Lake City, Florence Co. and Am. Bar Asns; S.C. Trial Lawyers Asn; Am. Judicature Soc; Mason; Florence Co. and Williamsburg Co. Field Trial Asns; secy, Lake City Jaycees, 60-61. Rel: Methodist. Mailing Add: Route 2, Lake City, S.C. 29560.

GODWIN, MILLS EDWIN, JR. D

Gov, Commonwealth of Va.

b. Nansemond Co, Va, 11/19/14; s. Mills Edwin Godwin and Otelia Darden G; m. 10/26/40 to Katherine Thomas Beale; c. Becky Katherine (deceased). Educ: Col. of William & Mary, 31-34; Univ. of Va, LL.D, 38. Hon. LL.D, Elon Col, 54, Col. of William and Mary, 66 and Roanoke Col, 69. Polit. & Govt. Pos: Former chmn, Va. Potomac River Cmn; former v.chmn, Va. Cmn. on Constitutional Govt; former mem, Cmn. Pub. Educ. and Va. Adv. Legis. Coun; Va. State Del, 48-52; chmn, Nansemond Co. Dem. Cmt, 48-58; Va. State Sen, 52-62; Lt. Gov, 62-66; Gov. of Va, 66-; del, Dem. Nat. Conv, 68. Bus. & Prof. Pos: Former asst. commonwealth's attorney, Nansemond Co; former Fed. Bur. of Invest. spec. agent; owner and operator 500 acre farm, Nansemond Co. Mem: Ruritan, past pres, Ruritan Nat; K. of P; Mason; Scottish Rite and Khedive Temple; Moose; Rotary; former chmn, Suffolk-Nansemond Red Cross, Tuberc. Asn, Cancer Soc. and United Fund. Rel: Christian Church; Former Chmn. Bd. of Deacons, Oakland Christian Church. Mailing Add: State Capitol, Richmond, Va. 23219.

GODWIN, PHILIP PITTMAN D

Majority Leader, N.C. House of Rep.

b. Gatesville, N.C; s. Adolphus Pilston Godwin and Mabel Claire Hayes G; m. 6/10/50 to Anita Thomas Freeman; c. Philip Pittman, Jr. Educ: Fishburne Mil. Sch, 43; Wake Forest, B.S, 53, Wake Forest Law Sch, LL.B, 56. Polit. & Govt. Pos: Former pres, Young Dem. Club, Wake Forest, N.C; N.C. State Rep, 61-, majority leader, N.C. House of Rep, 69-; mem, N.C. Legis. Research Cmn, 63-65 and N.C. Tax Study Cmn, 67-69. Bus. & Prof. Pos: Attorney-at-law. Mil. Serv: Staff Sgt, Air Force, 43-45; Pac. Theatre. Mem: Former pres, First Dist. Bar Asn; N.C. State Bar Asn; former mem, Judicial Coun. of State of N.C; AF&AM. Rel: Baptist. Mailing Add: Gatesville, N.C. 27938.

GODWIN, RUFFIN C. D

N.C. State Rep.

b. near Dunn, N.C, 2/10/91; s. Wiley Godwin and Harriett Elizabeth Parrish G; m. 6/2/57 to Mary Elizabeth Dixon; c. Robert C. Godwin. Educ: Buie's Creek Acad; Bus. Col, 10-11; night classes, Judge Pell's Law Sch, 12-13. Polit. & Govt. Pos: Mem, Co. Bd. Elec, N.C, 28; mem. bd, Aldermen, New Bern, 32-34; Vets. Employ. representative, N.C. and dir. employ. servs, 39-63; N.C. State Rep, 63- Bus. & Prof. Pos: Ins. salesman, 12-13; consult. on vets. affairs, 63- Mil. Serv: Army, Cpl, 17-18. Mem: Am. Fed. Govt. Employees; former pres, Int. Asn. Personnel Employ. Security; assoc. mem, N.C. State Employees Asn; Mason; Shrine; Elks; former post comdr, former dist. comdr, former state dept. v.comdr, former nat. v.comdr, currently v.chmn, Nat. Distinguished Guests Cmt, Am. Legion; former pres, Lions. Rel: Baptist. Mailing Add: 1118 National Ave, New Bern, N.C. 28560. (1967)

GODWIN, RUTH TICHI D

Committeewoman, Fla. Dem. Party

b. Isabell, S.Dak, 3/29/23; d. Samuel Tichi and Anna Oetken T; m. 2/6/42 to Venzie C. Godwin; c. Sharon Ann (Mrs. Jimmie D. Davis), John and Mike; grandchildren, Doug and Brian Davis. Educ: Ernest Ward High Sch, Walnut Hill, Fla, grad, 41; Pensacola Jr. Col. Polit. & Govt. Pos: Dem. committeewoman, Precinct 10, Davisville, Fla, 58-69; v.chmn, Escambia Co. Dem. Exec. Cmt, 62-69; mem, Tel-A-Friend Campaign, First Cong. Dist, 64; chmn, Ladies for Lyndon, Escambia Co, 64; mem, Ladybird Spec. Whistle Stop Cmt, Pensacola, Fla. and Flomaten, Ala, 64; mem, Escambia Co. Libr. Bd, 64, secy, currently; organizer and first pres, Dem. Woman's Clubs of N.W. Escambia Co, 64; woman's coordinator for Escambia Co, Robert King High for Gov. of Fla, 66; committeewoman, Fla. Dem. Party, Escambia Co, 66-; mem. adv. bd, Dem. Woman's Clubs of Fla, 66, publicity chmn. annual conv, 67, budget chmn, 68-69; del-at.lg, Dem. Nat. Conv, 68; chmn, Dem. Hq. for Escambia Co, Fla, 68. Bus. & Prof. Pos: Farmer and rancher, currently. Publ: 'I Am An American', 3/67 and 'Why I Support Hubert Humphrey for President', 11/68, Pensacola News J. Mem: PTA; Davisville Commun. Club; Fla. Farm Bur; Fla. Libr. Asn; Am. Libr. Asn. (assembly cmt, 66-68); W.Fla. Regional Libr; 4-H Club Leader; bd. dirs, Nat. Found; chmn, Mothers March for N.W. Escambia Co, 12 years; bd. dirs, Am. Cancer Soc. of Escambia Co, 6 years; chmn, Cancer Crusade for N.W. Escambia Co, 6 years. Conserv. Award, Fla. Farm Bur; Gold Clover Award for 10 Year Leadership, 4-H Clubs; Ten Year Pin and Plaque, Nat. Found. Rel: Presbyterian; Dist. Chmn. and Pres. of Women, Mobile Presbytery, Synod of Ala. Mailing Add: P.O. Box 8, Walnut Hill, Fla. 32568.

GODWIN, SAMUEL E. R

Chmn, Duplin Co. Rep. Exec. Cmt, N.C.

b. Dunn, N.C, 2/3/20; s. Edgar Judson Godwin and Kitty Elma G; m. 6/5/46 to Emma Francis Pridgen; c. Samuel E, Jr. Educ: Dunn High Sch, grad. Polit. & Govt. Pos: Del, Rep. Nat. Conv, 64; chmn, Duplin Co. Rep. Exec. Cmt, N.C, 66-; pres. elector, Third Cong. Dist, 68. Mil. Serv: Entered as Pvt, Army Air Corps, 42, released as Capt, 45, after serv. in Eighth Air Force, ETO, 44; Distinguished Flying Cross with Oak Leaf Cluster; Air Medal with Five Oak Leaf Clusters. Rel: Methodist. Mailing Add: 301 E. Chelly St, Warsaw, N.C. 28398.

GOE, WILLIAM ROBERT D

Chmn, Lewis Co. Dem. Exec. Cmt, W.Va.

b. Weston, W.Va, 8/7/18; s. Norval Douglas Goe and Madge Houghton G; single. Educ: Mountain State Bus. Col, Parkersburg, W.Va, grad, 36. Polit. & Govt. Pos: Mem, Lewis Co. Bd. Educ, W.Va, 49-55; chmn, Lewis Co. Dem. Exec. Cmt, 60-; mem, Weston Sanit. Bd, 65- Bus. & Prof. Pos: Acct, Danser Hardware & Supply Co, Weston, W.Va, 36- Mil. Serv: Entered as Pvt, Army, 42, released as Tech-4, 46, after serv. in 102nd Machine Records Unit, Seventh Corps, 46; Good Conduct Medal; Victory and Am. Campaign Medals. Mem: Past comdr, Weston Post 4, Am. Legion; past Third Dist. Comdr, of the Am. Legion Dept, W.Va; past pres, Weston Jr. C. of C; past pres, Weston Lions Club; Moose Lodge. Rel: Methodist. Mailing Add: 216 E. Third St, Weston, W.Va. 26452. (1967)

GOEBEL, ELDON E. R

b. Lehr, N.Dak, 9/26/24; married; c. 4. Educ: Univ. of N.Dak; Purdue Univ. Polit. & Govt. Pos: N.Dak. State Rep, 55-61. Bus. & Prof. Pos: Auto and implement dealer. Mem: Am. Legion; Elks; Masons; Shrine; Asn. Commerce. Mailing Add: Lehr, N.Dak. 58460. (1967)

GOEDECKE, HERBERT G. R

N.H. State Rep.

b. Berlin, Germany, 12/14/16; s. George Goedecke and Anna L. Koch G; m. 2/12/39 to Grace M. Goodwin; c. George, Carl, Alan R. and Marilynn G. Educ: Hesser Bus. Col, Manchester, N.H, 2 years. Polit. & Govt. Pos: Mem, Manchester Rep. Exec. Cmt, N.H, 64-69; N.H. State Rep, Dist. 25, 69- Bus. & Prof. Pos: Owner, George Goedecke & Son, 52- Mil. Serv: Entered as Pfc, Air Force, 45, released as Pfc, 45, after serv. in First, Second, Third and Eighth Air Corps; Good Conduct Medal. Mem: State, Regional and Nat. Painting & Decorating Asns. of Am; Rotary; Mason; Consistory; Shrine. Rel: Congregational. Mailing Add: 684 Varney St, Manchester, N.H. 03102.

GOEKEN, ROBERT LEE D
Chmn, Cass Co. Dem. Cent. Cmt, Iowa
b. Marne, Iowa, 2/13/20; s. Arthur G. Goeken and Jessie Polkingharn G; m. 6/23/46 to Lucile Gladys Reimer. Educ: Iowa State Univ, 38-39; LaSalle Exten. Univ, LL.B, 54. Polit. & Govt. Pos: Del, Dem. Co, State and Nat. Conv, 48-; treas. and finance chmn, Cass Co. Dem. Cent. Cmt, Iowa, 56-65, chmn, 65- Bus. & Prof. Pos: Pres, Marne Brighton Ins. Agency, Marne, Iowa, 50-; dir. and chmn. bd, Brighton Mortage Co, 54-; pres, R.L. Goeken Co. Inc, 55- Mil. Serv: Civilian flight instr, Civilian Pilots Prog, World War II. Publ: Land Use Changes, Am. Right of Way Asn, 66. Mem: Am. Right of Way Asn; Soc. Real Estate Appraisers(sr. appraiser); Mortgage Bankers Asn; Iowa Asn. Independent Ins. Agents; AF&AM; Jr. C. of C; Lions. Rel: Methodist. Legal Res: 300 Lincoln St, Marne, Iowa 51552. Mailing Add: 2 Washington St, Marne, Iowa 51552.

GOEMAERE, WARREN N. D
Mich. State Rep.
b. Detroit, Mich, 2/24/17; m. 1941 to Marian Kathryn Dallwitz; c. Warren Russell. Educ: High Sch, grad. Polit. & Govt. Pos: Mich. State Rep, 64- Bus. & Prof. Pos: Retired. Mil. Serv: 101st Airborne Div, World War II, 4 years serv. in Pac. and ETO. Mem: Elks; Warren 101st Airborne Div. Asn; Sacred Heart Dad's Club. Rel: Roman Catholic. Mailing Add: 27132 Demirick, Roseville, Mich. 48066. (1967)

GOEMANS, JOHN W. D
Polit. & Govt. Pos: Cand. for Hawaii State Sen; Hawaii State Rep, 64-66; dir, State Dept. Off. in Hawaii. Mem: Hawaii Bar Asn; Am. Bar Asn; State Adv. Coun. to Small Bus. Admin. 1967 Legal Res: 412 Trust Co. Bldg, 250 S. King St, Honolulu, Hawaii. No mailing address available. (1967)

GOETZ, JAMES B. 'JIM' R
Lt. Gov, Minn.
b. Freeport, Ill, 5/28/36; s. Thomas Goetz and Marian Isley G; m. to Ruth Elbert; c. James Jeffrey and Gregory Thomas. Educ: Univ. Wis; Mid-West. Broadcasting Sch, Chicago. Polit. & Govt. Pos: Former alderman, Winona, Minn, former Winona Co. Rep. Chmn, former First V.Chmn. and Chmn, State Exec. Rep. Party and State Cent. Rep. Cmts; del, Rep. Nat. Conv, 64; Lt. Gov, Minn, 67- Bus. & Prof. Pos: Pres. and co-owner, KAGE, Winona, Minn, 61. Mil. Serv: Army. One of Ten Outstanding Young Men in Minn, 65. Legal Res: Villa Seeblick, Lakeland Shores, Lakeland Minn. 55043. Mailing Add: State Capitol, Winona, Minn. 55101.

GOETZ, MYRA GAMBURG D
b. Phila, Pa, 2/26/32; d. David Gamburg and Beatrice Jacobson G; m. 1/31/54 to Victor J. Goetz; c. Judith Suzanne and Victoria Anne. Educ: Univ. N.Mex, B.A, 66, M.A, 68. Polit. & Govt. Pos: Del, Dem. Nat. Conv, 64; chairwoman, Young Dem. State Conv, 67; former mem. exec. cmt, Young Dem; former committeewoman, Precinct 44 E, N.Mex. Dem. Party. Mailing Add: 7070 W. Mercer Way, Mercer Island, Wash. 98040.

GOETZ, ROBERT LYNWOOD R
State Committeeman, Wash. State Rep. Party
b. York, Pa, 1/12/28; s. Paul P. Goetz and Reba Brenneman G; m. 7/20/52 to Doris Elaine Wanbaugh; c. Susan, Paul and Cynthia. Educ: Susquehanna Univ, B.A, 49; Temple Univ. Med. Sch, M.D, 53; Phi Mu Delta; Phi Chi. Polit. & Govt. Pos: Chmn, Goldwater Campaign, Island Co, Wash, 64; chmn, Island Co. Rep. Cent. Cmt, 64-66; state committeeman, Wash. State Rep. Party, currently; del, Rep. Nat. Conv, 68. Bus. & Prof. Pos: Partner, Whidbey Med. Clin, Oak Harbor, Wash, 59- Mil. Serv: Entered as Lt.(jg), Navy, 55, released as Lt, 57; Comdr, Naval Res, Marine Corps in Yakima, Wash, 63-65. Mem: Am. Acad. Gen. Practice; Am. Med. Asn; Wash. State and Skagit Co. Med. Socs; U.S. Power Sq. Rel: Methodist. Mailing Add: 113 Highland Dr, Oak Harbor, Wash. 98277.

GOETZE, RAY A. R
Ariz. State Sen.
b. Minneapolis, Minn, 7/2/97; s. C. Arther Goetze and Harriet A. Harrison G; m. 9/26/21 to Verona Marie Monahan; c. James E, Robert E. and Donna Marie. Educ: Univ. of Minn. Polit. & Govt. Pos: Ariz. State Rep, 63-66; State Sen, 67- Bus. & Prof. Pos: V.pres, Dawson Mfg. Co; West Coast mgr, Krause Plow Corp; gen. supt, Associated Pipe & Eng. Co. Mil. Serv: Entered as Pvt, Minn. Nat. Guard, 16, released as 2nd Lt, Army, 19; Mexican Border Ribbon. Mem: Mason; World War I Orgn. Rel: Methodist. Mailing Add: 12230 Augusta Dr, Sun City, Ariz. 85351.

GOFF, ABE McGREGOR R
b. Colfax, Wash, 12/21/99; s. Herbert William Goff and Mary Dorsey G; m. 8/24/27 to Florence L. Richardson; c. Timothy R. and Annie McGregor. Educ: Univ. of Idaho, LL.B, 24; Scabbard and Blade; Beta Theta Pi. Polit. & Govt. Pos: Prosecuting attorney, Latah Co, Idaho, 26-34; cmnr, Idaho State Bar Cmn, 39-41; Idaho State Sen, 41-43; U.S. Rep, Idaho, 47-48; gen. counsel, U.S. Post Off. Dept, 54-58; cmnr, Interstate Commerce Cmn, 58-67. Bus. & Prof. Pos: Lawyer, currently. Mil. Serv: Pvt, Army, 18; re-entered serv. as Maj, Army, 41, released as Col, 46, after serv. in Judge Adv. Corps, Africa, Europe, Pac, Gen. McArthur's Staff, Tokyo and Off. Under Secy. of War; Col. (Ret), Army Res; Legion of Merit; Commendation and Reserve Medals; World War I and World War II Victory Medals; Am. Defense, Am. Campaign, Africa-Europe-Middle East and Pac. Campaign Ribbons; Army of Occup. Medal. Mem: Bd. of dirs, Fed. Bar Found; Fed. Bar Asn.(nat. secy, 58-59); Am. Soc. Int. Law (mem. exec. coun, 54-57); Judge Adv. Asn.(mem. bd. of dirs, 50-54); Am. Bar Asn.(mem. house of del, 41-42); Idaho State Bar (pres, 40-41); Inter-Am. Bar Asn; Mil. Order of the Carabao; Am. Legion; VFW; Elks; Mason; Nat. Lawyers Club. 1921-23 Center and Guard Col. football. Rel: Episcopal. Mailing Add: 503 E. C St, Moscow, Idaho 83843.

GOFF, JOHN BRYSON D
N.H. State Rep.
b. Portland, Maine, 9/4/23; s. John Spinney Goff and Mary J. Bryson G; m. 4/30/49 to Sandra Frances Stefanelli; c. John Stefan, Gregory Michael, Eric James, Rolfe Andrew, James Francis, Cynthia Mary, Pamela Ann and Sandrina Lynn. Educ: Univ. Maine, 3 years; Sigma Chi. Polit. & Govt. Pos: Town clerk, Pembroke, N.H, 63-; N.H. State Rep, 69- Bus. & Prof. Pos: Sales promotion mgr, Plymouth Div, Chrysler Corp, 54-57; dealer develop. mgr, Ford Motor Corp, 57-58; gen. sales mgr, Saab Motors Inc, 58-61; gen. mgr, Chadwick Ba Ross Inc, 61-62; pres-owner, John B. Goff Ins. Inc, 62- Mil. Serv: Pvt, Army Signal Corps, 42-43. Mem: Bd. of dirs, Independent Mutual Agents of New England; K. of C; Lions Int; Elks; Am. Legion; Am. Bowling Cong; PTA. Rel: Roman Catholic. Legal Res: Pembroke, N.H. Mailing Add: P.O. Box J, Suncook, N.H. 03275.

GOFF, KENNETH HAROLD R
b. Spring Lick, Ky, 11/1/26; s. Tom Goff and Beualh Carter G; m. 8/11/56 to Florene Shain; c. Kenneth Harold, II, Thomas Herman, Laura Jane and John Hardin. Educ: West. Ky. State Col, A.B; Univ. of Ky, College of Law, LL.B, Polit. & Govt. Pos: Attorney, Grayson Co, Ky, 54-66; del, Rep. Nat. Conv, San Francisco, 64 and Chicago, 60. Mil. Serv: Entered as Pvt, Army, 45, released as Pfc, 46, after serv. in 19th Inf. Reg, 24th Div, Japan. Rel: Baptist. Mailing Add: R.R. 3, Leitchfield, Ky. 42754. (1967)

GOLDBERG, ARTHUR JOSEPH D
b. Chicago, Ill, 8/8/08; Joseph Goldberg and Rebecca Pearlstein G; m. 7/18/31 to Dorothy Kurgans; c. Barbara L, Robert M. Educ: Crane Jr. Col, B.S.L, 29; Northwest. Univ. J.D, 30. Polit. & Govt. Pos: Secy. of Labor, 61-62; Assoc. Justice, U.S. Supreme Court, 62-65; U.S. Ambassador to the UN, 65-68. Bus. & Prof. Pos: Attorney-at-law, 29-41 and currently; mem. law firm Goldberg, Devoe, Shadur & Mikva, Chicago, 45-61; gen. counsel, USW, 48-61; with Goldberg, Feller & Bredhoff, Wash, 52-61; gen. counsel, Indust. Union Dept, AFL-CIO, 55-61; sr. partner, Paul, Weiss, Goldberg, Rifkind, Wharton & Garrison, 68- Mil. Serv: Maj, Army, 42-44, OSS, 42-43, serv. in ETO. Publ: Ed-in-chief, Ill. Law Rev, 29; author, AFL-CIO Labor United, 56; The Defense of Freedom: The Published Papers of Arthur J. Goldberg, 66. Rel: Jewish. Legal Res: Hotel Pierre, Fifth Ave. and 61st St, New York, N.Y. 10022. Mailing Add: 345 Park Ave, New York, N.Y. 10022.

GOLDBERG, RICHARD W. R
N.Dak. State Sen.
b. Fargo, N.Dak, 9/23/27; s. Jacob H. Goldberg and Frances Gilles G; m. 4/24/64 to Mary B. Borland; c. Julie. Educ: Univ. Miami, B.B.A, 50 and J.D, 52; Phi Alpha Delta. Polit. & Govt. Pos: Attorney and adv, Fed. Communications Cmn, 57-58; mem, N.Dak. State Rep. Exec. Cmt. and N.Dak. State Rep. Cent. Cmt, 64-66; mem, N.Dak. State Rep. Platform Cmt, 66; N.Dak. State Sen, currently. Bus. & Prof. Pos: Private law practice, 56-57; v.pres. and dir, Goldberg Feed & Grain Co. and Gold Label Feeds, Inc, 59- Mil. Serv: 1st Lt, Air Force, 53-56. Mem: N.Dak. and Fla. Bar Asns; past pres, West Fargo C. of C. and N.Dak. Feed Mfrs. Asn; N.Dak. Grain Dealers Asn; Elks; Fargo Country Club. Mailing Add: 501 Seventh St. S, Fargo, N.Dak. 58102.

GOLDEN, ARNOLD MORTIMER D
Sen, V.I. Legis.
b. Frederiksted, St. Croix, V.I, 12/13/31; s. Louis Reitvelt Golden and Violet Pedersen G; m. 9/23/56 to Carmen Maria Encarnacion; c. Helen Marie, Violet Anne, Louis Mortimer, Peder Mark and Carmen Louise. Educ: Polytech. Inst, San German, P.R, 49-50; Collegio de Mayaguez, Univ. P.R, 50-51. Polit. & Govt. Pos: Soc. worker, Dept. Soc. Welfare, St. Croix, V.I, 56-59; appraiser, Dept. Tax Assessors, 60-68; Sen, V.I. Legis, 69- Bus. & Prof. Pos: Heavy Equip. supvr, V.I. Corp, 54-56; land surveyor, A.C. Samfords, 59-60; real estate broker, currently; appraiser, land surveyor, currently. Mil. Serv: Entered as Pvt, Army, 52, released as Cpl, 54, after serv. in Co. B, 179th Inf, 45th Div, Korea; Res, 54-66, 1st Lt; Nat. Defense Serv. and UN Medals; Korean Serv. Medal with One Campaign Star. Mem: St. Croix Asn. Architects, Engrs. and Land Surveyors; Int. Asn. Assessing Officers; Christian Family Movement; Nat. Exchange Club; Am. Legion. Rel: Roman Catholic. Legal Res: 107 Anna's Hope, Christiansted, St. Croix, V.I. 08820. Mailing Add: P.O. Box 152, Christiansted, St. Croix, V.I. 00820.

GOLDEN, JAMES STEPHEN R
b. Barbourville, Ky, 9/20/91; s. Benjamin B. Golden and Elizabeth Davis G; m. 9/29/15 to Ruth Decker; c. Richard Davis and Dr. James S, Jr. Educ: Univ. of Ky, A.B; Univ. Mich, LL.B; Delta Theta Phi. Polit. & Govt. Pos: U.S. Rep, Ky, 48-55; co. attorney, Knox Co, Ky, 19. Mem: Bd. of Dirs, Boy Scouts and Salvation Army; past pres, Pineville Commun. Hosp. Helped to write Social Security Act in Cong; obtained Flood Control for Ky. Communities. Rel: Methodist. Mailing Add: 402 Tennessee Ave, Pineville, Ky. 40977.

GOLDEN, JOHN HOLLISTER R
b. Goodland, Kans, 11/12/32; s. L. Dick Golden and Margaret Lynch G; m. 6/1/63 to Marcia Laing; c. Margaret Lynch and Jennifer Laing. Educ: Univ. of Kans, 54; spec. study, Univ. of Denver and Mexico City Col. Polit. & Govt. Pos: Secy, Sherman Co. Rep. Cent. Cmt, Kans, 59-60; v.pres, First Dist. Young Rep, 61-62; Kans. State Rep, 61-66; mem, Govt. Cmt. Sugar Beets, 65-66; chmn, Goodland City-Co. Planning Cmn. Mil. Serv: Entered as Pvt, Army, 55, released as SP-3, 57, after serv. in Seventh Eng. Brigade, Germany, Mem: Goodland C. of C.(v.pres, 59); v.chmn. Agr. Rels. Coun, Kans. State C. of C, 66; Mason; Shrine; Elks; Kiwanis; Farm Bur; Kans. Livestock Asn; Jaycees. Rel: Episcopal. Mailing Add: 1010 W. Tenth, Goodland, Kans. 67735.

GOLDEN, JOHN MATTHEW D
Mem. Dem. Nat. Cmt, Conn.
b. Old Saybrook, Conn, 11/4/95; s. Matthew J. Golden and Alice P. Strickland G; m. 4/7/20 to Margaret J. Stumpf; c. Margaret (Mrs. John A. Berges), Frances A.(Mrs. William Krenisky). Educ: Pub. schs, Old Saybrook, Conn. Polit. & Govt. Pos: Dir. pub. works, New Haven, Conn, 32-45; mem, Dem. Nat. Cmt, 52-; del, Dem. Nat. Conv, 68. Bus. & Prof. Pos: Supt, Greist Mfg. Co, 15-30; pres, Golden, O'Neill & Gebhardt Inc. ins. agency, 40; dir, Gen. Bank and Trust Co. and Winthrop Bank and Trust Co; trustee, St. Raphael Hosp, Albertus Magnus Col, Annhurst Col. and New Haven Found. Mem: Pres, Camp Palmer for Boys; Knights St. Patrick: K. of C; Hibernian; Eagle; Union League Club; Caths. of N.Y. Club. Rel: Roman Catholic; dir. Catholic Diocesan Bur. Mailing Add: 185 Church St, New Haven, Conn. 06510. (1967)

GOLDFARB, ALEXANDER A. D
Counsr, Dem. State Cent. Cmt, Conn.
b. Hartford, Conn, 10/27/28. Educ: Trinity Col, Conn, B.S, 46; Cornell Univ.

Sch. of Law, LL.B, 49; Yale Grad. Sch, 50-51; Pi Gamma Mu. Polit. & Govt. Pos: Asst. corp. counsr, City of Hartford, Conn, 54-56; counsr, Dem. State Cent. Cmt, 54-; counsr, Gr. Hartford Flood Cmn. of Conn, 56-; mem, Cmt. to Revise Elec. Laws of Conn, 61-63. Bus. & Prof. Pos: Faculty Mem, Univ. Nebr. Col. of Law, 49-50; sr. partner, Goldfarb & Spellacy Esquires, 62- Mil. Serv: Pvt, Army Inf, 44-45. Rel: Jewish. Mailing Add: 1 Lewis St, Hartford, Conn. 06103.

GOLDIN, HARRISON J. D
N.Y. State Sen.
b. N.Y.C, 2/23/36; s. Harry Goldin, M.D. and Anna E. Eskolsky G; m. 11/20/66 to Diana Stern. Educ: Princeton Univ, A.B. summa cum laude, 57; Woodrow Wilson fel, Harvard Univ, 57-58; Yale Law Sch, LL.B, 61; Phi Beta Kappa; Order of the Coif; Princeton Club of N.Y; Princeton Quadrangle Club. Polit. & Govt. Pos: Trial lawyer, U.S. Dept. Justice, 61-63; N.Y. State Sen, 66-, mem. finance, educ, ment. hygiene and civil serv. and pensions cmts, N.Y. State Senate, 66- Bus. & Prof. Pos: Lawyer, Davis Polk & Wardwell, 63- Mem: Asn. of the Bar of the City of N.Y; N.Y. State, Fed. and Bronx Co. Bar Asns; Coun. For. Rels; Am. Jewish Cong.(gov. cmt, former chmn. exec. cmt, Metrop. Coun); Am. Jewish Cmt.(bd. dirs, N.Y. Chap); B'nai B'rith. Rel: Jewish. Mailing Add: 1020 Grand Concource, New York, N.Y. 10451.

GOLDMAN, MACLYN S. D
married to Rhoda Goldman; c. Two. Polit. & Govt. Pos: Former N.J. State Sen; chmn. adv. bd. to Draft Registrants; chmn. Co. Cmt, West Orange; chief counsel to Supt. of Elecs; counsel to Fed. Agency-Home Owners Loan Corp; acting magistrate, West Orange, 12 years; del, Dem. Nat. Conv, 68. Bus. & Prof. Pos: Lawyer, co-owner The Goldman Hotel, West Orange. Mem: West Orange Jewish Center; Lions; Suburban Club, Pleasantdale Manor; B'nai B'rith; chmn. Red Cross; U.J.A. Commun. Coun; March of Dimes Drive; Mentally Retarded Children's Fund Drive. Mailing Add: 305 Pleasant Valley, West Orange, N.J. 07052. (1967)

GOLDSTEIN, HERBERT D
Chmn, Queen Anne's Co. Dem. State Cent. Cmt, Md.
b. Prince Frederick, Md, 11/18/14; s. Goodman Goldstein (deceased) and Belle Butcher G; m. 11/1/38 to Shirley Fox; c. Frances and Alan. Educ: Univ. Md, 34. Polit. & Govt. Pos: Alternate del, Dem. Nat. Conv, 60, del, 64 & 68; chmn, Queen Anne's Co. Dem. State Cent. Cmt, Md, 62-; dir. and mem, Adv. Cmt. on Wage Hours Law, Md. Phys. Fitness Cmn. and dir, Queen Anne's Co. Welfare Bd, 65. Bus. & Prof. Pos: Dir, Centreville Nat. Bank, 66. Mil. Serv: Pvt, Army, 45. Mem: Chmn, Queen Anne's Co. to Employ the Handicapped; co-dir, Ment. Health Asn; pres, Centreville C. of C, 65 and Upper Eastern Shore Heart Asn, 66; past pres, Centreville Rotary Club; chmn, Queen Anne's Co. March of Dimes, 46-; Am. Legion; dir, Red Cross; Shriner; Farm Bur; Boy Scouts; Col, Hon. Order of Ky. Colonels; Advert. Club of Baltimore; Great Oak Yacht Club. Rel: Jewish. Mailing Add: 305 Chesterfield Ave, Centreville, Md. 21617.

GOLDSTEIN, LEWIS HOWARD D
b. Bronx, N.Y, 4/1/43; s. Leo Goldstein and Gertrude Finger G; single. Educ: City Col. of N.Y, B.A, 64; Brooklyn Law Sch, 64-66; Alpha Phi Omega. Polit. & Govt. Pos: Secy, J.F.K. Reform Dem. Club, 64-65; del, N.Y. State Gubnatorial Conv, 66; del, First Judicial Dem. Conv, N.Y, 66-69; legis. aide to N.Y. State Assemblyman Robert Abrams, 66-, clerk, Joint Legis. Cmt. on Land Appropriation, 68-; v.pres, Bronx Pelham Reform Dem. Club, 67-; asst. campaign mgr, Dem. to Elect Robert Abrams Borough Pres, 68; del, Dem. Nat. Conv, 68. Mem: B'nai B'rith; NAACP; Am. Civil Liberties Union. Rel: Jewish. Mailing Add: 2230 Grand Concourse, Bronx, N.Y. 10457.

GOLDSTEIN, LOUIS L. D
State Comptroller, Md.
b. Prince Frederick, Md, 3/14/13; s. Goodman Goldstein and Belle Butcher G; m. 11/22/47 to Hazel Elizabeth Horton; c. Philip, Luisa and Margaret. Educ: Wash. Col, B.S, 35; Univ. Md, LL.B, 38; Omicron Delta Kappa; Zeta Beta Tau. Polit. & Govt. Pos: Md. State Del, 39-42; del. or alternate del, Dem. Nat. Conv, 40, 48, 52, 56, 60, 64 & 68; Md. State Sen, 47-58, Majority Leader 4 years, pres, 4 years and chmn, Chesapeake Bay and Tributaries, Exec, Nominations and Finance Cmts; chmn. legis. coun. and mem, Atlantic State Marine Fisheries Cmn; mem, Bd. Pub. Works, Bd. Revenue Estimates and Gov. Adv. Coun; mem, Employee's, Teachers' and State Police Retirement Systs; State Comptroller, Md, 59- Bus. & Prof. Pos: Lawyer, Prince Frederick, Md; ed, Calvert Journal-Gasette; real estate broker; mem. bd. visitors and gov, Wash. Col; ex-officio mem. bd. regents, Univ. Md. Mil. Serv: Entered as Pvt, Marine Corps, 42, released as 1st Lt, 46, after serv. in Asiatic and Pac. Theaters; Capt.(Ret), Marine Corps. Res. Mem: Md, D.C. and Am. Bar Asns; Am. Judicature Soc; Real Estate Bd. of Gr. Baltimore; Md. Real Estate Bd; Nat. Asn. of State Auditors, Comptrollers and Treas; Md. Pub. Finance Officers Asn; Munic. Finance Officers Asn. of U.S. and Can; Md. and Calvert Co. Hist. Socs; Hist. Soc. of Cecil Co; Hist. Annapolis, Inc; Md-Del. Press Asn; Advert. Club of Baltimore; Nat. Cong. of Parents and Teachers; Univ. Md. Alumni Asn; Md. Travel Coun; Chesapeake Bay Fishing Fair Asn; charter mem, Calvert Co. Lions and Calvert Co. Vol. Fire Dept; VFW; Am. Legion; Elks; Moose; B'nai B'rith; East Baltimore Boys Club; Sportsman's Club of Calvert Co; Calvert Co. Fox Hunters Club; Order of World Wars; Md. Vet. Asn. Rel: Jewish. Mailing Add: Oakland Hall, Prince Frederick, Md. 20678.

GOLDSTEIN, NATHANIEL LAWRENCE D
New York, N.Y, 6/9/96; s. Max Goldstein and Mollie Marayna G; m. 1931 to Etta May Brown; c. Lois Elaine (Mrs. Jerome Lowenstein), Stephen Martin. Educ: N.Y.U, B.C.S, 15; N.Y. Law Sch, LL.B, 18; LL.D, 57; Syracuse Univ, LL.D, 49; Yeshiva Univ, 52; Hobart and William Smith Cols, 50; Sigma Omega Psi (nat. pres.); Alpha Epsilon Pi. Polit. & Govt. Pos: Attorney Gen. N.Y. State, 42-54; civilian chief counsel, Dir. Selective Serv, N.Y.C, 40-42; pub. mem, Interboro Rapid Transit Depreciation Fund Bd, 38-40; Brooklyn Conf. (exec. nat. cmt), Christians and Jews; dir, Govt. Affairs Found, Inc; mem, U.S. del. to UN Narcotic Drug Control Cmn. Bus. & Prof. Pos: Mem. Goldstein, Judd and Gurfein, 55-; gen. counsel, Postal Life Ins. Co, 31-42. Mem: Am. and Bklyn. Bar Asns; Am. Legion (past post comdr.); Mason; Harmonie Club, N.Y.C; Capitol Hill Club, Wash, D.C. Vpres. & dir, Wilkie Mem. of Freedom House; trustee, N.Y. Law Sch; mem. bd. overseers, Fletcher Sch. Law and Diplomacy; pres, Am. Friends of Hebrew Univ. and dep. chmn. bd. gov, Hebrew Univ; holder chair forensic med, Albert Einstein Col. Med; trustee, Park Ave. Synagogue. Rel: Jewish. Legal Res: 737 Park Ave, New York, N.Y. 10021. Mailing Add: 655 Madison Ave, New York, N.Y. 10021. (1967)

GOLDSTEIN, NOAH D
b. Providence, R.I, 10/5/07; s. Jacob Goldstein and Anna Thaler G; m. 8/3/32 to Sylvia Chervin; c. Loretta (Mrs. Richard Lewis) and Eileen (Mrs. Theodore Rice); grandchildren, Geoffrey and Cheryl Rice and David and Gayle Lewis. Educ: Fordham Univ; Brooklyn Law Sch, LL.B, 30. Polit. & Govt. Pos: Referee, Small Claims Night Court of Civil Court, 53-63; N.Y. State Assemblyman, 63-66; N.Y. State Dem. Committeeman, 66-68; chmn. speakers bur, King Co. Dem. Party; judge, Civil Court City of N.Y, 69- Bus. & Prof. Pos: Attorney, 31- Mem: Jewish Center Nachlath Zion founder and past pres); K. of P.(past chancellor); Boy Scouts (dep. scout cmnr, 27-30); hon. chmn, Muscular Distrophy Asn. Brooklyn; Brooklyn Bar Asn; B'nai B'rith; Zionist Orgn. Am; Brooklyn Trial Lawyers Asn; commun. adv. bd, Coney Island Hosp; bd. dirs, Commun. Hosp. Brooklyn; admitted to Supreme Court U.S; lectr. on domestic rels. Recipient of Francis Salvador Award. Rel: Hebrew. Legal Res: 2150 E. 23 St, Brooklyn, N.Y. 11229. Mailing Add: Chamber Civil Court, 120 Schermerhorn St, Brooklyn, N.Y. 11201.

GOLDSUM, JOHN F. D
Chmn, Precinct 233, Travis Co. Dem. Party, Tex.
b. Victoria, Tex, 6/14/28; s. John F. Goldsum and Lillie A. Montag G; m. 8/24/51 to Shirley Anne Payne (deceased); c. Lynn Alice. Educ: Am. Univ, LL.B. Polit. & Govt. Pos: Secy, Rep. Clark W. Thompson, 50-53; legis. asst. to Sen. Daniel, 54-57; admin. asst. to Gov. Price Daniel, 57-62; admin. asst. to U.S. Rep. J.J. Pickle, Tex, 65-66; chmn, Precinct 233, Travis Co. Dem. Party, 68- Bus. & Prof. Pos: Reporter, Victoria Advocate, 48-49; attorney-at-law, Austin, Tex, 63-64 & 66- Mem: Travis Co. and Am. Bar Asns; State Bar of Tex; Delta Theta Phi; AF&AM; Scottish Rite; Tex. State Soc. of Wash. Rel: Lutheran. Mailing Add: 4110 Idlewild Rd, Austin, Tex. 78731.

GOLDSWORTHY, ROBERT F. R
Wash. State Rep.
b. Rosalia, Wash, 1917; m. to Jean G; c. two. Educ: Wash. State Univ, B.A. Polit. & Govt. Pos: Wash. State Rep, 7 terms. Bus. & Prof. Pos: Farmer. Mil. Serv: Air Force, World War II and Korean War. Mem: Mason; Am. Legion; Mil. Order of the World Wars; Order of Daedalians. Mailing Add: Route 2, Rosalia, Wash. 99170.

GOLDTHWAITE, ALFRED WITHERSPOON D
Chmn, Ala. Rep. Party
b. Montgomery, Ala, 8/12/21; s. Archibald Campbell Goldthwaite and Mary Goldthwaite Arrington G; m. 12/12/58 to Evelyn Adams; c. Alfred Witherspoon, Mary Arrington and Ellen Adams. Educ: Univ. Ala, B.A, 43, LL.B, 48. Polit. & Govt. Pos: Ala. State Rep, 59-66; chmn, Ala. Rep. Party, 67-; del, Dem. Nat. Conv, 68. Mil. Serv: World War II and Korea. Rel: Episcopal. Mailing Add: 436 S. Goldthwaite St, Montgomery, Ala. 36104.

GOLDWATER, BARRY, JR. R
U.S. Rep, Calif.
b. Los Angeles, Calif, 7/15/38; single. Educ: Univ. Colo; Ariz. State Univ, grad, 62; founder of col. bus. and mkt. newspaper. Polit. & Govt. Pos: Speaker, Barry Goldwater for President Campaign, 64; mem. adv. bd, Hank Arklin for Calif. State Assembly Campaign, 68; mem, Calif. Rep. State Cent. Cmt, currently; U.S. Rep, 27th Dist. Calif, 69- Bus. & Prof. Pos: Partner, Noble Cooke, Div. of Gregory & Sons, stock brokers. Mem: SAR; vol. worker, Southeast Los Angeles Youth Coun. Rel: Episcopal. Legal Res: Los Angeles, Calif. Mailing Add: House Office Bldg, Washington, D.C. 20515.

GOLDWATER, BARRY MORRIS R
U.S. Sen, Ariz.
b. Phoenix, Ariz, 1/1/09; s. Barron Goldwater and Josephine Williams G; m. 9/22/34 to Margaret Johnson; c. Barry Morris, Jr, Margaret Ann (Mrs. Holt), Joanne (Mrs. Ross) and Michael Prescott. Educ: Staunton Mil. Acad; Univ. Ariz, 1 year, hon. LL.D, 69; Sigma Chi. Polit. & Govt. Pos: Mem, Phoenix City Coun, 50-52; U.S. Sen, Ariz, 52-64 & 69-; Rep. cand. for President, 64. Bus. & Prof. Pos: Pres, Goldwater's, Inc, 37-50. Mil. Serv: Entered as 2nd Lt, Army Res, 30, serv. in Asiatic-Pac. and ETO, released as Maj. Gen, Air Force Res; Air Medal; China-Burma-India Campaign Star. Publ: Down the River of Canyons; Arizona Portraits; Conscience of a Conservative; plus 2 others. Mem: Assoc. mem, Royal Photog. Soc. of Gt. Brit; Am. Legion; Mason (32°); VFW. Rel: Episcopal. Legal Res: 6250 N. Hogan Dr, Phoenix, Ariz. 85251. Mailing Add: 240 Old Senate Office Bldg, Washington, D.C. 20510.

GOLDY, DANIEL LOUIS D
b. Butler, N.J, 8/7/15; s. Morris A. Goldy and Gussie Silverman G; m. 8/14/44 to Genevieve Beatrice Rustvold; c. Daniel Rustvold. Educ: Univ. of Wisconsin, Madison, B.A, summa cum laude, 1936; Grad. Sch, Univ. of Chicago, 36-37; Phi Beta Kappa; Phi Kappa Phi; Artus. Polit. & Govt. Pos: Asst. cmnr, Placement & Unemploy. Compensation, State Ill, 37-41; asst. regional dir, Off. Defense, Health & Welfare Serv, Fed. Security Agency Cleveland, Ohio, 41-42; asst. regional dir, War Manpower Cmn, Cleveland, 42-43; spec. asst. to dir, U.S. Employment Serv, Wash, D.C, 46-47; Dep. Asst. Secy. Interior, 47-48; regional adminstr, Bur. Land Mgt, Portland, Ore, 49-51; off. of the spec. rep. of the President, Econ. Coop. Admin, Paris, France, 51-52; regional dir, Bur. Employ. Security, Seattle, Wash. and N.Y.C, 52-58; dep. adminstr, Area Redevelop. Admin, U.S. Dept. Commerce, Wash, D.C, 61-62; adminstr, Bus. & Defense Serv. Admin. and Dep. Asst. Secy. Commerce, 62-64; President's Nat. Export Expansion Coordinator and Exec. Dir. of U.S. Cabinet Cmt. on Export Expansion, 64-65; alternate del, Dem. Nat. Conv, 68. Bus. & Prof. Pos: Lectr, grad. sch, Northwest. Univ, 38-41; gen. partner, Mt. Fir Lumber Co, Independence, Ore, 55-61 & 65-; v.pres, Pac. North. Lumber Co, Wrangell, Alaska & Portland, Ore, 59-61; v.pres. and dir, Int. Systs. & Controls Corp, Houston, Tex. and Wash, D.C, 65-69; pres, Rhodes Corp, Oklahoma City, Okla, 67-68; pres, ISC World Trade Corp, Wash, D.C, 68-; pres. and dir, Capital Shares, Inc, Investors Counsel, Inc.

and Int. Systs. & Controls Corp, Houston, Tex, 69- Mil. Serv: Entered as Ens, Navy, 43, released as Lt, 46, after serv. in Pac, 44-45. Mem: Am. Econ. Asn; Soc. Pub. Admin; Acad. Polit. & Soc. Sci; Int. Cmt. of C. of C. of U.S; U.S. Coun. of Int. C. of C.(v.chmn. commercial policy cmt); Machinery and Allied Prod. Inst.(int. opers. coun); Int. Club Wash; Nat. Capital Dem. Club. John Lendrum Mitchel Mem. Medal; hon. lectr, Am. Inst. For. Trade. Legal Res: R.R. 2 Box 1218, Bend, Ore. 97701. Mailing Add: 1875 Connecticut Ave. N.W, Washington, D.C. 20009.

GOLLBERG, WILLIAM LOUIS R
b. Milwaukee, Wis, 3/20/29; s. Louis Herman Gollberg and Emily Bremeier G; m. 9/9/50 to Betty Jane Buege; c. William L. Educ: Marquette Univ, 48. Polit. & Govt. Pos: V.chmn, West Allis Rep. Party, Wis, 61-63, campaign chmn, 62; Fourth Cong. Dist. Chmn, 63-67; del, Rep. Nat. Conv, 64; campaign chmn, Estkowski for Cong, 64; co-chmn, Warren for Attorney Gen. Cmt, 68. Bus. & Prof. Pos: Mfrs. rep, Kingsley Publ, Helm & Hann Co. and Leys Christie & Co. Mil. Serv: Entered as Pvt, Marine Corps, 51, released as Sgt, after serv. in Third Tank Bn, Third Marine Div, 53. Mem: Lutheran Men in Am; Eagles; Am. Legion. Rel: Lutheran. Mailing Add: 1111 S. 117th St, West Allis, Wis. 53214.

GOLLOB, JOSEPH D
b. Newark, N.J, 6/6/14; married; c. Three. Polit. & Govt. Pos: Dem. Precinct Committeeman, Colo; former Colo. State Rep. Bus. & Prof. Pos: Partner, B&G Enterprises, Investment Firm. Mem: Pres, Adams Co. Asn. for Ment. Health; Adams Co. Commun. Center for Retarded and Seriously Handicapped Persons Inc; co-founder, Adams Co. Ment. Hygiene Clin. Mailing Add: 6656 Birch St, Commerce City, Colo. 80022. (1967)

GOLLOTT, TOMMY ARLIN D
Miss. State Rep.
b. Biloxi, Miss, 9/29/35; s. Houston C. Gollott and Ida Quave G; m. 9/2/56 to Zelma Jackson; c. Tanya Denise, Lisa Michelle and Jennifer Beth. Educ: Notre Dame High Sch, grad; Jefferson Davis Jr. Col, 1 year. Polit. & Govt. Pos: Mem, Biloxi Recreation Bd, Miss, 61-68; Miss. State Rep, Harrison Co, 68- Bus. & Prof. Pos: Mgr, Gollott & Sons Transfer, Biloxi, Miss, 54-62; owner and operator, AAA Transfer & Storage, 62- Mil. Serv: Entered as Pvt, Army Nat. Guard, 52, released as S/Sgt, 62. Mem: Gulf Coast Movers Asn; Nat. Movers Conf. of Am; Nat. Defense Transportation Asn; life mem, Nat. Soc. of State Legislators; Jaycees (past pres); C. of C; Boys Club (first pres. and bd. dirs); bd. dirs, Ment. Health & Retardation for Harrison Co; K. of C; Fleur De Lise Soc; Gulf Coast Hunting & Fishing. Biloxi's Outstanding Young Man, 65; Outstanding Past Pres, Jaycees, 68-69, Outstanding Jaycee for Month, May, 69. Rel: Catholic. Mailing Add: 1390 E. Bay View Ave, Biloxi, Miss. 39530.

GOLMAN, JOE H.
Tex. State Rep.
b. Dallas, Tex, 3/13/24; s. Julius Golman and Esther Tobolowsky G; m. 1/31/43 to Frances Lee Goodman; c. Julie, Jon David, Edward Tim and Stanley Joshua. Educ: Tex. A&M. Polit. & Govt. Pos: Mem, Pub. Welfare Bd, Dallas, Tex, 47-49, City Planning Cmn, 49-53 and Citizens Housing Rehabilitation Cmt, 55-62, chmn, Zoning Bd. of Adjustment, 53-62, mem, Zoning Rev. Cmt, 60-64, city councilman, 62-67, dep. mayor-pro-tem, 65-69; Tex. State Rep, 69- Bus. & Prof. Pos: Partner, dir. sales and secy-treas. Goodman Produce Co, 46-62; pres, Julius Shepps Commun. Center, 60-62; pres, Circle T Foods Corp, Joe H. Golman and Co, Inc. and Serv, Roadway, Inc; dir, First Citizens Bank, Oak Cliff Baking Co. and Golman Baking Co; former pres, Carnation Charity Home for Aged. Mil. Serv: Entered as Pvt, Army, 43, released as M/Sgt, 46, after serv. in Inf; Army Res, 41-43; Good Conduct Medal; Am. Theater Ribbon. Mem: Dallas Citizens Coun; Rotary; charter mem. Dallas Assembly; Dallas and North Dallas and Oak Cliff C. of C; Hella Temple Shrine; chmn, Jewish Welfare Asn. UTA Drive, 66; dir, Nat. Jewish Welfare Bd. and pres, South Sect; dir, Golden Acres; Nat. Conf. Christians and Jews; v.pres, Jewish Welfare Fedn; Dallas Crime Cmn; United Fund; Commun. Chest Trust Coun. Adv. Cmts; exec. bd, Circle Ten Boy Scouts Coun; dir, United Fresh Fruit and Vegetable Asn; former mem. bd. dirs, Salesmanship Club. Distinguished Serv. Award, Jr. C. of C, 59. Rel: Jewish. Legal Res: 6530 North Port, Dallas, Tex. 75230. Mailing Add: P.O. Box 1151, Dallas, Tex. 75221.

GOLOMBEK, EUGENE W. D
b. Union City, N.J, 2/28/46; s. Morris Golombek and Estelle Rosen G; single. Educ: Queens Col, B.A, 68. Polit. & Govt. Pos: Alternate del, Dem. Nat. Conv, 68. Publ: 'Kierkkegaard as Applied to the Republican Party,' Changing Am. Philos, 9/68; 'The Effect of the Miniskirt on American Political Campaigns,' Living Circle, 1/69; 'The American Labor Party's New Role in Politics,' Contemporary Polit. Today, 7/69; 'Strom Thurmond and the New Politics,' Carolina Israelite, 8/69. Mailing Add: 144-31 78th Ave, New York, N.Y. 11367.

GOMER, PIERRE JACKSON R
b. Eunice, La, 3/12/09; s. Joseph E. Gomer and Amelia Chacheré G; m. 5/4/35 to Gladice De Launay; c. P.J, Jr. Educ: Univ. Southwest, 29-32; Pi Kappa Alpha. Polit. & Govt. Pos: Alternate del, Rep. Nat. Conv, 68; chmn, Seventh Cong. Dist. Rep. Polit. Action Coun, La; chmn, Parish of St. Landry Rep. Polit. Action Coun; mem, La. State Bd. Rep. Polit. Action Coun. Mem: Soc. Automotive Engrs; La. Tire Dealers Asn.(bd. dirs, 69-); Elks; Rotary Rel: Catholic. Mailing Add: 121 N. Ninth, Eunice, La. 70535.

GOMPERTS, ROBERT ELLIOT D
Cong. Dist. Co-Chmn, Calif. Dem. State Cent. Cmt.
b. San Francisco, Calif. 4/22/27; s. Jack Gomperts and Ro Fles G; m. 4/17/48 to Elizabeth Konstance Schneider; c. John Sarto, Mark Alexander and Rosan Elizabeth. Educ: Lowell High Sch, San Francisco, Calif, grad, 45. Polit. & Govt. Pos: Pres, Menlo Atherton Dem. Club, Calif, 68-; Cong. dist. co-chmn, Calif. Dem. State Cent. Cmt, 68. Bus. & Prof. Pos: V.Pres, Calagrex, Inc, San Francisco, 61-; pres, Idaho Sales Corp, 61-; pres, Nordisk Andelsforbund Calif. Inc, 62- Mil. Serv: Seaman 3/C, Navy Air Corps, 45, released as Seaman 1/C, 46, after serv. as a combat aircrewman. Mem: Sch. of World Bus. Adv. Coun, San Francisco State Col; World Affairs Coun. of North. Calif.(exec. cmt); Calif. Coun. for Int. Trade (dir); UN Asn. of San Francisco (dir). Rel: Unitarian; Bd. Dirs, Redwood City Unitarian Fel. Mailing Add: 132 Tuscaloosa Ave, Atherton, Calif. 94025.

GONG, EDMOND JOSEPH D
Fla. State Sen.
b. Miami, Fla, 10/7/30; s. Joe Fred Gong and Fayline G; m. 7/25/57 to Sophie Vlachos; c. Frances Fayline, Peter, Madeleine, Joseph Fred, II and Edmond Joseph, Jr. Educ: Harvard Col, A.B. cum laude, 52, Harvard Sch. of Law, 54-55; Univ. Miami Sch. of Law, LL.B, 60; Phi Alpha Delta; Iron Arrow; Pi Sigma Alpha. Polit. & Govt. Pos: Asst. U.S. attorney, South. Dist. of Fla, Dept. of Justice, 61-62; Fla. State Rep, 63-66; Fla. State Sen, 66- Bus. & Prof. Pos: Spec. writer, Hong Kong Tiger Standard, 55-56; staff writer, Miami Herald, 58-59; assoc. Helliwell, Melrose & DeWolf, 60-61; mem, Law Off. of Edmond J. Gong, 62- Mil. Serv: Entered as Lt, Air Force, 52, released as 1st Lt, 54; Capt, Air Force Res, at present. Publ: 'A Review of Current Court Decisions Relating to Collection of Delinquent Contributions to Taft-Hartley Joint Trusts,' Nat. Found. of Health, Welfare and Pension Plans, Inc, 66. Mem: Am, Fla, Dade Co. and Fed. Bar Asns; assoc. legal counsel, Jr. Chamber Int. Rel: Methodist. Legal Res: 7751 Southwest 78 Court, Miami, Fla. 33143. Mailing Add: 1617 Alfred I. duPont Bldg, Miami, Fla. 33131. (1967)

GONSALVES, JOE A. D
b. Holtville, Calif, 10/13/19; s. Jaoquin Gonsalves and Elvira G; m. 7/17/40 to Virginia Mello; c. Robert, James, Joe, Jr, Frank, Jack, Anthony, David, Timothy and John Kennedy. Educ: Excelsior High Sch. Polit. & Govt. Pos: Councilman and Mayor, Dairy Valley, Calif, 58-62; Calif. State Assemblyman, 66th Dist, 63-67 and chmn. cmt. on rules. Mem: Elks; Moose; Lions; K. of C. Rel: Catholic. Legal Res: 12414 Gottes Lane, La Mirada, Calif. 90638. Mailing Add: P.O. Box 614, Norwalk, Calif. 90650.

GONZALES, ARCENIE A. D
b. 1926. Educ: N.Mex. Highlands Univ, B.A. and 38 hours grad. work. Polit. & Govt. Pos: N.Mex. State Rep, 63-66; del, Dem. Nat. Conv, 68. Bus. & Prof. Pos: Teacher and bus. mgr, W. Las Vegas Schs, N.Mex. Mil. Serv: Army. Mem: Am. Legion; VFW; dir, Am. Legion Baseball; Alpha Zeta Iota. Rel: Catholic. Mailing Add: 9 Grand Ave, Las Vegas, N.Mex. 87701. (1967)

GONZALES, FIDEL C. D
N.Mex. State Rep.
b. 1906. Polit. & Govt. Pos: Mem, State Police, N.Mex, 7 years, Co. Cmnr, 3 years; City Councilman, 8 years; N.Mex. State Rep, 63-66 & 69-; del, Dem. Nat. Conv, 68; chmn, San Miguel Co. Dem. Party, N.Mex, 69- Bus. & Prof. Pos: Undertaker. Mil. Serv: Army, World War II. Rel: Catholic. Mailing Add: 2315 Hot Springs Rd, Las Vegas, N.Mex. 87701. (1967)

GONZALES, ROBERT EUGENE D
Mem, San Francisco Co. Bd. Supvr, Calif.
b. Fresno, Calif, 11/13/36; s. Bernard Louis Gonzales and Ramona Ortiz G; single. Educ: Univ. Calif, Berkeley, B.A, 59; Hastings Col. of Law, J.D, 62; Kappa Alpha; Big C Soc; Circle C Soc. Polit. & Govt. Pos: Pres, Mexican-Am. Polit. Asn. of San Francisco, 65-67, v.pres, Calif. Asn, 66-68; mem, Calif. Dem. State Cent. Cmt, 66-68; mem, Bd. of Permit Appeals, San Francisco City and Co, 68-69; mem, San Francisco City and Co. Bd. Supvr, 69- Bus. & Prof. Pos: Assoc, Gonzales and Mitchell, Attorneys. Mem: Calif. and Am. Trial Lawyers Asns; Calif. Bar Asn; adv.coun, Langley Porter Neuropsychiat. Inst; Juvenile Court Study Cmt; adv. cmt, Human Rights Cmn. of San Francisco; consult, Bilingual Educ, Calif. State Dept. of Educ, Centro Soc. Obreros, Off. of Econ. Opportunity on Nat. Legal Serv. Progs. and Mission Area Commun. Action Bd, Inc, an Econ. Opportunity Coun. Prog; Mission Coalition Orgn; Chinese-Am. Dem. Club; Mission Area Neighborhood Orgn; v.pres. and dir, Mexican-Am. Legal Defense and Educ. Fund; gen. counsel, Mexican-Am. Polit. Asn. of Calif; bd. dirs, Mission Eng. Lang. Center, Coun. for Civic Unity and San Francisco Neighborhood Legal Assistance Found, 65-67; Mission Coun. on Redevelop, 66; chmn, Spanish-Speaking Issues Conf, Sacramento, 67, San Francisco, 68. Rel: Catholic. Legal Res: 541 Missouri St, San Francisco, Calif. 94107. Mailing Add: 1231 Market St, San Francisco, Calif. 94103.

GONZALES, VICTOR, JR. D
b. 1925. Educ: Univ. of N.Mex, B.A. Polit. & Govt. Pos: N.Mex. State Rep, until 66. Bus. & Prof. Pos: Teacher. Mil. Serv: Army, 43-45, ETO. Mem: VFW; G.I. Forum; PTA. Rel: Catholic. Mailing Add: Box 934, Pico Rivera, Calif. 90660.

GONZALEZ, HENRY BARBOSA D
U.S. Rep, Tex.
b. San Antonio, Tex, 5/3/16; s. Leonides Gonzalez (deceased) and Genevieve Barbosa G; m. 11/10/40 to Bertha Cuellar; c. Henry Thomas, Rose Mary (Mrs. Ramos), Charles, Bertha Alice (Mrs. Denzer), Stephen, Genevieve, Francis and Anna Marie; two grandchildren. Educ: San Antonio Jr. Col; Univ. Tex; St. Mary's Univ. Sch. Law, LL.B, hon. LL.D, 65. Polit. & Govt. Pos: Probation officer, Bexar Co, Tex, 43-46; family relocation dir, San Antonio Housing Authority, 50-52; city councilman, San Antonio, 53-56, mayor pro-tem, 54; Tex. State Sen, 56-61; co-chmn, Viva Kennedy Orgn, 60, Viva Johnson Orgn, 64 and Arriba Humphrey, 68; U.S. Rep, Tex, 61- Publ: 'Bank Interest Rates and the Federal Law,' Personal Finance Law, winter, 65; 'The War Profiteers,' Progressive Mag, 8/67; 'Hope and Promise: Americans of Spanish Surname,' Am. Federationist, AFL-CIO Mag; plus others. Mem: Delta Theta Phi. Legal Res: 238 W. Kings Highway, San Antonio, Tex. 78212. Mailing Add: 116 Cannon House Office Building, Washington, D.C. 20515.

GONZALS, JOHN PETER R
Ward Chmn, Taunton Rep. City Cmt, Mass.
b. Taunton, Mass, 9/14/09; s. Albert Gonzals and Mary Szargowicz G; m. 1/16/41 to Pauline M. O'Neill; c. Virginia (Mrs. Walkey) and N. Peter. Educ: Univ. Maine, B.S, Elec. Eng, 33; Tau Beta Pi; Phi Kappa Phi; Theta Chi. Polit. & Govt. Pos: Construction Eng, Taunton Munic. Lighting, Mass, 39-60, asst. mgr, 60-; ward chmn, Taunton Rep. City Cmt, Mass, 68- Mem: Mass. Soc. Prof. Eng; Mass. Soc. Surveyors; Elec. Eng. Inst; K. of C. Rel: Catholic. Mailing Add: 103 School St, Taunton, Mass. 02780.

GOOCH, JAMES THOMAS D
Chmn, Clark Co. Dem. Cmt, Ark.
b. Vanndale, Ark, 12/10/13; s. Samuel Amos Gooch and Augusta Connelia Halk G; m. 3/9/40 to Edris Wyanna Lookadoo; c. Edris Johanna (Mrs. Quinn) and Marilyn Kay. Educ: Ark. State Univ. and Ark. Law Sch. Polit. & Govt. Pos: Ark. State Sen, 40-44; U.S. Attorney, East. Dist, Ark, 45-54; chmn, Clark Co. Dem. Cmt, Ark, 60- Bus. & Prof. Pos: Pres, U.S. Attorneys Conf, 50-52; pres, Clark Co. Bar Asn, 64-65. Mil. Serv: Entered as Ens, Navy, 42, released as Lt.(sg), 45, after serv. as Naval Gunnery Officer, ETO and Pac. Theater. Mem: Clark Co, Southwest. Ark, Ark. and Am. Bar Asns; Ark. Trial Lawyers Asn.(v.pres); Am. Trial Lawyers Asn; Am. Judicature Soc; Rel: Methodist; Chmn. of World Serv. and Finance of Little Rock Conf, Methodist Church. Legal Res: 1215 Richardson St, Arkadelphia, Ark. 71923. Mailing Add: P.O. Box 357, Arkadelphia, Ark. 71923.

GOOD, JAMES W, JR. R
b. Cedar Rapids, Iowa, 9/26/10; s. James W. Good and Lucy Deacon G; m. 4/11/36 to Virginia Foster; c. James W, III and Jane G.(Mrs. Kendall). Educ: Northwest. Univ, B.A, 32; J.D, 35; Phi Kappa Psi; Phi Delta Phi. Polit. & Govt. Pos: Committeeman, New Trier Twp. Rep. Party, Ill, 58-; v.chmn. exec. cmt, Rep. Cent. Cmt, Cook Co, 67-68; del, Rep. Nat. Conv, 68. Bus. & Prof. Pos: Secy. and dir, Arnar Stone Labs, Inc, 47-60, Fidelitone, Inc, 50-, Cherry Elec. Prod. Corp, 52- and Standard Pharmacal Corp, 62-; partner, Burchmore, Good & Robinette, Ill, 49- Mil. Serv: Entered as Lt.(jg), Naval Res, 44, released as Lt, 46, after serv. in Squadron VD-3, Pac. Theatre, 44-46; Res, Lt.(Ret). Mem: Am, Illinois State and Chicago Bar Asns. Rel: Presbyterian. Legal Res: 75 Indian Hill Rd, Winnetka, Ill. 60093. Mailing Add: 135 S. La Salle St, Chicago, Ill. 60603.

GOOD, JOSEPHINE LOUISE R
Conv. Dir. and Asst. to the Chmn, Rep. Nat. Cmt.
b. Denver, Colo, 3/10/18; d. George Washington Good and Pearl Wooley G; single. Educ: High Sch. and Blair's Bus. Col, Denver, Colo. Polit. & Govt. Pos: Secy, Trading & Exchange Div, Securities & Exchange Cmn, 40-42; admin. asst, exec. off. for price, Off. Price Admin, 42-43; cong. secy, House of Rep, 46-53; confidential and admin. aide, Postmaster Gen, Post Off. Dept, 53-56; conv. dir. and asst. to the chmn, Rep. Nat. Cmt, currently. Bus. & Prof. Pos: Secy. to pres, Fageol Motor Sales Co, 39-40. Mil. Serv: Entered as A/S, Coast Guard Women's Res, 43, released as Chief Yeoman, 45, after serv. in Mil. Morale Hq; Am. Theater Ribbon. Publ: The History of Women in Republican National Conventions and Women in The Republican National Committee. 1st and thus far only woman dir. of Presidential Nominating Convs. of either party. Rel: Catholic. Mailing Add: 3900 Tunlaw Rd. N.W, Washington, D.C. 20007.

GOOD, ROBERT CROCKER D
b. Mt. Vernon, N.Y, 4/7/24; s. Alfred Henry Good and Josephine Crocker G; m. 8/21/46 to Nancy Cunningham; c. Stephen, Karen and Kathleen. Educ: Haverford Col, B.A, 45; Yale Divinity Sch, B.D, 51, Yale Grad. Sch, Ph.D, 56; Phi Beta Kappa. Polit. & Govt. Pos: Research assoc, Wash. Center of For. Policy Research, Johns Hopkins Univ, 58-61; dir, Carnegie Endowment Seminars in Diplomacy, 60-61; coordinator, Kennedy's Task Force on Africa, 60-61; dir, Off. of Research and Analysis for Africa, State Dept, 61-65; U.S. Ambassador to Zambia, 65-69. Bus. & Prof. Pos: Dir, Am. Friends Serv. Cmt. Neighborhood Center, Frankfurt au Main, 47-48; adminstr, Int. Student Seminars in Phila, 48; faculty, Univ. Denver, 53-58; research assoc, Wash. Center of For. Policy Research, Johns Hopkins Univ, with a grant from Ford Found. to prepare a book on the Rhodesian Rebellion, 65- Publ: Co-auth, Alliance Policy in the Cold War, 59, co-auth, Neutralism and Non-Alignment; the New States in World Politics, Praeger, 62; co-ed, Reinhold Neibuhr on Politics (w. Harry R. Davis), Scribner, 60 and Foreign Policy in the Sixties: the Issues and the Instruments (w. Roger Hilsman), Johns Hopkins Univ, 65. Mem: Soc. of Relig. in Higher Educ; African Studies Asn. Superior Honor Award, Dept. of State, 64. Rel: Unitarian. Mailing Add: 1400 Iris St. N.W, Wash, D.C. 20012.

GOOD, THOMAS J, JR. D
N.Mex. State Rep.
b. 1921. Polit. & Govt. Pos: N.Mex. State Rep, 61-; co. cmnr, 4 years. Bus. & Prof. Pos: Rancher. Mem: Mason; Shrine. Rel: Episcopal. Mailing Add: Box 707, Ft. Sumner, N.Mex. 88119. (1967)

GOOD, VINAL G. R
Maine State Sen.
b. 1907; m. to Dorothy I. Anderson; c. James, Jeanette. Educ: Colby Col; Northeast. Univ. Law. Sch. Polit. & Govt. Pos: Past budget cmn. chmn, town meeting moderator and Rep. Town Cmt. chmn, Sebago, Maine; mem, Sebago Rep. Town Cmt. and Cumberland Co. Rep. Cmt; past v.chmn, State Rep. Platform Cmt; Maine State Rep, 99th and 100th Legis, Speaker, Maine State House of Rep, 100th Legis; Maine State Sen, 67- Bus. & Prof. Pos: Attorney; real estate and ins. bus; former teacher-coach, Vet. Admin. Adjudication Off. and U.S. Govt. Investigator. Mem: Cumberland Co. and Maine State Bar Asns; C. of C; Cumberland Club; Lincoln Club of Portland; Grange; Sebago-Long Lakes Region Asn; Standish Lodge; Am. Legion. Mailing Add: Box 8, East Sebago, Maine 04029.

GOODE, JAMES WALTOM R
Chmn, Calhoun Co. Rep. Party, Ga.
b. Albany, Ga, 3/11/50; s. James Lee Goode and Jeannine Knighton G; single. Educ: Calhoun Co. High Sch, grad, 68; Albany Jr. Col, currently. Polit. & Govt. Pos: Secy-treas, Calhoun Co. Rep. Party, Ga, 68, ballot security chmn, 68, co-chmn, 68, chmn, 69-; chief mgr, first Rep. primary in Calhoun Co, 68; polit. action and polit. educ. dir, TAR of Albany, 68; co-founder, Albany Jr. Col. Young Rep, 68, polit. educ. and polit. act. dir, 68, chmn, 68-, chmn. eight mem. del. to Ga. Fedn. of Young Rep. Clubs State Conv, 69; off. pole observer, gen. Elec, Calhoun Co, 68. Bus. & Prof. Pos: Carrier, Albany Herald, Leary, Ga, 61-67; swimming instr, summers 66-68. Publ: Ed, The War Hawk 1968, Taylor Publ, Co, 68. Cert. of Award for boys declamation and Cert. of Award for Annual Editorship, Calhoun Co. High Sch. Rel: Methodist. Mailing Add: P.O. Box 125, Leary, Ga. 31762.

GOODE, P. WAYNE D
Mo. State Rep.
b. St. Louis, Mo, 8/20/37; m. 7/27/63 to Jane Margaret Bell. Educ: Univ. Mo, B.S. Polit. & Govt. Pos: Mo. State Rep, currently; mem, Normandy Twp. Reg. Dem. Club, St. Louis Co. Young Dem. Bus. & Prof. Pos: Dir, Advert. and P.R, Be-Mac Transport Co, Inc. Mil. Serv: Army, Lt, grad. U.S. Army Artil. and Missile Sch; active reservist. Mem: Alpha Kappa Psi; Sigma Alpha Epsilon; St. Louis Jr. C. of C; Normandy C. of C; bd. mgrs, Mark Twain YMCA; Kiwanis. Mailing Add: 7335 Huntington Dr, Normandy, Mo. 63121. (1967)

GOODE, VIRGIL H. D
Mem, Franklin Co. Dem. Cmt, Va.
b. Franklin Co, Va, 7/31/02; s. Benjamin M. Goode and Fannie Mildred Ross G; m. 11/13/43 to Alice Elizabeth Besecker; c. Virgil H, Jr. and Elizabeth Ross. Educ: Univ. Richmond, B.S, 27, LL.B, 35; Omicron Delta Kappa; Sigma Delta Psi; Phi Alpha Delta; Lambda Chi Alpha; Pres, Law Sch. Student Body; Pres, Athletic Asn; Pres, Freshman Law Class. Polit. & Govt. Pos: Mem, Franklin Co. Dem. Cmt, Va, 32-; Va. State Del, Franklin Co, 40-48, commonwealth's attorney, Franklin Co, 48-; del, Va. State Constitution Conv, 56; state campaign dir, Va. Straight Dem. Ticket Elec, 60; del, Dem. Nat. Conv, 60, alternate del, 68; del, Am. Legion Nat. Conv; mem, Va. State Bar Coun, 67- Bus. & Prof. Pos: Teacher, coach and athletic dir, Ansted High Sch, W.Va, 26-31. Mil. Serv: Entered as Pvt, Army, 42, released as Capt, 45, after serv. in Qm. C; Commendation; Citation for Army Commendation Ribbon. Mem: Va. State Bar Asn; W.Va. and Va. Bars; Franklin Co. Bar Asn.(pres, 53-); Am. Legion; Rotary; Ruritan Club. Capt. undefeated track team and held four col. track records, mem. all varsity teams. Legal Res: R.F.D. 2, Rocky Mount, Va. 24151. Mailing Add: Courthouse, Rocky Mount, Va. 24151.

GOODELL, CHARLES ELLSWORTH R
U.S. Sen, N.Y.
b. Jamestown, N.Y, 3/16/26; s. Dr. Charles E. Goodell and Francesca Bartlett G; m. 8/28/54 to Jean Rice; c. William Rice, Timothy Bartlett, Roger Stokoe, Michael Charles Ellsworth and Jeffrey Harris. Educ: Williams Col, B.A. cum laude, 48; Yale Univ. Sch. of Law, LL.B, 51; Yale Univ. Grad. Sch. of Govt, M.A, 52; Phi Beta Kappa. Polit. & Govt. Pos: Asst. to Attorney Gen. and Cong. Liaison, Dept. of Justice, N.Y, 54-55; councilman, Ellicott Town Bd, 57; chmn, Chautauqua Co. Rep. Cmt, 58; U.S. Rep, 38th Dist, N.Y, 59-68; del, Rep. Nat. Conv, 68; U.S. Sen, N.Y, 68- Bus. & Prof. Pos: Law partner, Goodell, VanVlack & McKee, Jamestown, 56-58. Mil. Serv: Seaman, Navy, World War II; 1st Lt, Air Force, Korean Conflict. Mem: Am, N.Y. State and Jamestown Bar Asns; Univ. Club of Jamestown; Am. Legion; former mem. bd. dirs. and govt. affairs chmn, Jamestown Area C. of C; chmn, Cancer Drive, Jamestown. Five varsity letters in baseball and football at Williams Col; semi-pro baseball catcher. Rel: Episcopal. Legal Res: 504 Fairmount Ave. W.E, Jamestown, N.Y. 14701. Mailing Add: 3331 New Senate Office Bldg, Washington, D.C. 20510.

GOODELL, LAWRENCE D
b. 1915. Polit. & Govt. Pos: N.Mex. State Rep, 57-66. Bus. & Prof. Pos: Ins. agency mgr. Mem: Past pres, Rotary; C. of C; Masons; Elks; Shrine. Rel: First Christian. Mailing Add: 1408 W. 4th, Roswell, N.Mex. 88201. (1967)

GOODEN, WILLIAM JOSIAH R
Okla. State Rep.
b. Kingfisher, Okla, 2/28/34; s. Francis W. Gooden and Lillian Ruth Gardner G; m. 4/20/57 to LaDonna Jane Kramer; c. Mark William, Lori Karen and John Kramer. Educ: Okla. State Univ, B.S. in Indust. Eng, 57; Blue Key; Sigma Tau; Alpha Pi Mu; Alpha Phi Omega; Arnold Air Soc; Sigma Nu; Student Senate; Inter-Fraternity Coun; Eng. Student Coun; Toastmasters Club; Disciples Student Fel. Polit. & Govt. Pos: Precinct orgn. chmn, Kingfisher Co. Rep. Party, Okla, 62-63, chmn, 67-68; v.chmn, Kingfisher Co. Young Rep, 62-64; campaign chmn, Bud Wilkinson for U.S. Senate, Kingfisher Co, 64, chmn, bd. adjust, Kingfisher, 65; campaign chmn, James Smith for Cong, 66, campaign chmn, Dewey Bartlett for Gov, 66; Okla. State Rep, Dist. 42, Blaine and Kingfisher Co, 68- Mil. Serv: Entered as 2nd Lt, Air Force, 58, released as 1st Lt, 61, after serv. in Third Bomb Wing, Tactical Air Command, Japan, 60-61, Capt, Res, 66- Mem: Bowling Proprietor's Asn. Am.(dir, 64-69); Okla. State Bowling Proprietor's Asn.(secy-treas, 64-65, v.pres, 66-67, pres, 68-69); Lions (dir. and Tailtwister); Jaycees (pres, Kingfisher Br, 63-64); pres, Kingfisher Co. Artist Series; Mason; Eastern Star; Sportsman's Club; Quarterback Club; Men's Garden Club; Kingfisher Country Club; Boy Scouts (dist. chmn); C. of C.(pres, Kingfisher Br, 64). Distinguished Serv. Award as Outstanding Young Man in Kingfisher, 64; Outstanding Young Oklahoman, 64, Okla. Jaycees. Rel: Disciples of Christ; Elder and Treas, First Christian Church of Kingfisher. Mailing Add: 116 Thompson Dr, Kingfisher, Okla. 73750.

GOODFELLOW, ROBERT LAWSON D
Okla. State Rep.
b. Binger, Okla, 2/27/05; s. Ira Goodfellow and Gertrude Ruley G; m. 11/27/48 to Oma Jean Carr; c. Scott Witt, Robert, Jr, Roberta and Elizabeth. Educ: Gracemont High Sch; Anadarko Bus. Col. Polit. & Govt. Pos: Co. clerk, Caddo Co, Okla, 33-37; chmn, Sixth Cong. Dist. League of Young Dem, 36-37; dist. supvr, Nat. Youth Admin, 37-38; co. treas, Caddo Co, 41-47; Okla. State Rep, 54- Mem: Pres, Co. Clerks Asn. of Okla, 34 and Co. Treas. Asn. of Okla, 42; Anadarko C. of C; Lions; Okla. Farmers Union. Rel: Methodist. Mailing Add: P.O. Box 149, Gracemont, Okla. 73042.

GOODHEART, BERNARD J. 'SWEDE' D
Mont. State Sen.
b. Wagner, Mont, 8/27/23; s. Ervin Joseph Goodheart and Mildred Miller G; m. 8/10/46 to Lois Jean Baker; c. Dennis Lee, Dianne Lynn, Douglas Larry, and Dawn Lanette. Educ: Harlem High Sch, grad, 41. Polit. & Govt. Pos: City coun. alderman, Malta, Mont, 59-67, mayor, 67-69; Mont. State Sen, Dist. Ten, Phillips and Blaine Co, 69- Mil. Serv: Entered as Pvt, Army, 42, released as Sgt, 45, after serv. in Signal Serv. and Signal Engr. Bn, ETO, 43-45. Mem: Moose; VFW; Am. Legion; K. of C. Rel: Catholic. Legal Res: 25 S. Eighth West, Malta, Mont. 59538. Mailing Add: Box 1013, Malta, Mont. 59538.

GOODING, MARY ETTA D
b. Clayton, Del, 2/19/21; d. Earl Edwin West and Henrietta Cole W; m. 8/15/42 to William Lambert Gooding, III; c. Mary Lou (Mrs. David Stephens). Educ: Beacon Bus. Col, grad. Polit. & Govt. Pos: Former mem, New Castle Co. Dem. Exec. Cmt, Del. and Del. State Dem. Cmt; chief dep, New Castle Co. Sheriff's Off, 61-62; Del. State Rep, 64-69. Bus. & Prof. Pos: Secy, Hercules Powder Co, 39-46; Conrad High Sch, 58-60. Mem: Past pres, Suburban Century Club; state bd. mem, Del. Fedn. Women's Clubs; Conrad High Sch. PTA; Christiana Hundred Dem. Club; New Castle Co. Women's Dem. Club; Status of Women Cmn; adv. coun, Interagency Cmt. on Ment. Retardation; del, Educ. Cmt. of the States. Good Govt. Award, Cmt. of 39, 66. Rel: Methodist; mem, WSCS. Mailing Add: 400 Becker Ave, Woodcrest, Wilmington, Del. 19804. (1967)

GOODLING, GEORGE A. R
U.S. Rep, Pa.
b. Loganville, Pa, 9/26/96; s. R.A. Goodling and Jennie K.G; m. to Annetta J. Glatfelter (deceased); c. Three boys and three girls. Educ: Pa. State Univ, B.S. in Hort; Gamma Sigma Delta. Polit. & Govt. Pos: Pa. State Rep, 42-56; chmn, Joint State Govt. Subcmts; U.S. Rep, 19th Dist, Pa, 62-64, 67-; mem, Migratory Bird Conserv. Cmn. and Agr. and Merchant Marine and Fisheries Cmts. Bus. & Prof. Pos: Owner and operator, fruit farm, 23-; dir, Peoples Bank of Glen Rock; dir, White Rose Motor Club; dir, Stewartstown Mutual Ins. Co. Mil. Serv: Seaman 2/C, Navy. Mem: Pa. Hort. Asn.(past pres, exec. secy, currently); Agr. Exten. Asn; Pa. Farmers Asn; mem, Civil War Centennial Cmn; secy, Loganville Fire Co, 32 years; Grange; Am. Legion; Izaak Walton League; Blue Lodge (Past Master); Commandery; Consistory; Supreme Coun.(33°); Tall Cedars of Lebanon; Shrine; Elks; Alpha Tau Omega. Rel: Evangelical United Brethren Church; treas, 25 years. Legal Res: Loganville, Pa. 17342. Mailing Add: 1714 Longsworth House Office Bldg, Washington, D.C. 20510.

GOODMAN, ARTHUR D
b. New York, N.Y, 4/14/35; s. Jesse J. Goodman and Lillian Wisla G; m. 4/1/58 to Marian Edelson Van Loen; c. Loren and Drew. Educ: Hunter Col, Bronx, N.Y, 3 years; Dramatic Club. Polit. & Govt. Pos: Mem. exec. bd, New Dem. Coalition of Huntington, N.Y; chmn, Concerned Dem, 2nd Cong. Dist, 67-68; exec. bd, L.I. Dissenting Dem, 67-69; del, Dem. Nat. Conv, 68. Bus. & Prof. Pos: Pres, Argood Enterprises, Ltd, N.Y, currently. Rel: Jewish. Mailing Add: 39 Foxwood Dr. E. Huntington Sta, N.Y. 11746.

GOODMAN, ARTHUR JR. D
b. Mooresville, N.C, 9/17/26; s. Arthur Goodman; Katherine Cohen G; m. to Joyce Lyles; c. David, Beth, Beverly, Phillip, Arthur III. Educ: Duke Univ, B.A, 50; Duke Univ. Sch. of Law, LL.B, 59. Polit. & Govt. Pos: N.C. State Rep -66. Bus. & Prof. Pos: Lawyer. Mil. Serv: Navy, 44-46. Mem: N.C. Bar Asn; Mecklenburg Co. Bar Asn; B'nai B'rith. Rel: Jewish, mem, Temple Israel, former v.pres, Temple Israel Men's Club. Mailing Add: 6419 Morven Lane, Charlotte, N.C. 28211. (1967)

GOODMAN, CARLYLE WHITTIER, SR. D
S.C. State Rep.
b. Shiloh, S.C, 11/18/01; s. Adolphus Julious Goodman and Rebecca Ann Carraway G; m. 11/29/20 to Neva Julea Green; c. Carlyle W, Jr. and David Earle. Educ: Carlyle Mil. Acad, 3 years. Polit. & Govt. Pos: Mem. Bd. of Trustees and Bd. of Educ, Sumter Co, S.C; S.C. State Rep, 59-, chmn, Agr. and Conserv. Cmt, S.C. State House of Rep, 67- Bus. & Prof. Pos: Farmer; bank dir. Mem: Farm Bur.(dir, S.C. Chap); dir, S.C. Farm Bur. Fire Ins. Co. Rel: Methodist. Mailing Add: Route 1, Lynchburg, S.C. 29080.

GOODMAN, JAMES ANTHONY D
Pa. State Rep.
b. New Boston, Pa, 6/12/36; s. Cornelius Goodman and Anna Holzenthaler G; m. 7/4/64 to Joan Margaret Yonosky; c. Sharon. Educ: Pa. State Univ, B.S. in Bus. Admin, 61. Polit. & Govt. Pos: Pa. State Rep, currently; mgt. trainee, City of Philadelphia, Pa, 61-62. Bus. & Prof. Pos: Securities salesman, Waddell and Reed, Inc, 62-; owner and mgr, Independent Ins. Agency, 63-Mil. Serv: Entered as Airman Basic, Air Force, 54, released as Airman 1/C, 57, after serv. in Hq, Controllers Br, Wash, D.C, France and Morocco. Mem: Amvets; Elks; K. of C; Pa. State Univ. Alumni Asn; Young Dem. Rel: Roman Catholic. Legal Res: 726 E. Mahanoy St, Mahanoy City, Pa. 17948. Mailing Add: 534 Vermont Ave, Erie, Pa. 16505. (1967)

GOODMAN, JAY S. D
b. St. Louis, Mo, 1/16/40; s. Harold M. Goodman and Minnie Frumer G; m. 6/13/63 to Ellen Safier; c. Robert Francis. Educ: Beloit Col, B.A, 61; Stanford Univ, M.A, 63; Brown Univ, Ph.D, 66; Woodrow Wilson fel, 61 and dissertation fel, 64-65. Polit. & Govt. Pos: Chmn, R.I. Fedn. Col. Young Dem, 63-64; mem, R.I. Dem. Adv. Cmt, 67-68; chmn, R.I. Citizens for Kennedy, 68; alternate del, Dem. Nat. Conv, 68. Bus. & Prof. Pos: Asst. dir. research, R.I. Constitutional Conv, 65-67; assoc. prof. govt. and chmn. dept, Wheaton Col, 65-; research assoc. polit. sci, Brown Univ, 66- Publ: The Democrats and Labor in Rhode Island, Brown Univ, 67; co-auth, The American Democracy, Macmillan, 69; ed, Dimensions of Urban Political Behavior: A Reader, Allyn & Bacon, 70. Mem: Am, N.Eng. and South. Polit. Sci. Asns; Am. Asn. Univ. Prof. Rel: Jewish. Mailing Add: 33 Phillips St, Providence, R.I. 02906.

GOODMAN, ROY M. R
N.Y. State Sen.
b. N.Y.C, 3/5/30; s. Bernard A. Goodman and Alice Matz G; m. 6/28/55 to Barbara Furrer; c. Claire, Leslie and Randolph. Educ: Harvard Col, B.A. cum laude, 51; Harvard Grad. Sch. of Bus. Admin, M.B.A. with distinction, 53; Hasty Pudding Club. Polit. & Govt. Pos: Former treas, New York Co. Rep. Party, N.Y; v.chmn, Lindsay-for-Mayor Cmt; treas, New Yorkers for Lindsay; mem, Commun. Planning Bd. No. 8, 64; former pres, Ninth Assembly Dist. Rep. Club and the City Club; finance adminstr, N.Y.C, 66-68; N.Y. State Sen, 26th Dist, 68-, chmn, Housing Cmt. and mem, City of New York, Taxation, Civil Serv. and Pensions and Rd. and Pub. Works Cmts, N.Y. State Senate. Bus. & Prof. Pos: Assoc, Kuhn, Loeb & Co, investment bankers, 56-60; pres, drug co. including Ex-Lax, Inc, Roycemore, Inc. and Harcliffe Labs, Inc, 60- Mil. Serv: Officer, Navy, 53-56. Mem: N.Y.C. Banking Cmn; bd. trustees, N.Y.C. Police and Fire Dept. Pension Funds and the Fire Dept. Life Ins. Fund; trustee and chmn, exec. cmt, Brotherhood-in-Action; mem. bd. Carnegie Hall Corp, Dalton Schs, L.I. Col. Hosp, Columbia Univ. Col. of Pharmaceutical Sci, Anti-Defamation League of B'nai B'rith, Tel Aviv Univ, Am. Parents Cmt. and N.Y. Cmt. of Young Audiences; Harvard 1951 Permanent Class Cmt; Young Pres. Orgn, Inc; Wall St. Club; Harvard Clubs of New York and Boston; Century Country Club. Received Distinguished Serv. Award, Jr. C. of C. and named Young Man of the Year, 66; hon. mem, Omicron Delta Epsilon, St. John's Univ, 67; Mt. Scopus Citation, Hebrew Univ. of Jerusalem, 68. Rel: Jewish. Mailing Add: 1035 Fifth Ave, New York, N.Y. 10028.

GOODMAN, WILLIAM J. D
Md. State Del.
b. Poyen, Ark, 1/22/30; married. Educ: Los Angeles, Calif. pub. schs. Polit. & Govt. Pos: Pub. rels. dir, Co. Coun. Dem. Clubs, Md, 59-60; v.pres, Citizens Dem. Club, 59-61; mem, Palmer Park Dem. Club, 59-61; campaign adv. to R.E. Lankford, Cong. Elector, 60; Md. State Del, 63- Bus. & Prof. Pos: Tel. serv. engr. Mil. Serv: Marine Corps, 47-50. Mem: AFL-CIO. Mailing Add: 6408 Kalso Court, Hyattsville, Md. 20784. (1967)

GOODRICH, RAY C. R
b. Roulette Twp, Potter City, Pa, 4/1/13; s. Chauncey B. Goodrich and Ruth Jones G; m. to Marjorie Summers; c. three. Educ: Lycoming Col; Pa. State Univ, B.A. Polit. & Govt. Pos: Pa. State Rep, 56-67; Rep. State Cmt; Potter Co. Rep. Cmt. Bus. & Prof. Pos: Business and farming, sch. busses dir, First Nat. Bank of Couldersport. Mem: Past Pres, Potter City Fed. Sportsmen's Clubs; Roulette Fish and Game Club; Roulette C. of C; Dir, Potter City Recreation, Inc; Former Exec. Cmt, Potter City Agr. Ext. Asn; Masons; I.O.O.F; Grange, Exchange Club of Coudersport; L.O.O.M; Roulette Fire Dept; Past Dir. & Treas, Potter City Chap, Pa. Soc. Crippled Children and Adults. Mailing Add: R.D. 1, Box 111, Roulette, Pa. 16746. (1967)

GOODWIN, ALFRED THEODORE R
b. Bellingham, Wash, 6/29/23; s. Alonzo Theodore Goodwin and Miriam Haxel Williams G; m. 12/23/49 to Mary Ellin Handelin; c. Karl, James, Margaret and Sara. Educ: Univ. Ore, B.A, 47, Law Sch, J.D, 51; Order of the Coif; Phi Delta Phi; Sigma Delta Chi; Alpha Tau Omega. Polit. & Govt. Pos: Circuit judge, Ore. Circuit Court, Lane Co, 55-60; assoc. justice, Ore. Supreme Court, 60- Bus. & Prof. Pos: Partner, Darling, Vonderheit & Goodwin, 51-55. Mil. Serv: Entered as Pvt, Army, 42, released as Capt, 46, after serv in 342nd Inf, 86th Div, ETO and Philippines; ETO and Asia-Pac. Ribbons; Victory Medal; Occup. Medal; Combat Infantryman Badge; Lt. Col.(Ret), Army Res, 46-69. Mem: Am. Bar Asn; Am. Judicature Soc; ROA. Rel: Presbyterian. Mailing Add: 1999 High St. S.E, Salem, Ore. 97302.

GOODWIN, ERNEST E. R
Vt. State Rep.
b. Montreal, Can, 6/8/00; m. to Louise Fairbanks; c. Four sons; two daughters. Educ: Univ. Maine; West. State Teachers Col, Maine. Polit. & Govt. Pos: Former lister, Hyde Park, Vt, town agent, 6 years, sch. dir, Weathersfield and Hyde Park, 6 years; village trustee, Hyde Park, 48-; Vt. State Rep, 65- Bus. & Prof. Pos: Retired, businessman and teacher, Springfield, Vt. High Sch, 19 years. Mem: Odd Fellows; Rotary; Vt. Real Estate Bd; Vermont Appraisal Soc; v.pres. and dir, Vt. Cattle Dealers Asn. Rel: Congregational. Mailing Add: Hyde Park, Vt. 05655. (1967)

GOODWIN, JOHN WILLIAM D
b. Roger Mills Co, Okla, 1/1/35; s. Robert L. Goodwin and Obera Hatley G; m. 9/4/60 to Phoebe Jane Woodward; c. Thomas Hatley, Laura Elizabeth, Clariss Obera and John Ashley. Educ: Panhandle A & M Col, B.A, 56; Univ. Conn; Okla. State Univ, M.S, 59, Ph.D, 62; Alpha Zeta; Alpha Gamma Rho. Polit. & Govt. Pos: Secy-treas, Roger Mills Co. Dem. Cent. Cmt, 56-62; Dem. nominee, U.S. Rep, Okla, 68. Bus. & Prof. Pos: Res. asst, Univ. Conn, 56-57; res. asst, Okla. State Univ, 57-58, instr. agr. econ, 58-61; economist, Armour & Co, Chicago, 61-64; from asst. to assoc. prof. agr. econ, Okla. State Univ, 64- Mil. Serv: Entered as Pfc, Army Res, 57, released as Sgt, 63. Publ: Co-auth, 'Aggregation of Normative Microsupply Relationships for Dryland Crop Farms in the Rolling Plains of Oklahoma and Texas,' Okla. Agr. Exp. Sta, Tech. Bul. T-103, 8/63; auth, 'Cattle Feeding: An Analysis of Oklahoma's Opportunities,' Okla. Agr. Exp. Sta, Processed Series P-488, 1/65; co-auth, 'The Irreversible Demand for Beef,' Okla. Agr. Exp. Sta, Tech. Bul. T-127, 6/68; plus 31 others. Mem: Am. Agr. Econ. Asn; Mason; Farmers Union. Blue Key-Alumni Asn. Outstanding Teacher Award, 67; Alpha Zeta Outstanding Teacher Award, 69. Rel: Church of Christ. Mailing Add: 3324 N. Monroe, Stillwater, Okla. 74074.

GOODWIN, KATHLEEN WATSON D
Maine State Rep.
b. Bath, Maine, 11/13/40; d. Nathan Wilbur Watson and Kathleen Leonard W; m. 7/12/69 to John Raymond Goodwin. Educ: Univ. Maine, 60-62; Bliss Bus. Col, Lewiston, Maine, 63. Polit. & Govt. Pos: Secy, Bath City Dem. Cmt, Maine, 63-66; treas, Sagadahoc Co. Dem. Cmt, 64-65; committeewoman, Maine Dem. State Cmt, 66-, secy, 68-; secy, Gov. Task Force Govt. Reorgn, 67-68; Maine State Rep, 69-, mem. and secy, Joint Standing Cmt, State Govt, Maine House Rep, 69- Bus. & Prof. Pos: Secy, Pres. of Maine State Sen, 65, Cmnr. Forestry, 65-66 and Off. Gov, 67-68. Mem: Natural Resources Coun, Maine. Rel: Catholic. Legal Res: 848 Washington St, Bath, Maine 04530. Mailing Add: Box 190C, Bath Rd, Brunswick, Maine 04011.

GOODWIN, MARTIN BRUNE R
b. Vancouver, B.C, Can, 8/8/21; s. Ray S. Goodwin and Emma Agusta Brune G; m. 6/18/47 to Bette-Jane Hatton Wilson; c. Nancijane Emma Margo. Educ: Univ. B.C, B.S.A, 43; McGill Univ, M.D, C.M, 48; Nu Sigma Nu; Kappa Sigma. Polit. & Govt. Pos: Mem, State Radiation Tech. Adv. Coun, N.Mex, 60-; chmn, Curry Co. Rep. Cmt. and N.Mex. State Cent. Cmt, 63-64 & 65-67; chmn, N.Mex. Health and Soc. Serv. Bd, currently. Mil. Serv: Capt, Army Med. Corps, 53-55. Mem: Am. Col. Radiologists (coun, 65-); N.Mex. Tuberc. Asn.(dir, 58-) N.Mex. Thoracic Soc.(pres, 61-63); N.Mex. Radiol. Soc.(pres, 61-62); N.Mex. Cattlemen's Asn; Farm. Bur; AF&AM; Scottish Rite (32°); Shrine; Am. Legion; Lions; Mounted Patrol of Clovis; Air Force Asn. Intercollegiate basketball and rowing. Rel: Presbyterian. Legal Res: 1001 Pile, Clovis, N.Mex. 88101. Mailing Add: P.O. Drawer, 1628, Clovis, N.Mex. 88101.

GOODWIN, RICHARD N. D
m. 6/15/58 to Sandra Leverant; c. Richard Joseph. Educ: Tufts Univ, B.A, 53; Harvard Law Sch, LL.B, 58. Polit. & Govt. Pos: Asst. spec. counsr. to President of U.S, 61-62 and spec. asst. 64-65; dep. asst. secy. of state, 63-64; adv. to Sen Eugene McCarthy's Presidential Campaign, 68; del, Dem. Nat. Conv, 68. Mil. Serv: Entered as Pvt, Army, 54, released as Cpl, 56, after serv. in Ord. Corps, France; Good Conduct Medal. Publ: The Sower's Seed: A Tribute to Adlai Stevenson, New Am. Libr, 65; Triumph or Tragedy: Reflections on Viet Nam, Random House, 66. Mem: Mass. Bar Asn. Rel: Jewish. Legal Res: Pleasant St, Brookline, Mass. 01447. Mailing Add: 14 Chestnut St, Boston, Mass. 02108. (1967)

GOODWIN, ROBERT KINGMAN R
b. Des Moines, Iowa, 5/23/05; s. William J. Goodwin and Grace Kingman G; m. 8/24/32 to Marguerite Schoen; c. Ann (Mrs. Witmer) and Robert F. Educ: Drake Univ, A.B, 28; George Wash. Univ; Omicron Delta Kappa; Alpha Tau Omega; Alpha Phi Omega. Polit. Pos: Rep. Nat. committeeman, Iowa, 52-56; dir, Farm & Ranch Campaign, Rep. Party, 52; chmn, sixth dist, Rep. Party and state Rep. Cent. Cmt, 50-52; precinct chmn, Dallas Co. Rep. Party, 34-38. Govt. Pos: Civilian aide to Secy. of the Army, 52-56; U.S. Rep, Iowa, 40; mayor, Redfield, 38-40. Bus. & Prof. Pos: Chmn, Red Wing Sewer Pipe Corp, Minn, 65-; mem. of Bd, Stoner Co, 61-; chmn, Bd, Wash. Mfg. Co, Inc, 56-; chmn, Exec. Cmt, Cent. Nat. Bank, 62-66 and chmn, Bd, 58; chmn, Roll, Inc. and its predecessors. Mil. Serv: Entered as Lt, Navy, 42, released as Lt. Comdr, 45; Lt. Comdr, Inactive Naval Res. Publn: Contributor, 'The Articulates,' 57. Mem: Pres, Des Moines Rotary, 62-63; chmn. exec. cmt, Herbert Hoover Birthplace Found; dir, State Univ. Iowa Found; trustee, Iowa, 4-H Club Found; v.chmn, Region VIII, Boy Scouts, Silver Beaver, Silver Antelope; 1st pres, Jr. Achievement of Des Moines, 56, Nat. Bd; Mason (32°); Odd Fellows; Des Moines Club; Am. Legion; Iowa Farm Bur. Fedn; co-chmn, Des Moines United Campaign, 57; Des Moines Pioneer Club. Alumni Distinguished Serv. Award, Drake Univ, 65; polit. sci; natural sci. Rel: Christian. Legal Res: 415 Foster Dr, Des Moines, Iowa 50312. Mailing Add: 3810 Ingersoll Ave, Des Moines, Iowa 50312. (1967)

GOODWIN, THOMAS G. D
W.Va. State Del.
b. Kanawha Co, W.Va, 11/22/22; s. Charles A. Goodwin and Grace B. Hudnall G; m. 5/28/55 to Shirley Jo Stamper; c. Matthew Virlon. Educ: W.Va. Inst. Tech, B.S; Morris Harvey Col; W.Va. Univ; Univ. Miami. Polit. & Govt. Pos: W.Va. State Del, 64- Bus. & Prof. Pos: Teacher; coach. Mil. Serv: Marine Corps, 42-45, Pac. Theatre. Mem: Nat. Educ. Asn; W.Va. Educ. Asn; VFW; Am. Legion; Elks; Lions; PTA; Kanawha Co. Coon Hunters Asn; leader, Boy Scouts. Rel: Baptist. Mailing Add: Seth, W.Va. 25181. (1967)

GOODWYN, O. J. D
Pres. Pro-Tem, Ala. State Senate
b. Warrior, Ala, 12/12/20; s. Andrew Goodwyn; m. to Mary Chalmers Hair; c. Otis James, Jr. and Susan Anne. Educ: Univ. Ala, B.S. and LL.B. Polit. & Govt. Pos: Ala. State Rep, 54, 58 & 62-66; Ala. State Sen, 67-, pres. pro-tem, Ala. State Senate, currently. Bus. & Prof. Pos: Instr, Jones Law Sch; asst. gen. counsel, Dept. Indust. Rels. Mem: State and Co. Bar Asns; Phi Alpha Delta; South. Regional Educ. Bd; Nat. Coun. of State Govts. Bd; C. of C; Jaycees; Exchange Club; K. of P; Am. Legion. Rel: Presbyterian. Mailing Add: 325 Bell Bldg, Montgomery, Ala. 36104.

GOOGASIAN, GEORGE ARA D
Chmn, Oakland Co. Dem. Cmt, Mich.
b. Pontiac, Mich, 2/22/36; s. Peter Googasian and Lucy Chobanian G; m. 6/27/59 to Phyllis Elaine Law; c. Karen and Steven. Educ: Univ. Mich, B.A, 58; Northwest. Univ. Sch. of Law, J.D, 61; Phi Delta Phi; Sigma Nu. Polit. & Govt. Pos: Chmn, Pontiac Dem. Club, Mich, 62-63; mem, Oakland Co. Dem. Cmt, 62-63, chmn, 64-; asst. U.S. attorney, East. Dist, Mich, 63-64; del, Dem. Nat. Conv, 68. Bus. & Prof. Pos: Attorney-at-law, Marentay, Rouse, Selby, Fisher & Weber, Detroit, Mich, 62-63; attorney-at-law, Hartman, Beier, Howlett and McConnell, Pontiac, 64- Mem: Oakland Co. Bar Asn; State Bar of Mich; Pontiac Sch. Bd. Study Cmt; Speakers Bur; United Fund. Rel: Protestant. Mailing Add: 105 E. Iroquois Rd, Pontiac, Mich. 48053.

GORDON, BERNARD G. R
N.Y. State Sen.
b. Peekskill, N.Y; m. to Leila Mencher; c. Elise Ann. Educ: Syracuse Univ; Syracuse Col. of Law. Polit. & Govt. Pos: Corp. counsel, Peekskill, N.Y; counsel, Joint Legis. Cmt. to Study Assessments and Taxation of State Lands; Dep. Secy. of State in charge of N.Y.C. Off, 59; N.Y. State Assemblyman, 60-64; N.Y. State Sen, 64- Bus. & Prof. Pos: Attorney; assoc. dir, Co. Trust Co; mem. bd. of dirs, Peekskill Hosp. Mil. Serv: Lt. and Command Pilot, Navy, World War II. Mem: F&AM (Past Master, Dunderberg Lodge No. 1070); Jewish War Vets (Past Comdr, Peekskill Post). Mailing Add: 1420 Riverview Ave, Peekskill, N.Y. 10566.

GORDON, EDWARD D
b. Morrilton, Ark, 4/17/15; s. Edward Gordon and Ada Ruth Bearden G; m. 12/22/44 to Marjorie Foster; c. Edward Allen and Martha Ruth. Educ: Columbia Mil. Acad, Tenn, 31-33; Ark. Polytech. Col, 33-36; Univ. Ark, LL.B, 40. Polit. & Govt. Pos: Ark. State Rep, Conway Co, 41-43; bd. mem, Ark. War Mem. Stadium Cmn, 47-62; prosecuting attorney, Fifth Dist. of Ark, 53-59; chmn, Conway Co. Dem. Cent. Cmt. and Elec. Bd, 60-66; mem, Ark. Bd. of Educ, 62-64; mem, Ark. Game and Fish Cmn, 65- Bus. & Prof. Pos: Mem, Judiciary Cmn, Ark. Bar, 62-, chmn, 64- Mil. Serv: Entered as A/S, Navy, 42, released as Lt, 45, after serv. in Pac. Area, 43-45; Pac. Theater Ribbon. Mem: Conway Co, Ark. and Am. Bar Asns; Am. Judicature Soc; Ark. and Am. Trial Lawyers Asns; Mason (32°); Consistory; Shrine; VFW; Am. Legion; DAV. Rel: Methodist. Mailing Add: 300 S. St. Joseph, Morrilton, Ark. 72110.

GORDON, JAY H. D
Auditor of Accounts, Vt.
b. Bellows Falls, Vt, 10/10/30; s. Harry Gordon and Annie Mandel G; m. 6/28/64 to Joan Carolyn Plumpton; c. Harry Edward. Educ: Univ. Vt, B.S. in econ, 53; N.Y. Univ, Grad. Sch. Bus. Admin, M.A, 59; Phi Sigma Delta. Polit. & Govt. Pos: Chmn, Windham Co. Dem. Cmt, 63-65; mem, Vt. State Dem. Cmt. and exec. cmt, 63-65; mem, Bellows Falls Zoning Cmn, 63-64; Auditor of Accts, Vt, 65-; mem, Vt. Cmt. on Admin. Coord, Bd. of Acquiring Fed. Forest Lands, Vt. State Police & Motor Vehicle Inspectors' Retirement Bd, Vt. Employees' Retirement Bd, Vt. State Claims Cmn. and Vt. Indust. Bldg. Authority, at present. Bus. & Prof. Pos: Staff acct, Peat, Marwick, Mitchell & Co, CPA's, 56-59; CPA, Bliss, Lawlor & Co, Bellows Falls, 59-65; mem, Vt. Bd. Acct, 63-66. Mil. Serv: Entered as 2nd Lt, Air Force, 53, released as 1st Lt, 55 after serv. as Auditor Gen, Hq. Air Force. Publ: "Too Small to Budget?" NAA Bul, 4/64. Mem: Am. Inst. CPA's; Nat. Asn. Acct; Asn. of CPA Examiners; Vt. Soc. of CPA's; Munic. Finance Officers Asn. U.S. and Can; bd. trustees, Vt. Hist. Soc; Mason; Elks; Am. Legion; Rotary; state dir, Bellows Falls Jaycees, 62; past treas, Bellows Falls Country Club. Rel: Jewish. Legal Res: 2 Deerfield Dr, Montpelier, Vt. 05602. Mailing Add: P.O. Box 372, Montpelier, Vt. 05602. (1967)

GORDON, JEAN ELLA R
b. San Jose, Calif; d. William Douglas Gordon and Ella Grace Church G; single. Educ: San Jose State Col, B.A, 42; Alpha Chi Omega. Polit. & Govt. Pos: Secy, U.S. Rep. Jack Anderson, 49-52; admin. asst. to U.S. Rep. Gubser, Calif, 53- Bus. & Prof. Pos: Secy, Guaranty Savings & Loan Asn, San Jose, Calif, 43-44 and Magnuson Engrs, 44-49. Mem: Cong. Secretaries Club; Rep. Women of Capitol Hill. Rel: Presbyterian. Legal Res: San Jose, Calif. Mailing Add: 2373 Rayburn House Office Bldg, Washington, D.C. 20515.

GORDON, LINCOLN
b. N.Y.C, 9/10/13; married. Educ: Harvard Univ, B.A, 33; Rhodes Scholar, Oxford Univ, Ph.D, 36. Polit. & Govt. Pos: Technician and consult, Nat. Resources Planning Bd, Wash, D.C, 39-40; econ. analyst, Nat. Defense Adv. Cmn, 40; prog. v.chmn, War Prod. Bd, 42-45; bur. dir, Civil Prod. Admin, 45-47; U.S. del, UN Atomic Energy Cmn, 46-47; consult, Dept. of State, 47-48, 56 & 58-61; chief, Prog. Rev. Div, Econ. Coop. Admin, 49-51, asst. to dep. adminstr, 51-52; chief of missions, London, 52-55; U.S. Ambassador to Brazil, 61-66; Asst. Secy. of State for Inter-Am. Affairs, 66-67. Bus. & Prof. Pos: Instr, Harvard Univ, 36-39 & 40-42, prof. govt. and admin, 46-49, prof. int. econ. rels, 55-69; pres, Johns Hopkins Univ, 67- Mailing Add: Office of the President, Johns Hopkins University, Baltimore, Md. 21218. (1967)

GORDON, MARGARET SHAUGHNESSY D
Councilman, Berkeley, Calif.
b. Wabasha, Minn, 9/4/10; d. Michael James Shaughnessy and Mary O'Brien S; m. 8/15/36 to Robert Aaron Gordon; c. Robert James and David Michael. Educ: Bryn Mawr Col, B.A, 31; Radcliffe Col, Ph.D, 35. Polit. & Govt. Pos: Head res. unit, Export-Import Off, Off. Price Admin, Wash, D.C, 42-43; mem, Personnel Bd, Berkeley, Calif, 61-65; consult. unemployl ins, U.S. Dept. Labor, 62-; mem, Res. Adv. Cmt, U.S. Social Security Admin, 65-66, chmn, 66-67; councilman, Berkeley, Calif, 65- Bus. & Prof. Pos: Res. fel, Harvard-Radcliffe Bur. Int. Res, 36-39; asst. res. economist, Univ. Calif, Berkeley, 50-54, assoc. dir, Int. Indust. Rels, 54- Publ: Employment Expansion and Population Growth, 54; The Economics of Welfare Policies, 63; Retraining and Labor Market Adjustment in Western Europe, plus others. Mem: Am. Econ. Asn; Indust. Rels. Research Asn; fel. Gerontology Soc, Inc. Mailing Add: 984 Creston Rd, Berkeley, Calif. 94708. (1967)

GORDON, MILTON G. D
Mem, Dem. State Cent. Cmt, Calif.
b. Detroit, Mich, 6/1/22; s. Abe Gordon and Anna Pragg G; m. to Sandra Louise Driver. Educ: Wayne State Univ, A.B. in Pub. Admin; Univ. Calif. at Los Angeles, M.A. in Polit. Sci; Pi Sigma Alpha. Polit. & Govt. Pos: Mem, Los Angeles Co. Dem. Cent. Cmt, 58-66, treas, 63-66; mem, Real Estate Cmn, Calif, 62-63, Pub. Works Bd, 63-64 and Gov. Emergency Resources Planning Cmt, 64; adminstr, Bus. and Commerce Agency, State of Calif; mem, Dem. State Cent. Cmt, 69- Bus. & Prof. Pos: Pres, Milton-Gordon Co, Inc, 51-63; pres, Village-Gordon Co, 63; consult. and real estate counsr, 69- Mil. Serv: Pfc, Army, 42-44; Good Conduct Ribbon; Marksman. Publ: Race and Property, Univ. Calif. Mem: Elks; DAV; Am. Legion; B'nai B'rith; Beverly Hills and Los Angeles Realty Bds; Nat. Asn. License Law Off.(v.pres. and regional dir); head fund-raising drive, Northeast. Calif. Chap, Arthritis Found. Outstanding Alumnus Award, Wayne State Univ. Club of South. Calif, 63. Rel: Jewish. Mailing Add: 2700 Krim Dr, Los Angeles, Calif. 90064.

GORDON, ROBERT H. R
Asst. Attorney Gen, Commonwealth of Mass.
b. 1935; m. to Judith; c. Kim, Ian, Adam and Andrew. Educ: Syracuse Univ, B.A, 57, M.P.A, 58, Ph.D, 66; Harvard University, LL.B, 64; Hague Acad. of Int. Law, The Hague, Netherlands, law study; Phi Beta Kappa. Polit. & Govt. Pos: Chmn, Rep. Town Cmt; tax consult, Gov. Rockefeller's Tax Struct. Study Cmt; admin. pos, Mass. and N.Y. state govt. agencies; asst. attorney gen, Commonwealth of Mass, 67- Bus. & Prof. Pos: Attorney; col. instr, govt. Mem: former admin. chmn, United Fund; Kiwanis (past pres); Am. Soc. Pub. Admin; Am. Polit. Sci. Asn; Pi Sigma Alpha; Phi Kappa Phi; Mass. Bar Asn. Outstanding Young Man of Burlington, Mass, 66. Rel: Exec. Cmt, St. Mark's Episcopal Church. Mailing Add: 51 Lexington St, Burlington, Mass. 01803.

GORDON, ROBERT W. D
Polit. & Govt. Pos: Ind. State Rep, 63-64 & 67-69. Bus. & Prof. Pos: Machinist, McQuary-Norris Mfg. Co. Mil. Serv: Army. Mem: VFW; Odd Fellows. Rel: Methodist. Mailing Add: 2405 Virginia Ave, Connersville, Ind. 47331. (1967)

GORDON, S. RALPH R
Chmn, Davidson Co. Rep. Party, Tenn.
b. Nashville, Tenn, 8/1/38; s. Harry Gordon and Gladys Perlen G; m. 8/28/60 to Phyllis Lefkovitz; c. Gary Russell and Brad Alan. Educ: Univ. Tenn, B.S, 60; Vanderbilt Univ, LL.B, 63; v.pres, Omicron Delta Kappa; Scarabbean Sr. Soc; pres, Tenn. Interfraternity Coun; pres, Zeta Beta Tau; pres, Tenn. Pre-Legal Soc. Polit. & Govt. Pos: Exec. v.chmn, Davidson Co. Rep. Party, Tenn, 65, chmn, 66-; chmn, Fifth Dist. Rep. Cmt, 66- Bus. & Prof. Pos: Partner, Murphy & Gordon, Attorneys, 64-; secy, Fontaine Royale, Inc, 64-; pres, Import Sales & Serv. Inc, 64- and Affiliated Enterprises, Inc, 65- Mem: Tenn. and Nashville Bar Asns; Tenn. and Davidson Co. Trial Lawyers Asn; F&AM. Rel: Jewish. Mailing Add: 6660 Clearbrook Dr, Nashville, Tenn. 37205.

GORDON, VIRGIL R
Chmn, Austin Co. Rep. Party, Tex.
b. Campbellsburg, Ind, 10/15/89; s. Thomas Gordon and Sarah Catherine Wheat G; m. 10/21/14 to Josie Mae Miller. Educ: Ind. Univ, M.D; Delta Upsilon. Polit. & Govt. Pos: Chmn, Austin Co. Rep. Party, Tex, 62- Bus. & Prof. Pos: Owner, Sealy Hosp, Tex, 50-66. Mil. Serv: Entered as Lt, Army Med. Corps, 18, released, 19, after serv. in 103rd Inf, 26th Div. Mem: Austin, Waller and Grimes Co. Med. Socs; Tex. State and Am. Med. Asns; Am. Legion. Legal Res: 1031 Meyer St, Sealy, Tex. 77474. Mailing Add: 317 Fowlkes, Sealy, Tex. 77474.

GORDON, WILLARD FREMONT D
Chmn, Rankin Co. Dem. Exec. Cmt, Miss.
b. Hermanville, Miss, 7/29/88; s. Willard Fremont Gordon and Mary Henrietta Vanisson Gartman G; m. 10/27/12 to Mary Rhodes Nightingale; c. Slater Rhodes, Horatio 'Ray' Nightingale and Robert Tiffany. Educ: Brown Univ, 12; Psi Upsilon; Cammarian Club; Circle Francaise; Pi Kappa. Polit. & Govt. Pos: Justice of the peace, First Dist, Rankin Co. Miss, 28-44; chmn, Rankin Co. Dem. Exec. Cmt, Miss, 56- Mem: Mason; Miss. Farm Bur. Rel: Episcopal. Mailing Add: Rt. 2, Box 12, Florence, Miss. 39073. (1967)

GORDUS, MICHAEL R
b. Mt. Carmel, Pa, 1/2/02; s. Andrew Gordus and Mary Derbas G; m. 1/23/60 to Bernice Walenga Modla; c. Adon, Arnold and Diane (Mrs. Meier); stepchildren: Rita (Mrs. Smith), Renée (Mrs. Contento), Gloria (Mrs. Foley) and John Modla. Educ: Warren Ave. Trade Sch, 2 years; Armour Inst. of Tech, 2 years. Polit. & Govt. Pos: Alternate del, Rep. Nat. Conv, 68. Mem: Int. Operating Engrs; West Elsdon Civic Orgn. Rel: Catholic. Mailing Add: 3727 W. 56th St, Chicago, Ill. 60629.

GORDY, A. PERRY, II R
b. Columbus, Ga, 12/16/12; s. Arthur Perry Gordy, Sr. and Edna Spencer G; m. 2/1/48 to Martha Louisa Trimble; c. Layton Trimble, Louisa Denise and A. Perry, III. Educ: Univ. Ga; Univ. Fla; Ga. Inst. Tech; Harvard Univ; Ala. Polytech. Inst, 36; Alpha Tau Omega; Phi Psi. Polit. & Govt. Pos: Mem, Ga. Rep. State Cent. Cmt, 63-65; Ga. State Sen, 63-66, Rep. chmn, Ga. State Senate, 64-65; mem, Third Cong. Dist. Rep. Party, 65-69; mem, Muscogee Co. Rep. Party, 65-69. Bus. & Prof. Pos: Textile engr; advert. and pub. rels; owner credit bur, 5 years; dir, Columbus Tech, 65-69. Mil. Serv: Navy, Lt.(sg), 42-45. Mem: S.E. Resources Develop. Asn.(secy-treas, 47-48); Jaycees; C. of C. (mem. bd. dirs). First coordinator in Ga. for Diversified Coop. Training, Jordan High Sch, 38-40; Outstanding Young Man of the Year, Columbus Jaycees, 39; originator, Port Cities Day for Columbus, Ga. and Phenix City, Ala, 46; Silver Beaver Award, Outstanding Vol. Adult in Boy Scouts, 50; first Rep. chmn. of the Ga. State Senate in modern times and First Rep. elected to state polit. office from Columbus, Ga. and Muscogee Co. Rel: Methodist. Mailing Add: Columbus, Ga. 31902.

GORDY, WILLIAM J. D
b. Laurel, Del, 2/20/25; s. Reese O. Gordy and Mary Collins G; m. 11/25/44 to Marian Lee Hearne; c. Mary Ellen, Peggy, Cynthia, Michael, Judith and Philip. Educ: Laurel High Sch. Polit. & Govt. Pos: Chief clerk, Del. House of Rep, 57-58; committeeman, 4th and 32nd Rep. Dists, Sussex Co, Del, 57-66; chmn, Del. Indust. Accident Bd, 61-; del, Dem. Nat. Conv, 68. Bus. & Prof. Pos: Dir. and secy, Laurel Grain Co. Mem: Farm Bur; Exchange Club; leader, 4-H Club. Rel: Protestant. Mailing Add: R.D. 2, Box 139, Laurel, Del. 19956. (1967)

GORE, ALBERT ARNOLD D
U.S. Sen, Tenn.
b. Granville, Tenn, 12/26/07; s. Allen Gore and Margie Denny G; m. 4/17/37 to Pauline LaFon; c. Nancy and Albert. Educ: State Teachers Col, Tenn, B.S, 32; YMCA Night Law Sch, Tenn, LL.B, 36. Polit. & Govt. Pos: Cmnr. labor, Tenn, 36-37; U.S. Rep, Tenn, 39-53; U.S. del. UN Gen. Assembly; U.S. Sen, Tenn, 53-; del, Dem. Nat. Conv, 68. Bus. & Prof. Pos: Lawyer. Mem: Tenn. Educ. Asn. Rel: Baptist. Legal Res: Carthage, Tenn. 37030. Mailing Add: 100 Maryland Ave. N.E, Washington, D.C. 20002. (1967)

GORE, LOUISE R
Md. State Sen.
Single. Educ: Mt. Vernon Sem, Wash, D.C; Finch Jr. Col; Georgetown Univ; Bennington Col. Polit. & Govt. Pos: Mem, Rep. Nat. Finance Cmn; Md. State Del, 63-67; alternate del, Rep. Nat. Conv, 64, del, 68; Md. State Sen, 67-; U.S. Rep. to UNESCO, 69. Bus. & Prof. Pos: Hotel, restaurant and realty operator. Mem: Bd. dirs, Am. Health Found; Am. Good Govt. Soc. Mailing Add: 11300 River Rd, Potomac, Md. 20854.

GORE, MARION ADAMS R
b. Manchester, N.H, 6/12/02; d. James Edward Adams and Grace Gibson A; m. 5/2/30 to Harry Brigham Gore; wid; c. John Adams, James Edward and Judith (Mrs. Masten). Educ: Sweet Briar Col, 22-23; Katherine Gibbs secretarial Sch, 23-24; Boston Univ, 25-26; Boston Conservatory of Music; Glee Club, Sweet Briar Col. Polit. & Govt. Pos: V.pres, Souhegan Rep. Club, 55-57; alternate del, Nat. Rep. Conv, 64; advisor, Young Rep. Club, Univ. N.H, 66- Bus. & Prof. Pos: Secy. to Dr. Sherman, Columbia Univ, 27-28 and Mass. Investment Fund, 28-30; treas, Shoe Rep, 46-56 and Adams Bros, 58-61; head resident, Univ. N.H, 60- Mem: Boston Boot and Shoe Traveler's Asn; treas, The Women's Asn, Amherst, N.H. Rel: Congregational. Mailing Add: Box 482, Amherst, N.H. 03031.

GORE, NEY McKINLEY, JR. D
Miss. State Rep.
b. Quitman Co, Miss, 6/30/21; s. Ney McKinley Gore and Annie Lee Sparkman G; m. 9/19/42 to Robbie Lee Clark; c. Ney McKinley, III and Lee Partee. Educ: Miss. Delta Jr. Col, A.A, 40; Univ. Miss. Law Sch, LL.B, 46. Polit. & Govt. Pos: Miss. State Rep, 52-59 & 66- Bus. & Prof. Pos: Attorney-at-law, Marks, Miss, 46-47 & 68-; Denton & Gore, 48-68. Mil. Serv: Entered as Pvt, Army, 42, released as T/Sgt, 46, after serv. in Hq, Ft. Lawton, Wash, re-entered as M/Sgt, 50, released as WOJG, 51, after serv. in 301st Logistical Command. Mem: Quitman Co, Miss. State and Am. Bar Asns; Am. Judicature Soc; Miss. Judiciary Cmn; Gov. Cmt. on Law Enforcement Assistance; Mason; Am. Legion; Wilson Lake Country Club; Quitman Saddle Club; Grand Orator, Grand Lodge of Miss. F&AM, 68 & 69, past Master, Marks Lodge 435. Mem, Col. Gov. Staff and Spec. Asst. Attorney Gen, 56-60. Rel: Southern Baptist. Legal Res: Old Hwy. Six E, Marks, Miss. 38646. Mailing Add: P.O. Box 10, Marks, Miss. 38646.

GORE, TEAY NORLEY D
Chmn, Quitman Co. Dem. Exec. Cmt, Miss.
b. Embry, Miss, 8/28/90; s. William Wesley Gore, M.D. and Sarah Carver G; m. 7/28/18 to Lola Burkhart; c. T.N, Jr, Imogene (Mrs. Nobles), Carver Burkhart, Carol (Mrs. Little) and Esther (Mrs. Boykin, deceased). Educ: Freed-Hardeman Jr. Col; Valparaiso Univ; Milsaps Col. Law Sch. Polit. & Govt. Pos: Miss. State Rep, 28-32 & 36-40, chmn, Judiciary Cmt, Miss. State House of Rep, 36-40; del, Dem. State Conv, 28-64; mem, Co. Sch. Bd, 32-36 and pres. trustees, sch. bd, Lambert Consol. Sch. Dist; chmn, Quitman Co. Dem. Exec. Cmt, Miss, 32-; mem, Miss. State Dem. Exec. Cmt, 45-52. Mil. Serv: Entered as Pvt, Army, 17, released as Cpl, 19, after serv. in Co. A, 114th Engr. Combat Unit; Meuse-Argonne Medal. Mem: Pres, Quitman Co. Bar Asn, 62-; Miss. Bar; Am. Legion; VFW; Rotary; RAM. Rel: Methodist. Legal Res: 221 Chestnut St, Marks, Miss. 38646. Mailing Add: P.O. Box 232, Marks, Miss. 38646. (1967)

GORE, TRUMAN EARL D
Cmnr, Finance and Admin, State of W.Va.
b. Clarksburg, W.Va, 2/18/10; s. Truman Earl Gore and Pearl Post G; m. 11/13/34 to Eileen Williams; c. Beatrice Elizabeth, Truman Earl and Edmund Jude. Educ: W.Va. Wesleyan Col; Univ. Pa, B.S, 33 and M.A, 34; Cornell Univ; Sigma Phi Sigma; Chi Alpha Tau. Polit. & Govt. Pos: Chief dep. in charge of taxes, Harrison Co, W.Va, 45-52, chief dep. sheriff, 37-52, cmnr, 60- and dir. emergency planning, 62-; cmnr. of Finance and Admin, State of W.Va, secy, W.Va. Bd. Sch. Finance, budget dir, State of W.Va, state records adminstr. and state coords.emergency econ. stabilization, 60-; mem, State Teachers Retirement Bd, Pub. Employees Retirement Bd, Cmn. on Interstate Coop. and Gov. Coun. of Econ. Adv, 61- Bus. & Prof. Pos: Pres, Gore Hotel, Inc, Gore Corp; secy-treas, Appalachian Royalties, Inc; secy. and dir, Union Livestock Sales Co; dir, Weston Livestock Sales Co, G.A. Brown & Sons, Boca Raton Capital Corp. and Boca Raton Mgt. Corp; dir, Stonewall Jackson Life Ins. Co, 65-66. Mem: Nat. Asn. Auditors, Comptrollers and Treas; Fraternal Order of Police; Elks; Moose; VFW; Mason; Shrine. Rel: Methodist. Legal Res: Gore Hotel, Clarksburg, W.Va. 26301. Mailing Add: State Capitol Bldg, Charleston, W.Va. 25305. (1967)

GORHAM, AUSTEN C. R
b. New Bedford, Mass, 3/5/01; s. Robert Swain Gorham and Ella Beswick G; m. 3/5/32 to Dorothy A. McCarron; c. Robert L. and Deborah G. Educ: Conn. Literary Inst; Temple Bar Col, B.B.A, 23. Polit. & Govt. Pos: Mem. exec. res, U.S. Dept. Interior, 60-; chmn, Budget Cmt, Derry, N.H, 64-; former N.H. State Rep. Bus. & Prof. Pos: Dist. off. mgr, Mobil Oil Co, 25-62. Mem: Past nat. pres, Soc. of Am. Magicians; v.pres, Int. Brotherhood of Magicians; territorial v.pres, Magicians Alliance Eastern States; Mason, High Priest, Bell Chap, Derry, N.H, past master, Haverhill Coun, Mass, St. Mark's Lodge, Derry, N.H; pres, Merrimack Valley Region Asn; dir, Am. Auto Asn; dir, Advert. Club of N.H; past pres, N.H. Taxpayers Fedn; dir, N.H. Hwy. Users Conf. Has done weekly TV prog. each Monday, since 54. Rel: Central Congregational Church, Derry, N.H; Moderator. Mailing Add: 20 Boyd Rd, Derry, N.H. 03038. (1967)

GORHAM, BRADFORD R
R.I. State Rep.
b. Providence, R.I, 3/7/35; s. Sayles Gorham and Ruth Campbell G; m. 8/1/59 to Diann Gebow; c. Christopher, Nicholas, Joshua, Jane and Nancy. Educ: Dartmouth Col, A.B, 57; Harvard Law Sch, LL.B, 64. Polit. & Govt. Pos: Town solicitor, Foster, R.I, 64-; town solicitor, Exeter, 66-; del, R.I. Constitutional Conv, 64-68; R.I. State Rep, 53rd Dist, 69- Bus. & Prof. Pos: Lawyer, Gorham & Gorham, 64- Mil. Serv: Entered as 2nd Lt, Marines, 57, released as 1st Lt, 60, after serv. in Pioneer Bn, Okinawa and Camp Lejeune, N.C. Mem: R.I. and Am. Bar Asns. Mailing Add: Cucumber Hill Rd, Foster, R.I. 02825.

GORLIN, MARILYN ALPERN DFL
b. New York, N.Y, 3/27/25; d. Milton B. Alpern and Henrietta Nathanson A; m. 8/24/52 to Dr. Robert James Gorlin; c. Cathy Ellen and Jed Barron. Educ: Ethical Culture Sch; Adelphi Col, B.A. cum laude, 45; State Univ. of Iowa, grad study; Delta Tau Alpha. Polit. & Govt. Pos: Mem, Gov. Anderson's Fair Campaign Practices Cmn, 63-64; del, Dem. Nat. Conv, 64; mem, Gov. Rowaag's Status for Women Cmn, 64-; first v.chairwoman, Minn. State Dem-Farmer-Labor Party, 62-68; presidential elector, 68. Bus. & Prof. Pos: Ed. Asst, educ. dept, Nat. Found. for Infantile Paralysis, 45-46; asst. story ed, Warner Bros. Pictures, Inc, 46-52. Mem: Am. Civil Liberties Union; Americans for Dem. Action; NAACP. Rel: Jewish. Mailing Add: 4600 Chatelain Terr, Golden Valley, Minn. 55422.

GORMALLEY, JOAN PATRICIA R
V.chmn, Mass. Young Rep. Asn.
b. Salem, Mass, 5/11/38; d. Francis P. Gormalley and Edith Bates G; single. Educ: Mass. State Col, Salem, B.S. Educ, 59; Future Teachers Am. Polit. & Govt. Pos: Organizer, N.Shore Young Rep. Club, Mass, 61 and pres, 62-63; mem, Salem Rep. City Cmt, 61; young Rep. nat. committeewoman, Mass. Young Rep. Asn, 63-67, co-chmn, 65-67, chmn, 67-69 and v.chmn, 69-; signer, statewide petition drive, State Constitutional Conv, 68; alternate del, Rep. Nat. Conv, 68; pres, Salem Women's Rep. Club, 69- Bus. & Prof. Pos: Teacher, St. Pius V Sch, Lynn, 59- Mem: Int. Reading Asn; Salem State Col. Alumni Asn; North Shore Cath. Charity League; Cath. Daughters Am; NAACP; Mass. Cmt. Constitutional Reform. Rep. of the Year Award, North Shore Young Rep. Club, 65. Rel: Roman Catholic. Mailing Add: 236 Lafayette St, Salem, Mass. 01970.

GORMAN, FRANCIS JOHN D
Committeeman, Camden Co. Dem. Cmt, N.J.
b. Gloucester City, N.J, 11/19/24; s. John Francis Gorman and Mary M. Nowrey G; m. 8/19/50 to Margaret C. McHugh; c. Francis X, Regina M, John F, Edward, Bridget, James M, Robert T, Cecilia M. and Matthew P. Educ: LaSalle Col, B.A, 49. Polit. & Govt. Pos: Treas, Gloucester City Dem. Cmt,

N.J, 53-66, chmn, 67-; mem. city coun, Common Coun, Gloucester City, 54-57, city treas, 58-; committeeman, Camden Co. Dem. Cmt, 64-; del, Dem. Nat. Conv, 68. Bus. & Prof. Pos: Teacher, Mt. Ephraim Pub. Sch, 49-50; br. mgr, Seaboard Finance Co, Hartford, Conn. and Bound Brook, N.J, 52-57. Mil. Serv: Entered as A/S, Naval Res, 43, released as Yeoman 1/C, 46, after serv. in U.S.S. Wharton, Pac. Theatre, 43-46; recalled, 50-52. Mem: Munic. Finance Officers N.J; Tax Collectors, Treas. and Receivers N.J; VFW; K. of C.(4°); bd. dirs, Gloucester City Savings & Loan Asn; Custodian of Sch. Funds, Gloucester City Bd. of Educ. Rel: Roman Catholic. Mailing Add: 921 Hudson St, Gloucester City, N.J. 08030.

GORMAN, FRANK McGOWN D
b. Cleveland, Ohio, 9/19/21; s. Harold H. Gorman and Dorothy Bowman G; m. 6/8/54 to Mary Lou Martin; c. Peter, Mary, Matthew and Benjamin. Educ: Harvard Univ, A.B, 43; West. Reserve Univ. Law Sch, LL.B, 48. Polit. & Govt. Pos: Ohio State Rep, 51-58; mem, Cuyahoga Co. Dem. Exec. Cmt, 51-68; del, Dem. Nat. Conv, 56 & 68, alternate del, 64; cmnr, Cuyahoga Co, 59- Bus. & Prof. Pos: Attorney, 48- Mil. Serv: Entered as Aviation Cadet, Army Air Corps, 43, released as 1st Lt, 45, after serv. in Eighth Air Force, 445th Bomb Group, England, 44-45; Air Medal with four Oak Leaf Clusters. Mem: F&AM (32°). Rel: Protestant. Mailing Add: 2825 Coventry Rd, Shaker Heights, Ohio 44120. (1967)

GORMAN, GEORGE E. D
Chmn, Goodhue Co. Dem. Party, Minn.
b. Goodhue, Minn, 3/4/21; s. Ernest Gorman and Mary McNamara G; m. 1/30/46 to Josephine Heaney; c. Helen, Tom, Chas, Mike, Mary, Ernest, Patricia, Donna, Denise and Richard. Educ: High Sch. Polit. & Govt. Pos: Chmn, Goodhue Co. Dem. Party, Minn, 60- Mil. Serv: Entered as Pvt, Army, released as Cpl, 45, after serv. in 763rd Tank Div, Pac; Pac. Campaign Ribbon with 2 Stars; Good Conduct Medal. Mem: Am. Legion; VFW; K. of C; Farmers Union. Rel: Catholic. Mailing Add: Goodhue, Minn. 55027.

GORMAN, JIMMIE EDWIN D
b. Wewoka, Okla, 8/12/97; s. Jackson A. Gorman and Amey Bowlegs G; m. 12/6/19 to Exzetta A. Jones. Educ: Wewoka High Sch, 12-18. Polit. & Govt. Pos: Dem. chmn, Precinct Two, Ward Five, Wewoka, Okla, 62-; del, Dem. Nat. Conv, 68. Bus. & Prof. Pos: Electrician, motor winder, currently. Mil. Serv: Pvt, Army, serv. in 165th Inf. Div, 18-19. Mem: Mason; K. of P. Rel: Methodist. Mailing Add: 211 S. Ocheese, Wewoka, Okla. 74884.

GORMAN, REDMON HENRY Non-Partisan
b. Lemington, Vt, 11/19/98; m. to Madeline Owen; c. 4 sons; 2 daughters. Educ: Colebrook High Sch, N.H. Polit. & Govt. Pos: Dep. sheriff, Essex Co, N.H, 46-; town auditor, overseer of the poor and selectman, Colebrook, 56-; Vt. State Rep, 61-69. Bus. & Prof. Pos: Farmer. Mem: Pres, Essex Co. Farm Bur. Rel: Catholic. Mailing Add: R.F.D. 2, Colebrook, N.H. 03576. (1967)

GORMAN, ROBERT HERANCOURT D
b. Cincinnati, Ohio, 8/2/35; s. Robert Nestor Gorman and Mary Hartman G; m. 12/1/62 to Susan Elizabeth Deck. Educ: Brown Univ, A.B, 57; Univ. Cincinnati, LL.B, 60; Sigma Nu; Phi Alpha Delta. Polit. & Govt. Pos: Ohio State Rep, Hamilton Co, 65-67. Bus. & Prof. Pos: Assoc, Gorman, Davis & Hengelbrok, 60. Mil. Serv: Entered as 1st Lt, Air Force, 61, released as Capt, 64, after serv. in Hq. CONAC, 64; Air Force Commendation Medal; Outstanding Unit Award with 1 Cluster. Mem: Am, Ohio and Cincinnati Bar Asns; Am. Trial Lawyers Asn; Mason; Brown Alumni Club of Cincinnati. Rel: Episcopal. Mailing Add: 1010 Brayton Ave, Cincinnati, Ohio 45215. (1967)

GORRELL, FRANK D
Lt. Gov, Tenn.
Mailing Add: State Capitol, Nashville, Tenn. 37219.

GORTON, DONALD GRANT R
b. Chadron, Nebr, 9/27/05; s. L. W. Gorton and Maude Ira G; m. 10/4/30 to Margaret Moore; c. Mary Sue, Sara Jayne, Jay Moore and Linda Gay. Educ: Univ. of Nebr, B.S. in bus. admin, 30; Delta Upsilon. Polit. & Govt. Pos: Chmn, Johnson Co. Rep. Cmt, Nebr, 58-66. Bus. & Prof. Pos: Owner, Gortons Clothing, Nebr, 45-65 and Gortons Motel, 61-66. Mil. Serv: Entered as Capt, Army, 41, released as Col, 45, after serv. in 359th Inf, 90th Div, ETO; Col, Army Res, 45-66; Silver Star; Soldiers Medal; Bronze Star; Croix De Guerre; Purple Heart; Combat Inf. Badge; ETO Medal with 5 major Battle Stars; Pre-Pearl Harbor and Victory Medals; Germany Occupation Medal. Mem: Mason (32°); Am. Legion; VFW. Rel: Episcopal. Mailing Add: Box 390, Tecumseh, Nebr. 68450.

GORTON, SLADE R
Attorney Gen, Wash.
b. Chicago, Ill, 1/8/28; s. Thomas Slade Gorton, Jr. and Ruth Israel G; m. 6/28/58 to Sally Jean Clark; c. Tod, Sarah Jane and Rebecca. Educ: Dartmouth Col, A.B, 50; Northwest. Univ. Law Sch, Columbia Univ. Law Sch, LL.B, 53; Phi Beta Kappa; Gamma Delta Phi; Phi Delta Phi. Polit. & Govt. Pos: Pres, Young Rep. of King Co, Wash, 59-60; Wash. State Rep, 46th Dist, 59-69, Majority Leader, Wash. State House of Rep, 67-69; Attorney Gen, Wash, 69- Bus. & Prof. Pos: Assoc. and partner, Little, Gandy, Palmer, Slemmons & Holcomb and predecessors, 56-69. Mil. Serv: Entered as Pvt, Army, 46, released as Pfc, 47, re-entered as 1st Lt, Air Force, 53, released 56; Maj, Air Force Res, 58- Publ: 'Redistricting—a Proposal,' Nat. Munic. Rev, spring, 64. Mem: Seattle, Wash. State and Am. Bar Asns; Citizen's Planning Coun; Wash. Roadside Coun; trustee, Pac. Sci. Center; Forward Trust, Seattle Tennis Club. Rel: Episcopal. Mailing Add: 2622 S. Capitol Way, Olympia, Wash. 98501.

GOSMAN, ROBERT F. 'BOB' R
Chmn, Wyo. State Rep. Cmt.
b. Butte, Mont, 12/2/27; s. Frank Gosman and Ruth Weenik G; m. Barbara B; c. Jeffrey and Deborah. Educ: Mont. State Univ, B.A; Dartmouth Col, M.A. Polit. & Govt. Pos: Chmn, Natrona Co. Rep. Cmt, Wyo, 63-66; secy, Wyo. State Rep. Cmt, 64-66, chmn, 66- Mil. Serv: Entered as Pvt, Army, 46, released as Sgt, 47, after serv. in Sixth Engrs, Korea. Rel: Protestant. Legal Res: 3055 Hamilton Way, Casper, Wyo. 82601. Mailing Add: 150 N. Center St, Casper, Wyo 82601.

GOSSER, MARVEL G. R
b. Queen City, Mo, 1/21/07; m. to Hazel Spry; c. Pauline, Larry Dee, Bruce Marvel and twins, Betty Lou and Bobby Lee. Educ: Trade Sch, Chicago, Ill, 25. Polit. & Govt. Pos: Mem, Mo. Ration Bd, World War II; mem, Sch. Bd, Mo, 2 terms; sheriff, Schuyler Co, 41-44; Mo. State Rep, 62-66. Bus. & Prof. Pos: Auto mechanic and farmer, 27-34; sawmill and lumber bus, 34-40; Farm machinery dealer, Gosser Implement Co, 54-58; operator, coin-operated laundromat, 59-61; farmer, 60- Rel: Christian Church; Deacon, First Christian Church. Mailing Add: Lancaster, Mo. 63548.

GOSSETT, ED D
b. Sabine Parish, La, 1/27/02; s. Edward L. Gossett and Sarah Anne McKinley G; m. 5/20/39 to Mary Helen Mosley; c. Glenn, Judy, Jane, Melissa, Stephen and Murray. Educ: Univ. of Tex, A.B, 24, LL.B, 27. Polit. & Govt. Pos: Dist. Attorney, 46th Judicial Dist, Tex, 32-38; U.S. Rep, 13th Dist, 38-51; mem, Nat. Electoral Reform Cmt; judge, Criminal Dist. Court 5, Dallas Co, 68- . Bus. & Prof. Pos: Jr. mem, Berry, Stokes, Warlock and Gossett, Vernon, Tex, 27-32; gen. attorney for Tex, S.W. Bell Tel. Co, 51-67; counsel, to Strasburger, Price, Kelton, Martin & Unis, 67- Mem: Am. Bar Asn.(mem, House of Del, 2 terms); Dallas Bar Asn.(pres, 60); bd. dirs, Fed. Home Loan Bank Bd, Little Rock, Ark; former mem. bd. regents, Tex. Women's Univ. and Tex. Sr. Cols. Bd; former pres, Dallas Coun. on World Affairs; former state chmn, U.S. Savings Bond Prog, 15 years. Rel: Presbyterian. Mailing Add: 308 S. Akard St, Dallas, Tex. 75202.

GOSSETT, JAMES D. R
Chmn, Upton Co. Rep. Party, Tex.
b. Post, Tex, 9/16/24; s. Ed L. Gossett and Sarah McKinley G; m. 12/9/59 to Pauline Thompson; c. Annie (Mrs. Joe Shaffer), Tom, Bryan, Kitty Sue, Linda and Jamie Dee. Educ: Univ. Tex, M.D, 48; Theta Kappa Psi. Polit. & Govt. Pos: Chmn, Upton Co. Rep. Party, Tex, 61- Bus. & Prof. Pos: Pres, Rankin Sch. Bd, 60-69. Mil. Serv: 2nd Lt, Army, 42-45, 1st Lt, 48-53. Rel: Methodist. Legal Res: 1000 Elizabeth, Rankin, Tex. 79778. Mailing Add: Box 525, Rankin, Tex. 79778.

GOTCH, CLIFFORD ROY R
Chmn, Dixon Co. Rep. Party, Nebr.
b. Waterbury, Nebr, 10/3/24; s. Roy Edward Gotch and Loena Brownell G; m. 10/11/44 to Rose Von Minden; c. Dwight Eugene. Educ: Allen High Sch, Nebr, grad. Polit. & Govt. Pos: Treas, Galena Twp. Nebr, 52-60; mem, Agr. Soil Conserv. Bd, 56-60; financial secy, Dixon Co. Rep. Party, 62-66, chmn, 66- Bus. & Prof. Pos: Pres, Big Four Tel, 51-63; agr. researcher, Univ. Nebr, 57-58. Mem: Iowa Life Ins. Underwriters Asn; secy-treas, Dixon Co. Farm Bur, 50-59; mem. bd, Farmers Coop, 61-67; hon. mem, Future Farmers of Am; Shrine. Rel: Lutheran; Treas, 51-52, pres, 52-60. Mailing Add: Box B, Allen, Nebr. 68710.

GOTTLIEB, FRANK R
b. Gransville Township, N.Dak, 3/24/04; single. Educ: Commercial Col, 4 yrs. Polit. & Govt. Pos: N.Dak. State Rep, 45-61; Sch. clerk, 10 yrs. Bus. & Prof. Pos: Farmer; rancher. Mailing Add: Kief, N.Dak. 58747. (1967)

GOTTLIEB, ROY A. D
Dem. Nat. Committeeman, V.I.
Mailing Add: 61 Lindberg Bay, St. Thomas, V.I. 00801.

GOTTLIEB, STEPHEN STEWART D
N.Y. State Assemblyman
b. Boston, Mass, 6/4/36; s. Louis Irving Gottlieb and Anne Kartz G; m. 5/30/65 to Carol Ann Erbecker; c. Christine Elizabeth and Peter Stephen. Educ: Cornell Univ, B.A, 57; N.Y. Law Sch, LL.B, 59; Sigma Alpha Mu. Polit. & Govt. Pos: Mem, Dem. Co. Cmt, N.Y, 59-; del, Judicial Dist. Conv, 68; N.Y. State Assemblyman, 71st Dist, 69- Bus. & Prof. Pos: Partner, Gottlieb & Gottlieb, Attorneys, N.Y.C, 60- Mem: Am. Bar Asn; N.Y. State Bar Asn; Asn. of Lawyers of the Criminal Courts, N.Y.C. Rel: Jewish. Mailing Add: 159-34 Riverside Dr, New York, N.Y. 10032.

GOTTSCHALK, ARTHUR R. R
b. Chicago, Ill; m. to Norma; c. three daughters. Educ: Univ. Ill; Shrivenham Univ, Eng. Polit. & Govt. Pos: Police magistrate, Park Forest, Ill, 2 terms; chmn, Park Forest Police and Fire Cmt; Ill. State Sen, 60-68. Bus. & Prof. Pos: V.pres. and regional gen. counsel, Reuben H. Donnelley Corp; attorney-at-law. Mil. Serv: Normandy landing and three major battles during World War II; Purple Heart. Cited in Saturday Evening Post for handling juveniles while police magistrate. Mailing Add: 1705 Brookwood Dr, Flossmoor, Ill. 60422.

GOTTSCHALK, GERTRUDE RIORDAN D
Treas, Ormsby Co. Dem. Cent. Cmt, Nev.
b. Preston, Nev, 2/4/16; d. James C. Riordan and Jennie Susan O'Hare R; m. 12/31/37 to George L. Gottschalk; c. Kerry George, Mark Riordan. Educ: Grad. sec. sch, Notre Dame Col, 34. Polit. & Govt. Pos: Secy, Young Dem, West. Nev, 36-37; pres, Dem. Women's Club of Ormsby, Storey and Douglas Co, Nev, 57-59; mem, Ormsby Co. Dem. Cent. Cmt, 57-, treas, 60-; mem, Dem. Nat. Cmt, 60-; secy, West. States Dem. Conf, 62- Mem: Commun. Chest; Leisure Hour Club (past pres); Mark Twin Garden Club Carson City (past pres). Mailing Add: 10 Circle Dr, Carson City, Nev. 89701. (1967)

GOTTSTEIN, BARNARD J. D
Alaska State Dem. Finance Officer
b. Des Moines, Iowa, 12/30/25; s. Jacob Gottstein and Anna Jacobs G; m. 9/10/46 to Natalie Werner; c. Sandra, Ruth, James, Robert and David. Educ: Univ. Wash, B.A, 49; Zeta Mu Tau; Sigma Alpha Mu. Polit. & Govt. Pos: Del, Dem. Nat. Conv, 64 & 68; cmnr, Alaska State Human Rights Cmn, 63-69, chmn, 68-69; Alaska State Dem. Finance Officer and mem, Alaska State Dem. Cent. Cmt 64- Bus. & Prof. Pos: Pres, Alaska Food, Inc, 53-, Foodland Shopping Center, Inc, 57- and J.B. Gottstein & Co, Inc, 63-; treas, North. TV, Inc, 53-68. Mil. Serv: Entered as Pvt, Army Air Force, 44, released as Aviation Cadet, 45. Mem: Elks; Am. Legion. Rel: Jewish. Legal Res: 227 E. Seventh St, Anchorage, Alaska 99501. Mailing Add: 1301 Whitney Rd, Anchorage, Alaska 99501.

GOULD, GEORGE BENJAMIN D
b. Scotia, N.Y, 4/10/40; s. George Benjamin Gould, Jr. and Eleanor O'Meara G; m. 11/27/65 to Mary Diane Charuhas; c. George Benjamin, IV. Educ: El Camino Col, A.A, 60; Calif. State Col. at Long Beach, B.A, and grad. work; U.S. Dept. of Agr, grad. work; Int. Circle K (dist. treas). Polit. & Govt. Pos: Staff asst. to Jesse M. Unruh, Speaker of the Calif. State Assembly, 63, campaign dir. to, 64; asst. campaign coordinator for Assemblyman Carley V. Porter, 23rd Dist. Cong. Campaign, 63; asst. campaign coordinator for Billy G. Mills, Los Angeles City Coun. Campaign, 63; admin. asst. to Dir. Madale Watson, Dollars for Dem, Los Angeles Co, 63-64; admin asst. to Congressman Charles H. Wilson, 65-69; staff dir, Census and Statist. Subcmt, U.S. House of Rep. Post Off. and Civil Serv. Cmt, 69- Bus. & Prof. Pos: Admin. asst. to William T. White, gen. mgr, Los Angeles Area Econ. Develop. Agency, 64-65. Mil. Serv: Entered as Pfc, Army Nat. Guard, 63. Mem: Am. Pol. Sci. Asn; Young Dem; Nat. Dem. Club; Burro's Club. Rel: Protestant. Legal 2403 W. 77th St, Inglewood, Calif, 90305. Mailing Add: 15 Canterbury Sq. 303, Alexandria, Va. 22304.

GOULD, HAROLD D, JR. D
b. 1934. Educ: Holy Cross; Harvard Law Sch. Polit. & Govt. Pos: Chmn. selectmen, Blackstone, Mass; mem, town counsel, Millville, Mass; Mass. State Rep, 67-68. Bus. & Prof. Pos: Attorney, Maher, McCann & Talcott, Worcester. Mil. Serv: Capt, Army Res. Mailing Add: 10 Howard St, Blackstone, Mass. 01504. (1967)

GOULD, LORA IONE D
b. Grand Rapids, Mich, 4/7/18; d. Harry Baumunk and Bessie L. Robinson B; m. 3/20/40 to Carrol F. Gould; c. Connie (Mrs. Vaughn), Sally (Mrs. Evans), Bill and Rick. Educ: Kirtland Col, Psychol. Courses, currently. Polit. & Govt. Pos: Mem, Get Out and Vote Cmt, Mich, 56-; co. secy, Dem. Party, Mich, 61-63; co. chmn, 63-66; Secy. of State br. mgr, Mich, 61-69; exec. dir. for pub. housing, Grayling Housing Cmn, 65-; v.pres. for Upper Half of Lower Penninsular Campaign for Nahro. Bus. & Prof. Pos: Partner, Gould Dry Cleaners, 51-68; exec. dir. for Crawford Co, Multi Purpose Sr. Citizen Center. Mem: Grayling Woman's Club; St. Mary's Ladies Club; C. of C; Housing Cmn; chmn, City Clean Up Orgn; chmn, EOA Co. Cmt; Chmn, Crippled Children's Co. Cmt; mem. state bd. of dirs. for crippled children and adults, Easter Seal Soc, 69-70; Am. Legion Auxiliary. Rel: Catholic. Mailing Add: 308 Au Sable Court, Grayling, Mich. 49738.

GOURLAY, ISLAY MAE R
Mem, Calif. Rep. State Cent. Cmt.
b. Hastings, Nebr, 7/17/30; d. Joseph Clinton Hein and Mabel Schiffler H; m. 7/7/51 to Robert Dale Gourlay; c. Bruce Alan and Brian Robert. Educ: Mt. San Antonio Col, 49; Jr. Ebell. Polit. & Govt. Pos: Second v.pres, Canoga Park Rep. Women's Club. Fedn, Calif, 65, first v.pres, 66, pres, 67-68; 27th cong. dist. chmn, Los Angeles Co. Fedn. Rep. Women, 69; press chmn, 64th Assembly Dist. Rep. Precinct Orgn, 69; mem, Calif. Rep. State Cent. Cmt, 69- Bus. & Prof. Pos: Secy, Hughes Aircraft Co, Culver City, 50-53; Tech. Ed, Gen. Testing Lab, 54-55. Rel: First Christian Church. Mailing Add: 20756 Lull St, Canoga Park, Calif. 91306.

GOVE, WILLIAM P. R
N.H. State Sen.
b. Salem, Mass, 2/4/14; married; c. 5. Educ: William and Mary Col. Polit. & Govt. Pos: Alderman-at-lg, Concord, N.H, mayor, 68-; N.H. State Rep, 59-63; N.H. State Sen, 63- Bus. & Prof. Pos: Retired. Mil. Serv: Army Air Force, World War II, 42-45. Rel: Unitarian. Mailing Add: 321 South St, Concord, N.H. 03301. (1967)

GOWARD, RUSSELL D
Mo. State Rep.
b. St. Louis, Mo, 8/25/35; s. William Goward and Zenobia Askew G; m. 3/16/57 to Dolores Jean Thornton; c. Russell, II. Educ: Hubbard's Bus. Col, Cert, 59; Harris Teachers Col, currently. Polit. & Govt. Pos: Div. leader, 21st Ward Dem. Orgn, Mo, 63-66; Mo. State Rep, 76th Dist, 67-, v.chmn, License Cmt, Mo. House Rep, mem, Munic. Corp. Cmt. and Fees and Salaries Cmt, currently. Bus. & Prof. Pos: Spec. agent, Prudential Ins. Co, 64-65; pres. and treas, Goward's & Assoc. & Inc, 67-; ins. broker, 67-; real estate broker, 67- Mil. Serv: Entered as S/A, Navy, 52, released as QMSN, 56, after serv. in U.S.S. Libra and U.S.S. Cambria, Korea and ETO, 52-55; Nat. Defense Serv. Ribbon; European Occupation Medal; Good Conduct Ribbon. Mem: Mason; Boy Scout (cmt. mem, Troop 922 merit badge counsr, signaling and Morse code); Human Develop. Corp. Bd. Rel: Congregational. Mailing Add: 4210 A Holly, St. Louis, Mo. 63115.

GOWER, JOHN CLARK R
Dist. Attorney, Brown Co, Wis.
b. Chicago, Ill, 1/10/41; s. Benjamin Gray Gower and Julie Paradis G; m. 8/31/63 to Helen S. Coman; c. David Coman and Heather Kathleen. Educ: Marquette Univ, A.B, 63; Marquette Univ. Law Sch, J.D, 66; Delta Theta Phi. Polit. & Govt. Pos: Del, Annual Wis. Fedn. Young Rep. Conv, 59-; pres, Marquette Univ. Young Rep, Wis, 59-60; dep. col. dir, Wis. Fedn. Young Rep, 60-61, col. dir, 61-62, state committeeman, 66-67, state chmn, 67-69; del, Annual Midwest Fedn. Col. Rep. Clubs Conv, 61-65; alternate del, Young Rep. Nat. Conv, 61, del, 67 & 69; del, Wis. Rep. State Conv, 62, 63, 66, 67, 68 & 69, alternate del, 64; secy, Midwest Fedn. Col. Young Rep, 62-63; chmn, Milwaukee Co. Young Rep, 65-66; sixth v.chmn, Rep. Party, Wis, 67-69; alternate del, Rep. Nat. Conv, 68; dist. attorney, Brown Co, Wis, 69- Bus. & Prof. Pos: Asst. gen. attorney, Inland Steel Prod. Co, 66-67. Mem: Wis. and Brown Co. Bar Asns; Wis. Dist. Attorney's Asn; Nat. Dist. Attorney's Asn; Elks; Optimists; Kiwanis; Wis. Hist. Soc; Wis. Guides Asn; Jaycees; Commun. Coun. Drug Abuse. Dean's Award, Marquette Law Sch. Rel: Catholic. Mailing Add: 312 Terraview Dr, Green Bay, Wis. 54301.

GRABER, BEN J. D
V.Chmn, Greeley Co. Dem. Cmt, Kans.
b. Pretty Prairie, Kans, 8/8/97; s. Peter J. Graber and Anna Schwartz G; m. 4/15/20 to Martha Schwartz; c. Helen (Mrs. Kaufman), Leona (Mrs. Gehring), Ben, Jr, Harlan, Robert, Howard Dean and Katherine (Mrs. Stinson). Educ: Bethel Col, 2 years. Polit. & Govt. Pos: V.Chmn, Greeley Co. Dem. Cmt, Kans, 64- Bus. & Prof. Pos: Farmer. Rel: Mennonite. Legal Res: 801 Wichita St, Tribune, Kans. 67879. Mailing Add: Box 367, Tribune, Kans. 67879.

GRABER, WALTER W. D
Kans. State Rep.
b. Pretty Prairie, Kans, 1/22/07; s. Jacob K. Graber and Mary Graber G; m. 12/22/35 to Jean Arbuckle; c. Geraldine (Mrs. Neil Crane), Mary (Mrs. Mark Collins) and Helen (Mrs. Wayne Unruh). Educ: Bethel Col, Kans, A.B, 29. Polit. & Govt. Pos: Mem, Pretty Prairie Sch. Bd, Kans, 38-69; mem, State Bd. of Educ, 54-60; adminstr, Kans. Wheat Cmn, 57-63; Kans. State Rep, 69-, mem, Cmt. on Assessment and Taxation, Cmt. on Agr. and Livestock and Cmt. on Natural Resources, Kans. House of Rep, 69. Bus. & Prof. Pos: Exec. secy, U.S. Bulgur Processors, 63-64; state dir, Kans. State Wheat Growers, 67-; consult, African Land Develop. of World Homes, Subsidiary of Garvey Enterprises, Wichita, Kans, currently; dir, Kans. Asn. of Wheat Growers. Mem: Lions; Farm Bur; Kans. Livestock Asn. Farm Bur. Award for Serv; Award for 31 years Serv. on Sch. Bd. Rel: Mennonite. Mailing Add: Pretty Prairie, Kans. 67570.

GRABOWSKI, BERNARD F. D
b. New Haven, Conn, 6/11/23; m. to Anne Gorski; c. Carol Ann and Diane Marie. Educ: Univ. Conn, 49, Law Sch, LL.B, 52. Polit. & Govt. Pos: Councilman, Bristol, Conn, 53-55; judge, City Court of Bristol, 55-60; U.S. Rep, Conn, 63-66. Bus. & Prof. Pos: Coordinator redevelop, Bristol, Mass, 53-55; mem, law firm, Hanrahan, Grabowski & Hayes; admitted to practice before U.S. Supreme Court. Mil. Serv: Army. Mem: Bristol, Hartford Co. and Conn. State Bar Asns; DAV; Civitan; Elks; Bristol Polish Am. Citizens Club; Polish Legion of Am. Vets; K. of C. Rel: Roman Catholic. Legal Res: 57 George St, Bristol, Conn. 06010. Mailing Add: 683 Farmington Ave, Bristol, Conn. 06010.

GRADISON, WILLIS DAVID, JR. R
Vice Mayor, Cincinnati, Ohio
b. Cincinnati, Ohio, 12/28/28; s. Willis David Gradison and Dorothy Benas G; m. 6/25/50 to Helen Ann Martin; c. Ellen, Robin, Anne, Beth and Margaret. Educ: Yale Univ, B.A, 48; Harvard Univ, M.B.A, 51, D.C.S, 54. Polit. & Govt. Pos: Asst. to under secy, U.S. Treas. Dept, 53-55; asst. to secy, U.S. Dept. of Health, Educ. and Welfare, 55-57; city councilman, Cincinnati, Ohio, 61-67, vice mayor, 67- Bus. & Prof. Pos: Gen. partner, W.D. Gradison & Co, Mem. N.Y. Stock Exchange, 58- Publ: 'Key Questions in Pension Fund Investment,' Harvard Bus. Rev, 7-8/55. Rel: Jewish. Legal Res: 6 Elmhurst Place, Cincinnati, Ohio 45208. Mailing Add: 408 Dixie Terminal Bldg, Cincinnati, Ohio 45202.

GRADY, HOMER E. R
Secy. and Treas, Scott Co. Rep. Cent. Cmt, Ill.
b. Coffeyville, Kans, 3/21/85; s. Mike Grady and Ella Hutton G; m. 10/7/09 to Annis Lawson; c. Arthur. Educ: Pub. sch, 1890-1900. Polit. & Govt. Pos: Revenue investr, Springfield, Ill, 53-61; secy. and treas, Scott Co. Rep. Cent. Cmt, Ill, 68- Bus. & Prof. Pos: Secy, high sch, Bluffs, Ill, 32-34; owner, Grady Gravel Co, 30-53; retired, 68. Mil. Serv: Civilian employee, 43-44, as inspector of heavy equip, Corozal, C.Z, 42-44. Mem: AF&AM; life mem, Local 965, Hoisting and Operating Engrs. Rel: Methodist. Legal Res: South St, Exeter, Ill. 62621. Mailing Add: R.R, Bluffs, Ill. 62621.

GRADY, JOSEPH HAROLD D
b. Williamsport, Pa, 2/27/17; s. Thomas Leo Grady and Edythe Grange G; m. 5/26/42 to Patricia Grogan; c. Maureen Ann, Joseph Harold, Kathleen Ann and Thomas Leo. Educ: Loyola Col, B.A, magna cum laude, 38; Univ. Md, LL.B, 42; admitted to Md. bar, 42. Polit. & Govt. Pos: Spec. agent, Fed. Bur. Invest, 42-47; asst. states attorney, Baltimore, Md, 47-55, dep. states attorney, 55-56, states attorney, Baltimore, 56-59; mayor, Baltimore, 59-62; assoc. judge, Supreme Bench Baltimore, 62- Bus. & Prof. Pos: Instr. Univ. Md. Sch. Law, Mt. Vernon Law Sch, Baltimore, 49-58. Mem: Md. and Baltimore Bar Asns; States Attorneys Asns. Md. (pres, 57-59); Friendly Sons St. Patrick of Baltimore, (pres, 59); Order of Coif; K. of C. (4°). Rel: Roman Catholic. Legal Res: 209 Goodale Rd, Baltimore, Md. 21212. Mailing Add: Court House, Baltimore, Md. 21202.

GRAEN, FRED A. D
b. Kewanee, Ill, 12/20/26; s. Phil Graen and Dorothy Ratcliff Graen Fricke; single; c. David, Sandra and Douglas. Educ: Univ. Denver, B.S. in Pub. Admin; Alpha Kappa Psi. Polit. & Govt. Pos: Former Dem. precinct committeeman; Denver permit chief for zoning admin, currently; Dem. Capt, Dist. Eight, Denver, currently. Mil. Serv, Army, $7\frac{1}{2}$ years; Combat Infantry Badge; various campaign ribbons. Mem: West. Slavonic Asn; Mason; Denver City Employees Union; AFSCHE. Mailing Add: 1125 Columbia, Denver, Colo. 80206.

GRAF, AL N. R
Chmn, 20th Assembly Dist. Rep. Party, Calif.
b. San Francisco, Calif, 6/15/10; s. Leopold Graf and Lena Stienberg G; m. 1/17/37 to Lillian Novitzky; c. Carolyn Cecilia (Mrs. Arlan Kertz) and Leonard Paul. Educ: Mission High Sch, 25-29. Polit. & Govt. Pos: Chmn, 20th Assembly Dist. Rep. Party, Calif, 69- Mil. Serv: Entered as Seaman, Navy, 43, released as Specialist 3/C, 45, after serv. in Shore Patrol, San Francisco. Mem: Past Co. Coun. Comdr. of World War II in San Francisco; Mayor Robinson Vet. Housing Cmt; Mason; Shrine; assoc. mem, Press Club of San Francisco; bd. dir, Footprinter; v.pres, Parks Job Corps Coun; bd. dirs, Police Athletic League. Rel: Jewish. Mailing Add: 859 Bryant St, San Francisco, Calif. 94103.

GRAF, ROBERT E. R
Vt. State Rep.
b. Rupert, Vt, 11/5/15; married; c. 3 daughters. Educ: St. Lawrence Univ, Canton, N.Y, B.S, 38. Polit. & Govt. Pos: Auditor, justice of the peace, Pawlet, Vt, 47-; Bennington Soil Conserv. Dist. supvr, 50; Vt. State Rep, 59- Bus. & Prof. Pos: Dairy farmer. Mem: F&AM; Eastern Star; Scottish Rite; Alpha Tau Omega. Rel: Congregational. Mailing Add: Pawlet, Vt. 05761. (1967)

GRAFF, JOHN ROBERT R
b. Madison, S.Dak, 3/14/36; s. Ardean Erving Graff and Barbara Catherine Schneck G; m. 6/11/66 to Kay Arlene Ellsworth; c. Christopher Lyn. Educ: Univ. S.Dak, B.A, 58; Ind. Univ, M.A, 59; Phi Eta Sigma; Tau Kappa Alpha; Omicron Delta Kappa; Beta Theta Pi. Polit. & Govt. Pos: Exec. dir, S.Dak. Rep. Cent. Cmt, 63-69; minority counsel, U.S. Senate Subcmt. on Exec. Reorg,

69- Bus. & Prof. Pos: Research asst, S.Dak. Munic. League, 54-58; secy, Gr. S.Dak. Asn, 60-63; asst. to pres, North. State Col, 69. Mil. Serv: 2nd Lt, Army, 59-60. Mem: Rotary; Elks. Rel: Congregational Christian Church. Legal Res: 7826 Winona Court, Annandale, Va. 22033. Mailing Add: Room 162, Old Senate Office Bldg, Washington, D.C. 20510.

GRAGG, BILLY HARDIN R
Chmn, Anderson Co. Rep. Party, Tex.
b. Palestine, Tex, 10/10/28; s. Oscar Lee Gragg and Inez Hardin G; m. 11/22/58 to Jacquelyn Lockey; c. Holli Sue and Laura Lee. Educ: Univ, Tex, B.A. in Econ, 50, LL.B, 53; Alpha Phi Omega. Polit. & Govt. Pos: Bd. mem, Palestine Civil Serv. Cmn, Tex, 63-; chmn, Anderson Co. Rep. Party, 64-; Rep. state committeeman, 66. Bus. & Prof. Pos: Anderson Co. Bar Asn. (pres, 58); Tex. and Am. Bar Asns; Rotary. Rel: Methodist. Legal Res: 1020 Hilltop, Palestine, Tex. 75801. Mailing Add: P.O. Box 678, Palestine, Tex. 75801.

GRAHAM, ALFRED T. D
Wyo. State Rep.
b. Lincoln, Nebr, 12/22/09; m. to Ada; c. three. Polit. & Govt. Pos: Former Wyo. State Sen; Wyo. State Rep, 59-61 & 65- Bus. & Prof. Pos: Contractor. Mem: Elks; K. of C; Eagles. Rel: Catholic. Mailing Add: 1115 Clark St, Thermopolis, Wyo. 82443.

GRAHAM, ANNA R
Pres, Ala. Fedn. Rep. Women
b. New Orleans, La, 9/6/32; d. Jake Montalbano and Josephine Latino M. m. 6/9/56 to William Hardin Graham; c. Carol Anne, Michael David, Janet Lee, Patrick Hardin and Alan Gleason. Educ: La. State Univ, B.S.Ed, 54; Newman Club. Polit. & Govt. Pos: Treas. and pres, Huntsville Fedn. Rep. Women, Ala, 64; mem, Madison Co. Rep. Exec. Cmt, 64-65; membership chmn, Ala. Fedn. Rep. Women, 65-66, fourth v.pres, 66-67, pres. and mem. bd. dirs, 67- Bus. & Prof. Pos: Fifth grade teacher, Sacred Heart of Jesus Sch, 54-56; fourth grade teacher, Blessed Sacrament Sch, 56-57. Mem: Huntsville, Madison Co, Ala. and Nat. Fedn. Rep. Women; La. State Univ. Alumni Asn, Huntsville Chap; Fantasy Playhouse Sponsor; Huntsville Deanery Bwse Club; bd. dirs, Cath. Charities Bur. Alpha Omega Award, La. State Univ, 56; John Henry Newman Award, Nat. Newman Club, 56; Outstanding Rep. Woman of the Year, Ala. Fedn, 66. Rel: Roman Catholic. Mailing Add: 8318 Louis Dr, Huntsville, Ala. 35802.

GRAHAM, BETTY JUNE D
Chmn Cowley Co. Dem. Cent. Cmt, Kans.
b. Mt. Hope, Kans, 9/2/17; d. Harley L. Caffrey and May Wimp C; m. 3/23/41 to Eugene Holt Graham. Educ: Southwest. Col, A.B, 39. Polit. & Govt. Pos: Precinct committeewoman, Dem. Party, 48-; chmn, Cowley Co. Dem. Cent. Cmt, Kans, 60-; secy, Fifth Dist Dem. Party, 62-64; del, Dem. Nat. Conv, 64 and alternate del, 68; v.chmn, Jefferson Jackson Day Dinner, Kans, 66. Mem: Winfield Country Club Golf Asn; Snyder Research Found. Auxiliary. Rel: Methodist. Legal Res: 1515 E. 13th, Winfield, Kans. 67156. Mailing Add: P.O. Box 632, Winfield, Kans. 67156.

GRAHAM, CARROLL ADRIAN D
Mont. State Sen.
b. Hardin, Mont, 12/14/13; s. Joseph Allen Graham and Frances Robinson G; m. 6/28/39 to Nelle Yvette Pickard; c. Gary Joe and Carroll Allen. Educ: Lodge Grass High Sch; Billings Polytechnic. Polit. & Govt. Pos: Mont. State Sen, Big Horn Co, 61-; chmn, Livestock and Grazing Cmt, Mont. Senate, 4 sessions, Legis. Admin, Cmt, 3 sessions, chmn, Past Legis. Audit Interim Cmt, 69- Mem: Mason; RAM; Al Bedoo Shrine; Eastern Star; Elks; Mont. and Big Horn Co. Livestock Asns; Farmers Union; Nat. Farm Orgn. Rel: Baptist. Legal Res: 22 Miles S.W, Lodge Grass, Mont. 59050. Mailing Add: Drawer K, Lodge Grass, Mont. 59050.

GRAHAM, DAVID LIVINGSTONE D
b. Philadelphia, Pa, 8/26/04; s. John Graham and Florence Beale G; m. 10/20/56 to Mymie Warrell; c. Lani Florence Beale. Educ: Yale Univ, B.A, 27; Cambridge Univ, B.A. and M.A, 29; Zeta Psi; Wolf's Head Soc. Polit. Pos: Maine State Rep, 65-66. Bus. & Prof. Pos: English instr, Univ. Ga, 30-32. Mil. Serv: Entered as Lt.(jg), Navy, 41, released as Lt. Comdr, 45, after serv. in Southwest Pac, 44-45. Publn: 'The Rise of the Mexican Right,' Yale Review, Autumn, 62; 'What Progress in the Alliance?' Va. Quarterly Review, Autumn, 63; 'Government by Freshmen,' The Nation, 1/66. Mem: Authors League of Am; Am. Vets. Cmt. Water Polo, Boxing, Ice Hockey and Tennis. Rel: Protestant. Mailing Add: Flying Point Rd, Freeport, Maine 04032. (1967)

GRAHAM, DOLORES JEAN 'DEE' R
Chmn, Second Cong. Dist. Rep. Party, Nebr.
b. Bayard, Nebr, 7/23/22; d. Edward F. Carter and Vera Hofrichter C; m. 5/2/42 to William E. Graham; c. William E, Jr, Judith Marie and Julie Anne. Educ: Univ. Nebr, 3 years. Polit. & Govt. Pos: Secy, Omaha Rep. Womens Club, Nebr, 60-62; Rep. chmn, Precinct I, Ward 13, Douglas Co. Ward Orgn, 62-63, v.chmn, Ward 13, 63-64; mem, Douglas Co. Cent. Cmt, 64-65, campaign co-chmn, 64; mem, Nebr. State Rep. Cent. Cmt, 64-69; chmn, Douglas Co. Rep. Party, 66-69; chmn, Second Cong. Dist. Rep. Party, 68-; mem, Nebr. State Rep. Exec. Cmt, 69- Rel: Protestant. Mailing Add: 8119 Harney, Omaha, Nebr. 68114.

GRAHAM, ELWOOD R
Ill. State Rep.
b. Chicago, Ill, 4/10/02. Educ: Chicago pub. schs. Polit. & Govt. Pos: Dep. clerk, Probate Court; mem, State Dept. of Registrn. and Educ; pres. and secy, Sixth Ward Reg. Rep. Orgn; Ill. State Rep, 62-64 & 66- Bus. & Prof. Pos: DuSable Realty Co. Mem: VFW. Rel: Methodist; Mem. Finance Cmt, Woodlawn Methodist Church. Mailing Add: 6711 S. Langley Ave, Chicago, Ill. 60637. (1967)

GRAHAM, J. WESLEY R
Iowa State Rep.
b. Ida Co, Iowa, 1/19/02; s. John Robert Graham and Elizabeth. Educ: Cornell Col; Univ. Iowa, grad. Polit. & Govt. Pos: Iowa State Rep. Bus. & Prof. Pos: Farmer, 8 years; farm loan agent, 2 years; farm mgr, 28 years. Mem: Mason; C. of C; Farm Bur; Iowa and Nat. Asns. Farm Mgrs. and Rural Appraisers; past pres, Iowas Anns. Farm Mgrs. and Rural Appraisers; bd. of dir, Ida Grove Comm. Hosp. Rel: Methodist. Legal Res: 609 Moorehead Ave, Ida Grove, Iowa 51445. Mailing Add: State Capitol, E. Tenth and Grand Ave, Des Moines, Iowa 50319. (1967)

GRAHAM, JEAN CHARTERS D
b. Columbia, Mo, 12/31/14; d. W.W. Charters and Jessie Allen C; m. 12/27/41 to Charles Andrew Graham; c. Judi Allen, Andy and Margaret M. Educ: Univ. Wis, B.A, 35; Columbia Univ, M.A, 36; Univ. Chicago, Ph.D, 42; Mortar Bd; Pi Beta Phi. Polit. & Govt. Pos: Dem. Nat. Committeewoman, Colo, 60-68; del, Dem. Nat. Conv, 68; chmn, Colo. Dem. Equal Rights Cmn, 69- Bus. & Prof. Pos: Part time faculty mem, polit. sci. dept, Univ. Denver. Colo. Dem. Woman of the Year, 68. Mailing Add: 2345 Routt St, Denver, Colo. 80215.

GRAHAM, JOHN A. R
Ill. State Sen.
b. Irving, Ill, 12/3/11; m. to Inga G; c. Vickie Lynn, Steven. Educ: Fillmore High Sch; bus. schs, tech. schs; grad. acct. Polit. & Govt. Pos: Ill. State Sen, 54-; mem, Reg. Rep. Orgn. Bus. & Prof. Pos: Owner, appliance bus, 46- Mil. Serv: Army Air Force, T/Sgt, World War II, Pac. Theatre. Mem: C. of C.(past pres); Mason (past master); Lions; Am. Legion; Moose; Ill. Vets. Rep. League. Rel: United Church of Christ. Mailing Add: 715 S. Cook St, Barrington, Ill. 60010. (1967)

GRAHAM, LLOYD KENNETH 'LUKE' D
Mem, Dem. Nat. Cmt, Wash.
b. Cashmere, Wash, 7/1/06; s. Fred C. Graham and Clara Bollman G; div; c. James E, Carol Ann (Mrs. John S. Edgar) and Fred C. Educ: Int. Correspondence Schs. Polit. & Govt. Pos: First Chmn, Polit. Action Cmt, Clark, Skamamona and W. Klickitat Cent. Labor Coun, Wash, 34; chmn, Scale Cmt, W. Klickitat Cent. Labor Coun, 41; v.pres, Seattle Webb Local, 41; chmn, Clark Co. Dem. Cmt, 47-56; treas, Nine Counties Dem. League, 48-53, chmn, 53-54; del, Dem. Nat. Conv, 48-60 & 68, chmn, Wash. del, 60; chmn, Statewide Jefferson-Jackson Day Dinner, 51; mem, Wash. Dem. Finance Cmt, 53-54, chmn, 57-61; pres, Portland Webb's Pressmans Union, 55-56; mem, Sen. Magnuson's Dinner Cmt, 63; co-dir, Sen. Magnuson's Campaign, 62; mem, Gov. Rosellini's Dinner Cmt, 63; mem, Sen. Jackson's Dinner Cmt, 63; co-chmn, Jefferson-Jackson Dinner Cmt, 63; mem, King Co. Dem. Finance Cmt, 63-64; co-chmn, Wash. Cmt. Elec. Dem. House, 64; chmn, President Johnson's Wash. Finance Cmt, 64; mem, Dem. Nat. Cmt, Wash, 64- Bus. & Prof. Pos: Mem. staff, Astoria, Ore, Budget, 20-24, Columbian Daily, Vancouver, Wash, 24-25, San Francisco Exam, Calif, 24-25, Vancouver Columbian, 25-37, Ore. Jour, Portland, 37-41, Seattle Post Intelligencer, Wash, 41-42 & 51-55; pressman, Columbian Daily, Vancouver, 55-57; with Int. Correspondence Schs, 42-51, supt, Ore. Div, 45-51; staff mem, Bank of Tacoma, Wash, 61-63, secy, 63-64, mem. exec. bd, 64- Mem: Mason; Elks. Legal Res: 2649 Walnut St. S.W, Seattle, Wash. 98116. Mailing Add: 1312 Second Ave, Seattle, Wash. 98101.

GRAHAM, LORRAINE HUNT D
Vt. State Rep.
b. Burlington, Vt, 7/20/25; d. Elzor L. Hunt (deceased) and Leona M. Gelinas H; m. 9/2/46 to Foster J. Graham; c. Lealand Hunt, Foster J, II, Deborah Lorraine, Dana Scott, Darryl Kim and Bryan Keith. Educ: Burlington High Sch, grad, 44. Polit. & Govt. Pos: Vt. State Rep, 66-; membership chmn, Chittenden Co. Dem. Women, 67-; mem, Gov. Cmt. Children with Learning Disabilities. Bus. & Prof. Pos: Typist eng. dept, Bell Aircraft, 44-45; traffic dept, New Eng. Tel. & Tel, 45-52; investr, C.T.I-New Eng. Tel. & Tel, 62-65. Mem: State and Nat. Order of Women Legislators; Nat. Guard Officers Wives; Vt. A Child with Learning Disabilities; Fanny Allen Hosp. Auxiliary; Sch. and Home Asn, Rice Mem. High Sch; Home and Sch. Asn, St. Joseph's; Chittenden Co. Dem. Women; Vt. Fedn. Dem. Women; Dem. City and Ward Cmt. President's Award for Children with Learning Disabilities; del. from Vt. Nat. Support of Pub. Schs, 67. Rel: Roman Catholic. Mailing Add: 280 N. Winooski Ave, Burlington, Vt. 05401.

GRAHAM, MACK D
Miss. State Rep.
b. Sumrall, Miss, 6/12/24; married. Polit. & Govt. Pos: Miss. State Rep, 61- Bus. & Prof. Pos: Merchant; farmer. Mil. Serv: World War II. Mem: Am. Legion; VFW; 40 et 8; bd. dir, Miss. Asn. Retarded Children; PTA; Lions; v.pres, P.T. Coun. Miss. Sch. Blind. Rel: Baptist. Mailing Add: Box 205, Sumrall, Miss. 39482. (1967)

GRAHAM, MARVA FROST R
b. Neosho, Mo, 3/18/36; d. Jay Stone Frost and Vera Suttles F; m. 6/16/56 to Douglas Warner Graham. Educ: Lewis & Clark Col, B.A, 56; Reed Col, M.A.T, 62; Hist. Hon. Soc; Kappa Kappa Gamma. Polit. & Govt. Pos: Precinct committeewoman, Rep. Party, Portland, Ore, 61-66; Ore. State Rep, until 68. Bus. & Prof. Pos: Hist. teacher, Lake Oswego Pub. Schs, 63-66. Rel: Protestant. Mailing Add: 1812 S.W. High St, Portland, Ore. 97201. (1967)

GRAHAM, MILTON HENRY R
Mayor, Phoenix, Ariz.
b. Fairfield, Iowa, 3/23/19; s. Lonnie D. Graham and Bertha M. Coffman G; m. 7/6/69 to Charlotte S. Kelley; stepchildren, Brian and Melanie. Educ: Parsons Col, B.A, 40. Polit. & Govt. Pos: Mayor, Phoenix, Ariz, 64-; v.pres, Nat. Munic. League, 64-69; mem, Nat. League of Cities-Am. Asn. of Hwy. Off. Joint Hwy. Study Cmt, 66-69; mem. bd. dirs, Town Affiliation Asn, 66-69; mem. bd. adv, U.S. Conf. of Mayors, 67-69; mem. steering cmt, Nat. Urban Coalition, 67-69; v.pres, League of Ariz. Cities & Towns, 68-69; mem. bd. dirs, Nat. League of Cities, 69. Bus. & Prof. Pos: Owner, Milt Graham Distributing Co, 46-; Pres, Laundry Equipment Rentals, Inc, 58-; Secy-Treas, Guaranty Appliances, Inc, 59- Mil. Serv: Entered as Aviation Cadet, Air Force, 42, released as Capt, 46, after serv. in 8th Air Force, ETO. Mem: C. of C; Jaycees; Commun. Coun; Thunderbirds; advisory bd, Theodore Roosevelt Boy Scout Coun; Ariz. Country Club. Rel: Protestant. Legal Res: 207 W. Clarendon, Phoenix, Ariz. 85013. Mailing Add: 251 W. Washington, Phoenix, Ariz. 85003.

GRAHAM, MORTIMER ELLIOTT R
Chmn, Erie Co. Rep. Cmt, Pa.
b. Oil City, Pa, 10/18/01; s. Lyman Lincoln Graham and Luella Barnes G; m.

7/7/25 to Grace Budd; c. Douglas Hume and Nancy Lee (Mrs. Brown). Educ: Allegheny Col, A.B. cum laude, 22; Univ. Pa, LL.B, cum laude, 25; Phi Beta Kappa; Order of the Coif; Sigma Delta Rho; Phi Delta Theta. Polit. & Govt. Pos: Dist. Attorney, Erie Co, Pa, 32-40; chmn, Erie Co. Rep. Cmt, 32-34 & 66-; alternate del, Rep. Nat. Conv, 36, del, 64 & 68; mem, Cmn. on Constitutional Revision, Pa, 64-66; mem. exec. cmt, Pa. Rep. Primary Campaign Cmt, 66; mem, Pa. State Rep. Exec. Cmt, 66- Bus. & Prof. Pos: Attorney-at-law, 25-; secy, Hammermill Paper Co, 48-64, gen. counsel, 48-66, v.pres, 64- Mil. Serv: Entered as Lt, Navy, 42, released as Lt. Comdr, 45, after serv. in Naval Aviation; Comdr.(Ret), Naval Res, 52. Mem: Erie Co, Pa. and Am. Bar Asns; Mason (33°); pres, United Fund of Erie Co; v.pres, Pa. United Fund. Rel: Episcopal. Mailing Add: 322 Mohawk Dr, Erie, Pa. 16505.

GRAHAM, RALPH WARREN D
La. State Rep.
b. Shreveport, La, 7/7/37; s. James Warren Graham and Bess McClaran G; m. 3/7/59 to Carol Parker; c. Ginger Gay, Leslie Loris and Piper Elizabeth. Educ: La. State Univ, B.S, 59; Kappa Alpha; Samurai. Polit. & Govt. Pos: La. State Rep, 68- Bus. & Prof. Pos: Partner, Gen. Ins. Agency, Alexandria, La, 60- Mil. Serv: Entered as Pvt. E-1, Army, 59, released as Pvt. E-2, 60; Capt, La. Nat. Guard. Mem: Nat. and La. Asns. of Ins. Agents; Nat. Soc. State Legislators; Mason; Kiwanis; Jaycees. Rel: Presbyterian. Mailing Add: 4607 Wellington Blvd, Alexandria, La. 71301.

GRAHAM, ROBERT VINCENT D
State Auditor, Wash.
b. Pacific City, Wash, 4/12/21; s. Ralph Vincent Graham and Hazel M. Smith G; m. 8/12/45 to Lloydine C. Ryan; c. Randall V, Susan L, Paul R, James M. and Richard S. Educ: Grays Harbor Col. Polit. & Govt. Pos: Exam, Budget Dept, Wash, 47-48; chief exam, auditors munic. div, Wash, 48-59, dep. state auditor, 59-64, asst. state auditor, 64-65, state auditor, 65- Mil. Serv: Entered as Pvt, Air Force, 42, released as T/Sgt, 46, after serv. in Air Transport Command; Good Conduct Medal; Victory Medal; Am. and Asiatic-Pac. Theater Ribbons. Mem: Nat. Asn. of State Auditors, Controllers and Treasurers; Munic. Finance Officers of U.S. and Can; bd. mem, U.G.N. Rel: Presbyterian; Elder. Legal Res: 4600 Boulevard Rd, Olympia, Wash. 98501. Mailing Add: Legislative Bldg, Olympia, Wash. 98502.

GRAHAM, ROGER A. D
b. Dalles, Ore, 5/24/29; s. Henry H. Graham and Jeanie B. Barclay G; m. 6/28/57 to Jeanette Roberts; c. Janet L, Leslie A, Joel A. and Beth A. Educ: Univ. Portland, 48-50; Portland State Univ, 53-55. Polit. & Govt. Pos: Precinctman, Dem. Party, Linn Co, Ore, 60-; dist. finance chmn, Reelect Ullman Cong, 68; alternate del, Dem. Nat. Conv, 68; mem, Ore. State Dem. Finance Cmt, 69-; state finance chmn, Straub for Gov, 69- Bus. & Prof. Pos: Sales rep. Hallamark Card Co, Portland, Ore, 54-55; sales rep, Tubesales, 55-57; independent agent, Seattle, Wash, 58-59; sales rep, Wah Chang Corp, Albany, Ore, 59-67 and Wah Chang Albany Corp, 67- Mil. Serv: Entered as Seaman, Navy, 46, released as Lt. Comdr, 49, after serv. in Pac. and China, 46-48, recalled, 50-53, serv. in Korea; Campaign medals. Mem: Am. Soc. Metals; Am. Soc. Corrosion Engr; Elks; Linn Co. Ment. Health Asn.(past pres); Linn Co. Ment. Health Asn. Clin.(bd mem). Rel: Agnostic. Mailing Add: 914 W. Fifth Ave, Albany, Ore. 97321.

GRAHAM, SPENCER W. R
b. Crellin, Md, 1/7/94; married. Educ: Garret Co. pub. schs. Polit. & Govt. Pos: Mem, Garret Co. Rep. Cent. Cmt, Md; minority Clerk, Md. State House of Del, 29; Md. State Sen, 63-67. Bus. & Prof. Pos: Retired life ins. underwriter and fraternal ins. counselor. Mem: Lions; K. of P; Odd Fellows; WOW. Mailing Add: 433 N. Third St, Oakland, Md. 21550.

GRAHAM, THOMAS D. D
Mo. State Rep.
b. 10/14/22; m. 4/22/44 to Christine Wood; c. Thomas Christopher. Educ: Univ. Mo. Polit. & Govt. Pos: Mo. State Rep, 50-, Speaker, Mo. House of Rep, 61-67, chmn, House Ins. Cmt, 69-71; pres, Nat. Legis. Conf; mem, Mo. Reorgn. Cmt, Cmt. on Local Govt. and cmt. of the Nat. Conf. of Cmnrs. on Uniform State Laws; v.chmn, Mo. World's Fair Cmn. Bus. & Prof. Pos: Partner, law firm, Graham and Hawkins; law practice, 49. Mil. Serv: 1st Lt, Army Air Force, served in Judge Adv. Gen. Dept, Wright Field, released in 46. Mem: Cole Co, St. Louis and Mo. Bar Asns; Phi Gamma Delta; Phi Delta Phi; Mason; Shrine; Am. Legion; citizenship merit badge counsellor, Boy Scouts. Rel: Christian Church. Mailing Add: 312 Capitol Ave, Jefferson City, Mo. 65101.

GRAHAM, THOMAS ESTUS D
Miss. State Rep.
b. Ellisville, Miss, 11/10/04. Polit. & Govt. Pos: Miss. State Rep, 52-56 & 64- Bus. & Prof. Pos: Farmer. Mem: Mason; Eastern Star; Jones Co. Wild Life League. Rel: Baptist. Mailing Add: Route 2, Ellisville, Miss. 39437. (1967)

GRAHAM, WILLARD WOODROW D
Chmn, Wayne Co. Dem. Cmt, Mo.
b. Clubb, Mo, 12/11/12; s. William Monroe Graham and Elizabeth Durr G; m. 11/28/57 to Madalyne Armstrong Hollida; c. Carrie Elizabeth (Mrs. William G. Beckett), Imogene (Mrs. James R. Roach), B.G. Hollida, Judith (Mrs. Lavern Daves) and R. Dan Hollida. Polit. & Govt. Pos: Committeeman, Cowan Twp. Rep. Party, Mo, 40-56; chmn, Wayne Co. Dem. Orgn, 56- Bus. & Prof. Pos: Farmer, 28-69; Saw Mill Operator, 38-56, Grocery, 57-60, Egg Inspector, State of Mo, Dept. of Agri, 60- Mem: AF&AM; Scottish Rite. Rel: Missionary Baptist. Mailing Add: Clubb, Mo, 63934.

GRAHAM, WILLIAM CLYDE D
b. Coward, S.C, 12/31/97; s. W. Watson Graham and Knita Emma Matthews G; m. 11/30/22 to Marguerite Hyman. Educ: Clemson Col, B.S, 18. Polit. & Govt. Pos: S.C. State Rep, 66; S.C. State Sen, 51-64; S.C. State Rep, 35-38; 41-48. Bus. & Prof. Pos: Farmer, breeder reg. Jersey cattle and mgr. DeWitts Bluff Farms, dir, First Nat. Bank Florence, S.C, 25-31; bookkeeper, acct, 20-25; taught voc. agr, Pamplico, 23, Coward, 20 and Batesburg, 19. Mil. Serv: Plattsburg ROTC Camp, 18. Mailing Add: Route 1, Pamplico, S.C. 29583. (1967)

GRAHAM, WILLIAM EDGAR, JR. D
b. Jackson Springs, N.C, 12/31/29; s. William Edgar Graham and Minnie Autry G; m. 11/24/62 to Jean Dixon McLaurin; c. William McLaurin, John McMillan and Sally Faircloth. Educ: Univ. N.C, A.B, 52, LL.B, 56; Order of the Coif; Phi Delta Phi. Polit. & Govt. Pos: Mem, N.C. Dem. Exec. Cmt, 61; pres, Young Dem. of N.C, 62. Bus. & Prof. Pos: Attorney, Charlotte, N.C, 56- Mil. Serv: Entered as 2nd Lt, Air Force, 62, released as 1st Lt, 64, after serv. in Off. of Spec. Invest. Mem: Am. Bar Asn; N.C. Bar Asn; Mason; Civitan Int. Rel: Presbyterian. Mailing Add: 214 Manning Dr, Charlotte, N.C. 28209.

GRAHAM, WILLIAM HARDIN R
Mem-at-lg, Ala. Rep. Exec. Cmt.
b. Birmingham, Ala, 4/27/32; s. David Franklin Graham and Roberta Lee Hardin G; m. 6/9/56 to Anna Montalbano; c. Carol Anne, Michael David, Janet Lee Patrick Hardin and Alan Gleason. Educ: La. State Univ, B.S, 53, M.S, 55; Fla. State Univ, Ph.D, 58; Nat. Sci. Found. Predoctoral fel; Phi Lambda Upsilon; Newman Club (pres, La. State Univ. Chap, 53). Polit. & Govt. Pos: Area, precinct and ward chmn, Madison Co. Rep. Campaign Cmt, Ala, 63-64, asst. city chmn, 64; city chmn, Madison Co. Rep. Exec. Cmt, 65, dir. of orgn, 65-66, chmn, 66-68; chmn. of del, Madison Co. Del. to State Rep. Conv, 66 & 68; mem-at-lg, Ala. Rep. Exec. Cmt, 66-; Rep. presidential elector, State of Ala, 68; cand. recruitment chmn, Eighth Cong. Dist. Rep. Party, 69. Bus. & Prof. Pos: Arthur Amos Noyes research fel, Calif. Inst. Tech, 58-59; research chemist, Rohm & Haas Co, Huntsville, Ala, 59- Publ: About 20 sci. papers in J. Am. Chem. Soc, J. Organic Chem, J. Phys. Chem, J. Chem. Physics & Tetrahedron. Mem: Sigma Xi; Am. Chem. Soc; Am. Inst. of Chemists; Young Rep. Club; Citizens for Better Govt.(chmn, 68); Young Am. for Freedom. Rel: Catholic. Mailing Add: 8318 Louis Dr, Huntsville, Ala. 35802.

GRAHAM, WILLIAM M. D
Mem, Arlington Co. Dem. Cmt, Va.
b. Norfolk, Va, 2/12/24; s. William Snead Graham and Ruth Tunstall G; m. 9/4/48 to Nancy Alger; c. W. David, Margaret Wharton and Susan Tunstall. Educ: Univ. Va, B.A, 49; George Wash. Univ, postgrad. study, 50-53; Trigon; Phi Kappa Psi. Polit. & Govt. Pos: Mem, Arlington Co. Dem. Cmt, Va, 61-, v.chmn, 61-63, chmn, 63-65, treas, 65-67; del, Dem. Nat. Conv, 64; chmn, Arlington Del, Va. State Dem. Conv, 64, del, 68; mem, Sch. Bd, Arlington Co, 68- Bus. & Prof. Pos: Bus. economist, U.S. Bur. of Labor Statist, 49-53; opers. analyst, Fed. Res. Bd, 53-55; transportation economist, Am. Trucking Assocs, 55-63; transportation and econ. consult, 63- Mil. Serv: Entered as Pvt, Army, 43, released as S/Sgt, 46, after serv. in 465th FA Bn, S.W. Pac. Theater, 44-46. Mem: Am. Acad. Polit. & Soc. Sci; Transportation Research Forum; Am. Econ. Asn; Am. Statist. Asn; Econ. Develop. Round Table; former pres. and chmn. exec. cmt. and sch. cmt, Arlington Civic Fedn; Donaldson Run Civic Asn. and Recreation Asn. Rel: Episcopal. Mailing Add: 2778 N. Wakefield St, Arlington, Va. 22207.

GRAHAM, WILLIAM THOMAS R
Asst. Gen. Counsel for Legal Opinions and Research, Dept. of Housing and Urban Develop.
b. Waynesboro, Va, 10/24/33; s. James Monroe Graham and Margaret Virginia Goodwin G; m. 2/1/58 to Nancy Kent Hill; c. William Thomas, Jr. and Ashton Cannon. Educ: Duke Univ, A.B, 56; Univ. of Hawaii, 58; Wake Forest Col, 61; Univ. of Va, LL.B, 62; Beta Theta Pi; Phi Alpha Delta. Polit. & Govt Pos: Del, N.C. Rep. State Conv, 64, 66 & 68, N.C. Fifth Cong. Dist. Rep. Conv, 66 & 68 and Forsyth Co. Rep. Conv, 64, 66 & 68; mem. exec. cmt, Forsyth Co. Rep. Party, 64-69, chmn, 66-69; mem, Forsyth Co. Bd. Elecs, 64-66; alternate del, Rep. Nat. Conv, 68; asst. gen. counsel for legal opinions and research, Dept. of Housing and Urban Develop, Wash, D.C. currently. Bus. & Prof. Pos: Assoc, Craige, Brawley, Lucas & Horton, 62-65, partner, Craige, Brawley, Horton & Graham, 65-69. Mil. Serv: Entered as Pvt, Army, 57, released as Pfc, 58, after serv. on staff of the Judge Adv, Hq, Army Security Agency, Pac, in Tokyo, Japan and Helemano, Hawaii. Mem: Am, N.C, Forsyth Co. and Forsyth Co. Jr. Bar Asns; Va. and N.C. State Bars; Twin City Club; Old Town Club; Forsyth Co. Duke Alumni Asn. Rel: Methodist. Legal Res: 1000 Arbor Rd, Winston-Salem, N.C. 27106. Mailing Add: 3410 P St, N.W, Washington, D.C. 20007.

GRAHL, DANIEL KENDALL, SR. D
Ga. State Rep.
b. Jacksonville, Fla, 8/7/15; s. James Samuel Grahl, Sr. and Celia Elizabeth Shook G; m. 12/27/40 to Mildred Donnan; c. Mildred Anne and Daniel Kendall, Jr; one grandson. Educ: Ga. Southwest. Col, dipl. 37; Mercer Univ, A.B, 39; Sigma Upsilon; Alpha Psi Omega; Kappa Phi Kappa; Alpha Tau Omega; Blue Key. Polit. & Govt. Pos: Admin. asst. to Chief of Maintenance, Warner Robins Air Material Area, Ga, 44-47 and Chief of Flight Oper. Sect, 47-52; Ga. State Rep, Dist. 52, 66-67, Dist. 40, 68- Bus. & Prof. Pos: Reporter, Times-Recorder, Americus, Ga, 35-37; prin, Edison High Sch, 40-41; ed, Warner Robins Press, Ga, 46-52; ed-publisher, Leader-Tribune, Ft. Valley, 52- Mil. Serv: Pvt, Army, 45-46. Mem: Mason; F&AM, Ft. Valley; Am. Legion; 40 et 8; Kiwanis; Farm Bur; hon. mem, Future Farmers of Am. Rel: Methodist. Mailing Add: 1011 First St, Ft. Valley, Ga. 31030.

GRALIKE, DONALD J. D
Mo. State Rep.
b. St. Louis Co, Mo, 10/22/29; m. Feb. 1954 to Rita J. Simeone; c. Donald, David and twins Dennis and Daniel. Educ: Wash. Univ. Polit. & Govt. Pos: Mem, United Young Dem; mem, Regular Legis. Dem. Club; Mo. State Rep, 62-, majority whip, Mo. House Rep. Bus. & Prof. Pos: Instr, O'Fallen Tech. High Sch, 56-60; bus. rep, Inst. Brotherhood of Elec. Workers, 60-62; Sachs Elec. Contractors. Mil. Serv: Army, 52-54; 185th Engr. Combat Battery. Mem: Am. Legion. Rel: Catholic. Mailing Add: 648 Buckley Rd, St. Louis, Mo. 63125. (1967)

GRAMMES, LLOYD EDGAR R
Councilman, City of Allentown, Pa.
b. Allentown, Pa. 8/9/03; s. George P. Grammes and Jennie A. Wieder G; m. 9/65 to Florence A. Bartholomew; c. Roberta J.(Mrs. Daubenspeck). Educ: Allentown High Sch; LaSalle Univ. Exten. Polit. & Govt. Pos: Alderman, Pa. Magistrates Asn, 35-; dir, City Coun, Allentown, Pa, 49-, councilman, 56- Bus. & Prof. Pos: Weighmaster, U.S. Steel Corp, 24-27; acct, Mack Trucks, Inc, 27-30; dry cleaners, 30-34. Mem: Odd Fellows; Elks; Fraternal Order of

Police; hon. pres, Boys Club of Am; hon. pres, Magistrates Asn; Ocean City, Md. Marlin Club. Rel: Protestant. Legal Res: 836 N. 29th St, Allentown, Pa. 18104. Mailing Add: 716 Union St, Allentown, Pa. 18101.

GRANAHAN, KATHRYN ELIZABETH D
b. Easton, Pa; d. James B. O'Hay and Julia Reilly O; m. 11/20/48 to William Thomas Granahan (deceased). Educ: Mt. St. Joseph Col, Phila, grad. Hon. LL.D, St. Joseph's Col, Phila, 59. Polit. & Govt. Pos: Supvr. of pub. assistance, Auditor Gen. Dept, and liaison officer between Auditor Gen. Dept. and Dept. Pub. Assistance, Pa; U.S. Rep, Second Dist, Pa, 56-62; Treas. of U.S, 62-66; Mailing Add: Rittenhouse Savoy Apt, 1810 Rittenhouse Sq, Philadelphia, Pa. 19103. (1967)

GRANAI, CORNELIUS O. R
b. New York, N.Y, 7/11/97; m. to J. Ruth Carpenter; c. 2 sons; 1 daughter. Educ: Syracuse Univ, 20-23; Syracuse Law Col, LL.B, 25. Polit. & Govt. Pos: Mayor, Barre, Vt; state's attorney; justice of the peace; grand juror; chmn, Rep. Co. Cmt; Vt. State Rep, 47-49, 51-59 & 63-68. Bus. & Prof. Pos: Attorney. Mil. Serv: Army, Transport Hercules, coal passer and fireman, 17-18; Fifth Army, 2576 Regt, Co. J, Italy, and Seventh Army, Africa, World War II, Judge Advocate Maj. with Mil. Govt, 43-46; Army Res, 46-52. Mem: DAV; Am. Legion; VFW; Mason; Shrine; Fish & Game Club; former trustee, U.V.M. and Vt. Cols. Rel: Methodist. Mailing Add: 46 Beacon St, Barre, Vt. 05641. (1967)

GRANATA, PETER C. R
Ill. State Rep.
b. Chicago, Ill, 10/28/99; m. 1/6/45 to Johanna Wellner G; c. Peter, Jr. and Paul. Educ: Pub. and commercial schs. Polit. & Govt. Pos: Rep. committeeman, First Ward, Ill; chief dep. coroner, Cook Co, 25-27; chief clerk, Prosecuting Attorney for Chicago, 27-30; U.S. Rep, Ill, 30; Ill. State Rep, 33-42, 44-64 & 66-; del, Rep. Nat. Conv, 68; v.chmn, Ill. Rep. State Cent. Cmt, currently. Mailing Add: 1025 S. May St, Chicago, Ill. 60607. (1967)

GRANDYS, FRANCIS T. D
Polit. & Govt. Pos: Ind. State Rep, -66; clerk, Lake Circuit Court, 2 terms, chief dep. clerk, 47-56, dep. clerk, Lake Circuit Court, 32-47. Bus. & Prof. Pos: Real estate agent. Mem: Former pres, Ind. Asn. of Clerks of Circuit Courts; former dir, Lake Co. Chap, Nat. Found. Infantile Paralysis; Lions; Cath. Order of Foresters. Rel: Catholic. Mailing Add: 609 S. Main St, Crown Point, Ind. 46307. (1967)

GRANGER, HERBERT CURRY D
S.C. State Rep.
b. Greenville, S.C, 5/25/23; s. James H. Granger and Lula Myers G; m. 8/19/45 to Vera Taylor; c. Ronald L. and Russell C. Educ: Okla. State Teachers Col. Polit. & Govt. Pos: S.C. State Rep, 59- Bus. & Prof. Pos: Textiles, J. P. Stevens, Inc. Mil. Serv: Air Force, 42-45; 8th AF, 548th Bomb Sq, 385th Bomb Group, ETO. Mem: Treas, Carolina High Sch. Booster's Club; former trustee, W. Gantt High Sch; Mason; Am. Legion. Pres. Sr. Class W. Gantt High Sch; Citizenship Award, High Sch. Rel: Baptist; Gen. Supt. Sunday Sch, West Gantt Baptist Church, Past Chmn. Bd. of Deacons, Former Pres. Brotherhood. Mailing Add: R.F.D. 4, Greenville, S.C. 29605. (1967)

GRANGER, LESTER BLACKWELL R
b. Newport News, Va, 9/16/96; s. William Richard Randolph Granger, Sr. and Mary Louise Augusta Turpin G; wid. Educ: Dartmouth Col, A.B, 18; N.Y. Univ, 23-24; N.Y. Sch. of Soc. Work, 24-25. Hon. D.H.L, Dartmouth Col, 46, Wilberforce Univ, 47 and Columbia Univ, 54; hon. LL.D, Oberlin Col, 52, Morris Brown Col, 52 and Va. State Col, 53. Polit. & Govt. Pos: Secy. Negro welfare, Welfare Coun. of N.Y.C, 38-40; mem, President's Cmt. on Equal Opportunity in Armed Serv; chmn, Fed. Adv. Coun. Employ. Security; soc. serv. adminstr; spec. adv. and personal rep, Secy. of Navy, 45-47; spec. adv, Secy. of Defense, 47-48; mem, Fed. Adv. Cmt. on Employ. Security, 54-60, chmn, 60. Bus. & Prof. Pos: Teacher, Slater State Normal Sch, Winston-Salem, N.C, 19-20; exten. worker, State Manual Training Sch, Bordentown, N.J, 22-34; exec. secy, Los Angeles Urban League, 30-31; secy. for workers educ, Nat. Urban League, 34-37, exec. dir, 40-61. Mil. Serv: Entered as Officer Cand, FAOTS, 18, released as 2nd Lt, FA-AEF, 19, after serv. in 349th Regt, 92nd Div. AEF. Publ: Articles in Am. Acad. of Polit. and Soc. Sci; Columns in N.Y. Amsterdam News for 20 years and Denver Post; many articles contrib. to prfnl. jour. Mem: Int. Conf. Soc. Work (pres, 61-64); Am. Asn. Soc. Workers (v.pres, 42); Nat. Asn. Soc. Workers; Nat. Conf. on Soc. Welfare (v.pres, 50, pres, 52); trustee, Sch. Grad. Soc. Welfare, Brandeis Univ, Sch. of Soc. Work, Columbia Univ, State Univ. of N.Y. and St. Paul's Col; Am. Legion. Recipient, Navy Medal for Distinguished Civilian Serv. and President's Medal for Merit. Rel: Episcopal. Mailing Add: 6411 Congress Dr, New Orleans, La. 70126.

GRANQUIST, WAYNE G. D
b. New Britain, Conn, 11/1/35; s. George William Granquist and Ruth Johnson G; m. 8/31/57 to Marilyn Martha Gumbrecht; c. Leslie Ann, Andrea Briggs and Sarah Elizabeth. Educ: Harvard Col, 53-55; Tufts Univ, A.B, 57; Harvard Law Sch, LL.B, 60. Polit. & Govt. Pos: Admin. asst. to U.S. Sen. Abraham Ribicoff, Conn, 64-69. Bus. & Prof. Pos: For. serv. officer, Dept. of State, 60-62; chief prog. analyst, NASA, 62-64; pres, Norwalk Nat. Bank, Conn, 69- Mem: Mass. and Am. Bar Asns; Am. Polit. Sci. Asn; Nat. Lawyers Club, Wash, D.C. Am. Polit. Sci. Asn. Fel, 63. Rel: Unitarian. Legal Res: 99 Comstock Hill Rd, Norwalk, Conn. 06850. Mailing Add: R.R. 2, Silvermine, Norwalk, Conn. 06850.

GRANT, DAVID MARSHALL D
Dir. Legis. Research, St. Louis Bd. Aldermen, Mo.
b. St. Louis, Mo, 1/1/03; s. William Samuel Grant and Elizabeth Margaret Holliday G; m. 9/18/44 to Mildred Hughes; c. David Wesley and Gail Milissa. Educ: Univ. Mich; Howard Univ. Sch. Law, LL.B, 30; Omega Psi Phi. Polit. & Govt. Pos: Asst. city counselor, St. Louis, Mo, 33-40, asst. circuit attorney, 40-42 and mem, Bd. of Freeholders, 56-57; dir. Legis Research, St. Louis Bd. of Aldermen, 57-; mem. state adv. cmt, U.S. Cmn. on Civil Rights, 61-; U.S. del, Freedom Celebration, Kampala, Uganda, E.Africa, Oct, 62. Bus. & Prof. Pos: Practicing attorney, 30- Mem: Life mem, NAACP; Nat. Asn. Criminal Defense Lawyers; Lawyers Asn; Bar Asn. of St. Louis; Mound City Bar Asn. Rel: Episcopal. Mailing Add: 3309 Arsenal St, St. Louis, Mo. 63118.

GRANT, EDMUND GRIFFIN D
S.C. State Rep.
b. Chesterfield, S.C, 1/2/09; s. Jesse L. Grant and Mattie Peele G; m. 4/27/31 to Anna Brunson. Educ: Univ. of S.C. Polit. & Govt. Pos: S.C. State Rep, 59-64 & 69- Bus. & Prof. Pos: Gen. agent in S.C, Kans. City Life Ins. Co; owner and mgr, Edmund G. Grant & Assoc, Investments-Ins. Mem: Chmn. bd. of dirs, Bus. and Prfnl. Men's Finance and Investment Co; State and Nat. Underwriters Asns; past pres, Columbia Civitan Club; Kans. City Life's Pres. Club. Holder, Nat. Award for Quality Life Underwriting Serv. to the Pub, for 10 years; Cert. of Serv, Boy Scouts; Cert. of Pub. Serv, S.C. Munic. Asn. Rel: Episcopal. Mailing Add: 1929 Gervais St, Columbia, S.C. 29201. (1967)

GRANT, ERVIN EUGENE R
Kans. State Rep.
b. El Dorado, Kans, 3/14/24; s. E. W. Grant and Frankie Detrick G; m. 2/9/52 to Mary Jo Davis; c. Laurie Lynn and Randall Eugene. Educ: Kans. Univ, B.A, 48, Law Sch, LL.B, 51; Phi Alpha Delta. Polit. & Govt. Pos: Bd. Mem. and pres, El Dorado Bd. of Educ, Kans, 57-61; asst. co. attorney, Butler Co, 61-63; mem. bd, Bradford Mem. Libr, 63-; Kans. State Rep, 63rd Dist, currently. Mil. Serv: Entered as Seaman 3/C, Navy, 43, released as Ens, 46. Mem: Am. Bar Asn; charter mem, World Peace Through Law Center; El Dorado Kiwanis Club; Am. Legion; Big Brothers; People-to-People. Rel: Methodist. Legal Res: 525 Harvard, El Dorado, Kans. 67042. Mailing Add: Box 162, El Dorado, Kans. 67042.

GRANT, GARY S. D
Wash. State Rep.
b. Chippewa Falls, Wis, 9/18/34; s. Merrill E. Grant and Kathryn T. Lutgen G; m. 4/30/60 to Tanya C. Olson; c. Stephen, Leah and Daniel. Educ: St. Martin's Col, B.A, 56; Pi Kappa Delta. Polit. & Govt. Pos: Wash. State Rep, currently. Bus. & Prof. Pos: Pres, Bold Venture, Inc, 65-66. Mem: East-gate-Newport Jaycees; Renton 306, Toastmasters. Rel: Catholic. Mailing Add: 12835 S.E. 160th, Renton, Wash. 98055.

GRANT, GEORGE HENRY D
S.C. State Rep.
b. Ware Shoals, S.C, 10/4/17; s. John A. Grant and Pearl Elizabeth Schumpert G; m. 9/14/56 to Louise Foust; c. George H, Jr. and Kelli Reed. Educ: Wofford Col, 46-49; Univ. S.C, LL.B, 52; Lambda Chi Alpha; Phi Delta Phi; Omicron Delta Kappa. Polit. & Govt. Pos: Chmn, Aiken Co. Dem. Party, S.C, 66-68; state exec. committeeman, S.C. Dem. Party, 68-; S.C. State Rep, 69- Bus. & Prof. Pos: Circuit v.pres, S.C. Bar Asn, 66- Mil. Serv: Entered as Seaman 2/C, Navy, 42, released as PO 1/C, 46, after serv. in Navy Med. Corps, Pac. Theatre, S.Pac, Tenth Army, 42-46; Good Conduct, Pac. Theatre and Am. Oper. Medals; Distinguished Serv. with Combat Device. Mem: Am. and Aiken Co. Bar Asns; S.C. Bar Asn.(circuit v.pres, 66-); Am. Trial Lawyers Asn; Am. Judicature Soc; Elks; VFW; Am. Legion. Rel: Baptist. Legal Res: 111 Gregg Ave, Aiken, S.C. 29801. Mailing Add: Box 328, Aiken, S.C, 29801.

GRANT, GEORGE McINVALE D
b. Louisville, Ala, 7/11/97; s. Benjamin Giles and Fannie Gholson Stevens G; m. 12/5/38 to Matalie Carter; c. George McInvale Jr, Alicia Lee. Educ: Univ. of Ala, LL.B, 22; Bob Jones Univ, LL.D, (hon), 50. Polit. & Govt. Pos: U.S. Rep, Ala, 37-64; Co. solicitor, Pike Co, 27-37; Chmn, Pike Co. Dem. Exec. Comm, 27-38; State Dem. Exec. Comm, 35-38. Mil. Serv: U.S. Army, 18-19. Mem: Bd. of Trustees, Bob Jones Univ; Am. Legion, state comdr. 29; Pi Kappa Phi, nat. secy, 22; Kiwanis; Woodmen of the World; Elks; Moose; Mason, Shriner. Rel: Methodist. Legal Res: Court Sq, Troy, Ala. 36081. Mailing Add: 4801 Connecticut Ave. N.W, Washington, D.C. 20008.

GRANT, RAYMOND ARMAND D
Chmn, Custer Co. Dem. Cent. Cmt, Mont.
b. Licking, Mo, 7/25/97; s. John Charles Grant and Elizabeth Rathbone Dixox G; m. 6/18/19 to Fannie Maude Bryant; c. Raymond Armand, Jr, Juanita Lyonors (Mrs. Murnion) and Dorothy Elizabeth. Educ: Springfield Teachers' Col, Mo; Univ. Mo; Univ. Mont. Polit. & Govt. Pos: Clerk, Garfield Co, Mont, 31-42; Mont. State Rep, Custer Co, 54-56 and Mont. State Sen, 56-60; chmn, Custer Co. Dem. Cent. Cmt, currently. Bus. & Prof. Pos: Secy-mgr, Miles City PCA, 42-53; credit mgr, Beacon-Carter Serv, 53-59; v.pres, First Security Bank & Trust, 59- Mem: Elks; Eagles; MWA; C. of C. Rel: Presbyterian; Chmn, Bd. of Trustees. Mailing Add: 1502 Pleasant St, Miles City, Mont. 59301.

GRANT, ROBERT ELMER D
N.Dak. State Rep.
b. Lakota, N.Dak, 10/6/14; s. Robert Milton Grant and Gertrude Matthews G; m. 3/19/41 to Bernice Oleda Nelson; c. Sandra Kay (Mrs. Donald Oss) and Robert N. Educ: Tagus Pub. Sch, 12 years. Polit. & Govt. Pos: Precinct committeeman, Dem. Party, Egan Twp, N.Dak, 52-66; commun. committeeman, Agr. Stabilization & Conserv. Serv, Fourth Dist, 62-68; mem, Montrail Co. Fed. Housing Admin, 66-68; commun. committeeman, N.Dak. State Asn. Farmers, 68-; N.Dak. State Rep, 69- Mil. Serv: Entered as Pvt, Army, 41, released as S/Sgt, 45, after serv. in 753rd Field Artil, ETO, 44-45; Cert. Merit. Mem: Farmers Union; Elks; Am. Legion. Rel: Protestant. Mailing Add: R.R. 2, Box 36, Berthold, N.Dak. 58718.

GRANT, ROBERT WILLIAMS, JR. R
Chmn, Saginaw Co. Rep. Party, Mich.
b. Saginaw, Mich, 7/4/15; s. Robert W. Grant and Lucile Brewer G; m. 12/28/38 to Patricia Lord; c. Robert L, James M. and Carolyn. Educ: Northwest. Univ, B.S. in Commerce, 37; Lynx; Beta Theta Pi. Hon. degree in bus. admin, Saginaw Bus. Inst, 63. Polit. & Govt. Pos: Mem, Police-Fireman Civil Serv. Cmn, Saginaw, Mich, 44-50; mem. bd. educ, Saginaw, 50-62; chmn, Saginaw Co. Rep. Party, 66-; alternate del, Rep. Nat. Conv, 68. Bus. & Prof. Pos: Pres, Grant Grocer Co, Saginaw, 37-; pres, Brewer Co, 38-; dir, Cent. Warehouse Co, 40-; dir, Saginaw Properties, 45-; pres, Washington Ave. Co, 50-; dir, Brewer Neinstedt Lumber Co, Palmetto, La, 57-; pres, Golden Triangle Cold Storage Co, Saginaw, 59-; dir, Mich. Nat. Bank, 63-; dir, Midland Terminal Warehouse Co, 64-; partner, GSW Co, 64-

Mem: Nat. Frozen Food Asn.(pres, 59-60); Cent. States Frozen Food Asn. (pres, 56-57); Nat. Asn. Wholesalers; Saginaw Club; Kiwanis; United Fund; United Commercial Travelers; Jr. Achievement; C. of C; Zerocrats. Rel: Congregational. Legal Res: 429 Ardussi Ave, Saginaw, Mich. 48602. Mailing Add: 2700 Perkins St, Saginaw, Mich. 48605.

GRANT, VIRGINIA ANNE D
b. Mesa, Ariz, 7/25/26; d. Granville Ewing Dickinson and Lucy Anne Hollowell D; m. 5/29/45 to Harry J. Grant; c. Gregory Gary. Educ: High Sch; Bus. Col. Polit. & Govt. Pos: Dem. Nat. committeewoman, Ore, 56-60; candidate for Ore. State Rep, West. Suburban Dist. Mem: PTA; Nat. Ment. Health Asn; Local 305 Jane Jefferson Women's Club. Mailing Add: 4621 S.E. 50, Portland, Ore. 97206.

GRANT, WILLIAM D
b. Estes Park, Colo, 8/29/10; s. William West Grant and Gertrude Hendrie G; m. 6/6/38 to Helen Prindle. Educ: Dartmouth Col, A.B, 31; Harvard Law Sch, B.L, 38; Phi Beta Kappa. Polit. & Govt. Pos: Chmn, Dem. State Cent. Cmt, Colo, until 69; del, Dem. Nat. Conv, 68. Bus. & Prof. Pos: Chmn. bd, Metrop. TV Co, Colo. Mil. Serv: Entered as Lt.(jg), Naval Res, 42, released as Lt. Comdr, 46, after serv. in Pac; Bronze Star. Mem: Colo. and Am. Bar Asns. Rel: Episcopalian. Mailing Add: 101 S. Humboldt St, Denver, Colo. 80233.

GRANT, WILLIAM PATRICK D
b. Fall River, Mass, 11/5/06; s. William J. Grant and Ellen Lee G; m. 12/29/37 to Anna Duggan; c. Louise P.(Mrs. Brian Saltus). Educ: Wheeler Prep, 28-31; Staley Col, B.O, 32; Boston Univ, 33-34; Northeast. Univ. Law Sch, LL.B; Kappa Delta Kappa. LL.D, Bradford DurFee Col. Polit. & Govt. Pos: Mass. State Rep, 11th Dist, 34-36; Mass. State Sen, Second Dist, 37-46; mayor, Fall River, 46-51, chmn. sch. cmt, 46-51 and chmn, Dem. city cmt, 53-56; clerk of courts, Bristol Co, 55-; dir, Gr. Fall River Dem. Club, 66-; del, Dem. Nat. Conv, 68. Bus. & Prof. Pos: Trustee, Citizen's Savings Bank, 50- Mem: Bristol Co. Bar Asn.(dir, 59-); Fall River and Mass. Bar Asns; K. of C; Mass. Legis. Asn; Quequechan Club Fall River; Clover Club; Eire Soc. Boston. Award, DAV, 48; Award, U.S. Jr. C. of C, 49. Rel: Roman Catholic. Mailing Add: 312 Florence St, Fall River, Mass. 02720.

GRANT, WILLIAM S. R
b. Calif; m. 11/5/30 to Ethel Ada Walter G. Educ: S. Calif. Schs; hon. degree, Master of Humanities. Polit. & Govt. Pos: Calif. State Assemblyman, 47-52, 54-66. Bus. & Prof. Pos: Union Oil Co. Mem: NSGW; Masons; Elks; Moose; past Pres, Long Beach C. of C; Dir, Army and Navy YMCA; Los Altos YMCA; former dir, Commun. Chest Conv. Bur; Planning Cmt; Philharmonic Soc. Mailing Add: 2999 E. Ocean Blvd, Long Beach, Calif. 90803. (1967)

GRANTHAM, JASPER EDWARD 'JACK' R
b. Memphis, Tenn, 5/5/22; s. Ray Grantham and Saleta Frances Edwards G; m. 3/30/56 to Florence Harrington; c. Kevin Ray, Robin Frances, Fern, Kellie Lorraine, Stanley Douglas and David Charles. Educ: Univ. Md, B.S. Polit. & Govt. Pos: Mem, Ala. State Rep. Exec. Cmt. and platform sub-cmt, 62-63; v.chmn, Montgomery Co. Rep. Exec. Cmt, Ala, 62-63; alternate del, Rep. Nat. Conv, 64; precinct dir, Escambia Co. Citizens for Goldwater, Fla, 64; chmn, Fla. State Rep. Ballot Security Cmt; chmn, Escambia Co. Rep. Exec. Cmt, 65-68. Bus. & Prof. Pos: Dist. mgr, Waddell & Reed, Inc, Montgomery, Ala, 61-63, div. mgr, Pensacola, Fla, 63-64; regional mgr, Mutual Funds of Am, Inc, 64-65; v.pres. Dixie region, Planned Security Consult, Inc, 65- Mil. Serv: Entered as Pvt, Army Air Corps, 40, released as Maj, Air Force, 61, after serv. at Air Univ, Maxwell Air Force Base, Ala; Air, Am. Defense Serv. and Good Conduct Medals; Am. Theater Ribbon with Star; Pac. Theater Ribbon with Three Battle Stars; ETO Ribbon. Mem: Prfnl. mem, Am. Meteorol. Soc, 48-61; Kiwanis. Rel: Protestant. Mailing Add: 2233 Knoxville Ave, Pensacola, Fla. 32506.

GRANTHAM, ROY EMERY D
Okla. State Sen.
b. Fairfax, Okla, 1/26/07; s. Amos Dean Grantham and Flora Lillian McCarty G; m. 12/24/33 to Martha Elizabeth Young; c. Marcia Lea (Mrs. Moore) and Linda Roy (Mrs. McNew). Educ: Univ. Okla, A.B, 34, LL.B, 34; Ed.M, 38; Phi Delta Phi; Univ. Okla. Debate Team. Polit. & Govt. Pos: Co. attorney, Kay Co, Co, Okla, 41-42; Okla. State Sen, 50-, secy, State Sen. Dem. Caucus, 54, presiding officer, Okla. State Senate, sitting as Court of Impeachment, 65 and chmn, Cmt. on Committees and Rules, 65; del, all Dem. Convs, 62-; alternate del, Dem. Nat. Conv, 68. Bus. & Prof. Pos: Gen. practice of Law, 47- Mil. Serv: Entered as 1st Lt, Army, 42, released as Lt. Coll, 47, after serv. in 78th Div. and U.S. Army of Occupation, ETO, 45-47; Commendation Ribbon for Outstanding Serv. in Judge Adv. Sect. Hq, Berlin Command; Lt. Col, Army Res, 47- Publ: 'Introduction to Symposium on Commercial Code,' Okla. Law Review, 8/62. Mem: Kay Co. Bar Asn.(pres, 64); Okla. and Am. Bar Asns; Am. Legion; ROA; C. of C; Ponca City Lions Club (pres, 53-54). Rel: Christian Church N.Am. Legal Res: 325 S. 12th, Ponca City, Okla. 74601. Mailing Add: 313 N. Fourth, Ponca City, Okla. 74601.

GRASSLEY, CHARLES E. R
Iowa State Rep.
b. New Hartford, Iowa, 9/17/33; m. to Barbara Ann Spiecher; c. Lee, Wendy, Robin Lynn and Michelle Marie. Educ: State Col. of Iowa, B.A, 55, M.A, 56; Univ. of Iowa, work toward Ph.D. Polit. & Govt. Pos: Iowa State Rep. Bus. & Prof. Pos: Farmer; instr. polit. sci, Drake Commun. Col, 62. Mem: Farm Bur; State and Co. Hist. Socs; Pi Gamma Mu; Kappa Delta Pi; Mason; Eastern Star. Rel: Baptist. Legal Res: 305 Washington, New Hartford, Iowa 50660. Mailing Add: State Capitol, E. Tenth and Grand Ave, Des Moines, Iowa 50319. (1967)

GRASSO, ELLA TAMBUSSI D
Secy. of State, Conn.
b. Windsor Locks, Conn, 5/10/19; d. James Tambussi and Maria Oliva T; m. 8/31/42 to Dr. Thomas A. Grasso; c. Susane and James. Educ: Mt. Holyoke Col, B.A. magna cum laude, 40, M.A, 42; Phi Beta Kappa. Polit. & Govt. Pos: Asst. dir. of research, War Manpower Cmn. of Conn. World War II; Conn. State Rep, 53-57, mem, Educ, Pub. Personnel and Finance Cmts, Conn. State House of Rep, floor leader, 55; mem, Long Lane Farm Study Cmn. and Hwy. Finance Adv. Cmn; chmn, Dem. State Platform Cmt, 56-; Secy. of State, Conn, 59-; Cmnr. of Elec; del, Dem. Nat. Conv, 60, 64 & 68, mem, Platform Drafting Cmt, 60, co-chmn, Resolutions Cmt, 64 & 68; mem, Bd. of For. Scholarships, 61-66; chmn, Cmn. to Prepare for Constitutional Conv; del. and Dem. Floor Leader, Conn. State Constitutional Conv, 65; chmn, planning cmt, Gov. Cmn. on Status of Women; v.chmn. exec. cmt, Human Rights and Opportunities, 67; mem, bd. of dirs, Conn. Inst. for Blind; mem, Bd. of Educ. for Blind; mem, bd. of dirs, Proj. Cause, Off. Ment. Retardation, State Dept. Health. Publ: 'Canal Fever,' Hartford Courant, 5/69. Mem: Bd. of trustees, Conn. Col; Cent. Conn. Commun. Cultural, Civic and Charitable Corp; Conn. Educ. TV Corp; adv. bd, Hartford Chap, Am. Cmt. on Italian Migration; bd. of dirs, Windsor Locks Pub. Libr; bd, Austin Sch. and Cmt. of 100, Univ. of Hartford Libr; hon. mem, bd. of dirs, Urban League of Gr. Hartford; hon. trustee, Conn. Opera Asn; hon. chmn, Italian Flood Relief Cmt. of Conn. and Sicilian Earthquake Relief Cmt; gen. chmn, Conn. Children's Cystic Fibrosis Asn. of Conn; Loomis-Chaffee Challenge Fund Cmt; Cmt. of 1000 for St. Francis Hosp; dir, St. Mary's Cath. Youth Orgn; hon. chmn, Girl Scout Commun. Fund Drive; hon. chmn, Capitol Region Ment. Health Fund Drive, 69; Am. Asn. Univ. Women; Windsor Locks Cmt. of Symphony Soc. of Gr. Hartford; Mt. Holyoke Club of Hartford; Suffield League of Women Voters; Order of Sons of Italy in Am; Pilot Club; Regina Elena Soc; former mem, adv. bd, Serv. Bur. for Women's Orgn; past pres, Chaffee Sch. Alumnae Asn; Conn. Fedn. of Dem. Women's Clubs; Nat. Asn. of Secy. of State; assoc. mem, Int. Asn. Munic. Clerks. Amita Award; Cited at Second Annual Recognition Dinner of Cent. Conn. State Col. Chap, Kappa Delta Pi; Am. Heritage Award; Americanism Award, Conn. Valley Coun, B'nai B'rith; Citizenship Award, Bradley Field Kiwanis Club; Knight in the Order of Merit of the Italian Repub; Italian-Am. Gold Medal Award and Good Citizenship Award, Conn. Grand Lodge of the Order of Sons of Italy in Am; Leadership Award, Conn. Asn. for Retarded Children; Leadership Citation, Conn. Children's Cystic Fibrosis Asn; Humanitarian Award, Dramatic Order, Knights of Khorassan, 69; Woman of the Year Award, Bus. and Prfnl. Women's Club of Hartford; Silver Apple Award, Conn. Educ. Asn; Most Distinguished Serv. Citation, Am. Legion Auxiliary; Citation Award, Wilson Col. Club of Conn. Rel: Catholic; Elected mem. of church coun, St. Mary's Church, Windsor Locks. Legal Res: 13 Olive St, Windsor Locks, Conn. 06096. Mailing Add: State Capitol, Hartford, Conn. 06115.

GRATZ, H(OMER) TUCKER D
b. Louisville, Ky, 12/11/06; s. Hugh Turney Gratz and Ora Tucker G; m. to Julia Boyd; c. Barbara (Mrs. Parmlee) and Sherie (Mrs. Weiskittel). Educ: Greenville Col, 23-27; Nat. Training Sch. Scout Execs, grad, 28; Alpha Phi Omega. Polit. Pos: Party worker, Hawaii, 44-; former state v.chmn, Dem. nat. committeeman and treas, Dem. Party, 13 western states. Govt. Pos: Dir, Hawaii Field Office, U.S. Dept. Commerce, 64-; collector of customs, Honolulu, 50-52. Bus. & Prof. Pos: V.Pres, Windward Properties, 48-; pres, Pepsi Cola of Hawaii, 61-64; pres, Better Brands, Ltd. of Hawaii, 52-64. Mil. Serv: Navy, 37-; Commendation Ribbon; All Major Pac. Theater Campaign Ribbons; Capt, Naval Res, 56. Mem: Pres, Honolulu Rotary, 66-67; 1st v.pres, Navy League of Hawaii, 66; chmn, Pac. War Memorial Cmn, 49-; Pres. Coun, Aloha Boy Scouts, 63-66. Rel: Presbyterian. Mailing Add: Suite 202, 1022 Bethel St, Honolulu, Hawaii 96813. (1967)

GRAVEL, CAMILLE F, JR. D
b. Alexandria, La, 8/10/15; s. Camille F. Gravel, Sr. and Aline Delvaille G; m. 11/26/39 to Katherine David; c. Katherine A, Mary E.(Mrs. Richard B. Cappell), Martha L.(Mrs. Thomas A. Antoon, Jr.), Camille F, III, Grady D, Eunice H, Virginia M, Margaret L, Mark A. and Charles G. Educ: Univ. Notre Dame, 31-35; La. State Univ, 35-37; Catholic Univ. Am, 37-39; Kappa Sigma; Phi Delta Phi; winner Moot Court competition; mem, U.S. Capitol Police Force, 37-39. Polit. & Govt. Pos: Asst. dist. attorney, Rapides Parish, La, 42; attorney for Rapides Parish for Inheritance Tax Collector, 43-45; mem, Dem. State Cent. Cmt, La, 48-64; Presidential Elector, 52; Dem. Nat. Committeeman, La, 54-60; mem, exec. cmt, Dem. Nat. Cmt, 55-60; mem, Nat. Adv. Coun. of Dem. Party, 56-60; del, Dem. Nat. Conv, 56, 60 & 64, chmn, La. del, 56, chmn, Site Selection Cmt, co-chmn, Credentials Cmt. and mem, Arrangements Cmt, 60; co-chmn, La. Lawyers for Johnson-Humphrey campaign, 64; mem, Gov. Adv. Cmns. on Workmen's Compensation laws and Tax Laws, La, 64-65; mem, Nat. Citizens Cmt. for Commun. Rels, 64-68; mem, La. Adv. Cmt. on Civil Rights and Nat. Adv. Bd. on Commun. Rels, 65-67; mem, bd. dirs, La. Coun. on Human Rels, 65-68; spec. consult. on Medicare to Gov, La, 66-67. Bus. & Prof. Pos: Attorney-at-law; sr. partner, Gravel, Roy & Burnes; officer and dir, Payne-Gravel Corp, South. Ventures Corp. and MYCI Corp. Mem: La. and Am. Bar Asns; Alexandria Bar Asn, pres, 49-50; fel, Int. Acad. Trial Lawyers, bd. dirs, 60-; Law Sci. Acad; Int. Soc. Barristers; Am. Trial Lawyers Asn; assoc. ed, NACCA Law Jour; bd. dirs, Notre Dame Law Asn, 60-66, pres, 62-63; past exalted ruler, Elks, Alexandria Lodge 546; Alexandria-Pineville C. of C; Am. Legion; Pub. Affairs Research Coun; La. Civil Serv. League; bd. dirs, Cath. Charities and adv. bd, Cath. Young Orgn, Diocese of Alexandria; bd. advs, N.Cent. Cath. Register; nat. bd. gov, Cath. Univ. of Am. Alumni Asn. and pres, Alumni Chap. for Diocese of Alexandria; K. of C.(4°). Admitted to Fifth Circuit Court of Appeal, U.S. Dist. Courts of La. and all La. Coutrs; Invested Knight of St. Gregory by Pope Pius XII, 54; cited for Outstanding Achievements in Field of Politics by Cath. Univ. of Am, 62. Rel: Catholic. Legal Res: 3214 Carol Court, Alexandria, La. 71301. Mailing Add: 611 Murray St, Alexandria, La. 71301.

GRAVEL, MIKE ROBERT D
U.S. Sen, Alaska
b. Springfield, Mass, 5/13/30; s. Alphonse Gravel and Maria Bourassa G; m. 4/25/59 to Rita Jeannette Martin; c. Martin Anthony and Lynne Denise. Educ: Assumption Prep Sch, Worcester, Mass, 4 years; Assumption Col, Worcester, 1 year; Am. International Col, Springfield, 1 year; Columbia Univ, N.Y, 2 years. Polit. & Govt. Pos: Alaska State Rep, until 68, speaker, Alaska House Rep, 65-69; U.S. Sen, 69- Mil. Serv: Entered Army, 51, released as 1st Lt, 54. Legal Res: 468 Aurora Dr, Anchorage, Alaska 99503. Mailing Add: Senate Office Bldg, Washington, D.C. 20510.

GRAVEN, DAVID LAUREN DFL
Budget Dir, Minn. State Dem-Farmer-Labor Cent. Cmt.
b. Minneapolis, Minn, 7/22/29; s. Henry N. Graven and Helen T. Davis G; Educ: St. Olaf Col, B.A, 50; Univ. Minn. Law Sch, LL.B, 53; Phi Beta Kappa;

Order of Coif; Phi Delta Phi. Polit. & Govt. Pos: Asst. co. attorney, Freeborn Co, Minn, 57-62; uniform law cmnr, Minn, 58-61; del, Dem. Nat. Conv, 60, alternate del, 64 & 68; cand, U.S. House Rep, First Cong. Dist, 62; budget dir, Minn. Dem-Farmer-Labor Cent. Cmt, 63-65, 66-, policy adv. chmn, 65-66; mem, Gov. Human Rights Cmn, 65-67; secy, Minn. Judicial Coun, 65- Bus. & Prof. Pos: Attorney-at-law and partner, Olson & Graven, Albert Lea, Minn, 57-63; prof. law, Univ. Minn. Law Sch, 63- Mil. Serv: Entered as 1st Lt, Army, 54, released 57, after serv. in Claims Div, Judge Adv. Gen. Corps, Europe; Capt, Army Res. Publ: Minnesota Criminal Procedure, 2 Vols, Minn. Continuing Legal Educ, 68; 'The Minnesota Contract for Deed,' 5/65 and 'Pleading an Auto Defect Case,' 11/65, Minn. Continuing Legal Educ. Mem: Am. and Minn. Bar Asns; Am. Asn. Univ. Prof; Citizens League of Minn. and Hennepin Co. Rel: Lutheran. Mailing Add: 417 Tarrymore, Minneapolis, Minn. 55419.

GRAVES, CHARLES EDWARD D
Ga. State Rep.
b. Rome, Ga, 9/15/38; s. Rev. Yuell Emmett Graves and Alice Yarbrough G; m. 11/23/57 to Sara Brooks; c. Lisa Elaine, Tina Ann and Charles Terrell. Educ: Rome Center, Univ. Ga, 58-60; Shorter Col, 61-63. Polit. & Govt. Pos: Aide to U.S. Rep. John Davis, Ga, 63-65; Ga. State Rep, Post 2, 67- Bus. & Prof. Pos: Staff reporter, Rome News-Tribune, Ga, 57-63, city ed, 67-; pub. affairs dir, Radio Sta. WROM AM-FM, 65-67. Mil. Serv: Marines Res, 57-63. Mem: Breakfast Optimist Club, Rome; Floyd Co. Dem. Asn; Floyd Co. Young Dem. Asn. Numerous awards for newspaper and radio reporting plus com mun. serv. awards. Rel: Baptist. Mailing Add: 209 Billy Pyle Rd, Rome, Ga. 30161.

GRAVES, CURTIS MATTHEW D
Tex. State Rep.
b. New Orleans, La, 8/26/38; s. Joseph F. Graves and Mable Haydel G; single. Educ: Tex. Southern Univ, B.B.A, 63; Kappa Alpha Psi; Knights of St. Peter Claver. Polit. & Govt. Pos: Tex. State Rep, 67- del, Dem. Nat. Conv, 68. Bus. & Prof. Pos: Mgr, Standard Savings Asn, 64-66; Pub. rels. consult, currently. Mil. Serv: Entered as Pvt, Army, 63, released as Pfc, 64; Spec 4, Army Res. Rel: Catholic. Legal Res: 5417 Troost St. 1, Houston, Tex. 77020. Mailing Add: 4101½ Lyons Ave, Houston, Tex. 77020. (1967)

GRAVES, FRANCIS XAVIER D
s. Frank X. Graves; m. to Ethel; c. Carol, Linda and Nancy. Educ: Paterson State Teacher's Col; Univ. Va. Polit. & Govt. Pos: Alderman, Patterson, N.J, Mayor, 63-66; freeholder, Passaic Co, N.J; dir, Civil Defense. Mil. Serv: Army, 42-45; Purple Heart. Outstanding Young Man of the Year Award, Jaycees. Rel: Catholic. Legal Res: 454 E. 42nd St, Paterson, N.J. 07504. Mailing Add: City Hall, 155 Market St, Paterson, N.J. 07505.

GRAVES, G. EUGENE R
b. Gossett, Ill, 10/18/14; s. Charles Alexander Graves and Minnie Jane Bruce G; m. 6/29/46 to Catherine Lucille Sturgill; c. Carolyn Jean (Mrs. Keebler). Educ: High Sch, 4 years. Polit. & Govt. Pos: Rep. Precinct committeeman, Ill, 40-42, 50-; chmn, East St. Louis Rep. Cmt, 52-66; asst. supvr, St. Clair Co. Bd. of Supvrs, 53-; chmn, St. Clair Co. Rep. Cmt, 66-68. Mil. Serv: Entered as Pvt, Army, 43, released as T/Sgt, 46; after serv. in Second Mil. Rwy. Serv, ETO, 43-46; Normandy and Rhineland Ribbons with Three Battle Stars; Bronze Star; Three Overseas Bars; Good Conduct and Victory Medals; Mid. East-African-European Theater Ribbon with Three Bronze Battle Stars. Mem: BRT (past pres, Lodge 1086); Parimutuel Clerk 253A; AF&AM; Low Twelve Club; High Twelve Club; Terminal R.R. Compass Club; Terminal R.R. Employees Club; East St. Louis Exchange Club. Rel: Protestant. Mailing Add: 640 N. 61st St, East St. Louis, Ill. 62203.

GRAVES, HAZEL CAROLINE R
Chmn, Marblehead Rep. Town Cmt, Mass.
b. Cambridge, Mass, 3/1/02; d. John Axel Ohman and Annie Marie Black O; m. 12/2/23 to Emerson Arthur Graves; c. Jacqueline Mae (Mrs. Williams), Emerson Arthur, Jr. and Fred Lawrence, II. Educ: Lynn Burdett Col, 21-22. Polit. & Govt. Pos: Corresponding secy, Women's Rep. Club Essex Co, Mass, 54, fourth v.pres, 56, third v.pres, 58, second v.pres, 60, first v.pres, 62, pres, 64; legis. chmn, Marblehead Women's Club, 62-68; co-chmn, Bill Bates for Cong. Cmt. Marblehead, 63; mem, Marblehead Rep. Town Cmt, 64-, chmn, 68-; clerk, Clerk of Court's Off, Dist. Court. South. Essex; del, Mass. Rep. State Conv. Mem: Marblehead Women's Club; Eastern Star; Marblehead Hosp. Asn; St. Catherine's Guild (pres, thrift shop, 54-); Abbot Hall Assocs; Marblehead Vis. Nurse Asn; Mass. Women's Rep. Orgn. Rel: Episcopal; Vestry, St. Michael's Church. Mailing Add: 36 Evans Rd, Marblehead, Mass. 01945.

GRAVES, JAMES THOMAS R
Mem, Kans. State Rep. Cent. Cmt.
b. Salina, Kans, 11/14/34; s. Dwight Lyman Graves and Rita Lavonne Carlin G; m. 8/19/57 to Karen Larsen Milner; c. Leslie Ann, Sarah Carlin and Amy Katheryn. Educ: Kans. State Univ, B.S. Polit. Sci. & B.S. Bus. Admin, with honors, 57; Univ. Kans, J.D, with distinction, 60; Phi Kappa Phi; Order of Coif; Sigma Alpha Epsilon; Phi Delta Phi. Polit. & Govt. Pos: Chmn, Saline Co. Young Rep, Kans, 64-66; chmn, Cent. Kans, Avery for Gov. Cmt, 65-66; chmn, Saline Co. Rep. Cent. Cmt, Kans, 66-; mem, Kans. State Rep. Cent. Cmt, 66-; mem, Citizens Urban Renewal Adv. Cmt, 67-68. Bus. & Prof. Pos: Asst. instr. west. civilization, Univ. Kans, 58-60; and assoc. ed, Univ. Kans. Law Rev, 59-60; assoc, Morrison, Hecker, Buck and Cozad, Mo, 60-61; assoc, Clark, Mize and Lillard, Kans, 61-64 and partner, 64-; dir. and exec. secy, Graves Truck Line, Inc, 62-; dir, Nat. Bank Am. Salina, Kans, 67- Mil. Serv: 2nd Lt, Army Res, 61, serv. in 48th Transportation Croup, Ft. Eustis, Va; Distinguished Mil. Grad. of ROTC; Unit Comdr. Letter of Commendation. Mem: Am. Judicature Soc; Saline Co. Bar Asn.(pres, 66); Kans. and Am. Bar Asns; dir, Salina C. of C, 67-; dir, Salina Retail Credit Bur, 63-66 and chmn, 66; dir, Salina YMCA, 66-68; lay adv, St. John's Hosp, Salina, 66-68; dir, Salina Americanization Center, 65-66; dir, Salina Civic Orchestra, 64-65; trustee, Salina Co. Law Libr, 61-68. Outstanding Civic Serv. Award, Salina Jr. C. of C, 66. Rel: Presbyterian; chmn, bd. trustees, First Presbyterian Church, Salina. Legal Res: 740 Highland Ave, Salina, Kans, 67401. Mailing Add: Box 1343, Salina, Kans. 67401.

GRAVES, JAMES WILSON D
S.C. State Rep.
b. Okatee, S.C, 10/11/15; s. Williams Capers Graves and Daisy Louise Skinner G; m. 4/6/36 to Sadie Elizabeth Preacner. Educ: Bluffton High Sch, 36. Polit. & Govt. Pos: Chmn. bd. of trustees, Bluffton High Sch, S.C, 50-62; S.C. State Rep, 51-58 & 63- Bus. & Prof. Pos: Pres, Hilton Head Real Estate Co; Construction and Ins. Pepper-Hall Plantation. Mailing Add: Bluffton Star Route, Bluffton, S.C. 29910. (1967)

GRAVES, JOHN Independent
State Comptroller, Ala.
b. Jackson, Tenn, 5/28/07; s. Henry Norman Graves and Ann Smith G; m. 12/26/36 to Meredith Louise Seawell; c. Lucy Meredith and Louise Lynne (Mrs. Hammond). Educ: Univ. Ala, Montgomery Center. Polit. & Govt. Pos: Acct, Ala. State Serv, 25-32, prin. acct, 32-42 and asst. budget officer, 42-45; State Comptroller, 45-; mem, Coun. State Govt. Cmt. Automation, Tech. and Data Process, 64-66; mem, Gov. Resources Mgt. Cmt, Off. of Emergency Planning, 64-66; gen. chmn, Tenth and 11th Annual Data Processing Conf, Univ. Ala, 65-66. Bus. & Prof. Pos: Treas, Ala. State Employees Asn, 50-53; dir, Security Fed. Savings and Loan Asn, 61- Mil. Serv: Entered as Sgt, Ala. State Militia, 39, released as Lt. Col, Med. Corps, 50. Mem: Nat. Asn. State Auditors, Comptrollers & Treas.(past pres); Int. Data Processing Mgt. Asn.(int. dir); Nat. Soc. Pub. Accts; Munic. Finance Officers Asn; Fed. Govt. Accts. Asn; Nat. Asn. Accts; Kiwanis (past pres, Montgomery Chap); Montgomery Country Club; Beauvoir Club; Mason; Blue-Gray Cols; Mardi Gras Asn; Mystic Soc. Rel: Episcopal. Mailing Add: 2097 Myrtlewood Dr, Montgomery, Ala. 36111. (1967)

GRAVES, MARGUERITE EVERETT D
b. New Orleans, La, 1/11/09; d. Maurice Micheal Glapion and Anita Young G; m. 11/4/52 to Charles C. Graves; c. Geraldine E. (Mrs. Warrick), Monica E. (Mrs. Crowe), John E, Maurice M. and Marguerite C. (Mrs. Werts). Educ: Straight Col, 1 year. Polit. & Govt. Pos: Precinct committeeman, Dem. Party, 46-; 1st v.chairlady, Gary Dem. Party, 62-66. Bus. & Prof. Pos: Tel. operator, City Hall, Gary, Ind. Mem: NAACP; Urban League; Elks; Eastern Star; Court of Calanthe. Rel: African Methodist Church. Mailing Add: City Hall, 401 Broadway, Gary, Ind. 46402. (1967)

GRAVES, PARKER R
Chmn, Crawford Co. Rep. Cent. Cmt, Ill.
b. Champaign, Ill, 3/8/21; s. Perry H. Graves, Sr. (mother deceased); m. 2/15/44 to Betty Beryington Benjamin; c. John, David and Clifford. Educ: Ind. Univ, B.S, 42; Alpha Tau Omega. Polit. & Govt. Pos: Chmn, Crawford Co. Rep. Cent, Cmt, Ill, 62-; chmn, 55th Sen. Co. Cmt, 66- Mil. Serv: Entered as Officer candidate, Navy, 43, released as Lt.(jg), 45. Mem: Dir, exec. cmt, Ind. Univ. Alumni Asn, 65-; dir, Ill. Lumber and Material Dealers Asn, 58-64; lt. gov, Div. 13, Ill-E.Iowa Dist, Kiwanis, 58; dir, Ill. Fuel Merchants Asn, 54-56; Elks; Am. Legion. Rel: Methodist. Legal Res: 301 N. Allen St, Robinson, Ill. 62454. Mailing Add: Box 242, Robinson, Ill. 62454.

GRAVES, RALPH WAYNE D
Okla. State Sen.
b. Elmore City, Okla, 5/28/19; s. Luther Homer Graves and Wing Park G; m. 9/14/42 to Betty Collum; c. Barbi and Russ. Educ: Okla. Baptist Univ, B.A, 50. Polit. & Govt. Pos: City cmnr, Shawnee, Okla, 48-50, mayor, 50-54; Okla. State Rep, 54-60; Okla. State Sen, 60- Bus. & Prof. Pos:Owner and mgr, Ralph Graves Ins. Agency, 46. Mil. Serv: Entered as Pvt, Army, 42, released as S/Sgt, 46, after serv. in 96th Inf, Pac; Purple Heart; Bronze Star. Mem: Am. Legion; VFW; DAV; Elks; Okla. Baptist Univ. Alumni. Rel: Baptist. Legal Res: 716 W. Dewey, Shawnee, Okla. Mailing Add: 601 American Bldg, Shawnee, Okla. 74801.

GRAW, JOSEPH P.
Minn. State Rep.
b. Knoxville, Iowa, 1915; married; c. Three. Educ: Northwest. Univ; Chicago Tech. Polit. & Govt. Pos: Minn. State Rep, 62- Bus. & Prof. Pos: Ins. exec. Mil. Serv: Capt, Army, 41-45, Pac. Theatre. Mailing Add: 10730 Access Rd, W. Bloomington Freeway, Bloomington, Minn. 55431.

GRAY, ALEXANDER HARBERT D
Chmn. Haywood Co. Dem. Exec. Cmt, Tenn.
b. Brownsville, Tenn, 9/3/96; s. John Turner Gray and Ora Battle G; m. 7/4/42 to Vara Verner Rietz; c. Estelle Johnston and Marilyn Edwards. Educ: Southwest. Univ; Wash. and Lee Univ; Cumberland Univ; Alpha Tau Omega. Polit. & Govt. Pos: Tenn. State Sen, 29-30 & 49-60; chmn, Haywood Co. Dem. Exec. Cmt, Tenn, currently. Mil. Serv: Entered as Pvt, 73rd Artil, Coast Artil. Corps, 18, released as Cpl, 19. Mem: Am. and Tenn. Bar Asns; Am. Legion; VFW; Rotary; Farm Bur. Rel: Presbyterian. Mailing Add: Box 64, Brownsville, Tenn. 38012.

GRAY, BETTY JUNE D
V.chmn, Custer Co. Dem. Cent. Cmt, Colo.
b. Maple Park, Ill, 6/25/30; d. Oscar Friedlund and Julia Olson F; m. 7/10/48 to Alden Henry Gray; c. Julie Francine and Loel Loyd. Polit. & Govt. Pos: V.chmn, Custer Co. Dem. Cent. Cmt, Colo, 68- Mem: Beta Sigma Phi; Eastern Star (Past Matron's Club, Florence Chap); Fremont Co. Exten. Homemakers Club. Rel: Christian. Mailing Add: P.O. Box 11, Wetmore, Colo. 81253.

GRAY, CARRIE J. R
b. Derby, Vt, 7/5/91; m. to Carl E. Gray; c. 5 daughters. Educ: Johnson Normal Sch. Polit. & Govt. Pos: Sch. dir, Derby Line, Vt, justice of the peace, Vt. State Rep, 51-53, 55-63 & 65-68. Bus. & Prof. Pos: Retired teacher. Mem: M.E. Ladies Aid; Home Demonstration Club. Rel: Methodist. Mailing Add: Derby Line, Vt. 05830. (1967)

GRAY, CHARLES F. D
b. Rochester, Mich, 6/29/32; married; c. Charles Earl, Bruce Edward. Educ: Cleary Col; East. Mich. Univ; Detroit Col. of Law. Polit. & Govt. Pos: Mich. State Rep, 64-66. Bus. & Prof. Pos: Former Ypsilanti twp. clerk. Mil.

Serv: Army Med. Corps, 53-55, Panama Canal Zone. Mem: K. of P; Moose; Jr. C. of C. Rel: Methodist. Mailing Add: 1554 Wismer St, Ypsilanti, Mich. 48197. (1967)

GRAY, FREDERICK THOMAS D
Va. State Del.
b. Petersburg, Va, 10/10/18; m. to Evelyn Helms Johnson. Educ: Univ. of Richmond, B.A, LL.B; Phi Beta Kappa. Polit. & Govt. Pos: Mem, South. Bd. of Regional Educ; mem, Va. Constitutional Conv, 56; mem, Va. Cmn. on Constitutional Gov; attorney gen, Va, 61-62; Va. State Del, 66-; mem, Va. Code Cmn, 68- Bus. & Prof. Pos: Attorney-at-law. Mil. Serv: Army Air Force, 1st Lt, Navigator. Mem: Chesterfield Colonial Heights, Richmond and Va. State Bar Asns; past pres, Lions; Meadowbrook Country Club; past pres, Jordan Point Country Club; bd. of trustees, Randolph-Macon Col. Rel: Methodist. Mailing Add: 510 State-Planters Bank Bldg, Richmond, Va. 23219.

GRAY, GARLAND D
Va. State Sen.
b. Gray, Va, 11/28/01; s. Elmon L. Gray and Ella Darden G; m. to Frances Bage; c. Elmon T, Agnes E. (Mrs. Duff), Florence G. (Mrs. Tullidge), Mary G. (Mrs. Stettinius) and Mary Frances. Educ: Univ. Richmond, B.A; Wash. and Lee Univ, M.A; Omicron Delta Kappa. Polit. & Govt. Pos: Chmn, State Port Authority; mem, Co. Sch. Bd; chmn, Fourth Dist. Dem. Cmt; Va. State Sen, currently. Bus. & Prof. Pos: Chmn. bd, Gray Prods. Co; pres, Bank of Waverly, Va; mem. bd. First and Merchants Bank, Richmond, Va. Mem: Ruritan Nat.(past nat. pres); Rotary; Commonwealth Club of Richmond; Downtown Club-Richmond. Rel: Congregational. Mailing Add: Waverly, Va. 23890. (1967)

GRAY, GEORGE EDWARD R
Del. State Rep.
b. Selbyville, Del, 1/3/22; s. Everett Mitchel Gray and Annie Grise G; m. 4/11/42 to Anna Lee Long; c. Carolyn Lee, Ronald Everett and Annette Lisa. Educ: Selbyville High Sch, Del. Polit. & Govt. Pos: Del. State Rep, 67- Mem: Delmarva Poultry Indust; Mason; Shrine; Tall Cedar; Elks; pres, Little League. Rel: Methodist. Mailing Add: Selbyville, Del. 19975.

GRAY, JACK KENNETH D
b. Amite, La, 7/29/46; s. Henry Weston Gray and Norma Lanier G; m. 6/22/69 to Pamela Kathylne Hammond. Educ: Southeast. La. Col, B.A, 68; Nicholls State Col, 68-69, cand. M.B.A, 70; Delta Sigma Pi; student body pres, 67-68. Polit. & Govt. Pos: V.pres, Tangipahoa Parish Young Dem, La, 66-68; polit. research dir, Southeast. Research Inst, 67-68; pub. rels. dir. for Congressman Patrick Caffery, 63rd Dist, 69- Publ: 'Business & Interest Rates: The Louisiana Study,' Atlanta Econ. Rev, 9/69. Mem: Cong. Secretaries Club; Jaycees of Am; Jaycees. Rel: Church of Christ. Legal Res: P.O. Box 583, 302 Cedar St, Amite, La. 70422. Mailing Add: P.O. Box 2222, Thibodaux, La. 70301.

GRAY, JAMES H. D
Chmn, Ga. Dem. State Exec. Cmt.
b. Westfield, Mass; married; c. James H, Jr, Geoffrey and Constance. Educ: Dartmouth Col; Univ. Heidelberg; Phi Beta Kappa. Polit. & Govt. Pos: Temporary chmn. and keynote speaker, Ga. Dem. Conv, 58; chmn, Ga. Dem. Exec. Cmt, 60; delivered South. minority report to nation-wide TV audience, Dem. Nat. Conv, 60; chmn, Ga. Dem. State Exec. Cmt, 62-; Dem. Cand. Gov, 66. Bus. & Prof. Pos: Ed. and feature writer, Courant and New York Herald Tribune, Hartford, Conn; owner, Albany Herald, 46-; chmn. bd. and pres, Gray Commun. Systs. Inc. Mil. Serv: Entered as 2nd Lt, Army, 42, released as Maj, 46, after serv. in Sicily and Europe. Mem: Rotarian; C. of C.(pres). Citizens of the Year, Co. Cmnrs. Asn. Ga, 59. Rel: Episcopal; Vestryman. Legal Res: Albany, Ga. Mailing Add: 2501 Bank of Georgia Bldg, Atlanta, Ga. 30303.

GRAY, JO ANNE HASTINGS R
Rep. Nat. Committeewoman, Colo.
b. Birmingham, Ala, 12/1/21; d. Littleberry Byrd Haley and Virginia Irene Jenkins Haley Hastings; m. 4/29/46 to Daniel Gray; c. Daniel Allen and Robert Byrd. Educ: Univ. Colo, B.A, 43; Univ. Denver, grad. study, summer, 43; rush chmn, Delta Gamma. Polit. & Govt. Pos: Precinct committeewoman, Rep. Party, Colo, 60-; clerk, Colo. State Senate, 63-65; mem, Rep. Roundtable, Rep. Women's Club, 63-, pub. rels. chmn, 65-; state co-chmn, Goldwater Campaign, 64; Co. Rep. Training Chmn, City and Co. of Denver, 65-; Schauer campaign, 66; chmn, Reservations and Housing, Rep. West. Conf, 67; Rep. Nat. Committeewoman, Colo, 68- Bus. & Prof. Pos: Stewardess, Continental Airlines, 43-46, asst. chief stewardess and dir. stewardess training, 46; teacher stewardess training, Denver Univ, 47. Mem: Univ. Colo. Alumni Asn. (pres, 59 and bd. dirs, 58-60); Univ. Colo. Develop. Found. (bd. dirs, 61-63); behind scenes coordinator, Bus. & Indust. Polit. Action Cmt; Planned Parenthood of Colo. (info. and educ. chmn, 66 and bd. dirs, 64-66); Delta Gamma Alumnae (S.E. area recommendations chmn. and past pres); discussion leader, Great Books; leader, Jr. Great Books; legis. chmn, PTA. Inaugurated first Univ. Colo. Alumni Inst. Rel: Presbyterian. Mailing Add: 2850 E. Flora Place, Denver, Colo. 80210.

GRAY, JOHN DAVID D
Va. State Del.
b. Newport News, Va, 6/8/28; m. to Nancy Louise McMillan G. Educ: Univ. Va, B.S, LL.B. Polit. & Govt. Pos: City attorney, Hampton, 54-63; past chmn, Hampton Dem. Cmt; Va. State Del, 66- Bus. & Prof. Pos: Lawyer. Mil. Serv: Army. Mem: Mason; Shrine; Elks; Va. State Bar Asn. Rel: Methodist. Legal Res: 501 Harbor Dr, Hampton, Va. 23361. Mailing Add: Citizens and Marine Bank Bldg, Hampton, Va. 23369.

GRAY, JOHN NICHOLAS R
Chmn, Mo. Fedn. Young Rep.
b. Maryville, Mo, 7/2/33; s. John Borland Gray and Eunice Cox G; single. Educ: Northwest Mo. State Col, summer 53; Univ. Mo, B.S, 56; Delta Chi. Polit. & Govt. Pos: Chmn, Nodaway Co. Young Rep, Mo, 58-62; secy, Mo. Fedn. Young Rep, 59-62, mem. bd, 66-68 and chmn, 69-; committeeman, Polk Twp. Rep. Party, 66-; chmn, Nodaway Co. Rep. Cent. Cmt, 66-; v.pres, Mo. Asn. Rep, Sixth Dist, 69- Bus. & Prof. Pos: Salesman, Henry Bernhart & Co, Kansas City, Mo, 58-61; prin, J. Nick Gray and Assocs. Mfg. Rep, Maryville, 61- Mil. Serv: Entered as Pvt, Army, 56, released as Sp-3, 58, after serv. in Specialist Sch. Command, Ft. Chaffee, Ark, 56-58. Mem: Asn. Midwest Gift Orgn; United Commercial Travelers. Rel: Presbyterian. Mailing Add: 320 W. Cooper, Maryville, Mo. 64468.

GRAY, KENNETH ELWOOD D
b. Saginaw, Mich, 11/9/31; s. Carl Jennings Gray and Grace Lockwood G; m. 9/10/60 to Patricia Neal; c. Jefferson Morton and Douglas Humphrey. Educ: West. Mich. Univ, A.B, 53; Univ. Chicago, 55-61. Polit. & Govt. Pos: Legis. asst. to U.S. Sen. Paul H. Douglas, Ill, 61-65; prfnl. staff mem, Cmt. on Banking and Currency, U.S. Senate, Wash, D.C, 65-66; legis. asst. to Vice President Hubert H. Humphrey, 66-67; admin. asst. to U.S. Sen. Joseph D. Tydings, Md, 67- Mil. Serv: Entered as Pvt, Army, 53, released as Pfc, 55, after serv. in Hq, N.J. Mil. Dist, 54-55. Mailing Add: 7904 Park Overlook Dr, Bethesda, Md. 20034.

GRAY, KENNETH J. D
U.S. Rep, Ill.
b. West Frankfort, Ill, 11/14/24; m. 1943 to June Croslin; c. Diann. Educ: West Frankfort Commun. High Sch; Army Adv. Sch. during World War II. Polit. & Govt. Pos: U.S. Rep, Ill, 54- del, Dem. Nat. Conv, 68. Bus. & Prof. Pos: Auto bus; air serv, Benton, Ill, 6 years; licensed pilot; licensed auctioneer. Mil. Serv: Army, Air Forces World War II, overseas, Italy, N. Africa, Corsica and S. France. Mem: Am. Legion; 40 et 8; VFW; Kiwanis; Elks; Eagles; Past Comdrs. Club of Am. Legion; Ill. C. of C.(former state vice pres); founder, Walking Dog Found. for Blind. Rel: Baptist. Legal Res: 1603 E. Main St, West Frankfort, Ill. 62896. Mailing Add: U.S. House of Representatives, Washington, D.C. 20515. (1967)

GRAY, MARCUS J. D
Chmn, Third Cong. Dist. Dem. Party, Mich.
b. Kansas City, Mo, 9/22/36; s. Marcus O. Gray and Christina Kaigler G; m. 11/21/59 to Abbey Lynette Dowdy; c. Marcus III and Sean. Educ: Kellogg Commun. Col, currently. Polit. & Govt. Pos: Co. chmn, Young Dem, 59-60; mem, Dem. Exec. Cmt, 59-69; dir, Dem. Youth. Activities, 61-64; co. clerk, Calhoun Co, Mich, 64-; dir, Dem. Party Orgn, 66-68; chmn, co. Dem. campaign, 68; chmn, Third Cong. Dist. Dem. Party, 69- Bus. & Prof. Pos: Secy, Battle Creek Bus. & Prfnl. Men's Club, Mich, 69. Mil. Serv: Entered as E-1, Air Force 55, released as A/2C, after serv. in Strategic and Tactical Air Commands, Pac. Air Command; Good Conduct Medal; Airman of the Month. Mem: Nat. and United Co. Off. Asns; Mich. Co. Clerks' Asn; F&AM; Battle Creek Urban League (pres). Les Bon Amie Club Award for Outstanding Commun. Serv; Cert. of Merit, Mich. Dem. Party and Cert. of Merit, Dem. Women's Club for Outstanding Work in the Party. Rel: Protestant. Legal Res: 234 Parkway Dr, Battle Creek, Mich. 49017. Mailing Add: 315 W. Green St, County Bldg, Marshall, Mich. 49068.

GRAY, OREN LEE R
Kans. State Rep.
b. Parsons, Kans, 2/17/10; s. Orville Lester Gray and Grace Lorene Thompson G; m. 3/12/32 to Jean Mercedes McGuire; c. Jené Lee, Oren Lee, Jr. and Oené LaRee. Educ: Parsons Jr. Col; Parsons Bus. Univ; Kans. Univ, law. Polit. & Govt. Pos: Dep. clerk, Dist. Court, Labette Co, Kans, 37-41, clerk, 41-45, probate judge, 45-49, attorney, 51-55 & 61-65; Kans. State Rep, 24th Dist, 65-66, Sixth Dist, 67- Bus. & Prof. Pos: Lawyer, 48- Mem: Am. Trial Lawyers Asn.(serv. on the task force of Kans); Kans. State Trial Lawyers Asn.(serv. on bd. of gov); Kans. Peace Officers Asn; Kans. Bar Asn; Elks. Legal Res: 220 N. 31st St, Parsons, Kans. 67357. Mailing Add: 110 S. Central, Parsons, Kans. 67357.

GRAY, THEODORE MILTON R
Ohio State Sen.
b. Springfield, Ohio, 9/3/27; s. Theodore Milton Gray, Sr. and Dorothy Whittington G; m. 2/23/51; c. Scarlett Ann Lewis and Thackery Scott, Timothy Milton and Nathan Theodore Gray. Educ: Wabash Col, fall, 45; Ohio State Univ, B.A, 50. Polit. & Govt. Pos: Ohio State Sen, 11th & 12th dist, 51-; exec. secy, Ohio League Young Rep, 54-55; precinct committeeman, Miami Co. Rep. Party, 56-; pres. pro tem, Ohio Senate, 65-; co-chmn, Bi-Partisan Cmt. Reapportionment, 67; co-chmn, $750 Million bond issue, 68 and homestead exemption, 68; coordinator, Ohio United Citizens for Nixon, 68; del, Rep. Nat. Conv, 68. Bus. & Prof. Pos: Owner-operator, Gray Ins. Agency, 51-; pres, Howe-Simpson Co, 61-; pres, Fairview Mem. Park, 62- Mil. Serv: Entered as Seaman, Navy, 45-46, serving in Fifth Fleet, S.Pac, 46. Mem: Exec. cmt, Nat. Legis. Conf; Am. Legion. Jaycee's State and Local Distinguished Serv; Award, 60, Governor's Award for the Adv. of the Prestige of Ohio, 69. Rel: Presbyterian. Legal Res: 1108 Maplewood, Piqua, Ohio 45356. Mailing Add: Capitol Bldg, Columbus, Ohio 43216.

GRAYBILL, LEO CARLISLE D
b. Shelbyville, Ill, 7/23/94; s.George Roland Graybill and Henrietta May Laughlin G; m. 7/29/22 to Atta H. Hutchinson; c. Leo, Jr. and Helen Gene (Mrs. C.J. Millhouse). Educ: Millikin Univ, A.B, 16; Univ. Chicago, J.D, 20; Tau Kappa Epsilon. Polit. & Govt. Pos: Mont. State Rep, 43-55, Speaker of the House, Mont. House of Rep, 49 & 55; Dem. nominee, U.S. Rep, Mont, 45; Dem. nat. committeeman, 50-60; city attorney, Belt; city attorney, Great Falls; mem. adv. coun, Nat. Dem. Cmt, 55-60; del, Dem. Nat. Conv, 68. Bus. & Prof. Pos: Pres, Belt Valley Bank, 46- Mil. Serv: Entered as Pvt, Army Inf, 17, released as 2nd Lt, 18, after serv. in 163rd Inf. Mem: State of Mont. and Am. Bar Asns; Cascade Co. Bar Asn.(pres); Lions Int.(past dist. gov. and past int. dir); Mason; Shrine. Rel: Presbyterian. Mailing Add: 609 Third Ave. N, Great Falls, Mont. 59401.

GRAYS, LEWIS JAMES R
b. Plainfield, N.J, 9/5/07; s. James Grays and Elizabeth G; m. to Ruth Russell; c. Elizabeth Ann and Charles Alden. Educ: N.Y. Univ, 2 years. Polit. & Govt. Pos: Councilman, Borough of Watchung, N.J, 47-50, mayor, 50-61; mem, Middlesex Co. Sewer Authority, 52-55; pres, State League of Munic, 62-; chmn, Somerset Co. Rep. Cmt, until 68. Bus. & Prof. Pos: Mem, Somerset Co. Tax Bd, 49-; dir, Somerset Trust Co; exec. v.pres, Raritan Valley Hosp, Greenbrook, N.J. Mem: Elks; Mason; Eagles; Shrine;

N.J. Florists Asn; Nat. Orgn. of Assessors; N.J. Bankers Asn; Rotary N.J. Asn. Tax Bd. Cmnrs; Raritan Valley Country Club; Twin Brooks Golf Club. Mailing Add: 760 Johnston Dr, Watchung, N.J. 07060. (1967)

GREASER, WILLIE O. D
b. 1920. Polit. & Govt. Pos: N.Mex. State Rep, 59-68. Bus. & Prof. Pos: R.R. switchman. Mem: Boy Scouts; Little League; Girl Scouts; Brotherhood of R.R. Trainmen. Rel: Baptist. 1967 Legal Res: Tucumcari, N.Mex. No mailing address available. (1967)

GRECCO, JOSEPH D
b. 1915. Educ: Upsala Col, B.A; Montclair State Col, M.A. Polit. & Govt. Pos: Former N.J. State Assemblyman; councilman. Bus. & Prof. Pos: Teacher-prin, Sch. 13, Clifton; coach, Clifton football teams with three state championships, 45-64. Mem: Elks; Moose; K. of C; UNICO; Holy Name Soc. 1967 Legal Res: Trenton, N.J. No mailing address available. (1967)

GRECO, ANGELO F. D
b. Milwaukee, Wis, 3/19/25. Educ: Lawrence Col, B.A, 50; Marquette Univ, 1 year; Univ. of Wis. Law Sch, LL.B, 55; Delta Tau Delta. Polit. & Govt. Pos: Wis. State Assemblyman, 60-66; Majority caucus chmn; Gov. Cmt. on Loans and Scholarships, 65. Bus. & Prof. Pos: Practicing attorney, 55- Mil. Serv: Army Med. Corps, 3 years in China, Burma, India. Mem: DAV and China, Burma, India Vets; Elks; State and local bar asns; Shorewood Players; Holy Name Soc; pres, Holy Rosary Home and Sch. Asn. Mailing Add: 2021 E. Newberry Blvd, Milwaukee, Wis. 53211. (1967)

GRECO, MICHAEL JOHN D
b. N.Y.C, 5/22/29; s. Michael Greco and Florence Carlucci G; m. 7/15/58 to Joan Elizabeth Carroll; c. John, Michele, Carol Ann, Mary and Michael John, Jr. Educ: Iona Col, B.A, 51; N.Y. Law Sch, LL.B, 53. Polit. & Govt. Pos: Alternate del, N.Y. State Dem. Conv, 60; del-at-lg, Dem. Nat. Conv, 64; del, Judicial Conv, First Dept, 64 & 65. Bus. & Prof. Pos: Asst. Corp. Counsel, New York City, 55-59. Mil. Serv: Pvt, Army, 53-55. Mem: New York Co. and Bronx Co. Bar Asns; Progressive Era Asn. Rel: Catholic. Legal Res: 1515 Jarvis Ave, New York, N.Y. 10461. Mailing Add: 233 Broadway, New York, N.Y. 10007.

GRECO, STEPHEN R. D
N.Y. State Assemblyman
b. Buffalo, N.Y, 12/2/19; m. to Anne L. Cherre; c. three sons. Educ: Lafayette High Sch, Buffalo. Polit. & Govt. Pos: Judge, N.Y. State Athletic Cmn; mem, Erie Co. Bd. of Supvrs, 57; N.Y. State Assemblyman, 58- Bus. & Prof. Pos: Food broker, Joseph Greco & Sons. Mem: Del, Fedn. of Italian & Am. Socs; K. of C; West Side Rowing Club of Buffalo; West Side Businessmen's Asn; Forest Dist. Civic Asn; Romukes Club; Eagles; Nat. Narcotic Enforcement Officers Asn; Elmwood Businessmen's Asn; Holy Name Soc. of Nativity B.V.M; Elks; Nat. Cong. of PTA. Mailing Add: 795 Richmond Ave, Buffalo, N.Y. 14222. (1967)

GREELEY, STEPHEN ALONZO R
N.H. State Rep.
b. Franklin, N.H, 4/8/01; s. Loren B. Greeley and Clara Stevens G; single. Polit. & Govt. Pos: Chmn, Merrimack Co. Rep. Cent. Cmt. and Franklin Rep. Club, N.H; N.H. State Rep, currently. Mem: Nat, N.H, Merrimack Pomma and Franklin Grange; Odd Fellows; C. of C. Mailing Add: 26 Pleasant St, Franklin, N.H. 03235.

GREEN, ALLISON R
State Treas, Mich.
b. Caro, Mich, 10/28/11; s. James Edward Green and Evelyn Kiteley G; m. 12/26/34 to Marjorie Christina Denhoff; c. Shirley Joan (Mrs. Chapin), James Allison, Thomas Albert, Marjorie May and Robert Frederick. Educ: Cent. Mich. Univ, A.B, 35; adv. studies, Univ. Mich; Hon. LL.D, Cent. Mich. Univ. Polit. & Govt. Pos: Mich. State Rep, 50-64, Speaker, Mich. House of Rep, 63-64; Auditor Gen, Mich, 65; State Treas, Mich, 65- Bus. & Prof. Pos: Mem. of bd, Kingston State Bank, 54-65; teacher, prin. & supt. of schs, 14 years. Mem: Mich. Farm Bur; Lions; Mason; RAM. Rel: Methodist. Legal Res: Kingston, Mich. 48741. Mailing Add: 617 Farmstead Lane, Lansing, Mich. 48917.

GREEN, BEN CHARLES D
b. Cleveland, Ohio, 1/4/05; s. Isadore Green and Rose Mailman G; m. 11/20/40 to Sylvia E. Chappy; c. Rosemary A. Educ: West. Reserve Univ, A.B. cum laude, 28, LL.B, 30; Order of the Coif. Polit. & Govt. Pos: Attorney, Fed. Land Bank, Louisville, Ohio, 33-35; spec. counsel to Attorney Gen, Ohio, 37-38; mem, Law Dept, Cleveland, 44-50; del, Dem. Nat. Conv, 48 & 52; treas, Cuyahoga Co. Dem. Party, 48-61; chmn, Cuyahoga Co. Elec. Bd, 50-61; trustee, Ohio Asn. Elec. Off, 55-61; U.S. Dist. Judge, Ohio, 61- Bus. & Prof. Pos: Past dir, Progressive Mutual Ins. Co, Progressive Casualty Ins. Co. and Cleveland Broadcasting Co; attorney, Cleveland, 30-61; real estate consult, 44-50. Mem: Ohio, Cleveland and Cuyahoga Co. Bar Asns; Beechmont Country Club. Legal Res: 3280 Belvoir Blvd, Beachwood, Ohio 44122. Mailing Add: Federal Court Bldg, Cleveland, Ohio 44114.

GREEN, BRAXTON R
V.Chmn, Seventh Cong. Dist. Rep. Cmt, Va.
b. Daytona Beach, Fla. 9/30/29; s. Alfred Anderson Green and Agnes Braxton G; m. 4/16/55 to Judith Taylor; c. Braxton, Jr, Alexander, Craig and Carter. Educ: Va. Mil. Inst, B.A, 50; Kappa Alpha. Polit. & Govt. Pos: Campaign mgr, Staunton Rep. Cmt, Va, 62, chmn, 64-66; alternate del, Rep. Nat. Conv, 68; v.chmn, Seventh Cong. Dist. Rep. Cmt, Va, currently. Bus. & Prof. Pos: V.pres, Callison & Co, Ins, 52-; secy, Stanco, Inc, 55-; partner, Cabell & Story Ins. Agency, 67- Mil. Serv: Capt, Inactive Army Res. Mem: Staunton-Waynesboro Asn. of Ins. Agents (pres, 65-66); Staunton C. of C.(1st v.pres); YMCA (1st v.pres); Rotary; cubmaster, Cub Scout Pack 71; exec. cmt, Woodrow Wilson Birthplace Found; Staunton Jaycees (past pres); Va. Jaycees (past. v.pres. and nat. dir); past pres. and campaign chmn, Staunton United Fund; past pres, United Fund of Va; past pres, Shenandoah Valley, Inc; Country Club of Staunton (past pres). Outstanding Young Man of Staunton, 64. Rel: Episcopal; Past Vestryman, Trinity Episcopal Church. Mailing Add: 1422 Dogwood Rd, Staunton, Va. 24401.

GREEN CLINTON D
b. Worthington, Ind, 6/2/12; s. Byron T. Green and Bula Taylor G; m. 9/7/54 to Phyllis Yaggi. Educ: Ind. Univ, 1 year; Purdue Univ, B.S. in M.E, 32; Sigma Nu. Polit. & Govt. Pos: Engr, Ind. Dept. of Conserv, U.S. Dept. of Agr, 33-42 and Nat. Housing Admin, Wash, D.C, 46-47; training officer, Vet. Admin, Indianapolis, 47-49; dir, Ind. State Dept. of Vet. Affairs, 49-53 and Ind. State Dept. of Admin, 61-62; chmn, Ind. State Hwy. Dept, 61-62 and Ind. Great Lakes Cmn, 61-69; admin. asst. to the Gov. of Ind, 61-64; secy. and treas, Ind. Port Cmn, 61-64; del, Dem. Nat. Conv, 68. Bus. & Prof. Pos: Engr. assoc, Klein and Kohn, Indianapolis, 64-69. Mil. Serv: Entered as 2nd Lt, Ord. Dept, Army, 42, released as Maj, 46, after serv. in 614th Ord. Bn, ETO, 44-46; Army Res, 46-56. Mem: Indianapolis Athletic Club; Am. Legion; Ind. Soc. of Chicago. Rel: Christian. Mailing Add: 700 N. Alabama St, Apt. 1516, Indianapolis, Ind. 46204.

GREEN, DIANA BILLER D
Secy, Winnebago Co. Dem. Party, Wis.
b. Los Angeles, Calif, 2/5/38; d. Joseph Abraham Biller, Jr. and Marjory Farnham B; m. 12/27/58 to Dennis Curtis Green; c. Donna Elaine. Educ: Univ. Calif, Berkeley, A.B, 59; Kappa Phi; Nat. Methodist Women. Polit. & Govt. Pos: Chmn, Winnebago Co. Dem. Party, Wis, 67, prog. chmn, 68, secy, 68-; chmn, Winnebago Co. McCarthy for Pres. Campaign and staff mem, Ind. Ore. and Calif. Campaign, 68; mem. steering cmt, Wis. Dem. Coalition, 69. Bus. & Prof. Pos: Teacher, Berkeley Unified Sch. Dist, Calif, 60, Lincoln Dist, Stockton, 60-61, Pomona, 63-66 and Oshkosh, Wis, 68-; soc. worker, Los Angeles Co, Calif, 62-63; continuity dir, WMKC Radio, Oshkosh, 67-68. Mem: Oshkosh, Wis. & Nat. Educ. Asns; Am. Civil Liberties Union (Oshkosh bd. dirs); Am. Asn. Univ. Women; Wis. State Univ. Oshkosh Faculty Dames. Calif. Alumni Scholar. Mailing Add: 211 E. Lincoln Ave, Oshkosh, Wis. 54901.

GREEN, DOROTHEA MARIE D
Mem, Iowa State Dem. Cent. Cmt.
b. Dubuque, Iowa, 5/18/22; d. Joseph Edmund Hamel and Bertha Sebald H; m. 8/28/51 to James Stephen Green; c. Patrick, Kathy and Julie. Educ: St. Joseph Acad, grad, 40. Polit. & Govt. Pos: Treas, Dubuque Co. Dem. Cent. Cmt, Iowa, 62-64, committeewoman sixth precinct, 62-64 and v.chmn, 64-; first pres. and founder, Dubuque Dem. Women's Club, 63-64, v.pres, 64-; mem, Iowa State Dem. Cent. Cmt, Second Dist, 64-; mem, Dubuque Citizens Adv. Cmt, Dubuque City Coun, 67-; mem. platform cmt, Dem. State Conv, 68; del, Dem. Nat. Conv, 68; mem. apportionment cmt, Iowa State Legis, 69. Bus. & Prof. Pos: Admin. asst. to milk mgt. adminstr, U.S. Dept. Agr, 46-54. Mem: Dubuque Archdiocesan Coun. Cath. Women; B.V.M. Alumnae Fedn. Women's Doer Award, Dubuque Co. Dem. Party, 68. Rel: Roman Catholic. Mailing Add: 1855 Atlantic St, Dubuque, Iowa 52001.

GREEN, DOROTHY R
b. New York, N.Y, 7/15/11; married; c. Two. Polit. & Govt. Pos: N.H. State Sen, -67; Women's Rep. Club. Bus. & Prof. Pos: Housewife. Mem: Eastern Star; Grenier Air Base Wives' Club; Jewish Commun. Center. Rel: Jewish. Mailing Add: 55 Trenton St, Manchester, N.H. 03104. (1967)

GREEN, EDITH S. D
U.S. Rep, Ore.
b. Trent, S.Dak, 1/17/10; d. James Vaughn Starrett and Julia Hunt S; div; c. James S. and Richard. Educ: Willamette Univ; Univ. Ore, B.S; Stanford Univ, grad. work; Delta Kappa Gamma; Delta Sigma Theta. Hon. LL.D, Univ. Alaska, 56, Goucher Col, Linfield Col, Gonzaga Univ. and Seattle Univ, 64, Hood Col, Regis Col, Boston Col, St. Xavier Col, Keuka Col. and Yale Univ, 65; L.H.D, Culver-Stockton Col, 60 and Eureka Col, 62; D.P.A, Bethany Col, 64; also hon. degrees from Reed and Oberlin Cols, Georgetown and Miami Univs. and Univ. Portland. Polit. & Govt. Pos: U.S. Rep, Ore, 54-, mem, House Educ. and Labor Cmt. and chmn, Subcmt. on Educ; del-at-lg, Dem. Nat. Conv, 56, 60, 64 & 68, mem, Platform Cmt, 56, Credentials Cmt, 64, chmn, Ore. Del, 60 & 68, seconded nominations of Adlai Stevenson, 56 and John F. Kennedy, 60; del, Parliamentary Conf, Switz, 58, NATO Conf, London, Eng, 59 and UNESCO Gen. Conf, Paris, France, 64; mem, President Kennedy's Cmn. on Status of Women and U.S. Cmn. to UNESCO. Bus. & Prof. Pos: Teacher, Ore. Schs; commercial radio work. Mem: Dir. pub. rels, Ore. Educ. Asn; Bus. & Prfnl. Women's Club; Urban League; League of Women Voters; Am. Asn. of Univ. Women; hon. life mem, Ore. Libr. Asn; UN Asn. of U.S; Am. Fedn. of Radio Artists. Brotherhood Award, Portland B'nai B'rith, 56; Woman of Year, Nat. Amvets Auxiliary, 58; Distinguished Achievement Award, Nat. Asn. Colored Women's Clubs, 62 and Am. Col. Pub. Rels. Asn, 64; Code of Personal Commitment Award, Nat. Coun. Jewish Women and YWCA, 62; Outstanding Serv. to Handicapped Award, Goodwill Indust. Am, 64; Soc. Progress Contribution Award, South. Univ. Women's Club, 64; Parents Mag. Award, 64; Top Hat Award, Bus. & Prfnl. Women's Clubs of Am, 65; Distinguished Serv. Award, Univ. Ore, 67, Coun. of Chief State Sch. Officers and Nat. Educ. Asn; Outstanding Woman in the Field of Govt, Who's Who of Am. Women; Educ. Citizen of the Year, Ore. Educ. Asn; President's Award for 1967, Nat. Rehabilitation Asn. Rel: Christian Church. Legal Res: 1209 S.W. Sixth, Portland, Ore. 97204. Mailing Add: 2441 Rayburn House Office Building, Washington, D.C. 20515.

GREEN, HOWARD E, JR. R
b. Chicago, Ill, 4/14/29; s. Howard E. Green and Eva King G; m. 8/21/54 to Patricia Ann Erb; c. Laura Leslie and Arthur William, II. Educ: Williams Col, B.A, in English, 50; Psi Upsilon. Polit. Pos: Alternate del, Rep. Nat. Conv, 64; secy, Lake Co. Rep. Cent. Cmt, Ill, 62-64, committeeman, 60-65. Bus. & Prof. Pos: Dist. mgr, McGraw-Hill, Inc, 58- Mil. Serv: Entered as Air Cadet, Naval Res, 51, hon. discharged as Airman, 54. Rel: Presbyterian. 1967 Legal Res: Deerfield, Ill. No mailing address available. (1967)

GREEN, HOWARD LEMUEL D
b. Swenson, Tex, 1/24/21; s. Thomas Lemuel Green and Della Hall G; m. to Betty Bratton; c. Leslie Carole and Howard Lemuel, Jr. Educ: McMurry Col; Nat. Hon. Soc; Nat. Forensic League. Polit. & Govt. Pos: Tex. State Rep, 57-67; co. judge, Tarrant Co, Tex, 67- Bus. & Prof. Pos: Pres, Longhorn Baseball league, 46-49, Gulf Coast Baseball League, 50-52 and Big State Baseball League, 50-56. Mil. Serv: Entered as Pvt, Air Force, 43, released as

S/Sgt, 45, after serv. in 8th Air Force, ETO; Air Medal; ETO Ribbon. Mem: Am. Legion; VFW. Rel: Methodist. Legal Res: 7316 Oakland Lane, Fort Worth, Tex. 76118. Mailing Add: Box 13214, Fort Worth, Tex. 76118.

GREEN, JAMES ALLISON D
Chmn, Butler Co. Dem. Cmt, Pa.
b. Evans City, Pa, 10/24/30; s. Fred Allison Green and Ioda Pearl Barkey G; m. 2/14/58 to Margaret Loretta Beyer. Educ: Geneva Col, 2 years. Polit. & Govt. Pos: Committeeman, Dem. Party, Pa, 50-62, state committeeman, 54-56; asst. state dir, Bur. Standard Weights and Measures, Dept. Internal Affairs, Commonwealth of Pa, 55-59; co. cmnr, Butler Co, 59-67; chmn, Butler Co. Dem. Cmt, 65-; del, Dem. Nat. Conv, 68. Mil. Serv: Pvt, Air Force, 49-50. Mem: Mason; Grange; Elks; Eagles; Moose; Shrine; Bd. mem, Am. Cancer Soc; Crippled Children; Blind Asn. Man of the Year, Butler Co, 63. Rel: United Church of Christ. Mailing Add: 328 S. Washington St, Evans City, Pa. 16033. (1967)

GREEN, JAMES COLLINS D
N.C. State Rep.
b. Halifax Co, Va, 2/24/21; s. John Collins Green and Frances Sue Oliver G; m. 10/7/43 to Alice McAulay Clark; c. Sarah Frances, Susan Clark and James Collins, Jr. Educ: Wash. and Lee Univ. Polit. & Govt. Pos: Precinct v.chmn. and chmn, Dem. Party, 10 years; mem, Bladen Co. Dem. Exec. Cmt, N.C, formerly; mem, Bladen Co. Bd. Educ, 55-61; N.C. State Rep, 61- Bus. & Prof. Pos: Farmer and tobacco warehouse operator. Mil. Serv: Entered Marine Corps, 44, released as Cpl, 46, after serv. in the Iwo Jima invasion as machine gunner with 3rd Marine Div. Mem: Trustee and chmn. bldg. cmt, Commun. Col; past pres, Rotary; dir, Clarkton Commun. Develop. Corp; Clarkton Merchant Asn; pres, Brown March Develop. Corp. of Clarkton; French Lodge 270, AF&AM; Scottish Rite Mason (32°); WOW; trustee, Consol. Univ. N.C. Rel: Presbyterian; Deacon, Clarkton Presby. Church; past supt, Sunday Sch. Mailing Add: Box 185, Clarkton, N.C. 28433.

GREEN, JOSEPH THOMAS R
Chmn, Monroe Co. Rep. Cmt, Mich.
b. Whiting, Iowa, 8/7/16; s. John Carl Green and Mable Watson G; m. 8/24/38 to Madeline Langenberger (deceased); 5/23/64 to Opal A. Miller; c. John Carl, Marilyn Jo (Mrs. Monhollen) and Robert C. Miller. Educ: High Sch; Bliss Bus. Col, Columbus, Ohio. Polit. & Govt. Pos: Mem, Bd. Canvassers, Monroe Co, Mich, 66; chmn, Monroe Co. Rep. Cmt, 66- Bus. & Prof. Pos: Mgr. training, S.S. Kresge Co, 37-50, mgr, 50-51; mgr, Miller's Appliances, 51-54, owner, 54- Mil. Serv: Entered as Pvt, Army, 44, released as Pvt, 46, after serv. in 85th Div, Italy; Presidential Unit Citation; N. Appenines and Po Valley Campaigns. Mem: Am. Legion; Kiwanis; C. of C; bd. dirs, Monroe United Fund. Rel: Methodist. Legal Res: 710 Maple Blvd, Monroe, Mich. 48161. Mailing Add: 31 W. Front St, Monroe, Mich. 48161.

GREEN, MADGE MILLER R
b. Palestine, Ill; wid. of Sen. Herschel S. Green. Educ: East. Ill. Univ; Ind. State Univ, B.S, M.S.(Educ). Polit. & Govt. Pos: Ill. State Sen, 60-64, postmistress, Ill. State Senate, 65-; mem, Cmn. on Status of Women and Cmn. to Study Co. Govt, 63-64. Bus. & Prof. Pos: Teacher, Palestine, Ill; teacher, hist. and art, Richmond, Ind. Mem: Nat. Fed. Rep. Women; Wabash Valley Asn; DAR; Red. Bus. & Prfnl. Women's Club. Publ: Through the Years in Indiana, now used in Ind. schs. Named Woman of the Year, Robinson Bus. & Prfnl. Women's Club, 61. Mailing Add: 509 W. Grand Prairie, Palestine, Ill. 62451.

GREEN, MARSHALL
Asst. Secy, Bur. of E.Asian and Pac. Affairs, Dept. of State
b. Holyoke, Mass, 1/27/16; s. Addison Loomis Green and Gertrude Metcalf G; m. 2/14/42 to Lispenard Seabury Crocker; c. Marshall Winthrop, Edward Crocker and Brampton Seabury. Educ: Yale Univ, B.A, 39. Polit. & Govt. Pos: Private secy, Am. Ambassador to Japan, 39-41; career officer, U.S. Dept. of State For. Serv, 45-; third secy. and v.consul, Wellington, N.Z, 46-47; Officer in Charge of Japanese Affairs, Dept. of State, 47-50; first secy. and consul, Stockholm, 50-55; Nat. War Col, 55-56; Regional Planning Adv. for the Far East, 56-59; Acting Dep. Asst. Secy. of State for Far East. Affairs, 59-60; minister counsr, Seoul, 60-61; consul gen, Hong Kong and consul, Macao, 61-63; dep. asst. secy, Bur. of Far East. Affairs, 63-65; U.S. Ambassador to Indonesia, 65-69; detached to Viet Nam Peace Mission, Jan. to Mar. 69; asst. secy, Bur. of E. Asian and Pac. Affairs, 69- Mil. Serv: Entered as Ens, Navy, 42, released as Lt, 45, after serv. in Naval Intel. Mem: Metrop. and Chevy Chase Clubs, D.C. Received Meritorious Serv. Award, Dept. of State, 59. Rel: Episcopal. Mailing Add: 5063 Millwood Lane N.W, Washington, D.C. 20016.

GREEN, MARY LOUISE KATHERINE R
Mem, San Francisco Co. Rep. Cent. Cmt, Calif.
b. Fresno, Calif, 2/9/29; d. Edward Hilary Green and Elinor Mary Komes G; single. Educ: Univ. Calif, Davis and Berkeley, B.S, 50; Univ. San Francisco, Gen. Sec. Teacher's Credential, 56; Newman Club. Polit. & Govt. Pos: Precinct dir, 20th Assembly Dist. for Rep. Co. Cent. Cmt, Calif, 60-65; mem, Rep. State Cent. Cmt, 60-66 & 68-70; mem, San Francisco C. Rep. Cent. Cmt, 61-; pres, Golden Gate Rep. Women's Club, 65-67. Mem: Calif. Math. Coun; Nat. Educ. Asn; Calif. Teachers Asn; San Mateo Elem. Teachers Asn.(chmn. legis. cmt, parliamentarian and recording secy, 64-69); Tel. Hill Dwellers Orgn. Rel: Roman Catholic. Mailing Add: 566 Vallejo, Apt. 21, San Francisco, Calif. 94133.

GREEN, MAXINE WISE R
Mem, Calif. Rep. State Cent. Cmt.
b. Vincennes, Ind, 2/7/17; d. Raymond Franklin Wise and Iva Copple W; m. 4/16/38 to Alvin E. Green; c. William C. and Alvin E, Jr. Educ: Lincoln High Sch, Vincennes, Ind, grad, 34; Univ. Calif. exten. classes. Polit. & Govt. Pos: Hq. chmn, Congressman Bob Wilson, 58-60; campaign coordinator, Calif. State Assemblyman Clair W. Burgener, 62, secy, 63-66, campaign chmn, 64, coordinator, Calif. State Sen. campaign, 66, field rep, Calif. State Sen. Burgener, 68-; secy, Regional Off. for Gov. Ronald Reagan, 66-67; field rep, Calif. State Sen. Jack Schrade, 67-68; alternate mem, Rep. Cent. Cmt, San Diego Co, currently; mem, Rep. State Cent. Cmt, Calif, currently. Mem: Hon. life mem. PTA (past pres, Longfellow chap. and Marston Jr. High chap); past pres, Clairemont Woman's Club; past pres, Clairemont Rep. Women's Club; past residential chmn. and past chmn, co. coun, women's div, United Fund of San Diego Co. Woman of the Year, Clairemont Woman's Club, 58; Woman of Valor, City of San Diego, 59. Rel: Presbyterian. Mailing Add: 2847 Arnott St, San Diego, Calif. 92110.

GREEN, RICHARD J, JR. R
Pa. State Sen.
b. Johnstown, Pa, 7/26/25; s. Richard E. Green and Margaret Roberts G; m. to Alice L. Hite; c. two. Educ: Univ. Pittsburgh, B.S. & LL.B. Polit. & Govt. Pos: Chmn, Cambrial Co. Young Rep, 6 years; Pa. State Rep, 62-64; Pa. State Sen, 64- Bus. & Prof. Pos: Attorney. Mil. Serv: Sgt, Army Inf, 26th Div, 42-45; Purple Heart; ETO Ribbon. Mem: Cambria Co, Supreme and Superior Courts of Pa; Fed. Courts; past pres, Cambria Co. P.A.R.C (retarded children); Am. Legion; Elks. Mailing Add: 208 Cambria Savings Bldg, Johnstown, Pa. 15901.

GREEN, S. WILLIAM R
b. N.Y.C, 10/16/29; m. to Patricia Freiberg. Educ: Harvard Col, A.B, 50, Harvard Law Sch, 53. Polit. & Govt. Pos: Law secy. to Judge George T. Washington, U.S. Court of Appeals for D.C. Circuit, 55-56; counsel to Joint Legis. Cmt. on Housing & Urban Develop, 61-64; N.Y. State Assemblyman, 64-68. Bus. & Prof. Pos: Attorney. Mem: N.Y. State Bar Asn; New York Co. Lawyers Asn; Asn. of Bar of N.Y.C; Fed. Bar Asns. of N.Y, N.J. and Conn; Am. Bar Asn.(alternate observer to U.S. Mission to UN); trustee, Montifiore Hosp; dir, Manhattanville Commun. Centers; chmn. cmt. on commun. develop, Fedn. of Jewish Philanthropies of N.Y; v.pres, Jewish Asn. for Serv. to the Aged; dir, Citizens Union; Commun. Serv. Soc.(mem. cmt. on pub. affairs). Mailing Add: 55 Liberty St, New York, N.Y. 10005.

GREEN, VICTOR D
Ind. State Sen.
Educ: Ind. Univ. Sch. Journalism. Polit. & Govt. Pos: Ind. State Sen, currently. Bus. & Prof. Pos: Publisher, several weekly papers, 30 years; resort owner. Mem: Pres, Nat. Asn. of Advert. Publ; pres, Ind. Advert. Publ. Asn; Sigma Delta Chi. Rel: Methodist. Mailing Add: Banner Bldg, Pekin, Ind. 47165.

GREEN, WALTER GUERRY American Party
Interim State Chmn, American Party of N.C.
b. Charleston, S.C, 1/1/07; s. Walter Guerry Green and Daisie Holt G; m. 9/1/34 to Irma Camman; c. Walter Guerry, III. Educ: Univ. of the South; Oxford Univ; Phi Beta Kappa. Polit. & Govt. Pos: Alternate del-at-lg, Rep. Nat. Conv, 64; Rep. cand. for U.S. House of Rep, Sixth Dist, N.C, 64 and for N.C. State Senate, 66; mem, N.C. Rep. State Exec. Cmt, 64-68; interim state chmn, Am. Party of N.C, 69- Bus. & Prof. Pos: Attorney-at-law. Mil. Serv: Entered as Lt.(jg), Naval Res, 42, released as Lt. Comdr, 45; Am. and Asiatic-Pac. Theater Ribbons; Philippine Liberation and Victory Medals. Mem: N.Y. Bar, 33- and N.C. Bar, 34- Rel: Episcopal. Mailing Add: P.O. Box 621, Burlington, N.C. 27215.

GREEN, WALTER LeROY D
b. Graham, Tex, 7/2/04; s. The Rev. John H. Green and Myrtle Joblin G; m. 3/2/28 to Catherine Roe (deceased, 59); c. Anne (Mrs. Fotos), Carlton M. and Walter L, Jr. (deceased). Educ: Nat. Univ, now George Washington Univ, LL.B, 29. Polit. Pos: Del, Dem. Nat. Conv, 63; cand. for Congress, 61. Govt. Pos: Trial magistrate, Prince Georges County, Md, 39-45. Bus. & Prof. Pos: Dir, Allied Capital Corp, 59-; pres, Green Hotels, Inc, 51-; chmn. of bd, Metrop. Fed. Saving & Loan Asn, 51-; chmn. trust cmt. and dir, Suburban Trust Co, 33-; partner, Green Babcock and Dukes, 31- Mem: Pres, Prince Georges County Bar Asn. and v.pres, Md. State Bar Asn, 65-66; Am. Bar Asn; fel, Am. Col. Probate Lawyers; Terrepin Club; Nat. Lawyers Club; charter mem, Nat. Capital Dem. Club; Mason; Tall Cedars; Scottish Rite; Shrine; Lions; Elks; Moose; C. of C; Jefferson Island Club. Rel: Presbyterian. Mailing Add: 7002 Wake Forest Dr, College Park, Md. 20740.

GREEN, WARREN ERNEST R
Okla. State Rep.
b. Mannford, Okla, 12/23/21; s. Clarence Green and Millie P. Shoumake G; m. 7/13/41 to Betty J. Foster; c. Sharon Kay (Mrs. Cloyd W. Childers), Priscilla A.(Mrs. Kenneth W. Davidson), Roberta Susan and Marilyn L. Educ: Draughons Bus. Col, Tulsa, Okla, Grad, 42. Polit. & Govt. Pos: Precinct chmn, dist. dir. and mem. Tulsa Co. Rep. Exec. Cmt, Okla, several years; Okla. State Rep, 64- Bus. & Prof. Pos: Serv. supvr. and salesman, Fred Jones Ford and Leasing Co, 48-54; pres. and prin. owner, Green Auto Serv, Inc, Tulsa, 54- Mem: C. of C; Lions. Rel: Disciples of Christ. Mailing Add: 2260 E. 39th St, Tulsa, Okla. 74105.

GREEN, WILLIAM JOSEPH D
U.S. Rep, Pa.
b. Phila, Pa, 6/24/38; s. William Joseph Green and Mary Elizabeth Kelly G; m. 6/13/64 to Patricia Anne Kirk; c. William Joseph. Educ: St. Joseph's Col, Pa; Villanova Law Sch; Georgetown Univ. Polit. & Govt. Pos: U.S. Rep, Fifth Dist, Pa, currently; chmn, Dem. Co. Exec. Cmt, 67-; del, Dem. Nat. Conv, 68. Publ: The Congressman, McGraw Hill, 69. Mem: Bd. dirs, Frankford Hosp; bd. dirs, Neighborhood Center; adv. bd, Holy Family Col. Rel: Catholic. Legal Res: Wakeling St, Philadelphia, Pa. 19124. Mailing Add: Room 1128, Longworth House Office Bldg, Washington, D.C. 20515.

GREENAWALD, DOLORES ROSE R
Mem, Calif. Rep. State Cent. Cmt.
b. Bronx, N.Y, 6/22/34; d. Charles Gibson Whitehead and Theresa Albano W; m. 3/9/59 to Walter Harry Greenawald; c. Richard Jeffrey and Susan Ann. Educ: Greenbrier Col. for Women, Assoc. B.A, 54; Webber Col, B.B.S, 56; Zeta Mu Epsilon. Polit. & Govt. Pos: Asst. assembly dist. Rep. precinct chmn, Woodland Hills, Calif, 69-; alternate, 64th Assembly Dist. Rep. Cent. Cmt, 69-; mem, Calif. Rep. State Cent. Cmt, 69- Bus. & Prof. Pos: Tech. secy, N.Am. Aviation, Cape Canaveral, Fla, 56-57; data analyst, Gen. Elec, Fla, 57-59. Rel: Presbyterian. Mailing Add: 20709 Collins St, Woodland Hills, Calif. 91364.

GREENAWAY, ROBERT FRANCIS R
b. Aurora, Ill, 1/8/19; s. Francis Wallace Greenaway and Cora Ellen Wilkinson G; m. 5/2/42 to Mary Virginia Ann Plummer; c. Terri Ann (Mrs. Eugene Humes), Mary Noell (Mrs. Gripp), Michael Francis and Elizabeth Ann. Educ: De Kalb Township Sr. High Sch, grad, 36; Western Mil. Acad, grad, 38. Polit. & Govt. Pos: Mem. adv. cmt, Dept. Conserv, Ill, 8 years, Dept. of Personnel, 2 years, Dept. Ill. Toll Hwy. Cmn, 8 years, corresponding secy, past 3 years; alternate del, Rep. Nat. Conv, 68; dir, Ill. State Toll Hwy. Authority, 69- Bus. & Prof. Pos: Ed. and v.pres, De Kalb Daily Chronicle, 53- Mem: U.S. C. of C; Ill. State C. of C; Sigma Delta Chi; Am. Newspaper Publishers Asn; Inland Daily Press Asn; Ill. Daily Press Asn; Ill. Daily Mkt. Asn; North. Ill. Ed. Asn.(past pres); Ill. Ed-Publishers Safety Seminar (first pres, 58-61, mem. exec. bd. and bd. dirs, currently); past v.pres, De Kalb C. of C; Elks; Am. Legion; Kishwaukee Country Club (past bd. mem. and former v.pres). Rel: Catholic. Mailing Add: 225 Windsor Dr, De Kalb, Ill. 60115.

GREENAWAY, ROY FRANCIS D
Mem, Calif. Dem. State Cent. Cmt.
b. Takoma Park, Md, 7/9/29; s. Alfred Roy Greenaway and Lila F. Bartlett G; m. 3/18/51 to Carol Faye Wagle. Educ: Univ. Chicago, B.A, 50; Fresno State Col, M.A, 56. Polit. & Govt. Pos: Mem, Fresno Co. Dem. Cent. Cmt, 52-65; regional v.pres, Calif. Dem. Coun, 57-60, North. v.pres, 65-67; mem, Calif. Dem. State Cent. Cmt, 58-60 & 66-; inheritance tax appraiser, Fresno Co, 59-67; chief legis. counsel, to U.S. Sen. Alan Cranston, Calif, 69- Bus. & Prof. Pos: Teacher, Kerman Union High Sch, Calif, 55-59; appraiser, Fresno Co. and Los Angeles, 67-69. Mil. Serv: Entered as Pvt, Army, 52, released as Cpl, 54, after serv. in Casual Officers Detachment, Camp Drake, Far E. Command, Japan, Korean War; Good Conduct Medal. Mem: Calif. Teachers Asn; Nat. Educ. Asn; Am. Fedn. of Teachers; NAACP; VFW; Elks. Rel: Unitarian. Legal Res: 4325 E. Madison, Fresno, Calif. 93705. Mailing Add: 326 M St. S.W, Washington, D.C. 20024.

GREENBERG, JOEL SELIG D
Mass. State Rep.
b. New York, N.Y, 5/31/30; s. Meyer Greenberg and Gertrude Bauer G; m. 8/25/57 to Carol Selkowitz; c. Peter, Betsy Jane and Susan. Educ: Syracuse Univ, B.A, 51; Harvard Law Sch, LL.B, 54; Tau Delta Phi. Polit. & Govt. Pos: Councilman, Pittsfield, Mass, 62-63; Mass. State Rep, Fourth Berkshire Dist, 65- Mem: Am, Mass. and Berkshire Bar Asns; Asn. of Bar, City of New York; B'nai B'rith. Rel: Jewish. Mailing Add: 24 Waverly St, Pittsfield, Mass. 01201. (1967)

GREENBERG, MELVIN J. D
b. Phila, Pa, 8/2/33; s. Isidore J. Greenberg and Jean Meshman G; m. to Estelle M. Freedman; c. three. Educ: Temple Univ, B.S; Temple Univ. Sch. of Law, LL.B; Temple Law Quarterly; Temple Moot Court; Temple Legal Aid. Polit. & Govt. Pos: Pa. State Rep, 64-67. Bus. & Prof. Pos: Attorney; admitted to practice before Phila. Common Pleas, Orphans', Co. Crts, Supreme, Superior Crts. of Pa. Mil. Serv: U.S. Army, 54-56. Mem: Am. Bar Asn; Alpha Delta; B'nai B'rith. Rel: Jewish. Mailing Add: Suite 500, 1405 Locust St, Philadelphia, Pa. 19102. (1967)

GREENBERG, SAMUEL L. D
N.Y. State Sen.
b. New York, N.Y, 11/12/98; married. Educ: Columbia Col; N.Y. Univ. Law Sch, LL.B, 19; Phi Sigma Delta. Polit. & Govt. Pos: Govt. appeal agent local bd. 144, Selective Serv; chmn. bd. of dir, Flatbush Dem. Club, N.Y. State Sen, 42- Bus. & Prof. Pos: Lawyer; businessman. Mil. Serv: World War I, Naval Res. Mem: Pres, Flatbush Boy's Club; N.Y. Co. Lawyers Asn; N.Y. State, Brooklyn and Am. Bar Asns; K. of P; Am. Legion. Rel: Jewish; Pres, Temple Beth Emeth. Mailing Add: 1111 Ocean Ave, Brooklyn, N.Y. 11230. (1967)

GREENE, BILL D
Calif. State Assemblyman
Educ: Lincoln Jr. Col; Univ. Mich. Polit. & Govt. Pos: Clerk, Calif. State Assembly; labor consult. legis. advocate; legis. asst. to Assemblyman Mervyn Dymally; Calif. State Assemblyman, 67- Radio; television; journalism. Legal Res: 3809½ S. Flower Dr, Los Angeles, Calif. 90037. Mailing Add: 8563 S. Broadway, Suite 210, Los Angeles, Calif. 90003.

GREENE, CHARLES OLAND HASKELL D
Vt. State Rep.
b. Georgia, Vt, 3/22/03; married; c. 2 daughters. Educ: St. Albans High Sch; eve. courses, Columbia Univ; adult ed. in speaking, U.V.M. Polit. & Govt. Pos: Mem, Employ Security Bd; alderman, St. Albans, Vt, 52-61, Vt. State Rep, 65- Bus. & Prof. Pos: Retired rwy. clerk; mem. bd. dirs. and independent salesman, Transcontinental Bolt Co, Detroit, Mich, 65- Mem: F&AM. Rel: Congregational. Mailing Add: 62 Lincoln Ave, St. Albans, Vt. 05478.

GREENE, CLAUDE L, JR. R
b. Oak City, N.C, 7/9/20; s. Claude L. Greene and Essie Jones G; m. 7/8/53 to Marjorie Shepherd; c. Mike S. and Toni. Educ: Wake Forest Col. Polit. & Govt. Pos: Treas, N.C. Young Rep, 57-58; chmn, Martin Co. Rep. Cmt, N.C, 60-68; first div. chmn. and mem, N.C. Rep. Cent. Cmt, 62-64. Bus. & Prof. Pos: Farmer, 49- Mil. Serv: Entered as Pvt, Army, 42, released as T/Sgt, 46, after serv. in Transportation Corps. Mem: Farm Bur; Ruritan Club; Am. Legion; K. of P. Rel: Disciples of Christ. Mailing Add: Edge Hill Farm, Robersonville, N.C. 27871. (1967)

GREENE, EDWIN EUGENE R
Chmn, Marshall Co. Rep. Party, Miss.
b. Holly Springs, Miss, 7/9/22; s. Edwin E. Greene and Lilla Matthews G; m. 12/27/42 to Allie Jewell Boatwright; c. Edwin E, Jr, Kerry Lawrence, Allen Leroy and Patrice Elizabeth. Educ: Columbia Mil. Acad, Tenn, grad; Univ. Ala, Col. of Commerce and Bus. Admin, grad. Polit. & Govt. Pos: Mem, City Sch. Bd; chmn, Marshall Co. Rep. Party, Miss, currently. Mil. Serv: S/Sgt, Army, 42-45, serv. in 3rd Army, ETO; Normandy and 2 others. Mem: Secy, Rotary Club, 58-60 and bd. dirs, 66-67; Credit Men's Asn; Nat. Asn. of Cost Accts; Nat. Asn. of Pub. Accts; Miss. Cattlemen's Asn; Mason; Miss. C. of C; Miss. Farm Bur; Am. Legion. Rel: Presbyterian. Legal Res: Magnolia Gardens, Holly Springs, Miss. 38635. Mailing Add: Box 516, Holly Springs, Miss. 38635.

GREENE, ELIZABETH A. R
N.H. State Rep.
b. North Hampton, N.H; m. to Leroy Greene; c. Three. Educ: Univ. N.H. Polit. & Govt. Pos: N.H. State Rep, 61-; v.chmn, Rockingham City Del, 67; clerk, budget cmt, town of Rye. Mem: Trustee, Rye Libr; exec. bd, N.H. Pub. Libr. Trustee Asn; Order Women Legislators. Rel: Protestant. Mailing Add: 399 South Rd, Rye, N.H. 03870. (1967)

GREENE, HAROLD A. D
Co. Cmnr, Dade Co. Fla.
b. N.Y.C, 4/6/26; s. Sidney Greene and Rose Teich G; m; c. Stephen S, Robert D, Jonathan D. and Richard S. Educ: Univ. Miami, J.D, 53. Polit. & Govt. Pos: Libr. cmnr, North Miami Beach, Fla, 62-63; co. cmnr, Dade Co, Fla, 64-; del, Dem. Nat. Conv, 68. Bus. & Prof. Pos: Attorney-at-law, currently. Mil. Serv: Entered as Seaman 1/C, Navy, 44, released as RM 2/C, 46, after serv. in Com. Marines Hq, Pac. Theatre; Naval Res, currently; Good Conduct Medal; Pac. and Am. Theatre Awards. Mem: Am, Fla. and Dade Co. Bar Asns; Real Property, Probate and Trust Law Sect, Fla. Bar; Kiwanis; Optimist; Am. Legion; Toastmasters (past pres); Elks; Gr. Miami C. of C.(mass transit cmt, roads and hwy. cmt, oceanography cmt); Govt. Research Coun. South Fla, Inc; B'nai B'rith (past pres); state bd, Anti-Defamation League; Young Dem; campaign v.chmn. for govt, United Fund, 67-68. Legal Res: 18955 N.E. 21st Ave, Miami, Fla. 33162. Mailing Add: 3000 Biscayne Blvd, Miami, Fla. 33137.

GREENE, LEONARD ROBERT R
b. Auburn, N.Y, 10/29/13; s. John Joseph Greene and Jane Doyle G; m. 7/4/38 to Marian Theresa O'Donnell; c. Sister Leonardo S.S.G.(Judith Ann) and Robert Leonard. Educ: Auburn Commun. Col, 1 year; Acad. Lighting Arts, Cert. Lighting Consult. Polit. & Govt. Pos: City councilman, Auburn, N.Y, 64-67, mayor, 67; chmn, Cayuga Co. Rep. Cmt, N.Y, 65-69; cmnr. elec, Cayuga Co, 69- Bus. & Prof. Pos: Pres, O'Donnell Elec. Co. Inc, 38- Mil. Serv: Army, 43-45, Pvt, serv. in 13th F.A. Brigade, ETO; Am. Defense Medal; Five Battle Stars; Good Conduct Medal; French Citation. Mem: K. of C; Owasco-Fleming Kiwanis; Sportsman's Club; St. Mary's Men's Club; VFW; Mt. Carmel Men's Club; Builders Exchange Coun. Man of the Year, Home Builders Indust. Rel: Catholic. Legal Res: 45 Grove Ave, Auburn, N.Y. 13021. Mailing Add: 12 Market St, Auburn, N.Y. 13021.

GREENE, MERRILL KINGSLEY R
b. Wilmington, Vt, 5/16/99; widower; c. 1 son, 3 daughters. Educ: Norwich Univ. Polit. & Govt. Pos: Mem, Bd. Civil Authority; selectman, Wilmington, Vt, 32-45; Vt. State Rep, 43-49 & 65-68. Bus. & Prof. Pos: Merchant, partially retired. Mil. Serv: Hq. Co, 20th F.A, Sgt, 17-19. Mem: AF&AM. Rel: Protestant. Mailing Add: Wilmington, Vt. 05363. (1967)

GREENE, R. L. R
m. to Rose; c. 1. Polit. & Govt. Pos: Wyo. State Sen, 5 1/2 terms, -67; Wyo. State Rep, 1 term. Bus. & Prof. Pos: Livestock, rancher. Mailing Add: Buffalo, Wyo. 82834. (1967)

GREENE, ROY LOUIS D
b. Keswick, Iowa, 3/1/27; s. James J. Greene (deceased) and Bertha Nilles G. (deceased); m. 7/17/54 to Marilyn Weak; c. Anne, Margaret, Roy Kelly, Kevin, Mary, Sandra, Susan, Laura and Thomas. Educ: Creighton Univ, B.S. in finance; Am. Inst. Foreign Trade, B.F.T. Polit. & Govt. Pos: Precinct worker, Dem. Party, Iowa, 48-; chmn, Linn Co. Exec. Cmt, Citizens for Hughes and Culver, Iowa, 66. Bus. & Prof. Pos: Pres, Greene & Co. and United Exporters. Mil. Serv: Entered as Pvt, Army, 44, released as Pfc, 46, after serv. in Korean Theater; Good Conduct and Korean Occupation Medals. Mem: Bd. dirs, Jr. C. of C; chmn, Co. Heart Asn; pres, 10 Co. Heart Asns; bd mem, Cath. Charities; Speakers Burs; Juvenile Detention Home; ACCM; Investment Bankers Asn; Security Analyst, Int. Trade Club; Concord Club; K. of C. Rel: Catholic. Legal Res: 2425 18th S.W, Cedar Rapids, Iowa 52404. Mailing Add: P.O. Box 682, Cedar Rapids, Iowa 52406.

GREENE, SARAH MOORE R
Secy, Knox Co. Rep. Exec. Cmt, Tenn.
b. Madisonville, Tenn, 2/22/12; d. Isaac Moore and Mary Toomey M; div. Educ: Tenn. State Col, 2 years; Knoxville Adult Bus. Sch, 2 years. Polit. & Govt. Pos: Mem. and secy, Tenn. State Rep. Primary Bd, 58; v.chmn, M-14th Ward Rep. Party, 60-; mem, Knox Co. Rep. Primary Bd, 67; secy, Knox Co. Rep. Exec. Cmt, 67-; del. and secy. Tenn. del, Rep. Nat. Conv, 68. Bus. & Prof. Pos: Prin, Greene's Kindergarten, 49- Mem: NAACP (state pres); YWCA; Girl Scouts (sr. leader); Knoxville Area Urban League (bd. dir); Commun. Action Cmt. Outstanding Award for Civic Work in Commun; First Negro Voting Del. from Tenn. to Rep. Nat. Conv. Rel: Baptist. Mailing Add: 2453 Linden Ave. S.E, Knoxville, Tenn. 37917.

GREENE, SCOTT E. R
b. Fleischmanns, N.Y; m. to Helen Whitaker. Educ: Univ. Kans; Union Col; Albany Law Sch, LL.B, 49. Polit. & Govt. Pos: Former Asst. Dist. Attorney, Otsego Co, N.Y; N.Y. State Assemblyman, 64-68. Bus. & Prof. Pos: Attorney, law firm, Greene & Kepner, 49- Mil. Serv: Army Inf, 41-45. Mem: Am. Legion; VFW; Rotary; Elks; Mason; Grange. Rel: Presbyterian. Mailing Add: R.D. 1, Cooperstown, N.Y. 13326. (1967)

GREENE, THOMAS H. D
b. Jacksonville, Fla, 8/2/32; s. C. Ray Greene, Sr. and Irma Diliberry G; m. 10/21/61 to Virginia Elaine Akin; c. Thomas H, Jr. and Julia Betts. Educ: Univ. Fla, A.A, 53; Stetson Col. Law, LL.B, 58; Phi Delta Phi; secy. and v.pres, Student Body; Stetson Honor Court; pres, PDP. Polit. & Govt. Pos: Fla. State Rep, 63-65, v.chmn, Cmt. on Banks & Loans, Fla. House Rep, 63-65, mem, Cmt. on Constitutional Amendments, Cmt. on Finance and Taxation and Cmt. of Pub. Health and Pub. Utilities; Fla. State Sen, 66-68. Bus. & Prof. Pos: Attorney. Mil. Serv: Entered as Pvt, Army, 53, released as Sgt, 55, after serv. in 350th Regt. Combat Team, Austria; European Occupation and Good Conduct Medals; Expert Infantryman Award. Mem: Jack-

sonville, Fla. and Am. Bar Asns; Legal Aid Asn.(v.pres, currently); Am. Arbitration Asn.(nat. panel of arbitrators); Mason; Scottish Rite; York Rite; Shrine; Jr. C. of C; North Jacksonville Bus. Men's Club; Moose; Univ. Fla. Alumni Club; Lions; River Club; San Jose Country Club; Ponta Vedra Club; Seminole Club. Rel: Episcopal. Legal Res: 1148 Greenridge Rd, Jacksonville, Fla. 32207. Mailing Add: 812 American Heritage Life Bldg, Jacksonville, Fla. 32202. (1967)

GREENE, THOMAS WESLEY D
S.C. State Rep.
b. Greenville, S.C, 3/8/42; s. Dr. Oliver B. Greene and Aileen Collins G; m. July, 1963 to Carolyn Faye Conner; c. Thomas Scott. Educ: Emory Univ. Sch. of Law, LL.D, 65. Polit. & Govt. Pos: S.C. State Rep, Greenville Co, 69- Bus. & Prof. Pos: Attorney-at-law, Greenville, S.C. Mem: Am. Bar Asn; Am. and S.C. Trial Lawyers Asns. Rel: Baptist. Legal Res: 103 Chasta Ave, Greenville, S.C. 29607. Mailing Add: P.O. Box 10051, Federal Sta, Greenville, S.C. 29603.

GREENE, WILLIAM BERNARD D
b. Cartersville, Ga, 11/23/23; s. William M. Greene and Della Peavy G; m. 9/1/48 to Jane Stow; c. William Calvin, Randall Keith and Barry Bernard. Educ: Ga. Tech, transferred Univ. of Ga, LL.B, 51, intermittent studies at Emory Univ. and Ga. Exten. Div; Phi Alpha Delta. Polit. & Govt. Pos: Ga. State Rep, 57-64; city attorney, Adairsville and Kingston, Ga. Bus. & Polit. Pos: Attorney-at-law. Mil. Serv: Naval Res, storekeeper 1/C. Mem: Elks; Kiwanis. Rel: Protestant. Mailing Add: Cartersville, Ga. 30120.

GREENE, WILLIAM C. R
b. 1933; s. W. Leo Maker and Maude Larsson M; m. to Davis Crane; c. 3 sons, 3 daughters. Educ: Princeton Univ; Babson Inst; Harvard Bus. Sch. Polit. & Govt. Pos: Rep. Town Comm, Dover; del, Rep. State Conv; Rep. Club of Mass. Bus. & Prof. Pos: CPA, currently; instr. in tax planning, mgt. seminar, Small Bus. Admin. of New Eng. Publ: Col. case book in the field of acct. and finance; assoc. ed, Mass. CPA Rev. Mem: Am. Inst. of Cert. Pub. Acct.(mem, membership promotion cmt); Mass. Soc. Cert. Pub. Acct.(secy); Babson Alumni Athletic Cmt; Princeton Alumni Asn; Princeton Schs. Cmt; former chmn, Dover United Fund. Mailing Add: Meadowbrook Rd, Dover, Mass. 02030.

GREENE, WILMA ANN D
b. Siloam Springs, Ark, 8/8/18; d. Walter Clarence Taylor and Leona Freeman T; m. 4/25/54 to Robert Earl Greene. Educ: Local Grove High Sch, grad, 35. Polit. & Govt. Pos: Secy, Jane Jefferson Club, 68- Mem: Bus. and Prfnl. Women's Club; Eastern Star. Rel: Protestant. Mailing Add: Box 310, Steamboat Springs, Colo. 80477.

GREENHILL, JOE D
Justice, Supreme Court, Tex.
b. Houston, Tex, 7/14/14; s. Joseph Robert Greenhill and Violet Stanuell G; m. 6/15/40 to Martha Shuford; c. Joe Robert, IV and William Duke. Educ: Univ. Tex, B.A. and B.B.A, 36, LL.B, 39; Ed, Cactus; foreman, Cowboys; student mgr, Intramural Sports; Friar; Phi Beta Kappa; Beta Gamma Sigma; Phi Eta Sigma; Order of the Coif; ed, Tex. Law Rev; Phi Delta Phi; Phi Delta Theta. Polit. & Govt. Pos: First asst. to Attorney Gen, Tex, 49-50; Justice, Supreme Court, Tex, 57- Mil. Serv: Entered as Ens, Naval Res, 42, released as Lt.(sg), 46, after serv. in Cent. Pac. Publ: Articles published in Baylor Law Rev, Southwestern Law J. and Tex. Law Rev. Mem: Am. and Tex. Bar Asns; Lions; Philos. Soc. Tex; dir, Tex. Ex-Students Asn; bd. visitors, South. Methodist Univ; Mason (32°); KCCH. Rel: Episcopal. Legal Res: 3204 Bridle Path, Austin, Tex. 78703. Mailing Add: Supreme Court of Texas, Box J, Capitol Station, Austin, Tex. 78711.

GREENLEAF, HALE CARR, JR. R
b. Colfax, Iowa, 2/7/23; s. Hale Carr Greenleaf and Mary Bean G; m. 5/1/52 to Mary Winifred Nye; c. Stephen, Amy, John and William. Educ: Univ. Iowa, B.A, 47; Phi Kappa Psi. Polit. & Govt. Pos: Co. chmn, Young Rep, Iowa, 47-48; precinct committeeman, Rep. Party, 61-; chmn, Page Co. Rep. Cent. Cmt, 63-66. Bus. & Prof. Pos: In sales and analysis, Cent. Surveys, Inc, 64- Mil. Serv: Entered as A/S, Naval Res, 43, released as Lt.(jg), 46; Am. and Asiatic Pac. Theater Medals. Rel: Presbyterian. Legal Res: 601 Sixth Ave, Shenandoah, Iowa 51601. Mailing Add: Box 100, Shenandoah, Iowa 51601.

GREENO, MABEL EMERSON D
b. Steuben Co, Ind, 3/11/97; d. Abijah Dunnel Emerson and Clara Belle Spears E; m. 7/23/18 to Samuel Phillip Greeno; c. Virginia Eileen, Max Emerson and Gene Alice. Educ: Tri-State Col. Polit. & Govt. Pos: V.chmn, Steuben Co. Dem. Party, 58-66; charter mem, Dem. Women's Club. Mem: Farm Bur; Home Demonstration; Questor Club; Salem Study Club; Friends of the Libr. of Englewood, Fla; Home Demonstration of Englewood; Womans Club, Englewood; Englewood Gardens Club. Rel: Presbyterian. Mailing Add: R.R. 1, Hudson, Ind. 46747.

GREENWALD, JAMES LYON D
b. N.Y.C, 12/1/30; s. Stephen Greenwald and Agnes Lyon G; m. 6/15/57 to Caroline Meyer; c. Elaine and Geraldine. Educ: Cornell Univ, B.S, 52; Univ. Wis. Law Sch, LL.B, 57. Polit. & Govt. Pos: Asst. dist. attorney, Superior, Wis, 57-60; asst. family court cmnr, Madison, 60-61; attorney, Wis. Employ. Rel. Cmn, 62-65; alternate del, Dem. Nat. Conv, 68. Bus. & Prof. Pos: Attorney, private practice, Madison, 66- Mil. Serv: Entered as 2nd Lt, Air Force, 52, released as 1st Lt, 54, after serv. in AC & W Squadrons, Alaska, 53-54. Mem: State Bar of Wis; Dane Co. Bar Asn. Rel: Unitarian. Legal Res: 3400 Cross St, Madison, Wis. 53711. Mailing Add: 3010 E. Washington Ave, Madison, Wis. 53704.

GREENWOOD, BERNARD R
b. Rochdale, Eng, 9/9/93; m. to Ethel M. Ellor; c. two sons. Educ: Schs. in Rochdale, Eng. Polit. & Govt. Pos: Auditor, 23-29; selectman, 29-54; town agent; Vt. State Rep, 51-65; asst. judge, Co. Court, 67- Bus. & Prof. Pos: Carpenter. Mem: Mason; Grange. Rel: Baptist. Mailing Add: South Newfane, Vt. 05351.

GREENWOOD, DAVID COLBERT D
R.I. State Rep.
b. Pawtucket, R.I, 11/11/10; s. Joseph Henry Greenwood and Mary V. Grady G; m. 10/14/59 to Hellen Hall. Educ: Brown Univ, Exten. Courses. Polit. & Govt. Pos: Mem, R.I. State Dem. Cmt, 62-; chmn, 79th Dist. Rep. Party, 62-; R.I. State Rep, 79th Dist, Pawtucket, 62- Bus. & Prof. Pos: Policeman and acting Lt, vice squad, Pawtucket Police Dept, 33-54; asst. maintenance, Harry M. Stevens, 56-62. Mem: Blackstone Valley Retarded Childrens Asn; Paramount Civil Asn.(past. v.pres); Pawtucket Police Asn; Fraternal Order of Police; Erie Soc; Elks. Bronze Plaque for Outstanding Serv. to Pawtucket Police Dept. for 21 years. Rel: Catholic. Mailing Add: 216 Central Ave, Pawtucket, R.I. 02860.

GREENWOOD, EVELYN HANKE R
Secy, Del. Rep. State Cmt.
b. Brooklyn, N.Y, 5/13/38; d. Fritz Hans Hanke and Rosa Tausendfreund H; m. 6/20/59 to Dr. Albert Edward Greenwood, Jr; c. W. Page and Julie Ann. Educ: Fairleigh Dickinson Univ, 56-58. Polit. & Govt. Pos: Committeewoman, Kent Co. Rep. Cmt, Del, 62-; v.pres, Women's Rep. Club Dover, 67-69, pres, 69-; state conf. chmn, Nat. Rep. Women's Conf, 68; secy, Del. Rep. State Cmt, 69- Mem: Jr. Bd, Kent Gen. Hosp. Rel: Protestant. Mailing Add: 547 Pennsylvania Ave, Dover, Del. 19901.

GREENWOOD, GORDON HICKS
N.C. State Rep.
b. Black Mountain, N.C, 7/3/09; s. James Hicks Greenwood and Louella Ray G; m. 3/8/41 to Garnet Elizabeth Carder; c. George Gordon and Ricky Eugene. Educ: N.C. State Col, 28; Biltmore Col, 29-30; Univ. Ill, B.S, 41; Univ. London Eng, 45. Polit. & Govt. Pos: N.C. State Rep, 59-, chmn. House Appropriations Cmt, 67-; mem, State Board of Higher Educ, 64-65; mem, N.C. Adv. Budget Cmn, 67-; bd. dir, N.C. Sanatorium Sept. Bus. & Prof. Pos: Owner, publisher, Black Mountain News; asst. prof. journalism, Boston Univ, 51-52; faculty, Montreat Col, 52-58. Mil. Serv: Army, psychologist, Europe, 43-45. Mem: New Eng. Press Asn.(former mgr); Kappa Tau Alpha; AF&AM; York Rite. Rel: Methodist. Mailing Add: Black Mountain, N.C. 28711.

GREER, ALBERT R. D
b. 1922. Educ: N.Mex. Sch. of Mines, B.S. Polit. & Govt. Pos: N.Mex. State Sen, 61-66. Bus. & Prof. Pos: Petroleum engr. Mil. Serv: Navy submarine serv, WWII. Mem: Elks. Rel: Methodist. Mailing Add: 158 Petroleum Center Blvd, Farmington, N.Mex. 87401. (1967)

GREER, MICHAEL IRA D
Co. Cmnr, San Diego Co, Calif.
b. Detroit, Mich, 5/2/34; s. Claude Grasgreen and Faye Stellar G; m. 1/29/55 to June Lee; c. Jeffrey, Keri and Jennifer. Educ: Univ. Calif, Los Angeles, B.A, 57; Univ. Calif, Los Angeles Law Sch, J.D, 60; Phi Sigma Delta. Polit. & Govt. Pos: Asst. U.S. Attorney, Los Angeles, Calif, 60-62; mem, San Diego Co. Dem. Cent. Cmt, currently; mem, Calif. Dem. State Cent. Cmt, currently; del, Dem. Nat. Conv, 68; co. cmnr, San Diego Co, Calif, currently. Mil. Serv: Entered as Cadet, Air Force, 53, released as Airman 2/C, 55, after serv. in Texas. Mem: Am, Calif. and San Diego Bar Asns; Am. Trial Lawyers Asn; Big Brothers of San Diego Co; Mens Dem. Club. Rel: Jewish. Mailing Add: 5831 Madra St, San Diego, Calif. 92120.

GREER, WILLIAM CALVIN D
Md. State Del.
b. Harford County, Md. 2/26/24; s. Grover Cleveland Greer and Annie Osborne G; m. 5/8/48 to Mary Patricia Short; c. William C, Jr, Mary Elizabeth, Michael Dudley, Patricia Carroll, Marianne, Maureen, Timothy Shaun and John Terrence. Educ: Univ. of Md, 44-47; Kappa Alpha. Polit. & Govt. Pos: Md. State Del, 67- Bus. & Prof. Pos: General Manager, Greer Transportation Co, Bel Air, Md, currently. Mem: Bel Air Rotary; Churchville Raritan; Harford County Farm Bureau. Junior Chamber of Commerce Award for Outstanding State Physical Fitness Leadership. Rel: Catholic. Mailing Add: R.D. 1, Box 576, Churchville, Md. 21028.

GREGERSON, MARY PAT D
b. Cass County, Iowa, 5/25/38; d. John E. Amder and Mary A; m. 8/63 to Dallas Gregerson. Educ: Creighton Univ, B.A, 60, M.A, 65. Polit. Pos: Iowa State Rep, 66; 7th Dist. Committeewoman, Young Dems. Bus. & Prof. Pos: High Sch. Eng. Teacher. Rel: Catholic. Mailing Add: 106 Happy Hollow Blvd, Council Bluffs, Iowa. 51501.

GREGG, CHARLES STONE D
Committeeman, Bergen Co. Dem. Cmt, N.J.
b. N.Y.C, 5/27/28; s. William Burr Gregg and Dorothy Kilbourne G; m. 11/15/51 to Patricia Hagerty; c. Paul Laurent, John Francis, Peter Kevin, Dorothy Kilbourne, Catherine Patricia, James Burr and Thaddeus Bartholomew. Educ: Univ. Nanking, China, 48-49; Columbia Univ, 49-51. Polit. & Govt. Pos: Committeeman, Bergen Co. Dem. Cmt, N.J, 65-; finance chmn, 66-68, v.chmn, 66-68; munic. chmn, Ridgewood Dem. Party, 66-68 & 69-; trustee, Montclair State Col, 67-69; trustee, Bd. Libr. Trustees, Ridgewood, N.J, 67-, mem. transportation cmt, 68-; Dem. cand. U.S. House Rep, Seventh Cong. Dist, 68. Bus. & Prof. Pos: Staff reporter, Passaic Herald-News, N.J, 51-52; bur. chief, N.Y. Daily News, 52-58; pub. rels. dir, N.Y. Cent. Syst, 58-59; spec. proj. dir, NBC-TV Network, N.Y, 59-63; pres. and publisher, Gregg Press, Upper Saddle River, N.J, 63- Mil. Serv: Entered as Pvt, Army, 45, released as S/Sgt, 48, after serv. in Allied Translator and Interpreter Serv, Gen. Hq, SCAP, Tokyo, Japan, 46-48; Good Conduct Medal; Meritorious Serv. Citation; Victory Medal. Mem: Fel. Peabody Mus. Salem; fel. N.Y. Hist. Soc; Am. Libr. Asn; Citizens for Kennedy or Muskie in 1972; Rotary; Am. Vet. Cmt; C. of C; For. Policy Asn. Rel: Roman Catholic. Legal Res: 33 Maynard Court, Ridgewood, N.J. 07450. Mailing Add: 121 Pleasant Ave, Upper Saddle River, N.J. 07458.

GREGG, HUGH R
b. Nashua, N.H, 11/22/17; s. Harry A. Gregg and Margaret Richardson G; m. 7/24/40 to Catherine Marshall Warner; c. Cyrus W. and Judd A. Educ: Yale Univ, A.B, 39; Harvard Law Sch, LL.B, 42; Alpha Sigma Phi. Hon. degrees, Univ. N.H, New Eng. Col. and Dartmouth Col. Polit. & Govt. Pos: Al-

derman-at-lg, Nashua, N.H, 48-50, mayor, 50; Gov, N.H, 53-55. Bus. & Prof. Pos: Attorney-at-law, Sullivan & Gregg, 46-; pres. & treas, Gregg & Son, Inc, 47-; chmn. bd, Indian Head Nat. Bank, Nashua, 48-; pres, Nashua Fresh Air Camp, 48-; chmn. bd, Wildcat Corp, 58-, N.H. Bankshares, 64- and Indian Head Nat. Bank, Manchester, 65-; pres. & treas, Gregg Cabinets, Ltd, Can, 65-; dir, Can. Kitchen Cabinet Asn, 68- Mil. Serv: Entered as Air Force Cadet, 42, released as Spec. Agent, Counter Intel. Corps, 52, after serv. in Mil. Intel. Res, ETO, Mediterranean and China-Burma-India, 43-45 and Korea; usual campaign ribbons. Publ: Co-publisher, New Hampshire Profiles, 59-65. Mem: Nashua, N.H, Mass. and Am. Bar Asns; Nat. Kitchen Cabinet Asn.(former v.pres); former pres. and chmn. of bd, New Eng. Coun; VFW; Am. Legion; various police asns. Rel: Congregational. Mailing Add: R.F.D. 2, Nashua, N.H. 03060.

GREGG, JAMES ERWIN D
Mem, Butte Co. Dem. Cent. Cmt, Calif.
b. Harrisburg, Pa, 5/3/27; s. Clarence Richard Gregg, Sr. and Mabel Elicker G; m. 6/11/55 to Lyla Pauline Korb; c. William Jason, Richard James, Joan Nancy and Michael Eric. Educ: Lebanon Valley Col, B.A, 50; Univ. Calif, Berkeley, M.A, 54; Univ. Calif, Santa Barbara, Ph.D, 64; Pi Gamma Mu. Polit. & Govt. Pos: Admin. asst, U.S. Navy, China Lake, Calif, 51-52; staff secy. for Educ, Gov. Edmund G. Brown, Calif, 65-66; del, Dem. Nat. Conv, 68; mem, Butte Co. Dem. Cent. Cmt, 68- Bus. & Prof. Pos: Teacher, counsr. and head dept, Shasta Union High Sch. and Jr. Col, Calif, 52-59; asst. prof. journalism, Chico State Col, 59-62, assoc. prof. journalism and polit. sci, 64-68 and prof. and head dept. polit. sci, 68-; dir. student publ, Univ. Calif, Santa Barbara, 62-63 and teaching fel. polit. sci, 63-64. Mil. Serv: Entered as A/S, Navy, 45, released as Photo Mate 3/C, 46, after serv. in U.S.S. Cape Gloucester CVE-109, Pac. Theatre, 46. Publ: 'Newspaper Editorial Endorsements and California Elections,' Journalism Quart, autumn 65; 'Newspaper Endorsements and Local Elections in California,' Univ. Calif, Davis, 5/66; 'Journalism Advisor,' P. Wallace Pischel, spring 66. Mem: Am, West. and North. Calif. Polit. Sci. Asns; Am. Fedn. Teachers; Calif. Col. & Univ. Faculty Asn. Ford Found. Fel, 54-55; Wall Street J. Journalism fel, 59; Nat. Center for Educ. in Polit. fel, 65-66; Pub. Rels. Soc. Am. fel, 65. Mailing Add: 1655 Filbert Ave, Chico, Calif. 95926.

GREGG, MARIE ELLEN R
Chmn, Stevens Co. Rep. Cent. Cmt, Kans.
b. Cherokee Co, Okla, 3/10/14; d. Thomas Lafayette Manes and Irene Nations M; m. 9/15/34 to Elden Marion Gregg; c. John Elden, Keith Thomas and Carl Donald. Educ: High sch. grad; Nat. Honor Soc. Polit. & Govt. Pos: Precinct committeewoman, Kans, 64; v.chmn, Stevens Co. Rep. Cent. Cmt, 64-68, chmn, 68-; organized, Women's Rep. Club, 66; sponsor, Stevens Co. TAR, 66- Bus. & Prof. Pos: Cooperator and mgr, E.M. Gregg Truck Serv, 51-63, traffic mgr, E.M. Gregg, Inc, 63-68 and adv. and consult, 68-69; acct, Rowland Construction Co, 68-69. Mem: Kans. Acct. Coun, Kans. Motor Carriers; Nat. Acct. and Finance Coun, Am. Trucking Asns; Nat. Fedn. Independant Bus; Hugoton C. of C; Kans. C. of C; Home Demonstration Unit, Stevens Co. Knife and Fork Club; Stevens Co. TAR Club; Rep. Southwest Kans; Stevens Co. Rep. Women's Club; Kans. Rep. Five Score Club; Young Am. for Freedom; Rep. Nat. Cmt. Rel: Church of God. Mailing Add: 141 S. Madison, Hugoton, Kans. 67951.

GREGOIRE, EDWARD PAUL R
Chmn, Bannock Co. Rep. Cent. Cmt, Idaho
b. Pocatello, Idaho, 6/10/27; s. George H. Gregoire and Josephine Robison G; m. 10/30/60 to Maria Kallimopolou; c. Jeannine and Janette. Educ: Idaho State Univ. Polit. & Govt. Pos: Chmn, Bannock Co. Rep. Cent. Cmt, Idaho, currently; Rep. precinct committeeman, 63-64. Bus. & Prof. Pos: Mgr, Pioneer Motors, Pocatello, Idaho, 48-54; sales mgr, Staples-Dodge-Plymouth, Beverly Hills, Calif, 54-55; dist. sales mgr, Chrysler Corp, 55-57; sales mgr, Simmons Motor Co, Austin, Tex, 57-58; v.pres, City Motors, Inc, Pocatello, Idaho, 58-66, pres, 66-; v.pres, Parkin Auto Parts, 64- Mil. Serv: Entered as A/S, Navy, 45, released as Seaman 1/C, 46. Mem: Navy League; Idaho Automobile Dealers; Nat. Automobile Dealers; Elks. Private Pilots License. Rel: Catholic. Mailing Add: City Motors, Inc, Pocatello, Idaho 83201. (1967)

GREGORY, CARSON D
b. Harnett Co, N.C, 8/11/11; s. Alex Gregory, Carra Parrish G; m. 11/4/39 to Blanche Williams; c. Carson, Jr, Joe, Frances. Educ: Campbell Col. Polit. & Govt. Pos: N.C. State Rep, 51-66; mem, bd. of trustees and financial sec, cmnr, Harnett Co, 48-50; Coats Agr. Planning Cmn. Bus. & Prof. Pos: Farmer; dairyman; dealer in dairy cattle, breeder, reg. Spotted Poland China Swine; owner, Red Bird Cab Co; real estate bus. Mem: Pres, N.C. Spotted Breeders Asn; v.pres, Harnett Cty. Artificial Breeders' Asn; former mem, Agr. Found, Inc. of N.C. State Col; former local AAA Comm; former chmn, v.chmn. pres, Farm Bur; former Harnett Cty. Kellogg Comm; former chmn, Finance Comm. and dist. chmn, Finance Drive, Boy Scouts, Harnett Cty; W.O.W; Erwin Lodge, J.O.U.A.M; former state dep. councilor of N.C. Jr. Order, United Am. Mechs; Masons; v.pres, Shrine; Coats Fellowship Club. Rel: Baptist; former pres, Sunday Sch. class; former mem. bd. of deacons and brotherhood of First Baptist Church. Mailing Add: Route 2, Angier, N.C. 27501. (1967)

GREGORY, DICK Peace
Co-Chmn, New Party
b. St. Louis, Mo, 1932; m. 1959 to Lillian G; c. Michelle, Lynn, Paula, Pamela, Stephanie, Gregory and Miss. Educ: South. Ill. Univ, 51-53 and 55-56; outstanding athlete, 53. Polit. & Govt. Pos: Chmn, Nat. Conf. for New Polit, 67-; co-chmn, New Party, 69- Bus. & Prof. Pos: Nightclub, TV and recording artist; comedian, appearances at Playboy Club and Esquire Club, Chicago, master of ceremonies, Roberts Show Club, Chicago, Mil. Serv: Army, 53-55. Publ: What's Happening, 65; The Shadow That Scares Me, Doubleday, 68; Write Me In, Bantam Books, 68; weekly nationwide syndicated column; plus others. Mailing Add: 1451 E. 55th St, Chicago, Ill. 60615.

GREGORY, EDWIN PAUL D
Chmn, Dem. Party, Colchester, Conn.
b. Colchester, Conn, 2/21/08; s. Paul Gregor Kewich and Malvina G. Zywicki K; m. 6/22/41 to Ruth Anastasia Hury; c. Edwin Paul, Jr, Arthur and Gary. Polit. & Govt. Pos: Conn. State Rep, 55-56; judge, Colchester, Conn, 56-60; chmn, Dem. Party, Colchester, 62- Bus. & Prof. Pos: Owner, Gregory's Soda Shop, 36- Mil. Serv: Pvt, Army, 41-43. Mem: Lions (past pres); Am. Legion (past comdr, Donald A. Bigelow Post 54); St. Joseph Soc; Colchester Fish and Game Club. Rel: Catholic. Mailing Add: 14 Broadway, Colchester, Conn. 06415. (1967)

GREGORY, GEORGE WINFIELD, JR. D
b. Jefferson, S.C, 6/5/38; s. George W. Gregory, Sr. and Harriet Venters G; m. 6/29/62 to Sharon Bennett; c. Sharon Kristen. Educ: Univ. S.C, B.A, 59, Law Sch, LL.B, 62; Sigma Chi. Polit. & Govt. Pos: S.C. State Sen, Eighth Dist, until 68. Mil. Serv: Entered as 1st Lt, Army, 63, released as Capt, 66; Capt, Army Res. Mem: Am. and S.C. Bar Asns; Chesterfield Co. Bar; Am. Legion; Jr. C. of C. Rel: Presbyterian. Legal Res: 104 Clyde Ave, Cheraw, S.C. 29520. Mailing Add: 121 Chesterfield Rd, Cheraw, S.C. 29520.

GREGORY, HOWARD EVANS R
V.Chmn, Eighth Dist. Rep. Cmt, Va.
b. Newport News, Va, 12/29/28; s. Richeson Todd Gregory and Jennie Howard G; m. 9/2/50 to Sara Leonard Rowlett; c. Janet Lee and Susan Carol. Educ: Georgetown Col, B.S, 50; Tex. A&M Univ, D.V.M, 54; Gamma Sigma Epsilon; Kappa Alpha. Polit. & Govt. Pos: Chmn, Fredericksburg Rep. Cmt, Va, 62-65; city councilman, Fredericksburg, Va, 64-68; v.chmn, Eighth Dist. Rep. Cmt, 68- Mem: Am. and Va. Vet. Med. Asns; Farm Bur; Jr. C. of C.(local dir. and v.pres, 61-62). Distinguished Serv. Award, Fredericksburg Jaycees, 62. Rel: Baptist. Legal Res: 306 Chancellor Place, Fredericksburg, Va. 22401. Mailing Add: Jefferson Davis Blvd, Fredericksburg, Va. 22401.

GREGORY, JAMES R
b. Williamsport, Ind, 2/26/15; s. John Rupert Gregory and Daisy Haughton G; c. John R, Alison, James R, Martha Elizabeth and Marianne. Educ: DePauw Univ, A.B. in econ, 37; Sigma Delta Chi; Delta Kappa Epsilon. Polit. & Govt. Pos: Spec. Asst. to Secy. Navy, 53-54; Fla. State Sen, Dist. 48, 66-68. Bus. & Prof. Pos: Advert. mgr, Rough Notes Co, 38-42, v.pres. and ed, 45-54; pres, Dilley, Martin & Hess, Inc, 55-64; pres, Gregory & Sons, 64-66. Mil. Serv: Entered as Ens, Naval Res, 42, released as Lt. Comdr, 54, after serv. in LCT Group 23, Southwest Pac, Seventh Fleet; Silver Star; Legion of Merit with Combat V; Purple Heart; Five Naval Unit Commendations; Atlantic and Pac. Campaign Ribbons; Victory Medal. Mem: Am. Legion; Am. Farm Bur; Military Order of Purple Heart. Farming. Rel: Episcopal. Mailing Add: 102 S.E. 16th Ave, Ft. Lauderdale, Fla. 33301.

GREGORY, NOBLE JONES D
b. Mayfield, Ky, 8/30/97; s. William Jones Gregory and Rosa A. Boyd G; m. 6/22/25 to Marion Hale; c. Marion (Mrs. H. Foster Pettit). Educ: Mayfield High Sch. grad; Mayfield Bus. Col; Gardner Col, grad. Polit. & Govt. Pos: U.S. Rep, First Dist, Ky, 36-59, mem, For. Affairs Cmt, U.S. House Rep, until 43, mem, Ways and Means Cmt, Joint Cmt. on Internal Revenue Taxation, Joint Cmt. on Reduction of Nonessential Fed. Expenditures and Dem. Nat. Cong. Cmt; mem, Ky. Water Pollution Control Cmn, currently. Bus. & Prof. Pos: Dir, Ky-Tenn. Clay Co, Mayfield, Ky. and Commonwealth Securities Investors, Versailles; dir. and chmn. of bd, Bankers South, Louisville; pres, Gregory & Peal, Inc, Investments; former dir, Citizens Bank and Trust Co, Jeffersonville, Ind. Mem: Four Rivers Area Dir, Boy Scouts; Elks; Odd Fellows; MWA; WOW; Graves Co. Farm Bur; Ky. Hist. Soc; Filson Club; Pendennis Club; Keeneland Asn; Girl Scouts (area finance chmn, Bear Creek Coun). Rel: Presbyterian; Elder. Mailing Add: 518 S. Second St, Mayfield, Ky. 42066.

GREGORY, NORRIS PAIGE, JR. D
City Councilman, San Bernardino, Calif.
b. Ft. Riley, Kans, 4/6/26; s. Norris Paige Gregory, Sr. and Marion Miller G; m. 12/26/46 to Salena Tyree Conway; c. Norris Paige, III. Educ: Washburn Munic. Univ, B.A, 58; Univ. Kans, M.Ed, 58; Calif. State Col, Los Angeles, grad. study; Univ. Calif, Riverside, grad. study; Phi Delta Kappa; Kappa Alpha Psi. Polit. & Govt. Pos: City councilman, San Bernardino, Calif, 67-; mem, Calif. Dem. State Cent. Cmt, 68. Bus. & Prof. Pos: Elem. teacher, Topeka City Schs, Kans, 50-51; nat. sales dir, Lustrasilk Corp, Minneapolis, Minn, 52-53; v.pres. and counsr, Boys Indust. Sch, Topeka, Kans, 54-58; elem. teacher, San Bernardino City Unified Sch. Dist, Calif, 58-66 and Fed. Aid Adminstr, 68-69. Mil. Serv: Entered as Pvt, Army, 44, released as 1st Lt, 46, after serv. in 3062nd Engr. D.T. Co, ETO and S.E. Asian Theatre, 45-46; ETO Medal; S.E. Asian Theatre Medal; Japanese Invasion Medal; Good Conduct Medal. Mem: San Bernardino and Calif. Teachers' Asns; Nat. Educ. Asn; Am. Legion; VFW; NAACP; Inland Empire Urban League. Rel: Catholic. Legal Res: 1540 W. 16th St, San Bernardino, Calif. 92405. Mailing Add: City Hall, San Bernardino, Calif. 92401.

GREGORY, THORNE D
N.C. State Rep.
b. Halifax, N.C, 12/25/29; s. Fletcher Harrison Gregory and Boyd Thorne G; m. 2/23/57 to Hester Elizabeth Lockett; c. Hester Elizabeth, Boyd Wynn, Ann Harrison and Thorne, Jr. Educ: Univ. of N.C, A.B, 52, Sch. of Banking, grad, 60; Zeta Psi; Order of Ghimghoul; German Club. Polit. & Govt. Pos: Dir, Roanoke River Basin Asn; mem, Atlantic State Marine Fisheries Cmt. and Fed. and Interstate Coop. Cmt; N.C. State Rep, 60-, mem, Nat. Legis. Conf. on Rules and Procedure, Nat. Hwy. Policy Cmt, N.C. Bd. Higher Educ. and N.C. Adv. Budget Cmn. Bus. & Prof. Pos: Dir, Halifax Co. Hosiery Mills, N.C; dir. and v.pres, Bank of Halifax; dir. and v.pres, Br. Banking & Trust Co, currently. Mil. Serv: Entered as 2nd Lt, Air Force, 52, released as 1st Lt, 56, after serv. in Training Command, Fighter Pilot and Instr. Mem: Kiwanis; Am. Legion. All Air Force Tennis Championships, 56. Rel: Episcopal. Legal Res: 2318 Beechridge Rd, Raleigh, N.C. 27608. Mailing Add: Branch Banking & Trust Co, Raleigh, N.C. 27601.

GREGORZEK, JOSEPH D
Conn. State Rep.
b. Nanticoke, Pa, 7/25/36; s. Peter Gregorzek and Mary Orzechowski G; m. 5/30/69 to Gayle Wright Simpson. Educ: Cent. Conn. State Col, 1½ years. Polit. & Govt. Pos: Committeeman, Town Cmt, New Britain, Conn, 68; justice of peace, New Britain, 68; Conn. State Rep, 28th Dist, 69- Bus. & Prof. Pos: Asst. circulation mgr, New Britain Herald, 65- Mil. Serv: Entered as Re-

cruit, Army, 58, released as SP-5, 64, after serv. in Regular and Res. Units. Mem: Elks; pres, New Britain Press Club; Young Men's Indust. Forum, New Britain; Young Dem. of Conn; Pulaski Dem. Club; New Britain Ski Club. Rel: Roman Catholic. Mailing Add: 532 Church St, New Britain, Conn. 06051.

GREGSON, MARY POAGE R
Mem, Roanoke Co. Rep. Cmt, Va.
b. Roanoke Co, Va, 4/16/10; d. Harvey Claytor Poage and Lucy Dyer P; m. 12/30/44 to Carl Louis Gregson; c. Naomi (Mrs. Ramsey), Carol (Mrs. Mills), Carl L, Jr, Molly Poage and Jeff S. Educ: Radford Col, grad, 29. Polit. & Govt. Pos: Clerk, Va. precinct for 25 years; del, Rep. Nat. Conv, 64; mem, Co. Rep. Cmt; corresponding secy, Roanoke Valley Rep. Woman's Club, 65-66; pres, Roanoke Valley Rep. Club; mem, Roanoke Co. Rep. Cmt, currently; mem, Rep. State Cent. Cmt, Va, 68-; mem, Roanoke Co. Welfare Bd, 69- Bus. & Prof. Pos: Elem. sch. teacher, Va. for 18 years. Mem: Tuberc. Asn.(bd); PTA; bd. dirs, Mercy House Inc. Rel: Presbyterian. Mailing Add: Route 7, Box 327, Roanoke, Va. 24018.

GREIGG, STANLEY L. D
b. Ireton, Iowa, 5/7/31; s. Robert D. Greigg and Hattie M. Torwelle G; m. 6/26/65 to Cathryn Olivia Thomson; c. Valerie. Educ: Morningside Col, B.A, 54; Maxwell Grad. Sch, Syracuse Univ, fel. and M.A. in hist. Polit. & Govt. Pos: Mem. city coun, Sioux City, Iowa, 61-64, mayor, 64-65; U.S. Rep, Iowa, 65-67 and mem. cmt. on agr; exec. asst. to Asst. Postmaster Gen, U.S. Post Off. Dept, 67, dir, Off. of Regional Admin, 67-69. Mil. Serv: Navy, 57-59. Mem: Sponsor, Northwest Iowa Commun. Conf, Aug, 65 and Northwest Iowa Indust. Opportunities Conf, Nov, 65. Rel: Lutheran. Mailing Add: 1526 S. Helen St, Sioux City, Iowa 51106.

GREINER, KEITH ALLEN R
Chmn, Lyon Co. Rep. Cent. Cmt, Kans.
b. Hunter, Kans, 2/24/40; s. Wendell Whitson Greiner and Lois Jaeger G; m. 12/22/63 to Sarah Jane Steerman; c. Laura Elaine and Keith Allen, Jr. Educ: Wichita State Univ, 58-59; Kans. State Teachers Col, B.A, 62, study, 62-63; Univ. Va, Charlottesville, LL.B, 66; Blue Key; Pi Gamma Mu; Kappa Mu Epsilon. Polit. & Govt. Pos: Pres, Kans. Collegiate Young Rep, 62-63. Bus. & Prof. Pos: Lawyer, Steerman, Perkins & Greiner, Emporia, Kans, 66- Mem: Am, Kans. and Lyon Co. Bar Asns; Am. Judicature Soc; Rotary; C. of C; Jaycees; Am. Cancer Soc.(dir, Kans. Div); Emporia Country Club. Rel: Protestant. Mailing Add: 1033 Walnut, Emporia, Kans. 66801.

GREINER, WILLIAM MERLIN R
Chmn, Muskingum Co. Rep. Cent. Cmt, Ohio
b. Zanesville, Ohio, 1/31/26; s. William Martin Greiner and Mildred Eddy G; m. 5/2/49 to Phyllis C. Webster; c. William Mark (deceased), Lisa Karen, Jeff Jay, Erin Gale and Eric Martin. Educ: Zanesville High Sch, 4 years. Polit. & Govt. Pos: Committeeman, Washington Twp. Rep. Party, Ohio, 66; mem, Muskingum Co. Rep. Club, 66; chmn, Muskingum Co. Rep. Cent. Cmt, 68- Bus. & Prof. Pos: Agent, Prudential Ins. Co, 63- Mil. Serv: Entered as A/S, Navy, 42, released as Signalman 2/C, 46, after serv. in L.S.T, S.Pac, 43-46. Mem: Life Underwriters; AMROV Grotto; Charity Newsies; Old Timers Baseball; Muskingum Co. Fair Bd; Eagles; Layfette Lodge Masons; Union of Life Underwriters; Muskingum Co. Rep. Club. Rel: Protestant. Mailing Add: Route 4, East Pike, Zanesville, Ohio 43701.

GREIVE, R. R. 'BOB' D
Wash. State Sen.
b. West Seattle, Wash, 10/6/19; s. Raymond Greive and Kathleen G; m. 4/23/50 to Barbara Ann Cough; c. Bernadette Marie, Mary Janis, Kathleen Anne, Raymond Peter, James Joseph and Thomas John. Educ: Seattle Univ; Univ. Wash; Univ. Miami Sch. of Law. Polit. & Govt. Pos: Wash. State Sen, currently, Majority Leader, Wash. State Sen, 14 years. Bus. & Prof. Pos: Attorney, Greive & Law, Seattle. Mil. Serv: Coast Guard during World War II. Mem: Lions; Am. Legion; Elks. Rel: Catholic. Legal Res: 5116 S.W. Hudson, Seattle, Wash. 98116. Mailing Add: 4444 California Ave. S.W, Seattle, Wash. 98116.

GRELLNER, JOHN A. D
Mo. State Rep.
b. St. Louis, Mo, 11/29/37; single. Educ: St. Louis Univ, B.S. Polit. & Govt. Pos: Mo. State Rep, 64- Bus. & Prof. Pos: Ins. adjustor, Gen. Ins, Inc; staff asst. to dir, Civic Develop, C. of C, Metrop. St. Louis. Mem: Maplewood Fats & Leans Charitable Orgn; St. Louis Jr. C. of C; K. of C. Rel: Catholic. Mailing Add: 7380 Dale Ave, Richmond Heights, Mo. 63117. (1967)

GREMILLION, ALLEN CASTLE D
La. State Rep.
b. Crowley, La, 11/5/28; s. Curtis L. Gremillion and Beatrice Watson G; m. to Judith Childers. Educ: Univ. Southwest. La, 46-47; La. State Univ, 47-48, Law Sch, LL.B, 51. Polit. & Govt. Pos: La. State Rep, Acadia Parish, 64-68, 35th Dist, 68- Bus. & Prof. Pos: Oil well logging engr. and ore analyst, Core Lab, Inc, La, 51-52; attorney-at-law, 52- Mil. Serv: Entered as Seaman 1/C, Navy, 45, released as Seaman 2/C, 46, after serv. in LSU 247, Seventh Amphibious Fleet, S.Pac, 45-46; Asiatic, Pac, Am. Theatre and Victory Ribbons. Mem: Am, La. State, 15th Judicial Dist. and Acadia Parish Bar Asns; La. State Jr. Bar Asn; Am. Legion; Optimist; Cattlemen's Asn; Boy Scouts (Evangeline Coun. and Acadia Dist). Rel: Baptist. Legal Res: 625 E. Fourth St, Crowley, La. 70526. Mailing Add: 529 W. Court Circle, Crowley, La. 70526.

GREMILLION, JACK PAUL FAUSTIN D
Attorney Gen. of La.
b. Donaldsonville, La, 6/15/14; s. William Kossuth Gremillion and Genoa Henderson G; m. 1/12/42 to Doris McDonald; c. Jack Paul Faustin, William McDonald, Wayne Francis and Doris H. Polit. & Govt. Pos: Attorney, Dept. of Revenue, 40-42; second asst. dist. attorney, Parish E. Baton Rouge, La, 52-53, first asst. dist. attorney, 53-56; Attorney Gen. La, 56- Mil. Serv: Army, 42-45, 1st Lt, serv. in 106th and Third Inf. Div. Mem: Nat. Asn. Attorneys Gen; Am. Legion (past post pres); Mil. Order World Wars; C. of C; K. of C; Elks; Lions; Young Mens Bus. Asn.(pres, 40). Admitted to La. Bar, Fed. Courts, U.S. Supreme Court. Mailing Add: 5475 Capital Heights Ave, Baton Rouge, La. 70806. (1967)

GREMMINGER, JOHN E. D
b. Chester, Pa, 3/13/09; s. William Gremminger and Annie Mulrine G; m. to Alice Barraclough; c. two. Educ: Chester schs. Polit. & Govt. Pos: Pa. State Rep, 60-62, 64-67; Dem. Committeeman, 56-61; Dem. Ward Chmn; Constable, 56-59. Bus. & Prof. Pos: Secy, treas, Transport Workers Union. Mailing Add: 312 E. 22nd St, Chester, Pa. 19013. (1967)

GRENIER, JOHN EDWARD R
Mem, Ala. State Rep. Exec. Cmt.
b. New Orleans, La, 8/24/30; s. Charles Desire Grenier and Elizabeth Schaumburg G; m. 6/12/53 to Lynne Dea Youmans; c. John Beaulieu. Educ: Tulane Univ, LL.B, 53; N.Y. Univ, LL.M, 57; Omicron Delta Kappa; Delta Kappa Epsilon. Polit. & Govt. Pos: Chmn, Jefferson Co. Young Rep. Club, Ala, 60-61; chmn, Ala. Fedn. of Young Rep, 61-62; mem, Jefferson Co. Rep. Exec. Cmt, 62-; mem, Ala. State Rep. Exec. Cmt, 62-, chmn, 62-65; South. Regional dir, Goldwater for President Cmt, 63-64; exec. dir, Rep. Nat. Cmt, 64. Bus. & Prof. Pos: Assoc, Burke and Burke, 56-57; attorney, South. Natural Gas Co, 57-59; mem, Bradley, Arant, Rose & White, 59-66; mem, Lange, Simpson, Robinson and Somerville, currently. Mil. Serv: Entered as 2nd Lt, Marine Corps, 53, released as Capt, 56, after serv. in 121st Squadron, Korea, 55-56; Capt, Marine Corps Res. Mem: Ala, La. and N.Y. Bar Asns; Kiwanis. Rel: Episcopal. Legal Res: 3758 E. Fairway Dr, Birmingham, Ala. 35213. Mailing Add: 1800 City Federal Bldg, Birmingham, Ala. 35203.

GRESHAM, MILDRED MIRIAM R
Secy, Fremont Co. Rep. Cent. Cmt, Colo.
b. Canon City, Colo, 10/7/02; d. Ira Julian Faires and Alice Catherine Vaughn F; m. 6/24/24 to Bryan Collins Gresham. Educ: Canon City High Sch, grad; Canon City Bus. Col, 1 year. Polit. & Govt. Pos: Stenographer clerk, War Dept, Wash. D.C, 24-26; secy, Fremont Co. Rep. Cent. Cmt, Colo, 52- Mem: Am. Legion Auxiliary (past state pres); 40 et 8. Rel: Baptist. Mailing Add: 1304 N. Sixth St, Canon City, Colo. 81212.

GRESSETTE, LAWRENCE MARION D
S.C. State Sen.
b. St. Matthews, S.C, 2/11/02; s. J.T. Gressette and Rosa Wannamaker G; m. 8/18/27 to Florence Howell. Educ: Univ. of S.C, LL.B, 24. Polit. & Govt. Pos: S.C. State Rep, 25-28 & 31-32; S.C. State Sen, 37-, chmn. judiciary and rules cmt; Col, Gov. William's Staff; mem, State Dem. Exec. Cmt, S.C, 48, chmn, 53-54; chmn, S.C. Sch. Cmt, 51-66. Bus. & Prof. Pos: Lawyer. Mem: Fel, Am. Col. Trial Lawyers; Mason; Phi Kappa Phi; Blue Key. Rel: Baptist. Mailing Add: Box 346, St. Matthews, S.C. 29135.

GREWE, FRED A, JR. R
W.Va. State Del.
b. Wheeling, W.Va, 1/26/30; s. Fred A. Grewe, Sr. and Edith V. Stewart G; m. 11/24/51 to Shirley M. Stein; c. Fred A, III, Gail L, Elaine J. and Diane M. Polit. & Govt. Pos: Mem, Wheeling City Coun, 63-67; W.Va. State Del, 67- Bus. & Prof. Pos: Pres, Miracle Valley Broadcasting, 64-, Westmoreland Broadcasting, 66- and WPAR Inc, 68- Mil. Serv: Entered as Pvt, Marine Corps, 47, released as Sgt, 53, after serv. in Anglico & 11th Marines; Good Conduct Medal. Mem: Lions; Elks; Am. Legion; K. of C; Jaycees; Downtown Wheeling Assocs; Holy Name Soc. Named Outstanding Jaycee State of W.Va, 63. Rel: Catholic. Mailing Add: 24 Park View Lane, Wheeling, W.Va. 26003.

GREWE, ISABELLE McNAUGHTON R
Secy, Rep. Party of Wis.
b. Middleville, Mich, 5/10/10; d. Charles Peter McNaughton and Hazel Mitchell M; m. 6/24/33 to Raymond Howard Grewe; c. Thomas M. and John M. Educ: Univ. Minn, Minneapolis, B.S. in Health Supv. of Sch. Child, 31; Chi Omega. Polit. & Govt. Pos: Part-time vol. case worker, State Dept. of Pub. Instr, Local Pub. and Private Agencies and State Dept. of Pub. Welfare-Div. of Children and Youth, Wis, 33-39; mem. and officer, Eau Claire Co. Children's Bd, 33-53; mem, Eau Claire Co. Rep. Club, 50; pres, Eau Claire Co. Fedn. of Rep. Women, 53-57; mem, Wis. Rep. State Cent. Cmt, 54-60; alternate del, Rep. Nat. Conv, 56, 60 & 68; v.chmn, Ninth Cong. Dist. Rep. Party, Wis, 57-63; mem. exec. cmt, Rep. Party of Wis, 57-, secy, 63- Bus. & Prof. Pos: Dir, Health Educ, Hennepin Co. Anti-tuberc. Asn, Minneapolis, Minn, 31-33, part-time employ, 34-36. Mem: Wis. Conf. Soc. Work; Wis. Ment. Health Asn; Wis. Anti-tuberc. Asn; Wis. Children's Aid Soc; Sacred Heart and Luther Hosp. Guilds; Eau Claire Woman's Club. Rel: United Church of Christ. Mailing Add: 122 Wold Court, Eau Claire, Wis. 54701.

GREY, ROBERT THADDEUS, JR. D
b. Shirley, Mass, 1/14/36; s. Robert Thaddeus Grey and Marie Walsh G; m. 12/28/59 to Ann Kriegel Guilford; c. Anne-Marie, Robert Livingstone and Liv Erika. Educ: Dartmouth Col, B.A, 57; Univ. Mich, J.D, 60. Polit. & Govt. Pos: Third secy, Am. Embassy, Oslo, Norway, 61-63; second secy, Am. Embassy, Ouagadougou, Upper Volta, 63-65; spec. asst. to under-secy. of state for polit. affairs, Dept. of State, 66-69; admin. asst. U.S. Sen. Alan Cranston, Calif, currently. Legal Res: 857 Milldale Rd, Cheshire, Conn. 06410. Mailing Add: 925 N. Van Dorn St, Alexandria, Va. 22304.

GRICE, BENNING MOORE D
b. Hawkinsville, Ga, 9/16/09; s. Warren Grice and Clara Elberta Rumph G; m. 10/18/41 to Mary Flavia Calhoun; c. Benning M, Jr, Ann Victoria and Warren C. Educ: Mercer Univ, A.B, 31, LL.B, 32; Blue Key; Kappa Alpha Order. Polit. & Govt. Pos: Ga. State Rep, 39-42; part time judge, Juvenile Court of Bibb Co, 46-59; mem, Ga. Bd. of Bar Exams, 57-60; assoc. justice, Supreme Court of Ga, 61- Mil. Serv: Entered as Lt.(jg), Navy, 42, released as Lt. Comdr, 45, after serv. in Continental U.S, 42-44 and in Fifth and Third Fleets, Pac. Theater, 44-45; Lt. Comdr.(Ret), Naval Res, 45-56; Am. and Pac. Theater Ribbons; Japanese Victory Medal with Three Battle Stars. Mem: Macon, Ga. and Am. Bar Asns; pres, Macon Circuit Bar Asn, 53-54; Mason; Scottish Rite, KCCH; pres, Cent. Ga. Boy Scout Coun, 55-58; pres, Law Chap, Mercer Alumni Asn, 50-51; YMCA; trustee, Ga. Indust. Home, 37-42; pres, Kiwanis, 51. Selected Macon's Outstanding Young Man, 40. Rel: Baptist. Legal Res: 3065 High Point Dr, Macon, Ga. 31204. Mailing Add: 533 State Judicial Bldg, Atlanta, Ga. 30334.

GRIDER, GEORGE WILLIAM D
b. Memphis, Tenn, 10/1/12; s. John McGaveck Grider and Marguerite Samuels G; m. 1936 to Ann Curlin; c. Lt.(jg) George W. Jr, Gail Ann (Mrs. Gurley), Sally Elizabeth and Wilson Northcross. Educ: Memphis Univ. Sch; Southwest. at Memphis; U.S. Naval Acad, B.S, 36; Univ. of Va, LL.B, 50. Polit. & Govt. Pos: Mem, City Planning Cmn, 56-57; mem, Shelby Co. Quart. Court, Tenn, 59-64; U.S. Rep, Tenn, 64-67. Bus. & Prof. Pos: Lawyer, 50-64. Mil. Serv: Navy, 36-47; commanded the subs 'Flasher' and 'Cubera'; Navy Cross; retired as Capt. because of phys. disability. Publ: War Fish (w. Lydel Sims). Mem: Bar Asn; Engrs. Club; Navy League; Am. Legion; Pres, Coun. of Southwest. at Memphis; Memphis Acad. of Arts; helped found and served as officer and dir, Shelby United Neighbors; Memphis and Tenn. Coun. of Human Rels; local and nat. bd, United Serv. Orgn. Rel: Methodist. 1967 Legal Res: Memphis, Tenn. No mailing address available. (1967)

GRIECO, SALVATORE J. D
N.Y. State Assemblyman
b. Brooklyn, N.Y, 12/5/09; m. to Rose M. Buonadonna; c. Margaret, Jeanette and Andrew. Educ: St. Leonard's Bus. Acad, Brooklyn. Polit. & Govt. Pos: Past dep. cmnr, Dept. of Sanitation of NYC; v.pres, United Regular Dem. Orgn, Inc; N.Y. State Assemblyman, 64- Bus. & Prof. Pos: Real estate, ins, 28-; licensed real estate broker, 32-; licensed ins. broker, 46- Mem: Soc. of Residential Appraisers; Brooklyn and Bay Ridge Real Estate Bds; Nat. Asn. Real Estate Bds; Kings Lions Int. Club; Brooklyn Ins. Brokers Asn; K. of C. (past treas, Baron DeKalb Coun). Rel: Catholic; Trustee, 36- Mailing Add: 1861 W. Third St, Brooklyn, N.Y. 11223. (1967)

GRIER, FRANK R. R
Del. State Sen.
b. 1905. Educ: Univ. of Del. Polit. & Govt. Pos: Mem, State Labor Cmn; State Hwy. Cmn; Milford City Coun; Del. State Sen, 67- Bus. & Prof. Pos: V.Pres, Dentists' Supply Co, N.Y; L.D. Caulk Div. Mem: Bd. Mem, Milford City Hosp; Bd. Mem, Bo-Co. United Fund; AF&AM (past master). Mailing Add: 417 Kings Hwy, Milford, Del. 19963. (1967)

GRIER, J. D, JR. D
b. McDonough, Ga, 12/2/29; s. Joe Dell Grier and Josephine George G; m. 7/2/51 to Henrietta Johnson; c. Lisa Cherryle and Joseph D, III. Educ: Morris Brown, A.B; Gammon Theol. Sem, B.D. Polit. & Govt. Pos: Ga. State Rep, 132nd Dist, until 68. Bus. & Prof. Pos: Minister, Fort Street Mem. Methodist Church, currently. Mem: Ga. Annual Conf, NAACP; Call Man for Oper. Breadbasket; Methodist Ministers Interracial Alliance; past pres, Northeast Civic Commun. Coun. Rel: Methodist. Legal Res: 596 Glen Iris Dr. N.E, Atlanta, Ga. 30308. Mailing Add: 562 Boulevard N.E, Atlanta, Ga. 30308. (1967)

GRIFFEE, JOHN FRANKLIN R
Mem, Ark. State Rep. Exec. Cmt.
b. Ft. Smith, Ark, 8/16/29; s. John Franklin Griffee and Leda Mae Woodruff G; m. 9/17/68 to Pamela Naoma Busby; c. John, Jr, Jeffrey Mark, Karen Lynne and Kimberly Anne. Educ: Univ. Ark, B.A, 52; Wash. Univ. Sch. of Dent, D.D.S, 60; Lambda Chi Alpha; Xi Psi Phi. Polit. & Govt. Pos: Mem, Ark. State Rep. Exec. Cmt, 64-; chmn, Cross Co. and First Cong. Dist. Rep. Cmts, 64- Mil. Serv: Entered as 2nd Lt, Air Force, 51, released as 1st Lt, 56. Mem: Ark. and Am. Dent. Asns; Mason (32°), Ark. Consistory; pres, Wynne C. of C, 64; Lions Int; Univ. Club, Memphis. Rel: Methodist. Legal Res: 306 N. State, Wynne, Ark. 72396. Mailing Add: P.O. Box 24, Wynne, Ark. 72396.

GRIFFEN, DANIEL D
b. Kansas City, Mo, 11/4/00; s. Daniel Griffen and Phebe Mitchell G; m. 12/29/26 to Armeada Mary Werle; c. Esther Armeada, Ruth Mary, Eleanor Mae, Lee Daniel and John K. Educ: Cent. Mich. Univ; East. Mich. Univ; Wayne State Univ; Univ. Mich; Columbia Univ; v.pres, Douglas Debating Soc. Polit. & Govt. Pos: Chmn, Grand Traverse Co. Dem. Cmt, 65-66; nominee, U.S. Rep, Mich, 65; field auditor, Mich. Liquor Control Cmn, Civil Serv, 43-64; social worker, Mich. Social Welfare Dept, Newaygo and later, Lake Co, 37-43; Grand Traverse Co. Recreation Supvr, 34-37; census enumerator, 34; educ. adv, Civilian Conserv. Corps. Prof. Pos: Asst. to Resident Supt. of Building, Traverse City State Hosp. Cottages Construct, 33 and 35; high sch. prin, Williamsburg Consol. Dist, 32-33; attendance officer, Detroit Pub. Schs, Dist. D and F, 30-31; supt. of schs, Higgins-Garrish Twp. Unit Dist, 26-28, Tittabawassee Twp, 25-26 and Millersburg Pub. Schs, 24-25; rural teacher, Dist. 9, Norman Twp, 23-24. Mem: Eagles 383; Pres. and trustee, Local 1034 SC&ME AFL-CIO, Lansing, Mich; sgt. and 1st v.pres, Dads of Foreign Serv. Vet. Post 73, pres, 67-68, publicity chmn, Dept. of Mich, 68-70, dep. chief staff, Dept. of Mich. for Fourth Dist, 69-70. Rel: Catholic. Mailing Add: 321 W. 12th St, Traverse City, Mich. 49684.

GRIFFIN, BEN HILL, JR. D
b. Fort Meade, Fla, 10/20/10; m. to Frances Pearce; c. Harriet, Sarah Jane, Lucy Anne, Ben Hill, III and Francie. Educ: Univ. Fla; Pi Kappa Phi. Polit. & Govt. Pos: Mem. sch. adv. bd. and sch. trustee, Frostproof, Fla; Fla. State Rep, 56-62; Fla. State Sen, 64-68; del, Dem. Nat. Conv, 68. Bus. & Prof. Pos: Citrus growing, packing and processing; cattle; banking. Mem: Mason; Shrine; Elks; Dir, Scout Coun. Rel: Presbyterian. Mailing Add: P.O. Box 368, Frostproof, Fla. 33843. (1967)

GRIFFIN, C. FRANK D
b. Union Co, N.C, 7/22/26; s. N. Charlie Griffin and Mary Marian G; m. 5/30/53 to Betsy Lee; c. Pamela Lee and Tina Marie. Educ: Univ. N.C, B.S, Commerce, 47; Duke Univ. Sch. of Law, LL.B, 50. Polit. & Govt. Pos: N.C. State Sen, 64-68; alternate del, Dem. Nat. Conv, 68. Bus. & Prof. Pos: Lawyer. Mil. Serv: Seaman 2/C, Navy, 44-45. Mem: N.C. and Am. Bar Asns; Delta Sigma Pi; Delta Theta Phi. Rel: Methodist; Mem. Bd. of Stewards and Chmn. Cmt. on Stewardship and Finance, Cent. Methodist Church. Mailing Add: 1200 Lancaster Ave, Monroe, N.C. 28110.

GRIFFIN, CHARLES F. R
b. Mapleton, Iowa, 9/23/10; m. 1934 to Alice Krefta; c. Patricia. Educ: State Univ. of Iowa, Col. of Pharm, grad; Rho Chi. Polit. & Govt. Pos: Iowa State Sen. until 66; Iowa State Bd. of Pharm. Exams; Town Councilman. Bus. & Prof. Pos: Operator of Griffin Pharm. Mem: Masons; Rotary; House of Delegates, Iowa Pharm. Asn. Rel: Methodist. Mailing Add: Mapleton, Iowa. 51034. (1967)

GRIFFIN, CHARLES HUDSON D
U.S. Rep, Miss.
b. Utica, Miss, 5/9/26; s. Charles Farris Griffin and Nora Shelton G; m. 11/8/53 to Angelina Mary Pedrotti. Educ: Hinds Jr. Col, 43-44 and 46-47; Miss. State Univ, B.S. in Pub. Admin, 49; Barristers Club. Polit. & Govt. Pos: Admin. Asst. to U.S. Rep. John Bell Williams, Miss, 49-68; U.S. Rep, Miss, 68- Bus. & Prof. Pos: Dir, Cong. Employees Fed. Credit Union, 63-68. Mil. Serv: Entered as A/S, Navy, 44, released as Qm. 3/C, 46, after serv. in Asiatic-Pac. Theater, 45; Asiatic Pac. Campaign and Victory Ribbons. Mem: Miss. Hist. Soc; Mason; Am. Legion; VFW; Moose. Legal Res: Utica, Miss. 39175. Mailing Add: 1330 Longworth House Office Bldg, Washington, D.C. 20515.

GRIFFIN, EDWARD FOSTER D
N.C. State Sen.
b. Louisburg, N.C, 11/4/00; s. Paul B. Griffin and Frances Wilder G; m. 6/18/25 to Mildred Scott; c. Nancy (Mrs. Person). Educ: Univ. N.C, 1½ years; Wake Forest Col, Law. Polit. & Govt. Pos: Dir. Civil Defense, Raleigh, N.C, 13 years; Franklin Co. Attorney, Louisburg, 10 years; N.C. State Sen, 69- Mil. Serv: Entered as Lt. Col, Army, 40, released as Col, 47, after serv. in 30th Div. Artil, ETO as Commanding Officer, 113th Field Artil. Bn; Army Res, C.G. 30th Inf. Div, 47-61, Maj. Gen.(Ret); 5 Battle Stars, ETO; Oak Leaf Cluster with Bronze Star; Belgian Fourgarre. Mem: Past pres, Nat. Asn. of State Civil Defense Dirs, del. to Nat. Civil Defense Meeting, Paris, France, 60; Nat. Guard rep. on Dedication of ETO Mil. Cemeteries, Europe and N.Africa, 61; Mason; Shrine; Am. Legion; 40 et 8. Rel: United Methodist. Mailing Add: 105 Sunset Ave, Louisburg, N.C. 27549.

GRIFFIN, FRANCIS J. D
N.Y. State Assemblyman
b. Buffalo, N.Y; married; c. Margaret Mary. Educ: Canisius Col. Polit. & Govt. Pos: N.Y. State Assemblyman, 62-; Erie Co. Bd. of Supvrs, 15 years. Bus. & Prof. Pos: Ins. broker. Mem: K. of C; Am. Legion Post 721; Holy Name Soc. of St. Ambrose Parish; Knights of Equity; Brotherhood of Rwy. Clerks. Mailing Add: 38 Treehaven Rd, West Seneca, N.Y. 14224. (1967)

GRIFFIN, FRANK J. R
b. Warren, Vt, 7/18/92; m. to Maude Clough. Educ: Bliss Bus. Col, Lewiston, Maine. Polit. & Govt. Pos: Overseer of the poor, 54-; Vt. State Rep, 65-66. Bus. & Prof. Pos: Retired; granite plant worker. Mem: Mason; Odd Fellows; Grange; Farm Bur. Rel: Methodist. Mailing Add: RFD 2, Waterbury, Vt. 05676. (1967)

GRIFFIN, J. J, JR. D
b. Kissimmee, Fla, 1/16/13; m. to Gail Kinney; c. J. J. III. Educ: Riverside Mil. Acad, Gainesville, Ga. Polit. & Govt. Pos: Fla. State Rep, 52-66. Bus. & Prof. Pos: Ins; dir, Citizens State Bank of St. Cloud; v.pres, First Fed. Sav. & Loan Asn. of Osceola Co. Mem: C. of C. Rel: Presbyterian; Trustee. Mailing Add: P.O. Box 607, St. Cloud, Fla. 32769. (1967)

GRIFFIN, JAMES D. D
N.Y. State Sen.
b. 1929; single. Educ: Erie Co. Tech. Inst. Polit. & Govt. Pos: Ellicott Dist. councilman, Buffalo, 61-65; chmn, Council's Port Cmt; N.Y. State Sen, currently. Bus. & Prof. Pos: Engineer, Buffalo Creek R.R. Mil. Serv: Paratrooper, ranger, Korean War; discharged as Lt. Mem: Brotherhood of Locomotive Firemen and Engineers; St. Brigid Holy Name Soc; K. of C; Downtown YMCA. Mailing Add: 81 Parkview Court, Lackawanna, N.Y. 14218. (1967)

GRIFFIN, MARGARET A. R
N.H. State Rep.
b. Auburn, N.H, 4/1/88; widow; c. Two. Educ: Manchester. Polit. & Govt. Pos: Chmn, Women's Rep. Club; mem. sch. bd; town auditor, Auburn, N.H; mem, Constitutional Conv, 48, 56 & 64; N.H. State Rep, 49- Mem: Grange (past master, Massbesic Chap); Eastern Star (past matron Adah Chap); Ladies Auxiliary, Auburn VFW; Order Women Legislators; Libr. trustee. Rel: Congregational. Mailing Add: Auburn, N.H. 03032. (1967)

GRIFFIN, MARVIN COLLINS D
Secy, United Polit. Orgn. of Tex.
b. Wichita, Kans, 2/20/23; s. Jesse Griffin and Beulah Howell G; m. 8/5/44 to Lois Jesse King; c. Marva Lois, Gaynelle and Ria Joy. Educ: Bishop Col, B.A, 44; Oberlin Grad. Sch. of Theol, B.D, 47; Southwest. Baptist. Theol. Sem, M.R.E, magna cum laude, 55; pres, Col. YMCA. Polit. & Govt. Pos: Mem, Grass Roots Cmt, Waco, Tex, 54, pres, Progressive Voters League, 56-; treas, Action Cmt. to Implement Needs, Waco, 56-; secy, United Polit. Orgn, Tex, Austin, 63-; v.chmn. citizens adv. cmt, Waco Independent Sch. Dist, 64; first v.pres, Tex. Grand Jury Asn, Houston, 65; mem, Waco. Park Bd, 66-; v.chmn, Econ. Opportunity Adv. Corp, Waco, 67-68; alternate del, Dem. Nat. Conv, 68. Bus. & Prof. Pos: Chmn. bd. dirs, Tex. South. Univ, Houston, 63-; pastor, New Hope Baptist Church, Waco, 51-69. Mem: YMCA (chmn, Doris Miller Br, 57-68, v.chmn, 68-; dir, Waco United Fund, 66- Named Alumnus of the Year, Bishop Col; Recipient of Outstanding Leadership Award, West Tex. C. of C. Rel: Baptist. Legal Res: 915 N. Sixth, Waco, Tex. 76707. Mailing Add: 1324 N. Sixth, Waco, Tex. 76707.

GRIFFIN, OSCAR O'NEAL, JR. R
Dep. Info. Dir, Dept. of Transportation
b. Daisetta, Tex, 4/28/33; s. Oscar O'Neal Griffin and Myrtle Ellen Edgar G; m. 7/28/55 to Patricia Lamb; c. Gwendolyn and Amanda. Educ: Univ. Tex, Austin, B.J, 58. Polit. & Govt. Pos: Dep. info. dir, Dept. of Transportation, 69- Bus. & Prof. Pos: Pub. rels. dir, Liberty, Tex, 58-59; ed, Canyon News, 59-60 and Pecos Independent, 60-62; spec. assignments reporter, Houston Chronicle, 62-66, Wash. correspondent, 66-69. Mil. Serv: Entered as Pvt, Army, 53, released as Sgt, 55, after serv. as ed, Ft. Bliss News, 4052nd Area Serv. Unit, Ft. Bliss, Tex, 54-55; Armed Serv. Newspaper Award, 55. Mem: Nat. Press Club; Sigma Delta Chi. Tex. Newspaper Asn. Sweepstakes Award,

60; Pulitzer Prize, 63; Golden Plate Award, Am. Acad. Achievement for Journalism, 64; Tex. Headliners Club Award for Journalistic Reality, 65. Rel: Roman Catholic. Mailing Add: 6424 Woodridge Rd, Alexandria, Va. 22312.

GRIFFIN, RAYMOND P. D
Supvr, Grand Island, N.Y.
b. Buffalo, N.Y, 9/17/24; s. Raymond J. Griffin and Blanche Casper G; m. 11/27/48 to Noreen; c. Patricia, Paul, Laurie, Brian and Raymond. Educ: Univ. Buffalo, Sch. Pharm, B.S, 49; Beta Phi Sigma. Polit. & Govt. Pos: Supvr, Grand Island, N.Y, 64-; minority leader, Erie Co. Bd. Supvrs, 66-67; mem, Erie & Niagara Co. Regional Planning Bd, 67-69; del, Dem. Nat. Conv, 68; pres, Asn. Erie Co. Govt, 69. Bus. & Prof. Pos: Pharmaceutical sales, Parke Davis Co, Buffalo, N.Y, 49-51; pharmacist and store mgr, Miller Drug Co, 51-55, Lane Drug Co, Amherst, N.Y. and Batavia, N.Y, 55-57 and Lane Island Drugs, Grand Island, N.Y, 57-63. Mil. Serv: Entered as Pvt, Army, 42, released as Sgt, 46, after serv. in Co. L, 406th Inf. Regt, 43-46; Capt, Army Res; Silver Star; Bronze Star; Combat Inf. Badge. Mem: VFW; Am. Legion; C. of C; Rotary; K. of C. Grand Island C. of C. Citizen of the Year, 67. Rel: Roman Catholic. Mailing Add: 1421 Whitehaven Road, Grand Island, N.Y. 14072.

GRIFFIN, RICHARD EARL D
Ark. State Sen.
b. El Dorado, Ark, 3/13/39; s. Ervin Earl Griffin and Jo Ellen Posey G; m. 1/1/59 to Betty Marilyn Cutrer; c. Richard Gregory and Robert Edward. Educ: Univ. Ark, B.S.P.A. and LL.B, 63; Sigma Nu; Delta Theta Phi. Polit. & Govt. Pos: Mem, Planning Cmn, Crossett, Ark, 66-; Ark. State Sen, 19th Sen. Dist, 67- Mem: Am. and Ark. Trial Lawyers Asns; Am. and Ark. Bar Asns; Southeast Ark. Legal Inst; Kiwanis. Rel: Latter-day Saint. Legal Res: 1414 Cypress St, Crossett, Ark. 71635. Mailing Add: P.O. Box 777, Crossett, Ark. 71635.

GRIFFIN, ROBERT ALWYN 'CHENEY' D
b. Bainbridge, Ga, 8/20/14; s. Ernest Howard 'Pat' Griffin and Josie Butler G; m. 3/28/40 to Margaret Emily Daniels; c. Robert J. Educ: The Citadel, 31-32; Ga. Teachers Col, 34-38. Polit. & Govt. Pos: Ga. State Rep, 59-64; mayor, City of Bainbridge, 47-64; Bainbridge City Coun, 40-44. Bus. & Prof. Pos: Newspaper ed; realtor; ins. agent. Mil. Serv: Marine Corps, 2nd Lt, 44-46. Mem: Elk; Mason; Shriner; Moose. Rel: Presbyterian. Mailing Add: Bainbridge, Ga. 31717. (1967)

GRIFFIN, ROBERT PAUL R
Minority Whip, U.S. Senate
b. Detroit, Mich, 11/6/23; s. Julius A. Griffin and Beulah Childers G; m. 5/10/47 to Marjorie Jean Anderson; c. Paul Robert, Richard Allen, James Anderson and Martha Jill. Educ: Cent. Mich. Univ, A.B. and B.S, 47, LL.D, 63; Univ. Mich. Law Sch, J.D, 50; The Citadel; Shrivenham Univ, Eng; Tau Alpha Upsilon; Sigma Tau Delta. LL.D, East Mich. Univ, 69; L.H.D, Hillsdale Col, 69. Polit. & Govt. Pos: U.S. Rep, Ninth Cong. Dist, Mich, 57-66; U.S. Sen, Mich, 66-, Minority Whip, U.S. Senate, 69-, del, Rep. Nat. Conv, 68. Mil. Serv: Army, 3 years in World War II, serv. in Field Artil, ETO; Medal with 2 Battle Stars. Publ: 'The Labor Board and Section 8(b) (7),' Univ. Detroit Law J, 12/62; 'Federal Labor Policy and the NLRB,' Mich. State Univ. Bar J, 11/68; 'The Fortas Controversy: the Senate's Role of Advice and Consent,' Prospectus, a J. of Law Reform, 4/69. Mem: Am. and Mich. State Bar Asns; Alpha Kappa Psi; Phi Alpha Delta; Elks; Kiwanis; Am. Legion. Named one of the Ten Outstanding Young Men in America, 59. Rel: Congregational. Legal Res: 1320 Peninsula Court, Traverse City, Mich. 49684. Mailing Add: 353 Senate Office Bldg, Washington, D.C. 20510.

GRIFFIN, SAMUEL MARVIN D
b. Bainbridge, Ga, 9/4/07; s. Ernest Howard Griffin and Josie Butler G; m. 7/11/31 to Mary Elizabeth Smith; c. Samuel Marvin, Jr. Educ: The Citadel, A.B. Polit. & Govt. Pos: Ga. State Rep, 35-37; Adj. Gen, State of Ga, 44-47, Lt. Gov, 48-54 and Gov, 54-59. Bus. & Prof. Pos: Publisher, The Post-Searchlight, 33- Mil. Serv: Entered as Capt, Army, 40, released as Lt. Col, 44, after serv. in 101st Sep. Bn. (AA-AW), S.W. Pac. Theatre, 42; Unit Citation. Mem: V.pres, Ga. Press Asn, 46; Mason; Shrine; Lions (past pres); C. of C.(past pres, Bainbridge Chap); Elks; Moose; Jr. Order Am. Mech; Am. Legion; VFW; Sigma Delta Chi; Farm Bur. Man of the Year, Lions. Rel: Presbyterian. Mailing Add: 809 Lamar St, Bainbridge, Ga. 31717.

GRIFFIN, SAUNDRA LEE D
b. Detroit, Mich, 9/15/43; d. Lawrence Spencer Griffin and Ruth Majors G; single. Educ: Univ. Calif, Los Angeles, B.A, 69; Delta Sigma Theta. Polit. & Govt. Pos: Secy, 37th Cong. Dist, Dem. Cmt, Calif, 65-66; del, Calif. State Dem. Conv, 66, 67 & 68; alternate del, Dem. Nat. Conv, 68. Rel: Catholic. Legal Res: 3635 College Ave, Apt. B-49, San Diego, Calif. 92115. Mailing Add: 1516 S. Purdue Ave, Apt. 3, Los Angeles, Calif. 90025.

GRIFFIN, WALTER JOSEPH R
Chmn, Sudbury Rep. Town Cmt, Mass.
b. Brooklyn, N.Y, 8/12/26; s. Walter R. Griffin and Grace H. Kallighan G; m. 7/24/54 to Jean A. Oates; c. Barbara J. and Thomas M. Educ: Brooklyn Polytech. Inst, B.S.E.E, 52; Northeast. Univ, M.S.E.E, 62; Eta Kappa Nu; Tau Beta Pi; Pi Kappa Phi. Polit. & Govt. Pos: Chmn, Sudbury Rep. Town Cmt, Mass, 68- Bus. & Prof. Pos: Eng. sect. head, Raytheon Co, Waltham, Mass. Mem: Inst. Elec. and Electronics Engrs. Rel: Roman Catholic. Mailing Add: 25 Old Coach Rd, Sudbury, Mass. 01776.

GRIFFITH, EUGENE C. R
b. Newberry, S.C, 2/1/36; s. Steve C. Griffith and Bertie Lee Hambright G; m. to Anne Bruner; c. Leanne and Eugene C, Jr. Educ: Univ. S.C, B.S, 57, LL.B. Polit. & Govt. Pos: Alternate del, Rep. Nat. Conv, 68; S.C. State Sen, 22nd Dist, currently. Mil. Serv: Lt, Navy. Rel: Methodist. Mailing Add: Newberry, S.C. 29108. (1967)

GRIFFITH, GEORGE G. D
W.Va. State Del.
b. Wheeling, W.Va, 12/7/26; s. James P. Griffith, Sr. and Mary F. Ebbert G; m. 6/25/49 to Rita M. Schultz; c. Christine Lynn, George Geoffrey and Patricia Michelle. Educ: Col. of Steubenville; bus. training courses. Polit. & Govt. Pos: W.Va. State Del, 64- Bus. & Prof. Pos: Commercial rep, tel. co. Mil. Serv: World War II, Pac. Theatre; two battle stars. Mem: Elks; K. of C; Lions; adv, Jr. Achievement, Gr. Weirton Area, Inc. Rel: Catholic. Mailing Add: 3720 Collins Way, Weirton, W.Va. 26062. (1967)

GRIFFITH, JERRY L. D
b. Tulsa, Okla, 1/26/31; s. Bert O. Griffith and Corine Knollenberg G; m. 5/28/54 to Ann Study; c. Jeffrey, Bruce, Scot, Mark and Lynn. Educ: Southwest. Col, Kans, B.S; Washburn Univ, LL.B; Delta Theta Phi; Pi Gamma Mu. Polit. & Govt. Pos: City attorney, Derby, Kans, 57-; Kans. State Rep, 68th Dist, 60-68. Bus. & Prof. Pos: Sr. Partner, Griffith & Mize, 57- Mil. Serv: Entered as Pvt, Army, 53, released as Cpl, 55. Mem: Lions; Mason; Consistory; Shrine; Wichita, Kans. and Nat. Bar Asns; Am. Legion. Rel: Methodist. Mailing Add: 460 Springcreek, Derby, Kans. 67037. (1967)

GRIFFITH, MARGARET RUTH R
Chmn, Pike Co. Rep. Cent. Cmt, Mo.
b. Louisiana, Mo, 8/22/25; d. Lester I. Zumwalt and Marie Jones Z; m. 7/4/43 to Darwin Bartlett Griffith; c. Darwin Bartlett (Bart), Jerry Lester and Randall Lee. Educ: Louisiana High Sch, grad, 43. Polit. & Govt. Pos: Secy, Pike Co. Rep. Cent. Cmt, Mo, 58-68, chmn, 68-; pres, Federated Rep. Women Pike Co, 67-; treas, Ninth Cong. Dist. Rep. Women's Club, 69. Mem: Leader Willing Workers and pres. of coun, Pike Co. 4-H Clubs; Farm Bur. (citizenship and govt. chmn); PTA (Louisiana High Sch. hospitality chmn). Outstanding 4-H family, 57. Rel: Presbyterian. Mailing Add: McIntosh Angus Farm, R.R. 1, Clarksville, Mo. 63336.

GRIFFITH, RICHARD ALDEN R
Mem, Calif. Rep. State Cent. Cmt.
b. Oxnard, Calif, 5/23/22; s. Dean Allen Griffith and Christine Corbett G; m. 3/15/47 to Mary Sue Spiller; c. Richard Hollis and Leigh Ann. Educ: Ventura Col, 2 years; Travelers Ins. Sch, 1 year. Polit. & Govt. Pos: Pres, Oak View Sanit. Dist, 60-; mem, Calif. Rep. State Cent. Cmt, currently. Mil. Serv: Entered as Pvt, Air Force, 43, released as Capt, 46, after serv. in Ninth Air Force, ETO, 44-46. Mem: Ventura Co. Ins. Agents Asn.(pres, 54-55). Rel: Presbyterian. Legal Res: 240 Alto Dr, Oak View, Calif. 93022. Mailing Add: P.O. Box 1236, Ventura, Calif. 93001.

GRIFFITH, ROBERT R. D
Exec. Secy, Wash. Dem. Coun.
b. Hutchinson, Kans, 7/1/39; s. Cecil W. Griffith and Edith F. G; m. 9/2/61 to Beatrice D. Branch; c. Erinn. Educ: Univ. Wash, B.A, 64; Univ. Pittsburgh, M.P.A, 68. Polit. & Govt. Pos: Exec. secy, Wash. Dem. Coun, 69- Mil. Serv: Entered as Pvt, Marine Corps, 58, released as Cpl, 61, after serv. in Wash. and Calif. Rel: Unitarian. Mailing Add: 2122 S. Tacoma Way, Tacoma, Wash. 98409.

GRIFFITH, WILLIAM F, Jr. Conservative, N.Y.
Mem. State Exec. Cmt, Conservative Party, N.Y.
b. Pearl River, N.Y, 4/23/28; s. William F. Griffith and Marie Dexter G; m. 9/26/53 to Lillian Louise Kowatsch; c. William F, III, Todd Allan and Clark Dexter. Educ: Univ. Tenn, 45-46; Univ. Madrid, Spain, 47-50; Fairleigh Dickinson Univ. Eve. Div, 53-57. Polit. & Govt. Pos: Founding Chmn, Orangetown Young Rep. Club, N.Y, 60; mem, Conservative Party State Cmt, N.Y; past chmn, Conservative Party Club Rockland Co; past chmn, Rockland Co. Cmt, Conservative Party, N.Y. and mem. state exec. cmt, currently. Bus. & Prof. Pos: Partner, William F. Griffith Agency, 52-58; pres. and gen. mgr, Perillo-Griffith Travel Serv, Inc, 58- Mil. Serv: Entered Army, 50, released as Cpl, 52, after serv. in 160th Inf. Regt, 40th Div, Korea; Combat Infantryman's Badge; Korean Serv. Ribbon with 2 Battle Stars; UN Serv. Ribbon. Mem: Am. Soc. Travel Agents; Rotary Int; Am. Legion; Nat. Rifle Asn. Am. Rel: Methodist. Mailing Add: 171 Springsteen Ave, Pearl River, N.Y. 10965.

GRIFFITHS, ARTHUR H. D
Chmn, Yates Co. Dem. Cmt, N.Y.
b. Penn Yan, N.Y, 7/12/20; s. Albert J. Griffiths and Irene Harris G; m. 1/18/58 to Sally J. Brennan; c. Kelly Irene, Maxine Leigh, John Edward, Bridget Mary, Casey Charles and William Albert. Educ: Penn Yan Acad, grad. Polit. & Govt. Pos: Pres, Yates Co. Mens Dem. Club, N.Y, 60-64; chmn, Yates Co. Dem. Cmt, 64- Bus. & Prof. Pos: Adjuster and salesman, Retail Purchasing Corp, Penn Yan, 52-69. Mil. Serv: Entered as Pvt, Marine Corps, 42, released as M/Sgt, 46, after serv. in MAG 33, Pac. Theatre, 43-45. Rel: Catholic. Mailing Add: 310 Court St, Penn Yan, N.Y. 14527.

GRIFFITHS, MARTHA W. D
U.S. Rep, Mich.
b. Pierce City, Mo; m. to Hicks G. Griffiths. Educ: Univ. of Mo, B.A; Univ. of Mich. Law Sch, LL.B. Polit. & Govt. Pos: Mich. State Rep, 49-52; recorder and judge, Recorder's Court, 53; U.S. Rep, Mich, 54- Legal Res: 6603 Warwich, Detroit, Mich. 48219. Mailing Add: U.S. House of Representatives Office Bldg, Wash, D.C. 20510.

GRILLS, NELSON GROVER D
Ind. State Sen.
b. Decatur, Ill, 4/26/12; s. Garner Reagan Grills and Minnie Doolin G; m. 9/14/40 to Reva McMahan; c. Walter Reagan, Peter Hudson, Sarah Louise and Susan Mary. Educ: Ind. Univ, B.S. in bus. admin, 35, J.D, 37, LL.M, 40; Columbia Univ. Sch. Law, LL.M, 41; Order of the Coif; Sigma Alpha Epsilon; Phi Delta Phi. Polit. & Govt. Pos: Chmn, Marion Co. Dem. Cent. Cmt, Ind, 52-56; chmn, 11th Dist. Dem. Cent. Cmt, 54-56; Ind. State Sen, 59-61 & 65- Bus. & Prof. Pos: Gen. counsel, Am. Osteopathic Asn, 45-47; assoc. prof. of law, Ind. Univ, 46-52. Mil. Serv: Entered as Lt.(jg), Naval Res, 41, released as Lt. Comdr, 45, after serv. in Atlantic Sea Frontier, 42-45; Comdr.(Ret), Naval Res; Purple Heart; Distinguished Flying Cross. Rel: Presbyterian. Mailing Add: 1669 E. Kessler Blvd, Indianapolis, Ind. 46220.

GRIMBALL, JOHN D
b. Charleston, S.C, 3/10/14; s. William Heyward Grimball and Panchita Heyward G; m. 11/30/40 to Caroline Gordon Belser; c. John Berkley, Caroline Gordon, Maria Heyward, Mary Elliot and Ann Belser. Educ: Col. Charleston, B.S, 35; Univ. Va, LL.B, 39; Alpha Tau Omega; Phi Alpha Delta. Polit. & Govt. Pos: S.C. State Rep, 56-60; judge, Court of Common Pleas and Gen.

Sessions, S.C, 60-; alternate del, Dem. Nat. Conv, 68. Mil. Serv: Entered as Pvt, Army, 41, released as 1st Lt, 45, after serv. in 11th Armored Div. and Ninth Armored Div, ETO, 44-45; Res, 45-66, Lt. Col; Distinguished Serv. Cross; Silver Star Medal; Presidential Unit Citation; Three Battle Stars; Am. Campaign Medal; Am. Defense Serv. Medal; World War II Victory Medal; German Occup. Medal. Mem: Richland Co, S.C. and Am. Bar Asns; Am. Legion; 40 et 8; Mason; Lions; Forest Lake Country Club. Rel: Episcopal. Legal Res: 4000 Bloomwood Rd, Columbia, S.C. 29205. Mailing Add: P.O. Box 57, Columbia, S.C. 29202.

GRIMES, CECIL CLAYMON, JR. D
S.C. State Sen.
b. Greenville, Miss, 7/23/22; s. Cecil Claymon Grimes, Sr. and Sadie Ehlers G; m. 10/4/47 to Harriett Horry Pyatt; c. Harriet, Cecil Claymon III and John Pyatt. Educ: Univ. S.C, B.A, 46, LL.B, 47. Polit. & Govt. Pos: S.C. State Rep, 59-62; S.C. State Sen, 62- Bus. & Prof. Pos: Attorney-at-law. Mil. Serv: Air Force, 42-46, serv. in Pac. Theatre as fighter pilot, 21st Fighter Squadron, Seventh Fighter Command, 20th Air Force. Mem: Mason. Mailing Add: P.O. Box 556, Georgetown, S.C. 29440.

GRIMES, THOMAS PARNELL R
b. Cumberland, Md, 6/26/19; s. Harry P. Grimes and Mary C. Kelly G; m. 10/3/59 to Mary Lou Gingrich; c. Jean Marie, Kathleen Mary, Nancy Anne, Thomas Mathew, David Anthony, Jerome Francis and Mark Steven. Educ: Macomb Col, A.A, 69. Polit. & Govt. Pos: Precinct del, Rep. Party, Warren, Mich, 62-68; mem. exec. cmt, Macomb Co. Rep. Cmt, 66-68; chmn, Macomb Co. Rep. Conv, 67 & 68; alternate del, Rep. Nat. Conv, 68. Bus. & Prof. Pos: Mem. styling staff, Gen. Motors, 15 years. Mil. Serv: Entered as Pvt, Army, 44, released as 1st Lt, 46, after serv. in Ord. Dept, Mediterranean, 45-46; Army Commendation Medal. Rel: Catholic. Mailing Add: 29616 Fairfield Dr, Warren, Mich. 48093.

GRIMM, PETER R
b. N.Y.C, 1/12/86; s. Adam Grimm and Josephine Henry G; m. 2/11/22 to Harriet Lawrence; c. Peter and Laurie. Educ: Columbia Univ, B.S, 11. Polit. & Govt. Pos: V.pres. and trustee, Citizens Budget Cmt, N.Y.C; minister, U.S. Opers. Mission to Italy; chmn, Mayor's Cmt. on Taxation, N.Y.C, 32-54; mem, N.Y.C. Planning Cmn, 34; spec. asst. to Secy. of Treas. Dept, 35-36; mem, Real Estate Adv. Bd, War Dept, 41; mem. exec. cmt, Nat. Inst. Soc. Sci, 60-65; chmn, Mayor's Cmt. for Gracie Mansion, N.Y.C, 63, pres, 64-65; mem, Mayor's Fiscal Cmn, 63-64; mem, Race and Housing Cmn, Fund for Repub, 63-64. Bus. & Prof. Pos: Real estate broker with Stephen H. Tyng & Co, N.Y.C, 11-20; owner, real estate bus, 20-29; pres. and dir, William A. White & Sons, 29-44, dir. and chmn. bd, 44; pres. and dir, Grand Cent. Art Galleries; dir. of various companies. Mil. Serv: From Capt. to Maj, Army, 17-18. Mem: Trustee, N.Y. Zool. Soc; fel, Royal Soc. Fine Arts, London; trustee and chmn. real estate cmt, Presby. Hosp; pres, Sailor's Snug Harbor, 51-52; C. of C.(pres, N.Y. State Chap, 46-48); Am-Italy Soc. (pres, 58-65); chmn, Columbia Col. Coun, Netherland-Am. Found; dir, and mem. exec. cmt, United Cerebral Palsy Asn; pres, N.Y.C. Baseball Fedn, 63-65. Medal for Soc. Serv, Columbia Univ, 34, Alumni Medal, 54, Alexander Hamilton Gold Medal, 65; Man of the Year Award, Realty Found, 65; Citation for Distinguished Serv, Explorer's Club, 65; Plaque for Distinguished Serv, Munic. Art Soc, N.Y.C; decorated Grand Officer, Order Cristobal Colon, Dominican Repub; Comdr, Order of Orange-Nassau, Netherlands; Grand Officer Order of Merit, Repub. of Italy. Legal Res: 104 E. 68th St, New York, N.Y. 10021. Mailing Add: 51 E. 42nd St, New York, N.Y. 10017.

GRIMMETT, ORVILLE BAILEY R
Chmn, Monroe Co. Rep. Exec. Cmt, W.Va.
b. Hinton, W.Va, 4/3/13; s. Letcher Bailey Grimmett and Savine Frances Thompson G; m. 8/26/37 to Bernice Maud Dillon; c. Betty Louise (Mrs. Hinkle). Educ: Marchall Col, 2 years. Polit. & Govt. Pos: Sheriff, Monroe Co, W.Va, 57-61; Chmn, Monroe Co. Rep. Exec. Cmt, 65- Bus. & Prof. Pos: Automotive jobber, Union, 46- Mil. Serv: Entered as A/S, Navy, 44, released as Quartermaster 2/C, 45, after serv. in Amphibious Div, Pac. Theater, 44-45; Liberation of Philippines and Occupation of Japan Medals. Mem: Am. Legion (Comdr); Mason; C. of C.(past pres); Ruritan (past pres); Rotary (past pres). Rel: Baptist. Mailing Add: Union, W.Va. 24983.

GRIMSEY, J. HERBERT R
Dep. Dir, N.Y. State Rep. Campaign Cmt.
b. East Orange, N.J, 10/10/09; s. George H. Grimsey and Evelyn Terrien G; m. 12/12/42 to Ruth Marie Sheridan. Educ: Univ. Ky, B.S. in elec. eng, 30. Polit. & Govt. Pos: Cmnr, White Plains Elec. Bd, N.Y, 51-; campaign chmn, Westchester Co. Rep. Party, 52, 56, 58, 62 & 64; dep. dir, N.Y. State Rep. Campaign Cmt. and co. committeeman, Westchester Co, N.Y, 60-; del, Rep. Nat. Conv, 64; bd. of visitors, Wassaic State Sch, 64- Bus. & Prof. Pos: Pres, East. Elec. Corp, 48-52, chmn. and bd. dir, 52-; mem. bd. dirs, Rumarlin Corp, 59 and Windsor Life Ins. Co. of Am, 65- Mem: Nat. Pres, Nat. Exchange Clubs; Elks; Mason (32°); Third time pres, C. of C; dir, Red Cross and Commun. Chest. Rel: Protestant. Legal Res: 90 Bryant Ave, White Plains, N.Y. 10605. Mailing Add: 96-98 Fulton St, White Plains, N.Y. 10606.

GRIMSHAW, THOMAS T. R
Colo. State Rep.
b. Minneapolis, Minn, 10/31/32; s. Ulmont Leon Grimshaw and Judith Tollin G; m. 6/5/54 to Donna Rae Groniga; c. Scott Michael, Lynn Louise, Stephen Thomas, Lisa Ann and Shane Douglas. Educ: Hamline Univ, 49-51; Univ. of Minn, B.A, 53; Northwest. Univ, J.D, 56; Phi Delta Phi; Sigma Delta Chi; Alpha Sigma Chi. Polit. & Govt. Pos: Colo. State Rep, currently. Bus. & Prof. Pos: Attorney, Calkins, Kramer, Grimshaw & Carpenter, 56-70. Mem: Denver First Judicial Dist; Am. Bar Asn; Colo. Bar Asn.(mem. bd. of gov); bd. dirs, Colo. Baptist Conv; gen. bd, Nat. Coun. of Churches; Mason; Scottish Rite; C. of C; Jaycees. Rel: American Baptist. Mailing Add: 2419 S. Chase Lane, Jefferson City, Colo. 80456.

GRINDLE, WILLIAM L. D
m. to Ina Ruth Pulliam G; c. William Nicky. Educ: Law course; Aetna Casualty and Surety Sales Sch. Polit. & Gov. Pos: Ill. State Sen, 56-66; City Coun. Alderman; Dem. Precinct Committeeman; Dist. Supvr, U.S. Census Bur. Bus. & Prof. Pos: Chief boiler engr; owns, operates Gen. Ins. Agency. Mil. Serv: U.S. Navy, W.W. II, 6 1/2 years, Pac. Theatre; Chief P. O, U.S. Naval Ready Res. Mem: Past Pres, Herrin Jr. C. of C; past State Vice-Pres, Jaycees; Pres, Senior Teen Town Coun; A.F. & A.M; B.P.O.E; D.A.V; Am. Legion; VFW; Int. Union Operating Engrs. & Textile Workers. Mailing Add: 216 Circle Dr, Herrin, Ill. 62948. (1967)

GRINER, ADELINE CALTHA D
Committeewoman, Mich. Dem. State Cent. Cmt.
b. Buckley, Mich, 12/12/16; d. Earl Raymond Cook and Beulah Gibbs C; m. 1/21/36 to Burton Samuel Griner; c. Patricia (Mrs. Thomas Swanson), Burton Jay and James Earl. Educ: Northwest. Mich. Col, 56-58; Northwest. Mich. Col. Investment Club. Polit. & Govt. Pos: V.chmn, Grand Traverse Co. Dem. Party, Mich, 59-62 & 69-; committeewoman, Mich. Dem. State Cent. Cmt, 63-, secy, 69-; alternate del, Dem. Nat. Conv, 68; pres, Grand Traverse Co. Women's Organ, 69- Bus. & Prof. Pos: Admin. secy, Northwest. Mich. Col, 67- Rel: Presbyterian. 510 Woodland Dr, Traverse City, Mich. 49684.

GRINNELL, HAROLD C. R
b. Broadalbin, N.Y, 7/7/95; married; c. two daughters. Educ: Cornell Univ, B.S, M.S. and Ph.D. Polit. & Govt. Pos: Former mem, Durham Sch. Bd, N.H; former mem, Budget Cmn. and Zoning Adjust. Bd; del, Constitutional Conv, 64; N.H. State Rep. until 67. Bus. & Prof. Pos: Former col. adminstr. and prof. Mil. Serv: Lt, Coast Artil. Corps, World War I. Mem: F&AM (past Master); Phi Kappa Phi; Alpha Zeta; Durham Men's Club; Durham Civic Cmts. Rel: Protestant. Mailing Add: 24 Bagdad Rd, Durham, N.H. 03824.

GRINSTEIN, GERALD BATES D
b. Seattle, Wash, 6/26/32; s. Alexander Grinstein and Selma Wampold G; m. 5/9/59 to Rosalie Alhadeff; c. Blake, Keith David and Gerald Charles. Educ: Yale Univ, B.A, 54; Harvard Law Sch, LL.B, 57; Zeta Psi. Polit. & Govt. Pos: Chief counsel, U.S. Senate Cmt. on Commerce, 63-67; admin. asst. to U.S. Sen. Warren Magnuson, Wash, 67- Mem: Seattle Tennis Club; Wash. Athletic Club; Yale Club N.Y. Rel: Jewish. Legal Res: 1650 92nd N.E, Seattle, Wash. 98004. Mailing Add: 3551 Tilden St. N.W, Washington, D.C. 20008.

GRISWOLD, MARY BROOKS D
Conn. State Rep.
b. Scranton, Pa, 6/11/06; d. John H. Brooks and Augusta Archbald B; m. 6/10/30 to A. Whitney Griswold; wid; c. Sarah (Mrs. R.G. Leahy), Mary (Mrs. J.B. Baker) Susanna W. and A. Whitney, Jr. Educ: Smith Col, B.A, 28. Polit. & Govt. Pos: Del, Conn. Constitutional Conv, 65; Conn. State Rep, 67- Rel: Protestant. Mailing Add: 280 Livingston St, New Haven, Conn. 06511.

GRITTNER, KARL FREDERICK DFL
Minn. State Sen.
b. West St. Paul, Minn, 11/22/22; s. Joseph F. Grittner and Eva Olin G; m. 5/26/45 to Carolyn Cora Pierce; c. Linda, Frederick and Laura. Educ: Hamline Univ, B.A, 45; Univ. Minn, M.A, 59; Pi Gamma Mu; Phi Delta Kappa; Torch & Cycle. Polit. & Govt. Pos: Mem, Minn. Dem-Farmer-Labor Party Exec. Cmt; Minn. State Rep, 53-59; Minn. State Sen, asst. Minority Leader, Minn. Senate, 63-67, Minority Leader, 67- Bus. & Prof. Pos: Intern, Nat. Inst. of Pub. Affairs, Wash, D.C, 45-46; teacher and coach, St. Clair, Minn, 46-48; teacher, Cleveland Jr. High Sch, 48-60; asst. prin, Wilson High Sch, 60-64; prin, Mounds Park Jr. High Sch, St. Paul, 64-68; prin, Marshall Jr. High, 68; sch. adminstr, St. Paul Pub. Schs, 68- Publ: The Drop-out Studies-A Critical Analysis, Publ. 279, St. Paul Pub. Schs, 12/62. Mem: Scholia; St. Paul Principals' Forum; Nat. Asn. Secondary Sch. Prins; Am. Fedn. of Teachers 28; League of United Latin-Am. Citizens; steering cmt, Educ. Cmn. of the States, 66-67; Nat. Conf. State Legis. Leaders, 63- Rel: Presbyterian. Mailing Add: 824 Cherokee Ave, St. Paul, Minn. 55107.

GRIZZLE, MARY R. R
Fla. State Rep.
b. Lawrence Co, Ohio, 8/19/21; m. to Ben F. Grizzle; c. Henry, Polley, Lorena, Mary Alice, Betty and Jeanne. Educ: Portsmouth Interstate Bus. Col. Polit. & Govt. Pos: Former town cmnr; Fla. State Rep, 63-, mem, Govt. Reorgn. and Efficiency and Educ. and Pub. Schs. Cmts. and chmn, Group III, Cmt. on Appropriations; chmn, Pinellas Co. Del, 64-66, mem, Co. Civil Serv. Cmt. and Co. Planning Coun; Rep. Precinct Committeewoman; mem, Belleair Womens Rep. Club, Largo; past pres, Clearwater Women's Rep. Club and Fla. Fedn. of Rep. Women; chmn, Fla. Cmn. on Status of Women; Gov. Rep. to Nat. Conf. of Women Commun. Leaders for Hwy. Safety. Bus. & Prof. Pos: Housewife; bus. investments. Publ: Co-author and publisher, Thimbleful of History. Mem: Past pres, Anona PTA; Altrusa and Woman's Clubs of Clearwater; Bus. Indust. Polit. Cmt, N.Y; Nat. Soc. of Arts and Letters; Hon. Order of Ky. Col; Pinellas Schs. PTA. Selected Outstanding Woman of the Year, 66; One of Ten Outstanding Women in 1966 by St. Petersburg Times. Rel: Episcopal. Legal Res: 120 Gulf Blvd, Belleair Shore, Indian Rocks Beach, Fla. 33535. Mailing Add: Room 505, Coachman Bldg, 503 Cleveland St, Clearwater, Fla. 33515.

GROEN, EGBERT B. R
Ill. State Sen.
b. Pekin, Ill, 1/26/15; s. Klaas D. Groen and Bertha Bloompot G; m. 7/28/35 to Helen Marie Clary; c. Keith Clary and Karel Jeane. Educ: Knox Col, A.B, 37; Univ. of Ill. Col. of Law, LL.B, 40; Phi Gamma Delta; Phi Delta Phi. Polit. & Govt. Pos: Ill. State Sen, 48th Dist, 53- Bus. & Prof. Pos: Mem. bd. dirs, First Nat. Bank and Trust Co, 39-; chmn. of bd, Capital Security Life Ins. Co. and Superior Invest. Corp, 61- Mil. Serv: Entered as 2nd Lt, Air Force, 41, released as Lt. Col, 46, after serv. as Staff Judge Adv, Air Force Tech. Training Command. Mem: Mason; Elks; Am. and Ill. Bar Asns; Farm Bur; Union League Club, Chicago; Sangamo Club, Springfield, Ill. Rel: Protestant. Legal Res: 3 Rosewood Lane, Pekin, Ill. 61554. Mailing Add: 34 S. Fourth, Pekin, Ill. 61555. (1967)

GROENEN, JAN HENRY R
Mem, Calif. Rep. State Cent. Cmt.
b. Bladel, Noord Brabant, Netherlands 5/1/29; s. Henri Groenen and Wilhelmina Smetsers G. (deceased); single. Educ: Wash. State Univ, B.A, Soc. Sci, 52, for. study scholarship; Univ. South. Calif, M.A, Polit. Sci, 59, grad. study scholarship, teaching asst. and Rufus B. Van Kleinsmid fel; for. study scholarship, Vanderbilt Univ, grad. study scholarship and teaching and research asst,

Inst. Soc. Sci. Research; summer fel, Am. Friends Int. Affairs Inst, 49 and Am. Friends Int. Affairs Seminar, 52; San Diego State Col; Univ. Calif, San Diego; Pi Sigma Alpha; Alpha Kappa Delta; Cosmopolitan Club (pres); Collegia Int.(chmn); chmn. Wash. State Univ. Del, Model UN, 52. Polit. & Govt. Pos: Vol worker in Rep. campaigns at all levels; assoc. mem, Calif. Rep. State Cent. Cmt, 66-68, mem, 69-; polit. consult, Commun. Assocs, Los Angeles, 64-68; educ. adv, George Christopher Gubernatorial Campaign, 65-66; mem, Calif. Rep. League, 65-67; mem. exec. campaign cmt, Calif. Assemblyman George Milias, 65-; field oper. dir, Bill Treadwell for Congress, 66; chmn, Politics '66 and Politics '67, San Jose City Col, 66-67; mem, Sen. Thomas Kuchel's Santa Clara Co. Campaign Cmt, 67; chmn, Santa Clara Co. Educators for Nixon-Agnew Cmt, 68. Bus. & Prof. Pos: Budget supvr, Shell Oil Co, Calgary, Alta, Can, 54-56; owner-mgr, Field Off. Serv. Co, Vancouver, B.C, 56-57; instr. gen. studies, Univ. South. Calif, 58-61; teacher soc. studies, Los Angeles City Schs, 61-62; instr. govt. and hist, Southwest. Col, 62-65; vis. prof, Jr. Statesman of Am. Inst. Govt, summer 65; instr. U.S. Govt. and insts, San Jose City Col, 65- Publ: 'Our Duty as Foreign Students,' 1/50 and 'Far Reaching Experiment,' 4/52, News Bul, Inst. Int. Educ. Mem: Calif. Teachers Asn; San Jose City Col. Commun. Serv. Speakers Bur; Jr. Statesman Am. Found; Calif. Automobile Asn; Wash. State Univ. Alumni Asn; sustaining mem, Rep. Action Fund-Rep. Nat. Cmt. Commendation, Calif. Assembly, 68; Spec. Mention Cong. Record, 68. Rel: Roman Catholic. Legal Res: 78 Bentley, Apt. 11, Los Gatos, Calif. 95030. Mailing Add: P.O. Box 422, Los Gatos, Calif. 95030.

GROESBECK, ARTHUR JEROME, III R
Treas, Kans. Young Rep. Fedn.
b. Manhattan, Kans, 1/21/41; s. Arthur Jerome Groesbeck, Jr. and Dorothy Griffin G. Educ: Kansas State Univ, B.A. in polit. sci, 63; pres, Delta Sigma Rho; mem. nat. bd. of dirs, Collegiate Coun. for UN; pres, Integrity Party; founder, pres. of senate and chmn. of steering cmt, Model Cong. Polit. & Govt. Pos: Treas, Region VII Col. Young Rep, 61-62; pres, Kans. State Univ. Col. Young Rep, 62-63; dir, Riley Co. Young Rep, 62-63; mem, col. serv. cmt, and exec. secy, Young Rep. Nat. Fedn, 63-64; publicity chmn, Kans. Fedn. of Col. Young Rep, 63-65; campaign mgr, Mize for Cong. Cmt, 64 and admin. asst. to U.S. Rep. Chester L. Mize, Kans, 65-68; founder and first state dir, Teen-Age Rep. Fedn, 64-65; treas, Kans. Young Rep. Fedn, 65- Bus. & Prof. Pos: Mem. bd. dirs. and bus. mgr, Winter Atlas Prod, Inc; mem. bd. dirs. and exec. v.pres, Lil' Duffer Nebr, Inc; operational mgr, Goodwill Publishers, Inc, 58-61; mem. bd. dirs, Independence Hall Mgt. Corp, 65-; incorporator, Liberty Investors, Inc, 65-; registered rep, Columbian Securities Corp, 65- and Puritan Life Ins. Co, 66- Mil. Serv: Entered as Recruit, Army, 59, released as Pvt, 59, after serv. in Hq. and Hq. Co. USATC, Sixth Army, Ft. Ord, Calif; Specialist 4, Army Res, 59-62. Mem: Am. Acad. Polit. and Soc. Sci; Bull Elephants Club; Cong. Secy. Club; Elks; Asn. of U.S. Army; Jaycees; SAR; Kans. State Univ. Alumni Asn; Native Sons & Daughters of Kans; Kans. Day Club; Active 20-30 Club Int; C. of C; cmt. v.chmn, Shawnee Co. Cancer Crusade, 66. Number One Unit Mgr. in Nation Award, Goodwill Publishers, Inc, 61; Runner-up, Robert Taft Outstanding Col. Young Rep. Award, 63; Number One Salesman in Nation Award. Rel: Methodist. 1967 Legal Res: Topeka, Kans. No mailing address available. (1967)

GROFF, WILLIAM ALBERT D
Mont. State Sen.
b. Victor, Mont, 2/17/20; s. Houston Clay Groff and Julia Vic G; m. 4/7/46 to Phyllis Ann Wiesener; c. Ann and Kay. Educ: Kemper Mil. Sch, A.A, 40; Univ. Tex, 41; Univ. Mont, B.A, 42; Delta Tau Delta. Polit. & Govt. Pos: Mont. State Sen, 55-, chmn, Finance and Claims Cmt, Mont. State Senate, 57-63, 65-67 & 69-, Majority Leader, 63, Pres. Pro Tem. Ad Interim, 67-69; mem, Columbia River Compact Cmn, 57-; mem, White House Conf. Educ, 59; chmn, Mont. Legis. Coun, 63-64; del, Dem. Nat. Conv, 68. Bus. & Prof. Pos: Cashier, Farmers State Bank, 55-61, pres, 61- Mil. Serv: Entered as Pvt, Army, 42, released as 1st Lt, 46, after serv. in Hq, Base F, Quartermaster Corps, Southwest Pac; Asiatic-Pac. Serv. Medal with 2 Bronze Stars; Philippine Liberation Medal with 1 Bronze Star; World War II Victory Medal. Mem: Mason; Elks; Am. Legion; VFW; Grange; exec. mem. West. States Water Coun. Rel: Presbyterian. Mailing Add: Box 46, Victor, Mont. 59875.

GROMALA, JOHN ANTHONY R
Mem, Calif. State Rep. Cent. Cmt.
b. Meriden, Conn, 1/23/30; s. John Anthony Gromala and Anna Wojcik G; m. 6/16/56 to Suzanne Thornton Barrie; c. Ellen Suzanne, Margaret Ann and John Barrie. Educ: Quinnipiac Col, A.S, 49; Univ. San Francisco, B.S, 56, J.D, 58. Polit. & Govt. Pos: Chmn, San Francisco 22nd Dist. Young Rep, Calif, 55; co-chmn, Young Rep. Testimonial for Sen. Knowland, 55; treas, San Francisco Young Rep, 56; chmn, San Francisco Ike Day, 56; co-chmn, San Francisco Young Voters Cmt. for Sen. Kuchel, 56; chmn, San Francisco Knowland for Gov. Clubs, 57-58; campaign mgr, Athearn for Calif. State Sen, San Francisco, 58; mem. exec. cmt, Humboldt Co. Nixon for President, 60; pres, Eel River Valley Young Rep, 61; mem. exec. cmt. and parliamentarian, Humboldt Co. Rep. Cent. Cmt, 61-65; finance chmn, Clausen for Cong. Primary Campaign, Humboldt Co, 62; parliamentarian, First Cong. Dist. Rep. Cmt, 62-63; v.pres. of Region I, Calif. Young Rep, 62-63, gen. counsel, 63-64, pres. and mem. exec. bd, 64-65; del, Young Rep. Nat. Conv, 63 & 65; Rep. Presidential Elector Nominee and del, Rep. Nat. Conv, 64; mem, Calif. State Rep. Cent. Cmt, 64-; successor treas. in event of disaster, Calif, 67- Bus. & Prof. Pos: Partner, law firm, Mahan, Harland & Gromala, 60-68 and Mahan, Dunn, Harland & Gromala, 68-; dir, Bank of Loleta, Calif, 61- Mil. Serv: Entered as Pvt, Marine Corps, 51, released as S/Sgt, 54, after serv. in Continental U.S. Mem: Am, Calif. and Humboldt Co. Bar Asns; dir, Fortuna Rotary, 62-64, 67-60, pres, 67-68; dir, Humboldt Co. Cancer Soc, 61-64 & 67- and Humboldt Co. Crippled Childrens Soc, 62-63; chmn, Humboldt Co. Family Clin, 61-64 and Fortuna Cancer Soc, 63-64; v.pres, Fortuna C. of C. Rel: Roman Catholic. Legal Res: 22 Pinecrest Dr, Fortuna, Calif. 95540. Mailing Add: P.O. Box 626, Fortuna, Calif. 95540.

GRONHOVD, KENNETH D
b. Steele Co, N.Dak, 4/6/13; married; c. 3. Educ: N.Dak. Sch. of Sci. Polit. & Govt. Pos: N.Dak. State Rep, 57-61. Bus. & Prof. Pos: Farmer. Mem: Farmers Union. Rel: Lutheran. Mailing Add: Hatton, N.Dak. 58240. (1967)

GRONNEBECK, TREVA D. D
Mem, Calif. Dem. State Cent. Cmt.
b. 12/24/93; d. Chris Dowrson and Cristina Anderson Christensen D; wid; c. Christy L. Educ: Pub. schs, Wellington, Ohio, 2 years. Polit. & Govt. Pos: Pres, Uptown Huntington Park Dem. Club, Wellington, Ohio; Asst. campaign mgr. for Sen. Lawrence Walsh, 30th Dist, 67; mem, Calif. Dem. State Cent. Cmt, 68-; co-chmn, 23rd Dist. Dem. Party; v.chmn, 52nd Assembly Dist. Dem. Party. Mem: Rebekah Lodge; Neighbors of Woodcraft; 848 Poppy Circle; Pythian Sisters; Am. Asn. of Retired Persons. Rel: Protestant. Mailing Add: 2716 California St, Huntington Park, Calif. 90255.

GRONOUSKI, JOHN AUSTIN D
b. Dunbar, Wis, 10/26/19; s. John Austin Gronouski and Mary Riley G; m. to Mary Louise Metz, 1/24/48; c. Stacy and Julie. Educ: Univ. Wis, B.A, 42, M.A, 47 and Ph.D, 55. Polit. & Govt. Pos: Research dir, Wis. Dept. of Taxation, 59; mem, Wis. State Cmn. of Taxation, 60-63; Postmaster Gen. of U.S, 63-65; Presidential Rep, Int. Trade Fair, Poland, 64; U.S. Ambassador, Poland, 65-68; mem. bd. trustees, Nat. Urban League, 68- Bus. & Prof. Pos: Writer, lectr. and organizer of private bus; appointed dean, Lyndon B. Johnson Sch. Pub. Affairs, Univ, Tex, Austin, 69- Mil. Serv: Army, 42-45. Mem: Am. Econ. Asn; Nat. Tax Asn; Polish Inst. Arts and Sci. Legal Res: 1118 Tomahawk Trail, Madison, Wis. 53705. Mailing Add: 4915 30th Place N.W, Washington, D.C. 20008.

GRONVOLD, A. F. R
b. Rugby, N.Dak, 2/4/15; s. F. T. Gronvold and Alice Egeland G; m. 9/16/35 to Ellen Lund; c. William A. Educ: Dakota Bus. Col, study in bus. admin, 33-34; Univ. N.Dak, study in bus. admin, 34-35; Kappa Sigma. Polit. & Govt. Pos: Dir, Garrison Diversion, Bismarck, N.Dak, 54-59; N.Dak. State Sen, 53, 59 & 61. Bus. & Prof. Pos: Automobile dealer, Gronvold Motor Co, 36-48; farmer, 51-; registered rep, Waddell & Reed, Inc, 68- Mil Serv: Entered as 2nd Lt, Army, 42, released as Capt, 46, after serv. in 3142nd Air Ord. MAM Co, S.W. Pac. and Japan, 44-46. Mem: Durum Wheat Asn; Lions; VFW; Am. Legion; Farmers Union; Mason; Shrine; Odd Fellows. Rel: Lutheran. Mailing Add: 610 W. Third St, Rugby, N.Dak. 58368.

GROOM, JAMES HAYNES R
Mem, Calif. Rep. State Cent. Cmt.
b. Rocky Ford, Colo, 7/3/19; s. Elijah Moore Groom and Tina G; m. 4/5/46 to Pearl Daisy Andersen, c. Charlene (Mrs. Scott La Strange) and Ann. Educ: Santa Rosa Jr. Col, A.A, 39. Polit. & Govt. Pos: Mem, Calif. Rep. State Cent. Cmt, 67-; chmn. finance cmt, First Cong. Club, 67-; dir, Sonoma Co. Rep. Cent. Cmt, 67; chmn, Indust. Develop. Cmt, Rohnert Park, 67-69; dir, Eel River Asn; dir, Zone 1A Flood Dist; former mem, Santa Rosa City Coun. Bus. & Prof. Pos: Owner, Groom Equipment Co, Santa Rosa, Calif, 46- Mil. Serv: Entered as A/S, Navy, 42, released as CPO, 66, after serv. in Pac. Theatre; Letter of Commendation; seven combat stars. Mem: Calif. State Exchange Clubs (state pres, 62-63); Santa Rosa C. of C.(dir, 68-69); Mason; Scottish Rite; Shrine; First Cong. Club; Odd Fellows. Key to City, Santa Rosa, Calif. Rel: Protestant. Legal Res: 1625 Fair Oaks Court, Santa Rosa, Calif. 95404. Mailing Add: 85 Scenic Ave, Santa Rosa, Calif. 95401.

GROOVER, DENMARK,JR. D
b. Quitman, Ga, 6/30/22; s. Denmark Groover, Sr. and Mary McCall G; m. 4/14/45 to Kathryn Mc Caskell Terry, div. 63; c. Denmark III, Charles Terry. Educ: Univ. of Ga, LL.B, 48; Phi Delta Theta. Polit. & Govt. Pos: Ga. State Rep, 63-64, 53-56, elected floor leader, 55-56. Bus. & Prof. Pos: Attorney. Mil. Serv: Marine Corps Res, Maj, 42-45; Purple Heart; Air Medal. Mem: Admitted to bar, 47; practiced in Macon, Ga; admitted to practice in all State Courts of Ga. and the Fed. Courts including the Supreme Court of the U.S. Rel: Presbyterian. Mailing Add: Macon, Ga. 30008. (1967)

GROSBY, ELEANOR R
Chmn, 145th Legis. Dist. Rep. Party, Conn.
b. Boston, Mass, Sept, 2; d. Jacob Hurwitz and Minnie Slosberg H; m. 9/22/47 to Robert N. Grosby; c. Mark Jonathan and Craig Hollis. Educ: N.Y. Univ; Univ. Cincinnati. Polit. & Govt. Pos: Pres, Norwalk Women's Rep. Club, Conn, 56-60; co-chmn, Young Rep, 60; councilwoman, Norwalk Common Coun, 61-67, cand. for re-election, 67 & 69; chmn, Conserv. Cmn, 63-; Oak Hills Bd. of Gov, 65; spec. dep. sheriff, Fairfield Co, currently; chmn, 145th Legis. Dist. Rep. Party, 69- Bus. & Prof. Pos: Publisher, Rathkopfon Planning & Zoning, 48-50; realtor, 59-, treas, Norwalk Real Estate Bd, currently. Mem: Nat. Asn. of Real Estate Bds; Wilson Cove Yacht Club; Navy League U.S. Legal Res: East Rocks Rd, Norwalk, Conn. 06851. Mailing Add: 534 West Ave, Norwalk, Conn. 06850.

GROSE, JAMES H. R
m. to Eunice Gladen; c. Linda, Henry and Julia. Educ: Kenyon Col, grad; completed seminar in retailing at N.Y. Univ; Sigma Phi. Polit. & Govt. Pos: Ohio State Sen, 62-66; served as Hubbard precinct committeeman; mem, Trumbull Co. Rep. Exec. Cmt; field coordinator for N.E. Ohio, Ohio Off. Opportunity, 67- Bus. & Prof. Pos: Field rep. for Dept. of Hwy. Safety in northeast. Ohio; salesman; substitute teacher. Mil. Serv: Navy, Vet, overseas duty in S. Africa and New Guinea. Mem: Elks; Mason; Shrine; Youngstown C. of C; Ohio Coun-Retail Merchants Asn. Rel: Presbyterian. Mailing Add: 763 Mentor Ave, Painesville, Ohio 44077.

GROSECLOSE, JOHN ROBERT - 'BOB' R
Chmn, Tom Green Co. Rep. Party, Tex.
b. San Angelo, Tex, 2/8/38; s. William Buell Groseclose and Adelaide Colvard G; single. Educ: Univ. Tex, B.A. in math. Polit. & Govt. Pos: Precinct chmn, Tom Green Co. Rep. Party, Tex, 64-, chmn, 66- Mailing Add: 114 E. Twohig, San Angelo, Tex. 76901.

GROSHEK, LEONARD ANTHONY D
Wis. State Assemblyman
b. Stevens Point, Wis, 6/13/13; s. Leo Groshek and Helen Jablonski G; wid; m. June, 1968 to Regina T. Kirschling; c. Anita (Mrs. Gosh), Audrey (Mrs. Pieczynski) and Dalene. Educ: Col, 2 years, Teaching Cert, 30. Polit. & Govt. Pos: Town assessor, Stockton, Wis, 49-51, town clerk, 51-; chmn, Reynolds for Gov. Campaign, Portage Co, 64; 1st v.chmn, Portage Co. Dem. Party, 65, chmn, 66-; Wis. State Assemblyman, currently. Bus. & Prof. Pos:

Prod. worker & supvr, A.O. Smith Corp, Milwaukee, 42-48; storekeeper, Grosheks Trading Post, 48-; gen. ins. agent, 49-; cmnr, Land Condemnation, Portage Co, 60- Mem: Tomorrow River Conserv. Club. Rel: Catholic. Mailing Add: 2125 Indiana Ave, Stevens Point, Wis. 54481.

GROSS, BERNARD MORTON D
Pa. State Rep.
b. Phila, Pa, 5/22/35; s. Albert R. Gross and Ruth Checker G; m. 12/22/57 to Harriet Segal; c. David Michael, Susan Rachel and Deborah Ruth. Educ: Univ. Pa, Wharton Sch. Finance & Commerce, B.S. in econ, 56, Law Sch, LL.B, 59; Pi Gamma Mu; Tau Epsilon Rho. Polit. & Govt. Pos: Asst. city solicitor, Phila, 61-64; Pa. State Rep, 67- Mem: Phila. and Pa. Bar Asns; Am, Pa. and Phila. Trial Lawyers Asns; B'nai B'rith; Anti-Defamation League; Am. for Dem. Action; Am. Civil Liberties Union; Shomrim Soc. Rel: Jewish. Legal Res: 8206 Williams Ave, Philadelphia, Pa. 19150. Mailing Add: 11 North Juniper St, Philadelphia, Pa. 19107.

GROSS, FRED ALFRED, JR. R
N.Mex. State Sen.
b. Fulton, Mo, 4/2/23; s. Fred Alfred Gross and Florence Marie Hutsel G; m. 7/2/43 to Susan Kist; c. Joyce (Mrs. Michael Costello), Cheryl Ann, Fred A, III and Nara Sue. Educ: Westminister Col, chem, 41-42; Univ. Wis, B.S. in Physics and M.S. in Nuclear Physics; Univ. N.Mex, theoretical physics, 52-53; Indust. Col. Armed Forces, 59-60; Debate Team, Westminister Col; Alpha Phi Omega. Polit. & Govt. Pos: Chmn, Div. 44A, N.Mex, 3 years; del, co. and state nominating conv; mem, mil. lands conserv. cmt, Nat. Wildlife Fedn, 66-, wilderness subcmt, 68-69 and environ. qual. subcmt, 69-, resolutions cmt; wildlife rep, dist. adv. panel, Albuquerque Dist, Bur. of Land Mgt, 68; N.Mex. State Sen, Dist. 40, 68-, mem, educ. and conserv. cmts, N.Mex. State Senate. Bus. & Prof. Pos: House painter, carpenter's asst, gen. construction worker and stone mason, 37-42; asst. high sch. football coach and math. teaching asst, Westminister Col, 41-42; vis. scientist for N.Mex. Acad. of Sci, 60-67; staff mem, adv. syst. research dept, Sandia Corp, 63-66, supvr, exp. syst. div, 66-67; v.pres. and dir, Nuclear Defense Research Corp. of N.Mex, Inc, 67- Mil. Serv: Entered as Pvt, Army Air Corps, 42, released as Lt. Col, 63, after serv. as navigator, instr, briefing officer and post engr, Air Force, and as nuclear weapons research and develop. officer, 11 years; Distinguished Flying Cross; Air Medal with Seven Oak Leaf Clusters; Commendation Medal; Occup. of Japan Medal; Am. and European Mid. East Theatre Medals; World War II Victory Medal; Presidential Unit Citation; Korean Serv. Medal. Publ: Effects of Topography on Shock Waves in Air, PVIM-57, 57; Nuclear Weapons Employment Handbook, Air Force Manual 200-8, 58; System Applications of Nuclear Technology and Nuclear Weapon Effects on Air Force Systems, Air Force System Command Manual 500-1, 63. Mem: Bd. dir, Chaparral Coun, Girl Scouts, chmn, camping cmt, 58-62, active in camping and conserv. progs, Va. and N.Mex, 10 years; bd. dir, Albuquerque Wildlife and Conserv. Asn, 64-, first v.pres, 65, pres, 66 & 67; bd. dir, N.Mex. Wildlife and Conserv. Asn, 66-, exec. cmt. and parliamentarian, 67 & 68, resolutions cmt, 4 years, chmn, 67, 68 & 69, third v.pres, 68; Civic Beautification Cmt. of Albuquerque; charter mem, West. Hist. Soc; past cubmaster, Weblos leader, asst. scoutmaster, scoutmaster and explorer adv. and founder Explorer Post 144, Boy Scouts, v.chmn, Sandia Dist, Kit Carson Coun, currently; Wilderness Soc; Am. Forestry Asn; bd. dir, Albuquerque Chap, Am. Ord. Asn; provisional life mem. and rated instr. hunter safety and home safety, Nat. Rifle Asn; Am. Phys. Soc; Retired Officers' Asn; Nat. Geog. Soc; Vet. for Equalization of Taxes. Rel: Methodist. Mailing Add: 2916 Chama N.E, Albuquerque, N.Mex. 87110.

GROSS, H. R. R
U.S. Rep, Iowa
b. Arispe, Iowa, 6/30/99; m. 6/29/29 to Hazel E. Webster; c. Phil and Alan. Educ: Univ. Mo. Sch. Journalism. Polit. & Govt. Pos: U.S. Rep, Iowa, 48-; del, Rep. Nat. Conv, 68. Bus. & Prof. Pos: Newspaper reporter and ed, 21-35; radio news commentator, 35-48. Mil. Serv: AEF, World War I; Mexican Border Serv, 16. Mem: Mason; Elks; Am. Legion; VFW. Rel: Presbyterian. Legal Res: Waterloo, Iowa. Mailing Add: 1600 S. Joyce St, Arlington, Va. 22202.

GROSS, NELSON G. R
Chmn, State Rep. Party, N.J.
b. Englewood, N.J, 1/9/32; s. Albert Gross and Rose Nelson G; m. Aug. 1961 to Noël Love; c. Neil and Pinah. Educ: Yale Univ, B.A, 53; Columbia Univ, LL.B, 56; Chi Phi; Phi Delta Phi. Polit. & Govt. Pos: Asst. U.S. Attorney, N.J, 56-58; N.J. State Assemblyman, 62-63; co. counsel, Bergen Co, 63-66; chmn, Bergen Co. Rep. Party, 66-69; del, Rep. Nat. Conv, 68; chmn, State Rep. Party, N.J, 69- Bus. & Prof. Pos: Partner, Gross and Gross, Hackensack, 58- Mil. Serv: Entered as Lt, Naval Res, 67- Rel: Jewish. Legal Res: 2 Chestnut Ridge Rd, Saddle River, N.J. 07458. Mailing Add: 1 Essex St, Hackensack, N.J. 07601.

GROSSENBACHER, JEROME FRANCIS D
Chmn, Maverick Co. Dem. Exec. Cmt, Tex.
b. San Antonio, Tex, 7/8/28; s. Max Hubert Grossenbacher and Elenor Kathryn Biedeger G; m. 4/15/55 to Olga Elizondo; c. Jerome F, Jr, Cynthia Elaine, John S, Elenor Kathryn and Glenn T. Educ: Tex. A&M Col, ½ year; Schreiner Inst, 1½ years. Polit. & Govt. Pos: City cmnr, Eagle Pass, Tex, 64-66; chmn, Maverick Co. Dem. Exec. Cmt, 66- Bus. & Prof. Pos: Consignee, Texaco, Inc, Eagle Pass, Tex, 64-; secy-treas, Sin-Tex Develop. Co, 66- Mil. Serv: Entered as Pvt, Air Force, 46, released as S/Sgt, 49, after serv. in 301st Fighter Wing, Okinawa, 47-49; World War II Victory Medal; Pac. Theater Ribbon; Good Conduct Medal. Mem: Am. Legion. Rel: Catholic. Legal Res: 1442 Simpson Dr, Eagle Pass, Tex. 78852. Mailing Add: P.O. Box 787, Eagle Pass, Tex. 78852.

GROSSI, ANTHONY J. D
Chmn, Passaic Co. Dem. Party, N.J.
b. Haskell, N.H; m. to Ruth Berwald; c. Patricia. Educ: John Marshall Law Sch, LL.B, cum laude. Polit. & Govt. Pos: Mem, Cmt. Taxes and Assessments, Paterson, N.J, Dem. munic. chmn, 48-60; Dem. state committeeman, Passaic Co, until 57; N.J. State Sen, 57-68, pres. pro tem, N.J. State Sen, until 68; del, Dem. Nat. Conv, 68; chmn, Passaic Co. Dem. Party, N.J, currently. Legislator of the Year, State Asn. of Bd. of Freeholders, 63. Mailing Add: 14 Clark St, Paterson, N.J. 07505. (1967)

GROSSMAN, HOWARD M. D
b. N.Y.C, 4/18/22; s. Charles Grossman and Rose Unger G; m. 3/21/48 to Adele S. Stiller; c. Elizabeth, James and Andrew. Educ: Cornell Univ, A.B, 42; Columbia Law Sch, LL.B, 48; Alpha Epsilon Pi. Polit. & Govt. Pos: Pres, Greenburgh Dem. Club, N.Y, 60-63; del, N.Y. State Dem. Conv, 62; del, Dem. Nat. Conv, 64; chmn, Greenburgh Town Dem. Cmt, 63-67. Bus. & Prof. Pos: Attorney-at-law, 56-66. Mil. Serv: Entered as Aviation Cadet, Air Force, released as Cpl, 45, after serv. in European Civil Affairs Div, ETO; Normandy, France and Rhine Campaign Ribbons; Croix de Guerre, Grand Duchy of Luxembourg. Mem: Westchester Co. and Mt. Vernon Bar Asns; dirs, Philharmonic Symphony Soc. Westchester and Woodlands High Sch. Scholarship Bd; PTA (past pres, Greenburgh Chap, pres, Woodlands High Sch, 69, v.pres, Greenburgh Housing Coun, 69). Rel: Hebrew. Mailing Add: 27 Shaw Place, Hartsdale, N.Y. 10530.

GROSSMAN, LEON WOLFE D
b. Harbin, China, 12/3/10; s. David Grossman and Ethel Pento G; m. 2/7/47 to Dorothy Zauher. Educ: Univ. Calif, Berkeley, 33. Polit. & Govt. Pos: Del, Calif. Dem. Coun, 64, 65 & 66; del, Dem. Nat. Conv, 64 & 68; San Jose chmn, Johnson-Humphrey Campaign, Santa Clara Co, 64; mem. steering cmt, State Sen. Al Alquist Campaign, 64, 66 & 68, chmn, 68; chmn, Cmt. for Re-election Assemblyman John Vasconcellos, 66-68; treas, Dem. Century Club, 66-; treas, Bus. & Prfnl. Dem. Club, 66-; treas, Dem. Campaign for Gov. Brown, 68; finance chmn, Congressman Don Edwards Campaign, 68; treas, Humphrey-Muskie Campaign, Santa Clara Co, 68; finance chmn, Sen. Robert Kennedy Campaign, 68. Bus. & Prof. Pos: Owner, Grossman's Off. Equip, 53- Mil. Serv: Entered as Recruit, Army, 43, released as Cpl, 46, after serv. in Fourth Inf. Div, ETO, 44-45; Purple Heart; Presidential Citation; Four Battle Stars. Publ: 'Rise and Fall of an Empire,' 1/66, 'Pope Paul's Appeal Before the United Nations,' 5/66 and 'Robert Kennedy Memorial,' 6/68, Cong. Record. Mem. Nat. Off. Furniture Asn.(pres. North. Calif. Chap, 60-62, v.pres. and bd. dirs, Chicago, 61-64); Nat. Stationers and Off. Equip. Asn; Calif. Ment. Health Asn.(treas, 68-); Calif. C. of C; Optimist Club San Jose (bd. dirs, 64); Commonwealth Club Calif; San Jose C. of C.(legis. cmt, 65); Santa Clara Co. Ment. Health Asn.(bd. dirs, 64-, pres, 67-68); Elks; B'nai B'rith. Serv. Award, Nat. Off. Equip. Asn; Serv. Award, Ment. Health Asn; Ten and Fifteen Year Serv. Awards and Youth Leadership Develop. Award, San Jose Optimist Club. Rel: Jewish. Legal Res: 15120 Camden Ave, San Jose, Calif. 95124. Mailing Add: 842 S. First St, San Jose, Calif. 95110.

GROTHUS, EDWARD BERNARD D
b. Clinton, Iowa, 6/28/23; s. Edward T. Grothus and Regina Hebinck G; m. 9/1/51 to Margaret Jane Turnquist; c. Barbara, Thomas, Susan and Michael. Educ: St. Ambrose Col, 46; Univ. Iowa, 47. Polit. & Govt. Pos: Del, Dem. Nat. Conv, 68. Bus. & Prof. Pos: Mgr, Los Alamos Sales Co, 52- Mem: K. of C; IAMAW. Rel: Catholic. Legal Res: 208 Andanada, Los Alamos, N.Mex. 87544. Mailing Add: Box 795, Los Alamos, N.Mex. 87544.

GROUBY, EDWARD ARTHUR, SR. D
b. Abbeville, Ala, 9/20/02; s. Augustus Underwood Grouby and Jeannie Skipper G; m. 7/25/26 to Rose Saunders; c. Edward A, Jr, Betty (Mrs. Clarence T. Milldrum) and Dianne (Mrs. Juhan). Educ: High Sch, Abbeville Ala, grad, 19; Massey Bus. Col, 20. Polit. & Govt. Pos: Mem, Prattville City Coun, Ala, 41-47; chmn, Prattville Water Works, 48-54; Ala. State Rep, 51-66; chmn, Bd. of Revenue and Control, Autauga Co, 66-; judge of probate, Autauga Co, 66- Bus. & Pros. Pos: Owner and operator, Grouby Furniture Co, Prattville, Ala, 34-; railway express agency, 44- Mem: Lions; Mason (Master); Prattville Country Club; Peace Officers Asn; WOW; Farm Bur; Asn. of Co. Cmnr; Probate Judges Asn; dir, Coosa-Ala. River Develop. Asn. Rel: First Baptist. Legal Res: 327 Washington St, Prattville, Ala. 36067. Mailing Add: P.O. Box 388, Prattville, Ala. 36067.

GROVER, HERBERT J.
Wis. State Assemblyman
b. Fond du Lac, Wis, 2/5/37; s. Felix N. Grover and Helen Hardgrove G; m. 7/31/65 to Caroline J. Studach. Educ: St. Norbert Col, B.S. in Am. Hist, 59; Am. Univ, M.A. in Int. Rels. and Orgn, 63; Alpha Phi Omega. Polit. & Govt. Pos: Mem. staff, U.S. Sen. William Proxmire, 61-63; mgt. analyst, Wis. Dept. Voc. and Adult Educ. and Wis. State Motor Vehicle Dept, 64; Wis. State Assemblyman, 65- Mem: Rotary Int; Jaycees; Ment. Retardation Asn. Rel: Catholic. Mailing Add: Hartman Apts, Route 3, Shawano, Wis. 54166. (1967)

GROVER, JAMES R, JR. R
U.S. Rep, N.Y.
b. Babylon, N.Y, 3/5/19; m. to Mary Fullerton; c. Nancy L, Jean, James R. and Jill. Educ: Hofstra Col, A.B; Columbia Law Sch, LL.B. Polit. & Govt. Pos: Spec. counsel, Babylon, N.Y; N.Y. State Assemblyman, 57-62; U.S. Rep, Second Dist, N.Y, 63- Bus. & Prof. Pos: Attorney. Mil. Serv: Army Air Force Coast Artil, World War II, China Theater, discharged as Capt. Mem: Lions; K. of C; Holy Name Soc; VFW; Am. Legion; Am. Red Cross; Babylon Yacht Club. Rel: Roman Catholic. Legal Res: 185 Woodsome Rd, Babylon, N.Y. 11702. Mailing Add: 1234 Longworth House Office Bldg, Washington, D.C. 20515.

GROVES, ELWOOD S. R
b. McHenry, Md, 7/29/03; married. Educ: Garret Co. Pub. Schs. Polit. & Govt. Pos: Md. State House of Dels, 63-67. Bus. & Prof. Pos: Retired from dist. govt. Mil. Serv: 5th Marine Res, 31-35. Mem: K. of P; Oakland Co. Club. Mailing Add: 1006 Broadford Rd, Oakland, Md. 21550. (1967)

GROVES, G. MARK R
Mem, Calif. Rep. State Cent. Cmt.
b. Long Beach, Calif, 5/29/29; s. Gordon L. Groves, Jr. and Aimee K. Bryant G; m. 6/26/53 to Bette Jane Lummis; c. Keith L. Educ: El Camino Col, Los Angeles Co, 47-49; Ore. State Univ, B.S, 52. Polit. & Govt. Pos: Mem, Coffee Creek Elem. Sch. Dist, Calif, 59-69; mem, Trinity Co. Sch. Dist. Orgn. Cmt, 62-; mem, Trinity Co. Rep. Cent. Cmt, 64-65; mem, Calif. Rep. State Cent. Cmt, 69- Bus. & Prof. Pos: Forester, R & G Lumber Co, Trinity Co, 56-60; private timber consult, 60-64; v.pres, Wyntoon Develop. Co, 64- Mil. Serv: Entered as Pvt, Army, 53, released as Cpl, 55, after serv. in Mil. Police, Ft. Lewis, Wash. Mem: Soc. Am. Foresters; Am. Philatelic Soc. Mailing Add: Coffee Creek Route, Trinity Center, Calif. 96091.

GROW, DORAH LUCILE D
b. Jones, Okla, 3/6/05; d. Albert Monaghan Engel and Mary Norris Edmonson E; m. 11/6/26 to Russell Grow; c. Rose Marie (Mrs. Taylor) and Dr. Engel Eugene. Educ: Northeast. State Col, Tahlequah, Okla, A.B; Univ. of Okla, M.A. in bus. admin; Grad. work at N.Y, Wash. and Southern Ill. Univs; Delta Pi Epsilon. Polit. & Govt. Pos: Ill. State Rep, 65-67; chief clerk, Tulsa Co. Election Bd, Okla; asst.co. supt. of schs, Tulsa Co, Okla, and dep. co. clerk. Bus. & Prof. Pos: Asst. prof. of Bus, Robert Morris Col, at present; prof. of bus, Gem City Col, 61-65; dir. of personnel & off. mgr, Christian Freedom Found, N.Y, 58-60; asst. dir. of personnel, Spartan Aircraft Co, 41-45. Mem: Eastern Star; Am. Asn. of Univ. Women; Bus. and Prfnl. Women; YWCA; Gamma Phi Beta. Rel: Disciples of Christ. Legal Res: Christian Church Parsonage, Denver, Ill. 62331. Mailing Add: Box 74, Denver, Ill. 62331.

GROWNEY, KENNETH L. D
b. Maryville, Mo, 9/10/35; m. 8/8/64 to Nancy J. Faber. Educ: Rockhurst Col, Kans. City, Mo, B.S. Polit. & Govt. Pos: Fifth Dist. chmn, Young Dem. Clubs of Mo; pres, Kansas City Young Dem, 64; Mo. State Rep, 64-68. Bus. & Prof. Pos: Asst. v.pres, Home Savings Asn, Kansas City, Mo. Rel: Catholic. Mailing Add: 3707 Madison, Kansas City, Mo. 64111. (1967)

GRUBB, KENNETH PHILIP
b. Mauston, Wis, 9/14/95; s. George S. Grubb and Lucy Nuzum G; m. 12/27/21 to Marguerite Nuzum; c. Dr. Kenneth and Barbara (Mrs. William Weiner). Educ: Northwest Univ; Univ. Wis; Order of Coif, Univ. Wis. Law Sch; Sigma Chi; Phi Delta Phi. Polit. & Govt. Pos: U.S. Dist. Judge, East. Dist. Wis, 55- Bus. & Prof. Pos: Partner, Law Firm of Quarles, Spence & Quarles, 30-55. Mil. Serv: Entered Officers' Training Camp, Ft. Sheridan, 17, transferred to Air Force, released as 2nd Lt, 19, after serv. with 93rd Air Squadron Pursuit Group, France. Mem: State Bar of Wis; Milwaukee and Am. Bar Asns; Bar Asn. of Seventh Fed. Circuit; fel, Am. Col. of Trial Lawyers; Int. Asn. Ins. Counsel (pres, 48-49); Milwaukee Club; Milwaukee Athletic Club. Papers delivered to State Bar of Wis, Ohio and Nebr. Bar Asns, Ins. Sect. of Am. Bar Asn. and Int. Asn. of Ins. Counsel. Rel: Congregational. Mailing Add: 3410 N. Hackett Ave, Milwaukee, Wis. 53211.

GRUBB, ROBERT LAY D
b. Lexington, N.C, 1/17/34; both parents deceased; m. 6/7/58 to Rochelle Thomason; c. Robert Gordon, George Thomason and William Clay. Educ: Univ. N.C, LL.B, 58; N.Y. Univ, LL.M, 59; Phi Gamma Delta; Phi Delta Phi. Polit. & Govt. Pos: Co. Attorney, Davidson Co, N.C, 66; solicitor, Davidson Co. Court, 66-67; chmn, Davidson Co. Dem. Exec. Cmt, 66-69. Mem: N.C. and Davidson Co. Bar Asns; Kiwanis; C. of C. Distinguished Serv. Award, 62; Outstanding Young Layman Award, 68. Rel: United Church of Christ. Legal Res: 30 Williams Circle, Lexington, N.C. 27292. Mailing Add: Professional Building, Lexington, N.C. 27292.

GRUBBS, LAWTON EDISON D
Chmn, White Co. Dem. Cent. Cmt, Ark.
b. Sharpe, Ky, 9/19/98; s. Thomas Achel Grubbs and Jennie Johnston G; m. 12/22/51 to Louise Simerley. Educ: Ark. State Col, 2 years. Polit. & Govt. Pos: Alderman, Kensett, Ark, 32-34; ward committeeman, White Co. Dem. Cmt, 38-40; chmn, White Co. Welfare Bd, 38-42; committeeman, Ark. State Dem. Cmt, 40-44; chmn, White Co. Bd. Educ, 40-44; chmn, White Co. Dem. Cent. Cmt, 66- Bus. & Prof. Pos: Traveling salesman, Milburn Johnston Grocery Co, Searcy, 27-42; mgr, New Port Br, Plunkett Jarrell Grocery Co, Little Rock, 42-50, br. house supvr, 50-57; v.pres, Wood-Freeman Lumber Co, Searcy, 57-; mem, State Bd. Collection Agencies, Little Rock, 66; mem, White Co. Draft Bd, 66- Mil. Serv: Entered as Pvt, Army, 18, released as Pvt, 18, after serv. in Student Army Training Corp, St. Louis, Mo. Mem: Wholesale Grocery Asn; State Fair Asn; Searcy C. of C; dir, Newport C. of C; Mason; Rotary; Am. Legion; chmn, White Co. Chap, Red Cross; regional dir, Am. Red Cross. Awards from Am. Red Cross and Rotary. Rel: Protestant. Mailing Add: 1805 W. Center Ave, Searcy, Ark. 72143.

GRUENING, ERNEST D
b. New York, N.Y, 2/6/87; s. Emil Gruening and Phebe G; m. 11/19/14 to Dorothy Elizabeth Smith; c. Ernest Jr. (deceased), Peter Brown (deceased), Huntington Sander G; five grandchildren. Educ: Harvard, 07; Harvard Med, 12. Polit. & Govt. Pos: Adv. U.S. del, Seventh Inter-Am. Conf, Montevideo, 33; dir, Div. Territories and Island Possessions, Dept. Interior, 34-39; minister, P.R. Reconstruction Admin, 35-37; mem, Alaska Hwy. Cmn, 38-42; app. Gov. Alaska, 39-53; U.S. Sen, Alaska, 58-68; del, Dem. Nat. Conv, 68. Bus. & Prof. Pos: Doctor; former journalist. Mailing Add: P.O. Box 1001, Juneau, Alaska 99801. (1967)

GRUENWALD, MAX R
S.Dak. State Rep.
b. Mitchell, S.Dak, 11/4/31; s. Charles Gruenwald and Kathryn Anderson G; m. 10/1/54 to Dona Olson; c. Lane Scott, Mark Todd and Shari Ann. Educ: Yankton Col, 49-51; Univ. S.Dak, B.A, 54, LL.B, 56; Tau Kappa Alpha; Alpha Tau Omega. Polit. & Govt. Pos: Co. attorney, Grant Co, S.Dak, 62-66; city attorney, Milbank, 63-; S.Dak. State Rep, Grant-Deuel Dist, 69- Mil. Serv: Entered as Ens, Navy, 56, released as Lt.(jg), 59, after serv. in 14th Naval Dist, Pac. Theatre, 57-59. Mem: State Bar of S.Dak; Am. Trial Lawyers Asn; Mason; Eastern Star; Kiwanis; Milbank Commerce Commun. Club. Rel: Congregational. Mailing Add: 111 S. Viola, Milbank, S.Dak. 57252.

GRUHN, KARL DFL
Chmn, Third Dist. New Dem. Coalition, Minn.
b. Johnsonburg, Pa, 11/9/12; s. August Gruhn and Irene Deterling G; m. 12/22/43 to Eleanor Mae Outzen; c. Joel David, Janet Louise (Mrs. Smith) and Jodimae Ellen. Educ: Concordia Col, B.A, 34; Univ. Minn, 35-37; Northwest. Lutheran Theol. Sem, 37; mem. nat. exec. cmt, Col. and Univ. YMCA, 37. Polit. & Govt. Pos: Justice of the Peace, Mound, Minn, 52-57; dir, Civil Defense, 54-64; alternate del, Dem. Nat. Conv, 68; mem, Dem-Farmer-Labor State Cent. Cmt, 68-; chmn, McCarthy Caucus, 69-; chmn, 22nd Ward, Dem-Farmer-Labor Party, Mound, Minn, 69-; chmn, Third Dist. New Dem. Coalition, Minn, 69- Bus. & Prof. Pos: V.pres, Kozee-Kar, Inc, Minneapolis, Minn, 41-49; owner, Minnetonka Furniture, Mound, Minn, 49-66; pres, Tonka Mills, Inc, 67-; mem. bd. dirs, Minn. Summerhill Sch. Found, 68-; v.pres, Miller Peace Mem. Found, Fifty Lakes, Minn, 68- Mil. Serv: Entered as Pvt, Air Force, 42, released as S/Sgt, 46, after serv. in 27th Reconnaissance Squadron, Eighth Air Force, ETO, 44-46; Six Bronze Combat Stars. Mem: Am. Legion; VFW. Rel: Lutheran. Mailing Add: 6299 Birch Lane, Mound, Minn. 55364.

GRUMBACHER, RICHARD D
Md. State Del.
b. York, Pa, 4/10/14; m. to Marjorie Cohen; c. Steven, Robert, John and Nancy. Educ: Mercersburg Acad, Pa. Polit. & Govt. Pos: Md. State Del, 61- Bus. & Prof. Pos: Mem. bd. dirs, Wash. Co. Free Libr; pres, Hagerstown-Wash. Co. Indust. Found; bd. dir, Commun. Research Asn. Mil. Serv: Army Air Corps, 41-45. Mem: Elks; Mil. Order of World Wars; United World Federalists; Am. Civil Liberties Union. Mailing Add: 1151 The Terrace, Hagerstown, Md. 21740.

GRUNFELD, ROSELYN E. D
b. N.Y.C, 3/24/19; d. Benjamin Epstein and Mildred Lotheim E; m. 6/3/41 to Edwin Albert Grunfeld; c. Judith Ahern. Educ: N.Y. Univ, B.A, 39. Polit. & Govt. Pos: Committeewoman, Queens Co. Dem. Orgn, N.Y, 54-56, committeewoman, Nassau Co. Dem. Orgn, 57-60, exec. mem, 61-66; pres, New Hyde Park Dem. Club, 61-62; purchasing supvr, Bur. Purchase and Supply, 62-; State Committeewoman, Dem. Nat. Cmt, 66-68; alternate del, Dem. Nat. Conv, 68. Bus. & Prof. Pos: Purchasing agent, Gen. Purchasing Agency, 41-54. Mem: Manhasset Hills Civic Asn; Orgn. Adminstr. and Supvr. (pres, Chap. Civil Serv. Employees Asn). Gavel and Plaque, New Hyde Park Dem. Club; Onyx Desk Set, Presiding Manhasset Hills Civic Asn, 69. Rel: Jewish. Mailing Add: 117 Olive Lane, New Hyde Park, N.Y. 11040.

GRUNSKY, DONALD LUCIUS R
Calif. State Sen.
b. San Francisco, Calif, 10/19/15; s. Eugene Lucius Grunsky and Margaret Koch G; m. 8/16/43 to Mary Lou Meidl. Educ: Univ. Calif. at Berkeley, A.B, 36, LL.B, 39. Polit. & Govt. Pos: Calif. State Assemblyman, 47-52; Calif. State Sen, currently; del, Rep. Nat. Conv, 68. Bus. & Prof. Pos: Attorney-at-Law, Grunsky & Pybrum. Mil. Serv: Entered as Ens, Navy, 41, released as Lt. Comdr, 45. Mem: State Bar of Calif; Am. Bar Asn; Elks; Am. Legion; VFW. Rel: Protestant. Mailing Add: 130 Rogers Ave, Watsonville, Calif. 95076.

GRUNWALDT, DAVID CARL R
Chmn, Outagamie Co. Rep. Party, Wis.
b. Green Bay, Wis, 2/6/38; s. Carl August Grunwaldt (deceased) and Viola Wussow G; m. 11/22/63 to Diane Cory; c. Christine, Constance and Cathleen. Educ: Marquette Univ. Sch. Dent, D.D.S, 63; Delta Sigma Delta. Polit. & Govt. Pos: Chmn, Outagamie Co. Young Rep, Wis, 64-65; mem. exec. cmt, Outagamie Co. Rep. Party, 64-, chmn, 68-; mem. resolutions cmt, Wis. State Rep. Party, 69. Mil. Serv: Pvt. E-2, Army, 56; Army Res, 56-; Reservist of the Year, 84th Div, 58. Mem: Am. Dent. Asn; Wis. State and Outagamie Co. Dent. Socs; Am. Acad. Physiologic Dent; Kiwanis; Elks; F&AM. Rel: Methodist. Mailing Add: 1008 Hennes Court, Kaukauna, Wis. 54130.

GRUSSENDORF, WM. T. Conservative
City Councilman, Duluth, Minn.
b. Jordan, Minn, 09; m; c. Three daughters. Educ: Univ. Minn, B.S. Polit. & Govt. Pos: Pres, Duluth Efficient Govt. Asn; Minn. State Rep, 64-66; city councilman, Duluth, 67- Bus. & Prof. Pos: Area mgr, Fed. Land Bank Nat. Farm Loan Asn, 12 years; former sch. bd. mem, Foodwood, Minn; Carlton Co. Super Rural Rehabilitation, 2 years; Univ. Minn. Exten. Serv, 2 years; high sch. teacher, 6 years. Mailing Add: 7511 Grand Ave, Duluth, Minn. 55807.

GRUSSING, GEORGE P. Conservative
b. Clara City, Minn, 1905; married; c. 2 sons. Educ: Clara City Pub. Schs. Polit. & Govt. Pos: Minn. State Rep, 55-68. Bus. & Prof. Pos: Bldg. contractor; farmer. Mem: School, Creamery, Drainage, Flood, Soil Conserv. and Civic Orgns. Mailing Add: 727 S. Main St, Clara City, Minn. 56222. (1967)

GRUVER, WILLIAM RAND II D
b. N.Y.C, 6/18/27; s. Henry Gruver and Anne Lauer G; m. Sept. 1961 to Lila Jean Aharnian; c. Catherine Anne and Robin Marie. Educ: Columbia Univ, A.B. and M.A; grad. course, Am. Polit; Beta Sigma Tau. Polit. & Govt. Pos: Press secy, John F. Kennedy Calif. Campaign, 60 and President United States Lyndon B. Johnson South. Calif. Campaign, 64; mem, Calif. Dem. State Cent. Cmt, 64-65, press secy, 65-68; press secy, spec. events, Gov. Campaign, 66; media adv, Dem. Nat. Cmt, 68; campaign press secy, U.S. Sen. Robert F. Kennedy, and conv. press secy, U.S. Sen. George McGovern, 68; Adv, several U.S. Sen. Bus. & Prof. Pos: Pub. rels. counsel ed, William Gruver Pub. Rels, 62-65; ed, Beverly Hills Times, Calif, 64-66 and Mercury News Serv, 64-; polit. consult, TV Network, 67-; faculty mem, New Sch. Col, N.Y.C, 68 & 69; pub. rels.counsel ed, Fred Rosen Int, N.Y.C, 68- Mil. Serv: Entered as Seaman, Navy, 44, released as PO, 47, after serv. as Fleet Newspaper Ed, in Far East and Mediterranean; Naval Res, 47-50; Air Force Res, 50-62; Area Ribbons; United Commendations. Publ: Since 1792, 68, Facing Leaves of November, 68-69 and City Hall (in prep), Mermac Pub. Mem: Overseas Press Club of Am; Pub. Rels. Soc. of Am; Ed. Asn. of N.Am. Recipient of Bishop Buckley Award for Scholastic Achievement. Rel: Protestant. Legal Res: Calif. Mailing Add: 127 E. 59th St, New York, N.Y. 10022.

GRUYS, ARNOLD DFL
Minn. State Rep.
b. 1928; m. to Ruth Ostergren; c. Doug, Carol, Kenneth. Educ: Univ. of Minn, B.A. Polit. & Govt. Pos: Minn. State Rep, 67- Mil. Serv: Army, 46-48, Sgt; U.S. Army Res, 50, Lt. Mem: Annandale Commercial Club; Buffalo C. of C. Lions; Red Cross; PTA; Boy Scout Cmt; Am. Legion; Church Coun; Synod del. Mailing Add: Annandale, Minn. 55313. (1967)

GUARDINO, ALPHONSE PETER R
b. N.Y.C, 2/11/05; s. Vincenzo Guardino and Assunta Baldassano G; m. 6/29/30 to Mary Giusti; c. Marie (Mrs. Giusto). Educ: N.Y. Univ; Brooklyn Law Sch. Polit. & Govt. Pos: Assoc. counsel, N.Y. State Joint Legis. Cmt. on Indust. and Labor Rels; del, N.Y. Rep. State Conv, 42-58 and Rep. Nat. Conv,

48, 56 & 60; referee, assoc. counsel, secy, mem. and v.chmn, N.Y. State Workmen's Compensation Bd, 43-54; chmn, 11th Assembly Dist, Queens Co. Rep. Cmt, 44-54; law secy. to Co. Court Judge William B. Groat, 54-58; State Rep. Committeeman, 28th Assembly Dist, Queens Co, N.Y, 54-69; law secy. to Supreme Court Justice, Henry J. Latham, N.Y, 59-60 & 61-; Justice, City Court, Queens Co, 60; Justice, Family Court, N.Y, 69- Mem: Queens Co. and Am. Bar Asns; K. of C; Italian Charities of Am; Elks; Order Sons of Italy in Am. Admitted to practice law before U.S. Supreme Court and all Fed. and N.Y. State Courts. Rel: Roman Catholic. Mailing Add: 102-30 135th St, Richmond Hill, N.Y. 11419.

GUARINI, FRANK J, JR. D
N.J. State Sen.
Educ: N.Y. Univ. Sch. of Law, LL.B. and LL.M; Dartmouth Col; Hague Acad. Int. Law, Holland; Columbia Univ. Polit. & Govt. Pos: Pres, Commun. Charter Coun; N.J. State Sen, currently. Bus. & Prof. Pos: Counselor at law. Mil. Serv: Navy, Lt.(sg), Navig. Pac, Training Officer, Naval Training Center. Mem: Nat. bd. gov, Am. Red Cross; dir, C. of C; Rotary; Hudson Co. Bar Asn; Health and Tuberc. League and Ment. Health Asn; bd. of regents, St. Peter's Col; trustee, Christ Hosp, Jersey City, N.J. Admitted U.S. Supreme Court. Mailing Add: 610 Newark Ave, Jersey City, N.J. 07306.

GUASTELLO, THOMAS D
Mich. State Rep.
b. Detroit, Mich, 10/25/43; s. Peter James Guastello and Barbarose Shaw G; single. Educ: Mich. State Univ, B.A, 65; Detroit Col. of Law, 65-69; Alpha Tau Omega; Student Govt. J. Coun. Polit. & Govt. Pos: Chmn, Macomb Co. Young Dem, Mich, 67-68; Mich. State Rep, 69- Bus. & Prof. Pos: V.pres, Village Inns, Inc, 64- Mem: Student Bar Asn; Mich. State Univ. Alumni Club; Utica Sch. Adv. Cmt; Jaycees; Goodfellow; Macomb Co. Prosecuting Attorneys Asn. Ben Probe Moot Court Finalist; Poly Sci. Hon. Prog. Rel: Catholic. Mailing Add: 11165 Laurel Court, Sterling Heights, Mich. 48077.

GUBBINS, JOAN MARGARET R
Ind. State Sen.
b. N.Y.C, 7/2/29; d. Arthur L. Barton and Margaret Hedge B; m. 5/6/49 to Dale George Gubbins; c. Gregory Dale and Carol Jane. Educ: Univ. Ill, 47-49; Alpha Chi Omega. Polit. & Govt. Pos: Research chmn, Ind. Goldwater for Pres. Cmt, 64; del, Ind. Rep. State Conv, 66 & 68; Rep. precinct committeewoman, Indianapolis, 66-; Ind. State Sen, 69- Mem: Nat. Fedn. Rep. Women; Women's Club; Ind. State Legislators Club; Citizens' Forum; Nora Commun. Coun; PTO; hon. mem, Poet's Corner; Am. Contract Bridge League; Cent. Ind. Bridge Asn. Rel: Reformed Presbyterian. Mailing Add: 1000 E. 81st St, Indianapolis, Ind. 46240.

GUBBRUD, ARCHIE R
b. Alcester, S.Dak; 12/31/10; s. Maruis T. Gubbrud and Ella Rommeriem G; m. 8/15/39 to Florence Dexter; c. John D. and Maxine (Mrs. Roberts). Polit. & Govt. Pos: Mem, Twp. Bd, S.Dak, 34-50; mem, Local Sch. Bd, 47-53; S.Dak. State Rep, 51-60, Speaker of the House, 58-60; Gov, S.Dak, 61-64; del, Rep. Nat. Conv, 68. Bus. & Prof. Pos: Chmn. bd. dirs, Beefland Int, Council Bluffs, Iowa, 68-; dir, State Bank, Alcester, S.Dak, currently. Mem: Nat. Livestock Feeders (dir. for S.Dak); Mason (32°); Shrine; Farm Bur. Miss. Valley Asn. Award, Soil Conservation S.Dak. Rel: Lutheran. Mailing Add: R.F.D. 2, Alcester, S.Dak. 57001.

GUBSER, CHARLES S. R
U.S. Rep, Calif.
b. Gilroy, Calif, 2/1/16; s. Charles Henry Gubser and Ella Oma Matlack G; m. 1/8/39 to Joan Brimberry G; c. Mrs. Raymond Camino; three grandchildren. Educ: Univ. of Calif, A.B, 37; Kappa Alpha. Polit. & Govt. Pos: Calif. State Assemblyman, 50-52; U.S. Rep, Calif, 52- Bus. & Prof. Pos: Secondary sch. teacher, 39-43; operator, truck farm, 40-50; farmer. Mem: Mason; Elks; Rotary. Legal Res: 280 N. Princevalle, Gilroy, Calif. 95020. Mailing Add: 2373 Rayburn House Office Bldg, Washington, D.C. 20515.

GUDAJTES, EDWARD RAYMOND D
b. Warsaw, N.Dak, 7/28/11; s. Anton L. Gudajtes and Jane Byzewski G; m. 11/21/39 to Marie Slominski; c. James, John, Mary and Marjorie. Educ: Minto High Sch. Polit. & Govt. Pos: Twp. assessor, Harriston, N.Dak, 46-50, twp. supvr, 63-; sch. dir, Dist, 44, 46-58; N.Dak. State Rep, Dist. 4, Walsh Co, 65-67. Bus. & Prof. Pos: Pres, Minto Co-op Oil Co, N.Dak, 51-56; pres, Minto Farmers Elevator, 59-63; secy. and mgr, Walsh Co. Mutual Ins. Co. of Minto, 67- Mil. Serv: Mem, Walsh Co. Draft Bd, 51-53. Mem: Farm Bur; Farmers Union; Nat. Farmers Orgn; Nat. Malting Barley Growers; Walsh Co. Crop & Improvement Asn; Polish Nat. Alliance; Eagles. Rel: Roman Catholic. Mailing Add: Minto, N.Dak. 58261.

GUDE, GILBERT R
U.S. Rep, Md.
b. D.C, 3/9/23; s. Adolph E. Gude (deceased) and Inez Gilbert G; m. 6/19/48 to Jane Wheeler Callaghan; c. Sharon, Gregory, Adrienne, Gilbert, Jr. and Daniel. Educ: Cornell Univ, B.S, 48; George Wash. Univ, M.A, 58; Pi Kappa Phi; Phi Sigma Kappa. Polit. & Govt. Pos: Md. State Del, 52-58; mem, Montgomery Co. State Rep. Cent. Cmt, 58-62, chmn, 61-62; Md. State Sen, 62-66; U.S. Rep, Md, 67-; del, Rep. Nat. Conv, 68. Mem: Md. Nurserymens Asn, past pres; Rockville, Md. Rotary; Montgomery Co. Hist. Soc; Atlantic Naturalist. Rel: Catholic. Mailing Add: 5411 Duvall Dr, Bethesda, Md. 20016.

GUENZL, HERBERT FERDINAND R
Mem. Exec. Cmt, Lincoln Co. Rep. Party, Wis.
b. Lindau, Austria, 6/18/06; s. Ferdinand Guenzl and Stephanie Stiller G; m. 1/26/35 to Elizabeth Surrena. Educ: Univ. Wis, A.B, 27, LL.B, 30; Phi Delta Phi. Polit. & Govt. Pos: Dist. Attorney, Lincoln Co, Wis, 36-38, circuit court cmnr; alderman, Second Ward Rep. Party, 38-42; supvr, Merrill, Wis, 38-42; v.chmn, Lincoln Co. Rep. Party, 46-62, chmn, 62-67, mem. exec. cmt, 46-; del, Rep. Nat. Conv, 58. Bus. & Prof. Pos: Pres, Tiny-Tot Mfg. Co, Inc. and Surrena Enterprises Inc, Wis, 46- Mil. Serv: Entered as Lt.(jg), Navy, 42, released as Lt. Comdr, 46, after serv. in Atlantic and Pac. Theaters; Victory Medal; Am, European-African-Middle East and Asiatic Pac. Campaign Ribbons; Am. Defense Medal; Nine Invasion Stars. Mem: Wis. Bar Asn; Rotary (past pres, Merrill Chap). Rel: Methodist. Mailing Add: 1200 E. Sixth St, Merrill, Wis. 54452.

GUERARD, THEODORE BOGERT D
S.C. State Rep.
b. Charleston, 3/10/30; s. Russell B. Guerard and Margaret Walker G; m. to Elizabeth deRossett Maybank. Educ: Col. Charleston, A.B, 50; Univ. S.C, LL.B, 53. Polit. & Govt. Pos: S.C. State Rep, currently. Bus. & Prof. Pos: Lawyer, Firm of Sinkler, Gibbs & Simons. Mailing Add: Box 340, Charleston, S.C. 29402. (1967)

GUERRA, MARK R
Mem, Calif. Rep. State Cent. Cmt.
b. El Paso, Tex, 3/23/18; s. Jess M. Guerra and Catherine LuJan G; m. 2/12/44 to Anna Marie Tevlin; c. Joanne (Mrs. Williams), Mark Joseph, Theresa, Edward, Mary Lou, Daniel and Catherine. Educ: San Jose State, A.B, 49; Stanford Univ, M.A, 53; Phi Delta Kappa; Alpha Eta Rho. Polit. & Govt. Pos: Mem, Calif. Fair Employ. Practices Cmn, 67-; del, Rep. Nat. Conv, 68; assoc. mem, Santa Clara Co. Rep. Cent. Cmt, 69; mem, Calif. Rep. State Cent. Cmt, 69- Bus. & Prof. Pos: Teacher, Counsr. and Adminstr, East Side Sch. Dist, San Jose, 51-65; Dean Students, East Side Union High Sch. Dist, 65; dir, Santa Clara Neighborhood Youth Corps, 65-66; dep. dir, Santa Clara Co. Econ. Opportunity Cmn, 66, dir, 66-67; prin, Williams High Sch, 67- Mil. Serv: Entered as Pvt, Air Force, 42, released as 1st Lt, 47, after serv. in 74th Airways and Air Commun. Serv, S.Am, 44-46. Mem: Calif. Teachers Asn; Calif. Counseling & Guid Asn; Nat. Educ. Asn; Mexican Am. Lions Club; Goodwill Industs.(mem. bd); YWCA (mem. bd); Seventh Step Found.(mem. bd); Hornets, Nat. Youth Football (mem. bd). Calif. State Assembly Commending Resolution for Excellence in Sch. Prog, 69. Rel: Catholic. Mailing Add: 490 Sunnyoaks Ave, Campbell, Calif. 95008.

GUERRERO, MANUEL FLORES LEON D
b. Agana, Guam, 10/25/14; s. Jose L.G. Leon Guerrero and Maria Lujan Flores G; m. to Delfina Tuncap; c. Alfred, Lolita, Rudolpho, Evelyna, Teresita, Manuel and Patricia. Educ: High Sch. Polit. & Govt. Pos: Secy. of Guam, 61-63, Gov, 63-69; U.S. Cmnr, S.Pac. Cmn, 64-; del, Dem. Nat. Conv, 68. Mil. Serv: Civilian internee, 41-44. Mailing Add: P.O. Box 223, Agana, Guam 96910.

GUERRY, HENDERSON, SR. D
b. Bonneau, S.C, 5/3/06; s. J. Stephen Guerry and Amanda Hood G; m. 4/17/26 to J. Maude Morris. Educ: Bonneau High Sch, 25. Polit. & Govt. Pos: Mem town coun, Moncks Corner, S.C, 43-47; S.C. State Rep, 49-68. Bus. & Prof. Pos: Dist. mgr, Liberty Life Ins, 37- Mem: C. of C.(past pres, Moncks Corner Chap, bd. dir, currently); Lions; Masons; Teacher Young Men's Club. Rel: Baptist; Deacon. Mailing Add: Box 38, Moncks Corner, S.C. 29461. (1967)

GUESS, EUGENE D
Alaska State Rep.
b. Tutwiler, Miss, 12/30/32; s. Thomas Alazo Guess and Ralda Bailey G; m. 7/14/56 to Carolyn Bailey Suber; c. Carl Thomas, John Bailey and Phillip Mosby. Educ: Col. William and Mary, B.A, 55; Univ. Va, LL.B, 59; Sigma Alpha Epsilon. Polit. & Govt. Pos: Attorney, solicitors off, Dept. of Interior, 59-61; campaign mgr. for Gov. William A. Egan, Southcent. Alaska, 62; pres, Gr. Anchorage Dem. Club, 63; Alaska State Rep, 64-, Majority Floor Leader and chmn, Local Govt. Cmt. and Legis Coun, Alaska State House of Rep; del, Dem. Nat. Conv, 68. Bus. & Prof. Pos: V.chmn, Gov. Adv. Cmt. on Econ. Develop, 61-; mem, Alaska Export Expansion Coun, 65- Mil. Serv: Entered as 2nd Lt, Army, 56, released as Capt, 65, after serv. in 534th Fuel Artil Bn, Ft. Sill, Okla; Capt.(Ret), Army Res, 65. Mem: Fed. Bar Asn.(pres, 63); Va, Alaska and Anchorage Bar Asns. Rel: Protestant. Legal Res: 3835 Baxter Rd, Anchorage, Alaska 99504. Mailing Add: 202 Crawford Bldg, Anchorage, Alaska 99502.

GUESS, SAM C. R
Wash. State Sen.
b. Greenwood, Miss, 1909; m. to Dorothy G; c. Two. Educ: Univ. Miss, B.S. Polit. & Govt. Pos: Wash. State Sen, 62- Bus. & Prof. Pos: Civil Eng. Mil. Serv: Maj, Army, Mem: Sigma Nu. Mailing Add: W. 408 - 33rd Ave, Spokane, Wash. 99023. (1967)

GUEST, RAYMOND R. D
b. N.Y.C, 11/25/07; m. to Caroline Murat; c. Achille Murat and Laetitia. Educ: Yale Univ, B.A, 31. Polit. & Govt. Pos: Va. State Sen, 48-53; mem, Va. State Cmn. on Fisheries and Game, 59-65; U.S. Ambassador to Ireland, 65-68. Bus. & Prof. Pos: Operator farm, Front Royal, Va, 31-53; dir, Bessemer Securities, Inc, 48-; owner and operator, Powhatan Plantation, King George, 53- Mil. Serv: Navy, 41-47; spec. asst. to Fiscal Dir, 47; Comdr.(Ret), Naval Res, 52. Mem: Trustee, Va. Mus. Fine Arts, Richmond. Mailing Add: Powhatan Plantation, King George, Va. 22485.

GUFFEY, DOROTHY ANNE D
b. Watertown, S.Dak, 1/6/20; d. Nicholas J. Kranz and Anna Bierscheid K; m. 9/17/40 to Boyd Vernon Guffey; c. James V. and Michael B. Educ: Watertown Commercial Col. Polit. & Govt. Pos: Mem; Hosp. Adv. Coun, S.Dak, 60-65; secy-treas, Dem. Co. Orgn, 16 yrs, officer, Women's Fedn. Bus. & Prof. Pos: Various off. and bookkeeping positions; legal secy, several yrs; operator, income tax serv; dist. clerk, Northwest. Pub. Serv. Co, Clark, S. Dak, 58- Mem: Local 330, IBEW; Elks Auxiliary. Rel: Roman Catholic. Mailing Add: 313 N. Dakota St, Clark, S.Dak. 57225.

GUGGENHEIM, RICHARD E. D
b. Cincinnati, Ohio, 1/5/13; s. Eli F. Guggenheim and Eva Stransky G; m. 9/21/43 to Carol J. Rice, wid. 58; m. 2/27/67 to Alice W. Joseph; c. Jane, Polly and Richard R. Educ: Univ. Mich, A.B, 34; Harvard, LL.B, 37. Polit. & Govt. Pos: With U.S. Dept. Justice, 40-42, attorney, Civil & Anti-trust Div, 46-50; dep. gen. counsel, Econ. Stabilization Agency, 50-51; mem, Mayor of Cincinnati Friendly Rel. Cmt, 58-59; chmn, Ohio Civil Rights Cmn, 59-62; chmn, platform cmt, Ohio Dem. Party, 66; del, Dem. Nat. Conv, 68; dir, Fed. Home Loan Bank. Bus. & Prof. Pos: With U.S. Shoe Corp, 51-, v.pres, 60-, secy, 64- Mil. Serv: Entered Army, 42, released as Maj, 46. Mem: Am, Ohio & Cincinnati Bar Asns; Miami Soc; Fellowship House. Rel: Jewish. Legal Res: 1846 Keys Crescent, Cincinnati, Ohio 45206. Mailing Add: 1658 Herald Ave, Cincinnati, Ohio 45207.

GUGLIELMO, DUDLEY A. D
State Cmnr. of Ins, La.
b. Paulina, La, 4/21/09; s. Joseph F. Guglielmo, Sr. and Lucille Trudeau G; m. 11/30/33 to Nellie Theriot; c. Lucille (Mrs. William F. Roy), Carey J. and Dudley A, Jr. Educ: Jefferson Col, B.S, 29; Soule Bus. Col, New Orleans, La, 29-30. Polit. & Govt. Pos: Adminstr, personnel and finance, Off. Secy. of State, La, 30-40; exec. asst. to Secy. of State, 40-44; asst. to Secy. of State and Ins. Cmnr. of La, 44-49; dep. cmnr. of ins, La, 49-64, State Cmnr. of Ins, 64- Mem: Nat. Asn. Ins. Cmnrs; Gov. La. Hwy. Safety Cmn; Ins. Soc. N.Y; Fedn. Ins. Counsel; K. of C; C. of C. Mailing Add: State Capitol, Baton Rouge, La. 70804.

GUIDO, ROBERT NORMAN R
b. N.Y.C, 1/25/35; s. Robert Guido and Helen Vega G; m. 1/13/57 to Loretta LaRocca; c. Robert Christopher, Michele Helene, John David, Paul Andrew and Jane Susan. Educ: Columbia Univ, 1½ years. Polit. & Govt. Pos: Co. committeeman and chmn, Paramus Rep. Party, N.J, 64; parliamentarian, Bergen Co. Rep. Party, 66, assembly dist. chmn, 67-; recreation cmnr, Paramus, 67; alternate del, Rep. Nat. Conv, 68; chmn, Bergen Co. Young Rep, 69- Bus. & Prof. Pos: Actuarial asst, Mutual Ins. Adv. Asn, N.Y.C, 64. Mem: Jaycees; Elks; Holy Name Soc; Reeder Rd. Art and Cultural Soc. Rel: Roman Catholic. Mailing Add: 71 Knollwood Dr, Paramus, N.J. 07652.

GUILD, LAWRENCE W, SR. R
b. Roslindale, Mass, 11/25/02; married; c. three. Educ: Worcester Acad; Lowell Tech. Inst. Polit. & Govt. Pos: Gilford Welfare Officer; N.H. State Rep, until 68. Bus. & Prof. Pos: Textile mfr. Mem: Thompson Ames Hist. Soc.(pres); Alumni Asn. Lowell Tech. Inst.(dir); C. of C.(past pres, Laconia Chap); dir, Laconia Indust. Develop. Corp; Mason (32°). Rel: Protestant. Mailing Add: RFD 4, Laconia, N.H. 03256. (1967)

GUILES, SAMUEL EVERETTE R
Mem, Dist. of Columbia Rep. Cent. Cmt.
b. Pamplico, S.C, 10/1/21; s. William Samuel Guiles and Areta Green G; m. 12/17/49 to Anne Rowe. Educ: Allen Univ, A.B, 44; Howard Univ. Sch. Relig, B.D, 47, Sch. Law, 47-48; Phi Beta Sigma. Hon. D.D, Kittrell Col, 53. Polit. & Govt. Pos: Mem. President's Cmt. Govt. Contracts, Wash, D.C, 58-61; mem, D.C. Rep. Cmt, 64-68; mem, Dist. Columbia Rep. Cent. Cmt, 68- Bus. & Prof. Pos: Pastor, Campbell African Methodist Episcopal Church, Wash, D.C, 49-56; mem, Coord. Cmt. Anacostia, D.C. and Vicinity, 53-54; pastor, Turner, Mem. African Methodist Episcopal Church, 56-; mem. cmt. hosp. ministry, Wash. Coun. Church, 57-59; mem, bd. dirs, Wash. Urban League, 59-; mem. bd. dirs, Iona Whipper Home Unwed Mothers, 60-65; mem, Instnl. Chaplaincy Cmt, Coun. Church, Nat. Capitol Area, 60-; pres, Interdenominational Ministers' Alliance of Wash. and Vicinity, 60-65; mem. exec. bd, Wash. D.C. Br, NAACP, 64-68; trustee, Kittrell Col, 64-; mem. bd. dirs, Opportunities Industrilization Center, 66-, treas, currently; v.chmn. cmt. inquiry of the judicial coun, African Methodist Episcopal Church, 68-, mem. prog. cmt, Gen. Conf. Cmn, 68-; treas, Wash. Conf. African Methodist Episcopal Church, 69-; mem. adv. bd, Nat. Med. Asn. 69- Del, World Methodist Conf, London Eng, 66; Wash. Urban League Award, 57; Minister of the Year, Coord. Cmt. Asacostia and Vicinity, 54; Outstanding Vol. Leader, United Givers Fund, 57; Steve Taylor Int. Dance Studios, Award, 64; Award, Nat. Capitol Area Coun. Boy Scouts Am, 68. Rel: African Methodist Episcopal. Mailing Add: 1605 Crittenden St. N.W, Washington, D.C. 20011.

GUILFORD, FRANK E. D
Fla. State Rep.
b. Dothan, Ala, 7/1/28; m. to Mildred Jeanette Register; c. Dona Christine and Frank E. Jr. Educ: Fla. State Univ, B.S, 31, M.S, Educ, 56. Polit. & Govt. Pos: Fla. State Rep, 62-66. Bus. & Prof. Pos: Elem Supvr. in Teaching Profession. Mil. Serv: Army. Mem: Lions; C. of C.(secy. and past pres); Cancer Soc; Am. Legion (past adj). Rel: Methodist; Official Board. Mailing Add: Box 24, Blountstown, Fla. 32424. (1967)

GUILLIOT, OGDEN CLARENCE D
La. State Rep.
b. Youngsville, La, 2/14/12; s. Jerry J. Guilliot and Olive Leblanc G; m. 8/3/57 to Ruby Angelle; c. O.C, Jr, Janet (Mrs. Stien), Sally, Robert and William. Educ: Univ. Southwest. La, 30; Soule Col, New Orleans, 31. Polit. & Govt. Pos: La. State Rep, Lafayette Parish, 68- Bus. & Prof. Pos: Bus. mgr, Lafayette Charity Hosp, 56-64; real estate bus, 64-69. Rel: Catholic. Legal Res: 410 Landry Dr, Lafayette, La. 70501. Mailing Add: 311 W. University, Lafayette, La. 70501.

GUILMETTE, ALFRED J. D
b. Rollinsford, N.H, 3/7/92; m; c. four. Educ: St. Josephs High Sch. Polit. & Govt. Pos: Tax collector; former assessor, Dover City Bd. of Health, N.H, former N.H. State Rep. Bus. & Prof. Pos: Retired city clerk purchasing agent; v.pres, Granite State Coop. Bank. Mem: Cath. Order of Foresters; Order of St. Jean Baptist. Rel: Catholic. Mailing Add: 574 Central Ave, Dover, N.H. 03820.

GUINAN, JAMES J. D
Mem, Washoe Co. Dem. Cent. Cmt, Nev.
b. Evanston, Ill, 9/21/23; s. James J. Guinan and Marion Philbin G; m. 7/23/58 to Ernestine Treiterer; c. James A, Jennifer, Leslie, Erika and Patrick A. Educ: Yale Univ, B.A, 49; Harvard Law Sch, LL.B, 52. Polit. & Govt. Pos: Mem, Washoe Co. Dem. Cent. Cmt, Nev, 64-, chmn, 66-68; del, Dem. Nat. Conv, 68. Bus. & Prof. Pos: Partner, Thornton, Guinan & Griswold, Reno, 66- Mil. Serv: Entered as Pvt, Army, 43, released as Cpl, 46, after serv. in S.W. Pacific Theater, 44-46. Mem: State Bar of Nev; Washoe Co. Bar Assn; Am. Judicature Soc. Legal Res: 630 Sapphire Circle, Reno, Nev, 89502. Mailing Add: 227 Hill St, Reno, Nev. 89501.

GULLICKSON, DALE DEAN D
b. Bryant, S.Dak, 12/24/33; s. Leo B. Gullickson and Edla Johnson G; m. 3/5/55 to Beverly J. McLain; c. Douglas Dean, Randy Gene, Scott Bradley and Bonnie Lou. Educ: S.Dak. State Univ, Brookings, attending. Polit. & Govt. Pos: S.Dak. State Rep, 65-67. Mil. Serv: Entered as Pvt, Army, 56, released as Pfc, 58, after serv. in 14th Army Res. Mem: Farmers Union; Nat. Farmers Orgn. Rel: Lutheran. Mailing Add: Lake Preston, S.Dak. 57249.

GUMERINGER, BERT D
b. N.Dak, 5/13/25; s. Joe Gumeringer and Margret Klien G; m. 10/10/49 to Agnes Zacher; c. Donald, Bert, Jr, Bettyl Lynn, Wesley Jay, Julie Ann and Kristi Kay. Educ: Esmond High Sch, N.Dak, 40-43. Polit. & Govt. Pos: Treas, Strasburg Sch. Dist, N.Dak, 48-58; clerk, Alexanter Twp, 50-; chmn, Pierce Co. Dem. Non-Partisan League, 57-68; mem, exec. cmt, N.Dak. Dem. Party, 63-68; chmn, 12th Dist. Dem. Non-Partisan League, 68; secy, Esmond Rural Fire Dept, 69; dir, N.Cent. Med. Planning Cmt, Minot, 69. Bus. & Prof. Pos: Secy-treas, Farmers Union Oil, Harvey, N.Dak, 60-69; dir, Area Planning Cmt, Rugby, 68- Mem: Eagles; Buffalo Lake Sportsmen's Club (secy, 53-60); chmn, Pierce Co. Farmers Union, 68-69; dir, N.Dak. Farmers Union, 69-; N.Dak. Wildlife Fedn. Rel: Catholic. Mailing Add: Esmond, N.Dak. 58332.

GUNDERSEN, GUNNAR ADOLF D
b. La Crosse, Wis, 6/12/24; s. Gunnar Gundersen and Mary C. Baldwin G; m. 3/29/52 to Elizabeth D. Hanmer; c. Gunnar, Lincoln, Ralph, Sven and Per. Educ: Yale Univ, 42-43; Univ. N.H, 44; Harvard Med. Sch, M.D, 48; Boylston Soc. Polit. & Govt. Pos: Mem, State Bd. Med. Examiners, Wis, 59-63; Dem. cand, U.S. Rep, Wis, 68; mem, Bd. Educ, La Crosse, 68- Mil. Serv: Entered as Pvt, Army, 43, released as Pfc, 46, after serv. in ASTP; Capt, Air Force (MC), 51-53. Publ: 'Nocardiosis,' Radiology, 56. Mem: Campaign chmn, Commun. Chest, 62; C. of C.(bd. of dirs, La Crosse Chap, 62-65); Am. Col. of Radiology; Radiological Soc. of N.Am; La Crosse Co. Med. Soc.(secy, 67-68); Wis. State Med. Soc; Am. Med. Asn; Soc. of Nuclear Med. Distinguished Serv. Award, Commun. Chest, 62. Rel: Unitarian-Universalist. Legal Res: 121 S. 13, La Crosse, Wis. 54601. Mailing Add: 1836 S. Ave, La Crosse, Wis. 54601.

GUNDERSON, ALBERT B. R
S.Dak. State Rep.
b. Lesterville, S.Dak, 5/15/04; m. to Carie Helsa; c. five daughters. Educ: Augustana Col, 1 year. Polit. & Govt. Pos: Fed. Housing Admin. committeeman, 3 years, clerk, local sch. bd, 5 years; S.Dak. State Rep, 60- Bus. & Prof. Pos: Farmer. Mem: Yankton Co. Livestock Feeders (dir); Yankton Prod. Credit Asn.(dir). Mailing Add: Lesterville, S.Dak. 57040. (1967)

GUNDERSON, DEANE CHARLES R
b. Rolfe, Iowa, 9/16/18; s. John Christian Gunderson and DeElda Lighter G; m. 7/23/41 to Marion Abbott; c. Clara Jeanne (Mrs. Hoover), Charles Abbott, Helen DeElda, Martha Ann, Margaret Jane and Louise Joan. Educ: Iowa State Univ, B.S. Agr. Eng, 39, B.S. Mech. Eng, 40; Pi Kappa Alpha. Polit. & Govt. Pos: Precinct committeeman, Rolfe Rep. Party, Iowa, 50-; chmn, Pocahontas Co. Rep. Party, 54; alternate del, Rep. Nat. Conv, 68. Mem: Lions; Farm Bur. Rel: Presbyterian. Legal Res: Rural Free Delivery, Rolfe, Iowa 50581.

GUNDERSON, DEXTER H. R
Speaker, S.Dak. House of Rep.
b. Irene, S.Dak, 5/18/23; s. C. Henry Gunderson and Mae Dexter G; m. 6/24/51 to Marian Boekelheide; c. John and Mary. Educ: S.Dak. State Col, 41-42; Univ. S.Dak, 46-48; Delta Tau Delta. Polit. & Govt. Pos: Precinct committeeman, S.Dak, 46-55; mem. exec. cmt, Young Rep, 48-56, v.chmn, 52-53; S.Dak. State Rep, 56-, speaker protem, S.Dak. House of Rep, 67-68, Speaker of House, 69-70. Bus. & Prof. Pos: Implement dealer, Dexter H. Gunderson Inc, 48-; farmer—cattle feeder, 49-; dir, Irene Farmers State Bank, 55-; dir, Am. State, Yankton, S.Dak, 69. Mil. Serv: Entered as A/S, Navy, 43, released as PO 2/C, 45, after serv. in VPB 215, Naval Air Corp, ETO, 44-45. Mem: Midwest Coun. Higher Educ; rules cmt, Nat. Legis. Conf; S.Dak-Minn. Implement Dealers Asn; Am. Legion; VFW; Mason; Elks; Farm Bur; ELRIAD Shrine; Capitol Hill Club; Irene Commercial Club; Irene Vol. Fire Dept. Commun. Serv. Award, S.Dak-Minn. Implement Dealers, 67. Rel: Lutheran. Mailing Add: Irene, S.Dak. 57037.

GUNDERSON, JACK EDWARD D
b. Great Falls, Mont, 5/23/29; s. Ole S. Gunderson and Effie Bergman G; m. 1/20/49 to Corinne Francis Nelson; c. Stephen, Dana, Kari and Alan. Educ: Mont. State Univ. Polit. & Govt. Pos: Nat. del, Mont. Young Dem, 62 & 64; Mont. State Rep, 65-67 & 69; app. to Gov. Adv. Cmt. for Voc-Tech. Educ, currently. Bus. & Prof. Pos: Dir, Power Farmers Elevator Co, 60-65; pres, Farmers Union Coop. Creamery, 65-69. Mem: Elks Lodge 214, Great Falls, Mont; Mont. Farmers Union; Mont. Grain Growers Asn. Rel: Lutheran. Mailing Add: Power, Mont. 59468.

GUNDERSON, MAXINE DELORES DFL
b. Decorah, Iowa, 3/7/25; d. George Elbert Wright and Alette Strand W; m. 5/30/43 to Jerome Odell Gunderson; c. Gary, James, Tony, Jean and Jerry Wayne. Educ: High Sch, 42. Polit. & Govt. Pos: Pres, Dem-Farmer-Labor Fillmore Co. Women's Club, Minn, 61-65; chairwoman, First Cong. Dist, Fillmore Co. Dem-Farmer-Labor Party, Minn, 62-65, publicity dir, 62-68; del, Dem. Nat. Conv, 64. Mem: Dem-Farmer-Labor Women's Club (membership chmn); Fillmore Co. Cancer Soc.(v.pres, 65-66, pres, 66-67); Newburg-Tawney Farmers Union (secy-treas, 67); Am. Lutheran Church Women. Rel: Lutheran; Bethel Bible Study Teacher. Mailing Add: Route 2, Mable, Minn. 55954. (1967)

GUNN, CHARLES WESLEY, JR. D
Va. State Del.
b. Tallahassee, Fla, 7/31/22; m. to Mary Wilson Sheffied. Educ: Fla. State Univ; Wash. and Lee Univ, LL.B. Polit. & Govt. Pos: Va. State Del, 64-; chmn, Rockbridge Co. Dem. Party, Va, 65- Bus. & Prof. Pos: Lawyer. Mil. Serv: Navy. Mem: Am. Legion; Kiwanis; Mason; Lexington-Rockbridge Co. C. of C.(past pres); Rockbridge Co. Buena Vista Bar Asn; Va. State Bar (mem, Coun); Hickory Gun Club. Rel: Methodist. Mailing Add: P.O. Box 1033, Lexington, Va. 24450.

GUNN, GEORGE, JR. R
Mem, Wash. State Rep. Finance Cmt.
b. Tacoma, Wash, 4/10/91; s. George Gunn and Emma Howe G; m. 7/29/17 to Cleata Dyer; c. Cleata (Mrs. McIntoch), Nancy (Mrs. Tobiason), Gloria (Mrs. Hagen) and JoAnne (Mrs. Fennema). Educ: Univ. Wash, 12-13. Polit. & Govt. Pos: Mem, Wash. State and King Co. Rep. Finance Cmts, 30-52 and currently; treas, Wash. State Rep. Cent. Cmt, 52-64; alternate del, Rep. Nat. Conv, 68. Bus. & Prof. Pos: V.pres, White Motor Car Co, 25-30; pres,

Kirsten Pipe Co, 38-49, Pioneer, Inc, 40-44, Webster-Brinkley Co, 45-59 and Tote Eng, Inc, 48-61. Mem: Phi Gamma Delta (nat. pres, 2 years, bd. mem, 8 years); Mason; C. of C; past pres, Gr. Seattle, Inc; Wash. Athletic Club (past pres); Rainier Club; Seattle Golf Club. Rel: Protestant. Legal Res: 1111 University St, Seattle, Wash. 98101. Mailing Add: 3306 White Bldg, Seattle, Wash. 98101.

GUNN, JOHN O. D
b. Pelham, N.C, 12/27/92; s. Richard Griffin Gunn and Nannie Elizabeth Rudd G; m. 6/5/30 to Annie Warner Newman; c. Ann (Mrs. Layton J. Everitt) and J.O, Jr. Polit. & Govt. Pos: Chmn, Caswell City Dem. Exec. Cmt, N.C, 42-45; N.C. State Coun, 54; N.C. State Rep, 64-68. Bus. & Prof. Pos: Automobile dealer; farmer; hosiery mfr. Rel: Methodist. Mailing Add: Box 387, Yanceyville, N.C. 27379.

GUNNELL, FRANKLIN WYATT R
Utah State Rep.
b. Wellsville, Utah, 9/20/15; s. Franklin Lewis Gunnell and Annie Wyatt G; m. 4/28/37 to Florus Larsen; c. Franklin La Noel, Darien, Roxanne and Varsi Lu. Educ: Utah State Univ. Polit. & Govt. Pos: Utah State Rep, 58-, Rep. floor leader, Utah House Rep, 61-67; mem, Legis. Coun, 61-63; mem, State Air Pollution Cmn, 61-68; v.chmn, Utah State Budget-Audit Cmn, 66- Bus. & Prof. Pos: Mgr, Cache Co. Fair, 58-; farm owner and operator; sales mgr. and pub. rel, Cache Valley Dairy; owner drive-in restaurant; with West. Elec. Co, Mt. States Tel. & Tel. Co, Agr. Econ. Dept. and Utah State Univ. Mem: Farm Bur; Kiwanis; CWA-CIO; area chmn, Red Cross and Boy Scout Drives; chmn, Cache Valley Cmt. against Obscene Literature; Cache Valley Dairy Festival Cmt; chmn, Mountaire Park. Rel: Latter-day Saint; Mem, E. Cache Stake High Coun. Mailing Add: 1160 North 17th East, Logan, Utah 84321. (1967)

GUNNING, ROSEMARY RITA Conservative, N.Y.
N.Y. State Assemblyman
b. Brooklyn, N.Y, 2/7/05; d. Joseph James Gunning and Annie Carney G; m. 9/21/46 to Lester Thomas Moffett. Educ: Brooklyn Law Sch, St. Lawrence Univ, LL.B, 3 years; Phi Delta Delta. Polit. & Govt. Pos: Del, Constitutional Conv, N.Y, 67; N.Y. State Assemblyman, 69- Bus. & Prof. Pos: Attorney-at-law, N.Y.C. and Mineola, N.Y, 30-42 and Ridgewood, N.Y, 53-; attorney, N.Y. Ord. Dist, Dept. of Army, 42-53; attorney, Staff-Pres. Pro Tem, N.Y. State Senate, 68. Mem: Fed. and Queens Co. Bar Asns; Queens Co. Women's Bar Asn; Cath. Lawyers Guild; Ridgewood Property Owners and Civic Asn; Assoc. Orgn. of Gr. Ridgewood; Women's Auxiliary of VFW; Ladies Auxiliary Hibernians; Parents and Taxpayers; N.Y. State Coun. of Neighborhood Schs. Outstanding Serv. to Commun, Sgt. Edward Miller Post of VFW and Parent and Taxpayers of Ridgewood-Glendale; Exceptional Polit. Leader, Conservative Party of N.Y. State. Rel: Roman Catholic. Mailing Add: 1867 Grove St, Ridgewood, N.Y. 11237.

GUNTER, ROBERT SHARP D
b. Alton, Ill, 12/20/39; s. Russell Amos Gunter and Mildred Hubbel G; m. 8/17/61 to Bonnie Carolyn Bradshaw; c. Michelle Jenee and Robert Sharp, Jr. Educ: Southeast Mo. State Col, ½ year. Polit. & Govt. Pos: Councilman, Kennett, Mo, 68; del, Mo. Dem. Conv, 68; admin. asst, U.S. Rep. Bill D. Burlison, 69- Bus. & Prof. Pos: Ed, Gideon News, Gideon, Mo, 65-66; advert. dir, Daily Dunklin Dem, Kennett, Mo, 66-68. Mil. Serv: Entered as Pvt, Marine Corps, 58, released as Cpl, 61, after serv. in 1st Marine Div; Good Conduct Award. Mem: Mo. Press Asn; Jr. C. of C; Kiwanis Int; Gideon Jaycees (past pres); Am. Red Cross (past chmn, Dunklin Co. Chap). Rel: South. Baptist. Legal Res: 418 E. John St, Campbell, Mo. 63933. Mailing Add: 4421 Medford Dr, Annandale, Va. 22003.

GUNTER, WILLIAM B. D
b. Commerce, Ga, 4/20/19; s. Wm. Barrett Gunter and Helen Carson G; m. 6/7/46 to Elizabeth Parker; c. Marjorie Gay, Barrett and John H. Educ: Univ. Ga, A.B, and Law Sch, LL.B. Polit. & Govt. Pos: City Attorney, Gainesville, Ga, 59-; mem, Ga. State Dem. Exec. Cmt, 65 and 66; del, Dem. Nat. Conv, 64; Ga. State rep, 52-58. Bus. & Prof. Pos: Partner, Kenyon & Gunter, Attorneys, 46- Mil. Serv: Entered as 2nd Lt, Army, 42, released as 1st Lt, after serv. in 3rd Inf. Div, ETO; Silver Star; Purple Heart and 7 Campaign Stars, ETO. Mem: Am. Bar Asn; State Bar of Ga. Rel: Presbyterian. Mailing Add: 710 Hillside Dr, Gainesville, Ga. 30501. (1967)

GUNTER, WILLIAM D, JR. 'BILL' D
Fla. State Sen.
b. Jacksonville, Fla, 7/16/34; s. William D. Gunter, Sr. and Ruth Senterfitt G; m. 8/19/56 to Leslie Letitia Peaden, wid; c. Bartlett David and Joel Stephen. Educ: Univ. of Fla, B.S.A. with high honors, 56; Univ. of Ga, 57-58; Fla. Blue Key; Univ. Hall of Fame; Alpha Zeta; Alpha Tau Alpha; Gamma Sigma Delta; Phi Kappa Phi; Sigma Alpha Epsilon. Polit. & Govt. Pos: Mem, Orlando Rehabilitation and Develop. Adv. Cmt, 66; Fla. State Sen, 18th Dist, 66- Bus. & Prof. Pos: Teacher, Orange Co. Sch. Bd, 58-59; ins. agent, State Farm Ins. Co, 59-61, agency mgr, 61- Mil. Serv: Entered as Pvt, Army, 56, released as Specialist, 58; Outstanding Hon. Grad. of Basic Army Admin. Course. Mem: Cent. Fla. Asn. of Life Underwriters; Gen. Agents and Mgrs. Asn; past pres, Orlando Jr. C. of C; former dir, Kiwanis; former v.pres, Univ. Fla. Alumni Asn; past pres, Young Dem. of Orange Co; dir, Cent. Fla. Fair; Univ. Club of Orlando; Orlando Jaycee-Colonels Orgn. Rel: Baptist. Legal Res: 3206 Inverness Court, Orlando, Fla. 32806. Mailing Add: P.O. Box 14001, Orlando, Fla. 32807.

GUNTHER, GEORGE LACKMAN R
Conn. State Sen.
b. Bridgeport, Conn, 11/22/19; s. George Gunther and Gwendolyn Clift G; m. 6/5/41 to Priscilla Agnes Staples; c. Priscilla Karen, Karla Gwen and Lance Inder. Educ: Nat. Col. of Drugless Physicians, Chicago, Ill, N.D, 42; hon. mem, Theta Sigma. Polit. & Govt. Pos: Secy, Conn. Bd. of Natureopathic Exams, 46-49; mem, Bd. of Educ, Stratford, Conn, 57-61; Third Dist. councilman, Town Coun, Stratford, 59-65; chmn, Stratford Conserv. Cmn, 61-66 and Conn. Asn. Conserv. Cmns, 63-65; Conn. State Sen, 21st Dist, 67- Mem: Nat. Col. of Drugless Physicians Alumni; Sigma Phi Kappa Alumni; Univ. Bridgeport Bd. of Assocs; Lions (past secy, 1st, 2nd and 3rd v.pres, pres. and zone chmn, Stratford Club); AF&AM; hon. mem, Stratford Antique Gun Collectors Asn.(past pres); DeMolay (sr. mem, Int. Supreme Coun); New Eng. Family Campers Asn; hon. mem, Bridgeport Boat Owners Asn. Outstanding Serv. Award, Seymour Fish & Game Club for work in pollution abatement, 66; Conn. Water Conserv. Award, presented by Conn. State League of Sportsmen's and Conserv. Clubs in coop. with Nat. Wildlife Fedn. and Sears-Roebuck Found, 66; Nat. Water Conserv. Award, Nat. Wildlife Fedn. and Sears-Roebuck Found, 66; Conserv. Award. for outstanding work in water pollution abatement, Am. Motors Co, 67; Citation for Meritorius Serv. to Humanity & Chiropractic, Am. Chiropractic Asn. Rel: Methodist. Mailing Add: 890 Judson Place, Stratford, Conn. 06497

GURLEY, WILLIAM ARTHUR, JR. D
b. Belton, S.C, 10/9/15; s. William Arthur Gurley and Betty Campbell G; m. 3/16/46 to Carene Finch; c. William Arthur, III, Carole (Mrs. Sawyers) and Anna Belle. Educ: Self-educated. Polit. & Govt. Pos: Spec. asst. for info. and legis, U.S. Rep. W.C. Daniel, Va, currently. Mil. Serv: Entered as Photographer, U.S. Navy, 41, released as Photographer's Mate 1/C, 45. Rel: Baptist. Legal Res: 106 Woodland Ave, Galax, Va. 24333. Mailing Add: 1730 Longworth Bldg, Washington, D.C. 20515.

GURNEY, CHAN (JOHN CHANDLER) R
b. Yankton, S.Dak, 5/21/96; s. Deloss Butler and Henrietta Belle Klopping G; m. 7/4/17 to Evelyn Bordeno; c. Ida Elaine (Mrs. Morgan T. Smith), John Bordeno, Deloss Braddock. Educ: Pub. schs, Yankton, S.Dak. Polit. & Govt. Pos: U.S. Sen, S.Dak, 39-51; mem, Civil Aeronaut. Bd, 51-65, chmn, 54, v.chmn, 57-61. Bus. & Prof. Pos: Built and operated Radio Sta. WNAX, 27-32; secy-treas, Gurney Seed & Nursery Co, 32; pres, Chan Gurney Oil Co, Sioux Falls, 32-36. Mil. Serv: Army Engrs, Sgt, World War I, serv. in 34th Div, overseas. Mem: Am. Legion; VFW; Mason; Goethals Mem. Cmn, 47. Mailing Add: 802 W. Third St, Yankton, S.Dak. 57078.

GURNEY, EDWARD JOHN R
U.S. Sen, Fla.
b. Portland, Maine, 1/12/14; s. Edward John Gurney and Nellie Kennedy G; m. 8/1/41 to Eleanor Natalie Ahlborn; c. Sarah and Jill (Mrs. Lewis Tappen Holt). Educ: Colby, B.S, 35; Harvard Univ, LL.B, 38; Duke Univ, LL.M, 48; Alpha Tau Omega. Polit. & Govt. Pos: Cmnr, Winter Park, Fla, 52-58, Mayor, 61-62; U.S. Rep, Fla, 63-68; U.S. Sen, 68- Bus. & Prof. Pos: Lawyer, Barry, Wainwright, Thacher & Symmers, N.Y.C, 38-41 and Gurney, Skolfield & Frey, Winter Park, Fla, currently. Mil. Serv: Entered as Pvt, Army, Nat. Guard, 41, released as Lt. Col, 46, after serv. in Eighth Armored Div, ETO, 44-45; Silver Star; Purple Heart. Rel: Congregational. Legal Res: 800 Greentree Dr, Winter Park, Fla. 33880. Mailing Add: Senate Office Bldg, Washington, D.C. 20510.

GURNEY, HARRY C, JR. 'BUD' R
Wyo. State Rep.
b. Brooklyn, N.Y, 10/20/30; s. Harry C. Gurney, Sr. and Elizabeth Niver G; m. 3/27/53 to Virginia Dornan; c. Bruce L, Jonathan P. and Steven C. Educ: Grinnell Col, 49-51; George Wash. Univ, 54; Univ. Wyo, B.S, 58; Colo. State Univ, D.V.M, 64. Polit. & Govt. Pos: Chmn, Wyo. Young Rep, currently; Wyo. State Rep, 69- Bus. & Prof. Pos: Researcher, Georgetown Univ, 56-57; researcher, Battelle Mem. Inst, 58-60; owner and operator, Tristate Vet. Hosp, Clin. and Pine Bluffs Clin, currently. Mil. Serv: Entered as Pvt, Army, 54, released as SP-4, 56, after serv. in Medics, Ft. Belvoir, 55-56; Nat. Defense Medal. Mem: Wyo. and Am. Vet. Med. Asns; Am. Equine Practitioners Asn; Am. Asn. Vet. Allergists & Immunologists; Young Rep; Young Am. for Freedom; Found. for Econ. Educ; Nat. Asn. Independent Businessmen; Mason (32°); Rotary Int;(speakers cmt, Cheyenne, 68-); Wyo. Stockgrowers Asn. Rel: Episcopal; Vestryman. Mailing Add: 101 Meriden Route, Cheyenne, Wyo. 82001.

GUSTAFSON, CARL H. R
Colo. State Rep.
b. Eaton, Colo, 2/26/29; married; c. Four. Polit. & Govt. Pos: Colo. State Rep, 67- Bus. & Prof. Pos: Regent of Dana Col, Blair, Nebr; partner, mgr, Quinn and Co, investment securities firm. Mailing Add: 974 S. Franklin, Denver, Colo. 80209. (1967)

GUSTAFSON, EARL B. DFL
Minn. State Rep.
b. Duluth, Minn, 1927; m; c. Kim, Ben, Mary, Joseph, Brad, Peter and Sarah. Educ: Gustavus Adolphus Col; Univ. Minn. Law Sch; Univ. Col, grad. study. Polit. & Govt. Pos: Spec. munic. judge, Duluth, Minn, 61-62; Minn. State Rep, 62-, Asst. Minority Leader, Minn. House of Rep, 69- Bus. & Prof. Pos: Lawyer. Mil. Serv: Navy. Mailing Add: 1818 E. Third St, Duluth, Minn. 55812.

GUSTAFSON, JOEL KARL R
Fla. State Rep.
b. New Haven, Conn, 5/24/37; s. J. Arthur Gustafson and Jane Thompson G; m. 9/2/61 to Judyth Field; c. Kimberly Ann, Stacey Lynn and Scott Evan. Educ: Lafayette Col, B.A, 60; Tulane Univ. Law Sch, LL.B, 63; Kappa Sigma; Maroon Key. Polit. & Govt. Pos: Prosecutor, City of Ft. Lauderdale, Fla, 64-67, assoc. munic. judge, 67 & 68; Fla. State Rep, 67- Bus. & Prof. Pos: Attorney, Ward, Gustafson, Caldwell & Shailer, Law Off, Ft. Lauderdale, currently. Mem: Conn, Fla, Am. and Broward Co. Bar Asns; Fraternal Order of Police Asn; Ft. Lauderdale Jr. C. of C; Young Rep. Club, Rep. Citizen Cmt. Voted One of Five Most Outstanding Young Men in Ft. Lauderdale by Jr. C. of C, 67. Rel: Presbyterian. Legal Res: 1636 S.E. 12th Court, Ft. Lauderdale, Fla. 33316. Mailing Add: 2455 E. Sunrise Blvd, Apt. 307, Ft. Lauderdale, Fla. 33304.

GUSTAFSON, WALLACE F. Nonpartisan
Minn. State Rep.
b. Bird Island, Minn, 1925; married; c. 2 daughters. Educ: Univ. Minn, B.S.L, LL.B, B.B.A. Polit. & Govt. Pos: Minn. State Rep, 62- Bus. & Prof. Pos: Lawyer. Mil. Serv: Navy. Mailing Add: 900 Meadow Lane, Willmar, Minn. 56201.

GUSTE, WILLIAM JOSEPH D
La. State Sen.
b. New Orleans, La, 5/26/22; s. William Joseph Guste, Sr. and Marie Louise Alciatore G; m. 4/7/47 to Dorothy Elizabeth Schutten; c. William Joseph, III, Bernard Randolph, Marie Louise, Melanie Ann, Valerie Eve, Althea Maria,

Elizabeth Therese, James Patrick and Anne Duchesne. Educ: Loyola Univ, B.A, 42, LL.B, 43; Blue Key; pres, Sigma Alpha Kappa. Polit. & Govt. Pos: Del, Dem. Nat. Conv, 68; La. State Sen, 68- Bus. & Prof. Pos: Practicing attorney-at-law, 46- Mil. Serv: T/Sgt, Army Inf, serv. in ETO, 46. Mem: Am. and La. Bar Asns; Nat. Housing Coun; K. of C. Rel: Catholic. Legal Res: 4 Richmond Place, New Orleans, La. 70115. Mailing Add: 1624 National Bank of Commerce Bldg, New Orleans, La. 70112.

GUTHRIDGE, ESTHER BLANCH R
Pres, Ind. Fedn. of Rep. Women
b. Klemme, Iowa; d. James William Scott and Annette Klaus S; m. to Emmett O. Guthridge; c. Garry A. and David E. Educ: Ind. Bus. Col. Polit. & Govt. Pos: Precinct committeewoman, Rep. Party, Benton Co, Ind, 34-42; v.chmn, Benton Co. Rep. Party, 36-62; dist. dir, Second Dist, Ind. Fed. Rep. Women, del, conv, 52-, pres, 61-; alternate del, Rep. Nat. Conv, 56, del, 60, 64 & 68; secy, Second Dist. Rep. Cent. Cmt, 56-60, v.chmn, 60-; v.chmn, Ind. Rep. Cent. Cmt, 61- Bus. & Prof. Pos: Clerk circuit court, Benton Co, Ind, 63-67. Mem: Gov. Cmt. on Status of Women; Rep. State V.Chmn. Asn.(chmn, Midwest Regional Adv. Cmt); Eastern Star; Delta Sigma Kappa; Rebekah; Fowler Women's Club. Rel: Protestant. Legal Res: 105 N. Grant, Fowler, Ind. 47944. Mailing Add: 111 N. Capitol, Indianapolis, Ind. 46204.

GUTIERREZ, ROSENDO D
Mem, Ariz. Dem. State Exec. Cmt.
b. El Paso, Tex, 8/31/32; s. Rosendo C. Gutierrez and Caridad Muñoz G; m. 8/31/53 to Wanda Lynn; c. Rosendo Carlos and Armando. Educ: Tex. West. Col, B.S. in Civil Eng, 53. Polit. & Govt. Pos: Chmn, LEAP Cmn, Phoenix, Ariz, 65-68; Dem. nominee, State Senate, Dist. 8-I, 66; Dem. precinct committeeman, Madison Precinct 2, 66-; mem, Ariz. Dem. State Exec. Cmt, 66-; mem. exec. cmt, Phoenix Charter Govt. Cmt, 67 and Phoenix Forward Cmt, 69-; Dem. chmn, legis. dist, 8-I, 67-; mem, Maricopa Co. Dem. Exec. Cmt, 67-; initial chmn. and then exec. dir, City No Ward Campaign, Phoenix, 67; del, Dem. Nat. Conv, 68. Bus. & Prof. Pos: Proj. engr, L.H. Bell & Assoc, Phoenix, Ariz, 61-63 and Ken R. White Co, 63-66; eng. prin, PACE Consult, 66- Mil. Serv: Entered as A/S, Navy, 53, released as Lt.(j.g), 57, after serv. in Civil Eng. Corps, Japan and Miss; Lt. Comdr, Naval Res; Nat. Defense Medal; Korean Theatre Medal; UN Serv. Medal; Expert Pistol. Mem: Naval Res. Asn; Nat. and Ariz. Soc. Prfnl. Engrs; Am. Soc. Civil Engrs; Soc. Am. Mil. Engrs; Urban League (bd. dirs, Phoenix Chap); SER (bd. dirs, Phoenix Chap); NAACP (bd. dirs, phoenix Chap); VESTA Club; El Don Key Club. Rel: Methodist. Mailing Add: 4406 N. 18th Place, Phoenix, Ariz. 85016.

GUTMAN, PHILLIP EDWARD R
Ind. State Sen.
b. Ft. Wayne, Ind, 1/5/30; s. Froncie Gutman and Beulah M. Holman G; m. 9/3/55 to Mabel Carolyn Prickett; c. Phillip E, Jr, Gretchen K. and Kurt A. Educ: Ind. Univ, B.S. in Bus. Admin, 52, Law Sch, J.D, 57; Phi Delta Phi; Delta Upsilon. Polit. & Govt. Pos: Asst. to co. chmn, Rep. Party, Ind, 57-62; asst. to state chmn, Ind. Rep. Party, 62-64; precinct committeeman, Ft. Wayne, Ind, 64-68; ward chmn, 46-67; Ind. State Sen, 68- Mil. Serv: Air Force, 52-54, 1st Lt, serv. as, asst. finance officer, Park Air Force Base, Calif. and Ladd Air Force Base, Alaska. Mem: Allen Co. and Am. Bar Asns; Ind. State Bar Asn.(trial lawyers sect, probate trust and real property sect); Rotary; Am. Legion; Mason; Scottish Rite; York Rite; YMCA; C. of C. Rel: Methodist. Legal Res: 2840 Club Terrace, Ft. Wayne, Ind. 46804. Mailing Add: Mezzanine Floor, Indiana Bank Bldg, Ft. Wayne, Ind. 46802.

GUTOWSKI, STANLEY L. R
V.Chmn, Livingston Co. Rep. Cmt, N.Y.
b. Plymouth, Pa, 3/27/31; s. Stanley Gutowski and Catherine Stadts G; m. 5/23/53 to Edythe Mae Hank; c. Debra Ann, Darlene Marie and Doreen Sue. Educ: Plymouth High Sch, Pa, grad. Polit. & Govt. Pos: Pres, Livingston Co. Young Rep. Club, N.Y, 65-66, gov, 66-67, co-gov, 68; v.chmn, Livingston Co. Rep. Cmt, 66- Bus. & Prof. Pos: Plant mgr, Dynamic Components Corp, 63-68, v.pres, 68- Mil. Serv: Entered as Pvt, Air Force, 51, released as S/Sgt, 55, after serv. at Sampson Air Force Base. Named Outstanding Rep. of the Year by Livingston Co. Rep. Cmt, N.Y, 67 and Outstanding Gov. of N.Y. State by Young Rep. Club, 68. Rel: Catholic. Mailing Add: 67 North St, Caledonia, N.Y. 14423.

GUTTERSON, MILDRED E. R
b. Fair Haven, Vt. Educ: Univ. of Vt; Univ. of N.H. Polit. & Govt. Pos: Secy, Rep. Party, Keene, N.H; N.H. State Rep, until 68. Bus. & Prof. Pos: Retired pub. sch. teacher; bookkeeper. Mem: Cheshire Rep. Womens Club; League Women Voters; N.H. Educ. Asn; Delta Gamma; Am. Asn. Univ. Women; Eastern Star; Nat. Retired Teachers Asn. Rel: Unitarian. Mailing Add: 32 Washington St, Keene, N.H. 03431. (1967)

GUY, WILLIAM L. D
Gov. N.Dak.
b. Devils Lake, N.Dak, 9/30/19; m. to Jean Mason; c. William, James, Deborah, Nancy and Holly. Educ: N.Dak. State Univ, B.S, 41; Univ. of Minn, M.A, 46. Polit. & Govt. Pos: N.Dak. State Rep, 59-60; Gov, N.Dak, 60-, chmn. Mo. State Cmn. and Midwest Gov. Conf, 61-63; chmn, Nat. Gov. Conf. and Coun. of State Govts, 66; mem, President Johnson's Elec. Observer Team to S.Vietnam, 67; mem, President Johnson's Nat. Health Facilities Adv. Cmt, 68; del, Dem. Nat. Conv, 68. Bus. & Prof. Pos: Farmer; former teacher agr. econ. at N.Dak. State Univ. Mil. Serv: U.S. Navy, World War II. Mem: Past pres, Amenia Sch. Bd; Church trustee; Sunday Sch. teacher; past pres, N.Dak. State Univ. Alumni Asn; past pres, Gate City Toastmasters Club, Fargo. Mailing Add: Amenia, N.Dak. 58004.

GUYANT, GEORGE M. D
b. Milwaukee, Wis, 8/29/45; s. Wakefield M. Guyant and Evelyn Akey G; m. 7/24/65 to Patricia Ann Berto; c. Albert William. Educ: Wis. State Univ, Stevens Point, 68-69. Polit. & Govt. Pos: Chmn. and organizer, Portage Co. Young Dem, Wis, 62-63; del, Seventh Dist. Dem. Conv, 68; del, Wis. Dem. Conv, 68 & 69; alternate del, Nat. Dem. Conv, 68. Mil. Serv: Entered as E-1, Air Force, 63, released as E-4, 67, after serv. in First Combat Support Unit, First Fighter Wing, 64-67; E-4, Inactive Air Force Res, 69-, Nat. Defense and Good Conduct Medals. Rel: Christian. Mailing Add: 2143 Oak St, Stevens Point, Wis. 54481.

GUYER, TENNYSON R
Ohio State Sen.
b. Findlay, Ohio, 11/29/12; s. William Harris Guyer and Myrtle Emma Hartsock G; m. 6/10/44 to Edith Mae Reuter; c. Sharon Mae and Rosetta Kae. Educ: Findlay Col, A.B, 34, Hon. D.Litt, 53; Hon. D.Com.Sci, Tiffin Univ, 53; Alpha Club; Letter F Club. Polit. & Govt. Pos: Councilman, Celina, Ohio, 40-42, mayor, 42-44; mem, Ohio State Rep. Cent. and Exec. Cmts, 54-66; Ohio State Sen, 59- Publ: The Church—Institution or Destitution, Post Publishing Co, 40; Speech Record—'The Miracle Called America,' Queen City Record Co, 63. Mem: Life mem. Int. Platform Asn, pres, 56-58; hon. mem. Exchange Club; Ohio Press Club; zone chmn, Int. Lions Clubs, 38-39; Mason; York and Scottish Rites; Shrine; Eastern Star; Elks; K. of P; Rotary Int; YMCA; Teen-Center Bd; Winebrenner Theological Seminary Bd; Findlay Col. Bd. Govs; Speakers Assocs. Best Inspirational Speaker; Million Miler, United Air Lines; Amvets Commun. Serv. Award; Golden Deeds Award; Nat. Exchange Clubs; hon. chief Sa-Gee-Ya, Cherokee Indians; Ky. Col; Outstanding Alumnus Findlay Col, 66. Rel: Church of God. Mailing Add: 1196 East Sandusky St, Findlay, Ohio 45840.

GUYOT, LAWRENCE T, JR. D
b. Pass Christian, Miss, 7/17/39; s. Lawrence Guyot, Sr. and Margaret Piernas. Educ: Tougaloo Col, B.S, 61; Omega Psi Phi. Polit. & Govt. Pos: Recruiter, Student Nonviolent Coord. Cmt, Miss, 61-66; Fifth Cong. dir, Coun. of Fed. Orgn, 64-67; founder, Miss. Freedom Dem. Party, 64, chmn, 64-68, lobbyist, 69-; del, Dem. Nat. Conv, 68. Publ: 'Politics of Survival,' Freedomways, 66. Mem: Pres, NAACP Tougaloo Col. Chap, 58-59; mem. cmn, Delta Ministry of Nat. Coun. of Churches, 68-; Nat. Prfnl. Adv. Cmt, Mary Holmes Col, 68-; Int. Elks. Rel: Catholic. Mailing Add: 343 Davis Ave, Pass Christian, Miss. 39571.

GUZMAN, RALPH D
b. Moroleon, Guanajuato, Mexico, 10/24/24; s. Casildo Guzman-Yepez and Virginia Cortéz; m. 10/22/52 to Margaret Stella Tafoya; c. Christine. Educ: Calif. State Col, Los Angeles, B.A, 58, M.A, 60; Univ. Calif, Los Angeles, 60-62; Pi Sigma Alpha. Polit. & Govt. Pos: Assoc. dir, U.S. Peace Corps, Venezuela, 62-63, Peru, 63-65; adv, U.S. Off. Educ, 66-; consult, U.S. Info. Agency, 67-68; Cmnr. Compensatory Educ, State Calif, 67-68; consult, U.S. Dept. Labor, 68; consult, U.S. Dept. Commerce, 68; del, Dem. Nat. Conv, 68; co-chmn, Calif. Viva Kennedy, 68. Bus. & Prof. Pos: Asst. Prof. polit. sci, Calif. State Col, Los Angeles, 67-69; acting assoc. prof. govt, Univ. Calif, Santa Cruz, 69- Mil. Serv: Entered as Seaman, Navy, 44, released as Seaman 1/C, 46, after serv. in U.S.S. Breton, Pac, 44-46. Publ: The Mexican-American People, Free Press, 69; Ethnic Tenacity, Cummings, 69; 'The Mexican American Community,' In: California Politics and Policies, Addison-Wesley, 65. Rel: Roman Catholic. Mailing Add: 209 Calvin Place, Santa Cruz, Calif. 95060.

GUZZI, RALPH JOSEPH D
b. Bridgeport, Conn, 4/5/32; s. Salvatore Guzzi and Margaret Tempini G; m. 12/1/56 to Lorraine Bouchard; c. Sharon Marie, Charlene Ann and Allison Marie. Educ: Univ. Conn. Exten. Sch, 56-57; Univ. Purdue, 64. Polit. & Govt. Pos: Mem, Stratford Dem. Town Cmt, 57-; Justice of the Peace, Stratford, Conn, 57-58, chmn. zoning bd. of appeals, 60-63; mem, Gr. Bridgeport Regional Planning Agency, Bridgeport and Stratford, Conn, 64; Dem. Cand. State Legis, 66; mem, Redevelop. Agency, 67; del, Dem. Nat. Conv, 68. Bus. & Prof. Pos: Owner, The Ralph J. Guzzi Agency, Life Gen. Agent, part owner, West Haven Manor Convalescent Hosp, partner, The Ralton Agency Real Estate and partner, Jar Assocs. Develop. Co, currently. Mil. Serv: Entered as Airman, Air Force, 51, released as Airman 1/C, 55, after serv. on Patrol Squadron Duty, Iceland, 53-55; Good Conduct Medal; Spec. Unit Citation. Publ: Several articles in, The Ins. Salesman, 60-66. Mem: Bridgeport Life Underwriters; tailtwister, East Bridgeport Lions Club; dir, East Bridgeport Trade and Civic Asn. Qualifier Million Dollar Round Table, Nat. Asn. Life Underwriters, 5 times; Boss of the Year, Bridgeport Jr. C. of C, 68. Rel: Roman Catholic. Mailing Add: 100 Canary Place, Stratford, Conn. 06497.

GWATHMEY, ROBERT RYLAND, III D
Va. State Del.
b. Richmond, Va, 12/21/17; m. to Anne Spottswood Merritt. Educ: Randolph Macon, B.A; Univ. Va. Law Sch, LL.B. Polit. & Govt. Pos: Commonwealth attorney, Hanover Co, Va, 48-56; pres, Jamestown Festival Cmt, 56-58; past asst. co. judge, Hanover Co; Va. State Del, 58- Bus. & Prof. Pos: Lawyer. Mil. Serv: Navy. Mem: Ruritans; Hanover Farm Bur; Country Club, Va; Downtown Club Richmond; Va. State and Richmond Bar Asns. Rel: Episcopal. Legal Res: Hanover, Va. 23069. Mailing Add: Mutual Bldg, Richmond, Va. 23219.

GWIN, JOHN P. R
Mem, Representative Cmt, Ill. Rep. Cent. Cmt.
b. Springfield, Ill, 11/28/32; s. Edgar N. Gwin and Elizabeth A. Hiett G; m. 9/1/61 to Joene L. Guyer; c. Susan, Bobby and Beth. Educ: Univ. Ill, degree in finance, 55; Delta Tau Delta. Polit. & Govt. Pos: Rep. precinct committeeman, Ill, 60-64; mem, Representative Cmt, Ill. Rep. Cent. Cmt, 68-; legis. chmn, Nat. Cable TV Asn, Wash, 69- Bus. & Prof. Pos: Licensed real estate broker, Ill, 55-; partner, Gwin TV & Appliance Co, Robinson, Ill, 59-65; partner, Flat Rock Coin Laundry, 62-; pres. and dir, Robinson TV Cable Co, 64-; v.pres. and dir, Rustic Land Develop. Corp, 64-; pres, Ill-Ind. Cable TV Asn, 67 & 68; dir, Pro-Del Corp, 67-; dir, Crawford Co. Opportunities, Inc, 68-69; dir, Nat. Cable TV Asn, Wash, 68-; midwest regional mgr, Cox Cable Commun, Inc, Atlanta, 69- Mil. Serv: Entered as 2nd Lt, Air Force, 56, released as 1st Lt, 59, after serv. in Strategic Air Command as Instr. Navigator, Inflight Refueling Crew; Capt, Air Force Res; commendations for performance, 818th Air Div, Strategic Air Command. Publ: 'Strengthening State Associations,' TV Commun. Mag, 8/67; plus others. Mem: Springfield Bd. Realtors; Ill. Bd. Realtors; United Brotherhood of Carpenters & Joiners; treas. and trustee, Crawford Co. Country Club; Moose; Elks; C. of C.(pres. and dir, 68); various civic clubs. Various appreciation awards; profiled as a leader of cable TV indust. in CATV Mag, 68; cover photo and subject for Cable News mag, 8/22/69. Rel: Methodist. Legal Res: R.F.D. 1, Robinson, Ill. 62454. Mailing Add: 215 S. Cross St, Robinson, Ill. 62454.

GWYN, ALLEN HATCHETT, JR. D
Chmn, Rockingham Co. Dem. Exec. Cmt, N.C.
b. Yanceyville, N.C, 12/5/22; s. Allen Hatchett Gwyn and Janie Johnston G; m. 9/9/50 to Evelyn Worsham; c. Jane Carol and Mary Leslie. Educ: Duke Univ, A.B, 47, LL.B, 50; Sigma Alpha Epsilon; Phi Delta Phi. Polit. & Govt. Pos: Pres, Rockingham Co. Young Democrats, N.C, 55-56; mem, Gov. Cmn. Educ. TV, 62-64; mem, N.C. Bd.Higher Educ, 63-64 and educ. facilities, 64; presidential elector, 64; chmn, Rockingham Co. Dem. Exec. Cmt, 66-; del, Dem. Nat. Conv, 68. Bus. & Prof. Pos: Attorney, Gwyn, Gwyn, & Morgan, Reidsville, N.C. Mil. Serv: Entered as Ens, Naval Res, 43, released as Lt. (jg), 46, after serving in Atlantic and Pac. Theaters, 44-46; Lt. (jg), Naval Res, 46- Mem: Rockingham Co. and Am. Bar Asn; N.C. Bar Asn. (bd. gov, 63-66); N.C. State Bar; Nat. Asn. Defense Counsel in Criminal Cases; Am. Trial Lawyers Asn; Am Judicature Soc; Kiwanis; pres, Reidsville Jaycees, 53-54. Rel: Methodist. Legal Res: 108 S. Main St, Reidsville, N.C. 27320. Mailing Add: 509 Pennrington Circle, Reidsville, N.C. 27320.

GWYN, RUSH CROCKETT, JR. D
b. Chatham Hill, Va, 7/28/03; s. Rush Crockett Gwyn and Ida Walton G; m. to Louise Lambert. Educ: Univ. Va, B.S, 26, LL.B, 28. Polit. & Govt. Pos: Va. State Del, 60-68. Bus. & Prof. Pos: Lawyer; farmer; banker; v.pres, Bank, Marion, Va. Mem: Phi Delta Phi Omicron Delta Kappa; State and Am. Bar Asns; Masons; Shrine; Elks; Rel: Methodist. Legal Res: Lee Highway E, Marion, Va. 24354. Mailing Add: Box 26, Marion, Va. 24354.

GWYNNE, JOHN WILLIAMS R
b. Victor, Iowa, 10/20/89; s. Thomas Williams Gwynne and Katherine McGilway G; wid; c. Mary (Mrs. Carroll) and John Williams, Jr. Educ: State Univ. Iowa, B.A, 12 and LL.B, 14; Order of the Coif. Polit. & Govt. Pos: Judge, Munic. Court, Waterloo, Iowa, 20-26; co. attorney, Black Hawk Co, 29-34; U.S. Rep, Iowa, 35-59; mem, Fed. Trade Cmn, 53-59, chmn, 55-59. Bus. & Prof. Pos: Mem, Law Firm of Mears, Lovejoy, Jensen & Gwynne, 26-35. Mil. Serv: Entered as Trainee, 17, released as 2nd Lt, after serv. in 313th Trench Mortar Battery. Mem: Am. Legion; Elks. Rel: Epsicopal. Mailing Add: 255 Prospect Blvd, Waterloo, Iowa 50701.

H

HAAG, GEORGE A. R
b. San Antonio, Tex, 8/18/39; s. G. A. Haag and Dora Fehlis H; m. 6/23/63 to Geneva Ann Tresenriter; c. Amber Dawn. Educ: Tex. A & I Univ, B.A, magna cum laude, 61; Univ. of Mo-Columbia, Mo, M.A. & M.P.A, magna cum laude, 64; Alpha Chi; Phi Alpha Theta; Pres. & V.Pres. of Student body; South. Conf. Debate Champions; All State Baseball. Polit. & Govt. Pos: Guest speaker, Rep. Nat. Cmt. Campaign Mgt. Seminar; Admin. Asst, U.S. Rep. Jim Collins, Tex. 68- Bus. & Prof. Pos: V.Pres, First South. Inc, Dallas, Tex, 66-68. Mil. Serv: Entered as 2nd Lt, Air Force, 62, released as Capt. 66, after serv. as a Flight Training Officer, Squadron Comdr. and General's Aide in ADC & ATC, 62-66; Capt, Res, 66-; Air Force Commendation Medal; Outstanding Unit Award; Viet Nam Serv. Medal; Marksmanship Award; Selected as Outstanding Junior Officer for Air Defense Command, 64. Publ: "Joint Chiefs of Staff-Three Problems," Air Force J, 64. Mem: Dallas Junior C. of C. (Bd. of Dirs); Dallas Summer Job Fair Cmt. (Div. Comdr); Jaycee Chmn, 1967 Dallas Mile of Dimes. Outstanding Jaycee in Dallas, 67. Rel: Episcopal. Legal Res: 1114 Commerce St, Suite 1112, Dallas, Tex. 75202. Mailing Add: 12 Infield Court S, Rockville, Md. 20854.

HAAKENSON, ROBERT MELVIN D
Idaho State Rep.
b. Fargo, N.Dak, 5/16/35; s. Carl Melvin Haakenson and Elsie Mary Campbell H; m. 8/19/61 to Patricia Ann Pool; c. Eric Karl and Kristina Helene. Educ: N.Idaho Jr. Col, A.A, 58; Univ. Idaho, 58-59; Mont. State Col, B.S. in Indust. Arts Tech, 62; Phi Theta Kappa. Polit. & Govt. Pos: Idaho State Rep, Second Legis. Dist, 67- Mil. Serv: Entered as Pfc, Idaho Nat. Guard, released as S.P. 3, after serv. in Battery A, 148th Field Artil. Mem: Nat, Idaho and Coeur d'Alene Educ. Asns; Past Worshipful Master Kootenai Lodge 24, AF&AM, Idaho. Rel: Presbyterian. Mailing Add: 1102 N. 12th, Coeur d'Alene, Idaho 83814.

HAAS, AL H. D
Chmn, LaPlata Co. Dem. Party, Colo.
b. Hays, Kans, 6/4/24; s. Jacob Haas and Pauline Dechant H; m. 7/4/46 to Mary Lou Munson; c. Sue Anne, Michael Roy, Charles Jacob, Catherine Louise and Carol Elizabeth. Educ: Univ. Denver, B.A, 49; Denver Univ. Law Sch, LL.B, 51; Phi Alpha Delta; Sigma Tau Gamma. Polit. & Govt. Pos: Dist. attorney, Durango, Colo, 61-68; chmn, LaPlata Co. Dem. Party, Colo, 69- Bus. & Prof. Pos: Lawyer, Haas & Watts, 51- Mil. Serv: Entered as 2nd Lt, Army, 42, released as Capt, 46, after serv. in First Infantry Div, ETO, 42-43; Purple Heart with cluster; ETO Medal; 2 Arrowheads. Mem: Am, Colo. and Southwest. Colo. Bar Asns; Lions; Elks; K. of C; Am. Legion; VFW. Rel: Catholic. Legal Res: R.R. 1, Box 482, Durango, Colo. 81301. Mailing Add: P.O. Box 138, Durango, Colo. 81301.

HAAS, HARL H. D
Ore. State Rep.
b. Cape Girardeau, Mo, 12/24/32; s. Harl H. Haas and Mary Berneice Taylor H; single. Educ: Southeast Mo. State Col, 51-52 & 55-57; Willamette Univ, LL.B, 61; Phi Delta Phi. Polit. & Govt. Pos: Mem, criminal Law Revision Cmn, Ore, 69; orgn. chmn, State Dem. Party, 69; Ore. State Rep, Multnomah Co, 69-; Rep. of Elected Dem. Off, Multnomah Co. Dem. Cent. Cmt, 69- Bus. & Prof. Pos: Mem, Client Indemnity Fund Cmt, Ore. State Bar, 62-63, Procedure and Practice Cmt, 63-64 and Pub. Rels. Cmt, 68-69; lectr. on Workman's Compensation, Willamette Univ, 68-69. Mil. Serv: Entered as Pvt, Army, released as Pfc, after serv. in 716th Mil. Police Bn, 53-55; Good Conduct Medal; Nat. Defense Ribbon. Publ: 'Other Insurance Clauses,' Willamette Law J; author, Continuing Legal Educational articles on evidence, malicious prosecution and workman's compensation. Mem: Am. Bar Asn; Am. Trial Lawyers Asn; Nat. Judiciary Soc; City Club of Portland. Best Oral Argument, Am. Trial Lawyers West. Regional Moot and Contest, 60. Rel: Methodist. Legal Res: 255 S.W. Harrison, Portland, Ore. 97204. Mailing Add: 617 Corbett Bldg, Portland, Ore. 97204.

HAASE, ROBERT DUANE R
Cmnr. of Ins, Wis.
b. Marinette, Wis, 5/10/23; s. William Frederick Haase and Laura Schulze; single. Educ: Univ. Wis, LL.B, 51; Order of the Coif; Theta Delta Chi; Delta Theta Chi. Polit. & Govt. Pos: Wis. State Assemblyman, 59-65, Rep. Caucus Chmn, Wis. State Assembly, 59-60, Majority Leader, 61-62, Speaker, 63-64, and Minority Leader, 65; Cmnr. of Ins, Wis, 65- Mil. Serv: Entered as Pvt, Air Force, 43, released as Sgt, 46. Mem: Fedn. of Ins. Counsel; Wis. Bar Asn; Elks; Am. Legion; Amvets; Dane Co. Big Bros. Rel: Methodist. Mailing Add: 1221 Main St, Marinette, Wis. 54134. (1967)

HABENICHT, ROBERT JULIUS
V.Mayor, Richmond, Va.
b. St. Louis, Mo, 2/13/26; s. Walter A. Habenicht and Loretta Glenn H; m. 1/31/47 to Colette Winifred Pflanz; c. P. Geoffrey, Peter A, Christopher J, Mathew F. and Roberta Marie. Educ: St. Louis Univ, 45-47, St. Louis Univ. Law Sch, LL.B, 54; Ohio State Law Sch, summer, 50; Phi Alpha Delta. Polit. & Govt. Pos: Asst. circuit attorney, St. Louis, Mo, 55-56; v.mayor, Richmond, Va, 64- Bus. & Prof. Pos: Attorney, 56-66; dir. of Trade Relations, A.H. Robins Co, Inc, 66- Mil. Serv: Entered as Cadet, Air Force, 43, released as Cpl, 45. Mem: Fed, Mo, Va, St. Louis, and Richmond Bar Asns; Int. Asn. of Law & Sci; Pharmaceut. Mfr. Asn; Narcotics Cmt, Am. Pharmaceut. Asn; K. of C; Kiwanis; Press Club; Suburban Sertoma Club. Major League Baseball Pitcher for St. Louis Cardinals, St. Louis Browns and Baltimore Orioles. Rel: Catholic. Legal Res: 1500 Confederate Ave, Richmond, Va. 23227. Mailing Add: 1407 Cummings Dr, Richmond, Va. 23220.

HABER, RICHARD MICHAEL R
b. Bridgeport, Conn, 2/17/37; s. David Haber and Marion Robbins H; m. 1/8/64 to Judith Cernik. Educ: Univ. Fla, B.S, 59; Am. Univ. Law Sch, J.D, 67; Pi Lambda Phi; Alpha Delta Sigma; Phi Alpha Delta. Polit. & Govt. Pos: Admin. asst, U.S. Rep. William C. Cramer, Fla, 61-; dep. campaign mgr, Pinellas Co. Rep. Exec. Cmt, Fla, 64-68; mem. cong. rels. div, Nixon for President Campaign, Wash, D.C, 68; asst. to chmn. host cmt, Rep. Nat. Conv, 68. Mil. Serv: Entered as Pvt, Army Res, 59, released as Sp-4, 62, after serv. in Berlin Crisis. Publ: 'Circuit Court Power to Modify Sentence of District Court which is Within Statuatory Limits,' Am. Univ. Law Rev, 6/66. Mem: D.C. Bar; Am. Bar Asn; Fed. Bar Asn.(dep. chmn, annual conv, 69, nat. coun, 68-69); Capitol Hill Club; Nat. Lawyers Club; Fla. State Soc.(second v.pres, 67-68). Rel: Jewish. Legal Res: 3651 Manatee Dr, S.E, St. Petersburg, Fla. 33705. Mailing Add: 9222 Park Lane, Ft. Washington, Md. 20022.

HABERMAN, RUSSELL L, JR. D
Chmn, First Assembly Dist. Dem. Party, Wis.
b. Milwaukee, Wis, 4/14/42; s. Russell L. Haberman, Sr. and Margaret Wohlford H; m. 5/26/62 to Karen Ann Tennies; c. Kathleen Jean and Rita Rose. Educ: Spencerian Bus. Col, Milwaukee, Wis, 3 years. Polit. & Govt. Pos: Membership secy, Waukesha Co. Dem. Party, Wis, 66-67, chmn, Waukesha Co. Dem. Party, 67-68; treas, Ninth Cong. Dist. Dem. Party, 67-; chmn, First Assembly Dist. Dem. Party, 68- Bus. & Prof. Pos: Loan mgr, Family Finance Corp, 63-64; credit mgr, Allied Radio of Wis, 64-68; acct. mgr, Fine-Lando Clin, Cudahy, 68- Mem: Am. Civil Liberties Union; Milwaukee Consumer Credit Asn.(bd. dirs, 68-); Wis. Asn. Credit Granters' Humane Animal Welfare Soc Waukesha Co.(secy, 67-69). Hold Assoc. Credit Exec. designation, Int. Consumer Credit Asn. Mailing Add: 22172 Hillcrest Dr, Waukesha, Wis. 53186.

HABERMEYER, HOWARD WILLIAM R
Chmn, U.S. Railroad Retirement Bd.
b. Aurora, Ill, 3/26/15; s. William G. Habermeyer and Marie Schneider H; m. 7/2/38 to Helen Lorraine Braithwaite; c. Howard William and Kent Leigh. Polit. & Govt. Pos: Successively messenger, clerk, supvr, U.S. Railroad Retirement Bd, 36-47, asst. bur. dir, 47-52, dir, 52-56, chmn, 56- Mil. Serv: Army, 44-46. Mem: Am. Legion; Moose. Recipient, Arthur S. Flemming Award, U.S. Jr. C. of C, 55; scholarship to mgt. sch, Am. Mgt. Asn, 55. Rel: Lutheran. Legal Res: 175 Westlawn Ave, Aurora, Ill. 60506. Mailing Add: 844 Rush St, Chicago, Ill. 60611.

HACHMEISTER, ALBERT WILLIAM R
b. Chicago, Ill, 6/1/19; s. Walter Christian Hachmeister and Phoebe Thompson H; m. 7/14/46 to Jean M. Marx; c. Ann, David and Peter. Educ: Northwest. Univ, 36-38; Sigma Delta Chi. Polit. & Govt. Pos: Ill. State Rep, 53-67 and Minority Leader; v.chmn, Intergovt. Coop. Cmn, 53-67; chmn, Great Lakes Cmn, 54-60, Ill-Ind. Port Study Cmn, 57-59 and World's Fair Cmn, 63-67; pres, 44th Ward Rep. Orgn, 56; chmn, Cigarette Tax Adv. Cmt, Ill, 69. Bus. & Prof. Pos: Pres, Mkt. Devices Pub. Co, 40-; pres, Plymouth Agency, Advert-Pub. Rels, 54-; v.pres, Mkt. Decision Data, Ind, 68- Mil. Serv: Entered as Pvt, Corps of Engrs, 42, released as 1st Lt, 45, after serv. in Off, Chief of Engrs, U.S. Mem: Headline Club; Chicago Press Club; Am. Mkt. Asn; assoc. mem, Am. Inst. Mgt; Lincoln Park C. of C; German Club; life mem, Art Inst. and Field Mus; assoc, Bd. of Trustees, Shimer Col; dir, Better Govt. Asn, 68- Rel: Protestant. Legal Res: 2350 Lincoln Park West, Chicago, Ill. 60614. Mailing Add: 18 E. Huron St, Chicago, Ill. 60611.

HACKEL, DONALD H. D
Mem, Vt. State Dem. Cmt.
b. Boston, Mass, 8/1/25; s. Myer Jacob Hackel and Rose Milhender H; m. 8/14/49 to Stella Bloomberg; c. Susan Jane and Cynthia Anne. Educ: Univ. Vt; Middleburg Col, A.B. cum laude, 45; Boston Univ, 45; Harvard Law Sch, LL.B, 48. Polit. & Govt. Pos: Mem, Vt. State Dem. Cmt, 61-; mem, Bd. Sch. Cmnrs, Rutland, 67-, pres, 69-; del, Dem. Nat. Conv, 68. Bus. & Prof. Pos: Dir, Vt. Elec. Supply Co, Inc, 50-; partner, Loveland & Hackel, Attorneys, 50-69; partner, Dick, Hackel & Hull, Attorneys, 69- Mem: Am, Vt. and Rutland Co. Bar Asns; Am. Judicature Soc; Defense Res. Inst. Rel: Jewish. Mailing Add: 43 North St. Extension, Rutland, Vt. 05701.

HACKETT, HANLEY ANTON D
Treas, Wash. Co. Dem. Exec. Cmt, Ohio
b. Marietta, Ohio, 4/1/99; s. John Michael Hackett and Matilda Mary Borman H; m. 1/16/37 to Mary Clara Hiener; c. John Joseph. Educ: Marietta Col, B.A; Lambda Chi Alpha. Polit. & Govt. Pos: Investr, Div. of Pub. Welfare, Ohio, 37-40; city clerk, Marietta, 40-47; treas, Wash. Co. Dem. Exec. Cmt,

currently. Bus. & Prof. Pos: Mgr. and operator, Hackett Hotel, 25-63. Mil. Serv: Entered as Pvt, Army Air Corps, 17, released as Cpl, 19, after serv. in 242nd Ambulance Unit, 11 San. Train, 11th Div. Mem: Am. Legion; 40 et 8. Rel: Roman Catholic. Mailing Add: 801 Montgomery St, Marietta, Ohio 45750.

HACKETT, LEONA AMELIA D
Secy, Huron Co. Dem. Cent. and Exec. Cmt, Ohio
b. Norwalk, Ohio, 8/31/12; d. George Albert Hipp and Rose Kathryn Heitz H; wid. Educ: St. Paul's Cath. High Sch, Norwalk, Ohio, grad. Polit. & Govt. Pos: Dep. dir, Huron Co. Bd. of Elec, Ohio, 52-69; acting secy, Huron Co. Dem. Cent. and Exec. Cmt, 58-59, recording secy, 59-60 & 64-66, cent. committeewoman, 60-69 and secy, 60-64 & 66-; pres, Huron Co. Fireland's Dem. Women's Club, 64-67; trustee, Ohio Bd. of Elec. Off, 65-69; secy-treas, Dem. Citizens for Better Govt. Cmt, 69- Mem: Fireland's Bus. & Prfnl. Women's Club, Norwalk (recording secy, 60-62, first v.pres 67-69, pres, 69-); Huron Co. Dem. Women's Club; Fisher-Titus Mem. Hosp. Auxiliary; Willard Dem. Womens Club; Federated Dem. Women of Ohio; St. Paul's Boosters Club; Am. Asn. Retired Persons. Rel: Catholic. Mailing Add: 48 Milan Ave, Norwalk, Ohio 44857.

HACKETT, LUTHER FREDERICK R
Vt. State Rep.
b. Burlington, Vt, 6/20/33; s. Luther Chaffee Hackett and Barbara Stearns H; m. 6/23/55 to Sally Smith; c. L. Stephen and Elizabeth Lee. Educ: Univ. Vt, B.A, 55. Polit. & Govt. Pos: Chmn, Vt. Young Rep. Club, 62-63; Vt. State Rep, 65-, majority leader, Vt. House of Rep, 66-68, chmn. appropriations cmt, 69- Bus. & Prof. Pos: V.pres, The Hackett Agency Inc, 59- Mil. Serv: Entered as 2nd Lt, Air Force, 56, released as 1st Lt, 59, after serv. in 6920th Security Wing, Air Force Security Serv, 56-59, Capt, Res; Air Force Commendation Medal. Rel: Protestant. Mailing Add: 39 Laurel Hill Dr, South Burlington, Vt. 05402.

HACKETT, ROGER C. D
b. Marion, Ind, 3/15/00; s. Arthur Marion Hackett and Lola Thomas H; m. 6/5/26 to Miss Robert Henry Lyon; c. Martha Lucile. Educ: Ind. Univ, A.B, 23; Harvard Univ, A.M, 24; Oxford Univ, summer, 37; Univ. Colo, summer, 50; Phi Beta Kappa; Phi Delta Kappa. Polit. & Govt. Pos: Mem, C.Z. Del, Dem. Nat. Conv, 64. Bus. & Prof. Pos: Dean and instr, Pineland Jr. Col, 24-26; teacher, Bosse High Sch, Evansville, Ind, 26-30; teacher, Cristobal High Sch, C.Z, 30-35; instr, C.Z. Col, 35-41, dean and chief adminstr, 41-46. Publ: 'Geographical Availability of Presidential and Vice Presidential Candidates,' Hist. Outlook, 5/32; 'Some Aspects of Latin-American Politics and Government,' Ind. Univ. Alumni Quart, 10/32, 3/33, 4/33 and Oxford Univ, 10/38. Mem: Sojourners Lodge, AF&AM, AASR, South. Jurisdiction, KCCH (32°), AAONMS; C.Z. Civic Coun, Pac. Side, 57-, pres, 59-61; N.C. Lit. Club and Hist. Soc; Harvard Club of East. N.C; Raleigh Country Club. Rel: Unitarian. Mailing Add: 114 E. Drewry Lane, Raleigh, N.C. 27609.

HADAWAY, JOHN HENRY D
Ga. State Rep.
b. Hillsboro, Ga, 6/29/09; s. Thomas Roland Hadaway and Ola Avant H; m. 11/30/38 to Mildred Wynens; c. Carol, John R, Charles and Philip. Educ: Purdue Univ, Fraternal Ins. Course. Polit. & Govt. Pos: Ga. State Rep, Dist. 46, 66- Bus. & Prof. Pos: Dairy farmer, 38-69; with U.S. Forest Serv, 40-63; automobile salesman, 49-58; salesman, Woodmen of the World Life Ins. Co, 60- Mem: Kiwanis; Farm Bur; PTA; Boosters Club. Rel: Baptist. Mailing Add: Hillsboro, Ga. 31038.

HADDEN, CARL THOMPSON D
Ky. State Sen.
b. Elkton, Ky, 7/4/15; s. Joseph Newton Hadden and Nettie Latham H; m. 1/19/41 to Louise Willis; c. Molly Sue (Mrs. Mitchell), Peggy Ann and Carl Thompson, Jr. Educ: Univ. Ky, B.S, 39; Alpha Gamma Rho. Polit. & Govt. Pos: Ky. State Sen, 68-; committeeman, Cmt. Health, Educ. & Welfare, 68; committeeman, Cmt. Counties & Spec. Dist, 68; v.chmn, Cmt. Highways & Traffic, 68; cmnr, Ment. Health Cmn, 68; cmnr, Ky. Un-Am. Activities Cmt, 69. Mil. Serv: Entered Army, 43, released as Technician, 46, after serv. in Med. Corps Vet. Detached. Mem: F&AM; Shrine; C. of C.(pres, 54); Rotary (pres, 52); Farm Bur; Nat. Union; Univ. Ky. Alumni (pres, 67); Todd Co. Fair (pres, 55). Rel: Methodist. Mailing Add: Clarksville St, Elkton, Ky. 42220.

HADDICK, DEAN Z. R
Dep. Co. Treas, Rock Island Co, Ill.
b. Sherrard, Ill, 3/5/10; s. Robert Thompson Haddick and Millie Zude H; m. 8/20/38 to Nina Rachel Leuders; c. Dean William and Mark Leuders. Educ: Augustana Col, Rock Island, 28-30; Univ. Ill, Champaign, 30-32; Beta Kappa. Polit. & Govt. Pos: Twp. supvr, Moline Twp, Ill, 43-50; co. clerk, Rock Island Co, 50-54; admin. asst. to gov. Ill, Springfield, 54-61; health officer, Moline, 61-62; chief dep. co. clerk, Rock Island Co, 62-66; dep. co. treas, 66- Bus. & Prof. Pos: Salesman, Rath Packing Co, Rock Island Co, Ill, 33-36; produce salesman, Stanley Fruit Co, 36-38; partner, food mkt, Moline, 38-60; partner, ins. bus, Rock Island, 55-68. Mil. Serv: Seaman 3/C, Coast Guard Res, 43-45, serv. in Security Patrol. Mem: Life mem, Nat. Asn. Co. Officials; life mem, State Co. Officials; Twp. Officials, Ill; Ill. Police Asn; Ill. Press Club; Mason (32°); Tabala Shrine; Zal Grotto; Odd Fellows; Eagles; Blackhawk Shrine Club; C. of C. Rel: Congregational. Mailing Add: 720-11th St. A, Moline, Ill. 61265.

HADEN, CHARLES McINTYRE R
b. Timpson, Tex, 8/6/23; s. Charles Clinton Haden and Cecil McIntyre H; m. 12/20/44 to Cynthia Suzanne Tracy; c. Charles McIntyre, Jr, Susan Carol and Sharon Dianne (Mrs. Gordon A. Gabbert, Jr); grandchildren: Christopher Anthony Gabbert and Brian Haden Gabbert. Educ: Rice Univ, B.A. and Univ. of Tex, LL.B, 49; Football Letterman, R Asn; Phi Alpha Delta. Polit. & Govt. Pos: Chmn. Precinct 213, Harris Co. Rep. Party, Tex, 56-60, chmn. Cand. Cmt, 60-62; city judge, Hunter's Creek, Tex, 57-59, mayor, 59-61; chmn, Harris Co. Rep. Exec. Cmt, 64; del, Rep. Nat. Conv, 64. Bus. & Prof. Pos: Legal Counsel, Trans-Tex. Airways, 49-50; asst. dist. attorney, Houston, 50-52; assoc, Fulbright, Crooker, Freeman, Bates & Jaworski, 52-61, partner, 62- Mil. Serv: Entered as Student, Naval ROTC, Rice Univ, 41, released as Lt.(jg), 46, after serv. in Pac. Theater, 44-46; New Guinea, Peleliu, Philippines, Eniwetok, Guam, Japan, Okinawa and Iwo Jima Campaign Ribbons. Mem: Houston, Tex. and Am. Bar Asns; v.pres, Nat. Asn. of Railroad Trial Counsels; U.S. Dist. Court for the Southern Dist. of Tex; U.S. Court of Appeals for the Fifth Circuit; Memorial Drive Country Club; v.chmn, Govt. Affairs Cmt, Houston C. of C. Private pilot. Rel: Presbyterian; Elder. Legal Res: 10709 Old Coach Lane, Houston, Tex. 77024. Mailing Add: 8th Floor, Bank of the Southwest Bldg, Houston, Tex. 77002.

HADLEY, FRED B. R
Ohio State Rep.
b. Pioneer, Ohio, 7/2/11; s. F.W. Hadley and Ethel M. Grannis H; m. 8/19/35 to Jean Munro; c. James F; Betty. Educ: Hillsdale Col. Polit. & Govt. Pos: Former mem, Bd. Pub. Affairs, Pioneer, Ohio; Ohio State Rep, 64- Bus. & Prof. Pos: Hadley Dept. Store, 31-63. Mem: Mason; C. of C; Williams Co. Develop. Corp; Farm Bur. Rel: Methodist. Mailing Add: R.R. 2, Bryan, Ohio 43506.

HADSEL, FRED LATIMER
U.S. Ambassador to the Somali Repub.
b. Oxford, Ohio, 3/11/16; s. Fred Latimer Hadsel and Mary Perine H; m. 1/21/42 to Winifred Nelson; c. Mary C, Winifred R. and Jane L. Educ: Univ. Grenoble, grad. student, 33; Miami Univ, A.B, 37; Freiburg Univ, grad. student, 38; Clark Univ, M.A, 38; Univ. Chicago, Ph.D, 42. Polit. & Govt. Pos: With Dept. of State, 46; hist. researcher, German Affairs Off. and exec. secretariat, Bur. of Near East, S.Asian and African Affairs, 46-56; dir, Off. of S.African Affairs, 56-57; first secy, Am. Embassy, London, Eng, 57-61, dep. chief of mission, Addis Ababa, Ethiopia, 61-62; adv, Bur. of African Affairs, Dept. of State, 63-64, dir, Off. of Inter-African Affairs, 64-69; U.S. Ambassador to the Somali Repub, 69- Bus. & Prof. Pos: Prof. lectr. polit. sci, George Wash. Univ, 63-69; lectr. African affairs, Johns Hopkins Univ. and Howard Univ, 68-69. Mil. Serv: Entered as Pvt, Army, 42, released as Maj, 46. Publ: Contrib, articles, prfnl. jour. Mem: Phi Beta Kappa; Beta Theta Pi; Omicron Delta Kappa; Phi Eta Sigma. Rel: Protestant. Legal Res: 3432 Ashley Terr. N.W, Washington, D.C. 20008. Mailing Add: U.S. Embassy, Mogadishu, Somalia.

HAENEL, LOYOLA THERESA R
V.Chairlady, Dormont Rep. Cmt, Pa.
b. Pittsburgh, Pa, 3/6/27; d. Elmer G. Haenel, Sr. and Winifred V. Hearn H; single. Polit. & Govt. Pos: Mem, Young Rep, 12 years; past secy, Dormont Young Rep. Club, Pa; state committeewoman, 45th Sen. Dist. Young Rep, 59-62; del, Pa. Young Rep. Conv, 60 & 62; secy, Dormont Rep. Cmt, 60-62, vice chairlady, 62-; committeewoman, Dormont Sixth Dist. Rep. Party, 60-; prog. chmn, Dormont Coun. Rep. Women; secy, Dormont Rep. Finance Cmt; v.chmn, Allegheny Co. Young Rep, 61-63, mem. bd. of dirs, 3 years; co-v.chmn, Scranton for Gov. Cmt, 62; v.chmn, Pa. Young Rep, 62-64; del, Young Rep. Nat. Conv, 63; chmn. rally, East. Div, Young Americans for Goldwater, 64; alternate del, Rep. Nat. Conv, 64. Bus. & Prof. Pos: Employee, Prod. Planning Dept, Pittsburgh Steel Co, Pa. Mem: Dormont Civic League; Dormont Rep. Citizens League; Pittsburgh Hornet Booster Club; Int. Fedn. of Cath. Alumni; Elizabeth Seton High Sch. Alumni Asn. Rel: Roman Catholic. Mailing Add: 1300 Wisconsin Ave, Dormont, Pa. 15216. (1967)

HAERLE, PAUL RAYMOND R
Secy, Calif. Rep. State Cent. Cmt.
b. Portland, Ore, 1/10/32; s. George W. Haerle and Grace Soden H; m. 5/30/53 to Susan Ann Wagner; c. Karen Joyce and David Arthur. Educ: Yale Univ, A.B, 53; Univ. Mich. Law Sch, J.D, 56; Phi Delta Phi; Soc. of Barristers; Yale Key; Order of the Coif. Polit. & Govt. Pos: Mem, Marin Co. Rep. Cent. Cmt, Calif, 63-66; pres, Marin Rep. Coun, 65-66; mem, Calif. Rep. State Cent. Cmt, 65-, secy, 69-; chmn, Marin Co. Reagan for Gov. Cmt, 66; appointments secy, Gov. staff, State of Calif, 67-69. Bus. & Prof. Pos: Assoc, Thelen, Marrin, Johnson & Bridges, 56-64, partner, 65-67 & 69- Publ: Ed-in-Chief, Mich. Law Rev, 55-56. Mem: Am. and San Francisco Bar Asns; The Guardsmen, San Francisco. Rel: Protestant. Mailing Add: 32 Idlewood Place, San Rafael, Calif. 94901.

HAFLICH, EDWIN LURIE D
b. Bridgeport, Conn, 10/31/23; s. Samuel Haflich and Celia Lurie H; m. 4/8/51 to Barbara Ann Weiner; c. Jan Susan and Kim Meredity. Educ: Univ. Ill, 2 years; Yale Univ, B.A, 48. Polit. & Govt. Pos: Justice of the Peace, Bridgeport, Conn, 51-53, clerk, Trumbull, Conn, 57-63, mem. town coun, 65-67, bd. educ, 67-; dep. sheriff, Fairfield Co, 59-63; chmn, Trumbull Dem. Town Cmt, 66-68. Bus. & Prof. Pos: Auctioneer, S. Haflich, 48-57; admin. asst. to pres, Stevenson Lumber, 63-64; owner, Edwin L. Haflich, 64- Mil. Serv: Entered as Pvt, Army, 42, released as T-5, 46, after serv. in Mil. Police, 44-46. Mem: Assoc. mem, Am. Soc. Appraisers; Mason; Cerebral Palsy Asn; Am. Legion; Navy League. Rel: Jewish. Mailing Add: 30 Jog Hill Rd, Trumbull, Conn. 06611.

HAFSTAD, KATHARINE CLARKE R
Chmn, Emmet Co. Rep. Cmt, Mich.
b. Harbor Springs, Mich, 12/6/03; d. James Turner Clarke and Maud Hartness Bishop C; div. Educ: Northwest. Univ, B.S, 26; Clark Univ, M.A, 30; Kappa Delta. Polit. & Govt. Pos: Mem, Gov. Cmn. on the Status of Women, Mich, 63-65; mem. bd. trustees, Cent. Mich. Univ, 64-, chmn, 66; v.chmn, 11th Cong. Dist. Rep. Cmt, Mich, 65-69; chmn, Emmet Co. Rep. Cmt, 65-; fourth v.pres, Rep. Women's Fedn, 67-; mem. exec. cmt, Mich. State Rep. Cent. Cmt, 69- Bus. & Prof. Pos: Climatologist, Carnegie Inst. of Wash, 30-34; meteorologist, Soil Conserv. Serv, 34-40, U.S. Weather Bur, 40-42; research analyst, U.S. Air Force, 42-50; opers. analyst, Opers. Research Off, Johns Hopkins Univ, 50-58; owner and mgr, Snowberry Farm Lodge, 58- Mem: Am. Asn. of Univ. Women. Korean Theater Medal for serv. in Korea as civilian opers. analyst. Rel: Presbyterian. Mailing Add: Snowberry Farm Lodge, Route 2, Harbor Springs, Mich. 49740.

HAGAMAN, LLOYD CATES, JR. R
b. Toledo, Ohio, 5/14/28; s. Lloyd Cates Hagaman and Sarah Estelle Patrick H; m. 12/20/52 to Sylvia Joyce Sharp; c. John Chuck and Perry Lee. Educ: Univ. Tenn, 1 year. Polit. & Govt. Pos: Leader, DemoKirk movement, Brevard Co, Fla, 66; mem, Brevard Co. Finance Cmt. for Conressman Gurney, 66; campaign mgr. for U.S. Sen. C.S. Reuter, 67; exec. asst. to Gov. of Fla, 67-; nat. defense exec. reservist, Dept. Army, Wash, D.C, 68; mem, Fla.

Civil Defense Adv. Bd, 68; alternate del, Rep. Nat. Conv, 68. Bus. & Prof. Pos: V.pres, Hagaman Insulation, Knoxville, Tenn, 48; purchasing agent, Witt Lumber Co, 54; pres, Rocket Insulators, Brevard Co, 61; v.pres, Smith & Sapp Construction, Orlando, 67- Mil. Serv: Entered as Pvt, Army, 46, released as S/Sgt, 47, after serv. in Ninth Inf. Div. Mem: Mem. bd, Leon Co. Red Cross; v.pres, Four Community Fire Dept; pres, Fairglen PTA. Rel: Baptist. Mailing Add: 2916 Brandemere Dr, Tallahassee, Fla. 32303.

HAGAN, G. ELLIOTT D
U.S. Rep, Ga.
b. Sylvania, Ga, 5/24/16; m. to Frances Bryant; c. G. Elliott, Jr, Charles Franklin and Frances Bryant. Educ: Univ. of Ga; Emory Univ; John Marshall Law Sch. Polit. & Govt. Pos: Ga. State Rep, five terms; Ga. State Sen, one term; former secy-treas. and dep. dir, State Bd. Workmen's Compensation, 46; state mem, Nat. Coun. State Govt, two terms; dist. dir, Savannah Dist. Off, Off. Price Stabilization, 51-53, dep. regional dir, Atlanta Regional off, 53; U.S. Rep, Ga, 60- Bus. & Prof. Pos: Formerly engaged in life ins, estate planning and farming; former weekly newspaper ed. Mil. Serv: Signal Corps, Army, two years in World War II. Mem: Life mem, Million Dollar Round Table; Nat. Asn. Life Underwriters; Rotary; Am. Legion; Farm Bur; York Rite; Scottish Rite; Alee Temple of the Shrine; C. of C; Elks; Asn. of U.S. Army; Ga. Livestock Asn; Nat. Rivers and Harbors Cong; Peace Officers Asn. of Ga; Univ. of Ga. Alumni Asn; U.S. Capitol Hist. Soc; counselor to and mem. bd. dirs, Wash. Sect. Marine Tech. Soc; pres, Ga. State Soc; Moose; Gridiron Secret Soc; bd. dirs, Grace Home; bd. mgrs, Ga. Press Asn. Rel: Baptist; V.pres, Ga. Baptist Conv, 63. Legal Res: Sylvania, Ga. 30467. Mailing Add: 218 House Office Bldg, Washington, D.C. 20515.

HAGEDORN, GARRETT WILLIAM R
N.J. State Sen.
b. Midland Park, N.J, 9/16/10; s. John William Hagedorn and Jennie Klopman H; m. 10/5/35 to Hubrine M. Hamersma; c. Ruth Ann (Mrs. Knyfd), Donald W. and Dorothy M.(Mrs. Vander Guchte). Educ: East. Christian Sch. Syst, 12 years. Polit. & Govt. Pos: Councilman, Midland Park, N.J, 51-57 and mayor, 58-68; mem. exec. bd, N.J. League of Municipalities, 62-68; N.J. State Sen, 68- Rel: Christian Reformed. Mailing Add: 210 Vreeland Ave, Midland Park, N.J. 07432.

HAGEDORN, MERLE W. D
Iowa State Sen.
b. Clay Co, Iowa, 1911; s. George Hagedorn and Clara Christiansen H; m. to Lucile Weik; c. Marcel, Pauline and Dean. Educ: Dana Col. Polit. & Govt. Pos: Former assessor, Lincoln Twp, Iowa; former mem, Clay Co. Sch. Bd; Iowa State Rep, 55-65; Iowa State Sen, 65-69. Bus. & Prof. Pos: Farmer; real estate broker. Rel: Lutheran. Mailing Add: Royal, Iowa 51357. (1967)

HAGEMAN, ALVIN WILLIAM D
Mont. State Rep.
b. Wheatland, Ill, 2/6/14; s. William Jacob Hageman and Amanda Dannenberg H; m. 7/28/39 to Evelyn Marie Conover; c. Gayle (Mrs. Long), Richard and Carol. Educ: Billings Pub. High Sch, grad, 35. Polit. & Govt. Pos: Mem, sch. bd, Stillwater Co, Mont, 40-60, mem, Agr. Stabilization & Conserv. Serv, 50-58, co. cmnr, 59-64; Mont. State Rep, Stillwater and Carbon Co, 69- Bus. & Prof. Pos: Own and operate diversified wheat and cattle ranch, Stillwater Co, Mont, 39- Mem: Pres, Stillwater Grain Growers Asn, 56-58; dir. and secy, Mont. State Grain Growers Asn, 66-68; Mason; Scottish Rite; Shrine; Elks; Farmers Union; Cub Scout Leader. Rel: Am. Lutheran. Mailing Add: Broadview, Mont. 59015.

HAGEN, E. BRUCE D
Cmnr, N.Dak. Pub. Serv. Cmn.
b. Devils Lake, N.Dak, 6/21/30; s. Ernest W. Hagen and Mildred Bryn H; m. 12/28/68 to Sylvia Bergstrom; c. Jennifer. Educ: Devils Lake Jr. Col, 48-49; Univ. N.Dak, Ph.B. in Soc. Studies, 53, M.A. in Govt. and Econ, 55; Univ. Wis, Adv. study in Govt, 55-56; Phi Alpha Theta; Phi Delta Theta. Polit. & Govt. Pos: Dep. Motor Vehicle Registr, State of N.Dak, 61; cmnr, N.Dak. Pub. Serv. Cmn, 61-, pres, 69-; chmn, Gov. Cmt. on Dual Inspection of N.Dak. Grain by Minn. and Gov. Adv. Cmt. on Hold Points, 62-64; mem, Mkt. Res. Adv. Cmt, U.S. Dept. Agr, 65-67; v.pres, Mid-Am. Gov. Transportation Cmt, 67; mem, N.Dak. Safety Cmt, 67-69; cand. for U.S. Rep, Dem-Nonpartisan League, East Dist, N.Dak, 68; mem, Gov. Transportation and Rate Cmt. for Midwest. Gov. Conf; v.pres, Adv. Coun, Upper Great Plains Transportation Inst, 68; mem, Northwest Shippers Adv. Bd, 68. Bus. & Prof. Pos: Pres, 11-state Midwest Asn. R.R. and Utilities Cmnr, 68-69. Mil. Serv: Entered as Pvt, Army, 50, released as Sgt, 52, after serv. in 164th Inf. Regt, U.S. Mem: State Hist. Soc. N.Dak; N.Dak. Water Users Asn; Am. Asn. UN; Dakota Seminar; Elks; Sons of Norway. Selected as one of Outstanding Young Men of Am, 65. Rel: Lutheran. Mailing Add: 2908 Ave. B E, Bismarck, N.Dak. 58501.

HAGEN, HARLAN FRANCIS D
Mem, Calif. Dem. State Cent. Cmt.
b. Lawton, N.Dak, 10/8/14; s. Oluf Hagen and Carrie Swenson-Tofsrud H; m. 1937 to Martha Ritz. Educ: Long Beach, Calif. Jr. Col, 31-33; Univ. Calif, Berkeley, A.B. in econ, 36; Univ. Calif. Sch. of Jurisp, Berkeley, LL.B, 40; Phi Alpha Delta. Polit. & Govt. Pos: Mem, City Coun, Hanford, Calif, 48; Calif. State Assemblyman, 49-52; U.S. Rep, 18th Dist, Calif, 53-68; mem, Calif. Dem. State Cent. Cmt, currently. Bus. & Prof. Pos: Attorney-at-law, 40- Mil. Serv: Entered as Pvt, Army, 43, released as T/Sgt, 46, after serv. in Counter-Intel. Corps, U.S; Lt. Col, Army Res, 3 years. Mem: Calif. State Bar; Am. Legion; VFW; Amvets; DAV; Farm Bur; Grange; Elks; Eagles; Moose; Commonwealth Club of San Francisco. Rel: Protestant. Mailing Add: 1206 N. Kaweah St, Hanford, Calif. 93230. (1967)

HAGEN, JOHN WILLIAM R
Va. State Del.
b. Huntington, W.Va, 2/16/35; s. Karl B. Hagen and Frances Adkins H; m. 2/6/55 to Sondra Dell Sheppard; c. Karla M. and John W, Jr. Educ: Marshall Univ, A.B, 55; Lambda Chi Alpha; Young Rep. Club. Polit. & Govt. Pos: Va. State Del, 64- Bus. & Prof. Pos: Pres, Twin Ridge Marina, Inc, 62, Fire Control Co, Inc, 64 and Safety Control Co, 65. Mem: Elks; Mason. Outstanding Young Man of Am. Award, 65. Rel: Baptist. Legal Res: 6179 Steeplechase Dr, Route 2, Salem, Va. 24153. Mailing Add: P.O. Box 102, Roanoke, Va. 24002.

HAGEN, ORVILLE WEST Independent
Labor Cmnr, N.Dak.
b. Watford City, N.Dak, 9/26/15; s. Oscar Wilhelm Hagen and Carrie Scollard H; m. 11/24/39 to Astrid Berg; c. Orvis Wayne, Mylo LeRoy, Ellyn Marie and Lana Jo. Educ: Dickinson State Teachers Col, 37-38. Polit. & Govt. Pos: N.Dak. State Sen, McKenzie Co, 53 & 55; Lt. Gov, N.Dak, 60-62, Labor Cmnr, 67- Mem: Elks; Sons of Norway; Odd Fellows. Rel: Lutheran. Legal Res: Arnegard, N.Dak. 58835. Mailing Add: 1528 N. 19th, Bismarck, N.Dak. 58501.

HAGER, EARL B. D
W.Va. State Del.
b. Gill, W.Va, 4/10/11; s. Golden DeClifford Hager and Fannie Brumfield H; m. 6/14/64 to Mary Hutchinson Smith; c. David Shelton and Earl Bradley. Educ: Marshall Univ, A.B, 47, A.M, 53. Polit. & Govt. Pos: Mem, Dem. Cong. Cmt, 44; W.Va. State Del, 52-66 and currently. Bus. & Prof. Pos: Elem. sch. prin, Logan Co. Bd. Educ, W.Va, 33-66; mem, W.Va. Centennial Cmn, 56-63; mem, W.Va. State Teachers Retirement Bd, 65-66. Mil. Serv: Entered as Pvt, Army, 42, released as Cpl, 44; Army Res, 44-45. Mem: W.Va. and Nat. Educ. Asns; Nat. Elem. Prin. Asn; Red Men; Logan Co. Sportsman Asn; Am. Legion. Rel: Protestant. Mailing Add: Route 1, Box 374-A, Chapmanville, W.Va. 25508. (1967)

HAGER, ELLEN HUME WILLIAMS R
State Committeewoman, Fourth Sen. Dist, Tex. Rep. Party
b. New Orleans, La, 11/20/18; d. Charles Laval Williams, M.D. and Lewise Stratton McLaurine W; m. 12/27/41 to Dale Carroll Hager, M.D; c. Dale Carroll, Jr, Frederick Hume, Lewise McLaurine, Stephen Carroll, Gordon Orval and Peter Hobson. Educ: H. Sophie Newcomb Col, 35-36; George Washington Univ, 36-38; Strayer Bus. Col, 38-39. Polit. & Govt. Pos: V.chmn, Jefferson Co. Rep. Party, Tex, 61-62 & 64-66; del, Rep. Nat. Conv, 64 & 68; state committeewoman, Fourth Sen. Dist, Rep. Party, Tex, 66- Rel: Episcopal. Mailing Add: 4910 Gladys St, Beaumont, Tex. 77706.

HAGER, H. WILLIAM, JR. R
b. Narberth, Pa, 9/13/25; s. Harold William Hager and Marion Harris H; m. 9/6/46 to Ruth Long; c. Peggs, Jeanne, Bill, III and Beth. Educ: Wharton Sch, Univ. Pa, B.S. in Econ, 45; Kite and Key; Sigma Phi Epsilon. Polit. & Govt. Pos: Pres, Eighth Precinct, Rep. Party, S.C, 64-67; chmn, Darlington Co. Rep. Party, 67-68; Rep. cand. for Darlington Co. Cmnr, 68. Bus. & Prof. Pos: Salesman, J.E. Fricke Co, Phil, Pa, 57-69. Mem: Aircraft Owners & Pilots Asn; Mason (Master, Lodge 173); Hartsville Golf Club. Rel: South. Baptist. Legal Res: 1611 Golf Course Rd, Hartsville, S.C. 29550. Mailing Add: P.O. Box 813, Hartsville, S.C. 29550.

HAGERTY, JAMES C. R
b. Plattsburg, N.Y, 5/9/09; s. James A. Hagerty and Katherine S. Kearney H; m. 6/15/37 to Marjorie Lucas; c. Roger C. and Bruce C. Educ: Columbia Univ, B.A, 34; Delta Kappa Epsilon. Polit. & Govt. Pos: Exec. asst. to Gov. Thomas E. Dewey, 43-50, secy, 50-52; press secy. for President of U.S, 53-61. Bus. & Prof. Pos: Staff mem, Albany Bur, N.Y. Times, 34-42, legis. correspondent, 38-42; v.pres, ABC News, 61-63, v.pres. corp. rels, Am. Broadcasting Co, Inc, 63- Rel: Episcopal. Mailing Add: 7 Rittenhouse Rd, Bronxville, N.Y. 10708.

HAGGERTY, JUDSON FRANCIS D
b. Indianapolis, Ind, 3/19/25; s. Walter Francis Haggerty and Elsie Booher H; c. Marc, Kevin, Dana, Bryan and Darren. Educ: Butler Univ, 46-48; Ind. Univ. Sch. Law, LL.B, 51. Polit. & Govt. Pos: Ind. State Rep, 49-50; chmn, Marion Co. Young Dem, 50-52; dep. prosecutor, Marion Co, 59-60; chmn, Marion Co. Dem. Party, 62-64; del, Dem. Nat. Conv, 64, alternate del, 68; spec. rep. for dist. affairs to U.S. Rep. Andrew Jacobs, Jr, 64- Bus. & Prof. Pos: Pvt. law practice. Mil. Serv: Entered as A/S, Naval Air Corps, 43, released as Aviation Radioman 3/C, 46, after serv. in Patrol Bombing Squadron 112, European-African and Asiatic Pac. Theaters; European-African, Asiatic-Pac. and Am. Defense Ribbons; Good Conduct Medal; Combat Air Wings. Mem: Ind. and Indianapolis Bar Asns; Ind. Trial Lawyers Asn; Ind. Dem. Club. Rel: Protestant. Mailing Add: 3037 S. Meridian St, Indianapolis, Ind. 46217.

HAGGERTY, KENNETH M. R
b. New York, N.Y, 1/31/24; s. Thomas A. Haggerty and Martha A. Pearn H; m. 8/9/47 to Regina M. Alluise; c. Kevin Patrick, Peter Andrew, Brian Michael, Maura Patricia and Kelly Ann. Educ: Fordham Univ; Holy Cross Col; Georgetown Univ. Sch. of Dent; Omicron Kappa Upsilon. Polit. & Govt. Pos: Mem, Arlington Co. Bd. of Cmnrs, Va, 66-; mem, Exec. Cmt, Arlington Co. Rep. Party; del, Nominating Conv, Rep. Party, Va. Bus. & Prof. Pos: Assoc. prof. prosthetic dent, Georgetown Univ. Dent. Sch, 52- Mil. Serv: Entered as Seaman, Navy, 42, released as PO 2/C, 45, after serv. in Med. Corps, 11th Naval Dist. Publn: Editor-in-chief, Jour. of D.C. Dent. Soc, 56-57. Mem: Chmn. exec. coun, Va. State Dent. Asn; councilor, N. Va. Dent. Soc. and pres, 59; Am. Legion; Am. Dent. Asn; Fedn. Dentaire Internationale; fel, Int. Col. of Dentists. Honorable mention, Basketball All-American, 47; Capt, Nat. Championship Basketball Team, Holy Cross Col, 47. Rel: Roman Catholic. Mailing Add: 4954 Old Dominion Dr, Arlington, Va. 22207. (1967)

HAGGLAND, P. B. 'DOC' R
Alaska State Sen.
b. Seattle, Wash; married; c. three. Polit. & Govt. Pos: Mem, Fairbanks City Coun, Alaska, 55-57; Alaska Territorial Sen, 57; mayor, Fairbanks, 57-59; Alaska State Sen, 67- Bus. & Prof. Pos: Physican. Mem: Alaska Med. Soc; Am. Col. Surgeons; Am. Acad. Orthopedics; Rotary; nat. exec. cmt, Boy Scouts; Midnight Sun Boy Scouts; chmn, Friends of the Libr. Mailing Add: 502 Kellum, Fairbanks, Alaska 99701.

HAHN, GILBERT, JR. R
Chmn, D.C. City Coun.
b. Washington, D.C, 9/12/21; s. Gilbert Hahn and Hortense King H; m. 6/29/50 to Margot Hess; c. Gilbert, III, Amanda B. and Polly K. Educ: Princeton Univ, A.B, 43; Yale Law Sch, LL.B, 48; Cannon Club; Corbey Court; Fed. City Club. Polit. & Govt. Pos: Pres, D.C. Young Rep. Club, 49; alternate del, Rep. Nat. Conv, 52; finance chmn, D.C. State Rep. Cmt, 64-68; chmn, Rep. Party, D.C, 68-69; chmn, D.C. City Coun, 69- Bus. & Prof. Pos: Partner, Amram, Hahn & Sundlun, 54- Mil. Serv: Entered as Sgt, Army, 42,

released as 1st Lt, 46, after serv. in 558th Field Artil, ETO, 43-45; ETO Ribbon with Three Battle Stars; Metz and Verdun Medals; Purple Heart. Mem: D.C, Md. and U.S. Supreme Court Bar Asns. Rel: Jewish. Mailing Add: 3022 University Terr. N.W, Washington, D.C. 20016.

HAHN, RUBY VIRGINIA D
V.Chmn, Md. State Dem. Cent. Cmt.
b. Frederick Co, Md, 6/1/05; d. Philip Clark and Effie Snyder C; m. 11/8/23 to James Russell Hahn; c. Rebecca (Mrs. Windsor) and Mary C.(Mrs. Biser). Polit. & Govt. Pos: Pres, Women's Dem. League of Frederick Co, Md, 52-53; West. Md. chmn, United Dem. Women's Clubs of Md, 57-58, state pres, 58-59; mem, Frederick Dem. Cent. Cmt, 58-; chmn, New Market Dist. Dem. Cent. Cmt, 58-; v.chmn, Md. Dem. State Cent. Cmt, 59-; del, Dem. Nat. Conv, 64. Bus. & Prof. Pos: V.pres. and secy, Hahn Transportation, Inc, New Market, Md, 54- and Richmond, Va, 64- Mem: Bd. mem, Childrens Aid Soc. Frederick Co. and Salvation Army, Frederick Co; Frederick Mem. Hosp. Auxiliary; charter pres, Ladies Auxiliary, New Market Vol. Fire Dept; Cedarettes. Rel: Methodist. Mailing Add: 115 Fairview Ave, Frederick, Md. 21701. (1967)

HAIGHT, DAVID HENRY D
Chmn, Fannin Co. Dem. Party, Ga.
b. Sudbury, Ont, Can. 3/16/10; s. David H. Haight, Sr. and Grace Merwin H; m. 8/30/35 to Willa Allen; c. David H, III, Joe Allen and Lewis M. Educ: Syracuse Univ, B.S. in Forestry, 30; Scabbard and Sword; Alpha Phi Sigma. Polit. & Govt. Pos: Local fire chief, Blue Ridge, Ga, 50-68; mem. local sch. bd, 55-60; mem. local tax assessors, 57-65; chmn, Fannin Co. Dem. Party, currently. Mil. Serv: Lt, Navy, Pac. Theatre, 43-45. Mem: Appointed by Gov. to People-to-People tour of Russia as a bus. exec. in contracting; Kiwanis (Lt. Gov, 15th div, Ga). Several Kiwanis awards for outstanding work. Rel: Anglican. Mailing Add: E. Main, Box 696, Blue Ridge, Ga. 30513.

HAILEY, SALLIE D
Secy, Saline Co. Dem. Cmt, Mo.
b. Arrow Rock, Mo, 6/20/03; d. Charles James Wood and Myrtle Poindexter W; m. 10/24/29 to Ernest E. Hailey. Educ: High Sch. Grad. Polit. & Govt. Pos: Secy, Saline Co. Dem. Cmt, Mo, 48-; v.chmn, Mo. del. and mem. platform cmt, Dem. Nat. Conv, 56, del, 64 & 68, co-chmn. rules and order bus. cmt, 68; dir, State Dept. of Bus. and Admin, Mo, 57-64; chmn, Women's Div. of Stuart Symington Campaign for U.S. Sen, 58 & 64 and Edward Long Campaign for U.S. Sen, 62; Dem. Nat. Committeewoman, Mo, 61-68; judge, Saline Co. Court, 65-66. Bus. & Prof. Pos: Off. mgr, Waco Record, Tex, 30-39; cost acct, Aireon Mfg. Co, Slater, Mo, 43-47. Mem: Former pres, Mo. Fedn. of Women's Dem. Clubs; DAR; UDC; Zonta; Mo. and Saline Co. Hist. Socs. Rel: Christian Church. Legal Res: Box 10, Arrow Rock, Mo. 65320. Mailing Add: 155 S. Lafayette St, Marshall, Mo. 65340.

HAIN, B.V. D
Ala. State Rep.
b. Selma, Ala, 9/3/15; s. Jesse Bruce Hain and Ellen May H; m. 4/20/65 to Lilla Davenport Anderson; c. stepson, Marvin Williams Goodwyn, Jr. Educ: Vanderbilt Univ, A.B, 38; Univ. of Ala. Law Sch, LL.B, 41. Polit. & Govt. Pos: Ala. State Rep, 54- Bus. & Prof. Pos: Partner, Hobbs & Hain, Attorneys-at-Law; farmer. Mil. Serv: Lt, Naval Res, 42-46. Mem: Am, Ala. and Dallas Co. Bar Asns; Am. Judicature Soc; Delta Kappa Epsilon. Rel: Baptist. Mailing Add: Box 1190, Selma, Ala. 36701.

HAINES, DAVID GRAVES D
b. Waco, Tex, 7/3/30; s. Paul Graves Haines and Lydie Grabow H; m. 6/23/51 to Virginia Ann Hull; c. Carol Susan, Ellen Ann, Paula Lynn and John David. Educ: Tex. A&M Univ, B.B.A, 51; Sigma Delta Chi. Polit. & Govt. Pos: Tex. State Rep, 62-68. Mil. Serv: Entered as 2nd Lt, Army, 51, released as 1st Lt, 54, after serv. in Field Artil, ETO; 52-54; Army of Occup. Medal. Mem: Elks. Rel: Methodist. 1967 Legal Res: Bryan, Tex. No mailing address available. (1967)

HAINES, DON HUGH D
Chmn, Gila Co. Dem. Cent. Cmt, Ariz.
b. Winkelman, Ariz, 6/22/25; s. Charles Thomas Haines and Alma Scheier H; single. Educ: North. Ariz. Univ, 46-49; Kappa Sigma Sigma; Alpha Psi Omega; Ariz. Playmakers. Polit. & Govt. Pos: Former chmn, Gila Co. Active Dem, Ariz; former mem. exec. cmt, Ariz. State Dem. Party; former Dem. precinct committeeman; del, Dem. Nat. Conv, 68; mem, Steering Cmt, Ariz. Dem. Party, currently; chmn, Gila Co. Dem. Cent. Cmt, 68- Bus. & Prof. Pos: Employee, Christmas Mine Mill. Mil. Serv: Entered as A/S, Navy, 43, released as Seaman 1/C, 46, after serv. in CASU(F) 13, S.Pac, 43-46; Presidential Citation. Publ: 'Act of Compassion' (one act play), Monument, spring 59; 'Sister Bourne—Woman in Levi's,' Ariz. Hwy, 3/68. Mem: USW 586; VFW; Elks. Mailing Add: 519 Cuprite St, Globe, Ariz. 85501.

HAINES, JOAN RENSHAW D
Mem, Ohio State Dem. Exec. Cmt.
b. Phila, Pa, 7/29/34; d. Harry Francis Renshaw and Laura Hendricks R; m. 9/15/56 to John J. Haines; c. John P, Jason R. and Lauren A. Polit. & Govt. Pos: Mem, Geauga Co. Bd. of Elec, Ohio, 66-; exec. v.chmn, Geauga Co. Dem. Party, 66-; mem, Ohio State Dem. Platform Cmt, 68; alternate del, Dem. Nat. Conv, 68; state cent. committeewoman, 11th Cong. Dist. Dem. Party, Ohio, 68-; mem, Ohio State Dem. Exec. Cmt, 68-; mem, Ohio State Dem. Party Reform and Del. Selection Cmt, 69- Mem: League of Women Voters, Geauga Co; Progress Research Club, Chardon. Rel: Protestant. Mailing Add: 10666 Cedar Rd, Chesterland, Ohio 44026.

HAINKEL, JOHN JOSEPH, JR. D
La. State Rep.
b. New Orleans, La, 3/24/38; s. John Joseph Hainkel and Alida Bonnette H; m. 6/10/61 to Kathleen Roth; c. John Joseph, III, Juliet Roth and Alida Camors. Educ: Tulane Univ, B.A, 58, Law Sch, LL.B, 61; Order of Coif; Kappa Alpha. Polit. & Govt. Pos: La. State Rep, 29th Dist, 68- Bus. & Prof. Pos: Assoc. attorney, Porteous and Johnson, New Orleans, La, 61-65; partner, Porteous, Toledano, Hainkel & Johnson, 65- Mem: New Orleans, La. and Am. Bar Asns; New Orleans and La. Defense Counsel Asns; Exchange Club; Am. Farm Bur; Young Men's Bus. Club; K. of C. Most Distinguished Alumni, De La Salle High Sch, 68. Rel: Catholic. Mailing Add: 909 Arabella, New Orleans, La. 70115.

HALABY, NAJEEB E.
b. Dallas, Tex, 11/19/15; s. Najeeb Elias Halaby and Laura Wilkins H; m. 2/9/46 to Doris Carlquist; c. Lisa, Christian and Alexa. Educ: Stanford, A.B, 37; Mich. Univ. Law Sch, 37-38; Yale Univ, LL.B, 40. Hon. LL.D, Allegheny Col, 67 and Loyola Univ, Calif, 68. Polit. & Govt. Pos: Former mem, Chief Intel. Coord. Div, Dept. of State; for. affairs adv. ot Secy. of Defense, 48-53; dep, Mutual Security Affairs, Econ. Coop. Admin, 50-51; Dep. Asst. Secy. of Defense, 52-54; v. chmn, White House Aviation Facilities Study Group, 55-56; adminstr, Fed. Aviation Agency, 61-65. Bus. & Prof. Pos: Gov, Flight Safety Found; lectr, civil mil. rels, Nat. War Col, Air War Col. and Univ. Calif, Los Angeles; dir. and lectr, Aspen Inst; faculty lectr, Sch. Bus. Admin. and dir. defense studies prog, Univ. Calif, Los Angeles; v.pres, Janss Corp; trustee, Aerospace Corp; pres, Am. Tech. Corp; Attorney, O'Melveny & Meyers, Los Angeles, 40-42; attorney-at-law, 40-48 & 54-61; test pilot, Lockheed Aircraft Corp, Burbank, 42-43; assoc, L.S. Rockefeller & Bros, 53-56; exec. v.pres. and dir, Servomechanisms, Inc, 56-58 & 59; dir. and mem. exec. cmt, Pan Am. World Airways, Inc, 65-, pres, 68-; dir, Whirlpool Corp, 68-, UniRoyal, Inc, Bank of Am, San Francisco and Gimbel Bros. Dept. Store, 69- Mil. Serv: Aviator, Navy; Asst. Chief Fighter Sect, Naval Air Test Center, Patuxent River, Md. Mem: Am. Inst. Aeronaut. and Astronaut; Soc. Exp. Test Pilots; Corbey Court; Beta Theta Phi; Phi Delta Phi; Econ. Club of New York; For. Policy Asn; Stanford Assocs; bd. visitors, Stanford Law Sch; trustee, The LeeLanau Schs; bd, N.Y. Urban Coalition Planned Parenthood-World Population; Civil Serv. League; Conf. on Pub. Serv, Nat. Panel, Am. Arbit. Asn; Sky, River, Metrop, Chevy Chase, Burning Tree, Town Hall and Los Angeles Clubs. Legal Res: 1120 Fifth Ave, New York, N.Y. 10028. Mailing Add: Pan American Bldg, New York, N.Y. 10017.

HALACY, DANIEL STEPHEN, JR. R
Ariz. State Sen.
b. Charleston, S.C, 5/16/19; s. Daniel Stephen Halacy, Sr. and Pearl Edwards H; m. 6/2/46 to Beth Ann DeBolt; c. Jessie Ann and Deirdre Jean. Educ: Phoenix Col, A.A, 56; Ariz. State Univ, B.A, 57. Polit. & Govt. Pos: Dist. chmn, Ariz. Rep. Party, 60-64, precinct committeeman, 60-68; Ariz. State Sen, 66-; del, Rep. Nat. Conv, 68. Bus. & Prof. Pos: Number of pos. in aircraft and electronics indust, 39-62; mgr. tech. info, Motorola, 62; free lance writing, currently. Mil. Serv: Entered as Aviation Cadet, Army Air Corps, 43, released as 2nd Lt, 46, after serv. in various Air Force training commands, recalled for Korean serv, 51-52; Air Medal and various theatre ribbons. Publ: Published more than 40 books and several hundred articles and stories. Mem: Solar Energy Soc; Am. Geog. Soc. Rel: Protestant. Legal Res: 5804 W. Vista Ave, Glendale, Ariz. 85301. Mailing Add: Senate Wing, Capitol Bldg, Phoenix, Ariz. 85007.

HALBERT, HERSCHEL OGDEN D
b. Baltimore, Md, 2/17/16; s. Herschel Ogden Halbert and Rebecca Rosalie Buck; div; c. Sarah Innes, David Johns, Stephen Buck and Peter Fraser. Educ: Johns Hopkins Univ, A.B, 38; Gen. Theol. Sem, 39-42; Alpha Delta Phi; Tudor and Stuart Club. Polit. & Govt. Pos: Del, Dem. Nat. Conv, 68. Bus. & Prof. Pos: Secy. for Int. affairs and rep. to UN, Episcopal Church, 63- Mil. Serv: Lt, Naval Res. Publ: Author, articles on South. Africa, human rights and world peace. Rel: Episcopal. Mailing Add: 815 Second Ave, New York, N.Y. 10017.

HALBRITTER, ROBERT C. R
W.Va. State Del.
b. Grafton, W.Va, 5/28/30; s. Arden O. Halbritter and Gertrude Coffman H; m. 5/30/54 to Waneila C. Fisher; c. Marc Alan, Kevin Ashley and John Robert. Educ: Potomac State Col; W.Va. Univ, B.A, 53, Col. of Law, J.D, 54; Mt. Club. Polit. & Govt. Pos: Mem, City Coun, Kingwood, W.Va, 60-62; W.Va. State Del, Preston Co, 67- Mil. Serv: Entered as Pvt, Army, 54, released as Specialist 4/C, 56; Good Conduct Medal. Mem: Am, W.Va. and Preston Co. Bar Asns; v.pres, Kingwood Area C. of C, 63; gen. chmn, Preston Co. Buckwheat Festival, 64; pres, Preston Country Club, 65-66; past secy. & pres, Lions; Kingwood Vol. Fire Dept; past co. chmn, John Barton Payne Chap, Am. Red Cross; past co. fund chmn, March of Dimes; Mason. Rel: Episcopal. Legal Res: 311 Pleasant St, Kingwood, W.Va. 26537. Mailing Add: P.O. Box 55, Kingwood, W.Va. 26537.

HALBROOK, DAVID McCALL D
Miss. State Rep.
b. Belzoni, Miss, 8/8/27; s. John Cullum Halbrook and Ernestine McCall H; m. 10/1/49 to Rita Mary Robertshaw; c. Ann Loree, David McCall, Jr, Lynn Ernestine and Andrew Lee. Educ: Southwest. Ark. Agr. & Mech. Col, 1 semester; Southwest. Univ, 1 semester; Univ. Miss, B.A; Tau Kappa Alpha; Delta Psi. Polit. & Govt. Pos: Pub. rels. coordinator, Miss. State Bd. Health, 49; Miss. State Rep, Dist. 18, Humphreys Co, 68- Bus. & Prof. Pos: Mgr, Halbrook Motor Co, Belzoni, 50-54; mgr, Belzoni Ins. Agency, 54-; secy-treas-agent, Belzoni Realty Co, 58- Mil. Serv: Aviation Cadet, Fifth Div. Naval Air Corps, 45-46. Mem: Miss. Mutual Agents Asn.(exec. secy, 62-, pres); Nat. Asn. Mutual Agents; Mutual Ins. Communicators; Rotary Int; Farm Bur; Am. Legion; Humphreys Co. Country Club; C. of C; Aircraft Owners and Pilots Asn. Mr. Mutual Agent. Rel: Episcopal. Legal Res: 169 Cohn St, Belzoni, Miss. 39038. Mailing Add: P.O. Box 653, Belzoni, Miss. 39038.

HALE, EVERETTE R
Minority Whip, Del. House of Rep.
b. Middletown, Ohio, 7/13/20; s. Stanley F. Hale and Verne McQuinn H; m. 5/25/44 to Charlene Haynes; c. George and Cheryl. Educ: Va. Polytech. Inst, B.S. in chem. eng; Univ. of Del, grad. study in polit. sci. Polit. & Govt. Pos: Del. State Rep, 62-, Minority Whip, Del. House of Rep, 62- Bus. & Prof. Pos: Area supvr, E.I. Dupont, 48- Mil. Serv: Entered as Pvt, Air Force, released as Maj, 45, after serv. in ETO; Air Medal with 4 Oak Leaf Clusters; ETO Ribbon with 5 Battle Stars; Presidential Citation. Mem: AF&AM; K.T; Scottish Rite; Shrine. Rel: Methodist; Mem. Off. Bd. Mailing Add: 109 Meriden Dr, Fairfield, Newark, Del. 19711. (1967)

HALE, JOSEPH ROBERT R
Committeeman, Ill. Rep. Cent. Cmt.
b. Ridgway, Ill, 6/12/27; s. Everett Lee Hale and Grace Jackson H; m. 8/13/50 to Phyllis Ann Miner; c. Susan Lee, Sally Jo and Joseph R, Jr. Educ: Univ. Ill, Urbana, B.S, 50, LL.B, 52; Sigma Nu; Phi Delta Phi. Polit. & Govt. Pos: Co. judge, Gallatin Co, Ill, 54-62; Ill. State Rep, 59th Dist, 63-65; committeeman, Ill. Rep. Cent. Cmt, 21st Cong. Dist, 66- Bus. & Prof. Pos: Dir, First Nat. Bank, Shawneetown; former pres, Tri-Co. Bar Asn. Mil. Serv: Entered as Pvt, Army, 45, released as Pfc, 47, after serv. in Finance Corps, Fifth Army. Mem: Ill. State Bar Asn; Am. Judicature Soc; pres, Ridgway Lions; bd. dirs, Shawneetown C. of C; Am. Legion; 40 et 8. Honors Day, Univ. Ill. Rel: Presbyterian. Legal Res: Main St, Ridgway, Ill. 62979. Mailing Add: Lincoln Blvd. E, Shawneetown, Ill. 62984.

HALE, LOUIS DEWITT D
Tex. State Rep.
b. Caddo Mills, Tex, 6/10/17; s. Ernest Louis Hale and Ethel Massay H; m. 6/8/47 to Carol Gene Moore; c. Janet Sue and Nancy Carol. Educ: Univ. Tex, B.A, 37, M.A, 40; Pi Sigma Alpha; Sigma Iota Epsilon; Rusk Literary Soc. Polit. & Govt. Pos: Asst. dist. supvr, Work Proj. Admin, 40-41; classification analyst, Off. Emergency Mgt, 41-43; classification officer, Off. Defense Transportation, 43; Tex. State Rep, 39-40, 53-62 & 65-, mem, Tex. Legis. Coun, 54-55, Tex. Civil Judicial Coun, 61-65 & 69- and Speaker-Pro-Tem, 62, Tex. State House of Rep. Bus. & Prof. Pos: V.pres, Nueces Invest. Corp, 55-57; secy, Ulrich Bros, Inc, 60- Mil. Serv: Entered as Pvt, Army Air Force, 43, released as 1st Lt, 46, after serv. in Hq, Strategic Air Command; Lt. Col, Air Force Res, 46-66; Commendation Medal. Publ: 'Streamlining Classification,' 6/45 and 'Let's Rewrite the Classification Act,' 6/46, Personnel Admin. Mem: Am. Bar Asn; State Bar of Tex; Tex. State Teachers Asn; ROA; C. of C; Jr. C. of C; Am. Legion; Lions; Longhorn Club; Young Dem. Club. Rel: Baptist. Legal Res: 226 Lorraine Dr, Corpus Christi, Tex. 78411. Mailing Add: 205 Wilson Bldg, Corpus Christi, Tex. 78401.

HALE, MADDOX JEROME D
Ga. State Rep.
b. Trenton, Ga, 8/18/08; s. Shadrach Jerome Hale and Clara Street H; m. 4/06/47 to Mauline Morrison. Educ: Chattanooga Col. of Law, 31, LL.B, LL.D, 33; Sigma Delta Kappa. Polit. & Govt. Pos: City attorney, Trenton, Ga, 38-43 & 46-; Ga. State Rep, 49-54 & 59-; co. attorney, 50- Bus. & Prof. Pos: Attorney-at-law. Mem: Lions; dir, Coosa River Area Develop. Asn. Rel: Methodist; Steward, Trustee, former Sunday Sch. Supt, Trenton Church; Holston Conf. Mailing Add: Trenton, Ga. 30752. (1967)

HALE, PHALE DOPHIS D
Ohio State Rep.
b. Starksville, Miss, 7/16/15; s. Church Hale and Lee Ellen H; m. to Cleo Marian Ingram; c. Phale Dophis, Jr, Janice Ellen, Marna Amoretta and Hilton Ingram. Educ: Morehouse Col, A.B, 40; Gammon Theol. Sem, B.D, 44; Chapel Sch. Theol, D.D, 48. Polit. & Govt. Pos: Ohio State Rep, currently. Bus. & Prof. Pos: Pastor, Union Grove Baptist Church, 50- Mem: Inter-Denominational Ministers Alliance; Ohio Pastors Conf; Baptist Pastor's Conf; Columbus Area Coun. Pastor's Conf; Ohio Coun. of Churches; chmn, bd. dirs, Am. Baptist Theol. Sem; Ohio Baptist General Asn; Nat. Baptist Conv, USA, Inc; Nat. Sunday Sch. and B.T.U. Cong; exec. secy, Social Action Cmn, Ohio Baptist State Conv; bd. dirs, Ment. Health Asn; Mason; v.pres, Frontiers, Int; past pres, NAACP Leadership Conf; Columbus Urban League; Credit Union. Rel: Baptist. Mailing Add: 266 N. Champion Ave, Columbus, Ohio 43203. (1967)

HALE, PRESTON L. D
b. Carroll Co, Md, 10/15/10; married. Educ: Baltimore and Carroll Co. pub. schs. Polit. & Govt. Pos: Mem, Carroll Co. Bd. of Elec. Supvr, Md, 51-54; Md. State Del, 59-63 & 65-67. Bus. & Prof. Pos: Ins; real estate. Mem: Mason; past pres, Hampstead Lions. Mailing Add: Hampstead, Md. 21074.

HALE, ROBERT R
b. Portland, Maine, 11/29/89; s. Clarence Hale and Margaret Rollins H; m. 4/20/22 to Agnes Burke; c. Patricia. Educ: Bowdoin Col, A.B, 10; Oxford Univ, B.A. in Jurisp, 12; Harvard Law Sch; Phi Beta Kappa; Psi Upsilon. Polit. & Govt. Pos: Mem. of Mission Sent to Finland, Estonia, Latvia and Lithuania by Am. Cmn. to Negotiate Peace, 19; Maine State Rep, 23-30; U.S. Rep. Maine, 43-59. Bus. & Prof. Pos: Lawyer; secy, treas. and trustee of various Institutions; overseer, Bowdoin Col. Mil. Serv: Entered as Pvt, Army, 17, released as 2nd Lt, 19, after serv. in various units; Capt, Army Res. Publ: But I Too Hate Roosevelt, Harper, 36; 'The United States and the War,' Speeches printed in book form, 40; 'Congressional Farewell,' New Yorker. Mem: Am. Legion. Rel: Congregational. Legal Res: Portland, Maine. Mailing Add: 1000 Vermont Ave, Washington, D.C. 20005.

HALEY, FRANCES SHALLER R
Committeewoman, Sequoyah Co. Rep. Party, Okla.
b. Canadian, Tex, 12/18/32; d. Frank Jefferson Shaller and Lillian Pauliae McMordie S; m. 3/20/54 to James Evetts Haley, Jr; c. Mary Ann, James Evetts, III, Frank Jefferson and Frances Sabrina. Educ: Stephens Col, 1 year; Univ. Tex, Austin, 51-53; Delta Delta Delta. Polit. & Govt. Pos: V.pres, Sequoyah Co. Rep. Womans Federated Club, Okla, 67; committeewoman, Sequoyah Co. Rep. Party, 67-; alternate del, Rep. Nat. Conv, 68. Bus. & Prof. Pos: Owner and mgr, Book Shop, 65-68. Rel: Lutheran-Mo. Synod. Mailing Add: Route 4, Sallisaw, Okla. 74955.

HALEY, JAMES ANDREW D
U.S. Rep, Fla.
b. Jacksonville, Ala, 1/4/99; s. Andrew Jackson Haley and Mary Lee Stevenson H; m. to Aubrey B. Ringling. Educ: Univ. Ala, 19-20. Polit. & Govt. Pos: Chmn, Sarasota Co. Dem. Exec. Cmt, Fla, 32-52; Fla. State Rep, 48-52; U.S. Rep, Fla, 52-; del, Dem. Nat. Conv, 52 & 60. Bus. & Prof. Pos: Pres. and dir, Ringling Bros. Barnum & Bailey Circus, 46-48. Mil. Serv: Army, World War I. Mem: Am. Legion; 40 et 8; VFW; SAR; Mason; Elks. Rel: Methodist. Legal Res: Sarasota, Fla. Mailing Add: 20 Fifth St. S.E, Washington, D.C. 20003.

HALEY, K. DANIEL D
b. Ogdensburg, N.Y, 5/25/29; s. Leon Frank Haley and Virginia Baker H; div; c. Isabel Virginia. Educ: Harvard Col, A.B. cum laude. Polit. & Govt. Pos: V.consul, Am. Embassy, Saigon, 53; training officer, U.S. Aid Mission to Brazil, 58-60; cand, U.S. House Rep, 31st Dist, N.Y, 68. Bus. & Prof. Pos: Mgr, Underwood Dealership, Brazil, 60-62; mgr. Brazilian subsidiary, Mosler Safe Co, 62-64, distributor for Brazil, 64-68. Mil. Serv: Entered as Pvt, Air Force, 54, released as 1st Lt, 57, after serv. in Air Intel. Group, Far East Air Force, 55-57. Publ: The Rural Crisis, privately publ, 68. Mem: Harvard Club of N.Y. Rel: Episcopal. Mailing Add: Waddington, N.Y. 13694.

HALL, AMY EVELYN R
b. Avon, Mont, 12/24/23; d. William McGilluray and Jennie Elizabeth Nelson M; m. 12/26/50 to Richard E. Hall; c. Richard Daniel, Gilluray and Amy Elizabeth. Educ: Deaconess Hosp. Sch. Nursing, Spokane, Wash, R.N, 46. Polit. Pos: Chmn, Union Co. Cmt, Ore. Rep. Cent. Cmt, 64-66 and v.chmn, 62-64; precinct committeewoman, Union Co. Rep. Cmt, 62-66. Prof. Pos: Relief nurse in charge, Vet. Admin. Hosp, Helena, Mont, 49-50 and staff nurse, 46-48; supv. nurse and in-charge hosp. floor, S.Shore Hosp, Chicago, Ill, 48-49. Mem: Eastern Star. Rel: Methodist. Mailing Add: Route 1, Box 258, La Grande, Ore. 97850. (1967)

HALL, BILLY D
b. Henderson, Tex, 9/28/09; s. Homer Hall and Belle Turner H; single. Educ: W.Tex. Univ, 30-31; Cumberland Univ, LL.B, 34. Polit. & Govt. Pos: Alternate del, Dem. Nat. Conv, 68; Dem. chmn, Precinct 12, Littlefield, Lamb Co, Tex, 68-69. Mem: Tex. Asn. Plaintiff's Attorneys; Tex. Bar Asn; Odd Fellows; Elks. Rel: Methodist. Mailing Add: 306½ Phelps Ave, Littlefield, Tex. 79339.

HALL, CHARLES EDWARD D
Mem, Calif. Dem. State Cent. Cmt.
b. Plum, Tex, 4/28/30; s. H. Boyd Hall and Semoria Moore H; m. 9/8/57 to Wynona Toms; c. Apryl Wynee, H. Boyd and Arnice Natell. Educ: Fisk Univ, A.B, 54; Meharry Med. Col, D.D.S, 58; Omega Psi Phi. Polit. & Govt. Pos: 55th Assoc, 55th Assembly Dist, Los Angeles, Calif, 67; mem, Calif. Dem. State Cent. Cmt, 68-; mem, Commun. Develop. Agency, Los Angeles, 69. Bus. & Prof. Pos: Dentist, 58- Mil. Serv: Entered as Pvt, Army, 51, released as Cpl, 53, after serv. in 32nd Inf. Regt, Seventh Div, Far E. Korea, 52-53; Purple Heart; Commendation Ribbon with Metal Pendant; Combat Inf. Badge; Good Conduct Ribbon; various serv. ribbons. Mem: Nat. and Am. Dent. Asns; Angel City and South. Calif. Dent. Socs; Watts Med, Dent, Pharmaceutical Asn. Rel: Baptist. Legal Res: 4315 Olympiad Dr, Los Angeles, Calif. 90043. Mailing Add: 11504 S. Central Ave, Los Angeles, Calif. 90059.

HALL, CRAYTON GREEN R
Chmn, Rep. State Cent. Cmt, La.
b. Columbus, Ga, 3/24/25; s. Cecil Dempsey Hall and Lillian Green H; m. 9/5/48 to Ida Mae Crochet; c. Larry Michael, Cecil Edmond and Connie Marie. Educ: Northwest. State Col, La, B.S. in physics, 51; Sigma Tau Gamma. Polit. & Govt. Pos: Chmn. precinct orgn, East Baton Rouge, La, 63-64; campaign mgr, Sixth Dist. Cong. Cand, 64; chmn, precinct orgn. for Goldwater Campaign, 64; chmn, Rep. Polit. Action Coun, 65; Rep. nominee for Cong. Sixth Dist, 66; del, Rep. Nat. Conv, 68; Rep. nominee for Mayor of Baton Rouge, 68; state chmn. labor, La. Rep. Party, 68; chmn. Sixth Cong. Dist, Rep. State Cent. Cmt, 68- Bus. & Prof. Pos: Develop. engr, Ethyl Corp, 52- Mil. Serv: Entered as A/S, Navy, 42, released as Radioman 2/C, 46, after serv. in Armed Guard and 7th Fleet, all theatres including Philippines, 42-46. Mem: Am. Inst. Chem. Engrs; Am. Legion; Mason; Boy Scouts; SAR. Rel: Non-Denominational. Mailing Add: 12425 Castle Hill Dr, Baton Rouge, La. 70814.

HALL, DAVID McGIFFERT R
Chmn, Greene Co. Rep. Cmt, Ala.
b. Moundville, Ala, 1/8/10; s. Dr. David M. Hall and Louise Elliott H; m. 10/8/49 to Lida Meriwether; c. Lida Rogers. Educ: Birmingham-South. Col, A.B, 31; Univ. Ala, LL.B, 36; Omicron Delta Kappa; Phi Alpha Delta; Kappa Alpha. Polit. & Govt. Pos: Ala. State Rep, 35-39; Ala. State Sen, 57-59; chmn, Greene Co. Rep. Cmt, currently. Bus. & Prof. Pos: Attorney. Mil. Serv: Entered as Capt, Army, 41, released as Lt. Col, 46, after serv. in XV Corps, ETO; Am. Defense Medal; Am. Theater Serv. Medal; European African Medal; East. Theater Serv. Medal with Two Bronze Stars; Victory Medal; Army Commendation Ribbon; Col, Army Res, 46-61. Mem: Ala. Bar Asn; Am. Legion; VFW. Rel: Methodist. Legal Res: 314 Eatman Ave, Eutaw, Ala. 34562. Mailing Add: P.O. Box 596, Eutaw, Ala. 35462.

HALL, DURWARD GORHAM R
U.S. Rep, Mo.
b. Cassville, Mo, 9/14/10; s. Thomas C. Hall and Omah Neill H; m. 9/6/31 to Mary Elizabeth Turner; c. Linda Lea (Mrs. Ellison). Educ: Drury Col, A.B, 30; Rush Med. Sch, Univ. Chicago, M.D, 34; Theta Kappa Nu scholarship key; Beta Beta Beta; Alpha Omega Alpha; Lambda Alpha Chi. Polit. & Govt. Pos: U.S. Rep, Seventh Cong. Dist, Mo, 61- Bus. & Prof. Pos: Intern, St. Elizabeths Hosp, D.C, 34-36; physician and surgeon, 36-60. Mil. Serv: Entered as 1st Lt, Army, 40, released as Col, 46, after serv. as Asst. Surgeon Gen, Dept. Army and Chief, Personnel Serv, Med. Corps; Legion of Honor; Commendation Ribbon and Two Palms; Col.(Ret), Army, Res, 65. Publ: Personnel in World War II, Dept. of Army Med. Dept, 63 and Cong. Record. Mem: Life fel, Am. Col. of Surgeons; dipl, Am. Bd. of Surg; Mo. del, Am. Med. Asn, 51-66; bd. trustees, Drury Col; Springfield, Mo. and U.S. C. of C; MOWW; Nat. Coun, Boy Scouts; YMCA; Rotary. Cong. adv, XV World Health Assembly, Geneva, 62. Rel: Baptist. Legal Res: 2442 S. Fremont St, Springfield, Mo. 65804. Mailing Add: 2351 Rayburn House Office Bldg, Washington, D.C. 20515.

HALL, EARL WELLS R
Chmn, Jefferson Co. Rep. Cmt, Ala.
b. Haleyville, Ala, 12/6/24; s. Oliver Beauregard Hall and Alene Wells H; m. 6/27/47 to Mary Jacqueline Brislin; c. Earl W, Jr. and Murray O.B. Educ: Univ. Pittsburgh; Birmingham-South. Col, 3 years; Univ. Ala, LL.B, 51; Phi Alpha Delta; Kappa Alpha. Polit. & Govt. Pos: Munic. judge, Gardendale, Ala, 64-66; mem, Ala. State Rep. Cmt, 67; chmn, Jefferson Co. Rep. Cmt, Ala, 67-; del, Rep. Co, State and Nat. Conv, 68. Mil. Serv: Entered as Pilot Cadet, Air Force, 43, released as 2nd Lt, 45, after serv. in Air Transport Command, Am. Theater, 45. Mem: Ala. Munic. Judges Asn. (secy, 67); Ala. and Birming-

ham Bar Asns; Jefferson Co. Munic. Judges Asn.(secy, treas, v.pres and pres, 65-67); The Club; VFW; Am. Legion; Eagles. Rel: Methodist. Legal Res: 2210 Montreat Circle, Vestavia, Ala. 35216. Mailing Add: 825 Frank Nelson Bldg, Birmingham, Ala. 35203.

HALL, EDWARD THOMAS R
Minority Leader, Md. State Senate
b. Calvert County, Md, 8/15/16; s. Charles Wesley Hall and Bessie Virginia Bowen H; m. 1/12/59 to Irma Bernice Sweeney. Educ: Ottmar Mergenthaler Sch. of Printing, 34-37; spec. course Strayers Col, 35 and City Col, Baltimore, 36. Polit. & Govt. Pos: Md. State Sen, 59-, Minority Leader, Md. State Senate, 59-; del, Rep. Nat. Conv, 68. Bus. & Prof. Pos: Owner and publisher, Calvert Independent. Mem: Fire Dept; Lions; Hist. Soc; Farm Bur; Sportsmen Club; C. of C; Bd. of Trade; Yacht Club. Rel: Methodist. Mailing Add: Prince Frederick, Calvert County, Md. 20678. (1967)

HALL, EDWIN ARTHUR, JR. R
b. Binghamton, N.Y, 2/11/09; s. Edwin Arthur Hall and Harriet Babcock H; first wife deceased; m. 12/31/58 to Freida Stein; c. Eric Ashley, Charles Milton, George Richard, Marlyce, David Reginald, Edwin Arthur, III and Marriet Bowser. Educ: Cornell Univ, 27-28; Chi Phi. Polit. & Govt. Pos: Mem, Broome Co. Rep. Cmt, N.Y, 35-37; del, N.Y. State Rep. Conv, 36; city councilman, Binghamton, 37-39; U.S. Rep, N.Y, 39-53; admin. asst. to N.Y. State Assemblyman Richard Knauf, 53-54; acct. clerk, Syracuse State Sch, 54-56; admin. asst, U.S. Dept. Agr, N.Y, 56-58; dir, Silver Lake Twp. Sch. Bd, Pa, 62-65, pres, 63-65; dir, Montrose Area Sch. Bd, Pa, 65- Mem: Pres, Binghamton Chap, Am. Inst. Banking, 36; Preston Grange, N.Y, 45-61; Nat. Grange, 46-50; Lawsville Grange. Winner, N.Y-New Eng. Oratorical Contest and participant and rep. of N.Y-New Eng. Dist, Nat. Oratorical Competition, A.P. Gianinni Found, 35, served as U.S. Rep. from Broome Co, N.Y. longer than any other person in history. Rel: Episcopal. Mailing Add: Indian Mountain, Brackney, Pa. 18812.

HALL, EVELYN ELIZABETH R
b. Granby, Conn, 2/9/17; d. Lawrence J. Kupruck and Helen Y. K; m. 6/22/40 to Albert James Hall; c. Judson Edward, Judith Evelyn, Albert James, Jr. and John Douglas. Polit. & Govt. Pos: Mem, Town Rep. Cmt, Granby, Conn, 42-, secy, 52-60; Justice of the Peace, Granby, 52-60 & 67-; Conn. State Rep, 63-67; mem, Conn. Order of Women Legislators and Nat. Order of Women Legislators, 63-; pres, Women's Rep. Club of Granby, 67- Mem: Charter mem, Farmington Valley Bus. and Prfnl. Women's Club, 65; dir, Hartford Co. YWCA, 44-59, v.pres, 55-59; dir, Granby Hist. Soc; pres, Salmon Brook Hist. Soc, 68-; Granby chmn, Hartford Symphony; dir, Granby Civic Club. Rel: Protestant. Mailing Add: 41 Salmon Brook St, Granby, Conn. 06035.

HALL, F. RILEY R
Mem, Marion Co. Rep. Exec. Cmt, Ohio
b. Columbus, Ohio, 12/26/22; s. John H. Hall and Ila M. Secrest; m. 11/47 to Geraldine A. Jones; c. Virginia, Carol, Susan and Kevin. Educ: Ohio North. Univ, LL.B, 51; Sigma Delta Kappa. Polit. & Govt. Pos: Solicitor, Marion, Ohio, 56-60; mem, Marion Co. Rep. Exec. Cmt, currently, chmn, 62-64. Mil. Serv: Entered as Pvt, Army, 43, released as S/Sgt, 46 after serv. in 102nd Inf. Div, ETO; ETO Ribbon; Expert Infantryman. Mem: Pres, Marion Co. Bar Asn, 65; Lions; Mason; Marion County Club; Am. Legion; Toastmasters. Rel: Baptist. Mailing Add: 600 Summit St, Marion, Ohio 43302. (1967)

HALL, FERN L. R
Secy, Colo. Rep. State Cent. Cmt.
b. Rugby, N.Dak, 1/5/34; d. George R. Livingston and Sadie F. McCabe L; m. 7/26/56 to Richard P. Hall; c. Jennifer Ann. Educ: North. Mont. Col, 2 years. Polit. & Govt. Pos: Secy, United Rep. Fund of Colo, 61-62; secy, Speaker of Colo. House of Rep, 63-69; dist. capt, S.E. Jefferson Co. Rep. Party, Colo, 65-67; v.chmn, State Rep. Dist, 67-69; bd. mem, Rep. Workshops of Colo; secy, Colo. Rep. State Cent. Cmt, 69- Rel: Lutheran. Legal Res: 5405 Ridge Trail, Littleton, Colo. 80120. Mailing Add: Republican State Headquarters, Room 205, 1711 Pennsylvania, Denver, Colo. 80203.

HALL, FRED WILLIAM, JR. R
b. Franklin, N.H, 9/22/20; s. Fred W. Hall and Grace Canney H; m. 9/23/50 to Jane Fell Coe; c. Marcella, Susan and John. Educ: Univ. N.H, B.S, 41; Univ. Mich. Law Sch, LL.B, 48. Polit. & Govt. Pos: Solicitor, Strafford Co, N.H, 51 and Rochester, 61-62; mem; Gov. Coun, 63-64. Bus. & Prof. Pos: Pres, N.H. Bar Asn, 65-66; partner, Cooper, Hall & Walker, Rochester, N.H. Mil. Serv: Entered as 2nd Lt, Army, 41, released as Maj, 52, after serv. in 1st Inf. Div, 2nd Army Dist, Mediterranean-ETO; Combat Inf. Badge; Silver Star with Oak Leaf Cluster; Croix de Guerre with Silver Star; Dist. Unit Citation with 2 Oak Leaf Clusters; Bronze Star with 2 Oak Leaf Clusters; Lt. Col, Army Res, 52-66. Mem: Am. Bar Asn; chmn, bd. trustees, Univ. N.H; Rotary; Am. Legion. Rel: Episcopal. Legal Res: 5 Sunset Dr, Rochester, N.H. 03867. Mailing Add: 11 Wakefield St, Rochester, N.H. 03867.

HALL, GODFREY WORTH R
Chmn, Ward Four Rep. Party, Lowell, Mass.
b. Grafton, Vt, 10/1/14; s. George Washington Hall, II and Violet Turner H; m. 6/14/41 to Edna Dolly Osborne; c. Anthony Richard. Educ: Boston Univ, 33-36; Suffolk Law Sch, 37-40. Polit. & Govt. Pos: Notary Public, Mass, 53-; chmn, Ward Four Rep. Party, Lowell, Mass, 66- Mil. Serv: Entered as Pvt, Air Force, 42, released as Sgt, 46, after serv. in 1346th Army Air Force Base Unit, China-Burma-India, 44-46; Am. Serv, Good Conduct, World War II Victory and Asiatic-Pac. Serv. Medals. Mem: F&AM Most Worshipful Prince Hall Grand Lodge of Mass. Rel: Protestant. Mailing Add: 111 Inland St, Lowell, Mass. 01851.

HALL, HARBER HOMER R
Ill. State Rep.
b. Chicago, Ill, 9/24/20; s. Harry Hall and Dorothy Harber H; m. 1/27/59 to Jeanette Buttell. Educ: Univ. Miami, Fla, 39-41. Polit. & Govt. Pos: Co. treas, McLean Co, Ill, 62-66; Ill. State Rep, currently. Bus. & Prof. Pos: Pres, Brookside Farms, Inc. Mil. Serv: Entered as Aviation Cadet, Air Force, 42, released as Maj, 56, after serv. in Hq. Mil. Air Transport Serv; Distinguished Flying Cross with 1 Oak Leaf Cluster; Air Medal with 7 Oak Leaf Clusters; Medal for Humane Action; Berlin Air Life; Pac, European, Am. Theater Ribbons; Presidential Citation. Mem: Pres, Ill. Co. Treas. Asn, 66-67; v.pres, Co. Treas. Asn, 62-66; Mason; Consistory; Shrine; Am. Legion. Rel: Presbyterian. Mailing Add: 1202 E. Jefferson, Bloomington, Ill. 61701.

HALL, HENRY GOODWIN D
b. Kite, Ga, 4/13/06; s. Charlie L. Hall and Mary Kea H; m. 4/02/34 to Katybel Moore; c. Marinel (Mrs. Rhodes), Joyce Ann and James M. Educ: Newton High Sch. Polit. & Govt. Pos: Ga. State Rep, 57-69. Bus. & Prof. Pos: Farmer. Mem: Mason; Shrine; Lions. Rel: Baptist. Mailing Add: Leesburg, Ga. 31763. (1967)

HALL, JAMES BATTLE D
b. Swainsboro, Ga, 10/15/14; s. Bennett W. Hall and Mattie Waller H; m. 12/26/38 to Anna Whitlock; c. James Battle, Jr, Judy Ann. Educ: Berry Col, B.S, 38; Univ. Ga, M.Ed, 49. Polit. & Govt. Pos: Ga. State Rep, 51-62; Ga. State Sen, 63-67. Bus. & Prof. Pos: Gen. ins. Rel: Baptist. Mailing Add: Rome, Ga. 30161. (1967)

HALL, JAMES MERWIN R
Chmn, Stone Co. Rep. Cmt, Mo.
b. Clever, Mo, 12/15/11; s. James Allen Hall (deceased) and Mabelle Sherd H; m. 4/23/32 to Frances Dunivant; c. Connie Sue and Jane Ann (Mrs. Larry E. Cox). Educ: Southwest Mo. State Col, B.S. in Sci, 42; Mo. Univ, M.E, 47; Phi Delta Kappa. Polit. & Govt. Pos: Chmn, Stone Co. Rep. Cmt, Mo, 48- Bus. & Prof. Pos: Teacher rural schs, Stone Co, Mo, 33-39; supt. & prin. schs, Galena, 40-45; supt. schs, Spokane, 45-51 & 64-68; co. supt. schs, Stone Co, 51-55; supt. schs, Blue Eye, 55-56, Hurley, 56-63, Chadwick, 63-64 and Fordland Schs, 68- Mem: Webster Co. Teachers Asn.(chmn, 68-); Mason; Shrine; chmn, Polio Drive, 45-51; past chmn, Stone Co. Am. Red Cross, United Serv. Orgn; past scoutmaster, Galena Boy Scouts Am; chmn, Stone Co. Regional Libr, 51-; charter mem, Galena Lions Club; Clever Lions Club, plus others. Rel: Methodist. Mailing Add: Route 1, Clever, Mo. 65631.

HALL, JOHN CLEVELAND D
Minority Leader, Mont. House of Rep.
b. Great Falls, Mont, 11/4/30; s. H. Cleveland Hall and Georgia Coleman H; single. Educ: Univ. Mich, A.B, 52; Law Sch, J.D, 54; Sigma Delta Pi; Phi Kappa Phi; Phi Eta Sigma; Phi Beta Kappa; Order of the Coif. Polit. & Govt. Pos: Asst. to legal adv, U.S. Dept. State, 55-57; dep. co. attorney, Cascade Co, Mont, 58-62; mem. bd. trustee, Great Falls Pub. Libr, 62-65; Mont. State Rep, 64-, Minority Leader, Mont. State House Rep, 69-; chmn, Great Falls Fire Cmn, 67-; city-co. planning bd, Great Falls, 69- Bus. & Prof. Pos: Assoc, Hall, Alexander & Kuenning, Great Falls, Mont, 57-63; partner, Hall, Alexander & Kuenning, 63; partner, Alexander, Kuenning & Hall, 63- Mem: Am, Mont. and Cascade Co. Bar Asns; Elks; Rotary. Rel: Episcopal. Mailing Add: 1020 Third Ave. N, Great Falls, Mont, 59401.

HALL, JOHN EMORY R
Chmn, Whiteside Co. Rep. Party, Ill.
b. Rock Falls, Ill, 1/9/13; s. Emery John Hall and Ebal Osborn H; m. 8/29/37 to Esther Arlene Bley; c. Peggy (Mrs. Lawrence Dunlap), Ginny (Mrs. John Butzer) and John Fredric. Educ: Sterling Twp. High Sch, 4 years; Bus. and sales course under, Nat. Recovery Admin, 2 years; typing and shorthand course, 2 years. Polit. & Govt. Pos: Chief clerk, State Police Dist. 1, Ill, 41-49; precinct committeeman, Rep. Party, Sterling, 43-; investr, Ill. Commerce Cmn, 53-54; chief clerk, State Treas, 54-56; clerk circuit court, Whiteside Co, 56-68; chmn, Whiteside Co. Rep. Party, 66-; appellate court clerk, 3rd Dist, 69- Bus. & Prof. Pos: Employee bus. off. finance dept, Sterling Daily Gazette, Ill, 49-53; owner Restaurant and Lounge, N.Sterling, 52-54. Mem: Mason; Shrine; Elks; Moose; Hist. Soc. PTA; past pres, court clerk's of Ill; past pres, Co. Off. of Ill. Rel: Protestant. Mailing Add: 1506 Locust St, Sterling, Ill. 61081.

HALL, LEONARD WOOD R
b. Oyster Bay, N.Y, 10/2/00; s. Franklyn H. Hall and Mary Garvin H; m. 5/10/34 to Gladys Dowsey; stepchild: H.W. Carroll. Educ: Georgetown Univ. Law Sch, LL.B, 20; C.W. Post Col, LL.D. Polit. & Govt. Pos: N.Y. State Assemblyman, 27-28 & 34-38; sheriff, Nassau Co, 29-31, surrogate, 53; chmn, Nassau Co. Bd. of Ethics; U.S. Rep, N.Y, 39-53; chmn, Nat. Rep. Cong. Cmt, 47-53; chmn, Rep. Nat. Cmt, 53-57; campaign chmn, Nixon for Pres. Campaign, 60; chmn, Nassau-Suffolk Regional Planning Bd, 65-; mem, N.Y. State Banking Bd, 69- Bus. & Prof. Pos: Partner, Hall, Casey, Dickler & Howley; dir, Servo Corp. Am, 59- and Beneficial Nat. Life Ins. Co, 63-; mem, Mitchel Field Develop. Corp, currently. Publ: 'An Old Pro Describes How Politics in U.S. Has Changed,' Life, 4/60; 'What's Wrong with the Republican Party,' Newsday, 3/65. Mem: Nassau and N.Y. State Bar Asns; Mason; Elks; mem. exec. cmt, United Fund of L.I; Metrop. Club, Wash, D.C; Nassau Country Club. Rel: Episcopal. Legal Res: Feeks Lane, Locust Valley, N.Y. 11560. Mailing Add: 600 Old Country Rd, Garden City, N.Y. 11530.

HALL, LEWIS HARVEY, JR. D
b. Battery Park, Isle of Wight Co, Va, 10/5/07; s. Levin Henry Hall and Mary Elizabeth White H; m. 7/5/41 to Isabel Thomas; c. Isabel (Mrs. Atlee). Educ: Wofford Col, A.B, 37; Fordham Univ. Polit. & Govt. Pos: Chmn, York Co. Del, Va. State Conv, 64; del, Dem. Nat. Conv, 64, Bus. & Prof. Pos: Practice-of-Law, 45- Mil. Serv: Served in Merchant Marine, 42-45, leaving serv. with rank of Chief Officer Aboard Ship. Mem: Am, Va. State and Newport News Bar Asns; The Va. Bar; Int. Asn. of Ins. Counsel; Am. Judicature Soc; Va. and Am. Trial Lawyers Asns; Int. Soc. of Barristers; Elks; SAR; James River Country Club; Whitehall, Warwick and Old Point Clubs. Rel: Methodist. Legal Res: Route 4, Box 180, Yorktown, Va. 23490. Mailing Add: 219 27th St, Newport News, Va. 23607.

HALL, LILBOURNE PRESTON R
Mem, Exec. Cmt, Lauderdale Co. Rep. Cmt, Ala.
b. Florence, Ala, 2/3/22; s. Lamar Petway Hall and Maude Evelyn Murphree H; m. 7/23/49 to Helen Elizabeth Mattox; c. Gregory, Jeffrey, Zachary and Peri. Educ: N.C. Univ, Chapel Hill, 42-43; Florence State Univ, B.S, 45; Peabody Col, M.A, 47; Kappa Delta Pi; Kappa Mu Epsilon. Polit. & Govt. Pos: V.chmn, Lauderdale Co. Rep. Cmt, Ala, 58-62, mem. exec. cmt, 60-, chmn,

64-66, cand. recruitment chmn, 64-66; cand, Bd. of Educ, Lauderdale Co, 62, mem, Ala. State Rep. Exec. Cmt, 62-64. Bus. & Prof. Pos: Teacher, math. and sci, Leighton High Sch, 45-46 & 47-48; teaching fel, Peabody Col, 46-47; life underwriter, Pilot Life Ins. Co, Florence, 53-54; life underwriter, Jackson Life Ins. Co, 54-58, regional mgr, 58- Mil. Serv: Pvt, Army Air Force, 42-43. Publ: Various articles in Ins. Mag. Mem: Life Underwriter Asn. Ala Boy Scouts (field exec, Tenn. Valley Coun, 48-53). Silver Beaver Award, Bo. Scouts; Number One Sales Award, Jackson Life Ins. Co, 10 of last 11 years. Rel: Lutheran-Mo. Synod; Bd. Elders; pres. congregation; Sunday Sch. teacher, Our Redeemer Lutheran Church. Mailing Add: 2128 Old Cloverdale Rd, Florence, Ala. 35630.

HALL, LYLE GILLIS D
b. Ridgway, Pa, 11/2/29; s. Lyle Gillis Hall (deceased) and Jane Grube H. (deceased); m. 11/5/55 to Lisbeth Jordan; c. Alexander Gillis, Megan Eugenia, Charlotte Grube and Cara Catherine. Educ: Yale Univ. Polit. & Govt. Pos: Former Pa. State Sen, 26th Dist. Bus. & Prof. Pos: Treas. and dir, Stackpole Carbon Co, St. Marys, Pa; pres. and dir, Can. Stackpole Ltd, Toronto, Ont; treas. and dir, Phin, Inc, Bloomfield, N.J; treas. and dir, St. Marys Sewer Pipe Co, Pa; v.chmn. and dir, Elk Co. Bank and Trust Co, St. Mary; mem. exec. bd, Bucktail Coun, Boy Scouts Am; pres. and dir, Ridgway Publ. Co; dir, St. Marys Boys Club, St. Marys; pres. bd. trustees, Elk Co. Gen. Hosp, Ridgway; mem. bd. trustees, Episcopal Diocese, Erie. Mil. Serv: Sgt, Marine Corps, 51-54. Mem: Elk Co. Country Club, Ridgway, Pa; St. Marys Country Club, St. Marys; Pennhills Club, Bradford; Am. Legion, Ridgway; Elks; Yale Club, N.Y.C; Valley Hunt Club, Bradford. Rel: Episcopal. Legal Res: 602 Hyde Ave, Ridgway, Pa. 15853. Mailing Add: Stackpole Carbon Co, St. Marys, Pa. 15857.

HALL, MURIEL FISHER D
b. Miami, Fla, 9/9/28; d. Dr. Raymond Holmes Fisher and Muriel Mullinaux F; m. 11/4/50 to Miles Lewis Hall, Jr; c. Miles Lewis, III and Don Thomas. Educ: Ward-Belmont Jr. Col, 46-48; Univ. N.C, A.B, 50; Delta Delta Delta. Polit. & Govt. Pos: Del, Dem. Nat. Conv, 68. Mem: Jr. League Miami, Inc.(pres, 63); PEO; Ch Ak; bd, United Fund Women; bd, Coral Gables War Mem. Youth Center; bd. trustees, United Fund. Rel: Methodist. Mailing Add: 2907 Alhambra Circle, Coral Gables, Fla. 33134.

HALL, NANCY JOHNSON D
State Treas, Ark.
b. Prescott, Ark, 10/5/04; d. George Sim Johnson and Minnie Bryan J; m. 10/5/29 to Claris G. Hall; c. Nancy (Mrs. R. Bailey). Educ: High Sch, Little Rock, Ark. Polit. & Govt. Pos: Asst. Secy. of State, Ark, 37-61; Secy. of State, 61-63, State Treas, 63- Bus. & Prof. Pos: Formerly head steno, Ark. Hwy. Dept, 25-30. Mem: Secy, Ark. Bd. of Finance; secy-treas, Ark. Rural Endowment Fund, Inc; chmn. of investments, State Employees Retirement Syst; Teachers Retirement Syst; Ark. Hwy. Employees Syst; Daughter of 1812, Womens Dem. Club; Bus. & Prof. Womens Club; Zonta Int; UDC. Rel: Presbyterian. Mailing Add: 4206 Woodlawn St, Little Rock, Ark. 72205.

HALL, PAUL DAVIS R
Mayor, Dayton, Ohio
b. Miamisburg, Ohio, 7/13/06; s. Frank Smith Hall and Lillie Thirkield H; m. to Anna Rue Hess; c. Sam, Mike and Tony. Educ: Steele High Sch. Polit. & Govt. Pos: Mayor, Dayton, Ohio, 66- Bus. & Prof. Pos: Pres, Hall's Hand Laundry and Troy-Pearl Laundry, Inc. until 53; Real Estate Investor, currently. Mem: Dayton Bicycle Club; Dayton Country Club: Mason; Shrine. Rel: Protestant. Mailing Add: 104 E. Third St, Dayton, Ohio 45402.

HALL, RICHARD HAROLD D
b. Akron, Ohio, 1/12/27; s. John Silas Hall and Phoebe Mairet H; m. 10/16/54 to Wilma Jean Rush; c. Richard R. and Daniel F. Educ: Univ. Akron, 44 & 46; Case Inst. Tech, B.S.Ch.E, 50; Univ. Del, M.S. and Ph.D, 53; Pi Kappa Epsilon; Alpha Chi Sigma; Alpha Chi. Polit. & Govt. Pos: Chmn, Homer Twp. Dem. Party, Mich, 60-; mem, Midland Co. Dem. Cmt, 60-63; mem, Midland Co. Bd. Canvassers, 63-66, chmn, 63-64; del, Midland Co. Dem. Conv, 67; del, Dem. Nat. Conv, 68; mem. exec. cmt, Midland Co. Dem. Party, 69. Bus. & Prof. Pos: Chemist, BF Goodrich Research, Brecksville, Ohio, 52; research chemist, Dow Chem. Co, Midland, Mich, 53, group leader, 54 and sr. research engr, 68- Mil. Serv: Entered as Pvt, Marine Corps, 44, released as Pfc, 46, after serv. in U.S; Am. Theatre and Victory Medals. Mem: Sci. Research Soc. Am; Am. Chem. Soc; Am. Inst. Chem. Engrs; Brit. Chem. Soc; N.Y. Acad. Sci; Am. Inst. Chemists; Boy Scouts; Big Bros; Mich. Dem. Party; Little League. Rel: American Lutheran. Mailing Add: 1187 Stewart Rd, Route 2, Midland, Mich. 48640.

HALL, ROBERT, JR. R
Chmn, Bleckley Co. Rep. Party, Ga.
b. Cochran, Ga, 9/3/28; s. Robert Hall and Mary L. Dye H; m. 8/3/47 to Janie Dalton; c. Stanley, Jay and Martin. Educ: Middle Ga. Col, 45. Polit. & Govt. Pos: Supply officer, Civil Serv, 55-63; finance chmn, Eighth Dist. Rep. Party, 64-66; chmn, Bleckley Co. Rep. Party, Ga. 64- Bus. & Prof. Pos: Acct. and chmn. bd, Hall & Hall Assocs, 63- Mil. Serv: Entered as Aviation Cadet, Air Force, 45, released as T/Sgt, 49, after serv. in Air Transport Command, Pac; Good Conduct and Japanese and Korean Occup. Medals; Asiatic Pac. Ribbon. Mem: Am. Legion (comdr, Post 107); VFW; Moose; Baptist Brotherhood. Rel: Baptist. Legal Res: 213 Edmondson Dr, Cochran, Ga. 31014. Mailing Add: Box 182, Cochran, Ga. 31014.

HALL, STANLEY VERNON R
Maine State Rep.
b. Raymond, Maine, 6/15/16; s. George Herbert Hall and Matilda Pollard H; m. 8/7/37 to Mary Leonora Libby; c. George Vernon, Russell Edward and Karen Jo Anne. Polit. & Govt. Pos: Maine State Rep, 67- Bus. & Prof. Pos: Livestock dealer, 35-69; owner, Dairy Farm, 38-69; pres, Cumberland Farmers Club, Cumberland Co. Fair, 52-69. Mem: Pleasant River Grange; Mason; Eastern Star; Shrine. Rel: Protestant. Legal Res: Foster's Corner, Windham, Maine 04082. Mailing Add: R.F.D. 1, South Windham, Maine 04082.

HALL, THELMA NOBLE D
Mem, W.Va. Dem. State Exec. Cmt.
b. Lansing, W.Va, 1/6/10; d. Oscar Noble and Lillie McClung N; m. 6/24/30 to Attorney Earl Mason Hall; c. Edward Noble. Educ: Marshall Univ, B.S, 32; Kanawha Col, 34; W.Va. Univ, 35; Lambda Chi Omega. Polit. & Govt. Pos: Clerk, State of W.Va, 33-36; local and state officer, Young Dem. Clubs, W.Va 34-36; social worker, Boone Co. Dept. of Pub. Assistance, 37; pres, Boone Co. Dem. Women's Club, 40-46 & 56-60; mem, W.Va. Dem. State Exec. Cmt, Seventh Sen. Dist, Boone, Lincoln and Logan Co, 60-, state assoc. chmn. and dir, Women's Activities, 60-64; organized and chartered W.Va. Coun. Dem. Women, 62 and W.Va. Fedn. Dem. Women's Club, 64; alternate del, Dem. Nat. Conv, 64. Bus. & Prof. Pos: Certified Am. Red Cross First Aid and Water Safety Instr, Girl Scouts, summer, 54 and private camp, summer, 55. Publ: War Time Accomplishments, Boone Co. Chap, Am. Red Cross, 47; Handbook for Democrats, W.Va. State Dem. Exec. Cmt, 64; Annual Reports and Convention Programs, Women's Div, W.Va. State Dem. Exec. Cmt, 61, 62, 63 & 64. Mem: Exec. dir, Boone Co. Chap, Am. Nat. Red Cross, 39-50; W.Va. Welfare Conf; W.Va. Hist. Soc; mem-at-large, League of Women Voters, W.Va; co-chmn, Gov. Barron's Cmn. on the Status of Women; Gov. Adv. Cmt. for Ment. Health Planning; State Clean-up Cmt; Keep Am. Beautiful Prog; first v.pres, Woman's Club of Madison, 68-70; Boone Co. Civic League; founder, Boone Co. Coun. PTA and life mem, W.Va. Cong. PTA. Selected One of Top Ten Club Women of 1963 Centennial Year, Gazette-Mail Newspaper, Charleston, W.Va; spec. assignment to secure crystal reproduction in W.Va. glass for Mrs. Lyndon B. Johnson. Rel: Baptist. Mailing Add: P.O. Box 423, Madison, W.Va. 25130.

HALL, TONY P. D
Ohio State Rep.
b. Dayton, Ohio, 1/16/42; s. Paul Davis Hall and Anna Deve H; single. Educ: Denison Univ, B.A, 64; Sigma Chi. Polit. & Govt. Pos: Vol, U.S. Peace Corps, Thailand, 65-67; Ohio State Rep, 69- Bus. & Prof. Pos: Real estate agent, Paul Tipps Inc, 68; real estate investor. Mem: Sigma Chi Alumni; v.pres, Gem. City Dem. Club; YMCA; Agomis Club. All-State Football, Little All-Am. Football Team, Denison Univ, 63. Rel: Presbyterian. Mailing Add: 51 Grafton Ave, Dayton, Ohio 48406.

HALL, VIRGINIA McDANIEL D
Mem, Dem. Nat. Cmt.
b. Erwin, Tenn, 4/19/21; d. James Oscar McDaniel and Lillie M; m. 7/13/39 to Elmo Rush Hall, Jr; c. Nancy Kerrigan (Mrs. Cosby) and Lt. Thomas Elmo. Educ: Marshall Univ, 38-39; John Robert Powers Finishing Sch, 57. Polit. & Govt. Pos: Mem. adv. bd. for President Lyndon B. Johnson; alternate del, Dem. Nat. Conv, 68; Fifth Dist. chmn, Robert F. Kennedy Presidential Campaign, Va, 68; Martinsville chmn, Humphrey-Muskie Campaign, 68; mem, Martinsville Dem. Exec. Cmt; mem, Dem. Nat. Cmt. Bus. & Prof. Pos: Mem. staff, Martinsville Bul, 56-66; asst. publisher, Henry Co. J, currently. Publ: Columnist, 'Around Town With Virginia,' 12 years. Mem: Martinsville Retail Merchants Asn.(prog. dir. and mem. bd. of dirs); Forest Park Country Club (former mem. bd. of dirs); capt, Cancer Crusade, 66; chmn, Cerebral Palsy Fund, 66; Gray Ladies, Martinsville Gen. Hosp Auxiliary; Credit Women's Breakfast Club; Martinsville Asn. of Life Underwriters; former secy, Airport Develop. Asn; Elks Auxiliary; C. of C; Am. Bus. Women's Asn. Good Citizenship Medal, DAR. Rel: Protestant. Mailing Add: 711 Beechnut Lane, Martinsville, Va. 24112.

HALL, WALTER GARDNER D
b. Houston, Tex, 5/30/07; m. to Helen Lewis; c. W. G, Jr, Samuel L. and Charles F; number of grandchildren. Educ: Rice Univ, B.A, 28. Polit. & Govt. Pos: Bd. dirs. and pres, San Jacinto River Authority, Tex, 43-54; chmn, Galveston Co. Postwar Planning Cmt; chmn, Galveston Co. Dem. Exec. Cmt; mem, Tex. State Dem. Exec. Cmt; mem, Campaign Cmts. of Lyndon B. Johnson, Ralph W. Yarborough and other local cand; del, Dem. Nat. Conv, 68. Bus. & Prof. Pos: Cashier in clay mine for oil co, 28-31; cashier, Citizens State Bank, League City, Tex, 31-35, Dickinson, 35-43, pres, 43-, Alvin State Bank, 53-, League City State Bank, 56- and Webster State Bank, 63-; controlling interest, Bay City Bank and Trust Co, 67- Mem: Past pres, Mainland C. of C; past trustee, Rosenberg Libr, Galveston; past dir, Bay Area Boy Scouts; gov. bd, Lakewood Yacht Club, Seabrook; Houston Club; Philos. Soc. of Tex; Rice Assocs, Rice Univ; dir, Tex. Bill of Rights Found. Legal Res: P.O. Box 757, League City, Tex. 77573. Mailing Add: Drawer A, Dickinson, Tex. 77539.

HALL, WILLIAM CLARENCE D
b. St. Edward, Nebr, 3/9/93; s. Edward Chidester Hall and Elizabeth Alice Rengler H; m. 12/15/28 to Elsie Mae Vinden; c. Betty Lou (Mrs. Hopkins), Billie Mae (Mrs. Lindberg), Doris Irene (Mrs. Dennis), Alice Fay (Mrs. Alkire), Evelyn Grace (Mrs. Toth), Edna Christine (Mrs. Reese), Mildred Jean (Mrs. Graves) and Carolyn Marie (Mrs. Hood). Educ: St. Edward High Sch, grad, 12. Polit. & Govt. Pos: Mem, Wyo. State Dem. Cmt, Converse Co, 58-66; del, Wyo. Dem. State Conv, 60-66; del, West. States Dem. Conf, 63 and Dem. Nat. Conv, 64; mem. adv. coun, Wyo. Small Bus. Admin, 68- Bus. & Prof. Pos: Rancher, 16-59; ranch mgr, William C. Hall Livestock, 59-66; dir, First Nat. Bank, Douglas, Wyo, 65-66. Mil. Serv: Pvt, Coast Guard, 18. Mem: Am. Legion; Farmers Union; Farmers Grange. Rel: Methodist. Mailing Add: P.O. Box 153, Douglas, Wyo. 82633.

HALL, WILLIAM KEENY R
b. Hays, Kans, 10/1/42; s. Don S. Hall and Lucile Flickinger H; single. Educ: Baker Univ, A.B, 64; Univ. Kans, M.A, 66, Ph.D, 69; Pi Kappa Delta; Zeta Chi; Pi Sigma Alpha. Polit. & Govt. Pos: Kans. State Rep, 65-67. Bus. & Prof. Pos: Asst. instr, Univ. Kans, 67-69; asst. prof, Bradley Univ, 69- Mem: Am. Polit. Sci. Asn. Rel: Methodist. Mailing Add: 428 Smokyhill, Oakley, Kans. 67748.

HALL, WILLIAM O.
U.S. Ambassador to Ethiopia
b. Roswell, N.Mex, 5/22/14; s. William O. Hall and Margaret Barnard H; m. 9/19/43 to Jayne Bowerman; c. Sarah, William and Robert. Educ: Univ. Ore; Univ. Minn; Phi Beta Kappa. Polit. & Govt. Pos: Off. dir, Dept. of State, 47-51; sr. adv, U.S. Mission to the UN, 51-56; counselor, Am. Embassy, London, 56-57; dep. asst. secy. of state, 57-59; minister counselor, Am. Embassy, Karachi, Pakistan, 59-63; asst. admin, Agency for Int. Devlop, Dept. of State, 63-67; U.S. Ambassador to Ethiopia, 67- Mil. Serv: Entered as Ens, Navy, 44, released as Lt.(jg), 46, after serv. in ETO. Mem: Am. Soc. Pub. Admin; Am.

For. Serv. Off. Asn; St. James Int. City Mgr; Cosmos Club. Nat. Civil Serv. League Award, 65. Rel: Episcopal. Legal Res: R.D. 1, Joseph, Ore. 97846. Mailing Add: American Embassy, APO New York 09319.

HALLECK, CHARLES ABRAHAM R
b. Jasper Co, Ind, 8/22/00; s. Abraham Lincoln Halleck and Lura Luce H; m. 6/15/27 to Blanche White; c. Charles W. and Patricia (Mrs. Litchfield). Educ: Ind. Univ, A.B, 22, LL.B, 24; Phi Beta Kappa; Order of the Coif; Phi Delta Phi; Beta Theta Pi. Polit. & Govt. Pos: Prosecuting attorney, Jasper-Newton Judicial Circuit, Ind, 24-35; U.S. Rep, Ind, 35-68, former Minority Leader and Majority Leader, U.S. House of Rep; del, Rep. Nat. Conv, 68. Bus. & Prof. Pos: Assoc, Law Firm of Stuart, Branigin, Ricks & Schilling, Lafayette, Ind, currently. Mil. Serv: Army, Inf, World War I. Mem: Am. Legion; Elks. Rel: Methodist. Mailing Add: 600 Jefferson, Rensselaer, Ind. 47978.

HALLETT, LEWIS FRANCIS D
Chmn, Fulton Co. Dem. Exec. Cmt, Ohio
b. Swanton, Ohio, 7/24/17; s. Sherman Charles Hallett and Margaret Langenderfer H; m. 6/15/46 to Patricia Lucille Funkhouser; c. Timothy, Daniel, Michael and Maggie. Educ: Univ. Toledo, Ph.B; Univ. Cincinnati, J.D. Polit. & Govt. Pos: Chmn, Fulton Co. Dem. Exec. Cmt, Ohio, 67-; v.chmn, Fulton Co. Bd. of Elec, 67-; mem, Ohio State Dem. Exec. Cmt, 69- Bus. & Prof. Pos: Chmn, Fulton Co. Law Libr, Wauseon, Ohio, 56-; secy, Wauseon Develop. Co, 56-; mem, Ohio Law Found, 66- Publ: Ed. and publisher, 'Fulton County Democratic News,' monthly, 67- Mem: Fulton Co. and Ohio State Bar Asns; K. of C, Swanton; life mem. and Past Exalted Ruler, Elks, Wauseon; Holy Name Soc; Valleywood Golf Club, Swanton (past pres). Rel: Roman Catholic. Mailing Add: 629 Parkview, Wauseon, Ohio 43567.

HALLEY, HARRY LEE STUART D
b. Antlers, Okla, 9/5/94; s. John Henry Halley and Annie Stuart H; m. 9/6/23 to Fredrica Sabalt Probst; wid; c. Matilda (Mrs. J. R. Rummage). Educ: Univ. Okla, B.A, 15, LL.B, 17; Phi Delta Phi; Sigma Chi. Polit. & Govt. Pos: Asst. city attorney, Tulsa, Okla, 22-28; Dist. judge, Tulsa and Pawnee Counties, 31-47; Justice, Okla. Supreme Court, 47-53 & 54-65, chief Justice, 53-54 & 65-69. Mil. Serv: Entered as Student, Officers Training Camp, 17, released as Capt, Inf, 19, re-entered as Lt. Col, Army, 42, released as Col, 45, after serv. in Inf, N.Africa, Italy and France; Col.(Ret), Army Res, 45-54. Mem: Am, Okla. and Tulsa Co. Bar Asns; Conference of Chief Justices; pres, Okla. Soc. of SAR (past pres); Masons; K. of P; High Twelve; Okla. Farmer Union; Tulsa Farm Club; Am. Legion; VFW; Res. Officers Asn; Retired Officers Asn; Military Order of World Wars; Vets. of World War I. Rel: Methodist. Legal Res: 1618 S. Boulder, Tulsa, Okla. 74119. Mailing Add: P.O. Box 53302, Oklahoma City, Okla. 73105.

HALLEY, JAMES WINSTON R
Mem. Exec. Cmt, Calif. Rep. State Cent. Cmt.
b. San Francisco, Calif, 3/17/21; s. James Leopold Halley and Clara Kroehnke H; m. 5/6/49 to Isabelle Joyce Finlay; c. Janet Elizabeth, James F. and John A. Educ: Univ. Calif, Berkeley, A.B, 43, Law Sch, LL.B, 48; Harvard Bus. Sch, completion cert, 44; Officers Midn. Sch, 44; pres, Alpha Sigma Phi, 43. Polit. & Govt. Pos: V.chmn, Peninsula Div. Rep. Alliance, 61, chmn, 62; v.chmn, Bay Area Rep. Alliance, 63, chmn, 64; chmn, San Mateo Co. Rep. Party, Calif, 63-64; mem, Rep. Nat. Cmt. and chmn, Calif. Rep. State Cent. Cmt, 67-69; del. and v.chmn. Calif. Del, Rep. Nat. Conv, 68; mem. exec. cmt, Calif. Rep. State Cent. Cmt, 69- Bus. & Prof. Pos: Partner and founder, Halley & Cornell, Attorneys, 56-; secy. treas. and gen. counsel, Woodlawn Mem. Park Asn, 64- Mil. Serv: Entered as Midn, Naval Res, 43, released as Lt.(jg), 45, after serv. in Philippines aboard USS Robert F. Keller, Pac. Theater, 44-45; Philippines, Iwo Jima, Okinawa and Japan Campaign Ribbons. Publ: Weekly signed column on polit. and govt. commentary, San Mateo Times. Mem: Calif, San Francisco and San Mateo Bar Asns; past dir, San Francisco Barristers Club; arbitrator, Am. Arbit. Asn; Am. Legion; past sect. chmn, Commonwealth Club of Calif. and United Crusade; Past Master, Richmond Lodge 375, F&AM; Calif. Hist. Soc; past pres, San Mateo Park Improv. Asn. Rel: Episcopal. Legal Res: 529 W. Poplar Ave, San Mateo, Calif. 94402. Mailing Add: 351 California St, San Francisco, Calif. 94104.

HALLOCK, JOSEPH THEODORE 'TED' D
Ore. State Sen.
b. Los Angeles, Calif, 10/26/21; s. Joseph Homer Hallock and Mary Peninger H; m. 2/4/46 to Phyllis Eggert Natwick, div, Mar, 1968; c. Stephanie Elizabeth, Leslie Mary and Christopher. Educ: Univ. of Ore, B.S. in journalism, 48; Sigma Delta Chi. Polit. & Govt. Pos: Ore. State Sen, 62-; del, Dem. Nat. Conv, 68. Bus. & Prof. Pos: State coordinator, Ore. Centennial Cmn, 58-59; co-owner, Ted Hallock, Inc, pub. rels, 59-69, owner, pub. rels-advert, 69- Mil. Serv: Entered as Aviation Cadet, Army Air Corps, 42, released as Capt, 45, after serv. in 306th Heavy Bombardment Group, 8th Air Force, England, 43-44; Distinguished Flying Cross; Air Medal with 3 Oak Leaf Clusters; Purple Heart with Oak Leaf Cluster; Presidential Unit Citation; ETO Theater Ribbon with Battle Star; Capt, Army Res, 45-50. Mem: Press Club of Ore; Local 99, Am. Fedn. of Musicians; Portland Local, Am. Fedn. of TV and Radio Artists. Rel: Presbyterian. Mailing Add: 2445 N.W. Irving St, Portland, Ore. 97210.

HALPERN, SEYMOUR R
U.S. Rep, N.Y.
b. N.Y.C, 11/19/13; s. Ralph Halpern and Anna Swanton H; m. 12/27/59 to Barbara Margaret Olsen. Educ: Seth Low Col, Columbia Univ, 32-34. Polit. & Govt. Pos: Staff asst. to Mayor Fiorello LaGuardia, N.Y.C, 37; asst. to the pres, N.Y. City Coun, 37-40; N.Y. State Sen, 41-54, chmn, Senate Cmt. on Civil Serv, 41-46, Senate Cmt. on Motor Vehicles and Transportation, 46-47 and N.Y. State Joint Legis. Cmt. on Motor Vehicle Problems, 48-54; mem, Mayor's Cmt. on the Courts, 56-58; mem, Queens Co. Rep. Cmt, presently; U.S. Rep, N.Y, 59-; mem, Franklin D. Roosevelt Mem. Cmt, 62- Bus. & Prof. Pos: Reporter, Long Island Daily Press, 31-32; staff writer, Chicago Herald Examiner, 32-33; partner, Halpern & Stone, 45-64; impartial chmn, Moving & Storage Indust. of N.Y, 55-60; v.pres, John C. Paige & Co, Inc, N.Y, 64- Mem: Exec. bd, Citizens Union of N.Y, 54-58; Nat. Panel, Am. Arbitration Asn; dir, Nat. Aeronautics Asn, Queens Mental Health Soc, Queens Hosp. Center Cancer Research Soc. and North Queens Child Guidance Center; bd. chmn, Nat. Family Coun. on Drug Addiction; chmn, bd. sponsors, Queens Symphony Orchestra; Elks; Gavel Lodge, K. of P; B'nai B'rith; trustee, Franklin D. Roosevelt Lodge; Nat. Queens Village and John Foster Dulles Rep. Clubs; bd. dirs, Richmond Hill Rep. Club; North Queens Young Rep. Club, Inc; Capitol Hill Club. Rel: Jewish. Legal Res: 166-05 Highland Ave, Jamaica, N.Y. 11432. Mailing Add: District Office, 89-31 161st St, Jamaica, N.Y. 11432.

HALPIN, ROBERT J. D
Mem, Cumberland Co. Bd. of Freeholders, N.J.
b. Vineland, N.J, 12/8/22; married; c. five. Educ: S.Jersey Col; Rutgers Univ. Law Sch. Polit. & Govt. Pos: Former asst. prosecutor, Cumberland Co, N.J, 1½ years; former mem, Bd. Estimates Sch. Bd; former mem, Vineland City Planning Bd; pres, Vineland City Coun, 56; N.J. State Assemblyman, 60-68, Asst. Minority Leader, N.J. State Assembly, 65, Majority Leader, 66 and Speaker, 67; del, Dem. Nat. Conv, 68; mem, Cumberland Co. Bd. of Freeholders, 69- Bus. & Prof. Pos: Attorney-at-law. Mil. Serv: Navy, serv. in Atlantic and Pac. Mem: Vineland Co. and Cumberland Co. Bar Asns; secy-dir, Solicitor, Buena Vista Country Club; Solicitor, Vineland C. of C; K. of C.(4°); Navy Club; Cumberland Co. Bd. Realtors; Sacred Heart Varsity Club; Am. Legion; first v.comdr, Judge Adv. Vineland Cath. War Vet; past state trustee, N.J. Cath.War Vet. Outstanding Young Man, Vineland C. of C, 56. Mailing Add: 319 Landis Ave, Vineland, N.J. 08360.

HALPIN, STELLA D
V.Chmn, Herkimer Co. Dem. Cmt, N.Y.
b. Herkimer, N.Y, 9/22/19; d. Anthony Rockey and Sadie Sharpes R; m. 12/31/42 to Martin Glynn Halpin; c. Richard Martin and Kathleen Marla. Educ: Herkimer High Sch, N.Y, grad, 37. Polit. & Govt. Pos: Dem. co. committeewoman, Eighth Dist, Herkimer, N.Y, 54-69; v.chmn, Herkimer Dem. Town Cmt, 58-68; mem, N.Y. State Dem. Exec. Cmt, 60-62; del, N.Y. State Gubernatorial Conv, 62; secy, Herkimer Co. Dem. Cmt, N.Y, 64-66, mem. exec. cmt, 66-69 and v.chmn, 68- Mem: Herkimer Co. Women's Dem. Orgn. (past pres); Gr. Herkimer Dem. Club; Rosary Soc; charter mem, Herkimer Ladies Auxiliary Lodge 1439, Elks (past pres); Mil. Order of Purple Heart Auxiliary (past pres. and past state chaplain); chmn, Red Cross Drive, 59. Rel: Catholic. Mailing Add: 324 Marion St, Herkimer, N.Y. 13350.

HALSELL, FRANK BEN D
b. Clementsville, Tenn, 11/13/21; s. Benjamin Franklin Halsell and Effie Mae Woods H; m. 9/19/42 to Avos Boone; c. Lois G.(Mrs. Thompson), Frankie C.(Mrs. Scott) and Suzanne. Educ: Gamaliel High Sch, Ky, 2 years. Polit. & Govt. Pos: Rd. cmnr, Clay Co, Tenn, 46-48, conserv. officer, 48-49, trustee, 50-66, co. judge, 66-; del, Dem. Nat. Conv, 68. Mil. Serv: Entered as Pvt, Army, 42, released as Sgt, 45, after serv. in Ninth Armored Div, Battle of the Bulge, Germany; Purple Heart. Mem: Mason; Shrine; VFW; Am. Legion; Lions. Rel: Church of Christ. Mailing Add: Route 1, Moss, Tenn. 38575.

HALSETH, ELMER JOHANN D
b. Madison, S.Dak, 11/26/00; s. Andrew A. Halseth and Olina Holvick H; m. to Anna Elizabeth Laibly; c. John (deceased) and William L. Educ: Gen. Beadle Teachers, B.S, 24; Univ. of Wyo, M.S, 42; grad work, 46-; Kappa Delta Pi. Polit. & Govt. Pos: Former del, Nat. Cmn. Teacher Educ. and Prfnl. Standards; former state rep, West. Interstate Conf. Higher Educ; Wyo. State Rep, 57-63; mem, Interim Coun, Wyo, 59-61; Wyo. State Sen, 63-69, mem, Educ. and Labor Cmts, Wyo. State Senate, 63. Bus. & Prof. Pos: Broker and owner, Halseth Realty, 43- Mil. Serv: Pvt, Army, 18. Publ: 'Art in the Elementary Schools,' numerous newspaper articles and articles in Educ. News, Wyo. Mem: Nat. and Wyo. Educ. Asns; del, nat. conf, Nat. Educ. Asn; State Rep, Nat. Cmt, for Support of Pub. Schs; mem, Gov. State Interim Coun. on the Arts & Humanities; Rock Springs, Wyo. Coun. on the Arts & Humanities; dir, Fine Arts Center, Rock Springs, Wyo; Am. Legion; pres, Rock Springs Eagles Lodge; hon. Nat. Pres. of Eagles. Collector of paintings; led movement that created West. Wyo. Jr. Col, 59; received Gold Key Award, Wyo. Educ. Asn, 64. Rel: Lutheran. Mailing Add: 506 Second St, Rock Springs, Wyo. 82901.

HALSTEAD, FRED WOLF Socialist Workers Party
Anti-War Dir, Socialist Workers Party
b. Los Angeles, Calif, 4/21/27; s. Frank Harrison Halstead and Bloomah Buckholtz H; m. 5/20/57 to Virginia Garza; c. Laura Ellen, Celia Maria and Frank William. Educ: Univ. Calif, Los Angeles, 2 years. Polit. & Govt. Pos: Mem. Nat. Cmt, Socialist Workers Party, 62-, anti-war dir, 65-, Presidential cand, 68. Bus. & Prof. Pos: Garment cutter, shops in Los Angeles, Detroit and N.Y.C, 50-66; staff writer, The Militant, 55-66; anti-war organizer, Fifth Ave. Vietnam Peace Parade Cmt, 66-68. Mil. Serv: Entered as A/S, Navy, 45, released as Motor Machinist Mate 3/C, 46, after serv. in U.S.S. LST 897, Asiatic-Pac. Theatre. Publ: Harlem Stirs, Marzani-Munsell, 66; If This Be Revolution, Intercontinental Press, 5/67; Interviews With Anti-War GIs, Merit, 69. Mem: GI Civil Liberties Defense Cmt; steering cmt, New Mobilization Cmt. to End the War in Vietnam; Vet. for Peace. Legal Res: 288 Tenth Ave, New York, N.Y. 10001. Mailing Add: 873 Broadway, New York, N.Y. 10003.

HALSTED, CHARLES L. D
b. Ellendale, N.Dak, 9/23/94; s. Charles H. Halsted and Grace Harvey H; m. to Myrtle Gamble; c. Marjorie, Kathryn, Virginia, Lewis, Vivian, Donna and Charles, Jr. Educ: N.Dak. State Normal & Indust. Col. Polit. & Govt. Pos: Town clerk, Minn, 15-17, postmaster, 19-23; Minn. State Rep, 37-47 & 53-67; Dem. cand. for Gov, Minn, 48. Bus. & Prof. Pos: Hardware and forest prod, 23-28; retail grocery, 29-46; Ins, 46- Mem: Mason; Elks; Lions; Moose; Odd Fellows. Rel: Protestant. Mailing Add: 103 Fifth Ave, Brainerd, Minn. 56401.

HALVERSON, KENNETH SHAFER R
Pa. State Rep.
b. Somerset, Pa, 7/24/33; s. Kenneth Evan Halverson and Alma Shaffer H; m. 12/1/56 to Olive Mae Nibert; c. David, Daniel, Robert, Barry and William. Educ: Somerset High Sch, Pa, grad, 51; Univ. Pittsburgh. Polit. & Govt. Pos: Justice of the Peace, Somerset Twp, Somerset, Pa, 62-67; v.chmn, Young Rep, Somerset, 64, chmn, 66; Pa. State Rep, 69th Legis. Dist, 66- Bus. & Prof.

Pos: Spec. agent and underwriter, Selected Risks Ins. Co, Branchville, N.J, 56-59; owner, Ken Halverson Ins. Agency, 59- Mil. Serv: Entered as Pvt, Army, 53, released as S/Sgt, 56, after serv. in Army Security Agency, Germany. Mem: Magistrates Asn; Somerset Co. Develop. Coun; Laurel Highlands Inc, Ligonier; Somerset C. of C; Tri State Mutual Ins. Agents Asn; Jaycees; Am. Legion; Somerset Sportsmen; VFW; Red Men. Outstanding Jaycee Somerset, Pa, Jr. Chamber Int. Senate 6626. Rel: Protestant. Mailing Add: R.D. 5, Somerset, Pa. 15501.

HALVERSON, RONALD T. R
Utah State Rep.
b. Ogden, Utah, 12/18/36; s. Marlowe Halverson and Hilda Tomlinson H; m. 10/13/60 to Linda Kay Jenson; c. Brent Ronald, David J. and Jannette. Educ: Weber Col, A.S, 60; Univ. Utah, 60-61; Weber Col. Excellsior Club. Polit. & Govt. Pos: Voting dist. chmn, Rep. Nat. Conv, 60, del, 64; Utah State Rep, 67-, Majority Whip, Utah State House of Rep, 68- Bus. & Prof. Pos: Pres, Halverson Plumbing & Heating, currently; bd. mem, Joint Apprentice Cmt, 64- Mil. Serv: Entered as Pvt, Army, 60, released as Sgt, 66, after serv. in H/H Battery, 83rd Artil. Mem: Utah Plumbling & Heating Contractors Asn; Kiwanis. Rel: Latter-day Saint. Mailing Add: 1302 E. Halverson Dr, Ogden, Utah 84403.

HALVORSON, ALF HALVOR R
N.H. State Rep.
b. Berlin, N.H, 8/6/99; s. Otto Halvorson and Agnes Andersen; m. Aug. 1919 to Marjorie Dustin; March 1966 to Mary Hogencamp; c. William Halvor. Educ: Berlin Pub. Schs, 06-16. Polit. & Govt. Pos: Councilman, Berlin City Coun, N.H, 31-33; dir, Nat. Youth Admin, North, N.H, 36-41; mem, State Staff of Civil Defense, 42-65; chmn, Coos Co. Civil Defense, 42-65; indust. agent, City of Berlin, 58-63; N.H. State Rep, Cheshire, 69. Mem: Nansen Ski Club (pres); Easter Ski Asn.(founder); New Eng. Olympians (pres); Coach, Nordic Combined U.S. Olympic Team; Berlin C. of C.(founder pres. and secy, 10 years hon. pres); Berlin Indust. Corp (founder and hon. pres); Grange; Elks; Eagles; Hinsdale Raceway (founder, pres, 11 years). Nat. Ski Hall Fame 68. Rel: Lutheran. Mailing Add: Raceway Rd, Hinsdale, N.H. 03451.

HALVORSON, GEORGE CHARLES, SR R
Field Rep. Seventh Cong. Dist. Rep. Party, Minn.
b. Menahga, Minn, 6/22/24; s. Arthur B. Halvorson and Francis Gustafson H; m. 6/2/46 to Barbara T. Paulson; c. George C, Jr, Linda Sue and Barbara Jean. Educ: Concordia Col.(Moorhead, Minn), B.A, 51; Moorhead State Col; St. Cloud State Col; Univ. N.Dak; Mondamin Lit. Soc. Polit. & Govt. Pos: V.chmn, Wadena Co. Rep. Party, Minn, 62-66, 67-, chmn, 66-68; chmn, Educators for Langen, 64; mayor, Village of Menahga, 65-; chmn, Dist. Seven Resolutions, 66; mem, State Rep. Rules Cmt, 66; mem, Menahga Planning Cmn, Village of Menahga, 68-; field rep, Seventh Cong. Dist. Rep. Party, 68- Bus. & Prof. Pos: Secy, Menahga C. of C, 46-47; advisor, North. Minn. Educator, Newspaper, 65-68; chmn, Faculty Coun, 67-68. Mil. Serv: Entered as Pvt, Marines, 43, released as Cpl, 46, after serv. in Second Marine Div, S.Pac, 43-46; four combat awards for serv. in S.Pac; two Presidential Unit Citation Awards; Occupation of Japan Award. Publ: Numerous articles on polit. and civic subjects in area newspapers. Mem: Nat, Minn. and Wadena Co. Educ. Asns; Menahga Educ. Asn.(chmn, 58-59, chmn, legis. cmn, 61-67); Minn. Bus. Educator's Asn; Minn. Coaches Asn; North. Minn. Educ. Asn; Menahga C. of C; Wadena Co. Crow Wing Trails Asn; Menahga Sportsmen's Club; Lions; Am. Legion; VFW; Second Marine Div. Asn; Menahga Nursing Home Bd. Yearbook Dedication; Dist. Commendation; plus others. Rel: Lutheran. Mailing Add: Box 177, Menahga, Minn. 56464.

HAM, DONALD JAMIESON R
Chmn, Custer Co. Rep. Cent. Cmt, Mont.
b. Rapid City, S.Dak, 5/30/34; s. Ernest B. Ham and Nancy Hanum H; m. 12/27/56 to Arlene Frances Hansen; c. Jennifer Lynn and Grady Donald. Educ: S.Dak. State Univ, B.S, 54; Colo. State Univ, D.V.M, 58; Omicron Delta Kappa; Phi Zeta. Polit. & Govt. Pos: Pres, Colo. State Univ. Young Rep, 55-56; dep. state vet, Mont. Livestock Sanit. Bd, 60-; precinct committeeman, Custer Co. Rep. Cent. Cmt, 62-66, chmn, 66-; pres, Custer Co. Rep. Men's Club, 63-66; v.chmn, Mont. Young Rep, 66. Mil. Serv: Entered as 1st Lt, Army Vet. Corps, 58, released as Capt, 60, after serv. in Biol. Warfare Lab, U.S; Capt, Army Res, 66- Publ: 'Veterinary Topics,' Mont. Stockgrower Mag, 6/63, Mont. Farm Bur. Mag, 4/64 and Rocky Mt. Veterinarian, 10/65. Mem: Mont. Vet. Med. Asn.(v.pres, 66-68, pres, 68-); Mont. del, Am. Vet. Med. Asn. House of Del, 65-; East.Mont. Vet. Med. Soc; bd. dirs, Nat. Flying Vet. Asn; Mont. Polit. Action Cmt; Elks; Mason; Town and Country Club; Miles City and Mont. C. of C; Custer Co. and Mont. Farm Bur. Montana's Outstanding Young Man of the Year, Mont. Jaycees, 69. Rel: United Church of Christ. Legal Res: 1018 S. Stacy, Miles City, Mont. 59301. Mailing Add: West of City, Box 121, Miles City, Mont. 59301.

HAM, ERNEST BOLLMAN R
b. Farmingdale, S.Dak, 11/13/96; s. Charles Ham and Alice Denis H; m. 9/29/21 to Nancy Jane Hannum; c. Ruth Ann (Mrs. Anderson), Grace Ellen (Mrs. Neyens), Guy E, Ross C. and Dr. Donald J. Educ: S.Dak. Sch. Mines, 19. Polit. & Govt. Pos: Mem, Harmony Sch. Dist. Bd, S.Dak, 20-50; chmn, Meade Co. Rep. Cmt, 36-38; mem. S.Dak. State Brand Bd, 38-44; mem. bd, S.Dak. State Farm Home Admin, 54-57; mem. bd. supvr, Elk Creek Soil and Moisture Conserv. Dist, 16 years; S.Dak. State Rep, 57-66. Bus. & Prof. Pos: Mem. bd. dirs, First Nat. Bank, Black Hills, 51-68; mem. bd. dirs, West. S.Dak. Calf Show; mem. S.Dak. State Univ. Adv. Coun; mem. bd. trustees, Karl Mundt Libr; mem. bd, Nat. Cowboy Hall of Fame. Mil. Serv: Entered as Pvt, S.Dak. State National Guard, 14, released as Sgt, 19, after serv. at Mexican Border, 16-17 and in 147th Field Artil, France, 18-19. Mem: Farm Bureau; exec. cmt, Am. Nat. Cattlemen's Asn, 54-55, legis. cmt, 56; pres, S.Dak. Stock Growers Asn, 41-43; pres, S.Dak. Livestock Coun, 46-47; Mason; Am. Legion; Maka Sjrome Club. Honored at Little Int. State Col, 51; Eminent Farmer Award, S.Dak. State Col, 55; Founder Centenial Award for Outstanding Leadership in the Livestock and Meat Indust, Swift & Co, 55; Honored with Plaque by First Nat. Bank of the Black Hills, 68. Rel: Presbyterian. Mailing Add: Star Route, New Underwood, S.Dak. 57761.

HAM, EVERETT ADAMS, JR. R
Mem, Exec. Cmt, Ark. Rep. Party
b. Little Rock, Ark, 5/15/23; s. Everett A. Ham, Sr. and Lena Faisst H; div; c. Gretel Christine and Everett A, III. Educ: Univ, Dayton, 3 years; Univ. Ark, B.S.A, 50. Polit. & Govt. Pos: Rep. co. committeeman, Ark, 50-; exec. dir, Party for Two Parties, Little Rock, 61-69; Rep. nat. committeeman and asst. to Winthrop Rockefeller, 61-69; mem, exec. cmt, Rep. Party of Ark, 63-; Bolivian consul for Ark, 67-; del, Rep. Nat. Conv, 68. Mil. Serv: Entered as Aviation Cadet, Air Force, 42, released as Capt, 45, after serv. in Fifth Air Force, Southwest Pac, 43-44; Air Medal with Five Oak Leaf Clusters; Southwest Pac. Theatre Medal with Four Battle Stars. Mem: ROA; Little Rock Club; Top of the Rock Club; Ark. River Yacht Club; Am. Legion; VFW; Soc. for Preservation and Encouragement of Barbershop Singing in Am. Named Outstanding Barbershopper in the South, 63. Rel: Protestant. Mailing Add: 1007 Wildwood, North Little Rock, Ark. 72116.

HAM, GLEN D
Okla. State Sen.
b. Maysville, Okla, 4/1/19; s. Charles Ova Ham and Stella Melvina Reddell H; m. 10/24/64 to Ramona G. Garrison; c. Paul. Educ: Univ. Okla, 37-40; Univ. Tulsa Law Sch, 46-47; Okla. City Univ. Law Sch, LL.B, 49; Delta Theta Phi. Polit. & Govt. Pos: State exec. secy, Okla. League of Young Dem, 38, Fifth Dist. chmn, 39; Okla. State Rep, 50-60, Majority Leader, Okla. House of Rep, 53; Okla. State Sen, 60-, Majority Leader, Okla. State Senate, 63. Mil. Serv: Entered as Pvt, Army Air Corps, 42, released as Sgt, 45, after serv. in 5th Air Force, Australia, New Guinea, E.Indies, Philippines and Okinawa; New Guinea, South. Philippines and Luzon Campaign Ribbons; Good Conduct Medal; Philippines Liberation Ribbon with 1 Star. Mem: Garvin Co. and Okla. State Bar. Asns; Mason (32°); Am. Legion; VFW; C. of C. Rel: Southern Baptist. Legal Res: 412 N. Ash, Pauls Valley, Okla. 73075. Mailing Add: Box 198, Pauls Valley, Okla, 73075. (1967)

HAMBRIC, ALTON MARSHALL D
b. Jasper, Ala, 2/14/34; s. Marshall Hambric and Pauline Scott H; m. 11/12/57 to Doris Ann Bowen; c. Sherry, Terrie Ann, Marshela Dori, Darlene and Veronica. Educ: Walker Co. High Sch, Jasper, Ala, 1 year; Cordova High Sch, 2 years. Polit. & Govt. Pos: Mem, State Planning and Develop. Adv. Bd, Ala, 66; State Planning and Indust. Develop. Bd, 67-; del, Dem. Nat. Conv, 68; mem. Gov. Albert Brewer's Staff, 68- Bus. & Prof. Pos: Pres, Hambric Elec. Co, 61-; pres. and chmn. bd, Hambric Tel. & Comput. Serv. Corp, 65-; pres, Hambric Corp, 65-, Greenview Develop. Corp. and Frontier Recording Studios, 66-; v.pres, Journeyman Corp, 66-, Star Commun. Inc, 69- Mil. Serv: Entered as E-1, Army, 57, released as E-3, 58, after serving at U.S. Mil. Acad; Expert M-1 Rifle; Commendation Award, Army Signal Corps Sch; Good Conduct Medal. Publ: C.O.E. Installation & Testing, Heco Publ. Co, 67; wrote and recorded, 'Don't Forget The March For Freedom!,' Tribute to Martin Luther King. Mem: United Independent and Ala-Miss. Tel. Asns; Nat. Tel. Contractors Asn.(pres); Mason; Lions; Moose; Boy Scout Master; Jaycees. Various awards, Lions; hon. grad, U.S. Army Signal Corps Sch. Rel: Methodist. Mailing Add: Route 1, Box 118-F, Jasper, Ala. 35501.

HAMEL, STANLEY A. R
N.H. State Rep.
b. Haverhill, Mass, 8/4/27; s. Arthur A. Hamel and Pauline M. Little H; single. Educ: Harvard Col, A.B, 49. Polit. & Govt. Pos: N.H. State Rep, 65- Bus. & Prof. Pos: Investment Mgt, self-employed. Mil. Serv: Army, 51-53, served in Army Hq. Europe, Heidelberg, Germany. Mem: Soc. of Colonial Wars; Am. Legion. Antique car collector. Rel: Congregational. Mailing Add: Seabrook, N.H. 03874.

HAMER, ROBERT E. D
b. Brooklyn, N.Y, 8/13/30; s. William J. Hamer; m. to June Smith; c. Donna Marie, Robert Jr, Michael, Stephen and Susan. Educ: Manhattan Col, B.B.A, 51; Evening Div. Seton Hall Univ. Sch. of Law, LL.B, 63. Polit. & Govt. Pos: N.J. State Assemblyman, 65-69; mem, Elec. Law Rev. Cmn, N.J, mem, Co. Dem. Cmt. Bus. & Prof. Pos: Former dist. sales mgr, automobile firm; lawyer. Mem: Bergen Co, N.J. and Am. Bar Asns; K. of C; Commun. Chest; March of Dimes, bd. dirs, Sister Mary Eugene Found, Inc. Legal Res: 53 Wyncote Rd, Ho-Ho-Kus, N.J. 07423. Mailing Add: 215 E. Ridgewood Ave, Ridgewood, N.J. 07540.

HAMIL, DAVID ALEXANDER R
Adminstr, Rural Electrification Admin, Dept. of Agr.
b. Logan Co, Colo, 12/3/08; s. James Newton Hamil and Ada Walker H; m. 12/24/33 to Genevieve Robinson; c. Jo Ann (Mrs. Donald A. Ostwald), Donald William and Jack Robinson. Educ: Hastings Col, A.B, 30. Polit. & Govt. Pos: Colo. State Rep, 32nd-36th & 38th-40th sessions, chmn, Joint Budget Cmt, Colo. House of Rep, 34th & 36th sessions, speaker, 38th-40th sessions; adminstr, Rural Electrification Admin, Dept. of Agr, 56-61 & 69-; dir, Dept. of Insts, Colo, 63-69. Bus. & Prof. Pos: Owner and operator, Hamil Bros. Inc. and Hamil Bros. Land Co, Logan Co, Colo, 32- Mem: AF&AM (33°); Shrine; Elks (past exalted ruler, Sterling Lodge 1336, past dist. dep. and grand exalted ruler, Colo. N); hon. mem, Rotary; Univ. Club, Denver; bd. trustees, Sterling Col; bd. trustees, United Presby. Found; Colo. state chmn, Nat. $50 Million Fund Dr, Presby. Church, 65. Midwest. Cross-Country Champion, Amateur Athletic Union, 29; holder of seven letters in track and cross-country and recipient of Citizenship Award, Hastings Col; Cert. of Recognition, Colo. and U.S. Jr. C. of C; Merit of Honor Award, Colo. State Univ. Alumni Asn; Nat. 4-H Alumni Award. Rel: Presbyterian; Elder. Legal Res: Sterling, Colo. 80751. Mailing Add: 2000 S. Eads St, Arlington, Va. 22202.

HAMILTON, A. C. 'SCOTTY' R
Chmn, Second Cong. Dist. Rep. Party, Colo.
b. Dalmuir, Scotland, 1/5/18; s. William M. Hamilton (deceased) and Margaret Crawford H; m. 6/20/47 to Lea M. Suppes; c. Alwyn Charles and David Scott. Educ: Colo. State Col, B.A; Phi Mu Alpha; Kappa Kappa Psi; Phi Delta Pi. Polit. & Govt. Pos: Vet. Employ. Rep, Ft. Collins, Colo, 46-47; mem, sch. bd, Bayard, Nebr, 54-59, pres, 58-59; chmn, Merrill Co. Rep. Cent. Cmt, Nebr, 57-59; treas, Adams Co. Rep. Cent. Cmt, Colo, 61-; chmn, Second Cong. Dist. Rep. Party, Colo, 69- Mil. Serv: Entered as Pvt, Army, 41, released as M/Sgt, 45, after serv. in Hq. G-3, XVI Corps, ETO, 44-45; Bronze

Star; Victory Medal; Good Conduct Medal; European Theatre Medal. Mem: Beet Sugar Tech. Soc; Am. Legion; Kiwanis. Rel: Presbyterian. Mailing Add: 171 S. 15th Ave. Dr, Brighton, Colo. 80601.

HAMILTON, CLARENCE JAMES D
b. Detroit, Mich, 7/22/13; s. James Hamilton and Jane Ann Colclough H; m. 8/25/40 to Janice Oliver; c. Jill (Mrs. Jurvelin), Jack James and William Linton. Educ: Mich. State Univ, B.S. in Police Admin, 40; Univ. Idaho, LL.B, 48; Phi Kappa Tau; Phi Alpha Delta. Polit. & Govt. Pos: Prosecuting attorney, Kootenai Co, Idaho, 49-50, Dem. precinct committeeman, 54-; pres, Idaho Young Dem, 50; chmn, Kootenai Co. Dem. Party, Idaho, 54-56; del, Dem. Nat. Conv, 64 & 68. Bus. & Prof. Pos: Pres, Lincoln Mining Co, Wallace, Idaho, 40-; sr. mem, Law Firm of Hamilton and Hamilton, Coeur d'Alene, 48- Mil. Serv: Entered as 2nd Lt, Army, 41-46, 50-52, released as Capt, 52, after serv. in Provost Marshal Gen. Sch. and 41st Inf. Div, Pac. Far East Theatre, 41-44, Lt. Col, Army Res, 63; Purple Heart; Pac-Asiatic Theatre Ribbons; 3 Assault Landing Ribbons. Mem: Am, Idaho and First Judicial Dist. Bar Asns; Nat. Trial Lawyers Asn; Mason; Scottish Rite; York Rite; Shrine; Spokane Club; Hayden Lake Country Club; Kiwanis, Coeur d'Alene; Eagle Scout; VFW; Am. Legion; DAV; Mil. Order of World Wars; C. of C. Rel: Presbyterian. Legal Res: 104 S. Ninth St, Coeur d'Alene, Idaho 83814. Mailing Add: Box 606, Coeur d'Alene, Idaho 83814.

HAMILTON, DANIEL R
Chmn, Hanover Rep. Town Cmt, Mass.
b. Brookline, Mass, 8/19/37; s. Francis W. Hamilton, Jr. and Frances E. Godfrey H; m. 5/16/59 to Meredith A. Thomson; c. Katharine S, Julie A. and Janet L. Educ: Univ. Mass, Assoc, 58; Alpha Tau Gamma. Polit. & Govt. Pos: Mem, Mass. Rep. State Cmt, 65-; mem. exec. cmt, Plymouth Co. Rep. Club, 67-; chmn, Hanover Rep. Town Cmt, 68- Bus. & Prof. Pos: Salesman, Alden Electronics, 59-62; sales mgr, Feedback Controls Div, N.Y. Air Brake Co, 62-65; sales mgr, Precision Line Inc, 65-66; v.pres, R.H. Robinson Co, 66- Mem: Electronic Rep. Asn; AF&AM; Hanover Jaycees. Rel: Protestant. Mailing Add: 875 Main St, Hanover, Mass. 02339.

HAMILTON, DAVID McGREGOR D
Sen, V.I. Legis.
b. Toronto, Can, 10/25/25; s. Frank Campbell Hamilton and Audrey Vinton Leishman H; m. 5/28/50 to Dorothy Ann Gilliam; c. Robin Adair and David McGregor, Jr. Educ: Univ. Chattanooga, 46-47; Sigma Chi. Polit. & Govt. Pos: V.chmn, V.I. Planning Bd, 61-62; Sen, V.I. Legis, 67- Bus. & Prof. Pos: V.pres, Bd. Realtors, St. Croix, 65; overseer, Col. of the V.I, 62- Mil. Serv: Entered as Seaman, Coast Guard Res, 43, released as Rdm 3/c, 46, after serv. in U.S.C.G.C. Ingham, Pac. Theatre, 43-46; Am. Theatre, Pac. Theatre, Philippine Campaign, S.China Expeditionary Force and Victory Medals. Mem: C. of C.(pres, St. Croix Chap, 64-66). Rel: Protestant. Legal Res: 27 Orange Grove, Christiansted, St. Croix, V.I. 00820. Mailing Add: P.O. Box 279, Christiansted, St. Croix, V.I. 00820.

HAMILTON, DWIGHT ALAN R
Chmn, Arapahoe Co. Rep. Cent. Cmt, Colo.
b. Denver, Colo, 8/21/28; s. Alfred H. Hamilton, Jr. and Emily L. Loucks H; m. 5/4/52 to Elizabeth Folds; c. Camilla L, Dwight Alan, Jr, Elizabeth Ann and Scott Weston. Educ: Colo. Col, B.A, 50; Univ. Denver Col. Law, LL.B, 54; Beta Theta Pi. Polit. & Govt. Pos: Mem, Nat. Conf. of Cmnr. on Uniform State Laws, Colo, 65-; chmn, Patronage Cmt, Colo. Rep. Party, 68-; chmn, Arapahoe Co. Rep. Cent. Cmt, 69- Bus. & Prof. Pos: Attorney-at-law, partner, Fuller & Evan, 55- Mil. Serv: Entered as Cpl, Marines, 48, released as Capt, 62, after serv. in First Marine Div, Korea, 51; Purple Heart. Mem: Denver, Colo. and Am. Bar Asns; Denver Law Club; AF&AM; Rocky Mt. Consistory; Shrine. Rel: Christian Science. Mailing Add: 5005 S. Lafayette Lane, Englewood, Colo. 80110.

HAMILTON, ERNEST ROLL D
b. Chicago, Ill, 3/12/27; s. Ernest Frank Hamilton and Margarett Etta Stroud H; m. 6/19/49 to Dolores D. Meyer; c. Gary Stephen, Gail Louise, Dale Douglass and Cheryl Laurett. Educ: Ill. Inst. Tech, 44-45; Purdue Univ, Civil Eng, 53; Chi Epsilon; Delta Tau Delta. Polit. & Govt. Pos: Statistician, U.S. Dept. Army, 44; utility engr, Sanit. Dept, City of Indianapolis, Ind, 48; planning engr, Marion Co. Plan Cmn, 49-50; cand. co. engr, Marion Co, 52; precinct committeeman, Marion Co. Dem. Cent. Cmt, 53-64; del, Ind. State Dem. Conv, 62, 66 & 68; chmn, Washington Twp. Award, Indianapolis, 64-; del, Dem. Nat. Conv, 68. Bus. & Prof. Pos: Pres. and prfnl. engr, Ernest R. Hamilton Assocs, Inc, 55-; consult. prfnl. engr. and pres, Russell, Schubert, Hamilton & Assocs, Inc, 67- Mil. Serv: Entered as Pvt, Air Force, 45, released as Sgt, 46, after serv. in PACUSA, 13th and Fifth Air Force, Pac, 44-45; Pac. Theatre, Occup. and Good Conduct Medals. Publ: Water for Peace, Vol. 4, Industrial Reuse of Combined Sewage Treatment Plant Effluent, Supt. Documents, U.S, 67. Mem: Nat. Soc. Prfnl. Engrs; Am. Soc. Mech. Engrs.(incinerator div); Am. Water Works Asn; Water Pollution Control Fedn; Am. Pub. Works Asn. Rel: Lutheran. Mailing Add: 9420 N. Kenwood Ave, Indianapolis, Ind. 46260.

HAMILTON, GEORGE HENRY R
b. Marlboro, Vt, 10/10/83; m. to Frances Gillis. Educ: Wesleyan Univ, Ph.B, 06; Teachers Col, Columbia Univ, 28-29. Polit. & Govt. Pos: Mem, sch. bd, Vt, 43-55; cemetery cmnr, 48-54; Justice of Peace, 53-64; Vt. State Rep, 61-67. Bus. & Prof. Pos: Farmer, formerly. Mem: Farm Bur; Grange; Credit Union; Putney Hist. Soc, Civic Asn. Rel: United Church of Christ. Mailing Add: R.F.D. 3, Putney, Vt. 05346. (1967)

HAMILTON, HOWARD A. R
Iowa State Rep.
b. Hamilton Twp, Iowa, 4/5/09; s. Asbury T. Hamilton and Grace L. Bird H; m. 7/5/40 to Edna L. Hambright; c. Bryce H, Dennis R, James A. and Jerry L. Educ: Iowa State Univ, B.S, 32. Polit. & Govt. Pos: Iowa State Rep, 69- Bus. & Prof. Pos: Co. Exten Dir, Monroe Co, Iowa, 32-38; co. exten. dir, Cedar Co, Iowa, 38-66; dist. ins. dir, Hawkeye Nat. Life Ins. Co, 67- Mem: Iowa Co. Exten. Dirs. Asn; Million Dollar Round Table Ins. Orgn; Farm Bur. Distinguished Serv. Award, Nat. Co. Agr. Agency Asn. Rel: Methodist. Mailing Add: 122 W. Sixth St, Tipton, Iowa 52772.

HAMILTON, JOHN H, JR. R
Pa. State Rep.
b. Phila, Pa, 2/9/19; s. John H. Hamilton and Marie Holland H; m. to Doris V. Johnson; c. Two. Educ: Wharton Eve. Sch; N. Phila. Realty Sch. Polit. & Govt. Pos: Exec. v.pres. and treas, Pa. Rep. State Exec. Cmt, 17 years; Pa. State Rep, currently. Bus. & Prof. Pos: Ins. broker. Mil. Serv: Med. Corps, 75th Field Hosp, Okinawa, World War II. Mailing Add: 6916 Shalkop St, Philadelphia, Pa. 19128. (1967)

HAMILTON, JOHN ORVILLE D
b. Marathon City, Wis, 1/29/32; s. John Orville Hamilton and Mary Boucher H; single. Polit. & Govt. Pos: Del, Dem. Nat. Conv, 68. Mil. Serv: Air Force, 52, Pvt. Mem: Eagles. Mailing Add: 6109 Hamilton, Omaha, Nebr. 68132.

HAMILTON, JOSEPH T. D
Ark. State Rep.
b. Omaha, Ark, 1/27/37; s. Charles Ernest Hamilton and Emma Oliver H; single. Educ: Univ. Ark. Polit. & Govt. Pos: Coroner, Boone Co, Ark, 59-60; state committeeman, Young Dem. Club of Ark. and Ark. Dem. Party; Ark. State Rep, Third Dist, 61- Bus. & Prof. Pos: Farming interests, Boone Co, Ark, 55-; partner, Hamilton Land & Cattle Co, 59-; pres, Harrison-Hamilton Corp, 65- Mem: Mason (32°), F&AM, Boone Lodge 314, Ark. Consistory, Valley of Little Rock, Orient of Ark, RAM; Civitan Club. Rel: Christian Church. Legal Res: Highway 7 South, Harrison, Ark. 72601. Mailing Add: Box 459, Harrison, Ark. 72601. (1967)

HAMILTON, LEE HERBERT D
U.S. Rep, Ind.
b. Daytona Beach, Fla, 4/20/31; s. Frank A. Hamilton and Myra Jones H; m. 8/21/54 to Nancy Ann Nelson; c. Tracy Lynn, Deborah Lee and Douglas Nelson. Educ: DePauw Univ, A.B. cum laude, 52; Goeth Univ, Germany, study-travel scholarship, 52-53; Ind. Univ. Sch. Law, J.D, 56; Gold Key. Polit. & Govt. Pos: Chmn, Citizens for Kennedy Cmt, 60 and Bayh for Sen. Cmt, 62; treas, Bartholomew Co. Young Dem, Ind, 60-63, treas, 63-64; U.S. Rep, Ninth Dist, Ind, 65-, For. Affairs and Post Off. and Civil Serv. Cmts, U.S. House Rep, currently,and pres, 89th Cong. Club; del, Dem. Nat. Conv, 68. Bus. & Prof. Pos: Attorney, Wilkins Witwer & Moran, Chicago, 56-58; attorney and partner, Sharpnack & Bigley, Columbus, Ind, 58-64; instr, Am. Banking Inst, 60-61. Mem: Ind. Bar Asn; bd. dirs. Rotary, 61-62; DePauw Univ. Nat. Bequests Cmt; C. of C; Jr. C. of C. Nat. Collegiate Athletic Asn. Award for basketball and tennis in col, 65. Rel: Methodist. Mailing Add: 4216 Peach Tree Place, Alexandria, Va. 22304.

HAMILTON, MARY ELLEN R
Chmn, Coconino Co. Rep. Cent. Cmt, Ariz.
b. Great Bend, Kans, 8/4/21; d. Jay Abram Sitterley and Evelyn Buechner S; m. 3/20/43 to William H. Hamilton; c. Mary Ellen (Mrs. Joseph Lakin Lockett) and William H, III. Educ: Univ. Kans, 40-43. Polit. & Govt. Pos: Secy, Coconino Co. Rep. Women's Unit, Ariz, 60, pres, 63 & 64; asst. secy, Coconino Co. Rep. Cent. Cmt, 61-65, chmn, 66-; campaign off. mgr. for elections of 62, 64 & 68; state chmn, Mamie Eisenhower Libr. Proj, 65, 66 & 67; del, Rep. Nat. Conv, 68. Mem: Beta Sigma Phi. Rel: Protestant. Mailing Add: 24 W. Oak, Flagstaff, Ariz. 86001.

HAMILTON, MILTON HUGH, JR. D
Tenn. State Sen.
b. Union City, Tenn, 9/8/32; s. Milton Hamilton, Sr. and Novelle Rogers H; m. 3/29/53 to Dale White; c. Milton, III, Ann Barrett and David Blanton. Educ: Memphis State Univ, 3 years; Murray State Univ, B.A; Kappa Alpha; Inter Fraternity Coun. Polit. & Govt. Pos: Chmn, Union City Sch. Bd, Tenn, 60-64; v.chmn, Fiscal Rev. Cmt, State of Tenn; cmnr. from Tenn. on Educ. Compact of States; Tenn. State Rep, Obion, Weakley and Lake Co, 64-68; Tenn. State Sen, Obion, Weakley, Henry, Carroll and Lake Co, 24th Dist, 68- Mil. Serv: Entered as 2nd Lt, Army, 55, released as 1st Lt, 57, after serv. in Antiaircraft Artil. and Guided Missile Sch, Ft. Bliss, Tex; Maj, Army, Nat. Guard, 57-; Distinguished Mil. Student and Distinguished Mil. Grad. Mem: Mason; K.T; Rotary (dir, Union City Club, 65); C. of C.(bd. dirs, 64); Tenn. LP Gas Asn.(bd. dirs. and v.pres, 62-64); Eighth Dist. dir, Tenn. Sch. Bd. Asn, 62-64; pres, 230th Engr. Officers Club, 63. Selected Tenn. Outstanding Young Man of 64 by Tenn. Jaycees; Phillips Petrol. Co. Mr. Phil Award for Community Serv. Rel: Methodist; Mem, Bd. of Stewards. Mailing Add: 920 Whirmantler Dr, Union City, Tenn. 38261.

HAMILTON, PAT R. D
V.chmn, W.Va. State Dem. Exec. Cmt.
b. Oak Hill, W.Va, 2/14/23; s. James Clarence Hamilton and Ruth Gregory H; m. 6/10/50 to Helen Mae Packer; c. Patricia Leigh, Debra Lynn, Judith Ann and James Edward. Educ: W.Va. Univ. and George Wash. Univ; Phi Delta Theta; Phi Alpha Delta; bd. ed, Law Rev. Polit. & Govt. Pos: Spec. agent, Fed. Bur. Invest, 48-53; bd. govs, W.Va. Univ; former chmn, Fayette Co. Dem. Exec. Cmt; campaign dir, State & Co; v.chmn, State Dem. Exec. Cmt, currently; alternate del, Dem. Nat. Conv, 68; chmn, Platform Cmt, W.Va. Dem. State Conv, 68. Bus. & Prof. Pos: Lawyer, 53-; pres, Hamilton-Houck Realty Co. and Allegheny Realty Co, dir, New River Banking & Trust Co, Dunbar Metal & Supply Co, Brown-Hamilton, Inc. and Midway Contractors, Inc, plus others. Mil. Serv: Army Mil. Police, 43-45. Mem: Elks; Mason; Moose; pres, Oak Hill C. of C, 54-64; pres, New River Gorge Develop. Corp; dir, Laird Found, Inc; Fayette Co. Ment. Health Cmn; Fayette Co. Human Rights Cmt. Selected W.Va. Citizen of Year by W.Va. Jaycees, 64. Rel: Protestant. Legal Res: 10 Arbuckle Rd, Oak Hill, W.Va. 25901. Mailing Add: P.O. Box 115, Oak Hill, W.Va. 25901.

HAMILTON, PAUL L. D
Colo. State Rep.
b. Pueblo, Colo, 4/1/41; s. Robert Lee Price (stepfather) and Frances Susan Kittrell; single. Educ: Univ. of Denver, B.A. June, 1964; Phi Kappa Delta, Omicron Delta Kappa, Alpha Kappa Delta; Univ. of Denver Student YMCA. Polit. & Govt. Pos: Del, Denver Co. Assembly and Conv, 68; del, State Assembly and Conv, 68; mem, Colo. Dem. State Educ. Cmt, currently; mem, Colo. Dem. State Cmn. Equal Rights, currently; Colo. State Rep, 69- Bus. &

Prof. Pos: Teacher and minority hist. consult, Denver Pub. Schs, 64-; counsr, Neighborhood Youth Corps, N.Y.C, summer 65; asst. dir, Denver Head Start Family Camps, summer 67;instr. in-serv-training, Denver Pub. Schs, 68; assoc. dir, Denver Area Consortium for the Improvement of Teaching of Histories of Minorities, 69. Mem: Phi Kappa Delta; Am. Fedn. Teachers (organizer, Denver, spring 67). Traveled to Botswana, Rhodesia and Kenya, Oper. Cross Roads Africa, summer 63; and Hong Kong, Japan, Philippines, YMCA Int. Workcamp, 62. Mailing Add: 2770 California, Denver, Colo. 80205.

HAMILTON, ROBERT K. D
Pa. State Rep.
b. Roswell, N.Mex, 9/3/05; s. James C. Hamilton and Alma L. Ritchey H; m. 5/17/45 to Jean Hunt; c. William and James. Educ: Pa. State Univ, B.S; Duquesne Univ, J.D. Polit. & Govt. Pos: Former mem, Soil Conserv. Cmt, Beaver Co; Pa. State Rep, 40-, mem, Rules and Appropriations Cmts, Cmt. Higher Educ, Gen. State Authority, State Hwy. and Bridge Authority, State Pub. Sch. Bldg. Authority and Legis. Budget and Finance Cmt, Pa. House of Rep, chmn, Ins. Cmt, 55-57 and 61, v.chmn, Local Govt. Cmn. and Cmn. on Interstate Coop, 61-62, mem, Joint State Govt. Cmn, 65-66, Speaker of the House, 65-66, chmn, Policy Cmt, 67-68 and Ways and Means Cmt, 69-70. Bus. & Prof. Pos: Former farmer; ins. agent. Mil. Serv: 2nd Lt, ROTC Inf, 28-30; 2nd Lt, Battery B, 107th Field Artil, Officers Res. Corps and Pa. Nat. Guard Res. Mem: Mason; Grange; Elks; AFL; twp. chmn, Red Cross; bd. dirs, Beaver Co. Commonwealth Campus and Sch. Agr, Pa. State Univ. Outstanding Alumni Award, Pa. State Univ, 66, Dept. of Animal Indust. and Nutrition, 65. Rel: Methodist. Mailing Add: 917 Maplewood Ave, Ambridge, Pa. 15003.

HAMILTON, ROBERT WILLIAM D
Assoc. Justice, Supreme Court of Tex.
b. Nashville, Ark, 3/24/99; s. Charles P. Hamilton and Eddie Lassiter H; m. 5/4/29 to Lois Rogers; c. Robert W, Jr, Mrs. Tom Gunning and Mrs. Eddie Keetch. Educ: Lon Morris Col, Tex; Univ. Tex, A.B, and legal educ; Phi Alpha Delta. Polit. & Govt. Pos: Dist. Attorney, 70th Judicial Dist, Tex, 33-34, Dist. Judge, 51-53; del, Dem. Nat. Conv, 48; Chief Justice, Eighth Court of Civil Appeals, Tex, 53-59; Assoc. Justice, Supreme Court of Tex, 59- Mil. Serv: Pvt, Army, 18. Mem: Am, El Paso Co. and Travis Co. Bar Asns; Elks; Rotary; Am. Legion; Am. Judicature Soc; State Bar of Tex; Tex. Farm Bur; Austin Country Club. Rel: Episcopal. Legal Res: Austin, Tex. 78703. Mailing Add: Supreme Court of Texas, Austin, Tex. 78711.

HAMMACK, DEAN RAE D
b. Pinckneyville, Ill, [illegible]/9/01; s. William Hammack and Belle Trefftzs H; m. 7/1/25 to Matilda Dowty; c. Sylvia Dean (Mrs. Charles Carson) and John William. Educ: South. Ill. Univ, 21-23. Polit. & Govt. Pos: Off. tester, dairy dept, Univ. of Ill, 23-24; mem. staff, Dept. of Pub. Welfare, Ill, 37-40; Ill. State Rep, 44th dist, 50-57; cand, Ill. Constitutional Conv. Mem: Mason; Eastern Star; Blue Lodge; Shrine (32°); Scottish Rite; Farm Bur; Eagles; C. of C.(pres, Pinckneyville Chap, 48). Rel: United Methodist; past pres, Methodist Men's Orgn. Mailing Add: R.R. 2, Pinckneyville, Ill. 62274.

HAMMER, EDGAR THOMAS, JR. 'TACK' R
Chmn, Westmoreland Co. Rep. Cmt, Pa.
b. Greensburg, Pa, 10/5/32; s. Edgar Thomas Hammer and Ann Sorber H; m. 6/1/57 to Betty Jane Weaver; c. Edgar T. III and Theodore M. Educ: Lafayette Col, A.B, 55; Univ. Pittsburgh, LL.B, 58; Phi Delta Theta; Phi Delta Phi. Polit. & Govt. Pos: Chmn, Gr. Greensburg Young Rep. Club, 58-60; chmn, Westmoreland Co. Rep. Cmt, Pa, 64- Mem: Pa. Bar Asn; Westmoreland Co. Law Asn; F&AM; Elks; Lions. Rel: Presbyterian. Mailing Add: 46 Northmont St, Greensburg, Pa. 15601.

HAMMER, LUCY T. R
Conn. State Sen.
b. Washington, D.C, 4/27/04; d. Boyd Taylor and Marion Lilley T; m. 2/19/27 to Thorvald F. Hammer; c. Alexandra (Mrs. Richard M. Grave). Educ: Smith Col, B.A, 26; Yale Univ, M.A, 42; Phi Beta Kappa. Polit. & Govt. Pos: Secy, Bd. of Educ, Branford, Conn, 40-51; Conn. State Rep, 55-61; Conn. State Sen, 61-, asst. minority leader, Conn. State Senate, 67; co-chmn. for educ, Rep. Platform Cmt, 64, 66 and 68; pres, Third Cong. Dist. Rep. Women's Orgn, New Haven, Conn, 67; mem, Gov. Cmt. on Human Rights, 68. Bus. & Prof. Pos: Mem. bd. of gov, New Haven Col, West Haven, Conn, 62-65; v.chmn, Conn. Student Loan Found, Hartford, Conn, 67-; mem. exec. bd, Serv. Bur. for Women's Orgn, 68-; mem. adv. coun, S. Cent. Commun. Col. and Conn. Child Day Care Asn, 68- Mem: Bus. and Prfnl. Women's Club; Orgn. of Women Legis. Award for Outstanding Serv. to Voc. Educ, Instr. Orgn, Conn. Voc-Tech. Schs, 67; Raymond E. Baldwin Award for Outstanding Serv. in Advancing the Soc. and Econ. Ideals of the Trade Union Movement, Conn. Rep. Labor League, 69. Rel: Episcopal. Mailing Add: 95 Cherry Hill Rd, Branford, Conn. 06405.

HAMMER, WALTER BENJAMIN R
Iowa State Sen.
b. Newell, Iowa, 8/1/05; s. Louis H. Hammer and Mary Westmoreland H; m. 8/14/29 to Clara Margaret Gutel; c. Phyllis Karr and Lois Stright. Educ: Buena Vista Col, B.A, 28; Univ. Iowa, M.A, 35. Polit. & Govt. Pos: Iowa State Sen, 69- Bus. & Prof. Pos: High sch. prin, Luana Consol. Dist, 28-30 and supt. of schs, 30-34; supt. of schs, Mechanicsville, Iowa, 34-44; high sch. prin. and col. dean, Estherville, 44-57, high sch. prin, 55-67, Mem: Mason. Rel: Presbyterian. Mailing Add: W. 205 Central Ave, Estherville, Iowa 51334.

HAMMERSCHMIDT, JOHN PAUL R
U.S. Rep, Ark.
b. Harrison, Ark, 5/4/22; m. to Virginia Sharp; c. John Arthur. Educ: The Citadel; Univ. Ark; Okla. A&M. Polit. & Govt. Pos: Former Rep. State Committeeman, mem, Rep. Nat. Finance Cmn. and Harrison City Coun, Ark; del, Rep. Nat. Conv, 64; chmn, Rep. State Cent. Cmt, 64-; U.S. Rep, Ark, 66- Bus. & Prof. Pos: Bd. dirs, First Nat. Bank and Harrison Fed. Savings & Loan Asn; pres, Hammerschmidt Lumber Co; pres, Construction Prod. Co. Mil. Serv: Army Air Corps, 2nd Lt, 42; Maj, Air Force Res; Distinguished Flying Cross with 3 Oak Leaf Clusters; Air Medal with 4 Oak Leaf Clusters; 3 Battle Stars. Mem: Past pres, Rotary, Ark. Lumber Dealers Asn. and Southwest. Lumberman's Asn; bd. dir, Nat. Lumber and Bldg. Material Dealers Asn; Mason; Elks; Am. Legion; VFW. Harrison Man of the Year, 65. Rel: Presbyterian; Bd. of Elders. Mailing Add: End of Ridge Park Rd, Harrison, Ark. 72601.

HAMMETT, ROBERT A. D
b. Inman, S.C, 11/8/27; single. Educ: Wofford Col, A.B, 52; Univ. S.C, LL.B, 56. Polit. & Govt. Pos: Mayor, Inman, S.C, 59-60; S.C. State Rep, 61-68. Bus. & Prof. Pos: Lawyer, Burts, Turner & Hammett. Mil. Serv: Maj. Army Res. Mem: Lions; Am. Legion; S.C. and Am. Bar Asns; Mason (32°); WOW. Mailing Add: P.O. Box 172, Inman, S.C. 29349.

HAMMOND, EVERT NEWTON R
Chmn, Pike Co. Rep. Cent. Cmt, Ohio
b. Pike Co, Ohio, 8/17/17; s. Sherman Eli Hammond and Mary Alice Lowe H; m. 8/19/39 to Bernice Edith Dunlap. Educ: Wakefield High Sch, Ohio, 3 years. Polit. & Govt. Pos: Mem, Pike Co. Bd. Elect, Ohio; chmn, Pike Co. Rep. Cent. and Exec. Cmts, 66-; alternate del, Sixth Cong. Dist, Rep. Nat Conv, 68. Bus. & Prof. Pos: Farmer. Mem: Pike Co. Rep. Club; Farm Bur; Cattlemen's Asn. Rel: Protestant. Mailing Add: Box 416, R.R.1, Piketon, Ohio 45661.

HAMMOND, F. MELVIN D
Idaho State Rep.
b. Blackfoot, Idaho, 12/19/33; s. Floyd Milton Hammond and Ruby Hoge; m. 9/15/56 to Bonnie Sellers; c. Melanie, Lezlee, Stephanie, Todd and Lisa. Educ: Ricks Col, 51-53; Brigham Young Univ, B.A, 58, M.A, 62; Univ. of Colo, 63-67. Polit. & Govt. Pos: Idaho State Rep, 69- Bus. & Prof. Pos: Prof, Ricks Col, Rexburg, Idaho, 66-69. Rel: Latter-day Saint. Mailing Add: 149 Elm Ave, Rexburg, Idaho 83440

HAMMOND, GEORGE DONALD R
Mass. State Sen.
b. Westfield, Mass, 10/29/06; s. George Clinton Hammond and Emma Day H; m. 10/6/31 to Gwendolyn Rhoda Hanbury; c. Constance E.(Mrs. Henry Wakeman) and Donna M.(Mrs. Lawrence O'Brien). Educ: Northeast. Univ. Eve. Div; corporator, Am. Int. Col, Springfield, Mass. Polit. & Govt. Pos: Chmn, Mass. Rep. Finance Cmt, 60-61; mem, Rep. State Cmt. and chmn, Westfield Rep. City Cmt, Mass, 56-64; Mass. State Sen, currently. Bus. & Prof. Pos: Dir, Valley Bank & Trust Co, Westfield, Mass; trustee, Hammond Realty Trust, currently. Mem: Colony Club, Springfield, Mass; Ancient and Hon. Artil. Co. Mass; Moose; Elks. Rel: Episcopal. Mailing Add: 96 Western Ave, Westfield, Mass. 01085.

HAMMOND, JAY STERNER R
Majority Leader, Alaska State Senate
b. Troy, N.Y, 7/21/22; s. Morris A. Hammond and Edna Brown Sterner H; m. 9/25/52 to Bella Gardiner; c. Heidi and Dana. Educ: Pa. State Univ, 2 years; Univ. Alaska, B.S, 48; Triangle. Polit. & Govt. Pos: Alaska State Rep, Bristol Bay, 59-64; Alaska State Sen, 67-, Majority Leader, Alaska State Senate, 69- Bus. & Prof. Pos: Govt. hunter, U.S. Fish and Wildlife Serv, 49-56; mgr, Bristol Bay Borough, 65-66. Mil. Serv: Entered as Seaman 2/C, Naval Flight Cadets, 42, released as Capt, 46, after serv. in VMF 211 Fighter Pilot, S.Pac. Theatre, 45. Publ: Several outdoor articles; one book of verse. Mem: VFW. Rel: Protestant. Mailing Add: Naknek, Alaska 99633.

HAMMOND, MARGARET R
Vt. State Sen.
b. Springfield, Vt, 1/14/00; d. George L. Bibens and Lizzie A. Miller B; wid; c. Homer H, Hildreth M.(Mrs. Gilleran) and Frances H.(Mrs. Hunter). Educ: Springfield High Sch. Polit. & Govt. Pos: Town collector of taxes, Vt; chmn, Rep. Town Cmt; Justice of Peace, 36-; lister; town agent; overseer of poor; auditor; sch. dir; Vt. State Rep, 45-66; Vt. State Sen, 66- Bus. & Prof. Pos: Secy, 18-20; farming; housewife. Mem: Past pres, Order Women Legislators; Springfield Vis. Nurses Asn; dir, Vt. Cancer Soc; Farm Bur. Rel: Baptist. Mailing Add: R.F.D. 1, Chester Depot, Vt. 05144.

HAMMOND, REESE LEROY D
b. Whaleysville, Md, 7/18/07; s. Roy Hammond and Estella Armstrong H; m. 8/24/68 to Eloise Gauntt-Talia Fero. Educ: Cheyney State Normal; Charles Morris Price Sch, grad; N.Phila. Real Estate and Ins. Sch. Polit. & Govt. Pos: Del. State Rep, 65-66, 67-68, chmn, Temperance Cmt, Del. House of Rep, 65-66 and mem, Ways and Means and Revenue Cmts, 66-68. Bus. & Prof. Pos: Dir, Del. Nat. Surv. of Voc. Educ, Dept. of the Interior; Negro Specialist for Del. Fed. Writers Proj, Works Progress Admin; ed, Herald-Tribune newspaper; columnist, Wilmington Sunday Star; Chester Daily Times, 31-33; pres, Reese Hammond Inc, Real Estate & Ins, 68- Mem: Pres, Citizen's Dem. Alliance Inc, 68-69; YMCA; NAACP; Nat. Asn. Dem. Negro Bus. and Prfnl. Men and Women Inc. Rel: Roman Catholic. Legal Res: 1024 Christina Ave, Wilmington, Del. 19801. Mailing Add: 2015 Magellan Ave, Atlantic City, N.J. 08401.

HAMMONS, OTIS PARNELL D
Del, Ark. Constitutional Conv.
b. Bolivar, Tenn, 9/5/04; s. Thomas Redden Hammons and Lucy Belle Vaughan H.(deceased); m. 7/10/25 to Evalyn Elvira Pierce; c. Edward Parnell. Educ: Jackson Sch. of Bus, grad, 23; Union Univ, Jackson, Tenn, B.A, 28; Univ. of Okla, M.S, 37; Phi Delta Kappa. Polit. & Govt. Pos: Ark. State Rep, 59-69, mem, Legis. Coun, Ark. State Legis, 59 and Legis. Joint Audit Cmt, 60-69; del, Ark. Constitutional Conv, 69- Bus. & Prof. Pos: Supt. of schs, Talihina, Okla, 38-44; mgr, Forrest City Prod. Credit Asn, Ark, 43-44. Publ: Economic Conditions of Teachers, Pottawatamie Co, Okla, 37. Mem: Nat. Soc. of State Legis; Lions; Gov. Cmt. on Stream Preservation; Farm Bur; Rotary; C. of C; Huguenot Soc. of Founders of Manakin in Colony of Va; former mem, Young Men's Bus. Club. Hon. Chief, Choctaw Indian Tribe, Okla; Wild Life Preservation Award for State of Ark, C. of C; Nat. Award for Work in Distributive Educ. Rel: Southern Baptist. Legal Res: 1412 N. Washington, Forrest City, Ark. 72335. Mailing Add: Box 547, Forrest City, Ark. 72335.

HAMMONS, OWEN CECIL D
b. Horton, Ky, 12/19/22; s. Leslie Thompson Hammons and Ivy Taylor H; m. 1/4/40 to Martha Gray Peters; c. Martha Katherine (Mrs. Hay) and Cecilia Ann. Educ: Purdue Univ. Polit. & Govt. Pos: Mem, Dem. Nat. Cmt.

and Dem. Club. of Ky; del, Dem. Nat. Conv, 68. Bus. & Prof. Pos: Pres, Local 862, UAW, 48-61; int. rep. UAW, 61-66. Mil. Serv: Entered as Pvt, Marine Corps, 45, released as Pfc, 46, after serv. in 1st Div, S.Pac. Mem: F&AM; Eastern Star; Commun. Action; Ky. Col; bd. mem, Ky. State AFL-CIO; Bd. of Regents, West. Ky. Univ. Rel: Protestant. Mailing Add: 7307 Nottoway Circle, Louisville, Ky. 40214.

HAMNER, JAMES L. D
Chmn, Amelia Co. Dem. Cmt, Va.
b. Ammon, Va, 10/12/93; s. William Dabney Hamner and Nancy Harriet White H; m. 4/19/30 to Rebecca J. Sydnor; c. James L, Jr. Educ: Lynchburg Col; Med. Col, Va, M.D, 16; Phi Rho Sigma; Asn. of Professions. Polit. & Govt. Pos: Chmn, Amelia Co. Dem. Cmt, Va. 28- Bus. & Prof. Pos: Gen. practice of medicine, 20-; pres, Union Bank and Trust Co. of Amelia Co, 48- Mil. Serv: Entered as 1st Lt, Med. Corps, Army, 17, released as Capt, Med. Res. Corp, 20. Mem: Past pres, Med. Soc. of Va, Fourth Dist. Med. Soc, Amelia Co. Med. Soc, Va. Academy of Gen. Practice; Mason; Am. Legion; Ruritan; Farm Bur. Rel: Disciples of Christ. Mailing Add: Mannboro, Va. 23105.

HAMPTON, HAYES ALLEN D
Ky. State Rep.
b. Trenton, Ky, 3/25/03; s. Frank Wade Hampton and Mary Ellen Goens H; m. 8/20/30 to Hazel Belle Stokes; c. Glenn Dale, Allen Ray, Paul Reno and Dorothy (Mrs. William Sholar). Educ: Pembroke Elem. Sch, Ky, 9 years. Polit. & Govt. Pos: Magistrate, Todd Co, Ky, 38-60; Ky. State Rep, Todd Co, 60-64, Todd and Logan Co, 67- Bus. & Prof. Pos: V.Pres, People's Bank, Pembroke, Ky, 59- Mem: Farm Bur; Nat. Farmers Orgn. Award, Ky. Col. Rel: Christian Church of N.Am. Mailing Add: Route 2, Trenton, Ky. 42286.

HAMPTON, KEITH D
b. Jasper, Tenn, 7/16/11; m. 1933 to Annie Barker; c. Bill and Mary (Mrs. Bowen). Educ: Marion Co. High Sch. Polit. & Govt. Pos: Trustee, Marion Co, Tenn, 48-52; Marion Co. del, Tenn. Constitutional Conv, 53; dir, Chattanooga Div. of Finance and Taxation, 53; Cmnr. of Corrections, Tenn, 53-63, Cmnr. of Personnel, 63-67, dir, Div. of Pub. Works, 67-; Presidential Elector, 60. Mil. Serv: Army, World War II. Mem: Am. Legion; VFW. Rel: Presbyterian. Mailing Add: C2-201 Central Service Building, Nashville, Tenn. 37219.

HAMPTON, MASON LILLARD, JR. Conservative, N.Y.
V.Chmn, N.Y. State Conservative Party
b. Westgrove, Pa, 11/29/30; s. Mason Lillard Hampton and Nora Schuyler H; m. 6/25/57 to Jean Sprower; c. Linda Jean, John Wade and Katherine Lee. Educ: Va. Polytech. Inst, B.S, 51; Wash. & Lee Univ, LL.B, 56; Omicron Delta Kappa; Tau Kappa Alpha. Polit. & Govt. Pos: Nominee, U.S. Rep, N.Y, 68; v.chmn, N.Y. State Conservative Party, 68- Bus. & Prof. Pos: Assoc. lawyer, Townsend & Lewis, N.Y, 56-61; law partner, Gaylor & Hampton, Lynbrook, N.Y, 62- Mil. Serv: Entered as 2nd Lt, Army, 53, released as 1st Lt, 55, after serv. in 24th Inf. Div, Korea, 53-55. Mem: Phi Alpha Delta; Nassau Co. Bar Asn; Nassau-Suffolk Trial Lawyers. Rel: Lutheran. Mailing Add: 15 Margaret Blvd, Merrick, N.Y. 11563.

HAMPTON, ROBERT EDWARD R
Chmn, U.S. Civil Serv. Cmn.
b. Chattanooga, Tenn, 9/21/22; s. Charles Alfred Hampton (deceased) and Mary Lee Plemons H; m. 7/12/47 to Geraldyne A. Stivers; c. Adrienne Ann and Jeffrey Scott. Educ: Univ. Tenn, 46-48; Univ. Chattanooga, B.A. in Bus. Admin, 49. Polit. & Govt. Pos: Vice-consul, Munich, Germany, 50-52; for. affairs officer, Exec. Secretariat, State Dept, 52-53; staff asst. to Secy. of State, 53-55; asst. dep. manpower, personnel and orgn, Dept. Air Force, 55-57; spec. asst. to under secy. for admin, State Dept, 57-58; spec. asst. for personnel, White House, 58-61; cmnr, U.S. Civil Serv. Cmn, 61-69, chmn, 69- Bus. & Prof. Pos: Prin, Blackfox Sch, Cleveland, Tenn, 49-50. Mil. Serv: Army Air Force, 42-45, ETO. Mem: V.chmn, trustees, Fed. Womens Award Cmt, 61- Named Young Republican of Year, 60. Legal Res: 10 Savannah Ct, Bethesda, Md. 20034. Mailing Add: U.S. Civil Service Commission, Washington, D.C. 20415.

HAMPTON, WILLIAM PECK R
Minority Floor Leader, Mich. House of Rep.
b. Pontiac, Mich, 1/24/38; s. Vernon C. Hampton and Mildred Peck H; m. 7/22/61 to Elizabeth Taft Bradley; c. Mary Elizabeth. Educ: Mich. State Univ, B.A, 60; Wayne State Univ. Law Sch, LL.B, 63; pres, Excalibur; v.pres, Blue Key; Sigma Alpha Epsilon; Delta Sigma Phi; pres. of class; pres, Student Union; Law Sch. Bd. Gov; pres, Moot Court. Polit. & Govt. Pos: Mich. State Rep, 64-, Majority Leader, Mich. House of Rep, 66-68, Minority Floor Leader, 68- Bus. & Prof. Pos: Attorney, Hampton & Hampton, Pontiac, 63- Mem: Rotary Int; Oakland Co. and Mich. Bar Asn; Birmingham Jr. C. of C; bd. dirs. Camp Oakland and Mich. State Univ. Club of Oakland Co; United Fund; Young Rep. Club of Oakland Co. Commun. Serv. Citation, Birmingham Jr. C. of C; Outstanding Young Man in Am. Award, U.S. Jr. C. of C. Rel: Presbyterian. Legal Res: 2463 Hunt Club Dr, Bloomfield Hills, Mich. 48013. Mailing Add: Capitol Bldg, Lansing, Mich. 48901.

HAMRE, AL R
b. Willow Lake, S.Dak, 9/29/15; m. to Alice Eliason; c. Kay Frances. Educ: La Salle Exten. Univ, LL.B. Polit. & Govt. Pos: Mayor, alderman and treas, Willow Lake, S.Dak, 6 years; S.Dak. State Rep, 54-58 and mem. exec. bd. S.Dak. House Legis. Research Coun, 57; State Treas, 58-62; State Auditor, 62-66. Bus. & Prof. Pos: Businessman; farmer. Mil. Serv: Sgt, Army Inf, World War II; Purple Heart; Oak Leaf Cluster; Silver Star. Mem: Pres, S.Dak. Crippled Childrens Soc; Am. Legion; Commercial Club. 1967 Legal Res: Willow Lake, S.Dak. No mailing address available. (1967)

HAMRICK, CLAUDE MEREDITH D
b. Avondale, N.C, 7/27/26; s. Roland Bunyon Hamrick and Thelma Pauline Robbins H; m. 7/6/57 to Lena Mae Lewis; c. Kent Lewis and Roland Mont. Educ: Pfeiffer Jr. Col, 43-44; Wake Forest Col, 47-48, Sch. Law, 50; Phi Delta Phi; Theta Chi; Wake Forest Dem. Club. Polit. & Govt. Pos: Treas, Young Dem. Club, N.C, 55; N.C. State Rep, Forsyth Co, 61-69; alternate del, Dem. Nat. Conv, 68. Mil. Serv: Entered as Pvt, Army, 43, released as M/Sgt, 45, after serv. in 40th Inf. Div, Pac, 44-45, Re-entered as 1st Lt, Judge Adv. Gen. Corps, 50, released, 52, after serv. in ETO; Army Commendation Ribbon; Good Conduct Medal; Pac. Theater of Operations Ribbon. Mem: V.pres, Forsyth Jr. Bar Asn. and secy, Forsyth Bar Asn, 55; Jr. C. of C; C. of C; Lions. Rel: Baptist. Mailing Add: 2841 Holyoke Place, Winston Salem, N.C. 27106. (1967)

HAMZY, JOSEPH AMIN R
Chmn, Rep. Town Cmt, Falls Village, Conn.
b. Becket, Mass, 2/26/15; s. Amin Abu Hamzy and Friede H; m. 2/4/40 to Evelyn Ruth Goodrich; c. Joseph Amin, Jr. and Beth. Educ: Am. Univ, Beirut, Lebanon. Polit. & Govt. Pos: Chmn. bd. educ, Falls Village, Conn, 39-45, Justice of the Peace, 41-; Conn. State Rep, 43-47; co. treas, 49-60; chmn, Rep. Town Cmt. and Judge of Probate, Dist. Canaan, 60- Mem: Mason (32°); Consistory; Commandery; Shrine; Red Men. Rel: Protestant. Legal Res: Beebe Hill Rd, Falls Village Conn. 06031. Mailing Add: Box 264, Falls Village, Conn. 06031.

HANCHETT, JAMES GRANGER R
b. Evanston, Ill, 2/10/41; s. Harold G. Hanchett Jr. and Mary June Ballah H; m. 8/24/61 to Jo-Ann Dorothy Colburn; c. Janet Eileen and Jason Granger. Educ: Long Beach City Col, A.A, 60; San Fernando Valley State Col, B.A, 63; Sigma Delta Chi; Alpha Phi Gamma. Polit. & Govt. Pos: Exec. asst. to U.S. Rep. Craig Hosmer, 67- Bus. & Prof. Pos: Sports writer, Long Beach Independent, Press-Telegram, Calif, 57-60; asst. sports ed, Van Nuys News and Green Sheet, 60-62; pub. rels. rep, Atomics Int, Canoga Park, Calif, 62-65; correspondent, McGraw-Hill World News, Los Angeles, Calif, 65-66; Wash. ed, Nucleonics Week, 66-67. Publ: Author, numerous tech. and non-tech. articles for mag. Mem: Am. Nuclear Soc, Wash, D.C; Jaycees. Outstanding Journalist, Long Beach City Col, 59, and Man of the Year Award, 60. Rel: Protestant. Mailing Add: 12508 Canfield Lane, Bowie, Md. 20715.

HANCOCK, CLARA C. R
Chmn, York Co. Rep. Party, Va.
b. Lexington, Ky, 12/22/14; d. William Jefferson Clark and A. Katherine Snyder C; m. 12/23/39 to William Andrew Hancock; c. Mark J. Educ: Maryland Inst. Art, 35-36; Christopher Newport Col, 63-65; William & Mary Summer Col, 63-64. Polit. & Govt. Pos: Coordinator for census, Counties of York, Gloucester and Mathews, Va, 60; chmn, York Co. Rep. Party, 60-; pres, York Co. Rep. Women's Club, 61-63; rep, First Dist. Va. Fedn. Rep. Women, 63-64; v.chmn, First Sen. Dist. Rep. Orgn, 63-; cand, Va. State Sen, 65; mem, Va. Rep. State Cent. Cmt, 65-; mem, York Co. Prob. Study Group and York Co. Rep. to Hampton Roads Area Cmt, 68- Bus. & Prof. Pos: Off. mgr, Fuel Distributor, 32-39. Mem: V.pres, York High PTA, 60; Eastern Star; York Co. Rep. Assembly; bd, York Chap. Red Cross, 63-64; chmn, Jr. Red Cross. Rel: Lutheran. Mailing Add: R.R. 1, Robanna Shores, Yorktown, Va. 23428.

HANCOCK, DON D
Mo. State Rep.
b. Pine, Mo, 7/28/34; m. 9/7/53 to Avanell Jackson; c. Steve, Sherry and Stan. Educ: Southeast Mo. State Col; North. Ill. Univ; Ark. State Col. Polit. & Govt. Pos: Mo. State Rep, 64- Bus. & Prof. Pos: Salesman; sch. teacher. Mil. Serv: Army, Paratroopers, 54-56. Mem: Lions; C. of C. Rel: Protestant. Mailing Add: 906 Lafayette, Doniphan, Mo. 63935. (1967)

HANCOCK, FRANK ELLIS R
b. York, Maine, 6/19/23; s. William Patten Hancock and Hazel Ellis H; m. 4/27/46 to Kathleen Eleanor Matteo; c. Carolie, Emily, Joshua. Educ: Colby Col, 41-43, 46; Boston Univ, LL.B. Polit. & Govt. Pos: Attorney Gen, Maine, 59-65; Maine State Rep, 55-57; Moderator, York Town Meeting, 52-58. Bus. & Prof. Pos: Pvt. law practice, Levy & Hancock, 65-; Ogunquit, Maine, 50-57; partner, Hancock & Hutchins, Ogunquit, Maine, 59; Trustee, York Hosp. Mil. Serv: AUS, 43-46. Mem: Am, Maine, York Co. Bar Asns; Nat. Asn. Attorneys Gen. (Pres, 64-65); Navy League; Mason; Portland Club; Cumberland Club. Mailing Add: Cape Neddick, Maine 03902. (1967)

HANCOCK, OSCAR WALKER D
b. Ethelsville, Ala, 10/17/03; s. Thomas Jeremiah Hancock and Iva Pridmore H; m. 1/2/23 to Mary Eloise Sanders; c. Martha Jean (Mrs. William Lang), Oscar Walker, Jr, Charles Sanders and James Turiman. Educ: Birmingham South. Col, 22-23; Alpha Tau Omega. Polit. & Govt. Pos: Mem, Selective Service Bd, Pickens Co, Ala, 41-46; Mayor, Ethelsville, Ala, 56-; chmn, Pickens Co. Dem. Cmt, 54-69; mem, Pickens Co. Agr. Cmt, 61-69 and Pickens Co. Action Cmt, 67-69; legis. agent, Pickens Co, Ala, 68- Mem: Farm Bur.(pres, Pickens Co. Bur, 60-69); chmn, Pickens Co. 4-H Found, 63-; Rotary; Civitan Club; Mason; Yorkrite; Shrine; Eastern Star (past worthy patron). Rel: Methodist; Chmn. of Bd; Lay Leader; Sunday Sch. Supt. Mailing Add: P.O. Box 8, Ethelsville, Ala. 35461.

HANCOCK, RICHARD E. R
Okla. State Rep.
b. Tulsa, Okla, 4/10/40; s. Willard E. Hancock and Dorothy M. Parker H; m. 6/8/62 to Mary Lynn Huntington; c. Laura Ann. Educ: Okla. State Univ, B.S. in Acct; Univ. Tulsa, J.D. Polit. & Govt. Pos: Okla. State Rep, 69- Legal Res: 2828 E. 21st Place, Tulsa, Okla. 74114. Mailing Add: Suite 1302, Philtower Bldg, Tulsa, Okla. 74103.

HANCOCK, WILLIAM P. D
Cmnr, Ill. Indust. Cmn.
b. Chaffee, Mo, 3/15/16; s. Pat Hancock and Beatrice Howell H; m. 3/15/35 to Trutha Elizabeth Green; c. William P, Jr. and James Lee. Polit. & Govt. Pos: Supvr, Camargo Twp, Douglas Co, Ill, 57-; arbitrator, Ill. Indust. Cmn, 61-65, cmnr, 65-; del, Dem. Nat. Conv, 64. Mem: Past pres, Rotary; C. of C; Mason; Consistory; Eastern Star; Moose; Int. Asn. of Indust. Bd. Rel: Methodist. Legal Res: 160 N. LaSalle, Chicago, Ill. 60601. Mailing Add: 9 N. Main, Villa Grove, Ill. 61956.

HAND, BEULAH JOAN D
Ore. State Rep.
b. Baker, Ore, 5/12/17; d. Grover Thornton Caviness (deceased) and Ruby Rimbey C; m. 4/2/37 to Orville Floyd Hand. Educ: 3 years Col. Polit. & Govt. Pos: V.chmn, Ore. State Dem. Party, 58-59; Ore. State Rep, 58-; del,

Dem. Nat. Conv, 60 & 68. Mem: League of Women Voters; Farmers Union; Ore. Mycological Soc. Rel: Methodist. Mailing Add: 2515 Tenth Ave, Milwaukie, Ore. 97222.

HAND, LLOYD NELSON D
b. Alton, Ill, 1/31/29; s. Nelson T. Hand and Robbie Omega Taylor H; m. 2/23/52 to Lucy Ann Donoghue; c. Cathy, Lloyd, Susan, Bridget and Thomas. Educ: Univ. Tex, B.A, 52, LL.B, 57; Friar Soc. Polit. & Govt. Pos: U.S. Sen, Calif. and asst. to Vice President Lyndon B. Johnson, 57-61; financial coordinator for Calif. Johnson-Humphrey Campaign, 64; del, Dem. State Conv, 65; former mem, Calif. Dem. Cent. Cmn; Chief of Protocol, U.S. Dept. of State, 65-66. Bus. & Prof. Pos: Lawyer, 57-; v.pres. and dir, Pierce Nat. Life Ins. Co, Los Angeles; pres, Wilwesco Corp; dir, Valhalla Corp, Caltex Corp. and Perpetual Corp. Mil. Serv: Lt, Naval Res, 51-55. Mem: Univ. Tex. Ex-Students Asn; bd. dir, Los Angeles Symphony Asn; Bel-Air Country Club; Cong. Country Club. Mailing Add: 9808 Wilshire Blvd, Beverly Hills, Calif. 90212.

HAND, WILLIAM BREVARD R
Chmn, Mobile Co. Rep. Exec. Cmt, Ala.
s. Charles C. Hand and Irma Weems H; m. 6/17/48 to Allison Denby; c. Jane Connor, Virginia Alan and Allison. Educ: Univ. Ala, C.&B.A. and LL.B; Delta Kappa Epsilon. Polit. & Govt. Pos: Mem, Mobile Co. Rep. Exec. Cmt, Ala, 66-69, chmn, 68-; mem, Ala. State Rep. Exec. Cmt, 69. Mil. Serv: Pvt, Army, 43-46, serv. in ETO; Bronze Star. Mem: Nat. Asn. R.R. Trial Lawyers; Fedn. Ins. Coun; Ala. Defense Lawyers Asn; Am, Ala. State and Mobile Co. Bar Asns; Americans for Constitutional Action (state v.chmn). Rel: Methodist. Legal Res: 9 DeMouy St, Mobile, Ala. 36606. Mailing Add: P.O. Box 123, Mobile, Ala. 36601.

HANDLEY, WILLIAM J.
U.S. Ambassador to Turkey
b. Netherlands Guiana, 12/17/18; s. Am. citizens; married. Educ: Univ. London, 35-37; Univ. Md, B.A, 42; Am. Univ, 43-44. Polit. & Govt. Pos: Priority specialist, War Prod. Bd, 42-44; analyst, For. Econ. Admin, 44; econ. analyst, For. Serv. Auxiliary, 44; attaché, Cairo, Egypt, 45 and Addis Ababa, Baghdad, Beirut, Damascus, Jerusalem, Jidda and Teheran, 47; U.S. observer, 1st Int. Labor Orgn. meeting for Near E. govt, 47; assigned to Dept. of State, 48-49, labor adv, Bur. Near East, S.Asian and African Affairs, 49-51, labor adv, Off. of Asst. Secy. of State, 51; pub. affairs officer and attaché, New Delhi, India, 51-52, planning officer and attaché, 52-53; joined Info. Agency, New Delhi, 53, dep. chief pub. affairs officer and attaché, 54-55; assigned to Info. Agency, Wash, 55-61, chief, Near E. Policy staff, 55-56, dep. asst. dir, Near E, S.Asia and Africa, 56-57, asst. dir, 57-61; U.S. Ambassador to Mali, 61-64; dep. asst. secy. for Near East. Affairs, Dept. of State, 64-69; U.S. Ambassador to Turkey, 69- Bus. & Prof. Pos: Announcer and prog. writer, broadcasting sta, 36-39; mgr, import co, British Guiana, 37-39. Recipient of Superior Serv. Award, Info. Agency, 56. Mailing Add: U.S. Embassy, Ankara, Turkey.

HANDY, WENDELL TAYLOR R
b. Tyler, Tex, 1/28/28; s. Taylor Handy (deceased) and Lucy Johnson H; m. 1/9/60 to Adelaide Fisher; c. Wendell T, Jr, Anthony I. and Darryl H. Educ: Univ. Calif, Los Angeles Sch. Bus. Admin, 1 year; Metrop. Bus. Col, 1 year. Polit. & Govt. Pos: Mem. credentials and rules cmt, speakers' bur, Calif. Rep. State Cent. Cmt, 66; secy. and bd. mem, Compton Elem. Sch. Bd, Calif, 67; mem. and mem. del. assembly and legis. steering cmt, Calif. Sch. Bd. Asn, 67; chmn. youth employ. and recreation, Gov. Adv. Cmt. Children and Youth, 67-; del, Rep. Nat. Conv, 68; campaign dir, Nixon-Agnew Hq.(3), 68; mem. dist. attorney's adv. coun, Los Angeles Co. Legis. Cmt, 69; Calif. State chmn, Nat. Coun. Concerned Afro-Am. Republicans, 69; chmn, 55th Rep. Assembly Dist, 69; v.chmn, Mid-Cities Sch. Trustees Asn, 69; mem, 21st Rep. Cong. Dist. Cmt, currently; mem, Los Angeles Co. Rep. Cent. Cmt, currently. Publ: Watts Riot, privately publ, 66. Mem: Asst. coach and pub. rels. chmn, Willowbrook Athletic Youth Asn; Southeast Los Angeles Commun. Pride Cmt.(founder and chmn); NAACP (bd. mem, Compton Br); Compton Improv. Asn; Compton Bus. and Prfnl. Men's Asn. Recipient of Commun. Serv. Award for Outstanding Merits, Willowbrook Youth Athletic Asn; Compton Jr. Col. Award for Attendance and Participation in Class of Leadership Training; Award for Outstanding Achievement on Commun. Activities, Metrop. Gazette Newspaper, 68. Rel: Protestant. Legal Res: 13716 S. Wilmington Ave, Compton, Calif. 90222. Mailing Add: 13714 S. Wilmington Ave, Compton, Calif. 90222.

HANES, THOMAS C. D
Prosecuting Attorney, Darke Co, Ohio
b. Arcanum, Ohio, 9/29/30; s. Harry Russell Hanes and Marie Corwin H; m. 8/29/53 to Jean Staley; c. Catherine Marie, Richard David, Mark Staley and Lori Ann. Educ: Univ. Dayton, 48-52 & 55; Ohio North. Univ. Col. Law, J.D, 59; Sigma Delta Kappa. Polit. & Govt. Pos: Safety dir, Greenville, Ohio, 60-68; prosecuting attorney, Darke Co, 69- Mil. Serv: Entered as Pvt. E-1, Army, 51, released as 1st Lt, 55, after serv. in Germany, 51-52 and Korea, Far East, 53-55; Good Conduct Medal; Korean Serv. Medal; UN Serv. Medal. Mem: Am. Trial Lawyers Asn; Am, Ohio State and Darke Co. Bar Asns; Ohio Acad. of Trial Lawyers; Am. Judicature Soc; Nat. Dist. Attorneys Asn; Ohio Prosecutor's Asn; Rotary; Odd Fellows. Outstanding Young Man of the Year, Greenville Area Jaycees, 61. Rel: United Methodist. Legal Res: 1293 Parkway Dr, Greenville, Ohio 45331. Mailing Add: 220 Weaver Bldg, Greenville, Ohio 45331.

HANIFY, JOSEPH EDWARD, JR. D
Register of Deeds, Bristol Co, Mass.
b. Fall River, Mass, 9/2/22; s. Joseph E. Hanify and Ann E. Malady H; m. 9/1/47 to Claire M. Faucher; c. Pamela and Joseph. Educ: St. Anselm's Col, B.A, 43; Boston Univ, LL.B, 48; Phi Delta Phi. Polit. & Govt. Pos: Asst. corp. coun, Fall River, Mass, 52-55 and admin. asst. to Mayor, 55-58; pres, Fall River Young Dem, 55; alternate del, Dem. Nat. Conv, 56, 64 & 68, del, 60; register of deeds, Bristol Co, Mass, 60-; mem, Fall River Dem. City Cmt, 62. Bus. & Prof. Pos: Land Court Title Exam, Mass; mem, Fed. Court and U.S. Supreme Court; incorporator, Citizens Savings Bank, 61; dir, Corky Row Credit Union, 65. Mil. Serv: Entered as Pvt, Army, 43, released as Pfc, 46, after serv. in Hq. Div. Artil, 42nd Div, ETO; ETO Ribbon with Battle Star; Expert Infantryman Badge. Mem: Fall River, Bristol Co, Boston, Mass. and Am. Bar Asns; Past Exalted Ruler, Elks Lodge 118; pres, Past Exalted Rulers Asn; Exchange Club; C. of C; Fall River Clover Club; K. of C; Moose; Quequechan Club; Am. Legion; DAV; VFW; Corky Row Club; Fall River Dem. Club. Rel: Catholic. Legal Res: 369 Florence St, Fall River, Mass. 02720. Mailing Add: 214 Academy Bldg, Fall River, Mass. 02721.

HANKINS, DEWEY L. R
b. Barry Co, Mo, 5/6/98; m. 10/27/27 to Viola Gaige; c. Marjorie (Mrs. Boysen), Griffen, Georgia, Heeta Mae (Mrs. Seeley) and Peggy. Educ: Barry Co. High Sch. Polit. & Govt. Pos: Mo. State Rep, 56-67. Bus. & Prof. Pos: Retired teacher and farmer. Mem: Odd Fellows, Mason. Rel: Baptist. Mailing Add: R.F.D. 1, Cassville, Mo. 65625. (1967)

HANKINS, FREEMAN D
Pa. State Sen.
b. Brunswick, Ga, 9/30/18; s. Oliver Hankins and Anna Pyles H; m. to Dorothy Days; c. one. Educ: Friendship Sch, Pittsburgh, Selden Inst, Brunswick; Temple Univ; grad. Dolan's Col. of Embalming, 45. Polit. & Govt. Pos: Former Pa. State Rep; del, Dem. Nat. Conv, 68; Pa. State Sen, 69- Bus. & Prof. Pos: Funeral dir. Mil. Serv: Army Med. Corps, 44-47. Mem: Am. Legion; NAACP; Nat. Funeral Asn; Masonic bodies. Rel: Baptist. Mailing Add: 4075 Haverford Ave, Philadelphia, Pa. 19104.

HANLEY, JAMES MICHAEL D
U.S. Rep, N.Y.
b. Syracuse, N.Y, 7/19/20; s. Michael Joseph Hanley and Alice Gillick H; m. 8/12/50 to Rita Ann Harrington; c. Christine Mary and Peter J. Educ: Hon. LL.D, LeMoyne Col, 67. Polit. & Govt. Pos: U.S. Rep, N.Y, 64-; del, Dem. Nat. Conv, 68. Bus. & Prof. Pos: Funeral dir, Callahan-Hanley-Mooney Funeral Home. Mil. Serv: Army, World War II. Mem: C. of C; Am. Legion; K. of C.(grand knight); Elks; Syracuse Liederkranz; Ancient Order of Hibernians; Boys Town; Army and Navy Union; Onondaga Chap, Help for Retarded Children; Antique Auto Club of Am; Holy Name Soc; Order of the Alhambra; West End Soc. Club; St. Mary's Men's Club; hon. mem, Syracuse Police Benevolent Asn; nat, state and local funeral dirs. asns. Rel: Catholic. Mailing Add: 316 Coleridge Ave, Syracuse, N.Y. 13204.

HANN, JOHN ROBERT R
Chmn, Eighth Cong. Dist, Rep. Party, N.C.
b. Brazil, Ind, 2/11/23; s. John R. Hann and Jennie Teague H; m. 7/16/46 to Thelma Endicott; c. Stephen Endicott and Scott Thomas. Educ: Butler Univ, 3 years; Sales and Mgt. Inst, N.Y, 1 year; Phi Delta Theta. Polit. & Govt. Pos: Precinct chmn, Rep. Party, Indianapolis, Ind, 48-50; area orgn. chmn, Minneapolis, Minn, 52-56; mem. cmt, Nixon and Lodge Campaign, Seattle, Wash, 60; precinct organizer, Rep. Party, Houston, Tex, 64; chmn, Rowan Co. Rep. Party, 66 & 67; mem, Rep. State Exec. Cmt, 66-; chmn, Eighth Cong. Dist. Rep. Party, 67-; mem, Rep. State Cent. Cmt, 67-; mem. staff, Rep. Cand. for Gov, 68; mem, State Planning Orgn. Cmt, 68; del, Rep. Nat. Conv, 68. Bus. & Prof. Pos: Spec. rep, C.I.T. Corp, 50-58, James Talcott Inc, 58-60; self employed, 60-68; v.pres, Renn Enterprises Ltd, 69- Mil. Serv: Entered as Pvt, Air Force, 42, released as 1st Lt, 46, after serv. in Air Force Bombardier Command, Am. Theatre of Opers, 43-46; Theatre of Opers. and Unit citations. Mem: Sales and Mgt. Inst; Nat. Sales Execs; Kiwanis Int; C. of C; Salisbury Country Club. Rel: Methodist. Mailing Add: 518 W. Council St, Salisbury, N.C. 28144.

HANNA, DANIEL D. D
Wis. State Assemblyman
b. Milwaukee, Wis, 12/5/23; s. Frank Hanna and Marie H; m. to Lola L. Feldman; c. Michael, Nancy and Debra. Educ: Marquette Univ, 3 years. Polit. & Govt. Pos: Supvr, Lake, Wis, 54; Wis. State Assemblyman, currently. Bus. & Prof. Pos: Self-employed, Restaurant. Mil. Serv: Entered as Pvt, released as Sgt, after serv. in Army Medics, S. Pac; Regular Theater of Operation Ribbons. Mem: Am. Legion (past comdr, Post 505). Rel: Catholic. Legal Res: 2501 W. Henry Place, Milwaukee, Wis. 53221. Mailing Add: 615 W. Layton Ave, Milwaukee, Wis. 53221.

HANNA, MICHAEL A. D
Chmn, Washington Co. Dem. Party, Pa.
b. Joffre, Pa, 1/20/15; s. Samuel Hanna and Susan Albert H; m. 9/15/50 to Eliza Jane Gibson; c. Michael and Mark. Educ: Villanova Col, B.A, 38; Univ. Pittsburgh Law Sch, LL.B, 41. Polit. & Govt. Pos: Sch. dir, Smith Twp, Washington Co, Pa, 39-42; asst. co. solicitor, Washington Co, 47-53, chief co. solicitor, 53-56 and dist. attorney, 56-64; chmn, Washington Co. Dem. Party, 65- Bus. & Prof. Pos: Attorney-at-law, 42- Mil. Serv: Entered as Pvt, Army, 43, released as M/Sgt, 46, after serv. in ETO, 44-46; Five Battle Stars. Mem: VFW; Am. Legion; Elks; Eagles; Lions. Rel: Protestant. Mailing Add: R.D. 2, Washington, Pa. 15301.

HANNA, NILES EDWIN R
b. Enoree, S.C, 1/21/29; s. Paul Heath Hanna and Alpha Lenora Lanford H; m. 7/26/52 to Annie Pearl Larkin; c. Jerome Paul, Niles Edwin, Jr. and Patricia Ann. Educ: Wofford Col, A.B, 50; Kappa Alpha Order. Polit. & Govt. Pos: Pres, Lanford Rep. Precinct, S.C, 62, 64 & 66; del, Laurens Co. Rep. Conv, 62, 64 & 66; del, S.C. Rep. Conv, 62, 64, 66 & 68; chmn, Laurens Co. Rep. Party, 63-66; del, Spartanburg Co. Rep. Conv, 68, chmn. Credentials Cmt, 68; alternate del, Rep. Nat. Conv, 68; committeeman, Enoree Rep. Precinct, 68- Bus. & Prof. Pos: Owner, Hanna Oil Co, 53-; pres, P.H. Hanna & Son, 54-; owner, Enoree Washerette, 59-; dir, Southeast. Mag, Corp, 62- Mil. Serv: Entered as Pvt, Army, 51, released as Pfc, 53, after serv. in 481st Ord. Ammo. Co, Third Army. Mem: Mason; Sertoma Club (dir, Woodruff-Enoree Club); PTA (pres, Enoree); Good Citizenship Medal, DAR; State champions, Am. Legion Baseball, 46. Rel: Methodist. Legal Res: Parker Rd, Enoree, S.C. 29335. Mailing Add: P.O. Box 188, Enoree, S.C. 29335.

HANNA, RICHARD T. D
U.S. Rep, Calif.
b. Kemmerer, Wyo, 6/9/14; s. Robert Alexander Hanna and Martha Jane Thomas H; m. 4/1/45 to Doris Muriel Jenks; c. Pamela, Alexander Harris and Kimberly Grace. Educ: Univ. Calif, Los Angeles; Unif. Calif. Los Angeles Law Sch, LL.B, 52; Lambda Chi Alpha; Phi Delta Phi. Polit. & Govt. Pos:

Former mem, bd. dirs, Gemco Scholarship Found; recreation supvr, Works Progress Admin, W.Tex, 38-41, Calif, 46; Calif. State Assemblyman, 57-62; U.S. Rep, Calif, 62- Bus. & Prof. Pos: Newspaper reporter, Sweetwater Reporter, Tex, 37-38; gen. law practice, Orange Co, 52-; partner, Launer, Chaffee & Hanna, 58- Mil. Serv: Air Corps, Naval Res, 41-45. Mem: Am, Calif. and Orange Co. Bar Asns; Lions; VFW; Am. Legion; Elks; past pres, Westminster C. of C; area dir, W.Orange Co. Chap, Am. Red Cross; city-co. area dir, United Fund, Fullerton, 62. Rel: Latter-day Saint. Legal Res: 17071 Westport Dr, Huntington Beach, Calif. 92647. Mailing Add: House Office Bldg, Washington, D.C. 20515.

HANNA, WILLIAM SAWYER D
b. Baltimore, Md, 5/9/23; s. Edwin Fulton Hanna, Jr. and Mabel Hardy H; m. 6/3/45 to Betty Kruse; c. Gary William and Edwin Fulton, III. Educ: Mass. State Col, 43. Govt. Pos: Md. State Del, 63-67; exec. secy, Howard Co. Bd. of Trade, 57-59. Bus. & Prof. Pos: Coordinator for Appraisals & Surveys, Howard Co. Park Bd, Md, 64-66, appraiser & negotiator, Patapsco River Valley Park, 56-66; broker, Breckinridge & Hanna, Realtors, 46-66. Mil. Serv: Entered as Pvt, Army Air Force, 43, released as Sgt, 46, after serv. in 5th Air Force, S.Pac; Am. and S.Pac. Theater Ribbons; Good Conduct and Victory Medals; Sgt, Air Force Res, 46-50. Mem: Pres, Howard Co. Real Estate Bd, 61-63; dist. v.pres, Md. Asn. of Real Estate Bds, 62; Rotary; VFW; Howard Co. Hist. Soc; Friends of the Patapsco Inst; Hist. Ellicott Mills; Am. Right-of-Ways Asn. Achievements: Sponsored legis. for hwy. safety, driver educ. and safety belts in automobiles; proponent of enlargement of voc. training in Md, preservation of open spaces and protection of rivers; private pilot license, 42-66. Rel: Episcopal. Mailing Add: 703 S. St. John's Lane, Ellicott City, Md. 21043. (1967)

HANNAFORD, MARK WARREN D
Mem, Calif. Dem. State Cent. Cmt.
b. Woodrow, Colo, 2/7/25; s. William Townsend Hannaford and Ina Owen H; m. 4/20/48 to Sara Jane Lemaster; c. Mark William, Kim Karl and Robert Owen. Educ: Ball State Univ, B.A, 50; Yale Univ, John Hay fel, 61-62. Polit. & Govt. Pos: Mem, Planning Cmn, Lakewood, Calif, 60-61, city councilman, 66-68, mayor, 68-; mem, Los Angeles Co. Dem. Cent. Cmt, 62-67; mem, Calif. Dem. State Cent. Cmt, 66-; del, Dem. Nat. Conv, 68. Bus. & Prof. Pos: Teacher Govt, Lakewood High Sch, 56-67, Polit. Sci, Long Beach City Col, 67- Mil. Serv: Entered as Pvt, Air Force, 43, released as T/Sgt, 46, after serv. in 43rd Bomb Group, 5th Air Force, Pac. Theatre on Bomber Crew, 44-45. Rel: Protestant. Mailing Add: 4944 N. Stevely Ave, Lakewood, Calif. 90713.

HANNAFORD, PETER DOR R
Mem, Calif. Rep. State Cent. Cmt.
b. Glendale, Calif, 9/21/32; s. Donald Richardson Hannaford and Elinor Nielsen H; m. 8/14/54 to Irene Harville; c. Richard Harville and Donald R, II. Educ: Univ. Calif, Berkeley, A.B, 54; Order of the Golden Bear; Theta Xi. Polit. & Govt. Pos: Assoc. mem, Calif. Rep. State Cent. Cmt, 65-67, mem, 68-; treas, Rep. Alliance, E.Bay Div, Calif, 66, v.pres, 67, pres, 68, pres, Alameda Co. Div, 69; mem, Alameda Co. Rep. Cent. Cmt, 66-; chmn, 16th Assembly Dist. Rep. Coord. Coun, 69; managed several campaigns in Calif. Bus. & Prof. Pos: V.pres, Kennedy, Hannaford, Inc, 57-62, pres, Kennedy, Hannaford & Dolman, Inc, 62-67, Pettler & Hannaford, Inc, 67- Mil. Serv: Entered as 2nd Lt, Army Signal Corps, 54, released as 1st Lt, 56, after serv. in 24th Signal Bn, Ft. Devens, Mass, 55-56. Mem: Mutual Advert. Agency Network (nat. pres, 68-69); Advert. Club Oakland (pres, 61-62); Univ. Club, San Francisco; The Guardsmen; Athenian-Nile Club, Oakland; Rotary; Sierra Club; bd. dirs, Oakland Symphony Orchestra Asn; Children's Hosp. Med. Center; bd. trustees, Piedmont Commun. Church. Rel: Protestant. Mailing Add: 2083 Oakland Ave, Piedmont, Calif. 94611.

HANNAH, JOHN HENRY, JR. D
Tex. State Rep.
b. Nacogdoches, Tex, 6/30/39; s. John Henry Hannah and Velma Youngblood H; m. 1/22/65 to Susan Rebecca Denton; c. John Henry, III. Educ: Sam Houston State Col, B.S, 64; Pi Gamma Mu; Young Dem. Polit. & Govt. Pos: Mem, State Exec. Cmt, Young Dem. Tex, 63-64; Tex. State Rep, 67- Bus. & Prof. Pos: Teacher, Sam Houston State Col, 64-65. Mil. Serv: Entered as Seaman, Navy, 58, released as PO 3/C, 61, after serv. in Destroyers; Good Conduct Medal. Mem: Jr. mem, Am. Asn. of Univ. Profs. Rel: Baptist. Mailing Add: 202 Scarbrough, Lufkin, Tex. 75950.

HANNAY, ALLEN BURROUGHS D
b. Hempstead, Tex, 2/14/92; s. Robert Edwards Hannay and Katherine Allen H; m. 7/16/18 to Frances Johnson; c. Allen B, Jr. and Helen (Mrs. Dixon). Educ: Tex. A&M; Univ. of Tex, LL.B, 13; Delta Sigma Phi; Phi Delta Phi. Prof. Pos: Dist. judge, Harris Co, Tex, 30-45 and S. Dist. of Tex, 45-; co. judge, Waller Co, Tex, 15-17. Mil. Serv: 1st Lt, Air Force, 17-19. Mem: Life mem, Elks; Woodmen of the World; Mason (32°); KCCH; River Oak Country Club. Rel: Episcopal. Mailing Add: 4001 Ellalee Lane, Houston, Tex. 77027. (1967)

HANNAY, ESTHER E. D
b. Morris, Minn, 5/23/24; d. Emil Frederick Kroening and Margaret Puckta K; m. 2/27/53 to Edmund Alexander Hannay; c. Patrick Dorr, Elizabeth Gwynne (Mrs. Kroening) and James Walter Maxwell. Educ: Santa Monica Col, A.A, 43; Univ. Calif, Los Angeles, 44-45; Univ. Ala, 64. Polit. & Govt. Pos: Alternate del, Dem. Nat. Conv, 60, 64 & 68; Dem. cand. for Secy. of State, Ala, 62; dep. dir, Civil Defense, Lawrence Co, 62, mem, Indust. Develop. Bd, 65, pub. safety dir, 65-66; Dem. cand. for Ala. State Rep, 66. Mem: Bd. trustees, Econ. Opportunity Act, Lawrence Co, 65; gold card mem. and pres, Valley Bus. & Prfnl. Women's Club; Am. Legion Auxiliary. Hon. State Auditor, Ala, 65-66. Rel: Lutheran and Episcopal. Mailing Add: Route 2, Hillsboro, Ala. 35643. (1967)

HANNEMAN, PAUL A. R
Ore. State Rep.
b. Portland, Ore, 7/20/36; s. Karl Hanneman and Mary Doerfler H; m. 9/15/62 to Sandra Siltanen; c. Kurtis and John. Educ: Portland State Col. Polit. & Govt. Pos: Ore. State Rep, 65, 67 & 69; del, Rep. Nat. Conv, 68. Mem: Two C. of C; Kiwanis. Distinguished Serv. Award, Jaycees, 61; Outstanding Young Man of Ore, 67. Rel: Congregational. Mailing Add: R.R. 2, Cloverdale, Ore. 97112.

HANNEN, MARGARET E. D
V.Chmn, Coffey Co. Dem. Cent. Cmt, Kans.
b. Ellinwood, Kans, 12/17/12; d. Henry Edward Hagen and Katherine Apel H; m. 6/16/36 to Louis Robert Hannen; c. Louis Edward and Lois Ann (Mrs. Smith). Educ: Kans. Univ, A.B. and Univ. Teacher's Dipl, 34; Nat. Collegiate Players. Polit. & Govt. Pos: Dem. precinct committeewoman, Second Ward, Burlington, Kans, 20 years; v.chmn, Coffey Co. Dem. Cent. Cmt, 56-; Fifth Dist. v.chmn, Woodrow Wilson Women's Luncheon Club, 68 and twice previously; mem, Gov. Cmn. on Status of Women, 68; mem, bd. dirs, Kans. Women for Hwy. Safety, 69. Mem: Local study clubs; Grange. Rel: Roman Catholic. Mailing Add: 118 S. Eighth St, Burlington, Kans. 66839.

HANNON, BARRY THOMAS D
Mass. State Rep.
b. Boston, Mass, 11/21/35; s. Edwin F. Hannon and Marguerite Barry H; m. 11/21/59 to Deborah K. Smith; c. Amy, Barry, Jr. and Kathryn. Educ: Holy Cross Col, Worcester, Mass, B.S, 58; Boston Univ. Law Sch, LL.B, 61. Polit. & Govt. Pos: Mass. State Rep, Fifth Norfolk Dist, 67-; mem, Braintree Dem. Town Cmt, 68-69, chmn, 69. Bus. & Prof. Pos: Partner, Hannon and Hurley, 65- Mil. Serv: Entered as 2nd Lt, Air Force, 63, released as Capt, 65, after serv. in 831st Combat Support Group, Tactical Air Command, 63-65; Capt, Res, 65- Mem: Mass. and Norfolk Co. Bar Asns; Elks; K. of C; Jaycees; Sons of Union Vet. of Civil War. Rel: Roman Catholic. Mailing Add: 305 West St, Braintree, Mass. 02184.

HANNON, GEORGE WILLIAM, JR. D
Majority whip, Conn. House of Rep.
b. Hartford, Conn, 12/29/32; s. George W. Hannon Sr. and Mary Stanton H; m. 4/11/53 to Doris Elaine Davy; c. Patricia L, David R, Margaret E, Elizabeth J, Kathleen M, Colleen J, Thomas K, James S. and Mary Catherine. Educ: St. Bonaventure Univ, 2 years; Univ. Conn, 1 year. Polit. & Govt. Pos: Conn. State Rep. and Majority Whip, Conn. House of Rep, 69- Mem: Elks (charter mem. Lodge 2063); Lions (pres, East Hartford Club, 65-66). Distinguished Serv Award, East Hartford Lions Club, 62. Rel: Roman Catholic. Mailing Add: 9 Ellsworth St, East Hartford, Conn. 06108.

HANNUM, ROBERT JOHN R
Secy, Montgomery Co. Rep. Cmt, Pa.
b. Phila, Pa, 3/19/21; s. Edwin Pennell Hannum and Frances Smith H; m. 1/29/38 to Esther Nichols; c. Robert J, Jr. and Sandra Lee (Mrs. Dockstader). Polit. & Govt. Pos: Chmn, Cheltenham Twp. Rep. Orgn, 64-; secy, Montgomery Co. Rep. Cmt, 66-, area leader, 66-; alternate del, Rep. Nat. Conv, 68; 1st v.pres, Montgomery Co. Asn. Twp. Off, 68. Bus. & Prof. Pos: Bunting Co, Inc, Phila, Pa, 46 and Poloron Prod, Inc, New Rochelle, N.Y, 66- Mil. Serv: Entered as Pvt, Army, 42, released as 1st Lt, 45, after serv. in Fourth Armored Div, ETO; Two Purple Hearts; 2 ETO Stars. Mem: Am. Legion; Mason; Consistory; Shrine; East. Montgomery Co. Profession-Bus. Coun; Rep. League of Montgomery Co. Rel: Lutheran. Mailing Add: 37 Dewey Road, Cheltenham, Pa. 19012.

HANSEN, CARL R. R
V.Chmn, Cook Co. Rep. Cent. Cmt, Ill.
b. Chicago, Ill, 5/2/26; s. Carl M. Hansen and Anna Roge H; m. 12/31/52 to Christa Marie Loeser; c. Lothar. Educ: Univ. Chicago, M.B.A, 54. Polit. & Govt. Pos: Resident officer, U.S. High Cmn. for Germany, 48-52; chmn, Young Rep. Orgn. of Cook Co, Ill, 57-58; mem. bd, United Rep. Fund of Ill, 58-; del, Ill. State Rep. Conv, 62, 64, 66 & 68; Rep. committeeman, Elk Grove Twp, Cook Co, 62-; primary campaign mgr, Percy for Gov. Cmt, 63-64; v.chmn, Cook Co. Rep. Cent. Cmt, 64-66 & 68-, chmn. patronage cmt, 66-, chmn. inner city cmt, 68-; chmn, Third Rep. Dist. Rep. Party, 64-; spec. campaign adv, Ogilvie for Gov. Cmt, 68; del, Rep. Nat. Conv, 68; chmn, Third Sen. Dist. Rep. Party, 68- Bus. & Prof. Pos: Serv. v.pres, Mkt. Research Corp. Am, dir. mkt. research, Earle Ludgin & Co. and Kitchens of Sara Lee, 56-67; pres, Chicago Assocs, Inc, 67- Mil. Serv: Entered as Pvt, Army, 44, released as 1st Lt, 48, after serv. in European Command, Res, Maj.(Ret). Mem: Am. Mkt. Asn; Am. Statist. Asn; Shrine; Scottish Rite; Mason; ROA; Lions; Am. Legion; Danish Club Chicago; Dania Soc; Swedish Club Chicago; Am. Scandinavian Found; Univ. Chicago Alumni Asn; John Ericsson Rep. League. Rel: Lutheran. Mailing Add: 110 S. Edward St, Mt. Prospect, Ill. 60056.

HANSEN, CLIFFORD PETER R
U.S. Sen, Wyo.
b. Zenith, Wyo, 10/16/12; s. Peter Christoffersen Hansen and Sylvia Irene Wood H; m. 9/24/34 to Martha Elizabeth Close; c. Mary (Mrs. Mead) and Peter Arthur. Educ: Univ. Wyo, B.S, 34; Alpha Zeta; Delta Sigma Rho; Sigma Nu. Hon. LL.D, Univ. Wyo, 65. Polit. & Govt. Pos: Chmn. adv. cmt. livestock research and mkt, Secy. of Agr; Teton Co. Cmnr, Wyo, 43-51; trustee, Univ. Wyo, 46-, pres, 56-63; Gov. Wyo, 63-67; mem. exec. cmt, Nat. and West. Gov. Conf, 65-; U.S. Sen, Wyo, 67-; Del, Rep. Nat. Conv, 68. Bus. & Prof. Pos: V.pres, Jackson State Bank, Wyo, 53- Mem: Am. Nat. Cattlemen's Asn.(second v.pres, 56-57); Wyo. Stock Growers Asn.(pres, 53-55); Rotary; Newcomen Soc; AF&AM; Shrine; Mason (33°); Am. Soc. Range Mgt. Rel: Episcopal. Mailing Add: Jackson, Wyo. 83001.

HANSEN, CONNOR THEODORE
Assoc. Justice, Wis. Supreme Court
b. Freeman, S.Dak, 11/1/13; s. William Dayton Hansen and Gladdus G. Hall H; m. 6/17/39 to Annette P. Ferry; c. Annette H.(Mrs. Benjamin E. Olson), Peter C, David P. and Jane H.(Mrs. Richard LaRonge). Educ: Wis. State Univ, B.S, 34; Univ. Wis. Law Sch, J.D, 37; Sigma Nu; Phi Delta Phi. Polit. & Govt. Pos: Dist. attorney, Eau Claire Co, Wis, 39-43; spec. agent, Fed. Bur. Invest, Dept. Justice, Wash, D.C, 43-45; co. judge, Eau Claire Co, 58-67; assoc. justice, Wis. Supreme Court, currently. Bus. & Prof. Pos: Lawyer, Eau Claire, Wis, 39-58. Mem: Eau Claire, Dane and Milwaukee Co, Wis. State and Am. Bar Asns; Am. Law Inst; Inst. of Judicial Admin; Wis. Dist. Attorney Asn.(past pres); Wis. State Bd. Juvenile Court Judges (past pres). Rel: Protestant. Mailing Add: 2873 Kingston Dr, Madison, Wis. 53713.

HANSEN, GEORGE V. R
Dep. Adminstr, Agr. Stabilization and Conserv. Serv, U.S. Dept. Agr.
b. Tetonia, Idaho, 9/14/30; m. to Connie Camp; c. Steven George, James Vernon, Patricia Sue, William Dean and Joanne. Educ: Ricks Col, B.A, 56;

Idaho State Univ; Grimms Bus. Col, Pocatello, Idaho. Polit. & Govt. Pos: Former pres, Bannock Co. Young Rep. Club, Idaho; former v.chmn, publicity chmn. and precinct committeeman, Bannock Co. Rep. Cent. Cmt; mayor, Alameda, 61-62; city cmnr, Pocatello, 62-65; U.S. Rep, Idaho, 65-69; dep. adminstr, Agr. Stabilization and Conserv. Serv, U.S. Dept. Agr, 69- Bus. & Prof. Pos: Agent, life ins. Mil. Serv: Air Force, 3½ years; Naval Res. Officer. Mem: Dir, Idaho Munic. League, 61-63; past pres, 20-30 Club; past dir, Kiwanis; C. of C; Farm Bur; Am. Legion; chmn, Co. Heart Fund. Rel: Latter-day Saint. Mailing Add: 2792 N. Quebec St, Arlington, Va. 22207.

HANSEN, GRANT LEWIS R
Asst. Secy. of Air Force for Research and Develop.
b. Bancroft, Idaho, 11/5/21; s. Paul Ezra Hansen and Leona Sarah Lewis H; m. 4/21/45 to Iris Rose Heyden; c. Alan Lee, Brian Craig, Carol Margaret, David James and Ellen Diane. Educ: Ill. Inst. Tech, B.S. in Elec. Eng, 48; Univ. Calif, Los Angeles; Calif. Inst. Tech; Tau Beta Pi; Eta Kappa Nu. Polit. & Govt. Pos: Asst. Secy. of Air Force for Research and Develop, 69- Bus. & Prof. Pos: Former test conductor, Nike Prog, White Sands Proving Grounds, N.Mex, launched 74 of the earliest Nike research and develop. vehicles, responsible for design of Nike Launch Control and Test Equipment, later responsible for all elec. and electronic eng. for Nike Ajax, Nike Hercules, Honest John, Sparrow, MB-1, Thor, Thor-Delta, Nike Zeus and Skybolt and former tech. mgr, Sparrow flight test, Naval Air Missile Test Center, Point Mugu, Calif; former participant, research and develop. flight test progs, Holloman and Vandenberg Air Force Bases and Cape Kennedy; assisted in deployment of the Thor weapon system in Eng; asst. chief design engr, Douglas Aircraft Co, 58-60; chief engr, Convair Div, Gen. Dynamics Corp, San Diego, Calif, 60-62, v.pres. and prog. dir, Centaur, 62-65, v.pres, Launch Vehicle Prog, 65-69. Mil. Serv: Entered as A/S, Navy, 40, released as Chief Radio Tech, 45; Purple Heart; Asiatic-Pac. Area Campaign Medal with Nine Bronze Stars; Am. Defense Serv. Medal with One Star; Am. Area Campaign Medal; Good Conduct Medal. Mem: Assoc. fel, Am. Inst. of Aeronaut. and Astronaut; sr. mem, Inst. of Elec. and Electronics Engrs; Nat. Soc. of Aerospace Prfnl; sr. mem, Am. Astronaut. Soc; Grossmont-Mt. Helix Improv. Asn. Pub. Serv. Award, NASA, 66; Recognition Award for leadership and exceptional sci. and tech. accomplishment in connection with NASA's Surveyor I mission, Ill. Inst. Tech. Alumni Asn, 67. Rel: Latter-day Saint. Legal Res: San Diego, Calif. Mailing Add: 4 E. 968, The Pentagon, Washington, D.C. 20330.

HANSEN, JAMES MAGNUS D
b. Laurel, Nebr, 1/21/31; s. Magnus V. Hansen and Olivia W. Vorum H; m. 1/8/55 to Suzanne Miller; c. Gregory Alan, Lorie Annette, Eric James and Jeffrey Douglas. Educ: Dana Col, 54-55; Wayne State Col, B.A, 58; Univ. Wis-Milwaukee, 66-67. Polit. & Govt. Pos: Chmn, Kenosha-McCarthy for Pres, 68; del, Dem. Nat. Conv, 68. Bus. & Prof. Pos: Teacher, Britt Community Schs, Iowa, 58-61 and Kenosha Pub. Schs, Wis, 61- Mil. Serv: Entered as Airman, Air Force, 50, released as Airman 2/C, 53, after serving in 6400 Air Depot Wing, Far East Theater, 51-53. Rel: Lutheran. Mailing Add: 3401 104th St, Kenosha, Wis. 53140.

HANSEN, JOHN ROBERT D
b. Manning, Iowa, 8/24/01; s. Herman P. Hansen and Laura Karstens H; m. 6/21/29 to Mary Louise Osthoff, wid. 3/5/67; remarried 5/19/69 to Dorothy Meyer; c. Robert and John. Educ: State Univ. Iowa, 19-21; Alpha Sigma Phi. Polit. & Govt. Pos: Mem, Carroll Co. Dem. Cent. Cmt, Iowa, 32-52, chmn, 44-52; alternate del, Dem. Nat. Conv, 44 & 64 and del, 48 & 68; former mem, Iowa Cmn. on Interstate Coop. and exec. coun, Gov. Cmn. on Alcoholism; dist. chmn, State Dem. Cent. Cmt, 52-57; mem, Bd. Control State Insts, 57-60; West. Iowa area mgr, Savings Bonds Div, U.S. Treas. Dept, 61-62; U.S. Rep, Seventh Dist, Iowa, 64-66; mem, Iowa State Hwy. Cmn, 67-69. Bus. & Prof. Pos: Majority owner and pres, Dultmeier Mfg. Co, Manning, Iowa, 32-62; gen. mgr. and prin. partner, Dultmeier Sales Co, Omaha, 34-57. Mem: Charter mem. and past pres, Manning Rotary; Manual Lodge 450 AF&AM; Sioux City Consistory; Za Ga Zig Shrine; Salona Chap. Eastern Star; Izaak Walton League; Lions; former mem, Red Cross Cmt. and S.W. Iowa Coun, Boy Scouts; Nat. Farm Equip. Mfrs. Asn; Manning Gen. Hosp. Bd; bd of trustees, Col. of Osteopathic Med. and Surg, Des Moines; Manning League; Iowa Ment. Health Asn. Rel: Presbyterian; Elder. Mailing Add: 69 E. Lane, Winterset, Iowa 50273.

HANSEN, JULIA BUTLER D
U.S. Rep, Wash.
b. Portland, Ore, 6/14/07; m. to Henry A. Hansen; c. David K. Educ: Univ. Wash, B.A. Polit. & Govt. Pos: Wash. State Rep, 39-60, speaker pro tem, Wash. House Rep, 55-60; U.S. Rep, Wash, 60-, chmn. House Appropriations Subcmt. on Dept. Interior and Rel. Agencies, U.S. House Rep, mem, House Appropriations Subcmt. For. Oper; del, Dem. Nat. Conv, 68. Mem: Bus. & Prfnl. Women's Clubs, Longview, Wash; Eastern Star; past pres, local Red Cross, Polio Found, Crusade for Freedom and War Fund. Recipient Certificate of Merit, Wash. State Chap, Road Building; Wash. Outstanding Serv. Plaque; Good Roads Assoc. Award. Legal Res: Cathlamet, Wash. Mailing Add: 201 Cannon Bldg, Washington, D.C. 20515.

HANSEN, MARVIN E. D
b. Eugene, Ore, 6/4/27; s. Edwin M. Hansen and Mary H; single. Educ: Univ. Ore, B.S. in Law, 53; Willamette Univ, LL.B, 59. Polit. & Govt. Pos: Chmn, Lane Co. Dem. Cent. Cmt, Ore, 64-68. Bus. & Prof. Pos: Dairyman, 45-65; assoc, Johnson, Johnson & Harrang, 59-62; sole practitioner, 62- Mil. Serv: 2nd Lt, Air Force, 54-56; Cert. of Admin. Achievement. Mem: Elks; Ore. State, Lane Co. and Am. Bar Asns; Am. Judicature Soc; Very Little Theater. Rel: Lutheran. 1967 Legal Res: Eugene, Ore. No mailing address available. (1967)

HANSEN, MELVIN E. 'MEL' R
Minn. State Sen.
b. Russell, Minn, 9/20/15; s. Ludvig Hansen and Clara Petersen H; m. 1937 to Ethel E. Long; c. Sharon (Mrs. James C. Beckstrom), Judy C. and Kerry M. Educ: Univ. Minn, correspondence, 33-34; Univ. Minn, Minneapolis, 34-37; B.A, 40, exten, 37-60. Polit. & Govt. Pos: Treas, 12th Ward Rep. Orgn, Minneapolis, Minn, 60-62; Minn. State Sen, 34th Dist, 63- Bus. & Prof. Pos: Chief acct. and off. mgr, Fiber Div, Archer Daniels, Midland, Minn, 40-52; cost analyst, Ford Motor Co, St. Paul, 53-54; off. mgr. and credit mgr, Buttrey Stores, Minneapolis, 55-57; v.pres, Minn. Employ. Agencies Asn, 66-68; mgr, Careers Placement Serv, 57-65, pres, Careers, Inc, 65- Mil. Serv: Entered as Ens, Naval Res, 44, released as Lt.(jg), 46, after serv. in DD 614, asst. to legal assistance officer, Sixth Naval Dist, ETO. Mem: YMCA(chmn. Minn. YMCA youth in govt. prog); Boy Scouts; Int. Inst. St. Paul (bd. mem); RAM (3°); Roosevelt PTA (legis. chmn); Roosevelt Area Commun. Asn; Longfellow Field Activities Coun; Lake Hiawatha Recreation Coun; Toastmaster Int.(past area gov); Metro Clean Air Cmt.(corps of the founders); Danebo; Hennepin Co. Respiratory Disease Asn.(bd.mem). Rel: Lutheran; Secy. Bd. Pensions, Lutheran Church in Am; Past Pres, St. Peders Lutheran Church. Mailing Add: 4505 28 Ave. S, Minneapolis, Minn. 55406.

HANSEN, ORVAL HOWARD R
U.S. Rep, Idaho
b. Firth, Idaho, 8/3/26; s. Farrell Lawrence Hansen and Lily Walquist H; m. 12/31/55 to June Duncan; c. Margaret, Elizabeth, James, Katherine, John, Mary and Sarah. Educ: Univ. Idaho, B.A, 50; George Wash. Univ, J.D, 54; London Sch. Econs. and Polit. Sci, Univ. of London, 54-55; Phi Beta Kappa; Sigma Delta Chi; Phi Alpha Delta; Sigma Chi. Polit. & Govt. Pos: V.chmn, Idaho Young Rep. League, 50; Idaho State Rep, Bonneville Co, 56-62 & 64-66; mem, Rep. Cent. Cmt, Bonneville Co, 56-66; nominee, U.S. House Rep, 62; chmn, Idaho Manpower Adv. Cmt, 63-; mem, Idaho Cmn. Constitution Rev, 66; Idaho State Sen, Dist. 30, 67-68; U.S. Rep, Second Dist, 69- Mil. Serv: Entered as A/S, Navy, 44, released as Seaman 1/C, 46, after serv. in Pac, 45-46; Am. and Asiatic-Pac. Theater Ribbons; Victory Medal; Capt, Air Force Res. Mem: Ninth Dist. Bar Asn.(pres, 66-67); Am. and Idaho State Bar Asns; Rotary; Am. Legion; Idaho Farm Bur. Fedn; C. of C. Awarded Rotary Found. Fellowship for study at Univ. of London, 54-55. Rel: Latter-day Saint. Legal Res: 385 12th St, Idaho Falls, Idaho 83401. Mailing Add: 1321 Longworth House Office Bldg, Washington, D.C. 20515.

HANSEN, OTHELLO TANNER R
Inspector of Mines, Idaho
b. Collinston, Utah, 12/15/05; s. Jame Christian Hansen and Sarah Tanner H; m. 8/12/36 to Margaret Pratt; c. Mary Lucile (Mrs. Leslie Anderson) and Carol Jean (Mrs. Charles Blake). Educ: Brigham Young Univ, 24-26; Utah State Univ, B.S, 29; Univ. of Mo, M.S, 30. Polit. & Govt. Pos: Asst. land cmnr, Idaho, 50-58, inspector of mines, 63- Bus. & Prof. Pos: Analyst, War Prod. Bd, 42-45; chief lay-out engr, Idaho Power Co, 45-47; prfnl. engr, 47-63. Mem: Nat. Soc. of Prfnl. Engrs; Am. Inst. of Mining, Metallurgical and Petroleum Engrs; Idaho Safety Coun; Nat. Safety Coun; Idaho Soc. of Prfnl. Engrs; Mine Inspectors' Inst. of Am. Rel: Latter-day Saint. Mailing Add: 2301 N. 13th St, Boise, Idaho 83702.

HANSEN, PHIL L. D
Attorney Gen, Utah.
b. Park City, Utah, 9/5/23; s. Henry Hansen and Hazel Marie Sharp H; div; c. Jane Marie, Steven La Marr and David Alan. Educ: Carroll Col; Mont. State Sch. Mines; Univ. Utah; Phi Alpha Delta. Polit. & Govt. Pos: Prosecuting attorney, Murray City, Utah, 51 and Judge, 52-56; Attorney Gen, Utah, 65-68. Mil. Serv: Entered as A/S, Navy, 43, released as Specialist 2/C, 45, after serv. in Pac. Mem: Pres, C. of C, 51; Kiwanis; Eagles; Elks; VFW; Am. Legion; Salt Lake Co, Utah State and Am. Bar Asns. Admitted to practice law before U.S. Supreme Court; football, basketball, baseball and tennis. Rel: Latter-day Saint. Mailing Add: 1205 East South Temple St, Salt Lake City, Utah. 84102. (1967)

HANSEN, REED ROBERT D
b. Seattle, Wash, 10/23/18; s. Jacob Sigurd Hansen and Ruth Reed H; m. 6/5/45 to Emma Jane Dakan; c. Rolf and Barbara. Educ: Univ. of Wash, B.A, 43 and M.S, 52; Univ. of Wis, Ph.D, 60. Polit. & Govt. Pos: Mem, Whitman Co. Dem. Cmt, Wash, 60-64, chmn, 65-67; chief personal income tax sect, Off. Tax Anal, Off. of Secy, U.S. Treasury, until 67, del, Dem. Nat. Conv, 68; mem, Co. Dem. Exec. Bd, currently; Bus. & Prof. Pos: Prof. econ, Wash. State Univ, 56-; tax consult, Gov. Tax Adv. Coun, 58 & 66; vis. scholar, Brookings Inst, Wash, D.C, 63; vis. lectr, Univ. Khartoum, Sudan, 64. Mil. Serv: Entered as Ens, Navy, 43, released as Lt, 45, after serv. in S.Pac. Fleet; S.Pac. Campaign Ribbons. Publ: Current Readings in Economics, Irwin Co, 60; 'Retail Sales Tax Evaluation', Nat. Tax J, 3/62; 'The Diminishing Exemption', Quart. Rev. of Econ. and Bus, 11/62. Mem: Am. Econ. Asn; Am. Finance Asn; Nat. Tax Asn; Alaska Fisherman's Union; Am. Asn. of Univ. Prof. Mailing Add: 2109 Orion Dr, Pullman, Wash. 99163.

HANSEN, RODNEY ALTON R
b. Goshen, Idaho, 1/25/11; s. Hiram Knudt Hansen and Esther Peterson H; m. 6/9/37 to Jean Belnap; c. Karen Beth, Laureen, Margaret, Lowell A, Bruce E, David A. and Thayne R. Educ: Univ. Idaho, B.S. in agr; Wash. State Col; Alpha Zeta. Polit. & Govt. Pos: Chmn, Joint Senate Finance and House Appropriations Cmt, Idaho, 63-66, Idaho State Sen, 54-66; dist. conservationist, U.S. Dept. Agr, 42-47, asst. agronomist, 39-42 and jr. agronomist, 38-39. Rel: Latter-day Saint. Mailing Add: R.R. 2, Paul, Idaho 83347.

HANSEN, WILLIAM C. D
b. Neenah, Wis, 7/4/91. Educ: Univ. of Wis, B.S, 15, M.S, 25 and additional grad. work. Polit. & Govt. Pos: Mem, Whiting Plover Sch. Bd, 8 years; mem, Stevens Point Area Sch. Bd, Portage Co. Sch. Cmt, Wis. State Sen, 64-68. Bus. & Prof. Pos: Formerly high sch. teacher and prin. and supt. of schs, Neillsville, Oconto and Stoughton, Wis; pres, Wis. State Col, Stevens Point, 40-62. Mem: Pres, Northwest. Wis. Educ. Asn. at Eau Claire, 29; South. Wis. Educ. Asn, 39, Wis. Educ. Asn, 43 and Stevens Point C. of C, 57-58; past local pres, Kiwanis and Rotary. Jaycees Distinguished Citizens Award, Jaycees, 59. Mailing Add: Route 1, Box 274, Stevens Point, Wis. 54481.

HANSON, ARNOLD PHILIP R
b. Berlin, N.H, 7/11/24; s. Arnold H. Hanson and Evelyn Renaud H; m. 6/26/48 to Della Ann Lavernoich; c. Arnold P, Jr. Caryl S. and Julie E. Educ: Univ. N.H, B.A, 48; Boston Univ. Sch. of Law, LL.B, 51; Sigma Beta. Polit. & Govt. Pos: Chmn, Berlin City Rep. Cmt, N.H, 51; attorney, Coos Co, 52-56; del, Rep. Nat. Conv, 64; former mem. exec. cmt, N.H. State Rep. Cmt. Bus. & Prof. Pos: Partner, Law Firm of Bergeron and Hanson, Berlin, N.H, N. Country TV Cable Co, 62-; dir, Berlin Coop. Bank, 64-, Tri-Co.

Legal Serv, 67- Mil. Serv: Naval Submarine Serv, Pac. Theater, 43-46. Mem: Am. Bar Asn; Am. Trial Lawyers Asn; dir, N.H. Coun. on World Affairs; N.H. Bar Asn.(mem. exec. cmt, 65); Coos Co. Bar Asn.(Pres, 60); pres, Kiwanis Club of Berlin, 66; v.pres, C. of C, 64; judge advocate, VFW; former judge advocate, Am. Legion; Univ. of N.H. Alumni; Boston Univ. Alumni; Elks; Eagles; Mason; Shriners; Androscoggin Valley Country Club. Rel: Lutheran. Mailing Add: 119 Prospect St, Berlin, N.H. 03570.

HANSON, BERNICE ZILPHA R
b. Fitchburg, Mass, 12/11/01; d. Herbert Greenwood Bonney and Annie Amiott B; m. 7/19/23 to Howard Hartley Hanson; c. Virginia A.(Mrs. George Stackpole), Robert A. and Arthur W. Educ: High Sch; Exten. course in pub. speaking, Univ. N.H. Polit. & Govt. Pos: Moderator, Lebanon Town Meetings, 50-65; Maine State Rep, 51-52, 59-62 & 65-68, mem, Interim Legis. Cmts. Educ. and Appropriations to Study Sch. Construct, Maine House of Rep, 60; chmn, Lebanon Town Rep. Cmt, Maine, 53-; pres, Maine State Fedn. Rep. Women, 59-61; mem, Resolution Cmt. Educ, Rep. Nat. Conv, 60. Bus. & Prof. Pos: Part-time secy, YMCA, 44-45; clerk, Off. Price Admin, Bath Iron Works, Maine, 46. Mem: Ruth Chap, Eastern Star; pres, Arundel York Co. Rep. Women's Club, 55-56; Lebanon Hist. Soc; Grange. Rel: Congregational. Mailing Add: East Lebanon, Maine 04027.

HANSON, CAMILLA RUTH D
Treas, Tenth Dist. Dem. Party, Wis.
b. Lexington, Ky, 1/25/28; d. Edgar Zavitz Palmer and Ruth Opal Yarbrough P; m. 8/7/65 to J. Louis Hanson; c. Eric K, Stephen E. and Philip J. Sorensen. Educ: Univ. Wis, 45-46; Univ. Nebr, B.A, 49; YWCA. Polit. & Govt. Pos: Treas, Tenth Dist. Dem. Party, Wis, 67-; chmn, Ashland Co. Dem. Party, 67- Bus. & Prof. Pos: Proj. asst, Peace Corps, 62-63; spec. asst, Univ. Wis, 64-65. Mem: Headstart Parent Adv. Bd; League of Women Voters. Legal Res: 137 Tyler Ave, Mellen, Wis. 54546. Mailing Add: Box 707, Mellen, Wis. 54546.

HANSON, DEAN P. R
Chmn, Montezuma Co. Rep. Cent. Cmt, Colo.
b. Cortez, Colo, 11/15/22; s. Hazel Kirk Hanson (father deceased); m. Feb. 1953 to Shirley Kirk. Educ: Univ. Denver, B.S. in Bus. Admin, 50; Alpha Kappa Psi. Polit. & Govt. Pos: Chmn, Montezuma Co. Rep. Cent. Cmt, Colo, currently. Bus. & Prof. Pos: Indust. rels, Union Carbide Nuclear Co, 56-61; owner, Hanson Realty, 61- Mil. Serv: Entered as Pvt, Army, 43, released as S/Sgt, 46, after serv. in Qm. Corps, Pac. Theatre. Mem: Mgr, Cortez C. of C, 51-55; asst. secy, Colo. Mining Asn, 55-56; Nat. Asn. of Real Estate Bds; secy, Elks Lodge 1789. Rel: Protestant. Mailing Add: 803 Memorial Dr, Cortez, Colo. 81321. (1967)

HANSON, DONALD PAUL R
Chmn, Jackson Co. Rep. Party, Colo.
b. Laramie Wyo, 2/3/23; s. Victor Hanson Sr. and Sigrid Lindhal H; m. 5/4/47 to Anna Marie Van Valkinburg; c. Kent A, Kirk L, Kelly E, Kevin W, and Kale V. Educ: Iowa State Univ. Polit. & Govt Pos: Vet. serv. officer, Jackson Co, Colo, 3 years, civil defense dir, 15 years; chmn, Jackson Co. Rep. Party, 63- Bus. & Prof. Pos: Owner, Cattle Ranch. Mil. Serv: Entered as Pvt, Marine Corp, 43, released as Pfc, 45, after serv. in 28th Marines, Fifth Marine Div, Pacific Theatre, 44-45; Bronze Star; Purple Heart; Presidential Unit Citation; Am. Theatre and Pacific Theatre Medals. Mem: Odd Fellows; North Park Stockgrowers Asn; VFW; DAV. Rel: Methodist. Mailing Add: Box 428 Walden, Colo. 80480.

HANSON, DOYLE ROBERT D
Chmn, Dixon Co. Dem. Party, Nebr.
b. Thurston, Nebr, 7/14/03; s. George Lynn Elias Hanson and Jennie H; m. 5/9/32 to Katherin Carmen Hull; c. Wendall Hull. Educ: Morningside Col, 24-25. Polit. & Govt. Pos: Chmn, Dixon Co. Bd. Supv, 50-, chmn, Dixon Co. Welfare Bd, 50-; mem, State Welfare Rehabilitation, 62-69; pres, State Asn. Co. Officials, 64-; dir, Law Enforcement and Criminal Justice State Nebr; chmn, Dixon Co. Dem. Party, 68- Bus. & Prof. Pos: Pres, Newcastle Chevrolet Co, 26-32. Mil. Serv: Entered as Pvt, released as Cpl, Civilian Mil. Training Camp, 23. Mem: Odd Fellows; MWA. Good Sports Award, World Herald, Omaha, Nebr. Rel: Protestant. Mailing Add: New Castle, Nebr. 68757.

HANSON, FRED BYRON R
Iowa State Rep.
b. Inwood, Iowa, 11/20/88; s. Henry J. Hanson and Olive Johnson H; m. 1/12/63 to Grace M. Thompson; c. Merle A, Virgil S. and Delmar C. Educ: Lenox Col, 10; Iowa State Univ, Cert. in Agr, 12. Polit. & Govt. Pos: Co. exten. dir, Harrison Co, Iowa, 25-36; commun. proj. mgr, Farm Security Admin, Granger, 36-43, Fed. Pub. Housing Authority, Waukegan, Ill, 43-48; Iowa State Rep, 61-63 & 67- Bus. & Prof. Pos: Agency mgr, Farm Bur. Ins. Co, 49-55; secy-mgr, Mitchell Co. Fair, Osage, Iowa, 55-69. Mil. Serv: Entered as Pvt, Ill. Res. Militia, 44, released as Sgt, 47, after serv. in Third Inf. Mem: Mason; Eastern Star; MWA; Rotary; Farm Bur; Iowa and Mitchell Co. Hist. Socs. Rel: United Methodist. Mailing Add: 203 S. Fifth, Osage, Iowa 50461.

HANSON, HARLEY SVEN D
b. Vinton, Iowa, 6/20/16; s. Sven Olaf Hanson and Belle McLhaney H; m. 4/30/41 to Ina Mae Wiese; c. Barbara (Mrs. Franks) and Robert. Educ: Vinton High Sch, grad, 33. Polit. & Govt. Pos: Iowa State Rep, Benton Co, 67-69. Mil. Serv: Entered as A/S, Navy, 35, released as Machinists Mate 2/C, 39. Mem: Benton Co. Farm Bur.(treas, 3 years, pres, 1 year); Benton Co. Farm Serv. Co. Bd, 6 years; 4-H Leader, 5 years; co-chmn, Benton Co. Christian Rural Overseas Prog, 5 years. Rel: First Christian Church; Elder, 15 years. Mailing Add: R.R. 2, Vinton, Iowa 52349. (1967)

HANSON, HELEN WHEILAND D
V.Chmn, N.Dak. Dem. Non-Partisan League
b. Lemmon, S.Dak, 2/24/10; d. George C. Wheiland and Georgia M. Phelps W; m. 6/26/30 to Harold Ralph Hanson; c. Georgia (Mrs. Gutensohn) and Janice (Mrs. Christian). Educ: Valley City State Col, 27-29, life prfnl. teaching cert; grad with highest honor; Delta Zeta; Atheneum Soc. Polit. & Govt. Pos: Dist. chmn, N.Dak. Dem. Non-Partisan League Women, 58-, state v.pres, 58-60 & 63-65; del, N.Dak, Dem. Nat. Conv, 60; state v.chmn, N.Dak. Dem. Non-Partisan League, 63-67. Bus. & Prof. Pos: Sch. Teacher, 39-40. Mem: Order Eastern Star; Mo-Slope Shrine Auxiliary; N.Dak. Farmers Union. Dem. Woman of the Year Award, 65, Dem. Non-Partisan League Women's Conv. Rel: United Church of Christ. Mailing Add: R.R, New England, N.Dak. 58647.

HANSON, HENRY ELIAS D
b. Loon Lake Twp, Pequot Lake, Minn, 2/2/01; s. Fredrick Hanson and Emelia Bye H; m. 2/8/21 to Annie Jensen and m. 8/6/49 to Anna Peterson; c. Ruth, Helen, Kenneth and Darlene. Polit. & Govt. Pos: Cass Co. Agr. Inspector, 67; v.pres, Cass Co. Dem-Farmer-Labor Cmt, 66, pres, 61-66. Bus. Pos: Farmer. Mem: Chmn, Farmers Union, 60-; Cass Co. Wild Life Asn, 65 and ASCS, 61. Honored as Farmers Union Worker. Rel: Lutheran; previous chmn, Our Saviors Lutheran Church. Mailing Add: R.R. 1, Pequot Lakes, Minn. 56472. (1967)

HANSON, HERBERT L. R
Chmn, Somerset Rep. City Cmt, Maine
b. Weymouth, Mass, 3/6/25; s. Ludwig Hanson and Helga Nelson H; m. 6/1/45 to M. Shirley Thompson; c. Shirley Anne, Cheryl Lynne and H. Bradley. Educ: Univ. of Maine. Polit. & Govt. Pos: Moderator, Solon, Maine, 55-61, tax collector and constable, 56-61; commun. committeeman, Somerset Agr. Stabilization and Conserv. Cmt, 56-62; chmn, Solon Rep. Town Cmt, 56-66; mem, State Rep. Resolution Cmt, 60; chmn, Somerset Young Rep, 60-61; chmn, State Soil and Water Conserv. Div, Assoc. Educ. Cmt, 64-; chmn, Somerset Soil and Water Conserv. Div, 65; chmn, Somerset Rep. City Cmt, 65-; mem, Second Cong. Dist. Rep. Cmt, 66; Maine State Rep, 67-69. Bus. & Prof. Pos: Owner and operator, Poultry and egg bus, produce bus. and store, 46-53 and Brookvale Farm, 53-66; owner, real estate bus. Mil. Serv: Entered as Pvt, Army Air Force, 43, released as Capt, 45, after serv. as Pilot, 87th Fighter Squadron, 79th Fighter Group, 12th Air Force, ETO, 44 & 45; Capt, Air Force Res, 45-49; Distinguished Flying Cross; Three Air Medals; Two Presidential Unit Citations; ETO Ribbon with Six Battle Stars; Expert Aerial Gunnery Medal; Expert Small Arms Medal. Mem: Master, North Somerset Grange; pres, NEMPA Local; dir, Farm Bur; Dirigo; RAD Cmt. Received War Bond as Most Physically Fit Aviation Cadet, 43. Mailing Add: Brighton Rd, Solon, Maine 04979. (1967)

HANSON, J. LOUIS D
b. Chicago, Ill, 9/25/25; s. Hans Martin Johan Hanson and Ann Carroll H; m. 8/7/65 to Camilla R. Palmer Sorensen; stepchildren, Eric K, Stephen E. and Philip J. Sorensen. Educ: Northwest. Univ. Polit. & Govt. Pos: Chmn, Tenth Dist. Dem. Party, 61-63; v.chmn. Wis. Del, Dem. Nat. Conv, 64; mem, Legis. Coun, 65 & 66; chmn, Wis. State Dem. Party, formerly; spec. asst. to U.S. Sen. Gaylord A. Nelson, Wis, currently. Bus. & Prof. Pos: Pres, Bad River Lumber Co, 45; v.pres, Louis Hanson Co, 45- and Phillips Plastics Corp, 65-66. Mailing Add: Box 707, Mellen, Wis. 54546.

HANSON, JOSEPH LYLE R
b. Dolliver, Iowa, 10/2/26; s. Andros O. Hanson and Sylvia Heggen H; m. 12/20/48 to Verna Lavon Richardson; c. Randy Sprout, Thomas, Rebecca, Eric and Jennifer. Educ: State Univ. Iowa, B.A, 49, J.D, 51; Gamma Eta Gamma. Polit. & Govt. Pos: Precinct committeeman, Young Rep, Iowa, 52-53, co. chmn. and state committeeman, 54-55; precinct committeeman, Rep. Party, 60-; chmn, Palo Alto Co. Rep. Party, 62-68. Bus. & Prof. Pos: Attorney, Iowa-Ill. Gas & Elec. Co, 51-53; attorney-at-law, Smith & Hanson, 53-67, Hanson & Boumann, 68- Mil. Serv: Entered as Pvt, Army, 46, released as Pfc, 47, after serv. in 19th Inf. Regt, Army of Occup. Japan, 46-47; Victory Medal; Japanese Occup. Medal. Mem: Am, Iowa and Palo Alto Asns; Iowa Acad. of Trial Lawyers; Am. Trial Lawyers Asn; C. of C; Emmetsburg Indust. Corp; Farm Bur. Rel: Lutheran. Mailing Add: 606 Palmer, Emmetsburg, Iowa 50536.

HANSON, P. EMERY R
Chmn, Rep. City Cmt, Leominster, Mass.
b. Brockton, Mass, 7/15/22; s. Emil W. Hanson and Gladys A. Cook H; m. 6/26/43 to Merrilyn J. Carlson; c. Mark E, Gale M, Glenn D. and Joan C. Educ: N.Park Col; Univ. Minn. Sch. of Eng, B.S.M.E. Polit. & Govt. Pos: Chmn, Ward 5, Rep. Cmt, Mass, 58-60; chmn, Rep. City Cmt, Leominster, 60- Bus. & Prof. Pos: Foreman, Materials Control Dept, Allis Chalmers Mfg. Co, West Allis, Wis, 46-50, gen. foreman, 50-53, asst. supt, 53; pres. and treas, Gould Indust. Supply Co, Inc, Leominster, Mass, 54- Mil. Serv: Entered as Ens, Navy, 44, released as Lt.(jg), 46, after serv. in Pac. Area. Mem: Rotary; C. of C; United Fund; treas, Pilgrim Pines Bible Camp, W. Swanzey, N.H. Chmn. of Bd, Pilgrim Covenant Church, Lunenburg, Mass, chmn, Montachusett Coun. of Churches Laymen's Cmt. Mailing Add: 784 Merriam Ave, Leominster, Mass. 01453.

HANSON, RICHARD D. R
N.H. State Rep.
b. Bow, N.H, 6/12/27; s. Oscar V. Hanson and Lillian Morgan H; m. 7/9/49 to Betty Mae Morse; c. Susan C, Tina J, Richard D, Jr, Jonathan K. and Heidi E. Educ: Concord High Sch, 4 years. Polit. & Govt. Pos: Selectman, Bow, N.H, 54; N.H. State Rep, 58-; Chmn, Merrimack Co. Rep. Party, 60-62, del. chmn, 62; pres, N.H. Assessors Asn, 64; alternate del, Rep. Nat. Conv, 68; cmt. chmn, Munic. and Co. Govt, N.H, 69. Bus. & Prof. Pos: Owner, Hanson Bldg. Co, 59-; owner, Bow Trucking Co, 60- Mil. Serv: Entered as Seaman, Navy, 45, released as 1/C PO, 46, after serv. in Fleet No. Seven, S.Pac, 45-46. Mem: Bow Commun. Men's Club; Bow Vol. Fire Dept; N.H. Archaeol. Asn; Am. Legion; Mason; Grange; Pat's Peak Ski Club (pres). Rel: Methodist. Mailing Add: 14 Grandview, Bow, N.H. 03301.

HANSON, RICHARD H. Conservative
b. 1932. Educ: Duluth Pub. Schs. Polit. & Govt. Pos: Minn. State Rep, 67-69. Bus. & Prof. Pos: Pres. and co-owner, Arrowhead Off. Machines Co. Mem: Jaycees; Rotary. Mailing Add: 1618 Maple Grove Rd, Duluth, Minn. 55811. (1967)

HANSON, ROGER LEON R
Minn. State Rep.
b. Pelican Rapids, Minn, 11/26/25; s. Henry Jacob Hanson and Anna Larson H; m. 6/29/52 to Dona Marie Schermerhorn; c. Charles, Cynthia, Timothy,

Cheryl and Hans. Educ: Dakota Bus. Col, 44-45. Polit. & Govt. Pos: Minn. State Rep, Dist. 55, Otter Tail Co, 69- Bus. & Prof. Pos: Partner and owner, Vergas Hardware Co, 45; spec. dep. sheriff, Otter Tail Co; fire chief, Vergas Fire Dept. Mem: Lions; Vergas-Frazee Sch. Bd.(dir); Otter Tail Empire Resort Asn.(pres); Rel: Lutheran. Mailing Add: Box 86, Vergas, Minn. 56587.

HANSON, ROYCE D
b. Oklahoma City, Okla, 9/2/31; s. Chester Garfield Hanson and Ila Mae Quier H; m. 2/8/58 to Mary Byrd Gesler; c. Royce B, Mark C. and Juliette. Educ: Cent. State Col, Okla, B.A, 53; Am. Univ, M.A, 57 and Ph.D, 63; Pi Kappa Delta; Pi Sigma Alpha; Alpha Chi. Polit. & Govt. Pos: Pres, Md. Cmt. for Fair Representation, 60-66, secy-treas, Nat. Cmt, 65-; cand. for U.S. Rep, Sixth Dist, Md, 64, Eighth Dist, 66. Bus. & Prof. Pos: Prof. govt, Am. Univ, 57- and pres, Wash. Center for Metropolitan Studies, 67- Mil. Serv: Entered as Recruit, Army, released as Cpl, 55, after serv. in Artil, Fire Direction Cmt, Camp Chaffee, Ark. Publ: The Politics of Metropolitan Cooperation, Wash. Center for Metrop. Studies, 64; Fair Representation Comes to Maryland, McGraw-Hill, 64; The Political Thicket, Prentice-Hall, 66. Mem: D.C, South. and Am. Polit. Sci. Asns; Am. Soc. Pub. Admin; Ancient & Beneficent Order of the Red Red Rose. Rel: Presbyterian. Mailing Add: 7804 Cindy Line, Bethesda, Md. 20034.

HANSON, RUDOLPH NP
Minn. State Sen.
b. Freeborn Co, Minn, 5/30/03; s. Hans L. Hanson and Gustina M. Alm H; single. Educ: Univ. Minn, B.A, 35 and LL.B, 37. Polit. & Govt. Pos: Co. attorney, Freeborn Co, Minn, 47-55; Minn. State Sen, 55- Mil. Serv: Entered as Seaman 1/C, Naval Res, 42, released as Sp. Q 2/C (RP), 45. Mem: Am, Minn. and Dist. and Co. Bar Asns; Lions Club; Am. Legion; VFW; C. of C. Legal Res: 607 W. Clark St, Albert Lea, Minn. 56007. Mailing Add: Box 568, Albert Lea, Minn. 56007.

HANSON, WARREN EUGENE R
b. Osage City, Kans, 1/13/12; s. Peter Nelson Hanson and Grace M. Walthall H; m. 4/10/36 to Vera Louise Bennett; c. Patricia Louise (Mrs. Harper). Educ: Wichita Univ, Pre-Med, 29-32; Carver Col, D.C, 36 and Ph.D, 38; Phi Sigma Epsilon. Polit. & Govt. Pos: Chmn, Wichita Univ. Collegiate Rep. Club, Kans, 31, Harvey Co. Young Rep, 46, Harvey Co. Rep. Vet, 58, and Harvey Co. Rep. Cent. Cmt, 60-69; pres, Kans. State Bd. Chiropractic Exam, 40; presidential elector, Fourth Cong. Dist, Kans, 68. Mil. Serv: Entered as Pvt, Army, 42, released as Capt, 46, after serv. in ETO, 43-46; Europe-Africa-Middle East Theater Ribbon with two Bronze Stars; Am. Theater Ribbon; Victory Medal. Mem: Kans. Chiropractic Soc.(secy, 50-58); Mason; Am. Legion; 40 et 8; VFW; Elks; Optimists Int. Rel: Methodist. Mailing Add: 416 N. Pine, Newton, Kans. 67114.

HANSTEDT, AUGUSTUS ERNEST R
Chmn, Oconto Co. Rep. Party, Wis.
b. Gillett, Wis, 7/13/06; s. Henry Carl Hanstedt and Martha Kirchoff H; m. 6/20/29 to Marie L. Larsen; c. Betty Jane (Mrs. Jack Tessier), Noreen Marie (Mrs. Clyde Johnson) and Pastor Bruce Wallace. Educ: Gillett High Sch, Wis, grad, 24. Polit. & Govt. Pos: Mayor, Gillett, Wis, 62-; chmn, Oconto Co. Rep. Party, 68- Bus. & Prof. Pos: Pres, Gillett State Bank, 25-68, chmn. bd, 68. Mem: F&AM; Mason (32°); Shrine; Elks; Gillett Civic Club. Rel: Lutheran. Legal Res: 123 Eschner St, Gillett, Wis, 54124. Mailing Add: P.O. Box 186, Gillett, Wis. 54124.

HAPNER, JON CLARK R
Secy, Highland Co. Rep. Cent. Cmt, Ohio
b. Hillsboro, Ohio 11/10/34; s. William Ralph Hapner and Kathryn Hendrickson H; m. 4/10/65 to Suzanne Evans; c. Priscilla, Jonda and Jon. Educ: Ohio State Univ, B.A, 56, J.D, 58; Mexico City Col, 53; Univ. Cincinnati, 64. Polit. & Govt. Pos: Pres, Young Rep. of Highland Co, Ohio, 60-65; secy, Highland Co. Rep. Cent. Cmt, 65-; city solicitor, Hillsboro, 68- Mil. Serv: 2nd Lt, Army Artil, RFA, Cpt, Army Res, 67. Mem: Am, Ohio and Highland Co. Bar Asns; pres, Hillsboro Rotary, 64-65; Exalted Ruler, Elks, 64-65; treas, Jaycees, 62. Rel: Protestant. Legal Res: 130 Willow St, Hillsboro, Ohio 45133. Mailing Add: 100 S. High St, Hillsboro, Ohio 45133.

HARA, STANLEY IKUO D
Hawaii State Sen.
b. Honolulu, Hawaii, 5/23/23; s. Kurazo Hara and Senyo Fujiwara H; m. 12/1/45 to Diane Hisako Yamashita; c. Glenn Shoichi and Bradley Shoji. Educ: Honolulu Bus. Col; Univ. Hawaii. Polit. & Govt. Pos: Hawaii State Rep, 54-69, chmn Finance Cmt, 59-65 and v.chmn, Govt. Financing and Appropriations, 65-69; trustee, Health Facilities Planning Coun, Hawaii; Hawaii State Sen, First Sen. Dist, 69-, chmn, Educ. Cmt, Hawaii State Senate. Bus. & Prof. Pos: Owner, Glenbradia Farms, Hilo Factor and Kilauea Preserve Center; secy-treas, Akahi Painting Corp; dir, Hilo Develop, Inc; trustee, Vacationland Assocs. and Kaumana-Lani Assocs. Mem: Hawaii Farm Bur. Fedn; Produce Dealers Asn; Hilo Contractors' Asn; Native Sons & Daughters of Hawaii; Two Ten Golf Club; Hawaiian Island Archery Club; Foresters; Court Mauna Kea 8854; Japanese C. of C. and Indust. Hawaii. Grizzly Bear Award as Legis. Conservationist of Year, Nat. Wildlife Fedn. and Sears-Roebuck Found, 66. Mailing Add: 740 Kalanikoa St, Hilo, Hawaii 96720.

HARABEDIAN, MICHAEL THOMAS D
Mem, Steering Cmt, 19th Cong. Dist. Dem. Party, Calif.
b. Kars, Armenia, 9/15/14; s. Thomas Harabedian and Noono Davidian H; m. 1/14/56 to Eleanore Burger; c. Diana (Mrs. Vanus Frederickson); David T, Dennis S, Dick M, Deborah and Michael Thomas, II. Educ: James A. Garfield High Sch, 6 years. Polit. & Govt. Pos: Mem, Ways and Means Cmt, 30th Sen. Dist. Dem. Party, Calif, 67-; del, Dem. Nat. Conv, 68; mem, Steering Cmt, 19th Cong. Dist. Dem. Party, Calif, 68- Bus. & Prof. Pos: V.pres, Operating Industs, Inc, 48-, Pomona Valley Reclamation, 54- and A & A Feeding, Inc, 56-; dir. and organizer, Cerritos Valley Bank, 58- Mem: One of founders, East Los Angeles Jr. Col; F&AM; Al Malaikah Temple; YMCA (bd. dirs, 18 years); Shrine (past pres, Rio Hondo Club); Lions Inc.(past pres. and zone chmn, East Los Angeles Club, dep. dist. gov, Dist. 4L2). Lion of the Year Award, 66. Rel: Armenian Apostolic; Dir, Relig. Conf. Bldg. and chmn. bd. Saint Sarkis Church. Legal Res: 1800 Victoria Ave, Montebello, Calif. 90640. Mailing Add: 2425 S. Garfield Ave, Monterey Park, Calif. 91754.

HARBER, W. ELMER D
b. Pineville, Ark, 7/3/92; s. Thomas W. Harber and Cynthia Franks H; m. 10/14/65 to Lisbeth C. Patton. Educ: Pub. Schs, Seminole, Okla. Polit. & Govt. Pos: Dem. Nat. Committeeman, Okla, 48-50; chmn. bd, Reconstruction Finance Corp, 50-51; del, Dem. Nat. Conv, 68; mem, Bd. Econ. Warfare. Bus. & Prof. Pos: Pres, First Nat. Bank, Seminole, Okla, 21-; dir, Liberty Nat. Bank and Trust Co, Oklahoma City, 30-; pres, Am. Nat. Bank and Trust Co, Shawnee, Okla, 35- Mil. Serv: Inf, Army, World War I. Mem: Shawnee and U.S. C. of C; The President's Club. Mailing Add: c/o Am. Nat. Bank and Trust Co, Shawnee, Okla. 74801.

HARBISON, MAUREEN M. D
Mem, Ohio Dem. State Exec. Cmt.
b. Collingswood, N.J, 12/15/28; d. John J. Monroe and Helen R. Dillon M; m. 2/20/52 to Edward F. Harbison; c. Leslie Anne, Patricia, Lisa, Tracy and Kerry. Polit. & Govt. Pos: Mem, Montgomery Co. Dem. Exec. and Cent. Cmt, 65-; ward leader, 20 precincts, Centerville-Wash. Twp, 65-; alternate del-at-lg, Dem. Nat. Conv, 68; mem, Nat. Cmt. Party Struct. and Reorgn, Ohio, 69-; mem, Ohio Dem. State Exec. Cmt, currently. Bus. & Prof. Pos: Owner restaurant, Carriage House, Centerville, Ohio. Rel: Catholic. Mailing Add: 6060 Mad River Rd, Dayton, Ohio 45459.

HARBOR, WILLIAM H. R
Iowa State Rep.
b. Henderson, Iowa, 10/28/20; s. Ora Lee Harbor and Pearl Wilkerson; single. Educ: State Univ. Iowa, B.A, 43. Polit. & Govt. Pos: Mem, Town Coun, Iowa, 50-54; Iowa State Rep, 54-56 & 67-, Speaker, Iowa State House of Rep, 69-; Iowa State Sen, 56-60. Mil. Serv: Entered as A/S, Navy, 43, released as Lt.(jg), 46, after serv. in Pac; Pac. and Am. Theater Ribbons. Mem: Pres, Vol. Firemen, 50-; dir, Iowa Grain & Feed Asn, 59-62; co. comdr, Am. Legion, 54; Farm. Bur; Lions; Elks. Rel: Methodist. Mailing Add: Henderson, Iowa 51541.

HARCOURT, J. PALMER R
b. Albany, N.Y, 1/4/07; s. Samuel Charles Harcourt and Lois Palmer H; m. 4/5/35 to Anne Lee George; c. John P, Jr. Educ: Union Col, $1\frac{1}{2}$ years; Alpha Delta Phi; Tiger's Eye. Polit. & Govt. Pos: Mem, N.Y. State Rep. Cmt; committeeman, State and Town Rep. Orgn; dep. dir, div. safety, N.Y. State, asst. admin. dir, Div. Vet. Affairs and asst. admin dir, Civil Serv. Dept; alternate del, Rep. Nat. Conv, 68; chmn, Colonie Rep. Orgn, currently. Bus. & Prof. Pos: Ins. broker, Albany, N.Y; dir, Ten Eyck Insuring Agency, Inc. Mil. Serv: Entered as 2nd Lt, Army, 42, released as Capt, 44, after serv. in Qm. Corps. Mem: Ft. Orange Club; Elks; Am. Legion. Rel: Episcopal. Mailing Add: 6 Cherry Tree Rd, Loudonville, N.Y. 12211.

HARCOURT, RICHARD LLOYD R
b. San Francisco, Calif, 8/5/39; s. Harold Standley Harcourt and Lavina Speier H; m. 12/4/65 to Nancy Delagnes. Educ: Univ. San Francisco, B.S. in polit. sci, 61; Alpha Sigma Nu; Scabbard & Blade; Alpha Phi Gamma; Kappa Lambda Sigma; St. Ives Law Soc. Polit. & Govt. Pos: Admin. asst. to U.S. Rep. William S. Mailliard, 6th Dist, Calif, 65-69; mem. exec. cmt, Young Rep. San Francisco, 58-60. Bus. & Prof. Pos: Ed, San Francisco Progress, 63-65. Mil. Serv: 2nd Lt, Army Res, 61-63, serv. in 2nd Armored Div. Artil, Ft. Hood, Tex. and Germany and Hq, Presidio of San Francisco, Calif, 1st Lt, Army Res, at present. Mem: Res. Officers Asn; Officers' Club, Presidio of San Francisco; Palace of Fine Art League; Rep. Alliance San Francisco; Calif. State Soc, Wash, D.C; Cong. Secretaries Club. Rel: Presbyterian. Legal Res: 65 Cervantes Blvd, San Francisco, Calif. 94123. (1967)

HARDEN, CECIL MURRAY R
Rep. Nat. Committeewoman, Ind.
b. Covington, Ind; d. Timothy Murray and Jennie Clotfelter M; m. 12/22/14 to Frost R. Harden; c. Dr. Murray Harden. Educ: Ind. Univ. Polit. & Govt. Pos: U.S. Rep, Ind, 48-56; Rep. Nat. Committeewoman, Ind, 64-; del, Rep. Nat. Conv, 68. Mem: DAR; former mem, Post War Planning Cmt; charter mem, Bus. & Prfnl. Women's Club. Mailing Add: 302 Fifth St, Covington, Ind. 47932. (1967)

HARDEN, ROSS ULLMAN D
Chmn, Burke Co. Dem. Exec. Cmt, Ga.
b. Rockford, Ala, 4/20/09; s. James Elzie Harden and Eunice Ward H; m. 12/14/38 to Ann Bates; c. Sydney (Mrs. Wynne) and Annette (Mrs. Daniel) Educ: Mercer Univ, A.B. and LL.B; Blue Key. Polit. & Govt. Pos: Law clerk, Ga. Supreme Court, 36-43; asst. attorney gen, Ga, 43-47; attorney, Burke Co, 52-65; chmn, Burke Co. Dem. Exec. Cmt, 60-; solicitor, City Court of Waynesboro, 65- Mil. Serv: Entered as 2nd Lt, Marine Corps, 44, released as 1st Lt, 45. Mem: Ga. State Bar; Am. Legion. Rel: Baptist. Legal Res: Waters St, Waynesboro, Ga. 30830. Mailing Add: 221 E. Sixth St, Waynesboro, Ga. 30830.

HARDER, JOSEPH C. R
Kans. State Sen.
b. Hillsboro, Kans, 2/1/16; s. David E. Harder and Margaret Flaming H; m. 12/24/39 to Maryan Lee Brooks; c. Joseph Brooks. Educ: Bethel Col, 33, 35, 43; Tabor Col, 34. Polit. & Govt. Pos: City councilman, Moundridge, Kans, 54-58; precinct committeeman, McPherson Co. Rep. Party, 54-; bd. mem, McPherson Co. Hosp, 56-58; Kans. State Sen, 61-; state chmn, Rep. Legis. Campaign Cmn, 64-66. Bus. & Prof. Pos; Mgr, Harder Furniture Co, 50-60, secy-treas, Moundridge Tel. Co, 55-, mgr, 60-; pres, Ami Inc, 59- Mem: Masons; Elks; Lions. Winner of Local Golf Club Tournaments on several occasions. Rel: United Methodist. Mailing Add: 532 Becker Ave, Moundridge, Kans. 67107.

HARDER, ROBERT CLARENCE D
b. Horton, Kans, 6/4/29; s. Clarence Leslie Harder and Olympia Kubik H; m. 7/31/53 to Dorothy Lou Welty; c. Anne and James David. Educ: Baker Univ, A.B, 51; South. Methodist Univ, B.D, 54; Boston Univ, Th.D, 58; Zeta Chi. Polit. & Govt. Pos: Secy, Dem. Conf. on Issues, Kans, 61; Kans. State Rep, 61-67; mem. bd. dirs, Shawnee Co. Dem. Action Cmt, Kans, 64-; spec. adv. to Gov. Docking, 67-68; dir. commun. resources develop, League of Kans. Munic, 68-69; Kans. State Dir. of Soc. Welfare, 69- Bus. & Prof. Pos: Pastor, East Topeka Methodist Church, Kans, 58-64; research assoc,

Menninger Found, 64-65; dir, Topeka Off. of Econ. Opportunity, 65-67. Publ: 'The State's Responsibility to its Youth, ' Attorney Gen. Off, summer, 63; 'Small Church Big Student Ministry,' Christian Advocate, 1/64; 'State Government and Youth,' Concern, 12/65. Rel: Methodist. Mailing Add: 408 Leland, Topeka, Kans. 66607.

HARDIE, THORNTON, JR. D
b. El Paso, Tex, 12/2/17; s. Thornton Hardie and Mabelle Bryan H; m. 12/26/42 to Mary Elizabeth Whitaker; c. Mary (Mrs. Charles S. Teeple, IV), Ann Elizabeth and Thornton, III. Educ: Univ. Tex, Austin, LL.B, 47; Sigma Alpha Epsilon. Polit. & Govt. Pos: Trustee, Midland Independent Sch. Dist, Midland Co, Tex, 51-53; chmn, Midland-Odessa Dist. Grievance Cmt, 57; chmn, Midland Co. Dem. Exec. Cmt, 66-69; del, Dem. Nat. Conv, 68. Bus. & Prof. Pos: Attorney-at-law, currently. Mil. Serv: Entered as A/S, Naval Res, 41, released as Lt.(sg), 45, after serv. in Destroyer Serv, S.Pac. Theatre, 42-45. Mem: Fel, Int. Acad. Trial Lawyers; admitted to practice before Supreme Court of U.S; State Bar of Tex; Am. Bar Asn; Midland Co. Bar Asn. (past pres); past v.pres, Tex. Asn. Defense Counsel. Rel: Presbyterian. Mailing Add: 1908 N. L St, Midland, Tex. 79701.

HARDIN, CLIFFORD MORRIS R
Secy. of Agr.
b. Knightstown, Ind, 10/9/15; s. James Alvin Hardin and Mabel Macy H; m. 6/28/39 to Martha Love Wood; c. Susan Carol (Mrs. Larry Wood), Clifford W, Cynthia Wood (Mrs. Robert Milligan), Nancy Ann and James Alvin. Educ: Purdue Univ, B.S, 37, M.S, 39, Ph.D, 41; Farm Found. fel, Univ. Chicago, 39-40; Gamma Sigma Delta; Phi Kappa Phi; Sigma Xi; Alpha Zeta; Alpha Gamma Rho. Hon. D.Sc, Purdue, 52 and N.Dak. State Univ, 69, LL.D, Creighton Univ, 56, Hon. Doctorate, Nat. Univ. Columbia, 68. Polit. & Govt. Pos: Secy. of Agr, 69- Bus. & Prof. Pos: Grad. asst, Purdue Univ, 37-39; instr. and asst. prof, Univ. Wis, Madison, 41-44; from assoc. prof. agr. econ. to prof. and chmn. dept, Mich. State Col, 44-48, asst. dir. agr. exp. sta, 48, dir, 49-53, dean col. agr, 53-54; dir. Detroit br, Fed. Reserve Bank Chicago, 53-54; chancellor, Univ. Nebr, 54-69; mem. bd, Nat. Asn. State Univ. and Land-Grant Col, 57-62, pres, 60, chmn. exec. cmt, 61; mem. bd. trustees, Bankers Life Ins. Co, Nebr, 58-59; mem. educ. cmt, W.K. Kellogg Found, 60; mem. nat. adv. coun. on arthritis and metabolic diseases, U.S. Pub. Health Serv, 60-63; mem. Africa liaison cmt, Am. Coun. Educ, 60-64, dir. coun, 62-66; dir. Omaha br, Fed. Reserve Bank Kansas City, 61-66, chmn, 62-66; trustee and mem, Rockefeller Found, 61-69; mem, President's Cmn. Strengthen Security in the Free World, 63; trustee, Col. Retirement Equities Fund, 63-65; dir, Behlen Mfg. Co, Columbus, Nebr, 63-69; mem, Exec. Cmt. Higher Educ. Am. Repub, 64-69; mem. nat. sci. bd. Nat. Sci. Found, 66- Publ: Ed, Overcoming World Hunger, Prentice-Hall, 69; numerous articles and bulletins in the fields of agr. adn educ. Rel: Congregational. Legal Res: Lincoln, Nebr. Mailing Add: Office of the Secretary, U.S. Dept. of Agriculture, Washington, D.C. 20250.

HARDIN, RUSSELL R
b. Charlotte, N.C, 6/28/13; s. Edward Berkley Hardin and Hattie Russell H; m 2/17/35 to Mary Agnes Weatherly; c. Mrs. John C. Hinson, Russell, Jr. and Edward J. Educ: Cent. High Sch, Charlotte, N.C. Polit. & Govt. Pos: Chmn, Union Co. Exec. Cmt, N.C, until 68; chmn, Rep. Precinct Cmt, 68. Bus. & Prof. Pos: Secy-treas, Durham Pub. Warehouses, 42-45, South. Cotton Storage, Inc, 47-63, pres-treas, 63- Mem: Pres, Monroe Lions, 59-60; chmn, Monroe Park and Recreation Cmt, 54 & 55; assoc, Am. Inst. of Mgt; past pres, Carolinas Cotton Warehouse Asn; dir, South Atlantic Warehouse Asn; past pres, Nat. Cotton Compress and Cotton Warehouse Asn; dir, Nat. Cotton Coun; Atlantic Cotton Asn; Am. Cotton Shippers Asn; Rolling Hills Country Club; Moose; Monroe C. of C. Rel: Methodist. Legal Res: 606 E. Green St, Monroe, N.C. 28110. Mailing Add: P.O. Box 546, Monroe, N.C. 28110.

HARDIN, WILLIAM HENDERSON D
b. Gadsden, Ala, 8/4/34; s. William Farrell Hardin and Mildred Henderson H; m. 8/6/61 to Annita Jane Gibson; c. Brett Henderson and Scott Gibson. Educ: State Col, Jacksonville, Ala; Giffin Col; Howard Col; Univ. Ala; Univ. Detroit; Alpha Phi Omega. Polit. & Govt. Pos: Del, Dem. Nat. Conv, 64. Bus. Pos: News dir, WDAK, Ga, 65. Mil. Serv: Entered as Pvt, Army, 57, released as Specialist 5, after service in Army Security Agency, Europe, 58-59; Expert Badge for carbine and M-1 Rifle; Marksman Badge for .45 calibre pistol; Parachutists Badge; S/Sgt, Spec. Forces, Army Res, currently. Mem: Dir, Ala. Jaycees and state cmt. chmn, 64, bd. mem, 63-65; Reserve Asn. U.S. Army; Farm Bur. Achievements: Several journalism awards; selected 1 of Outstanding Young Men in Am, 65. Rel: Baptist. Mailing Add: 4137 Cainwood Court, Columbus, Ga. 31904. (1967)

HARDING, DOROTHY MAE R
Mem, Franklin Co. Rep. Exec. Cmt, Ohio
b. Columbus, Ohio, 7/12/19; d. William Irvin Hoxworth and Almeda Mae McDaniel H; m. 9/17/41 to Dr. Charles Weaver Harding; c. Abigail (Mrs. Daniel B. Jackson), Charles Hoxworth, Deborah, Jennifer (deceased) and Suzannah. Educ: Ohio State Univ, B.Sc, Educ, Nursing and Pub. Health Nursing. Polit. & Govt. Pos: Mem, Women's Div Rep. Finance Cmt, Worthington, Ohio, 60-66; Franklin Co. chmn, Neighbor to Neighbor, 66-; co-founder and first pres, Worthington Rep. Women, 64; mem, Franklin Co. Rep. Exec. Cmt, 67-; alternate del-at-lg, Rep. Nat. Conv, 68. Bus. & Prof. Pos: Charge nurse obstetrics, Univ. Hosp, Cols, Ohio, 42-43. Mem: Childhood League; Women's Auxiliary, Acad. Med; Women's Serv. Bd, Grant Hosp; Capitol Hill Rep. Club; Franklin Co. Women's Rep. Club; Worthington Area Rep; Worthington Rep. Women; Am. Cancer Soc. Crew IV. Rel: Presbyterian. Mailing Add: 970 High St, Worthington, Ohio 43085.

HARDING, EDWARD PERRY R
b. Boston, Mass, 2/8/23; s. Francis A. Harding and Dorothy Warner H; m. 1/19/46 to Suzanne Eckfeldt; c. Anna Laurence, Edward P, Jr, Susan, Linda and Michael S. Educ: Harvard Univ, B.S, 45; A.D. Club. Polit. & Govt. Pos: Asst. Nat. dir, Nat. Vol. for Nixon-Lodge, 60; chmn, Portland 'Reed for Gov' Cmt, 66; nominee, Rep. state chmn, Maine Rep. State Cmt, 67; mem, South Freeport, Maine Rep. Town Cmt, 68; finance chmn, Cumberland Co. Rep. Cmt, 68; del, Maine Rep. State Conv, 68; alternate del, Rep. Nat. Conv, 68; chmn, Maine Nixon for Pres. Cmt, 68; chmn, Maine United Citizens for Nixon-Agnew Cmt, 68; chmn, GOP Action Cmt, Maine, 69- Bus. & Prof. Pos: Pres. and chmn. bd, Harding-Glidden, Inc, Westwood, Mass, 46-60; pres. and chmn. bd, The Edson Corp, New Bedford, 56-61; pres. and dir, Mastercolor of New Eng, Boston, 61-63; pres, Ft. Hill Corp, 63-64; pres. and chmn. bd, Bicknell Photo Serv, Inc, Portland, Maine, 64-; pres, Maine Forum Corp, 68- Mem: Master Photo Dealers' & Finishers' Asn.(territorial v.pres, 67-68); Master Photo Finishers New Eng.(secy-treas, 66-68); Cumberland Club; Portland Club; C. of C; Harraseeket Yacht Club; Dedham Country and Polo Club. Rel: Protestant. Mailing Add: P.O. Box 4, South Freeport, Maine 04078.

HARDING, FLOYD L. D
Chmn. Aroostook Co. Dem. Cmt, Maine
b. Albion, Maine, 8/26/23; s. Judson J. Harding and Grace Hunt H; m. 5/26/63 to Jean Donovan; c. Jerry, Daniel, Dwight, Alan, Mark, Dolores, Ronda, Dolly and Linda. Educ: Colby Col, 41-43; Ala. Polytech. Inst, 43-44; Boston Univ. Law Sch, LL.B, 49. Polit. & Govt. Pos: Chmn, Presque Isle Dem. Cmt, Maine, 60-66; treas, Aroostook Co. Dem. Cmt, 62-66, chmn, 68-; former Maine State Sen. and Majority Leader, Maine State Senate. Bus. & Prof. Pos: Attorney-at-law, 49- Mil. Serv: Entered as Pvt, Army, 43, released as Cpl, 45, after serv. in 106th Inf. Div, ETO, 44-45. Mem: Am, Maine, Aroostook and Presque Isle Bar Asns; Kiwanis. Rel: Protestant. Mailing Add: P.O. Box 207, Presque Isle, Maine 04769.

HARDING, FORREST ASHBY D
Tex. State Rep.
b. Roanoke, Va, 11/4/13; s. Marion Lewis Harding and Maggie Pace H; m. 5/19/42 to Genelen Markham Flynn; c. Genest, Michelle and Therese. Educ: San Angelo Col, A.A, 50; Baylor Univ, LL.B, 53; Phi Delta Phi; Phi Theta Kappa. Polit. & Govt. Pos: Corp. Court Judge, San Angelo, Tex, 53-57; Tex. State Rep, 61- Mil. Serv: Entered as Pvt, Air Force, 41, released as Maj, 46, after serv. in Am-African Theaters and China-India-Burma; Maj, Res. Mem: Am. Judicature Asn; Tex. Bar Asn; Mason; Scottish Rite; Am. Legion; Elks. Distinguished Serv. Award Tex. Safety Asn, 57. Rel: Episcopal. Legal Res: 621 N. Madison, San Angelo, Tex. 76901. Mailing Add: 307 N. Van Buren St, San Angelo, Tex. 76901.

HARDING, FRANK EMIL R
Chmn, Hooker Co. Rep. Cmt, Nebr.
b. Mullen, Nebr, 2/15/22; s. Lester Lloyd Harding and Pearl Crain H; m. 3/17/56 to Iva Darlene Tucker; c. Patricia Ann and Karen Marie. Educ: Mullen Pub. Schs, 12 years. Polit. & Govt. Pos: Mem, Grant-Hooker-Thomas Exten. Bd, 50-54; Secy, Hooker Co. Agr. Soc, 56-59; Secy-Treas, Mullen Rural Fire Dist, 57-67; Treas, Mullen Bd. of Educ, 62-68; Chmn, Hooker Co. Rep. Cmt, 66-; Chmn, Co. Bd, 68- Mil. Serv: A/S, Navy, 42, released as Radioman 2C, 45, after serv. in Seventh Fleet, S. Pac. Theatre, 43-45; Asiatic-Pac. Medal with two Battle Stars; Am. Theatre Medal; Philippine Liberation with two Battle Stars; Victory Medal; Good Conduct Medal. Mem: Am. Legion; Nebr. Stock Growers Asn; Elks; Mullen Vet. Club; Ambassador, Knights of Ak-Sar-Ben. Nebr. Centennial Grasslands Award; Nebr. Centennial Tree-Planting Award; Grant-Hooker Conservation Award. Rel: Episcopal. Mailing Add: Mullen, Nebraska 69152.

HARDING, FRANKLIN DANIEL BOONE R
Mayor, Yadkinville, N.C.
b. Yadkinville, N.C, 6/29/04; s. Thomas Renny Harding and Effie M. Kelly H; m. 4/10/31 to Laura Milliner Bowman; c. Laura Frances (Mrs. Casstevens). Educ: Univ. N.C, A.B, 25 and 2 years law. Polit. & Govt. Pos: Former co. attorney, Yadkin Co, N.C; former town attorney, Yadkinville; N.C. State Rep, 49-50 & 61-64; N.C. State Sen, 65-66; mem, Rep. Cent. Cmt, N.C, currently; mayor, Yadkinville, 23rd Judicial Bar, 67- Mem: Am. and N.C. State Bar Asns; N.C. Bar; pres, Yadkin Co. Bar, 67; AF&AM 162; Yadkin Masonic Lodge, past master. Rel: Methodist. Mailing Add: P.O. Box 96, Yadkinville, N.C. 27055.

HARDING, KENNETH R. D
Asst. Sgt. at Arms, U.S. House of Rep.
b. Medina, N.Y, 3/28/14; s. Victor Hunt Harding and Edith Falk H; m. 1/28/38 to Jane S. Wedderburn; c. Kenneth Roberts, Richard Hunt, Bruce Addison and Victor Hunt. Educ: George Wash. Univ, LL.B, 37. Polit. & Govt. Pos: Mem, Dem. Nat. Cong. Cmt, 46-54, exec. dir, 54-; Asst. Sgt. at Arms, U.S. House of Rep, 54- Mil. Serv: Col, Air Force Res. Mem: Nat. Press Club. Rel: Protestant. Mailing Add: 3434 Greentree Dr, Falls Church, Va. 22041.

HARDING, MARGARET KATHERINE 'MARTY' D
b. Fredericksburg, Va, 10/29/36; d. Irvin Thomas Harding and Octavia Coppage H; m. 6/7/56 to Trewitt DeLano Harding. Educ: Strayer Jr. Col, Legal Secretarial Dipl, 55; George Wash. Univ, B.A. with spec. honors, 67; scholarship, class pres. and valedictorian, Strayer Jr. Col. Polit. & Govt. Pos: Admin. asst, U.S. Rep. George Grant, 56-64; admin. asst, U.S. Rep. Frank A. Stubblefield, Ky, 65- Mem: Cong. Secy. Club; North. Va. Art League. Valedictorian, Culpeper Co. High Sch, Culpeper, Va, 55; honor student, George Wash. Univ. Rel: Protestant. Mailing Add: 3822 12th St. S, Arlington, Va. 22204.

HARDING, RALPH RAY D
b. Malad City, Idaho, 9/9/29; s. Ralph W. Harding and Kathryn Olson H; m. 8/11/54 to Willa Conrad; c. Ralph David, Cherie, Charlene and John Kennedy. Educ: Brigham Young Univ, B.S, polit. sci, 55, studied acct, 55-56. Polit. & Govt. Pos: Idaho State Rep, 55-56; U.S. Rep, Idaho, 61-64, mem, Agr. Cmt; del, Dem. Nat. Conv, 64 & 68; spec. asst. for pub. legis. affairs to Secy. of the Air Force, 65-66. Bus. & Prof. Pos: Staff auditor, Touche, Niven, Bailey & Smart, CPA's, San Francisco, Calif, 56-57; controller, Am. Potato Co, Blackfoot, Idaho, 57-60, former dir. corp. develop, v.pres, currently. Mil. Serv: Off, Army, Korea, 51-53. Mem: Am. Legion; Blackfoot C. of C. Rel: Latter-day Saint; Mission to Cent. States, 49-51. Mailing Add: Route 4, Box 164, Blackfoot, Idaho 83221.

HARDING, RAY MURRAY R
b. Salt Lake City, Utah, 1/20/34; s. William Dean Harding and Jessie Brydson H; m. 6/12/52 to Martha Rasmussen; c. Raymond M, Jr, Douglas B, Darrell M, Matthew S. and Roxanne. Educ: Utah State Univ; Univ. Utah; Delta Theta Phi. Polit. & Govt. Pos: Utah State Rep, 63-69. Bus. & Prof. Pos:

Partner, Stewart, Topham & Harding, Attorneys-at-law, 60-66. Mil. Serv: Entered as Pvt, Army, 54, released as Cpl, 56, after serv. in 53rd Inf. Regt, Alaska; Good Conduct Medal. Mem: Am. and Utah State Bar Asns. Rel: Latter-day Saint. Mailing Add: 2203 E. 3205 S, Salt Lake City, Utah 84103. (1967)

HARDWICK, ARTHUR, JR. D
b. 1916; married to Essie Clarke. Educ: Buffalo Pub. Schs. Polit. & Govt. Pos: N.Y. State Assemblyman, 64-67; mayor's cmt. on Recreation for Elderly; chmn. bd, Dems. Unlimited. Bus. & Prof. Pos: Operator Sportsman's Liquor Store, 18 years; v.pres. Doris Records, Inc. Mil. Serv: WWII, D.A.V. Mem: Exec. bd, life mem, NAACP; Jessie Clipper Post 430, Paramount Lodge F&AM; exec. bd, Neighborhood House. Rel: Lloyds Memorial United Church of Christ Congregational. Mailing Add: 83 Locust St, Buffalo, N.Y. 14204. (1967)

HARDWICK, TED H. R
Mem, Ky. Rep. State Cmt.
b. Stanton, Ky, 2/13/08; m. to Jene; c. Two. Educ: Univ. Ky, A.B, 29; Harvard Bus. Sch, M.B.A, 31. Polit. & Govt. Pos: Mgr, Fayette Co. Eisenhower-Cooper Campaign, 52; past chmn, Ky. Rep. State Cmt. and mem, currently; Rep. Fayette Co. Cmnr, 53-; del, Rep. Nat. Conv, 68. Bus. & Prof. Pos: Farmer; bd. of dirs, New Union Savings & Loan Asn. Mem: Bd, United Commun. Fund; trustee, YMCA; former v.pres, Lexington C. of C. Rel: Central Christian Church. Mailing Add: 224 Queensway Dr, Lexington, Ky. 40505. (1967)

HARDWICKE, JOHN W. R
b. Winston-Salem, N.C, 4/10/27; married. Educ: Univ. N.C, B.A, 50; George Washington Univ. Sch. of Law, LL.B, 53. Polit. & Govt. Pos: Md. State Del, 63-67. Bus. & Prof. Pos: Lectr. in law, Mt. Vernon Sch. of Law, 55-60; instr. in law, Johns Hopkins Univ, 55- Mem: Am, Md, Baltimore and Jr. Bar Asns; Baltimore Bar Libr; Baltimore Asn. of Commerce; Johns Hopkins Club; Merchants Club; pres. Ment. Health Asn, Hartford Co. Mailing Add: 101 N. Charles St, Baltimore, Md. 21201. (1967)

HARDY, HELEN COLEMAN D
b. Steelville, Mo, 10/20/04; d. William C. Coleman and Hettie Huitt C; m. 2/24/24 to W. Clyde Hardy; c. Marcy (Mrs. Bowen) and Frances (Mrs. Hoxworth). Polit. & Govt. Pos: Treas, Maries Co. Dem. Cmt, Mo, 48-52, v.chmn, 52-54; Mo. State Rep, 55-66; v.chmn, Maries Co. Regional Planning Cmn. Mem: Mem. bd, Maries Co. Hist. Soc; co-chmn, Cancer Soc; Eastern Star; White Shrine; Exten. Club; Fair Bd; 1st v.pres, Belle Bus. & Prfnl. Women's Club; exec. cmt, Mo. Basin Asn; Gov. Task Force on Probs. of the Older Missourian; co-chmn, Nat. Found. March of Dimes; del, Nat. Rivers and Harbors Cong, Wash, D.C, 69. Rel: Christian. Mailing Add: Belle, Mo. 65013.

HARDY, JOEL CECIL 'JACK' D
Ga. State Sen.
b. Jefferson, Ga, 4/21/16; s. Charles Edward Hardy and Ada Tolbert H; m. 5/25/35 to Eleanor Harris; c. Joel C, Jr. and Daniel H. Educ: Univ. Ga, B.S. in Bus. Admin, 40. Polit. & Govt. Pos: Councilman-at-lg, Jefferson, Ga, 60-62; Ga. State Rep, Fulton Co, 69- Bus. & Prof. Pos: Exec. v.pres, Burke, Dowling, Adams, Inc, Div, Batton, Barton, Durstine & Osborne, Inc, Atlanta and N.Y, 52- Publ: Numerous financial papers. Mem: Kiwanis; many local civic clubs. Rel: Protestant. Mailing Add: 3714 Peachtree Rd. N.E, Atlanta, Ga. 30319.

HARDY, PORTER D
b. Chesterfield Co, Va, 6/1/03; s. The Reverend Porter Hardy and Jane Mahood H; m. 1939 to Edna Lynn Moore; c. Mrs. Paul M. Yeakel and Porter, III. Educ: Randolph-Macon Col, B.A, 22, LL.D, 55; Sch. of Bus. Admin, Harvard Univ, 24; Kappa Alpha; Tau Kappa Alpha. Polit. & Govt. Pos: U.S. Rep, Va, 46-68. Bus. & Prof. Pos: Businessman; farmer; retired. Mem: Hon. mem, Circus Saints and Sinners Club of Am. and Norfolk Rotary; Hampton Roads Post, Am. Soc. Mil. Engrs; Hampton Roads Maritime Asn; Ahepa; Moose. Recipient, Commerce Builder Award, Hampton Roads For. Commerce Club; Distinguished Alumni Award, Tau Kappa Alpha, 64; Brotherhood Citation, Nat. Conf. Christians and Jews, 69. Rel: Methodist. Mailing Add: Box 6248, Portsmouth, Va. 23703.

HARDY, RAYMOND H. R
Co-Chmn, Scott Co. Rep. Exec. Cmt, Ky.
b. Scott Co, Ky; s. S. R. Hardy and Letha Frances Robey H; single. Educ: Scott Co. Pub. Schs. Polit. & Govt. Pos: Election officer, precinct committeeman and elec. cmnr, Scott Co, Ky, 30-40; campaign mgr, King Swope for Gov, 35; chmn, Scott Co. Rep. Exec. Cmt, 49-69, co-chmn, 69-; campaign mgr, Gene Syler for Gov, 51; Rep. Patronage Chmn, 53-61; campaign chmn, John Sherman Cooper and Thruston B. Morton. Bus. & Prof. Pos: Real estate broker, 25 years; appraiser, The Equitable Life Assurance Soc. of the U.S, 7 years. Mil. Serv: Army, Pvt. Mem: Am. Legion. Rel: Baptist. Legal Res: 629 S. Broadway, Georgetown, Ky. 40324. Mailing Add: 112 E. Main St, Georgetown, Ky. 40324.

HARDY, SARAH FRANCES 'FANNIE' D
b. Amity, Ark, 6/21/97; d. Paulineus T. Hardy (deceased) and Senie V. Adams H. (deceased); single. Educ: High Sch. and Bus. Univ, grad; Atlanta Conservatory of Music. Polit. & Govt. Pos: Exec. Asst. State Ins. Cmnr, Ark, 53-; mem, Ark. Civil Defense Adv. Bd, 53-; adv, Gov. Cmn. on Status Women; mem, Cmt. on Soc. Ins. and Taxes, President Kennedy's Cmn. on Status Women; del, Dem. Nat. Conv, 64; mem. adv. cmt, Ark. Ins. Code Cmn, 58. Bus. & Prof. Pos: Head, casualty and marine dept, gen. ins. agency, Little Rock, Ark; underwriter, Williams and Rosen, Inc, Little Rock and Fidelity and Deposit Co, Memphis, Newark and Atlanta; music teacher. Mem: Int. Fedn. Bus. & Prfnl. Women's Clubs, Inc; chmn. bd. trustees, Bus. & Prfnl. Women's Found, 60-61; pres, Nat. Fedn. Bus. & Prfnl. Women's Clubs, Inc, 60-61, bd. dirs, 61-62, 1st, 2nd and 3rd v.pres. and chmn. pub. affairs, 2 year terms each; Nat. Fedn. Rep, Int. Fedn. Cong, Conf. and bd. meetings; pres, Ark. Fedn. Bus. & Prfnl. Women's Clubs and Little Rock Club; chmn. bldg. cmt, Dr. Minnie L. Maffett Nurses Residence, Taipei, Taiwan; E.Ark. Urban Policy Conf, 66; Am. Asn. for UN; Am. Legion Auxiliary; Ins. Women of Little Rock; Zonta Int; Int. Platform Asn; YWCA. Selected Bus. Woman of Year in Little Rock, 58; Little Rock's Woman of Year, 52. Rel: Methodist. Mailing Add: 5223 G St, Little Rock, Ark. 72205. (1967)

HARE, CLEVE THOMAS R
b. Coburg, Ky, 7/24/05; s. James Thomas Hare and Eliza Massey H; wid; c. Deloris (Mrs. Braswell) and James. Educ: Adair Co. Grade Sch, Ky, 8 years. Polit. & Govt. Pos: Committeeman, Adair Co. Rep. Party, Ky, 46-68, chmn, 48 & 68. Bus. & Prof. Pos: Former farmer and carpenter, Adair Co, Ky; truck driver, currently. Rel: Cumberland Presbyterian. Mailing Add: Cave Valley, Ky. 42720.

HARE, JAMES McNEIL D
Secy. of State, Mich.
b. Racine, Wis, 7/31/10; s. James McNeil and Sarah Wilson M; m. 11/9/67 to Catherine Hurley; c. Patricia, Michael and Bruce. Educ: Wayne State Univ, A.B, 32; Univ. Mich, M.A, 36; Wayne State Univ. Alumni Award; Phi Delta Kappa. Hon. H.H.D, Lawrence Inst. Tech. Polit. & Govt. Pos: Mgr, Mich. State Fair, 52-55; Secy. of State, Mich, 55-; chmn, Mich. State Safety Cmn, 15 years; mem, Nat. Hwy. Safety Adv. Cmt, 67-69; del, Dem. Nat. Conv, 68. Rel: Unitarian. Legal Res: 1216 Blake, Lansing, Mich. 48912. Mailing Add: Treasury Bldg, Lansing, Mich. 48918.

HARE, WILLIAM ROSS D
S.C. State Rep.
b. Chester, S.C, 8/6/34; s. Robert Lee Hare and Maggie Yongue H; m. 8/30/56 to Elizabeth Rudell Maffett; c. Elisa Maffett. Educ: Univ. S.C, A.B, 56; Univ. S.C. Law Sch, LL.B, 58; Wig and Robe; Lambda Chi Alpha. Polit. & Govt. Pos: Mem, Dist. Ment. Health Cmn, S.C, 66-; mem, Co. Airport Cmn, 67-68; S.C. State Rep, 68- Mil. Serv: Entered as 2nd Lt, Air Force, 58, released as Capt, 63, after serv. in 3909th Combat Supply Group, Seventh Air Div, 60-63, Air Force Res, 63- Mem: S.C. Bar Asn.(Sixth Circuit v.pres, 67-68); S.C. State Bar; dir, Co. C. of C, 68-; Moose; Am. Legion. Rel: Baptist. Mailing Add: Center St, Chester, S.C. 29706.

HARFF, HELEN G. R
Pres, Wis. Fedn. of Rep. Women
b. Sheboygan, Wis, 2/1/03; d. Henry C. Gruebner and Anna Knauf G; m. 2/20/37 to Ben W. Harff; c. Luanne Burchinal and James Warren. Educ: Milwaukee State Teacher's Col, 2 years; Girl Scout Exec. Training, Nat. Training Centers. Polit. & Govt. Pos: Precinct committeewoman, Rep. Party, Wis, 56; pres, Sheboygan Co. Women's Rep. Club, 58-61; attended Nat. Rep. Women's Conf, Wash, D.C, 58 & 66; chmn, Sixth Dist. Rep. Women, 61-65; mem. at large and v.chmn, Sheboygan Co. Rep. Party, 63-65; first v.pres, Wis. Fedn. of Rep. Women, 65-67, pres, 67-; del, Nat. Fedn. of Rep. Women's Conv, Wash. D.C, 67; alternate del, Rep. Nat. Conv, 68. Bus. & Prof. Pos: Kindergarten teacher, Sheboygan Pub. Schs, 23-26 and Lansing, Mich. Schs, 26-28; Girl Scout dir, Lansing Coun, 28-30 and Sheboygan, Wis. Coun, 30-37. Mem: Life mem, Wis. PTA (pres, Sheboygan Coun); pres, Sheboygan Girl Scout Coun; state treas, King's Daughters; v.pres, Sheboygan Women's Club. Rel: Protestant; Pres, Zion United Church of Christ Women's Guild, 67-68. Mailing Add: 2606 Wilgus Rd, Sheboygan, Wis. 53081.

HARFF, JAMES WARREN R
Mem, Sixth Dist. Rep. Exec. Cmt, Wis.
b. Sheboygan, Wis, 12/5/40; s. Ben Walter Harff and Helen Gruebner H; single. Educ: Northwest. Univ, B.S.J, 63, M.S.J, 65; Sigma Delta Chi; Chi Phi. Polit. & Govt. Pos: Chmn, Sheboygan Co. Young Rep, Wis, 58-59; v.pres, Northwest. Univ. Young Rep, 59-60, pres, 61; co-chmn. col. activities, Rep. Nat. Conv, 60; mem. nat. steering cmt, Youth for Nixon-Lodge, 60; campaign asst. to Philip G. Kuehn, Rep. gubernatorial cand, Wis, 60 & 62; treas, Midwest Col. Young Rep. Fedn, 61; Rep. del, NATO Nations Study Tour of Eng, France, Germany and Belgium, 61; chmn, Col. Rep. Nat. Cmt, 61-63; nat. dir, Youth for Goldwater-Miller, 64; staffmem, Rep. Nat. Cmt, 64; mem, Sixth Dist. Rep. Exec. Cmt, 66-; alternate del, Rep. Nat. Conv, 68; chmn, Sheboygan Co. Nixon for Pres. Cmt, 68. Bus. & Prof. Pos: Reporter and ed. writer, Radio Sta. WHBL, Sheboygan, 63-68; reporter, Evanston Review, Evanston, Ill, 65; asst. to the pres, Plastics Eng. Co, Sheboygan, 65- Mil. Serv: Entered as Pvt, Army Res, 65, released as Specialist 4, 68, after serv. in Co. C First Bn. 334th Regt. Mem: Econ. Club; Rotary; Sheboygan Arts Found. (bd. dirs); Sheboygan Co. Red Cross (bd. dirs). Rel: Protestant. Mailing Add: 2606 Wilgus Rd, Sheboygan, Wis. 53081.

HARGIS, GERROLL D
b. Lafayette, Tenn, 11/7/11; d. Joe Lee Carter and Jean Craighead C; m. 9/9/33 to Harold Wilson Hargis. Educ: Middle Tenn. State Univ, 2 years; Cumberland Univ, 1 year. Polit. & Govt. Pos: Pres, Davidson Co. Dem. Women's Club, 63; co-dir, Tenn. Women's Div. Presidential Campaign, 64; v.pres, Tenn. Fedn. Dem. Women, 64-66, pres, 66-68, mem. bd. dir, 68-; del, Dem. Nat. Conv, 68. Bus. & Prof. Pos: Teacher, Macon Co. Sch. Syst, 23 years, supvr, 53-55. Mem: Eastern Star; Past Matrons Asn; New Century Club; Colemere Country Club; Davidson Co. Dem. Women; Tenn. Fedn. Dem. Women. Rel: Baptist. Mailing Add: 5041 Villa Crest Dr, Nashville, Tenn. 37220.

HARING, NICK J. D
b. Denver, Colo, 8/31/38; s. John J. Haring and Edith Johnson H; m. 6/28/61 to Barbara L. McCormick; c. Debra Jo and John Leighton. Educ: Univ. Colo. Polit. & Govt. Pos: Dir, Adams Co. Young Dem, Colo, 65-68, secy, 68; chmn, Rep. Dist. 31, Colo. Dem. Party, 67-68; dir, Second Cong. Dist, Colo. Young Dem, 67-69; alternate del, Dem. Nat. Conv, 68; dir, Adams Co. Dem. Club, Colo, 68 & 69. Bus. & Prof. Pos: Eng. technologist, Stearns Roger Corp, Denver, Colo, 61-64, State of Colo, 64-66; MLC analyst, Int. Bus. Machine Corp, Boulder, 66- Mil. Serv: Entered as Pvt, Colo. Army Nat. Guard, 57, Sgt. 1/C, 221st Mil. Police Co, 57-; 10 Year Fed. Serv. Medal; 10 Year Colo. Serv. Medal. Mem: Northglenn Civic Asn.(past dir, 4 years, past secy, 2 years). Mailing Add: 1367 W. 101st Place, Denver, Colo. 80233.

HARING, PAUL BYRNE D
b. Beeville, Tex, 1/18/37; s. Paul Haring and Grace Von Dohlen H; m. 7/13/68 to Georgia Ann Kainer. Educ: Victoria Col, Tex, 53-54; Univ. St. Thomas, Houston, B.A, 57; Univ. Tex, Austin, LL.B, 64. Polit. & Govt. Pos:

Tex. State Rep, 61-66. Bus. & Prof. Pos: Teacher, 57-61; attorney, 64- Mil. Serv: Tex. Air Nat. Guard; Air Force Res. Mem: Am, Tex, Houston and Galveston Bar Asns; Lions. Rel: Roman Catholic. Mailing Add: 4390 Wheeler, Houston, Tex. 77004.

HARKER, JACQUELINE NUGENT R
Mem, Calif. Rep. State Cent. Cmt.
b. Tacoma, Wash, 10/27/24; d. Robert W. Nugent and Audrey Perry N; m. 6/22/45 to Richard Upson Harker; c. Richard Upson, Jr, Edward William and Kenneth Nugent. Educ: Univ. Calif, Los Angeles, A.B, 45; Mortar Board, Zeta Phi Eta, Eta Sigma Phi; Kappa Kappa Gamma. Polit. & Govt. Pos: Mem, Nixon for Senate Cmt, Los Angeles, Calif, 50; co-chmn, 22nd Cong. Dist. Citizens for Eisenhower, 56; co-chmn, Citizens for Nixon, San Fernando Valley, 60; chmn, Bell for Cong, 28th Cong. Dist, 62; precinct chmn, 57th Assembly 63-67; alternate mem, Los Angeles Co. Rep. Cent. Cmt, 63-; precinct chmn, Reagan for Gov, 57th Assembly Dist, 66; mem, Calif. Rep. State Cent. Cmt, 67-; chmn, Women for Nixon-Agnew, San Fernando Valley, 68; pres, Encino Rep. Women's Club, Federated, 69. Bus. & Prof. Pos: V.chmn, United Way, Inc, San Fernando Valley, 63-67; pres, San Fernando Valley Welfare Planning Coun, 64-65. Mem: Vol. League San Fernando Valley (pres, 60-62). Merit Leadership Award, Los Angeles Co. Rep. Cent. Cmt; Ann Schlarb Award, Women's Div, United Way, Inc. Rel: Protestant. Mailing Add: 4500 Densmore Ave, Encino, Calif. 91316.

HARKINS, BERNARD JOSEPH D
Pres, City Coun, Erie, Pa.
b. Erie, Pa, 10/5/15; s. John P. Harkins, Jr. and Jennie Dunne H; m. 8/7/48 to Rita A. Dill; c. Rita Jane, John C, Nora, Ann and Patrick J. Educ: Findlay Col, B.A.; St. Bonaventure Univ, M.A; grad.study, Univ. Pa, Syracuse Univ, Allegheny Col, Univ. of Pittsburgh and Edinboro State Col; Courses taken at Inst. for Training in Munic. Admin. of Int. City Mgr. Asn. Polit. & Govt. Pos: Pres. bd. trustees, Pa. Soldiers' and Sailors' Home, 56-63; Dem. coordinator, W.City, Erie, 59-60; pres, S.Erie Dem. Club, 60-63; pres, City Coun, Erie; v.chmn, Northwest. Pa. Region, Pa. League Cities, 69-70, chmn, 70- Bus. & Prof. Pos: Head Dept. of Health Instrs. and athletic coach, Erie Tech. Mem. High, Pa, 48-66; prin, John C. Diehl Sch, 66- Mil. Serv: CPO, Navy, 42-46. Mem: Pa. State Educ. Asn; Erie Teachers' Asn; past pres, Erie Fedn. Teachers Local 337, AFL-CIO; past Comdr, Am. Legion Post 11, Erie, Pa; K. of C. (4°); Moniuszko Singing Soc; Polish Falcons; pres, Pa. Chap, Pa. Sports Hall of Fame. Rel: Catholic. Mailing Add: 2639 Schley St, Erie, Pa. 16508.

HARKINS, MICHAEL EUGENE R
b. Wilmington, Del, 4/23/41; s. Eugene Francis Harkins and Aline Harrison H; m. 9/12/64 to Helen White; c. Christine and Kelly Ann. Educ: Holy Cross, B.S. in Hist, 63; St. John's Univ. Law Sch, 64-65. Polit. & Govt. Pos: Campaign co-ordinator, U.S. Rep. William Roth, Del, 66; research dir, Rep. State Cmt, Del, 66-68; campaign mgr, Hal Haskell for Mayor, Wilmington, Del, 68; spec. asst. to mayor Harry G. Haskell, Jr, Wilmington, 69- Rel: Catholic. Legal Res: 208 Village Road, Lancaster Village, Wilmington, Del. 19805. Mailing Add: 1112 King St, Wilmington, Del. 19801.

HARLAMON, GEORGE PETER R
Mayor, Waterbury, Conn.
b. Waterbury, Conn, 2/5/19; s. Peter Harlamon and Agnes Hanzakos H; m. 10/5/47 to Katherine Konstant; c. Peter and James. Educ: Fordham Univ, B.S. in Acct, 55; Univ. Con, M.B.A, 60; Beta Gamma Sigma. Polit. & Govt. Pos: Mem, Bd. of Finance, Waterbury, Conn, 64-65, mem, Rep. Town Cmt, 65-67, mem, Bd. of Aldermen, 66-67, pres, 68, acting mayor, 68, mayor, 68- Bus. & Prof. Pos: Pub. acct, 53-55; auditor, U.S. Gen. Acct. Off, 55; controller, Chase Metal Works Div, Chase Brass & Copper Co, Inc, 56-66, Waterbury Nat. Bank, 66-68. Mil. Serv: Entered as Pvt, Army, 42, released as Sgt, 46, after serv. in 29th Engrs, Pac. Theatre, 43-46. Mem: Nat. Asn. Acct; Mason; Shrine; Am. Hellenic Educ. Progressive Asn. Rel: Greek Orthodox. Legal Res: 132 Forest Ridge Rd, Waterbury, Conn. 06708. Mailing Add: 236 Grand St, Waterbury, Conn. 06702.

HARLAN, DALE MORGAN D
b. Glendale, W.Va, 9/5/24; s. H.H. Harlan and Lulu May Calvert H; m. 6/20/48 to Joyce Dolores Niedermeyer; c. Janice Marie, David Otto, James Dale and Nancy Ann. Educ: Univ. Ore, B.S, 48; Stanford Univ. Sch. Law, 48-50; Univ. Colo. Sch. Law, LL.B, 52; Phi Alpha Delta. Polit. & Govt. Pos: Ore. State Rep, 65-69. Bus. & Prof. Pos: Attorney-at-law, Allstate Ins. Co, 53-58, private practice, 58- Mil. Serv: Entered as Pvt, Army, 42, released as S/Sgt, 45, after serv. in 101st Airborne Div, Pac. and ETO; Purple Heart; Air Medal; Pac. Theater Ribbon with 2 Battle Stars; ETO Ribbon with 2 Battle Stars. Mem: Elks; Kiwanis; Am. Legion; Knife & Fork Club; Ore. State and Am. Bar Asns. Rel: Presbyterian. Mailing Add: 11717 Linwood Ave, Milwaukie, Ore. 97222. (1967)

HARLAN, JOHN MARSHALL
Assoc. Justice, U.S. Supreme Court
b. Chicago, Ill, 5/20/99; s. John Maynard Harlan and Elizabeth Palmer Flagg H; m. 11/10/28 to Ethel Andrews; c. Eve (Mrs. Frank Dillingham); Educ: Princeton Univ, A.B, 20; Rhodes Scholar, Oxford Univ, Balliol Col, B.A. in jurisprudence, 23 and M.A, hon. fel, 55; New York Law Sch, LL.B, 24. Hon. LL.D, Brandeis Univ, Evansville Col, New York Law Sch. and Princeton Univ, 55, Columbia Univ. and Oberlin Col, 56, Univ, Mich, 59, Northwest. Univ, 60, Univ. Pa, 63 and Harvard Univ, 64; Hon. Bencher, Inner Temple Inn, London, Eng, 69. Polit. & Govt. Pos: Asst. U.S. Attorney, South. Dist. of New York, 25-27; spec. asst. attorney gen, N.Y, 28-30; chief counsel, N.Y. State Crime Cmn, 51; judge, U.S. Court of Appeals, Second Circuit, 54-55; assoc. justice, U.S. Supreme Court, 55- Bus. & Prof. Pos: Admitted to N.Y. Bar, 25, Circuit Court of Appeals, 25, U.S. Dist. Court, 25 and U.S. Supreme Court, 45; mem, Root, Ballantine, Harlan, Bushby & Palmer, 31-54. Mil. Serv: Col, Army Air Force, Chief of Opers. Anal. Sect, Eighth Air Force, Eng, 43-45 and mem, Planning Sect. for occupation of Germany, U.S. Startegic Air Forces in Europe; U.S. Legion of Merit; French and Belgium Croix de Guerre. Mem: Am. and N.Y. State Bar Asns; Asn. of the Bar of the City of New York; Am. Law Inst; dir, Nat. Legal Aid Asn; and New York Co. Lawyers Asn; Century Asn. and Univ. Clubs, N.Y.C; Country Club of Fairfield, Conn; Ivy Club, Princeton, N.J. Legal Res: Weston, Conn. 06880. Mailing Add: U.S. Supreme Court, Washington, D.C. 20543.

HARLESS, RICHARD FIELDING D
b. Kelsey, Tex, 8/6/05; s. William Crousin Harless and Mary Pennington H; m. 11/28/48 to Meredith Howard; c. Glen Richard. Educ: Univ. Ariz, B.A, 28 and J.D, 33; Phi Alpha Delta; Delta Sigma Rho; Phi Delta Phi; Sigma Nu. Polit. & Govt. Pos: U.S. Rep, Ariz, 42-49; co. attorney, Maricopa Co, 38-42; asst. attorney gen, Ariz, 36-37; asst. city attorney, Phoenix, 35-36. Rel: Latter-day Saint. Mailing Add: 2323 N. Central Ave. Apt. 204, Phoenix, Ariz. 85004. (1967)

HARLLEE, JOHN D
Chmn, Fed. Maritime Cmn.
b. Washington, D.C, 1/2/14; s. William Curry Harllee and Ella Fullmore H; m. 9/10/37 to Jo Beth Carden; c. John. Educ: U.S. Naval Acad, B.S, 34; Naval War Col, grad, 50. Polit. & Govt. Pos: Chmn, Citizens for Kennedy and Johnson, North. Calif, 60; counsr, Under Secy. of Commerce for Transportation, 61; mem. and predecessor, Fed. Maritime Cmn, 61-63, chmn, 63- Bus. & Prof. Pos: Dir. and past pres, Peter Tare, Inc; prod. planner, AMPEX Corp, 60; v.pres, Edward I. Farley & Co, Inc, N.Y.C, 60-61. Mil. Serv: Ens. to Rear Adm, Navy, 34-59; Comdr, Motor Torpedo Squadron 12, 43-44; mem, Naval Cong. Liaison Unit, 48-49; Comdr, USS Dyess, 49-50 and USS Rankin, 58; Silver Star; Legion of Merit, Commendation Ribbon. Mem: Trustee, Am. Merchant Marine Libr. Asn; Nat. Cargo Bur; Sons of Repub. of Tex; Tex. Soc. of Wash; Tex. Breakfast Club; Chevy Chase Club; Army-Navy Country Club; N.Y. Yacht Club; hon. mem, Delta Theta Phi. Selected Man of the Year, N.Y. For. Freight Forwarders Asn, 64; Golden Quill Award, Rudder Club, Brooklyn, N.Y. Hon. Port Pilot Award, Port Long Beach, Calif, 68; Commendation, Fed. Bar Asn, 69. Mailing Add: 2950 Legation St. N.W, Washington, D.C. 20015.

HARLOW, ALLEN S. R
b. 1916; m. to Dorothy Beattie; c. Jane, Richard and David. Educ: Dean Acad; Univ. of Mass. Polit. & Govt. Pos: Mem, Town Coun, Middletown, R.I, 53-56, pres, 56-58; R.I. State Sen, 58-67. Bus. & Prof. Pos: Pres, Aquidneck Island Creamery. Mil. Serv: Maj, U.S. Army, World War II. Mem: Lions; VFW; Boys Clubs of Newport Co; trustee, Newport Hosp. Mailing Add: 414 Mitchell Lane, Middletown, R.I. 02840. (1967)

HARLOW, PAUL KIDDER D
Mont. State Rep.
b. Okobojo, S.Dak, 8/25/04; s. Arthur I. Harlow and Martha Bunch H; m. 7/21/29 to Margaret Barto; c. Arthur Allen and Ruth Marie. Educ: Stanford Univ, B.A, 30. Polit. & Govt. Pos: Mem, Sch.Bd, Thompson Falls, Mont, 40-43 & 52-55; Mont. State Rep, Dist. 27, 45-50 & 67-; chmn, Green Mt. Soil and Water Conserv. Dist, 50-65; committeeman, Dem. Party, 52-65; chmn, Sanders Co. Dem. Cent. Cmt, 54-64; crew leader, Agr. Census, 64. Bus. & Prof. Pos: Sch. teacher, 30-36, 43-44 & 49-50. Mem: Chmn, Mont. Citizens Cmt. for Pub. Schs, 47-49; Nat. Cmt. for Pub. Schs; Nat. Cmt. for the Support of Pub. Schs. Rel: Protestant. Mailing Add: Box 277, Thompson Falls, Mont. 59873. (1967)

HARLOW, W. M. 'MONTY' R
b. Springfield, Mo, 8/2/34; m. 6/5/57 to Marie Maupin; c. two daughters. Educ: Drury Col; Wash. Univ, A.B; Sigma Nu. Polit. & Govt. Pos: Mo. State Rep, 58-67; former state chmn, Mo. Young Rep. Club. Bus. Pos: Investment broker; formerly television announcer. Mil. Serv: Marine Corps, 8 years; Mo. Nat. Guard. Mem: Mason. Rel: Christian; lay minister. Mailing Add: 3324 Laclede, St. Louis, Mo. 63103. (1967)

HARMAN, CHARLES WILLIAM D
Mem, Nebr. Dem. State Cent. Cmt.
b. Granum, Alta, Can, 2/25/03; s. James Robert Harman and Emma Summer H; m. 5/31/38 to Eunice Pauline Rood. Educ: York Bus. Col, York, Nebr, 2 years. Polit. & Govt. Pos: Chmn, Furnas Co. Dem. Party, Nebr, 59-; mem, Nebr. Dem. State Cent. Cmt, 60- Bus. & Prof. Pos: Farmer and lifestock producer, 13- Mem: Odd Fellows; Mason (Worshipful Master); Shrine; Nat. Grange. Rel: Protestant. Mailing Add: 820 Tenth St, Beaver City, Nebr. 68926.

HARMAN, CHARLTON NEWTON R
W.Va. State Del.
b. Davis, W.Va, 8/16/15; s. Charlie Newton Harman and Stella May Kimble H; m. 8/11/47 to Harriet Jane Dempsey; c. James Kyle, John Duglas and Charlene Jane. Educ: Packard Merlin Sch, Warrington, Eng, 2 years; New Eng. Aircraft Sch; Bell Aircraft Sch; completed drawing and design course, Col. Eng, 42 and state and local govt. course, 69, W.Va. Univ. Polit. & Govt. Pos: W.Va. State Del, 69- Bus. & Prof. Pos: Gen. mgr, Harman Construction, 46- Mil. Serv: Entered as Pvt, Air Force, released as T/Sgt, 46, after serv. in 479th Fighter Group, Eighth Air Force, ETO, 42-46; 5 Bronze Stars; Good Conduct Medal; Europe-Africa-Middle East Serv. Ribbon; Am. Theater Serv. Ribbon; World War II Victory Ribbon; Air Medal. Mem: Mason; Grand Chap. RAM; DeMolay (Commandery Noll); K.T; Elks; VFW. Rel: Methodist; Sunday Sch. Supt, United Methodist Blueville Church. Mailing Add: 4 Harman Ave, Grafton, W.Va. 26354.

HARMAN, JAMES HARVEY R
State Committeeman, Ala. Rep. Party
b. Birmingham, Ala, 12/17/32; s. Harvey Harman and Mabel Johnston H; m. 6/18/54 to Barbara Ann Plunkett; c. Leigh Ann, James H, Jr. and Heather Kathryn. Educ: Auburn Univ, B.S, 57. Polit. & Govt. Pos: Co. pres, Jefferson Co. Rep. Workshops, Ala, 62-63; precinct capt, Jefferson Co. Rep. Party, 62-66; co. committeeman, Jefferson Co. Rep. Cmt, 62-67; state committeeman, Ala. Rep. Party, 62-, mem. finance cmt, 67-, mem. legis. recruitment cmt, 69-; state pres, Rep. Workshops, 63-65; mem, Jefferson Co. Rep. Exec. Cmt, 63-67; ballot security officer, Jefferson Co, 64-66; Rep. chmn, 25th Precinct, Jefferson Co, 66-; alternate del, Rep. Nat. Conv, 68; Justice of the Peace, Jefferson Co, currently. Bus. & Prof. Pos: Pres, AAA Air & Hydraulics, Birmingham, Ala, 68-; sales engr, Air & Hydraulics Engr. Mil. Serv: Entered as Pvt, Air Force, 51, released as A 3/C, 52, after serv. in 117th Air Tact Group. Rel: Methodist. Mailing Add: 3628 Leslie Ann Rd, Birmingham, Ala. 35243.

HARMAN, RICK R
b. Leon, Kans, 3/30/28; s. Walter George Harman and Lucy Souders H; m. 8/27/49 to Susanne Green; c. Sally, Betsy and Richard. Educ: Kans. State

Univ, B.S. in Indust. Chem, 50; Blue Key; Scabbard and Blade; Am. Chem. Soc; Beta Theta Pi. Polit. & Govt. Pos: Finance chmn, Johnson Co. Rep. Cent. Cmt, Kans, 64-66, chmn, 66-68; Rep. nominee for Gov. of Kans, 68. Bus. & Prof. Pos: Pres, Myron Green and Assocs, 57-, Myron Green Bldg. Co, currently. Mil. Serv: Entered as 2nd Lt, Air Force, 51, released as 1st Lt, 53, after serv. at Westover Air Force Base. Publ: 'Manpower Utilization,' Insts. Mag, 58. Mem: Pres, Kansas City Restaurant Asn, 60; pres, Mo. Restaurant Asn, 58-60; dir, Nat. Restaurant Asn, 63-; pres, Kans. State Univ. Alumni Asn, 57; dir, Kans. State Univ. Endowment Asn, 57-; Pub. Accomodations Cmt, Kansas City (v.chmn, 62); Mission Hills Country Club. Mo. Restaurant Man of Year, 59; Beta Theta Pi Man of Year, Metrop. Kansas City, 68. Rel: Presbyterian. Mailing Add: 6224 Mission Rd, Shawnee Mission, Kans. 66205.

HARMAN, ROBERT DALE R
W.Va. State Del.
b. Keyser, W.Va, 10/7/37; s. Herbert Roscoe Harman and Lillian Miller H; m. 6/8/58 to Phyllis Ann Sanders; c. Kelley Ann, Robert Craig, Tracy Dawn and Stephen Kirk. Educ: Potomac State Col, A.A, 57; Shepherd Col, B.A, 59; Frostburg State Col, 64; W.Va. Univ, M.A, 69; Theta Sigma Chi; Col. Thespians; Potomac State Col. Newspaper; Shepherd Col. Newspaper and Yearbook; Shepherd 4-H Club. Polit. & Govt. Pos: W.Va. State Del, Mineral Co, 64-, secy, Rep. Legis. Coord. Cmt, 67; chmn, Mineral Co. Rep. Exec. Cmt, 65-; state adult adv, W.Va. Fedn. Teenage Rep, 66-; pres. bd. dirs, W.Va. GOP Camp Inc, 68- Bus. & Prof. Pos: Exten. Serv, W.Va. Univ, 54-59; teacher of govt. and hist, Mineral Co. Schs, 59-66; mgr. and owner, Harman's West End Grocery, 61-63; radio sportscaster, Sta. WKYR, 64-65; assoc. prof, W.Va. Univ. Exten. Serv, 67-68; radio sportscaster, Sta. WKLP, 68- Mil. Serv: ROTC, Potomac State Col. Publ: Polit. column, 'Capitol Views,' Mineral Daily News, 65-69 and Piedmont Herald, 67-69. Mem: Nat. and W.Va. Educ. Asn; Mineral Co. Educ. Asn.(pres, 67-69); Asn. Classroom Teachers; DeMolay (Chevalier); Moose; Jaycees; Kiwanis; Farm Bur; 4-H All Star Asn; chmn. Mineral Co. Chap, Nat. Found. for Polio and Birth Defects. 4-H All Star; Outstanding Freshman Legislator, Charleston Daily Mail, W.Va, 65. Rel: Methodist. Mailing Add: 1090 Carolina Ave, Keyser, W.Va. 26726.

HARMER, JOHN L. R
Calif. State Sen.
b. 1934; m. to Carolyn J; c. five. Educ: Univ. Utah, grad; George Wash. Univ, law degree. Polit. & Govt. Pos: Former spec. aide to U.S. Sen. Wallace Bennett, Utah; mem, Rep. State Cent. Cmt; Calif. State Sen, 67- Mem: Former pub. affairs dir, Nat. Asn. of Mfrs, 62-64. Mailing Add: 1621 Vista Dr, Glendale, Calif. 91201.

HARMODY, RICHARD M. D
City Councilman, Cleveland, Ohio
b. Cleveland, Ohio, 4/8/30; s. Michael L. Harmody and Mary A. Gasper H; m. 6/7/58 to Elsie J. Smith; c. Matthew R, Ellen M. and Mark R. Educ: Fenn Col, B.B.A, 57; West. Reserve Univ. Sch. Law, LL.B, 60; Phi Alpha Delta. Polit. & Govt. Pos: Ward leader and precinct committeeman, Cleveland Dem. Party, Ohio, 63-; city councilman, Cleveland, 64- Bus. & Prof. Pos: Attorney-at-law, 60- Mil. Serv: Entered as Pvt, Army, 51, released as Sgt, 53; Combat Infantryman's Award; Korean Serv. Unit Citations. Mem: Cleveland and Ohio Bar Asns; Polish Legion of Am. Vet; Slovenian Nat. Benefit Soc. Rel: Roman Catholic. Mailing Add: 4824 W. 14th St, Cleveland, Ohio 44109.

HARMON, GEORGE McKINLEY R
Chmn, Avery Co. Rep. Party, N.C.
b. Beech Creek, N.C, 6/12/98; s. William Monroe Harmon and Mary Marinda Harmon H; m. 2/24/24 to Rosa Ann Palmer; c. Betty Lou (Mrs. Elbert Stansberry). Educ: Kellersville Elem. Sch, N.C, 7 years. Polit. & Govt. Pos: Postmaster, Beech Creek, N.C, 48-64; chmn, Avery Co. Rep. Party, N.C, 67- Bus. & Prof. Pos: Merchant, Beech Creek, 20-48. Mil. Serv: Entered as Pvt, Army, 17, released as Pfc, 19, after serv. in Co. D, Fifth Div, AEF, France, 18-19; Purple Heart. Rel: Protestant. Mailing Add: Route 1, Box 162, Sugar Grove, N.C. 28679.

HARNED, HORACE HAMMERTON, JR. D
Miss. State Rep.
b. State College, Minn, 7/27/20; s. Horace Hammerton Harned and Harriet Rice H; m. 6/19/49 to Nellie Howell; c. Margaret Ann, Helen, Alice and Horace H, III. Educ: Miss. State Univ, B.S, 42; Blue Key; Kappa Sigma. Polit. & Govt. Pos: Miss. State Sen, 52-56; Miss. State Rep, 60-; Presidential Elector, Am. Independent Party, 68. Bus. & Prof. Pos: Dairy and livestock farmer, 46- Mil. Serv: Entered as Aviation Cadet, Air Force, 42, released as Capt, 46, after serv. in 311th Photo Mapping Group, Am. Theater, 43-44, 45-46 and China-Burma-India Theater, 44-45; Asiatic Combat Ribbon with 2 Battle Stars; Am. Theater of Opers. Ribbon. Mem: State Bldg. Cmn; State Sovereignty Cmn; Dist. Law Enforcement Coun; Rotary; Mason; Am. Legion; 40 et 8. Rel: Baptist. Mailing Add: Route 1, Box 27, Starkville, Miss. 39759.

HARNETTY, CHARLES SAMUEL D
Chmn, Perry Co. Dem. Exec. and Cent. Cmts, Ohio
b. Junction City, Ohio, 5/18/37; s. William A. Harnetty and Florence G. Paxton H; m. 6/19/65 to Barbara Elaine Eckard. Educ: U.S. Navy Hosp. Corps Sch, grad; Ohio Univ, Lancaster Br, 2 years. Polit. & Govt. Pos: Chmn, Perry Co. Dem. Exec. and Cent. Cmts, Ohio, 68; v.chmn, Dem. Co. Chmn. Ohio, 69- Bus. & Prof. Pos: Foreman, Ludowici-Celadon Co, New Lexington, Ohio, 61- Mil. Serv: Entered as Airman 3/C, Air Force, 55, released as Airman 1/C, 59, after serv. in 36th Tactical Wing, Germany; Good Conduct Medal; Unit Citation Award. Mem: Elks; K. of C.(3°); Tenth Dist. Dem. Action Club; chmn, Perry Co. Dem. Action Club; Father Flanagan's Boys Town, Nebr. Rel: Catholic. Mailing Add: Box 234 Logan St, Junction City, Ohio 43748.

HARP, JOSEPH ROBERT D
Mayor, Sebring, Ohio
b. Salem, Ohio, 5/30/24; s. Joseph H. Harp and Miriam Steiner H; m. 10/19/46 to Alice Louise Miller; c. Mary Josephine, Richard Paul, Barbara Louise, James Joseph, David Francis and Theresa Marie. Educ: Salem High Sch, grad, 42. Polit. & Govt. Pos: Councilman, Sebring, Ohio, 59-60, mayor, 63-; alternate del, Dem. Nat. Conv, 68. Bus. & Prof. Pos: Pres, Sebring Trade & Labor Coun, 56-61. Mil. Serv: Entered as Pvt, Army, 43, released as T-5, 46, after serv. in 28th Tank Bn, Southwest Pac. Theatre, 45-46. Mem: VFW; K. of C; Am. Legion; Int. Brotherhood Oper. Potters (secy-treas, Local Union 59, 55-63). Rel: Roman Catholic. Mailing Add: 103 W. Carolina, Sebring, Ohio 44672.

HARPER, C. LEM D
S.C. State Rep.
b. Ocilla, Ga, 5/28/18; s. James J. Harper and Willie Middlebrooks H; m. 3/10/44 to Rebecca Hayes Roddey; c. Lynne Delene, C. Lem, Jr, Laurie Charmel and Darrell William. Educ: Univ. S.C. Exten. Div. Polit. & Govt. Pos: S.C. State Rep, 66- Bus. & Prof. Pos: Pres. and owner, C. Lem Harper, Ltd, 46-; exec. v.pres, Preferred Am. Life, 58-63; pres, Exec. Investment Asn, 58- Mil. Serv: Pvt, Army, 41-42. Mem: Past pres, S.C. Jr. C. of C, Columbia, S.C. Jr. C. of C. and South. Conf. Football Off. Asn; Jr. C. of C. Palmetto Sertoma Club; Richland Masonic Lodge 39; Scottish Rite Mason; Shrine; Omar Temple; Am. Legion; Columbia Country Club; Columbia Tip-Off Club; Univ. S.C. Century Club. Conducted 2 European and 1 Far-East Football Clin. for U.S. Air Force Personnel. Rel: Methodist. Legal Res: 6705 Skii Lane, Lake Arcadia, Columbia, S.C. 29206. Mailing Add: 1226 Washington St, Columbia, S.C. 29201.

HARPER, GEORGE EDWARD R
Chmn, Lenoir Co. Rep. Party, N.C.
b. Lynn, Mass, 3/26/38; s. Andrew Earl Harper and Mary Morgan H; m. 4/8/61 to Eileen Alana MacLean; c. George Edward, Jr, Michael Joseph and Karen Marie. Educ: Stevens Inst. Tech, M.E, 60; Delta Tau Delta. Polit. & Govt. Pos: Mem, exec. cmt, Lenoir Co. Rep. Party, N.C, 68 and chmn, 68- Bus. & Prof. Pos: Exec, E.I. DuPont, Kinston, N.C, 64- Mil. Serv: Entered as 2nd Lt, Marine Corps, 60, released as 1st Lt, 63, after serv. in 3rd LAAM Bn, Cuban Crisis and FMF Pac, 62-63, Maj, Res, 63-69; Nat. Defense Ribbon; Armed Forces Expeditionary Medal. Mem: N.C. Soc. Engrs; Moose; Jaycees. Spoke Award, Jaycees. Rel: Catholic. Mailing Add: 2902 Ginger Rd, Kinston, N.C. 28501.

HARPER, KENNETH FRANKLIN R
Mem, Kenton Co. Rep. Exec. Cmt, Ky.
b. Covington, Ky, 1/15/31; s. Kenneth Wellington Harper and Elizabeth Brickler H; m. 5/16/53 to Eileen Ann Kathman; c. Gregory, Scott, Glenn, Bryan and Lesley Ann. Educ: Univ. Ky, 49-51; Pi Kappa Alpha. Polit. & Govt. Pos: Mem, Kenton Co. Rep. Exec. Cmt, Ky, 61-; Ky. State Rep, 63rd Dist, 64-68, Asst. Minority Floor Leader, Ky. State House of Rep, 66; mem, Cmt. Hwy. Policy Problems, S.Region, Coun. State Govts, 66-67; asst. cmn, Ky. Dept. Child Welfare, mem. exec. cmt, Ky. Crime Cmn. and chmn, Juvenile Delinquency Subcmt, 68- Bus. & Prof. Pos: V.pres, Assoc. Credit Bur. Ky, 62; pres. and treas, Prfnl. Bus. Serv. Ky, Inc, 66- dir, First Nat. Bank & Trust Co, 68- Mil. Serv: Entered as Pvt, Air Force, 51, released as Airman 1/C, 53, after serv. in 5th Commun. Group, 5th Air Force, Korean Theater; Korean and UN Serv. Medals; Good Conduct Medal. Mem: Dir, Campbell Kenton Asn. for Retarded Children; pres. of bd, Campbell Lodge Home Adv. Cmt, 61-62; Ad Hoc Cmt, for Ment. Health, Mental Retardation Reg. Bd; Legis. Cmt, Ky. Asn. for Retarded Children; Kenton Co. Rep. Mens Club; Kenton Co. Young Rep. Club; pres, Covington Rotary, 59-60 and Covington Kenton Co. Jaycees, 62-63; Ky. Jaycees; Covington-Kenton-Boone C. of C; chmn, Kenton Co. Heart Fund, 65-66; dir, N.Ky. Coun. Retarded Children and pres, 61-62. Outstanding Young Man of Ky, 1963. Rel: Roman Catholic. Mailing Add: 33 Arcadia, Lakeside Park, Fort Mitchell, Ky. 41017.

HARPER, ROY W. D
b. Gibson, Mo, 7/26/05; s. Marvin H. Harper and Minnie Brooks H; m. 7/30/41 to Ruth Butt; c. Katherine Brooks and Arthur Murray. Educ: Univ. Mo, A.B. and LL.B, 29; Delta Theta Phi. Polit. & Govt. Pos: Chmn, Mo. Dem. State Cmt, 46-47; U. S. Dist. Judge, East. and West. Dist, Mo, 47-59; Chief Judge, East. Dist, 59-; mem, U.S. Judicial Conf, currently. Bus. & Prof. Pos: Private law practice, 31-34; mem, Law Firm of Ward, Reeves & Western, 34-47. Mil. Serv: Entered as Pvt, Army Air Force, 42, released as Maj, 45, after serv. in Southwest Pac; Col, Air Corps Res; Bronze Star Medal. Mem: Am, Mo. and St. Louis Lawyers Asns; Pemiscot Co. Bar Asn; Grand Orator, Grand Lodge of Mo, 65; AF&AM, Steele, Mo; Scottish Rite; KCCH; Shrine; DeMolay (Legion of Honor, 57); Order of the Coif, 58. Citation of Merit, Univ. Mo. Law Sch, 63. Rel: Presbyterian. Legal Res: 3 Woodcliffe Rd, Ladue, Mo. 63124. Mailing Add: 315 U.S. Court House and Custom House, St. Louis, Mo. 63101.

HARPER, THOMAS D
Dem. Nat. Committeeman, Ark.
b. Greenwood, Ark, 11/23/08; s. Robert Atlas Harper and Merton Harrell H; wid; c. Thomas, Jr, Granville, Blake and Kay. Educ: Univ. Ill, 27-28; Delta Upsilon; Phi Eta Sigma. Polit. & Govt. Pos: Chmn, Sebastian Co. Dem. Cent. Cmt, Ark, 42-44; chmn, Ark. Dem. State Cmt, 54-63; del, Dem. Nat. Conv, 56, 60, 64 & 68; Dem. nat. committeeman, Ark, 63- Bus. & Prof. Pos: Attorney-at-law, 30- Mil. Serv: Entered as Seaman 1/C, Naval Res, 44, released as Lt.(jg), 46, after serv. at Norfolk Navy Yard and Treasure Island, Calif, 44-46; Am. Theater Ribbon. Mem: Am, Ark. and Sebastian Co. Bar Asns; Am. Col. of Trial Lawyers; Motor Carrier Lawyers Asn; Am. Legion. Rel: Methodist. Legal Res: 5001 S. Cliff Dr, Fort Smith, Ark. 72901. Mailing Add: P.O. Box 43, Fort Smith, Ark. 72901.

HARPER, VIRGINIA MAUGHAN D
Mem, Calif. Dem. State Cent. Cmt.
b. Wood River, Nebr, 5/31/21; d. John Patrick Maughan and Florence Maus M; c. Carl Brian. Polit. & Govt. Pos: Mem, Yolo Co. Dem. Cent. Cmt, Calif, 60, 62, 64 & 66, mem, Calif. Dem. State Cent. Cmt, 62-; dir, Fourth Cong. Dist, Calif. Dem. Coun, 63-66; del, Dem. Nat. Conv, 64. Mem: Am. Civil Liberties Union; NAACP. Mailing Add: 606 Radcliffe Dr, Davis, Calif. 95616.

HARPER, WARREN WAYNE, SR. D
b. Livingston, Mont, 8/4/30; s. Willard B. Harper (deceased) and Emma McKinney H; m. 8/15/54 to Annabelle Desta Mercer; c. Desta Mona, Warren Wayne, Jr. and Dawn Maureen. Educ: High Sch, 44-48. Polit. & Govt. Pos: Mont. State Rep, 61-67. Bus. & Prof. Pos: Conductor-brakeman, North. Pac. Rwy, 52-65, trainmaster, 65- Mil. Serv: Entered as Pvt, Army Air Corps, 46, released as Sgt, 56, after serv. in Intel. and Reconnaissance, Korea, 50-51;

Parachute Inf. Badge; Combat Inf. Badge; Bronze Star Medal with Valor V; Purple Heart; Victory Medal; Korean Serv. Ribbon with Four Stars and Arrowhead; UN Serv. and Japan Occupation Ribbons; Good Conduct Medal. Mem: Lions Int; State Comdrs. Asn, DAV; VFW; Am. Legion; Mil. Order of Purple Heart; Elks; Traffic Club. Mailing Add: 318 N. Ninth St, Staples, Minn. 56479. (1967)

HARPHAM, ELMER DEE R
Chmn, Camden Co. Rep. Cent. Cmt, Mo.
b. Newtown, Mo, 8/20/92; s. Charles Wesley Harpham and Charlotte Long H; m. 5/21/19 to Neva Lynn Miller; c. Charlotte (Mrs. Bonner), Mary H.(Mrs. Wille), Dorothy (Mrs. Whillen) and Neva Dee (Mrs. Brown). Educ: Northeast Mo. State Teachers Col, Kirksville, B.S; Univ. Mo, Columbia, A.M; Colo. Col. of Educ, Greeley, 2 terms. Polit. & Govt. Pos: Treas, Camden Co. Cent. Cmt, Mo, 64-66; secy. and treas, 7th Cong. Dist. Rep. Party, 64-66; chmn, Camden Co. Rep. Cent. Cmt, 66-; del, Rep. Nat. Conv, 68. Bus. & Prof. Pos: Sch. administrator, 53 years; supt. schs, Windsor and Imperial, Mo, 68. Mil. Serv: Entered as Pvt, Army, 17, released as Bn. Supply Sgt, after serv. in 164th Brigade. Publ: 'Granby turns to Consolidation,' Mo. Ruralist. Mem: Life mem, Nat. Educ. Asn; Mason; Shrine; Rotary; Am. Legion (past dept. chaplain of Mo). Rel: Reorganized Latter-day Saint. Mailing Add: 126 Panoramic Dr, Camdenton, Mo. 65021.

HARPSTRITE, BEN C. R
Ill. State Rep.
b. Trenton, Ill, 6/10/26; s. Ben Anton Harpstrite and Ella Bossler H; m. 6/19/47 to Eleanor Schmidt; c. Janice (Mrs. Dale Zellers), Karen, Sheryl and Janine. Educ: High sch, 4 years. Polit. & Govt. Pos: Trustee, Clinton Co. Sch. Bd, Ill, 6 years; twp. supvr, Lookingglass Twp, 6 years; twp. assessor, 8 years; Ill. State Rep. 53rd Dist, 67- Bus. & Prof. Pos: Farmer; secy, Sugar Creek Mutual Ins. Co, 4 years; pres, Trenton Coop. Equity Elevator Exchange, 6 years. Mem: Mason; C. of C; Lions; Farm Bur. Rel: Methodist. Mailing Add: R.R, New Baden, Ill. 62265.

HARRELL, AUBREY HEWLETTE D
Ga. State Rep.
b. Fayetteville, Ga, 7/24/27; s. Aubrey T. Harrell and Pauline Williams H; m. 10/05/46 to Hariette Dean Morgan; c. Gregory Morgan and Diana Lucy. Educ: Fayette Co. High Sch, 44. Polit. & Govt. Pos: Ga. State Rep, 61- Bus. & Prof. Pos: Auto and truck dealer; Ready Mix Concrete. Mil. Serv: Merchant Marines, 45-47. Mem: Mason; Civil Defense Dir; Clayton City C. of C; Kiwanis; Lakeshore Country and Quarterback Clubs; PTA; Am. Legion. Rel: Baptist. Mailing Add: 440 Kelly Dr, Fayetteville, Ga. 30214.

HARRELL, JAMES H. D
Ark. State Rep.
b. Bearden, Ark, 7/3/37; s. L.V. Harrell and Audrey Means H; m. 12/27/58 to Zella Keener; c. William Bradford and Timothy Douglas. Educ: Ark. Tech, B.A, 62. Polit. & Govt. Pos: Pres, Pope Co. Young Dem, 58; Ark. State Rep, Fourth Dist, 67- Bus. & Prof. Pos: Pres, Harrell & Co, currently. Mem: Lions; C. of C; Russellville Jaycees (past pres). Rel: Protestant. Legal Res: 205 S. Pasadena, Russellville, Ark. 72801. Mailing Add: P.O. Box 188, Russellville, Ark. 72801.

HARRELSON, JAMES P. D
S.C. State Sen.
b. Mullins, S.C, 6/28/19; s. Carson A. Harrelson and Bertha Mae H; m. 6/24/43 to Hazel H. Richardson. Polit. & Govt. Pos: Mem. gen. bd, Young Dem. Club of S.C, 48-53, nat. committeeman, 52-57; S.C. State Rep, 57-60; S.C. State Sen, 63-; del, Dem. Nat. Conv, 68. Bus. & Prof. Pos: Lawyer, practicing in state, Fed. and U.S. Supreme Courts. Mil. Serv: Army Air Corps, 40; disabled. Mem: Mason; York Rite; Shrine; WOW; Elks; VFW; Am, S.C. and Colleton Bar Asns. Rel: Baptist. Mailing Add: Walterboro, S.C. 29488. (1967)

HARRELSON, JOSEPH EDWARD D
b. Equality, Ill, 2/3/25; s. Thurman Louis Harrelson and Lydia Uselton H; m. 12/22/46 to Dorothy Clark. Educ: Equality Pub. Sch, 8 years. Polit. & Govt. Pos: Committeeman, Ill. Dem. Cent. Cmt, until 69. Mil. Serv: Entered as Seaman 2/C, Navy, 43, released as PO 3/C, 46, after serv. in S.Pac. Theatre; Two Stars in Asian and Pac; Philippines and European Theatre Ribbons; Philippine Liberation Medal; Japanese Victory Ribbon. Mailing Add: Box 246, Equality, Ill. 62934.

HARRELSON, WILLIAM L. D
State Cmnr. of Agr, S.C.
b. Mullins, S.C, 7/25/13; s. Maxey C. Harrelson and Dora Page H; m. 3/29/56 to Grace Hough; c. Cynthia Page and William Louis, Jr. Educ: The Citadel; Univ. S.C, LL.B, 37. Polit. & Govt. Pos: Mem, S.C. Dairy Cmn. and Mkt. Cmn; S.C. State Rep, 41-42; S.C. State Sen, 53-55; State Cmnr. of Agr, S.C, 56- Bus. & Prof. Pos: Former attorney. Mil. Serv: Coast Guard, World War II. Legal Res: Mullins, S.C. Mailing Add: S.C. Dept. of Agriculture, Hampton Office Bldg, 5th Floor, Columbia, S.C. 29201.

HARRIGAN, ALICE ANNA D
Dem. Nat. Committeewoman, Alaska
b. Orwigsburg, Pa, 12/2/09; d. Clarence Brown and Myrtle Newhard B; m. 8/7/33 to James F. Harrison; c. Alice Ann (Mrs. Charles Stedman), Patricia (Mrs. James Gallian) and James Joseph. Educ: Beckley Commercial Teachers Col, 29; Pa. State Col, B.A, 31. Polit. & Govt. Pos: Mem, Gov. adv. cmt, Alaska Centennial; mem. exec. cmt, Alaska Centennial Cmt; mem, Active Dem. Party, 33-; Dem. nat. committeewoman, Alaska, 39- Bus. & Prof. Pos: Commercial teacher, West Hazelton, Pa, 29-33; teacher, Mt. Edgecumbe Voc. Sch, Sitka, Alaska, 39-41. Mem: Exec. secy, Alaska Day Festival Cmt. Club, Sitka, Emblem (past pres). Mailing Add: P.O. Box 196, Sitka, Alaska 99835.

HARRIMAN, JOHN H. R
Treas, Los Angeles Co. United Rep. Finance Cmt, Calif.
b. Buffalo, N.Y, 4/14/20; s. Lewis G. Harriman and Grace Bastine H; m. 6/12/43 to Barbara Ann Brunmark; c. Walter B, Constance B. and John H, Jr. Educ: Dartmouth Col, A.B, 42; Stanford Law Sch, LL.B, 49; Phi Beta Kappa; Theta Delta Chi; Phi Alpha Delta. Polit. & Govt. Pos: Mem. or assoc. mem, Calif. State Rep. Cent. Cmt, 56-; mem, Los Angeles Co. Rep. Cent. Cmt, 58-, v.chmn, 62; chmn, 58th Assembly Dist. Rep. Cent. Cmt, 59-60, Los Angeles Co. Rep. Precinct Orgn, 60, 15th Cong. Dist. Rep. Cent. Cmt, 60-62 and 30th Cong. Dist. Rep. Cent. Cmt, 62; trustee, Rep. Assocs, Los Angeles, 62-; treas, Los Angeles Co. United Rep. Finance Cmt, 69- Bus. & Prof. Pos: Attorney, Lawler, Felix & Hall, 49-55; asst. v.pres, Security Pac. Nat. Bank, Calif, 55, v.pres, 61 & 65, secy, 65. Mil. Serv: Entered as Aviation Cadet, Army Air Force, 43, released as Capt, 46, after serv. in 5th and 8th Air Forces, Pac. Theater, 45-46. Mem: State Bar of Calif; Am. and Los Angeles Co. Bar Asns; Town Hall; Lincoln Club; Calif. Club; Beach Club. Rel: Episcopal. Mailing Add: 245 S. Plymouth Blvd, Los Angeles, Calif. 90004.

HARRIMAN, W. AVERELL
Ambassador at Large
b. N.Y.C, 11/15/91; m. to Marie Norton; c. Mrs. Shirley C. Fisk and Mrs. Stanley G. Mortimer, Jr. Educ: Yale Univ, B.A, 13. Polit. & Govt. Pos: Mem, Bus. Adv. Coun, Dept. of Commerce, 33-39, chmn, 37-39; adminstr, Nat. Recovery Admin, 34-35; mem, Off. of Prod. Mgt, 40-41; spec. rep. of the President, Gt. Brit, 41; U.S. Ambassador, Russia, 43-46 and Gt. Brit, 46; Secy. of Commerce, 46-49; U.S. Rep. in Europe, 48-50; Spec. asst. to the President, 50-51; dir, Mutual Security Admin, 51-53; Gov, N.Y, 54-58; U.S. Ambassador-at-lg, 61 & 65-; Asst. Secy. of State for Far East. Affairs, 61-63; Under Secy. of State for Polit. Affairs, 63-65; Rep. of the President to Peace Talks in Paris, 68-69. Bus. & Prof. Pos: Dir, Ill. Cent. R.R, 15-31, chmn. exec. cmt, 31-46; v.pres, Union Pac. R.R, 15-32, chmn. bd, 32-46; founder, W.A. Harriman and Co, 20-31; Ltd. partner, Brown Bros, Harriman and Co, 31- Legal Res: 16 E. 81st St, New York, N.Y. 10028. Mailing Add: 3038 N St. N.W, Washington, D.C. 20007.

HARRINGTON, DONALD SZANTHO Liberal Party, N.Y.
State Chmn, Liberal Party, N.Y.
b. Newton, Mass, 7/11/14; s. Charles Elliot Marshall Harrington and Leita Hersey H; m. 3/28/39 to Rev. Vilma Szantho; c. Ilona Vilma (Mrs. Joseph G. Hancock, Jr) and Francis David. Educ: Antioch Col; Univ. Chicago, A.B, 36; Meadville Theol. Sch, Chicago, B.D, 38; Starr King Sch. for the Ministry, Berkeley, Calif, S.T.D, 59; Meadville Theol. Sch, D.D, 64. Polit. & Govt. Pos: Cand, Lt. Gov, N.Y, 66; state chmn, Liberal Party, N.Y, 66- Bus. & Prof. Pos: Sr. Minister of the Commun. Church, N.Y, 44- Mem: Mason. Rel: Unitarian Universalist. Mailing Add: 10 Park Ave, New York, N.Y. 10016.

HARRINGTON, EDWARD DENNIS, JR. R
Mass. State Rep.
b. Worcester, Mass, 8/11/21; s. Edward Dennis Harrington and Alice Beeso H; m. 9/3/43 to Jean Thomas; c. Janet Elisabeth, James Thomas, Edward Dennis, III and Alison Jean. Educ: Holden High Sch. Polit. & Govt. Pos: Tax assessor, Holden, Mass, 49-59; Mass. State Rep, 57- Bus. & Prof. Pos: Material expediter, Heald Machine Co, 40-42 & 46-50; foreman, security dept, Wyman Gordon Co, Mass, 50- Mil. Serv: Entered as Pvt, Marine Corps, 42, released as Sgt, 46, after serv. in Fourth Marine Div, Pac; Letter of Commendation. Mem: Dir, Holden Dist. Hosp; Am. Legion; VFW. Rel: Catholic. Mailing Add: 170 South Rd, Holden, Mass. 01520. (1967)

HARRINGTON, EDWARD F. D
Mayor, New Bedford, Mass.
b. New Bedford, Mass, 5/16/27; s. Michael J. Harrington and Margaret H; m. 11/11/60 to June A. Lang; c. Michael J, II. Educ: Boston Col, 47-49; Ark. Law Sch, LL.B, 52. Polit. & Govt. Pos: Mem, New Bedford City Coun, Mass, 57-61; Mayor, New Bedford, 62- Mil. Serv: Entered as A/S, Navy, 45, released as Seaman, 46; Naval Res. Mem: Dir, Citizens Credit Union; bd. of dirs, Am. Red Cross and Volunteers of Am; incorporator, New Bedford Inst. Savings Bank, Pub. Admin. for Bristol Co. Rel: Catholic. Legal Res: 27 Milton St, New Bedford, Mass. 02740. Mailing Add: 133 William St, New Bedford, Mass. 02740.

HARRINGTON, JAMES ELMER, JR. R
Mem, N.C. Rep. State Exec. Cmt.
b. Bethlehem, N.H, 12/14/27; s. James Elmer Harrington and Berenice Morrill H; m. 6/10/64 to Harriett Lee Whitmore; c. Nancy, Mary, Harry Alexander, David and Molly. Educ: Va. Mil. Inst, B.S, 49. Polit. & Govt. Pos: Precinct chmn, Rep. Party, Moore Co, N.C, 52-60; chmn, Moore Co. Rep. Exec. Cmt, 60-64; secy, N.C. Rep. State Exec. Cmt, 62-64, mem, 68-; dist. chmn, Eighth Cong. Dist. Rep. Party, 64-66; chmn, Cong. Campaign Cmt, Fourth Cong. Dist, N.C, 66- Bus. & Prof. Pos: Exec. asst, Pinehurst, Inc, 52-58, asst. secy, 58-64, secy-treas, 64-67, pres, 67- Mil. Serv: Entered as 2nd Lt, Army, 49, releasedas 1st Lt, 52, after serv. in 82nd Airborne Div; Maj, Army Nat. Guard at present. Mem: Kiwanis; Elks; Asn. of U.S. Army; Nat. Guard Asn; Young Pres. Orgn. Rel: Episcopal. Legal Res: Midland Rd, Pinehurst, N.C. 28374. Mailing Add: Box 1151, Pinehurst, N.C. 28374.

HARRINGTON, JOHN FLOYD D
Ga. State Rep.
b. Milledgeville, Ga, 7/18/29; s. Glenn Terrell Harrington and Mary Williams H; m. 3/27/54 to Laura Nell Lawrence; c. John Floyd, Jr. Educ: Ga. Mil. Col, Univ. Ga, B.B.A, 51. Polit. & Govt. Pos: Ga. State Sen, 61-62; Ga. State Rep, 63- Bus. & Prof. Pos: Owner, farm supply and cotton warehouse. Mil. Serv: Pfc, Army, 46-48; Ga. Nat. Guard, 54- Rel: Methodist. Mailing Add: 6340 Aberdeen Dr. N.E, Atlanta, Ga. 30328. (1967)

HARRINGTON, MARGARET ELIZABETH D
b. St. Charles, Mo, 6/22/16; d. Joseph Benton and Mary Blaeser B; m. 6/6/35 to Ralph Deneen Harrington; c. Barbara (Mrs. William Schoeneweis). Educ: Jersey Twp. High Sch, grad, 33; McDowell Sch. of Music, Chicago; Schola Cantorum, San Francisco. Polit. & Govt. Pos: Precinct committeeman, Dem. Party, Ill, 60-; pres, Alton-Godfrey Dem. Club, two terms; financial secy. and treas, Alton-Godfrey Dem. Voter's League; del, Dem. Nat. Conv, 68. Bus. & Prof. Pos: Acct. clerk, Olin-Mathieson Chem. Co, 52-63. Mem: Choreophonic Singers of South. Ill. Univ. at Edwardsville; Kay Shanahan Singers of Acton; Bach Soc. of St. Louis, Mo. Rel: Roman Catholic. Mailing Add: 928 Washington Ave, Alton, Ill. 62002.

HARRINGTON, MICHAEL JOSEPH D
U.S. Rep, Mass.
b. Salem, Mass, 9/2/36. Educ: Harvard Col, A.B, 58; Harvard Law Sch, LL.B, 61; Harvard Grad. Sch. of Pub. Admin, 62-63. Polit. & Govt. Pos: City coun, 60-61, coun-at-lg, 62-63; Mass. State Rep, 65-69; U.S. Rep, Mass, 69- Bus. & Prof. Pos: Attorney-at-law. Legal Res: 7 Beach Ave, Salem, Mass. 01970. Mailing Add: U.S. House of Representatives, Washington, D.C. 20015.

HARRINGTON, PATRICK H. D
b. 1920; m. to Eleanor S. Spillane; c. Patrick H, Jr. Educ: Bates Col, A.B, Boston Univ. Law Sch, LL.B. cum laude, 48; case ed, BU Law Rev. Polit. & Govt. Pos: Chmn, Fall River Indust. Cmn, Mass; past pres, State Sheriff's Asn; mem, Gov. Adv. Cmt. Mass. Maritime Acad; del. to Nat. and State Polit. Convs; mem, Bristol Co. Bd. Cmnrs, 56-; nominee, U.S. House Rep, Tenth Cong. Dist, 66. Bus. & Prof. Pos: Lawyer. Mil. Serv: Navy, Lt. Comdr, 41-46; USNR Officers Schs, S.Weymouth, Otis AFB, Fall River, Naval Res, 60-, Capt, Comdr-Capt, Navy Selection Bd, 65. Mem: Fall River Indust. Develop. Corp. Participant, U.S. State Dept. Seminars For. Policy, Communist Strategy and Nat. Defense. Mailing Add: 56 N. Main St, Fall River, Mass. 02722.

HARRIS, DAVE T. R
Mem, Calif. State Rep. Cent. Cmt.
b. Reading, Pa, 5/19/20; s. John Edward Harris and Pauline Moore H; m. 9/4/43 to Rose Romaine Mather; c. David T. Harris, Jr. Educ: Yale, A.B, 42; Alpha Sigma Phi. Polit. & Govt. Pos: Nominee, U.S. Rep, Calif, 68; mem, Fresno Co. and Calif. State Rep. Cent. Cmts, 68- Bus. & Prof. Pos: Mgr, Radio Station KWG, Stockton, Calif, 50-53; mgr, Radio Station KMJ, Fresno, 53-58; owner and mgr, Radio Station KBIF, 58-59; realtor and owner, Dave Harris Real Estate, 59- Mil. Serv: Entered as Aviation Cadet, Air Force, 42, released as 1st Lt, 45, after serving in Eighth Air Force, ETO, 43-45; ETO Ribbon with six Bronze Stars; Presidential Unit Citation with two clusters. Mem: Fresno Realty Bd; Calif. Real Estate Asn; Nat. Asn. Real Estate Bd; Rotary (pres, Fresno Club, 65); Elks; Fresno Trade Club (bd. dirs). Rel: Episcopal. Mailing Add: 5745 N. Lafayette, Fresno, Calif. 93705.

HARRIS, EDWARD F. R
Wash. State Rep.
b. Harrison, Idaho; married; c. two. Educ: Univ. Idaho Bus. Sch; Gonzaga Law Sch. Polit. & Govt. Pos: Wash. State Rep, 54-, asst. Rep. Floor Leader, 57, Rep. caucus chmn, 59. Recipient Superior Qualifications Rating, Munic. League. Mailing Add: 716 Old National Bank Bldg, Spokane, Wash. 99203.

HARRIS, ELMER O. R
b. Baltimore, Md, 7/9/16; s. Elmer Francis Harris and Catherine Robinson H; m. 9/30/37 to Ora Ann Carey; c. Otis, Charles Richard, Marion Esther and Betty Lee (Mrs. Leroy McCardell). Educ: Douglass High Sch, Baltimore, Md. Polit. & Govt. Pos: Chmn, Baltimore Rep. State Cent. Cmt, Seventh Dist, 67-68, secy, 68; cmnr, Liquor Bd, 67-; del, Rep. Nat. Conv, 68; exec, 33rd Elec. Dist, Baltimore, 68. Bus. & Prof. Pos: Life underwriter, Mutual Benefit, Baltimore, 49-58; real estate rep, Manning Shaw Realty, Baltimore, 58-59 and Crocket Realty Inc, 60-69; pres, El Vio Inc. Investment Rentals, 68-69. Mem: Citizens Housing and Planning Asn; Urban League; NAACP; Rep. Coun. for Baltimore City. Rel: Baptist. Mailing Add: 3025 Wolcott Ave, Baltimore, Md. 21216.

HARRIS, FRANK CARLETON D
Chief Justice, Ark. Supreme Court
b. Pine Bluff, Ark, 12/31/09; s. Frank Alexander Harris and Johnnie Ada Rodgers H; m. 4/20/34 to Marjorie Allison Wilson; c. Eugene Starke. Educ: Union Univ, 29-31; Cumberland Univ, LL.B, 32; Alpha Phi Epsilon; Phi Alpha Delta; Alpha Tau Omega. Hon. LL.D, Ouachita Baptist Univ, 60. Polit. & Govt. Pos: Ark. State Rep, 33-38; prosecuting attorney, 11th Judicial Dist, 47-48; chancery and probate judge, Fourth Chancery Dist, 49-57; chief justice, Ark. Supreme Court, 57- Bus. & Prof. Pos: Nat. chmn, Conf. Chief Justices, 66-67; mem. nat. coun, Boy Scouts. Mil. Serv: Entered as Pvt, Marines, 44, released as Pfc, 45, after serv. in Hq. Co, Recruit Depot, San Diego, 44, and overseas duty, 45; Asiatic-Pac. Theatre Ribbon; Good Conduct Award. Mem: Am. and Ark. Bar Assns; Soc. Crippled Children (former mem. adv. bd); Mason; F&AM (Past Grand Orator); Shrine (Past Potentate); Cen. State Shrine Asn.(past pres); Lions (past pres); Am. Legion; past bd. mem, Ark. Baptist Hosp, Ouachita Baptist Univ, and State Hist. Cmn. Rel: Baptist; Mem. Exec. Cmt, Southern Baptist Conv, 67- Mailing Add: 2005 Laurel St, Pine Bluff, Ark. 71601.

HARRIS, FRANK H. D
b. Cecil Co, Md, 11/30/19; married. Educ: Northeast pub. schs. Polit. & Govt. Pos: Mem, Cecil Co. Dem. Cent. Cmt, Md, 54-58; pres, Young Dem. Club, Cecil Co, 56-58; Md. State Del, 59-67; admin. asst. to Gov, Md, currently. Mem: Brotherhood Locomotive Engrs; Mason; Lions; Cecil Co. Hunter's Asn. Mailing Add: Blythdale Rd, Perryville, Md, 21903.

HARRIS, FRANK W. R
Alaska State Sen.
b. Seattle, Wash, 3/13/20; s. Samuel Rhodes Harris and Judith Marie Eeckhoudt H; m. to Mona M. Ward; c. Judith Marie, Catherine Ann, Gerald Jay, Matthew Joseph and Mary Beth. Educ: High Sch, grad. Polit. & Govt. Pos: Dist. chmn, Alaska Rep. Party, 63-64, state chmn, 65-66; alternate del, Rep. Nat. Conv, 68; Alaska State Sen, currently. Mil. Serv: Entered as Pvt, Army Signal Corps, 42, released as T/Sgt, 46, after serv. in Alaskan Theater. Mem: Elks; Lions; Am. Legion. Rel: Catholic. Mailing Add: 1805 Scenic Way, Anchorage, Alaska 99501.

HARRIS, FRED R. D
U.S. Sen, Okla.
b. Walters, Okla, 11/13/30; m. to LaDonna; c. Kathryn, Byron and Laura. Educ: Univ. Okla, B.A. in govt. and hist, LL.B, 54; Future Farmers Am; Phi Beta Kappa. Polit. & Govt. Pos: Okla. State Sen, 56-64, former chmn, Dem. Caucus, Okla. State Sen; U.S. Sen, Okla, 64-, chmn, Okla. Cong. Del, mem, Govt. Opers. Cmt. and Permanent Subcmt. on Investigations, Subcmts. on Exec. Reorgn. and Nat. Security and Int. Opers, chmn, Govt. Research Subcmt, mem, Finance Cmt, Select Cmt. on Small Bus. and subcmts. on Retail Distribution and Mkt. Practices and Taxation, U.S. House of Rep; del, Dem. Nat. Conv, 68; chmn, Dem. Nat. Cmt, 68- Bus. & Prof. Pos: Founder and sr. partner, law firm, Lawton, Okla, until 64. Outstanding Young Man in Okla, Okla. Jr. C. of C, 59; One of Ten Outstanding Young Men in U.S, U.S. Jr. C. of C, 65. Legal Res: Lawton, Okla. 73501. Mailing Add: U.S. Senate Office Bldg, Washington, D.C. 20510.

HARRIS, GENEVIEVE IRENE R
Chmn, 23rd Dist. Rep. Party, N.Dak.
b. Walnut Grove, Minn, 7/18/36; d. George Anderson and Gladys Purvis A; m. 5/29/65 to Robert A. Harris; c. Pauline Marie, Denise Rene and Daniel James. Educ: Windom High Sch, Minn, grad, 54. Polit. & Govt. Pos: Conv. recording secy, N.Dak. Young Rep, 63-67, v.chairwoman, 64-67, nat. committeewoman, 67-68 & 69-, state chmn, 68-69; mem, 23rd Dist. Women's Fedn, 66-; mem. exec. cmt, N.Dak. Rep. Party, 67-; mem. exec. cmt, Young Rep. Nat. Fedn, 67-, speaker and grad, Leadership Training Sch, 68; chmn, Young Rep. for Doherty Campaign, 68; chmn, N.Dak. Absentee Voter Campaign, 68; mem, N.Dak. Rep. Campaign, Cmt, 68; del, N.Dak. State Rep. Conv, 68; del, Rep. Nat. Conv. and mem. platform cmt, 68; v.chairwoman, N.Dak. Rep. Orgn. Sub-Cmt, 68-69; chmn, 23rd Dist. Rep. Party, N.Dak. 69- Bus. & Prof. Pos: Exec. secy, Neuropsychiatric Inst, Fargo, N.Dak. 59-60, Harold E. Flint & Assocs, 60-65 and Melroe Co, Cooperstown, 66- Publ: North Dakota Young Republican Organizational Manual, privately publ, 67; contrib, Young Republican National Federation Club Extension Handbook, 68. Mem: Nat. Secretaries Asn; Griggs Co. 4-H Coun.(secy. coun. and 4-H leader); Cooperstown Homemaker's Club. Secy. of the Year, Red River Chap, Nat. Secretaries Asn, 63; Outstanding Young Rep. in N.Dak, 67-68; Distinguished Serv. Award, Leadership Training Sch, Nat. Young Rep. Fedn, 68, Bronze, Silver & Gold Harcharger Awards, 69. Rel: Lutheran. Mailing Add: Cooperstown, N.Dak. 58425.

HARRIS, GLENN H. R
N.Y. State Assemblyman
b. Gloversville, 12/31/19; m. to Nora Larkins Avery; c. Linda Michele (Mrs. Martin Tallon), Glynn Kelli; two grandchildren. Educ: Univ. of Miami, Fla; Utica Col. Polit. & Govt. Pos: Councilman, Arietta, N.Y, 11 years; N.Y. State Assemblyman, 64- Bus. & Prof. Pos: Owner, operator, Christmas Tree Lodge (hotel and restaurant). Mil. Serv: Navy Air Corps, 3 years, World War II. Mem: F&AM; Ziyara Temple; Am. Legion; VFW; Caroga Lake Vol. Fire Dept; dir, Adirondack Improv. Coun, Inc; N.Y. State Conserv. Coun, Inc; Fulton Co. Chap, March of Dimes; Fulton Co. Ment. Health Asn.(v.pres). Rel: Lutheran. Mailing Add: Route 10, Arietta, Canada Lake, P.O, N.Y. 12030.

HARRIS, J. EDMOND R
Mass. State Rep.
b. Brooklyn, N.Y, 11/17/16; s. Joseph L. Harris and Hilda A. Woeckener H; m. 2/24/43 to Eleanor Barbara Graziadei; c. Eleanor F.(Mrs. John D. MacDougall, Jr). Educ: Clark Univ, A.B, 48; Univ. Mass. Grad. Sch. Econ, Amherst, 48-49; Kappa Phi; Glee Club; Deutsche Gesangverein. Polit. & Govt. Pos: Water cmnr. and chmn. bd, North Brookfield, Mass, 48-51; mem, Worcester Rep. Club, 50-69; chmn, Second Ward Eisenhower for Pres. Cmt. and mem. steering cmt, Worcester, 52; mem, Tenth Ward Rep. Club, Worcester, 67-69; mem. bd, Worcester Co. Men's Rep. Club and mem, Rep. State Finance Cmt, 68-69; Mass. State Rep, 69- Bus. & Prof. Pos: Sales rep. and area mgr. Worcester Co, J.I. Holcomb Mfg. Co, Indianapolis, Ind, 49-65; registered rep, Investor's Diversified Serv, Worcester, 65-66; dist. mgr, Channing Co, Inc, Worcester, 66- Mil. Serv: Entered as Pvt, Army Inf, 43, released as Sgt, 46, after serv. in 48th Reinf. Bn, ETO, 43-46; Merchant Marine Silver Star; European Campaign Medal with Four Serv. Stars. Mem: Am. Legion; Alhambra Coun, K. of C.(4°); Worcester Hort. Soc, Aquarium Club, Sci. Mus, Art Mus; Y2 Athletic Asn; Co. Fish and Game Asn. and Striper Club. Rel: Catholic. Mailing Add: 128 Russell St, Worcester, Mass. 01609.

HARRIS, J. MERVYN R
b. Johnstown, Pa, 10/28/33; s. Joseph Harris and Mae Williams H; m. 7/13/63 to Margaret Horn; c. J. Lloyd. Educ: Pa. Mil. Col, B.S, 57; pres, student body. Polit. & Govt. Pos: Former chmn, Rep. Finance Cmt; former mem. co. bd, Young Rep; Pa. State Rep, 65-67; Rep. committeeman, Second Ward, Nether Providence Twp, Pa, 58-68; chmn, Nether Providence Rep. Twp. Exec. Cmt, 67-; mem, Del. Co. Campaign Cmt, 67-; del, Rep. Nat. Conv, 68. Bus. & Prof. Pos: Assoc. dir. admissions, PMC Cols, 60- Mil. Serv: Entered as Pvt, Army Res, 54, released as Capt, 65. Mem: 446 Civil Affairs Co; ROA; Mil. Govt. Asn; Nat. Gymanea Ganu Asn; Co. Bd. Dir, Nat. Found; Am. Acad. Polit. & Soc. Sci; adv. bd, Pa. State Univ. Del. Co. Campus; chmn. Southeast. Pa. Commonwealth Rels. Cmt, Pa. Asn. Cols. and Univs; Welsh Soc. Phila. Rel: Episcopal. Mailing Add: 300 Copples Lane, Wallingford, Pa. 19086.

HARRIS, JAMES MONROE R
Committeeman, Bronx Co. Rep. Party, N.Y.
b. New York, N.Y, 8/2/22; s. Robert Eugene Harris and Annie Hall H; div. Educ: N.Y. Univ, 46-48; Col. Ins, N.Y.C, 60. Polit. & Govt. Pos: Committeeman, Bronx Co. Rep. Party, 78th assembly dist, N.Y, 67-; Rep. nominee for U.S. Rep, N.Y, 68. Bus. & Prof. Pos: Compensation claims supvr, State of N.Y. Workmen's Compensation Bd, N.Y.C, N.Y, 46-59, Markhoff, Gottlieb and Harkins, Esq, 59-60, Consolidated Mutual Ins. Co, Brooklyn, 60-64, General Fire and Casualty Ins. Co, N.Y.C, 64-65, Hartford Accident and Indust. Ins. Co, Jamaica, 65-66 and Mich. Mutual Liability Ins. Co, N.Y.C, 66- Mil. Serv: Entered as Pvt, Army, 42, released as Cpl, 45, after serv. in qm, ETO, 44-45; Good Conduct Medal; European-Middle East. Medal; 4 battle stars. Mem: NAACP; 369th Vet. Asn, Inc; Am. Legion (Comdr, Post 1782, N.Y. Co.). Meritorious Serv. Award, Am. Legion. Rel: Methodist. Mailing Add: 865 East 167th St, Bronx, N.Y. 10459.

HARRIS, JAMES ROBIN D
b. DeKalb Co, Ga, 7/5/25; s. Lucien Harris, Jr. and Virginia Nichols H; m. 3/12/48 to Rheta Helble; c. Linda Louise, Annette LaRose. Educ: The Citadel, 42-43; Emory Univ, LL.B, 48, J.D, 49; Delta Tau Delta; Phi Delta Phi. Polit. & Govt. Pos: Mem, Decatur City Cmn, Ga, 59-60; Ga. State Rep, 63- Bus. & Prof. Pos: Attorney-at-law, Decatur, Ga, 49- Mil. Serv: Pfc, Army, 44-45; 137th Inf. Regt, 35th Div, ETO. Mem: Elks (Exalted Ruler, Dacatur, 56-57, Dist. Dep. Grand Exalted Ruler, Northeast Ga, 57-58); pres, Decatur Rotary Club, 61-62. Rel: Presbyterian. 1967 Legal Res: Decatur, Ga. No mailing address available. (1967)

HARRIS, JOHN MATHEW WADE R
Committeeman, Md. State Rep. Cent. Cmt, Harford Co.
b. Covington, Va, 7/21/09; s. Joseph Benjamin Harris and Marianna Crockett Harper H; m. 3/21/31 to Florence Dorothy Johnson; c. John M, Jr, Thomas G, James R, Marianna J.(Mrs. Cooper) and Gloria R.(Mrs. Terlouw). Educ: Urbana Col. Polit. & Govt. Pos: Mem. personnel, Dept. of Army, 42-43 & 48-50; housing mgr, Fed. Pub. Housing Authority, 44-47; committeeman, Md. State Rep. Cent. Cmt, Harford Co, 59-; campaign mgr, Harford Co. Rep. Party, 60, 62, 64 & 68; alternate del, Rep. Nat. Conv, 60, del, 64. Bus. & Prof. Pos: Serv. supvr, Minn. Power & Light Co, Cloquet Div, Minn, 36-42; coast acct. and acct, Consolidated Eng. Co, Bainbridge, 50-51; acct, Zimmerman & Zimmerman, Indian Head, 52-53; mgr, Aberdeen Oil Co, 55-57; off. mgr, Thomas Blackson, Contractor, Md, 57- Mem: Eagles; Moose; life mem, Young Rep. Club, Harford Co; polit. lectr, 60- Rel: Christian Church of N.Am. Mailing Add: 114 Anderson Ave, Havre de Grace, Md. 21078.

HARRIS, LEN R
Nev. State Sen.
b. Sacramento, Calif, 8/4/09; s. Len Harris and Lillian Westkamper H; m. 2/15/46 to C. Dorothy Cremins; c. Sheila C, Leonard H, Jr. and Thomas Edward. Educ: Fremont High Sch, grad, 28; Healds Bus. Col, grad, 30. Polit. & Govt. Pos: Mayor, Reno, Nev, 55-59; dir, Dicentennial Census, State of Nev, 60; Nev. State Assemblyman, 62-68; Nev. State Sen, 68- Bus. & Prof. Pos: Mkt. mgr, Jenny Wren Stores, Oakland, Calif, 30-34; gen. mgr, Standard Meat Co, 34-41; owner, Len Harris Wholesale Meat Co, 46-69. Mil. Serv: Entered as PO 3/C, Naval Res, 42, released as PO 1/C, 45, after serv. as Diver, Pac. Theatre. Mem: Elks; Mason; Lions (past pres); VFW; Am. Legion; life mem, Young Rep; past chmn, Salvation Army Adv. Bd. Man of the Year Award, 67. Rel: Protestant. Mailing Add: 2600 S. Virginia, Reno, Nev. 89502.

HARRIS, LYLE D
Alderman, Church Hill, Tenn.
b. Hawkins County, Tenn, 6/16/25; s. John William Harris and Grace Marshall H; m. 6/8/50 to Hazelle Christian; c. Anthony Scott and Stephen Craig. Educ: Church Hill High Sch, 4 years. Polit. & Govt. Pos: De , Tenn. Dem. State Conv, 60 & 64; alderman, Church Hill, Tenn, 65-; chmn, Hawkins Co. Dem. Party, 66-68; mem, Church Hill Planning Cmn, 67-69; chmn, Hawkins Co. Dem. Party for Humphrey, 68; chmn. del, Hawkins Co. Dem. Conv, 68. Bus. & Prof. Pos: Research Dept, Tenn. Eastman Co, 42-69. Mil. Serv: Entered as Pvt, Army, 43, released as Pfc, 46, after serv. in 115th Field Artil, ETO, 44-46; Am. Theatre Ribbon; European Ribbon with Two Battle Stars; Good Conduct Medal; World War II Victory Medal. Mem: Elks; Eastern Star; Am. Legion; Ruritan Club; Mason; VFW. Rel: Protestant. Mailing Add: Route 6, Church Hill, Tenn. 37642.

HARRIS, MARSHALL S. D
Fla. State Rep.
b. Detroit, Mich, 2/2/32; s. David Harris and Dorothy Karol H; m. 6/29/58 to Harriet I. Lipton; c. Steven Matthew, Jennifer Lisa and Andrew David. Educ: Harvard Col, B.S, 53; Harvard Law Sch, LL.B, 56. Polit. & Govt. Pos: Fla. State Rep, currently. Bus. & Prof. Pos: Attorney and partner, Harris & Robinson, 60 and Harris and Sirkin, 66- Mil. Serv: Entered as Pvt, Army, 56, released as Specialist 3/C, 58, after serv. in Korean Mil. Adv. Group, Korea, 57-58. Mem: Dade Co, Fla. and Am. Bar Asns; v.pres, Jewish Occupational Coun; Gr. Miami Jewish Fedn; Jewish Voc. Serv; Anti-Defamation League of B'nai B'rith; YM-YWHA; United Fund of Dade Co; Jewish War Vet; Am. Jewish Cmt. Rel: Jewish. Legal Res: 4725 Pine Dr, Miami, Fla. 33143. Mailing Add: 12th Floor, Dade Federal Building, 101 E. Flagler St, Miami, Fla. 33131. (1967)

HARRIS, MAX BROOKS R
Committeeman, Macomb Co. Rep. Party, Mich.
b. Detroit, Mich, 8/24/30; s. Max Brooks Harris and Christine Ward H; m. Elizabeth Ann Hushon; c. Katherine A, Steven B, David P, Eileen E, Margaret M. and Madeline P. Educ: Wayne State Univ, B.S, 56, M.S, 65. Polit. & Govt. Pos: Chmn, 12th Dist. Rep. Cmt, Mich, 68, committeeman, 69; Rep. cand, U.S. Rep, 12th Cong. Dist, Mich, 68; committeeman elec, Macomb Co, 69; committeeman, Macomb Co. Rep. Cmt, 69- Bus. & Prof. Pos: Sci. chmn, Van Dyke Pub. Schs, currently. Mil. Serv: Entered as Pvt, Army, 48, released as Cpl, 52, after serv. in Gen. Hq. Far East Command, Signal Training Command, 48-50; Occup. Medal; Good Conduct Medal; Victory Medal. Mem: Nat. Sci. Teachers Asn; Van Dyke Fedn. of Teachers, AFL-CIO. Rel: Methodist. Mailing Add: 8135 Republic, Warren, Mich. 48089.

HARRIS, MERRILL R
b. Montpelier, Vt, 5/10/94; m. to Genevieve B. Damon; c. one daughter. Educ: Montpelier High Sch. Polit. & Govt. Pos: Vt. State Rep, 39-40, 44-45 & 65-68; Vt. State Sen, 49-52. Bus. & Prof. Pos: Dir. and v.pres, Montpelier Savings Bank and Trust Co; dir. and pres. bd. dirs, Vt. Junior Col. Mil. Serv: 101st Ammunition Train, 26th Div, World War I. Mem: VFW; Am. Legion; Masonic York Rite bodies; Shrine. Rel: Episcopal. Mailing Add: 24 Clarendon Ave, Montpelier, Vt. 05602. (1967)

HARRIS, MORRAN DENVER D
b. Benton Co, Mo, 10/17/21; s. Pressa Denver Harris and Elberta May Breshears H; m. 6/4/49 to Artalee Wheeler; c. Sheryl Lee, Lila Gayl (deceased), Denver Wesley, Julie Kay, Marita Ann and Mark Wheeler. Educ: N.Dak. State Col, 43-44; Cent. Mo. State Col, A.B, 46; Wash. Univ, 46-47; Univ. of Mo, LL.B, 49 and M.A, 56. Polit. & Govt. Pos: Mayor, Osceola, Mo, 53-59 & 67-69; prosecuting attorney, St. Clair Co, 51-53 & 55-63; Mo. State Rep, St. Clair Co, 63-68. Mil. Serv: Entered as Pvt, Army, 43, released as T-5, 45, after serv. in 90th Inf. Div, ETO, 44-45; numerous campaign ribbons; 3 Battle Stars. Publ: Political Trends in Missouri 1900-54, master's thesis, 56. Mem: Mo. Bar; Am. Bar Asn; State Hist. Soc. of Mo; Rotary Int; pres, Osceola Rotary Club, 61-62, 66-67. Hobby: Missouriana. Rel: Southern Baptist. Mailing Add: P.O. Box, 330, Osceola, Mo. 64776.

HARRIS, OREN D
b. Belton, Ark, 12/20/03; s. Homer Harris and Bettie Lee H; m. 5/9/34 to Ruth Ross; c. Carolyn Marie (Mrs. George McLeod) and James Edward. Educ: Henderson-Brown Col, A.B, 29; Cumberland Univ, LL.B, 30; Sigma Alpha Epsilon. Polit. & Govt. Pos: Dep. prosecuting attorney, 13th Judicial Dist, Ark, 33-35, prosecuting attorney, 36-40; U.S. Rep, Ark, 40-66, chmn, Cmt. on Interstate and For. Commerce, U.S. House of Rep, 57-66; U.S. Judge, East. and West. Dist, Ark, 66- Bus. & Prof. Pos: Attorney-at-law. Mem: Am. and Ark. Bar Asns; Mason; Shrine; K. of P; Lions Int.(dist. gov, 39-40). Saturday Rev. and Pub. Serv. Awards; Award of Merit; Distinguished Pub. Serv. Citation; Presidential Citation; Nat. Transportation Award; Spec. Citation of Broadcast Pioneers; Albert Lasker Pub. Serv. Award; George Wash. Award. Rel: Baptist. Mailing Add: P.O. Box 1733, El Dorado, Ark. 71730.

HARRIS, ORLAND HAROLD 'IKE' R
Tex. State Sen.
b. Denton, Tex, 6/5/32; s. Orland Harris and Rebecca Yarbrough H; m. 11/12/55 to Ann Landrum; c. Wynn and Gillian. Educ: N.Tex. Univ, B.S, 54; South. Methodist Univ, LL.B, 60, pres, Law Sch. and Student Body; Cycen Fjodr. Polit. & Govt. Pos: Asst. dist. attorney, Dallas Co, Dallas, Tex, 60-62; Tex. State Rep, 62-64; Tex. State Sen, 67- Bus. & Prof. Pos: Attorney and assoc, Burt Barr, Dallas, Tex, 62-66, Harris & Miller, 66-68 and Braecklein & Mitchell, 68- Mil. Serv: Entered as Lt, Air Force, 54, released as Lt, 57, after serv. in Air Training Command, Capt, Inactive Res. Mem: Dallas and Tex. Bar Asns; Admitted to Practice before U.S. Dist. Court and U.S. Court of Appeals; C. of C. Rel: Methodist. Legal Res: 3425 Amherst, Dallas, Tex. 75225. Mailing Add: 2271 First National Bank Bldg, Dallas, Tex. 75202.

HARRIS, PATRICIA ROBERTS D
b. Mattoon, Ill, 5/31/24; m. to William Beasley Harris. Educ: Howard Univ, A.B. summa cum laude, 45; Univ. Chicago; Am. Univ; George Wash. Univ. Sch. of Law, J.D, John Bell Larner Prize as First in Class, 60; Phi Beta Kappa; Order of the Coif; assoc. ed, George Wash. Univ. Law Rev. Hon. LL.D, Lindenwood Col, 67 and Morgan State Col, 67; D.H.L, Miami Univ, 67; D.C.L, Beaver Col, 68. Polit. & Govt. Pos: Mem. staff, Dem. Nat. Cmt, 56; attorney, criminal div, U.S. Dept. of Justice, 60-61; del, Dem. Nat. Conv, 64, seconded nomination of President Johnson; presidential elector, D.C, 64; mem, P.R. Study Cmn, 64-65; U.S. Ambassador, Luxembourg, 65-67; U.S. alternate del, 21st and 22nd Gen. Assemblies, UN, 66 & 67; U.S. alternate del, 20th Plenary Meeting, Econ. Cmn, Europe, 67; mem, Nat. Adv. Cmt. Reform Fed. Criminal Laws; mem, Admin. Conf. U.S; mem, Nat. Cmn. Causes and Prev. Violence. Bus. & Prof. Pos: Prog. dir. for work with indust. women, YWCA, Chicago, 46-49; asst. dir, Am. Coun. on Human Rights, 49-53; exec. dir, Delta Sigma Theta Inc, 53-59; assoc. dean students and lectr. law, Howard Univ, 61-63, asst. prof. law, 63-65, assoc. prof, 65-67, prof, 67-69, dean sch. of law, 69. Mem: Am. and Fed. Bar Asns; Kappa Beta Pi; Am. Asn. Univ. Prof; Delta Sigma Theta; Carnegie Cmn. Future Higher Educ; Cmn. Found. and Private Philanthropy; Atlantic Inst.(bd. gov); UN Asn. U.S.(bd. gov); Nat. Educ. TV (bd. dirs); Wash. Educ. TV (bd. dirs); Urban Coalition (steering cmt. and policy coun); exec. bd, NAACP Legal Defense Fund; bd. dirs, Twentieth Century Fund. Distinguished Alumni Award, Howard Univ, 66; Distinguished Serv. Award, Wash. Alumnae Chap, Delta Sigma Theta; Order of the Oaken Crown, Luxembourg, 67; Distinguished Achievement Award, Women's Cmt. Yeshiva Univ, 68; Woman of the Year, Women's Auxiliary Jewish War Vet, 68; Emma V. Kelley Award, Daughter Elks, 68; Centennial Citation, Wilson Col, 69. Mailing Add: 1742 Holly St. N.W, Washington, D.C. 20012.

HARRIS, RAYMOND ALEXANDER R
Chmn, S.C. Rep. Party
b. Wake Forest, N.C, 2/3/27; m. to Vi Barringer; c. Belva John, Vi Haynsworth, Raymond A, Jr, Laurence Barringer, Mary Barringer and James Gill. Educ: Wake Forest Col, B.A, 50. Polit. & Govt. Pos: Spec. agent, Fed. Bur. Invest, 51-52; spec. invest. work, U.S. Defense Dept, 56-61 & 62-63; mem, Workman for Senate Campaign Cmt, 61; organizer, Darlington Co. Rep. Party, S.C, 63; exec. dir, S.C. Rep. Party, 65-68, chmn, 68- Bus. & Prof. Pos: Supvr, Atlantic Coast Line R.R, 53-54; partner, Barringer-McKeel Hardware Co, Darlington, S.C, 55-; real estate broker, 68-69. Mil. Serv: Naval Air Corps, 44-46, serv. in Far East. Theatre. Mem: Darlington C. of C.(past pres); past mem, Darlington Co. Boy Scout Coun; Kiwanis. Rel: Presbyterian. Legal Res: Oakview Dr, Darlington, S.C. Mailing Add: P.O. Box 5247, Columbia, S.C. 29205.

HARRIS, REID WALKER D
Ga. State Rep.
b. Brunswick, Ga, 7/6/30; s. Augustus Myddelton Harris and Edna Walker H; m. 11/24/55 to Doris Latrelle Nelms; c. Reid Walker, Jr, Michael Myddelton and Douglas Howell. Educ: Univ. N.C, A.B. in Polit. Sci; Presidio of Monterey Army Language Sch, Russian; Emory Univ. Law Sch, LL.B; Phi Mu Alpha; Phi Delta Phi. Polit. & Govt. Pos: Mem, Ga. State Dem. Exec. Cmt, 64-66; Ga. State Rep, 65-, chmn, Cmts. on Trial Practice and Procedure, Strip Mining Legis, Estuarine Areas and Corp. Code Revision, Ga. State House of Rep, 67. Bus. & Prof. Pos: Partner in Law Firm. Mil. Serv: Entered as Pvt, Army Security Agency, 52, released as Cpl, 55, after serv. in Japan. Mem: Am. Bar Asn; Ga. Bar Asn.(cmt. chmn, dist. rep, Younger Lawyers Sect, 59-64); Asn. Ins. Attorneys; dir, Brunswick Glynn Co. C. of C; Kiwanis; Sea Palms Golf & Country Club. Rel: Presbyterian. Legal Res: Frederica Rd, St. Simons Island, Ga. 31522. Mailing Add: P.O. Box 1762, Brunswick, Ga. 31520.

HARRIS, ROBERT OBERNDOERFER D
b. N.Y.C, 11/11/29; s. Samuel Doran Harris and Miriam Sonneborn H; m. 3/30/58 to Ritalou Rogow; c. Peter Oberndoerfer and Gail. Educ: Columbia Col, A.B, 51; Yale Law Sch, LL.B, 54; Georgetown Univ, LL.M, 61. Polit. & Govt. Pos: Mem. staff, Off. of the Gen. Counsel, Dept. of Health, Educ. and Welfare, 57-59 and Off. of the Solicitor, Dept. of Labor, 59-61; spec. asst. to the chmn, Nat. Labor Rels. Bd, 61-67; counsel and staff dir, Cmt. on Labor and Pub. Welfare, U.S. Senate, 67- Mil. Serv: Entered as Cpl, Army, 54, released as SP-5, 56, after serv. in 4447th Army Unit, Germany, 55-56. Publ: Several law rev. articles. Rel: Jewish. Mailing Add: 3665 Upton N.W, Washington, D.C. 20008.

HARRIS, RUTH ROBERTS R
Mem, Washington Co. Rep. Women's Club, Tenn.
b. Roswell, N.Mex, 3/15/21; d. Simon Jones Roberts and Mildred Park R; m. to Capt. C. Meierhoff (deceased); m. 1/4/47 to Allen Harris, Jr; c. Allen, III and Stanley. Educ: Amarillo Jr. Col, 38-39; W.Tex. State Col, 39-40; Alpha

Omicron Pi. Polit. & Govt. Pos: Secy, War Prod. Bd, 41-42; women's chmn, Johnson City Cong. Campaign for James H. Quillen, 62; mem, Wash. Co. Rep. Women's Club, Tenn, 62-; secy, Wash. Co. Rep. Exec. Cmt, 63-65; alternate del, Rep. Nat. Conv, 64. Bus. & Prof. Pos: Writer feature articles, Amarillo Globe News, Amarillo, Tex, 38-39; stewardess, Am. Airlines and hosp secy. and recreation worker, Am. Red Cross, China-Burma-India Theatre, 45-46. Mil. Serv: Am. Red Cross Overseas Meritorious Serv. Award. Mem: Charter mem. Jr. Serv. League, Johnson City; Ment. Health Asn.(pres); State Bd. Ment. Health, Tenn; Ment. Health Clin. Bd, Johnson City; past regent, John Sevier Chap DAR; Girl Scouts (past cmnr); Gov. Cmt. Employ. Handicapped; President's Cmt. Employ. Handicapped; bd. gov, B.Carroll Reece Mus, E.Tenn. State Univ; Johnson City Country Club; Monday Club (past chmn. educ. cmt); Johnson City Garden Club. Rel: Episcopal. Mailing Add: 230 Gilmer Park N, Johnson City, Tenn. 37601.

HARRIS, THOMAS ALAN D
b. Chattanooga, Tenn, 9/27/33; s. Freeman R. Harris and Marjorie Williams H; m. 6/13/64 to Sally D. Hoover; c. Thomas Alan, Jr. and Timothy Freeman. Educ: Vanderbilt Univ, B.A, LL.B; pres, Phi Kappa Sigma; Student Senate; Phi Delta Phi. Polit. & Govt. Pos: Tenn. State Rep, 62-66; Tenn. State Sen, 67-69. Bus. & Prof. Pos: Partner, Milligan, Hooper & Harris, Attorneys, 63- Mil. Serv: Entered as Ens, Navy, 55, released as Lt.(jg), Naval Res, 57. Mem: Am, Tenn. and Chattanooga Bar Asns. Rel: Presbyterian. Legal Res: 911 Crown Point Rd. W, Signal Mountain, Tenn. 37377. Mailing Add: 1118 Hamilton National Bank Bldg, Chattanooga, Tenn. 37402.

HARRIS, THOMAS JESSE R
b. Chicago, Ill, 3/16/15; s. Elijah George Harris and Sarah Stewart Wright H; m. 3/14/42 to Marilynn Lois Tenny; c. Thomas Elijah, Kendra Jane, Elizabeth Anne and Jefferson Wright. Educ: Crane Jr. Col, 32-33; Northwest. Univ. Sch. Commerce, eve, 33-38; Alpha Kappa Psi. Polit. & Govt. Pos: Regional chmn, Rep. State Finance Cmt, Okla, 60-62, v.chmn, Rep. State Budget Cmt, 62-64; cmnr, Okla. Indust. Develop. Cmn, 63; del. and mem, Cmt. on Permanent Arrangements, Rep. Nat. Conv, 64. Bus. & Prof. Pos: European cargo mgr, Am. Overseas Airlines Inc, 47-49; dir. cargo sales, Am. Airlines Inc, 54-57; v.pres, gen. mgr. and dir, Aero Comdr. Inc, 57-64; pres. and dir, Mgt. Enterprises Inc, 63- and United Tech. Industs. Corp, 65- Mil. Serv: Entered as Lt.(jg), Navy, 42, released as Lt. Comdr, 46, after serv. in Okinawa, 42-45; Lt. Comdr, Naval Res, (Ret). Publ: Mag. articles on air freight and corporate aircraft, 54-65. Mem: Am. Inst. Aeronaut. and Astronaut; founding mem, Am. Soc. Traffic and Transportation; indust. coun, Okla. Univ. Research Inst. adv. bd. dirs, Asn. of U.S. Army; Navy League; Air Force Asn; Res. and Develop. Cmt. and chmn, Transportation Adv. Cmt, Nat. Security Indust. Asn; chmn, Asn. of Local Transport Airline Suppliers; bd. dirs, Nat. Right to Work Legal Aid Found; Metrop. and Marco Polo Clubs, N.Y; New York Traffic Club; Army-Navy Club, Wash; Indianapolis Athletic Club, Ind. Rel: Congregational. Mailing Add: 327 N.W. 18th St, Oklahoma City, Okla. 73103.

HARRIS, THOMAS MURRAY R
Committeeman, Ill. Rep. State Cent. Cmt.
b. Lincoln, Ill, 5/14/23; s. Homer Blinn Harris and Renee Murray H; m. 4/15/50 to Britta Borgeson; c. Janet, Jean, John, Julie and Thomas M, Jr. Educ: Northwest. Univ, 41-43; Northwest. Univ. Law Sch, LL.B, 48; Sigma Chi; Phi Delta Phi. Polit. & Govt. Pos: Committeeman, Ill. Rep. State Cent. Cmt, 22nd Cong. Dist, 66-; chmn, Logan Co. Planning Cmn, Lincoln, Ill, 68 & 69; mem, Selective Serv. Syst, 68 & 69. Bus. & Prof. Pos: Licenced attorney-at-law, Ill, 49- Mil. Serv: Entered as Cadet, Naval Air Corps, 43, released as Ens, 45, after serv. as Carrier Based Fighter Pilot. Mem: Am. and Ill. State Bar Asns; Am. Judicature Soc; Am. Legion; Elks. Lincoln Daily Courier Man of the Month. Rel: Methodist. Legal Res: 1 Deer Creek Lane, Lincoln, Ill. 62656. Mailing Add: Griesheim Bldg, Lincoln, Ill. 62656.

HARRIS, VIRGINIA MARY D
Dem. Nat. Committeewoman, C.Z.
b. Newark, N.J, 8/27/22; d. William Charles Happel and Mary A. Busteed H; m. 1/29/43 to Earl Donovan Harris; c. Donovan and Craig L. Educ: Drake Jr. Col, 2 years. Polit. & Govt. Pos: V.pres. Citizens Adv. Bd, Monmouth Co, N.J, 57-61; spec. asst. to exec. dir, Nat. Capital Housing Authority, Wash, D.C, 63-68; coordinator neighborhood and spec. projs, Mrs. Lyndon Johnson's Cmt. for a More Beautiful Nat. Capital, 66-68; Dem. Nat. Committeewoman, C.Z, 68- Rel: Catholic. Mailing Add: P.O. Box 115, Ft. Clayton, C.Z.

HARRIS, WILLIAM BIRCH R
Co. Committeeman, Rep. Party, Tex.
b. Loveland, Colo, 9/26/19; s. William Birch Harris and Julia Ann Longan H; m. 12/26/42 to Mary Kloiber; c. William B. and Mary Ann. Educ: Univ. Colo, B.S.Ch.E, 41; Tex. A&M Univ, M.S.Ch.E, 60; Phi Lambda Upsilon; Tau Beta Pi; Sigma Xi. Polit. & Govt. Pos: Dir, Brazos Co. Rep. Coun, Tex; del, Rep. Nat. Conv, 64; co. committeeman, Rep. Party, Tex. Bus. & Prof. Pos: Research chemist, Allied Chem. Corp, 41-46; tech. dir, Apache Powder Co, 46-53; prof, Tex. A&M Univ, 56- Publ: 'Engineering Design of Aeration Systems,' 2/61, 'Gaseous Ammonia as Refining Agent,' 7/63 and 'Deterioration of Cottonseed During Storage', 66, J. Am. Oil Chemists' Soc. Mem: Am. Inst. Chem. Engrs; Am. Chem. Soc. Amateur radio; photography. Rel: Latter-day Saint. Mailing Add: Route 3, Box 293A, Bryan, Tex. 77843. (1967)

HARRIS, WILLIAM CULLEN R
Ill. State Sen.
b. Pontiac, Ill, 5/7/21; s. Raleigh J. Harris and Bernadine Cullen H; m. 5/31/47 to Jeanne Kathryn Turck; c. Charles Matthew and Barbara Ann. Educ: Mich. State Univ, 2 years. Polit. & Govt. Pos: Ill. State Rep, 55-61; Ill. State Sen, 61-, asst. majority leader, Ill. State Sen, 67-; del, Rep. Nat. Conv, 68. Bus. & Prof. Pos: Dist. agent, State Mutual of Am, 58- Mil. Serv: Entered as A/S, Navy, 42, released as Aviation Chief Ordnanceman, 45, after serv. in the Solomons, Asiatic-Pac; Asiatic-Pac. Campaign Ribbon. Mem: Elks; Moose; Am. Legion; VFW. Rel: Episcopal. Legal Res: 706 S. Walnut St, Pontiac, Ill. 61764. Mailing Add: 201 W. Water St, Pontiac, Ill. 61764.

HARRISON, ALBERTIS SYDNEY, JR. D
b. Brunswick Co, Va. 1/11/07; s. Albertis Sydney Harrison and Lizzie Goodrich H; m. 5/8/30 to Lacey Virginia Barkley; c. Albertis Sydney, III and Antoinette (Mrs. Jamison). Educ: Univ. of Va, LL.B, 28; LL.D, William and Mary Col, 63; Omicron Delta Kappa; Delta Sigma Phi; Phi Delta Phi; Order of the Coif; Va. Law Rev. Polit. & Govt. Pos: Town attorney, Lawrenceville, Va, 29-31; commonwealth's attorney, Brunswick Co, 31-48; Va. State Sen, 48-59; Attorney Gen, Va, 59-62; Gov, Va, 62-66; Justice, Supreme Court of Appeals, Va, 66- Bus. & Prof. Pos: Dir, Farmers and Merchants Bank of Lawrenceville. Mil. Serv: Lt.(jg), Navy. Mem: Am. and Va. State Bar Asns; Va. State Bar; Am. Inst. of Trial Lawyers. Rel: Episcopal. Mailing Add: Farmers and Merchants Bank Bldg, Lawrenceville, Va. 23868.

HARRISON, BURR POWELL D
b. Winchester, Va, 7/2/04; s. Thomas Walter Harrison and Nellie Cover H; m. to Dorothy W. Green. Educ: Woodberry Forest Sch, 18-20; Va. Mil. Inst, 20-21; Hampden-Sydney Col, 21-22; Univ. of Va, 22-23; Georgetown Univ, 23-26; LL.D, Hampden-Sydney Col, 49. Polit. & Govt. Pos: Mem, Va. Cmn. on Constl. Govt, 63-; U.S. Rep, Va, 45-64; Judge, 17th Jud. Circuit, 42-46; Va. State Sen, 40-42; Atty. for Commonwealth Fredrick Co, Va, 32-40. Bus. & Prof. Pos: Mem, firm of Harrison & Johnston, 46-; Rector, Madison Col, Harrisonburg, Va, 64-; Gen. Law Practice, Winchester, Va, 26-42; practiced before the Supreme Court of the U.S, 37; before Supreme Court of Appeals of Va, 28; admitted to Fredrick Co. Bar, 26. Mailing Add: Graichen Bldg, Winchester, Va. 22601. (1967)

HARRISON, CLAYTON S, JR. R
State Chmn, Del. Rep. Party
b. Wilmington, Del; m. to Gertrude Sullivan; c. Patricia and Sherron. Polit. & Govt. Pos: Mem, Del. Rep. Party, 64- and state chmn, 66- Bus. & Prof. Pos: Owner, Clayt-Harrison Parking Syst; secy, Wilmington Bldg. Trades Coun; trustee, Cent. Labor Union, 1st v.pres, Del. State Fedn. of Labor. Mem: Eagles; Elks; Labor Lyceum Asn; Serra Club; Plasterers Union, Local 38. Rel: Catholic. Legal Res: Woodland Dr, North Hills, Wilmington, Del. 19809. Mailing Add: 1510 W. 14th St, Wilmington, Del. 19806. (1967)

HARRISON, DAVID ELDRIDGE D
Mass. State Rep.
b. Gloucester, Mass, 6/19/33; s. Lester W. Harrison and Hazel Eldridge H; single. Educ: Tufts Col, B.A, 55; pres, Tower Cross. Polit. & Govt. Pos: Mass. State Rep, 62-; alternate del, Dem. Nat. Conv, 64, del-at-lg. and co-chmn, del. for Sen. George McGovern for Pres, 68; mem, Mass. State Dem. Cmt, 64-66 & 68-, chmn, 68-, v.chmn, Legis. Cmt. Pub. Welfare, 65; chmn, Legis. Cmt. Harbors and Pub. Lands, 65-66; chmn. Legis. Cmt, Natural Resources, 68; mem, Tufts Alumni Coun, 68-; mem. Dem. Nat. Cmt. Rules, 69- Bus. & Prof. Pos: Owner, D.E. Harrison Ins. and Real Estate Agency, 61- Mil. Serv: Entered as Pvt, Army, 55, released as Specialist 4/C, 57, after serv. in Third Armored Div, Germany, 56-57. Mem: Dir, Am. Red Cross, Cape Ann Savings Bank and Addison Gilbert Hosp; trustee, Gilbert Home for Aged and Indigent Persons; chief referee, New Eng. Lacrosse Off. Asn; East. Intercollegiate Football Off. Asn; Univ. Boat Club, Boston. All-New Eng. Lacrosse Player, 55; One of Ten Outstanding Young Men, Boston Jr. C. of C, 67. Rel: Episcopal. Legal Res: 2 Haskell Court, Gloucester, Mass. 01930. Mailing Add: P.O. Box 16, Gloucester, Mass. 01930.

HARRISON, DWIGHT ALLEN R
b. Hampton, Iowa, 10/31/32; s. Dallas M. Harrison and Ruth Artley H; m. 8/50 to Delores Guldberg; c. Charles Allen, Teresa Christine, John Philip, Thomas Bradley, Pamela Sue and Paul David. Educ: Cornell Col, Iowa. Polit. & Govt. Pos: Former chmn, Franklin Co. Rep. Cmt, Iowa; finance chmn, Franklin Co. Rep. Orgn; mem, Sch. Bd. Bus. & Prof. Pos: Pres, Lil' Red Barn Inc. Mem: Rotary; Farm Bur; Jaycees. Rel: Methodist. Mailing Add: Central Ave. E, Hampton, Iowa 50441. (1967)

HARRISON, GORDON F. D
b. Providence, R.I, 9/20/14; s. Albert V. Harrison and Ella Morralley H; m. 7/18/39 to Phyllis Swanson; c. Naomi (Mrs. John H. Opdycke) and Peter Gordon. Educ: Providence Col, Ph.B, 35; Georgetown Univ, LL.B, 41; George Wash. Univ, LL.M, 52. Polit. & Govt. Pos: Legis. asst, Gov. Theodore Francis Green, R.I, 36, U.S. Sen. Theodore F. Green, R.I, 37-41; trial attorney, U.S. Dept. Justice, 41-42 & 46-54; staff dir, Cmt. on Rules and Admin, U.S. Senate, 55- Mil. Serv: Entered as Lt.(jg), Naval Res, 42, released as Lt. Comdr, 46, after serv. in Naval Aviation, U.S.S. Franklin CV-13, Pac. Theatre; Capt, Naval Res, 60. Mem: Am. Soc. of Int. Law; Am. and Fed. Bar Asns; Alexander Wilbourne Weddell Award related to world peace, George Wash. Univ, 52; Order of Ky. Col. Mailing Add: 6007 Softwood Trail, McLean, Va. 22101.

HARRISON, HAROLD D
b. Bethlehem, Ga, 4/29/20; s. Robt. Luther Harrison and Susie Tanner H; single. Educ: Univ. Ga, B.S.A, 41. Polit. & Govt. Pos: Ga. State Sen, 63-64; chmn, Winder-Barrow Hosp. Authority, 51-; chmn, Barrow Co. Bd. of Educ, 50- Bus. & Prof. Pos: Poultry bus, hatchery, growing and processing. Mil. Serv: Army, Capt, Inf, 4 years; 3 years in ETO. Rel: Methodist. Mailing Add: Box 202, Bethlehem, Ga. 30620.

HARRISON, IRVING D
b. N.Y.C, 4/6/20; s. Henry Z. Harrison and Edna Boas H; m. 6/7/42 to Ruth Wolfert; c. Lisabeth (Mrs. Mitrany) and Daniel Paul. Educ: City Col. N.Y, B.A; Pratt Inst, 2 years. Polit. & Govt. Pos: Fifth Cong. Dist. committeeman, Nassau Co. Dem. Party, N.Y, 10 years; del, Dem. Nat. Conv, 68. Bus. & Prof. Pos: Self-employed architect, L.I, 15 years. Mil. Serv: Entered as Pvt, Army, 43, released as S/Sgt, 46, after serv. in U.S. Mil. Intel, S.E. Asia; Am. Medal. Rel: Hebrew. Mailing Add: 2303 Howes St, Merrick, N.Y. 11566.

HARRISON, IVAN R
Chmn, Clayton Co. Rep. Party, Ga.
b. Fostoria, Ohio, 3/3/23; s. Ivan L. Harrison and Ruby L. Werner H; m. 9/21/47 to Marjorie M. Strawbridge; c. Michael T, Marsha L, Mindy L. and Merri M. Educ: Bowling Green State Univ, 40-42. Polit. & Govt. Pos: Mem, bd. educ, Clayton Co, Ga, 56-60, 62-64; chmn, Clayton Co. Rep. Party, 68- Mil. Serv: Entered as 2nd Lt, Marine Corp, 42, released as 1st Lt, 46, after serv. in Marine Fighter Squadron Unit 115, S.Pac, 44-45; Capt, Res.(Ret);

Air Medal with 6 stars; Distinguished Flying Cross with 1 star. Mem: Riverdale Lions Club (pres, 57-). Rel: Episcopal. Mailing Add: 2850 Emerald Dr, Jonesboro, Ga. 30236.

HARRISON, JAMES A. D
Officer-At-Lg, Mich. Dem. State Cent. Cmt.
b. Topeka, Kans, 5/10/38; s. Russell N. Harrison 'Hap' and Ruth Keck H; m. 2/1/58 to Beverly Hoffmeister; c. Douglas Keith and Bryan Wade. Educ: Kans. State Univ, B.S. in TV-Radio, 60; Mich. State Univ, M.A. in TV-Radio, 65; Alpha Epsilon Rho; Phi Kappa Phi. Polit. & Govt. Pos: Dir. Pub. Rel, Mich. Dem. State Cent. Cmt, 65-67, officer-at-lg, 69-; chmn, East Lansing Dem. Club, 66; chmn, McCarthy for Pres. Cmt. of Mich, 67-68; chmn, Ingham Co. Dem. Cmt, 67-; Dem. nominee, U.S. Rep, Mich, 68; v.chmn, New Dem. Coalition of Mich, 68-69; v.chmn, Mich. Cmt. on Polit. Reform, 69- Bus. & Prof. Pos: Info. Specialist, Mich. State Univ, 60-65; Commun. Consult, 67-69; consult, Shepard Systems, Inc, 69- Rel: United Church of Christ. Legal Res: 923 Huntington, East Lansing, Mich. 48823. Mailing Add: 818 S. Harrison Rd, East Lansing, Mich. 48823.

HARRISON, JAMES EDWARD, III R
Chmn, McDuffie Co. Rep. Party, Ga.
b. Thomson, Ga, 2/25/40; s. James Edward Harrison, Jr. and Sara Bryant H; m. 12/28/66 to Ellen Reynolds Tipton; c. James Edward, IV. Educ: Univ. of Ga, B.B.A, 62; Kappa Alpha; Gridiron Secret Soc. Polit. & Govt. Pos: Mem, Ga. State Rep. Exec. Cmt, 64-66; chmn, McDuffie Co. Rep. Party, 64- Bus. & Prof. Pos: V.Pres, Harrison Farms, Inc, 62- Mem: Rotary; Farm Bur; Belle Beade Country Club; Plantation Club, Hilton Head Island, S.C. Rel: Methodist. Mailing Add: Route 2, Thomson, Ga. 30824.

HARRISON, JAMES LERLIE
Pub. Printer of U.S.
b. Greer, S.C, 6/3/05; s. John D. Harrison and Sallie Pitts H; m. 12/31/60 to Margaret Scott; c. Joan (Mrs. Albert D. Silbaugh). Polit. & Govt. Pos: With the Bur. of Census, 34-42; liaison officer at Capitol, Off. Price Admin, 42-47; staff dir, Joint Cong. Cmt. on Printing, 49-61; Pub. Printer of U.S, 61- Bus. & Prof. Pos: Wholesale, retail food bur, 27-33. Publ: Biographical Dir. of Am. Congress—1774-1949, 50; ed, compiler, Congressional Directory 49-; Govt. Printing and Binding Regulations, 49-; Govt. Paper Specification Standards, 59- Rel: Christian Church of N.Am. Legal Res: 4000 Massachusetts Ave. N.W, Washington, D.C. 20016. Mailing Add: c/o Government Printing Office, Washington, D.C. 20401.

HARRISON, JAMES THOMAS
b. Hankinson, N.Dak, 4/4/03; s. Edward Charles Harrison and Karen Marie Anderson H; m. 8/26/26 to Leah Lambert; c. Barbara Louise (Mrs. R. J. Losleben, Jr), Beverly Ann (Mrs. Stanley J. Hould) and James T, Jr. Educ: St. Paul Col. of Law. Polit. & Govt. Pos: Court reporter, 17th Judicial Dist, Mont, 29-38; city attorney, Malta, intermittently, 39-56; co. attorney, Phillips Co, 49-52; chmn, State Bd. of Pardons, 55-56; chief justice, Mont. Supreme Court, 57- Bus. & Prof. Pos: Attorney-at-Law, 26-29 & 38-56. Mem: Past Grand Master Mont, Masons, 58-59, AF&AM, Past Potentate, Algeria Shrine, 60; Elks; Moose; Eagles; Gov, Mont. Dist, Kiwanis Int, 50. Silver Beaver and Silver Antelope Awards, Boy Scouts; occasional mem. Awards Jury, Freedoms Found, Valley Forge. Rel: Methodist. Mailing Add: 1616 Highland, Helena, Mont. 59601.

HARRISON, JAMES THOMAS, JR. R
Mont. State Rep.
b. Glasgow, Mont, 7/1/39; s. James Thomas Harrison and Leah Lambert H; m. 12/10/66 to Carol Ellen Hansen; c. Jana Terese and Jodi Tamara. Educ: Univ. of Mont, B.S, bus, 61 and LL.B, 64; Phi Delta Phi; Sigma Phi Epsilon; Mont. Student Bar Asn. Polit. & Govt. Pos: Spec. asst. attorney gen, State of Mont, 64-66; Mont. State Rep, 21st Dist, 67- Bus. & Prof. Pos: Partner, Harrison, Leondorf and Poston, currently. Mil. Serv: 1st Lt, Mont. Nat. Guard. Mem: Am. and Mont. Bar Asns; Mont. Trial Lawyers Asn; Jaycees; Elks; Univ. of Mont. Alumni Asn; Mason; Algeria Shrine; Capital City Quarterbacks Club. Rel: Methodist. Legal Res: 1100 Chotean, Helena, Mont. 59601. Mailing Add: 820 N. Montana Ave, Helena, Mont. 59601.

HARRISON, JOHN CONWAY D
b. Grand Rapids, Minn, 4/28/13; s. Francis Randall Harrison and Ethelyn Conway H; m. 8/28/41 to Virginia Flanagan; c. Nina Lyn, Robert Charles, Molly McKinley, John Conway, Frank Randall and Virginia Lee. Educ: Mont. State Col, 31-34; Univ. Mont. Law Sch, 35-37; George Wash. Univ, LL.B, 40; Sigma Chi. Polit. & Govt. Pos: Asst. co. attorney, Lewis and Clark Co, 47-50, co. attorney, 54-60; city attorney, East Helena, 51-60, assoc. justice, Mont. Supreme Court, 61- Mil. Serv: Entered as 1st Lt, Army, 40, released as Lt. Col, 45, after serv. in Seventh Corps Hq, ETO; 5 Battle Stars; Bronze Star; Croix de Guerre with Star. Mem: Am. Bar Asn; Mont. Bar Asn.(secy-treas, 47-49); Mont. Tuberc. Asn.(pres, 51-53); Am. Legion (comdr, 53); VFW; Kiwanis; Ment. Health Asn; Elks. Rel: Protestant Episcopal. Mailing Add: 516 N. Park, Helena, Mont. 59601.

HARRISON, JOHN RAY D
b. Abilene, Tex, 8/2/30; s. John Weldon Harrison and Carrie Palmour H; m. 12/24/48 to Barbara Grace Hale; c. John, Jr, Donna, Michael, Kipper, Nikki, Robert and Nancy. Educ: McMurry Col, Abilene, Tex, B.S; South Tex. Col. of Law, LL.B; Delta Theta Phi. Polit. & Govt. Pos: Tex. State Rep. until 67. Mem: Optimist; Elks; State, Local and Nat. Bar Asns. Rel: Methodist. Mailing Add: 240 Crescent, Pasadena, Tex. 77502. (1967)

HARRISON, JOSEPH WILLIAM R
Ind. State Sen.
b. Chicago, Ill, 9/10/31; s. Roy Joseph Harrison and Gladys Greenman H; m. 6/9/56 to Ann Hovey Gillespie; c. Holly Ann, Tracy Jeanne, Thomas Joseph, Amy Beth, Kitty Lynne and Christy Jayne. Educ: Purdue Univ, 49-52; U.S. Naval Acad, B.S, 56; Ind. Univ. Law Sch, 67-69; Sigma Chi. Polit. & Govt. Pos: Pres, Attica Consolidated Sch. Bd, Attica, Ind, 64-67; Ind. State Sen, 66-, chmn. Senate Finance Cmt, Ind. State Senate, 69- Bus. & Prof. Pos: Asst. to pres, Harrison Steel Castings Co, Attica, Ind, 60-64, sales research engr, 64-66 and asst. secy, 66- Mil. Serv: Entered as Midn, Navy, 52, released as Lt.(jg), 60, after serv. in Naval Intel, Wash, D.C, 56-60; Naval Res, Lt.(jg), 69. Mem: Am. Legion, C. of C; Wabash Valley Asn; Rotary Int. Rel: Methodist. Legal Res: 504 E. Pike St, Attica, Ind. 47918. Mailing Add: P.O. Box 60, Attica, Ind. 47918.

HARRISON, JOSEPH WYLIE R
Spec. Asst. to the Asst. Postmaster Gen.
b. Pasadena, Calif, 11/9/37; s. Joseph Wylie Harrison (deceased) and Myra Sumption H; single. Educ: Univ. Notre Dame, A.B, 59; Univ. Tenn, Knoxville, M.A, 61; Pi Sigma Alpha; Student Govt. Polit. & Govt. Pos: Research assoc, Rep. Nat. Cmt, Wash, D.C, 63-64, research specialist, campaign, 66; legis. asst. to U.S. Rep. Ed Reinecke, Calif, 65-66; admin. asst. to U.S. Rep. Garry Brown, Mich, 67-68; field rep, Nixon Presidential Campaign, Wash, D.C, 68; Spec. Asst. to the Asst. Postmaster Gen, 68- Bus. & Prof. Pos: Instr. polit. sci, Univ. Tenn, Knoxville, 60-61; research dir, Nat. Employ. Asn, Wash, D.C, 62-63. Mil. Serv: Army Res, 61-67. Publ: 'The Bible, The Constitution and Public Education,' Tenn. Law Rev, spring 62. Mem: Am. and South. Polit. Sci. Asns; life mem, Calif. Scholarship Fedn. Rel: Roman Catholic. Mailing Add: 2827 N. Quebec St, Arlington, Va. 22207.

HARRISON, LILLIAN LUELLA R
b. Topeka, Kans, 4/15/09; d. Thomas Major Reynolds and Luella Jordan R; m. to Charley Spencer Harrison, wid; c. Frederica L. (Mrs. Tipton), Edna V. (Mrs. Rogers) and Edgar Theodore. Educ: Washburn Col; Alpha Kappa Alpha. Polit. & Govt. Pos: V.chmn, Wyandotte Co. Rep. Cent. Cmt, 62-66; committeewoman, 56-66; alternate del-at-large, Rep. Nat. Conv, 64. Bus. & Prof. Pos: Staff nurse, surg. tech. and licensed practical nurse, Bethany Hosp, Kansas City, Kans, 62-; PBX Operator, Topeka, Kans, 35-48. Mem: Past Ancient Matron, Heroines of Jericho; treas, Mayme J. Ewing Chap, Eastern Star; Order of Cyrenes; Order of Golden Circle. Winner of 7 track medals, Shawnee Co. Meets. Rel: Methodist; mem. church choir, Trinity A.M.E. Church. Mailing Add: 2720 N. Seventh, Kansas City, Kans. 66101. (1967)

HARRISON, MARK I. D
V.chmn, Dem. Party, Ariz.
b. Pittsburgh, Pa, 10/17/34; s. Coleman Harrison and Myrtle Seidenman H; m. 6/15/58 to Ellen R. Gier; c. Lisa and Jill. Educ: Antioch Col, A.B, 57; Harvard Law Sch, LL.B, 60. Polit. & Govt. Pos: V.chmn, Maricopa Co. Dem. Cent. Cmt, Ariz, 67-68; del, Dem. Nat. Conv, 68; v.chmn, Dem. Party, Ariz, 68- Bus. & Prof. Pos: Law clerk, Justices Lorna E. Lockwood and Charles C. Bernstein, Ariz. Supreme Court, 60-61; assoc, Kramer, Roche, Burch, Streich & Cracchiolo, 61-64; assoc, Langerman, Begam & Lewis, 64-66; partner, Harrison, Strick, Myers and Singer, Attorneys, 66- Publ: 'Arizona Appellate Briefs,' 62 and 'Arizona Appellate Practice,'' 66, Ariz. Weekly Gazette. Mem: Maricopa Co. Bar Asn.(bd. dirs, 66-; treas, 67, secy, 68, v.pres, 69-); State Bar Ariz; Am. Bar Asn; Am. Trial Lawyers Asn.(bd. dirs, Phoenix chapter, 65-); Am. Judicature Soc; bd. dirs, Careers for Youth, 63-67, pres, 66-67; Phoenix Exec. Club; coop. attorney, Ariz. Civil Liberties Union. Rel: Jewish. Legal Res: 326 E. Kaler Dr, Phoenix, Ariz. 85020. Mailing Add: 1200 Arizona Title Bldg, 111 W. Monroe, Phoenix, Ariz. 85003.

HARRISON, REUEL EMMETT D
Chmn, Dist. 29 N.Dak. Dem. Non-Partisan League Cmt.
b. Minneapolis, Minn, 8/4/14; s. William Henry Harrison and Annie M. Horner H; single. Educ: Valley City State Teachers Col, one term. Polit. & Govt. Pos: Mem. co. exec. cmt, N.Dak. Dem. Non-Partisan League, 51- and precinct committeeman, 60-; farm census enumerator, 55; twp. assessor, Edmunds, 55-; N.Dak. State Rep, 65-67; chmn, Dist. 29 N.Dak. Dem. Non-Partisan League Cmt, currently. Bus. & Prof. Pos: Farmer; secy-treas, Dakota Cent. Tel, 60- Mil. Serv: Entered as Pvt, Air Force, 42, released as S/Sgt, 45, after serv. in Am. Theater, Newfoundland, 42-44; Am. Theater Ribbon; Good Conduct Medal. Mem: Am. Legion; VFW; Air Force Asn; Toastmasters; past dist. dep, N.Dak. Odd Fellows; pres, Stutsman Co. Farmers Union and supvry. cmt, Jamestown Farmers Union Credit Union; pres, N.Dak. Credit Union League, 63-65; pres, Foster Co. Coop. Credit Union, secy-treas, Edmunds Mem. Asn. Rel: Protestant. Mailing Add: Edmunds, N.Dak. 58434. (1967)

HARRISON, ROBERT DINSMORE R
Chmn, Madison Co. Rep. Party, Nebr.
b. Panama, Nebr, 1/26/97; s. Herbert Harrison and Jennie Dinsmore H; m. 9/8/21 to Mary Arra Sutton; c. Nancibelle (Mrs. Lingenfelter). Educ: Peru State Teachers Col, A.B, 26; Univ. Calif, summer 28; Univ. Nebr, M.A, 34. Polit. & Govt. Pos: Chmn, Madison Co. Rep. Party, Nebr, 47-50 & 68-; U.S. Rep, Nebr, 51-59; Civilian Conserv. Corps consult, U.S. Dept. Agr, 59-60; state dir. Fed. Crop Ins, Lincoln, 60-62; del, Rep. Nat. Conv, 68. Bus. & Prof. Pos: Supt. pub. schs, Bradshaw, 3 years; supt. pub. schs, Dewitt, 26-35; marketer, Sinclair Refining Co, Norfolk, 35-60. Mil. Serv: Entered as Pvt, Army, 18, released as Sgt, 19, after serv. in 22nd Engrs, St. Mihiel and Muese Argonne, 18. Mem: Elks; Mason; Kiwanis; Sch. Bd; Am. Legion; Vet. World War I; C. of C. Aksarben Good Neighbor Award; Man of the Year Award; Jr. C. of C; Man of the Year; Norfolk C. of C, 66; Man of the Year, Class of 1926, Peru State Teachers Col. Rel: Methodist. Mailing Add: 408 N. 11th St, Norfolk, Nebr. 68701.

HARRISON, ROBERT WARD, JR. D
Ga. State Rep.
b. Fernandina, Fla, 6/26/22; s. Robert Ward Harrison, Sr. and Eva Bunkley H; m. 10/28/48 to Joanne Gawthrop; c. Suzanne. Educ: Charlton Co. High Sch, Folkston, Ga; Ga. Mil. Col; Glenville State Col; Cumberland Univ. and Law Sch. Polit. & Govt. Pos: City attorney, St. Marys, Ga, 51-, Kingsland, 52- and Woodbine, 55-; co. attorney, Camden Co, 53-; Ga. State Rep, 66th Dist, Brantley-Camden-Charlton Counties, 65- Bus. & Prof. Pos: Pres, C. of C, St. Marys, 52-55; chmn, St. Marys Airport Authority, 63- Mil. Serv: Entered as Pvt, Army, 41, released as M/Sgt, 45, after serv. in ETO; ETO Ribbon; Combat Infantryman's Badge. Mem: Am. and Ga. Bar Asns; St. Marys Masonic Lodge 109, F&AM; Delta Theta Phi; Grafton Green Senate; Am. Judicature Soc; Am. Trial Lawyers Asn; Nat. Pilots Asn. Rel: Methodist. Legal Res: 804 Alexander St, St. Marys, Ga. 31558. Mailing Add: P.O. Box 207, St. Marys, Ga. 31558.

HARRISON, WILLIAM HENRY R
b. Terre Haute, Ind, 8/10/96; s. Russell Benjamin Harrison and Mary Saunders H; m. 10/19/20 to Mary Elizabeth Newton; c. Maribeth Brewer and William Henry, Jr. Educ: Univ. Nebr; Sigma Chi; Sigma Delta Kappa. Hon. LL.D, Vincennes Univ. Polit. & Govt. Pos: Wyo. State Rep, 45-51; U.S. Rep. at Large, Wyo, 51-54, 61-64 & 67-69; regional adminstr, Atlanta, 55-56; liaison officer, Housing & Home Finance Agency, Wash, D.C, 57-58, mem, Renegotiation Bd, currently. Bus. & Prof. Pos: Attorney, 25- Mil. Serv: Pvt, Signal Enlisted Res. Corps, Army, World War I, serv. in U.S. Mem: Mason (33°); Scottish Rite; Shrine; Elks; Moose; Am. Legion; hon. mem. VFW; Rotary; Am. Farm Bur; Wyo. Stockgrowers Asn. Rel: Presbyterian. Mailing Add: Box 725, Sheridan, Wyo. 82801.

HARROD, M. MERLE R
Mem, Ohio Rep. Finance Cmt.
b. Wapakoneta, Ohio, 12/30/06; s. Walter L. Harrod and Carrie L. Wagstaff H; m. to Doris Marie Fischer; c. Mahlon M, Jr. and Barbara (Mrs. Olds). Educ: Ohio State Univ, B.S. in Econ; pres, sr. class and Sigma Chi; Alpha Kappa Psi; charter mem, Frontliners, Athletic Dept. Polit. & Govt. Pos: Del, Rep. Nat. Conv, 56, 60, 64 & 68; mem. finance, cent. and exec. cmts, Auglaize Co. Rep. Cmt, Ohio; mem, Ohio Rep. Finance Cmt, currently. Bus. & Prof. Pos: Pres. and dir, Wapakoneta Machine Co, Ohio; chmn. bd, chief exec. officer and dir, Calif. Saw Knife and Grinding, Inc, San Francisco; trustee, Ohio Info. Cmt; dir, First Nat. Bank, Wapakoneta. Mem: Machine Knife Trade Asn. (pres, 52-53); Metal Cutting Knife Trade Asn.(pres, 60-61); Nat. Asn. Mfrs. (indust. probs. cmt); trustee, Ohio Mfrs. Asn; Ohio C. of C.(dir); Wapakoneta C. of C; Nat. C. of C; Scioto Country Club; Shawnee Country Club (bd. gov. and pres, 65); Wapakoneta Country Club (bd. gov); Wequetonsing Country Club; Capitol Hill Club; TWA Ambassadors Club; 500,000 Mile Club, United Airlines; Admirals Club, Am. Airlines; life mem, Ohio State Univ. Asn; charter mem. Pres. Club, Ohio State Univ; Ohio State Univ. Alumni Asn. (v.pres, 54, bd. dirs, 6 years); Rotary Int; Newcomer Soc; Mason; Scottish Rite; Shrine; Elks. Rel: United Church of Christ. Mailing Add: Glynwood Rd, Wapakoneta, Ohio 45895.

HARROUN, HAROLD FRANKLIN R
Chmn, Richardson Co. Rep. Party, Nebr.
b. Nebraska City, Nebr, 12/26/33; s. C. Howard Harroun and Ruth Russell H; m. 1/5/60 to Barbara Jo Wiltse; c. John H, David F, Sharol R. and Marcia J. Educ: Univ. Nebr, 51-52; Univ. Md. Overseas Prog, 1 semester. Polit. & Govt. Pos: Councilman, Falls City, Nebr, 63-64, mem, park bd, 64-67, mem. sch. bd, Dist. 56, 68-; chmn, Richardson Co. Rep. Party, 68- Bus. & Prof. Pos: Mgr, Norman's IGA, Nebraska City, Nebr, 60; asst. mgr, Falls City Fed. Savings & Loan, 60-67, mgr. and treas, 67- Mil. Serv: Entered as Pvt, Army, 56, released as Sgt, 60, after serv. in Inf, Germany, 56-58. Mem: Nebr. and U.S. Leagues of Savings & Loan Asns; U.S. Savings and Loan Inst; Elks; C. of C; VFW; Am. Legion. Named Jaycee of the Year, 64. Rel: Methodist. Mailing Add: 2614 Abbott St, Falls City, Nebr. 68355.

HARROWER, LEONTINE LYLE 'TINA' R
Rep. Nat. Committeewoman, Conn.
b. N.Y.C, 2/12/26; m. 1945 to Norman Harrower, Jr; c. Mimi, Norman, III and Mary Stuart. Educ: Private schs. Polit. & Govt. Pos: Conn. chmn, Rep. Women's Conf, Wash, 63; mem. exec. cmt, Rep. Nat. Coun. of Women's Rep. Club, 63; alternate del, Rep. Nat. Conv, 64, del. and mem. platform cmt, 68; mem, Young Rep. Nat. Fedn. Exec. Bd, 65-69; Rep. Nat. Committeewoman, Conn, currently. Mem: Former mem, United Fund, League of Women Voters and New Haven Symphony. Mailing Add: 144 Edgehill Rd, New Haven, Conn. 06511.

HARSH, LESTER R
Nebr. State Sen.
b. Indianola, Nebr, 3/13/10; s. Jacob A. Harsh and Anna Brahmer H; m. 4/27/32 to Elizabeth Mills; c. Delwyn, Stephen and Philip. Educ: Univ. Nebr, 3 years. Polit. & Govt. Pos: Mem, Agr. Adjustment Agency Prog, 34-40 and Farmers Home Admin. Adv. Cmt, 62-64; Nebr. State Sen, 64- Publ: 'Farm Prattle,' McCook Daily Gazette, 57-64. Mem: Rotary; pres, Indianola Club, 62; Farm Bur; Wheat Growers Asn; Mason. Rel: Methodist. Mailing Add: McCook, Nebr. 69001.

HARSHA, WILLIAM H. R
U.S. Rep, Ohio
b. Portsmouth, Ohio, 1/1/21; m. to Rosemary Spellerberg; c. Bill, Mark, Bruce and Brian. Educ: Kenyon Col, A.B; West. Reserve Univ, LL.B. Polit. & Govt. Pos: Asst. city solicitor, Portsmouth, Ohio, 47-51; Scioto Co. prosecutor, 51-55; U.S. Rep, Ohio, 60- Bus. & Prof. Pos: Attorney-at-law. Mil. Serv: Marine Corps, World War II. Mem: U.S. Supreme Court Bar; Ohio State and Portsmouth Bar Asns; Exchange Club; Elks, Past Exalted Ruler; Masons; YMCA; Bus. and Prfnl Men's Club; Am. Legion; DAV; 40 et 8; past dir, Scioto Co. Red Cross and Scioto Co. Cancer Soc; past chmn, Scioto Co. Tuberc. and Health Asn; life mem, Amateur Trapshooting Asn. Rel: Presbyterian. Legal Res: Portsmouth, Ohio 45662. Mailing Add: 1102 Delf Dr, McLean, Va. 22101.

HARSHBARGER, HELEN MARGARET R
Treas, Knox Co. Rep. Cent. Cmt, Ill.
b. Galesburg, Ill, 5/5/01; d. William R. Hendryx and Margaret Anna Bonney H; m. 6/21/19 to Guy Allan Harshbarger; c. Jean Margaret (Mrs. Seckler Alves) and Louise Helen (Mrs. Frederick Walker Cline). Educ: Galesburg High Sch, grad, 18; Carl Sandburg Jr. Col. Adult Educ, 68-69. Polit. & Govt. Pos; Precinct committeewoman, Knox Co. Rep. Cent. Cmt, Ill, 54-69, secy, 64-69, treas, 69-; precinct committeewoman, Peoples Party, Galesburg, 55-, secy, 59, temporary secy. for caucus and reorgn, 69. Bus. & Prof. Pos: Substitute teacher, Grade Sch, Knox Co, Ill, 20; dep. tax appraiser, Galesburg, Ill, 68-69. Mem: PTA (pres, Weston Chap, 33-35); Red Cross (chmn, motor serv, Galesburg Chap, 49-50, nurses aide at blood cent, first aide instr. and mem. of exec. bd); Oliver Wendell Holmes Club (pres, 52-54); pink lady, vol. serv, Galesburg State Res. Hosp, 57-58; Citizens Adv. Cmt. on Disposition of the Old High Sch. and to Study Measures to Take to Alleviate Crowded Conditions in the Dist. Elem. Schs, 58-59; bd. mem, Carl Sandburg Birthplace Asn, 68-69, chmn. penny parade, 69; Eastern Star; Ladies Auxiliary to the Brotherhood of Rwy. Trainmen; Burlington Vet. Asn; Galesburg Musician's Club; Local Organ Club. Resolution passed by Ill. House of Rep. Honoring our 50th Wedding Anniversary, June 21, 1969. Rel: Methodist. Mailing Add: 358 S. Pearl St, Galesburg, Ill. 61401.

HART, ADELAIDE JULIA D
b. Saginaw, Mich, 4/24/00; d. Malachi Patrick Hart and Margaret Hogan H; single. Educ: West. Mich. Col, Teachers Cert, 23; Marygrove Col, Ph.B, 30, M.A, 37. Polit. & Govt. Pos: Mem. bd. of supvrs, Wayne Co, Mich, 48-50, and rent adv. bd, 48-51; mem. exec. bd, 17th Cong. Dist. Dem. Party and precinct del, 48-; v.chmn, Mich. Dem. State Cent. Cmt, 51-61 & 63-67; del, Dem. Nat. Conv, 52-64, alternate del, 68, mem. platform cmt, 52 & 64; mem, State Ment. Health Cmn, 60-63; del. and Dem. caucus chmn, Constitutional Conv, Mich, 61-62; chmn, Mich. Fedn. Dem. Women, 63-67; co-chmn, Wayne Co. Fedn. Dem. Women, 69-; chmn, registrn. of voters, Wayne Co. Dem. Cmt, currently. Bus. & Prof. Pos: Music teacher and head of fine arts dept, Detroit Bd. of Educ, Mich, 23-63. Mem: Exec. bd, v.pres. and exec. secy, Detroit Fedn. of Teachers; exec. bd. and past pres, Marygrove Col. Alumnae Asn; Synod Implementation Cmt, Archdiocese of Detroit Co. Rel: Catholic. Mailing Add: 17323 Ward Ave, Detroit, Mich. 48235.

HART, EMMETT C. D
N.Mex. State Sen.
b. Springer, N.Mex, 8/2/28; s. Curtis B. Hart and Maude Stephens H; c. Kathryn Ann, Steven Curtis, Marshall John and Mark Randal. Educ: Univ. N.Mex, LL.B, 54. Polit. & Govt. Pos: N.Mex. State Sen, 61-65 & 67- Mil. Serv: Entered as Pvt, Army, 46, released as Cpl, 47, after serv. in Med. Corps. Mem: Lions; Elks. Rel: Presbyterian. Mailing Add: 1623 S. Fourth, Tucumcari, N.Mex. 88401.

HART, FLOYD HENRY R
b. Medford, Ore, 12/30/31; s. Floyd H. Hart, Sr. and Leah C. Walther H; m. 6/7/52 to Jo Ann Barbara Larsen; c. Pamela, Andrea and Margretha. Educ: Univ. Colo, 49-50; Ore. State Univ, 54; South. Ore. Col, 55-56; Sigma Nu. Polit. & Govt. Pos: Pres. and cmnr, City Planning Cmn, Medford, Ore, 62-66; Ore. State Rep, 19th Dist, 67-69; alternate del, Rep. Nat. Conv, 68. Bus. & Prof. Pos: Partner, Security Ins. Agency, 59-; dir, Crater Nat. Bank and Rogue Valley Mem. Hosp, 64- Mil. Serv: Entered as Pvt, Air Force, 51, released as S/Sgt, 54, after serv. in 307th Air Refueling Squadron, Hydrogen Bomb Tests, Marshall Islands, Mid.Pac, 52; Airman of the Year Award, 53; Good Conduct Medal. Mem: Ore. Asn. of Ins. Agents; dir, Medford C. of C, 60-62; Rogue River Valley Univ. Club; Rogue Valley Country Club; Air Force Asn. Rel: Episcopal. Mailing Add: 116 Black Oak Dr, Medford, Ore. 97501.

HART, FRED J. R
Ill. State Sen.
b. Steator, Ill, 3/8/06; s. John Hart, Sr. and Jennie Champley H; m. 10/5/32 to Katheryne Crowl; c. Craig C, Bruce F. and Nan J. Educ: Rice Inst. Polit. & Govt. Pos: City clerk, Streator, Ill, 31-38; co. treas, 38-42; Ill. State Rep, 42-50; Ill. State Sen, currently. Rel: Episcopal. Legal Res: 501 W. Bluff St, Streator, Ill. 61364. Mailing Add: 114 N. Monroe St, Streator, Ill. 61364.

HART, HARRIE E. R
Colo. State Rep.
Educ: Brown Univ, B.A. Polit. & Govt. Pos: Campaign mgr, Gov. Love, Colo, 62; exec. secy. to Gov. Love, 63-65; Colo. State Rep, 65- Bus. & Prof. Pos: Formerly, corp. exec. N.Y; formerly with Harris-Upham Brokers and Danield Motors Co, Colorado Springs, Colo. Mil. Serv: Navy, World War II. Mem: Chmn, Ind. Develop. Cmt; C. of C. Mailing Add: 1260 Mesa Ave, Colorado Springs, Colo. 80906. (1967)

HART, HUGH GLEN, JR. D
b. Borger, Tex, 12/10/40; s. Hugh Glen Hart, Sr. and Dorothy Myers H; singel. Educ: South. Methodist Univ, B.A, 63, Law Sch, J.D, 65; Blue Key; Delta Sigma Phi; Phi Alpha Delta. Polit. & Govt. Pos: Admin. asst. to U.S. Rep. Earle Cabell, Tex, 67- Mil. Serv: 1st Lt, Army Res, 65- Mem: Tex. State and Dallas Bar Asns; South. Methodist Univ. Alumni Asn.(bd. of dirs); Jr. C. of C. Rel: Methodist. Legal Res: 4300 Grassmere, Dallas, Tex. 75205. Mailing Add: 418 House of Representatives Bldg, Washington, D.C. 20515.

HART, JEROME THOMAS D
Mich. State Sen.
b. Saginaw, Mich, 7/23/32; s. Bernard V. Hart and Florence D. Stevens H; single. Polit. & Govt. Pos: Treas, Saginaw Co. Dem. Cmt, 54-58; exec. asst. to Treas, Mich, 62-64; chmn, Eighth Cong. Dist. Dem. Party, 62-64; Mich. State Sen, 34th Dist, 65-; del, Dem. Nat. Conv, 68. Bus. & Prof. Pos: Secy-treas, Quality Seal Oil Co, Saginaw, Mich, 54-58 and Saginaw Catholic Cemetery Cmt, 59-62; owner-mgr, Tiny Town Clothing, 58-61. Mem: K. of C. Rel: Roman Catholic. Legal Res: 2244 Woodbridge, Saginaw, Mich. 48602. Mailing Add: Box 240, Capitol Bldg, Lansing, Mich. 48902. (1967)

HART, JOHN C. R
Ind. State Rep.
b. Indianapolis, Ind, 4/26/21; s. Edgar Hart (deceased) and Elma Logsdon H; m. 8/5/50 to Mary Haselmire; c. Barbara (Mrs. Wolkhoff), Susan, John C, Jr, Victoria, James, Molly, Amy, Peggy and Joseph. Educ: Butler Univ, 40-42. Polit. & Govt. Pos: Ind. State Rep, 69- Bus. & Prof. Pos: Chmn. legis. cmt, Local-State Builders, 63-69; pres, Marion Co. Residence Builders, 66; pres, Ind. State Home Builders, 70. Mem: IAC; bd. dirs, CYO; Hoosier Motor Club (bd. dirs); Jr. Baseball Inc. Builder of Year, 68; CYO, John Bosco Award, Presby-Dawson Award. Rel: Presbyterian. Legal Res: 5141 N. Meridian, Indianapolis, Ind. 46208. Mailing Add: 3643 Mission Dr, Indianapolis, Ind. 46224.

HART, MARK FIELDING D
Idaho State Rep.
b. Preston, Idaho, 3/30/04; s. Arthur William Hart and Ada Doney Lowe H; m. 8/26/33 to Clara Walburger; c. Jo Ann (Mrs. Perry T. Roberts), Mark Dean, David Fielding, Carolyn (Mrs. Wallace F. Bennett), Beverly (Mrs. James Robinson), Bonnie (Mrs. John H. Murray), Shelley, Ruth and Reed Kenneth. Educ: Utah State Univ, B.S, 35; Univ. Wash, M.Ed, 42; Phi Delta Kappa. Polit.

& Govt. Pos: Supt. pub. instr, Franklin Co, Idaho, 2 terms; Idaho State Rep, Franklin Co, 37th Session and Dist. 32, Bear Lake, Caribou and Franklin Co, currently. Bus. & Prof. Pos: High sch. teacher, Utah, Idaho and Wash, 21 years; band dir, famous marching bands; owner, Markhart Educ. Serv, currently. Mil. Serv: Citizens Mil. Training. Publ: 3-Star Spelling and Vocabulary Enrichment Testers and Builders, Grades Four Through Nine; 4-Star Collegiate Word Power, Grades 9-12; 6-Star College Entrace Books; Apple Blossom Daze; plus others. Won honors as band dir, in Portland Rose Festival, Pasadena Tournament of Roses Parade, Wenatchee Apple Blossom Festival, Puyallup Daffodil Festival, Seattle Potlatch of Progress Parades and others. Rel: Latter-day Saint. Legal Res: 161 S. Third E, Preston, Idaho 83263. Mailing Add: Box 274, Preston, Idaho 83263.

HART, NATHANIEL IRWIN DFL
Chmn, Stevens Co. Dem-Farmer-Labor Party, Minn.
b. New York, N.Y, 3/4/30; s David Hart and Ruth Feldman H; m. 3/2/57 to Joanne Therese Velz; c. John, Thomas, Marya, Naomi, Agnes, Natalie, Joseph and David. Educ: Tulane Univ, B.A, 52; Univ. Conn, M.A, 54; Univ. Minn, Ph.D, 68. Polit. & Govt. Pos: V.Chmn, Stevens Co. Dem-Farmer-Labor Party, Minn, 62-66, chmn, 66-, mem, State Cent. Cmt, 64-, State Policy Adv. Cmt, 66-67 and mem-at-lg, State Exec. Cmt, 66-68; v.chmn, Morris Pub. Housing Authority, 66- Bus. & Prof. Pos: Asst. prof. Eng, Univ. Minn, Morris, 61- Mil. Serv: Entered as Pvt, Army, 54, released as SP3, 56, after serving in Hq. Co, North. Area Command, Germany, 55-56. Mem: Am. Asn. Univ. Prof; Nat. Coun. Teachers Eng; Minn. Coun. Teachers Eng; Mod. Lang. Asn; Midwest Mod. Lang. Asn; Conf. Col. Composition & Commun; Am. Civil Liberties Union. Nat. ROTC scholarship, 48-51; Am. Chem. Soc. Essay Award, 48; Grant-in-aid, grad. sch, Univ. Minn, 69-70. Rel: Jewish. Mailing Add: 309 E. Second St, Morris, Minn. 56267.

HART, PARKER THOMPSON
Dir, For. Serv. Inst, Dept. of State
b. Medford, Mass, 9/28/10; s. William Parker Hart and Ella Louisa Thompson H; m. 4/23/49 to Jane Constance Smiley; c. Margaret Alice and Judith Ella. Educ: Dartmouth Col, B.A, 33; Harvard Univ, M.A, 35; L'Inst. des Hautes Etudes Int, Geneva, 36; Georgetown Univ. Sch. For. Serv; Phi Kappa Sigma. Polit. & Govt. Pos: Career officer, U.S. Dept. of State For. Serv, 38-, interpreter French, State Dept, 37-38, overseas serv. in Vienna, Para, Rio de Janeiro, Cairo, Jidda, Dhahran and Damascus, with Div. of For. Serv. Planning, 47-49, attended Nat. War Col, 51-52, dir. Off. Near East. Affairs, 52-53, dep. asst. secy. of state for Near East. and S.Asian Affairs, 58-61, minister to Yemen, 61-62; U.S. Ambassador, Saudia Arabia, 61-65, Ambassador, Kuwait, 62-63, U.S. Ambassador, Turkey, 65-68, Asst. Secy. of State for Near East. and S.Asian Affairs, 68-69, and dir, For. Serv. Inst, Dept. of State, 69- Publ: 'Hanbalite and Decree Law in Saudi Arabia,' Wash. For. Law Soc, 53. Mem, Cosmos Club and Am. For. Serv. Asn, Wash, D.C; former mem, Coun. of the Harvard Univ. Grad. Soc. for Adv. Study and Research; bd. gov, Mid.E. Inst, pres, 69-; Mid. East. Civilizations Vis. Cmt. of The Bd. of Overseers of Harvard Col; Royal Geog. Soc; Royal Cent. Asian Soc; Am. Research Center in Egypt; Rotary. Nat. Civil Ser. League Citation, 57. Rel: Protestant. Legal Res: 830 Lincoln St, Evanston, Ill. 60201. Mailing Add: 4201 Cathedral Ave. N.W, Washington, D.C. 20016.

HART, PETER D. D
Dir. Polit. Research, Dem. Nat. Cmt.
b. San Francisco, Calif. 1/3/42; s. James D. Hart and Ruth Arnstein H; single. Educ: Colby Col, Waterville, Maine, B.A, 64. Polit. & Govt. Pos: Polit. analyst, Louis Harris & Assocs, N.Y, 64-68; mem. staff, John J. Gilligan for U.S. Senate, Ohio, 68; dir. polit. research, Dem. Nat. Cmt. and spec. asst. to Sen. Fred R. Harris, chmn, 69- Mil. Serv: Pvt, Army, 65; Pfc, Army Res, 69. Legal Res: 740 San Louis Rd, Berkeley, Calif. 94707. Mailing Add: 311 A St. N.E, Washington, D.C. 20002.

HART, PHILIP A. D
U.S. Sen, Mich.
b. Bryn Mawr, Pa, 12/10/12; m. 1943 to Jane C. Briggs; c. 4 sons and 4 daughters. Educ: Georgetown Univ, A.B, cum laude, 34; Univ. Mich. Law Sch, J.D, 37; Phi Delta Phi. Polit. & Govt. Pos: Cmnr, Mich. Corp. and Securities Cmn, 49-50; dir, Off. Price Stabilization, 51; U.S. Attorney, East. Mich, 52; legal adv. to Gov. Williams, Mich. 53-54; Lt. Gov, Mich, 54-58; U.S. Sen, Mich, 58-; del, Dem. Nat. Conv, 68. Mil. Serv: Army, 41-46. Mem: Trustee and past pres, Mich. Bar Found; Lansing World Affairs Coun; Am. Judicature Soc; Am. Soc. Inst. Law. Legal Res: Mackinac Island, Mich. 49757. Mailing Add: 362 Senate Office Bldg, Washington, D.C. 20510. (1967)

HART, RICHARD ODUM D
Ill. State Rep.
b. Benton, Ill, 12/13/27; s. Marion Murphy Hart and Constance Skinner H; m. 12/23/51 to Carolyn Margaret Coddington; c. Murphy Coddington and Paul Richard. Educ: Univ. Ill, A.B, 51; Wash. Univ, J.D, 54; Theta Chi. Polit. & Govt. Pos: Ill. State Rep, 58th Dist, 69- Mil. Serv: Entered as Seaman 3/C, Navy, 45, released as Seaman 1/C, 46, after serv. in Pac. Mem: Am, Ill. State and Franklin Co. Bar Asns; Am. Trial Lawyers Asn; Am. Judicature Soc; Rotary; VFW; Am. Legion; Mason; Farm Bur. Rel: Protestant. Legal Res: 301 W. Reed, Benton, Ill. 62812. Mailing Add: P.O. Box P, Benton, Ill. 62812.

HART, RICHARD T, JR. R
Chmn, Carlton Co. Rep. Cmt, Minn.
b. Moose Lake, Minn; s. Richard T. Hart and Mabel Anderson H; single. Educ: Univ. of Minn, B.A, 42, LL.B, 48; Phi Kappa Psi; Phi Delta Theta; M Club. Polit. & Govt. Pos: Munic. judge, Moose Lake, Minn, 56-; chmn, Carlton Co. Rep. Cmt, currently. Mil. Serv: Entered as 2nd Lt, Army, 42, released as Capt, 45, after serv. in ETO, reentered serv. as Capt, 51, released as Capt, 53, after serv. in 504th Anti-Aircraft Artil, Combat Infantryman's Badge; Bronze Star; ETO Ribbon with 5 Campaign Stars. Mem: Carlton Co, Eleventh Dist. and Minn. State Bar Asns; AF&AM; Scottish Rite; Shrine; Moose; Am. Legion; VFW. Rel: Episcopal. Legal Res: 333 Lakeshore Dr, Moose Lake, Minn. 55767. Mailing Add: Box 396, Moose Lake, Minn. 55767.

HART, ROYAL D
Md. State Sen.
b. Jefferson, Ore, 3/14/26; married. Educ: Willamette Univ, B.A, 48; Univ. of Wash; Univ. of Ore. Polit. & Govt. Pos: Md. State Del, 63-67; Md. State Sen, 67- Bus. & Prof. Pos: Photographer. Mil. Serv: Navy, 43-46. Mem: Prfnl. Photographers of Am, del. to nat. coun, 59-60. Mailing Add: 6326 60th Place, Riverdale, Md. 20840. (1967)

HART, WALTER DEAN D
b. Pauls Valley, Okla, 10/3/16; s. Walter L. Hart and Charlotte Blackwood H; m. 11/2/43 to Lucille Grenier; c. Walter Dean, Lucinda Antoinette, Charlotte Clara, Laura Beth, Anastaia Germaine and Simone Berniece. Educ: Va. Mil. Inst; Univ. Okla. Law Sch; Beta Theta Pi. Polit. & Govt. Pos: Chmn, Co. Dem. Cent. Cmt, Okla, 58-62; del, Dem. Nat. Conv, 64; cmt. mem, Dem. Party, 66. Bus. & Prof. Pos: Trial lawyer. Mil. Serv: Entered as 2nd Lt, Army, released as Maj, 45, after serv. in 602 Tank Destroyers, Third Army, ETO; Silver Star; Bronze Star; Purple Heart with Oak Leaf Cluster; Croix de Guerre with Silver Star. Mem: Okla. and Am. Bar Asns; Southwest Legal Inst; Farmers Union; Elks; K. of P; Rotary. Rel: Methodist. Mailing Add: P.O. Box 177, Pauls Valley, Okla. 73075.

HART, WILLIAM F. R
Del. State Sen.
b. 1927. Educ: Univ. of Del. Sch. of Eng. Polit. & Govt. Pos: Del. State Rep, 67-69; Del. State Sen, 69- Bus. & Prof. Pos: Mgr, Ronson Corp, Ogletown, Del; research engr. Mem: Past pres, Tennie E. Smith, ATA; Chestnut Hill Estates Civic Asn; Gr. Newark Recreation Asn. Mailing Add: 16 Marlyn Rd, Chestnut Hills Estate, Newark, Del. 19711. (1967)

HARTE, HELEN C. D
b. Witherbee, N.Y, 2/20/09; married; c. 6 daughters. Educ: Addison, Vergennes, Castleton State Teachers Col; Univ. Vt. Polit. & Govt. Pos: Vt. State Rep, 65-66. Prof. Pos: Sch. teacher. Mem: Lady of Mt. Carmel Altar Soc; Nat. Educ. Asn; Vt. Educ. Asn; Classroom Teachers' Asn; Vt. Cath. Women's Asn; League of Women Voters; Addison Sch. Cmt, 37-44; chmn, Addison Co. PTA, 40-44. Rel: Roman Catholic. Mailing Add: R.F.D, Charlotte, Vt. 05445. (1967)

HARTEL, ARTHUR PAUL, JR. R
b. N.Y.C, 9/22/33; s. Arthur P. Hartel and Ethel Kovacs H; m. 6/29/57 to Patricia Woodward Vauthier Seitz; c. Arthur Paul, III, Alexander Woodward, Austin Stewart and Juliette Elizabeth. Educ: Duke Univ, A.B, 55, Law Sch, LL.B, 58; Phi Delta Phi Sigma Phi Gamma; Alpha Phi Omega. Polit. & Govt. Pos: Alternate del, Rep. Nat. Conv, 68. Bus. & Prof. Pos: Attorney, Off. of Gen. Coun, Commercial Credit Corp. Publ: 'And Justice For All...,' N.C. Bar Asn, 59. Mem: Am. and N.C. Bar Asns. Rel: Lutheran. Mailing Add: 5622 Sherrier Place N.W, Washington, D.C. 20016.

HARTIG, JUDITH MARTIN R
Secy, La Porte Co. Rep. Cent. Cmt, Ind.
b. Cleveland, Ohio 3/17/38; d. John B. Martin and Helen Hickam M; m. 10/30/57 to Richard William Hartig; c. Tracy Lynne and Stephen Martin. Educ: Univ. Mich, 55-58; Univ. Wis, Milwaukee, B.S, 63; Chi Omega. Polit. & Govt. Pos: Precinct committeeman, Rep. Party, Racine, Wis, 60; chmn, Assembly Dist. Registrn, Whittier, Calif, 62; precinct chmn, Rep. Party, Whittier, 63-64; cong. dist. chmn, Calif. Rep. Assembly, 64; precinct chmn, Paducah Co, Ky, 64; pres, McCracken Co. Young Rep. Club, 65-66; pres, La Porte Young Rep. Club, Ind, 66-67; secy, La Porte City Campaign Cmt, 67; v.chmn, Third Dist. Young Rep, 67-68; alternate del, Rep. Nat. Conv, 68; secy, La Porte Co. Rep. Cent. Cmt, 68-; v.chmn, Second Dist. Young Rep, 69- Mailing Add: 102 Evergreen Dr, La Porte, Ind. 46350.

HARTIGAN, MARGARET D
Dem. Nat. Committeewoman, Vt.
Mailing Add: 23 Hickok Place, Burlington, Vt. 05401.

HARTIGAN, WINIFRED E. D
Dem. Nat. Committeewoman, N.H.
b. Somersworth, N.H, 7/4/14; m. to John L. Hartigan; c. Peter, Mary Ann and Noreen. Polit. & Govt. Pos: Dem. Nat. Committeewoman, N.H, currently; del, Dem. Nat. Conv, 68. Mailing Add: 145 Charles St, Rochester, N.H. 03867. (1967)

HARTKE, VANCE D
U.S. Sen, Ind.
b. Stendal, Ind, 5/31/19; s. Hugo Hartke and Ida Egbert H; m. 6/43 to Martha Tiernan; c. 7. Educ: Evansville Col, A.B; Ind. Univ. Law Sch, J.D; ed, Ind. Law J; Lambda Chi Alpha; Phi Delta Phi; Tau Kappa Alpha. Polit. & Govt. Pos: Attorney, Evansville, Ind, 48-58 and Mayor, 56-58; dep. prosecuting attorney, Vanderburg Co, 50-51; U.S. Sen, Ind, 58-; del, Dem. Nat. Conv, 68. Bus. & Prof. Pos: Dir, Evansville's Future, Inc. Mil. Serv: Navy and Coast Guard, World War II. Mem: Wabash Valley Asn; Ohio Valley Improv. Asn; Exchange Club; Cent. Turners; Lutheran Laymen's League. Rel: Lutheran. Legal Res: Evansville, Ind. Mailing Add: 6500 Kerns Court, Falls Church, Va. 22044. (1967)

HARTLE, DEAN PICKETT R
Chmn. Steele Co. Rep. Cmt, Minn.
b. Owatonna, Minn, 7/19/31; s. Herbert J. Hartle and Helen I. Pickett H; m. 7/26/52 to Marsha Jane Werhan; c. Leslea Irene, Allyson Jane, Daniel W, Bradley D, Joel F, Meredith C. Educ: Hamline Univ, 49-50; Univ. Minn, B.S, 53; Alpha Gamma Rho. Polit. & Govt. Pos: Alternate del, Rep. State Conv, Minn, 64-65; chmn, Steele Co. Rep. Cmt, currently; mem, Steele Co. Planning Cmn, 64- Mem: Minn. Farm Mgrs. Asn; Star in East Lodge 33; AF&AM; RAM; K.T; Farm Bur; C. of C. Rel: Methodist; Sunday Sch. Teacher and Past Chmn. Educ. Cmn; Past Chmn, Off. Bd; Past Mem, Bldg. Cmt. Mailing Add: Route 4, Box 178, Owatonna, Minn. 55060. (1967)

HARTLEY, FRED D. R
V.chmn, Wis. Rep. Party
b. Superior, Wis, 7/10/19; s. Clarence J. Hartley and Marie Damon H; m.

m. 9/18/46 to Carolyn Buck; c. Tom, Steve, Fritz and Mary. Educ: Carleton Col, B.A, 40; Univ. Mich. Law Sch, 40-41; Univ. Wis. Law Sch, LL.B, 47; Phi Delta Phi. Polit. & Govt. Pos: Treas, Kenosha Co. Rep. Party, Wis, 52-56, chmn, 56-60; chmn, First Dist. Rep. Party, 60-66, chmn, grievance cmt, 68-; del, Rep. Nat. Conv, 64 & 68; v.chmn, Wis. Rep. Party, 66- Bus. & Prof. Pos: Circuit court cmnr, Kenosha Co, 51- Mil. Serv: Entered as Midn, Navy, 41, released as Lt. Comdr, 46, after serving in N.Atlantic and S.Pac. Theaters, 42-45. Mem: Kenosha Co. Bar Asn.(chmn, 50-51); Wis. Bar Asn.(treas, bd. gov, 54); Am. Bar Asn; Racine-Kenosha Estate Planning Coun; Elks; Kenosha Country Club; C. of C; Goodfellows. Rel: Congregational. Mailing Add: 202 69th St, Kenosha, Wis. 53140.

HARTLEY, GEORGE B. D
b. Phila, Pa. 1/17/02; s. Howard Hartley and Rebeca Carman H; m. to Mary C. Haley; c. two sons. Educ: Holy Family Sch. and Cent. High Sch. Polit. & Govt. Pos: Pa. State Rep, 60-66; former treas, 22nd Ward Dem. Exec. Cmt. Bus. Pos: Tool and die maker. Mem: Former mem, Auxiliary Police; past pres, Cliveden Improv. Asn; Holy Name Soc. Mailing Add: 620 Vernon Rd, Philadelphia, Pa. 19119. (1967)

HARTLEY, MINNIE MATILDA R
b. Grayling, Mich, 1/20/94; d. John A. Love and Henrietta Fuller L; wid; c. Virginia E. (Mrs. Selesky). Educ: High Sch, Grayling, Mich. Polit. & Govt. Pos: Co-chmn, Crawford Co. Rep. Party, Mich, 57-65. Bus. & Prof. Pos: Owner, Black & White Grocery, 34-54; stock mgr, Ben Franklin Variety Store, 60-65. Mem: Rebekah. Rel: Lutheran. Mailing Add: Apt. 31, Amyra Acres, Grayling, Mich. 49738.

HARTMAN, HERVIE FRANKLIN D
b. Greene Co, Tenn, 10/4/13; s. James Lawrence Hartman and Bessie Kelton H; m. 12/24/45 to Marie Easterly; c. Hervie Franklin, Jr, Mary Anise and Marie Anne (Mrs. Tyrone Frye). Educ: Greenville High Sch, Grad. Polit. & Govt. Pos: Asst. chief clerk, Tenn. House of Rep, 57-; del, Tenn. State Conv, 52-; col. on Gov. of Tenn. Staff, 52-; mem, Ellington for Gov. Cmt. and Clement for Sen. Cmt, 66; mem, Clement for Gov. Cmt, 62; mgr. Co. Campaigns, Ellington for Gov, 58 and Clement for Gov, 52 & 54; chmn, Co. Dem. Party, 52-54; mem, various Dem. State Cmts, including Credentials Cmt, 58. Bus. Pos: Inspector, Dept. of Ins. and Banking, State of Tenn, 53- Mil. Serv: Entered as Pvt, Air Force, 42, released as S/Sgt, 45, after serv. in 19th Troop Carrier Squadron, Asiatic-Pac. Theater, 7th Air Force, 45; Asiatic-Pac. Ribbon; Allied, Good Conduct and Am. Defense Medals. Mem: VFW; Am. Legion; DAV; York Rite; Scottish Rite; Mason (32°); Shrine; Eastern Star; Lions; Elks; Moose; Ruritan; Quarterback Club. Capt. of All-Am. Team of Post Comdrs, VFW, 60-61, 63-64; mem, All-Am. Team, 62-63. Legal Res: Crockett Lane, Greeneville, Tenn. 37743. Mailing Add: P.O. Box 46, Greenville, Tenn. 37743. (1967)

HARTMAN, RALPH D. D
N.Mex. State Rep.
b. Berino, N.Mex, 3/16/30; s. Carl G.T. Hartman and Thelma Avalos H; m. 6/12/54 to Alice Valdiviez; c. Richard Frank, Yvonne Marie and Michael Ralph. Educ: N.Mex. State Univ, 49; N.Mex. Highlands Univ, 50-51; Univ. Colo. Sch. of Banking, grad, 61; Alpha Chap. of Kappa Theta. Polit. & Govt. Pos: N.Mex. State Rep, Dist. Two, Dona Ana Co, 65- Bus. & Prof. Pos: Petroleum mgr, Farmer's Supply Coop, 54-55; asst. v.pres, First Nat. Bank, La Cruces, N.Mex, 55-; agent, Great Am. Reserve Ins. Co, 68- Mil. Serv: Entered as Pvt, Army, 52, released as Sgt, 54, after serv, in 246th Field Artil, Missile Bn, Fort Bliss, Tex; Good Conduct Medal. Mem: Mason; Optimist Club; C. of C. Football Scholarship, Highlands Univ. Rel: Protestant. Mailing Add: Box 73, Berino, N.Mex. 88024.

HARTMAN, ROGER L. R
Chmn, Buffalo Co. Rep. Party, Wis.
b. Manchester, Iowa, 1/28/29; s. Carl Edward Hartman and Lucille Ann Nordurft H; m. 7/11/54 to Dolores Elaine Palmiter; c. Kevin Lee. Educ: Univ. Idaho, B.S. in Bus. Admin, 54; Univ. Wis, Madison, J.D, 59; Scabbard and Blade; Phi Delta Phi. Polit. & Gov. Pos: City attorney, Alma, Wis, 60-; secy, Buffalo Co. Rep. Party, 62-66, chmn, 66-; village attorney, Pepin, Wis, 63-65; dist. attorney, Buffalo Co, 65-; v.chmn, Minn-Wis. Boundary Cmn, 67- Mil. Serv: Entered as Pvt, Air Force, 51, released as 1st Lt, 55, after serv. in 433rd Fighter Interceptor Squadron, Am. Defense Command, 52-55; Maj. and Gen. Area Rep, Judge Adv. Gen. Corps, Air Force Res, 69; Am. Defense Medal. Mem: Tri-Co, Wis. and Am. Bar Asns; Nat. Dist. Attorney's Asn; Lions Int.(secy); Am. Legion (chaplain); Alma Booster Club (chmn); Elks. Rel: Lutheran. Legal Res: 1301 River View Dr, Alma, Wis. 54610. Mailing Add: P.O. Box 337, Alma, Wis. 54610.

HARTMANN, ROBERT TROWBRIDGE R
b. Rapid City, S.Dak, 4/8/17; s. Miner Louis Hartmann and Elizabeth Trowbridge H; m. 1/17/43 to Roberta Edith Sankey; c. Roberta (Mrs. Charles Frederick Brake) and Robert Sankey. Educ: Stanford Univ, B.A, 38; Delta Chi; Delta Sigma Rho; Hammer & Coffin; Sigma Delta Chi. Polit. & Govt. Pos: Ed, Rep. Conf, U.S. House of Rep, 66-69, sgt-at-arms to minority and legis. asst. to Minority Leader Gerald R. Ford, Mich, 69-; asst. to permanent chmn, Rep. Nat. Conv, 68. Bus. & Prof. Pos: Mem. ed. staff, Los Angeles Times, Calif, 39-64, chief, Wash. Bur, 54-63, Mediterranean and Mid.E. Bur, Rome, 63-64; N.Am. Regional Info. Adv, Food and Agr. Orgn, 64-65. Mil. Serv: Entered as Ens, Naval Res, 41, released as Lt. Comdr, 45, after serv. in 11th Naval Dist. & Pac. Fleet; Capt, Naval Res, at present. Mem: Nat. and Overseas Press Clubs; Int. Club of Wash; Capitol Hill Club; Mil. Order of the Carabao. Sigma Delta Chi Nat. Distinguished Serv. Award for Wash. Correspondence, 58; Overseas Press Club Citation, 61; Vigilant Patriot Award, 60; English Speaking Union Better Understanding Award, 59; Freedoms Found. Citation, 62. Rel: Protestant. Legal Res: 5001 Baltimore Ave, Washington, D.C. 20016. Mailing Add: HB-25, U.S. Capitol, Washington, D.C. 20515.

HARTNETT, JAMES JOSEPH D
b. Medford, Mass, 4/26/03; s. Jeremiah James Hartnett and Mary McCool H; 9/15/31 to Elinor M. Holland; c. James, Jr, Mary Lou (Mrs. Robert Whitty), Grace Ann (Mrs. Charles Leffel) and Joan. Educ: Boston Univ, BB.A, 23; Delta Mu Delta; Delta Sigma Pi. Polit. & Govt. Pos: Conn. State Rep, Windsor, 61-67, mayor, 53-59, councilman. 47-53, mem. Bd. of Educ, 41-47, and justice of the peace, 43-47. Mem: Exchange Club of Windsor; K. of C. Rel: Roman Catholic. Legal Res: 71 Hillcrest Rd, Windsor, Conn. 06095. Mailing Add: P.O. Box 172, Windsor, Conn. 06095. (1967)

HARTNETT, ROBERT C. D
Fla. State Rep.
b. Coral Gables, Fla, 9/3/38; s. Fred B. Hartnett and Elizabeth Grace Hartnett H; single. Educ: Univ. Miami, B.B.S, 61; Alpha Kappa Psi; Iota Nu Sigma; Phi Delta Theta. Polit. & Govt. Pos: Admin. asst. to Secy. of Fla. State Senate, 61; mem, Dade Co. Dem. Exec. Cmt, Fla, currently; v.chmn, Banks and Loans Cmt, currently; Fla. State Rep, 66-; mem, Dade Co. Young Dem, Fla, currently. Bus. & Prof. Pos: V.pres. and dir, Cove Inn Hotel, Naples, Fla, currently, U.S. Truck Leasing Corp, currently; exec. v.pres, Commercial Div, Hartnett Realty, Inc, currently; mem. adv. bd, Dixie Nat. Bank, Dade Co, currently; chmn. bd, Mid-Fla. Equities, Securities and Real Estate Investment Trust, currently. Mil. Serv: A/S, Coast Guard Res, 61. Mem: Fla. Asn. of Realtors; Soc. of Real Estate Appraisers; Nat. Soc. of Legislators; Children's Psychiat. Center of Dade Co.(dir); United Fund Speakers Bur; Coral Gables Jr. C. of C; Bachelors Club; Metrop. Club. Rel: Roman Catholic. Legal Res: 1721 S. Bayshore Lane, Miami, Fla. 33131. Mailing Add: 2820 Ponce de Leon Blvd, Coral Gables, Fla. 33134.

HARTNETT, THOMAS FORBES D
S.C. State Rep.
b. Charleston, S.C, 8/7/41; s. Thomas C. Hartnett and Catherine Forbes H; m. 12/18/65 to Bonnie Lee Kennedy. Educ: Charleston Col, 60-61. Polit. & Govt. Pos: S.C. State Rep, 65- Bus. & Prof. Pos: Realtor, v.pres, Hartnett Realty Co. Mil. Serv: Air Force, active duty; Air Force Res, currently. Mem: Charleston Optimist Club; K of C; Scout master, Troop 7, Boy Scouts; pres, Bishop England Alumni Asn; Hibernian Soc. Legal Res: 447 Geddes Ave, Charleston, S.C. 29407. Mailing Add: Box 221, Charleston, S.C. 29401.

HARTRICK, GORDON DEAN R
Chmn, Ashley Co. Rep. Party, Ark.
b. Stettler, Alta, Can, 5/13/15; s. Maver Steven Hartrick and Lila M. Dean H; m. 6/10/40 to Alma L. Seely; c. Holly (Mrs. Ves Childs), Susan (Mrs. Jerry MacDonald), Alice (Mrs. Mike McBee), Heather (Mrs. Dave Bevil), Nancy (Mrs. Ken Stafford), Frank Dean, Fred Gordon, Jean Margaret, Robin Edmund and Betsy. Educ: Univ. Mich, B.S, 40, M.S.F, 41. Polit. & Govt. Pos: Chmn, Ashley Co. Rep. Party, Ark, 65- Bus. & Prof. Pos: Area forester, Ga. Pac. Corp, Crossett, Ark. Mem: Soc. Am. Foresters (chmn, Ozark sect); chmn, Ashley Co. Develop. Coun; Southeast Ark. Resource and Conserv. Develop. Coun. Rel: Methodist. Mailing Add: Route 3, Box 194, Hamburg, Ark. 71646.

HARTUNG, THOMAS FREDERICK R
Ore. State Rep.
b. Eugene, Ore, 6/11/27; s. Frederick Elmer Hartung and Claudia Broders H; m. 9/15/50 to Beverly May Tice; c. Kurt, Julie, Elizabeth, Marcia and Mary. Educ: Ore. State Univ, B.S, 50; Univ. Ore. Exten, grad. study; Blue Key; Alpha Zeta; Phi Kappa Phi; Phi Delta Theta. Polit. & Govt. Pos: Dir, Ore. Sch. Dist, 48 & 61-66; Ore. State Rep, Fourth Dist, 66- Bus. & Prof. Pos: V.pres, West. Div, Nat. Asn. of Meat Purveyors, 64-66. Mil. Serv: Entered as A/S, Navy, 45, released as Storekeeper 3/C, 46, after serv. in Pac; S.Pac. Ribbons. Mem: Ore. and Nat. Restaurant Asns; Food Serv. Exec. Asn; Rotary; Wash. Co. Pub. Affairs Forum; Mason; dir, Ore. State Alumni Asn; Ore. Indoor Track Meet Asn; Col. for Ore. Future. Rel: United Church of Christ. Mailing Add: 2280 N.W. 143rd Ave, Portland, Ore. 97229.

HARTVIGSEN, LESTER A. D
Idaho State Rep.
b. Downey, Idaho, 5/8/11; s. Joakim F. Hartvigsen and Ellen Amelia Eilertsen H; m. 1/1/42 to Evelyn Jardine Williams; c. James L, Rulon Eric and Kim Ray. Educ: Utah State Univ, B.S. in econ, 36; Pi Gamma Mu. Polit. & Govt. Pos: Supvr, Bannock Co. Agr. Conserv. Asn, Idaho, 38-41; asst, Power Co. War Bd, 41-44; secy, Power Co. Agr. Conserv. Asn, 41-44; Idaho State Rep, Dist. 33, 67- Bus. & Prof. Pos: Owner-operator, Wheat Farms, 36-66. Mem: Lions Int. Rel: Latter-day Saint. Mailing Add: 255 E. 155 S, Malad, Idaho 83252.

HARTWIG, ASA CHARLS R
Chmn, Cullman Co. Rep. Party, Ala.
b. Cullman, Ala, 1/17/40; s. George Theodore Hartwig and Wilhelmina Schuman H; m. 1/29/63 to Susanne Louisa Smith; c. Elizabeth and Amy. Educ: Univ. Ala, B.S, 62; Univ. Ala. Sch. of Law, LL.B, 64; Phi Tau Chi; Sigma Delta Kappa; Alpha Kappa Psi; Gamma Delta; Young Rep. Polit. & Govt. Pos: V.pres, Univ. Ala. Young Rep, 61-62, pres, 62-63; organizational chmn, Cullman Co. Rep. Party, Ala, summer 62 & 66-67, chmn, 67- Bus. & Prof. Pos: Attorney-at-law, Cullman, Ala, 66- Mil. Serv: Entered as 2nd Lt, Army, 64, released as 1st Lt, 66, after serv. in Army Sch. Training Center, Ft. McClellan, Ala, Hq. Commandant, Capt. Army Res, currently. Mem: Ala. Bar Asn; Am. Trial Lawyers Asn; Lutheran Layman's League; Rotary Int. Jaycees. Rel: Lutheran; Mo. Synod. Mailing Add: 713 Second Ave. E, Cullman, Ala. 35055.

HARUTUNIAN, ALBERT THEODORE, JR. R
b. Pasadena, Calif, 8/4/25; s. Ardash Harutunian, Sr. and Virginia Goorgenian H; m. 7/18/54 to Elsie Ruth Tomboulian; c. Albert T, III, Arthur and Robert Haig. Educ: Col. of William & Mary; Princeton Univ; Col. of Pac; Univ. Calif, Los Angeles, B.S, 47, M.S, 48; Delta Sigma Rho; Gamma Sigma Delta; Phi Kappa Tau. Polit. & Govt. Pos: Mem, World Nutrition Coun. of the President, 58-; planning cmnr, San Diego, Calif, 64-65; mem, Calif. State Rep. Cent. Cmt, 65; founding chmn, San Diego Stadium Authority, Calif, 66-; Calif. State chmn, Citizens For Nixon, 68. Mil. Serv: Entered as A/S, Navy, 43, released as Student Officer, 46, after serv. in Found. World Power Seminar, Univ. Calif; World War II and Am. Theatre Medals. Publ: 'N.P.K—Food For Billions.' Univ. Calif, 1/48; 'National Defense Aspects of Agriculture,' 9/59 and 'Sea Farming,' 7/62, Nat. Plant Food Review. Mem: Fel, Am. Soc. of Agronomy; Nat. Plant Food Inst.(dir, Region IV); Calif, Fertilizer Asn. (secy. and dir); C. of C.(v.pres. and dir, San Diego C. of C, 60-62); founder of proj, Try San Diego First, 62-; proj. chmn, Drive to Build A Stadium, San Diego, 65; chmn. Bob Hope USO Show, 68; Rotary; Los Angeles Athletic Club;

Kona Kai Club; La Jolla Country Club; Univ. Club; Cuyamacha Club. Man of the Year Award, San Diego C. of C, 62-63. Rel: Protestant. Mailing Add: 1715 Grand Ave, San Diego, Calif. 92109.

HARVEY, DARYL PRESTON R
Mem, Ky. State Rep. Cent. Exec. Cmt.
b. Willow Shade, Ky, 11/24/14; s. O.P. Harvey and Mary Enna Alexander H; m. 10/20/50 to Mary Jeannette Banet; c. Prentice Alexander. Educ: West. Ky. Univ, B.S, 39; Tulane Univ, M.D, 43; Kappa Alpha Order; Phi Chi. Polit. & Govt. Pos: V.chmn, White House Conf. on Children and Youth and mem, Pres. Adv. Cmt. on Youth Fitness, 59-60; chmn, Doctors for Nixon, 60 and Doctors for Morton, Ky, 62; mem, Physicians for Goldwater Cmt, 64; former chmn, Barren Co. Rep. Exec. Cmt. and former v.chmn, Second Cong. Dist. Exec. Cmt; mem, Ky. State Rep. Cent. Exec. Cmt, 64- Publ: Article on cuts, Parade, 59. Mem: Am. Asn. Physicians and Surgeons; Am. Acad. Gen. Practice (v.speaker, 55-56, mem, nat. cmn. on legis. and pub. policy, 57-60); Am. Med. Asn.(alternate del, Am. Med. Asn. House of Del, Ky, 68-69); former mem. exec. cmt, Ky. Med. Polit. Action Cmt; legis. coun, Ky. Med. Asn, 61-67; Farm Bur; Lions. Rel: Methodist. Legal Res: R.R. 6, Glasgow, Ky. 42141. Mailing Add: Box 667, Glasgow, Ky. 42141.

HARVEY, DAVID CHRISTENSEN D
Utah State Rep.
b. Pleasant Grove, Utah, 9/2/34; s. Leo Paul Harvey and Arvilla Christensen H; m. 8/8/59 to Dixie Renee Timons; c. Craig David, Julie Ann, Mark Thomas and Stanley William. Educ: Brigham Young Univ, $1\frac{1}{2}$ years; Athenians. Polit. & Govt. Pos: Chmn, Fourth Dist. Dem. Party, Pleasant Grove, Utah, 60, secy, Peoples Party, 62; mem, Utah Co. Dem. Cent. Cmt, 62; Utah State Rep, 38th Dist, Utah Co, 65-66 & 69-, mem, Legis. Coun. and chmn, Econ. Develop. Cmt, Utah House of Rep, 69-; mem, Interstate Pact Cmt, representing State of Utah in Agr, 69; del, Utah State Dem. Conv, 67 & 69. Bus. & Prof. Pos: Self-employed farmer, currently. Mil. Serv: S/Sgt, Army Res, 60-66, serv. in Inf. Mem: Farm Bur. Orgn; Farmers Union. Distinguished Serv. Award, City of Pleasant Grove, 67. Rel: Latter-day Saint; Bishop, 65- Mailing Add: R.F.D. 1, Box 417, Pleasant Grove, Utah 84062.

HARVEY, EDWARD D
b. Lewiston, Maine, 3/14/17; s. John Edward Harvey and Eva Langelier H; m. 8/30/39 to Alice Savina Wilson; c. Diana (Mrs. Gerald M. Clarke), Janet and James. Educ: Bates Col, B.A, 37; Middlebury Col, M.A, 46; Harvard Univ, M.A, 46, Ph.D, 52; Phi Beta Kappa; Phi Sigma Iota; fel. inst. int. educ, Lycee, Angers, France, 37-38. Polit. & Govt. Pos: V.chmn, Knox Co. Dem. Cent. and Exec. Cmts, Ohio, 56-64, chmn, 64-65; mem. Platform Cmt, Ohio State Dem. Conv, 58 & 60; precinct committeeman, Knox Co. Dem. Cent. Cmt, Ohio, cent. committeeman, 56-, chmn, 64. Bus. & Prof. Pos: Sch. Teacher, Rochester, N.H, 38-42; wire-maker, Rome Cable Corp, Rome, N.Y, 42-45; teaching fel, Harvard Col, 44-48; Samuel Mather Prof. French, Kenyon Col, 48-, chmn. dept. French, 62-; mem. cmt. advan. placement prog, Col. Entrance Exam. Bd, 52-61; vis. prof, Colby Col, 62 & 66, Colo. Col, 63 and Ohio State Univ, 65; asst. managing ed, Mod. Lang. J, 65-; prof-in-charge, Jr. Year in France, Sweet Briar Col, 66-67. Publ: Contributor to prfnl. journals. Mem: Modern Lang. Asn; Am. Asn. Teachers of French; Am. Asn. Univ. Prof; Cent. States Modern Lang. Teachers Asn.(v.pres, 62); Ohio 17th Dist, Cmt. on Polit. Educ. Rel: Roman Catholic. Mailing Add: Box 123, Gambier, Ohio 43022.

HARVEY, ELLERY HALE R
b. Lewisburg, Pa, 1/13/95; s. E. Hale Harvey and Mary Conrad H; m. to L. Maye Lundquist; c. Ellery H, III and Glenn W. Educ: Ph.C. and Ph.M, Phila Col. Pharm, 21; A.B, Bucknell Univ, 23, A.M, 24 and Ch.E, 29; LL.B, John Marshall Law Sch, 32; Ph.D. in Chem, Wis, 26; Sigma Xi; Delta Theta Phi. Polit. & Govt. Pos: Past Justice of Peace; past chmn, M-O-R-E Campaign, First Cong. Dist, Fla; founder Walton Co. Non-Partisan League for Constitutional Govt; past chmn, Nat. Draft Goldwater Cmt. of Fla. First Cong. Dist; past chmn, Walton Co. Rep. Exec. Cmt, Fla; past v.chmn, Rep. State Exec. Cmt; v.chmn, Ormond Beach Rep. Club, currently. Bus. & Prof. Pos: Dir, Bur. of Standards, Montgomery Ward & Co, Chicago, Ill; dir. of research, Anheuser-Busch, St. Louis, Mo, Sun Chem. Co, N.Y; prof, Ill. Inst. Tech, Chicago, Ill. Mil. Serv: 1st Lt, Chem. Warfare Serv.(Ret). Publ: Elements of Food Engineering, 3 vols, Reinhold; 40 articles in magazines. Mem: Am. Chem. Soc; Am. Inst. Chem. Engrs; Inst. Food Tech; Nat. Genealogical Soc; Am. Hist. Soc; Genealogical Soc. of Pa; Mason; Consistory and Shrine; pres, WALCO Develop. Coop, Inc; pres, WALCO Commun. Action, Inc; pres, Mossy Head Commun. Center; v.pres, RAD; trustee, Daytona Beach Jr. Col, 4 years. Genealogist. Rel: Protestant. Mailing Add: 484 Wild Olive Ave, Ormond Beach, Fla. 32074.

HARVEY, JAMES R
U.S. Rep, Mich.
b. Iron Mountain, Mich, 7/4/22; s. Martin Harvey, Sr. and Agnes Thomas H; m. 4/1/48 to June Elizabeth Collins; c. Diane Elizabeth and Thomas Martin. Educ: Univ. Mich, 40-43; Univ. Mich. Law Sch, LL.B, 46-49. Polit. & Govt. Pos: Asst. city attorney, Saginaw, Mich, 49-53, mem, city coun, 55-57 and mayor, 57-59; U.S. Rep, Mich, 61- Bus. & Prof. Pos: Attorney, Bauer & Williams, 53-56; partner, Nash, Nash & Harvey, 56-59 and Smith, Brooker, Harvey & Cook, 59- Mil. Serv: Entered ROTC, Army Air Corps, 43, released as 2nd Lt, 45. Mem: Am. and Mich. Bar Asns; hon. mem, Saginaw Rotary; Germania Club; Congressional Country Club; Capitol Hill Club. Rel: Presbyterian. Legal Res: 2746 W. Genesee Ave, Saginaw, Mich. 48602. Mailing Add: 5002 Nahant St, Washington, D.C. 20016.

HARVEY, JAMES FERGUSON, JR. R
Chmn, Jackson Co. Rep. Exec. Cmt, Miss.
b. Simon, W.Va, 6/21/16; s. James Ferguson Harvey and Viola Morgan H; m. 1/26/46 to Mary Lyons; c. James F, III, Chester Lyons and Patricia Lynn. Educ: Bowling Green Col. Commerce, B.S. in commerce, 40; Pi Tau Nu. Polit. & Govt. Pos: Alternate del, Rep. Nat. Conv, 68; chmn, Jackson Co. Rep. Exec. Cmt, Miss, 68- Bus. & Prof. Pos: Dist. chmn, Singing River Dist, Boy Scouts, 64-66 and camping and activities chmn, Pine Burr Coun, 67-69. Mil. Serv: Entered as Pvt, Army, 41, released as Maj, 46, after serv. in Continental Advance Sect, ETO, 43-45. Mem: Shrine; F&AM; Scottish Rite Mason; Rotary. Silver Beaver, Boy Scouts. Rel: Methodist. Mailing Add: 1500 Dantzler St, Moss Point, Miss. 39563.

HARVEY, RALPH R
b. New Castle, Ind, 8/9/01; s. Eli M. Harvey and Bessie Bouslog H; m. 6/16/25 to Charline Bowers. Educ: Purdue Univ, B.S.A, 23; Alpha Zeta; Tau Kappa Alpha; Alpha Gamma Rho. Polit. & Govt. Pos: Mem, Co. Coun, Ind, 32-42; Ind. State Rep, 43-47; U.S. Rep, Ind, 47-59 & 61-66. Mem: Mason. Rel: Disciples of Christ. Mailing Add: Route 4, New Castle, Ind. 47632.

HARVEY, WILLIAM BRANTLEY, JR. D
S.C. State Rep.
b. Walterboro, S.C, 8/14/30; s. W. Brantley Harvey and Thelma Lightsey H; m. 12/30/52 to Helen Coggeshall; c. Eileen, William B. III, Helen, Margaret and Warren. Educ: The Citadel, A.B. in Polit. Sci, 51; Univ. S.C. Law Sch, LL.B, 55; Phi Beta Kappa; Wig & Robe; Kappa Alpha Order; Phi Delta Phi. Polit. & Govt. Pos: S.C. State Rep, Beaufort Co, 59-, chmn. Rules Cmt, S.C. State House of Rep, 67-, mem, Ways & Means Cmt. and Cmt. for Revision of S.C. Constitution. Bus. & Prof. Pos: Partner, Harvey, Harvey & Battey, 55-; dir. and secy, Tidewater Investment & Develop. Co, 58-; dir, Peoples Bank, Beaufort, 66- Mil. Serv: Entered as 2nd Lt, Army, 52, released as 1st Lt, 54, after serv. on Staff and Faculty AA&GM Br, Artil. Sch, Ft. Bliss, Tex. Mem: Am, S.C. and Beaufort Co. Bar Asns; Am. Trial Lawyers Asn; Am. Legion; Sertoma; C. of C. Rel: Presbyterian; Elder, teacher adult Sunday sch. class. Legal Res: 121 N. Hermitage Rd, Beaufort, S.C. 29902. Mailing Add: P.O. Box 1107, Beaufort, S.C. 29902.

HARVEY, WILLIAM EDWARD R
Chmn, Campbell Co. Rep. Exec. Cmt, Ky.
b. Cincinnati, Ohio, 6/26/30; s. Edward George Harvey and Janice Marion Clause H; m. 6/11/60 to Marilyn Ellen Kuhn; c. William Edward, Jr, John Charles and Jeanne Ellen. Educ: Harvard Col, A.B, 52; Univ. of Cincinnati Col. of Law, LL.B, 58; Phi Delta Phi; Bat Club, Harvard. Polit. & Govt. Pos: Elec. cmnr, Campbell Co, Ky, 65-66; chmn, Campbell Co. Rep. Exec. Cmt, 66- Bus. & Prof. Pos: Attorney, Nieman, Aug, Elder and Jacobs, 64- Mil. Serv: Entered as Officer Cand, Naval Res, 52, released as Lt, 55, after serv. in Amphibious Force, Atlantic Fleet; Lt, Naval Res, currently. Mem: Ohio, Ky, Cincinnati and Campbell Co. Bar Asns; chmn. elec, Campbell Co. Kiwanis. Rel: Methodist. Mailing Add: 33 N. Ft. Thomas Ave, Ft. Thomas, Ky. 41075. (1967)

HARWARD, ROYAL THOMAS R
Utah State Rep.
b. Aurora, Utah, 11/15/10; s. Thomas Franklin Harward and Sarah Jeanette Harding H; m. 3/15/34 to Donna Pauline Bagley; c. Donna Carol (Mrs. Dwight Williams), Carvel Royal, Ronald Vermont, Newell Edward, Thomas Kendall and Layne Bagley. Educ: Snow Col, 31-32. Polit. & Govt. Pos: Mem, Local Sch. Bd, 40-, pres, 47-69; pres, Utah Sch. Bd. Asn, 56; Utah State Sen, 57-61; regional dir, Nat. Sch. Bd. Asn, 59-63; Utah State Rep, 61-65 & 67-, mem, Utah Legis. Coun, 63-65 & 67-69. Bus. & Prof. Pos: Self-employed rancher and merchant, currently. Mem: Lions (pres, local club, 43); South. and East. Utah Assoc. Civic Clubs (pres, 55 & 56); Farm Bur. Utah Sch. Bd. Asn. Distinguished Serv. Award, 63 & 67; Phi Delta Kappa Man of the Year Award, 68. Rel: Latter-day Saint. Mailing Add: Loa, Utah 84747.

HARWELL, DAVID WALKER D
S.C. State Rep.
b. Florence, S.C, 1/8/32; s. Baxter Hicks Harwell and Lacy Rankin H; m. 3/12/55 to Nell Miles; c. David W, Jr, Robert Bryan and William Baxter. Educ: Univ. S.C, LL.B, 58; Phi Delta Phi; Beta Theta Pi. Polit. & Govt. Pos: S.C. State Rep, 63-; chmn, S.C. Agr. Study Cmt, 66- Bus. & Prof. Pos: Sr. partner, Harwell & Harwell, 58-; mgr, rental property partnership, 60-; pres, Farm Corp, 66-; pres, dry cleaning bus, 67. Mil. Serv: Enlisted man, Navy, 52-54; 2nd Lt, Air Force Res; Good Conduct Medal. Publ: Article in S.C. Law Quart, 58. Mem: S.C, Am. & Co. Bar Asns; Am. Trial Lawyers Asn; Am. Legion; Mason; PTA; Lions; WOW; Jr. C. of C; S. C. Farm Bur; Shrine; C. of C; S.C. Heart Asn. Rel: Presbyterian. Legal Res: 186 N. Irby St, Florence, S.C. 29501. Mailing Add: P.O. Box 107, Florence, S.C. 29501.

HARWOOD, MADELINE BAILEY R
Vt. State Sen.
b. Newbury, Vt, 7/7/14; d George Allen Bailey and Maude Smith B; m. 7/4/36 to Dr. Clifford Burr Harwood; c. Clifford B, Jr, Catherine A, Richard D. and Roger B. Educ: Mary Fletcher Hosp. Sch. of Nursing, R.N, 36. Polit. & Govt. Pos: Secy, Vt. State Rep. Cmt, 61-63 & 64-67; mem. drafting bd, State Platform Cmt, 64, 66 & 68; del, Rep. Nat. Conv, 64 & 68, mem. Drafting Cmt, 64 and secy, Platform Cmt, 68; pres, Vt. Fedn. Rep. Women, 65-67; v.chmn, Rep. State Cmt, 67-69; Vt. State Sen, 68-; mem, Gov. Coun. Civil Defense, 69- Mem: Pres, Vt. State Med. Soc. Auxiliary, 61-63; Regional legis. chmn, Am. Med. Asn. Auxiliary, 60-65, pres. auxiliary, 61-63; pres, Vt. Legis. Coun, Inc, 63-65; secy, Vt. Heart Asn, 66-68; dir, Mt. Laurel Sch. Ment. Retarded; past dir, Bennington Co. Red Cross; del, Am. Heart Asn, 68-69; del, Med. Polit. Action, 68-69; Past Matron, Eastern Star. Rel: Congregational. Mailing Add: Village View Rd, Manchester Center, Vt. 05255.

HARWOOD, STANLEY D
N.Y. State Assemblyman
b. Brooklyn, N.Y, 6/23/26; s. Benjamin Harwood and Hannah Schwartz H; m. 6/18/50 to Deborah Weinerman; c. Richard B, Ellen S, Michael C. and Jonathan R. Educ: Columbia Col, N.Y.C, B.A, 49; Columbia Univ. Law Sch, LL.B, 52. Polit. & Govt. Pos: Co. committeeman, Dem. Party, N.Y, 55-65; law secy. to Justice N.Y. State Supreme Court, 61-65; del, Dem. State Conv, 62 & 66; N.Y. State Assemblyman, 11th Assembly Dist, Nassau Co, 66- Bus. & Prof. Pos: Attorney-at-law, private practice, Levittown, N.Y, 56-65; Mishkin, Miner, Harwood & Semel, Mineola, 65-69; Shayne, Dachs, Weiss, Kolbrener & Levy, 69- Mil. Serv: Entered as Cadet-Midn, Merchant Marine Acad, 44, released, 47, after serv. in Acad. and Merchant Vessels, Eng, Africa, India and Belgium, 45-46. Mem: Nassau Co. and N.Y. State Bar Asns; Criminal Courts Bar Asn. of Nassau; Lions; K. of P; Jewish War Vet. Rel: Jewish. Mailing Add: 43 Grace Lane, Levittown, N.Y. 11756.

HASBROOK, THOMAS CHARLES R
Pres, City Council, Indianapolis, Ind.
b. Ft. Wayne, Ind, 7/29/20; s. Harold L. Hasbrook (deceased) and Charlotte Hensel H. (deceased); m. 2/13/43 to Mary Jane Thompson; c. Carol (Mrs.

Jack Holmes), Dan, Bill, Charles, Nancy and David. Educ: Ind. Univ, B.S, 42 Kappa Sigma; Riviera Club. Polit. & Govt. Pos: Mem, Ind. Legis. Cmt. to Study Laws Relating to Cities and Towns; Ind. State Rep, 50-54; Ind. State Sen, 54-58; City Councilman, First Dist, City Coun, Indianapolis, Ind, 60-, pres, 68- Bus. & Prof. Pos: Clerk, Eli Lilly & Co, 45-46, writer, 46-56, head employee commun. dept, 56-66, head employee benefit dept, 66- Mil. Serv: Entered as Pfc, Marine Corps Res, 42, released as 2nd Lt, 44. Mem: Dir. and founder, Hoosier Star-Light, publn. for blind, Indianapolis Star Blind Fund; sponsor, Crossroads Rehabilitation Center; past dir. and past chmn, Easter Seal Drive, Ind. Soc. Crippled Children and Adults; Nat. Soc. Prev. Blindness (past dir); Ind. Soc. Prev. Blindness (campaign chmn. and past pres); Blinded Vet. Asn.(past nat. pres. and dir); Health and Rehabilitation Sect, Coun. Soc. Agencies (past dir); Army-Navy Club; Riviera Club; Cath. Youth Orgn.(adv); Parents Club Cathedral High Sch.(past pres); Indianapolis Jaycees (past dir); Kappa Sigma Alumni Asn; Little League Baseball (former mgr); Rep. Vet. of World War II; adv. bd, Ind. Sch. Blind; Ind. Cmn. Spec. Inst; former mem, President's and Ind. Gov. Cmt. Employ. Handicapped; Boy Scouts (counsr. and troop cmt. mem). Outstanding Young Man of Good Govt. Awards, U.S. Jaycees; Grand Prize in Oper. Comeback, Am. Legion; Blind Father of Year, Nat. Fathers' Day Cmt; Sagamore of the Wabash from Gov. Welsh. Rel: Catholic. Mailing Add: 5541 Central Ave, Indianapolis, Ind. 46220.

HASKELL, FLOYD K. R
b. Morristown, N.J, 2/7/16; married; c. three. Polit. & Gov. Pos: Colo. State Sen. Bus. & Prof. Pos: Lawyer. Mem: Pres, United Rep. Fund, 62. Mailing Add: 2711 Willamette St, Littleton, Colo. 80120. (1967)

HASKELL, HARRY GARNER, JR. R
Mayor, Wilmington, Del.
b. Wilmington, Del, 5/27/21; s. Harry Garner Haskell and Elizabeth Scott Denham H; m. 5/3/47 to Mary Carey Foster; c. Malcolm Wells, Christopher Denham, Laurie Amory, Mary Carey, James Foster, Harry Garner, III, Elizabeth Patch and David Nathaniel. Educ: Princeton Univ, 40-42; Ivy Club; Polit. & Govt. Pos: Del, Rep. Nat. Conv, 52 & 68; secy. departmental coun, Dept. of Health, Educ. and Welfare, 53-55; consult, Exec. Off.of the President, Off. of Nelson A. Rockefeller, Spec. Asst. to President Eisenhower, 55; U.S. Rep, Del, 57-58; former v.pres, State Fedn. Young Rep; former treas, New Castle Co. Rep. Exec. Cmt. and Young Rep. of New Castle Co; Rep. Nat. Committeeman, Del, currently; mayor, Wilmington, Del, 69- Bus. & Prof. Pos: Personnel mgr, Speakman Co, 47-48; owner and chmn bd, Greenhill Dairies, Inc, 48-53; former dir, Abercrombie & Fitch Co, Wilmington Trust Co. and Brown & Scott Packing Co. Mil. Serv: Entered as Seaman 1/C, Coast Guard Res, 42, released as Lt.(jg), 46, after serv. in Pac. Theater, 44-45; Asiatic-Pac. Theater Campaign Ribbon with 1 Bronze Star; Am. Theater Campaign Ribbon; Philippine Liberation Medal; Victory Medal. Mem: Am. Guernsey Cattle Club; Phila. Soc. for Promoting Agr; VFW; Wilmington Country Club; Del-Mar-Va Coun, Boy Scouts; YMCA. Rel: Episcopal. Legal Res: 1600 Brinckle Ave, Wilmington, Del. 19806. Mailing Add: 1300 Market St, Wilmington, Del. 19801.

HASKELL, REUBEN L. R
b. Brooklyn, N.Y, 10/5/78; s. Robert B. Haskell and Monrovia Grayson; wid. Educ: Cornell Univ, LL.B, 98. Polit. & Govt. Pos: Cmnr, N.Y. State Transit Cmn, 32-43; judge, Kings Co. Court, Brooklyn, N.Y, 20-25; del, Rep. Nat. Convs, 20 and 08; U.S. Rep, 10th Dist, N.Y, 15-19; mem, N.Y. State Rep. Cmt, 07-19; asst. cmnr, Pub. Works, Borough Pres. Off, Brooklyn, N.Y, 14 and borough secy, 10-13; counsel for Co. Clerk, Kings Co, N.Y, 08-09. Prof. Pos: Retired Lawyer. Mil. Serv: Pvt, Army, Spanish-Am. War. Mem: Am. and Brooklyn Bar Asns; Mason; Elks; Odd Fellows; K. of P; Moose; Royal Arcadian; Soc. of Old Brooklynites. Rel: Congregational. Mailing Add: 19 Brookside Pl, Hillsdale, N.J. 07642. (1967)

HASS, EWING R
b. Palms, Calif, 3/14/10; s. Ernest S. Hass and Girlie Jenison H; m. 10/24/31 to Gervais Prentiss; c. Susan G. Educ: Univ. South. Calif, B.F.S, 29; Pi Kappa Alpha. Polit. & Govt. Pos: Chief Dep. State Controller, Calif, 46-55; Calif. state inheritance tax appraiser, 55-59; admin. asst. to U.S. Sen. Kuchel, Calif, 60-69. Bus. & Prof. Pos: Co-publisher, Arcadia Tribune & News, Calif, 39-65; asst. v.pres, Crocker-Anglo Bank, 59-60. Mil. Serv: Lt, Navy, 43-45, serv. in Pac. Area. Mem: Mason, Shrine; Jesters; Press & Union League Clubs of San Francisco; Sutter Club, Sacramento; Am. Legion; Native Sons of the Golden West. Rel: Methodist. Mailing Add: 1331 Ridgeway Dr, Sacramento, Calif. 95822. (1967)

HASSELBALCH, HAL BURKE R
b. St. Edward, Nebr, 8/2/32; s. Earl Hasselbalch and Nellie Burke H; m. 6/13/54 to Marilyn Jean Campfield; c. Kurt Campfield, Eric Burke, Peter Nels and Ane Catherine. Educ: Univ. Nebr, A.B. in Journalism, 54, Col. Law, LL.B, 59; Phi Delta Phi; Alpha Tau Omega. Polit. & Govt. Pos: Examiner, Nebr. Rwy. Cmn, 59-61; asst. city attorney, Lincoln, Nebr, 61-62; del, Nebr. Young Rep. Conv, 61-66; alternate del, Nat. Young Rep. Fedn. Conv, 61, del, 63; mem, Lancaster Co. Young Rep. Club, 61-; del, Lancaster Co. Rep. Conv, 62, 64, 66 & 68; mem, Nebr. Fedn. Young Rep, 63-; co-campaign mgr. for Mayor, 63; campaign mgr. for City Councilman, 63 and for Co. Cmnr, 64; alternate del, Rep. Nat. Conv, 64; Nebr. rep, U.S. Rep. Ralph F. Beermann and mem. steering cmt, Lancaster Co. Rep. Party, 64-65; chmn. exec. cmt, Lancaster Co. Young Rep, 64-65, mem, 64-66; del, Nebr. Rep. Conv, 64 & 66; cand, City Coun, 69. Bus. & Prof. Pos: Lawyer, self-employed, 62- Mil. Serv: Entered as Ens, Navy, 54, released as Lt.(jg), 56, after serv. on West Coast. Mem: Nebr. and Lancaster Co. Bar Asns; pres, Lancaster Co. Barristers' Club, 64-65; Int. Y's Men, pres, Capital City Y's Men, 65-66; camp cmt, YMCA, 63-; Danish Brotherhood of Am; life mem. Culver Alumnae Asn; Jacobins Club; Mayor's Cmt. for Int. Friendship, 68-69. Actor and stage crewman, Lincoln Commun. Playhouse; lectr, Nebr. Boys' State, 9 years. Rel: Presbyterian. Mailing Add: 4705 South St, Lincoln, Nebr. 68506.

HASSENPLUG, RICHARD DOSS R
Mem, Calif. Rep. State Cent. Cmt.
b. Johnstown, Pa, 8/7/27; s. Homer H. Hassenplug and Margaret E. Coley H; m. 5/31/63 to Carla R. Lappin; c. Gunnar Wolfgang. Educ: Tulane Univ, B.A, 53, LL.B, 55; Order of Coif; Tulane Law Rev. Polit. & Govt. Pos: Mem, Calif. Rep. State Cent. Cmt, 69- Bus. & Prof. Pos: Partner, law firm, Hassenplug & Higuchi, 64-; dir, Southwest Criminal Bar Asn, 69. Mil. Serv: Entered as Seaman, Navy, 44, released as EM 3/C, 46, after serv. in U.S.S. Strickland DE 333, European & Pac. Theaters; entered Marines, 47, released as Cpl, 50. Mem: Calif. State and South Bay Bar Asns; Southwest Criminal Bar Asn. Rel: Protestant. Legal Res: 5034 Deelane St, Torrance, Calif. 90503. Mailing Add: 1515 Redondo Beach Blvd, Gardena, Calif. 90247.

HASSLER, JOHN DAVID D
Chmn, Pickett Co. Dem. Exec. Cmt, Tenn.
b. Byrdstown, Tenn, 9/15/19; s. Landon B. 'Spike' Hassler and Laura Gunnels H; m. 6/1/43 to Robbie C. Wells. Educ: Pickett Co. Elem. Schs. and Putnam Co. Inst. Polit. & Govt. Pos: Field supvr, State Hwy. Dept, Tenn. and chmn, Pickett Co. Dem. Exec. Cmt, Tenn, 53- Bus. & Prof. Pos: Co-owner, Hassler-Baker Hardware and Implement Co; cattle farmer. Mil. Serv: Entered as Pvt, Army, 42, released as Sgt, 46, after serv. in Serv. Command Unit 1474. Mem: Army adv. cmt, 3rd U.S. Army, 52-; chmn, Cordell Hull Mem; past Post Comdr, past Adj. and past Dist. Comdr, Am. Legion; past Master, Masonic Lodge; K.T. York Rite Mason; Scottish Rite (32°); Shrine. Rel: Christian Church. Mailing Add: P.O. Box 1, Byrdstown, Tenn. 38549.

HASTE, JAMES FRANCIS R
Committeeman, Ill. Rep. State Cent. Cmt.
b. Rockford, Ill, 8/7/07; s. Richard Haste and Sarah Kelley H; m. 6/24/39 to Marion Worden. Educ: High sch grad; 1 year of col. Polit. & Govt. Pos: Alderman, Third Ward, Rockford, Ill, 29-45; secy, Winnebago Co. Rep. Cent. Cmt, 36 years, precinct committeeman, 31-67; chmn, Police and Fire Cmn. of Rockford, 55-59; committeeman, Ill. Rep. State Cent. Cmt, 60- Bus. & Prof. Pos: Sales rep, Smith Oil Corp, 35 years, asst. v.pres. in charge fuel oil sales, currently. Mil. Serv: Pvt, Army, 43-45. Mem: Pres, Oil Fuel Inst. Ill; Am. Legion; Elks; 40 et 8; K. of C; Univ. Club; C. of C.(former dir, 8 years, v.pres, 2 years). Rel: Roman Catholic. Mailing Add: 1919 Hillside Dr, Rockford, Ill. 61107.

HASTINGS, JAMES FRED R
U.S. Rep, N.Y.
b. Olean, N.Y, 4/10/26; s. Glenn Tracy Hastings and Ruth Elizabeth Trail H; m. 9/24/47 to Barbara Louise Gaylor; c. Linda Ann, Karen Diane, James Robert, David Michael and Tracy Eileen. Educ: High Sch. Polit. & Govt. Pos: Mem, Town Bd, Allegany, N.Y, 53-62; police justice, Allegany, 56-62; N.Y. State Assemblyman, 63-65; N.Y. State Sen, 66-68; alternate del, Rep. Nat. Conv, 68; U.S. Rep, N.Y, 38th Dist, 69- Bus. & Prof. Pos: Advert. and sales, Proctor & Gamble Distributing Co, 48-51; mgr. and v.pres, Radio Sta. WHDL, 52-67; nat. advert. mgr. and secy, Olean Times Herald Corp, 57-67. Mil. Serv: Entered as A/S, Navy, 43, released as PO 2/C, 46. Mem: Am. Legion; Amvets; Mason; dir, Ment. Health Asn, Children Asn. and Recreation Cmn. Rel: Methodist. Legal Res: 124 Second St, Allegany, N.Y. 14706. Mailing Add: 1107 Longworth House Office Bldg, Washington, D.C. 20515.

HASTINGS, JOSEPH HENRY R
Chmn, Lake Co. Rep. Cmt, Mich.
b. Luther, Mich, 6/3/24; s. John Percy Hastings, Sr. and Irene Sibary; m. 12/25/43 to Mary Ellen Foster; c. Sharon Kay (Mrs. Floyd Coon), Joseph H, Jr. and Mark S. Educ: Luther Agri. Sch, grad, 44. Polit. & Govt Pos: Village councilman, Luther, Mich, 46-47 & 50-60, village marshal and fire chief, 47-49; mem, Luther Commun. Sch. Bd, 56-62 and pres, 2 years; chmn, Lake Co. Rep. Cmt, 67- Mem: Mason; F&AM; committeeman, Luther Boy Scouts; Luther Cub Scouts. Originator and Dir, Recreational Prog. for Luther Area, 20 years; Organized Benefits for Crippled Children; numerous other civic activities. Rel: Protestant. Mailing Add: 310 State St, Luther, Mich. 49656.

HASTINGS, WILMOT REED R
Exec. Asst. to Under Secy. of State
b. Salem, Mass, 5/29/35; s. Abner Horace Hastings and Florence Leslie Hylan H; m. 8/30/58 to Joan Amory Loomis; c. W. Reed, Jr, Melissa Hylan and Claire Amory. Educ: Harvard Col, A.B. magna cum laude, 57; Univ. Paris, 57-58; Harvard Law Sch, LL.B. magna cum laude, 61; ed, Harvard Law Rev. Polit. & Govt. Pos: Law clerk to Chief Justice Raymond S. Wilkins, Mass, 61-62; first asst. and dep. attorney gen, Mass, 68-69; spec. asst. and exec. asst. to Under Secy. of State, Wash, D.C, 69- Bus. & Prof. Pos: Assoc. lawyer, Bingham, Dana & Gould, Boston, Mass, 62-68. Publ: Book rev, Harvard Law Rev, 62. Rel: Protestant. Mailing Add: 4866 Reservoir Rd. N.W, Washington, D.C. 20007.

HASWELL, FRANK I.
Assoc. Justice, Montana Supreme Court
b. Great Falls, Mont, 4/6/18; s. Irvin A. Haswell and Laura Cool H; m. 5/5/51 to June Arnold; c. Frank Warren, Bruce Douglas and John Richard. Educ: Univ. Montana, 37-39, LL.B, 47; Univ. Wash, B.A, 41; Phi Sigma Kappa. Polit. & Govt. Pos: City Attorney, Whitefish, Mont, 48-51; Dist. Judge, 11th Judicial Dist, Mont, 58-67; Assoc. Justice, Montana Supreme Court, 67- Mil. Serv: Entered as Pvt, Marines, 43, released as Cpl, 46, after serv. in various units in Pacific, 43-46. Mem: Montana Judges Asn.(pres, 69-); Am. and Mont. Bar Asns; Am. Judicature Soc; Elks, Eagles, Rotary. Rel: Protestant. Mailing Add: 1370 Munger Lane, Helena, Mont. 59601.

HATCH, FRANCIS WHITING, JR. R
Mass. State Rep.
b. Cambridge, Mass, 5/6/25; s. Francis W. Hatch and Marjorie H; m. 10/25/52 to Serena Merck; c. Timothy, Serena, Francis W, III, George and Olivia. Educ: Harvard Col, B.A, 44. Polit. & Govt. Pos: Alderman, Beverly, Mass, 57-62; committeeman, Mass. Rep. State Cmt, 60-64; Mass. State Rep, Third Essex Dist, 62-; del, Rep. Nat. Conv, 68. Bus. & Prof. Pos: Reporter, Minneapolis Star and Tribune, 46-48, nat. advert. salesman, 48-50; v.pres, Subwsan Centers Trust, 51-54; dir. advert. and pub. rels, New Eng. Mutual Life Ins, 54-62. Mil. Serv: Navy, 44-46, Ens, serv. in U.S.S. Pensacola, Pac; Two Campaign Stars; Purple Heart. Sears Roebuck Found, Regional Conserv. Award, 66; New Eng. Wildflower Soc. Conserv. Medal. Rel: Protestant. Mailing Add: Preston Place, Beverly Farms, Mass. 01915.

HATCH, MIKE W. D
b. Bancroft, Idaho, 4/8/31; s. Asa F. Hatch and Elizabeth Whitworth H; m. 8/5/53 to Donna Marie Hogan; c. Terry Mike, Lisa Marie, Chris W. and Mike

W, Jr. Educ: Ricks Col, 49-50 & 54-56; Utah State Univ, B.S, 57; Univ. Utah, M.S, 66. Polit. & Govt. Pos: Chmn, Caribou Co. Dem. Party, Idaho, 66-68. Mil. Serv: Entered as E-2, Army, 53, released as Sgt, 54, after serv. in Second Inf. Div, Qm. Co, Sixth Army; Good Conduct Medal. Mem: Pres, King Creek Grazing Asn, Inc, 68-; Farm Bur. Fedn. Rel: Latter-day Saint. Mailing Add: Bancroft, Idaho 83217.

HATCH, STANLEY CRAIG D
Chmn, Santa Barbara Co. Dem. Cent. Cmt, Calif.
b. Logan, Utah, 1/16/34; s. Adrian William Hatch and Marjorie Webb H; m. 2/7/58 to Anne Lorraine Burnham; c. Christine Elizabeth. Educ: Utah State Univ, B.S, 55; Harvard Law Sch, J.D, 58; Marriner S. Eccles scholarship, 54; Harvard Law Sch. scholarship, 55-58; Phi Kappa Phi; Pi Sigma Alpha; Blue Key; Sigma Chi. Polit. & Govt. Pos: Dep. dist. attorney and dep. co. counsel, Santa Barbara Co, Calif, 61-65, legis. advocate, 62-65; mem, Calif. State Dem. Cent. Cmt, 64-, chmn. bylaws cmt. and mem. steering cmt. of exec. cmt, 66-68, mem. exec. cmt, 66-; mem, Santa Barbara Co. Dem. Cent. Cmt, 64-, chmn, 66-; del, Dem. Nat. Conv, 68. Bus. & Prof. Pos: Research attorney, U.S. Dept. Justice, Wash, D.C, 57; attorney, Hatch, Parent & Abbott, Santa Barbara, Calif, 65- Mil. Serv: Entered as 2nd Lt, Air Force, 58, released as Capt, 60, after serving in Strategic Air Command-8th Air Force, Can. and Air Defense Command, West. Air Defense Command, Calif, 58-60; Capt, Air Force Res, 60-; Distinguished mil. student, 58. Mem: Santa Barbara Co. Bar Asn; State Bar of Calif, Bar U.S. Supreme Court, Calif. Supreme Court, Ninth Circuit Court of Appeals and Fed. Dist. Court, North. Dist. Calif; Santa Barbara Young Attorney's Club; Channel City Club. Named Outstanding Young Men of Am, Compilation, 67. Rel: Protestant. Legal Res: 959 Cheltenham Rd, Santa Barbara, Calif. 93105. Mailing Add: Box 838, Santa Barbara, Calif. 93102.

HATCHER, JAMES GERALD D
b. Peoria, Ill, 6/18/34; s. James Gregson Hatcher and Helen Cannon H; m. 3/25/61 to Joan Margaret-Mary Glückert; c. Julia Catherine and Maria Elizabeth. Educ: Harvard Col, B.A, 56; Columbia Law Sch, LL.B, 63; Columbia Univ. int. fel; Hasty Pudding Club. Polit. & Govt. Pos: Law clerk, U.S. Dist. Court, Portland, Ore, 63-64; asst. states attorney, Tazewell Co, Ill, 65; asst. U.S. attorney, Peoria, 65-68; Dem. cand. for U.S. Cong, 18th Cong. Dist, Ill, 68; precinct committeeman, Dem. Party, Morton, currently. Bus. & Prof. Pos: Attorney, 68- Mil. Serv: Entered as Pvt, Officers Cand. Sch, Marines, 56, released as 1st Lt, 59, after serv. in 1st Marine Air Wing, Japan, 57-59; Capt, Marine Res, 59- Mem: Peoria, Tazewell Co. and Ill. Bar Asns; Am. Acad. Polit. Sci; Optimist; Morton Active Citizens; Jaycees. Rel: Protestant. Mailing Add: 608 E. Adams, Morton, Ill. 61550.

HATCHER, RICHARD G. D
Mayor, Gary, Ind.
b. Michigan City, Ind, 7/10/33; s. Carlton Hatcher and Catherine H. Educ: Ind. Univ, B.A; Valparaiso Univ, LL.B. Hon. doctorates, Duquesne and Fisk Univs. Polit. & Govt. Pos: Former dep. prosecutor, Lake Co, Ind; councilman-at-lg, city coun, Gary, Ind, 63-66, mayor, 67-; chmn, Nat. Cmt. on Inquiry and mem, Nat. Steering Cmt, Urban Coalition. Bus. & Prof. Pos: Admitted to Ind. bar and practiced in East Chicago, Ind. Mem: Muigwithania. Mailing Add: City Hall, 401 Broadway, Gary, Ind. 46402.

HATCHETT, TEXANNA L. R
Okla. State Rep.
b. Skiatook, Okla, 1/19/26; d. Elsie Raymond Smith (deceased) and Lona Sisson S; m. to Don Hatchett; c. Cynthia Leigh and Donna Ann. Educ: Okla. City Univ, B.S. in Econ, 62; Univ. Okla, M.A. in Econ, 64, Ph.D. cand; scholarships and grad. asst, Univ. Okla; Beta Gamma; Omicron Delta Epsilon (secy, 63). Polit. & Govt. Pos: Chmn. subcmt. on revenue, Mayors Cmt, Oklahoma City, 62; Rep. area chmn, Okla. Co, 62-66, precinct chmn, 62-68, div. chmn, 66-68; secy. to Rep. Caucus, Okla. House of Rep, 66-67; Okla. State Rep, Dist. 84, 67- Mem: Am. Econ. Asn; Nat. Order of Women Legislators; Am. Asn. Univ. Women; Am. Acad. Polit. and Soc. Sci; Okla. PTA. Dr. David P. Delorme Mem. Award in Econ, Okla. City Univ; First Woman to be Mem. of Okla. House of Rep. Leadership. Rel: Baptist. Mailing Add: 3133 N.W. 12th St, Oklahoma City, Okla. 73107.

HATFIELD, MARK ODOM R
U.S. Sen, Ore.
b. Dallas, Ore, 7/12/22; s. Charles Dolan Hatfield and Dovie Odom H; m. 7/8/58 to Antoinette Kuzmanich; c. Elizabeth, Mark O, Jr, Charles Vincent and Theresa. Educ: Willamette Univ, B.A, 43; Stanford Univ, A.M, 48; Beta Theta Pi. Polit. & Govt. Pos: Ore. State Rep, 51-55; del, Rep. Nat. Conv, 52, 56, 60, 64 & 68, mem, Conv. Resolutions Cmt, 52 & 56, chmn, Ore. Del, 60, 64 & 68, keynoter, 64, nominator for Richard M. Nixon, 60 and seconded Nixon's nomination, 68; Ore. State Sen, 55-57; Secy. of State, Ore, 57-59, Gov, 59-67; U.S. Sen, Ore, 67- Mil. Serv: Entered as Midn, Navy, 43, released as Lt.(jg), 46, after serv. at Iwo Jima and Okinawa, S.Pac. & Far East Theaters, 45; Pac. Theater Ribbon. Mem: Mason; Shrine; Am. Legion; Grange. Rel: Baptist. Legal Res: P.O. Box 2308, Salem, Ore. 97308. Mailing Add: 6809 Selkirk Dr, Bethesda, Md. 20034.

HATFIELD, MARSHAL JOE R
Chmn, McLean Co. Rep. Cmt, Ky.
b. Livermore, Ky, 3/8/38; s. J. B. Hatfield and Josephine Porter H; m. 8/16/57 to Elizabeth Sue Nantz; c. Steven Lynn and David Allan. Educ: Livermore High Sch. Polit. & Govt. Pos: Chmn, McLean Co. Rep. Cmt, 64- Bus. & Prof. Pos: Cashier, Farmers & Merchants Bank, 68- Mem: C. of C; Livermore Loin Club (pres). Rel: Baptist. Mailing Add: R.R. 3, Utica Ky. 42376.

HATHAWAY, DONALD H. R
Mem, N.Dak. Rep. State Cent. Cmt.
b. Kingsley, Iowa, 12/18/14; s. Ray Hathaway and Anna Brewster H; m. 12/28/46 to Helen Wyman; c. Thomas and Richard. Educ: Beach High Sch. Polit. & Govt. Pos: Co-chmn, Rep. Cmt, 59-60; mem, N.Dak. Rep. State Cent. Cmt, 60-; chmn, Twp. Bd, 61-66 and Bd. of Educ, 62-66; mem, N.Dak. Rep. State Exec. Cmt, 63-65; alternate del, Rep. Nat. Conv, 64; mem, N.Dak. Sch. Bds. Legis. Cmt, 68-69. Bus. & Prof. Pos: Farmer, 36- Mil. Serv: Entered as Pvt, Army, 42, released as Capt, 46, after serv. in 42nd Rainbow Inf, ETO; Combat Inf. Badge; ETO Ribbon with Two Clusters; Good Conduct Medal; Army Occupation Medal; Letter of Commendation. Mem: Mason; Am. Legion. Rel: Congregational. Mailing Add: Beach, N.Dak. 58621.

HATHAWAY, LOIS EILEEN D
V.Chmn, Porter Co. Dem. Cmt, Ind.
b. Valparaiso, Ind, 1/2/22; d. Louis Clarence Henderlong and Mary Finn H; m. 6/12/48 to J. Paul Hathaway. Educ: Liberty High Sch, Valparaiso, Ind. Polit. & Govt. Pos: Precinct committeeman, Porter Co, Ind, 60-; secy, Porter Co. Dem. Party, 60-64; v.chmn, Porter Co. Dem. Cmt, 64- Mem: North Porter Co. Dem. Women's Club; Westchester Dem. Women's Club. Mailing Add: 414 Bowser Ave, Chesterton, Ind. 46304.

HATHAWAY, MICHAEL DAVID R
Mem, Prince Georges Co. Rep. Cent. Cmt, Md.
b. Washington, D.C, 1/5/37; s. George Edward Hathaway and Jeanette Forsythe H; m. 9/7/57 to Ellen Louise Hagedorn; c. Michael Stuart, David Brian and Edward John. Educ: Univ. Md, B.S. in Aeronaut. Eng, 59; Scabbard and Blade. Polit. & Govt. Pos: Mem, Prince Georges Co. Rep. Cent. Cmt, Md, 66-, chmn, 68. Bus. & Prof. Pos: Engr, Douglas Aircraft Co, Santa Monica, Calif, 59-60; sr. engr, Space Div, Chrysler Corp, New Orleans, La, 62-65; pres, United Int. Corp, Wash, D.C, 65- Mem: Opers. Research Soc. Am; Inst. Elec. and Electronic Engrs; Am. Ord. Asn; Air Force Asn. Mailing Add: 9535 Nottingham Dr, Upper Marlboro, Md. 20870.

HATHAWAY, ROBERT RICHARD D
b. Nogales, Ariz, 7/31/30; s. William Harrison Hathaway and Mary McIntyre H; m. 12/23/50 to Laura Ellen Hill; c. Diane Susan, Mary Ellen, Evangeline Anne, Rosalie Lorraine and Robert William. Educ: Univ. Ariz, 1 year. Polit. & Govt. Pos: Former mem. sch. bd, Dist. 28, Santa Cruz Co, Ariz; Ariz. State Rep, 55-64; Ariz. State Sen, 65-67; co. assessor, Santa Cruz Co, 68- Bus. & Prof. Pos: Dir, Security Savings & Loan Asn, Nogales, Ariz, 66- Mil. Serv: Entered Nat. Guard, 48, released as Capt, Army Res. Mem: Dir, South. Ariz. Cattle Protective Asn. Rel: Protestant. Legal Res: Duquesne Rd, Nogales, Ariz. 85621. Mailing Add: Box K, Nogales, Ariz. 85621.

HATHAWAY, STANLEY K. R
Gov, Wyoming
b. Osceola, Nebr, 7/19/24; s. Franklin E. Hathaway and Velma Holbrook H; m. 11/25/48 to Roberta Harley; c. Susan and Sandra. Educ: Univ. Wyo, 42-43; Univ. Nebr, A.B, 48, LL.B, 50; Delta Theta Phi; Sigma Chi. Polit. & Govt. Pos: Prosecuting attorney, Goshen Co, Wyo, 54-62; nat. committeeman, Young Rep. Fedn, 58-60; committeeman, Wyo. State Rep. Party, 60-62, chmn. and secy, 62-64; chmn, Goshen Co. Rep. Party, 62-64; Gov, Wyo, 67-; del, Rep. Nat. Conv, 68. Mil. Serv: Entered as Pvt, Air Force, 43, released as T/Sgt, 45, after serv. in 8th Air Force, ETO, 44-45; 5 Air Medals and ETO Campaign Ribbon. Mem: Am. and Wyo. Bar Asns; pres, Wyo. Co. Attorneys Asn, 61; Am. Legion; VFW; Lions Int; AF&AM; Elks; Moose. Rel: Episcopal. Mailing Add: 219 Linda Vista, Torrington, Wyo. 82240.

HATHAWAY, WILLIAM DODD D
U.S. Rep, Maine
b. Cambridge, Mass, 2/21/24; m. Aug. 1945 to Mary Lee Bird; c. Susan Louise and Fred William. Educ: Harvard Col, grad, 49, Harvard Law Sch, grad, 53. Polit. & Govt. Pos: Asst. co. attorney, Androscoggin Co, Maine, 55-57; hearing exam. for State Liquor Cmn, 57-61; del, Dem. Nat. Conv, 64 & 68; U.S. Rep, Maine, 65- Mil. Serv: Army Air Force, 42-46. Mem: Am, State and Co. Bar Asns; Maine Med-Legal Soc; bd. dir, Lewiston-Auburn Chap. of Am. Red Cross and Lewiston-Auburn Asn. for Retarded Children; div. chmn, Lewiston-Auburn United Fund. Rel: Episcopal. Legal Res: Auburn, Maine 04210. Mailing Add: 6707 Wemberley Way, McLean, Va. 22101.

HATHORN, BYRON C. R
Mem, Windsor Co. Rep. Cmt, Vt.
b. Hartford, Vt, 7/1/28; s. George B. Hathorn and Elizabeth Cope H; m. 8/21/48 to Jean W. Gates; c. Byron C, Jr, Patricia J, Roberta E, Robert E. and Mary E. Educ: Norwich Univ, 47-48. Polit. & Govt. Pos: Mem, Hartford Rep. Town Cmt, 56-; mem, Bd. of Selectmen, Hartford, 58-64 and chmn, 60-64; Vt. State Rep, 61-69, chmn, Ways and Means Cmt, Vt. House of Rep, 65 and State and Court Expenses Cmt, 66, v.chmn, Rules Cmt, 66; mem, Vt. Young Rep, 61-; exec. secy, Vermonters for Rockefeller, 63-64; chmn, Munic. Corp, 63-64; campaign dir, Ralph Foote for Gov, 64; consult, Vt. Tax Dept, 65; mem, Emergency Bd, 65; mem, Windsor Co. Rep. Cmt, 65- Bus. & Prof. Pos: Dir, Coop. Ins. Co. of Vt, 64- Mem: Elks; past pres, PTA; Holstein Friesian Asn. of Am; dir, New Eng. Holstein Asn, 63-65; pres, Vt. Holstein Club, 63-65; Farm Bur. Rel: Congregational. Mailing Add: R.F.D. 1, White River Junction, Vt. 05001. (1967)

HAUF, OTTO D
b. Max, N.Dak, 12/11/08; s. Christian Hauf and Helena Henchel H; m. 6/11/34 to Alice M. Wolter; c. Marion Jane (Mrs. Dick Burgess), Edward, Ronald, Kenneth, Margaret and Darlene. Educ: McLean Co. Schs. Polit. & Govt. Pos: Popular Twp. Clerk, N.Dak, 44-52; N.Dak. State Rep, 59-66, chmn, Legis. Research Coun. Cmt. on Educ, mem, Subcmt. on Taxation and mem. Full Cmt. State Legis. Research Coun, N.Dak. State House of Rep; bin storage supvr, Agr. Stabilization & Conserv. Serv, State Dept. Agr, Minot, N.Dak, currently. Bus. & Prof. Pos: Life-time farmer; dir, McLean Elec. Coop, 42-; secy. and dir, Equity Farmers Elevator, 48- Publ: 'Tension Breakers, and other poems relating to kind of debate in N.Dak. House of Rep, 59-65. Mem: Leader, 4-H, 48-54; Max Civic Club. Presented mkt. plan to U.S. Senate Agr. Cmt, 59. Rel: Lutheran. Mailing Add: 1108 Seventh St. S.W, Minot, N.Dak. 58701.

HAUGEN, DONNELL WILFRED D
b. Roseglen, N.Dak, 1/24/07; s. John Nels Haugen and Christine Severina Jacobson H; m. 6/12/38 to Anna Marie Fines; c. Bernard Jon, Ronald Kent and Barbara Ann (Mrs. Ziegler). Educ: Ryder High Sch, N.Dak, grad. Polit. & Govt. Pos: N.Dak. State Rep, 41-53, N.Dak. Dem. Non-Partisan League Floor Leader, N.Dak. House of Rep, 47-53; legis. asst. to Congressman Usher

L. Burdick, Wash, D.C, 49-50; del, Dem. Nat. Conv, 68. Bus. & Prof. Pos: Secy, Farmers Union Oil Co, Ryder, N.Dak, 36-49, Farmers Union Elevator Co, 38-49; pres, Reservation Tel. Coop, Parshall, 51-; secy-treas, West McLean Co. Farmers Mutual Ins. Co, Roseglen, 53- Mem: Sons of Norway; Farmers Union; Nat. Farmers Orgn; Roseglen Commun. Club. Rel: Lutheran. Mailing Add: Roseglen, N.Dak. 58775.

HAUGEN, ROY S. D
Mem, Cumberland Co. Dem. Cmt, Maine
b. Portland, Maine, 9/10/33; s. Hans A. Haugen and Elfrida T. Seterdal H; single. Educ: Ind. Inst. Tech, Ft. Wayne, Ind, B.S. in math, 62. Polit. & Govt. Pos: Mem, S. Portland Dem. City Cmt, Maine, 63-; mem, Cumberland Co. Dem. Cmt, 64-; Maine State Rep, 65-67. Mil. Serv: Entered as A/S E-1, Navy, 52, released as Electronics Tech. 3/C E-4, 56. Rel: Lutheran. Mailing Add: 254 Pine St, South Portland, Maine 04106.

HAUGERUD, NEIL SHERMAN D
Minn. State Rep.
b. Canton Twp, Fillmore Co, Minn, 7/3/30; s. Allen Sherman Haugerud and Anna Armstrong H; m. 6/5/54 to Helen Arlene Anderson; c. Renee Lynn, Susan Kay, Thomas Neil and Karen Marie. Educ: Winona State Teachers Col; Univ. Minn, Minneapolis. Polit. & Govt. Pos: Co. Sheriff, Fillmore Co, Minn, 58-66; Minn. State Rep, Dist. 1A, Preston, 68- Bus. & Prof. Pos: Ins. agent, Haugerud Ins. Agency, 56-58; investment broker, John G. Kinnard & Co, Minneapolis, 66- Mil. Serv: Entered as Pvt, Marines, 48, released as Sgt, 52, after serv. in Ord. Div, Second Marines, 51-52. Mem: Hon. life mem, Minn. State Sheriffs Asn; Am. Legion; Lions; Toastmasters. Rel: Lutheran. Mailing Add: Preston, Minn. 55965.

HAUGH, JOHN H. R
Ariz. State Rep.
b. Clinton, Iowa, 11/1/10; s. John Aloyisus Haugh and Paula Harms H; m. 12/2/39 to Emilie Loucille Johnson; c. William and Emilie and stepsons Clyde and Carl Skinner. Educ: Lake Forest Col, 27-29; Univ. Calif, Los Angeles, 31; Univ. Ariz; Nat. Forensic League; Kappa Sigma. Polit. & Govt. Pos: Precinct committeeman, Rep. Party, Ariz, 50-66; del, Rep. Nat. Conv, 56, 60 & 64, participant, 68, mem. platform cmt, 60; Ariz. State Rep, 52-, Rep. Floor Leader, Ariz. House Rep, 56-62, Asst. Majority Floor Leader, 63-64, Majority Leader, 65-66, Speaker of the House, 69-; Rep. Nat. Committeeman, Ariz, currently; mem, Rep. Nat. Cmt. Task Force Constitutional Rev. at State Level, 67-68. Bus. & Prof. Pos: Dir, Fats & Protein Research Inc, 62-; dir, Tucson Gas & Elec. Co; pres, Tucson Tallow Co, Inc; trustee, Lake Forest Col. Mem: Nat. Renderers Asn.(pres, 62-63); Rotary. Rel: Episcopal. Mailing Add: 5705 N. Campbell Ave, Tucson, Ariz. 85718.

HAUGHEY, JAMES McCREA R
Minority Leader, Mont. State Senate
b. Courtland, Kans, 7/8/14; s. Leo E. Haughey and Elizabeth Stephens H; m. 9/8/38 to Katherine Hurd; c. Katherine Loo, Bruce Stephens and John Caldwell. Educ: Univ. Kans, LL.B, 39; Phi Delta Theta; Phi Delta Phi. Polit. & Govt. Pos: Mont. State Rep, 61-65; Mont. State Sen, 67-, Minority Leader, Mont. State Senate, 69- Bus. & Prof. Pos: Lawyer and partner, Crowley, Kilbourne, Haughey, Hanson & Gallagher, 43- Publ: Examination of Title to Federal Oil and Gas Leases, First Annual Rocky Mt. Mineral Law Inst, 55; 'Calligraphy, the Gracile Art of the Broad Pen,' Mont. Arts, 8/67. Mem: Rocky Mt. Mineral Law Found.(pres, 57-58); Am. Watercolor Soc; Am. Artists Prfnl. League; Lions; Yellowstone Art Center Found.(pres, 69-). Permanent Collection and Fel. Awards, Mont. Inst. Arts. Rel: Episcopal. Legal Res: 2205 Tree Lane, Billings, Mont. 59102. Mailing Add: P.O. Box 2529, Billings, Mont. 59103.

HAUGLAND, BRYNHILD R
N.Dak. State Rep.
b. Minot, N.Dak, 7/28/05; d. Nels Haugland and Sigurda Ringoen H; single. Educ: Minot State Col, B.A; Delta Kappa Gamma. Polit. & Govt. Pos: N.Dak. State Rep, 39-, chmn, Cmt. on Soc. Welfare, mem, Legis. Research Cmt; mem, Ward Co. Zoning Cmn, 9 years; mem, Gov. Cmn. on Status of Women; v.chmn, State Adv. Coun. for Hosp. and Related Construction; chmn. Adv. Coun. to State Unemployment Compensation Div. and State Employ. Serv. Div, Workmen's Compensation Bur. Mem: Quota Club; Bus. & Prfnl. Women's Club; 1st v.pres, Int. Peace Garden and bd. mem, 10 years; bd. dir, Minot State Col. Alumni Asn, Lutheran Home, Inc. and Ward Co. Ment. Health Asn; Adv. Coun. to Minot Area Soc. Serv. Cent. Named Minot Woman of Year, 56. Rel: Lutheran. Legal Res: Farm Harrison Twp, Ward Co, Minot, N.Dak. 58701. Mailing Add: P.O. Box 1684, Minot, N.Dak. 58701. (1967)

HAUKAP, EDWARD RALPH D
Chmn, Clinton Co. Dem. Cmt, Ill.
b. Germantown, Ill, 6/14/16; s. Frank Haukap and Helen Korte H; m. 11/23/43 to Marcella Kues; c. Edward J, Connie M, Michael J. and Dale. Polit. & Govt. Pos: Chmn, Clinton Co. Dem. Cmt, Ill, currently; secy, State Drivers License Div, 64-65; mem, Ill. Dem. State Cent. Cmt, currently. Bus. & Prof. Pos: Mem. staff, State Hwy. Dept, Dist. Eight, Ill, 61-64, maintenance foreman, 65- Mem: K. of C; Moose. Rel: Roman Catholic. Mailing Add: Oak St, Aviston, Ill. 62261. (1967)

HAUSBECK, ALBERT J. D
N.Y. State Assemblyman
b. Buffalo, N.Y, 2/15/18; s. Joseph J. Hausbeck and Manetta Van Dusen H; m. 10/7/39 to Rita Ross; c. Joseph J, Jr. and Patricia Ann. Educ: Hurst Bus. Sch; Univ. Buffalo. Polit. & Govt. Pos: Dir, Cmt. on Recreation for Elderly, Buffalo, N.Y, 57-61; N.Y. State Assemblyman, 60-67 and currently. Bus. & Prof. Pos: Merchandise mgr, Sattlers Dept. Store, 51-54 and S.M. Flickinger Co, 54-57; exec. v.pres, Airway Hotels, Inc, BAW Construction Co. and Cent. Park Shopping Center, currently. Mem: Past pres, Buffalo Lions; Buffalo Trap & Field; Elks; Buffalo Eye Bank; Schuhplatters Gebirgstracten Berein Edelweiss; Buffalo Athletic Club; C. of C; Fillmore-Cent. Park Businessmen's Asn; hon. chmn Cent. Park Little League Baseball and Football and Jr. Buffalo Bills Football League. Rel: Roman Catholic. Mailing Add: 315 Dartmouth Ave, Buffalo, N.Y. 14215. (1967)

HAUSER, FREDERICK HOWARD D
N.J. State Sen.
b. Brooklyn, N.Y, 5/15/00; m. 1925 to Edna Weihe. Educ: N.Y. Univ, B.A, M.A. and J.D; Phi Kappa Alpha; pres, N.Y. Univ. Athletic Asn. and N.Y. Univ. YMCA Coun; ed-in-chief, univ. newspaper, New Yorker. Polit. & Govt. Pos: N.J. State Assemblyman, 47-66, Speaker, N.J. Gen. Assembly, 66; chmn, N.J. Law Rev. and Legis. Serv. Cmt, 60-67; Acting Gov, N.J, 66; N.J. State Sen, 67- Bus. & Prof. Pos: Counsr-at-law, N.J. and N.Y; former reporter, N.Y. World; former v.prin. and asst. to supt, Hoboken Pub. Schs, N.J; former instr. Am. hist, Hoboken High Sch; prof. law of property, John Marshall Law Sch, 29-49. Mil. Serv: Army, World War I and World War II, serv. in Staff Judge Adv, 78th Inf. Div, 44th Inf. Div. and Coastal and Harbor Defenses of N.Y, Phila, Chesapeake Bay and Southeast. U.S, acting chief of mil. justice, Off. of Judge Adv. Gen; Col, Judge Adv. Gen. Dept, Army Res, currently; World War I and World War II Victory Medals; Am. Defense and Am. Theatre Medals; Army Commendation Medal. Mem: Hudson Co. and N.J. Bar Asns; U.S. Judge Advocate Asn; Am. Legion (comdr, Hoboken Post, 26-28, comdr, Hudson Co. Cmt, 28-29, state v.chmn, 30-31, mem. nat. distinguished guests cmt, 36-, exec. cmt, nat. legis. conf, 61-66, nat. v.pres, 63-64, nat. pres, 64-65); Mason; Elks; N.J. Educ. Asn; ROA. Rel: Episcopal. Mailing Add: 1000 Hudson St, Hoboken, N.J. 07030.

HAUSEY, WILLIE ROBERT D
b. McManus, La, 1/26/33; s. Joseph Burnell Hausey and Eva D. Mathews H; m. 5/6/61 to Bettye Jean Ponton-Nixon; c. Frond Geleé and Rodney Keith. Educ: South. Univ. Polit. & Govt. Pos: Pres, Dem. Club, Sacramento, Calif, 62, 65 & 69; mem, Co. Dem. Cent. Cmt, 67-68; mem, Calif. Dem. State Cent. Cmt, 67-69; pres, Del Paso Heights Dem. Club, 68; mem, Welfare Cmn, Sacramento, 69. Bus. & Prof. Pos: Owner, Standard Sta, 61-69, Coop Rock Liquor Store, 67-69, Commun. Coop. Orgn, 67-69, and Thirty Store, 68-69. Mil. Serv: Entered as Pvt, Army, 53, released as Sgt, 55, after serv. in Eighth Army; Service, Conduct and Korean War Medals. Mem: Businessmen's Cmt; Optimist; Toastmasters; W.Coast South. Univ. Alumni; Am. Legion; Mason. Five year Certificate, Standard Oil; Neighborhood Sch. Awards; Commun. Serv. Award. Rel: Methodist. Mailing Add: 3844 Alder St, Sacramento, Calif. 95838.

HAUSMAN, HOWARD E. R
Chmn, Rep. State Cent. Cmt, Conn.
Educ: Grad. Yale Col, 29 and Yale Law Sch, 31. Polit. & Govt. Pos: Exec. dir, Employ. Security Div, State Labor Dept, 39-55; research chmn, Mayor Edward B. Scott, 54, Mayor Thomas J. Meskill, 62, Mayor Paul J. Manafort, 65 and Representative Thomas J. Meskill, 66; State Legis. Cmnr, 61-67; committeeman, Rep. State Cent. Cmt, Conn, until 67, chmn, 67-; del, Rep. Nat. Conv, 68; mem, Rep. Nat. Cmt, 68- Bus. & Prof. Pos: Attorney, New Britain, Conn, 55-; dir, Savings Bank New Britain, currently. Mil. Serv: Army Air Corps, 42-46. Mem: Trustee, Am. Cancer Soc, New Britain Chap; corporator, New Britain Gen. Hosp. Rel: Lutheran; Chmn. bldg. cmt, St. Matthew's Lutheran Church. Mailing Add: 410 Asylum St, Room 315, Hartford, Conn. 06103.

HAUSMAN, SAMUEL R
b. Austria, 11/14/97; s. Morris Hausman and Berthe Hoffman H; m. 5/4/24 to Vera Kuttler; c. Bruce Alan, Merna (Mrs. Richard Miller) and Alice (Mrs. Morton I. Davidson). Polit. & Govt. Pos: Alternate del, Rep. Nat. Conv, 68. Bus. & Prof. Pos: Chmn. bd, Belding Heminway Co. Inc, N.Y, 63 and Belding Hausman Fabrics, Inc, currently; dir, L.I. Lighting Co, Mineola, L.I. Mem: Hon. chmn. bd. United Jewish Appeal of Gr. N.Y; 1st v.pres, Beth Israel Med. Cent; trustee, Fedn. Jewish Philanthropies; dir, Nat. Jewish Welfare Bd; chmn, bd. Gov, Brotherhood In Action; dir, Am. Jewish Cmt; mem, N.Y. State Manpower Adv. Coun, 63; mem, Bus. Adv. Coun, Urban Develop. Corp, 68. Rel: Hebrew. Legal Res: 930 Fifth Ave, New York, N.Y. 10021. Mailing Add: 10 E. 32nd St, New York, N.Y. 10016.

HAUSMANN, C. STEWART R
Freeholder, Essex Co, N.J.
b. Orange, N.J, 10/18/22; s. Charles F. Hausmann and Christina Becker H; m. 8/6/44 to Lillian D'Addario; c. Charles S, Steven C. and Christine C. Educ: Upsala Col, A.B; Montclair State Col, M.A. Polit. & Govt. Pos: Mem, Bd. of Educ, Irvington, N.J, 58-64; freeholder, Essex Co, 67-, dir, Bd. of Freeholders, 68; del, Rep. Nat. Conv, 68. Bus. & Prof. Pos: Teacher, Irvington Pub. Schs, 47-53; self-employed mortician, 53- Mil. Serv: Entered as Aviation Cadet, Air Force as Pilot, 42, released as Lt, 45, after serv. in Air Transport Command, European and Am. Theatres, 44-45. Mem: Essex Co, N.J. and Nat. Funeral Dirs. Asns; Am. Legion; Lions; Elks; Mason; Shrine; Human Rels. Coun; Hist. Soc; PTA. Outstanding Young Man in N.J, Jaycees, 54; Civic Award, Irvington C. of C; Churchman of Year Award, Irvington Coun. Churches; Citizen of Year, B'nai B'rith; Layman's Award for Contributions to Educ, Essex Co. Educ. Asn; Jewish War Vet, Citizenship Award. Rel: Reformed Church. Mailing Add: 191 Park Place, Irvington, N.J. 07111.

HAVEN, IVAN BYRON D
b. Palmyra, Ill, 5/3/14; s. Issac B. Haven and Jennie Solomon H; m. 10/15/37 to Camella R. Bottini; c. Sandra Lee and Jeffrey L. Educ: Greenfield High Sch, Ill, grad, 33. Polit. & Govt. Pos: Del, Dem. Nat. Conv, 68; del. Tex. Dem. Conv, 68. Bus. & Prof. Pos: Union rep, OCAWIU-AFL-CIO, 46- Mem: OCAWIU-AFL-CIO; Jefferson Co. Dem. Rel: Baptist. Legal Res: 1021 Washington, Port Neches, Tex. 77651. Mailing Add: Box 762, Port Arthur, Tex. 77640.

HAVENS, FLORENCE L. R
Chmn, Stanton Co. Rep. Cmt, Nebr.
b. Stanton, Nebr, 11/7/31; d. Gus Bremer, Sr. and Anne Reiss B; m. 5/30/53 to Richard Lee Havens; c. Randy, Shelly, Joni Kay and James. Educ: Lindenwood Col, St. Charles, Mo; Drake Univ. Polit. & Govt. Pos: V.chmn, Stanton Co. Rep. Cmt, Nebr, 62-64 and chmn, 64- Mem: Pres, Stanton PTA, 65-67. Rel: Congregational. Mailing Add: 1205 Kingwood, Stanton, Nebr. 68779. (1967)

HAVER, MILDRED ALLISON 'MIDDY' R
Pres, Colo. Fedn. Rep. Women
b. McPherson, Kans, 8/12/26; d. John Benjamin Allison and Marn Jensen A;

m. 6/22/50 to Robert Thompson Haver; c. Frances Ann and Robert Thompson, Jr.(Tom). Educ: Kansas State Univ, B.S, 48; Claremont Grad. Sch, 49; Pi Beta Phi. Polit. & Govt. Pos: Mem. campaign staff, Robert T. Haver for State Rep, 60; Pueblo chmn, Door Bell Ringers for Dominick, 62; co-chmn, Pueblo Door to Door Campaign for Barry Goldwater, 64 and for Love, Allott, Enoch and Shoemaker, 66; mem, Pueblo Co. Rep. Exec. Cmt. and del, Nat. Fedn. Conv, 68; del, Rep. Nat. Conv, 68; mem. campaign staff, Rep. Party, Colo, 68; pres, Colo. Fedn. of Rep. Women and mem. bd, Nat. Fedn. of Rep. Women, 68- Bus. & Prof. Pos: Third grade teacher, Somerlid Sch, Pueblo, Colo, 50. Mem: Altar Guild of Ascension Episcopal Church, PEO, Pueblo Service League (life member), Bel Nor Rep. Women's Club, United Fund. Rel: Episcopal. Mailing Add: 1526 Alexander Circle, Pueblo, Colo. 81001.

HAVERFIELD, ROBERT METCALFE D
Fla. State Sen.
b. Cadiz, Ohio, 10/26/18; s. J. Craig Haverfield and Elizabeth Metcalfe H; m. to Shirley O'Connor; c. Betty Ann, Carol Lee and Jill O'Connor. Educ: Ohio State Univ, 39-42; Univ. Miami, B.B.A. & LL.B, 47; Phi Alpha Delta; Sigma Chi. Polit. & Govt. Pos: Legal aid attorney, Dade Co, Fla, 49-51; asst. city attorney, Miami, 51-56; mem, Dade Co. Cmn, 58-60, chmn, 60-62; Fla. State Sen, 13th Dist, 64-69, 41st Dist, 69- Bus. & Prof. Pos: Sr. partner, Law Firm, Aronovitz & Haverfield, 57- Mil. Serv: Civilian Technician with Army Engrs, 42-44. Mem: Am, Dade Co. and Fla. Bar Asns; Am. Judicature Soc; Fla. Bar Aeronaut. Law Cmt; Kiwanis; Pilots Asn; past pres, Gr. Miami Aviation Asn. Rel: Lutheran; past pres, St. Matthews Lutheran Church, Miami and mem. Bd. Trustees, Eastride Lutheran Sr. Citizens Retirement Village. Legal Res: 10701 S.W. 62nd Ave, Miami, Fla. 33156. Mailing Add: 1117 City National Bank Bldg, Miami, Fla. 33130.

HAVERKAMP, WARREN FRANKLIN R
Mayor, Glendale, Calif.
b. Brazil, Ind, 4/2/26; s. Edwart Haverkamp and Pearl Roberts H; m. 10/12/50 to Anna Lee Wright; c. Lance Warren. Educ: Rose Polytech. Inst, B.S. in Chem. Eng, 46; Lambda Chi Alpha. Polit. & Govt. Pos: Councilman, Glendale, Calif, 65-69, mayor, 69- Bus. & Prof. Pos: Partner and chmn. bd, Columbia Wax Co, Glendale, Calif, 50-62; owner, Haverkamp Investment Co, 63-; tech. dir, Am. Inst. of Maintenance, 65-68, pres, 68- Mem: Fel, Am. Inst. of Chemists; Am. Inst. of Chem. Engrs; Am. Asn. for Adv. of Sci; Mason; Rotary; Verdugo Club. Distinguished Serv. Award for Outstanding Commun. Serv, U.S. Jr. C. of C, 61. Rel: Assembly of God. Mailing Add: 519 Meadows Dr, Glendale, Calif. 91202.

HAVERLUK, STEVE D
b. Gorham, N.Dak, 3/18/26; s. Mike Haverluk and Mary Drebnenki H; single. Polit. & Govt. Pos: Chmn, Billings Co. Dem. Cmt, N.Dak, 60-69. Mil. Serv: Entered as Recruit, Army, 44, released as T/Sgt, after serv. in 24th Inf. Div; Army of Occupation Medal; Distinguished Unit Badge; Philippine Liberation Medal with One Bronze Serv. Star; Asiatic Pac. Serv. Medal; Good Conduct Medal; Victory Medal. Mem: Am. Legion; K. of C; Eagles; CWV. Rel: Catholic. Mailing Add: Fairfield, N.Dak. 58627. (1967)

HAWBAKER, D. ELMER R
Pa. State Sen.
b. Mercersburg, Pa, 11/30/16; s. Daniel M. Hawbaker and Ada B. Hege H; m. to Blanche A. Highlands; c. two. Educ: Chambersburg Bus. Col. Polit. & Govt. Pos: Pa. State Sen, 60- Bus. & Prof. Pos: Dairy farming. Mil. Serv: Cpl, Army Air Force, 43-46. Mem: Pa. Farmers Asn; Am. Legion; VFW. Mailing Add: 125 Linden Ave, Mercersburg, Pa. 17236. (1967)

HAWES, AARON EDWARD D
Chmn, Pawnee Co. Dem. Party, Kans.
b. Larned, Kans, 4/21/18; s. Aaron Edward Hawes and Anna Bell Booker H; m. 2/25/51 to Mary Alice Crawford; c. Deborah Kay and Donald Aaron. Educ: Kans. State Teachers Col, B.S. in admin. bus. and teaching credential, 41; Army Officers Sch, Ft. Benning, Ga, 42; Kappa Sigma. Polit. & Govt. Pos: Committeeman, Pawnee Co. Dem. Cmt, Kans, 48-, chmn, 54-60; crew chief, Govt. Census, 50; co. chmn, Docking for Gov. Campaign, 66; former del, Dem. Nat. Conv; chmn, Pawnee Co. Dem. Party, 66- Bus. & Prof. Pos: Committeeman, Kans. Livestock Asn, 48-; mem. adv. staff, Centennial Life Ins. Co, Pittsburg, 64- Mil. Serv: Entered as Pvt, Army, 40, released as Capt, 46, after serv. in 475th Composite Burma, 43-45; Silver Star and Unit Citation, Frank Merrils Marauders, Mars Task Force; China-Burma-India Campaign Ribbons; Hon. Capt, Army Res, 46-56. Mem: VFW; Am. Legion; Shrine, Mason; Elks; Livestock Asn, Kans; Kans. Wheat Cmn, 66-; bd. dirs, Great Plains Wheat Asn; chmn, For. Mkt. Cmt, Great Plains Wheat and West. Wheat Asns; dir, Gulf Ports Agr. Export Asn. Rel: Presbyterian. Mailing Add: 308 Martin, Larned, Kans. 67550.

HAWES, BRYAN D
Chmn, Edwards Co. Dem. Party, Kans.
b. Davis Co, Ind, 5/26/96; s. Aaron Edward Hawes and Anna Belle Booker H; m. 5/24/22 to Ona Muriel McCandless; c. Betty Jean (Mrs. Thomas L. Dittman) and Bryana Muriel (Mrs. Calvin Hefner, Jr). Educ: Salt City Bus. Col, Kans. Polit. & Govt. Pos: Clerk of bd, Belpre, Kans, 28-34, trustee, 42-45 and mayor, 63-; dist. supvr, Nat. Farm Census, 34-35; dist. supvr, Nat. Farm and Population Census, Dodge City, Kans, 50; del, Dem. Nat. Conv, 52 & 68; mem, Kans. Real Estate Bd, 57-60; bd. mem. and trustee, Laird Libr. Fund, 61-; adv. mem, Farmers Home Admin, 62-65; chmn, Edwards Co. Dem. Party, currently. Bus. & Prof. Pos: Farmer and stockman, Edwards, Haskell and Greeley Cos, Kans. Mem: Mason (32°); Kiwanis. Rel: Baptist; Deacon and Moderator. Legal Res: P.O. Box 82, Belpre, Kans. 67519. Mailing Add: Belpre, Edwards Co, Kans. 67519. (1967)

HAWES, JUDITH MAYS D
b. N.Y.C, 10/16/13; d. Edward Harris Mays and Lester Baker M; m. 6/6/36 to John Hawes, Jr; c. John, Amanda (Mrs. Fisher), Jane and Lester Ann. Educ: Vassar Col, A.B, 34; Paterson State Col. and Newark State Col, certification to teach mentally retarded. Polit. & Govt. Pos: Alternate del, Dem. Nat. Conv, 68; Dem. representative, Dist. 8, Glen Rock, N.J, 69- Bus. & Prof Pos: Teacher, Waldwick Pub. Schs, N.J, 61-69. Publ: Fireflies in the Night, 61, Bees and Beelines, 63 and Why Frogs are Wet, 68, T.Y. Crowell Co; plus 5 others. Mem: Coun. on Exceptional Children. N.J. Teachers of Eng. Award for books. Rel: Dutch Reformed. Mailing Add: 79 Abbington Terr, Glen Rock, N.J. 07452.

HAWES, PEYTON SAMUEL, JR. D
Ga. State Rep.
b. Elberton, Ga, 6/27/37; s. Peyton Samuel Hawes and Virginia Smith H; m. 6/10/61 to Mary Gregory; c. David Cooper, Gregory Battle, Elizabeth Claiborne and Peyton Samuel III (deceased). Educ: Univ. N.C, Chapel Hill, B.A, 60; Univ. Va, Charlottesville, LL.B, 63; Sigma Alpha Epsilon; Order of Old Well; Order of Gimghoul; Phi Alpha Delta. Polit. & Govt. Pos: Asst. attorney gen, Dept. Law, Atlanta, Ga, 63-66; mem. reorgn. cmt, Ga. State Dem. Party, 69; Ga. State Rep, 69- Bus. & Prof. Pos: Attorney, Jones, Bird & Howell, Atlanta, Ga, 66- Mem: Am, Ga. and Atlanta Bar Asns; Lawyers Club of Atlanta. Rel: Episcopal. Mailing Add: Haas-Howell Bldg, Fourth Floor, Atlanta, Ga. 30303.

HAWFIELD, SAMUEL GLENN D
b. Monroe, N.C, 4/21/91; s. William Dallas Hawfield and Julia Houston H; m. to Kate Clark; c. Samuel Glenn, Jr, William Dallas and Harold Houston. Educ: Duke Univ, A.B, 15; Univ. of N.C, M.A, 26; 9019, Scholarship Orgn. Govt. Pos: N.C. State Rep, 59-67. Publns: History of Stonewall Jackson Training School, Concord, N.C, 1947; History of the Development of Public High Schools in North Carolina, 1926. Mem: Pres, Union Co. Historical Asn, 57-66; life mem, N.C. Ed. Asn. and pres, 40-41, pres, Union Co. Unit, 49-50; Mason; Boy Scouts, Silver Beaver Award since 45. Rel: Methodist. Mailing Add: 604 W. Franklin St, Monroe, N.C. 28110. (1967)

HAWK, ELIZABETH B. D
b. Phila, Pa, 7/24/14; d. Horace W. Brooks and Margaret Nichols B; m. 5/26/34 to Harold Robert Hawk; c. Judith Ann (Mrs. Williams) and Robert B. Educ: Camden High Sch, 1 year; Camden Commercial Sch, 1 year. Polit. & Govt. Pos: Dem. councilwoman, Camden City, N.J, 61-; pres, Camden City Coun, 66-; alternate del, Dem. Nat. Conv, 68. Mem: Chmn, Camden City Red Cross; secy, Tuberc. Respiratory Disease Asn. of Camden Co; life mem, N.J. PTA. Rel: Catholic. Mailing Add: 1337 Argos Rd, Camden, N.J. 08104.

HAWKE, ROBERT DOUGLAS R
Chmn, Gardner Rep. City Cmt, Mass.
b. Gardner, Mass, 7/20/32; s. Arthur Eugene Hawke and Gladys Waite H; m. 7/20/58 to Nancy Moschetti; c. Linda, Cynthia, Heather and Dean. Educ: Northeast. Univ, A.B, 54; Boston Univ, LL.B, 56; Gamma Phi Kappa. Polit. & Govt. Pos: Chmn, Gardner Rep. City Cmt, Mass, 67-; adv. bd, Wachusett Commun. Col, 69- Bus. & Prof. Pos: Chmn. soc. studies dept, Murdock High Sch, 56-66; teacher, Gardner High Sch, 66- Mem: Mass. Teacher's Asn; Polish-Am. Citizens Club. Rel: Baptist; Deacon, First Baptist Church. Mailing Add: 12 Winslow St, Gardner, Mass. 01440.

HAWKES, ELIZABETH D
Co. Statutory Chmn, Wis. Dem. State Cent. Cmt.
b. Washburn, Wis, 11/22/06; d. Richard Hawkes and Maria Louisa Von Frank H; single. Educ: Boston Univ; Nat. Univ. Polit. & Govt. Pos: V.chmn, Wis. Dem. State Cent. Cmt, 41-50, Co. Statutory Chmn, presently; alternate del, Dem. Nat. Conv, 52 & 56, del, 60 & 64. Bus. & Prof. Pos: Practicing attorney, Wis, 37- Mem: Wis. State Bar Asn. Rel: Catholic. Mailing Add: Washburn, Wis. 54891.

HAWKINS, ALICE TENNESON R
Mem. Exec. Cmt, Los Angeles Co. Rep. Cent. Cmt, Calif.
b. Portland, Ore, 11/23/84; d. Tennes C. Tenneson and Emma Carlson T; m. 6/17/24 to Alvin Hawkins (deceased). Educ: Univ. Wash, A.B, 06; Columbia Univ. Grad. Sch, M.A, 24; Debating Club. Polit. & Govt. Pos: Chmn, San Pedro Rep. Hq, 56-63, Calif. campaign chmn, 66 & 68; pres, San Pedro Women's Rep. Club, Federated, 59, 60, 61 & 67; assoc. mem, Calif. Rep. State Cent. Cmt, 60-68, mem, 69; chmn, Cong. Dist. Rep. Party, 62-67 & 68; secy, 17th Cong. Dist. Rep. Cent. Cmt, 62-68; mem. exec. cmt, Los Angeles Co. Rep. Cent. Cmt, 62-; secy, Assembly Dist, 68 Rep. Party, 69. Bus. & Prof. Pos: Hist. and govt. teacher, Clarkston, Wash, 06-09; hist. and econ. teacher, Yakima, Wash, 09-23, head dept, 17-23; hist. teacher, San Pedro High Sch, Los Angeles Schs, Calif, 24-50, head dept, 47-50; chmn, Los Angeles Schs. Heads of Soc. Studies Dept, 48-50. Publ: Mountain, Desert, and Sea, poetry, Badger, 30; 'Music Festival,' 48; 'Jacaranda Trees are Blooming,' 65; poetry, 62; plus others. Mem: Am. Asn. Univ. Women (pres, 42); Nat. League Am. Penwomen; Eastern Star; Nat. Assistance League; Woman's Div, San Pedro C. of C; San Pedro Art Asn; San Pedro Writers' Guild. Ribbons for watercolors entered in art shows; lit. prizes; first prize for 'Music Festival,' Phi Delta Kappan Nat. Contest. Rel: Episcopal. Mailing Add: 1081 Tenth St, San Pedro, Calif. 90731.

HAWKINS, AUGUSTUS F. D
U.S. Rep, Calif.
b. Shreveport, La, 8/31/07; s. Nyanza Hawkins and Hattie H. Freeman H; m. 8/28/45 to Pegga A. Smith. Educ: Univ. Calif, Los Angeles, B.A; Univ. South. Calif, Inst. of Govt. Polit. & Govt. Pos: Calif. State Assemblyman, 34-62; U.S. Rep, Calif, 62- Bus. & Prof. Pos: Real estate and retail bus, Los Angeles, 45- Mem: Mason. Rel: Methodist. Legal Res: 4251½ Avalon Blvd, Los Angeles, Calif. 90011. Mailing Add: 125 North Carolina Ave. S.E, Washington, D.C. 20003.

HAWKINS, CLYDE E. R
Secy, Monroe Co. Rep. Exec. Cmt, Ohio
b. Stafford, Ohio, 9/27/07; s. William E. Hawkins and Minnie Craig H; m. 6/16/36 to Lillian Luburgh; c. John W. Educ: Muskingum Col, Elem. Dipl; Wilmington Col, B.S. in Ed, 34. Polit. & Govt. Pos: Mayor, Antioch, Ohio, 40-64; cent. committeeman, Perry Twp. Rep. Party, 57-; secy, Monroe Co. Rep. Exec. Cmt, 64-; bd. elec, Monroe Co, 65- Bus. & Prof. Pos: Elem. teacher, Stafford, Ohio, 27-34, high sch. teacher, 34-38, Antioch, Ohio, 39-56 and New Matamoras, 56-68. Mem: Ohio, Southeast. Ohio and Local Educ. Asns; F&AM; Scottish Rite. Rel: Methodist. Mailing Add: Box 116, Antioch, Ohio 43710.

HAWKINS, DONALD ANDREW D
City Councilman, Birmingham, Ala.
b. Birmingham, Ala, 9/30/17; s. Robert Llewellyn Hawkins and Katie Mae Davis H; m. 9/20/38 to Mary Lou Eads; c. Donald Lelias, Robert Larry, Brenda Lou and Janet Lynn. Polit. & Govt. Pos: Financial chmn, Park and Recreation Bd, Birmingham, Ala, 63-; city councilman, Birmingham; del, Dem. Nat. Conv, 68. Bus. & Prof. Pos: Dist. sales mgr, Coatings & Resins Div, Pittsburgh Plate Glass Co, Ala, 64- Mil. Serv: Entered as Seaman, Navy, 44, released as Chief Qm, 46, after serv. in Amphibious Forces, Pac. Theater, 45; Okinawa Campaign Ribbon. Mem: Pres, Painting & Decorating Contractors, 61; Birmingham Paint Club; Lions; Crestwood Civic Club; Mason; Zamora Shrine Chanters; Am. Legion. Rel: Methodist; Choir Dr. Mailing Add: 4817 Clairmont Ave, Birmingham, Ala. 35222. (1967)

HAWKINS, DONNA KAY D
b. Birmingham, Ala, 9/3/44; d. N.F. Black and Polly Strickland B; m. 6/14/63 to Don L. Hawkins; c. Jennifer Reneé. Educ: Univ. Fla. Polit. & Govt. Pos: Del, Dem. Nat. Conv, 68; nat. committeewoman, Ala. Young Dem, 68-; v.pres, Jefferson Co. Young Dem, 69- Mem: Jr. Womens League; Birmingham Symphony Asn; Birmingham Festival of Arts Bd; Birmingham Music Club. Rel: Methodist. Mailing Add: 761 Meadowbrook Dr, Birmingham, Ala. 35215.

HAWKINS, HENRY C. R
b. Glocester, R.I, 12/10/03. Polit. & Govt. Pos: Mem, Glocester Town Coun, R.I, 23 years; dep. town clerk, Glocester, 3 years; mem, Chepachet and Glocester Rep. Town Cmts; R.I. State Rep, 59-63; R.I. State Sen, 63-67. Bus. & Prof. Pos: Lumberman. Mem: Mason; chief, West Glocester Fire Dept, 3 years. Mailing Add: R.F.D. 1, West Glocester, R.I. 02814. (1967)

HAWKINS, HERB CLAY, JR. D
b. Forsythe Co, Ga, 6/10/33; s. Herbert Clay Hawkins, Sr. and Elizabeth Smith H; m. 11/4/61 to Mary Elizabeth Richards; c. Mary Elizabeth. Educ: Univ. Ga, B.S; Alpha Gamma Rho. Polit. & Govt. Pos: Former Ga. State Rep, Dist. 139. Bus. & Prof. Pos: V.pres, Hawkins Feed & Seed, Inc. Mil. Serv: Entered as 2nd Lt, Air Force, 55, released as Capt, 58, after serv. in 376 ARS, Strategic Air Command; Viet Nam Medal; Ga. Air Nat. Guard, at present. Mem: F&AM; Rotary; Jaycees. Rel: Baptist. Legal Res: Crossville Rd, Roswell, Ga. 30075. Mailing Add: P.O. Box 68, Roswell, Ga. 30075. (1967)

HAWKINS, JACK ROSS D
Tex. State Rep.
b. Stephensville, Tex, 9/1/05; s. Wade Hampton Hawkins and Martha Ware H; m. 1/29/31 to Euleta Ruth Sharp; c. Martha Elizabeth (Mrs. Jack Stone), Jack Wade and Thomas Earl. Educ: Tarleton State Col, 2 years. Polit. & Govt. Pos: Bd. trustees, Groesbeck Sch. Dist, Tex, 44-49; chmn, Limestone Co. Dem. Cmt, 44-50; mem, State Bd. Educ, Tex. Educ. Agency, 49-59; mem, City Coun, Groesbeck, Tex, 62-64; Tex. State Rep, Dist. 26, 65- Bus. & Prof. Pos: Assoc. ed, The Stephenville Empire, 26-30; ed, owner and publisher, The Groesbeck Jour, 30-69. Mil. Serv: Tex. Nat. Guard, 24-28, Cpl, serv. in Co. D, 36th Div; Capt, Co. C, Tex. State Guard, 42-45. Mem: Lions (past pres); C. of C.(past pres); Tex. Press Asn.(bd. dirs); North and East Tex. Press Asn.(past pres). Rel: Baptist. Legal Res: 501 E. Cobb St, Groesbeck, Tex. 76642. Mailing Add: P.O. Box 440, Groesbeck, Tex. 76642.

HAWKINS, JEFFREY LADEN D
Mem, Ark. State Dem. Cmt.
b. Ashley Co, Ark, 4/28/05; s. Abner Hawkins and Celia Hughes H; m. 8/28/27 to Ora Mae Smith; c. Jeffrey Laden, Jr, Bobbie (Mrs. Johnson), Robert Lee, Eloise (Mrs. Rodgers), Alsea, Don Horace, Maurice, Raymond, Brenda (Mrs. Trotter), Jacquelyn (Mrs. Paxton) and Reginal Dwight. Educ: High sch. Polit. & Govt. Pos: Pres. and founder, East End Civic League, Little Rock, Ark, 48-; mem. adv. bd, Finance Cmt, Little Rock, 63-; del, President's Civil Rights Conf, Wash, D.C, 65; mem, Pulaski Co. Dem. Exec. Bd, 66-; mem, Ark. State Dem. Cmt. 67-; del, Dem. Nat. Conv, 68. Bus. & Prof. Pos: Adv. bd, Urban League, Little Rock, Ark, 58-; chmn. exec. bd, NAACP, 60-62; mem. bd. dirs, Industrialization Opportunities, 67- Mem: Leadership Roundtable; PTA; Voter Registrn. Proj; Mason. Plaque for Outstanding Commun. Serv: Miles Chapel Church; Honor Cert, Carver-Pfeifer; hon. mem. Teamster's Union. Rel: Baptist; Chmn. Trustee Bd, First Baptist Church. Mailing Add: 1022 Inez St, Little Rock, Ark. 72202.

HAWKINS, JESSE F. D
b. Newberry Co, S.C, 11/21/87; s. Pierce M. Hawkins and Mary Jane Swindler H; m. 2/12/20 to Anna Louise Dickert. Educ: Clemson Col, 16-17. Polit. & Govt. Pos: S.C. State Rep, 57-60; S.C. State Sen, 61-67. Bus. & Prof. Pos: Dairy farmer. Mem: Past master and charter mem, Hartford Grange; Farm Bur; dir, Clinton Prod. Credit Asn; charter mem. and dir, Newberry Co. Bank; life mem, Newberry Co. Fair Asn; pres, Newberry Co. Breeder's Asn; Bd. Visitors, Columbia Col. Newberry Co. Citizen of the Year, 55; First Annual Award, Newberry Lodge 1718, Moose; Award of Merit, Clemson Col. Extension Serv, Newberry Co. Agr. Cmt, 52; Cert. of Appreciation, Newberry Co. Breed Asn, 66; Recorded in Book of Golden Deeds, Newberry Exchange Club, 67; S.C. Dairy Hall of Fame, Clemson Univ, 66-67. Rel: Methodist; chmn. bd. stewards, Ebenezer Methodist Church; Jesse F. Hawkins Appreciation Day, 9/18/18 in honor of lifetime serv. Mailing Add: R.D. 4, Newberry, S.C. 29108.

HAWKINS, JOHN H, JR. D
Ala. State Sen.
b. Birmingham, Ala, 9/27/26; s. John Harper Hawkins and Sara Wager H; m. to Betty Clair Hudson; c. John Harper, III, William Hudson and Davis Heath. Educ: Marion Mil. Col, grad; Univ. Ala. Polit. & Govt. Pos: Ala. State Rep, 59-63; Ala. State Sen, 64- Bus. & Prof. Pos: Owner, Hawkins Book & Mag. Co, Birmingham, Ala. Mil. Serv: Seaman 1/C, Navy. Mem: Mason; Shrine. Rel: Methodist. 1967 Legal Res: Birmingham, Ala. No mailing address available. (1967)

HAWKINS, MARLIN C. D
Sheriff, Conway Co, Ark.
b. Center Ridge, Ark, 4/22/13; s. John Carl Hawkins (deceased) and Nettie Mae Dockins H; m. 4/11/48 to Catherine Marvine Treadwell; c. Elizabeth Kaye, John Robert and Donald Bruce. Educ: Nemo-Vista High Sch, Center Ridge, Ark, grad, 33; Harding Col, Morrilton, Bus. Course, 33-34. Polit. & Govt. Pos: Sheriff and collector, Conway Co, Ark, 51-; bd. mem, Ark. Retirement Syst, 64-68; del, Dem. Nat. Conv, 68. Mil. Serv: Entered as Pvt, Army, 43, released as Sgt, 45, after serv. in Hq. Co, Camp Qm, Camp Joseph T. Robinson, Little Rock, Ark. Mem: Ark. Sheriff's Asn.(pres, 61); Ark. Law Enforcement Asn; Nat. Sheriff's Asn.(bd. gov, 59-64); pres, Ark. Peace Officers Asn, 60; Am. Legion (serv. officer, Luther Bradley Post 39, Morrilton, 45-50); Farm Bur. Rel: Church of Christ. Mailing Add: 807 N. Oak St, Morrilton, Ark. 72110.

HAWKINS, PAULA F. R
Rep. Nat. Committeewoman, Fla.
b. Salt Lake City, Utah, 1/24/27; m. 9/5/47 to Walter Eugene Hawkins; c. Genean, Kevin Brent and Kelley Ann. Educ: Schs. in Atlanta, Ga; Utah State Univ. Polit. & Govt. Pos: Precinct committeewoman, Orange Co. Rep. Exec. Cmt, 64-, mem, Finance Cmt, 66-; coordinator, E.J. Gurney for Cong. Campaign, 66; chmn. speakers bur, Fla. Rep. State Exec. Cmt, 67-; del, Rep, Nat. Conv, 68; co-chmn, Fla. Nixon Campaign Activities, 68; mem, Cmn. on Status of Women, 68-; Inaugural Coordinator for Fla, 69; Rep. Nat. Committeewoman, Fla, currently. Mem: Maitland Civic Center; Cent. Fla. Mus; Maitland Woman's Club; C. of C; charter mem. and secy-treas, Am. for Constitution Action Cmt. of 100, Fla, 66- Received State Chmn. Award for Serv, 66-67; Outstanding Woman in GOP Polit. Chmn. Award, 68. Rel: Latter-day Saint. Mailing Add: 241 Dommerich Dr, Maitland, Fla. 32751.

HAWKINS, REGINALD ARMISTICE D
b. Beaufort, N.C, 11/11/23; s. Charles C. Hawkins and Lorena Smith H; m. 9/8/45 to Catherine Elizabeth Richardson; c. Lorena Bernice, Wayne Beauregard, Reginald Armistice, Jr. and Pauletta Charlene. Educ: Johnson C. Smith Univ, B.S, 48, B.D, 56 and hon. LL.D; Howard Univ, D.D.S, 48; Beta Kappa Chi; Kappa Alpha Psi. Polit. & Govt. Pos: Precinct chmn, Mecklenburg Co. Dem. Party, N.C, 54-64; mem. bd, Men's Dem. Club, Mecklenburg Co, 56-; chmn, Mecklenburg Orgn. on Polit. Affairs, 56-; mem, Nat. Speakers Bur. Dem. Party, 60-64; mem. bd. trustees, N.C. Col. at Durham, 61-66; mem, N.C. Good Neighbor Coun, 63-65; First Black Cand. for Gov. of N.C; del, Dem. Nat. Conv, 68; chmn, N.C. Cmt. for More Polit. Rep. for Blacks, 68- Bus. & Prof. Pos: Practicing dentist, Charlotte, N.C, 48-; ordained minister, United Presby. Church, U.S.A, 56-; chmn, Southeast. Regional Investment Corp, 67-, Parker Heights Ltd, 68-; mem, Nat. Black Econ. Develop. Coun, Small Business Admin, 68-; v.chmn, East. N.C. Develop. Corp, Goldsboro, 69- Mil. Serv: Entered as 1st Lt, Army Dent. Corps, 51, released as Capt, 53, after serving in Korean Theatre, 51-53. Publ: 'Status of Negro Doctor in Municipal Hospitals,' J. Nat. Med. Asn, 58; 'Peripatetic Reflections on a Black Man's Gubernatorial Campaign,' RAM, Winston-Salem, N.C, 68. Mem: Am. and Nat. Dent. Asns; N.C, Old N. State and Second Dist. Dent. Socs; Charlotte Med. Soc; Counc. on Church & Race of United Presby. Church, U.S.A; Mason. Named Dentist of the Year, Old N. State Dent. Soc, 61 and Nat. Dent. Soc, 62; Cited by Interracial Coun. of United Presby. Church, U.S.A, and sev. clubs and fraternities. Rel: Presbyterian. Legal Res: 1703 Madison Ave, Charlotte, N.C. 28208. Mailing Add: 1218 Beatties Ford Rd, Charlotte, N.C. 28208.

HAWKINSON, JOHN W. R
Chmn, Knox Co. Rep. Party, Ill.
b. Galesburg, Ill, 4/30/14; s. Carl O. Hawkinson and Francis Elizabeth H; m. 10/13/46 to Marilyn J. Peterson; c. Carl E. and Judy E. Educ: Command & Gen. Staff Col, grad, 53; Officer Cand. Sch, Ft. Lee, Va, grad, 42; Army Br. Career Courses, completed. Polit. & Govt. Pos: Precinct committeeman, Galesburg, Ill, 62-; chmn, Knox Co. Rep. Party, 68- Bus. & Prof. Pos: Mgr, Peoria Off, Pittsburgh & Midway Coal Co, Subsidiary of Gulf Oil Corp, 64-; admission rep, North Park Col, Chicago, Ill, 65- Mil. Serv: Entered as Pvt, Army, 41, released as Maj, 46, after serv. in 14th Armored Div. & others, Asiatic-Pac. Theater, 44-46; Asiatic-Pac. Theaters, Carolines and Okinawa Campaigns with Battle Stars; Victory Medal; Res. Medal; Am. Defense Medal; Col, Army Res, 65. Mem: Key mem, Lions Int.(pres, Galesburg Club, zone chmn. and dept. dist. gov); John Erickson Rep. League; Lake Bracken Country Club; Am. Legion; Creve Coeur Club, Peoria. Rel: Evangelical Covenant; Mem, Bd. of Trustees. Mailing Add: 458 E. Grove St, Galesburg, Ill. 61401.

HAWKS, BOB D
Tenn. State Rep.
b. Memphis, Tenn, 8/1/26; s. Arthur Gilbert Hawks, Sr. and Myrtie Hames H; m. 6/21/44 to Margaret Elizabeth Holland; c. Doris (Mrs. Burress), Janet Kaye and Robert E. Educ: Treadwell High Sch, grad, 43; Memphis Baptist Col, 1 year. Polit. & Govt. Pos: Held various pos. in State Wide Campaigns in Shelby Co, 'Tip' Taylor for Gov, Estes Kefauver for Sen, 48-60 and Frank Clement for Gov, 62; Tenn. State Rep, Shelby Co, 66- Bus. & Prof. Pos: Part-owner, A-1 Transfer Co, 50-55; pres, Bob Hawks Movers, Inc, 55-; agent, Real Estate, 69- Mil. Serv: Entered as A/S, Navy, 44, released as TEM 2, 46, after serv. in Sixth and Eighth Naval Dist. Mem: Optimist; YMCA Bd, T. Walker Lewis; Shrine. Outstanding Spoke, Jaycees, 59-60. Rel: Baptist. Mailing Add: 3596 Mayfair, Memphis, Tenn. 38122.

HAWKSLEY, RAYMOND H. D
Gen. Treas. of R.I.
b. East Providence, R.I, 8/13/09; m. to Helen B. Educ: Bryant Col, B.A, 29; Brown Univ, R.I. Col. of Educ, exten. courses; Am. Inst. of Banking, pre-standard, standard, grad. cert; Beta Sigma Chi. Hon. M.Sc. in Bus. Admin, Bryant Col, 57. Polit. & Govt. Pos: Gen. Treas. of R.I, 49-; chmn, East Providence Dem. City Cmt, 56-; del, Dem. Nat. Conv, 68. Bus. & Prof. Pos: Banker, Providence Inst. for Savings, R.I. Mil. Serv: Navy, Pac. Theatre, World War II; Navy Cross. Mem: Past pres, Bryant Col. Alumni Asn, East Providence Boys' Club and Nat. Treas. Asn; chief, East Providence Auxiliary Police; exec. cmt. and past pres, R.I. Pub. Finance Officers Asn; bd. of dirs, Muscular Dystrophy Asn. of Am; dir, Rising Sun Lodge; hon. chmn, Oakland Beach Real Estate Asn; Ans. Emotionally Disturbed Children; Craftsmen Club; Odd Fellows; Am. Legion; VFW; RAM. Rel: Methodist; Pres. and Financial Secy, Bd. of Trustees, Providence Haven Methodist Church. Mailing Add: 15 Mary Ave, East Providence, R.I. 02914. (1967)

HAWLEY, DWIGHT SPENCER R
Wash. State Rep.
b. Seattle, Wash, 7/2/96; s. Lucien Spencer Hawley and Emeline Margaret Young H; m. 7/16/23 to Dorothy Youngblood; c. Dwight S. Jr, Robert W, Barry M, Helen (Mrs. Smith), Lorreta and Valorie (Mrs. Masters). Educ: Univ. Wash, 3 years. Polit. & Govt. Pos: Dist. leader, 44th Dist. Rep. Party, 30-49; Wash. State Rep, 50-59 & 61- Bus. & Prof. Pos: Owner and operator, Dwight S. Hawley Ins. Inc, 34-; owner and operator, Dwight S. Hawley Real Estate, 40-67; assoc. broker, Hawley Realty, 67- Mil. Serv: Army, 16, Pvt, serv. in 161 Inf, Mex. Border; recalled, Pvt, 17-18, serv. in 23rd Inf. Div; Good Conduct Medal; Purple Heart. Mem; Elks (past state pres); Eagles (second div. asn); Am. Legion (past Comdr); Ballard C. of C.(past secy); Seattle C. of C.(past trustee); Seattle King Co. Bd. Realtors; Ballard Kiwnais Club (past pres); Shilshole Breakwater Asn.(past pres); secy, Ballard Commun. Hosp, 15 years. King Co. Am. Legion Merit Award Commun. Leadership, 54; Lathan Goble Award Leadership, Shilshole Breakwater Develop, 58; Ballard Eagles Civic Award, 61-65 & 68; Ballard Commun. Appreciation Award, 63; VFW Voice Democracy Award, 69; Wash. State Elks Cert. Merit. Rel: Protestant. Legal Res: 1569 N.W. 80th St, Seattle, Wash. 98107. Mailing Add: P.O. Box 5201, Ballard Station, Seattle, Wash. 98107.

HAWLEY, W. KERMIT D
S.Dak. State Rep.
b. Deuel Co, S.Dak, 11/19/19; m. 6/24/44 to Gladys Hubbard; c. John, Roger and Thomas. Educ: Bus. Col. Polit. & Govt. Pos: Mem, Brandt Sch. Bd. and Town Bd; dir, Deuel Co. Civil Defense; S.Dak. State Rep, 64-; del, Dem. Nat. Conv, 68. Bus. & Prof. Pos: Businessman. Mem: Kiwanis; Izaak Walton League. Rel: Lutheran. Mailing Add: Brandt, S.Dak. 57218. (1967)

HAWLEY, WAYNE V. D
b. Armour, S.Dak, 11/25/28; s. Dice E. Hawley and Arietta Shearer H; m. 4/19/52 to Delores J. Schonher; c. Spencer L, Susan Jo, Ann Marie and Gregory T. Educ: Armour High Sch, grad. Polit. & Govt. Pos: Chmn, Brookings Co. Dem. Party, S.Dak, 66-69; del, Dem. Nat. Conv, 68; campaign mgr. for Frank Denholm, Cand. First Cong. Dist, 68. Mil. Serv: Entered as Pvt, Air Force, 49, released as S/Sgt, 52, after serv. in 19th Bomb Group, Far East, 50-51; Korean Serv. and Good Conduct Medals. Mem: Comdr, Armour S.Dak. VFW, 53 and jr. v.chmn, Lake Norden VFW, 55; pres, Brookings Jaycees, 62-63; v.pres, S.Dak. Jaycees, 63-64; mem, S.Dak. Small Bus. Adv. Counc, 68-70; pres, Brookings Independent Ins. Agents, 68; alternate dir, S.Dak. Independent Ins. Agents Asn; Huron Independent Ins. Agents Asn; VFW; Am. Legion; Kiwanis, Elks; Isaac Walton League. Distinguished Serv. Award, Brookings Jaycees, 63; Outstanding Air Force Reservist, S.Dak, 66. Rel: Catholic. Mailing Add: 554 Fifth, S.W, Huron, S.Dak. 57350.

HAWN, JOE D
Tex. State Rep.
b. Sherman, Tex, 5/8/15; s. Peter L. Hawn and Clara Beechy H; m. 10/7/37 to Mary Elizabeth Ross; c. Fred Joseph, Charles Richard and Roger Paul. Educ: Sherman High Sch, Tex. Polit. & Govt. Pos: Tex. State Rep, 69- Bus. & Prof. Pos: Capt, Dallas Fire Dept, 42-64. Mem: Pleasant Grove Civitan Club; Pleasant Grove C. of C.(exec. v.pres, 62-69). Southeast Citizen of the Year, 65. Rel: Baptist. Mailing Add: 8922 Rockledge, Dallas, Tex. 75217.

HAWORTH, ROGER LEE R
Chmn, Jay Co. Rep. Cent. Cmt, Ind.
b. Portland, Ind, 2/17/16; s. Laurence Haworth and Delcie Sackett H; m. 11/14/40 to Mabel M. Tharp; c. David P. and Cathy L.(Mrs. Layman). Polit. & Govt. Pos: Twp. trustee, Pike Twp, Jay Co, Ind, 59-67; chmn, Jay Co. Rep. Cent. Cmt, 66-; commodity auditor, Sch. Lunch Div, Ind. Dept. Pub. Instr, 67-69; dist. supvr, License Br, Bur. Motor Vehicles, 69- Mil. Serv: Entered as Pvt, Army, 44, released as Sgt, 46, after serv. in Co. K, 260th Inf, 65th Div, ETO; Combat Inf. Medal with 2 Battle Stars. Mem: Farm Bur; UAW. Rel: United Church of Christ. Mailing Add: R.R. 1, Portland, Ind. 47371.

HAWSE, THOMAS JACKSON D
W.Va. State Del.
b. Rock Oak, W.Va, 7/27/11; s. Thomas Jackson Hawse and Celia Davidson H; m. 8/14/41 to Chloe W. Halterman; c. Dixie H. (Mrs. Keller), Thomas J, III, Marion H. (Mrs. Tanner) and Herbert Edwin. Educ: Potomac State Col, W.Va, 2 yrs. Polit. & Govt. Pos: Sheriff, Hardy Co, W.Va, 56-60; W.Va. State Del, 63-64 & 67- Bus. & Prof. Pos: Pres, Hawse Food Mkt, Inc. Mem: Farm Bur; Moose; Lions; Rod & Gun Club. Capt, Potomac State Col. football team, 33. Rel: Presbyterian. Mailing Add: 216 Washington, Moorefield, W.Va. 26836.

HAY, MALCOLM D
b. Pittsburgh, Pa, 5/19/07; s. Southard Hay and Eleanor Humbird H; m. 5/2/68 to Jessie F. Bruckart; c. Eleanor Anne (Mrs. Thomson), Malcolm, Jr. and Thomas S. Educ: Yale Univ, B.A, 30; Univ. Pittsburgh, LL.B, 33; Phi Delta Phi. Polit. & Govt. Pos: Adj. gen, Pa, 61-63; chmn, Pa. Aeronaut. Cmt, Pa. Armory Bd. and Gettysburg Centennial Cmt, 61-63; civilian aide to Secy. Army, 63-65; del, Dem. Nat. Conv, 64; treas, Allegheny Co, Pa, 64-68; judge, court of common pleas, Orphans Court Div, Allegheny Co, 68- Bus. & Prof. Pos: Partner, Miller, Hay, Entwisle & Duff, 57-67. Mil. Serv: Entered as Pvt, Army Res, 29, released as Lt. Gen, Pa. Army Nat. Guard, 63; Legion of Merit; 5 Theater Ribbons in ETO; Pre-Pearl Harbor. Mem: Chancellor, Episcopal Diocese of Pittsburgh, 50 and Standing Cmt, 60-; dep. to Gen. Conv. Episcopal Church, 52-; pres, C. of C, 62-63, Family & Childrens Serv. of Allegheny Co, 55-56 and 66- and United Ment. Health Serv. of Allegheny Co, 65-; bd. trustees, St. Margaret Mem. Hosp, Pittsburgh, 56- and Family Serv. Asn. of Am, 69-; Syria Shrine; Fox Chapel Lodge, F&AM; Fox Chapel Golf Club; Univ. Club of Pittsburgh; Harvard-Yale Princeton Club; Pittsburgh Club. Rel: Episcopal. Legal Res: 705 Fairview Rd, Pittsburgh, Pa. 15238. Mailing Add: 802 City-County Bldg, Pittsburgh, Pa. 15219.

HAYDEN, CARL TRUMBULL D
b. Hayden's Ferry, Ariz, 10/2/77; s. Charles Trumbull Hayden and Sallie Calvert Davis H; m. 2/14/08 to Nan Downing, wid. 6/25/61. Educ: Ariz. Territorial Normal Sch, grad, 96; Stanford Univ, 96-00. Polit. & Govt. Pos: Mem. town coun, Tempe, Ariz, 02; treas, Maricopa Co, 04, sheriff, 07-12; U.S. Rep, Ariz, 12-27; U.S. Sen, Ariz, 27-69. Mil. Serv: Maj, Army, 18. Mem: Am. Legion; Rotary; Boy Scouts; Tempe Lodge 15, F&AM; Phoenix Lodge 335, Elks; Ariz. Pioneers' Hist. Soc. Legal Res: Tempe, Ariz. 85281. Mailing Add: Arizona State University Library, Tempe, Ariz. 85281.

HAYDEN, GERALD C. D
R.I. State Rep.
b. Central Falls, R.I, 10/12/22; single. Educ: Holy Trinity Sch; Central Falls Trade Sch. Polit. & Govt. Pos: R.I. State Rep, 61- Bus. & Prof. Pos: Serv. sta. owner. Mil. Serv: Army Air Corps. Mailing Add: 101 Perry St, Central Falls, R.I. 02863. (1967)

HAYDEN, MILDRED MARY R
Vt. State Rep.
b. Barre, Vt, 5/31/95; d. Richard E. Churchill and Emma L. Buck C; m. 5/23/17 to Earle C. Hayden, wid; c. Robert C, Patricia E. (Mrs. King) and Barbara J. (Mrs. Dufresne). Educ: Spaulding High Sch, grad, 13. Polit. & Govt. Pos: Town auditor, Berlin, Vt, 39, tax collector, 41-, overseer, 47- and mem. sch. study cmt, 63-; Vt. State Rep, 43-45, 63-66 & 69-; Vt. State Sen, 47-55. Mem: State Order Women Legislators (pres, 55); Nat. Order Women Legislators (treas, 64-65); Bus. & Prfnl. Women's Club (past pres); Barre Fed. Woman's Club (past pres). Rel: Methodist. Legal Res: Berlin, Vt. 05641. Mailing Add: Route 1, Barre, Vt. 05641.

HAYDON, JOHN M.
Gov, Am. Samoa
b. Billings, Mont, 1920; m. to Jean Parker; c. Four. Educ: Univ. Wash. Polit. & Govt. Pos: Chmn, Oceanographic Cmn, Wash, pres, Oceanographic Inst. and mem, Gov. Adv. Cmts, Dept. of Commerce and Econ. Develop. and State Dept. of Fisheries, currently; mem, Port of Seattle Cmn, 60-, pres, currently; Gov, Am. Samoa, 69- Bus. & Prof. Pos: Mem. staff, Port of Seattle and Bardahl Int. of Seattle, Wash, formerly; owner, Marine Digest, 56- Mil. Serv: Air Force, World War II. Mem: Exec. cmt. and bd, Wash. State Int. Trade Fair; bd, Seattle Traffic Asn; bd. and past pres, Pac. Coast Asn. of Port Authorities; Seattle Mayor's Maritime Adv. Bd; curriculum adv. bd, Shoreline Commun. Col. and Seattle Commun. Col. Legal Res: Seattle, Wash. Mailing Add: Office of the Governor, Pago Pago, American Samoa 96920.

HAYDUK, ALBERT T. R
Chmn, Yonkers Rep. City Cmt, N.Y.
b. Yonkers, N.Y, 2/26/07; m. to Margaret Pasuch; c. Albert T, Jr, Robert, Richard and Deborah. Educ: Columbia Univ; Alexander Hamilton Inst. Polit. & Govt. Pos: Rep. Co. committeeman, Tenth Ward, Yonkers, N.Y, 33-; former ward leader, Tenth Ward Rep. Co. Cmt; del, Rep. State Gubernatorial and Rep. Nat. Convs; pres, Yonkers Rep. Orgn, 40-44, former v.pres; mem, Rep. Club Tenth Ward; mem. and hon. pres, Slavonian-Am. Rep. Club Yonkers; co-chmn, Yonkers Rep. City Cmt, 58, chmn, 59-; dir, N.Y.C. Off, N.Y. State Dept. Commerce, until 59; mem, Rep. Coun. Leaders, Westchester Co. and mem. exec. cmt, Westchester Rep. Co. Cmt, currently; mem, N.Y. State Pure Waters Authority, 67-69; del, Rep. Nat. Conv, 68; cmnr, Westchester Co. Bd. Elec, 69- Bus. & Prof. Pos: Secy-treas, White City Linen Supply Co, Inc, 37-54; pres, White City Laundry Co, Inc, N.Y.C, 50-54; consult, Cascade Linen Supply Co. Inc. and Gen. Linen Supply Co, Inc, 54-58; pres, Hayduk Linen Supply, Inc, currently. Mil. Serv: Marine Corps, 43-45, serv. in Aviation Supply; N.Y. State Guard, Capt. Mem: Rotary Int.(dist. gov, dist. 257, 55-56); Yonkers Rotary Club (pres, 51-52); City Club Yonkers (pres, 53-54); Salvation Army (adv. bd); Boy Scouts Am.(former exec. bd, Wash. Irving Coun. Westchester Co, finance chmn, Yonkers Div); charter mem. Am. Inst. Mgt. (adv. bd); Am. Legion; K. of C.(4°); Yonkers Tuberc, Heart and Health Asn. (former mem. bd. dirs); 25 Club Yonkers (former pres); co-chmn. mem. gifts, St. Bartholomew's Sch. Bldg. Fund Dr; mem. annual campaign, United Givers Fund, chmn, coord. coun. Yonkers, 36-37; Red Cross Fund Raising Campaigns; Leewood Golf Club; Westchester Hunter's Asn. Rel: Roman Catholic. Legal Res: 377 N. Broadway, Yonkers, N.Y. 10706. Mailing Add: 1021 Saw Mill River Rd, Yonkers, N.Y. 10710.

HAYES, ALBERT J. D
married; c. Nine. Polit. & Govt. Pos: Pres, Waltham City Coun; Waltham City councilor, 4th term. Mem: Little League Progs; past pres, Waltham Retarded Children Asn. Mailing Add: 308 Lake St, Waltham, Mass. 02154. (1967)

HAYES, ARTHUR C. R
Ind. State Rep.
b. Ft. Wayne, Ind, 8/24/18; s. Walter F. Hayes and Marie P. Hardesty H; m. 2/1/46 to Miriam E. Peck (deceased); c. Arthur C, Jr, Bethany Marie and Gayle Wynne. Educ: Ind. Univ, B.S, 48. Polit. & Govt. Pos: First ward chmn, Young Rep, Ind, 38-41; chmn, Allen Co. Vet, 48; del, Ind. State Rep. Conv, 48-; chmn, Fourth Dist. for Eisenhower Cmt, 52; supvr. budget, State Hwy. Dept, 55-58; Ind. State Rep, 63-; chmn, Interstate Coordn. Cmt, 67 & 69; chmn, Resolution Cmt, Midwest Conf. States, 68; chmn, Recodification of Cities and Towns. Bus. & Prof. Pos: Ins. exec. Mil. Serv: Entered as Pvt, Army, 41, released as Sgt, 45, after serv. in 148th Gen. Hosp. Asiatic-Pac, 42-45; 1st Lt, Ind. Guard Res; Good Conduct Medal; Meritorious Unit Emblem; Am. Defense Serv. Medal; Asiatic-Pac. Campaign Medal with Bronze Serv. Star; World War II Victory Medal. Mem: Int. Platform Asn; Ind. State Young Rep; Ft. Wayne C. of C; Ind. Farmers Asn; Fraternal Order of Police; PTA; Ind. Univ. Club of Allen Co; Ind. State Legis. Club; Am. Legion; mem, Ind. Sesquicentennial Cmn; Am. Negro Emancipation Centennial Cmn. Rel: Lutheran. Mailing Add: 2001 Oakland St, Ft. Wayne, Ind. 46808.

HAYES, DAVID SAYRE R
Pa. State Rep.
b. Erie, Pa, 12/31/41; s. A.J. Hayes, Sr. (deceased) and Pauline F. Hennen H; single. Educ: Gannon Col, B.S. in Finance, 63; Univ. Miami, J.D, 67; Finance chmn, Blue Key; treas, Tau Kappa Epsilon; treas, Inter-Fraternity Coun; Phi Delta Phi; Int. Law Club; Student Bar Asn; Am. Inst. Taxation and Law; Bar and Gavel. Polit. & Govt. Pos: Pres, Young Rep. Gannon Col. and Students for Scranton, 62; mem, Erie Co. Exec. Cmt. Young Rep, 62-63; staff aide to Gov. Scranton, 63; del, Young Rep. Leadership Conf, 64; page, Rep. Nat. Conv, 64; co-chmn, West. Co. Rep. Camp, 68; Pa. State Rep, Fifth Dist, 69- Bus. & Prof. Pos: Pres, Student Investment Trust and treas, Delta Chi Housing Corp,

62-63; dir, Jackburn Mfg. Co, 63-; dir, Hayes Corp, 67- Mem: Jaycees; Gannon Col. Alumni Asn.(treas); Erie Co. Sportsmen's League. Rel: Methodist. Legal Res: 140 W. Main St, Fairview, Pa. 16415. Mailing Add: Box 33, Fairview, Pa. 16415.

HAYES, ERNEST A. R
Chmn, Iowa Rep. Finance Cmt.
b. New London, Iowa, 1/20/04; s. A.D. Hayes and Margaret Elizabeth Ferrel H; m. 2/13/37 to Ruth Anita Irons; c. Janet Elizabeth (Mrs. Dougherty) and Ruth JoAnn (Mrs. Farrell). Educ: Iowa Wesleyan Col, B.A. and L.H.D; Wash. Univ, M.S. in commerce and finance; Delta Sigma Chi; Omicron Delta Gamma. Polit. & Govt. Pos: V.chmn, Henry Co. Mem. Hosp. Bd, Mt. Pleasant, 41-; regional dir. savings div, U.S. Treasury Dept, 41-; chmn, Iowa Develop. Cmn, 62-; chmn, Iowa Rep. Finance Cmt. and mem. Nat. Rep. Finance Cmt, currently. Bus. & Prof. Pos: Pres, A.D. Hayes Co, Mt. Pleasant, Iowa, 26-; chmn. bd, New London State Bank, 33-; chmn. bd, Ins. Plan Savings and Loan Asn, 37-; pres, Hillsboro Savings Bank, 50-; dir, Henry Co. Savings Bank, Mt. Pleasant, 56-; pres, Henry Co. Indust. Develop. Corp, Mt. Pleasant, 58-; dir, Iowa Blue Cross Asn, Des Moines, 62-; pres, Hawkeye Nat. Life. Ins. Co. and Hawkeye Nat. Invest. Co, Des Moines, 65-; dir, Burlington Bank and Trust Co, 66; dir, Dyresville Nat. Bank, dir, Steel Valley Inc, Davenport and state chmn, Radio Free Europe, currently. Mem: Inst. Am. Democracy, D.C.(bd); chmn. bd, Iowa Wesleyan Col; Navy League Club; Boy Scouts (v.chmn, S.E. Iowa Coun); Sigma Phi Epsilon; Mason; Shrine; Moose; Elks; Kiwanis; Des Moines Club; Flint Hills Club. Rel: Methodist. Mailing Add: 400 Broadway, Mt. Pleasant, Iowa 52641.

HAYES, FLORENCE M. R
Mem, Okla. State Rep. Exec. Cmt.
b. Pretty Prairie, Kans, 9/12/13; d. Peter G. Stucky and Elizabeth Kaufman S; m. 7/24/35 to Ernest James Hayes, wid; c. Jeanine Ann (Mrs. Zenge) and Sherry Elizabeth. Educ: Hutchinson, Kans. Jr. Col, grad; McPherson Col, Kans; Southwest. State Col, Okla. Polit. & Govt. Pos: Campaign coordinator for Clyde Wheeler, Cong. Cand, 60; task force chmn, Okla. Rep. State Cmt, 61-62; v.chmn, Sixth Dist. Rep. Cong. Cmt, Okla, 61-; mem. exec. cmt, Custer Co. Rep. Party, 61-63 & 65-; mem, Okla. State Rep. Exec. Cmt, 61 & 65-; del, Rep. Nat. Conv, 64. Bus. & Prof. Pos: Tax Acct. Mem: Bd. mem, Miss Okla. Pageant Corp, 64-; pres, Bus. & Prfnl. Women's Club, 64, state corresponding secy, 66; Wesleyan Serv. Guild. Rel: Methodist; bd. trustees, First Methodist Church. Legal Res: 1021 Avant, Clinton, Okla. 73601. Mailing Add: Box 141, Clinton, Okla. 73601.

HAYES, FREDRIC GRANISON D
La. State Rep.
b. Lafayette, La, 1/2/37; s. Jack Alison Hayes and Jewell Baggett H; m. 4/13/57 to Patricia Anne Lafargue; c. Eric Alison, Jack Alvan and Charlotte Mariah. Educ: Univ. Southwest. La, 54-57; Tulane Univ, B.A, 60, LL.B, 61; Theta Xi. Polit. & Govt. Pos: La. State Rep, Lafayette Parish, 68-; chmn. bd. mgr, La. State Weapons Mus, 69; mem, Cmn. on Law Enforcement and Admin. of Criminal Justice, La, 69. Bus. & Prof. Pos: Self-employed attorney, 64- Mem: Am, La. State and Lafayette Bar Asns; Am. Judicature Asn; La. Trial Lawyers Asn; Rotary; Attakapas Area Tuberc. Asn; La. Kidney Found; hon. dir, La. Gulf Coast Oil Expos; Commun. Concert; Krewe of Gabriel; Krewe of Zeus; Lafayette Town House Order of Troubadours; C. of C. Rel: Southern Baptist. Mailing Add: 404 Parkside Dr, Lafayette, La. 70501.

HAYES, JAMES A. R
Calif. State Assemblyman
Educ: Hastings Col. of Law, Univ. Calif, J.D. Polit. & Govt. Pos: Former v.chmn, Court Reorgn. Cmt, League of Calif. Cities; former v.mayor of Long Beach, Calif; Calif. State Assemblyman, 39th Dist, 67-, chmn, Assembly Judiciary Cmt, mem, Assembly Revenue and Taxation Cmt, Assembly Health and Welfare Cmt, Judicial Coun. of Calif, Select Cmt. on Admin. of Justice, Calif. Coun. on Criminal Justice and Joint Legis. Cmt. on Pub. Domain, currently. Mem: Bd. gov, Hastings Col. of Law Alumni Asn. Described by the press in 1968 as 'The Calif. Legis. most adamant smog fighter'. Mailing Add: The International Tower, 666 E. Ocean Blvd, Suite 2104, Long Beach, Calif. 90802.

HAYES, JESSE C. D
Ark. State Rep.
b. Ingram, Ark, 10/16/14; s. Agustus Hayes and Melvia Estell Tiner H; m. 5/12/35 to Jewel Dean Shaver; c. Jesse Dean, Doris Jeanne (Mrs. Johnson) and L.A. Educ: Col. of the Ozarks, polit. sci, 57. Polit. & Govt. Pos: Ark. State Rep, Dist. Six, 63- Mil. Serv; Entered as Pvt, Army Res, 38, released as Maj, 60, after serv. in Inf. and Artil. in ETO, Far East and Korea; Combat Inf. Badge; Bronze Star; Commendation Medal; ETO Ribbon with 3 Battle Stars; Korean Campaign Ribbon with 3 Battle Stars. Mem: Elks (Past Exalted Ruler, Lodge 1871; VFW (past post comdr, post 2036 and Post 4556, past dist. comdr, dist 3, 62 & 65 present comdr); Farm Bur; C. of C; Am. Legion. Rel: Protestant. Mailing Add: R.R.5, Box 90, Pocahontas, Ark. 72455.

HAYES, JOHN DONALD R
N.H. State Rep.
b. Paterson, N.J, 10/18/10; s. John Hayes and Charlotte Strickland H; m. 9/19/33 to Dorothy Violet Dean. Educ: Paterson State Col, B.S. Polit. & Govt. Pos: Auditor, Madison, N.H, 53-54, clerk, 55-; N.H. State Rep, Dist. Three, 65- Bus. & Prof. Pos: Supvr. spec. process div, Wright Aero. Corp, N.J, 33-48; plant supt, Boonton Metallurgical Corp, N.J, 48-52; owner, Hayes Gen. Store, Madison, N.H, 52-; mem. bd. dirs, N.H. Retail Grocers Asn, 65- Publ: Outdoor ed, N.J. News, 45-52. Mem: Am. Electroplaters Soc; Grange; Mason; Shrine; Carroll Co. Fish and Game Club. Nat. Outstanding Citizen's Award, 69. Rel: Protestant Episcopal. Mailing Add: Main St, Silver Lake, N.H. 03875.

HAYES, JOHN FRANCIS R
Kans. State Rep.
b. Salina, Kans, 12/11/19; s. John Francis Hayes and Helen Dye H; m. 8/10/50 to Elizabeth Ann Ireton; c. Carl Ireton and Ann Chandler. Educ: Washburn Col, A.B, 41; Washburn Law Sch, LL.B, 46; Phi Delta Theta. Polit. & Govt. Pos: Del, Rep. Nat. Conv, 52; Kans. State Rep, 53-55 & 67- Bus. & Prof. Pos: Partner, Gilliland, Hayes & Goering, Attorneys, Hutchinson, Kans; dir, Cent. State Bank and May Abstract & Title Co, Inc. Mil. Serv: Entered as Pvt, Army, 42, released as Capt, 46, after serv. in Qm. Corps, U.S. and Pac. Theatre. Publ: 'Kansas Marriage Laws,' 46 and 'Kansas Automobile Insurance Laws,' 53, Kans. Bar J. Mem: Delta Theta Phi; Reno Co, Kans. and Am. Bar Asns; Elks; Am. Legion; K. of C; Hutchinson C. of C. (pres, 61); Kans. C. of C.(v.pres, 65); Hutchinson Rotary (pres, 64). Rel: Roman Catholic. Mailing Add: 106 Crescent Blvd, Hutchinson, Kans. 67501.

HAYES, JOHN S.
b. Phila, Pa, 8/21/10; m. to Donna Gough; c. Jonathan, Peter O, Rhea and Laurie. Educ: Univ. of Pa, A.B, 31. Polit. & Govt. Pos: U.S. Ambassador to Switz, 66-69; mem, U.S. Del. Int. Conf. Satellite Commun, 69- Bus. & Prof. Pos: Mem. staff, N.Y. Times Co, 45-48; mem, Wash. Post Co, 48-66, v.pres, 53-61, exec. v.pres, 61-66; pres, Post-Newsweek Sta; mem, Cmn. Educ. TV, Carnegie Corp, N.Y, 65- Mil. Serv: Commanding Officer, Am. Forces Radio Network, ETO; Order of British Empire; French Croix de Guerre; Am. Bronze Star. Publ: Co-auth, Both Sides of the Microphone. Mem: bd, Nat. Asn. Broadcasters; bd. dirs, U.S.O; pres, United Commun. Funds and Coun. of Am, Inc, 62-64; bd. dirs, Asn. Maximum Serv. Telecasters; founder, United Givers Fund in Gr. Nat. Capital Area, 56; pres, Commun. Chest Fed, Wash, D.C; trustee,Springfield Col; trustee, Urban League; bd. dirs, Nat. Symphony Orchestra Asn. Mailing Add: 4625 Garfield St. N.W, Washington, D.C. 20007.

HAYES, PATRICK O'N. D
R.I. State Sen.
b. 1918; married to Marilyn Morrissey; c. Patrick, Jr, Michael, Christopher, Ellen and Peter. Educ: De La Salle Acad; Col. of Holy Cross; Georgetown Law Sch. Polit. & Govt. Pos: City councilman, Newport, R.I, 55-59 & 61-65; R.I. State Sen, 67- Bus. & Prof. Pos: Attorney-at-law; mem. bd.of dirs, Newport Elec. Corp. and Viking Hotel. Mem: Bd. of dirs, Visiting Nurses Asn. Mailing Add: 565 Spring St, Newport, R.I. 02840. (1967)

HAYES, ROBERT WESLEY D
b. Mullins, S.C, 1/20/16; s. John Walton Hayes and Mary Love H; m. 11/27/37 to Wilbur Ruth Kirkland; c. Ruth Kirkland, Betsy Catherine and Robert Wesley, Jr. Educ: Univ. S.C, B.S, 37; Univ. S.C. Law Sch, LL.B, 40; Clariosophic Literary Soc; chmn, Soc. Cabinet, Univ. S.C, 37. Polit. & Govt. Pos: Mem, City Coun, Rock Hill, S.C, 53-56, mayor-pro-tem, 54-56; S.C. State Sen, York Co, 57-66; Circuit Judge, 16th Judicial Circuit, S.C, 66- Bus. & Prof. Pos: Mem. law firm, Hayes, Hayes & Brunson, 49-66. Mil. Serv: Entered as Pvt, Army, 43, released as 1st Lt, 46, after serv. in Ninth Eng. Command, 44-46; Lt. Col.(Ret), Res; ETO Campaign Medal; Army Occupation Medal; Am. Theatre Medal; Reserve Forces Medal; Good Conduct Medal; Am. Army Victory Medal. Mem: York Co. and S.C. State Bar Asns; S.C. Judicial Conf; Kiwanis; Elks; Am. Legion; 40 et 8; VFW. Civitan Man of the Year in Govt. Rel: Baptist. Legal Res: 636 Ascot Ridge, Rock Hill, S.C. 29730. Mailing Add: P.O. Box 529, Rock Hill, S.C. 29730.

HAYES, ROGER W. R
Secy, DeKalb Co. Rep. Cent. Cmt, Ill.
b. Farmington, Minn, 4/28/16; s. Marion Cleveland Hayes and Hattie Belle Rodgers H; m. 3/9/68 to Carolyn Eulass; c. Carol Sue (Mrs. Larry Cadle) and Roger W, Jr. Educ: Univ. Ill, Urbana, B.A, 39; Univ. Ill, Urbana, Law Sch, LL.B, 46; Phi Delta Phi. Polit. & Govt. Pos: State's attorney, McDonough Co, Ill, 48-56; Rep. committeeman, Precinct 14B, DeKalb Co, 62-; secy, DeKalb Co. Rep. Cent. Cmt, 62-; spec. attorney for People of State of Ill, Fulton Co, 67-; spec. asst. to Attorney Gen. of Ill, 69- Bus. & Prof. Pos: Self employed lawyer, 46- Mil. Serv: Entered as Aviation Cadet, Navy, 41, released as Lt. Comdr, 45, after serv. in Composite Squadron 97 as Carrier Fighter Pilot in Pac. Theatre, 43-45, Comdr, Naval Res, 54-; Distinguished Flying Cross; Air Medal with 5 Stars. Mem: Am. Trial Lawyers Asn; Am, Ill. State and DeKalb Co. Bar Asns; Am. Legion; VFW; Elks; Moose; Eagles. Rel: Protestant. Legal Res: 1105 Garden Rd, DeKalb, Ill. 60115. Mailing Add: 150 E. Lincoln Hwy, DeKalb, Ill. 60115.

HAYES, THOMAS LAWLOR R
Lt. Gov, Vt.
b. Fair Haven, Vt, 5/30/26; s. Harold John Hayes and Mary Lawlor H; m. 12/8/51 to Jennie Christy; c. Richard, James, Leslie and Kevin. Educ: Univ. Vt, B.A, 50; Georgetown Univ. Law Center, LL.B, 55; Nat. Champion Intercol. Debate; Wilbur Fund Scholar and Law Rev. Eligible; Lawrence Debate Club; Tau Kappa Alpha. Polit. & Govt. Pos: Nat. committeeman, Vt. Young Rep, 51; exec. asst. and legal counsel to U.S. Sen. Winston L. Prouty, 51-66; chmn. exec. assts, Rep. U.S. Sen, 66; mem, State Rep. Platform Cmt, 66; mem, Addison Co. Rep. Cmt, 68; mem, Gov. Cmt. Children with Learning Disabilities; Lt. Gov. Vt, 69-; co-auth, Vermont Law to Aid Children with Learning Disabilities. Bus. & Prof. Pos: Attorney-at-law, 12 years; assoc, Conley & Foote, Attorneys, Middlebury, 67-69. Mil. Serv: Entered as Pvt, Army, 44, released as T/5, 46, after serv. in 3159th Signal Serv. Bn, Asiatic-Pac. Theater; Good Conduct, World War II Victory, Army of Occupation and Asiatic-Pac. Campaign Medals. Mem: Vt. Bar Asn; VFW; Am. Legion; K. of C; Vt. Asn. for Children with Learning Difficulties. Lawrence Debating Prizes. Rel: Roman Catholic. Mailing Add: 29 Chipman Park, Middlebury, Vt. 05753.

HAYMOND, FRANK C. D
b. Fairmont, W.Va, 4/13/87; s. William Stanley Haymond and Agnes Cruise H; m. 1/25/22 to Susan Watson Arnett; c. William S, II and Thomas A. Educ: Harvard Col, A.B. cum laude, 10, Law Sch, 10-12; Triangle Club. Hon. LL.D, Morris Harvey Col. and W.Va. Univ, 63. Polit. & Govt. Pos: Chmn, Marion Co. Dem. Exec. Cmt, W.Va, 16; W.Va. State Del, 16-18; judge, circuit court of Marion Co, 39-45, Supreme Court of Appeals, 45- Bus. & Prof. Pos: Dir, Peoples Nat. Bank of Fairmont, W.Va, 12-30, Union Nat. Bank of Fairmont, 30-32 and Liberty Holding Co, 35- Mil. Serv: Entered as Pvt, Army, 18, released as Capt, 19, after serv. in Am. Expeditionary Forces; commissioned Capt, Judge Adv. Gen. Dept, France, 18; Chateau-Thierry, St. Mihiel and Meuse-Argonne Campaign Ribbons. Publ: 'Certified Cases Under the Statutes and the Rules of Civil Procedure,' 2/62 and 'Law Day Address,' 2/66, W.Va. Law Rev; 'The Supreme Court of Appeals of West Virginia,' W.Va. State Bar News, 5-6/66. Mem: W.Va. State Del, Am. Bar Asn, chmn, ins. sect, 35 and bd. gov, 43-46 & 67-68; pres, Marion Co. Bar Asn, 29 and W.Va. Bar Asn, 35; Elks; VFW; Am. Legion; 40 et 8. Rel: Catholic. Legal Res: 227 Jefferson St, Fairmont, W.Va. 25311. Mailing Add: State Capitol, Charleston, W.Va. 25305.

HAYNE, JACK McVICAR R
Chmn, Pondera Co. Rep. Cent. Cmt, Mont.
b. Great Falls, Mont, 11/22/20; s. George Roy Hayne and Effie McVicar H; m. 4/3/46 to Harriet Ann Danielsen; c. Mary Joan, John David, Alice Sue and Nancy Ann. Educ: Grays Harbor Jr. Col, 2 years; Wash. State Univ, B.A, 42; Lambda Chi Alpha. Polit. & Govt. Pos: Precinct committeeman, Pondera Co. Rep. Cent. Cmt, 60-69, chmn, 66-; committeeman, Mont. Rep. State Cent. Cmt, 62-66. Bus. & Prof. Pos: Owner, cattle ranch, Pondera Co, Mont, 53-69. Mil. Serv: Entered as A/S, Navy, 42, released as Lt, 46, after serving Navy Amphibious Force, Pac. Theatre. Mem: Am. Legion; Mont. Farm Bur. Fedn. Rel: Presbyterian. Mailing Add: Box 26, Dupuyer, Mont. 59432.

HAYNES, CLYDE, JR. D
Tex. State Rep.
b. Silsbee, Tex, 11/23/24; s. Jessie Clyde Haynes, Sr. and Viola Lindsey H; m. to LaVelle; c. Lanny. Educ: Lamar State Col. Tech, Beaumont, Tex, B.B.A. Polit. & Govt. Pos: Tex. State Rep, Dist. Eight, Orange Co, 61- Bus. & Prof. Pos: Owner, Haynes Gas & Oil. Mil. Serv: Entered as Pvt, Army, 42, released as T/3, after serv. in Far East, S.Pac; Oak Leaf Cluster. Mem: V.pres, Vidor Jaycees and Vidor C. of C, 55-58; secy, Vidor Sch. Bd, 55-58; Grass Roots Study Cmn. Tex. Educ, 51; VFW; Mason. Rel: Baptist. Mailing Add: P.O. Box 1235, Vidor, Tex. 77662. (1967)

HAYNES, DONALD D
b. Sedgwick, Kans, 10/31/25; s. Roy E. Haynes and Myrtle Hare H; m. 6/24/44 to RoseMary Franklin; c. Donald, Jr. and Mary Catherine. Educ: Tex. A&I Univ, B.B.A, 49; Alpha Chi. Polit. & Govt. Pos: Del, Dem. Nat. Conv, 68. Bus. & Prof. Pos: Jr. dist. clerk, Humble Oil & Refining Co, Pleasanton, Tex, 49-50; auditor, J.H. Robinson Truck Lines, Corpus Christi, 50; internal revenue agent, Internal Revenue Serv, Corpus Christi and San Antonio, 50-62; partner, Donald Haynes & Son, Cattle Ranchers, Jourdanton, 59-; partner, Brite & Haynes, Tax Acct, 62- Mil. Serv: Entered as A/S, Navy, 43, released as Pharmacist's Mate 2/C, 46, after serv. in U.S.S. Mifflin, Pac. Theatre, 45-46; Iwo Jima and Okinawa Campaign Ribbons. Mem: Am. Brahman Breeders Asn; S.Tex. Brahman Asn; Am. Legion. Rel: Protestant. Legal Res: 610 Bensdale Ave, Pleasanton, Tex. 78064. Mailing Add: P.O. Box 575, Pleasanton, Tex. 78064.

HAYNES, GLENN JOHNSON R
Chmn, Itawamba Co. Rep. Party, Miss.
b. Burnsville, Miss, 1/14/10; s. Robin Alexander Haynes and Ollie Johnson H; m. 9/25/47 to Marcelle League. Educ: Miss. State Univ, B.S. in Bus, 42, B.S. in Eng, 47; Marine Club; Latin Am. Club; Itawamba Co. Club. Polit. & Govt. Pos: Chmn, Itawamba Co. Selective Serv. Bd, 48-53; del, Rep. Nat. Conv, 50; mem, Miss. State Rep. Exec. Cmt, 50-51; chmn, Itawamba Co. Rep. Party, Miss, 50-52 & 58- Bus. & Prof. Pos: Dir, Itawamba Co. Develop. Coun, 60-67; dir, Itawamba Co. Fair Asn, 60-, v.pres, 62-66. Mil. Serv: Entered as Pvt, Marine Corps, 42, released as Cpl, 46, after serv. in 4th Marine Div, Central Pac; Marshal Islands, Saipan-Tinian and Iwo-Jima Campaign Ribbons; Presidential Unit Citation. Mem: Dist. chmn, Nat. Fedn. of Independent Bus; pres, Fulton Lions, 61; 40 et 8; State Exec. Cmt, Am. Legion; VFW; Miss. State Univ. Alumni Asn. Received the Int. Lions Exten. Award for organizing a Lions Club in Tremont, Miss. Rel: Methodist. Mailing Add: 101 Adams St, Fulton, Miss. 38843.

HAYNES, JETER L. R
N.C. State Rep.
b. Jonesville, N.C, 12/26/02; s. Roscoe Haynes and Mary Vestal H; m. 12/13/35 to Cleo Harrell; c. Peggy Joyce (Mrs. Eskridge). Educ: Appalachian Teachers' Col, B.S, 33; Catawba Col, A.B, 39; Univ. N.C, M.A, 54; Int. Rels. Club; Philomathian Literary Soc. Polit. & Govt. Pos: Precinct chmn, Rep. Party, N.C, 35; N.C. State Rep, 37-38 & 67-; alternate del, Rep. Nat. Conv, 60; del, State Rep. Conv, N.C, 60. Bus. & Prof. Pos: Prin, Reeds High Sch, 42-48, Townsville High Sch, 56-57 and Benham Elem. Sch, 57-66. Publ: 'Geometry Made Practical,' N.C. Educ, 45. Mem: N.C. and Nat. Educ. Asns; Little Mt. Grange; chmn, Math. Group, Northwest. Educ. Asn, 37. Mailing Add: 112 Williams St, Jonesville, N.C. 28642.

HAYNES, WILLIAM G, JR. R
Chmn, Ouachita Parish Rep. Party, La.
b. Chatham, La, 2/14/12; s. William G. Haynes and Eva Pilkinton H; m. 9/3/39 to Erlene Honeycutt; c. Alice A. and Kathleen J. Educ: Sch. of Banking of the South, La. State Univ, grad, 55. Polit. & Govt. Pos: Chmn, Ouachita Parish Rep. Party, La, 63-; chmn, Fifth Dist. Rep. Party, 64-; mem. bd. dirs, Rep. Polit. Action Coun. of La, 64-; mem, La. Rep. State Cent. Cmt, 65- Mil. Serv: Entered as Pvt, Air Force, 42, released as T/Sgt, 46, after serv. in Training Command. Mem: Am. Legion. Rel: Christian Science. Legal Res: 200 Slack St, West Monroe, La. 71291. Mailing Add: P.O. Box 1215, West Monroe, La. 71291.

HAYNSWORTH, CLEMENT FURMAN, JR.
b. Greenville, S.C, 10/30/12; s. Clement Furman Haynsworth and Elsie Hall H; m. 11/25/46 to Dorothy Merry Barkley; c. Rufus C. Barkley, Jr. and Joseph G. Barkley. Educ: Furman Univ, A.B. summa cum laude, 33 and hon. LL.D, 64; Harvard Law Sch, LL.B, 36; Kappa Alpha Order; Lincoln's Inn, Harvard; Phi Alpha Delta. Polit. & Govt. Pos: Alternate mem, Regional Wage Stabilization Bd, 51-52; mem, Judicial Coun. State of S.C, 56-57; judge, U.S. Court of Appeals, Fourth Circuit, 57-; chief judge, U.S. Court of Appeals, Fourth Circuit, 64-; chief judge, Fourth Judicial Circuit of the U.S, 64-; nominated Assoc. Justice, U.S. Supreme Court by the President, 69. Bus. & Prof. Pos: Former dir, S.C. Nat. Bank, Liberty Life Ins. Co, Southeast. Broadcasting Co, Greenville Hotel Co, Greenville Commun. Hotel Co, South. Weaving Co. and Pickens R.R. Co; assoc, Haynsworth and Haynsworth, 36-40, partner, 40-46; exec. partner, Haynsworth, Perry, Bryant, Marion & Johnstone, 46-57. Mil. Serv: Entered as Ens, Navy, 42, released as Lt, 45, after serv. in Amphibious Forces, Pac, 45. Publ: Numerous opinions, Fed. Reporter, 2d, 57 and opinions in Federal Supplement, 57. Mem: Judicial Conf. U.S; Am. Law Inst; Am. Judicature Soc; Am, S.C. and Fed. Bar Asns; Commonwealth Club, Richmond, Va; Green Valley Country Club; Poinsett Club; Nat. Lawyers Club, Wash, D.C; S.C. State C. of C.(former v.pres. and mem. exec. cmt). Rel: Episcopal. Legal Res: 415 Crescent Ave, Greenville, S.C. 29605. Mailing Add: Federal Bldg, Greenville, S.C. 29603.

HAYS, DAVID WITHEROW R
Dir, Off. of Intergovt. Rels, Dept. of Transportation
b. Boston, Mass, 6/12/35; s. William E. Hays and Edna Charlton H; m. 7/9/61 to Charlotte V. Blanchet; c. Deborah A. Educ: Lafayette Col, A.B, 57; Boston Univ. Law Sch, LL.B, cum laude, 61; Alpha Chi Rho. Polit. & Govt. Pos: Mem. legal staff, Off. of Attorney Gen, Boston, Mass, 63-66 and Commonwealth of Mass, 66-69; dir, Off. of Intergovt. Rels, U.S. Dept. of Transportation, 69- Bus. & Prof. Pos: Mem, legal staff, Holland, Johnson & Hays, Boston, Mass, 61-63. Mil. Serv: 2nd Lt, Army, 57-58; Capt, Judge Adv. Gen. Corps, Army Res. Mem: Boston, Mass. and Am. Bar Asns. Rel: Protestant. Legal Res: Waltham, Mass. Mailing Add: 3527 Laurel Leaf Lane, Fairfax, Va. 22030.

HAYS, GUYTON B. D
b. Siminole, Tex, 5/18/12; s. Eugene Hays and Ora Hackler H; m. 10/28/38 to Marie Jenson; c. Cliff, Dan and Gary. Educ: Univ. N.Mex, grad, 35; Kappa Alpha Order. Polit. & Govt. Pos: Land Cmnr, State Land Off, N.Mex, 65- Bus. & Prof. Pos: Farmer and rancher, Estancia Valley, 38-53; sch. teacher, Univ. N.Mex, 35-38. Mem: Cattlemans Asn; Oil Conserv. Cmn; State Investment Coun; State Forestry; Oil and Gas Acct. Cmn. Rel: Methodist. Mailing Add: 1319 Bryn Mawr N.E, Albuquerque, N.Mex. 87106. (1967)

HAYS, JACK D. H. R
Justice, Ariz. Supreme Court
b. Lund, Nev, 2/17/17; s. Charles Hays (deceased) and Thelma Savage H; m. 8/31/44 to Priscilla Harvey; c. Eugene Harrington, Rory Cochrane, Bruce Harvey and Victoria Wakeling. Educ: South. Methodist Univ, B.S, 39, LL.B, 41; Lambda Chi Alpha; Pi Alpha Delta. Polit. & Govt. Pos: Asst. city attorney, Phoenix, Ariz, 49-52; Ariz. State Rep, 52; state chmn, Eisenhower for Pres, 52; U.S. Attorney, Phoenix, Ariz, 53-60; superior court judge, Maricopa Co, 60-69; Justice, Ariz. Supreme Court, 69- Bus. & Prof. Pos: Attorney, Hays & Webster, 46-, Myers, Whitlow & Hays, 52- Mil. Serv: Entered as Pvt, Army, 41, released as Maj, 46, after serv. in Field Artil, Ital. Theatre, 44-45; Bronze Star. Mem: Am. Judicature Soc; Fed, Am. and Ariz. Bar Asns; Ariz. Judges Asn; Ariz. Acad; Ariz. Inst; Rotary; Boy Scouts; adv. bd, Salvation Army; Maricopa Co. Jr. Col. Found.(bd. dirs); adv. bd, Valley Big Bros. Recipient of Big Brother of the Year Award. Rel: Episcopal. Legal Res: 727 W. Palo Verde Dr, Phoenix, Ariz. 85014. Mailing Add: Room 230, Capitol Bldg, Phoenix, Ariz. 85007.

HAYS, PRISCILLA HARVEY R
b. Boulder, Colo, 1/22/23; d. Eugene Cochrane Harvey and Helen Newhall H; m. 8/31/44 to Jack D.H. Hays; c. Eugene, Rory, Bruce and Victoria. Educ: Univ. Calif, Berkeley, 41; Univ. Ariz, B.A, 44; Alpha Phi. Polit. & Govt. Pos: Precinct committeewoman, Ariz. Rep. Party, 48-66; Rep. state committeewoman, 52-66; Ariz. State Rep, 58-66. Mem: Chmn, Legis. Water Cmt, Western Region, Coun. of State Govts; bd, Interstate Conf. on Water Problems. Rel: Episcopal. Mailing Add: 727 W. Palo Verde Dr, Phoenix, Ariz. 85013. (1967)

HAYS, WAYNE L. D
U.S. Rep, Ohio
b. Bannock, Ohio, 5/13/11; s. Walter Lee Hays and Bertha Mae Taylor H; m. 6/3/37 to Martha Judkins; c. Martha Brigitte. Educ: Ohio State Univ, B.S, 33; Duke Univ, 35, grad. work; hon. LL.D, Ohio Univ, 66 and Col. Steubenville, 68. Polit. & Govt. Pos: Dep. auditor, Belmont Co, Ohio; mayor, Flushing, Ohio, 39-45; Ohio State Sen, 41-42; mem. Bd. Educ; mem, Belmont Co. Bd. Cmnrs, 45-49; U.S. Rep, Ohio, 48-; chmn. House Rep. del, N.Atlantic Assembly Conf, 55-68, pres. conf, 56 & 57, v.pres, currently; U.S. rep, N.Atlantic Assembly Standing Cmt, currently. Bus. & Prof. Pos: Chmn. bd. dir, Citizens Nat. Bank, Flushing. Mem: Rotary. Rel: Presbyterian. Mailing Add: Rayburn House Office Bldg, Washington, D.C. 20515.

HAYWARD, CHANNING WAYNE R
b. Brockton, Mass, 11/7/29; s. Eliot Aron Hayward and Alda Hildegard H; m. 12/24/53 to Mary Helen Correia; c. Wayne. Polit. & Govt. Pos: Chmn, Fairhaven Rep. Town Cmt, Mass, 63-68; mem, Fairhaven Planning Bd, 68- Mil. Serv: Pvt, Army, 47-48, and 50-51, released as Pfc, after serv. in Third Signal Co, Third Inf. Div, Korea, 51; Good Conduct Medal; Korean Serv. Medal with four Bronze Stars; Nat. Defense Serv. Medal; United Nations Serv. Medal; Repub. of Korea Presidential Unit Citation Badge. Mem: Local 17, Int. Brotherhood Tel. Workers; Bristol Co. Rep. Club; VFW; Am. Legion; RAM; AF&AM. Rel: Unitarian. Mailing Add: 582 Washington St, Fairhaven, Mass. 02719.

HAYWARD, WILLIAM R
Mich. State Rep.
b. Detroit, Mich, 7/5/06; s. William Wellington Hayward and Dolly E. Wixom H; m. 2/12/38 to Madelon Bernice Land; c. Mary Helen (Mrs. Thomas Kaser), Susan (Mrs. Leonard Siudara), Nancy (Mrs. Raymond Howard) and William Hayward. Educ: Rutger's Univ, Grad. Sch. Banking, 40-42. Polit. & Govt. Pos: City Cmnr, Royal Oak, Mich, 39-45 & 51-59, mayor, 45-49 & 59-63; Mich. State Rep, 59- Bus. & Prof. Pos: Exec. positions in financial and banking insts, 42-59. Mailing Add: 1839 Sycamore, Royal Oak, Mich. 48073.

HAYWOOD, ISAAC HENRY D
City Councilman, Chesapeake, Va.
b. Gloucester Co, Va, 6/7/03; s. George Washington Haywood and Lula West H; m. 5/27/25 to Cottie Bright; c. Evelyn J.(Mrs. Hardison) and Virgil H. Educ: Portsmouth High Sch. Polit. & Govt. Pos: Mem, Norfolk Co. Bd. of Supvrs, Va, 43, West. Br. Mosquito Control Cmn, 51, Elizabeth River Tunnel Cmn, 54 and Va. State Milk Cmn, 66; city councilman, Chesapeake, 61- Bus. & Prof. Pos: Dir, Bank of Chesapeake, Va, 56-; pres, Tidewater Feed & Seed Co. Mem: Masonic Lodge 276; Port Norfolk RAM; Portsmouth Commandery 8 and Khedive Shrine Temple. Rel: Westhaven Baptist. Legal Res: Bruce Station Rd, Chesapeake, Va. 23321. Mailing Add: P.O. Box 155, Churchland, Chesapeake, Va. 23321. (1967)

HAYWORTH, DON D
b. Toledo, Iowa, 1/13/98; s. Charles LeRoy Hayworth and Mae Wilkinson H; m. 6/17/34 to Frances Knight; c. Donna Lou, Francene and Barbara. Educ: Grinnell Col, A.B, 18; Univ. Chicago, A.M, 21; Univ. Wis, Ph.D, 29. Polit. & Govt. Pos: Dir, Victory Speakers Prog, Off. of Civilian Defense, 42-43; info. specialist, Dept. of Interior, 43-45; U.S. Rep, Mich, 55-56; consult, Dept. of

Agr, 63-64 and Soc. Security Admin, 65-67. Bus. & Prof. Pos: Prof, Penn Col, Iowa, 23-27, Univ. Akron, 28-37, Mich. State Univ, 37-63; established Plastics Mfg. Co, Lansing, Mich, 52-63. Mil. Serv: Pvt, Army, 18. Publ: Several books and articles in prfnl. speech jour; mag. articles. Mem: Kiwanis; Torch Club; NAACP. Rel: Protestant. Mailing Add: 1311 Delaware Ave. S.W, Washington, D.C. 20024.

HAZELETT, JOHN MARTIN R
Cmnr, Ariz. State Tax Cmn.
b. Phoenix, Ariz, 4/22/15; s. Earl Tuttle Hazelett and Willie Barnes Martin H; m. 8/26/44 to Jean Dendinger; c. Judith Diane (Mrs. Rhorer), Susan Louise and Carol Ann. Educ: Phoenix Jr. Col, grad, 35; Univ. Calif, Berkeley, B.S. in Commerce, 37; Letterman's Club; Iota Sigma Alpha; Sigma Nu; Phi Alpha Chi; Barry M. Goldwater Cup, 33. Polit. & Govt. Pos: Cmnr, Ariz. State Tax Cmn, 64- Bus. & Prof. Pos: Auditor, Harmon Audit Co, Phoenix, Ariz, 38-40; acct. and head tax dept, Consolidated Vultee Aircraft Corp, San Diego, Calif, 40-46; sr. acct, Tagus Ranch, Tulare, Calif, 47; prin. founder, v.pres, pres. and gen. mgr, Superior Equip. Co, Phoenix, 48-; v.pres. and dir, Ariz. Gypsum Corp, 53- Publ: 'Tax Accounting for the Aircraft Industry,' In: Handbook of Tax Accounting Methods, Lasser, 46; 'Proceedings of Interim Committee Concerned with Activities of Public Land Law Review Commission,' West. States Asn. Tax Adminstr, 11/68; 'Present Status of Arizona's Mine Taxation,' Univ. Ariz. Symposium on Mine Taxation, 3/69. Mem: Am. Inst. Cert. Pub. Acct; Assoc. Equip. Distributors Am; Phoenix Country Club. Rel: Christian Science. Mailing Add: 1905 W. Cambridge, Phoenix, Ariz. 85009.

HAZLEWOOD, GRADY D
Tex. State Sen.
b. Ft. Chadbourne, Tex, 8/18/01; s. William Temple Hazlewood and Lula Douglas H; m. to Andrine Smith. Educ: W.Tex. State Univ, B.A; Univ. Tex, Austin, LL.B. Polit. & Govt. Pos: Dist. attorney, 47th Judicial Dist, Tex, 33-37; Tex. State Sen, 39- Mem: Amarillo Optimist Club (pres); C. of C; State Bar, Tex; Panhandle Plains Hist. Soc.(pres). Annual Commun. Serv. Award, 65; Man of the Year, 65. Rel: Presbyterian. Legal Res: Route 2, Box 224, Canyon, Tex. 79015. Mailing Add: Senate Chamber, Austin, Tex. 78701.

HEABERLIN, STANLEY M. D
b. Tenn, 9/4/08; s. J. W. Heaberlin and Eliza H; m. 1932 to Jessie Core; c. Gene and Bruce. Educ: Pleasantville High Sch. Polit. & Govt. Pos: Iowa State Sen, 65-69. Bus. & Prof. Pos: Trucking bus; farmer; livestock raiser. Mem: Marion Co. Exten. Coun; dir, State Hereford Asn; Des Moines Coop. Dairy. Rel: Methodist. Mailing Add: Pleasantville, Iowa 50225. (1967)

HEAD, DOUGLAS M. R
Attorney Gen, Minn.
b. Minneapolis, Minn, 4/14/30. Educ: Yale, B.A. in Polit. Sci, 52; Univ. Minn. Law Sch, LL.B, 56; assoc. ed, Minn. Law Rev; Order of the Coif; Nat. Legal Scholastic Honor Soc. Polit. & Govt. Pos: Minn. State Rep, 60-64; Attorney Gen, Minn, 66-; alternate del, Rep. Nat. Conv, 68. Bus. & Prof. Pos: Attorney-at-law, Minneapolis, 57-66. Named One of Two Outstanding First Term Legislators, 61. Legal Res: Minneapolis, Minn. Mailing Add: State Capitol, St. Paul, Minn. 55101.

HEADLEE, RICHARD HAROLD R
b. Ft. Dodge, Iowa, 5/16/30; s. William Clark Headlee and Violet Rebecca Lunn H; m. 10/17/49 to Mary Elaine Mendenhall; c. Michael S, William D, Mary K, Richard B, Natalie A, Carolyn, Laura, Howard and Elaine. Educ: Utah State Univ, B.S, 53; Blut Key; Alpha Sigma Nu; Sigma Nu. Polit. & Govt. Pos: Private consult, George Romney and Mich. Dir. of Dept. of Commerce, 66; asst. to Leonard Hall, Romney For Pres, 67; nat. chmn, Young Bus. & Civic Leaders For Nixon-Agnew, 68; mem, Isabella Co. Rep. Exec. Cmt, 68-69. Bus. & Prof. Pos: Pres, Morbark Industs, 68; dir, Alexander Hamilton Life Ins. Co. and NORCAP, 69. Mil. Serv: Entered as 2nd Lt, Army, 53, released as 1st Lt, 56, after serv. in Qm. Corps, Europe. Mem: Pres, Bountiful Jr. C. of C, Utah, 59; pres, Utah Jr. C. of C, 61; dir, U.S. Jr. C. of C, 60, v.pres, 63; dir, U.S. C. of C, 64-65; pres, U.S. Jaycees, 63-64. Distinguished Serv. Award, 60; Outstanding Alumnus, Utah State Univ, 64. Rel: Latter-day Saint. Mailing Add: Route 1, Rosebush, Mich. 48878.

HEADLEY, LEWIS W. D
Ala. State Rep.
b. Clanton, Ala, 12/31/23; s. J.C. Headley and Sallie H; m. 12/28/47 to Dot Wesson Patterson; c. Sally Jane (Mrs. Tom Underwood), Ginger Ann and Melanie Jo. Educ: Chilton Co. High Sch, Clanton, grad, 42. Polit. & Govt. Pos: Ala. State Rep, Chilton Co, 67- Bus. & Prof. Pos: Owner, supermkt; dir, First Fed. Savings & Loan. Mil. Serv: Entered as Pvt, Marines, 42, released as Platoon Sgt, 45, after serv. in Third Marines, S.Pac. Theater, 42-45. Mem: VFW; Am. Legion; Lions; Mason; C. of C.(pres). Rel: Baptist; Deacon, First Baptist Church, Clanton. Legal Res: Mt. Pleasant Rd, Clanton, Ala. 35045. Mailing Add: P.O. Box 471, Clanton, Ala. 35045.

HEADRICK, WILLIAM MOORE R
Mem, Finance Cmt, Miss. Rep. Party
b. Laurel, Miss, 2/14/29; s. James Dewey Headrick and Helen Moore H; m. 6/18/49 to Helen Jean Trotter; c. Helen Hope, William M, Jr. and Albert T. Educ: Bowling Green Col. Commerce, B.S, 51; Alpha Kappa Psi. Polit. & Govt. Pos: Mem, Forrest Co. Rep. Exec. Cmt, Miss, 52-56; mem, Miss. Rep. Cand. Cmt, Miss. Rep. Party, 56-60; finance chmn, Forrest Co. Rep. Party, 60-; alternate del, Rep. Nat. Conv, 68; mem, Nixon for Pres. Nat. Finance Cmt, 68; mem, finance cmt, Miss. Rep. Party, 68. Bus. & Prof. Pos: Salesman, Moore Bus. Forms, Inc, 52-57; sales mgr, Hub City Off. Supply Co, Inc, 57-62; pres, Med. Records Co, Inc, 62- Mil. Serv: Entered as Pvt, Marines, 46, released as 2nd Lt.(R), 48 after serv. in Spec. Serv. Rel: Episcopal. Mailing Add: Woodland Hills, Hattiesburg, Miss. 39401.

HEADY, MARION BENJAMIN R
Chmn, Jasper Co. Rep. Orgn, Ill.
b. Newton, Ill, 12/5/08; s. Joe Heady and Nora Pulliam H; m. 5/30/31 to Iva F. Staley; c. Duane and Nora (Mrs. Mansur). Polit. & Govt. Pos: State oil well inspector, Ill, 53-59; Justice of the Peace, Newton, 54-58; treas, Jasper Co. Rep. Cmt, 54-64; chmn, Jasper Co. Rep. Orgn, 64-; mem, Ill. Rep. Cent. Cmt, 68-; chmn, 54th Representative Dist. Rep. Party, currently. Mem: Jasper Co. Farm Bur; Moose. Mailing Add: P.O. Box 1, Newton, Ill. 62448.

HEALEY, JAMES CHRISTOPHER D
b. Bronx, N.Y.C, 12/24/09. Educ: Univ. Pa, 33; Fordham and St. John's Law Sch, 36. Polit. & Govt. Pos: U.S. Rep, 56-64; counsel to borough pres. of Bronx, 49-56; asst. corp. counsel for N.Y.C, 46-49; asst. U.S. Attorney, South. Dist. of N.Y, 41-43; attorney for N.Y. State Labor Rels. Bd, 38-40. Mil. Serv: Navy, 43-46. Legal Res: 1535 Undercliff Ave, Bronx, N.Y. 10453. Mailing Add: 1405 Edward L. Grant Hwy, Bronx, N.Y. 10452. (1967)

HEALEY, JAMES THOMAS D
Conn. State Rep.
b. Waterbury, Conn, 10/15/18; s. Patrick Healey and Kathleen Coughlan H; m. 1/12/46 to Marie D. Tedeschi; c. Patrick. Educ: Yale Univ, B.A, 40 and LL.B, 47. Polit. & Govt. Pos: Conn. State Rep, 87th Dist, 67- Bus. & Prof. Pos: Assoc, Healey & Healey, 47-52, partner, 52- Mil. Serv: Entered as 2nd Lt, Army, 41, released as Capt, 45, after serv. in 25th Field Artil. Bn, Caribbean and Europe; Bronze Star; Am. Serv. Ribbon with Overseas Clasp; ETO Serv. Ribbon; Victory Medal. Mem: Am. Bar Asn; Waterbury Club; Country Club of Waterbury; Univ. Club. of Waterbury; incorporator and ex-dir, Waterbury Area Crippled Children Soc; ex-dir, Waterbury Chap, Am. Red Cross; mem. adv. bd, Waterbury Br, Salvation Army. Rel: Roman Catholic. Legal Res: 165 Hillside Ave, Waterbury, Conn. 06710. Mailing Add: c/o Healey & Healey, Box 2299, Waterbury, Conn. 06720.

HEALEY, JANICE FARRELL D
b. Hastings, Nebr, 6/25/34; d. Dr. Chester Harvey Farrell and Margaret Louise Cathers F; m. 3/5/60 to Patrick William Healey; c. Christopher William and Michael Terry. Educ: Wellesley Col, 53-55; Univ. Nebr, 55-57; Univ. Nebr. Law Sch, part-time, 65-66; Kappa Kappa Gamma. Polit. & Govt. Pos: Del, Dem. Nat. Conv. and mem. credentials cmt, 68. Bus. & Prof. Pos: Guidette, Nat. Broadcasting Co, New York, 58-59, receptionist, Steve Allen Show, 59; publicity writer, Gr. N.Y. Fund, 59; reporter, Sun Newspapers, Omaha, 59-60 & 62-63, Lincoln J, 60-62. Mem: Pub. rels dir, Lincoln Commun. Chest, 63-64; bd. dirs, Southeast Br, YMCA; mem. bd, Lincoln Co. Y Cmt; pres, Theatre Inc, Lincoln; Jr. League; Country Club; NAACP; bd. dirs, Lincoln Commun. Playhouse Found; YWCA; Nebr. Art Asn. Several acting awards, Lincoln Commun. Playhouse. Rel: Unitarian. Mailing Add: 5845 Saylor St, Lincoln, Nebr. 68506.

HEALEY, MARIE D
b. Highland, Kans, 3/17/04; d. Thomas William Lawhon and Pauline Ganzer L; m. 6/29/29 to Herbert Thomas Healey; c. Thomas Martin and Joyce Marie (Mrs. Hilbert). Educ: Browns Bus. Col, Davenport, Iowa. Polit. & Govt. Pos: Co. v.chmn, Dem. Cent. Cmt, Iowa, 48-60; dist. committeewoman, First Cong. Dist, 56-62; v.chmn, Iowa Dem. State Cent. Cmt, 58-62; del, Dem. Nat. Conv, 60 & 64, mem, Permanent Orgn. Cmt, 60 and Rules and Order of Bus. Cmt, 64. Mem: Am. Red Cross; Catholic Woman's League; Parent Teachers Orgn; Girl Scout Leader; United Crusade. Rel: Catholic. Mailing Add: 2122 N. Fairmount St, Davenport, Iowa 52804.

HEALY, ELLEN D
Dem. Nat. Committeewoman, Idaho
b. Coeur d'Alene, Idaho; single. Educ: Univ. Idaho. Polit. & Govt. Pos: Former state v.chmn, Idaho Dem. State Cent. Cmt; del, four Dem. Nat. Conv, mem, Platform and Resolutions Cmts, 64 & 68; Dem. Nat. Committeewoman, Idaho, 60-; mem. exec. cmt, Dem. Nat. Cmt; mem, City Planning Cmn, Coeur d'Alene, 63-69; mem. exec. cmt, West. State Dem. Conf. Bus. & Prof. Pos: Pres. and gen. mgr, Graham Investment Co. Inc, Real Estate & Ins. Mem: Univ. of Idaho Alumni Asn; Nat. Asn. of Ins. Women; Cath. Daughters of Am; bd. regents, Gonzaga Univ. Mailing Add: 1221 E. Lakeshore Dr, Coeur d'Alene, Idaho 83814.

HEALY, H. E. PAT R
Kans. State Sen.
b. Wichita, Kans, 4/12/15; s. John Patrick Healy and Margaret Irene Hooper H; m. Mary Celestine Grob. Educ: Wichita Univ, arts and sci, 4 years; Washburn Univ, LL.B; Delta Theta Phi. Polit. & Govt. Pos: Rep. precinct committeeman, Kans, 40-42 & 46-66; spec. asst. to co. attorney, Sedgwick Co, 41-42, dep. sheriff, 46-68; mem, Kans. Bur. of Invest, 48-51; counsel, Kans. Real Estate Cmn, 52-53 and Small Bus. Asn, Udall Kans. Disaster, 55-56; spec. counsel, Sedgwick Co. Bd. of Cmnrs, 67-69; Judge-Pro-Tem, Police and Traffic Courts and Court of Common Pleas, various dates; Kans. State Sen, 19th Dist, 69- Bus. & Prof. Pos: Attorney-at-Law, Wichita, Kans, 50- Mil. Serv: Entered as Pvt, Air Force, 42, released as 1st Lt, 46, after serv. as Ninth Troop Carrier Command Glider Pilot, 20th Air Force, Staff of Provost Marshall, S.Pac, 46. Mem: Am, Kans. and Wichita Bar Asns; Kans. Peace Officers Asn; Cowtown; Lancers Asn, Inc; VFW. Rel: Catholic. Mailing Add: 715 Union National Bldg, Wichita, Kans. 67202.

HEALY, JOHN EDWARD 'JACK' D
Mont. State Rep.
b. Butte, Mont, 9/23/07; s. Dennis Healy and Julia McCarthy H; m. 2/8/38 to Irene Leary; c. John E, Jr. Educ: Mont. Tech, 2 years; Univ. Wash, grad. Polit. & Govt. Pos: Engr, Mont. State Hwy, 32-33 & 34-35, Forest Serv, 33-34, Co. surveyor and engr, Silver Bow Co, Mont, 35-51; Mont. State Rep, 61- Bus. & Prof. Pos: Engr, Anaconda Co, 51- Mem: K. of C; Elks; past pres, Mont. Soc. Engrs. Athletics in Col. Rel: Catholic. Mailing Add: 624 W. Granite St, Butte, Mont. 59701.

HEALY, WINSTON R
Mass. State Rep.
b. Chicago, Ill, 11/11/07; s. John Jay Healy and Katharine Andrews H; m. 12/29/31 to Margaret Lee; c. Winston, Jr, Cynthia (Mrs. Peter Ellis) and Jonathan. Educ: Williams Col, A.B, 29; Phi Beta Kappa; Sigma Phi; Gargoyle Soc; Purple Key Soc. Polit. & Govt. Pos: Auditor, Charlemont, Mass, 38, selectman, 39-42 & 49-56, assessor, 56-60, mem. sch. cmt, 47 and moderator, 65-; Mass. State Rep, 63- Bus. & Prof. Pos: Owner, Hall Tavern Farm, 36-; dir, Shelburne Falls Nat. Bank, 48- Mil. Serv: Entered as Lt, Naval Res, 42, released as Cmdr, 45, after serv. in U.S, Pac. and Africa areas aboard U.S.S. Wasp and HMS Victorious; Bronze Star; Unit Citation and theatre medals. Legal Res: Charlemont, Mass. 01339. Mailing Add: R.D, Shelburne Falls, Mass. 03170.

HEARD, FRED W. D
Ore. State Rep.
b. Prineville, Ore, 9/9/40; s. Darrell L. Heard and Wilma E. Straube H; m. 6/11/66 to Adair E. Flann; c. one. Educ: Univ. Ore, 58-60; South. Ore. Col, B.S, 61, M.S, 63. Polit. & Govt. Pos: Chmn, Klamath Co. Dem. Cent. Cmt, Ore, 66-69; Ore. State Rep, 69- Bus. & Prof. Pos: Teacher, Klamath Union High Sch, Klamath Falls, Ore, 63- Mem: Ore. Educ. Asn; Moose; Grange (officer, co. Grange). Rel: Congregational. Legal Res: 825 Lincoln St, Apt. 4, Klamath Falls, Ore. 97601. Mailing Add: P.O. Box 613, Klamath Falls, Ore. 97601.

HEARD, ROLAND SHAEFER D
b. Lanett, Ala, 10/07/95; s. George Heard and Mary Shaefer H; m. 10/28/25 to Janie Lovelace. Educ: Bus. Col. in Atlanta, course in bookkeeping and acct, 16. Polit. & Govt. Pos: Lt. Col, Staff of Gov. Carl E. Sanders, Gov. S. Ernest Vandiver and Gov. Eugene Talmadge, 40-41; mem, Sixth Dist. Dem. Exec. Cmt, 54-; mem. city coun, West Point, Ga, 56-62; Ga. State Sen, 29th Dist, 63-64. Bus. & Prof. Pos: Cashier and off. mgr, gen. off, West Point Mfg. Co; Heard-Williams Co; v.pres, Valley Nat. Bank, Lanett, Ala, retired; pres, Mid. Chattahoochee River Develop. Asn, 58-; mem, Cmt. on Navigation, Nat. Rivers and Harbors Cong, D.C, 61-; mem, State Cmn. for Develop. of Chattahoochee River, 67-71; chmn, Parks and Recreation, Troup Co. Planning Cmn, LaGrange, Ga. and dir. and chmn, West Point Dam and Reservoir Cmt, Valley Chamber of Commerce, West Point, 67- Mil. Serv: Naval Res, 18-21; active duty Charleston, S.C, Yeoman 3/C; Victory Medal. Mem: Past Master, West Point Lodge, F&AM; Chap, Commandery, Shrine; charter mem. with perfect attendance, West Point Lions Club, 36-, pres. and dist. gov, 44-45; Am. Legion; pres, Middle Chattahoochee River Develop. Asn, 58; dir, Valley C. of C. Silver Beaver Award, Boy Scouts, 44; Outstanding Civilian Serv. Award, U.S. Corps of Army Engrs, 68; Achievement Award, West Point Lions Club, 51; Citation of Merit, Valley C. of C, West Point. Rel: Baptist; lifetime deacon. Mailing Add: P.O. Box 246, West Point, Ga. 31833.

HEARN, CLIFFORD BURTON, JR. D
Del. State Rep.
b. Raspesburg, Md, 10/18/37; s. Clifford Burton Hearn and Margaret Addison H; m. 8/31/63 to Kerin Bertl. Educ: Univ. Del, B.A, 59; Univ. Va. Law Sch, LL.B, 62. Polit. & Govt. Pos: Mem, Ninth Ward Dem. Club, Del. and Young Dem. Wilmington; asst. city solicitor, Wilmington, 66-67; Del. State Rep, 68- Bus. & Prof. Pos: Attorney, Morris, Nichols, Aesht and Tunnel, 65-68; Biggs and Battaglia, 69- Mil. Serv: Entered as 1st Lt, Army, 62, released as Capt, 65, after serv. in Army Judiciary; Capt, Res; Army Commendation Medal. Mem: Am, Va. State and Del. Bar Asns. Legal Res: 917 W. 22nd St, Wilmington, Del. 19802. Mailing Add: 401 Farmers Bank Bldg, Wilmington, Del. 19801.

HEARN, GEORGE HENRY D
N.Y. State Dem. Committeeman
b. Brooklyn, N.Y, 7/4/27; s. Henry G. Hearn and Grace A. Flaherty H; m. 6/28/52 to Cecelia Anne Philbin; c. Annemarie Jude, Margaret Mary and George Henry. Educ: Fordham Univ. Sch. of Bus. Admin, 48; St. Francis Col, B.A, 50; St. John's Univ, LL.B, 54. Polit. & Govt. Pos: N.Y.C. Coun, 58-61; chmn, Kings Co. Speakers Cmt. for Pres. Elec, 60; v.chmn, cmt. nationalists and intergroup rels, N.Y. State Dem. Cmt, 60-; cmnr, Fed. Maritime Cmn, 64- Bus. & Prof. Pos: Lawyer, Haight, Gardner, Poor & Havens, N.Y.C, 54-61. Mil. Serv: Naval Res, World War II, Pac. Theater; Distinguished Serv. Award. Mem: Dist. cmnr, Boy Scouts, 58-; U.S. Jr. C. of C, 58; past pres, St. Patrick's Soc, Brooklyn; Am. Cmt. Italian Migration, recording secy, Brooklyn Div; K of C. Legal Res: 423 Bay Ridge Parkway, Brooklyn, N.Y. 11209. and 1414 Dilston Rd, Silver Spring, Md. 20903. Mailing Add: 1405-I St. N.W, Washington D.C. 20005.

HEARN, GEORGE J.
Adj. Gen. and Dir, Civil Defense, Ga.
m. 9/18/29 to Nell Potts; c. George J, III; grandchildren, Cheryl Ann, Vicki Lynn and George J, IV. Polit. & Govt. Pos: Former mayor, Monroe, Ga; mem, Dept. Army Gen. Staff Cmt. on Army Nat. Guard and Army Res. Policy; Adj. Gen. and dir, Civil Defense, Ga, currently. Bus. & Prof. Pos: Owner, Hearn Hardware Co, currently. Mil. Serv: Ga. Nat. Guard, 25-, commissioned 2nd Lt, 32; Fed. Serv, 40-46 and Brig. Gen, Korean War, 52; Maj. Gen, Atlanta's Hq. and Hq. Detachment Ga. Army Nat. Guard, currently. Mem: Am. Legion (past Comdr, Ga. Dept); Mason; F&AM (Past Worshipful Master, Generous Warren Lodge 20); Walton Co. Hosp. Bd; Atlanta Consistory; VFW; 40 et 8; U.S. and Ga. Nat. Guard Asns. Rel: Christian Church; Elder. Mailing Add: Monroe, Ga. 30655. (1967)

HEARN, IRENE FINNERTY R
Mem, Calif. Rep. State Cent. Cmt.
b. Glendale, Calif, 10/21/32; d. Robert Emmet Finnerty and Margaret Flautt F; m. 2/13/65 to Frederick William Hearn. Educ: Immaculate Heart Col, B.A, 54; Delta Chi Phi. Polit. & Govt. Pos: Campaign staff, Sen. Thomas H. Kuchel, 56; admin. asst. to U.S. Rep. H. Allen Smith, Calif, 57-66; field rep, 66-; mem, Los Angeles Co. Rep. Cent. Cmt, 43rd Assembly Dist. Rep. Cent. Cmt. and Calif. Rep. State Cent. Cmt, currently. Mem: Rep. Buck & Ballot Brigade (dir); Jr. Auxiliary of Flower Guild Charities for Children; 43rd Rep. Assembly; Glendale Rep. Women's Workshop. Rel: Catholic. Mailing Add: 1245 Imperial Dr, Glendale, Calif. 91207.

HEARNES, WARREN EASTMAN D
Gov, State of Mo.
b. Moline, Ill, 7/24/23; s. Earle B. Hearnes and Edna Eastman H; m. 1948 to Betty Sue Cooper; c. Lynn, Leigh and Julia B. Educ: U.S. Mil. Acad, West Point, B.S, 46; Univ. Mo. Sch. of Law, A.B. and LL.B, 52; Phi Delta Theta; Phi Delta Phi. Polit. & Govt. Pos: Former city attorney, E. Prairie, Mo; Mo. State Rep, 50-61, Majority Floor Leader, Mo. State House of Rep, 57-61; Secy. of State, Mo, 61-65; Gov, State of Mo, 65- Bus. & Prof. Pos: Mem, State Bd. of Dirs, Mo. Ment. Health Asn, 60-; Bd. of Dirs, Am. Royal Exposition, Kansas City, Mo. Mil. Serv: Enlisted in Army and served in Hq. Co, 140th Inf, 35th Div, 77th Anti-Aircraft, released as 1st Lt, 49. Mem: Scottish Rite, York Rite, Shrine, Mason; Mo. Bar Asn; Lions; Elks; Eagles; Am. Legion; VFW. Rel: Baptist. Mailing Add: Executive Mansion, Jefferson City, Mo. 65101.

HEARST, WILLIAM CURTIS R
b. Cedar Falls, Iowa, 11/11/03; s. Dr. William L. Hearst and Jennie Curtis H; m. 8/15/51 to Harriet Skaggs; c. William Skaggs. Educ: DePauw Univ, Greencastle, Ind; Univ. Iowa, B.S. in commerce, 26; Acacia. Polit. & Govt. Pos: Mem, Clarion Co. Rep. Exec. Cmt, Pa, 56-60; del, Rep. Nat. Conv, 64. Bus. & Prof. Pos: Co-owner, Radio Station WWCH; publisher, Rep. Newspaper, 42-65, Dem. Newspaper, 48-65 and Clarion Newspapers, 48-65. Mem: Pa. Newspaper Publishers Asn.(state exec. cmt); Knox Rotary Club (past pres); charter mem. Clarion Rotary Club (past pres); founder, Clarion C. of C.(past dir). Rel: Methodist. Mailing Add: 117 S. Eighth Ave, Clarion, Pa. 16214.

HEARTWELL, HENRY LIGHTFOOT D
b. Lawrenceville, Va, 12/11/21; s. Herbert Harrison Heartwell and Cornelia Walsh Mich H; m. 3/25/49 to Jane Hamilton Adams; c. Karen Adams. Educ: Lawrenceville High Sch, 37-41. Polit. & Govt. Pos: Halifax Co. Mt. Carmel Dist. rep, Fifth Dist. Dem. Party, Va, 59-; del, Dem. Nat. Conv, 68. Mem: Jr. C. of C; C. of C; Halifax Country Club; Cancer Society; Ruritan Club; PTA; United Fund; Red Cross. Rel: Presbyterian. Mailing Add: Route 3, Box 101, South Boston, Va. 24592.

HEASLIP, GEORGE JOSEPH R
b. N. Benningham, Vt, 9/1/11; m. to Mary Lombardy; c. 1 son, 1 daughter. Educ: St. Francis de Sales Acad; Benningham High Sch. Polit. & Govt. Pos: Vt. State Rep, 63-67. Bus. & Prof. Pos: Distributor of Mobil Prod. Rel: Catholic. Mailing Add: Manchester Center, Vt. 05255. (1967)

HEATER, ELLIOTT VERMONT, JR. R
b. Grandview, Wash, 5/22/25; s. Elliott Vermont Heater and Bernice Wilson H; m. 11/7/47 to Winifred Gemmell; c. Monica, Stephen, Robert and Gregg. Educ: Spokane Commun. Col, 67-69. Polit. & Govt. Pos: Chmn, Stevens Co. Rep. Club, Wash, 67- Bus. & Prof. Pos: Farming, 43-52; custom contract farming, 52-54; heavy duty mech, 54-66; retired, 66. Rel: Protestant. Mailing Add: Route 2, Box 56A, Colville, Wash. 99114.

HEATH, DONALD E. R
Fla. State Rep.
b. Waukegan, Ill, 6/20/29; s. Clarence L. Heath and Anne McVennon H; m. 9/11/66 to Carol Reese; c. Karen, Donald E, Jr. and Michael. Educ: Gen. Educ. Develop, Army, courses in surg. tech. and air transportability, 2 years; LaSalle Exten. Univ, law course, at present. Polit. & Govt. Pos: Mem, Bd. of Adjusters, Sarasota Co, Fla, 65; legis. asst, Fla. State Legis, 65; Fla. State Rep, Dist. 118, 68- Bus. & Prof. Pos: H & R Construction Co, Ill, 53-57; Customline Home Builders, Inc, Venice, Fla, 57- Mil. Serv: Entered as Pvt, Army, 45, released as T/Sgt, 51 after serv. in Medics; Pacific Theatre, 46-49. Mem: Venice Home Builders Asn.(past pres), National Home Builders Asn.(past nat. dir); Elks; dir, Venice C. of C. Rel: Presbyterian. Legal Res: 513 Peach St, Venice, Fla. 33595. Mailing Add: P.O. Box 246, Nokomis, Fla. 33555.

HEATH, JOSEPH BRYAN, JR. D
Committeeman, La. Dem. State Cent. Cmt.
b. Baton Rouge, La, 3/10/20; s. Joseph Bryan Heath and Alice Acy H; m. 11/9/39 to Helen Hanna; c. Ted Ray and Sue (Mrs. Richard E. Faires). Educ: Baton Rouge Bus. Col, Bookkeeping, 2 years. Polit. & Govt. Pos:Committeeman, La. Dem. State Cent. Cmt, 60-; del, Dem. Nat. Conv, 68. Bus. & Prof. Pos: Employee, Humble Oil & Refining, 42-57; mgr. and owner, Heath Ins. Agency, 57-; notary pub. Mem: Nat. and La. Asns. Ins. Agents; F&AM; C. of C; Jr. Achievement. Rel: Baptist. Legal Res: Route 1, Box 13 D, St. Amant, La. 70774. Mailing Add: P.O. Box 307, Gonzales, La. 70737.

HEATH, RALPH LEWIS R
b. Waterville, Que, Can, 2/9/90; s. John P. Heath and Emma M. Gero H; m. 6/18/55 to Elsie Marion Richardson; c. by 1st m. Lewis C. Polit. & Govt. Pos: Postmaster, U.S. Post Off. Dept, 51-60; Vt. State Rep, East Haven, 65-68; former chmn, Town Civil Defense. Mem: F&AM. Rel: Methodist. Mailing Add: East Haven, Vt. 05837.

HEATH, TIM RAY R
Mem, Ware Co. Rep. Exec. Cmt, Ga.
b. Homerville, Ga, 5/6/35; s. Hezekaih K. Heath, Sr. and Elizabeth Kirkland H; m. 8/6/61 to Mary Anne Kennedy; c. Mary Anne and Tim Ray, Jr. Educ: N.Ga. Col; Med. Col. of Ga. Polit. & Govt. Pos: Mem, Ware Co. Rep. Exec. Cmt, Ga, 62- Rel: Protestant. Mailing Add: Box 1131, Waycross, Ga. 31501. (1967)

HEATLY, CONSTANCE A. R
State Chmn, Young Rep. of N.J.
b. Summit, N.J, 10/26/38; d. John Heatly and Phyllis Mary Williams; single. Educ: Ohio Univ, B.F.A, 60; Sigma Kappa. Polit. & Govt. Pos: Secy, Westfield Area Young Rep, N.J, 61, co. del, 62 & 63, v.chmn, 63-64; alternate state del, Union Co. Young Rep, 62-63, state del, 64-65, co. chmn, 66-68; committeewoman, Westfield Rep. Cmt, 65-; alternate del, Rep. Nat. Conv, 68; state chmn, Young Rep. N.J, 69- Bus. & Prof. Pos: Commercial artist, Venet Advert, Union, N.J, 61-65 & 68- and Scheer Advert, Newark, 67-68. Rel: Presbyterian. Mailing Add: 728 Fairacres Ave, Westfield, N.J. 07090.

HEATLY, WILLIAM STANFORD, JR. D
Tex. State Rep.
b. Mart, Tex, 9/3/12; s. William Stanford Heatly and Byrta Rogers H; m. 1/10/46 to Jonnie Green Hawkins; c. Eugene Newcomb, William Hawkins and William Stanford, III. Educ: Decatur Baptist Col, 31-33; Baylor Univ, A.B. and LL.B, 36, Law Sch. Foreman, Baylor. Hon. LL.D, Howard Payne Col, Tex. and Dallas Baptist Col. Polit. & Govt. Pos: City attorney, Paducah, Tex, 50-52; Tex. State Rep, 54-, mem, Legis. Budget Bd, Tex. House of Rep, 55-60 & 63-66, chmn, State Affairs Cmt, 57-58, mem, State Audit Cmt, 59-60 & 63-66 and chmn, Appropriations Cmt, 59-60 & 63-66. Bus. & Prof. Pos: Farmer; rancher; oil and banking interests; attorney-at-law, Paducah, Tex, 47-; owner, Jones and Renfrow, Abstractors, 50- Publ: 'Alcohol-Public Enemy #1,' Baptist Standard, 58. Mem: Am. Bar Asn; mem, legis. cmt, Tex. State Bar Asn; past pres, Lions; former dir, C. of C; K. of P; Scottish Rite; Mason (33°); Cattle King Farmers Union; Crippled Childrens Easter Seals; Distributive Edc. in Tex; Cmn. on Alcholism; State Bar of Tex. All State Jr. Col. quarterback, Deca-

tur Baptist Col, 32 and 33; Clarendon Jr. Col. Award. Rel: Christian Church; former chmn. bd. of deacons and elders, First Christian Church of Paducah. Mailing Add: Drawer 1, Paducah, Tex. 79248.

HEAVEY, PATRICIA W. DURBIN D
Mem, Calif. Dem. State Cent. Cmt.
b. Oakland, Calif, 4/7/27; d. Charles W. Wallace and Enid L. Remick W; m. 12/6/58 to James T. Heavey; c. Leonore. Educ: Univ. of Calif, Berkeley, B.S, 48, Ph.D, 53; Sigma Xi; Iota Sigma Pi; Alpha Gamma Delta. Polit. & Govt. Pos: Pres, Berkeley Young Dem, 56-57; Secy. North div, Calif. Fedn. of Young Dem, 57-58, nat. committeewoman, 58-59; chmn, Seventh Cong. Dist. Dem. Coun, 59; alternate del, Dem. Nat. Conv, 60; grand juror, Alameda Co, 67; mem, Calif. Dem. State Cent. Cmt, 68. Bus. & Prof. Pos: Research physiologist, Lawrence Radiation Lab, 46- Publ: 'Metabolic Characteristics within a Chemical Family,' 60 and 'Distribution of the Transuranium Elements in Mammals,' 62, Health Physics; 'Development of Spontaneous Mammary Tumors over the Life Span of the Female Rat,' Cancer Research, 66. Mem: Radiation Research Soc; Health Physics Soc; Am. Asn. Adv. Sci; Fedn. of Am. Scientists; Univ. of Calif. Alumni Asn; Calif. Tomorrow; Nat. Parks Asn; Am. Civil Liberties Union. Rel: Protestant. Mailing Add: 3433 Boston Ave, Oakland, Calif. 94602.

HEBARD, EMORY R
b. Carmel, Maine, 9/28/17; m. to Irma M. Mills; c. two daughters. Educ: Middlebury Col, A.B, 38. Polit. & Govt. Pos: Vt. State Rep, 61-67; Trustee, Glover Fire Dept; Dir, Orleans Co. Fair and Vt. Fairs Asn; Town Moderator; twice served as Asst. Mgr; Dir of Ind. Develop. for Vt. Develop. Dept; Chmn, Repub. Co. Cmt; State Repub. Cmt. Mil. Serv: WW II and Korea, Lt. Comdr, U.S. Coast Guard Reserve. Mem: Grange; Masons; Eastern Star; 100F; Am. Legion; Phi Beta Kappa. Rel: Congregational. Mailing Add: Glover, Vt. 05839. (1967)

HEBBLE, HARRY HAROLD D
Chmn, Adams Co. Dem. Cent. Cmt, Ind.
b. Decatur, Ind, 7/13/10; s. John Perry Hebble and Estella Bell Niblich Hebble Coffee; m. 4/4/36 to Mildred Marilee Gause; c. John Cecil and Harry Harold, Jr. Educ: Ball State Univ; North.Ill. Col. of Optom. Polit. & Govt. Pos: Chmn. and precinct committeeman, Decatur Dem. Cmt, Ind, 40-44; councilman, Decatur, 43-47; mem, Sch. Bd, 50-55; chmn, Adams Co. Dem. Cent. Cmt, 52-66 and currently. Mem: Red Men; Moose; Mason. Rel: Protestant. Mailing Add: 1233 Adams St, Decatur, Ind. 46733. (1967)

HEBERT, F. EDWARD D
U.S. Rep, La.
b. New Orleans, La, 10/12/01; s. Felix Joseph Hebert and Lea Naquin H; m. 8/1/34 to Gladys Bofill; c. Dawn Marie (Mrs. John Malcolm Duhe Jr.). Educ: Tulane Univ, 20-24; Delta Sigma Phi (nat. v.pres, 37-49). Polit. & Govt. Pos: U.S. Rep, La, 41- Bus. & Prof. Pos: Dir, Cent. Homestead Asn; asst. sports ed, New Orleans Times-Picayune, 19-20; asst. sports ed, New Orleans States, 20-25; dir publicity, Loyola Univ, New Orleans, 26-29; polit. ed. and columnist, 27-37; city ed, New Orleans States, 37-40; dir, Bank La, New Orleans, currently. Publ: 'I Went, I Saw, I Heard'. Mem: Young Men's Bus. Club New Orleans (pres, 32). Mailing Add: 5367 Canal Blvd, New Orleans, La. 70124.

HEBERT, PERCY DANIEL D
Sheriff, St. John the Baptist Parish, La.
b. Lions, Louisiana, 7/13/07; s. Emile Joseph Hebert and Oralie Ory H; m. 11/5/35 to Leona Montz; c. Sheila Kathryn (Mrs. Adams). Educ: Leon Godchaux High Sch, 4 years; La. State Police Sch, 3 months. Polit. & Govt. Pos: La. State Police, 35-40; Sheriff, St. John Baptist Parish, La, 41- Mem: Nat. and La. Sheriff's Asns; K. of C; WOW; C. of C. Rel: Catholic. Legal Res: 900 Main St, Laplace, La. 70068. Mailing Add: P.O. Drawer Q, Laplace, La. 70068.

HEBERT, ROLAND ARTHUR, JR. R
Mem, Oakdale Rep. Town Cmt, Conn.
b. Fall River, Mass, 3/23/33; s. Roland Arthur Hebert and Ruth Bradley H; m. 4/18/59 to Doris Marie Cabral; c. Roland Manuel, Steven Edward and Richard Andrew. Educ: Westport High Sch, Mass, grad, 55. Polit. & Govt. Pos: Campaign chmn, Oakdale Rep. Town Cmt, Conn, 67-68, chmn, 67- Bus. & Prof. Pos: Div. mgr, Sears, Roebuck & Co, Fall River, Mass, 61-64, New London, Conn, 64-68 and Norwich, Conn, 68- Mil. Serv: Entered as E-1, Army, 51, released as E-4, 53, after serv. in 192nd R.C.T, Korea and Alaska. Mem: Montville Jaycees; Oakdale Fire Co; Oakdale Water Asn; Neighborhood Dump Cmt. Distinguished Serv. Award, Montville, Conn; Three Presidential Awards, Keyman Award, Sparkplug Award and Spoke Award, Jaycees. Rel: Roman Catholic. Mailing Add: 11 Glendale Rd, Oakdale, Conn. 06370.

HECHLER, KEN D
U.S. Rep, W.Va.
b. Roslyn, N.Y, 9/20/14; s. Charles Henry Hechler and Catherine Elizabeth Hauhart H. Educ: Swarthmore Col, A.B, 35; Columbia, A.M, 36, Ph.D, 40. Polit. & Govt. Pos: Research asst. to Judge Sam I. Roseman on President Roosevelt's Pub. Papers, 39-50; sect. chief, Bur. of Census, 40; personnel technologist, Off. for Emergency Mgt, 41; admin. analyst, Budget Bur, 41-42 & 46-47; spec. asst. to President Truman, 49-53; research dir, Adlai Stevenson Campaign, 56; U.S. Rep, W.Va, 59-; del, Dem. Nat. Conv, 68. Bus. & Prof. Pos: Govt. lectr, Barnard Col, Columbia Univ, 37-41; asst. prof. polit. sci, Princeton Univ, 47-49; assoc. prof. polit. sci, Marshall Col, 57; radio-TV commentator, 57-58. Mil. Serv: Maj, Army, 42-46; Col, Army Res, currently. Publ: Insurgency: Personalities and Policies of Taft Era, 40; The Bridge at Remagen, 57; West Virginia Memories of President Kennedy, 65. Mem: Am. Legion; VFW; DAV; Elks; Am. Polit. Sci. Asn. Rel: Episcopal. Legal Res: 917 Fifth Ave, Huntington, W.Va. 25701. Mailing Add: U.S. House Office Bldg, Washington, D.C. 20515. (1967)

HECHT, BURTON D
N.Y. State Assemblyman
b. New York, N.Y, 12/30/27; m. to Isabel H; c. Mindy, Audrey and Allen. Educ: N.Y. Univ; N.Y. Univ. Law Sch. Polit. & Govt. Pos: Asst. Dist. Attorney, Bronx Co, N.Y; N.Y. State Assemblyman, 62- Bus. & Prof. Pos: Lawyer Mem: Decatur Dem. Club; chmn, Fedn. of Jewish Philanthropies, 61-63; Gen, Israel Orphanage Home for Girls; counsel, Parkside Tenants League; speakers cmt, United Jewish Appeal; F&AM; Zionist Orgn. of Am; Bronx Co. Bar Asn; bd. dirs, Kingsbridge Heights Jewish Center; Muscular Dystrophy Asn. of Am; Beth Sharaga Inst; Bedford Park Civic Asns; speakers cmt, Anti-Defamation League, B'nai B'rith. Rel: Jewish. Mailing Add: 2715 Grand Concourse, Bronx, N.Y. 10460. (1967)

HECHT, CHIC R
Nev. State Sen.
b. Cape Girardeau, Mo, 11/30/28; s. Louis Hecht and Anna Sigoloff H.(deceased); m. 7/23/59 to Gail Sharon Kahn; c. Lori Ann and Leslie Lyn. Educ: Mo. Univ, 45-46; St. Louis Univ, 46-47; Wash. Univ, B.S. in Bus. Admin, 49; Sigma Alpha Mu. Polit. & Govt. Pos: Nev. State Sen, 67-, Minority Leader, Nev. State Senate, 69-; alternate del, Rep. Nat. Conv, 68. Mil. Serv: Entered as Pvt, Army, 51, released as Cpl, 53, after serv. as Spec. Agent, Counter Intel, Berlin, Germany, 51-53; Army Occupation Medal. Mem: Pres, Retail Merchants Asn, Las Vegas, 63; dir, C. of C, 63; Elks; Am. Legion; Jewish War Vets; B'nai B'rith. Rel: Jewish. Legal Res: 47 Country Club Lane, Las Vegas, Nev. 89109. Mailing Add: 413 Fremont, Las Vegas, Nev. 89101.

HECHT, CHRISTINE SIGRID D
Mem, Fairfax Co. Dem. Cmt, Va.
b. Chicago, Ill, 1/22/43; d. Lothar H. Schroeder and Theresa Wailand S; m. 3/18/61 to Stephen J. Hecht; c. Victoria Lynn and Lisa Katherine. Educ: Chicago City Col, 1 year. Polit. & Govt. Pos: Precinct chmn, Fairfax Co. Dem. Cmt, Va, 65-; del, Fairfax Co. Dem. Conv. and Dem. Nat. Conv, 68. Mem: League of Women Voters. Rel: Unitarian. Mailing Add: 6611 E. Wakefield Dr, Alexandria, Va. 22307.

HECHT, HENRY DEL BANCO, JR. R
b. New Orleans, La, 11/9/01; s. Henry Del Banco Hecht and Sarah Rohrbacher H; m. 12/6/23 to Harriet Jay; c. Harriett (Mrs. Rousseau) and Henry D, III. Educ: Warren Easton Sch, New Orleans, 4 years; Soule Bus. Col, 3 years. Polit. & Govt. Pos: Asst. campaign mgr, Rep. Party, La, 48-54; mem, La. State Rep. Cent. Cmt, 60-68; secy-treas, Jefferson Parish Rep. Exec. Cmt, 60-68, asst. campaign mgr. for Hugh Exnicious for Dist. Attorney's Off, 67- Bus. & Prof. Pos: Gen. Ins, retired, 60. Mem: F&AM (Past Master, Ideal Lodge 367, Dep. Grand Lectr, 65-67, dist. Dep. Grand Master, 68); Mason (secy-treas, Cert. Asn. of New Orleans, 8 years). Rel: Methodist. Mailing Add: 123 Midway Dr, New Orleans, La. 70123.

HECHT, W. ARTHUR R
Mem, Calif. State Rep. Cent. Cmt.
b. Bielefeld, Germany, 12/13/23; s. Leo Hecht and Herta Lewinski H; m. 11/22/51 to Doris Ida Goldstein; c. Stephen Thomas. Educ: Columbia Univ, B.S, 48; Tau Beta Pi; Alpha Phi Omega. Polit. & Govt. Pos: Dir. East Bay Div, San Francisco Bay Area Rep. Alliance, Calif, 65-, v.pres, 66, pres, 67, treas, 68, v.chmn, 69-; co. campaign worker, Christopher for Gov, 66, Kelley for State Senate, 66, Sherman for State Senate, 66 & 70, Finch for Lt. Gov, 66, Kuchel for U.S. Senate, 68 and Hillburn for Cong, 68; mem, Calif. State Rep. Cent. Cmt, 67-; mem, Alameda Co. Rep. Finance Cmt, 67-; cand, Piedmont Bd. of Educ, 68. Bus. & Prof. Pos: Indust. Engr, various companies, 48-53; plant chief indust. engr, Continental Can Co, Oakland, Calif, 53-60; v.pres, Allwork Mfg. Co, 60-66; agent, New York Life Ins. Co, 67- Mil. Serv: Entered as Pvt, Army, 42, released as Sgt, 46, after serv. in 656th Engr. Topographic Bn, European Theatre, 45-46, Capt, Army Intel. Res, 46-49. Mem: Am. Inst. Indust. Engrs; Soc. Adv. of Mgt; Nat. Asn. Life Underwriters; Boy Scouts (Piedmont Coun. Exec. Bd, formerly Oakland Area Coun. Exec. Bd); Piedmont Swim Club (co-founder and dir, 64-, pres, 67-68); Am. Jewish Cmt.(dir, Oakland Chap). Silver Beaver, Boy Scouts. Rel: Jewish. Mailing Add: 71 Wildwood Ave, Piedmont, Calif. 94610.

HECK, WILFRED HENRY D
Chmn, Union Dem. Town Cmt, Conn.
b. Union, Conn, 2/10/27; s. Albert Monroe Heck and Leila Willis H; m. 2/15/58 to Shirley Elaine Newton; c. Elaine Irene and David Monroe. Educ: Windham Tech, 4 years. Polit. & Govt. Pos: Chmn, Union Dem. Town Cmt, Conn, 61- Legal Res: Wales Rd, Union, Conn. 06076. Mailing Add: R.F.D. 2, Box 155, Stafford Springs, Conn. 06076.

HECKARD, WILLIAM NORMAN R
Chmn, Martin Co. Rep. Party, Ind.
b. Bicknell, Ind, 2/17/22; s. Darwin Manuel Heckard and Grace M. McClure H; m. 8/8/47 to Delphia Doris; c. Norman Wayne, William Malcolm, Grace Diane, Cathy Lynn, Ricky Lee and Darwin Ivan. Educ: Shoals High Sch, Ind, grad, 40. Polit. & Govt. Pos: Mem, Martin Co. Selective Bd, Ind, 58-65; chmn, Halbert Twp. Agr. Stabilization & Conserv. Cmt, 65-66; chmn, Martin Co. Rep. Party, 68- Bus. & Prof. Pos: Timber dealer and farmer, 47- Mil. Serv: Entered as A/S, Navy, 42, released as SSM-2/C, 45, after serving in Pac. Seventh Fleet, 42-45. Mem: Mason; Shrine; Eastern Star; Moose; Elks; Eagles; Am. Legion; VFW; Farm Bur; Lions; PTA. Rel: Methodist. Mailing Add: P.O. Box 36, Shoals, Ind. 47581.

HECKEMEYER, ANTHONY JOSEPH D
Majority Whip, Mo. House of Rep.
b. Cape Girardeau, Mo, 1/20/39; s. Paul Quenton Heckemeyer and Frances Goetz H; m. 2/13/65 to Elizebeth Faye Littleton; c. Anthony Joseph, III and Matthew Paul. Educ: Mo. Univ, B.S. in agr, 61; Sigma Nu. Phi Delta Phi. Polit. & Govt. Pos: Pres, Scott Co. Young Dem. and dir, State Young Dem, Mo, 65-66; Mo. State Rep, 157th Dist, 65-, majority whip and v.chmn, Agr. Cmn, Mo. House of Rep, currently; mem, Gov. Task Force on Aging, 68-69. Bus. & Prof. Pos: Owner, The Sportsman; cattleman. Mil. Serv: Entered as Pvt, Nat. Guard, 60, released as E-3, 66. Mem: Elks; Jaycees; adv. cmt, Mo. Crippled Children Asn. Rel: Catholic. Mailing Add: 526 Vernon, Sikeston, Mo. 63801.

HECKERT, CLARICE UPSON R
Del. State Rep.
b. Marion, Conn, 11/11/10; d. Robert Ellsworth Upson and Helen Nickerson U; m. 9/9/33 to Dr. Winfield Walter Heckert; c. John Upson, Frances (Mrs. Pane), Rowena (Mrs. Gasser) and Clark Webster. Educ: Geneva Sch. of Int. Studies, Switz, summer, 31; Wheaton Col, Mass, A.B, 32. Polit. & Govt. Pos: Mem, Brandywine Hundred Rep. Policy Cmt, 58-64; asst. secy, Del. State Rep. Cmt, 64; Del. State Rep, 64-, chmn, House Educ. Cmt, Del. House of Rep, 67- Mem: Exec. cmt, Greater Wilmington Develop. Coun; bd. dirs, Del. Citizens Crime Cmn; nat. legis. prog. cmt, Am. Asn. of Univ. Women. Rel: Unitarian. Mailing Add: 16 Ravine Rd, Wilmington, Del. 19803.

HECKLER, MARGARET M. R
U.S. Rep, Mass.
married. Educ: Boston Col. Law Sch; Albertus Magnus Col; U.S. student rep, Univ. Leiden, Holland. Polit. & Govt. Pos: Mem, Mass. Gov. Coun, 4 years; U.S. Rep, Mass, 67-; del, Rep. Nat. Conv, 68. Bus. & Prof. Pos: Attorney-at-law, 10 years. Mem: Past v.pres, Women's Rep. Club of Mass; Boston Bar Asn; Mass. Trial Lawyers Asn. Named an Outstanding Young Woman of Am, 65. Legal Res: 30 Colburn Rd, Wellesley, Mass. 02181. Mailing Add: 318 Cannon House Office Bldg, Washington, D.C. 20515.

HECTOR, ROBERT C. D
Fla. State Rep.
b. Ft. Lauderdale, Fla, 4/16/18; s. Harry H. Hector and Grace Kellerstrass H; m. 6/3/42 to Alice Guyton; c. Mrs. Bryan H. Lamb, Alice Guyton, Robert C, Jr. and Emily C. Educ: Princeton Univ, A.B. cum laude in Econ, 40; Charter Club; Triangle Club. Polit. & Govt. Pos: Fla. State Rep, 104th Dist, 66- Bus. & Prof. Pos: Employee, Hector Supply Co, 40-42, v.pres, 46-55, pres, 55-66, chmn. bd, 66- Mil. Serv: Entered as 2nd Lt, Army Res. Artil, 42, released as Capt, 46, after serv. in 415th Field Artil. Group; Lt. Col.(Ret), Army Res, 62. Mem: Chief Exec. Forum; Rotary; Orange Bowl Cmt.(pres, 66); Crippled Children's Soc. U.S. Jr. C. of C. Distinguished Serv. Award, 52-53; Voted one of five Outstanding Young Men in Fla, 53. Rel: Episcopal. Legal Res: 7830 Erwin Rd, South Miami, Fla. 33143. Mailing Add: 3445 N.W. Seventh St, Miami, Fla. 33125.

HEDBERG, ARTHUR CARL, JR. D
b. Chicago, Ill, 4/11/28; s. Arthur C. Hedberg and Hazel Weir H; m. 8/13/55 to Janet Kathryn Terry; c. Eric Garland, Mark Terry, Christopher Lee and Kathryn Jean. Educ: State Univ. Iowa, B.A, 52, LL.B, 54. Polit. & Govt. Pos: Asst. Co. Attorney, Polk Co, Iowa, 56-58; state pres, Young Dem. of Iowa, 57-59; chmn, Polk Co. Dem. Party, 61-69; del, Dem. Nat. Conv, 68. Bus. & Prof. Pos: Attorney at Law, 54- Mil. Serv: Entered as Pvt, Army, 46, released as Sgt, 48, after serv. in 7th Div, Korea, 47-48. Publ: Iowa Probate Practice System, Asn. Law Libraries, Lincoln, Nebr, 63. Rel: Methodist. Mailing Add: 1706 E. 31st Court, Des Moines, Iowa 50317. (1967)

HEDGES, EDWARD EUGENE 'ED' R
Idaho State Rep.
b. Almena, Kans, 9/13/32; s. Charles Edward Hedges and Winifred Gishwiller H; m. 10/26/57 to Cynthia Pearl Ball; c. Christianne K. and Barton Stabe. Educ: Boise Jr. Col, Idaho, dipl, 52; Wash. State Col, B.A, 54, grad. study, 56-57; Sigma Iota; Pi Sigma Sigma (local pres, 52). Polit. & Govt. Pos: Co. chmn, Ada Co. Young Rep, Idaho, 67-68; Idaho State Rep, 15th Legis. Dist, 68- Bus. & Prof. Pos: Treas, Pitkin & Assocs, Inc, 65- Mil. Serv: Entered as E-1, Army Security Agency, 54, released as E-4, 56, after serv. in Security in Mass. and Alaska, 55-56; Non-Combat Ribbons. Mem: Nat. Asn. of Real Estate Bd; Idaho Asn. of Realtors; Boise Bd. of Realtors (dir, 66); AF&AM; PTA; Youth Employ. Serv. Adv. Bd; Toastmasters Int; Boy Scouts. Boise Realtor of the Year, 66; commencement speaker. Rel: Methodist. Mailing Add: 1825 Broadmoor Dr, Boise, Idaho 83705.

HEDGES, VIRGINIA LEE MAHON R
b. San Jose, Calif, 7/14/27; d. Norton Jasper Mahon and Leola Myra Stammer M; div; c. Kelly Paul. Educ: San Jose State Col, 45-47; Univ. of Ore, B.S. in journalism, 49; Gamma Alpha Chi; Alpha Chi Omega. Polit. & Govt. Pos: Secy, Josephine Co. Rep. Cent. Cmt, Ore, 58-60, v.chmn. and chmn, 60-62; secy, State Party Growth Cmt, 62-64; state secy, Ore. Rep. State Cent. Cmt, 62-65, acting exec. dir, 63, letters-to-the ed. chmn, 63-65; secy, First Cong. Dist. Nominating Cmt, 64; cand. for Presidential Elector, 64; staff asst. to U.S. Rep. Wendell Wyatt, Ore, 65- Bus. & Prof. Pos: Advert. promotion asst, Register Publ, Boston, 49-50; secy. and asst. to Northwest Serv. Mgr, Foote, Cone & Belding Advert. Agency, Portland, Ore, 50-52; women's news reporter and continuity writer, Radio Sta. KAGI, Grants Pass, 59-60; secy. and asst. to pres, Adolph L. Bloch Advert. Agency, Portland, 65; freelance advert. and pub. rels, 67-69. Publ: Oregon G.O.P. County Leaders Manual, Ore. Rep. State Cent. Cmt, 68. Mem: PEO; past mem, Am. Asn. of Univ. Women, pres, Grants Pass Br, 54-55; Portland Pub. Rels. Round Table. Rel: Protestant. Mailing Add: 6210 S.W. Pomona, Portland, Ore. 97219.

HEDRICK, CLAY E. R
Kans. State Auditor
m. to Florance L. Greenway; c. Clay E, John E. and Georgianne (Mrs. Robert A. Mercer). Educ: Fairmont Col. Polit. & Govt. Pos: Mem. bd. educ, Newton, Kans, 45-56; mem, State Munic. Acct. Bd, 3 years; clerk, Harvey Co, 3 terms; Kans. State Auditor, currently. Bus. & Prof. Pos: Secy. treas, Gen. Distributing Co, Newton; Union Nat. Bank. Mem: Lions; Mason; past pres, Kans. Co. Clerks Asn; past dist. dep. and past state treas, Elks. Rel: Episcopal; lay reader. Legal Res: P.O. Box 205, Newton, Kans. 67114. Mailing Add: Statehouse, Topeka, Kans. 66612.

HEDRICK, COLEENA WADE 'ANN' R
Mem, Calif. Rep. State Cent. Cmt.
b. Healdsburg, Calif, 5/30/28; d. Charles Henry Wade and Marion Milroy Stewart W; m. 6/17/49 to Joseph Watson Hedrick, Jr; c. Joseph Wade and Robert Stewart. Educ: Univ. Calif, Berkeley, 46-47. Polit. & Govt. Pos: V.pres, Fresno Co. and City Rep. Women, Calif, 63-66, pres, 67-68; chmn, Fresno Co. Women for Ronald Reagan, 66; mem, Calif. Rep. State Cent. Cmt, 69- Bus. & Prof. Pos: Saleswoman, Roos Bros, San Francisco and Oakland, 47-51; serv. rep, Pac. Tel. & Tel, 51-53; buyer, women's clothing, Hedrick's Dept. Stores, Fresno, 60-69. Mem: C. of C.(Women's Branch, Fresno Chap); Heart Asn.(vol); Cerebral Palsy Asn.(area capt); PTA (pres; Alice Birney and Wawona Chaps). Rel: Christian Science. Mailing Add: 4853 N. Warren, Fresno, Calif. 93705.

HEDRICK, O. G. D
W.Va. State Sen.
b. Elkins, W.Va, 12/18/12; s. Soloman Garrett Hedrick and Orpha Rebecca Moyer H; m. 4/5/42 to Yvonne Ruth Little; c. Olana Lynn and Janet Yvonne. Educ: Fairmont State Col, A.B; W.Va. Univ; Phi Sigma Kappa. Polit. & Govt. Pos: W.Va. State Sen, 52- Bus. & Prof. Pos: Racing off. Mil. Serv: Army, World War II, 18 months Gen. Patton's 3rd Army, tank driver; Purple Heart; Bronze Star. Mem: Mason; Shrine; Moose; VFW. Mailing Add: Fairmont, W.Va. 26554. (1967)

HEEGAARD, PETER ANKER R
V.Chmn, Hennepin Co. Rep. Party, Minn.
b. Minneapolis, Minn, 3/3/36; s. William R. Heegaard and Dorothy Goddard H; m. 6/12/58 to Anne Mintener; c. Susan, Peter, Jr. 'Kip' and Kate Educ: Dartmouth Col, B.A, 58; Amos Tuck Sch. Bus. Admin, M.B.A, 59; Distinguished Military Student; Alpha Delta Phi. Polit. & Govt. Pos: Rep. precinct chmn, Minnetonka Village, Minn, 62-63; chmn, Minnetonka Village Rep. Party, 64-66; mem, Minn. State Rep. Exec. Cmt, 66-; mem, Charter Cmn, Minnetonka Village, 66-; v.chmn, Hennepin Co. Rep. Party, 67-; pres, Hennepin Co. Libr. Bd, 68- Bus. & Prof. Pos: V.pres. and dir. investment res, Northwest. Nat. Bank of Minneapolis, 69- Mil. Serv: Entered as 2nd Lt, Army, 59, released as 1st Lt, 60 after serv. in Finance Corp, Fifth Army, 59-60; Res, 60-69, Capt. Publ: 'U.S. Economic Growth and the Common Market,' 62 and 'The International Monetary System and the U.S. Balance of Payments,' 63, Northwest Nat. Bank of Minneapolis. Mem: Financial Analysts Fed. of USA; Inst. Chartered Financial Analysts; Am. Inst. Banking; Citizens League of Hennepin Co; For. Policy Asn. Minn. Rel: Presbyterian; Elder, St. Luke Presbyterian Church. Mailing Add: 2434 Sherwood Hills Rd, Minnetonka, Minn. 55343.

HEEKE, DENNIS H. D
Ind. State Rep.
Polit. & Govt. Pos: Rep, Wabash Valley Interstate Compact, Ind; Ind. State Rep, currently. Bus. & Prof. Pos: Farmer; poultryman. Mem: K. of C; Dubois Commun. Club; Dubois Co. Soil Conserv; Wabash Valley Asn; Ind. State Poultry Asn; pres, Dubois Vol. Fire Dept. Rel: Catholic. Mailing Add: R.R. 2, Dubois, Ind. 47527.

HEEN, WALTER MEHEULA D
b. Honolulu, Hawaii, 4/17/28; s. Ernest Nalani Heen and Jeannette Hanapi H; m. 3/29/58 to Norma Kumiko Tada; c. Cameron Kealani. Educ: Univ. Hawaii, B.A, 53; Gerogetown Law Sch, LL.B, 55. Polit. & Govt. Pos: V.chmn, Co. Dem. Cmt, Hawaii, 56-60, chmn, 62-64; dep. attorney, Honolulu, 57-58; Hawaii Territorial Rep, 58-59; Hawaii State Rep, 59-64; councilman, Eighth Precinct, 16th Dist, 62-66; Hawaii State Sen, 67-68; chmn. and presiding officer, Honolulu City Coun, 69- Mem: Hawaii and Am. Bar Asns; Univ. Hawaii Alumni Asn; Hawaiian Civic Club of Honolulu; Big Brothers of Hawaii, Inc. Outstanding Young Man of Year, Jr. C. of C, 62. Rel: Catholic. Legal Res: 365 Kaumakani St, Honolulu, Hawaii 96821. Mailing Add: Room 810, Melim Bldg, 333 Queen St, Honolulu, Hawaii 96813.

HEFFERNAN, NATHAN STEWART D
Justice, Wis. Supreme Court
b. Frederic, Wis, 8/6/20; s. Jesse Eugene Heffernan and Pearl Kaump H; m. 4/27/46 to Dorothy Hillemann; c. Katie, Michael and Thomas. Educ: Univ. Wis, B.A, 42; Harvard Grad Sch. Bus. Admin, 43; Univ. Wis. Law Sch, LL.B, 48; Phi Eta Sigma; Order of the Coif; Phi Delta Phi. Polit. & Govt. Pos: Admin. asst. to Gov. of Wis, 48-49; asst. dist. attorney, Sheboygan, Co, 51-53; city attorney, Sheboygan, 53-59; Dep. Attorney Gen, Wis, 59-62; parliamentarian, Wis. State Dem. Conv, 60, chmn, 61 & 62; U.S. Attorney, Dept. of Justice, 62-64; Justice, Wis. Supreme Court, 64- Bus. & Prof. Pos: Assoc. Schubring, Ryan, Peterson & Sutherland, Madison, Wis, 48-49; partner, Law Firm of Buchen & Heffernan, 50-62; lectr, Univ. Wis. Law Faculty, 60-64. Mil. Serv: Entered as A/S, Navy, 42, released as Lt.(sg), 46, after serv. in ETO and Pac. Theaters; Lt.(Ret), Naval Res. ETO, Pac. and Am. Theater Ribbons; Naval Reserve and Victory Medals. Mem: Fed, Am. and Wis. Bar Asns; Am. Judicature Soc; Am. Law Inst; Appellate Judges Seminar; Military Order of World Wars; Am. Legion; Madison Club; VFW. Rel: Congregational; Deacon. Mailing Add: 17 Veblen Place, Madison, Wis. 53705.

HEFFNER, GEORGE W. R
b. Pottsville, Pa, 5/3/25; s. George S. Heffner and Helen Moyer H; m. to Barbara Richards; c. Kimberly Jane and George W, Jr. Educ: Dickinson Col, B.S; Dickinson Sch. of Law, LL.B. Polit. & Govt. Pos: Mem, Schuylkill Co. Rep. Exec. Cmt. and Rep. Club, Pa; Pa. State Rep, 56-67; Judge, Court of Common Pleas, Schuylkill Co, 68- Bus. & Prof. Pos: Partner, Burke, Bowe, Dolbin and Heffner, Attorneys. Mil. Serv: Pharmacist Mate 2/C, Navy, 43-46. Mem: Bd. of dir, United Cerebral Palsy of Schuylkill Co; Pottsville Children's Home; Elks; Mason; Lions; Tall Cedars of Lebanon; Am. Legion; Amvets. Rel: Lutheran. Mailing Add: 1310 Howard Ave, Pottsville, Pa. 17901.

HEFLIN, DAN HUGH, JR. R
b. Norfolk, Va, 9/26/31; s. Dan Hugh Heflin and Ann Taylor H; m. 9/12/53 to Jeanne Graham. Educ: Va. Polytech. Inst, B.S. in mech. eng, 53; Scabbard and Blade. Polit. & Govt. Pos: Rep. Precinct Capt, Va. Beach, Va, 60-64; chmn, Va. Beach City Rep. Cmt, 64-; mem, State Party Plan, 65-66. Bus. & Prof. Pos: Design supvr, Newport News Shipbldg. and Drydock, 55-66. Mil. Serv: Entered as 2nd Lt, Army Corps Eng, 53, released as 1st Lt, 55, after serv. in Spec. Category, Army with Air Force, Eng. Mem: Soc. Am. Mil. Engrs; Soc. Naval Architects and Marine Engrs; U.S. Jr. C. of C. Rel: Protestant. 1967 Legal Res: Virginia Beach, Va. No mailing address available. (1967)

HEFLIN, HENRY GRADY D
b. 4/25/02; s. James Henry Heflin and Cora Pickens H; m. 11/7/23 to Mary Duke; c. Twigg, Leila Duke (Mrs. Spinks). Educ: Lawrence Co. Schs. Polit. & Govt. Pos: Ala. State Rep, 63-66; City Coun. of Clanton, 30-48. Bus. & Prof. Pos: Banking; Peoples Savings Bank of Clanton, pres, 50-59; employed since 1919. Rel: Baptist, deacon and trustee. Mailing Add: Box 1057, Clanton, Ala. 35045.

HEFT, DOYLE J. D
b. Coldwater, Kans, 4/28/14; c. Clyde E. Heft and Ruth Latas H; m. 6/1/35 to Jessie L. Williams; c. Jerry L. and Dayle A. Polit. & Govt. Pos: Cmnr, Kans. Livestock Brand, Cmn, 68- Mem: Conserv. Materials and Serv. Elec. Bd. Dir, 46-69; Am. Nat. Livestock Asn; Kans. Livestock Asn; Farm Bur. (pres, Comanche Co. Chap, 46); Farmers Union (pres, Comanche Co. Chap, 66); Mason; Wichita Consistory; Shrine. Rel: Protestant. Mailing Add: 200 N. Frisco, Coldwater, Kans. 67209.

HEFT, FRANCIS J. R
b. Lewisville, Ohio, 10/10/11; s. Lewis Heft and Minnie Christman H; m. to Vivian B. Harper; c. Karl, Ruth, David, Nina, Eric and Marjorie. Educ:

Ohio Univ, 29-37. Polit. & Govt. Pos: Mem. and pres. village coun, 42-44; Ohio State Rep, Monroe Co, 47-49 & 53-67, chmn, Cmt. on Conserv, Ohio House of Rep, 57-59 & 61-67; mem. and pres. local bd. educ, 49-53; probation officer of Monroe Co. Court of Common Pleas, 67- Bus. & Prof. Pos: Teacher and prin, Graysville Sch, 67- Mem: Masons; Scottish Rite (32°). Rel: Methodist. Mailing Add: Route 2, Lewisville, Ohio 43754.

HEFTON, DON WARREN D
b. Sherman, Tex, 9/17/27; s. Robert L. Hefton and Alice Ritchie H; m. 11/1/68 to Alta M. Edmonds; c. Randy, Darin and Jeff. Educ: Austin Col, B.A, 49; Alpha Chi. Polit. & Govt. Pos: Tex. State Rep, 61-67; tax assessor-collector, Sherman, Tex, 67-68. Mil. Serv: Pvt, Army, 45-46. Rel: Church of Christ. Legal Res: 900 W. College, Sherman, Tex. 75090. Mailing Add: P.O. Box 1202, Sherman, Tex. 75090.

HEGARTY, EUGENE D. D
b. New York, N.Y, 6/30/11; s. John C. Hegarty and Madeline V. O'Hara H; m. 4/22/42 to Marie Harton; c. Eugene D, Jr, Patricia, Madelyn Ann, John Thomas and Michelle. Educ: Pa. State Univ, B.S, 33. Polit. & Govt. Pos: Admin. asst, Rep. Daniel J. Flood, Pa, currently. Bus. & Prof. Pos: Landscape and civil engr, private practice. Mil. Serv: Entered as Lt, Marine Corps Res.(Ret). Mem: VFW; Marine Corps League; Marine Corps Reserve Officers Asn; Am. Legion; K. of C; Pa. State Soc. of Wash; Wash. Soc. Engrs. Rel: Catholic. Mailing Add: 6936 Alpine Dr, Annandale, Va. 22023.

HEGE, JOE H, JR. R
N.C. State Rep.
b. Lexington, N.C, 1/28/26; s. Joe H. Hege, Sr. and Ellen Josephine Hilliard H; m. 11/27/48 to Pallie Jane Owen; c. Joe H, III, Karen Lynne and Edwin Lamar. Polit. & Govt. Pos: Vet. Serv. officer, Davidson Co, N.C, 48-50; N.C. State Rep, 67- Bus. & Prof. Pos: V.pres. and purchasing agent, Siceloff Mfg. Co, Inc, Lexington, 53- Mil. Serv: Entered as Pvt, Army, 44, released as T/Sgt, 46, after serv. in 80th Reconnaissance Troop, 80th Inf. Div, 3rd Army, ETO, Germany, Austria and Czech, 45-46; Europe-Africa-Mid. East Serv. Medal with 2 Bronze Stars; Good Conduct Medal; Victory Medal; Occup. Medal. Mem: Airport Cmn, Lexington; Am. Legion; VFW; Aircraft Owners & Pilots Asn. Private pilot. Rel: Pilgrim Reformed Church. Mailing Add: 1526 Greensboro St, Lexington, N.C. 27292. (1967)

HEHL, LAMBERT LAWRENCE, JR. D
Mem. Policy Cmt, Ky. State Dem. Cent. Exec. Cmt.
b. Newport, Ky, 7/22/24; s. Lambert Lawrence Hehl, Sr. and Martha Daly H; m. 5/25/46 to Helyn Mae Bathiany H; c. Barbara Lynn and Susan Helyn. Educ: Salmon P. Chase Col. Commerce, 46-48, Col. Law, 48-52; Kappa Xi Delta. Polit. & Govt. Pos: Dep. tax cmnr, Campbell Co, Ky, 53-56; city attorney, Crestview, 56-59; Ky. State Sen, 59-63; del, South. Regional Educ. Bd, 61-63; cmnr, Campbell Co. Fiscal Court, 63-; trustee, N.Ky. Area Planning Coun, 63-; dir, N.Ky. Commun. Action Cmt, 66; trustee, Ohio-Ky-Ind. Regional Authority, 66-; Fourth Cong. Dist. Committeeman, Ky. State Dem. Cent. Cmt, 68-, mem. policy cmt, 69- Bus. & Prof. Pos: Lawyer, 52- Mil. Serv: Entered as Pvt, Marine Corps, 43, released as Sgt, 46, after serv. in 3rd Island Command, FMF Pac; Asiatic Theater Ribbon. Mem: Adv. coun, Campbell Coun. of Govt; pres, Campbell Co. Bar Asn, 56-57; Campbell Co. Jaycees; Campbell Co. C. of C; Am. Legion; VFW. Rel: Catholic. Mailing Add: 46 Madonna Dr, Thomas, Ky. 41075.

HEID, JAMES K. R
b. Browerville, Minn, 2/23/29; s. Leo E. Heid and Lulu C. Woell H; m. 6/20/53 to Barbara Ann Hadley; c. Gail, David, Elizabeth, John and Lucy. Educ: Univ. Minn, B.S. and M.D; Phi Chi. Polit. & Govt. Pos: Chmn, Morrison Co. Rep. Party, Minn, 64-68. Bus. & Prof. Pos: Physician. Mil. Serv: Entered as 1st Lt, Army, 53, released as Capt, 56, after serv. in Med. Corps, Alaskan Theater. Mem: K. of C; Am. and Minn. Med. Asns. Rel: Catholic. Mailing Add: 3 Edgewater Dr, Little Falls, Minn. 56345.

HEIDE, WALTER JOHN R
Chmn, Smith Co. Rep. Cent. Cmt, Kans.
b. Harlan, Kans, 10/31/11; s. Fredrick John Heide and Sallie DuVall H; m. to Opal Pearl Grimes; c. Robert Kay. Educ: Harlan High Sch, grad, 30. Polit. & Govt. Pos: Trustee, Harlan Twp, Kans, 41-47; dir, Harlan Sch. Bd, 40-46; councilman, Smith Center City Coun, 57-63; chmn, Smith Co. Rep. Cent. Cmt, 67- Bus. & Prof. Pos: Pres, Heide-Christolear Inc, 59- Mem: Mason; Elks; Shrine; Smith Center Develop. Asn. Rel: Methodist. Mailing Add: 114 W. Third, Smith Center, Kans. 66967.

HEIDEL, FINIS LEROY D
N.Mex. State Rep.
b. 1913. Educ: Tex. Tech, A.B; Georgetown Univ. Law Sch, LL.B and LL.M. Polit. & Govt. Pos: N.Mex. State Rep, 59- Bus. & Prof. Pos: Attorney-at-Law. Mil. Serv: Lt. Col, Corps of Engrs, Army Res, World War II. Mem: Lions; Am. Legion; C. of C; Odd Fellows. Rel: Protestant. Mailing Add: P.O. Box 1298, Lovington, N.Mex. 88260.

HEIDEPRIEM, HERBERT A. R
b. Custer, S.Dak, 3/24/22; m. to Roberta Nelson; c. Steve, Nicolette, Scott and Rebecca. Educ: Univ. S.Dak, B.A, LL.B, 48; Lambda Chi Alpha. Polit. & Govt. Pos: States Attorney, Hand Co, S.Dak, 51-54; S.Dak. State Sen, 56-60 & 62-69; chmn, Court Study Cmn, S.Dak, 62-63. Bus. & Prof. Pos: Lawyer; pres, S.Dak. Title Asn; dir, First Nat. Bank of Miller. Mil. Serv: Army, 4 years; Purple Heart. Mem: Mason; Oriental Consistory; Kiwanis; Am. Legion; VFW (Post Comdr, 65); Yelduz Shrine; Am. and S.Dak. Bar Asns; finance drive chmn, Pheasant Coun. Boy Scouts, 65; chmn. bd, Prairie Center Nursing Home. Rel: Presbyterian. Mailing Add: Miller, S.Dak. 57362.

HEIL, WALLACE LEE D
Mem, Finance Cmt. and Exec. Bd, Christian Co. Dem. Cent. Cmt, Ill.
b. Mt. Vernon, Ill, 6/6/20; s. Samuel Edward Heil and Ruby Louise Wallace H; m. 8/28/39 to Guinevere Barret Spillman; c. Wallace Lee, Jr. and Pamela. Polit. & Govt. Pos: Mem, Finance Cmt. and Exec. Bd, Christian Co. Dem. Cent. Cmt, Ill, currently. Bus. & Prof. Pos: Pres. and mem. Bd. of Dirs, Asn. of Commerce, 62; past v.pres, St. Vincent Hosp. Lay Bd, pres, 69- Mil. Serv: Entered as Pvt, Army, 44, released as Pfc, 44, after serv. in Co. B, 22nd Armored Inf. Bn, ETO; Victory Medal; European-African-Middle East. Theater Ribbon with 3 Bronze Battle Stars; 2 Overseas Serv. Bars; Good Conduct Medal; Purple Heart; Combat Inf. Badge. Mem: Christian Co. Shrine Club; Elks; VFW; Am. Legion. Rel: Methodist. Mailing Add: Lincoln Trail, Taylorville, Ill. 62568.

HEIMKE, KARL FREDERIC R
b. Sheboygan, Wis, 3/4/24; s. William Karl Heimke and Amanda Steen H; m. 10/4/52 to E. Elizabeth Herold; c. Susan Elizabeth, Sally Ann, William Karl and Robert Herold. Educ: Ripon Col, A.B; Univ. Wis. Law Sch, Madison, J.D; Pi Kappa Delta; Theta Chi; Acacia. Polit. & Govt. Pos: Mayor, Wheaton, Ill, 63-68; v.pres, Ill. Munic. League, 64-68; representative committeeman, DuPage Co. Rep. Party, 65-68; pres, DuPage Co. Mayors Asn, 66; mem, exec. cmt, Governor's Cmn. on Local Govt, 68. Bus. & Prof. Pos: Attorney-at-law, Sheboygan, Wis, 52-54, Potosi, Wis, 54-57; attorney, U.S. Dept. Agr, Chicago, 58-59; v.pres, Chicago Mercantile Exchange, 60-68; asst. mgr, Certified Livestock Mkts. Asn, Kansas City, Mo, 69. Mil. Serv: Entered as Pvt, Army, 42, released as Lt, 46, after serv. in Ninth Air Force, ETO, 44-46; Maj, Air Force Res; Air Medal; Unit Citation; European Campaign Medal; three battle stars. Mem: Wis. Bar; Mo. Asn. Independent Ins. Agents; Mason; Scottish Rite; Shrine; Am. Legion; VFW; ROA; Wis. Farm Bur. Rel: Lutheran. Mailing Add: 9912 Wedd, Overland Park, Kans. 66202.

HEIN, SIDNEY S. R
Chmn, Queen's Co. Rep. Cmt, N.Y.
b. New York, N.Y, 4/16/07; s. Hugo Hein and Regina Pulitzer H; m. 8/28/37 to Frederica Elizabeth Clark; c. Orrin M.C. and Holly Clark. Educ: St. Johns Univ, LL.B, 28, LL.M, 29. Polit. & Govt. Pos: Co. committeeman, Queens Co. Rep. Cmt, N.Y, 28-; del, Rep. State Conv, 32-; del, Judicial Conv, 32-; Rel. chmn, 12th Assembly Dist, 48-51; del, Rep. Nat. Convs, 48-68; state committeeman, 19th and 12th Assembly Dist, 51-; mem, N.Y. State Rep. Exec. Cmt, 62-; chmn, Queens Co. Rep. Cmt, 68- Bus. & Prof. Pos: Partner, Hein, Bradie, Waters & Klein, Attorneys, 37-; dir, First Nat. Bank of Inwood, 43-54; dir, Franklin Nat. Bank, 61-; cmnr, Port of New York Authority; dir, Am-Swiss Credit Corp. Mem: Dir, Peninsula Gen. Hosp. and Brunswick Hosp. Center; Am. Cancer Soc; French Univ. N.Y; Lotos Club; Manhattan Club; Montauk Club; Inwood Country Club; F&AM; Elks; Am. Soc. Legion Honor. Chevalier, French Legion Honor. Legal Res: 2518 Deerfield Rd, Far Rockaway, N.Y. 11691. Mailing Add: 1600 Central Ave, Far Rockaway, N.Y. 11691.

HEINE, RALPH ROBERT R
Ind. State Rep.
b. Auburn, Ind, 4/8/28; s. Herbert H. Heine and Margaret Schlup H; m. 6/27/53 to Mildred Lucille Candler; c. Cynthia Leigh, Janelle and Robin. Educ: Purdue Univ, B.S. in Agr, 50; Beta Sigma Psi. Polit. & Govt. Pos: Ind. State Rep, currently, chmn, Co. and Twp. Bus. Cmt, Ind. State House of Rep, 69-; chmn, Whitley Co. Young Reps; mem, Rep. Finance Cmt, 4 years; organizer, Teen-Age Reps; del, State Rep, Conv. Bus. & Prof. Pos: Owner-mgr, Gobbler's Retreat Turkey and Dairy Farm. Mil. Serv: Entered as 2nd Lt, Army, 51, released as 1st Lt, 53, after serv. in Korea. Mem: State dir, Ind. State Poultry Asn, Turkey Div; Am. Legion; Whitley Co. Farm Bur, chmn. 3 years; C. of C, chmn, Polit. Action Cmt. 3 years; v.pres, Co. Agr. Ext. Coun; state tax cmn. for Farm Bur, Inc. Active in 4-H and Future Farmers of Am. affairs. Rel: Lutheran-Mo. Snyod; chmn, congregation. Mailing Add: R.R. 2, Columbia City, Ind. 46725.

HEINEMANN, DAVID JOHN R
Kans. State Rep.
b. West Point, Nebr, 7/18/45; s. Lester Otto Heinemann and Rita Charlotte LaNoue H; single. Educ: Augustana Col, B.A. Polit. Sci. and German, cum laude, 67; Univ. Kans, 67-68. Polit. & Govt. Pos: Kans. State Rep, 117th Dist, 69- Rel: Lutheran. Mailing Add: 627 Fleming, Garden City, Kans. 67846.

HEINTZELMAN, ROSS GARFIELD R
Ohio State Rep.
b. Greensburg, Pa, 1/2/17; s. Ross Garfield Heintzelman and Bertha Acklin H; m. 3/17/45 to Margery Isabel Major; c. Christian Lee and Diane Kay. Educ: Kent State Univ, 40; Ohio State Univ, B.Sc, 48, M.A, 50; Indust. Mgt. Soc; Dean's Hon. Citation. Polit. & Govt. Pos: Councilman, Canton, Ohio, 57-69, served on all coun. cmts. and chmn. traffic cmt, five terms; Ohio State Rep, Dist. 89, Stark Co, 69- Bus. & Prof. Pos: Asst. to factory mgr, Timken Roller Bearing Co. Mil. Serv: Entered as Pvt, Air Force, 43, released as Sgt, 45, after serv. in Ord. Units; S. Atlantic Anti-Submarine Campaign Ribbon. Mem: Polit. Sci. Acad; Am. Econ. Found; Indust. Mgt. Soc; Mason; Moose; Eagle; Am. Legion; VFW; Canton Police Boys Club; YMCA; Wilderness Center; Stark Hist. Soc. Rel: Methodist. Mailing Add: 206 Grandview Ave. N.W, Canton, Ohio 44708.

HEINZ, HENRY JOHN, III R
Mem. Exec. Cmt, Allegheny Co. Rep. Finance Cmt, Pa.
b. Pittsburgh, Pa, 10/23/38; s. Henry John Heinz and Joan Diehl H; m. 2/4/66 to Maria Teresa Thierstein Simoes-Ferreira; c. Henry John, IV. Educ: Yale Univ, B.A, 60; Harvard Grad. Sch. Bus. Admin, M.B.A, 63; Chi Psi. Polit. & Govt. Pos: Spec. asst. to U.S. Sen. Hugh Scott, Pa, 64; mem. exec. cmt, Allegheny Co. Rep. Finance Cmt, 65-; mem, Allegheny Rep. Coun, 67-; del, Rep. Nat. Conv, 68. Bus. & Prof. Pos: Mgt. consult, private practice, 64-65; asst. mgr. profit planning, H.J. Heinz Co, 65, assoc. mgr. grocery prod. mkt, 65-66, mgr, 66-68, gen. prod. mgr. grocery mkt, 68- Mil. Serv: Entered as Airman Basic, Air Force, 63, released as Sgt, Air Force Res, 69, after serv. in 911th Troop Carrier Group. Mem: Am. Mgt. Asn; Am. Mkt. Asn; mem. bd. trustees, Univ. Pittsburgh and Childrens Hosp. of Pittsburgh; mem. exec. cmt, Urban League of Pittsburgh. Rel: Episcopal. Legal Res: 1950 Squaw Run Rd, Pittsburgh, Pa. 15238. Mailing Add: 1062 Progress St, Pittsburgh, Pa. 15230.

HEINZ, LYLE KENNETH D
Chmn, Emmet Co. Dem. Party, Mich.
b. Matchwood, Mich, 6/27/21; s. Frank Heinz and Mae Higgins H; m. 6/14/42 to Anna Mae Lanterman; c. Michael K, James L. and David L. Educ: Harbor Springs High Sch. Polit. & Govt. Pos: Chmn, Emmet Co. Dem. Party, Mich, currently. Mil. Serv: Entered as Seaman, Navy, 42, released as Fire Controlman, 45, after serv. in Pac. Mem: Pres, Local Mich. Bell Tel, 56-64. Rel: Presbyterian. Mailing Add: 629 E. Lake, Harbor Springs, Mich. 49740. (1967)

HEINZE, JAMES HENRY R
Mich. State Rep.
b. Clarksburg, W.Va, 9/4/14; s. H. Arthur Heinze and Helene Devore H; m. 8/12/39 to Mary Frances Gibbs; c. Frances (Mrs. Wm. P. Winslow) and Margaret Jane. Educ: W.Va. Univ, A.B, 36, Law Sch, LL.B, 38; Phi Beta Kappa; Phi Delta Phi; Delta Tau Delta; Sphinx; Mountain. Polit. & Govt. Pos: Munic. attorney, West Union, W.Va, 40-42 and Zionsville, Ind, 52-60; del, Ind. State Rep. Conv, 52 & 56; Mich. State Rep, 45th Dist, 66- Bus. & Prof. Pos: V.pres. and gen. counsel, Secured Ins. Co, 46-54, pres, 54-65; pres, Riverside Ins. Co. of Am, 58-66; secy. and gen. corp. counsel, Wolverine Ins. Co, 64- Mil. Serv: Entered as Ens, Naval Res, 42, released as Lt, 45, after serv. in Naval Commun, 15th Naval Dist, Panama Canal Zone, 43-45; Lt. Comdr.(Ret), Naval Res, 42-62. Am. Theater Campaign Ribbon; Victory Ribbon. Mem: Mich, Ind. and W.Va. and Am. Bar Asns; Young Presidents Orgn, 55-63; Mason (32°); Lions; Battle Creek Country Club. Rel: Presbyterian. Hon. Cert, Freedom Found. of Valley Forge, 68. Mailing Add: 130 Edgebrook Dr, Battle Creek, Mich. 49015.

HEINZEN, RAYMOND FRANK R
Wis. State Sen.
b. Marshfield, Wis, 5/11/18; s. Jacob Heinzen and Rosa Schuler H; m. 10/25/41 to Reba Weichmann; c. Ann Marie (Mrs. Peter Fisher) and Paul Ben. Educ: Univ. Wis, 36-39; Alpha Zeta. Polit. & Govt. Pos: Clerk, Dist. Sch. Bd, Wis, 53-58; mem, State Bd. of Voc. and Adult Educ, 56-63; Wis. State Assemblyman, 61-68; Wis. State Sen, 69- Bus. & Prof. Pos: Pres, Marshfield Coop. Dairymen's Asn, 49-53; secy-treas, Hub Dairy Coop, 55-63; farm columnist, Times Rev, LaCrosse, Wis, 57-59; bd. mem, St. Joseph Hosp. Adv. Bd, 60- Mem: Rotary; Farm Bur; Nat. Cath. Rural Life Conf. Outstanding Young Farmer Award, Jaycees, 53. Rel: Roman Catholic. Mailing Add: Route 5, Marshfield, Wis. 54449.

HEIPLE, JAMES DEE R
Secy, Tazewell Co. Rep. Cent. Cmt, Ill.
b. Peoria, Ill, 9/13/33; s. Rae Crane Heiple and Harriet Birkett H; m. 7/28/56 to Virginia Duffield Kerswill; c. Jeremy, Jonathan and Rachel. Educ: Bradley Univ, B.S, 55; Univ. of Louisville, LL.B, 57; Delta Theta Phi; Pi Kappa Delta; Sigma Nu; Alpha Pi. Polit. & Govt. Pos: Pres, Bradley Univ. Young Rep. Club and Univ. of Ill. Young Rep. Club; treas, Midwest Fedn. of Col. Young Rep. Clubs; v.pres, Young Rep. Orgn. of Ill; Rep. precinct committeeman, Pekin, 60-; secy, Tazewell Co. Rep. Cent. Cmt, 66- Bus. & Prof. Pos: Partner, Heiple & Heiple Attorneys, Ill, 57- Mil. Serv: Nat. Guard and Army Res, 57-63. Mem: Tazewell Co. Bar Asn.(pres, 67-68); Ill. Bar Asn. (legal educ. cmt, 66-); Ky. and Am. Bar Asns; Mason; Shrine; Scottish Rite; Nat. Rifle Asn; life mem. Filson Club; life mem. Union League Club of Chicago. Rel: Methodist. Mailing Add: 707 S. Fifth St, Pekin, Ill. 61554.

HEISER, KARL FLORIEN D
b. Hamilton, Ohio, 6/30/04; s. Karl William Heiser and Alta Dell Harvey H; m. 7/9/54 to Ruth Bishop; c. Karl Robert and John Vail. Educ: Oberlin Col, A.B, 26, M.A, 27; Columbia Univ, Ph.D, 32. Polit. & Govt. Pos: Dir. research, Conn. Pub. Welfare Coun, 43-45; br. chief, U.S. Element, Allied Cmn. for Austria, 45-47; cand. for State Bd. of Educ, Ohio, 67; cand, U.S. House of Rep, First Dist, Ohio, 68; alternate del, Dem. Nat. Conv, 68; chmn, Glendale Village Dem. Party, Ohio, 68- Publ: Our Backward Children, W.W. Norton, N.Y, 55; Research studies in psychol. and articles on prfnl. probs. of educ. in various jour. Mem: Am. Psychol. Asn.(assoc. exec. secy, 49-51, Coun. of Rep, 66-69); pres, Am. Bd. for Psychol. Serv, 59-61; pres, Ohio Psychol. Asn, 64-65; pres, Conn. Valley Psychol. Asn, 43-44; Sigma Xi; Kiwanis; Cincinnati Women's City Club (assoc); Little Miami, Inc; Resident Home for Retarded Children. Rel: Unitarian. Mailing Add: 60 E. Sharon Ave, Glendale, Ohio 45246.

HEISKELL, JOHN N. D
b. Rogersville, Tenn, 11/2/72; s. Carrick White Heiskell and Eliza Ayre Netherland; m. 6/28/10 to Wilhelmina Mann; c. (Mrs. George Whitfield Cook), (Mrs. Hugh B. Patterson, Jr). Educ: Univ. of Tenn, B.A, 93; Little Rock Col, Litt.D, 29; Ark. Col, LL.D, 34; Univ. of Ark, LL.D, 38; Colby Col, LL.D, 58; Sigma Delta Chi; Sigma Alpha Epsilon. Polit. & Govt. Pos: U.S. Sen, Ark. by app. 13; pres. bd. trustees Little Rock Pub. Libr; former chmn. Little Rock City Planning Cmn; former mem. State Planning Bd. Bus. & Prof. Pos: Ed. Ark. Gazette, 02-; pres. Gazette Pub. Co. Mem: 2nd v.pres. Assoc. Press, 26-27. John Peter Zenger Award, Dept. Journalism, Univ. of Ariz; Univ. Mo. Sch. of Journalism, Distinguished Serv. Medal, 62; Lovejoy Award, Colby Col, 58; Annual Award, Columbia Sch. of Journalism, 58; Medal and Citation, Syracuse Univ. Sch. Journalism, 58; recipient Citation, A.L.A, 57. Mailing Add: 6015 Greenwood Rd, Little Rock, Ark. 72207. (1967)

HEISLER, DONALD EUGENE D
b. Rockford, Ill, 4/28/29; s. Samuel Young Heisler and Elizabeth Frances Collman H; m. 1/24/48 to Patricia Louise Fenelon; c. Michael Eugene, Steven Lee, Linda Louise, David Alan, Susan Marie, Debra Frances and James Edward. Educ: High Sch. Polit. & Govt. Pos: Pres, Third Ward Dem. Club, Ill, 59-60; secy, Winnebago Co. Young Dem, 61-62; secy, Open Dem. Primary, 62-63; chmn, Winnebago Co. Dem. Cent. Cmt, 64-69. Mil. Serv: Entered as Pvt, Air Force, 47, released as Sgt, 50, after serv. in Training Command. Mem: Local 592, UAW-CIO Union. Rockford C. of C. Commun. Appreciation Award, 60 & 64. Rel: Protestant. Mailing Add: 726 Locust St, Rockford, Ill. 61103. (1967)

HEITMAN, BETTY GREEN R
Pres, La. Fedn. Rep. Women
b. Malvern, Ark, 11/27/29; d. George Anderson Green and Inell Cooper G; m. 4/3/51 to Henry Schrader Heitman; c. Donna Inell, Thomas Haile, Perry Schrader and Paul Anderson. Educ: Tex. State Col. for Women, B.S. in foods and nutrition, 49; Dietetic Internship, Charity Hosp, New Orleans, 49-50. Polit. & Govt. Pos: V.chmn, Sixth Cong. Dist. Rep. Action Coun, 64-66; membership chmn, La. Fedn. Rep. Women, 65-66, pres, 67-; del, Rep. Nat. Conv, 68; mem, E. Baton Rouge Parish Rep. Exec. Cmt, 69. Bus. & Prof. Pos: Admin. dietitian, Hotel Dieu Hosp, New Orleans, La, 50; therapeutic dietitian, Clarkson Hosp, Omaha, Nebr, 51; pediatric dietitian, Charity Hosp, La, 53- Mem: Am. Dietetic Asn; E. Baton Rouge Parish Med. Auxiliary. Rel: Episcopal. Mailing Add: 655 Waverly Dr, Baton Rouge, La, 70806.

HEITMAN, KATHRYN J. R
Vt. State Rep.
b. Weybridge, Vt, 5/28/02; m. to Henry G. Heitman, wid; c. 1 son, 2 daughters. Educ: Plattsburg State Teachers Col. Polit. & Govt. Pos: Addison Co. del. chmn. to Vt. House of Rep; secy, Addison Co Exten. Serv. Adv. Bd, Vt; mem, Addison Co. Rep. Cmt; mem, Shoreham Town Rep. Cmt; clerk and dir, Shoreham Sch. Bd; Vt. State Rep, 63- Bus. & Prof. Pos: Teacher; secy; libr. trustee. Mem: Homemakers' Club; Women's Club; Women's Fel; Eastern Star (Grand Warden, Vt. Chap); Addison Co. Homemaker's Coun.(past secy, v.pres. and pres); Vt. Homemaker's Coun.(pres). Rel: Congregational. Mailing Add: Shoreham, Vt. 05770. (1967)

HELBING, STEPHEN COUCH R
N.Mex. State Rep.
Educ: Tex. A&M, B.S. Polit. & Govt. Pos: Appraiser for Bur. of Revenue, N.Mex, 60-62; N.Mex. State Rep, currently. Bus. & Prof. Pos: Oil and ranching. Mil. Serv: Navy, 45-46, destroyer duty. Rel: Presbyterian. Mailing Add: Box 568, Roswell, N.Mex. 88201. (1967)

HELD, GERALD S. R
State Committeeman, N.Y. Rep. Party
b. N.Y.C, 12/9/32; s. Albert Held and Rose Korman H; m. 3/30/58 to Carol E; c. Jonathan Lawton, Rhonda Meryl and Lindsay Mason. Educ: Brooklyn Col, B.A, Law Sch, LL.B. Polit. & Govt. Pos: Alternate del, Rep. Nat. Conv, 68; leader, 45th Assembly Dist. Rep. Party, N.Y, currently; state committeeman, N.Y. Rep. Party, currently; arbitrator, Kings Co. Civil Court, currently. Mil. Serv: Entered as Pvt, Army, 54, released as Specialist, 55, after serv. in 52nd AAA Brigade. Mem: Am, Brooklyn and other local Bar Asns; VFW; Jewish War Vet; B'nai B'rith; Mason; K. of P. Rel: Jewish. Legal Res: 2080 Ocean Ave, Brooklyn, N.Y. 11230. Mailing Add: 16 Court St, Brooklyn, N.Y. 11201.

HELD, JAMES EDWARD R
b. Racine, Wis, 2/16/38; s. William Francis Held and Eleanor Thielen H; single. Educ: Marquette Univ, B.A. in Speech, 60, B.A. in Journalism, 61; Georgetown Univ, LL.B, 64; Phi Alpha Theta; Pi Gamma Mu; Sigma Delta Chi; Phi Delta Phi; Alpha Phi Omega. Polit. & Govt. Pos: Legal and legis. asst. to Milwaukee Co. Rep. Exec. Cmt, Wis, 64-66; former Wis. State Assemblyman, 18th Dist. Mem: Wis. and Milwaukee Bar Asns; Milwaukee Jr. Bar Asn; Jaycees; Holy Name Soc. Rel: Roman Catholic. Mailing Add: 8723 W. Mill Rd, Milwaukee, Wis. 53225. (1967)

HELGESON, DONALD KEITH R
Wis. State Assemblyman
b. Manitowoc, Wis, 5/30/32; s. Gordon T. Helgeson and Olivia Thompson H; m. 9/12/53 to Della Hansen; c. Karin, Katherine and Constance. Educ: Univ. Wis, B.A; Alpha Gamma Rho. Polit. & Govt. Pos: Wis. State Assemblyman, 69- Mil. Serv: Entered as Ens, Navy, 54, released as Lt.(jg), 57, after serv. in Pac, Lt. Comdr, Res, 57-69. Mem: Elks. Rel: Protestant. Mailing Add: 937 N. Fifth St, Manitowoc, Wis. 54220.

HELLBAUM, HAROLD R
Wyo. State Rep.
b. Wheatland, Wyo, 9/26/26; s. Herman Hellbaum and Lydia Lust H; m. 9/17/50 to Margaret L. Otis; c. Rebecca, Holly, Robert and Bruce. Educ: Univ. Wyo, 46-47; Sigma Nu. Polit. & Govt. Pos: Wyo. State Rep, 62-, mem, Gov. Agr. Adv. Cmt, Med. Assistance & Serv. Adv. Cmt, Educ. Cmn. State, Wyo. Educ. Coun, Gov. Motor Pool Coun, Wyo. State House of Rep; alternate del, Rep. Nat. Conv, 64, del, 68; treas, Platte Co. Rep. Party, 66-; state chmn, Nixon Campaign, Wyo, 68. Bus. & Prof. Pos: Chmn, Sch. Dist. Four, Wyo, 59-; Farmer, Rancher and Investments. Mem: Pres, Wyo. Grain Feed-Seed Dealers Asn. and Wyo. Wheat Growers Asn; Lions; Farm Bur; State Stock Growers Asn. Rel: Protestant. Legal Res: Chugwater, Wyo. 82210. Mailing Add: Box 55, Route 1, Chugwater, Wyo. 82210.

HELLER, FRANK JOHN R
Mem, Okla. Rep. State Cmt.
b. Newark, N.J, 4/29/17; s. Gilbert Nelson Heller and Jay MacLagan H; m. 11/20/41 to Lucille Virginia John; c. J. Scott and R. Page. Educ: Univ. Okla, B.S. Ch.E, 40; Tau Beta Pi; Sigma Tau; Alpha Chi Sigma; Sigma Alpha Epsilon. Polit. & Govt. Pos: Rep. precinct chmn, Bartlesville, Okla, 50-58; mem, Washington Co. Rep. Exec. Cmt, 56-; mem, Okla. Rep. State Cmt, 58-; mem, Rules Cmt, Okla. State Rep. Conv, 60, mem, Resolutions Cmt, 62 and Credentials Cmt, 66; chmn, Rep. State Budget Cmt, 60-67; mem, Rep. State Finance Cmt, 66-; finance chmn, Garrison For Cong, Dist. Two, 66; alternate del, Rep. Nat. Conv, 68. Bus. & Prof. Pos: Sr. Research Engr, Phillips Petroleum Co, 40-42 & 46-49, dir. of personnel, 49-52, dir. eng. standards cmt, 52- Mil. Serv: Entered as 2nd Lt, Air Force, 42, released as Lt. Col, 46, after serv. in Air Materiel Command, Am. and Pac. Theatres, 44-46; Lt. Col. (Ret), Air Force Res. Publ: 'How to Size Relief Valves,' Oil & Gas J, 51; 'Tank Trucks are made Safe,' Butane-Propane News, 60; 'Prophesy of Future for Liquefied Petroleum Gas,' LP Gas Times, 62. Mem: Bd. dirs, Compressed Gas Asn, 60-; chmn, Int. People to People Photographic Cmt, 60-; admin. cmt. co. mem. coun, Am. Standards Asn, 60-62; exec. standards bd, USA Standards Inst, 68-; fel, Royal Photog. Soc. of Gr. Brit. and Photog. Soc. of Am; Hillcrest Country Club; Lakeview Country Club, Morgantown, W.Va. Rel: Presbyterian. Mailing Add: 400 Denver Rd, Bartlesville, Okla. 74003.

HELLER, MAX M. D
City Councilman, Greenville, S.C.
b. Vienna, Austria, 5/28/19; s. Israel Heller and Lea Hirsch H; m. 8/2/42 to Trude Schonthal; c. Francie (Mrs. Hurvitz), Susan (Mrs. Moses) and Steven N. Educ: Real Gymnasium, Vienna, 4 years; Handels Bus. Sch, 3 years. Polit. & Govt. Pos: Treas. and finance chmn, Greenville Co. Dem. Party, S.C, 66-68; del, Dem. Nat. Conv, 68; city councilman, Greenville, S.C, 69- Bus. & Prof. Pos: Pres, Williamston Shirt Co, 45-48, Maxon Shirt Co, Greenville, S.C, 48-68, Helco Inc, 57-68 and Trumax Inc, 57-; dir. and co-founder, First Piedmont Bank & Trust, 68- Mem: Chmn, St. Francis Commun. Hosp; mem. adv. bd, Furman Univ; bd, United Fund; bd, Co. Health Coun; chmn. housing cmt, C. of C; Mason; City Club; Elks; Federated Jewish Charities. Rel: Jewish. Mailing Add: 36 Pinehurst Dr, Greenville, S.C. 29609.

HELLER, WALTER WOLFGANG D
b. Buffalo, N.Y, 8/27/15; s. Ernst Heller and Gertrude Warmburg H; m. 9/16/38 to Emily Karen Johnson; c. Walter P, Eric and Kaaren Louise. Educ: Oberlin Col, B.A, 35; Univ. Wis, M.A, 38, Ph.D, 41; Phi Beta Kappa; Beta Gamma Sigma; Alpha Kappa Psi. Hon. LL.D, Oberlin Col, 64; hon. Litt.D, Kenyon Col, 65; hon. LL.D, Ripon Col, 67; hon. L.H.D, Coe Col, 67; hon. LL.D, Long Island Univ, 68 and Univ. Wis, 69. Polit. & Govt. Pos: Fiscal economist and consult, Treas. Dept, 42-53; chief internal finance, U.S. Mil. Govt, Germany, 47-48; consult, Cmt. of Econ. Develop, 48-49 & 54-57; consult, UN, 52-60; consult, Minn. Dept. of Transportation, 55-60; tax adv, Gov, Minn, 55-60; consult, Nat. Educ. Asn, 58; chmn, Coun. Econ. Adv, 61-64; consult. to Exec. Off. of the President, 65-69. Bus. & Prof. Pos: Assoc. prof. econ, Univ. Minn, 46-50, prof, 50-67, regents' prof, 67-, chmn. dept, 57-61. Publ: New Dimensions of Political Economy, Harvard Univ. Press, 66 and W. W. Norton & Co, 67; co-auth, Revenue Sharing and the City, Resources for the Future, 68; ed, Perspectives in Economic Growth, Random House, 68; co-auth, Monetary vs. Fiscal Policy, W. W. Norton & Co, 69; plus others. Mem: Am. Econ. Asn; Nat. Tax Asn; Am. Finance Asn; Am. Acad. Arts & Sci; Dir. and v.chmn, Nat. Bur. Econ. Research; Fed. City Club, D.C; dir, Int. Milling Co, Nat. City Bank of Minneapolis, Northwest. Nat. Life Ins. Co. and Fed. Nat. Mortgage Asn; trustee, Oberlin Col, Col. Retirement Equities Fund. Legal Res: 2203 Folwell St, St. Paul, Minn. 55108. Mailing Add: Dept. of Economics, University of Minnesota, Minneapolis, Minn. 55455.

HELLMAN, OTIS D
V.Chmn, Greenwood Co. Dem. Party, Kans.
b. Eureka, Kans, 11/9/90; s. Oscar Hellman and Carrie Wiggins H; m. to Lydia Yates (div); c. Lila (Mrs. Fast) and Phillip. Educ: High Sch, Eureka, Kans, 4 years. Polit. & Govt. Pos: Twp. trustee, Salm Twp, Kans; v.chmn, Greenwood Co. Dem. Party, currently. Bus. & Prof. Pos: Farmer-stockman, 19- Mil. Serv: Entered as Pvt, Army, 17, released as Pvt, 19, after serv. in Belgium and France. Mailing Add: Star Route, Eureka, Kans. 67045.

HELLMAN, RUSSELL D
Mich. State Rep.
b. Dollar Bay, Mich; m. 1938 to Edith Kaarlela; c. Kathleen, Gene and Nancy. Educ: High Sch. Grad. Polit. & Govt. Pos: Former twp. supvr, Mich; Mich. State Rep, 60- Bus. & Prof. Pos: Mgr, Copper Country Fruit Growers, Inc. Mem: Mason. Rel: Lutheran. Mailing Add: Dollar Bay, Mich. 49922. (1967)

HELLMANN, CLAUDE BERNARD
b. St. Denis, Md, 11/2/90; s. John Joseph Hellmann and Regina Rex H; m. 3/28/32 to Alvina Haggerty. Polit. & Govt. Pos: Secy. of State, Md, 56-59; chmn, Indust. Develop. Cmn. of Baltimore Co, Md, 59-61. Bus. & Prof. Pos: Pres, Claude B. Hellmann Co, Baltimore, 19-30; mgr. lighting dept, Baltimore Gas & Elec. Co, 30-56; pres, Roland Park Apts, Baltimore, Md, currently. Mil. Serv: Asst. Supt, Naval Aircraft Factory, Phila, World War I. Mem: Illuminating Eng. Soc.(chmn, Baltimore-Wash. D.C. Chap, 38-40); bd. dirs, Nat. Conf. on Citizenship, Wash, D.C; Kiwanis Int.(pres,51-52); Rel: Catholic. Mailing Add: 6 Upland Rd, Baltimore, Md. 21210.

HELLMUTH, JAMES GRANT R
Treas, N.Y. Rep. State Cmt.
b. Wash, D.C, 7/31/25; s. William Frederick Hellmuth and Sybil Grant H; m. to Daphne Preece; c. James G, Jr. and Timothy P. Educ: Yale, B.S, 48; George Wash. Univ. Law Sch, LL.B, 53; St. Elmo Soc. Polit. & Govt. Pos: Treas, Lefkowitz for Mayor, N.Y, 61, Lindsay for Mayor, 65, Rockefeller for Gov, 66 and Rockefeller for President, 68; treas, N.Y. Rep. State Cmt, 66- Bus. & Prof. Pos: V.pres, Empire Trust Co, 60-67 and Morgan Guaranty Trust Co. of New York, 67- Mil. Serv: Entered as Pvt, Army, 43, released as 1st Lt, 46, after serv. in Pac. Theatre. Publ: Ed, Atomic Energy Law J, 60; author, Modern Trust Forms, 65. Mem: Yale Club; Rockaway Hunt Club; Lawrence Beach Club. Legal Res: 1105 Park Ave, New York, N.Y. 10028. Mailing Add: 522 Fifth Ave, New York, N.Y. 10036.

HELM, JOSEPH BURGE D
b. Louisville, Ky, 9/2/31; s. Blakey Helm and Catherine Burge H; m. 8/11/58 to Louise Wile; c. Joseph B, Jr, Lucy Ware, Sarah Wile and John Blakey. Educ: Princeton, 50-53; Univ. Ky. Col. Law, LL.B, 58; Polit. & Govt. Pos: Dem. precinct capt, Louisville, Ky, 60-63; Dem. cand, Ky. State Rep, 63; co-chmn, Jefferson Co. Citizens for Johnson, 64; chmn, Jefferson Co. Humphrey-Muskie Campaign, 68; alternate del, Dem. Nat. Conv, 68. Bus. & Prof. Pos: Partner, Law Firm of Helm, Eddelman & Jay, 61- Mil. Serv: Entered as Pvt, Army, 53, released as Cpl, 55, after serv. in France, 54-55. Mem: Am. and Louisville Bar Asns; Ky. State Bar Asn.(House of Del); Kiwanis; Ky. Civil Liberties Union. Rel: Presbyterian. Legal Res: 4201 Maryknoll Lane, Louisville, Ky. 40207. Mailing Add: 606 Louisville Trust Bldg, Louisville, Ky. 40202.

HELM, W. STUART R
b. Cowansville, Pa, 4/8/08; s. Fred H. Helm and Jennie L. Clark H; m. to Geraldine Rearick; c. two daughters. Educ: Pa. State Univ; Duquesne Univ. Polit. & Govt. Pos: Mem, Kittanning Borough Sch. Bd, Pa, 17 years; Pa. State Rep, 40-65, Speaker, Pa. House of Rep, 57-58 & 63-64, chmn, House Rep. Party Policy Cmt, 59-62, second v.pres, Coun. State Govt, 62 and pres, Nat. Legis. Conf, 62-63; spec. asst. to Gov, Pa, 65; secy, Commonwealth of Pa, 65-67. Mem: Kiwanis (past pres. and past Lt. Gov); Mason; Elks. Mailing Add: 940 N. McKean St, Kittanning, Pa. 16201. (1967)

HELMS, JAMES MARVIN, JR. R
Va. Dir, Arts and Sci. Div, Rep. Nat. Cmt.
b. Rock Hill, S.C, 9/4/27; s. James Marvin Helms and Almetta Moss H; m. 3/2/46 to Josephine Alice Goodman; c. James Marvin, III and Kelly Elizabeth. Educ: Emory Univ, 44-45; Clemson Col, B.S, 48; Univ. Va, M.A, 55, Ph.D, 62; Delta Tau Delta. Polit. & Govt. Pos: Organizer, Prince Edward Co. Rep. Party, Va, 64, co. committeeman, 64-; secy, Fourth Dist. Rep. Party, 64-; organizer and adv, Longwood Col. Young Rep. Club, 64-; Va. dir, Arts and Sci. Div, Rep. Nat. Cmt, 64-; legis. research, writing and pub. rels. work, U.S. House of Rep, 66-68; campaign coordinator for five counties, Nixon Campaign, 68; alternate del, Rep. Nat. Conv, 68; mem, Va. State Rep. Cent. Cmt, 68-; Fourth Dist. campaign coordinator, Gubernatorial Campaign, Va, 69. Bus. & Prof. Pos: Mgr. retail jewelry store with branches, 48-52; asst. archivist, Alderman Libr. Manuscripts Div, Univ. Va, 53-54; prof. hist, Longwood Col, 54-; mgr. resort motel, summers 55-60; educ. adv, Humphries Assocs, 66- Mem: Am. Hist. Asn; Orgn. of Am. Historians; Va. Soc. Sci. Asn; Asn. for Preservation of Va. Antiq; Am. Asn. of Univ. Prof; Rotary; Moose. Rel: Methodist. Mailing Add: 412 Fourth Ave, Farmville, Va. 23901.

HELMS, JULIAN DEAN D
Chmn, Hansford Co. Dem. Party, Tex.
b. Arkadelphia, Ark, 2/22/32; s. Palmer Dale Helms and Rosie Pollard H; m. 1/24/53 to Donna Brown; c. Brent, Conner and Blake. Educ: Tex. Tech. Col, B.B.A, 54; Univ. Tex, LL.B, 57; Phi Eta Sigma. Polit. & Govt. Pos: Mem, Sch. Bd, Spearman Independent Sch. Dist, Tex; chmn, Hansford Co. Dem. Party, currently. Mil. Serv: Entered as Pvt, Air Force, 50, released as S/Sgt, 53. Mem: Jr. C. of C.(pres, 63-64); Lions (pres, Spearman Club, 59-60); N.E. Panhandle Bar Asn.(pres); Am. Legion; Am. and Tex. State Bar Asns. Nominee for Outstanding Young Men of Am, 65. Rel: Baptist. Legal Res: 11 W. Kenneth, Spearman, Tex. 79081. Mailing Add: P.O. Box 38, Spearman, Tex. 79081. (1967)

HELMS, WILLIAM J, JR. D
Md. State Del.
b. Anne Arundel Co, Md, 9/3/29; s. William J. Helms and Mary A. Donnelly H; m. 3/21/52 to Marilyn Pinocher; c. William, Karen, Lisa and LeRoy. Educ: Univ. Va; Baltimore Inst. Polit. & Govt. Pos: Mem, Zoning Bd. of Appeals, Md, 59-62; Md. State Del, 62-; del, Dem. Nat. Conv, 68. Bus. & Prof. Pos: Ins. broker, William Helms, Ins, 53- Mil. Serv: Entered as Pvt, Air Force, 50, released as Cpl, 53. Mem: K. of C; Elks. Rel: Roman Catholic. Mailing Add: 193 McKinsey Rd, Severna Park, Md. 21146. (1967)

HELSTOSKI, HENRY D
U.S. Rep, N.J.
b. Wallington, N.J, 3/21/25; s. Heyonim Helstoski and Margaret Spiek H; m. to Victoria Ubaldo; c. Henry and Andrea. Educ: Patterson State Col; Montclair State Col, M.A, 49. Polit. & Govt. Pos: Councilman, East Rutherford, N.J, 56, Mayor, 57-64; U.S. Rep. N.J, 64- Bus. & Prof. Pos: Teacher and high sch. prin; supt. of schs, 49-62; mgt. consult, advert, 62-64. Mil. Serv: Army Air Force, Control Neto Syst, 43-45. Mem: N.J. Teachers Asn; Nat. Educ. Asn; N.J. Teachers Vets. Asn; active in many civic, fraternal, vet. and prfnl. orgn. Legal Res: 84 Cottage Place, East Rutherford, N.J. Mailing Add: 326 Cannon House Office Bldg, Washington, D.C. 20515.

HELTON, JAMES CARTER R
Chmn, Bell Co. Rep. Exec. Cmt, Ky.
b. Pineville, Ky, 5/16/27; s. James Skidmore Helton and Frances Kinningham H; m. 3/20/53 to Mary Cathern Napier; c. Jimmy and Jeffery. Educ: Univ. Ky, LL.B, 50; Kappa Sigma; Phi Delta. Polit. & Govt. Pos: Chmn, Bell Co. Rep. Exec. Cmt, Ky, 64- Bus. & Prof. Pos: Chmn, Ky. Mountain Theatre, Inc, 62-64. Mil. Serv: Entered as A/S, Navy, 45, released as Pharmacist Mate 3/C, 46. Mem: Bell Co, Ky. and Am. Bar Asns; Middlesboro Country Club. Rel: Baptist. Legal Res: Sycamore St, Pineville, Ky. 40977. Mailing Add: Asher Bldg, Pineville, Ky. 40977.

HEMBREE, GERRY P. R
b. Atlanta, Ga, 12/6/35; d. Fred William Phillips, Sr. and Rubye Hawkins P; m. 7/2/60 to Dr. William L. Hembree; c. William L, Jr, Russell R, Karen Leigh and Kimberly Ann. Polit. & Govt. Pos: Alternate del, Rep. Nat. Conv, 64 & 68; precinct committeewoman, Duval Co. Rep. Exec. Cmt, Fla, 64-66, finance coordinator, 65-66; TAR page coordinator, Young Rep. Nat. Conv, 65; 1st v.pres, Young Rep. Club of Duval Co, Fla, 65; Rep. cand. for Fla. State Rep, 66. Bus. & Prof. Pos: Cert. dent. asst, Am. Dent. Asst. Asn, 66. Rel: Episcopal. Mailing Add: 2948 Park St, Jacksonville, Fla. 32205. (1967)

HEMBREE, WILLIAM LASATER R
b. Bridgeport, Ala, 6/19/28; s. Gordon Hembree and Kathleen Lasater H; m. 7/2/60 to Gerry Phillips; c. Rusty, Russell, Karen and Kim. Educ: Univ. of Ala, B.A, 51, D.M.D, 57; Pi Kappa Alpha. Polit. & Govt. Pos: Finance chmn, Duval Co. Rep. Exec. Cmt, Fla, 64-65, chmn, 65-68. Mil. Serv: Entered as A/S, Navy, 45, released as Lt, 54. Rel: Episcopal. Legal Res: 2948 Park St, Jacksonville, Fla. 32205. Mailing Add: 1510 Willow Branch Ave, Jacksonville, Fla. 32205. (1967)

HEMENWAY, ROBERT BRUCE R
Chmn, Rep. 16th House Dist. of Alaska
b. South Weymouth, Mass, 1/28/40; s. William Andrew Mitchell and Constance Duncan Mitchell H. adopted by Floyd Norman Hemenway; m. 11/5/60 to Shirley Lorraine McFadden; c. Robert Bruce, Jr. and Ronald John. Educ: Mass. Radio & Tel. Sch, Boston, Dipl, 57; various electronics sch. and Rep. Campaign Schs. Polit. & Govt. Pos: Rep. campaign chmn, Tok Precinct, 16th House Dist, Alaska, 65-67, Delta Area chmn, Dr. McKinley for U.S. Sen, 66; Rep. committeeman, Seventh Precinct, 16th House Dist, 67-; orgn. chmn, 16th House Dist, 67-68, chmn, 68-; alternate del, Rep. Nat. Conv, 68. Bus. & Prof. Pos: Electronics field engr, RCA Serv. Co, Cherry Hill, N.J, 61-62 and electronics site rep, Murphy Dome, Alaska, 62- Mil. Serv: Entered as Airman, Air Force, 57, released as Airman 2/C, 61, after serv. in Hq. Bangor Air Defense Sector, Air Defense Command, 57-61; Res, 61-63; Good Conduct Medal. Mem: Tok Businessman's Asn.(secy-treas); Jr. C. of C; Tok Rod & Gun Club (pres); IBEW. Rel: Episcopal. Mailing Add: 128 Kantishna Way, Fairbanks, Alaska 99701.

HEMENWAY, RUSSELL DOUGLAS D
Nat. Dir, Nat. Cmt. for an Effective Cong.
b. Leominster, Mass, 3/24/25; s. Alan E. Hemenway and Bessie Picard H; div; c. Anne. Educ: Dartmouth Col, A.B, 49; Inst. d'Etudes Politiques, Paris, France, 49-50; Chi Phi. Polit. & Govt. Pos: Mem, U.S. For. Serv, Paris, France and Athens, Greece, 50-53; dir, N.Y. State Dept. of Commerce for N.Y.C, 57-58; Dem. campaign mgr, state and local off, 56-66; dep. nat. campaign mgr, Adlai E. Stevenson, 60; del, Dem. State and Nat. Conv, 60-68; pres, Lexington Dem. Club, N.Y.C, 63-64; exec. dir, N.Y. Cmt. for Dem. Voters, 64-66; nat. dir, Nat. Cmt. for an Effective Cong, 66- Bus. & Prof. Pos: Pres, Russell D. Hemenway & Co, N.Y.C, 58-61, St. Martins Develop. Co, Inc, 61- and Mt. Vernon Co. Ltd, 69. Mil. Serv: Entered as Seaman, Navy, 43, released as Qm. 1/C, 46, after serv. in U.S.S. Pittsburg, Pac. Theatre. Publ:

Cong. Report, Nat. Cmt. for an Effective Cong, four times yearly. Mem: Munic. Arts Soc; Cmt. on Housing and Urban Develop, Commun. Serv; Sierra Club; Wilderness Soc; Nat. Capital Dem. Club. Rel: Episcopal. Legal Res: 871 First Ave, New York, N.Y. 10017. Mailing Add: 10 E. 39th St, New York, N.Y. 10016.

HEMPHILL, JOE PAUL D
b. Monroe, Okla, 9/6/26; s. Joseph Braxton Hemphill and Bertha Mae Cagle H; m. 8/28/48 to Wilma Marceil Barentine; c. Joe Paul, Jr, Dennis Keith, Suanna, Rodney Braxton and Roger Burton. Educ: Poteau Commun. Col, A.A, 49; Southeast. State Col, B.S, 50; Okla. State Univ, M.S, 56; Tex. Tech, Okla. State and South. Ore, grad. study; O-Club. Polit. & Govt. Pos: Dem. precinct chmn, Monroe Precinct, Okla, 60-66; Leflore Co. chmn, Raymond Gary For Gov, 62 & 66 and Raymond Gary For U.S. Senate, 64; chmn, Leflore Co. Dem. Cent Cmt, 67-69. Bus. & Prof. Pos: Prin, Monroe Pub. Schs, 55-60, supt, 60-65; supt, Wister Pub. Schs, 65-67; dean, Poteau Commun. Col, 67- Mil. Serv: Entered as A/S, Navy, 44, released as Seaman First Class, 46, after serv. in Base Security Div, Coronado Naval Base. Mem: Okla. Col. Deans; Math Teachers Asn; Okla. and Leflore Co. Educ. Asns; Mason; McAlester Consistory; Am. Legion. Honor grad, Southeast. State Col. Rel: Baptist. Mailing Add: 206 Hillcrest, Poteau, Okla. 74953.

HEMPHILL, PAUL, JR. D
b. Chester, S.C, 11/27/30; s. Paul Hemphill and Isabel Hardin H; m. 5/26/56 to Lucy Ann Robinson. Educ: The Citadel, B.A, 51; Univ. of S.C, LL.B, 57. Polit. & Govt. Pos: S.C. State Sen, 64-66; succeeded Wilbur G. Grant, who died 6/15/64. Bus. & Prof. Pos: Lawyer, Hemphill & Hemphill. Mil. Serv: Army, Artil. Officer, 52-55; 25th Inf. Div. Mailing Add: Box 687, Chester, S.C. 29706. (1967)

HEMPHILL, ROBERT WITHERSPOON D
b. Chester, S.C, 5/10/15; s. John McLure Hemphill and Helen Witherspoon H; m. 6/20/42 to Forrest Isabelle Anderson; c. Forrest Richardson, Harriet Witherspoon and Robert Witherspoon. Educ: Univ. S.C, A.B, 36 and LL.B, 38; Omicron Delta Kappa; Kappa Alpha; Phi Delta Phi. Polit. & Govt. Pos: Chmn, Chester Co. Dem. Conv, S.C, 46-47; S.C. State Rep, 46-48; solicitor, Sixth Judicial Circuit, 50-56; U.S. Rep, Fifth Cong. Dist, S.C, 56-64; U.S. Dist. Judge, S.C. 64- Mil. Serv: Entered as Flying Cadet, Army-Air Force, 41, released as Maj, 45, serv. in Judge Adv. Gen. Dept, D.C, until 64; Lt. Col, Air Force Res. Publ: Capitol Punishment, Am. Legion, 62. Mem: Am. Judicature Soc; Am. and S.C. Bar Asns; Nat. Lawyers Club; Am. Legion; 40 et 8; K. of P; Elks; Moose; Army and Navy Club; Palmetto Club. Rel: Presbyterian. Legal Res: 167 York St, Chester, S.C. 29706. Mailing Add: U.S. Courthouse, Columbia, S.C. 29202.

HENDERSON, CHARLES D. R
N.Y. State Assemblyman
b. Beloit, Wis, 1/1/11; m. 1939 to Carolyne Brown. Educ: Alfred Univ, B.A, 36. Polit. & Govt. Pos: N.Y. State Assemblyman, 54-; chmn, Steuben Co. Rep. Party, N.Y, 68- Bus. & Prof. Pos: Pres, Hornell Broadcasting Corp; owner, Radio Sta. WLEA; licensed ins. agent. Mil. Serv: Nat. Guard, 4 years. Mem: Grange; F&AM; Moose; Elks; Eagles; KT; Damascus Temple of Rochester; RAM; RSM; AASR; Hornell Rep. Club; Rotary; Univ. Club; Auto Old Times; N.Y. Athletic Club; dir, C. of C. Rel: Episcopal. Mailing Add: 39 Church St, Hornell, N.Y. 14843. (1967)

HENDERSON, CHARLES ROBERT R
W.Va. State Del.
b. St. Marys, W.Va, 12/12/32; s. Charles Russell Henderson and Irene McKeny H; m. 9/2/61 to Mary Deloris Gibson; c. Robert Sean. Educ: Marshall Univ, 51. Polit. & Govt. Pos: Pres, Putnam Co. Young Rep, W.Va, 66-67; mem, Putnam Co. Bd. of Educ, 67; W.Va. State Del, 69- Bus. & Prof. Pos: Salesman, bldg. materials, 60-68; pres, Hurricane Heating & Supply Corp, 68- Mil. Serv: Army Res, 51-60. Mem: AF&AM; Royal Arch Mason; K.T; Scottish Rite; Shrine; Lions; Civitan Club. Ky. Colonel. Rel: Protestant. Mailing Add: 2828 Virginia Ave, Hurricane, W.Va. 25526.

HENDERSON, DAVID NEWTON D
U.S. Rep, N.C.
b. Hubert, N.C, 4/16/21; s. I. N. Henderson and Virginia Boney H; m. to Mary Knowles; c. David Bruce, Wiley Bryant and Wimbric Boney. Educ: Davidson Col, B.S, 1942; Univ. N.C. Law Sch, L.L.B, 1949. Polit. & Govt. Pos: Asst. gen. counsel, Cmt. on Educ. and Labor, U.S. House of Rep, 51-52; solicitor, Duplin Co. Gen. Court, N.C, 54-58, judge, 58-60; U.S. Rep, N.C, 60-, mem, Pub. Works Cmt, Post Off. and Civil Serv. Cmt. and chmn, Subcmt. Manpower Utilization. Bus. & Prof. Pos: Attorney-at-law. Mil. Serv: Entered as 2nd Lt, Air Corps, released as Maj, 46, after serv. in India, China and Okinawa. Mem: Mason; Am. Legion; VFW; Duplin Co. Bar Asn; Wallace Squadron Air Patrol; Lions. Rel: Presbyterian. Legal Res: Wallace, N.C. 28466. Mailing Add: 217 Cannon House Office Building, Washington, D.C. 20515.

HENDERSON, DOUGLAS
U.S. Rep. to Inter-Am. Cmt. for Alliance for Progress
b. Newton, Mass, 10/15/14; s. William Joseph Henderson and Nellie Kalloch H; m. 2/12/42 to Dorothy Frances Henderson (deceased 10/21/68); c. Peter, Bruce, Lee, Jennifer, Karen and Mark. Educ: Boston Univ. Col. of Liberal Arts, B.S, 40; Fletcher Sch. of Law and Diplomacy, M.A, 41; Phi Beta Kappa. Hon. D.H.L, Boston Univ, 69. Polit. & Govt. Pos: V.consul, Nogales, Mex, Arica, Chile, Cochabamba, Boliva, 42-47; career officer, U.S. Dept. of State For. Serv, 42-; Dept. of Commerce, 47-50; consul, Bern, 50-56; asst. chief, Econ. Defense Div, 56-58; Sr. Seminar in For. Policy, 59-60; counselor, consul, Lima, 60-63; U.S. Ambassador, Bolivia, 63-69; consultant policy planning staff, Dept. of State, 68-69; U.S. Rep. to Inter-Am. Cmt. for Alliance for Progress, 69- Rel: Episcopal. Mailing Add: 2329 Nebraska Ave. N.Y, Washington, D.C. 20016.

HENDERSON, FRANCES R
b. N.Y.C; d. Charles F. Henderson and Mary Parker H; single. Educ: Barnard Col, B.A, 37; George Wash. Univ; Rutgers Law Sch, J.D, 55. Polit. & Govt. Pos: Asst. to chmn, Atomic Energy Cmn, 47-49; mem, tech. assistance staff, Int. Bank for Reconstruction & Develop, 51-53; exec. asst. to U.S. Sen. Clifford P. Case, N.J, 55-65, admin. asst, 65- Bus. & Prof. Pos: Field secy, N.Y. League of Women Voters, 38-40; research and assoc. ed, Time Mag, N.Y.C, 41-45 and Wash. correspondent, Wash, D.C, 45-47; asst. to pres, Fund for the Repub, N.Y.C, 53-54. Mem: Wash, D.C. Bar; Am. and Fed. Bar Asns; Am. Newspaper Women's Club; Admin. Asst. and Secy. Asn. of U.S. Senate; Rep. Women of Capitol Hill; Barnard and Rutgers Law Alumni. Mailing Add: Yonder House, Indian Head, Md. 20640.

HENDERSON, FRANK E. R
S.Dak. State Sen.
b. Miller, S.Dak, 4/7/28; m. to Norma Johnson; c. Seven. Educ: Univ. S.Dak. Law Sch, 51. Polit. & Govt. Pos: Rep. precinct committeeman, Rapid City, S.Dak, 4 years; U.S. Cmnr, 63-64; mem, bd. dir, Nat. Asn. of U.S. Cmnrs; S.Dak. State Sen, 64-66 and currently. Bus. & Prof. Pos: Teacher law, Rapid City, S.Dak; owner and operator, Pine Rest Motel, Hill City; Henderson Law Office; lawyer, 53- Mem: Pres, Black Hills Bar Asn, 64; State Bar S.Dak; Nat. Legal Cmt, VFW; Elks; Am. Legion; DAV. Admitted to practice before the Supreme Court, 51 and Fed. Dist. Court, S.Dak, 54. Rel: Catholic. Mailing Add: 629 Quincy St, Rapid City, S.Dak. 57701.

HENDERSON, DR. J. H, JR. 'JACK' D
Ga. State Rep.
b. Marietta, Ga, 3/11/32; s. John H. Henderson and Evelyn York H; m. 2/7/57 to Martha Jayne; c. John H, III, Hanley Scott and Keith York. Educ: Univ. Ga; Gridiron; Omega Tau Sigma; Chi Phi; Student Coun; Inter Fraternity Coun. Polit. & Govt. Pos: Ga. State Rep, currently. Bus. & Prof. Pos: Dir, South Cobb Bank. Mem: Pres, Jaycees; pres, N.Ga. Vet. Med. Asn; dir, YMCA and Cobb Co. Fair Asn; Elks; Farm Bur; Kiwanis; Boys Club; C. of C; Am. and Ga. Vet. Med. Asns. Rel: Baptist. Legal Res: 1525 Powder Springs Rd, Marietta, Ga. 30060. Mailing Add: 1290 Gresham Rd, Marietta, Ga. 30060. (1967)

HENDERSON, JAMES H. R
Treas. and Committeeman, Mass. Rep. State Cmt.
b. Canada, 4/15/94; s. Robert C. Henderson and Anne Cody H; m. 6/24/67 to Joan A. Patterson. Educ: High Sch. Polit. & Govt. Pos: Chmn, Bd. of Assessors, Brookline, Mass, 37-; mem, Mass. Dept. of Pub. Safety, 46-56; secy. and mem, Selective Serv. Bd, 56-; treas. and committeeman, Mass. Rep. State Cmt, currently. Bus. & Prof. Pos: Pres, Rental Housing Asn, 60-61; pres, Greater Boston Real Estate Bd, 64-65; dir, Nat. Asn. of Real Estate Bd, 65. Mil. Serv: Entered as Pvt, Army, 17; released as Sgt. 1/C, 19. Mem: Am. Legion; Odd Fellows; Elks; Rotary; Middlesex Club; Rep. Club of Mass. Rel: Presbyterian. Legal Res: 65 Hilltop Rd, Brookline, Mass. 02167. Mailing Add: 1318 Beacon St, Brookline, Mass. 02146.

HENDERSON, JAMES MARVIN R
Spec. Asst. to the Postmaster Gen.
b. Atlanta, Ga, 3/28/21; s. Isaac Harmon Henderson and Ruth Ashley H; m. 4/28/45 to Donna Fern Baade; c. Linda Dee, James Marvin, Jr. and Deborah Fanchon. Educ: Furman Univ, 39-40; Clemson Col, 40-42; N.Y. Univ, 44; Univ. Denver, B.S.C, 46; Harvard Univ, A.M.P, 56; Omicron Delta Kappa; Alpha Kappa. Polit. & Govt. Pos: Chmn, Eisenhower Campaign, Greenville Co, S.C, 52; Spec. Asst. to the Postmaster Gen, 69- Bus. & Prof. Pos: Sales supvr, Gen. Foods Corp, N.Y, 42-44; acct. exec, Curt Frieberger Advert. Agency, Denver, Colo, 44-46; pres, Henderson Advert. Agency, Greenville, S.C, 46-69. Mil. Serv: Entered as Pvt, Army, 42, released as Sgt, 43. Mem: Chmn. Southeast Chap, Greenville Advert. Coun; Am. Asn. Advert. Agencies (past pres, Southeast Chap); mem. bd. dir, Citizens and South. Nat. Bank; pres, Greenville Heart Asn; Greenville Youth Cmn; past dir, Greenville Ment. Hygiene Clin; dir, United Fund; past dir, Greenville Jr. C. of C; past pres, Gr. Greenville C. of C; past pres, Young Pres. Orgn; past dir, Kiwanis. Young Man of the Year. Rel: Methodist. Legal Res: Route 7, Hickory Lane, Greenville, S.C. 29609. Mailing Add: 2650 Virginia Ave. N.W, Washington, D.C. 20037.

HENDERSON, JOHN EARL R
b. Crafton, Pa, 1/4/17; s. William Clinton Henderson and Edna Vessels H; m. 4/17/43 to Wilma Maxine Gill; c. James Clinton and Nancy Gill. Educ: Ohio Wesleyan, A.B, 39; Univ. Mich, LL.B, 42; Pi Sigma Alpha; Phi Mu Alpha; Phi Gamma Delta. Polit. & Govt. Pos: Ohio State Rep, 51-54; U.S. Rep, Ohio, 55-60. Bus. & Prof. Pos: Attorney-at-law, 46- Mil. Serv: Entered as Pvt, Army, 42, released as Capt, 46, after serv. in 29th Div, 9th Army, ETO; Bronze Star; Army Commendation Medal; Combat Infantry Ribbon. Mem: Ohio and Guernsey Co. Bar Asns; Elks; Mason, Scottish Rite; Am. Legion; C. of C; Lions. Rel: Methodist. Legal Res: 1301 Foster Ave, Cambridge, Ohio 43725. Mailing Add: 126 N. Ninth St, Cambridge, Ohio 43725.

HENDERSON, MARY WARNER R
City Councilman, Redwood City, Calif.
b. Fresno, Calif, 3/26/27; d. Conrad Maupin Warner and Merle Allen W; m. 11/4/50 to Howard Randall Henderson; c. Laura and Bruce Warner. Educ: Univ. Calif, Berkeley, A.B, 48; Delta Gamma. Polit. & Govt. Pos: Assoc. mem, San Mateo Co. Rep. Cent. Cmt, Calif, 56-; assoc. mem, Calif. Rep. State Cent. Cmt, 62-68, mem, 69-; city councilman, Redwood City, Calif, 66- Mem: Univ. Calif. Alumni Asn; Sierra Club; Cmt. Green Foothills; Children's Home Soc; San Mateo Co. Hist. Asn; Save San Francisco Bay Asn; C. of C; commun. adv. cmt, Jr. League Palo Alto; past pres, Kennedy Sch. PTA; hon. chmn, 1969 Am. Cancer Crusade, Redwood City. Rel: Episcopal. Mailing Add: 3098 Muller Court, Redwood City, Calif. 94061.

HENDERSON, OPAL MAE D
V.Chmn, Woodson Co. Dem. Party, Kans.
b. Neosho Falls, Kans, 12/2/33; d. Alex B. McCullough and Neva Opal Stephens M; m. 5/3/53 to Clarence Wesley Henderson, Jr; c. Terri L. Educ: Neosho Falls High Sch, Kans, grad, 51. Polit. & Govt. Pos: City clerk, Neosho Falls, Kans, 60-64; Dem. committeewoman, First Ward, Yates Center, 68-; v.chmn, Woodson Co. Dem. Party, 68- Bus. & Prof. Pos: Secy, J.M. Powell Ins. Agency, Iola, Kans, 51-52; ins. agent, Opal M. Henderson Ins. Agency, Neosho Falls, 63-68. Mem: Eastern Star; Womens Christian Soc. Rel: Methodist. Mailing Add: 111 E. Mary, Yates Center, Kans. 66783.

HENDERSON, ROBERT EARL R
Chmn, Ashland Co. Rep. Exec. Cmt, Ohio
b. Cleveland, Ohio, 8/16/27; s. Earl R. Henderson and Elsie Sydenstricker H;

m. 6/30/51 to Ruth Elaine Jones; c. Robert J, Rebecca E. and Elizabeth A. Educ: Baldwin Wallace Col, A.B, 48; Western Reserve Univ, LL.B, 51; Phi Beta Kappa. Polit. & Govt. Pos: V.chmn, Ashland Co. Rep. Exec. Cmt, Ohio, 56-60, chmn, 60-; mem. bd. of elections, Ashland Co, 62-; Common Pleas Judge, Ashland Co, 67- Bus. & Prof. Pos: Pres, United Appeal, Ashland, Ohio, 60; dir, Mohican Rubber Co, 60-; pres, Ashland C. of C, 62; dir, Philway Prod. Inc, 65- Mil. Serv: Entered as Pvt, Air Force, 51, released as 1st Lt, 53, after serv. in Mil. Air Transport Serv. Mem: Am, Ohio and Ashland Co. Bar Asns; Ashland and Valley of Columbus Masonic Lodges; Am. Legion; Grange. Rel: Methodist. Mailing Add: 231 N. Countryside Dr, Ashland, Ohio 44805.

HENDERSON, ROBERT EMMET D
b. Newark, N.J, 11/16/06; m. to Ann Denny; c. four sons. Educ: Univ. of Buffalo and Brown Univ. Polit. & Govt. Pos: Mayor, Rahway, N.J, 7 years and councilman-at-lg, 4 years; N.J. State Assemblyman, 2 terms. Bus. & Prof. Pos: Asst. to the chmn, East. R.R. Mem: Elks; Moose; Sideliners; Ramblers; Kiwanis; bd. of mgrs, Rahway Savings Inst. and Rahway Mem. Hosp. 1967 Legal Res: Trenton, N.J. No mailing address available. (1967)

HENDERSON, ROBERT G. R
Chmn, Cheboygan Co. Rep. Cmt, Mich.
b. Detroit, Mich, 8/5/18; s. Robert Henderson and Elizabeth Ambrose H; m. 10/22/38 to Patricia Haylor; c. Barbara (Mrs. Deeter) and Robert G, II. Educ: Univ. Detroit, 48-50. Polit. & Govt. Pos: Training specialist, Vet. Admin, 46-49; secy-treas, Cheboygan Recreation Cmt, Mich, 57-; chmn, Cheboygan Co. Rep. Cmt, 64-; supvr, Cheboygan Co, 69- Bus. & Prof. Pos: Owner-mgr, Royal Linen of Cheboygan Inc, 57- Mil. Serv: Entered as Pvt, Army Air Force, 40, released as Chief Warrant Officer, 46, after serv. in Flying Training Command, San Marcos, Tex. Mem: F&AM; Mason; Kiwanis; Am. Legion; C. of C.(Mil. Affairs Cmt). Rel: Methodist. Mailing Add: 304 Riverside Dr, Cheboygan, Mich. 49721.

HENDERSON, STUART D
b. Scio, Ohio, 7/12/05; s. John William Henderson and Mary Whitehead H; m. 7/5/31 to Katherine Sherlock; c. Stuart, Jr, Barbara, William B. and Marsha. Educ: High Sch, Ohio. Polit. & Govt. Pos: Cmnr, Ohio, 50-62; former Ohio State Rep. Bus. & Prof. Pos: Farmer. Mem: Lions; Eagles; Grange; Farm Bur; Hist. Soc. Rel: Methodist. Mailing Add: R.R. 1, Scio, Ohio 43988. (1967)

HENDERSON, WALDO D
b. Ocilla, Ga, 7/03/93; s. J.A.J. Henderson and Martha Paulk H; m. 7/03/22 to Lynda Leigh Thorpe. Educ: Gordon Inst, 13. Polit. & Govt. Pos: Ga. State Rep, 61-66, 49-56; Ga. State Sen, 57-58. Bus. & Prof. Pos: Naval stores operator. Mil. Serv: WWI, Pvt. Mem: Mason; Shriner. Rel: Methodist. Mailing Add: Lakeland, Ga. 31635. (1967)

HENDERSON, WARREN S. R
Fla. State Sen.
b. Exeter, N.H, 11/14/27; m. to Polly Ann Schurr; c. Warren C, Susan D. and Wendy L. Educ: Denison Univ, B.A, 51; Phi Delta Theta. Polit. & Govt. Pos: Mem, Sarasota Co. Planning and Zoning Cmn, Fla, 57-58; chmn, Sarasota Co. Cmn, 61-63; chmn, Manatee/Sarasota Airport Authority, 61-63; chmn, West Coast Inland Navig. Dist, 62-63; Fla. State Sen, currently; del, Rep. Nat. Conv, 68. Bus. & Prof. Pos: Investments. Mil. Serv: Navy, World War II. Mem: C. of C.(past pres); Elks (Past Exalted Ruler); Mason. Rel: Presbyterian. Mailing Add: P.O. Box 1358, Venice, Fla. 33595.

HENDERSON, WILLIAM BRUCE R
b. Athens, Ala, 6/7/27; s. James Richard Henderson and Ila Merle McDole H; m. 12/21/50 to Mary Rita Kimbrough; c. William Luther and Randall Warren. Educ: Ga. Inst. of Tech, B.Ch.E, 53; Kappa Mu Epsilon; Independent Students Orgn. Polit. & Govt. Pos: V.chmn, Morgan Co. Young Rep, Ala, 61-62; secy, Morgan Co. Rep. Exec. Cmt, 62-64, v.chmn. and orgn. dir, 64-66 and chmn, 66-; mem-at-lg, Ala. State Rep. Exec. Cmt, 66- Bus. & Prof. Pos: Develop. proj. leader, Monsanto Chem. Co, 63- Mil. Serv: Entered as A/S, Navy, 45, released as PO 2/C, TE-2, 48; Good Conduct, Asian Theater and Victory Medals. Mem: Am. Inst. Chem. Engrs; Registered Prfnl. Engr, Ala; Civitan Club; Boy Scouts. Rel: Methodist. 1967 Legal Res: Decatur, Ala. No mailing address available. (1967)

HENDERSON, WILLIAM H. D
b. Salt Lake City, Utah, 11/13/08; s. Evan B. Henderson and Florence Jarman H; m. 6/7/33 to Dorothy Ann Robinson; c. W. Ben and Robin G. Educ: Univ. Utah, B.S; Stanford Univ, LL.B. Polit. & Govt. Pos: Law clerk, Sr. Circuit Judge, U.S. Circuit Court of Appeals, 35; chief, Claims and Leasing Secy, Div. of Eng, Pac. Div, War Dept, 44; chief, W.Coast Antitrust Div, U.S. Dept. of Justice, 46; dep. adminstr, Philippine Alliance Property Admin, 48-49; Dem. cand. for Attorney Gen. of Utah, 60 & 62; del, Dem. Nat. Conv, 64; attorney, Fed. Trade Cmn, currently. Publ: Articles on antitrust law in Nebr. Law Rev, Calif. Law Rev. and Fed. Bar J; 'The Race to Oligopoly,' Duke Law J, 68. Mem: Fed. Bar Asn; Businessmen's Alliance; Nat. Lawyers Club; C. of C. Rel: Latter-day Saint. Legal Res: 2139 Sherman Ave, Salt Lake City, Utah. 84108. Mailing Add: 8510 16th St, Apt. 718, Silver Spring, Md. 20910.

HENDREN, WILLIAM FOSTER D
Chmn, Greene Co. Dem. Cmt, Ind.
b. Indianapolis, Ind, 1/14/29; s. William Foster Hendren and Fannie Williams H; m. 7/1/51 to Sue Ellen Flater; c. William Mark and Tammy Ann. Educ: Ind. Univ, Bloomington, B.S, 51; Ind. Univ. Law Sch, J.D, 61; Phi Kappa Psi; Phi Delta Phi. Polit. & Govt. Pos: Dep. Ind. Securities Cmnr, 58-59, Ind. Securities Cmnr, 60; Chief Dep. Ins. Cmnr, Ind, 61-64; precinct committeeman, Precinct Two, Bloomfield, 62-; chmn, Greene Co. Dem. Cmt, 64-; dep. prosecuting attorney, 63rd Judicial Dist. of Ind, 65-67, prosecuting attorney, 67-; city attorney, Linton and Jasonville, 66- Bus. & Prof. Pos: V.pres, H. & H. Motors, Inc, Ford dealership, Bloomfield, Ind, 51-58; secy-dir. and counsel, United Presidential Life Ins. Co, Kokomo, 64-; trustee and counsel, Founder Real Estate Investment Trust, Bloomfield, 67- Mil. Serv: Entered as 2nd Lt, Army, 51, released as 1st Lt, 53, after serv. in Inf, Korea; Lt. Col, Ind. Nat. Guard, J.A.G, 60-; Combat Inf. Badge; Korean Serv. Badge. Publ: Municipal Cooperation, Ind. Univ. and Ind. Dept. of Commerce, 59; History of Bail and the Bondsman, Ind. Univ. and United Bonding Ins. Co, 62. Mem: Am, Ind. and Greene Co. Bar Asns; Ind. Prosecuting Attorneys Asn; Trial Bar of Ind; pres, Tri-Co. Bar Asn, 68-; Am. Legion; Elks; VFW; Odd Fellows; Mason; Shrine; Nat. Farmers Orgn. Rel: Protestant. Mailing Add: 202 W. Main, Bloomfield, Ind. 47424.

HENDRICKS, CHARLES O. R
b. Speed, Ind, 2/9/14; s. Asbury Hendricks; m. to Mary Elizabeth Popp; c. Charles and Marilyn Sue. Educ: Cent. Normal Col; Ind. Univ. Polit. & Govt. Pos: Precinct committeeman, Clark Co. Rep. Party, Ind, 14 years; del, Rep. State Conv, 44-66; Secy. of State, Ind, 60 & 62; former chmn, Ind. Rep. State Cent. Cmt. Bus. & Prof. Pos: Employee, pub. rels, Louisville Cement Co. Mem: Mason; Scottish Rite; Shrine; Elks; lifetime mem, Jaycees; Rep. Nat. Cmt. Sr. Citizens Cmt. Rel: Nondenominational. Mailing Add: 574 Edgewood Dr, Sellersburg, Ind. 47172. (1967)

HENDRICKS, JOSEPH EDWARD D
b. Lake Butler, Fla, 9/24/03; s. Joseph Edward Hendricks and Mary Ellinor Andrews H; div. Educ: Montverde Acad; John B. Stetson Univ, A.B, 30, LL.B, 34; Phi Alpha Delta; Pi Kappa Phi. Polit. & Govt. Pos: Attorney, legal tax surv, Fla, 34; U.S. Rep, Fifth Dist, Fla, 37-49. Bus. & Prof. Pos: Head of tax and ins. dept, South. Div, Am. Oil Co, 35; practiced law, 35-36; pres, Hendricks Industs. Inc, 49- Publ: Little Joe, Cody Publ. Co, 67. Mem: Elks; Kiwanis. Rel: Presbyterian. Mailing Add: 504 N. Dort St, Plant City, Fla. 33566.

HENDRICKS, LEONARD MONROE, JR. R
Mem, La. Rep. State Cent. Cmt.
b. Algiers, La, 11/25/28; s. Leonard Monroe Hendricks, Sr. and Elizabeth Hotard H; m. 12/17/46 to Mary Rochetti; c. Donn David. Educ: Loyola Univ. of South, D.D.S. Polit. & Govt. Pos: Mem, La. Rep. State Cent. Cmt. and chmn, Terrebonne Parish Rep. Exec. Cmt, 63- Mil. Serv: Entered as A/S, Navy, 46, released as Seaman 1/C ETM, Pac, 48; Good Conduct Medal; Victory Medal; Pacific Theater Ribbon. Mem: Am. Dent. Asn; Int. Dent. Fedn; VFW; Aircraft Owners & Pilots Asn; Chicago Dent. Soc; Am. Soc. Clin. Hypnosis; Tex. Asn. Magicians; Am. Soc. Dent. for Children; Mason; F&AM; Elks. Rel: Presbyterian. Mailing Add: 1350 E. Main, Houma, La. 70360. (1967)

HENDRICKS, LEWIS S. R
Chmn, Calhoun Co. Rep. Cent. Cmt, Iowa
b. New Salisbury, Ind, 9/30/19; s. Solomon Charles Hendricks and Flora Temple H; m. 11/24/49 to Marguerite Macke; c. Steven and John. Educ: Univ. Iowa, B.A, 41; Col. Law, J.D, 42; Beta Theta Pi; Phi Delta Phi. Polit. & Govt. Pos: Govt. appeal agent, Calhoun Co. Selective Serv, Iowa, 47-; co. attorney, Calhoun Co, 49-55; mem, numerous dist. and state conv. cmt. and del, 49-; mem. and attorney, Calhoun Co. Hosp, Cmt, 58-; chmn, Calhoun Co. Rep. Cent. Cmt, 59-; committeeman, Rockwell City Precinct, 62-66; mem, Rockwell City Zoning and Planning Cmn, 67-; mem, State Platform Cmt, 68; alternate del-at-lg, Nat. Rep. Conv, 68. Bus. & Prof. Pos: Attorney-at-law, L.S. Hendricks, 46-; dir. and gen. counsel, Nat. Bank of Rockwell City, 52-; mem, 16th Dist. Judicial Nominating Cmn, 63-; dir, North Cent. Iowa Ment. Health Asn, 64- Mil. Serv: Entered as Aviation Cadet, Naval Air Corps, 42, released as Lt.(jg), 46, after serv. in Patrol Bombers, Atlantic and Pac, 43-46. Mem: Calhoun Co, 16th Judicial Dist, Iowa State and Am. Bar Asns; Am. Judicature Soc; Iowa Acad. Trial Lawyers; Am. Legion; Farm Bur; Twin Lakes Golf Club; Iowa Alumni Asn. Rel: Methodist. Legal Res: 110 E. Main, Rockwell City, Iowa 50579. Mailing Add: 516-A Fourth, Rockwell City, Iowa 50579.

HENDRICKS, MALVIN LEON, SR. R
Committeeman, Pulaski Co. Rep. Party, Ark.
b. Magnolia, Ark, 1/28/21; s. Clayton Hendricks and Maggie Easter H; m. 6/7/46 to Della Mae Graham; c. Geneice H.(Mrs. Center), Barbara Ann, Malvin Leon, II and Michael Eugene. Educ: A.M.&N. Col, B.A, 60; Jackson Theol. Sem, B.D, 65; Sociol. Club; Vet. Club; Alumni Club. Polit. & Govt. Pos: Field coordinator and asst. mgr. for Congressman Brock, Chattanooga, Tenn, 62; field coordinator for Gov. Rockefeller, Little Rock, Ark, 64; committeeman, Pulaski Co. Rep. Party, 65-; asst. campaign mgr, State of Ark. Minority Group, 66; originator of plans used by minority group, 66-; gov, Ark. Coun. Human Rels, 66-; mem, Ark. State Screening Cmt, 66-; gov, Ark. Coun. Human Resources, 66-; field coordinator for Mr. Ed. Allison in a spec. elec, 67; field coordinator in voter's registrn, nine co, 67-68; field coordinator, Pulaski, Saline, Garland and Hot Spring Co, 68; Rep. cand, Ark. State Rep, Pulaski and Perry Co, Pos. One, 68; del, Rep. Nat. Conv, 68; seconded nomination for Winthrop Rockefeller, Gov. Ark, for President of U.S, 68; mem, Ark. State Rep. Platform Cmt, 68-; mem, Ark. State Police Cmn, 69- Bus. & Prof. Pos: Minister, Christian Methodist Episcopal Church, Little Rock, 47-, dist. supt, 47- Mil. Serv: Entered as Pvt, Air Force, 42, released as Sgt, 46, after serv. in 805th Air Force Base; World War II Victory Ribbon; Good Conduct Medal; Am. Theater Ribbon. Publ: TRI, Intercollegiate Press, 53. Mem: NAACP; Urban League; Little Rock Christian Methodist Episcopal Minister's Alliance; Interdenominational & Interracial Minister's Alliance; YMCA; F&AM (32°); Consistory; Am. League. Pastor of the Year, 62. Rel: Protestant. Mailing Add: 1311 W. 15th St, Little Rock, Ark. 72202.

HENDRICKSON, CONSTANCE COOPER D
Mem, Montgomery Co. Dem. Cmt, Md.
b. New York, N.Y, 8/12/26; d. Samuel Cooper and Frances Planinsek C; m. 10/25/58 to Adolph Carl Hendrickson; c. Christopher R, Kenneth C. and Nicholas A. Holt; Philip A. and Kirsten F. Hendrickson. Educ: Univ. Md, B.A, 69; Alpha Kappa Delta. Polit. & Govt. Pos: Dem. Precinct chmn, Silver Spring, Md, 59-66; mem, Montgomery Co. Dem. Cmt, 66-; alternate del, Dem. Nat. Conv, 68; mem, Md. Gov. Cmn. on Childhood Nutrition, 69- Rel: Unitarian. Mailing Add: 2202 Richland Place, Silver Spring, Md. 20910.

HENDRYX, GENE R. D
b. Perryton, Tex, 7/16/27; s. Earl A. Hendryx and Lillian Mallett H; m. 3/15/50 to Lucille Easterwood Kempen; c. Gene Ray, Jr, Forrest George and Houston Bowie. Educ: Sul Ross State Col, B.A. and M.A, 49; Alpha Chi; Kappa Delta Pi. Polit. & Govt. Pos: Precinct chmn, Brewster Co. Dem. Party, Tex, 48-52, chmn, 52-56; cmnr, Brewster Co, 56-62; Tex. State Rep,

62-69. Bus. & Prof. Pos: Pres. and owner, Radio Sta. KVLF, 50- Mil. Serv: Entered as Pvt, Marine Corps, 43, released as Pfc, 45, after serv. in 3rd Marine Div; Presidential Citation; Guam and Iwo Jima Campaign Ribbons. Publ: Semper Fil, Pageant, 59. Mem: Tex. Asn. Broadcasters; Am. Legion; VFW; Rotary; Mason. Rel: Baptist. Mailing Add: Box 779, Alpine, Tex. 79830. (1967)

HENKIN, DANIEL Z. D
Asst. Secy. of Defense for Pub. Affairs, Dept. of Defense
b. Washington, D.C, 5/10/23; m. to Hannah Ronen; c. Doron, Leora and Tamar. Educ: Univ. Calif, grad. Polit. & Govt. Pos: Dir. Opers, Off. of the Asst. Secy. of Defense for Pub. Affairs, Dept. of Defense, 65-67, Dep. Asst. Secy. of Defense for Pub. Affairs, 67-69, Acting Asst. Secy. of Defense for Pub. Affairs, 69- Bus. & Prof. Pos: Former staff mem, Buffalo Evening News, Wash, D.C; mem. staff, J. of the Armed Forces, then the Army-Navy J, 41, asst. ed. and ed, 48-65. Mil. Serv: Enlisted and serv. as Coast Guard Combat Correspondent covering amphibious opers. in the Pac. Theatre, including D-Day landings at Saipan and the Philippines, World War II; released as Chief PO. Awarded Secy. of Defense Meritorious Civilian Serv. Medal for outstanding serv. to the Dept. of Defense, 65-69. Legal Res: 2306 Washington Ave, Chevy Chase, Md. 20015. Mailing Add: Dept. of Defense, Pentagon, Washington, D.C. 20301.

HENLEY, JOHN TANNERY D
N.C. State Sen.
b. Wadesboro, N.C, 8/10/21; s. Frank C. Henley and Melissa Hamilton H; m. 7/28/43 to Rebecca Beddingfield; c. John T, Jr, Robert Ray and Douglas Eugene. Educ: Univ. of N.C, B.S. in pharm, 43; Kappa Psi. Polit. & Govt. Pos: N.C. State Rep, 57-63; state purchasing officer, N.C, 63-65; N.C. State Sen, 66- Mil. Serv: Entered as Pvt, Army, 43, released as S/Sgt, 45, after serv. in Europe; Bronze Star; Purple Heart. Mem: Bd. of Sci. & Tech, N.C; N.C. Pharmaceut. Asn; Mason; Kiwanis; Am. Legion. Rel: Methodist. Mailing Add: 216 Lakeshore Dr, Hope Mills, N.C. 28348.

HENLEY, LELAND R
Chmn, Searcy Co. Rep. Cent. Cmt, Ark.
b. Marshall, Ark, 7/10/02; s. Jackson Franklin Henley and Emma McBride H; m. 3/6/46 to Mary Ellen Ratchford. Educ: Little Rock Col, 1 year. Polit. & Govt. Pos: Chmn, Searcy Co. Rep. Cent. Cmt, Ark, 52-60 & 68- Bus. & Prof. Pos: Farmer and stockman, to 52; grocery owner, 52-57; owner and mgr, Searcy Co. Creosoting Co, 57-68; retired. Mil. Serv: Entered as Pfc, Army, released as Pfc, 18, after serv. in Mil. Police Hdq. Troops, Camp Pike, Little Rock, Ark, 4 months. Mem: Am. Wood Preservers Asn; Farm Bur. Rel: Protestant. Mailing Add: St. Joe, Ark. 72675.

HENLEY, ROBERT L. R
Councilman, Fourth Ward Rep. Party, Calif.
b. Kansas City, Mo, 7/20/28; s. Miles Jack Henley and Cleo Arvilla Carter H; m. 1/7/50 to Barbara Alice Perry; c. Susan, Larry, George, Melinda and Joel Dean. Educ: Univ. of Mo, B.S. in Speech Educ, 51; Cert. YMCA Secy; Sigma Chi Xi. Polit. & Govt. Pos: Councilman, Fourth Ward Rep. Party, Calif, 65- Publ: Hike Football Fundamentals for Boys, Sunset Press, 57. Mem: Rotary. George Wash. Medal, Freedom Found. Rel: Christian Scientist. Mailing Add: 179 W. 49th St, San Bernardino, Calif. 92407. (1967)

HENNEBERGER, ROBERT LAWRENCE R
Mem, Wabash Co. Rep. Cent. Cmt, Ill.
b. Mt. Carmel, Ill, 1/6/13; s. Lawrence Francis Henneberger and Elmima Utter H; single. Educ: Notre Dame Univ, B.A; Georgetown Law Sch; Northwest. Univ. Polit. & Govt. Pos: Coordinator, Vols. for Nixon, 60 & 68; coordinator, 23rd Cong. Dist. Vols. for Goldwater, 64; mem, Ill. Rep. Work Group, Rep. Nat. Conv, 64 & 68, cand. for del, 68; mem. resolutions and platform cmt, Rep. State Conv, Ill. and one of three mems. commended for outstanding work, 66; chmn, Wabash Co. Rep. Cent. Cmt, Ill, 66-68, mem, 68-; mem, Rep. Exec. Cmt, 21st Cong. Dist, 66-68. Mil. Serv: Entered as Pvt, Army Med. Dept, 41, released as 2nd Lt, 45, after serv. in MAC, 20th Sta. Hosp. and 2 years overseas in Etousa Theater. Mem: Mt. Carmel Sch. Bd, 46-47; Buffalo Trace Coun, Boy Scouts, chmn. camping and activities, 50-53, Brotherhood Mem. Order Arrow, Orgn. and exten. chmn, Buffalo Trace Coun, 56-58; C. of C.(bd. dirs, 38-40); Rotary (pres, Mt. Carmel, 52-53); Am. Legion; VFW; Elks; Civic Theatre Group. Silver Beaver Award for Distinguished Serv. to Boyhood, Nat. Coun. Boy Scouts Am, 55; writing background and experience in numismatics. Rel: Catholic; Instr. church youth groups, 58-62; host instr. Oper. Understanding, St. Mary's Church, 62. Legal Res: 126 E. Fourth St, Mt. Carmel, Ill. 62863. Mailing Add: P.O. Box 689, Mt. Carmel, Ill. 62863.

HENNEN, JAMES ALLEN R
b. Minneapolis, Minn, 11/15/38; s. Hubert L. Hennen and Velma Degendorfer H; m. 10/9/65 to Patricia Louise Doyle. Educ: St. Cloud State Col, Minn, B.A. Bus. Admin. & Mgt. Polit. & Govt. Pos: Chmn, Chisago Co. Young Rep, Minn, 67-68; chmn, Eighth Dist. Young Rep, 67-69; cand, U.S. Rep, Minn, 68. Bus. & Prof. Pos: Assoc. partner, Hennen Chevrolet Co, Forest Lake, Minn; owner and pres, Construction Trucking Co. Mil. Serv: Entered as Pvt. E-1, Marine Corps, 56, released as Cpl. E-4, 59, after serv. in First Marine Div, First Tank Bn, Calif. and Third Marine Div, Third Tank Bn, Okinawa; Commanding Officers' Meritorious Mast, 59; Meritorious Proficiency Pay Award (two time consecutively, one of the first Marines to ever be so honored) promoted Meritoriously to Cpl. E-4. Mem: Cook Co. Hist. Soc; Jaycees (former dir. Chisago Lakes Jaycees); Chisago Co. Farm Bur; Finland Conserv. Club. Nominated Outstanding Young Man for Chisago Co, 68. Rel: Roman Catholic. Mailing Add: Lindstrom, Minn. 55045.

HENNESSY, ARTHUR L, JR. D
Chmn, Eighth Dist. New Dem. Coalition, Pa.
b. Malden, Mass, 4/23/25; s. Arthur L. Hennessy, Sr. and Rose Lyons H; m. July 1953 to Maude McColl; c. Kevin M, Patricia L. and Arthur L, III. Educ: Cath. Univ, B.A, 50; Harvard Univ, M.A, 52; Georgetown Univ, Ph.D, 57; Phi Alpha Epsilon; Phi Alpha Theta; Utopia; Grant from LaSalle Col. for study at Columbia Univ, 67. Polit. & Govt. Pos: V.pres, Southampton Dem. Club, Pa, 63-65; co-chmn, Cmt. of Concerned Polit. of Southeast Pa, 67-68; del, Dem. Nat. Conv, 68; mem, Pa. State Cmt. for McCarthy, 68; Sponsor of Cmt. of Col. Prof. for the Elec. of Humphrey and Muskie, 68; co-chmn, McCarthy for Pres, Orgn. Eighth Dist, Pa, 68; mem, State Cmt. of Pa. New Dem. Coalition, 68-; chmn, Eighth Dist. New Dem. Coalition, 68- Bus. & Prof. Pos: Research analyst, Nat. Security Agency, Ft. Meade, Md, 53-57; asst. prof. hist, Univ. Notre Dame, 57-61 and LaSalle Col, Phila, Pa, 61- Mil. Serv: Entered as A/S, Navy, 43, released as Qm. 2/C, 46, after serv. in Fleet, S.Pac. Theatre, 44-46; Good Conduct Medal; Pac. Overseas Medal. Publ: 'The School and the World Outside,' Cath. Educ. Rev, 4/64; two articles on Francia Egan and the Storers, In: New Catholic Encyclopedia, 66; two articles on Am. Polit. Parties and Relig. as a Factor in Am. Polit, In: Catholic Home and School Encyclopedia, 67. Mem: Am. Asn. Univ. Prof; Am. Cath. Hist. Asn; Nat. Cmt. for Sane Nuclear Policy (bd. mem, Phila. Chap). Rel: Roman Catholic. Mailing Add: 168 Forrest Ave, Southampton, Pa. 18966.

HENNESSY, FRANCIS XAVIER D
Chmn, Windsor Dem. Town Cmt, Conn.
b. New York, N.Y, 9/11/30; s. Gervais Hennessy and Margaret O'Connor; m. 8/17/57 to Mary Frances Callery; c. Maura and Mark. Educ: Fordham Col, B.S.S.S, 57; Univ. Conn. Sch. Law, LL.B, 61; Student Govt. Vet. Club; French Club. Polit. & Govt. Pos: Chmn, Windsor Dem. Town Cmt, Conn, 66- Bus. & Prof. Pos: Partner, Platt & Hennessy, Attorneys-at-Law. Mil. Serv: Entered as Pvt, Army, 51, released as Cpl, 53, after serv. in 32nd Inf. Regt, Seventh Div, Korea, 52; Purple heart, combat infantrymans badge; Good Conduct Medal; UN Medal; Korean Medal with two battle stars. Mem: Windsor Bar Asn.(secy); Hartford Co, Conn. State and Am. Bar Asns; K. of C; Gr. Hartford Heart Asn; Conn. Heart Asn.(bd. dirs); C. of C; Windsor Youth Hockey League. Rel: Roman Catholic. Mailing Add: 45 Darwyn Dr, Windsor, Conn. 06095.

HENNING, H. J. Conservative
b. Germany, 1896. Polit. & Govt. Pos: Co. Treas, Minn, 51-57; Minn. State Rep, 58-69. Bus. & Prof. Pos: Food bus. Mailing Add: Pelican Rapids, Minn. 56572. (1967)

HENNING, JOHN FRANCIS
b. San Francisco, Calif, 11/22/15; s. William Henry Henning and Lulu Frances McLane H; m. 11/25/39 to Marguerite Morand; c. John Francis, Brian H, Patrick W, Nancy R, Daniel M, Thomas R. and Mary J. Educ: St. Mary's Col. Calif, B.A, 38. Hon. LL.D, St. Anselm's Col, 65; hon. D.C.S, St. Bonaventure Univ, 66. Polit. & Govt. Pos: With U.S. Dept. of Agr, 38-42; research dir, Calif. Fedn. of Labor, 49-59; dir, Calif. State Dept. Indust. Rels, 59-62; Under Secy, U.S. Dept. of Labor, 62-67; U.S. Ambassador to New Zealand, 67-69. Bus. & Prof. Pos: Mem, pub. rels. staff, West. Pipe & Steel Co, 42-47, Cath. Monitor, Weekly, 46-47 and Cath. Bishops of Calif, 47-49. Mem: Past pres, San Francisco Bd. of Permit Appeals, St. Mary's Col. Alumni Asn. and San Francisco Irish Lit. and Hist. Soc; NAACP. Rel: Roman Catholic. Mailing Add: c/o U.S. Dept. of State Foreign Service, Washington, D.C. 20521. (1967)

HENNING, WILLIAM LEWIS D
b. Hicksville, Ohio, 1/4/00; s. George Frederick Henning and Elizabeth Brinck H; m. 1942 to Dr. Harriet Marcella Harry; c. William Lewis, Jr. and George Frederick, III. Educ: Ohio State Univ, B.S. in Agr, 21; Pa. State Univ, M.S, 23; Univ. Wis, Ph.D, 37; Alpha Zeta; Gamma Sigma Delta; Phi Kappa Phi; Phi Sigma; Sigma Xi; Acacia. Polit. & Govt. Pos: Secy. Agr, Commonwealth of Pa, 55-63; del, 23rd Cong. Dist. Dem. Nat. Conv, 68. Bus. & Prof. Pos: Grad. asst, Dept. Animal Husbandry, Ohio State Univ, 21-22; from asst. instr. to assoc. prof, Pa. State Univ, 22-53, prof. and head dept. animal husbandry, 53-55, prof. animal indust. and nutrition, 63-65, prof. emer, 65- Mil. Serv: Entered as A/S, Navy Res, 17, released, 18, after serv. in Naval Unit SATC, Ohio State Univ. Mem: Fel. Am. Asn. for the Adv. of Sci. and Am. Soc. of Animal Sci; Am. Genetic Asn; Am. Soc. Animal Prod; secy-treas, Am. Southdown Breeders Asn, 24-; bd. trustees, Pa. State Univ, 55-63; chmn, Pa. State Farm Show Cmn. and Cmt, State Soil Conserv. Cmn; exec. cmt. and past pres, Nat. Asn. State Depts. of Agr; Mason; Centre Hill, State Col. Country Club; Am. Legion; Shrine; Rotary. Award for Promoting Agr. and for Meritorious Serv. in Field of Agr, Phila. Soc, 56. Rel: Presbyterian. Mailing Add: 718 W. Nittany Ave, State College, Pa. 16801.

HENNINGTON, BURNETTE YARBROUGH D
b. Hickory, Miss, August 17; d. Lewis Hutchins Yarbrough and Bertha Everett Y; div. Educ: Baylor Univ, B.J, 30; Sigma Phi. Polit. & Govt. Pos: Chief clerk, Selective Serv. Syst, Draft Bd, Miss, 40-46; mem, President's Water Pollution Control Adv. Bd, 64-68; Dem. Nat. Committeewoman, Miss, 64-68. Bus. & Prof. Pos: Owner, Burnette Y. Hennington, Realtor, 46-; parliamentarian, Jackson Bd. of Realtors. Mem: Miss. Asn. of Realtor Bd; past Miss. Gov, Women's Coun, Nat. Asn. of Realtor Bd; Multiple Listing Serv. of Jackson; past pres, Jackson Bus. & Prfnl. Women's Club, parliamentarian, 67-68, pres, 69-; Zonta Int; nat. civic participation chmn, Nat. Fedn. Bus. & Prfnl. Women Clubs, 62-63, nat. recording secy, 64-65; parliamentarian, Miss. Fedn. Bus. & Prfnl. Women's Clubs, 66-68; past pres, Jackson League Women Voters; past pres, Miss. Women's Cabinet Pub. Affairs, parliamentarian, 69-; trustee, Bus. & Prfnl. Women's Found, 64-65; C. of C; pres, Miss. Asn. for Ment. Health; past pres, Hinds Co. Asn. for Ment. Health; past dir, Am. Cancer Soc, Soc. for Crippled Children and Adults, United Givers Fund and Cerebral Palsy of Cent. Miss. Organizer, Nation's First Water Pollution Control Conf. for Women, Miss, 61; spec. citation for orgn. ability, U.S. Pub. Health Serv, 63. Rel: Baptist. Legal Res: 4840 Sheridan Dr, Jackson, Miss. 39206. Mailing Add: P.O. Box 9712, Northside Station, Jackson, Miss. 39206.

HENRICHS, ULRIC H. R
Polit. & Govt. Pos: Ind. State Rep, 61-67. Bus. & Prof. Pos: Life Ins. Agent. Mil. Serv: Tech. Adv. to Army Air Force, 43-45. Mem: Past Master, Wheatfield Lodge, F&AM. Rel: Methodist. Mailing Add: Demotte, Ind. 46310. (1967)

HENRIOD, FREDERIC HENRI R
Justice, Utah Supreme Court
b. American Fork, Utah, 1/26/05; s. Frederic Augustus Henriod and Melissa Greenwood H; m. 4/28/33 to Wilma Ellen Savage; c. Richard Henri. Educ: Univ. Utah, A.B; Georgetown Univ, 1 year; Harvard Law Sch, LL.B, 32; Sigma

Nu Phi. Polit. & Govt. Pos: Pres, Young Rep. Club, 38; chmn, Salt Lake Co. Rep. Party, Utah, 41-42; campaign mgr. for Gov. J. Bracken Lee, 48; Justice, Utah Supreme Court, 51- Bus. & Prof. Pos: Utah State Bar Cmnr, 8 years. Mil. Serv: Entered as 2nd Lt, Air Corps, Intel. Officer, 42, released as Capt, 45, after serv. in Air Corps and Judge Adv. Gen. Dept, Africa, Sicily, Italy and Corsica, 43-45. Mem: Am. Legion; VFW; DAV; Elks; Ft. Douglas Club. Rel: Latter-day Saint. Mailing Add: 235 E. Capitol, Salt Lake City, Utah 84103.

HENRY, AARON EDD D
Chmn, Miss. Dem. Party
b. Coahoma Co, Miss, 7/2/22; s. Edd Henry and Mattie Logan H; m. 6/10/50 to Noelle Michael; c. Rebecca. Educ: Xavier Univ, La, B.S, 50; Omega Psi Phi; pres. student body, Xavier Univ. 50. Polit. & Govt. Pos: Del, Dem. Nat. Conv, 68; chmn, Miss. Dem. Party, 68-; mem. cmt. party reform, Nat. Dem. Party, 69. Bus. & Prof. Pos: Secy, Miss. State Pharmaceutical Soc, 54- Mil. Serv: Entered as Pvt, Army, 43, released as S/Sgt, 46, after serv. in Pac. Theater, 45-46; Good Conduct Medal; plus several Co. and Bn. awards. Mem: Nat. Pharmaceutical Asn. (pres, 63); Am. Pharmaceutical Asn; Coahoma Co. C. of C; Am. Legion; Am. Vet. Cmt; VFW. Rosa Parks award, South. Christian Leadership Conf; Outstanding Citizens award, Off. Econ. Opportunity. Rel: Methodist. Legal Res: 636 Page St, Clarksdale, Miss. 38614. Mailing Add: 213 Fourth St, Clarksdale, Miss. 38614.

HENRY, AILEE M. R
Chmn, Jefferson Co. Rep. Cent. Cmt, Kans.
b. Oskaloosa, Kans, 9/26/03; d. Charles E. Decker and Monica Lowman D; m. 9/25/26 to R. Glenn Henry; c. Jane (Mrs. Michner). Educ: Kans. Univ; Gamma Phi Beta. Polit. & Govt. Pos: V.Chmn, Jefferson Co. Rep. Cent. Cmt, Kans, 45-66, chmn, 66-; state v.chmn, Kans. Rep. State Cmt, 55-59; mem, Kans. Rep. State Exec. Cmt, 55-65; v.chmn, Rep. Cong. Dist, 59-65; del, Rep. Nat. Conv, 60, alternate del, 64; dist. dir, Women's Rep. Clubs, 60-62; sponsor, Jefferson Co. TAR Group, 68- Bus. & Prof. Pos: Teacher, Jefferson Co. Schs, 24-25; part-time asst. to husband, R. Glenn Henry, D.D.S, 28-33, 38- Mem: Am. Legion Auxiliary; Eastern Star; Dent. Auxiliary; past pres, Native Daughters of Kans; Kans. Coun. of Women; auditor, Women's Kans. Day Club; C. of C; Study Club; Steering Cmt. for Commun. Proj. Develop; hon. mem, Topeka Girl Scouts. Award from Great Navy of Nebr, 62; Distinguished Jayhawker Award, 64; Outstanding Commun. Leader, 68; Established First Hist. Mus. in Co. Rel: Presbyterian; Elder and Clerk of Session. Mailing Add: Oskaloosa, Kans. 66066.

HENRY, AL D
Wash. State Sen.
b. Ness Co, Kans, 4/12/11; s. Bert A. Henry and Ethel Strobel H; m. 9/28/65 to Anne Boss Karr. Educ: Bus. educ. Polit. & Govt. Pos: Wash. State Rep, 41-57; mayor, White Salmon, Wash, 53-67; Wash. State Sen, 57- Bus. & Prof. Pos: Admin. asst, United Tel. Syst, Hood River, Ore, 54- Mil. Serv: World War II. Mem: Elks; Eagles (past pres). Mailing Add: Rio Vista, White Salmon, Wash. 98672.

HENRY, EDGERTON L. D
La. State Rep.
b. Jonesboro, La, 2/10/36; s. Dallas E. Henry and Ruby Lewis H; m. 4/4/58 to Frances Turner; c. Patrick E. and Lori Martiel. Educ: Baylor Univ, B.A, 58; La. State Univ, Baton Rouge, LL.B, 61; Gamma Eta Gamma; Alpha Tau Omega; Circle K. Polit. & Govt. Pos: La. State Rep, 68- Bus. & Prof. Pos: Partner, Emmons & Henry Law Firm, Jonesboro, La, 61- Mem: Lions; Jaycees. Rel: Baptist. Mailing Add: P.O. Drawer 726, Jonesboro, La. 71251.

HENRY, EDWARDS C. D
b. Algoma, Miss, 11/3/19; married. Polit. & Govt. Pos: Miss. State Sen, 61-69. Bus. & Prof. Pos: V.pres, First Fed. Savings & Loan Asn, Canton. Mil. Serv: Pilot, Air Force. Mem: Lions (past pres); Canton C. of C. (bd. dirs. and past pres); VFW; Am. Legion; Citizen's Coun. Rel: Baptist; Deacon. Mailing Add: 442 Lyon St, Canton, Miss. 39046. (1967)

HENRY, EMIL WILLIAM D
b. Memphis, Tenn, 3/4/29; s. John Philips Henry and Elizabeth Tschudy H; m. 12/21/55 to Sherrye Eileen Patton; c. Elizabeth Tschudy, Sherrye Patton and Emil William. Educ: Yale Univ, B.A, 51; Vanderbilt Univ, LL.B, 57; Order of the Coif; assoc. ed, Vanderbilt Law Review; Phi Delta Phi; Chi Psi. Polit. Pos: Mem, Tenn. Adv. Cmn, U.S. Cmn. on Civil Rights, 62. Govt. Pos: Chmn, Fed. Commun. Cmn, 63-66 and cmnr, 62-63. Bus. & Prof. Pos: Mem, Arnold and Porter, attorneys, Wash, D.C; partner, Chandler, Maneir & Chandler, Memphis, 58-62. Mil. Serv: Entered as Ens, Navy, 51, released as Lt.(jg), 54, after serv. in Korea, 52-53. Mem: Am. Bar Asn; v.pres, Family Serv. Asn, Memphis, 60-62; bd. dirs, Memphis Chap, Am. Red Cross; Rel: Episcopal. Legal Res: 3464 Macomb St, N.W, Washington, D.C. 20016. Mailing Add: 1229 19th St, N.W, Washington, D.C. 20036. (1967)

HENRY, FOREST THOMAS D
Pres. and Exec. Dir, Greater Fifth Ward Dem. Citizens League, Tex.
b. Houston, Tex, 8/1/12; s. John Johnson Henry and Arilla Smith H; m. 12/12/31 to Belzora Butler; c. Bettye Joyce, Jennie Ruth, Wiley Eldridge, Alvin Leon, Erma Lucille, Forest T, Jr. and Rosa Mary (Mrs. Monroe Doyle, Jr). Educ: Prairie View A&M Col, 30; hon. LL.B, Tex. Col, 56. Polit. & Govt. Pos: Secy. Harris Co. Del, State Dem. Conv, Tex, 48, v.chmn, 64; pres. and exec. dir, Greater Fifth Ward Dem. Citizens League, 48-; alternate del, Dem. Nat. Conv, 64, del, 68. Bus. & Prof. Pos: Staff rep, USW, 44-49; mem, Human Resources & Develop. Prog. for Houston, Tex, 65. Mem: F&AM; NAACP; YMCA; Wheatley Alumni Asn; Houston Citizens C. of C. Rel: Baptist. Legal Res: 5609 Perkins St, Houston, Tex. 77020. Mailing Add: 4218 Lyons Ave, Houston, Tex. 77020. (1967)

HENRY, HAROLD EUGENE D
Mem, Calif. Dem. State Cent. Cmt.
b. Springfield, Mass, 11/9/28; s. Paul Lawrence Henry and Louise Chisholm H; m. 4/14/56 to Janet Elizabeth Peterson. Educ: Yale Univ, B.E, 50, M.Eng, 57, D.Eng, 59; Sigma Xi. Polit. & Govt. Pos: Dem. cand, Calif. State Assembly, 35th Dist, 68; mem, Scientists and Engrs. for Humphrey-Muskie, 68; mem, Calif. Dem. State Cent. Cmt, 68- Bus. & Prof. Pos: Mem, tech. staff, Space Tech. Labs, Redondo Beach, Calif, 60-62; eng. mgr, Autonetics, Anaheim, Calif, 62- Publ: 'Analysis of Non-linear Feedback Systems with Random Inputs,' Inst. Radio Engrs, 6/62. Mem: Inst. Elec. and Electronic Engs; Nat. Mgt. Asn; Sci. Res. Soc. Am. Rel: Roman Catholic. Mailing Add: 5331 Kentwater Place, Yorba Linda, Calif. 92686.

HENRY, HERMANN RUSSELL D
Chmn, Johnson Co. Dem. Party, Ind.
b. Whiteland, Ind, 2/12/17; s. William Floyd Henry and Christena Wilde H; m. 9/28/40 to Rachel Saunders; c. Pamela (Mrs. Norman Stucker), Diane (Mrs. Joseph Sooy) and David S. Educ: Franklin Col, 36-38; Purdue Univ, 40; Kappa Delta Rho. Polit. & Govt. Pos: Councilman, Johnson Co, Ind, 54-58; Ind. State Rep, 58-60; chmn, Johnson Co. Dem. Party, 64-; co. clerk, Johnson Co, 65-68; treas, Sixth Cong. Dist. Dem. Party, 66-67; del, Dem. Nat. Conv, 68; chief enforcement div, Pub. Serv. Cmn. of Ind, 68-69. Bus. & Prof. Pos: Farm owner and mgr, Johnson Co, 40-; store owner and mgr, Franklin, 52- Mem: Ind. Implement Dealers Asn; Ind. Purebreed Livestock Asn; Mason; Elks; Ind. Dem. Club; Farm Bur. Distinguished Serv. Award, Jr. C. of C; Country Life Award for Outstanding Commun. Serv, Kiwanis. Rel: United Church of Christ. Mailing Add: R.R. 2, Box 57, Franklin, Ind. 46131.

HENRY, JOE W, JR. D
b. Lynnville, Tenn, 9/20/16; s. Joseph W. Henry and Louise Ward H; m. 6/28/43 to Marjorie Royster Clark; c. Joe W, III and Robert C. Educ: Mid. Tenn. State Univ; Cumberland Univ. Law Sch. Polit. & Govt. Pos: City attorney, Pulaski, Tenn, 47-53; Tenn. State Rep, 49; Adj. Gen, Tenn, 53-59; alternate del, Dem. Nat. Conv, 56, del, 64. Bus. & Prof. Pos: Sr. partner, Moore, Henry, Henry, Lewis & Cain, Attorneys, currently. Mil. Serv: Entered as Pvt, Army, 41, released as Maj, 46, after serv. in Mediterranean Theater; Bronze Star; Combat Infantryman Badge. Mem: Pulaski, Tenn. and Am. Bar Asns; Am. and Tenn. Trial Lawyers Asns; Am. Legion; VFW; Elks. Rel: Methodist. Legal Res: 313 Rose St, Pulaski, Tenn. 38478. Mailing Add: 121 S. First St, Pulaski, Tenn. 38478.

HENRY, JOHN J. D
Chmn, Stearns Co. Dem-Farmer-Labor Cmt, Minn.
b. St. Cloud, Minn, 9/16/17; s. John A. Henry and Rose Kraker H; m. 8/26/46 to Muriel C. Lund; c. Marguerite Kurr, John, Jr, James, Thomas, Charles, Patricia and William. Educ: St. John's Univ, B.A. in Econ. Polit. & Govt. Pos: Treas, Stearns Co. Young Dem, Minn, 36-37; treas, Stearns Co. Dem-Farmer-Labor Cmt, 58-62, chmn, 62- Bus. & Prof. Pos: Asst. cashier, Northwest. Bank and Trust Co, St. Cloud, Minn, 46-55, cashier, 55- and v.pres, 64- Mil. Serv: Entered as Pvt, Marine Corps, 42, released as S/Sgt, 46; New Brit. Campaign Ribbon with Combat Star. Mem: St. Cloud C. of C; Kiwanis; Elks; Eagles; VFW; treas, Elks; treas, Stearns Co. Nat. Found; St. Cloud Country Club. Rel: Catholic. Mailing Add: 117-17th Ave. S, St. Cloud, Minn. 56301. (1967)

HENRY, WILLIAM KEITH D
Ky. State Rep.
b. Georgetown, Ky, 9/15/17; s. Dudley Davis Henry and Alice Sublett H; m. 7/31/63 to Sarah Tabb. Educ: Georgetown Col, A.B, 41; Pi Kappa Alpha. Polit. & Govt. Pos: Ky. State Rep, 62nd Dist, currently; chmn, Scott Co. Young Dem. Club, Ky, 52; alternate del, Dem. Nat. Conf, 52 & 60; dist. chmn, Sixth Cong. Dist. Young Dem, Ky, 54; del, Young Dem. Nat. Conv, 54, 56 & 58; asst. and Sgt. at Arms, Ky. State Senate, 54 & 64; chmn, Scott Co. Dem. Party, 68- Bus. & Prof. Pos: Real estate bus. and farmer, currently. Mil. Serv: Serv. in Army during World War II, 3 years. Mem: Rotary Int. (past. pres, Georgetown Club and past dist. gov); Am. Legion; 40 et 8; Farm Bur; VFW; Odd Fellows. Rel: Presbyterian; Deacon and Elder. Mailing Add: 201 Montgomery Ave, Georgetown, Ky. 40324.

HENSHAW, EDMUND LEE, JR. D
Research Dir, Dem. Nat. Cong. Cmt.
b. Bowling Green, Va, 12/11/25; s. Edmund Lee Henshaw and Edna Earle Carter H; m. 8/5/50 to Barbara Louise Hanby; c. Carol Lynne, Richard Edmund and Scott Frederick. Educ: Univ. Md, B.S, 54; George Wash. Univ. Law Sch, 55-56; Sigma Chi. Polit. & Govt. Pos: Research dir, Dem. Nat. Cong. Cmt, 55- Mil. Serv: Army Air Force, 43-46. Publ: Co-ed, Who's Who in American Politics, Bowker Assocs, 67 & 69. Rel: Episcopal. Mailing Add: 1111 Westbriar Court, Vienna, Va. 22180.

HENSLER, CHARLES MORRIS R
Chmn, Jefferson Co. Rep. Party, Ind.
b. Jefferson Co, Ind, 12/22/24; s. Joseph Morris Hensler and Clara Belle Davis H; m. 5/8/46 to Pauline Sams; c. Robert Joseph and Deborah Anne. Educ: Hanover High Sch, grad, 42. Polit. & Govt. Pos: Del, Ind. State Rep. Conv, 60, 62, 64, 66 & 68; chmn, Jefferson Co. Rep. Party, Ind, 65-; del, Rep. Nat. Conv, 68. Bus. & Prof. Pos: Pres, Kreeger-Hensler, Inc, Hanover, Ind, 60- Mil. Serv: Entered as Pvt, Army Air Force, 43, released as Pfc, 46, after serv. in 806th Aviation Eng. Bn, Pac. Theatre, 44-46; Asiatic-Pac. Theatre Ribbon with 2 Bronze Stars; Good Conduct Medal; Victory Medal. Mem: Jefferson Co. Farm Bur; Mason; Scottish Rite; Hanover Vol. Fire Dept; Shrine; Am. Legion; VFW; Hon. Order Ky. Col; Moose; Fraternal Order of Police; Conserv. Club. Rel: Methodist. Mailing Add: Box 85, Hanover, Ind. 47243.

HENSLEY, WILLIAM L. D
Alaska State Rep.
b. Kotzebue, Alaska, 6/17/41; s. John Hensley, Sr. and Priscilla H; single. Educ: Wash. Univ, B.A, 66; Univ. Alaska, 60-62, grad. work, 66; Alpha Kappa Psi. Polit. & Govt. Pos: Mem, Bd. for State Land Use, representing Alaskan native interests, Bur. of Land Mgt, 67-; Alaska State Rep, Dist. 17, currently; del, Dem. Nat. Conv, 68. Mem: V.chmn, Alaska Fedn. of Native Asns; exec. dir, Northwest Alaska Native Asn. John F. Kennedy Mem. Award from the Experiment in Int. Living for Trip to Poland and Russia. Mailing Add: Kotzebue, Alaska 99752. (1967)

HENSON, BURT MARTIN D
b. Oakland, Calif, 5/28/26; s. Dewey Henson and Edith Anderson H; m. 7/6/56 to Nancy Gleichmann; c. Lynn, Julie, Charlene, Alisa and Deborah.

Educ: Modesto Jr. Col, Stanford Univ, Stanford Law Sch; Alpha Gamma Sigma; Theta Delta Chi; Phi Delta Phi. Polit. & Govt. Pos: Calif. State Assemblyman, 37th Assembly Dist, 63-67; mem, Ventura Co. Dem. Cent. Cmt, 63-66 and State Dem. Cent. Cmt, 63-66; del, Dem. Nat. Conv, 64; pres, Ventura Dem. Club, 61-62; dep. dist. attorney, Ventura Co, 54-58. Bus. & Prof. Pos: Attorney, Johnston, Lucking and Henson, 60-66; attorney, Ruffner and Henson, 58-60. Mil. Serv: Entered as A/S, Navy, 44, released as Radioman 2/C, 46; North Am, Asiatic-Pac. and Philippine Liberation Medals. Mem: Mason; Am. Legion; Sunrise Optimist Club; Calif. and Ventura Co. Bar Asns. Rel: Presbyterian. Mailing Add: 534 Via Cielito, Ventura, Calif. 93003. (1967)

HENSON, JAMES HARVEY R
b. Wynne, Ark, 8/19/31; s. Herman Fredrick Henson and Lucy Cross H; m. 7/14/49 to Clara Boone; c. Linda Carol, Sharon (Mrs. Caldwell) and Tracie Ann. Educ: Wynne High Sch, Ark, grad, 48. Polit. & Govt. Pos: Chmn, Cross Co. Rep. Party, Cook, 66; mem, Elec. Cmn, Cross Co, 66. Bus. & Prof. Pos: V.pres, H.F. Henson & Son, Inc, 59; Henson Lumber Co, 59; Henson Ready Mix, Inc, 59; Spencer Motor Co, 66. Mil. Serv: Pvt, Army Nat. Guard, 48; Maj, Ark. Nat. Guard Res, 64. Mem: Gov. bd, Small Bus. Admin; gov. bd, Off. Econ. Opportunity, Cross Co; Rotary; pres, Crowley Ridge Country Club. Rel: Baptist. Legal Res: 11 Sunset Dr, Wynne, Ark. 72396. Mailing Add: Box 370, Wynne, Ark. 72396.

HENSON, JOHN R. D
Asst. Dir, Dept. Financial Institutions, Ill.
b. Villa Grove, Ill, 1/23/01; s. Shelton C. Henson and Alice M. Hanson H; m. 12/18/25 to Avis B. Murphy (deceased); c. Mary H. (Mrs. Pieske) and Jean H. (Mrs. Ryan); m. 1/25/67 to Imogene M. Baer. Educ: Mo. Mil. Acad, 20; Univ. Mo, B.S, 24. Polit. & Govt. Pos: Mayor, Villa Grove, Ill, 38-64; Dem. precinct committeeman, Camargo Twp, 48-66; chmn, Douglas Co. Dem. Orgn, 50-66; dir, State Co. Chairmens Dem. Orgn, 61-66, secy, 63-66; asst. dir, Dept. Financial Inst, Ill, 61- Bus. & Prof. Pos: Pres. and dir, Villa Grove 1st Nat. Bank, 28-61. Mem: Mason; Elks; Moose; Rotary; C. of C; Jr. C. of C. Rel: Methodist. Legal Res: Room 121, Capitol Bldg, Springfield, Ill. 62706. Mailing Add: 202 Henson Rd, Villa Grove, Ill. 61956.

HENSRUD, INGMEN O. R
N.Dak. State Rep.
b. Mekinock, N.Dak, 4/9/07; s. John I. Hensrud and Maline Dock H; m. 11/27/30 to Adelaide Myrtle Brusegaard; c. Neil B, John I. and David W. Educ: High Sch. and Bus. Col. Polit. & Govt. Pos: Sgt, N.Dak. State Hwy. Patrol, 41-60; sheriff, Grand Forks Co, 61-66; N.Dak. State Rep, 67- Mem: Kiwanis; Elks; Mason; Shrine; N.Dak. Sheriffs and Peace Officers. Rel: Lutheran. Mailing Add: 711 13th Ave. S, Grand Forks, N.Dak. 58201.

HENSS, DONALD ALLEN R
Ill. State Rep.
b. Moline, Ill, 12/24/30; s. Paul Lawrence Henss and Geneva Runkel H; m. 6/8/52 to Joline Carolyn Schieberl; c. Wendy Ann, Mark Douglas and Kimberly Sue. Educ: Univ. Ill. Col. Commerce, B.S, 53; Univ. Ill. Col. Law, LL.B, 55; Phi Delta Phi; Beta Theta Pi. Polit. & Govt. Pos: Asst. States Attorney, Rock Island Co, Ill, 56; Ill. State Rep, 67- Bus. & Prof. Pos: Partner, Moran, Klockau, McCarthy, Schubert & Henss, 57-63, Bozeman, Neighbour, Patton & Henss, 63- Mem: Rock Island Co. Bar Asn; chmn, Ins. Law Sect, Ill. State Bar Asn, 67-; mem, Nat. Panel of Arbitrators, Am. Arbit. Asn, 64-; bd. dirs, Moline YMCA; secy, Citizens Cmt. on Athletics for Moline Sch. Dist; pres, Moline Football Alums; Elks; Optimist. Rel: Presbyterian. Mailing Add: 935 26th Ave, Moline, Ill. 61265.

HEPBRON, PERCY M. D
b. Still Pond, Md, 11/30/98; married. Educ: Kent Co. pub. schs. Polit. & Govt. Pos: Md. State Sen, 61-67; chmn. Joint Comm. on Investment since 63; Co. Cmnr, Kent Co, 50-58, chmn, 58-60; Kent Co. Welfare Bd, 50-58; chmn. Kent Co. Bd. of Elec. Supvrs, 46-50; Kent. Co. Sch. Bldg. Cmn, 46-50. Bus. & Prof. Pos: Farmer; dir, Peoples Bank of Chestertown. Mem: Rock Hall Vol. Fire Dept; Farm Bur; Masons; Lions. Mailing Add: Rock Hall, Md. 21161. (1967)

HEPFORD, H. JOSEPH R
Pa. State Rep.
b. Harrisburg, Pa, 7/1/24; s. Ross Earl Hepford and Hilda Elizabeth Hassler H; m. 8/16/52 to Grace E. Miller; c. Diane Elizabeth and Marcia Elaine. Educ: Dickinson Col, 42-46, Sch. of Law, LL.B, 48; Phi Delta Theta. Polit. & Govt. Pos: Dir, Dauphin Co. Young Rep, Pa, 49-51; Pa. State Rep, 63- Bus. & Prof. Pos: Admitted to practice before Pa. Supreme Court, 49, U.S. Supreme Court, 60. Mil. Serv: Entered as Pvt, Air Corps, 42, released as 2nd Lt, 45. Mem: Am, Pa. and Dauphin Co. Bar Asns; Am. Trial Lawyers Asn; past dist. gov, Lions Int; past chmn. bd, Cent. Pa. Multiple Sclerosis Soc; past comdr, Olmsted Squadron, Air Force Asn; Supreme Guide, U.S. and Can, Royal Arcanum; Mason; Am. Legion. Rel: Protestant. Mailing Add: 3408 Canby St, Harrisburg, Pa. 17109.

HERBENER, LLOYD WAYNE R
b. Mitchell, S.Dak, 2/26/29; s. Adam Hennes Herbener and Alyce Dagle H; m. 8/26/50 to Julia Ann Bardens; c. Catherine, Stephen Richard, Wendy Ann, David Lloyd and Jeffry Merrill. Educ: Pomona Col, B.A, 51; Claremont Grad Sch, M.A. in Hist, 52. Polit. & Govt. Pos: 19th Cong. Dist. gov, Ill. Young Rep, 57-61, state pres, 61-63; committeeman and 46th dist. rep, Rep. Party, Ill, 58-60; chmn, Traffic Cmt. and alderman, Canton, Ill, 59-63, chmn, Finance Cmt, 61-63 and mayor-pro-tem, 62-63; former campaign mgr. cand, Nat. Young Rep. Conv; awards chmn. and mem. exec. cmt, Nat. Young Rep, 61-63, co-chmn. of vet. cmt, 63-65; chmn, Fulton Co. Rep. Party, 63-69; coordinator for five cong. dists, Rep. State Ticket Motor Caravan, 66. Bus. & Prof. Pos: Prin, Little York Elem. Sch, 52-55 and Cent. Sch, Canton, Ill, 54-55; chief probation officer, Ninth Judicial Circuit, Ill, 55-; asst. prof. polit. sci. and dean of students, John F. Kennedy Col, 67- Mil. Serv: 2nd Lt, Army, 51-54, serv. at Ft. Lewis, Wash. Mem: Nat. Coun. on Crime and Delinquency; Ill. State Probation and Parole Asn; Ill. State Hist. Soc; Elks; John Erickson Rep. League; Ill. Police Asn. Rel: Presbyterian; Elder. Mailing Add: 1258 N. Linden, Wahoo, Nebr. 68066.

HERBERT, DOROTHY FESS R
Committeewoman, Ohio Rep. State Cent. and Exec. Cmt.
b. Springfield, Ohio, 6/12/17; d. Lehr Fess and Dorothy Davis F; m. 9/13/41 to Josiah T. Herbert (deceased); c. Jane Hall, Hannah Davis and Nancy Belle. Educ: Conn. Col. for Women, 34-35; Denison Univ, 35-36; Toledo Univ, B.A, 38; Kappa Alpha Theta. Polit. & Govt. Pos: Pres, Maumee Women's Rep. Club, 52-53; chairwoman, Lucas Co. Rep. Party, Ohio, 66-; v.chmn, Lucas Co. Rep. Exec. Cmt, 66-; alternate del, Rep. Nat. Conv, 68; mem, Bd. of Elec, Lucas Co, Ohio, 68-; committeewoman, Ohio Rep. State Cent. & Exec. Cmt, 68- Mailing Add: 228 E. Broadway, Maumee, Ohio 43537.

HERBERT, EDWARD N. R
b. Fairmont, W.Va; married; c. two. Polit. & Govt. Pos: N.H. State Rep, 63-67; Chmn, Bd. of Selectmen; overseer of poor; Selectman; Exec. Bd, Co. Del; pres, N.H. Munic. Asn, 65-66. Bus. & Prof. Pos: Surveyor. Mil. Serv: S/Sgt, World War II, Italy, Army Air Force; S/Sgt, Korean Conflict, 51 (recalled) Okinawa, Air Force. Mem: Church Bldg. Cmt; Am. Legion; Presco Club; Planning Bd; exec. bd, Am. Munic. Asn; Bowling League. Rel: Presbyterian; Elder. Mailing Add: Londonderry Rd, Windham, N.H. 03087.

HERBERT, JOHN DAVID R
State Treas, Ohio
b. Columbus, Ohio, 9/8/30; s. Thomas J. Herbert and Jeannette Judson H; m. 12/16/55 to Joan Hoiles; c. John David, Jr, Kathleen Hoiles, Martha Elizabeth, Megan Jean and Susan Joan. Educ: Culver Mil. Acad, grad, 48; Princeton Univ, A.B, 52; Univ. Mich. Law Sch, LL.B, 57; Phi Delta Phi; Tower Club. Polit. & Govt. Pos: Asst. attorney gen, Ohio, 57-59, state treas, 63-; del-at-lg, Rep. Nat. Conv, 64, alternate del, 68. Bus. & Prof. Pos: Attorney, Schwenker, Teaford, Brothers & Barnard, Attorneys, Columbus, 59-60, George, Greek, King & McMahon, 60-63; pres, Mausoleum Builders Corp, Youngstown, 61- Mil. Serv: Entered as 2nd Lt, Army, 52, released as 1st Lt, 54, after serv. in 7th Div, Far East. Theater, 53-54; Capt, Nat. Guard, 59-67; Bronze Star; Korean Serv, UN and Nat. Defense Ribbons. Mem: Am, Ohio and Columbus Bar Asns; v.pres, Nat. Asn. State Auditors, Comptrollers and Treas; Humboldt Masonic Lodge 476; Columbus Consistory, Mason (32°); Am. Legion; Amvets; Elks; Moose; Optimists. Award of Merit, Ohio Legal Center Inst, 63; Serv. Award, Ohio Ment. Health Asn; One of Top Ten Outstanding Young Men, Columbus Jr. C. of C. Rel: Methodist. Legal Res: 2528 Lytham Rd, Columbus, Ohio 43220. Mailing Add: State House, Columbus, Ohio 43216.

HERBERT, RICHARD JOHN D
Cmnr, Ariz. Corp. Cmn.
b. Chicago, Ill, 12/20/37; s. John Herbert and Helen Drimba H; m. 12/31/55 to Carol Diane Workman; c. John David, Robert Michael, Cheryl Anne and Gary Allen. Educ: Univ. Ariz. Law Sch, LL.B, 62; Phi Delta Phi. Polit. & Govt. Pos: Ariz. State Rep, 63 & 64; cmnr, Ariz. Corp. Cmn, 65- Bus. & Prof. Pos: Pres, Herbert Develop. Co, 62- Rel: Catholic. Legal Res: 1928 W. Whitton Ave, Phoenix, Ariz. 85015. Mailing Add: State Capitol Annex, Phoenix, Ariz. 85007.

HERBST, ANN C. D
V.Chmn, St. Louis Co. Dem. Cmt, Mo.
b. St. Louis, Mo, 12/14/18; d. Leo Holaus and Anna Blassie H; m. 4/27/46 to Joseph H. Herbst, Jr; c. Mary Alline and Jo Ann. Educ: Madison High Sch, 1 year. Polit. & Govt. Pos: Committeewoman, Dem. Club of Cravois Twp, Mo, 62-; del, Dem. Nat. Conv, 68; v.chmn, St. Louis Co. Dem. Cmt, Mo, 68- Bus. & Prof. Pos: Forelady, Canvas Prod, 35-42; govt. inspector, Army, 42-46. Rel: Catholic. Mailing Add: 7638 Genesta, Affton, Mo. 63123.

HERBST, ED D
b. Davidson Co, S. Dak, 4/4/01; m. to Merle Speelman; c. Virginia Fern, Margaret Ruth, Carroll Mildred, Helen Marie, Romana Mae. Polit. & Govt. Pos: S. Dak. State Sen, 64-66; S. Dak. State Rep, 58-62; Sch. Bd.(14 years); Twp. Assessor (3 yrs.). Bus. & Prof. Pos: Farmer. Rel: Lutheran, Lutheran Brotherhood. Mailing Add: Mt. Vernon, S. Dak. 57363. (1967)

HERGENROEDER, HENRY ROBERT, JR. D
Md. State Del.
b. Baltimore, Md, 10/26/43; s. Henry R. Hergenroeder, Sr. and Ann A. Reymann H; single. Educ: Univ. Baltimore, B.S, 67. Polit. & Govt. Pos: Md. State Del, currently. Bus. & Prof. Pos: Treas, Hergenroeder's Bakery Inc, 65- Mem: Red Cross. McCormick Unsung Hero, Lacrosse and Earnest B. Marx Memorial Award, swimming. Rel: Roman Catholic. Mailing Add: 5336 Perring Pkwy, Baltimore, Md. 21214.

HERING, GEORGE C, III R
Speaker, Del. House of Rep.
b. 1930. Educ: Dickinson Col, 53; Dickinson Law Sch, 59. Polit. & Govt. Pos: Del. State Rep, 67-, Speaker, Del. House of Rep, 67-; alternate del, Rep. Nat. Conv, 64 & 68. Bus. & Prof. Pos: Attorney, Morris, James, Hitchens & Williams, 59-; dir. and secy, Old Brandywine Village, Inc. Mil. Serv: Army. Mem: Pres, Del. Chap, UN Asn, 63; dir, YMCA Camp Tockwogh; Alumni Coun, Dickinson Col. Wilmington Jaycee Young Man of the Year, 65. Rel: Episcopal. Mailing Add: 1905 Field Rd, Wilmington, Del. 19806.

HERITAGE, JOHN MAULL D
b. Washington, D.C, 9/16/38; s. David Maull Heritage and Christine West H; m. 11/2/63 to Roselyn Anderson; c. John Down and Steven. Educ: Univ. Wash; Wash. State Univ; Univ. Mo, B.S; Cong. fel, Am. Polit. Sci. Asn, 63-64. Polit. & Govt. Pos: Admin. asst. to U.S. Rep. James Mackay, 65-66; campaign asst. to Vice President H. H. Humphrey, 68; legis. dir. to U.S. Sen. Gaylord Nelson, Wis, 69- Bus. & Prof. Pos: Polit. reporter, Atlantic Constitution, 62-63; environ. qual. reporter, Minneapolis Tribune, 67. Mil. Serv: Sgt, Marine Corps Res, 67. Mem: Delta Upsilon. Pub. Affairs Reporting Award; Hon. Mention, Stokes Award. Mailing Add: 4740 Lafitte Court, Alexandria, Va. 22312.

HERLONG, ALBERT SYDNEY, JR. D
Mem: Securities and Exchange Cmn.
b. Manistee, Ala, 2/14/09; s. Albert Sydney Herlong and Cora Knight H; m. 12/26/30 to Mary Alice Youmans; c. Mary Alice (Mrs. Pattillo), Margaret

(Mrs. Mayfied), Dorothy (Mrs. Hay and Sydney (Mrs. Johnson). Educ: Univ. Fla, LL.B, 30; Fla. Blue Key; Omicron Delta Kappa; Phi Delta Phi; Pi Kappa Phi. Polit. & Govt. Pos: Acting postmaster, Leesburg, Fla, 35-36, city attorney, 47-48; Judge, Lake Co, Fla, 37-48; U.S. Rep, Fla, 49-69; mem, Securities and Exchange Cmn, 69- Bus. & Prof. Pos: Consult, Asn. Southeast. R.R, currently. Mil. Serv: Capt, Army, 41. Mem: Mason (33°); Elks; Kiwanis; Moose; Odd Fellows; former pres, Fla. State Baseball League. Rel: Methoodist. Legal Res: 1009 Shore Acres Dr, Leesburg, Fla. 32748. Mailing Add: 4201 Massachusetts Ave. N.W, Washington, D.C. 20016.

HERLONG, WILLIAM FREDERICK, JR. R
b. Leesburg, Fla, 8/16/33; s. William Frederick Herlong, Sr. and Louise Bourlay H; m. 6/18/55 to Margaret Ann La Borde; c. Ann Louise, Mary Frances and William Frederick, III. Educ: Univ. Fla, B.S.B.A, 55; Fla. Blue Key; Alpha Tau Omega. Polit. & Govt. Pos: Cand, U.S. Rep, Fla, 68. Bus. & Prof. Pos: Dir. and gen. mgr, A.S. Herlong Packing Co, Leesburg, Fla, 57- Mil. Serv: Entered as Sgt. E-5, Army, 55, released as Specialist 2, E-5, 57, after serv. in Army Training Center, Inf, Ft. Jackson, S.C; Good Conduct Medal. Mem: Citrus Indust. Coun; Fla. Citrus Mutual; Fla. Fruit & Vegetable Asn; Elks; C. of C.(past pres); Lake Co. Farm Bur. Rel: Episcopal. Legal Res: Shore Acres Dr, Leesburg, Fla. 32748. Mailing Add: P.O. Box 657, Leesburg, Fla. 32748.

HERMAN, DONALD LOUIS D
b. Brooklyn, N.Y, 10/13/28; s. John Herman and Rose Pokorny H; m. 1/10/60 to Bluma Lupa; c. Deborah, Raymond and Jeffrey. Educ: Univ. Mich, B.A, 50; Ph.D, 64; Wayne State Univ, M.A, 59. Polit. & Govt. Pos: Chmn, Kent Co. Dem. Party, Mich, 66-68; del, Dem. Nat. Conv, 68. Bus. & Prof. Pos: Assoc. prof, polit. sci, Grand Valley State Col, 64- Mil. Serv: Entered as Pvt, Army, 53, released as Sgt, 56, after serving in Adj. Gen. Corps, Far E. Theatre, Japan, 54-56. Publ: 'Left Wing and the Communists in Mexico,' J. Mich. Acad. Arts and Sci, 69; 'Communism in Latin America,' forthcoming. Rel: Jewish. Mailing Add: 1510 Laurel Ave, S.E, Grand Rapids, Mich. 49506.

HERMANIES, JOHN HANS R
Secy, Hamilton Co. Rep. Cent. & Exec. Cmts, Ohio.
b. Cincinnati, Ohio, 8/19/22; s. John Hermanies and Lucia Eckstein H; m. 1/3/53 to Dorothy Steinbrecher. Educ: Univ. Cincinnati, 40-43; Pa. State Univ, B.A, 44; Univ. Cincinnati Col. of Law, J.D, 48; Phi Alpha Delta; Theta Chi. Polit. & Govt. Pos: Pres, Hamilton Co. Young Rep. Club, Ohio, 50-52; Asst. Attorney Gen, Ohio, 51-57; chmn, Ohio League of Young Rep, 52; admin. asst. to Gov. of Ohio, 57-58; pres, Hamilton Co, Rep. Club, 63-65; mem, Ohio State Bd. of Bar Exam, 63-68; secy, Hamilton Co. Rep. Cent. & Exec. Cmts, 65- Bus. & Prof. Pos: Law firm partner, Hoover, Beall & Eichel, 59- Mil. Serv: Entered as Pvt, Marines, 43, released as Pvt. 1/C, 45. Mem: Am. Judicature Soc; Cincinnati, Ohio State and Am. Bar Asns; Ohio State Bar Found; Am. Trial Lawyers Asn; Cincinnati Lawyers Club. Rel: Protestant. Legal Res: 2110 Columbia Pkwy, Cincinnati, Ohio 45202. Mailing Add: 519 Main St, Cincinnati, Ohio 45202.

HERMANN, ALBERT BARTHOLOMEW R
Spec. Asst. to Chmn, Rep. Nat. Cmt.
b. Milltown, N.J, 3/28/07; s. Charles Joseph Hermann and Ida Jeanette Bosse H; m. 7/4/37 to Sylvia B. Bernstein; c. Ellen Barbara and Jo Ann. Educ: Colgate Univ, B.S, 29; N.Y. Univ. Sch. of Ins, 32; Skull & Scroll; Delta Upsilon. Polit. & Govt. Pos: Rep. munic. chmn, Milltown, N.J, 34-36; state pres, N.J. Young Rep. Fedn, 34-37; exec. secy. to Gov. Harold G. Hoffman and Clerk of N.J. Court of Pardons, 35-38; admin. asst. to U.S. Sen. W. Warren Barbour, N.J, 38-44, U.S. Sen. H. Alexander Smith, N.J, 44-49 & 52-55; exec. dir, Polit. Orgn, Rep. Nat. Cmt, 49-52 & 57-61, campaign dir, 55-57, dir, 61-64, spec. asst. to chmn, Rep. Nat. Cmt, 64- Bus. & Prof. Pos: Prfnl. baseball in major and minor league for 9 years; pres, Berkshire Life Ins. Co, 29-39 and Herman Baking Co, Milltown, N.H, 31-35. Mem: JOUAM; Order of Redmen Lodge; Grange; Kenwood Golf and Country Club. Colgate Univ, All Am. in Baseball and Basketball, won 11 letters in 3 sports; Lawrence Scholarship Prize for best student-athlete. Rel: Protestant. Legal Res: 6900 Barrett Lane, Bethesda, Md. 20014. Mailing Add: Republican National Committee, 1625 Eye St. N.W, Washington, D.C. 20006.

HERMANN, ROBERT LAMBERT R
Chmn, North Andover Town Rep. Cmt, Mass.
b. Melrose, Mass, 10/21/25; s. Frederick Hunt Hermann and Ida Lambert H; m. 9/17/46 to Kathleen McMullen; c. Robert L, Jr. and Karen Sue. Educ: Harvard Univ, ASTP, 43; Suffolk Univ, 46-49 and Law Sch, LL.B, 53. Polit. & Govt. Pos: Pres. and organizer, Gr. Lawrence Young Rep, Mass, 60-62; del, Rep. State Conv, 62, 64 & 66; dir, Essex Club; co. chmn. for several statewide cand. and officeholders; asst. attorney gen, 63-; chmn, North Andover Town Rep. Cmt, currently. Bus. & Prof. Pos: Claim rep, Aetna Casualty and Surety Ins. Co, 51-63; chmn. and organizer, Gr. Lawrence Hwy. Safety Cmn, Mass, 60-; attorney-at-law, Lawrence, 63- Mil. Serv: Entered as Pvt, Combat Intel. Sch, Army Air Force, 43, released as Sgt, 46, after serv. in India-China Theater; Asiatic-Pac. Ribbon with 3 Stars; Presidential Unit Citation; China and Am. Theater Ribbons; Victory and Good Conduct Ribbons. Mem: VFW; Hermann's Hall; Lawrence and Mass. Bar Asns; Lions; Grange; dir, Jaycees, 59-61; PTA; Boy Scouts. Chmn. of Year Award, Jaycees, 60-61. Rel: Congregational. Mailing Add: 124 Hillside Rd, North Andover, Mass. 01810.

HERMANN, SYLVIA R
V.Chmn, Md. Rep. State Cent. Cmt.
b. Newark, N.J; m. 7/4/37 to Ab Hermann; c. Ellen (Mrs. William Warfield) and Jo Ann Educ: Barringer High Sch, Newark, N.J. Polit. & Govt. Pos: Pres, Rock Creek Women's Rep. Club, Montgomery Co, Md, 51-53; campaign chmn, Nat. Fedn. Rep. Women, 53-60, second v.pres, 60-62; campaign chmn, Md. Fedn. Rep. Women, 56-59, Wash. Liaison, 59-63, state pres, 64-; polit. educ. chmn, Montgomery Co. Fedn. Rep. Women, 62-64; v.chmn, Md. Rep. State Cent. Cmt, 66-; del-at-lg, Rep. Nat. Conv, 68. Publ: (Campaign Manuals), Plan of Action for Precinct Womanpower, Operation Coffee Cup and Republican Roundtables. Mem: Am. Newspaper Women's Club. Rel: Unitarian. Mailing Add: 6900 Barrett Lane, Bethesda, Md. 20014.

HERN, LESTER MONROE R
b. Argillite, Ky, 6/15/21; s. Joseph Henry Hern and Hattie Poynter; m. 7/4/46 to Faye Hall; c. Diana Kay, Anita Gail and Towana A. Educ: Greenup Co. Pub. Schs. Polit. & Govt. Pos: Precinct committeeman, Rep. Party, 66-; chmn, Collier Co. Rep. Exec. Cmt, Fla, 62-66. Bus. & Prof. Pos: Pres, Hern Construct. Inc, 63-; v.pres, R & L Roofing Co, 59-62. Mil. Serv: Entered as Pvt, Air Force, 42, released as Cpl, 45, after serv. in 386th Air Serv. Group, Asiatic-Pac. Theater, 44-45; Victory Medal; Meritorious Unit Award; Asiatic-Pac. Theater Ribbon with Bronze Star; Good Conduct Medal. Mem: Mason; Moose; VFW. Rel: Protestant. Mailing Add: 1117 Milano Dr, Naples, Fla. 33940. (1967)

HERNANDEZ COLON, MIGUEL Popular Dem, P.R.
Rep. P.R. House of Rep.
b. Moca, P.R, 11/25/28; s. Juan Hernandez and Nicolasa Colón H; m. 6/8/62 to Milagros López; c. Lourdes Milagros; Lizette and Carlos Miguel. Educ: Univ. P.R, B.A, 52, LL.B, 62. Polit. & Govt. Pos: V.pres, Mayaguez Popular Dem. Party, P.R, 68; Popular Dem. rep, Local Elec. Bd, 68; Rep, P.R. House of Rep, 69- Bus. & Prof. Pos: Attorney-at-law and notary pub, 62. Mil. Serv: Entered as 2nd Lt, Army, 52, released as 1st Lt, 54, after serv. in 25th Inf. Div, Far East Command, 53-54; Nat. Defense Ribbon; Korean Serv. Ribbon; UN Serv. Ribbon. Mem: P.R. Bar Asn; Lions. Rel: Catholic. Legal Res: 4 Santervas St, Urb. Ponce de Leon, Mayaguez, P.R. 00708. Mailing Add: P.O. Box 1731, Mayaguez, P.R. 00708.

HERNANDEZ, EDMA SANTIAGO de Popular Dem, P.R.
Sen, P.R. Senate
b. Santurce, P.R, 7/3/21; d. Enrique Santiago and María Eugenia Montijo S; m. 12/22/44 to Luperino H. Hernández; c. Humberto L. Educ: Univ. P.R, B.A, 52; N.Y. Univ, M.A, 63. Polit. & Govt. Pos: Pres, Popular Dem. Party Women's Cmt, Aguada, P.R, 60-68; v.pres, Popular Dem. Party Munic. Cmt, 64-68; Sen, P.R. Senate, 69- Bus. & Prof. Pos: Rural teacher, Cobo Rojo, Aguada, P.R, 41-52; dir. sch, Aguada, 52-60; asst. supt. schs, Moca and Rincón, 60-63; supt. sch, Rincón, 63-68. Mem: P.R. Teachers Asn; Nat. Educ. Asn; pres, Aguado Rotary Club Women. Various honors and awards for work as teacher and supt. of schs. Legal Res: Pilar 112, Urbanizacion García, Aguadilla, P.R. 00603. Mailing Add: Box 575, Aguada, P.R. 00602.

HERNANDEZ, SANCHEZ JESUS MANUEL New Progressive, P.R.
Sen, P.R. Senate
b. Vega Baja, P.R; s. Santiago Hernández and Dolores Sânchez H; m. to Laura Esther Santana; c. Claribel, Amibal and Ariel. Educ: Univ. P.R, B.S.C. and LL.B; Phi Delta Gamma. Polit. & Govt. Pos: V.pres, New Progressive Party, P.R, 68; sen, P.R. Senate, 69- Bus. & Prof. Pos: Attorney-at-law. Mil. Serv: Entered as 1st Lt, Army, 52, released, 55, after serv. in 24th Inf. Div, Korea; UN, Nat. Defense and Korean Serv. Medals; Repub. of Korea Presidential Unit Citation; Commendation Ribbon with Pendant. Mem: U.S. and P.R. Bar Asns. Rel: Catholic. Legal Res: Sarasate 923, Villa Serilla, Rio Piedras, P.R. 00924. Mailing Add: Puerto Rico Senate, Capitol Bldg, San Juan, P.R. 00903.

HERNANDEZ-COLON, RAFAEL Popular Dem, P.R.
Pres, P.R. Senate
b. Ponce, P.R, 10/24/36; s. Rafael Hernández Matos Colón and Dorinda C; m. 10/24/59 to Lila Mayoral; c. Rafael, José Alfredo, Dora Mercedes and Juan Eugenio. Educ: Johns Hopkins Univ, A.B, 56; Univ. P.R, LL.B; Phi Beta Kappa; Phi Eta Mu. Polit. & Govt. Pos: Assoc. cmnr. pub. serv, P.R. Pub. Serv. Cmn, 60-62; attorney gen, P.R. Dept. of Justice, 65-67; mem. presidential cmn, Popular Dem. Party of P.R, 68-; Dem. Nat. committeeman, P.R, 68-; Sen. and Pres, P.R. Senate, 69- Bus. & Prof. Pos: Partner, Hernandez Colon & Bauza, Law Off, 67-69. Publ: Manual of Civil Procedure, Equity, 69; 'The Commonwealth of Puerto Rico: Territory or State,' P.R. Bar Asn. Law Rev. Rel: Catholic. Legal Res: Sol 1, Ponce. P.R. Mailing Add: The Capitol, San Juan, P.R. 00903.

HERNDON, CHESLEY COLEMAN, JR R
Chmn, Midland Co. Rep. Party, Tex.
b. Tulsa, Okla, 1/18/27; s. Chesley Coleman Herndon and Ethel Alta Dunn H; m. 7/2/49 to Sarah Rose Ann Evans; c. Chesley Coleman III, Mary Jane, James Noel and Anne Elizabeth. Educ: Univ. Tex, Austin, 44-46; Univ. Tulsa, B.S, 48; Univ. Mich, M.A, 52; Sigma Gamma Epsilon; Beta Theta Pi. Polit. & Govt. Pos: Block chmn, Midland Co. Rep. Party, Tex, 60-63 & 66, precinct chmn, 63-66, Goldwater motorcade co-chmn, 64, co. orgn. chmn, 68, gen. chmn. of Spiro T. Agnew Rally, 68, chmn, 68-; sergeant at arms, Midland Co. Rep. Conv, 64 and chmn. nominating cmt, 68; del, Tex. State Rep. Conv, 64 & 66; mem, cmt. fed. employ, Tex. State Rep. Party, 69- Bus. & Prof. Pos: Trainee and landman, Carter Oil Co, Denver, Colo, 48-50, geologist, Grand Rapids, Mich. and Carmi, Ill, 52-55; geologist and dist. geologist, Kirby Petroleum Co, Tulsa, Okla, 55-58; sr. geologist, Skelly Oil Co, Midland, Tex, 59-65, dist. geologist, 65- Mem: Am. Asn. Petroleum Geologists; cert, Am. Inst. Prfnl. Geologists; Soc. Econ. Paleontologists & Mineralogists; W.Tex. and Tulsa Geol. Socs; dir, Permian Basin Civic Ballet Asn; Midland Co. Citizens Col. Cmt; mem, Episcopal Diocesan Christian Educ. Cmt; SAR; Midland Co. Rep. Men's Club; Midland Young Rep. Club; Nat. Rifle Asn. Cited by Resolution of Midland Co. Precinct 8, 66. Rel: Episcopal. Mailing Add: 3108 Humble, Midland, Tex. 79701.

HERNDON, CURTIS C. D
b. Surrency, Ga, 8/14/25; s. John Herndon and Ruth Mann H; m. 6/09/45 to Eta Mae Herrington; c. Cindy Gail. Educ: Surrency High Sch, 43. Polit. & Govt. Pos: Ga. State Rep, 63-66. Bus. & Prof. Pos: Ins; farming. Mil. Serv: Air Force, Pvt. Rel: Baptist. Mailing Add: Surrency, Ga. 31563. (1967)

HERNETT, GAIL H. R
N.Dak. State Sen.
b. Herman, Minn, 1/9/09; s. Charles Hernett and Jennie Schram H; m. 9/4/36 to Juanita Junge; c. Charles. Educ: Univ. N.Dak, 28. Polit. & Govt. Pos: Alderman, Ashley, N.Dak, 46-50, mayor, 50-64; mem. bd, N.Dak. State Banking Bd, 51-58; N.Dak. State Sen, 30th Dist, 55-; alternate del, Rep. Nat.

Conv, 68. Mem: Am. Bankers Asn. (mem. exec. coun, 53-59); N.Dak. Bankers Asn.(pres, 57); N.Dak. State C. of C.(pres, 60-61); Elks; Mason; Shrine; Lions. Rel: Lutheran. Mailing Add: Ashley, N.Dak. 58413.

HERR, GORDON D
Wash. State Sen.
b. Seattle, Wash, 1926; m. to Patricia; c. Five. Educ: Univ. of Wash. Polit. & Govt. Pos: Former Wash. State Rep; Wash. State Sen, currently. Bus. & Prof. Pos: Mfg. and Retail Lumber Bus. Mil. Serv: Air Force, World War II. Mem: Elks; K. of C; Am. Legion. Rel: Catholic. Mailing Add: 10617 21st S.W, Seattle, Wash. 98146. (1967)

HERR, HELEN E. D
Nev. State Sen.
Educ: N.Dak. State Teacher's Col. Polit. & Govt. Pos: Secy, State Hwy. Adv. Bd, Nev; pres, Boulder Hwy. Asn; chmn, Town Bd. of Whitney; Nev. State Assemblywoman, 4 terms; Nev. State Sen, 67- Bus. & Prof. Pos: Real estate agent. Mem: Past pres, Soroptimists. Mailing Add: 4620 Meredith St, Las Vegas, Nev. 89109. (1967)

HERREMA, LAVONNE JUNE D
Mem, Calif. Dem. State Cent. Cmt.
b. Chandler, Minn, 6/3/33; d. Henry J. Westerhof and Henrietta L. Moret W; m. 7/6/52 to Gordon G. Herrema; c. Deborah Kay. Educ: Long Beach City Col, 1 semester; Cerritos Jr. Col, 1 semester. Polit. & Govt. Pos: Mem, Calif. Dem. State Cent. Cmt, 68- Mem: Artesia Cerritos Lady Lions Club. Rel: Protestant. Mailing Add: 17910 Summer Ave, Artesia, Calif. 90701.

HERRIN, RALPH HERMAN D
Miss. State Rep.
b. Sanford, Miss, 12/3/08; married. Polit. & Govt. Pos: Miss. State Rep, 56-60 and currently. Bus. & Prof. Pos: Businessman; farmer. Mem: Rotary; Collins Bus. and Prfnl. Club; pres, Covington Co. Baptist Brotherhood; Farm Bur. Rel: Baptist. Mailing Add: Route 4, Box 185, Collins, Covington Co, Miss. 39428. (1967)

HERRING, EDGAR DALE R
Chmn, Coleman Co. Rep. Cmt, Tex.
b. Santa Anna, Tex, 11/20/31; s. Edgar Otto Herring and Cora Dancer H.(deceased); m. 6/13/64 to Arletta Jane Sides; c. Andy Dale and Angelita. Educ: Tex. Tech. Col, B.S, 59; Alpha Zeta. Polit. & Govt. Pos: Chmn, Coleman Co. Rep. Cmt, Tex, 66- Bus. & Prof. Pos: Sheep and cattle rancher, 59- Mil. Serv: Entered as Pvt, Air Force, 51, released as A-1/C, 55, after serving in 3700th Mil. Training Wing, Air Training Command, 51-55. Mem: Am. Soc. Range Mgt; Farm Bur; Tex. Sheep & Goat Raisers Asn; Am. Suffolk Sheep Soc; Debouillet Sheep Breeders Asn; mem. bd. supvr, Cent. Colo. Soil & Water Conserv. Dist; Tex. State and W.Tex. Genealogical Socs. Runner up Star Young Farmer of Area IV in Tex, 67; Tex. Conserv. Farmer-Rancher, Ft. Worth Press Awards Prog, 69. Rel: Methodist. Mailing Add: Route 2, Box 4, Talpa, Tex. 76882.

HERRING, ROBERT F. D
b. Newnan, Ga, 6/11/11; s. Robert Freeman Herring and Christine Arnold H; m. to Hazel Lipscomb; c. Robert F, III. Educ: Univ. of the South; Kappa Alpha Order. Polit. & Govt. Pos: Registr, Coweta Co, Ga; former chmn, Coweta Co. Dem. Exec. Cmt. Bus. & Prof. Pos: Employee, State Motor Vehicle Dept, Newnan, Ga. Mil. Serv: Pvt, Army. Mem: Civitan Club; Vet. Club. Rel: Methodist Episcopal. Legal Res: 48 W. Washington St, Newnan, Ga. 30263. Mailing Add: P.O. Box 294, Newnan, Ga. 30263. (1967)

HERRING, WILLIAM H. 'BILL' D
Educ: Canterbury Episcopal Col, 47; Ind. State Col; Ind. Univ. Polit. & Govt. Pos: Ind. State Rep, 55-66. Bus. & Prof. Pos: Teacher. Mem: Ind. State Teachers Asn; Int. Operating Engrs; Elks; Masons; Shrine; Scottish Rite. Rel: Episcopal. Mailing Add: P. O. Box 86, Linton, Ind. 47441. (1967)

HERRMAN, GREGORY JOSEPH D
Chmn, Ellis Co. Dem. Party, Kans.
b. Hays, Kans, 3/15/27; s. Henry F. Herrman and Margaret Schaefer H; m. 10/15/56 to Nancy Crabtree; c. Mary, Elizabeth, Gregory, John, Christopher and David. Educ: Ft. Hays Kans. State Col, 46-47; St. Louis Univ, B.S, 50; St. Louis Univ. Law Sch, LL.B and J.D.S, 53; Phi Delta Phi. Polit. & Govt. Pos: Co. attorney, Ellis Co, Kans, 61-63; chmn, Ellis Co. Dem. Party, 68- Mailing Add: 1610 Elm St, Hays, Kans. 67601.

HERRMANN, KARL V. D
b. Granite Falls, Wash, 8/24/15; m. to Beatrice; c. Four. Educ: Univ. of Puget Sound; Washington State Univ; Gonzaga Univ, LL.B. Polit. & Govt. Pos: Former Wash. State Sen; State Ins. Cmnr, Wash, 69- Mailing Add: 9417 E. Grace, Spokane, Wash. 99206.

HERRON, JAMES HENRY R
Chmn, Frio Co. Rep. Party, Tex.
b. Junction, Tex, 12/12/41; s. Jim Herron, Jr. and Stella May Grobe H; single. Educ: Abilene Christian Col, B.S.E, 65. Polit. & Govt. Pos: Chmn, Frio Co. Rep. Party, Tex, 68- Bus. & Prof. Pos: Soc. studies teacher, Pearsall Jr. High, Tex, 65- Mem: Tex. State Teachers Asn; Frio Co. Hist. Surv. Cmt. Rel: Church of Christ. Mailing Add: Box 188, Pearsall, Tex. 78061.

HERSCHLER, ED D
Wyo. State Rep.
b. Kemmerer, Wyo, 10/27/18; s. Edgar F. Herschler and Charlotte Jenkins H; m. 5/3/44 to Kathleen Colter; c. Kathleen Sue and James C. Educ: Univ. Colo, 36-41; Univ. Wyo, LL.B, 49. Polit. & Govt. Pos: City attorney, Kemmerer, Wyo, 50-; co. and prosecuting attorney, Lincoln Co, 51-59; Wyo. State Rep, 61- Mil. Serv: Entered as Pvt, Marine Corps, 42, released as Platoon Sgt, 45, after serv. in Third Raider Bn, S.Pac, 42-44; Purple Heart; Silver Star. Mem: Wyo. State Bar (pres, 68-); Am. Bar Asn; Int. Soc. Barristers; Mason; Am. Legion (Judge Adv, Dept. of Wyo, 66-); VFW. Rel: Episcopal. Mailing Add: 823-Third West Ave, Kemmerer, Wyo. 83101.

HERSEY, RALPH BERTRAM, JR. R
b. Boston, Mass, 1/2/25; s. Ralph Bertram Hersey and Eunice Clogston H; m. 4/3/48 to Edith Eklund; c. Diane, Richard and Mark. Educ: Dartmouth Col, A.B, 46; Phi Sigma Kappa. Polit. & Govt. Pos: Mem, Rep. Town Cmt, Norwood, Mass, 52-, chmn, 64-69. Bus. & Prof. Pos: Asst. trust officer, Boston Safe Deposit & Trust Co, 53-55, trust officer, 55-61, sr. trust officer, 61-64, v.pres, 64- Mil. Serv: Entered as A/S, Naval Res, 43, released as Ens, 46, after serv. in V-12 Col. Training Program. Mem: Chmn. interviewing cmt, Dartmouth Col, Norwood, Mass. area; trustee, Norwood Hosp; v.pres. & finance chmn, Greater Boston Coun. Camp Fire Girls; bd. trustees, Medfield State Hosp, 67- Rel: Episcopal; former Jr. Warden, Grace Episcopal Church, Norwood, Mass. 02062. Mailing Add: 30 Chatham Rd, Norwood, Mass. 02062.

HERSHBERGER, ROSS EDWARD D
b. Wolfsburg, Pa, 6/17/13; s. Edward Austin Hershberger and Sue Bixler H; single. Educ: Univ. Va, Charlottesville, 50-51. Polit. & Govt. Pos: Del, Dem. Nat. Conv, 56, 60 & 64, alternate del, 68; dir. of personnel, Pa. Turnpike, 58-68. Bus. & Prof. Pos: Acct, 45-69. Mil. Serv: Entered as Pvt, Marines, 41, released as Sgt, 45. Mem: Am. Legion; VFW; Elks; Mason. Rel: United Church of Christ. Mailing Add: R.D. 2, Bedford, Pa. 15522.

HERSHEY, LEWIS BLAINE
Dir, Selective Serv. Syst.
b. Jamestown Twp, Ind, 9/12/93; s. Latta Freleigh Hershey and Rosetta Richardson H; m. 11/29/17 to Ellen Dygert; c. Kathryn Elizabeth (Mrs. A. Alvis Layne, Jr), Gilbert Richardson, George Frederick and Ellen Margaret (Mrs. Sam Lewis Barth). Educ: Tri-State Col, B.S, 12, B.P.D. and A.B, 14; Ind. Univ, 17; Field Artil. Sch. of Fire, war course, 18 & 23; Command and Gen. Staff Col, 33; Army War Col, grad, 34; Univ. Hawaii, 35; Omicron Delta Kappa; Phi Beta Kappa. Polit. & Govt. Pos: Dep. sheriff, Steuben Co, Ind, 13-17; secy. and exec. officer, Army-Navy Selective Serv. Cmt, 36-40; dep. dir, Selective Serv. Syst, 40-41, dir, 41-47, & 48-, dir, Off. of Selective Serv. Records, 47-48. Bus. & Prof. Pos: Teacher, country sch, Jamestown Twp, Steuben Co, Ind, 10-11; prin, Flint Pub. Sch, 14-16; asst. prof. mil. sci. and tactics, Ohio State Univ, 23-27. Mil. Serv: Serv. successively as Pvt, Cpl, Sgt, 2nd Lt. and 1st Lt, Ind. Nat. Guard, 11-16, Platoon Comdr, Co. B, Third Ind. Inf, 11-16; Entered as 1st Lt, Army, 16, released as Lt. Gen, 56, after serv. as Bn. Adj, Battery Exec. Regt. Adj, Third Ind. Inf. and 137th Field Artil, 16-18, Troop Movement Officer, Brest, France, 18-19, Battery Comdr, Regt. Supply Officer, Tenth Field Artil, 19-22, Battery Comdr, Bn. Exec. and Bn. Commanding Officer, 82nd Field Artil, 27-31; asst. chief of staff, Hawaiian Dept, 34-36, and mem, War Dept. Gen. Staff, 27-31; Army, Navy and Mexican Border Distinguished Serv. Medals; World War I Victory Medal with Serv. Clasp (France); Am. Defense Serv. Medal; Am. Campaign Medal; World War II Victory Medal; Nat. Defense Serv. Medal with Oak Leaf Cluster. Publ: Off To College, Huntington Col, 69; Selective Service, 69 and Military Draft, 69, World Publ. Co. Mem: Chmn, Montgomery Co. Civil Defense Asn, Md, 50; chmn, Montgomery Co. Chap, Am. Red Cross, 52-68; pres, Nat. Capital Area Coun, Boy Scouts, 61-67; trustee, Tri-State Col; life mem, Am. Legion; Nat. Guard Asn; VFW; Mason. Distinguished Serv. Medal, Am. Legion, Nat. Guard Asn. of the U.S. and State of Ind; Distinguished and Meritorious Serv. Cert, Regular Vet. Asn. of the U.S; Annual Citation, Haim-Parnes Post 151, Jewish War Vet. of the U.S, 53; Distinguished Serv. Award, Mil. Chaplains Asn. of the U.S; Spec. Award, Freedoms Found; Medal of Merit, N.Dak; Medal and Citation, La; Magnolia Cross, Miss; Distinguished Serv. Medal and Oak Leaf Cluster, Ala; Minute Man of 1964, Reserve Officers Asn. of the U.S; Silver Beaver Award, Boy Scouts, 61, Silver Antelope Award, 64, Silver Buffalo Award, 66, Scouter of the Year Award, Nat. Capital Area Coun, 68; Pres. Gold Medal for outstanding serv. to the Army, Asn. of the U.S. Army; Bernard Baruch Award, VFW, Loyalty Day Award, D.C. Dept; Distinguished Serv. Award, Mil. Order of the World Wars; Gold Good Citizenship Medal, Wash, D.C. Chap, SAR; Caleb B. Smith Masonic Award, Ind, Gold Medal for 50 years as a Mason; Award, Nat. Rifle Asn; Gold Pin, Northeast. Lodge 210, Fremont, Ind; Gen. Benedict Crowell Gold Medal, Am. Ord. Asn, Cleveland, Ohio; Silver Helmet Defense Award, Amvets; 1968 Serv. to Mankind Award, Sertoma Club of Wash. Legal Res: Angola, Ind. Mailing Add: 5500 Lambeth Rd, Bethesda, Md, 20014.

HERSHMAN, RICHARD JOSEPH R
Chmn, Ashtabula Co. Rep. Cent. and Exec. Cmt, Ohio
b. Coshocton, Ohio, 2/24/33; s. Charles O. Hershman and Glendora Phillips H; single. Educ: Kent State Univ. Polit. & Govt. Pos: Cmnr, Ashtabula Co. Jury Cmn, Ohio, 61-63; co. chmn, Rhodes for Gov. Cmt, 62; chmn, Ashtabula Co. Rep. Cent. and Exec. Cmts, 63- Rel: Roman Catholic. Legal Res: 11 Lakehurst Dr, Lake Rd. W, Ashtabula, Ohio 44004. Mailing Add: P.O. Box 1658, Ashtabula, Ohio 44004.

HERTZ, GOTHOLD D
Chmn, 38th Legis. Dist. Dem. Party, N.Dak.
b. Mott, N.Dak, 1/14/11; s. Johan Hertz and Justina Stotz H; m. 9/6/32 to Lydia B. Schurr; c. Milton, William, Marie and Daniel. Polit. & Govt. Pos: Judge, Dem. Party, N.Dak, 34-62, precinct committeeman, 66; pres, Sch. Bd, Highland Twp, 54-66; pres, Co. Sch. Bd, 61; mem, Agr. Stabilization Conserv. Cmt; chmn, 38th Legis. Dist. Dem. Party, 62- Bus. & Prof. Pos: Owner and operator of farm, 43-66. Mem: Farmer's Coop; Grand Cross of Color; Mason; Eastern Star; Shrine; El Zagal of Fargo. Rel: Congregational; Mem, Church Coun, 12 years; financial dir, United Church of Christ, 2 years. Mailing Add: Highland Acres, Mott, N.Dak. 58646. (1967)

HERTZ, JOSEPH HAROLD D
Chmn, Jefferson Co. Dem. Party, Ind.
b. Madison, Ind, 5/4/16; s. Joseph John Hertz and Anna Cisco H; m. 10/1/41 to Stella Collins; c. Joseph John and Peggy Collins. Educ: Ill. Col. Podiatry, Chicago, D.P.M, 37. Polit. & Govt. Pos: City councilman, Madison, Ind, 59-63; chmn, Jefferson Co. Dem. Party, 60- Mil. Serv: Entered as Pvt, Army, 41, released as Cpl, 46, after serv. in 558th Signal Air Warning, China-Burma-India, 44-46. Mem: Elks; Moose; Am. Legion; VFW. Rel: Catholic. Mailing Add: 1322 Michigan Rd, Madison, Ind. 47250.

HERTZBERG, STUART E. D
Treas, Mich. State Dem. Cent. Cmt.
b. Detroit, Mich, 11/24/26; s. Barney Hertzberg and Rae Horowitz H; m.

6/10/50 to Marilyn Jean Cohen; c. Cathy Lee, Robert Steven and John David. Educ: Univ. Mich, B.A, 50, J.D. with distinction, 51. Polit. & Govt. Pos: Del-at-lg, Dem. Nat. Conv, 60, 64 & 68; finance dir, Mich. State Dem. Cent. Cmt, 63-66, treas, 66- Mil. Serv: Entered as Pvt, Army, 45, released as Sgt, 46, after serv. in Hq. Detachment, West.Pac. Theater, 45-46; Good Conduct Award; Expert Infantryman Badge; Philippine Independence Ribbon ; Asiatic Pac. Campaign Medal; World War II Victory Medal. Mem: Am, Mich, Detroit and Fed. Bar Asns; Am. Judicature Soc; Commercial Law League Am; Mason; VFW; NAACP (life mem); Archives of Am. Art; Founders Soc. and Friends of Modern Art, Detroit Inst. of Arts; Men's Club; Temple Emanu-El (bd. trustees); Detroit Hist. Soc; PTA; Old Newsboy's Goodfellow Fund. Rel: Hebrew. Legal Res: 10100 Burton Ave, Oak Park, Mich. 48237. Mailing Add: 1530 Buhl Bldg, Detroit, Mich. 48226.

HESKETT, BILL LEON D
b. Enid, Okla, 12/17/33; s. Ralph Leon Heskett and Pearl Green H; m. 6/14/52 to Janice Joy Newburn. Educ: Okla. State Univ, B.S. in Agr, 56; Univ. Tulsa Law Sch, J.D, 60; Phi Beta Gamma; Student Sect, Am. Soc. Agr. Economists. Polit. & Govt. Pos: Pres, Wash. Co. Young Dem, Okla, 61-62; chmn, Wash. Co. Dem. Cent. Cmt, 62-64; mem, Okla. State Dem. Party Platform Cmt, 64; del, Dem. Nat. Conv. and Young Dem. Nat. Conv, 64; former mem, Okla. Dem. Exec. Cmt; chmn, Second Cong. Dist. Dem. Cent. Cmt, Okla, 64-69. Bus. & Prof. Pos: Clerk, Phillips Petroleum Co, 52; asst. prof, Okla. State Univ, 55-56; attorney, Heskett & Heskett, 60-64, Tillman, Heskett & Heskett, Pawhuska and Bartlesville, Okla, 64- Mil. Serv: Entered as Pfc, Army Res. and Okla. Nat. Guard, 54, released as Sp-5, 62. Mem: Osage Co, Wash. Co, Okla. and Am. Bar Asns; Am. Trial Lawyers Asn; pres, E. Bartlesville, Kiwanis, 64. Admitted to practice before U.S. Dist. Court, North. Dist. of Okla, 62 and U.S. Supreme Court, 64. Rel: Baptist. Legal Res: 910 Keeler, Bartlesville, Okla. 74003. Mailing Add: 940 Price Tower, Bartlesville, Okla. 74003. (1967)

HESLER, HARRY RAY R
Chmn, Parke Co. Rep. Cent. Orgn, Ind.
b. Montezuma, Ind, 3/17/23; s. Harry Roscoe Hesler and Elanor Susan Pruett H; m. 1/30/61 to Marjorie Jane Walsh; c. Kendall W, Elizabeth A. and Charles M. Educ: Ind. State Teacher's Col. Polit. & Govt. Pos: Chmn, Parke Co. Rep. Cent. Orgn, Ind, 61-; del, Rep. Nat. Conv, 68. Mil. Serv: S/Sgt, Army, 46, ETO. Mem: VFW; Mason; Scottish Rite, Zorah Shrine; Elks. Rel: Presbyterian. Mailing Add: R.R. 1, Montezuma, Ind. 47862.

HESLIN, HELEN ELAINE D
b. Wallingford, Conn; d. James F. Heslin and Helen Sutton H; single. Educ: Larson Jr. Col, grad, 42. Polit. & Govt. Pos: Exec. secy. to U.S. Rep. Wayne Hays, Ohio, 49- Bus. & Prof. Pos: Employee, Fed. Bur. Invest, 42-46, Vet. Admin, 46-48. Rel: Catholic. Mailing Add: 620 S. 2111 Jefferson David Hwy, Arlington, Va. 22202.

HESS, ARTHUR EMIL
Dep. Cmnr, Soc. Security Admin.
b. Reading, Pa. 6/18/16; s. Emil Hess and Rose Brunner H; m. 3/14/42 to Ann McKeown Davis; c. Jean Elizabeth, Ann McMaster and Elizabeth Carol. Educ: Univ. Munich, summer 38; Princeton Univ, A.B, 39; Univ. Md. Sch. Law, LL.B, 48; Phi Beta Kappa; Order of the Coif. Polit. & Govt. Pos: Field rep. and mgr, Soc. Security Admin, Pa. and N.J, 39-44, admin. pos, Baltimore, Md, 44-50, dep. asst. dir, 50-54, dir. disability opers, 54-65, dir. health ins, 65-67, dep. cmnr, 67- Mem: Am. Pub. Welfare Asn; Nat. Rehabilitation Asn; Int. Soc. for Disabled; Princeton Alumni Asn. of Md. Recipient of Arthur S. Flemming Award for Outstanding Fed. Serv, Wash, D.C. Jr. C. of C, 55; Nat. Civil Serv. League Award, 67; President's Award for Distinguished Fed. Civilian Serv, 67. Rel: Presbyterian. Mailing Add: 4805 Woodside Rd, Baltimore, Md. 21229.

HESS, EVELYN A. D
b. Birdseye, Ind, 6/7/13; d. Harry Travis Chestnut and Letty Coble C; m. 12/25/41 to James William Hess; c. James W, Jr. Educ: Univ. Ky, Lexington, 2 years. Polit. & Govt. Pos: Committeewoman, Clifton Hts. Dem. Party, Pa, 48-; pres, Clifton Heights Dem. Womens Club, 56-60; chmn, Civil Serv. Cmn, Clifton Heights, 56-60; Dem. state committeewoman, Delaware Co, 56-68; registration chmn, Delaware Co. Dem. Party, 56-; Dem. councilman, Clifton Heights, 56-; instr, Polit. Action Precinct Sch, currently; secy, Robert Casey for Gov. Campaign, 66; alternate del, Dem. Nat. Conv, 68. Bus. & Prof. Pos: Investr, Pa. Dept. Revenue, 55-63; field auditor, Auditor Gen, Commonwealth of Pa, 63- Mem: Del. Co. Dem. Club. Serv. to Humanity Award, Four Chaplains Soc. Rel: Protestant. Mailing Add: 132 Academy Rd, Clifton Heights, Pa. 19018.

HESS, JAMES DOUGLAS R
b. Richlands, Va, 7/10/38; s. George Perry Hess and Bessie Clara Higginbotham H; m. 6/15/66 to Nancy Ann Horton. Educ: Nat. Bus. Col, B.A. in Acct; X-Phalanx. Polit. & Govt. Pos: Del, Rep. Nat. Conv, 68. Bus. & Prof. Pos: Staff acct, Cook Assocs, 60-66, partner, Cook Assocs. CPA, 66-67; self-employed CPA, 67- Mil. Serv: Entered as E-1, Army Nat. Guard, 60, released as E-4, 66, after serv. in Ft. Knox, Ky, 6 months and res, 5½ years. Mem: Jaycees; Lions; Moose; Tazewell Co. Country Club; Am. and Va. Inst. of CPA. Rel: Baptist. Mailing Add: Box 386, Tazewell, Va. 24651.

HESS, STEPHEN R
Dep. Asst. to the President for Urban Affairs
b. N.Y.C, 4/20/33; s. Charles Hess and Florence Morse H; m. 8/23/59 to Elena Shayne; c. Charles and James. Educ: Johns Hopkins Univ, B.A, 53; assoc. fel, Inst. for Policy Studies, Wash, 64-65; fel, Inst. of Polit, Harvard Univ, 67-68; Phi Beta Kappa. Polit. & Govt. Pos: Admin. asst. to field dir, Rep. Cong. Cmt, Wash, D.C, 56; mem, pub. rels. staff, Rep. Nat. Cmt, fall 58; staff asst. to the President, 59-61; asst. to minority whip, U.S. Senate, winter 61; speechwriter, Richard M. Nixon Gubernatorial Campaign, Calif, 62; speechwriter, Spiro T. Agnew Vice Presidential Campaign, 68; Dep. Asst. to the President for Urban Affairs, 69- Mil. Serv: Entered as Pvt, Army, 56, released as Pfc, 58, after serv. in Third Armored Div, Germany, 57-58. Publ: The Republican Establishment (with D. Broder), 67 and Nixon (with E. Mazo), 68, Harper & Row; The Ungentlemanly Art (with M. Kaplan), MacMillan, 68; plus 2 others. Mailing Add: 3705 Porter St. N.W, Washington, D.C. 20016.

HESS, W. DALE D
Md. State Del.
b. Fallston, Md, 8/17/30; married. Educ: Harford Co. Pub. Schs. Polit. & Govt. Pos: Mem, Harford Co. Real Estate Bd, Md; mem, Produce Mkt. Authority; Md. State Del, 55-, Majority Leader, Md. House of Del, 63-; del, Dem. Nat. Conv, 68. Bus. & Prof. Pos: Farmer. Mem: Elks; Lions; Moose; Bush River Boat Club; W. Nottingham Livestock Mkt, Inc; Grange; Farm Bur; former nat. v.pres, FF of Am; past pres, Harford Co. Dem. Club. Mailing Add: Fallston, Md. 21047. (1967)

HESS, WILLIAM E. R
Mem: Exec. Cmt, Hamilton Co. Rep. Party, Ohio
b. Cincinnati, Ohio, 2/13/98; s. William F. Hess and Rose Youngman H; m. 6/8/27 to Stella Ostendorf; wid. Educ: Univ. of Cincinnati; Cincinnati Law Sch; Phi Delta Phi. Polit. & Govt. Pos: Mem, Cincinnati City Coun, Ohio, 21-25; U.S. Rep, Ohio, 29-61; mem, exec. cmt, Hamilton Co. Rep. Party, currently; alternate del, Rep. Nat. Conv, 68. Mil. Serv: Pvt, Army, 18. Mem: Mason; Shrine; Elks; Am. Legion. Rel: Protestant. Mailing Add: 5751 Pine Hill Lane, Cincinnati, Ohio 45238.

HESSER, WOODROW CLEVELAND D
Committeeman, Ariz. Dem. State Cent. Cmt.
b. Stillwater, Okla, 4/1/18; s. Peter Cleveland Hesser and Lucy Adeline Mathews H; m. 5/19/39 to Rosemary Mahanay; c. Captain William Andrew, 1st Lt. Peter Mac, Sharon Kay (Mrs. Peters) and Neal Patrick. Educ: Okla. State Univ, 3 years. Polit. & Govt. Pos: Precinct committeeman, Dem. Party, Benson, Ariz, 56-, precinct area chmn, 58-; chmn. recreation cmt, Benson, 57-, city councilman, 69-; v.chmn, Cochise Co. Dem. Party, 64-66, chmn, 67-68, exec. committeeman, 67-; committeeman, Ariz. Dem. State Cent. Cmt, 64-, state exec. committeeman, 67-68; del, Dem. Nat. Conv, 68. Mem: Mason (officer); Benson Lions Club (third v.pres). Rel: Presbyterian. Legal Res: 100 Bonita St, Benson, Ariz. 85602. Mailing Add: Box 215, Benson, Ariz. 85602.

HESTER, J. WALSTON D
b. Russellville, Ala, 9/2/12; s. Amos Benton Hester and Lucy Jane Hendrix H; m. 8/25/43 to Jewel Chenault; c. Judy Joy. Educ: Auburn Univ, B.S. Polit. & Govt. Pos: Chmn, Franklin Co. Dem. Party, Ala, 49-57; finance chmn, Seventh Cong. Dist. for Kennedy, 60; Ala. State Rep, Franklin Co, 63-67. Mem: Pres, Lions, 43 and C. of C, 48. Rel: Baptist. Mailing Add: P.O. Box D, Russellville, Ala. 35653. (1967)

HESTER, LAWRENCE LAMAR D
S.C. State Rep.
b. Mt. Carmel, S.C, 12/17/91; s. James T. Hester and Adalina Hester H; m. 6/2/17 to Carrie Roser McCelvey. Educ: Pub. schs, Mt. Carmel; Greenwood Graded Sch, 08. Polit. & Govt. Pos: Mayor, Mt. Carmel, S.C, 16-20 & 30-40; chmn, Dem. Club, Mt. Carmel, 24-; S.C. State Sen, 41-69; S.C. State Rep, 69- Bus. & Prof. Pos: Farmer; business man; trustee, John de la Howe, 35- Rel: Episcopal. Mailing Add: Mt. Carmel, S.C. 29840.

HESTER, ROBERT JAMES, JR. D
Chmn, Bladen Co. Dem. Exec. Cmt, N.C.
b. Elizabethtown, N.C, 2/5/04; s. Robert James Hester and Rena Gaston Melvin H; m. 6/1/27 to Mary Pitkin Thomas; c. Robert James, III and Herbert Thomas. Educ: Wake Forest Col, 23-26. Polit. & Govt. Pos: Mayor, Elizabethtown, N.C, 27-29; judge, Gen. Court, Bladen Co, 29-33, solicitor, 37-39, co. attorney, 55-; chmn, Bladen Co. Dem. Exec. Cmt, 45-; N.C. State Sen, 15th Sen. Dist, 45-47 & 49-51; N.C. State Rep, Bladen Co, 47-49; trustee, Fayetteville State Col, 53-65; del, Dem. Nat. Conv, 60. Mem: Bladen Co. Bar Asn.(pres); 13th Judicial and N.C. Bar Asns; N.C. State Bar; pres, Dist. Bar Asn; Mason. Rel: Presbyterian. Mailing Add: P.O. Box 176, Elizabethtown, N.C. 28337.

HESTER, WILLIAM H. R
Chmn, Grady Co. Rep. Party, Ga.
b. Cairo, Ga, 6/18/36; s. W.B. Hester and Evelyn Gainous H; m. 11/13/60 to Betty Jeanette Nowell; c. William H, II, Hannah Eliseabeth and Joseph Mathew. Educ: Cairo High Sch, grad, 54. Polit. & Govt. Pos: Chmn, Grady Co. Rep. Party, Ga, 66- Bus. & Prof. Pos: Ins. Agent, State Farm Ins. Co, 61- Mil. Serv: Entered as Pvt, Army, 56, released as Pfc, 59, after serving in Army Security Agency, Europe and Middle E. Theatre, 56-58. Mem: Life Underwriter Asn; Jaycees; Cairo Country Club. Rel: Methodist. Legal Res: 1173 Sixth St. S.E, Cairo, Ga. 31728. Mailing Add: 807 First Ave. N.E, Cairo, Ga. 31728.

HESTERBERG, ALEXANDER GEORGE D
State Committeeman, 44th Assembly Dist, Kings Co. Dem. Party, N.Y.
b. Brooklyn, N.Y, 6/11/11; s. Henry Hesterberg and Wilhelmina Schimpf H; m. 11/19/40 to Ruth Tooley; c. Ann H.(Mrs. Derby), Frances, Henry, Alex G, Jr, Winifred and Gregory. Educ: Georgetown Univ, A.B, 33; St. John's Law Sch, LL.B, 36. Polit. & Govt. Pos: Secy. to Judge John J. Fitzgerald, 39-42; secy. to Nathan Sobel, 42-56; state committeeman, 44th Assembly Dist, Kings Co. Dem. Party, N.Y, 50-; cmnr, Tax Cmn, City of N.Y, 56-60; alternate del, Dem. Nat. Conv, 68. Bus. & Prof. Pos: Practicing attorney, 38-; counsel to Pub. Adminstr, Kings Co, 60- Mem: Brooklyn Bar Asn; Catholic Lawyers' Guild; past pres. and dir, Flatbush Boys Club; dir. and counsel, Anthonian Hall, Inc. Rel: Catholic. Legal Res: 478 Argyle Rd, Brooklyn, N.Y. 11218. Mailing Add: 32 Court St, Brooklyn, N.Y. 11201.

HESTRES, LOUIS PHILLIPPE D
Sen, V.I. Legis.
b. Charlotte Amalie, St. Thomas, V.I, 5/26/24; s. Jean Baptiste Hestres and Lucille Bernard H; m. 3/12/47 to Alice O. Wallace; c. Louis Philippe, Jr. and Gloria A.(Mrs. Cole). Educ: City Col. N.Y, B.B.A, 64. Polit. & Govt. Pos: Internal revenue agent, Tax Div, Govt. of V.I, 55-62, chief enforcement br, 62-65; chmn. finance cmt, Dem. Party, V.I, 66-68; chmn, V.I. Bd. Educ, 67-68; Sen, V.I. Legis, 69-, chmn, Cmt. on Commerce, 69- Bus. & Prof. Pos: Mgr. and owner, Louis P. Hestres & Assocs, Pub. Acct, 65- Mil. Serv: U.S. Maritime Serv, 40-49. Mem: Lions Club St. Thomas (charter treas); Jaycees Int; Tau Beta Alpha. Rel: Roman Catholic. Legal Res: 22 Ninth St, St. Thomas, V.I. 00801. Mailing Add: P.O. Box 1603, St. Thomas, V.I. 00801.

HETERICK, ROBERT CARY, JR. R
Chmn, Sixth Cong. Dist. Rep. Cmt, Va.
b. Washington, D.C, 4/9/36; s. Robert Cary Heterick and Barbara Harrison H; m. 1/16/60 to Mollie Elizabeth Miller; c. Robert Bruce, Dawn Elizabeth and Catherine Paige. Educ: Va. Polytech. Inst, B.S. in Civil Eng, 59, M.S. in Struct. eng, 61, Ph.D. in Civil Eng, 68. Polit. & Govt. Pos: Chmn, Montgomery Co. Rep. Cmt, Va, 65-68; chmn, Sixth Cong. Dist. Rep. Party, 68- Bus. & Prof. Pos: Consult. engr, 61-; asst. prof. struct. eng, Va. Polytech. Inst, 61- and dir. comput. center, 69-; mem. bd. dirs, Hufford Ins. & Investment Agency, 65- Publ: An Introduction to Computers and Elementary FORTRAN, W.C. Brown Co, 68. Mem: Am. Soc. Civil Engrs.(mem. bd. dirs, Va. Sect); Am. Soc. for Eng. Educ; Am. Concrete Inst; Nat. Soc. Prfnl. Engrs; Int. Asn. for Bridge & Struct. Eng; Va. Soc. Prfnl. Eng.(v.pres, Southwest. Chap); Sigma Xi; Va. Adv. Coun. on Educ. Date Processing; Blacksburg Young Rep. Club (pres, 64-66); Blacksburg Rep. Club (pres, 65-66); Va. Polytech. Inst. Young Rep. Club (faculty adv, 64-65). Rel: Episcopal. Mailing Add: 416 Owens St, Blacksburg, Va. 24060.

HETLAND, JAMES L, JR. R
Chmn, Metrop. Coun, Minneapolis, Minn.
b. Minneapolis, Minn, 6/9/25; s. James L. Hetland and Evelyn Lundgren H; m. 9/19/49 to Barbara Taylor; c. Janice E, James E, Nancy L. and Steven T. Educ: Univ. Minn. Law Sch, Minneapolis, J.D, 50; Order of the Coif; Phi Delta Phi; Psi Upsilon. Polit. & Govt. Pos: Block worker and precinct worker, Rep. Party, Minneapolis, Minn, 51, ward chmn, 53; del, Rep. Ward, Co, Dist. and State Conv, Minn, 52-68; v.chmn, Hennepin Co. Rep. Party, 55-57; Rep. campaign mgr. for Mayor Campaign, Minneapolis, 59, Fifth Cong. Dist. Campaign, 60; chmn, Minneapolis Charter Cmt, 60-67; chmn, Fifth Cong. Dist. Rep. Party, 65-68; chmn, Metrop. Coun, Minneapolis, 67-; alternate del, Rep. Nat. Conv, 68. Bus. & Prof. Pos: Attorney, Mackall, Crounse, Moore, 50-56; prof. law, Univ. Minn, 56- Mil. Serv: Entered as Pvt, Army, 43, released as 2nd Lt, 46, after serv. in 376 Inf, ETO. Legal Res: 5850 Irving S, Minneapolis, Minn. 55419. Mailing Add: Law School, University of Minnesota, Minneapolis, Minn. 55455.

HETRICK, W. BRADY D
Pa. State Rep.
b. Harrisburg, Pa, 2/3/07; s. Jerome I. Hetrick and Laura Caveny H; m. to Helen Lauver; c. One daughter. Educ: Port Royal High Sch. Polit. & Govt. Pos: Pa. State Rep, 62- Mem: Bd. of dirs, Ment. Health; Commun. Coun; United Fund; Kiwanis; Mason; Elks; Moose; United Commercial Travelers; Brooklyn and City Fame Fire Co; past pres. and secy, Miffin Co. New Car Dealers; dist. cmnr, Boy Scouts; C. of C. Rel: Presbyterian. Mailing Add: 804 W. Fourth St, Lewistown, Pa. 17044.

HETTRICH, E. DANIEL, JR. R
Mem, Richmond City Rep. Cmt, Va.
b. Buffalo, N.Y, 11/15/26; s. E. Daniel Hettrich and Cali Rothweiler H; m. 2/13/52 to Dolores Petra Lupejkis; c. Drucelle L, Darcy L, E. Daniel III, David L, Dena L, Dawn L. and Devon Lee, Dale Lincoln and Dirk Lindy. Educ: Univ. Rochester, B.S.M.E, 47. Polit. & Govt. Pos: Pres, Lynchburg-Campbell Co. Young Rep, Va, 60-62; mem, Sixth Dist. Rep. Cmt, 62-64; chmn, Campbell Co. Rep. Cmt, 62-66; mem, Fifth Dist. Rep. Cmt, 65-66; mem, Va. State Rep. Cent. Cmt, 65-66; mem, Richmond City Rep. Cmt, currently. Bus. & Prof. Pos: Mgr. eng. and sales, Old Dominion Iron & Steel. Mil. Serv: Entered as A/S, Naval Res, 44, released as Ens, 47. Rel: Presbyterian. Legal Res: 4201 Forest Hills Ave, Richmond, Va. 23225. Mailing Add: Belle Isle, Richmond, Va. 23219.

HEUER, WILLIAM C. F. D
Mem, Todd Co. Dem-Farmer-Labor Exec. Cmt, Minn.
b. Bertha, Minn, 11/19/05; s. William Heuer and Anna Sonnenberg H; m. 6/29/27 to Selma C. Rosenberg; c. Donald, Gerald, Maxine (Mrs. Lawrence Truax), Ramona (Mrs. Warren Truax), James, Waldemar, Charles and Carolyn (Mrs. Jim Tonneson). Educ: Co. elem. dist. 85, eight years. Polit. & Govt. Pos: Town clerk, Bertha, Minn, 32-54, sch. clerk, Dist. 85, 33-46; sch. treas, Bertha Consolidated, 47-54; chmn, P.M.A, Todd Co, 41-54; Minn. State Sen, Todd-Wadena Co, 55-67; mem, Todd Co. Dem-Farmer-Labor Exec. Cmt, 67- Mem: Farmers Union; Lions; Commercial Club. Rel: Lutheran. Mailing Add: Route 1, Bertha, Minn. 56437.

HEWES, RICHARD DAVID R
Maine State Rep.
b. Biddeford, Maine, 8/16/26; s. Clyfton Hewes and May Frances Libbey H; m. 9/25/54 to Betsey Shaw; c. Nancy D, Richard N, James S, Anne K. and Carolyn C. Educ: Univ. Maine, B.A, 50; Boston Univ. Sch. Law, LL.B, 53; v.pres, Intra Fraternity Counsel; Beta Theta Pi. Polit. & Govt. Pos: Mem, Ord. Rev. Cmt, Cape Elizabeth, Maine, 61-65, Sch. Study Cmt, 64-67 and Superintending Sch. Cmt, 65-67; Maine State Rep, 67- Bus. & Prof. Pos: Attorney, Saco, Maine, 53-54 and Portland, Maine, 60-; attorney, Liberty Mutual Ins. Co, Boston, 54-60. Mil. Serv: Entered as Pvt, Army, 45, released as Capt, 60, after serv. in 32nd Ft. Bn, Korea Base Command, Asiatic Pac. Theatre, 45-46. Publ: 'The Evolution of Contribution Among Joint Tortfeasors in Maine,' Boston Univ. Law Rev, winter 64. Mem: Am. Bar Asn; Cumberland Co. and York Co. Bar Asns; Maine State Bar Asn.(mem. cmt. gen. liability law and miscellaneous casualty ins. law); Odd Fellows; YMCA (mem. exec. cmt, Maine State YMCA and dir. Portland YMCA); The Portland Club; Portland Country Club. Rel: Episcopal. Mailing Add: 38 Ocean View Rd, Cape Elizabeth, Maine 04107.

HEWGLEY, JAMES MARION, JR. R
Mayor, Tulsa, Okla.
b. Gallatin, Tenn, 11/7/16; s. James Marion Hewgley and Margaret Corbett H; m. 11/3/67 to Eileen Rooney Warren; c. Mimi (Mrs. Bashaw), Joan (Mrs. Yoakum), James M, III, Robert W. and Fred C. Hewgley and Thomas E. Warren. Educ: Okla. Univ, B.A, 38; Phi Kappa Psi; Touchdown Club. Polit. & Govt. Pos: Mayor, Tulsa, Okla, 66-; alternate del, Rep. Nat. Conv, 68. Bus. & Prof. Pos: Mem. bd. trustees, Holland Hall Sch, Tulsa, Okla, 60-; chmn, Alcoholic Beverage Control Bd, Oklahoma City, 61-64; mem. bd. trustees, Children's Med. Center, Tulsa, 64-; v.pres. bd. regents, Col. Lib. Arts, Chickasha, Okla, 65-66. Mil. Serv: Entered as Pvt, Army, 42, released as 1st Lt, 46. Mem: South. Hills Country Club; Summit Club; Tulsa Club; Dallas Petrol. Club. Rel: Episcopal. Mailing Add: 2454 E. 30th, Tulsa, Okla. 74114.

HEY, JOHN D
b. Providence, R.I, 4/8/31; s. John Hey and Mary Reynolds H; single. Educ: Boston Univ, A.B, 58; W.Va. Univ. Col. Law, 67- Polit. & Govt. Pos: Town clerk, Lincoln, R.I, 59-60; mem, Lincoln Dem. Town Exec. Cmt, 59-60; asst. city mgr, Wheeling, W.Va, 60-62; W.Va. rep, Housing of Urban Develop, Charleston, 62-65; asst. coordinator, Gov. Econ. Opportunity Agency, 65-66; proj. rev. officer, Econ. Develop. Agency, U.S. Commerce, Huntington, 66-67; alternate del, Dem. Nat. Conv, 68. Mil. Serv: Entered as Pvt, Army, 48, released as Sgt. 1/C, 55, after serv. in Transportation, ETO, 50-52. Mem: Mason; Shrine; Jesters; Elks; Army-Navy Club of Charleston, W.Va. Rel: Protestant. Mailing Add: 16 Diamond Ave, Wheeling, W.Va. 26003.

HEYDE, JAMES WALLACE R
Chmn, Fulton Co. Rep. Party, Ind.
b. Kosciusko Co, Ind, 7/8/33; s. Forest Russell Heyde and Esther Knox H; m. 8/29/54 to Lalla Jane Boswell; c. Edwin F, David B. and Robert H. Educ: Ind. Univ. Sch. of Bus, B.S. in mkt, 56; Alpha Tau Omega. Polit. & Govt. Pos: Del, Rep. State Conv, Ind, 60 & 64; city finance chmn, Rep. Party, 63; chmn, Fulton Co. Rep. Party, 64- Bus. & Prof. Pos: Exec. v.pres, McMahan Construct. Co, 60- Mil. Serv: Seaman, Navy, 56-57. Mem: Rochester C. of C; Elks; Ind. Univ. Alumni Asn; Ind. Soc. of Chicago; F&AM Lodge, Scottish Rite, Mizpah Temple; Asn. of Ind. Officials, Inc; pres, Jaycees, 61; U.S. Jaycees; Ind. State and Fulton Co. Young Rep; life mem, Ind. DeMolay Found, Inc. Rel: Methodist. Legal Res: 728 Jefferson, Rochester, Ind. 46975. Mailing Add: P.O. Box 378, Rochester, Ind. 46975.

HEYING, HILARIUS L. D
b. Winneshiek Co, Iowa, 8/19/14; s. John Heying; Elizabeth H; m. to Josephine M. Langreck; c. Terry, Ames, Sondra, Charles, Tresa. Educ: Columbia Acad, 1936. Polit. & Govt. Pos: Iowa State Sen, -66. Bus. & Prof. Pos: Businessman; Farmer; dir, Holy Name Cath. Church, 20 yrs. Mem: Rotary; K. of C; Country Club; C. of C; Holy Name Soc; Nat. Hatchery Fedn. Rel: Catholic. Mailing Add: 115 Jefferson St, West Union, Iowa 52175. (1967)

HIBBARD, HENRY SIEBEN R
Mont. State Sen.
b. Helena, Mont, 11/15/19; s. Alfred Tyler Hibbard and Margaret Sieben H; m. 10/5/45 to Jane Goodsill; Chase Tyler, Scott Goodsill and Whitney Sieben. Educ: Dartmouth Col, 37-39; Mont. State Univ, B.S, 41; Harvard Univ. Bus. Sch, M.B.A, 49; Beta Theta Pi. Polit. & Govt. Pos: Mont. State Rep, 61-65; Mont. State Sen, 65- Bus. & Prof. Pos: Pres, Sieben Livestock Co, Helena, Mont, 55; dir, Union Bank & Trust Co, 58; v.pres, Am. Sheep Prod. Coun, Denver, Colo, 68. Mil. Serv: Entered as Pvt, Army, 42, released as Capt, 45, after serv. in 20th Armored Div, ETO, 45; Bronze Star Medal. Mem: Am. Soc. Farm Mgt. and Rural Appraisers (Accredited Rural Appraiser); v.pres, Nat. Wool Growers Asn, 61-68; pres, Mont. Wool Growers Asn, 62-63; dir, Young Men's Christian Asn; dir, Salvation Army; Rotary; Coun. of 50, Univ. Mont; adv. coun, Mont. State Univ. Livestock Man of the Year, Little Int. Livestock Show, Mont. State Univ, 68. Rel: Episcopal. Legal Res: 618 Madison, Helena, Mont. 59601. Mailing Add: Box 835, Helena, Mont. 59601.

HIBBERD, LUCY REED D
Mem, Colo. Dem. State Exec. Cmt.
b. Austin, Tex, 1/2/41; d. Malcom Hiram Reed and Roberta Farish Purvis R; m. 2/22/61 to Frederick Hyde Hibberd, Jr; c. Frederick Hyde, III. Educ: Finch Col, 1 year; Univ. Tex, Austin, B.A, 61. Polit. & Govt. Pos: Dist. Chmn, Denver Co. Dem. Party, Colo, currently; mem, Colo. Dem. State Exec. Cmt, currently. Bus. & Prof. Pos: Dir, Dickson Properties, Austin, Tex, 62-; dir, Colo. River Develop. Co, Austin, 62- Rel: Protestant. Mailing Add: 1937 E. Alameda Ave, Denver Colo. 80209.

HIBLER, WILLIAM D, JR. D
Mo. State Rep.
b. Brunswick, Mo, 7/22/05; m. 5/19/35 to Jennie L. Friesz; c. Ina Kay and William D, III. Educ: Platte Commercial Col. Polit. & Govt. Pos: Mo. State Rep, 56-; state chmn, Farmers for Symington; mem, Mo. Dem. State Cmt, 64. Bus. & Prof. Pos: Farmer, worked in Fed. Agr. Progs, 34-54; ed, The Brunswicker, 54-55. Mem: Mason; Brunswick Club; Brunswick Lions Club. Rel: Methodist. Mailing Add: Brunswick, Mo. 65236.

HIBNER, ROY HENRY R
Ind. State Rep.
b. Michigan City, Ind, 11/5/03; s. William M. Hibner and Minnie Miller H; m. 6/16/31 to Florence H. Hildebrandt. Educ: Purdue Univ, Indust. Eng. Polit. & Govt. Pos: Councilman, Michigan City Coun, Ind, 48-52; pres, Michigan City Common Coun, 64-68; Ind. State Rep, 69- Bus. & Prof. Pos: Coordinator indust. eng, Weil-McLain Co, Inc, 45-68, asst. to v.pres. mfg, currently. Publ: 'Article on Human Relations,' Research Inst. of Am, 54. Mem: Lions (past pres); Michigan City Symphony Orchestra (past pres); Salvation Army (past pres. Adv. Bd); Toastmasters' Club (past pres). Awarded life mem. in Ind. PTA; awarded Bronze Medallion by Research Inst. of Am. Rel: Lutheran. Mailing Add: 418 School St, Michigan City, Ind. 46360.

HICHENS, WALTER WILSON R
Maine State Rep.
b. Lynn, Mass, 3/8/17; s. Walter G. Hichens and Mary Norton H; m. 11/8/41 to Elmira A. Ballard; c. Walter W, Jr, Mary E, Jared C, Janice E, Judith I, Kathy A, Bethany L, Myra C.(deceased) and Laurie J.(deceased). Educ: Essex Agr. & Tech. Inst, Hathorne, Mass, 37. Polit. & Govt. Pos: Selectman, Eliot, Maine, 52-55, water dist. dir, 56-59; Maine State Rep, 67- Mem: State pres, Gideons Int, 57-60; field dir, Maine Christian Civic League, 64-; York Co. Poultry Asn; pres, Eliot C. of C, 65-68. Rel: American Baptist. Legal Res: N. Main St, Eliot, Maine 03903. Mailing Add: Box 211, Eliot, Maine 03903.

HICKEL, WALTER J. R
Secy, Dept. of the Interior
b. Claflin, Kans, 8/18/19; s. Robert A. Hickel and Emma Zecha H; m.

11/22/45 to Ermalee Strutz; c. Theodore J, Robert J, Walter J, Jr, Jack Edward, Joseph W. and Karl. Educ: Claflin High Sch, Kans, grad. Polit. & Govt. Pos: Rep. Nat. Committeeman, Alaska, 54-64; Gov, Alaska, 66-68; del, Rep. Nat. Conv, 68; Secy, Dept. of the Interior, 69- Bus. & Prof. Pos: Pres. and owner, Hickel Investment Co, Anchorage, Alaska, 57-66. Mem: Capitol Hill Club; Arctic Club, Harbor Club, Wash. Athletic Club and Town & Country Club, Seattle; Petroleum Club and Elks, Anchorage; Navy League of U.S; K. of C; Pioneers of Alaska. Alaskan of the Year, 69. Rel: Catholic. Legal Res: Anchorage, Alaska. Mailing Add: 6151 Interior Bldg, Washington, D.C. 20240.

HICKENLOOPER, BOURKE BLAKEMORE R
b. Blockton, Iowa, 7/21/96; s. Nathan O. Hickenlooper and Margaret A. Blakemore H; m. 1927 to Verna E. Bensch; c. Mrs. Russell Oberlin and David B. Educ: Iowa State Col, B.S; Univ. Iowa Law Sch, J.D. Hon. LL.D, Parsons Col, Loras Col. and Upper Iowa Univ; hon. D.C.L, Elmira Col. Polit. & Govt. Pos: Iowa State Rep, 34 & 36; Lt. Gov, Iowa, 38 & 40, Gov, 42; U.S. Sen, Iowa, 44-69; del, Rep. Nat. Conv, 68. Bus. & Prof. Pos: Attorney-at-law. Mil. Serv: First Officers Training Camp, Ft. Snelling, Minn, 17; 3339th Field Artil, U.S. and France; discharged 19. Mem: Many fraternal and prfnl. orgns. Rel: Methodist. Mailing Add: 200 First Ave. N.E, Cedar Rapids, Iowa. 52401.

HICKERSON, MARCUS R. D
b. Waco, Tex, 9/10/26; s. Marcus C. Hickerson and Emily Sparks H; m. 7/6/51 to Renda Louise Morgan; c. Marcus Neale, Lisa Annette and Stephen Rea. Educ: N.Tex. State Univ, B.B.A, with honors. Polit. & Govt. Pos: Mem, Tex. Dem. Adv. Coun, 52-56; chmn, Ellis Co. Del, Dem. State Conv, 56; alternate del, Dem. Nat. Conv, 64. Bus. & Prof. Pos: Pres. and dir, Holly Corp, 61- Mil. Serv: Midn, Merchant Marine, 44; Pvt, Air Force, 50; Capt.(Ret), Air Material Command Res, 52. Legal Res: 929 Miramar, Claremont, Calif. 91711. Mailing Add: 1111 W. Foothill, Azusa, Calif. 91702.

HICKEY, JAMES CLYDE D
Mem, Jefferson Co. Dem. Exec. Cmt, Ky.
b. Big Sandy, Tenn, 9/25/36; s. R.G. Hickey and Clara York H; single. Educ: Vanderbilt Univ, B.A, 59; Duke Univ, LL.B, 65; Phi Kappa Psi; Phi Alpha Delta. Polit. & Govt. Pos: Del, Dem. Nat. Conv, 68; chmn, 32nd Legis. Dist. Dem. Party, Ky, 68-69; mem, Jefferson Co. Dem. Exec. Cmt, Ky, 68- Bus. & Prof. Pos: Asst. dir, Ky. Cmn. Human Rights, Frankfort, 65-66; assoc, Erwin A. Sherman, Attorney, Louisville, 66-68; assoc, Jones, Ewen, MacKenzie & Peden, Attorneys, 68-69. Mil. Serv: Entered as Ens, Navy, 59, released as Lt.(jg), 62, after serv. in U.S.S. Lexington, CVA-16, West. Pac, 59-62; Lt. Res. Mem: Louisville, Ky, and Am. Bar Asns. Rel: Presbyterian. Mailing Add: 2701 Brownsboro Rd, Louisville, Ky. 40206.

HICKEY, JOHN JOSEPH D
b. Rawlins, Wyo, 8/22/11; s. John J. Hickey and Brigid O'Meara H; m. 1/14/46 to Winifred Espy; c. John David and Paul Joseph. Educ: Univ. of Wyo, LL.B, 34; Sigma Alpha Epsilon. Polit. & Govt. Pos: City treas, Rawlins, Wyo, 35; co. prosecuting attorney, Carbon Co, 38 & 46; former U.S. Attorney, Cheyenne; Gov, Wyo, 59-61; U.S. Sen, Wyo, 61-63; Judge, U.S. Court of Appeals, Tenth Circuit, currently. Bus. & Prof. Pos: Admitted to Wyo. Bar, 34; law practice in Rawlins, 34-42. Mil. Serv: Capt, Army, 42-45. Mem: Bd. dirs, Carbon Co. Mem. Hosp, 35-42; dir. and treas, Hosp. Bd, 36-42; VFW (Comdr, Wyo. Dept, 49-50); K. of C; Elks; Lions, Serra (Cheyenne). Rel: Roman Catholic. Mailing Add: 3418 Central Ave, Cheyenne, Wyo. 82001.

HICKEY, PATRICK JOSEPH D
Mo. State Rep.
b. St. Louis, Mo, 9/25/28; m. 11/25/50 to Delores Marie Slawson; c. Maureen, Deborah, Kathleen, Patrick Joseph, Jr. and Mary Ann. Educ: Blewett High Sch. Polit. & Govt. Pos: Alderman, St. Ann, Mo; v.chmn, Mo. State Rep. Cmt; chmn, Mo. Labor Cmt; Mo. State Rep, 58- Bus. & Prof. Pos: Pipefitter. Mil. Serv: Army, 82nd Airborne Div. Mem: Officer, St. Louis Co. Young Dem; Pipefitters Local 562. Rel: Catholic. Mailing Add: 4508 St. Leo Lane, St. Ann, Mo. 63074. (1967)

HICKEY, WILLIAM, JR. D
Conn. State Sen.
b. Stamford, Conn, 1931; married. Polit. & Govt. Pos: Conn. State Sen, 61- Bus. & Prof. Pos: Attorney. Mailing Add: 30 Parry Rd, Springdale, Conn. 06907. (1967)

HICKEY-EVANS, TERRI R. R
Mem, Calif. Rep. State Cent. Cmt.
b. Los Angeles, Calif, 9/27/34; d. Raymond Ellis Tronsgard and Jeri McQuire Wofford T; div; c. Michael, Jerilyn, Randyl and Scott. Educ: Citrus Jr. Col, Calif, 2 years; Mt. San Antonio Jr. Col, working on A.A. in Polit. Sci, currently. Polit. & Govt. Pos: Asst. chmn, 25th Cong. Dist. for Spencer Williams, Calif, 66; regional dir, Ronald Reagan Campaign, 66; assoc. mem, Calif. Rep. State Cent. Cmt, 66-68, mem, 68-; alternate, Los Angeles Co. Rep. Cent. Cmt, currently; exec. confidential secy, Henry Quevedo Campaign for Calif. State Assemblyman, 68; exec. confidential secy. to exec. dir, Inter-Agency of Mex. Am. Affairs, Wash, D.C, 69- Bus. & Prof. Pos: Exec. Admin. Secy, Day & Night Mfg. Co, 63-66; legal secy, 66-69. Mem: Legal Secy. Asn; Prof. Secy. of Today; Calif. Rep. Assembly (Past v.pres. and secy); Young Rep.(pres); Women's Rep. Federated; Pueblos of Los Angeles Rep. Asn.(corresponding secy); Covina Jr. Football Conf; Covina Pony League Asn. Rel: Episcopal. Legal Res: 2228 Chapman Rd, Hyattsville, Md. 20783. Mailing Add: Inter-American Agency Mexican-American Affairs, 1800 G St. N.W, Washington, D.C. 20506.

HICKLE, RALPH R
N.Dak. State Rep.
b. Sanger, N.Dak, 2/18/04; s. Sherman Hickle and Nellie Lamb H; m. 2/19/46 to Doris Christenson; c. Rodney, Janice, Arlene, Crystal, Carmen and Robert. Educ: Night Col. Classes. Polit. & Govt. Pos: Committeeman, Co. Agr. Stabilization and Conserv. Serv, N.Dak, 36-45; chmn, Co. Soil Conserv. Serv, 46-69; N.Dak. State Rep, 33rd Dist, 64-; chmn, 33rd Dist. Rep. Party, 66-, mem, exec. cmt, currently. Mem: Treas and dir, Co. Livestock & Crops Asn, 40-66; co. pres, Farm Bur, 48-64, state dir, 57-60; N.Dak. del. to Am. Sheep Producers, 56-69. Rel: Lutheran; Mem. Church Coun. until 64. Mailing Add: Center, N.Dak. 58530.

HICKLIN, EDWIN ANDERSON R
b. Wapello, Iowa, 6/13/22; s. Edwin R. Hicklin and Irene Anderson H; m. 6/21/47 to Carolyn Woods; c. Kathryn, Martha and Elizabeth. Educ: State Univ. Iowa, B.A, 46 and J.D, 48; Sigma Nu; Phi Delta Phi. Polit. & Govt. Pos: Co. attorney, Louisa Co, Iowa, 53-56; Iowa State Rep, 67 & 68; mem, State Bd. of Tax Rev, 69- Mil. Serv: Entered as Pvt, Army Air Force, 43, released as 1st Lt, 45, after serv. in 307th Bomb Group, 370th Squadron, Southwest Pac, 44-45; Air Medal with 3 Clusters; Pac. Theater and Philippine Liberation Medals. Mem: Louisa Co, Iowa State and Am. Bar Asns; AF&AM; Elks; Iowa Farm Bur. Rel: Episcopal. Mailing Add: Wapello, Iowa 52653.

HICKMAN, ANNE KENT R
b. Lenoir, N.C, 5/13/19; d. Robert Alexander Kent and Zella Anderson K; m. 8/7/44 to Malcolm Vance Hickman. Educ: Hudson High Sch, grad, 35; Lenoir Bus. Col, 36. Polit. & Govt. Pos: Nat. committeewoman, N.C. Young Rep, 48-51; dir, Region IV and auditor, Nat. Fedn. of Young Rep; precinct chmn, Forsyth Co. Rep. Exec. Cmt, 48-66, past secy. and v.chmn; v.chmn, N.C. Rep. Party, 52; organized, N.C. Fedn. of Rep. Women, 53, chmn. pub. rels. cmt, 65, pres, 66-69; past pres, Forsyth Co. Young Rep; past pres, Forsyth Co. Fedn. of Rep. Women; mem. bd. dirs, Nat. Fedn. of Rep. Women; chmn, Elec. Tellers Cmt, Nat. Fedn. Conv, 67; del, Rep. Nat. Conv, 68. Bus. & Prof. Pos: Serv. rep, Pa-N.Y. Cent. Transportation Co, Winston-Salem. Mem: Past pres, Pilot Club of Winston-Salem; past Lt. Gov. and Gov, Dist. Six and bd. dirs, Pilot Int; past v.chmn, Women's Group Action Coun, Winston-Salem; Forsyth Co. Cmt. on Pub. Solicitation and Forsyth Co. Civil Defense Bd. Dirs; past regional dir. and bd. dirs, East. States Women's Traffic Conf; past pres. and bd. dirs, Women's Traffic Club of Winston-Salem; bd. dirs, Assoc. Traffic Clubs and Fred Hooper Mem. Scholarship Fund. Hon. Life Membership, Forsyth Co. Young Rep. Club and N.C. Fedn. of Rep. Women; Outstanding Rep. Woman of Year in N.C, 68. Rel: Presbyterian. Mailing Add: 2700 Tudor Rd, Winston-Salem, N.C. 27101.

HICKMAN, CARTER MALCOLM D
Md. State Del.
b. Felton, Del, 8/25/10; s. Willard Hickman and Annie Killen H; m. 8/21/37 to Marion Elizabeth Hardesty; c. David Hardesty and Marion Suzanne (Mrs. John DeWitt Pratt). Educ: Wash. Col, B.S, 31; Columbia Univ, M.A, 34; Univ. Del. and Univ. Md, additional courses; Lambda Chi Alpha. Polit. & Govt. Pos: Md, State Del, Queen Anne's Co, 63-; mem, Md. Rep. Agr. Cmt, Coun. of State Govt, 64-; mem, Md. Gov. Cmt, to Study Drug Addiction, 65- Bus. & Prof. Pos: High sch. supvr, teacher and prin, Queen Anne's Co. Bd. Educ, 31-54; owner and mgr, Greensboro Supply Co, Inc, 54-65; real estate salesman, Anthony & Co, 60- Mem: Mason; Lions; Farm Bureau. Rel: Methodist; Bd. Trustees and Lay Del, Church Hill Methodist Church. Mailing Add: Walnut Hill Farm, Church Hill, Md. 21623.

HICKMAN, MARCUS TOBIAS R
b. Hudson, N.C, 10/2/22; s. Marcus Tobias Hickman and Claudia Cline H; m. 9/16/48 to Mary Kensing Currie Frey; c. Mary Stuart, William Davidson and Marcus Tobias. Educ: Duke Univ, A.B, 43, Law Sch, LL.B, 48; Phi Beta Kappa; Order of the Coif; Phi Delta Phi; Tau Kappa Alpha; Kappa Alpha Order. Polit. & Govt. Pos: Mem. exec. cmt, Young Rep. Nat. Fedn, 53-57; mem, N.C. Rep. Exec. Cmt, 53-68; chmn, N.C. Fedn. Young Rep. Clubs, 54-55; chmn, Mecklenburg Co. Rep. Exec. Cmt, N.C, 55-68; del, Rep. Nat. Conv, 56 & 64, alternate-at-large, 60. Bus. & Prof. Pos: Mem, Law Firm, Kennedy, Covington, Lobdell & Hickman, Charlotte, N.C. Mil. Serv: Entered as Ens, Navy, released as Lt, after serv. in Supply Corps; Am. Theater Ribbon; European-African-Mid. East Theater Ribbon; Asiatic-Pac. Theater Ribbon; Victory Medal; Naval Res. Medal; Lt. Comdr, Naval Res, discharged, 65. Mem: Am, N.C. and Mecklenburg Co. Bar Asns; Charlotte City Club; Myers Park Country Club; Pinehurst Country Club; Houds Ears Golf & Ski Club; Charlotte Exec. Club. Rel: Episcopal. Legal Res: 2225 Sanford Lane, Charlotte, N.C. 28211. Mailing Add: 1210 North Carolina National Bank Bldg, Charlotte, N.C. 28202. (1967)

HICKMAN, RUSSELL ORLANDO D
Md. State Del.
b. Showell, Md, 2/5/08; s. Charles H. Hickman and Eva Floyd H; m. 1/3/31 to Sadie Katherine Donaway; c. Herman William. Educ: High Sch. Polit. & Govt. Pos: Md. State Del, Worcester Co, 54-; del, Dem. Nat. Conv, 68. Bus. & Prof. Pos: Collection mgr, Mardelvia Finance Corp, Salisbury, Md, 25-29; field rep, Universal Credit Co, Phila, Pa, 29-31; farmer, assoc. with father, 31-40; mgr, U.S. Finance Co, Berlin, Md, 40- Mem: Lions; Farm Bur; dir, Worcester Co. Chap. Am. Red Cross. Rel: Methodist; chmn. off. bd, Whaleysville Methodist Church. Mailing Add: Whaleysville, Md. 21872.

HICKMAN, THOMAS EDWIN, JR. R
Del. State Sen.
b. Ocean View, Del, 9/6/15; s. Thomas Edwin Hickman and Nettie E. Melson H; m. 10/13/37 to Kathryn Mae Williams; c. Anita H. (Mrs. Evans), Susan H. (Mrs. West) and Deborah Ann. Educ: Randolph-Macon Col, A.B, 36; Sigma Phi Epsilon. Polit. & Govt. Pos: Del. State Sen, 18th Dist, 69- Bus. & Prof. Pos: High Sch. teacher, John M. Clayton Sch, 36-41; Salesman and Plant mgr, Consolidated Products Co, 41-49; Mgr. and partner, Hickman & Willey, Inc, 49- Mem: AF&AM (Past Master, Doric Lodge 30); Lions (past pres, Lord Baltimore Club). Rel: Methodist, Trustee, Mariners Bethel Methodist Church. Mailing Add: R.D. 2, Frankford, Del. 19945.

HICKS, ARCH R, JR. R
b. Le Vanna, Ohio, 10/13/15; s. Arch. R. Hicks, Sr. and Nellie Pangburn H; m. 10/17/37 to Monica Brown; c. Carol (Mrs. Cooper) and Linda Kay. Educ: Ohio State Univ, LL.B, 37; Delta Theta Phi. Polit. & Govt. Pos: Mayor, Ripley, Ohio, 40; prosecuting attorney, Brown Co, 41-49; alternate del, Rep. Nat. Conv, 48, 52 & 60; village solicitor, Ripley, Aberdeen, Higginsport and Russellville, Ohio, currently. Mem: Pres, Brown Co. Bar Asn, 62-63; Ohio

State and Am. Bar Asns; Am. Judicature Soc; trustee, Brown Co. Gen. Hosp; pres, Ripley Pub. Libr; Kiwanis (pres, Ripley Club, 45). Rel: Church of Christ. Mailing Add: 417 Main St, Ripley, Ohio, 45167.

HICKS, DAVID L. R
Chmn, Eaton Co. Rep. Party, Mich.
b. Alma, Mich, 10/4/39; s. Mervin L. Hicks and Charlotte Vernon H; m. 12/30/61 to Sally J. Severson; c. Jane and Jynell. Educ: Ferris State Col. Polit. & Govt. Pos: Finance chmn, Eaton Co. Rep. Party, Mich, 65, chmn, 66-; del, Rep. Nat. Conv, 68. Bus. & Prof. Pos: Mgr, Radio Stas. WCER & WCER-FM, Charlotte, Mich, 64- Mem: Kiwanis (past pres, Charlotte Club). Man of the Year Award, 65. Rel: Protestant. Mailing Add: 206 Cambridge Dr, Charlotte, Mich. 48813.

HICKS, DICK WALTON D
b. Bandera, Tex, 7/10/15; s. Elvious Hicks and Pearl Harriss H; m. 6/23/40 to Carmen Connally; c. Jeanine, Charmen, Dick Walton, Jr. and David Connally. Educ: Tex. A&M Univ, B.S. Bus. & Prof. Pos: Rancher. Mil. Serv: Entered as Pvt, Army, 42, released as Capt, 46, after serv. in ETO; Battle Star; N.Africa and Italy Campaign Ribbons. Mem: Tex. Sheep & Goat Raisers Asn; Tex. and Southwest. Cattle Raisers Asn. Rel: Baptist. Mailing Add: Bandera, Tex. 78003. (1967)

HICKS, ERNEST LEE D
b. Ionia, Mich, 9/15/92; s. John Thomas Hicks and Gazella Clark H; m. 5/3/20 to Susan Garth Bible; c. John Darwin, Marilee Clark (Mrs. John N. McLaughlin) and Suzanne Jones (Mrs. James P. Rickards). Educ: Olivet Col; Univ. Mich. Polit. & Govt. Pos: N.C. State Rep, 53-69. Bus. & Prof. Pos: Pres, Pettit Motor Co. Mil. Serv: Ens, Naval Res. Mem: Charlotte Merchants Asn. (mem. legis. cmt, pres, 52); Charlotte Auto Dealers Asn. (past pres. and dir); N.C. Auto Dealers Asn.(mem. legis. cmt, 50); Nat. Ford Dealer Coun, 52; Charlotte C. of C.(dir); AF&AM (past Master, 30-31); Carolina Consistory; Charlotte Oasis Temple; Charlotte Exec. Club; Charlotte City Club; Myers Park Country Club; Charlotte Rotary (pres, 51-52, mem. bd. dirs, 49); past dir. bd, Commun. Chest. Rel: Presbyterian; Deacon, 27. Mailing Add: 500 Clement Ave, Charlotte, N.C. 28204.

HICKS, FLOYD V. D
U.S. Rep, Wash.
b. Prosser, Wash, 5/29/15; s. J.Otis Hicks and Ruth I. Crofutt; m. 6/20/42 to Norma Jeanne Zintheo; c. Tracie and Betsie. Educ: Cent. Wash. State Col, B.Ed, 38; Univ. Wash. Law Sch, LL.B, 48. Polit. & Govt. Pos: Judge, Pierce Co. Superior Court, Wash, 61-63; U.S. Rep, Wash, 64-; del, Dem. Nat. Conv, 68. Bus. & Prof. Pos: Teacher, 35-42; lawyer, 48- Mil. Serv: Capt, Army Air Force, 42-46. Mem: Am. Bar Asn; Kiwanis. Mailing Add: 3301 N. 30th St, Tacoma, Wash. 98407.

HICKS, HARLEY IRVING R
Mem, Iowa Co. Rep. Co. Exec. Cmt, Wis.
b. Linden, Wis, 9/21/97; s. Thomas Hicks and Elizabeth Wearing H; m. 11/26/20 to Vera Fish. Educ: Valparaiso Univ; Alpha Epsilon. Polit. & Govt. Pos: Mem, Iowa Co. Bd. Supvrs. Wis. and chmn, 58-59; chmn, Iowa Co. Rep. Orgn, until 68; mem, Iowa Co. Rep. Co. Exec. Cmt, currently; mem, Bd. of Vet. Affairs, Wis, currently. Bus. & Prof. Pos: Pres. and chmn. bd, Dodgeville State Bank, Wis. Mil. Serv: Entered Army, 18, Hosp. Unit Base 131, served at Mars-sur-Allier-A.P.O. 780 France. Mem: Former post comdr, Co. comdr, dist. comdr, 3rd Dist, Wis. Am. Legion and Dept. v.comdr. of State; chmn. bd. trustees, Camp Am. Legion; past chmn, Finance Cmt, Legion and v.chmn, Nat. Econ. Cmn. of Nat. Legion; pres, Dodgeville Kiwanis, 47; Dodgeville Blue Lodge, Masonic, Consistory and Ambassador-at-lg, Zor Shrine, Madison; past chmn, Park Bd, past pres, Athletic Asn. Rel: Methodist. Mailing Add: 415 W. Merrimac St, Dodgeville, Wis. 53533.

HICKS, HENRY NICHOLS Independent
Vt. State Rep.
b. Weathersfield, Vt, 8/13/06; m. to Helen LaVenture; c. 1 daughter. Educ: Cushing Acad; N.Y.M.A. Polit. & Govt. Pos: Trustee, Village of Perkinsville, Vt, 46; selectman, Weathersfield, 47-55; Vt. State Rep, 63- Bus. & Prof. Pos: Retired bus. agent, U.E. 218, Springfield, Vt. Rel: Protestant. Mailing Add: Perkinsville, Vt. 05151. (1967)

HICKS, HERVEY OWINGS D
Miss. State Rep.
b. Benton, Miss, 8/9/00; married. Polit. & Govt. Pos: Miss. State Rep, 32-36, 48-64 and currently. Bus. & Prof. Pos: Planter; livestock dealer. Mem: Mason; dir, Yazoo City Farm Bur; Methodist Mens Club; Benton Farmers Club. Rel: Methodist. Mailing Add: Route 1, Box 64, Benton, Yazoo Co, Miss. 39039. (1967)

HICKS, JOHN THOMAS, SR. D
Tenn. State Rep.
b. Nashville, Tenn, 8/5/25; s. John George Hicks and Rhoea Briley H; m. 3/27/48 to Peggy Tomlin; c. Donna Joyce and John Thomas, Jr. Educ: Univ. Tenn, adv. acct. cert. Polit. & Govt. Pos: Tenn. State Rep, 11th Legis. Dist, 67- Mil. Serv: Navy, 42-46, Machinist Mate 2/C. Mem: Nat. Soc. Pub. Acct; Tenn. Asn. Pub. Acct; Al Menah Temple; McQuirtersville Lodge; Lions; VFW; Am. Legion. Outstanding Pub. Acct. of Year 67-68. Rel: Methodist. Legal Res: 2820 Windemerd Dr, Nashville, Tenn. 37214. Mailing Add: 2517 Lebanon Rd, Nashville, Tenn. 37214.

HICKS, PAUL EDWARD D
W.Va. State Del.
b. Logan, W.Va, 10/20/23; s. Cecil L. Hicks and Almeta Bryant H; m. 6/12/53 to Betty Lou Rayburn; c. Paula Lou, Mary Susan and David Edward. Educ: Logan High Sch, grad, 42. Polit. & Govt. Pos: Recorder, West Logan, W.Va, 51, mayor, 52-55 & 58-59; W.Va. State Del, 68- Bus. & Prof. Pos: Motor tank salesman, Esso Standard Oil Co, 47-49, serv. sta. owner and operator, 49-54; plant mgr, Ashland Oil & Refining Co, 54- Mil. Serv: Entered as Pvt, Air Force, 43, released as T/Sgt, 46, after serv. in Fifth Air Force, S.Pac. Theatre, 43-45; Am. Theatre and S.Pac. Theatre Ribbons; Philippine Liberation Award; Five Bronze Stars; Presidential Unit Citation; Asiatic Pac. Oper. Ribbon; Good Conduct Medal; Bismarc Archipelago Medal. Mem: VFW, Logan, W.Va; Mason; Moose. Rel: Baptist. Mailing Add: 308 Ninth St, West Logan, W.Va. 25601.

HICKS, VANCE DODSWORTH R
Mem, Town Rep. Cmt, Weston, Conn.
b. Brooklyn, N.Y, 2/8/15; s. Oscar Penn Hicks and Flora Dodsworth Holland H; m. to Miriam Anna Provost; c. Karen Elizabeth, Curtis Vance Dodsworth and Neal Provost. Educ: Ohio Univ. Polit. & Govt. Pos: Chmn, Town Rep. Cmt, Weston, Conn, 64-68, mem, 64-; mem. bd, Aspetuck Valley Health Dist, Weston-Westport, 66-; dep. sheriff, Fairfield Co, 68- Bus. & Prof. Pos: Media rels. expert, Young & Rubicam, Inc, 38-68 (Ret). Mil. Serv: Entered as Pvt, Army, 41, released as 1st Sgt, 46, after serv. in 43rd AAA Brigade, ETO; Europe-Africa-Middle East. Ribbon with 2 Battle Stars and Am. Defense Serv. and Am. Campaign Ribbons; Good Conduct Medal; Victory Medal. Mem: DeMolay (Legion of Honor); F&AM. Rel: Congregational. Mailing Add: P.O. Box 1255, Weston, Conn. 06880.

HICKSON, ROBERT C. R
b. Mount Gilead, Ohio, 8/24/28; s. Charles C. Hickson and Marian Sampson H; m. 2/13/54 to Mary Jean Sturrock; c. Robert C, Jr. and Thomas M. Educ: Ohio Wesleyan Univ, A.B, 50; Ohio State Univ, M.B.A, 52; Phi Mu Alpha; Alpha Kappa Delta; Alpha Tau Omega. Polit. & Govt. Pos: Committeeman, Morrow Co. Rep. Cent. Cmt, Ohio, 63-68, chmn, 64-68. Bus. & Prof. Pos: Auditor, Ohio Bell Tel. Co, 52-54; partner, Hickson-Ins-Realty, 54-; chmn, The Peoples Bank, 65-, pres, 67- Mem: Kiwanis (past pres, Mt. Gilead Kiwanis); C. of C.(past pres); Mason (32°). Young Man of the Year Award, Jr. C. of C, Morrow Co, Ohio. Rel: Methodist. Mailing Add: 371 N. Main St, Mount Gilead, Ohio 43338.

HIERING, WILLIAM THOMAS R
N.J. State Sen.
b. Seaside Heights, N.J, 12/27/15; s. Albert C. Hiering and Phoebe M. McGann H; m. 5/31/40 to Marie R. Lame; c. William T, Jr, Marea Christine, Robert and Carol. Educ: Wharton Sch. of Finance & Commerce, Univ. Pa, B.S. in Econ; Georgetown Law Sch; Rutgers Law Sch, LL.B. Polit. & Govt. Pos: N.J. State Assemblyman, 60-65; N.J. State Sen, Fifth Dist, 66-; del, Rep. Nat. Conv, 68. Bus. & Prof. Pos: Sr. partner, Hiering, Grasso & Gelzer, Law Firm, 52- Mil. Serv: Entered as Ens, Navy, 42, released as Lt, 46, after serv. in Supply Corps, Aleutian Islands; Battle Attu Ribbon; Navy Commendation Ribbon. Mem: Elks; Rotary; K. of C; VFW; Am. Legion; Navy League. Rel: Catholic. Mailing Add: 9 Central Ave, Toms River, N.J. 08753. (1967)

HIESTAND, EDGAR WILLARD R
b. Chicago, Ill, 12/3/88; s. Henry Hiestand and Sarah Willard H; m. 7/21/11 to Berenice Craft; c. Barbara (Mrs. Fred H. Bragassa), Mary (Mrs. D. McCoy), Janet (Mrs. Norman E. Watts). Educ: Dartmouth, A.B, 10. Polit. & Govt. Pos: U.S. Rep, Calif, 53-64; pres, Bd. Educ, San Marino, Calif. Bus. & Prof. Pos: Dir, Better Bus. Bur; stores mgr, Sears, Roebuck & Co, Los Angeles, 39-49, Tulsa, 32-39, Atlanta, 32-32; various pos. with Filene's, Boston, Hudson's, Detroit, The Broadway, Los Angeles, Pogue's, Cinn, 12-31. Mem: Gen. Staff War Col, World War I; Rotary (past dist. gov, pres, dir.); Calif. Univ. Club (Los Angeles); Calif. Club, Los Angeles; Univ. Club, Pasadena. Mailing Add: 101 N. Grand Ave, Pasadena, Calif. 91103.

HIESTAND, JOSEPH FRANKLIN R
Ohio State Rep.
b. Hillsboro, Ohio, 11/28/06; s. Harry C. Hiestand and Ella Gabriel H; m. 3/18/38 to Mary Roselyn Custer; c. James Edwin, Linda (Mrs. Dennis) and Marilyn Ruth. Educ: Officers' Training Sch, Commercial Pilot. Polit. & Govt. Pos: Cmnr, Highland Co, Ohio, 57-64; Ohio State Rep, 20th Dist, 65-, mem, Agr. Conserv, Govt. Opers. and Hist. Cmts, Ohio State House of Rep. Bus. & Prof. Pos: Farm owner and mgr; dir, N.Am. Life Assurance Co, 66; shooting instr. Mil. Serv: 1st Lt, Army Air Force, 41-45; Lt. Col, Air Force Res, until 66. Publ: 'Clues by Joe,' Rifleman; 'Shooting Tips,' Trap and Field. Mem: Rotary; Mason (32°); C. of C; Elks; Am. Trapshooting Asn; Farm Bur. N.Am. Trapshooting Champion; mem, All American Trapshooting Team, 20 times; holder of World Record in Trapshooting. Rel: Methodist; Trustee. Legal Res: Route 5, Box 31, Hillsboro, Ohio 45133. Mailing Add: Ohio State Capitol Bldg, Columbus, Ohio 43215. (1967)

HIGGINS, JOSEPH J. D
N.J. State Assemblyman
b. Elizabeth, N.J, 10/12/29; married; c. three. Educ: Seton Hall Univ, B.S; Georgetown Law Center, LL.B. Polit. & Govt. Pos: N.J. State Assemblyman, currently. Bus. & Prof. Pos: Attorney; former exec. secy. to U.S. Sen. Harrison A. Williams, Jr. Mil. Serv: Navy. Mem: K. of C. Mailing Add: State House, Trenton, N.J. 08625.

HIGGINS, MARION WEST R
b. New York, N.Y, 1/9/15; d. Dr. James Edward West (deceased) and Marion Speaks W; m. 8/16/41 to William Francis Higgins; c. William Francis, Jr. and Robert Kevin. Educ: Mt. Holyoke Col, B.A, 36; Katharine Gibbs Secretarial Sch, 37; St. John's Law Sch, 41. Polit. & Govt. Pos: Mem, Recreation Cmn, Hillsdale, N.J, 54-56; committeewoman, Bergen Co. Rep. Cmt, 54-68; mem, Bergen Co. Park Cmn, 56-59; N.J. State Assemblyman, 59-65, Majority Leader, N.J. Gen. Assembly, 64, Speaker of House, 65; mem, exec. cmt, N.J. Rep. Platform Cmt, 61 & 63; mem, exec. cmt, N.J. State Rep. Cmt, 64-65; Acting Gov, N.J, 65; former v.pres, N.J. Fedn. Rep. Women; former v.pres, Bergen Co. Women's Rep. Club. Bus. & Prof. Pos: Real estate and ins. broker; v.pres, William F. Higgins Agency, Inc, 45- Mem: Hillsdale Rep. Club; Col. Club of Ridgewood; Woman's Clubs of Hillsdale, Ridgewood and Westwood. Golf, women's tournament play, Westchester-Fairfield Counties, 1940's. Rel: Roman Catholic. Mailing Add: 90 Werimus Rd, Hillsdale, N.J. 07642.

HIGGINS, MARTIN JOSEPH D
b. New York, N.Y, 5/18/38; s. Walter J. Higgins and Aileen T. Walsh H; m. 5/15/65 to Evan Kathrine Larocque; c. Melissa Marie. Educ: Tufts, B.A, 60; N.Y. Univ. Grad. Sch. of Bus. Admin; Delta Upsilon. Polit. & Govt. Pos: Co-chmn. cmt, N.Y. State Young Dems, 60; alternate del, Dem. Nat. Conv,

64; aide to Abraham D. Beame, Mayoral Campaign, 65. Bus. & Prof. Pos: Dir, Gold Medallion Vending Corp, Inc, 64-; pres. and dir, Evan Realty Co, 64-; dir. mgt. real estate investments, Wien, Lane, Klein and Malkin, 66-; dir, Higwil Matrix Co, 66- Mil. Serv: Airman 1/C, N.Y. State Air Nat. Guard, 66- Mem: Nat. Dem. Club, N.Y. Co-capt, Tufts Univ. football, 59. Rel: Roman Catholic. Mailing Add: 60 E. 42nd St, New York, N.Y. 10017.

HIGGINS, MARY CLAIRE R
b. Tulsa, Okla, 10/6/26; d. William Henry Higgins and Agnes Josserand H. Educ: Univ. of Tulsa. Polit. & Govt. Pos: Former exec. secy. to U.S. Rep. Page Belcher, Okla, admin. asst, currently. Bus. & Prof. Pos: Legal Secy, Ungerman, Whitebrook, Grabel & Ungerman, Attorneys at Law, Tulsa, Okla, 45-46. Mem: Kappa Delta; Pro-Am; Young Rep.(Col); Tulsa Co. Young Rep; Rep. Women's Club; Fedn. of Rep. Women; D.C. Young Rep. Alumni rush adv, Kappa Delta. Mailing Add: 1427 N. Nash St, Apt. 23, Arlington, Va. 22209. (1967)

HIGGINS, NED PRESTON R
Mem, Morrow Co. Rep. Cent. Cmt, Ohio
b. Mt. Gilead, Ohio, 8/11/23; s. Clark Higgins and Josie Fogle H; m. 12/18/49 to Roberta Geyer; c. Robert, Dale, John and Nancy. Educ: Mt. Gilead High Sch, Ohio, grad, 43. Polit. & Govt. Pos: Mem, Morrow Co. Rep. Cent. Cmt, Ohio, 58-; mem, Morrow Co. Elec. Bd, 68- Bus. & Prof. Pos: Farmer, 49; milk tester, Ohio State Univ, 63. Mil. Serv: Entered as Pvt, Air Force, 43, released as Sgt, 45, after serv. in Ninth Air Force, ETO, 44-46. Mem: Farm Bur; Morrow Co. Bd. for the Retarded. Efficient Prod. Award, State of Ohio, 65. Rel: Protestant. Mailing Add: Route 3, Fredericktown, Ohio 43019.

HIGGINS, RAYMOND J Conservative
Minn. State Sen.
b. Duluth, Minn, 1919; m. to Mary Helen Butler; c. Five. Educ: Georgetown Univ, Wash, D.C, B.S, Chem. Polit. & Govt. Pos: Minn. State Sen, 64- Bus. & Prof. Pos: Property mgt. and bus. investments; dir, Minn. Arrowhead Asn; dir, North. City Nat. Bank of Duluth. Mil. Serv: Inf. Officer, Army. Mem: Am. Inst. of Mining, Metallurgical & Petroleum Engrs. Legal Res: 420 Hawthorne Rd, Duluth, Minn. 55801. Mailing Add: 735 First American National Bank Bldg, Duluth, Minn. 55802. (1967)

HIGGINS, SAMMIE L. R
Mem, Calif. Rep. State Cent. Cmt.
b. Ft. Worth, Tex, 5/11/23; s. Leon Higgins and Elnora Evans H; m. 1951 to Vicki Ricks; c. Benita and Donald. Educ: Air Force Admin. Sch, Ft. Logan, Colo, 44; Univ. Denver, B.S. in Bus. Admin, 54; Merritt Col, Assoc. Arts in Sociol, 67; Univ. Utah; Utah State Univ; San Francisco State Col; West Theol. Sem; mem. bd. dirs, Collegiate C. of C; secy, Student Christian Asn; mem. judicial coun, Student Senate; keeper of the records and seal, Omega Psi Phi. Polit. & Govt. Pos: Mem, Collegiate Young Rep, Denver, Colo, Box Elder Co. Rep. Cent. Cmt, Utah and exec. cmt, Shelby Co. Rep. Cent. Cmt, Tenn; mem, Alameda Co. Rep. Cent. Cmt, Calif, Calif. Rep. State Cent. Cmt. and exec. cmt, San Francisco Co. Young Rep, currently; chmn, Southwest Berkeley United Rep. Precinct Orgn, Alameda Co, Calif, currently; cand. develop. cmt, 17th Assembly Dist. Rep. Coord. Coun, Calif, currently; dir, North Berkeley Rep. Assembly, Calif. Rep. Assembly, currently; del, Alameda Co. Coordinating Rep. Assembly, Calif. Rep. Assembly, currently; secy. Rep. coun. for equal opportunity, San Francisco Co. Rep. Cent. Cmt, currently. Bus. & Prof. Pos: Accountant, San Francisco, Calif, 55-61; youth coordinator, Memphis Juvenile Cmn, 65-66; sr. minister, Mt. Marks Methodist Church, Oakland, Calif, Amos Temple Methodist Church, Ogden, Utah, Coleman Chapel Methodist Church, Memphis, Tenn. and Warren Chapel Methodist Church, Milan Tenn; asst. minister, Phillips Temple Methodist Church, Oakland, Calif. Mil. Serv: Entered as Pvt, Army, released as Cpl, after serv. in 92nd Inf. Div; Am. Defense and Good Conduct Medals; Purple Heart. Mem: Methodist Clergymans Coun.(secy); Rel. Educ. Press Club; Nat. Notary Pub. Asn; Denver Real Estate Bd; Colo. Tax Consult. Asn; Boy Scouts (dist. cmnr); Men of Tomorrow (bd. dirs); YMCA (mgt. cmt); Urban League (bd. dirs); Metrop. Methodist Men's Coun.(bd. dirs); Am. Legion educ. cmt; Mason; Elks. Named Outstanding Citizen of Ogden, Utah, 64. Rel: Methodist. Mailing Add: 1810 Ward St, Berkeley, Calif. 94703.

HIGGINS, THOMAS S. D
Solicitor, Camden Co. Dem. Party, N.J.
b. Camden, N.J, 4/23/35; s. John B. Higgins (deceased) and Katherine M. Keane H.(deceased); m. 12/16/61 to Kathleen M. Murphy; c. Kathleen, Colleen, Thomas, Daniel and Sean. Educ: St. Joseph's Col, B.S, 58; Villanova Univ, J.D, 62; Villiger Debating Soc. Polit. & Govt. Pos: Munic. judge, Gloucester Twp, N.J, 62-63; asst. prosecutor, Camden Co, 63-65; dep. attorney gen, N.J, 65-67; solicitor of borough, Stratford, 68; Dem. nominee, U.S. Rep, N.J, 68; solicitor, Camden Co. Dem. Party, 69- Bus. & Prof. Pos: Attorney-at-law, N.J, 62- Mil. Serv: Cadet, AFROTC, 54-56. Mem: Am, N.J. and Camden Co. Bar Asns; K. of C. Rel: Catholic. Legal Res: 14 Sunnybrook Rd, Stratford, N.J. 08084. Mailing Add: 14 E. King's Hwy, Mt. Ephraim, N.J. 08059.

HIGGS, RUFUS FRANKLIN, JR. D
Chmn, Erath Co. Dem. Exec. Cmt, Tex.
b. Stephenville, Tex, 1/31/26; s. Rufus Fielding Higgs and Johnnie Mae Sullivan H; m. 12/27/57 to Janice Carolyn Wood; c. Frances Kelly and John Tiner. Educ: Tarleton State Col, 44 and 46-47; Univ. Tex, 47-51; capt, Tarleton State Col. Track Team, 47. Polit. & Govt. Pos: Chmn, Erath Co. Dem. Exec. Cmt, Tex, currently; pres, Erath Co. Young Dem, 59. Mil. Serv: Pvt, Army Air Corps, 44-46. Mem: W.Tex. Press Asn; dir, Tex. Good Roads Asn, 65-66; Mason; Shrine; adj, Turnbow-Higgs Am. Legion Post 240, 53; Kiwanis (secy, 52, v.pres, 58 and pres, 59); dir, C. of C. Rel: Methodist. Mailing Add: 478 N. Belknap, Stephenville, Tex. 76401. (1967)

HIGH, MARY ELLEN R
V.Chmn, Second Cong. Dist. Rep. Cent. Cmt, Colo.
b. Topeka, Kans, 8/5/32; d. John William Nelson and Gertrude Elsena Shoaf N; m. 6/9/58 to John Meredith High; c. Clifton Nelson, Mary Ann and Christopher Alan. Educ: Washburn Univ, 1½ years; Zeta Tau Alpha. Polit. & Govt. Pos: Belle chmn, Brotzman Campaign, Jefferson Co, Colo, 66, co-chmn, 68; Rep. committeewoman, Precinct 605, Jefferson Co, 66-; second v.pres, Rep. Elephant Stompers, Women's Fedn, 69; bonus mem, Colo. Rep. State Cent. Cmt, 69-; v.chmn, Second Cong. Dist. Rep. Cent. Cmt, Colo, 69- Mem: Columbine Hills Civic Asn.(treas, 3 years); Columbine Hills Elem. PTA (bd. mem, 3 years); Parent Teachers Orgn.(treas, 69-70). Woman of the Year Award, Columbine Hills Civic Asn, 67. Rel: Protestant. Mailing Add: 7953 Chestnut Way, Littleton, Colo. 80120.

HIGH, ROBERT KING D
b. Tullahoma, Tenn; s. Lester High and Kate Holt H; m. 3/30/54 to Sara Faith Price; c. Robert King, Jr, Cindy, Holiday, Bonnie Lou, Valerie and Susan Jill. Educ: Univ. Miami, 47; Stetson Univ. Law Sch, LL.B, 49; Llamba Chi; Iron Arrow; Omicron Delta Kappa; Alpha Kappa Psi. Polit. & Govt. Pos: Mayor, Miami, Fla, 57-69. Bus. & Prof. Pos: Sr. Partner, High, Stack and Davis, 49- Mil. Serv: Entered Army Air Force, 42, released as Air Force Engr, 44. Mem: Alianza Interamericana; Am, Fla. and Dade Co. Bar Asns; Am. Legion; Am. Munic. Asn; Boy Scouts; Dade League of Municipalities; Fla. League of Municipalities; Interamerican Center Authority; Moose; Mason; Miami Dade Co. C. of C; Miami Police Benevolent Asn; PTA; Supervisors Coun, City of Miami; U.S. Conf. of Mayors. Named One of 100 Outstanding Young Americans by Life Magazine; selected as One of America's Most Important Young Men and Women by Acad. of Achievement, San Diego, Calif. Rel: Baptist. Mailing Add: 2131 S. Bayshore Dr, Miami, Fla. 33133. (1967)

HIGH, THOMAS WILLIAM R
Mem, Calif. Rep. State Cent. Cmt.
b. Oakland, Calif, 12/7/47; s. William Alfred High and Vera D. Blumann H; m. 6/8/69 to Nancy Jane Hughes. Educ: Univ. of Calif, Berkeley, B.A. in Polit. Sci, 68. Polit. & Govt. Pos: Research analyst, Newman for Cong, 14th Cong. Dist, Calif, 66; asst. to the chmn, Alameda Co. Rep. Finance Cmt, 68; campaign mgr, Chefsky for Assembly, 15th Assembly Dist, 68; mem, Calif. Rep. State Cent. Cmt, currently. Bus. & Prof. Pos: Orgn. mgr. and exec. v.pres, Data Research Inc, San Francisco, Calif, 68- Mem: Am. Polit. Sci. Asn; Commonwealth Club of Calif. Mailing Add: 420 Bellevue Ave, Oakland, Calif. 94610.

HIGHAM, JUSTUS CHARLES D
b. Trenton, N.J, 10/26/08; s. Charles Higham and Mary Gribbin H; wid; c. Mary Lou (Mrs. Sheppard), Carol Elizabeth (Mrs. White), Gerald William, Justus C, Jr, William Yard, Michael Edward, Eleanor Ann, Kathleen T. (Mrs. Iavarone), Timothy Patrick, Anthony Peter, Jane Ellen, Stephen Kevin, Susan Patricia, Dennis Sean and Terrance Brian. Educ: Seton Hall Univ, B.A, 53. Polit. & Govt. Pos: Secy, N.J. Dem. State Cmt, 54-69. Mem: Elks; Ancient Order of Hibernians. Rel: Roman Catholic. Legal Res: 871 Revere Ave, Trenton, N.J. 08610. Mailing Add: 31-33 N. Willow St, Trenton, N.J. 08608. (1967)

HIGHAM, WILLIAM ROLSTON D
Mem, Calif. Dem. State Cent. Cmt.
b. New York, N.Y, 8/28/26; s. William Harry Marcus Higham and Alice Fonde H; m. 12/19/47 to June N. Hoskinson; c. Mary Bethyl and Jeaneane Alice. Educ: Ore. State Univ, B.S, 49; Hastings Col. of Law, LL.B, 52; Delta Sigma Rho. Polit. & Govt. Pos: Dep. dist. attorney, Contra Costa Co, Calif, 58-66, pub. defender, 66-; mem, Calif. Dem. State Cent. Cmt, 68- Bus. & Prof. Pos: Secy-treas, Calif. Pub. Defenders Asn, 69- Mil. Serv: Entered as A/S, Navy, 45, released as Seaman 2/C, 46, after serv. on Naval Detachment, Naples, Italy, 45 & V-12, Naval ROTC, Corvallis, Ore, 45-46, Lt.(jg), Naval Res. Mem: State Bar of Calif; Contra Costa Co. Bar Asn; Concord Elks; Diablo Squadron, U.S. Power Squadrons; Diablo Dem. Club; past pres, Local 1675, Am. Fedn. State, Co. & Munic. Employees, AFL-CIO. Rel: Episcopal. Legal Res: 101 Wayne Court, Walnut Creek, Calif. 94596. Mailing Add: 901 Pine St, Box 1029, Martinez, Calif. 94553.

HIGHTOWER, CAMERON D
b. Liberty, Tex, 7/12/37; s. Thomas J. Hightower and Opal LaFour H; single. Educ: Univ. Tex, B.A. with honors, 58, LL.B, 62; Phi Eta Sigma; Phi Alpha Theta; Pi Sigma Alpha; Delta Sigma Rho; Phi Beta Kappa; Silver Spurs; Friar Soc. Polit. & Govt. Pos: Tex. State Rep, 65-67. Bus. & Prof. Pos: Legal officer, Tex. R.R. Cmn, 62-64; attorney-at-law, private practice, 64- Mem: Charter mem, Nat. Soc. State Legislators; Tex. and Am. Bar Asns; Tex. Jr. Bar Asn.(bd. of dirs); nat. dir, U.S. Jaycees; state v.pres, Tex. Jaycees; Tex. Good Rd. Asn; dir, Big Thicket Asn; Tex. Water Conserv. Asn; Elks: Named Outstanding V.Pres, Tex. Jaycees; Named Outstanding Nat. Dir. and Received Clint Dunagan Award, U.S. Jaycees. Rel: Catholic. Legal Res: 1711 Cos, Liberty, Tex. 77575. Mailing Add: Box 1317, Liberty, Tex. 77575.

HIGHTOWER, JACK ENGLISH D
Tex. State Sen.
b. Memphis, Tex, 9/6/26; s. Walter Thomas Hightower and Floy English H; m. 8/26/50 to Colleen Ward; c. Ann, Amy and Alison. Educ: Baylor Univ, B.A, 49, LL.B, 51; Phi Alpha Delta. Polit. & Govt. Pos: Tex. State Rep, 53-54; dist. attorney, 46th Judicial Dist, Tex, 55-61; mem. and v.chmn, Bd. Regents, Midwest. Univ, 62-64; Tex. State Sen, 65-; del, Dem. Nat. Conv, 68. Mil. Serv: Entered as A/S, Naval Res, 44, released as Yeoman 2/C, 46. Mem: Mason; Lions. Rel: Baptist. Mailing Add: 2719 Mansard St, Vernon, Tex. 76384.

HILBRECHT, NORMAN TY D
Nev. State Assemblyman
b. San Diego, Calif, 2/11/33; s. Norman Titus Hilbrecht and Elizabeth Lair H; div; c. Bonnie Jean. Educ: Northwest. Univ, B.A, 56; Yale Law Sch, LL.B, 59; Phi Beta Kappa; Phi Delta Phi; Delta Phi Epsilon; past pres, Theta Chi. Polit.& Govt. Pos: Chmn. trustees, Clark Co. Law Libr, Nev, 63-; v.chmn, Clark Co. Dem. Cent. Cmt, 66-68; Nev. State Assemblyman, 67-; del, West. Conf. on Ombudsman, 68; del, First Nat. Conf. on Abortion Reform, 69; del, Rutgers State Legislator Seminar, 69. Mil. Serv: Entered as 2nd Lt, Army, 58, released as Capt, 66, after serv. in various Judge Adv. Gen. and Mil. Govt. Units; Capt. Army Res, 66- Publ: 'The Colby Case and Full Faith and Credit,' 7/63 and 'Farnham vs. Farnham-Variations on a Theme,' 1/65, Nev. Bar Jour; Nevada Public Defender Act, 1/64. Mem: Chmn, Cmt. on Legal Aid and Indigent Defense, Am. Bar Asn, 63-; Nev. Bar Asn; chmn, Pub. Defender Cmt, Clark Co. Bar Asn, 63-64; pres, Las Vegas Chap, Am. Trial

Lawyers Asn, 67 and Clark Co. Legal Aid Soc, 64; Elks Lodge 1468; Rotary; Jr. C. of C; Nat. Conf. Christians and Jews; Las Vegas Young Dem; v.pres, Fraternal Order of Police Assocs, 68. Rel: Unitarian. Mailing Add: 5729 Idle Ave, Las Vegas, Nev. 89107.

HILBUN, BENJAMIN FRANKLIN, JR. D
Miss. State Sen.
b. Starkville, Miss, 8/20/34; single. Polit. & Govt. Pos: Miss. State Sen, 60-64 & 66- Bus. & Prof. Pos: Lawyer. Mem: Mason; Farm Bur; Sigma Alpha Epsilon; Omicron Delta Kappa; Phi Delta Phi; Delta Sigma Pi. Rel: Baptist. Mailing Add: Box 332, Starkville, Miss. 39759. (1967)

HILDEBRAND, GEORGE H. R
Dep. Under Secy. for Int. Affairs, Dept. of Labor
b. Oakland, Calif, 7/7/13; m. to Margaret Boardman; c. George, Stephen and Richard. Educ: Univ. Calif, Berkeley, B.A, 35; Harvard Univ, M.A, 41; Cornell Univ, Ph.D, 42. Polit. & Govt. Pos: Prin. economist, Nat. War Labor Bd. and tech. adv, President's Cost of Living Cmn, World War II; labor arbitrator, 51-; consult. and mem. cmt. to guide the Secy. of Labor's study of the basic steel indust, Dept. of Labor, 59-60, Dep. Under Secy. for Int. Affairs, 69-; pub. mem, Minimum Wage Bd. for restaurant indust, N.Y. and consult, Dept. of Health, Educ. and Welfare, 61-62; former chmn, adv. cmt. on research, Soc. Security Admin. Bus. & Prof. Pos: Asst. prof. econ, Univ. Tex, 41-43; instr, Univ. Calif, Berkeley, 45-47, vis. prof, 59-60; from asst. prof. to prof, Univ. Calif, Los Angeles, 47-60, dir, Inst. of Indust. Rels, 56-60; Fulbright fel, 52-53; Guggenheim fel, 52-53 & 57-58; prof. econ. and indust labor rels, Cornell Univ, 60-69. Publ: Co-auth, Pacific Coast Maritime Shipping Industry, 1930-1948, 52 and Manufacturing Production Functions in the United States, 57 & 65; auth, Growth and Structure in the Economy of Modern Italy, 65. Mem: Bd. dirs, Soc. Sci. Research Coun; Comitato per le Scienze Politiche e Sociali; Am. Econ. Asn; Indust. Rels. Research Asn; Nat. Acad. of Arbitrators; Phi Beta Kappa. Mailing Add: Dept. of Labor, 14th St. & Constitution Ave. N.W, Washington, D.C. 20210.

HILDRETH, HORACE A, JR. R
b. 1932; m. to Alison Derby; c. four sons. Educ: Bowdoin Col; Columbia Univ. Sch. of Law. Polit. & Govt. Pos: Maine State Sen, 67-69; cand, U.S. Rep, Maine, 68. Bus. & Prof. Pos: Attorney; Corporator, Maine Med. Center and Maine Savings Bank. Mem: Co. chmn, Maine 4-H Club Found; trustee, N.Yarmouth Acad. and Radio Parish Church; dir, Maine State C. of C; Kiwanis; United Commun. Servs. Mailing Add: 465 Congress St, Portland, Maine 04111.

HILGEMANN, CALVIN C. R
b. McPherson Co, S.Dak, 2/2/01; m. to Christine Kammerer; c. Fred and Harry. Educ: High Sch. Polit. & Govt. Pos: Local assessor and mem. sch. bd, Co. Assessor, Auditor and Treas, City Auditor and Mayor, formerly; S.Dak. State Rep, 62-66; fieldman, Dept. of Sch. and Pub. Lands, 66- Bus. & Prof. Pos: Former farmer; businessman and ins. agent. Rel: Lutheran. Mailing Add: Box 200, Leola, S.Dak. 57456.

HILL, ALBERT ALAN R
b. Palo Alto, Calif, 2/1/38; s. Albert Andrew Hill and Margaret Silver H; m. 6/17/61 to Mary Jeanette Smith; c. Andrew Alan, Timothy Brewster and Michael Ralph. Educ: Col. of the Pac, A.B, 60; Univ. Calif, Berkeley, 60-61; Golden Gate Col, 63-64 & 67-68; Blue Key; Alpha Kappa Phi. Polit. & Govt. Pos: Asst. to Minority Leader, Calif. State Senate, 62-64; state. info. officer, Calif. Rep. State Cent. Cmt, 65-69; asst. to Secy. for Resources, Calif, 69- Rel: Episcopal. Mailing Add: 102 Coleman Dr, San Rafael, Calif. 94901.

HILL, ARTHUR ROSS R
b. Greensboro, Vt, 6/4/05; m. to Doris Sprague; c. 1 son; 2 daughters. Educ: Univ. Vt, B.S, 32. Polit. & Govt. Pos: Selectman, Brookfield, Vt, 42-46, town moderator, 49-; Vt. State Rep, 53-57 & 65-66. Bus. & Prof. Pos: Equipment sales and serv. Mem: Mason; Barre Rotary Club; Eastern Star. Rel: Congregational. Mailing Add: East Brookfield, Vt. 05036. (1967)

HILL, BENJAMIN HARRISON D
Okla. State Rep.
b. Nova Scotia, Can, 11/1/03; s. Joseph Lee Hill and Anna Edmund H; m. 6/20/32 to Fannie Johnson; c. George F. and Norma (Mrs. Smallwood). Educ: Wilberforce Univ, B.S, 25; Lincoln Nebr. Univ, 26-28; Lincoln Univ, Sociol, 48-49; Alpha Phi Alpha. Polit. & Govt. Pos: Okla. State Rep, 69- Bus. & Prof. Pos: Minister, Vernon African Methodist Episcopal Church, 49-68, mag. ed, African Methodist Episcopal Church, 68-; editorial ed, Okla. Eagle, 53-69. Publ: 'Truth Must Come Out,' column, Okla. Eagle, 53-69. Mem: Mason (32°). Tulsa Urban League Award, 62. Rel: Methodist. Mailing Add: 3004 N. Cincinnati, Tulsa, Okla. 74106.

HILL, BOBBY L. D
Ga. State Rep.
b. Athens, Ga, 7/24/41; s. Birl Hill and Fannie Hubbard H; m. 4/21/66 to Dolores Clarke. Educ: Savannah State Col, B.S, 63; Howard Univ, Sch. Law, LL.B, 66; Alpha Phi Alpha; Sigma Delta Tau; Thespian Dramatics Club. Polit. & Govt. Pos: Ga. State Rep, 94th Dist, 69- Publ: 'Low Income and Poor Educational Status of One Party is Basis for Holding a Contract Unconscionable,' Howard Law J, Vol. 1, No. 12. Mem: Am. Bar Asn; bd. dirs, Nat. Assembly for Soc. Policy and Develop; Nat. Voter Educ. Proj, U.S. Youth Coun; coop. counsel, NAACP Legal Defense & Educ. Fund, Inc. Man of the Year Award, Savannah State Col. and Alpha Phi Alpha; Achievement Award, Omega Psi; Alumnus Award, Howard Univ. Sch. Law Student Bar Asn. Rel: Baptist. Legal Res: 923 W. 37th St, Savannah, Ga. 31401. Mailing Add: 458½ W. Broad St, Savannah, Ga. J1401.

HILL, CLYDE R
Kans. State Rep.
b. Yates Center, Kans 11/18/12; s. George Hill, Jr. and Edie Crumrine H; m. 6/9/51 to Mildred Landes. Educ: Emporia State Col, 35-36; Washburn Col, Ph.B, 38; Washburn Univ. Law Sch, LL.B, 40. Polit. & Govt. Pos: Co. attorney, Woodson Co, Kans, 47-51; Kans. State Rep, Woodson Co, 55-67, Woodson and Wilson Co, 67-, Speaker, Kans. House Rep, 65-66, Speaker-Pro-Tem, 67-68. Bus. & Prof. Pos: Private practice of Law, 46- Mil. Serv: Entered as Pvt, Army, 40, released as 2nd Lt, 46 after serv. in 28th Replacement Depot, Pac. Mem: V.F.W; Am. Legion; Kans. Farm Bur; Mason; Past pres. Rotary. Rel: Episcopal. Legal Res: 504 N. State, Yates Center, Kans. 66783. Mailing Add: Box 202, Yates Center, Kans. 66783.

HILL, DENNIE LEE D
W.Va. State Del.
b. Seth, W.Va, 10/8/25; s. Dennie E. Hill and Gertrude M. Norris H; m. 4/14/49 to Elaine Hadveck; c. Robert Edison and David Lee. Educ: W.Va. Univ, B.S; Sigma Chi. Polit. & Govt. Pos: Former mem, Young Dem. Club; chmn. bd. trustees, Boone Co. Hosp, W.Va; mem, Town Coun, Madison, 54-; W.Va. State Del, 58- Bus. & Prof. Pos: Operated gen. ins. and real estate agency. Mil. Serv: Navy, 44-46. Mem: Mason; VFW; Am. Legion; former pres, Rotary Club; PTA, Madison Grade Sch. Rel: Baptist. Mailing Add: 212 Riverside Dr, Madison, W.Va. 25130. (1967)

HILL, DONNELLEY JOSEPH R
Tenn. State Rep.
b. Chicago, Ill, 12/12/38; s. Kenneth Horace Hill and Mary Louise Karsch H; m. 6/4/61 to Anita Jo Adair; c. Joseph Sean, Mary Karsch and Patrick Shane. Educ: Univ. Tenn, Knoxville, 57-59; Christian Bros. Col, B.S, 62; Memphis State Univ, J.D, 65; Sigma Alpha Epsilon; Delta Theta Phi. Polit. & Govt. Pos: Tenn. State Rep, 69- Bus. & Prof. Pos: Assoc. attorney, Apperson, Crump, Duzane & Maxwell, 66- Mem: Am, Tenn, Memphis and Shelby Co. Bar Asns; Memphis and Shelby Co. Jr. Bar Asns; Am. and Tenn. Trial Lawyers Asns; K. of C; Optimist Club; Elks; Phoenix Club; Memphis Athletic Club; Univ. Club. Rel: Catholic. Legal Res: 4354 Walnut Grove Rd, Memphis, Tenn. 38117. Mailing Add: 2610 100 N. Main Bldg, Memphis, Tenn. 38103.

HILL, EDWARD POLK, III D
Judge, Supreme Court, Ky.
b. Bonanza, Ky, 9/2/04; s. Edward Polk Hill, Jr. and Adda Davis; m. 6/14/29 to Maria Doss; c. Carolyn Doss (Mrs. Coleman), Edward Polk, IV, John Josiah and Sarah Noel (Mrs. Stumbo). Educ: Berea Col, 21-22; Bowling Green Bus. Univ, 23; Jefferson Law Sch, 25-27. Polit. & Govt. Pos: Judge, Floyd Co. Court, Ky, 38-45; Circuit Judge, 31st Dist, 45-63; Appellate Judge, Seventh Appellate Dist, Commonwealth of Ky, 65-69; Judge, Supreme Court, Ky, 69- Bus. & Prof. Pos: Bank teller, 24; attorney, 28-38. Mem: Am. Judicature Soc; Ky. Bar Asn, Floyd Co. Bar Asn; Kiwanis; Odd Fellows; Mason. Rel: Baptist. Legal Res: Prestonsburg, Ky. 41653. Mailing Add: Kentucky Supreme Court, Frankfort, Ky. 40601. (1967)

HILL, EUGENE MARSHALL D
Iowa State Sen.
b. Newton, Iowa, 10/24/13; s. George R. Hill and Minnie Rees H; m. 10/17/46 to Ruth Ryburn; c. David, Robert, Patricia, Kathleen and John. Educ: Iowa State Univ, B.S, 37; Univ. Ill, post grad. work, 41; Alpha Zeta; Sigma Upsilon. Polit. & Govt. Pos: Supvr, Farm Security Admin, Dept. Agr; Iowa State Sen, currently. Bus. & Prof. Pos: Instr. voc. agr, Col. Springs and Coin, Iowa High Schs, 46-49; farmer, Newton, Iowa, 50- Mil. Serv: Marine Corps, World War II; 4th Tank Bn, Battles of Roi Namur, Saipan, Tinian and Iwo Jima; Maj, Marine Corps Res, currently; Letter of Commendation with Ribbon, Secy. of Navy, 45; Presidential Unit Citation, Saipan, 44; Navy Unit Commendation, Iwo Jima, 45. Mailing Add: Route 3, Newton, Iowa 50208.

HILL, GEORGE BARKER D
Chmn, Coal Co. Cent. Cmt, Okla.
b. Sulphur Springs, Tex, 7/9/15; s. John B. Hill and Grace Martha Summers H; m. 9/19/43 to Margaret Ellen Culbertson; c. John Carl, Judith Ann (deceased) and Mary Lynn (deceased). Educ: Ardmore Bus. Col, 31-33; Okla. Baptist Univ, 33-34; Sigma Delta Chi. Polit. & Govt. Pos: Secy, Johnston Co. Cent. Cmt, Okla, 40-41 & 46-49; mem. credentials cmt, Okla. State Dem. Conv, 52, platform cmt, 64, 66 & 68; chmn, Coal Co. Cent. Cmt, Okla, 52-53 & 67-; del, Dem. Nat. Conv, 64; mem, state and dist. resolutions and spec. studies cmts; mem, State Constitution Revision Cmt, Okla. State Dem. Cent. Cmt, 64 & 66, party revision cmt, 69. Bus. & Prof. Pos: Publisher, Coalgate Record Register, 49- Mil. Serv: Entered as Pvt, Army, 41, released as T-3, 45, after serv. in Panama Mobile Force, Caribbean Defense Command, 42-44. Mem: Okla. Press Asn.(chmn. of various cmts, 48-69, pres, 56-57); Selected Weeklies of Okla; Nat. Publishers Asn; pres, Southeast Okla. Water Rights Asn, 67-69; AF&AM (Past Master, Past Dist. Dep. Grand Master, past chmn. and mem. pub. rels. cmt, past mem, publ. cmt. and educ. cmt, Grand Lodge, Okla); Odd Fellows; Lions (pres, Goalgate Club, 66-67); Am. Legion; VFW; Coal Co. C. of C.(pres, 68). 50 Awards in State Press Contests; Nat. Ed. of the Week, 54; Hon. Col, Maj. and Comdr; Spec. Presentations, 4-H, Soil Conserv. Serv, Mason, C. of C, Okla. Press Asn, Secy. of Navy and Prime Minister of Ont. Rel: Baptist. Legal Res: 503 S. Byrd, Coalgate, Okla. 74538. Mailing Add: Box 327, Coalgate, Okla. 74538.

HILL, GEORGE HOWARD D
b. Mount Hope, Va, 8/22/03; m. to Emily Parks Ames H. Educ: William and Mary, exten. Polit. & Govt. Pos: Va. State Del, 54-69. Bus. & Prof. Pos: Banker, v.pres, First and Merchants Nat. Bank, Newport News, Va. Mem: Past pres, Newport News Kiwanis; past pres, James River Country Club; Warwick Ruritan Club; bd. mem, Peninsula C. of C; Am. Inst. of Banking (past pres, Peninsula Chap); Bd. of Jamestown Found; Peninsula Mem. Park; past pres, Peninsula Exec. Club. Rel: Baptist. Mailing Add: 900 River Rd, Newport News, Va. 23601. (1967)

HILL, GEORGE LESTER, JR. R
b. Crossville, Tenn, 5/26/23; s. George Lester Hill and Susie Ellen Kemmer H; m. 12/16/46 to Martha Ruth Brock; c. Richard Brock, Rebecca S. and David James. Educ: Univ. Tenn, 42-43 & 46; Alpha Tau Omega. Polit. & Govt. Pos: Chmn, Cumberland Co. Rep. Party, Tenn, 66-67; del, Rep. Nat. Conv, 68. Bus. & Prof. Pos: Partner, Hill's Dept. Store, Crossville, 47, owner and mgr, 64; secy. and treas, Catousa Knitting Mill, 58; dir, First Nat. Bank, 60. Mil. Serv: Entered as A/S, Coast Guard, 43, released as Aviation Cadet, 45, after serv. in Caribbean Theatre, 43-45; Caribbean Theatre Ribbon. Mem: VFW; Am. Legion; C. of C; Optimist Int; Shrine. Rel: Methodist. Mailing Add: 412 Brown Ave, Crossville, Tenn. 38555.

HILL, GLENDA R
Committeewoman, Tex. Rep. Party
b. San Antonio, Tex, 11/7/28; d. James P. Ferrell and Clyde Parchman F; m.

5/3/47 to Edward T. Hill; c. Terri and Laura. Educ: Trinity Univ, San Antonio, Tex, 2 years. Polit. & Govt. Pos: Rep. Precinct chmn, Bexar Co, Tex, 56-60; nat. elector, State of Tex, 60; pres, Rep. Women, Bexar Co, 60; dist. committeewoman, Bexar Co. Rep. Party, 61-65; absentee vote chmn, Rep. State Campaign Cmt, 62; del, Rep. Nat. Conv, 64, alternate del, 68; v.chmn, Bexar Co. Nixon Campaign, 68; committeewoman, 26th Sen. Dist, Tex. Rep. Party, 68- Mem: Inner Wheel; CPA Auxiliary; PTA. Rel: Presbyterian. Mailing Add: 1119 Haltown, San Antonio, Tex. 78213.

HILL, HAROLD EUGENE 'GENE' D
b. Brazil, Ind, 7/6/34; s. Harold Hill and Nellie Smith H; m. 8/26/56 to Amelia Flores; c. Ernest Harold, Rodney Charles and Jeffrey Scott. Educ: Ind. Univ, 2 years; Univ. N.Mex, 1½ years; Delta Sigma Pi. Polit. & Govt. Pos: Precinct chmn, Dona Ana Co. Dem. Party, N.Mex, 62-66, v.chmn, 63-66, chmn, 66-69. Bus. & Prof. Pos: Secy-treas, Assoc. Credit Bur, N.Mex, 61-65, v.pres, 65-66, pres, 66- Mil. Serv: Entered as Pvt, Army, 54, released as Sgt, 56; Good Conduct Medal; Expert Rifle Medal. Mem: Elks; Jaycees; C. of C. Rel: Methodist. Legal Res: 1525 Camino Del Rex, Las Cruces, N.Mex. 88001. Mailing Add: Drawer DD, Las Cruces, N.Mex. 88001. (1967)

HILL, IZORA R. D
b. Boley, Okla, 3/25/15; d. William Callahan and Birdie Manyard C; m. 8/30/46 to McKinley Hill; c. Sidney R, Richard, Alvin, Dovie and Eric. Educ: Ariz. State Univ, 1 year. Polit. & Govt. Pos: Precinct committeewoman, Phoenix, Ariz, 48-; state committeewoman, 60; Nat. committeewoman, 68; del, Dem. Nat. Conv, 68. Bus. & Prof. Pos: Teacher's aide, Maricopa Co. Accommodation Sch, 59-69. Mem: Am. Educ. Asn; Eastern Star; Ariz. Southside Dem. Club; NAACP; Am. Educ. Asn. Credit Union. Rel: Baptist. Mailing Add: 1414 S. 11th Ave, Phoenix, Ariz. 85007.

HILL, J. MORRIS R
b. Lebanon, Mo, 2/28/03; m. 9/8/46 to Frances Davis; c. Sandra Mae, Ronald Davis. Educ: Drury Col; Southwest Mo. State Col, Springfield; Univ. of Mo, B.S. Polit. & Govt. Pos: Mo. State Sen, 54-66; Mo. State Rep, 3 terms. Bus. & Prof. Pos: Ins. rep, Franklin Life Ins. Co. of Springfield, Ill; sch. teacher, 13 years. Mil. Serv: Army, Capt, 42-46; served in New Guinea, Philippines. Mem: Rotary; VFW; Am. Legion; Odd Fellows. Rel: Christian Church. Mailing Add: 15 Belwood Dr, Lebanon, Mo. 65536. (1967)

HILL, JACK HOWARD D
b. Franklin, Ind, 3/25/11; s. Harry D. Hill and Floy Hendricks H; m. 4/4/59 to Frances Caroline Vaughn; c. Elizabeth Ann (Mrs. McTurnan) and Thomas Howard. Educ: Cent. Normal Col; Purdue Univ. Polit. & Govt. Pos: Del, Dem. Nat. Conv, 64; U.S. Forest Service, 34. Bus. & Prof. Pos: Pres, Hill Bros. Veneer, Inc, 52-; dir, Franklin State Bank, 50- Mem: Mason (32°), Scottish Rite; Elks; Indianapolis Athletic Club. Rel: Presbyterian. Mailing Add: R.R. 1, Edinburg, Ind. 46124. (1967)

HILL, JAMES DEAN R
Utah State Rep.
b. Ucon, Idaho, 2/19/23; s. Robert E. Hill and Fanny M. Monsen H; m. 6/8/45 to Virginia Mae Burtenshaw; c. Carolyn, Michelle, Sharyl, Janene and Von. Educ: Ricks Jr. Col, A.A, 46; Univ. Utah, B.S. in Civil Eng, 48, M.S, 49; Tau Beta Pi. Polit. & Govt. Pos: Hydraulic engr, U.S. Geol. Surv, 49-56; dist. chmn, Rep. Party, Utah, 63; del, State Rep. Conv, 63-65; Utah State Rep, Davis Co, 65- Bus. & Prof. Pos: Pres, Great Basin Eng. & Surv, Inc, 61-68; rep, Utah Eng. Coun, 63; consult. engr, Eng. Assocs, Inc, 68- Mil. Serv: Entered as Aviation Cadet, Air Corps, 43, released as 2nd Lt, 45, after serv. in 398th Bomb Group, 8th Air Force, ETO, 45; Air Medal & 3 Oak Leaf Clusters; ETO Ribbon & 2 Battle Stars; Victory Medal; Am. Defense Medal; Res. Ribbon with Hour Glass; Maj, Air Force Res, 45- Mem: Secy, Utah Chap, Am. Soc. Civil Engrs, 60-62, pres, 62; Consult. Engrs. Coun; Utah Coun. Land Surveyors. Registered Civil Engr, Idaho, Utah and Ariz; Licensed Civil Eng, Mont. Rel: Latter-day Saint. Mailing Add: 274 West, 1350 North, Bountiful, Utah 84010.

HILL, JAMES HENRY, JR. D
b. Hickory, N.C, 4/8/22; s. James Henry Hill and Sadie Salvo H; m. 8/28/43 to Mavis Ailean Peace; c. Mavis Helena (Mrs. W.E. Tulluck, Jr). Educ: Capitol Page Boys' Sch, D.C, 37; The Citadel, 40-42; Newberry Col, 44; Northwest. Univ, 44; Lenoir Rhyne Col, 42-44, 58-59, A.B; Gamma Beta Chi. Polit. & Govt. Pos: Page boy, U.S. Rep. A.L. Bulwinkle, 37; organizer, Young Dem. Club, Tenth Cong. Dist. N.C, 46, chmn, United Dem. Club, 47; pres, Catawba Co. Young Dem. Club, 48-49; v.chmn, Catawba Co. Dem. Party, 50; del, Dem. Nat. Conv, 52; N.C. mem, South. Regional Educ. Bd, 59-61; trustee, N.C. Confederate Women's Home, Fayetteville, 59-61; N.C. State Rep, 59-66. Bus. & Prof. Pos: Partner, Hill & Johnson Realty Co; partner, Little Bros. Construction Co, 67- Mil. Serv: Pharmacist Mate 2/C, Navy, 43-46. Mem: N.C. Restaurant Asn, dir, 50-54; past pres. and state dir, Jr. C. of C; Lake Hickory Country Club; Lenoir Rhyne Col. Bldg. Fund Cmt; Hickory Toastmasters Club; Elks; Moose; VFW; past v.comdr. and head of exec. cmt, Am. Legion; 40 et 8, chaplain, 50-51. Rel: Presbyterian; Presby. Men's Club; past pres, Usher's Guild. Mailing Add: 850 Fourth St. Dr. N.W, Hickory, N.C. 28601.

HILL, JAMES RENDER D
b. Greenville, Ga, 3/16/23; s. O. Warner Hill and Mary Render H; m. 3/30/46 to Mary Estes; c. James R, Jr. Educ: Univ. Ga, 44; Chi Phi. Polit. & Govt. Pos: Former Ga. State Sen, 29th Dist; Ga. State Rep, Meriwether Co, 59-65. Bus. & Prof. Pos: Self-employed. Mem: Kiwanis; C. of C; Agr. Stabilization & Conserv. Cmt. Rel: Baptist. Mailing Add: Greenville, Ga. 30222. (1967)

HILL, JESSE EDWIN R
Chmn, Alamosa Co. Rep. Cent. Cmt, Colo.
b. Lamar, Colo, 2/5/37; s. Jesse Emory Hill and O'Leta Spikes H; m. 5/28/59 to Jayne Southard; c. Nancy Lenn and Susan Lynn. Educ: Univ. Colo, B.A, 59; Univ. Colo. Young Rep. Polit. & Govt. Pos: Precinct committeeman, Alamosa Co. Rep. Cent. Cmt, Colo, 66, chmn, 67- Bus. & Prof. Pos: Asst. cashier, Alamosa Nat. Bank, 65-67, asst. v.pres, 67-68, v.pres, 68- Mem: Bank Admin. Inst; Elks; Kiwanis; Jaycees. Distinguished Serv. Award, Alamosa, Colo, 68. Rel: Protestant. Mailing Add: 722 Douglas, Alamosa, Colo. 81101.

HILL, JOHN JEROME 'JACK' D
Ill. State Rep.
b. Aurora, Ill, 10/27/18; m. to Belva Mae Satterlee; c. Patti Anne. Educ: St. Ambrose Col. Polit. & Govt. Pos: Ill. State Rep; former mem, Aurora Civil Serv. Bd; alderman. Bus. & Prof. Pos: Grievance committeeman, v.pres, Local 3672, United Steel Workers. Mil. Serv: Second Armored Div, 4 years; Am. Defense Serv. Ribbon; European-African-Middle East. Theatre Ribbon with One Silver Star and Two Bronze Stars; Bronze Serv. Arrowhead for Beach Head Landing in Sicily, Bronze Star Medal and the Oak Leaf Cluster to the Bronze Star Medal; Cert. of Merit; Distinguished Unit Badge; Presidential Citation; Belgium Croix De Guerre. Mem: DAV; VFW; St. Joseph Holy Name Soc. Rel: Catholic. Mailing Add: 741 Sheridan, Aurora, Ill. 60505. (1967)

HILL, JOSEPH WAYNE R
Mo. State Rep.
b. Des Moines, Iowa, 3/19/07; s. Joseph Byrd Hill and Grace Robertson H; m. 12/25/35 to Ann Marie Ochiltree; c. Margaret. Educ: Drake Univ, 26-29; Am. Univ, LL.B, 38; Southeast. Univ, acct, 38-39; Sigma Alpha Epsilon. Polit. & Govt. Pos: Clerk, House Off. Bldg, 35-37; auditor and spec. auditor, U.S. Gen. Acct. Off, 37-46, investr, 46-51, supvry. investr, 51-65; Mo. State Rep, 67- Mem: Iowa and Fed. Bar Asns; Mason; Nat. Asn. Retired Civil Employees. Golf, has taken local honors. Rel: Presbyterian. Mailing Add: 1438 E. 78th St, Kansas City, Mo. 64131.

HILL, (JOSEPH) LISTER D
b. Montgomery, Ala, 12/29/94; s. Luther Leonidas Hill and Lilly Lyons H; m. 2/20/28 to Henrietta Fontaine McCormick; c. Henrietta (Mrs. Charles C. Hubbard) and Luther Lister. Educ: Univ. Ala, B.A, 14, LL.B, 15; Columbia Univ, LL.B, 16; Phi Beta Kappa; Delta Kappa Epsilon. Hon. LL.D, Univ. Ala, 39, Auburn Univ, 39; Nat. Univ, 41, Woman's Med. Col. Pa, 56, Columbia Univ, 60, Wash. Univ, 61, Univ. Pa, 65, N.Y. Univ, 66 and Gallaudet Col, 66; D.Sc, Hahnemann Med. Col. Pa, 58, N.Y. Med. Col, 61 and Jefferson Med. Col, 66. Polit. & Govt. Pos: Pres, Montgomery Co. Bd. Educ, Ala, 17-22; U.S. Rep, Ala, 23-38; U.S. Sen, Ala, 38-68, sponsor, Hill-Burton Act, 46 and Hill-Harris Act, 63, chmn, Labor and Pub. Welfare Cmt, U.S. Senate, 55-68. Mil. Serv: Entered as 2nd Lt, Army, 17, released as 1st Lt, 19, after serv. in 17th and 21st U.S. Inf. Regts. Mem: Am. Asn. Dent. Schs; Am. Dent. Asn; Am. Thoracic Soc; Med. Sect, Nat. Tuberc. Asn; Birmingham Dent. Soc; hon. fel. Am. Col. Physicians and Am. Col. Surgeons; Int. Med. Club of Wash, D.C; Med. Soc. D.C; Montgomery Dist. Dent. Soc; Omicron Kappa Epsilon Dent. Soc; Phi Alpha Delta; Mason; Am. Legion; Alexander Graham Bell Asn. for the Deaf; Am. Hosp. Asn; Am. Libr. Asn; Am. Vocational Asn; Gargas Mem. Inst. of Tropical and Preventive Med; Am. Cancer Soc; Nat. Asn. for Ment. Health; Nat. Rehabilitation Cmt, Johns Hopkins Univ; Am. Psychiat. Asn; Lister Hill Nat. Center for Biomed. Commun. Albert Lasker Award, 59; Award of Honor, Am. Hosp. Asn, 66; Pub. Welfare Medal, Nat. Acad. Sci, 69; City of Hope Salute to Med. Prog. Award. Mailing Add: 1618 Gilmer Ave, Montgomery, Ala. 36104.

HILL, LOUIS G. D
Pa. State Sen.
b. Palm Beach, Fla, 3/10/24; s. Crawford Hill and Ann Kaufman H; m. 7/7/51 to Jane Cox; c. Crawford, III, Leslie, Jessie B, Thomas G, Michael C, Charlotte and Ann. Educ: Harvard Col, B.S, 44; Univ. Pa, LL.B, 49; Delta Psi; Fly Club; Delta Kappa Epsilon. Polit. & Govt. Pos: Pa. State Sen, 67- Bus. & Prof. Pos: Lawyer, Dilworth, Paxson, Kalish, Kohn & Levy, Phila, Pa, 50- Mil. Serv: Entered as 2nd Lt, Marine Corps Res, 44, released as Capt, 52, after serv. in Pac. Theatre; Asiatic-Pac. Ribbon; Korean Emergency Ribbon; China Serv. Ribbon; Atlantic Defense Ribbon; World War II Victory Ribbon. Mem: Sierra Club; W. Mt. Airy Neighbors; dir, Coun. for Int. Visitors; trustee, Springside Sch; trustee, St. Christophers Hosp. for Children. Rel: Episcopal. Mailing Add: 6610 Wissahickon Ave, Philadelphia, Pa. 19119.

HILL, MARY BERTHA D
Conn. State Rep.
b. Shelburne Falls, Mass, 5/24/96; d. William Henry Mandeville and Alexina Saulnier M; m. 1/15/19 to Braxton Wilbur Hill, wid; c. Alyce (Mrs. O'Connor) and Marilyn (Mrs. Kelly). Educ: Drury High Sch, grad, 15. Polit. & Govt. Pos: Conn. State Rep, 59-, mem, Appropriations, Rules, Pub. Welfare, Humane Inst, Claims, Water Resources, Educ, Pub. Health and Safety Cmts, Conn. House Rep; mem, Dem. Town Cmt, 59- Bus. & Prof. Pos: Asst. administr, New London Co. Jail, 55-58. Mem: Am. Legion Auxiliary (pres); 40 et 8 (Madam Chapeau Dept); Order Women Legislators Conn.(pres). Rel: Catholic. Mailing Add: 5 Maxson Place, New London, Conn. 06320.

HILL, ROBERT CHARLES R
U.S. Ambassador, Spain
b. Littleton, N.H, 9/30/17; s. Allen Frank Hill and Katharine Lyle Morse; m. 12/1/45 to Cecelia Gordon Bowdoin; c. W. Graham Bowdoin and James Bowdoin. Educ: Dartmouth Col, 42; Alpha Delta Phi. Hon. LL.D, Dartmouth Col, St. Mary's Univ, San Antonio, Tex, Univ. of Dallas, New Eng. Col. and Mexican Acad. of Int. Law. Polit. & Govt. Pos: Vice consul, For. Serv, India, China and Burma, 43-45; clerk, Senate Banking and Currency Cmt, 46-47; U.S. Ambassador, Costa Rica, 53-54, El Salvador, 54-55, Mex, 57-61 and Spain, 69-; spec. asst. to Under Secy. of State for Mutual Security Affairs, 55-56; Asst. Secy. of State for Cong. Rels, 56-57; N.H. State Rep, 61-62; chmn, Task Force on For. Policy, Rep. Nat. Cmt, 65-68 and mem, Task Force on Nat. Security, 67-68. Bus. & Prof. Pos: Mgr, Wash. Off, Nat. Confectioner's Asn, 48; asst. v.pres, W.R. Grace & Co, 49-53; consult. on int. affairs and dir, United Fruit Co, 61-69; dir, Can. Int. Power Co, Ltd, Montreal, 62, Merck & Co, Inc, Rahway, N.J, 62-69, Northeast Airlines, Boston, Mass, 65 and Todd Shipyards Corp, N.Y, 66. Mem: Newcomen Soc. of N.Am; Am. Soc. Int. Law; C. of C; North Co. YMCA; Metrop. Clubs of N.Y. and Wash; Univ. Club of Wash; Chevy Chase Club; Elkridge Club, Baltimore, Md. Aztec Eagles, First Class, Repub. of Mex; Peruvian Grand Order of Merit, Repub. of Peru; First Annual Fraternitas Award, Mex. City Col; Cuerpo de Defenso-

res de la Republica, Mex; La Orden Mexicana del Derecho y la Cultura, Mex; Americas Award, Rollins Col, Winter Park, Fla. Rel: Episcopal. Legal Res: The Boulders, Littleton, N.H. 03561. Mailing Add: American Embassy, Madrid, Spain.

HILL, ROBERT McCLELLAN, JR. D
Ala. State Rep.
b. Florence, Ala, 4/16/32; s. Judge Robert M. Hill and Ratchel Fitzgerald H; m. 6/16/62 to Patsy Lynne Graydon; c. Alicia Michelle. Educ: Florence State Col; Univ. Ala, B.S, 57, LL.B, 59; Sigma Gamma Epsilon: Phi Alpha Delta; Phi Gamma Delta. Polit. & Govt. Pos: Law clerk, Ala. Supreme Court, 59-60; asst. attorney gen, Ala, 60-63; munic. judge, Florence, 63-66; Ala. State Rep, Lauderdale Co, 66- Mil. Serv: Entered as Seaman, Navy, 51, released as Seaman 1/C, 53. Mem: Am, Ala. and Lauderdale Bar Asns; Am. Judicature Soc; first v.pres, Ala. Munic. Judges Asn, 65, pres, 66; Ala. Citizen's Judicial Conf. Rel: Methodist. Legal Res: 321 Palisade Dr, Florence, Ala. 35630. Mailing Add: P.O. Box 687, Florence, Ala. 35630.

HILL, ROWLAND LESTER D
Chmn, Tuscola Co. Dem. Cmt, Mich.
b. Kent Co, Mich, 8/11/02; s. Rowland Snowden Hill and Maryanne Snowden H; m. 4/17/32 to Leona Ames; c. Ronald A, Janet M. (Mrs. Harper), Roger M. and Russell S. Educ: Mich. State Univ, 25-26. Polit. & Govt. Pos: Mem, bd. dirs, Tuscola Co. Soil Conserv. Dist, 43-63; mem, Mich. State Soil Conserv. Cmt, 45-63; chmn, Mich. State Asn. Soil Conserv. Dists, 46-47; chmn, Tuscola Co. Dem. Cmt, 67-; alternate del, Dem. Nat. Conv, 68. Bus. & Prof. Pos: Owner and operator, Fruit Farm, Caro, Mich, 33- Mem: Nat. Soil Conserv. Soc; Caro Exchange Club; Mich. Farm Bur. Spec. serv. award, Nat. Asn. of Soil and Water Conserv. Dists, 69; numerous other awards for serv. in the soil conserv. movement. Rel: Presbyterian. Mailing Add: 2029 S. Fenner Rd, Caro, Mich. 48723.

HILL, SHERMAN L. R
Pa. State Rep.
b. Lancaster Co, Pa, 12/4/11; s. Ellsworth F. Hill and Mabel Lehman H; m. to Kathryn Bender; c. one. Educ: Millersville State Col. Polit. & Govt. Pos: Organizer, Lancaster Co. Young Rep, Pa; div. chmn, Lancaster Co. Rep. Finance Cmt; mem, Gov. Adv. Cmt. on Children and Youth, Pa; Rep. committeeman, 53-55; Pa. State Rep, currently. Mem: Exec. dir, Boys Club, Lancaster, Inc; Civil Defense; Police Auxiliary; Nat. Bd, Boys Club Am; former mem. bd, Child Develop. Sch; chmn, Lancaster Clean Up-Paint Up Week; past pres, C. of C; Lions; Millersville Fire Co; Boys Club Prfnl. Asn; Mason; solicitor for charities. Rel: United Church of Christ. Legal Res: 201 Manor Ave, Millersville, Pa. 17551. Mailing Add: 545 Pershing Ave, Lancaster, Pa. 17602. (1967)

HILL, THOMAS E. D
Ohio State Rep.
b. W.Va, 1932; married; c. three. Educ: W.Va. State Col; West. Reserve Univ. Polit. & Govt. Pos: Ohio State Rep, 67- Bus. & Prof. Pos: Printing salesman. Mem: Pres, N.E. Glenville Civic Asn. Legal Res: 11706 Iowa Ave, Cleveland, Ohio 44108. Mailing Add: State Capitol Bldg, Columbus, Ohio 43215. (1967)

HILL, THOMAS JEFFERSON, III D
Chmn, Lincoln Co. Dem. Cent. Exec. Cmt, Ky.
b. Stanford, Ky, 6/5/29; s. Thomas Jefferson Hill, Jr. and Pearl FieldsTudor H; m. 12/27/58 to Nancy Miller; c. T.J, IV, and Virginia Carol. Educ: Centre Col. Ky, 47-48; Wash. and Lee Univ, A.B, 51, LL.B, 54; Phi Alpha Delta; Pi Kappa Alpha. Polit. & Govt. Pos: Ky. State Rep, 20th Dist, 60-63; chmn, Lincoln Co. Dem. Cent. Exec. Cmt, Ky, 64- Bus. & Prof. Pos: Master cmnr, Lincoln Circuit Court, 64- Mil. Serv: Entered Navy, 54, released as Lt.(jg), 58, after serv. in Pac; Lt, Naval Res, 60-; China Serv. Ribbon. Rel: Methodist. Legal Res: 101 Danville Ave, Stanford, Ky. 40484. Mailing Add: P.O. Drawer 387, Stanford, Ky. 40484.

HILL, W. W, JR. R
b. Kinard, Fla, 4/14/27; s. W. W. Hill and Carrie Clements H; m. 3/6/51 to Ellen Curry; c. Sue Ellen, William Douglas and Carol Lynne. Educ: Fla. State Univ, B.S, 49 and M.S, 51; Ind. Univ, D.B.A, 52 and J.D, 55. Polit. & Govt. Pos: Ind. State Rep, 61-62; ward chmn. and precinct committeeman, Rep. Party, Ind, 62-64; attorney, Ind. House of Rep, 63; Ind. State Sen, until 68; cand. for U.S. Rep, 11th Dist, 68; Cmnr. of Admin, Ind, 69- Bus. & Prof. Pos: Asst. prof, Univ. N.Dak, 52-54; educ. dir, Ind. State C. of C, 54-58; investments mgr, Col. Life Ins. Co, 58- Mil. Serv: S 2/C, Navy. Mailing Add: 6532 Wyman Court, Indianapolis, Ind. 46220.

HILL, WILLIAM R
Iowa State Rep.
b. Lynch, Nebr, 4/28/30; s. Ralph William Hill and Hazel Meachen H; m. 12/26/51 to Esther Lorraine Gulliver; c. Cathryn, Charles and Edward. Educ: Phillips Univ, B.A, 53; Drake Univ, B.D, 57 and J.D, 65. Polit. & Govt. Pos: Iowa State Rep, 67- Bus. & Prof. Pos: Pastor, First Christian Church, Cement, Okla, 51-53, Liscomb Church of Christ, 53-56 and Bethel Grove Christian Church, 56-63; lawyer, Marshalltown, Iowa, 65-; assoc. pastor, Garwin-Bethel Grove-Whitten Christian Church Parish, 68- Mil. Serv: Capt, Chaplain with Iowa Army Nat. Guard, 58-69. Mem: Iowa State Bar Asn; Marshalltown Ministerial Alliance; Local 176, Am. Fedn. of Musicians, AFL-CIO; Mason; Iowa Farm Bur. Fedn. Prfnl. pianist. Rel: Christian Church. Legal Res: 307 Park St, Marshalltown, Iowa 50158. Mailing Add: Woodbury Bldg, Marshalltown, Iowa 50158.

HILL, WILLIAM LANIER, II D
b. Wilmington, N.C, 5/21/31; s. John Bright Hill and Katherine Taylor H; m. 1/28/56 to Virginia Ashburn; c. William L, III and Taylor A. Educ: Univ. N.C, B.S. in bus. admin, 53, Law Sch, LL.B, 55; Delta Kappa Epsilon; Phi Delta Phi. Polit. & Govt. Pos: Former N.C. State Rep; Asst. U.S. Attorney, Eastern Dist, N.C, 61-62. Mil. Serv: Entered as 2nd Lt, Air Force, 55, released as 1st Lt, 57; former Capt, Air Force Res. Mem: Nat, State and Local Bar Asns. Rel: Presbyterian. Mailing Add: 2602 Parmele Dr, Wilmington, N.C. 28401. (1967)

HILLEBOE, PETER STUART R
N.Dak. State Rep.
b. Minneapolis, Minn, 9/24/21; s. Christian Hilleboe and Mabell Johnson M. H; m. 11/26/46 to Sarah A. Fleck; c. Laura, Stuart, Kristina and Amy. Educ: N.Dak. State Univ, B.S, 43; Univ. N.Dak, M.S, 46; Delta Sigma Pi; Sigma Chi. Polit. & Govt. Pos: Precinct committeeman, Rep. Party, N.Dak, 49-, mem, Co. Exec. Cmt, 58-64; del, N.Dak. Rep. Conv, 58, 60, 62, 64, 66 & 68; mem, Dist. 21, Rep. Finance Cmt, 59-; state chmn. for Nixon, 60; alternate del, Rep. Nat. Conv, 64; N.Dak. State Rep, 21st Dist, 64-, chmn, State and Fed. Govt. Cmt, 69-, and State Fiscal Audit and Rev. Cmt, 69-, N.Dak. State House of Rep; state chmn. for Rockefeller, 68. Bus. & Prof. Pos: Registered Rep, N.Y. Stock Exchange, 65- Mil. Serv: Entered as Aviation Cadet, Navy, 43, released as Airman 3/C, 46; Lt.(jg), Naval Res. Mem: Nat. Asn. Securities Dealers; N.Dak. Cattlemans Asn; Am. Legion; VFW; C. of C; Elks; Shrine; Fargo Country Club. Rel: Protestant. Mailing Add: 1622 Ninth St. S, Fargo, N.Dak. 58102.

HILLELSON, JEFFREY P. R
Mem, City Coun, Kansas City, Mo.
b. Springfield, Ohio, 3/9/19; s. Henry Hillelson and Ann Morrison H; m. Dec. 1952 to Alice Moore Goetz; c. Debra Ann and Jan. Educ: Univ. Mo. at Kansas City, Mo, B.A; Univ. Mo. Law Sch, 2 years. Polit. & Govt. Pos: U.S. Rep, Mo, 53-55; exec. asst. Postmaster Gen. of U.S, 55; del-at-lg, Rep. Nat. Conv, 56; acting postmaster, Kansas City, Mo, 57-61; mem, City Coun, Kansas City, 63- Bus. & Prof. Pos: Contract Sales mgr, The Vendo Co, 61- Mil. Serv: Entered as Pvt, Army, 42, released as Capt, 46, after serv. in Transportation Corps, Alaskan Depot; ETO, Am. Theater and Pac. Theater Ribbons; Victory Medal. Mem: Mil. Order World War I and II; Am. Legion; Shrine; Carriage Club, Kans. City, Mo; De Molay Legion of Honor. Rel: Episcopal. Mailing Add: 5322 Sunset Dr, Kansas City, Mo. 64112.

HILLEREN, RICHARD H. DFL
Chmn, Swift Co. Dem-Farmer-Labor Party, Minn.
b. Willmar, Minn, 7/8/28; s. Jens J. Hilleren and Ruby Marietta Teigen H; m. 6/25/61 to Marianne Kulstad; c. Mark Richard. Educ: St. Olaf Col, 49-50; Univ. Wash, B.A, 51; Yale Law Sch, LL.B, 54; Theta Delta Chi; Corby Court. Polit. & Govt. Pos: Treas, Dist. Dem-Farmer-Labor Party, Minn, 56-57; co. attorney, Swift Co, 58-66; chmn, Sixth Dist, Vol. for Rolvaag, 62; chmn, Swift Co. Dem-Farmer-Labor Party, 65- Bus. & Prof. Pos: Secy, 12th Judicial Dist, Minn, 60; pres, 12th Judicial Dist. Bar Asn. Mil. Serv: Entered as Pvt, Army, 46, released as T-5, 48, after serv. in Alaskan Commun. Syst, Seattle, Wash, 46-48; Victory Medal; Spec. Commendation from the Commanding Officer, Alaskan Commun. Syst. Mem: Am. Trial Attorney's Asn; Am, Minn. and 12th Judicial Dist. Bar Asns; Kiwanis; Northwest Yale Asn. Rel: Lutheran. Mailing Add: 618 12th St. S, Benson, Minn. 56215.

HILLERY, THOMAS J. R
b. Boonton, N.J; s. Thomas J. Hillery. Educ: Georgetown Univ; Columbia Univ, B.A; Seton Hall Univ, LL.D, 61. Polit. & Govt. Pos: Former alderman, Boonton, N.J, mayor, 2 terms; N.J. State Assemblyman, 46-53; former acting gov, N.J; N.J. State Sen, 53-69, Pres, N.J. State Senate, 59. Bus. & Prof. Pos: Pres. of George Benda, Inc, Boonton; pres. Valley Molding Co, Inc, Boonton; ins. broker, Hillery-Franke Asn, W.Milford, N.J; dir. Boonton Mt. Lakes Savings and Loan Asn. Mem: Rotary; Am. Cancer Soc; dir, All Souls Hosp; St. Claire's Hosp. Mailing Add: 195 N. Main St, Boonton, N.J. 07005. (1967)

HILLGREN, RALPH OLIVER R
b. Minneapolis, Minn, 2/7/97; s. John Hillgren and Nettie Paulsrud H; m. 6/26/29 to Priscilla Adaline Mannes; c. John Albert, Annette (Mrs. Marchiafava) and Sonja Dorothy. Educ: Univ. Minn, Minneapolis, B.A, 21; Sigma Delta Chi; Chi Phi. Polit. & Govt. Pos: S.Dak. State Rep, 31-35 & 55-69, chmn, 50th Anniversary Cmn, 39; census supvr, Dept. Commerce, 59-60. Bus. & Prof. Pos: Reporter and ed, Argus-Leader, 23-28, state ed, 28-52; teacher journalism, Augustana Col, 46-67; securities salesman, Imperial Financial Servs, 52-57; proprietor, Hillgren & Co. Mutual Funds, 57- Mil. Serv: Entered as Officer Cand, Army, released as 2nd Lt, Inf, 18 after serv. in Cent. Machine Gun, Officers Training Sch. Publ: Co-auth, Modern Journalism, Pittman, 62. Mem: S.Dak. State Hist. Soc. Rel: Lutheran. Mailing Add: 2021 S. Phillips Ave, Sioux Falls, S.Dak. 57105.

HILLIARD, ROBERT LEE D
b. Dracut, Mass, 12/21/35; single. Educ: Univ. of N.H. Polit. & Govt. Pos: N.H. State Rep, -67. Bus. & Prof. Pos: Appraiser. Mil. Serv: USMC, 56-58. Mem: Bellamy Chap, D.A.V. Rel: Episcopalian. 1967 Legal Res: 2 Oak Hill Dr, Dover, N.H. No mailing address available. (1967)

HILLING, HENRY BOYCE, SR. R
b. Flaville, Mont, 4/11/15; s. Arthur Earl Hilling and Sena Olson H; m. c. Sandra Jean Tilton, Henry B, Jr, Kathleen Louise (Mrs. James Burns) and Stanley Charles. Educ: Univ. Mont, B.S. in pharmacy, 38; Kappa Psi; Alpha Tau Omega. Polit. & Govt. Pos: Mont. State Sen, Yellowstone Co, 63-66; Mont. State Rep, 61-62; city councilman, Billings, 59-60. Bus. & Prof. Pos: Pres. and adminstr, Valley Convalescent Nursing Home, 62-; pres. and pharmacist, Hillings Pharmacy, 56-; salesman, E.R. Squibb & Sons, 43-55; pharmacist and mgr, City Drug, Anaconda, 42-43; pharmacist, 4 stores, various locations, 38-42. Mil. Serv: Pvt, Mont. Nat. Guard, 31-34. Mem: Squibb Adv. Coun, 59-64; Mont. State Pharmaceutical Asn, pres, 58-59; pres, Mont. Drug Travelers Asn, 55; Nat. Asn. Retail Druggists; Mason; Blue Lodge; Scottish Rite; York Rite; Shrine; Kiwanis; Elks. Mont. Pharmacists of the Year Award, 63; A.H. Robbins Award for Outstanding Commun. Serv. in Pharmacy, 61. Rel: Presbyterian. Legal Res: 1214 Ninth St, West Billings, Mont. 59102. Mailing Add: 3311 Fourth Ave. North, Billings, Mont. 59101.

HILLINGS, PATRICK J. R
Mem, Los Angeles Co. Rep. Cent. Cmt, Calif.
b. Hobart Mills, Calif, 2/19/23; s. Edward John Hillings and Evangeline Murphy H; m. 10/5/47 to Phyllis K. Reinbrecht; c. Pamela Jane, David Michael and Jennifer Ann. Educ: Univ. of Southern Calif, B.A, 47, J.D, 49; Delta Theta Phi; Blue Key; Trogan Knights; Skull & Dagger. Polit. & Govt.

Pos: Pres, Los Angeles Co. Young Rep, 49; field asst. to U.S. Rep. Richard Nixon, Calif, 49-50; U.S. Rep, 25th Dist, Calif, 51-59; del, Rep. Nat. Conv, 52, 56, 60 & 64; chmn, Los Angeles Co. Rep. Cent. Cmt, 60; spec. asst. to John Mitchell, Nixon Campaign Mgr, 68; mem. bd. trustees, Rep. Assocs, Los Angeles; past mem, Calif. State Rep. Cent. Cmt; mem, Los Angeles Co. Rep. Cent. Cmt. and RN Assocs, currently. Bus. & Prof. Pos: Attorney-at-law, 49-; owner and pres, Pat Hillings Travel Agency, 62-; civic and govt. affairs mgr, Ford Motor Co, West. U.S, currently; counsel, Reeves and Harrison, Wash, D.C, currently. Mil. Serv: Entered as Pvt, Army, 43, released as Sgt, 46, after serv. in Signal Intel. Serv, S.Pac; S.Pac. Campaign Ribbons and Three Battle Stars; Presidential Unit Citation. Publ: Series of articles on Tour of Russia, Hearst Press, 55; 'California Federal Judicial Districts,' State Bar J. of Calif, 57. Mem: Bar of Supreme Court of U.S; Am, Calif, Los Angeles Co, Fed. and Inter-Am. Bar Asns; Bar of D.C; Am. Soc. Travel Agents; Legion Lex; Am. Legion; VFW; Calif. Club; Capitol Hill Club; Commonwealth Club of San Francisco; 82nd Club of Capitol Hill; Cong. Chowder & Marching Soc; Kiwanis; K. of C. Rel: Catholic. Legal Res: 1130 Fallen Leaf Rd, Arcadia, Calif. 91006. Mailing Add: 3921 Wilshire Blvd, Suite 518, Los Angeles, Calif. 90005.

HILLIS, ELWOOD H. R
Ind. State Rep.
b. Kokomo, Ind, 3/6/26; s. Glen R. Hillis and Bernice Haynes H; m. 6/12/49 to Carol Hoyne; c. Jeffrey H, Gary L. and Bradley R. Educ: Ind. Univ, B.S, 49 and J.D, 52; Sigma Nu; Phi Delta Phi; Alpha Kappa Psi. Polit. & Govt. Pos: Mem, Kokomo Housing Authority, Ind, 58-66, chmn, 62-66; Ind. State Rep, Tipton & Howard Co, 67- Bus. & Prof. Pos: Dir, Union Bank & Trust Co, 56-; pres, Hillis Enterprises, Inc. Mil. Serv: Entered as Pvt, Air Force, 44, released as 2nd Lt, 46, after serv. in 9th Inf. Div, 39th Regt, ETO, 46; Capt, Inf. Res, until 54; Am. Theater and Army of Occupation Ribbons; Victory and Good Conduct Medals. Mem: Rotary; Elks; Am. Legion; VFW; Mason; Shrine; asst. chmn, United Fund Drive, 66, chmn, 67; pres, Elwood Haynes Mem. Charitable Trust; pres, Howard Co. United Fund, 69. Rel: Presbyterian. Legal Res: 2331 South Wabash Ave, Kokomo, Ind. 46901. Mailing Add: P.O. Box 847, Kokomo, Ind. 46901.

HILLMAN, ELSIE HILLIARD R
Mem, Pa. State Rep. Exec. Cmt.
b. Pittsburgh, Pa, 12/9/25; d. Thomas Jones Hilliard and Marianna Talbott H; m. 5/10/45 to Henry L. Hillman; c. Juliet Lea, Audrey Hilliard, Henry L, Jr. and William Talbott. Educ: Westminster Choir Col. Polit. & Govt. Pos: Chmn, v.chmn, and mem. of many cmts. for campaigns and candidates, 52-; secy, Alleghany Co. Rep. Exec. Cmt, Pa, 62-66, chmn, currently; mem, State Rep. Women's Adv. Cmt, 62-; chmn, 14th Ward Rep. Cmt, Pittsburgh, 63-; mem, Pa. State Rep. Exec. Cmt, and State Finance Cmt; del, Rep. Nat. Conv, 68. Mem: Secy, Health and Welfare Asn, Alleghany Co; bd. of dirs, Women's Asn. of Pa. Symphony Soc; bd. dirs, Hill House Asn; bd. of trustees, Carlow Col. Women in Politics Award, Nat. League of Woman Voters, given at Worlds Fair. Rel: Episcopal. Mailing Add: Morewood Heights, Pittsburgh, Pa. 15213.

HILLS, JOHN PARKER R
Chmn, Tenn. Fedn. Young Rep. Clubs.
b. Cambridge, Mass, 4/18/35; s. Isaac Hills and Hilda Susan Sawyer H; m. 3/8/58 to Marian Sue Hellernan; c. Mary Alice. Educ: Brown Univ, A.B. cum laude, 57; Wash. & Lee Sch. of Law, LL.B, 60; Phi Delta Theta; Phi Delta Phi. Polit. & Govt. Pos: Mem. bd, Memphis and Shelby Co. Young Rep. Club, Tenn, 61-67, pres, 63; treas, Tenn. Fedn. Young Rep. Clubs, 63, chmn, 67-; chmn, Shelby Co. Primary Bd, 64-66. Bus. & Prof. Pos: Mem, Dann Hills & Blackburn, Attorneys, 67- Mem: Va, Am, Memphis and Shelby Co. Bar Asns; Delta Sailing Club; Young Exec. Club; Int. Lightning Class Asn. Mailing Add: 1624 Harbert St, Memphis, Tenn. 38104.

HILLYER, WILLIAM HUDSON R
Chmn, Tuscarawas Co. Rep. Exec. Cmt, Ohio
b. Uhrichsville, Ohio, 7/28/28; s. Edgar Evans Hillyer and Louise Coldren H; m. 7/2/50 to Marie Cowan; c. Blair, Brad, Beth and Becky. Educ: Ohio State Univ, B.S, 50, J.D, 52; Phi Delta Phi; Phi Kappa Tau. Polit. & Govt. Pos: Mem, Ohio Dept. Develop, 56-58; mem, Civil Serv. Cmn, Uhrichsville, 64-; mem, bd. elec, New Philadelphia, 66-; chmn, Tuscarawas Co. Rep. Exec. Cmt, 66- Bus. & Prof. Pos: Dir, Clay City Pipe Co, Uhrichsville, Ohio, 56-, Bowerston Shale Co, Bowerston, 56-, Union Country Club, New Philadelphia, 62-66; United Clay Pipe Co, Seminole, Okla, 63- and Ross Clay Prod. Co, Gnadenhutten, Ohio, 64- Mil. Serv: Entered as Ens, Naval Res, 46, released as Lt.(sg), 59, after serv. in Supply Corps, U.S. Mem: Ohio State Alumni Asn; Eagles; Elks; Mason. Rel: Methodist. Legal Res: 405 Park Dr, Uhrichsville, Ohio 44683. Mailing Add: 201 N. Main St, Box 272, Uhrichsville, Ohio 44683.

HILTON, IVAN JAY D
V.Chmn, N.Mex. State Dem. Party
b. Springfield, Ill, 1/31/98; s. Albert Hilton and Rosa K. H; m. 12/25/26 to Elizabeth J. Klauser; c. Joyce. Educ: Univ. of Ill, 15-19. Polit. & Govt. Pos: N.Mex. State Sen, 36-38; chmn, N.Mex. State Hwy. Cmn, 38-45; mayor, Las Vegas, 40-46 & 50-54; v.chmn, N.Mex. State Dem. Party, currently. Mil. Serv: 2nd Lt, Army, 18. Mem: Pres. bd. of regents, N.Mex. Highlands Univ; Elks; Am. Legion; pres, C. of C, 64-65. Rel: Presbyterian. Mailing Add: 702 Lee Dr, Las Vegas, N.Mex. 87701.

HIMSL, MATHIAS A. R
Mont. State Rep.
b. Bethune, Sask, Can, 9/17/12; s. Victor S. Himsl and Clara Engels H; m. 7/18/40 to Lois L. Wohlwend; c. Allen, Marilyn, Louise, Kathleen and Judith. Educ: St. John's, Minn, B.A, 34; Univ. Mont, M.A, 40. Polit. & Govt. Pos: Rep. co. chmn, Mont, 52-64; Rep. nominee for State Rep, 64; del, Rep. Nat. Conv, 64; Mont. State Rep, Flathead Co, 67-, mem, Legis. Coun, 69- Bus. & Prof. Pos: Secy-mgr, Himsl-Wohlwend Motors, Inc, 45-; dir, Conrad Nat. Bank, 48; pres, Skyline Broadcasters, Inc, 58-; pres, Mont. Auto Dealers' Asn, 68-; polit. sci. instr, Flathead Valley Commun. Col, 69- Mem: Elks; Kiwanis; C. of C. Editorial writer for KGEZ radio prog. Rel: Roman Catholic. Legal Res: 305 Fourth Ave. E, Kalispell, Mont. 59901. Mailing Add: P.O. Box 838, Kalispell, Mont. 59901.

HINCHEY, FRANCIS NATHANIEL D
b. Rutland, Vt, 12/15/93; m. to Katherine F. Culliney; c. One son; two daughters. Educ: Middlebury Col; Yale Univ, Ph.B, 21; Univ. Vt, M.Ed, 39; Chi Psi. Polit. & Govt. Pos: Vt. State Rep, 65-69. Bus. & Prof. Pos: Retired supv. prin, W.Rutland, Vt. Mil. Serv: M.S.E. Aviation Sect, Signal Corps, 17-19, 496th Aero Squadron. Rel: Catholic. Mailing Add: 45 Park St, Rutland, Vt. 05701.

HINE, ROBERT WALTER R
b. New Milford, Conn, 12/6/24; s. Raymond Arthur Hine and Cora Ferriss H; m. 8/7/48 to Vera Mae Rogers; c. Linda Jean and Mary Alice. Educ: West. State Col, B.A, 62. Polit. & Govt. Pos: Committeeman, Precinct 402, Colo. Rep. Party, 64-; mem, Colo. State Rep. Cent. Cmt, 66-68; chmn, Sen. Dist. 31 Rep. Party, 66-69; capt, Dist. 3 Adams Co. Rep. Party, 66-; del, Rep. Nat. Conv, 68; chmn. audit cmt, Adams Co. Rep. Party, 68- Bus. & Prof. Pos: Teacher, Aurora Schs, 63- Mil. Serv: Entered as Pvt, Air Force, 43, released as SM Sgt, 63, after serving in Guam, 48-49, and Germany, 52-56. Mem: Nat, Colo. and Aurora Educ. Asns; VFW. Rel: Protestant. Mailing Add: 1741 Havana St, Aurora, Colo. 80010.

HINEMAN, EDWIN S. R
Chmn, Del. Co. Rep. Exec. Cmt, Pa.
b. Beaver, Pa, 12/18/16; s. Oliver Hineman and Flora Sharp H; m. Anna L. Litz; c. Richard E, Edwin S, Jr, Clifford O, Suzanne, Martin and Donald. Educ: Univ. Pa, B.S, 37; Nat. Mil. Honor Soc; Sigma Phi Sigma. Polit. & Govt. Pos: Rep. committeeman, Birmingham Twp, Pa, 56 & 60-; chmn, Upper Chichester Twp. Rep. Orgn, 56-68; supvr, Birmingham Twp, 6 years, chmn, 5 years; chmn, Birmingham Twp. Rep. Orgn; mem, Del. Co. Planning Cmn, 56-, v.chmn, 61-64, chmn, 64-68; treas, Del. Co, 63-67; treas, Del. Co. Inst. Dist; mem, Del. Co. Retirement Bd; exec. dep. secy, Pa. Dept. Revenue, 67-; mem. bd. supvrs, Del. Co, 68-; chmn, Del. Co. Rep. Exec. Cmt, 68- Bus. & Prof. Pos: Owner, Fox Hollow Farm, Breeder of Thoroughbred Horses and Racing Stable; secy-treas, Delaware Co. Supply Co, Boothwyn, Pa, Tri-Co. Supply Co, Glen Mills and Eddo Corp, Boothwyn; adv. bd, Fidelity Bank. Mem: Pa. Planning Asn; Am. Soc. Planning Officials; Co. Treas. Asn. Pa.(legis. cmt, 64-65, dir, 66-67); F&AM; Consistory (32°); Shrine; Lions Int.(past pres, Brandywine Hundred Lions Club, past zone chmn, Dist. 22D, past dep. dist. gov); Pa. Horse Breeder's Asn; Horsemen's Benevolent and Protective Asn; Pa. Mfg. Asn; Nat. Asn. Tax Adminstr; Mid. Atlantic Lumber Dealer's Asn; Concordville Fire & Protective Asn; United Hunts. Rel: Methodist. Mailing Add: Fox Hollow Farm, Webb Rd, Chadds Ford, Pa. 19317.

HINES, ARTHUR SNOW R
Chmn, Templeton Co. Rep. Party, Mass.
b. Baldwinville, Mass, 11/14/32; s. Ronald Hines and Elizabeth Snow Hines Thompson; m. 7/14/56 to Kathleen Lilleen Hunter; c. Cynthia May, Debra Ann, Michael Arthur and James Arthur. Educ: Worcester Trade Sch, Machine Trade Cert; Worcester Jr. Col, A.I.E. Polit. & Govt. Pos: V.chmn, Templeton Co. Rep. Party, Mass, 66, chmn, 68- Bus. & Prof. Pos: Methods engr, Heald Machine Co, 56-63; sales engr, Lindeo Inc, 63- Mil. Serv: Entered as Pvt, Army, 53, released as Cpl, 54, after serv. in 623 F.A.B, Korea; Korean Medal. Mem: Am. Soc. Tool and Mech. Engrs; Am. Legion; Mason. Rel: Episcopal. Mailing Add: 6 Athol Rd, Baldwinville, Mass. 01436.

HINES, LEON C. D
Chmn, Dundy Co. Dem. Orgn, Nebr.
b. Benkelman, Nebr, 6/10/22; s. Leon L. Hines and Keturah E. Sipe H; m. 8/12/46 to Anne E. Rosser; c. Elizabeth Susan, Patricia Ann and Barbara Ellen. Educ: Univ. Nebr, B.Sc, 43, J.D, 48; Phi Delta Phi; Kappa Sigma. Polit. & Govt. Pos: Mem, Nebr. State Dem. Cent. Cmt, 54-56; co. attorney, Dundy Co, Nebr, 54-58; pres, Nebr. Asn. Housing & Renewal Authorities, 65-67; dir, Nat. Asn. Housing & Renewal Off, 66-68; chmn, Dundy Co. Dem. Orgn, 66- Mil. Serv: Entered as Pfc, Army, 42, released as 1st Lt, 46, after serving in 106th Inf. Div, ETO. Mem: Mason; Elks; Am. Legion; C. of C. Rel: Methodist. Mailing Add: 631 First Ave. W, Benkelman, Nebr. 69021.

HINES, PAULENA LININGER R
V.Chmn, Teller Co. Rep. Party, Colo.
b. Savannah, Mo, 9/3/09; d. Atlee Burpee Lininger and Ollie Howard L; m. 2/21/31 to Ralph Everette Hines; c. Marvin Eugene and Victor Burpee. Educ: Platt Bus. Col, 29. Polit. & Govt. Pos: V.chmn, Teller Co. Rep. Party, Colo, 60- Bus. & Prof. Pos: Secy. and bookkeeper, Mo. Livestock Cmn. Co, 29-32. Mem: Ladies Auxiliary, VFW; Parent-Teacher Orgn; Lioness Club; Teller Co. Rep. Womens Club. Rel: Baptist. Mailing Add: Box 502, Woodland Park, Colo. 80863.

HINES, PETER FRANCIS D
City Councillor, Boston, Mass.
b. Boston, Mass, 11/30/27; s. Colonel Paul H. Hines and Margaret Galvin H; m. 6/30/62 to Dorothy Marie Hicks; c. Peter, Jr. and Elizabeth. Educ: Boston Col, Pre-Legal, Boston Col. Law Sch, LL.B, 52. Polit. & Govt. Pos: City Councillor, Boston, Mass, 58-; mem, Dem. Ward Cmt, 64- Bus. & Prof. Pos: Practicing attorney, Boston, Mass. Mil. Serv: Entered as Pvt, Army, 46, released as Sgt, 47, after serv. as City Ed, Pac. Stars and Stripes, under Army of Occup, Far East Command, Gen. Hq, Tokyo, Japan. Mem: Mass. Trial Lawyers Asn. Rel: Roman Catholic. Mailing Add: 9 Hobson St, Roslindale, Mass. 02131. (1967)

HINIG, WILLIAM E. D
Ohio State Rep.
b. New Philadelphia, Ohio, 5/24/19; s. Floyd W. Hinig and Florence M. Stilgenbauer H; m. 1/15/46 to Clara M. Aldergate; c. Judith L, Richard W. and Jill. Educ: LaSalle Exten. Univ. Polit. & Govt. Pos: Councilman-at-lg, New Philadelphia, Ohio, 62-63, pres. city coun, 64; Ohio State Rep, Tuscarawas Co, currently. Bus. & Prof. Pos: Registered pub. acct, Hinig & Miller Co, 53-66. Mil. Serv: Entered as Pvt, Army, 41, released as Sgt, 46, after serv. in Inf, ETO, 45; Purple Heart; ETO Ribbon. Mem: Pub. Acct. Soc. of Ohio; Nat. Soc. of Pub. Accts; Elks; DAV; VFW; Exchange Club; Toastmasters. Rel: Protestant. Mailing Add: 835 Hardesty Ave. N.W, New Philadelphia, Ohio 44663.

HINKINS, MARILYN C. D
V.Chmn, Salt Lake Co. Dem. Cmt, Utah
b. Manti, Utah, 11/11/35; d. Wilbur L. Christensen and Lou Brady Lundberg C; div; c. Arthur Lee and Ryan Tay. Educ: Col. East Utah, A.S, 65; Univ. Utah, B.A, 66, grad. study, 66-; Phi Rho Pi; Phi Theta Kappa; Block C Medallion. Polit. & Govt. Pos: Co-chmn, East. Utah Rampton for Gov. Cmt, 64; chmn, East. Utah Dem. Hq, 64; pres, Carbon Co. Young Dem, 64-65; pres, Col. East. Utah Young Dem, 64-65; v.pres, Utah Young Dem, 65-67, acting pres, 66 and nat. committeewoman, 67-; chmn, Nat. Young Dem. Cmt. Meeting, 67; co-chmn, Jefferson-Jackson State Fund Raising Dinner, 67; v.chmn, Salt Lake Co. Dem. Cmt, 67-; chmn, Utah Young Citizens for Humphrey Campaign, 68; del, Dem. Nat. Conv, 68. Bus. & Prof. Pos: Exec. secy, Kaiser Steel Credit Union, Sunnyside, Utah, 55-56; and Carbon Co. Nursing Home, Price, Utah, 64-65; admin. asst. pub. rels. specialist, Utah State Dept. of Hwys, Salt Lake, 65-67; asst. dir. advert. and pub. rels, Eimco Corp, Salt Lake City, 67-69; state mgr. pub. rels, Glenmore Distilleries, 68-; pub. rels. consult, Hinkins Pub. Rels. and Counseling, 68-. Publ: 'Mountain America's Interstate 15,' Rocky Mt. Construction, 11/65; 'Progress Report on the West's Route 15,' Better Roads, 3/66; 'Unusual Bridge Goes Over River But Not Across,' Pac. Rd. Builder, 7/66. Mem: Assoc. mem. Utah Press Asn; assoc. mem. Intermt. Chap, Pub. Rels. Soc. Am; Intermt. Asn. Indust. Ed; Theta Sigma Phi; Gen. Fedn. Women's Clubs; Eagles Women Auxiliary; Epsilon Sigma Omicron; Kiwaniannes. Outstanding Speech Student, Col. East. Utah, 64-65, Outstanding Woman Student, and Valedictorian of Class, 65; Honors Student, Univ. Utah (Master's Honors Prog); Outstanding Young Woman of Am, 65. Rel: Presbyterian. Mailing Add: Sunset Towers Suite 15A, 40 S. Ninth E, Salt Lake City, Utah 84102.

HINKLE, ALLEN BROOKS D
Ky. State Rep.
b. Paris, Ky, 1/18/13; s. Thurman Hinkle and Elizabeth Parsons H; m. 5/28/41 to Elaine Brierly. Educ: Esat. State Univ, B.A, 35; Univ. Ky, M.A, 52. Polit. & Govt. Pos: Ky. State Rep, 72nd Dist, 56- Bus. & Prof. Pos: Teacher, Bourbon Co. Schs, Ky, 35-42, principal, 46-63; teacher, Franklin Co. Schs, 63- Mil. Serv: Entered as Pvt, Army, 42, released as Maj, 46, after serv. in Transportation Corps; Army Res, 46-68. Mem: Bourbon Co. Farm Bur; Franklin Co. Teachers Orgn; Nat. and Ky. Educ. Asns; Mason; Am. Legion. Rel: Christian. Mailing Add: Route 3, Paris, Ky. 40361.

HINKLE, DORIS McCASTLAIN D
Cmnr. of Revenues, Ark.
b. Graysonia, Ark, 1/23/18; d. Earl L. Wagner and Flossie Meeks W; m. Hugh Marvin McCastlain, wid; remarried 11/24/66 to Col. Carl Hinkle, Jr, c. Hugh Marvin, Mary Lynn (Mrs. Nelson), Julia Ann and Laura Adams. Educ: Glenwood High Sch, Ark, grad; Beta Delta. Polit. & Govt. Pos: Asst. secy, Ark. House of Rep, 41-52; Ark. State Rep, Monroe Co, 61-65, mem, Audit Cmt, Ark. House of Rep, 61-65; chmn, Ark. Revenue Dept. Bldg. Cmn, 65-; secy, Ark. State Racing Cmn, 65-; cmnr. of revenues, Ark, 65-; secy, Ark. Gov. Traffic Safety Adv. Cmt, 66- Bus. & Prof. Pos: Mem, Nat. Asn. Tax Adminstrs. and Am. Asn. of Motor Vehicle Adminstrs, 65- Mem: Charter mem, Nat. Soc. State Legislators; South. and Nat. Coun. State Govt, 61-65; Nat. Order Woman Legislators (state pres, 61-65); Woman Civil Defense (state pres, 61-65); Altrusa; state v.pres, Am. Red Cross; past pres, PTA and Womens Soc. of Christian Serv; State Fedn. Women's Clubs; Farm Bur; past pres, Brinkley Country Club; Mercy Hosp. Auxiliary. Hon. Ky. Col. Rel: Methodist; former bd. mem, 1st Methodist Church of Brinkley. Legal Res: Brinkley, Ark. Mailing Add: 1701 Sundale Rd, Johnson City, Tenn. 37601.

HINKLE, JOE THOMAS D
Chmn, Fremont Co. Dem. Cent. Cmt, Wyo.
b. Purcell, Okla, 1/17/21; s. John Earl Hinkle and Mary V. Spence H; m. 10/3/48 to Aly Maxine Brandon; c. David, Dana and Donald. Educ: Univ. Denver. Polit. & Govt. Pos: Chmn, Fremont Co. Dem. Cent. Cmt,Wyo, 62- Bus. & Prof. Pos: Mem, Bd. of Dirs, Lander Livestock Cmn. Co, 56- and pres, 60-64; Bd. of Dirs, Lander C. of C, 58-60. Mil. Serv: Entered as Aviation Cadet, Navy, 42, released as Lt.(sg), 45, after serv. as Naval Aviator in Units in S.Pac, 44 and 45; Air Medal; Unit Citation; S.Pac. Theater Ribbon. Mem: Mason, Consistory, Shrine; Elks; Am. Legion; VFW. Rel: Episcopal; mem. of the Vestry. Legal Res: 290 Adams St, Lander, Wyo. 82520. Mailing Add: 494 Main St, Lander, Wyo. 82520. (1967)

HINKLE, PAUL DAVID D
b. Cherokee, Kans, 9/21/38; s. Proctor K. Hinkle (deceased) and Elsie M. Perry H; m. 5/29/69 to Carole Mary Dupuis. Educ: East Contra Costa Col, A.A, 58; Sacramento State Col, B.A, 60; Blue Key; Alpha Phi Gamma; Phi Kappa Tau; Editor, The State Hornet, Sacramento State Col; World Univ. Serv; Sacramento State Col. Press Club. Polit. & Govt. Pos: Precinct Capt, Stevenson for President Campaign, Antioch, Calif, 56; Press aide, Calif. State Assemblyman Jerome R. Waldie, 60; hq. mgr, Kennedy - Johnson Campaign, Antioch, Calif, 60; admin. asst. to Calif. State Assemblyman Leroy Greene, 63-65; pub. coordinator, Johnson-Humphrey Campaign, Sacramento Co, 64; legis. asst. to U.S. Rep. John E. Moss, Calif, 65-66, admin. asst, 66- Bus. & Prof. Pos: Ed, The Rancho Cordovan, 63. Mil. Serv: Entered as Pvt, Army Nat. Guard, Calif, 62, released as Sp-4, 65, after serv. in 49th Inf. Div. Mem: Cong Secy. Club; Calif. State Soc. Norseman Award in Journalism, 58. Rel: Protestant. Legal Res: 2417 38th Ave, Sacramento, Calif. 95822. Mailing Add: 2185 Rayburn Office Bldg, Washington, D.C. 20515.

HINMAN, EDNA JANE R
b. York, Mont, 11/27/02; d. Richard McCreanor and Margaret Lyle M; m. 5/19/23 to Dewey Morgan Hinman, wid; c. Suzanne (Mrs. R.M. Bateman) and Lucille (Mrs. Wm. E. Samson). Educ: High Sch. grad. Polit. & Govt. Pos: Asst. secy, Senate or asst. chief clerk, House of Rep, 29-47; secy, Rep. Party State Hq, various intervals, 39-42; receptionist, Gov. Off, 53; state treas, Mont, 53-57 & 61-65; clerk of Supreme Court, 57-59 and employed by State Controller, 59-61; chief clerk, Mont. House of Rep, 67-; former co. v.chmn, Rep. Cent. Cmt, Mont. Bus. & Prof. Pos: Stenographer, Mountain States Tel. & Tel. Co, Helena, Mont, 20-23; cashier, Union Oil Co, Portland, Ore, 26-28; legal secy, Off. of Charles E. Pew, 34-36 and Off. of Weir, Gough & Matson, Helena, Mont, 42-51; mem. staff, Mont. Girls State. Mem: Chmn, Mont. Gov. Cmn. Status Women; Gov. Cmt. on the Mont. Centennial Train; Gov. Joint Cmt. on Ment. Health and Ment. Retardation; past Nat. Officer, Women of the Moose; past matron and grand officer, Eastern Star; past mother advisor, Rainbow Girls; Rebekahs; Am. Legion Auxiliary (past pres; pres, Dist. 6, currently); past chap. chmn, Red Cross; pres. bd. dir, YWCA; pres. Helena Camp Fire Girls; secy, Helena Commun. Chest Bd; secy, Helena Commun. Coun; past pres, Bus. and Prfnl. Women's Club, Helena; bd. dir, United Givers; treas. and mem. bd. dir, Mont. Asn. for Ment. Health Adjudged Montana's Woman of the Year by the Bus. and Prfnl. Women, 64. Rel: Presbyterian; Elder and trustee, financial secy. and youth advisor, First Presbyterian Church of Helena. Mailing Add: 562 Fifth Ave, Helena, Mont. 59601.

HINMAN, GEORGE L. R
Rep. Nat. Committeeman, N.Y.
b. Binghamton, N.Y, 9/25/05; s. Harvey D. Hinman and Phebe Brown H; m. 9/12/29 to Barbara Davidge; c. Constance (Mrs. Getz), Martha (Mrs. Vaughn), Virginia (Mrs. Robinson) and Harvey D, II. Educ: Princeton Univ, A.B, 27; Harvard Univ, LL.B, 30; Quadrangle Club. Hon. D.H.L, Elmira Col, 50; hon. LL.D, Union Univ, 62; hon. L.C.D, Colgate Univ, 68. Polit. & Govt. Pos: Regent, State Univ. N.Y, 48-50; mem, Lt. Gov. Cmt. on Teachers Salaries, 51; mem, N.Y. Attorney Gen. Cmt. on Ethical Standards in Govt, 55-59; counsel, N.Y. State Temporary Cmn. on Constitutional Conv. and Spec. Legis. Cmt. on Rev. and Simplification of Constitution, 56-58; exec. asst. to Gov. Nelson A. Rockefeller, N.Y, 58-59; Rep. Nat. Committeeman, N.Y, 59-; del-at-lg, Rep. Nat. Conv, 60 & 64. Bus. & Prof. Pos: Partner, Hinman, Howard & Kattell, Binghamton, N.Y; spec. counsel, Rockefeller Family and Assocs, N.Y.C; dir, Int. Bus. Mach. Corp, N.Y. Tel. Co, Security Mutual Life Ins. Co. of N.Y, First-City Nat. Bank of Binghamton, Arlington Hotel, Inc. and Lincoln First Banks, Inc. Mem: Trustee, State Univ. N.Y. and Colgate Univ; exec. cmt, Salvation Army N.Y. State Adv. Conf; The Pilgrims; Harvard Club; Univ. Club; Century Asn; The Links; Binghamton City Club; Cypress Point Club; Edgartown Yacht Club, Mass; Capitol Hill Club, D.C. Rel: Presbyterian. Legal Res: Hawleyton Rd, Binghamton, N.Y. 13901. Mailing Add: Room 5600, 30 Rockefeller Plaza, New York, N.Y. 10020.

HINMAN, KEITH DFL
b. Grey Eagle, Minn, 1925; Married; c. Five. Educ: Grey Eagle Pub. Schs. Polit. & Govt. Pos: Minn. State Rep, 60-66; Sch. Bd. Mem, 57-60. Bus. & Prof. Pos: Owner and operator, grocery store. Mem: Pres, Grey Eagle Commercial Club; former pres, PTA; chmn, Grey Eagle Centennial Celebration, 58. Mailing Add: Grey Eagle, Minn. 56336. (1967)

HINMAN, WALLACE PORTER R
Colo. State Rep.
b. Nelson, Nev, 6/16/14; s. Mark Merrit Hinman and Pearl Menhennett H; m. 9/2/40 to Ione Virginia Trantham; c. Marian (Mrs. Walton) and Jeanne. Educ: Kremmling High Sch, grad. Polit. & Govt. Pos: Colo. State Rep, 69- Mem: Mid. Park Woolgrowers Asn, 41-42; pres, Colo. Hereford Asn, 53-54; pres. and dir, Nat. West. Stock Show, 58-70; pres, Routt Co. Stock Growers, 61-62; centennial pres. and pres. of centennial cmn, Colo. Cattlemens Asn; 67; mem, Colo. State Fair Cmn, 67 & 68; Elks, Idaho Springs, Colo; Aviation Club, Denver; Petroleum Club. Livestock Judging Awards; Serv. Awards, State Fair Cmn. and Colo. Cattlemens Asn. Rel: Protestant. Mailing Add: P.O. Box 48, Yampa, Colo. 80483.

HINSON, CALDWELL THOMAS D
S.C. State Rep.
b. Lancaster, S.C, 8/1/20; s. Alexander M. Hinson and Lula Barker H; m. 7/3/43 to Myrtle Louise Moore; c. Caldwell T, Jr, Sarah (Mrs. McCants), Donald M, Wanda E. and Angela L. Educ: Buford High Sch. grad, 40. Polit. & Govt. Pos: S.C. State Rep, 69- Bus. & Prof. Pos: Owner, grocery & meat market, 46-51; owner, Hinson Motors, 51-69. Mil. Serv: Entered as Pvt, Army, serv. as Rifleman and Machine Gunner, Tenth Mt. Inf, Italy, 44-45; Combat Inf. Medal; Good Conduct Medal; Bronze Star with One Cluster; Purple Heart with Two Clusters. Mem: Past Master Jackson Lodge 53, A&FM; Past High Priest, Keystone Chap. 19, RAM; Past Illustrious Master, Witherspoon Coun. 33, RSM; Shrine (past pres, Jackson Club, charter mem, Hejaz Temple Color Guard); AAONMS; Jackson Realty Co; Eastern Star; Green Dragons; Royal Order of Fleas; Demolay adv, Am. Legion; VFW; DAV. Rel: Baptist. Mailing Add: 1115 Chesterfield Ave, Lancaster, S.C. 29720.

HINTON, GRANVILLE R
Tenn. State Rep.
b. Savannah, Tenn, 2/10/29; s. Isom G. Hinton and Lucille Stansell H; m. 6/29/46 to Willie Mae Barker; c. Jeanne Lynn and Robert Granville. Educ: Florence State Col, B.S, 49. Polit. & Govt. Pos: Mayor, Savannah, Tenn, 53-57 & 61-65, city cmnr, 57-61 & 65-66; Tenn. State Rep, Hardin and McNairy Co, currently. Mem: Mason; Scottish Rite; Shrine; Moose; Rotary. Rel: Methodist. Legal Res: 604 Patterson Rd, Savannah, Tenn. 38372. Mailing Add: 109 Gwinn St, Savannah, Tenn. 38372. (1967)

HIPKINS, STELLA A. D
b. Flint, Mich, 1/1/22; d. John Sujak and Rosie Sutorik S; m. 3/22/41 to Walter L. Hipkins; c. Sondra (Mrs. Spivack), Larry S, Marsha Jon and Jeffrey W. Educ: Flint Northern High Sch, Mich, 38-41. Polit. & Govt. Pos: Genesee Co. campaign mgr, Mich. Court of Appeals, Judge O'Brian, 64; trustee, Flint Twp. Dem. Club, 65-67, v.chmn, 67-; v.chmn, Genesee Co. Dem. Exec. Cmt, 66; campaign mgr, Edward Suski, Mich. State Rep, 66; campaign mgr, Dick Wood, Co. Treas, 68; del, Dem. Nat. Conv, 68; mem, exec. bd, Genesee Co. Dem. Women's Div, 69- Mem: State Dem. Party; Flint Twp. Dem. Club; Dem. Womens Div, Genesee Co. Mailing Add: 4290 Calkins Rd, Flint, Mich. 48504.

HIRAI, SEICHI D
b. Waihee, Maui, Hawaii, 7/29/23; s. George Choei Hirai and Shizue Sakamoto H; m. 1/11/47 to Beverly Hideko Yamaguchi; c. Colleen Kazumi. Educ: Univ. Hawaii, B.A, 50; George Wash. Univ. Law Sch, J.D, 58; Phi Alpha Delta. Polit. & Govt. Pos: Research asst. to Del. J.A. Burns, Wash, D.C, 56-58; asst. clerk, Hawaii Senate, 59; clerk, Hawaii State Senate, 63-; del, Dem. Nat. Conv, 68. Bus. & Prof. Pos: Attorney, Honolulu Redevelop. Agency, 60-62. Mil. Serv: Entered as Pvt, Army, 43, released as Pfc, 46, after serv. in 442nd Inf. Regt, ETO, 44-45; Rome-Arno Campaign, Europe-Africa-Middle-East Serv, Asiatic-Pac. Serv, Po Valley Campaign, Rhineland Campaign, Good Conduct, Purple Heart, Bronze Star and World War II Victory Medals; Distinguished Unit Badge. Mem: Hawaii Bar Asn; Am. Judicature Soc; Phi Alpha

Delta. Rel: Methodist. Legal Res: 1408 Kaminaka Dr, Honolulu, Hawaii 96816. Mailing Add: Room 421, Central Pacific Bank Bldg, Honolulu, Hawaii 96817.

HIRSCH, HILDA R
V.Chmn, Richmond Co. Rep. Orgn, N.Y.
b. N.Y.C, 6/23/11; d. Ignatz Kessler and Sadie Klein K; m. 1930 to Samuel Hirsch. Educ: Staten Island Acad; West End Finishing Sch; Metrop. Ballet Sch; N.Y. Univ; Wagner Col. Polit. & Govt. Pos: Chmn. and hostess for various polit. activities; chmn, Annual Dance of Rep. Orgn; chmn, Annual Rep. Picnics; chmn. of Store Fronts for Friends of Rockefeller, Javits, Keating and Lefkowitz; secy, N.Y.C. Rep. Conv; mem, N.Y.C. Mayoralty Cmt; mem, N.Y.C. Rep. Adv. Cmt; mem, Local, City, State and Nat. Rep. Finance Cmts; del, N.Y. State Rep. Conv; mem, N.Y. State Rep. Cmt; Elec. Dist. Capt; mem, Richmond Co. Rep. Orgn, N.Y, v.chmn, 62- Bus. & Prof. Pos: Mgr, buyer and seller for local dept. store; owner and mgr. of real estate. Mem: Coun. Jewish Women; dir, Staten Island Cancer Soc; dir, Staten Island Ment. Health Soc; dir, N.Y.C. Coun. of Ment. Health Soc; v.pres. and legis. cmt, N.Y. State Ment. Health Soc; Red Cross; Commun. Chest; Jewish Commun. Center; Temple Emanuel. Rel: Jewish. Mailing Add: 700 Victory Blvd, Staten Island, N.Y. 10301.

HIRSCH, ROBERT WILLIAM R
S.Dak. State Sen.
b. Tripp, S.Dak, 10/12/25; s. Raymond Theophil Hirsch and Linda Schmiedt H; wid; c. John Scott, James Robert and Jayne Marie; m. 2/16/68 to Lyla Ruth Voorhees. Educ: Miss. Col; Univ. S.C, B.A. in Math; Univ. S.Dak. Law Sch, LL.B; Phi Kappa Delta; Phi Delta Phi; Sigma Alpha Epsilon; Phi Mu. Polit. & Govt. Pos: Chmn, Hutchinson Co. Young Rep, S.Dak, 49-59; states attorney, Hutchison Co, 52-56; del, Rep. State Conv, 54-56; S.Dak. State Sen, 14th Dist, 56-, mem. exec. bd, Legis. Research Coun, 57-62, chmn, 62-63 and mem, Court Study Cmn, 63-65, S.Dak. State House of Rep. Mil. Serv: Entered as Seaman 2/C, Naval Res, 43, released as Lt.(jg), 47, after serv. in Serv. Force, Atlantic Fleet, 46-47; 1st Lt, S.Dak. Army Nat. Guard, 59-62; Good Conduct and Victory Medals. Mem: Exec. secy, Bi-Co. Bar; Judicial Coun, S.Dak. Bar Asn; Am. Bar Asn; Am. Trial Lawyers Asn; former pres. and former bd. mem, Int. Lutheran Laymen's League. Nat. Debate Champion. Rel: Lutheran Mo-Synod. Mailing Add: Tripp, S.Dak. 57376.

HIRSCHI, FRANK WILLIAM R
b. Montpelier, Idaho, 2/2/25; s. William Hirschi and Marianna Seiler H; m. 11/26/46 to Carol Price; c. Frank Craig, David Price, Carol Lyn, Scott William, Laura and Janet. Educ: Utah State Univ, B.S, 50, M.S, 62 and Ph.D, 69; Alpha Zeta; Alpha Tau Alpha; Phi Delta Kappa. Polit. & Govt. Pos: Former Idaho State Rep, chmn, House Agr. Cmt, 61-63 and mem, House Educ. Cmt, 63-67. Bus. & Prof. Pos: Owner, 500 acre ranch, 49-66; voc. agr. instr, State of Idaho, 50-55; adminstr. and prin, Latter-day Saint Sem, 55-66; dir. and part owner, Realty Ins. Mart, Inc, 63-66; dir. relig. educ, Church of Jesus Christ of Latter-day Saints, Los Angeles, 69- Mil. Serv: Entered as Seaman, Navy, 44, released as Radioman 3/C, 46; Pac.Campaign Ribbon. Publ: 'Civic Responsibilities,' Impact, 68; 'Reflective Teaching,' The Growing Edge, 69. Mem: Am. Legion; Kiwanis Int. Rel: Latter-day Saint. Mailing Add: 12792 Longden St, Garden Grove, Calif. 92641.

HIRST, OMER LEE D
Va. State Sen.
b. Annandale, Va, 8/30/13; m. to Ann Horton Palmer H. Educ: Wash. and Lee Univ, B.S; Phi Beta Kappa. Polit. & Govt. Pos: Mem. Adv. Cmt. of George Mason Col; Va. State Del, 54-59; Va. State Sen, 64- Bus. & Prof. Pos: Realtor; bd. of trustees, Sibley Mem. Hosp; bd. of trustees, Wash. Center for Metro. Studies; bd. of trustees, Va. Found. of Independent Col; dir, Arlington Trust Co, Arlington, Va. Mil. Serv: Lt, Marines. Mem: Gr. Annandale C. of C; Alexandria C. of C; Hist. Soc. of Fairfax Co; North. Va. Bd. of Realtors, Inc; Fairfax Co. C. of C; Commonwealth Club; Farmington Country Club; North. Va. Adv. Bd. of AAA. Evening Star Trophy, 62. Rel: Methodist. Mailing Add: 7215 Little River Turnpike, Annandale, Va. 22003.

HISLOPE, LEONARD RUSSELL R
b. 1913. Educ: West. Ky State Col, B.S. Polit. & Govt. Pos: Former mem. Speakers Bur, Rep. State Cent. Cmt, Ky; former mem, Pulaski Co. and Lincoln Rep. Club; past pres, Pulaski Co. Young Rep. Club; Ky. State Rep, 56-69, Caucus Chmn, 58 and Minority Leader, 60 & 64, Ky. State House of Rep. Bus. & Prof. Pos: Indust. Prom; former teacher, instr. Mil. Serv: Air Corps. Mem: Odd Fellows; C. of C; Regional Dir, Ky. Hist. Soc; State Dir, Sites and Shrines Cmt. Rel: Methodist. Mailing Add: 107 Church St, Somerset, Ky. 42501. (1967)

HITCHCOX, FORREST L. D
Treas, Anderson Co. Dem. Exec. Cmt, Tenn.
b. Pikeville, Tenn, 9/10/24; s. John Marion Hitchcox and Elizabeth Tate H; m. 12/24/45 to Gwendolyn England; c. Michael Forrest. Educ: Am. Univ. D.C, 9 months. Polit. & Govt. Pos: Secy, Oak Ridge Young Dem. Club, Tenn, 52-54; Second Dist. Chmn, Young Dem. Club Tenn, 52-54; treas, Anderson Co. Dem. Exec. Cmt, 62-; del, Dem Nat. Conv, 68. Bus. & Prof. Pos: Mgr, Powell Clinch Utility Dist, 67- Mil. Serv: Entered as A/S, Navy, 43, released as Pho.M. 2C, 45, after serv. in Bomb and Mine Disposal Unit, S.Pac. Theatre, 44-45; Navy and Presidential Unit Citations. Mem: Am. Legion; Optimist Club. Rel: Protestant. Mailing Add: 114 Kingfisher Lane, Oak Ridge, Tenn. 37830.

HITE, F. RICHARD R
b. Lafayette, Colo, 6/22/14; s. Arleigh Dempster Hite and Mae Daniels H; m. 4/7/46 to Alice Marjorie Brennan; c. Richard Garth and Janis Ruthellen. Educ: Univ. of Colo, B.A, 38, LL.B, 41; Phi Delta Theta. Polit. Pos: Precinct committeeman, Jefferson Co. Rep. Party, Colo, 60-; del, Rep. Nat. Conv. and chmn, Jefferson Co. Rep. Conv, 64; secy, United Rep. Fund, Colo, 62-64; chmn, Jefferson Co. Rep. Finance Cmt. and mem. exec. cmt, Jefferson Co. Rep. Cent. Cmt, 56-60. Govt. Pos: Asst. dist. attorney, Jefferson Co, Colo, 61-66; chmn, Colo. Racing Cmn, 52-60; asst. attorney gen. and dir, Colo. Legis. Reference Bur, 50-52; dep. dist. attorney, City & Co. of Denver, 47-48. Bus. & Prof. Pos: Private practice of law, 46- Mil. Serv: Entered as Pvt, Army, 42, released as Capt, 46, after serv. in 7th Div, Asiatic-Pac. Theater, 43-46; Okinawa and Leyte Ribbons; Mariannas Campaign Ribbon. Mem: Criminal Law Sect, Am. Bar Asn; Lions; Mason (32°); Nat. Rules Cmt, Thoroughbred Horse Racing. Rel: Methodist. Mailing Add: 3705 Garland, Wheatridge, Colo. 80033.

HITT, PATRICIA REILLY R
Asst. Secy. for Commun. and Field Serv, Dept. of Health, Educ. and Welfare
b. Taft, Calif, 1/24/18; d. John B. Reilly and Vera Hearle R.(deceased); m. 9/26/47 to Robert J. Hitt; c. John and Patrick Hamilton. Educ: Univ. South. Calif, B.S. in Educ, 39; Delta Gamma. L.H.D, Chapman Col. Polit. & Govt. Pos: Mem. and v.chmn, Orange Co. Rep. Cent. Cmt, Calif, 55-62; mem. bd, Calif. Fedn. Rep. Women, South. Div, 55-65; pres, Orange Co. Fedn. Women's Clubs, 56-60; mem. exec. cmt, Calif. Rep. State Cent. Cmt, 58-; Rep. Nat. Committeewoman, Calif, 60-64; chmn. women's activities, George Murphy Campaign, 64 and Robert Finch Campaign, 66; co-chmn, Nixon-Agnew Campaign, 68; Asst. Secy. for Commun. and Field Serv, Dept. Health, Educ. and Welfare, 69-; cmnr, U.S. Cmn. for U.S-Mex. Border Develop. and Friendship, 69- Bus. & Prof. Pos: Partner, Miller-Hitt; part owner, Reilly Holdings. Mem: Assistance League; Villa Park Property Owners Asn; C. of C; bd. gov, Chapman Col; Orange Co. Trojan League; Chapman Col. Town & Gown; El Niguel Country Club; chmn, Fed. Woman's Award Bd. Trustees, 69- Los Angeles Times Woman of the Year, 68. Rel: Methodist. Legal Res: 101 Mc-Knight Dr, Laguna Beach, Calif. 92651. Mailing Add: 3113 Woodley Rd, Washington, D.C. 20008.

HITT, ROBERT JAMES R
Exec. Adminstr, Rep. Nat. Cmt.
b. Los Angeles, Calif, 4/22/15; s. Raymond Edwin Hitt and Gladys O'Bert H; m. 9/26/47 to Patricia Vera Reilly. Educ: Univ. South. Calif, B.S. in B.A, 38; Univ. South. Calif. Law Sch, 38-39; Sigma Nu; Blue Key; Skull and Dagger. Polit. & Govt. Pos: Dir. admin, Nixon Campaign Cmt, Wash, D.C, 68-69; mgr, Nixon Conv. Off, Rep. Nat. Conv, 68; exec. adminstr, Rep. Nat. Cmt, 69- Bus. & Prof. Pos: Br. mgr, Repub. Van Lines, Santa Ana, Calif, 53-59; sr. v.pres, Cleary, Hitt & Co. Ltd, mgt. counsr, 59- Mil. Serv: Entered as Pvt, Army, 40, released as Maj, 45, after serv. in Second Inf. Div, ETO, 43-45; Army Res, 45-59, Maj.(Ret); Bronze Star with Four Oak Leaf Clusters with V Devise for Valor; Purple Heart; European Cert. of Merit; Presidential Unit Citation. Mem: Pres. adv. bd, St. Josephs Hosp, Orange, Calif; bd. dirs, Florence Crittenton Home, Orange Co; bd. mem. and treas, Goodwill Industs, Orange Co; pres, Villa Park Property Owners Asn. Rel: Methodist. Legal Res: 101 Mc-Knight Dr, Laguna Beach, Calif. 92651. Mailing Add: 3113 Woodley Rd. N.W, Washington, D.C. 20008.

HIX, JOHN DENHAM R
b. Lake Charles, La, 11/19/32; s. Irl Richard Hix and Alice Denham H; m. 8/31/52 to Carol Yvonne Denty, div. 9/13/69; c. John D, Jr, Yvonne Richelle, Richard Marshall and Patrice Renée. Educ: Southwest Tex. State Col, 50-52. Polit. & Govt. Pos: Chmn, Fresno Co. Young Rep, Calif, 65-66; co-coordinator, 33rd Assembly dist. campaign, Mobley for Assembly Cmt, 66; del, Calif. Young Rep. State Conv, 66, 67, 68 & 69; mem, Fresno Co. Rep. Cent. Cmt, 66- and treas, 67 & 68; state pres, Calif. Young Rep, 67; chmn. Calif. Young Rep. del, Nat. Conv. Young Rep. Nat. Fedn, 67; mem. cent. and exec. cmts. and secy. youth affairs cmt, Calif. Rep. State Cent. Cmt, 67 & 68; del, Rep. Nat. Conv, 68; mem. campaign staff, 16th Dist. Harris for Cong. Cmt, 68. Bus. & Prof. Pos: Asst. mgr. cotton dept, Producers Cotton Oil Co, Fresno, 63-; mgr, Prodco Warehouse Co, 67- Mem: Fresno Cotton Exchange; West. Cotton Shippers Asn; Fresno Transportation Club; Am. Mensa Soc; Am. Carnival Glass Asn; North. Calif. Golf. Asn; Commonwealth Club of Calif. Rel: Protestant. Mailing Add: 544 E. Clinton, Fresno, Calif. 93704.

HO, STUART T. K. D
Hawaii State Rep.
b. Manila, Philippine Islands, 11/18/35; s. Chinn Ho and Betty Ching H; m. 6/17/61 to Mary Lois Lee; c. Peter Samuel and Cecily. Educ: Claremont Men's Col, B.A, 57; Univ. Mich, J.D, 63; Phi Delta Phi. Polit. & Govt. Pos: Dep. corp. counsel, City and Co. of Honolulu, Hawaii, 64 and spec. coun, City Coun, 66; Hawaii State Rep, 67-, Majority Floor Leader, Hawaii House of Rep, 69-; del, State Constitutional Conv, 68. Bus. & Prof. Pos: Assoc, Proskauer Rose Goetz & Mendelsohn, N.Y, 64-65; v.pres. and dir, Capital Investment of Hawaii, Inc, 65-; asst. secy, Honolulu Star-Bulletin, 67-; dir, Honolulu Symphony Soc, 68-; dir, Honolulu Stadium, Ltd, 68- Mil. Serv: Entered as 2nd Lt, Army, 58, released as 1st Lt, 60 after serv. in 28th Transportation Bn, COMZEUR, Europe, 58-60; Commendation Medal. Mem: Am. and Hawaii Bar Asns; Am. Judicature Soc. One of Three Outstanding Young Men, Hawaii State Jaycees, 66. Legal Res: 1777 Ala Moana Blvd, Honolulu, Hawaii 96815. Mailing Add: 239 Merchant St, Honolulu, Hawaii 96813.

HOAGLAND, DONALD W.
b. New York, N.Y, 8/16/21; s. Webster Comly Hoagland and Irene Wright H; m. 4/14/49 to Mary Tiedeman; c. Peter, Mary, Sara, Ann. Educ: Yale Univ, B.A, 42; Columbia, LL.B, 48. Polit. & Govt. Pos: Asst. Admin, AID, 64-66. Bus. & Prof. Pos: Lawyer, 48-; Dir, Cent. Fund, Inc; Gryphon Fund, Inc, 59-63; Bd. of Dir. & V.Pres, Denver Art Museum, 59-63; Bd. Dir, Colo. Urban League, 60-63. Mil. Serv: Navy Res, 43-45. Mem: Am, Colo. and Denver Bar Asns; Am. Judicature Soc; Am. Soc. Int. Law; Trustee, Phillips Exeter Acad. Mailing Add: 2250 S. Columbia St, Denver, Colo. 80210. (1967)

HOAK, BERTRAND H. D
b. Buffalo, N.Y, 1/29/17; m. to Nora Theresa Beasley; c. Five. Educ: N.Y. State Forest Ranger Sch; Canisius Col. Polit. & Govt. Pos: N.Y. State Sen, 64-67. Bus. & Prof. Pos: Grader inspector, U.S. Forest Serv, 39; mem, Buffalo Fire Dept, N.Y, 46-; co-owner and mgr, Hoak's Restaurant, Athol Springs; pres. and past chmn, Inn Keepers Asn. of West. N.Y. Mil. Serv: Air Force, 42-46; Gr. Air Force Combat Intel. Sch, Harrisburg, Pa, 43; Combat Intel. Officer, Pac. Theatre, 31 months. Mem: S. Buffalo Am. Legion Post 721; 4° K. of C. Coun. 184, 3° K. of C. Coun. 2220; Hamburg Jr. C. of C; Syracuse Club of Buffalo; Holy Name Soc, St. Martin's Church; AFL Local 282; Capitol Hill Club; Nat. Conf. of Christians and Jews. Founder of Erie Co. Sheriff's Identification Syst. Mailing Add: 102 Turner Ave, Buffalo, N.Y. 14220.

HOARD, CLIFFORD BROOKS D
W.Va. State Del.
b. Hoard, W.Va, 9/4/11; s. William U. Hoard and Mary F. Cunningham H; m. 5/8/47 to Evelyn F. Chapman; c. Betty Lynn, Gloria Jean and William Earl. Polit. & Govt. Pos: W.Va. State Del, 67- Bus. & Prof. Pos: Self employed salesman; genealogist. Mil. Serv: Entered as Pvt, Army, 42, released as T/3 Sgt, 45, after serv. in 865 Rehabilitation Unit, ETO, 44-45. Mem: VFW; SAR; Toastmasters. Rel: Protestant. Mailing Add: Hoard Road, Route 4, Box 331, Morgantown, W.Va. 26505.

HOBBS, FREDERICK HOWARD R
Pa. State Sen.
b. Pottsville, Pa, 1/6/34; s. Blake Hobbs and Marian Hause H; m. 11/18/67 to Pamela Watkins. Educ: Amherst Col, B.A, 55; Georgetown Univ, LL.B, 58; Delta Kappa Epsilon; Delta Theta Phi. Polit. & Govt. Pos: Attorney, Bur. Operating Rights, Interstate Commerce Cmn, 59-60; chmn, Young Rep. of Schuylkill Co, Pa, 62-64; state dir, Young Rep, 64-66; Pa. State Sen, 29th Dist, 66- Mil. Serv: Pvt, Army, 59; Army Res. until 65. Mem: Schuylkill Co, Pa. and Am. Bar Asns; Lions; bd. dirs, Schuylkill Co. Cancer Soc; Schuylkill Co. Tuberculosis Soc; Schuylkill Co. Heart Asn. Rel: Presbyterian. Legal Res: 1423 Mahantongo St, Pottsville, Pa. 17901. Mailing Add: Plaza Bldg, 118 E. Norwegian St, Pottsville, Pa. 17901.

HOBBS, HENRY GRADY D
Chmn, Webster Parish Dem. Exec. Cmt, La.
b. Minden, La, 5/1/23; s. Grady Hobbs and Minnie Chancelor H; m. 11/19/50 to Laulie Thibaut; c. Emily Anne, David Chancelor, Henry Grady, Jr. and William Winship. Educ: La. Polytech. Inst, B.A, 47; Tex. Tech. Col; La. State Univ, LL.B, 50. Polit. & Govt. Pos: Mem, Bd. of Supvrs. of Elecs, Minden, La, 53-, city attorney, 55-; mem, Libr. Bd. of Control, Webster Parish, 62-; chmn, Webster Parish Dem. Exec. Cmt, 63- Mem: Pres, Webster Parish Bar Asn, 60-; La. and Am. Bar Asns; Webster Parish Farm Bur; past comdr, Am. Legion Post; past pres, Minden Jaycees and Civitan Club; past judge advocate, La. Dist. Civitan Club; 40 et 8. Rel: Episcopal. Legal Res: 1501 E. Todd St, Minden, La. 71055. Mailing Add: P.O. Box 912, Minden, La. 71055.

HOBBS, HORACE EASTOW D
b. Hampton, N.H, 9/13/99; s. Oliver W. Hobbs and Ardenia I. Blake H; m. 4/10/25 to Miranda E. Brooks; c. Kendall E. and Jacquelyn D. Educ: Univ. N.H, B.S, 21; Columbia Univ, M.A, 26; Univ. Chicago, Harvard Univ, Univ. Tenn, Univ. Tex. and George Wash. Univ. summer schs; Casque & Casket; Phi Mu Delta. Polit. & Govt. Pos: Former mayor, Warwick, R.I; cand. for Gov, 66. Bus. & Prof. Pos: Teacher-coach, Mapleton, Maine, 21-22, Cornwall-on-Hudson, N.Y, 22-23, Westwood, N.J, 23-27; prin, high sch, Chelmsford, Mass, 27-30; prin. and asst. supt. high sch, Warwick, R.I, 30-60; instr. Univ. N.H. summer sch, Brown Univ. Exten, 5 years and R.I. Col. Educ, 12 years. Mil. Serv: Entered as Pvt, Army, 18, released as Cpl, 18. Publ: Articles in Educational Digest. Mem: Henry Barnard Club; R.I. Secondary Sch. Principals' Asn; Munic. Execs. Asn. of R.I; Warwick Hist. Asn; Elks; Mason; YMCA; cmnr, Boy Scouts. Rel: Congregational. Legal Res: 105 Oak Tree Ave, Warwick, R.I. 02886. Mailing Add: City Hall, Warwick, R.I. 02887. (1967)

HOBBS, RUTH JOSEPHINE R
Treas, Nat. Fedn. Rep. Women
b. Wilmette, Ill, 1/24/13; d. Samuel Cohen and Ronald Hilmer C; m. 11/5/32 to Wendell Wilson Hobbs; c. Robert S. and William S. Educ: Rockford Col, 30-32; Univ. Mich, 40-43. Polit. & Govt. Pos: Pres, Ann Arbor Women's Rep. Club, Mich, 54; mem, State Rep. Cent. Cmt, 55-, v.chmn. women's activities, 64-65 and dir, 65-66; alternate del, Rep. Nat. Conv, 56 & 64, alternate del-at-lg, 68 and chmn, Transportation to Nat. Conv, State Rep. Cent. Cmt, 64 and chmn, Transportation to Nat. Conv, 68; asst. campaign coordinator, Second Cong. Rep. Cmt, 60-63; co-chmn, Gov. Inauguration, 64-65; pres, Rep. Women's Fedn, 66-69; treas, Nat. Fedn. Rep. Women, 68-; cmnr, Ann Arbor Human Rels. Cmn, 68-, chmn, Housing Div, 69- Bus. & Prof. Pos: Corp. secy, Hobbs, Caldwell Spaly & Co, 62-68, sales mgr, 68-; pres, Ann Arbor Bd. of Realtors and dir, Mich. Real Estate Asn, 62; v.pres, Hobbs-Schmidt & Co, 58. Mem: Women's City Club; secy, Ann Arbor's Workable Prog; League of Women Voters; Ann Arbor Golf and Outing Club. Rel: Protestant. Mailing Add: 3000 Overridge Dr, Ann Arbor, Mich. 48104.

HOBBS, WENDELL WILSON R
Treas, Mich. Rep. State Cent. Cmt.
b. Detroit, Mich, 6/8/08; s. W. Scott Hobbs and Castara L. Brooks H; m. 11/5/32 to Ruth Josephine Cohen; c. Robert Scott and William S. Educ: Northwest. Univ, 26-30; Univ. Mich, 46-49; Phi Kappa Sigma. Polit. & Govt. Pos: Mem, Chmn. Adv. Cmt, State Cent. Cmt, Mich, 56-66; chmn, Washtenaw Co. Rep. Cmt. and campaign coordinator, Second Cong. Dist, 60-64; chmn, State Cent. Elec. Laws Cmt, 61-65; mem, Mich. Almanac Cmt, State Finance Cmt, 61-66; alternate del-at-lg, Rep. Nat. Conv, 64 & 68; chmn, Rep. State Conv, 64; chmn, Second Cong. Dist. Rep. Cmt, 65-; treas, Mich. Rep. State Cent. Cmt, 67- Bus. & Prof. Pos: Pres, Hobbs, Caldwell, Spaly & Co, Realtors, 48- Mem: Mich. C. of C. Polit. Action Cmt, 63-66; dir, Ann Arbor C. of C. and Greater Ann Arbor Res. Park, 62-65; mem, Enlarged Realtor's Wash. Cmt, 60-66 and Ann Arbor Planning Cmn, 59-62; pres, Ann Arbor Bd. of Realtors, 50-51, Detroit Econ. Club; Elks; Ann Arbor Golf and Outing Club. Rel: Protestant. Mailing Add: 3000 Overridge Dr, Ann Arbor, Mich. 48104.

HOBBY, OVETA CULP R
b. Killeen, Tex, 1/19/05; d. I.W. Culp and Emma Hoover C; m. 2/23/31 to William P. Hobby (deceased); c. William and Jessica (Mrs. Henry E. Catto, Jr). Educ: Mary Hardin-Baylor Col. Hon. LL.D, Baylor Univ, Sam Houston State Teachers Col. and Univ. Chattanooga, 43, Bryant Col. and Ohio Wesleyan Univ, 53, Columbia Univ, Smith Col. and Middlebury Col, 54, Univ. Pa. and Colby Col, 55, Fairleigh Dickinson Univ. and West. Col, 56; L.H.D, Bard Col, 50 and Lafayette Col, 54; Litt.D, Colo. Women's Col, 47 and C.W. Post Col, 62; HH.D, Mary Hardin-Baylor Col, 56. Polit. & Govt. Pos: Parliamentarian, Tex. House of Rep, 26-31, 39, 41; chief, Women's Interest Sect, Bur. Pub. Rels, War Dept, 41-42, appt. dir. WAAC, 42, WAC, 43-45; consult, Alternate UN Freedom of Info. Conf, Geneva, Switz, 48; consult, Cmt. on Orgn. of Exec. Br. of Govt, 48; Fed. Security Adminstr, 53; Secy, Dept. Health, Educ. and Welfare, 53-55; mem, President's Cmt. on Employ. of Physically Handicapped and President's Cmt. on Civilian Nat. Honors; mem, Cmt. for White House Conf. on Educ, 54-55; mem, Nat. Adv. Cmt, Citizens for Eisenhower, 56; trustee, Am. Assembly, 57-66 and Eisenhower Exchange Fels, 57-; mem, Carnegie Cmn. on Educ. TV, 65-67, Vietnam Health Educ. Task Force, Dept. Health, Educ. and Welfare, 66 and Nat. Adv. Cmn. on Selective Serv, 66-67. Bus. & Prof. Pos: Research ed, Houston Post, 31, lit. ed, asst. ed, v.pres, exec. v.pres, ed. and publisher, 31-53, pres, 55-65, ed, 55-; chmn. bd, Houston Post Co, 65-; dir, Sta. KPRC and KPRC-TV, 45-53, 55-; mem. bd. dirs, Gen. Food Corp. and Gen. Aniline and Film Corp, 65-67 and Corp. for Pub. Broadcasting, 68- Mil. Serv: Col, WAC, 42-45; Distinguished Serv. Medal, 44; Philippine Mil. Merit Medal, 47. Publ: Mr. Chairman, parliamentary law textbook; syndicated column, Mr. Chairman. Mem: Bd. gov, Am. Red Cross and adv. cmt, fund campaign, 50; nat. v.chmn, Am. Cancer Soc. Campaign, 49; former dir, Nat. Conf. Christians and Jews and Advert. Fedn. of Am; nat. cmt, Am. Mus. Immigration, 56; pres, South. Newspapers Publishers Asn, 49; Am. Design Awards Cmt; sponsor, Clark Sch. for the Deaf; Col. Cmn, Episcopal Diocese of Tex, 56, bd, Adv. Cmt. on Econ. Develop, 56-; Continental Oil Co. Scholarship Award Cmt; nat. adv. bd, Navy-Marine Corps Mem. Stadium, 57-58; Cmt. of 75, Univ. Tex, 58-; trustee, Eisenhower Birthplace Mem. Park; South. Regional Cmt. for Marshall Scholarships, 57-; hon. v.chmn, Gamma Alpha Chi; bd. dirs, Houston Symphony Soc; Southwest Adv. Bd, Inst. Int. Educ: trustee, Mutual Ins. Co. of N.Y, 56-; Spec. Studies Proj, Rockefeller Bros. Fund; Crusade for Freedom Inc, 58-; cmt. 50th Anniversary, Sch. Journalism, Univ. Mo; vis. cmt, Grad. Sch. Educ, Harvard; adv. bd, George C. Marshall Research Found; trustee, Soc. Rehab. of Facially Disfigured; Century Coun, Tex. A&M; Cuban Freedom Cmt; nat. bd. develop, Sam Rayburn Found; bd. dirs, Tex. Heart Asn; former trustee, People to People; nat. coun, Eleanor Roosevelt Mem. Found; trustee, Rice Univ, 67-; Bus. Cmt. for the Arts, Inc, 67-; charter mem, Acad. Tex, 69; Houston Country Club; Bayou and Ramada Clubs; Jr. League Club, Houston. Publisher of the Year Award, Headliners Club, 60; Living Hist. Award, Research Inst. of Am, 60; Honor Award, Nat. Jewish Hosp, 62; Carnegie Corp. Award for the Advan. and Diffusion of Knowledge and Understanding, 67. Rel: Episcopal. Mailing Add: Houston, Tex. 77001.

HOBDY, CLARENCE CHESTER R
Mem. Exec. Cmt, Los Angeles Co. Rep. Cent. Cmt, Calif.
b. Alvord, Tex, 11/28/02; s. Herbert Hobdy and Mainna Cornelia Sossaman H; m. 6/15/39 to Dorothy Dee Book; c. Clarence Jr, Vida Delorez, Robert Raymond and David Darryll. Educ: Chillicothe Bus. Col, Mo, 22; Tenor Soloist, College Male Quartet and Glee Club. Polit. & Govt. Pos: Dir, Vol. for Eisenhower-Nixon, 52; mem. and alternate, Los Angeles Co. Rep. Cent. Cmt, 52-, mem, Co-Wide Rules Cmt. and chmn, Subcmt. on Personnel Develop, 58-61 and mem. exec. cmt, 69-; precinct chmn, 40th Assembly Dist. Rep. Cent. Cmt, 52-54, chmn, 55-61; capt, home precinct, 52-68; chmn, Cmt. to Elect Norris Poulsen Mayor, 53; mem, State Rep. Cent. Cmt, 54-60, assoc. mem, 61-62; mem, U.S. Sen. Kuchel's Cmt, 56; v.chmn, 19th Cong. Dist. Rep. Cent. Cmt, 56-61, polit. educ. chmn, 62-64 and chmn, 64 & 69-; co-chmn, Mex-Am. Serv. Center, E.Los Angeles, 60-61; asst. sgt-at-arms, Rep. Nat. Conv, 60 & 64; presidential elector and chmn, Norwalk Rep. Hq, 64; polit. hobbyist and adv. to cand. for many years. Bus. & Prof. Pos: Various clerical and jr. officer assignments, Gen. Mgrs. Off, Atchison, Topeka & Sante Fe Rwy. Co, Los Angeles, 22-39, personnel asst, 39-43, chief clerk to div. supt, 43-49; asst. supvr. wage agreements, Sante Fe Rwy. Syst, 49-50; supvr. wage agreements, Los Angeles Junction Rwy. Co, 50-69, retired. Mil. Serv: Entered as Pvt, Tex. Nat. Guard, 33, released as S/Sgt, 35; Sharpshooter. Mem: Master Mason, Sante Fe Masonic Club; past Patron, Eastern Star. Rel: Baptist. Mailing Add: 14513 Dumont Ave, Norwalk, Calif. 90650.

HOBSON, LEATHEL JAMES R
b. Bedford, Ind, 1/8/98; s. John D. Hobson and Estella McKnight H; m. 9/4/26 to Martha May Mark; c. Kenneth Dale, Wanda May, Wilma Jean and Mary Jane. Educ: Heltonville High Sch, grad. Polit. & Govt. Pos: Mem, Lawrence Co. Liquor Bd, Ind, 45 & 46; chmn, Lawrence Co. Rep. Cmt, 54-66; mem, Ind. Ins. Coun. Bd, 57-61; br. mgr, Bur. Motor Vehicles, 57-61. Bus. & Prof. Pos: Ins. agent, 26-60; farmer, 61- Mem: Lawrence Co. Women's Rep. Club; Lawrence Co. Young Rep; Marion Twp. and Lawrence Co. Rep. Club. Rel: Presbyterian. Mailing Add: R.R. 1, Heltonville, Ind. 47436.

HOBSTETTER, ELIZABETH ALICE R
Secy, Meigs Co. Rep. Cent. and Exec. Cmts, Ohio
b. Gallipolis, Ohio, 2/15/19; d. Rufus Andrew Pitchford and Callie Lee Johnston P; m. 12/31/40 to William Jacob Hobstetter; c. James William. Educ: Gallia Acad. High Sch, Gallipolis, Ohio dipl, 37. Polit. & Govt. Pos: Committeewoman, Rutland Village, Meigs Co. Rep. Party, Ohio, 65-; secy, Meigs Co. Rep. Cent. and Exec. Cmts, 68- Bus. & Prof. Pos: Dep. clerk, Meigs Co. Clerk of Courts, Ohio, 55- Rel: Methodist. Legal Res: Salem St, Rutland, Ohio, 45775. Mailing Add: Box 22, Rutland, Ohio 45775.

HOCHMAN, WILLIAM RUSSELL D
b. New York, N.Y, 8/28/21; s. Julius Cornelius Hochman and Ruth H. H; m. 8/21/41 to Margaret Dean Schloss; c. Abigail, Dean, Meg and John. Educ: Columbia Col, A.B, 42; Columbia Univ, A.M, 48 and Ph.D. in hist, 55. Polit. & Govt. Pos: State Dem. Secy, 61-65; del. and mem, Platform Cmt, Dem. Nat. Conv, 64, del. and mem, Credentials Cmt, 68. Bus. & Prof. Pos: From instr. to prof, hist, Colo. Col, 55- Mil. Serv: Entered as Ens, Naval Res, 42, released as Lt.(jg), after serv. in Mediterranean and N.Atlantic Theaters; ETO and Atlantic Theater Ribbons and 4 Battle Stars. Mem: Am. and Mississippi Valley Hist. Asns. Mailing Add: 1237 Terrace Rd, Colorado Springs, Colo. 80904.

HOCKER, BLAINE C. R
b. Oberlin, Pa, 8/25/08; c. Clinton Hocker and Mary Brown H; m. to Frances E. Baker. Educ: Swatara Twp. Pub. Schs. Polit. & Govt. Pos: Pa. State Rep, 46-67; Secy, Bd. Cmnrs, Swatara Twp, 41. Bus. & Prof. Pos: Farming; Dairy bus, 32-43; Bethlehem Steel Co, 25-32. Mil. Serv: U.S. Coast Guard, 43-45. Mem: Interstate Coop. Cmn, treas. 1967 Legal Res: 42 Harrisburg St, Oberlin, Pa. No mailing address available. (1967)

HOCKER, IRAH EAVES D
b. Bismarck, Mo, 8/12/14; d. James Eaves and Mary L. Watson E; m. 7/26/41 to Thomas H. Hocker. Educ: Akron Univ, 2 years. Polit. & Govt. Pos: Secy, Works Progress Admin, Farmington, Mo, 34-41; analyst, Corps of Engrs, Wash, D.C, 41-44; admin. asst. to U.S. Rep. A.S.J. Carnahan, Mo, 49-61 and to U.S. Rep. William J. Randall, Mo, 61- Mem: Eastern Star. Rel: Protestant. Legal Res: Farmington, Mo. Mailing Add: 3000 Arizona Ave. N.W, Washington, D.C. 20515.

HOCKING, BERT WHITMAN R
Secy, Winnebago Co. Rep. Cent. Cmt, Ill.
b. Darlington, Wis, 10/10/91; s. Henry M. Hocking and Martha Whitman H; m. 6/19/18 to Esther M. Baumgarten; c. Martha (Mrs. James Davis) and Dorothy (Mrs. Donald Kiesbuy). Educ: Lawrence Col, 11-13; Univ. Wis, Madison, B.A, 15; Delta Iota. Polit. & Govt. Pos: Precinct committeeman, Third and Fourth Wards, Rockford, Ill, 20 years; committeeman, Seventh Precinct, Third Ward, currently; secy, Winnebago Co. Rep. Cent. Cmt, 68- Bus. & Prof. Pos: Partner, Rockford Mercantile Agency, Retired, 67. Mil. Serv: Entered as Pvt, Army, released as Band Sgt, 19, after serv. in 13th Field Artil. Band, 86th and Fourth Div, ETO, 18-19; Serv. Medal. Mem: Kiwanis; Mason; Freeport Consistory; Tebala Temple. Rel: United Methodist. Mailing Add: 517 Fisher Ave, Rockford, Ill. 61103.

HOCKING, SYDNEY BURDETTE D
b. Casselton, N.Dak, 9/20/02; s. Edmund Hocking and Ida Thoemke H; m. 5/19/62 to Mary H. Hicks. Educ: Loyola Univ. Dent. Sch, D.D.S, 29; Delta Sigma Delta. Polit. & Govt. Pos: Pres, N.Dak. Young Dem, 36-40; mem, State Bd. of Health, 41-47; chmn, Ramsey Co. Dem. Party, 48-54; del, Dem. Nat. Conv, 56, 60, 64 & 68; Dem. Nat. Committeeman, 60-68. Mem: Int. Acad. Orthodontics; Dist, State and Am. Dent. Asns; Past Exalted Ruler, Elks; Mason. Rel: Presbyterian. Mailing Add: Sweetwater Apts, Devils Lake, N.Dak. 58301.

HODEL, DONALD PAUL R
b. Portland, Ore, 5/23/35; s. Philip E. Hodel and Theresia Rose Brodt H; m. 12/10/56 to Barbara Beecher Stockman; c. Philip Stockman and David Beecher. Educ: Harvard Col, B.A, 57; Univ. Ore. Law Sch, J.D, 60; Phi Delta Phi. Polit. & Govt. Pos: Treas, Harvard Young Rep. Club, 55-56, pres, 56-57; precinct orgn, Clackamas Co. Rep. Cent. Cmt, Ore, 64, secy, 64-65 and chmn, 65-66; former chmn, Ore. Rep. State Cent. Cmt; alternate del, Rep. Nat. Conv, 68; dep-adminstr, Bonneville Power Admin, currently. Bus. & Prof. Pos: Attorney, Davies, Biggs, Strayer, Stoel and Boley, 60-63; Georgia-Pacific Corp, 63- Publ: 'The Doctrine of Exemplary Damages in Oregon,' Ore. Law Rev, 4/65. Mem: Am, Ore. and Multnomah Bar Asns. Rel: Lutheran. Mailing Add: 2825 Dellwood Dr, Lake Oswego, Ore. 97034.

HODES, RICHARD S. D
Fla. State Rep.
b. New York, N.Y, 4/24/24; s. Stanley Hodes and Rosabel Palley H; m. 5/19/46 to Marjorie Cohen; c. Marilyn. Educ: Tulane Univ, B.S, 44 and M.D, 46; Univ. Minn, Fel, 51; Phi Delta Epsilon; Sigma Alpha Mu. Polit. & Govt. Pos: Fla. State Rep, currently; chmn, Cmt. Pub. Health and Welfare, currently. Bus. & Prof. Pos: Dir, Dept. of Anesthesia, Tampa Gen. Hosp. and clin. asst. prof, Univ. Fla. Sch. Med, currently. Mil. Serv: Entered as Pfc, Army, 43, released as Capt, 49, after serv. in Med. Dept, Tech. Training Command Air Force, 49. Publ: 'Auxiliary Myocardial Revascularization,' Surg, Gynecology and Obstetrics, 3/60. Mem: Hillsborough Co. and Fla. Med. Asns; del, Am. Med. Asn; Am. and Fla. Socs. of Anesthesiologists (Fla. pres, 60); Am. Legion; Mason; Elks; Kiwanis. Rel: Jewish. Mailing Add: 116 Ladoga Ave, Tampa, Fla. 33606.

HODGDON, S. FOX R
b. Victory, Vt, 1/6/08; m. to Jennie E. Wilson; c. Three sons and two daughters. Educ: Victory and Granby Schs. Polit. & Govt. Pos: Lister, 12 years; road cmnr, 10 years; sch. dir, 17 years; former Vt. State Rep; chmn, Rep. Party, Granby, currently. Bus. & Prof. Pos: Farmer. Mem: Farm Bur. (pres, Essex Co. Bur). Rel: Protestant. Mailing Add: Granby, Vt. 05840.

HODGE, FRANK S. R
Kans. State Sen.
b. Sterling, Kans, 7/17/03; s. U.S. Hodge and Bertha Knouse H; m. 6/24/34 to Betty G. Burriss; c. Frank Galen and David Stanton. Educ: Sterling Col, A.B; Kans. Univ, LL.B; Order of the Coif. Polit. & Govt. Pos: Chmn, Reno Co. Rep. Cent. Cmt, Kans, 44-52; del, Rep. Nat. Conv, 48; Kans. State Sen, 57- Bus. & Prof. Pos: Sr. partner, Hodge, Reynolds, Smith & Peirce, 68- Mem: Mason. Rel: Methodist. Legal Res: R.F.D. 4, Hutchinson, Kans. 67501. Mailing Add: Box 432, Hutchinson, Kans. 67501.

HODGE, KENNETH KENNEDY R
Chmn, Eighth Assembly Dist. Precincts, Calif.
b. Florin, Calif, 3/29/22; s. Kenneth William Hodge and Evelyn Kennedy H; m. 9/29/45 to Vivian Esther Nygren; c. Corolyn, Denise, Jacqueline, Vicki and Kenneth. Educ: Sacramento Jr. Col, 39-42; Stanford Univ, 43-45; St. Louis Univ. Sch. of Med, M.D, 49; Phi Chi. Polit. & Govt. Pos: Alternate del, Rep. Nat. Conv, 64; chmn, Sacramento Co. Goldwater Orgn, Calif, 64; assoc. mem, Calif. State Cent. Cmt, mem, Sacramento Co. Rep. Cent. Cmt. and chmn, Eighth Assembly Dist. Precincts Cmt, Calif, 65-; mem, Sacramento Co. Rep. Fund, 66- Bus. & Prof. Pos: Chief, Anesthesia Dept, Sacramento Co. Hosp, 58-60 and Mercy Hosp, 63. Mil. Serv: Entered as 1st Lt, Army, 50, released as Maj, 56, after serv. in 21st Inf. Regt, Korea, 51-52; Bronze Star; Presidential Unit Citation; Five Campaign Ribbons. Mem: Am. Bd. Anesthesiologists; Am. Med. Asn; Am. Soc. Anesthesiologists. Rel: Methodist. Mailing Add: 3820 Silver Spur Way, Sacramento, Calif. 95841.

HODGE, OLIVER D
State Supt. of Pub. Instr, Okla.
b. Exeter, Mo, 9/24/01; s. George W. Hodge and Cordie Antle H; m. 6/8/24 to Faye Hall. Educ: Tulsa Univ, B.A, 29; Okla. Univ, Ed.M, 33, Ed.D, 37; Kappa Delta Pi; Phi Beta Sigma; Iota Lambda Sigma. Polit. & Govt. Pos: Co. Supt. of Schs, Tulsa Co, Okla, 37-47; State Supt. of Pub. Instr, Okla, 47- Mem: Pres, Coun. of Chief State Sch. Officers, 59-60; Nat. Educ. Asn; Nat. Asn. of Sch. Adminstrs; Okla. Educ. Asn; Okla. Asn. of Sch. Adminstrs. Publ: Doctor's dissertation, History of Oklahoma School Land Department. Rel: Christian Church. Mailing Add: 6800 Trenton Rd, Oklahoma City, Okla. 73116. (1967)

HODGE, WILLIAM SNEED D
Mem, Exec. Cmt, Ariz. State Dem. Orgn.
b. Belton-Bell County, Tex, 6/13/05; s. William Richard Hodge and Ella Morris H; m. 8/16/24 to Ruby Leona Biggs; c. Bonnie May, (Mrs. Morrill), Wanda Fay (Mrs. Russell), Joy Oleda (Mrs. Miller), Audine Fern (Mrs. Wyrick) and Donnie Bill. Polit. & Govt. Pos: Precinct committeeman, Winslow, Ariz, 44 & 68-69; v.chmn, Co. Dem. Party, 63-67 and chmn, 67-68; del, Dem. Nat. Conv, 68; mem. exec. cmt, Ariz. State Dem. Orgn, 68- Bus. & Prof. Pos: Brakeman, Santa Fe Railroad, 20 years, conductor, 25 years. Mem: Brotherhood of Railroad trainmen; Order Railway Conductors, United Transportation Union. Rel: Baptist. Mailing Add: 900 Apache Ave, Winslow, Ariz. 86047.

HODGES, CHARLES EDWARD D
S.C. State Rep.
b. Tabor City, N.C, 4/2/31; s. Joseph Judson Hodges and Mada Lee Cox H; m. 10/1/51 to Patty Macon Nobles; c. Charles Joseph and Charissa Dean. Educ: Tabor City High Sch, grad, 49; Kings Bus. Sch, 1 year, Bus. Admin. Polit. & Govt. Pos: S.C. State Rep, Horry Co, 68- Bus. & Prof. Pos: Pres, Hodges, Inc, 59-; farmer, 64-; cmt. chmn, Indust. Developers, 66-67; treas, United Investors, Inc, currently. Mil. Serv: Pfc, Air Force, 51. Mem: Nat. Asn. of Accredited Talent and Beauty Pageant Judges, S.C. Retail Grocerymen Asn; Loris Libr. Bldg. Cmt; pres, Loris Merchants Asn, 60 & 66; bus. mgr, Miss Loris contest, several years; past pres. and dir, for 8 years, Carolina Country Club; Civitan Club; Am. Legion; Booster Club; WOW; charter mem, Loris Jaycees; Mason; Shrine. Jaycee of the Year, 65 & 66, Spark-Plug Award, Jaycees, 66 & 67; Loris Distinguished Serv. Award, 67. Rel: Baptist. Mailing Add: Eoxbay Rd, Loris, S.C. 29569.

HODGES, HAROLD YOUNG R
Chmn, Surry Co. Rep. Party, N.C.
b. Surry, N.C, 7/14/19; s. Delmar Decauter Hodges and Lelia Dickens H; m. 7/14/48 to Dorothy June Klutz; c. Harold Y, Jr, Richard Dale and Gene Daywalt. Educ: Wake Forest Col, 44-46; Appalachian State Col, 47; Sigma Pi. Polit. & Govt. Pos: Chmn, Surry Co. Rep. Party, N.C, 55- Bus. & Prof. Pos: Partner, WKSP Radio, Kingstree, S.C. and Dixie Tobacco Warehouse, Mt. Airy, 47-62, owner and operator, 62-; partner, Farmers Tobacco Warehouse, Kingstree, 53-63; farmer, Tobacco, Grain and Cattle. Mil. Serv: 45-46. Publ: Farm News Prog, WPAQ Radio, 62-69. Mem: Past Master, Mason; Shrine; past gov, Moose; Past Exalted Ruler, Elks; dist. gov. Ruritan; Am. Legion; Farm Bur. Rel: Baptist; Deacon and Sunday Sch. Supt. Legal Res: RFD 6, Box 267, Mt. Airy, N.C. 27030. Mailing Add: P.O. Box 547, Mt. Airy, N.C. 27030.

HODGES, J. ALEX R
Exec. Dir, Rep. Party of Ga.
b. Decatur, Ga, 3/5/41; s. Thomas Lumpkin Hodges and Lillian Powell H; div. Educ: Mercer Univ, B.A, 63; Walter F. George Sch. Law, 1 year; Phi Delta Theta; Scabbard and Blade. Polit. & Govt. Pos: Field rep, Ga. Draft Goldwater Cmt, 64; orgn. dir, Bibb Co. Rep. Party, Ga, 64; field rep, Rep. Nat. Cmt, 64; exec. dir, Rep. Party of Ga, 64-65 & 68-; mem. campaign mgt. cmt, Thompson for Mayor, Macon, 67; mem, Human Rels. Cmt, Macon, 67-68. Bus. & Prof. Pos: Bus. and personnel mgr, Phil Walden Artists and Promotions, Macon, Ga, 67-68; secy. and mem. bd. dirs, Glendora Develop. Corp, Atlanta, 67-; licensed real estate salesman, 68- Mil. Serv: Entered as 2nd Lt, Army, 65, released as 1st Lt, 67, after serv. in Finance Corp, SASCOM, 65-66 and Sixth Army, 66-67, Army Res, 66-69; Cert. of Achievement, Ft. Irwin, Calif. Publ: Author, County Chairmen's Manual, 65, Prospectus, Republican Party of Georgia, 1960-70, 68 and ed, The Candidate and the Press, Manual, 68, Rep. Party of Ga. Mem: Ga. Sheriffs Asn; Phi Delta Theta Alumni Asn; Mercer Univ. Alumni Asn. Rel: Methodist. Mailing Add: 3030 Old Decatur Rd, No. 107-B, Atlanta, Ga. 30305.

HODGES, LLOYD JAMES R
Colo. State Sen.
b. Julesburg, Colo, 11/14/14; s. Hurley H. Hodges and Adelphia A. Vest H; m. 11/17/36 to Frances Jo Miles; c. James and Marianne. Educ: Colo. State Univ, 32-36; Sigma Phi Epsilon. Polit. & Govt. Pos: Colo. State Sen, 67- Bus. & Prof. Pos: Partner, Hodges Mfg. Co, 46-50 and Hodges & Sons Farms, 40-66; pres, Hodges-Kinnie Grain Co, 58-66; pres, Colo. Seed Growers Asn, 64-65, secy, 65-67. Mem: Rotary Int; Elks; Farm Bur. Rel: Methodist. Mailing Add: Box 448, Julesburg, Colo. 80737. (1967)

HODGES, LUTHER HARTWELL D
b. Pittsylvania Co, Va, 3/9/98; s. John James Hodges and Louicia Gammon H; m. 6/24/22 to Martha E. Blakeney; c. Betsy (Mrs. Donald Bernard, Jr), Nancy (Mrs. John C. Finlay) and Luther H, Jr. Educ: Univ. N.C, A.B, 19. Hon. degree, Univ. N.C, 46 and hon. degrees from 16 other univs. and cols. Polit. & Govt. Pos: Former dir, South. Regional Educ. Bd; head textile div, Off. Price Admin, 44; consult. to Secy. of Agr, 45; head indust. div, Econ. Coop. Admin, W. Germany, 50; consult. on Int. Mgt. Conf, Dept. of State, 51; Lt. Gov, N.C, 52-54; Gov, N.C, 54-60; Secy. of Commerce, 61-65; del, Dem. Nat. Conv, 68. Bus. & Prof. Pos: Various capacities in prod. and mgt. in textile indust, 19-50, retired as v.pres, Marshall Field & Co; chmn. bd, Research Triangle Found, 65-; dir, Drexel Enterprises, Inc. and Servomation Corp, 65-; chmn. bd, Financial Consult, Int, S.A, 65-; mem, several corporate bd, currently. Mem: Rotary Int.(pres, 67-68); Univ. Club. Rel: Methodist. Mailing Add: Box H, Research Triangle Park, N.C. 27709.

HODGES, WILLIAM HOWARD D
Va. State Sen.
b. Hickory, Va, 4/18/29; m. to Ann Turnbull Harding H. Educ: Randolph-Macon Col, B.A; Wash. and Lee U, LL.B; Phi Kappa Sigma; Phi Delta Phi. Polit. & Govt. Pos: Former mem, Young Dem. Club, Chesapeake, Va; Va. State Del, 62-66; Va. State Sen, 66-; v.chmn, Va. Crime Cmn, 66-; mem. exec. cmt, Va. Dem. Cent. Cmt, 66- and mem, Fourth Dist. Cmt, 68-; v.chmn, Va. Code Cmn, 68- Bus. & Prof. Pos: Attorney-at-law; chmn. bd. dirs, People's Bank, Chesapeake, Va, 67- Mil. Serv: Coast Guard, 51-53. Mem:

Portsmouth-Norfolk Co. Bar Asn; Norfolk-Portsmouth Bar Asn; Am. Legion; Cedar Point Club; Farm Bur; Commonwealth Club; Harbor Club. Rel: Methodist; trustee and past chmn. off. bd, Centenary Methodist Church. Mailing Add: P.O. Box 15508, Chesapeake, Va. 23320.

HODGES, WILLIAM L. D
Md. State Sen.
b. Baltimore, Md, 12/8/07. Educ: Baltimore City Col. Polit. & Govt. Pos: Former pres, Allied Dem. Clubs, Inc, Baltimore, Md; hon. pres, Vet. Dem. Coun; Md. State Del, 51-59; mem, Baltimore City Coun, 59-62; Md. State Sen, 63-; del, Dem. Nat. Conv, 68. Bus. & Prof. Pos: Real estate salesman. Mil. Serv: Navy, 44-45. Mem: Sixth Ward Holy Name Soc; Am. Legion; VFW; Friendly Sons of St. Patrick; Eagles; Moose. Mailing Add: 1225 W. Cross St, Baltimore, Md. 21230. (1967)

HODGSON, JAMES DAY D
Under Secy. of Labor, U.S. Dept. of Labor
b. Dawson, Minn, 12/3/15; s. Fred Arthur Hodgson and Casaraha Day H; m. 8/24/43 to Maria Denend; c. Nancy (Mrs. Richard J. Nachman) and Fredric. Educ: Univ. Minn, Minneapolis, A.B, 38, 40; Univ. Calif, Los Angeles, 47-48; Phi Sigma Kappa. Polit. & Govt. Pos: Supvr. youth employ, State of Minn. Dept. Employ, 40-41; mem. exec. cmt, Los Angeles Mayor's Labor-Mgt. Cmt, Calif, 62-69; consult, State of Calif. Cmt. Automation and Manpower, 65-67; under secy. of labor, U.S. Dept. of Labor, 69- Bus. & Prof. Pos: Jr. exec. trainee, Dayton Co, Minneapolis, Minn, 38-40; personnel clerk, Lockheed Aircraft Corp, Burbank, Calif, 41-43, numerous indust. rels. positions including corporate dir. indust. rels, 46-68 and corporate v.pres. indust. rels, 68-69. Mil. Serv: Entered as Ens, Navy, 43, released as Lt, 46, after serv. in Naval Air Corps, Pac, 42-46. Publ: 'Automation,' Univ. Mich. Quart, 63; 'Employing the Unemployables,' Harvard Bus. Rev, 9/68. Mem: Aerospace Indust. Asn. Indust. Rels. Cmt; Nat. Indust. Conf. Bd; Am. Mgt. Asn; Town Hall Indust. Rels. Planning Cmt. Los Angeles. Rel: Presbyterian. Legal Res; Los Angeles, Calif. Mailing Add: 2801 New Mexico Ave. N.W, Apt. 301, Washington, D.C. 20007.

HODSON, GERALD K. R
Chmn, Tenth Cong. Dist. Rep. Party, Ind.
b. Delaware Co, Ind, 12/8/25; s. Walter E. Hodson and Mae E. Scott H; m. 6/27/65 to Betty Helen Loay. Educ: Ind. Univ, Bloomington, B.S, 49, J.D, 51. Polit. & Govt. Pos: Del, Rep. Nat. Conv, 68; chmn, Tenth Cong. Dist. Rep. Party, Ind, 69- Bus. & Prof. Pos: Attorney, 51- Mil. Serv: Army, 44-46, Pfc, serv. in 86th Inf. Div. Mailing Add: R.R. 2, New Castle, Ind. 47362.

HODSON, RICHARD W. D
b. 11/20/23; m. 1952; c. two sons, one daughter. Educ: Martin High Sch; S.Dak. State Univ. Polit. & Govt. Pos: S.Dak. State Sen, 64-66. Bus. & Prof. Pos: V.pres, fieldsman, Blackpipe State Bank; rancher; auctioneer. Mil. Serv: Marine Corps, Fighter Pilot, 42-46; Korean Conflict, 52. Mem: S.Dak. Dept. Comdr. Am. Legion, 62-63; Mason; Oriental Consistory; S.Dak. Auctioneers Asn; S.Dak. Stockgrowers; dir, S.Dak. Angus Asn; secy-treas, Bennett Co. Stock Growers Asn; Volunteer Fire Dept; Martin Commercial Club. Mailing Add: Martin, S.Dak. 57551.

HOE, HARRY MORGAN R
Ky. State Rep.
b. Middlesboro, Ky, 5/25/25; s. Harry Allen Hoe and Ethel Morgan H; m. 12/21/48 to Mary Bob Hale; c. Priscilla Hale, Harry Hale and Marilyn Morgan. Educ: Univ. Tenn, B.S, 49; Phi Gamma Delta. Polit. & Govt. Pos: Mem, Ky. Rep. State Cent. Cmt, 64-; mem, Ky. Legis. Research Cmn, 66-67; Ky. State Rep, 87th Dist, currently, minority whip, Ky. House of Rep, asst. minority floor leader, 68. Bus. & Prof. Pos: V.pres, J.R. Hoe & Sons, Inc; past pres, Assoc. Industs. of Ky. Mil. Serv: Entered as Pvt, Army, 43, released as Sgt. T-4, 45, after serv. in 4th Inf. Div, ETO, 44-45; Silver Star; Bronze Star with Oak Leaf Cluster; ETO Campaign Ribbon with 4 Battle Stars. Mem: Past pres, Kiwanis and Little League; past chmn, Salvation Army; pres, Ky. Mountain Laurel Festival Bd, 68-70; Ky. Crime Cmn; trustee, Clear Creek Baptist Sch. Gen. Chmn, Cumberland Gap Nat. Hist. Park Dedication, 59; One of Three Outstanding Young Men in Ky, 53. Rel: Baptist. Mailing Add: 413 Dorchester Ave, Middlesboro, Ky. 40965.

HOEFS, RUDOLPH HERMAN R
Finance Chmn, 25th and 26th Dist. Rep. Party, N.Dak.
b. Hankinson, N.Dak, 4/17/96; s. August Hoefs and Emelie Tews H; m. 6/2/32 to Marjorie Scribner; c. Lloyd, Kenneth and Ronald. Educ: Hankinson High Sch, 4 years. Polit. & Govt. Pos: Precinct committeeman, Rep. Party, N.Dak, 41-69; chmn, Richland Co. Rep. Party, 43-68; Mayor, Hankinson, N.Dak. 44-52; finance chmn, 25th and 26th Dist. Rep. Party, 67-; del, Rep. Nat. Conv, 68. Bus. & Prof. Pos: Farm mgr, John R. Jones Co, 27-64; owner, Hoefs Farm Store, 47-64. Mil. Serv: Entered as Pvt, Army, 18, released as Musician 2/C, 19, after serving in 345th Field Artiliary Band; Good Conduct Medal. Mem: Am. Legion; VFW; Int. War Veterans Alliance, U.S. and Can; Am. Legion Playing Mem. Orgn; N.Dak. Farm Bur. Loyalty and Service Award, N.Dak. State Band, 61; Richland Co. Rep. Appreciation Award for 20 years Serv. as Rep. Co. Chmn, 64. Rel: Immanual Lutheran. Mailing Add: 510 First Ave. S.W, Hankinson, N.Dak. 58041.

HOEGH, LEO ARTHUR R
b. Audubon Co, Iowa, 3/30/08; s. William Hoegh and Annie K. Johnson H; m. 6/29/36 to Mary Louise Foster; c. Kristin F. and Janis. Educ: Univ. Iowa, B.A, 29 and J.D, 32; Omicron Delta Kappa; Pi Kappa Alpha; Delta Theta Phi. Polit. & Govt. Pos: Iowa State Rep, 37-42; city attorney, Chariton, Iowa, 41-42; chmn, Co. Rep. Finance Cmt, 48-50; chmn, Iowa Rep. Cmt, 50-53; mem, Iowa for Eisenhower Cmt, 51-52; Attorney Gen, Iowa, 53-55; Gov, 55-57; nat. dir, Off. of Civil and Defense Mobilization, 57-61. Bus. & Prof. Pos: Attorney-at-law, self-employed, 32-66; dir, Iowa Fund, Inc, 61-66; dir. and gen. counsel, Soypro, Int, 63-66; dir, Minutemen Industs, Inc, 63-66; mgt. consult, George Jensen & Assocs, 64-66. Mil. Serv: Entered as 1st Lt, Army, 42; released as Lt. Col, 46, after serv. in 104th Inf. Div, ETO, 44-45; Col.(Ret), Army, Res, 59; Legion of Honor; Croix de Guerre; Bronze Medal; 3 Campaign Ribbons. Publ: 'Timberwolf Tracks,' Infantry J, 46. Mem: Iowa, Colo. and Am. Bar Asns; Am. Legion; Amvets; Rotary; VFW. Rel: Methodist. Mailing Add: Chipita Park, Colo. 80811.

HOEH, DAVID CHARLES D
Mem, N.H. Dem. State Cmt.
b. Boston, Mass, 12/1/37; s. Robert Y. Hoeh and Priscilla Smith H; m. 2/9/63 to Sandra Unterman; c. Christopher and Jeffrey. Educ: Univ. N.H, B.A, 60; Boston Col. Law Sch, 61; Boston Univ, A.M, 66; Univ. Mass, Ph.D. cand; Pi Gamma Mu; Pi Sigma Alpha; Tau Kappa Epsilon. Polit. & Govt. Pos: Organizer, Rockingham Co. Dem. Cmt, N.H, 60; treas, Strafford Co. Dem. Cmt, 62; campaign coordinator, King for Gov, 62; commun. planning technician, State of N.H, 63-65, prin. planner, 65-67; campaign mgr, Officer for Cong, 64; N.H. chmn, McCarthy for President Campaign, 67-68; cand. for U.S. Rep, N.H, Second Cong. Dist, 68; del, Dem. Nat. Conv. & chmn. N.H. del, 68; mem. steering cmt, New Dem. Coalition; mem, N.H. Dem. State Cmt, 68- Bus. & Prof. Pos: Assoc. dir, Pub. Affairs Center, Dartmouth Col, 67-69, Planners Collaborative, 69- Publ: Ed, Collective Bargaining in the Public Sector, Public Affairs Center, Dartmouth Col, 69; 'Where Do We Go from Here,' New Republic, 10/68. Mem: Am. Soc. of Planning Off; Am. Polit. Sci. Asn; Am. Civil Liberties Union (bd. dirs. for N.H); N. Country Resources Conserv. and Develop. Project (bd. dirs); Soc. for the Protection of N.H. Forests; ACTION for N.H.(bd. dirs); N.H. Coun. of World Affairs. Mailing Add: 2 Ridge Rd, Hanover, N.H. 03755.

HOEH, GEORGE CHARLES D
b. Brooklyn, N.Y, 9/12/27; s. George Ferdinand Hoeh and Evelyn Thelma Lang H; single. Educ: St. John's Univ, 49-53; Berkeley Divinity Sch, 54-57. Polit. & Govt. Pos: Del, Dem. Nat. Conv, 68. Bus. & Prof. Pos: Chaplain, Vet. Admin. Hosp, Brooklyn, N.Y, 60-; mem. Youth Cmn, Diocese of L.I, 66-67, Diocesan Coun, 66- and M.R.I. Cmn, 67-68; mem. exec. cmt, Archdeaconry of Brooklyn, 66- Mil. Serv: Entered as Pvt, Army, 46, released as Cpl, 48, after serv. as Mil. Police and Chaplain's Asst. in 29th Engrs. Corps, 1st Army, Phillipine Islands, 47-48. Mem: Brooklyn Club; Officers Club, Ft. Hamilton. Rel: Episcopal. Mailing Add: 98-19 Ft. Hamilton Pkwy, Brooklyn, N.Y. 11209.

HOEH, SANDRA U. D
Treas, Hanover Dem. Town Cmt, N.H.
b. Baltimore, Md, 10/8/41; d. Milton Unterman and Semah Zinsher U; m. 2/9/63 to David Charles Hoeh; c. Christoper D. and Jeffrey D. Educ: Univ. N.H, B.A, 63; Phi Beta Kappa; Phi Kappa Phi; Pi Sigma Alpha; Pi Gamma Nu; Alpha Chi Omega. Polit. & Govt. Pos: Chmn, Concord Dem. Women Club, N.H, 65-67; chmn, Concord McIntyre for Senate Cmt, 66; mem. platform cmt, N.H. Dem. State Conv, 66; chmn, Second Cong. Dist. Dem. Party, 66-68; treas, Hanover Dem. Town Cmt, 67-; alternate del. and mem. credentials cmt, Dem. Nat. Conv, 68. Mem: N.H. Soc. Welfare Coun.(bd. dirs); N.H. Coun. World Affairs (bd. dirs); Upper Valley Human Rights Coun; League of Women Voters. Mailing Add: 2 Ridge Rd, Hanover, N.H. 03755.

HOEHN, ELMER L. D
b. Memphis, Ind, 12/19/15; s. Louis Hoehn and Agnes Goss H; m. 6/10/43 to Frances Cory; c. Kathleen and Patrick. Educ: Canterbury Col, B.S, 36; Univ. Louisville, LL.B, 40; Sigma Delta Kappa. Polit. & Govt. Pos: Ind. State Rep, 45-49, chief clerk, Ind. House of Rep, 49; chmn, Clark Co. Dem. Cmt, Ind, 46-52; dir, Ind. Div. of Oil and Gas, 49-52; Ind. Gov. Off. Rep, Interstate Oil Compact Cmn, 49-52 & 60-64; chmn, Eighth Cong. Dist. Dem. Cmt, 52-58; chmn, Ind. for Lyndon B. Johnson for President, 60; adminstr, U.S. Oil Import Admin, 65-69; energy, fuel and environment counselor, Wash, D.C, 69- Bus. & Prof. Pos: Teacher, Jeffersonville High Sch, 35-41; farmer, 36-; teacher, Ind. Univ, 40-42; lawyer, 40-; real estate broker, 46-; exec. secy, Tri-State Independent Oil Producers, 54-65. Mem: Am. Petroleum Institute; Evansville Petroleum Club; Am, Fed. and Ky. State Bar Asns; Nat. Lawyers Club, D.C; Elks; Lions. Rel: Catholic. Legal Res: 101 Sparks Ave, Jeffersonville, Ind. 47130. Mailing Add: 1523 L St. N.W, Washington, D.C. 20005.

HOELLEN, JOHN JAMES R
Alderman, Chicago, Ill.
b. Chicago, Ill, 9/24/14; s. John James Hoellen, Sr. and Mame Skellinger H; m. 4/24/48 to Mary Jane McMeans; c. Elizabeth and Robert. Educ: Northwest. Univ, B.A, 35, J.D, 38; Phi Beta Kappa; Eta Sigma Phi; Delta Theta Phi. Polit. & Govt. Pos: Alderman, 47th Ward, Chicago, Ill, 47-; mem, Cook Co. Rep. Cent. Cmt, 64-, v.chmn, 68-; Rep. cand, U.S. House Rep, 68. Bus. & Prof. Pos: Lawyer, Hoellen & Seyferth, Chicago; dir, Lincoln Sq. Savings and Loan Asn, 59-; dir, Bank of Ravenswood, Chicago, 62-; pres, Sulzer Family Found, 63- Mil. Serv: Entered as Ens, Naval Res, 41, released as Lt, 46, after serv. in Naval Intel. Serv. and on U.S.S. Chester T. O'Brien, Seventh Fleet, Atlantic, Mediterranean and Pac; Theatre Ribbons; Philippine Liberation Medal. Publ: Various newspaper articles. Mem: Am, Ill. and Chicago Bar Asns; Am. Judicature Soc; Am. Acad. Polit. Sci; Kiwanis; Chicago Execs; Chicago Asn. Commerce and Indust; YMCA (dir); VFW; Am. Legion; Orphei; Germania; Chicago Hist. Soc; Chicago Coun. For. Rels. Awards from Trinity Col. and Chicago Col. Indust. Eng; VFW and Amvets awards for sponsoring vet. legis; Kiwanis for original sponsorship of Peanut Day; Man of the Year, Lions. Rel: Methodist. Legal Res: 1842 W. Larchmont Ave, Chicago, Ill. 60613. Mailing Add: 1940 W. Irving Park Rd, Chicago, Ill. 60613.

HOEPPEL, JOHN HENRY D
b. Tell City, Ind, 2/10/81; s. John M. Hoeppel and Barbara Zoll H; m. 11/11/07 to Anna Seitz; c. Raymond, Charles and Mildred (Mrs. Ruddick). Educ: Grade Sch, 93. Polit. & Govt. Pos: Postmaster, Arcadia, Calif, 23-31; U.S. Rep, Calif, 32-36. Mil. Serv: Entered as Pvt, 1st Artil, Army, 98, retired as M/Sgt, Signal Corps, 21; served 10 years in Alaska between 00 and 17 and with 1st Div, France, 17-18; many letters of commendation; 1st Lt.(Ret), Air Force. Publ: Initiator and vol. publisher, National Defense, 28-63. Mem: Organizer and 1st comdr, Post of Am. Legion, also comdr, Arcadia Post 247; organizer and 1st comdr, Post of VFW and Camp of United Spanish War Vets. Was operator in charge of U.S. Tel. Off, Ft. Egbert, Eagle, Alaska who reported success of Roald Amundsen's Sailing of the Northwest Passage, 03-05; obtained transfer of World War I Balloon Sch. to Co. of Los Angeles and funds for develop. of the sch, plaque honoring this achievement erected in Los Angeles Co. Park, Arcadia. Mailing Add: P.O. Box 687, Arcadia, Calif. 91006.

HOEVEN, CHARLES BERNARD R
b. Hospers, Iowa, 3/30/95; s. Gerrit Hoeven and Lena Weiland H; m. June, 1919 to Velma Ruth Pike; c. Pauline Ruth (Mrs. Marshall) and Charles Pike. Educ: State Univ. Iowa, B.A, 20, Col. Law, LL.B, 22; Phi Alpha Delta. Cert. of Accomplishment, State Univ. Iowa, 47; Cert. of Merit, Northwestern Col, 64; hon. LL.D, Westmar Col, 56, Morningside Col, 65 and Buena Vista Col, 68. Polit. & Govt. Pos: Attorney, Sioux Co, Iowa, 25-37; Iowa State Sen, 37-41, Pres. Pro-Tem, Iowa State Sentate, 39-41; permanent chmn, Iowa State Rep. Conv, 40 and Iowa State Judicial Conv, 42; U.S. Rep, Sixth and Eighth Cong. Dists, Iowa, 43-65, chmn, Rep. Conf. and mem. Rep. Policy Cmt, U.S. House of Rep, 57-62, Dep. Rep. Whip, 57-65, mem, Ranking Rep. Cmt. on Agr, 58-65; cong. del, Food & Agr. Orgn, Rome, 57; U.S. Del, Interparliamentary Union, London, 57, Brussels, 61, Belgrade, 63 and Copenhagen, 64. Bus. & Prof. Pos: Dir. and v.pres, Alton Savings Bank, Iowa, 32- Mil. Serv: Entered as Pvt, Army, 17, released as Sgt, 19, after serv. in 350th Inf, 88th Div, U.S, Eng. and France; Victory Medal; Meuse-Argonne Medal. Mem: Past pres, Sioux Co. Bar Asn, 21st Judicial Bar Asn. and Iowa Co. Attorney's Asn; Maxonic Blue Lodge; Consistory; Shrine; Am. Legion; VFW; DAV; Vet. of World War I; Rotary; Sioux Golf & Country Club. Honor Iowans Award, Buena Vista Col, 66. Rel: Presbyterian; moderator, Presbytery of Northwest Iowa, 67. Mailing Add: Box 290, Alton, Iowa 51003.

HOFF, ARTHUR R
b. Eureka, S.Dak, 2/14/19; s. John Hoff and Lydia Weixel H; m. 10/5/51 to Betty Ray Smart; c. Dennis Ray and Christy Lee. Educ: High sch. Polit. & Govt. Pos: Co. chmn, Nutter for Gov, Mont, 60; chmn, Fergus Co. Rep. Cent. Cmt, 62-69. Mil. Serv: Entered as Pvt, Army, 41, released as S/Sgt, 45, after serv. in ETO. Mem: Dir, C. of C, 60 & 62; Elks. Rel: Lutheran. Mailing Add: 511 E. Montana, Lewistown, Mont. 59457.

HOFF, PHILIP HENDERSON D
b. Greenfield, Mass, 6/29/24; s. Olaf Hoff, II and Agnes E. Henderson H; m. to Joan P. Brower; c. Susan Brower, Dagny Elizabeth, Andrea Clark and Gretchen Henderson. Educ: Williams Col, A.B, 48; Cornell Law Sch, LL.B, 51. Hon. degrees from, Am. Int. Col, Middlebury Col, Norwich Univ, Williams Col, Windham Col, Univ. Vt. Polit. & Govt. Pos: Precinct worker, Dem. Party, Vt, 51; Vt. State Rep, Burlington, 61-62; Gov. of Vt, 62-69; cmnr, Pub. Land Law Rev. Cmn, 65-; del, Dem. Nat. Conv, 68. Bus. & Prof. Pos: Former partner, Black, Wilson & Hoff; attorney, Philip H. Hoff, currently; chmn. adv. cmt, States Urban Action Center of Urban Am, Wash, D.C, currently. Mil. Serv: Entered Navy, 43, released as Seaman 1/c, 46, after serv. in Submarine Serv. Mem: Am, Vt. and Chittenden Co. Bar Asns; former trustee, Vt. Rehab. Center; former dir, Vt. Children's Aid Soc, Lake Champlain C. of C. and Gr. Burlington Indust. Corp; Elks; K.T; Grange; Eagles; YMCA; Moose; Children's Assocs. United for Spec. Educ, Inc; sponsor, Atlantic Coun. U.S; hon. mem, United Serv. Orgn; hon. chmn, Vt. Chap. Arthritis and Rheumatism Found; Burlington Country Club; Ethan Allen Club. First Dem. Gov. in 109 years. Rel: Episcopal. Legal Res: 214 Prospect Pkwy, Burlington, Vt. 05401. Mailing Add: 109 S. Winooski Ave, Burlington, Vt. 05401.

HOFFELDER, WALTER P. R
Ill. State Sen.
b. Chicago, Ill, 12/25/00; m. 10/14/62 to Loretta Semrow; c. daughter. Educ: Metrop. Bus. Col. Polit. & Govt. Pos: Ill. State Sen, 62-; former Ill. State Rep. Bus. & Prof. Pos: Owner, operator, interstate truck lines, Suburban motor serv, 20-; part owner, automotive sales bus; Universal Heating Supply Co; Zander Jeep Sales Co; Hoffelder Road Maintenance Co; Superior Coach Sales Co; farmer. Mem: Higgins-Norwood Lions Club, Dania Soc, Chicago; Pier 66 Yacht Club, Ft. Lauderdale, Fla. Mailing Add: 5730 N. Menard Ave, Chicago, Ill. 60646. (1967)

HOFFER, GILES G. R
Chmn, Kosciusko Co. Rep. Cent. Cmt, Ind.
b. Atwood, Ind, 1/11/05; s. Charles Hoffer and Charlotte Rarick H; m. 12/29/34 to Mary Poor; c. Jerry B. and Judy (Mrs. Lovering). Educ: Manchester Col, 24-27; Univ. Miss, B.A.E, 38, M.A, 41. Polit. & Govt. Pos: Town bd. mem, Etna Green, Ind, 48-51; Rep. precinct committeeman, Kosciusko Co, 49-, co. chmn, Kosciusko Co. Rep. Cent. Cmt, 59- Bus. & Prof. Pos: Foreman, Planada Fruit Farms, Calif, 29-31; sch. teacher, Kosciusko Co, Ind, 38-50; teacher, Warsaw Commun. Schs, 50-58, chmn, soc. studies dept, 59- Mem: Nat. Coun. for the Soc. Studies; Nat. Educ. Asn; Ind. State Teachers Asn; Lions; Mason; Scottish Rite; Shrine; Nat. Farm Orgn; co. chmn, Cancer Soc. Rel: United Methodist. Mailing Add: 715 N. Union St, Warsaw, Ind. 46580.

HOFFMAN, BENJAMIN FRANKLIN D
b. Tremont, Ill, 11/23/11; s. John M. Hoffman and Edith Fornoff H; m. 4/9/39 to Lulu Irene Oelker; c. Jay Thomas, Anita Kay and Jeanine Marie. Educ: Tremont High Sch, 4 years. Polit. & Govt. Pos: Dem. precinct committeeman, Ill, 60-69; hearing officer, Secy. State, 64- Bus. & Prof. Pos: Owner, Nu-Cafe-Restaurant, 46-65. Mem: Lions Int. Rel: Baptist. Mailing Add: 212 Chestnut, Tremont, Ill. 61568.

HOFFMAN, GENE LOUIS R
Ill. State Rep.
b. Canton, Ill, 9/26/32; s. Wilbur Merle Hoffman and Helen Randolph H; m. 11/21/54 to Diane Wilma Thorton; c. Mark, Lynn, Susan and Gregory. Educ: Ill. State Univ, B.S, 54; North. Ill. Univ, M.S, 62; Pi Gamma Mu; capt, football team, 53 and wrestling team, 54. Polit. & Govt. Pos: Secy, Elmhurst Young Rep, Ill, 65-66, v.pres, 66-67; Ill. State Rep, currently. Bus. & Prof. Pos: Chmn, Social Studies Dept, Fenton High Sch, Bensenville, Ill, 59- Mil. Serv: Entered as Pvt, Army, 54, released as Cpl, 56, after serv. in 130th Sta. Hosp, Europe; Good Conduct and European Occup. Medals. Mem: Nat. and Ill. Educ. Asns; Elmhurst Jaycees. Rel: Unitarian. Mailing Add: 255 Niagara, Elmhurst, Ill. 60126.

HOFFMAN, HARRY S. Conservative, N.Y.
Chmn, Ulster Co. Conservative Party, N.Y.
b. Philadelphia, Pa, 4/9/25; s. Harry S. Hoffman and Evelyn Buckman H; m. 7/23/49 to Elizabeth Tallman; c. Barbara, Robert, Sharon, Marilyn, William and James. Educ: Case Inst. Tech, B.S.E.E, 47; Alpha Phi Omega. Polit. & Govt. Pos: Mem. bd. educ, Saugerties Cent. Schs, N.Y, 58-63; town committeeman, Fourth Dist, Saugerties, 64-66; v.chmn, Ulster Co. Conservative Party, 64-66, chmn, 66- Bus. & Prof. Pos: Engr, Int. Bus. Machines, 50-61, sr. engr, 61-66. Mil. Serv: Entered as A/S, Naval Res, 44, released as Seaman 2/C, 46. Mem: Jaycees; Boy Scouts Exec. Bd. Rel: Religious Society of Friends. Mailing Add: R.D. 5, Box 8, Saugerties, N.Y. 12477. (1967)

HOFFMAN, IRWIN F. D
Md. State Del.
b. Cumberland, Md, 1/10/27; married. Educ: Hagerstown pub. schs. Polit. & Govt. Pos: Md. State Del, 63- Bus. & Prof. Pos: Gen. ins. agent. Mil. Serv: Navy, 45. Mem: Past Exalted Ruler, Elks, Lodge 378. Mailing Add: 262 S. Potomac St, Hagerstown, Md. 21740. (1967)

HOFFMAN, JOHN STANLEY D
Ky. State Rep.
b. 1936. Educ: Centre Col, A.B; Univ. Ky, LL.B. Polit. & Govt. Pos: Ky. State Rep, currently. Bus. & Prof. Pos: Lawyer. Mil. Serv: Naval Res, 54-62. Mem: Ky. and Am. Bar Asns; state dir, Henderson Co. Jaycees. Rel: Methodist. Mailing Add: 2547 Honeysuckle Lane, Henderson, Ky. 42420. (1967)

HOFFMAN, JUDITH LINDA D
V.Chmn, Doniphan Co. Dem. Party, Kans.
b. Jackson, Mich, 2/6/39; d. Lawrence Meidinger and Winnetta Brady M; m. 4/23/61 to Wallace Gene Hoffman; c. Catherine Sue and Scott Brady. Educ: Highland Jr. Col, 2 years; Northwest Mo. State Col, B.S. in Educ; Student Nat. Educ. Asn; Am. Home Econ. Asn. Polit. & Govt. Pos: Dem. committeewoman, Wathena, Kans, 64-; v.chmn, Doniphan Co. Dem. Party, 64-; co-chmn, Bob Swan for Cong. Cmt, 68; chmn, Robert Kennedy for Pres. Campaign, 68. Mem: V.pres, USD 406 PTA, 68-69, pres, 69-; Am. Legion Auxiliary. Rel: Catholic. Legal Res: 410 Fremont, Wathena, Kans. 66090. Mailing Add: Box 66, Wathena, Kans. 66090.

HOFFMAN, PAUL JEROME D
b. San Francisco, Calif, 6/25/23; s. Louis Hoffman and Bessie Brodofsky H; m. 3/18/43 to Elaine Stroll; c. Valerie, Jonathan Marshall and Elizabeth. Educ: Univ. Calif, 40-42; Stanford Univ, B.A. in psychol, 49, M.A. in educ, 52 and Ph.D. in psychol, 53; Pi Lambda Phi; Sigma Xi. Polit. & Govt. Pos: Chmn, Subcmt. on World Peace and mem, Platform and Resolutions Cmt, Ore. State Dem. Conv, 62; alternate del, Dem. Nat. Conv, 64 & 68; campaign mgr. for Successful Dem. State Treas, 64; alternate chmn, Lane Co. Dem. Cent. Cmt, 66, 67. Bus. & Prof. Pos: Instr. and asst. prof, Wash. State Univ, 53-57; research consult, Maintenance Systs. Research Lab, Air Force, 54 & 55; consult. clin. psychol, Vet. Admin, 56-; asst. prof. psychol, Univ. Ore, 57-60; consult. weapons systs, Dept. of Navy, 60-64 and Systs. Develop. Corp, 61; pres, Ore. Research Inst, 60- Mil. Serv: Entered as Pvt, Air Force, 42, released as 2nd Lt, 46, after serv. in 31st Squadron, 5th Bomb Group, 13th Air Force, Southwest Pac. Area, 45; 2nd Lt, Air Force Res, 46-52; Distinguished Unit Badge with Oak Leaf Cluster; Victory, Asiatic-Pac. Serv. and Am. Theater Serv. Medals; Philippine Liberation Ribbon. Publ: Decision Processes, Thrall, Coombs, Davis, Wiley and Sons, 54; 'Tendencies Toward Group Comparability in Competitive Bargaining,' Human Rels, 54; 'The Paramorphic Representation of Clinical Judgement,' Psychol. Bul, 60; 'Psychological Approaches to Problems of National Security,' Ore. Research Inst. Research Bul, 61. Mem: Pres, Ore. Psychol. Asn, 66; Asn. Comput. Machinery; Human Factors Soc; Am. Psychol. Asn; Psychometric Soc; Psychonomic Soc; Coun. Basic Educ; Am. Statist. Asn; Ment. Health Asn; Nat. Asn. Retarded Children; fel. Soc. for Psychol. Study Soc. Issues; pres, Ore. Inventors Coun. and Ore. Research Inst; Moose; Metrop. Civic Club; C. of C. Rel: Unitarian. Legal Res: 3248 Bryceler Dr, Eugene, Ore. 97403. Mailing Add: Oregon Research Institute, Eugene, Ore. 97403.

HOFFMAN, QUINCY R
Mich. State Rep.
b. Applegate, Mich, 5/30/13; married; c. Howard, Janice. Educ: Col, two years. Polit. & Govt. Pos: Mich. State Rep, 64-; sheriff, Sanilac Co, 5 terms; former pres, village and sch. bd. Bus. & Prof. Pos: Owner and operator, purebred beef farm, Sanilac Co. Mich. Mem: Lions; F&AM; RAM; pres, Sanilac Unit, Am. Cancer Soc; cmnr, Boy Scouts; Farm Bur. Rel: Methodist. Mailing Add: Box 127, Applegate, Mich. 48401. (1967)

HOFFMAN, RONALD KENNETH R
Ill. State Rep.
b. Chicago, Ill, 4/5/32; s. Arthur Hoffman and Lillian Popa H; m. 7/11/53 to Marilyn Ella Roth; c. Donna Lynn and Sharon Lee. Educ: Morton Col, 2 years. Polit. & Govt. Pos: Pres, Westchester Park Dist, Ill, 65-69; Ill. State Rep, 69- Bus. & Prof. Pos: Br. mgr, Sunbeam Appliance Serv. Corp, 55-69. Mil. Serv: Entered as A/S, Navy, 51, released as PO, 55, after serv. in Amphibious Unit, Korean Conflict; Good Conduct Medal; China Serv. Medal; Nat. Defense Medal; Korean Serv. Medal: UN Serv. Medal Letter of Commendation. Man of the Year Award, Italian Cath. Fedn, 69. Rel: Protestant. Mailing Add: 10838 Windsor Dr, Westchester, Ill. 60153.

HOFFMANN, FRANK NORDY D
Exec. Dir, Dem. Sen. Campaign Cmt.
b. Seattle, Wash, 12/19/09; s. Henry Hoffmann and Helen Nordhoff H; m. 2/27/65 to Joanne Eileen Amnott; c. Eileen Joanne, Patricia Ann and Mary Frances. Educ: Notre Dame Univ, LL.B, 33; pres, Monogram Club. Polit. & Govt. Pos: Exec. dir, Dem. Sen. Campaign Cmt, 67- Bus. & Prof. Pos: Legis. dir, USW, 45-67. Mil. Serv: Entered as Lt.(jg), Navy, 43, released as Lt, 45, after serv. in Armed Guard, Atlantic and Pac. Theatres. Publ: Legis. Manual, 53. Mem: Am. Polit. Sci. Asn; Am. Asn. of Polit. Consult. Rel: Catholic. Mailing Add: 6602 Karlson Court, Hyattsville, Md. 20783.

HOFFNER, S. F. 'BUCKSHOT' D
N.Dak. State Rep.
m. to Pat. Polit. & Govt. Pos: N.Dak. State Rep, 62-, asst. majority floor leader, N.Dak. House of Rep, 65; Dem. cand. for U.S. Rep, N.Dak; del, Dem. Nat. Conv, 68; mem, N.Dak. Dem. Non-Partisan League State Exec. Cmt, currently. Bus. & Prof. Pos: Farmer. Mil. Serv: Inf, France and Germany, World War II. Mem: VFW. Mailing Add: Esmond, N.Dak. 58332. (1967)

HOFFSES, ALBERT WINSTON R
Maine State Sen.
b. Waldoboro, Maine, 11/2/13; s. Clarence T. Hoffses and Bessie May Hanna H; m. 10/16/38 to Marjorie Taylor; c. Elaine (Mrs. Davis). Polit. & Govt. Pos: Mem, Camden Town Rep. Cmt, Maine, 40-66; mem, Knox Co. Rep. Cmt, 48-52; town moderator, Camden, 59-69; Maine State Sen, Knox Co, 63- Bus. & Prof. Pos: Owner and mgr, Poultry Farming, 39-66; Bldg. Construction, 60-69. Mem: Rotary; Camden Hosp. Incorporator; past presiding officer, all York Rite Masonic Bodies; past grand comdr, K.T, Kora Shrine; Red Cross of Constantine. Rel: Baptist. Mailing Add: Washington St, Camden, Maine 04843.

HOFLER, WILLIAM HANCE D
N.C. State Rep.
b. Gatesville, N.C, 3/29/04; s. James Luther Hofler and Annie Brown H; m. 8/26/26; to Winnie Davis Oliver; c. Barbara. Educ: Lincoln Mem. Univ; Univ. N.C; Wake Forest Col. Polit. & Govt. Pos: Rationing exec. and asst. state dir, Off. Price Admin, 42-45; N.C. State Rep, 65- Bus. & Prof. Pos: Lawyer. Mem: Pres, Durham Co. Bar Asn, 55-56; N.C. Bar Asn; N.C. State Bar Asn; pres, Durham C. of C, 57-58. Rel: Baptist. Mailing Add: 1532 Hermitage Court, Durham, N.C. 27707.

HOFSTETTER, EDWIN THOMAS R
b. Huntsburg, Ohio, 8/12/18; s. Kaspar Hofstetter and Augusta Kresin H; m. 3/28/41 to Anna May Booth; c. Beth Marie (Mrs. Milliken), Edwina Kay and William Clay. Educ: Ohio State Univ, B.S. in Rural Econ, 41; Cleveland-Marshall Law Sch, LL.B, 52; Delta Theta Phi; Stadium Scholarship Dormitories, Ohio State Univ. Polit. & Govt. Pos: Justice of the peace, Chardon Twp, Ohio, 54-56; cmnr, Geauga Co, 57-60, prosecuting attorney, 61-66; Ohio State Rep, 36th Dist, 67-68; presiding judge, 11th Dist. Court of Appeals, Ohio, 69- Mem: Secy-treas, Geauga Co. Bar Asn, 61-66; Ohio State Bar Asn; Ohio Prosecuting Attorneys Asn; Nat. Dist. Attorneys Asn; Am. Judicature Soc; Geauga Co. Trustees and Clerks Asn; past mem, Chardon Jr. C. of C; Geauga Co. Farm Bur. Fedn; Ohio Farm Bur. Fedn; Rotary; treas. and chmn, Methodist Church Bldg. Cmn. Selected Outstanding Young Man of Year by Chardon Jr. C. of C, 53. Rel: Methodist. Legal Res: 11169 Aquilla Rd, Chardon, Ohio 44024. Mailing Add: Geauga Co. Courthouse, Chardon, Ohio 44024.

HOFSTRAND, HAROLD R. R
b. Churchs Ferry, N.Dak, 11/19/15; married; c. four. Educ: Iowa State Col. Polit. & Govt. Pos: Mem, Econ. Develop. Cmn, 57-61; N.Dak. State Rep, 61-66; N.Dak. State Sen, 67-69. Bus. & Prof. Pos: Farmer. Mem: Mason; Shrine; Elks. Rel: Lutheran. Mailing Add: Leeds, N.Dak. 58346. (1967)

HOGAN, CHARLES V. D
Mass. State Sen.
b. Lynn, Mass, 4/12/97. Educ: Suffolk Univ. Law Sch. Polit. & Govt. Pos: Mass. State Rep, 35-40; Mass. State Sen, 41- Bus. & Prof. Pos: Attorney-at-law. Mem: Pres. bd, Lynn Cath. Charities Center. Rel: Catholic. Mailing Add: 36 Baltimore St, Lynn, Mass. 01901.

HOGAN, ELWOOD LEON D
Ala. State Rep.
b. Mobile, Ala, 7/13/30; s. Walter Leroy Hogan and Mary Rosana Batchelor H; m. 12/15/56 to Patricia Russell; c. Patricia Lauren, Elwood Leon, Jr, Russell Lindsay and Leslie Rose. Educ: Univ. Ala, B.S, 51, LL.B, 56. Polit. & Govt. Pos: Law clerk, Ala. Supreme Court, 56; Ala. State Rep, 63- Bus. & Prof. Pos: Lawyer. Mil. Serv: Lt, Army. Mem: VFW; Am. Legion. Rel: Methodist. Mailing Add: Suite 1201, Merchants National Bank Bldg, Mobile, Ala. 36601. (1967)

HOGAN, FRANK SMITHWICK D
b. Waterbury, Conn, 1/17/02; s. Michael F. Hogan and Ann Smithwick H; m. 11/11/36 to Mary Egan. Educ: Columbia Col, A.B, 24; Columbia Univ. Law Sch, LL.B, 28. Hon. LL.D, Columbia Univ, 52 and Suffolk Law Sch, 55. Polit. & Govt. Pos: Asst. to the spec. prosecutor, Spec. Invest. of Organized Crime, N.Y. Co, N.Y, 35-39, admin. asst, Dist. Attorney, 38-41, Dist. Attorney, 42-; del, Dem. Nat. Conv, 44, 52, 56, 60 & 64; Dem. cand. for U.S. Sen, 58. Bus. & Prof. Pos: Attorney-at-Law, 29-35. Mem: Am. and N.Y. State Bar Asns; exec. cmt, Bar Asn. of the City of N.Y, 59-63; Dist. Attorneys' Asn. of the State of N.Y; Nat. Prosecutors' Asn; trustee, Columbia Univ, Knickerbocker Hosp. and St. Luke's Hosp. Rel: Catholic. Legal Res: 404 Riverside Dr, New York, N.Y. 10025. Mailing Add: 155 Leonard St, New York, N.Y. 10013.

HOGAN, JOHN J. D
R.I. State Rep.
b. Cumberland, R.I, 1/29/35. Educ: LaSalle Acad, 52; Providence Col, 62. Polit. & Govt. Pos: R.I. State Rep, 63-; chmn, R.I. State Dem. Party, currently. Bus. & Prof. Pos: Pres-treas, Three-R. Corp, Pawtucket, R.I. Mil. Serv: Navy Electrician, 52-56 in U.S.S. Gilbert Islands. Mem: K. of C; Friendly Sons of St. Patrick; Lions; Pawtucket Bd. of Realtors. Rel: Catholic. Mailing Add: 200 Curran Rd, Cumberland, R.I. 02864.

HOGAN, LAWRENCE JOSEPH R
U.S. Rep, Md.
b. Boston, Mass, 9/30/28; m. 1947 to Nora Elizabeth Maguire; c. Mary Theresa (Mrs. Wm. Robert Lazarus) and Lawrence J, Jr. Educ: Georgetown Univ. Col, A.B, 49, Georgetown Univ. Law Sch, LL.B, 54; Am. Univ, M.A, 66. Polit. & Govt. Pos: Alternate del, Rep. Nat. Conv, 64, del, 68; U.S. Rep, Fifth Dist, Md, 69- Bus. & Prof. Pos: Spec. agent, Fed. Bur. Invest, 48-58; asst. dept. mgr, U.S. C. of C, 58-59; pres, Larry Hogan Assocs, Inc, 59-69; part-time prof, Univ. Md, 60-68. Publ: Weekly article, 'In the Nation's Capital,' Telephony Mag, 61-69. Mem: D.C. Bar Asn; Nat. Press Club; Former Spec. Agents of Fed. Bur. Invest. Admitted to practice before U.S. Supreme Court. Rel: Roman Catholic. Mailing Add: Box 1231, Landover, Md. 20785.

HOGAN, MARK ANTHONY D
Lt. Gov, Colo.
b. Chicago, Ill, 1/27/31; s. Mark Anthony Hogan (deceased) and Alice Glavin H. (deceased); m. 2/6/54 to Nancy Stevenson; c. Cary Lucile, Mark A, Jr, Lisa Ann, Matthew J. and Michael J. Educ: Georgetown Univ, A.B, 52. Polit. & Govt. Pos: Colo. State Rep, 63-66, Asst. Majority Leader, Colo. House of Rep, 65-66; Lt. Gov, Colo, 67-; del, Dem. Nat. Conv, 68. Bus. & Prof. Pos: Pres, Hogan-Stevenson Real Estate Co. Mil. Serv: Entered as Ens, Naval Res, 52, released as Lt.(jg), 54. Denver and Colo. Young Man of the Year, Jr. C. of C, 58. Rel: Catholic. Mailing Add: 1861 S. Niagara Way, Denver, Colo. 80222.

HOGAN, MORRIS BERNARD R
Conn. State Rep.
b. Harwinton, Conn, 2/22/02; s. Patrick James Hogan and Marion Martha Morris H; m. 6/9/32 to Mabel M. Casson. Polit. & Govt. Pos: Chmn, Rep. Town Cmt, Burlington, Conn, 32-, selectman, 49-57, mem. bd. finance, 57-; Conn. State Rep, 177th Dist, 55- Bus. & Prof. Pos: Farm owner and mgr, 19- Mem: Grange; Farm Bur; C.M.P.A. Rel: Catholic. Mailing Add: Route 4, Burlington, Conn. 06085. (1967)

HOGAN, ROBERT GEORGE D
b. Waukegan, Ill, 2/9/11; s. Andrew Vincent Hogan and Marie Hinrichs H; m. 4/12/55 to Margaret Adams; c. Robert G, Jr. and Anne Marie. Educ: La. State Univ, B.A, 35; Univ. Wash, 37-38; Univ. Ark, LL.B, 39; Zeta Psi. Polit. & Govt. Pos: Dep. attorney gen, Territory of Hawaii, 46-47, mem, Hawaii Statehood Cmn, 50-51, mem, Bd. of Harbor Cmnrs, 50-53; del, Dem. Nat. Conv, 64 & 68; Dem. pres, Eighth Precinct, 16th Dist, Hawaii, 67- Bus. & Prof. Pos: Partner, Hogan, Howell & Rother, Attorneys, and its predecessor firms, 39- Mil. Serv: Entered as 2nd Lt, Army, 41, released as Lt. Col, 45, after serv. in Hq, Army Res, Pac. Theater, 41-45; Res, Lt. Col.(Ret); Bronze Star; plus others. Publ: 'A Proposal for the Adoption of the Doctrine of Comparative Negligence in Hawaii by Judicial Declaration,' Hawaii Bar J, 68; plus others. Mem: Bar. Asn. of Hawaii; Am. Bar Asn; Am. Trial Lawyers Asn; Outrigger Canoe Club; Waialae Country Club; Nat. Lawyers Club; Zeta Psi. Legal Res: 2957 Kalakaua Ave, Honolulu, Hawaii 96815. Mailing Add: 320 Dillingham Bldg, Honolulu, Hawaii 96813.

HOGAN, ROSEMARIE D
V.Chmn, Ulster Co. Dem. Cmt, N.Y.
b. East Kingston, N.Y, 4/22/24; d. Santo F. Amato and Mary Fuscardo A; m. 9/8/46 to John J. Hogan; c. Jay F. Educ: Kingston High Sch, grad, 42; Muran's Sch. of Business; High Sch. Secy. of Manning Chap, Nat. Honor Soc. Polit. & Govt. Pos: Secy, Ulster Co. Dem. Women's Club, N.Y, 52-54, v.pres, 54-56; committeeman, First Dist, 11th Ward, Kingston, 53-; mem, Civil Serv. Cmn, Kingston, 58-63, pres, 61-63; v.chmn, Ulster Co. Dem. Cmt, 63- Bus. & Prof. Pos: Office Mgr, Zwick & Schwartz, Kingston, 43-55, Washington Growers & Distributors, Poughkeepsie, N.Y, 59- Mem: Ulster Co. Business & Prof. Womens' Club; Ulster Co. Dem. Womens' Club; Rapid Hose Ladies Auxiliary. Rel: Roman Catholic. Mailing Add: 47 German St, Kingston, N.Y. 12401.

HOGBEN, ANNE D
b. New York, N.Y, 8/6/22; d. Van Beuren Stanbery and Hazel Morey S; m. 11/1/48 to C. Adrian M. Hogben; c. Leslie and Lynn. Educ: Ore. State Col, 40-42; Univ. Calif, Berkeley, A.B. summa cum laude, 44; Phi Beta Kappa. Polit. & Govt. Pos: Secy, precinct 7-11, Montgomery Co, Md, 59-61; mem. hospitality cmt, Nat. Inaugural Cmt. for President Kennedy, 60-61; alternate del, Dem. Nat. Conv, 64 & 68; registrn. and canvassing chmn, Johnson Co. Dem. Cent. Cmt, 64-66, precinct committeewoman, 64-68; pres, Johnson Co. Dem. Women's Club, 66-67; Iowa chmn, Nat. Conf. of Concerned Dem, 67; first dist. co-chmn, Iowa McCarthy-for-President Campaign, 68; mem. exec. bd, East. Iowa Chap, Am. for Dem. Action, 69; mem-at-lg, state exec. cmt, Iowa Dem. Conf, 69. Bus. & Prof. Pos: Tech. asst. in eng, Standard Oil Co. of Calif, 44-48; statist. asst, div. of biometry and med. statist, Mayo Clinic, Minn, 49-50. Mem: League of Women Voters. Mailing Add: 910 Rider St, Iowa City, Iowa 52240.

HOGG, ROBERT LYNN R
b. Point Pleasant, W.Va, 12/30/93; s. Charles Edgar Hogg and Nancy Berden Hawkins H; m. 6/24/26 to Mary Louise Holliday; c. Mary Lynn (Mrs. John E. Shackelford), Charles Edgar, II. Educ: W.Va. Prep. Sch; Morgantown, W.Va; W.Va. Univ, A.B, 14, LL.B, 16; Morris Harvey Col, Dr. of Laws, 56. Polit. & Govt. Pos: U.S. Rep, W.Va, (unexpired term 30-31 and 31-33); W.Va. State Sen, 24-28 (chmn. com. on taxation and fin); prosecuting attorney, Mason Co, W.Va, 20-24. Bus. & Prof. Pos: Counsel Jackson, Kelley, Holt & O'Farrell, Charleston, W.Va, 60-; Equitable Life Assurance Soc, bd. mem, 59-, v.chmn, bd, 56-59, dir, 55, sr. v.pres. adv. counsel, 54-56; exec. v.pres. and gen. counsel, Am. Life, 46-54; mgr. and gen. counsel Am. Life Conv, Chicago, 44-46; assoc. gen. counsel Life Ins. Assoc. of Am, 43-45, asst. gen. counsel, 35-43; began practice Point Pleasant, W.Va, 16. Mil. Serv: Army, 17-19; overseas 15 months. Mem: Am, W.Va. Bar Asns; Asn. Life Ins. Counsel, U.S, N.Y. (chmn. ins. com) Cs. of C; Ins. Soc. N.Y. (dir); Clubs: Cong. Country; Buring Tree; Nat. Press; Metrop. (N.Y.C); Kenwood Golf and Country (Bethesda, Md); Masons. Published Hogg's Pleadings and Forms. Rel: Presbyterian. Legal Res: Lewisburg, W.Va. 24901. Mailing Add: Kanawha Valley Bldg, Charleston, W.Va. 25301. (1967)

HOGGINS, DALE EDWIN R
Wash. State Rep.
b. White Swan, Wash; 4/25/32; s. James Ralph Hoggins and Leba Duke H; m. 7/19/51 to Donna Lee Allen; c. Vicki Lee, Kerry Lynn and Robert Dale. Educ: West. Wash. State Col, B.A, 54; Univ. Wash, M.Ed, 66; Phi Delta Kappa. Polit. & Govt. Pos: Wash. State Rep, 21st Legis. Dist, 67- Bus. & Prof. Pos: Elem. teacher, Edmonds Sch. Dist. 15, Wash, 54-59, elem. prin, 59-69. Mem: Nat, Wash. and Edmonds Educ. Asns; Nat. and Wash. Elem. Prin. Asns; Boiler makers' Union; Elks; Mid-City Athletic Asn. Citation for commun. serv, United Good Neighbors; 500 Hour Award, Wash. Educ. Asn. Rel: Methodist. Mailing Add: 21826-95th Ave. W, Edmonds, Wash. 98020.

HOH, PAUL JACOB D
b. Lancaster, Pa, 9/27/34; s. Ernest J. Hoh and Ruth C. Kirsch H; m. 6/17/56 to Mary C. Houseman; c. Christopher John and Robyn Adelle. Educ: Denison Univ, B.A, 55; Psi Chi; Phi Alpha Theta; Lambda Chi Alpha. Polit. & Govt. Pos: Former Pa. State Rep; mem, Exec. Cmt, Berks Independent Dem, 63- and v.pres, 64-65. Bus. & Prof. Pos: Pastor, Christ Lutheran

Church, 59-66. Mem: Bd. dirs, Fel. House of Reading, 3 years; Cmn. on World Missions; Nat. Student Christian Fedn; Nat. Coun. of Churches; Cmt. on Religion and Race; Eastern Pa. Synod, Lutheran Church in Am. Rel: Lutheran. Mailing Add: 118 W. Windsor St, Reading, Pa. 19601. (1967)

HOHMAN, GEORGE H, JR. D
Alaska State Rep.
b. St. Louis, Mo, 6/2/32; s. George Harold Hohman, Sr. and Margaret Church H; m. 3/29/53 to Nancy Lou Mead; c. Margaret Carrie, Laura Marie, Sally Anne, Catherine Ann and George H, III. Educ: Michigan State Univ, B.A, 59. Polit. Pos: Alaska State Rep. Mil. Serv: Entered as Pvt, Army, 52, released as Cpl, 55. Mem: Kuskokwim Native Asn; Alaska Educ. Asn. Rel: Protestant. Mailing Add: Box 233, Bethel, Alaska 99559. (1967)

HOHN, MAYME R. R
V.Chmn, Hutchinson Co. Rep. Party, S.Dak.
b. Dimock, S.Dak, 1/5/14; d. Gottlieb F. Metzger and Lucy Reinsbach M; m. 12/30/43 to Leonard J. Hohn; c. Lee Ann (Mrs. Smith). Educ: Parkston High Sch, grad. Polit. & Govt. Pos: Secy, Agr. Adjust. Admin. Off, Parkston, S.Dak, 34-43, Civil Serv. Sect. and Intel. Div, U.S. Army, Camp Grant, Rockford, Ill, 43-45; v.chmn, Hutchinson Co. Rep. Party, S.Dak, 61- Bus. & Prof. Pos: Secy, Bldg. Fund Drive, Parkston, S.Dak, 62; saleslady, Coast to Coast Store, 66-67; admin. secy, St. Benedict Hosp, 66-; rep. mutual funds, stocks and bonds, Westamerica Securities, Inc, Emporia, Kans, 67- Mem: Am. Legion Auxiliary; Hosp. Auxiliary. Rel: Catholic. Mailing Add: Parkston, S.Dak. 57366.

HOILES, WILLIAM McHENRY R
b. Alliance, Ohio, 6/19/36; s. Arthur Jones Hoiles and Martha McHenry H; m. 12/22/59 to Susan Fralich; c. William McHenry, Melissa Lawson and Peter Beakley. Educ: Culver Military Acad, 51-55; Mount Union Col, 55-57; Univ. of Pennsylvania, B.S. Econ, 59; Univ. of Pittsburgh, LL.B, 65; Sigma Alpha Epsilon. Polit. & Govt. Pos: Asst. attorney gen. to Attorney Gen. William B. Saxbe, Ohio, 65-66, Admin. Asst, 67-68; Admin. Asst, U.S. Sen. William B. Saxbe, Ohio, 69- Legal Res: 4347 Mumford Dr, Columbus, Ohio 43220. Mailing Add: 1107 Flor Lane, McLean, Va. 22101.

HOIUM, VERNON STANLEY D
b. Minneapolis, Minn; s. Ole N. Hoium and Helmi M. Johanson H; m. 12/16/61 to Nancy Kay Watrud; c. Elizabeth Jane. Educ: Univ. Minn, B.A, 55; Univ. Minn. Law Sch, J.D, 59; Delta Sigma Rho; Beta Theta Pi. Polit. & Govt. Pos: Minn. State Sen, 63-67. Bus. & Prof. Pos: Dir, Columbia Heights C. of C, 65-, v.pres, 66-67, pres, 67- Mil. Serv: Entered as Recruit, Army, 48, released as S/Sgt, 52, after serv. in Army Security Agency, ETO, 50-51. Mem: Am, Minn. State, Hennepin Co. and Anoka Co. Bar Asns; Am. Trial Lawyers Asn; Zuhrah Temple Shrine, Free Mason. Rel: Lutheran. Mailing Add: 4163 Stinson Blvd. N.E, Columbia Heights, Minn. 55421.

HOLADAY, T.W. 'BILL' R
Okla. State Rep.
b. Oklahoma City, Okla, 4/16/21; s. Noble Austin Holaday and Mary Agnes Walker H; m. 6/29/47 to Mary Adeline MaGuire; c. Holly Diane. Educ: Okla. Univ, 41. Polit. & Govt. Pos: Mem. state reapportionment cmt, Okla. Co. Rep. Cmt, Okla, 62; precinct chmn, 63-64; organizer and pres, Northwest Rep. Club, 62-64; Okla. State Rep, 82nd Dist, 64-, mem, Bus. & Indust, Elec. & Privileges, Prfnl. & Occupational Regulations, Pub. Safety and Roads & Hwys. Cmts, Okla. State House of Rep; mem. adv. cmt, Young Rep. Action Cmt, 65-66; mem, Okla. State Rep. Cmt, 65-66. Bus. & Prof. Pos: Owner, T.W. Holaday and Assocs, Designers, 55- Mil. Serv: Entered as Pvt, Air Force, 42, released as Sgt, 45, after serv. in 62nd Troop Carrier Squadron, 314th Group, ETO, 43-45; recalled as S/Sgt, 50-51, Tinker Air Force Base; Distinguished Unit Badge with 1 Bronze Oak Leaf Cluster; Europe-Africa-Middle East Serv. Ribbon with 1 Silver Serv. Star and 2 Bronze Serv. Stars. Mem: Lions; Okla. City C. of C; Northwest C. of C; Nat. Fedn. Independent Bus, Inc. Rel: Episcopal. Mailing Add: 3844 N.W. 64th St, Oklahoma City, Okla. 73116. (1967)

HOLAND, DONALD C. R
N.Dak. State Sen.
b. Mckinley, Minn, 4/25/13; s. Peter Holand and Camilla Berger H; m. 10/19/47 to Lenore Jensen; c. Stephen and David. Educ: Univ. N.Dak, B.S. in Educ, 34, LL.B, 47; George Washington Univ. Law Sch, 46-47; Phi Delta Kappa; Phi Delta Phi; Blue Key; Theta Chi. Polit. & Govt. Pos: Secy. to U.S. Sen. Milton R. Young, 47-48; N.Dak. State Sen, 55-, Majority Leader, N.Dak. State Sen, 59, 61, 63 & 65. Bus. & Prof. Pos: Prin, high sch, Drayton, N.Dak, 34-36; supt. schs, Drayton, 37 and Lancaster, 37-40. Mil. Serv: Entered as Pvt, Army Air Force, 42, released as Capt, 46, after serv. in 2nd Weather Reconnaissance Sq, China-Burma-India; 5 Bronze Stars; Air Offensive, Japan, Cent. Burma and India-Burma and China Defensive Campaigns. Mem: N.Dak. State and Am. Bar Asns; Kiwanis; Am. Legion; VFW. Rel: Lutheran. Mailing Add: 311 Rose St, Lisbon, N.Dak. 58054.

HOLAND, P.J.
married; c. one. Polit. & Govt. Pos: Minn. State Sen, 54-66. Mem: Dir, Nat. Swine Shows; secy, Mower Co. Fair; secy, Midwest Livestock Show; pres, Mower Co. Pioneer and Hist. Soc; Moose; Elk; Rotary; Shrine. Mailing Add: 100 20th St. S.W, Austin, Minn. 55912.

HOLBEL, DIANE ERICKSON R
V.chmn, Genesee Co. Rep. Exec. Cmt, Mich.
b. Iron River, Mich, 6/29/39; d. Leslie C. Erickson and Lydia Tadey E; m. 8/27/60 to James B. Holbel; c. James B, Jr. and David James. Educ: Ferris State Col, A.A.S, 59. Polit. & Govt. Pos: Precinct del, Genesee Co. Rep. Exec. Cmt, Mich, 60-68, v.chmn, 69-; mem, bd. dirs. and area coordinator, Rep. Women's Fedn. Mich. Bus. & Prof. Pos: Secy, Dow Corning Corp, Midland, Mich, 59, Gen. Motors Research Labs, Warren, 60 and Consumers Power Co, Flint, 60-67. Mem: Genesee Co. Rep. Women's Club; Republic-Anns Club; mem. bd. dirs, Ferris State Col. Alumni Asn, 69- Outstanding Woman of the Year, Ferris State Col, 59. Rel: Catholic. Mailing Add: 1311 Greenway, Flint, Mich. 48504.

HOLBERT, SALIN R
b. Owenton, Ky, 4/10/98; s. Farmer Reese Holbert and Nannie Belle Wilbur H; div. Educ: Univ. Ky, A.B. Polit. & Govt. Pos: Teacher, Ky. House of Reform, 25-31 and Owen Co, 26-27; chmn, Owen Co. Rep. Cmt, Ky, 40-58 & 60-66; auditor, Ky. Dept. Revenue, 45-48. Bus. & Prof. Pos: Farmer, 18-; asst. shipping clerk, Belknap Hardware, 41; timekeeper, Mengel Co, 43-44. Mem: Odd Fellows; Mason. Rel: Christian Church; Deacon and teacher, bible class, El Bethel Christian Church. Mailing Add: R.R. 3, Owenton, Ky. 40359.

HOLBROOK, DONALD E, JR. R
Mich. State Rep.
b. Grand Rapids, Mich, 10/29/31; m. to Evelyn Archbold; c. Donald E, III, Gregg Bradford and Christopher Todd. Educ: Albion Col, B.A, 53; Wayne State Univ. Law Sch, LL.B, 56. Polit. & Govt. Pos: Friend of the Court, Clare Co, Mich, 61-64; Mich. State Rep, 64- Bus. & Prof. Pos: Attorney. Mil. Serv: Air Force, 57-61. Mem: State Bar of Mich; Am. Bar Asn; Mason; Kiwanis Int. Rel: Methodist. Mailing Add: 520 Helen St, Clare, Mich. 48617. (1967)

HOLCOMB, S. RICHARD D
Tenn. State Rep.
b. Chattanooga, Tenn, 10/30/35; s. Starlan Richard Holcomb and Irene Lingerfelt H; m. 12/30/56 to Nona Brotherton; c. Starlan Richard, III and Lora Lee. Educ: Univ. Chattanooga, A.B. Econ, 59; Univ. Cincinnati, LL.B, 62; Blue Key; Order of Coif; Kappa Sigma. Polit. & Govt. Pos: Tenn. State Rep, 66-; city judge, East Ridge, Tenn. Bus. & Prof. Pos: Attorney, 62- Mil. Serv: Entered as recruit, Navy, 54, released as FP/3, 56, after serving in U.S.S. Columbus, U.S.S. Northampton. Mem: Elks; VFW. Rel: Episcopal. Legal Res: 3807 Northview Ave, Chattanooga, Tenn. 37412. Mailing Add: 201 Professional Bldg, Chattanooga, Tenn. 37402.

HOLDEN, CREIGHTON DAVIDSON R
b. Detroit, Mich, 1/19/17; s. Creighton Holden and Belinda Davidson H; m. 3/24/41 to Rebecca Jean Harshbarger; c. Holly, Creighton, Jr, Belinda, Becky and Heather. Educ: Dartmouth Col, B.A, 40; Dragon Sr. Soc; Phi Gamma Delta. Polit. Pos: Mem, Gov. Cmt. on Higher Educ, 64-65; dir, Citizens for Mich, 61-64. Bus. & Prof. Pos: V.pres, Am. Hotel and Motel Asn, at present; past pres, Mich. Hotel Asn, 58. Mil. Serv: Entered as Pvt, Army, 43, released as Pfc, 46, after serv. in Inf, ETO; Combat Inf. Award; ETO Ribbon with 3 Battle Stars; Purple Heart. Mem: V.pres, Mich. State C. of C; v.pres, Southeast. Tourist Asn; Detroit Athletic Club; St. Clair River Country Club; Rotary; VFW; DAV; Otsego Ski Club; Great Books Club. Rel: Protestant. Mailing Add: 710 Brown St, St. Clair, Mich. 48079. (1967)

HOLDEN, DOROTHY ALMOND D
b. Wayne, Nebr, 9/14/16; d. Jacob Robert Almond and Alice Hill A; m. 5/19/44 to Theodore Albon Holden; c. Theodore Albon, Jr. and Glenn Almond. Educ: Tex. State Col. for Women, B.A, 38; Alpha Lambda Delta. Polit. & Govt. Pos: Mem, Fairfax Co. Dem. Cmt, Va, 56-69; v.chmn, Falls Church Dist. Dem. Cmt, 58-60; v.chmn, Mason Dist. Dem. Cmt, 62-66; del, Dem. Nat. Conv, 68; v.chmn, Annandale Dist. Dem. Cmt, 68-69. Bus. & Prof. Pos: Teacher, Sugarland Schs, Sugarland, Tex, 40-43; teacher, Fairfax Co. Schs, Va, 54-57 & 60- Mil. Serv: Entered as Pvt, Women's Army Corps, 42, released as Cpl, 44; Good Conduct Medal. Mem: Fairfax, Va. and Nat. Educ. Asns; Hillbrook Civic Asns. Rel: Unitarian. Mailing Add: 4803 Kingston Dr, Annandale, Va. 22003.

HOLDEN, EDGAR H. R
Iowa State Rep.
b. Tama, Iowa, 3/24/14; s. Glenn B. Holden and Laura M. Warner H; m. 1/1/37 to Rachel O. Brown. Educ: Davenport High Sch, grad. Polit. & Govt. Pos: Iowa State Rep, 67- Bus. & Prof. Pos: Mgr, Coop. Oil Co, Farm Serv. Co, Davenport, Iowa, 37-49; pres, Propane Gas Co, 49-64, Cent. Scott Tel. Co, Eldridge, 60- and Holdens Inc, Davenport, 64-; secy-treas, Holdens Oil Co, 59- Mil. Serv: Entered as Pvt, Army, 43, released as T-5, 45, after serv. in 946th Qm. Salvage and Repair Co, ETO, 44-45; ETO Medal with 4 Stars; Unit Citations. Mem: Am. Legion; Rotary; C. of C; Farm Bur; Gideons. Rel: United Presbyterian. Mailing Add: Route 3, Davenport, Iowa 52804.

HOLDEN, WALTER A. D
W.Va. State Sen.
b. Bristol, W.Va, 10/25/10; s. Arden J. Holden and Ila Harden H; m. 1960 to Helen Davisson; c. Thomas Harden and Mrs. George C. Finly. Educ: Salem Col, A.B; Univ. Pittsburgh, M.A; Delta Pi Epsilon. Polit. & Govt. Pos: W.Va. State Del, 47; W.Va. State Sen, 50-; del, Dem. Nat. Conv, 64. Bus. & Prof. Pos: Camp supvr, Erie R.R. Co, summers 44-45; mercantile bus; guest instr, Univ. Pittsburgh, summer 50; teacher coordinator of distributive educ, Victory and Bridgeport High Schs, 15 years; sch. teacher, Harrison Co, W.Va. for past 35 years. Mem: Former pres, Harrison Co. Classroom Teachers Asn; Elks; Eagles; Lions. Rel: Methodist. Mailing Add: 342 Lee Ave, Clarksburg, W.Va. 26301.

HOLDER, ELMO D
Polit. & Govt. Pos: Former Ind. State Sen. Bus. & Prof. Pos: Self employed, production of oil and gas. Mem: C. of C; Indept. Petroleum Asn. of Am; Interstate Oil Compact Cmn; Am. Petroleum Inst; Ind. Oil and Gas Asn; Elks; Evansville Petroleum Club; Evansville Country Club; Evansville Kennel Club; pres, Dem. for Better Govt. Rel: Baptist. Mailing Add: 520 Scenic Dr, Evansville, Ind. 47715. (1967)

HOLDERMAN, SAMUEL JAMES R
Chmn, Grundy Co. Rep. Cent. Cmt, Ill.
b. Morris, Ill, 12/21/01; s. Samuel D. Holderman and Mae E. Wilcox, wid; c. Gordon B, Helen (Mrs. Schmult) and James B. Educ: Univ. Ill. Col. of Law, LL.B, 25; Phi Alpha Delta; Square and Compass. Polit. & Govt. Pos: State's attorney, Grundy Co, Ill, 32-48; chmn, Grundy Co. Rep. Cent. Cmt, Ill, 52-, Indust. Cmn, Ill, 53-63. Mem: Ill. State Bar Asn; pres, Grundy Co. Bar Asn, 57; Cedar Lodge AF&AM, Orient Chap, RAM, Blaney Commandery, Mohammed Temple, Morris Shrine Club; Eagles; Elks; C. of C; Grundy Co. Farm Bur. Rel: Presbyterian. Mailing Add: 302½ Liberty St, Morris, Ill. 60450. (1967)

HOLDSTOCK, RICHARD S. D
Mem, Yolo Co. Dem. Cent. Cmt, Calif.
b. Southampton, Eng, 6/30/34; s. John E. Holdstock and Lilian Jury H; m. 12/13/53 to Jacqueline May; c. Kenneth A, Daniel A. and Marcia D. Educ: John Muir Col, A.A, 54; Univ. Calif, Los Angeles, B.Sc, 58, M.Sc, 60; Bruin Pub. Health Asn. Polit. & Govt. Pos: Mem, Econ. Opportunity Cmn, Yolo Co, Calif, 67; mem, Calif. Dem. State Cent. Cmt, 68; mem, Yolo Co. Dem. Cent. Cmt, 68-; mem. adv. bd. of sanitation standards, Calif. State Health Dept, 69. Bus. & Prof. Pos: Pub. health sanitarian, Los Angeles Co. Health Dept, 58 and Placer Co. Health Dept, 59; environ. health and safety officer, Univ. Calif. Davis, 62. Mil. Serv: Entered as Pvt, Army, 54, released as Sp-3, 56, after serv. in Med. Corps, Army Optical Activity, St. Louis, Mo; Good Conduct Medal. Publ: Public Health Effects of Microwave Radiation, J. Environ. Health, 59. Mem: Health Physics Soc; Nat. Asn. of Sanitarians; Am. Conf. of Govt. Indust. Hygienists; pres, Calif. Asn. of Sanitarians; Davis Human Rels. Coun; Calif. Dem. Coun; United Word Federalists. Named Humanitarian of the Year by Davis Human Rels. Coun, 68. Rel: Protestant. Mailing Add: 933 K St, Davis, Calif. 95616.

HOLDSWORTH, EARL THOMAS R
Conn. State Rep.
b. Bridgeport, Conn, 10/11/10; s. Clement J. Holdsworth and Jessie M. Hammond H; m. 8/13/34 to Bella B. Brown; c. Earl T, Jr. and Susan L. (Mrs. Maxey). Educ: New Haven Col, 32-36. Polit. & Govt. Pos: Rep. Town Meeting, Conn, 53-62 and moderator, 61-62; police cmnr, Trumbull, Conn, 62-68; Conn. State Rep, 125th Dist, 69- Bus. & Prof. Pos: Mem, exec. bd, Conn. Union Tel. Workers, 38-46; splicers helper, S. New Eng. Tel. Co, 29, cable testing supvr, 46-54, construction methods supvr, 54-57 and dist. construction supt, 57- Mem: Mason (32°). Rel: Methodist. Mailing Add: 15 Hemlock Trail, Trumbull, Conn. 06611.

HOLE, RICHARD EUGENE, II. R
Exec. secy, Darke Co. Rep. Party, Ohio
b. Greenville, Ohio, 4/26/37; s. Richard Eugene Hole and Harriett Watson H; m. 12/3/65 to Barbara Davenport; c. Elizabeth Jane and Amy Lynn. Educ: Ohio North. Univ, B.A, 59, J.D, 65; Alpha Sigma Phi; Delta Theta Pi. Polit. & Govt. Pos: Exec. secy, Darke Co. Rep. Party, Ohio, 67-; safety dir, Greenville, 68- Bus. & Prof. Pos: Attorney-at-law, Spidel, Staley, Hole & Hanes, Greenville, 66- Mil. Serv: Entered as Pvt, Army, 61, released as Specialist, 4/C, 63, after serv. in Garrison, Ft. Sam Houston, Tex, 61-63. Mem: Elks; Greenville Country Club. Rel: United Church of Christ. Mailing Add: 622 Chestnut St, Greenville, Ohio 45331.

HOLGATE, FRANKLIN WESLEY D
Mass. State Rep.
b. Boston, Mass, 5/3/29; s. Daniel Augustus Holgate and Lavina Pearce H; m. 11/25/50 to Ethany Lorine Garner; c. Franklin, Jr. and Lorine Lynne. Educ: Boston Pub. Sch. Syst. Polit. & Govt. Pos: Mass. State Rep, currently; 12th Ward Dem. Committeeman, 60- and former chmn; mem, Mass. Dem. Cmt; area del, Wash. Park Citizens Urban Renewal Action Cmt; mem, Adv. Coun, Small Bus. Admin, Mass; bd. dirs, Metrop. Coun. for Educ. Opportunity and gen. adv. cmt. on educ. research and develop. for Boston Pub. Schs; del, Dem. State Conv, 60 & 64 and mem. rules cmt, 64; del, Dem. Nat. Conv, 68. Bus. & Prof. Pos: Pres, Robate, Inc. Mem: Exec. bd, Boston br. NAACP; State Club of Boston; Gr. Boston C. of C; Roxbury Commun. Coun; Urban League; Int. Elks; bd. dirs, Resthaven Inc; treas, REHAB, Inc; hon. trustee, African Methodist Episcopal Zion Church; treas, Dorchester Meeting House Bldg. Fund. Rel: Protestant. Mailing Add: 39 Hutchings St, Boston, Mass. 02121. (1967)

HOLIFIELD, CHET D
U.S. Rep, Calif.
b. Mayfield, Ky, 12/3/03; s. Ercie V. Holifield and Bessie Brady H; m. to Vernice Caneer; c. Lois Anita (Mrs. William Mulholland), Betty Lee (Mrs. Robert H. Feldman), Willa Mae (Mrs. Donald Lee Douglas) and Jo Ann (Mrs. Robert Ward); grandchildren, 15. Educ: Ark. Pub. Schs. Polit. & Govt. Pos: Del, Dem. Nat. Conv, 40-64; U.S. Rep, Calif, 42-; chmn, Joint Cmt. on Atomic Energy, Pres. Spec. Eval. Cmn. on Atomic Bomb Tests at Bikini Atoll, Cmt. on Govt. Opers, Cmn. on Orgn. of the Exec. Br. of the Govt, cong. adv. on U.S. Del. to Int. Conf. on the Peaceful Uses of Atomic Energy, Geneva, 55, rep, Joint Cmt. Atomic Energy, Int. Atomic Energy Agency, Vienna, 57, cong. adv. Am. Del. Conf. in the Discontinuance of Nuclear Weapons Tests, Geneva, 59 & 61, cong. adv. U.S. Del. Seventh Gen. Conf. Int. Atomic Energy Agency, Vienna, 63, chmn, Joint Cmt. on Atomic Energy, 69-, U.S. House of Rep. Bus. & Prof. Pos: Mfg. and selling of men's apparel. Rel: Christian Church. Legal Res: 2001 Lincoln Ave, Montebello, Calif. 90640. Mailing Add: 2469 Rayburn Bldg, Washington, D.C. 20515.

HOLL, EDWIN G. R
Pa. State Sen.
b. Chester, Pa; s. Paul T. Holl and Margaret Rupp H; married; c. Sandra K. and Paul E. Educ: Taylor Sch; Temple Univ. Polit. & Govt. Pos: Del-at-lg, Mont. Coun. Health & Welfare Coun; mem, Montgomery Co. Rep. Adv. Cmt; Pa. State Rep, 61-66; Pa. State Sen, 66- Bus. & Prof. Pos: Indust. equip. and supplies, E.G. Holl Co; trustee, YMCA. Mem: Moose; Mason (32°); Lansdale Lions Club (past pres); North Pa. YMCA (founder, charter pres, mem. dist. gov. cabinet) mem. exec. bd, Valley Forge Coun. Boy Scouts; pres, U.S. Navy League; pres United Fund; C. of C; Mfrs. Golf & Country Club, Oreland; Union League. Assisted in develop. of Lansdale Youth and Adult Recreation Prog. and Munic. Swimming Pool. Lansdale Lions Club Award; Lansdale Jr. C. of C. Award; YMCA Award; Boys Scouts Award; Outstanding Citizens Award, C. of C, 68. Rel: Lutheran. Mailing Add: 426 Perkiomen Ave, Lansdale, Pa. 19446.

HOLLADAY, HUGH EDWIN D
Ala. State Rep.
b. Ashville, Ala, 1/6/23; m. to Patty Nell Stines; c. four. Educ: Univ. Ala, LL.B. Polit. & Govt. Pos: Ala. State Rep, 63- Bus. & Prof. Pos: Lawyer. Mil. Serv: 1st Lt, Army Air Corps, World War II, 3 years. Mem: VFW; Mason; Am. Legion; C. of C; Jr. C. of C. Rel: Baptist. Mailing Add: P.O. Box 646, Pell City, Ala. 35125.

HOLLAHAN, GEORGE LOVETT, JR. D
Fla. State Sen.
b. Pittsburgh, Pa, 5/1/19; s. George Lovett Hollahan and Margaret Ames H; m. to Anne Thompson; c. Kathleen Ames, George L, III, Linley Anne and Michael Scott. Educ: Univ. Miami, B.S.B.A, 42, LL.B, 49; Student Govt; Intramural Athletic Chmn; varsity and freshman football teams; Pi Kappa Alpha. Polit. & Govt. Pos: Munic. Judge, South Miami, 7 years; govt. appeal agent. and Asst. State Attorney, Fla, 53-54; Fla. State Rep, 56-62; Fla. State Sen, 43rd Dist, 63-, chmn, Gov. Reorgn. and Efficiency, Corps, Legis. Coun. and Gen. Legis. Cmts, v.chmn, Resolutions and Memorials Cmt, mem, Constitutional Rev. Cmn. and Appropriations and Banking Cmt, Fla. State Senate. Bus. & Prof. Pos: Attorney, Hollahan & Russo, Miami, currently. Mil. Serv: Entered as Ens, Naval Res, World War II, released as Lt.(sg), after serv. in Pac. Theater; Presidential Unit Citation, Task Force, 72. Mem: Munic. Judges Asn. Dade Co.(past v.pres); Dade Co, Fla. and Am. Bar Asns; VFW; Eagles; Rotary Int. (past pres); Jaycees (past pres, South Miami Chap); Elks; Moose; Am. Legion. Rel: Episcopal. Legal Res: 5409 Riviera Dr, Coral Gables, Fla. 33146. Mailing Add: 7211 S.W. 62nd Ave, Suite 208, South Miami, Fla. 33143.

HOLLAND, ARTHUR JOHN D
b. Trenton, N.J, 10/24/18; s. Joseph F. Holland and Helen Groh H; m. 7/28/62 to Elizabeth Anne Jackson; c. Cynthia, Elise, Christopher and Timothy. Educ: St. Francis Col, N.Y; Rutgers Univ, A.B. in soc. studies, M.A. in pub. admin. Polit. & Govt. Pos: Dep. dir, Dept. of Pub. Affairs, Trenton, N.J, 51-52, dir, 55-62; dep. dir, Dept. of Parks and Pub. Property, 52-55; mayor, Trenton, N.J, 59-66; past mem. bd. dirs, Young Dem. of Mercer Co, N.J. Bus. & Prof. Pos: Res. analyst, Opinion Res. Corp, 45-49; assoc. dir, Princeton Research Serv, 49-51; adj. research specialist, Urban Studies Center and Bur. Commun. Serv, Rutgers, The State Univ, 66-69, adj. research prof, Urban Studies Center, 69-, lectr. polit. sci, Univ. Col, 67-; consult, Dept. of Housing and Urban Develop, July-Dec, 66 and Nat. Inst. of Pub. Affairs, 66- Publ: 'The Professional Mayor,' Proc. Cong. of Cities, Nat. League of Cities, 66; 'The Study of the Metropolitan Desk Concept from the Viewpoint of the Mayor,' Dept. of Housing and Urban Develop, 66; 'The Changing Functions of Urban Government,' Wash. Exec. Conf. held at Brooklyn Inst, sponsored by Am. Univ, 67. Mem: Former mem. adv. coun. and chmn. commun. facilities cmt, Nat. League of Cities; former pres. exec. cmt Regional Conf. of Elec. Off; former pres, Mercer Co. League of Munic; former treas, Mercer Co. Soc. Welfare Club; Nat. Munic. League; Torch Club; Trenton Hist. Soc; former 3rd v.pres, N.J. State League of Munic; former v.pres, Rutgers Club, Mercer Co; hon. mem, Kiwanis; Polish-Am. Club of Cent. N.J; Hibernians; Cath. Slovak Union; K. of C; St. Stephen's Aid Soc; Am-Hungarian Civic Asn; former city employee chmn. and former pub. div. chmn, Del. Valley United Fund; chmn, Del. Valley Citizens Transportation Cmt; v.pres. for N.J, Del. Valley Citizens Coun. for Clean Air; bd, Soc. Welfare Research Found. of N.J. Inc, Del-Raritan Tuberc. and Respiratory Disease Asn, Inc. and Human Rels. Coun. Serv. Gr. Trenton area; bd. mem, Urban League Metrop. Trenton; former chmn, Trenton Soc. Serv. Exchange; hon. bd. mem, Mercer Co. Soc. for Prevention of Cruelty to Animals; former pres, Jr. C. of C; hon. mem, Trenton Asn. of the Blind; former Penn-Jersey Adv. Coun. on Naval Affairs, Fourth Naval Dist; NAACP. Young Man of the Year, Trenton Jr. C. of C, 54; Cath. Interracial Coun. of N.Y. Award for Interracial Justice, 64; N.J. Americanization Conv. Citizenship Award, 64; del, White House Conf, To Fulfill These Rights, 66; Commendation for meritorious achievement in furthering the cause of international understanding through the town affiliation prog. of the President's People to People Prog. Rel: Roman Catholic. Mailing Add: 138 Mercer St, Trenton, N.J. 08611.

HOLLAND, EVELYN FAUCETTE D
b. Lillington, N.C, 9/11/27; d. Henry Bethune Faucette, Sr. and Virginia Stegall F; m. 4/28/46 to Sherman William Holland, Jr; c. Karen (Mrs. Charles Wilfred Shaffer), Sherman William, III and Michael Edward. Educ: Charron-Williams Commercial College, 45-46; Univ. Miami Ins. Prog, 48. Polit. & Govt. Pos: V.pres, Miami Int. Allied Printing Trades, 65-68; pres, local 11, Int. Brotherhood Bookbinders, 66-68; Cmt. on Polit. Educ. del, Dade Co. Fedn. Labor, 66-68; mem. alcoholism cmt, Dade Co. Welfare Coun, 67-68; co. coun. mem, Dade Co. Dem. Women's Club, 67-68; cmnr, Hialeah Housing Authority, 67-; mem. and v.chmn, Dade Co. Personnel Adv. Bd, 67-; alternate del, Dem. Nat. Conv, 68; mem, Brotherhood Cmt, 68- Bus. & Prof. Pos: Owner, ATSCO Tractor Co, Miami, 54-; pres, Videon Corp, Hialeah, 60; secy-treas, Falco Printing, Inc, 62, and pres, Falco Printing, Inc, 69; pres, Falco & Assoc, Inc, 69- Publ: The Student, Falco & Assocs, Inc, 69. Mem: Int. Brotherhood of Bookbinders; Dade Co. Dem. Women's Club; Dade Co. Allied Trades Coun; Dade Fedn. of Labor, AFL-CIO; Gr. Miami Dem. Woman's Club; Hialeah Sr. Citizens Club; Miami Edison Alumni Club; Young Dem. of Dade Co. Received Service Award, Dept. of Veteran's Affairs, 64; Appreciation Award, Lions Club, 65. Rel: Catholic. Legal Res: 330 W. 54th St, Hialeah, Fla. 33012. Mailing Add: 675 N.W. 90th St, Miami, Fla. 33150.

HOLLAND, HORTON FAYE R
Mo. State Rep.
b. Redding, Iowa, 11/4/98; s. Charles Edward Holland and Effie Ebarr H; m. 3/6/43 to Bernice Pence; c. Darrell W, Bobby B, Shrley (Mrs. Hopkins) and Ruth (Mrs. Galigher). Educ: High Sch; Bus. Sch. Polit. & Govt. Pos: Mo. State Rep, currently. Mil. Serv: Entered as Pvt, Army, 17, released as Sgt, 20, after serv. as Gun Comdr, Artil. Mem: Mason; Am. Legion; Lions. Rel: Methodist. Mailing Add: Sheridan, Mo. 64486.

HOLLAND, JOHN D
Dem. Nat. Committeeman, N.H.
Mailing Add: 5 Glenn Rd, Bedford, N.H. 03102.

HOLLAND, SPESSARD LINDSEY D
U.S. Sen, Fla.
b. Bartow, Fla, 7/10/92; s. Benjamin Franklin Holland and Fannie V. Spessard H; m. 2/8/19 to Mary Agnes Groover; c. Spessard Lindsey, Jr, Mary Groover, William B. and Ivanhoe. Educ: Emory Col, Ph.B. magna cum laude, 12; Univ. Fla, LL.B, 16; Phi Beta Kappa; Phi Kappa Phi; Alpha Tau Omega; Phi Delta Phi. Hon. LL.D, Rollins Col, Fla. South. Col, Emory Univ, Fla. State Univ. and Univ. Miami; D.C.L, Univ. Fla; H.H.D, Univ. Tampa. Polit. & Govt. Pos: Prosecuting attorney, Polk Co, Fla, 19-20, judge, 21-29; Fla.

State Sen, 32-40; Gov, Fla, 41-45; U.S. Sen, Fla, 46- Bus. & Prof. Pos: Teacher, Warrenton, Ga, 12-14; attorney-at-law, Bartow, 16- Mil. Serv: Capt, Coast Artil. Corp, World War I; Aerial Observer, 24th Squadron, Army Air Corps, France; Distinguished Serv. Cross. Mem: Am. Legion; VFW; Kiwanis; Mason; Shrine; Elks; SAR; trustee, Emory Univ, Atlanta and Fla. South. Col; Fla. State and Am. Bar Asns; past pres. and exec. coun, Univ. Fla. Alumni Asn. Rel: Methodist. Legal Res: Bartow, Fla. 33830. Mailing Add: 421 Old Senate Office Bldg, Washington, D.C. 20008.

HOLLAND, W. LAMOINE D
Tex. State Rep.
b. San Antonio, Tex, 3/8/33; s. W. Lamoine Holland, Jr. and Nancy Jane Davenport H; m. to Carol Jean Fulton; c. Nancy Carol and Michael. Educ: Rice Univ, B.S. in Educ, 55; St. Marys Univ; Delta Theta Phi. Polit. & Govt. Pos: Tex. State Rep, 67- Mil. Serv: Entered as Pvt, Army, released as Specialist 2/C, after serv. in Third Armored Div, Germany, 56-57. Mem: Am, Tex. State and San Antonio Jr. Bar Asns; Northeast Optimist Club. Rel: Episcopal. Legal Res: 508 Garraty Rd, San Antonio, Tex. 78209. Mailing Add: 1135 Majestic Bldg, San Antonio, Tex. 78205.

HOLLAND, WILLIAM K. D
Chmn, Stanley Co. Dem. Cmt, S.Dak.
b. Pierre, S.Dak, 1/24/08; s. John Holland and Kate Harvey H; m. 11/08/38 to Helen Marie Hayes; c. Dennis Harvey and John Hayes. Educ: Columbus Col, S.Dak, 3 years; North. State Col, grad, 31. Polit. & Govt. Pos: Inheritance tax dir, S.Dak, 33-37; co-dir, Farm Security Admin, 37-40 and food stamp plan, U.S. Dept. Agr, 40-45; relocation officer, U.S. Dept. Interior, 45-48; chmn, Stanley Co. Dem. Cmt, 53- Mem: K. of C. Rel: Catholic. Mailing Add: 319 W. Capitol, Pierre, S.Dak. 57501.

HOLLANDER, SANFORD LLOYD D
b. Paterson, N.J, 4/1/32; s. Edward Hollander and Fay Dobinsky H; m. 2/16/58 to Roslyn Theresa Turkin; c. Joseph E, Andrew B, David A. and Elizabeth A. Educ: Brown Univ, A.B, 54; Columbia Univ. Law Sch, LL.B, 57. Polit. & Govt. Pos: Staff mem, N.J. Attorney Gen. Off, 57-58; asst. to Hon. Vito A. Concilio, 58-59; chmn, Dem. Munic. Orgn, Newton, N.J, 60-67; munic. counsel for Twp. of Andover and Hampton, 63-; del, Dem. Nat. Conv, 64; del, N.J. Constitutional Conv, 66. Bus. & Prof. Pos: Attorney, self-employed, 59-64; partner, Trapasso, Dolan & Hollander, 64- Mil. Serv: Entered as Pvt, N.J. Army Nat. Guard, 58, released as Specialist, 64. Mem: Pres, Sussex Co. Chap. Am. Cancer Soc, 62-64; N.J. Regional Bd. Anti-defamation League, B'nai B'rith (chmn. exec. cmt. N.J. Regional Bd); chmn bd. trustees, Sch. of Arts; secy. bd. trustees, Jewish Cent. Sussex Co; chmn, Annual United Jewish Appeal, Sussex Co; mem. young leadership cabinet, United Jewish Appeal. Rel: Jewish. Mailing Add: 5 Dogwood Dr, Newton, N.J. 07860.

HOLLANDER, THOMAS D
b. Monessen, Pa, 3/9/36; s. Edward Hollander and Edith Bergstein H; m. 8/8/60 to Barbara Ann Stone; c. Scott Michael, Leslie Rachel and David Louis. Educ: Pa. State Univ, B.A, 58; Univ. Pittsburgh, J.D, 61; Omicron Delta Kappa; Phi Epsilon Pi. Polit. & Govt. Pos: Committeeman, Mt. Lebanon Twp. Dem. Cmt, Pa, 66-; del, Dem. Nat. Conv, 68; chmn, Allegheny Co. Dist. Orgn. Cmt. to Reelect Sen. Joseph S. Clark, 68. Bus. & Prof. Pos: Partner, Evans, Ivory & Evans, Attorneys, Pittsburgh, 69- Mem: Allegheny Co. Bar Asn.(mem. exec. cmt, young lawyers sect, 64-68 and treas, young lawyers sect, 67); Pa. Bar Asn.(cmt. presidential inability and v.pres. succession); Am. Trial Lawyers Asn; arbitrator, Am. Arbit. Asn; South Hills Asn. Racial Equality (past pres); Am. Civil Liberties Union; Am. Dem. Action; YMCA. Undergrad. of the year, Phi Epsilon Pi, 57; Blackburn Mem. Award; The Samuel Wagner Prize, 61. Rel: Jewish. Legal Res: 272 Vee Lynn Dr, Pittsburgh, Pa. 15228. Mailing Add: 711 Frick Bldg, Pittsburgh, Pa. 15219.

HOLLANDER, WALTER G. R
Wis. State Sen.
b. Fond du Lac, Wis, 9/8/96. Educ: Omro High Sch. Polit. & Govt. Pos: Local elective office, Rosendale, Wis, 29-; mem, Fond du Lac Co. Bd, 38-53, chmn, 53-; Wis. State Sen, 56- Bus. & Prof. Pos: Ins. agent and farmer, Springvale, Wis; retired. Mailing Add: Route 1, Rosendale, Wis. 54974. (1967)

HOLLAR, CHARLES HAYS R
Co-chmn, Dyer Co. Rep. Exec. Cmt, Tenn.
b. Custer, Okla, 12/3/97; s. Charles Ruth Hollar and Laura Viola Pierce; m. 7/21/21 to Orbyn Ruth Craddock; c. Orbyn Sunshine (Mrs. Davis). Educ: High Sch, Bus. Col. and Govt. Tax Course. Polit. & Govt. Pos: Dir, Population Census, Eighth Dist, Tenn, 60; former chmn, Dyer Co. Rep. Exec. Cmt, co-chmn, currently. Bus. & Prof. Pos: Owner, C. Hays Hollar Seed Co, Newbern, Tenn, 31- Mem: Tenn. Seedmen's Asn.(secy-treas, 59-); Rotary (past pres); Farm Bur; Mason; Commandery; Shrine. Rel: Methodist; dist. trustee, Methodist Church properties. Legal Res: 503 W. Main, Newbern, Tenn. 38059. Mailing Add: P.O. Box 279, Newbern, Tenn. 38059.

HOLLEMAN, HARLAN HARMON R
Mem, Ark. State Agr. Stabilization & Conserv. Serv. Cmt.
b. Hickory Ridge, Ark, 1/23/27; s. Herman H. Holleman (mother deceased); m. 12/26/48 to Emaline Moore; c. Nancy and David. Educ: N.Mex. Col. Agr. & Mech. Arts, 1 year; Tex. A & M Univ, 1 year. Polit. & Govt. Pos: Del, Rep. Nat. Conv, 68; mem, Ark. State Agr. Stabilization & Conserv. Serv. Cmt, 69- Mil. Serv: Entered as Pvt, Air Force, 44, released as Sgt, 47, after serv. in East Air Force, Pac. Theater. Mem: Cross Co. Farm Bur. (pres, 64); Ark. Seed Growers Asn.(pres, 64); Ark. Seed Dealers Asn.(v.pres); v.pres, Wynne Sch. Bd; Girl Scouts (v.pres, Crowby's Ridge Coun); Rel: Methodist. Mailing Add: Route 1, Box 130, Wynne, Ark. 72396.

HOLLENBECK, HAROLD CAPISTRAN R
N.J. State Assemblyman
b. Passaic, N.J, 12/29/38; s. Harold J. Hollenbeck and Hazel Howell; single. Educ: Fairleigh Dickinson Univ, B.A, 61; Univ. Va. Law Sch, LL.B, 64; Phi Delta Epsilon; Phi Gamma Delta. Polit. & Govt. Pos: Prosecutor, Carlstadt, N.J, 66, 67; councilman, E. Rutherford, 67-; alternate del, Rep. Nat. Conv, 68; N.J. State Assemblyman, 68- Bus. & Prof. Pos: Attorney-at-law, private practice, 65- Mem: Am, N.J. and Bergen Co. Bar Asns; Kiwanis Int; Lions. Dean's List, Fairleigh Dickinson Univ; Selected as Outstanding Young Man, 69. Rel: Roman Catholic. Mailing Add: 27 Lincoln Place, E. Rutherford, N.J. 07073.

HOLLEY, HUBERT LEE D
Exec. Chmn, First. Dist. Dem. Party, Mich.
b. Carrollton, Ga, 11/1/14; s. Ernest Holley and Mabel Williams H; m. 10/11/52 to Marjorie Jacqueline Holly; c. Hubert Lee, Jr. Educ: Wayne State Univ, 57-60. Polit. & Govt. Pos: Del, Mich. State AFL-CIO, 58-; Mich. state legis. agent, div. 26, Amalgamated Transit Union, AFL-CIO, 59-; mem. exec. bd, Mich. Voters League, 66-; mem. exec. bd, Wayne Co. AFL-CIO, 67-; exec. chmn, First Dist. Dem. Party, 67-; alternate del, Dem. Nat. Conv, 68. Bus. & Prof. Pos: V.pres, div. 26, Amalgamated Transit Union, AFL-CIO, 57-58, financial secy-treas, 58-; financial secy-treas, Mich. Legis. of Busdrivers, 61-; br. mgr, fee br, off. of secy. of state, Mich, 68- Mem: Urban Alliance, Booker T. Washington Asn; Dem. Centre Club; Lancers Club; NAACP; Mason (32°); Shrine; Trade Union Leadership Coun. Good Citizenship Award, Mayor's Cmt. on Human Rels. Rel: Protestant. Mailing Add: 4084 Glendale, Detroit, Mich. 48238.

HOLLEY, THOMAS PHILLIP R
Asst. to the Secy, Dept. of Interior
b. Billings, Mont, 1/19/31; s. Thomas W. Holley and Mabel C. Noble H; m. 8/25/54 to Patricia Ann Todd; c. Mary Kellene, Sandra Kay, Kevin Michael, Timothy Patrick, Mary Margaret and Amy Kathleen. Educ: Gonzaga Univ, B.A, 55. Polit. & Govt. Pos: Admin. asst. to U.S. Rep. Walt Horan, Wash, 56-64; info. dir, Wash. Pub. Power Supply Syst, 65-66; asst. to dir, Bur. Outdoor Recreation, Dept. of the Interior, 66-68, asst. to the secy, 69- Bus. & Prof. Pos: Info. dir, Gonzaga Univ, 55-56. Mil. Serv: Entered as Recruit, Army Corps of Engrs, 50, released as Sgt, 52, after serv. in 453rd Engr. Bn, Korea, 51-52. Rel: Catholic. Mailing Add: 2500 Quebec St. N, Arlington, Va. 22201.

HOLLIDAY, HAROLD L. D
Mo. State Rep.
b. Muskogee, Okla, 6/28/18; m. 5/31/42 to Margaret Louise Garrett; c. Harold L. Jr. and Bertha G. Educ: Lincoln Univ; Univ. of Mich; Univ. of Mo, A.B, M.A. and LL.B; Omega Psi Phi. Polit. & Govt. Pos: Former case worker, Mo. State Dept. of Welfare; formerly with U.S. Employ. Serv; former Vet. Employ. Rep; former contact rep, U.S. Vet. Admin; former economist, Off. of Price Stabilization; Mo. State Rep, 64- Bus. & Prof. Pos: Attorney-at-law. Mil. Serv: Army, 2nd Lt, 42-45, ETO. Mem: Pres, Mo. State Conf. of NAACP Br; bd. dirs, Freedom Inc. Rel: Presbyterian. Mailing Add: 2907 Cleveland, Kansas City, Mo. 64128.

HOLLIDAY, ROBERT KELVIN D
W.Va. State Sen.
b. Logan, W.Va, 2/11/33; s. James Kelvin Holliday (deceased) and Helen Kathleen Harris H; m. 12/23/56 to Lillian Sylvia Lawson; c. Kelvin Edward, Kathleen Edna, Stephen Kerr and Robert Lawson. Educ: W.Va. Tech, A.B, 54; Marshall Univ, M.A, 55; Phi Sigma Alpha; Psi Delta. Polit. & Govt. Pos: Pres, Fayette Co. Young Dem. Club, 62-64; del, Dem. State Conv, 62, 64, 66 & 68; W.Va. State Del, Fayette Co, 62-68; W.Va. State Sen, 69- Bus. & Prof. Pos: Publisher, Montgomery Herald and Fayette Tribune, Oak Hill, 56-; publisher, Meadow River Post, Rainelle, 66. Mil. Serv: Sgt, Army. Publ: Politics in Fayette County, 56; Portrait of Fayette County, 60; Tests of Faith, 66. Mem: AF&AM; pres, Fayette Needy Asn, Minden; Fayette Co. Develop. Asn; chmn, Fayette Co. Ment. Health Cmn, Inc; dir, New River Gorge Develop. Corp; chmn, Fayette Heart Asn, 6 years; dir, Davis-Stuart Home, Lewisburg; Cmn. of Minister and His Work, Kanawha Presbytery. Successfully co-sponsored bill which abolished capital punishment in W.Va; successfully sponsored Good Samaritan Bill, PKU testing for new-born Babies, mandatory immunization for pre-sch. children, upgrading practical nurses profession through legislation and improved Workmen's Compensation benefits for coal workers. Rel: Presbyterian. Mailing Add: 1709 Edgewood Dr, Oak Hill, W.Va. 25901.

HOLLING, BING R
Mem. Rules Cmt, Mont. State Rep. Cent. Cmt.
b. Townsend, Mont, 2/1/39; s. Charles Fane Holling and Hazel Sitton H; m. 6/26/65 to Connie R. Dillon; c. Brett Kyle and Brian Kieth. Educ: Univ. Mont, 58-59; Carroll Col, 59-64; Young Rep. Club. Polit. & Govt. Pos: Chmn, Lewis & Clark Rep. Party, Mont, 66-68; mem. rules cmt, Mont. State Rep. Cent. Cmt, 66-; adv, Helena TAR, Mont, 67; mem, Urban Renewal Cmt, Helena, 67-68; first v.chmn, Great Falls Young Rep. Party, 69- Mil. Serv: Entered as Pvt, Army Res, 56, released as SP-5, 61, after serv. in 396th Sta. Hosp. Mem: Lions; YMCA; Toastmasters; Int. Bartenders Union; Jaycees. Rel: Episcopal. Mailing Add: 756 33rd Ave. N.E, Great Falls, Mont. 59401.

HOLLINGER, JOHN FIELDING D
b. Meadville, Miss, 5/25/17; married. Polit. & Govt. Pos: Miss. State Rep, 64-68. Bus. & Prof. Pos: Merchant; farmer; sawmill operator. Mem: Am. Legion; Farm Bur; Citizens Coun; Miss. State Alumni Asn; State Forestry Asn; Civitan. Rel: Methodist. Mailing Add: Route 1, Meadville, Miss. 39653.

HOLLINGS, ERNEST FREDERICK D
U.S. Sen, S.C.
b. Charleston, S.C, 1/1/22; s. Adolph G. Hollings and Wilhelmine D. Meyer H; m. 3/30/46 to Martha Patricia Salley; c. Michael Milhous, Helen Hayne, Patricia Salley, Ernest Frederick III. Educ: The Citadel, B.A, 42; Univ. S.C, LL.B, 47. Polit. & Govt. Pos: S.C. State Rep, 48-54, Speaker-Pro-Tem, S.C. State House of Rep, 50-54; mem, Hoover Cmn. on Intel. Activities, 54-55; mem, Pres. Adv. Cmn. on Intergovt. Rels, 59-63; Lt. Gov, S.C. 55-59, Gov, 59-63; U.S. Sen, S.C, 67-, mem, Commerce, Banking and Currency, Post Off. and Civil Serv. Cmts, U.S. Senate, chmn, Senate Commerce Cmt. Spec. Study on UN Suboceanic Lands Policy. Bus. & Prof. Pos: Attorney-at-law. Mem: Asn. Citadel Men; Hibernian Soc; Phi Delta Phi; Sertoma Club. One of Ten Outstanding Young Men, U.S. Jr. C. of C, 54. Rel: Lutheran; Mem. Exec. Coun; Bd. Adjudication, Lutheran Church of Am. Legal Res: 120 S. Battery, Charleston, S.C. 29401. Mailing Add: 432 Senate Office Bldg, Washington, D.C. 20510.

HOLLINGSWORTH, WILLIAM RIGHT R
City Councilman, Manhattan Beach, Calif.
b. Washington, D.C, 5/8/27; s. William Right Hollingsworth and Thelma Stallworth H; m. 6/17/52 to Joanne McGarry; c. William, Lee, Sherrel and Julia. Educ: Pomona Col, B.A, 49; Stanford Univ, LL.B, 52. Polit. & Govt. Pos: Mem, Sch. Bd, Manhattan Beach City Sch. Dist, Calif, 54-88; mem, Bd. of Zoning Adjust, Manhattan Beach, 62-65, mem, Planning Cmn, 65-66, city councilman, 67-; mem, Calif. Rep. State Cent. Cmt, 67- Mem: State of Calif. Bar Asn; Los Angeles Co. and South Bay Bar Asns. Rel: Episcopal. Legal Res: 857 Eighth St, Manhattan Beach, Calif. 90266. Mailing Add: 1203 Highland, Manhattan Beach, Calif. 90266.

HOLLINGTON, RICHARD R, JR. R
Ohio State Rep.
b. Findlay, Ohio, 11/12/32; s. Richard R. Hollington and Annett Kirk H; m. 4/4/59 to Sally Stecher; c. Lorie, Julie, Richard, III and Peter. Educ: Williams Col, B.A, 54; Harvard Univ, LL.B, 57; trustee, Alpha Delta Phi. Polit. & Govt. Pos: Spec. counsel, Ohio Attorney Gen, 63-; v.pres, Shaker Heights Rep. Club, 64-; mem. exec. cmt, Cuyahoga Co. Rep. Orgn, 64-; Ohio State Rep, 56th Dist, 67- Bus. & Prof. Pos: Partner, Law Firm of McDonald, Hopkins, Hardy & Hollington, 57-; dir, Ohio Bank & Savings Co, 57- Mil. Serv: Entered as Pvt, Ohio Nat. Guard, 57, released as 1st Lt, 63. Mem: Am, Ohio, Cuyahoga and Cleveland Bar Asns; Citizens League; City Club; Cleveland Grays; Newcomer Soc; Ripon Club; St. Luke's Hosp. Asn; Commun. Serv, Div. of Welfare Fedn; Bluecoats, Inc; adv. coun, Natural Sci. Mus; trustee, Cuyahoga Co. Hosp. Found. Rel: Episcopal. Mailing Add: 2950 Attleboro Rd, Shaker Heights, Ohio 44120.

HOLLINS, WILBUR HUGO D
b. Birmingham, Ala, 2/26/09; s. David Hollins and Lula Wells H; m. 8/17/31 to Mary S. Warren. Educ: Ala. State Col, B.S, 31; Miles Col, spec. course, 51; Univ. of Ala, spec. course, 67-68; Alpha Phi Alpha. Polit. & Govt. Pos: Dem. chmn, precinct nine, Dist. 17, Ala, 47-; cmnr, Birmingham Planning Cmn, 65-; del, Dem. Nat. Conv, 68; v.pres, Jefferson Co. Progressive Dem. Coun, 69. Bus. & Prof. Pos: Press and real estate broker, Hollins & Shores Realty Co, 39; mgr, real estate and secy, Jones Valley Finance Co, Inc, 45-; exec. v.pres, Alamar Realty and Ins. Co, Inc, 62- Mem: Pres, Magic City Real Estate Bd, Birmington, Ala, 47-; treas, Nat. Asn. of Real Estate Brokers, 47-50; Elks; Free and Accepted Prince Hall Mason. First Negro Appointed on Maj. City Bd. by the Mayor and City Coun. of Birmingham, Ala. Rel: United Church of Christ; Church Sch. Supt, First Congregational Christian Church of Birmingham. Mailing Add: 24 Tenth Court W, Birmingham, Ala. 35204.

HOLLIS, HERBERT BROWN R
Mass. State Rep.
b. Braintree, Mass, 9/10/99; s. Albert Frank Hollis and Bridget Maria Nugent H; m. 10/14/25 to Bertha Alice Gertrude Marquardt; c. Donald Alfred. Educ: Northeast. Col, 2 years. Polit. & Govt. Pos: Mem. finance cmt, Braintree, Mass, 41-45, mem, bd. health, 47-52, mem, selectman, 51-57, mem, bd. of pub. welfare, 51-63, town meeting mem, 42-69 and mem, Rep. Town Cmt, 51-69; Mass. State Rep, 53- Bus. & Prof. Pos: Off. mgr, Old Colony Gas Co, Braintree, Mass, 33-43; tax acct, East. Gas and Fuel Assoc, Boston, 43-60; v.pres, Braintree Savings Bank, 69- Mil. Serv: Entered as Pvt, Marines, 18, released as Cpl, 19, after serv. in 13th Marines, Co. I, France, 18-19; Good Conduct Medal. Mem: Mason (Master, 37); Scottish Rite; Shrine; Kiwanis (pres, 42); Norfolk Co. Selectmens' Asn.(pres, 55-57); Mass. Legislators Asn.(pres, 65-66); All Soul's Mens' Club (pres, 69); Charitable Irish Soc; charter mem, Am. Legion; hon. mem, Braintree Jr. C. of C, 58. Recipient Brotherhood Citation, Beth Israel Synogogue, 65. Rel: Protestant. Mailing Add: 607 Washington St, Braintree, Mass. 02184.

HOLLISTER, CHARLES AMMON D
b. Newport, Nebr, 6/15/18; s. Grover Clarence Hollister and Clara Belle Ammon H; m. 5/31/47 to Mary Jane Marsteller; c. Robdon Dean and Michaela Jean. Educ: Nebr. State Col, Chadron, A.B, 40; Univ. Ariz, M.A, 46; Univ. Pa, Ph.D, 57; Omicron Delta Kappa; Pi Sigma Alpha; Sigma Tau Delta; Phi Alpha Theta; Psi Beta Sigma; Lambda Chi Alpha. Polit. & Govt. Pos: Field rep, Pa. State Dem. Cmt, 50-67; asst. dir, Bur. of Munic. Affairs, Dept. Internal Affairs, Commonwealth of Pa, 57-59; chmn, air pollution control bd, 62-64; chmn, Union Co. Dem. Cmt, 62-67; campaign mgr, Hayes for Cong, Pa, 64; admin. asst. auditor gen. off, Commonwealth of Pa, 65 & 66; staff mem, Make Shapp Gov, 66; chmn, Coles Co. Cmt. for Humphrey and Muskie, 68; mem. adv. cmt. legis. coun, State of Ill. and Univ-State Agency Coun, 69- Bus. & Prof. Pos: Instr, Muhlenberg Col, Allentown, Pa, 46-50; prof. Bucknell Univ, Lewisburg, Pa, 50-67, prof, East. Ill. Univ, Charleston, Ill, 67- Publ: Adjusting Municipal Boundaries: Law and Practice, Nat. League of Cities, 66; Some Political Realities, Bucknell Univ. Press, 67; 'School Boards and the United States Constitution,' Am. Sch. Bd. J, 69. Mem: Am. Econ. Asn; Midwest and Am. Polit. Sci. Asns. Commun. Leader of Am, 68. Rel: Lutheran. Mailing Add: 2515 S. 4th St, Charleston, Ill. 61920.

HOLLISTER, JOHN BAKER R
b. Cincinnati, Ohio, 11/7/90; s. Howard Clark Hollister and Alice Keys H; m. 8/15/17 to Ellen W. Rollins (deceased), remarried 6/28/62 to Florence B. Wigglesworth; c. Mrs. Anne H. Stevenson; Alice (Mrs. D. Scott) and John B, Jr. Educ: St. Paul's Sch, Concord; Yale, A.B, 11; Univ. Munich, 11-12; Harvard, LL.B, 15. Hon. LL.D, Univ. Cincinnati, 61. Polit. & Govt. Pos: In charge of relief in Lithuania; Am. Relief in Poland, 19; U.S. Rep, Ohio, 31-36; del, Rep. Nat. Conv, 40-52; chmn, Mission to Netherlands, UNNRA, 45; pres, Little Miami R.R. Gov. Nat. A.R.C, 47-51; exec. dir, Hoover Cmn, 53; consult, Secy. of State, 54-55; dir, Int. Coop. Admin, 55-57. Bus. & Prof. Pos: Dir. of several corp; partner, Taft, Stettenius & Hollister, 24-55, 57-67, sr. partner, 41-67. Mil. Serv: Capt, 46th Artil, C.A.C, 17-19. Mem: Cincinnati Bd. Educ, 21-29; trustee, Cincinnati Art Mus, N.Y. and Spring Grove Cemetery; Am. Ohio and Cincinnati Bar Asns; Psi Upsilon; Queen City and Camargo Country Clubs; Yale Club; Metrop. Club, Wash; Links Club, N.Y.C; Bohemian Club, San Francisco; Myopia Club, Hamilton, Mass. Rel: Presbyterian. Mailing Add: 603 Dixie Terminal Bldg, Cincinnati, Ohio 45202.

HOLLISTER, WILLIAM HILLMAN D
Mem, Chittenden Co. Dem. Cmt, Vt.
b. Washington, D.C, 7/8/29; s. Joseph Hillman Hollister and Katharine Lauder H; m. to Joan Schaaff; c. Jody, Mark, Hillman, Kristen Kay, Kip Elizabeth and Chad Joseph. Educ: Williams Col, B.A, 51; Union Theological Sem, N.Y, B.D, 54; Beta Theta Pi. Polit. & Govt. Pos: Vt. State Rep, 66-68, mem, Insts. Cmt. and Dem. Steering Cmt, Vt. House of Rep, 66-68; mem, Legis. Coun. Penal Study Cmt, 66-67; mem, Burlington Dem. City Cmt, 67-; del, Dem. Nat. Conv, 68; mem, Chittenden Co. Dem. Cmt, 68-; mem, Vt. State Bd. Corrections, 69- Bus. & Prof. Pos: Pastor, Presbyterian Church, Burlington, 54-; dir, Burlington Ecumenical Action Ministry, 68- Mil. Serv: Marine Corps Res, 48-50, Sgt, Serv. in P.L.C. Prog, Quantico, Va. Publ: 'Recovery in Suburbia,' Union Seminary Quarterly Review, 4/61. Rel: Presbyterian. Mailing Add: 909 North Ave, Burlington, Vt. 05401.

HOLLOMON, JOHN HERBERT Independent
b. Norfolk, Va, 3/12/19; s. John Herbert Hollomon and Pearl Twiford H; m. 8/12/41 to Margaret Knox Wheeler; c. Jonathan Bradford, Elizabeth Wheeler, James Martin and Duncan Twiford. Educ: Mass. Inst. of Tech, B.S, 40, D.Sci, 46. Hon. Ph.D. in Eng, Worcester Polytech. Inst, 64 and Mich. Tech. Univ, 65; hon. Dr. Eng, Rensselaer Polytech. Inst, 66. Polit. & Govt. Pos: Asst. Secy. for Sci. and Tech, U.S. Dept. of Commerce, 62-67; mem, Fed. Coun. for Sci. and Tech, consult, President's Sci. Adv. Cmt. and chmn, Interdept. Cmt. for Atmospheric Sci, 62-67. Bus. & Prof. Pos: Researcher, research lab, elec. co, 46-52, mgr. metallurgical and ceramics research, 52-60, gen. mgr. gen. eng. lab, 60-62; pres-designate, Univ. Okla, 67-68, pres, 68- Mil. Serv: Entered as Lt, Army, 41, released as Maj, 46, after serv. in Watertown Arsenal; Army Legion of Merit. Publ: Ed. of tech. series pub. by John Wiley & Sons; Ferrous Metallurgical Design, Wiley, 47. Mem: Fel, Am. Phys. Soc; Am. Inst. Metallurgical Engrs.(former dir); Am. Soc. Metals (former trustee); Am. Acad. Arts and Sci; Am. Asn. for Adv. of Sci; Am. Soc. Mech. Engrs; Sigma Xi; Soc. Hist. of Tech; founding mem, Nat. Acad. of Engrs; fel, N.Y. Acad. Sci. Raymond W. Rossiter Award, Am. Inst. of Mech, Engrs; Alfred Nobel Award, Combined Eng. Socs; Rosenhain Medal, Brit. Inst. of Metals; Edward DeMille Campbell Mem. Lectr, Am. Soc. Metals, 65. Rel: Episcopal. Mailing Add: 1200 S. Pickard, Norman, Okla. 73069.

HOLLOMAN, JOHN HOLLIDAY, III D
b. Columbus, Miss, 3/5/37; s. John Holliday Holloman, Jr. and Rosa Tate H; m. to Ann Scales Klaus; c. Edith Ann and Rosa Haley. Educ: Univ. Miss, B.A, 59, LL.B, 61; Phi Alpha Delta; Phi Delta Theta. Polit. & Govt. Pos: Del, Dem. Nat. Conv, 60; Miss. State Rep, 60-64; mem. bd. dirs, Tombigbee Water Mgt. Dist, Miss, 63-69; prfnl. staff mem, U.S. Senate Judiciary Cmt, 64-66, chief counsel and staff dir, 67- Bus. & Prof. Pos: Partner, Holloman & Holloman, Columbus, Miss, 61-64; instr, Miss. State Col. for Women, 61-64. Mem: Miss. and Am. Bar Asns; Kiwanis; Miss. Jr. C. of C.(pres, 63); U.S. Senate Staff Club. Outstanding Young Man of the Year, Columbus, Miss. Jr. C. of C, 63. Rel: Episcopal. Legal Res: Ridge Rd, Columbus, Miss. 39701. Mailing Add: Room 2226, New Senate Office Bldg, Washington, D.C. 20510.

HOLLORAN, MARK RICHARD D
Mem, Dem. Nat. Cmt, Mo.
b. St. Louis, Mo, 5/15/05; s. Patrick J. Holloran and Margaret E. Robinson H; m. to Ceil Ann Murdock; c. Mark R, Jr, Cecilia, Ruth (Mrs. Tighe) and Phillip. Educ: St. Louis Univ, B.A; Phi Sigma Tau. Polit. & Govt. Pos: Mem, Dem. Nat. Cmt, Mo, 52-; del, Dem. Nat. Conv, 68. Bus. & Prof. Pos: Pres, P.J. Holloran Co. and Cahokia Investors; secy, Pierre Laclede Fur Co; dir, Jefferson Bank & Trust Co. and Utilities Ins. Co. Mem: Knight of Malta; Knight of the Holy Sepulchre; Racquet Club; Media Club; Press Club; Mo. Athletic Club; Elks; Belvedere Club; Doctor's Med. Found. Blue Shield Bd. Rel: Roman Catholic. Legal Res: 6115 Lindell Blvd, St. Louis, Mo. 63112. Mailing Add: 222 S. 21st St, St. Louis, Mo. 63103. (1967)

HOLLOWAY, ALBERT WESTON D
Majority Leader, Ga. State Senate
b. Poquoson, Va, 11/04/18; s. John P. Holloway and Octavia Weston H; m. 3/19/50 to Ethel Hilsman Edmondson; c. Judith Warren. Educ: William and Mary Col, Norfolk, Va. Polit. & Govt. Pos: Ga. State Rep, 57-58; Ga. State Sen, 63-, Majority Leader, Ga. State Senate, 69- Bus. & Prof. Pos: Pres. and gen. mgr, Eng. and Equip. Co; pres. and dir, Albany First Fed. Savings and Loan. Mil. Serv: Air Force, OCS, Capt, 42-45; Air Medal, 5 Clusters; Distinguished Flying Cross, 1 Cluster; Presidential Unit Citation. Mem: Elks; Rotary; Am. Legion; C. of C; Ga. State C. of C; South. Wholesalers Asn; Dougherty Co. Pub. Solicitations; Cancer Soc; past gen. chmn, Commun. Chest; Chehaw Coun, Boy Scouts. Rel: Episcopal; Vestry, St. Pauls Episcopal Church. Mailing Add: Box 588, Albany, Ga. 31702.

HOLLOWAY, EAGER LOUIS D
b. Blues, Tenn, 12/18/17; s. Eager Holloway and Pearl H; m. 9/15/43 to Delores Lee Guy; c. Patrick, Mike, Cheryl Jane and Delores Lee. Educ: Freed Hardeman Jr. Col, 2 yrs; George Pepperdine Col, 1 yr. Polit. & Govt. Pos: Mem, State of Alaska Liquor Bd; chmn, Southeast Alaska Dem. Party, 62-64; precinct chmn, Juneau, Alaska, 62-64, precinct committeeman, 58-; chmn. for President Johnson Campaign, Southeast Alaska, 64; Gov. William Campaign mgr, Southeast Alaska, 62. Bus. Pos: Private bus. for 22 yrs. Mil. Serv: Seaman 1/C, Qm. Corps, Coast Guard; served in Asiatic-Pac. Theater, 45; Asiatic-Pac. Theater Ribbon; Good Conduct Medal. Mem: Elks; VFW; Am. Legion; Capt, Basket Ball Team, Freed Hardeman Jr. Col, 36 and George Pepperdine Col, 37. Rel: Church of Christ. Mailing Add: 135 Douglas Hwy, Juneau, Alaska 98801. (1967)

HOLLOWAY, HERMAN MONWELL D
Del. State Sen.
b. Wilmington, Del, 2/4/22; s. William Holloway and Hennie Hawk H; m. 9/9/41 to Ethel Mae Johnson; c. Marlene, Sandra, Herman, John and Mercedes. Educ: Hampton Inst, 40-41. Polit. & Govt. Pos: Fifth dist. committeeman, Second Ward Dem. Party, Del, 58-66; chief, Custodial and Maintenance Dept, Del. State Tax Dept, 60-62; Del. State Sen, 64-; alternate del, Dem. Nat. Conv, 68; mem, Govt. Merit Syst. Study Cmn, Wilmington Urban Renewal Cmt. and Del. Citizens for Open Housing Legis. Bus. & Prof. Pos:

Co-owner with sons, Convenient Janitorial Service, 62-66. Mem: AF&AM; Elks; Monday Club of Del. Legion of Honor, Chapel of the Four Chaplains, Mt. Jay Church. Rel: Methodist. Mailing Add: 636 Townsend St, Wilmington, Del. 19801. (1967)

HOLLOWAY, JAMES D. D
Ill. State Rep.
b. Granite City, Ill, 9/8/31; s. Donald R. Holloway and Elvira Massmann H; m. to Doris Cundiff. Educ: Wash. Univ. Polit. & Govt. Pos: Assessor and treas, Randolph Co, Ill, 54; Ill. State Rep, 58- Bus. & Prof. Pos: Admin. asst. to mgr, Egyptian Elec. Coop. Asn, 58- Mem: Mason, Miss. Valley Consistory, Ainad Temple. Rel: Presbyterian. Mailing Add: Grant Place, Sparta, Ill. 62286. (1967)

HOLLOWAY, VERNON CARLYLE D
Fla. State Rep.
b. Richmond, Va, 9/5/19; s. Samuel Lee Holloway and Maude Estelle Powell H; m. 7/28/60 to Roberta Mae Galbraith; c. Jean Estelle, Vernon C, Jr. and Lee Anthony. Educ: Va. Mech. Inst, Univ. Miami. Polit. & Govt. Pos: Chmn, Metrop. Dade Co. Elec. Exam. Bd, Fla, 54-66; mem, Dade Co. Mediation Bd, 57-66; mem, Dade Co. Bd. Rules and Appeals, 64; Fla. State Rep, Dade Co, 66- Bus. & Prof. Pos: Pres. and founder, Interstate Elec. Co, Miami, Fla, 49- Mem: Nat. Elec. Contractors Asn.(past pres, S.Fla. Chap. and mem. Code Making Panel); past pres, Fla. State Elec. Masters Asn; past pres, Fla. Asn. Elec. Contractors; past pres, Fla. Elec. Coun; mem, Inst. Elec. & Electronics Engrs, Inc; Past Potentate, Mahi Shrine Temple AAONMS; mem, F&AM; Scottish Rite; York Rite; Red Cross of Constantine; Jesters; Eastern Star; DeMolay; past pres, Rotary. Rel: Lutheran. Mailing Add: 6444 N.E. Fourth Ave, Miami, Fla. 33138.

HOLLOWELL, LINWOOD BRANTON D
b. Kinston, N.C, 11/21/04; s. Hugh Linwood Hollowell and Virginia Coleman Branton H; m. 7/23/35 to Evelyn Fitch; c. Linwood Branton, Jr, Linda Fitch, Samuel Hugh. Educ: Duke Univ, A.B, 26; Duke Univ. Law Sch, LL.B, 29. Polit. & Govt. Pos: Chmn, Gaston Co. Bd. of Elecs, 34-46; Judge, Gastonia Munic. Court, 45-48; alternate del, Dem. Nat. Conv, 48, del, 52; chmn, Gaston Co. Dem. Exec. Cmt, 48-56; mem, N.C. Dem. State Exec. Cmt, 48-56; N.C. State Sen, 63-66. Bus. & Prof. Pos: Lawyer. Mem: Gaston Co, N.C. and Am. Bar Asns; pres, Dist. Bar Asn, 50-51; Elks; pres, Kiwanis, 38; Eagles; pres, Gaston Country Club, 44; Local Govt. Cmn, 48-61; Bd. of Stewards, 48-; Bd. of Trustees, 56- Rel: Methodist. Mailing Add: Box 995, Gastonia, N.C. 28052.

HOLM, EDITH MURIEL R
Pres, Alaska Fedn. of Rep. Women
b. Takoma Park, Md, 1/30/21; d. Henry LeRoy Transtrom and Hannah Howarth H; m. 6/10/41 to John Holm; c. Stuart and James. Educ: La Sierra Col, Arlington, Calif, 38-40. Polit. & Govt. Pos: Secy, Fairbanks Rep. Women's Club, Alaska, 57-58, v.pres, 60-61 and pres, 65-66; precinct committeewoman, Fairbanks 12th Precinct, 60-61 & 67; Alaska del, Nat. Fedn. of Rep. Women Conv, 64; state chmn, Rep. Women's Conf, 66; campaign chmn, Rep. Cent. Dist. of Alaska, 66; del, Cent. Dist. Rep. Conv, 66; del, State Rep. Conv, 68; del. and mem. platform cmt, Rep. Nat. Conv, 68; mem, Alaska Rep. State Cent. Cmt, 68-; pres, Alaska Fedn. of Rep. Women, 68-; pres, Alaska Legis. Wives Club, 69- Bus. & Prof. Pos: Clerk typist, Dept. of Pub. Exam, Minn, 43-44; lab. technician, Dr. John Saur, Glendale, Calif, 45; secy, Tanana Valley Fair Asn, 50; admin. asst. to the cmnr, Alaska Dept. of Agr. and ed, The Alaska Farmer, 51-52; secy. to the mgr and advert. mgr, Northern Commercial Co, Fairbanks, 58-60; mgr. and co-owner, Garden Store and Nursery, Fairbanks, 60- Mem: Mem. and past pres, Fairbanks Garden Club; mem. and former v.pres, Alaska Fedn. of Garden Clubs; mem. bd, United Good Neighbors; mem, Fairbanks Asn. for the Arts; mem. Nat. Bd, People to People, Inc. Rel: Protestant. Legal Res: 208 Kody Dr, Fairbanks, Alaska 99701. Mailing Add: Box 1196, Fairbanks, Alaska 99701.

HOLM, JEANNE ANTOINETTE D
Secy, McHenry Co. Dem. Cent. Cmt, Ill.
b. Chicago, Ill, 6/10/36; d. Arthur O. Jensen and Hazel Oster J; m. 9/7/65 to Vernon Lawrence Holm; c. Dale L, David A. and Margaret L. Hillstrom and Christopher F. Holm. Educ: Steinmetz High Sch, 4 years. Polit. & Govt. Pos: Precinct capt, McHenry Co. Dem. Party, Ill, 61-64; secy-treas, McHenry Co. Dem. Woman's Orgn, 62-64; Dem. precinct committeeman, McHenry Co, Ill, 64-; secy, McHenry Co. Dem. Cent. Cmt. and McHenry Twp. Dem. Orgn, 66- Bus. & Prof. Pos: Reporter, Fox Lake Press, Grayslake, Ill, 62-69; commercial artist, free lance, currently. Publ: Articles written for weekly newspaper column, Fox Lake Press. Mem: Pistakee Regular Dem. Orgn; Pistakee Highlands Commun. Asn. Rel: Catholic. Mailing Add: 5611 Meadowhill Lane, McHenry, Ill. 60050.

HOLMAN, ALLAN W. JR. R
Pa. State Rep.
b. Hazleton, Pa, 7/28/29; s. Allan W. Holman Sr. and Alma Schwartz H; m. to Joan Robinson; c. Three. Educ: Gettysburg Col, A.B; Dickinson Sch. of Law, LL.B; Phi Delta Theta, pres, Beta Chap. Polit. & Govt. Pos: Pa. State Rep, 60- Bus. & Prof. Pos: Attorney. Mil. Serv: 1st Lt., Air Force, 51-53; Korean Conflict. Mem: Gravel Club; secy-treas, Perry Co. Bar Asn; pres, bd. of dirs, Perry Co. YMCA; past chmn, Perry Co. Cancer Crusade; bd. of dirs, Perry Co. Cancer Soc; Pa. Bar Asn. Selected for Who's Who in Am. Cols. & Univs, 51; winner, Annual Franklin Moore Award at Gettysburg Col. Rel: Methodist; official bd. mem and trustee, Newport Methodist Church. Mailing Add: 14 E. Main St, New Bloomfield, Pa. 15224.

HOLMAN, CLAUDE W. B. D
b. Topeka, Kans, 1/31/04; s. Joseph Johnson Holman and Lillian Stevens H; single. Educ: Crane Jr. Col, 23; Loyola Univ, 32; John Marshall Law Sch, LL.B, 33; Kappa Alpha Psi. Polit. & Govt. Pos: Secy. to U.S. Rep. A.W. Mitchell, 35-37; secy, Chicago City Draft Bd, 3, Ill, 40-45; former chmn, Judiciary Cmt; Senate committeeman, 50-54; ward committeeman, Fourth Ward Dem. Orgn, 53- and chmn, Health Cmt; alderman, Fourth Ward, Chicago, currently; del, Dem. Nat. Conv, 68. Mem: Cook Co. Bar Asn. Legal Res: 4800 Chicago Beach Dr, Chicago, Ill. 60615. Mailing Add: 54 W. Randolph St, Chicago, Ill. 60601.

HOLMAN, GEORGE, JR. D
b. Moncks Corner, S.C, 12/24/10; s. George Holman, Sr. and Laura Spann H; m. 2/28/65 to Francine Gourdin. Educ: S.C. State Col, B.S, 36; Omega Psi Phi. Polit. & Govt. Pos: Del, Dem. Nat. Conv, 68. Bus. & Prof. Pos: Funeral Dir, Moncks Corner, S.C, currently. Mem: S.C. State Bd. of Funeral Serv; S.C. Morticians Asn. (bd. mem); Berkeley Co. Hosp. Bd; Mason; AF&AM; S.C. State Col. Club; Willing Workers Club; Coming Light Soc; Christian Aid Soc; Berkeley United Corp; McGowan United Corp; past chmn, Berkeley Voter Educ. Prof; life mem, NAACP. Award for being first Negro on State Bd. of Funeral Serv, S.C. Morticians Asn. Rel: Episcopal. Legal Res: Hwy. 17A, 1, Moncks Corner, S.C. 29461. Mailing Add: P.O. Box 97, Moncks Corner, S.C. 29461.

HOLMAN, HASKELL D
State Auditor, Mo.
b. Moberly, Mo, 11/29/08; foster parents William Otis Doyle and Ethel Holman D; m. 10/12/46 to Beverly Virginia Stone; c. Michael Hodge. Educ: Univ. Mo, Columbia, A.B, 31, Pi Sigma Alpha. Polit. & Govt. Pos: With State Auditor's Off, Mo, 33-46; supvr. income tax, Dept. of Revenue, 46-49; chief clerk, State Treas. Off, 49-53; state auditor, Mo, 53- Mil. Serv: Entered as Pvt, Army, 41, released as Pfc, 41, after serv. in DEML Jefferson Barracks. Mem: Nat. Asn. State Auditors, Comptrollers and Treas.(pres, 62); Am. Soc. Pub. Adminstrs; Hist. Sites Adminstrs; Munic. Finance Officers Asn; Nat. Tax Asn, Coun. State Govt; Gov. Cmt. Interstate Coop; Mason; Scottish Rite; York Rite; Shrine; Elks; Eagles; Lions (past pres, Jefferson City Lions Club); Mo. Hist. Soc; Conserv. Fedn. Mo.(bd. dirs, chmn, ways and means cmt. and mem. Cole Co. Chap); past pres, Cole Co. Chap, Am. Red Cross; life mem. AMVETS; past pres, Jefferson City Fellowship Club; Lake of the Ozarks Coun, Boy Scouts. Rel: Protestant. Legal Res: 114 Elizabeth, Moberly, Mo. 65270. Mailing Add: Old Gibler Rd, Jefferson City, Mo. 65101.

HOLMAN, KINGSLEY DAVID DFL
Treas, Minn. State Dem-Farmer-Labor Party
b. Chicago, Ill, 3/13/22; s. Hans J. Holman and Leona Hookland H; m. 10/15/49 to Elaine Teresa Fischer; c. David Lowell, Craig Byron and Dirk Whittier. Educ: Univ. Minn, B.S.L, 49, LL.B, 49. Polit. & Govt. Pos: Spec. munic. judge, Bloomington, Minn, 52-58; State Finance Dir, Dem-Farmer-Labor Party and rural Hennepin Co. chmn, 54-58; chmn, Gov. Adv. Cmn. on Suburban Probs, 54-60; chmn, Minn. Third Dist. Dem-Farmer-Labor Party, 56-62; del, Dem. Nat. Conv, 64, alternate del, 68; treas, Minn. State Dem-Farmer-Labor Party, currently. Mil. Serv: Entered as Pvt, Army, 42, released as S/Sgt, 46, after serv. in 13th Armored Div, 3rd Army, ETO; Overseas Serv. Bar; Am. Campaign Medal; European-African-Middle East Medal with 2 Bronze Stars; Good Conduct and Victory Medals. Publ: Columnist, Political Patter,' Chicago Lerner Newspapers, 63. and 'Partisan Patter,' Minn. Dem.-Farmer-Labor News, 63-; weekly newspaper column, 'Lets get involved.' Mem: Minn. and Hennepin Co. Bar Asns; pres, Bloomington C. of C, 56-58; Mason. Legal Res: 10009 Drew Ave. S, Bloomington, Minn. 55431. Mailing Add: 220 W. 98th St. Bloomington, Minn. 55420.

HOLMBERG, R(OY) HOPKINS DFL
Chmn, Fifth Cong. Dist. Dem-Farmer-Labor Party, Minn.
b. Oak Park, Ill, 4/11/39; s. Roy Harold Holmberg and Katherine Dolce Hopkins H; m. 8/23/62 to Judith Vandell; c. Beth Bonnet and Daniel Hopkins. Educ: Dartmouth Col, A.B, 61; Univ. Minnesota, Minneapolis, M.H.A, 63, res. fel, 63-65; Casque & Gauntlet; Gamma Delta Chi. Polit. & Govt. Pos: Mem, Hennepin Co. Dem-Farmer-Labor Cent. Cmt, Minn, 66; mem. steering cmt. and coordinator, Minn. Conf. of Concerned Dem, 67-68; v.chmn, McCarthy for President Cmt, Minn, 68; alternate del, Dem. Nat. Conv, 68; mem, Dem-Farmer-Labor Constitutional Reform Cmn, 68-69; mem, Hennepin Co. Dem-Farmer-Labor Cent. Cmt, Fifth Cong. Dist, Minn, 68-; mem, Minn. State Dem-Farmer- Labor Exec. Cmt, 68-; chmn, Fifth Cong. Dist. Dem-Farmer-Labor Party, Minn, 68- Bus. & Prof. Pos: Admin. resident, Johns Hopkins Hosp, 62-63; coordinator rehabilitation ecology, Am. Rehabilitation Found, Minneapolis Minn, 65-66, dir. health syst. div, 66-68, asst. exec. dir, 68- Mem: Am. Hosp. Asn; Am. Pub. Health Asn; Am. Acad Polit. & Soc. Sci; Group Health Asn. Am; Opers. Res. Soc. Am; World Future Soc; Urban and Regional Info. Syst. Asn; Pub. Choice Soc. Mailing Add: 2708 Irving Ave. S, Minneapolis, Minn. 55408.

HOLMDAHL, JOHN W. D
b. San Francisco, Calif, 1924; married; c. Four. Educ: Univ. of Calif, 1948; U.C. Sch. of Law, 1951. Polit. & Govt. Pos: Calif. State Sen, 58-66; Oakland City Councilman, 55-58. Bus. & Prof. Pos: Attorney. Mil. Serv: WWII, Combat Inf, 99th Inf. Div. Mem: Alameda Co. Bar Asn; State Bar of Calif; Lawyers Club of Alameda Co; Daniel Webster Dad's Club; Fannie Wall Children's Home, Bd. of Dir. Mailing Add: 5484 Fernhoff Rd, Oakland, Calif. 94619. (1967)

HOLMER, JOHN KENNETH R
m. to Barbara Kimball; c. John, Jr, James and Jean. Educ: Univ. Mass. Polit. & Govt. Pos: Selectman, Littleton, Mass, 3 terms; chmn, Local Bd. of Pub. Welfare; finance chmn, Rep. Town Cmt, formerly, v.chmn, 68-69. Bus. & Prof. Pos: Mem. financial staff, Gen. Motors Corp, Framingham, Mass, 57-69; comptroller, Katahdin Industs, Natick, 69- Mil. Serv: Command staff, Atlantic Submarine Fleet. Mailing Add: 41 New Estate Rd, Littleton, Mass. 01460.

HOLMES, ALVIN ADOLF D
b. Montgomery, Ala, 10/26/39; s. John H. Holmes and Willie Ann Stinson H; m. 8/28/63 to Corrie Nelson; c. Veronica A. Educ: Ala. State Col, B.S, 62; Atlanta Univ, 66-67; Univ. Ala, Cand. for M.A, 69; Kappa Alpha Psi. Polit. & Govt. Pos: Exec. committeeman, Ala. Dem. Conf, Inc, 67-; del, Dem. Nat. Conv, 68; pres, Montgomery Co. Young Dem, Ala, 68-; Nat. alternate committeeman, Ala. Young Dem, 68- Bus. & Prof. Pos: Teacher, East Newton Sch, Covington, Ga, 62-63; asst. registr, Ala. State Col, Montgomery, 65-66, asst. dir. pub. rels, 67-68, admin. asst, 68-69; dir, Holmes' Agency, Pub. Rels. Firm, 69- Mil. Serv: Entered as Pvt, Army, 63, released as SP-4, 65, after serv. in Fifth Inf. Div, Ft. Carson, Colo; Good Conduct Medal. Mem: Ala. State Teachers Asn; NAACP (first v.pres, E. Montgomery, state dir. pub-

licity and info, Ala); Elks,Int. Outstanding Young Man of Am, 68; Outstanding Personality of the South, 68. Rel: Baptist. Legal Res: 2855 Milton Rd, Montgomery, Ala. 36110. Mailing Add: P.O. Box 6064, Montgomery, Ala. 36106.

HOLMES, DAVID H. R
Chmn, Woodbury Co. Rep. Cent. Cmt, Iowa
b. Omaha, Nebr, 1/3/28; s. Allen W. Holmes and Mary Wigton H; m. 3/21/51 to Beverly Ann Kaiser; c. David Allen and Thomas Dwight. Educ: Iowa State Univ, B.S, 51; Phi Delta Theta. Polit. & Govt. Pos: Pres, Woodbury Co. Young Rep. Club, Iowa, 65; chmn, Wiley Mayne for Cong. Campaign Cmt, 66 & 68; chmn, Woodbury Co. Rep. Cent. Cmt, 68- Bus. & Prof. Pos: Pres, Holmes Co, Food Brokers, Sioux City, Iowa, 69- Mem: Lions. Rel: Presbyterian. Mailing Add: 4542 Manor Circle, Sioux City, Iowa 51104.

HOLMES, DAVID S, JR. D
Mich. State Rep.
b. Covington, Ky, 8/11/14; s. Sanford Holmes and Elizabeth Cain H; m. 1962 to Avis Ernestine Greene. Educ: Va. State Col, B.S; Univ. Mich; Alpha Phi Alpha. Polit. & Govt. Pos: Mich. State Rep, 58-; chmn, Mich. Black Caucus, 66-; del, Dem. Nat. Conv, 68. Bus. & Prof. Pos: Former sch. teacher, Va; former social worker and union organizer, Mich. Mem: Mason; Bus. & Prfnl. Men's Club; Trade Union Leadership Coun. Rel: Protestant. Mailing Add: 654 E. Kirby, Detroit, Mich. 48202.

HOLMES, DAVID WILLIAM R
Mem, Calif. Rep. State Cent. Cmt.
b. Woonsocket, S.Dak, 11/24/25; s. David Lyle Holmes and Marie Smith H; m. 1/19/50 to Maxine Arnold; c. Sheila, Hilary, Leslie and David William, Jr. Educ: San Francisco City Col, A.A, 47; Univ. San Francisco, B.S, 49; Alpha Beta Tau; Mu Iota Epsilon. Polit. & Govt. Pos: Mem, Calif. Rep. State Cent. Cmt, 66-; mem, Calif. Rep. State Finance Cmt, 66-; chmn, Madera Co. Rep. Finance Cmt, 66-; chmn, Cmn. on Calif. State Govt. Orgn. and Econ, 67-; mem, Madera Co. Rep. Cent. Cmt, 69- Bus. & Prof. Pos: Proprietor, D.W. Holmes & Co, 54- Mil. Serv: Entered as Pvt, Marines, 43, released as Cpl, 46, after serv. in Corps Artil, Fifth Amphibious Corps, Pac. Theatre, 43-45; Unit Citation. Mem: Nat. Asn. Securities Dealers; Elks (Past Exalted Ruler and Past Trustee, Madera Lodge 1918); Boy Scouts; 20-30 Club (past active); Commonwealth Club of Calif. Rel: Episcopal. Legal Res: 29181 Rd. 26, Madera, Calif. 93637. Mailing Add: 110 S. A St, Madera, Calif. 93637.

HOLMES, GORDON CONANT R
Chmn, Inyo Co. Rep. Cent. Cmt, Calif.
b. Los Angeles, Calif, 1/20/15; s. Carston F. Holmes and Mary Conant H; m. 1/15/46 to Virginia Koster; c. Andrew, Sally Jane and Heidi Ann. Educ: Univ. Calif, Berkeley. Polit. & Govt. Pos: Chmn, Inyo Co. Rep. Cent. Cmt, Calif. Bus. & Prof. Pos: Consult. Civil Engr, 6 yrs, with South. Calif. Edison Co, 16 yrs. and South. Calif. Gas Co, 7 yrs. Mem: Am. Soc. of Civil Engrs. Rel: Presbyterian. Mailing Add: 106 Main St, Bishop, Calif. 93514. (1967)

HOLMES, HAROLD HUBERT D
Chmn, Carroll Co. Dem. Party, Ill.
b. Kinsman, Ill, 5/28/08; s. Myron Hubert Holmes and Blanche Trotten H; m. Feb. 1930 to Lucille Evelyn Calkinn; c. Ronald Gene, Hoyt Elloit and Vicki Sue (Mrs. Imel). Educ: Carthage Col, B.A, 36; Loyola Univ, D.D.S, 40; Beta Beta Beta; Delta Sigma Delta. Polit. & Govt. Pos: Tax investigator, Carroll Co, Ill; chmn, Carroll Co. Dem. Party, 50-; mem, Carroll Co. Chmn. Orgn, 60-; mem, Carroll Co. Bd, Medicare, 66- Bus. & Prof. Pos: Mem. Village Bd, 47-55; v.chmn, Northwest. Dent. Soc, 50. Mil. Serv: Lt, Navy, 46-47. Mem; Mason; Shrine; Am. Legion; Elks; State and Am. Dent. Socs; pres, Commercial Club, 54. Rel: Protestant. Legal Res: Fourth St, Chadwick, Ill. 61014. Mailing Add: Box 178, Chadwick, Ill. 61014.

HOLMES, HERBERT HADLEY D
Chmn, Major Co. Dem. Cent. Cmt, Okla.
b. Mannford, Okla, 3/10/15; s. Robert Exum Holmes and Edna Kindred H; m. 6/8/41 to Eleanor Murray; c. Stephen Robert, Gayle Ann and Susan Murray. Educ: Okla. State Univ, B.S. in Agr, 38; Dean's Honor Roll; Alpha Zeta. Polit. & Govt. Pos: Chmn, Major Co. Dem. Cent. Cmt, Okla, 60- Bus. & Prof. Pos: Voc. agr. instr, Seiling, Okla, 38-39; co. supvr, Farmers Home Admin, 39-54; rancher and custom combiner, Okla, 54- Mil. Serv: Entered as A/S, Naval Res, 44, released as Lt.(jg), 46, after serving as Armed Guard Officer on U.S.S. Timberhitch, S.W. Pac, 44-46, Res, 46-52. Mem: Scottish Rite; Mason; Am. Legion; Okla. and Int. Flying Farmers; Farmers Union. Rel: Disciples of Christ. Mailing Add: 808 N. Eighth, Fairview, Okla. 73737.

HOLMES, HERBERT UNDERWOOD R
R.I. State Rep.
b. Branford, Conn, 12/17/14; s. Herbert Holmes and Elizabeth Bridge H; m. 12/12/42 to Elsie Anna Schade; c. Douglas Peter, Philip Alan, Stephen Paul and Victoria Lynn. Educ: William Hall High Sch, West Hartford, Conn, grad, 33. Polit. & Govt. Pos: Chmn, Barrington Rep. Town Cmt, R.I, 56-; R.I. State Rep, 89th Dist, 69- Bus. & Prof. Pos: Salesman, Curtis 1000, Inc, 45- Mil. Serv: Entered as Seaman, Naval Res, 40, released as Seaman 1/C, 45, after serv. in Atlantic and Pac. Theaters, 40-45; Purple Heart. Mem: Mason; Rotary. Rel: Protestant. Mailing Add: 15 Anchorage Way, Barrington, R.I. 02806.

HOLMES, JAMES LOREN R
b. Dover, Okla, 7/10/03; m. 12/28/27 to Margaret Ruth Gerlach H. Educ: Exten. Course, Bus. Admin, LaSalle Univ, Ill. Polit. & Govt. Pos: Calif. State Assemblyman, 54-66, v.chmn, Joint Cmt. on Fairs, Allocation and Classification, Calif. State Legislature, mem, Cmts. on Mfg, Oil and Mining Industs, Agr, Pub. Health and Pub. Utilities and Corp. Bus. & Prof. Pos: Real estate and Ins; Nat. Cash Register Co, 25-46. Mil. Serv: Okla. Nat. Guard; Naval Res, Wash, D.C. and San Jose, Calif. Mem: Masons; Elks; Shrine; Sons of Am. Revolution; Santa Barbara Real Estate Bd; Calif. Real Estate Asn; Nat. Asn. Real Estate Bds; Horseless Carriage Club; Channel City Club; Toastmasters; S.F. Commonwealth Club; Hon. Dir, Old Spanish Days, Inc; Adv. to State Coordinator of Air Force Mil. Affil. Radio Syst. Mailing Add: 209 E. Anapamu, Santa Barbara, Calif. 93104. (1967)

HOLMES, JOHN A. D
b. St. Louis, Mo, 1/10/12; s. Ray Eli Holmes and Mary Armstrong H; m. 1934 to Freda K. Levsen; c. Mary K. (Mrs. Ronald Andrews), Jerry A, Jane (Mrs. Donald Cox) and Martha. Educ: Cornell Col, 30-31. Polit. & Govt. Pos: Former chmn, Jones Co. Dem. Party, Iowa; Iowa State Rep, 66. Bus. & Prof. Pos: Farmer 35- Mem: Wyoming Community Club; Farm Bur; AF&AM; K. of P. Rel: Methodist. Mailing Add: RFD, Wyoming, Iowa 52362.

HOLMES, JOHN PAUL, JR. R
Chmn, Jasper Co. Rep. Party, Ga.
b. Goldsboro, N.C, 3/21/40; s. John Paul Holmes and Cammie Pickett H; m. 3/17/62 to Mary Susan Dykes; c. John Paul, III, Samuel Dykes and Cammie Truitt. Educ: Univ. Ga, B.B.A, 63; Sigma Alpha Epsilon. Polit. & Govt. Pos: Chmn, Jasper Co. Rep. Party, Ga, 66-; v.chmn, Tenth Cong. Dist. Rep. Party, 68-; alternate del, Rep. Nat. Conv, 68; mem. rules cmt, Ga. State Rep. Party, 69; cmnr, Jasper Co, 69- Bus. & Prof. Pos: Owner, Holmes Dairy and Blackwell Merc Co, 65-, Holmes Mobile Homes, 68-; dir, Am. Dairy Asn. Ga, 69. Mem: Piedmont Beef Cattle Asn; Piedmont Real Estate Bd; Jasper Co. C. of C; Jaycees; Kiwanis; Farm Bur. Rel: Baptist. Mailing Add: Farrar, Ga. 31027.

HOLMES, LAURENCE STREET D
Kans. State Rep.
b. Wichita, Kans, 7/6/16; s. H. Claude Holmes and Ardelle Street H, both deceased; m. 6/19/41 to Lois E. Langenwalter; c. Marilyn Ruth (Mrs. Orrin P. Rugen), John L. and James H. Educ: Friends Univ, A.B, 37; Washburn Col, LL.B, 39. Polit. & Govt. Pos: Parliamentarian, Dem. Cent. Cmt, Kans, 64-66, precinct committeeman, 56-; Kans. State Rep, 80th Dist, 67- Mem: Kans. State Bar; Tenth Circuit Court Bar; Kans. Fed. Dist. Court Bar; Wichita Bar Asn; Kans. State Bar Asn; Kiwanis; mem, State Bd, Kans. Civil Liberties Union; Kans. Inst. of Int. Rels. Rel: Quaker. Mailing Add: 1138 Amidon, Wichita, Kans. 67203. (1967)

HOLMES, ROBERT EDWARD R
b. Columbus, Ohio, 11/14/22; s. Harry Barclay Holmes and Nora Birney H; m. 8/23/55 to Margery Jean Wren; c. Robert E, Jr. and Hamilton Barclay. Educ: Ohio Univ, A.B, 44; Ohio State Univ, LL.B, 49; Phi Kappa Tau. Polit. & Govt. Pos: Ohio State Rep, 61-69, speaker-pro-tem, Ohio House of Rep, 67-68; judge, Tenth Dist. Court of Appeals, 69- Mil. Serv: Entered as A/S, Navy, 43, released as Ens, 46. Mem: Kiwanis; Ohio State and Columbus Bar Asns; Agonis; C. of C. Outstanding Young Man in Franklin Co, Jr. C. of C, 57. Rel: Methodist. Mailing Add: 4200 Dublin Rd, Columbus, Ohio 43221.

HOLMES, THOMAS HOWARD D
Tex. State Rep.
b. Granbury, Tex, 5/31/35; s. Cora Shackelford Holmes Harkins; m. 6/26/53 to Patsy Ann McCarty; c. Vickie, Tommy and Charles. Educ: Weatherford Jr. Col; Tarleton State Col. Polit. & Govt. Pos: Tex. State Rep, Dist. 51, 64- Mil. Serv: Airman 1/C, Air Force, 54-57. Mem: Jaycees; Mason; Scottish Rite; Shrine; C. of C. Outstanding Citizen Award. Rel: Methodist. Mailing Add: 1117 Penrod St, Granbury, Tex. 76048.

HOLMES, ZAN W, JR. D
Tex. State Rep.
b. San Angelo, Tex, 2/1/35; s. Zan Wesley Holmes, Sr. and Naomi Ruth Blakley H; m. 6/25/69 to Dorothy Burse. Educ: Huston-Tillotson Col, B.A, 56; South. Methodist Univ, B.D, 59, S.T.M, 68; Alpha Phi Alpha. Polit. & Govt. Pos: Tex. State Rep, 69- Bus. & Prof. Pos: Pastor, Hamilton Park United Methodist, 58-68; dist. supt, Dallas Dist. United Methodist Church, 68- Rel: United Methodist. Legal Res: 6910 Robin Rd, Dallas, Tex. 75209. Mailing Add: P.O. Box 7170, Dallas, Tex. 75209.

HOLMQUIST, CLAIRE WALFRED R
Nebr. State Sen.
b. Oakland, Nebr, 10/4/06; s. August C. Homlquist, Sr. and Ora D. Minier H; m. 6/12/35 to Mildred Ruth Romberg; c. Cynthia Ann (Mrs. Fitchett), Nancy Claire (Mrs. Diekman) and Jean Carol. Educ: Univ. Nebr; Phi Gamma Delta. Polit. & Govt Pos: Chmn, City Coun, Oakland, Nebr, 58-62; Nebr. State Sen, 65-, chmn, Nebr. Legis. Coun. Exec. Bd, Nebr. State Senate, 69-70. Bus. & Prof. Pos: V.pres, Holmquist Grain & Lumber Co, Nebr, 28, secy-treas, 57 and secy-treas and gen. mgr, 62- Mem: Mason; Omaha Athletic Club; Inter-Commun. Club; C. of C; Univ. Nebr. Alumni Asn; Oakland Country Club; Farm Bur; Wash. Co. Hist. Soc; Eagles; Elks; Univ. Club. Rel: Methodist. Mailing Add: 115 E. 2nd, Oakland, Nebr. 68045.

HOLMQUIST, STANLEY W. Conservative
Minn. State Sen.
b. Hallock, Minn, 8/23/09; s. Victor Holmquist and Hilma Truedson H; m. 10/28/38 to Edith M. Johnson; c. Mary E. (Mrs. James O. Saboe), Willard and Charles. Educ: Univ. Minn, B.S, 36, M.A. in Admin, 40. Polit. & Govt Pos: Minn. State Rep, 46-54; Minn. State Sen, 54-; Majority Leader and chmn. Cmt. on Rules and Legis. Expense, Minn. State Senate, 67- Bus. & Prof. Pos: Retail lumber merchant; supt, Grove City Schs, 39-46; v.chmn, Bd. of Soc. Ministry for Lutheran Churches of Am; chmn, Bethesda Lutheran Hosp. Bd, 52-58. Rel: Lutheran. Mailing Add: Grove City, Minn. 56243.

HOLMSTROM, ANDREW BIRGER R
b. Worcester, Mass, 4/10/95; s. Andrew Holmstrom and Emily W. Olson H; m. 6/30/21 to Jennie Elizabeth Lofgren; c. Barbara E. (Mrs. Adams), Carol A.(Mrs. Narbeshuber), Nancy E.(Mrs. Oakes) and Joan P.(Mrs. Spence). Educ: Worcester Polytech. Inst, B.S. in Civil Eng, 17; Harvard Cadet Sch, 18; Middlebury Col. Summer Sch, 21; Chi Epsilon. Hon. D.Sc, Worcester Polytech. Inst, 68. Polit. & Govt. Pos: Supt. of sewers, Worcester, Mass, 25-29, mayor, 50-54, city coun, 50-67. Bus. & Prof. Pos: Plants eng, Norton Co, 19-25, tech. secy, 31-34, v.pres. and gen. mgr, 40-60 and consult, 60-66; research engr, Norton Grinding Wheel Co, Ltd, 30-31, gen. mgr, 34-39; pres. and chmn, Coun. for Int. Progress in Mgt, 60-66, chmn, incinerator cmt, Worcester, 68. Mil. Serv: Entered as Chief Machinist Mate, Naval Res, 17, retired as Lt. Comdr, 39; World War I Medal with One Bar; Order of Vasa, King of Sweden, 60. Mem: Sr. bd. mem, Nat. Indust. Conf. Bd; pres, Cent. Mass. Chap, Nat. Safety Coun; pres, Rehabilitation Center, Worcester; bd.

trustees, Fairlawn Hosp; pres, Worcester Econ. Club, 56-57; Am. Legion; Mason. Recipient of Citation for Outstanding Contribution to Hwy. Safety, 54. Rel: Baptist. Legal Res: 43 Metcalf St, Worcester, Mass. 01609. Mailing Add: Norton Co, 1 New Bond St, Worcester, Mass. 01606.

HOLROYD, ROBERT E. D
b. Princeton, W.Va, 9/15/31; s. Dr. Frank J. Holroyd and Virginia D. Lazenby H; m. 1/24/53 to Emily Norwood Adams; c. Virginia E, William F. and Mary J. Educ: W.Va. Univ, LL.B, 58; Pi Kappa Alpha; Phi Delta Phi. Polit. & Govt. Pos: Asst. prosecuting attorney, Mercer Co, W.Va, 61-64, prosecuting attorney, 65-66; W.Va. State Del, 64-66. Bus. & Prof. Pos: Attorney-at-law. Mil. Serv: Marine Corps, 51-54. Mem: Elks; VFW; Am. Legion; Rotary; Jaycees; Princeton Park Asn; Princeton Area Bus. Develop. Corp. Rel: Baptist. Mailing Add: 1438 Main St, Princeton, W.Va. 24740.

HOLSCLAW, DOUGLAS STANLEY R
Ariz. State Sen.
b. Grangeville, Idaho, 7/31/98; s. John Cling Holsclaw and Abbie Oliver H; m. 8/5/31 to Alice Young; c. Dr. Douglas Stanley, Jr. Educ: Univ. Ariz, B.S, 25; Stanford Univ, summers, 23-25; Harvard Med. Sch, 25-28; Univ. Ariz. Law Sch, part time, 50-56; Phi Delta Phi; Phi Beta Pi; Delta Chi; Phi Kappa Phi; Phi Lamdba Upsilon; Kappa Kappa Psi. Polit. & Govt. Pos: Rep. cand, Ariz. State Sen, Pima Co, 30; mgr, Rep. City Write-In Campaign, 48; party worker in Tucson for 40 years; state, ward and precinct committeeman; Ariz. State Rep, 52-66; Ariz. State Sen, 66-, chmn, Health and Welfare Cmts, Ariz. State Senate, 69-, mem, Appropriations, Rules, Educ. and State Cmts, 69-; mem, Legis. Coun, 69- Bus. & Prof. Pos: With New York Life Ins. Co, 30-36; owner, Pima Realty & Ins, Co, 36-47; Capital Investments, 47- Mil. Serv: Entered as Pvt, ROTC, 18, released as Cpl, 18; later commissioned as 2nd Lt. Mem: Vet. World War I; DAV; Am. Legion; Univ. Ariz. Found. and Alumni Asn; Towncats; Rotary; C. of C; YMCA; Commun. Coun; bd. dirs, Ariz. Ment. Health Asn, Tucson Guid. Clin, Tucson Boys Club and Boys Chorus and Tucson Conf. Christians and Jews; Tucson chmn, Nat. Brotherhood Week and Nat. Citation, 49; Tucson Cmn. Human Rels; Mason (32°); El Sabbar Shrine; Ariz. Pioneers' Hist. Soc; Harvard Club; Pima Co. Coun. Alcoholism; Tucson chmn, Premarital Blood Test and Waiting Period Initiative Petition Drive, 56; Pima Co. Jr. Col. Steering Cmt. Carnegie Human Rels. Award, 62; writer, Univ. Ariz. Fight Song; donor, 5 annual band scholarships in honor Jack Lee; State Health Dept. Award, 67; Ariz. Asn. Retarded Children Award, 68; Phi Delta Kappa Award, 69. Rel: Congregational. Mailing Add: 925 Foothills Dr, Tucson, Ariz. 85718.

HOLSHOUSER, JAMES EUBERT JR. R
N.C. State Rep.
b. Boone, N.C, 10/8/34; s. James Eubert Holshouser; Virginia Dayvault H; m. 1961 to Patricia Hollingsworth; c. Virginia Walker. Educ: Davidson Col, B.S, 56; Univ. N.C. Law Sch, LL.B, 60; Phi Delta Theta; Phi Alpha Delta. Polit. & Govt. Pos: N.C. State Rep, currently; chmn, N.C. Rep. Party, currently; del, Rep. Nat. Conv, 68. Bus. & Prof. Pos: Lawyer. Mem: Boone Jaycees. Rel: Presbyterian; deacon, treas. Mailing Add: Westbrook Exten, Boone, N.C. 28607. (1967)

HOLSINGER, GALEN WRIGHT 'JOE' D
North. Calif. Chmn, Dem. State Cent. Cmt, Calif.
b. Bellwood, Pa, 11/24/21; s. Virgil Clair Holsinger, Sr. and Bessie Wright H; div; c. Joseph G. (deceased), Michael B, Thomas M, William H. and Matthew W. Educ: Univ. Pittsburgh, 38-41; Univ. Calif, Santa Barbara, B.A, 47. Polit. & Govt. Pos: Pos: Pres. and founder, San Francisco Federated Young Dem, 49; chmn. credentials cmt, Founding Conv. of Calif. Dem. Coun, 53; v.chmn, Marin Dem. Assembly, 53-54; mem. exec. cmt, Clem Miller for Cong. Campaigns, 56 & 58; San Mateo Co. chmn, Pierre Salinger for Sen. Campaign, 64; mem, Dem. State Cent. Cmt, Calif, 64-, North. Calif. chmn, 68- and co-chmn, 11th Cong. Dist, 67-68; North. Calif. chmn, McCarthy for Pres. Campaign, 68; del, Dem. Nat. Conv, 68. Bus. & Prof. Pos: Pres, Holsinger Inc, Calif, 61-; legis. chmn, Calif. Distributors Cmt, 69-; legis. chmn, Educ. Suppliers of Calif, 69- Mil. Serv: Entered as Pvt, Army, 42, released as 1st Lt, 46, after serving in 96th Inf. Div, Far E. Theatre, 45-46. Mem: Nat. Sch. Supply & Equip. Asn; Commonwealth Club of San Francisco. Rel: Church of the Brethren. Mailing Add: 1901 Ray Dr, Burlingame, Calif. 94010.

HOLSTEAD, GEORGE B. D
La. State Rep.
b. Ruston, La, 7/31/24; s. George B. Holstead and Lois Oliver H; m. 6/13/47 to Mary Ellen Cochran; c. Nancy Ellen, Helen Lois, Mary Kate and George B, III. Educ: La. Polytech. Inst, B.A. in econ; La. State Univ, LL.B; Gamma Eta Gamma. Polit. & Govt. Pos: La. State Rep, Lincoln Parish, 64- Mil. Serv: Entered as Pvt, Army Air Force, 43, released as Sgt, 46, after serv. in 43rd Bomb Group, 5th Air Force; Asiatic Pac. Campaign Medal with 5 Bronze Stars; Philippine Liberation Medal with 2 Bronze Stars; World War II Victory Medal; Air Medal. Mem: Am. Legion; VFW; Lincoln Parish and La. State Bar Asns. Rel: Methodist. Legal Res: Woodlawn Dr, Ruston, La. 71270. Mailing Add: P.O. Box 609, Ruston, La. 71270.

HOLSTINE, LORETTA MARGUERITE D
b. Newberry, Ind, 10/28/08; d. Everet Aden Jolliff and Della Bynum J; m. 4/17/27 to Alva Holstine; c. Anna Mae (Mrs. Andrick), Versie Louise (Mrs. Hitt) and Bonnie Jean. Educ: Newberry High Sch. Polit. & Govt. Pos: Pres, South. Daviess Co. Women's Dem. Club, Ind; v.chmn, Daviess Co. Dem. Cmt, 64-66; precinct v.committeewoman, Bogard Twp. Dem. Cmt, 32-64. Bus. Pos: Stanley Home Products dealer, 53- Mem: Epsom Home Demonstration Club; Cornettsville Women's Soc. Christian Serv. Rel: Evangelical United Brethren. Mailing Add: R.R. 1, Plainville, Ind. 47568. (1967)

HOLT, MARJORIE SEWELL R
b. Birmingham, Ala, 9/17/20; d. Edward R. Sewell and Alice Felts S; m. 12/26/40 to Duncan McKay Holt; c. Rachel (Mrs. Kenneth Tschantre), Edward Sewell and Victoria. Educ: Jacksonville Univ, 40-41; Univ. Fla, 43-47; Univ. Fla. Col. Law, LL.B, 49; Phi Kappa Phi; Phi Delta Delta. Polit. & Govt. Pos: Precinct leader, Anne Arundel Co. Rep. Party, Md, 61; supvr. elections, Anne Arundel Co, 63-66, clerk, circuit court, 66-; del, Rep. Nat. Conv, 68. Bus. & Prof. Pos: Attorney at law, Severna Park, Md. Publ: 'When is Doctrine of Comparative Rectitude Applied in Florida?' spring 49 and 'Spendthrift Trusts,' fall 49, Univ. Fla. Law Rev. Mem: Anne Arundel Co, Md, and Am. Bar Asns; Md. Court Clerks Asn. Rel: Presbyterian; Elder. Mailing Add: 151 Boone Trail, Severna Park, Md. 21146.

HOLT, W. STULL D
Mem. Exec. Bd, King Co. Dem. Cent. Cmt, Wash.
b. N.Y.C, 10/2/96; s. Byron W. Holt and Elizabeth Kinsella H; m. 2/12/21 to Lois Crump; c. Jocelyn (Mrs. Marchisio) and Enid (Mrs. Dolstad). Educ: Cornell Univ, A.B, 20; Johns Hopkins Univ, Ph.D, 26. Polit. & Govt. Pos: Chmn, 47th Dist. King Co. Dem. Orgn, Wash, 66-69; del. and mem. platform cmt, Dem. Nat. Conv, 68; del, Wash. State Dem. Conv, 68; del, previous Wash. State and King Co. Dem. Conv; precinct committeeman, Dem. Party, currently; mem. exec. bd, King Co. Dem. Cent. Cmt, 68- Bus. & Prof. Pos: Asst. prof. hist, George Wash. Univ, 27-30; prof. hist, Johns Hopkins Univ, 30-40; prof. hist. and head dept, Univ. Wash, 40-67; vis. prof, Harvard, Columbia Univ, Stanford Univ, Univ. Calif, Berkeley, plus others. Mil. Serv: Entered Army, 17, released as 1st Lt, 19, after serv. in 20 Day Bombardment Squadron, France, 17-19, recalled as Lt. Col, 42, released in 45, after serv. as Commanding Officer, PW and X Detachment, Mil. Intel. Serv, Eng, France and Belgium, 42-45; Silver Star; Bronze Star; French Croix de Guerre; Officer of the Order of the British Empire. Publ: Treaties Defeated by the Senate, Johns Hopkins, 33; Historical Scholarship in the United States, Univ. Wash, 67; plus six others. Mem: Am. Hist. Asn; Orgn. Am. Historians. Mailing Add: 5221 148th Ave. S.E, Bellevue, Wash. 98004.

HOLTZOFF, ALEXANDER
b. 11/7/86; s. Lazarus Holtzoff and Mary Holtzoff H; m. to Louise Cowan. (wid, 66). Educ: Columbia Univ, A.B, 08, M.A, 09, LL.B, 11; Phi Beta Kappa; Phi Delta Phi. Polit. & Govt. Pos: Spec. asst. to Attorney Gen. of U.S, 42-45, exec. asst, 45; U.S. Dist. Judge, 24th Dist, D.C, 45- Bus. & Prof. Pos: Lectr, Wash. Col. Law and Sch. Law, Cath. Univ; attorney, N.Y, 11-24. Mil. Serv: Pvt, Army, 18. Publ: New Federal Procedure and the Courts, 41; co-auth, Federal Procedural Forms, 41 and Federal Practice and Procedure. Mem: Am. Bar Asn. (chmn. sect. judicial admin, 55-56); Fed. Bar Asn; Bar Asn. D.C; Asn. of Bar of City of N.Y; Am. Legion (past comdr. dept. justice post and past parliamentarian, dept. D.C); Nat. Press Club; Columbia Univ. Club, N.Y. Navy Distinguished Pub. Serv. Award, 48. Legal Res: 3601 Connecticut Ave. N.W, Washington, D.C. 20008. Mailing Add: U.S. District Court, Washington, D.C. 20544.

HOLUB, CARL JAMES D
Md. State Del.
b. Baltimore, Md, 7/25/23; s. Charles Holub and Frances Brill H; c. Charles Michael, Carol Paula, Catherine Francine and Carl Clayton. Educ: U.S. Mil. Acad, 43-46; Johns Hopkins Univ, 46-52; Kappa Alpha. Polit. & Govt. Pos: Dep. dir. civil defense, Baltimore, Md, 59-63; del, Md. Dem. State Conv, 64-65; Md. State Del, 67- Mil. Serv: Entered as Cadet, Army, 43, released as 2nd Lt, 47, after serv. in 32nd Inf, Seventh Div, Far East Command, 46-47; Parachute Infantryman's Badge; Overseas Theater Ribbon; Good Conduct Medal; Maj, Army Res, until 66. Mem: Past pres, Md. Cent. Dist. Bd. of Basketball Off; James C. Ludwig Post 139, Am. Legion. All Md. high sch. and all Md. collegiate basketball teams. Rel: Roman Catholic. Legal Res: 2634 Ashland Ave, Baltimore, Md. 21205. Mailing Add: Route 1, Box 19E, Severna Park, Md. 21146.

HOLUM, KENNETH
b. Groton, S.Dak, 8/30/15; s. Knute Holum and Gusta Olson H; m. 3/7/37 to Solveig Myrwang; c. (Mrs. J. Josephson), Kenneth, John, Robert, Charles, Knute. Educ: Augustana Col, B.A, 36. Polit. & Govt. Pos: S.Dak. State Rep, 49-53; chmn, West States Water and Power Conf, 56-61; mem, Pres. Miss. Basin Surv. Cmn, 51-52; secy, Water and Power Develop, Dept. of Interior, 61, former asst. secy. for Water and Power. Bus. & Prof. Pos: V.pres, North. Elec. Coop, 48-60; secy, E. River Elec. Power Coop, 50-54; pres, James Valley Coop. Tel, 52-60; v.pres, S.Dak. Rural Tel. Asn, 54-60; pres, Midwest Elec. Consumers Asn, 57, exec. dir, 57-61. Mem: Elks. Rel: Lutheran. Mailing Add: 8132 W. Beach Dr, Washington, D.C. 20012. (1967)

HOLYFIELD, ROBERT LEE D
b. Meridian, Miss, 7/4/22; married. Educ: Northwest. Univ, B.S.B.A. Polit. & Govt. Pos: Former Miss. State Rep. Bus. & Prof. Pos: Exec. dir, Southeast Miss. Indust. Develop. Coun. Mem: V.pres, Miss. Indust. Coun; South. Indust. Develop. Coun; Am. Indust. Develop. Coun; Pi Kappa Alpha. Rel: Methodist. Mailing Add: 725 Northwood Dr, Laurel, Miss. 39440.

HOMAY, ALAN D
b. Iran, 10/1/19; s. A.B. Homayounpour and F.S. H; m. to Barbara Hayes; c. Darius and Patrick. Educ: Univ. of Calif. at Los Angeles, grad. study in microbiology, 48; Univ. of Geneva, Switzerland, M.D, 58. Polit. & Govt. Pos: Med. officer, Federal Aviation Agency, 59; alternate del, to Dem. Nat. Conv, 68; pres, Dem. Club, Anchorage, Alaska, 68-69. Bus. & Prof. Pos: Doctor of Medicine, 60-; bd. of dirs, NAACP, 69-. Mil. Serv: Served as volunteer physician, Vietnam, 67. Publ: Anatomic Variations of Round Window in Normal Temporal Bones (Microphotographic Study), 59. Mem: Am, Anchorage, Aerospace and Alaska Med. Asns; Acad. of General Practice; Rotary Int; Elks. Humanitarian Service Award, Am. Med. Asn, 67; Service Award from Repub. of S.Vietnam, 67. Rel: Presbyterian. Legal Res: 1951 Stanford Dr, Anchorage, Alaska 99504. Mailing Add: 1815 South Bragaw St, Anchorage, Alaska 99504.

HOMEIER, CHRISTIAN HENRY R
Ill. State Rep.
b. Springfield, Ill, 12/27/34; s. Christian Henry Homeier and Lena Kupisch H; m. 2/13/65 to Sheryl V. Bantell; c. Renee C, Heidi L. and Christian H, IV, Educ: Ill. State Univ, B.A. in Educ. Polit. & Govt. Pos: Ill. State Rep, 51st Dist, 69- Bus. & Prof. Pos: Corporate officer, Homeier Dairy, Inc, 48-, Europa Travel, Inc, 68- Mil. Serv: Entered as Pvt, Army, 56, released as Sgt, 59, after serv. in Army Security Agency, Europe, 57-59. Mem: Elks; Toastmasters; Mason; Lakewind Improv. Club. Rel: Lutheran. Mailing Add: 314 Toronto Rd, Springfield, Ill. 62707.

HOMER, MAX H. D
Pa. State Rep.
b. Stowe Twp, Pa, 5/20/35; s. Max Homer and Josephine Poliwczak H; m. to Patricia Ann Musmanno; c. three. Educ: Thiel Col, B.S; Duquesne Univ, M.Ed; W.Va. Univ. Polit. & Govt. Pos: Pa. State Rep, 64- Bus. & Prof. Pos: Educator. Mem: Chmn, Boy Scouts and Red Cross local cmts. As College Quarterback, led U.S. in passing and total offense, 1955. Mailing Add: 137 William Circle, McKees Rocks, Pa. 15136. (1967)

HOMER, PORTER WYMAN
Co. Mgr, Dade Co, Miami, Fla.
b. Oxford, N.Y, 4/7/23; s. Willis Heald Homer and Grace Katherine Wyman H; m. 11/10/49 to Laura Magdalen McHale; c. Katherine, Peter, Gregory, Andrew and Pierce. Educ: Univ. Conn, B.A, 48; Syracuse Univ, grad. study, 48-49. Polit. & Govt. Pos: Dir. research, budget, Kansas City, Mo, 49-55; city mgr, Tucson, Ariz, 55-62 and Rochester, N.Y, 62-65; co. mgr, Dade Co, Miami, Fla, 65- Mil. Serv: Army, 43-46, Inf, ETO. Mem: Int. City Mgrs. Asn; Am. Soc. Pub. Admin; Nat. Asn. Co. Officials; Munic. Finance Officers Asn; Nat. League Cities, chmn. personnel policy cmt; past pres, L.P. Cookingham Alumni Asn. Legal Res: 11710 S.W. 67th Court, Miami, Fla. 33156. Mailing Add: County Court House, 73 W. Flagler, Miami, Fla. 33130. (1967)

HONAMAN, JUNE N. R
V.Chmn, Rep. State Cmt, Pa.
b. Lancaster, Pa, 5/24/20; d. Lester W. Newcomer and Maud Stauffer N; m. 11/20/48 to Peter K. Honaman. Educ: Beaver Col, B.F.A, 41. Polit. & Govt. Pos: Committeewoman, 13th Dist, Pa, 60-64; v.chmn, Rep. State Cmt, Pa, 63-; del-at-lg, Rep. Nat. Conv, 64 & 68, mem, Platform Cmt, 68. Bus. & Prof. Pos: Teacher, Lancaster City Sch. Dist, 48-54. Mem: Am. Asn. Univ. Women; Disaster Cmt. and Home Serv, Am. Red Cross; Bus. and Prfnl. Women; Pa. Gov. Cmn. on Status of Women. Rel: Episcopal. Mailing Add: 400 Main St, Landisville, Pa. 17538.

HONE, SUSAN MEADOWS D
Mem, Calif. Dem. State Cent. Cmt.
b. San Francisco, Calif, 38; d. Edward Meadows, Jr. and Hazel Boling M; m. 9/12/59 to Michael Curran Hone; c. Elizabeth A. and Michael E. Educ: Univ. Calif, Berkeley, B.A, 60; Alpha Delta Pi. Polit. & Govt. Pos: Mem, Calif. Dem. State Cent. Cmt, 68- Rel: Episcopal. Mailing Add: 3 Tanglewood Rd, Berkeley, Calif. 94705.

HONNOLD, JOHN OTIS, JR. D
b. Kansas, Ill, 12/5/15; s. John Otis and Louretta Wright H; m. 6/26/39 to Annamarie Kunz; c. Carol (Mrs. Vinton Deming), Heidi (Mrs. David Spencer) and Edward. Educ: Univ. Ill, B.A, 36; Harvard, J.D, 39; Phi Beta Kappa; Phi Kappa Phi; Guggenheim Fel, 58; Fulbright Sr. Research Scholar, Univ. of Paris, 58. Polit. & Govt. Pos: Adv, U.S. del, Diplomatic Conf. on Unification of Int. Sales Law, The Hague, Holland, 64; del, Dem. Nat. Conv, 68; U.S. del, UN Cmn. on Int. Trade Law, Geneva, Switz, 69. Bus. & Prof. Pos: Attorney-at-law, Wright, Gordon, Zachry & Parlin, N.Y.C, 39-41; attorney, Security Exchange Cmn, 41; chief court review br, Off. Price Admin, 42-46; mem. of faculty, Univ. Pa. Law Sch, 46-52 and prof. law, 52-; mem. bd. ed, Am. J. Comp. Law, 59-; mem. faculty law session, Salzburg Seminar Am. Studies, Austria, 60 and chmn, 63 & 66. Publ: Life of the Law, 64; Commercial Law (with E. Allen Farnsworth), second ed, 68; Unification of the Law Governing International Sales of Goods, 66; plus others. Mem: N.Y. and Pa. Bars; Practice before U.S. Supreme Court; Am. and Phila Bar Asns; Soc. de Législation Comparée; v.pres. and mem. bd, Gr. Phila Br, Am. Civil Liberties Union, 65-; mem. bd. S.E. Pa. Br, Am. for Dem. Action, 65-; chief counsel, Miss. Off, Lawyers Cmt. for Civil Rights Under Law, 65; bd. dirs, Am. Friends Serv. Cmt, 66-; U.S. rep, int. practices cmt, Int. C. of C, 64- Rel: Society of Frineds. Legal Res: 524 Rutgers Ave, Swarthmore, Pa. 19081. Mailing Add: 3400 Chestnut St, Philadelphia, Pa. 19104.

HOOD, ELIZABETH HANNA R
V.Chmn, West Feliciana Parish Rep. Polit. Action Coun, La.
b. Newport, R.I, 3/31/47; d. William Alexander Hood, Jr. and Ola Mae Reeve H; single. Educ: Randolph-Macon Women's Col, 64-66; Newcomb Col, B.A, 68; Chi Omega; mem, cosmopolitan cmt, Int. Rels. Club. Polit. & Govt. Pos: V.chmn, West Feliciana Parish Rep. Polit. Action Coun, La, 69- Bus. & Prof. Pos: Secy, Alfa Enterprises, Inc, New Orleans, La, 69; dir, Richardson King Industs, 69- Mem: West Feliciana Parish Justice of the Peace and Constable Asn; Causerie du Lundi; Chi Omega Alumnae Club; Newcomb and Randolph-Macon Alumnae Clubs; La. Coun. for Music and the Performing Arts; Jeunesse d'Orleans; La. Rep. Asn; West Feliciana Parish Develop. Asn; Cmt. for a Pro-Am. For. Policy. Am. Woman of the Year Award, Cmt. for a Pro-Am. For. Policy, 69. Rel: Episcopal. Legal Res: Hwy. 61, Bains, La. 70713. Mailing Add: 37 Colony Rd, Gretna, La. 70053.

HOOD, JACK C. R
b. Ferndale, Wash, 1919; m. to Suzanne H; c. three. Educ: Whitman Col; Phi Delta Theta. Polit. & Gov. Pos: Wash. State Rep, until 66. Bus. & Prof. Pos: Banker. Mil. Serv: Navy. Mem: Elks. 1967 Legal Res: Route 3, Ferndale, Wash. No mailing address available. (1967)

HOOD, RAYMOND W. D
Mich. State Rep.
b. Detroit, Mich, 1/1/36; married. Educ: Fullerton Jr. Col, Fullerton, Calif, 2 years. Polit. & Govt. Pos: Mich. State Rep, 64- Bus. & Prof. Pos: Assembler, Ford Motor Co, Wixom. Mem: 13th Cong. Dist. Dem. Orgn; Mich. Young Dem; NAACP; Trade Union Leadership Coun; Metrop. Detroit Labor Commun. Asn; YMCA; UAW, AFL-CIO. Mailing Add: 16209 Baylis, Detroit, Mich. 48221. (1967)

HOOD, VERNON A. R
b. Fairlee, Vt; 9/6/14. Educ: Cornish, N.H. High Sch; Windsor High Sch, Windsor, Vt. Polit. & Govt. Pos: N.H. State Rep, 63-67; Selectman, Trustee of Trust Funds; Collector of Taxes; Supvr. of Check List. Bus. & Prof. Pos: Real Estate Rentals and Sexton of Cemeteries. Mem: N.H. Hist. Soc; Subordinate and Pomona Granges. Rel: Congregational. Mailing Add: P.O. Box 65, Plainfield, N.H. 03781. (1967)

HOOK, FRANK EUGENE D
b. L'Anse, Mich, 5/26/93; s. Michael Hook and Mary Smith H; m. 6/20/28 to Elsie C. Schneider; c. Emmae (Mrs. Meyer) and Mary Louise (Mrs. Allen). Educ: Valparaiso Univ, LL.B, 18; Sigma Delta Kappa. Polit. & Govt. Pos: Cmnr, Wakefield, Mich, 22-25, munic. judge, 24-25; U.S. Rep, Mich, 35-42 & 45-47; dir, Farm Employ. Practices Cmt, 43; mem, Motor Carrier Claims Cmn, 50-51. Bus. & Prof. Pos: Pres, WJMS Radio Sta, Ironwood, Mich, 33-35. Mil. Serv: Entered as Pvt, Army, 18, released as 2nd Lt, 18; Army Res. Mem: Am. Legion; DAV; Vets. of World War I; Mich. and Wis. Bar Asns; Gogebic-Ontonagan Bar Asn. Rel: Lutheran. Mailing Add: 208 E. Coolidge Ave, Ironwood, Mich. 49938.

HOOK, ROBERT FRANKLIN R
Chmn, Duval Co. Rep. Exec. Cmt, Fla.
b. Raleigh, N.C, 4/10/33; s. Frank Walter Hook and Margaret Francis Jordan H; m. 9/19/64 to Carol Marshall Driggs. Educ: Univ. N.C, B.S, 54, Med. Sch, M.D, 58; N.Y. Univ, 61-62; Phi Beta Kappa; Kappa Sigma; Phi Chi. Polit. & Govt. Pos: Mem, adv. hosp. coun, State Bd. Health, Fla, currently; chmn, Duval Co. Rep. Exec. Cmt, Fla, 68- Bus. & Prof. Pos: Head, opthalmology, Mem. Hosp, Jacksonville, Fla, currently; chmn. legis. cmt, Duval Co. Med. Soc, currently. Mil. Serv: Air Force, 59-61, Capt, serv. in 804th Med. Group, Strategic Air Command. Publ: A weekly polit. commentary, Jacksonville Chronicle, newspaper. Mem: Am, Fla. and South. Med. Asns; Duval Co. Med. Soc.(chmn. legis. cmt); Contact Lens Asn. Opthalmologists; Asn. Am. Physicians and Surgeons; Fla. Med. Polit. Action Cmt; Asn. Seaboard Coast Line R.R. Surgeons; Musicians Union; Fla. Cattlemans Asn; C. of C.(cultural cmt); Jaycees; Aircraft Owners and Pilots Asn. Rel: Presbyterian. Legal Res: 9752 Scott Mill Rd, Jacksonville, Fla. 32217. Mailing Add: 836 Miami Rd, Apt. 405, Jacksonville, Fla. 32207.

HOOKER, EDWIN WILBURN SR. D
b. New Orleans, La, 7/17/13; married. Educ: Phi Delta Theta. Polit. & Govt. Pos: Miss. State Rep, 56-64. Bus. & Prof. Pos: Farmer; cattleman; gen. ins. Mem: Mason; Shrine; Lexington C. of C; dir, Delta Coun; Rotary; Am. Legion; VFW; Farm Bur. Rel: Methodist. Mailing Add: 103 Wall St, Lexington, Holmes Co, Miss. 39095. (1967)

HOOKER, ROGER WOLCOTT R
b. Blue Island, Ill, 3/30/97; s. Albert Huntington Hooker and Ambolena Maria Jones; m. 7/13/35 to Grace Celeste Garden; c. Roger W, Jr. and Henry Garden. Educ: Cornell Univ, 21; Harvard Bus. Sch, A.M.P, 54; pres, N.Y. State Citizens Cmt. for Pub. Schs; Cornell Univ. Coun. Polit. & Govt. Pos: Mem, Rockefeller for Gov. Finance Cmt; chmn, United Rep. Finance Cmt, N.Y, 63-65. Bus. & Prof. Pos: Retired sr. v.pres, Hooker Chem. Corp, and dir; chmn bd, Estate Welcome; chmn. of bd, Alemco; dir, P.E. Int; dir, Occidental Petroleum Corp; mem, Nat. Industrial Conf. Bd; dir, Lohwood, Kessler & Bartlett. Mil. Serv: Flying Instr. 2nd Lt, 17-19; Aeronautics Sect. Signal Enlisted Res. Corps. Mem: A&FM 132, Niagara Falls; Am. Legion; Chemists. Club; Univ. Club; St. Andrews Golf Club. Boy Scouts of America Silver Beaver, Silver Antelope. Rel: Presbyterian. Mailing Add: 563 Park Ave, New York, N.Y. 10805.

HOOKS, JAMES C. D
b. Horry Co, S.C, 10/15/98; s. J. T. Hooks and Eliza J. H; m. 3/13/23 to Bonnie B. Coward; c. Marjorie H. (Mrs. Bethea), James C. Jr, William Thomas, Miriam H. (Mrs. Benefield). Educ: Univ. of S.C, A.B, 20; LL.B, 22. Polit. & Govt. Pos: S.C. State Rep, 47-52; 55-60; 63-64; 64-66; Co. Dem. chmn, 28; 54-56; State exec. committeeman, 30; 56-57; mayor of Mullins, S.C, 36-46; del, State Dem. Conv, 36; 48; 50; 62; 64; State Reorganization Cmt, 51-52; Marion Co. Adv. Bd. during WWII; chmn, Mullins War Bond Drs; v. chmn. Marion Co. War Bond Drs. during WWII; chmn, Mullins Civil Defense, WWII. Bus. & Prof. Pos: Lawyer, Hooks & Hooks, 22- Mil. Serv: S.A.T.C, U.S.C, 18-18. Mem: Shriner (Omar Temple); comdr, Mullins Am. Legion Post 89, 53-54; pres, Co. Bar Asn, 56. Rel: Baptist; Chmn. bd. of deacons, 1st Baptist Church, Mullins, 53-55. Mailing Add: 234 E. Wine St, Mullins, S.C. 29574. (1967)

HOOKS, PATRICK F. D
Chmn, Broadwater Co. Dem. Party, Mont.
b. Bozeman, Mont, 4/30/26; s. Frank T. Hooks and Myrtle Vaughn H; m. 6/25/55 to Mary F. Kieckbusch; c. Susan, William and Michael. Educ: Univ. Idaho, 44; Univ. Colo, B.A, 48; Georgetown Univ. Law Sch, LL.B, 51; Beta Theta Pi. Polit. & Govt. Pos: Mont. State Rep, 55-58; secy, Mont. Dem. State Cent. Cmt, 64-68, cong. committeeman, 68-; chmn, Broadwater Co. Dem. Party, 65- Mil. Serv: Entered as Seaman, Navy, 44, released as Ens, 47. Mem: Am. and Mont. Bar Asns; Rotary; Am. Legion. Rel: Roman Catholic. Mailing Add: 701 Broadway, Townsend, Mont. 59644.

HOOKS, VENDIE H, JR. D
b. Lexsy, Ga, 10/4/21; s. Vendie H. Hooks and Frances Youmans H; m. 7/23/44 to May Jones; c. Vendie H, III and Jones. Educ: Univ. of Ga; Gupton Jones Col. of Mortuary Sci. Polit. & Govt. Pos: Coroner, Candler Co, Ga, 59-; mem, Ga. Dem. Exec. Cmt, 62-66. Bus. & Prof. Pos: Mem. bd. of dirs, Peniland State Bank and United Family Life Ins. Co. Mil. Serv: Coast Guard, 41-43. Mem: Univ. Ga. Alumni Soc; Ga. Funeral Dirs. Asn; Kiwanis; Masonic Lodge 435; Am. Legion Post 108; Farm Bur; policy bd, Statewide Voc. Rehabilitation. Rel: Primitive Baptist. Mailing Add: 223 Broad St, Metter, Ga. 30439.

HOOLEY, QUENTIN R
b. Wyo, 8/23/25; single. Educ: Univ. of Colo, B.S. Polit. & Govt. Pos: Wyo, State Rep, until 67. Bus. & Prof. Pos: Registered Pharmacist. Mem: Wyo. Pharmaceutical Asn.(pres); Lions; C. of C.(pres); Shrine; Masonic Lodge; Elks; Moose; Am. Legion; VFW; Farm Bur. Rel: Methodist. Mailing Add: 43 Mesa Verde Dr, Glenrock, Wyo. 82637. (1967)

HOOPER, JAMES FULLERTON, III R
Mem, Miss. Rep. State Exec. Cmt.
b. Selma, Ala, 9/2/15; s. James Fullerton Hooper, Jr. and Kathleen Browning H; m. 1/29/43 to Virginia Reid Fite; c. Cynthia (Mrs. Rood), James Fullerton, IV and Ped Fite. Educ: Auburn Univ, Eng. Graphics, 39; Phi Psi; Sigma Nu. Polit. & Govt. Pos: Del, Dixiecrat Conv, 48; mem. Citizens Cmt. for Ike,

52 & 56; del, Rep. Nat. Conv, 60, 64 & 68; chmn, Rep. Cand. Cmt, 62-64; mem, Miss. Rep. Exec. Cmt, 63, 64 & 68-; chmn, Lowndes Co. Rep. Party, Miss, 68- Bus. & Prof. Pos: Owner, Hooper Farms, 45- Mil. Serv: Entered as Cadet, Air Force, 41, released as Maj, 45, after serving as instr, tech. lab, 44-45; invented and perfected the crash helmet now worn by all pilots. Mem: Farm Bur; Magowa Hunt Club; Columbus Country Club; Lowndes Co. Chowder and Marching Soc; Miss. Rivers and Harbors Asn.(pres, 62-63, bd. dirs, 63-); Tombigbee Valley Asn.(v.chmn, 64-66). Rel: Presbyterian. Mailing Add: 800 Eighth St, North Columbus, Miss. 39701.

HOOPER, PERRY O. R

b. Birmingham, Ala, 4/8/25; s. Ernest J. Hooper and Mary Lou Pery H; m. 5/16/53 to Marilyn Yost; c. Perry, Jr, Walter, Conwell and John. Educ: Univ. Ala, B.S, 49, LL.B, 53; Phi Alpha Delta; Sigma Alpha Epsilon. Polit. & Govt. Pos: Law clerk, Ala. Supreme Court, 53-56; secy, Ala. State Rep. Exec. Cmt; judge, Probate Court, Montgomery Co, 65-; Rep. Cand, U.S. Sen, 68. Mil. Serv: Entered as Pvt, Marine Corps, 43, released as Cpl, 46; Capt, Judge Adv. Gen. Corps, Army Res. Mem: Mason; Shrine; pres, Capital City Kiwanis and Bear Sch. PTA, 66; pres, Dixie Youth Baseball South. League, 68; mem. be. dir, Montgomery Country Club. Rel: Presbyterian. Mailing Add: 3221 Warrenton Rd, Montgomery, Ala. 36111.

HOOPER, THOMAS BERTRON D

b. Macon, Ga, 12/20/09; s. Thomas Neal Hooper and Bertha Barnes H; m. 1/21/39 to Martha Catherine Wilkins. Educ: Morehouse Col; Fla. A&M Col. Polit. & Govt. Pos: Pres, Middle Ga. Dem. Club; v.pres, Asn. of Citizens Dem. Clubs; mem, Southern Dem. Conf. and State and Nat. Dem. Parties; mem, Urban Renewal Cmt; mem, Ga. Dem. Party Forum. Bus. & Prof. Pos: Agent supvr, Atlanta Life Ins. Co, Ga, 54- Mem: Homosophian Club; Ga. Coun. on Human Rels; C. of C; chmn, Boy's Club. Rel: Methodist; Steward, Holsey Temple CME Church. Legal Res: 1970 Viking Circle, Macon, Ga. 31204. Mailing Add: 827 Cotton Ave, Macon, Ga. 31201.

HOOPER, VIRGINIA FITE R

Mem. Exec. Cmt, Rep. Nat. Cmt.

b. Byhalia, Miss, 9/23/17; d. Dr. Pleasant LaFayette Fite and Nell Brooks F; m. 1/29/43 to James Fullerton Hooper; c. Cynthia Merriman (Mrs. Ralph E. Rood), James Fullerton, IV and Pleasant Fite. Educ: Southwest. Univ, 36-37; Univ. Miss, 37-38; Univ. Ala, 38-40; Chi Omega; Pi Intersorority; Five Crown. Polit. & Govt. Pos: Del, Nat. State Rights Conv, 48; co. chmn, Eisenhower Publicity Cmt, 60; v.chmn, State Rep. Party, 60-62; Rep. Nat. committeewoman, Miss, 62-69; mem. exec. cmt, Rep. Nat. Cmt, 69- Mem: DAR; UDC; Nat. Parliamentarian; Eastern Star; Am. Legion Auxiliary; Cherokee Garden Club; Columbus Country Club; Lowndes Co. Hist. Soc; Lowndes Co. Soc. for the Preservation of Anitq; Magowa Gun and Hunt Club; Nat. Asn. of Jr. Auxiliaries (nat. pres). Miss. Outstanding Chi Omega Alumna Award. Rel: Presbyterian; 1st v.pres, Women of the Church. Mailing Add: 800 Eighth St. North, Columbus, Miss. 39701.

HOOPES, DARLINGTON Socialist

Hon. Nat. Chmn, Socialist Party

b. Vale, Md, 9/11/96; s. Price Hoopes and Elizabeth L. Tucker H; m. 10/16/25 to Hazelette Miller; c. Darlington, Rae and Delite. Educ: Univ. Wis, 14-15; studied law in off. of G. Herbert Jenkins, Norristown, Pa, 17-21. Polit. & Govt. Pos: Mem, Nat. Socialist Party, 14-, mem. exec. cmt, 32-36 & 44-68, nat. chmn, 46-57 & 60-68 and hon. nat. chmn, 68-; asst. city solicitor, Reading, Pa, 28-32, city solicitor, 36-40; Pa. State Rep, 30-36; cand, V.Pres, U.S, 44; mem. exec. cmt, State Coun. Fair Employ. Practices Cmt, 48-58, v.chmn, 54-58; cand. Pres, U.S, 52 & 56. Bus. & Prof. Pos: Attorney-at-law, Norristown, Pa, 21-27, Reading, 27-; dir, East. Coops, Inc, 47-51. Mem: Am, Pa. and Berks Co. Bar Asns; Commercial Law League Am; Am. Fedn. Teachers; NAACP; YMCA; Boy Scouts. Rel: Society of Friends. Mailing Add: 1521 Greenview Ave, Reading, Pa. 19601.

HOOPES, ROBERT 'BOB' D

b. Ariz, 1902. Polit. & Govt. Pos: Mayor, Fairbanks, 50-52; Fairbanks City Coun, 49; Alaska Terr. Rep. to 49. Bus. & Prof. Pos: Retired auto dealer. Mem: Pioneers of Alaska; Elks; Alaska Yukon Pioneers; Masons; Tanana Valley Sportsmen Asn. Mailing Add: P.O. Box 673, Fairbanks, Alaska. 99701. (1967)

HOOVER, JOHN EDGAR

Dir, Fed. Bur. of Invest.

b. Washington, D.C, 1/1/95; s. Dickerson N. Hoover and Annie M. Scheitlin H. Educ: George Wash. Univ, LL.B, 16 and LL.M, 17; Kappa Alpha; Omicron Delta Kappa; Delta Theta Phi; Alpha Phi Omega; Zeta Sigma Pi. Hon. LL.D, George Wash. Univ, 35, Pa. Mil. Col. and N.Y. Univ, 36, Westminster Col, 37, Okla. Baptist Univ, 38, Georgetown Univ, 39, Drake Univ, 40, Univ. Notre Dame and St. John's Univ. Law Sch, 42, Rutgers Univ. and Univ. Ark, 43, Seton Hall Col. and Holy Cross Col, 44, Marquette Univ, 50, Pace Col, 54, Morris Harvey Col, 59 and Cath. Univ. of Am, 64; D.Sc, Kalamazoo Col, 37; D.C.L, Univ. of South, 41. Polit. & Govt. Pos: Spec. asst. Attorney Gen. of U.S, 19-21; asst. dir, Bur. Invest, Dept. of Justice, 21-24, dir, 24- Publ: Persons in Hiding, 38; Masters of Deceit, 58; A Study of Communism, 62; J. Edgar Hoover on Communism, 69. Mem: Bars of U.S. Dist. Court, D.C, U.S. Court of Claims, U.S. Supreme Court; Nat. Bd. of Boys' Clubs of Am, 43; Nat. Court of Honor; Nat. Adv. Coun, Girl Scouts; hon. mem, Nat. Coun. of Boy Scouts; trustee, George Wash. Univ; hon. life mem, Int. Asn. for Identification, Chief Constables Asn. of Can; Mason (33°, K.T. Shriner); DeMolay. Recipient, Nat. Americanism Award (Gold Medal), VFW, 63; Pro Deo et Juventute Award, Nat. Cath. Youth Orgn, 63; Gold Medal Merit, Jewish War Vets, U.S, 62; George Wash. Honor Medal, Freedoms Found, 62; Criss Award, Mutual of Omaha, 61; U.S. Sen. Resolution of Commendation for Distinguished Serv. to U.S, 61; Am. Citizenship Award, Jr. Order United Am. Mechanics, 59; Great Living Americans' Award, U.S. C. of C, 58; President's Award for Distinguished Fed. Civilian Serv, 58. Rel: Presbyterian. Mailing Add: Federal Bureau of Investigation, U.S. Dept. of Justice Bldg, Washington, D.C. 20535.

HOOVER, LAWRENCE HAROLD D

b. Timberville, Va, 3/27/06; s. John Henry Hoover and Annie Rebecca Flory H; m. 6/18/27 to Ola May; c. Rebecca Anne (Mrs. Milam) and Lawrence H, Jr. Educ: Bridgewater Col, B.A, 27; Univ. Va, LL.B, 30; Tau Kappa Alpha; Phi Delta Phi. Polit. & Govt. Pos: Asst. cmnr. of accts, Circuit Court, Rockingham Co, Va, 60-; city attorney, Harrisonburg, 48-; mem, Harrisonburg City Dem. Cmt, 34-; Va. State Del, 52-66; commonwealth's attorney, Rockingham Co. and Harrisonburg, 40-48. Bus. & Prof. Pos: Pres, Harrisonburg Grocery Co, Inc; v.pres, Farmers & Merchants Bank of Timberville and Lincoln-Miller, Inc; dir, Wetsel Seed Co, Inc. Mem: Past pres, Harrisonburg-Rockingham Bar Asn. and Va. State Elks, Americanism Cmt, Grand Lodge of Elks; Downtown Club of Richmond; Masons, Shrine. Collegiate honors in debate and oratory; pub. speaker; coin collector; world-traveller. Rel: Church of the Brethren. Mailing Add: 231 Grace Street, Harrisonburg, Va. 22801. (1967)

HOOVER, THOMAS WARREN R

N.Mex. State Rep.

b. Washington, Iowa, 6/25/32; s. Leo Hoover and Rhea Warren H; m. 4/23/60 to Bettye Ruth Garrard; c. Kurt Thomas and Craig William. Educ: Iowa State Univ, B.S.M.E, 54; Tau Beta Pi; Pi Tau Sigma; Phi Mu Alpha. Polit. & Govt. Pos: N.Mex. State Rep, 65-, mem, Rep. State Cent. Cmt. and Rep. Co. Cent. Cmt, 65- Bus. & Prof. Pos: Staff mem, Sandia Corp, Albuquerque, 54- Mil. Serv: 2nd Lt, Army Corps. of Engrs, 24th Armored Eng. Bn, 56. Rel: Methodist. Mailing Add: 8524 Las Camas N.E, Albuquerque, N.Mex. 87111.

HOPE, CLARENCE CALDWELL, JR. D

b. Charlotte, N.C, 2/5/20; s. Clarence Caldwell Hope and Margaret Boyd Kidd H; m. 2/5/44 to Mae D. Duckworth; c. Stephen Douglas, C. C, III and Joan Jennings. Educ: Mars Hill Col, 41; Wake Forest Col, B.S. in bus. admin, 43; Harvard Univ, Grad. Sch. of Bus, M.A, 44; Rutgers Univ, Grad Sch. of Banking, Commercial 53, Invest. 56; Omicron Delta Kappa; Sigma Phi Epsilon. Polit. & Govt. Pos: Precinct secy-treas. and former precinct chmn, Dem. Party, N.C; asst. state chmn, N.C. State Emergency Planning Cmn. and mem, Gov. Cmn. on Libr. Resources, 64-65; del, Dem. Nat. Conv, 68. Bus. & Prof. Pos: First exec. v.pres, First Union Nat. Bank, 63- Mil. Serv: Lt, Navy; serv. in Pac. Theater. Mem: Asn. of Reserve City Bankers; bd. dirs, Robert Morris Asn, C. of C, Mecklenburg Co. Red Cross, Exec. Club, Cent. Charlotte Asn; bd. trustee, Charlotte-Mecklenburg Pub. Libr; Newcomen Soc; treas, Charlotte Merchants Asn; Army-Navy Club; Charlotte City Club; Myers Park Country Club. Rel: Baptist. Legal Res: 3807 Pomfret Lane, Charlotte, N.C. 28211. Mailing Add: P.O. Box 10498, Charlotte, N.C. 28201.

HOPE, CLIFFORD RAGSDALE R

b. Birmingham, Iowa, 6/9/93; s. Harry M. Hope and Olive Armitta Ragsdale H; m. 1/8/21 to Pauline E. Sanders; c. Edward Sanders (deceased), Clifford Ragsdale and Martha (Mrs. Frank West). Educ: Washburn Law Sch, Topeka, Kans, LL.B, 17. Hon. LL.D, Washburn Munic. Univ, 51; hon. D.C.L, Sterling Col, 52; hon. D.Agr, Kans. State Col, 56. Polit. & Govt. Pos: Kans. State Rep, 21-27, Speaker, Kans. State House of Rep, 25-27; U.S. Rep, Kans, 27-57; Cong. adv. to U.S. Del, Food and Agr. Orgn, UN, 45, 46, 48, 49, 51 & 55; chmn, Cmt. Agr, U.S. House of Rep, 47-48 & 53-54; chmn, Rep. Conf. House of Rep, 49-57; U.S. del, Inter-Parliamentary Union Meeting, Stockholm, 49 and Istanbul, 51; mem, Mo. Basin Survey Cmn, 52. Bus. & Prof. Pos: Admitted to Kans. Bar, 17; began law practice with William Easton Hutchinson, Garden City, Kans, 19; mem, Hutchinson, Hope & Fleming, 21-27; former mem, Hope, Haag, Saffels & Hope; pres, Great Plains Wheat, Inc, 59-63, consult, 64-66. Mil. Serv: Army, 17-19, O.T.C, Ft. Riley, Kans. and commissioned 2nd Lt. served in 35th and 85th Div, France. Mem: Am. Legion; Kans. State Hist. Soc; Soil Conserv. Soc. of Am; Mason; Elks. Hon. Am. Farmer, Future Farmers of Am, 52; Hugh Bennett Gold Medal, Friends of Land, 54; Founders Award for Distinguished Serv. and Outside Achievement toward Furthering Conserv. of America's Natural Resources, Izaak Walton League, 57. Rel: Presbyterian. Legal Res: 905 Lyle St, Garden City, Kans. 67846. Mailing Add: Box 1093, Garden City, Kans. 67846.

HOPE, CLIFFORD RAGSDALE, JR. R

Chmn, Finney Co. Rep. Cent. Cmt, Kans.

b. Garden City, Kans, 12/21/23; s. Clifford Ragsdale Hope and Pauline Sanders H; m. 12/30/48 to Dolores Mary Sulzman; c. Christine, Nancy, Quentin, Holly and Rosemary. Educ: George Wash. Univ, 42-43; Harvard Col, A.B, 47; Washburn Univ. Law Sch, LL.B, 50; Sigma Nu. Polit. & Govt. Pos: Chmn, Finney Co. Rep. Cent. Cmt, Kans, 52-56 & 68-; Kans. State Sen, 57-63; mem, Kans. Interstate Coop. Cmn, 61-63; v.chmn, Kans. Commun. Jr. Col. Adv. Coun, 65-69; chmn, Rep. Assocs. of Southwest Kans, 66-68, dir, 65-; mem, Garden City Libr. Bd, 67-; mem, Kans. Citizens Cmt. on Constitutional Rev, 68-69. Mil. Serv: Entered as Pvt, Army, 43, released as Sgt, 45, after serv. in 16th FA Observation Bn, ETO, 44-45; ETO Ribbon; Five Battle Stars. Mem: Pres, Garden City C. of C, 54-55; first v.pres, Finney Co. Hist. Soc, 68; Finney Co, Southwest Kans, Kans. and Am. Bar Asns; Am. Col. Probate Counsel; World Peace Through Law Center; Lions (pres, Garden City Club, 55-56); Am. Legion; VFW; Elks. Rel: Presbyterian. Legal Res: 1112 Gillespie, Garden City, Kans. 67846. Mailing Add: Box 439, Garden City, Kans. 67846.

HOPE, LEIGHTON A. R

b. Washington, D.C, 12/9/21; m. to Polly Pierce Gochenour; c. Leighton Jr, Peter and Steven. Educ: DePauw Univ, 46. Polit. & Govt. Pos: N.Y. State Sen, 62-66; Secy, N.Y.S. Conserv. Dept, 66-68, Dep. Cmnr, 68- Bus. & Prof. Pos: Sub acct. and auditor, San Juan, P.R. Br, First Nat. City Bank of N.Y, 46-50; dir, First Nat. Bank of Cortland, N.Y; v.pres, Cort Lanes, Inc; owner, and operator, Sta. WKRT, Cortland. Mil. Serv: Air Force, World War II; B-24 Pilot, 15th Air Force, 25 Missions. Mem: Cmnr, Cortland Co. Youth Cmn; secy, Cortland Co. Develop. Co; dir, Cortland YMCA; chmn, U.S. Savings Bond Sales, Cortland Co; past pres, Cortland Rotary; past pres. and dr. chmn, Cortland Co. United Fund; Am. Legion; VFW. Legal Res: 39 Prospect Terr, Cortland, N.Y. 13045. Mailing Add: New York State Conservation Dept, Albany, N.Y. 12226.

HOPF, PETER S. D

b. Nuremberg, Germany, 4/26/29; s. Henry S. Hopf and Elizabeth Homburger H; m. 12/18/54 to G. Edith Hutzler; c. Russell S. and Suzanne A. Educ: Columbia Univ, 48-50; Pratt Inst, B.Arch, 54; Pratt Archit. Club. Polit. & Govt. Pos: Del-at-lg, Dem. Nat. Conv, 68; zone leader, New Dem. Coalition, Huntington, N.Y, 68-69; committeeman, Fifth Elec. Dist. Dem. Orgn, 69- Bus. & Prof. Pos: Partner, Brodsky, Hopf & Adler, Architects & Engrs, N.Y.C, currently. Mil. Serv: Entered as Pvt, N.Y. Nat. Guard, 48, released as 1st Lt, 58, after serv. in 104 FA Bn. Mem: Corporate mem, Am. Inst. Architects; N.Y. State Asn. Architects; nat. panel, Am. Arbit. Asn; Wings Club, N.Y.C. Several awards for archit. design by Queens C. of C. Rel: Jewish. Mailing Add: 11 Anondale Dr, Huntington, N.Y. 11743.

HOPFINGER, RAYMOND B. D
b. Montrose, Mo, 8/24/06. Educ: St. Louis Univ, St. Louis, Mo. Polit. & Govt. Pos: Mo. State Rep, 48-58; Mo. State Sen, 58-66. Mil. Serv: Marine Corps. Mem: K. of C. (4°); Elks; Lions Club. Rel: Catholic. Mailing Add: 8751 Argyle Ave, St. Louis, Mo. 63114. (1967)

HOPKINS, CHARLES A. PORTER R
Md. State Del.
b. Baltimore, Md, 3/12/30; s. David Luke Hopkins and Katherine Porter H; m. 9/5/52 to Mary Wanamaker; c. Alexandra W, Mary D. and Lindsay D. Educ: Princeton Univ, 48-50; Johns Hopkins Univ, A.B, 52, M.A, 54; Phi Beta Kappa. Polit. & Govt. Pos: Mem, Fifth Dist. Rep. Exec. Cmt, Baltimore, Md, 63-; mem, Baltimore Co. Park Bd, 63-; Md. State Del, 67- Bus. & Prof. Pos: Teacher, Gilman Sch, Baltimore, Md, 55-58; asst. dir, Md. Hist. Soc, 58-65; ed, Maryland Conservationist, 66. Mil. Serv: Entered as Pvt, Army, 51, released as Sgt. 1/C, 55, after serv. in various training units and 175th Inf, Md. Nat. Guard. Publ: Asst. ed, Md. Hist. Mag, 58-65. Mem: Chesapeake Bay Found; Isaak Walton League; Ducks Unlimited; Md. Farm Bur. Rel: Episcopal. Mailing Add: Falls Rd, Glyndon, Md. 21071.

HOPKINS, RICHARD D
Ky. State Rep.
b. 1915. Educ: West. Ky. State Col, B.S; Univ. Ky, M.A; Kappa Delta Pi. Polit. & Govt. Pos: Ky. State Rep, 58- Bus. & Prof. Pos: Teacher; farmer. Mem: S.D.E.A; K.E.A; K.V.A; Lions; Farm Bur. Rel: Methodist. Mailing Add: Seventh and Center Sts, Calhoun, Ky. 42327. (1967)

HOPKINS, ROBERT E. D
Okla. State Rep.
b. Tulsa, Okla, 2/2/29; s. Harry L. Hopkins and Mildred I. Kitchen H; m. 7/28/67 to Frances L. Yandell; c. Marvin L. and Michael L. Educ: Daniel Webster High Sch, Tulsa. Polit. & Govt. Pos: Okla. State Rep, Dist. 68, 59-63 & 65- Bus. & Prof. Pos: Employee, Tex. Oil Co, Tulsa and Real Estate and Ins. Broker, currently. Mil. Serv: Entered as Pvt, Marine Corps, 46, released as Pfc, after serv. in 1st Marine Air Wing, Pac. Theatre. Mem: Mason (32°); AFL-CIO; Southwest Tulsan's and Tulsa Co. Dem. Rel: Protestant. Mailing Add: 6103 W. 39th St, Tulsa, Okla. 74107.

HOPKINS, WILLIAM BENJAMIN D
Va. State Sen.
b. Richmond, Va, 4/16/22; m. to Virginia George. Educ: Roanoke Col; Wash. and Lee Univ, A.B; Univ. Va, LL.B. Polit. & Govt. Pos: Va. State Sen, 60-; Dem. Nat. Committeeman, 68; del, Dem. Nat. Conv, 68. Bus. & Prof. Pos: Lawyer. Mil. Serv: Marine Corps; Distinguished Serv. Award. Mem: Am. Legion; Pythians; VFW; DAV. Rel: Episcopal. Mailing Add: 1102 Oakwood Dr, S.W, Roanoke, Va. 24015.

HOPPE, VERNON T. Conservative
Minn. State Rep.
b. 1923. Educ: Univ. Minn, 51-53, exten. courses, 64-66; Am. Tech. Soc. Union Leadership Acad, 59-60. Polit. & Govt. Pos: Minn. State Rep, currently. Bus. & Prof. Pos: Engr. draftsman, Hennepin Co. Auditor. Mil. Serv: Army, 1 year; Air Force, 3 years. Mem: Cooper Sch, PTA.(pres, 64-66); Am. Fedn. of State, Co. and Munic. Employees (trustee and ed. Local 9 publn, 56-); Gopher Post Am. Legion. Rel: Lutheran. Mailing Add: 3212 44th St, Minneapolis, Minn. 55406. (1967)

HOPPER, HUBERT CARSON R
Chmn, Russell Co. Rep. Party, Ky.
b. Russell Springs, Ky, 11/4/10; s. David Carson Hopper and Victoria Frances Wade H; m. 10/11/31 to Mary Gladys Kimble; c. Barbara Jean (Mrs. Douglas Hemby), Betsy Carol (Mrs. Vaughn Sharp) and Kenton Wayne. Educ: East. Ky. Univ, 2 years; played basketball and football; on debating team and wrestling team. Polit. & Govt. Pos: Chmn, Russell Co. Rep. Party, Ky, currently. Bus. & Prof. Pos: Asst. postmaster, Russell Springs, Ky, 29-32; sch. teacher, 30-36; farmer and lumberman, 36- Mem: Nat. Farmers Orgn; Odd Fellows. Rel: Protestant. Mailing Add: R.R. 2, Box 278, Russell Springs, Ky. 42642.

HOPPING, WADE LEE R
b. Dayton, Ohio, 8/12/31; s. Paul Wade Hopping and Mildred VanScoyk H. m. 6/11/53 to LiAnne Heckman; c. Stephen Wade, Judson Stuart and Henry Lee. Educ: Ohio State Univ, B.A. in Polit. Sci, 53; Ohio State Univ. Law Sch, LL.B, 55; Pi Sigma Alpha; Nat. Polit. Sci. Hon; Ralph D. Mershon Honor Soc; pres, Pre-Law Club; Student Senate; Sigma Chi; Phi Delta Phi. Polit. & Govt. Pos: Research asst. to Justice, Supreme Court of Fla, 58-60 & 62-64, Justice, 68-69; legis. asst. and constitutional law adv. to Gov, State of Fla, 67-68; mem, Fla. Law Revision Cmn, 68- Bus. & Prof. Pos: Attorney-at-law, Adams & Hopping, Columbus, Ohio, 57-58 and Law Offices of M.F. Baugher, Palm Beach, Fla, 60-61; dir, continuing legal educ, Fla. Bar, Tallahassee, 64-67; partner, Mahoney, Hadlow, Chambers & Adams, Jacksonville, 69- Mil. Serv: Entered as 2nd Lt, Army, 55, released as 1st Lt, 57, after serv. in Sixth Tank Bn, 24th Inf. Div, 56-57. Publ: Co-author, The Attorney-Client Relationship, Florida Civil Practice Before Trial. Mem: Nat. Cmt. for Support of Pub. Schs; Fla. Cmn. on Constitutional Govt; Tallahassee, Am. and Fla. Govt. Bar Asns; Am. Judicature Soc; Elks; Sigma Chi Alumni Ans; Kiwanis; past pres, Toastmasters Club, N.Palm Beach, Fla. and Timberlane PTA. Rel: Episcopal. Legal Res: 900 Barnett Bank Bldg, Jacksonville, Fla. 32201. Mailing Add: 3305 Oak St, Jacksonville, Fla. 32205.

HORAN, MICHAEL FRANCIS D
R.I. State Sen.
b. Pawtucket, R.I, 8/9/42; s. Willard Vincent Horan and Mary Campbell H; m. 7/1/67 to Mary Monica Coogan. Educ: Providence Col, A.B, 63; Cath. Univ. Law Sch, LL.B, 66; Delta Epsilon Sigma. Polit. & Govt. Pos: R.I. State Sen, 69- Mil. Serv: Lt.(jg), Naval Res. Mem: Am. and R.I. Bar Asns; Pawtucket Bar Asn.(treas, 68-69). Rel: Roman Catholic. Legal Res: 36 Fillmore St, Pawtucket, R.I. 02860. Mailing Add: 393 Armistice Blvd, Pawtucket, R.I. 02860.

HORAN, RICHARD HENRY R
N.H. State Rep.
b. Manchester, N.H, 6/29/88; s. Thomas Horan and Winifred Campbell H; wid; c. Richard J. and Justin T. Educ: St. Joseph's Christan Bros. High Sch, 4 years. Polit. & Govt. Pos: Del, N.H. Constitutional Conv, 13-14; N.H. State Rep, 15-18 & 69-; N.H. State Sen, 19-20. Bus. & Prof. Pos: Principle acct. and supvr. bus. admin, N.H. State Bd. of Educ, Concord, 18-60; teacher and prin, adult educ, Manchester, currently. Rel: Roman Catholic. Mailing Add: 6 Holt St, Concord, N.H. 03301.

HORBAL, KORYNE EMILY DFL
State Chmn, Democrat-Farmer-Labor Party of Minn.
b. Minneapolis, Minn, 2/11/37; d. Stanley Raymond Kaneski and Emma Jamtoos K; m. 2/1/58 to William Orin Horbal; c. Steven Ray and Lynn Rae. Educ: Gustavus Adolphus Col, 2 quarters; Univ. Minn, 1 quarter. Polit. & Govt. Pos: Mem, Young Democrat-Farmer-Labor Party, Minn, 53-55; precinct chmn, Brooklyn Center Democrat-Farmer-Labor Party, 60; Democrat-Farmer-Labor chmn, 20th Ward, Hennepin Co, 61-; third v.chmn, Hennepin Co. Democrat-Farmer-Labor Party, 61-63, first v.chmn, 63-65; chmn, Anoka Co. Democrat-Farmer-Labor Party, 66-68; del, Dem. Nat. Conv, 68; state chmn, Democrat-Farmer-Labor Party of Minn, 68-; mem, Mayor's Citizen Cmt, Fed. Progs, Coon Rapids. Bus. & Prof. Pos: V.pres. and treas, Am. Contracting Corp, 64- Rel: Lutheran. Mailing Add: 8380 Palm St. N.W, Coon Rapids, Minn. 55433.

HORN, AMOS D
Chmn, Montgomery Co. Dem. Party, Ark.
b. Caddo Gap, Ark, 2/3/04; s. James Thornton Horn and Loucinda Elizabeth Davis H; m. 11/29/33 to Hazel Lucille McLean. Educ: Col, 2 years. Polit. & Govt. Pos: Co. and circuit clerk, Montgomery Co, Ark, 33-42, co. judge, 43-46; chmn, Montgomery Co. Dem. Party, currently. Bus. & Prof. Pos: Cashier, Bank of Montgomery Co, Ark, 48-53. Mem: Mt. Ida Masonic Lodge; Scimita Shrine; past pres, Montgomery Co. Farm Bur. Rel: Methodist. Mailing Add: Mt. Ida, Ark. 71957. (1967)

HORN, CARL LEWIS R
Chmn, Arenac Co. Rep. Cent. Cmt, Mich.
b. Highland Park, Mich. 8/18/28; s. Casper Smith Horn and Marie Beckman H; m. 2/15/55 to Ann Barton; c. Craig W, Marjorie A. and Karen J. Educ: Univ. Mich, A.B, 50, J.D, 52; Delta Theta Phi. Polit. & Govt. Pos: Prosecuting attorney, Arenac Co, Mich, 60-; chmn, Arenac Co. Rep. Cent. Cmt, 69- Bus. & Prof. Pos: Attorney-at-law, 59-; city attorney, Standish, Mich, 60-; pub. adminstr, Arenac Co, 62- Mil. Serv: Entered as Basic Airman, Air Force, 52, released as S/Sgt, 56; Nat. Defense Medal. Mem: Am. and Mich. Bar Asns; 34th Judicial Circuit Bar Asn; Nat. Inst. Munic. Law Officers; Nat. Asn. Dist. Attorneys; Kiwanis (past pres); F&AM; Mason; Boy Scouts; bd, Arenac Co. Sr. Citizens; bd. dirs, Prosecuting Attorneys Asn. of Mich. Rel: Methodist; past chmn. bd, Methodist Church. Legal Res: 617 Orchard, Standish, Mich. 48658. Mailing Add: Courthouse, Standish, Mich. 48658.

HORN, JOHN J. D
Asst. Minority Leader, N.J. State Assembly
b. Philadelphia, Pa, 11/2/17. Educ: S. Jersey Ext, Rutgers Univ. Polit. & Govt. Pos: Dem. committeeman, 11th Ward, N.J; pres, Camden City Coun; chmn, Charter Study Cmn; mem. bd. educ, Camden, 9 years, pres, 2 years; N.J. State Assemblyman and asst. minority leader, N.J. State Assembly, currently; del, Dem. Nat. Conv, 68. Bus. & Prof. Pos: Asst. dir, U.R.C.L.P.W.A-AFL-CIO. Mem: Legis cmt, N.J. League Munic; K. of C; bd. gov, Merchantville Country Club; chmn, N.J. Youth Cmn; Camden Juvenile Conf. Cmt; pres, Cramer Hill Boys Club; bd. dirs, Union Orgn. for Soc. Serv. Mailing Add: 375 W. State St, Trenton, N.J. 08618.

HORN, RAYMOND LEE D
Okla. State Sen.
b. Pawnee, Okla, 11/3/16; s. Vilas Lee Horn and Josie Hestand H; m. 2/8/35 to Lucile La Verne Palmer; c. Jimmie Lee, Gary Raymond and Brenda Lee. Educ: Pub. Schs. Polit. & Govt. Pos: Okla. State Sen, 64- Bus. & Prof. Pos: Automobile, implement and hardware owner and dealer; oil well drilling contractor, 42- Mem: Mason; Shrine; Kiwanis (pres, 64). Rel: Christian Church of N.Am. Mailing Add: Main and She She, Hominy, Okla. 74035.

HORNBAKER, LEE VAUGHN D
Chmn, Geary Co. Dem. Party, Kans.
b. Castleton, Kans, 7/31/16; s. Charles Hornbaker and Mabel Logan H; m. 12/30/41 to Alma Wacha; c. David and Steven. Educ: Hutchinson Jr. Col, 33-35; Washburn Col, Ph.B. and LL.B, 40. Polit. & Govt. Pos: Acct. clerk, cmn. acct. deposits, U.S. Treas. Dept, 35-39; organizer, surplus mkt. admin, U.S. Dept. Agr, 40-42; asst. to regional dir, U.S. War Labor Bd, Kansas City, 43-44; treas, Geary Co. Dem, Kans, 48-56 & 61-65; co. attorney, Geary Co, Kans, 49-53; chmn, Geary Co. Dem. Party, 56-60 & 66-; del. Dem. Nat. Conv, 68. Mailing Add: 102 Bunker Hill Dr, Junction City, Kans. 66441.

HORNE, ALICE M. R
Chmn, Salem Rep. City Cmt, Mass.
b. Salem, Mass, 12/20/16; d. William Henry Horne and Bertha I. Jones H; single. Educ: Hawthorne Inst, Salem, 2 years, Bus. Finishing; Boston Univ, 4 years. Polit. & Govt. Pos: Pres, Women's Rep. Club Salem, Mass, 67-69; chmn, Salem Rep. City Cmt, 68-; mem, Essex Co. Women's Rep. Club, 68- Bus. & Prof. Pos: Owner and pres, Horne Bus. Serv, Advert. and Acct, 27 years; off. mgr, I.M. Kaplan, Inc, Danvers, Mass, 64- Mem: Armed Forces Writers League, Hawthorne Br; Bus. & Prfnl. Women's Club; Women's Rep. Club (past pres); Wesleyan Serv. Circle, Wesley United Methodist Church (treas). Rel: Methodist. Mailing Add: 42 Howard St, Salem, Mass. 01970.

HORNE, JOHN ELMER D
b. Clayton, Ala, 3/4/08; s. John Eli Horne and Cornelia Thomas H; m. 7/27/38 to Ruth F. Kleinman; c. Linda L. (Mrs. Richard L. Clark) and Susan Elizabeth (Mrs. James K. Ewart). Educ: Troy State Univ; Univ. Ala, A.B, 33, M.A, 41; Phi Beta Kappa; Kappa Delta Pi; Phi Delta Kappa; Pi Kappa Alpha; Omicron Delta Kappa. Polit. & Govt. Pos: Admin. asst. to U.S. Sen. John Sparkman, Ala, 47-51 & 53-61; from dep. adminstr. to adminstr, Small Defense Plants Admin, 51-53; staff dir, Dem. Sen. Campaign Cmt, 54; exec.

dir, Citizens for Stevenson-Kefauver, 56 and Citizens for Kennedy-Johnson, 60; adminstr, Small Bus. Admin, 61-63; mem. bd, Fed. Home Loan Bank, 63-65, chmn. bd, 65-68. Bus. & Prof. Pos: Teacher, Shelby Co. High Sch, Columbiana, Ala, 28-31; fel. in hist, Univ. Ala, 33-35; Southeast. rep, McMillan Pub. Co, 35-38 and Rowe, Peterson & Co, 38-43 & 46; pres, Investors Mortgage Ins. Co, Boston, Mass, 68- Mil. Serv: Entered as Lt.(jg), Navy, 43, released as Lt.(sg), 47, after serv. as Commun. Watch Officer, Puerto Rico, 43-44 and Commun. Officer, Naval Air Base, San Julian, Cuba, 44-46; Capt, Naval Res, 47-65; Letter of Commendation for Meritorious Navy Serv. Mem: Nat. Educ. Asn; Nat. Press Club; Post Mortem Club; Am. Legion; VFW; Sons of Confederate Vet; Elks; bd. dirs, Nat. Capital Dem. Club; Algonquin Club, Boston; Metrop. Club, Wash, D.C. Man of the Year Award, Long Island Univ. Sch. Bus. Admin, 63; Alumni of the Year, Troy State Univ, Capital Chap, Univ. of Ala. Alumni, 65; Distinguished Achievement Award, Nat. Asn. Small Bus. Investment Co, 64; Distinguished Achievement Award, Pi Kappa Alpha, 66. Rel: Episcopal. Legal Res: Clayton, Ala. 36016. Mailing Add: 770 Boylston St, Apt. 17 B, Boston, Mass. 02199.

HORNE, RUFUS LEE R
b. Scott Co, Va, 12/5/26; s. Drew Lee Horne and Elizabeth Smith H; m. 7/5/47 to Helen Jo Pierson; c. Gloria Jane. Educ: East Tenn. State Univ. Polit. & Govt. Pos: Chmn, Scott Co. Rep. Party, Va, 59-69; Ninth Dist. chmn, Rep. Party, 64. Mil. Serv: 2 years in Armed Forces. Mem: Secy. and past master, Fincastle Masonic Lodge 33, Shrine; Royal Arch Chap. Rel: Baptist. Mailing Add: Fort Blackmore, Va. 24250. (1967)

HORNER, JACK B. R
Pa. State Rep.
b. York, Pa, 3/24/22; s. Galen B. Horner and Gladys Coleman H; m. 6/21/45 to Nancy Joan Schlosser; c. Deborah Gail. Educ: Colgate Univ, B.A, 43; Dickinson Sch. of Law, LL.B, 48; Theta Chi. Polit. & Govt. Pos: Committeeman, Lancaster Co. Rep. Party, Pa, 56-64; sch. dir, Elizabethtown Area Sch. Bd, 59-64; Pa. State Rep, 65- Mil. Serv: Entered as Pvt, Army Air Force, 43, released as Pfc, 3rd Air Force, 46. Mem: Rotary. Rel: Church of Brethren. Legal Res: 545 Groff Ave, Elizabethtown, Pa. 17022. Mailing Add: 23 A. S. Market St, Elizabethtown, Pa. 17022. (1967)

HORNIG, DONALD FREDERICK D
B. Milwaukee, Wis, 3/17/20; s. Chester Arthur Hornig and Emma Knuth H; m. 6/17/43 to Lilli Schwenk; c. Joanna Gail, Ellen Constance, Christopher Wayne and Leslie Elizabeth. Educ: Harvard Univ, B.S, 40, Ph.D, 43. Polit. & Govt. Pos: Mem, President's Sci. Adv. Cmt, 60-69; spec. asst. to the President for Sci. and Tech, 64-69. Bus. & Prof. Pos: Research assoc, Woods Hole Oceanographic Inst, 43-44; group leader, Los Alamos Lab, Univ. Calif, 44-46; prof. chem. and dir, Metcalf Research Lab, Brown Univ, 46-57; Donner prof. sci. and chmn. dept. chem, Princeton Univ, 57-64; prof. chem, Univ. Rochester, 69-; v.pres, Eastman Kodak Co, 69- Publ: Over 80 sci. papers publ. Mem: Nat. Acad. Sci; Am. Asn. Adv. Sci; Am. Phys. Soc; Am. Philos. Soc; Am. Chem. Soc; Optical Soc. of Am; Faraday Soc; Cosmos Club, Wash, D.C; Sakonnet Golf Club, Little Compton, R.I; Chemists Club, NYC. Eng. Centennial Award, PMC Cols, 67; Charles Lathrop Parsons Award, Am. Chem. Soc, 67; the first Mellon Inst. Award, 68; Order of Civil Merit, Korean Govt, 68. Rel: Lutheran. Mailing Add: 1 Huxley Lane, Pittsford, N.Y. 14534.

HORNSBY, DAVID HUGO R
Chmn, McIntosh Co. Rep. Cmt, Ga.
b. Hammond, Ind, 6/11/44; s. Hugo Virgil Hornsby and Louise McGuffin H; m. 9/18/65 to Wilma Ann Bolin; c. David Hugo, II. Educ: S. Ga. Col, 2 years; Ga. South. Col, B.B.A, 69; Phi Beta Lambda; Mkt. Club; Soc. Adv. Mgt. Polit. & Govt. Pos: Chmn, McIntosh Co. Rep. Cmt, Ga, 68- Bus. & Prof. Pos: Coordinator, Altamaha Farms, Inc, Hazelhurst, Ga. Mem: Jaycees (regional v.pres, currently. Rel: Southern Baptist. Legal Res: Altamaha Farms, Inc, Hazelhurst, Ga, 31539. Mailing Add: Box 326, Hazelhurst, Ga. 31539.

HORNSBY, ERNEST CLAYTON D
b. E. Tallassee, Ala, 10/8/36; s. Ernest Arnold Hornsby and Kate Clayton H; m. 5/27/61 to Judith Ellen O'Daniel; c. Ernest Clayton Jr. Educ: Ala. Polytech. Inst, 58; Univ. of Ala, 60, Law. Polit. & Govt. Pos: Del, Dem. Nat. Conv, 60; Ala. State Sen, 63-66. Bus. & Prof. Pos: Exec. asst. to Supt. of Ins, 60-63; exec. v.pres. and mgr, First Fed. Savings and Loan Asn, Tallassee; attorney-at-law. Mem: Mason. Rel: Disciples of Christ. Mailing Add: Natasulga Rd, East Tallassee, Ala. 36023.

HORRIGAN, ALBERT R. D
Mich. State Rep.
b. Mount Morris Twp, Mich, 3/16/09; married; c. Patrick, Alice, Margaret. Educ: Univ. Detroit, 2 years; Gen. Motors Inst. of Tech, 1 year. Polit. & Govt. Pos: Mich. State Rep, 52- Bus. & Prof. Pos: Employed at Buick Motor Car Co. Mem: K. of C; First Friday Club; Notre Dame Club of Flint; Eagles; Buick Local 599. Rel: Catholic. Mailing Add: 4030 Brownell Blvd, Flint, Mich. 48504. (1967)

HORSLEY, GEORGE WILLIAM, SR. R
Ill. State Sen.
b. Creal Springs, Ill, 7/15/10; s. Otto Horsley and Della Schafer H; m. 11/12/66 to Dorothy Von Dera; c. Judith K. (Mrs. Richard Lott) and George William, Jr. Educ: Univ. Ill, 28-31; Lincoln Col. of Law, LL.B, 35. Polit. & Govt. Pos: Ill. State Rep, 46-66; Ill. State Sen, 66- Bus. & Prof. Pos: Attorney-at-Law, Springfield, Ill, 35-; pres, Hawaiian Village Motels Corp, 63- Mil. Serv: Entered as Lt.(jg), Navy, 44, released as Lt, 65, after serv. in Navy, Gunnery Officer, Atlantic and Med. Theater. Mem: Am, Ill. State and Sangamon Co. Bar Asns; Am. Trial Lawyers Asn; Navy Club; Amvets; Am. Legion; VFW; Cosmopolitan Club; Mason; Shrine; Elks; Odd Fellows. Rel: Methodist. Legal Res: 1402 W. Lake Dr, Springfield, Ill. 62707. Mailing Add: 316 East Adams St, Springfield, Ill. 62701.

HORST, DONALD J. D
Colo. State Rep.
b. Chicago, Ill, 12/27/32; s. William F. Horst and Mary G. Snyder H; m. 6/11/66 to Nancy Ann Whyte. Educ: Univ. Colo, B.S. in bus. admin. and LL.B, 56. Polit. & Govt. Pos: Colo. State Rep, currently. Bus. & Prof. Pos: Trust officer, The Colo. Nat. Bank of Denver, 60- Mil. Serv: Entered as 2nd Lt, Air Force, 57, released as 1st Lt, 60, after serv. in Judge Adv. Gen. Off, ETO; Capt, Air Force Res, 66. Mem: Am, Colo. and Denver Bar Asns. Rel: Roman Catholic. Mailing Add: 1255 Ogden, Apt. 205, Denver, Colo. 80218. (1967)

HORSTMAN, ALICE LOU R
Dep. Committeewoman, Wheeling Twp. Rep. Party, Ill.
b. Lincoln, Nebr, 8/24/36; d. Francis J. Hoag and Ada A. Engelhart H; m. 2/22/54 to Ronald R. Horstman; c. Katheryn Ann, Rhonda Lee, Mary Alice and Barbara Diane. Educ: High Sch. grad. Polit. & Govt. Pos: Co-sponsor, 'Go Girl' and you name it, Nebr, 60-65; alternate del, Rep. Nat. Conv, 64; co-chmn, Nebr. State Young Rep. and mem. nat. prog. cmt, 64-65; campaign chmn, Wheeling Twp. Rep. Women, Ill, TAR chmn. Wheeling Young Rep. and precinct capt, Wheeling Rep. Party, 66-; dep. committeewoman, Wheeling Twp. Rep. Party, 68-; treas, Wheeling Twp. Young Rep, 69. Bus. & Prof. Pos: Small column writer, local subdivision news, Prospect Heights Herald, Ill, 66. Mem: Bd, Lincoln Mrs. Jaycees, 63-65; founding and charter mem. E-Hart Girls, pres, 67- Outstanding Lancaster Co. Young Rep, Nebr, 64. Rel: United Church of Christ. Mailing Add: 315 Columbine Dr, Prospect Heights, Ill. 60070.

HORSTMAN, ROBERT ANTHONY D
Chmn, Montgomery Co. Dem. Exec. Cmt, Ohio
b. Dayton, Ohio, 5/2/09; s. Albert Adam Horstman and Julia Kost H; m. 4/20/29 to Betty Mayer; c. Betty Ann (Mrs. E.C. Sanders). Educ: Chaminade High Sch. of Dayton, Grad; Univ. Dayton Prep. Sch. Polit. & Govt. Pos: Chmn, Montgomery Co. Dem. Exec. Cmt, Ohio, 61-; mem, Bd. Elec, Montgomery Co, 61-; pres, Ohio Asn. Elec. Officials, 63-64; del, Dem. Nat. Conv, 68; mem, Ohio Dem. State Cent. Cmt, 68- Bus. & Prof. Pos: Pres, Wayne Invest. Co, 60-; v.pres, Horstman Printing Co, 60-65, pres, 65-; mem. bd. dirs, Home Savings and Loan Asn, 61- Mem: Past pres, E.Dayton Businessmen's Asn, Dayton Optimists, Coun. of Optimist Clubs, Dayton Bicycle Club, Chaminade Alumni Asn, Ky-Ind-Ohio Bowling Asn; vice high chief ranger and past pres, Cath. Order of Foresters 549, past pres, Cent. Chap; lay bd, Good Samaritan Hosp; bd. trustees, Dayton Boy's Club; Miami Valley Golf Club; E.Dayton Commun. Coun; Newcomen Soc; Gem. City Dem. Club. Rel: Catholic. Mailing Add: 2189 Willowgrove Ave, Kettering, Ohio 45429. (1967)

HORSTMAN, RONALD RALPH R
b. Lincoln, Nebr, 12/31/64; s. Ralph William Horstman and Rose A. Runge H; m. 2/22/54 to Alice L. Hoag; c. Katheryn Ann, Rhonda Lee, Mary Alice and Barbara Diane. Educ: Univ. Nebr, $3\frac{1}{2}$ years. Polit. & Govt. Pos: Precinct capt, Lancaster Co. Rep. Party, Nebr, 60; del, Nebr. Young Rep. Conv, 62-65; initiated drive to bring nat. conv. to Nebr. in 1967, 63; mem, Lancaster Co. Rep. Cent. Cmt, 63; chmn, Lancaster Co. Young Rep, 63-64; alternate del, Nat. Young Rep. Conv, 63 & 67; hon. sgt-at-arms, Rep. Nat. Conv, 64; mem, Nebr. Finance and Budget Cmt, 64-65; publicity dir, Nebr. Fedn. Young Rep, 64-65; mem, Nat. Young Rep. Urban Club Cmt, 64-65; del, Ill. Rep. Conv, 67; n. area chmn, Cook Co. Young Rep, Ill, 67-68; mem, Wheeling Twp. Exec. Bd, Ill, 67-; pres, Wheeling Twp. Young Rep, 68; pub. rels. dir, Ill. Young Rep, 68-69. Bus. & Prof. Pos: Advert. sales rep, Nebr. Farmer Mag, 62-64 and Farm J, Inc, 54- Mil. Serv: Entered as Seaman Recruit, Naval Res, 52, released as Hospitalman 1/C, 64, after serv. in 11th Naval Dist. San Diego Naval Hosp, Calif, 55-57. Mem: Nat. Agr. Advert. Mkt. Asn. Nebr. Jaycees SPOKE Award, 63; Recipient of Keyman Award, Lincoln Nebr. Jaycees, 64; Outstanding Govt. Affairs Chmn, Nebr. Jaycees, 64-65; Outstanding Young Rep, Lancaster Co, 64-65; Outstanding Area Chmn, Cook Co, Ill. Young Rep, 67-68; Top Sales Award, Farm J, Inc, 68. Rel: United Church of Christ; Pres, Church Coun, 67- Mailing Add: 315 Columbine Dr, Prospect Heights, Ill. 60070.

HORTING, RUTH GRIGG D
b. Lancaster, Pa, 1/31/00; d. J. Edgar Grigg and Annie Walker Powell; m. 11/9/22 to John Francis Horting; c. Arthur Lionel. Educ: Millersville Normal Sch, 18-20; Gettysburg Col, hon. L.H.D, 61; Delta Kappa Gamma. Polit. & Govt. Pos: Pa. State Rep, 36-38; v.chmn, Pa. Dem. State Cmt, 42-54 and former mem; Secy. of Pub. Assistance, Pa, 55-59, Secy. of Pub. Welfare, 59-63; alternate del, Dem. Nat. Conv, 68. Mem: Federated Woman's Club; Iris Club of Lancaster; Quota Club, Soroptimist Asn. Rel: Lutheran. Legal Res: 2101 West Ridge Dr, Lancaster, Pa. 17604. Mailing Add: Box 332, Lancaster, Pa. 17604.

HORTON, FRANK R
U.S. Rep, N.Y.
b. Cuero, Tex, 12/12/19; m. to Marjorie Wilcox; c. Frank, Steven. Educ: La. State Univ, B.A, 41; Cornell Univ. Law Sch, LL.B, 47; Phi Kappa Phi. Polit. & Govt. Pos: Councilman-at-lg, Rochester, N.Y, 55-61; U.S. Rep, N.Y, 63-; del. from U.S. Cong. to dedication of Israeli Parliament, Israel, 66; del. to Ditchley Conf. on Anglo-Am. Affairs, Eng, 67. Bus. & Prof. Pos: Former exec. v.pres, Int. Baseball League; attorney, Johnson, Reif & Mullan; pres, Rochester Commun. Baseball. Mil. Serv: Entered as 2nd Lt, Army, 41, released as Maj, 45, after serv. in N.Africa and Italy, 42-45; Lt. Col, Army Res; Legion of Merit; Bronze Star. Publ: How to End the Draft, Nat. Press, Inc, 67; Study in Urban Education, 68 and Air Safety, 69, Policy Memorandum. Mem: Order of the Coif; Monroe Co, N.Y. State and Am. Bar Asns; VFW; Am. Legion; Res. Officers Asn; Master, Seneca Lodge 920, F&AM; pres, Masonic Serv. Bur, 55-56; Rochester Consistory; Scottish Rite; Damascus Temple, Shrine; Hamilton Chap. 62, RAM; Doric Coun. 19, RSM; Monroe Commandery 12, K.T; Mason (32°); past pres, Fedn. of Bar Asns. of West. N.Y; secy, Rochester Bar Asn, 53-57. Rel: Presbyterian; Elder and trustee, Cent. Presbyterian Church. Legal Res: 2123 East Ave, Rochester, N.Y. 14610. Mailing Add: 407 House Office Building, Washington, D.C. 20515.

HORTON, ISAAC JOSEPH D
b. Walstonburg, N.C, 9/18/23; s. Isaac Joshua Horton; Annie Hamilton H; m. 9/3/49 to Agnes Galloway; c. Barbara Jo, Cynthia, Sheila. Educ: Presbyterian Jr. Col, 41-43; Atlantic Christian Col, A.B, 47; Wake Forest Law Sch, LL.B, 50; Phi Alpha Delta. Polit. & Govt. Pos: Solicitor, Green Co. Court, N.C, 50-60; chmn, Greene Co. Econ. Develop. Cmn; N.C. State Rep, 63-69. Bus. & Prof. Pos: Lawyer. Mil. Serv: Army, Pvt. 43-46. Mem: Greene Co,

N.C. State and Am. Bar Asns; Rotary; Am. Legion; Mason (32°); Shrine. Rel: Baptist, trustee, deacon, teacher in adult men's class. Mailing Add: Snow Hill, N.C. 28580.

HORTON, JAMES EDWIN, JR. D
s. James Edwin Horton and Anna Echols Hobbs H; m. 11/9/46 to Ann Williams. Educ: Univ. of Tex, 47. Polit. & Govt. Pos: Ala. State Sen, -66; mem, State Bd. of Agr. and Industs, 58-62. Bus. & Prof. Pos: Farmer and cattle raiser. Mil. Serv: Army, 43-46, capt, 66th Inf. Regt. Rel: Supt, Belle Minor Methodist Church. Mailing Add: Route 1, Madison, Ala. 35758. (1967)

HORTON, NEVILS DUDLEY, JR. D
b. Eatonton, Ga, 5/04/34; s. N.D. Horton, Sr. and Maude Matthews H; m. 8/17/55 to Jacquelyn Pickron. Educ: Mercer Univ, 56. Polit. & Govt. Pos: Ga. State Rep, 59-64. Bus. & Prof. Pos: Pres, Horton Develop. Corp. and Putnam Co. Indust. Develop. Corp. Mil. Serv: 1st Lt, 57. Selected as one of the Outstanding Young Men of Am. by Nat. Outstanding Young Men Cmt. of Jaycees. Rel: Baptist. Mailing Add: Eatonton, Ga. 31024.

HORTON, SEAB SANFORD, JR. R
Chmn, Polk Co. Rep. Party, Ga.
b. Rome, Ga, 5/14/32; s. Seab Sanford Horton, Sr. and Martha McKinney H; m. 8/9/59 to Jane Adelia Reeves; c. Martha Adelia and Lydia Reeves. Educ: Univ. Ga, B.B.A, 54; Univ. Munich, 56; Phi Delta Theta. Polit. & Govt. Pos: Secy, Polk Co. Rep. Party, Ga, 60-63, chmn, 64-; mem, Seventh Cong. Dist. Rep. Exec. Cmt, 64- Bus. & Prof. Pos: V.pres, Spar Oil Co, 56-61; owner and pres, Ideal Oil Co, 61- Mil. Serv: Entered as 2nd Lt, Army, 54, released as 1st Lt, 56, after service in Comptroller Div, South. Area Army Command, Germany, 55-56; Occupation Ribbon. Mem: Jr. C. of C; Lions. Rel: Episcopal. Legal Res: 126 Jule Peck Ave, Cedartown, Ga. Mailing Add: Box 151, Cedartown, Ga. 30125.

HORWITZ, ERWIN R. D
Pres, 24th Ward Dem. Orgn, Chicago, Ill.
b. Chicago, Ill, 3/9/11; s. Jacob Horwitz and Celia Schwartz H; m. 12/7/41 to Mary Davis (deceased); m. 1/9/67 to Florence Peters; c. Howard. Educ: Northwest. Univ, 29-33. Polit. & Govt. Pos: Supvry. engr, Cook Co. Hwy. Div, Ill, 34-47; first dep. chief bailiff, Munic. Court, 47-50; capital stock assessor, Gov. Stevenson's Cabinet, 51-55; dir. of research, Co. Assessors Off, 55-59; del, Dem. Nat. Conv, 60 & 64, alternate del, 68; bldg. cmnr, Cook Co, 62-64; pres, 24th Ward Dem. Orgn, Chicago, currently. Bus. & Prof. Pos: Ins. broker, Chicago, Ill; publisher, Todays Lawndale, A Commun. Newspaper; dir. and v.pres, Steinway-Ford Hopkins Drug Co; dir, Bankers Bldg. Chicago; publisher, Northwest Community Advertiser, A Commun. Newspaper. Mem: Registered mem, Chicago Real Estate Bd, Nat. Asn. Real Estate Bd. and Nat. Asn. Appraisers; dir, Chicago Press Club, Hebrew Theol. Col, Jewish Bd. Educ, Beth Am. and Lake Shore Dr. Temples, Chicago Israel Bond Cmt, Research Found. for Mentally Ill and Retarded Children, Little City and Portes Cancer Prev. Center; Cancer Prev. Coun; trustee, Faulkner Sch; Covenant Club; Chicago Chap, Hebrew Univ; Chicago Red Cross; Chicago Boy Scouts; Jewish Home for Aged; Adlai Stevenson and Near N.Side B-nai B'rith Lodges. Registered prfnl. civil engr, State of Ill. Rel: Jewish. Legal Res: 77 W. Washington St, Chicago, Ill. 60602. Mailing Add: 1000 Lake Shore Dr, Chicago, Ill. 60611.

HORWITZ, LARRY D
b. Hollywood, Calif, 5/1/40; s. Alexander Horwitz and Gertrude Anzis H; single. Educ: Harvard Col, 57-59 and 61-62; Univ. Calif, Los Angeles, 60-61. Polit. & Govt. Pos: Admin. Asst. to U.S. Rep. John Conyers, Jr, Mich, 65-; asst. to dep. campaign mgr, Calif. Johnson-Humphrey Campaign, 64; legis. asst. to U.S. Rep. Al Ullman, Ore, 63, summer interne, 62; mem, Mich. 1st Dist. Dem. Party Orgn, Mich. Voters Coun, 1st Dist. Club, D.C. Young Dem. Club and Calif. Dem. Coun. Mil. Serv: Entered as Pvt, Army, 63, 4 months active duty, presently in Active Army Res. Control Group. Mem: Am. Jewish Cmt, B'nai B'rith; NAACP; Retail Clerks Int. Asn, Local 770; Americans for Dem. Action. Recipient of Nat. Merit Scholarship, 57. Rel: Jewish. Legal Res: 11512 Duque Dr, Studio City, Calif. 91604. Mailing Add: c/o Congressman John Conyers, U.S. House Office Bldg, Washington, D.C. 20515. (1967)

HOSE, JACOB W, SR. R
b. York, Pa, 5/17/05; s. Charles E. Hose and Maude M. Emig H; m. Sept. 1938 to Beatrice A. Gross; c. Jacob W, Jr. and William M. Polit. & Govt. Pos: Patrolman, lt. of police and capt. of police, York, Pa, 34-56, chief of police, 56-, dir, Dept. of Pub. Safety, 62. Bus. & Prof. Pos: Security Officer, Am. Chain, 58-59. Mem: Cent. Pa. Chap, Am. Soc. of Safety Engrs; Fraternal Order of Police; Pa. Chiefs of Police Asn; Int. Asn. Chiefs of Police; Elks; Moose; Yankee A.A; Viking A.A; Prince A.A; Union Fire Co. and Club. Rel: Protestant. Legal Res: 627 W. Princess St, York, Pa. 17404. Mailing Add: City Hall, 50 W. King St, York, Pa. 17405.

HOSEA, NORMA KATHERINE D
b. Scottsburg, Ind, 3/10/40; d. Bernice Lee Dismore and Mae Cook D; m. 5/23/59 to John William Hosea; c. Jeffrey, Jennifer and David. Educ: Scottsburg High Sch. Polit. & Govt. Pos: V.chmn, Scott Co. Dem. Cent. Cmt, Ind, 63-69; former mem, Scott Co. Dem. Womens Club and Scott Co. Young Dem. Mem: Scott Co. Exten. Homemakers Club. Rel: Christian Church. Mailing Add: 733 Lucas St, Scottsburg, Ind. 47170. (1967)

HOSKING, MARY KATHERINE R
Mem, Calif. Rep. State Cent. Cmt.
b. Bakersfield, Calif, 2/9/27; d. Walter Charles Jaynes and Mary E. Young J; div; c. Geoffrey Richard, Timothy William and Meredith Katherine. Educ: Bakersfield Col. Polit. & Govt. Pos: Mem, Calif. Rep. State Cent. Cmt, 56 & 62-; mem, Charity Bd. of Appeals, Bakersfield City Coun, Calif, 59-65; mem, Kern Co. Rep. Cent. Cmt, 56-60 & 64-66; state secy, Area 9, United Rep. of Calif, 63-64, state v.chmn, 64-65, gov, 65-66; del, Rep. Nat. Conv, 64; pub. mem, Calif. State Bd. of Archit. Exam, 68- Bus. & Prof. Pos: Ed, Bakersfield News Bul, Calif, currently. Publ: 'How to Win,' Leadership Manual, United Rep, Calif, 64. Mem: Woman's Club of Bakersfield; DAR; Colonial Dames of 17th Century; Bakersfield Racquet Club; Kern Co. Hist Soc; Kern Press Club. Mailing Add: 2900 19th St, Bakersfield, Calif. 93301.

HOSKING, RICHARD R
b. Taft, Calif, 8/24/23; s. Ronald Richard Hosking and Catherine Cattani H; div; c. Geoffrey Richard, Timothy William and Meredith Katherine. Educ: Univ. of Santa Clara, J.D, 49. Polit. & Govt. Pos: Mem, Young Rep. Club, 51-63 and Calif. Rep. Asn, 55-65; mem, Calif. Rep. State Cent. Cmt, 60-62; mem, Kern Co. Rep. Cent. Cmt, 60-64, v.chmn, 60-62, co-chmn, 63; gen. counsel, United Rep. Calif, 63-64; mem. city coun, Bakersfield, Calif, 65-69, police cmnr, 69- Bus. & Prof. Pos: Mem. bd. dirs, Kern Co. Bar Asn, 60-62, secy-treas, 63, second v.pres, 64, first v.pres, 65 and pres, 66; mem, Cmt. for the State Bar Jour, State Bar of Calif, 65-68. Mil. Serv: Entered as Pvt, Army Air Force, 43, released as 1st Lt, 46, after serv. in 7th and 5th Air Force, Cent. Pac. Command and Far East Air Force; Air Medal; Campaign Ribbons; 7 Battle Stars. Publ: 'The Morality of Law,' Jour. of State Bar of Calif, 65. Mem: Calif. and Am. Bar Asn; Am. Arbit. Asn; Elks; Lions; Am. Legion; 40 et 8; Kern Co. Hist. Soc, pres, 63; Calif. Hist. Soc. Rel: Catholic. Legal Res: 1408 18th St, Bakersfield, Calif. 93301. Mailing Add: P.O. Box 2507, Bakersfield, Calif. 93303.

HOSKINS, ROBERT GERALD D
Chmn, Waukesha Co. Dem. Party, Wis.
b. Milwaukee, Wis, 10/29/35; s. Gerald Hoskins and Isabel Johann H; m. 11/13/54 to Janet Ruth Strike; c. Robert, Elizabeth, Pamela, Rebecca, Gerald and James. Educ: Carroll Col, Wis, B.S, 57; Univ. Iowa, 57-58; Univ. Wis-Milwaukee, M.S, 69; Sigma Tau Delta; Kappa Delta Pi; Beta Pi Epsilon. Polit. & Govt. Pos: Precinct committeeman, Waukesha Co. Dem. Statutory Cmt, Wis, 62-69; v.chmn, Ninth Cong. Dist. Dem. Party, 64; bd. mem, Waukesha Co. Dem. Admin. Cmt, 67-69; chmn, Waukesha Co. Dem. Party, 67-; treas, Waukesha Co. McCarthy for Pres. Cmt, 68; alternate del, Dem. Nat. Conv, 68. Bus. & Prof. Pos: Caseworker, Waukesha Co. Welfare Dept, 58-60; Eng. teacher, Oconomowoc High Sch, 61-69. Mil. Serv: Sgt, Marine Corps Res. Mem: Wis, Oconomowoc and South. Wis. Educ. Asns; Wis. Coun. Teachers of Eng; Oconomowoc Jaycees; IBT; Am. Civil Liberties Union. Sigma Tau Delta Award. Rel: Catholic. Legal Res: Delafield, Wis. 53018. Mailing Add: Route 1, Box 402, Nashotah, Wis. 53058.

HOSMER, CRAIG R
U.S. Rep, Calif.
b. Brea, Calif, 5/6/15; s. Chester Cleveland Hosmer and Mary Jane Craig H; m. to Marian Caroline Swanson; c. Susan Jane and Craig Larkin. Educ: Univ. Calif, A.B, 37; Univ. South. Calif, J.D, 40; Phi Kappa Psi; Phi Alpha Delta. Polit. & Govt. Pos: Spec. asst, U.S. Dist. Attorney for Atomic Energy Cmn, Los Alamos, N.Mex, 48, adv, Int. Atomic Energy Agency Del, 59-; U.S. Rep, Calif, 52-, adv, U.S. Del. to 18 Nation Disarmament Conf, 65-, Joint Cmt. on Atomic Energy, Interior Insular Affairs and adv, U.S. Atoms for Peace Del, Geneva, 58, 63, U.S. House of Rep. Bus. & Prof. Pos: Ed, Univ. South. Calif. Rev, 39-40; lawyer, Long Beach, Calif, 46- Mil. Serv: Navy, 41-46, Capt, Naval Res. Legal Res: 4130 Cedar Ave, Long Beach, Calif. 90807. Mailing Add: House Office Bldg, Washington, D.C. 20515.

HOSMER, LARRY F. R
Chmn, Yankton Co. Rep. Cent. Cmt, S.Dak.
b. Fedora, S.Dak, 2/2/40; s. Harold Martin Hosmer and Naomi Pearl Shumaker H; m. 7/27/63 to Carol Lynne Tisher; c. David. Educ: Univ. S.Dak, 58-65, B.A. and J.D; Sigma Alpha Epsilon; Delta Theta Phi. Polit. & Govt. Pos: Chmn, Yankton Co. Rep. Cent. Cmt, S.Dak, 67-; state attorney, Yankton Co, 69- Mem: S.Dak, Am. and First Circuit Bar Asns; Yankton Co. Bar Asn. (secy, 66-69); Am. Judicature Soc; S.Dak. States Asn; Sertoma; Mason; Consistory; Shrine; Eastern Star; Elks; Odd Fellows; Yankton Jaycees (pres, 67); S.Dak. Jaycees (v.pres, 68). Rel: Methodist. Mailing Add: 2008 Burleigh, Yankton, S.Dak. 57078.

HOSMER, LUCILE CALLAN R
First V.Chmn, San Mateo Co. Rep. Cent. Cmt, Calif.
b. San Francisco, Calif, 8/15/08; d. Edward Joseph Callan and Lucy Ellen Helm C; m. to Merritt Reynolds Hosmer (deceased); c. William McAulay. Educ: San Mateo Jr. Col, A.A, 28; Univ. Calif, 1½ years. Polit. & Govt. Pos: Mem, San Mateo Co. Rep. Assembly, Calif, 44; mem, San Mateo Co. Fedn. of Rep. Women, 45-, secy, 46, prog. chmn, 47, co. campaign chmn, 48, v.pres, 48-52, pres, 52-56; San Mateo Co. women's chmn. for Calif. Assemblyman Richard J. Dolwig, 46, 48 & 50; mem, Calif. Rep. State Cent. Cmt, 48-, mem, principles cmt, 63, chmn, polit. educ. cmt, mem, exec. cmt; mem, San Mateo Co. Cmt, Richard Nixon for U.S. Sen, 50; San Mateo Co. women's chmn, Eisenhower-Nixon, 52, San Mateo Co. precinct chmn, and women's chmn, 56; precinct chmn, San Mateo Co. Rep. Party, 52-66 & 67-68; mem, Nat. Asn. of Pro Am, 52-, speaker, nat. bd. meeting, 69, third nat. v.pres, 69-; mem, San Mateo Co. Rep. Cent. Cmt, 53-, first v.chmn, 54-; Americanism chmn, North. Div, Calif. Fedn. of Rep. Women, 54-56, pres, 56-60, state Americanism chmn, 58-60, state pres, 60-63, jr. pres, state bd, 63-65, resolutions chmn, 65-67, hospitality chmn, North. div. bd, 63-65, resolutions chmn, 65-69; North. Calif. women's chmn, William F. Knowland for Gov, 58; North. Calif. cmt, Nixon for Pres, 60; elector, Electoral Col, Calif, 60; mem, exec. bd, Nat. Fedn. of Rep. Women, 60-63, state pres, 63-65; Americanism chmn, exec. bd, 63-65, legis. chmn, 65-68; del, Rep. Nat. Conv, 60 & 64, secy, Calif. Del, 60, alternate del, 68; mem, North. Calif. cmt, Nixon for Gov, 62; mem, Cmt. to Elect Dr. Max Rafferty State Supt. of Pub. Instr, 62; wrote principles statement for Calif. State Rep. Party, 63, readopted, 68; Nat. Women's Cmt. liaison to Calif. to elect Goldwater-Miller, 64; state women's chmn, Dr. Max Rafferty's reelection, 66; co. co-chmn. and mem, North. Calif. exec. cmt, Reagan for Gov, 66; mem, Calif. Women's Bd. of Terms and Parole, 68- Bus. & Prof. Pos: Speaker, constitutional govt, Am. Heritage, hist, polit. sci. and state and nat. legis. Mem: Bus. and Prfnl. Women's Club, San Carlos and Belmont, Calif; San Mateo Co. Grand Jury, 51; PTA. Rel: Protestant. Legal Res: 520 Elm St, San Carlos, Calif. 94070. Mailing Add: Box 846, San Carlos, Calif. 94070.

HOSTETLER, H. RICHARD D
Dep. State Chmn, Dem. State Cmt, Pa.
b. Mifflintown, Pa, 5/15/39; s. John Blair Hostetler and Klara Parnell H; single. Educ: Lycoming Col, A.B.A, 62. Polit. & Govt. Pos: Pres, Juniata Co. Young Dem. Club, Pa, 58-64; state dir, Young Dem. Clubs Pa, 60-62, v.pres, 62-64; registration chmn, Juniata Co. Dem. Party, 63-65, mem. exec. cmt, 63-; dep. state chmn, Pa. Dem. State Cmt, 65-; del, Constitutional Conv, 67-

68; state registration chmn, Pa. Dem. Party, 68; alternate del, Dem. Nat. Conv, 68; cand, U.S. Rep, Pa, 68; state campaign chmn, Manderino for Supreme Court, 69. Bus. & Prof. Pos: Owner-operator, Hostetler Eggs and dealer, Dekalb Agr. Asn, 62- Mem: VFW; Am. Legion; Lions; Jaycees; Future Farmers Am. Rel: Lutheran. Mailing Add: R.D. 2, Mifflintown, Pa. 17059.

HOSTETTLER, DORIE McFETRIDGE R
Rep. State Committeewoman, Lake Co, Fla.
b. Creighton, Pa, 9/4/10; d. George Edwin McFetridge and Ida Stacy Smith M; m. to Donald Cook Hostettler (deceased); div; c. Donna (Mrs. J.H. Dickson). Educ: Marjorie Webster Sch. Speech, B.E, 33; Rollins Col, A.B, 49; Univ. Fla, M.A, 53; Sigma Alpha Eta; Comus; Delta Delta Delta. Polit. & Govt. Pos: Pres, Golden Triangle Rep. Womens Club, Fla, 60-62 & 67-69, secy, 63, prog. chmn, 69-; Fla. del, White House Conf. on Children and Youth, 60; del, Rep. Nat. Conv, 64 & 68; precinct committeewoman; Rep. State Committeewoman, Lake Co, currently. Bus. & Prof. Pos: Teacher speech and drama, Eustis High Sch, Fla, 49-55 and Howley Acad, 56-59; chmn. speech and drama dept, Brenau Col, 55-56. Mem: Speech Asn. Am; Fla. Coop. Coun. on Children and Youth; PEO; Int. Platform Asn. Rel: Christian Scientist. Legal Res: Old Mt. Dora Rd, Eustis, Fla. 32726. Mailing Add: P.O. Box 775, Eustis, Fla. 32726.

HOUCK, CHARLES WESTON D
b. Florence, S.C, 4/16/33; s. W. Stokes Houck and Charlotte Weston H; m. 8/2/58 to Elizabeth Bland Ariail. Educ: Univ. of N.C; Univ. of S.C, LL.B, 56. Polit. & Govt. Pos: S.C. State Rep, 63-66. Bus. & Prof. Pos: Lawyer, Willcox, Hardee, Houck, Palmer & O'Farrell. Mil. Serv: Army, JAGC, 57-58; Army Res, Capt. Mem: Florence Kiwanis Club; Jr. C. of C. Rel: St. John's Episcopal Church. Mailing Add: Box 909, Florence, S.C. 29501. (1967)

HOUCK, WILLIAM M. D
Md. State Del.
b. Keyser, W.Va, 3/14/20; s. George C. Houck and Lula E. Barncord H; m. 9/21/43 to Ruth Howard Wachtel; c. William W, John M. and Jean. Educ: Frostburg State Teachers Col, 39-41. Polit. & Govt. Pos: Town councilman, Thurmont, Md, 52-54; Md. State Del, 58-, v.chmn, House Ways and Means Cmt, 64-66; chmn, 67-, Majority Leader, 69- Mil. Serv: Entered as Pvt, Army, released as Sgt, Security Intel. Corp, 3rd Serv. Command, 45. Mem: Am. Legion; Elks; Lions; Thurmont Sportsmans and Conserv. Club. Rel: Lutheran. Legal Res: Emmitsburg Rd, Thurmont, Md. 21788. Mailing Add: Box 121, Thurmont, Md. 21788.

HOUGEN, CHESTER ORLAN R
Iowa State Sen.
b. McCallsburg, Iowa, 4/10/07; s. Ole Cornelius Hougen and Carrie Malmin H; m. 8/23/29 to Louise Weber Montgomery; c. Maj. Howard Montgomery. Educ: State Univ. of Iowa, B.A, 28, Law Col, J.D, 32; Gamma Eta Gamma. Polit. & Govt. Pos: Attorney, Fed. Land Bank, 33-36 and Off. Price Admin, 42-45; Iowa State Rep, 61-64; Iowa State Sen, 67- Bus. & Prof. Pos: Owner, Hougen's Kitchens, Iowa. Mem: Mason, Scottish Rite; Shrine (32°); Elks; Rotary Int; C. of C. Rel: Protestant. Mailing Add: 3215 Waterloo Rd, Cedar Falls, Iowa 50613.

HOUGEN, JAMES RICHARD R
N.Dak. State Rep.
b. Larimore, N.Dak, 3/8/29; s. Leonard A. Hougen and Gladys Mae Larson H; m. 8/1/51 to Vella Caroline Olson; c. John, Jane, Ardis, Charles, David, Paul and Susan. Educ: Concordia Col, Moorhead, Minn, 1 year. Polit. & Govt. Pos: Mem, Bd. of Educ, Larimore, N.Dak, 65-; N.Dak. State Rep, 69- Bus. & Prof. Pos: Mem, mens wear cmt, V.S.C, Clara City, Minn, 68-69. Mem: Larimore Commercial Club; Lions. Rel: Lutheran. Mailing Add: Larimore, N.Dak. 58251.

HOUGH, CASS SHEFFIELD R
Mem. Exec. Cmt, Ark. Rep. State Cmt.
b. Plymouth, Mich, 10/4/04; s. Edward Cass Hough (deceased) and Louise Sheffield H. (deceased); m. 6/6/60 to Beth Brogdon; c. Emily Louise (Mrs. Egan), Cass S. and Christopher B. Educ: Univ. Mich, A.B. cum laude, 25, A.M, 26; Cleary Col, M.B.A, 52; John Brown Univ, LL.D, 66; Alpha Kappa Psi; Pi Delta Epsilon; Sigma Alpha Epsilon; Sphinx; Druids; hon. mem. Beta Gamma Sigma. Polit. & Govt. Pos: Mem, Mich. Aeronautics Cmn, 47-51, chmn, 47-51, acting dir, 68; city cmnr, Plymouth, Mich, 49-51, Mayor, 50-51; finance chmn, Rockefeller for Gov. Campaigns, Ark, 66 & 68; mem, Ark. Indust. Develop. Cmn, 67-; del, Rep. Nat. Conv, 68; mem. exec. cmt, Ark. Rep. State Cmt, 69- Bus. & Prof. Pos: Exp. engr, Daisy Mfg. Co, Plymouth, Mich, 26-27, asst. prod. mgr, 27-28, mgr. King Mfg. Co. Subsidiary, 29-31, sales and advert. mgr, 31-37, v.pres, 31-45, dir, companies, Plymouth and Rogers, Ark, 32-67, dir. sales, Plymouth, Mich, 37-41, exec. v.pres. and secy, Plymouth and Rogers, Ark, 45-49 and pres. and treas, Rogers, Ark, 59-67; pres, Daisy/Heddon, Rogers, Ark, 67-; pres, Recreation Prod. Group, Victor Comptometer Corp, 69- Mil. Serv: Entered as 1st Lt, Air Force, 41, released as Col, 45, after serv. in Eighth Air Force, ETO, 41-45, Res, 45-61, Col.(Ret); Legion of Merit; Air Medal with 3 clusters; Distinguished Flying Cross with cluster; Pre-Pearl Harbor Medal; Am. Theatre Medal; ETO Medal with 6 battle stars; Commendation Ribbon with 2 clusters (8 times); Belgian Croix de Guerre with Palm. Mem: Elks; Bus-Indust. Polit. Action Cmt; Meadowbrook Country Club; South. Hills Country Club; Union League of Chicago; Detroit Athletic Club; Tulsa Club; Prairie Creek Country Club; VFW; Am. Legion; Air Force Asn; Vet. Air Pilots; Quiet Birdmen; Sportsman Pilots Asn; Mich. Aeronautics & Space Asn; Nat. Pilots Asn; Rogers C. of C; Nat. Conf. Christians & Jews. Outstanding Boss of the Year Award, Ark. State Jaycees, 66. Rel: Episcopal. Mailing Add: P.O. Box 220, Rogers, Ark. 72756.

HOUGH, JOHN E. R
Rep. Nat. Committeeman, Wis.
b. Janesville, Wis, 7/5/16; s. Azel Clarence Hough and Dorothy Whitehead H; m. 12/28/40 to Vivian Swensson; c. Gordon Richard and Lawrence A. Educ: Cornell Univ, B.A, 37. Polit. & Govt. Pos: Rep. City chmn, Janesville, Wis, 48-52; chmn, Rock Co. Rep. Orgn, 53-55; chmn, First Dist. Rep. Orgn, 58-61; treas, Rep. Party of Wis, 61-68; alternate del, Rep. Nat. Conv, 68; Rep. Nat. Committeeman, Wis, 68- Bus. & Prof. Pos: Pres, Hough Mfg. Corp, 37- Mem: Dir, Wis. C. of C; Chief Execs. Forum; Rotary; Cornell Club. of N.Y.C. Rel: Episcopal. Legal Res: 1901 Ruger Ave, Janesville, Wis. 53545. Mailing Add: P.O. Box 591, Janesville, Wis. 53545.

HOUGH, JOHN HOWARD D
b. Magnolia, Miss, 12/22/00; married. Educ: Miss. State Univ; Stetson Univ; Chi Psi. Miss. State Rep, 60-64. Bus. & Prof. Pos: Farmer; ginner; realtor-developer. Mil. Serv: Miss. State Guard, Col. Mem: Past pres, Indianola Rotary and Indianola C. of C; dir, Delta Coun. Rel: Baptist. Mailing Add: Indianola, Miss. 38751. (1967)

HOUGHTELING, JOSEPH CANNON D
b. San Francisco, Calif, 12/7/24; s. William Houghteling and Virginia Le Seure H; wid; c. Anne, Elizabeth and Mary. Educ: Col. of the Holy Cross, Worcester, Mass, B.S, 45; Yale, B.A, 47. Polit. & Govt. Pos: Mem, Calif. Dem. State Cmt, 50-67; del, Dem. Nat. Conv, 56 & 60; mem, Calif. State Park Cmn, 59-61, chmn, 61-62; v.chmn, San Francisco Bay Study Cmn, 63; mem, Calif. Hwy. Cmn, 64-65. Bus. & Prof. Pos: Pres, Gilroy Evening Dispatch, Calif, 49-; pres, Los Gatos Times-Observer, 53-; pres, Pleasanton Times, 55-; ed-publisher, Sunnydale Daily Standard, 56-65; pres, Diablo Press Inc, 67- Mil. Serv: Entered as A/S, Naval Res, 43, released as Ens, 46, after serv. in NROTC then U.S.S. Ocklawaha, Pac, 45-46. Publ: 'Confessions of a Highway Commissioner,' Cry Calif, 66. Mem: Sigma Delta Chi. Legal Res: 5 Fenwood Dr, Atherton, Calif. 94025. Mailing Add: 440 Pacific Ave, San Francisco, Calif. 94133.

HOUGLAND, GERALD LEE R
Kans. State Rep.
b. Olathe, Kans, 3/19/32; s. Howard F. Hougland and Lois Allison H; m. 11/25/53 to Elizabeth Jane Turner; c. Steven C, Michael B, Blaine A. and Allison L. Educ: Washburn Univ, B.A, 58, LL.B, 59; Alpha Phi Omega; Delta Theta Phi. Polit. & Govt. Pos: Dep. prosecuting attorney, Johnson Co, Kans, 60-67; Kans. State Rep, 16th Dist, 69- Bus. & Prof. Pos: Private law practice, 59-60, 67- Mil. Serv: Entered as Pvt, Army, 53, released as Cpl, 55, after serv. as Spec. Agent, Counter-Intel. Corps, Continental U.S, 53-55; Nat. Defense and Good Conduct Medals. Mem: Am, Kans. and Johnson Co. Bar Asns; Am. Trial Lawyers Asn; Am. Legion; Optimist; Johnson Co. Navy League; troop cmt. chmn, Boy Scouts. Rel: Methodist. Legal Res: 1900 W. Hwy. 56, Olathe, Kans. 66061. Mailing Add: P.O. Box 373, Olathe, Kans. 66061.

HOULEY, ROBERT D. D
Conn. State Sen.
b. Berlin, N.H, 11/20/27; s. James Feeney Houley and Val Marquis H; m. 10/27/57 to Helen M. Daly; c. James Feeney, Kathleen Anne and Elizabeth Ruth. Educ: Univ. N.H, B.S, 53; Theta Kappa Phi; Newman Club; N.H. Club; Senior Skulls. Polit. & Govt. Pos: Secy, Zoning Cmn, Vernon, Conn, 65-66, chmn, Econ. Develop. Cmt, 65-67, mem, Dem. Town Cmt, 65- and bd of rep, 67-69; Conn. State Sen, 69- Bus. & Prof. Pos: Sales rep, L.G. Balfour Co, Mass, 53-59, sales mgr, 59-61 and dist. sales mgr, commercial, 61- Mil. Serv: Entered as Pvt, Marine Corp, 46, released as Cpl, 48, after serving in 8th Marines, 2nd Div. Mem: Nat. Soc. State Legislators. Rel: Roman Catholic. Legal Res: 75 Mercine Rd, Vernon, Conn. 06086. Mailing Add: P.O. Box 0035, Vernon, Conn. 06086.

HOUSE, BYRON O. R
b. St. Louis, Mo, 9/27/02; s. Harold H. House and Olive Edwards H; m. 6/9/25 to Mildred Holston; c. James B, Marilyn (Mrs. Enwright) and Dorothy Holston. Educ: Univ. Ill, LL.B, 26; Phi Alpha Delta; Pi Kappa Phi. Polit. & Govt. Pos: States attorney, Wash. Co, Ill, 45-46; Judge, Third Circuit Court, 56-57; Justice, Ill. Supreme Court, 57-; mem. adv. cmt, Nat. Cmn. Reform Fed. Criminal Laws, 67- Mem: Univ. Club, Chicago; Mo. Athletic Club. Rel: Presbyterian. Mailing Add: 320 W. St. Louis St, Nashville, Ill. 62263.

HOUSE, LEVERETTE D. D
b. Tex; m. 1929 to Hazel Cassatt H; c. Helen (Mrs. Seabolt), Pauline, Jane. Polit. & Gov. Pos: Calif. State Assemblyman, 56-66. Bus. & Prof. Pos: Wholesale Oil Distributor. Mem: Past pres, Brawley Rotary; Imperial Lions; Del Rio Country Club; past Master, Masonic Imperial Lodge No. 390, Royal Arch Mason; 32nd Degree Mason; former DeMolay Chap. Dad; Brawley Elks Club; former Dir, Brawley C. of C; Chmn, Brawley Polio Drive, 2 yrs; Co. Polio Bd. Rel: First Methodist Church, Brawley. Mailing Add: Brawley, Calif. 92227. (1967)

HOUSE, LLOYD LYNN D
Ariz. State Rep.
b. Winslow, Ariz, 10/24/31; s. Albert House and Elizabeth H; m. 7/31/52 to Victoria Elena Monsegur; c. Josephine Victoria, Electa Elena, Margaret Melanie and Lloyd Lynn, II. Educ: Bacone Col, 49-50; North. Ariz. Univ, B.Ed, 58. Polit. & Govt. Pos: Teacher adv, Bur of Indian Affairs, 58-59, proj. develop. officer, 63; resident rep, Social Security Admin, 59-63; Ariz. State Rep, Third Dist, 67- Bus. & Prof. Pos: Dir. Social Security, Navajo Tribe, Window Rock, Ariz, 63- Mil. Serv: Entered as Pvt, Marine Corps, 50, released as Pfc, 54; Korean Presidential Unit Citation; Korean Serv. Medal with 3 Stars; UN Serv. Medal; A/1st, Air Force Res, 64-67. Publ: A History of the Navajo for the Elementary School (unpublished), 55. Mem: VFW; Lions; PTA; Marine Corps League. Rel: Episcopal. Legal Res: 301 Shonto Blvd, Window Rock, Ariz. 86515. Mailing Add: P.O. Box 98, Window Rock, Ariz. 86515.

HOUSE, LUTHER PORTER, SR. D
b. Adolphus, Ky, 9/30/96; s. M.C. House and Ella Read Dalton H; m. to Lucy Moss Harris; c. Luther Porter, Jr. Educ: Scottsville High Sch, Ky, 4 years. Polit. & Govt. Pos: Ky. State Rep, Frankfort, Dist. Four, 32-33; asst. state tax cmnr, 34-35; rural letter carrier, 67-68; del, Dem. Nat. Conv, 68. Mil. Serv: Pvt, Marine Corps, 18-19. Mem: Mason; Am. Legion; Rotary. Rel: Methodist. Mailing Add: 218 W. Main, Scottsville, Ky. 42164.

HOUSE, MARY CORBIN D
Committeewoman, Ark. State Dem. Cmt.
b. Clay, Ky, 4/7/25; d. Lonnie James Corbin and Georgia Alma Clark C; m. 10/2/48 to Howard Leland House; c. Dianne Lee. Educ: St. Anthony's Sch.

Nursing, Louisville, Ky; Nazareth Col, Ky. Polit. & Govt. Pos: Committeewoman, Ark. State Dem. Cmt, 66-; third v.pres, Dem. Women's Club Ark, 67-68; del, Dem. Nat. Conv, 68. Mem: Nat. Asn. Jr. Auxiliaries, Inc; Dem. Women's Club of Independence Co.(treas); Eastern Star; Batesville Jr. Auxiliary (pres). Rel: Methodist. Mailing Add: 1775 Highland Rd, Batesville, Ark. 72501.

HOUSE, MITCHEL PATRIE, JR. D
b. Macon, Ga, 11/30/34; s. Mitchel Patrie House, Sr, and Mamie O'Cain H; m. 10/4/59 to Elizabeth Glennelle Bryant; c. Laura Elizabeth and Mitchel Patrie, III. Educ: Mercer Univ, B.A, 56; Walter F. George Sch. of Law, LL.B, cum laude, 59; Sigma Alpha Epsilon; Delta Theta Phi; Outstanding Freshman Law Student, 56; Outstanding Sr. Law Student, 59. Polit. & Govt. Pos: Spec. legal counsel, City of Macon, Ga, 59-63; Ga. State Rep, 63-64. Bus. & Prof. Pos: Attorney-at-law, Macon, 58- Mil. Serv: Ga. Army Nat. Guard, Maj, asst. staff judge adv. Mem: 40 et 8; Am. Legion; Blue Key; Ga, Am, Macon Bar Asns; Ga. Asn. of Plaintiffs' Trial Attorneys; Macon Legal Aid Soc; Am. Trial Lawyers Asn; Nat. Guard Asn. of the U.S. and Ga; Exchange Club of Bibb Co.(pres, 61-62); bd. of control, Ga. State Exchange Clubs, 62-63. Publ: Author of Contracts Title, Ga. Encyclop. of Law. Rel: Episcopal. Mailing Add: Macon, Ga. 32104.

HOUSE, RAYMOND DURWARD D
Chmn, Laurel Co. Dem. Exec. Cmt, Ky.
b. Laurel Co, Ky, 5/26/22; s. Matt House and Emma Young H; m. 3/21/48 to Zula House; c. Raymond Durwood and Darrell Edwin. Educ: Sue Bennett Col, Ky. Polit. & Govt. Pos: Chmn, Laurel Co. Dem. Exec. Cmt, 64-; Laurel Co. campaign chmn, Johnson for President. Bus. & Prof. Pos: Owner, House's Garage, 46- Mil. Serv: Entered as Seaman, Navy, 43, released as Gunners Mate 1/C, 46, after serv. in 5th Amphibious Forces; Letter of Commendation; Am. Theater and European-African-Middle East Ribbons; Asiatic-Pac. Ribbon with 4 Battle Stars; Philippine Liberation Medal with 2 Battle Stars; Victory Medal with 1 Battle Star. Mem: Am. Legion; VFW. Rel: Baptist. Mailing Add: Box 424, West Fifth St, London, Ky. 40741. (1967)

HOUSE, VAL A, JR. D
Chmn, Allen Co. Dem. Exec. Cmt, Ky.
b. Scottsville, Ky, 6/22/29; s. Val A. House and Elsie Siegrist H; single. Educ: Centre Col, B.A, 50; Univ. Louisville, LL.B, 54; Phi Delta Theta; Phi Alpha Delta. Polit. & Govt. Pos: Master Cmnr, Circuit Court, Allen Co, Ky, 58-65; Chmn, Allen Co. Dem. Exec. Cmt, 58- Bus. & Prof. Pos: Smith & Smith, Attorneys, Louisville, Ky, 57-58; attorney-at-law, Scottsville, 58- Mil. Serv: Entered as E-2, Army, 54, released as Specialist 3/C, 56, after serv. in U.S. Army Terminal Command, Atlantic Theatre, Ft. Knox, Ky. Mem: Pres, Allen Co. Jaycees, 65; chmn, Allen Co. United Givers Fund, 65. Rel: Methodist. Legal Res: 510 E. Cherry St, Scottsville, Ky. 42164. Mailing Add: Box 454, Scottsville, Ky. 42164.

HOUSE, VINCENT F. R
Secy, 50th Assembly Dist, Los Angeles Co. Rep. Cent. Cmt, Calif.
b. Salt Lake City, Utah, 1/5/38; s. Vincent H. House and Bernadine Marron H; m. 5/31/58 to Thekla Lamberty; c. Liana, Kevin and Leslie. Educ: Rosemead High Sch, Calif, 2 years. Polit. & Govt. Pos: Secy, 50th Assembly Dist, Los Angeles Co. Rep. Cent. Cmt, Calif, 69-, 25th Cong. Dist, currently. Bus. & Prof. Pos: Field rep, Hycon Mfg, Monrovia, Calif, 62-66, acting proj. engr, 66-68; pres, V & T Enterprises, La Puente, Calif, currently. Mil. Serv: Entered as Pvt, Air Force, 55, released as A 2/C, 59, after serv. in 405th Tactical Air Command Missile Wing, ETO, 56-59; Good Conduct Medal; Outstanding Unit Citation; Presidential Unit Citation; Guided Missile Insignia. Mem: U.S. Jaycees; La Puente Valley Jaycees. Jaycee of the Month; Key Man Award. Rel: Catholic. Mailing Add: 358 Dalesford, La Puente, Calif. 91744.

HOUSE, WILLIAM H. DFL
b. Rainy Lake, Ontario, Canada; married; c. three. Educ: Univ. Minn, B.S; Univ. Minn, Duluth, M.A. Polit. & Govt. Pos: Minn. State Rep, 59-69. Bus. & Prof. Pos: Instr, Two Harbors High Sch. Mem: First pres, Am. Fedn. of Teachers, 737; Minn. Educ. Asn; v.pres, Lake Co. Centennial Cmt; adv. cmt, Great Lake Fisheries, 56-61; Moose; Lake Co. Sportsmen's Club; AF&AM. Rel: Lutheran; pres, Bethlehem Lutheran Church. Mailing Add: W. Star Route, Two Harbors, Minn. 55616. (1967)

HOUSER, THOMAS JAMES R
Chmn, Exec. Cmt, Cook Co. Rep. Cent. Cmt, Ill.
b. Chicago, Ill, 6/28/29; s. Tom Houser and Mayme Mikulecky H; m. 10/28/54 to Jo-Ann Ochsenhirt; c. Deborah Ann, Deneen Jo and David Gerad. Educ: Hanover Col, B.A, 51; Adv. Sch. of Int. Studies, Wash, D.C, 52; Northwestern Univ. Law Sch, J.D, 59; Gamma Sigma Phi; Beta Theta Phi. Polit. & Govt. Pos: Rep. committeeman, Wheeling Twp, Ill, 62-66; campaign mgr, Percy for Gov, 64 and Percy for Sen. Cmt, 66; chmn, exec. cmt, Cook Co. Rep. Cent. Cmt, 64- Bus. & Prof. Pos: Commerce attorney, Asn. of Western R.R, 59-62. Mil. Serv: Entered as Pvt, Army, 54, released as Sgt, 56, after serv. in Counter-Intel. Corps, Germany. Mem: Am, Ill. and Chicago Bar Asns; Exec. Club; Chicago Cmt; Union League Club of Chicago; Tavern Club of Chicago; Counter-Intel. Club. of Chicago. All conf. col. halfback, Hanover Col, 50; all city high sch. football, Chicago, 46. Rel: Christian Church. Mailing Add: 219 N. Hickory, Arlington Heights, Ill. 60004.

HOUSER, WILLIAM FREEMAN R
Chmn, Exec. Cmt. Webb Co. Rep. Party, Tex.
b. Staunton, Va, 3/6/03; s. Richard Lavier Houser and Carrie Freeman Parrish H; m. 8/15/36 to Rosabel Bunn; c. Philip Stuart and William Freeman, Jr. Educ: Va. Polytech. Inst. Polit. & Govt. Pos: Chmn, Exec. Cmt. Webb Co. Rep. Party, Tex, 66-; minor posts, Rep. Party. Bus. & Prof. Pos: Geologist, Cities Serv. Oil Co, 25-27; independent oil operator, 27-33 & 36-; landman, Superior Oil Co, 33-36. Mem: Am. Asn. Petrol. Landmen; Corpus Christi Landman's Asn; Am. Soc. Mining Engrs; Elks; Kiwanis. Rel: Methodist. Legal Res: 2100 Meadow Apt. 106, Laredo, Tex. 78040. Mailing Add: Box 846, Laredo, Tex. 78040.

HOUSLEY, GRADY EUGENE D
Ga. State Rep.
b. Copperhill, Tenn, 12/19/37; s. Grady Melvin Housley and Charlotte Stymus H; m. 7/25/60 to Mary Dupree; c. Julie Desiree and Zachary Eugene. Educ: John Marshall Univ, LL.B, 59. Polit. & Govt. Pos: Pres, Young Dem. Cobb Co, Ga, 58-60; mem, Cobb Co. Bd. of Educ, 64-68, pres, 67-68; mem, State Dem. Exec. Cmt, 66-; mem. and Lt. Col, Aide-de-Camp, Gov. Staff, Ga, 67-; Ga. State Rep, Dist. 117, Post 1, 69- Bus. & Prof. Pos: Mem, City of Marietta Employees Retirement Bd, Ga, 63-64; referee, Juvenile Court, Cobb Co, 64-69; pub. rels. dir, Housley Riding Equip, Marietta, 69- Publ: 'Juvenile Delinquency: A National Problem,' 64 and 'Your Child's Future Depends On You,' Communities Newspapers Inc, 68. Mem: Lions; Marietta-Cobb Boys Club; Ga. Sheriff's Boys Ranch; Jaycees; Nat. Sch. Bd. Asn; Ga. Peace Officers Asn. Distinguished Citizen Award, Marietta Jaycees, 68; Outstanding Serv. Award, Cobb Co. Bd. of Educ, 69. Rel: Baptist. Mailing Add: 1011 Housley Rd, Marietta, Ga. 30060.

HOUSMAN, KENNETH ALFRED R
Asst. Postmaster Gen. for Personnel, Post Off. Dept.
b. N.Y.C, 11/16/25; s. A.J. Housman and Ruth Sorely H; m. 7/31/49 to Patricia Eagan; c. Pamela Ann and Jeffrey. Educ: Harvard Univ, B.A. cum laude, 47. Polit. & Govt. Pos: Mem, Gov. Reagan's Task Force to Study Efficiency and Cost Control of the Exec. Br, Calif, 67; Asst. Postmaster Gen. for Personnel, Post Off. Dept, 69- Bus. & Prof. Pos: V.pres. opers, Englander Co, Union Carbide Corp, Chicago, Ill, 64-66; mgr. indust. rels, fibers and fabrics div, Union Carbide Corp, N.Y.C, 66-67, mgr. pub. affairs, 67-69. Mem: Mason; Am. Philatelic Soc; Soc. of Bur. Issues Assoc. Nominee, Bus. Citizenship Award, Nat. Businessmen Coun, 68. Rel: Presbyterian. Legal Res: New Canaan, Conn. Mailing Add: 7104 Arrowood Rd, Bethesda, Md. 20014.

HOUSTON, FRANCIS D
b. Waycross, Ga, 12/20/26; s. Charley Thomas Houston and Beckian Kimmons H; m. 11/26/64 to Jacqueline Copland; c. Tony Lynn. Educ: Grad, Ga. Teachers Col; Univ. Ga; Atlanta Law Sch, LL.B, LL.M. Polit. & Govt. Pos: Judge, City Court of Blackshear, 67-; Ga. State Rep, 63-66. Bus. & Prof. Pos: Attorney, Blackshear, 54- Mil. Serv: Army, Sgt; Expert Inf. Badge and overseas medals. Mem: Am. Legion, comdr, Post 181, 58-61; Mason, worshipful master, Blackshear Lodge 270, F&AM, 62. Rel: Baptist. Mailing Add: Blackshear, Ga. 31516. (1967)

HOUSTON, HAROLD J. D
b. Near Dow City, Iowa, 3/10/17; s. John T. Houston and Susan Kelly H; m. 1939 to Jeanne Buss; c. Michael, Stephen, Nancy and Kathleen; grandchildren, David Houston and Gregory Houston. Educ: Dow City High Sch, 1933. Polit. Pos: Iowa State Rep, 66; Crawford Co. Bd. of Supvrs. Bus. & Prof. Pos: Farming and Trucking. Mem: Crawford Co. Fair Bd; 4H Club; ASA Committeeman. 1967 Legal Res: Dow City, Iowa 51528. No mailing address available. (1967)

HOUSTON, HENRY ERVIN 'HANK' R
City Councilman, San Dimas, Calif.
b. Montgomery, Ala, 5/6/28; s. Henry H. Houston and Annie M. Gibbons H; m. 2/19/50 to Margarett A. Austin; c. Lori Ann and Henry Michael. Educ: Draughons Bus. Col, Memphis, Tenn; Memphis Col. of Accountancy. Polit. & Govt. Pos: Mem, Planning Cmn, San Dimas, Calif, 65, city councilman, 66-; mem, Calif. Rep. State Cent. Cmt, 67- Bus. & Prof. Pos: Acct, Lumber Indust, 50-52; auditor, Standard Oil Co, Denver, Colo, 52-57; acct, Mobil Oil Co, Los Angeles, Calif, 57-59; P.U.C. analyst, Surburban Water Co, 59-60; sales agent, Allstate Ins. Co, Pasadena, 60- Mil. Serv: Entered as Pvt, Army and Air Force, 46, released as Sgt, 49, after serv. in Air Transport Command and Strategic Air Command, Far East, Philippines, U.S. and Europe. Mem: AF&AM; League of Calif. Cities; Eastern Star; Contract Cities Asn; Rotary. Rel: Protestant. Legal Res: 1215 Valebrook, Glendora, Calif. 91740. Mailing Add: Box 521, San Dimas, Calif. 91773.

HOUSTON, HOWARD EDWIN R
b. Ryan, Iowa, 11/2/10; s. Frederick Lincoln Houston and Ida Woodard H; m. 9/9/39 to Frances Gregory Crawford; c. Frederick Woodard and Molly Crawford. Educ: Columbia Univ, A.B, 32; Psi Upsilon (pres). Polit. & Govt. Pos: Mayor, Meriden, Conn, 47-51 & 62-63; chmn, Gov. Cmt. on Med. Schs, 52; chmn, Rep. Town Cmt, Meriden, 52; cmnr, State Welfare Dept, 53-54; dep. dir, U.S. Aid Mission to India, 55-57, dir. and minister, 57-59; mem, Mutual Security Prog. Eval. Team to Peru; chmn, Rep. State Cmt, Health and Welfare; mem, Rep. State Cent. Cmt, Conn, 60-66; del, Conn. Const. Conv, Fifth Cong. Dist, 65. Bus. & Prof. Pos: Dir, Meriden Savings Bank, Meriden Trust and Safe Dep, Co. and Morningside House of N.Y; dir, Bradley Home for Aged, Meriden, 35-54; chmn, Meriden-Wallinford Region Health Coun, 54; chmn, India Cmt. of Asia Soc. of N.Y, 61; mem. assoc. bd, Conn. Bank & Trust Co, 68-; trustee, Colby Jr. Col, New London, N.H, 68-; mem. coun, S.Cent. Commun. Col, Conn, 68-; corporator, Marine Biol. Lab, Woods Hole, Mass, 68- Mil. Serv: Entered as Pvt, Army, 43, released as 1st Lt, 46, after serv. in Med. Serv. Corps, S.W. Pac, 44-46. Mem: Am. Legion; Elks; Mason; Eagles; Rotary; Shuttle Meadow Country Club; Woods Hole Golf Club, Mass; Quissett Yacht Club, Mass; N.Y. Univ. Club; Meriden Home Club, Conn; Hartford Club. Rel: Episcopal. Mailing Add: 691 Preston Ave, Meriden, Conn. 06450.

HOUSTON, NEAL J. R
b. Barre, Vt, 8/22/26; s. Ira Nathaniel Houston and Alice Clyde Quinn H; m. 7/2/49 to Marilyn Mills; c. Deborah Ann, Neal J, Jr, Rebecca Hadley, Virginia Gale, Laura Lee, Alison Joan. Educ: Univ. of Vt, 46-49; Kappa Sigma. Polit. & Govt. Pos: Admin. Asst, Rep. Stafford, R-Vt, 60-; Vt. State Budget Dir, 59; Asst, Gov. of Vt, 55-58. Bus. & Prof. Pos: Reporter, 48-55. Mil. Serv: U.S. Army Air Corps, WW II, 43-45. Mem: Plainfield Village Trustees, Past Pres; Montpelier Rotary Club; Past Pres, Windsor, Vt, Jr. C. of C. Rel: Episcopal, St. Lukes Vestry; Treas, St. Luke's Episcopalian Church. Mailing Add: 1124 Cameron Rd, Alexandria, Va. 22314. (1967)

HOUSTON, NORMAN OLIVER D
b. San Jose, Calif, 10/16/93; s. Oliver James Houston and Lillian L; m. to Edythe L. Pryce; c. Norman B, Ivan J, Elizabeth Jean. Educ: Univ. of Calif; Univ. of South. Calif; Bethune-Cookman Col, LL.D, 51; Wilberforce Univ, LL. D, 51; Kappa Alpha Psi; Sigma Pi Phi. Polit. & Govt. Pos: Exec. Cmt. Gov. Calif. Adv. Coun; Mem, Town Hall, Los Angeles; Trustee, Los Angeles Zoo. Bus. & Prof. Pos: Pres, Golden State Mutual Life Ins. Co, 45-; Controller,

45-49; Dir, Co-founder, 25-; Adv. Bd, Riverside Nat. Bank, Houston. Mil. Serv: U.S. Army, 17-19, Lt, 92nd Div, A.E.F. in France. Mem: Bd. Dir, Crippled Children's Soc, Children's Home Soc; Citizens Com. Commun. Rels; Co-Chmn, Inter-racial Coun. for Business Opportunities; Am. Cancer Soc; Int. Student Center; Int. Exec. Serv. Corps, Wilson-Andrews Found; V.Pres, Dir, Nat. Conf. Christians and Jews; Chmn. Bd, Men of Tomorrow; Bd. Mgrs, Los Angeles YMCA; Am. Mgt. Asn; Life Off. Mgt. Asn. Inst; Ins. Accounting and Statist. Asn; Past Pres, Nat. Ins. Asn; NAACP; Am. Legion; VFW. Rel: Trustee, A.M.E. Church. Mailing Add: 4230 Parva Ave, Los Angeles, Calif, 90027. (1967)

HOUSTON, WILLIAM KYLE R
b. Tacoma, Wash, 1/1/16; m. 7/16/38 to Bunnie Stokes; c. Kyla (Mrs. Medigovich) and William K, Jr. Educ: Univ. Wash, B.A, 37; Harvard Sch. Bus, grad, 38; Sigma Alpha Epsilon. Polit. & Govt. Pos: Chmn, Reagan for Gov. Cmt, Contra Costa Co, Calif, 66; del, Rep. Nat. Conv, 68; chmn, Calif. State Athletic Cmn, 68- Bus. & Prof. Pos: Partner and pres, Conklin Bros, Oakland, San Francisco, Hayward and Santa Rosa, Calif, 47-69; regent, John Kennedy Univ, 67- Mil. Serv: Entered as 2nd Lt, Air Force, 41, released as Lt. Col; Res, 46-62, Lt. Col.(Ret). Mem: Rotary; Mason (32°); Shrine. Rel: Unitarian. Mailing Add: 1 Robert Rd, Orinda, Calif. 94563.

HOUTCHENS, DELTON LOUIS D
Chmn, State Dem. Party, Mo.
b. Deepwater, Mo, 1/14/18; s. Emmet Houtchens and Bessie Lowderman H; m. 11/26/38 to Betty Jo Kirkwood; c. Richard K. and Joyce Sue. Educ: Westminster Col, 36-38; Univ. Mo, LL.B, 41. Polit. & Govt. Pos: Prosecuting attorney, Henry Co, Mo, 43-44; Mo. State Rep, 48-52, Majority Floor Leader, Mo. House of Rep, 50-52; mem, Personnel Adv. Bd. of Mo, 59-64; state wide campaign mgr. for Gov. Warren E. Hearnes, 64; chmn, Mo. State Dem. Party, 65-; del, Dem. Nat. Conv, 68. Mil. Serv: Entered as Pvt, Army, 43, released as 1st Lt, 45, after serv. in Med. Admin. Corps. Mem: Bd. gov, Mo. Bar Asn, 60-64; Shrine; Scottish Rite; Mason; Elks; Am. Legion. Rel: Baptist. Legal Res: 406 S. Eighth St, Clinton, Mo, 64735. Mailing Add: Carney Bldg, Clinton, Mo. 64735.

HOUTHAKKER, HENDRIK SAMUEL R
Mem, Coun. Econ. Adv, Exec. Off. of the Pres.
b. Amsterdam, The Netherlands, 12/31/24; s. Bernard Houthakker and Marion Lichtenstein H; m. 9/8/55 to Anna-Teresa Tymieniecka; c. Louis, Isabella and Jan Nicholas. Educ: Univ. Amsterdam, Drs. Econ, 49. Polit. & Govt. Pos: Consult, Joint Econ. Cmt, U.S. Cong, 57-62; consult, U.S. Treas. Dept, 61-67; sr. staff econ, Coun. Econ. Adv, Exec. Off. of the Pres, 67-68, mem, 69- Bus. & Prof. Pos: Research staff, Univ. Cambridge, 49-51; research staff, Univ. Chicago, 52-53; prof. econ, Stanford Univ, 54-60; prof. econ, Harvard Univ, 60- Publ: Analysis of Family Budgets (with S. J. Prais), Cambridge Univ. Press, 55; Consumer Demand in the United States (with Lester D. Taylor), Harvard Univ. Press, 66; Economic Policy for the Farm Sector, Am. Enterprise Inst, 67. Mem: Am. Econ. Asn; Am. Statist. Asn; Economet. Soc.(past pres); Int. Statist. Inst; Am. Acad. of Arts and Sci. John Bates Clark Medal, Am. Econ. Asn, 63. Legal Res: 348 Payson Rd, Belmont, Mass. 02178. Mailing Add: Council of Economic Advisers, 315 Executive Office Bldg, Washington, D.C. 20506.

HOVEN, GORDEN ELSWORTH D
b. Antelope, Mont, 8/12/13; s. O.B. Hoven and Eleanora Anderson H; m. 11/15/41 to Madeline Daly; c. Gorden, Jr, Mary Virginia, James Daniel and Renee. Educ: Univ. Mont, LL.B, 37; Sigma Alpha Epsilon. Polit. & Govt. Pos: Former chmn, Hill Co. Dem. Cmt, Mont; attorney, secy, Hill Co. Water Dist, 63-; exec. secy. and attorney, Hill Co. Commun. Action, 65-; city attorney, Havre, 65- Mil. Serv: Entered as Pvt, Air Force, 44, released as Cpl, 45. Mem: Mont. Bar Asn; Elks. Rel: Lutheran. Legal Res: 1225 Seventh Ave, Havre, Mont. 59501. Mailing Add: Box 55, Havre, Mont. 59501. (1967)

HOVERMALE, RALPH BEN D
b. Berkeley Springs, W.Va, 3/29/09; s. O.B. Hovermale and Edna Unger H; m. 11/28/35 to Anna Hunter; c. Anna Jo (Mrs. Crosby) and Cynthia Ann. Polit. & Govt. Pos: W.Va. State Del, 62-66; mem, Bd. of Educ, 9 years; former pres, Sch. Bd. Bus. & Prof. Pos: Pres. and mgr, Berkeley Club Bottling & Mfg. Co, Ind; bd. of dir, Citizens Nat. Bank. Mem: Kiwanis; C. of C; Moose; Morgan Co. Wildlife Asn; pres, Morgan Co. Econ. Develop. Corp. Rel: Methodist. Mailing Add: Berkeley Springs, W.Va. 25411.

HOWARD, CHARLES ALLEN, JR. R
Chmn, S.Dak. State Rep. Cent. Cmt.
b. Aberdeen, S.Dak, 8/11/04; s. Charles Allen Howard and Grace Brown H; single. Educ: North. State Col; Princeton Univ, A.B; Harvard Law Sch, LL.B; Phi Beta Kappa; Delta Sigma Rho; Pi Kappa Delta. Polit. & Govt. Pos: Mem, S.Dak. State Rep. Cent. Cmt, 50-65, chmn, 65-; del, Rep. Nat. Conv, 56 & 64; mem, S.Dak. State Rep. Chmn. Adv. Cmt; mem, Rep. Nat. Cmt, currently. Bus. & Prof. Pos: Pres, Howard & Hedger Co, 33-; trustee, Huron Col. Mil. Serv: Entered as 1st Lt, Army Air Force, 42, released as Maj, 46, after serv. in 56th and 357th Fighter Group, ETO; Lt. Col.(Ret), Army Air Force Res; Bronze Star; Victory Medal ; Distinguished Unit Citation and Cluster; ETO Ribbon with 6 Battle Stars; German Occupation Ribbon. Mem: Asn. Bar, City of New York; Mason; Scottish Rite; Shrine; DeMolay; Elks; Rotary; Am. Legion; Aberdeen Country Club; Nassau Club; Princeton Club, N.Y. S.Dak. Amateur Golf Champion, 33. Rel: Episcopal. Legal Res: 1201 N. Main St, Aberdeen, S.Dak. 57401. Mailing Add: Box 248, Aberdeen, S.Dak. 57401.

HOWARD, CHARLES BILLY R
Educ: Butler Univ; Phi Delta Theta. Polit. & Govt. Pos: Ind. State Rep, 63-69; co-chmn, Econ. Develop. Study Cmn, 64. Bus. & Prof. Pos: Ins; real estate; investments; chartered property casualty underwriter, Mem: Ind, Nat. Asns. of Ins. Agents; State, U.S, City C. of C; Mason; Toastmasters; Elks; Columbia Club; Culver Mil. Acad. Rel: Christian Church. Mailing Add: Route 1, Box 300C, Noblesville, Ind. 46060. (1967)

HOWARD, DURHAM W. R
b. Pineville, Ky, 9/24/02; s. Jasper Howard and Mary V. H; m. 9/20/30 to Katherine Morgan; c. Jasper B, John G. and Vivi-Jo (Mrs. John M. Bingham). Educ: Union Col, Ky, 27-29; East. Ky. Univ, 30. Polit. & Govt. Pos: Ky. State Rep, 48, 50, 56 & 58, minority leader, Ky. House of Rep; Ky. State Sen, 60, 62, 64 & 66, minority leader, Ky. State Senate. Bus. & Prof. Pos: Sch. teacher and prin, 28-35; dir. and mgr, First Fed. Savings & Loan Asn, 35-, now exec. v.pres. Mem: Past pres, Ky. Bldg. Savings and Loan League; F&AM; Scottish Rite (32°); past pres, Rotary. Conserv. Award of Merit, awarded by Gov, 66. Rel: Baptist. Mailing Add: 186 Summit Dr, Pineville, Ky. 40977.

HOWARD, ED D
Tex. State Rep.
b. Hot Springs, Ark, 4/13/37; s. Verna Elisha Howard and Ruth Moryne Jackson H; m. 1/15/60 to JoAnn Jay; c. Eric, Jay and Lee. Educ: Abilene Christian Col, B.S, 59; South. Methodist Univ, 60-61. Polit. & Govt. Pos: Tex. State Rep, Bowie Co, 69- Bus. & Prof. Pos: V.pres, Gibson Wholesale Distributors, Inc, Texarkana, Tex, 59-; exec. v.pres, Howard-Gibco Corp, 69- Mem: Bd. dirs, Texarkana Red Cross; bd. dirs, United Way Fund; Tex. Soc. Welfare Asn. (bd. mem); Kiwanis; C. of C.(cmt. of 100). Rel: Church of Christ. Mailing Add: 4007 Potomac, Texarkana, Tex. 75501.

HOWARD, EDWIN MOREY, JR. R
Chmn, Hamilton Rep. Town Cmt, Mass.
b. Winthrop, Mass, 4/4/38; s. Edwin Morey Howard and Dorothy Penney H. (deceased); m. to Laura Harris; c. Channing B. and Catherine G. Educ: Burdett Col; Northeast. Univ; twice pres, Delta Nu Omega. Polit. & Govt. Pos: Chmn, Hamilton Rep. Town Cmt, Mass, 67-; pres, Essex Co. Rep. Club, 69- Bus. & Prof. Pos: Dir, Whitman & Howard, Inc, Engrs. and Architects, Boston, Mass, 58-59; pres, Howard Cem. Corp, 68-; owner and dir, Alonzo B. Reed, Inc, Engr, Planners & Architects, 69-; trustee, Seaside Develop. Trust, Quincy, 69-; owner and dir, Commun. Planning Serv, 69- Mil. Serv: Entered as Airman, Air Force, 62, released as Staff Sgt, 67, after serv. in 619th Air Force Hosp, Chief Nursing Serv. Mem: YMCA (chmn. finance cmt); founder, Learning Center. Rel: Protestant. Legal Res: 10 Meyer Lane, Box 344, Hamilton, Mass. 01936. Mailing Add: 177 Milk St, Boston, Mass. 02109.

HOWARD, FLORENCE C. R
V.Coordinator, Milwaukee Co. Rep. Party, Wis.
b. Milwaukee, Wis, 7/9/95; d. Nick Barbian and Katherine Grossbier B; m. 6/4/21 to Martin Farley Howard; c. Shirley (Mrs. Dudgeon), Patricia (Mrs. Nigh) and Lorayne (Mrs. Karweik). Polit. & Govt. Pos: Organizer and past pres, South Side Rep. Women's Club, Wis; del, State, Dist. and Co. Conv. and Caucus, 46-; mem. exec. cmt, 17th Ward Milwaukee Co. Rep. Party, 56-66; mem. exec. cmt, Milwaukee Co. Rep. Party, 60-62, v.chmn, 62- and mem. Constitution Revision Cmt, 65 & 66; alternate del, Rep. Nat. Conv, 64. Bus. & Prof. Pos: Editorial and instr, Internal Revenue Dept, 45-55. Mem: Am. Legion Auxiliary; 4th of July Cmt; Christian Mothers. Rel: Catholic. Mailing Add: 2500 S. Howell Ave, Milwaukee, Wis. 53207.

HOWARD, GENE C. D
Okla. State Sen.
b. Perry, Okla, 9/26/26; s. Joe W. Howard and Nell Lillian Brown; m. 3/10/51 to Marian Ruth Berg; c. Jean Ann and Joe Ted. Educ: Univ. Okla, LL.B, 51; Phi Delta Phi. Polit. & Govt. Pos: Pres, Young Dem. Okla, 54; secy, Tulsa Co. Elec. Bd, 54; Okla. State Rep, 58-62; del, Dem. Nat. Conv, 64; Okla. State Sen, 64- Mil. Serv: Entered as Pvt, Army, 44, released as Sgt, 46, after serv. in Gen. Hq, Army, Pac, World War II, Asiatic-Pac. Theatre, 45-46; re-entered as Capt, Air Force during Berlin Crisis, 61-62; Maj, Air Force Res, 69; Asiatic-Pac. Ribbon with Two Battle Stars; Philippine Liberation with One Battle Star. Mem: Okla. Bar Asn; Mason (32°); Okla. Cattleman's Asn; Tulsa Consistory; Tulsa Club. Named Outstanding Young Attorney, Tulsa Co. Bar Asn, 53. Rel: Christian Church. Legal Res: 1738 S. Erie Place, Tulsa, Okla. 74112. Mailing Add: 4815 S. Harvard, Tulsa, Okla. 74135.

HOWARD, HENRY SEYMOUR R
Chmn, St. Lawrence Co. Rep. Cmt, N.Y.
b. Waddington, N.Y, 6/22/10; s. Joel Manning Howard and Gertrude Crapser H; m. 9/19/59 to Lilian Gould Cheshire. Educ: Univ. Mich, A.B, 31; Albany Law Sch, LL.B, 37, J.D, 68; Delta Sigma Pi; Scabbard and Blade. Polit. & Govt. Pos: Supvr, Waddington, N.Y, 48-51; dir. of Civil Defense, St. Lawrence Co, 51-54; mem, St. Lawrence Co. Rep. Cmt, 48-, chmn, 65- Mil. Serv: Entered as Capt, Army Air Corp, 41, released as Col, 46, after serving in various Army Air Corp.Units, Asiatic-Pac. Theatre, 45-46; Col, Air Force Reserves, 46-61, Retired; Bronze Star Medal; Am. Defense Serv. Medal; Am. Theatre Medal; Asiatic-Pac. Theatre Medal; Occup. Medal; World War II Victory Medal; Armed Forces Res. Medal. Mem: St. Lawrence Co. and N.Y. State Bar Asns; F&AM; Shrine; Waddington, N.Y. and Nat. Grange; Am. Legion; VFW. Rel: Presbyterian. Mailing Add: Waddington, N.Y. 13694.

HOWARD, JAMES J. D
U.S. Rep, N.J.
b. Irvington, N.J, 7/24/27; s. George P. Howard and Bernice M. H; m. to Marlene Vetrano; c. Kathleen (Mrs. Lowther), Lenore, Marie. Educ: St. Bonaventure Univ, B.A, 52; Rutgers Univ, M.Ed, 58. Polit. & Govt. Pos: Pres, Monmouth Co. Educ. Asn; mem, Del. Assembly of N.J. Educ. Asn; mem, Nat. Educ. Asn; U.S. Rep, N.J, 64-; del, Dem. Nat. Conv, 68. Bus. & Prof. Pos: Teacher and acting prin. in Wall Twp. Sch. Syst, 52-64. Mil. Serv: Navy; S. Pac. Theatre. Mailing Add: U.S. House of Representatives, Washington, D.C. 20515.

HOWARD, JOHN MELL D
b. Stephens, Ga, 7/9/06; s. Charles Lewis Howard and Carrie Susan Young H; m. to Lucy Gertrude Moore. Polit. & Govt. Pos: Chmn, Oglethorpe Co. Dem. Cmt, Ga, 67-69. Bus. & Prof. Pos: Owner, Howard Merc.Co. Rel: Methodist. Mailing Add: Stephens, Ga. 30667. (1967)

HOWARD, KENITH RAYMOND, JR. R
Kans. State Rep.
b. Kansas City, Kans, 10/23/31; s. Kenith Raymond Howard, Sr. and Margaret Brinkmeier H; m. 12/19/53 to Jean Marie Almon; c. Gregory, Jeffrey and Mark. Educ: Univ. Kans, A.B. and LL.B, 55; Phi Delta Phi; Alpha Tau Omega. Polit. & Govt. Pos: Treas, Prairie Village Rep. Club, Kans, 60; committeeman, Johnson Co. Rep. Cent. Cmt, 62-68; city attorney, Westwood, 62-; v.chmn, Johnson Co. Young Rep, 63-64; committeeman, Gr. Overland

Park Rep. Asn, at present; mem, Rep. State Party Coun, 64, 66 & 68, mem. resolutions cmt, 68; Kans. State Rep, 11th Dist, 64-66 and 23rd Dist, 66-; mem, Lewis and Clark Trail Cmt. in Kans, 65- Bus. & Prof. Pos: Attorney and sr. partner, Keach, Howard & Hursh, 57- Mil. Serv: Entered as 2nd Lt, Air Force, Judge Adv. Gen. Corps, 55; Capt, Air Force Res, at present. Publ: 'There Ought To Be A Law,' Johnson Co. Herald, 2/17/66 and 3/3/66; newspaper column, Loyd Neff and Son, Publishers, 64-67. Mem: Am, Kans, Mo. and Johnson Co. Bar Asns; Am. and Kans. Trial Lawyers Asns; Am. Judicature Soc; C. of C; Rotary; Nat. Soc. of State Legislators. Rel: Methodist. Mailing Add: 6510 W. 67th, Overland Park, Kans. 66202.

HOWARD, LAURENCE EDWARD D
Chmn, Fifth Dist. Dem. Party, Mich.
b. Ionia, Mich, 2/15/34; s. Leo Eugene Howard and Marion Burtch H; m. 8/23/58 to Marilyn Mueller; c. Michael Laurence, Timothy Leo, Nancy Ann and Thomas Patrick. Educ: Northwest. Univ, 54-56; Univ. Notre Dame, B.S, 58; Univ. Notre Dame Law Sch, J.D, 61. Polit. & Govt. Pos: Asst. city attorney, Grand Rapids, Mich, 62-64; cand, U.S. Rep, Fifth Cong. Dist, Mich, 68; alternate del, Dem. Nat. Conv, 68; chmn, Fifth Dist. Dem. Party, 69- Bus. & Prof. Pos: Partner, Law Firm of VanderWerff, Howard & Addison, 67- Mil. Serv: Entered as Pvt, Army, 54, released as Specialist 3/C, 56 after serv. at Fifth Army Hq, Chicago, Ill, 54-56. Mem: State Bar of Mich; Grand Rapids Bar Asn; K. of C; St. Paul the Apostle Sch. Bd. Rel: Catholic. Mailing Add: 1917 Woodcliff, S.E, Grand Rapids, Mich. 49506.

HOWARD, NELSON E. R
b. Sanbornton, N.Y, 5/24/03; married; c. 1 son. Polit. & Govt. Pos: N.H. State Sen, 63-69. Bus. & Prof. Pos: Retired businessman; wholesale grocery; textile and real estate; pres, K M H Corp. Mem: Trustee, N.H. State Sanatorium; past trustee, exec. cmt, Franklin Hosp. Asn; Franklin C. of C; Bd. of Incorporators of the Franklin Savings Bank; Franklin Home for the Aged Asn; Farm Bur; N.H. Holstein-Friesian Club; Fish and Game Club; Mojalaki Country Club; Past Exalted Ruler, Franklin Lodge, Elks; Franklin Rotary Club; Franklin Grange; Franklin K. of C. Rel: Catholic. Mailing Add: Webster Lake, N.H. (1967)

HOWARD, RAYMOND D
Mo. State Sen.
b. St. Louis, Mo, 3/13/35; s. Raymond Howard and Geneva Howard H; single. Educ: Univ. of Wis, B.S, 56; St. Louis Law Sch, LL.B, 61; Kappa Alpha Psi. Polit. & Govt. Pos: Mo. State Rep, 65-69; Mo. State Sen, 69- Mil. Serv: Entered as 2nd Lt, Army, 56, released as 1st Lt, 58, after serv. in 82nd Air Borne Inf. Div; Parachute Wings. Publ: 'Abolition of Capital Punishment,' 65 and 'Racial Protests,' 66, St. Louis Bar J. Mem: Chmn, Criminal Cmn, St. Louis Bar Asn, 65; Am. and Nat. Bar Asns; Am. Trial Lawyer Asn; Nat. Asn. of Defense Law in Criminal Cases; bd. dirs, St. Louis NAACP, 60-62; Jr. C. of C. Distinguished Award as Member of Mo. Legis, St. Louis Bar Asn. Rel: Protestant. Legal Res: 200 Manion House Center, St. Louis, Mo. 63101. Mailing Add: 705 Chestnut, St. Louis, Mo. 63101. (1967)

HOWARD, RHEA D
Mem, State Dem. Exec. Cmt, Tex.
b. Wichita Falls, Tex, 7/25/92; s. Ed. Howard and Jettie Lee Maloney H; m. 10/22/13 to Kathleen Benson; c. Anna Katherine (Mrs. Barnett). Educ: Trinity Univ, Waxahachie, Tex; Eastman Col, Poughkeepsie, N.Y; Sigma Delta Chi. Polit. & Govt. Pos: Mem, Wichita Falls Sch. Bd, 14 years; del, Dem. Nat. Conv, 52, 56, 60, 64 & 68; committeeman, 23rd Senatorial Dist, Tex, 58-66 and 30th Senatorial Dist, 66; mem, State Dem. Exec. Cmt, Tex, currently. Bus. & Prof. Pos: Pres, publisher and ed, Wichita Falls Times and Wichita Falls Record News. Mil. Serv: 1st Lt, Army Nat. Guard, Adjutant on Col.'s staff, World War I. Mem: Nat. Press Club, Wash, D.C; Headliners Club; Assoc. Press; Tex. Daily Newspaper Asn; Am. Soc. of Newspaper Ed; Am Newspapers Publishers Asn; South. Newspaper Publishers' Asn; President's Club; Wichita Falls Country Club; Wichita Club; Air War Col, Maxwell Air Force Base; v.pres. and dir, Indust. Develop, Inc; YMCA Adv. Bd; Mason (32°), Scottish Rite, K.T, Shrine; United Fund, first pres, chmn. and Scott-White Adv. Bd. Wichita Falls Art and Museum; Area Health Facility Planning Cmn; Woman's Forum; dir, Red Cross; bd, Midwest. Univ. Found, Wichita Co. Child Welfare and Youth Develop, Wichita Falls Symphony, Burlington Lines; N. Tex. Oil and Gas Asn; Tex. Law Enforcement and Youth Develop. Found; C. of C. Red River Valley Asn. Elected Publisher of Year by Headliners Club, Austin, Tex, 60. Rel: Presbyterian. Legal Res: 2105 Berkley Dr, Wichita Falls, Tex. 76308. Mailing Add: P.O. Box 120, Wichita Falls, Tex. 76307.

HOWARD, WALTER BOIVIN D
Pub. Rels. Dir, Hamilton Co. Dem. Party, Ohio
b. Carbondale, Pa, 12/20/27; s. Frank Walter Howard and Philomena Donato H; m. 3/19/53 to Jeanne E. Thomas; c. Marc Walter, Melissa Jean, George Gregory, Paul Francis, Marybeth and Patricia Lorraine. Educ: Hobart Col, B.A. cum laude with honors in Econ, 53; Columbia Univ, 53-54; Maxwell Sch. of Citizenship and Pub. Affairs, Syracuse Univ, M.A. with honors, 55; Phi Beta Kappa; Chi Eta Sigma; Sigma Chi; Baccia. Polit. & Govt. Pos: Precinct exec. Clermont Co. Dem. Party, Ohio, 58-62; chmn. speakers bur, Hamilton Co. Dem. Party, 58-62, pub. rels. dir, 62- and mem. steering cmt, currently; mem, Dem. State Platform Cmt, 62, 64 & 66; chmn. election cmt, Young Dem. for Ohio, 66, Citizens for Reams Campaign Cmt, 66 and Hamilton Co. Citizens for Humphrey, 68; del-at-lg, Young Dem. of Ohio, 66-68; del, Dem. Nat. Conv, 68; co-chmn, Businessmen for Humphrey, 68; mem, Hamilton Co. Young Dem, currently. Bus. & Prof. Pos: Gen. commercial supvr, Cincinnati and Suburban Bell Tel. Co, 66-67, gen. pub. rels. supvr, 67-68; pres, B.H.W, Inc, 66-; exec. v.pres, Wabash Consol. Corp, 68. Mil. Serv: Entered as Pvt, Air Force, 45, released as Sgt, 58, after serv. in Air Transport Command, ETO, 45-48. Publ: 'The Economic Impact of the St. Laurence Seaway Power Project,' Mimeograph, 54; 'The Image of Cincinnati,' Images, 69. Mem: Am. Mkt. Asn; Univ. of Cincinnati Tech. Adv. Coun; Advert. Club of Cincinnati; bd. mem, Cancer Coun. of Cincinnati; Census Tract Cmt. of Gr. Cincinnati; C. of C.(chmn. econ. research cmt; bus. indust. dir. cmt); pub. rels. cmt, Cincinnati Symphony Orchestra; Civic Club of Cincinnati; Determined Young Men; Jr. Achievement (bd. mem); del. bd, Pub. Health Fedn. of Gr. Cincinnati; Queen City Asn; Sigma Chi Alumni Chap.(former pres). Recipient of Distinguished Serv. Award, Gr. Cincinnati C. of C; Outstanding Citizen of the Year Nominee, Cincinnati, Ohio. Rel: Catholic. Mailing Add: 846 Ackley Dr, Cincinnati, Ohio, 45230.

HOWARTH, NELSON OLIVER R
Mayor, Springfield, Ill.
b. Bloomfield, Ind, 7/10/11; s. William Edward Howarth and Agnes Hand H; m. 3/2/35 to Mary Prindiville; c. William L, David N, Susan (Mrs. Eastman), Mary Jo and Lydia Ann. Educ: Univ. Ill, A.B, 32, LL.B, 34; Phi Beta Kappa; Order of Coif; Phi Alpha Delta. Polit. & Govt. Pos: Asst. state's attorney, Sangamon Co, Ill, 48-51; legal adv, Dept. Aeronauts, Ill, 52-55; mayor, Springfield, Ill, 55-59 & 63- Bus. & Prof. Pos: First asst. resident attorney, mortgage loan dept, Prudential Ins. Co, 36-40, resident attorney, 40-43; practicing attorney, Ill, 34- Mil. Serv: Entered as Lt.(jg), Navy, 43, released as Lt, 46, after serv. as Fighter Dir. Officer, Third and Fifth Fleets; Am. and Pac. Theater Ribbons and Six Battle Stars; Philippine Seas Ribbon; Presidential Unit Citation; Philippine Liberation Medal with Two Stars. Publ: Contrib, Munic. Magazines. Mem: Am, Ill. and Sangamon Co. Bar Asns; v.pres, Ill. Munic. League; Mason; Amvets; Am. Legion; VFW; Sangamon Club; Elks; Eagles; divers & other social and athletic orgns. Rel: Presbyterian. Legal Res: 1340 S. State St, Springfield, Ill. 62704. Mailing Add: Mayor's Office, Municipal Bldg, Springfield, Ill. 62701.

HOWAT, CAROL L. D
V.Chmn, Pulaski Co. Dem. Orgn, Ind.
b. Tremont, Ill, 4/5/24; d. Samuel Fred Getz and Ann Swing G; m. 12/25/40 to W. Fred Howat; c. Terry F, Rebecca Sue and Dennis F. Polit. & Govt. Pos: V.chmn, Pulaski Co. Dem. Orgn, Ind. Rel: Christian Apostolic. Mailing Add: R.R. 1, Francesville, Ind. 47946.

HOWATT, LESTER A. Conservative
b. Wabasha Co, Minn, 1909; married; c. Two. Educ: Univ. Minn; Seminar on Pub. Affairs. Polit. & Govt. Pos: Sch. Bd. Clerk, 6 years; Minn. State Rep, 64-66. Bus. & Prof. Pos: Real estate agent; farmer until 59; dir, Lake City State Bank, Minn, currently. Mem: Leader, 4-H; former officer, Co. Farm Bur. Rel: Congregational. Mailing Add: RFD, Lake City, Minn. 55041.

HOWE, CARROL B. R
Ore. State Rep.
b. Brownsville, Ore, 9/25/10; s. John Bernard Howe and Lillian Bruce H; m. 4/30/33 to Marjorie Dee Reeder; c. George Carrol. Educ: Univ. Ore, B.S, 36, M.S, 42; Phi Delta Kappa. Polit. & Govt. Pos: Ore. State Rep, 61- Bus. & Prof. Pos: Secondary Supvr. State Dep. of Educ, 47-48; Supt. of Schools, Klamath Co, Sch. Dist, 48-60. Publ: Ancient Tribes of the Klamath Country, Binfords & Mort, 68; 'Conservation Education,' The Nation's Schools, 5/50. Mem: Rotary; C. of C; Farm Bur. Rel: Protestant. Mailing Add: Route 2, Box 697B, Klamath Falls, Ore. 97601.

HOWE, CHARLES BRYAN D
Mem, Boulder Co. Dem. Cent. Cmt, Colo.
b. Ft. Lupton, Colo, 11/16/35; s. Charles Daniel Howe and Elizabeth Bryan H; m. 11/16/61 to Joan Merle Satter; c. Charles Scott and Mary Elizabeth. Educ: Univ. Denver, B.S, 58, LL.B, 60, M.S. in Pub. Admin, 60. Polit. & Govt. Pos: Attorney and govt. consult, Gov. Local Affairs Cmt, State of Colo, 63-65; precinct coordinator, Boulder Co. Dem. Party, 66 and committeeman, Precinct 22, 67; munic. judge, City of Boulder, 67-; del, Dem. Nat. Conv, 68; mem, Boulder Co. Dem. Cent. Cmt. Colo, 69- Bus. & Prof. Pos: Gen. counsel, Colo. Munic. League, 65-68; attorney, Kohn and Howe, Boulder, 68- Mil. Serv: Entered as 1st Lt, Army, 60, released as Capt, 62, after serving in Judge Adv. Gen. Crops, Ft. Monmouth, N.J, 60-62; Distinguished mil. grad, Univ. Denver, 59. Publ: Numerous articles and publications, Colo. Munic. League, Boulder. Mem: Toastmasters (pres, Boulder Club, 64). Rel: Unitarian. Legal Res: 4605 Talbot, Boulder, Colo. 80302. Mailing Add: 2040 14th St, Boulder, Colo. 80302.

HOWE, DENNIS R
N.Mex. State Rep.
b. Belleville, Kans, 11/11/40; s. Louis Taft Howe and Alice Francis H; m. 11/20/65 to Mary Belden; c. Elizabeth and Janice. Educ: Univ. N.Mex, B.A. in Govt, 67. Polit. & Govt. Pos: Pres, Univ. N.Mex. Young Rep, 63-64 and Bernalillo Co. Young Rep, 65-66; N.Mex. State Rep, Dist. 11, 67-68, Dist. 14, 69- Mil. Serv: Entered as Airman Basic, Air Force, 58, released as Airman 1/C, 62; Good Conduct Medal. Rel: Methodist. Mailing Add: 5909 Ponderosa N.E, Albuquerque, N.Mex. 87110.

HOWE, EUNICE P. R
Rep. Nat. Committeewoman, Mass.
b. Belmont, Mass, 4/24/18; m. 2/9/47 to Henry Dunster Howe; c. Eunice Dunster and Mary Alice Boardman. Educ: Geneva Col, Switz, 36-37; Mount Holyoke Col, A.B, 38; Boston Univ. Sch. of Law, LL.B, 41. Polit. & Govt. Pos: Mem, Mass. Bar, 41-; asst. attorney gen, Mass, 41, 44 & 46; counsel, Div. of Employ. Security, 46-47; pres, Brookline Women's Rep. Club, 63-65; mem, Mass. Consumers Coun, 65-; v.pres, New Eng. Citizens Crime Cmn, 66-; chmn, Brookline Rep. Town Cmt, 67-69; mem, Mass. Coun. on Crime and Correction and chmn, Cmt. on Consumer Educ, 68-; hon. pres, Mass. Fedn. of Rep. Women, 68-; Rep. Nat. Committeewoman, Mass, currently. Bus. & Prof. Pos: Attorney-at-law. Mil. Serv: Lt.(jg), Naval Res, World War II. Mem: Chmn, Bequest and Annuities Cmt, Mount Holyoke Col, 60- Rel: Episcopal; Mem. of Vestry, Church of our Saviour, Brookline. Mailing Add: 6 Woodbine Rd, Belmont, Mass. 02178.

HOWE, GORDON A. R
b. Rochester, N.Y, 1/19/04; s. Frank Ballou Howe and Agnes Marrow H; m. 11/27/37 to Lois Speares; c. Gordon, II, Gretchen and David S. Polit. & Govt. Pos: Justice of the Peace, 29-34; town supvr, Greece, N.Y, 33-60; chmn. bd. of supvrs, Monroe Co, N.Y, 48-60, mgr, 60-; founding dir, Ken Keating Rep. League, 60; del, Rep. Nat. Conv, 60, 64 & 68; chmn, Monroe Co. Rep. Cmt, 60-62; committeeman, N.Y. State Rep. Cmt; cand. for Presidential Elector, 68. Bus. & Prof. Pos: Gov. appointee, N.Y. State Fire Adv. Bd; chmn. adv. bd, Monroe Co. Mutual Aid Plan for Fire Protection, 44; mem, Joint City-Co. Cmt. on Elimination of Overlapping Functions of Govt. in Roch-

ester & Monroe Co, 55, chmn, Joint City-Co. Civic Center Cmn, N.Y, 55- Mem: Pres, N.Y. Asn. of Towns, 55; Masons; Damascus Temple, Shrine; Elks; life mem, West. N.Y. Vol. Firemen's Asn; mem. since incorporation and past Lt, Barnard Fire Dept; former dist. cmnr, Red Jacket Coun, Boy Scouts; past towns chmn, Community Chest-Red Cross Drive; organizing mem, Barnard Exempt Firemen's Asn; past trustee, Town and Co. Officers' Sch. Speaker, Urban Co. Cong. of Nat. Asn. of Co. Officers, 59; Outstanding Rep. of Year, Lincoln Rep. League, 61. Rel: Presbyterian; Elder. Legal Res: 402 Beach Ave, Rochester, N.Y. 14612. Mailing Add: 39 W. Main St, Rochester, N.Y. 14614.

HOWE, HUGH FARNHAM R
b. Tunbridge, Vt, 10/24/02; wid; c. Three. Educ: S. Royalton High Sch. Polit. & Govt. Pos: Town road cmnr, Tunbridge, Vt, 31-34, sch. dir, 47-, selectman, 6 years, auditor, grand juror and town agent, formerly; Vt. State Rep, 61-66. Bus. & Prof. Pos: Farmer. Mem: Mason; Eastern Star; Farm Bur; Grange. Rel: Methodist. Mailing Add: Tunbridge, Vt. 05077. (1967)

HOWE, MARIE ELIZABETH D
Mass. State Rep.
b. Somerville, Mass, 6/13/39, d. William Andrew Howe and Amelia Gertrude McCauley H; single. Educ: Brooks Jr. Col, Dipl, 60; Suffolk Univ; New Eng. Sch. of Law, Boston, J.D, 69. Polit. & Govt. Pos: Mem, Somerville Sch. Cmt, Mass, 62-65, v.chairlady, 63, chairlady, 64; mem, Ward and City Dem. Cmts, 62-; staff, Dist. Attorney's Off, Middlesex Co, 63-64; Mass. State Rep, 65- Bus. & Prof. Pos: Exec. secy, Tech. Res. Group, Inc, 60-63. Publ: 'Administrators Forum,' Sch. Mgt, 3/66. Mem: Mass. Legislator's Asn; Nat. Cong. of Parents & Teachers; Nat. and Mass. Asns. of Sch. Cmts; Somerville Commun. Coun; Youth Serv. Cmt; St. Ann's Womens Club; organizer, Somerville Dem. Women's Club; Howe Associates. Woman Doer of Mass. in 65, Mass. Fedn. Women's Dem. Clubs, Inc. Rel: Roman Catholic. Mailing Add: 19 Pembroke St, Somerville, Mass. 02145.

HOWE, MARILYN ANN D
b. Ada, Okla, 4/24/42; d. John Morley Martyn and Margaret McMillan M; m. 7/8/67 to Benjamin Ramsey Howe. Educ: Univ. Colo, B.A, 66. Polit. & Govt. Pos: Chmn, Adams Co. McCarthy for Pres. Cmt, Colo, 67-68; alternate del, Dem. Nat. Conv, 68; mem, Young Dem. of Adams Co, Colo, 68-; Nat. Committeewoman, Young Dem. of Colo, 69-70; Dem. committeewoman, Precinct 240, Adams Co, 69-; mem, Colo. Cmt. on Nat. Priorities, 69-; mem, Am. for Dem. Action, 69- Bus. & Prof. Pos: Asst. ed, N.Y. ed, TV Guide Mag, 63-64; Eng. teacher, Highland High Sch, Thornton, Colo, 67-68; Eng. teacher, Westminster High Sch, Westminster, currently. Mem: Am. Fedn. Teachers. Mailing Add: 1001 Milky Way, Denver, Colo. 80221.

HOWELL, CHARLES ROBERT D
b. Trenton, N.J, 4/23/04; s. Robert W(ilson) Howell and Harriet Bumsted H; m. 10/3/28 to Inez W. Howe. Educ: Princeton Univ, 23-25; Univ. Pa, spec. ins. courses, 37-38; chartered life underwriter, Am. Col. Life Underwriter. Polit. & Govt. Pos: N.J. State Assemblyman, two terms, 44 & 45; U.S. Rep, N.J, 49-55; cand. for U.S. Sen, N.J, 54; cmnr, Banking and Ins, N.J, 55-69. Bus. & Prof. Pos: Ins. agent, 28-55; consult, The Ramapo Bank, Wayne, N.J, 69- Mem: Bd. mgrs, U.S. Savings Bank, Newark, N.J; trustee, Assoc. for the Arts N.J. State Mus; bd. trustees, N.J. Hosp. Serv. Plan; assoc. trustee, Inst. Applied Politics, Trenton, N.J; Trenton Club; pres, Nat. Asn. of Supvrs. of State Banks, 64-65; pres, Nat. Asn. Ins. Cmnr, 68-69. Golden Deed Award, N.J. Asn. Real Estate Bd, 63; General Comenfort Medal; Lacruz and Placa from Mex. Mailing Add: 56 E. Curlis Ave, Pennington, N.J. 08534.

HOWELL, HARRY U. D
W.Va. State Del.
b. Morgantown, W.Va, 10/9/23; s. William G. Howell and Dove Hinebaugh H; m. 11/9/56 to Evelyn Deloris Stephens; c. Linda Anne and William Doss. Educ: W.Va. Univ. Polit. & Govt. Pos: Mem, Monongalia Co. Young Dem, W.Va; mem, Morgantown Traffic Cmn. and Bd. of Adjustment for Zoning; W.Va. State Del, 64- Mil. Serv: W.Va. Nat. Guard, 38-41; Army, 42-46; Army Res, 46-56. Mem: VFW; Am. Legion; Odd Fellows; Moose; Painters Local Union 850; Laborers Local Union 814; exec. bd, W.Va. Fedn. of Labor; Morgantown Cent. Labor Union; Morgantown Bldg. Trades; chmn, Monongalia Co. March of Dimes, 61-62; charter mem, bd. of dir, Sundale Rest Home; dir, Monongalia Co. United Fund; Monongalia Co. Labor Day Celebration Cmt. Rel: Protestant. Legal Res: 419 Harding Ave, Morgantown, W.Va. 26505. Mailing Add: P.O. Box 76, Morgantown, W.Va. 26505.

HOWELL, HENRY EVANS, JR. D
Va. State Sen.
b. Norfolk, Va, 9/5/20; m. to Elizabeth McCarty. Educ: Col. William and Mary, 2 years; Univ. Va, LL.B. Polit. & Govt. Pos: Va. State Rep, 60-66; Va. State Sen, 66-; cand. for Gov, Va, 69. Bus. & Prof. Pos: Attorney-at-law. Mem: Va. Trial Lawyers Asn; Norfolk C. of C; Mace Club; Izaak Walton League; Hampton Rds. For. Commerce Club; Propeller Club; Hampton Rds. Maritime Asn; Ocean View Dem. Club. Rel: Episcopal. Mailing Add: 808 Maritime Tower, Norfolk, Va. 23505.

HOWELL, HERBERT HUGH R
Mem. exec. cmt, Wayne Co. Rep. Party, N.C.
b. Goldsboro, N.C, 8/7/29; s. Hubert Myrle Howell and Helen Wilkinson H; m. 6/12/54 to Cleta Joan Friedmann; c. Heidi Ann, Melissa Ann, Andrea, Stephanie Allison and Tina Suzanne. Educ: Univ. N.C, Chapel Hill, B.S, 52; Kappa Alpha Order. Polit. & Govt. Pos: Regional campaign mgr, Goldwater for President, 63-64; dist. campaign mgr, Sherman Rock for Cong, 63-64; dist. v.pres, N.C. Fedn. of Young Rep, 65; mem. exec. cmt, Wayne Co. Rep. Party, N.C, 65-; cand. for Cong, 68. Bus. & Prof. Pos: Secy-treas, Howell Oil Co, Inc, 66- Mil. Serv: Entered as Aviation Cadet, Air Force, 52, released as 1st Lt, 56, after serving in 551st Aircraft Early Warning Wing, Air Defense Command, 55-56. Mem: N.C. Oil Jobbers Asn.(pres, 57); Roanoke Island Hist. Asn; Wayne Citizens for Decent Lit; Boy Scouts; Am. Legion; Civitans; N.C. Symphony. Rel: Methodist. Mailing Add: 704 Park Ave, Goldsboro, N.C. 27530.

HOWELL, JOHN E. D
Sgt. at Arms, W.Va. State Senate
b. Little Rock, Ark, 7/21/08; s. John H. Howell and Myrtle Thompson H; m. 12/3/37 to Evelyn Hurst; c. John, Jr. Polit. & Govt. Pos: Doorkeeper, W.Va. State Senate, 57-, sgt. at arms, 61- Bus. & Prof. Pos: Salesman and baseball umpire. Mem: Lions; Elks; Moose; Eagles; United Commercial Travelers; Am. Asn. of Prof. Baseball Clubs. Rel: Baptist. Mailing Add: 3803 Venable Ave. S.E, Charleston, W.Va. 25304. (1967)

HOWELL, MAX D
Ark. State Sen.
b. Lonoke, Ark, 12/22/15; s. Flavius Josephus Howell and Margaret Anthony H; m. 2/7/67 to Inez Donham; c. Max, Jr, Patricia (Mrs. Tate), Rachel, William, Katrina and Don. Educ: Ark. Law Sch, 37-40. Polit. & Govt. Pos: Ark. State Rep, 46-50; Ark. State Sen, 18th Dist, 50- Mil. Serv: Entered as Pvt, Air Force, 42, released as Maj, 46; Col, Army Res, currently. Mem: Ark, Am. and Pulaski Co. Bar Asns; Am. Legion; Mason; Consistory; Shrine; Jesters; Elks; Eagles; C. of C; Farm and Ranch Club. Rel: Presbyterian. Legal Res: Singley Rd, Little Rock, Ark. Mailing Add: 211 Spring St, Little Rock, Ark. 72201.

HOWELL, THOMAS MADISON JR. D
S.C. State Rep.
b. Walterboro, S.C, 2/5/26; s. Thomas Madison Howell and Margaret Gelzer H; m. 9/2/49 to Harriott Kinloch Barnwell; c. Thomas M, III, Margaret Middleton, Harriott Kinloch and Joseph Barnwell. Educ: Univ. S.C, B.S, 46, LL.B, 49; Sigma Alpha Epsilon; Omicron Delta Kappa; Kappa Sigma Kappa. Polit. & Govt. Pos: Secy, Co. Dem. Party, S.C; S.C. State Rep, 61- Bus. & Prof. Pos: Lawyer. Mem: Co. Develop. Bd; dir, Lions Club; pres, Forest Hills PTA; pres, Jr. C. of C; dir, C. of C. Rel: Episcopal; Vestryman, St. Judes Episcopal Church. Mailing Add: Drawer 1115, Walterboro, S.C. 29488.

HOWELL, WILLIAM MOBLEY D
Ga. State Rep.
b. Blakely, Ga, 8/18/20; s. William Omar Howell and Lottye Smith H; div; c. William Omar and Charlotte Frances. Educ: South Ga. Col. Polit. & Govt. Pos: Ga. State Sen, 9th Dist, 57-58; Ga. State Rep, 86th Dist, 65- Mil. Serv: Entered as A/S, Navy, 40, released as CPO, 46, after serv. in Fleet Air Wing Three, Caribbean; Am. Theater Ribbon; Good Conduct and Victory Medals; Am. Serv. Prior Pearl Harbor Medal. Mem: Exec. dir, Blakely-Early Co. C. of C; Mason; Rotary; Am. Legion; VFW. Rel: Methodist. Mailing Add: P.O. Box 348, Blakely, Ga. 31723.

HOWELL, WILLIAM THOMAS R
Chmn, Burleson Co. Rep. Cmt, Tex.
b. Plainview, Tex, 1/1/24; s. L. V. Howell and Minnie B. Lawrence H; m. 4/10/45 to Edna Mae Lehde; c. Glenn A, and Don W. Educ: Olton High Sch, Tex, 3 years. Polit. & Govt. Pos: Chmn, Burleson Co. Rep. Cmt, Tex, 63- Bus. & Prof. Pos: Farmer-Rancher, currently. Mil. Serv: Entered as Pvt, Air Force, 42, released as Pfc, 46, after serv. in 1090th Guard Squadron, Bryan Field, Tex, 43-45. Mem: Farm Bur; Am. Legion. Rel: Baptist. Mailing Add: Route 3, Box 33, Caldwell, Tex. 77836.

HOWERTON, JAMES WILLIAM R
b. Paducah, Ky, 10/22/31; s. Walter C. Howerton and Nell Bass H; m. 8/24/57 to Hunter Blackburn; c. John B, Jane Hunter and Walter Clay. Educ: Univ. Ky, B.S. in Commerce, 53 and LL.B, 61; Phi Delta Phi; Sigma Alpha Epsilon. Polit. & Govt. Pos: Rep. Gubernatorial Campaign Chmn, Univ. Ky, 59; prosecution attorney, Paducah, Ky, 61-66; Rep. Senatorial Campaign Chmn, McCracken Co, 62, First Cong. Dist, 66; chmn, McCracken Co. Rep. Exec. Cmt, 64-68; corp. counsel, Paducah, 67- Bus. & Prof. Pos: Attorney-at-Law, 61- Mil. Serv: Entered as 2nd Lt, Air Force, 54, released as 1st Lt, 55, after serv. in Far East, Japan; Maj, Air Force Res; Nat. Defense Medal; Korean Serv. Ribbon; UN Serv. Ribbon; Res. Medal. Publ: 'Occupational Diseases: Interpretation and Need for Statutory Revision of the Illinois, Indiana and Kentucky General Definition,' 49, Ky. Law J. 563, 1961. Mem: Am, Ky. and McCracken Co. Bar Asns; Rotary (pres, 69-); Toastmasters (pres, 69). Rel: Episcopal. Legal Res: 1212 Lone Oak Rd, Paducah, Ky. 42001. Mailing Add: 616 Citizens Bank Bldg, Paducah, Ky. 42001.

HOWLETT, MICHAEL J. D
State Auditor of Pub Acct, Ill.
b. Chicago, Ill, 8/30/14; m. to Helen Geary H; c. Michael, Robert, Edward, Catherine, Mary Christine and Helen Marie. Educ: DePaul Univ, 34. Polit. & Govt. Pos: Chicago Area Dir. of Nat. Youth Admin, 40-42; Ill. State Bank Exam; exec. dir, Off. Orgn. and Admin, Chicago Park Dist; regional dir, Off. of Price Stabilization, 51; Ill. State Auditor, 60-; del, Dem. Nat. Conv, 68. Bus. & Prof. Pos: V.pres, Sun Steel Co, Chicago, 52-60; Ins. Bus, 37-40. Mil. Serv: U.S. Navy, 42-45. All-Am. Water Polo Player (in his youth); mem. 10 championship teams, Ill. Athletic Club; 3-time winner Chicagoland Tribune 100-yd. swimming championships; winner many A.A.U. gold medals and Inter-Ocean Swimming championships; Citation by Nat. Restaurant Asn. for invest. which smashed a sensational horsemeat racket and broke up a ring of swindlers; Citation by an Ill. Vet. Orgn. for leadership in fight against indecent lit. in N. Ill. Mailing Add: 123 N. Park Ave, Springfield, Ill. 62702.

HOWRIGAN, JAMES E. D
b. Fairfield, Vt, 10/26/87; wid; c. One son (deceased). Polit. & Govt. Pos: Sch. dir, 6 years; Vt. State Rep, 62-65. Bus. & Prof. Pos: Field buyer, Cary Maple Sugar Co, 27 years; retired. Mem: Elks; United Commercial Travelers; Cath. Order of Foresters. Rel: Catholic. Mailing Add: Fairfield, Vt. 05455. (1967)

HOWSDEN, ARLEY LEVERN D
Co. Supvr, Butte Co. Calif.
b. Huntley, Nebr, 10/17/26; s. Harry Ray Howsden and Hattie K. Donley H; m. 12/12/47 to Vivian May McCready; c. Jo Ann (Mrs. Alsey), Jean, Harry Scott, Karen, Kathie and Jan. Educ: Univ. Nebr, B.S, 48, M.A, 52 and Ed.D, 58. Polit. & Govt. Pos: Pres, Chico Dem. Club, Calif, 63; mem, Butte Co. Dem. Cent. Cmt, 64-65; co. supvr, Butte Co, 65-; Butte Co. chmn. for McCarthy Cmt, 68; alternate del, Dem. Nat. Conv, 68. Bus. & Prof. Pos: Supt. and coach, Axtell, Nebr, 48-52; high sch. coach and teacher, North Platte, 52-54; dir. of educ, Am. Samoa, 54-55; supt. of schs, Oxford, Nebr, 55-56; commun. educ. coordinator, Univ. Nebr, 56-58; prof. educ, Chico State Col, 58-69. Mil. Serv: Pvt, Army Specialized Training Prog, Army, 44-45. Mem: Life

mem, Nat. Educ. Asn; Calif. Teachers Asn; Far West. Philos. of Educ; Rotary; Farm Bur; Mason; C. of C; Toastmasters (past Gov, Dist. 39); Calif. Col. Univ. Faculty Asn.(past pres). Rel: Unitarian. Legal Res: Route 2, Box 480, Chico, Calif. 95926.

HOY, REX BRUCE F
Kans. State Rep.
b. Lincoln, Nebr, 7/27/28; s. Les B. Hoy and Mabel Gilliland H; m. 5/15/48 to Lillian Kathryn Roth; c. Sharon Rae. Educ: Univ. Nebr, Lincoln, B.S, 52; Purdue Univ. Life Ins. Mkt. Inst, 62-63. Polit. & Govt. Pos: Mem, City of Mission Planning Coun, Kans, 65-66; Kans. State Rep, 24th Dist, 69- Bus. & Prof. Pos: V.pres, Metrop. Aviation, 68-69. Mil. Serv: Entered as Pfc, Army Engrs, 45, released as T-5, 46, after serv. in Hq. Co. 123 Eng. Surv. Bn, Ft. Belvoir and Japan; World War II Victory Medal; Army of Occup. Medal, Japan. Mem: Life Underwriters Asn; Mission C. of C.(pres, 66 & 67); Optimists; Mason; Univ. Nebr. Alumni Asn; bd. dirs, Johnson Co. YMCA, 61-; pres, Johnson Co. Area C. of C. Pres. Coun, 67-68. Rel: Methodist. Mailing Add: 3801 Johnson Dr, Fairway, Kans. 66205.

HOYER, STENY HAMILTON D
Md. State Sen.
b. N.Y.C, 6/14/39; s. Steen Hamilton Hoyer and Jean Baldwin H; m. 6/17/61 to Judith Elaine Pickett; c. Susan and Stefany. Educ: Univ. Md, B.S, 63; Georgetown Univ. Law Sch, LL.B, 66; Omicron Delta Kappa; Phi Sigma Alpha; Kalegethos; Sigma Chi. Polit. & Govt. Pos: Exec. asst. to U.S. Sen. Daniel B. Brewster, 62-66; pres, Young Dem. Clubs of Md, 64-65; Md. State Sen, 67-; del, Dem. Nat. Conv, 68. Bus. & Prof. Pos: Attorney, Haislip & Yewell, 66-68; attorney, gen. practice, 68- Mem: Am, Md. and Prince George's Co. Bar Asns; Am. Trial Lawyers Asn; Am. Judicature Soc; Crescent Cities Jaycees. Outstanding Male Grad, Univ. Md, 63. Rel: Baptist. Legal Res: 7408 Gateway Blvd, District Heights, Md. 20028. Mailing Add: 6108 Old Silver Hill Rd, District Heights, Md. 20028.

HOYLAND, FRANCES BURNS D
Polit. & Govt. Pos: Admin. asst. to U.S. Rep. George H. Fallon, Md, 44- Mailing Add: 4000 Cathedral Ave. N.W, Apt. 624 B, Washington, D.C. 20016.

HOYT, CHARLES RICHARD R
Ore. State Sen.
b. Portland, Ore, 1/15/05; s. Charles Elfred Hoyt and Minerva Wolf H; m. 3/24/33 to Esther LaVerne Taylor; c. Charles Taylor and Thomas Herbert. Educ: Univ. Ore, B.A; charter mem. Alpha Sigma Chap, Theta Chi. Polit. & Govt. Pos: Ore. State Rep, 59-67; Ore. State Sen, 67- Mem: Pres, Corvallis C. of C, 54; chmn, Corvallis Library Bd, 58; pres, Corvallis Lions Club, 36; bd. trustees, Corvallis Gen. Hosp, 45-48; hon. mem, Farm Bur; Scottish Rite; Elks; Lions. Rel: Unitarian. Mailing Add: 1105 Buchanan St, Corvallis, Ore. 97330.

HOYT, EUGENE R. D
Beaumont, Tex, 6/12/26; s. Joseph V. Hoyt and Edna Mae Wentz H; m. 4/29/61 to Mary Lee Ainsworth; c. Scott, Evangalan, Helen, Eugene, Jr, Gina and Jenny. Educ: Lamar Col, A.A, 47; Univ. Miami, $1\frac{1}{2}$ years; Univ. Tex. Law Sch, LL.B, 50. Polit. & Govt. Pos: Judge, 163rd Dist. Court, State of Tex, 63-68; alternate del, Dem. Nat. Conv, 68. Bus. & Prof. Pos: Dir, Sabine Insulation Co, 58- Mil. Serv: Cadet, Air Force, 44-45. Mem: Am. and Tex. Bar Asns; Orange Co. Bar Asn.(pres, 57); Exchange Club; Optimist. Rel: Methodist. Mailing Add: 1 Canterbury Dr, Orange, Tex. 77630.

HOYT, HERMAN E. R
Vt. State Rep.
b. Barnet, Vt, 10/3/01; m. to Elsie E. Darling; c. Three. Educ: McIndoes Acad, McIndoes Falls, Vt. Polit. & Govt. Pos: Vt. State Rep, 65-; mem, Bd. of Civil Authority, St. Johnsbury; exec. cmt, Vt. Rep. State Cmt. Bus. & Prof. Pos: U.S. Postal Serv, retired. Mem: F&AM; hon. life mem, Nat. Asn. of Postal Supvrs; Long Trail Coun; Boy Scouts. Rel: Methodist. Mailing Add: 20 Perkins St, St. Johnsbury, Vt. 05819.

HOYT, MERLYN HAROLD D
Dist. Attorney, White Pine Co, Nev.
b. Ely, Nev, 6/13/33; s. Harold Jerome Hoyt and Hazel Newman H; m. 3/21/59 to Carol Lamphere; c. Michael Harold, Barbara Gail and Tracy Ann. Educ: Univ. Nev, B.S. in Bus. Admin, 57; Am. Univ, Wash. Col. of Law, J.D, 63; Lambda Chi Alpha. Polit. & Govt. Pos: Employee, Solicitor's Off, Nat. Park Serv, Dept. of Interior, Wash, D.C, 63-64; Asst. U.S. Attorney, U.S. Dept. of Justice, Reno, Nev, 64-66; Dist. Attorney, White Pine Co, Ely, 67-; alternate del, Dem. Nat. Conv, 68. Mem: Am, Nev. and D.C. Bar Asns; Am. Judicature Soc; Lions Int; U.S. Jaycees; C. of C; White Pine Co. Dem. Club. Rel: Methodist. Legal Res: 479 Cedar St, Ely, Nev. 89301. Mailing Add: P.O. Box 729, Ely, Nev. 89301.

HRUSKA, ROMAN LEE R
U.S. Sen, Nebr.
b. David City, Nebr, 8/16/04; s. Joseph C. Hruska and Caroline L.H; m. 1930 to Victoria E. Kuncl; c. Roman L, Jr, Quentin J. and Jana L. Educ: Univ. Omaha; Univ. Chicago Law Sch, 28; Creighton Univ. Col. of Law, LL.B, 29. Hon. LL.D, Creighton Univ. and Doane Col; hon. HH.D, Coe Col. Polit. & Govt. Pos: Chmn. bd. of co. cmnrs, Douglas Co, Nebr, 45-52; mem. adv. cmt, Nebr. Bd. of Control, 47-52; pres, Nebr. Asn. of Co. Off, 50-51; mem. bd. of regents, Univ. Omaha, 50-57; v.pres, Nat. Asn. of Co. Off, 51-52; U.S. Sen, Nebr, 54-; del, Rep. Nat. Conv, 68. Bus. & Prof. Pos: Attorney-at-law. Mem: Nebr. State and Am. Bar Asns; Kiwanis; Shrine; Nat. v.pres. and gen. counsel, West. Bohemian Fraternal Asn; past pres, Nebr. Fraternal Cong. Rel: Unitarian. Legal Res: 2139 S. 38th St, Omaha, Nebr. 68105. Mailing Add: Senate Office Bldg, Washington, D.C. 20510. (1967)

HUBBARD, CARROLL, JR. D
Ky. State Sen.
b. Murray, Ky, 7/7/37; s. Dr. Carroll Hubbard, Sr. and Addie Beth Shelton H m. 8/20/66 to Joyce Lynn Hall. Educ: Georgetown Col, B.A, 59; Univ. Louisville, LL.B, 62; Delta Omicron Kappa; Kappa Alpha. Polit. & Govt. Pos: V.pres, Young Dem. Ky, 60, state col. chmn, 60 & 62; Ky. State Sen, First Dist, 68- Mil. Serv: Entered as Airman Basic, Air Force Nat. Guard, 62, Capt, 69-, Army Nat. Guard Selective Serv. Hq, Legal Adv. for Ky. Selective Serv, 67- Mem: Ky. and Nat. Bar Asns; Phi Alpha Delta; Rotary (pres, Mayfield Club, 65-66); Jaycees (v.pres, 68-69); Graves Co. Young Dem. Club. For three years selected as Outstanding Young Man of Graves Co, Ky; One of Three Outstanding Young Men of Ky, Ky. Jaycees, 68. Rel: Southern Baptist. Legal Res: 410 Macedonia Rd, Mayfield, Ky. 42066. Mailing Add: P.O. Box 462, Mayfield, Ky. 42066.

HUBBARD, CHESTER R. R
W.Va. State Sen.
b. Wheeling, W.Va, 12/4/05; s. Arthur G. Hubbard and Mary Paul H; m. 11/14/44 to Joan D. Holloway; c. Joan Dana, Nancy P, Cynthia R and Mary P. Educ: Lafayette Col, B.A, W.Va. Univ, LL.B; Sigma Nu; Phi Alpha Delta. Polit. & Govt. Pos: W.Va. State Del, formerly; W.Va. State Sen, 62- Bus. & Prof. Pos: Lawyer. Mil. Serv: Entered as Pvt, Army, 41, released as 1st Lt, 45; 1st Lt, Army Res. Mem: Ft. Henry Club; SAR; Am. Legion; Elks; Eagles; Moose; Fraternal Order of Police; dir, Woodsdale Childrens Home; Wheeling Symphony Soc. Inc; Ohio Valley Gen. Hosp; Blue Shield; chmn, Arterial Hwys. Cmt. of Wheeling Area Conf; former pres, Wheeling Coun. of Soc. Agencies, Children and Family Serv. Asn; Wheeling Country Day Sch; Commun. Chest; Seeing Hand Soc; local Boy Scout Coun; Wildlife League; Oglebay Inst; Ohio Co. Ment. Health Asn. Rel: Presbyterian. Legal Res: Route 4, Wheeling, W.Va. 26003. Mailing Add: 88 14th St, Wheeling, W.Va. 26003.

HUBBARD, DONALD D
Wyo. State Rep.
b. Wabash, Ind, 9/27/02; m. to Lilian; c. Two. Educ: Univ. Wyo, B.A. Polit. & Govt. Pos: Wyo. State Rep, currently; del, Dem. Nat. Conv, 68; mem, Nat. Exec. Reserve Off. Emergency Transportation, currently. Bus. & Prof. Pos: Cashier, Rwy. Express Co. Mem: Masonic Blue Lodge; York Rite; Shrine; Moose; treas, R.R. Employers Fed. Credit Union; pres, Snowy Range Chap. of Fed. Credit Unions; dir, State League Fed. Credit Unions. Rel: Episcopal. Mailing Add: 1600 Kearney, Laramie, Wyo. 82070.

HUBBARD, KENNETH DEAN D
Chmn, Pitkin Co. Dem. Cent. Cmt, Colo.
b. Glenwood Springs, Colo, 10/15/34; s. Erle E. Hubbard and Ruby Clarke H; m. 6/23/57 to Eleanor Graves; c. Kenneth Dean, Jr, Randall Emerson, Edward Roy and Curtis Andrew. Educ: Harvard Col, A.B. magna cum laude, 56, Law Sch, LL.B, 59; Phi Beta Kappa; Sigma Alpha Epsilon. Polit. & Govt. Pos: West. Slope coordinator, Colo. John F. Kennedy for Pres. Cmt, 60; Jefferson Co. publicity dir, McVicker for Cong, Second Dist, 64; campaign mgr, Cmt. to Reelect McVicker, 66; regional coordinator, Fourth Dist, Ken Monfort Primary Campaign, 68; chmn Pitkin Co. Dem. Cent. Cmt, 69- Bus. & Prof. Pos: Assoc. and partner, Holland & Hart, Attorneys, 59- Publ: 'Application of State Conservation Laws to Federal Lands,' Colo. Univ. Law Rev, 60; 'Extensions and suspensions-Federal Oil and Gas Leases, 63 and'Access and Prospecting Problems in Wilderness Ares,' 69, Rocky Mt. Mineral Law Found. Mem: Dener Bar Asn.(dir, young lawyers's sect, 60); Colo. Bar Asn.(v.chmn, 68); Pitkin Co. Bar Asn.(Pres, 69-); Lions; Rocky Mt. Harvard Club (past pres). Rel: Episcopal. Legal Res: 9 Snowbunny Court, Aspen, Colo. 81611. Mailing Add: P.O. Box 2092, Aspen, Colo. 81611.

HUBBARD, ORVILLE L. R
Mayor, Dearborn, Mich.
b. Batavia Twp, Mich, 4/2/03; s. Ralph Star Hubbard (deceased and Sylvia Elizabeth Hart H; m. 7/20/27 to Fay Cameron; c. four sons, one daughter. Educ: Marine Corps Inst; Int. Correspondence Schs; U.S. Army exten. courses; Detroit Inst. Tech; Ferris Inst; Detroit Col. Law, LL.B, 32; Univ. Mich. and Henry Ford Commun. Col, exten. courses. Polit. & Govt. Pos: Cand, Mich. State Senate, 32; Rep. precinct del, Dearborn, Mich, 32-; asst. attorney gen, Mich, 39-40; alternate del. Rep. Nat. Conv, 40, del, 52; mem. Wayne Co. Bd. Supvr, 42-68 and former mem. airport and ways and means cmts. mayor, Dearborn, 42- Bus. & Prof. Pos: Factory worker, cement factory, Union City, Mich; mem. serv. dept, Dodge Bro, Hamtramck, Mich; laborer, Clerk and stenographer purchasing dept, Ford Motor Co, Detroit, Mich, 25; reporter, Wall St. J, N.Y.C, 29-34; Mich. State Trooper, 42-45. Mil. Serv: Marine Corps, Sgt, 22-25; Army Res, officer, 30-37. Publ: Government-In-Exile, 50. Mem: Dearborn Bar Asn.(past pres); Marine Corps Vet.(first commandant). Recipient of Distinguished Citizen Award, Dearborn C. of C, 62. Legal Res: 7055 Mead, Dearborn, Mich. 48126. Mailing Add: Office of the Mayor, Dearborn, Mich. 48126.

HUBBARD, ROBERT WILLIAMS R
b. Logan, Utah, 4/24/16; s. Alma E. Hubbard and Mana Williams H; m. 7/26/39 to Aileen Ashbaker; c. Robert Brent, Cheryl (Mrs. Arbuckle), Margene (Mrs. Snow), Evelyn (Mrs. Banks), David A. and Randall A. Educ: Utah State Univ, 1 year. Polit. & Govt. Pos: Idaho State Rep, 63-66. Bus. & Prof. Pos: Pres, Soda Springs Elevator, Inc. and Robert W. Hubbard & Sons, Inc, 55- Mem: Pres, Soda Springs Farm Bur, 56; mem. tax cmt, Idaho State Farm Bur, currently. Rel: Latter-day Saint; Bishop, Williams Ward, Idaho, 45-54 and Soda Springs Ward, 57-59, pres, Idaho Stake, currently. Mailing Add: Star Route, Soda Springs, Idaho 83276.

HUBENAK, JOE ADOLPH D
Tex. State Rep.
b. Frenstat, Tex, 7/2/37; s. John Joe Hubenak and Rosemary Polansky H; single. Educ: Alvin Jr. Col, A.A, 63; Univ. Houston, B.B.A. in Acct, 65; Phi Beta Kappa (pres, 62). Polit. & Govt. Pos: Tex. State Rep, Dist. 20, 69- Bus. & Prof. Pos: Partner, Hubenak and Webb, 63- Mil. Serv: Entered as Pvt, Army, 55, released as Sgt 1/C, 62, after serv. in Tex. Nat. Guard, 36th Div. Mem: Lions; C. of C.(Rosenberg-Richmond Br); Jr. C. of C.(Rosenberg-Richmond Br); Farm Bur; K. of C. Rel: Catholic. Legal Res: 1214 Austin St, Rosenberg, Tex. 77471. Mailing Add: P.O. Box 688, Rosenberg, Tex. 77471.

HUBER, ARTHUR P. R
b. 1911. Educ: New Haven Pub. Schs. Polit. & Govt. Pos: Conn. State Rep, -67; Orange Bd. of Educ, 2 years; Orange Rep. Cmt 10 years, chmn, 1 year. Bus. & Prof. Pos: Gen. credit mgr, Armstrong Rubber Co, West Haven. Mailing Add: 51 Old Tavern Rd, Orange, Conn. 06477. (1967)

HUBER, AUGUST C. D
Polit. & Govt. Pos: Ind. State Rep, -66; Indianapolis City Coun, 59-63; Ind. Dem. Club. Bus. & Prof. Pos: Retired warehouse supt, 38 yrs. Mem: Charter mem, Indianapolis Zool. Soc; assoc. mem, Fraternal Order of Police, Lodge No. 86. Rel: Protestant. Mailing Add: 1407 S. N.J. St, Indianapolis, Ind. 46227. (1967)

HUBER, LeROY JAMES D
Chmn, Perry Co. Dem. Cmt, Mo.
b. Perryville, Mo, 7/5/27; s. Edwin F. Huber and Inice Colin H; m. 7/24/48 to Velma Lee Gibbar. Educ: Univ. Mo, 1 year; Rubicam Bus. Sch, grad. Polit. & Govt. Pos: Committeeman, Perry Co. Dem. Party, Mo, 63-; comnr. spec. rd. dist. 1, Perry Co, 15 years, pres, 7 years; chmn, Perry Co. Dem. Cmt, 63- Bus. & Prof. Pos: Real estate broker, Huber & Beeson Real Estate, 48-50; farmer, Perry Co, Mo, 50-60; salesman, Perryville Steel, Butler Bldgs, 60-62; owner and operator, Hubers House of Color, 60- Mil. Serv: Entered as A/S, Navy, 45, released as Yeoman 3/C, 46, after serv. on U.S.S. Ellyson DMS 19. Publ: Ed, 'Voice', Dem. Quart, Perry Co. Dem. Cmt, 69. Mem: Carpenters Union; Farmer Elected Committeeman Orgn; Mo. Construction Orgn; Am. Legion; VFW; K. of C. Rel: Catholic. Mailing Add: Route 3, Box 263A, Perryville, Mo. 63775.

HUBER, OSCAR EDWIN R
S.Dak. State Rep.
b. Bowdle, S.Dak, 8/22/17; s. Richard F. Huber and Rosina Schlaht H; single. Educ: North. State Col, Aberdeen, S.Dak, B.S, 41; Univ. Minn, grad. credits, 52-53; North State Col, grad. credits, 59-60; Sigma Delta Epsilon; Kappa Delta Pi. Polit. & Govt. Pos: S.Dak. State Rep, 60-; mem, Local Govt. Study Comn, 66-67; chmn. munic. and mil. affairs cmt, S.Dak. House of Rep, 67-68, chmn. cmt. on educ, 69-70. Bus. & Prof. Pos: Prin. and teacher, Roscoe High Sch, 46-57; teacher, Hosmer High Sch, 57-58. Mem: S.Dak. Educ. Asn, 46-58. Rel: Lutheran. Mailing Add: Bowdle, S.Dak. 57428.

HUBER, RAY ARLEN D
b. Quakertown, Pa, 6/23/33; s. Percy Dubbs Huber and Pearl Fluck H; m. 7/6/57 to Karin Margarete Mathiesen; c. Ray Alan, Jr, Kent Brian, Scott Kevin, Dirk Michael and Cindy Michelle. Educ: Moravian Col, 3½ years; Pi Delta Epsilon. Polit. & Govt. Pos: Fed. proj. coordinator, Mayor's Off, Bethlehem, Pa, 66; admin. asst. to U.S. Rep. Fred B. Rooney, Pa, 66- Bus. & Prof. Pos: Ed, Moravian Col. Student Newspaper, 54-55; staff writer and columnist, Bethlehem, Pa. Globe-Times Newspaper, 58-66. Mil. Serv: Entered as Pvt, Army, released as SP-3, after serv. in Army Security Agency, Europe, 55-58. Four Keystone Press Awards for News Writing, Pa. Newspaper Publishers Asn. Rel: United Church of Christ. Legal Res: Bethlehem, Pa. 18017. Mailing Add: 3612 Paul St, Alexandria, Va. 22311.

HUBER, ROBERT DANIEL R
Mem, Marin Co. Rep. Cent. Cmt, Calif.
b. Charlotte, Mich, 12/20/23; s. Charles Huber and Maybel Holden H; m. 7/27/46 to Jean Murray; c. Ann, David, Jane, Timothy and Mary. Educ: Univ. Mich, A.B, 47; Univ. San Francisco, J.D, 50; Tau Kappa Epsilon. Polit. & Govt. Pos: City councilman, Mill Valley, Calif, 54-62, mayor, 56-62; mem, Marin Co. Rep. Cent. Cmt, 61-; mem, Calif. State Rep. Cent. Cmt, 64- Bus. & Prof. Pos: Partner, Hassard, Bonnington, Rogers and Huber, San Francisco, 50- Mil. Serv: Entered as A/S, Navy, 42, released as Ens, 46, after serv. on Tanker, Pac. Theatre, 42-44. Mem: Calif, Am. and San Francisco Bar Asns. Rel: Protestant. Mailing Add: 245 Tamalpais, Mill Valley, Calif. 94941.

HUBER, ROBERT J. R
Mich. State Sen.
b. Detroit, Mich, 8/29/22; married. Educ: Culver Mil. Acad; Yale Univ, B.S. Polit. & Govt. Pos: Mayor, Troy, Mich, 2 terms; Mich. State Sen, 64- Bus. & Prof. Pos: Pres, Mich. Chrome and Chem. Co; past pres. and dir, Plating Inst. of Mich. Mil. Serv: Army, 43-46. Mem: Econ. Club of Detroit; Rotary Club; Elks; Am. Legion; Detroit Bd. of Commerce; Detroit Athletic Club; Univ. Club; Yale Club of N.Y; Otsego Ski Club; Young Pres. Orgn, former chmn. of Mich. Chap. Rel: Roman Catholic. Mailing Add: 4909 Beach Rd, Troy, Mich. 48084. (1967)

HUBER, ROBERT T. D
Wis. State Assemblyman
b. Eckelson, N.Dak, 8/29/20; s. Theodore J. Huber and Rose Ziebert H; m. 8/26/44 to Beatrice Bartlein; c. John Michael and Robert Thomas. Educ: West Allis High Sch, Wis, grad, 38. Polit. & Govt. Pos: Mem, Gov. Cmt. on Wis. Water Resources; Wis. State Assemblyman, 22nd Dist, 48-, Minority Floor Leader, Assembly, 55, 57, 61, 63, 67 & 69, Speaker Pro-Tem, 59, Speaker, 65; del, Dem. Nat. Conv, 68; Dem. Nat. Committeeman, Wis, 68- Bus. & Prof. Pos: Former contractor, 44-48; auto parts and serv. salesman; merchandising salesman. Mem: Holy Name Soc; Local 9, Brewery Workers' Union; K. of C. Rel: Catholic. Mailing Add: 2228 S. 78th St, West Allis, Wis. 53219.

HUBER, WILLIAM IRVIN D
b. West Reading, Pa, 1/20/21; s. James Huber and Margaret Leader H; m. 2/8/47 to Marion Reider; c. David, Ruth (Mrs. James Ford) and Margaret (Mrs. Donald Koch). Educ: West Reading High Sch, 11 years. Polit. & Govt. Pos: Dep. game protector, Pa, 54-58; Dem. committeeman, Ninth Ward, Reading, Pa, 54-60 and constable, 58-; del, Dem. Nat. Conv, 64 & 68; asst. health adminstr, Reading, Pa, 68- Bus. & Prof. Pos: Self-employed paper hanger. Mil. Serv: Entered as Pvt, Air Force, 43, released as Pfc, 46, after serv. in Second Photographic Tech. Unit, Ninth Air Force, Mediterranean & ETO Theatres, 44-46. Mem: Ivy Leaf Asn; Jackson Dem. Asn; Vet. Firemen's Asn; 1900 Beneficial Asn; Berks Co. Constables Asn; Travelers Protective Asn; Beneficial Soc. Victor Emmanuel II; Polish Falcons' Alliance, Berks Co, Pa, Inc; Francis J. Adams Post No. 876; Rainbow Fire Co. Relief Asn. Rel: Lutheran. Mailing Add: 1124 Elm St, Reading, Pa. 19604.

HUBERTY, DOROTHEA HILL WITTER R
Mem, Calif. Rep. State Cent. Cmt.
b. Neodesha, Kans, 5/26/02; d. Arthur Lloyd Hill and Hattie Cross H; m. 6/15/68 to Linus Ambrose Huberty; c. Charles Witter, Jr. Educ: Mills Col, 19-23; Ore. Univ, 23; Kappa Alpha Theta. Polit. & Govt. Pos: Pres, Rep. Women, Santa Rosa, Calif, 60-64 and v.pres, Walnut Creek, 65-69; mem, Sonoma Co. Rep. Cent. Cmt, 60-64 and Calif. Rep. State Cent. Cmt, 60- Mem: Am. Red Cross (past exec. secy. and vol, Santa Rosa); Co. Probation Cmt, Sonoma Co, 44-52. Rel: Episcopal. Mailing Add: 2416 Tice Creek Dr, Apt. 1, Walnut Creek, Calif. 94595.

HUDDLESTON, GEORGE, JR. D
b. Birmingham, Ala, 3/19/20; s. George Huddleston and Bertha Baxley H; m. 3/13/53 to Alice Jeanne Haworth; c. George, III, Margaret and Nancy. Educ: Birmingham-Southern Col, A.B, 41; Univ. Ala. Law Sch, LL.B, 48; Phi Beta Kappa; Phi Delta Phi; Farrah Order of Jurisprudence. Polit. & Govt. Pos: Asst. U.S. Attorney, North. Dist, Ala, 49-52; U.S. Rep, Ala, 55-65. Bus. & Prof. Pos: Attorney-at-law, Birmingham Ala, 52-55; spec. asst. govt. affairs, N.Am. Aviation, Inc, 64- Mil. Serv: Entered as Seaman, Naval Res, 42, released as Lt, 46, after serv. in Pac; Capt, Naval Res: Asiatic-Pac. Theater Ribbon; 8 Battle Stars; Am. and European Ribbons. Mem: Ala, D.C. and U.S. Supreme Court Bars; Mason; Shrine; VFW; Am. Legion (past dept. comdr, Ala). Rel: Episcopal. Mailing Add: Kinross Farm, Middleburg, Va. 22117.

HUDDLESTON, WALTER 'DEE' D
Ky. State Sen.
b. 1926. Educ: Univ. Ky, B.A. Polit. & Govt. Pos: Ky. State Sen, currently. Bus. & Prof. Pos: Gen. mgr, Radio Sta. WIEL. Mil. Serv: Army, World War II. Mem: Former pres, Ky. Broadcasters Asn; C. of C; Rotary. Rel: Methodist. Mailing Add: Seminole Rd, Elizabethtown, Ky. 42701. (1967)

HUDGENS, JOE F. D
Dir, Div. of Vet. Affairs, Tenn.
b. Putnam Co, Tenn, 9/18/07; m. to Theresa Wallace. Educ: Tenn. Polytech. Inst. Polit. & Govt. Pos: Past pres, Putnam Co. Young Dem, Tenn; claims specialist, Tenn. Dept. of Vet. Affairs, 45-58; asst. dir, Div. of Vet. Affairs, 61-63, dir, 63- Mil. Serv: Army, World War II. Mem: Am. Legion; F&AM; RAM; Shrine; 40 et 8. Rel: Methodist. Mailing Add: 323 Seventh Ave. N, Nashville, Tenn. 37219.

HUDGINS, EDWARD MORTON D
Mem, Va. Dem. State Cent. Cmt.
b. Chase City, Va, 12/19/14; s. Edward Wren Hudgins and Lucy Morton H; m. 3/10/45 to Mary Atherton Howard; c. Edward Wren, II and Frank Howard. Educ: Univ. Va, B.S. and LL.B; Phi Delta Phi; Beta Theta Pi. Polit. & Govt. Pos: Va. State Del, 52-66; mem, Va. Adv. Legis. Counsel, 58-66; past chmn, Va. Jefferson-Jackson Day Activities; past pres, Fourth Cong. Dist. Young Dem; mem, Va. State Dem. Cent. Cmt. and Chesterfield Co. Dem. Cmt, currently. Bus. & Prof. Pos: Gen. Claims Attorney, Chesapeake and Ohio Rwy. Co. and Baltimore and Ohio R.R. Co. Mil. Serv: Entered as Capt, Army, released as Col, after serv. in Inf, 29th Div. and 3 overseas theaters of war; Brig. Gen, Va. Army Nat. Guard, currently; Bronze Star Medal; Three Battle Stars; Pac-Asiatic Theater Ribbon. Mem: Past pres, Chesterfield Co. Bar Asn; Am, Va. and Richmond Bar Asns; Nat. Guard Asn. of U.S; past chmn, Gen. Claims Div, Asn. of Am. R.R; Am. Legion; Ruritan; Commonwealth Club; Country Club of Va. Rel: Episcopal. Legal Res: 8061 Riverside Dr, Richmond, Va. 23225. Mailing Add: 1500 First National Bank Bldg, Richmond, Va. 23219.

HUDGINS, FLOYD D
Ga. State Sen.
b. Gadsden, Ala, 3/11/30; s. William L. Hudgins and Ollie Hudgins H; m. 6/10/50 to Margie Louise Hand; c. Floyd Wayne, Wanda Lynne and Sharon Janelle. Educ: St. Clair Co. High Sch, Odenville, Ala. Polit. & Govt. Pos: Ga. State Rep, 64-66; Ga. State Sen, currently. Bus. & Prof. Pos: Operating engrs, Columbus, Ga, 50- Mil. Serv: Ga. Nat. Guard, 52-60. Mem: Mason. Rel: Methodist. Mailing Add: 3034 Emory St, Columbus, Ga. 31903. (1967)

HUDSON, DOUGLAS R
N.Y. State Sen.
m. to Mildred Purdy; c. one son. Educ: Albany Bus. Col. Polit. & Govt. Pos: Appointed Co. Welfare Cmnr, N.Y, 42, elected 3 terms; sheriff, Rensselaer Co, 2 terms; former N.Y. State Assemblyman; N.Y. State Sen, 67- Mailing Add: 116 Green Ave, Castleton-on-Hudson, N.Y. 12033.

HUDSON, EUGENE TALMADGE 'TED' D
Ga. State Rep.
b. Ocilla, Ga, 2/8/23; s. Dee Dudley Hudson and Ella F. Williams H; m. 12/1/57 to Anne Bass; c. Julianne and Mike Harris. Educ: Univ. Ga, B.S.A. in Agronomy, B.S.A. in Animal Husbandry and B.S.A. in Agr. Econ. Polit. & Govt. Pos: Ga. State Rep, Post 2, 48th Dist, 69- Bus. & Prof. Pos: Registered prfnl. sanitarian, State Health Dept, 63- Mil. Serv: Entered as Pvt, Army, 43, released as Lt, 46, after serv. in Armor Cavalry, Southwest Pac. Theatre, 44-46; Combat Inf. Badge; Battle Stars; Cmn. Ribbon. Mem: Elks; Mason; RAM; Shrine; Farm Bur; Nat. Farmers Orgn; VFW. Gov. Staff, Congressman Stuckey's Staff. Rel: Methodist. Mailing Add: 301 Glynn Ave, Fitzgerald, Ga. 31750.

HUDSON, GLEN GARY R
Exec. Dir, Rep. Party of Hawaii
b. Knoxville, Tenn, 11/2/37; s. Dr. George Donald Hudson and Nellie Ruckelhausen H; m. 8/7/67 to Carol Anne Berntsen; c. Debra Lynn, Terri Ann and Kristin Leigh. Educ: Hamilton Col, B.A, 60; Cornell Univ, 62; Theta Delta Chi. Polit. & Govt. Pos: Rep. committeeman and area chmn, 43rd Dist, Wash, 63-65; dist. coordinator, Dan Evans Campaign, 64; mem. bd. trustees, King Co. Young Rep, 64-65; asst. dir, Gov. Off. of Econ. Opportunity, 65-66; admin. asst. to Secy. of State A. Ludlow Kramer, 66-67; pres, Thurston Co. Young Rep, 67; exec. dir, Rep. Party of Hawaii, 68- Mil. Serv: Coast Guard Res, 60-68. Mem: Adv, Youth Group, Univ. Congregational Church; Big Bros; Seattle and Honolulu; football and basketball coach, Jr. Athletic Progs, Seattle, player and mem, Olympia, Wash. Soccer Club, 67-68. Rel: Episcopal. Mailing Add: 7102 Pilaa Place, Honolulu, Hawaii 96821.

HUDSON, JAMES AUBREY R
b. Austin, Tex, 7/25/30; s. Horace Seymour Hudson and Margaret Harkness H; m. 6/8/51; c. Elizabeth Harkness and James Aubrey, Jr. Educ: Univ.

Tex, B.A, 51; Church Divinity Sch. of the Pac, B.D, 54; Phi Eta Zeta; Delta Kappa Epsilon. Polit. & Govt. Pos: Chmn, Jackson Co. Rep. Party, Tex, 64-66; del, Rep. State Conv, 66 & 68; precinct chmn, Caldwell Co. Rep. Party and co. treas, currently. Bus. & Prof. Pos: Rector, St. John's, Columbus, 54-56; asst. minister, St. Alban's Church, Waco, Tex, 56-57; curate, St. Andrew's Church, Amarillo, 57-59; minister-in-charge, Trinity Church, Edna, Tex. and St. James' Church, Hallettsville, 60-66; rector, Emmanuel Church, Lockhart, 66- Mem: Lions; United Steelworks, 59-60; YMCA, 56-60; Rotary, 54-56. Rel: Episcopal. Mailing Add: Box 662, Lockhart, Tex. 78644.

HUDSON, JAMES WEISSINGER R
Co. Chmn, Pocahontas Co. Rep. Party, Iowa
b. Des Moines, Iowa, 8/31/25; s. Fred M. Hudson and Anne E. Weissinger H; m. 6/25/49 to Frances Leone Whisler; c. James C, Carol Ann, David Carl and Thomas Edwin. Educ: Univ. of Iowa, B.A, 48, LL.B, 50; Sigma Nu, Phi Delta Phi. Polit. & Govt. Pos: Co. Attorney, Pocahontas Co, Iowa, 55-60; city attorney, Pocahontas, currently; co. chmn, Pocahontas Co. Rep. Party, 60- Bus. & Prof. Pos: Pres, Pocahontas C. of C; mem. bd, Pocahontas Commun. Found. Mil. Serv: Entered as Pvt, Army Air Corps, 44, released as 2nd Lt, 46. Mem: Pres, Pocahontas Co. Bar Asn; secy, 14th Judicial Dist. Bar Asn; Iowa State and Am. Bar Asns; Mason; Am. Legion; Farm Bur; Rotary. Rel: Methodist. Mailing Add: 1000 Sunset Dr, Pocahontas, Iowa 50574.

HUDSON, MORLEY ALVIN R
V.Chmn, N.W. Region Rep. Party, La.
b. San Antonio, Tex, 3/31/17; s. Oscar Alvin Hudson and Ruth Morley H; m. 11/11/44 to Lucy Worthington North; c. Nancy, Lucy and Courtney. Educ: Ga. Tech, B.S. in Mech. Eng, 38; Tau Beta Pi; Omicron Delta Kappa; Phi Kappa Phi. Polit. & Govt. Pos: La. State Rep. and Minority Leader, La. House of Rep, 64-68; campaign mgr, Nixon-Agnew Campaign, 68; del, Rep. Nat. Conv, 68; state v.chmn, N.W. Region Rep. Party, La, 68- Bus. & Prof. Pos: Pres. and gen. mgr, Hudson-Rush Co, 52-; v.pres, McElroy Metal Mills, Inc, 62- Mil. Serv: Entered as Lt, Army, 38, released as Capt, 42, after serv. in Inf. Mem: Am. Soc. Mech. Engrs.(sport power sq). Rel: Presbyterian. Mailing Add: 4609 Gilbert Dr, Shreveport, La. 71106.

HUERTA, JOSEPH LOPEZ D
b. El Paso, Tex, 2/17/29; s. Refugio Martinez Huerta and Juana Reyes Lopez H; m. 8/17/68 to Maria Luisa Leon Arredondo. Educ: Univ. Ariz, B.P.A, 57; Phi Kappa Alpha. Polit. & Govt. Pos: Chmn, Pima Co. Dem. Party, 61-63; original mem, Viva Kennedy Orgn, 63-65; v.chmn, Ariz. Dem. State Cmt, 63-67; del, Dem. Nat. Conv, 64 & 68; South. Ariz. campaign chmn, Sen. Robert Kennedy, 68. Bus. & Prof. Pos: Dep. assessor, Tucson, Ariz, 54-57; owner and operator, La Fuente Restaurant and Cocktail Lounge, 59- Mil. Serv: Entered as Pvt, Army, 51, released as Sgt, 53, after serv. in 24th Div, Korea, 51-52; UN Medal; Far East Command Medal; Korea Ribbon; Inf. Combat Badge. Mem: Elks; Moose; Bartenders Union; Bishops Fund; K. of C. Rel: Roman Catholic. Mailing Add: 3832 E. Calle Ensenada, Tucson, Ariz. 85716.

HUETT, ORVIL E. D
Polit. & Govt. Pos: Ind. State Rep, formerly. Bus. & Prof. Pos: Welder set-up, Bucyrus Erie Co; mem, Local 5352, USW, v.pres, 2 years, pres, 7 years, mem, Legis. Cmt, 4 years and trustee, Welfare and Educ. Cmt, 2 years. Mil. Serv: 36th Inf. Div, World War II. Mem: Mason; Scottish Rite; Am. Legion; VFW. Rel: Baptist. Mailing Add: 7112 Pollack Ave, Evansville, Ind. 47715. (1967)

HUETTEL, WILLIAM LePRINCE R
Tenn. State Rep.
b. Memphis, Tenn, 9/7/33; s. Wilfred Joseph Huettel and Alice LePrince H; m. 2/2/57 to Martha Janet Alford; c. Laura Jane, Cathryn Alford, William L, Jr. and Sarah Whitley. Educ: Tex. A&M Univ, B.A, 55. Polit. & Govt. Pos: Tenn. State Rep. Bus. & Prof. Pos: V.pres, United Paint Co, 55- Mil. Serv: 2nd Lt, Army, 56, serv. in 894 Tank Bn, Sch. Troops, Ft. Knox, Ky; Capt, Army Res. Mem: Memphis Paint, Varnish & Lacquer Asn.(pres, 65). Rel: Roman Catholic. Mailing Add: 5889 Brierdale, Memphis, Tenn. 38117.

HUETTL, CARL W. R
Chmn, Forest Co. Rep. Orgn, Wis.
b. Wabeno, Wis, 6/17/21; s. Erhard A. Huettl and Florence Voelz H; m. 8/9/41 to Esther Ruth Buttke; c. Gerald W, Larry C, James D, Dona Mae (Mrs. Funk), David A, Ronald L. and Mark A. Educ: Wabeno High Sch, 4 years. Polit. & Govt. Pos: Chmn, Forest Co. Rep. Orgn, Wis, 61- Bus. & Prof. Pos: Rural sales rep, Wis. Pub. Serv. Corp, 45-; dir, Forest Co. Civil Defense, 61-69. Mem: Lions (pres, Wabeno Club, 56-57); C. of C.(v.pres, Wabeno chap, 60-61). Rel: Lutheran. Mailing Add: P.O. Box 131, Wabeno, Wis. 54566.

HUEY, ARTHUR TICKNOR R
Chmn, Leelanau Co. Rep. Party, Mich.
b. Traverse City, Mich, 2/15/41; m. 9/7/63 to Joan Elaine Seafuri; c. Mark. Educ: Middlebury Col, A.B; Mich. State Univ, M.B.A; Beta Gamma Sigma; Tau Kappa Alpha; Beta Alpha Psi. Polit. & Govt. Pos: Chmn, Leelanau Co. Rep. Party, Mich, currently. Bus. & Prof. Pos: Bus. mgr, Leelanau Schs. Mem: Rotary. Mailing Add: c/o Leelanau Schools, Glen Arbor, Mich. 49636.

HUFF, BEATTIE EUGENE D
S.C. State Rep.
b. Greenville, S.C, 5/21/11; s. Beattie G. Huff and Lora Edwards H. m. 11/26/42 to Gladys L. Rainey; c. Glenda, Eugenia, Greg, Vicki and Libby. Educ: Lincoln Mem. Univ. Polit. & Govt. Pos: S.C. State Rep, 61- Bus. & Prof. Pos: Farmer and contractor; real estate. Mem: Lions; WOW; Farm Bur; C. of C; former trustee Berea High Sch; Mason. Rel: Berea First Baptist Church. Mailing Add: White Horse, Rd, Route 1, Greenville, S.C. 29611.

HUFF, GENE R
Ky. State Rep.
b. Franklin, Ohio, 10/6/29; s. Adam Huff and Maud H; m. 7/4/52 to Ethel Delores Dayberry; c. Georgia Arlene, Martin Blaine, Marsha Gail, Anna Marie and Roberta Jean. Educ: Union Col, B.A; Miami Univ, 61-62. Polit. & Govt. Pos: Ky. State Rep, 85th Dist, 68- Bus. & Prof. Pos: Minister, Pentecostal Churches, 49- Mem: Mason (32°); Scottish Rite. Rel: Pentecostal. Mailing Add: 231 E. Fourth St, London, Ky. 40741.

HUFF, IRA LU R
Chmn, Morgan Co. Rep. Cent. Cmt, Mo.
b. Gravois Mills, Mo, 10/23/19; d. Ira B. Williams and Mary Lucetta Holst W; m. 6/3/39 to Elmer Gregory Huff; c. Robert G, Rebecca Ann (Mrs. Claude Joy) and Racher Lynn (Mrs. Michael McDorman). Polit. & Govt. Pos: Treas, Morgan Co. Rep. Club, Mo, 56-60; mem, Morgan Co. Rep. Cent. Cmt, 56-, treas, 58-62, v.chmn, 62-68 and chmn, 68-; mem, State Cmt, Mo, 66- Bus. & Prof. Pos: Dep. Circuit clerk and recorder, Morgan Co, Mo, 67- Mem: Past matron, Eastern Star; past pres, Evening Sorosis Federated Club; Women's Civic Club; past pres, Westminister Presby. Women's Asn; mem. bd, Versailles Cemetery Asn, Inc; mem, bd, Morgan Co. Chap. of Tuberculosis. Rel: Presbyterian. Mailing Add: Rt. 3, Versailles, Mo. 65084.

HUFF, RICHARD LEE R
b. Madison, Wis, 5/6/27; s. Forrest Gibbs Huff and Lucille Beimborn H; m. 7/26/58 to Harriet Willis; c. Molly (Mary Lee), William Gibbs and Peter Bashford. Educ: Univ. Wis, B.S, 51, grad. work in Eng. and hist, 65; Phi Eta Sigma. Polit. & Govt. Pos: Chmn, Second Dist. Nixon-Agnew Cmt, 67-; del, Rep. Nat. Conv, 68. Bus. & Prof. Pos: Owner, Elec. Utilities TV, 58-65; partner, Huff and Waterman, 65-67 and pres, 67-; pres, Concept Visuals, Inc, 68- Mil. Serv: Merchant Marine Serv, 44-45 & 51. Publ: 'Paul Siefert: Wisconsin Pioneer Artist,' Wis. Tales and Trails, winter 67. Mem: Pub. Utilities Advert. Asn; v.chmn, Children Serv. Soc; Scottish Rite; Rotary; Maple Bluff Country Club. Rel: Lutheran. Mailing Add: 820 Kings Way, Madison, Wis. 53704.

HUFF, SARA ELLEN D
Mem. Exec. Bd, Pa. Dem. State Cmt.
b. Warren, Pa, 11/14/07; d. Forest Albert Huff and Mary McAdoo H; single. Educ: Clarion State Col, 27-36; Wharton State Col. Exten. and Pa. State Col. Exten; private lessons in pub. speaking. Polit. & Govt. Pos: Supvr. bonds and ins, Pa. State Liquor Control Bd, Harrisburg, 36-42; supvr, U.S. Navy, Mechanicsburg, Pa, 42-55; mem, Forest Co. Dem. Cmt, 55-56, v.chmn, 56; cand, Pa. State Rep, 56; Forest Co. mem, mem. Dem. policy cmt. and mem. exec. bd, Pa. State Dem. Cmt, 58-; mem, Gov. Cmt. on Children and Youth, 59; del. and secy. Pa. Del, Dem. Nat. Conv, 68; regional dir, Pa. Fedn. Dem. Women, 4 years; Bus. & Prof. Pos: Elem. sch. teacher, Forest and Jefferson Co, Pa, 27-36; pres, Clarington Sand and Gravel Co, Clarington, Pa, 55-56; mem. and secy. bd, Polk State Sch, Pa, 58-63. Mem: Bethlem Star Chap; Joppa Shrine; Clarion Co. Women's Club; Forest Co. Dem. Women's Club; Clarion Co. Dem. Women's Club. Rel: Presbyterian. Mailing Add: 111 Locust St, Harrisburg, Pa. 17101.

HUFF, WILLIAM HENRY, III R
Iowa State Rep.
b. Davenport, Iowa, 6/24/37; s. William Henry Huff Jr. and Estelle Evelyn Joseph H; m. 9/9/67 to Judith Ann Ewing; c. Amy Christine. Educ: Wis. State Univ, Eau Claire, B.S, 59; Drake Univ, J.D, 67. Polit. & Govt. Pos: Iowa State Rep, 69- Bus. & Prof. Pos: Attorney at law, Des Moines, Iowa, 67- Mil. Serv: Entered as 2nd Lt, Army, 59, released as Capt, 64, after serv. in Brooke Gen. Hosp, Ft. Sam Houston, Tex, 2 years and Europe, 3 years. Mem: Am, Iowa State and Polk Co. Bar Asns; Phi Alpha Delta; Urbandale Jaycees. Iowa State Bar Asn. Cert. of Merit; Martin Tollefson Mem. Award; Am. Law Student's Asn. Silver Key Award. Rel: Methodist. Mailing Add: 4209 65th St, Apt. 1, Des Moines, Iowa 50322.

HUFFAKER, WILLIE CALLOWAY D
Chmn, Lynn Co. Dem. Party, Tex.
b. Stamford, Tex, 3/7/14; s. Willie C. Huffaker and Maud Schofner H; m. 12/22/34 to Nina Ruth Scott; c. Wayne, Gerald and John. Educ: Tex. Tech. Col, B.A, 37; Univ. Tex, Austin, 37-39. Polit. & Govt. Pos: Co. attorney, Tahoka, Tex, 40-44; dist. attorney, 106th Judicial Dist, 44-48; chmn, Lynn Co. Dem. Party, 66- Bus. & Prof. Pos: Attorney, Tahoka, 48- Mem: Tex. State Bar Asn; Mason; Eastern Star. Rel: United Methodist. Legal Res: 2309 N. Second, Tahoka, Tex. 79373. Mailing Add: P.O. Box 416, Tahoka, Tex. 79373.

HUFFER, ROY HENRY, JR. D
b. Circleville, Ohio, 3/12/35; s. Roy Henry Huffer and Margaret Settles H; m. 7/27/57 to Marilyn Joan Crawford; c. Cynthia Kay, Roy Henry, III, Johnna Lynn, Steven Todd and Mark Edward. Educ: Ohio State Univ, B.A. in polit. sci, 57; Franklin Univ, J.D, 64; Sigma Nu. Polit. & Govt. Pos: Ohio State Rep, Pickaway Co, 65-66; prosecuting attorney, Pickaway Co, 69- Bus. & Prof. Pos: Partner, Huffer & Huffer, Attorneys, currently. Mem: Ohio State Bar Asn; v.pres, Pickaway Co. Bar Asn; Am. Bar Asn; Am. Judicature Asn; Elks; K. of C; Rotary; Farm Bur; C. of C; Pickaway Country Club. Rel: Catholic. Legal Res: 210 S. Court, Circleville, Ohio 43113. Mailing Add: 975 Circle Dr, Circleville, Ohio 43113.

HUFFMAN, BILL S. D
Mich. State Rep.
b. Estelle, Ga, 12/27/24; married; c. Sherry, Marvin, Krisaundra and Beth. Educ: Spec. courses, Lawrence Inst. of Tech. Polit. & Govt. Pos: Mem. city coun, Madison Heights, Mich, 2 terms and mayor, 1 term; Mich. State Rep, 62- Bus. & Prof. Pos: Sales rep, Assoc. Metals. Mil. Serv: Navy, 42-47; participated in Navy V-12 prog. Mem: Kiwanis Club. Rel: Protestant. Mailing Add: 615 W. Barrett, Madison Heights, Mich. 48071. (1967)

HUFFMAN, DONALD WISE R
Mem. City Cmt, Roanoke Rep. Party, Va.
b. Staunton, Va, 12/5/27; s. Thomas Elmer Huffman and Virginia Wise H; m. 8/12/50 to Colleen James; c. Teresa Lynn and Kelly Virginia. Educ: Va. Polytech. Inst, B.S, 50; Wash. & Lee Univ, LL.B, 66; Phi Beta Kappa; Omicron Delta Kappa; Scabbard & Blade; Alpha Pi Mu; Order of the Coif; Sigma Phi Epsilon. Polit. & Govt. Pos: V.chmn, Lexington-Rockbridge-Buena Vista Rep. Party, Va, 64-65, former chmn; mem. city cmt, Roanoke Rep. Party, 68- Mil.

Serv: Entered as Pvt, Army, 46, released as Pfc, 47; Army Res, 49-60. Mem: Pres, Lexington C. of C; chmn, Lexington Merchant's Cmt; Jaycees; Rotary. Rel: Presbyterian. Mailing Add: 3002 Burnleigh Rd. S.W, Roanoke, Va. 24014.

HUFFMAN, FRANK HOWARD D
Secy, Hancock Co. Dem. Cent. and Exec. Cmts, Ohio
b. Rawson, Ohio, 12/28/95; s. Darius Edward Huffman and Teresa Ellen Hartman H; m. 11/1/23 to Grace Marie Inbody. Educ: Rawson High Sch, Ohio, grad, 13. Polit. & Govt. Pos: Dep. Clerk of Courts, Hancock Co, Ohio, 13-19, Dep. Co. Auditor, 19-35, Co. Auditor, 35-43; committeeman, Hancock Co. Dem. Cent. Cmt, 30-; State Exam, Bur. of Inspection and Supv. of Pub. Off, State Auditor's Off, 43-53; treas, Hancock Co. Dem. Party, 58-64; mem, Hancock Co. Bd. Elec, 61-; secy, Hancock Co. Dem. Cent. and Exec. Cmts, 68- Mem: Ohio Asn. of Elec. Officials; Co. Auditors Asn; Mason; Elks. Twenty-five year Pin, Findlay Elks; Twenty-five year Pin, Findlay Masonic Lodge. Rel: Methodist. Mailing Add: 1125 S. West St, Findlay, Ohio 45840.

HUFFMAN, JAMES WYLIE D
b. Chandlersville, Ohio, 9/13/94; s. John Alexander Huffman and Tacy Careins H; c. Margaret (Mrs. Graff) and James W, Jr. Educ: Ohio Wesleyan Univ; Ohio State Univ; Univ. Chicago, LL.B; Phi Gamma Delta; Delta Phi. Polit. & Govt. Pos: Secy. to Gov. Vic Donahey, 24-26; mem, Pub. Utilities Cmn, 26-30; State Dir. of Commerce, 45; U.S. Sen, Ohio, 45-47. Bus. & Prof. Pos: Attorney-at-Law, Columbus, Ohio, 30-65; v.pres, Logan Clay Prod, Logan, 50-; pres, Motorists Mutual Ins. Co, 58- and Motorists Life Ins. Co, Columbus, 65- Mil. Serv: Entered as 2nd Lt, Army, 17, released as 1st Lt, 19, after serv. in 329th Inf, 83rd Div, Ohio, 17 and 120th Machine Gun Bn, 32nd Div, France, 18-19; Vesle Aisne, Soissons, Argonne and Dun-sur Meuse Campaign Ribbons; Army of Occp. Medal. Publ: The Legend of Ducan Falls. Mem: Am. Legion; 40 et 8; VFW; Mason, Scottish Rite, Shrine; Am, Ohio and Columbus Bar Asns; Athletic Club. Trustee Emer, Ohio State Univ, Distinguished Serv. Award, 58. Rel: Presbyterian. Mailing Add: 2620 E. Broad St, Columbus, Ohio 43209.

HUFFMAN, ODELL HAMPTON D
W.Va. State Del.
b. Wyco, W.Va, 2/18/23; s. Mitchell Odell Huffman and Callie Whittington H; m. 8/5/50 to Geraldine Cline; c. Katherine Anne, David Hampton, William Odell and John Bruce. Educ: Concord Col, 40-43 & 46-47; W.Va. Univ. Col. Law, J.D, 50; Phi Delta Phi. Polit. & Govt. Pos: Mem, Princeton City Coun, W.Va, 63-67; mayor, Princeton, 65-66; W.Va. State Del, 69- Bus. & Prof. Pos: Secy, Princeton Commun. Hosp. and Princeton Extended Care Asn. Mil. Serv: Entered as Pvt, Air Force, 43, released as Sgt, 46, after serv. in Third Air Force. Mem: W.Va. State Bar (bd. dirs); W.Va. Trial Lawyers Asn.(bd. dirs); W.Va, Mercer Co. and Am. Bar Asns; Am. Trial Lawyers Asn; Elks; Moose; Mercer Co. Vet. Coun; Rotary. Rel: Methodist. Mailing Add: Law Bldg, Princeton, W.Va. 24740.

HUFFSMITH, JUDITH ANN R
V.chmn, Arapahoe Co. Rep. Cent. Cmt, Colo.
b. Cedar Rapids, Iowa, 2/20/34; d. George Merrill King and Agatha Nielson K; m. 1/30/53 to Richard Reeves Huffsmith; c. Thomas Guinn, Gretchen and Melissa. Educ: Univ. Colo, 53. Polit. & Govt. Pos: Block worker, Arapahoe Co. Rep. Cent. Cmt, Colo, 60-66, committeewoman, 61-66, area chmn, 66-69, v.chmn, 69-; bd. mem, Cherry Creek Rep. Women, 62-65; campaign chmn, Hugh Fowler, Colo. State Sen, 68. Mem: Denver Assistance League. Rel: Episcopal. Mailing Add: 4601 S. Lafayette, Englewood, Colo. 80110.

HUFSMITH, GEORGE W. R
Wyo. State Rep.
b. Omaha, Nebr, 8/27/24; m. to Betty; c. Four. Educ: Yale Univ, B.A, M.A. Polit. & Govt. Pos: Wyo. State Rep, currently. Bus. & Prof. Pos: Independent Ins. Agent. Mem: Elks; Mason; Shrine. Rel: Episcopal. Mailing Add: P.O. Box 325, Jackson, Wyo. 83001.

HUG, PROCTER RALPH, SR. D
Nev. State Sen.
b. Elgin, Ore, 10/25/02; s. Charles Hug and Ella Procter H; m. to Margaret Beverly; c. Procter R, Jr, Beverly (Mrs. Sharp) and Patricia (Mrs. Durham). Educ: Univ. Nev, B.A, 27, M.A, 44; Phi Kappa Phi; Alpha Tau Omega. Hon. Dr, Univ. Nev, 66. Polit. & Govt. Pos: Nev. State Sen, currently. Bus. & Prof. Pos: Teacher, Sparks High Sch, Nev, 27-32, v.prin, 32-37, prin, 37-40; supt, Sparks City Schs, 40-56, asst. supt, 56-59; Supt. of Schs, Washoe Co, 59-66. Mem: Lions; Mason; Shrine. Rel: Episcopal. Mailing Add: 1055 Sonora Dr, Reno, Nev. 89502.

HUGGINS, HARRY F. R
N.H. State Rep.
b. Pittsburg, N.H, 8/13/02; married; c. Three. Educ: Plymouth Teachers Col. Polit. & Govt. Pos: Sexton, auditor, supvr, selectman and mem. sch. bd, formerly; N.H. State Rep, 65- Mem: Dir, Guides Asn; Patrons of Husbandry; Odd Fellows. Rel: Protestant. Mailing Add: Pittsburg, N.H. 03592.

HUGHES, CALISTA COOPER R
b. Humboldt, Nebr, 4/27/14; d. Guy Lester Cooper, Sr. and Josephine Lovina Bruun C; m. 10/3/36 to Morris Nelson Hughes; c. Calista Mary (Mrs. Kenneth Solari), Judith Cooper (Mrs. Keith Reagan Leech) and Morris Nelson, Jr. Educ: Univ. Nebr, A.B, 35; Delta Omicron; Mortar Bd; Pi Beta Phi; Vestals; YWCA. Polit. & Govt. Pos: Del, Rep. Co. Conv, 62; alternate del, Rep. State Conv, Nebr, 64; Nebr. State Sen, First Dist, 64-68; mem, Gov. Cmn. on Status of Women; dir, Comprehensive Health Planning, Off. of Gov, 69- Bus. & Prof. Pos: French teacher, Humboldt Pub. Schs, Nebr, 63-64. Mem: Bus. and Prfnl. Women's Club; Nat. Rehab. Asn; Nebr. Rehab. Asn; Nebr. State Welfare Asn; Nat. Cmt. Supporting Pub. Schs; trustee, Univ. Nebr. Found; League of Women Voters; PEO; Am. Legion Auxiliary; past mem, Jr. League, Mexico City Chap; Alpha Club; Delphian Soc; Nebr. and Brownville Hist. Socs; Lincoln Univ. Club; Presby. Women's Asn; Omaha Athletic Club; Humboldt's Hopeful Gardeners; Nebr. Art Asn. Rel: Presbyterian. Legal Res: 815 Fifth St, Humboldt, Nebr. 68376. Mailing Add: State Capitol, Lincoln, Nebr. 68509.

HUGHES, CHARLES E. D
Co. Chmn, Dem. Party, Tex.
b. Sherman, Tex, 4/30/27; s. Roy E. Hughes and Mary Fowler H; m. 12/25/54 to Wilma Haralson. Educ: Univ. Tex, B.A. and LL.B; Phi Delta Phi. Polit. & Govt. Pos: Tex. State Rep, 51-62; Co. Chmn, Dem. Party, Tex, 64- Bus. & Prof. Pos: Attorney-at-Law, self-employed, 51- Mil. Serv: Entered as Recruit, Merchant Marine, released as Commun. Officer, after serv. in Pac. and Atlantic. Mem: Elks. Rel: Baptist. Legal Res: 326 W. Belden, Sherman, Tex. 75020. Mailing Add: 104 S. Crockett St, Sherman, Tex. 75020.

HUGHES, CHARLES LENDALL R
b. Desoto, Ill, 11/20/21; s. George W. Hughes and Mary Williams H; m. 9/17/60 to Janet Louise Kesel; c. Charles Scott and Karen Louise. Educ: Univ. Mo, LL.B, 51, J.D, 69; Delta Theta Phi. Polit. & Govt. Pos: Asst. state attorney, Kane Co, Ill, 57-64, state attorney, 64-65; village attorney, Maple Park, 65-; former Ill. State Rep. Bus. & Prof. Pos: Mem. law firm, Edwards, Brunnemeyer and Hughes, Aurora, Ill, currently. Mil. Serv: Entered as A/S, Navy, 39, released as Fireman 1/C to enter Naval Academy, 41; Good Conduct and Defense Medals. Mem: Ill. and Kane Co. Bar Asns; AF&AM 855; Elks Lodge 705. Rel: Presbyterian. Legal Res: 216 South Evanslawn, Aurora, Ill. 60506. Mailing Add: Aurora National Bank Bldg, Aurora, Ill. 60504.

HUGHES, DOUGLAS WILLIAM R
b. Duluth, Minn, 1/28/01; s. Robert Luther Hughes and Jennie Sundberg H; m. 6/22/25 to Eunice L. Norstrom, wid; c. Douglas W, Jr. and Donald R. Educ: Univ. Minn, B.S. in bus. admin, 22. Polit. & Govt. Pos: Pres, Rep. Cmt. of 200, 60; campaign mgr, 22nd Assembly Dist. Rep. Party, 60, co. committeeman, 62-; cand. for pres, Borough of Queens, 62; pres, 22nd Assembly Dist. Rep. Club, N.Y, 66. Mem: Mason; Scottish Rite; Shrine; Elks; C. of C; pres, Queensboro Rotary, 52-53; Nat. Conf. of Christians and Jews; chmn, Cent. Chap. of Queens, Am. Red. Cross, 54-60; Utopia Improvement Asn. Rel: Protestant Episcopal. Mailing Add: 193-14 48th Ave, Flushing, N.Y. 11365.

HUGHES, EDWARD JOSEPH, JR. D
b. Phila, Pa, 7/19/22; s. Edward Joseph Hughes and Ellen McCloskey H; m. 12/12/42 to Margaret Brendana Burns; c. Annette Marie (Mrs. Marcozzi) and Edward J, III. Educ: Drexel Inst. Tech, Mech. E. Polit. & Govt. Pos: Committeeman, Third Dist. Dem. Party, 5 years; alternate del, Dem. Nat. Conv, 68. Bus. & Prof. Pos: Consult. engr, 47-51; pres. and founder, Hughes Industs, 51- Mil. Serv: Pvt, Signal Corp, Army, 43. Mem: Engrs. Club Phila; Am. Soc. Tool & Mfg. Engrs; Inst. Elec. & Electronics Eng; Am. Soc. Mech. Eng; Navy League; Air Force Asn; Kiwanis; Army Ord. Asn; Holy Name Soc; K. of C; Moose. Rel: Roman Catholic. Mailing Add: 1103 Cherry Lane, Cinnaminson, N.J. 08077.

HUGHES, EVA FRANCES R
Chmn, Osage Co. Rep. Cent. Cmt, Kans.
b. Quenemo, Kans, 9/24/08; d. Walter Anderson Cates and Lulu McGuire C; m. 2/8/30 to Rollo Glenn Hughes; c. Max Leon. Polit. & Govt. Pos: Committeewoman, Osage Co. Rep. Cent. Cmt, Kans, 50-59, chmn, 59-; secy, Fifth Cong. Dist. Rep. Party; pres, Osage Co. Womens Rep. Clubs, 57-60; alternate del, Rep. Nat. Conv, 64. Bus. & Prof. Pos: Owner and operator, cafe, 45-49 and supermarket, 52-58. Mem: Past Matron, Eastern Star; Past Noble Grand, Rebekah; Demolay Mothers; Sunflower-Fidelas; Womens Christian Serv; Farm Bur; H.D.U. Rel: Methodist. Mailing Add: 227 S. Eighth, Quenemo, Kans. 66528.

HUGHES, GEORGE RAYMOND, JR. R
b. Cumberland, Md, 7/12/25; s. George Raymond Hughes and Anna Fahey H. (deceased); m. 12/28/49 to Patricia Lou Funk; c. Frances Anne, Mary Lou, Patricia Lee, Georgia Rae and George R, III. Educ: Univ. of Md, A.B, 50, Law Sch, LL.B, 52. Polit. & Govt. Pos: Md. State Del, 55-58, minority floor leader, Md. House of Del, 56-58; mem, Legis. Coun, Md, 56-58; dist. dir, U.S. Census Bur, 60; Md. State Sen, 63-69; judge, Md. Tax Court, 69- Mil. Serv: Entered as Aviation Cadet, Navy, 43, released as Qm. 3/C, 46, after serv. in Amphibious Forces, Group 75, Philippine Sea Frontier, 45-46; Philippine Liberation and American and Pacific Theater Ribbons; Victory and Good Conduct Medals. Publ: Several newspaper articles, Baltimore Sun, 58 & 63. Mem: Treas, Allegany Co. Bar Asn, 52-55; Am. Legion Post 13; former pres, PTA. Rel: Episcopal. Legal Res: 1008 Greene St, Extended, Cumberland, Md. 21502. Mailing Add: Clark-Keating Bldg, Cumberland, Md. 21502.

HUGHES, HAROLD EVERETT D
U.S. Sen, Iowa
b. Ida Grove, Iowa, 2/10/22; s. Lewis C. Hughes and Etta Kelly H; m. 8/23/41 to Eva Mae Mercer; c. Connie (Mrs. Dennis Otto), Carol (Mrs. Matthew Fatino) and Phyllis. Educ: Univ. Iowa, 40-41. Hon. D.Sc.Govt, Col. of Osteopathic Med. and Surgery, 65; hon. LL.D, Cornell Col, 66, Buena Vista Col, 67, Graceland Col, 67, Loras Col, 68, Lehigh Univ, 69 and Grinnell Col, 69; hon. D.H.L, Marycrest Col, 67; hon. D.C.L, Simpson Col, 69. Polit. & Govt. Pos: Mem, Interstate Commerce Cmn. Joint Bds, 59-62; mem, Iowa State Commerce Cmn, 59-63, chmn, 59-60 & 61-62; Gov, Iowa, 63-69; del, Dem. Nat. Conv, 64 & 68; cmts. on state planning, fed-state rels, state and local revenue, health and welfare, and transportation, Nat. Gov. Conf, mem, exec. cmt, 65-67; chmn, Dem. Gov. Conf, 66-68; mem. pub. off. adv. coun, U.S. Off. Econ. Opportunity, 66-68; trustee, States Urban Action Center, 67-68; chmn, Cmn. on Dem. Selection of Presidential Nominees, 68; v.chmn, Spec. Dem. Cmn. on Party Structure and Del. Selection, 69-; U.S. Sen, Iowa, 69-, mem, U.S. Senate Cmts. on Banking and Currency and Labor and Pub. Welfare, 69-, chmn, Subcmt. on Alcoholism and Narcotics, 69- Bus. & Prof. Pos: With motor transportation industry, 46-58; mgr, Hinrich's Truck Line, Ida Grove, Iowa, 50-53; field rep, Iowa Motor Truck Asn, 53-55; founder and mgr, Iowa Better Trucking Bur, 55-58. Mil. Serv: Pvt, Army, 42-45, with serv. in 83rd Chem. Bn, North Africa, Sicily, and Italy, 43-45. Mem: Am. Legion; K. of P; Mason; RAM; Mizpah Commandery; Shrine. Rel: Methodist. Legal Res: Ida Grove, Iowa 51445. Mailing Add: Senate Office Building, Wash, D.C. 20510.

HUGHES, HARRY ROE D
Md. State Sen.
b. Easton, Md, 11/13/26; s. Jonathan Longfellow Hughes and Helen Roe H;

m. 6/30/51 to Patricia Ann Donoho; c. Ann D. and Elizabeth R. Educ: Mt. St. Mary's Col, 44-45; Univ. of Md, B.S, 49; George Wash. Univ. Sch. of Law, LL.B, 52. Polit. & Govt. Pos: Md. State Del, 55-59; Md. State Sen, 59-, mem, Gov. Cmn. on City-Co. Fiscal Rels, Md. State Senate, 59, Gov. Reapportionment Cmn, 62, chmn, Standing Cmt. on Taxation and Fiscal Matters, 62-64, chmn, Exec. Nominations Cmt, 62-64, Cmn. Revise Condemnation Laws of Md, 63-64, spec. legis. cmt, State-Local Fiscal Rels, 65, Legis. Coun. Md, 65-, chmn, Gov. Cmt. on Taxation and Fiscal Reform, 67 and chmn, Joint Budget and Audit Cmt, Md. Gen. Assembly, 68-69; alternate del, Dem. Nat. Conv, 68. Mil. Serv: Entered as A/S, Naval Air Corps Training Prog, 44, released as Aviation Cadet, 45. Mem: Md. State Bar Asn.(pres, 65-66); Am. and Caroline Co. Bar Asns; Am. Legion; Rotary. Rel: Episcopal. Legal Res: Sunset Dr, Denton, Md. 21629. Mailing Add: P.O. Box 70, Denton, Md. 21629.

HUGHES, H(ENRY) STUART D
b. N.Y.C, 5/7/16; s. Charles Evans Hughes, Jr. and Marjory Stuart H; m. 3/26/64 to Judith B. Markham; c. Sandra, Kenneth and David. Educ: Amherst Col, A.B, 37; Harvard Univ, M.A, 38, Ph.D, 40; Phi Beta Kappa. Hon. L.H.D, Amherst Col, 67. Polit. & Govt. Pos: Chief div. of research for Europe, Dept. of State, 46-48; independent cand, U.S. Sen, 62; co-chmn, Nat. Cmt. for Sane Nuclear Policy, 63-67, chmn, 67- Bus. & Prof. Pos: Asst. prof, Harvard Univ, 48-52, prof, 57-; vis. mem, Inst. Advanced Study, 50; assoc. prof, Stanford Univ, 52-55, head dept. hist, 55-56. Mil. Serv: Entered as Pvt, F.A, Army, 41, released as Lt. Col, Off. of Strategic Serv, 46; Commendatore dell'Ordine della Corona D'Italia; Cavaliere Officiale al Merito della Repubblica Italiana. Publ: Consciousness and Society, 58; An Approach to Peace, 62; The Obstructed Path, Harper & Row, 68; plus others. Mem: Am. Hist. Asn; Am. Civil Liberties Union; NAACP; Urban League; Am. Acad. Arts and Sci. Recipient Guggenheim Fel, 55 & 58. Mailing Add: Dept. of History, Harvard University, Cambridge, Mass. 02138.

HUGHES, JEROME MICHAEL D
Minn. State Sen.
b. St. Paul, Minn, 10/1/29; s. Michael Joseph Hughes and Mary Malloy H; m. 8/11/51 to Audrey Magdalene Lackner; c. Bernadine, Timothy, Kathleen, Rosemarie, Margaret Mary and John. Educ: Col. St. Thomas, Minn, B.A, 51; Univ. Minn, Minneapolis, M.A, 58; Wayne State Univ, 67-68; Phi Delta Kappa. Polit. & Govt. Pos: Precinct chmn, Dem. Party, Maplewood, Minn, 59-65; legis. dist. coordinator, 50th Dist, 64-66; chmn, Village Maplewood Police Cmn, 64-66; Minn. State Sen, 50th Dist, 67- Bus. & Prof. Pos: Pres, St. Paul Counsr. Asn, 63-64; bd. dirs, Minn. Counsr. Asn, 63-66. Mem: Minn. and Am. Personnel and Guid. Asns; Twin City Voc. Guid. Asn; Minn. Educ. Asn; Parkside Recreation Asn.(former pres); Boy Scouts (dist. v.chmn). Rel: Catholic. Mailing Add: 1978 Payne Ave, St. Paul, Minn. 55117.

HUGHES, JERRY MILES, JR. R
b. Orangeburg, S.C, 5/21/17; s. Jerry Miles Hughes and Oressie Collier H; m. 12/28/52 to Jean Hardwick; c. Jerry Miles, III and Jennings H. Educ: Univ. S.C, A.B, 39, LL.B, 41; pres, Student Body, 38; Omicron Delta Kappa; Sigma Alpha Epsilon. Polit. & Govt. Pos: S.C. State Rep, 53-58 & 61-68, Minority Leader, S.C. State House of Rep, 67-68. Bus. & Prof. Pos: Attorney-at-law, Orangeburg, S.C, 46- Mil. Serv: Entered as Pvt, Marine Corps, 41, released as Capt, 45, after serv. in Seventh Marines and others in Pac; Maj, Marine Corps Res; Presidential Unit Citation. Mem: Am. and S.C. Bar Asns; Kiwanis; Elks; VFW; Am. Legion; Chef de Gare, 40 et 8; Moose; Orangeburg Country Club; Orangeburg Rifle and Gun Club. Rel: Methodist. Legal Res: Jackson Dr, Orangeburg, S.C. 29115. Mailing Add: P.O. Box 615, Orangeburg, S.C. 29115.

HUGHES, JOHN HENRY R
N.Y. State Sen.
b. Syracuse, N.Y, 4/1/04; s. Thomas P. Hughes and Susan Eagan H; m. 2/26/38 to Mary Loraine Porter; c. Mary L.(Mrs. Thomas Francis Dolan, III), Suzanne (Mrs. Thomas Francis Quinlan) and Thomas Porter. Educ: Syracuse Univ. Col. of Law, LL.B, 28; Phi Delta Phi; Sigma Nu. Polit. & Govt. Pos: N.Y. State Sen, 47-, chmn, Judiciary Cmt. and Ethics and Guid. Cmt, N.Y. State Senate; chmn, Onondaga Co. Rep. Cmt, 60-63; alternate del, Rep. Nat. Conv, 68. Bus. & Prof. Pos: Mem. firm, Mackenzie, Smith, Lewis, Michell & Hughes; dir, Syracuse Transit Corp. and Onondaga Co. Savings Bank. Mem: Past pres, Onondaga Co. Bar Asn; Am. and N.Y. State Bar Asns; past pres, Fedn. of Bar Asns. for Fifth Judicial Dist; fel. Am. Col. Trial Lawyers; United Cerebral Palsy Asn. Syracuse; Commun-Gen. Hosp; Onondaga Co. Chap, Asn. for Help of Retarded Children; Univ, Century and Onondaga Golf and Country Clubs. Rel: Roman Catholic. Legal Res: 311 Brookford Rd, Syracuse, N.Y. 13224. Mailing Add: Onondaga County Savings Bank Bldg, Syracuse, N.Y. 13202.

HUGHES, JOHN WILLIAM R
Conn. State Rep.
b. Stratford, Conn, 7/9/26; s. James Henry Hughes and Irene Lucey H; m. 8/21/48 to Mary Louise Madigan; c. James Prescott, Alexandria Mary, Jeffrey Clarke and John Britton. Educ: South. Conn. State Col, B.S. in Educ, 50; Univ. Bridgeport, M.S. in Educ, 56. Polit. & Govt. Pos: Mem, Stratford Town Rep. Cmt, Conn, 55-; mem, Stratford Bd. Educ, 56-61; cmnr, Stratford Housing Authority, 64-69; Conn. State Rep, 67- Bus. & Prof. Pos: Teacher, Stratford, Conn, 50-54; compensation coordinator, United Aircraft Corp, 54- Mil. Serv: Entered as Seaman, Navy, 43, released as Qm, PO, 45, after serv. in Motor Torpedo Boat Sq, Mediterranean; ETO and Atlantic Theater Ribbons. Rel: Roman Catholic. Mailing Add: 415 Housatonic Ave, Stratford, Conn. 06497.

HUGHES, KEITH F. Conservative
Minn. State Sen.
b. St. Cloud, Minn, 1936; married; c. Four. Educ: St. John's Univ, B.A; Univ. Minn. Law Sch, LL.B. Polit. & Govt. Pos: Minn. State Sen, 64-, special elec. for vacancy. Bus. & Prof. Pos: Lawyer. Mil. Serv: Army Res. Mailing Add: 1269 12th Ave. N, St. Cloud, Minn. 56301.

HUGHES, LAWRENCE EDWARD R
Ohio State Rep.
b. Columbus, Ohio, 4/13/22; s. Frank S. Hughes and Florence Powell H; m. 6/3/50 to Ruth Eileen Keller; c. Lawrence E, Jr, John Bradford, David James and James Michael. Educ: Ohio State Univ, B.S, 48; Sigma Alpha Epsilon. Polit. & Govt. Pos: Ohio State Rep, 69- Bus. & Prof. Pos: Rep, Ohio Bell Tel. Co, 56-60, coordinator Southwest area, 60-64, nat. acct. exec, 64-69, asst. directory supvr, 69- Mil. Serv: Entered as Naval Air Cadet, Navy, 42, released as Pilot, 45, after serv. in Naval Air Corps and Naval Intel. Mem: Downtown Civitan Club (past founding pres); Sigma Alpha Epsilon Alumni (past pres); Clintonville Conserv. Club; Alladin Shrine; F&AM (past master, Goodale Lodge); Masonic Orgn; Rep. Clubs. Rel: Lutheran. Mailing Add: 4319 Fairoaks Dr, Columbus, Ohio 43214.

HUGHES, MILDRED BARRY D
b. Elizabeth, N.J; m. to Peter L. Hughes, Jr; c. Three sons. Educ: Georgian Court Col, A.B; N.Y. Univ. Polit. & Govt. Pos: Chmn, Assembly Cmt. on Inst. Pub. Health Welfare, 59; N.J. State Assemblyman, 4 terms; N.J. State Sen, 1 term, asst. Majority Leader, N.J. State Assembly, 60 & 61; mem, Joint Cmt. on Interstate Coop, 64; mem, N.J. Cmn. on Aging; chmn, N.J. Senate Inst. Pub. Health, 66 & 67; mem, N.J. Cmn. to Study Obscenity and Depravity in Pub. Media, currently. Bus. & Prof. Pos: Teacher. Mem: Bus. & Prof. Women's Club; former pres, Cath. Woman's Club; exec. bd, Am. Asn. Univ. Women, N.J. Asn. for Ment. Health, Union Co. Ment. Health Asn, Homemaker's Serv. Inc. and St. Elizabeth's Hosp. Maternity Guild; Urban League; Union Co. Children's Serv. Cmt; past pres, Union Co. Dem. Women's Club; former v.pres, Elizabeth League Women Voters and ed. of their handbook; adv. cmt, N.J. Hist. Trust. First Woman elected to N.J. State Sen. Rel: Catholic. Mailing Add: Blue House, Morris Ave, R.F.D, Union, N.J. 07083.

HUGHES, OLIVER H. R
b. Chanute, Kans, 1/19/21; s. John Francis Hughes and Ione White H; m. 7/31/48 to Melba V; c. Marilyn S, Stephen R. and Melinda Ann. Educ: Kans. Univ. Sch. of Bus, B.S. in Bus. Admin; Kans. Univ. Sch. of Law, LL.B; Phi Delta Phi; Sigma Alpha Epsilon. Polit. & Govt. Pos: Former Rep. precinct committeeman and former mem. various polit. cmts; chmn, Kans. State Rep. Cmt, 64-66. Bus. & Prof. Pos: Dir, Educators Investment Co. of Kans, Inc. and Augusta State Bank, 60-; chmn. bd, Wichita State Bank, 65-; pres, Citizens Nat. Bank, Emporia, 66- Mil. Serv: Entered as Pvt, Army, 43, released as Capt, 46, after serv. in ETO. Publ: Co-auth, Thornton on the Law of Oil and Gas, 48. Mem: Rotary; Wichita Estate Planning Coun; Kans. Chap, Nat. Conf. Christians and Jews. Rel: Presbyterian. Legal Res: 1966 Morningside Dr, Emporia, Kans. 66801. Mailing Add: P.O. Box 459, Emporia, Kans. 66801.

HUGHES, PEASTER LEO D
Miss. State Rep.
b. West, Miss, 8/28/10; married. Educ: Univ. Miss. Polit. & Govt. Pos: Cmnr, Madison Co. Soil Conserv. Dist; Miss. State Rep, 60- Bus. & Prof. Pos: Farmer; cattleman. Mem: Elks; Optimist Club; Lions; Citizens Coun; Miss. Cattlemens Asn; Canton C. of C; pres, Madison Co. Farm Bur, affiliated with Miss. and Am. Farm Bur. Fedn. Rel: Baptist. Mailing Add: Mannsdale Rd, Madison, Miss. 39110. (1967)

HUGHES, PHYLLIS JOSEPHINE D
Pres, Iowa Fedn. of Dem. Women's Clubs
b. The Dalles, Ore, 3/7/15; d. Edward M. Hughes and Elizabeth Rowe H; single. Educ: Marquette Univ, Ph.B, 33, J.D, 35; Theta Rho; Delta Sigma Rho; Kappa Beta Pi. Polit. & Govt. Pos: Unemployment compensation exam, Indust. Cmn. of Wis, 36-37; secy, Milwaukee Co. Young Dem, 36-40 and Young Dem. of Wis, 40-42; mem, Bd. of Appeals, Milwaukee, 40-44; pres, Jane Jefferson Club of Del. Co, Iowa, 49-51, 67-; advisor Second Dist, Iowa Fedn. of Dem. Women's Club, 54-64, secy, 62-64, pres, 64-; v.chmn, Del. Co. Dem. Cent. Cmt, 60-64, chmn, 64-68, proj. dir, 68- Bus. & Prof. Pos: Private practice of corporation law, 35-; pres, E.M. Hughes Dept. Store, Manchester, Iowa. Publ: Poetry, Lyrical Iowa, 63. Mem: Wis. State Bar Asn; Bus. & Prfnl. Women's Club; Marquette Univ. Alumni Asn; hon. life mem, Am. Flag Asn; C. of C; past pres, Federated Women's Club; Manchester Country Club; Nat. Coun. of Cath. Women; Rotary Anns; Book Hour; hon. likfe mem, Manchester Newcomers Club. Rel: Catholic. Legal Res: 501 E. Main, Manchester, Iowa 52057. Mailing Add: 112 S. Franklin, Manchester, Iowa 52057.

HUGHES, RICHARD J. D
Gov, N.J.
b. Florence, N.J, 8/10/09; m. 1954 to Betty Murphy; c. Ten. Educ: St. Joseph's Col; N.J. Law Sch; Rutgers Univ, LL.B. Polit. & Govt. Pos: Dem. cand. for Cong. from Fourth Dist, N.J, 38; Asst. U.S. Attorney for N.J, 39-45; judge, Mercer Co, 48-52; chmn, Supreme Court's Cmt. on Juvenile and Domestic Rels. Courts; judge, Superior Court of N.J, 52-61, Appellate Div, 57-61; Gov. of N.J, 61-; del, Dem. Nat. Conv, 68. Bus. & Prof. Pos: Lawyer. Mem: Chmn, St. Francis Hosp. Fund-Raising Campaign, 60; chmn, Del. Valley United Fund, 58; former chmn, Citizens Adv. Cmt. to Investigate Welfare Practices in Trenton; adv. cmt, Who's Who in Am. Politics, 69; Past Exalted Ruler, Elks; Past Grand Knight, K. of C. Rel: Catholic. Mailing Add: State House, Trenton, N.J. 08625.

HUGHES, ROBERT E. R
b. Twin Falls, Idaho, 4/29/28; s. Ralph E. Hughes and Jessie Siders H; m. 12/23/50 to Georgia C. Burgess; c. Leslie, Diane, Jerry and Nancy. Educ: Ore. State Col. Polit. & Govt. Pos: Chmn, Columbia Co. Rep. Cent. Cmt, Wash, 62-68. Bus. & Prof. Pos: Employ. supvr, Green Giant Co, 54-59, agr. supt, 59-60 and regional personnel mgr, 60- Mil. Serv: Entered as Pvt, Army, 45, released as S/Sgt, 47, re-entered as S/Sgt, 50, released as Sgt. 1/C, 51. Mem: Pac. Northwest Personnel Mgt. Asn; Gov. Subcmt. on Migratory Labor; finance chmn. camp fire, Dayton Vol. Fire Dept; Elks; Am. Legion; Kiwanis. Rel: Methodist. 1967 Legal Res: Dayton, Wash. No mailing address available. (1967)

HUGHES, ROBERT EARLE D
b. Greenville, S.C, 9/17/17; s. John Robert Hughes and Metta Good H; m. 4/3/46 to Mary Eugenia Cary; c. Robert Earle, Jr. and Phillip Rivers. Educ: Furman Univ, B.A. in Econ, 38. Polit. & Govt. Pos: Mem. bd, Greenville Co. Family Serv. Center, S.C, 58; states rep, Appalachian Regional Cmn, Wash, 65-69; chmn, S.C. Appalachian Adv. Cmn, 65-; del, Dem. Nat. Conv, 68. Mil. Serv: Entered as A/S, Coast Guard, 42, released as Lt, 45, after serv. as

exec. officer, Coast Guard Cutter Bedloe and as Hq. Unit Syst. Analyst for LORAN, 42-45; Theater of War Ribbons. Publ: System Checking for LORAN, U.S. Govt, 45. Mem: Greenville Real Estate Bd.(first v.pres, 41); charter mem, Greenville Home Guilders Asn.(nat. dir, 46); Nat. Urban Land Inst; Nat. and S.C. Home Builders Asns; Am. Legion; Greenville Country Club (chmn. house cmt, 56, mem. bd, 57, chmn. membership cmt, 58, chmn. greens cmt, 59); West. Carolina Sailing Club; Jr. C. of C.(first v.pres, 37). Rel: Baptist. Legal Res: 619 E. Faris Rd, P.O. Box 1821, Greenville, S.C. 29602. Mailing Add: P.O. Box 1821, Greenville, S.C. 29602.

HUGHES, ROBERT HIGGINS D
b. Dallas, Tex, 11/26/25; s. Maury Hughes and Ann Louise Higgins H; m. 6/26/48 to Ann Hanszen; c. Ann, Robert, Jr. and Melinda. Educ: Univ. of Tex, M.A, 46; South. Methodist Univ, LL.B, 49; Phi Alpha Delta; Sigma Alpha Epsilon. Polit. & Govt. Pos: Asst. attorney gen, Tex, 51-52; Tex. State Rep, 55-63; dist. judge, Dallas, 63-69; nominee, U.S. Rep, 68. Mil. Serv: Entered as Pvt, Air Force, 43, released as Capt, 45, after serv. in Judge Adv. Gen. Corps. Mem: Am. and Tex. Bar Asns; Am. Judicature Soc; Trial Lawyers Asn.(chmn, family law sect); Highland Park Lodge; Scottish Rite; Shrine. Rel: Episcopal. Legal Res: 3643 West Lake, Austin, Tex. 78746. Mailing Add: 313 Perry Brooks Bldg, Austin, Tex. 78701.

HUGHES, SARAH TILGHMAN D
b. Baltimore, Md, 8/2/96; d. James Cooke Tilghman and Elizabeth Haughton T; m. 3/13/33 to George E. Hughes, wid. Educ: Goucher Col, A.B, 17; George Wash. Univ, LL.B, 22; Phi Beta Kappa; Delta Sigma Rho; Delta Kappa Gamma; Delta Gamma; Kappa Beta Pi. Govt. Pos: U.S. Dist. Judge, 61-; Judge, 14th Dist. Court, 35-61; Tex. State Rep, 31-35. Bus. & Prof. Pos: Instr, Southern Methodist Univ, 43, YMCA, Dallas, 39-42 and Jefferson Sch. of Law, 23-31; policewoman, Metrop. Police Dept, Wash, D.C, 19-22; teacher, Salem Acad. Col, Winston-Salem, N.C, 17-19. Publn: 'Judicial Selection and Tenure,' Women Lawyers Jour, 64; 'The Unfortunate One Per Cent Our Responsibility,' Tex. Study of Secondary Educ, 1/59; 'World Peace Through World Law,' Tex. Observer, 65. Mem: Coun. on World Affairs; Dallas United Nations Asn; Bus. & Prfnl. Women's Club; Zonta; League of Women Voters. Rel: Episcopal. Legal Res; 3816 Normandy, Dallas, Tex. 75205. Mailing Add: Box 1019, Dallas, Tex. 75221. (1967)

HUGHES, SHELBY BOND D
Chmn, Henry Co. Dem. Cent. Cmt, Mo.
b. Clinton, Mo, 6/4/03; s. Robert Lee Hughes and Alice Frances Bond H; m. 12/8/28 to Aetna Mary Jeude; c. Robert Shelby, William Bond and James Lawrence. Educ: Univ. Mo, A.B, 26, B.S. in Med, 27; St. Louis Univ, M.D, 29; Alpha Kappa Kappa. Polit. & Govt. Pos: Coroner, Henry Co, Mo, 36-40, dep. state health cmnr, 56-, mem, State Bd. Registrn. for Healing Arts, 65-; chmn, Henry Co. Dem. Cent. Cmt, 38-42 & 60- Bus. & Prof. Pos: Gen. practice of med, 30-; mem. staff, Clinton Gen. Hosp, Mo, 40- Mil. Serv: Entered as 1st Lt, Army, 42, released as Capt, 45, after serv. in Med. Corps, World War II, Continental U.S. Mem: Am, South. and Mo. State Med. Asns; Henry Co. Med. Soc; Am. Astronomical Asn. Rel: Methodist. Legal Res: 210 E. Wilson, Clinton, Mo. 64735. Mailing Add: 106 S. Third, Clinton, Mo. 64735.

HUGHES, THOMAS RAYMOND D
b. St. Paul, Minn, 12/6/25; s. Thomas Raymond Hughes and Inga Hoyer H; m. 8/14/58 to Barbara Dale Lynch; c. Jane Marie, Jacqueline Lee and Andria Carol. Educ: Macalester Col, 43-45; Univ. Minn, 45-48. Polit. & Govt. Pos: Exec. Asst. to Secy. of Agr, 61-; secy. to Gov. Minn, 55-60; exec. secy, Minn. Dem-Farmer-Labor Party, 49-50, 53 and 54; staff asst, Humphrey for Senator Volunteer Cmt, 48. Mil. Serv: Entered as Pvt, Army, 50, released as Pfc, after serv. in Japan. Mailing Add: 3103 Kent St, Kensington, Md. 20735. (1967)

HUGHES, WAYNE R
Educ: Tri-State Col; Manchester Col, A.B; Ind. Univ, M.S; Phi Delta Kappa. Polit. & Govt. Pos: Mem. twp. adv. bd, 42-50 and co. coun, 50-60; Ind. State Rep, 61-67. Bus. & Prof. Pos: Farmer; former teacher and sch. prin. Mem: Mason; Eastern Star; White Shrine of Jerusalem. Rel: Protestant. Mailing Add: Hudson, Ind. 46747. (1967)

HUHTALA, RALPH E. R
b. Ishpeming, Mich, 1/6/20; s. Otto E. Huhtala (deceased) and Jennie Kurin; single. Educ: Univ. Ark; Mich. Tech. Univ. Polit. & Govt. Pos: Dist. finance chmn, Rep. Party, Mich, 58-; mem, Mich. Cmn. on Legis. Apportionment, 63-; del-at-lg, Rep. Nat. Conv, 64; chmn, 11th Cong. Dist. Rep. Party, Mich, formerly. Bus. & Prof. Pos: Mem. eng. dept, Cliffs Dow Chem. Co, 41-49; indust. rels. asst, Cleveland Cliffs Iron Co, 49-54; mgr. personnel and pub. rels, Lake Shore, Inc, 54- Mil. Serv: Entered as Pvt, Army Air Force, 42, released as Lt, 45, after serv. as a Pilot Officer in U.S. Mem: Rotary; Am. Legion; YMCA; Jr. Achievement; v.pres, Mich. United Fund; v.chmn, Mich. State C. of C; past officer, local, state and nat. Jr. C. of C. and C. of C. Rel: Lutheran. Mailing Add: 400 Hamilton, Kingsford, Mich. 49801. (1967)

HUIET, BEN TILLMAN D
b. Edgefield Co, S.C, 3/01/95; s. Joseph Eugene Huiet and Mary Bradley H; m. 11/6/19 to Edythe Maude Rudder; c. Edythe Florence and Ben F, Jr. Educ: Richmond Acad; Clemson Col; Cent. Night Sch-Winder Law Sch, LL.B, 33. Polit. & Govt. Pos: Mem, Atlanta Dem. Exec. Cmt, Ga, 22-25; councilman, Atlanta, 25-28, alderman, 28-33, pub. serv. cmnr, 33-36; Cmnr. of Labor, Ga, 38-68. Mil. Serv: Lt, World War I. Mem: Mason; Shrine; 40 et 8; Am. Legion; Elks, Jr. Order; WOW; Ga. Bar Asn; treas, Interstate Conf. of Employ. Security Agencies of U.S; past pres, Int. Asn. of Govt. Labor Off. Admitted to all bars, 34, U.S. Supreme Court, 38. Rel: Methodist. Mailing Add: 5901 Peachtree Dunwoody Rd. N.E, Atlanta, Ga. 30328. (1967)

HUIRAS, MARVIN HENRY D
Chmn, Ozaukee Co. Dem. Party, Wis.
b. Port Washington, Wis, 6/12/25; s. Henry George Huiras and Louise Jungers H; single. Educ: Univ. Wis, Madison, B.S, 50. Polit. & Govt. Pos: Dem. campaign coordinator, Sixth Representative Dist, Wis, 62; v.chmn, Ozaukee Co. Dem. Party, 65-67, chmn, 67-; village trustee, Belgium, Wis, 66- Bus. & Prof. Pos: Mem. staff prod. control, Consol. Vultee Aircraft, 53-58; admissions counsr, Milwaukee Sch. of Eng, 58-62; tavern owner and real estate operator, 62- Mil. Serv: Entered as Seaman, Navy, 43, released as MMR 3/C, 45, after serv. in 138th Naval Commun. Bd, N.Pac. Theatre; Merchant Marines, 51-53. Mem: Am. Asn. of Admissions Counsr; Lions; Elks; VFW; Am. Legion. Rel: Catholic. Mailing Add: 787 Main, Belgium, Wis. 53004.

HULBERT, GERALD ERICKSON D
Chmn, Salt Lake Co. Dem. Party, Utah
b. Salt Lake City, Utah, 1/1/31; s. Arthur Davies Hulbert and Effie Erickson H; m. 8/12/59 to Lois Steffensen; c. Thomas Arthur, Wendy Lyn and Kimberly. Educ: Univ. Utah, B.S, 56, grad. sch, 1 year; Sigma Chi. Polit. & Govt. Pos: Chmn, Salt Lake Co. Dem. Party, Utah, 67-; del. and mem. rules cmt, Dem. Nat. Conv, 68. Mem: Nat. Asn. Independent Ins. Adjusters; Ft. Douglas-Hidden Valley Country Club. Rel: Latter-day Saint. Mailing Add: 4964 Waimea Way, Salt Lake City, Utah 84117.

HULETT, STANLEY WILLIAM R
b. San Francisco, Calif, 7/31/38; s. Leo Stanley Hulett and Isabelle Francis Walker H; m. 6/15/68 to Mary Ann Minenna; c. Gregory Allen. Educ: Menlo Sch. and Col, A.A, 58; Stanford Univ, A.B, 60; El Toro Club, Stanford Univ. Polit. & Govt. Pos: Chmn, bd. of trustees, Willits Unified Sch. Dist, Calif, 66-69; v.chmn, Mendocino Co. Rep. Cent. Cmt, 69; asst. to U.S. Rep. Don H. Clausen, Calif, 69- Mem: Nat. Asn. Lumber Salesman; pres, Willits C. of C, 66-68; Hoo-Hoo Int; pres, Mendocino Co. C. of C, Ukiah, 68-69; research cmt, Calif. Redwood Asn; chmn. bd. dirs, Calif. Lumberman's Accident Prev. Asn, Oakland, 68-69; Mason; Rotary Int; Commonwealth Club San Francisco. Man of Year Award, Willits Jaycees. Rel: Protestant. Legal Res: 248 Pine St, Willits, Calif. 95490. Mailing Add: 1010 N. Rochester, Arlington, Va. 22205.

HULL, ANN REMINGTON D
Md. State Del.
b. Seattle, Wash, 2/24/25; d. Arthur Ernest Remington and Marian Knowlton R; m. 4/16/49 to Gordon Crittenden Hull; c. Suzanne and Peter Crittenden. Educ: Univ, Washington, B.A, 45; Syracuse Univ, M.A, 48; Phi Beta Kappa. Polit. & Govt. Pos: Md. State Del, 67- Bus. & Prof. Pos: Geographer, U.S. Govt, 48-54. Mem: Asn. of Am. Geographers; League of Women Voters. Rel: Protestant. Mailing Add: 1629 Drexel St, Takoma Park, Md. 20012.

HULL, JAMES M. JR. D
b. Augusta, Ga, 3/3/23; s. James M. Hull and Marion Phinizy H; m. 9/3/47 to Frank Mays; c. Frank M; James M, III; Carol De l'Aigle. Educ: Va. Mil. Inst, 43; Univ. of Ga. Lumpkin Law Sch, 48; Kappa Alpha Order. Polit. & Govt. Pos: Ga. State Rep, 61-66. Bus. & Prof. Pos: Mem. of law firm of Hull, Willingham, Towill & Norman, 48- Mil. Serv: Sgt; awarded combat citations. Rel: Episcopalian. Mailing Add: Augusta, Ga. 30903. (1967)

HULL, M. CORDELL D
Tex. State Rep.
b. Ft. Worth, Tex, 7/21/40; s. Henry Anton Hull and Josephine Daugherty H; m. 12/21/67 to Sharon Harwell; c. Lyndell Anne. Educ: Univ. Tex, 3 years; Tex. Wesleyan Col, 1 year. Polit. & Govt. Pos: Tex. State Rep, 65- Mem: Bd. dir, Ex-Student Asn, Northside High Sch, Ft. Worth, 68; bd. dir, Austin Jaycees, 63; state bd. dir, Jaycees, 64; charter mem. and dir, Northwest Optimist Club, 67. Rel: Methodist. Mailing Add: 4707 Alwood Court, Ft. Worth, Tex. 76135.

HULL, W.R, JR. D
U.S. Rep, Mo.
b. Weston, Mo, 4/17/06; wid; c. W.R. Hull, III, Mrs. Susan Hudson. Educ: Pub. schs. Polit. & Govt. Pos: U.S. Rep, Mo, 54-; former mayor, Weston, Mo. Bus. & Prof. Pos: Dir, First Nat. Bank, Leavenworth, Kans; co-owner, Hull's Tobacco Warehouse, Weston, Mo. Mem: Past v.pres. and dir, Kansas City Area Coun. Boy Scouts; past pres, C. of C. Rel: Christian Church, Deacon. Legal Res: Weston, Mo. 64098. Mailing Add: House Office Bldg, Washington, D.C. 20515.

HULLINGER, ARLO D
b. Decatur Co, Iowa, 1921; s. Earl Hullinger; m. 1941 to Betty Sage; c. Five. Educ: Iowa State Univ. Polit. & Govt. Pos: Iowa State Rep, formerly. Bus. & Prof. Pos: Farmer and cattleman. Mem: Farm Bur. Rel: Baptist. Mailing Add: R.D, Leon, Iowa 50144.

HULSE, JAMES WARREN D
b. Pioche, Nev, 6/4/30; s. James Gordon Hulse and Berene Cutler H; m. 6/20/62 to Betty Kay Wynkoop; c. Jane and James Charlton. Educ: Univ. Nev, B.A, 52, M.A, 58; Stanford Univ, Ph.D, 62; Phi Alpha Theta; Phi Kappa Phi; Kappa Tau Alpha. Polit. & Govt. Pos: Mem, Washoe Co. Dem. Cent. Cmt, Nev, 64-68; mem, Nev. Equal Rights Cmn, 66-68; del, Dem. Nat. Conv, 68. Bus. & Prof. Pos: Polit. reporter, Nev. State Jour, Reno, 54-58; asst. prof, Cent. Wash. Col, 61-62; asst. prof, Univ. Nev, 62-66, assoc. prof, 66- Mil. Serv: Entered as Pvt, Army, 52, released as Cpl, 54, after serv. in 83rd Eng. Bn, France, 53-54. Publ: The Forming of the Communist International, Stanford Univ. Press, 64; The Nevada Adventure: A History, Univ. Nev. Press, 65; Revolutionists in London, Oxford Univ. Press, autumn 69. Mem: Am. Hist. Asn; Am. Civil Liberties Union; Am. Asn. for Adv. Slavic Studies; Odd Fellows. Rel: Unitarian. Mailing Add: 940 Grandview Ave, Reno, Nev. 89503.

HULSEY, RANDI TORGESEN R
Chmn, Habersham Co. Rep. Party, Ga.
b. Teaneck, N.J, 3/16/41; d. Walter T. Torgesen and Elizabeth Creel T; m. 4/27/58 to Garnett Richard Hulsey; c. Goodney Miranda, Garnett R, Jr. and Gia Heather. Educ: South Habersham High Sch, Ga, grad. cum laude, 58. Polit. & Govt. Pos: Rep. precinct chmn, Habersham Co, Ga, 66-68; mem, State Rep. Cmt. and chmn, Habersham Co. Rep. Party, 68- Mailing Add: Route 1, Cornelia, Ga. 30531.

HULSHIZER, R. DALE D
b. Parsons, Kans, 8/23/29; s. L. Stanford Hulshizer, Sr. and Emily P. Frazier H; m. 10/9/54 to Julia Ann Wendling; c. Rebecca Jo, Ronald Dale, Jr, Daniel Joseph and Ann Marie. Educ: Drake Univ, B.A, 53; South. Calif. Univ, 53; pres, Sigma Alpha Epsilon. Polit. & Govt. Pos: Chmn, El Paso Co. Stewart

for Cong. Cmt, Colo, 60; v.pres, Colo. Springs Young Dem, 62, pres, 63; staff dir, Dem. Party of Colo, 63-65; asst. to U.S. Rep. Frank E. Evans, Colo, 65-67, admin. asst, 67- Bus. & Prof. Pos: Admissions counsr, Drake Univ, Des Moines, Iowa, 53-56; rep, New Eng. Life Ins, 56-58; rep, KRDO-TV, Colorado Springs, Colo, 58-60; res. mgr, KOAA-TV, 60-61, KKTV, 61-63. Mil. Serv: Entered as Pvt, Air Force, 48, released as Cpl, 49, after serv. at Lackland, San Marcos and Randolph Air Force Bases, Tex. Res, 49-55. Rel: Protestant. Legal Res: Colorado Springs, Colo. Mailing Add: 4321 Cedarlake Court, Alexandria, Va. 22309.

HULSTRAND, GEORGE EUGENE DFL
Chmn, Kandiyohi Co. Dem-Farmer-Labor Party, Minn.
b. Cannon Falls, Minn, 8/3/18; s. John G. Hulstrand and Alice E. Holm H; m. 9/7/46 to Mabel E. Ericson; c. George E, Jr, Brian D, Darlene L. and Jeanne L. Educ: Gustavus Adolphus Col, B.A, 43; Yale Law Sch, LL.B, 46; Epsilon Pi Alpha; pres, Student Senate, Senior Year. Polit. & Govt. Pos: Asst. co. attorney, Kandiyohi Co, Minn, 47-50; mem, Willmar City Coun, 53-56; secy, Seventh Dist. Dem-Farmer-Labor Party, 53-57; chmn, Willmar Planning Cmn, 57-67; chmn, Kandiyohi Co. Dem-Farmer-Labor Party, 57- Publ: 'Communism vs. Christianity,' The Lutheran Outlook, 47; 'Get Ready for March 15 Now,' Capper's Farmer, 51; 'Willmar Establishes Annexation Policy,' League of Munic. Mag, 65. Mem: Exec. cmt, 12th Dist, Bar Asn, 60-66; pres, Kandiyohi Co. Bar Asn, 61; Am. and Minn. Bar Asns; Gr. Gustavus Asn; former chmn. bd, Gustavus Adolphus Col; C. of C; Lions. Rel: Lutheran. Mailing Add: 325 N. Seventh St, Willmar, Minn. 56201.

HULTEN, JOHN JAMES D
Hawaii State Sen.
b. San Francisco, Calif, 11/2/13; s. Augustin Anthony Hulten and Margaret Trosak H; m. 5/29/37 to Helen Salopek; c. John James, Jr, Stephen Paul, Virginia Marie and Thomas Anthony. Educ: Univ. San Francisco, evening div, 3 years. Polit. & Govt. Pos: Tax adv, Pub. Housing Admin, 45-46, regional tax adv, 46-47; chief appraisal sect, U.S. Vet. Admin, 48-51; precinct chmn, Dem. Party, Hawaii, 57-58, dist. chmn, 59; Hawaii State Sen, currently; del, Dem. Nat. Conv, 68. Publ: Land Reform in Hawaii, Land Econs, Univ. Wis, 5/66; 'The Appraisal Report,' Prentice-Hall's Encyclopedia on Appraising, 57. Mem: Pres, Honolulu Chap, Am. Inst. of Real Estate Appraisers, 55 and Honolulu Chap, Soc. of Residential Appraisers; Kiwanis. Rel: Roman Catholic. Legal Res: 631 Paopua Loop, Kailua, Oahu, Hawaii 96734. Mailing Add: 810 Richards St, Suite 703, Honolulu, Hawaii 96813.

HUME, EDMUND TERRENCE R
Mayor, Maplewood, N.J.
b. Newark, N.J, 10/29/20; s. Robert Hume and Bridget Brennan H; m. 11/10/44 to Lois T. Johnson; c. Edmund T, Jr, Kristin (Mrs. Louis Provenzano), Robert and John. Educ: Newark Col. Eng, Newark, N.J, 46; Rutgers Univ, Cert. in Bus. Mgt, 53; Univ. Alumni Asn. Polit. & Govt. Pos: Chmn, Maplewood Citizens Budget Cmt, N.J, 56-59; chmn, Maplewood Planning Bd, 57-63; v.chmn, Maplewood Bd. Adjust, 58-64; mayor and committeeman, Maplewood, 60-; mem, N.J. League Munic, 60-; v.pres, N.J. Conf. Mayors, 64-; pres, League of Suburban Munic, 65-68; del, N.J. Constitutional Conv, 66; del, Rep. Nat. Conv, 68. Bus. & Prof. Pos: Lineman, N.J. Bell Tel. Co, 41, installer, 45-47, customer sales rep, 47-50, asst. staff supvr, 50-51, serv. engr, 51-52, sales mgr, 52-53, staff supvr, 53-54, bus. off. mgr, 54-60 and exec. asst. to v.pres. pub. affairs, 60- Mil. Serv: Entered as Pvt, Marine Corps, 41, released as Sgt. Wire Chief, 45, after serv. in First and Third Div, Solomon Island Campaign, Guadalcanal and Bougainville, 42-44. Mem: N.J. Coun. Research and Develop; Am. Legion; VFW. Man of the Year, Maplewood C. of C, 62; Americanism Award, B'nai B'rith, 68. Rel: Roman Catholic. Mailing Add: 710 Prospect St, Maplewood, N.J. 07040.

HUME, JAQUELIN HOLLIDAY R
Mem, Rep. Nat. Finance Cmt.
b. Harbor Point, Mich, 7/17/05; s. George E. Hume and Lucy Holliday H; m. 2/20/35 to Caroline Elizabeth Howard; c. William J, Patricia (Mrs. Highberg), Carol E. and George H. Educ: Princeton Univ, A.B, 28; Harvard Bus. Sch, M.B.A, 30. Polit. & Govt. Pos: V.chmn, Citizens for Eisenhower, North. Calif, 52; dep. chmn, Nat. Citizens for Eisenhower, Wash, D.C, 54; finance chmn, Goldwater-for-president, North. Calif, 64, Reagan-for-Gov, 66 and Nixon-Agnew Cmt, Region II, 68; del, Rep. Nat. Conv, 64 & 68; mem, Calif. Rep. State Finance Cmt, 64-; mem, Calif. Rep. State Cent. Cmt, 66-; chief of protocol, Rep. Party North. Calif, 67-; mem, Rep. Nat. Finance Cmt, 68- Bus. & Prof. Pos: Pres. and dir, Basic Vegetable Prod, Inc, San Francisco, Calif, 33-; chmn. and dir, Am. Potato Co, 55-; dir, Leslie Salt Co, 68-; dir, KUDO Channel 38 TV, 69- Rel: Unitarian. Legal Res: 3355 Pacific Ave, San Francisco, Calif. 94118. Mailing Add: 120 Montgomery St, San Francisco, Calif. 94104.

HUMES, THEODORE LEON R
b. Pittsburgh, Pa, 2/1/23; s. Casimir Huminski and Martha Kraus H; m. 6/17/48 to Betty Jane Iams; c. Linda Frances; Paul Michael, Robert Gary, Barbara Ann, Teresa Lynn and Theodore L, Jr. Educ: Univ. Pittsburgh, A.B, 48; George Washington Univ, LL.B, 52; Delta Tau Delta. Polit. Pos: Del, Rep. Nat. Conv, 64; field dir, Nationalities Div. Rep. Nat. Cmt, 64; state chmn, Pa. Citizens for Goldwater/Miller, 64. Govt. Pos: Intel. officer, Cent. Intel. Agency, 50-52; econ. officer, Dept. of State, 48-50. Bus. & Prof. Pos: V.pres, Chatham Communs. Inc, 65-; res. economist, Kennametal Inc, 61-65; lectr. econ, Seton Hill Col, 61-62; bus. analyst, Consolidation Coal Co, Pittsburgh, Pa, 55-61. Mil. Serv: Entered as PO 3/C, Navy, 42, released as PO 1/C, 45, after serv. in Naval Amphibious Forces Unit, European, Mediterranean, Cent. and South Pacific Theaters; All Theaters of Operations Ribbons. Publn: Various articles published in Human Events, National Review, The Wanderer and The Freeman. Mem: Pittsburgh Press Club; Econ. Club. of Pittsburgh; Am. Econ. Asn; Edmund Burke Found. Rel: Roman Catholic. Mailing Add: 242 Dan Dr, Pittsburgh, Pa. 15216. (1967)

HUMISTON, HOMER R
b. Chicago, Ill, 1903; m. to Katharine H; c. Three. Educ: Univ. Ill; Harvard Med. Sch. Polit. & Govt. Pos: Wash. State Rep, formerly; alternate del, Rep. Nat. Conv, 68. Bus. & Prof. Pos: Physician; med. dir, Pierce Co. Med. Bur. Mil. Serv: Maj, Med. Corps. Mem: Elks. Mailing Add: 607 N. Stadium Way, Tacoma, Wash. 98403. (1967)

HUMMEL, LOWELL HAROLD R
b. Fairbury, Nebr, 12/1/35; s. Harold H. Hummel and Alma Blobaum H; m. 1/17/59 to Luana Jeanne Roberts; c. Michael Robert and Erich Paul. Educ: Univ. Nebr, B.S, 56; Sigma Xi; Alpha Zeta; Gamma Sigma Delta; Farm House. Polit. & Govt. Pos: Nat. committeeman, Nebr. Fedn. Young Rep, 63-64, chmn, 64-66; former regional v.chmn, Young Rep. Nat. Fedn; mem, Nebr. State Agr. Stabilization & Conserv. Serv. Cmt, currently. Bus. & Prof. Pos: Chmn, Nebr. Young Farmers Educ. Asn, 66- Mil. Serv: Entered as Pfc, Marine Corps, 56, released as 1st Lt, 59, after serv. in First Marine Brigade, Fleet Marine Force, Pac. Theater; Capt, Marine Res, 59-66. Mem: Soil Conserv. Soc. Am; Farm Bur. Rel: Lutheran, Mo. Synod. Mailing Add: R.R. 1, Box 92, Fairbury, Nebr. 68352.

HUMMER, FANNIE MAY D
b. Tipton, Ind, 5/16/06; d. Henry Wilhelm Rediger and Annie May Hinkle R; m. 6/12/25 to Herbert Garrett Hummer; c. Georgia L. (Mrs. Warner), Rita J. (Mrs. McAninch), Joseph H. and Herbert H. Polit. & Govt. Pos: Mgr, State Auto License Br, Kokomo, Ind, 61-; v.chmn, 5th Dist, Dem. Party, 60-66, precinct committeeman, 40-63, v.precinct committeeman, 34-40; alternate del, Dem. Nat. Conv, 64, del, 60; active worker in Birch Bayh's sen. campaign, 62; pres, Howard Co. Womens Dem. Club, 54-58 and Howard Co. Young Dem, 40-44; secy, 5th Dist. Young Dem, 34-38. Mem: Moriah Rebekah Lodge; Women of Moose; Women's Soc. Christian Serv; Garden Club; PTA. Rel: Methodist. Mailing Add: 419 Lincoln Rd, Kokomo, Ind. 46901. (1967)

HUMPHREY, GEORGE F. Conservative
Minn. State Rep.
b. Greenwood, Miss, 1917; married; c. Four. Educ: Southwestern, B.A; Univ. Minn, M.A. Polit. & Govt. Pos: Mem. sch. bd, Minneapolis, Minn, 63-64; Minn. State Rep, 64- Bus. & Prof. Pos: Life ins. salesman. Mil. Serv: Navigator, Air Force, World War II and Korea. Mem: Church, bus, and civic orgns. Mailing Add: 1936 Irving Ave. S, Minneapolis, Minn. 55403.

HUMPHREY, HUBERT HORATIO D
b. Wallace, S.Dak, 5/27/11; s. Hubert Horatio Humphrey and Christina Sannes H; m. 9/3/36 to Muriel Fay Buck; c. Nancy (Mrs. C. Bruce Solomonson), Douglas Sannes, Hubert Horatio III and Robert Andrew. Educ: Denver Col. Pharm, 33; Univ. Minn, B.A, 39; La. State Univ, M.A, 40; Phi Beta Kappa. Polit. & Govt. Pos: State dir, War Prod. Training and Employment, 42; asst. dir, War Manpower Cmn, 43; mayor, Minneapolis, Minn, 45-48; U.S. Sen, Minn, 49-64; Vice President, United States, 65-69; del, Dem. Nat. Conv, 68; Dem. cand.for President, United States, 68. Bus. & Prof. Pos: Mem. faculty, Macalester Col. and Univ. of Minnesota, Minneapolis, 69- Publ: The War on Poverty, McGraw-Hill, 64; School Desegregation: Document and Commentary, Thomas Y. Crowell, 64; The Cause is Mankind, Frederick Praeger Co, 64. Rel: United Church of Christ. Legal Res: Waverly, Minn. 55390. Mailing Add: 550 N St. S.W, Washington, D.C. 20024. (1967)

HUMPHREY, ISAAC BAILEY D
b. Salina, Utah, 3/7/95; s. William Bird Humphrey and Elizabeth Bailey H; m. 9/12/24 to Twila Heiner; c. Roswell Marlin, William Donald, Darlene (Mrs. Fred J. Anderson), Geraldine (Mrs. Gordon R. Smith) and Twila May (Mrs. Samuel Glade Isaacson). Educ: Univ. Utah, B.A, 22, M.A, 36. Polit. & Govt. Pos: Del, Dem. State and Co. Conv, 34-; Utah State Rep, 64-67, Speaker, Third House Spec. Sessions, v.chmn, State and Nat. Affairs Cmt. and mem, Appropriations and Hwy. Cmts, 66; mem, State Dem. Platform Cmt, 60 and 56. Bus. & Prof. Pos: Teacher, soc. studies, South and West High Schs, Salt Lake City, Utah, 28-60, Jordan High Sch, 23-28 and N.Sanpete High Sch, 22-23. Mil. Serv: Entered as Pvt, Army, 17, released, 19, after serv. in Co. G, 18th Inf, 1st Div, Am. Exped. Forces; Divisional Citation. Mem: Nat. Educ. Asn; co-chmn, joint cmt, Nat. Educ. Asn-Am. Legion; v.pres, exec. cmt. mem. and chmn. retirement cmt, Utah Educ. Asn; pres, v.pres. and exec. bd. mem, Salt Lake Teachers Asn; Am. Legion; DAV. Rel: Latter-day Saint. Mailing Add: 1777 S. Fifth East St, Salt Lake City, Utah 84105. (1967)

HUMPHREY, JOSEPH W. H. R
b. 1930; married; c. Four. Polit. & Govt. Pos: City attorney and munic. judge, Boynton Beach, Fla; Fla. State Rep, 67-68; co. judge, Palm Beach Co, 69- Bus. & Prof. Pos: Attorney. Mem: C. of C; past pres, PTA. Rel: Presbyterian; Trustee and Elder, Presby. Church. Mailing Add: P.O. Box 190, Boynton Beach, Fla. 33435.

HUMPHREY, LOUISE B. R
Rep. Nat. Committeewoman, S.Dak.
b. White Lake, S.Dak; d. August Adolph Beutner and Louise Nihart B; m. to Bert Humphrey, wid; c. Mary Louise (Mrs. R.K. Stanley); grandchildren, Lee Scott, Clint and Sally. Educ: Yankton Col, B.A, 27; Aristonian. Polit. & Govt. Pos: Assessor, Mellette Co, S.Dak, 31-32; del, Rep. Nat. Conv, 48; Rep. precinct committeewoman, Mellette Co, S.Dak, 50-54; v.chmn, Mellette Co. Rep. Party, 50-54; mem, Gov. Adv. Cmt, 52-56; State Cent. Committeewoman, 54-64; supvr. agr. census, Westriver, 55; S.Dak. State Rep, 42nd Dist, Bennett and Mellette Counties, 58-62; mem, State Court Study, Joseph Ward and S.Dak. Centennial Cmns, 61; Rep. Nat. Committeewoman, S.Dak, 64- Bus. & Prof. Pos: Teacher, White River High Sch, S.Dak, 27-28, Rural Sch, White River, 34-35. Mem: Mem. corp. bd. and bd. trustees, Yankton Col, 69; Am. Asn. Univ. Women; Bus. & Prfnl. Women's Club; Am. Legion Auxiliary; Federated Women's Club; Cowbelles Art Club; Sandhills Badlands Earth Sci. Club; Rep. Womens Fedn. Rel: Lutheran. Mailing Add: White River, S.Dak. 57579.

HUMPHREY, LUCIE KING R
Rep. Nat. Committeewoman, Nev.
b. Mokelumne Hill, Calif, 2/23/11; d. Ralph Mower King and Mabel Plumb K; m. 9/14/32 to Marvin Bender Humphrey; c. Joseph King, Barbara (Mrs. Redman), Sara (Mrs. White) and Ellen. Educ: Lassen Jr. Col, 27-29; Univ. Nev, A.B, 31; Gamma Phi Beta. Polit. & Govt. Pos: Mem, Washoe Co. Rep. Cent. Cmt, Nev, 49-; mem, Rep. Women's Club, Reno, 49-, bd. pres, 63-67; pres, Nev. Fedn. Rep. Women, 50-53, mem. bd, 50-; mem, Nev. Rep. State Cent. Cmt, 63-; Rep. Nat. Committeewoman, 68- Bus. & Prof. Pos: Teacher, 31. Rel: Episcopal. Mailing Add: 30 Suda Way, Reno, Nev. 89502.

HUMPHREY, NELSON HINE D
Chmn, Ashtabula Co. Dem. Party, Ohio
b. Ashtabula, Ohio, 8/24/19; s. Russell Clark Humphrey, Jr. and Zoe Hine H; m. 4/22/46 to Shirley Jean Kemmer; c. Brian K, Kay A, Wendy S. and Todd L. Educ: Ashtabula High Sch, Ohio, grad, 38. Polit. & Govt. Pos: V.chmn, Ashtabula Co. Dem. Party, 56-58, secy, 58-60, chmn, 60-; mem, Ashtabula Co. Elect. Bd, 62-; del, Dem. Nat. Conv, 64 & 68. Bus. & Prof. Pos: Real estate salesman, C. Berry Realty, 66- Mem: Ashtabula Co. Bd. Realtors; Ohio Asn. Elect. Off; Ashtabula Co. Dem. Club; Farmers Union. Rel. Protestant. Mailing Add: 6413 Jefferson Rd, Ashtabula, Ohio 44004.

HUMPHREY, PRESTON ADOLPH D
b. Muskogee, Okla, 3/12/10; s. Ed Humphrey and Maria Jackson H; m. 11/26/36 to Arvella Peacox; c. Elizabeth. Educ: Muskogee High Sch, Okla, grad, 30. Polit. & Govt. Pos: Coordinator, Vote Registrn. for Kennedy, Okla, 60; Dem. chmn, Precinct 208, 66-67; Dem. coordinator of 14 precincts in Area 3, 67-; coordinator for Mike Monroney, 68; del, Dem. Co, State and Nat. Conv, 68; mem, Tulsa Co. Dem. Cent. Cmt, 68; mem, United for Humphrey Cmt, 68; bd. mem, Econ. Opportunity Task Force, 69; chmn, Tulsa Task Force Fed. Credit Union Loan Cmt. Bus. & Prof. Pos: Real estate broker and pres. of local realty co, 69-; exec. v.pres, McIntosh & Humphrey Realty Co, currently. Mem: Local and nat. real estate orgn; Commun. Rels. Cmn, Tulsa; Nat. Asn. of Real Estate Brokers; Mason (32°); YMCA. Citation of Congratulations from Rex Privett, Speaker, Okla. House of Rep, 67. Rel: Baptist; mem, Bd. of Trustees, First Baptist Church, North Tulsa. Mailing Add: 2028 E. Young Place, Tulsa, Okla. 74110.

HUMPHREY, W. HUGH R
b. Wilmington, N.C, 8/18/14; s. Wayne Hugh Humphrey and Mary Chinnis H; m. 5/17/36 to Mary Louise Frady; c. Linda (Mrs. William Henry) and Martha (Mrs. Glen Norling). Polit. & Govt. Pos: Pub. affairs officer, Fed. Civil Defense Admin, 56-59; dir. pub. rels, Mich. State Rep. Cent. Cmt, 65-68; pub. info. exec, Off. of Secy. of State Mich, currently. Bus. & Prof. Pos: Managing ed, Morning Star, Wilmington, N.C, 39-43; copy ed, Baltimore Eve. Sun, 43-44; writer and desk ed, Eve. Star, D.C, 44-45; ed-in-chief, Great Am. Publ, 54-56; ed, Editorial Page, Enquirer and News, Battle Creek, Mich, 59-65. Publ: Weekly syndicated column on space sci. for Cent. Press Asn, 59-64. Mem: Nat. Conf. of Ed. Writers; Mich. Pub. Rels. Asn; Econ. Club of Detroit. Rel: Unitarian. Legal Res: 504 Laurel Lane-Apt. 1, East Lansing, Mich. 48823. Mailing Add: Office of the Secretary of State, State Capitol, Lansing, Mich. 48903.

HUMPHREY, WILLIAM HOWARD D
Chmn, Williamson Co. Dem. Party, Ill.
b. Tolu, Ky, 12/7/23; s. Corbett Humphrey and Mary Lou Stone H; m. 5/2/40 to Helen Hatfield; c. Jerry Dale. Polit. & Govt. Pos: Precinct committeeman, Precinct 8-2-8, Williamson Co, Ill, 60-69; Dem. nominee for Sheriff, 65; dep. sheriff, Williamson Co, 65-66; employee, State Hwy. Dept, Williamson Co, 66-68; Chief of Police, Herrin, currently; chmn, Williamson Co. Dem. Party, 68- Bus. & Prof. Pos: Bus. rep, IBT, 50-65; bus. agent, Herrin Trades Coun, 55-65. Mem: Elks; Eagles. Rel: Baptist. Mailing Add: 1320 N. 14th St, Herrin, Ill. 62948.

HUMPHREYS, FREDERICK M. R
Chmn, Clark Co. Rep. Cmt, Kans.
b. Sterling, Kans, 2/18/22; s. John Ephraim Humphreys and Vinette Hutchinson H; m. 7/19/46 to Carrie May Arnold; c. Karen, Iras, John, Tom and Fred. Educ: Kans. Univ, B.S, 43; Phi Mu Alpha; Pi Kappa Delta; Sigma Alpha Epsilon. Polit. & Govt. Pos: Rep. precinct committeeman, Kans, 56-60; city councilman, Ashland, 60-66; chmn, Clark Co. Rep. Cmt, currently. Bus. & Prof. Pos: Gen. mgr, Home Lumber and Supply Co, 64- Mil. Serv: Entered as A/S, Navy, 43, released as Lt, 45, after serv. in Motor Torpedo Boat Squadron 33, S.Pac, 44-45; Campaign Ribbons. Mem: Am. Legion; VFW; AF&AM; C. of C; Kiwanis. Rel: Presbyterian. Mailing Add: Ashland, Kans. 67831.

HUMPHREYS, GEORGE DOUGLASS D
Mem, Calif. State Dem. Cent. Cmt.
b. Custer City, Okla. 9/29/37; s. Lloyd Frank Humphreys and Helen McAdoo H; div; c. Douglass B, Jennifer and Carolyn. Educ: Univ. Calif, Berkeley, A.B, 59, J.D, 63; Alpha Chi Rho. Polit. & Govt. Pos: Pres, Sacramento Co. Young Dem, Calif, 65-66; regional dir. and chmn. bylaws cmt, Calif. Fedn. Young Dem, 65-68; pres, Sacramento Co. Dem. Coun, 66-67; parliamentarian, Sacramento Co. Dem. Cent. Cmt, 66-; mem, Calif. State Dem. Cent. Cmt, 67- Bus. & Prof. Pos: Dep. Corp. Cmnr, Calif. Div. Corp, 63-65; partner, Russell, Humphreys & Estabrook, Attorneys, Sacramento, Calif, 65- Mem: Am, Calif. and Sacramento Co. Bar Asns; Calif. and Am. Trial Lawyers Asns; Elks; Sacramento Co. Safety Coun; Citizens for Better Govt. Legal Res: 8797 Winding Way, Fair Oaks, Calif. 95628. Mailing Add: 3815 Marconi Ave, Sacramento, Calif. 95821.

HUMPHREYS, PRISCILLA FAITH R
Rep. Nat. Committeewoman, W.Va.
b. Huntington, W.Va, 4/28/12; d. James Edward Cobb and Bertie Esque C; m. 2/9/36 to Irvin Wendell Humphreys; c. David Wendell, Bertie Anne and John Edward. Educ: Marshall Univ. Polit. & Govt. Pos: Pres, Huntington-Cabell Rep. Womens Club, W.Va, 61-63; v.chmn, Cabell Co. Rep. Exec. Cmt, 63-66; Rep. Nat. Committeewoman, W.Va, currently. Mem: Huntington Mothers Club; Women's Club of Huntington; past pres, Alpha Delta Mothers Club. Rel: Baptist. Mailing Add: 1546 16th St, Huntington, W.Va. 25701. (1967)

HUMPHREYS, RAYMOND V. R
Dir. Educ. and Training, Rep. Nat. Cmt.
b. Huntington, W.Va, s. Edward Humphreys and Zelda Henson H; single. Educ: Marshall Univ, 31-34. Polit. & Govt. Pos: W.Va. State Del, 50-52; dir. educ. and training, Rep. Cong. Cmt, 57-63, Rep. Nat. Cmt, 63- Bus. & Prof. Pos: Pres, Assoc. Underwriters, 38-42 and Raymond V. Humphreys Assocs, 46-51; exec. v.pres, Nat. Sales, 54-57. Mil. Serv: Entered as Pvt, Army, 42, released as Maj, 52, after serv. in Gen. Staff, AA Command, Gen. MacArthur Command; S.W. Pac. Theater, 43-45. Rel: Baptist. Legal Res: Lonesome Cedar Farm, Hurricane, W.Va. 25526. Mailing Add: P.O. Box 81, Haymarket, Va. 22069. (1967)

HUMPLEBY, TWYLA JEAN R
b. Creston, Iowa, 8/14/33; d. Emmett H. Worthington and Edna Anna Hocke W; m. 8/27/51 to Edwin Albert Humpleby; c. Bobbie Lynn, Kim Denise and Nicole Jean. Educ: Mascatine High Sch, grad, 51. Polit. & Govt. Pos: Finance chmn, Johnson Co. Rep. Womans Club, Iowa, 63-65, pres, 66-67; committeewoman, Rep. Party, 63-; v.chmn, First Dist. Young Rep, 64-; chmn. campaign activities, First Dist. Rep. Women, 67-, first v.pres, 68-; alternate del, Rep. Nat. Conv, 68; co-chmn, Iowa State Rep. Rev. Cmt, 68- Mem: Univ. Athletic Club; Iowa City Christian Woman's Club; Iowa City Woman's Club; Johnson Co. Rep. Women. Outstanding Rep. Women in Johnson Co, Johnson Co. Rep. Woman's Club. Rel: Evangelical Free Church of Am. Mailing Add: 5 Highview Knoll, Iowa City, Iowa 52240.

HUNCOCK, D. HOWITT Independent
b. East Norwich, N.Y, 10/31/15; s. Edward Erving Huncock and Dorothy Fanny H; m. 9/28/35 to Joanna Coulter Chambers; c. John Dale Coulter and Rachel Christina; 1 granddaughter. Educ: Exeter Col, Oxford. Polit. & Govt. Pos: Spec. asst. to N.Y. State Assemblyman, 3 years; former mem. Tax Study Cmt. Bus. & Prof. Pos: Lawyer, 25 years; dir, Bluecoat Life Ins. Co; chmn. bd, Bentinck Wool Corp. Mil. Serv: Navy, 41-45. Rel: Episcopal. Mailing Add: 8554 E. Mackenzie Dr, Scottsdale, Ariz. 85251.

HUNGATE, WILLIAM LEONARD D
U.S. Rep, Mo.
b. Benton, Ill, 12/14/22; s. Leonard Wathen Hungate and Maude Irene Williams H; m. to Dorothy Nell Wilson; c. William David and Margie Kathryn. Educ: Univ. Mo, A.B, 43; Harvard Law Sch, LL.B, 48. Polit. & Govt. Pos: Prosecuting attorney, Lincoln Co, Mo, 51-56; asst. attorney gen, Mo, 59-64; U.S. Rep, Ninth Dist, Mo, currently. Bus. & Prof. Pos: Sr. partner, Hungate and Grewach, Attorneys, 56-68. Mil. Serv: Entered as Pvt, Army, 43, released as Pfc, 46, after serv. in Co. L, 377th Inf. Regt, 95th Inf. Div, ETO, 44-45; Bronze Star; 3 Battle Stars; Combat Inf. Badge; Medal of Metz. Publ: 'Administration of Criminal Justice,' Chieftain, 57; 'Rules Are Made to Be,' Mo. Law Rev, 4/66. Mem: Mo, Ill, Am. and Fed. Bar Asns; bd. trustees, William Woods Col; Lewis and Clark Trail Cmn; Mason; VFW; Am. Legion; Amvets; Kiwanis. Musical composer. Rel: Disciples of Christ. Legal Res: 755 Cap-au-Gris St, Troy, Mo. 63379. Mailing Add: U.S. House Office Bldg, Washington, D.C. 20515.

HUNKER, JOSEPH FREDERICK D
Mem, Nebr. State Dem. Cent. Cmt,
b. West Point, Nebr, 4/18/11; s. Fred D. Hunker and Stella Jarrett H; m. 4/18/39 to Frances Armbruster; c. Mary Josephine (Mrs. Rief) and Fred D. Educ: St. Mary's Col, Kans, 28-30; Creighton Univ. Law Sch, 30-31, LL.B, 63; Alpha Sigma Nu; Phi Alpha Delta; Creighton Student Bd. of Govs, 61-63, v.pres, 62-63. Polit. & Govt. Pos: Mem, Nebr. State Dem. Cent. Cmt, and chmn, Cuming Co. Dem. Party, 64- Bus. & Prof. Pos: Co. attorney, Cuming Co, Nebr, 66-; private practice of law, West Point. Mil. Serv: Entered as A/S, Navy, 32; transferred to Army Air Corps, 36; released as Col, Air Force, 58, after serv. in Am. and Pac, Theaters, ETO, Philippines and Far East Command, 32-58; Navy Good Conduct Medal; Pre-Pearl Harbor, Pearl Harbor, Pac. and Am. Theater Ribbons; ETO Medal with one Battle Star; Legion of Merit, Air Force Commendation Medal; Victory Medal; Korean War Medal; Am. Defense Serv. Medal. Mem: Am. Judicature Soc; Am. Trial Lawyers Asn; Am, Nebr. and Ninth Judicial Dist. Bar Asns; Elks; DAV; K. of C. (3° and 4°). Rel: Catholic. Mailing Add: 237 S. Farragut St, West Point, Nebr. 68788. (1967)

HUNNINGS, R. H. R
Chmn, Fayette Co. Rep. Party, Ind.
b. Attica, Ind, 9/9/14; s. Raymond Harrison Hunnings and Kate Henson H; m. 5/23/42 to Viola Isabell Shultz; c. R.H, II and Virginia Jo. Educ: Ind. Univ, 33-35; Ind. State Univ, B.S, 48; Miami Univ, grad. work, 50-51. Polit. & Govt. Pos: Young Rep. chmn, Clinton Co, Ind, 30-33; Rep. precinct committeeman, Fayette Co, 56-62; chmn, Fayette Co. Rep. Party, 66- Bus. & Prof. Pos: Teacher, Connersville Pub. Schs, Ind, 45-53; real estate broker, 51- Mil. Serv: Entered as Pvt, Army, 41, released as Capt, 46, after serv. in Second Armored Div, ETO, 44-45; Capt.(Ret), Army Res; Purple Heart; Bronze Star. Mem: Am. Inst. Real Estate Appraisers; sr. mem, Am. Soc. Real Estate Appraisers; Nat. Asn. of Real Estate Bd; Ind. Real Estate Asn; Elks; Mason; York Rite; Scottish Rite; Shrine; Lions; Am. Legion. Rel: Methodist. Mailing Add: R.R. 3, Connersville, Ind. 47331.

HUNSAKER, ROGER CLYDE R
Chmn, Tarrant Co. Rep. Party, Tex.
b. LeRoy, Ill, 6/19/20; s. Clyde Hunsaker and Cora Smith H; m. 4/9/46 to Joan Wilson; c. David, Steve and Nancy. Educ: High Sch. Grad. Polit. & Govt. Pos: Rep. precinct chmn, Tex, 63-66; chmn, Redistricting Cmt, Rep. Party, 65; chmn, Tarrant Co. Rep. Party, 65-; del, Rep. Nat. Conv, 68. Bus. & Prof. Pos: Pres, Ft. Worth Pressed Steel Corp, Tex, 47-; v.pres, Machined Parts Corp, 56- and Com-Tech Agency, 64- Mil. Serv: Entered as Cadet, Navy, 42, released as Ens, 45. Mem: Shrine, Lions; Mason; Tex. Mfg. Asn; Ft. Worth and U.S. C. of C. Rel: Southern Baptist. Mailing Add: 3309 Mt. Vernon Ave, Fort Worth, Tex. 76103.

HUNSICKER, CARL T. R
Ill. State Rep.
b. Rooks Creek Twp, Ill, 11/8/04; m. to Elsie Vissering. Polit. & Govt. Pos: Alderman, Pontiac City Coun, Ill, 33-47, chmn, Finance Cmt, 10 years; supvr. of Pontiac Twp, Livingston Co. Bd. of Supvr, 51-61, chmn, Finance Cmt, 4 years; mem, Pontiac Area Planning Cmn, 56-61; pub. mem, State and Co. Probs. Cmn, 57-61; Ill. State Rep, fourth term, currently. Bus. & Prof. Pos: Formerly in outdoor advert. and sign bus, 26-49; farm owner and mgr, 24 years; retired. Mem: Livingston Co. Farm Bur; Mason; Lions; Elks. Rel: Presbyterian. Mailing Add: 905 N. Main St, Pontiac, Ill. 61764.

HUNSINGER, JOSEPHINE D. D
Mich. State Rep.
b. Acosta, Pa; d. Joseph Drivinsky and Kathryn Moskal D; m. 5/29/30 to Raymond L. Hunsinger; c. Irene K.(Mrs. Ramauld B. Locher, Jr); grandchildren, Mark R, Brent R. and Kathleen Kimberley. Educ: Mich. State Univ.

Polit. & Govt. Pos: Jury cmnr, Wayne Co, Mich, 53-54; Mich. State Rep, 54-; chmn, Wayne Co. Del, 65- Mem: 17th Cong. Dist. Dem. Party Orgn; Nat. Order of Women Legislators; Int. Platform Asn; Nat. Fedn. of Bus. and Prfnl. Women's Clubs, Inc; Athena Club and Women's City Club, Detroit; Detroit Press Club; League of Women Voters; Eastern Star. Only woman in Mich. to receive the Mich. Agr. Conf. Award in recognition of distinguished serv. Legal Res: 24414 Frisbee St, Detroit, Mich. 48219. Mailing Add: State Capitol, Lansing, Mich. 48933. (1967)

HUNT, ARLINE PAT BRUSH R
b. N.Y.C, 1/23/28; d. Donald Linsley Brush and Arline Camp B; m. 8/20/49 to Paul Henry Hunt; c. Stuart Gerald, Donald Porter and Andrew Loren. Educ: Univ. Vt, A.B, 49; Kappa Alpha Theta. Polit. & Govt. Pos: V.chmn, Vt. Young Rep. Club, 58-60, nat. committeewoman, 60-64; mem, Vt. State Bd. Historic Sites, 60-63; sch. dir, Brighton, Vt, 61-69; committeewoman, Vt. Rep. State Cmt, 66-67; pres, Tri-Co. Sch. Dirs, 67-69; mem. and legis. chmn, Vt. State Sch. Dirs. Asn, 67-69; alternate del, Rep. Nat. Conv, 68; sch. dir, North Country Union High Sch, Newport, Vt, 69-; mem, Vt. State Bd. of Educ, 69- Bus. & Prof. Pos: Teacher, Kensington, Conn, 49-51; news correspondent, Burlington Free Press, Newport Daily Express and Caledonian Record, 56- Publ: 'Rockefeller Center Christmas Tree,' N.Y. Herald Tribune, 12/57; 'Two Sides to the Picture,' Rural Vermonter, spring 64; 'Pueblo Crewman Writes Parents,' Burlington Free Press, 4/68. Mem: Island Pond Woman's Club; trustee, North Region United Fund. Mrs. Vt, 64; Vt. Educ. Asn. Layman's Award, 66; Creative Writing Awards, Vt. Fedn. Womans Clubs, 66 & 68. Rel: United Church of Christ. Mailing Add: Morgan, Vt. 05853.

HUNT, BILLY R
Chmn, Shelby Co. Rep. Exec. Cmt, Tex.
b. Beckville, Tex, 1/19/25; s. Arthur E. Hunt and Pellie McLeroy; single. Educ: Univ. of Tex, Austin, LL.B, 48. Polit. & Govt. Pos: Tex. State Rep, 55-56; chmn, Shelby Co. Rep. Exec. Cmt, 62- Bus. & Prof. Pos: Partner, Fairchild & Hunt, Attorneys, Center, Tex, 56- Mem: Tex. Bar Asn. Mailing Add: P.O. Box 666, Center, Tex. 75935.

HUNT, HOWARD P, JR. D
Ky. State Rep.
b. 1930. Educ: Grad. from Bus. Sch. Polit. & Govt. Pos: Ky. State Rep, 62-; alternate del, Dem. Nat. Conv, 68. Bus. & Prof. Pos: Farmer; merchant; ins. agent. Mem: 4-H Coun. Rel: Baptist. Mailing Add: Perryville Rd, Danville, Ky. 40422. (1967)

HUNT, JAMES BAXTER, JR. D
b. Greensboro, N.C, 5/16/37; s. James Baxter Hunt and Elsie Brame H; m. 8/20/58 to Carolyn Joyce Leonard; c. Rebecca Joyce, James Baxter, III, Rachel Henderson and Elizabeth Brame. Educ: N.C. State Univ, B.S, 59, M.S, 62; Univ. N.C, Chapel Hill, LL.B, 64; Phi Kappa Phi; Gamma Sigma Delta; Kappa Phi Kappa; Golden Chain; Blue Key; Thirty & Three; Alpha Zeta; Phi Alpha Delta; ed, The Agriculturist; two terms, student government pres. Polit. & Govt. Pos: V.pres, N.C. Young Dem. Clubs, 60; chmn, N.C. Young Voters for Terry Sanford, 60; col. dir, Dem. Nat. Cmt, 62-63; pres, Wilson Co. Young Dem. Club, 66-67; pres, N.C. Young Dem. Clubs, 68; del. and mem. rules cmt, Dem. Nat. Conv, 68; asst. to state Dem. chmn, N.C. Dem. Party, 68-; chmn, State Jefferson-Jackson Dinner, 69; mem, Nat. Dem. Party Cmn. Rules, 69- Bus. & Prof. Pos: Econ. adv, His Majesty's Govt. of Nepal, employed by Ford Found, 64-66; mem. firm, Kirby, Webb & Hunt, Attorneys at Law, 66-; training consult. to Peace Corps, 66-67. Publ: 'Acreage Controls and Poundage Controls for Flue Cured Tobacco,' N.C. Agr. Tech. Bul, 62; numerous articles on land reform and agr. development, H.M.G. Press, 64-66; 'Rally Around the Precinct,' N.C. Dem. Party Precinct Manual, 68. Mem: Wilson Co. and N.C. Bar Asns; Sertoma Club; Jaycees; N.C. State Univ. Alumni Asn; Wilson Good Neighbor Coun; Coastal Plains Develop. Asn, Inc; Wilson Arts Coun; Grange. Rel: Presbyterian; Deacon, First Presby. Church, Wilson, N.C. Mailing Add: 1806 Windsor St, Wilson, N.C. 27893.

HUNT, JAMES E. R
b. 1922. Educ: Pikeville Col; East. Ky. State Col, A.B. Polit. & Govt. Pos: Ky. State Rep, formerly. Bus. & Prof. Pos: Coal operator. Mil. Serv: Army; Two Bronze stars. Rel: Baptist. Mailing Add: Fedscreek, Ky. 41524. (1967)

HUNT, JAMES IRVING R
Ohio State Rep.
b. Newbury, Ohio, 7/27/08; s. Lee J. Hunt and Emma O. Harrington H; m. 8/10/33 to Frances Lillian Moss; c. Judith Ann (Mrs. Ward), Gary Lee and Frances Lynn (Mrs. Frank). Educ: Ohio State Univ, 1 year. Polit. & Govt. Pos: Mem, Middlefield Coun, Ohio, 47-53; mem, Middlefield Sch. Bd, 53-55; co. cmnr, Geauga Co, 55-69; Ohio State Rep, 36th Dist, 69- Bus. & Prof. Pos: Pres. and mgr, Home Tel. Co, Middlefield. Mem: Mason; Kiwanis; K. of P. Rel: Methodist. Legal Res: 16810 Kinsman Rd, Middlefield, Ohio 44062. Mailing Add: P.O. Box 338, Middlefield, Ohio 44062.

HUNT, JOE B. D
State Ins. Cmnr, Okla.
b. Mammoth Spring, Ark, 1/23/07; s. John Hunt and Iuka Woodall H; m. 10/8/35 to Anna Maude Dial; c. Jo Ann. Educ: Univ. Okla; Pi Kappa Alpha. Polit. & Govt. Pos: Pres, State Bd. Property and Casualty Rates, Okla, 54-59; state ins. cmnr, Okla, 55-; zone five chmn, Nat. Asn. Ins. Cmnrs, 59-65; mem, State Burial Bd, bd. trustees, Teachers Retirement System; state dir, Firemen's Relief & Pension Fund; state dir, Policemen's Pension & Retirement System; state dir, Motor Vehicle Assigned Risk Plan; statutory receiver for the liquidation of insurance co; serv. agent, ins. co. of other states; mem, Dem. nominee for presidential elector. Bus. & Prof. Pos: Mgr. rating dept, State Ins. Bd, Okla, 42-54. Mem: C. of C; Blue Goose; 3 Lion Clubs; hon. mem, Chickasaw Nation of Indians; Int. Asn. Fire Chiefs; hon. life mem, Okla. Firemens Asn; Fedn. Ins. Counsel. Rel: Presbyterian; past pres. bd. trustees, Capitol Presbyterian Church. Legal Res: 4309 N.W. June, Oklahoma City, Okla. 73112. Mailing Add: Will Rogers Memorial Bldg, Oklahoma City, Okla. 73105.

HUNT, JOHN E. R
U.S. Rep, N.J.
b. Lambertville, N.J, 11/25/08; m. to Doris R. Foster; c. Deborah. Educ: Bus. Sch, 3 years; U.S. Army Air Force Intel. Sch; Fed. Bur. of Invest. Police Acad; Harvard Sch. of Police Sci. Polit. & Govt. Pos: Sheriff, Gloucester Co, N.J, 59 & 62; former N.J. State Policeman and exec. officer; former N.J. State Sen; U.S. Rep, N.J, currently. Mil. Serv: Entered as 2nd Lt, Army, World War II, released as Maj, 46, after serv. as Combat Intel. Officer, Africa, Sicily, Italy, France, Germany, Yugoslavia, Bulgaria and Roumania; Bronze Star Medal; Air Medal with 2 Oak Leaf Clusters; Purple Heart; Presidential Unit Citation with 1 Oak Leaf Cluster; EAME Campaign Medal with 8 Bronze Stars; Am. Theatre, Victory and Army Res. Medals. Legal Res: 508 Pitman Ave, Pitman, N.J. 08071. Mailing Add: U.S. House Office Bldg, Washington, D.C. 20515. (1967)

HUNT, JOHN JOSEPH, JR. D
Mem, Minn. Dem-Farmer-Labor State Cent. Cmt.
b. Arlington, Minn, 5/21/31; s. John J. Hunt and Kathryn Collins H; m. 2/12/55 to Rita Marie Zeck; c. Thomas L, Nancy Jo, Susan Kay and John Joseph, III. Educ: St. Johns Univ, 50; Univ. Minn, B.S. in pharmacy, 53; Rho Chi; Phi Delta Theta; Phi Delta Chi. Polit. & Govt. Pos: Mem, Dem-Farmer-Labor Co. Cmt, 64-, spec. events officer, 66-68, sustaining fund chmn, 68-; mem, Rochester Jr. Col. Adv. Cmt. and ACRE Educ. Cmt, 66-; chmn, mayors adv. cmt. on urban renewal, 68-69; mem, Minn. Dem-Farmer-Labor State Cent. Cmt, 68- Bus. & Prof. Pos: Pres, Hunt Drugstore, Inc, 63- Mil. Serv: Entered as Pvt, Army, 54, released as Cpl, 56, after serv. in 98th Gen. Hosp, ETO and Neubrucke, W.Germany, 55-56; Army of Occupation Good Conduct Medal. Mem: Minn. State Pharmaceutical Asn.(chmn. first dist, 66-68); Nat. Asn. Retail Pharmacists; Am. Pharmaceutical Asn; bd. dirs, Rochester C. of C, 67; K. of C; Sertoma Club; NAACP. Knight of the Year, K. of C, 68. Rel: Catholic. Mailing Add: 2115 Eighth Ave. N.E, Rochester, Minn. 55901.

HUNT, LLOYD EDWARD D
S.C. State Rep.
b. Pickens Co, S.C, 11/22/02; s. Luthes E. Hunt and Mary Ella Bowen H; m. 3/13/30 to Mattie Lee Meares. Educ: N. Greenville Acad. Polit. & Govt. Pos: Mayor, Greer, S.C, 55-66; S.C. State Rep, currently. Bus. & Prof. Pos: Dir, S.C. Peach Festival Asn; dir, First Nat. Bank of Greer; retired. Mem: Former pres, Lions Club; dist. chmn, Greer-Paris Mt. Boy Scouts, 59-63; former pres, Munic. Asn. of S.C, 60; dir, Blue Ridge Coun, Boy Scouts; Mason (32°); Shrine; W.O.W. Mailing Add: 110 Oakdale Ave, Greer, S.C. 29651. (1967)

HUNT, LYMAN CURTIS R
Vt. State Rep.
b. Fairfax, Vt, 1/3/91. Educ: Univ. Vt, A.B, 12; Columbia Univ, M.A, 38. Polit. & Govt. Pos: Vt. State Rep, 65-; alternate del, Rep. Nat. Conv, 68. Bus. & Prof. Pos: Supt. of schs, 22-57, retired. Rel: Congregational. Mailing Add: 7 Church St, Essex Junction, Vt. 05452. (1967)

HUNT, McPHERSON WILLISS 'MACK' R
State V.Chmn, Okla. Young Rep.
b. Lincoln, Nebr, 5/30/33; s. Burt Williss Hunt and Elizabeth Julia McPherson H; m. 6/1/53 to Audrey Fae Alexander; c. Mark Alan, Scott Willis, Julia Fae, Kevin Roy and Eric Earl. Educ: Nebr. Wesleyan Univ, A.B, 55; Univ. Nebr, M.S, 57; Phi Lambda Upsilon; Sigma Xi; Crescent Fraternity. Polit. & Govt. Pos: Publicity chmn, Kay Co. Young Rep, Okla, 58-59, co. chmn, 64-66; precinct v.chmn, Kay Co. Rep. Party, 59-60, precinct chmn, 61-62, co. chmn, 67-; conv. chmn, Okla. Fedn. Young Rep, 65, state v.chmn, 69- Bus. & Prof. Pos: Assoc. research chemist, Continental Oil Co, Ponca City, 57-60, research chemist, 60-63, sr. research chemist, 63-67, research group leader, 67- Mil. Serv: Electrician 3/C, Naval Res, 58- Publ: 'Benzene 3-nitro and 3-amino-Cinnolines,' 59 and 'Sulfonates as Dye Sites in Polypropylene,' 69, Am. Chem. Soc. Mem: Am. Chem. Soc; Instrumental Music Soc.(first v.pres); YMCA (bd. dirs); team capt, United Fund; cmnr, explorer adv. & asst. cubmaster, Boy Scouts; football coach, Little League. Outstanding Young Man of Am, 68; Young Alumni award, Nebr. Wesleyan Univ, 68; Personality of the South, 69; plus local awards; fourteen U.S. and several for. patents in fields ranging from detergents to rocket fuels. Rel: Presbyterian. Mailing Add: 903 E. Cleveland, Ponca City, Okla. 74601.

HUNT, OCIE D
Chmn, Nolan Co. Dem. Party, Tex.
b. Moro, Tex, 4/22/93; s. Meno Hunt and Julia Brewer H; m. 4/21/17 to Nell Irvin; c. Olivia (Mrs. Bill Horn). Educ: Tex. Tech, Correspondence course in Eng; Air War Col. and Air Univ, grad, 66. Polit. & Govt. Pos: Chmn, Nolan Co. Dem. Party, Tex, 45- Bus. & Prof. Pos: Owner and operator, local fire and casualty ins. agency, 12-; dep. collector, N.Tex. div, Internal Revenue Serv, currently. Mem: Elks, Sweetwater, Tex; AF&AM, Ft. Worth; Dallas Consistory; Suez Shrine, San Angelo; Odd Fellows, Big Springs. Rel: Methodist. Legal Res: 1708 Pease St, Sweetwater, Tex. 79556. Mailing Add: 105 W. Third, Sweetwater, Tex. 79556.

HUNT, ROBERT RICHARD, SR. R
Chmn, Farmington Rep. Town Cmt, Conn.
b. Buffalo, N.Y, 2/1/28; s. Albert H. Hunt and Esther Richards H; m. 3/28/53 to Audrey Ann Carlson; c. Andrea Louise and Robert Richard, Jr. Educ: Rensselaer Polytech. Inst. B.Sc. in Eng, 52; Pi Delta Epsilon; Theta Chi; Scalp and Blade. Polit. & Govt. Pos: Cmnr, Farmington Indust. Develop. Cmn, Conn, 57-60; pres, Farmington Young Rep, 57-60; chmn, Farmington Rep. Town Cmt, 60-; cmnr, Farmington Town Planning and Zoning Cmn, 67- Bus. & Prof. Pos: Sales engr, United Aircraft Corp, 52-56, sr. sales engr, 56-57; asst. to pres, New Brit. Tool & Mfg. Co, Inc, 57-61, v.pres, 61-66; secy, Winsted Container Co, Inc, 64-; chmn. bd. and treas, New Eng. Cup Co, Inc, 68-; pres, New Brit. Tool & Mfg. Co, Inc, 68- Mil. Serv: Entered as Pvt, Army, 46, released as Technician, 47, after serv. in 181st Signal Depot Co, Second Army, 47; Good Conduct Medal. Mem: Wyllys Lodge 99 AF&AM. Rel: Episcopal. Mailing Add: 4 Parish Rd, Farmington, Conn. 06032.

HUNT, ROGER L. D
N.H. State Rep.
b. 1/23/99; married; c. Three. Educ: Northumberland, N.H. Polit. & Govt.

Pos: Trustee of Trust Funds; former Police Chief; health officer; N.H. State Rep, currently. Mem: Grand master at arms, K. of P; Mason. Rel: Protestant. Mailing Add: North Stratford, N.H. 03590. (1967)

HUNT, WILLIAM EDWARD D
State Committeeman, Mont. Dem. Party, Liberty Co.
b. Tacoma, Wash, 2/28/23; s. William Clyde Hunt and Ann Nolan H; m. 8/25/52 to Mary Veronica Fassler; c. James G, Joseph R, Kathryn E, Patricia A. and William E, Jr. Educ: Univ. Mont, B.A. and LL.B, 55. Polit. & Govt. Pos: Secy, Hill Co. Dem. Cent. Cmt, Mont, 56-57; co. attorney, Liberty Co, 57-62 & 64-; chmn, Liberty Co. Dem. Cent. Cmt, 64-67; mayor, Chester, 67-69; state committeeman, Mont. Dem. Party, Liberty Co, 67- Bus. & Prof. Pos: Judicial v.pres, Mont. Bar Asn, 56-57 & 68-69; dir. and secy, Westland Mutual Ins. Co, Mont, 60-; chmn, N.Cent. Mont. Circuit Rider Cmt, Havre, 66-; pres, Mont. Consumer Coun, Helena, 68- Mil. Serv: Entered as Pvt, Army, 41, released as Sgt, 45, after serv. in 286th Assault Signal Co, N.Africa and ETO, 42-45; Bronze Arrowhead; Good Conduct Medal. Mem: Am. and Mont. Bar Asns; Section on Mineral Law; Elks; Am. Legion; VFW; K. of C. Rel: Roman Catholic. Mailing Add: P.O. Box C, Chester, Mont. 59522.

HUNT, WILLIAM J. D
b. Macon, Ga, 4/6/12; s. Letcher B. Hunt, Sr. and Gertrude Smith H; m. 8/27/38 to Nell Elizabeth Wilder; c. Claude J, Laura L. Educ: Winter Park High Sch, 29; spec. courses, Am. Univ. Polit. & Govt. Pos: Ga. State Sen, 63-66; Army Adv. Cmt, 56-; dir, Civil Defense, Macon, 56-58. Bus. & Prof. Pos: Merchant, retail appliances. Mil. Serv: Army. Mem: Elk; Am. Legion; VFW; Amvets; pres. Macon Appliance, Radio, TV dealers, 58-59; dir. Macon USO, 57- ed, Optimists Bul, 58-60; Nat. Cmt. Americanism, Am. Legion, 62-63; Americanism Chmn, Elks, 63-; Rehabilitation Nat. Cmt, Am. Legion, 55-56. Rel: 1st Baptist Church, pres. Baraca Sunday Sch. Class. 1967 Legal Res: Macon, Ga. No mailing address available. (1967)

HUNTER, DONALD H. R
Judge, Supreme Court, Ind.
b. Anderson, Ind, 10/21/11; s. Carl Edward Hunter and Mary Samuels H; m. 10/11/41 to Violet K. Oemler; c. Samuel E. and Jean Ellen. Educ: Lincoln Univ. Sch. of Law, LL.B, 37; Phi Delta Phi. Polit. & Govt. Pos: Ind. State Rep, Madison Co, 43; dep. attorney gen, Indianapolis, 43 & 46-47; hearing exam, Ind. Pub. Serv. Cmn, 48; judge, LaGrange Circuit Court, 48-62; judicial mem, Statewide Cmt. Rev. Adoption Laws, 50-52; judicial mem, Adv. Cmt. Probation and Parole, Ind. Citizens Coun, 53-55; judge, Appellate Court Ind, 63-66; chmn. exec. cmt, Ind. First Judicial Conf, 67; judge, Supreme Court Ind, 67- Mil. Serv: Entered as Pvt, Army, 43, released as Cpl, 46, after serv. in 47th Inf, Ninth Inf. Div, ETO, 43-46; Five Campaign Stars; Combat Inf. Badge; Combat Medic Badge; Bronze Star; Purple Heart; Belgique Fouragere; Four Presidential Unit Citations. Mem: Ind. State, Indianapolis and Madison Co. Bar Asns; Mason; Am. Legion; VFW; 40 et 8. Rel: Protestant. 1719 Costello Dr, Anderson, Ind. 46011.

HUNTER, GEORGE PATRICK, JR. D
N.C. State Rep.
b. Charlotte, N.C, 1935; m. to Annette Shaw; c. Patrick, Michael and Amy. Educ: Univ. of N.C, B.S, 57, LL.B, 62. Polit. & Govt. Pos: N.C. State Rep, 67-; mem, Dem. Adv. Cmn, Dem. Co. Exec. Cmt. Dem. Precinct Cmt; Past Pres, Mecklenburg Co. Young Dem. Club. Bus. & Prof. Pos: Attorney; Pres, South Distributors, Inc; app.legal adv. to Charlotte Police Dept. Mil. Serv: Navy 2 years, Lt; Naval Res. Mem: Dem. Men's Club; C. of C. Rel: Baptist. Mailing Add: 3123 Cloverfield Rd, Charlotte, N.C. 28211.

HUNTER, HAROLD V. R
b. Waukomis, Okla. 8/14/17; s. V.J. Hunter and Minnie Houghkirk H; m. 5/15/41 to Ruth Irene Hyde; c. Losco N. and Ramona (Mrs. Loewen). Educ: Univ. Okla, 35-36; Phi Eta Sigma. Polit. & Govt. Pos: Okla. State Rep, 63-69, Asst. Minority Floor Leader, Okla. House Rep, 67-69; chmn, Gov. Task Force Agr-Bus; State exec. dir, Agr. Stabilization and Conservation Serv, 69- Mem: Okla. Polled Hereford Breeders Asn.(state pres, 52, 57, 66-); Okla. Hereford Breeders Asn.(bd. dirs, 65-66); state cmt, Agr. Res. & Educ. Asn, Okla. State Univ. Sch. Agr; Mason; Lions; Farm Bur; Grange. Agricultural Hall of Fame, Enid C. of C; Farm Family of the Year, Garfield Co. Farm Bur, 62. Rel: Baptist. Mailing Add: 1001 S. Western, Stillwater, Okla. 74074.

HUNTER, JACK J. D
Chmn, Elko Co. Dem. Cent. Cmt, Nev.
b. Elko, Nev, 5/22/15; s. John J. Hunter and Viola Beaulieu H; m. 3/24/38 to Jean Nicol; c. Jack J, III. Educ: N.Mex. Mil. Inst. and Univ. of Nev, 2 years; Sigma Alpha Epsilon. Polit. & Govt. Pos: Nev. State Assemblyman, 2 terms; chmn, Elko Co. Dem. Cent. Cmt, 62- Bus. & Prof. Pos: Pres, Elko C. of C, 63. Mil. Serv: Entered as Aviation Student, Air Force, 42, released as Pvt, 44. Mem: Rotary Int. Rel: Presbyterian. Legal Res: 237 Pine St, Elko, Nev. 89801. Mailing Add: Box 208, Elko, Nev. 89801.

HUNTER, JAMES S. D
Polit. & Govt. Pos: Ind. State Rep, 41-66; House Dem. Caucus Chmn, 65; Pres, Co. Welfare Bd, 62-63; E. Chicago Redevelop. and Housing Bd; Dem. Caucus Chmn, 49-55. Bus. & Prof. Pos: Chmn, Hunter's Real Estate & Ins. Brokerage. Mil. Serv: WW I. Mem: E. Chicago and Gary Chaps, Frontiers of Am, Inc. Rel: Catholic. Mailing Add: 3910 Carey St, E. Chicago, Ind. 46312. (1967)

HUNTER, JEAN LORRAINE MAJOR R
Mem, Calif. Rep. State Cent. Cmt.
b. Kansas City, Kans, 2/24/22; d. Everett Ora Major and Uhla W. Hinds M; m. 4/29/46 to William Frank Hunter; c. Diana, Frank and Bonnie. Educ: Kans. State Col, 40-42; Abbott Art Sch, 49-50; El Camino Jr. Col, 60-61. Polit. & Govt. Pos: Rep. precinct div. chmn, 67th assembly dist, Los Angeles Co. Rep, Cent. Cmt. Precinct Orgn, Calif, 66-68 and Rep. precinct area chmn, 68-; hq. chmn, 67th Assembly Dist. Rep. Cent. Cmt, 66; alternate mem, Los Angeles Co. Rep. Cent. Cmt, 67-68 and 69- and mem, 68-69, research chmn. hq. cmt, 17th Dist, 69-; mem, Calif. Rep. State Cent. Cmt, 68 and 69- Mem: Los Angeles Co. Fedn. of Rep. Women; United Rep. of Calif; Int. Toastmistress Clubs; Calif. Fedn. of Gem & Mineral Socs; Northrup Gem & Mineral Club; North Torrance Property and Homeowners Asn. Blue Ribbon and Cert. of Merit, Tech. Illustrators Mgt. Asn, 61. Rel: Presbyterian. Mailing Add: 17122 Spinning Ave, Torrance, Calif. 90504.

HUNTER, ROBERT EDWARD D
b. New Orleans, La, 6/11/12; s. Joseph Cooper Hunter and Alice C. Sporl H; m. 1/2/35 to Marie Le Blanc; c. Rev. Patrick Joseph, S.J. Educ: Loyola Univ. of the South, Ph.B, 48; Alpha Pi; past pres, D.C. Chap, Loyola Alumni. Polit. & Govt. Pos: Admin. asst. to U.S. Sen. Russell B. Long, La, currently. Mil. Serv: Entered as Pvt, Army, 44, released as 2nd Lt, 45; Maj, Army Res, 59- Mem: Past pres, La. Post, Soc. Am. Mil. Engrs, Commercial Athletic Asn. of New Orleans and Fed. Bus. Asn. of New Orleans. Rel: Catholic. Legal Res: New Orleans, La. Mailing Add: 2400 36th St. S.E, Washington, D.C. 20020.

HUNTER, WILLIAM A. D
Mem, Chittenden Co. Dem. Cmt, Vt.
b. Newfane, N.Y, 5/10/34; s. John Hunter and Mary W. Drummond H; m. 9/27/57 to Carol Dussault; c. David John, William A, Jr. and Barbara Carol. Educ: Ithaca Col, B.A, 56. Polit. & Govt. Pos: Mem, Chittenden Co. Dem. Cmt, Vt, 67-; chmn, State Dem. Party, 68; cand, Lt. Gov, Vt, 68; del, Dem. Nat. Conv, 68. Bus. & Prof. Pos: Pres, Hunter Broadcasting Inc, WDAT, Burlington, Vt, 63-; pres, Hunter Broadcasting Group, WBAZ, Kingston, N.Y, 66- Mil. Serv: Entered as Pvt, Marine Corps, 57, released as 1st Lt, 60, after serv. in MACS-6, Cherry Point, N.C, 57-60; Capt, Res, 63-69. Mem: Vt. Asn. Broadcasters; F&AM; Elks; Ethan Allen Club. Rel: Unitarian. Mailing Add: 95 Rivermount Terr, Burlington, Vt. 05901.

HUNTER, WILLIAM HARVEY R
Mem. Exec. Cmt, S.C. Rep. Party
b. Anderson, S.C, 9/13/23; s. Samuel Eugene Hunter, III and Ruth McCarrell H; m. 3/28/45 to Jane Minter Gardner; c. Samuel Eugene, V, Loucelle Gwin, William Harvey, Jr, James Madison Gardner and John Mark McCarrell. Educ: Clemson Univ, B.S, 48; Med. Col. of S.C, M.D, 52; Phi Rho Sigma. Polit. & Govt. Pos: Campaign chmn, Third Cong. Dist. Rep. Party, 61-62, chmn, 65-; mem. exec. cmt, S.C. Rep. Party, 61-, secy, 62-64, mem. cent. adv. cmt, 62- and state campaign adv. cmt, 65-66; chmn, Oconee Co. Rep. Party, 64; del, Rep. Nat. Conv, 64. Bus. & Prof. Pos: Chmn. cmt. on continuing educ, S.C. Regional Med. Prog, 69. Mil. Serv: Entered as Naval Aviation Cadet, Marine Corps, 42, released as 1st Lt, 46, after serv. as air group intel. officer and fighter pilot, Pac. Theater, Publ: 'Conditioning of Athletes,' Coach and Athlete, 59;'The Politics of a Fanatic ,' Liberty Letter, 64; 'Osteoarthritis,' J. S.C. Med. Asn, 66. Mem: Am. and South. Med. Asns; v.pres, S.C. Med. Asn, 65-66, chmn, Cmt. on Careers in Med, 65-66, House of Del, 54-; Am. Academy General Practice; Anderson Co. Medical Soc; former chmn, Keowee Dist. Boy Scouts; exec. cmt, Am. Red Cross Pickens Co; Planning Cmt, S.C. Heart Asn; prfnl. adv. cmt, Pickens Co. Ment. Health Asn; former mem, Rotary; state chmn, Educ. Cmt, S.C.R.M.P, 68-69. All State Football Team, S.C; South. Conf. Boxing Finalist, Heavy Weight Div, 47; Distinguished Serv. Award as Outstanding Young Man of Year, Clemson, 56. Rel: Methodist; mem. bd. trustees, Anderson Dist. Methodist Church former mem. off. bd, Clemson Methodist Church; lay speaker. Legal Res: Pendleton Rd, Clemson, S.C. 29631. Mailing Add: Hunter Court, Clemson, S.C. 29631.

HUNTINGTON, JOHN WILLARD D
Mayor, West Hartford, Conn.
b. Hartford, Conn, 10/19/10; s. Robert Watkinson Huntington and Constance Willard H; m. 6/20/36 to Patricia Hannah Shaffer; c. John Willard, Jr, Sara B. and Derek Updegraf. Educ: Yale Univ, B.A, 32; Columbia Univ. Sch. Archit, B.Arch. and M.Arch, 36; Chi Psi. Polit. & Govt. Pos: Mem, West Hartford Town Coun, Conn, 61-, minority leader, 63-; Mayor, West Hartford, 67- Bus. & Prof. Pos: Sr. partner, Huntington, Darbee & Dollard, Architects, 46-; pres, Hartford Stage Co, 63- Mem: Trustee and v.pres, Wadsworth Atheneum, 51-; Conn. Chap, Am. Inst. of Architects. Rel: Episcopal. Legal Res: 159 Bloomfield Ave, West Hartford, Conn. 06105. Mailing Add: 41 Lewis St, Hartford, Conn. 06103.

HUNTINGTON, LAWRENCE SMITH R
b. N.Y.C. 6/13/35; s. Prescott Butler Huntington and Sarah Powell H; m. 12/19/59 to Olivia Hallowell; c. Matthew H, C. Stewart B. and Christopher B. Educ: Harvard, A.B, 57; N.Y. Law Sch, LL.B, 64. Polit. & Govt. Pos: Del, Rep. Nat. Conv, 68. Bus. & Prof. Pos: Exec. v.pres, Fiduciary Trust Co. of N.Y, 61- Mil. Serv: Entered as Seaman Recruit, Coast Guard Res, 57, released as Lt(jg), 61; Lt, Coast Guard Res, 61- Mem: Trustee, Burke Found, St. Luke's Hosp, Lower Eastside Narcotics Center, West Side Montessori Sch. and Women's Prison Asn; v.chmn, N.Y. Local Planning Bd. Rel: Episcopal. Mailing Add: 895 West End Ave, New York, N.Y. 10025.

HUNTINGTON, PRESCOTT BUTLER R
N.Y. State Assemblyman
b. St. James, N.Y, 7/26/05; s. Francis C. Huntington and Susan Butler H; m. 1/11/30 to Sarah H. Powell; c. Francis C, Samuel, Sarah P.(Mrs. Dugald A. Fletcher), Susan B. and Lawrence S. Educ: Harvard Col. and Law Sch. Polit. & Govt. Pos: Mayor, Nissequogue, N.Y, 34-41; Justice of the Peace, Smithtown Bd, 53-56; N.Y. State Assemblyman, Fourth Dist, 57- Bus. & Prof. Pos: Pres, Garden City Co, N.Y, 41-42 & 46-56; partner, Lord & Huntington and predecessor firm, Lawyers, 35-53, Choate, Reynolds, Huntington & Hollister and predecessor firms, Lawyers, 53-65. Mil. Serv: Entered as Lt, Naval Res, 42, released as Lt. Comdr, 45, after serv. in Secretariat, Joint Chiefs of Staff; Victory Medal; Am. Theater and Navy Commendation Ribbons. Mem: Asn. of Bar of City of N.Y; Suffolk Co. Bar Asn. Rel: Episcopal. Legal Res: Long Beach Rd, St. James, L.I, N.Y. 11780. Mailing Add: 38 Landing Ave, Smithtown, L.I, N.Y. 11787.

HUNTLEY, ELMER C. R
Wash. State Sen.
b. St. John, Wash, 1915; m. to Necia. Educ: Wash. State Univ. Polit. & Govt. Pos: Wash. State Rep, Fifth term to 66; chmn, Wash. State Hwy. Cmn, 2 years; Wash. State Sen, 67- Bus. & Prof. Pos: Grain and Livestock Farmer; mem. bd. dir, Old Nat. Bank, Wash. and mem. bd, Gen. Telephone. Mailing Add: Thornton, Wash. 99176.

HUNTLEY, LOUIS L. D
b. Doctor's Inlet, Fla, 1/8/28; m. to Mary Wand; c. Frank Dewyatt, Elizabeth and Ward Louis. Educ: Univ. Fla, B.S. and B.A, 50; Sigma Chi. Polit. & Govt. Pos: Mem. bd. cmnrs, Clay Co, Fla, 62-64; Fla. State Rep, formerly. Bus. & Prof. Pos: Grocery retailing; hardware and air conditioning; farming; cattle raising. Mil. Serv: Maj, Signal Corps, Army Nat. Guard, Fla. Mem: Pres, C. of C, 56; Jaycees; Lions; Moose; Elks; exec. bd, N. Fla. Coun, Boy Scouts. Rel: Methodist. Mailing Add: 1632 Plainfield Ave, Orange Park, Fla. 32073. (1967)

HUNTLEY, WILLIAM LEONARD D
Chmn, San Bernardino Co. Dem. Cent. Cmt, Calif.
b. San Bernardino, Calif, 7/15/38; s. Wright H. Huntley and Cecile Mary Kerr H; div; c. Leonard S, Leslie G. and Lori Jean. Educ: Claremont Men's Col, 4 years. Polit. & Govt. Pos: Finance chmn, Ken Dyal for Cong. Campaign, Calif, 66; pres, San Bernardino Downtown Dem. Club, 67; campaign chmn, Nancy Smith for Supvr. and Jim Evans for Calif. State Assembly, 68; chmn, San Bernardino Co. Dem. Cent. Cmt, 68- Bus. & Prof. Pos: Realtor, San Bernardino Bd. Realtors, 63-; contractor and v.pres, I.C. Minium Corp, 65-66; pres, Arrowhead Construction Corp, 68- Mem: Elks; Argonaut Club of San Bernardino (past pres). Rel: Methodist. Mailing Add: 247 E. Highland Ave, San Bernardino, Calif. 92404.

HUNTON, BENJAMIN LACY R
Job Corps Prog. Officer, Dept. of the Interior
b. Washington, D.C, 11/25/19; s. Benjamin H. Hunton and Evelyn Lacy H; m. 6/10/61 to Kelsy Jean Cooper; c. Benjamin Lorimer. Educ: Howard Univ, A.B. 40, M.A, 42; Am. Univ, Ph.D, 54; Gamma Tau. Polit. & Govt. Pos: Supv, dir, Pub. Schs, Wash. D.C, 51-58, asst. to asst. supt, jr. sr. high schs, 58-66; area dir, Equal Educ. Opportunity Prog, Dept. of Health, Educ. and Welfare, 66-69; Job Corps Prog. Officer, Dept. of the Interior, 69- Bus. & Prof. Pos: Teacher, Wash, D.C. Pub. Schs, 42-51. Mil. Serv: Entered as Platoon Leader/Supply Officer, Army, 42, released as asst. prof. of mil. sci. and tactics, Howard Univ, 49, after serv. in U.S; Brigade Comdr, First Brigade, 80th Div, Army Res, 61-; World War II Victory and Am. Theater Medals, 20-Year Res. Ribbon. Publ: Budget of the Department of War 22-32, Am. Univ, 54; Basic Track in Junior High Schools, 62, and Study of Selected School Drop-outs 63-66, 67, D.C. Pub. Schs. Mem: Asn. of U.S. Army; ROA; Am. Fedn. of Govt. Employees; Amvets. Rel: Catholic. Mailing Add: 7737 Ardmore-Ardwick Rd, Hyattsville, Md. 20784.

HUNTOON, MAXWELL C. R
b. Providence, R.I, 6/13/96. Educ: Dartmouth Col; Phila. Textile Inst. Polit. & Govt. Pos: Mem, town coun, Little Compton, R.I, 3 years; R.I. State Sen, 63-67. Bus. & Prof. Pos: Trustee, People's Savings Bank; dir, Fireman's Mutual Ins. Co; v.pres, Marshall & Williams Corp, Providence, R.I. and Marshall & Williams South. Corp, Greenville, S.C. Mil. Serv: Chem. Warfare Serv. and State Decontamination Officer, World War II. Mailing Add: Little Compton, R.I. 02837. (1967)

HUOT, J. OLIVA D
b. Laconia, N.H, 8/11/17; s. Amedee Huot and Marie Bibiane Decelles H; m. 10/1/38 to Irene R. Fournier; c. David O. Educ: High Sch. Polit. & Govt. Pos: Mem. sch. bd, Laconia, N.H, 53-59, mayor, 59-63; nominee for N.H. House of Rep, First Dist, 62; del, Dem. Nat. Conv, 64; U.S. Rep, First Dist, N.H, 65-67. Bus. & Prof. Pos: Supvr, Tabulating Dept, Scott & Williams, Inc, 35-56; advert. mgr, Laconia Eve. Citizen, 56-64; gen. mgr, Lakes Region Trader, 59-64; trustee, City Savings Bank, Laconia, 65- and Gustock Jr. Col, 66- Mem: New Eng. Daily Newspapers Asn; K. of C; Elks; Lakes Region Sled Dog Asn; Kiwanis; Moose; Laconia St. Jean-Baptiste Soc. Rel: Roman Catholic. Mailing Add: 32 Adams St, Laconia, N.H. 03246. (1967)

HUPE, LAWRENCE LOUIS R
Mem, Fourth Dist. Rep. Cmt, Ill.
b. Blue Island, Ill, 3/10/09; s. Ernest H. Hupe and Katherine Knierium H; m. 2/24/34 to LaVerna M. Zebell; c. Carol (Mrs. Marvin Redemske) and Lawrence E. Educ: Univ. Ill, Champaign-Urbana, B.S, 31; Chicago Normal Sch, 32; Univ. Chicago, 33; Polit. & Govt. Pos: Mem, Worth Twp. Rep. Orgn, Ill, 35-; committeeman, Worth Twp. Rep. Party, 57-; mem, Fourth Dist. Rep. Cmt, 68- Bus. & Prof. Pos: Treas, Worth Twp. Sch, Ill, 48- Mem: Lions. Rel: Lutheran. Mailing Add: 12821 Elm St, Blue Island, Ill. 60406.

HURD, ELIOT PROVOOST R
b. N.Y.C, 10/25/22; s. Edward Augustus Hurd and Elise P. Smith H; m. 4/17/43 to Marian Poultney Handy; c. Ellen Preston (Mrs. George Meredith Fitz-Hugh), Eliot P, Jr. and Susan P. Educ: Johns Hopkins Univ, nights, 50-58; Inst. of Investment Banking; Wharton Sch. Finance, Univ. Pa, 58-60. Polit. & Govt. Pos: Precinct capt, Baltimore Co. Rep. Cmt, Md, 58-60, area exec, 60-62 and chmn, 63-64; treas, Md. State Rep. Cent. Cmt, 62-66. Bus. & Prof. Pos: Staff asst, Chesapeake and Potomac Tel. Co, Md, 41-56; pres. and dir, Tidewater Indust. Leasing Co, 58-; partner, Hurd Mgt. Co, 61-; chmn. bd. and treas, Machinery Systs, Inc, 64-66. Mem: Eng. Soc. Baltimore; Bond Club of Baltimore; Baltimore Asn. of Credit Mgt; past pres, Baltimore chapter and nat. dir, Soc. for Advancement of Mgt; North. Lake George Yacht Club; Merchants Club; Chesapeake Bay Yacht Racing Asn; Green Spring Valley Hunt Club; Windjammers of Baltimore; Green Spring and Worthington Valley Planning Coun. Ocean Yacht Racing. Rel: Episcopal. Legal Res: Garrison Forest Rd, Owings Mills, Md. 21117. Mailing Add: 306 N. Charles St, Baltimore, Md. 21201.

HURD, ESTHER THOMPSON R
Asst. Treas, N.H. Rep. State Cmt.
b. Concord, N.H, 8/2/04; d. Augustine P. Thompson and Melinda Story T; m. 9/10/27 to Vinal Ray Hurd; c. Beverley (Mrs. Headberg), Cynthia (Mrs. Kirby) and Vinalrae (Mrs. McBride). Educ: Concord High Sch, grad, 23. Polit. & Govt. Pos: Secy, U.S. Army Los Angeles Port of Embarkation, 46; recorder, N.H. State Sen, 47-; asst. treas. and office secy, N.H. Rep. State Cmt, 47-; treas. women's div, N.H. Rep. Party, 52-; vol, Women for Nixon, 68. Mem: Bus. & Prfnl. Women's Club. Rel: Episcopal. Legal Res: 13 Thomas St, Concord, N.H. 03301. Mailing Add: 134 N. Main St, Concord, N.H. 03301.

HURD, HOWARD D
Chmn, Terry Co. Dem. Cmt, Tex.
b. Vera, Tex, 5/30/13; s. William Perrin Hurd and Gertrude Sanders H; m. 2/26/38 to Bettye Holmes; c. Mrs. Rex Lee Wilkes and Howard, Jr. Polit. & Govt. Pos: Campaign mgr, Terry Co. for Lyndon B. Johnson, Tex, 60 & 64, for John Connelly, 62 & 64 and for Rep. George Mahon, 64; chmn, Terry Co. Dem. Cmt, 62- Mem: Adm, Tex. Navy; retired Vol. Fireman, Brownfield; life mem, Dads Club, South. Methodist Univ; Masonic Lodge 903; Khiva Temple, Amarillo, Scottish Rite, Dallas Consistory; Brownfield Country Club; Lubbock Club; committeeman, Troop 749, Boy Scouts. Rel: Methodist; bd. mem, First Methodist Church, Brownfield. Mailing Add: 1008 E. Tate, Brownfield, Tex. 79316. (1967)

HURLEY, JAMES RICHARDSON R
N.J. State Assemblyman
b. Seaford, Del, 1/29/32; s. Victor Elzey Hurley and Annabel Jarman H; m. 8/18/56 to Walda Lou Reed; c. Leslie, Jamie and Kerri Anna. Educ: Wesley Col, Dover, Del, A.A, 53; Univ. N.C, Chapel Hill, A.V, 55; Sigma Nu. Polit. & Govt. Pos: Freeholder, Cumberland Co, N.J, 66-67; N.J. State Assemblyman, Dist. 1, 67- Bus. & Prof. Pos: Broadcaster, WBOC, Salisbury, Md, 57-59; teacher, Millville Sr. High Sch, N.J, 59-61; news dir, WMUB, Millville, 61-63; asst. v.pres, Millville Nat. Bank, 63- Mil. Serv: Entered as E-1, Army, 55, released as E-3, 57, after serv. in Signal Corps. Mem: Bank Pub. Rels. & Mkt. Asn; N.J. Bankers Asn; Kiwanis; YMCA; United Fund. Distinguished Serv. Award, Millville Jr. C. of C, 64. Rel: Presbyterian. Mailing Add: 2 Elizabeth Ave, Millville, N.J. 08332.

HURLEY, MRS. JOSEPH E. D
Wash. State Rep.
b. Winnebago, Minn; m. to Joseph E; c. Four. Educ: Holy Names Col, B.A. Polit. & Govt. Pos: Wash. State Rep, currently. Bus. & Prof. Pos: Teacher; homemaker. Mem: Spokane Co. Bar Asn. Auxiliary. Mailing Add: 730 E. Boone Ave, Spokane, Wash. 99202. (1967)

HURST, ELLA BLANCHE D
b. Dallas, Ark, 6/17/85; d. Holder Hightower Hudgens and Ella Blanche Petty H; m. to Geo. A. Hurst. Educ: Univ. of Ark, 01-05. Polit. Pos: Mem, Ark. State Dem. Party; Ark. State Rep, 45, 43 and 35; former pres, Co. Dem. Club. Govt. Pos: Enrolling Clerk, Ark. House of Rep, five yrs. Rel: Baptist. 1967 Legal Res: 531 Fayetteville, Oakland, Ark. 72701. No mailing address available. (1967)

HURST, GLYNN J. D
Chmn, Ziebach Co. Dem. Party, S.Dak.
b. St. Lawrence, S.Dak, 8/19/10; s. Levi C. Hurst and Julia Petersen H; m. 7/17/37 to Sybil Bird; c. Phyllis Rose. Educ: Dupree High Sch. Polit. & Govt. Pos: Chmn, Ziebach Co, Dem. Party, S.Dak. Bus. & Prof. Pos: Treas, Ziebach Co. Dem. Party, for five terms and auditor for two. Mil. Serv: Entered as Pvt, Army, released as T/Sgt, 40, after serv. in 975th Field Artil. Bn, ETO; Four Major Campaign Ribbons. Mem: Pres, S.Dak. Asn. of Co. Off; Odd Fellows; Mason; Am. Legion; VFW; Farmers Union. Rel: Congregational. Mailing Add: Dupree, S.Dak 57623.

HURST, JOHN RAYMOND R
b. Wilhurst, Ky, 4/22/99; s. Harden B. Hurst and Ida Murphy H; m. 6/28/32 to Willa Mae Poynter; c. Joan Rae (Mrs. Robert C. Smith). Educ: Hazel Green Acad, teacher cert. Polit. & Govt. Pos: Chmn. bd, Montgomery Co. Rep. Party, Ky, 60-64, finance chmn, 66-69; former chmn, Registration Purgation Bd, ten years. Bus. & Prof. Pos: Salesman, Mutual Benefit Life Ins. Co, Newark, N.J, 44- Mem: Mason; Kiwanis. Rel: Protestant. Mailing Add: Route 2, Mt. Sterling, Ky. 40353.

HURST, JOSEPH J. D
b. Louisville, Ala, 12/11/00; s. John J. Hurst and Leona Bickley H; m. 1/21/33 to Mary Castellow (deceased); c. Mary Jo (Mrs. Beech), Edith Frances (Mrs. Hammond) and Sandra Arnall (Mrs. Dunaway); grandchildren: Ray Marshall Beech, Jr, Hutchen Morgan Hammond, Jr, Joseph Michael Hammond and Lena Gayle Beech. Educ: Barbour Co. Schs. Polit. & Govt. Pos: Quitman Co. Cmnr, Ga, 35-45; employed by State Hwy. Dept, 43-47, Revenue Dept, 47-49; inspector, Ga. State Dept. of Agr; Ga. State Rep, 49-50 & 53-64. Mem: Mason; Shriner. Rel: Methodist. Mailing Add: Georgetown, Ga. 31754.

HURST, JULIUS R
b. McNair Co, Tenn, 1919; m. 1947 to Mary Louis Nipp; c. Suzanne, David. Educ: Univ. of Tenn, B.A, 40, M.A, 50. Polit. & Govt. Pos: Supvr, McNair Co. Schs, 59-66; chmn, Rep. State Exec. Cmt, 65; McNair Co. Rep. Campaign Chmn, 60, 56 and 52; McNair Co. Rep. Exec. Cmt, 54. Bus. & Prof. Pos: Dir, Tenn. Farm Bur, 52-53; Jr. High Sch. Prin, 40. Mil. Serv: Army, WW II. Mem: Rotary; Co, State and Nat. Educ. Asns. Misc: C. of C. Outstanding Citizen, 65. Rel: First Presbyterian Church. Mailing Add: 1252 E. Poplar, Selmer, Tenn. 38375. (1967)

HURST, QUINCY BYRUM D
Pres. Pro-Tem, Ark. State Senate
b. Hot Springs, Ark, 9/21/18; s. Floyd Leroy Hurst and Alva Cash H; m. 11/6/44 to Hazel Earline Barham; c. Nancy (Mrs. John Harmon), Lezah (Mrs. Ronald Stenger), Q. Byrum, Jr. and Byretta. Educ: Anderson Col; Ark. Law Sch, LL.B, 39; LaSalle Univ, LL.B, 42. Polit. & Govt. Pos: U.S. West. Dist. Cmnr, Hot Springs, Ark, 42-44; co. judge, Garland Co, Ark, 46-50; Ark. State Sen, Seventh Dist, 51-, Pres. Pro-Tem, Ark. State Senate, currently. Mil. Serv: Entered as Pvt, Army, 44, released as Cpl, 45. Mem: Am, Ark. and Judge Advocate's Bar Asns; Am. Angus Asn; Optimist (past pres, dist. gov); Am. Legion (Judge Advocate); Elks; K. of P; 40 et 8. Hot Springs C. of C. Legis. Award of Appreciation, 68-69; Assoc. Press Most Influential Legislator, 68. Rel: Church of God. Mailing Add: 14 Conway, Hot Springs, Ark.. 71901.

HURST, RONALD ALAN R
Ill. State Rep.
b. Milwaukee, Wis, 4/16/30; s. Charles Edmund Hurst and Victoria Wojciechowski H; m. 12/11/54 to Jean Elizabeth Hunt; c. Gregory, Pamela, Scott

and Teresa. Educ: Marquette Univ, B.S, 51; Univ. Wis, M.S, 56; Kappa Tau Alpha; Sigma Delta Chi. Polit. & Govt. Pos: Ill. State Rep, currently. Bus. & Prof. Pos: Staff writer, United Press, 55-56; sales rep, Caterpillar Tractor Co, Peoria, Ill, 56-60, legis. affairs rep, 60-63, mgr, Caterpillar Found, 63-65, mgr. col, prfnl. and tech. recruiting, 65- and labor rels. rep, 68- Mil. Serv: Entered as A/S, Navy, 51, released as Lt. Comdr, 55, after serv. in Admiral's Staff, Hawaii; Lt. Comdr, Naval Res, currently; Coding, Aleutian Islands; Commun. Officer Aboard Destroyer, Far East; Formosa Patrol, Korean Conflict, UN and Am. Defense Ribbons. Mem: Col. Placement Asn; United Health Found; Peoria Jr. Col. Steering Cmt; Catholic Church Lay Coun; Gifted Children's Parents' Club; adv, Newman Student Club, Bradley Univ, Peoria. Rel: Roman Catholic. Mailing Add: 2822 N. Elmcroft, Peoria, Ill. 61604.

HURST, THURMAN SCOTT D
b. Cassville, Mo, 4/28/89; s. Winfield Scott Hurst and Emma Jane Frost H; m. 11/5/15 to Mary Elizabeth Stevens; c. Helen Louise (Mrs. Thompson), Edwin Scott and Robert Thurman. Educ: Univ. Okla. Sch. Law; Order of the Coif; Phi Delta Phi. Polit. & Govt. Pos: Attorney, Okfuskee Co, Okla, 15-19; Judge, Tulsa and Pawnee Co, Okla, 31-37; Assoc. Justice, Supreme Court, Okla, 37-47, Chief Justice, 48-49; dir, Off. Price Stabilization, East. Okla, 51-52. Mil. Serv: Govt. Appeal Agent, Okfuskee Co, Okla, World War I. Mem: Mason. Rel: Disciples of Christ. Legal Res: 1357 Sixth St, Pawnee, Okla. 74058. Mailing Add: 631 Sixth St, Pawnee, Okla. 74058.

HURSTON, CHARLES ANDREW D
b. Memphis, Tenn, 8/9/27; s. James Thomas Hurston and Kathryn Louise Ashurst H; m. 10/24/55 to Henrietta Keller; c. Vicki Louise, Charles Robin and Charlene Lenora. Educ: Miss. State Col, 46-47. Polit. & Govt. Pos: Mem, La. State Hosp. Bd, 64-68; del, Dem. Nat. Conv, 68; secy. bd. rev, Dept. Employ. Security, 68- Mailing Add: Covington, La. 70433.

HUSFLOEN, ABRAHAM 'ABE' D
Mem, State Cent. Cmt, N.Dak. Dem. Non-Partisan League
b. Osterdalen, Norway, 12/31/93; s. Ole Halvorson Husfloen and Johanna Moen H. Polit. & Govt. Pos: Mem, State Cent. Cmt, N.Dak. Dem. Non-Partisan League, at present and former chmn, 4 yrs; precinct committeeman, 66-; co. chmn, Rep. Party, 4 yrs. Bus. & Prof. Pos: Rancher, Hereford Cattle, 25- Mil. Serv: Pvt, Army, 18-19. Mem: Am. Legion; Farmers Union; Vets. World War I. Rel: Lutheran. Mailing Add: P.O. Box 101, Mandan, N.Dak. 58554. (1967)

HUSKINS, JOSEPH PATTERSON D
b. Burnsville, N.C, 6/23/08; s. Joseph Erwin Huskins and Mary Etta Peterson H; m. 9/29/34 to Mildred Amburn; c. Mrs. Judson Durward Watson, III. Educ: Univ. N.C, Chapel Hill, A.B, 30. Polit. & Govt. Pos: Area Rent Control Bd, N.C, 47-51, Statesville Zoning Bd, 60-62 and N.C. Bd. Higher Educ, 66- Bus. & Prof. Pos: Pres. & gen. mgr, Statesville Daily Record, Inc, 46-; pres, N.C. Asn. Afternoon Dailies, 48-49 and Assoc. Dailies of N.C, 65-66; chmn. bd. trustees, Mitchell Col, 62- Mil. Serv: Entered as Lt.(jg), Naval Res. 43, released as Lt.(sg), 46, after serv. in Air Navig. Sect, Hydrographic Office, Wash, D.C. Mem: Pres, Statesville C. of C, 60; Past Exalted Ruler, Statesville Elks; v.pres, Statesville City Club; Am. Legion; Statesville Arts & Sci. Mus; N.C. Art Soc. Rel: Methodist. Legal Res: Our Dell, Statesville, N.C. 28677. Mailing Add: 220 E. Broad St, Statesville, N.C. 28677.

HUSKY, MILTON J. D
Chmn, Ariz. State Corp. Cmn.
b. Evansville, Ind, 3/3/22; s. George D. Husky and Marie Gonterman H; div; c. Milton E, George H, Marsha A. and John A. Educ: Phoenix Col, 47; Ariz. State Univ, B.S, 49. Polit. & Govt. Pos: Mem. and past pres, Creighton Elem. Sch. Dist, 56-65; treas, State of Ariz, 62-64; chmn. and cmnr, Ariz. State Corp. Cmn, 65- Bus. & Prof. Pos: Controller, Sunland Life Ins. Co, Scottsdale, Ariz, 52-55; owner, Husky Bros. Real Estate & Ins. Co, Phoenix, 55-62. Mil. Serv: Entered as Reservist, Naval Air Res, 40, released as 1/c Bombardier, 45, after serv. in Patrol Bomber Squadron, S.Pac, Solomons and Philippines; Distinguished Flying Cross; Air Medals; Navy Unit Citation. Mem: West. Conf. Pub. Serv. Cmnrs.(first v.pres); Nat. Water & Sewer Cmt, Nat. Asn. of Regulatory and Utility Cmnrs.(exec. cmt); Cong. Am. Indians; Am. Legion; VFW; Fraternal Order of Police; Mason; Shrine; Elks; Jesters. Rel: Protestant. Mailing Add: 3324 E. Osborn Rd, Phoenix, Ariz. 85016.

HUSSEY, DANIEL JAMES R
N.H. State Rep.
b. Rochester, N.H, 4/30/47; s. Robert D. Hussey and Matilda Cebula H; single. Educ: Univ. N.H, B.A, 69; N.H. chmn, Coun. Int. Rels. and UN Affairs, 67-68. Polit. & Govt. Pos: V.chmn, N.H. TAR Clubs, 66-67; v.pres, Univ. N.H. Young Rep. Club, 67; chmn, N.H. Col. Rep, 67-68; N.H. rep, Nat. Col. Young Rep. Exec. Bd, 67-68; exec. bd. mem, N.H. Fedn. Young Rep. Clubs, 67-68; N.H. State Rep, 69- Mil. Serv: Army ROTC, 2nd Lt, 69- Mem: N.H. Coun. World Affairs. Rel: Catholic. Mailing Add: Flagg Rd, Box 481, Rochester, N.H. 03867.

HUSTEAD, D.W. 'BILL' R
S.Dak. State Sen.
b. 6/22/27; married; c. Rick, Ted, Jon, Pat, Kelly, Sue and Jamie. Educ: S.Dak. State Univ, B.S. Polit. & Govt. Pos: Former v.pres, Young Rep, Pennington Co, S.Dak; del, Rep. Nat. Conv, 60 & 62; S.Dak. State Rep, 63-66; S.Dak. State Sen, 67- Bus. & Prof. Pos: Registered pharmacist; mem. adv. bd, Mt. Marty Col; v.pres, Wall Drug, Inc; pres, Wall Auto Livery, Inc. Mil. Serv: Navy Vet; discharged in 46; served as aviation radioman. Mem: Am. Legion; Bd. of Dirs, 'Keep South Dakota Green' Asn. Rel: Catholic. Mailing Add: Wall, S.Dak. 57790.

HUSTON, MARY THELMA D
b. Glenwood, Mich, 6/25/15; d. Carry Lee Craig and Charlottie M. Morford C; m. 9/29/34 to Harold Thomas Huston. Polit. & Govt. Pos: Treas, Cass Co, Mich, 65-68; v.chmn, Fourth Dist. Dem. Party, 66 & 67; cand. chairwoman, Fourth Cong. Dist. Congress, 66, 67 & 68; Dem. cand, Mich. State Rep, 42nd Dist, 66; del, Dem. Co. and State Conv, 65, 66, 67, 68 & 69; del, Dem. Nat. Conv, 68. Bus. & Prof. Pos: Purchasing and inventory control clerk, Kaiser, Frazer Corp, Dowaigac, Mich, 45-49; unit control mgr, Sears Roebuck & Co, Niles, 50-52, interviewer, cashier, collection, asst. credit mgr, South Bend, Ind, 52-64. Mem: Dowagiac Bus. & Prfnl. Women (past legis. chmn, pres. elect, currently); Cass Co. Med. Facility Auxiliary (v.chmn, currently); Sumnerville Grange (chmn. commun. improv, Jr. Grangers Master). Rel: Methodist. Mailing Add: 1300 Barron Lake Rd, Niles, Mich. 49120.

HUSTON, TEDD CLARK R
Chmn, Custer Co. Rep. Cent. Cmt, Nebr.
b. Grand Island, Nebr, 4/10/26; s. Paul C. Huston and Hazel F. Colwell H; m. 8/23/49 to Barbara Jean Stearns; c. David C, Charles D, Ann D. and Thomas C. Educ: St. Mary's Col, 44-45; Univ. Nebr, B.A, 49; Univ. Nebr. Law Col, LL.B. & J.D, 52; Phi Alpha Theta; Phi Delta Phi. Polit. & Govt. Pos: Chmn, Custer Co. Rep. Cent. Cmt, currently. Bus. & Prof. Pos: Chmn, Nebr. State Law Day USA, 69. Mil. Serv: Entered as A/S, Navy, 44, released as Ensign, 57, after serv. in Pac. Mem: Am. and Nebr. Bar Asns; Cent. Nebr. Bar Asn. (pres, 69); Custer Co. Bar Asn. (pres, 56); Am. Legion; Custer Co. Farm Bur; VFW; Broken Bow Jaycees; Elks; C. of C. Rel: Protestant. Legal Res: 1105 North Sixth, Broken Bow, Nebr. 68822. Mailing Add: 426 S. Tenth, Broken Bow, Nebr. 68822.

HUSTON, W. GLENN D
Ore. State Sen.
b. Seattle, Wash, 3/19/11; s. Roscoe C. Huston and Hattie Dempsey H; m. to Willa E. Forbis; c. Walter F. and Wilma (Mrs. Grill). Educ: Bus. Col. Polit. & Govt. Pos: Coroner, Linn Co, Ore, 46-63; city councilman, Lebanon, 48-50; Ore. State Sen, Linn Co, 62-66 and currently. Mem: Pres, Linn Co. C. of C, 66; Odd Fellows; Elks Lodge 1663; Mason, Shrine; Farm Bur; Grange; Santiam Fish & Game Cmt. Rel: Protestant. Mailing Add: Route 2, Box 176, Lebanon, Ore. 97355. (1967)

HUTAR, PATRICIA R
b. Minneapolis, Minn; d. George Hansom Miller and Selma Barge M; m. 5/9/53 to Laddie Frank Hutar. Educ: Univ. Minn, 46-49; Memphis State Col, B.S, 50. Polit. & Govt. Pos: Pub. chmn, group work and recreation div, Commun. Welfare Coun. of San Diego, Calif, 52; Vol. Young Rep, San Diego, 52; precinct capt, 39th precinct, 43rd Ward, Ill, 55-; playground proj. chmn, and v.pres, 43rd Ward Young Rep. Orgn, Inc, 55-56, pres, 56-57, del, 57-; spec. activities chmn, Young Rep. Orgn. of Cook Co, Inc, 56-57, v.chmn-at-lg, 57-; co-dir, Region V, Nat. Fedn. Young Rep, 57-, co-chmn, publicity, 59-; co-chmn, Cook Co. membership dr, United Rep. Fund, 59-; bd. gov, 62-65; v.pres, Rep. Citizens League, Ill. and former asst. chmn, Rep. Nat. Cmt. Bus. & Prof. Pos: Group soc. worker, Girl Scout Coun. of San Diego Co, Inc, 51-52; recorder, First Annual Conf. of Group Leadership, San Diego State Col, 52; fashion photographers model and fashion lectr, 54-58; with Beveridge Orgn, Inc, pub. rels, 58-; partner, Investment Club Counsrs, 59-; dir, Nuscope Co, Inc, Chicago; free lance writer. Mem: Art Inst, Chicago; Metrop. Opera Guild, Chicago; staff adv. to residential chmn, Girl Scouts and supvt, Day Camps, 52; vol, Girl Scout Coun. of Oak Park, Ill, 53, YMCA, 56; donations chmn, Chicago Arden Shore Asn, 56-; recording secy, Women's Bd, Metrop. YMCA; Great Books discussion leader, 51-52, 55-, v.chmn, Great Books Coun, Gr. Chicago, 56- Named Most Outstanding Young Rep. Woman of Ill, 55-57. Mailing Add: 511 Brompton Place, Chicago, Ill. 60657. (1967)

HUTCHCRAFT, JAMES EDWIN R
Chmn, Hamilton Co. Rep. Cmt, Ill.
b. Dahlgren, Ill, 8/2/20; s. Martin Luther Hutchcraft and Mary Learned H; m. 10/11/47 to Mary Louise Bancroft; c. Roy Howard. Polit. & Govt. Pos: Twp. assessor, 53-57; chmn, Hamilton Co. Rep. Cmt, Ill, 63- Bus. & Prof. Pos: Farmer. Mil. Serv: Entered as Pvt, Army, 45, released as S/Sgt, 46, after serv. in 25th Div, Pac. Area; Pac. Theater Ribbon. Mem: Past Master, Masonic Lodge, Andrew Webb Chapter, RAM, Palton Commandery, KT; Odd Fellows. Rel: Baptist. Mailing Add: R.R. 1, Dahlgren, Ill, 62828. (1967)

HUTCHENS, CHARLES KUNKLE D
b. Radford, Va, 1/22/96; m. to Anne E. McEnlaine. Educ: Newport News Pub. Schs. Polit. & Govt. Pos: Mem, Va. State House of Del, 38-68. Bus. & Prof. Pos: Sr. partner, Chevrolet Agency; dir. and v.chmn. of bd, Citizens Marine Bank; pres, Riverside Hosp. Mem: Dir, Va. Penninsula Asn. of Commerce; Khedive Temple Shrine; Mason; Rotary; Elks; dir. and v.pres, Tidewater Auto Asn; Commonwealth Club; Propellor Club; James River Country Club. Rel: Methodist. Mailing Add: P.O. Box 516, Newport News, Va. 24507. (1967)

HUTCHENS, DAVID PAUL D
Okla. State Rep.
b. Hobart, Okla, 12/27/38; s. Gilbert B. Hutchens and Exa Henderson H; m. 8/14/59 to Rita Leonore Gutierrez; c. Tamara Sue, Ramona Lynn and Douglas Paul. Educ: Phillips Univ, B.A, 61; Univ. Okla, 61-64; Pi Sigma Alpha; Varsity Club, Phillips Univ. Polit. & Govt. Pos: Pres, Kiowa Co. Young Dem, Okla, 61-62; col. coordinator, Okla. Young Dem, 62; Okla. State Rep, 65-, asst. floor leader, Okla. State House of Rep, 69- Bus. & Prof. Pos: Instr. polit. sci, Hardin-Simmons Univ, 62; pres, Cosmopolitan Trading Co, 63-66; agent, Colonial Life & Accident Ins. Co, 65-; secy, Am. Engraving, Inc, 68- Mem: Elks; C. of C. Rel: Disciples of Christ. Legal Res: 201 S. Hitchcock, Hobart, Okla. 73651. Mailing Add: P.O. Box 744, Hobart, Okla. 73651.

HUTCHENS, JAMES ALBERT R
b. East Bend, N.C, 12/20/20; s. David Harrison Hutchens and Julia Phillips H; m. 6/7/52 to Thelma Lucille Dinkins. Educ: Univ. N.C, A.B. in hist, 50, M.A. in govt, 60. Polit. & Govt. Pos: Acct, tax supvr. and contracting officer for co. watershed, Yadkin Co, 60-68; precinct worker, Rep. Party, 62-68; chmn, Yadkin Co. Rep. Exec. Cmt, N.C, 66-68. Bus. & Prof. Pos: Payroll clerk, Taylor Bros. Tobacco Co, 52; teacher, N.C. Pub. Schs, 53-60; mem. faculty polit. sci, Surry Commun. Col, 68- Mil. Serv: Entered as Pvt, Army, 43, released as S/Sgt, 46; Purple Heart; Cent. European Campaign Ribbon. Mem: Am. Hist. Asn; Nat. Asn. of Counties. Student of Hist. and Govt. Rel: Baptist. Mailing Add: R.F.D. 2, Box 227, Yadkinville, N.C. 27055.

HUTCHENS, JOHN GROVER R
Mem. Exec. Cmt, Guilford Co. Rep. Party, N.C.
b. High Point, N.C, 11/28/28; s. George Elijah Hutchens and Elizabeth Line-

back H; m. 12/23/50 to Jane Campbell Davis; c. John G, Jr, Julia, James and Jane Campbell. Educ: Davidson Col, B.S, 51; Univ. N.C, Chapel Hill, LL.B, 54; Univ. N.C. Law Review; Sigma Alpha Epsilon; Phi Delta Phi. Polit. & Govt. Pos: Chmn, High Point Rep. Party, N.C, 65; mem. exec. cmt, Guilford Co. Rep. Party, 65-; del, Rep. Nat. Conv, 68; campaign chmn, James C. Gardner for Gov, 68. Bus. & Prof. Pos: V.pres and treas, Big Bear of N.C, Inc, 56-; secy. and treas, ORD Enterprises, Inc, 59-; dir, Wachovia Bank & Trust Co, 64-; dir, Life Assurance Co. of Carolina, 65- Publ: 'Taxation of Trusts,' Univ. N.C. Law Review, 54. Mem: N.C, Am. and High Point Bar Asns; Emerywood Country Club (pres, 68); Willow Creek Golf Club; String & Splinter Club. Rel: Presbyterian. Mailing Add: 803 Country Club Dr, High Point, N.C. 27262.

HUTCHERSON, NATHAN B, JR. D
b. Rocky Mt, Va, 8/24/18; s. Nathan B. Hutcherson, Sr. and Sallie Divers H; m. 2/22/47 to Ellen E. Lamberth; c. Ellen Divers, Virginia Peyton and Sallie Elizabeth. Educ: Hampden Sydney Col, 36-37; William & Mary Col, A.B, 40, B.C.L, 42. Polit. & Govt. Pos: Secy, Franklin Co. Electoral Bd, Va, 54-58; chmn, Franklin Co. Dem. Cmt, 54-68; Va. State Del, 59-64; chmn, Bd. Pub. Welfare, 60- Bus. & Prof. Pos: Trustee, Franklin Mem. Hosp, 59-63; v.pres, and dir, Bankers Trust Co, 60- Mil. Serv: Entered as Pvt, Army, 42, released as Sgt, after serv. in ETO; Purple Heart; Oakleaf with Cluster; ETO Ribbon with 5 Battle Stars; Combat Inf. Badge; Paratrooper Badge. Mem: V.pres, Franklin Co. Bar Asn, 52- and Va. Trial Lawyers Asn, 64-65; Am. and Va. Bar Asns; Law Sci. Acad; Rotary; VFW; Am. Legion. Rel: Christian Church. Mailing Add: 284 Knollwood Dr, Rocky Mount, Va. 24151. (1967)

HUTCHESON, JOHN WILLIAMS R
Chmn, Polk Co. Rep. Cent. Cmt, Mo.
b. Bolivar, Mo, 12/7/15; s. Zenas Willard Hutcheson and Sue Farmer H; m. 8/4/40 to Lillian Faye Hicks; c. John Williams, Jr. and Sue Ann (Mrs. Cansler). Educ: Southwest Baptist Jr. Col, A.A, 35; Univ. Mo, B.S. in Agr, 37; Alpha Gamma Rho. Polit. & Govt. Pos: Chmn, Polk Co. Rep. Cent. Cmt, Mo. and Seventh Cong. Cmt, 62-; del, Rep. Nat. Conv, 68; chmn, Mo. State Agr. Stabilization & Conserv. Serv, 69- Mem: Mason; Rotary; Mo. Farmers Asn. Rel: Baptist. Mailing Add: 602 E. Broadway, Bolivar, Mo. 65613.

HUTCHESON, JOHN YOUNG D
Chmn, Mecklenburg Co. Dem. Party, Va.
b. Mecklenburg Co, Va, 7/7/96; s. Herbert Farrar Hutcheson and Mary Young H; single. Educ: William & Mary Col. and Univ. Va. Law Sch. Polit. & Govt. Pos: Chmn, Mecklenburg Co. Dem. Party, Va, currently. Rel: Episcopal. Mailing Add: P.O. Box 14, Boydton, Va. 23917.

HUTCHESON, R. H. D
b. Henning, Tenn, 3/11/00; s. J. A. Hutcheson and Rosa B. H; m. to Elizabeth Ford; c. one son. Educ: Univ. Tenn, Southwest; Univ. Tenn. Sch. Med, M.D; postgrad. work pub. health, Johns Hopkins Sch. Hygiene; internship, C.S. Marine Hosp, Norfolk, Va; Alpha Omega Alpha; Kappa Alpha. Polit. & Govt. Pos: Asst. dir, Rutherford Co. Health Dept, Tenn, 31; asst. dir, Williamson Co. Health Dept, 32, dir, 32-34; dir, local health serv, Tenn. Dept. Pub. Health, 35-40; asst. cmnr. pub. health, Tenn, 40-43, cmnr, 43-69. Bus. & Prof. Pos: Former assoc. prof. prev. med, Vanderbilt Univ. Mem: Am, Co. and State Med. Asns; State and Territorial Health Officers Asn.(former pres); Am. Pub. Health Asn.(former pres. South. br); Tenn. Pub. Health Asn.(former secy); Mason. Mailing Add: Cordell Hull Bldg, Nashville, Tenn. 37219.

HUTCHINS, CHARLES EUGENE D
b. Oskaloosa, Iowa, 1910; m. to Margaret Ferguson; c. Larry, Ann England, Carol. Educ: Penn Col; Univ. of Ill, 1932. Polit. & Govt. Pos: Iowa State Rep, -66; State Cmn. on Alcoholism; Mayor, Bell Plaine, 3 Terms; Bd. of Dirs, Iowa League of Munic. Bus. & Prof. Pos: Attorney. Mem: State Bar Asn; Former Pres, Oskaloosa Bar Asn. Rel: Methodist. Mailing Add: 1308 10th Ave, Belle Plaine, Iowa 52208. (1967)

HUTCHINS, CHRISTOPHER R
V.Chmn, Bangor City Rep. Cmt, Maine
b. Boston, Mass, 11/15/37; s. Curtis Marshall Hutchins and Ruth Rich H; m. 9/10/60 to Sandra Manee; c. Charles Manee and James Britton. Educ: Wash. and Lee Univ, B.A, 60; Sigma Chi. Polit. & Govt. Pos: V.chmn, Bangor City Rep. Cmt, Maine, 67-; del. and mem. platform cmt, Rep. Nat. Conv, 68. Bus. & Prof. Pos: Asst. to mkt. dir, Dead River Co, Bangor, Maine, 62-67, v.pres. and dir, 67- Mil. Serv: Entered as 2nd Lt, Army, 60, released as 1st Lt, 62, after serv. in Sixth Missile Bn; 60th Artil, Hawk, Seventh Army, 61-62. Rel: Congregational. Mailing Add: 49 Bruce Rd, Bangor, Maine 04401.

HUTCHINS, ELIZABETH DENNIS R
Mem, Columbia Rep. Town Cmt, Conn.
b. Cliffside Park, N.J, 5/5/14; d. Edward LeRoy Dennis and Elizabeth Wilson D; m. 9/21/40 to Carlton Winslow Hutchins; c. Lawrence Dennis and Sally (Mrs. Slonski). Educ: Conn. State Col, A.B, 36, Univ. Conn. Law Sch, LL.B, 39. Polit. & Govt. Pos: Justice of the Peace, Conn, 50-; trial justice, Columbia Justice Court, 53-61; mem, Columbia Rep. Town Cmt, 53-, v.chmn, 53-58, chmn, 58-68; secy, Conn. Trial Justice Assembly, 59; town counsel, Columbia, 66-68. Bus. & Prof. Pos: Attorney-at-law, 39-; with Dennis & Dennis, 39-46; secy, Multiple Listing Serv, Willimantic Bd. of Realtors, 61-64. Mem: Conn. and Tolland Co. Bar Asns; trustee, Saxton B. Little Free Libr, Inc; charter mem, Willimantic Soroptomists, 66; secy, Willimantic Dist. Heart Asn, 56-60, pres, 60-62; Columbia Grange; bd. dirs, East. Chap, Conn. Heart Asn, 67-, secy, 68-; Eastern Star; DAR; troop cmt, Girl Scouts, 58; Den Mother, Cub Scouts, 50-51; charter mem, Columbia Women's Rep. Club and Columbia Hist. Soc; Windham Co. Young Rep, 39-40. Rel: Congregational. Mailing Add: Lake Rd, Columbia, Conn. 06237.

HUTCHINS, FRANK A. R
b. Cambridge, Mass, 9/22/99; m. to Vera Phillips; c. One. Educ: Lyndon Inst. Polit. & Govt. Pos: Former town treas. and overseer of the poor; chmn, Temperance Cmt; town moderator, selectman, justice of the peace and fire warden; Vt. State Rep, 31, 51, & 65; chmn, Rep. Town Cmt, 41- Bus. & Prof. Pos: Farmer, semi-retired. Mem: Farm Bur; Wash. Elec. Coop. Rel: Methodist; Trustee and Sunday Sch. Supt, Greensboro Bend Methodist Church. Mailing Add: East Hardwick, Vt. 05836. (1967)

HUTCHINSON, DONALD PAUL D
Md. State Del.
b. Baltimore, Md, 12/31/45; s. Preston Amidon Hutchinson and Evelyn Gartside H; m. 3/28/69 to Margaret Louise Hoffman. Educ: Frostburg State Col, B.S, 67; Univ. Md. Grad. Sch. of Govt. and Polit, 68-69. Polit. & Govt. Pos: Del, Md. Constitutional Conv, 67-68; Md. State Del, 68- Bus. & Prof. Pos: Life ins. agent, Fidelity Union Life Ins. Co, 68-69; div. dir, United Fund of Cent. Md, 69- Mem: Jr. C. of C. Rel: Methodist. Mailing Add: 331 Lorraine Ave, Baltimore, Md. 21221.

HUTCHINSON, EDWARD R
U.S. Rep, Mich.
b. Fennville, Mich, 10/13/14; married. Educ: Univ. of Mich, A.B, 36, LL.B, 38. Polit. & Govt. Pos: Mich. State Rep, 46-50; Mich. State Sen, 51-60; del. and v.pres, Mich. Constitutional Conv, 61-62; U.S. Rep, Mich, 62- Bus. & Prof. Pos: Attorney. Mil. Serv: U.S. Army, 41-46, discharged as Capt. Legal Res: Fennville, Mich. Mailing Add: 417 House Office Bldg, Washington, D.C. 20515.

HUTCHINSON, ESTHER MAU R
Pres, Lincoln Co. Fedn. Rep. Women, Wyo.
b. Rock Springs, Wyo, 7/9/32; d. William F. Mau and Barbara Von Orff M; m. 6/10/51 to Paul William Hutchinson; c. W. Michael and Barbara Carol. Educ: St. Mary-of-the-Wasatch, Utah, pres, sr. class; v.pres, student body. Polit. & Govt. Pos: Chmn, Lincoln Co. Rep. Cmt, Wyo, 64-65; pres, Lincoln Co. Fedn. Rep. Women and precinct committeewoman, 65-; del, Citizens Conf. on Wyo. Courts, 66. Bus. & Prof. Pos: Secy-treas, Mau-Hutchinson Sand & Livestock Co, at present; working partner, livestock-ranching operation, 52- Mem: Past dist. pres, Am. Legion Auxiliary; Wyo. Wool Grower Auxiliary; Altar Soc; Wyo. Stockgrowers; Farm Bur. Art and Music. Rel: Catholic. Legal Res: H Ranch, Cokeville, Wyo. 83114. Mailing Add: Box 63, Cokeville, Wyo. 83114. (1967)

HUTCHINSON, FLAVOUS LEO D
Chmn. Educ. and Sch. Personnel Cmt, Dem. Party Miss.
b. Guntown, Miss, 8/5/23; s. Lawrence E. Hutchinson and Rennie Lee Bates H; m. 9/16/45 to Mamie Ruth Sullivan; c. Richard Sullivan, Flavia Ruth, Lawrence Patrick and Charles Christopher. Educ: Univ. Miss, LL.B, 50, M.Ed, 57, J.D, 68. Polit. & Govt. Pos: Chmn, Oktibbeha Co. Action Cmt. for Lyndon Baines Johnson, Miss, 64; faculty adv, Miss. State Univ. Chap, Young Dem. Clubs Miss, 64-69; del, Dem. Nat. Conv, 68; mem, State Exec. Cmt. Robert Kennedy, 68; chmn, Educators for Hubert Humphrey, Miss, 68; treas, Oktibbeha Co. Dem. Party, 68-; chmn. educ. and sch. personnel cmt, Dem. Party of Miss, 68- Bus. & Prof. Pos: Attorney-at-law, Tupelo, Miss, 50-69; research asst, Univ. Miss, 55-56; lectr. bus. law, South. Ill. Univ, 56-57; asst. prof. law, Valparaiso Univ, 57-58, assoc. prof. bus. law, Miss. State Univ, 58-64, prof, 64- Mil. Serv: Entered as Cadet, Navy, 42, released as Seaman 1/C, 45, after serv. in Naval Air Force Aerology, Pac, 44-45. Publ: 'Experts and the Constitution,' 62, 'Of Men and Mules and the Retailers' Liability,' 62 and 'Usury: Insurance Premium as Interest,' 63, Miss. Bus. Rev. Mem: Am. and Miss. Bar Asns; Am. Bus. Law Asn; S.Cent. Regional Bus. Law Asn; Am. Trial Lawyers Asn; Int. Platform Asn. Kellog Found. Research Fel, 55. Rel: Baptist. Legal Res: 1300 Fillmore St, Tupelo, Miss. 38801. Mailing Add: P.O. Box 317, Verona, Miss. 38879.

HUTCHINSON, RICHARD SHIRLEY D
Ga. State Rep.
b. Harris Co, Ga, 10/19/01; s. Thomas Rolan Hutchinson and Annie Rebecca O'Neal H; m. 12/16/33 to Lula Voyles; c. Sara Etta. Educ: Ga. Inst. Tech, grad, 22. Polit. & Govt. Pos: Ga. State Rep, Dist. 61, 65- Bus. & Prof. Pos: Life and gen. ins, 41 years. Mem: Mason; Exchange Club Methodist Church. Rel: Methodist. Mailing Add: 915 Sixth Ave, Albany, Ga. 31705.

HUTCHINSON, WARREN CLARK R
b. New York, N.Y, 11/24/98; m. to Eleanor Jones; c. One. Educ: Princeton, A.B; Columbia Law Sch, 20; Univ. Wash. Law Sch, 46-47; Phi Beta Kappa. Polit. & Govt. Pos: Former lister, auditor, selectman, town grand juror, town clerk and treas, Hancock, Vt; former justice of the peace and auditor, Rochester; Vt. State Rep, 61-67. Bus. & Prof. Pos: Former mfr. of charcoal and pallets; farmer; retired. Mil. Serv: Pvt, Marine Corps, 18; Seaman 1/C, Coast Guard, 42-45. Mailing Add: Rochester, Vt. 05767. (1967)

HUTCHISON, CARL MAHLON R
Supvr, Crawford Co. Bd. Supvr, Wis.
b. Readstown, Wis, 11/16/01; s. William E. Hutchison and Rose Crook H; m. 6/1/33 to Ann Violet Smith; c. Deane Rose and William Carl. Educ: La Crosse Teachers Col, 2 years. Polit. & Govt. Pos: Supvr, Crawford Co. Bd. Supvr, Wis, 40-; village trustee, Bell Center, 5 years; chmn, Crawford Co. Rep. Party, 54-69; chmn, Five Co. Libr. Bd, Fennemore, 58-69; mem, Gays Mills Sch. Bd, 60-64; mem, Crawford Co. Civil Defense Cmt, 60-69; mem, Crawford Co. Sesquicentennial Cmt, 69; v.chmn, Coulee Region Commun.Action Coun, 65-69; mem, Kickapoo Valley Barbers Apprentice Bd, 64-69; adv. mem, Crawford Co. Draft Bd, currently. Mem: Kickapoo Valley Defense Asn. (v.pres, 37-42); Barbers Asn; Crawford Co. Tavern League (trustee, 66); Odd Fellows; Mason; Consistory; Shrine; Farm Bur; Lions (dir, Gay Mills Club, 69-). Outstanding Tavern Owner in Wis, 64. Rel: Protestant. Legal Res: Bell Center, Wis. Mailing Add: Box 53, Gays Mills, Wis. 54631.

HUTCHISON, ERVIN A. R
b. Sioux City, Iowa, 6/27/07; s. Arthur M. Hutchison and Edna E. Purcell H; m. 6/1/35 to Elizabeth A. Popham; c. Mrs. Kurt Smith. Educ: State Univ. Iowa, LL.B, 39. Polit. & Govt. Pos: Precinct committeeman and co. finance committeeman, Rep. Party, 46-66; chmn, Woodbury Co. Rep. Cent. Cmt, Iowa, 60-68; chmn, Rules Cmt, Iowa Rep. State Conv, 64. Mil. Serv: Entered as Pvt, Army, 44, released as Sgt, 45, after serv. in 749th Field Artil. Bn, Hq. Battery; Good Conduct Medal and others. Mem: Pres, secy. and treas, S.C. Bar Asn, 47; bd. gov, Iowa Bar Asn, 50; Am. and Sioux City Bar Asns; sustaining mem, Rep. Party; Mason (32°), Knight Comdr. of Court of Honor, Shrine, pres, Shrine White Horse Mounted Patrol, Sioux City, 59-61; S.C. Country Club; S.C. Brat Club; Farm Bur; Lions; S.C. Bus. Leaders Club; C. of C; Red Shield Boys Club; Boy's Town, Omaha, Nebr. Rel: Methodist; Trustee,

First Methodist Church of Sioux City. Legal Res: 3927 Country Club Blvd, Sioux City, Iowa 51101. Mailing Add: 420 Security Bldg, Sioux City, Iowa 51101. (1967)

HUTNIK, WILLIS J. R
Wis. State Assemblyman
b. Elk, Wis, 3/23/15; married. Educ: Cent. State Col, Ohio; Univ. of Wis, Madison. Polit. & Govt. Pos: Chmn, Rusk Co. Conserv. Cong; exec. coun, Northwest Wis. Conserv. Cong; Wis. State Assemblyman, 52-, Speaker Pro-tem, Wis. State Assembly, 61, chmn, Assembly Labor Cmt, 63, mem, Plumbing License Law Cmt, 65-67, chmn, Assembly Highways Cmt. and co-chmn, Joint Interim Cmt, 67-69, chmn, Rules Cmt, mem, Educ. Cmt. and Joint Interim Cmt, mem, Legis. Coun, serv. on Legis. Coun. Highway Adv. Cmt, v.chmn, Reapportionment Cmt, mem, Assembly Commerce and Mfrs, Pub. Welfare and Vet. Affairs Cmts. Bus. & Prof. Pos: Former teacher and prin; former personnel mgr, Camp Grant, Ill; owner, sch. and off. supply bus, presently. Mem: Ladysmith Community Club; past pres, Price Co. Educ. Asn. Mailing Add: 716 E. Third St. N, Ladysmith, Wis. 54848.

HUTSON, FRANK LORING, JR. D
Finance Chmn, Ohio State Dem. Exec. Cmt.
b. Washington Court House, Ohio, 1/24/19; s. Frank Loring Hutson and Jessie E. Thompson H; m. 1/19/49 to Marjorie Lee Cockerill; c. Frank Loring, Patricia Ann, Kathryn Elizabeth and David Harrison. Educ: Univ. Miami, 39-42; Rollins Col, Theater Arts, 46-48. Polit. & Govt. Pos: Former sustaining mem, Dem. Nat. Cmt; finance chmn, Ohio Dem. State Exec. Cmt, 63-; alternate del-at-lg, Dem. Nat. Conv, 64; pres, Fayette Co. Dem. Club, 64-65; chmn, Fayette Co. Dem. Cent. and Exec. Cmts, Ohio and mem, Adv. Cmt, Ohio State Dem. Cmts, 64- Bus. & Prof. Pos: Pub. rels. consult, Hallmark Prod, Hollywood, Calif, 49-53, Investment Corp. of Fla, Ft. Lauderdale, 55-58 and Haiti Rhum Co, S.A. and Mex, D.F, 58-61. Mil. Serv: Entered as Pvt, Army, 42, released as 1st Lt, 46; Capt, Inactive Army Res; North. France and Rhineland Campaign Ribbons; European-African-Middle East. Serv. Medal; Victory Medal; Am. Serv. Medal. Mem: SAR; v.pres, Culver Summer Schs. Alumni Asn, Ind. and Columbus Culver Club, Ohio; committeeman, Cent. Ohio Coun, Boy Scouts; Staunton Mil. Acad. Alumni Asn; Franklin Forum; Wash. Country Club. Rel: Methodist. Legal Res: 230 N. Hinde St, Washington Court House, Ohio. 43160. Mailing Add: Neil House Hotel, Columbus, Ohio 43215. (1967)

HUTSON, H. KEITH R
Chmn, Guadalupe Co. Rep. Party, Tex.
b. Hereford, Tex, 3/4/31; s. Rufus B. Hutson and Beatrice Dennis H; m. 9/27/52 to Phyllis Buehler; c. Leslie Brooke and Whiney Rae. Educ: Tex. Tech. Col, B.S, 56; Phi Psi. Polit. & Govt. Pos: Asst. chmn, Guadalupe Co. Rep. Party, Tex, 62-67, chmn, 68- Bus. & Prof. Pos: V.pres, Seguin Jr. C. of C, 58-59; pres, Seguin and Guadalupe Co. C of C, 63-64. Mil. Serv: Entered as Airman Basic, Air Force, 51, released as Airman 1/C, 54 after serv. in 20th Air Force Div, Far East and Okinawa, 53-54. Mem: Am. Inst. Indust. Engrs; v.chmn, Lone Star Chap, Tex. Mfrs. Asn, 69-; Am. Legion; Kiwanis (pres, Seguin Club, 59-60). Rel: Lutheran. Mailing Add: 531 Berkeley, Seguin, Tex. 78155.

HUTT, STANLEY LOWELL Independent
b. Pittsfield, Vt, 9/6/11; s. Giddion Hutt and Grace Lowell H; m. 10/12/34 to Amy Irene Merriam; c. Betty (Mrs. Joel Moore), Nelson, Beverly (Mrs. Louis Potwin), Paul, Donald and Virginia (Mrs. Arnold Powell). Educ: Pittsfield Pub. Schs. Polit. & Govt. Pos: Former Vt. State Rep. Bus. & Prof. Pos: Custodian and bus driver, Bridgewater Sch, 44-66; Star Route Mail Carrier, 66- Mem: Mason; Fire Dept. Laymons Award, Windsor Sch. Dist. Rel: Protestant. Mailing Add: Box 320, Bridgewater, Vt. 05034.

HUTTE, ROBERT EMMETT D
b. Escanaba, Mich, 10/22/17; s. Albert Hutte and Mary Peiffer H; m. 10/27/42 to Marjorie Waller; c. John Robert, Mary Margot and Michael Delano. Educ: Wis. Sch. of Mines. Polit. & Govt. Pos: Chmn, Clarke Co. Dem. Cent. Cmt, Iowa, 52-60; campaign mgr, U.S. Rep. Carter, 56 & 58; alternate del, Dem. Nat. Conv, 56, 60 & 64; Dem. Cand. for State Auditor, 60; chmn, Iowans for Johnson, 64. Bus. & Prof. Pos: Pres, J.M.M. Corp, 59-, Ins. Advs. Inc, 63-, Midwest Nursing Homes, 65-66 and Leisure Homes Inc, 66- Mil. Serv: Pvt, Army, 42. Mem: Lions; Am. Legion; Rotary; K. of C; Variety Int; Allied Theater Owners of Iowa, Nebr, N.Dak. and S.Dak. Rel: Roman Catholic. Mailing Add: 530 N. Fillmore St, Osceola, Iowa 50213.

HUTTON, LOUISE PHILLIPS R
Asst. Secy, Calif. Rep. State Cent. Cmt.
b. Los Angeles, Calif, 8/18/18; d. Edwin Roscoe Phillips and Blanche Wakeham P; m. 2/15/41 to John Hampton Hutton; c. James Hampton and John Phillips. Educ: Mills Col, B.A, 40. Polit. & Govt. Pos: Pres, South Pasadena Rep. Women's Club. Fedn, Calif, 54-56; mem, Calif. Rep. State Cent. Cmt, 54- and chmn, educ. and promotion cmt, asst. secy, currently; mem, Electoral Col, 56; chmn, 54th Dist. Co. Cmt, 58-59 and 54th Dist. Coord. Coun, 62-64; v.chmn, Los Angeles Co. Cent. Cmt, 58-62 and 64-66; supvr, 1960 Census, Los Angeles Off, 60; pres, Huntington Harbour Rep. Women's Club, 66 and Orange Co. Fedn. of Women's Clubs, 67-; chmn. campaigns, South Div, Fedn. Rep. Women, 66- Mem: C. of C. Rel: Protestant. Mailing Add: 16622 Somerset Lane, Huntington Beach, Calif. 92646. (1967)

HUVAERE, VALERE D
b. Detroit, Mich, 7/23/23; s. Victor Huvaere and Alida Cafemeyer H; m. 7/13/46 to Grace Oilive Morenz; c. Kerin Anne, Lawrence Joseph, Valerie Ann and John Francis. Educ: Sheet Metal Trade Sch, grad. Journeyman, 47. Polit. & Govt. Pos: Precinct del, 14th Dist. Dem. Party, Mich, 66, bd. mem, 66; mem, Wayne Co. Bd. Supvrs, 66-68; del, Dem. Nat. Conv, 68; br. mgr. License Plates, Secy. of State, 69-; exec. bd. mem, Br. Mgrs. Asn. Bus. & Prof. Pos: Secy-treas, Grosse Point Heating Co, 54-; v.pres, Sheet Metal Contractors Detroit; trustee, Local 281 Pension and Welfare Fund; mem. local joint adjustment bd, Sheet Metal Contractors & Local 80. Mil. Serv: Entered as Pvt, Air Force, 43, released as Sgt, 45, after serv. in 445th Bomb Group, ETO, 43-45; Presidential Unit Citation; Qua De Guere; Six Battle Citations. Mem: Sheet Metal Contractors Metrop. Detroit; Better Heating and Cooling Bur; Nat. Asn. Sheet Metal and A/C Contractors; Sgt. & Lt. Asn; Grosse Pointe Crisis Club; 14th Dist. Dem. Club; Grosse Pointe Dem. Club. Rel: Catholic. Mailing Add: 1353 Wayburn Ave, Grosse Pointe Park, Mich. 48230.

HUYETT, MILDRED C. D
b. Hagerstown, Md, 12/31/99; single. Educ: Hagerstown pub. schs. Polit. & Govt. Pos: Md. State Rep, 44-67. Bus. & Prof. Pos: Housewife and former teacher. Mem: Wash. Co. Dem. Women's Orgn; Clear Spring Fire Dept. Aux; Dry Run Homemaker's Club. 1967 Legal Res: Route 1, Clear Spring, Md. 21722. No mailing address available. (1967)

HYATT, DONALD M. D
Mayor, Newport News, Va.
b. Waynesville, N.C, 6/7/09; s. William A. Hyatt and Evelyn McIntosh H; m. 7/29/33 to Julia May; c. Donald M, Jr. Educ: Duke Univ, 28-32; Varsity Club. Polit. & Govt. Pos: Mayor, Newport News, Va, currently. Bus. & Prof. Pos: Supt, Newport News Shipbuilding & Dry Dock Co, 34- Mem: Mason; Shrine; Jester; James River Country Club; dir, C. of C; Lions Club. Rel: Methodist. Mailing Add: 54 Maine St, Newport News, Va. 23601. (1967)

HYATT, GEORGE SIMPSON D
Treas, Spartanburg Co. Dem. Party, S.C.
b. Ft. Lawn, S.C, 10/19/13; s. Isaac Lyle Hyatt and Ruby Sloan H; m. 5/28/41 to Emma Hale; c. George S, Jr, Walter Hale and Katherine Sloan. Educ: Wofford Col, A.B, 35; Univ. S.C. Law Sch, LL.B, 38; Phi Kappa Sigma. Polit. & Govt. Pos: Treas. and mem. exec. cmt, Spartanburg Co. Dem. Party, S.C, 39-; del, State Dem. Conv, 56, 58, 60, 61, 64, 66 & 68, mem. platform and rules cmt; pres, Spartanburg City Dem. Club, 61-; del, Dem. Nat. Conv, 64 & 68. Bus. & Prof. Pos: Mem, Law Firm, Hyatt & Creal, Spartanburg, S.C, 62- Mil. Serv: Entered as 1st Lt, Army, 41, released as Lt. Col, 46, after serv. in 82nd, 98th and 81st Inf. Div, 24th and First Corps Hq, Asiatic-Pac. Theatre, 41-46; Army Res, 46-55, Col.(Ret); Philippine Liberation Ribbon with One Bronze Star; Am. Defense, Asiatic-Pac. Theatre and Am. Theatre Serv. Medals; World War II Victory Medal. Mem: Spartanburg Co. Bar Asn.(pres, 67); S.C. Bar Asn.(law sch. cmt); S.C. State Bar; Am. Bar Asn; S.C. Trial Lawyers Asn; life mem, Am. Businessmen's Club (past pres, Spartanburg Chap); YMCA; VFW; K. of P; AFM (past master, Spartan Lodge No. 70); Grand Lodge No. 70); Grand Lodge of S.C.(officer); Scottish Rite (32°, Americanization Cmt); KCCH. Rel: Baptist. Legal Res: 100 Calhoun Ave, Spartanburg, S.C. 29302. Mailing Add: 188 W. Main St, Spartanburg, S.C. 29301.

HYDE, DeWITT STEPHEN R
b. Washington, D.C, 3/21/09; s. Burr Hamilton Hyde and Ethel Holland Larrick H; m. 10/19/35 to Mildred Sullivan. Educ: George Wash. Univ, J.D, 35; Kappa Sigma. Polit. & Govt. Pos: Law clerk, Farm Credit Admin, 33-38; Md. State Del, 47-50; Md. State Sen, 51-52; U.S. Rep, Md, 53-58; assoc. judge, D.C. Court of Gen. Sessions, 59- Bus. & Prof. Pos: Partner, Hilland & Hyde, 38-59; prof. law, Benjamin Franklin Univ, 46-52 & 60-; chmn. bd. dirs, Christ Church Child Center, 61- Mil. Serv: Entered as Lt.(jg), Navy, 43, released as Lt. Comdr, 46, after serv. in S.Pac. Command, Am. Theater and S.Pac. Theater; Lt. Comdr, Naval Res, 46, Victory Ribbon; Am. Area Campaign Ribbon; Asiatic-Pac. Area Campaign Ribbon. Mem: Am. and D.C. Bar Asns; The Barristers; Columbia Country Club; George Wash. Univ. Alumni Asn. Legal Res: 5606 McLean Dr, Bethesda, Md. 20014. Mailing Add: D.C. Court of General Sessions, Fourth and E St. N.W, Washington, D.C. 20001.

HYDE, FLOYD H.
Asst. Secy. for Model Cities and Govt. Rels, Dept. of Housing and Urban Develop.
b. Fresno, Calif, 1921. Educ: Fresno State Col, 42; Univ. South. Calif. Law Sch, LL.B, 49. Polit. & Govt. Pos: Mayor, Fresno, Calif, 65-69; Asst. Secy. for Model Cities and Govt. Rels, Dept. of Housing and Urban Develop, 69- Bus. & Prof. Pos: Lawyer, 50- Mil. Serv: Capt, Marine Corps, World War II, Pac. Theater. Mem: Fresno Citizens' Cmt. for Commun. Improv, 62-63; Fresno Commun. Coun; bd. of dirs, YMCA, 60-61. Legal Res: Fresno, Calif. Mailing Add: Room 8100, Dept. of Housing and Urban Development, Washington, D.C. 20410.

HYDE, HENRY JOHN R
Ill. State Rep.
b. Chicago, Ill, 4/18/24; s. Henry Clay Hyde and Monica Kelly H; m. 11/8/47 to Jeanne Marie Simpson; c. Henry, Jr, Robert, Laura and Anthony. Educ: Georgetown Univ, 42-43, B.S.S, 47; Duke Univ, 43-44; Loyola Univ. Sch. of Law, J.D, 49; Sigma Chi; Phi Alpha Delta. Polit. & Govt. Pos: Ill. State Rep, 67- Bus. & Prof. Pos: Pres, Trial Lawyers Club of Chicago, 62. Mil. Serv: Entered as A/S, Navy, 42, released as Lt.(jg), 46, after serv. in Seventh Fleet, S.Pac. Theatre, 44-46; Comdr, Res, 61-69. Mem: Am, Illinois State and Chicago Bar Asns; Ill. Defense Counsel; K. of C. Best Freshman Rep, 75th Gen. Assembly, Ill. Polit. Reporters. Rel: Roman Catholic. Legal Res: 6841 N. Tonty Ave, Chicago, Ill. 60646. Mailing Add: 111 W. Washington St, Chicago, Ill. 60602.

HYDE, HENRY VAN ZILE, JR. R
Asst. to the Secy, Dept. of Health, Educ. and Welfare
b. Syracuse, N.Y, 9/10/36; s. Henry Van Zile Hyde, M.D. and Ellen Tracy H; m. 6/26/65 to Eveline Zoppi. Educ: Hamilton Col, A.B, 58; Cornell Law Sch, 61-63; Delta Kappa Epsilon. Polit. & Govt. Pos: Mem, Staff of U.S. Rep. Bray, Ind, 59; mem, Staff of Vice President Richard Nixon, 59-61; Asst. to the Secy, Dept. of Health, Educ. and Welfare, 69- Bus. & Prof. Pos: Mem. staff, United Rep. Fund, Chicago, Ill, 63-64; buyer and br. supvr, Ill. Power Transmission, Inc, 65-68. Mil. Serv: Entered as Pvt, Army Res, 59, released as Cpl, 65, after serv. in U.S; Spec. Letter of Commendation. Mem: Phi Delta Phi. Rel: Protestant. Mailing Add: 5807 Aberdeen Rd, Bethesda, Md. 20034.

HYDE, HERBERT LEE D
b. Bryson City, N.C, 12/12/25; s. Ervin M. Hyde and Alice Medlin H; m. 12/25/49 to Kathryn Long; c. Deborah, Lynn, Karen and Benjamin. Educ: West. Carolina Teachers Col, A.B, 51; N.Y. Univ. Sch. of Law, LL.B, 54; Phi Delta Phi; Alpha Phi Sigma. Polit. & Govt. Pos: N.C. State Sen, 63-66. Bus.

& Prof. Pos: Lawyer. Mil. Serv: PO 3/C, Naval Res, 44-46. Mem: N.C. State Bar; N.C. and Am. Bar Asns; pres, Candler Lions, 59. Rel: Baptist. Mailing Add: 93 East View Circle, Asheville, N.C. 28806. (1967)

HYDEN, JESSE L. 'JACK' R
Chmn, Floyd Co. Rep. Party, Ky.
b. Prestonburg, Ky, 3/29/27; s. Chauncey L. Hyden and Clora Adams H; m. 6/29/51 to Doris Anne Clark; c. Jack Clark and Judy Anne. Polit. & Govt. Pos: Chmn, Floyd Co. Rep. Party, Ky, 64- Bus. & Prof. Pos: Mgr, Prestonburg Lincoln-Mercury, Ky, 51-53; owner, Jack Hyden Auto Sales, Prestonsburg, 53- Mil. Serv: Entered as A/S, Navy, 44, released as Seaman 1/C, 46, after serv. in Pac. Theatre. Mem: Mason; VFW; Am. Legion. Rel: Baptist. Mailing Add: 202 Third Ave, Prestonsburg, Ky. 41653. (1967)

HYLAND, RICHARD STEPHEN D
b. Camden, N.J, 12/14/35; s. Theodore J. Hyland and Margaret Gallagher H; m. 6/28/69 to Anne M. D'Arcangelo. Educ: St. Joseph's Col, Pa, B.S, 57; Univ. Pa. Law Sch, LL.B, 60. Polit. & Govt. Pos: Attorney, Cherry Hill Twp. Planning Bd, N.J, 62-63 and Audubon Park Bd. of Educ, 62-65; N.J. State Assemblyman, Camden Co, 66-68; attorney, South Jersey Port Corp, 69- Bus. & Prof. Pos: Partner, Hyland, Davis & Reberkenny, Esqs, 64-; mem. bd. mgrs, Camden Co. Bar Asn, 67- Mil. Serv: Entered as Pvt, N.J. Nat. Guard, 60, released as Sgt, 66, after serv. in 63rd Army Band. Mem: Camden Co, N.J. and Am. Bar Asns; Am. Arbit. Asn; Cherry Hill Dem. Club (pres, 64-65); dir. and counsel, Big Brothers of Camden Co; treas. and dir, Commun. Child Guid. Clin. Young Man of Year, Gr. Camden Jaycees, 66. Rel: Roman Catholic. Legal Res: 614 Colonial Apt. W, Cherry Hill, N.J. 08034. Mailing Add: 499 Cooper Landing Rd, Cherry Hill, N.J. 08034.

HYLAND, WILLIAM FRANCIS D
b. Burlington, N.J, 7/30/23; s. Theodore J. Hyland and Margaret Gallagher H; m. 4/20/46 to Joan E. Sharp; c. William, Jr, Nancy, Stephen, Emma, Margaret and Thomas. Educ: Univ. Pa, Wharton Sch, B.S, 44, Law Sch, LL.B, 49; Phi Kappa Psi. Polit. & Govt. Pos: N.J. State Assemblyman, 54-60, Minority Leader, N.J. State Assembly, 55-57 and Speaker, 58; acting gov, N.J, 58; pres, N.J. Bd. Pub. Utility Cmnrs, 61-68; del, Dem. Nat. Conv, 64 & 68; mem. exec. cmt, Nat. Asn. R.R. and Utilities Cmnrs, 65-68; chmn, N.J. State Atomic Energy Coun, 68; chmn, N.J. State Cmn. of Invest, 69- Bus. & Prof. Pos: Assoc. trustee, Univ. Pa, 58-; attorney, Hyland, Davis and Reberhenary, Esquires, Cherry Hill, N.J, currently. Mil. Serv: Entered as A/S, Naval Res, 43, released as Lt.(jg), 46, after serv. in Atlantic and Pac; Atlantic, Pac. and Philippine Theater Ribbons; ETO Ribbon. Mem: Knights of St. Gregory. Rel: Roman Catholic. Legal Res: 201 Horse Shoe Court, Cherry Hill, N.J. 08034. Mailing Add: 499 Cooper Landing Rd, Cherry Hill, N.J. 08034.

HYLTON, TRACY W. D
W.Va. State Sen.
b. Crab Orchard, W.Va, 7/4/22; s. Arthur M. Hylton and Grace Snutter H; m. 12/9/47 to Betty Jo Foster; c. Tracy II, Robert Steven and Harry McKinley. Educ: Pub. Schs. and Col. Polit. & Govt. Pos: City cmnr. and pres, Planning and Zoning Cmn, Mullens; W.Va. State Sen, 64- Bus. & Prof. Pos: Coal operator. Mil. Serv: Army. Mem: Mason; Shrine; Commandery, Masonic Orders; Elks; Moose; Am. Legion. Rel: Presbyterian. Mailing Add: 1104 Davis St, Mullens, W.Va. 25882. (1967)

HYMAN, ALBERT H. D
Alderman, Meriden, Conn.
b. Meriden, Conn, 2/19/21; s. Max Hyman and Sarah Wall H; m. 9/21/43 to Nancy Hill; c. Alison K, Peter I. and John N. Educ: Univ. of Conn, B.A. in Econ, 42. Polit. & Govt. Pos: Alderman, Third Ward, Meriden, Conn, currently. Mil. Serv: Entered as 2nd Lt, Army, 42, released as Capt, 46, after serv. in ETO, 46; Am. Theater Ribbon; ETO Ribbon with 3 Combat Stars. Mem: Civitan; C. of C; Retail Bd. of Trade. Rel: Jewish. Mailing Add: 223 Allen Ave, Meriden, Conn. 06450.

HYMAN, LESTER SAMUEL D
b. Providence, R.I, 7/14/31; s. Carl Hyman and Alice Adelman H; m. 9/9/59 to Helen Reeder Sidman; c. David Anthony, Andrew Theodore and Elizabeth Alice. Educ: Brown Univ, A.B, 52; Columbia Univ, LL.B, 55; Phi Alpha Delta. Polit. & Govt. Pos: Counsel, Corp. Finance Div, U.S. Securities and Exchange Cmn, 55; campaign mgr, Peabody for Gov, 61-62; asst. to Gov, 63-64; del, Dem. Nat. Conv, 64 & 68; cmnr. of Commerce and Develop, Mass, 64-65; cand. for Dem. Nomination for Attorney Gen, Mass, 66; chmn, Mass. Dem. State Cmt, 67-69. Bus. & Prof. Pos: Lectr, John F. Kennedy Sch. of Govt, Harvard Univ, 68-69; partner, Leva, Hawes, Symington, Martin and Oppenheimer, Law Firm, Wash, D.C, 69- Mil. Serv: Entered as Seaman Recruit, Navy, 55, released as Yeoman 3/C, 56. Publ: 'Constitutional Reform in Massachusetts,' Portia Law J, 65. Mem: Dir, Big Brother Asn. of Boston. Rel: Jewish. Mailing Add: 3414 Lowell St. N.W, Washington, D.C. 20016.

HYMAN, PETER DeWITT D
S.C. State Rep.
b. Florence, S.C, 7/11/27; s. Cannie E. Hyman and Ethel Harrell H; m. 9/18/54 to Vera Jane Church; c. Helen Sheffield, Martha Elizabeth and Peter D, Jr. Educ: Univ. S.C, LL.B, 53; pres. Freshman Class, 46, Junior Class, 48; v.pres, Am. Law Students Asn, 52; assoc. ed, S.C. Law Quart, 53; pres. Law Sch. Student Body, 53; Omicron Delta Kappa; Kappa Sigma Kappa; Phi Kappa Sigma. Polit. & Govt. Pos: Magistrate, 55-59; S.C. State Rep, 61- Bus. & Prof. Pos: Partner, Hyman, Morgan and Brown, Attorneys, 55-; dir, Peoples Bank of S.C, 65- Mil. Serv: Entered as A/S, Navy, 43, released as AL2, 46, after serv. in VPB-142, Asiatic and Pac. Theatre, 44-45; Lt. Col, Army Res, 65-; Distinguished Flying Cross; Air Medal with Two Stars; Navy Letter of Commendation. Publ: 'Substantial Performance of Builders Contracts,' S.C. Law Quart, 53. Mem: Am. and S.C. Bar Asn; dir, Am. Trial Lawyers Asn; Optimist Club; Amity Lodge; AFM; AANOMS; Elks. Listed in Who's Who Among Students in Am. Univs. and Cols. from Univ. S.C, 52-53. Rel: Lutheran; mem. church coun, St. Johns Evangelical Lutheran Church. Legal Res: 1104 Wentworth Dr, Florence, S.C. 29501. Mailing Add: P.O. Box 1186, Florence, S.C. 29501.

HYMEL, GARY GERARD D
b. 4/25/33; s. Andrew Joseph Hymel and Elise Carrière H; m. 8/21/54 to Alice Fox; c. Amy Marie, Margaret Mary, Gregory Paul, Elizabeth Ann, Madelene Teresa, Kevin Michael, Joy Odile and Judith Ann. Educ: Loyola Univ, 50-54; La. State Univ, M.A, 59; Blue Key; Thirty Club; Beggars Fraternity; ed, Loyola Maroon. Polit. & Govt. Pos: Admin. asst. to Majority Whip, U.S. House of Rep, currently. Bus. & Prof. Pos: Sports; polit. reporter. Mil. Serv: Lt, Army, 54-56; Capt, Army Res. Mem: Press Club of New Orleans. Rel: Catholic. Legal Res: New Orleans, La. Mailing Add: 4111 Rosemary St, Chevy Chase, Md. 20015.

I

IBANEZ, FRANCISCO BARRERAS R
b. Morovis, P.R, 4/11/12; s. José Barreras and Petra Ibáñez B; m. 9/9/49 to Joseff del Rio; c. Sandra Clotilde, Petra Esther and Susana Raguel. Educ: High sch. Polit. & Govt. Pos: V.pres, Arecibo Dist. Statehood Rep. Party, 48-; Sen, P.R. Senate, 64-68, mem, Agr, Indust. and Commerce, Pub. Order and Pub. Finance Cmts, P.R. Senate, pres, Contact and Polit. Action Cmts, 64-66. Bus. & Prof. Pos: Owner, Barreras Texaco Station, P.R, 58- Mil. Serv: Entered as Pvt, Army, 43, released as M/Sgt. 1/C, 46, after serv. in 766th Anti-Aircraft Artil, Caribbean Defense, Panamá; Am. Theater Serv. Medal; Victory Medal; Five Serv. Bars; Good Conduct Medal. Mem: Exec. cmt. and v.pres, Arecibo Dist, Am. Legion; Asn. Agr. P.R; pres, Fathers Asn. Morovis Sch. Rel: Catholic. Legal Res: Bo. Morovis Norte, Morovis, P.R. 00717. Mailing Add: Box 1, Morovis, P.R. 00717. (1967)

IBBOTSON, GORDON MACKENZIE D
Chmn, Weld Co. Dem. Cent. Cmt, Colo.
b. Brooklyn, N.Y, 10/23/05; s. Benjamin M. Ibbotson and Emily Mackenzie I; m. 7/20/27 to Marguerite Mae Ainsworth; c. Robert Dean and Judy (Mrs. Holub). Educ: Univ. Mich, 3 years; Mich. Mimes; Hermitage. Polit. & Govt. Pos: Chmn, Weld Co. Dem. Party, Colo, 55-56; dep. state treas, 58-66; chmn, Weld Co. Dem. Cent. Cmt, 69- Bus. & Prof. Pos: Mem, A.E. Kusterer & Co. Grand Rapids; Brown Cress & Co, Ann Arbor, First Nat. Bank; G.M. Ibbotson & Co. and Kidder Peabody Inc, N.Y, 27-33; from salesman to mgr, Kaffee Hag Sales, Kellogg Sales Co, Battle Creek, Mich, 33-41; partner, Harley F. Jones Co, food brokers, Chicago, 41-46; mgr, Consumers Oil Co, Roggen, Colo, 46-48; owner, Farm & Town Agency, 49-60. Rel: Episcopal. Mailing Add: 1315 12th Ave, Apt. 1, Greeley, Colo. 80631.

ICHORD, RICHARD H. D
U.S. Rep, Mo.
b. Licking, Mo, 6/27/26; c. Richard H, III, and Pamela. Educ: Univ. Mo, B.S, 49 and LL.B, 52; Phi Eta Sigma; Delta Sigma Pi; Alpha Pi Zeta; Beta Gamma Sigma; Phi Delta Phi. Polit. & Govt. Pos: Mo. State Rep, 52-60, speaker pro tem, Mo. House of Rep, 57-58, speaker, 59-60; U.S. Rep, Mo, 60-, mem, Armed Servs. and Un-Am. Activities Cmts. and Cmts. on Interior and Insular Affairs and Post Off. and Civil Serv, U.S. House of Rep. Bus. & Prof. Pos: Attorney-at-law. Mil. Serv: Naval Air Corps, World War II, Pacific Area, 2 years. Mem: VFW; Lions; Am. Legion; Odd Fellows; Masons. Rel: Baptist. Mailing Add: 116 Main St, Houston, Mo. 65483. (1967)

IDE, RAYMOND F. R
27th Ward Rep, Phila. City Rep. Cmt, Pa.
b. Phila, Pa, 5/18/20; s. Raymond Ide and Marie De Dominicis I; div; m. to Helen Ryan; c. Christina. Educ: Temple Univ; Air Force Cadet Training, Pilot. Polit. & Govt. Pos: Leader, 27th Ward and rep, Phila. City Rep. Cmt, Pa, 61-; candidate, Pa. State Sen, 62; alternate del, Rep. Nat. Conv, 64 & 68. Bus. & Prof. Pos: Owner, Raymond F. Ide Agency, 50- Mil. Serv: Entered as Pvt, Army Air Force, 41, released as Capt, 46. Mem: C. of C.(dir, West Phila. Chap); Lions (past pres, West Phila. Club); Am. Legion. Rel: Catholic. Legal Res: 4401 Spruce St, Philadelphia, Pa. 19104. Mailing Add: 4003 Chestnut St, Philadelphia, Pa. 19104.

IDSO, RUSSELL R
b. Pringhar, Iowa, 4/09/04; married; c. Five. Educ: Pub. Schs. Polit. & Govt. Pos: N.Dak. State Rep, 57-61, -66; sch. bd, 17 years; Twp. bd, 4 years. Bus. & Prof. Pos: Farmer. Mem: Farm Bur. Mailing Add: Amenia, N.Dak. 58004. (1967)

IGO, IRMA L. D
State Chairwoman, South. Dist. Ill. Dem. Party
b. Mt. Olive, Ill, 8/22/05; d. Bruno Fred Heusler and Margaret Falke H; m. 2/11/22 to Aubrey E. Igo; wid; c. Mary M.(Mrs. John Garry). Educ: Litchfield Bus. Col. Polit. & Govt. Pos: Clerk, War Price and Rationing Bd, 42-44; chairwoman, Jefferson Co. Dem. Party, Ill, 48-54; 23rd Dist. Dem. committeewoman, 50-54; inspector, Women's and Children's Div, Ill. Dept. of Labor, 52-54; dep. clerk, Appellate Court, Fourth Dist, 54-61; State chairwoman, South Dist. of Ill. Dem. Party, 54-; del-at-lg, Dem. Nat. Conv, 56, 64 & 68 and mem, Credentials Cmt, 68; admin. asst, State Auditor's Off, Ill, 61-67; chief clerk, Appellate Court, Fifth Dist, 67- Bus. & Prof. Pos: Owner and mgr, Igo Tire Sales and Serv, 44-47. Mem: Chmn, Jefferson and Marion Co. Commun. Action Cmt, Ill, 65- Rel: Lutheran. Mailing Add: P.O. Box 495, Mt. Vernon, Ill. 62864.

IHNEN, H. B. R
b. Golden, Ill, 7/19/95; s. Behrend G. Ihnen and Bertha Kohlman I; m. 5/12/17 to Ethel Laura Keppner; c. Ernel Dean. Educ: Camp Point High Sch. Polit. & Govt. Pos: Precinct committeeman; Twp. supvr, 12 years; chmn, Adams Co. Bd. of Supvrs, 3 years; chmn, Adams Co. Bd. of Rev, 3 years; Ill. State Rep, 18 years; chmn, Ill. Motor Vehicles Law Cmn, 67-69; mem, Gov. Adv. Cmt. and Ill. Dept. Agr. Adv. Coun. Bus. & Prof. Pos: Farm mgr, E.A. Meyer, Highland Park, Ill, 20 years. Mem: Farm Bur; Lions; Eagles; Mason; Shrine; Hi Twelve; active in commun. and church affairs. Rel: Lutheran. Mailing Add: 330 East Ave, Quincy, Ill. 62301.

IMHOFF, LAWRENCE EDWARD
Dep. Asst. Secy. for Admin, Dept. of Commerce
b. Elkville, Ill, 7/25/08; s. Wiley B. Imhoff and Laura E. Castelton I; m.

7/26/30 to Maybelle B. Carroll; c. Larry C. and Maren E. Educ: Oberlin Col, A.B, 30; Manchester Col, 34-35; Purdue Univ, M.P.E, 40. Polit. & Govt. Pos: Budget analyst, Dept. of Commerce, 46-51; dir. minerals and fuels div. and staff asst. to asst. secy. mineral resources, Dept. of Interior, 51-60; dep. dir. off. budget and mgt, Dept. of Commerce, 60-62, dep. dir. off. of budget and finance, 62-65, Dep. Asst. Secy. of Commerce for Admin, 65- Bus. & Prof. Pos: Investment banker, 30-32; family bus, 32-35; teaching, 35-42. Mil. Serv: Capt, Army Air Force, World War II; Pac. Theater Opers. Ribbon; Purple Heart; Bronze Star. Mem: Am. Soc. Pub. Admin; past chmn, Budget Off. Conf; Conglist; Mason (32°); Nat. Civil Serv. League; Kenwood Golf and Country Club, Bethesda, Md. Meritorious Serv. Award, Dept. of Interior, 60; Distinguished Serv. Award, Dept. of Commerce, 65. Legal Res: 4540 Chesapeake St, Washington, D.C. 20016. Mailing Add: Dept. of Commerce, Washington, D.C. 20230.

IMLE, ALBERT ROBERT D
Mem, Ill. State Dem. Cmt.
b. Marshall, Ill, 12/25/13; s. Christopher Carl Imle and Alta Mae Finkbinder I; m. 9/2/39 to Mary Virginia Brinton; c. Carroll Ann, Deborah and Barclay. Educ: Univ. Ill, 32-36; Lincoln Col. Law, LL.B, 40. Polit. & Govt. Pos: Spec. agent, Fed. Bur. Invest, 41-48; nominee for Cong, 23rd Cong. Dist, Ill, 54 & 56; chmn, Montgomery Co. Dem. Party, 56-60; asst. dir. revenue, Ill, 61-64, asst. dir. finance, 65-66; mem, Ill. State Dem. Cmt, 62-; extradition secy. to Gov. Otto Kerner, 65-66; mem. bd. govs, State Cols. and Univs, Ill, 65- Mem: Montgomery Co. and Ill. State Bar Asns; Mason; Shrine; Consistory; Rotary; pres, Hillsboro C. of C, 58-60. Rel: Lutheran. Mailing Add: 608 Ridgely Bldg, Springfield, Ill. 62701.

IMM, VAL DFL
married; c. Six. Polit. & Govt. Pos: Mem, Mankato City Coun, Minn, 31-33; Minn. State Rep, 33-35; Minn. State Sen, 35-66, pres. pro-tem, Minn. State Senate, 55. Bus. & Prof. Pos: Ed. and publisher, Mankato News. Mil. Serv: World War Vet. Mailing Add: Mankato News, Mankato, Minn. 56001. (1967)

INABA, MINORU D
Hawaii State Rep.
b. Holualoa, Hawaii, 2/20/04; s. Jentaro Inaba and Hatsuyo Miyamoto I; m. 12/17/55 to Sumie Mizuno; c. Jeanette (Mrs. Tinnel), Mae (Mrs. Kawahara) and Annette (Mrs. Sato). Educ: Univ. Hawaii, B.A, 29. Polit. & Govt. Pos: Hawaii State Rep, 68- Bus. & Prof. Pos: V.prin, Konawaena High & Intermediate Sch, Kealakekua, Hawaii, 56-66; v.pres. and Kona br. mgr, Great Hawaiian Financial Corp, Holualoa, 66- Mem: Nat, Hawaii and Kona Educ. Asns; Kona Mauka Trollers; Holualoa Athletic Asn. Sportsman of the Year Award, Island of Hawaii. Mailing Add: P.O. Box 233, Kealakekua, Hawaii 96750.

INGALLS, GEORGE LEWIS R
Trustee, State Power Authority, N.Y.
b. Danielson, Conn, 6/7/14; s. Louis Sessions Ingalls and Mary Ethel Gallup I; m. 12/12/42 to Dorothy M. Joggerst; c. Bryan, Robert, John and Janet. Educ: Amherst Col, 35; Syracuse Univ. Col. Law, LL.B, 39; Phi Beta Kappa; Phi Kappa Phi; Phi Delta Phi; Justinian Soc. Polit. & Govt. Pos: N.Y. State Assemblyman, 53-66, Majority Leader, 61-64, Minoirty Leader, 65; trustee, State Power Authority, N.Y, currently. Bus. & Prof. Pos: Pres, New Industs. for Broome, Inc, 50-53; mem, adv. bd, Marine Midland Trust Co. South N.Y, 63- Mem: Dir, Binghamton Commun. Chest, 44-47; v.pres, N.Y. State Jr. C. of C, 45; pres, Binghamton Jr. C. of C, 43-44; Am, N.Y. State and Broome Co. Bar Asns; Rotary; Binghamton Club; Binghamton Country Club. Rel: Congregational. Legal Res: 38 Beethoven St, Binghamton, N.Y. 13905. Mailing Add: 709 Marine Midland Bldg, Binghamton, N.Y. 13901.

INGALLS, JAMES W. D
Mem, Exec. Cmt, Idaho State Dem. Cent. Cmt.
b. Aberdeen, S.Dak, 9/3/25; s. James L. Ingalls and Ila A. Knott I; m. 8/26/51 to Beverly D. Evans; c. Jan V, David J. and Jon W. Educ: Univ. Idaho, LL.B, 51; Phi Alpha Delta; Delta Tau Delta. Polit. & Govt. Pos: State committeeman, Idaho State Dem. Cent. Cmt, 52-55 & 66-, mem. exec. cmt, 65-; prosecuting attorney, Kootenai Co, Idaho, 55-61; del, Dem. Nat. Conv, 60; chmn, Kootenai Co. Dem. Cent. Cmt, 61-66. Mil. Serv: Entered as Pvt, Air Force, 43, released as S/Sgt, 45, after serv. in Eighth Air Force, ETO, 44-45; Air Medal with 5 Clusters; Bronze Star; European-African-Middle East Ribbon with 3 Bronze Stars. Mem: Am. and Idaho State Bar Asns; Idaho Prosecuting Attorneys Asn.(pres, 59-60); Univ. Idaho Col. Law Alumni Asn.(pres, 60-61); VFW; Elks; Eagles; Mason; Scottish Rite; Shrine; Kiwanis. Rel: Methodist. Legal Res: 203 Bruce Dr, Fernan Lake Village, Idaho. Mailing Add: Box 427, Coeur d'Alene, Idaho 83814.

INGE, HUTCHINS F. D
m. to Evelyn Timmons. Educ: Univ. Minn. Col. of Pharm; Howard Univ. Sch. of Med. Polit. & Govt. Pos: Former N.J. State Sen. Bus. & Prof. Pos: Staff physician, Presby. Hosp. and Div. of Child Hygiene, Newark Bd. of Health; dir, N.J. Asn. for Retarded Children. Mem: Dir, Essex Urban League; N.J. Med. Soc; Am. Med. Asn. Rel: Episcopal. Mailing Add: 221 S. Orange Ave, Newark, N.J. 07103. (1967)

INGLE, JOHN R. D
Chmn, Mecklenburg Co. Dem. Exec. Cmt, N.C.
b. Siler City, N.C, 2/13/32; s. Joseph B. Ingle and Lillie Clark I; single. Educ: Univ. N.C, Chapel Hill, A.B, 54; Univ. N.C. Law Sch, Chapel Hill, J.D, 59; Phi Beta Kappa; Phi Alpha Theta; Delta Theta Phi; Richardson Found. Fel, 59. Polit. & Govt. Pos: Pres, Mecklenburg Co. Young Dem. Club, N.C, 62 & 63; mem, Mecklenburg Co. Dem. Precinct Cmt, 65-67; chmn, Mecklenburg Co. Dem. Exec. Cmt, 66- Mil. Serv: Entered as 2nd Lt, Air Force, 54, released as 1st Lt, 56, after serv. in Mil. Air Transport Command, Capt. Res. Mem: 26th Judicial Dist. Bar Asn; N.C. Bar Asn; Am. Bar Asn; Am. Judicature Soc; Charlotte Civitan Club. Ted Williams Award for Outstanding Young Dem. in Mecklenburg Co, 68. Rel: Methodist. Mailing Add: 208 Hillside Ave, Charlotte, N.C. 28209.

INGLISH, JOHN WILLIAM D
b. Centertown, Mo, 5/8/21; s. John Inglish and Bessie Longan I; m. 6/15/47 to Myra Jane Jacobs; c. Janice Ann, Sarah Beth, John Stephen and William Stuart. Educ: Cent. Col, Mo, 38-40; Juilliard Sch. of Music, 40-42; Univ. Mo, A.B. and LL.B, 50; Phi Mu Alpha; pres, Phi Alpha Delta, 49; Beta Sigma Rho. Polit. & Govt. Pos: Asst. Attorney Gen, Mo, 53-60; city attorney, California, Mo, 53-61; dist. chmn, Young Dem. Clubs of Mo, 55-56, recording secy, 56-57; chmn, Mo. Dem. State Cmt, 60-63; spec. hearing officer, U.S. Dept. of Justice, 64-68. Bus. & Prof. Pos: Pres, Calif. Foods, Inc, 59-, Xtra Valu Stamp Co, 60- and Mem. Commun. Hosp, 64-65. Mil. Serv: Entered as Pvt, Army, 42, released as Telegrapher, 45, after serv. in Signal Corps, ETO, 43-45; Two Battle Stars; ETO and Am. Theater Ribbons. Mem: Mo. and St. Louis Bar Asns; Cole Co. Bar Asn.(pres, 60-61); Rotary Int; VFW; Am. Legion; Mason; Shrine; Eagles; pres, Heart of Mo. Girl Scout Coun, 58-60. Rel: Christian. Legal Res: 115 W. Versailles Ave, California, Mo. 65018. Mailing Add: 211 E. Capitol, Jefferson City, Mo. 65101.

INGRAM, JOHN W. R
b. New Brighton, Pa, 1915; m. to Marjorie Brown; c. Barbara and John. Educ: Miami Univ, undergrad. degree, 38; Univ. Denver, M.A, 41; Alfred P. Sloan Found. fel. Polit. & Govt. Pos: Comptroller, Maywood, Ill; mem, Exec. Reorgn. Surv, Ill. and Civic Fedn, Chicago; mgt, research and admin, City and Co. of Denver, Colo; mem, Colo. Expenditure Coun, Denver; coordinator, co. activities and dir. of research, Pa. Econ. League, dir. state div, 68-; State Secy. of Admin, Pa, 63-67; exec. dir, Pa. Constitutional Conv, 67-68. Bus. & Prof. Pos: Former dir, grad. prog. in govt. mgt, Univ. Denver; with, Ernst and Ernst, Cleveland and Eastman Corp, Kingsport, Tenn. Mem: Am. Soc. Pub. Admin.(former pres, Cent. Pa. Chap); Govt. Research Asn.(past pres). Mailing Add: 9 Clemson Dr, Camp Hill, Pa. 17011.

INGRAM, KENNETH FRANK D
b. Ashland, Ala, 7/7/29; s. Earnest Frank Ingram and Alta Mary Allen I; m. 9/3/54 to Judith Louise Brown; c. Jennifer Lynn and Kenneth Frank, Jr. Educ: Auburn Univ, B.S, 51; Jones Law Sch, LL.B, 63; Alpha Gamma Rho; Delta Sigma Kappa. Polit. & Govt. Pos: Mem, Ashland Town Coun, Ala, 56-59; Ala. State Rep, 59-67; circuit judge, 18th Judicial Circuit, 68- Bus. & Prof. Pos: Attorney at Law, Kenneth F. Ingram, 63- Mil. Serv: Entered as Pvt, Marine Corps, 52, released as Lance Cpl, 54, after serv. in Support Unit for 3rd Marine Div, Camp Lejeune, N.C, 52-54; Good Conduct Medal; Certificate as Outstanding Member of Platoon during Recruit Training at Parris Island, S.C. Mem: Am, Ala. and Clay Co. Bar Asns; State Bar Cmt. on Trial Court Congestion, 65-; Mason, RAM. Rel: Methodist. Legal Res: 311 N. First St, Ashland, Ala. 36251. Mailing Add: P.O. Box 486, Ashland, Ala. 36251.

INGRAM, ROBERT L. D
b. Mt. Sterling, Ill, 12/1/30; s. Owen R. Ingram and Carlene Wemhoener I; m. 12/17/50 to Deloris Joan Dorsey; c. Deborah Lynn, Bradford Byron and Deanna Denise. Educ: Pekin Commun. High Sch, 44-48. Polit. & Govt. Pos: Dem. precinct committeeman, Tazewell Co, Ill, 62-; del, Dem. Nat. Conv, 68; mem. exec. bd, Tazewell Co. Dem. Cent. Cmt, 69. Bus. & Prof. Pos: Mem. staff, Caterpiller Tractor Co, 48-, design engr, 64- Mem: Mason (32°). Rel: Christian Church of N.Am. Mailing Add: R.R. 1, Pekin, Ill. 61554.

INGRAM, VERNER MERRITT R
b. Potsdam, N.Y, 8/27/11; s. Harry M. Ingram and Edna B. Keyes; m. 7/24/39 to Ethel K. Mason; c. Verner M, Jr. Educ: Cornell Univ, A.B, 33; Albany Union Univ. Law Sch, LL.B-J.D, 34-36; Pi Kappa Phi. Polit. & Govt. Pos: Justice of the Peace, Potsdam, N.Y, 40-56; spec. surrogate, St. Lawrence Co, 52-55; N.Y. State Assemblyman, 57-66. Bus. & Prof. Pos: Attorney-at-Law, Potsdam, N.Y, 37-; partner, Heartland Develop. Co, 55-; partner, Col. Park Develop. Co, Cooklands, Inc, 45- Publ: Pastor's Legal Advisor, Abingdon-Cokesbury. Mem: N.Y. State Bar; U.S. Dist. Court North. Dist. of N.Y. Bar; U.S. Court of Appeals Second Circuit Bar; Practicing Law Inst; N.Y. State and Am. Bar Asns; Am. Trial Lawyer's Asn; St. Lawrence Co. Bar Asn; Mason; Shrine; Potsdam Vol. Rescue Squad, Inc; Rotary; Potsdam Town and Country Club. Rel: Episcopal. Legal Res: 15 State St, Potsdam, N.Y. 13676. Mailing Add: 19 Market St, Potsdam, N.Y. 13676.

INGVALSON, ELLIOTT LOUIS 'PADDY' R
S.Dak. State Rep.
b. Flandreau, S.Dak, 11/5/11; s. Alfred Ingvalson and Anna Hart I; m. 6/7/34 to Margaret Mae Williams; c. Sybil (Mrs. Strain), Thomas, Margo (Mrs. Goodman) and Jean (Mrs. Davis). Educ: Minn. Univ, 2 years; S.Dak. State Univ, 1 year. Polit. & Govt. Pos: S.Dak. State Rep, Pennington Co, 69- Bus. & Prof. Pos: Retired as exec. ed, Rapid City J, 66. Mem: Am. Soc. Newspaper Ed; Sigma Delta Chi; pres, Keep S.Dak. Green Asn. Rel: Catholic. Legal Res: 3639 Jefferson, Rapid City, S.Dak. 57701. Mailing Add: P.O. Box 1691, Rapid City, S.Dak. 57701.

INHOFE, JAMES MOUNTAIN R
Okla. State Sen.
b. Des Moines, Iowa, 11/17/34; s. Perry D. Inhofe and Blanche Mountain I; m. 12/19/59 to Kay Kirkpatrick; c. James Mountain, II, Perry Dyson, II, Molly Marie and Kay Kirkpatrick. Educ: Tulsa Univ, Lib. Arts degree, 57. Polit. & Govt. Pos: Okla. State Rep, 66-68; Okla. State Sen, 68- Bus. & Prof. Pos: V.pres, Mid-Continent Casualty Co, Quaker Life Ins. Co. and Okla. Surety Co, 57- Mil. Serv: Pfc, Army. Mailing Add: 2139 E. 32nd, Tulsa, Okla. 74105.

INKLEY, RONALD WALTER R
Utah State Rep.
b. Salt Lake City, Utah, 5/12/29; s. Walter Barnes Inkley and Helen Mackay I; m. 4/20/56 to Ethal Zaugg. Educ: High Sch. grad. Polit. & Govt. Pos: Pres. and co-founder, Weber Co. Rep. 500 Club, 61-65; Utah State Rep, 67- Bus. & Prof. Pos: Pres, Inkley Photo Centers, 58-; mem. bd. of dirs, Photo. Res. Orgn, 61- Mil. Serv: Entered as Sgt, Army, 50, released as 1st Lt, 62, after serv. in 653rd Field Artil. Observation Bn, Korea, 61-62. Mem: Master Photo Dealers' and Finishers Orgn; Ogden C. of C; Rotary. Rel: Latter-day Saint. Mailing Add: 1734 24th St, Ogden, Utah 84401.

INMAN, W. M. D
b. Greensboro, Fla, 9/12/95; m. to Clara Strickland. Educ: Pub. Schs, Gadsden Co, Fla. Polit. & Govt. Pos: Cmnr, Gadsden Co, Fla, 29-32, sheriff, 33-41; Fla. State Rep, 50-68. Bus. & Prof. Pos: Auto dealer; farmer; cattleman;

dir, Co. Hosp. Mil. Serv: Qm. Corps, World War I. Mem: Mason; Am. Legion; Farm Bur.(state dir, 6 years, co. dir, 20 years). Rel: Methodist. Mailing Add: Quincy, Fla. 32351. (1967)

INNES, ALLAN C. R
b. Thomaston, Conn, 4/13/01; s. Robert Innes and Elizabeth Anderson I; m. 2/14/25 to Agda Sandell; c. Marion (Mrs. DePecol), Helen (Mrs. Titus) and Elaine A. Educ: Eastman Bus. Col. Polit. & Govt. Pos: Chmn, Appropriations Cmt, Conn. House of Rep, 61-66, Conn. State Rep, 52-66 and 42-46; chmn, Finance Bd, Thomaston, 40-58, mem, 34-66; mem, Town Rep. Cmt, 30-66. Bus. & Prof. Pos: Treas, Waterbury Ready Mixed Concrete Co, Conn, 66, dir, 31-66; pres. and treas, Innes Bros. Inc, Gen. Contractors, 28-66; v.pres, Innes Realty Inc, 54; dir, Thomaston Savings Bank, 48. Mem: Union Lodge 96, F&AM; Rotary. Rel: Congregational. Mailing Add: 78 High St, Thomaston, Conn. 06787. (1967)

INNES, GEORGE BARR R
Finance Exec. Secy, Rep. Party, Wis.
b. Ashland, Wis, 3/15/38; s. Marvin A. Innes and Barbara Barr I; m. 8/21/65 to Sheila Jane Giese. Educ: Superior State Univ, Wis, B.S, 66; Univ. Wis. Law Sch, Madison, 66-67. Polit. & Govt. Pos: Field rep, Rep. Party, Wis, 67, finance exec. secy, 68- Mil. Serv: Entered as Airman Basic, Air Force, 57, released as Airman 2/C, 61. Mem: Elks; Big Bros. of Dane Co, Wis. Mailing Add: 567 Marigold Dr, Madison, Wis. 53713.

INOUYE, DANIEL KEN D
U.S. Sen, Hawaii
b. Honolulu, Hawaii, 9/7/24; s. Hyotaro Inouye and Kame Imanaga I; m. 6/12/49 to Margaret Shinobu Awamura; c. Daniel Ken, Jr. Educ: Univ. Hawaii, B.A, 50; George Wash. Univ. Law Sch, J.D, 52. Polit. & Govt. Pos: Asst. pub. prosecutor, City and Co. of Honolulu, Hawaii, 53-54; Hawaii Territorial Rep. and Majority Leader, Hawaii Territorial House of Rep, 54-58; Hawaii Territorial Sen, 58-59; U.S. Rep, Hawaii, 59-62, U.S. Sen, 63-, mem, Armed Serv. Cmt, U.S. Senate, 63-, Asst. Majority Whip, 64-, mem, Commerce Cmt. and chmn, Dem. Sen. Campaign Cmt, 69-; temporary chmn. and keynoter, Dem. Nat. Conv, 68. Bus. & Prof. Pos: Attorney-at-law, 53- Mil. Serv: Entered as Pvt, Army, 43, released as Capt, 47, after serv. in 442nd Inf. Regt. Combat Team, ETO, 43-47; Distinguished Serv. Cross; Bronze Star; Purple Heart with Cluster; Five Battle Stars; Four Distinguished Unit Citations, and others. Publ: Journey to Washington, Prentice-Hall, 67. Mem: Phi Delta Phi; Am. and Hawaii Bar Asns; George Wash. Law Rev; Lions Int; YMCA; Boy Scouts; Honolulu C. of C; Am. Legion; DAV; VFW; 442nd Vet. Club; Legion of Valor. Selected as One of the Ten Outstanding Young Men of the Year by the U.S. Jr. C. of C, 60, One of the 100 Most Important Men and Women in the U.S. by Life Mag, 62 and for the 1967 Golden Plate Award, Am. Acad. of Achievement; Alumnus of the Year Award, George Wash. Univ, 61. Rel: Methodist. Legal Res: 1777 Ala Moana Blvd, Honolulu, Hawaii 96815. Mailing Add: Room 442, Old Senate Office Bldg, Washington, D.C. 20510.

INOUYE, ROY Y. R
b. Stockton, Calif, 7/15/16; s. Yoshiye Inouye and Shio Nakagawa I; m. 8/15/41 to Yoshiko Nakayama; c. Ronald. Educ: Denver Univ. Polit. & Govt. Pos: Chmn, Conejos Co. Rep. Party, Colo, 62-69. Mem: Colo. Farm Bur.(state dir, 58-64, mem. adv. cmt. on water, 67-; Conejos Co. Farm Bur.(pres, 56-57); Am. Farm Bur.(mem. hort. adv. cmt, 59-64); secy, Colo. Potato Processors Corp, 64-; pres, San Luis Valley Resource Develop. Cmt, 63; Rotary (pres, La Jara Club, 54); San Luis Valley Japanese Am. Citizens League (pres, 49, 51, 53 and 69); Agr. and Livestock Cmn, Colo. Asn. of Commerce and Indust, 66; Colo. State Agr. Stabilization & Conserv. Serv. Cmt, 69-; dir, Nat. Potato Coun, 67-69; Colo. Ground Water Cmn, 67-69. Rel: Buddhist; pres, bd, Buddhist Church, 61-66, pres, church, 63-69. Mailing Add: La Jara, Colo. 81140.

INSKEEP, JOHN JERRY R
Ore. State Sen.
b. Bryan, Tex, 8/16/96; s. Henry Carter Inskeep and Pearl Newman I; m. 2/3/23 to Beatrice Carrie Holt; c. Bettie (Mrs. Washington) and John Jerry II. Educ: Purdue Univ, B.S.A, 21; Ore. State Univ, M.S, 41; Scabbard and Blade; Alpha Zeta; Lambda Chi Alpha. Polit. & Govt. Pos: Ore. State Sen, 63- Bus. & Prof. Pos: Co. Exten. agent, Kansas State Col, 21-26; co. exten. agent, Clackamas Co, Ore, 26-61. Mil. Serv: Army, 18; Res, 21-31. Publ: Numerous newspaper columns and magazine articles. Mem: Mason; Elks; Rotary (past dist. gov, 67-68). Superior Serv. Award, U.S. Dept. Agr, 57; Distinguished Serv. Award, Rotary, 68. Rel: Episcopal. Mailing Add: 810 Center, Oregon City, Ore. 97045.

INZETTA, JAMES WILLIAM D
b. Brooklyn, N.Y, 8/18/32; s. Louis Inzetta and Anna Torrisi I; m. 6/13/53 to Rose Dolores Cirnigliaro; c. Mark Stephen and Bruce James. Educ: Hofstra Univ, B.B.A, 58; Am. Inst of Banking, N. Bergen, Completion Cert; Savings and Loan Inst, Newark, Completion Cert. Polit. & Govt. Pos: Del, Dem. Nat. Conv, 68; financial aide to exec. cmt, Ohio Dem. Party, 69- Mil. Serv: Entered as Pvt, Army, 53, released as Sgt. 1/C on 54 after serv. in 40th & 24th Inf. Div., Finance Unit, Korea, 53-54; Korean Ribbon, Nat. Defense Ribbon, U.N. Ribbon, Presidential Unit Citation; Korean Presidential Unit Citation. Mem: Am. Savings and Loan Inst; Am. Legion; Rotary; Elks; Moose; Order of Sons of Italy, K. of C. Rel: Roman Catholic. Mailing Add: 118 Pine Lane, Barnesville, Ohio 43713.

IPPOLITO, ANDREW VINCENT D
b. New York, N.Y, 3/6/30; s. Andrew Vincent Ippolito and Antoinetta Emmanuele I; m. 5/31/54 to Constance Mary Di Mitrio; c. Jenette, Andrew, Paul and Michael. Educ: Queens Col, N.Y, 2 years; Georgetown Univ, B.S.F.S, 55; Pratt Inst, M.L.S, 59; founder, Student Vet. Orgn. Polit. & Govt. Pos: Del, Dem. Nat. Conv, 68. Bus. & Prof. Pos: Law clerk, Berg, Mezansky & Mendes, N.Y. City, 58; dir, Lindenhurst Pub. Libr, L.I, 59-60, N. Babylon Publ Libr, 60-62 and Merrick Pub. Libr, 62-65; dir. libr. and research, Newsday, Garden City, 65- Mil. Serv: Hosp. Corps, Navy, 50-52. Publ: 'Electronic Frisk,' Odds & Book Ends, fall 64; 'Library Without Books,' Suffolk Co. Libr. Asn. Data, winter 68. Mem: Admin. Mgr. Soc; mem. documentation div. and chmn. newspaper div, Spec. Libraries Asn; N.Y, Nassau Co. and Suffolk Co. Libr. Asns; Beta Phi Mu; Dem. for New Polit; pres, Pub. Sch. 130 PTA, Bayside; Queens Cmt. for Commun. Involvement; Georgetown Univ. Club. of Metrop. New York. Legal Res: 42-46 209th St, Bayside, N.Y. 11361. Mailing Add: Newsday, 550 Stewart Ave, Garden City, N.Y. 11530.

IPSEN, PAUL MARTIN R
Chmn, Grant Co. Rep. Orgn, Wis.
b. Cuba City, Wis, 12/30/22; s. Henry William Ipsen and Eva Rosetta Evansen I; m. 2/21/59 to Mary Jane MacCulloch. Educ: Univ. Dubuque, 40-41; Univ. Wis, B.A, 45; Delta Sigma Pi. Polit. & Govt. Pos: Citizen mem, Wis. Higher Educ. Aids Bd, 65, chmn, 68-; chmn, Grant Co. Rep. Orgn, Wis, 67- Bus. & Prof. Pos: Partner and mgr, Cuba City Creamery, Wis, 60- Rel: United Church of Christ. Mailing Add: 947 Union St, Platteville, Wis. 53818.

IRELAND, ARTHUR PIERCE R
Ore. State Sen.
b. Forest Grove, Ore, 4/3/93; s. John Preston Ireland and Clarissa Pierce I; m. 4/3/16 to Ada Miria Snook, wid. 4/5/66; m. 12/12/68 to Alice Schulmerich; c. Glen. Educ: Pac. Univ; Alpha Zeta. Polit. & Govt. Pos: Ore. State Sen, 33-34 & 63-; chmn, Wash. Co. Rural Sch. Bd, 46-58; mem. and chmn, Wash. Co. Planning Zoning Bd, 48-66; Ore. State Rep, 55-63. Bus. & Prof. Pos: Pres. and dir, May Flower Farms, 31-60; mem, State Selective Serv. Appeals Bd, 49-66. Mem: Nat. Milk Producers Fedn.(dir); Farm Bur; Mason; Elks; Pac. Univ. Alumni Bd. Athletic letterman in baseball, football and basketball; received 15 year placque, State Selective Serv. Appeals Bd. Rel: Congregational. Mailing Add: 1845 N. Elm St, McMinnville, Ore. 97128.

IRELAND, THOMAS ROBERT R
b. Middletown, Ohio, 4/26/42; s. Robert Ebel Ireland and Luella Pratt I; m. 7/27/64 to Marilyn Jean Schleue; c. Lee Tera. Educ: Miami Univ, B.A, 64; Univ. Va, Ph.D, 68; Phi Eta Sigma. Polit. & Govt. Pos: Rep. nominee, U.S. Cong, Second Dist, Ill, 68; dep. dist. gov, Ill. Young Rep. Orgn, 69. Bus. & Prof. Pos: Instr, Univ. Va, 65-66; research asst, Nat. Bank of Detroit, Mich, summer 65; asst. prof. econ, Loyola Univ, 66-69, Purdue Univ, 69- Mem: Am. and Midwest Econ. Asns. Richard Weaver fel, 64; Thomas Jefferson Center fel, 64; Phillip Dupont fel, 65. Rel: Presbyterian. Mailing Add: 7125 Missouri Ave, Hammond, Ind. 46323.

IREY, DON F. D
Co. Dem. Chmn, Iowa
b. Iowa City, Iowa, 12/16/17; s. John H. Irey and Laura Schooley I; m. 10/8/56 to Vera Elaine Dimler; c. Mark C, Donna F, S. Kay and Denise L. Polit. & Govt. Pos: Co. Dem. Chmn, Iowa, 62- Mil. Serv: Entered as Pvt, Air Force, 41, released as S/Sgt, 52, after serv. in Ferry Command, ETO, Middle East, and Asiatic Pac. Theaters; Five Bronze Stars. Mem: Moose; Am. Legion; VFW; Cedar Co. Bd. Health; Cedar Co. Fair Asn; Lions Int; Am. Cancer Soc. (state cmt). Rel: Protestant. Mailing Add: 408 Ninth Ave, Clarence, Iowa 52216.

IRICK, GETHER D
Ky. State Rep.
b. 1912. Educ: East. Ky. State Col, B.A. and M.A; Univ. Ky, grad. work. Polit. & Govt. Pos: Ky. State Rep, 60- Bus. & Prof. Pos: Dir. of Pupil Personnel, Pike Co. Sch, Ky. Mil. Serv: Army, World War II; Nat. Guard. Mem: Mason; Eastern Ky, Ky, and Nat. Educ. Asns; Ky. and Nat. Chap. Dirs. of Pupil Personnel. Rel: Church of Christ. Mailing Add: Stone, Ky. 41567. (1967)

IRISH, AARON D. D
Vt. State Rep.
b. Jericho, Vt, 6/10/03; m. to Leona Whitehead; c. 3 sons; 1 daughter. Educ: Jericho Schs. Polit. & Govt. Pos: Vt. State Rep, 63- Bus. & Prof. Pos: Retired farmer. Mem: PTA. Rel: Methodist. Mailing Add: Hinesburg, Vt. 05461.

IRVING, DON D
Chmn, Pike Co. Dem. Cmt, Ill.
b. Chambersburg, Ill, 9/20/98; s. Wade Hampton Irving and Martha Hume I; m. 11/25/20 to Marjorie Lindsey; c. Mary Frances (Mrs. Christenson), Brice Lindsey and Roger Wade. Educ: James Millikin Univ, 18; Eureka Col, 19; Gem City Bus. Col, 20. Polit. & Govt. Pos: Sch. dir, local grade and high sch, 28-51; chmn, Pike Co. Bd. Supvrs, Ill, 37-52; chmn, Pike Co. Defense Cmt, 40-52; automobile investigator, 45-52; chmn, Pike Co. Dem. Cmt, 49-65 and currently; cattle quarantine inspector, 61-; mem, Ill. Dem. State Cent. Cmt, currently. Bus. & Prof. Pos: Farmer, 21-45; ins. agency owner, Ill, 57- Mil. Serv: Pvt, Army, 18, serv. in Students Army Training Corps. Publ: Weekly column for five co. newspapers, 50- Mem: Am. Legion Post 152; Farm Bur; Farmers Union. Mem, Co. All Star Basketball Second Team, 17; mgr, local baseball team, 41 years. Rel: Christian; Bd. Mem. Mailing Add: Chambersburg, Ill. 62323. (1967)

IRVIS, K. LEROY D
Pa. State Rep.
b. Saugerties, N.Y, 12/27/19; s. Francis H. Irvis and Harriet Cantine I; Educ: N.Y. State Teachers Col, A.B. and M.A; Univ. Pittsburgh, LL.B; teaching fel. in master's year; Owens fel. in law; Signum Laudis; Pi Gamma Mu; Order of the Coif; Phi Delta Phi. Polit. & Govt. Pos: Civilian attache, Aviation Training Div, War Dept; mem, Juvenile Court Adv. Cmt; mem. exec. cmt, Allegheny Co. Dem. Cmt; asst. dist. attorney, 57-63; Pa. State Rep, 58-, Minority Whip, Pa. House Rep; del, Dem. Nat. Conv, 68. Bus. & Prof. Pos: Attorney, mem. of fed. dist, all Commonwealth Courts; author; former ed. and teacher; former secy, pub. rels, Urban League of Pittsburgh; steel chipper, Crucible Steel, Pittsburgh; newscaster, Pittsburgh Courier. Mem: Bd, YMCA; legal redress cmt, NAACP. Mailing Add: 2170 Centre Ave, Pittsburgh, Pa. 15219. (1967)

IRWIN, BETTY J. R
Mem, Lake Co. Rep. Cent. Cmt, Calif.
b. Fresno, Calif, 11/7/22; d. Olen Hanks Carter and Gladys Wotton C; m. 5/29/45 to James E. Irwin, Jr; c. Nancy Hanks, James Carter and William Stuart. Educ: Col. Pac, grad. B.A, Nat. Debate Soc; Kappa Alpha Theta. Polit. & Govt. Pos: Secy, Calif. State Young Rep, 52; pres, Young Rep. Contra

Costa Co, 54; mem, Calif. Rep. State Cent. Cmt, 54- co. dir, Young Rep, 56-59; mem, Bd. Rep. Women, Orinda, 56-59; v.chmn, Contra Costa Cent. Cmt, 57; secy, Lake Co. Rep. Cent. Cmt, Calif, 62-64, chmn, 64-68, mem, currently; N.W. coast dir, Rep. Co. Chmn. Asn, 66. Mem: Mother's Club (pres). Rel: Episcopal. Mailing Add: Route 1, Box 874, Lakeport, Calif. 95453.

IRWIN, CHARLES G. R
b. Belvidere, Nebr, 11/20/92; m. Ruth; c. Two Sons. Polit. & Govt. Pos: Wyo. State Sen, 10 Years, -67; Pres. Sen, '37th Wyo. Legis; Wyo. State Rep, 4 Terms; Pres, Douglas High Sch. Dist. Bus. & Prof. Pos: Merchant; Banker; Former R.R. Sta. Agent. Mem: Masonic Lodge; Moose; C. of C; Kiwanis Club; VFW; Am. Legion; Pres, Thunder Basin Grazing Asn. Rel: Episcopalian. Mailing Add: 234 North 4th, Douglas, Wyo. 82633. (1967)

IRWIN, DONALD JAY D
b. Rosario, Argentina, 9/7/26; s. Montrose Wellington Irwin and Marion Reynolds I; m. 8/23/52 to Mary Stapleton; c. Patrick, Marion, Lucile and Stephen. Educ: Yale Univ, B.A. in Am. Hist, 51 and LL.B, 54. Polit. & Govt. Pos: Mem, Norwalk Bd. of Educ, 55; U.S. Rep, Fourth Dist, Conn, 58-60 & 64-68; gen. counsel, U.S. Info. Agency, 61; Conn. State Treas, 62. Bus. & Prof Pos: Attorney, Relihan & Irwin. Mil. Serv: Entered as Pvt, Army, 45, released as Pfc, 47. Mem: Rowayton Vol. Hose Co; Norwalk Stamford Inter-Racial Coun; K. of C. Yale Swimming Team; Soccer & Rugby; Distinguished Serv. Award, Jr. C. of C. Rel: Catholic. Mailing Add: 3 Topsail Rd, Norwalk, Conn. 06853.

IRWIN, JAMES ELLIS D
Chmn, Shelby Co. Dem. Exec. Cmt, Tenn.
b. Memphis, Tenn, 5/1/20; s. Robert L. Irwin, Sr. and Ethel Farris I; m. 4/29/46 to Nada Saskor; c. Gwyneth Ann. Educ: U.S. Coast Guard Acad; Univ. Tenn. Exten. Div; Univ. Memphis Law Sch, LL.B; Delta Theta Phi. Hon. LL.B, Memphis State Univ. Law Sch. Polit. & Govt. Pos: Co-chmn, Orgill for Mayor Campaign, Memphis, Tenn, 55; chmn, Independent Dem, 56-59; mem, Shelby Co. Dem. Exec. Cmt, 56-62, chmn, 62-; co-chmn, Orgill for Gov. Campaign, 58; co-chmn, Kennedy-Johnson Campaign, 60; Field counsel, Fed. Nat. Mortgage Asn, 61-; chmn, Dem. Campaign, 62; chmn, Johnson-Humphrey Campaign, 64; del, Dem. Nat. Conv, 64 & 68; Dem. nominee for U.S. Rep, Ninth Dist, Tenn, 68; Mem, Annexation Cmt, Memphis. Mil. Serv: Entered as A/S, Coast Guard, 41, released as Lt.(jg), 46, after serv. in N.Atlantic, S.Pac, New Guinea, Philippines and Okinawa, 43-46; Philippine and New Guinea Theaters, China Sea and N.Atlantic Patrol Ribbons; Pre-Pearl Harbor and Victory Medals; Commendation Ribbon for bravery off Mindanao, 44. Mem: Memphis & Shelby Co. Bar Asn.(mem. judicial selections cmt); Am. and Tenn. Bar Asns; Memphis Trial Lawyer's Asn.(dir, pres, 68-69); adv. bd, Memphis League of Women Voters; dir, Good Local Govt. League, 56; Mason (32°); Scottish Rite; Boy Scouts (troop comdr); Am. Legion. Rel: Presbyterian. Legal Res: 3496 McCorkle Rd, Memphis, Tenn. 38116. Mailing Add: Suite 1904, 100 N. Main Bldg, Memphis, Tenn. 38103.

ISAACKS, MAUD D
b. Austin, Tex; d. Samuel Jackson Isaacks and Minnie Willard Rutledge I; single. Educ: Univ. Tex, B.A, 27 and M.A, 40; Delta Kappa Gamma. Polit. Pos: Tex State Rep, 54-67. Bus. & Prof. Pos: Mem, State Textbook Cmt, Tex, 45-47 and El Paso High Sch. faculty, 16-54. Mem: C. of C; Bus. & Prfnl. Women's Club; DAR. Rel: Christian. Mailing Add: 3021 Federal, El Paso, Tex. 79930. (1967)

ISAACS, JOHN DONALD R
Del. State Sen.
b. Milford, Del, 4/8/32; s. Earle Lofland Isaacs and Sara Stayton I; m. 11/17/51 to Clydia Drucilla McGinnes; c. Lisa Drucilla, Nicholas Waldon and Melissa Elaine. Educ: Milton High Sch, grad, 50. Polit. & Govt. Pos: Pres, Lower New Castle Co. Asn. Young Rep, Del, 59, v.pres, Del. State Asn. Young Rep, 60, pres, 61; Del. State Sen, 62- Bus. & Prof. Pos: Mem. state bd, Del. Farm Bur, 60; pres, New Castle Co. Farm Bur, 60-62; chmn, South. State Bd, 60-64. Mem: Mason; Farm Bur; Shrine; Grange; Rotary. Outstanding Young Farmer Del, Jaycees; Nat. Robert S. Kerr Award. Rel: Methodist. Mailing Add: R.D. 2, Townsend, Del. 19734.

ISAACS, JOSEPH W. R
b. Edwardsville, Felton, Del, 10/23/03; s. Joseph. H. Isaacs and Laura Laramore I; m. to Winifred V. Thomas. Educ: Beacon Bus. Col; Pub. Serv. Inst. Polit. & Govt. Pos: Pa. State Rep, 54-67; Justice of the Peace, Folcroft, 44-62; Rep. Committeeman. Bus. & Prof. Pos: Farmer; Capt. of Police, P.R.R. 21- Mem: Delaware Co. Police Chiefs Asn; Police Chiefs Asn. of Southeast. Pa; Masonic Bodies; former pres, Magistrates Asn. of Delaware Co; former ex-ec-legis. chmn, now hon. pres, Magistrates Asn. of Delaware Co. and Pa. Rel: Former vestryman, St. Johns' Evangelical Lutheran Church, Folcroft. Mailing Add: 1547 Baltimore Ave, Folcroft, Pa. 19032. (1967)

ISAACS, M. MARTIN D
b. Georgetown, Del, 2/4/22; s. Miles M. Isaacs and Clara Gordy I; m. 10/1/50 to Susanne Phillips; c. Nancy Clara, Grace K, Lynne S, M. Steven, W. Delbert and Thomas Martin. Educ: Univ. Del, B.S. in bus. admin; Phi Kappa Tau. Polit. & Govt. Pos: Del. State Rep, 63-66, majority leader, Del. House of Rep, 65 and 66; Secy. Agr, State Del, 67-69. Bus. & Prof. Pos: Farmer, 46- Mil. Serv: Entered Intel. Div, Mil. Police Corps, 42, released as Sgt, 46; ETO Ribbon. Mem: Kiwanis Club; VFW. Rel: Methodist. Mailing Add: R.R. 2, Box 100, Georgetown, Del. 19947.

ISACSON, LEO D
b. New York, N.Y, 4/20/10; s. Hyman Isacson and Laura Nager I; m. 2/17/37 to Rose Roxon; c. Jill and Dale. Educ: N.Y. Univ, B.S, 31; N.Y. Univ. Law Sch, J.D, 33; N.Y. Univ. Letter Club; Alpha Epsilon Pi. Polit. & Govt. Pos: N.Y. State Assemblyman, 44-46; U.S. Congressman, Labor Party, 48; del, Dem. Nat. Conv, 68. Mem: Vernon Hills Country Club. Rel: Jewish. Legal Res: 84 Lake Shore Dr, Yonkers, N.Y. 10707. Mailing Add: 59 E. 161st St, Bronx, N.Y. 10451. (1967)

ISENBERG, JOE D
b. Atlanta, Ga, 5/24/08; s. Sol Isenberg and Sadie Smith I; m. 1/12/36 to Edith Wise; c. Sandra Joan, Rosalyn, Marvin. Educ: Ga. Tech, 24-25. Polit. & Govt. Pos: Mem, Port Authority, Brunswick, Ga, 47-60, chmn, 55-59; Ga. State Rep, 63-64. Bus. & Prof. Pos: Merchant. Mem: Elks; Mason (32°); Scottish Rite; Shrine; Brunswick Rotary Club (dir, 52-53). Rel: Jewish; B'nai B'rith. Mailing Add: Brunswick, Ga. 31520.

ISENHOUR, GEORGE MYRON, JR. R
b. New London, N.C, 10/1/21; s. George Myron Isenhour and Mary Menius I; m. 7/22/42 to Mary Maxine Cashatt; c. George Myron, III, Cynthia and Mary Annette. Educ: Oak Ridge Mil. Inst; N.C. State Univ. Polit. & Govt. Pos: Chmn, Bd. Co. Cmnrs, N.C, 57-58; chmn, Stanly Co. Planning Bd, 62-63; chmn, Stanly Co. Rep. Party, 64-66, precinct chmn, currently; v.chmn, Stanly Co. Indust. Develop. Cmn, 60- Bus. & Prof. Pos: V.pres. and treas, Yadkin Brick Co, N.C, 46-; mem. bd. dirs, Home Savings & Loan Asn, 58- Mil. Serv: Entered as Cadet, Air Force, 42, released as Capt, 45, after serv. as Pilot, Air Transport Command, North Africa and ETO. Mem: C. of C; U.S. C. of C; Nat. Asn. of Mfrs. Rel: Baptist. Mailing Add: Route 2, New London, N.C. 28127.

ISLER, JOHN J. D
Ky. State Rep.
b. 1908. Polit. & Govt. Pos: Secy. and former pres, Dem. Club; Ky. State Rep, 56- Bus. & Prof. Pos: Rwy. clerk; acct. Mem: Eagles; Cent. Covington Civic Club; Crusaders East End Club; Peaselburg Liars Club; St. Augustine Holy Name Soc. Rel: Catholic. Mailing Add: 1813 Jefferson Ave, Covington, Ky. 41014. (1967)

ISON, DONALD R
Chmn, Breathitt Co. Rep. Cmt, Ky.
b. Oscaloosa, Ky, 6/22/39; s. Edgar Ison and Lona Hampton I; m. 5/16/62 to Marsha Allen; c. Cheryl Anne. Educ: Morehead State Univ, B.S, 61. Polit. & Govt. Pos: Chmn, Breathitt Co. Rep. Cmt, Ky, 68- Mil. Serv: Entered as Pvt, E-1, Army Nat. Guard, 61, released as Sgt. E-6, 68, after serving in 201st Engr. Bn; Merit Award, 68. Mem: Breathitt-Jackson Airport Bd; Breathitt Co. Indust. Bd; Jaycees; Kiwanis. Jaycee of the Year, 66. Rel: Protestant; Deacon, Christian Church. Mailing Add: Panbowl Rd, Jackson, Ky. 41339.

ISSAC, MACK STEWART R
b. Newland, N.C, 5/28/21; s. Benjamin H. Issac and Loretta Banner I; single. Educ: Lees-McRae Col. Polit. & Govt. Pos: N.C. State Rep, 59-68. Bus. & Prof. Pos: Farmer; bd. dirs, Avery Co. Bank. Mil. Serv: Tech. Sgt, 101st Airborne Div, 43-45. Mem: Avery Co. C. of C; Am. Legion. Rel: Presbyterian; Deacon, 41- Mailing Add: Box 395, Newland, N.C. 28657. (1967)

IVASCYN, JOHN PETER D
Mass. State Rep.
b. Austria-Poland, 10/29/09; s. Peter J. Ivascyn and Pauline I; m. 5/24/41 to Stephanie Marion Chmura; c. John Paul, Daniel Walter and Lee Anthony. Educ: New Eng. Sch. of Acct, courses in polit. and govt, ins. and real estate. Polit. & Govt. Pos: Selectman, Webster, Mass, 17 years; Mass. State Rep, Sixth Dist, 51- Bus. & Prof. Pos: Broker and agent, John Ivascyn Ins. Mil. Serv: Classified work, World War II. Publ: Articles for local newspapers on town and state govt, legis. and effects and town and state finances as pertaining to Sixth Worcester Dist, Mass. Mem: Mass. Selectmen's Asn; State Rep. Asn; K. of C; Elks; Eagles; 200 Sportsmen's Club; plus others. Sponsored and voted for legis. for Vet. benefits, aid to educ. and aid to police; baseball and basketball player; Eagles Award; Citizen of Year; Polish-Am. Citizens Award. Rel: Roman Catholic. Mailing Add: 17 Lincoln St, Webster, Mass. 01570.

IVERSON, DONALD L. D
b. St. Croix Falls, Wis, 2/3/23. Educ: River Falls State Univ, B.S; Chicago Col. of Optom, Dr. of Optom. Polit. & Govt. Pos: Wis. State Assemblyman, 64-66; Alderman 61-63; Co. Bd. Supvr, 62- Bus. & Prof. Pos: Optometrist, High Sch. Sci. Teacher 53-54. Mil. Serv: WWII Vet, 43-45, Mid. East Theater. Mem: Am. & Wis. Optom. Asns; Int. Bd. of Exams. in Optom; Indianhead Optom. Asn; VFW; Am. Legion; C. of C; St. Croix Cty. Hist. Soc; Hudson Boosters (Little League); St. Croix Cty. Welfare Bd. & Co. Ment. Health Com; State Bd. of Exams. in Optom, 59-64, Formerly Pres. Mailing Add: 822 Summer St, Hudson, Wis. 54016. (1967)

IVES, ALDEN ALLEN R
Conn. State Sen.
b. Torrington, Conn, 5/21/25; s. Sherman Kimberly Ives and Lida Skilton I; m. 3/26/51 to Janet Reed Stiles; c. Richard Allen, Russell Reed and Tracey Jean. Educ: Univ. Conn, B.S. in Bus. Admin. and Law Sch, 1 yr. Polit. & Govt. Pos: Treas, Morris, Conn, 52-58; Conn. State Rep, Morris, 57-59; Conn. State Sen, 32nd Dist, 61- Bus. & Prof Pos: V.pres. and treas, Ives Ins, Inc, 60-64; exec. v.pres, Patrons Mutual Ins. Co, 64- Mil. Serv: Entered as Recruit Army, 43, released as S/Sgt, 46, after serv. in Co. L, 302nd Inf, 94th Inf. Div, ETO; European Theater Ribbon with three Battle Stars; Silver Star; CWO-3, Army Res, 46- Mem: Am. Legion; VFW; AF&AM; Grange; Volunteer Fire Dept. Rel: Congregational. Legal Res: Morris, Conn. Mailing Add: 769 Hebron Ave, Glastonbury, Conn. 06033.

IVES, TIMOTHY READ D
b. Chicago, Ill, 4/9/28; s. Ernest L. Ives and Elizabeth D. Stevenson I; m. 6/23/54 to Adrienne A. Osborne; c. Alison A, Sandra R. and Timothy O. Educ: Univ. Va, 47-51; Phi Gamma Delta; V Club. Polit. & Govt. Pos: Precinct committeeman, Dem. Party, Bloomington, Ill, 58-; del, Ill. State Conv, 64 and 68; secy, Ill. Sch. Bldg. Cmn, 65-; del, Dem. Nat. Conv, 68. Bus. & Prof. Pos: Radio sales, WBT, Charlotte, N.C, 55-56, WJBC, WJBC-FM, Bloomington, Ill, 56-60; radio sta. mgr, WJBC-WBNQ, 60- Mil. Serv: Entered as enlisted man, Air Force, 51, released as 1st Lt, 55, after serving in 5th Air Force, Korea, and Training Command in U.S, 53-55; Capt, Air Force Res, Retired; Air Medal. Mem: Nat. Asn. Broadcasters; Ill. Broadcasters Asn; Nat. Asn. FM Broadcasters; Rotary; Am. Legion; VFW; SAR; Bloomington Grad. Chap, Phi Gamma Delta; Soc. of the Cincinnati; Bloomington Country Club; Bloomington Club; Asn. of Commerce; Citizens Commun. Improv. Cmt. Mailing Add: 1504 E. Washington St, Bloomington, Ill. 61701.

IVINS, HEBER GRANT D
b. Salt Lake City, Utah, 6/15/21; s. Heber Grant Ivins and Bertha Hamblin I; m. 7/23/43 to Virginia Woodhouse; c. Cathleen (Mrs. Stanley Street), Les-

lie (Mrs. Gary Beardall), Christine, Jeffrey, Timothy and Anthony W. Educ: Brigham Young Univ, 39-41 & 46; George Wash. Univ, 42; Univ. Utah, J.D, 49; Phi Alpha Delta. Polit. & Govt. Pos: Asst. dist. attorney, Fourth Judicial Dist, Utah, 60-67, dist. attorney, 67-68; alternate del, Dem. Nat. Conv, 68. Mil. Serv: Entered as Pvt, Air Force, 42, released as Sgt, 45; Capt. Res, 45-55. Rel: Latter-day Saint. Legal Res: 1040 N. First E, American Fork, Utah 84003. Mailing Add: Box 397, American Fork, Utah 84003.

IZAC, EDOUARD VICTOR MICHEL D
b. Cresco, Iowa, 12/18/91; s. B. Michel Izac and Mathilda Geuth I; m. 6/5/15 to Agnes Elmer Cabell; c. Cabell, Edouard, Jr, Charles, Suzanne, Forrest and Andre. Educ: Sch. of the Assumption, Cresco, Iowa; U.S. Naval Acad. Polit. & Govt. Pos: U.S. Rep, 20th and 23rd Dists, Calif, 37-47. Mil. Serv: Entered as Midshipman, Navy, 11, retired as Lt. Comdr, 21; Cong. Medal of Honor; Croce di Guerra, Italy; Cross of Montenegro. Publ: Prisoner of the U 90, Houghton Mifflin; The Holy Land Then and Now, Vantage Press. Rel: Catholic. Mailing Add: 2901 29th St. N.W, Washington, D.C. 20008.

J

JAAKOLA, RAYMOND THEODORE R
Chmn, Beltrami Co. Rep. Cmt, Minn.
b. Iron River, Wis, 6/5/14; s. Matt Jaakola and Jennie Marie Neiminan J; m. 11/9/45 to Una Monette White; c. Michelle Marie and Una Ashby. Educ: Univ. Minn, Duluth, 2 years; Ill. Col. Optometry, Chicago, O.D; Tomb and Key; Omega Epsilon Phi. Polit. & Govt. Pos: Chmn, Beltrami Co. Rep. Cmt, Minn, 67- Bus. & Prof. Pos: Committeeman, Oper. Manpow, Am. Optom. Asn; 67-; mem. cabinet, N. Cent. States Optom. Conf, 68- Mil. Serv: Entered as Pvt, Air Force, 42, released as Sgt, 45, after serving in 317 Troop Carrier Group, S.W. Pac, 44-45; 5 battle ribbons; Presidential Unit Citation. Mem: Optom. Exten. Prog; Am. Optom. Found; Am. Pub. Health Asn; Better Vision Inst; Minn. Optom. Asn.(pres, 69-70); Mason; Am. Legion; VFW; Elks; Rotary. Rel: Lutheran. Legal Res: 1019 Park, Bemidji, Minn. 56601. Mailing Add: Box 547, Bemidji, Minn. 56601.

JACHENS, NORMAN H.W. R
Chmn, Alameda Co. Rep. Cent. Cmt, Calif.
b. San Francisco, Calif, 12/16/35; s. John Adolph Jachens and Anna Louise Domeir J; m. 6/2/63 to Camille T. Salpetro; c. Karen Camille. Educ: Univ. Calif, Berkeley, B.A; Hastings Col. Law, San Francisco, 1 year. Polit. & Govt. Pos: Mem, Young Rep. Nat. Exec. Cmt, 57-59; chmn, West. Fedn. Col. Young Rep. Clubs, 57-59; mem, Calif. Rep. State Cent. Cmt, 58-, mem. exec. cmt, 69-; mem, Alameda Co. Rep. Cent. Cmt, 58-, chmn, 69-; asst. to chief clerk, Calif. State Assembly, 59; eighth dist. dir, Calif. Rep. Assembly, 63-65, state v.pres, 65-68; chmn, N.Alameda Co. Reagan for Gov. Campaign, 66; foreman pro-tem, Alameda Co. Grand Jury, 68. Bus. & Prof. Pos: Field rep, Duggan Investment Co, 61-62; loan officer, Am. Savings and Loan Asn, 63- Mil. Serv: Entered as Pvt, Calif. Nat. Guard and Army Res, 53, released as 1st Lt, 63, after serv. in 159th Inf. Regiment, 49th Div, Exec. Officer Inf. Co, 62-63. Mem: Kiwanis; Jr. C. of C.(pres, Alameda Chap, 65). Rel: Lutheran. Mailing Add: 2051 Shoreline Dr, Alameda, Calif. 94501.

JACKMAN, LAWRENCE McLAM R
Vt. State Rep.
b. East Corinth, Vt, 6/14/03; married; c. One son and one daughter. Educ: Goddard Sem, 22; U.V.M; Baypath Inst, 24. Polit. & Govt. Pos: Vt. State Rep, 57-61 and currently; mem. adv. bd, Unemploy. Compensation Cmn, 60-63; Vt. State Sen, 61; mem, Town Rep. Cmt; trustee, Blake Mem. Libr; dir, Valley Sch. for Retarded Children; pres, Valley Health Center, East Corinth; sch. dir; asst. chmn, Orange Co. Rep. Cmt, 64. Bus. & Prof. Pos: Bobbin mfr. Mem: Mason; Shrine. Rel: Congregational. Mailing Add: East Corinth, Vt. 05039. (1967)

JACKSON, AMOS D
b. Detroit, Mich, 6/13/16; s. John J. Jackson and Lula Johnson J; m. 3/4/50 to Cora I. Livingston; c. Sheila and Denise. Polit. & Govt. Pos: Alternate del, Dem. Nat. Conv, 68. Mem: Ohio State Union Label and Serv. Trades Coun.(pres); Ohio AFL-CIO (v.pres); Laborers' Int. Union N.Am.(pres, Local 265); Nat. Found. Health, Welfare and Pension Plans; Buckeye State Sheriffs Asn. Mailing Add: 26 Burton Woods Lane, Cincinnati, Ohio 45229.

JACKSON, AMOS WADE D
Justice, Ind. Supreme Court
b. Versailles, Ind, 6/25/04; s. Rowland H. Jackson and Georgia W. Frohliger J; m. 8/20/27 to Lola M. Raper; c. Ann Louise (Mrs. Stanley) and Jeanette (deceased). Educ: Hanover Col, A.B, 26; Lambda Chi Alpha; Phi Alpha Delta. Polit. & Govt. Pos: Prosecuting attorney, Ripley Co, Ind, 37-40; assoc. attorney, War Dept, 42-43; justice, Ind. Supreme Court, 59- Bus. & Prof. Pos: Practice of law, 25-59; pres, Bank of Versailles, Ind, 58- Mem: Am, Ind, Ripley Co. and Indianapolis Bar Asns; Southeast. Ind. Park Asn; Mason; Shrine; Hoosier Hills Coun, Boy Scouts, 28-29. Rel: Baptist. Legal Res: Versailles, Ind. Mailing Add: Room 306, State House, Indianapolis, Ind. 46204.

JACKSON, BARRY WENDELL D
Alaska State Rep.
b. Long Branch, N.J, 1/27/30; s. Rodney H. Jackson and Marion Englebright J; m. 6/4/55 to Susan Braddy Shields; c. Stacy Ann, Leslie Barry, Bruce Edward, Sydney Elise and Morgan Susan. Educ: Stanford Univ, A.B. in Polit. Sci, 52, J.D, 58; Delta Theta Phi. Polit. & Govt. Pos: City attorney, Fairbanks, Alaska, 59-63; staff dir, Borough Study Group, 62-63; Alaska State Rep, 65-67 & 69-, chmn. judiciary cmt, Alaska State House of Rep, 69- Bus. & Prof. Pos: Mem, Coun. of Advice, Missionary Dist. Alaska, 66-67, exec. bd, 67-68. Mil. Serv: Entered as 2nd Lt, Marine Corps, 52, released as 1st Lt, 55; Maj, Marine Corps Res, currently; commanding officer, Composite Co, 17-3, Naval Res, 66-68; Korean and UN Serv. and Am. Defense Medals. Mem: Am. Bar Asn.(state chmn. local govt. law sect and cmt. on state legis); Tanana Valley Bar Asn.(pres, 61-63); Alaska Bar Asn; state chmn, Nat. Inst. Munic. Law Officers, 60-63; Am. Trial Lawyers Asn; Alaska Acad. Trial Lawyers; Fairbanks Dem. Club; Marine Corps Res. Officers Asn; PTA; Alaska Conserv. Soc; NAACP; Am. Civil Liberties Union; United Good Neighbors of Nanana Valley (chmn. budget cmt); Boy Scouts (mem. exec. bd, Midnight Sun Coun, 65-68); Kiwanis; Elks. Rel: Episcopal. Mailing Add: 1140 Sunset Dr, Fairbanks, Alaska 99701.

JACKSON, CLEVELAND D
b. Culloden, Ga, 2/16/12; s. Kinchen Jackson and Carrie Belle Washington J; m. 7/18/48 to Sarah Marion Connally. Educ: Howard Univ, Wash, D.C, 30-34; Miami Univ, Oxford, summer, 36; Cleveland-Marshal Law Sch, 47-51; Omega Psi Phi. Polit. Pos: Dem. leader, 18th Ward, Cleveland, Ohio, 52- Govt. Pos: Asst, Law Dir. Criminal Div, City of Cleveland, Ohio, 63-65; asst. attorney gen, State of Ohio, 59-63. Mil. Serv: Entered as Pvt, Army, 41, released as Capt, Air Force, 46; after serv. in Qm. Truck Co, 5th Air Force, S.Pac. Area; Am. Defense Ribbon; Asiatic-Pac. Ribbon with 2 Battle Stars; ATO Ribbon; Victory Medal with 3 Overseas Serv. Bars; Maj.(Ret), 46. Mem: John Harlan Law Club, Cleveland; Cuyahoga Co. and Ohio Bar Asns; Am. Legion; NAACP; Citizens League, Cleveland; Howard Univ. Alumni Club. Rel: Methodist. Legal Res: 3668 East Blvd, Cleveland, Ohio 44105. Mailing Add: 10506 Cedar, Cleveland, Ohio 44106. (1967)

JACKSON, DONALD LESTER R
Cmnr, Interstate Commerce Cmn.
b. Ipswich, S.Dak, 1/23/10; s. Cyrus Lester Jackson and Betina Ames J; separated; c. Donald C. Educ: Pub. Schs, S.Dak. and Calif. Polit. & Govt. Pos: U.S. Rep, 47-61; cmnr, Interstate Commerce Cmn, 69- Bus. & Prof. Pos: Dir. of publicity, City of Santa Monica, Calif, 41. Mil. Serv: Entered as 2nd Lt, Marines, 42, released as Maj, 45, after serv. in Second Marine Div, Pac. Theatre; Col, Marine Corps Res. Mailing Add: 2800 Wisconsin Ave. N.W, Washington, D.C. 20007.

JACKSON, E(DWARD) FRANKLIN D
Mem, Dem. Nat. Cmt, D.C.
b. Pensacola, Fla, 7/19/11; s. Charles Wesley Jackson and Phoebe Hart J; m. 9/1/37 to Mildred Dodson; c. Edward Franklin, II, Cameron Wesley, Gloria Jean and Darryl Joseph. Educ: Fla. Agr. & Mech. Univ, 32-33; Edward Waters Col, B.Th, 36; Tuskegee Inst, 36-37; Livingstone Col, Hood Sem, D.D, 49; Omega Psi Phi. Polit. & Govt. Pos: V.chmn, D.C. Cent. Dem. Cmt, 60-64; mem, Dem. Nat. Cmt, D.C, 64-; del, Dem. Nat. Conv, 68. Bus. & Prof. Pos: Pastor, Price Mem, 37-41, Harris Chapel, 41-43, St. Luke's, 43-52 and John Wesley AME Zion Church, 52- Publ: The Full Grown Minister, Rozen, 50; My Church, Brown, 53; 'Why I Believe In God,' Ebony, 60. Mem: Redemption Lodge 24, F&AM, Jonothan Davis Consistory 1, AASR, Supreme Coun.(33°); Columbia Lodge 85; Int. Elks. Rel: African Methodist Episcopal Zion Church. Legal Res: 1736 Webster St. N.W, Washington, D.C. 20011. Mailing Add: 1615 14th St. N.W, Washington, D.C. 20009. (1967)

JACKSON, ELLEN M. D
b. Boston, Mass, 10/29/35; d. David Swepson and Marguerite Booker S; m. to Hugh L. Jackson; c. Ronica, Darryl, Sheryl, Troy and Stefani. Educ: State Teachers Col. at Boston, 2 years. Polit. & Govt. Pos: Alternate del, Dem. Nat. Conv, 68. Bus. & Prof. Pos: Parent group coordinator, North. Student Movement, 63-64; soc. serv. supvr, First Head Start Prog, 64-65; exec. dir, Operation Exodus, Inc, 65-; exec. dir, Black Women's Commun. Develop. Found, 68- Publ: 'Family Experiences in Operation Exodus,' (co-author), Community Health J, Columbia Univ. Press, 67. Mem: Mass. exec. bd, Cmn. on Church and Race; nat. bd. of dirs, Crusade Against Poverty; bd. of dirs, Roxbury Fedn. of Neighborhood Centers; citizens educ. adv. bd. of A.B.C.D; bd. of Opportunities Industrialization Center, Metrop. Coun. for Educ. Opportunity and Roxbury Commun. Coun; Mass. State Adv. Cmt. on Civil Rights; adv. bd, Civil Liberties Union of Mass; Mass. adv. bd, Legal Defense and Educ. Fund, Inc; bd. of trustees, Mass. State Cols; Nat. Coun. of Women of the U.S. Zeta Phi Beta Award, 65; NAACP Award, 65; Freedom House Award, 65; Kiwanis Recognition Award, 65; Lambda Kappa Mu Award, 66; Nat. Coun. of Women of the U.S. Award, 67; Sojourner Truth Awards, Nat. Asn. of Negro Bus. and Prfnl. Women's Clubs, Inc, 68; Simon Gutman Found. Award, 69. Rel: African Methodist. Legal Res: 27 Brookledge St, Boston, Mass. 02121. Mailing Add: 378 Blue Hill Ave, Roxbury, Mass. 02121.

JACKSON, GEORGE R
Colo. State Sen.
b. Governor's Island, N.J; married; c. three sons. Polit. & Govt. Pos: Mem, Mayor's Watershed Cmt; Colo. State Rep; Colo. Springs Parks and Recreation Adv. Bd, 3 years; Colo. State Sen, 66- Bus. & Prof. Pos: Trucking bus, operator, Mountain Express Truck Line, at present. Legal Res: Colorado Springs, Colo. 80907. Mailing Add: 2903 N. Tejon St, Colorado Springs, Colo. 80907. (1967)

JACKSON, GEORGE WINFIELD R
Chmn, Person Co. Rep. Party, N.C.
b. Belhaven, N.C, 11/17/37; s. Clarence Benjamin Jackson and Lillian Winfield J; m. 11/24/62 to Dorothy Ann Freeman; c. Burton Winfield and John Gregory. Educ: Univ. N.C, A.B, 60; Univ. N.C. Sch. Law, LL.B, 66; Chi Psi; Delta Theta Phi. Polit. & Govt. Pos: Attorney, Second Cong. Dist. Person Co. Selective Serv, N.C, 67-; mem. bd. dir, Second Cong. Dist. Rep. Party, 68-; chmn, Person Co. Rep. Party, 68-; pres, Person Co. Young Rep, 68, dir, 68-; city attorney, Roxboro, 69- Bus. & Prof. Pos: Assoc, Ramsey & Long, 66-67, partner, Ramsey, Long & Jackson, 67- Mil. Serv: Entered as Pvt, Army, 60, released as S/Sgt, 63, after serving in 112th Intel. Corps Group, Fourth Army Area, 61-63; Good Conduct Medal; Marksmanship Medals. Mem: N.C. and Person Co. Bar Asns; Ninth Judicial Dist. Bar Asn. of N.C.(bd. dir, 68 & 69); Jaycees; Person-Orange Ment. Health Authority. Rel: Baptist. Legal Res: 409 Reams Ave, Roxboro, N.C. 27573. Mailing Add: Box 601, Roxboro, N.C. 27573.

JACKSON, GUY CADE, III D
Chmn, Chambers Co. Dem. Exec. Cmt, Tex.
b. San Antonio, Tex, 8/16/31; s. Guy Cade Jackson, Jr. and Katherine Cook J; m. 11/24/61 to Linda Cummins; c. Guy Robert, Linda Ann and Steven Lynn. Educ: Tex. A&M Col, B.B.A, 52; Univ. Tex, Austin, LL.B, 58; Delta Theta Phi. Polit. & Govt. Pos: Chmn, Chambers Co. Dem. Exec. Cmt, Tex, 58-61

& 63-; mem. bd. dirs, Trinity River Authority of Tex, 67- Bus. & Prof. Pos: Asst. secy, Anahuac Hardware Co, Tex, 66-; secy-treas, Chambers Co. Abstract Co, Anahuac, 66- Mil. Serv: Entered as 2nd Lt, Army, 52, released as 1st Lt, 54, after serv. in Third Armored Cavalry Regt, Camp Pickett, Va. and 72nd Tank Bn, Second Inf. Div, Korea; Recalled, 61-62, serv. in 49th Armored Div, Ft. Polk, La; Tex. Army Nat. Guard, Maj. Mem: State Bar of Tex; Am. Bar Asn; Am. Judicature Soc.(bd. mem); Nat. Guard Asn. of Tex. and U.S. chmn, Chambers Co. Hist. Surv. Cmt; Tex. Water Conserv. Asn; Nat. Reclamation Asn; chmn, Chambers Co. Imported Fire Ant Cmt, 67-; Am. Legion (Comdr, Anahuac Chap, Tex); Lions; AF&AM; Shrine. Rel: Methodist. Legal Res: 101 Lynn St, Anahuac, Tex. 77514. Mailing Add: P.O. Box 308, Anahuac, Tex. 77514.

JACKSON, HARLEY TAYLOR R
Chmn, Delta Co. Rep. Cent. Cmt, Colo.
b. Topeka, Kans, 2/10/28; s. Howard Taylor Jackson and Nettie Stover J; m. 7/2/49 to Ethel Fairlamb; c. Catherine Ruth, Charles Howard and Haley Annette. Educ: Kans. State Col, 46. Polit. & Govt. Pos: Co-campaign mgr, Mayors Race, Topeka, Kans, 52; co. chmn, Gov. Race Dave Hamit, Colo, 62, Goldwater Campaign, 64 and Gov. Love Campaign, 66; chmn, Delta Co. Rep. Cent. Cmt, 68- Bus. & Prof. Pos: Pres, Delta Co. Develop. Co. Inc, Delta, Colo, 67-68. Mil. Serv: Entered as Pvt, Air Force Aviation Cadets, 48, released as Cpl, 49, after serv. in 96th Fighter Squadron. Publ: 'Three the Infinite Number, the Key to Infinity,' privately publ, 63. Mem: Bd. dirs, Jr. C. of C, Topeka, Kans, 52; state chmn. nat. conv. cmt, Kans. Jr. C. of C, 53-54; Delta C. of C.(pres, 62); bd. dirs, Delta Co. Golf Course Asn, 67-68; Nat. Elec. Contractors Asn.(bd. dirs, Intermountain Group, 69-); IBEW; Aircraft Owners & Pilots Asn; Mason; Elks; Kiwanis; Delta Golf Club; 4-H; Future Farmers of Am. Rel: Protestant. Legal Res: 740 Leon, Delta, Colo. 81416. Mailing Add: 520 Main, Delta, Colo. 81416.

JACKSON, HARRY COOK D
Ga. State Sen.
b. Columbus, Ga, 7/23/15; s. Stonewall Jackson and Emmie Herndon J; m. 10/5/41 to Helen Lovein; c. Helen Lovein, Harry Stonewall. Educ: Auburn Univ, B.S. in Mech. Eng; admission to practice law granted in 52; Sigma Phi Epsilon. Polit. & Govt. Pos: Ga. State Sen, 61-66 & 69-, pres. pro tem, Ga. State Sen, 63. Bus. & Prof. Pos: Registered prof. engr; attorney; pres, Morton Machine Works, Inc. Mil. Serv: Air Force, Lt. Col. Rel: Methodist. Mailing Add: 2120 Country Club Rd, Columbus, Ga. 31906.

JACKSON, HENRY M. D
U.S. Sen, Wash.
b. Everett, Wash, 5/31/12; m. 12/16/61 to Helen Eugenia Hardin J; c. Anna Marie and Peter Hardin. Educ: Univ. of Wash. Law Sch, LL.B, 35. Polit. & Govt. Pos: Prosecuting Attorney, Snohomish Co, Wash, 38; U.S. Rep, 41-52; U.S. Sen, 53-; chmn, Dem. Nat. Cmt, 60-61; del, Dem. Nat. Conv, 68. Bus. & Prof. Pos: Mem, law firm of Black & Rucker, Everett, Wash, 35-38. Legal Res: Everett, Wash. 98201. Mailing Add: Room 137 Senate Office Bldg, Washington, D.C. 20510.

JACKSON, ISABEL HOPE R
V.Chmn, Del. State Rep. Cmt.
b. Dover, Del, 7/17/05; d. William Malcolm Hope and Amy Louise Stanford H; m. 10/1/38 to Harry Richardson Jackson; c. William A. Hughes, Jr. Educ: Wesley Col. Polit. & Govt. Pos: Mem, Kent Co. Rep. Cmt, Del, 58-62; del, Del. Rep. Conv, 60; v.pres, Kent Co. Rep. Women's Club, 62-64; mem, Del. State Rep. Cmt, 62-, v.chmn, 66; del. and mem, rules cmt, Rep. Nat. Conv, 64. Mem: Women's Nat. Rep. Club; Women's Rep. Club of Dover; Del. Fedn. Rep. Women's Clubs; Kent Co. Rep. Women's Club; Mapledale Country Club. Rel: Episcopal. Mailing Add: 144 King's Hwy, Dover, Del. 19901.

JACKSON, J. ELVIN D
Finance chmn, Moore Co. Dem. Party, N.C.
b. West End, N.C, 3/17/38; s. William Elias Jackson and Helen Sullivan J; m. 3/20/60 to Iris Ann Baldwin. Educ: Am. Inst. of Banking, 58-59; Carolina's Sch. of Banking, Univ. N.C, summers, 64, 65. Polit. & Govt. Pos: Co. mgr, Young Voter's Prog. for Terry Sanford for Gov, N.C, 60; v.pres, Moore Co. Young Dem. Club, 61, pres, 62-63, dir, 64-66; chmn, Eighth Cong. Dist. Young Dem. Club, 63; state organizer, Young Dem. Club of N.C, 63 & 64; state co-campaign mgr, H. Clifton Blue for Lt. Gov, 64; mem, Moore Co. Agr. Exten. Adv. Bd, 64-66; chmn, Moore Co. Dem. Exec. Cmt, 64-68; Finance Chmn, Moore Co. Dem. Party, 68- Bus. & Prof. Pos: Loan mgr, Carolina Bank, Pinehurst, N.C, 58-62, asst. cashier, Carthage, N.C, 62-63, cashier, Vass, 63-66, asst. v.pres. and cashier, 66-67, v.pres. and mgr, Carthage, 67- Mil. Serv: Sgt, Army Res, 61- Mem: Am. and N.C. Bankers Asns; Vass. Indust. Develop. Cmt; Sandhills Area Develop. Asn; Sandhill Commun. Col. Adult Basic Educ. Adv. Bd; N.C. Health Ins. Bd, 67-; N.C. Voc. Educ. Bd, 69-; Farm Bur; Mason (Master, Carthage Lodge 181, 68); Elks; Jaycees; Boy Scouts (mem. state treas. cmt). Named one of ten outstanding Young Dem. in N.C, 63; Distinguished Serv. Award, Carthage Jaycees, 68; Rotary Found. two month travel grant to represent N.C. in Israel, 69; politics and stock mkt. Rel: Presbyterian; Deacon and treas. of church. Legal Res: Vass Rd, Carthage, N.C. 28327. Mailing Add: Box 372, Carthage, N.C. 28327.

JACKSON, J. RUPERT, JR. D
b. Baird, Tex, 6/13/14; s. J. Rupert Jackson and Anna Faust J; single. Educ: Univ. Tex, B.A, 36, LL.B, 45. Polit. & Govt. Pos: Chmn, Callahan Co. Dem. Exec. Cmt, 38-41. Mil. Serv: Entered as Ens, Naval Res, 42, released as Lt.(sg), 45; Asiatic-Pac, Philippine Liberation, Victory and Am. Ribbons; 7 Combat Stars. Mem: Tex.and Am. Bar Asns; Masons; Am. Legion; C. of C; Callahan Co. Luncheon Club. Rel: Presbyterian. Legal Res: 915 Cherry St, Baird, Tex. 79504. Mailing Add; Box 878, Baird, Tex. 79504.

JACKSON, JAMES H. D
b. Waterloo, Iowa, 4/24/39; s. James V. Jackson and Wilma J; m. 1958 to Janet L. Norman; c. Denise, Jacqueline, Stephanie. Educ: State Col. of Iowa, B.A. Polit. & Govt. Pos: Iowa State Rep, -66. Bus. & Prof. Pos: Head, Sci. Dept, McKinstry Jr. High Sch, Waterloo, Iowa. Mem: Phi Sigma Epsilon; I.S.E.A; N.E.A; Int. Civitan; Bd. Mem, Family Serv. League; Bd. Mem, NAACP; K. of P, Past Chancellor, Present Grand Lectr. Rel: Antioch Baptist Church, Waterloo. Mailing Add: Science Dept, McKinistry Junior High School, Waterloo, Iowa 50701. (1967)

JACKSON, JAMES WILLIAM R
Chmn, Gallatin Co. Rep. Cent. Cmt, Ill.
b. Ridgway, Ill, 9/21/19; s. Will Jackson and Martha Downen J; m. 1/15/46 to Lorene Stoponi; c. James W, Jr, Joseph M. and John M. Educ: High Sch. Polit. & Govt. Pos: Chmn, Gallatin Co. Rep. Cent. Cmt, Ill. and treas, Ill. Rep. Co. Chmn. Asn, currently; mem, Ill. Rep. Cent. Cmt, 69- Mil. Serv: Entered as Pvt, Army Air Force, 42, released as S/Sgt, 45, after serv. in 454th Bomb Group, Second Air Force; Am. Theater Ribbon; European-African-Middle East.Theater Ribbon with One Silver Battle Star and Three Bronze Battle Stars; Four Overseas Serv. Bars; Two Presidential Unit Citations. Mem: AF&AM; Scottish Rite; VFW; Am. Legion. Rel: Methodist. Mailing Add: P.O. Box 66, Ridgway, Ill. 62979. (1967)

JACKSON, JAY WAYNE D
Conn. State Sen.
b. Albany, N.Y, 1/30/31; s. J. Wayne Jackson and Catherine McDonald J; m. 10/29/60 to Francoise de Chabert-Ostland; c. Francoise and Stephanie. Educ: Washington & Lee Univ, B.A, 53; Washington & Lee Sch. of Law, LL.B, 55; Phi Alpha Delta; Sigma Nu. Polit. & Govt. Pos: Conn. hearing officer, Justice Dept, 63-; mem, West. Hartford Town Coun, 64-66; Conn. State Sen, 66- Bus. & Prof. Pos: Partner, Law Firm of Manion, Egan, Eagan and Jackson, Hartford Conn, 58- Mil. Serv: Entered as Cpl, Army, 54, released as 1st Lt, 57, after serv. in 594th Movement Control Group, Orleans, France, 56-57; Maj, Judge Adv. Gen. Corps, Army Res, at present. Mem: Am, Hartford Co. and Conn. Bar Asns; Kiwanis (past pres, West Hartford Club); K. of C.(past grand Knight, West Hartford Chap). Rel: Roman Catholic. Mailing Add: 74 Mohawk Dr, West Hartford, Conn. 06117.

JACKSON, JESSE ERNEST D
Ala. State Sen.
b. Flomaton, Ala, 8/14/14; s. Ernest H. Jackson and Jessie White J; m. 1/11/36 to Pearl Jones (deceased); c. Robert H; m. 11/20/64 to Ruth Rigby; stepchildren, John M. Locklier, II and Judy Ann. Educ: High sch. and bus. col, 33-39. Polit. & Govt. Pos: City Councilman, Flomaton, Ala. 48-62; mem. adv. bd, State Indust. Cmt, 62-66; alternate del, Dem. Nat. Conv, 64; Ala. State Sen, 67- Bus. & Prof. Pos: Owner, Jackson's Ben Franklin Stores, 46-66; dir, Mercantile Life Ins. Co, 56-60; mem. adv. bd, Brewton Jr. Col, 64-66; trustee, Ala. Indust. Sch, 64- Mem: Farm Bur; C. of C.(dir. and pres, Tri City Chap, 63-66); Mason; Lions; Boy Scouts Coun; 4-H Club; pres, Indust. Develop. Bd, 66- Rel: Baptist. Legal Res: Highland Ave, Flomaton, Ala. 36441. Mailing Add: P.O. Box 614, Flomaton, Ala. 36441.

JACKSON, LEO ALBERT D
Councilman, Cleveland, Ohio
b. Lake City, Fla, 3/10/20; s. William Jackson and Hattie Howard J; m. 5/31/45 to Gilberta Jackson; c. Linda Adelle and Leonard Alan. Educ: Morehouse Col, A.B, 43; Atlanta Univ, M.A, 46; Cleveland-Marshall Law Sch, LL.D, 50; Kappa Alpha Psi. Polit. & Govt. Pos: Councilman, Ward 24, Cleveland, Ohio, 58-; mem, Cuyahoga Co. Dem. Exec. Cmt, 63-69; mem, policy cmt, Cuyahoga Co. Dem. Orgn, 67-69; mem, Electoral Col. from Ohio, 68; del, Dem. Nat. Conv, 68. Bus. & Prof. Pos: Attorney-at-law, Cleveland, Ohio, 50-69. Mil. Serv: Pvt, Army, 42-43, serv. at Ft. Benning, Ga. Publ: Wartime Adjustment of Labor Disputes Involving Negro Workers in the Railway Express Industry of the Southeast, 46. Mem: Cleveland and Cuyahoga Bar Asns; exec. bd. or bd. trustees, Cleveland Music Sch. Settlement, Forest City Hosp, Cleveland Legal Aid Soc; Cent. and Glenville YMCA, Glenville Neighborhood Center, Consumers League of Ohio, Commun. Housing Corp, Better Homes for Cleveland Found, Aim-Jobs and Cleveland Manpower Prog; Citizens League of Gr. Cleveland; Lions; Glenville Area Commun. Coun; NAACP; juvenile delinquency cmt. and legis cmt, Cleveland Welfare Fedn. Hon. life membership, PTA; Outstanding Leadership Plaque, Maj. John Fulton Post 3362, VFW, 61; radio documentary, 'Leo A. Jackson—The Making of a Councilman,' KYW Radio, 11/63; Testimonial Dinner and Plaque by Citizens of Gr. Cleveland, 11/22/63; Outstanding Leadership Plaque, Nat. Coun. of Negro Women, Cleveland, 67; Leadership Citation, Cleveland Diocesan Union of Holy Name Socs, 69; Cleveland Bus. League Award of Honor. Rel: Baptist. Mailing Add: 10315 Marlowe Ave, Cleveland, Ohio 44108.

JACKSON, LLOYD G. D
b. Clinton, Iowa, 9/14/26; s. Earl and Viola J; m. 7/31/48 to Ruth Blake; c. David, Carolyn, Jeffrey, James and Scott. Educ: State Univ. of Iowa, B.A, 50, J.D, 55; Phi Beta Kappa. Polit. & Govt. Pos: Mem, Co. Sch. Bd, Iowa, 56-58; asst. co. attorney, 59-60; Iowa State Rep, until 65; secy, State Exec. Coun, 65-67; dep. state ins. cmnr, 67- Bus. & Prof. Pos: Lawyer, Clinton, Iowa. Mil. Serv: Army, Germany, 45-46, Korea, 51-52. Mem: Bar Asns; YMCA (mem. bd. of dirs); Elks; Izaak Walton League. Outstanding Young Man Award, Jr. C. of C, 59; Clinton Man of the Year Award, 61. Rel: Congregational. Mailing Add: 1300 Pleasant Dr, West Des Moines, Iowa 50265.

JACKSON, LLOYD GEORGE D
Pres, W.Va. State Sen.
b. Yawkey, W.Va, 5/30/18; s. Guy H. Jackson and Ella Johnson J; m. 12/16/48 to Pauline Adkins; c. Suzanne and Lloyd G, II. Polit. & Govt. Pos: W.Va. State Sen, Seventh Dist, 46-, pres, W.Va. State Sen, 69-; alternate del, Dem. Nat. Conv, 68. Bus. & Prof. Pos: Drilling contractor, Jackson Drilling Co, 51-; construction contractor, L & R Construction Co, 62-; producer of natural gas, Orbit Producing Co, 65- Mil. Serv: Entered as Pvt, Army, 41, released as M/Sgt, 45, after serv. in 150th Inf. Reg, Carribean, 41-45. Mem: Mason; Shrine; Elks; Moose; Am. Legion; VFW. Rel: Methodist. Legal Res: Sycamore St, Hamlin, W.Va. 25523. Mailing Add: P.O. Box 498, Hamlin, W.Va. 25523.

JACKSON, M. MORRIS D
Ohio State Sen.
b. Georgia, 1920; married; c. two sons. Educ: Cleveland Col. Polit. & Govt. Pos: Ohio State Sen, 67- Bus. & Prof. Pos: Real estate broker. Mailing Add: 1717 E. 70th St, Cleveland, Ohio. 44103. (1967)

JACKSON, MARY HILLARD R
b. St. Paul, Minn, 10/13/18; d. Thomas Jones Hilliard and Marianna Talbott H; m. 7/4/38 to Donald Eldredge Jackson, Jr; c. D. Eldredge, III, Marianna Hilliard and Mary (Mrs. Holiday). Educ: Sarah Lawrence Col, 40. Polit. & Govt. Pos: Pres, Red Bridge Coun. Rep. Women, R.I, 53-55; finance chmn, R.I. Fedn. Rep. Women, 55-58; past mem. exec. cmt, Rep. State Cent. Cmt; Rep. Nat. Committeewoman, R.I, 60-69; del, Rep. Nat. Conv, 68. Rel: Episcopal. Mailing Add: 99 President Ave, Providence, R.I. 02906.

JACKSON, MATTHEW ERNEST D
Chmn, Carroll Co. Dem. Cent. Cmt, Ind.
b. Delphi, Ind, 9/27/21; s. Matthew Elliot Jackson and Elva Trittipo J; wid; c. Sandra L.(Mrs. Joe Schaffer), Alan D, Stephen D, David Scott and Marilyn J. Educ: Delphi High Sch, Ind, 4 years. Polit. & Govt. Pos: Chmn, Carroll Co. Dem. Cent. Cmt, Ind, 62- Mil. Serv: Entered as A/S, Navy, 44, released as Signalman 3/C PO, 46, after serv. in Armed Guard, ETO, 45; Good Conduct Medal. Mem: Am. Legion; 40 et 8; Flora Commun. Club (v.pres, 66-67). Rel: Baptist. Legal Res: 1½ S. Center, Flora, Ind. 46929. Mailing Add: Box 27, Flora, Ind. 46929.

JACKSON, MILDRED KATE C. R
b. Sevierville, Tenn, 4/23/38; d. Lee Anderson Cardwell and Lula Lamons C; m. to Ernest W. Jackson, Jr; c. Mark Wesley and Ernest Wesley III. Educ: Draughon's Business College, Knoxville, Tenn. Polit. & Govt. Pos: Exec. secy. to U.S. Rep. James H. Quillen, First Dist, Tenn, 63-68; secy. to U.S. Rep. James C. Cleveland, N.H, 69- Bus. & Prof. Pos: Secy, Cincinnati Cordage & Paper Co, 55-58; secy. to pres, Cherokee Textile Mills, 58-63. Mem: Cong. Secy. Club; Tenn. State Soc. Rel: Southern Baptist. Legal Res: Route 1, Seymour, Tenn. 37865. Mailing Add: 3405 Gallows Rd, Falls Church, Va. 22042.

JACKSON, MURRAY EARL D
Chmn, First Dist. Dem. Party, Mich.
b. Philadelphia, Pa, 12/21/26; s. Murray Jacob Jackson and Mabel Steele J; m. 8/16/52 to Dauris Gwendolyn Smart; c. Linda and Murray David. Educ: Adrian Col, 49; Wayne State Univ, B.A, 54, M.A, 59; Kappa Alpha Psi; Am. Commoners Club; Letterman's Club. Polit. & Govt. Pos: Chmn, Wayne State Univ. Chap, Dem. Acad. Resources Cmt, Mich, 66-69; chmn, first dist. Dem. Party, Mich, 67-; del, Dem. Nat. Conv, 68. Bus. & Prof. Pos: Group leader, Wayne Co. Youth Home, 51-55; acad. adv, Wayne State Univ, 55-64, exec. asst. to Dean Lib. Arts, 65-, asst. to v.pres. student affairs and asst. dean, student urban affairs, 69; coordinator, spec. projs, Univ. Mich, 64-65. Mil. Serv: Entered as Seaman, Navy, 45, released as Seaman 1/C, 46, after serving in Seabees. Publ: 'Helping to Educate the Disadvantaged,' Kappa Alpha Psi J, 5/65. Mem: Mich. Col. Asn; Jr. Commun. Col. President's Asn; Urban Alliance; Big Brothers-Big Sisters; Varsity Club; Draft Bd; NAACP; Higher Educ. Opportunities Cmt; Work Adjust. Prog; Tuberc. Health Soc; Detroit Bd. Educ. Citizens Adv. Cmt. on Finance; Neighborhood Serv. Orgn. Ted R. Owens award, Kappa Alpha Psi. Rel: Episcopal. Mailing Add: 19398 Stratford Rd, Detroit, Mich. 48221.

JACKSON, NYLE MERINGO R
Exec. Asst. to the Asst. Postmaster Gen.
b. Bradleyville, Mo, 3/27/14; s. James Richard Jackson and Emma Huntsman J; m. 9/4/38 to Ina Elaine Hutcheson. Educ: Westminster Col, B.A, 35; Southwest Mo. State Col, 35; Nat. Univ. Law Sch, 46. Polit. & Govt. Pos: Exec. secy. to U.S. Rep. Earl Wilson, Ind, 41-53; admin. asst. to U.S. Sen. William E. Jenner, Ind, 53-59; spec. staff mem, U.S. Sen. Homer E. Capehart, Ind, 59; legis. asst. to U.S. Sen. Thruston B. Morton, Ky, 59; exec. asst. to the Postmaster Gen, 59-61, asst. to the Exec. Asst. Postmaster Gen, 61-63, asst. dir, Customer Rels. Div, U.S. Post Off. Dept, 62-69, exec. asst. to the Asst. Postmaster Gen, Bur. of Opers, 69- Bus. & Prof. Pos: Advert. mgr, daily and weekly newspaper, Seymour, Ind, 38-41. Mil. Serv: Entered as Ens, Navy, 42, released as Lt.(sg), 46, after serv. in Armed Guard and Amphibious Forces, Am, European and Asiatic Theatres; Naval Res. Mem: Am. Legion; Senate Asst. Asn; VFW; Order of the Carabao; Orgn. of Cabinet Asst; Capitol Hill Club. Distinguished Serv. Award, 60 and Meritorious Serv. Award, 67 & 68, U.S. Post Off. Dept. Rel: Baptist. Legal Res: Seymour, Ind. 47274. Mailing Add: 4429 35th St. N.W, Washington, D.C. 20008.

JACKSON, RANDALL CALVIN D
b. Baird, Tex, 3/21/19; s. J. Rupert Jackson and Anna C. Faust J; m. to Betty Johnson; c. Randall C, Jr. Educ: Univ. of Tex, B.B.A, 42 and LL.B, 46. Polit. & Govt. Pos: Mem, 22nd Sen. Dist, Tex. State Dem. Exec. Cmt, 60-64; alternate del, Dem. Nat. Conv, 60 & 64; mem. bd. of regents, Tex. Woman's Univ, 61-66, chmn. bd, 65-66; mem, State Securities Bd, 66- Bus. & Prof. Pos: Mem. bd. dirs, First Nat. Bank, Baird, Tex, 52- and T.S. Lankford & Sons, 62-; gen. counsel, Bank of Commerce, Abilene, 65- Mil. Serv: Entered as Pvt, Army Air Force, 42, released as M/Sgt, 43, for cmn. at Harvard Statist. Control Sch, released as Capt, 46, after serv. in Statist. Control Unit Detachment, Guam; 5 Campaign Stars. Mem: Taylor Co, Tex. and Am. Bar Asns; Am. Col. of Probate Counsel; Southwest. Legal Found; charter mem, Tex. Bar Found; Southwest Cattle Raisers Asn; bd. dirs, Abilene Boys Ranch; exec. cmt, Boy Scouts; chmn. bldg. cmn, Sears Methodist Center; Mason (32°); Shrine; Headliners Club, Austin; Abilene Country Club; Petroleum Club. Rel: Methodist. Legal Res: 1406 Tanglewood, Abilene, Tex. 79605. Mailing Add: Bank of Commerce Bldg, Abilene, Tex. 79605.

JACKSON, ROSELLA MILDRED R
Treas, Alpine Co, Calif.
b. Clinton Co, Ohio, 9/10/16; d. Martin William Cole and Edith Meyers C; m. 6/30/48 to Robert Milton Jackson; c. Jeanette Ann (Mrs. Turnbeaugh), Judith K. and John Robert. Educ: Millers Col. of Bus, Cincinnati, Ohio, 2 years; Univ. Nev, exten. Polit. & Govt. Pos: Mem. and secy-treas, Alpine Co. Rep. Cent. Cmt, Calif, 6 years, chmn, 1 year; chief dep, co. clerk, auditor and recorder, Alpine Co, 9 years, treas, 68- Mem: Am. Red Cross (secy-treas, Alpine Co. Chap, 48-59, chmn, 59-); charter mem. Alpine Mother's Club (past pres). Rel: Protestant. Legal Res: Laramie St, Markleeville, Calif. 96120. Mailing Add: P.O. Box 236, Markleeville, Calif. 96120.

JACKSON, SAMUEL CHARLES R
Asst. Secy. for Metrop. Develop, Dept. of Housing and Urban Develop.
b. Kansas City, Kans, 5/8/29; s. James C. Jackson and Mattie Webber J; m. 1/27/52 to Judy Bradford; c. Marcia Lyn and Brenda Sue. Educ: Washburn Univ, A.B, 51, Law Sch, LL.B, 54; Sagamore; Kappa Alpha Psi; Arnold Air Soc; Press Club. Polit. & Govt. Pos: V.chmn, Kans. Collegiate Rep, 50-54; v.chmn, Kans. Young Rep, 57-59; precinct committeeman, Shawnee Co. Rep. Cmt, Kans, 60-63; mem, Shawnee Co. Rep. Exec. Cmt, 60-63; dep. gen. counsel, Kans. Dept. Soc. Welfare, 62-65; cmnr, Equal Employ. Opportunity Cmn, 65-68; asst. secy. for metrop. develop, Dept. of Housing and Urban Develop, 69- Bus. & Prof. Pos: Practicing attorney, Scott, Scott and Jackson, Topeka, Kans, 57-65; v.pres. and dir, Center for Dispute Settlement, Am. Arbitration Asn, 68-69. Mil. Serv: Capt, Air Force, 54-57, with serv. in Judge Adv. Dept, Eighth Strategic Air Command. Publ: 'EEOC vs. Discrimination, Inc,' Crisis Mag, 1/68; 'Using the Law to Attack Discrimination in Employment,' Washburn Law J, winter 69. Mem: Nat, Am, Fed. and Topeka Bar Asns; Nat. Conf. Black Lawyers; NAACP; Am. Legion; Nat. Lawyer's Club. Man of the Year, Topeka, 65; numerous honors and awards for civil rights activities. Rel: Protestant. Legal Res: 2603 Pinehurst Rd, Topeka, Kans. 66606. Mailing Add: 1855 Upshur St. N.W, Washington, D.C. 20011.

JACKSON, STEPHEN BERNARD D
Committeeman, Iowa State Dem. Cent. Cmt.
b. Cedar Rapids, Iowa, 7/9/36; s. Wilbur Elgar Jackson and Winnifred Driscoll J; m. 9/5/64 to Kay Lynn Bellows; c. Stephen Bernard, II and Andrea Lynn. Educ: Coe Col, B.A, 59; George Wash. Grad. Sch, 59; Univ. Iowa Law Sch, J.D, 64; Phi Kappa Tau. Polit. & Govt. Pos: Legis. asst. to Congressman Len Wolf, 59-60; precinct committeeman, Linn Co. Dem. Polit. Orgn, Iowa, 64-68; asst. co. attorney, Linn Co, 64-; del, Dem. Nat. Conv, 68; committeeman, Iowa State Dem. Cent. Cmt, 68- Mil. Serv: Entered as Pvt. E-2, Army, 59, released as Sgt. E-7, 65, after serving in Res. Mem: Linn Co. Bar Asn. (treas, 65-68); Iowa and Am. Bar Asns; Jaycees; Toastmasters. Iowa Polit. Internship, 58. Rel: Catholic. Mailing Add: 512 41st St, N.E, Cedar Rapids, Iowa 52402.

JACKSON, THOMAS EDWIN D
Mayor, Huntington Park, Calif.
b. Lumberton, N.C, 2/1/36; s. David Bryant Jackson and Ruth Marie Gregory J; m. 5/3/58 to Janice Marie Lanza; c. Thomas Edwin, II, Timothy John, Andrew David, Mary Jane and Sharon Marie. Educ: Our Lady of Hope Mission Sem, Newburgh, N.Y, A.A; Calif. State Col, Los Angeles, 1 year. Polit. & Govt. Pos: City councilman, Huntington Park, Calif, 68-69, mayor, 69- Bus. & Prof. Pos: Indust. salesman, Calif. Hardware Co, 56- Mem: Past pres, Huntington Park Jaycees. Nominated for Distinguished Serv. Award as Outstanding Young Man in Commun. Rel: Catholic. Mailing Add: 6910 Hood Ave, Huntington Park, Calif. 90255.

JACKSON, WALTER FRANK D
Ala. State Rep.
b. Wilsonville, Ala, 3/13/15; s. William Jones Jackson and Ida McEwen J; m. 7/5/40 to Mary Etta Brown; c. Judy Lee (Mrs. Scofield), Mary Frances (Mrs. Bryan) and Martha Sue. Educ: Shelby Co. High Sch, Columbiana, Ala, grad, 33. Polit. & Govt. Pos: Mem, Opp City Bd. of Educ, Ala, 51-52; mem, Opp City Coun, 52-60; Ala. State Rep, Dist. 40, 67- Bus. & Prof. Pos: Warehouse foreman-salesman, Int. Harvester Co, Birmingham, 37-45, dealer, Opp, 45-61; v.pres. and gen. mgr, Morgan Distributing Co, 61- Mem: Charter mem, Opp Lions Club (pres, 49-50); Mason (Worshipful Master, Opp Lodge, 49-51); C. of C.(pres, Opp Br, 50-51 & 62-63); McArthur Trade Sch. Cmt. Outstanding Young Man of Year, Opp Lions Club, 50. Rel: Baptist; Deacon and past supt, Sunday sch, First Baptist Church. Legal Res: Forest Park, Opp, Ala. 36467. Mailing Add: P.O. Box 209, Opp, Ala. 36467.

JACOB, J. LAIRD, JR. D
b. Morganton, N.C, 1/31/40; s. John Laird Jacob, Sr. and Jeanne Verreault J; m. 8/14/65 to Sarah Wilson; c. John Laird, III. Educ: Wake Forest Col, B.B.A, 62, Law Sch, LL.B, 65; Pi Kappa Alpha; Alpha Kappa Psi; Phi Delta Phi. Polit. & Govt. Pos: Pres, Burke Co. Young Dem, N.C, 67-; alternate del, Dem. Nat. Conv, 68. Mem: N.C. and Burke Co. Bar Asns; N.C. State Bar; Jaycees. Rel: Presbyterian. Legal Res: 409 Mountain View Ave, Valdese, N.C. 28690. Mailing Add: P.O. Box 8, Valdese, N.C. 28690.

JACOBETTI, DOMINIC J. D
Mich. State Rep.
b. Negaunee, Mich, 7/20/20; m. 1942 to Marie D. Burnettee; c. Judith K, Colin K, Dominic J, Jr. Educ: High Sch. Grad. Polit. & Govt. Pos: Mich. State Rep, 54- Bus. & Prof. Pos: Rep, United Steelworkers of Am. Mem: Moose; Eagles; K. of C; Elks; Rod and Gun Club; Young Dem. Club; Druids; North. Mich. Athletic Club; Marquette Co. Hist. Soc; Lions Club. Presented Distinguished Serv. Award by Mich. Practical Nurses Asn, 4/6/61. Rel: Catholic. Mailing Add: 1017 Owaissa, Negaunee, Mich. 49866. (1967)

JACOBS, ANDREW, JR. D
U.S. Rep, Ind.
b. Indianapolis, Ind, 2/24/32; s. Andrew Jacobs, Sr. and Joyce Wellborn J; single. Educ: Ind. Univ, B.S, 55, LL.B, 58; Phi Alpha Delta. Polit. & Govt. Pos: Safety dir, Marion Co. Sheriff's Dept, Ind, 55-56; Ind. State Rep, 59-61; U.S. Rep, Ind, 65-; del, Dem. Nat. Conv, 68. Bus. & Prof. Pos: Lawyer, Jacobs & Jacobs, 58- Mil. Serv: Entered as Pvt, Marines, 50, released 52, after serv. in First Marine Div, Korea, 51. Publ: 'The Jury System,' Am. Co. Govt, 3/66. Mem: Am. Legion. Rel: Catholic; Parishioner of S.S. Peter and Paul Cathedral. Legal Res: 3630 Watson Rd, Indianapolis, Ind. 46205. Mailing Add: 1029 Longworth Office Bldg, Washington, D.C. 20515.

JACOBS, EARL BRYAN R
b. Waynesburg, Pa, 10/2/08; s. Joseph Warren Jacobs and Emma Dulany J; m. 6/18/34 to Blanche Louise Widdup. Polit. & Govt. Pos: Chmn, Greene Co. Rep. Cmt, Pa, 62-67; cmnr, Greene Co, 64- Bus. & Prof. Pos: Owner-mgr, Jacobs Oil Prod, 36-; past v.chmn, Greene Co. Soil & Water Conserv. Dist. and Wheeling Creek Watershed. Mem: Pa. Petroleum and Fuels Asn.(past dir); past dir, Green Co. Mem. Hosp; chmn, Green Co. Chap, Am. Red Cross; chmn, Greene Co. U.S. Savings Bonds Cmt; Pa. Motor Truck Asn; Pittsburgh Petroleum Club; State Coun. of Civil Defense; F&AM (Past Master, Waynesburg Lodge 153); Elks (Past Exalted Ruler, Waynesburg Lodge 757); Scottish

Rite; AAONMS; SAR (pres, Ft. Jackson Chap, currently); Boy Scouts (chmn, Greene Dist, Allegheny Trails Coun). Mailing Add: 424 S. Washington St, Waynesburg, Pa. 15370.

JACOBS, FRANCIS R
Kans. State Rep.
b. Phillipsburg, Kans, 4/20/96; s. Thomas Marida Jacobs and Bertha Cathrine Snay J; m. 12/26/17 to Zora Laughery; c. Lorraine (Mrs. Lesh, wid) and Lois (Mrs. Dale Rogers). Educ: Phillipsburg High Sch, Kans, grad. Polit. & Govt. Pos: Mem, City Coun, Kans, 4 years; mayor, Phillipsburg, 6 years; mem, Bd. of Educ, 12 years; Kans. State Rep, Dist. 113, 48-; mem. and chmn, Kans. Turnpike Authority, 3 years; mem, Kans. Legis. Coun, 8 years; chmn, Kans. Reciprocity Cmn, 2 years and State C. of C. Hwy. Coun, 4 years. Mem: Mason; Odd Fellows; Elks; Farm Bur; Lions; pres, Phillipsburg Rodeo Asn. Rel: Methodist; mem. Church Bd. Mailing Add: 575 F St, Phillipsburg, Kans. 67661.

JACOBS, HARRY MICHAEL D
Mem, Calif. Dem. State Cent. Cmt.
b. Bridgeport, Conn, 9/15/41; s. Robert Bernard Jacobs and Lillian Roselyn Spaner J; m. 8/14/66 to Susan Ann Berlin. Educ: Los Angeles City Col, A.A, 62; Los Angeles State Col, B.A, 64; Calif. State Col, Los Angeles, M.A. in Govt, 67; Alpha Phi Omega; Zeta Beta Tau; B'nai B'rith Hillel Found. Polit. & Govt. Pos: Notary pub, 63-; dep. registrar of voters, Los Angeles Co, Calif, 67-; mem, Calif. Dem. State Cent. Cmt, 68- Bus. & Prof. Pos: High sch. teacher, Los Angeles City Sch. Dist, 65-67; coordinator student activities, Calif. State Col, Los Angeles, 67-68, financial aids counsr, 68-69; admin. asst, Int. Prog. Div, Off. of the Chancellor, Calif. State Cols, San Francisco Br, 69- Mem: Am. Acad. Polit. and Soc. Sci; West. Asn. Student Financial Aid Adminstrs; Boy Scouts; Alhambra Dem. Club; Beverly Hills Young Dem; Calif. Notary Asn. Rel: Jewish. Mailing Add: 1600 Holloway Ave, San Francisco, Calif. 94132.

JACOBS, WILLIAM CLYDE R
b. Olympia, Wash, 6/17/28; s. William Clyde Jacobs, Sr. and Sadie Cales J; m. 11/15/57 to Patricia Elaine Rongey; c. William Cole (Chip) and Lisabeth Anne (Libby). Educ: St. Martins Col, 3 years. Polit. & Govt. Pos: Campaign chmn, various legis. and cong. cand, 56-66; chmn, Thurston Co. Rep. Cent. Cmt, Wash, 64-66; del, Wash. State Rep. Conv, 64, 66 & 68; spec. asst. to Gov. Daniel J. Evans, Wash, 67-69; alternate del, Rep. Nat. Conv, 68; dir, Dept. Labor & Indust, Wash, D.C, 69- Bus. & Prof. Pos: Acct. trainee, Puget Sound Power & Light Co, 52-54; admin. officer, Sunset Life Ins. Co. of Am, Olympia, Wash, 54-65; pub. rels. dir, Asn. Wash. Industs, 65-67. Mil. Serv: Entered as Pvt, Army, 50, released as Sgt, 52, after serving in 7th Inf. Div, Far E. Theatre, Korea, 52; Bronze Star Medal. Mem: Wash. Asn. of Young Men's Bus. Clubs; Elks; Kiwanis; C. of C; Olympia Fine Arts Guild; Olympia Golf & Country Club. Distinguished serv. award, Jr. C. of C, 64. Rel: Baptist. Mailing Add: 2626 Hillside Dr, Olympia, Wash. 98501.

JACOBSEN, ERNIE R.
Minn. State Rep.
b. Denmark, 9/2/05; Married; c. Four. Educ: Denmark. Polit. & Govt. Pos: Minn. State Rep, 2 terms. Bus. & Prof. Pos: Retail businessman. Mem: Lions (past pres); Masons; Shrine. Rel: Lutheran; past pres, Lutheran Brotherhood, Wooddale Church. Mailing Add: 3410 Aquila Lane, St. Louis Park, Minn. 55426.

JACOBSEN, GLENN EUGENE D
b. Phoenix, Ariz, 1/22/28; s. Paul Jacobsen and Anne Pedersen J; (deceased); m. 9/16/51 to Bernice Lorraine Brenteson; c. Bruce Lind, Diane Rae, Brian Paul and Glenn Arne. Polit. & Govt. Pos: Committeeman, Sheridan Co. Dem. Cent. Cmt, Mont, 59-, chmn, 64-68. Bus. & Prof. Pos: V.chmn, Commun. Oil Co, 64- Mil. Serv: Entered as Pvt, Air Force, 46, released as Pfc, 49, after serv. in 11th and 82nd Airborne Divs, Japan and Pac. Areas, 46-48; Occup. and World War II Victory Medals. Mem: Past. mem. adv. cmt, Eastern Mont. Br. Exp. Sta, Sidney, Mont, adv. cmt. agron, Mont. State Univ, Bozeman, Mont. and adv. cmt, Cereal Quality Lab; dir. and past secy, Mont. Grain Growers Asn; dir. and past pres, Sheridan Co. Grain Growers Asn; Mont. Farmers Union; dist. supvr. and past chmn, Sheridan Co. Soil & Water Conserv; dir, Sheridan Co. Planning & Improv. Coun; VFW; Century Invest. Club; Plentywood Recreational Cmt; past secy-treas, Coalridge Flying Club. Rel: Lutheran. Mailing Add: Reserve, Mont. 59258. (1967)

JACOBSON, ALF EDGAR R
N.H. State Sen.
b. Spokane, Wash, 4/4/24; s. Carl Magnus Jacobsson and Emmy Bjoresson J; m. 12/8/51 to Sonja Ruth Torstenson; c. Kurt Torsten and Brent Burgess. Educ: Northwest. Univ, B.S, 52; Tufts Univ, M.A, 54; Harvard Univ, S.T.B, 54, S.T.M, 55, Ph.D, 63. Polit. & Govt. Pos: Libr. trustee, New London, N.H, 60-63, mem. planning bd, 65-, chmn, 67-69; moderator, Kearsarge Regional Sch. Dist, 68-; N.H. State Sen, Seventh Dist, 69-, Asst. Majority Leader. Bus. & Prof. Pos: Prof, Colby Col. Women, 58- Mil. Serv: Entered as Pvt, Marine Corps, 43, released as Sgt, 46, after serv. in Joint Intel. Center, Pac. Ocean Area and 2nd Bn, 27th Marines, Pac. and Occupation Force Japan, 44-46. Mem: Bibliog. Soc. Am; Am. Econ. Asn; Am. Soc. of Church Hist; Am. Philatelic Soc; Manuscript Soc; Swedish Pioneer Hist. Soc; Rotary. Brewer Prize, Am. Soc. Church Hist. Rel: Swedish Congregational. Legal Res: Burpee Hill Rd, New London, N.H. 03257. Mailing Add: Box 188, New London, N.H. 03257.

JACOBSON, HOWARD O. D
Chmn, Clay Co. City Coun, Minn.
b. Moorhead, Minn, 10/14/34; s. Henry Jacobson and Matilda Anderson J; m. 6/11/58 to Anne J. Jesten; c. Tracy. Educ: Moorhead State Col, Minn, M.Sc. Polit. & Govt. Pos: Chmn, Clay Co. City Coun, Minn, currently; mem, City Coun, Moorhead, Minn, 62- Bus. & Prof. Pos: Alumni pres, Moorhead State Col, 65-66. Mil. Serv: Entered as Pvt, Army, 58, released as E-4, 60. Mem: Elks; Bd. Dir, Jr. C. of C; Am. Legion. Rel: Lutheran. Mailing Add: 223 N. 12th, Moorhead, Minn. 56560. (1967)

JACOBSON, IRVEN JULIAN D
V.Chmn, West Dist. Dem. Party, N.Dak.
b. Corinth, N.Dak, 6/29/20; s. Andrew James Jacobson and Karen Sateren J; m. 7/18/43 to Carol Leone Wilson; c. Karen (Mrs. Dale Lucas), Irven Julian, Jr, Marjorie (Mrs. Paul McPhail), Jeanine, Marilyn, Laurie and Luann. Educ: Williston High Sch, N.Dak. Polit. & Govt. Pos: Dem. precinct committeeman, 40th Legis. Dist, N.Dak, 56-66; state cent. committeeman, Divide Co. Dem. Party, 64-66; chmn, Redlin for Cong. Club, West Dist, 64 & 66; chmn, Dist. Two Dem. Party, 66, 67 & 68; v.chmn, West Dist. Dem. Party, 67-; mem. bd. dirs, N.Dak. Century Club, 69-; mem, N.Dak. Non-Partisan League State Exec. Cmt, currently. Mem: Crosby Country Club; Moose; Farmers' Union. Rel: Lutheran. Mailing Add: Corinth, N.Dak. 58841.

JACOBSON, ROBERT LEE R
Chmn, Oldham Co. Rep. Party, Tex.
b. Amarillo, Tex, 3/31/32; s. Norman Lee Jacobson and Hattie Edith Moore J; m. 12/1/56 to Priscilla Baumgardner; c. Paul Randall, Jo Ellen, Diana Leigh and Janet Carrol. Educ: Tex. Tech. Col, B.S, 54; Alpha Phi Omega. Polit. & Govt. Pos: Chmn, Oldham Co. Rep. Party, Tex, 62-69. Bus. & Prof. Pos: Farmer and Rancher, 57-69. Mil. Serv: Entered as 2nd Lt, Air Force, 54, released as 1st Lt, 56, after serving in Aviation Eng. Force, Tex; Capt, Air Force Res, 56-69. Mem: Tex. Farm Bur; scoutmaster and cubmaster, Boy Scouts. Rel: Methodist. Mailing Add: P.O. Box 5, Adrian, Tex. 79001.

JACOBSON, THOMAS MICHAEL D
Chmn, Fifth Cong. Dist. Dem. Party, Wis.
b. Bomberg, Germany, 5/8/38; s. Eric Jacobson and Greta Simon J; single. Educ: Univ. Wis-Milwaukee, 55-58; Univ. Wis-Madison, B.A, 59, LL.B, 62. Polit. & Govt. Pos: Mem, Platform Cmt, Milwaukee Co. Dem. Party, Wis, 65-66, parliamentarian, 67; del, Milwaukee Co. Coun. Dem. Party, 65-66; v.chmn, Third Ward Dem. Unit, Milwaukee Co, 67; spec. asst. Attorney Gen. on Consumer Affairs to Attorney Gen. Bronson C. La Follette in Milwaukee Cent. City Area, 67-68; chmn, Fifth Cong. Dist. Dem. Party, 67-; del, Dem. Nat. Conv, 68. Bus. & Prof. Pos: Private practice of law, Milwaukee, 62- Mem: Wis. State and Milwaukee Sr. Bar Asns; Milwaukee Jr. Bar Asn.(chmn, Human Rights and Constitutional Law Cmt, 66-67, secy, 68); pres, Univ. Wis-Madison Student Civil Rights, 61; NAACP (organized sit-in at Capitol of Madison to achieve fair housing legis, 61, state legal redress chmn, 63 & 66-67, state polit. action chmn, 64-65, Milwaukee polit. chmn, 65-66, gen. counsel, Milwaukee Youth Coun, 66-67); Am. for Dem. Action (organized and first pres, Univ. Wis-Madison, 62, organized and first chmn, Milwaukee Chap, 64-65, organized and first chmn, State Chap, 65); Univ. Wis-Madison student rep. on Mayor's Cmn. for Human Rights, 62; gen. counsel, Milwaukee CORE, 63-64; action coordinator, Milwaukee Sch. Boycott, Milwaukee United Sch. Integration Cmt, 64, gen. counsel, 65-66; B'nai B'rith (3rd v.pres, Gillead Lodge, 65, 1st v.pres, 66-67); bd. dirs, United Migratory Serv. Inc, 67. Rel: Jewish. Legal Res: 1505 N. Franklin Place, Milwaukee, Wis. 53202. Mailing Add: 110 E. Wisconsin Ave. 1010, Milwaukee, Wis. 53202.

JACOBY, WILLIAM ROY R
b. Schleicher Co, Tex, 7/9/27; s. Thomas John Jacoby and Letha Ann Menzies J; m. 6/16/50 to Martha Ann Bannowsky; c. Jane, Jamie, Nancy and Letha. Polit. & Govt. Pos: Chmn, Menard Co. Rep. Party, Tex. until 67. Bus. & Prof. Pos: Pres, Menard Independent Sch. Dist, 60-61. Mil. Serv: Entered as A/S, Navy, 45, released as Seaman 2/C, 46. Mem: Menard Rotary (pres, 59-60); Menard C. of C.(pres, 61-62); Sheep & Goat Raisers Asn. Rel: Church of Christ. Mailing Add: Gen. Delivery, Menard, Tex. 76859.

JACQUART, BEATRICE LENORA. See WILLIAMS, BEATRICE JACQUART.

JACQUES, NORMAN JOSEPH D
b. Pawtucket, R.I, 8/31/43; s. Dominique Jacques and Gilverte Guilbeault J; single. Educ: Emerson Col; Portia Law Sch, currently. Polit. & Govt. Pos: Student-intern to U.S. Sen. Claiborne Pell, 61, Dept. of Labor, 62, and Anthony J. Celebrezze, Secy. of Health, Educ. and Welfare, 63; student-mem, President Kennedy's White House Seminar Prog, 62-63; R.I. State Rep, 64-66; R.I. State Sen, 67-68; Dem. primary cand, U.S. Rep, First Dist, R.I, 68. Bus. & Prof. Pos: Dir. housing develop. corps, Urban America, Inc, 69- Elected Boy of the Year, St. Jean's Cath. Youth Coun, 61; First Bronze Medal for Citizenship, Sacred Heart Acad, 61. Legal Res: Pawtucket, R.I. Mailing Add: Urban America Inc, 1717 Massachusetts Ave. N.W, Washington, D.C. 20036.

JACQUIN, WILLIAM C. R
Ariz. State Sen.
b. Peoria, Ill, 9/1/35; s. W.C. Jacquin and Kathryn Niehaus J; m. 8/21/59 to Deborah Young; c. Susan, Gregg and Lisa. Educ: Wabash Col, A.B, 57; Univ. Ariz. Law Sch; Sphinx Club; Beta Theta Pi. Polit. & Govt. Pos: Chmn, Ariz. State Young Rep. Conv, 62; del, Rep. Nat. Conv, 64; Ariz. State Rep, Pima Co, Dist. Ten, 65 & 66; mem, Ariz. Rep. Legis. Campaign Cmt, 65-, v.chmn, currently; Ariz. State Sen, Pima Co, Dist. Seven-F, 67-, Majority Whip, Ariz. State Senate, 67 & 68, Majority Leader, 69-; precinct committeeman, state committeeman; past v.pres, Pima Co. Young Rep. League; past secy, Pima Co. Rep. Club. Bus. & Prof. Pos: Retail mgr, Jacquin & Co, Peoria, Ill, 57-58; ins. salesman, Conn. Mutual Life, Peoria, Ill. and Tucson, Ariz, 59-61, Aetna Life & Casualty, Tucson, 62 and Tucson Realty & Trust Co, 62- Mem: South. Ariz. Estate Planning Coun; South. Ariz. Life Underwriters Asn; El Con Club; Tucson Press Club; YMCA (bd. dirs. and coach swimming team, Lighthouse Br); Tucson Commun. Coun.(children's code cmt); United Commun. Campaign (vol). Rel: Presbyterian. Legal Res: 5202 E. Alhambra Place, Tucson, Ariz. 85711. Mailing Add: Capitol Bldg, Senate Wing, Phoenix, Ariz. 85007.

JAHNKE, FRANKLIN M. R
b. Marquette, Wis, 4/20/00. Educ: Green Lake Co. Pub. Schs. Polit. & Govt. Pos: Chmn, Green Lake Co. Bd, 44-65; town chmn, Marquette, Wis, 33-65, pres, Wis. Asn. Soil Conserv. Dist. Supvr, 54-56; Wis. State Assemblyman, 56-68; pres, Wis. Co. Bds. Asn, 63-65. Bus. & Prof. Pos: Farmer; owner Dairy and Hog Farms. Mem: Kiwanis Club; State Banking Rev. Bd; Coop. Educ. Agency Study Cmt; Dist. Comprehensive Ment. Health Cmt, 64-65; former pres. and dir, Coop. Asn. Mailing Add: Route 3, Markesan, Wis. 53946. (1967)

JALBERT, LOUIS D
Maine State Rep.
b. Lewiston, Maine, 5/7/12; s. Arthur J. Jalbert and Celina Simard J; m.

7/30/38 to Yvonne Sproul. Educ: Portland Jr. Col, B.A, 51; Portland Law Univ, $1\frac{1}{2}$ years. Polit. & Govt. Pos: Finance agent, Dem. Party, 44; Maine State Rep, 45-, Dem. leader, Maine House of Rep, 47-49; ranking mem, Legis. Research Cmt, 14 years, chmn, 65-67, mem, currently; del, Dem. Nat. Conv, 68. Mailing Add: 83 Elm St, Lewiston, Maine 04240.

JAMBOR, LOUISE IRMA R
Chmn, Ford Co. Rep. Cent. Cmt, Kans.
b. San Francisco, Calif; d. Jean Louis Hintermann and Fannie Schlesinger H; m. 4/13/47 to James John Jambor; c. Christopher Noel, Ann and Jonathan Jean. Educ: San Francisco Jr. Col, 2 years. Polit. & Govt. Pos: Pres, Ford Co. Rep. Women's Club, 64; precinct committeewoman, Dodge City, Kans, 64; treas, First Dist. Rep. Women's Clubs, 66; chmn, Ford Co. Rep. Cent. Cmt, 66-; bd. mem, Rep. Assocs, West. Kans, 66-69; v.chmn, First Cong. Dist, 68; alternate del-at-lg, Rep. Nat. Conv, 68. Bus. & Prof. Pos: Bd. Dirs, Dodge City Commun. Concert Asn, 68-70. Mem: PEO; pres, Ford Co. Med. Auxiliary, 64; Trinity Hosp. Auxiliary; St. Anthony Hosp. Auxiliary; Ford Co. Hist. Soc; Ford Co. Ment. Health Asn; Young Rep. Club Ford Co; pres, Cent. Sch, PTA, Dodge City, 64; pres, Am. Field Serv, Kans, 68-; bd. dirs, Dodge City Commun. Concert Asn. Commun. Leader Award, 69. Rel: Episcopal. Mailing Add: 1707 Ave. A, Dodge City, Kans, 67801.

JAMES, BOBBIE McFEE R
Historian, Fla. Rep. Exec. Cmt.
b. Jacksonville, Fla, 1/19/33; d. John Robert McFee and Ena Maxine Gissendanner M; m. 11/24/51 to William Godfrey James; c. Amy Michele, Mark William and George Andrew. Educ: Palm Beach Jr. Col, 2 years; Fla. State Univ, 1 year; Alpha Omicron Pi. Polit. & Govt. Pos: Secy, Goldwater for Pres, Palm Beach Co, Fla, 64; v.pres, Women's Rep. Club of Delray Beach, 65, pres, 66 & 68; campaign dir, William G. James for State Rep. Exec. Cmt, 66 and William G. James for Fla. House Rep, 67 & 68; area coordinator, Rep. Campaign Coord. Cmt, 67-69; historian, Fla. Rep. Exec. Cmt, 67-; del, Rep. Nat. Conv, 68; del, Fla. Fedn. Rep. Women Conv, 69. Mem: Eastern Star; Palm Beach Co. Alpha Omicron Pi Alumni Chap. Rel: Presbyterian. Mailing Add: 136 Coconut Rd, Delray Beach, Fla. 33444.

JAMES, DAVID FARNHAM D
Mont. State Sen.
b. Thornton, Iowa, 12/6/05; s. John L. James and Martha Farnham J; m. 1/5/29 to Lillian Meldrum; c. Lysle Allen, Angela Dawn (Mrs. Eldridge), Doris Helen (Mrs. Nelson) and Dorathy Mae (Mrs. Keough). Educ: Mason City Jr. Col, Iowa, 23-25; Iowa State Teachers Col, 25-26; Mont. State Univ. at Missoula, 27. Polit. & Govt. Pos: Mont. State Rep, 39-49, Minority Leader, Mont. House of Rep, 45-47; Mont. State Sen, Liberty Co, 49-65 and Dist. 19, 67-, Majority Leader, Mont. State Sen, 57 and 59, pres. of Sen, 63. Mem: Mason; Elks; Farmers Union. Rel: Lutheran. Mailing Add: Joplin, Mont. 59531.

JAMES, EARL DANIEL
Mayor, Montgomery, Ala.
b. Florala, Ala, 8/10/14; s. Walter Home James and Atha Daniel J; m. to Dorothy Goggans; c. Walter Thomas and Kathleen Sue. Educ: Ala. Polytech. Inst, B.S. Polit. & Govt. Pos: Former assoc. city comnr, Montgomery, Ala, mayor, currently. Bus. & Prof. Pos: Former teacher, athletic instr. and athletic dir, Pub. Schs, Montgomery. Mil. Serv: Army Air Force, World War II. Mem: Phi Delta Kappa; Optimist. Rel: Methodist. Legal Res: 26 Oak Forest Dr, Montgomery, Ala. 36109. Mailing Add: Office of the Mayor, Montgomery, Ala. 36604.

JAMES, EDWARD 'DOC' D
b. Memphis, Tenn, 12/8/21; s. Randle Ben James and Eddie Clower J; m. 12/4/65 to Violet Hower; c. Edward James, Jr, 'Doc.' Educ: West. Mich. Teachers Col. Polit. & Govt. Pos: Secy, Lake Co. Dem. Cent. Cmt, Ind, 48-52; alternate del, Dem. Nat. Conv, 48-68; probation officer, Lake Co. Juvenile Court, 50-54; v.chmn, Dem. Precinct Cmt, 51-56; Dem. cand, U.S. Rep. Ind, Lake Co, 56; supt. sanit. Bus. & Prof. Pos: Owner, grocery store, fish mkt. and bleach mfg. co; owner and salesman, ins. co; owner and ed, newspaper. Mil. Serv: Entered as Seaman, Navy, 42, released as Seaman 1/C, after serv. in Great Lakes, 42-45. Mem: Negro Bus. Asn.(pres, 46); Ol' Timers Club (pres); VFW; Am. Legion; NAACP. Rel: Methodist. Mailing Add: 3150 W. 19th Place, Gary, Ind. 46404.

JAMES, HENRY PARKER D
b. Brent, Ala, 3/10/02; s. John Eldridge James and Amanda Ward J; m. 1/3/34 to Neva LeVert. Educ: Bibb Co. High Sch; Univ. of Ala.(Summer Sch). Polit. & Govt. Pos: Ala. State Sen, 54-66. Bus. & Prof. Pos: Farmer; cattleman. Rel: Bethel Baptist Church, Brent, Ala. Mailing Add: Brent, Ala. 35034.

JAMES, ISABEL BRENNER R
b. Butte, Mont, 9/1/21; d. Charles P. Brenner and Beth Yearian B; m. 5/27/44 to Robert Herschel James; c. William Charles, Robert Alexander, Catherine Anthony and Julie Isabel. Educ: Col. of William & Mary, 38-39; Univ. of Mont, B.A, 42; Kappa Kappa Gamma. Polit. & Govt. Pos: Mem. bd. trustees, Sch. Dist. Seven, Mont, 48-, chmn, 51-61; mem, Gov. Cmn. Status of Women, 65-66; Mont. State Rep, Beaverhead Co, until 68. Bus. & Prof. Pos: Partner, Horse Prairie Livestock, 54- Mil. Serv: Entered as A/S, WAVES, 43, released as Ens, 44, after serv. in Commun, 13th Naval Dist. Hq. Mem: Mont. Stockgrowers; Farm Bur; Mont. Cow Belles (pres, Beaverhead Cow Belles, 62-64). Rel: Episcopal. Mailing Add: Grant, Mont. 59734. (1967)

JAMES, L. ELDON D
Chmn, Hampton Dem. Town Exec. Cmt, Va.
b. Dendron, Va, 1/1/13; s. Leonard Wallace James and Lillian Noyes J; m. 2/17/39 to Aurelia Mitchell; c. Nancy J.(Mrs. Buhl), Quinby J.(Mrs. Amory), Sally L. and L. Eldon, Jr; four grandchildren. Educ: Col. William & Mary, B.S, 34, Law Sch, 34-35; George Wash. Univ. Law Sch, J.D, 37; George Wythe Law Club; Sigma Phi Epsilon. Polit. & Govt. Pos: Mem, Va. State Bar Coun, 61-67; mem, U.S. Vet. Adv. Cmn, 67-68; U.S. observer, S.Vietnam Elec, 67; chmn, Hampton Dem. Town Exec. Cmt, Va, 67-; del, Dem. Nat. Conv, 68; nat. chmn, Vet. for Humphrey-Muskie, 68. Mil. Serv: Entered as Lt.(jg), Naval Res, 44, released as Lt, 46, after serv. in Assignments in Wash, D.C. and Portsmouth, N.H. Publ: Articles in Nat. Educ. Asn. J; Am. Legion Mag. and Parade. Mem: Am. and Va. State Bar Asn; Hampton Bar Asn.(pres, 68); Am. and Va. Trial Lawyers Asn; Am. Legion (nat. comdr, 65-66); Lions Int. Distinguished Alumni Award, George Wash. Univ; Distinguished Citizen Award, City of Hampton; Distinguished Serv. Award, Col. William & Mary; Honor Cert. Award, Freedoms Found; Two Citations, President U.S; Nat. Police Officers Asn. Pub. Serv. Award; Distinguished Alumni Award, Sigma Phi Epsilon. Rel: Baptist. Legal Res: 9 Terrace Rd, Hampton, Va. 23361. Mailing Add: P.O. Box 38, Hampton, Va. 23369.

JAMES, LOUIS EARL R
b. Santa Monica, Calif, 6/11/23; s. Louis Archibold James and Margaret Wickel J; m. 4/11/46 to Lida Faye 'Pat'; c. Louis Earl, II, Michael Bruce, Leslie Faye and Judy Lynn. Educ: Los Angeles Col. of Optom, B.S, 48, O.D, 49. Polit. & Govt. Pos: Mil. adv, Calif. State Selective Serv, 67-69; mem, Calif. Rep. State Cent. Cmt, 68-69; campaign chmn, Nixon, Reagan and Keichel, Mar Vista-Los Angeles, Calif; mem, Los Angeles Mayor's Adv. Cmt; mem. adv. cmt, 11th coun. dist, Los Angeles. Bus. & Prof. Pos: Optometrist; dir, Fidelity Bank, Beverly Hills, Calif, currently. Mil. Serv: Entered as Air Cadet, Navy, 42, released as Lt. Comdr, 68, after serv. in Naval Air Corps; Lt. Comdr, Naval Res; Am. Theatre Ribbon; World War II Victory Medal; Naval Res. Medal. Mem: Am. Optom. Asn.(mil. affairs cmt); Calif. Optom. Asn.(chmn. mil. affairs cmt); Los Angeles Co. Optom. Soc; Navy League of U.S.(nat. dir); chmn, 11th Region Navy League Ball; C. of C; Mar Vista Optimist Club; Am. Legion. Rel: Latter-day Saint. Legal Res: 5605 Chariton Ave, Los Angeles, Calif. 90056. Mailing Add: 12577 Venice Blvd, Los Angeles, Calif. 90066.

JAMES, RONALD R. R
Mayor, San Jose, Calif.
b. San Jose, Calif, 6/11/28; s. W. Ray James and Mina Pelton J; m. 8/3/47 to Laurel L. Schuetz; c. Laurie L, Cynthia R, Charles W, Alexander D. and William R. Educ: Stanford Univ; Phi Delta Theta. Polit. & Govt. Pos: Planning cmnr, San Jose, Calif, 62-65, chmn. planning cmn, 64-65, v.mayor, 65-66, mayor, 66-; dir, League of Calif. Cities, 66- Bus. & Prof. Pos: V.pres. and mgr, James Transfer & Storage Co, 51-; v.pres, Orth Van & Storage Co, Pasadena, Calif. and James & Neal Moving & Storage Co, Sunnyvale, Calif. Mil. Serv: Entered as Lt, Air Force, 52, released as Capt, 60. Mem: Nat. Furniture Warehouseman's Asn.(dir, 65-); Rotary. Rel: Protestant. Legal Res: 1225 Koch Lane, San Jose, Calif. 95125. Mailing Add: Office of the Mayor, San Jose, Calif. 95110. (1967)

JAMES, TROY LEE D
Ohio State Rep.
b. Texarkana, Tex; s. Samuel W. James and Anniebell J; m. to Betty Jean Winslow; c. Laura M. Educ: Bethany Col, W.Va, degree, Bldg. Legis; West. Reserve Univ, $2\frac{1}{2}$ years; Fenn Col, $1\frac{1}{2}$ years. Polit. & Govt. Pos: Precinct committeeman, Ward 11 Dem. Orgn, 8 years and pres, 7 years; Ohio State Rep, 46th Dist, 67- Bus. & Prof. Pos: Businessman, self-employed, 17 years; employee, Ohio Crankshaft, 12 years. Mil. Serv: Serv. in World War II and Korean War. Mem: 11th Ward Dem. Club (pres); 40th and 43rd St. Neighborhood Block Club (pres); Ohio Soc. State Legis; Dem. Exec. Coun; Mayor's Cmt. Housing; Phyllis Wheatly Asn; chmn, March of Dimes Drive; mem. bd, Eliza Bryant Home for the Aged; NAACP; Boy Scouts; YMCA (mem. cent. area coun); VFW; Prince Hall Lodge. Rel: Baptist. Mailing Add: 4216 Cedar Ave, Cleveland, Ohio 44103.

JAMES, VERDA I. R
Speaker, Wyo. State House of Rep.
b. Stratford, Ont, Can; d. William Henry James and Sara Ann Nice J; single. Educ: Univ. Iowa, B.A; Univ. Denver, M.A; Mortar Bd; Delta Zeta. Polit. & Govt. Pos: Dep. state supt. of schs, Wyo, 40-50; Wyo. State Rep, 53-, Speaker, Wyo. State House of Rep, 69- Bus. & Prof. Pos: Teacher, high sch, Casper, Wyo, 27-39; reading consult, Casper Elem. Schs, 52-55; asst. supt. of schs, Casper, 58-68; instr, Casper Col, 68- Mem: Delta Kappa Gamma; Nat. Educ. Asn; Am. Asn. Univ. Women; Wyo. and Cent. Wyo. Ment. Health Asns; Bus. & Prfnl. Women's Club; Wyo. Fedn. Women's Rep. Club; Eastern Star. Golden Key Award, Wyo. Educ. Asn; First Woman Speaker in Wyo. House of Rep. Rel: Episcopal. Mailing Add: 314 E. Tenth St, Casper, Wyo. 82601.

JAMES, VERNON M. R
b. Protem, Mo, 1/5/89; m. 3/6/15 to Sibyl O'Brien; c. Jack A. Educ: Southwest Mo. State Col, B.S. Polit. & Govt. Pos: Mem, City Coun, 6 years; co. collector, 8 years; Mo. State Rep, 60-66, mem. educ, fees and salaries, rds. and hwys. and ways and means cmts, Mo. House Rep; co. judge, Taney Co, 67- Bus. & Prof. Pos: Teacher; ins. bus. Mem: Mason. Rel: Christian Church N.Am. Mailing Add: 210 Walnut Lane, Branson, Mo. 65616.

JAMES, WILLIAM S. D
Md. State Sen. and Pres. of the Sen.
b. Aberdeen, Md, 2/14/14; married. Educ: Tome Sch, 28-32; Univ. of Del, 32-34; Univ. Md. Law Sch, LL.B, 37. Polit. & Govt. Pos: Md. State Rep, 47-55; Md. State Sen, 55-; chmn, Legis. Coun. Cmt. on Taxation, Fiscal Matters, 59-62, pres. of the Sen, chmn, Rules Cmt. and chmn, Legis. Coun, 63-; del, Dem. Nat. Conv, 68. Mem: Bd. Libr. Trustees, Harford Co, 45-53; Rotary (past pres, Havre de Grace Club). Mailing Add: Old Bay Farm, Havre de Grace, Md. 21078.

JAMESON, JOHN HENRY R
Maine State Rep.
b. Bangor, Maine, 6/8/98; s. Joseph D.M. Jameson and Catherine Gehan J; m. 6/22/27 to Mildred Cleveland; c. Charles J. Educ: Mass. Agr. Col. Polit. & Govt. Pos: Maine State Rep, 61- Bus. & Prof. Pos: Licensed tree surgeon, John H. Jameson's Tree Experts, 45 years. Mil. Serv: Entered as A.P, Navy, 17, released as G.M. 2/C, 18, after serv. in Grand Fleet, ETO. Mem: VFW (past comdr); Am. Legion; World War I Vet.(past comdr). Rel: Catholic. Mailing Add: 780 Union St, Bangor, Maine 04401.

JAMIEL, MORPHIS A. Independent
b. Warren, R.I, 12/19/21. Educ: Univ. of R.I, B.S, 43; Boston Univ. Law Sch, LL.B, 48. Polit. & Govt. Pos: R.I. Sen, 63-66; Probate Judge, 13 years;

Town Solicitor Warren, R.I, 2 years; mem, Planning Bd. of Warren, 4 years. Bus. & Prof. Pos: Lawyer; judge; enrolled to practice before U.S. Supreme Court and U.S. Court of Mil. Appeals; real estate agent; auctioneer; mortgage loans; chem. engr. Mil. Serv: Army, Europe Seventh Armored Div, World War II, 43-46; 43rd Inf, Germany, Korea, 50-52; Army Engr. Sch, 50; Army Gen. Sch, 51; Command and Gen. Staff Col, 55; R.I. Army Nat. Guard, Lt. Col; Purple Heart; Bronze Star with Three Oak Leaf Clusters. Mem: Nat. Guard Asn; Bristol Lions Club (past pres); Warren Scholarship Found; R.I. and Mass. Bar; Am. Bar Asn; Massasoit Hook and Ladder Fire Co; Am. Legion; life mem. VFW; life mem. DAV; life mem. Seventh Armored Div. Asn; life mem. E. Warren Rod and Gun Club. Mailing Add: 8 Market St, Warren, R.I. 02885.

JAMIESON, NORMAN LESLIE R
Chmn, Livingston Co. Rep. Cmt, Mich.
b. Howell, Mich, 8/5/34; s. Norman Richard Jamieson and Mary Burns J; div. Educ: Mich. State Univ, B.A, 56; Pre-law club; Officer's club. Polit. & Govt. Pos: Voter identification chmn, Livingston Co. Rep. Cmt, Mich, 61-63, orgn. chmn, 63-67, chmn, 67-; v.chmn, Livingston Co. Young Rep, 62; justice of the peace, Marion Twp, 65-69; mem. exec. cmt, Second Cong. Dist, Rep. Party, 67-; del, Rep. Nat. Conv, 68. Bus. & Prof. Pos: Casualty underwriter, Citizen's Mutual Ins. Co, Howell, 59-63, sr. commercial lines underwriter, 63-66; asst. v.pres. and ins. mgr, Howell Town & Country, Inc, 66-; substitute teacher, Howell-Livingston Co. Int. Sch. Dist, 69. Mil. Serv: Entered as Pvt, Army, 56, released as Sp-4, 58, after serv. in Intel. Sect, Hq, Second Missile Command, Fifth Army, 56-58. Mem: Independent Ins. Agents Mich; Elks (Past Exalted Ruler); Howell Area C. of C; Econ. Club Detroit; Mich. State Univ. Livingston-Washtenaw Alumni Club (exec. cmt); Livingston Co. Chap. Chmn, Nat. Found, March of Dimes, County Chmn, Michigan Week, 65. Rel: Presbyterian. Legal Res: 922 Hadden Ave, Howell, Mich. 48843. Mailing Add: 1002 E. Grand River, Howell, Mich. 48843.

JAMISON, CHARLES HAYDEN D
b. York, Pa, 10/27/21; s. Earnest Gates Jamison and Evelyn P. J; m. 12/28/46 to Sarah Moore Von Nieda; c. Van Courtney, Scott Keene, Kent Hayden and Craig Allen. Educ: Drexel Inst. Tech, B.S, 42; Univ. Exeter, M.A, 47; Univ. Pa, Ph.D, 52; Phi Kappa Phi; Drexel Bourse; Blue Key; Lambda Chi Alpha. Polit. & Govt. Pos: Trustee, State Wis. Investment Bd, 60-63, exec. dir, 63-68; del, Dem. Nat. Conv, 68; del, Dem. State Conv, 68 & 69. Bus. & Prof. Pos: Exec. v.pres. and economist, Beloit State Bank, 57-63; pres, C. Hayden Jamison & Assocs, 68- Mil. Serv: Entered as 2nd Lt, Army, 42, released as Capt, 46, after serv. in 290th Inf, 75th Div, ETO, 44-46; Bronze Star; Silver Star; Unit Commendation; European Theater Ribbon with Three Campaign Stars. Mem: Rotary; Salvation Army (treas, Beloit Chap). Rel: Presbyterian. Mailing Add: 3610 Sunset Dr, Madison, Wis. 53705.

JAMISON, JOHN WILLIAM D
Chmn, Gilmer Co. Dem. Exec. Cmt, W.Va.
b. Glenville, W.Va, 12/7/32; s. Coy Russell Jamison and Rosa Chapman J; m. 6/17/61 to Wilma Furr. Educ: Glenville State Col. Polit. & Govt. Pos: Chmn, Gilmer Co. Dem. Exec. Cmt, W.Va, 64- Bus. & Prof. Pos: Store mgr, W.Va. ABCC, 61- Mil. Serv: Entered as Pvt, Air Force, 50, released as Sgt, 63, after serv. in 11th Radar Calibration Squadron. Mem: Immediate past pres, Lions; Farm Bur, Gilmer Co; Am. Legion. Rel: Methodist. Legal Res: 12 Whiting Ave, Glenville, W.Va. 26351. Mailing Add: Box 302, Glenville, W.Va. 26351. (1967)

JAMISON, LESLIE D. R
Chmn, Pickens Co. Rep. Party, S.C.
b. Charleston, S.C, 9/23/26; d. Daniel William Dukes and Sarah Massenburg D; m. 6/25/46 to Dr. Elmer Alvis Jamison (deceased); c. William Robert and John Charles. Educ: Sch. Nursing, Med. Col. S.C; The Citadel, night sch, Charleston. Polit. & Govt. Pos: Women's campaign chmn, Citizens for Nixon-Lodge, 60; Rep. precinct secy, Pickens Co, S.C, 62-64, 66 & 68, Rep. campaign chmn, 62, 64, 66 & 68; chmn, Pickens Co. Rep. Party, 64-; S.C. Conv. chmn, Rep. Women's Conf, Wash. D.C, 66; S.C. State publicity chmn, Rep. Women's Conf, Little Rock, Ark, 67; S.C. State co-chmn, Women for Nixon-Agnew, 68. Mem: Pickens Co. Med. Auxiliary (past pres); Pickens Co. Friends of the Libr.(v.pres). Rel: Episcopal. Mailing Add: 122 Lakeview Dr, Easley, S.C. 29640.

JANCZAK, LOUIS R
Ill. State Rep.
b. Chicago, Ill, 8/25/96. Educ: St. Stanislaus Koska Sch. Polit. & Govt. Pos: Mem, Dept. Registrn. & Educ, Bd. Local Improv, Sheriff's Off, and Co. Treas. Off; Ill. State Rep, currently. Bus. & Prof. Pos: Real estate & ins. 1967 Legal Res: Chicago, Ill. No mailing address available. (1967)

JANEWAY, EDWARD G. R
Vt. State Sen.
b. New Rochelle, N.Y, 8/25/01; s. Dr. Theodore Caldwell Janeway and Eleanor Alderson J; m. 5/23/25 to Elinor White; c. five and 17 grandchildren. Educ: Yale Col, 22. Polit. & Govt. Pos: Chief conservation, Tin & Lead Div, War Prod. Bd, 41-42; chmn, Vt. for Eisenhower Cmt, 51-52; Vt. State Rep, 51-57; Rep. Nat. Committeeman, Vt, 52-; mem, Vt. Little Hoover Cmn, 57-58; Vt. State Sen, 59- Bus. & Prof. Pos: Investment bus, N.Y, 24-41; dairy farming and purebred cattle breeding, Vt, 45-; chmn. bd. trustees, Experiment in Int. Living, Putney, Vt; chmn, Conserv. Soc. South. Vt; dir, Stratton Corp, Vt. and Catamount Nat. Bank. Mil. Serv: Entered Navy, 42, released as Lt, 46, served in Amphibious Forces, Africa and Eng, Lt. Comdr, Naval Res; Bronze Star; Croix de Guerre. Mem: Grange; Am. Legion; Links Club, N.Y; Tavern Club, Boston; Ekwanok Club, Vt. Rel: Congregational. Legal Res: Middletown Farm, South Londonderry, Vt. 05155. Mailing Add: Stratton Corp, Stratton Mountain, South Londonderry, Vt. 05155.

JANOVIC, JOHN PETER D
b. Harrison, N.J, 5/6/08; s. John Janovic and Isabel Stenkiewicz J; m. 6/24/29 to Sophie M. Levandoski; c. Barbara J.(Mrs. Fialkoski), Robert J. and Karen M. Polit. & Govt. Pos: Probation officer, Adult Police Court, New London, Conn, 52-54; mem, City Coun, New London, 54-64 and Mayor, 57-58; former Conn. State Sen, 20th dist. Mem: New London Bd. of Realtors (pres, 57-58); Realtors Wash. Cmt, 60; Conn. Polish Am. Cong; Elks (trustee, New London Lodge); Kiwanis (dir); K. of C.(4°); Moose. Rel: Catholic. Legal Res: 185 Norwood Ave, New London, Conn. 06320. Mailing Add: 625 Colman St, New London, Conn. 06320.

JANSEN, LEONARD FRANCIS D
b. Lind, Wash, 3/12/17; s. August Carl Jansen and Gertrude Bogk J; m. 11/26/42 to Jean Driver; c. Judith Ann and Laurence Douglas. Educ: Whitman Col, A.B. cum laude with hon. in polit. sci, 40; Columbia Univ. Sch. Law, LL.B, 47; Phi Delta Theta; Phi Beta Kappa; Phi Delta Phi. Polit. & Govt. Pos: Chmn, Adams Co. Dem. Cent. Cmt, Wash. and mem, 4th Dist. Dem. Coun, 64-66; dem. area campaign coordinator and Wash. state chmn, Rural Am. for Johnson & Humphrey, 64. Mil. Serv: Entered as Ensign, Navy, 42, released as Lt(sg), 46, after serv. at Naval Air Station, Pensacola, Fla; Am. Theater Ribbon; Victory Medal. Mem: Am, Wash. and Spokane Co. Bar Asns; Mason (32°); Shriner; Pres, Lind and Retzville C. of C, 57; exec. bd, Boy Scout Coun. and troop cmt. chmn, Boy Scouts, 64-66; Am. Legion; Nat. Grange (7°); Presidents Club. Mem, People to People Tour, Iron Curtain Lands, 60. Rel: Episcopal. Legal Res: 4307 S. Madelia, Spokane, Wash. 99203. Mailing Add: P.O. Box 324, N. 711 Lincoln, Spokane, Wash. 99210. (1967)

JANSSEN, JACK WESLEY D
Kans. State Sen.
b. Lyons, Kans, 7/6/23; s. Juanita Hughes J, father deceased; m. 8/14/43 to Dorothy Link. Educ: Univ. Okla, 2½ years. Polit. & Govt. Pos: Co. cmnr, Rice Co, Kans, 59-65; Kans. State Sen, 33rd Dist, 65-69, 23rd Dist, 69- Bus. & Prof. Pos: Pres, Rice Co. Develop. Corp, 64-68; bd. mem, Gov. Nuclear Energy Coun, 66-, Alliance for Progress Cmt, 68- Mil. Serv: Entered as Cadet, Army Air Force, 42, released as 1st Lt, 45, after serv. as Bomber Pilot, Eighth Air Force, ETO, 44-45; Lt. Col, Air Force Res, 69-, Liaison Officer for Air Force Acad, currently; Air Medal with 7 Oak Leaf Clusters; European-African-Middle East. Serv. Medal; North. France-Germany Serv. Medal; Victory Medal; Air Force Res. Medal. Mem: Eagles; Odd Fellows; Optimists; C. of C; Am. Legion; VFW. Rel: Christian Church of N.Am. Legal Res: Route 1, Lyons, Kans. 67554. Mailing Add: P.O. Box 326, Lyons, Kans. 67554.

JARBOE, JOHN BRUCE D
Secy-Treas, First Dist, Okla. Dem. Party
b. Tulsa, Okla, 3/28/40; s. Joseph Ralph Jarboe and Mildred Maguire J; m. to Sally. Educ: Univ. Okla, B.A, 62; Univ. Tulsa, J.D, 65; Sigma Chi; Phi Alpha Delta. Polit. & Govt. Pos: Nominee, U.S. Rep, First Dist. Okla, 68; Secy-treas, First Dist, Okla. Dem. Party, 69- Bus. & Prof. Pos: Research asst, U.S. Dist. Court, Tulsa, 63-65; trial attorney, U.S. Dept. Justice, Wash, D.C, 65-66; private law practice and cattle bus, Tulsa, 68- Mil. Serv: Entered as Pvt, Army, 66, released as SP-5, 68, after serving in Staff Judge Adv. Off, Ft. Polk, La, 66-68; SP-5, Army Res; Nat. Serv. Medal; Army Commendation Medal. Publ: 'Taxation,' Tulsa Law J, 64. Mem: Okla, La, Am, Fed. and Tulsa Co. Bar Asns; Nat. Lawyers Club; Am. Legion. Ed-in-chief, Tulsa Law J. and Outstanding Law Grad, Univ. Tulsa, 65. Rel: Catholic. Mailing Add: 3305 E. 45th, Tulsa, Okla. 74135.

JARBOE, JOSEPH BENJAMIN, JR. D
b. Lebanon, Ky, 1/7/09; s. Joseph Benjamin Jarboe, Sr. and Rose Ellen Hilpp J; m. 12/30/35 to Jennie Elizabeth Kelly; c. Joseph Kelly and Thomas McElroy. Educ: St. Augustine's High Sch, Lebanon, Ky, grad. Polit. & Govt. Pos: Ky. State Rep, 40-44; judge, Marion Co, 58-66; chmn, Marion Co. Dem. Party, 64-68. Bus. & Prof. Pos: Retail furniture dealer, 35 years. Mem: K. of C. Rel: Roman Catholic. Legal Res: 245 Kobert Ave, Lebanon, Ky. 40033. Mailing Add: 209 W. Main St, Lebanon, Ky. 40033.

JARMAN, JOHN D
U.S. Rep, Okla.
b. Sallisaw, Okla, 7/17/15; s. John H. Jarman and Lou N. Jones; m. 2/25/42 to Ruth Bewley, wid. Sept, 1964; m. 2/19/68 to Marylin Grant; c. Jay, Susan and Steve. Educ: Yale Univ, B.A, 37; Harvard Law Sch, LL.B, 41; Westminster Col, Mo. Polit. & Govt. Pos: Okla. State Rep; Okla. State Sen; U.S. Rep, Okla, 50-; del, Dem. Nat. Conv, 68. Bus. & Prof. Pos: Lawyer. Mil. Serv: Army, 42-45. Legal Res: 1805 Huntington, Oklahoma City, Okla. 73112. Mailing Add: 2416 Rayburn House Office Bldg, Washington, D.C. 20515.

JARUSSI, JOHN MATTHEW D
Chmn, Carbon Co. Dem. Cent. Cmt, Mont.
b. Red Lodge, Mont, 2/2/08; s. Louis Jarussi and Carmela Maschio J; m. 8/22/43 to Margaret Feldman; c. Louis, Franklin, Lorraine, Kathleen, Eileen, Rose Ann and Anthony. Educ: Univ. Mont, B.Sc. in Pharm, 28; Kappa Psi. Polit. & Govt. Pos: Mont. State Rep, Carbon Co, 46-50; precinct committeeman, Dem. Party, 58-65; chmn, Carbon Co. Dem. Cent. Cmt, currently. Mil. Serv: Entered Navy, 44, released as Pharmacist Mate 2/C, 45. Mem: Mont. State Pharmaceutical Asn; Rotary; Lions; Am. Legion; C. of C; Holy Name Soc. Rel: Catholic. Mailing Add: 9 S. Platt, Red Lodge, Mont. 59068.

JARVIS, ARTHUR J. R
b. Isle LaMotte, Vt, 3/21/93; m. to Florence LaBombard; c. 1 son; 1 daughter. Educ: Pub. Schs, Isle, La Motte, Vt. Polit. & Govt. Pos: Town selectman; justice of the peace; town moderator; sch. dir; Vt. State Rep, 33-37, 44-45 & 53-66; Draft Number 7, draft bd. Bus. & Prof. Pos: Retired. Rel: Roman Catholic. Mailing Add: Isle La Motte, Vt. 05463. (1967)

JARVIS, NORMAN O. R
Mem. Exec. Adv. Cmt, D.C. Rep. Cmt.
b. Washington, D.C, 11/3/08; s. William Ernest Jarvis and Elva Catherine Minor J; m. 6/2/28 to Mary Hallie Jackson; c. Norman W, W. Ernest, Richard Wilson, Anne Elizabeth (Mrs. Bennett), Sidney Jackson, Stephen Daniel, Mary Constance (Mrs. Dixon) and Charlotte Marie (Mrs. Allen). Educ: Denver Univ, 29-30; Howard Univ, 30-33; Frelinhysen C.O.E, D.S.S, 36. Polit. & Govt. Pos: Asst. to chmn, D.C. Forward Looking Rep; alternate del, Rep, Nat. Conv, 64; mem. exec. adv. cmt. and bd. dirs. and special asst. to chmn, D.C. Rep. Cmt. and mem. bd. dirs. and spec. asst. to chmn, Cmt. 68, N.Y.C, 64- Bus. & Prof. Pos: Pres, W. Ernest Jarvis Co, 45-66. Mem: Undertakers Bd, D.C, 60-66; Int. Elks; Mason; DePriest 15; Pigskin Club of D.C; Urban League

NAACP; Oldest Inhabitants of D.C; Cape Cod Golf Club; Royal Golf Club; YMCA. Won Sr. Championship, United Golf Asn, 62. Rel: Episcopal. Mailing Add: 1778 Verbena St. N.W, Washington, D.C. 20012. (1967)

JASPER, CLAUDE J. R
B. Alma, Iowa, 8/23/05; s. John K. Jasper and Julia Brost J; m. 6/14/46 to Shirley Tholen; c. William, Thomas and Julia. Educ: St. Thomas Col; Univ. Wis. Law Sch. Polit. & Govt. Pos: Treas, Taft for President Campaign, 52; treas, Wis. Rep. Party, 52-58, chmn, 58-62; alternate del, Rep. Nat. Conv, 52, 56 & 60, del, 64; mem, Rep. Nat. Cmt, 58-62. Bus. & Prof. Pos: Attorney, Jasper, Winner, Perina & Rouse. Mem: Wis. and Am. Bar Asns; Elks. Rel: Catholic. Legal Res: 1630 Sherman Ave, Madison, Wis. 53704. Mailing Add: 111 S. Fairchild, Madison, Wis. 53703.

JASPER, NORBERT J. D
Mo. State Rep.
b. Washington, Mo, 4/2/13; m. to Dorris Crowder; c. John N. Educ: Wash. High Sch. Polit. & Govt. Pos: Mem, City Coun. and Bd. Pub. Works, Washington, Mo; Mo. State Rep, 56-, mem. legis. inaugural cmt, Mo. House Rep, chmn. ways and means cmt. appropriations, mem. ins. and rds. and hwys. cmt. Bus. & Prof. Pos: Owner Serv. Sta; ins. bus. Mil. Serv: Air Corps, S.Pac. Mem: Elks; K. of C; Am. Legion; VFW; Lions; Jr. C. of C.(pres, 42); C. of C.(pres, Washington Chap, 58-59). Rel: Catholic. Mailing Add: 819 W. Second St, Washington, Mo. 63090. (1967)

JASPER, WILLIAM N, JR. D
b. Sun, Fayette Co, W.Va, 10/13/06; s. William N. Jasper and Ida Johnson J; m. 10/18/44 to Eloise Van Stavern; c. Mary Nichols Welch. Educ: Pub. schs; Greenbriar Mil. Sch. Polit. & Govt. Pos: W.Va. State Sen, 54-66; chmn, Greenbrier Co. Dem. Exec. Cmt; mayor and councilman, Lewisburg, W.Va. Bus. & Prof. Pos: Merchant. Mem: Elks; Rotary; Moose; Greenbrier Co. Country Club; Greenbrier Co. Farm Bur. Rel: Presbyterian. Mailing Add: Lewisburg, W.Va. 24901. (1967)

JASTAD, ELMER D
Wash. State Rep.
b. Chehalis, Wash, 1906; m. to Edna Mae; c. 1 son. Educ: Wash. State Univ, Sch. of Pharm. Polit. & Govt. Pos: Wash. State Rep, currently. Bus. & Prof. Pos: Pharmacist. Mem: Mason; Shrine; Scottish Rite; Eagles; Elks; Moose. Mailing Add: Box 38, Morton, Wash. 98356. (1967)

JAVITS, JACOB KOPPEL R
U.S. Sen, N.Y.
b. N.Y.C, 5/18/04; s. Morris Javits and Ida J; m. 11/30/47 to Marion Ann Borris; c. Joy, Joshua and Carla. Educ: N.Y. Univ. Law Sch, LL.B, 26. Hon. degrees, N.Y. Univ, Hartwick Col, Yeshiva Univ, Hebrew Union Col, L.I. Univ, Ithaca Col, Colgate Univ, Niagara Univ, Jewish Theol. Sem, Lincoln Univ. and Dartmouth Col. Polit. & Govt. Pos: Mem, Ivy Rep. Club, 18th Cong. Dist, 32; U.S. Rep, 21st Dist, N.Y, 46-54, mem. for. affairs cmt, U.S. House Rep; attorney gen, N.Y, 54-56; chmn, NATO Parliamentarians' Conf. Spec. Cmt. on Econ. Develop. Less-Develop. NATO Nations, Rapporteur, NATO Polit. Cmt; U.S. Sen, N.Y, 56-, mem, for. rels, govt. opers, selec. cmt. on small bus, cmt. of labor and pub. welfare, joint econ. cmt. and select cmt. on nutrition and human needs, U.S. Senate; del, Rep. Nat. Conv, 68. Bus. & Prof. Pos: Counsel, Law Firm, Javits, Trubin, Sillcocks and Edelman. Mil. Serv: Entered as Maj, Army, 42, released as Lt. Col, 45, after serv. as Asst. to Chief Opers. Chem. Warfare, ETO, 43, Pac. Theatre, 44; Legion of Merit; Army Commendation Ribbon. Publ: Order of Battle, A Republican's Call to Reason, Atheneum, 64, rev, 66; Discrimination, U.S.A, 60, rev, 62. Mem: Am. Legion; VFW; Jewish War Vets. Rel: Jewish. Legal Res: 375 Park Ave, New York, N.Y. 10022. Mailing Add: Room 326, Old Senate Office Bldg, Washington, D.C. 20510.

JAYNE, EDWARD JAMES R
b. Exira, Iowa, 2/15/34; s. Edward Boyer Jayne and Martha Andreasen J; single. Educ: Univ. Omaha and Creighton Univ, Night Sch. Polit. & Govt. Pos: Precinct chmn, Audubon Co. Rep. Cent. Cmt, Iowa, 59-64, chmn, 64-68; dist. chmn, Seventh Cong. Dist. Young Rep, 60; mem, Young Rep. Iowa State Cent. Cmt, 60; city clerk, Exira, 60-61, city councilman, 63-65; staff auditor, State of Iowa, 61-64; field supvr, Iowa State Auditor's Off, 68- Bus. & Prof. Pos: Staff acct, Dutton, Schmidt, Upp & Co, 65-68. Publ: Various political editorials for local newspapers. Mem: Order of the Arrow, Boy Scouts (scoutmaster, Boy Scout Troop 65, 10 years and Troop 51, currently). Rel: Lutheran. Legal Res: 627 Clinton, Des Moines, Iowa 50313. Mailing Add: Box 92, E.D.M. Station, Des Moines, Iowa 50309.

JAZOWSKI, J. PETER, JR. R
Chmn, Wayland Rep. Town Cmt, Mass.
b. Quincy, Mass, 12/16/35; s. Dr. Joseph Peter Jazowski and Helena Jagielski J; m. 11/20/59 to Elizabeth Ann Adams; c. Kim Adams and Kristen Brooks. Educ: Harvard Col, 57; D.U. Club; Pi Eta. Polit. & Govt. Pos: Finance chmn, Wayland Rep. Town Cmt, Mass, 66, chmn, 67-; dir, Middlesex Club, 68- Bus. & Prof. Pos: Spec. agent, Ins. Co. of N.Am, 57-59; acct. exec, John Liner Assocs, Ins. Consult, 59-60; pres, Neelon Ins. Assocs, 60- Mem: Mass. Ins. Agents and Brokers Asn; Kiwanis; Harvard Club of Boston. Award of Merit, Mass. Rep. State Cmt, 66. Rel: Episcopal. Mailing Add: 31 Sedgemeadow Rd, Wayland, Mass. 01778.

JEANMARD, FUCHSIA LEONTEEN R
Secy, Pueblo Co. Rep. Cent. Cmt, Colo.
b. Pueblo, Colo, 8/23/19; d. George Nelson Womack and Clara Bybee W; m. 12/25/53 to Herbert John Jeanmard; c. Julian Terry Mitchell. Educ: Pueblo Jr. Col, A.A, 39; Tillotson Col, B.A, 41; Alpha Kappa Alpha. Polit. & Govt. Pos: Exec. secy, Colo. Rep. State Cent. Cmt, 62-68; stenographer, State Legis, 63; secy, Steel City Rep. Women's Club, 67-; secy, Pueblo Co. Rep. Cent. Cmt, 69- Bus. & Prof. Pos: Secy, psychiat. team and Region X, Colo. State Hosp, 64- Mem: NAACP; Am. Bus. Women's Asn.(corresponding secy, Pride City Chap, 67-68); Iota Phi Lambda; Colo. State Hosp. Labor Union; Colo. State Employees' Asn. Rel: Protestant. Mailing Add: 1213 Cypress, Pueblo, Colo. 81004.

JEBENS, JOHN HERMAN R
Mayor, City of Davenport, Iowa
b. Davenport, Iowa, 6/6/18; s. John H. Jebens and Mathilde Looges J; m. 5/29/48 to Marian I. Blank; c. John H. Jebens, III. Educ: St. Ambrose Col, B.A, 39. Polit. & Govt. Pos: Alderman-at-lg, Davenport, Iowa, 57-66, mayor, currently. Mil. Serv: Entered as Ens, Navy, 44, released as Lt.(jg), 46, after serv. in Mediterranean and Pacific. Mem: Elks; Turners; Eagles; Moose; I.T.U; Optimist, A.B.C. Rel: Episcopal. Mailing Add: 3203 Arlington Ave, Davenport, Iowa 52803. (1967)

JEFFERS, MARY L. D
Committeewoman, Calif. Dem. State Cent. Cmt.
b. Lebanon, Tenn; d. Preston C. Lloyd and Lillie Officer L; m. 10/1/60 to Clifton R. Jeffers. Educ: Spelman Col, 51-53; Tenn. State Univ, A.B, 56, M.A, 57; Wayne State Univ. and Univ. Calif, Berkeley, grad. work; Sigma Rho Sigma; Pi Sigma Alpha. Polit. & Govt. Pos: Committeewoman, Calif. Dem. State Cent. Cmt, 68- Bus. & Prof. Pos: Sec. Eng. and hist. teacher, Detroit Unified Sch. Dist, Mich, 57-59; polit. sci. instr, Col. San Mateo, 63- Mem: Acad. of Polit. Sci; North. Calif. Polit. Sci. Asn; Am. Fedn. of Teachers; Am. Asn. Univ. Prof; Phi Delta Kappa; NAACP; Charles Houston Law Club Auxiliary. Rel: Protestant. Mailing Add: 36 Thrift St, San Francisco, Calif. 94112.

JEFFERS, WOODROW WILSON D
Chmn, Vinton Co. Dem. Exec. Cmt, Ohio
b. Radcliff, Ohio, 11/3/12; s. Delmont Henry Jeffers and Emma Esteline Webb J; m. 11/8/30 to Dena Olive Cooper; c. Harlan Woodrow and Loretta Maude (Mrs. Saylor). Educ: Vinton Twp. High Sch, grad, 30. Polit. & Govt. Pos: Mem, sch. bd, Vinton Twp, Vinton Co, Ohio, 42-54; co. cmnr, Vinton Co, 56-60; co. cetn. committeeman, Vinton Co. Dem. Party, 60-; chmn, Vinton Co. Dem. Exec. Cmt, 60-; chmn, Vinton Co. Bd. Elections 64-; del, Dem. Nat. Conv, 68; mem. bd. of trustees and treas, Jackson-Vinton Community Action Prog. Bus. & Prof. Pos: Self-employed, 30-59; pres, W.W. Jeffers, Inc, 59-69. Mem: Grange; Ohio Asn. Election Off; Tenth Dist. Dem. Action Club; Eagles; Eastern Star; Mason (32°); K.T; Shrine. Rel: Latter-day Saint. Mailing Add: 105 S. Pearl St, McArthur, Ohio 45651.

JEFFORDS, JAMES MERRILL R
Attorney Gen, Vt.
b. Rutland, Vt, 5/11/34; s. Olin Merrill Jeffords and Marion Hausman J; m. 8/26/61 to Elizabeth C. Daley; c. Leonard Olin and Laura Louise. Educ: Yale Univ, B.S, 56; Harvard Law Sch, LL.B, 62. Polit. & Govt. Pos: Rep. Town Chmn, Shrewsbury, Vt, 63-, town agent, 64, town grand juror, 64; chmn, Vt. Rep. Fund Raising Dinner, 67; Vt. State Sen, 67-68, mem, Judicial Selection Bd, spec. cmt, Admin. Procedures Act, 67, Finance Cmt, Gen. Cmt. and chmn, Hwy. Invest. Cmt, 68, Vt. State Senate; Attorney Gen, Vt, 69- Bus. & Prof. Pos: Law clerk, Judge Ernest W. Gibson, U.S. Dist. Court, 62; partner, Crowley, Bishop and Jeffords, 63-66; partner, Kinney, Carbine and Jeffords, 66- Mil. Serv: Entered as Ens, Navy, 56, released as Lt.(jg), 59, after serv. in Naval Res. Surface Div, Burlington, Vt; Lt. Comdr, Naval Res, 65; Naval Expeditionary Medal for Lebanon Crisis. Mem: Vt. Bar Asn.(pres, Young Lawyers Sect, 66-67 and mem. bd. trustees); Am. Judicature Soc.(panelist, 67, voting mem, 68); trustee, Legal Aid, 66-; Lions; Elks. Rel: Congregational. Mailing Add: 5 Heaton St, Montpelier, Vt. 05602.

JEFFREY, HARRY PALMER R
b. Dayton, Ohio, 12/26/01; s. Samuel E. Jeffrey and Grace S. Wilson J; m. 9/11/35 to Susan Virginia Gummer; c. Harry P, Jr, Juliet L. (Mrs. Jacobs) and Susan J. (Mrs. Seifert). Educ: Ohio State Univ, B.A, 24, J.D, 26; Phi Beta Kappa; Order of Coif; Phi Delta Phi. Polit. & Govt. Pos: Spec. Asst. Attorney Gen, Ohio, 33-36; U.S. Rep, Third Cong. Dist, Ohio, 43-44. Bus. & Prof. Pos: Secy. and gen. counsel, Foremanship Found, 45-; mem, bd. dirs. of numerous corps; partner, Law Firm of Iddings, Jeffrey & Donnelly. Mil. Serv: 2nd Lt, Army Res, 27-31. Mem: Dayton Bar Asn.(past pres); past co-chmn, Cmt. on Rev. of Fed. Laws; Am. Bar Asn.(mem. Labor sect); Ohio Bar Asn; Am. Judicature Soc; fel, Am. Col. Trial Lawyers; adv. cmt, Wright State Univ; Mason (33°); C. of C. (past pres, Dayton Area Chap); bd. of numerous civic and philanthropic orgn. Rel: Presbyterian. Legal Res: 4433 Lotz Rd, Dayton, Ohio 45429. Mailing Add: 1212 Third National Bldg, Dayton, Ohio 45402.

JEFFREY, MILDRED D
Dem. Nat. Committeewoman
b. Alton, Iowa, 12/29/11; d. Bert David McWilliams and Bertha Merritt M; m. 11/27/36 to Homer Newman Jeffrey; c. Sharon Rose and Daniel Balfour. Educ: Univ. Minn, B.A, 32; Bryn Mawr Col, 34. Polit. & Govt. Pos: Investr, NRA, 35-36; del, White House Conf. Children and Youth 50 & 60; chmn. platform cmt, Mich. Dem. Party, 55-60, alternate nat. committeewoman, 57-; mem, Nat. Platform Cmt, 56-60; mem, Citizens Adv. Cmt. Sch. Needs, 57-59; v.chmn, Mich. Consumers Asn, 59; mem, Detroit Libr. Cmn, 59-; v.chmn, Nat. Cmt. Employ. Youth, 59-; Dem. Nat. Committeewoman, 61- del, Dem. Nat. Conv, 68. Bus. & Prof. Pos: Dir. women's bur, Int. Union United Automobile, Aircraft and Agr. Implement Workers Am, 44-49, dir. radio dept, 49-50 and dir. commun. rels. dept, 51-; mgr, Sta. WDET-FM, Detroit, 50-51; secy, Metrop. Detroit Relig. and Labor Conf, 54-59; labor rep. chmn, Adult Educ. Study United Commun. Serv, 58-60. Received Distinguished Commun. Serv. Award; Workmen's Circle, 55; St. Cyprian's Award, P.E. Church of Diocese, Mich, 59; Outstanding Layman of the Year Award, Detroit Coun. Churches, 60; Human Rights Liberty Award, 68. Mailing Add: 8000 E. Jefferson, Detroit, Mich. 48214.

JELBERT, JAMES D. R
S.Dak. State Rep.
b. Sundance, Wyo, 4/6/17; m. to Margery Curnow; c. Judith Ann. Educ: Univ. Wash, B.A. Polit. & Govt. Pos: Del, Rep. State Conv, 54; S.Dak. State Rep, 56-, Speaker-Pro-Tem, S.Dak. House of Rep, 65-66, Speaker, 67-68. Bus. & Prof. Pos: V.pres. and mgr, 1st Nat. Bank of the Black Hills, Spearfish, S.Dak. Mem: Phi Delta Theta; Mason; Lions; VFW; Am. Legion; Elks; C. of C. Rel: Lutheran. Mailing Add: 1421 Canyon, Spearfish, S.Dak. 57783.

JELINEK, GEORGE JOSEPH D
b. Chicago, Ill, 8/7/07; s. Joseph Jelinek and Anna Bezemek J; m. 8/20/33 to Goldie M. Schroeder; c. Joseph Eugene. Educ: Kans. State Univ. Polit. & Govt. Pos: Kans. State Rep, 80th Dist, 59-62, 99th Dist, 65-67. Publ: Ellsworth Story; Land of Quivira; The Butterfield Trail. Mem: Archeol. Soc;

Kans. State and Ellsworth Co. Hist. Socs; state campaign chmn, United Cerebral Palsy; all Masonic bodies; C. of C.(pres, Ellsworth Chap, 61). Rel: Methodist. Mailing Add: 107 W. Tenth, Ellsworth, Kans. 67439.

JEMISON, HOWARD ALLAN R
N.C. State Rep.
b. Chicago, Ill, 9/15/99; s. Thomas Jemison and Carrie Vawter J; m. 9/25/20 to Caroline Elmore Bishop; c. Howard A, Jr, M.D, Grace J.(Mrs. Rohrer) and Edward T. Educ: Tech. High Sch, Chicago, Ill, 4 years. Polit. & Govt. Pos: N.C. State Rep, 66- Bus. & Prof. Pos: Supvr, West. Elec. Co, Inc, 26-63. Mil. Serv: Pvt, Army, 17. Mem: Telephone Pioneers of Am; Vienna Civic Club and Vienna Volunteer Fire Dept, Pfafftown, N.C. Rel: Methodist. Mailing Add: R.R. 8, Winston-Salem, N.C. 27106.

JENDZEJEC, STANLEY MICHAEL D
Chmn, Coventry Dem. Town Cmt, R.I.
b. Coventry, R.I, 6/16/34; s. Frank M. Jendzejec and Bertha S. Szarek J; m. 10/2/54 to Jessie F. Iwuc; c. Stephen M, Mark A. and Thaddeus. Educ: Univ. R.I. Exten, 2 years. Polit. & Govt. Pos: Chmn, Coventry Dem. Town Cmt, R.I, 67-; pres, Coventry Town Coun, 68- Bus. & Prof. Pos: Sales adminstr, H.P. Hood & Sons, Providence, R.I, 55- Mil. Serv: Yeoman 1/C, Naval Res, 16 years. Mem: Polish Nat. Alliance; Boy Scouts; Polish Am. Cong; K. of C; Fraternal Order of Police; Coventry Jaycees; Pawtuxet Valley Polish Am. Citizens Club; Int. Inst. of Providence. Rel: Roman Catholic. Mailing Add: 12 Apple Blossom Lane, Coventry, R.I. 02816.

JENISON, EDWARD HALSEY R
b. Fond du Lac, Wis, 7/27/07; s. Ernest Manley Jenison and Laura Hinsey J; m. 9/14/29 to Barbara Weinburgh; c. Edward Hinsey. Educ: Univ. Wis, 3 years. Polit. & Govt. Pos: U.S. Rep, Ill, 47-52; Ill. State Rep, 65-66; alternate del, Rep. Nat. Conv, 68. Bus. & Prof. Pos: Ed. and publisher, Daily Beacon News, Paris, Ill, 31- Mil. Serv: Entered as Lt.(jg), Navy, 43, released as Lt. Comdr, 46, after serv. in Naval Aviation. Mem: Sigma Delta Chi. Rel: Protestant. Mailing Add: 711 Shaw Ave, Paris, Ill. 61944.

JENKINS, ALICE ELAINE BROWN R
Mem, D.C. Rep. Cmt.
b. Butte, Mont, 4/2/16; d. The Rev. Russell S. Brown and Floy Smith B.(deceased); m. 6/24/40 to Howard Jenkins, Jr; c. Judith Elaine, Howard, III and Lawrence Coleman. Educ: Denver Univ, B.A, 37; Ohio State Univ, M.A, 38; Philos. Acad; Delta Sigma Theta. Polit. & Govt. Pos: Teacher, Children's Center, Bd. Pub. Welfare, D.C, 48-49, asst. supt, Nat. Training Sch. for Girls, 49-51; mem. campaign staff, Rep. Nat. Cmt, 60; mem, D.C. Rep. Cmt, 60-, v.chmn, 64-69; part-time consult. to asst. chmn, Women's Div, Rep. Nat. Cmt, 69- Bus. & Prof. Pos: Teacher, Denver Pub. Schs, 38-46; substitute teacher, D.C. Pub. Schs, 46-48; founder and dir, Summer Private Schs. in Cultural Subjects, 51-54; teacher in D.C. Schs, 54-69; consult, Univ. Md. Head Start Training Prog. for Teachers, 66; Tri-Sch. Commun. Coordinator, 66-69. Publ: Column, School for Thought, Afro-Am. Newspaper, 62-63; Student's Guide to Washington, Etzell Publ, 61. Mem: Nat. and D.C. Educ. Asns; D.C. Teachers Asn; area co-chmn, Wash. Urban League; Barristers Wives; League of Rep. Women; educ. cmt, Brightwood Civic Asn; Neighbors Inc. Educ. Cmt; League of Women Voters; D.C. Citizens for Better Educ. Urban League Appreciation Award, Membership Campaign, 65. Rel: Congregational; Founder of Plymouthites Club for new mem, now in 12th year, Plymouth Congregational Church. Mailing Add: 1333 Tuckerman St. N.W, Washington, D.C. 20011.

JENKINS, CLYDE DAVID, JR. 'PETE' D
b. Fork Shoals, S.C, 1/31/23; s. Clyde D. Jenkins, Sr. and Floride Austin J; m. 9/27/46 to Mary Elizabeth Rainey; c. Mary Deck, Susan, Clyde III. Educ: Clemson Col, B.S.C.E, 43. Polit. & Govt. Pos: S.C. House of Reps, 53-66; trustee, Fork Shoals High Sch, 51. Bus. & Prof. Pos: Farmer; ins. - real estate - investments. Mil. Serv: Army, Engr. Basic and Engr. O.C.S, Ft. Belvoir, Va, 43-44; training officer 9th Group, 44; Fort Leonard Wood, Mo, 44-45. Mem: Rotary; Elks. Rel: Fork Shoals Baptist Church. Mailing Add: 602 E. Wash.St, Greenville, S.C. 29601. (1967)

JENKINS, EDWARD GERRARD R
Idaho State Rep.
b. Salt Lake City, Utah, 1/2/26; s. Elmer Cutler Jenkins and Mildred Gerrard J; m. 6/11/48 to Billye Virginia Olsen; c. Jennifer, Jessica, Jerilyn, William Edward, Jamie and Robert Olsen. Educ: Univ. of Utah, B.S, 49; Univ. of Hawaii, 46-47; Beta Theta Pi. Polit. & Govt. Pos: Idaho State Rep, Dist. 12, 69- Mil. Serv: Maritime Serv. Mem: Chmn. of bd, Mercy Hosp; fund raising chmn, Idaho Ment. Health Asn, 68-69; lay mem, Idaho Blue Cross; Rotary; Elks; Nat. Farmers Orgn. Rel: Latter-day Saint. Mailing Add: Route 3, Caldwell, Idaho 83605.

JENKINS, FRANK WILLIAMSON R
Treas, Montgomery Co. Rep. Cmt, Pa.
b. Phila, Pa, 5/8/26; s. Harry L. Jenkins and Caroline K. Williamson J; m. to Edith Witte; c. four. Educ: Univ. of Pa, B.S, Law Sch, LL.B; Nat. Merit Honor Soc. Polit. & Govt. Pos: Committeeman and twp. chmn, Rep. Cmt; Pa. State Rep, 64-66; co. cmnr, Montgomery Co, Pa, 66-; treas, Montgomery Co. Rep. Cmt, currently. Bus. & Prof. Pos: Attorney. Mil. Serv: Lt.(jg), Navy. Mem: Lions (Dir, Oreland Club). Legal Res: 1101 Country Club Dr, Oreland, Pa. 19075. Mailing Add: 140 E. Butler Ave, Ambler, Pa. 19002.

JENKINS, JACQUELINE ANN D
Secy, Miami Co. Dem. Cent. and Exec. Cmt, Ohio
b. Piqua, Ohio, 2/13/29; d. John J. Thompson and Salome Kaiser T; m. 8/29/46 to Robert E. Jenkins; c. John O, Robert E, II and Patricia A. Educ: Piqua Cent. High Sch. Polit. & Govt. Pos: Secy, Miami Co. Dem. Cent. and Exec. Cmt, Ohio, currently. Mailing Add: 1381 Sussex Rd, Troy, Ohio 45373.

JENKINS, R. DAVID R
b. Johnson City, Tenn, 7/10/32; s. Robert O. Jenkins and Pauline Connor J; m. 1/5/53 to Nancy Jane Miller; c. Pamela, Deborah, David and Sally. Educ: Univ. Tenn, 50-53; E.Tenn. State Univ, B.S, 54; Sigma Alpha Epsilon. Polit. & Govt. Pos: Secy, Washington Co. Rep. Party, Tenn; alternate del, Rep. Nat. Conv, 68. Mem: Johnson City Country Club. Rel: Methodist. Mailing Add: 1906 Sherwood Dr, Johnson City, Tenn. 37601.

JENKINS, THOMAS M. D
Mayor, San Carlos, Calif.
b. Benton, Ill, 3/7/21; s. Thomas M. Jenkins and Ruby Lasley J; m. 7/13/44 to Anne W. Oakhill; c. Thomas Mark, Jo Anne and Dirk Allison. Educ: Chicago Teachers Col, B.E, 43; Univ. Calif. Hastings Col. Law, LL.B, 49. Polit. & Govt. Pos: Mem, San Mateo Dem. Cent. Cmt, 48-56; mem, Planning Cmn, San Carlos, 58-62, city councilman, 62-, Mayor, 64-65 & 69-; chmn, San Mateo Co. Dem. Campaign, 60, 62, 64 & 68. Mil. Serv: Army, 43-46. Mem: Am. Bar Asn.(mem, House of Del); State Bar of Calif.(chmn, exec. cmt; bd. gov, 69); pres, Am. Asn. Homes for Aging, 66-68; pres, United Commun. Fund of San Francisco, 62-64; v.chmn, Nat. Bd. Dirs, Camp Fire Girls, 64; Lawyers' Club of San Francisco (pres); Mason. Rel: Protestant. Legal Res: 711 Terrace Rd, San Carlos, Calif. 94070. Mailing Add: 1 Kearney St, San Francisco, Calif. 94108.

JENKINS, WILLIAM GREEN R
Chmn, Barnwell Co. Rep. Party, S.C.
b. Kline, S.C, 12/12/21; s. Basil Manly Jenkins and Effie Green J; m. 1/19/54 to Ellen Dunbar Bush; c. William G, Jr, St. Julien Bush, Perry Manly and Mary K. Educ: Clemson Univ, B.S, 42. Polit. & Govt. Pos: Chmn, Barnwell Co. Rep. Party, S.C, 64- Mil. Serv: Entered as 2nd Lt, Air Force, 42, released as 1st Lt, 45, after serv. in 98th Bomb Group, Middle East. Theater; Two Unit Citations; Three Campaign Ribbons. Mem: Ellenton Agr. Club. Rel: Baptist. Mailing Add: 1806 Burr St, Barnwell, S.C. 29812. (1967)

JENKINS, WILLIAM LEWIS R
Speaker, Tenn. House of Rep.
b. Detroit, Mich, 11/19/36; s. Lewis C. Jenkins and Maud Wilson J; m. 6/12/59 to Mary Kathryn Myers; c. Rebecca, Georgeanne, William Lewis, Jr. and Douglas. Educ: Univ. Tenn. Col. Law; Phi Alpha Delta. Polit. & Govt. Pos: Tenn. State Rep, 62-66 and currently; Speaker, Tenn. House of Rep, currently. Bus. & Prof. Pos: Partner, Hyder, Jenkins & Boyd, Attorneys, 62- Mil. Serv: 2nd Lt, Army Res, 59, Capt, currently. Mem: Hawkins Co. and Tenn. Bar Asns; Mason; Kiwanis. Rel: Baptist. Mailing Add: Box 209, Rogersville, Tenn. 37857.

JENKS, DAVIDSON R
b. 1910. Polit. & Govt. Pos: Former Ariz. State Rep. Bus. & Prof. Pos: Retired resort owner. Mailing Add: 3945 E. Desert Cove, Phoenix, Ariz. 85028. (1967)

JENNINGS, JANET ROBERTS R
b. Chicago, Ill, 6/18/33; d. James E. Roberts and Minnette Brewington J; div; c. Joy Isabelle. Educ: Roosevelt Univ, B.A, 52, M.A, 59. Polit. & Govt. Pos: Campaign secy. for U.S. Sen. Everett M. Dirksen, 50 & 56; nominee, U.S. Rep. First Dist. Ill, 68. Bus. & Prof. Pos: Teacher, Chicago Pub. Schs, 52-; caseworker, Cook Co. Dept. Pub. Aid, Chicago, summer 60. Mem: Nat. Educ. Asn; Teachers Union; mem, gov. bd, Roosevelt Univ, 3 years; United Rep. Fund; Prfnl. Women's Auxiliary of Provident Hosp.(founder and first pres); United Negro Col. Fund; YWCA. Del, White House Conf. Children & Youth; Women's Day at Monumental Baptist Church; hostess at Rep. Nat. Conv, 60. Rel: Episcopal; mem. St. Veronica Guild, St. Edmund's Church. Mailing Add: 400 E. 81st St, Chicago, Ill. 60619.

JENNINGS, LYNDON BARGER D
b. Statesville, Tenn, 10/15/10; s. John Wiley Jennings and Sarah Elizabeth Caledonia Patterson J; m. 11/12/41 to Elizabeth Chenault; c. Lynda Young (Mrs. Shelton), Tom Patterson, Jack Harding and Susan Elizabeth. Educ: Cumberland Univ, B.S, pres, Sr. Class. Polit. & Govt. Pos: Tenn. State Sen, 53-55 & 57-59; Tenn. State Rep, 55-57; mem, Gov. Cabinet, Tenn, 59-63; del, Dem. Nat. Conv, 68. Bus. & Prof. Pos: High sch. teacher, Pikeville and Tullahoma, 36-40; businessman, Tullahoma, Tenn, 40- Mem: Rotary. Rel: Baptist. Mailing Add: Rutledge Falls, Tullahoma, Tenn. 37388.

JENNINGS, RENZ DIXON D
Ariz. State Rep.
b. Phoenix, Ariz, 8/4/41; s. Renz L. Jennings and Leola Lesueur J; single. Educ: Ariz. State Univ, B.A, 64. Polit. & Govt. Pos: Dem. committeeman, Palmcroft Precinct, Ariz, 64-65; Ariz. State Rep, 69- Mailing Add: 1311 E. McKinley, Phoenix, Ariz. 85006.

JENNINGS, RUDOLPH DILLON D
Mem, Mercer Co. Dem. Club, W.Va.
b. Bluefield, W.Va, 10/28/23; s. William Webb Jennings and Vangie Francisco J; m. 7/30/49 to Maymie Jean Hubbard; c. Nigel Lewis, Laura Lee, Maxine Elizabeth and James Webb. Educ: Morris Harvey Col, B.S. in Acct, 54; Blackfriers. Polit. & Govt. Pos: Del-at-lg, Dem. Nat. Conv, 64 & 68; cong. candidate, Dem. Primary Election, W.Va, 66; mem, Mercer Co. Dem. Club, 66- Bus. & Prof. Pos: Owner, R.D. Jennings, Acct, 55; secy, Kearns Ins. Agency, Inc, 62-; instr, W.Va. Bus. Col, 64-65; pres, Acct. Systs, Inc, 64-67. Mil. Serv: Entered as Pvt, Army Air Force, 42, released as Sgt, 45, after serv. in 405th Fighter Squadron, ETO, 44-45; Sharpshooter Medal; Distinguished Unit Badge; Normandy and Rhineland Campaign Stars; European-African-Mid. East Theater Ribbons. Publ: News articles in Waverly News and Waverly Watchman, 59. Mem: Toastmasters; VFW; Am. Legion; Air Force Asn; Morris Harvey Col. Alumni Asn; Ind. Univ. Alumni Asn. Award of Merit, Blackfriers; Personality of the South, 68. Rel: Presbyterian. Legal Res: 608 College Ave, Bluefield, W.Va. 24701. Mailing Add: P.O. Box 647, Bluefield, W.Va. 24701.

JENNINGS, WILLIAM PAT D
b. Camp, Va, 8/20/19; m. to Annabelle Cox; c. Grover C, Pat, Jr, Mary Ann and Richard Joel. Educ: Va. Polytech. Inst, B.S, 41. Polit. & Govt. Pos: U.S. Rep, Va, 54-66, clerk, U.S. House of Rep, 67 and currently; del, Dem. Nat. Conv, 68. Bus. & Prof. Pos: Mem. bd. dir, Bank of Marion, Va; sheriff, Smyth Co, 48-54; v.pres, Marion Pub. Co; bus. and farm interests, Marion. Mil. Serv: Maj, Army, 41-46, Europe; Lt. Col, Army Res. Mem: Kiwanis; Mason; Shrine; Am. Legion; VFW; Elks; Alpha Zeta; Sigma Phi Epsilon; ODK. Rel: Methodist. Legal Res: Marion, Va. 24354. Mailing Add: 900 Fairway Dr, Vienna, Va. 22180. (1967)

JENNINGS, WILLIAM WEBB D
b. Hillsville, Va, 8/12/00; s. Lewis Alexander Jennings and Ruth A. Webb J; m. 6/4/21 to Vangie L. Francisco; c. Rudolph D. and Dr. Maxine I.(Mrs. Funk). Educ: W.Va. Univ. Polit. & Govt. Pos: Del, Dem. Nat. Conv, 48, alternate del, 64 & 68. Bus. & Prof. Pos: Elec. trouble shooter, N.Am. C.C, 32-54 and Charleston Elec. Co, 55-62; with Joy Mfg. Co, currently. Mem: UMW,AFL; JOUAM; K. of P. Rel: Presbyterian. Mailing Add: 1225 Woodland Ave, Bluefield, W.Va. 24701.

JENNISON, HAROLD STEWART R
Chmn, Lane Co. Rep. Party, Kans.
b. Scott City, Kans, 11/24/22; s. Herlan Stewart Jennison and Katherine Ehmke J; m. 6/18/49 to Yvonne Siegrist; c. Pamela F. and Lois D. Educ: Ft. Hays Kans. State Col, 3 semesters. Polit. & Govt. Pos: Precinct committeeman, Cheyenne Twp. Rep. Party, Kans, 52-; dir, Common Sch. Dist, 56-65; chmn, Lane Co. Rep. Party, 56-; treas, Kans. Rep. Cmt, 58-60; pres, Unified Sch. Dist, 65- Bus. & Prof. Pos: V.pres, First State Bank, Healy, Kans, 46-49, cashier, 49-; Mil. Serv: Entered as Pvt, Army and transferred to Air Force, 43, released as 2nd Lt, 45, after serv. as B-24 navigator. Rel: Methodist. Mailing Add: Healy, Kans. 67850.

JENRETTE, JOHN WILSON, JR. D
S.C. State Rep.
b. Conway, S.C, 5/19/36; s. John Wilson Jenrette, Sr.(deceased) and Mary Herring Jenrette Housand; m. 12/20/60 to Sara Louise Jordan; c. Elizabeth and Harold. Educ: Wofford Col, A.B, 58; Univ. S.C. Sch. Law, LL.B, 62; Kappa Sigma. Polit. & Govt. Pos: City judge, Ocean Drive Beach, S.C, 62-68, city attorney, 62-69; S.C. Rep, Horry Co, 65- Mil. Serv: Entered as 2nd Lt, Army, 59, released as 1st Lt, 59, after serv. in Co. A, 18th Bn, First Training Regt; Capt, Commanding Officer, A Co, 263rd Armored Div, S.C. Nat. Guard, currently. Mem: S.C, Horry Co. and Am. Bar Asns; S.C. Munic. Asn; Farm Bur; Lions; C. of C; Elks. Distinguished Serv. Award, S.C. Munic. Asn. Rel: Methodist. Legal Res: Eighth Ave, Ocean Drive Beach, S.C. 29582. Mailing Add: P.O. Box 362, Ocean Drive Beach, S.C. 29582.

JENSEN, A.J. R
b. Denmark, 1893; m. 2/25/14 to Bernice Roda; c. four. Educ: Pub. schs, Columbia Co, Wis; home law course. Polit. & Govt. Pos: N.Dak. Cmnr. of Ins, 50-68. Bus. & Prof. Pos: Farmer; dir. of Weights & Measures, Dept. of N.Dak. Mem: Shrine; Eagles; Elks. Rel: Lutheran. 1967 Legal Res: Jamestown, N.Dak. No mailing address available. (1967)

JENSEN, ANNA GERTRUDE BATES R
Women's V.Pres, Fresno Co. Rep. Cent. Cmt, Calif.
b. Redmond, Ore, 2/19/17; d. William Robert Bates and Anna Donlavy B; m. 8/19/35 to Arnold Winther Jensen; c. Robert William and Ronald Clyde. Educ: Selma Union High Sch, grad. Polit. & Govt. Pos: Secy. to exec. dir, Fresno Co. Rep. Cent. Cmt, Calif, 63-64 and Central Valley Rep. State Cent. Cmt, Calif, 64-65; secy, Fresno Co. Rep. Cent. Cmt, 64-65, mem, 64-69 and women's v.pres, 66-69; bd. mem, Fresno Co. Rep. Assembly, Calif. Rep. Assembly, 64-68; mem, Goldwater for Pres. Campaign, 64, mem, Calif. Rep. State Cent. Cmt, 64-69; acting exec. secy, Calif. Rep. State Cent. Cmt. and Fresno Co. Rep. Cent. Cmt, 65-66; mem, Floyd Hyde for Mayor of Fresno Campaign, 66; mem. Rep. campaign cmt, 16th Cong. Cand, 66 & 68; mem. bd. dirs, Rep. Women of Fresno Co. and City, 66-69; secy. to two area field dirs, Calif. Rep. State Cent. Cmt, 67-68; mem. Rep. campaign cmt, Fresno Co. for Controller Houston Flournoy, 68; mem. bd. dirs, Cent. Div. Rep. Women, 68-69; secy. to area rep, Gov. Reagan, 68-69. Mem: Farm Bur. of Fresno Co. Rel: Baptist. Mailing Add: 738 N. Ninth St, Fresno, Calif. 93702.

JENSEN, BEN FRANKLIN R
b. Marion, Iowa, 12/16/92; s. Martin Jensen and Gertrude Anna Anderson J; m. 12/13/17 to Charlotte Elizabeth Hadden; c. Betty Lorraine (Mrs. Donald G. Fitzpatrick). Educ: Exira (Iowa) High Sch. Polit. & Govt. Pos: U.S. Rep, Iowa, 39-64. Bus. & Prof. Pos: Green Bay Lumber Co, Exira, Iowa, 14-38, yard mgr, 19-38. Mil. Serv: Dist. Command, 2d Lt, U.S. Army, Camp Pike, Ark, 18. Mem: Am. Legion (7th Dist. Comdr, 36-37); Mason. Rel: Lutheran. Mailing Add: Exira, Iowa. 50076.

JENSEN, CARL ARTHUR R
Minn. State Sen.
b. Sleepy Eye, Minn, 12/11/20; s. Jens Jensen and Hulda Hansen J; m. 1/3/48 to Lorraine Johnson; c. Steven, Karen, Scott, Paul and Bruce. Educ: Univ. Minn, B.S.L, 48, LL.B, 49; Acacia. Polit. & Govt. Pos: Del, State Rep. Conv. and Brown Co. Rep. Conv, Minn, 50-; Minn. State Rep, Brown Co, 51-61; mem, Co. Rep. Cmt, 60-66; attorney, Minn. Asn. of Twp. Officers; city attorney, Sleepy Eye, 58-; Minn. State Sen, 67- Bus. & Prof. Pos: Attorney, Sleepy Eye, Minn, 49- Mil. Serv: Entered as Pvt, Army Air Force, 44, released as S/Sgt, 46. Mem: Minn, Am. and Dist. Bar Asns; bd. dir, Sleepy Eye Indust. Develop. Corp; attorney, Sleepy Eye United Fund; Lions; Sleepy Eye Golf Club; Ishtakhaba Investment Club; PTA; Servicemens Club; Am. Legion; Mason; Sportmens Club; C. of C. Rel: Lutheran. Legal Res: 209 South Fifth St, Sleepy Eye, Minn. 56085. Mailing Add: 127 East Main St, Sleepy Eye, Minn. 56085.

JENSEN, DONALD HUGO D
Chmn, Crawford Co. Dem. Cent. Cmt, Iowa
b. Denison, Iowa, 3/26/20; s. Hugo P. Jensen and Grace Mullen J; m. 2/15/50 to Ann Caryle; c. Linda Ann, Mary Lisa and Andrea Kay. Educ: Denison High Sch, grad, 38. Polit. & Govt. Pos: Chmn, Third Ward Dem. Cmt, Iowa, 60; chmn, Crawford Co. Dem. Cent. Cmt, 65- Bus. & Prof. Pos: Receiving mgr, Montgomery Ward, 39-69. Mem: K. of C. Rel: Catholic. Mailing Add: 1339 Fifth Ave. N, Denison, Iowa 51442.

JENSEN, ELMER R
b. Dwight, Ill, 1/16/07; s. Martin C. Jensen and Katherine Jepsen J; m. 8/18/29 to Louise Pauline Anderson; c. Kenneth C, Richard E. and Keith E. Polit. & Govt. Pos: Precinct committeeman, Rep. Party, Ill, 54-; chmn, Livingston Co. Rep. Party, 63-66. Mem: Odd Fellows; Danish Brotherhood Lodge; Men's Club, St. Peter's Lutheran Church; Farm Bureau; C. of C. Rel: Lutheran; Councilman, St. Peter's Lutheran Church. Mailing Add: Route 1, Box 4, Dwight, Ill. 60420.

JENSEN, GLORIA NATALIE R
Chairwoman, Polk Co. Rep. Party, Minn.
b. Brooten, Minn, 1/20/28; d. Herbert Benoni Baalson and Thresa Kjeldahl B; m. 11/5/55 to John Arnold Jensen, M.D, c. Karla, Terry, John Richard, Judy and Nancy. Educ: St. Lucas Deaconess Sch. Nursing, Fairbault, Minn, R.N, 48. Polit. & Govt. Pos: Blockworker, Crookston, Minn, 58-68; del. and alternate, Rep. Co, Dist. and State Conv, 58-69; chairwoman, West Polk Co. Young Rep. League, 63-65 and Seventh Dist, 64; adv. TAR, Crookston, 64- and dir. Second State Camp, White Earth Lake, 66; area I chairwoman, North. 9 Counties, 65-67; v.chairwoman, Polk Co. Rep. Party, 65-67, chairwoman, 67-; alternate del, Rep. Nat. Conv, 68; v.chairwoman, Seventh Dist. Cong. Langen Vol. Cmt, 68-; leadership consult, Seventh Dist. Rep. Party, 69. Bus. & Prof. Pos: Gen. duty nurse, Nursery, Miller Hosp, St. Paul, Minn, 48-50; head nurse pediatrics, Anchor Hosp, 50-53 and 54-55; gen. duty nurse, premature infants, Charity Hosp, New Orleans, La, 53-54; head night nurse, contagion, Touro Infirmary, 53-54; surg. nurse, Bethesda Hosp, Crookston, Minn, 55-56; housewife, 56- Mem: Former mem, Minn. Nurses Asn; Red River Valley Med. Auxiliary; past pres, Crookston Commun. Theater; past pres, Agassiz Study Club; Am. Field Serv.(local chap. pres); PTA; Minakawa Country Club. Outstanding Young Rep. League Award, Seventh Dist. Rep. Party, Minn, 64 & 65. Rel: Lutheran; past pres, Am. Lutheran Church Women, St. Pauls Lutheran Church, Crookston, Minn. Mailing Add: 717 Thorndale, Crookston, Minn. 56716.

JENSEN, HANS OTTO D
b. Marquette, Nebr, 4/18/98; s. Carl Jensen and Elisa Hansen J; m. 4/5/22 to Helen Christensen; c. Maynard W, Shirley (Mrs. Hansen) and Grace (Mrs. Potter). Educ: Kearney State Teachers Col, 1 year; Nebr. Univ, 1 year. Polit. & Govt. Pos: Chmn, Co. Agr. Adjust. Admin. Cmt, Dept. of Agr, Nebr, 36-38, area fieldman of 9 counties, 39-41, Northwest Area dir, Agr. Stabilization & Conserv. Serv, 61 & 62, chmn, Nebr. State Agr. Stabilization & Conserv. Serv. Cmt, 63-67; Nebr. State Sen, 57-61; del. and chmn. Nebr. del, Dem. Nat. Conv, 68. Bus. & Prof. Pos: Mem, Local Sch. Bd, 28-42. Mil. Serv: Pvt, Army, 18, serv. in Strategic Air Command. Mem: Am. Legion (Comdr. and Chaplain, Lester S. Harter Post 42, Hamilton Co); Lions (past officer); C. of C.(past officer); Nebr. Farmers Union; policy cmt, Nat. Farmers Union. Honored by Aurora C. of C. for Map Makers Award, honored by Nebr. Soil and Water Conserv. for Outstanding Serv. to Nebr; honored by Kiwanis of Lincoln for Outstanding Serv. to Youth. Rel: Lutheran; Mem, Church Coun, St. Johns Lutheran Church, Marquette, Nebr. Mailing Add: 1711 Main St, Aurora, Nebr. 68818.

JENSEN, JOHN CALVIN R
Mem, Exec. Bd, Wayne Co. Rep. Party, N.C.
b. Cincinnati, Ohio, 7/4/25; s. John Jensen and Mary Pederson J; m. 4/10/45 to Agnes Jakob; c. Marcia, Nina K. and John C, Jr. Educ: Wharton Sch, Univ. Pa, 46-48; C.L.U, Am. Col. Life Underwriters, 62. Polit. & Govt. Pos: Pres, Wayne Co. Young Rep, N.C, 61-63; U.S. Cmnr, East. Dist. N.C, 63-66; chmn, Wayne Co. Rep. Party, 66-69; mem. exec. bd, 69- Bus. & Prof. Pos: Asst. to pres, C.F. Simonin's Sons, Inc, Phila, Pa, 48-56; sales, Wing's Inc, 57; sales, Nat. Advert. Co, Goldsboro, N.C, 58-59; agent, Equitable Life Assurance Soc, 60-67; supvr, Jefferson Standard Life Ins, 67- Mil. Serv: Entered as Aviation Cadet, Army Air Force, 43, released as 2nd Lt, 45, recalled as 1st Lt, Pa. Nat. Guard, 50-52. Mem: Wayne Co. Life Underwriters Asn; Wayne Action Group for Econ. Solvency; Wayne Co. Life Underwriters Asn.(pres, 61-62); Goldsboro Area C. of C.(bd. dirs). Outstanding Mem, Wayne Co. Life Underwriters Asn, 63-64; Nat. Qual. Award, Nat. Asn. Life Underwriters. Legal Res: 502 S. Pineview, Goldsboro, N.C. 27530. Mailing Add: Box 166, Goldsboro, N.C. 27530.

JENSEN, LEONA SCHROEDER R
b. Huron, S.Dak, 12/31/19; s. Fred W. Schroeder and Ella S. Vetterman S; m. 9/21/47 to William Robert Jensen; c. Barbara J.(Mrs. John B. Ahrens). Educ: Huron Bus. Col, 39-40. Polit. & Govt. Pos: Rep. precinct committeewoman, Cheyenne, Wyo, 47-52; Rep. State committeewoman, Laramie Co, 54-57; v.chmn, Rep. State Cent. Cmt, 57-60; Rep. Nat. committeewoman, Wyo, 60-64. Mem: Wyo. Girl Scouts (past chmn. area div); Cheyenne Little Theatre (past pres). Rel: Episcopal. Mailing Add: P.O. Box 30, Teton Village, Wyo. 83025.

JENSEN, MILLO R
b. Glendive, Mont, 7/18/11; s. Nels M. Jensen and Mathilda Frandsen J; m. 9/24/38 to Fern Bertha Bertelson; c. Osa Hensine, Nels H, Sigrid Ann and Peder L. Educ: High Sch, grad, 30. Polit. & Govt. Pos: City councilman, Ronan, Mont, 39-44, mayor, 44-50; precinct committeeman, Lake Co. Rep. Party, 40-52, chmn, 54-56; mem, Lake Co. Joint Airport Bd. and chmn, 49-65; Rep. state committeeman, Mont, 56-60; Mont. State Rep, Lake Co, 61-68. Bus. & Prof. Pos: Gen. merchandise bus. with father, Lindsay, Mont, 30-31, wholesale and retail oil bus, Circle, Mont, 32-37, Ford automobile agency, Roundup, 37-39; wholesale oil bus, Ronan, 39- Mem: C. of C.(past pres, Ronan Chap); miscellaneous trade orgns; Elks; Lions. Rel: Lutheran. Mailing Add: Ronan, Mont. 59864. (1967)

JENSEN, ROBERT N. D
Electronic Data Processing Coordinator, Arapahoe Co. Dem. Party, Colo.
b. Racine, Wis, 5/26/21; s. Nels C. Jensen and Emily Musilek J; m. 9/26/46 to Gladys M. Zitka; c. Dane Alan. Educ: Union Grove High Sch, Wis, Gen. Educ. Develop. Dipl. Polit. & Govt. Pos: Precinct committeeman, Aurora Dem. Party, Colo, 64-65; Aurora dist. coordinator, Arapahoe Co. Dem. Party, 65-67, chmn, 67-69, electronic data processing coordinator, 69- Bus. & Prof. Pos: Civil defense dir, Aurora, 65-67. Mil. Serv: Entered as Pvt, Army, 39, released as Maj, 62, after serv. in Army and Air Force, ETO, 39-62; Air Force Res, Maj.(Ret), 62; Purple Heart; Air Force Commendation Medal; Air Medal; Good Conduct Medal; N.Am. Campaign Medal; World War II Victory Medal; Korean Victory Medal; Am. Defense Serv. Medal; Europe-Africa-Middle East Campaign Medal. Mem: Mensa; Am. Rifle Asn. Mailing Add: 14063 E. Dakota Ave, Aurora, Colo. 80010.

JENSEN, THOMAS LEE R
Tenn. State Rep.
b. Knoxville, Tenn, 10/28/34; s. Irving Oscar Jensen and Christine Scarbrough J; m. 6/17/60 to Carolyn Frances Carter; c. Lucinda Anne and Thom-

as Carter. Educ: Univ. Tenn, 52-58. Polit. & Govt. Pos: Tenn. State Rep, 66-, majority whip, Tenn. House of Rep, 68- Bus. & Prof. Pos: Pres, Jensen Corp, 58-; owner, Indust. Leasing Co, 60-; v.pres, Delta Cleaning Contractors, 64-68; pres, Delta Develop. Corp, 65- Mem: Nat. Asn. Independent Businessmen; C. of C; Better Bus. Bur; Jaycees (pres, Fountain City, 64, v.pres, Tenn, 65, secy-treas, 67); Knoxville Exec. Club; adv. cmt, YWCA; trustee, Knoxville Children's Mus. Jaycee of the Year, 66; Tenn. Jaycees Key Man, 67. Rel: Baptist. Legal Res: 2323 Juniper Dr, Knoxville, Tenn. 37912. Mailing Add: P.O. Box 3272, Knoxville, Tenn. 37917.

JENSEN, VERNON K. DFL
Minn. State Sen.
b. Montevideo, Minn, 1912; m. to Irene Warnke; c. Becky, Patty. Educ: Ontario Vet. Col, Guelph, Ontario, 33. Polit. & Govt. Pos: Minn. State Sen, 65-; Montevideo Sch. Bd, 13 years. Bus. & Prof. Pos: Vet, 40- Mem: W. Cent. Vet. Asn; Minn. Vet. Asn.(pres). 4-H award for outstanding serv. Mailing Add: 320 N. Ninth St, Montevideo, Minn. 56265. (1967)

JENSEN, WILLIAM MARTIN R
S.Dak. State Rep.
b. Omaha, Nebr, 10/31/03; s. Martin Christian Jensen and Marie Nelsen J; m. 7/1/29 to Agnes Marie Stromer; c. Clifford Wayne, Janet Jeanine (Mrs. Krogman) and Barry Marlin. Polit. & Govt. Pos: S.Dak. State Rep, 67- Bus. & Prof. Pos: Pres. and dir, Fed. Land Bank Asn, Winner, S.Dak, currently, Cherry Todd Elec, Mission, currently; dir, S.Dak. Asn. of Coop, currently. Mem: Farmers Coop. Oil Asn, Winner, S.Dak; Sch. Bd; Twp. Bd; Mason; Oriental Consistory; Shriners; Eastern Star; Farmers Union. Agr. Conserv. Plaque. Rel: Methodist. Mailing Add: Route 1, White River, S.Dak. 57579.

JENSEN, WILLIAM OWEN, JR. D
Md. State Del.
b. Baltimore, Md, 8/17/29; s. William Owen Jensen and Myrtle Eva Gibson J; m. 4/17/54 to Patricia Hale Harrington; c. William Owen, III, Christopher Michael, Susan Louise, Jacqueline Hale and Patti Jo. Educ: Univ. Baltimore, LL.B, 56; Sigma Delta Kappa. Polit. & Govt. Pos: Precinct exec, Baltimore Co. Dem. Party, Md, 60-66; Md. State Del, 67-, chmn. tourism, Md. House Del, 68- Bus. & Prof. Pos: Home off. correspondent, Calvert Fire Ins. Co, 50-52; claim rep, Ins. Co. N.Am, 52-61 and Md. Casualty Co, 62-; Attorney, 58- Mil. Serv: Entered as Seaman Recruit, Navy, 48, released as Seaman 1/C, 50. Mem: Am. and Md. State Bar Asns; Joppa Rd. Civic League (pres); Intercommun. Coun.(v.pres); Fourth Councilmanic Dem. Club (v.pres); Triangle Dem. Club; Bi-Partisian Cmn. to Defeat Parallel Bay Bridge; Kiwanis. Layman of the Year, Teachers Asn. Baltimore Co, 69. Rel: Methodist. Mailing Add: 2417 Bradford Rd, Baltimore, Md. 21234.

JEPHSON, EVELYN S. D
Mem, State Cmt, Maine Dem. Party
b. Bristol, Conn, 8/16/27; d. Karl Scheschinski and Pauline Doplestein S; m. 12/29/50 to George Hastings Jephson; c. Leslie Carla. Educ: Waterbury Sch. Nursing, 46. Polit. & Govt. Pos: Mem, Waldoboro Sch. Bd, Maine, 62-64; del, Dem. Nat. Conv. and mem, Platform Cmt, 64 & 68; justice of the peace, Maine, 66; mem, Maine Water and Air Environ. Improv. Cmn, 67-; mem, Gov. Adv. Coun. on the Status of Women, 67-; v.chmn, Waldoboro Dem. Town Cmt, 68; treas, Waldoboro Dem. Women's Club, 68; secy, Maine Asn. Dem. Women's Clubs, 68; dedimus justice, Maine, 68; mem. state cmt, Maine Dem. Party, Lincoln Co, 68- Bus. & Prof. Pos: Owner, Shop of Folly Farm, 68- Mem: Knox-Lincoln Co. Exten. Club. Rel: Lutheran. Legal Res: Bremen Rd, Waldoboro, Maine 04572. Mailing Add: R.F.D. 4, Waldoboro, Maine 04572.

JEPSEN, ROGER W. R
Lt. Gov, Iowa
Mailing Add: State Capitol, Tenth & Grand Ave, Des Moines, Iowa 50319.

JEPSON, ALAN HERBERT D
Mayor, Milford, Conn.
b. Hartford, Conn, 5/28/26; s. Chauncey Albert Jepson and Alice Piercy J; m. 9/11/48 to Mary Elizabeth Pettingell; c. Linda Caroline, Susan Emily, Margot Elizabeth, Nancy Ellen and Paula Leslie. Educ: Boston Univ, B.S; Lambda Chi Alpha. Polit. & Govt. Pos: Mayor, Milford, Conn, 63- Bus. & Prof. Pos: Exec. dir, Citizens Action Cmn. and Jr. Achievement of Greater New Haven; prog. dir, Jr. Achievement of Boston and Jr. Achievement of West. Conn. Mil. Serv: Entered as A/S, Navy, 43, released as Seaman 1/C, 46, after serv. in Pac; Am. Theater Ribbon; Philippine Liberation Medal with One Star; Asiatic-Pac. Ribbon with Six Stars. Mem: Elks; Am. Legion; VFW; Rotary; Conn. Chiefs of Police Asn; Deputy Sheriffs Asn. of New Haven Co. Rel: Episcopal. Legal Res: 118 Springdale St, Milford, Conn. 06460. Mailing Add: City Hall, Milford, Conn. 06460.

JERNEGAN, JOHN DURNFORD
b. Los Angeles, Calif, 6/2/11; s. Edward Skinner Jernegan and Ida Latham Hollingsworth J; m. to Mary Margaret Brownrigg; c. Jeffrey L, Joan A, John B. and Jeremy H. Educ: Stanford Univ, A.B, 33, A.M, 35; Georgetown Univ. Sch. of For. Serv, 33-34; Phi Beta Kappa. Polit. & Govt. Pos: V.counsul, Mexico City, Mex, 36-38; v.consul, Barcelona, 38-41; with State Dept, 41-43; third secy, v.consul and second secy, Tehran, 43-46; asst. chief, Div. Near East. Affairs, 46; chief, Div. Greek Turkish Iranian Affairs, 48; dir, Off. of Greek, Turkish Iranian Affairs, 49; consul gen, Tunis, 50-52; dep. asst. secy. of state for Near East, South Asian and African Affairs, 52-55; minister-counsr, Rome, 55-58; U.S. Ambassador to Iraq, 58-63; dep. asst. secy. of state for Near East. and South Asian Affairs, 63-65; U.S. Ambassador to Algeria, 65-67; diplomat in residence, Emory Univ, 67-68; polit. adv, Comdr. in Chief Atlantic, Norfolk, Va, 68- Bus. & Prof. Pos: Newspaper reporter, Oakland,(Calif) Tribune, 36. Mem: Am. For. Serv. Asn; Mid.E. Inst; Acad. Polit. Sci; Acad. Polit. & Soc. Sci. Nat. Civil Serv. League Award, 61. Legal Res: Palo Alto, Calif. Mailing Add: 1211 Langley Rd, Norfolk, Va. 23507.

JERNIGAN, ROBERTS HARRELL, JR. D
N.C. State Rep.
b. Ahoskie, N.C, 11/24/15; s. Roberts Harrell Jernigan and Jessie Garrett J; m. 5/14/49 to Linda Williams; c. Roberts III, Elizabeth, Clawson. Educ: Naval Acad. Prep Sch, 32-33; Wake Forest Col, 33-36; Univ. of N.C, A.B, 37, Law Sch, 37-39. Polit. & Govt. Pos: Chmn, Hertford Co. Dem. Exec. Cmt, N.C, 58; N.C. State Rep, 63- Bus. & Prof. Pos: Farmer; Pres. & treas, Ahoskie Meat & Provision Co, Inc; Standard Vacuum Oil Co, Mgr, Peiping Off, China, pre-World War II. Mil. Serv: Prisoner of Japanese, 23 months, World War II; Ensign, USN, 43-46; Invasion of S.France. Mem: Sigma Nu; Rotary (pres, Ahoskie Club, 55); Hertford Co. Young Dem. Club. Rel: Episcopal; Sr. Warden. Mailing Add: 401 N. Curtis St, Ahoskie, N.C. 27910.

JERNIGAN, WALLACE LAWSON D
b. Jesup, Ga, 6/23/25; s. Fred Wallace Jernigan and Sammie Bishop J; m. 11/25/51 to Carolyn Moore; c. Nancy Elizabeth. Educ: Ga. Inst. Tech, B.S.C.E, 46; Am. Soc. Civil Engrs; Sigma Phi Epsilon (treas); Interfraternity Coun. Polit. & Govt. Pos: Co. surveyor, Clinch Co, Ga, 49-53; Ga. State Sen, 59-60, chmn. educ. cmt, Ga. State Senate, 59-60; Ga. State Rep, 61; admin. asst. to Gov. S. Ernest Vandiver, Ga, 61 and exec. secy, 62; mem, Gov. Carl Sanders' Cmn. to Improve Educ, 63; admin. asst. to U.S. Rep, W.S. Stuckey, Jr, Ga, 67- Mem: Ga. Funeral Dirs.(pres, Eighth Dist, 61); Ga. Beekeepers Asn.(past pres); Mason; Lions; Ga. Sportsman Fedn. Rel: Baptist. Legal Res: 215 Peagler St, Homerville, Ga. 31634. Mailing Add: 4818-301 Kenmore Ave, Alexandria, Va. 22304.

JESK, JAMES WILBERT D
Committeeman, Ill. Dem. Cent. Cmt.
b. Chicago, Ill, 5/14/07; s. Michael Jesk and Bertha Bartels J; m. 6/15/29 to Mary Ruth Lyons; c. James W, Jr, Mary (Mrs. Rust), Dale Edward, Terrance, Sharon (Mrs. Poe), John and Robin. Educ: Chicago Law Sch, LL.B, 33. Polit. & Govt. Pos: U.S. Postmaster, Oak Forest, Ill, 42-45; supvr, Bremen Twp, Ill, 49-69; committeeman, Ill. Dem. Cent. Cmt, 64- Bus. & Prof. Pos: Dir, Interstate Bank of Oak Forest, 69- Mem: Lions; Twp. Off. Ill. Rel: Catholic. Mailing Add: 15146 Cicero Ave, Oak Forest, Ill. 60452.

JESSE, NORMAN GALE D
Iowa State Rep.
b. Des Moines, Iowa, 11/9/37; s. James Rollin Jesse and Helen Grace Mahan J; single. Educ: Iowa State Univ, B.S, 61; Drake Univ. Law Sch, Des Moines, Iowa, LL.B, 64; Theta Xi Soc. Fraternity; Phi Alpha Delta Legal Fraternity. Polit. & Govt. Pos: Iowa State Rep, Polk Co, 69- Bus. & Prof. Pos: Attorney at Law, Jesse, LeTourneau & Johnston; Des Moines, Iowa, 64- Mem: Polk Co, Iowa State and Am. Bar Asn; Iowa Dem. Conf; Iowa Civil Liberties Union. Rel: Lutheran. Legal Res: 2016 Avalon Road, Des Moines, Iowa 50314. Mailing Add: 917 Savings & Loan Bldg, Des Moines, Iowa 50309.

JESSEN, GUDMUND BENDIX, JR. D
b. Hennepin, Ill, 3/15/33; s. Gudmund Bendix Jessen and Ethel Ester Coleman J; m. 5/28/55 to Billie Adele Brown; c. Debra Lee, Cheryl Lynn and Craig Alan. Educ: Hennepin High Sch, grad; Govt. Approved Agr. Course, 3 years. Polit. & Govt. Pos: Deputy sheriff, Putnam Co, Ill, 58-61; Justice of the Peace, Senachwine and Hennepin, 61-65; precinct committeeman, Hennepin Twp. Dem. Party, 62- Bus. & Prof. Pos: Farmer, grain and livestock oper, 55- Mil. Serv: Entered Army, 53, released as S/Sgt, 55, after serv. in Hq. U.S. Army, Europe, in Heidelburg, Germany with G-2 Intel, and the Korean War, 53-55; Army of Occupation Medal; Nat. Defense Serv. Medal; Good Conduct Medal. Mem: Odd Fellows; Am. Legion; Farm Bur; Putnam Co. Dem. Orgn; Hennepin Betterment Asn; Village of Hennepin Planning Bd; Hennepin Sportsmen Club; Ill. Sheriff Asn; Nat. Farmers Orgn. Rel: Methodist. Mailing Add: Box 205, Hennepin, Ill. 61327.

JESSEN, HERBERT HENRY D
b. Charleston, S.C, 9/19/98; s. Frederick W. Jessen and Minnie Torck J; m. 10/6/20 to Lillian A. McDougal. Educ: Clemson Col, 15-17. Polit. & Govt. Pos: S.C. State Sen, 61-64, 65-66; Sheriff, Dorchester City, 29-60; Mayor, Summerville, S.C, 25-29; Alderman, Summerville, S.C, 23-25. Bus. & Prof. Pos: Gen. Servs. Admin. Contractor. Mem: S.C. Sheriffs Asn. (Secy. & Treas, 32 yrs.) Bd. of Govs, Nat. Sheriffs Asn, 54-56; State Dir, 58-60; Lutheran Brotherhood (life mem.); K. of P, past chancellor comdr. Rel: Lutheran. Mailing Add: 710 S. Main St, Summerville, S.C. 29483. (1967)

JESSUP, ROGER L. R
Ind. State Rep.
b. 2/23/29; married; c. four. Educ: Purdue Univ, B.S; Ball State Univ, M.A. Polit. & Govt. Pos: Ind. State Rep, 67- Bus. & Prof. Pos: Owner & operator of farm; high sch. teacher. Mem: Fairmount Masonic Lodge; Am. Legion. Mailing Add: R.R. 2, Summitville, Ind. 46070. (1967)

JETER, JAMES CLAY R
W.Va. State Del.
b. Morgantown, W.Va, 10/1/34; s. James Garrett Jeter, Jr. and Lucille Chenoweth J; m. 11/24/61 to Nancy Eileen Chapman; c. Garrett Chapman, Clay Chenoweth and David Spafford. Educ: Wash. & Lee Univ, B.A, 56 and LL.B, 59; Phi Alpha Delta; Kappa Sigma; Student Bar Asn. Polit. & Govt. Pos: W.Va. State Del, Kanawha Co, 67- Bus. & Prof. Pos: Partner, Jeter, Jeter & Jeter, law firm, 61-; asst. ed, Advocate, W.Va. Trial Lawyer's Newspaper, 66. Mil. Serv: Entered as A/S, Naval Res, 59, released as Seaman, 61; Naval Res, 65. Publ: 'Reopening Workmen's Compensation Cases,' Advocate, 66. Mem: W.Va. Bar Asn; W.Va. and Am. Trial Lawyers Asns; Press Club; Army-Navy Club; The Charleston Tennis Club. Rel: Episcopal. Legal Res: 16 Norwood Rd, Charleston, W.Va. 25314. Mailing Add: P.O. Box 855, Charleston, W.Va. 25323.

JEVITZ, JOHN LOUIS R
Exec. Secy, Will Co. Rep. Cent. Cmt, Ill.
b. Chicago, Ill, 4/24/01; s. John J. Jevitz and Cecelia Hren J.(deceased); m. 1/11/25 to Lottie Marie Witczak; c. Dorothy M.(Mrs. Reno Sartori), Geraldine A.(Mrs. Stuart Christensen), John D. and Eugene J. Educ: St. Joseph's Parochial, Seventh Grade; Farragut Pub. Sch, Eighth grade grad. Polit. & Govt. Pos: Dep. twp. assessor, Joliet, Ill, 27-33; precinct committeeman, Rep. Town and Co. Cent. Cmts, Ill, 27-38 & 48-69; asst. supvr, Will Co. Bd. Supvr, 29-33; dep. sheriff, Will Co, 38-42, off. and chief dep. sheriff, 48-52; exec. secy, Will Co. Rep. Cent. Cmt, 50-; supt. forest preserves, Will Co, 56-69; Slovenian adv. nationalities div, Rep. Nat. Cmt, 60-; town clerk, Joliet, 69-; campaign mgr, several successful Rep. local off. cand. Mem: Am. Slovenian

Cath. Union; St. Joseph's Slovenian Cath. Parish; Am. Fraternal Union (past Supreme V.Pres); West. Slavonic Asn; Slovenia Cultural Soc, Triglav; St. Joseph's Parish Singing Soc; Am. Slovenian Home; Slovenian Radio Hour Club of Chicago; organizer and conductor, first Slovenian Radio Hour, 30-33; pres. and chmn, first Slovenian Day in Joliet, Ill, 34; Men's Holy Name Soc.(pres, St. Joseph's Parish Chap, 60); Eagles; Joliet Rivals Athletic and Soc. Club; Northwest Recreation and Soc. Club; City Baseball League (pitcher, 20's, pres, 36); Old Timers Baseball Asn. of Joliet and Will Co.(organizer, 49, pres, first 10 years, hon. pres, currently); Old Timers Baseball Asns. of Milwaukee, Wis. and Chicago, Ill; Am. Cancer Soc.(crusade chmn, Will Co. Chap, 64); Match Workers Union (pres, local chap, 22). Recipient of the only Gold Life Time Presidency, Old Timers Baseball Asn, Joliet and Will Co, Ill, recipient of 5 keep-sake gavels in recognition of presidency in various Slovene and other groups. Rel: Catholic. Mailing Add: 810 Oakland Ave, Joliet, Ill. 60435.

JEWELL, FLAVE M. R

b. Monticello, Maine, 12/18/92; s. George W. Jewell and Almeda Good J; m. to Respa Hare; c. Robert M. Educ: Monticello Pub. Schs. Polit. & Govt. Pos: Maine State Rep, 63-64 & 66-67. Mem: Mason; Kiwanis. Mailing Add: Box 100, Monticello, Maine 04760. (1967)

JEWETT, DONALD W. R

Wyo. State Sen.

b. Kimball, Nebr, 5/1/09; m. Ethel. Educ: Univ. Wyo, B.S. Polit. & Govt. Pos: Wyo. State Rep, 1 term; co. cmnr, $14\frac{1}{2}$ years; mem. sch. bd. 9 years; mem, Bur. of Farm Land Mgt, 4 years; Wyo. State Sen, 64- Bus. & Prof. Pos: Rancher. Mem: AF&AM; RAM (Knight Templar); Shrine; Lions; Wyo. Farm Bur; Wyo. Stock Growers Asn; Wyo. Taxpayers Asn. Rel: Episcopal. Mailing Add: Big Piney, Wyo. 83113. (1967)

JIACOLETTI, RAYMOND N. D

Chmn, Wasatch Co. Dem. Party, Utah

b. Frontier, Wyo, 12/4/13; s. James F. Jiacoletti and Mary Rhoades J; m. 9/2/39 to Rachel Fortie; c. Raymond N, Jr, Phyletta J.(Mrs. Gardner) and Maria J. (Mrs. Hilton). Educ: Univ. Wyo, B.S, 35; Brigham Young Univ, M.S, 40; Utah State Univ, Grad. Work, 40-65; Univ. Utah, Grad. Work, 45-60; Iron Skull; Sigma Nu. Polit. & Govt. Pos: Educ. adv, Civil Conserv. Corps, U.S. Army, Ft. Douglas, Utah, 36-38, camp Comdr, 38-39; chmn, Wasatch Co. Dem. Party, 45-; mayor, Heber, 46-66; dir, Utah Munic. League, State of Utah, 55-66. Bus. & Prof. Pos: Employ. supvr, State of Wyo, Kemmerer, 35-37; pub. acct. and tax consult, R.N. Jiacoletti, Heber, Utah, 38-69; off. mgr, Fryn Eng. Co, Chicago, Ill, 38-42; control acct. supvr, Columbia Steel Co, Geneva, Utah, 42-45; pres, Heber Light and Power Plant, Heber City Corp, 46-66; dairy processing partnership, Fortie-Jiacoletti Dairy, Heber, 47-53; jr. high sch. prin, Wasatch Co. Sch. Dist, 53- Mil. Serv: Entered as 2nd Lt, Army, 38, released as 1st Lt, 41, after serv. in Inf. and Air Corps; Commanding Officer, Civil Air Patrol, 55-61. Publ: Civil Conservation Corps Work Procedures Handbook, U.S. Bur. of Reclamation, 39. Mem: Nat, Utah State and Wasatch Co. Educ. Asns; Nat. and Utah State Asns. of Sec. Prin; pres, Utah State Voc. Asn; Phi Delta Kappa; charter mem, Wasatch Co. C. of C. and Wasatch-Summit Dining Club; past pres, Heber Lions; Capt, Blackhawk Asn; pres, Wasatch Co. Libr. Valley Forge Found. Award, 59-60; Second Place, Utah Mayor of the Year, 65. Rel: Latter-day Saint. Mailing Add: 176 W. Second South, Heber City, Utah 84032.

JINDRA, ROY I. R

Committeeman, Tex. State Rep. Exec. Cmt.

b. Omaha, Nebr, 10/25/20; s. Joseph George Jindra and Ruth Kutscher J; m. 9/22/52 to Lou Cele Rice; c. Michael Scott. Educ: Univ. Kans, B.S, 48; Sigma Gamma Epsilon. Polit. & Govt. Pos: Committeeman, Tex. State Rep. Exec. Cmt, 21st Sen. Dist, 64-66 & 68-; alternate del, Rep. Nat. Conv, 68. Bus. & Prof. Pos: Geologist, Amerada Petroleum Corp, Tyler and San Antonio, Tex, 48-51, Kirkwood & Co, Alice, 51-60; chief geologist, Harkins & Co, Alice, Tex, 60- Mil. Serv: Entered as Pvt, Marines, 42, released as Cpl, 45, after serv. in 22nd Marine Regt, Pac. Theatre, 42-44. Mem: Corpus Christi Geol. Soc; Am. Geol. Inst; Am. Asn. Petroleum Geologists. Rel: Protestant. Legal Res: 1220 Washington St, Alice, Tex. 78332. Mailing Add: Box 1490, Alice, Tex. 78332.

JIROLANIO, JUSTIN DI D

Chmn, Bethlehem Dem. City Cmt, Pa.

b. N.Y.C, 5/11/04; s. Joseph Di Jirolanio and Filomena J; m. to Dorothy Elizabeth Fawber; c. Mary Louise (Mrs. Harrison Wright). Educ: Franklin & Marshall Col, B.S; Temple Univ. Law Sch. Polit. & Govt. Pos: Rep, CIO-USW and Amalgamated Clothing Workers; Pa. State Rep, 37-41; Asst. Dist. Attorney, Northampton Co, Pa, 40-43; Pa. State Sen, 63-67; chmn, Bethlehem Dem. City Cmt, currently. Bus. & Prof. Pos: Attorney; mem, local courts, Pa. Supreme and Superior Courts, U.S. Dist. Court of East. Pa. Mem: Mason (mem. all lodges). Rel: United Church of Christ. Mailing Add: 2854 Linden St, Bethlehem, Pa. 18017.

JOELSON, CHARLES S. D

b. Paterson, N.J, 1/27/16; s. Harry Joelson and Jennie Ellenstein J; c. Susan. Educ: Cornell Univ, B.A, 37; LL.B, 39; Phi Beta Kappa. Polit. & Govt. Pos: City counsel, Paterson, N.J, 49-52; dep. attorney gen, State of N.J, 55-60; U.S. Rep, N.J, Eighth Dist, 61-68; Judge, Superior Court N.J, currently. Mil. Serv: Entered as Yeoman 2/C, Navy, released as Ens, after serv. in Off. of Naval Intel, Far East. Branch. Mem: N.J. Bar Asn; Am. Legion. Rel: Jewish. Mailing Add: 599 Broadway, Paterson, N.J. 07514.

JOERG, DAVID ALLEN R

b. Spring Grove, Minn, 4/27/32; s. Leslie Eugene Joerg and Luverne Lien J; m. 12/26/64 to Trudy A. Spaetgens; c. Christopher John. Educ: Univ. Minn. and Univ. Minn Law Sch, B.S.L, 54; Univ. Minn. Law Sch, LL.B. magna cum laude, 56; Kappa Sigma. Polit. & Govt. Pos: Chmn, Fillmore Co. Rep. Party, Minn, 67-69; village attorney, Preston, currently; govt. appeal agent, Selective Serv. Syst, Fillmore Co, currently. Mem: Fillmore Co. Bar Asn.(secy, 57-63); Tenth Judicial Dist. Bar Asn.(pres, 68-69); Minn. State and Am. Trial Lawyers Bar Asns; Mason; Lions Int; Toastmasters Int. Rel: Unitarian Universalist. Mailing Add: Preston, Minn. 55965.

JOHANNESON, HELGI R

Attorney Gen, N.Dak.

b. Gardar, N.Dak, 6/21/06; s. Benedict Johanneson and Hildur Gudjonson J; m. 11/27/30 to Ann K. Prokosch; c. Carole (Mrs. Miller), Jeanne (Mrs. Cummings), Kent and Robert J. Educ: Univ. of N.Dak; St. Paul Col. of Law; Phi Beta Gamma. Polit. & Govt. Pos: State attorney, Pembina Co, Minn, 33-37; dir. sch. dist, Newfolden, Minn, 48-50; asst. attorney gen, N.Dak, 52-62, Attorney Gen, 63- Bus. & Prof. Pos: Mem, Judicial Coun, N.Dak; secy, Marshall Co. Locker Asn; owner and mgr, Newfolden Machine Co, Minn. Mem: Newfolden Civic Club; Lions. Rel: Catholic. Mailing Add: 1315 Mohawk St, Bismarck, N.Dak. 58501. (1967)

JOHANSON, LOUIS CARL D

b. Phila, Pa, 1/4/29; s. Nils G. Johanson and Emma E. Sonderschafer J; m. to Kathleen Rodden; c. three. Educ: Univ. of Pa, B.A; Univ. of Pa. Law Sch, LL.B. Polit. & Govt. Pos: Pa. State Sen, 64-67; Secy, Ward Cmt; Admin. Asst, Pres. of City Coun; Exec. Asst, Mayor, Phila. Bus. & Prof. Pos: Attorney, Supreme, Superior Courts, Pa, and Fed. Courts; Dist. Dir, United Fund, 62-63. Mil. Serv: U.S. Navy, Electronic Technician 3, 46-47; U.S. Marine Corp, Korean Conflict, 51-53; 2nd Btn. 7th Marines, 1st Lt, Commendation with Combat 5; U.S. Marine Corps, Maj, 53-; Marine Corp Res. Officers Asn. Misc: High Sch. Football, 150 lb. E.C.A.C. Football. Mailing Add: 4348 N. Franklin St, Phila, Pa. 19140. (1967)

JOHN, LOUISE MOSES D

V.Chmn, Pa. Dem. State Cmt.

b. West Chester, Pa, 10/8/10; d. George Joseph Moses and Mabel Rupert M; m. 6/26/35 to James John. Educ: Pa. Sch. Occup. Therapy, grad, 34. Polit. & Govt. Pos: Dem. precinct committeewoman, 40-; Dem. state committeewoman, 42-55; v.chmn, Pa. Fedn. Dem. Women, 48-52; del-at-lg, Dem. Nat. Conv, 56, 60, 64 and 68; v.chmn, Pa. Dem. State Cmt, 56-; inspector, Chester Co. Prison, 57-59; mem, Pa. Welfare Cmn, 57-60; presidential elector, 60; mem, State Employees Retirement Bd, 61-64; secy. bd. trustees, West Chester State Col, 61-68. Bus. & Prof. Pos: Occup. therapist, Pennhurst State Sch, 34. Mem: Bd. dirs, hosp. and hist. groups, 53-; Bus. & Prfnl. Women's Club; Am. Legion Auxiliary; Salvation Army Auxiliary. Rel: Presbyterian; mem, Bd. of Deacons. Legal Res: 829 S. High St, West Chester, Pa. 19380. Mailing Add: 510 N. Third St, Harrisburg, Pa. 17101.

JOHNS, CHARLEY EUGENE D

b. Starke, Fla, 2/27/05; s. Everett Earnest Johns and Annie Pettit J; m. 4/21/27 to Thelma Brinson; c. Charley Jerome and Markleyann (Mrs. Cash). Educ: Univ. Fla. Polit. & Govt. Pos: Fla. State Rep, 35-37; Fla. State Sen, 38-65; Acting Gov, Fla, 53-55. Bus. & Prof. Pos: Owner, Charley F. Johns Ins. Agency, Starke, Fla, 30-; pres, Commun. State Bank of Starke, 57- Mem: Fla. Educ. Asn; Fla. Ins. Agents Asn; BRT; Order of R.R. Conductors; Elks; Mason; Shrine; C. of C. Rel: Baptist. Legal Res: 415 E. South, Starke, Fla. 32091. Mailing Add: 131 S. Walnut, Starke, Fla. 32091.

JOHNS, GEORGE PETER R

b. Howells, Nebr, 1/5/06; m. to Betsy Morton; c. George Peter, Jr, Thomas M. and Christopher. Polit. & Govt. Pos: Ill. State Sen, 28th Dist, 56-60; Ill. State Rep, 47th Dist, 62-64 and 52nd Dist, 66-68. Bus. & Prof. Pos: Chmn. bd, Credit Bur. of Decatur. Mem: Asn. of Commerce; Mason; YMCA; Elks; Country Club of Decatur; Decatur Club; Kiwanis; Shrine. Rel: Presbyterian. Legal Res: 150 N. Oakdale, Decatur, Ill. 62552. Mailing Add: 260 E. Wood St, Decatur, Ill. 62523.

JOHNS, JOHN S. D

b. Beaver Falls, Pa, 3/4/15; s. George Johns and Rose Abraham J; m. 6/15/41 to Emma Dager; c. Robert and Irene. Polit. & Govt. Pos: Del, Dem. Nat. Conv, 64 & 68. Mil. Serv: Entered as Pvt, Army, 42, released as Sgt, 45; Marksmanship and Good Conduct Medals; Pac. Theater Ribbon and others. Mem: USW staff rep, 41-52, dir, Dist. 27, 52-; Indust. Develop. Corp; United Fund; Commun. Improv. Corp; Citizens Cmt. Pub. Schs; Moose; Eagles; Urban League. Public speaking. Rel: Syrian Orthodox. Legal Res: 2118 University Ave. N.W, Canton, Ohio 44709. Mailing Add: 1330 Market Ave. N, Canton, Ohio 44714.

JOHNS, MERRILL BLAINE, JR. R

b. Chicago, Ill, 4/9/16; s. Merrill Blaine Johns and Ellen Davis J; m. 12/26/40 to Claire Golden, separated; c. Gail and Jennifer. Educ: Cornell Univ, 33-34; Univ. Chicago, 34-35; Psi Upsilon. Polit. & Govt. Pos: N.Mex. State Rep, 52-54; mem, N.Mex. State Bd. Finance, 52-54 & 56-58; committeeman, Rep. Nat. Cmt, 54-56 & 66-67; chmn, N.Mex. Rep. Party, 54-56 & 66-67; state treas, N.Mex, 68; mem, Pub. Employees Retirement Bd, State Invest. Coun, and Educ. Retirement Bd, 68. Bus. & Prof. Pos: Rep, Leo Burnett, Inc, 37-40; rep, Time Mag, 40-46; owner, Santa Fe Real Estate and Invest. Co, N.Mex, 46-; dir. Storer Broadcasting Co; v.pres, U.S. Uranium Corp, 52-55; pres, Strata Corp. Mil. Serv: Entered as 2nd Lt, Army, 41, released as Maj, after serv. in Adj. Gen. Dept, 41-46. Mem: Am. Nat. Cattlemen's Asn; Colo. Cattlemen's Asn; Wyo. Stock Growers Asn; Am. Quarter Horse Asn; Chicago Athletic Club; Denver Club; Old Baldy Club, Saratoga, Wyo; Kiva, Santa Fe; Foundation, El Paso. Rel: Protestant. Mailing Add: Old Baldy Club, Saratoga, Wyo. 82331.

JOHNS, ROY WILLIAM R

b. Wakefield, Mich, 7/29/00; s. James Oates Johns and Mary J; m. 8/30/24 to Lempi Katherine Hill; c. Kenneth Roy, Norma (Mrs. Rigotti), Neal William, Rosemary (Mrs. Farrington) and Marcia (Mrs. Vogel). Educ: Wakefield High Sch, 4 years. Polit. & Govt. Pos: City employment dir, Wakefield, Mich, 31-35, assessor of taxes, 39-43, cmnr. of pub. works, 44-47, mayor, 61-68; state cmnr. of labor, 63-66; pres, Wakefield Housing Authority, 66- Mil. Serv: Entered as Pvt, Army, 20, released as Spc. 4/C, 21, after serv. in Eighth Engrs, Ft. Bliss, Tex. Mem: USW; Wakefield C. of C.(pres, 36-39). Rel: Lutheran. Mailing Add: 1504 Putnam St, Wakefield, Mich. 49968.

JOHNS, WILLIAM CAMPBELL R

b. Ames, Iowa, 9/4/25; s. Erwin William Johns and Maria Jongewaard J; m. 3/17/51 to Madge Hazlett; c. Donald William, Janice Ruth, Lawarence Campbell and Maria Josephine. Educ: Univ. N.Mex, 43 & 46-47; Wheaton Col, Ill,

47-48; Northwest. Univ. Med. Sch, B.S. in Med, 48, M.D, 52; Phi Chi. Polit. & Govt. Pos: Chmn, Redman Cmt. for Cong. Cand, N.Mex, 62 & 64; chmn, N.Mex. Rep. State Finance Cmt, 66-67, co-chmn, 67-69; del, Rep. Nat. Conv, 68. Bus. & Prof. Pos: Pres. med. staff, Presby. Hosp. Center, Albuquerque, N.Mex, 64-65; mem, N.Mex. Bd. of Med. Exam, 67- Mil. Serv: Entered as Pvt, Army, 43, released as S/Sgt, 46, after serv. in 86th Inf. Div, ETO. Mem: Fel, Am. Col. of Obstetricians & Gynecologists; Am. and N.Mex. Med. Asns. Civic Serv. Award, Albuquerque Jr. C. of C, 64. Rel: Presbyterian. Legal Res: 1726 Notre Dame N.E, Albuquerque, N.Mex. 87106. Mailing Add: 717 Encino Place N.E, Albuquerque, N.Mex. 87106.

JOHNSON, ALBERT SIDNEY SR. D
b. Gainesville, Ga, 7/11/88; s. George W. Johnson and Elizabeth Watson J; m. 11/6/14 to Elas E. Gunther; c. Dr. Albert Sidney Jr, Carl, Frieda (Peggy) and Estes. Educ: N.Ga. Col; Emory Univ, M.D, 13; Pi Kappa Alpha. Polit. & Govt. Pos: Councilman, Elberton, Ga, 31-32, Ga. State Rep, 63-68. Bus. & Prof. Pos: Physician, Elberton, Ga, 13- Mil. Serv: World War I Med. Bd. Mem: Mason; Elks; Elberton Rotary (dir). Rel: Methodist. Mailing Add: Elberton, Ga. 30635. (1967)

JOHNSON, ALBERT W. R
U.S. Rep, Pa.
b. Smethport, Pa, 4/17/06; s. John A. Johnson and Edla Marie Ostrom J; m. 6/23/26 to Virginia Balsley; c. Richmond, David, Ronald and Karen. Educ: Univ. Pa. Wharton Sch, 26-28; John B. Stetson Univ, LL.B; Alpha Tau Omega. Polit. & Govt. Pos: Pa. State Rep, 46-63, Rep. Party Whip, Pa. House of Rep, 51-59, Floor Leader, 53-55 & 57-63, chmn, House Cmt. on Rules, mem, Legis. Budget and Finance and Interstate Coop. Cmts; chmn, Pa. Rep. Platform Cmt, 58 & 62; U.S. Rep, 23rd Dist, 63-, asst. to Rep. Floor Leader and mem, Banking and Currency and Post Off. and Civil Serv. Cmts, U.S. House of Rep; mem, Joint State Govt. Cmn, Gen. State Authority, State Pub. Sch. Bldg. Authority, State Hwy. and Bridge Authority and State Coun. Civil Defense. Bus. & Prof. Pos: Dir. and counsel, Smethport Nat. Bank, Pa, 42-62. Mem: Pa. and McKean Co. Bar Asns; Moose. Rel: Protestant. Mailing Add: 409 Franklin St, Smethport, Pa. 16749.

JOHNSON, ALLEN LEVI D
Chmn, Fifth Congression Dist. Dem. Party, Miss.
b. Meridian, Miss, 8/31/17; s. Levi Evans Johnson and Verina Hollman J; m. 7/30/37 to Vanilla Antoinette Davis; c. Allene (Mrs. Sylvester Tucker), Allen, Jr, Marcia (Mrs. Robert Hall), Sandra (Mrs. James Hester), Nathaniel, Glenda, Linda, Henry and Jerome. Educ: Rust Col, B.S, 40; Gammon Theological Seminary; B.D, 43; Harvard Univ, summer, 43; Phi Beta Sigma. Polit. & Govt. Pos: Chmn, Political Action; chmn, Fifth Cong. Dist. Dem. Party, Miss, currently. Bus. & Prof. Pos: Pastor, St. Paul United Methodist Church, June, 1967. Mil. Serv: 1st Lt, Army, 45, released as Maj, 49, after serv. in 92nd Div, Regimental Chapter European and S.Pacific, 45-49; Silver Star with Oak Leaf Cluster; Purple Heart. Mem: Council on Evangelism (v.pres); Nat. Bd. Mem, South. Christian Leadership Conf; Elks; Mason; Int. Frontiersmen. Man of Year, Phi Beta Sigma, 65; Man of Year, Omega Psi Phi, 69. Rel: United Methodist. Legal Res: 517 Jefferson St, Laurel, Miss. 39440.

JOHNSON, ANICE WISMER R
Ohio State Rep.
b. Lumber City, Ga, 2/22/19; d. Adelbert Jesse Wismer and Kathryn Harwell W; m. 4/12/43 to George C. Johnson, Jr; c. Michael Anne, George C, III, Anice W, Jr, Doan Burgess and Wismer A. Educ: Brenau Col, A.B, 39; Tau Kappa Alpha; Alpha Delta Pi. Polit. & Govt. Pos: Ohio State Rep, 35th House Dist, 69- Bus. & Prof. Pos: Continuity writer and newscaster, WRBL Radio, Ga, 40-46; reporter, Record-Courier Ravenna, Ohio, 65-66. Mem: Sustaining mem, Jr. League of Cleveland; Aurora Study Club. Rel: Episcopal. Legal Res: 286 Eggleston Rd, Aurora, Ohio 44202. Mailing Add: Ohio House of Representatives, Columbus, Ohio 43215.

JOHNSON, ARTHUR LLOYD, JR. D
b. Lawrence, Kans, 12/5/14; s. Arthur Lloyd Johnson and Olda Lottie Anderson J; m. 4/23/43 to Gladys Mainese McClain. Educ: Hampton Inst, B.S, 37, M.A, 49. Polit. Pos: Ky. State Rep, 40th Dist, 64-66. Bus. & Prof. Pos: Teacher, Wood High Sch, Indianapolis, Ind, 65-; teacher, Cent. High Sch, Louisville, Ky, 46-65; teacher, Navy, Chicago, carpenter, Thompkins Construction Co, Bainbridge and carpenter, Wingate Construction Co, Camp Butner, N.C, 42; teacher, Warren Co. Training Sch, N.C, 41-42 and Richmond High Sch, Ky, 37-41. Mil. Serv: Entered as Pvt, Army, 42, released as T/Sgt, 45, after serv. in Field Artillery, 92nd Buffalo Div, ETO; Good Conduct Medal and Oak Leaf Cluster. Mem: Am. Fedn. of Teachers; Ky. Teachers Asn; Ky. Educ. Asn; Ky. and Louisville Coaches Asns; Ind. Indust. Arts Asn. Rel: Baptist. Mailing Add: 1736 Dumesnil St, Louisville, Ky. 40210. (1967)

JOHNSON, ARTIS VISANIO D
Okla. State Rep.
b. Chandler, Okla, 3/10/41; s. Clarence Odell Johnson and Bernice Humphress Johnson Roper; m. 8/16/64 to Alice Christine Leonard; c. Alicia Rochelle and Andrea Nicole. Educ: Lincoln Univ, Mo, 58-62; Okla. Univ. Sch. Law, LL.B, 65; Alpha Phi Alpha; Delta Theta Phi. Polit. & Govt. Pos: Okla. State Rep, 98th Dist, 66- Bus. & Prof. Pos: Attorney-at-Law, Okla, 65- Mem: Am, Nat, Okla. State and Okla. Co. Bar Asns; NAACP; YMCA; Urban League. Rel: Baptist. Legal Res: 2237 N.E. 22nd St, Oklahoma City, Okla. 73111. Mailing Add: 2116 N.E. 23rd St, Oklahoma City, Okla. 73111.

JOHNSON, AUGUSTUS CLARK D
Chmn, Tenth Dist. Dem. Cmt, Va.
b. Covington, Ky, 4/12/14; s. Augustus Clark Johnson and Elizabeth Brown J; m. 12/24/48 to Constantia Hommann; c. Muriel T. Educ: George Wash. Univ, A.B. in Math, 46, A.M. in Math, 48; Sigma Xi; Omicron Delta Kappa; Pi Delta Epsilon; Sigma Chi. Polit. & Govt. Pos: Fed. Civil Serv, Govt. Printing Off, Tariff Cmn, Selective Serv. Systs, Dept. of Defense, 31-43; mem, Fairfax Co. Dem. Cmt, Va, 55-, chmn, 58-64; del, Va. State Dem. Conv, 56, 60, 64 & 68; Dem. cand. for Cong, Tenth Dist, Va, 62 & 64, del, Dem. Nat. Conv, 64; mem, Dem. State Cent. Cmt, Va, 66- Bus. & Prof. Pos: Instr, George Wash. Univ, 46-48, mem. faculty and research staff, 51-57; asst. prof, Robert Col, Istanbul, Turkey, 48-51; partner, Appl. Math. Serv, 57-59; research dir, Booz-Allen Appl. Research, Inc, 59-67; mem. tech. staff, Mitre Corp, 67-69; mgr, comp. urban studies, Doxiadis-Syst. Develop. Corp, 69- Mil. Serv: Entered as Pvt, D.C. Nat. Guard, 31, released as Capt, 41. Mem: Am. Asn. for the Adv. of Sci; Nat. Cmt. for Support of Pub. Schs; Nat. Capital Dem. Club; UN Asn.(mem. bd); Gr. Wash. Citizens for Clean Air (mem. bd); Am. Civil Liberties Union (mem. bd, Va. Br). Rel: Unitarian. Mailing Add: 7012 Woodland Dr, Springfield, Va. 22151.

JOHNSON, BEN(JAMIN) F(RANKLIN) D
b. Carrollton, Ga, 9/30/14; s. Ben F. Johnson and Grace Veal J; m. 6/8/38 to Stella Byrd Darnell; c. Ben F, III and Sherman D. Educ: Univ. of Ga, A.B, 37; Emory Univ, J.D, 39; Duke Univ, LL.M, 49; Omicron Delta Kappa; Phi Delta Phi; Sigma Pi. Polit. & Govt. Pos: Spec. asst. attorney gen, Ga, 55-61; Ga. State Sen, 42nd Dist, 63-68. Bus. & Prof. Pos: Private practice of law, Sutherland, Tuttle & Brennan, Atlanta and Washington, 40-43; mem. faculty, Emory Univ, 46-; dean sch. law, 61- Mil. Serv: Entered as Ens. Naval Res, 43, released as Lt.(sg), 46; Am. Theater Ribbon; Philippine Liberation Medal; Pac. Theater Ribbon with Iwo Jima and Okinawa Battle Stars. Mem: Am, Ga, Atlanta and Decatur-DeKalb Bar Asns; Atlanta Lawyers' Club; Rotary. Rel: Baptist. Mailing Add: 1035 Clifton Rd. N.E, Atlanta, Ga. 30307.

JOHNSON, BETH R
Fla. State Sen.
m. to Peter Johnson (deceased); c. Blair, Dinah and Brayton. Polit. & Govt. Pos: Mem, Cocoa Beach and St. Lucie Woman's Rep. Clubs; mem, Fla. Steering Cmt, President's White House Conf. on Youth; Fla. State Sen, 37th Dist, 66-67, 29th Dist, 67-, mem. Pub. Schs. and Ment. Health and Retardation Subcmts. and Ethics Cmt, Fla. State Senate, 69-; del-at-lg. and mem. platform cmt, Rep. Nat. Conv, 68; del. chmn, Martin Co. Rep. Party, currently. Bus. & Prof. Pos: Pres, Cape Canaveral Unlimited, Cocoa Beach, Fla, currently. Mem: Adv. bd, Salvation Army; Nat. Soc. Legislators; bd. dir, United Fund; Nat. Order of Women Legislators; Zonta Int; Bus. & Prfnl. Women; adv. bd, Day Care Centers; Cocoa Beach Woman's Club; Cape Canaveral Hosp. Auxiliary; bd. dir, Family Serv. Coun; bd. dir, Commun. Achievement Center. Chosen by legis. correspondents and ed. of state's nespapers to receive St. Petersburg Times Award as one of the most valuable legislators of 67 session; chosen by Ray Starr to receive Keyhole Award as one of state's most outstanding freshman legislators for work in cmts. and knowledgeable presentation before Senate and in cmts; U.S.A. Award, 70 Annual Awards Soc, 69. Mailing Add: P.O. Box 1016, Cocoa Beach, Fla. 32931.

JOHNSON, BETH McCOLLOUGH D
Mem, Orlando Planning Bd, Fla.
b. Butler, Pa, 11/21/09; d. Newton C. McCollough and Amelia Sherman M; m. 7/26/30 to George W. Johnson, Jr; c. Winifred (Mrs. Sharp), Margaret Phillips and George W, III. Educ: Vassar Col, A.B, 30. Polit. & Govt. Pos: Del, Dem. Nat. Conv, 52 & 68; chmn, Orlando Planning Bd, Fla, 51-55, mem, 67- Fla. State Rep, Orange Co, 57-62; Fla. State Sen, 19th Dist, 62-67. Mem: League of Women Voters; Jr. League; Fla. Asn. Ment. Health (exec. cmt); Coun. Continuing Educ. Women; Bus. & Prfnl. Women's Club; Altrusa; life mem, Fedn. Women's Club; life mem, PTA; hon. mem. Fla. Nurses Asn. First woman elected to Florida Senate; citations from Fla. Psychiatric Asn, Fla. Nurserymen's Asn. and Fla. Agr. Coun; Good Govt. Award, Orlando Jaycees, 58 & 66. Rel: Disciple of Christ. Mailing Add: 505 Peachtree Rd, Orlando, Fla. 32804.

JOHNSON, BEVERLY ADELE R
Mem, Calif. Rep. State Cent. Cmt.
b. West Allis, Wis, 10/24/22; d. Wellington Clark and Gladys Cushing C; m. 9/15/40 to Carl Ernest Johnson; c. Carolyn (Mrs. Douglas) and Steven. Educ: Univ. Calif, Los Angeles. Polit. & Govt. Pos: Brentwood chmn. for Gov. Reagan, Calif, 66; pres, Brentwood Rep. Women's Club, Federated, 66-67, first v.pres, 69; mem. bd. dirs, Los Angeles Co. Fedn. of Rep. Women, 66-68; mem, Calif. Rep. State Cent. Cmt, 67-; Brentwood chmn. for President Nixon, 68; cmt. chmn. for Assemblyman Paul Priolo, 69. Bus. & Prof. Pos: Real estate broker and appraiser, Brentwood Off, Coldwell, Banker & Co, Los Angeles, Calif, 68- Mem: Pres, Palisades High Sch. PTA; pres, Brentwood Guild for John Tracy Clin; Footlighter's for Child Guid. Clin, Hollywood Presby. Hosp. Citizen of the Year, Brentwood Savings & Loan, 67; Woman of the Year, Brentwood Rep. Women's Club, Federated, 67. Rel: Presbyterian. Mailing Add: 134 N. Bowling Green Way, Los Angeles, Calif. 90049.

JOHNSON, BOBBY WARE D
Ga. State Rep.
b. Warrenton, Ga, 1/12/30; s. Mashburn Columbus Johnson and Josie Dye J; single. Educ: Warrenton High Sch, 47. Polit. & Govt. Pos: Ga. State Rep, Dist. 29, 63- Bus. & Prof. Pos: Exec. Dir, Ga. Concrete & Prod. Asn, Inc, currently. Mil. Serv: Nat. Guard, Sgt, 6 years. Mem: Mason; Scottish Rite; Augusta Consistory (32°); Kiwanis; Moose. Chosen one of the outstanding men of Am. by Jr. C. of C; Award for Man of the Year, Ga. Mobile Home Asn, 64. Rel: Baptist. Mailing Add: P.O. Box 122, Warrenton, Ga. 30828.

JOHNSON, BYRON JERALD D
V.Chmn, Ada Co. Dem. Cent. Cmt, Idaho
b. Boise, Idaho, 8/2/37; s. Arlie Johnson and V. Bronell Dunten J; m. 6/26/60 to Marie Elizabeth Rauseo; c. Matthew, Ethan, Elaine and Laura. Educ: Harvard, A.B, 59, LL.B, 62. Polit. & Govt. Pos: Pres, Ada Co. Young Dem, Idaho, 64-65; regional v.pres, Col. Young Dem, 65-66; nat. committeeman, Idaho Young Dem, 66; registration chmn, Ada Co. Dem. Cent. Cmt, 67-68, v.chmn, 68-; del, Dem. Nat. Conv, 68. Bus. & Prof. Pos: Northwest regional v.pres, Nat. Asn. Estate Planning Coun, 68-69; prog. chmn, Gr. Boise C. of C, 69. Mem: Idaho, Boise and Am. Bar Asns; pres, Boise Art Asn; mem. bd. dirs, Red Cross, Boise Philharmonic and Salvation Army; second v.pres, Boise United Fund. Rel: Unitarian. Mailing Add: 1021 Glen Haven Dr, Boise, Idaho 83705.

JOHNSON, BYRON LINDBERG D
b. Chicago, Ill, 10/12/17; s. Theodore Johnson and Ruth Lindberg J; m. 10/22/38 to Catherine Elizabeth Teter; c. Steven, Christine and Eric. Educ: Univ. Wis, Madison, B.A, 38, M.A, 40, Ph.D, 47; Phi Kappa Phi; Artus; Delta

Sigma Rho. Polit. & Govt. Pos: In-serv. training apprentice, Wis. State Bd. of Health, 38-39, statistician, 40-42; pub. utility rate analyst, Pub. Serv. Cmn, Wis, 39-40; fiscal analyst, U.S. Bur. of the Budget, Exec. Off. of the President, 42-44; economist, Soc. Security Admin, 44-47; Colo. State Rep, Arapahoe Co, 55-56; cand. for Cong, Second Dist, Colo, 56; admin. asst. to Gov. Steve McNichols, Colo, 57-58; U.S. Rep, Second Dist, 59-60; del, Dem. Nat. Conv. and mem. platform cmt, 60; consult, Agency for Int. Develop, 61-64; del, Co, Dist, State Dem. Conv. and Dem. Nat. Conv, 68; mem. adv. cmt. to state dem. chmn, 69- Bus. & Prof. Pos: Prof. econ, Univ. Denver, 47-56; pres, Mile High Housing Asn, 48-51; exec. secy, Sr. Homes of Colo, 53-58; prof. econ, Univ. Colo, 65-, assoc. chmn. of dept. econ. and dir. center for urban affairs, Denver Center, 68- Publ: The Principle of Equalization Applied to the Allocation of Grants in Aid, Soc. Security Admin, 47; Need is Our Neighbor, Friendship Press and United Church Press, 66; Chap. in Christianity Among Rising Men and Nations, Asn. Press, 66. Mem: Am. Econ. Asn; Nat. Tax Asn; Rocky Mt. Soc. Sci. Asn; Peace Research Asn; Regional Research Asn; Am. Fedn. of Teachers; Int. House, Denver; Metro Denver Coalition for Action (first v.chmn); v.moderator, Colo. Coun. of Churches; dept. of int. affairs, Nat. Coun. Churches. Herfurth Efficiency Award, 38; Ky. Col, 60. Whitehead Award, Colo. Chap, Am. Civil Liberties Union, 60. Rel: United Church of Christ. Mailing Add: 2451 S. Dahlia Lane, Denver, Colo. 80222.

JOHNSON, C.A. 'GUS' Conservative
Minn. State Rep.
Polit. & Govt. Pos: Minn. State Rep, 62- Bus. & Prof. Pos: Lawyer. Mailing Add: 130 Crocus Place, Mankato, Minn. 56001. (1967)

JOHNSON, C. MONTGOMERY R
Chmn, Rep. State Cent. Cmt, Wash.
b. Seattle, Wash, 6/6/23; s. C. Montgomery Johnson and Helena Mason J; m. 6/9/48 to Bette Ann Maples; c. Randy, Heidi, Melissa and Shana. Educ: Univ. Wash, B.S.F. and M.F. in Forestry, 47; Stanford Univ, exec. develop. prog, 59; fel, Inst. Polit, Harvard Univ, 69. Polit. & Govt. Pos: Del, King Co. and Wash. State Rep. Conv, 52-62; mem. bd. gov, King Co. Cent. Cmt, 59-60, area chmn, 61-62; mem. and chmn, Vashon Island Sch. Bd, 60-64; chmn. steering cmt, John Stender for Sen. Cmt, 62; chmn. cand. cmt, Seventh Cong. Dist, 62; state chmn. steering cmt, Dan Evans for Gov. Cmt, 63-64; chmn, Rep. State Cent. Cmt, Wash, 65-; chmn, Wash. Rep. Party, 65-; mem, Rep. Nat. Conv, 65-, mem. exec. cmt, 69-; del, Rep. Nat. Conv, 68. Bus. & Prof. Pos: Wash. mgr. pub. affairs, Weyerhaeuser Co, 56-64. Mem: Keep Wash. Green Asn.(field dir, 49-50); Wash. Educ. Asn.(dir. pub. rels, 50-56); Pub. Rels. Soc. Am; Soc. Am. Foresters. Widely known speaker on pub. affairs and govt. rels. Rel: Unitarian. Mailing Add: Route 6, Box 210, Olympia, Wash. 98501.

JOHNSON, CARL CLIFFORD R
b. Clear Lake, S.Dak, 2/24/27; s. Oscar W. Johnson and Maria Parson J; m. 6/18/50 to Lillian Arlene Edwards; c. Jenifer and Julie. Educ: S.Dak. State Univ, B.S, 50; Blue Key; Camera Club. Polit. & Govt. Pos: Chmn, Stevens Co. Planning Cmn, Minn, 58-; co-chmn, Sixth Cong. Dist. and finance chmn, Odegaard for Cong, 65; chmn, Stevens Co. Rep. Cmt, Minn, 65-68. Bus. & Prof. Pos: Pres, Carl C. Johnson Drug Co, Inc, 64- Mil. Serv: Entered as Pvt, Air Force, 44, released as Sgt, 46, after serv. in 16th Commun. Squadron, S.Pac, 45-46; S.Pac. and Air Force Ribbons. Mem: C. of C.(pres, Morris Chap, 63); Dist. Pharm. Asn.(secy, 65); Nat. Asn. Retail Druggists; Am. and Minn. Pharmaceutical Asns; Mason; Shrine; Am. Legion; VFW; Morris Flyers; Lions Club; Pomme De Terre Country Club. Rel: Lutheran. Legal Res: 305 W. Ninth St, Morris, Minn. 56267. Mailing Add: 616-618 Atlantic Ave, Morris, Minn. 56267. (1967)

JOHNSON, CARL MARCUS DFL
Minn. State Rep.
b. St. Peter, Minn, 9/12/33; s. Chester M. Johnson and Lena Renneke J; m. 6/7/57 to Adele Elizabeth Ellen Johnson; c. Cameron Matthew, Anita Elizabeth and Martha. Educ: Mankato State Col, B.S. Polit. & Govt. Pos: Treas, Co. Democrat-Farmer-Labor Party, Minn, 64-66; Minn. State Rep, 67- Bus. & Prof. Pos: Farmer, 56-; owner and operator, Home Improv. Co, 58- Mil. Serv: Entered as Pvt, Army, 54, released as SP-4, 56, after serv. in Mil. Police, Korea, 54-56. Mem: Am. Legion; Farmers Union; Farm Bur. Rel: Lutheran. Mailing Add: Route 3, St. Peter, Minn. 56082.

JOHNSON, CHARLES CLAYTON R
Del, Minn. State Rep. Exec. Cmt.
b. Minneapolis, Minn, 7/26/24; s. George A. Johnson and Hanna A. J; m. 9/13/47 to Barbara Brazier; c. Jennifer, Mark, Charles Andrew, Samuel and James. Educ: Mankato State Col; Univ. Minn; Univ. Minn. Law Sch; Delta Theta Phi. Polit. & Govt. Pos: Attorney, Blue Earth Co, Minn, 55-; chmn, Blue Earth Co. Rep. Party, 56-60; v.chmn, Second Cong. Dist. Rep. Party, 59-61, chmn, 61-64; alternate del, Rep. Nat. Conv, 60, del, 64; del, Minn. State Rep. Exec. Cmt, 65-; dist. prosecutor, Fifth Judicial Dist, Minn, 67-69. Mil. Serv: Entered as A/S, Navy, 43, released as ETM 3/C, 46, after serv. in S.Pac; U.S. Defense Serv. Medal; Philippine Liberation Medal with Battle Star; S.Pac. Medal with Battle Star; Good Conduct Medal; Am. Theater Ribbon. Publ: Cooperation Between Police and Prosecutor, 'FBI Law Enforcement Bul, 9/57. Mem: Am. and Minn. Bar Asns; Nat. Dist. Attorneys Asn.(state dir, 69-); Minn. Co. Attorneys Asn.(pres, 67); VFW; Am. Legion; Exchange Club; Elks; Mason. Distinguished Serv. Award, Mankato Jr. C. of C, 58. Rel: Methodist. Mailing Add: 617 Baker Ave, Mankato, Minn. 56001.

JOHNSON, CHARLES RICK R
Chmn, Gregory Co. Rep. Cent. Cmt, S.Dak.
b. Gregory, S.Dak, 7/29/42; s. G.F. Johnson and Corrine Spicknall J; m. 6/12/65 to Frances Ellen Driscoll; c. Stephanie and Sara. Educ: Univ. S.Dak, J.D, 66; Phi Beta Kappa; Eta Sigma Phi; Omicron Delta Kappa; Phi Eta Sigma; Govt. Hon. Soc; Delta Theta Phi. Polit. & Govt. Pos: Chmn, Gregory Co. Rep. Cent. Cmt, S.Dak, 67- Bus. & Prof. Pos: Attorney, Johnson & Johnson, Gregory, 66- Publ: 'The Jury Voir Dire—Useless Delay or Valuable Technique,' S.Dak. Law Rev, 66. Mem: Am. and S.Dak. Bar Asns; Am. Trial Lawyers Asn.(state committeeman, 68-); S.Dak. Trial Lawyers Asn; Elks. Outstanding Sr. Law Student, Univ. S.Dak, 66. Rel: Episcopal. Mailing Add: 114 Felton, Gregory, S.Dak. 57533.

JOHNSON, CHRISTOPHER T. 'CHRIS' R
Majority Whip, Ariz. State Senate.
b. Parker Dam, Ariz, 6/11/38; s. Tom Royce Johnson and Gertrude Rutt J; m. 6/12/61 to Mary Monroe; c. Kristin Lee and Tom Royce. Educ: Univ. Ariz, B.A, 61, LL.B, 63; Phi Gamma Delta. Polit. & Govt. Pos: Ariz. State Rep, Dist. 33, 64-66; Ariz. State Sen, 66-, majority whip, Ariz. State Senate, 69- Mil. Serv: Pfc, Marines, 56-57. Mem: Ariz. State and Maricopa Co. Bar Asns. Rel: Presbyterian. Legal Res: 2007 W. Montebello, Phoenix, Ariz. 85015. Mailing Add: 316 Luhrs Bldg, Phoenix, Ariz. 85003.

JOHNSON, CONSTANCE ADA R
V.Chmn, Washington Co. Rep. Party, Vt.
b. South Fayston, Vt, 4/16/34; d. Guy Boyce Folsum and Harriet Spooner F; m. 8/17/52 to Larry West Johnson; c. Russell Kendall, Lauren Jeanne, Erika Leigh, Kerrick Lance, Robin Winona and Marilyn Margaret. Educ: Univ. Vt, 1 year. Polit. & Govt. Pos: V.pres, Federated Rep. Women's Club, Highland, Ind, 58-60; v.chmn, Barre City Rep. Party, Vt, 67-; v.chmn, Washington Co. Rep. Party, 67-; chmn, Washington Co. Women for Nixon, 68; chmn, Washington Co. Nixon Now, 68; del, Vt. Rep. State Conv, 68; del, Rep. Nat. Conv, 68- Rel: Congregational. Mailing Add: 18 Bridgeman St, Barre, Vt. 05641.

JOHNSON, CYRUS R
Mem, Calif. Rep. State Cent. Cmt.
b. Milledgeville, Ga, 11/2/23; s. Jesse C. Johnson and Jessie Tucker J; m. 3/8/46 to Edna P. Hill; c. Debbie, Cy Duane and Janet. Educ: Mid. Ga. Col, dipl, 41; Univ. of Mo, 43-44; Univ. of Hawaii, 63. Polit. & Govt. Pos: Mem, Ventura Co. Rep. Cent. Cmt, 68-69; mem, Calif. Rep. State Cent. Cmt, 69- Mil. Serv: Entered as Pvt, Air Force, 42, released as Lt. Col, 64, after serving in Hq, Pac. Air Forces, ETO and Korea, 61-64; Distinguished Flying Cross; Air Medal with Four Oak Leaf Clusters. Mem: Exec. Bd, Calif. Lutheran Col. Commun. Leaders' Club, Thousand Oaks, Calif, 66-69; chmn, Conejo Valley Days, 66, mem. steering cmt, 67-69; Ventura Co. Life Underwriters Asn.(v.pres, 68-69); C. of C.(exec. bd, Conejo Valley Chap, 68-69); chmn, Cancer Crusade, 68-69. Outstanding Serv. to the Commun. Award, Conejo Valley C. of C; Outstanding New Agent, 65 and Outstanding Career Agent, 67, Ventura Co. Life Underwriters. Rel: Protestant. Mailing Add: 1595 Kirk Ave, Thousand Oaks, Calif. 91360.

JOHNSON, DANNY D. D
b. Midvale, Ohio, 11/23/21; m. to Lucy E. Adamowicz; c. Danny D, Jr, Michael C, Susan Gaye, David E. and Mark E. Educ: Ohio State Univ, LL.B, 49; Delta Theta Phi. Polit. & Govt. Pos: Prosecuting attorney, Tuscarawas Co, Ohio, 51-57; Ohio State Sen, 59-60 & 65-66. Mil. Serv: Entered as Air Cadet, Army Air Force, 42, released as Capt, 56, after serv. in 303rd Bomb Group, ETO; Air Medal. Mem: Ohio State Bar Asn.(chmn. criminal law cmt, 57-64); Nat. Defense Lawyer in Criminal Cases; Am. Trial Lawyers Asn; The Pittsburgh Inst. of Legal Med; hon. life mem, Nat. Asn. Dist. Attorneys; F&AM; RAM; Tuscarawas Coun. 109 RSM; K.T; Elks; Eagles; Moose; VFW. Rel: Methodist. Mailing Add: 515 Union, New Philadelphia, Ohio 44663.

JOHNSON, DEWEY E. D
Educ: W. Tex. State, B.S; Baylor Univ. and N. Tex. State, M.S. Polit. & Govt. Pos: N.Mex. State Rep. Bus. & Prof. Pos: High sch. prin. Mil. Serv: Marine Corps. Mem: Kiwanis; N.Mex. High Sch. Coaches Asn. Rel: Baptist. Mailing Add: 1200 W. Summit St, Roswell, N.Mex. 88201.

JOHNSON, DEWEY M. D
b. Quincy, Fla, 4/6/07; m. to Margie Kimbrough; c. Sandra Ann. Educ: Univ. of Fla, LL.B, 30; Delta Sigma Phi; Phi Alpha Delta. Polit. & Govt. Pos: Fla. State Rep, 38, 44, 46 & 48; Fla. State Sen, 41-43 & 50-67, pres, Fla. State Senate, 59; judge, Dist. Court Appeals, First Dist, Fla, 65- Bus. & Prof. Pos: Attorney; cattleman; farmer. Rel: Baptist. Mailing Add: Quincy, Fla. 32351.

JOHNSON, DONALD L. R
Ky. State Sen.
b. 1931. Educ: Univ. Cincinnati, B.A, LL.B; Phi Alpha Delta. Polit. & Govt. Pos: Ky. State Sen, 64- Bus. & Prof. Pos: Attorney. Mil. Serv: Air Force. Mem: Campbell Co. Jaycees; VFW; Campbell Co. Bar Asn.(past pres. and past. v.pres); legal coun, Campbell Co. Boys Club of Am. Mailing Add: 69 S. Crescent, Ft. Thomas, Ky. 41075. (1967)

JOHNSON, DORIS J. D
b. Wash; m. to Harold W; c. one daughter. Educ: West. Wash. State Col, M.A. Polit. & Govt. Pos: Wash. State Rep, until 68. Bus. & Prof. Pos: Teacher. Mem: Am. Asn. Univ. Women; Delta Kappa Gamma, Psi Chap; Kennewick-Riverview, Wash. & Nat. Educ. Asns. Mailing Add: 737 Tacoma Place, Kennewick, Wash. 99336. (1967)

JOHNSON, DOROTHEA ALICE R
Chairwoman, Martin Co. Rep. Cmt, Minn.
b. Minneapolis, Minn, 1/21/12; d. Harry Peter Bradt and Jewel Wolfgang B; div. Educ: Univ. of Minn, Minneapolis, 4 years; Alpha Gamma Delta. Polit. & Govt. Pos: V.Chairwoman, Martin Co, Rep. Cmt, Minn, 61-65, Chairwoman, 65-, Alternate Del, Rep. Nat. Conv, 68. Bus. & Prof. Pos: Clerk, Pollard Mfg. Co, Sherburn, Minn, 57-59; Secy. to Pres, Fairmont Railway Motors, Inc, Fairmont, Minn, 59- Mem: Eastern Star. Rel: Methodist. Legal Res: 302 W. Third St, Sherburn, Minn. 56171. Mailing Add: Box 321, Sherburn, Minn. 56171.

JOHNSON, DORR A. R
Chmn, Manistee Co. Rep. Party, Mich.
b. Reed City, Mich, 10/21/14; s. Gust Johnson and Hilda J; m. 5/5/36 to Esther Oehlke; c. Susan (Mrs. Hodde) and Jane (Mrs. Clausen). Educ: Mich. State Univ, 1 year. Polit. & Govt. Pos: Mem, Manistee Sch. Bd, Mich, 48-63, pres, 11 years; finance chmn, Manistee Co. Rep. Party, 66-68, chmn, 69-; mem, Manistee City Coun, 68- Bus. & Prof. Pos: Owner, Dorr's Food Shop, 48-68; mgr, Nat. Car Rental, 69- Mem: Elks; past pres, Jr. C. of C. and Kiwanis. Rel: Protestant. Mailing Add: 457 Cedar, Manistee, Mich. 49660.

JOHNSON, E. G. 'TED' R
Chmn, Trumbull Co. Rep. Party, Ohio
b. Cortland, Ohio, 7/6/25; s. Fred G. Johnson and Blanche Byrnes J; m.

10/10/47 to Ruth L. Sipple; c. Kathleen (Mrs. Love) and Ted David. Educ: Youngstown Univ, LL.B, 52, J.D, 69; Gessner Law Club. Polit. & Govt. Pos: Twp. solicitor, Howland Twp, Ohio, 60-64; Rep. precinct committeeman, Howland Twp. Precinct J, Trumbull Co, 62-; chmn, Trumbull Co. Rep. Party, 66-; mem, Trumbull Co. Bd. of Elec, 68-; city law dir, Newton Falls, Ohio, 68-. Bus. & Prof. Pos: Attorney-at-law, Warren, Ohio, 52- Mil. Serv: Entered as A/S, Navy, 43, released as Aviation Elec. Technician 1/C, 46, after serving in Naval Air Corps in the Carribbean and Pac, 44-46; Theatre Ribbons. Mem: Trumbull Co. and Ohio State Bar Asns; Ohio Asn. Elec. Off; Sports Car Club of Am. Rel: Protestant. Legal Res: 5875 Mines Rd, Warren, Ohio 44484. Mailing Add: 501-2 Union Savings and Trust Bldg, Warren, Ohio 44481.

JOHNSON, E. ORVILLE R
b. Straughn, Ind, 12/29/11; s. Myrton L. Johnson (deceased) and Bessie Jefferis J; m. 6/21/37 to Mary Finch; c. Mary Anne (Mrs. Beam), David O, Rita (Mrs. Pardieck), Patricia and James. Educ: Earlham Col, A.B, 33; Univ. Mich, A.M, 37, Ph.D, 57; Tau Kappa Alpha; scholarship, Earlham Col; fel, Univ. Mich. Polit. & Govt. Pos: Rep. precinct committeeman, Richmond, Ind, 52-62; mem, Common Coun, Richmond, Ind, 58-62; admin. asst, U.S. Rep. David W. Dennis, Ind, 69- Bus. & Prof. Pos: Field secy, Earlham Col, 34-36, asst. to pres, 37-39 & 44-46, prof. speech, 37-, dean of men, 45-47, dir. East. Ind. Center, 62-68. Mem: Speech Asn. Am; Adult Educ. Asn; Rotary. Rel: Society of Friends. Legal Res: 830 S.W. Fifth St, Richmond, Ind. 47374. Mailing Add: 20 Wessex Rd, Silver Spring, Md. 20910.

JOHNSON, EARL D
b. Vale, N.C, 11/13/31; s. Wayne George Johnson and Nannie Lefevers J; m. 8/24/58 to Evelyn Hudson; c. Vicki Renee. Educ: Lenoir Rhyne Col, A.B, 58. Polit. & Govt. Pos: Revenue collector, N.C. Dept. Revenue, 58-; pres, Catawba Co. Young Dem. Club, 63; del, Dem. Nat. Conv, 68. Mil. Serv: Entered as Pvt, Army, 52, released as Sgt, 54, after serv. in Second Inf. Div, 37th Field Artil, Korea, 53-54, Good Conduct, Presidential, S.Korea Presidential and Armed Forces Far East Ribbons; one Battle Star with Ribbon; Commendation Ribbon with Metal Pendant. Mem: Mason; Lions; Elks; Moose; Young Dem. Club. Rel: Methodist. Mailing Add: 713 W. Sixth St, Newton, N.C. 28658.

JOHNSON, EDWARD A. D
Mont. State Rep.
b. Butte, Mont, 8/13/17; s. Andrew Johnson and Hilda Niemia J; m. 3/24/46 to Irene Elizabeth Hoehne; c. Scarlett M, Edward Ford, Bonnie I, Irene L. and William A. Educ: Correspondence course, I.A.S. Acct. Polit. & Govt. Pos; Mont. State Rep, currently; sch. bd. trustee, Sch. Dist. 10, Deer Lodge Co, Mont. Bus. & Prof. Pos: Financial secy, Anaconda Mill & Smeltermen's Union, 54-58. Mil. Serv: Entered as Pvt, Army, 42, released as S/Sgt, 46, after serv. in Pac; Good Conduct Medal; Asiatic-Pac. Theater Ribbon; Leyte and Luzon Campaign Ribbons. Mem: USW (pres, local 6002, currently); Lions; Am. Legion. Rel: Methodist. Mailing Add: 710 W. Sixth St, Anaconda, Mont. 59711.

JOHNSON, EDWARD ALFRED R
N.H. State Rep.
b. Springfield, Mass, 1/1/02; s. William Johnson and Ida Olson J; m. 12/27/28 to Doris E. MacLean; c. Doris E.(Mrs. Bruce A. Adams). Educ: Springfield High Sch, Mass; Andover Acad, Phillips, N.H. Polit. & Govt. Pos: Sch. cmt. mem, Agawam, Mass, 46-50; N.H. State Rep, Dist. One, 69- Bus. & Prof. Pos: V.pres. and mgr, J.H. Dunning Corp, Windham Div, 51- Mem: Rotary; Elks; corporator, Bellows Falls Hosp, Vt. Rel: Protestant. Mailing Add: Prospect Hill, Walpole, N.H. 03608.

JOHNSON, EDWIN CARL D
b. Scandia, Kans, 1/1/84; s. Nels Johnson and Anna Bell Lunn J; m. 2/17/07 to Ferne Claire Armitage; c. Janet Grace (Mrs. Robert Lee Howsam) and Gladys Marie (Mrs. Harold Marshall). Educ: High Sch. Grad; Sigma Phi Epsilon. Polit. & Govt. Pos: Colo. State Rep, 22-30; co. assessor, Colo; Lt. Gov, 30-32; Gov. Colo, 32-36 & 55-57; U.S. Sen, 37-55, mem. commerce cmt, U.S. Senate, 37-45, mil. affairs cmt, 37-47; del, Dem. Nat. Conv, 68. Mem: Mason; Odd Fellows; Elks; Grange; Farmers Union; Order of Railroad Telegraphers; Train Dispatchers Asn. Rel: Lutheran. Legal Res: Craig, Colo. Mailing Add: 901 Sherman St, Denver, Colo. 80203.

JOHNSON, ELIZABETH JEAN 'BETH' R
b. Catskill, N.Y, 12/12/32; d. John Walter Wheeler and Helen Jean Cary W; m. 9/19/53 to Peter Lane Johnson; c. Blair Bette, Dinah Sue and Brayton Douglas. Polit. & Govt. Pos: Fla. State Sen, 37th Dist, Brevard Co, until 68. Mem: Cocoa Beach Womens Rep. Club; YMCA; Cocoa Beach Womens Club; Cape Canaveral Young Rep; Cape Canaveral Hosp. Auxiliary; Surfside Players. Rel: Methodist. Mailing Add: 489 S. Atlantic Ave, Cocoa Beach, Fla. 32931. (1967)

JOHNSON, ELMORE THOME R
Nebr. State Sen.
b. Broken Bow, Nebr, 1/4/05; s. Henry Albert Johnson and Ella Thome J; m. 2/14/30 to Jean Claney; c. William and Howard. Educ: Univ. Nebr, B.S, 27; Alpha Gamma Rho. Polit. & Govt. Pos: Supvr, Dodge Co, Nebr, 67-69; Nebr. State Sen, 15th Dist, 69- Bus. & Prof. Pos: Mem. bd. dirs, South Omaha Prod. Credit Asn, 48-56, pres. bd, 52-56; mem. bd. dirs, Fremont Nat. Bank, 69- Mem: Mason; Golf Club. Rel: United Methodist. Mailing Add: 2120 Parkview Dr, Fremont, Nebr. 68025.

JOHNSON, ELSTON LOWE D
Treas, Tift Co. Dem. Cmt, Ga.
b. Alma, Ga, 8/25/14; s. James Monroe Johnson and Ina Jackson J; m. 7/15/47 to Nell Virginia Davis; c. Elston L, Jr, James Davis and Joel Monroe. Educ: Univ. Ga, B.S.C; Emory Univ, 1 year; Pi Kappa Alpha; Glee Club. Polit. & Govt. Pos: Chmn, Tift Co. Dem. Cmt, Ga, 51-68, treas, 68-; pres, Tift Co. Sch. Bd, 61- Bus. & Prof. Pos: Ga. Planing Mill Co. and Alma Gin Co, 34-41; pres, Johnson Motors, Tifton, 47-54; pres, Johnson Oil Co. and Johnson Farm Serv, 54-; v.pres, Natala Corp, 61-; v.pres, Interstate Motor Hotels, 64-; pres, Stafford Oldsmobile Co, 66- Mil. Serv: Entered as Midn, Navy, 42, released as Lt, 46, after serv. in Southwest Pac, 42-45; Res, 45-55, Lt.(Ret); Am, Asiatic, Philippines and Three Major Campaign Ribbons; Southwest Pac. Ribbon with Three Bronze Stars; Unit Citation. Mem: Lions Club (pres); Boy Scouts (pres, Chehaw Coun); Springhill Country Club (pres); Am. Legion; Elks; C. of C; United Givers; Boy's Ranch (sheriff's asn). Silver Beaver, Boy Scouts. Rel: Methodist. Mailing Add: 602 20th St, Tifton, Ga. 31794.

JOHNSON, ELTON F. R
b. Rock Rapids, Iowa, 5/28/21; m. to Donna Lee Richards; c. Kandace, Karla Lee, Karman. Educ: Iowa State Col. (1 yr.); Cornell Col. (1 yr.). Polit. & Govt. Pos: S. Dak. State Rep, 58-66 and majority leader, 65-66. Bus. & Prof. Pos: Elec. contractor; real estate. Mem: Past pres, Sioux Falls Sertoma Club, chmn. of the bd, 62; gov, Sertoma Intl, Dakotas-Manitoba Dist, 62-63; past dir, S. Dak. Elec. Coun; Am. Legion; Shrine; Elks; Masons. Rel: Methodist. Mailing Add: 1602 Carter Place, Sioux Falls, S.Dak. 57105. (1967)

JOHNSON, ERNEST N. R
N.Dak. State Rep.
b. Cooperstown, N.Dak, 5/9/15; married; c. Two. Educ: Pub. schs. Polit. & Govt. Pos: Mem, local twp. and sch. bd; N.Dak. State Rep, 59-61 and currently. Bus. & Prof. Pos: Farmer. Mem: Farm Bur. Rel: Lutheran. Mailing Add: Dazey, N.Dak. 58429. (1967)

JOHNSON, ERNEST RAYMOND D
b. Glenwood, Minn, 1/25/16; s. Carl S. Johnson and Inga Rosten J; m. 6/6/39 to Inez Gilbertson; c. Carolyn (Mrs. Gary Jonson and Martha (Mrs. Gary Sirguy). Educ: Carpio High Sch, 30-34. Polit. & Govt. Pos: Alternate del, Dem. Nat. Conv, 68; Dem. committeeman, Third Precinct, Ferndale, Wash, 69- Bus. & Prof. Pos: Owner-operatcr, Johnson's Fine Food Restaurant, 46-; dir, Ferndale First Nat. Bank, 65. Mil. Serv: Entered as draftee, Navy, 45; released as M.M 1/C, 46 after serving in 2nd Marine Div, 31st Bn, C.B's, Pac-Asiatic Theaters. Mem: Wash. State Restaurant Asn; Whatcom Dem. Party; Sons of Norway; Bellingham & Ferndale C of C; Am. Legion; Kiwanis; Whatcom Co. Mus. Found; North Cross State Hwy. Asn; Wash. Good Rd. Asn. Rel: Lutheran. Legal Res: 775 Malloy Dr, Ferndale, Wash. 98248. Mailing Add: P.O. Box 1065, Ferndale, Wash. 98248.

JOHNSON, FAIRIS D
b. 1927. Educ: Morehead State Col, A.B; Univ. of Ky, M.A. Polit. & Govt. Pos: Ky. State Sen, until 68. Bus. & Prof. Pos: Coal bus; former sch. teacher. Mem: Mason; PTA; Ky. Educ. Asn. Mailing Add: Martin, Ky. 41649. (1967)

JOHNSON, FREDERIC D
Chmn, San Patricio Co. Dem. Exec. Cmt, Tex.
b. Sinton, Tex, 7/13/23; s. Charles Frederic Johnson and Clara Barnard J; m. 12/20/47 to Alice Eloise Fraser; c. Mary Ann and Charles Frederic, III. Educ: Univ. Tex, LL.B, 50; Phi Eta Sigma. Polit. & Govt. Pos: Mem. rules cmt. and 18th Dist, Tex. State Dem. Exec. Cmt, 60-62; chmn, San Patricio Co. Dem. Exec. Cmt, Tex, 58-; v.pres, San Patricio Co. Cmt. on Youth Educ. & Job Opportunity, 65-67. Bus. & Prof. Pos: Partner, Johnson Ins. Agency, 46-65, owner, 65-; lawyer, 50-; dir. and secy-treas, People's Lumber Co, 50-62, Surety Title & Abst. Co, 52-65, Plumbing & Elec. Co, 53-62, San Pat Lumber Co, 55-62 and Sinton Savings Asn, 63-64. Mil. Serv: Entered as Seaman 2/C, Navy, 42, released as Capt, Marine Corps Res, 46, after serv. in second Marine Aircraft Wing, Pac. Theater; discharged Res, Maj, 58; Air Medal; Japan Occupation Medal; Asiatic Pac. Ribbon with 1 Star; Am. Theater Ribbon. Publ: 'An Equal Minimum Share,' The Texas Observer, 64. Mem: Tex. and Am. Bar Asns; Asn. Defense Lawyers in Criminal Cases; Am. Asn. for the Advancement of Sci; Rotary; Sinton Swimming Club; Colony Club. Rel: Episcopal. Legal Res: 808 N. Bowie Ave, Sinton, Tex. 78387. Mailing Add: 111 N. Oden Ave, Sinton, Tex. 78387.

JOHNSON, FRIDOLF D
Chmn, Mecosta Co. Dem. Cmt, Mich.
b. North Easton, Mass, 2/18/13; s. William T. Johnson and Hilda C. Johnson J; m. 9/4/48 to Janine A. Dziejowski; c. J. Janfrid and Truse Anne. Educ: Cent. Mich. Univ, B.S. with honors, 40; Univ. Mich, M.A, 46, grad. work, 48-53. Polit. & Govt. Pos: Del, Mecosta Co. Dem. Conv, 54-; del, Dem. State Conv, Mich, 54-; chmn, Mecosta Co. Dem. Cmt, Mich, 56-61 & 68-, co-chmn, 61-66; mem, Mich. Dept. Conserv. Citizens' Adv. Cmt. Deer, 66-69; mem, steering cmt, Tenth Cong. Dist. Dem. Party, 69- Bus. & Prof. Pos: Pres, Ferris State Col. Men's Club, 53-55, chmn, Representative Faculty Adv. Coun, 57-60 and mem, 68-69. Mil. Serv: Entered as Pvt, Army Air Force, 42, released as Sgt, 46, after serv. in Weather Squadron, ETO, 43-46. Mem: Am. Legion; Elks; Citizens Cmt. Promote Fluoridation of City Water, Big Rapids; Citizens Cmt. Promote Qual. Educ, Big Rapids (organizer); Mecosta Co. Rod and Gun Club (pres, 66-68); Citizens Sch. Study Cmt, Big Rapids; dir, Big Rapids City Cmn. Campaign Cmt. for City Income Tax. Citation, Representative Faculty Adv. Coun, Ferris State Col; Citation, City Cmn. Big Rapids. Mailing Add: 716 Woodward, Big Rapids, Mich. 49307.

JOHNSON, G. GRIFFITH, JR. R
b. New York, N.Y, 8/15/12; s. Gove Griffith Johnson and May Francelia Russell ; m. 1936 to Janet Clementson Young; c. Carol Lynne and Gove Griffith, III. Educ: Harvard Univ, B.A, 34, M.A, 36, Ph.D, 38; Delta Upsilon. Polit. & Govt. Pos: With U.S. Treas. Dept, 36-39, Nat. Defense Adv. Cmn, 40-41 and Off. Price Admin, 41-46; dir. econ. stabilization div, Nat. Security Resources Bd, 48-49; asst. chief fiscal div. and chief economist, U.S. Bur. of the Budget, 49-50; asst. adminstr. econ. policy, Econ. Stabilization Agency, 50; asst. secy. econ. affairs, Dept. of State, 62-65. Bus. & Prof. Pos: Consult. economist, Nathans Asn, 46-47; economist, Motion Picture Asn. of Am, 52, v.pres, 52-62, exec. v.pres, 65-; consult. economist, currently. Publ: Auth, The Treasury and Monetary Policy, 39; Economic Effects of Federal Public Works Expenditures (with J.K. Galbraith), 40. Mem: Coun. Harvard Found. Adv. Study and Research; vis. cmt, Harvard Sch. Pub. Admin; Am. Econ. Asn; Am. Polit. Sci. Asn; Am. Statist. Asn. Mailing Add: 6412 Garnet Place, Chevy Chase, Md. 20015.

JOHNSON, GARDINER R
Mem, Rep. State Cent. Cmt, Calif.
b. San Jose, Calif, 8/10/05; s. George W. Johnson and Izora Carter J; m. 9/28/35 to Doris Louise Miller; c. Jacqueline Ann and Stephen Miller. Educ:

Univ. Calif, A.B, 26; Univ. Calif. Sch. Jurisprudence, J.D, 28; Phi Delta Phi; Phi Beta Kappa; Kappa Delta Rho. Polit. & Govt. Pos: Mem, Alameda Co. Rep. Cent. Cmt, Calif, 34-47 & 59-; mem, Rep. State Cent. Cmt, Calif, 34-; Calif. State Assemblyman, 35-47, Speaker Pro Tem, Calif. State Assembly, 40; alternate del, Rep. Nat. Conv, 40, del, 56, 60, 64 & 68; mem, Nat. Drafting Cmt, Coun. of State Govts, 44-47; chmn, Calif. Del. to White House Conf. on Educ, 55; chmn, Gov. Conf. on Educ, 55; pres, Calif. Rep. Assembly, 59-60; mem, Rep. Nat. Cmt, 64-68. Bus. & Prof. Pos: Law practice, San Francisco, 28-; partner, Johnson & Stanton, Attorneys, 52- Mem: Bar Asn. of San Francisco (pres, 58); State Bar of Calif.(chmn, Conf. of State Bar Dels, 57); Am. Bar Asn; Am. Col. Trial Lawyers; Commonwealth Club of Calif.(pres, 58-59); Univ. Calif. Hospitals Auxiliary (pres, 61, 64 & 65); Calif. Hist. Soc.(pres, 68-69); pres, Florence Crittenton Home of San Francisco, 68-69; San Francisco Heart Asn.(v.pres, 65-66, chmn. bd, 67-69). Rel: Episcopal. Legal Res: 329 Hampton Rd, Piedmont, Calif. 94611. Mailing Add: Johnson & Stanton, 221 Sansome, San Francisco, Calif. 94104.

JOHNSON, GEORGE ALFRED R
b. New Haven, Conn, 4/17/19; s. George G. Johnson and Nellie Buffert J; m. 7/25/44 to Mabel Morris; c. Lezetta J, George A, Mabel D. and Charles R. Educ: Boston Univ, B.S, M.Ed; Boston State Col, Grad. Studies, 2 years. Polit. & Govt. Pos: Mem, Ward 12 Rep. Cmt, Mass, 60, & 69, chmn, 64 & 68; mem. Boston Rep. City Cmt, 64, mem. exec. cmt, 64 & 68; del, Mass. State Rep. Conv, 64 & 68. Mil. Serv: Entered as Pvt, Army, 41, released as Capt, 46, after serv. in 92nd Inf. Div, ETO, 41-46, Res, 46-, Lt. Col; Letter of Commendation; Two Bronze Stars North Appenines and Po Valley; Combat Med. Badge; Bronze Star Medal; World War II Victory Medal. Mem: Am. and Mass. Asns. Phys. Educ, Health and Recreation; Am. Fedn. Teachers; ROA. Rel: Church of Christ. Mailing Add: 152 Ruthven St, Boston, Mass. 02121.

JOHNSON, GEORGE R. R
Pa. State Rep.
b. West Haven, Conn, 10/19/29; s. George N.R. Johnson and Evelyn Gibson J; m. 11/19/55 to Rosemary A. Doyle; c. George R, Jr, Mark Doyle and Margaret Mary. Educ: St. Joseph's Col, B.S, 52; Temple Univ. Law Sch, LL.B, 55; Phi Delta Phi. Polit. & Govt. Pos: Pa. State Rep, 67- Bus. & Prof. Pos: Attorney-at-law, Crawford, Graham & Johnson, Media, Pa, 56-64, Lynch & Johnson, Upper Darby, 64-68 and Feeney, Guiliano & Johnson, 68- Mem: Delaware Co. and Pa. Bar Asns; Rolling Green Golf Club; Jr. C. of C. Rel: Roman Catholic. Legal Res: 44 Rodman Ave, Havertown, Pa. 19083. Mailing Add: Feeney, Guiliano & Johnson, 8246 West Chester Pike, Upper Darby, Pa. 19082.

JOHNSON, GEORGE THOMAS R
Chmn, White Co. Rep. Party, Ga.
b. Cleveland, Ga, 6/22/07; s. Julius Glorer Johnson and Alice Black J; m. 6/16/31 to Ollie Ilene McGugin; c. Barbara Lanette (Mrs. Perry Painter), George Randolph, Julus Dallas and Charles Ashford. Educ: Cent. Hight High Sch, Atlanta, 2 years, bus. course. Polit. & Govt. Pos: Chmn, White Co. Rep. Party, Ga, 63- Bus. & Prof. Pos: Speciality type setter for various prod, Atlanta, 20 years; owner, George T. Johnson Co, Atlanta, 5 years. Mil. Serv: Entered as Seaman 2/C, Navy, released as Seaman 1/C. Publ: Articles in U.S. News & World Report, Reader's Digest and Good Housekeeping. Mem: F&AM; Chattchoochu Wild Life Club; Helen Glee. Rel: Baptist. Mailing Add: P.O. Box 374, Cleveland, Ga. 30528.

JOHNSON, GRADDY WILLIAMS R
Ky. State Rep.
b. Lexington, Ky, 8/11/40; s. Joseph Eversole Johnson, Jr.(deceased) and Margaret Williams J; m. 9/5/60 to Mary Dillard Marr; c. Jennifer Carlisle, Graddy Williams, Jr. and John Wesley. Educ: Williams Col, B.A, 62; Univ. Ky. Col. Law, LL.B, 65; Alpha Delta Phi. Polit. & Govt. Pos: Ky. State Rep, 54th Dist, Fayette Co, 68- Bus. & Prof. Pos: Lawyer, Anggelis & Vimont, Lexington, Ky, 68- Mem: Am, Fayette Co. and State Bar Asns. Dean's List in Col; Legal Aid Soc. Award, Law Sch. Rel: Presbyterian. Legal Res: 333 Kingsway Dr, Lexington, Ky. 40502. Mailing Add: 139 Market St, Lexington, Ky. 40507.

JOHNSON, GREGORY HAMILTON R
City Comptroller, Denver, Colo.
b. Denver, Colo, 9/14/40; s. Earl H. Johnson and Jeanne L. Stoecker J; m. 8/12/63 to Mary Turnevall. Educ: Univ. Colo, B.S. in Acct, 68; Pi Lambda Nu; pres, Young Am. for Freedom, 61. Polit. & Govt. Pos: Block worker, Rep. Party, Colo, 60-; city comptroller, Denver, 65-; pres, Young Rep. Mil. Serv: Entered as Pfc, Marine Corps, 55, released as Sgt, 58, after serv. in 12th Div, 42nd Bn, Seoul, Korea; Marine Corps Res, 58-69; Purple Heart. Publ: 'Life in New Orleans,' 'Time for Some Water' and 'Once I Had to Leave, I Couldn't Stop,' Acct. Rev, 61. Mem: Union of City Comptrollers; Mason; Eagles. Best Improv, City of Denver, 55. Rel: Catholic. Mailing Add: 3346 Milwaukee, Denver, Colo. 80205.

JOHNSON, HAROLD R
Pres, San Luis Obispo Co. Chap, Calif. Rep. Assembly
b. Syracuse, N.Y, 10/8/28; s. Harold Oscar Johnson and Betty Kittell J; m. 6/24/50 to Kay Reilly Blair; c. Michael Robert, Kevin Harold, Kristin Lee and Linda Kay. Educ: Northwest. Univ, B.S, 51; Univ. Calif, Los Angeles, B.Ed, 54; Southwest. Univ. Law Sch, LL.B, 61; Zeta Psi. Polit. & Govt. Pos: Dep. dist. attorney, San Luis Obispo Co, 63-64 & 65-66; co-chmn, San Luis Obispo Co. Citizens for Goldwater and Goldwater for Pres. Cmts, 64; city attorney, San Luis Obispo, Calif, 66-; pres, San Luis Obispo Co. Chap, Calif. Rep. Assembly, 66- Bus. & Prof. Pos: Teacher, Simi Valley Unified Sch. Dist, Calif, 54-56; contract admin. and contract analyst, Atomics Int. Div, N.Am. Aviation, Inc, 56-63; attorney, Muller & Woolpert 64-65; instr. bus. law, Cuesta Jr. Col, San Luis Obispo, 65-66. Mil. Serv: Entered as A/S, Navy, 46, released as Electronics Technician 3/C, 49, after serv. in Fleet Underway Training Unit, Guantanamo Bay, Cuba, 48; Victory Medal. Mem: San Luis Obispo Co, Calif. State and Am. Bar Asns. Tennis, lettered in high sch. Rel: Presbyterian. Legal Res: 832 Virginia Dr, Arroyo Grande, Calif. 93420. Mailing Add: P.O. Box 1112, San Luis Obispo, Calif. 93401. (1967)

JOHNSON, HAROLD N. Non-Partisan
b. Wheelock, N.Da, 1906; married; c. one daughter. Educ: Concordia Col, B.A. Polit. & Govt. Pos: Minn. State Rep, 62-66. Bus. & Prof. Pos: High sch. sci. teacher. Mailing Add: 612 N. Main St, Park Rapids, Minn. 56470. (1967)

JOHNSON, HAROLD T. 'BIZZ' D
U.S. Rep, Calif.
b. Calif; m. to Albra I. Manuel; c. One Son, One Daughter. Educ: Univ. of Nev. Polit. & Govt. Pos: Calif. State Sen, 48-58; U.S. Rep, Calif, 58-; mayor, Roseville Calif, 7 years, sch. trustee, city councilman; dist. chmn, Brotherhood of Rwy. Clerks; mem, Calif. Dem. State Cent. Cmt, currently. Bus. & Prof. Pos: Supvr, Pac. Fruit Express Co. Mem: Lambda Chi Alpha; Eagles; Moose; Elks; Brotherhood of Rwy. Clerks. Am. River Develop. League (pres). Legal Res: 423 Grove St, Roseville, Calif. 95678. Mailing Add: 110 D St. S.E, Washington, D.C. 20003. (1967)

JOHNSON, HARRY S. R
b. Haverhill, Mass, 4/20/83; married; c. 3 girls, 1 boy. Educ: pub. schs, Haverhill, Mass. Polit. & Govt. Pos: N.H. State Rep, 59-67; Mem, City Coun; former city treas; Selectman. Bus. & Prof. Pos: Retired, N.E. Tel. & Tel. Mem: Mason (32°); Knight Templar; Eastern Star, Life Mem; Tel. Pioneers of Am. Rel: Protestant. Mailing Add: 161 N. Main St, Rochester, N.H. 03867. (1967)

JOHNSON, HARVEY MYERS D
Calif. State Assemblyman
b. Sabetha, Kans, 12/13/04; s. William Edward Johnson and Adella Myers; m. 6/12/27 to Margaret Boomer; c. Bettie (Mrs. Culleton), Richard L. and William. Educ: Univ. Kans, B.S; Southwest. Univ; Los Angeles Col. Law, LL.B, Delta Sigma Pi. Polit. & Govt. Pos: Mem, Potrero Sch. Bd, 6 years; mem, El Monte Bd. Educ, 10 years and chmn. 2 years; cmnr, Eagle Bd. Rev; mem. finance cmt. of the late Sen. Clair Engle; Calif. State Assemblyman, 62- Bus. & Prof. Pos: Attorney. Mem: Am. Right of Way Asn; Los Angeles Co. Bar Asn; Boy Scouts (cub and scout master); life mem. PTA; Rotary (past pres); Pomona Valley Bar Asn.(past pres); bd. trustees, City of Hope; Mason. Golden Apple Award. Rel: Methodist. Legal Res: 5110 La Madera Ave, El Monte, Calif. 91732. Mailing Add: P.O. Box 268, El Monte, Calif. 91732.

JOHNSON, HARVEY WILLIAM R
Iowa State Rep.
b. Exira, Iowa, 1/22/04; s. Lawrence William Johnson and Mary Esbeck J; m. 9/22/28 to Beulah Anna Larsen; c. Keith William and Lynn William. Educ: Elk Horn Public Sch. Polit. & Govt. Pos: Iowa State Rep, currently. Bus. & Prof. Pos: Pres, Danish Mutual Insurance Asn, Elk Horn, Iowa. Mem: Farm Bur. Rel: Lutheran. Mailing Add: Exira, Iowa 50076.

JOHNSON, HELEN CHAFFIN R
State Prog. Chmn, Mont. Rep. Women's Club.
b. Corvallis, Mont, 6/7/05; d. Balem Sigel Chaffin and Rilla Jane Walls C; m. 1/5/29 to Melvin A. Johnson; c. Carol (Mrs. Norman Strong). Educ: Univ. Mont, B.A, 27; Mortar Board; Tanan; Alpha Chi Omega. Polit. & Govt. Pos: Precinct committeewoman, Gallatin Co. Rep. Cent. Cmt, Mont, 46-69; pres, Rep. Women of Gallatin Co, 51-53; state v.chmn, Mont. Cent. Rep. Cmt, 57-60; Mont. State Rep, 61-62; state co-chmn. for Goldwater, 64; dist. co-chmn. for Dick-Smiley, 66; state campaign acct, Mont. Rep. Women's Club, state prog. chmn, 66- Bus. & Prof. Pos: Teacher, 7 years; home econ. supvr, Farm Security Admin, 34-41; mem. bd, State Bd. of Health, Iowa, 53-60 and Hosp. Adv. Bd, 66-69; realtor and broker, 60- Mem: Bd. of Realtors (chmn, 63); Soroptomists (pres, Bozeman Chap, 66); Univ. Mont. Exec. Bd. (chmn, 68); dir, Bozeman Deaconess Hosp, 61-69; C. of C.(dir. Bozeman Chap, 66-67); Eastern Star; Daughters of the Nile; White Shrine; Farm Bur. Woman of the Year, Jaycees, 66. Rel: Presbyterian. Mailing Add: 619 S. Willson, Bozeman, Mont. 59715.

JOHNSON, HOUSTON K. D
Chmn, Owen Co. Dem. Cmt, Ind.
b. Lafayette, Tenn, 1/11/09; s. George A. Johnson and Mildta Weems J; m. 11/26/30 to Willie B. Willams; c. Kenneth, Judy (Mrs. Thomas Ray) and Wilma (Mrs. Harvey Jerry). Educ: Macon Co. High Sch, Tenn, 3 years; Bus. Col, $1\frac{1}{2}$ years. Polit. & Govt. Pos: Precinct committeeman, Owen Co. Dem. Cmt, Ind, 52-60, chmn, 60-; del, Ind. State Dem. Conv, 58-60; del, Dem. Nat. Conv, 60. Bus. & Prof. Pos: Employee, DuPont Rayon, 28-38; grocery bus, 38-43; mgr, Govt. Post Exchange, 43-46; restaurant bus, 46-50; tool and cutter grinder, Allison Div, Gen. Motors Corp, 50-; farmer, 50- Mem: Mason; Eastern Star; AFL-CIO; Farm Bur. Rel. Methodist. Mailing Add: R.R. 1, Poland, Ind. 47868.

JOHNSON, HUGH STEWART, JR. D
N.C. State Rep.
b. Rose Hill, N.C, 12/12/20; s. Hugh S. Johnson; Ethel Southerland J; m. 1944 to Evelyn Furr; c. Five. Educ: Oak Ridge Mil. Inst, 37; Motte's Bus. Sch. of Wilmington, N.C, 38. Polit. & Govt. Pos: Mem. town cmn, Rose Hill, N.C, 47-49; N.C. State Rep, 56-; chmn, Legis. Coun, 63-64. Bus. & Prof. Pos: Retail hardware merchant. Mil. Serv: Naval Res, Lt.(jg), Naval aviator, 3 years. Mem: AF&AM (32°, master, Rehobeth Lodge, 53); Am. Legion. Man of Year Award, English-Brown Post 9161, VFW, Wallace, N.C, 56. Rel: Presbyterian; Deacon, 40- Mailing Add: Rose Hill, N.C. 28458. (1967)

JOHNSON, JACOB EDGAR 'JAKE' D
b. Kingsville, Tex, 1/5/33; s. Clarence Sylvester Johnson and Frances Edna White J; m. 5/28/66 to Carolyn Annette Marks; c. by previous marriage, Jacob Dwight, Cheryl Lynn, Cynthia Louise and Frances Marie. Educ: Perkinson Jr. Col; Univ. Houston; S.Tex. Col. Law. Polit. & Govt. Pos: Asst. city attorney, Houston, Tex, 63-64; Tex. State Rep, 64-68. Bus. & Prof. Pos: Attorney at Law and sch. teacher. Mil. Serv: Entered as Cadet, Marine Corps, 52, released as Capt, Marine Corps Res, 66. Mem: Mason; Tex. State and Houston Bar Asns. Rel: Protestant. Legal Res: 8626 Ruthby St, Houston, Tex. 77017. Mailing Add: 1010 Houston Bar Center Bldg, Houston, Tex. 77002. (1967)

JOHNSON, JAKE D
Tex. State Rep.
b. Midland, Tex, 5/12/31; s. General Harry H. Johnson and Rose Marie Morriseau J; m. 3/19/66 to Ann Clair Schafer; c. Rebecca Ann and Sarah Ann. Educ: Univ. St. Thomas. Polit. & Govt. Pos: Tex. State Rep, 61- Mem: Bexar Co. Dem. Study Group; Nat. Dem. Party. Rel: Catholic. Mailing Add: Route 7, Box 219, San Antonio, Tex. 70221.

JOHNSON, JAMES BUFORD DFL
b. St. Cloud, Minn, 1/25/38; s. Buford Donvan Johnson and Lucille Waverek J; m. 8/11/65 to Marilu Belanger; c. Steven Anthony and Sue Marie. Educ: St. John's Univ, Minn, B.A. in Polit. Sci, 60; Ariz. State Univ, M.A. in Polit. Sci, 67. Polit. & Govt. Pos: Dem-Farmer-Labor cand, U.S. Rep, Sixth Cong. Dist, Minn, 68; Dem-Farmer-Labor precinct chmn, Fourth Cmnr. Dist, Stearns Co, 69- Bus. & Prof. Pos: Admin. trainee, Tempe, Ariz, 66; polit. sci. instr, Mankato State Col, 67-68; dir. sheltered workshop study proj, Tri-Co. Commun. Action Prog, St. Cloud, Minn, 69- Mil. Serv: Entered as 2nd Lt, Army, 60, released as Capt, 65, after serv. in Third Inf. Div, Germany and Tenth Spec. Forces, Bad Tolz, Germany and as a U.S. Army Adv, Vietnam, 60-65, Capt. Res, 65-67; Bronze Star; Armed Forces Expeditionary Medal; Combat Infantryman Badge; Parachutist Badge; Ranger Tab. Mem: Am. Legion; VFW; K. of C. Rel: Catholic. Legal Res: 1022 31st Ave. N, St. Cloud, Minn. 56301. Mailing Add: 334 33rd Ave. N, Apt. 2, St. Cloud, Minn. 56301.

JOHNSON, JAMES CALVIN, JR. R
N.C. State Rep.
b. Greensboro, N.C, 6/5/35; s. James Calvin Johnson and Juanita Hill J; m. 8/27/60 to Linda Henry; c. James Calvin, III, Kay Lynn and Jenny. Educ: Spartanburg Jr. Col, 54-56; East Tenn. State Univ, B.S, 58; Wake Forest Sch. Law, LL.B, 62; Phi Delta Phi. Polit. & Govt. Pos: Law clerk and res. attorney, U.S. Dist. Court, N.C, 62-63; Judge, Domestic Rels. & Juvenile Court, 63-66; attorney, Cabarrus Co, 66-; N.C. State Rep, currently. Mil. Serv: Active Res, U.S. Nat. Guard, 51st Div, 53-56, 30th Armor Div, Tenn, 56-58, 30th Inf. Div, N.C, 56-62. Publ: Ed, 'The Guardian,' a legal news jour. in the domestic and juvenile field, 64-65. Mem: N.C. State and Cabarrus Co. Bar Asns; N.C. Juvenile Court Judges Asn. (pres, 64-66); Concord Jaycees. Distinguished Serviceman's Award, Concord Jaycees, 65; One of three Outstanding Young Men of N.C, 66. Legal Res: 335 Eastcliff Dr, Concord, N.C. 28025. Mailing Add: 31 Corban Ave. S.W, Concord, N.C. 28025.

JOHNSON, JAMES DOUGLAS 'JIM' D
b. Crossett, Ark, 8/20/24; s. Thomas William Johnson and Maude Myrtle Long J; m. 12/21/47 to Virginia Morris; c. Mark Douglas, John David and Joseph Daniel. Educ: Cumberland Univ, LL.B, 47; Lambda Chi Alpha. Polit. & Govt. Pos: Ark. State Sen, 50-54; former Assoc. Justice, Ark. Supreme Court. Bus. & Prof. Pos: Attorney, Crossett, Ark, 48-58. Mil. Serv: Marine Corps, World War II. Mem: Ark. Judiciary Coun; Mason; Shrine. Rel: Methodist. Mailing Add: 601 Union Life Bldg, Little Rock, Ark. 72201.

JOHNSON, JAMES EDWARD R
V.Chmn, Civil Serv. Cmn.
b. Madison, Ill, 3/3/26; s. Richard Johnson and Veola Thompson J; m. 9/25/48 to Juanita Virginia Butler; c. Kenneth Edward, Janice Vernea, Kurtis James and Juan Eric. Educ: George Wash. Univ, 58-59; Md. Univ, 60-61; Chapman Col, 62-65; Santa Ana Col, 65-67. Polit. & Govt. Pos: Chmn, Rep. interested minority cmt, Orange Co. Rep. Cent. Cmt, 65-66; dir, Calif. Dept. of Vet. Affairs, Sacramento, 67-69; v.chmn, Civil Serv. Cmn, Wash, D.C, currently. Bus. & Prof. Pos: Exec. spec. agent, Prudential Ins. Co, Anaheim, Calif, 65-67. Mil. Serv: Entered as Pvt, Marine Corps, 44, released as Commissioned Warrant Officer, 65, after serv. in Third Marine Div, Okinawa, 60-61; Am. Theatre, Nat. Defense and Good Conduct Medals; Victory Award. Mem: Amvets; Am. Legion; VFW; nat. exec. bd, adv. bd, Nat. Capitol Area Coun. and bd. dir, Golden Empire Coun, Boy Scouts; bd. gov, Anaheim YMCA; area gov, Toastmasters Int; finance chmn, Planned Parenthood Asn; dir, Youth Leadership Prog; pres, Orange Co. Chap, Childrens Asthma Research Inst. and Hosp; bd. dir, United Christian Centers; bd. dir, Sacramento Safety Coun. God and Country Award. Rel: Baptist. Legal Res: 12731 Dean St, Tustin, Calif. 92680. Mailing Add: 2816 Blue Spruce Lane, Wheaton, Md. 20802.

JOHNSON, JAMES VERNOR D
Chmn, N.C. Dem. Exec. Cmt.
b. Statesville, N.C, 6/14/23; s. Frank Link Johnson and Ruby Fraley J; m. 10/16/48 to Mary Geitner Thurston; c. Mary Geitner, Ann Vernor. Educ: Univ. N.C, B.S. in Commerce, 46. Polit. & Govt. Pos: Chmn, Ninth Cong. Dist, Young Dem. Club, N.C, 52-53; chmn, Statewide Sch. Bd. Selection Study Cmn, 61-62; N.C. State Sen, 61-66; adv, Budget Cmn, 63-64; mem, State Bd. of Ment. Health, 64-69; del, Dem. Nat. Conv, 68; chmn, N.C. Dem. Exec. Cmt, 68- Bus. & Prof. Pos: Pres, Carolina Coin Caterers Corp, Charlotte, N.C; exec. v.pres, Charlotte Coca-Cola Bottling Co. Mil. Serv: Sgt, Army Armored Div, 43-45; German Prisoner of War, 44-45; Purple Heart. Mem: N.C. Bottlers Asn. (mem. exec. bd, 57-59 & 64, v.pres, 60, pres, 61); Kappa Sigma; Robert L. Doughton Mem. Cmn, 61-64; C. of C. (mem. bd. of dirs, 54-56 & 60-62, second v.pres, 56); VFW; Elks; (Leading Knight, 56, Loyal Knight, 57); Rotary (past pres); Am. Legion (past comdr, Post 65). Young Man of the Year, Jaycees, 51. Rel: Methodist; mem. off. bd, 58-60 & 62-64 and chmn, 64-65, finance chmn, 58-63, lay leader, 64-66. Mailing Add: 3200 Wickersham Rd, Charlotte, N.C. 28211.

JOHNSON, JED, JR. D
b. Washington, D.C, 12/27/39; s. Jed Joseph Johnson and Beatrice Luginbyhl J; m. 9/25/65 to Sydney Herlong. Educ: Univ. Okla, B.A, 61; Phi Eta Sigma; Omicron Delta Kappa; Pi Sigma Alpha; Pe-et. Polit. & Govt. Pos: U.S. Rep, Sixth Dist, Okla, 64-66, ranking freshman mem, House Armed Serv. Cmt; spec. asst. to Sargent Shriver, Dir, Off. Econ. Opportunity, 67-68; mem. educ. prog, Equal Employ. Opportunity Cmn, 68- Mem: Nat. field rep, Col. Div. of Am. Asn. for UN, 61-62; pres, U.S. Youth Coun, 62-64. Rel: Protestant. Legal Res: 1228 S. Eighth St, Chickasha, Okla. 73018. Mailing Add: 4447 Davenport St. N.W, Washington, D.C. 20016.

JOHNSON, JEWELLE RICHARDSON D
Chmn, Hot Spring Co. Dem. Cent. Cmt, Ark.
b. Prescott, Ark, 1/15/12; d. Sylvester Richardson and Mattie Clark R; wid; c. Robert O. Browning, Jr. and Betty (Mrs. Conover). Educ: High Sch. and Bus. Sch. Polit. & Govt. Pos: Chmn, Hot Spring Co. Dem. Cent. Cmt, Ark, currently; chmn, Co. Elec. Cmn. Bus. & Prof. Pos: Publisher and ed, Newspaper, 64-66; partner, cosmetic co. Mem: Eastern Star; Bus. & Prfnl. Women's Club; Press Asn; Hot Spring Co. Farm Bureau. Rel: Presbyterian. Legal Res: 704 E. Highland, Malvern, Ark. 72104. Mailing Add: P.O. Box 68, Malvern, Ark. 72104.

JOHNSON, JOHN DAVE D
Chmn, Beadle Co. Dem. Party, S.Dak.
b. Hetland, S.Dak, 8/22/19; s. John David Johnson and Mary Austed J; m. 12/29/41 to Margaret Gilmore; c. Gary Davis, Kimeron Jill and Pamela Jean. Educ: Dakota Wesleyan Univ, B.A, 42. Polit. & Govt. Pos: Mem. city recreation bd, Huron, S.Dak, 62-66; chmn, Beadle Co. Dem. Party, 67- Bus. & Prof. Pos: Principal, Highmore Sch. Syst, S.Dak, 42-45. Mem: Sertoma; Elks; Mason. Mailing Add: 1701 McDonald Dr, Huron, S.Dak. 57350.

JOHNSON, JOHN EDWARD D
b. Monroe, Ind, 10/26/37; s. Floyd Franklin Johnson and Osie Lenora Striker J; m. 2/10/59 to Carolyn Joyce Seifried; c. Coleen Jenét, Johnny Edward, James Eric and twins, Heidi Michelle and Jill Renét. Educ: Heidelberg Col, B.A, 59; Univ. Heidelberg, Germany, 57; West. Mich. Univ. Grad. Sch, 61-62; Ind. Univ. Grad. Sch, 62; Kent State Univ, M.Ed, 63; Univ. Akron Col. Law, 67-; Phi Kappa Delta; Sigma Tau Nu. Polit. & Govt. Pos: Del, Dem. State Conv, Mich. Dem. Party, 64; cand, Nomination to Cong, Ninth Dist. Dem. Primary, Mich, 64; publicity dir, Leelanau Co. Dem. Cmt, Mich, 64, chmn, 65; exec. cmt. mem, Ninth Cong. Dist. Cmt, 65; Wayne Co. campaign mgr. for Bob Secrest for Cong, Ohio, 66; city councilman, Orrville City Coun, 68-69; pres, Wayne Co. Dem. Club, 69- Bus. & Prof. Pos: Sportscaster, WSTR Radio Sta, Sturgis, Mich, 60-62; teacher, Eng. and speech and debate coach, Sturgis High Sch, 61-62; teacher hist. & speech, Traverse City High Sch, Mich, 63-65; speech instr, Mich. State Univ. Sch. of Labor and Indust. Rels. Spring Workshop, 64; teacher, German, Wooster High Sch, Ohio, 65-66; speech and govt. teacher and debate coach, Orrville High Sch, 66-69; speech instr, Univ. Akron Eve. Div, 68; pub. rels. dir, Smith Dairy, Orrville, 68-69; real estate salesman, McConnel Realty, Smithville, 68-; self-employed commun. consult, Wayne Co, 69- Mem: Educ. Asns; Orville Acad. Br. Cmt. for Higher Educ. Intercollegiate Debate Champion of Ohio, 56-58. Rel: United Church of Christ. Legal Res: R.R. 2, Orrville, Ohio 44667. Mailing Add: 1791 Lynn Dr, Orrville, Ohio 44667.

JOHNSON, JOHN J. D
Mo. State Sen.
b. St. Louis, Mo, 10/10/26; m. 1948 to Louise M. Hahn; c. Alane M. and John Jr. Educ: Wash. Univ, St. Louis, A.B, polit. sci, 52. Polit. & Govt. Pos: Committeeman, Dem. Party, Concord Twp, Mo, 58-; chmn, St. Louis Co. Dem. Cent. Cmt, 60 & 64; del, Dem. Nat. Conv, 64 & 68; mem, State Dem. Cmt; Mo. State Sen, 60- Bus. & Prof. Pos: Ins. broker; real estate bus. Mil. Serv: Navy, S.Pac. Theatre, 44-46. Mem: Gravois Kiwanis; Khoury Leagues; Shrine; Scottish Rite. Rel: St. John's Evangelical and Reformed Church, Mehlville, Mo. Mailing Add: 11001 Patrina Court, Affton, Mo. 63126. (1967)

JOHNSON, JOHN WARREN R
Minn. State Rep.
b. Minneapolis, Minn, 1/29/29; s. Walter E. Johnson and Eileen Hemphill J; m. 11/18/50 to Marion Louise Myrland; c. Daniel, Karen and Nancy. Educ: Univ. Minn, B.A, 51; M Club. Polit. & Govt. Pos: 13th ward alderman, Minneapolis City Coun, 63-67; Minn. State Rep, 67- Bus. & Prof. Pos: Exec. v.pres, Am. Collectors Asn, 55-; mem. bd. dirs, First Nat. Bank of Edina, currently. Mil. Serv: Entered as Seaman Recruit, Naval Res, 48, released as Tradesman 3/C, 53 after serv. in Korean Conflict, 2 years. Mem: Minn. Soc. Asn. Exec. (pres, 61-62); Am. Soc. Asn. Execs. (dir, 60-62, v.pres, 68-69); C. of C. (pres, Edina Chap, 61 and mem, Minneapolis Chap. Speakers Bur); Am. Legion; AF&AM; Citizens League of Minneapolis. Nat. Key Man Award, Am. Soc. Asn. Execs, 65. Rel: Lutheran. Mailing Add: 5101 Irving Ave. S, Minneapolis, Minn. 55409.

JOHNSON, JOSEPH EARL D
b. Ann Arbor, Mich, 8/14/46; s. Earl Cedric Johnson and Leila Micheel J; single. Educ: Kearney State Col, 64-65; Nebr. Wesleyan Univ, 65-; Sigma Tau Gamma; Student Senate, Nebr. Wesleyan Univ; Young Dem. Nebr. Wesleyan; Nat. Honor Soc; Elks Scholarship. Polit. & Govt. Pos: Pres, Custer Co. Teen Dem, Nebr, 63-64; co-chmn, Kearny State Col. Young Dem, 64-65; state committeeman, Young Dem. Nebr, 66-68, exec. secy, 68, treas, 68-69; third dist. committeeman, 69-; pres, Young Dem. Nebr. Wesleyan Univ, 67-68; alternate del, Dem. Nat. Conv, 68; alternate del, Nebr. Dem. State Conv, 68; pres, Citizens for Debate, 68-; third dist. chmn, Spec. Cmt. Young Dem. Affairs, 68- Bus. & Prof. Pos: Foreman, Johnson Ranch, Anselmo, Nebr, 64-; campus rep, Time, Inc, 66-67; campus rep, Braniff Int. Airline, 66-67; Publ: 'Of the Universe, God and Men (poem), Anthology-Songs of Youth, 5/64; 'A History of the Nebraska Dem. Party,' Nebr. Dem. Party, 5/67; 'Shall Earth and Man Survive,' Nebr. Wesleyan Univ, 5/69. Mem: DeMolay. Rel: Episcopal. Mailing Add: Route 1, Box 16, Anselmo, Nebr. 68813.

JOHNSON, JOSEPH PICKETT, JR. D
Va. State Del.
b. Washington Co, Va, 12/12/31; s. Joseph Pickett Johnson, Sr. and Gray Buchanan Henderson J; m. 2/17/58 to Mary Ann Allison; c. Mary Jo and Joseph P, III. Educ: Emory & Henry Col, B.A, 57; Univ. Richmond Law Sch, LL.B, 60; Phi Alpha Delta. Polit. & Govt. Pos: Pres, Washington Co. Young Dem. Club, Va, 63; mem, Washington Co. Dem. Cmt, 64-66; Va. State Del, 66- Bus. & Prof. Pos: Attorney-at-law, 60- Mil. Serv: Entered as Pvt, Air Force, 51, released as S/Sgt, 55 after serv. in Far East and Pac, 53-54. Mem: Va. State and Wash. Co. Bar Asns; Va. Trial Lawyers Asn; Va. State Bar; VFW (all state post comdr, 64-65, ninth dist. comdr, 66-67, Dept. Judge Adv, 67-68, Dept. Chief-of-Staff, 68-69); Am. Legion; Mason (Past Master); Shrine; Eastern Star; Odd Fellow; Rotary. Young Man of the Year, Abingdon Jaycees, 66. Rel: Presbyterian; Deacon. Mailing Add: 131 E. Main St, Abingdon, Va. 24210.

JOHNSON, KARL C. D
b. Cleveland, Ohio, 6/2/34; s. Harvey J. Johnson and Helene Clinthorne J; m. 5/14/56 to Muriel Cole; c. Karl, Jr. and Kerrick Scott. Educ: Cent. State Univ, A.B, 62; Alpha Kappa Mu. Polit. & Govt. Pos: Del, Young Dem. Ohio Conv, 60; alternate del, Dem. Nat. Conv, 64. Bus. & Prof. Pos: Publisher and ed, Cleveland Ohio Forum (weekly), 63-64. Mil. Serv: Entered as A/B, Air Force, 56, released as Airman 2/C, 60, after serv. as Korean Linguist, Security Serv, Pac, 57-58. Rel: Presbyterian. Mailing Add: 12600 Revere Ave, Cleveland, Ohio 44105.

JOHNSON, KAY R
b. Ogden, Utah, 6/26/14; d. James H. Wardleigh and Zina Hansen W; m. 8/7/33 to Kenneth Fred Johnson; c. Hazel Kay, Sharon Virginia and Kenneth F, II. Educ: Univ. Nev, 31-33. Polit. & Govt. Pos: Mem, Rep. Nat. Cmt, Nev, 52-60; v.chmn, Rep. West. Conv, 57-60; nat. dir, United Vol. Serv, 60-; coordinator, Rockefeller for Pres, 64. Mem: Young Rep. Club (past nat. cmt, Nev, past dir, Nev, Ariz. and Calif); VFW (past dept. pres, Nev); Rep. Nat. Speakers Bur. Nev; Hidden Valley Country Club. Rel: Latter-day Saint. Mailing Add: 2460 Piping Rock Dr, Reno, Nev. 89502. (1967)

JOHNSON, LANCE FRANKLIN R
Chmn, Dodge Co. Rep. Party, Nebr.
b. Topeka, Kans, 8/5/38; s. Harry Franklin Johnson and Dorothea Anne Simons J; single. Educ: Univ. Kans, A.B, 60; Univ. Denver, M.B.A, 63; Omicron Delta Kappa; Sigma Chi. Polit. & Govt. Pos: Chmn, Fremont City Rep. Party, Nebr, 67; chmn, Dodge Co. Rep. Party, 68-; committeeman, Nebr. State Rep. Party, 68-; mem, Nebr. Equal Employ. Opportunities Cmn, 68- Mil. Serv: Nebr. Air Nat. Guard, 63-, S/Sgt; Am. Spirit Honor Medal. Mem: Rotary; Jaycees. Rel: Methodist. Legal Res: 711 William, Fremont, Nebr. 68025. Mailing Add: 325 S. Main St, Fremont, Nebr. 68025.

JOHNSON, LARRY ALAN D
b. Farmington, Ill, 7/17/35; s. Kenneth C. Johnson and Merle Record J; m. 3/18/56 to Phyllis Mohn; c. Perry Alan, Lori Rae, Denise Lynn and Scott Fitzgerald. Educ: Bradley Univ, 57 & 58. Polit. & Govt. Pos: Dem. precinct committeeman, Ill, 62-69; pres, Limestone Dem. Club, Limestone Twp, 63-; alternate del, Dem. Nat. Conv, 64 & 68. Mem: V.pres, Limestone Human Rels. Coun; v.pres, Oak-Grove PTA. Rel: Presbyterian. Mailing Add: 4817 Rusty Lane, Bartonville, Ill. 61607.

JOHNSON, LAWRENCE H. R
Wis. State Assemblyman
b. Nadeau, Mich, 4/26/08. Educ: Sturgeon Bay High Sch. Polit. & Govt. Pos: Secy. dairy coop; v.pres, Wis. Soil Conserv. Dist. Supvrs. Asn; pres, Northeast. Wis. Soil Conserv. Dist. Asn; pres, Wis. Co. Hwy. Cmt. Mems. Asn; pres, Wis. Co. Bds. Asn; town clerk, Algoma, Wis, 30-47, chmn, 64-, co. bd. chmn, 55-; Wis. State Assemblyman, 60- Bus. & Prof. Pos: Farmer. Mem: Door-Kewaunee Co. Col. Bd. Active in many coops. and farm orgns; and soil conserv. work. Mailing Add: Route 2, Algoma, Wis. 54201. (1967)

JOHNSON, LAWRENCE H. R
Chmn, Lea Co. Rep. Party, N.Mex.
b. Cedar Rapids, Iowa, 5/30/26; s. Harry S. Johnson and Florence Wagner J; m. 11/21/62 to Joyce Howard; c. Regina. Educ: Okla. State Univ, 45; Coe Col, A.B.(econ), 49; Univ. Mich. Law Sch. LL.B, 52; Tau Kappa Epsilon; Phi Kappa Phi; Phi Delta Epsilon; Delta Theta Phi. Polit. & Govt. Pos: Pres, Coe Col. Young Rep, 48; treas, Lea Co. Rep. Party, N.Mex, 56-67, chmn, 67-; mem, N.Mex. Rep. State Cent. Cmt, 67- Bus. & Prof. Pos: Assoc, U.M. Rose, Attorney, Hobbs, N.Mex, 53; partner, Rose & Johnson, Attorneys, 54- Mil. Serv: Entered as Seaman 1/C, Navy, 44, released as Electronic Technician's Mate 3/C, 46. Mem: Lea Co, N.Mex. State and Am. Bar Asns; Am. Trial Lawyers Asn; Am. Legion; VFW; Hobbs Community Players; Hobbs C. of C; bd. trustees, Hobbs Pub. Libr. Tom Mason award for outstanding serv. to Hobbs Community Players, 68. Rel: United Presbyterian; mem. bd. trustees, First Presbyterian Church, Hobbs. Legal Res: 702 Seco Dr, Hobbs, N.Mex. 88240. Mailing Add: Box 159, Hobbs, N.Mex. 88240.

JOHNSON, LEROY REGINALD D
Ga. State Sen.
b. Atlanta, Ga, 7/28/28; s. Leroy Johnson and Elizabeth Heard J; m. 9/13/48 to Nydia Cleopatra Whittington; c. Michael Vince. Educ: Morehouse Col, A.B, 49; Atlanta Univ, M.A, 51; N.C. Col. Law Sch, LL.B, 57; Phi Beta Sigma. Polit. & Govt. Pos: Criminal investr, Solicitor Gen. Off, 57-61; v.pres, South. Conf. Dem, 62; Ga. State Sen, 38th Dist, 62-; spec. ambassador, Independence Celebration of Zanzibar, 63; pres, Ga. Asn. Citizens Dem. Clubs, 64-; pres, Fulton Co. Citizens Dem. Clubs, 66- Bus. & Prof. Pos: Attorney-at-Law, Johnson and Jordan, 61- Publ: United States Foreign Policy Towards Germany Since the Potsdam Conference, 51. Mem: Gate City Bar Asn; Am. Polit Sci. Asn; Mason; Shrine; Atlanta Cmt. for Coop. Action; C. of C; Atlanta Summit Conf; Parthenon Club. Selected One of Five Outstanding Young Men of Year, Atlanta C. of C, 64; Recipient Elks Lovejoy Award. Rel: Baptist. Legal Res: 372 Larchmont Dr. N.W, Atlanta, Ga. 30318. Mailing Add: 1014 Gordon St. S.W, Atlanta, Ga. 30310. (1967)

JOHNSON, LESTER ROLLAND D
b. Brandon, Wis, 6/16/01; s. John E. Johnson and Ella M. Paine J; m. to Violet F. Graunke, wid. 1953; m. 11/9/54 to Marjorie M. Gray; c. Mary Lynn (Mrs. Lindow), Jane Laura (Mrs. Siefert) and Jone Lee (Mrs. Hoffman). Educ: Lawrence Col, 19-21; Univ. Wis, Ph.B, 23, LL.B, 41. Polit. & Govt. Pos: Chief clerk, Wis. State Assembly, 35-39; Dist. Attorney, Jackson Co, Wis, 43-47 & 53; U.S. Rep, Ninth Dist, Wis, 53-65. Bus. & Prof. Pos: Owner, Johnson Lumber and Fuel Co, Brandon, 24-35; liquidated banks trusts, 41-45; practice of law, Black River Falls, Wis, 43-53. Mem: Masons; Odd Fellows. Rel: Lutheran. Mailing Add: R.F.D. 1, Box 222, Augusta, Wis. 54722.

JOHNSON, LEWIS JAMES, SR. D
b. Reader, Ark, 11/7/09; s. Tom Johnson and Maude Henley J; m. 3/28/32 to Elizabeth Neal; c. Julianne (Mrs. Coffman), Lewis J, Jr. and John Thomas. Educ: Univ. Ark, B.S. in Agr, 33; Kappa Sigma. Polit. & Govt. Pos: Supvr, Farm Security Admin, 34-41; mem, Ark. Water Control Cmn, 55-67; mem, Ark. Voc. Sch. Adv. Cmn, 61-67; mem, President's Cmn. on Rural Poverty, 66-69; Ark. co-chmn, Humphrey for Pres, 68; del, Dem. Nat. Conv, 68. Bus. & Prof. Pos: Mgr, Farmers Union Mutual Ins. Co, currently. Mil. Serv: Instr, Army Air Corps, Officers Training Corps, 41-44. Mem: bd. dirs, Nat. Farmers Union; pres, Ark. Farmers Union (past v.pres). Mailing Add: 1920 Wright Ave, Little Rock, Ark. 72204.

JOHNSON, LOUIS L. 'ROY' R
S.Dak. State Sen.
b. 5/25/15; married; c. one son. Educ: Watertown High Sch. Polit. & Govt. Pos: Former mem, Farm Home Admin. Co. Cmt. and Grant City Town Bd, La Bolt, S.Dak; S.Dak. State Sen, 64- Bus. & Prof. Pos: Implement bus. Mil. Serv: Army Air Corps, World War II, Flight Instr. Mem: Farm Home Admin, Grant Co; Am. Legion. Rel: Am. Lutheran; Former Mem, Church Coun. Mailing Add: 217 E. Eighth Ave, Milbank, S.Dak. 57252. (1967)

JOHNSON, LOUIS THOMAS D
Tax Assessor-Collector, Jones Co, Tex.
b. Anson, Tex, 2/10/09; s. Clarence Johnson and Bettie Tucker J; m. 7/10/32 to Juanita Foy; c. Wilma Jane (Mrs. H.H. Huddleston) and Louis Eugene. Polit. & Govt. Pos: Chmn. bd. trustees, Anson Sch. Dist, Tex, 44-45; chmn, Jones Co. Dem. Exec. Cmt, 46-52 & 60-; chmn. bd. trustees, Anson Gen. Hosp, 51-53; mayor, Anson, 54-58; tax assessor-collector, Jones Co, 69- Bus. & Prof. Pos: Mgr, retail lumber yard, 32-41; mgr. and owner, Johnson Feed Store, 41-66. Rel: Methodist. Legal Res: 1401 19th St, Anson, Tex. 79501. Mailing Add: Box 152, Anson, Tex. 79501.

JOHNSON, LOWELL BERTHEN D
Mem, Seymour Dem. Town Cmt, Conn.
b. Foley, Minn, 12/12/28; s. Oscar Berthen Johnson and Amanda C. Johnson J; m. 9/4/54 to Janet Mabel Christianson; c. Cynthia Elaine, Randall Paul, Kent Lowell and Lynn Carol. Educ: North Park Jr. Col, A.A, 47; Univ. Minn, Minneapolis, B.A, 51; Hartford Theol. Sem, B.D, 56; Trinity Col, M.A, 64. Polit. & Govt. Pos: Cong. Dist. coordinator McCarthy for Pres, Fifth Cong. Dist, Conn, 67-68; alternate del, Conn. Dem. State Conv, 68; alternate del, Dem. Nat. Conv, 68; mem, Seymour Dem. Town Cmt, 68-; mem. adv. bd, Commun. Develop. Action Plan, 69- Bus. & Prof. Pos: Pastor, Queen St. Congregational Church, Bristol, Conn, 53-57, Pleasant Valley Methodist Church, 57-61 and Seymour Methodist Church, 61-; supv. pastor, Ministerial Training, Divinity Sch, Yale Univ, 69- Mem: Lower Naugatuck Valley Clergy Asn. (past pres); N.Y. Conf. Methodist Church (dist. dir, Bd. Christian Soc. Concerns); Valley Asn. Counseling Clergymen, Griffin Hosp; Seymour C. of C.(secy); Naugatuck Valley Citizens League (v.pres); NAACP (chmn. exec. bd, Valley Br, Ansonia). Rel: Methodist. Mailing Add: 92 Pearl St, Seymour, Conn. 06483

JOHNSON, LYNDON BAINES D
b. Stonewall, Tex, 8/27/08; s. Sam Ealy Johnson and Rebekah Baines J; m. 11/17/34 to Claudia Alta (Lady Bird) Taylor; c. Lynda Bird (Mrs. Charles S. Robb) and Luci Baines (Mrs. Patrick Nugent). Educ: Southwest Tex. State Teachers Col, B.S, 30; Georgetown Univ. Law Sch, 34. Hon. LL.D, Southwest. Univ, 43, Howard Payne Col, 57, Brown Univ. and Bethany Col, 59, Univ. Hawaii, Univ. Philippines, Gallaudet Col, East Ky. State Col. and William Jewell Col, 61, Elon Col. and Southwest Tex. State Teachers Col, 62, Wayne State Univ, Jacksonville Univ, MacMurray Col, Univ. Md. and Tufts Univ, 63, Univ. Calif, Los Angeles, Univ. Tex, Swarthmore Col, Syracuse Univ. and Georgetown Univ, 64, Univ. Ky, Baylor Univ, Howard Univ. and Catholic Univ, 65, Princeton Univ. and Univ. Denver, 66, Tex. Tech. Col, 67, Tex. Christian Univ, Thomas More Col. and St. Francis Col, 68; hon. L.H.D, Okla. City Univ, 60 and Yeshiva Univ, 61; hon. Litt.D, St. Mary's Col. Calif, 62 and Glassboro Col, 68; hon. D.Civil Law, Col. Holy Cross and Univ. Mich, 64 and Univ. R.I, 66; hon. D.Sc. Pol, Chulalongkorn Univ, Thailand, 66. Polit. & Govt. Pos: Secy, U.S. Rep. Richard Kleberg, 31-35; Tex. Dir, Nat. Youth Admin, 35-37; U.S. Rep, Tex, 37-48; U.S. Sen, Tex, 49-61, minority leader, U.S. Senate, 53-55, majority leader, 55-60; V.President, United States, 61-63, chmn, Nat. Aeronaut. & Space Coun, President's Cmt. on Equal Employ. Opportunity and Peace Corps Adv. Coun; President, United States, 63-69. Bus. & Prof. Pos: Teacher, pub. schs, Cotulla and Houston, Tex, 30-31. Mil. Serv: Comdr, Naval Res, active duty, 41-42, resigned Cmn, 64; Silver Star, 42. Rel: Christian Church. Mailing Add: LBJ Ranch, Stonewall, Tex. 78671.

JOHNSON, MALCOLM KIRKLEY D
S.C. State Rep.
b. Hartsville, S.C, 7/14/23; s. Maxie Johnson and Letha Morrison J; m. 6/9/51 to Emodene Davis; c. Malcolm Kirkley, Jr, Melody Ann, Fletcher James and Rodney Preston. Educ: Emory Univ, B.S. in Eng, 44; Univ. S.C, LL.B, 49. Polit. & Govt. Pos: Magistrate, Darlington, S.C, 51; Judge of Civil and Criminal Court, Darlington Co, 51-60, co. attorney, 60-62; mem, Darlington Co. Tax Bd. of Rev, 64-67; S.C. State Rep, 69- Mil. Serv: Entered as Ens, Navy, 44, released as Lt.(jg), 46, after serv. as Commanding Officer, U.S.S. YMS, 44-46; Atlantic and Pac. Theatre Ribbons. Mem: Darlington Co, S.C. State and S.C. Bar Asns; Am. Trial Lawyers Asn; Mason; Shrine; Scottish Rite; C. of C; Grange; VFW. Rel: Methodist. Legal Res: 105 Circle Dr, Darlington, S.C. 29532. Mailing Add: 1225 College Ave, Hartsville, S.C. 29550.

JOHNSON, MARCO R
b. Spokane, Wash, 1919; s. Kirk E. Johnson and Etta S. Pettigren J; m. to LaVonne Winnifred Lakey; c. Brooks Allen, Bruce Eric, Peter Bryan, Barry David and Marc Ome. Educ: Spokane Jr. Col; Univ. Wash. Polit. & Govt. Pos: Del, Rep. Nat. Conv, King Co. Rep. Conv. and Wash. State Rep. Conv, chmn, First Cong. Dist. Orgn, King Co. Rep. Party, chmn, 45th Dist. and precinct committeeman and area chmn. Bus. & Prof. Pos: Budget Adminstr, Boeing Aero Space Group. Mem: Inst. Mgt. Sci; Boeing Mgt. Asn; Soc. Adv. Mgt; Inst. Gen. Semantics; Elks; F&AM; First Legis. Dist. Rep. Club; Lake City Rep. Toastmasters Club. Rel: Congregational. Mailing Add: 666 N.W. 178th Place, Seattle, Wash. 98177.

JOHNSON, MARY CATHERINE D
b. Dilworth, Minn, 9/7/20; d. Charles W. Coryell and Sarah Duffy C; div; c. Catherine (Mrs. Larry Anderson). Educ: High Sch, grad, 37; Tel. Sch. and R.R. Acct, summer 45. Polit. & Govt. Pos: Treas, Stutsman Co. Dem. Women, N.Dak, 58-64, campaign dir, 64-66; secy. and regional dir, Dist. 29 Dem. Women, 66-68, secy, 68; del, N.Dak. State Dem. Non-Partisan League

Conv, 66 & 68; del, Dem. Nat. Conv, 68; dir, N.Dak, Cmt. on Polit. Educ-WAD, 68. Bus. & Prof. Pos: Direct serv. agent, North Pac. Rwy. Co, N.Dak. and Minn, 45-69. Mem: PTA; VFW Auxiliary; Transportation-Commun. Union. Rel: Catholic. Mailing Add: 354 E. Main St, Valley City, N.Dak. 58072.

JOHNSON, MELVIN D
Chmn, Charles Mix Co. Dem. Party, S.Dak.
b. Hudson, S.Dak, 6/24/02; s. Olaf Johnson and Sinava J; m. 8/6/26 to Margrat Nelson; c. Joseph, Clifford and Norman. Educ: Geddes High Sch. Polit. & Govt. Pos: Pres, Charles Mix Co. Weed Bd, S.Dak, 62-69; committeeman, Agr. Stabilization Conserv. Cmt, 63-64 & 65; chmn, Charles Mix Co. Dem. Party, 64-; chmn, Dem. Party, S.Dak, 64-66; Dem. nominee, S.Dak. State Sen, 66. Mem: Charles Mix Co. Farmers Union (pres, 58-67); Dist. One Farmers Union (v.pres, 67-); Mason (Master, 54, Dist. Master, 54-59, bd. custodians, 59 & 68-); RAM; Consistory; Shrine. Rel: Lutheran; Past Pres, Luther League. Mailing Add: Geddes, S.Dak. 57342.

JOHNSON, MINNIE BUGG D
b. Roanoke, Va, 6/22/01; d. William Lee Weaver and Blanche J. Gearheart W; m. 9/17/49 to John M. Johnson; c. Mozelle E. (Mrs. Jones), Ethelleen (Mrs. Evans), James S. Bugg, Jr. and Donald A, Norman D. and William Lee Bugg. Educ: Lee Jr. Col, Roanoke, Va; Bus. Col, Canton, Ohio. Polit. & Govt. Pos: Mem, Credentials Cmt, Dem. State Conv, Utah, 66, mem, Platform Cmt, 56; co-chmn, Blanding Precinct Dem. Party, 61-66; del, Dem. Nat. Conv, 64 and 56; chmn, San Juan Co. Dem. Party, 42-60. Bus. & Prof. Pos: Curator, Minnie's Doll House Mus, Blanding, Utah, at present; owner, Bugg's Hotel, 40-51. Mem: V.pres, Blanding C. of C, 61-63; dir, Civil Defense, Womens Div, San Juan Co; pres, Blanding Garden Club. Rel: Latter-Day Saint. Mailing Add: 64 W. Third, S, Blanding, Utah 84511. (1967)

JOHNSON, NEAL SOX R
Mem, Ark. State Rep. Exec. Cmt.
b. Murfreesboro, Ark, 2/14/33; s. John Olvy Johnson and Elsie Faye Kelling J; m. 1/15/56 to Carmen Louise Webb; c. Tena Elizabeth, Neal Steven and Olvy Lynn. Educ: Henderson State Teachers Col, B.S.E, 55; Hendrix Col; Univ. Ark; Little Rock Univ; Lamar Tech. Col; summers, Am. Bridge Div, U.S. Steel training course struct. steel drafting, 55, Nat. Soc. Found. stipend, Univ. Ark, 60. Polit. & Govt. Pos: Chmn, Howard Co. Goldwater for President Cmt, Ark, 64; mem, Howard Co. Elec. Cmn, 66, chmn, 67; chmn, Howard Co. Rockefeller for Gov, 66; chmn, Howard Co. Rep. Cmt, 66-; mem, Ark. State Rep. Exec. Cmt, 66-; del, Nat. Rep. Campaign Mgr. Seminar, 67; mem, Ark. Game and Fish Cmn, 67; chmn. two political rallies for Gov. Winthrop Rockefeller Campaign, 68; mem, Gov. Rockefeller Rep. Patronage Cmt, 69- Bus. & Prof. Pos: Owner, Johnson's Texaco Serv. Sta, Ark, 46-51; hwy. construct. eng. dept, Ark. Hwy. Dept, 52; archit. drafting and estimating, Lollar Construct. Co, 52-55; struct. steel draftsman, Am. Bridge Co, Gary, Ind. and Orange, Tex, 55-56 & 56-57; design draftsman, Shipbuilding Div, Bethlehem Steel Corp, Tex, 57; gen. drafting and surv, Stowers & Boyce, Architects, Ark, 58; gen. drafting and supvn. of jr. draftsmen, Swaim & Allen, Architects, 59; instr, Bryant High Sch, 57-60; supvr. pub. rels. and sales construct. supvr, Stanley Brown, Architect, 60-62; partner and mgr, Carroll Bldg. & Appliance Co, 62-66; partner and gen. mgr, Nashville Bldg. Specialties, 66- Mil. Serv: Army Res, 56-64, Capt, serv. in Inf. and Combat Engrs. Mem: F&AM (Master Mason); Sigma Phi Epsilon; Rotary (dir); C. of C.(v.pres); Nashville City Planning Cmn. Rel: Baptist. Legal Res: 311 W. College St, Nashville, Ark. 71852. Mailing Add: Nashville Bldg. Specialties, P.O. Box 234, Nashville, Ark. 71852.

JOHNSON, NEWMAN NEWTON R
Chmn, Carroll Co. Rep. Cmt, Ga.
b. Cleburne Co, Ala, 10/16/77; s. Wesley Whitfield Johnson and Mary Elizabeth Lovvorn J; m. 2/12/05 to Lillian Inez Smith, wid. Educ: Bowden Col, 99; South. Bus. Col, Atlanta, Ga, Dipl, 01; Clay and Calhoun Debating Soc. Polit. & Govt. Pos: Chmn, Carroll Co. Rep. Cmt, Ga. and secy, 08-42; councilman and Mayor pro tem, Carrollton, 25-31. Bus. & Prof. Pos: Secy, Mandeville Mills, Carrollton, Ga, 06-14; v.pres. and secy, C.M. Tanner Grocery Co, 14-32; Fire and Casualty Ins. Agency, N.N. Johnson Ins. Agency, 33-54. Mem: Mason; York Rite; Scottish Rite; Shrine; Lions; Moose; WOW. Rel: Presbyterian; Elder. Mailing Add: Carrollton Hotel, Carrollton, Ga. 30117.

JOHNSON, NINA SIDLER D
State Committeeman, N.Y. Dem. Cmt.
b. North Rose, N.Y, 4/13/27; d. Harry Eugene Sidler and Lena Belle Sears S; m. 8/30/52 to Robert S. Johnson; c. Susan Sidler. Educ: Rochester Inst. of Tech. Sch. for Am. Craftsmen, 1 year. Polit. & Govt. Pos: Secy, Wayne Co. Dem. Cmt, N.Y, 60-; secy. to chmn, Wayne Co. Dem. Party, 63-69; state committeeman, N.Y. Dem. Cmt, 68- Bus. & Prof. Pos: Secy. to pres, William C. Moore & Co, Newark, N.Y, 51-63. Mem: Nat. Rural Letter Carrier's Auxiliary, N.Y. State Hist. Asn; Wayne Co. Hist. Soc. Rel: United Methodist. Mailing Add: Glenmark Rd, North Rose, N.Y. 14516.

JOHNSON, NORMAN AARON, JR. D
Chmn, Miss. Pub. Serv. Cmn.
b. Philadelphia, Miss, 6/8/21; s. Norman A. Johnson, Sr. and Bobbie Jasper J; m. May 1946 to Mary Grace Stringer; c. Norman A, III and Amanda. Educ: Miss. State Univ, B.S; Sigma Phi Epsilon. Polit. & Govt. Pos: Mayor, Philadelphia, Miss, 53-55; chmn, Miss. Pub. Serv. Cmn, 56- Bus. & Prof. Pos: Pres, Miss. Arthritis Found, 66-67, chmn. bd, 68-69. Mil. Serv: Entered as Pvt, Marines and Army, 42, released as Cpl, 45, after serv. in 30th Engrs. Corps, ETO, 43-45. Mem: Am. Legion (state comdr, 52); VFW; Sons of Confederate Vet; Mason; Shrine; Farm Bur. Rel: Baptist. Mailing Add: 506 Peebles Ave, Philadelphia, Miss. 39350.

JOHNSON, NORVAL STANLEY DFL
Chmn, Fillmore Co. Dem-Farmer-Labor Party, Minn.
b. Harmony, Minn, 9/22/30; s. Hellick Johnson and Ronnaug Sather J; m. 10/2/51 to Eleanor King; c. Randell, Raynard, Leslie, Beverley and John. Educ: Elem. Sch. Polit. & Govt. Pos: Del, Dem. Nat. Conv, 68; chmn, Fillmore Co. Dem-Farmer-Labor Party, Minn, 68-; mem, First Dist. Dem-Farmer-Labor Exec. and Cent. Cmts, 68-; mem, Minn. State Dem-Farmer-Labor Cent. Cmt, 68- Mem: Nat. Farm Orgn; Minn. Farmers Union. Rel: Protestant. Mailing Add: Lanesboro, Minn. 55949.

JOHNSON, O.S. D
b. Lamberton, Minn, 2/10/93; married; c. 3. Educ: Pub. Schs. Polit. & Govt. Pos: N.Dak. State Sen, 55-61; Legis. Research Comm, 55-59; City Auditor, 30-53; City Cmn, mem. Bus. & Prof. Pos: Real Estate; farmer. Mailing Add: Langdon, N.Dak. 58249. (1967)

JOHNSON, ORIE CARTER D
V.Chmn, Fremont Co. Dem. Cent. Cmt, Colo.
b. Paris, Ark, 3/22/94; d. Frederick Newton Carter and Annie Gunter C; m. 10/18/14 to David Eugene Johnson; c. Harlan David and Eugenia (Mrs. Crosby). Educ: High Sch, Paris, Ark, 1899-1911. Polit. & Govt. Pos: Treas, Jane Jefferson Club of Fremont Co, Colo. and v.chmn, Fremont Co. Dem. Cent. Cmt, 69- Rel: Protestant. Mailing Add: 903 Allison Ave, Canon City, Colo. 81212.

JOHNSON, OZ R
b. 1926. Educ: Univ. Louisville, B.A. and M.A. Polit. & Govt. Pos: Ky. State Rep, 62-67. Bus. & Prof. Pos: Adminstr. commun. schs, Off. Econ. Opportunity, Jefferson Co. Mil. Serv: Navy. Rel: Christian. Mailing Add: 5106 Princewood Place, Louisville, Ky. 40216. (1967)

JOHNSON, PAUL BURNEY D
b. Hattiesburg, Miss, 1/23/16; s. Gov. Paul B. Johnson (deceased) and Corrine Venable J; m. to Dorothy E. Power; c. Patricia, Paul B, III 'Chipper' and Shelby Venable. Educ: Univ. Miss, LL.B, 40, pres, Student Body; Blue Key; Omicron Delta Kappa; Membership, Hall of Fame. Polit. & Govt. Pos: Asst. U.S. Attorney, South. Dist, Miss, 48-51; Lt. Gov, Miss. and pres, Miss. State Senate, 60-64; Gov, Miss, 64-69. Bus. & Prof. Pos: Lawyer. Mil. Serv: Entered as Pvt, Marine Corps, 42, released as Capt, 46, after serv. in S.Pac; Maj, Marine Corps Res. Mem: Am, Miss. State and Forrest Co. Bar Asns; Sigma Alpha Epsilon; Am. Legion; VFW; Moose; Mason (32°); Scottish Rite; Shrine. Distinguished Serv. Award, Am. Vet. of World War II, 49. Rel: Methodist. Mailing Add: c/o Governors Mansion, Jackson, Miss. 39205. (1967)

JOHNSON, RALEIGH WEST R
Chmn, Navajo Co. Rep. Cent. Cmt, Ariz.
b. Phoenix, Ariz, 8/11/34; s. Charles Edgton Johnson and Julia Gwendolyn West J; M. 12/27/61 to Margene Symons; c. Grant Brian, Shauna Leigh, Lori Jean and Mark Eric. Educ: Brigham Young Univ, B.S, 60; Columbia Univ. Sch. Law, J.D, 63; Columbia Univ. Grad. Sch. Bus, M.B.A, 63; Blue Key. Polit. & Govt. Pos: Town attorney, Snowflake, Ariz, 65-, Holbrook, 66-, Taylor, 67-; precinct committeeman, Navajo Co. Rep. Party, Ariz, 66-; chmn, Navajo Co. Rep. Cent. Cmt, 68-; mem, Ariz. State Rep. Exec. Cmt, 68-; mem, Gov. Adv. Coun, 69- Bus. & Prof. Pos: Law partner, Axline & Johnson, Holbrook, Ariz, 64- Mem: Ariz. and Am. Bar Asns; Am. Trial Lawyers Asn; Rotary. Rel: Latter-day Saint. Legal Res: 806 N. Seventh St, Holbrook, Ariz. 86025. Mailing Add: P.O. Drawer 160, Holbrook, Ariz. 86025.

JOHNSON, RAY C. R
Nebr. State Auditor of Pub. Acct.
b. Oakland, Nebr, 3/21/93; m. 10/10/19 to Lenore Nixon; c. four. Educ: Boyles Bus. Col, Omaha. Polit. & Govt. Pos: Nebr. State Auditor of Pub. Acct, 38- Bus. & Prof. Pos: Clerk, Omaha Nat. Bank, 10-15; asst. cashier, 1st Nat. Bank, Oakland, 15-17 & 19-20; mgr, Swanson Land Bank, Burlington, Colo, 20-27; v.pres, Continental Nat. Bank, Lincoln, 27-36. Mem: Am. Legion; Mason. Rel: Presbyterian. Mailing Add: 3911 A St, Lincoln, Nebr. 68510. (1967)

JOHNSON, RAY EUGENE R
Calif. State Assemblyman
b. Oroville, Calif, 10/8/11; s. August Johnson and Emma Snyder J; m. 12/28/35 to Lorraine Christian; c. Mary Lou and Ray E, Jr. Educ: Univ. Calif, 32. Polit. & Govt. Pos: Mem, Butte Co. Bd. of Educ, Calif, 56-57; Calif. State Assemblyman, Fourth Dist, 65- Bus. & Prof. Pos: Founder and owner, Christian & Johnson Co, 40-60. Mem: Mason; Elks; K. of P; Rotary. Rel: Protestant. Legal Res: 1056 Vallombrosa Ave, Chico, Calif. 95926. Mailing Add: 352 Valombrosa Ave, Chico, Calif. 95926. (1967)

JOHNSON, RAYMOND ALLAN R
Chmn, Marlboro Rep. City Cmt, Mass.
b. Marlboro, Mass, 7/18/36; s. Herbert Gottfrid Johnson and Theresa Pietras J; m. 11/27/66 to Carolyn Gates Whithed. Educ: Worcester Polytech. Inst, Mass, B.S.M.E, 58; v.pres, The Shield. Polit. & Govt. Pos: V.pres, Young Rep. Club Marlboro, Mass, 63-64, treas, 64-66, ed. and founder, Newsletter, 64-66, pres, 66-68; ward one chmn, Marlboro Rep. Ward Cmt, 64-68; hq. coordinator, Frank Walker's Marlboro Mayorality Campaign, 65 & 67; del, Mass. Rep. State Conv, 66; chmn, City of Marlboro Inaugural Ball, 66; trustee, City Marlboro Pub. Libr, 66-; chmn, Marlboro Rep. City Cmt, 68- Bus. & Prof. Pos: Indust. engr, Johnson-Claflin Corp, Marlboro, Mass, 58-59 & 61-65, v.pres. and sales mgr, 69-; safety engr, Buckler, Irvin & Graf, Winchester, 65-69. Mil. Serv: Entered as Pvt, Army, 59, released as SP-5, 61, after serv. in Ord. Missile Command, Redstone Arsenal, Huntsville, Ala, 59-61. Mem: Am. Soc. Mech. Engr; Mason (Master). Cyrus Felton Medal, Rensselaer Polytech. Medal and Marlboro Rotary Club Scholarship, 54. Rel: Unitarian Universalist; Asst. Dir. Sr. High, Unitarian-Universalist Rowe Camp, summer 59, incorporator, 64-68, Mem. Parish Cmt, Marlboro Unitarian-Universalist Church, 64-67 & 69-, Finance Chmn, 65 & 67. Mailing Add: 206 Bolton St, Marlboro, Mass. 01752.

JOHNSON, RAYMOND BLAIR R
Mem, Cambria Co. Rep. Exec. Cmt, Pa.
b. Johnstown, Pa, 9/17/09; s. Stewart William Johnson and Marcella Grace O'Neil J; m. 6/16/38 to Louise Amelia Thiele; c. Stewart William and Raymond Blair, Jr. Educ: Lebanon Valley Col, A.B, 34; grad. study, Univ. Md, 34 and Univ. Pittsburgh, 37. Polit. & Govt. Pos: Chmn, Civil Serv. Fire Dept, Johnstown, Pa, 55-56, publicity chmn, Cambria Co. Rep. Finance Cmt, 56, mem, 58-; mem, Cambria Co. Rep. Exec. Cmt, 57-; del, 22nd Cong. Dist, Rep. Nat. Conv, 56 & 64; mem, City Coun, Johnstown, 58-62; chmn, Cambria Co. Rep. Presidential Campaign, 64; mem, Bd. Cambria Co. Cmnr, 64- Bus. & Prof. Pos: Teacher soc. sci, Cochranville High Sch, 36-41; pres, Johnson's Heating and Air Conditioning, Inc, 47- Mem: Am. Soc. Heating, Refrigeration and Air Conditioning Engrs; past nat. dir. and nat. v.pres, Travelers

Protection Asn. of Am; Soil Conserv. Dist; Johnstown Advert. Club (past pres); dir, Asn. of Blind; Gov. Cmt. on Ment. Health; bd. mem, Co. Ment. Health and Ment. Retardation Asn, currently; dir, Cambria Co. War Mem; Mason; Shrine; Rotary. Rel: Lutheran. Mailing Add: 347 Elknud Lane, Johnstown, Pa. 15905.

JOHNSON, RAYMOND C. R
Wis. State Sen.
b. Chicago, Ill, 8/20/36; s. Benjamin W. Johnson and Elsie Betz J; m. 9/15/62 to Ellen Nelson; c. Sarah. Educ: Wis. State Univ, Eau Claire, B.S, George Wash. Univ. Law Sch, D.C. and J.D. Polit. & Govt. Pos: Wis. State Sen, 31st Dist, 67-, asst. majority leader, Wis. State Sen, 69, v.chmn, Cmt. on Judiciary and Cmt. on Interstate Coop, 69, mem, Judicial Council, 69. Bus. & Prof. Pos: Attorney, Adler, La Fave & Johnson, Eau Claire. Mil. Serv: Entered as Seaman Recruit, Navy, 58, released as Lt, 65, after serv. as a legal officer, Aircraft Carrier Essex, Lt, Res. Mem: Wis. and Va. State Bar Asns; Am. Legion. Rel: Protestant. Mailing Add: 221 North 12th, Eau Claire, Wis. 54701.

JOHNSON, REX DUANE R
b. Oneida, Ill, 12/15/21; s. Delbert E. Johnson (deceased) and Alice McKie J. (deceased); m. 8/15/44 to Paula K. Shaver; c. Kathy Dee and Kris Alice. Educ: Univ. Mich; Yale Univ; Monmouth Col, B.S. in math. and physics, 46; Phi Eta Mu; Theta Chi; Debate Club; Monmouth Col. Choir. Polit. Pos: Precinct committeeman, Sparta Twp, Ill, 65-; bd. dirs, John Ericsson Rep. League Ill, 65-66, chmn, State Finance Cmt, 64-65, pres, Knox Co, 62-63; chmn, mid-state area, United Rep. Fund Ill, 65; mem, Knox Co. Rep. Vet. League, Rep. Cent. Cmt, United Rep. Fund and Monmouth Col. Young Rep; coordinator, Dist. 17-24, Downstate Ill. Citizens for Goldwater-Miller; alternate del, Rep. Nat. Conv, 64; co-chmn, 19th Cong. Dist, Ill. Goldwater for Pres. Cmt; secy-treas, McLoskey for Cong. Club. Bus. & Prof. Pos: Owner and operator, Johnson Grain Co, Oneida and Wataga, Ill. and Johnson Grain Co. Fertilizer Plant, Wataga. Mil. Serv: Entered as Pvt, Air Force, 42, released as 1st Lt, 46, after serv. in ETO; Good Conduct Medal; Am. Campaign Ribbon; ETO Medal with 2 Bronze Stars; Victory Medal; Medal of Army of Occupation, Germany; Armed Servs. Res. Medal; Air Force Longevity Serv. Award; Continental Air Command Cert. of Recognition, 59 and 62: Outstanding Liaison Officer Award, 62; Most Outstanding Liaison Officer Coordinator in U.S.A. Award, 65; Lt. Col, Air Force Res, 46-65. Mem: Knox Co. 4-H; Future Farmers Am; Adj, Am. Legion; comdr, Amvets; VFW; Air Force Asn; past pres, West. Ill. Chap, Res. Officers Asn; Mason Lodge 337, Eastern Star, Petitions Cmt, Consistory, Murga Grotto, Shrine, Mohammed Temple, dir, El Bon Shrine Club; Prairie Coun, Boy Scouts; Lions; Exec. Club; Oneida Centennial Cmt; dir, Knox Co. United Fund and area chmn, 64, co. chmn, 65; Big Bros. Knox Co; dir, Knox Co. YMCA; finance and citizens cmts, ROVA Sch. Dist; chmn, spec. fund drive, Galesburg-Kewanee Area, Monmouth Col. Alumni Asn, 65; Farm Bur; Farm Grange Ill; Agr-Bus. Rels. Cmt. and Foreign Trade Subcmt, Ill. State C. of C; Nat. Feed and Grain Dealers Asn; legis. cmt, Ill. Grain Dealers' Asn; Tri-State Truckers Asn; Ill. Anhydrous Ammonia Asn. Rel: Presbyterian; Bd. Deacons, elder and mem. session, chmn, bldg. fund, Oneida Presbyterian Church, 65. Mailing Add: P.O. Box A, Oneida, Ill. 61467.

JOHNSON, ROBERT ANTHONY D
b. Phila, Pa, 8/18/25; s. John Johnson and Agnes Harkins J; m. 6/17/50 to Peggy Clarke; c. Mary Beth, Frances, Robert, Meg and Patricia. Polit. & Govt. Pos: Pa. State Rep, 67-69. Bus. & Prof. Pos: V.pres, Poquessing Corp, Realtors, 60- Mil. Serv: Entered as Trainee, Marine Corps, 43, released as Sgt, 45, after serv. in Sea-Going Craft, Atlantic, Pac. and Japan Theaters, 43-45. Mem: Gov, Phila. Bd. Realtors, 58-65; Realtors Cmt. with City Planning Cmn; dir. and v.pres, Northeast Realty Bd; Torresdale-Frankford Country Club; Am. Legion. Rel: Catholic. Mailing Add: 4610 Fitler St, Philadelphia, Pa. 19114. (1967)

JOHNSON, ROBERT GEORGE
Minn. State Sen.
b. Hector, Minn, 3/24/25; s. Horace Johnson and Gladys Otness J; m. 6/16/49 to Dorothy Jean Warner; c. Peter, Thomas, Charles, Jane, Christopher and Ann. Educ: Univ. Minn, B.S.L, 48, LL.B, 49; Sigma Nu. Polit. & Govt. Pos: Mem, Willmar Sch. Bd. of Educ, Dist. 347, Minn, 65-; Minn. State Sen, 23rd Legis. Dist, currently. Mil. Serv: Entered as Aviation Cadet Seaman 2/C, Navy, 43, released as Ens, Naval Aviator, 45; Pilot, Naval and Marine Corps Res, 46-52. Mem: Pres, Kandiyohi Bar Asn, 64-65; treas, 12th Judicial Dist. Bar Asn, 50-57; Am. Bar Asn; Kiwanis; Am. Legion; C. of C. Rel: Episcopal. Mailing Add: Knollwood Dr, Willmar, Minn. 56201. (1967)

JOHNSON, ROBERT HENRY D
Wyo. State Sen.
b. Denver, Colo, 8/16/16; s. Henry Johnson and Ellen Haines J; m. 7/11/49 to Helen M. Hamm; c. Susan M, Glen R. and Leslie Ellen. Educ: Univ. Wyo, B.A, 38 and J.D, 63; Univ. Colo, 62; Alpha Tau Omega. Polit. & Govt. Pos: Precinct committeeman, Sweetwater Co. Dem. Cmt, Wyo, 48-49 & 51-; committeeman, Wyo. State Dem. Cmt, 66-; chmn. educ. subcmt, Wyo. Statute Rev. Cmn, 67-69; Wyo. State Sen, 67-; alternate del, Dem. Nat. Conv, 68; mem. libr. bd, Sweetwater Co, 68-; mem, State Cmn. Intergov. Coop, 69- Bus. & Prof. Pos: State ed, Wyo. State Tribune, Cheyenne, 37-38; news ed, North. Wyo. Daily News, Worland, 38-41, gen. mgr, 45-48; ed, Rock Springs Daily Rocket, 48-49, gen. mgr, 51-61, state mgr, United Press Asns, Cheyenne, 49-51; attorney-at-law, Rock Springs, 63- Mil. Serv: Entered as Pvt, Army, 41, released as Maj, 45, after serv. in Eighth Air Force, ETO, 44-45; Air Force Res, Lt. Col; Distinguished Flying Cross; Air Medal with Four Oak Leaf Clusters; Good Conduct Medal; Am. Defense Serv. Medal; Am. Campaign Medal; European Campaign Ribbon with Four Battle Stars; World War II Victory Medal; Air Force Res. Medal. Mem: Wyo. State Bar; Am. Bar Asn; pres, Wyo. Press Asn, 60; Elks; Am. Legion; West. Wyo. Col. Adv. Coun; dist. chmn, Boy Scouts; pres, Univ. Wyo. Alumni Asn, 58. Rel: Protestant; Chmn. Bd. of Trustees, First Congregational Church, 65-66. Mailing Add: 207 Hay St, Rock Springs, Wyo. 82901.

JOHNSON, ROBERT IVER R
b. Mondovi, Wis, 5/24/28; s. Albert Johnson and Goldene Rosenow J; single. Educ: Univ. Wis, 47. Polit. & Govt. Pos: Chmn, Ninth Cong. Dist. Young Rep, Wis, 58-60; Wis. State Assemblyman, Buffalo, Pepin and Pierce Co, 61-65; Chmn, Buffalo Co. Rep. Club, 65-67; candidate for U.S. Sen, 68. Bus. & Prof. Pos: Owner, Double 'J' Dairy Farm, 65. Mil. Serv: Pvt, Army, 52; UN and Korean Serv. Medals. Mem: Am. Jersey Cattle Club; Am. Legion; Lions; K. of P. Rel: Lutheran. Mailing Add: R.R. 2, Mondovi, Wis. 54755.

JOHNSON, ROBERT LIVINGSTON R
b. N.Y.C, N.Y, 3/25/94; s. Frank Russell Johnson and Grace Hazelton Bell J; m. 8/20/17 to Anna Talcott Rathbone; c. Robert Livingston and Albert Rathbone; grandchildren. Robert Livingston, III, Peter Rathbone, Linda Fitzgerald, Sally Edgerton and Carol Schilthuis. Educ: Yale Univ, A.B, 18; Univ. Pa, LL.D, 41; Franklin & Marshall Col, 41; Wisinus Col, 46; Bucknell Univ, 48; Univ. Denver, hon. L.H.D, 50; Univ. Pittsburgh, 51; Syracuse Univ, West. Reserve Univ, Trinity Col. and Rutgers Univ, 53; Beta Theta Pi. Polit. & Govt. Pos: Chmn, Citizens Cmt. for Reorgn. Govt, Pa, 49-53; adminstr, Int. Info. Admin, State Dept, 53; mem, Rep. Nat. Cmt, Pa, 60-68. Bus. & Prof. Pos: V.pres, Time, Inc, 22-37; pres, Temple Univ, 41-59, chancellor, 59-61; dir, Armstrong Cork Co, Girard Trust Corn Exchange Bank, Pa. Mutual Life Ins. Co, Bell Tel. Co, Avco Mfg. Co, Aitkin-Kynett Co, Inc, Esterbrook Pen Co. and Gen. Grinding Wheel Corp. Mil. Serv: 1st Lt, Army, 7th Field Artil, 1st Div, World War I. Mem: Nat. Civil Serv. Reform League (pres, 36-38); Pa. Asn. of Cols. & Univs; hon. mem, Int. Col. Surgeons; World Affairs Coun. (pres, 58); East. Psychiat. Inst.(pres, 58); Eng-Speaking Union (pres, Phila. Chap); Americans for Competitive Enterprise Syst.(nat. pres); Yale Univ. Club of N.Y.C; Contemporary; Poor Richard; Rotary; Midday; Franklin Inn; Sunday Breakfast; Gulph Mills; Golf Union League; Racquet Club of Phila; trustee, int. cmt, YMCA; trustee, Temple Univ; Boys Club of N.Y. Mailing Add: 134 Cherry Lane, Wynnewood, Pa. 19096. (1967)

JOHNSON, ROBERT LLOYD R
Chmn, Fergus Co. Rep. Cent. Cmt, Mont.
b. Lidgerwood, N.Dak, 5/16/27; s. Alfred W. Johnson and Mildred Boxeth J; m. 11/14/52 to Anita Zimmerman; c. Stanley W, Neal L, Alan W. and Robin L. Educ: Mont. State Univ, B.S, 55; Willamette Univ, J.D, 58; Phi Delta Phi. Polit. & Govt. Pos: Chmn, Fergus Co. Rep. Cent. Cmt, Mont, 68- Bus. & Prof. Pos: Attorney at Law, 58- Mil. Serv: Vet, World War II and Korean Conflict, Air Force, Overseas. Mem: Mont. and Am. Bar Asns; Mason; Shrine; Elks; Eagles; Farm Bur; Rotary; C. of C. Rel: Presbyterian. Legal Res: Route 1, Lewistown, Mont. 59457. Mailing Add: 507 Montana Bldg, Lewistown, Mont. 59457.

JOHNSON, ROBERT M. L. R
b. Des Moines, Iowa, 1/6/21; s. Max Louis Johnson and Nell Lanphear J; m. to Edna Mae Haldy; c. R. Kimberlee and Kristine K. Educ: Coe Col. Polit. & Govt. Pos: Cmnr. of Pub. Safety, Cedar Rapids, Iowa, 57-59, mayor, 62-68. Bus. & Prof. Pos: News ed, WMT Stas; Newspaper reporter and columnist, Waterloo, Iowa and Eldora Herald Ledger. Mil. Serv: Entered as Pvt, Army, 42, released as 2nd Lt, 46, after serv. in 8th Army, Pac. Theater. Publ: 'Well Planned Signs,' St. Eng, 2/59; 'Young Adults in Action,' Law and Order, 5/59; 'Promoting Public Safety in Cedar Rapids,' Munic. Signal Engr, 9/59. Mem: Am. Legion; Consistory; Shrine; Optimists; Goodfellows; High 12; Execs. Club; bd. dirs, United Commun. Serv. and Cerebral Palsy Asn; Vet. Mem. Cmn; chmn, Pub. Info. Cmt, League Iowa Munic, 63, chmn, Large Cities Group, 65; Gov. Cmn. State and Local Govt, Am. Pub. Works Admin. Distinguished Serv. Award, Sales Execs. Club, 63; Recognition Award, Optimists, 63; Upper Case Award, Cedar Rapids Press Club, 63; Boss of Year, Criabwa Chap, Am. Bus. Women's Asn, 65; DeMolay Legion of Honor, 66. Rel: Presbyterian. Mailing Add: 3811 Northwood Dr. N.E, Cedar Rapids, Iowa 52402. (1967)

JOHNSON, ROBERT PETER R
b. Phila, Pa, 9/7/26; s. William Barton Johnson and Ethel R. Bonsor J; m. 9/14/57 to Marilyn Joan Murray; c. Robert Peter, Jr. and Kathleen Marie. Educ: St. Joseph's Col, Phila, Pa, B.S, 54. Polit. & Govt. Pos: Magistrate, Lower Merion Twp, Montgomery Co, Pa, 54-; Pa. State Rep, 59-64; Pa. State Sen, 65-66. Mil. Serv: Navy, 44-46. Mailing Add: 287 Meeting House Lane, Merion Station, Pa. 19066. (1967)

JOHNSON, ROBERT WARREN Conservative
Minn. State Rep.
b. St. Paul, Minn, 5/4/24; s. Axel J. Johnson and Evelyn Swanson J; m. to E. Elizabeth Bremer; c. Elizabeth E, Susan B, Mari Leigh, Edward R, David S. and Richard W. Educ: Univ. Minn, Minneapolis, B.S.L, 48, LL.B. and B.B.A, 49; Delta Theta Phi. Polit. & Govt. Pos: Secy, Port Authority, St. Paul, 61-63; Minn. State Rep, Dist. 47A, St. Paul, 63- Bus. & Prof. Pos: Partner, Fisher, Johnson, Vieno & Evans, Attorneys, 58- Mil. Serv: Navy, 41-46, Pac. Theatre. Mem: Town and Country Club; St. Paul Athletic Club. Rel: Lutheran. Legal Res: 1950 Bayard Ave, St. Paul, Minn. 55116. Mailing Add: 624 Endicott on Fourth, St. Paul, Minn. 55101.

JOHNSON, ROGER D
b. Grass Lake, Mich, 12/3/14; married; c. Thomas, Robert, Laura, John, Sally. Educ: Albion Col; West. Mich. Univ; Battle Creek Col; Univ. Mich. Law Sch. Polit. & Govt. Pos: Mich. State Sen, 64-66; former Dem. State Cent. Cmt; exec. asst. to Calhoun Co. Chmn, 3rd Dist. Chmn. Bus. & Prof. Pos: Salesman. Mil. Serv: Army Air Corps. Rel: Presbyterian. Mailing Add: 632 Birch St, Marshall, Mich. 49068. (1967)

JOHNSON, ROY M. D
b. 8/26/08; married; c. Two sons and two daughters. Educ: Ruthland High Sch. Polit. & Govt. Pos: Former S.Dak. State Rep; Rutland Twp. Bd; Rutland Bd. of Educ, 9 years. Bus. & Prof. Pos: Farmer; chmn. and dir, Madison Farmers Coop Elevator Bd. and Madison Farmers Coop Creamery; treas. and dir, Sioux Valley Empire Elec. Asn, Inc. Rel: Lutheran, v.pres. Mailing Add: Box 12, Wentworth, S.Dak. 57075. (1967)

JOHNSON, SAMUEL HENRY D
N.C. State Rep.
b. Sampson Co, N.C, 9/13/27; s. Elliott W. Johnson and Katie Burnett J; m. 8/30/52 to Anne Latham; c. Leslie and William. Educ: Univ. N.C, A.B, 50, LL.B, 53. Polit. & Govt. Pos: Pres, Wake Co. Young Dem, N.C, 56; town attorney, Garner, 58-67; state organizer, N.C. Young Dem, 60, pres,61; mem,

Dem. Nat. Cmt, 62; state chmn, Proj. Victory, 62; N.C. State Rep, 63-; co-chmn, N.C. Local Govt. Study Cmn, 67-69; chmn, House Cmt. on Appropriations, 69-; mem, N.C. Adv. Budget Cmn, 69-; trustee, Univ. N.C, 69- Bus. & Prof. Pos: Lawyer. Mil. Serv: Electronics Technician, Navy, 46-48. Mem: N.C, Wake Co and Am. Bar Asns; N.C. State Bar; Phi Delta Phi; hon.mem, Delta Sigma Phi. Co-chmn, Jefferson-Jackson Day Dinner, 62. Rel: Presbyterian; Deacon, West Raleigh Presbyterian Church. Mailing Add: P.O. Box 1777, Raleigh, N.C. 27602.

JOHNSON, SEYMOUR BENNETT R
Chmn, Sunflower Co. Rep. Party, Miss.
b. Quincy, Ill, 6/4/28; s. Vivion Arvid Johnson and Emily Kay Seymour J; m. 9/1/51 to Joan Lee Dorsett; c. Leslee Kay, Lynn Annette and Gay Dorsett. Educ: Iowa State Univ, B.S, 50; Harvard Bus. Sch, M.Bus, 52; Beta Theta Pi. Polit. & Govt. Pos: Chmn, Sunflower Co. Rep. Party, Miss, 60-; v.chmn, Miss. Del, Rep. Nat. Conv, 64. Mil. Serv: Entered as 2nd Lt, Air Force, released as 1st Lt, after serv. in Air Transport Command, 53-55. Mem: Dir, Miss. Soybean Asn, 60-68, pres, 64-68; dir, Miss. Seed and Cattle Improv. Asns. and Farmer Grain Mkt. Terminal; charter mem. bd. dir, Am. Soybean Inst, 69- Rel: Presbyterian. Legal Res: 8 Seymour Dr, Indianola, Miss. 38751. Mailing Add: P.O. Box 7, Indianola, Miss. 38751.

JOHNSON, SHIRLEY CHASE R
b. Bradford, Vt, 12/2/17; m. to Daniel; c. 1 daughter. Educ: Lyndon Normal Sch, 38. Polit. & Govt. Pos: Town clerk and treas, Vershire, Vt, 56-, secy, Town Cmt; Vt. State Rep, 57-61 & 63-66. Bus. & Prof. Pos: Former elem. sch. teacher. Mem: Women's Club; PTA; Valley Schs, Inc.(retarded children); Vt. Town Clerks & Treas. Asn; Vt. Folklore Soc; Vt. Order Women Legislators, pres, 66 and secy, 65. Rel: Congregational. Mailing Add: Vershire, Vt. 05079. (1967)

JOHNSON, STANLEY ARTHUR R
S.Dak. State Rep.
b. Mitchell, S.Dak. 1/13/25; s. S.R. Johnson and Erma Larson J; m. 6/12/50 to Marjorie E. Barnhart; c. Dale Allen, Cherie Louise, Leila Marie, Carmen Lea, Debra Rena and Kimberly Kay (deceased). Educ: Dakota Wesleyan Univ, 43-44; S.Dak. State Univ, 47-49; Alpha Zeta. Polit. & Govt. Pos: Supvr. and treas, Davison Co. Conserv. Dist, S.Dak, 52-, pres, S.Dak. Asn. Conserv. Dist, 57-59; cmnr, S.Dak. Water Resources Cmn, 61-64; twp. clerk, Mitchell Twp; S.Dak. State Rep, Davidson Co, 68- Mil. Serv: Entered as Pvt, Army Engrs, 45, released as T/5, 47, after serv. in 1151st Combat Engrs, ETO, 46; Victory Ribbon; Commendation Award. Mem: Davison-Hanson Co. Farm Bur; C. of C; Davison Co. 4-H Leader. Rel: Presbyterian; Elder. Mailing Add: R.R. 2, Mitchell, S.Dak, 57301.

JOHNSON, THATCHER R
Chmn, Webster Co. Rep. Cent. Cmt, Iowa
b. Gowrie, Iowa, 8/3/28; s. Axel Emanuel Johnson and Laura Mollenhoff J; m. 3/29/56 to Sherrill Lynn McCarty; c. Tyra Lynn, Kelly Lane, Shane Thatcher and Courtney McCarty. Educ: State Univ. Iowa, 47-50; Sigma Alpha Epsilon. Polit. & Govt. Pos: Mem, Webster Co. Conserv. Bd, Iowa, currently; mem, Fifth Cong. Dist. Rep. Cent. Cmt, 68-; chmn, Webster Co. Rep. Cent. Cmt, 68- Bus. & Prof. Pos: Owner and operator, Johnson Lumber Co, Gowrie, Iowa, currently. Mil. Serv: Entered as Pvt, Army, 46, released as Tech-5, 47, after serv. in Hq. Serv. Record Detachment. Mem: Iowa Lumbermens Asn.(pres, 69-71); Toastmasters; Gowrie Commercial Club; Kiwanis. Rel: Lutheran. Mailing Add: Gowrie, Iowa 50543.

JOHNSON, THEODORE D
Pa. State Rep.
b. Mt. Vernon, Ga; s. William Edward Johnson and Mary Collins J; m. to Marietta Horne; c. four. Educ: Pa. State Col. Polit. & Govt. Pos: Pa. State Rep, 64- Mem: Teamster's Local Union 609 (secy-treas). Mailing Add: 7136 Hermitage St, Pittsburgh, Pa. 15208. (1967)

JOHNSON, THEODORE AUGUST R
b. Braddock, Pa, 9/22/03; s. Claus Albert Johnson and Hilda Holmgren J; m. 9/17/27 to Eleanor Hazel Park; c. Dale A. and Don P. Educ: Youngstown State Univ, 1 year; Univ. Wis, grad. work; Dartmouth Col, grad. work. Polit. & Govt. Pos: Precinct committeeman, Rep. Party, Mahoning Co, Ohio, 32-69, mem, Mahoning Co. Bd. Elec, 64-68; alternate del, Rep. Nat. Conv, 68; trustee, Broadman Twp, 68- Bus. & Prof. Pos: Credit mgr, The Youngstown Sheet and Tube Co, Ohio, retired, 69. Mem: Nat. Asn. Credit and Financial Mgt; Four Square Club. Rel: Lutheran. Mailing Add: 140 Meadowbrook Ave, Youngstown, Ohio 44512.

JOHNSON, THOMAS A. D
Exec. Dir, Legis. Coun. of Tenn.
b. Manchester, Tenn, 12/6/15; m. 7/17/37 to Helen Roddy. Educ: Cumberland Univ, LL.B. Polit. & Govt. Pos: Exec. dir, Legis. Coun. Cmt. of Tenn, 53-; Tenn. State Rep. Bus. & Prof. Pos: Lawyer, Bar 47; asst. cashier, Peoples' Bank & Trust Co. Mil. Serv: Army Air Corps, 42-45. Mem: Lambda Chi Alpha; Delta Theta Phi; Elks; Am. Legion; VFW; DAV; Mason. Rel: Methodist. Legal Res: Coffee Co, Tenn. Mailing Add: State Capitol Bldg, Nashville, Tenn. 37219.

JOHNSON, THURMAN CLEOPHUS D
Co-Chmn, 31st Dist. Dem. Cent. Cmt, Calif.
b. Antlers, Okla, 8/6/28; s. Blake Johnson and Cleo Dillard J; m. 10/21/51 to Juanita Jackson; c. Ronald Anthony; Andrea Denise; Alan Fitzgerald and Linda Yvonne. Educ: Tex. Col, B.A, 48; Calif. State Col. at Los Angeles, M.A, 60; Univ. South. Calif, 2 years; Alpha Phi Alpha. Polit. & Govt. Pos: Mem, Gov. Adv. Cmt. on Compensatory Educ, Calif, 62-64; co-chmn, 31st Dist. Cmt. to Elect Salinger to U.S. Senate, 64; pres, West. Knolls Dem. Club, 64-66; co-chmn, 31st Dist. Dem. Cent. Cmt, Calif, 67-; chmn, 31st Dist. Acad. Selection Cmt, 67-; chmn, 31st Dist. Educ. Cmt. for Congressman Charles Wilson, 68. Bus. & Prof. Pos: Teacher and v.prin, Willowbrook Sch. Dist, Los Angeles, Calif, 53-64, sch-commun. coordinator, 64-66 and asst. supt, 66- Mem: Asn. Calif. Adminstr. in Compensatory Educ; Nat. Educ. Asn; Calif. Teachers Asn; Los Angeles Co. Sch. Adminstr. and Supvr. Asn; Urban League; NAACP; Cmt. on Interracial Understanding. Annual Conf. Chmn. Award, Asn. Calif. Admin. on Compensatory Educ; Cong. Cert. of Appreciation for serv. as a mem. of Acad. Selection Cmt. Rel: Protestant. Mailing Add: 1858 W. 69th St, Los Angeles, Calif. 90047.

JOHNSON, U. ALEXIS
Under Secy. of State for Polit. Affairs
b. Falun, Kans, 10/17/08; s. Carl Theodore Johnson and Ellen Forsse J; m. 3/21/32 to Patricia Ann Tillman; c. Judith (Mrs. Mason S. Zerbe), Stephen Tillman, William Theodore and Jennifer (Mrs. Maitri Mojdara). Educ: Occidental Col, A.B, 31, LL.D, 57; Georgetown Univ. Sch. of For. Serv, 31-32. Polit. & Govt. Pos: Career officer, U.S. Dept. of State For. Serv, 35-; lang. attache, Am. Embassy, Tokyo, Japan, 35-37; v.consul, Seoul, Korea, 37-39, Tientsin, China, 39 and Mukden, Manchuria, 40-42; second secy, Am. Embassy, Rio de Janeiro, 42-44; U.S. Army Civil Affairs Training Sch, Univ. Chicago, 44; Am. Consul, Manila, Philippines, 45; Gen. Hq. Supreme Comdr. Allied Powers, Tokyo, Japan, Aug. 45; Am. Consul, Yokohama, 46, Am. Consul Gen, 47-50; dir, Off. of Northeast Asian Affairs, Dept. of State, 50-51, Dep. Asst. Secy. of State for Far East. Affairs, 51-53; U.S. Ambassador, Czech, 53-58 and Thailand, 58-61; Dep. Under Secy. of State for Polit. Affairs, 61-64 & 65-66; dep. ambassador, Vietnam, Saigon, 64-65; U.S. Ambassador, Japan, 66-69; Under Secy. of State for Polit. Affairs, 69- Mem: Japan-Am. Soc; Phi Beta Kappa; Am. For. Serv. Asn. Nat. Civil Serv. League's Career Serv. Award; Rockefeller Pub. Serv. Award; Appt. Rank Career Ambassador; Medal of Freedom. Legal Res: Calif. Mailing Add: 2101 Connecticut Ave. N.W, Washington, D.C. 20008.

JOHNSON, VERNON LEE, JR. R
Chmn, Boyle Co. Rep. Exec. Cmt, Ky.
b. Williamsburg, Ky. 8/13/33; s. Vernon Lee Johnson, Sr. and Myrtle Haun J; m. 1/22/57 to Mattie Clay Cartmill. Educ: Univ. Ky, 51; Pikeville Col, 52; Transylvania Col, 53; Univ. Ky. and Transylvania Col. Young Rep. Clubs. Polit. & Govt. Pos: Pres, Pendleton Co. Young Rep. Club, Ky, 63; campaign chmn, Boyle Co. Rep. Cmt, 67; chmn, 14th Sen. Dist. Rep. Exec. Cmt, 50th Legis. Dist. Rep. Exec. Cmt. and 13th Judicial Dist. Rep. Cmt, 68-; exec. officer, Ky. Dept. of Ins, 68-; chmn, Boyle Co. Rep. Exec. Cmt, 68- Bus. & Prof. Pos: Owner, Johnson Floral Co, Falmouth, Ky, 57-63; supvr, Retail Credit Co, Danville, 63-68. Mil. Serv: Entered as Pvt, Army, 54, released as Pfc, 56, after serv. in Adj. Gen. Corps, Caribbean Theatre, 55-56. Publ: Newspaper Features. Mem: Blue Grass Lincoln Club. Rel: Southern Baptist. Mailing Add: 610 Logan Ave, Danville, Ky, 40422.

JOHNSON, VICTOR L. DFL
Chmn, Kittson Co. Dem. Party, Minn.
married; c. Four. Educ: Concordia Col, Moorhead, Minn. Polit. & Govt. Pos: Mem, Sch. Bd, Minn; village coun. mem; Minn. State Rep, 58-66; chmn, Kittson Co. Dem. Party, currently. Bus. & Prof. Pos: Publisher, two Kittson City weeklies; dir, N.W. Minn. Develop. Asn; chmn, Ninth Dist. Ed. Asn. Mem: Kittson Co. Park Bd; chmn, Kittson Co. Centennial Cmt. Rel: Evangelical Mission Covenant Church. Mailing Add: Lake Bronson, Minn. 56734. (1967)

JOHNSON, WALTER KIRBY R
b. Franklin, Minn, 4/1/07; s. Oscar Johnson and Lydia Rieke J; m. 8/18/45 to Gloria Natalie Rymerson; c. Wanda Karen (Mrs. M. O. Lee, Jr.), Paul H, Harriet Emily (Mrs. Donald E. Scott); Cynthia Ann and David Walter. Educ: Mankato Commercial Col, 31. Polit. & Govt. Pos: Chmn, Hamlin Co. Rep. Party, S.Dak, 56-68; S.Dak. State Sen, 57-61; mem. and secy, S.Dak. Banking Cmn, 62-68. Bus. & Prof. Pos: Pres, Farmers State Bank, Estelline, 44-, Security State Bank, Canistota, 63-65. Mem: V.pres, S.Dak. Bankers Asn, (53-54, pres, 54-55 and mem, Legis. Cmt, 69-); Am. Bankers Asn.(v.pres. for S.Dak, 55-56, and mem. exec. coun, 65-68); pres, Estelline Commercial Club, 2 Terms. Rel: Lutheran. Legal Res: 702 N. Fourth St, Estelline, S.Dak. 57234. Mailing Add: 211 N. Main St, Estelline, S.Dak. 57234.

JOHNSON, WARREN O. R
Chmn, Aitkin Co. Rep. Cmt, Minn.
b. Duluth, Minn, 6/8/21; s. Oscar Linus Johnson and Bertha Groth J; m. 1953 to Regina McFarlane; c. Nevin, Theodore and Timothy. Educ: Concordia Col, Moorhead, Minn; Journalistic Fraternity. Polit. & Govt. Pos: Postmaster, U.S. Post Off, McGregor, Minn, 54-62; mem, McGregor Village Coun, 62-65; chmn, Aitkin Co. Rep. Cmt, currently. Bus. & Prof. Pos: Gen. mgr, Pineland Tel. Co, 65- Mil. Serv: Entered as A/S, Navy, 42, released as Lt.(jg), 46, after serv. in Underwater Demolition Team 24, S. Pac; Am. and Pac. Theater Ribbons; Victory Medal; Capt, Minn. Nat. Guard, 53- Mem: Past comdr, VFW Post 2747; Am. Legion; McGregor Merchants Club; past pres, McGregor Develop. Corp. Outstanding Athlete's Award, High Sch, 40; Varsity Football, Concordia Col, 41-43. Rel: Lutheran. Mailing Add: McGregor, Minn. 55760. (1967)

JOHNSON, WILLIAM A. D
Wis. State Assemblyman
b. Michigamme, Mich, 11/3/22. Educ: Riverside High Sch. Polit. & Govt. Pos: Del. and v.pres, Milwaukee Co. Labor Coun, Wis; mem, State Adv. Cmt. on Workmen's Compensation; mem. exec. bd, Seventh Ward Dem. Unit; Wis. State Assemblyman, 65- Bus. & Prof. Pos: Machinist. Mil. Serv: Navy, 43-45. Mem: Pres, Local 248, UAW. Mailing Add: 3403 N. 22nd St, Milwaukee, Wis. 53206. (1967)

JOHNSON, WILLIAM POTTER R
b. Peoria, Ill, 5/4/35; s. William Zweigle Johnson and Helen Marh Potter J; m. 5/18/68 to Pauline Ruth Rowe. Educ: Univ. Mich, B.A, 57; Sphinx; Beta Theta Pi. Polit. & Govt. Pos: Alternate del, Rep. Nat. Conv, 68. Bus. & Prof. Pos: Gen. mgr, Bureau Co. Republican, Inc, 61- Mil. Serv: Entered as Officer Cand, Navy, 58, released as Lt.(jg), 61, after serving as exec. officer in U.S.S. Bittern; Lt, Naval Res, 61- Mem: Sigma Delta Chi; Bureau Valley Country Club; Elks. Rel: Roman Catholic. Legal Res: 505 Park Ave. W, Princeton, Ill. 61356. Mailing Add: 316 S. Main St, Princeton, Ill. 61356.

JOHNSON, WILLIAM R. R
N.H. State Rep.
b. 10/21/30; married; c. Two daughters. Educ: Tuck Sch. of Bus, Dartmouth Col; Harvard Law Sch. Polit. & Govt. Pos: V.chmn, Legis. Coun, N.H; chmn, N.H. Rep. State Cmt; Majority Leader, N.H. House of Rep, N.H. State Rep,

currently; former N.H. State Sen. Bus. & Prof. Pos: Attorney-at-law; instr. of law. Mil. Serv: Army, 2 years. Mailing Add: 14 Rayton Rd, Hanover, N.H. 03755. (1967)

JOHNSON, ZEAKE W, JR.
Sgt-at-Arms, U.S. House of Rep.
b. Dyersburg, Tenn, 4/2/10; m. 11/4/65. Polit. & Govt. Pos: Sgt-at-Arms, U.S. House of Rep, 55- Mil. Serv: Coast Guard, 42-45. Legal Res: Jackson, Tenn. Mailing Add: 1200 N. Nash, Apt. 530, Arlington, Va. 22209.

JOHNSTON, ALAN R. R
Ill. State Rep.
b. Chicago, Ill, 4/21/14; m. to Eleanor Cope Smith; c. three. Educ: Princeton Univ, B.S. in Mech. Eng; Univ. Mich. Law Sch, LL.B. Polit. & Govt. Pos: Ill. State Rep, 62- Bus. & Prof. Pos: Lawyer, 41-; partner, Jenner & Block, 51- Mem: Chicago, Ill. State and Am. Bar Asns; former secy. and mem. bd, Chicago Crime Cmn; Legal Club Chicago (pres, 67-68); Law Club (mem. exec. cmt, 64-66); mem, Election Laws Cmn; Intergovt. Coop. Cmn; Ill. Crime Invest. Cmn; Princeton Club of Chicago (pres, 56). Mailing Add: 206 Cumberland Ave, Kenilworth, Ill. 60043.

JOHNSTON, DAN L. D
b. Montezuma, Iowa, 4/6/38; s. Orie Daniel Johnston and Vera Dunwoody J; single. Educ: Iowa State Univ, 58-59; Westmar Col, A.B, 60; Drake Univ, LL.B, 64; Phi Alpha Delta; Pi Kappa Phi. Polit. & Govt. Pos: Asst. Attorney Gen, Iowa, 65-66; Iowa State Rep, 67-68. Bus. & Prof. Pos: Dir, Des Moines Pre-Trial Release Proj, Hawley Found, 64; partner, Law Firm of Jesse, LeTourneau & Johnston, 66- Publ: 'Des Moines Pre-Trial Release Project,' Proc. Nat. Conf. on Bail & Criminal Justice, U.S. Dept. of Justice, 4/65; 'Problems in Pre-Trial Release Projects,' Bail & Summons, Nat. Conf. on Bail & Criminal Justice, 8/66. Mem: Polk Co. and Iowa State Bar Asns. Rel: Episcopal. Legal Res: 4501 N.E. 26th St, Des Moines, Iowa 50313. Mailing Add: 917 Savings & Loan Bldg, Des Moines, Iowa 50309. (1967)

JOHNSTON, EDWARD ELLIOTT R
High Cmnr, Trust Territory of the Pac. Islands
b. Jacksonville, Ill, 1/3/18; s. Leonard Edward Johnston and Erma Lytle Elliott J; m. 8/26/50 to Clara Margaret Stacey; c. Janice Linell and Karen Elleen. Educ: Ill. Col, Jacksonville, A.B. in Psychol. and Econ, 39; C.P.C.U, 64; Phi Beta Kappa. Polit. & Govt. Pos: Del, Hawaii State Rep. Conv, 53-68; chmn, Honolulu Co. Rep. Cmt, Hawaii, 55-58; Lt. Gov, Hawaii, 58-59; del. and mem. platform cmt, Rep. Nat. Conv, 60, alternate del, 64 and del, 68; chmn, Hawaii State Bd. of Econ. Develop, 60-63; state chmn, Rep. Party of Hawaii, 65-69; high cmnr, Trust Territory of the Pac. Islands, 69- Bus. & Prof. Pos: Pres, 50th State Ins. Assocs, Inc, 60-66; v.pres, Hawaiian Ins. & Guaranty Co, Ltd, 66-69. Mil. Serv: Entered as Pvt, Army Air Corps, 42, released as Maj, 52, after serv. in World War II and Korea, Continental U.S. and Pac. Area. Mem: Pres, Honolulu Easter Seal Soc; v.pres, Bd. of Ins. Underwriters of Hawaii; YMCA; PTA; Kiwanis; Waikiki Athletic Club; The Pac. Club. Received many awards, debating, high sch. and col, state high sch. champion, Ill, finalist in 2 nat. tourneys. Rel: Congregational. Mailing Add: P.O. Box 116, Capitol Hill, Saipan, M.I. 96950.

JOHNSTON, ELMER E. R
b. Oaksdale, Wash, 1898; m. to Lillian; c. two. Educ: Notre Dame; Georgetown. LL.B, LL.M. Polit. & Govt. Pos: Wash. State Rep, tenth term - resigned, 1966. Bus. & Prof. Pos: Attorney; O. P. A. Enforcement Attorney, WW II. Mil. Serv: WW I vet. Mem: World War Vets; Serah Club; Elks; K. of C. Mailing Add: Box 38, Morton, Wash. 98356. (1967)

JOHNSTON, ELTON ANDREW R
Chmn, Wayne Co. Rep. Cent. Cmt, Iowa
b. Diagonal, Iowa, 6/27/08; s. George Andrew Johnston and Sadie Fisher J; m. 6/19/39 to Beatrice Helena Bradley; c. John Andrew, Mary Lynn (Mrs. Dodds), Kathleen Ann, Jane Ellen and Paul Bradley. Educ: Creston Jr. Col, 33-35; Drake Univ, LL.B, 38; Delta Theta Phi. Polit. & Govt. Pos: Chmn, Drake Univ. Young Rep, 36; attorney, Wayne Co, Iowa, 47-51; chmn, Iowa Rep. State Conv, 62; chmn, Wayne Co. Rep. Cent. Cmt, currently. Mil. Serv: Marine Corps, 27-31; re-entered as Lt.(jg), Navy, 44, released as Lt, 46, after serv. in U.S. Naval Armed Guard, 44-45; African-European, American and S.Pac. Ribbons; Second Nicaraguan Campaign Ribbon. Mem: Wayne Co. Bar Asn.(pres); Third Judicial Dist, Iowa State and Am. Bar Asns; Am. Legion. Rel: Protestant. Mailing Add: Corydon, Iowa 50060.

JOHNSTON, HAROLD RALPH D
b. Prairieton, Ind, 1/23/26; s. Harold James Johnston and Martha Henderson Smith J; m. 7/18/48 to Joyce Ellen Thomas; c. Christina Marie, Cynthia Ellen and Harold Ralph II. Educ: Ind. Univ, B.S, 48, Sch. Law, J.D, 51. Polit. & Govt. Pos: Mem, Jefferson-Jackson-Kennedy Club; Dem. of Am; Vigo Co. Young Dem. Club; mem, Twp. Adv. Bd, Terra Haute, Ind, 56-60; circuit judge, 43rd Judicial Circuit Court, 63-; del, Dem. Nat. Conv, 68. Bus. & Prof. Pos: Mem. staff, Chicago, Milwaukee, St. Paul and Pac, R.R. Co; asst. pub. serv. cmnr, State of Ind; gen. practice law; secy. bd. dirs, Illiana Telecasting Corp; pres, Sycamore Land Develop, Inc. Mil. Serv: Navy, 44-46, PO 3/C, serv. in Am. and S.Pac; Am. Serv. Ribbon; Philippine Liberation Ribbon. Mem: Am, Ind. and Terre Haute Bar Asns; Ind. Judges Asn; Am. Judicature Soc; Rotary; Vigo Co. Coordinating Coun.(bd. dirs); YMCA; Wabash Valley Asn; Boy's Club (bd. dirs); chmn, Am. Cancer Crusade Vigo Co, 65; Am. Cancer Soc.(bd. dirs); bd. dirs, Terre Haute Adult & Child Guid. Clin; bd. dirs, United Fund; Prairieton Col. Fire Dept; Big Bros-Sister Terre Haute (bd. dirs); bd. dirs, Swope Art Gallery; bd. assocs, Rose Poly; Eagle Scout Bd. Rev; F&AM; Jesters; Shrine; AASR; Hon. Order of Ky. Colonels (Col); Wabash Valley Press Club; Honorable Order Strawberry Cannoneers; Am. Legion (past chaplain and past second v.comdr); VFW; Ind. Asn. Pioneers; Navy League Terre Haute; Vigo Co. Asn. Retarded Children; Regional Adv. Cmt. Ment. Health and Retardation. Award H.E.L.P. Orgn, Terre Haute, Jr. C. of C, Boy Scouts Am. and Vigo Co. Youth Coun, 64; Award, Am. Cancer Soc, 65; Notre Dame Man of the Year, Univ. Notre Dame and Notre Dame Club Terre Haute, 66; Award, Exchange Club Terre Haute, 66, Jr. Achievement, 67 and Boy Scouts Am, 67. Rel: Methodist; Teacher, Sunday Sch. Supt, Trustee, Mem. and Chmn. Gen. Bd, Mem, Ind. Conf. Bd. Educ. for Ind. Conf. Methodist Church. Legal Res: R.R. 21, Terre Haute, Ind. 47802. Mailing Add: Vigo Circuit Court, Court House, Terre Haute, Ind. 47801.

JOHNSTON, IMOGENE BANE R
Chmn, Harford Co. Rep. Cent. Cmt, Md.
b. Lundale, W.Va, 7/7/22; d. Augustus Fulweider Bane and Ellamae Rollins B; m. 7/17/48 to Drexel Marion Johnston. Educ: Marshall Col, 40-41; W.Va. Univ, 45-48; Alpha Sigma Alpha. Polit. & Govt. Pos: Rep. precinct chmn, Harford Co, Md, 58-62, dist. chmn, 62-66; chmn, Harford Co. Rep. Cent. Cmt, 66-; pres, Harford Fedn. Rep. Women, 68- Bus. & Prof. Pos: Statistician, Army Air Forces, D.C, 42-45; admin. asst, sales dept, Sterling Faucet, Morgantown, W.Va, 49-51; tea room mgr, Hutzler's, Baltimore, Md, 51-55; dent. asst. to Dr. Drexel Johnston, Perry Hall, 55-60. Mem: Md. State Dent. Asn Women's Auxiliary (pres, 65-67); Baltimore Co. Dent. Asn.(Women's Auxiliary pres, 63-64); Federated Garden Clubs of Md.(pres, Hill & Stream Garden Club, 65 & 66); charter mem, Baltimore Civic Opera Guild. Rel: Protestant. Mailing Add: 2006 Mountain Rd, Joppa, Md. 21085.

JOHNSTON, KENNETH R. D
Treas, Sierra Co. Dem. Cent. Cmt, N.Mex.
b. Los Angeles, Calif, 7/7/27; s. Benjamin Bynum Johnston and Doshie May Hedrick J; m. 1/31/49 to Jacqueline McKinney; c. Mark Kevin and Jana Rae. Educ: N.Mex. State Univ, 1 year. Polit. & Govt. Pos: N.Mex. State Sen, 57-60 & 65-66; treas, Sierra Co. Dem. Cent. Cmt, N.Mex, 69- Bus. & Prof. Pos: Pres, Elephant Butte Boat Co, Inc, N.Mex, 60-68; Partner, Elephant Butte Lodge, 63-68; owner, Johnston Oil Co. and Aviation Publ, Elephant Butte, 66- Mil. Serv: Entered Army, 50, released as Cpl, 52, after serv. in 716th AAA. Rel: Protestant. Legal Res: Lots 7 & 8, Block J, Hot Springs Landing, Elephant Butte Lake, Sierra County, N.Mex. 87935. Mailing Add: P.O. Box 11, Elephant Butte, N.Mex. 87935.

JOHNSTON, RAY S. DFL
b. Albert Lea, Minn, 4/3/34; s. Floyd Johnston and Harriet Smalling J; m. 8/3/57 to Madeline Virginia Gallihugh; c. Joy and Sally. Educ: State Col. of Iowa, B.A, 59, M.A, 64; Pi Gamma Mu; Kappa Delta Pi. Polit. & Govt. Pos: Councilman, Blaine City Coun, Minn, 63-66, pres. pro tem, 64-66; chmn, Anoka Co. Dem-Farmer-Labor Cent. Cmt, 63-66; mem, Blaine Charter Cmn, 63-68; trustee, N.Suburban Sanit. Sewer Dist, 64-66; Minn. State Rep, Dist. 57B, 67-68. Bus. & Prof. Pos: Instr. Am. hist, jr. high sch, 60-62, sr. high sch, 62-65 and Anoka-Ramsey Jr. Col, 65-67; partner, Haynes-Johnston Recreational Properties, Front Royal, Va, 68; pres, Sleepy Hollow, Inc, 68- Mil. Serv: Entered as Seaman Recruit, Navy, 53, released as Personnel Man 3/C, 55, after serv. in Wash, D.C. Mem: Am. Fedn. of Teachers; Minn. Jr. Col. Faculty Asn; Oak Park Civic League; Jaycees. Rel: Methodist. Mailing Add: 1823 Wainwright Dr, Reston, Va. 22070.

JOHNSTON, RONALD DALE R
b. Seattle, Wash, 7/3/31; s. Alph West Johnston and Gladys Elizabeth Butler J; m. 6/21/56 to Barbara Lee Fannon; c. Susan Lee and Diana Dale. Educ: Univ. Idaho, B.S. in Bus, 57. Polit. & Govt. Pos: Del, Idaho State Rep. Conv, 60, 62 & 64, parliamentarian, 66; chmn, Clearwater Co. Rep. Cent. Cmt, Idaho, 60-68; del, Rep. Nat. Conv, 64. Bus. & Prof. Pos: Off. mgr, Alph Johnston Lumber Co, 58- Mil. Serv: Entered as Pvt, Army, 50, released as Sgt, 53, after serv. in 59th Ord. Depot Co, Ryukyus Command, Okinawa, 51-53; Far East Occup. Ribbon; Good Conduct Medal. Mem: AF&AM; Elks; Lions Int. Rel: Lutheran. Mailing Add: Route 2, Box 128, Orofino, Idaho 83544. (1967)

JOHNSTON, RONALD VERNON D
Del, Calif. Dem. State Cent. Cmt.
b. Los Angeles, Calif, 12/27/42; s. Arthur Vernon Johnston and Lillian K. Nelson J; m. 9/8/63 to Patricia Joan Westerlind. Educ: Pasadena City Col, A.A, 63; LaSalle Univ, 4 years; Phi Kappa Tau. Polit. & Govt. Pos: Chmn, 43rd Assembly Dist, Dem. Vol. Cmt, Calif, 64-65; nominee, 43rd Assembly Dist, Dem. Party, 68; chmn, 43rd Assembly Dist. Del, Los Angeles Co. Dem. Cent. Cmt, 68-; del, Calif. Dem. State Cent. Cmt, 68-; publicity chmn, Glendale Dem. Club Forum, 68- Bus. & Prof. Pos: Packaging engr, Owen-Illinois Inc, 63-67; mgt-consult, Boise-Cascade Corp, 67-68; stockbroker, Hornblower & Weeks, Hemphill-Noyes, 68- Mem: Registered Rep, N.Y. Stock Exchange; Am. Stock Exchange; Nat. Asn. Securities Dealers. Rel: Methodist. Mailing Add: 1239 Berkeley Dr, Glendale, Calif. 91205.

JOHNSTON, THOMAS SHULL D
Chmn, Ashe Co. Dem. Exec. Cmt, N.C.
b. Jefferson, N.C, 1/14/25; s. Ira Thomas Johnston and Mary Adelaide Shull J; m. 8/21/48 to Nancy Cooper Kennickell; c. Jeffrey Allen, Thomas Mark, and John Cooper. Educ: Wake Forest Col, B.S, 47, LL.B, 49; Phi Beta Kappa; Phi Delta Phi; Kappa Alpha. Polit. & Govt. Pos: Mayor, Jefferson, N.C, 51-53; chmn, Ashe Co. Dem. Exec. Cmt, 58- Bus. & Prof. Pos: Practice of general law. Mil. Serv: Aviation Cadet, Air Force, 43-45. Mem: Rotary; Am. Legion. Rel: Methodist. Mailing Add: Jefferson, N.C. 28640.

JOHNSTONE, LOUISE MOFFIT 'PEG' R
Bonus Mem, Colo. Rep. State Cent. Cmt.
b. Morganfield, Ky, 5/10/21; d. James William Moffit and Daisy Hindle Spear M; m. 8/24/46 to James George Johnstone; c. Nancy Louise. Educ: West. Ky. Univ, B.S, 42; Purdue Univ, M.S, 53. Polit. & Govt. Pos: Rep. committeewoman, Precinct 411, Jefferson Co, Colo, 59-; mem. exten. adv. bd, Jefferson Co, 62-; dist. capt, Jefferson Co. Rep. Party, 63-65; bonus mem, Colo. Rep. State Cent. Cmt, 63-65 & 67-; co. supt. schs, Jefferson Co, 65-67, mem. libr. bd, 65-67; pres, Jefferson Co. Women's Rep. Club, 66- Bus. & Prof. Pos: Homemaking teacher, Taylorsville High Sch, Ky, 42-44, Morganfield High Sch, Ky, 44-46, Arvada High Sch, Colo, 46-48 and Dayton High Sch, Ind, 55-56; coordinator, Jefferson Co. Commun. Center for the Retarded, 65- Publ: 'Its up to You,' Colo. Prfnl. Engr, 3/68. Mem: Colo. and Ky. Educ. Asns; Am. Home Econ. Asn; Colo. Asn. Commun. Centered Bd; Jefferson Co. Asn. Retarded Children; Auxiliary, Prfnl. Engrs. Colo; Rocky Mt. Unit, Nat. Asn. Parliamentarians; PTA; Jefferson Co. 4-H Leaders; Colo. Sch. of Mines Faculty Wives; Auxiliary, Am. Soc. Civil Engrs; chmn, Ladies Auxiliary Adv.

Cmt, Nat. Soc. Prfnl. Engrs. Plaque for orgn. of ladies auxiliary to Prfnl. Engrs. Colo. Rel: Methodist. Mailing Add: 6535 W. 26th Ave, Denver, Colo. 80214.

JOINER, W. PAUL D
b. Kent Co, Md, 6/12/99; married. Educ: Kent Co. pub. schs. Polit. & Gov. Pos: Md. State Del, 51-67; Registr. of Wills, Kent Co, 42-45. Bus. & Prof. Pos: Farmer; Adv. Bd, Md. Nat. Bank, Kent Co. Br. Mailing Add: Chestertown, Md. 21620. (1967)

JOLLY, DAN D
Wash. State Rep.
b. Leahy, Wash, 1907; m. to Harriet; c. three daughters. Educ: High Sch. Polit. & Govt. Pos: Mayor, 13 years; Pub. Utility Dist. Cmnr, 22 years; Wash. State Rep, Fourth term, currently. Bus. & Prof. Pos: Farmer. Mem: Grange. Mailing Add: 353 E. Borah, Connell, Wash. 99326.

JOLLY, HENRY LEVI D
b. Gaffney, S.C, 5/17/37; s. Joe Dean Jolly and Winnie Anthony J; m. 6/19/66 to Mary Mason McConnell; c. Mary Christian, Sarah Lisa and Henry L, Jr. Educ: Limestone Col, A.B, in Econ. and Govt; Converse Col, grad work; Lambda Mu Sigma. Polit. & Govt. Pos: Chmn, Young Dem. of Cherokee Co, S.C, 61; S.C. State Rep, 62-68. Bus. & Prof. Pos: Teacher, Gaffney Sr. High Sch, 65-66; realtor, Henry L. Jolly Co, Gaffney, S.C. Mil. Serv: Naval Res.(Ret). Mem: Cherokee Co, S.C. and Nat. Asn. of Real Estate Bds; Civitan Club; Life Scout; RSM; past dir, Jr. C. of C. Rel: Baptist. Mailing Add: 104 Pinewood Dr, Gaffney, S.C. 29340.

JOLOVITZ, HERBERT ALLEN D
b. Canton, Ohio, 8/28/30; s. Louis Jolovitz and Dora Shapiro; m. 7/3/58 to Reva Feldman; c. Paul Adam and Jennifer Susan. Educ: Ohio State Univ, B.S, 48, LL.B, 53. Polit. & Govt. Pos: Admin. Asst. to Sen. Young, Ohio, currently; del, Dem. Nat. Conv, 68. Mil. Serv: Entered as 2nd Lt, Air Force, 54, released as 1st Lt, 56, after serv. in Judge Advocate Gen. Corp. Mem: Beta Gamma Sigma; Phi Eta Sigma. Legal Res: Canton, Ohio. Mailing Add: 7531 Sebago Rd, Bethesda, Md. 20034.

JOLY, CYRIL MATTHEW, JR. R
Chmn, Maine Rep. State Cmt.
b. Waterville, Maine, 5/22/25; s. Cyril M. Joly and Lorette LaPointe J; single. Educ: Colby Col, B.A, 48; Boston Univ. Law Sch, LL.B, 51; pres, Newman Club, Delta Upsilon and Interfraternity Coun. Polit. & Govt. Pos: City chmn, Rep. City Cmt, Waterville, Maine, 52 & 66-; Cent. Maine chmn, Eisenhower for President Campaign, 52; mem. staff, Rep. Nat. Cmt, Wash, D.C, 54; Spec. asst. to Secy. of Health, Educ. and Welfare, 55-57; mem. staff, Rep. Cong. Cmt, fall 56; mem. staff, Inaugural Cmt, winter 56; mem, Manhattan Rep. Cmt, N.Y.C, 59; Mayor, Waterville, Maine, 62-65; mem, Kennebec Co. Rep. Cmt, 62-; chmn, Maine Goldwater for Pres. Cmt, 64; chmn, Main State Rep. Cmt, 67- Bus. & Prof. Pos: Attorney at Law, Waterville, Maine, 51-53 & 61-; pub. affairs dir, Nat. Asn. Mfg, N.Y.C, 57-61. Mil. Serv: Entered as Pvt, Army, 43, released as S/Sgt, 46, after serv. in 66th Inf. Div, ETO, 44-46. Mem: Local, Co. and State Bar Asns; Elks; Am. Legion; Rotary Int; VFW. Rel: Roman Catholic. Legal Res: 63 Mayflower Hill Dr, Waterville, Maine 04901. Mailing Add: 222 Main St, Waterville, Maine 04901.

JONAS, ALLAN K. D
b. Richmond, Va, 6/13/21; s. Murray J. Jonas and Pearl Kaminsky J; m. 8/19/60 to Dorothy Nelle Briscoe; c. Larry, Bonnie, Anderson and Anthony. Educ: Univ. Pa, Wharton Sch. of Finance, B.S.E, 42; Pi Lambda Phi. Polit. & Govt. Pos: Chmn, 46th Assembly Dist. Dem. Coun. Calif, 54-55; mem, Calif. State Dem. Cmt, 54-58; mem, Los Angeles Co. Dem. Cmt, 54-60; dir, Calif. Disaster Off, 60-64; alternate del, Dem. Nat. Conv, 64 & 68; treas, State Cmt. and Humphrey Campaign, 68; chmn, Spec. Elec. Cmt, 69. Bus. & Prof. Pos: Pres, Jonas Corp, 48-; pres, Jonas, Goodglick & Beesley, 67; exten. instr, prin. of indust. real estate, Univ. Calif, Los Angeles, 69. Mil. Serv: Entered as Ens, Navy, 41, released as Lt, 45, after serv. in S.Pac. Area, 44-45. Publ: 'Beware that Overlooked Detail!,' J. Am. Indust. Realtors Asn, 66 & 68. Mem: Calif. Real Estate Bd; Am. Indust. Realtors Asn; C. of C; Am. Cancer Soc.(pres); Hillcrest Country Club; F&AM; Al Malaikah. Legal Res: 5429 W. Slauson Ave, Los Angeles, Calif. 90056. Mailing Add: 11203 S. La Cienega, Los Angeles, Calif. 90045.

JONAS, CHARLES RAPER R
U.S. Rep, N.C.
b. Lincolnton, N.C, 12/9/04; s. Charles Andrew Jonas and Rosa Petrie J; m. 8/28/28 to Annie Elliott Lee; c. Charles Raper, Jr. and Richard Elliott. Educ: Univ. N.C, A.B, 24, Law Sch, J.D, 28; LL.D, Elon Col; Chi Phi; Phi Delta Phi Order of the Coif. Polit. & Govt. Pos: U.S. Rep, Ninth Dist, N.C, 53- Mil. Serv: Entered as Capt, N.C. Nat. Guard, 40, released as Lt. Col, 46, after serv. in Judge Adv. Gen. Dept; Commendation Medal. Mem: Am, D.C. and N.C. Bar Asns; Am. Legion. Rel: Methodist. Legal Res: 301 W. Main St, Lincolnton, N.C. 28092. Mailing Add: Rayburn House Office Bldg, Washington, D.C. 20515.

JONAS, MILTON R
N.Y. State Assemblyman
b. New York, N.Y, 12/14/26; s. Jack Jonas and Miriam Sherman J; m. Jan, 1953 to Zelda Coon; c. Lisa Ann and Ilaina Ruth. Educ: Pace Col, B.B.A, 50; Brooklyn Law Sch, LL.B, 53; Debating Soc; co-capt, Swimming Team. Polit. & Govt. Pos: Rep. committeeman, Uniondale, N.Y, 55-56 and North Bellmore, 58-66; mem. bd. dirs, North Bellmore Rep. Club, 59-61, first v.pres, 62-63; alternate del, Rep. Judicial Conv, 63; legis. counsel to Assemblyman Francis P. McCloskey, 63-64; counsel, Joint Legis. Cmt. on Probs. of the Aged, 64-65; N.Y. State Assemblyman, Tenth Dist, Nassau Co, currently. Bus. & Prof. Pos: Attorney, self-employed. Mil. Serv: Entered as Enlisted Man, Air Force, released as Sgt, 46, after serv. in 308th Bombardment Wing, Asian Theater. Mem: Am. and Nassau Co. Bar Asns; South Nassau Lawyers Asn; Fedn. Lawyers Club of Nassau Co; Lions; Cancer Crusade; Boy Scouts; Civil Defense; Multiple Sclerosis Found. Rel: Jewish. Mailing Add: 1854 Zana Court, North Merrick, N.Y. 11566.

JONCAS, GRACE LUCILLE D
N.H. State Rep.
b. Rollinsford, N.H, 12/22/23; d. Hector L. Senechal and Emelia B. Bisson S; m. 10/12/46 to Richard J. Joncas; c. Richard J, Jr. Educ: St. Joseph's Acad, South Berwick, Maine, four years, bus. course. Polit. & Govt. Pos: Chmn, Bd. Supvrs, Rollinsford, N.H, 56-; secy, Rollinsford Dem. Town Cmt, 58-; N.H. State Rep, 69- Bus. & Prof. Pos: Owned and operated dept. store, Rollinsford, 59-61; presently in catering bus. Mem: Auxiliary mem, Am. Legion; Nat. and State Owl Orgn. Rel: Catholic. Mailing Add: Prospect St, Rollinsford, N.H. 03869.

JONES, A. CLIFFORD R
Mo. State Sen.
b. St. Louis, Mo, 2/13/21; m. 6/22/50 to Janet McAfee; c. A. Clifford, Jr, Irene C, Wesley McAfee and Janet. Educ: Princeton Univ, 42; Wash. Univ, 48. Polit. & Govt. Pos: City clerk, Ladue, Mo, 48-50; Rep. nominee for St. Louis City Supvr, 58; Mo. State Rep, 50-58, Majority Chmn, Mo. State House of Rep; Mo. State Sen, 64-, Minority Floor Leader, currently. Bus. & Prof. Pos: Bus. exec; lawyer; pres, Aluminum Truck Bodies, Inc. and Mo. Polaris Corp; secy-treas, Hewitt-Lucas Body Co, Inc, St. Louis. Mil. Serv: Navy, World War II, sea duty in Atlantic, Pac. and Indian Oceans. Mem: Mo. and St. Louis Bar Asns; Mo. Asn. for Soc. Welfare (past state pres); Ment. Health Asn. of St. Louis; United Fund of Gr. St. Louis; Ambassadors & Agency Rels. Coun; Rotary; AF&AM; Scottish Rite; Shrine; Am. Legion; John Marshall Club. Gold Key Award for distinguished serv. to city, state & nation, 52; Outstanding Young Man, Gr. St. Louis, 52; St. Louis Globe-Dem. Award, Outstanding Mem. of the Mo. State House of Rep, 58. Mailing Add: 9 Clermont Lane, Clayton, Mo. 63124.

JONES, ARTHUR H. D
N.C. State Rep.
b. Phila, Pa, 1902; m. to Gertrude; c. three. Educ: Oberlin Col, B.A, 29; Northwest. Univ, 50. Polit. & Govt. Pos: Supt, Charlotte Park and Recreation Cmn, N.C, 48; mem, Charlotte-Mecklenburg Planning Cmn, 2 terms; N.C. State Rep, 67- Bus. & Prof. Pos: Sr. v.pres, N.C. Nat. Bank. Mil. Serv: Commun. Liaison Officer of 5th Naval Dist. for all Mil. Serv. Mem: Charlotte Rotary (bd. dirs); Nat. Recreation and Park Asn. and United Commun. Funds and Coun. of Am; C. of C.(past mem. bd. dirs). Mailing Add: 6510 Sharon Hills Rd, Charlotte, N.C. 28210. (1967)

JONES, ARTHUR HENRY R
Vt. State Sen.
b. Hartford, Conn, 2/10/12; s. Richard F. Jones and Grace Mulrooney J; m. 1/17/42 to Arline Helen Thieme. Educ: Princeton Univ, B.S. in Elec. Eng, 34; Harvard Univ, grad, 41; Mass. Inst. Tech, grad, 42. Polit. & Govt. Pos: Consult, Off. Secy. of Defense, 47-57; Vt. State Sen. and mem. educ. and natural resources cmt, Vt. State Senate, currently; mem, Vt. Constitution Cmn, currently. Bus. & Prof; Pos: V.pres. and gen. mgr, Gray Research Develop. Co, 46-52; v.pres, Frank C. Brown & Co, 52-56; gen. mgr, Motorola, 56-58; v.pres, Avco, 58-61; pres, Newport Cable TV Co, Inc, 62- Mil. Serv: Entered as Pvt, Army, 40, released as Lt. Col, 46 after serv. in Hq. First Army Artil, ETO and Philippines; Legion of Merit; Bronze Star; Victory Ribbon with 5 Stars and Arrowhead. Mem: Trustee, Univ. Vt; Rotary; Elks; Am. Legion; VFW; Border Curling Club. Mailing Add: Box 56, Morgan, Vt. 05853.

JONES, ARTHUR LAUREL R
S.Dak. State Sen.
b. Mobridge, S.Dak, 4/23/24; s. Frank Arthur Jones and Elouise E. Bliss J; m. 6/21/46 to Bette Jane Grizzell; c. Roberta. Educ: S. Dak. Sch. Mines & Tech, B.S, 49; Triangle. Polit. & Govt. Pos: S.Dak. State Sen, Pennington Co, 66-; chmn, Gov. Interstate Indian Coun, 69; chmn, Interim Cmt. Govt. Affairs, 69-70; mem, S.Dak. Constitutional Rev. Cmt, 69-70; chmn, S.Dak. Senate Standing Invest. Cmt, 69-70. Bus. & Prof. Pos: Prog. dir, KOTA-TV, Rapid City, S.Dak, 55-59; owner mgr, Radio Stas. KEZU, Rapid City and KGFX, Pierre, 59-66; registered rep, Mick Vickers & Assocs, 66- Mil. Serv: Entered as Aviation Cadet, Army Air Force, 42, released as Cpl, 46, after serv. in Second Air Force, Continental U.S, 43-47. Mem: Nat. Speleological Soc; Nat. Asn. Securities Dealers; Elks; Boy Scouts; Kiwanis; Radio Free Europe. Silver Beaver, Boy Scouts, 60; Boss of the Year, 63. Rel: Protestant. Mailing Add: 5215 Pinedale Heights, Rapid City, S.Dak. 57701.

JONES, ARTHUR W. D
S.Dak. State Sen.
b. Britton, S.Dak, 4/24/04; m. to Wilma Wallace; c. Maurice, Curtis, Owen and Leon. Educ: S.Dak. State Col. Sch. of Agr. Polit. & Govt. Pos: Field man, Agr. Conserv. Prog, U.S. Dept. of Agr, 41-43; former mem, Sch. Bd, Britton, S.Dak; S.Dak. State Sen, 50-52 & 54-, mem. exec. bd, S.Dak. State Legis. Research Coun, 57-61, Agr. Prog. committeeman, currently. Bus. & Prof. Pos: Farming; livestock feeding. Mem: Pres, Basin Elec. Power Coop; pres, E. River Power Coop; charter dir, Lake Region Elec. Asn. Mailing Add: Britton, S.Dak. 57430. (1967)

JONES, AUBREY ELROY R
b.Sydney, N.S. Can, 9/10/33; s. Alexander Z. Jones and Margaret MacInnis J; m. 9/11/59 to Lois Chamberlain; c. Sabre-Lu. Educ: Colby Col, A.B, 58; Boston Univ. Sch. Law, LL.B, 61; Phi Delta Theta. Polit. Pos: Chmn, Weston Rep. Town Cmt, Mass, 65-66; co-chmn, Weston Citizens for Goldwater, 64; co-coordinator, Perry for Gov, 64; del. and mem, Credentials Cmt, Rep. State Conv, 64. Bus. & Prof. Pos: Asst. Counsel, Prudential Ins. Co. of Am, 63-66; attorney, Bernkopf, Goodman, Houghton and Dimond, 61-63. Mil. Serv: Entered as Pvt, Army, 54, released as Pfc, 56, after serv. in Spec. Serv, 8th Army, Inchon, Korea, 55-56. Mem: Mass. Bar Asn; Boston Estate Planning Coun; dir, Weston Rotary Club. Rel: Episcopal. Mailing Add: 650 Boston Post Rd, Weston, Mass. 02193. (1967)

JONES, BILL R
Finance chmn, 51st Assembly Dist. Rep. Cent. Cmt, Calif.
b. N.Y.C, 1/25/29; s. William E. Jones and Carolyn E. Pulici J; m. 11/5/60 to Anne L. Butler; c. Lawrence, Carolyn, Timothy and Daniel. Polit. & Govt. Pos: Finance chmn, 51st Assembly Dist. Rep. Cent. Cmt, Calif, 69- Mem:

Whittier chmn, Nat. Fed. of Independent Businessmen, 65-66; chmn, speakers bur, Whittier C. of C, 67-68. Rel: Lutheran. Mailing Add: 13730 Terrace Place, Whittier, Calif. 90601.

JONES, BOBBY S. R
Chmn, Jackson Co. Rep. Cmt, Okla.
b. Altus, Okla, 8/30/21; s. John I. Jones and Irene Cross J; m. 4/8/48 to Myrtle Barton; c. Shirley and Gary. Educ: U.S. Marine Corps Inst; Weaver Sch. Real Estate. Polit. & Govt. Pos: Co. chmn, Okla. Goldwater Club, 64; precinct leader, Jackson Co. Rep. Cmt, Okla, 64, chmn, 66- Bus. & Prof. Pos: Owner and mgr, Jonesville Serv. Center, Okla, 48-66. Mil. Serv: Entered as Pvt, Marine Corps, 40, released as Cpl, after serv. in 4th Marines, S.W. Pac; Japanese Prisoner of War for 3½ years; Presidential Unit Citation for Defense of Bataan and Corregidor. Mem: Am. Legion; DAV; Blinded Vet. Asn; Elks; Moose; Am. Ex-Prisoners of War. Rel: Christian Church. Mailing Add: 1909 Willard Dr, Altus, Okla. 73521.

JONES, BRERETON CHANDLER R
Minority Leader, W.Va. House of Del.
b. Point Pleasant, W.Va, 6/27/39; s. Edward Bartow Jones and Nedra Wilhelm J; single. Educ: Univ. Va, B.S; pres, Univ. Va. Sch. of Commerce. Polit. & Govt. Pos: W.Va. State Del, 64-, minority leader, W.Va. House of Del, currently. Bus. & Prof. Pos: Land develop. and construction bus; pres, Brereton Builders, Inc, Cavalier Enterprises, Inc. and Marshall Apt, Inc. Mem: Honor Court; Eli; I.M.P; Delta Sigma Pi; Omicron Delta Kappa; Beta Theta Pi; Nat. Asn. of Home Builders. Rel: Episcopal. Mailing Add: Point Pleasant, W.Va. 25550.

JONES, CASEY C. D
Ohio State Rep.
b. Paducah, Ky, 6/15/15; s. Clarence Jones and Boydie Brandon J; m. 2/29/36 to Lovell Barber; c. LaVerne (Mrs. Zackary Redden), Casey, Jr, Clarence, Sarah, Marsha (Mrs. Lamont Williams), Marylan, Curtis and Carlton. Educ: Toledo Univ, 37-39 & 64-65. Polit. & Govt. Pos: Inspector, Lucas Co. Sanit. Eng. Dept, Ohio, 49-65; personnel dir, Lucas Co, 65-66; pupil personnel dir, Miami Children Center, 66-68; Ohio State Rep, Dist. 78, 69- Bus. & Prof. Pos: Prfnl. basketball player, Toledo Nat. Basketball Asn, Globe Trotters and N.Y. Komidy Kings. Mem: Pub. Personnel Asn. of Am; bd. dirs, Ind. YMCA (gen. prog. secy, 42-44); Nat. Soc. State Legislators; Commun. Planning Coun. Northwest. Ohio, Inc; Frontiers Int; Elks; UAW Local 12, Bldg. Laborers & Hod Carriers Local 500; Lucas Co. Port Coun; Am. Fedn. State, Co. and Munic. Employees. Rel: Methodist. Mailing Add: 733 Vance St, Toledo, Ohio 43602.

JONES, CHARLES J. R
Ky. State Rep.
Educ: Sacred Heart Jr. Col; Univ. Louisville; Bellarmine Col. Polit. & Govt. Pos: Ky. State Rep, 64- Bus. & Prof. Pos: Buyer, E.I. DuPont Co; editor, Louisville Engr. and Scientist. Mil. Serv: Navy. Mem: Cane Run Improv. Club; Engrs. and Arthitects Club; Shively Gun Club. Rel: Catholic. Mailing Add: 4204 Lake Dreamland Rd, Louisville, Ky, 40216. (1967)

JONES, CHARLES MAURY D
Majority Whip, Ga. House of Rep.
b. Riceboro, Ga, 9/27/30; s. Maury Bancroft Jones and Catherine Dean J; m. 12/21/57 to Carole Lilly; c. Maury Eve and Charles Jay. Educ: Presby. Col, S.C, 48-50; Univ. Ga, B.B.A, 56, Sch. of Law, LL.B, 59; Blue Key; Sigma Nu; Phi Delta Phi. Polit. & Govt. Pos: Ga. State Rep, 61-, Majority Whip, Ga. House of Rep, 67- Bus. & Prof. Pos: Sr. partner, Jones, Kemp & Osteen, Attorneys, 59-; pres, Fairbrook Develop. Corp, Hinesville, Ga, 65-; dir, Coastal Bank, 67- Mil. Serv: Entered as Pvt, Army, 51, released as 1st Lt, 53, after serv. in 279th Inf. Regt, Korea, 52-53. Mem: Am. and Ga. Bar Asns; Am. Trial Lawyers Asn; Am. Legion; VFW. Young Man of the Year Award, Jaycees, 66. Rel: Presbyterian. Legal Res: 601 S. Main St, Hinesville, Ga. 31313. Mailing Add: 206 E. Court St, Hinesville, Ga. 31313.

JONES, CHARLOTTE THRALL R
Vt. State Rep.
b. Poultney, Vt, 2/24/04; d. Luther G. Thrall and Elsie Farr T; m. 8/3/33 to George F. Jones; c. Richard B, Barbara (Mrs. Vivian) and Joseph C. Educ: Ithaca Conservatory, N.Y. Polit. & Govt. Pos: Vt. State Rep, Dist. 2-1, 66- Mem: Pres, Rutland Missionary Asn; Am. Legion Auxiliary (past pres, Rutland Post 31); past princess, Airoc Court, Ladies of Oriental Shrine. Rel: Episcopal. Mailing Add: 77 Bellevue Ave, Rutland, Vt. 05701.

JONES, CLARENCE BENJAMIN D
b. Phila, Pa, 1/8/31; s. Goldsborough Benjamin Jones (deceased) and Mary Elizabeth Toliver J; m. 6/3/56 to Anne Aston Warder Norton; c. Christine Toliver, Alexia Norton; Clarence Benjamin, Jr. and Dana Nicholas Goldsborough. Educ: Columbia Col, Columbia Univ, B.A, 53; Boston Univ. Law Sch, LL.B, 59. Polit. & Govt. Pos: Del, Dem. Nat. Conv, 68; state co-chmn, Coalition for a Dem. Alternative, N.Y, 68-69. Bus. & Prof. Pos: Partner, Lubell, Lubell & Jones, Esquire, N.Y.C, 62-67; chmn. bd. and pres, Intramerican Life Corp, 64-67; v.pres. and dir, Cogan, Berlind, Weill & Levitt, Inc, 67- Mil. Serv: Entered as Pvt, Army, 53, released as Pvt, 55, after serv. in 47th Regt, First Army; Good Conduct Medal. Mem: Allied mem, N.Y. and Am. Stock Exchanges; N.Y. Bar; U.S. Dist. Court, South. Dist. N.Y; U.S. Court of Appeals, Second Circuit; Columbia Col, Columbia Univ. and Boston Univ. Law Sch. Alumni Asns. Legal Res: 4635 Douglas Ave, Riverdale, N.Y. 10471. Mailing Add: 767 Fifth Ave, New York, N.Y. 10022.

JONES, CLEO SATTIS R
W.Va. State Del.
b. Sissonville, W.Va, 11/17/17; s. William Marshall Jones and Estella J; m. 3/24/40 to Agatha Matilda Miller; c. Dale C, Denise and Becky. Educ: Morris Harvey Col; W.Va. Univ, LL.B, 50. Polit. & Govt. Pos: Dir. of orgn, State Young Rep. Club, W.Va, 52-54, pres, 54-55; city prosecutor, Charleston, 55-; del-at-lg, Rep. Nat. Conv, 60, del, Rep. Nat. Conv, 64; chmn, Kanawha Co. Rep. Exec. Cmt, 62-64; v.chmn, W.Va. State Rep. Exec. Cmt, 64-; W.Va. State Del, currently. Mil. Serv: Entered as Seaman, Navy, 43, released as 1/C PO, 45, after serv. in Pac; Pac. Theater Campaign Ribbon. Mem: Kanawha Co. and W.Va. Bar Asns; W.Va. State Bar. Rel: Baptist. Mailing Add: 911 Valley Rd, Charleston, W.Va. 25302.

JONES, D. LEE R
Ariz. State Rep.
b. 1903. Polit. & Govt. Pos: Ariz. State Rep, 67- Bus. & Prof. Pos: Semi-retired cattle and feed grain rancher. Mailing Add: 1201 E. Windsor, Phoenix, Ariz. 85006.

JONES, DAVID CAMPBELL D
b. Sylvester, Ga, 10/18/28; s. Charles Sidney Jones, Sr. and Margaret Maddux J; m. 3/11/55 to Rita Burke; c. David C. Jr. Educ: Southwest. Col; Univ. of Ga, LL.B, 50; Phi Alpha Delta. Polit. & Govt. Pos: Ga. State Rep, 53-64; dep. indust. loan cmnr, State Ga, 67- Bus. & Prof. Pos: Attorney; farmer; ins. Mem: Ga. Bar Asn; Tifton Circuit Bar Asn; Kiwanis; Jaycees. Rel: Methodist. Mailing Add: Sylvester, Ga. 31791.

JONES, DAVID LLOYD R
Cmnr, Bennett Co, S.Dak.
b. Sioux Falls, S.Dak, 11/21/22; s. David Henry Jones and Una Jannette Goodrich J; m. 5/25/46 to Marjorie Ethel Jobst; c. Susan (Mrs. Brassfield), Jannette (Mrs. Waller) and David Paul. Educ: Mitchell Bus. Col, Mitchell, S.Dak. Polit. & Govt. Pos: Chmn, Bennett Co. Rep. Party, S.Dak, 60-69; cmnr, Bennett Co, 62-65 & 69- Bus. & Prof. Pos: Cattle rancher, Bennett Co, S.Dak, 41-65; mgr, Markota Acres Recreation Asn, 66-67; owner, Martin Drugstore, Martin, 68- Mem: S.Dak. Retailers Asn; Nat. Asn. Retail Druggists; Martin Commercial Club; AF&AM; Scottish Rite. Rel: Presbyterian. Mailing Add: Box R, Martin, S.Dak. 57551.

JONES, DELWIN L. D
Tex. State Rep.
b. Lubbock, Tex, 4/2/24; s. Robert Elson Jones and Cordelia M. Boothe J; m. 10/18/46 to Reta Aloyce Womack; c. Lanny Del and Melodie Aloyce. Educ: Tex. Tech. Col, Lubbock, B.B.A, 49; Tex. Tech. Century Club; Tex. Tech. Ex-Students; Tex. Tech. Red Raider Club. Polit. & Govt Pos: Tex. State Rep, 65- Mil. Serv: Entered as Pvt, Air Force, 42, released as 2nd Lt, 45, after serv. in U.S. Mem: Am. Legion; Farm Bureau; Am. Bus. Club; Tex. Asn. for Retarded Children. Rel: Methodist. Mailing Add: 2129 54th St, Lubbock, Tex. 79412.

JONES, DORIS JOAN R
Ohio State Rep.
b. Morgantown, Ky, 8/5/31; d. Therion Hocker and Ann Pendley Brown H; m. to Robert G. Jones (deceased); c. Grace Ann, Lydia Ruth and Lance Peyton. Educ: Georgetown Col, B.A, 53; Delta Omicron; Alpha Beta Pi; Women's Self-Governing Bd; French Club; Chapel Choir. Polit. & Govt. Pos: Ohio State Rep, 69- Mem: Franklin Co. Rep. Women's Club; Cap City Young Rep. Club; Buckeye Rep. Club; PTA. Ky. Colonel, 69. Rel: Methodist. Mailing Add: 1165 W. First Ave, Columbus, Ohio 43212.

JONES, EDMUND EUGENE 'SONNY' R
Tex. State Rep.
b. Houma, La, 10/27/37; s. Edmund Eugene Jones, Sr. and Nida Smith J; m. 6/5/58 to Judith Howell; c. Melinda Holt and Michael Howell. Educ: Univ. Houston, B.S, 60. Polit. & Govt. Pos: Precinct chmn, Rep. Party, Tex, 62-65, area chmn, 63; del, Rep. Co. and State Conv, 62, 64, 66 & 68; mem, Goldwater Adv. Cmt, 63-64; dist. chmn, Bush for Sen. Campaign, 64; mem, Eighth Cong. Dist. Rep. Credentials Cmt, 64; dir, Harris Co. Young Rep. Club, 64, v.pres, 65, pres, 66; v.chmn, Northwest Texans for Tower, 66; Tex. State Rep, Harris Co, Dist. 22, Position Seven, currently. Mil. Serv: Entered as Airman Basic, Tex. Air Nat. Guard, 61, released as Airman 2/C, 64, after serv. in 147th Fighter Group, Airman 2/C, Air Force Res, 64-67. Mem: Soc. Explor. Geophysicists; Houston Asn. Health Underwriters (dir, 68-); Tex. and Nat. Asns. Life Underwriters; Jaycees; Oak Forest Civic Club; Univ. Houston Alumni Asn; Candlelight Civic Club; Nat. Rifle Asn. Guardian of Freedom, Tex. Young Am. for Freedom, 69. Rel: Episcopal. Legal Res: 5019 Forest Nook Court, Houston, Tex. 77008. Mailing Add: 4507 San Jacinto, Suite 324, Houston, Tex. 77004.

JONES, EDWARD D
U.S. Rep, Tenn.
b. Yorkville, Tenn, 4/20/12; m. to Llewellyn Wyatt; c. Mary Llew and Jennifer. Educ: Univ. Tenn, B.S, Dairy Husbandry, 34; Hon. Lit.D, Bethel Col. Polit. & Govt. Pos: Inspector, Div. Insect and Plant Diseases Control, Tenn. Dept. Agr, 34; mem. staff, Tenn. Dairy Prod. Asn, 41-43; agr. agent, Ill. Cent. R.R, 44-69, leave of absence to serv. as Tenn. Cmnr. Agr, 49-52; U.S. Rep, Eighth Dist, Tenn, 69- Bus. & Prof. Pos: Pres, Yorkville Tel. Coop; assoc. farm dir, Radio Sta. WMC, Memphis; mem. bd. trustees, Bethel Col, 17 years, pres. bd. several years. Mem: W.Tenn. Artificial Breeding Asn.(organizer and former pres). Man of the Year Award, Progressive Farmer, 51; Man of the Year in Agr, Memphis Agr. Club, 57. Rel: Presbyterian. Legal Res: Yorkville, Tenn. 38389. Mailing Add: 1118 Longworth House Office Bldg, Washington, D.C. 20515.

JONES, ELLIOTT VEDDER R
b. Amsterdam, N.Y, 8/8/94; m. to Edith Bernard; c. 2 sons. Educ: Union Col, B.E, 17. Polit. & Govt. Pos: Selectman, Ripton, Vt, 6 years, Overseer of Poor, 4 years; Vt. State Rep, 63-66. Bus. & Prof. Pos: Former rate engr, N.Y. Tel. Co, retired. Mil. Serv: Officers Training Sch, Madison Barracks, 17, N.Y, Nitrate Plant, Muscle Shoals, Ala. Mem: Mason; Rotary; Tel. Pioneers; Phi Gamma Delta. Rel: Congregational. Mailing Add: Box 17, Ripton, Vt. 05766. (1967)

JONES, ELMER FILLMORE R
Mem, Ohio State Rep. Cent. and Exec. Cmt.
b. Glouster, Ohio, 4/29/15; s. Herman Elmer Jones and Ora Mae Kasler J; m. 7/11/37 to Laura Elizabeth Heck; c. Thomas Fredric and Diana Sue (Mrs. Begg). Educ: Glouster High Sch, grad, 33. Polit. & Govt. Pos: Chmn, Athens Co. Rep. Cent. and Exec. Cmt, 52-69; exec. chmn, Athens Co. Rep. Party, 56-57 & 68-69; mem, Ohio State Rep. Cent. and Exec. Cmt, 62-; del, Rep. Nat. Conv, 68; presidential elector, Rep. Party, 69. Bus. & Prof. Pos: Pres, Elmer Jones Realty, Inc, Athens Ohio, 53-68; partner, Elmwood Co. and owner, Elmer F. Jones & Assocs, 60-; pres, Southeast. Ohio Develop. Co, Inc, 66- Mem: Nat. and Ohio Asn. Real Estate Bds; Athens-Hocking Co. Bd.

Realtors; Ohio Realtor Cmt; Athens Country Club; Athens Bus. Asn. Rel: First Christian Church; former deacon. Legal Res: 8 Terrace Dr, Athens, Ohio 45701. Mailing Add: 63 W. Carpenter St, Athens, Ohio 45701.

JONES, EVELYN ROSE D
Secy, Holmes Co. Dem. Cent. & Exec. Cmt, Ohio
b. Loudonville, Ohio, 7/12/04; d. William Herbert Mohler and Anna Maria Leidheiser M; m. 8/27/33 to Thomas Paul Jones. Educ: High sch, grad. Polit. & Govt. Pos: Secy, Holmes Co. Dem. Cent. and Exec. Cmt, currently. Bus. & Prof. Pos: Operator, chief operator tel, chief operator cashier and bookkeeper, Loudonville Tel. Co, 24-39; mem. eng. dept, Flxible Co, Loudonville, Ohio, 41-45; surv. work for Holmes Co. Commun. Action Cmt. Mem: Am. Red Cross; Grange; Womens Federated Dem. Asn, Ohio; DAR; Pythian Sisters; Holmes Co. Hist. Soc; Village Coun; Holmes Co. Planning Cmn. Rel: Lutheran; Assoc. mem. Methodist Church, Nashville, Ohio. Legal Res: East Millersburg St, Nashville, Ohio 44661. Mailing Add: Box 2, Nashville, Ohio 44661.

JONES, FANNIE GWENDOLYN D
b. East St. Louis, Ill, 11/22/22; d. Henry Jones (deceased) and Rosie McGee J; single. Educ: Tuskegee Inst, B.S; St. Louis Univ, adv. studies, 49; Univ. Ill. Exten, 62-63 & 66-67; Sigma Gamma Rho. Polit. & Govt. Pos: Mem, Paramount Dem. Club Women's Orgn; Dem. cand, Clerk of Supreme Court, Mo, 68; del, Dem. Nat. Conv, 68. Bus. & Prof. Pos: Pub. sch. teacher, East St. Louis Bd. of Educ, 46-69. Mem: Nat. Educ. Asn; Am, Ill. and East St. Louis Fedn. Teachers; Int. Elks. Woman of the Year Award, 65. Rel: Baptist. Mailing Add: 2442 Illinois Ave, East St. Louis, Ill. 62201.

JONES, FRANCES R. D
b. Mt. Holly Springs, Pa, 5/18/11; d. Rev. Walter R. Ward and Mrs. Ward; wid; c. four. Educ: Milton Schs. Polit. & Govt. Pos: Pa. State Rep, 59-67. Mailing Add: 2233 Christian St, Phila, Pa. 19146. (1967)

JONES, FRANCIS A, III 'MIKE' R
Chmn, Berrien Co. Rep. Party, Mich.
b. Iowa City, Iowa, 10/9/35; m. 8/9/58 to Judith Hartman; c. Deborah Ann and Francis A, IV. Educ: Univ. Colo, B.A; Wayne State Univ, LL.B; pres, Student Bar Asn; exec. v.pres, Am. Law Student Asn; Gold Key Scholarship; McKenzie Honor Soc. Polit. & Govt. Pos: Chmn, Berrien Co. Rep. Party, Mich, currently. Bus. & Prof. Pos: Assoc, Hartwig, Crow & Jones, Attorneys; Law Day Chmn, 67; Legal Aid Chmn; treas, Berrien Co. Bar Asn. Mem: Past pres, Humane Soc; dir, Planned Parenthood; div. chmn, Commun. Fund; Delta Tau Delta; Berrien Hills Country Club. Rel: Episcopal. Legal Res: 179 Higman Park, Benton Harbor, Mich. 49022. Mailing Add: Hartwig, Crow & Jones, P.O. Box 476, Benton Harbor, Mich. 49022.

JONES, FRED E. R
Mem, Ohio State Rep. Cent. Cmt.
b. Detroit, Mich, 8/22/26; s. Fred M. Jones and Thelma Riddell J; m. 7/19/48 to Colleen Cranmer; c. Jennifer L, Daniel F, Matthew C. and Barbara. Educ: Miami Univ; Ohio State Univ; Chase Col. Law, LL.B; Order of the Curia. Polit. & Govt. Pos: Mem, Bd. Elec. and prosecuting attorney, Warren Co, Ohio, 56-60; chmn, Warren Co. Rep. Party, 62-68; mem, Ohio State Rep. Cent. Cmt, 62-; del, Rep. Nat. Conv, 64 & 68. Bus. & Prof. Pos: Trial attorney and partner, Young and Jones, Lebanon, Ohio, 51- Mil. Serv: Entered as Pvt, Army, 45, released as Cpl, 46. Mem: Elks; Sycamore Creek Country Club. Rel: Baptist. Legal Res: R.R. 1, Drake Rd, Lebanon, Ohio 45036. Mailing Add: Box 280, Lebanon, Ohio 45036.

JONES, FREDERICK CARL, JR. D
b. Broxton, Ga, 3/11/21; s. Fred C. Jones, Sr. and Ada Magnolia J; m. 8/14/46 to Frances Elizabeth Conner; c. Frederick Carl III, Frank Stanley, George Christopher. Educ: Lumpkin Co. High Sch; N.Ga. Col. Polit. & Govt. Pos: Mem, Lt. Col, Gov. Staff, Ga, 46-56 & 63-67; mayor, Dahlonega, Ga, 47-50; mem, State Dem. Exec. Cmt, 49-52, 55-56 & 59-62; Ga. State Rep, 49-66; mem, State Game and Fish Cmn, 53-60, chmn, 56; state dir, Ninth Dist, GADA, 54-55. Bus. & Prof. Pos: Owner-dealer, Fred Jones Chevrolet Co, 45- Mil. Serv: Navy, Chief Pharmacist Mate, 41-45; received presidential citation 'for meritorious performance beyond the line of duty.' Mem: WOW; Am. Legion; Lions; Odd Fellows; Elks; Chattahoochie Country Club, Gainesville, Ga; Atlanta Athletic Club; Dahlonega C. of C.(past pres). Rel: Methodist; Bd. of Stewards. Mailing Add: 707 N. Grove St, Dahlonega, Ga. 30533.

JONES, G. PAUL, JR. R
b. Florence, S.C, 6/28/30; m. 7/2/55 to Dallis; c. G. Paul, III, Mary Sanford and Louise Hollis. Educ: Ga. Inst. of Tech, B.S. in Mech. Eng, 52. Polit. & Govt. Pos: Del-at-lg, Rep. Nat. Conv, 64, del, 68; first v.chmn, Rep. Party, Ga, 64; state chmn, 65; Ga. State Rep, 64-66; cand. for U.S. Rep, Sixth Dist, Ga, 66. Bus. & Prof. Pos: Pres, Macon Prestressed Concrete Co. Mil. Serv: Army, 52-54, Korea; Capt, Army Res, Corps of Engrs. Mem: Ga. Soc. of Prfnl. Engrs; Assoc. Indust. of Ga.(dir, 67). Rel: Presbyterian. Mailing Add: Old Forsyth Rd, Macon, Ga. 31201.

JONES, GARY L. D
Educ: Butler Univ, B.A, 63; Ind. Univ. Law Sch. Polit. & Govt. Pos: Ind. State Rep, -66; treas, Butler Young Dems, 62. Bus. & Prof. Pos: Law student; former supvr, refund sect, State Revenue Dept. Mem: Student Bar Asn, 63-64; Indianapolis Human Rels. Coun; Sigma Chi; Phi Delta Phi, Indianapolis Athletic Club; Marion Cty. Young Dems; Ind. Dem. Club. U.N. Study Group, 60. Rel: Protestant. Mailing Add: 1339 Fenwick, Indianapolis, Ind. 46219. (1967)

JONES, GLENN ROBERT R
Mem, Colo. Rep. State Cent. Cmt.
b. Jackson Center, Pa, 3/2/30; s. Alvin Robert Jones and Viola Jenkins J; m. 12/2/53 to Aldene Beagle; c. Christine Elaine, Suzanne Meredith and Glenn Michael. Educ: Findlay Col, 48-49; Allegheny Col, B.A. in Econ, 52; Univ. of Pa. Law Sch, 56-57 & 58-59; Univ. of Colo. Law Sch, J.D, 60; Phi Gamma Delta. Polit. & Govt. Pos: Rep. cand, U.S. Rep, First Cong. Dist. of Colo, 64; finance chmn, Arapahoe Co. Rep. Party, 68-69; mem, Arapahoe Co. Rep. Exec. Cmt, 68-69; mem, Colo. Rep. State Cent. Cmt, 69- Bus. & Prof. Pos: Attorney-at-law, private practice, Denver, Colo, 61-66; pres, Silver King Cable Co, 66-; pres, Data Transmission, Inc. and Silver King Co, 68- Mil. Serv: Entered as A/S, Navy, 52, released as Lt.(jg), 56, after serv. in Amphibious Corps, Pac. and frogman, Explosive Ord. Disposal, Far East, 54-56; Navy Res, 56-66, 1st Lt; Am. Spirit Honor Medal. Rel: Congregational. Mailing Add: 4555 Wagon Trail, Littleton, Colo. 80120.

JONES, GLORIA LEE R
V.Pres. Seventh Dist, Tenn. Fedn. of Rep. Women
b. Rochester, N.Y; 9/22/23; d. Benjamin Court Lee and Florence Hutchinson L; m. to Dr. Chester Kawel Jones; c. Lucinda Lee, Karen Kawel and Owen Chester, II. Educ: Geneseo State Teachers Col, 41-42; Alpha Chi Omega. Polit. & Govt. Pos: Pres, Madison Co. Fedn. of Rep. Women, Tenn, 62-64; chmn, Madison Co. Rep. Exec. Cmt, 62-; v.pres, Seventh Dist, Tenn. Fedn. of Rep. Women, 63-; state co-chmn, Goldwater for Pres. Campaign, 64; del, Rep. Nat. Conv, 64; state chmn. for women's conv, Nat. Fedn. of Rep. Women, 64. Mem: Jackson Serv. League; Jackson Symphony League; Jackson Art Asn. Rel: Episcopal. Mailing Add: Tinker Hill Rd, Jackson, Tenn. 38301.

JONES, GRANT D
Tex. State Rep.
b. Abilene, Tex, 11/11/22; s. Morgan Jones and Jessie Wilder J; m. 8/21/48 to Anne Smith; c. Morgan Andrew and Janet Elizabeth. Educ: South. Methodist Univ, B.B.A; Wharton Sch. Finance and Commerce, Univ. Pa, M.B.A. Polit. & Govt. Pos: Tex. State Rep, 65- Bus. & Prof. Pos: Casualty underwriter, Trezevant & Cochran, 50-54; partner, Abtex Ins, 54- Mil. Serv: Entered as Aviation Cadet, Army Air Corps, 43, released as 1st Lt, after serv. in Troop Carrier Command, Italy; ATC, S.Am. Mem: Soc. Chartered Property and Casualty Underwriters; Kiwanis. Rel: Methodist. Legal Res: 1509 Woodridge, Abilene, Tex. 79605. Mailing Add: P.O. Box 2777, Abilene, Tex. 79604.

JONES, GUY HAMILTON, SR. D
Ark. State Sen.
b. Conway, Ark, 6/29/11; s. Charles Carroll Jones and Cora Henry J; m. 12/28/41 to Rena Elizabeth Relyea; c. Guy H, Jr. and Robert Relyea 'Casey.' Educ: Hendrix Col, A.B, 32; Ark. Law Sch, 32-33. Polit. & Govt. Pos: City attorney, Conway, Ark, 38-42; Ark. State Sen, 14th Sen. Dist, 47-60, 64- Bus. & Prof. Pos: Secy, Conway Young Bus. Men's Asn, Ark, 37-42; secy, Conway C. of C, 38-42. Mil. Serv: Entered as Pvt, Army, 42, released as Capt, 46, after serv. in Fifth Inf. Regt, ETO, 45-46; Combat Infantryman's Badge. Mem: F&AM; Little Rock Consistory; Shrine; VFW; Am. Legion; Kiwanis. Rel: Methodist. Legal Res: 1238 Front St, Conway, Ark. 72032. Mailing Add: Jones Bldg, Conway, Ark. 72032.

JONES, HAROLD KINSMAN R
Chmn, Wilbraham Rep. Town Cmt, Mass.
b. Wilkes-Barre, Pa, 9/21/26; s. Llewellyn Jones and Harriet Kinsman J; m. 7/14/51 to June Collette ; c. Douglas Harold, Daniel Collette, Richard Albert and Dohn Llewellyn. Educ: Bucknell Univ, Lewisburg, Pa, B.S. in Commerce and Finance, 49; Lambda Chi Alpha. Polit. & Govt. Pos: Tax Assessor, Wilbraham, Mass, 59-68; chmn, Wilbraham Rep. Town Cmt, 68- Bus. & Prof. Pos: Mem. staff, Mass. Mutual Life Ins. Co, 49-66, asst. financial secy, 66- Mil. Serv: Entered as A/S, Navy, 44, released as Seaman 1/C, 46, after serv. in U.S.S. Princeton, Atlantic Theatre. Mem: Fel. Life Off. Mgt. Asn; Springfield Jr. C. of C.(former v.pres). Rel: Congregational. Mailing Add: 10 Birch St, Wilbraham, Mass. 01095.

JONES, HELEN B. D
b. Hiwanee, Miss, 5/10/18; d. John Mobley Brown and Evelyn Broadway B; m. 9/1/40 to Marvin Cannon Jones; c. Marvin C, Jr. and Melissa (Mrs. Thomas E. Childers). Educ: Univ. Ala, B.S. in Secondary educ, 62; Alpha Beta Alpha. Polit. Pos: Alt. del, Dem. Nat. Conv, 64. Mem: Nat. Educ. Asn; Am. Educ. Asn; C.T.A; Am. Asn. Univ. Women. Rel: Methodist. Mailing Add: Box 307, Oakman, Ala. 35579. (1967)

JONES, HENRY LEE D
Miss. State Rep.
b. Richton, Miss, 10/28/04; s. Thomas Eugene Jones and Emma Williams J; m. 6/12/29 to Nina Barrett; c. Thomas Henry, Frank Harold and Sue (Mrs. Scott). Educ: Newton Co. Agr. High Sch, 4 years. Polit. & Govt. Pos: Co. supvr, Perry Co, 52-68; Miss. State Rep, Greene and Perry Co, 68- Mem: Rotary; C. of C; Farm Bur. Rel: Baptist. Mailing Add: P.O. Box 449, Richton, Miss. 39476.

JONES, HERSCHEL ALBERT R
b. Mt. Zion, Ill, 3/15/00; s. Albert G. Jones and Nancy Ryan J; m. 8/19/20 to Carol Irene Elizabeth Barker; c. Howard R, Richard B, Betty Irene (Mrs. David B. Marshall) and Louise Nancy (Mrs. Harvey Lee Cox). Educ: Univ. S.C, 18; Syracuse Univ, 20. Polit. & Govt. Pos: Rep. committeeman, Hereford Precinct, Ariz, 59-69; chmn, Cochise Co. Rep. Party, 67-68; alternate del, Rep. Nat. Conv, 68. Bus. & Prof. Pos: Employee, mgr. and owner of various and numerous businesses, retired, 59. Mil. Serv: Entered as Pvt, Army, 18, released as Pfc, 18, after serv. in Student Army Training Corps, Univ. S.C. Rel: Baptist. Mailing Add: Star Route, Box 97, Hereford, Ariz. 85615.

JONES, IDWAL D
Chmn, Marshall Co. Dem. Party, S.Dak.
b. Britton, S.Dak, 7/25/08; s. John S. Jones and Mary A. Jones J; m. 9/16/40 to Elaine G. Emberson; c. Craig D, Mayren Elaine and David L. Educ: S.Dak. State Univ, B.S, 31; Alpha Zeta. Polit. & Govt. Pos: Mem, Rural Sch. Bd, S.Dak, 54-64; twp. supvr, Lowell Twp, 56-62; cent. committeeman, Marshall Co. Dem. Party, 58-62, chmn, 62-; sch. bd. mem, Britton Independent Sch. Dist, 66- Bus. & Prof. Pos: Exten. agent, Carson Co, S.Dak, 33-38; planning specialist, Bur. Agr. Educ, 38-42; soil conservationist, N.S. Soil Conserv. Serv, 42-52; farmer, 52- Mem: Soil Conserv. Soc. Am.(pres, S.Dak. Chap, 51); Mason. Rel: Presbyterian. Mailing Add: R.R, Britton, S.Dak. 57430.

JONES, J. FLETCHER D
b. Miami, Fla, 2/10/27; s. Clarence Julian Jones and Willie Maud Wood J; m. to Sara Jean Bradley; c. Lydia Karen, John Fletcher Jr. and Susan Ellen. Educ: Livingston St. Col; Univ. of Ala, LL.B, 53. Polit. & Govt. Pos: Ala.

State Rep, 59-66. Bus. & Prof. Pos: Lawyer. Mil. Serv: Navy, 44-46. Mem: VFW; Masons; Civitan; Covington City, Am. and Fed. Commun. Bar Asns. Rel: Methodist. Mailing Add: Drawer 1128, Andalusia, Ala. 36420.

JONES, J. L. D
Treas, Second Cong. Dist. Dem. Coun, Wash.
b. Harris Co, Tex, 7/4/16; s. Sean P. Jones and Annie Laura Lester J; m. Dec, 1948 to Anne Maxinchuk; c. Elizabeth and Barbara. Educ: Univ. Tenn, 33-35. Polit. & Govt. Pos: Del, Dem. Nat. Conv, 64; treas, Second Cong. Dist. Dem. Co, Wash, state committeeman, Whatcom Co. Dem. Party and precinct committeeman, currently. Bus. & Prof. Pos: Br. and div. mgr, Norman G. Jensen, Inc, 48- Mem: Elks; K. of C.(4°); C. of C; Bd. of Trade, Vancouver, Can. Rel: Roman Catholic. Legal Res: 2200 Iron St, Bellingham, Wash. 98225. Mailing Add: Box 327, Blaine, Wash. 98230.

JONES, JACK C. D
b. Carrollton, Mo, 4/5/18; m. 4/4/48 to Virginia Rowland. Educ: Washington and Lee Univ; Univ. of Colo; Univ. of Mo, A.B, LL.B. Polit. & Govt. Pos: Mo. State Sen, 54-66. Bus. & Prof. Pos: Asst. prosecuting attorney, Carroll Cty, Mo; legal consult, Office of War Mobilization Reconversion; law clerk. Mil. Serv: Air Force, 3 years, 1 year Far East. Mem: Masons. Rel: Baptist. 1967 Legal Res: 408 W. Third St, Carrollton, Mo. No mailing address available. (1967)

JONES, JAMES ELLYSON D
b. Roanoke, Va, 3/13/22; s. James Harry Jones and Pearl Via J; m. 4/5/47 to Shirley Anna Welsh; c. Anna Leigh and James Kimberly. Educ: Bus. Sch, Roanoke, Va; Mgt. Sch, Univ. of Mich. Polit. & Govt. Pos: City councilman, Roanoke, Va, 62-69. Bus. Prof. Pos: Elec. engr, Appalachian Power Co, 50-56, div. area develop. rep, 56-65, exec. asst. to v.pres. and gen. mgr, 65-66 and admin. asst. to div. mgr, 66- Mil. Serv: Entered as Pvt, Army Air Force, 42, released as S/Sgt, 46, after serv. in Air Transport Command, China-Burma-India; Campaign Ribbons; Presidential Citation with Cluster. Mem: State v.pres, Jaycees; chmn, M.O.D. & Chap; chmn, Roanoke Indust. Authority; mem. bd, several local and nat. civic orgns. Rel: Methodist. Mailing Add: 1810 Mt. Vernon Rd. S.W, Roanoke, Va. 24015.

JONES, JAMES FRED D
Assoc. Justice, Ark. Supreme Court
b. Mount Ida, Ark, 1/12/07; s. Ira Seward Jones and Ella Tyler J; m. 9/5/37 to Walta Lorea Hoback; c. James Voland, Vanda (Mrs. Crocker) and Lyn. Educ: Univ. Ark, LL.B, 37. Polit. & Govt. Pos: Ark. State Rep, 35-39; asst. prosecuting attorney, 18th Judicial Dist, 36-38; munic. judge, Little Rock, 50-51; assoc. justice, Ark. Supreme Court, 67- Mem: Pulaski, Ark. and Am. Bar Asns; Am. Judicature Soc; Inst. Judicial Admin; Inter Am. Bar Asn; Mason. Rel: Methodist. Legal Res: 1208 Silverwood Trail, North Little Rock, Ark. 72116. Mailing Add: Justice Bldg, Little Rock, Ark. 72201.

JONES, JAMES LOCKE D
Mem, Miss. Dem. State Exec. Cmt.
b. West Point, Miss, 11/1/34; s. William M. Jones and Mabel Locke J; m. 4/11/59 to Ann Carolyn Stevens; c. Sheri Lyn and Terri Ann. Educ: Millsaps Col, A.B, 56; Emory Univ, M.A, 57; South. Methodist. Univ, B.D, 62; Kappa Sigma. Polit. & Govt. Pos: Co-chmn, Lafayette Co. Dem. Party, Miss, 68; del, Dem. State Conv, 68; del, Rep. Nat. Conv, 68; mem, Miss. Freedom Dem. Exec. Cmt, 69-; mem, Miss. Dem. State Exec. Cmt, 69- Bus. & Prof. Pos: Methodist minister, Tupelo, Miss, Mobile, Ala, Southaven, Miss, Dallas, Tex, 57-69; campus minister, Univ. Miss, 65-69; assoc. exec. secy, Cmn. on Relig. and Race, United Methodist Church, 69- Rel: United Methodist. Mailing Add: 10547 Tolling Clock Way, Columbia, Md. 21043.

JONES, JAMES PAUL R
b. Slaton, Tex, 12/13/22; s. Braxton B. Jones and Nellie Heifner J; m. 8/4/46 to Patricia Groves; c. Frederick Braxton and Paul Stanley. Educ: Tex. Tech. Col, B.S, 50; Block and Bridle Club; Future Farmers of Am. Polit. & Govt. Pos: Commun. chmn, Swisher Co. Rep. Party, Tex, 61-65, co. chmn, 65-69; chmn, Farmers and Ranchers for U.S. Rep. Bob Price, 68; chmn, Tex. Farmers and Ranchers for Nixon-Agnew, 68; Southwest area dir, Agr. Stabilization and Conservation Serv, 69- Bus. & Prof. Pos: Teacher voc. agr, Cotton Center High Sch, 50 and Kress High Sch, Tex, 52-53; farmer, cotton, grain, sorghum, wheat and livestock, 51-69. Mil. Serv: Entered as Pvt, Marines, 43, released as Cpl, 46, after serv. in Marine Air Group 14, S.Pac, Philippines and Okinawa, 44-46; Unit Citation. Mem: Lion Club; Am. Legion; Am. Farm Bur. Rel: Methodist. Mailing Add: Box 212, Kress, Tex. 79052.

JONES, JAMES ROYDICE R
Chmn, Calhoun Co. Rep. Exec. Cmt, W.Va.
b. Big Bend, W.Va, 1/11/36; s. Homer Jacob Jones and Icy Bell Kemp J; m. 1/17/64 to Brenda Lou Starcher. Educ: Glenville State Col, A.B, 60; W.Va. Univ, grad. work, 64-65; Int. Rels. Club; Polit. Sci. Club; Col. 4-H Club. Polit. & Govt. Pos: Pres, Calhoun & Gilmer Young Rep. Club, 58-60; dir. col. activities, Young Rep. League, W.Va, 58-60; dir. first voters activities, 61-62 and dir. Rep. Youth Camp, 64-66; dir, region three, Col. Young Rep. Nat. Fedn, 58-60; W.Va. State Del, 63-64; pres. bd. dirs, W.Va. Rep. Youth Training Camp, Inc, 65-; chmn, Calhoun Co, Rep. Exec. Cmt, W.Va, 65-; supvr, State Rd. Cmn, Calhoun Co, currently. Mil. Serv: Entered as Pvt, Marine Corps, 61, released as Lt. Col, 62, after serv. in First Marine Div, Camp Pendleton, Calif. Publ: Youth in Politics, Young Rep. League of W.Va, 61. Mem: Calhoun Co. Educ. Asn.(pres, 65-66); Classroom Teachers Asn; del, W.Va. Educ. Asn, 65; Nat. Educ. Asn; Odd Fellows; W.Va. 4-H All Stars; admiral of line, Cherry River Navy; PTA; Calhoun Co. Young Rep. Club. Rel: Church of Christ. Legal Res: Big Bend, W.Va. 26136. Mailing Add: P.O. Box 381, Grantsville, W.Va. 26147.

JONES, JAMES SAMUEL D
State Land Cmnr, Ark.
b. Lonoke, Ark, 3/26/13; s. Samuel Allen Jones and Bertha Tygart J; m. 9/23/65 to Helen Beane Monroe; c. Judith Ann (Mrs. David Hopper). Educ: Ouachita Baptist Col, 31-32; Univ. Ala, 33. Polit. & Govt. Pos: State land cmnr, Ark, 57- Bus. & Prof. Pos: Cmn. agent, Standard Oil Co; contractor, Int. Paper Co; contractor, Crossett Lumber and Paper Co; sales rep, Dierks Lumber & Coal Co. Mil. Serv: ROTC, Ouachita Col. Mem: Small Bus. Asn. Rel: Protestant. Legal Res: 34 Nob View Circle, Little Rock, Ark. 72205. Mailing Add: P.O. Box 1531, Little Rock, Ark. 72203.

JONES, JEAN BOSWELL R
V.Chmn, Mo. State Rep. Cmt.
b. Baxter Springs, Kans, 6/27/20; d. Dr. James Henry Boswell and Maud Cramer B; m. 8/31/41 to Dr. Edward S. Jones; c. Stephen Edward, Pamela Jane and Bradley Boswell. Educ: Univ. Kans, A.B; Chi Omega. Polit. & Govt. Pos: Pres, Cass Co. Rep. Fedn. Womens Clubs, Mo, 64-65 & 68-69; chmn, Cass Co. Rep. Party, 64-; secy, Fourth Cong. Dist. Rep. Women's Club, 65-66; secy, Fourth Cong. Dist. Rep. Cmt, 66-68; mem. & v.chmn, Mo. State Rep. Cmt, 68- Mem: PEO (past pres); PTA; Youth Center Bd; v.pres, Hosp. Auxiliary; former mem, City Zoning Bd. Rel: Episcopal; mem, Vestry Bd, 69. Mailing Add: 301 Price Ave, Harrisonville, Mo. 64701.

JONES, JENIVER JAMES R
b. Sutton, W.Va, 9/24/15; s. Lee Jackson Jones and Mary Ida Lewis J; m. 10/6/39 to Maxine Hickman; c. Gary Keith, Glendon Kent and Ronnie Dale. Educ: Glenville State Col, 38; W.Va. Univ. Col. Law, LL,B, 47. Polit. & Govt. Pos: Secy, Braxton Co. Rep. Exec. Cmt, W.Va, 48-56, chmn, 64-66. Bus. & Prof. Pos: Attorney, Home Nat. Bank of Sutton, W.Va, 56-, Heater Oil Co, 65-; town attorney, Sutton, 59-, Burnsville, 64-66 and Gassaway, 66- Mem: W.Va. State Bar, (Cmt. on Grievances); charter mem, Sutton Lions Club, 48; dist. gov, Dist. 29-N, Lions Int, 63-64 and int. counsr, 64-66; chmn, Braxton Co. Red Cross; pres, Braxton Co. Coun. of Churches. Rel: Methodist. Legal Res: Gassaway, W.Va. 26624. Mailing Add: P.O. Box 578, Sutton, W.Va. 26601.

JONES, J(ESSE) FRED D
b. Inverness, Miss, 8/11/93; s. Jesse Floyd Jones and Callie Franklin J; m. to Ellyette Wilhite Jones, wid; m. 8/11/53 to Irene Hatten; c. Kathleen (Mrs. Lewis Poindexter, deceased) and Mary Ellyette (Mrs. Jack Williams); grandchildren, Scott, Fred, Will, Robert, John and Kathy. Educ: Millsaps Col; Univ. Miss. Polit. & Govt. Pos: Mem. and pres. for four terms, Sunflower Co. Bd. of Supvrs, Miss; supt, Miss. State Penitentiary; Miss. State Rep, one term; Miss. State Senate, 2 terms; mem, Miss. Dem. Exec. Cmt. Bus. & Prof. Pos: Owner, cotton plantation, 55 years. Mem: Delta Power Elec. Asn. (first pres); Newcomen Soc. Am; Miss. State chmn, Am. Cancer Soc; v.chmn, Am. Red Cross Drive, 52; Shrine; Sons of Confederate Vet; Scottish Rite. Rel: Methodist. Mailing Add: Box 45, Inverness, Miss. 38753.

JONES, JIMMIE 'RED' D
State Auditor, Ark.
b. Magnolia, Ark, 3/14/20; s. Stephen Herbert Jones and Ethel May Stevens J; m. June, 1957 to Bonnie Inez Smith. Educ: Southern State Col; Ark. Law Sch. Polit. & Govt. Pos: Tax collector, Columbia Co, Ark, 50-55; state land cmnr, 55-57; state auditor, 57- Bus. & Prof. Pos: Commercial mgr, Radio Sta. KVMA, Magnolia, Ark. Mil. Serv: Entered as 1st Lt, Air Corps, 42, released as Maj, 45, after serv. in Eighth Air Force; ETO Ribbon with Eight Battle Stars; Distinguished Flying Cross with Two Oak Leaf Clusters; Air Medal with Six Oak Leaf Clusters; Lt. Col, Ark. Nat. Guard, 45- Rel: Methodist. Legal Res: Magnolia, Ark. Mailing Add: State Capitol Bldg, Little Rock, Ark. 72201.

JONES, JOHN DAVID R
Ill. State Rep.
b. Springfield, Ill, 1/3/12; s. Oscar David Jones and Sally Boyd J; m. 9/19/34 to Marjorie Gale; c. Gale (Mrs. Jack P. Fixmer) and David B. Educ: Springfield High Sch; Col. Exten. Courses. Polit. & Govt. Pos: Rep. precinct committeeman; chmn, Sangamon Co. Rep. Cent. Cmt; Ill. state cent. committeeman from 20th Cong. Dist. Rep. Party; chmn, Springfield Airport Authority, 45-64; Ill. State Rep, 65- Bus. & Prof. Pos: Secy-treas, Ill. Pub. Airports Asn, 58-64; pub. rels. officer, United Theater Owners of Ill. Mem: Mason; Consistory; Ansar Shrine; Eagles; Jaycees (pres, Springfield Chap, 42-43). Rel: Methodist; Off. del, Ill. Methodist Church Conf. Legal Res: 6 Walnut Court, Springfield, Ill. 62704. Mailing Add: 104 N. Sixth St, Springfield, Ill. 62704.

JONES, JOHN DOUGLAS (J.D.) D
Chmn, Chesterfield Co. Dem. Exec. Cmt, S.C.
b. Chesterfield, S.C, 9/10/16; s. Neal Crawford Jones and Lana Melton J; m. 9/10/46 to Sarah Alliene Fields. Educ: Univ. S.C, B.S, 39. Polit. & Govt. Pos: Mem, Co. Bd. of Pub. Welfare, S.C, 52-59; v.pres, Chesterfield Dem. Club, 58-60, pres, 60-; chmn, Chesterfield Co. Dem. Exec. Cmt, 62-; cmnr, Chesterfield Co, 66-69. Mil. Serv: Entered as Pvt, Army, 43, released as T/Sgt, 46, after serv. in 42nd Gen. Hosp, S.W. Pac, 43-46; Battle of Luzon Medal and Battle Star; Meritorious Occup. of Japan Medal. Mem: Am. Legion; VFW; 40 et 8. Rel: Southern Baptist; Chmn. Bd. Deacons, Douglas Mill Church. Legal Res: 331 Laurel Ave, Chesterfield, S.C. 29709. Mailing Add: Jones Pharmacy, 146 Main St, Chesterfield, S.C. 29709.

JONES, JOHN J. J. D
Mem. Exec. Cmt, Suffolk Co. Dem. Cmt, N.Y.
b. Brooklyn, N.Y, 6/30/26; s. Joseph J. Jones and Helen V. Fatthauer J; m. 12/27/47 to Margaret A. Clancy; c. John J.J, Margaret A, Joan M, Denise M. and Brian G. Educ: Trinity Col, 45; N.Y. Univ. Grad. Sch. Law, 50; St. John's Univ. Sch. Law, LL.B, 49. Polit. & Govt. Pos: Dep. receiver of taxes, Brookhaven, N.Y, 59-60, spec. town attorney, 60-; del, Judicial Dist. Dem. Conv, 61-68; del, N.Y. State Dem. Conv, 62-68; del, Dem. Nat. Conv, 64 & 68; mem. exec. cmt, Suffolk Co. Dem. Cmt, 65-; chmn, Brookhaven Town Dem. Cmt, 66-68. Bus. & Prof. Pos: Attorney, 50- Mil. Serv: Navy, 44-45. Mem: Suffolk Co. and N.Y. State Bar Asns; Am. Legion (past Comdr and co. exec. mem); K. of C.(past Grand Knight); St. George Golf and Country Club; Stony Brook Yacht Club. Rel: Catholic. Legal Res: Cedar St, Stony Brook, N.Y. 11790. Mailing Add: Box J, Stony Brook, N.Y. 11790.

JONES, JOHN MARTIN D
b. Sweetwater, Tenn, 12/11/14; s. Oliver King Jones (deceased) and Byrd Browder J; m. 6/29/40 to Martha Arnold Susong; c. John Martin, Alex Susong, Gregg King, Edith Susong and Sarah Ingles. Educ: Wash. & Lee Univ, A.B,

37; Kappa Sigma. Polit. & Govt. Pos: Del, Dem. Nat. Convs, 56, 60, 64 & 68; chmn, Gov. Emergency Traffic Safety Cmt, Tenn; mem. State Armory Cmn, 58-; mem, Great Smoky Mt. Nat. Park Cmn, 60-; mem, Tenn. Cmn. Higher Educ, currently. Bus. & Prof. Pos: Dir, Hamilton Nat. Bank, Knoxville, First Nat. Bank Greeneville and Sweetwater Hosier Mills; mem. adv. bd, Downtowner Motor Inns; v.pres. and dir, Tenn. Electro-Minerals Corp. and Agr. Lime Co, Inc; publisher, Newport Plain Talk & Tribune; pres; Newport Pub. Co, Daily Post Athenian Co. and Etowah Enterprise, Inc; advert. mgr, Gilman Paint & Varnish Co, 38-41; ed. and gen. mgr, Greeneville Daily Sun, 46-; trustee, Tenn. Tuberc. Hosp, 57-61; pres, Greeneville Pub. Co, 57-; trustee, Tenn. Dept. Ment. Health and Tenn. Cmt. Physically Handicapped, 61- Mil. Serv: Entered as 2nd Lt, Army, 42, released as Lt. Col, 45, after serv. in Merrill's Marauders, China-Burma-India, 43-45; aide-de-camp to Lord Louis Mountbatten, Supreme Allied Comdr, S.E. Asia Command; exec. officer to Lt. Gen. R.A. Wheeler, India-Burma Theater Comdr; Legion of Merit; Soldier's Medal; Presidential Unit Citation. Mem: Greeneville C. of C.(pres, 50); Greene Co. Found.(pres, 52); Tenn. Press Asn.(pres, 62); Boy Scouts (dist. chmn, 52, v.pres, Sequoyah Coun, 56-64); Nat. Press Club; Greeneville Exchange Club; Elks; Gatlinburg Ski Club; Like Hills Country Club; VFW; Am. Legion; Wash. & Lee Univ. Alumni Asn.(bd. dirs. and v.pres). Rel: Episcopal. Legal Res: Hilltop, Greeneville, Tenn. 37743. Mailing Add: 202 S. Main St, Greeneville, Tenn. 37743.

JONES, JOHN MORTON R
Secy, Vermilion Co. Rep. Cent. Cmt, Ill.
b. Danville, Ill, 2/16/27; s. Paul Fouts Jones and Edith Fairchild J; m. 6/30/48 to Mary Elizabeth Jones; c. David Morton, Molly, Paula and Sarah. Educ: Bowling Green State Univ, 2 years; Univ. Mich, A.B, 47, J.D, 50; Bowling Green State Univ. math. honors; Zeta Alpha Epsilon; Phi Delta Phi. Polit. & Govt. Pos: Asst. states attorney, Vermilion Co, Ill, 50-53, states attorney, 68-; chmn, Citizens for Eisenhower, Vermilion Co, 52 & 56; precinct committeeman, Vermilion Co. Rep. Party, 52-; asst. U.S. dist. attorney, E. Dist, 53-56; secy, Vermilion Co. Rep. Cent. Cmt, 56-; supvr, Newell Twp, 59-62; chmn, Vol. for Nixon, Vermilion Co, 60; city attorney, Danville, 63-66; asst. supvr, Danville Twp, 65-68; chmn, Vermilion Co. OEO, 66-68. Mil. Serv: Entered as Recruit, Navy, 44, released as Seaman 1/C, 46, after serv. in Am. Theater, 44-46. Mem: Fed, Ill. State and Vermilion Co. Bar Asns; Am. Legion (past Comdr, Post 210); Danville Country Club; Vermilion Co. Red Cross (past chmn); C. of C.(dir, Danville Br, 60-62). Jr. C. of C. Distinguished Serv. Award, 59. Rel: Catholic. Legal Res: 5 Maywood Dr, Danville, Ill. 61832. Mailing Add: Court House, Danville, Ill. 61832.

JONES, JOSEPH E. D
Wis. State Assemblyman
b. Antigo, Wis, 6/29/14. Educ: Univ. of Wis; Bowlby Bus. Col; Northwest. Univ. Polit. & Govt. Pos: Mem, Milwaukee Co. Dem. Coun, Wis; mem, Milwaukee Co. Labor Coun; Wis. State Assemblyman, 62- Bus. & Prof. Pos: Former ins. agent; machinist, currently. Mil. Serv: Army, 44-46. Mem: Pres, Int. Asn. of Machinists, 60-64; Am. Legion; VFW; Eagles; K. of C; Holy Name Soc. Rel: Catholic. Mailing Add: 4285 N. 26th St, Milwaukee, Wis. 53209. (1967)

JONES, JOSEPH HILLIS R
b. Ainsworth, Iowa, 8/3/13; s. Joseph H. Jones and Mary Thomas J; m. 5/1/38 to Elsie Belle Stoakes; c. Gwyneth Ann, Joseph Hugh and Miriam Ruth. Educ: Iowa State Univ. Polit. & Govt. Pos: Mem, Sch. Bd, Crawfordsville, Iowa, 42-60; mem, Co. Rep. Cmts, 60-62; chmn, Wash. Co. Rep. Cent. Cmt, 63-68. Bus. & Prof. Pos: Owner and operator of farm, 34-63; farm supply salesman, Farm Serv, 63- Mem: Lions; Y's Men; Farm Bur. Rel: Methodist. Mailing Add: 718 S. Ninth, Washington, Iowa 52353. (1967)

JONES, LAWRENCE F. D
Chmn, Fond du Lac Co. Dem. Party, Wis.
b. Belvidere, Ill, 5/15/99; s. Fredric W. Jones and Carrie Alfreda Longley J; m. 2/2/29 to Anna Irene Russell; c. Caroline Ekvall (deceased). Educ: Wis. Univ, B.Ed, 32; Ruralete Soc; Debate Squad. Polit. & Govt. Pos: City cmnr, Fond du Lac, Wis, 36-53; chmn, Fond du Lac Co. Dem. Party, 65- Bus. & Prof. Pos: Instr, Fond du Lac Voc. Sch, 29-35; pub. rels. dir, Wis. Asn. of Coop, 58-61, exec. secy, 61-64. Mil. Serv: Capt, Army, 43-47, serv. in Mil. Govt; Maj.(Ret), Army Res, 54; ETO and 3 Campaign Ribbons. Mem: Coop. League of U.S; Eagles; Mason; Farmers Union; United Commercial Travelers; Eastern Star; K.T. Rel: Presbyterian. Mailing Add: 123 E. Division, Fond du Lac, Wis. 54935.

JONES, LAWRENCE LAWSON R
b. Hyde Park, Vt, 2/28/90; s. Alvah H. Jones and Jane Emerson J; m. 5/21/12 to Hazel Dell Utton; c. Leola (Mrs. Merton McLean); and Elvern A. Educ: Hyde Park Pub. Schs, 8 years. Polit. & Govt. Pos: Selectman, Vt, 42-59; Vt. State Rep, 51-55 & 59-63. Bus. & Prof. Pos: Store clerk, 14 years; farmer, retired 58; truck driver, Socony Oil Co, 15 years. Mem: WOW; Farm Bur. Rel: Protestant. Mailing Add: Eden, Vt. 05652.

JONES, LAWRENCE MICHAEL 'LARRY' New Party
b. Boonville, Mo, 6/4/35; s. Louis Verne Jones and Mary Appleman J; m. 5/31/58 to Dorice Elaine Willoughby; c. Scott Louis, Kenneth Paul, Todd Alan and Lisa Michele. Educ: Univ. of Geneva, Geneva, Switz, 55-56; Mo. Valley Col, B.A, 57; McCormick Theol. Sem, B.D, 61. Polit. & Govt. Pos: Mem, Eagle Co. Bd. of Educ, Colo, 64-66; chmn, Clark Co. Citizens for McCarthy, Wash, 68; del, Dem. Nat. Conv, 68; chmn, Clark Co. Dem. Coun, 68- Bus. & Prof. Pos: Minister, Minturn United Presby. Church, Colo, 61-66; minister of educ, First United Presby. Church, Vancouver, Wash, 66- Mem: Moderator, Columbia River Presbytery, 68; Portland Presbytery; NAACP (mem. bd. dirs, Clark Co. Chap); bd. dirs, Vancouver Head Start; Am. Civil Liberties Union (chmn, Ft. Vancouver Chap); Interfaith Broadcasting Cmn. Rel: United Presbyterian. Mailing Add: 6114 N.W. Cherry St, Vancouver, Wash. 98663.

JONES, LAWRENCE WALTER R
Utah State Rep.
b. Monroe, Utah, 8/16/96; s. Lewis William Jones and Sarah Nilsson J; m. 6/10/25 to Edna Marguerite Hansen; c. Lawrence Paul, Lewis Kimball and Janice. Educ: Utah State Univ, B.S. in Agr, 24; Phi Kappa Phi; Alpha Delta Epsilon. Polit. & Govt. Pos: Mem. bd. dirs, Sevier Co. Welfare Bd, Utah, 44-52; cmnr, Sevier Co, 44-56; pres, Utah Counties Asn, 55; v.pres, Utah State Fair Bd, 57-61; Utah State Rep, currently. Bus. & Prof. Pos: Pres, Monroe South Bend Canal Co, 62-66. Mem: Sevier Co. Hist. Soc; Lions; Sevier Co. Farm Bur; Utah State Alumni Asn; Sevier Co. Fair Bd. Rel: Latter-day Saint. Mailing Add: R.F.D, Monroe, Utah 84754.

JONES, LEE RICHARDSON R
b. Patesville, Ky, 3/23/34; d. Robert Gayle Richardson and Bess Hale R; m. 12/13/57 to Leonard Ralph Jones; c. Lenda Ruth, Lynn Cherie Lemmon, Leslie Rebecca, Leonard Ralph, II and Loren Robert. Educ: West. Mich. Col, 51-52. Polit. & Govt. Pos: Precinct committeewoman, Boulder Co. Rep. Cent. Cmt, Colo, 66-67, secy, 67-68 and v.chmn, 68-; secy, Second Cong. Dist. Rep. Party, Colo, 67- Bus. & Prof. Pos: Rep, Inheritance Tax Dept, 69- Mem: Boulder Women's Rep. Club; Morning Forum of Rep. Women; Boulder Co. Young Rep. Rel: Episcopal. Mailing Add: 7449 Crannell Dr, Boulder, Colo. 80302.

JONES, LEM T. R
Mem, Mo. Rep. Cent. Cmt.
b. Ebensburg, Pa, 1/23/96; s. Thomas D. Jones and Mary Ann Hughes J; m. 12/22/21 to Jessie E. Stover; c. Lem T, Jr, Russell S, Thomas D.(deceased), Sally Jacquelyn, Mary Ann and John Paul. Educ: Univ. Iowa, A.B. Hon. LL.D, Parsons Col; hon. L.H.D, Tarkio Col. Polit. & Govt. Pos: Mem. adv. cmt, Regional Health and Welfare Coun; mem, Rep. Nat. Finance Cmt; mem, Kansas City Crime Cmn, Mo, 51-; chmn. finance cmt, Mo. State Rep. Cmt, 60-62, chmn, currently; mem, Mo. State Rep. Cent. Cmt, currently. Bus. & Prof. Pos: Teacher, rural elem. schs, Iowa; instr. and head dept. commerce, Anamosa Reform Sch, Iowa; instr. and bus. mgr, J. Sterling Morton High Sch. and Jr. Col, Cicero, Ill; instr. principles of acct, Ottumwa High Sch, Iowa; exec. and partner, Russell Stover Candies, Inc, 28-60, pres, 60-; v.pres, Empire State Bank, Kansas City, Mo, 62-; sr. v.pres, Logistics Research Inc, 68-; sr. v.pres, Aviation Research Inc, 69- Mil. Serv: Entered as Fireman 3/C, Navy, 17, released as Ens, 19, after serv. in Pay Corps, First Naval Dist. Mem: Pres, Nat. Coun. Presbyterian Men, 50-52 and United Church Men Am, Dept. of Nat. Coun. Churches, 50-54; gen. bd, Nat. Coun. Churches; former v.pres, Mo. Coun. Churches; exec. cmt, Kansas City Coun. Churches; former mem, Bd. For. Missions, Presbyterian Church U.S.A; Laymen's Cmt, Rel. in Am. Life; chmn. for Kansas City, Am. Bible Soc, 43-50; hon. v.pres, Am. Sunday Sch. Union; Nat. Capital Bible Observance Sponsoring Cmt; bd. mem, Nat. Coun. Commun. Chests Am; bd. dirs, United Funds Kansas City and Helping Hand Inst; Kansas City Cmn. on Charitable Solicitation; former mem. bd. dirs, Kansas City and Mo. Tuberc. Socs; Neighborhood Cmnr, Boy Scouts; Nat. Coun, United Negro Col. Fund, Inc; founding mem. and bd. dirs, Kansas City Conf. Christians and Jews; former mem. nat. bd, Nat. Conf. Christians and Jews; bd. trustees, Baptist Mem. Hosp, Kansas City, Kansas City Conservatory Music and Mo. Bible Col; pres, bd. trustees, Mo. Valley Col. and State Univ. Iowa Found; bd. dirs, Starlight Theater, Am. Humanics Found, Urban League Kansas City and Assoc. Industs. Mo; bd. gov, Am. Royal; Nat. Asn. Mfrs; Mason; K. of P; pres, Kansas City and W.Cent. Area YMCA, 46-50, bd. dirs, Estes Park Conf, former mem, Nat. Bd, former v.pres, Nat. Coun. and mem, Int. Cmt. and Adv. Cmt, World Alliance; Kansas City and U.S. C. of C; bd. dirs, Mo. State C. of C; Indust. Promotion Cmt. and Adv. to State Dept, Nat. Confectioners Asn. Nat. Red Feather Award, Commun. Chests Am, 51; Silver Beaver Award, Boy Scouts. Rel: Presbyterian, Elder. Legal Res: 803 W. 54th Terrace, Kansas City, Mo. 64112. Mailing Add: 700 Waltower Bldg, Kansas City, Mo. 64106.

JONES, LEONA BROMWELL R
Speaker, Mass. State Rep. Cmt.
b. Boston, Mass, 7/4/18; d. Charles L. Bromwell and Marcella Boland B; m. 8/25/43 to Harold F. Jones. Educ: Boston Univ. Bus. Col, spec. course; Simmons Sch. of Social Work; Portia Law Sch, LL.B, 46. Polit. & Govt. Pos: Asst. moderator, Hull, Mass, 59; del, Mass. State Rep. Conv, 64; alternate del, Rep. Nat. Conv, 64; legis. chmn. and past pres, Women's Rep. Club, Norwell and South Shore, Mass; legis. chmn, Mass. Fedn. Women's Clubs; speaker, Mass. State Rep. Cmt, currently; former mem, Hull Rep. Town Cmt, Mass. Bus. & Prof. Pos: Practicing attorney, Mass, over 20 years; spec. title exam, Mass. Land Court, currently; teacher, Every Day Law, Mass. Dept. of Adult Educ. Mem: Past pres, Mass. Asn. of Women Lawyers; Prfnl. Women of Mass; Plymouth Co. Bar Asn; past pres, Hull Woman's Club; Past Pres. Club; bd. mem. and past chmn, Red Cross; dir, Girl Scouts; Sch. Study Cmt. Achievements: Instructing Red Cross classes; conducting and directing church jr. choir on tours and TV and making robes for them. Rel: Pope Mem. Church. Mailing Add: 62 Salisbury St, Hull, Mass. 02045. (1967)

JONES, LEWIS D
b. Urbanna, Va, 7/23/28; s. Lewis Jones and Lillian Farinholt J; m. 12/30/53 to Laura Walker; c. Laura Lillian, Lewis, III, Stephen Farinholt, and Robert Healy. Educ: Va. Military Inst, 45-48; Univ. of Va, B.S. in commerce, 50; L.L.B, 55; Phi Alpha Delta; Phi Kappa Sigma; Eli Banana. Polit. & Govt. Pos: Mem, Va. Constitutional Conv, 56; commonwealth's attorney, Middlesex Co, Va, 58-; mem, Va. Cmn. Fisheries, 60-68; mem, Potomac River Fisheries Cmn, 62-68, chmn, 2 years; del, Dem. Nat. Conv, 68; chmn. bd. admin, Va. Inst. Marine Sci, 68- Mil. Serv: Entered as Pvt, Army, 50, released as Sgt 1/C, 52, after serv. in Eighth Inf, Fourth Div, ETO, 50-52. Va. State Bar; 13th Judicial Circuit Bar Asn.(chmn, 60); Commonwealth Attorney Asn; Va. Trial Lawyers Asn; Ruritan Club; Am. Legion; Lions; PTA; Local Fire Dept. Rel: Episcopal. Mailing Add: Urbanna, Va. 23175.

JONES, LLOYD RAYMOND D
b. Stanley, N.Dak, 5/24/17; s. Tilmon Jones and Mary Elizabeth Marlet J; m. 1/13/50 to Caroline Louise Smart; c. Carol Ann and Tilman L. Polit. & Govt. Pos: Precinct committeeman, McGahan Twp, N.Dak, 54-; chmn, Mountrail Co. Non-Partisan League, 56-68; v.chmn, Mountrail Co. Dem. Party, 58-60, chmn, 60-66; cmnr, N.Dak. State Wheat Cmn, 63-; chmn, Mountrail Co. Commun. Action Cmt. and v.chmn, 5 Co. Commun. Action Cmts, N.Dak, 65-66; v.chmn, Fourth Legis. Dist. Dem. Party, 66-68. Mil. Serv: Entered as Pvt, Army, 42, released as Cpl, 45, after serv. in 254 Sig. Construction, Asiatic-Pac; Good Conduct Medal; Marksman Medal; Asiatic-Pac. Ribbon; Guam Medal with Battle Star. Mem: Am. Legion; PTA; chmn, Palermo Farmers Union Local, 51-63 & 65-66; chmn, Mountrail Co. Farmers Union, 54-63;

mem. bd. gov, N.Dak. Farmers Union, 54-63, state dir, 61; chmn, Mountrail Co. Human Rels. Cmt. of Rural Area Develop, 62-63. Rel: Lutheran; Chmn, Parish Coun. Mailing Add: Palermo, N.Dak. 58769. (1967)

JONES, MARJORIE CORNELIA R
V.Chairwoman, Minn. State Rep. Cent. Cmt.
b. Osseo, Wis, 6/29/09; d. Rev. John C. Hjelmervik and Olga Marie Sando H; m. 6/2/39 to Frank O. Jones. Educ: St. Olaf Col, B.A, 30; Univ. Minn, M.A, 36; Iota Chi Sigma; Phi Kappa Phi. Polit. & Govt. Pos: Mem, Gov. Citizens Ment. Health Cmt, Minn, 47-51, mem, State Adv, Cmt. on Libr. Serv, 48-51, mem, Gov. Adv. Coun. on Youth, 48-54, mem. exec. cmt, Minn. Ment. Health Coun, 51-54 and mem, Minn. Coun. on Human Rights, 55-; state chairwoman, Minn. Gubernatorial Campaign, 50, U.S. Senate Campaign, 60; co. VIP chmn, 60-61; co. chairwoman, 61-65; dep. v.chmn, Minn. Rep. Finance Cmt. and state chmn, Rep. Neighbor-to-Neighbor Fund Drive, 61-; v.chairwoman, Minn. State Rep. Cent. Cmt, 61-; del, Rep. Nat. Conv, 64. Bus. & Prof. Pos: High sch. instr. Eng. and hist, Grass Range, Mont, 30-32, Eng. and speech, Alberton, 34, Eng. and journalism, Malta, 34-35 and Eng. and speech, Hardin, 35-36; head speech dept, Sr. High Sch, Fairmont, Minn, 36-39; interviewer, Daniel Starch & Staff, Mkt. Research, 48-; secy. and treas, Frank O. Jones & Assocs, Consult. Engrs, 51-65. Mem: Am. Asn. of Univ. Women (v.pres, Minn. Div, 46-48, pres, 48-50). Rel: Lutheran. Mailing Add: 1375 Oak Beach Dr, Fairmont, Minn. 56031. (1967)

JONES, MARK PERRIN, III D
Mem, Ark. State Dem. Cmt.
b. Searcy, Ark, 1/19/32; s. Mark Perrin Jones, Jr. and Jamie Baugh J; m. 6/27/53 to Tommie Jean Cautrell, div; c. Mark Perrin, IV. Educ: Univ. Ark, B.S. in Journalism, 53, M.A. in Govt, 64; Omicron Delta Kappa; Alpha Phi Omega; Sigma Chi; Lambda Tau; ed, Traveler and Razorback; chmn, Bd. of Student Publ. Polit. & Govt. Pos: Chmn, Searcy Civil Serv. Cmn, Ark, 58-; mem, Ark. State Bd. Educ, 59-; secy, White Co. Dem. Cmt, Ark, 59-; mem, Ark. State Dem. Cmt, 68-; v.pres, Ark. Constitutional Conv, 69. Bus. & Prof. Pos: Publisher, Searcy Daily Citizen and White County Citizen, 59- Mem: Sigma Delta Chi (v.pres, 65); dir, secy. and treas, Nat. Asn. of State Bd. Educ, 68-; C. of C.(pres, Searcy Chap, 60); Rotary (pres, Searcy Club, 60); Mason (32°); Consistory; Shrine. Americanism Editorial Award, Continental Oil Co, 59; Ark. Young Man of the Year, Jr. C. of C, 65. Rel: Presbyterian; v.pres, Men of the Church of East Arkansas Presbytery, 65. Legal Res: 709 W. Academy Ave, Searcy, Ark. 72143. Mailing Add: 209 W. Arch Ave, Searcy, Ark. 72143.

JONES, MARSHALL P.
U.S. Ambassador to Malawi
b. Columbus, Ind, 4/7/15; m. to Virginia Spitler; c. three sons. Educ: Univ. of Colo; DePauw Univ, B.A, 37; Harvard Bus. Sch. Polit. & Govt. Pos: With Vet. Admin, 46-50; orgn. and methods examiner, Dept. of State, 51-55; career officer, U.S. Dept. of State For. Serv, 55-; first secy, Tel Aviv, 54-56, Belgrade, 56-58; dep. dir. and dir, Off. of Budget, 58-61, spec. asst. to Asst. Secy. for Admin, 61; counsr, Korea, 61-63; exec. dir, Bur. Far East. Affairs, 63-65; U.S. Ambassador to Malawi, 65- Bus. & Prof. Pos: Salesman wholesale foods co, 37-38; sales supvr, rubber co, 39-42. Mil. Serv: Maj, Army, 42-46. Legal Res: Bethesda, Md. 20016. Mailing Add: U.S. Embassy, Blantyre, Malawi.

JONES, MARSHALL WILLIAM, JR. R
Treas, Rep. State Cent. Cmt, Md.
b. Columbia, S.C, 2/3/32; s. Marshall William Jones and Viola Brown J; m. 3/20/54 to Gloria Delores Adams; c. Iris Romaine and Sharon Anita. Educ: Temple Univ. Community Col, Assoc. in Tech, 52; Eckels Col. Mortuary Sci. Polit. & Govt. Pos: Mem, Ninth Ward Civic Orgn, Md; mem, Baltimore Commun. Rels Cmn, 63-64; mem, Bur. Recreation & Parks, Baltimore, 64-65; mem, Bd. of Supvrs. of Elec, Baltimore, 65-67, secy, 69-; treas, Model Cities Commun. Coun-Area B, East. Terrace Commun. Coun, Inc, 69-; treas, Rep. State Cent. Cmt, currently. Bus. & Prof. Pos: Owner, Marshall W. Jones, Jr. Funeral Home, 61- Mil. Serv: Entered as Pvt, Air Force, 52, released as S/Sgt, 56; Nat. Defense, UN and Korean Serv. Medals; Good Conduct Medal. Mem: Nat. Funeral Dirs. & Morticians Asn.(dist. gov, dist. 2 and mem. bd. dirs); v.pres. exec. bd, Eastside Commun. Cmt; Baltimore Urban League & Urban Guild; Citizens Planning & Housing Asn; Am. Legion; F&AM; Odd Fellows. Rel: Baptist. Mailing Add: 1735 Harford Ave, Baltimore, Md. 21213.

JONES, MARVIN D
b. (near) Valley View, Cooke Co, Tex; s. H.K. Jones and Dosia J. Educ: Southwest. Univ, A.B, 05; Univ. of Tex, LL.B, 07; Tex. A.&M. Col, LL.D. Polit. & Govt. Pos: Sr. Judge, U.S. Court of Claims, 64-; app. Chief Justice, U.S. Court of Claims, July 47-64; War Mobilization Com, U.S. Food Admin, 43-45; Pres, 44 Nation Int. Conf. on Food & Agr, 43; asst. to Hon. James F. Byrnes, 43; app. Judge U.S. Court of Claims, 4/9/40, confirmed by U.S. Sen, 4/10/40, assumed duties 11/20/40, following resignation from U.S. House Rep, leave of absence, 43-45; Chmn, House Cmt. on Agr, Dec. 1931-11/20/40; U.S. Rep, Tex, 17-41; app. Chmn, Bd. Legal Examiners, 7th Supreme Jud. Dist. of Tex, 13; admitted to Tex. Bar, 07. Mem: Am. Legion; Order of Coif (Hon.); Mason; Woodman; Elk. Misc: Publications: How War Food Saved American Lives; Should Uncle Sam Pay--When and Why?. Rel: Methodist. Mailing Add: 2807 Hughes St, Amarillo, Tex. 79109. (1967)

JONES, MARY GARDINER R
Cmnr, Fed. Trade Cmn.
b. New York, N.Y, 12/10/20; d. Charles Herbert Jones and Anna Livingston Short; single. Educ: Wellesley Col, B.A, 43; Yale Univ, LL.B, 48; Order of the Coif. Polit. & Govt. Pos: Research analyst, Off. of Strategic Serv, 44-46; trial attorney, Dept. of Justice, 53-61; cmnr, Fed. Trade Cmn, 64- Bus. & Prof. Pos: Attorney and spec. asst. to Gen. William J. Donovan, Donovan, Leisure, Newton & Irvine, 48-53; attorney, Webster Sheffield, Fleischmann, Hitchcock & Chrystie, 61-64. Publ: 'Program for a Democratic Counter-Attack to Communist Penetration of Government Service,' with William J. Donovan, Yale Law J, 49; 'National Minorities: A Case Study in International Protection,' Law and Contemporary Probs, 49; 'Marketing Strategy and Government Regulation in Dual Distribution Practices,' The George Wash. Law Rev, 66. Mem: Panel mem, Am. Arbit. Asn. Rel: Episcopal. Legal Res: 1 E. 66th St, New York, N.Y. 10021. Mailing Add: 3037 West Lane Keys. N.W, Washington, D.C. 20007.

JONES, MILTON D
Ga. State Rep.
b. Columbus, Ga, 8/13/36; s. Robert Vance Jones and Thea Gamble J; m. 7/3/55 to Jeanette Beaird; c. Janice, Eleanor, Carolyn and Michael. Educ: Emory at Oxford, Emory Univ. and Law Sch; Phi Alpha Delta; Alpha Tau Omega. Polit. & Govt. Pos: Ga. State Rep, Muscogee Co, Dist. 112, Post 2, 63- Bus. & Prof. Pos: Lawyer, self-employed, 59-61; partner, Grogan & Jones, Attorneys, 61- Mil. Serv: Army Res, 54-62. Mem: Ga. Bar Asn; Columbus Lawyers Club; Scottish Rite; Mason; Kiwanis; Jaycees. Rel: Baptist. Mailing Add: 3438 Sue Mack Dr, Columbus, Ga. 31906.

JONES, MORTON EDWARD R
Mem, State Rep. Exec. Cmt, Tex.
b. Alhambra, Calif, 4/12/28; s. Edward Palmer Jones and Bonnibel Sanford J; m. 3/18/51 to Patricia L. Walker; c. Shelley, Steven, Kent and Jay. Educ: Univ. Calif, Berkeley, B.S, 49; Calif. Inst. Tech, Ph.D, 53; Sigma Xi; Kappa Alpha. Polit. & Govt. Pos: Alternate del, Rep. Nat. Conv, 68; mem, state Rep. Exec. Cmt, Tex, 68- Bus. & Prof. Pos: Mem, tech. staff, Tex. Instruments Inc, 53-61, sr. scientist, 61-65, lab. dir, 65- Publ: 'The Structure of Pentaborane,' Proc. Nat. Acad. Sci. U.S, 52; 'Transistors Intermetaliques,' L'Onde Eletrique. t. 61; 'The Growth of Crystals from Compounds with Volatile Components,' J. Electrochemical Soc, 63. Mem: Sr. mem, Inst. Elec. and Electronics Engrs; Tex. Acad. Sci; Electrochemical Soc; Park and Recreation Cmn, Richardson; Richardson and Dallas Co. Rep. Men's Clubs. Rel: Episcopal. Mailing Add: 619 Northill, Richardson, Tex. 75080.

JONES, NAPOLEON D
V.Chmn, San Joaquin Co. Dem. Cent. Cmt, Calif.
b. Holden, W.Va, 5/28/35; s. Samuel Jones and Lou Alma Phelps J.(deceased); adopted by Odessa Crook (Mrs. Follins); m. 6/28/57 to Comalene Evangeline Holman; c. Rosalind Georgette, Christopher Allen and Lorraine Monique. Educ: Stockton Jr. Col, A.A, 57; Univ. of the Pac, B.A, 61; Humphrey's Col. Sch. of Law, 65. Polit. & Govt. Pos: Mem, Calif. State Dem. Cent. Cmt, 68-; secy-treas, Coun. Dem. Clubs, 30th Assembly Dist, 68-; v.chmn, San Joaquin Co. Dem. Cent. Cmt, 68-; v.chmn, Stockton Redevelopment Agency, 67- Bus. & Prof. Pos: Acting chmn. Eng. dept, Franklin Sr. High Sch, 64, reading coordinator, 67 & 68; mem, bd. dirs, Delta Col. Eve. Div, 66. Mil. Serv: Entered as Pvt, Army, 52, released as Cpl, 55, after serv. in 160th and 15th Inf. Regt, 40th and Third Div, Korea, 53-54; UN Serv. Medal; Nat. Defense Serv. Medal; Korean Serv. Medal with 1 Battle Star. Mem: Stockton Teachers Asn. (membership chmn, 65); Calif. and Nat. Teachers Asns; Franklin Sr. High Teachers Asn.(pres, 65-66). Rel: Protestant. Mailing Add: 1854 Nightingale Ave, Stockton, Calif. 95206.

JONES, ORTON ALAN R
W.Va. State Del.
b. Spencer, W.Va, 1/24/38; s. French Smith Jones and Myrtle Ashley J; m. 8/20/61 to Mary Jo Chisler; c. Rebecca Sue. Educ: Glenville State Col, 56-58; W.Va. Univ, LL.B, 61; Alpha Psi Omega; Phi Delta Phi; Kappa Sigma Kappa. Polit. & Govt. Pos: Prosecuting attorney, Roane Co, W.Va, 65-68; W.Va. State Del, 68- Bus. & Prof. Pos: Partner, Hedges and Jones, Law Firm, Spencer, W.Va, 61- Mil. Serv: Entered as 1st Lt, Air Force, 61, released as Capt, 64, after serv. in Off. of the Staff Judge Adv, Keesler Tech. Training Center, Air Training Command, 61-64; Capt, Air Force Res. Publ: 'Immortality Enough,' (with Dr. C. Trent Busch), South. Speech J, spring 68. Mem: Am, Fed. and W.Va. Bar Asns; Am. Trial Lawyers Asn; W.Va. State Bar; Am. Acad. Soc. & Polit. Sci; Rotary (past pres, Spencer Club); Jaycees; C. of C; Am. Legion; past chmn, Roane Co. Heart Asn; Am. Numismatic Asn. Rel: Protestant. Legal Res: Ridgemont Rd, Spencer, W.Va. 25276. Mailing Add: P.O. Box 16, Spencer, W.Va. 25276.

JONES, PAUL C. D
b. Kennett, Mo, 3/12/01; m. 8/2/23 to Ethel Rockholt; c. Betty Anne (Mrs. Joe D. Cash), Paul C, Jr. and Nell (Mrs. Tom B. Mobley). Educ: Univ. Mo, B.J, 23. Polit. & Govt. Pos: Mem. City Coun. and Mayor, Kennett, Mo; pres. and mem, Kennett Bd. of Educ; Mo. State Rep, 35-37; Mo. State Sen, 37-44; chmn, State Hwy. Cmn, 45-48; U.S. Rep, Mo, 48-68. Bus. & Prof. Pos: Co-publisher, Dunklin Dem, 28-53; gen. mgr, Radio Sta. KBOA, 47-66. Mil. Serv: Dir. of orgn. of Sixth Mo. Inf, Mo. State Guard, Commanding Officer, Vol. Regt, 40-46. Mem: Miss. Valley Flood Control Asn.(pres, 58-60); Lions Int.(past dist. gov); Mason. Mo. Squire, 67. Rel: Christian Church of N.Am; mem. off. bd, 20 years; supt. of Sunday sch. Legal Res: 444 W. Washington Ave, Kennett, Mo. 63857. Mailing Add: P.O. Box 527, Kennett, Mo. 63857.

JONES, PAUL F. R
b. Rochelle, Ill, 8/26/12; m. to Ruth Gustavson; c. Pauline (Mrs. Fred Nehrer, Jr), Peter Alan. Educ: Iowa State Univ. (Ind. Science). Polit. & Govt. Pos:Ill. State Rep, 62-64; Chmn, Ogle Cty Rep. Cent. Comm, 4 years; Republican Precinct Chmn, 20 years; Bd. of Educ, Rochelle Twp. High Sch; Mayor of Rochelle, 59-63. Bus. & Prof. Pos:Real estate bus, 46-; farming. Mem: C. of C; Rotary. Rel: Presbyterian, First United Presbyterian Church, Rochelle. Mailing Add: 502 N. 11th St, Rochelle, Ill. 61068. (1967)

JONES, PHA L. R
Secy, Seneca Co. Rep. Cent. and Exec. Cmt, Ohio
b. New Castle, Ind, 10/1/01; s. Charles H. Jones and Anna Huffman J; m. 7/13/27 to Mabel Wagner; c. Barbara Ann (Mrs. R.G. Ingerham). Educ: Earlham Col, B.A, 24. Polit. & Govt. Pos: Precinct committeeman, Seneca Co. Rep. Cent. Cmt, Ohio, 50-, secy, 64-; mem, Seneca Co. Rep. Exec. Cmt, and adv. cmt, Eighth Cong. Dist, 64-; alternate del, Rep. Nat. Conv, 64; mem, Seneca Co. Bd. of Elec, 64- Bus. & Prof. Pos: Mgr, Kresge Store, 28-41; prod. mgr, Fostoria Corp, 42- Mem: Mason; Shrine; Kiwanis. Rel: Methodist. Mailing Add: 1398 N. Union St, Fostoria, Ohio 44830.

JONES, PLEAS E. R
Chmn, Fifth Cong. Dist. Rep. Party, Ky.
b. Williamsburg, Ky, 12/23/12; s. Nathaniel B. Jones and Rachel Lundy J;

m. 4/11/42 to Nancy Marie White; c. Pleas D. and Gorman Stanley. Educ: Cumberland Col, A.B, 34; Univ. Ky. Col. Law, LL.B, 52; Nat. Col. of State Trial Judges; Phi Delta Phi. Polit. & Govt. Pos: Circuit court clerk, Whitley Co, Ky, 40-51, judge, 54-57; commonwealth attorney, Whitley and McCreary Co, 59-63; circuit judge, Whitley and McCreary, 34th Judicial Dist, 64-; chmn, Fifth Cong. Dist. Rep. Party, 64- Bus. & Prof. Pos: Teacher, Whitley Co, 32-36; teacher, Williamsburg Independent Sch. Dist, 36-39. Mil. Serv: Entered as Pvt, Army, 42, released as Pfc, 45, after serv. in 113th Inf, East. Defense Command, 42-45. Mem: Lions (pres); Am. Legion (Comdr); Mason; Shrine; Univ. Ky. Law Alumni (pres). Rel: Protestant. Mailing Add: Box 157, Williamsburg, Ky. 40769.

JONES, RALPH LEE D
b. Frisco City, Ala, 7/26/99; s. James Wiley Jones and Mary Frances Hughes J; m. 2/22/24 to Lula Hixon; c. Nan (Mrs. McMurphy) and Sue (Mrs. Philipp). Educ: Univ. Ala, A.B, 18, LL.B, 19; Phi Beta Kappa; Pi Kappa Phi. Polit. & Govt. Pos: Co. solicitor, Ala, 24-35; state circuit solicitor, 35-46; Ala. State Sen, 54-59; Ala. State Rep, 59-65; Ala. state dist. attorney, 65-; alternate del, Dem. Nat. Conv, 68. Bus. & Prof. Pos: Lawyer, Barnett, Bugg, Lee & Jones, C.L. Hybart & R.L. Jones and B.E. Jones & R.L. Jones, Monroeville, Ala, 21- Mil. Serv: Army, Field Artil. Officers Training Sch, Camp Zachary Taylor, Louisville, Ky. Rel: Baptist. Mailing Add: Box 7, Monroeville, Ala. 36460. (1967)

JONES, RAY CHARLES D
Chmn, Okla. Corp. Cmn.
b. Yale, Okla, 4/11/99; s. Harry Jones and Anna Laura Abercrombie; m. 7/22/22 to Sarah Louise Beeler; c. Georgianna (Mrs. Moore), Dr. Harry B, Sally Lou (Mrs. Rawls) and Patricia Ann (Mrs. Zahler). Educ: Okla. State Univ, 3 1/2 years; Sigma Chi. Polit. & Govt. Pos: Okla. State Sen, 34-46; mem, Okla. Corp. Cmn, 46- and chmn, 47- Mil. Serv: Entered as Pvt, Army, 18, released 18, after serving in Off. Training Sch, Camp McArthur, Tex. Mem: Mason; Am. Legion; Lions. Rel: Christian Church. Mailing Add: 2708 N.W. 60th, Oklahoma City, Okla. 73112.

JONES, REX KENTON D
Miss. State Rep.
b. Hattiesburg, Miss, 11/16/33; s. Roy B. Jones and Ruth P. J; single. Educ: Univ. South. Miss, B.S, 54; Univ. Miss, LL.B, 59; Phi Alpha Delta. Polit. & Govt. Pos: City prosecuting attorney, Hattiesburg, Miss, 63. Miss. State Rep, Forest Co, 64- Bus. & Prof. Pos: Claims adjuster, USF&G Ins. Co, 61-63; attorney-at-law, self-employed, 63- Mil. Serv: Entered as Pvt, Army, 54, released as SP-3, 56, after serv. in Signal Sch, Ansbach, Germany; Good Conduct Medal. Mem: Metropolitan Club; Jaycees; bd. dirs, Am. Red Cross. Rel: Methodist. Mailing Add: 211 Chevy Chase Dr, Hattiesburg, Miss. 39401.

JONES, RICHARD R. 'DICK' R
Wyo. State Sen.
b. Huntley, Mont, 9/5/10; m. to Estes; c. 3. Educ: Worden High Sch, Mont. Polit. & Govt. Pos: Town councilman, Powell, Wyo, 4 years, mayor, 4 years; Wyo. State Rep, 2 years; Wyo. State Sen, currently. Bus. & Prof. Pos: Trucker. Rel: Methodist. Mailing Add: Box 773, Powell, Wyo. 82435. (1967)

JONES, ROBERT ALDEN D
N.C. State Rep.
b. Forest City, N.C, 6/8/31; s. Basil Thomas Jones, Jr. and Rosagray Chesson J; m. 4/3/54 to Nancy Hardwick; c. Pamela, Robert A, Jr. and John H. Educ: Wake Forest Col, 48-50; Wake Forest Univ, B.A, 59, Law Sch, LL.B. cum laude, 60; Alpha Sigma Phi; Phi Alpha Delta. Polit. & Govt. Pos: Research asst. to Justice Higgins, N.C. Supreme Court, 60-61; Rutherford Co. Civil Defense Dir, N.C, 67-; N.C. State Rep, 68- Mil. Serv: Entered as Pvt, Air Force, 50, released as 1st Lt, 56, after serv. in Newfoundland, 51-53 and France, 54-56, Maj, Res; usual theater awards. Mem: Rutherford Co. Bar Asn.(pres, 66-68); 29th Judicial Dist. Bar Asn.(pres, 67); N.C. State Bar; N.C. Bar Asn; VFW; Farm Bur; life mem, Forest City Jaycees (pres, 65); N.C. Jaycees (v.pres, 67); Forest City PTA (pres, 66-68); N.C. PTA (parliamentarian, 68-). Distinguished Award, Forest City Jaycees, 67. Rel: Baptist, Sunday Sch. Teacher and Jr. Deacon, First Baptist Church. Mailing Add: 122 Woodland Ave, Forest City, N.C. 28043.

JONES, ROBERT EMMET, II D
U.S. Rep, Ala.
b. Scottsboro, Ala, 6/12/12; s. Robert Emmet Jones, Sr. and Augusta Smith J; m. 4/9/38 to Christine Frances; c. Robert E, III. Educ: Univ. Ala, LL.B, 35; Kappa Alpha. Polit. & Govt. Pos: Judge, Jackson Co, Ala, 41-43 and 46; U.S. Rep, Ala, 47- Mil. Serv: Entered as Ens, Navy, 43, released as Lt, 46. Rel: Methodist. Legal Res: Old Larkinsville Rd, Scottsboro, Ala. 35768. Mailing Add: 2426 Rayburn House Office Bldg, Washington, D.C. 20515.

JONES, ROBERT G. D
La. State Rep.
b. Lake Charles, La, 5/9/39; s. Sam H. Jones and Louise Gambrell J; m. 9/8/61 to Sarah Quinn; c. Sam Houston, II, Anna Gambrelle and Genin Quinn. Educ: La. State Univ, 56-57; Tulane Univ, B.S. in Eng, 60; Harvard Bus. Sch, M.B.A, 62; Tau Beta Pi; Omicron Delta Kappa; Phi Eta Sigma; Sigma Alpha Epsilon. Polit. & Govt. Pos: La. State Rep, 18th Dist, 68- Bus. & Prof. Pos: Stock broker, Kohlmeyer & Co, 62-65, asst. mgr, Lake Charles Off, 65-69, mgr, 69- Mem: Young Men's Bus. Club (past pres, 65). Rel: Methodist. Mailing Add: 301 Shell Beach Dr, Lake Charles, La. 70601.

JONES, ROBERT W. D
Chmn, Shelby Co. Dem. Party, Ind.
Polit. & Govt. Pos: Dem. precinct committeeman, Ind, 48-64; mem, Morristown Town Bd, 51-63; former Ind. State Sen; chmn, Shelby Co. Dem. Party, Ind, currently. Bus. & Prof. Pos: Owner, fertilizer sales and manufacturing corp. Mem: Adv. bd, Madison State Hosp, 60-64; Lions; Elks; Hist. Soc; Conserv. Club; Farmers Union; Methodist Men; Ind. Univ. Alumni (life mem); Shelby Co. Dem. Club; Am. Automobile Asn; C. of C. Rel: Quaker. Mailing Add: Morristown, Ind. 46161. (1967)

JONES, ROY J. D
b. Longview, Tex, 11/15/25; s. Sam Jones, Jr. and Evangeline Fury J; m. 9/16/46 to Pauline Carol Finley; c. Roderick, Arliss and Valerie. Educ: Morgan State Col, B.S, 51; Howard Univ, M.S, 54; The Am. Univ, Ph.D, 61; Psi Chi. Polit. & Govt. Pos: Del, Nat. Dem. Conv, 68. Bus. & Prof. Pos: Dir. of training, Wash. Action for Youth, Wash, D.C, 64; asst. clin. prof. psychiat. and dir. research, inst. youth studies, Howard Univ, 64-67, asst. dean grad. sch. and dir, center for commun. studies, 67- Mil. Serv: Entered as Pvt, Army, 44, released as Sgt. Maj, 46, after serv. in Signal Corp, ETO and Pac. Theatre, 44-46; Bronze Star. Publ: 'Intellectual and Psychomotor Performance of Preschool Children from Low Income Families' (with David Terrell and James I. DeSheilds), Psychol. in Schs, 7/67; 'Home Environment and Child-Rearing Practices of Low-Income Mothers,' J. Marriage and the Family, (in press); 'Perception of the Opportunity System and Value Orientation of High and Low Risk Youth from Low-Income Families,' (in prep). Mem: Bd. dirs, Dag Hammarskjold Col; Dem. Cent. Cmt, Wash. D.C; bd. dirs, Wesley Found; Alpha Kappa Mu. Mailing Add: 1342 Kalmia Rd. N.W, Washington, D.C. 20012.

JONES, RUTH THOMPSON D
b. Hurricane, W.Va, 7/26/14; d. William Earl Thompson and Rose Queck T; m. 10/25/47 to E. Forrest Jones; c. Ruth Ellen, E. Forrest, Frances Madeline and Florence Thompson. Educ: Marshall Univ, A.B, 36; Columbia Univ, M.A, 46; Kappa Delta Pi. Polit. & Govt. Pos: Alternate del, Dem. Nat. Conv, 68. Bus. & Prof. Pos: Teacher, Hurricane, 32-34; mem. staff, Workmens Compensation Off, Charleston, 35-38; admin. secy, W.Va. State Tax Cmn, 38-39; sr. interviewer and personnel rep, West. Elec, 42-44; mem. staff personnel rels, Am. Tel. and Tel, 44-47. Mil. Serv: Red Cross Nurses Aide Vol, World War II. Publ: 'The Art of Interviewing,' Nat. Asn. Deans of Women Periodical, 45. Mem: Am. Asn. Women (bd. dirs); Am. Cancer Soc. (bd. dirs, Kanawha Co. Unit); bd. dirs, W.Va. Creative Arts Festival; W.Va. Flower Show Judges Coun; Japan Int. Christian Univ. Found.(women's cmt); nat. accredited flower show judge; Goodwill Industs.(past mem. bd. dirs); Kanawha Welfare Coun; United Fund (leader, past chmn, Women's Div); Marshall Univ. Alumni (area v.pres, past pres. Kanawha Co. Chap); W.Va. Hist. Soc; Am. Mothers' Cmt.(state chmn); past state chmn. and mem. adv. bd, W.Va. Centennial; Columbia Univ. Club of W.Va.(pres); Eastern Star (past matron); W.Va. Garden Clubs (past mem. state bd, past Blue Star Mem. chmn); Belmont Garden Club (past pres); DAR (past Regent); Morris Harvey Women Builders; Charleston Gen. Hosp. Auxiliary; women's cmt, Charleston Symphony Orchestra; Charleston Rose Soc; United Church Women of Charleston (pres, past mem. bd. Christian educ. and leadership training). One of W.Va. Outstanding Women and Spec. Award, Charleston-Gazette-Mail Newspaper Agency. Rel: Baptist; Past deaconess; active in student counselling and guidance. Mailing Add: 1502 Louden Heights Rd, Charleston, W.Va. 25314.

JONES, SEBY BROWN D
Mayor, Raleigh, N.C.
b. Franklin Co, N.C, 8/14/16; s. Lonnie Jones and Leta Stallings J; m. 5/5/35 to Christina Brown; c. Robert Lonnie, Alice (Mrs. Harrod), James Russell and Seby Brown, Jr. Educ: Franklin Co. Pub. Schs. Polit. & Govt. Pos: City councilman, Raleigh, N.C, 67-69, mayor, 69- Bus. & Prof. Pos: Partner, Davidson & Jones, Raleigh, N.C, 41-61, pres, 61-; partner, Carolina Venture Co, 54-; pres, Gateway Plaza, Inc, 61-, Boulevard Investment Co, 63- and Heart of Durham Motel, Inc, 66- Mem: Mason; Lions; C. of C.(mem, Raleigh Bd); Travel Coun. of N.C; trustee, Meredith Col. and Toccoa Falls Inst. Rel: Baptist. Mailing Add: 3936 Blue Ridge Rd, Raleigh, N.C. 27605.

JONES, STANLEY OSCAR R
Chmn, Elmore Co. Rep. Financial Cmt, Idaho
b. Corral, Idaho, 3/17/24; s. Thomas Harvey Jones and Daisy Thompson J; m. 8/14/46 to Maxine Miller; c. Kathy, Connie, Mike and Nathan. Educ: Camas Co. High Sch; Col. Idaho. Polit. & Govt. Pos: Precinct committeeman, Rep. Party, Idaho, 60-62; chmn, Elmore Co. Rep. Cent. Cmt, 62-66; alternate del, Rep. Nat. Conv, 64; chmn, Elmore Co. Rep. Financial Cmt, 66- Bus. & Prof. Pos: Mem. adv. bd, West. Idaho Prod. Credit Asn, 64-65. Mem: Lions; Grange. Rel: Episcopal. Mailing Add: Box 40, Glenns Ferry, Idaho 83623. (1967)

JONES, STEPHEN R
b. Lafeyette, La, 7/1/40; s. Leslie W. Jones and Gladys William J; m. 12/2/61 to Virginia Elizabeth Hadden; c. John Chapman. Educ: Univ. Houston, 60-61; Univ. Tex, Austin, 61-63; Univ. Okla, LL.B, 66; Phi Alpha Delta. Polit. & Govt. Pos: Dir. research, Rep. Party of Tex, 62; secy, minority conf, Tex. Legis, 63; asst. to Hon. Richard M. Nixon, 64; admin. asst. to Cong. Paul Findley, 66 & 68-69; legal asst. to Gov. Bartlett, Okla, 67. Bus. & Prof. Pos: Attorney, Otjen and Carter, 66- Publ: 'P.C. Simons, Attorney General,' 65 and 'Govenor Frank Frantz,' 65, Chronicles of Okla; 'Gaullism in the East,' Ripon Forum, 68. Mem: Okla. and Garfield Co. Bar Asns; Am. Bar Asn.(sect. on criminal, int, corporate and pub. utility law); Am. Judicature Soc; Oakwood Country Club. Rel: Episcopal. Legal Res: 1315 Vinita, Enid, Okla. 73701. Mailing Add: Otjen and Carter, Bass Bldg, Enid, Okla. 73701.

JONES, STEPHEN WHITCOMB R
Chmn, Brookings Co. Rep. Cent. Cmt, S.Dak.
b. Spencer, S.Dak, 3/1/05; s. Clarence Augustus Jones and Mertie Catherine Whitcomb J; m. 1/1/29 to Ruby La Vone Finnie; c. Lee Stephen and Allan Rudy. Educ: S.Dak. State Univ, B.S; Iowa State Univ, M.S; Alpha Zeta; Pi Kappa Delta; Lambda Gamma Delta; Blue Key; Alpha Gamma Rho. Polit. & Govt. Pos: Co. Agr. Agent, Howard, S.Dak, 28-31; farm mgt. specialist and dir. agr. planning, State Agr. Exten. Serv, Brookings, 31-44; dir. pub. rels, Univ. S.Dak, 47-54; chmn, Brookings Co. Rep. Cent. Cmt, S.Dak, 68- Bus. & Prof. Pos: Secy and dir. research and agr, Gr. S.Dak. Asn, Huron, S.Dak, 44-47; account exec, Phillip Leslie Co, Chicago, Ill, 54; field serv. mgr, Land O'Lakes Creameries, Inc, Minneapolis, Minn, 54-69; retired. Mil. Serv: ROTC in col, 2 years. Publ: 'A Graphic Summary of Land Use, Physical and Economic Features of South Dakota, S.Dak. State Exten. Serv, 38; 'A Job For Every Hand,' Successful Farming Mag, 10/44; 'This Business of Soil and Moisture Conservation,' Gr. S.Dsn, 46. Mem: Epsilon Sigma Phi; Mason. Rel: Presbyterian. Mailing Add: 1227 Second St, Brookings, S.Dak. 57006.

JONES, TEDDY ALBERT R
b. Mt. Vernon, Ill, 5/24/03; s. Wm. Perry Jones and Minerva Clark J; m. 7/2/21 to Maggie Nichelson; c. Betty Ruth (Mrs. Storme). Polit. & Govt.

Pos: Rep. Co. Chmn, 64-65; Precinct Committeeman, 16 yrs. Bus. & Prof. Pos: Owner of Bus. Rel: Baptist. Mailing Add: 502 S. Aikman, Marion, Ill. 62959.

JONES, THELMA D. D
Committeewoman, Ohio Dem. State Cent. Cmt.
b. Newark, Ohio, 3/16/05; d. William H. Kislingbery and Emma M. Kinney K; m. Leland W. Jones (deceased); c. Wanda Keith. Educ: Alexandria High Sch, grad, 23. Polit. & Govt. Pos: Mem, Licking Co. Dem. Women's Club, Ohio, 36-; precinct committeewoman, Dem. Party, Licking Co, 52-; secy, Licking Co. Dem. Cent. and Exec. Cmt, 66-; mem, Ohio Dem. State Exec. Cmt, 66-; committeewoman, 17th Dist. Dem. Cent. Cmt, 66-; mem, Federated Women's Dem. Club Ohio, 66-; alternate del, Dem. Nat. Conv, 68. Mem: Am. Red Cross; YWCA; Women's Auxiliary, Am. Legion; Women's Circle Druids. 25 Year Pin for Vol. Serv, Am. Red Cross. Rel: Methodist. Mailing Add: 100 N. 21st St, Newark, Ohio 43055.

JONES, THEODORE A. D
b. Pueblo, Colo, 11/14/13; s. Adam Jones and Nellie Gant J; m. 6/17/39 to Beatrice Mae Howard; c. Janice (Mrs. Morris) and Lynn. Educ: Univ. Ill, B.S, 33; Northwest. Univ, 47-49; Beta Gamma Sigma. Polit. & Govt. Pos: Mem, Parole and Pardon Bd, State of Ill, 61-63, mem, Pub. Aid Cmn, 63-65 and dir, Dept. of Revenue, 66-69; trustee, Univ. Ill, 63-; mem, President's Cmt. on Equal Opportunity in Housing, White House, Washington, D.C, 63-68; regional dir, Off. of Econ. Opportunity, Chicago, Ill, 65-66; del, Dem. Nat. Conv, 68. Bus. & Prof. Pos: Partner, Jones, Anderson & Co, CPA's, 45-; treas. and dir, Serv. Fed. Savings, 51-, Chicago Burr Oak Cemetery, 51-; v.pres, Supreme Life Ins. Co, 55-65. Mem: Am. Inst. of Certified Pub. Acct; Nat. Ins. Asn.(pres, 62-63); Nat. Asn. Tax Admin. Thomas Crowe Award, Cath. Interracial Coun; Waltham Man of Year; Cmt. of 100 Man of Year. Rel: Episcopal. Mailing Add: 5028 S. Ellis, Chicago, Ill. 60615.

JONES, THEODORE TANNER R
Chmn, Geauga Co. Rep. Cent. and Exec. Cmts, Ohio
b. Cleveland, Ohio, 6/23/34; s. Paul Vincent Jones and Winifred Lemmon J; m. 9/19/59 to Alison Trabue Corning; c. Warren Tanner and Edith Trabue. Educ: Yale Univ, B.A, 57; Phi Gamma Delta. Polit. & Govt. Pos: Pres, Young Rep. Club, Geauga Co, Ohio, 62; del, Ohio State Rep. Conv, 62 & 64; precinct committeeman, Rep. Cent. Cmt, 62-64; alternate del, Rep. Nat. Conv, 64, del, 68; chmn, Geauga Co. Rep. Cent. and Exec. Cmts, Ohio, 64-; mem, Ohio Rep. State Exec. Cmt, currently. Mil. Serv: Entered as Pvt, Army, 57, released as 2nd Lt; 2nd Lt, Army Nat. Guard, 66. Rel: Protestant. Mailing Add: R.R. 2, Kirtland-Chardon Rd, Chardon, Ohio 44024. (1967)

JONES, THOMAS APPLEWHITE, JR. D
Ala. State Rep.
b. Montgomery, Ala, 9/16/28; s. Thomas Applewhite Jones and Effie Tuttle J; m. 2/2/52 to Margaret Elizabeth Monroe; c. Janice Irene, Thomas Applewhite, III and Monroe Tuttle. Educ: Auburn Univ, B.Arch, 51; Sigma Nu. Polit. & Govt. Pos: Ala. State Rep, Third Dist, 67- Bus. & Prof. Pos: Draftsman, Paul W. Hofferbert, Architect, 51-53, Warren, Knight & Davis, 53-56 and Lawrence S. Whitten, Architect, 56-57; off. mgr, Hofferbert & Ellis, Architects, 57-62; proprietor, Thomas A. Jones, Registered Architect, 62-65; partner, Jones, Crow, Mann & Assocs, 66- Mil. Serv: Entered as A/S, Navy, 46, released as Aviation Photographer's Mate 3/C, 48; Naval Inactive Res. Mem: Pres, Cent. City Asn, 2 years; pres. N. Ala. Chap, Am. Inst. of Architects; dir, Better Bus. Bur; trustee, Arts Coun; Commun. Ment. Health Center Cmt; chmn, Madison Co. Cancer Crusade, 63; Huntsville Indust. Expansion Cmt; C. of C; Kiwanis. Rel: Episcopal. Legal Res: 1319 Governors Drive S.E, Huntsville, Ala. 35801. Mailing Add: P.O. Box 472, Huntsville, Ala. 35804. (1967)

JONES, THOMAS ROBERT R
Chmn, Cameron Co. Rep. Party, Tex.
b. Utopia, Tex, 10/24/24; s. Robert Newton Jones and Ada Lavalee J; m. 10/13/45 to Dorothy V. Marshall; c. Cindy and Marilyn. Educ: Rice Univ. Polit. & Govt. Pos: Chmn, Cameron Co. Rep. Party, Tex, 64- Mil. Serv: Entered Navy Res, 42, released as Comdr; Naval Res. Medal; Am, Asiatic-Pac. and Korean Areas Medals; Victory and UN Medals. Legal Res: 418 Retama Place, Harlingen, Tex. 78550. Mailing Add: P.O. Box 1006, Harlingen, Tex. 78550.

JONES, VIRGIL CARRINGTON D
b. Charlottesville, Va, 6/7/06; s. Alonzo Lewis Jones and Virginia Graves J; m. 7/28/34 to Geneva Carolyn Peyton; c. Virgil Carrington, Jr. and Judith Watkins. Educ: Va. Polytech. Inst, 24-26; Wash. and Lee Univ, A.B. in journalism, 30; Sigma Delta Chi; Pi Delta Epsilon; Square and Compass; Phi Beta Kappa; Alpha Chi Rho. Polit. & Govt. Pos: Exec. secy. to Gov. Wm. M. Tuck, Va, 46; admin. asst. to U.S. Rep. Wm. M. Tuck, Fifth Dist, Va, 63-68. Bus. & Prof. Pos: Mgr, D.C. Off, Curtis Publ. Co, 45-61; liaison officer, U.S. Civil War Centennial Cmn, 58-63. Publ: The Hatfields and The McCoys, Univ. N.C. Press, 48; The Civil War at Sea, Holt, Rinehart and Winston, Inc, 59-61; Birth of Liberty, Holt, Rinehart and Winston, Inc, 62; plus 3 others. Mem: Mason; Civil War Round Table. Rel: Christian Church. Mailing Add: 15000 Lee Highway, Centreville, Va. 22020. (1967)

JONES, WALTER BEAMAN D
U.S. Rep, N.C.
b. Fayetteville, N.C, 8/19/13; s. Walter G. Jones; Fannie M. Anderson J; m. 4/26/34 to Doris Long; c. Mrs. Bob Moye and Walter B, II. Educ: N.C. State Col, B.S. in Educ, 34. Polit. & Govt. Pos: Mem, Bd. of Cmnrs, Farmville, N.C, 47-49; Mayor pro tem, Farmville, 47-49; Mayor, Farmville and judge, Farmville Recorder's Court, 49-53; N.C. State Rep, 55-61; N.C. State Sen, 61-66; U.S. Rep, N.C, 67- Bus. & Prof. Pos: Off. equip dealer; dir, Farmville Savings & Loan Asn. Mem: Trustee, Campbell Col; Masons; Scottish Rite; Rotary (pres, 49); Moose; Jr. Order; Elks. Rel: Baptist; Deacon, 45- Legal Res: Farmville, N.C. Mailing Add: 130 Cannon House Office Bldg, Washington, D.C. 20515.

JONES, WALTON MORRIS (W. M.) D
b. 12/18/14; married. Polit. & Govt. Pos: Miss. State Senate, 60-64. Bus. & Prof. Pos: Partner & Mgr, Radio Station WCHJ, Brookhaven. Mem: Mason; Shriner; Lions; C. of C; Miss. Broadcasting Asn. Rel: Baptist. Mailing Add: Box 711, 899 Josephine St, Brookhaven. Miss. 39601. (1967)

JONES, WILFRED DENTON R
Chmn, Greene Co. Rep. Exec. Cmt, Ohio
b. Xenia, Ohio, 11/14/22; s. Clinton Arthur Jones and Amy Long J; m. 9/19/44 to Louise Faye Kendig; c. Frank Arthur. Educ: Univ. Dayton, 43; Miss. State Col, 44. Polit. & Govt. Pos: Committeeman, Greene Co. Rep. Cent. Cmt, Ohio, 60-; v.chmn, Greene Co. Rep. Exec. Cmt, 64, chmn, 64-; committeeman, Seventh Cong. Dist. Rep. Party, 64-; mem. bd. elec, Greene Co, 66- Bus. & Prof. Pos: Mgr, Jones Mgts, Xenia, Ohio, 46-60; salesman, Gen. Motors Langs Inc, 60-61; bus. mgr, Greene Co. Automobile Club, Inc, 62-67, secy-mgr, 67- Mil. Serv: Entered as Aviation Cadet, Army Air Force, 42, released as Flight Officer, 46, after serv. in Third Combat Cargo Group, Tenth Air Force, China-Burma-India, 45; Air Medal with clusters; Am. Campaign Serv. Medal; Victory Medal; Asiatic-Pac. Serv. Medal. Mem: Charter mem, Young Rep. Club; York Rite; Scottish Rite; Kiwanis (dir); Am. Legion (past adj. and past comdr); Eastern Star (past patron); Xenia High Parents Music Asn.(pres); Xenia Citizens on Pub. Schs.(past pres). Rel: Protestant. Mailing Add: 343 N. King St, Xenia, Ohio 45385.

JONES, WILLIAM D
Committeeman, Dem. State Cent. Cmt, Conn.
b. Youngstown, Ohio, 9/14/34; s. Harry Jones and Johnnie Mae White J; m. to Eunice Louise Rogers; c. Lowell Irving and Diane Marie. Educ: St. Phillips Col, A.S, 59; Huston-Tillotson Col, B.A, magna cum laude, 61, Trinity Univ; South. Conn. State Col, summer 69; Alpha Kappa Mu; Alpha Phi Alpha. Polit. & Govt. Pos: Pres, Progressive Dem, 67-; del, Dem. State Conv, 68; del, Dem. Nat. Conv, 68; exec. v.pres, Conn. Dem. Caucus, 68- Bus. & Prof. Pos: Off. Prod. Div, Int. Bus. Machines Corp, 65-67; salesman, Xerox Corp, 67-68; exec. dir, Commun. Anal. & Develop, Conn, 68-; pres, Serv, Inc, New Haven, 68-; v.chmn, Opportunities Indust. Center, 66-69; prof, S. Cent. Conn. Col, 69. Mil. Serv: Entered as Airman, Air Force, 54, released as Airman 1/C, 58, after serv. in AEC Command. Mem: Bus. & Prfnl. Men's Club; Black Coalition, New Haven; Black Arts Theater; bd. of dirs, Tuberc. and Respiratory Disease Asn. and Florence Virtue Housing Coop. Rel: Protestant. Legal Res: 60 Orchard Place, New Haven, Conn. 06511. Mailing Add: 206 Dixwell Ave, New Haven, Conn. 06511.

JONES, WILLIAM BEATY R
b. Glasgow, Ky, 12/12/22; s. William H. Jones, Jr. and Nina Beaty J; m. 12/14/47 to Jeanne Powell; c. William Powell and Janna Susan. Educ: Univ. Ky, B.S. in commerce, 48, LL.B, 51; Phi Delta Phi; Phi Mu Alpha. Polit. Pos: Alternate del, Rep. Nat. Conv, 64; secy, Barren Co. Rep. Cmt, Ky, 51-53. Govt. Pos: U.S. Attorney, 59-61, 1st asst, 53-59. Bus. & Prof. Pos: Master Comnr, Barren Circuit Court, 65-; publisher, The Glasgow Rep, 59- Mil. Serv: Entered as Pvt, Army-Air Force, 43, released as Sgt, 46. Publn: Weekly editorials, The Glasgow Rep. Mem: Ky. Press Asn; Ky. and Am. Bar Asns; Newcomen Soc; Nat. Press Club; Am. Judicature Soc; Am. Legion; C. of C; Glasgow Country Club. Rel: Disciples of Christ. Mailing Add: Box 465, Glasgow, Ky. 42141. (1967)

JONES, WILLIAM LAYMAN R
b. Eldorado, Ill, 1/28/21; s. W.J. Jones and Myrtle Layman J; m. 2/14/42 to Julia Aileen Tolbert; c. Billy Lynn. Educ: Eldorado Twp. High Sch, 4 years. Polit. & Govt. Pos: Rep. precinct committeeman, East Eldorado Twp, Ill, 52-, asst. supvr, 69-; state labor conciliator, Ill, 56-60. Mil. Serv: Entered as A/S, Navy, 42, released as EM 2/C, 45, after serv. in Submarine Serv, Asiatic-Pac. and Am. Area; Asiatic-Pac. Medal with one Bronze Star; Am. Area Medal. Mem: Odd Fellows; AF&AM; Am. Legion. Rel: Missionary Baptist. Mailing Add: R.R. 1, Eldorado, Ill. 62930.

JONES, WILLIAM TOWNES D
b. Ware Shoals, S.C, 1/29/22; s. William Townes Jones and Helen Sims J; m. 11/21/50 to Selma Singleton Gilland; c. William Townes, Howard Gilland, Selma Thorne, Nelson Logan and Caroline Gibbes. Educ: Univ. S.C; Omicron Delta Kappa; Sr. Superlative; pres, Student Body; Hon. Bd. Polit. & Govt. Pos: S.C. State Rep, Greenwood Co, 49-52; solicitor, Eighth Judicial Circuit, S.C, 52-; del, Rep. Nat. Conv, 68. Bus. & Prof. Pos: Lawyer, S.C, 49- Mil. Serv: Entered as A/S, Naval Res, 42, released as Lt.(jg), 46, after serv. in Amphibious Unit, Atlantic Theater. Mem: S.C. and Am. Bar Asns; Mason; Shrine; Lions; Am. Legion; 40 et 8. Rel: Episcopal. Legal Res: 302 Janeway, Greenwood, S.C. 29646. Mailing Add: P.O. Box 186, Greenwood, S.C. 29646.

JONES, WILLIAM VALENTINE, JR. D
Miss. State Sen.
b. Waynesboro, Miss, 8/13/32; div; c. Virginia Lynn and Valerie Anne. Educ: Jones Co. Jr. Col, 52-53; Univ. Miss, 51-52 & 53-55; Cumberland Univ. Sch. Law, LL.B, 57. Polit. & Govt. Pos: Miss. State Sen, currently. Bus. & Prof. Pos: Attorney. Mem: Alpha Tau Omega; Phi Alpha Delta; Moose; Mason (32°); Shrine; Wayne Co. and Miss. State Bar Asns; Wayne Co. C. of C. Rel: Protestant. Mailing Add: P.O. Box 96, Waynesboro, Miss. 39367.

JONSSON, JOHN ERIK R
Mayor, Dallas, Tex.
b. Brooklyn, N.Y, 9/6/01; s. John Peter Jonsson and Charlotte Palmquist J; m. 2/8/23 to Margaret Elizabeth Fonde; c. Philip R, Kenneth A. and Margaret Ellen (Mrs. George V. Charlton). Educ: Rensselaer Polytech. Inst, M.E, 22; Phi Beta Kappa; Alpha Tau Omega. Hon. D.E, Rensselaer Polytech. Inst, 59; D.Sc, Hobart and William Smith Col, 61 and Austin Col, 63; LL.D, South. Methodist Univ, 64; D.C.L, Univ. of Dallas, 68. Polit. & Govt. Pos: Mayor, Dallas, Tex, 64- Bus. & Prof. Pos: Managerial positions, Aluminum Co. of Am, N.J. and Dumont Motor Car Co, Inc, 23-30; officer, Geophys. Serv, Inc, Dallas, 30-42; v.pres, Tex. Instruments Inc, 42-58, pres, 58-66, hon. chmn. of bd, 67-; dir, Equitable Life Assurance Soc. of U.S, N.Y, 67-; dir, Repub. Nat. Bank of Dallas, 67- Publ: Of Time and the Cities, Gantt Medal Bd. of Award, 69; 'Avalanche: the Cities and the Seventies,' FBI Law Enforcement Bul, 3/69 and Mech. Eng, 6/69; 'Days of Decision,' Goals for Dallas, Vols. I and II. Mem: Former mem, bd. of trustees, Nat. Indust. Conf. Bd; bd. of trustees, Nat. Planning Coun. and Bus. Cmt, Nat. Planning Asn; Soc. of Exploration Geophysicists; life mem, Am. Mgt. Asn.(v.pres, gen. mgt. div, 56-59; bd. of dirs, 56-64; exec. cmt, 62-64); chmn. of bd, Dallas-Ft. Worth Regional Airport; proposer and chmn, Planning Cmt, Goals for Dallas; chmn,

bd. of gov, Dallas Found; bd. of dirs, Dallas Co. United Fund, 61- (pres, 61-62); bd. of dirs, Dallas Citizens Coun.(v.pres, 62; pres, 63); bd. of trustees, Southwest. Med. Found; chmn, exec. cmt, Southwest. Legal Found; bd. of trustees, Tex. Research Found; bd. of dirs, Dallas Symphony Orchestra, 58-; bd. of trustees, Am. Assembly, N.Y; founder and former chmn. of bd. of gov, Southwest Center for Adv. Studies, Univ. of Tex, Dallas; adv. bd, Univ. of Dallas; Gov. Cmt. on Educ. Beyond the High Sch, 63-64; hon. mem, bd. of trustees, The Hockaday Sch.(chmn, 54-64); Am. Newcomen Soc; Philos. Soc. of Tex; hon. mem, Am. Inst. of Architects. Am. Soc. of Metals Adv. of Research Award, 64; Soc. of Indust. Realtors Industrialist of the Year Award, 65; Bene Merenti Medal, 66; Gantt Medal, 68; Horatio Alger Award, 69. Rel: Methodist. Legal Res: 4831 Shadywood Lane, Dallas, Tex. 75209. Mailing Add: 3300 Republic Bank Tower, Dallas, Tex. 75201.

JOPP, RALPH P. Conservative
Minn. State Rep.
b. Hollywood Twp, Minn, 1913; Married; c. Three. Educ: Watertown Pub. High Sch. Polit. & Govt. Pos: Mem, Twp. Zoning and Planning Bd, Minn; Minn. State Rep, 60- Mem: Bd. dirs, Carver Co. Fair Asn. Rel: Lutheran; pres, St. John Lutheran Congregation. Mailing Add: Mayer, Minn. 55360. (1967)

JORDAN, B. EVERETT D
U.S. Sen, N.C.
b. Ramseur, N.C, 9/8/96; s. Rev. Henry Harrison Jordan and Annie Elizabeth Sellers J; m. 11/29/24 to Katherine McLean; c. Benjamin Everett, Rose Ann Gant and John McLean. Educ: Rutherford Col, N.C, Prep. Sch, 12-13; Trinity Col, 14-15. Polit. & Govt. Pos: Chmn, N.C. Dem. Exec. Cmt, 49-54; Dem. Nat. Committeeman, N.C, 54-58; appointed, U.S. Sen, N.C, to fill vacancy of deceased W. Kerr Scott, 58, elected, 58- Bus. & Prof. Pos: Secy. and gen. mgr, Organized Sellers Mfg. Co, 27 and has served in several other textile mfg. cos. Mil. Serv: U.S. Army Tank Corps, 18-19; Occupation Forces in Germany, 1919. Mem: N.C. Peace Officers Benefit and Retirement Cmn, 43-58; Officer, Alamance Co. Tuberc. Asn; Alamance Co. Red Cross; chmn. bd. of trustees, Alamance Co. Gen. Hosp; Rotary; Masons; trustee, Duke Univ, Am. Univ. and Elon Col; v.pres, Bd. Methodist Cols, 52-56. Alamance Co. Man of the Year, 55. Rel: Methodist; Adult Bible Class Teacher, 27-28, Chmn. Bd. Stewards, 30-50, Lay Leader, 35-40. Legal Res: Saxapahaw, N.C. Mailing Add: Calvert-Woodley Apts, Washington, D.C. 20008.

JORDAN, BEN CARLTON R
V.Chmn, Seventh Dist. Rep. Party of Ga.
b. Mableton, Ga, 12/21/29; s. Carl Thomas Jordan and Ruby L. J; m. 6/1/50 to Mary Leola Eldredge; c. Larry Carlton, Marion David and Richard Craig. Educ: Ga. State Col, B.B.A, 59. Polit. & Govt. Pos: First v.pres, Cobb Young Rep, Ga, 60-61, pres, 61-62; Cobb Co. chmn, Draft Goldwater for Pres, 63-64; first v.chmn, Cobb Co. Rep. Party, 64-65, chmn, 65-; Ga. State Rep, 103rd Dist, 64-65; alternate del, Rep. Nat. Conv, 68; v.chmn, Seventh Dist. Rep. Party of Ga, 68- Bus. & Prof. Pos: Purchasing agent, Fulton Cotton Mills, 47-56; sales exec, Sloan Paper Co, 56- Mil. Serv: Entered as Pvt, Army, 50, released as Sgt. 1/C, 56. Mem: F&AM; Jaycees; Lions. Rel: Baptist. Mailing Add: 143 Andrew Dr, Mableton, Ga. 30059.

JORDAN, CLIFFORD HOMER R
b. Des Moines, Iowa, 10/17/10; s. Talley E. Jordan and Lillian S. Tilton J; m. 11/22/31 to Vena June Russell; c. Richard Talley, Dennis Edward and Linda (Mrs. Rice). Educ: Univ. Minn, 28. Polit. & Govt. Pos: Finance chmn, Second Dist. Rep. Party, Iowa, 66-67; alternate del, Rep. Nat. Conv, 68. Bus. & Prof. Pos: Dir. bd. dirs, Merchants Nat. Bank, Cedar Rapids, Iowa; mem, Bd. Trustees, Coe Col; bd. of trustees, St. Luke's Hosp; pres, Jordan Bldg. Corp, 53-; pres, Hwy. Equipment Co, 58-; chmn. of bd, Kilborn Photo Paper Co, 66- Mem: Nat. Asn. Acct. Rel: Presbyterian. Legal Res: 1834 First Ave. N.E, Cedar Rapids, Iowa 52402. Mailing Add: 2911 First Ave. S.E, Cedar Rapids, Iowa 52406.

JORDAN, DAVID DAVOE R
b. Dillon, S.C, 12/12/38; s. Harvie Cabbel Jordan, Sr. and Liza Jane Calcutt J; m. 4/12/59 to Madelyn Iris Dedmondt; c. Robert Arthur. Educ: Duke Univ, 57-58. Polit. & Govt. Pos: V.Chmn, Buncombe Co. Young Rep. Club, N.C, 64-65, chmn, 66; chmn, 11th Dist, N.C. Fedn. Young Rep, 64-65, treas, N.C. Fedn. Young Rep, 66-; N.C. State Rep, 45th Dist, 66-68. Mil. Serv: Entered as Recruit E-1, Army, 58, released as Specialist E-4, P-1, 61, after serv. in Hq, First Logistical Command, Ft. Bragg, N.C; Cert. of Achievement; Good Conduct Medal. Mem: Chmn, Data Processing Mgt. Asn, 65-66; AF&AM; AASR. Legal Res: 22-A Westall Dr, Asheville, N.C. 28804. Mailing Add: P.O. Box 8117, Asheville, N.C. 28804. (1967)

JORDAN, DONALD WELLER, JR. D
Mem, Calif. Dem. State Cent. Cmt.
b. San Bernardino, Calif, 4/21/37; s. Donald Weller Jordan and Meredyth Savage J; div; c. Kenneth Ogle. Educ: Univ. Colo, A.B, 59; Univ. Calif. Law Sch, Berkeley, LL.B, 62; Kappa Sigma; Phi Delta Phi. Polit. & Govt. Pos: Mem, San Bernardino Co. Dem. Cent. Cmt, Calif, 66-68; mem, Calif. Dem. State Cent. Cmt, 68- Bus. & Prof. Pos: Peace Corps vol, Philippines, 62-64; dep. dist. attorney, Dist. Attorney's Off, San Bernardino, Calif, 64-66; staff attorney, Defender's Inc, San Diego, 68-69; attorney-at-law, Garza & Kassel, San Bernardino, 69- Mem: Am, Calif. and San Bernardino Co. Bar Asns; various Dem. orgn. Rel: Protestant. Mailing Add: 222 E. 17th St, San Bernardino, Calif. 92404.

JORDAN, FRANK MORRILL R
Secy. of State, Calif.
b. Alameda, Calif, 8/6/88; s. Frank C. Jordan and Emma Dudley Morrill J; m. 1955 to Alberta Stuzmann; c. Mary Jane (Mrs. Robert Law); grandchildren, Peggy Ann Law and Mrs. Nancy Jordan Law Tate. Educ: Pub. schs, Oakland, Calif. Polit. & Govt. Pos: Dep. Secy. of State, Calif, formerly, Secy. of State, 42-; del, Rep. Nat. Conv, 68. Bus. & Prof. Pos: With R.R. surv. gang; mining, Ariz. and Shasta Co, Calif; with eng. dept, Automobile Club of South. Calif, 11-17; gen. ins. bus, Calif, Ore. and Wash. Mil. Serv: Entered as Pvt, 144th Field Artil, World War I, released as Lt. Mem: Mason; Shrine; Elks; Native Sons of the Golden West; Am. Legion; VFW; 144th Field Artil. Asn; Jonathan, Balboa Bay and Grandfathers Clubs; past pres, Nat. Asn. Secy. of State. Rel: Protestant. Legal Res: 3720 Robertson Ave, Sacramento, Calif. 95821. Mailing Add: State Capitol, Sacramento, Calif. 95814.

JORDAN, GEORGE D
Ga. State Rep.
b. Broxton, Ga, 7/30/28; s. James B. Jordan and Aletha Morrison J; m. 1/8/54 to Helena Jaskiewicz; c. Jonathan, Mary Elizabeth, Peter Marshall, James and Paul. Educ: Mercer Univ, LL.B, 49; Sigma Alpha Epsilon. Polit. & Govt. Pos: Ga. State Rep, 55th Dist, 66- Mil. Serv: Entered as Pvt, Army, 50, released as First Lt, 54, after serv. in Korea, 53-54. Mem: Bar Asn. of Ga; Am. Legion; Farm Bur. Rel: Protestant. Mailing Add: Box 916, Douglas, Ga. 31533.

JORDAN, HUBERT BRUCE D
Tenn. State Rep.
b. Halls, Tenn, 2/20/21; s. Robert Horance Jordan and Pearl Trabue J; m. 6/3/43 to Emily Frances Gee; c. Emily Frances (Mrs. Grant Chambers). Educ: South. Law Univ, LL.B, 48; Univ. Tenn, 48-49. Polit. & Govt. Pos: Shelby Co. Cmnr, roads, bridges and penal farm, Memphis, Tenn, 62-65; mem, Tenn. Dem. Exec. Cmt, 64-; Tenn. State Rep, Dist. 3, 68- Bus. & Prof. Pos: Owner, Jordan Ins. Agency, 59-69, real estate and ins, 69- Mil. Serv: Entered as Pvt, Army, 44, released as Sgt, 46, after serv. in Ord. Sect, Hq. Co, 13th Maj. Port, Antwerp, Belgium, ETO; Army Res, 46-50; Good Conduct Ribbon; ETO Ribbon; Spec. Commendation Award. Mem: Am. Real Estate Orgn; dir, YMCA, 60-; Mason; Scottish Rite; Shrine; Am. Legion; Whitehaven Dem. Club; Lions. Rel: Methodist. Mailing Add: 1093 Chambliss Rd, Memphis, Tenn. 38116.

JORDAN, INGERSOLL D
b. New Orleans, La, 2/28/41; s. Thomas L. Jordan and Corneila I. J; single. Educ: Univ. of the South. Polit. & Govt. Pos: Staff asst, Off. of Majority Whip, U.S. Rep. Hale Boggs, La, 65-67; del, Dem. Nat. Conv, 68. Bus. & Prof. Pos: V.pres, Thomas Jordan, Inc, New Orleans, La, Timber Ridge Develop. Co, Miss. and Gilreath Hydraulics, Inc, Houston, Tex. Mil. Serv: Entered as Seaman, Coast Guard Res, 63, released as AG 3, 69. Mem: Pres, Sewanee Club New Orleans. Rel: Episcopal. Legal Res: 1415 Third St, New Orleans, La. 70130. Mailing Add: 800 Whitney Bank Bldg, New Orleans, La. 70130.

JORDON, JAMES ALONZO D
City Councilman, Pittsburgh, Pa.
b. Pittsburgh, Pa, 10/13/23; s. James Jordon and Adelaide E. Graves J; m. 9/10/59 to Marion O. Bond. Educ: Univ. Pittsburgh, B.S, 47, M.Litt, 48; Duquesne Univ, LL.B, 61; pres, Alpha Phi Alpha. Polit. & Govt. Pos: Pres, Dem. for United Action, 51-55; mem, Mayor's Cmn. on Human Rels, Pittsburgh, Pa, 51-55, mem, Mayor's Tax Adv. Cmt. and Youth Serv. Cmt, Allegheny Co, 52 and chmn, Mayor's Cmt. on Econ. Develop, 60-61; v.pres, Young Dem. Allegheny Co, 52-56; alternate del, Dem. Nat. Conv, 60, del, 64; city councilman, Pittsburgh, Pa, 60-; mem, Pittsburgh Pub. Parking Authority, 64- Bus. & Prof. Pos: Chmn. bd, Jordon Supply Co, 50-55; admin. asst, Koppers Co, Inc, 55-57, mgr. transportation research develop, 57-63 and attorney, 63-65 & 66; chmn. bd, Bus. & Job Develop. Corp, 65-66; gen. mgr, Commercial and Indust. Div, Westinghouse Learning Corp, 67- Mil. Serv: Pvt, Army, 43-46, serv. in Engrs. and Paratroops. Mem: Allegheny Co. Bar Asn; C. of C; nat. and local bd, YMCA; Am. Legion; bd. trustees, Carnegie Libr. and Carnegie Inst; bd. mem, Action Housing, Inc, World Affairs Coun, Health and Welfare Asn, Urban League, Coun. of Churches, Nat. Conf. Christians and Jews and Pittsburgh Br, NAACP. Selected 1 of 100 Most Promising Men in Pittsburgh, Pittsburgh C. of C. and Time Mag, 53; 1 of 3 Outstanding Men in Pa, Pa. Jr. C. of C, 57. Rel: Protestant. Mailing Add: 4301 Andover Terr, Pittsburgh, Pa. 15213. (1967)

JORDAN, JAMES E. (RED) D
b. Dalton, Ga, 12/22/22; s. John W. Jordan and Jewie Robinson J; m. 6/28/46 to Mildred Cowart Jordan; c. Miriam, James L, Kelly E, Alan R. Educ: Univ. of Ga, B.S.A, 43. Polit. & Govt. Pos: Ga. State Rep, 63-64. Bus. & Prof. Pos: Farmer, poultry, cattle; real estate. Mil. Serv: Army, Capt, Inf, Co. Comdr. Mem: Mason; Elk. Rel: Methodist. Mailing Add: Rome, Ga. 30161. (1967)

JORDAN, JOHN C. R
Mem. Exec. Cmt, Rep. Nat. Cmt.
m. to Joya J; c. John Jr, Langford, Charles, Grace Joya and Benjamin James. Educ: Grove City Col, grad; Ford Motor Co. Merchandising Sch; Marine Corps Missiles Sch. Polit. & Govt. Pos: Former mem, Resolution Cmt. of U.S. Conf. of Mayors and Pa. League of Cities; former mayor, New Castle, Pa; state chmn, Pa. Rep. Nat. Cmt, currently; del, Rep. Nat. Conv, 68; mem. exec. cmt, Rep. Nat. Cmt, 69- Mem: Am. Inst. of Banking; Am. Legion; Elks; YMCA. Mailing Add: P.O. Box 1624, Harrisburg, Pa. 17105.

JORDAN, JOHN W. R
Fla. State Rep.
b. Danville, Ind, 1/4/26; s. S. Paul Jordan and Ada Weaver Christenson J; single. Educ: Butler Univ, 46-48. Polit. & Govt. Pos: Fla. State Rep, 80th Dist, 68- Bus. & Prof. Pos: Bus. Exec. and Entrepreneur. Mil. Serv: Entered as Pvt, Army Air Force, 44, released as Cpl, 46. Mem: Scottish Rite; bd. dir. indust. for blind, Lions; Palm Beach Islanders (past pres); mem. bd, Ment. Health Asn; Jr. C. of C; West Palm Beach, Lake Worth and North. Palm Beach C. of C; Ky. Col. Rel: Baptist. Legal Res: 218 Butler St, West Palm Beach, Fla. 33407. Mailing Add: P.O. Box 1603, West Palm Beach, Fla. 33402.

JORDAN, LEON M. D
Mo. State Rep.
b. Kansas City, Mo, 5/6/05; m. 8/15/32 to Orchid Nee Ramsey. Educ: Washburn Univ; Wilberforce Univ, B.S. in Commerce. Polit. & Govt. Pos: Mo. State Rep, 64- Bus. & Prof. Pos: Businessman; has taught sch. and served as police officer. Mil. Serv: Army, Co E, 24th Regular Inf. Mem: Elks; Kappa Alpha Psi; Freedom, Inc. Rel: Episcopal. Mailing Add: 2548 Prospect, Kansas City, Mo. 64127. (1967)

JORDAN, LEONARD BECK R
U.S. Sen, Idaho
b. Mt. Pleasant, Utah, 5/15/99; s. Leonard Eugene Jordan and Irene Beck J; m. 12/30/24 to Grace Edgington; c. Joseph, Stephen and Patricia (Mrs. Charles Story). Educ: Univ. Ore, B.A, 23; Phi Beta Kappa; Alpha Tau Omega. Polit. & Govt. Pos: Idaho State Rep, Idaho Co, 47-49; Gov, Idaho, 51-55; chmn, Int. Joint Cmn. U.S-Can, 55-58; mem, U.S. Develop. Adv. Bd, 58-59; U.S. Sen, Idaho, 62-; del, Rep. Nat. Conv, 68. Bus. & Prof. Pos: Self employed, bus, livestock and farming. Mil. Serv: Entered as Pvt, Army, 18, released as 2nd Lt, 19. Mem: Mason; Scottish Rite (33°); Shrine; Rotary; Am. Legion. Rel: Methodist. Legal Res: 2 Hulbe Rd, Boise, Idaho 83705. Mailing Add: Senate Office Bldg, Washington, D.C. 20510.

JORDAN, LOIS E. D
Committeewoman, Davidson Co. Dem. Exec. Cmt, Tenn.
b. Nashville, Tenn, 8/4/40; d. John H. Jordan, Jr.(deceased) and Camilla Eddings J; single. Educ: Tenn. A&I State Univ, B.S. in Sociol; Univ. of Tenn. Exten. in Nashville, studies in Criminology and Real Estate, 67-68. Polit. & Govt. Pos: Committeewoman, Davidson Co. Dem. Exec. Cmt, Tenn, 64-; Tenn. rep. and chmn. workshop on youth, Nat. Dem. Women's Conv, 66; chmn, Prog. Cmt, co-chmn, Financial Cmt. and mem, Constitutional Bylaws Cmt, Dem. Party, Tenn; alternate del, Dem. Nat. Conv, 68. Bus. & Prof. Pos: Juvenile probation counsel, Dept. of Correction, Tenn, 66-; licensed real estate saleslady, 68- Mem: Nashville Bd. of Realtors; League of Women Voters; Dem. Women's League; Negro Bus. & Prfnl. Women's League; YMCA (chmn, polit. affairs cmt, Nashville); Tenn. Personnel and Guidance Asn; Tenn. Correction Asn; secy, Southeast Civic League; charter mem, Dudley Park Day Care Center; prog. chmn, Tenn. Fedn. Dem. League; Davidson Co. Young Dem. Club; Nashville Urban League. Rel: Catholic. Legal Res: 1249 Second Ave. S, Nashville, Tenn. 37210. Mailing Add: P.O. Box 7002, Nashville, Tenn. 37210.

JORDAN, ROBERT DEAN R
N.Mex. State Rep.
b. Amarillo, Tex, 10/31/30; s. Earl L. Jordan and Ruby Loe J; m. 2/3/66 to Carolyn Jean Raymond; c. Jaymie Lynn, Drue Henry and Melanie Earl. Educ: Univ. N.Mex, B.A, 58, grad. work in Pub. Finance, 61; Pi Kappa Alpha. Polit. & Govt. Pos: Chmn, Otero Co. Rep. Party, N.Mex, 59-60; exec. dir, N.Mex. State Tax Cmn, 61-62; dir. orgn. and finance, N.Mex. Rep. Party, 63; chmn, N.Mex. Citizens for Goldwater-Miller, 64; N.Mex. State Rep, 67-; chmn, N.Mex. Rep. Sch. and Tax Study Cmt, 67-68; treas, Manuel Lujan for Cong. Cmt, 68. Bus. & Prof. Pos: Off. mgr, F.P. Llewellyn Inc, Alamogordo, 59-60; owner and operator, Robert Jordan Co, Corporate Tax Consult, 64- Mil. Serv: Entered as Pvt, Army, 51, released as 1st Lt, 53, after serv. in 11th Airborne Inf. Div, Korea, 52-53. Publ: The Jordan Report, N.Mex. State Tax Cmn, 61; How State and Local Assessments Can Be Equalized, West. States Asn. of Tax Adminstrs, 62. Mem: West. States Asn. of Tax Adminstrs.(exec. cmt); Int. Asn. of Assessing Officers. Chosen by Eagleton Inst. of Polit, Rutgers Univ, to Represent N.Mex. House of Rep. at a Nat. Legis. Seminar, Naples, Fla, 69. Rel: Protestant. Mailing Add: 1100 Alvarado S.E, Albuquerque, N.Mex. 87108.

JORDAN, ROBERT LANSING R
Chmn, New Canaan Town Rep. Cmt, Conn.
b. Brooklyn, N.Y, 7/21/18; s. Robert B. Jordan and Katherine Lansing J; m. 7/4/42 to Elizabeth MacKenzie; c. Robert L, Jr, Marion L. and Martha L. Educ: Princeton Univ, grad, 40; Tiger Inn; Varsity Club. Polit. & Govt. Pos: Mem, various local and state Rep. Party Cmts, 52-; chmn, New Canaan Town Rep. Cmt, Conn, 62- Bus. & Prof. Pos: V.Pres, Palmer, Willson & Worker Inc, Advertising & Pub. Rels. Agency, 65-; also with McCann-Erickson, Benton & Bowles. Mil. Serv: Entered as Pvt, Army, 40, released as Capt, 46, after serv. in Inf, ETO; Five Campaign Ribbons. Publ: Feature article in Rep. Nat. Conv. program, 60. Mem: Soc. of Military Historians. Rel: Congregational. Mailing Add: Indian Rock Rd, New Canaan, Conn. 06840.

JORDAN, RUSSELL CLINGER, JR. D
b. Kansas City, Mo, 10/28/26; s. Russell C. Jordan and Lois Van Evera J; m. 2/27/49 to Margaret Joan McBride; c. Robert Michael. Educ: Kans. City Univ, 1 year; Rose Polytech. Inst, 1 year; Ind. Univ, ½ year. Polit. & Govt. Pos: Committeeman, Sarasota Co. Dem. Cmt, Fla, 60-; Fla. State Rep, Sarasota Co, 62-64. Bus. & Prof. Pos: Pres, Russ Jordan Ins, Inc, Sarasota, Fla, 50- and Russ Jordan Property, Inc, 55- Mil. Serv: Pvt, Air Corps, 43-48 with serv. in Field Artil, 24th Inf. Div, Far East Theatre, 47-48; Lt. Col, Army Res, 68- Mem: Secy-treas, Sarasota Asn. Independent Ins. Agents; Fla. Asn. Independent Ins. Agents; dir, Sarasota Life Underwriters; Sertoma; Elks; Am. Legion; C. of C; Power Squadron, SAR. Rel: Christian; Secy. Bd, First Christian Church. Legal Res: 3647 San Remo Terr, Sarasota, Fla. 33577. Mailing Add: 2101 Ringling, Sarasota, Fla. 33577.

JORDAN, WILLIAM HARVEY D
b. Leary, Ga, 6/24/14; s. Willie Duncan Jordan and Maggie Harvey J; m. 7/27/34 to Marjorie McClelland; c. Jean (Mrs. Webb), William Harvey, Jr. and Barbara. Educ: Leary High Sch, grad, 31; Norman Jr. Col, 1 year. Polit. & Govt. Pos: Mayor, Leary, Ga, 8 years; Ga. State Rep, 59-68. Bus. & Prof. Pos: Fertilizer bus; farmer; banker, Jordan Banking Co. Rel: Missionary Baptist. Mailing Add: Leary, Ga. 31762. (1967)

JORDAN, WILLIAM OSBORNE R
Committeeman, Conn. Rep. State Cent. Cmt.
b. Meriden, Conn, 3/8/08; m. 5/14/48 to Alice Springer; c. William L. Polit. & Govt. Pos: Pres, Willimantic Rep. Club, Conn, 40; treas, Windham Co. Young Rep, 40; former Registr. of Voters, Windham; mem, Windham Rep. Town Cmt, several years; committeeman, Conn. Rep. State Cent. Cmt, 29th Sen. Dist, 60-; alternate del, Rep. Nat. Conv, 64, del, 68; del, Conn. Constitutional Conv, 65. Bus. & Prof. Pos: Formerly in bldg. bus; employee, John Hancock Life Ins. Co, 35; owner, gen. ins. agency, 37-61, Ashton, Jordan & Blish, Ins. and Real Estate, 61- Mem: Eastern Star (Past Master, Lodge 44, Past Patron, Radiant Chap. 11); AF&AM; Shrine; past pres, Willimantic Asn. of Independent Ins. Agents, Inc; past pres, Willimantic Bd. of Realtors; former head, Willimantic Br, Pratt & Whitney Aircraft Fed. Credit Union; past pres, Vis. Nurses Asn; former dir, Am. Red Cross Chap, Willimantic; past treas, Congregational Men's Brotherhood; former instr, Nat. Rifle Asn. for Conn. State Bd. of Fisheries and Game; Fin, Fur and Feather Club; Windham Fish and Game Club; Setter Club of New Eng; Rotary Int. Rel: Protestant. Legal Res: Corner Routes 6 and 203, North Windham, Conn. 06256. Mailing Add: 702 Main St, Willimantic, Conn. 06226.

JORDAN, WILLIAM R, JR. 'BILL' D
b. 1934. Educ: Univ. Ky, B.S. Polit. & Govt. Pos: Ky. State Rep, 1962-68. Bus. & Prof. Pos: Automobile bus. Mem: Mason; Shrine; Young Dem. Club. Rel: Methodist. Mailing Add: Jenkins, Ky. 41537. (1967)

JORGENSEN, FRANK E. R
b. Bristol, Colo, 5/2/03; s. Fred Jorgensen and Effie Fenimore J; m. 12/25/26 to Mary E. Kimball; c. Frank Kimball. Educ: Drake Univ, 21-24. Polit. & Govt. Pos: Mem, Los Angeles Co. Rep. Cent. Cmt, 46-54, Calif. Rep. State Cmt, 47-58; chmn. campaign to elect Richard M. Nixon to U.S. House of Rep, 46 & 48; chmn. exec. cmt. to elect Richard M. Nixon to U.S. Senate, 50 and President of U.S, 68; chmn. exec. cmt, Calif. for George Murphy, currently. Bus. & Prof. Pos: V.pres, Metrop. Life Ins. Co, 29- Mem: Union League Club, N.Y.C. Mailing Add: 1570 Kingswood Dr, Hillsborough, Calif. 94010.

JORGENSEN, HARRY V. D
b. Jordan, S.Dak, 6/14/26; s. Anthony L. Jorgensen and Gladys E. Whitehorn J; m. 1/20/55 to Marian R. Swenkner; c. Terry A, Nancy L, Mary Ann and Anthony H. Educ: S. San Francisco High Sch, grad, 44. Polit. & Govt. Pos: Chmn, Tripp Co. Dem. Cent. Cmt, S.Dak, 62-68; mem, S.Dak. State Dem. Adv. Cmt, 63-68; del, Dem. Nat. Conv, 64; del. and mem. platform cmt, S.Dak. State Dem. Conv, 64 & 66. Bus. & Prof. Pos: Construction foreman, Johnson Builders; owner-operator, Jorgensen Construction Co, 54- Mil. Serv: Entered as Pvt, Calif. Nat. Guard, 43; entered Naval Res. as Seaman, 44, released as 2/C PO, 46, after serv. in Pac; Asiatic-Pac. Theater Ribbon; Victory Medal; Philippine Campaign Ribbon. Mem: VFW; Am. Legion; Mason; Elks; pres, Christian Mens Fel; AFL-CIO, BMPIUA. Private survey on 50 states problems in taxation and education. Rel: Christian Church. Mailing Add: 601 E. Third St, Winner, S.Dak. 57580. (1967)

JORGENSEN, JACK J. DFL
b. Enderlin, N.Dak, 7/25/14; s. Hans Jorgen Jorgensen and Anna Melin J; m. 8/31/40 to Florence V. Kinrade; c. Jack J, Jr, James Alan and Sandra Lee. Polit. & Govt. Pos: Fifth dist. chmn, Dem. Party, Minneapolis, Minn, 52; alderman, 13th Ward, Minneapolis, 55; del, Dem. Nat. Conv, 68; cmnr, Hennepin Co. Park Reserve, currently. Mem: Mason; Elks; Golden Valley Golf Club; Childrens Hosp. of Minneapolis; Teamsters. Rel: Lutheran. Legal Res: 216 E. 135th St, Burnsville, Minn. 55378. Mailing Add: 706 First Ave. N, Minneapolis, Minn. 55403.

JORGENSEN, LEONARD E. R
b. Viburg, S.Dak, 8/21/05; s. Neils Anton Jorgensen and Laura J; m. 8/14/30 to Edith Aggergaard; c. Janet J.(Mrs. Jerry Whitman) and Brenda R. (Mrs. Richard Buck). Educ: S.Dak. State Univ, B.S.M.E. Polit. & Govt. Pos: Chmn, McCook Co. Rep. Party, S.Dak, 63-68. Bus. & Prof. Pos: Owner, Regale Theatre, 30-69. Mem: Mason; Shrine; Oriental Consistory; Progressive Men's Asn; Salem Fire Dept; McCook Country Club (pres); Rel: Methodist. Mailing Add: 331 N. Minn, Salem, S.Dak. 57058.

JORGENSEN, NATALIE SMITH R
Pub. Rels. Chmn, Madison Co. Rep. Exec. Cmt, Ala.
b. St. Paul, Minn, 2/15/34; d. Dr. Howard Ripley Smith and Maxine Johnson S; m. 9/4/54 to Harry Kenneth Jorgensen; c. Drew Michael, Dacia Lyn and Dana Ann. Educ: Univ. Wyo, 52-54; Kappa Kappa Gamma. Polit. & Govt. Pos: Asst. co-dir. women, Goldwater Campaign Cmt, La, 64; alternate del-at-lg, Rep. Nat. Conv, 64; v.chmn, Metrop. Dist. Rep. Party, New Orleans, 64-66, Ninth Ward leader, 64-65; campaign chmn, Madison Co. Tax Assessor, Ala, 66; finance chmn, Madison Co. Rep. Exec. Cmt, 66-67, pub. rels. chmn, 69-; del, Ala. Rep. State Conv, 68; North. Ala. Campaign Chmn, Seventh and Eighth Cong. Dist, Hooper for U.S. Senate, 68. Mem: Madison Co. Fedn. Rep. Women (pres, 66); Huntsville Fedn. Rep. Women; exec. secy-dir, Madison Co. Asn. Ment. Health, 67; Willowbrook Civic Asn.(secy, 67-69); Cath. Charities Bd. of Dirs.(treas, 69); PTA (first v.pres, 68); South Huntsville Entrepreneurs Investment Club (pres, 68-69); St. Stephens Churchwomen; Boeing Wives Club. Distinguished Young Woman nominee, Jayceettes, 67 & 68; Vol. Award, Madison Co. Asn. Ment. Health, 68. Mailing Add: 8031 Navios Dr. S.E, Huntsville, Ala. 35802.

JORGENSON, LLOYD R
b. Hayti, S.Dak, 10/17/03; s. James Theadore Jorgenson and Annie Johnson J; m. 2/10/24 to Gladys Ellsworth; c. Mary Ann, William Lloyd, Glenn LeRoy, Ruby Ardell, Larry Lee and Nancy Rochelle. Educ: East. State Col, S.Dak, 24-25. Polit. & Govt. Pos: Secy-treas, Rep. Party, 37-39; co. official, Hamlin Co, S.Dak, 37-53; chmn, Hamilton Co. Rep. Party, 39-52; asst. state dir, Farmers Home Admin, 54-60; state soc. security dir, S.Dak, 61-63, state treas, 63-67, state auditor, 67-69. Bus. & Prof. Pos: Pub. sch. teacher, S.Dak, 24-37; independent ins. agent, 40-54. Publ: Thoughts While Thinking, Mod. Press Ind, Sioux Falls, S.Dak, 66. Mem: S.Dak. Poetry Soc; Elks; Kiwanis; Mason. Rel: Lutheran. Legal Res: Hayti, S.Dak. Mailing Add: Box 302, Pierre, S.Dak. 57501.

JOSEFSON, J. A. R
Minn. State Sen.
b. Minneota, Minn, 3/5/15; s. Johann A. Josefson and Winnie Hoftieg J; m. 4/6/50 to Gladys O. Coover; c. Lois Eileen. Polit. & Govt. Pos: Chmn, Lyon Co. Prod. and Mkt. Admin, Fed. Farm Prog, 46-54; Minn. State Sen, currently. Bus. & Prof. Pos: Dir. and chmn. bd. dirs, Farmers and Merchants Supply Co, 45- Mem: AF&AM; All York and Scottish Rites; Mason; Am. Farm Bur. Fedn; Toastmasters Int. Rel: Lutheran. Mailing Add: Minneota, Minn. 56264.

JOSEPH, GERALDINE M. 'GERI' D
V.Chmn, Dem. Nat. Cmt.
b. St. Paul, Minn, 6/19/23; d. Samuel S. Mack and Edith Berkovitz M; m. 4/2/53 to Burton M. Joseph; c. Shelley M, I. Scott and Jonathan P. Educ: Univ. Minn, B.A, 45; Theta Sigma Phi; Delta Phi Lambda. Polit. & Govt. Pos: State women's chmn, Vol. for Stevenson, Minn, 56; nat. committeewoman, Dem-Farmer-Labor Party, Minn. and state chairwoman, 58-60; mem, Presi-

dent's Cmt. on Youth Employ, 62-64; mem. prog. cmt, Anti-Defamation League and Gov. Coun. on Youth Training, Inc; mem. adv. coun, Nat. Inst. Ment. Health, 63-; mem, President's Cmn. on Income Maintenance Progs, 68-; v.chmn, Dem. Nat. Cmt, 69- Mem: Nat. Asn. for Ment. Health (pres, 68-). Only woman to win Sigma Delta Chi award, 50. Rel: Jewish. Mailing Add: 5 Red Cedar Lane, Minneapolis, Minn. 55410.

JOSEPH, MAURICE FRANKLIN D
Chmn, St. Clair Co. Dem. Cent. Cmt, Ill.
b. Freeburg, Ill, 9/29/05; s. Frank Henry Joseph and Ruth Carr J; m. 8/15/25 to Viola Mae Sterling; c. Robert F. and Virginia (Mrs. Gordon). Educ: High Sch. Polit. & Govt. Pos: Ill. State Police, 33-41; precinct committeeman, Dem. Party, Ill, 34-; supvr, New Athens Twp, 41-50; treas, St. Clair Co, 50-54 & 66-, dep. sheriff, 58-62 and sheriff, 62-66; chmn, St. Clair Co. Dem. Cmt, 50-; chmn. and treas, Ill. Dem. Cmt, 60-; del, Dem. Nat. Conv, 68. Bus. & Prof. Pos: Appliance and Furniture Bus, 41-58. Mem: Mason; Shrine; Jesters; Eastern Star; Moose; plus many civic orgns. Rel: Methodist. Legal Res: 906 Mill St, New Athens, Ill. 62264. Mailing Add: Court House, Belleville, Ill. 62220.

JOSEPH, PETER ANTHONY D
Vt. State Rep.
b. Island Pond, Vt, 8/13/19; single. Educ: St. Marys High Sch, Island Pond, Vt. Polit. & Govt. Pos: Mem, Town Planning Bd. and Budget Cmt, Brighton, Vt, 63-, town moderator, 64; Vt. State Rep, 65- Bus. & Prof. Pos: Owner and mgr, outdoor movie theatre. Mil. Serv: Technician Fifth grade, Army Signal Corps, 44-46. Mem: K. of C; Am. Legion; Northeast Vt. Fish & Game Club; Brighton Bd. of Trade. Rel: Catholic. Mailing Add: Island Pond, Vt. 05846. (1967)

JOSEPH, WILLIAM D
b. Franklin Borough, Pa, 8/28/26; s. Charles Joseph and Geraldine Jaber J; m. 11/29/47 to Helen Leschock; c. Theresa Ann, Norman P, William G, Mary Frances, Karen D. and David Brian. Polit. & Govt. Pos: Mem, Franklin Borough Coun, 56-65, pres, 60-65; counsr, Pa. State Workmen's Ins. Funds, 57-63; pres, Cambria Co. Young Dem, 58-64; secy, Young Dem. Clubs of Pa, 58-66; mem, exec. and policy cmts, Cambria Co. Dem. Cmt, 58-66; dist. chmn, Franklin Borough Dem. Cmt, 59-66; tax collector, Franklin Borough, 61; sealer of weights and measures, Cambria Co, 63-66; del, Dem. Nat. Conv, 68. Bus. & Prof. Pos: Partner, Royal Candy Co, 49-50; sales mgr, Conrad Wholesale Co, 51-56; treas, Cambria-Johnstown East. Prfnl. Basketball Team, 65- Rel: Syrian Orthodox. Mailing Add: 221 Bridge St, Conemaugh, Pa. 15909.

JOSEPH, WILLIAM FRANCIS, JR. R
Mem, Ala. State Rep. Exec. Cmt.
b. Montgomery, Ala, 6/15/29; s. William Francis Joseph, Sr. and Alice Pelzer J; m. 8/29/51 to Florence Hall; c. William F, III, Thomas Taylor and Charles Kinloch. Educ: Auburn Univ, B.A. in Archit, 52; Sigma Alpha Epsilon. Polit. & Govt. Pos: Mem, Montgomery Co. Rep. Exec. Cmt, Ala, 64-; cmnr, Montgomery Co. Bd. of Revenue, 64-, pres, 64-68, mem, 68-; mem, Ala. State Rep. Exec. Cmt, 65-; alternate del, Rep. Nat. Conv, 68. Bus. & Prof. Pos: Designer and draftsman, Morton & McElhaney, Montgomery, 54-61, partner, Morton, McElhaney & Joseph, Architects and Engrs, 61-62, Morton & Joseph, 62- Mil. Serv: Entered as Pvt, Army, 52, released as Sgt, 54, after serv. in 682nd Eng. Bn. Mem: Ala. and Nat. Am. Insts. of Architects; Am. Rd. Builders Asn; Ala. and Am. Asns. of Co. Cmnr; Capital City Kiwanis Club; Montgomery Co. Cattlemen's Asn. Rel: Presbyterian. Legal Res: 3230 Thomas Ave, Montgomery, Ala. 36106. Mailing Add: 429 S. Decatur St, Montgomery, Ala. 36104.

JOSLIN, ROGER R
Chmn, McLean Co. Rep. Cent. Cmt, Ill.
b. Bloomington, Ill, 6/21/36; s. James Clifford Joslin (deceased) and Doris McLaflin J; m. 6/14/58 to Stephany Moore; c. Scott and Jill. Educ: Miami Univ, B.S. in Bus, 58; Univ. Ill. Col. Law, Urbana, J.D, 61; Phi Beta Kappa; Omicron Delta Kappa; Beta Alpha Psi; Beta Sigma Pi; Phi Eta Sigma; Phi Delta Phi; Sigma Phi Epsilon. Polit. & Govt. Pos: Pres, McLean Co. Young Rep. Club, Ill, 64-66; dir, Rep. Workshops of Ill, 65-67; dist. gov, Ill. Young Rep, 65-67; chmn, McLean Co. Rep. Cent. Cmt, 66-; del, Rep. Nat. Conv, 68; v.pres, Ill. Rep. Co. Chmn. Asn, 68- Bus. & Prof. Pos: Attorney, Davis, Morgan & Witherell, Peoria, Ill, 61-63; controller, Union Ins. Group, Bloomington, 63-64; dir, Normal State Bank, 64-67; asst. v.pres, State Farm Mutual Automobile Ins. Co, Bloomington, 64- Mem: Am, Ill. State and McLean Co. Bar Asns; Ill. Soc. CPA; Dir, Bloomington Asn. Commerce, 67- Rel: Methodist. Mailing Add: 2001 E. Cloud St, Bloomington, Ill. 61701.

JOSSERAND, ROBERT WARREN R
Chmn, Pratt Co. Rep. Cent. Cmt, Kans.
b. Gray Co, Kans, 8/31/96; s. John F. Josserand and Anna Dulin J; m. 10/7/23 to Helen Douglas; c. Robert Douglas and James Rolf. Educ: Cimmeron High Sch, Kans, grad. Polit. & Govt. Pos: Chmn, Pratt Co. Rep. Cent. Cmt, Kans, 59-; del, Rep. Nat. Conv, 60; mem-at-lg, Electoral Col, 68. Bus. & Prof. Pos: Sch. teacher, 20-21 & 22; retail bus, 23-40; land owner and livestock, 40-69. Mil. Serv: Entered as Pvt, 20th Inf, Army, 18-19. Mem: Mason; Shrine; Elks; Lions Int; Am. Legion; C. of C; Farm Bur. Yearly State Awards for polit. achievement in leadership and finances, past 10 years. Rel: Methodist. Mailing Add: 1001 Random Rd, Pratt, Kans. 67124.

JOVA, JOSEPH JOHN
U.S. Ambassador to the Orgn. of Am. States
b. Newburgh, N.Y, 11/7/16; s. Joseph Luis Jova and Maria Josefa Gonzalez-Cavada; m. 2/2/49 to Pamela Johnson; c. Henry Christopher, John Thomas and Margaret Ynes. Educ: Dartmouth Col, A.B, 38; Sigma Phi Epsilon. Polit. & Govt. Pos: Career Officer, U.S. Dept. of State For. Serv, 47-; v.consul, Basra, 47-49; second secy, v.consul, Tangier, 49-52; consul, Oporto, 52-54; first secy, Lisbon, 54-57; officer-in-charge, French-Iberian Affairs, 57-58; attended Sr. Sem. in For. Policy, For. Serv. Inst, 58-59; asst. chief personnel opers. div, 59-60, chief, 60-61; counselor, Santiago, Chile, 61-65; U.S. Ambassador to Honduras, 65-69 and Orgn. of Am. States, 69- Bus. & Prof. Pos: Asst. overseer and div. inspector, fruit co, Guatamala, 38-41. Mil. Serv: Entered as Ens, Naval Res, 42, released as Lt, 46, after serv. in Am. and European Theaters. Mem: U.S. For. Serv. Asn; Am. Soc. Pub. Admin; Rotary; K. of M; Order of Morazan, Honduras. Rel: Roman Catholic. Legal Res: c/o First National Bank, Ft. Lauderdale, Fla. 33310. Mailing Add: ARA/OAS, Dept. of State, Washington, D.C. 20520.

JOY, MICHAEL BILL D
b. Las Vegas, N.Mex, 3/16/44; s. Minus Berg Joy and Ruth Boatwright Johnson J. Educ: Univ. South Carolina, 62-66, B.A, Econ, 66; Nat. Collegiate Press Asn; Chi Psi Euphradian Debating Soc. Polit. & Govt. Pos: Legis. asst, U.S. Senator Ernest F. Hollings, S.C, 66-68, admin. asst, 69- Mem: Asn. Admin. Assts. Outstanding Collegiate Columnist, 66. Legal Res: 901 Sumter St, Columbia, S.C. 29201. Mailing Add: 432 Senate Office Bldg, Washington, D.C. 20510.

JOYCE, ALBERT JOHN, JR. D
Chmn, C.Z. Regional Dem. Cent. Cmt.
b. Ancon, C.Z, 9/19/32; s. Albert John Joyce and Mary Gertrude Mulrey J; m. 12/19/59 to Maria Victoria Faraudo; c. Albert John, III and Richard Michael. Educ: The Citadel, Mil. Col. S.C, B.A, 54; Univ. S.C. Sch. Law, LL.B, 60; Pi Sigma Alpha; Phi Alpha Delta; Int. Rel. Club, The Citadel. Polit. & Govt. Pos: Intel. analyst, Dept. of Army, U.S. Army Caribbean, 56-57; v.chmn, C.Z. Regional Dem. Cent. Cmt, 60-62, chmn, 62-; acting Pub. Defender, C.Z. Govt, 66; del, Dem. Nat. Conv, 68. Bus. & Prof. Pos: Attorney at law, C.Z, 60- Mil. Serv: Entered as 2nd Lt, Army, 54, released as 1st Lt, 56, after serv. in Ft. Amador, C.Z, Far East Command, 55-56; Maj, Army Res, currently. Publ: Acting sports page ed, Star & Herald, 56-57; contributing sports writer, Panama Am, 60- Mem: ROA; Am. Bar Asn; Fed. Bar Asn.(third v.pres, C.Z. Chap, 70); C.Z. Bar Asn.(secy, 65-66, v.pres, 68, pres, 69). Legal Res: Nuevo Campo Alegre, Panama. Mailing Add: P.O. Box 615, Balboa, C.Z.

JOYCE, DANIEL L, JR. D
Mass. State Rep.
b. Woburn, Mass, 5/14/34; s. Daniel L. Joyce, Sr. and Mary E. Logan J; m. 4/23/60 to Beverly F. Hubert; c. Colleen, Daniel L, III, Patricia and Michael. Educ: Boston Col, B.S. and B.A; Suffolk Law Sch, LL.B. Polit. & Govt. Pos: Mass. State Rep, 22nd Middlesex Dist, 69- Bus. & Prof. Pos: Claims adjuster, Gen. Accident Co, Boston, 64; attorney, self employed, Woburn, 64- Mil. Serv: Entered as Pvt, Army, 53, released as Cpl, 55, after serv. in Eighth Army. Mem: Am, Middlesex and Mass. Bar Asns; Lions; K. of C. Rel: Catholic. Legal Res: 10 Revere Rd, Woburn, Mass. 01801. Mailing Add: 269 Main St, Woburn, Mass. 01801.

JOYCE, ROBERT H. D
Chmn, Grant Co. Dem. Cmt, Kans.
b. Ulysses, Kans, 4/25/18; s. Richard H. Joyce and Estell E. Towler; m. 8/28/39 to Myrna E. Reeves; c. Robert H, Jr, Richard M. and Rebecca. Educ: Kans. State Univ, B.S. in eng, 40; Theta Chi. Polit. & Govt. Pos: Mem, Grant Co. Dem. Cmt, Kans, 58-64; chmn, 64- Bus. & Prof. Pos: Draftsman, Navy, 40-41; engr, Soil Conserv. Serv, 41-43; commun. committeeman, Agr. Stabilization & Conserv. Serv, 54-64. Mil. Serv: Entered as Pvt, Army Corps Eng, 43, released as T-4, 45, after serv. in 1375th Engr. Petrol. Dist. Co, EAME, 44-45; EAME Theater Ribbon with Four Bronze Serv. Stars; Victory and Good Conduct Medals. Mem: Am. Soc. of Agr. Engrs; Mason; Am. Legion; VFW. Rel: Methodist. Mailing Add: Star Route 2, Hugoton, Kans. 67951.

JOYNER, CONRAD FRANCIS R
City Councilman, Tucson, Ariz.
b. Connersville, Ind, 10/21/31; s. Hubert Williams Joyner and Louise Ariens J; m. 7/9/55 to Arabella Ann Maxey; c. Conrad Francis, Jr, Michael Joseph and Mark Maxey. Educ: Earlham Col, B.A, 53; Univ. Fla, M.A, 54, Ph.D, 57; Univ. Sydney, 55-56; Phi Beta Kappa; Phi Eta Sigma; Tau Kappa Alpha; Pi Sigma Alpha. Polit. & Govt. Pos: Rep. precinct committeeman, Fayette Co, Ind, 52-54; 10th Dist. Young Rep. Chmn, Ind, 52-54; mem, Gov. and Sen. Mark O. Hatfield's Staff, Ore, 60-61 and summers 64 & 68;mgr, Richard Burke's Cong. Campaign, Ariz, 62; co-mgr, Lew Davis' Campaign for Mayor, Tucson, Ariz, 63; Rep. ward committeeman, Tucson, 63-; dir. arts and sci. div, Ariz. Rep. State Cent. Cmt, 63-; mem, Congressman Ogden Reid's Staff, Wash. D.C, summer 65; Rep. precinct committeeman, Pima Co, Ariz, 66-; mem, Ariz. Rep. State Cent. Cmt, 66-; city councilman, Tucson, 67-; alternate del, Rep. Nat. Conv, 68. Bus. & Prof. Pos: Instr, W.Va. Univ, 56-57; from asst. prof. to assoc. prof, Univ. Southwest. La, 57-61; from assoc. prof. to prof, Univ. Ariz, 61- Publ: The Republican Dilemma, Univ. Ariz, 63; The Commonwealth and Monopolies, F.W. Cheshire, Melbourne and London, 63; The American Democratic Politician, Nat. Press, 69. Mem: Am. Polit. Sci. Asn; South. Polit. Sci. Asn; West. Polit. Sci. Asn; Am. Asn. Univ. Prof; Ariz. League Cities and Towns; NAACP; Coun. on Orgn. Ariz. State Govt; Tucson Coun. Civic Unity; Lighthouse YMCA; mem. bd, Holy Cross House; Ariz. Acad. Fulbright Scholar, 55-56; John Henry Newman Honor Soc; Outstanding Young Men Am, Jr. C. of C, 64; Outstanding Male Faculty Mem, Univ. Ariz, 65; E. Harris Harbison Prize, Danforth Found, 67. Rel: Catholic. Mailing Add: 5322 E. Second St, Tucson, Ariz. 85711.

JOYNT, JOHN WILLIAM D
Mo. State Sen.
b. St. Louis, Mo, 1/3/99; s. John William Joynt and Nan Norris J; m. 1/24/20 to Helen Raines; c. Marilyn Frances (Mrs. Arthur F. Boettcher, Jr). Educ: Wash. Univ; City Col. of Law, LL.B. Polit. & Govt. Pos: Circuit Judge, St. Louis, Mo, 35-40; Mo. State Sen, 54-, Majority Leader, Mo. State Senate, 61-64, Pres. Pro Tem, 65-68. Bus. & Prof. Pos: Mem. firm, Bishop and Claiborne, 22-34; lawyer, 22- Mil. Serv: Army Training Corps. Rel: Protestant. Mailing Add: 3438 Russell Blvd, St. Louis, Mo. 63104.

JUAREZ, OSCAR F. R
b. Guatemala City, Guatemala, 6/28/40; s. Oscar A. Juárez and Helen D. J; m. Oct, 1964 to Nancy Plapp; c. Julia Elena. Educ: Stetson Univ, B.A, 63; Univ. Tenn, 64; Spanish Fraternity; Lambda Chi Alpha; Student Govt. Asn; Newman Club. Polit. & Govt. Pos: Treas, Young Rep. Club, Orange Co, Fla, 67-68; admin. asst. to U.S. Rep. Lou Frey, Jr, Fla, 69- Mil. Serv: Entered Army, 57, released as SP-3, 65, after serv. in Army Res. Mem: Civitan Club; Int. Jaycees; Fla. State Soc; Young Rep. Club; Am. for Constitutional Action;

bd. dirs, Lambda Chi Alpha. Ford Found. Scholarship, Grad. Assistantship. Rel: Roman Catholic. Legal Res: 2012 Merritt Park Dr, Orlando, Fla. 32803. Mailing Add: 7676 Tiverton Dr, Springfield, Va. 22150.

JUCKETT, ROBERT S. R
Ill. State Rep.
b. Evanston, Ill, 8/14/32; s. Harold F. Juckett and Gladyce Sewright J; m. 8/30/52 to Janet Taverner; c. Linda Kathryn, Robert S, Jr, William Howard and Pamela Ann. Educ: Oberlin Col, 49-51; Univ. Ill, B.S, 54, J.D, 58; Phi Delta Phi; Theta Delta Chi. Polit. & Govt. Pos: Asst. state attorney, Cook Co, Ill, 59-61; alternate del, Rep. Nat. Conv, 60; alderman, Park Ridge, Ill, 65; Ill. State Rep, 67- Bus. & Prof. Pos: Attorney-at-law; officer and dir, numerous corps. Mil. Serv: Entered as 2nd Lt, Army, released as 1st Lt, after serv. in ETO. Mem: Ill. and Am. Bar Asns; C. of C; Kiwanis; pres, Cent. Grad. Asn, Theta Delta Chi. Rel: Episcopal. Legal Res: 1823 W. Crescent, Park Ridge, Ill. 60068. Mailing Add: 720 Garden St, Park Ridge, Ill. 60068.

JUDD, C. DeMONT, JR. D
Utah State Rep.
b. Kanab, Utah, 8/26/28; s. Clarence DeMont Judd, Sr. and Elizabeth DeLong J; m. 8/6/55 to Ramona Fay Stoven Covey; c. RoseMarie, Michelle, Jefferson DeMont, Jennifer Caye, Spencer Mark and Christopher Jourdan. Educ: Univ. Utah, J.D, 56. Polit. & Govt. Pos: Utah State Rep, 69- Mil. Serv: Entered as Pvt, Army, 51, released as Pfc, 53, after serv. in Med. Corps. Mem: Am. Bar Asn; Nat. Asn. Defense Counsel in Criminal Cases. Rel: Latter-day Saint. Mailing Add: 1018 Fifth St, Ogden, Utah 84404.

JUDD, FRANK CASE R
Hawaii State Rep.
b. Honolulu, Hawaii, 5/30/15; s. Henry Pratt Judd and Martha Case J; m. 9/16/47 to Sarah Frances Mann; c. Laura Mann and Frank C, Jr. Educ: Univ. Hawaii, 32-36; Stanford Univ, 36-37; Phi Delta Theta. Polit. & Govt. Pos: Hawaii Territorial Rep, 58-59; Hawaii State Rep, 59-, Minority Floor Leader, Hawaii State House of Rep, 66-68. Mil. Serv: Entered as 1st Lt, Army, 42, released as Capt, 45, after serv. in Pac. Wing, Air Transport Command, Pac; Bronze Star. Rel: Congregational. Mailing Add: 951 Makaiwa St, Honolulu, Hawaii 96815.

JUDD, WALTER HENRY R
b. Rising City, Nebr, 9/25/98; s. Horace Hunter Judd and Mary Elizabeth Greenslit J; m. 3/13/32 to Miriam Louise Barber; c. Mary Lou (Mrs. Norman R. Carpenter), Carolyn Ruth and Eleanor Grace (Mrs. Paul Quinn). Educ: Univ. Nebr, B.A, 20, M.D, 23; Mayo Found, Univ. Minn, fel. in surg, 32-34; Phi Beta Kappa, Alpha Omega Alpha; Phi Rho Sigma; Omicron Delta Kappa; Alpha Kappa Psi. Hon. Doctorate degrees, including LL.D, D.S, D.Litt, L.H.D, D.C.L, D.S.W, D.H.S. and D.D. from 26 univs. and cols. Polit. & Govt. Pos: U.S. Rep, Fifth Dist, Minn, 43-62; U.S. del. to UN 12th Gen. Assembly; founder of Rep. Workshops. Bus. & Prof. Pos: Instr. zool, Univ. Omaha, 20-24, intern, Univ. Omaha Hosp, 22-24; traveling secy, Student Vol. Movement in cols. and univs, 24-25; med. missionary, Nanking, China, 25-26, Shaowu, Fukien, 26-31 and Fenchow, Shansi, 34-38; lectr. in U.S, 39-40; physician and surgeon, Minneapolis, 41-42; contributing ed, Readers Digest, 63-; commentator, Wash. Report of the Air, Am. Security Coun, 64- Mil. Serv: Entered as Pvt, Army, 18, released as 2nd Lt, 19, after serv. in Field Artil. Mem: Am. Med. Asn.(mem. judicial coun); Minn. Med. Asn; Am. Acad. Gen. Practice; hon. fel, Int. Col. Surgeons; China Soc; founder, Aid Refugee Chinese Intellectuals, Inc; co-founder, World Neighbors, Inc; v.chmn, Am. Emergency Cmt. for Tibetan Refugees, Inc; v.pres, Am. Bur. for Med. Aid to China; dir, Goodwill Industs, Inc; chmn. bd. of adv, Augsburg Col; Am. Legion; Mason (33°); YMCA (dir. Metrop. Bd, Wash, D.C); hon. mem, Rotary. Distinguished Serv. Awards, Univ. Nebr, 45 and Am. Med. Asn, 61; George Washington Hon. Medals, Freedom Found, 61 & 62; CARE-MEDICO World Humanitarian Award, 62; Great Living Am. Award, U.S. C. of C. and Silver Buffalo Award, Boy Scouts, 63. Mailing Add: 3083 Ordway St. N.W, Washington, D.C. 20008.

JUDE, VICTOR N. Non-Partisan
Minn. State Sen.
b. 3/11/23; married; c. nine. Educ: St. Thomas Col, B.A. in Bus. Admin; Univ. Minn, grad. work. Polit. & Govt. Pos: Minn. State Rep, 57-67; Minn. State Sen, 67-; alternate del, Dem. Nat. Conv, 68. Bus. & Prof. Pos: Wholesale candy and tobacco distributor. Mem: Bd, Wright Co. Retirement Asn; Lions; K. of C; PTA; Sportsmen, Wright Co; Agr. Asn, Wright Co; Am. Legion; VFW; Am. Asn. of UN (former bd. mem, Minn. Br). Mailing Add: Maple Lake, Minn. 55358.

JUDGE, JIM ERVIN R
State Committeeman, Idaho State Rep. Cent. Cmt.
b. Springfield, Idaho, 4/1/09; s. William Patrick Judge and Anna Battle J; m. 9/14/35 to Priscilla Marriott. Educ: Idaho State Col. Polit. & Govt. Pos: Chmn, Idaho State Rep. Cent. Cmt, Bonner Co, 60-68, State Committeeman, 68-; del. Rep. Nat. Conv, 64, alternate del, 68. Bus. & Prof. Pos: Instr, Farragut Col, 47-49 and Idaho State Col, 49-55. Mem: Elks; Nat. Farm Bureau; Int. Brotherhood Elec. Workers; v.chmn, Soil Conservation Dist. Bd. Rel: Catholic. Mailing Add: Route 1, Sagle, Idaho 83860.

JUDGE, THOMAS LEE D
Lt. Gov, Mont.
b. Helena, Mont, 10/12/34; s. Thomas Patrick Judge (deceased) and Blanche Guillot J; m. 1/19/66 to Carol Ann Anderson; c. Thomas Warren. Educ: Univ. Notre Dame, B.A, 57; Univ. Louisville, Advert. Cert, 59. Polit. & Govt. Pos: Mont. State Rep, Lewis and Clark Co, 61-67, Mont. State Sen, 67-69; Lt. Gov, 69- Bus. & Prof. Pos: Pres, Judge Advert, 60-; exec. secy, Mont. Broadcasters Asn, 61-, Mont. Chap, Am. Ins. Asn, 65-, Mont. Savings & Loan League, 65- and Mont. Optom. Asn, 67; advert. and sales mgr, Glacier Park Inc, 65- Mil. Serv: 2nd Lt, Army, Adj. Gen. Corps, Ft. Benjamin Harrison, Ind, 58, Capt, Res. Mem: Pub. Rels. Soc. Am; Elks; Eagles; K. of C; Exchange Club; Jaycee; C. of C. Distinguished Serv. Award, 63; Notre Dame Man of the Year, 66; Outstanding Young Man of Year, Mont. Jaycees, 67. Rel: Catholic. Legal Res: 219 Geddis Ave, Helena, Mont. 59602. Mailing Add: State Capitol Bldg, Helena, Mont. 59601.

JUEDEMAN, RUDOLPH F. R
b. Bristow, Okla, 5/11/08; s. William Henry Juedeman and Caroline Stienbeck J; m. 6/10/33 to Ithai M. Isbell; c. Lynne Carol. Polit. & Govt. Pos: Mont. State Rep, 52-58, Minority Leader, Mont. House of Rep, 56-58; chmn, Mont. State Rep. Party and nat. committeeman, 56-58; dep. chmn, Tex. State Rep. Party and state committeeman, 29th Sen. Dist, 64-68; del, Rep. Nat. Conv,68. Mem: Mason (32°); Shrine; Elks; Kiwanis; Farm Bur; U.S. C. of C; Odessa C. of C. Rel: Methodist. Legal Res: 1506 Idlewood Lane, Odessa, Tex. 79760. Mailing Add: 300 First National Bank, Odessa, Tex. 79760. (1967)

JUEL, ORRIN PERRINE R
b. Canton, S.Dak, 9/25/17; s. Melvin P. Juel and Clara Ellefson J; m. 7/7/51 to Mildred Aurelia Skyberg; c. Alan Paul, Perry Rolf and Karen Elizabeth. Educ: S.Dak. State Univ, 35; Westminster Choir Col, N.J, B.M; Acad. Adv. Traffic, N.Y, Traffic Mgt; Alpha Psi Omega. Polit. & Govt. Pos: Chmn, Planning Cmn, Brookings, S.Dak, 65, Rep. precinct committeeman, 67-; alternate del, Rep. Nat. Conv, 68. Mem: Shrine; Mason; Elks; pres, C. of C, 64; pres, Rotary, 67. Rel: Lutheran. Mailing Add: 621 Eighth St, Brookings, S.Dak. 57006.

JUELFS, STANLEY R. R
Chmn, Kimball Co. Rep. Cmt, Nebr.
b. Cheyenne Co, Nebr, 10/17/28; s. Lloyd A. Juelfs Sr. and Doris Hagemeister J; m. 8/6/50 to Donna L. Terman; c. Dallen R, Julie A. and Lori S. Educ: Nebr. Wesleyan Univ, 1 year; Theta Chi. Polit. & Govt. Pos: Mem. city coun, Potter, Nebr, 54-60; mem, Airport Authority Bd, Kimball, 62-64; mem. agr. bd, Kimball Co, 67-; chmn, Kimball Co. Rep. Cmt, 68- Bus. & Prof. Pos: Owner and operator, Stan's Propane Co, Potter, Nebr, 50-57, Buffalo Bend Motel & Cafe, 57-60; operator and builder, Motel Kimball, Kimball, 60-64; owner and mgr, Juelfs Ins. Agency, 64-67; pub. rels. officer and ins. dir, Am. Nat. Bank, 67- Mem: exec. v.pres, of the bd, Nebr. Panhandle Resource Conserv. and Develop. Proj; Aircraft Owners & Pilots Asn. Nebr. Thoroughbred Breeders Asn; Rotary Int; Mason; past pres, Kimball C. of C; Kimball Country Club (pres, 69). Rel: Methodist. Legal Res: 1110 E. Third, Kimball, Nebr. 69145. Mailing Add: Box 81, Kimball, Nebr. 69145.

JUELING, HELMUT L. R
Wash. State Rep.
b. Loup City, Nebr, 1913; m. to Ruth; c. Two daughters. Educ: Univ. of Puget Sound, B.A. Polit. & Govt. Pos: Wash. State Rep, currently. Bus. & Prof. Pos: Owner, laundry and linen supply bus. Mailing Add: 215 Contra Costa, Tacoma, Wash. 98409. (1967)

JUERGENS, WILLIAM G. R
b. Steeleville, Ill, 9/7/04; s. H.F. William Juergens and Mathilda Nolte J; m. 12/14/29 to Helen A. Young, wid; m. 3/18/67 to Charlotte Louise Mann; c. Jane (Mrs. Donald L. Hays) and William G, M.D. Educ: Carthage Col, A.B, 25; Univ. Mich, J.D, 28. Polit. & Govt. Pos: City attorney, Chester, Ill, 30-38; Co. judge, Randolph Co, Ill, 38-50; judge, Third Judicial Circuit Court, Ill, 51-56; U.S. dist. judge, East. Dist, Ill, 56-65, chief judge, 65- Mem: Randolph Co. and Ill. Bar Asns; Fed. Bar Asn; Bar Asn. of the Seventh Judicial Circuit; Mason; Scottish Rite; Shrine; Eastern Star; Lions. Rel: Presbyterian. Mailing Add: 1836 Swanwick St, Chester, Ill. 62233.

JULIA, GILDA R
Rep. Nat. Committeewoman, P.R.
b. San Juan, P.R, 11/18/27; d. Enrique Juliá and Emily Martinez J; div; c. Maria Emilia, Luis Esteban, Jr, Mario Enrique, Maria Luisa, Andrés Eduardo, Miguel Antonio and Maria Alexandra. Educ: Col. of Sacred Heart, 44-46; Univ. Va, 47-48. Polit. & Govt. Pos: Del, Rep. Nat. Conv, 68; Rep. Nat. Committeewoman, P.R, 69- Bus. & Prof. Pos: Mem. staff, Condominium Enterprises, Inc, Castle Enterprises, Inc, San Juan Realty Corp, City Enterprises, Inc, Center Enterprises Inc, Caparra Enterprises, Inc. and Ceramic Enterprises, Inc. Mem: Sleepy Hollow Country Club, N.Y; Boulder Brook Club, N.Y. Rel: Catholic. Legal Res: 37 Mallorca St, Hato Rey, P.R. 00917. Mailing Add: Box 11605, Santurce, P.R. 00910.

JUMANI, BETH VIRGINIA R
Mem, Calif. Rep. State Cent. Cmt.
b. Peoria, Ill, 3/26/34; d. Howard M. Marshall and Jessa Sopher M; m. 5/14/60 to Zamir 'Zim' Ahmed Jumani; c. Shahzadee 'Dee Dee' and Daud 'Bubby'. Educ: Marycrest Col, 2 years; Univ. of Kans. City, 1 year. Polit. & Govt. Pos: Secy, West Orange Co. Young Rep, Calif, 64-65 & 69-, press and pub. rels. secy, 66- and second v.pres; mem, Calif. Rep. State Cent. Cmt, 69- Publ: Various press releases and by-lines. Mem: Los Angeles Co. Legal Secy; Nat. Secy. Asn. Rel: Presbyterian. Mailing Add: 8422 Denni, Cypress, Calif. 90630.

JUMP, HARRY V. R
b. Bellevue, Ohio, 11/7/14; s. Otto V. Jump and LuLa C. Bell J; m. 11/26/37 to Leora Victoria Jacobs; c. James R, Michael M, David A, Deborah V. and Leora Ann. Educ: Bluffton Col, A.B, 36. Polit. & Govt. Pos: Mem, Huron Co. Rep. Exec. Cmt, Ohio, 47-69; co. cmnr, Huron Co, 49-56; Ohio State Rep, Huron Co, 57-66, Majority Whip, Ohio House of Rep, 61-66; Ohio State Sen, 13th Dist, 67-68. Bus. & Prof. Pos: Owner of gen. ins. agency, 46- Mem: Pres, Ohio Asn. of Co. Cmnr, 52; dir, Huron Co. Automobile Club, 65-; Ohio Asn. of Ins. Agents; Ohio Asn. of Real Estate Bd; Rotary (past pres); Mason (32°); Shrine; Willard Golf Club; Elks; Eagles; Moose. Rel: Methodist. Mailing Add: 221 E. Howard St, Willard, Ohio 44890. (1967)

JUNGCLAUS, WALTER C. Conservative
married; c. Three. Polit. & Govt. Pos: Clerk and constable, Glencoe Twp, Minn, 12 years, Co. Cmnr, 8 years, clerk, Sch. Dist. 60, 11 years, mem, Co. Welfare Bd, 7 years, mem, Pub. Health Bd, 8 years, mem, City Coun, Glencoe, 3 years and mayor, 2 years; Minn. State Rep, 59-68. Bus. & Prof. Pos: Pres, Glencoe Tile Co; charter mem, dir, v.pres-chmn, secy, McLeod Coop. Power Asn, 16 years. Mem: Glencoe Civic and Commerce Asn; Izaak Walton League; Glencoe Game Protective League; Gopher Campfire Club; Brownton Rod and Gun Club. Rel: Lutheran. Mailing Add: 1627 Greeley, Glencoe, Minn. 55336. (1967)

JUNGHANS, ROBERT WILLIAM D
b. Petaluma, Calif, 3/5/43; s. William Paul Junghans and Olga Applebee J; m. 5/2/64 to Eilseen Gaye Swenson; c. Heidi Jo. Educ: Univ. Minn, Duluth, 65; Winona State Col, B.A, 69; Harvard Law Sch, 69- Polit. & Govt. Pos: Wis-Minn. coordinator for Eugene McCarthy, 68; alternate del, Dem. Nat. conv, 68; co. coordinator, Gunnar Gundersen Cong. Campaign, 68. Bus. & Prof. Pos: Newspaper writer, Mankato Free Press, Minn, 64, News-Tribune, Duluth, 65 and Winona Daily News, 66-69. Mailing Add: Route 1, Trempealeau, Wis. 54661.

JUNGROTH, JAMES RALPH D
b. Jamestown, N.Dak, 9/10/25; s. W. Jungroth and Florence Baenen J; m. 6/9/61 to Dolores R. Taszarek; c. Eric James. Educ: Presby. Col. S.C, 43; Jamestown Col, 46-47; Univ. N.Dak, Ph.B. and LL.B, 50; Phi Delta Phi. Polit. & Govt. Pos: Stutsman Co. Chmn, N.Dak. Non-Partisan League, 58-61, N.Dak. State chmn, 61-67; Stutsman Co. States attorney, 61-63; chmn, N.Dak. Dem-Non-Partisan League State Cent. Cmt, 62-67; N.Dak. State Rep, 65-66. Bus. & Prof. Pos: Partner, Mackenzie & Jungroth, 52- Mil. Serv: Entered as Pvt, Army Air Force, 43, released as Pfc, 46. Mem: Elks; Am. Legion. Rel: Unitarian. Legal Res: 910 Eighth Ave. N.W, Jamestown, N.Dak. 58401. Mailing Add: P.O. Box 1367, Jamestown, N.Dak. 58401.

JUNKIN, JOHN RICHARD D
Miss. State Rep.
b. Natchez, Miss, 12/16/96; married. Polit. & Govt. Pos: Mem, Bd. of Supvr, Natchez, Miss, 28-36; Miss. State Rep, 44- Bus. & Prof. Pos: Contractor; Planter. Mem: Am. Legion. Rel: Catholic. Mailing Add: 311 N. Wall St, Natchez, Miss. 39120. (1967)

JUNKINS, F. LeROY R
N.H. State Rep.
b. Chester, Vt; 8/14/98; married. Educ: Univ. of N.H. Polit. & Govt. Pos: Treas, Exeter, N.H, 32 years; N.H. State Rep, currently. Bus. & Prof. Pos: Pres, Exeter Indust. Develop. Corp. Mil. Serv: World War I. Mem: Mason; Am. Legion; World War I Vet; trustee, Tri-Co. Hosp, Kittery, Maine. Rel: Protestant. Mailing Add: Hampton Rd, Exeter, N.H. 03833. (1967)

JURCICH, FRANK JOHN D
Mont. State Rep.
b. Anaconda, Mont, 1/4/31; s. Frank John Jurcich and Anna Butko J; single. Educ: Anaconda Central High Sch, 4 years. Polit. & Govt. Pos: Mont. State Rep, Dist. 22B, 67- Bus. & Prof. Pos: Railroad Conductor. Mil. Serv: Entered as Pvt, Air Force, 48, released as Cpl, 49, after serv. in Fourth Air Force. Mem: United Transportation Union; K. of C. (4°). Rel: Roman Catholic. Legal Res: 1006 East Third, Anaconda, Mont. 59711. Mailing Add: P.O. Box 257, Anaconda, Mont. 59711.

JURGELLA, RICHARD EDWARD D
b. Stevens Point, Wis, 6/6/40; s. Joseph John Jurgella and Mary Lucey Pestka J; single. Educ: High Sch; Col. Exten. Courses. Polit. & Govt. Pos: Treas, Portage Co. Dem. Party, Wis, 63-64, chmn, 64-69. Mil. Serv: Entered as Airman Basic, Air Force, 59, released as Airman 1/C, 62, after serv. in 497th Reconnaissance Tech. Squadron, 60-62; Good Conduct Medal. Mem: Izaak Walton League of Wis; Moose; Elks; K. of C; Lions; Jaycees. Selected for the Outstanding Young Man of Am. Award. Rel: Roman Catholic. Mailing Add: R.R. 2, Box 569, Stevens Point, Wis. 54481. (1967)

JURICH, ANTHONY J. R
Spec. Asst. to the Secy. of Treas. for Nat. Security Affairs
b. Floral Park, N.Y, 10/15/26; s. Anthony Jurich and Julia Mustapich J; m. 7/1/50 to Florence G. Anselmo; c. Julia Marie. Educ: St. Bonaventure Col, 1 year; Hofstra Univ, B.S. Polit. & Govt. Pos: Mem. prfnl. staff, Nat. Security Affairs, U.S. House of Rep, 63-66; for. and defense policy adv, Rep. Platform Cmt. and Campaign Staff, 64; staff dir, Nat. Security Affairs Key Issues Cmt, Nixon Campaign, 68; mem, White House Transition Staff, 69; spec. asst. to the Secy. of Treas. for Nat. Security Affairs, 69- Bus. & Prof. Pos: Mgt. staff. eng, planning and mgt, Sperry Gyroscope Co, 50-61; sr. assoc, Robert C. Sellers & Assocs, 61-64; pres, Pramac Assocs, 66-68. Mil. Serv: Army, with serv. in 43rd and First Cavalry Inf. Div, Pac. Theatre, 44-46. Rel: Roman Catholic. Legal Res: Springfield, Va. Mailing Add: Dept. of the Treasury, Washington, D.C. 20220.

JUSTICE, CLARENCE WAYNE D
b. Ree Heights, S.Dak, 8/28/23; s. Charles Emmett Justice and Anna Zemlicka J; m. 10/22/55 to Phyllis Catherine Dolan. Polit. & Govt. Pos: Secy-treas, Grant Co. Dem. Cent. Cmt, S.Dak, 58-61, chmn, 61-69. Bus. & Prof. Pos: Asst. ed, Grant Co. Rev, 57- Mil. Serv: Entered as A/S, Navy, 42, released as Radioman 3/C, 45, after serv. in Great Lakes-Patuxent River Naval Air Sta. and Am, African, European and Asiatic Theaters; Am, ETO and Pac. Theater Ribbons; Good Conduct and Victory Medals. Mem: Sigma Delta Chi (v.pres, S.Dak. Chap); Milbank Commerce and Commun. Club (past pres); Kiwanis Int.(mem. bd. dirs); Am. Legion (first v.comdr); VFW; dir, Co. Red Cross Bd; K. of C.(ed. of State KC Bul, 60-67); Rel: Catholic. Mailing Add: 802 S. Fourth St, Milbank, S.Dak. 57252.

JUSTICE, WILLIAM WAYNE D
b. Athens, Tex, 2/25/20; s. William D. Justice and Jackie May Hanson J; m. 3/16/47 to Sue Tom Ellen Rowan; c. Ellen Rowan. Educ: Univ. Tex, LL.B, 42. Polit. & Govt. Pos: V.Pres, Young Dem, Tex, 48; Athens City Attorney, 48-50 & 52-58; mem. adv. coun, Dem. Nat. Cmt, 54; alternate del, Dem. Nat. Conv, 56; presidential elector, 60; U.S. attorney, East. Dist, Tex, 61-69; U.S. Dist. Judge, East. Dist. Tex, 69- Bus. & Prof. Pos: Partner law firm, Justice & Justice, 46-61. Mil. Serv: Served as 1st Lt, FA, AUS, 42-46. Mem: VFW; Rotary; Mason. Rel: Baptist. Legal Res: 4001 Old Bullard Rd, Tyler, Tex. 75701. Mailing Add: P.O. Box 330, Tyler, Tex. 75701.

JUTRAS, PHILIP L. D
Maine State Rep.
b. Amesbury, Mass, 6/23/16; s. A. Jutras (deceased) and M. Roy J. (deceased); m. to Harriett McGrath; c. Phyllis (Mrs. Broyer), Sandra, David, P. and Corinne. Educ: Univ. Montreal, 6 years; St. Bernard's Sem, Rochester, N.Y, 2 years; Univ. Paris, 1 year. Polit. & Govt. Pos: Maine State Sen, 65-67, chmn, Cmt. on Sea and Shore Fisheries and Lobster Interim Study and mem, Joint Legis. Cmt. on Claims and on Vet. and Mil. Affairs and Intergovt. Rels. Cmn, Maine State Senate; mem, Maine Mil. Defense Cmn, 67-; justice of the peace and notary pub, Sanford, Maine, currently; Maine State Rep, 69-, mem, Cmt. on Sea and Shore Fisheries, Maine House of Rep. Bus. & Prof. Pos: Former funeral dir, Mass, Maine and N.H; theatre mgr, currently. Mil. Serv: Entered as recruit, Army, 41, released as Chief Warrant Officer, 61, after serv. in Eighth Coast Artil. Corps, Ft. Preble, Maine, and in Normandy, summer 44 and Korea, 46-48 and as Persia mem, U.S. Mil. Mission, Tehran, Iran, 49-50, instr, Adj. Gen. Sch. and Capt, Adj. Gen. Corps, 50-53; Chief Warrant Officer, Army Res, 48-61; ETO Medal with Three Battle Stars; Six Serv. Ribbons. Publ: 'Education on Grange Project', Sanford Tribune, 68- Mem: Serv. officer, Cole Post 19, Am. Legion; legis. officer, Post 9935, VFW; educ. cmt, Maine State Grange. Legal Res: 23 School St, Sanford, Maine 04073. Mailing Add: P.O. Box 329, Sanford, Maine 04073.

JYMM, MONROE M. D
b. Tohatchi, N.Mex; 2/7/33; s. Dan White Jim, Jr. (deceased) and Marie Cinnajinnie J; m. 10/12/57 to Teresa B. Reil; c. Eleanor. Educ: St. Josephs Col, Ind, 54-56; Univ. N.Mex, 63. Polit. Pos: N.Mex. State Rep, 1st Dist, 65-67. Rel: Roman Catholic. Mailing Add: Tohlakai Trading Post, Gallup, N.Mex. 87301. (1967)

K

KAAN, NICOLAAS, JR. D
State Committeeman, Niobrara Co. Dem. Cent. Cmt, Wyo.
b. Lusk, Wyo, 8/20/30; s. Nick T. Kaan and Edith M. Eikenberry K; m. 7/14/62 to Anne Benner Pierce; c. Stephanie, Tracy and Christopher. Educ: Univ. Wyo, 48-49; Woodbury Col, B.B.A, 52; Phi Theta Pi. Polit. & Govt. Pos: Town clerk-treas, Lusk, Wyo, 62, town supvr, 66; mem, Resolution cmt. Wyo. State Conv, 64 & 66; co. chmn, Niobrara Co. Dem. Cent. Cmt, 64-66, state committeeman, 65-; alternate del, Dem. Nat. Conv, 64 & 68. Bus. & Prof. Pos: Mem. adv. bd, Univ. Wyo. Adult Educ. and Community Serv, currently. Mem: Univ. Wyo. Alumni Asn.(dir, 65-). Rel: Episcopal. Legal Res: 424 S. Main St, Lusk, Wyo. 82225. Mailing Add: P.O. Box 831, Lusk, Wyo. 82225.

KAAPU, KEKOA DAVID D
Councilman, City and Co. of Honolulu, Hawaii
b. Honolulu, Hawaii, 2/2/37; s. David M. Kaapu and Myrtle King K; m. to Diana; c. Kekoa, Jr. and Carole. Educ: Harvard Col, A.B. in Hist, 58; Pi Eta. Polit. & Govt. Pos: Admin. asst. to Gov. John A. Burns, Hawaii, 62-64; state pres, Young Dem. Clubs of Hawaii, 63-65; councilman, City and Co. of Honolulu, 65- Mil. Serv: Entered as 2nd Lt, Marine Corps, 58, released as Capt, 62. One of Hawaii's Three Outstanding Young Men, Jr. C. of C, 65. Rel: Unitarian. Legal Res: Kualoa, Kaaawa, Oahu, Hawaii 96730. Mailing Add: Star Route 450, Kaaawa, Hawaii 96730. (1967)

KADISH, PAUL YALE D
Mem. Exec. Bd, 19th Cong. Dist. Dem. Cmt, Mich.
b. Detroit, Mich, 7/16/36; s. Jack Kadish and Rose Fox K; m. 1/27/57 to Lorraine Estelle Londer; c. Ross Howard, Debra Ann and David Paul. Educ: Santa Monica City Col, 54; Wayne State Univ. B.S, 58; Detroit Col. Law, 69-; Kappa Nu (past pres). Polit. & Govt. Pos: Del, Dem. State Conv, since 64; campaign mgr, 14th State Sen. Dist, Mich, 66; chmn, Livonia Mich. Dem. Club, 66-69; alternate del, Mich. Dem. State Cent. Cmt, 67-69; mem. exec. bd, 19th Dist. Cong. Dem. Cmt, 67-; campaign mgr, 19th Dist. Cong. Campaign 68; alternate del, Dem. Nat. Conv, 68. Bus. & Prof. Pos: State gen. agent, Am. Income Life Ins. Co, 63-; partner, Kadish-Friedman Ins. Assoc, 68- Mem: Gen. Agents and Mgr. Asn; Nat, State and City Life Underwriters Asns; Ins. Workers Int. Union; Jaycees. Rel: Jewish. Mailing Add: 18687 Purling Brook, Livonia, Mich. 48152.

KADLEC, LUDGER D
b. Pisek, N.Dak, 3/26/12; s. Frank J. Kadlec and Mary Hodney K; m. 11/26/42 to Elaine Horejsi; c. Lawrence, Rodney and Kathren. Polit. & Govt. Pos: Sgt-at-arms, N.Dak. State Senate, 55, N.Dak. State Sen, 65-66; N.Dak. State Rep, 59-60; del, Dem. Nat. Conv, 68. Mem: K. of C; Eagles; Farmers Union; N.Dak. Stockmens Asn. Rel: Catholic. Mailing Add: Pisek, N.Dak. 58273. (1967)

KADUK, FRANK J. D
Chmn, Van Wert Co. Dem. Cent. Cmt, Ohio
b. Van Wert, Ohio, 11/14/16; s. Andrew Kaduk, Sr. and Anna Hritz K; m. 1/29/38 to Betty Joe Huston; c. Nancy Grayce, Paul Dean and Charles Lynn. Educ: Van Wert Pub. Schs, 12 years. Polit. & Govt. Pos: Third Ward Dem. councilman, Van Wert, Ohio, 58-60; city serv. dir, 60-62; Dem. precinct committeeman, Precinct 2-A, currently; chmn, Van Wert Co. Dem. Cent. Cmt, 67-; mem, Election Bd, Van Wert Co, 68- Bus. & Prof. Pos: Sales mgr, Frederick Dodge, 63-69; truck sales mgr, Bruce Symons Chevrolet-Oldsmobile, 69; employed in sales dept, Kennedy Mfg. Co, Van Wert, Ohio, 69- Mil. Serv: Entered as Pvt, Ohio Nat. Guard, 35, released as Sgt, 42, after serv. in B Co, 112th Med. Regt, 37th Div, Camp Shelby, Miss, 40-42. Mem: Chmn, Van Wert Auto Dealers; mem. bd. trustees and legis. action coun, C. of C; area 8 gov, Toastmasters Int; chmn. orgn. and exten. cmt, Boy Scouts; chmn, United Fund Cmt. Scouter of the Year award. Rel: Lutheran; Mo. Synod. Mailing Add: 628 N. Jefferson St, Van Wert, Ohio 45891.

KAESS, FRED W. R
b. Detroit, Mich, 12/1/10; s. Fred C. Kaess, Jr. and Dorothy Koch K; m. 12/31/31 to Phyllis Marie Danckmeyer; c. Fred Charles, III. Educ: Univ. Mich, 4 years; Detroit Col. Law, LL.B, 32; Wayne State Univ, hon. J.D, 61; Sigma Delta Kappa. Polit. & Govt. Pos: Justice of the Peace, St. Clair Shores, Mich, 32-33; pres, Lansing Young Men's Rep. Club, 36-40; nat. committeeman, Mich.Fedn. of Young Rep, 38-40; dep. cmnr, Workmen's Compensation Cmn. of Mich, 39-40; gen. counsel, Nat. Fedn. of Young Rep. and chmn, Midwest Conf. Young Rep, 40-42; Wayne Co. Rep. chmn, 48-52; U.S. Attorney, E Dist, Mich, 48-52, U.S. Dist. Judge, 60- Bus. & Prof. Pos: Lawyer, Mt. Clemens, Mich, 32-33; attorney and claims mgr, Mutual Liability

Co, Lansing, 33-45; attorney, Workmen's Compensation Cmn. and mem. law firm of Davidson, Kaess, Gotshall & Kelly, Detroit, 45-53. Mem: State Bar of Mich; Am. Bar Asn; Int. Asn. of Ins. Counsel; Fed. Bar Asn.(pres, Detroit Chap, 55-59); Econ. Club; Caravan Shrine Club; Noontide Club; Detroit Press Club; Crisis Club; F&AM; Consistory; Shrine; K.T. Outstanding Fed. Adminstr, 59; Award for Outstanding Achievement, Crisis Club, 60. Legal Res: 971 N. Oxford Rd, Grosse Pointe, Mich. 48236. Mailing Add: 851 Federal Bldg, Detroit, Mich. 48226.

KAESS, HELEN MARIE R
V.Chmn, Chaffee Co. Rep. Cent. Cmt, Colo.
b. Salida, Colo, 8/23/11; d. Frank Stewart Albright and Blanche Collins A; m. 2/1/30 to Cecil Walten Kaess; c. Louise (Mrs. Armstrong), Preston Frank and Louella (Mrs. Fitch). Educ: Salida High Sch, grad, 26. Polit. & Govt. Pos: V.chmn, Chaffee Co. Rep. Cent. Cmt, Colo, 52-; pres, Chaffee Co. Rep. Women's Club, 56-57 & 59-64, v.pres, 58; v.chmn, 59th Representative Dist. Rep. Party, 63-67, secy, 69-; v.chmn, 30th Sen. Dist. Rep. Party, 63-; v.chmn, Fourth Cong. Dist. Rep. Party, 63- Mem: Tuesday Eve. Club; Colo. Fedn. Women's Clubs (secy, 67, bd. dirs, 69); Sangre de Cristo Elec. Asn.(mem. bd, 42-53, secy, currently); 4-H (Chaffee Co. leader, 32-38). Rel: Methodist. Mailing Add: Adobe Park, R.R. 1, Box 346, Salida, Colo. 81201.

KAFKA, LADA JAMES D
b. Havre, Mont, 8/23/22; s. George Kafka and Josephine Rypal K; m. 6/7/44 to Sylvia Sara Schafer; c. Ladene Mae, Deitra Ann, Kim James and Dorcie Della. Educ: North. Mont. Col, 39-41. Polit. & Govt. Pos: Mem, co. cmt, Mont, 54-55, chmn, 56; mem, State Rev. Cmt, Agr. Stabilization & Conserv. Serv, 57-61; Mont. State Sen, Hill Co, 65-68. Bus. & Prof. Pos: Farmer and rancher, 41. Mem: Farmers Union; C. of C; Mason. Rel: Methodist. Mailing Add: Shambo Route, Havre, Mont. 59501. (1967)

KAFKA, LAWRENCE J. R
Wis. State Assemblyman
b. Denmark, Wis, 3/16/98. Educ: Langes Sch. Polit. & Govt. Pos: Mem, Brown Co. Sheriff's Cmt, Wis; supvr, New Denmark, 27-42, chmn, 42-; mem, Brown Co. Bd, 42-; chmn, Hwy. Cmt, 59-; chmn, Denmark War Mem. Bd; Wis. State Assemblyman, 64- Bus. & Prof. Pos: Farmer; pres, Trucking Firm. Mem: Elks; Holy Name Soc; Vet. Cmt; Steering and Advice Cmt; Health and Welfare Cmt. Heart Fund Drive. Mailing Add: Route 3, Denmark, Wis. 53208. (1967)

KAGAN, SAMUEL C. D
R.I. State Rep.
b. Russia, 11/11/08; m. to Ruth G. Polit. & Govt. Pos: Mem, Spec. Cmt. Study Ins. Laws, R.I; mem, Providence City Coun, 35-38; R.I. State Rep, 41-, Dep. Majority Leader, R.I. House Rep, 62-; del, Dem. Nat. Conv, 68. Bus. & Prof. Pos: Ins. Mem: Past pres, Order Hebraic Comradeship; Hebrew Free Loan Asn; bd. dirs, Congregation, Sons of Jacob; Ahavath Sholom Synagogue; Elks; AF&AM; RAM; Providence Hebrew Sheltering Soc; Jewish Home for Aged; Zionist Orgn. Am; B'nai B'rith; Roger Williams Lodge 1184. Rel: Hebrew. Mailing Add: 161 Orms St, Providence, R.I. 02908. (1967)

KAGLE, JOHN HENRY D
Committeeman, Ohio Dem. Cent. Cmt.
b. Canton, Ohio, 3/26/11; s. Michael Kagle and Mary Vogt K; m. 8/25/36 to Amelia Mildred Crock. Educ: McKinley High Sch, grad, 28; Business Col, 28-29. Polit. & Govt. Pos: Committeeman, Stark Co. Cent. Cmt, Ohio, 20 years; mem. exec. bd, Stark Co. Dem. Party, 10 years; del, Dem. Nat. Conv, 68; Committeeman, Ohio Dem. Cent. Cmt, currently. Bus. & Prof. Pos: Owner, The Kagle Agency, Canton, Ohio, 50- Mil. Serv: Entered as Pvt, Army, 43, released as Sgt, 46, after serv. in Ordinance Corp; Good Conduct Medal; Sharp Shooter. Mem: Bd. of Dirs, Catholic Community League; Catholic Mens Business Club; Am. Legion; 40 et 8; Elks; Jackson Dem. Club. Rel: Catholic. Mailing Add: 1338 19th St. N.E, Canton, Ohio 44714.

KAHALLEY, JAMEAL A. D
b. Bay Minette, Ala, 3/27/22; s. Assad Kahalley and Lydia A. Rayes K; m. 10/30/59 to Sondra Boykin; c. Laura, Diana and Paul. Educ: Gulf Coast Mil. Acad; Marion Inst; Univ. Ala; Phi Kappa Phi. Polit. & Govt. Pos: Mem, Dem. Nat. Cmt, 50-58; del, Dem. Nat. Conv, 64 & 68. Bus. & Prof. Pos: Real estate broker, J.A. Kahalley Co, 47-; v.pres, Mobile Warehousing Co, 62-; exec. mgr, Abeta Travel Serv, 65-; pres, JAK Hotel Corp, currently. Mil. Serv: Entered as Pvt, Army Air Force, 43, released as S/Sgt, after serv. in Third Air Force, 46. Mem: Mason; Shrine; York Rite; Elks; Am. Legion; C. of C; past pres, South Fedn. of Syrian-Lebanon-Am. Clubs. Rel: Episcopal. Legal Res: 310 McDonald Ave, Mobile, Ala. 36604. Mailing Add: P.O. Box 503, Mobile, Ala. 36601.

KAHLE, ALVIN R
Pa. State Rep.
b. Clarion Co, Pa, 11/7/09; s. Alexander E. Kahle and Myrtle Kribbs K; m. to Margaret Segui; c. Two. Educ: Edenburg High Sch. Polit. & Govt. Pos: Mem, Borough Coun, Pa, 55; mem, Venago Co. Cmt, 59-64; pres, N.W. Co. Cmnr. Asn, 64; Pa. State Rep, 64- Mem: Boy Scout Orgn, 30 years; pres, Col. Drake Coun, Oil City, 63-64. Mailing Add: Emlenton, Pa. 16373. (1967)

KAHN, ALBERT B. D
b. Trenton, N.J, 3/6/00; s. Samuel M. Kahn and Emma K; m. 6/15/44 to Catherine Loll; c. Albert B, Jr, Joseph H, Edward S. and William E. Educ: Univ. Pa, A.B, 21; Harvard Univ, LL.B, 24; Phi Sigma Delta. Polit. & Govt. Pos: Treas, Independents for Stevenson for Pres, 56; chmn, Mercer Co. Lawyers for Hughes, N.J, 61 & 64; v.pres. bd. mgrs, N.J. State Prison, 62-; state treas, Citizens Cmt. for the Bond Issue, 63; del, Dem. Nat. Conv, 64; state chmn, Lawyers for Johnson and Humphrey, 64; cmnr, Del. River Joint Toll Bridge Cmn, 64-69, chmn, 69-; treas, Mercer Co. Commun. Col, trustee, 66- Bus. & Prof. Pos: Sr. partner, Kahn Schildkraut & Levy, Lawyers. Mil. Serv: Pvt, Army, 18, serv. in Student's Army Training Corps, Phila. Mem: Appointed by N.J. Supreme Court to Mercer Co. Ethics Cmt, 67-; Mercer Co. Bar Asn.(trustee and mem. judiciary cmt. and scholarship cmt); N.J. and Am. Bar Asns; chmn. scholarship cmt. and life trustee, Jewish Fedn. of Trenton, Shein Found. and Kramer Found; trustee, Harvard Law Sch. Asn. of N.J; Mercer Co. Voc. Educ. Study Cmt; bd. trustees, St. Francis Hosp, Trenton Symphony Orchestra, Jewish Commun. Center, Jewish Fedn. Found. and Har Sinai Temple; Mason; B'nai B'rith; nat. committeeman, Am. Jewish Joint Distribution Cmt. and Harvard Law Sch. Scholarship Cmt; mem. and former pres, Har Sinai Temple Men's Club; treas, Mercer Co. Commun. Col; co. chmn, United Serv. Orgn, 42-46; former pres, Jewish Commun. Center. Rel: Jewish. Mailing Add: 830 Riverside Ave, Trenton, N.J. 08618.

KAHOUN, RAYMOND J. R
Ill. State Rep.
b. Chicago, Ill, 12/28/36. Educ: Quincy Col; Univ. Chicago. Polit. & Govt. Pos: Mem, Beverly Forum, Ill; chmn, 18th Ward Rep. Orgn; Ill. State Rep, 62-; mem, Ill. Rep. State Cent. Cmt, 68-69. Bus. & Prof. Pos: Ins, real estate and pub. rels. Mil. Serv: Army, Artil. Mem: Local 150, I.U.O.E, Beverly Forum. Mailing Add: 8600 S. Winchester Ave, Chicago, Ill. 60620. (1967)

KAINRAD, JOSEPH ROBERT D
b. Wayland, Ohio, 5/29/33; s. Christian Kainrad and Kathryn Amstadt K; m. 6/6/64 to Judith Ann Kreinbihl; c. Christian Anthony and Joseph Robert, Jr. Educ: Kent State Univ, B.A, 55; Ohio State Univ, LL.B, 58; Theta Chi. Polit. & Govt. Pos: Mem, Portage Co. Parks Cmn, Ohio, 62-; Ohio State Rep, 63-69. Mem: Portage Co. and Ohio State Bar Asns; Kiwanis; Ruritan; past chmn, Portage Co. Cancer Crusade. Rel: Roman Catholic. Mailing Add: 8827 Newton Falls Rd, Ravenna, Ohio 44266. (1967)

KAIRIT, ELEANOR JESSIE R
Chmn, Bridgewater Town Rep. Cmt, Mass.
b. North Abington, Mass, 5/1/24; d. Elmer Edwin Colburn and Jean Alma Maclean C; m. 10/26/45 to John Walter Kairit; c. Judith Elaine and William John. Educ: Abington High Sch, 38-42. Polit. & Govt. Pos: Chmn, Bridgewater Town Rep. Cmt, Mass, 66-; asst. clerk, Town Hall, Bridgewater, 68-69. Mem: Womens Club; Garden Club; Red Cross; pres, Church Groups; pres, Visiting Nurse Asn. Rel: Congregational. Mailing Add: 1760 South St, Bridgewater, Mass. 02324.

KAISER, GEORGE CHAPIN R
Treas, Rep. Party, Wis.
b. Chicago, Ill, 1/20/33; s. George Chapin Kaiser, Sr. and Grace Betz K; m. 4/10/52 to Jeanne Aurelius; c. Mark Aurelius, Richard Alan and Charles Moore. Educ: Univ. Ill, Urbana, B.S, 54; Kappa Sigma. Polit. & Govt. Pos: Cmnr, Wis. Dept. Admin, 65-67; mem, Wis. Reorgn. Cmn, 65-67; mem, Mayor's Cmt. Reorgn. Milwaukee City Govt, 68; treas, Rep. Party, Wis, 68-; mem. adv. cmt, Dept. Local Affairs and Develop, 68-; mem, Milwaukee Co. Planning Cmn, 69-; mem. policy cmt, Gov. Cmn. Educ, 69- Bus. & Prof. Pos: Employee, Arthur Andersen & Co, Milwaukee, 57- Mil. Serv: Entered as Ens, Naval Res, 54, released as Lt.(jg), 56, after serv. in Amphibious Fleet, West. Pac, 54-56. Mem: Am. Inst. CPA; Wis. Soc. CPA; Am. Soc. Pub. Admin; Jaycees (past secy); adv, Jr. Achievement Southeast. Wis; Univ. Club Milwaukee; Madison Club; Delavan Lake Yacht Club. Rel: Presbyterian. Legal Res: 6265 N. Bay Ridge Ave, Milwaukee, Wis. 53217. Mailing Add: 795 N. Van Buren St, Milwaukee, Wis. 53202.

KAISER, ROLAND GLENN R
b. Meyersburg, Mont, 6/16/96; s. William J. Kaiser and Edna Browning Fay K; m. 3/23/27 to Elizabeth Louise Evans; c. Robert Glenn and Karen Elizabeth. Polit. & Govt. Pos: Sr. econ. analyst, U.S. Dept. State, Lima, Peru, 42; del, Rep. State Conv, 62 & 64; asst. sgt-at-arms, Utah House Rep, 63; dir, Utah State Fair, 63-64; Utah State Rep, 65-66. Bus. & Prof. Pos: Salesman, auditor and mgt, Int. Harvester Co, 17-57. Mil. Serv: Eng. 1/C, Navy, 18-19; serv. in Army G-2, counter-intel, various Latin Am. Countries, 43-45; World War I Victory Medal with Clasp; Cross of Eloy Alfaro, Ecuador, 49. Publ: Swiss Family Kaiser, 1962; Our Fay Lineage, 1964. Mem: AF&AM; Vets. of World War I; Am. Acad. Polit. Sci; Int. Platform Asn; Bonneville Knife & Fork Club, Salt Lake City, Utah; Copper Golf Club; former mem: Club Del Progreso, Buenos Aires; Club Internacional, Lima; Saddle and Sirloin, Chicago. Won a number of golf club tournaments in the S.Am. Countries. Rel: Latter-day Saint. Mailing Add: Canyon Crest Apts, Apt. 1408, 875 Donner Way, Salt Lake City, Utah. 84108.

KALBFLEISCH, GIRARD EDWARD R
b. Piqua, Ohio, 8/3/99; s. Oscar Conrad Kalbfleisch and Magdalena Gerstmeyer K; m. 5/1/29 to Chattie Lenora Spohn. Educ: Ohio Northern Univ, LL.B, 23, LL.D, 60. Polit. & Govt. Pos: Prosecuting attorney, Richland Co. Ohio, 29-33; munic. judge, City of Mansfield, Ohio, 36-42; common pleas judge, Richland Co, 42-59; Dist. Judge, U.S. Courts, 59- Mil. Serv: Pvt, Army, 18. Legal Res: 13801 Shaker Blvd, Apt. 3A, Cleveland, Ohio 44120. Mailing Add: Room 106, Federal Bldg, Cleveland, Ohio 44114.

KALENAK, NICHOLAS PAUL D
b. Nanty Glo, Pa, 12/2/31; s. Michael Kalenak and Anna Gmiter K; m. 6/22/54 to Irene Sienty; c. James P, Peter R. and Wendy Lynne. Educ: Columbia Col, B.A, 53; Columbia Univ. Law Sch, LL.B, 57. Polit. & Govt. Pos: Attorney, Town of Ledyard, Conn, 61-64; asst. prosecutor, Tenth Circuit Court, 63-65; chmn, Ledyard Dem. Town Cmt, 66-69. Mil. Serv: Entered as Pvt, Army, 53, released as Pfc, 55, after serv. in Europe, 54-55. Mem: Conn. and New London Co. Bar Asns; Am. Trial Lawyers Asn. Rel: Episcopal. Mailing Add: Nugget Hill Dr, Gales Ferry, Conn. 06335.

KALER, IRVING K. D
V.Chmn, Ga. State Dem. Exec. Cmt.
b. Pittsburgh, Pa, 10/2/19; s. Sam Kaler and Dora Skigen K; m. 11/24/60 to Sylvia Kanter; c. Jonathan, Dina, Amy, Matthew and Michael Jefferson. Educ: Wash. and Lee Univ; Emory Univ. Lamar Sch. Law, LL.B; Alpha Epsilon Pi. Polit. & Govt. Pos: V.chmn, Ga. State Bd. for Children and Youth, 63-; del, Dem. Nat. Conv, 64, mem, Credentials Cmt, 64, mem, Rules Cmt, 68; mem, Cmt. on Permanent Orgn. of Dem. Party of Ga, 64, chmn, steering cmt, 64; mem, Atlanta Juvenile Coun, 66-; mem, bd. dirs, Fulton Co. Dem. Party; chmn, Commun. Rels. Cmn, Atlanta, 67-; v.chmn, Ga. State Dem. Exec. Cmt, currently; mem, Nat. Rules Cmn. of Dem. Party, 69- Mem: Grievance cmt, Ga. State Bar Asn, 63; legal aid soc, Atlanta Bar Asn, 59, grievance cmt, 61; pub. rels cmt, Coun. Fedn. Jewish Welfare Funds, 66; govt. affairs cmt, Atlanta C. of C, 59; del. assembly, Atlanta Jewish Commun. Coun, 66; Com-

merce Club; Lawyers Club of Atlanta; State Bar of Ga; cmt. for legacy develop, B'nai B'rith Dist. 5; nat. serv. officer, Jewish War Vet. of U.S.; past pres, Gate City Lodge of B'nai B'rith; former pres, Atlanta Jr. C. of C; chmn, Southeast. Adv. Bd, Anti-Defamation League of B'nai B'rith. Selected Outstanding Young Man of Year, Atlanta Jr. C. of C, 46; Distinguished Serv. Award, Atlanta Gate City Lodge of B'nai B'rith, 67. Rel: Jewish. Legal Res: 960 W. Kingston Dr. N.E, Atlanta, Ga. 30305. Mailing Add: Suite 1820, Fulton National Bank Bldg, Atlanta, Ga. 30303.

KALICH, HUGH EDWARD D
Wash. State Rep.
b. Toledo, Wash, 6/6/21; s. Joseph L. Kalich and Annie Noble K; m. 6/4/43 to Mildred Norma Taylor; c. Gary and Gordon. Polit. & Govt. Pos: Councilman, Toledo, Wash, 52-54; cmnr, Lewis Co, 58-62; committeeman, Wash. Dem. State Cmt, 58-64; Wash. State Rep, 65-67 and currently. Bus. & Prof. Pos: Owner, Kalich Logging Co, 46-66. Mil. Serv: Entered as Pvt, Army, 44, released as Pfc, 46; ETO Ribbons with two Battle Stars; Combat Infantryman's Badge. Mem: Elks; Eagles; Moose; Lions; Am. Legion; VFW. Rel: Catholic. Mailing Add: P.O. Box 278, Toledo, Wash. 98591. (1967)

KALINA, HAROLD DFL
Minn. State Sen.
b. Minneapolis, Minn, 1928; married; c. Three. Educ: Univ. Minn, B.S.L, LL.B. Polit. & Govt. Pos: Minn. State Sen, 54- Bus. & Prof. Pos: Lawyer, Scholle, Schweiger and Kalina. Mil. Serv: Army. Mailing Add: 731 Columbia Blvd. N.E, Minneapolis, Minn. 55418. (1967)

KALISH, LOUIS D
b. Kings Co, N.Y; m. to Bertha Nacht; c. Myron. Polit. & Govt. Pos: Mem. exec. cmt, N.Y. State Dem. Party; N.Y. State Assemblyman, 46-66. Bus. & Prof. Pos: Ins. and real estate broker. Mil. Serv: Army, World War I. Mem: Am. Legion. Mailing Add: 4001 Sixth Ave, Brooklyn, N.Y. 11215. (1967)

KALMAN, THOMAS J. D
Pa. State Sen.
b. Perryopolis, Pa, 12/12/17; s. Joseph A. Kalman and Susan Danko K; m. to Clare E. Reagan; c. Mary Ann and Maureen. Educ: Notre Dame, A.B; Univ. of Pa. Law Sch, LL.B. Polit. & Govt. Pos: Asst. dist. attorney, Fayette Co, Pa, 48-52; first dist. attorney, 52-56; Pa. State Sen, 56-; chmn, Pa. Cmn. Interstate Coop, 67-; mem, bd. dirs, Coun. State Govt, hq, Ky, 67-, v.chmn. nat. fed. state rels. cmt, 67- and v.chmn, east. region, N.Y, 68-; mem, Nat. Legis. Hwy. and Transportation Cmt, 69- Bus. & Prof. Pos: Attorney, Uniontown, Pa; dir, Perryopolis Land Co. & Perryopolis Auto Auction. Mil. Serv: Navy, World War II, ETO; Capt, Res. Mem: ROA; VFW; Elks; Perryopolis Gold Star Post 7023; Amvets; Am. Legion; Fayette Co, Pa, Am. Bar Asns. Mailing Add: 2 Mayflower Dr, Uniontown, Pa. 15401.

KALTENBACHER, PHILIP DAVID R
N.J. State Assemblyman
b. Orange, N.J, 11/7/37; s. Joseph C. Kaltenbacher and Helen Lowy K; m. 6/21/62 to Nancy Stein; c. Laura Jean and Gail Ellen. Educ: Yale Univ, B.A. in Polit. & Econ. with honors, 59, Law Sch. LL.B, 63; admitted to Conn. State Bar, 63 and N.J. State Bar, 64. Polit. & Govt. Pos: Legis. Secy, N.J. Gen. Assembly, 64-65, N.J. State Assemblyman, 68-, mem. commerce, indust. and professions, and state govt. cmts, chmn. subcmt. on prfnl. and bus. licensing. Bus. & Prof. Pos: Attorney, law firm, Newark, N.J, 63-64; v.pres. corp. secy. and gen. counsel, Seton Co, Newark, 64-, Radel Leather Mfg. Co, Newark, Wilmington Enameling Co. and Wilmington Chem. Corp, Del. Mil. Serv: Army Intel. Corps, until 67. Mem: Am, N.J. and Essex Co. Bar Asns; corp. law cmt, Essex Co. Bar Found; Am. Mgt. Asn; Bus. and Indust. Coord. Cmt; Nat. Conf. Christians and Jews; trustee, Boys' Club of Newark and Beth Israel Hosp, Newark; former mem. alumni bd. of Gov, Newark Acad; Yale Club. Legal Res: 52 Troy Dr, Short Hills, N.J. 07078. Mailing Add: 849 Broadway, Newark, N.J. 07104.

KAMAKA, HIRAM K. D
Dir. Finance, State of Hawaii
b. Honolulu, Hawaii, 10/13/27; s. William Keliiahonui Kamaka and Ana Tilton K; single. Educ: Creighton Univ. Sch. Law, Omaha, Nebr, J.D, 52; Phi Alpha Delta. Polit. & Govt. Pos: Hawaii State Rep, 58-68; dir. Finance, State of Hawaii, 69- Mil. Serv: Entered as Pvt, Army, 45, released as T-4, 47, after serv. in Pac. Area. Mem: Am, Nebr. State and Hawaii Bar Asns; Liliuokalani Trust Adv. Bd; life mem, Koolaupoko Hawaiian Civic Club. Rel: Roman Catholic. Mailing Add: State Capitol, Honolulu, Hawaii 96813.

KAMAS, LEWIS MELVIN R
Okla. State Rep.
b. Knowles, Okla, 10/24/21; s. Frank Munsor Kamas and Mabel Francis Shalloup K; m. 10/23/43 to Mary Darlien Cohlmia; c. Leslie Allan and Carol Jeanne. Educ: Northwest. State Col, 39-40; Okla. State Univ, 40-41; Farm House. Polit. & Govt. Pos: Supvr, Woods Co. Soil and Water Conserv. Dist. 70, Okla, 48-66; Okla. State Rep, Dist. 58, currently, mem, Okla. House of Rep. Appropriations and Budget, Agr. and Conserv. and Econ. Develop. Cmts, Currently. Bus. & Prof. Pos: Pres, Cimmaron Watershed Counsel of Soil and Water Dist. of Okla, Kans, N.Mex. and Colo, 50. Mil. Serv: Entered as Pvt, Army Air Force, 42, released as 2nd Lt, 45, prisoner of war, 45, Stalagluft 1, Barth, Germany; Good Conduct and Air Medals; Purple Heart; Caterpillar Club; Europe-Africa-Middle East. Theater Ribbon with 4 Bronze Stars. Mem: Comdr, Am. Legion Hatch-Vincent Post 47, 63; pres, Freedom C. of C, 60; Mason (32°); Shrine; Elks; VFW; Am. Legion. Mem. State Champion Livestock Judging Team, Okla, 37; 4th Nat. Livestock Judging Contest, Kansas City, Mo, Am. Royal 1938. Rel: Orthodox. Mailing Add: Box 146, Freedom, Okla. 73842.

KAMPEN, PAUL D. D
Chmn, Humboldt Co. Dem. Party, Iowa
b. Ft. Dodge, Iowa, 11/14/42; s. Fred Dee Kampen and Edna Leist K; m. 2/26/62 to Marcia Kay Hart; c. Brett, Jeffery and Joel. Educ: Twin Rivers High Sch, Bode, Iowa, 4 years; Educated in Bus, Quincy, Ill, 63. Polit. & Govt. Pos: Served on cmts. for Congressman Stanley Greigg, Iowa State Treas. Paul Franzenburg and former Gov. Harold E. Hughes; Dem. precinct chmn, Wacousta Twp, 62-69; co. treas, Humboldt Co, Iowa, 64-66; co. chmn, Humboldt Co. Dem. Party, 66- Bus. & Prof. Pos: Farmer, 61-; mgr. several houses, Humboldt and Ottosen, Iowa, 62-; salesman, Moormans Feed Co, 63-66; owner of hotel, Humboldt, 69- Mem: 4-H leader; Ottosen Commercial Club; bd. mem, Livermore Lakes Region Bd; dir, Humboldt Sq. Dance Club; Farmers Union; publicity chmn, Farm Bur; Ottosen, Bode and Humboldt Coop. Elevators; state dir, Jaycees (dir. Humboldt chap. and pres. Dakota City chap). Nominated as Outstanding Young Farmer in Humboldt Co, 66 & 68; Outstanding Feed Salesman Plaque, 67; President Plaque, 68; Key Man Award, 68; Outstanding Jaycee, 68. Rel: Catholic. Mailing Add: R.R. 1, Ottosen, Iowa 50570.

KAMPMANN, FLORA CAMERON R
Mem, Rep. Nat. Finance Cmt.
b. Waco, Tex; d. William Waldo Cameron and Helen Evelyn Miller C; m. 11/1/47 to Ike Simpson Kampmann, Jr; c. Ike Simpson, III and Megan Cameron. Educ: Sweet Briar Col, A. B, 46. Polit. & Govt. Pos: Mem, Hq. Cmt, Tex, 57-58; v.chmn, Tex. Rep. State Exec. Cmt, 58-60; mem, Rep. Nat. Cmt. for Prog. and Progress, 59; del, Rep. Nat. Conv, 60 & 64, alternate del, 68, secy, Platform Cmt, 60, mem, Arrangements Cmt. for Theme and Entertainment, 64; mem, Rep. Nat. Cmt, 60-65; mem, Rep. Nat. Finance Cmt, 65-; mem, Presidential Mission to Latin Am, 69. Bus. & Prof. Pos: Pres, Kamko Found. Mem: Bd. of trustees, Sweet Briar Col; bd. of trustees and first chmn. pres. cmt, Trinity Univ; exec. cmt, San Antonio World's Fair, 68; Bexar Co. Legal Aid Soc; Nat. Coun. Metrop. Opera; Jr. League San Antonio Colonial Dames Am. Legal Res: 315 Westover Rd, San Antonio, Tex. 78209. Mailing Add: 4600 Broadway, San Antonio, Tex. 78209.

KAMYK, WALTER THOMAS D
Councilman, Pittsburgh, Pa.
b. Pittsburgh, Pa, 1/18/13; s. Anthony Kamyk and Anna Kopera K; m. 6/21/47 to Wanda A. Plucinski; c. Rita Theodora, Felicia Genevieve and Constance Amelia. Educ: Duquesne Univ, B.A. Polit. & Govt. Pos: Constable, Ninth Ward, Pittsburgh, Pa, 39-50; Pa. State Rep, 49-63; councilman, Pittsburgh, Pa, 63- Bus. & Prof. Pos: Investr, Pa. Dept. of Pub. Assistance, 38-39. Mil. Serv: Entered as Pvt, Army, 42, released as S/Sgt, 45, after serv. in Ord. Corps, Aberdeen, Md. and Newf; Army Ribbon of Commendation; Victory Medal; Good Conduct Medal. Mem: Various Vet, Fraternal and Civic Orgn. Rel: Roman Catholic. Mailing Add: 1665 Morningside Ave, Pittsburgh, Pa. 15206.

KANBARA, BERTRAM D
Attorney Gen, Hawaii
Mailing Add: State Capitol Bldg, Honolulu, Hawaii 96813.

KANDARAS, HOMER MICHAEL D
Chmn, Pennington Co. Dem. Cent. Cmt, S.Dak.
b. Aberdeen, S.Dak, 8/23/29; s. William D. Kandaras and Hallie Ferguson K; m. 6/24/58 to Alice Johnson Ahrendt; c. stepdaughter, Gwenythe (Mrs. Roy Thompson) and 2 stepsons, Devin Ahrendt and Gregory Ahrendt and Brian. Educ: Univ. S.Dak, LL.B, 54, grad. study, 56-58; Pi Sigma Alpha. Polit. & Govt. Pos: V.pres, S.Dak. Young Dem, 59-61; chmn, Pennington Co. Dem. Cent. Cmt, S.Dak, 59-; del. and mem. platform cmt, Nat. and State Dem. Conv, 60, del. and mem. rules cmt, Dem. Nat. Conv, 64 & 68, del, Dem. State Conv, 68; chmn, S.Dak. State Adv. Cmt, Dem. Party, 63-69; chmn. S.Dak. Greek Sect, All Am. Coun, Dem. Nat. Cmt, 64-69; Dist. 10 Capt, S.Dak. Dem. Party, 69- Mil. Serv: Entered as Pvt, Army, 54, released as Specialist 3/C, 56, after serv. in 37th AAA Bn, Japan, 55-56. Mem: S.Dak. Bar Asn; Pennington Co. Heart Asn; Assoc. Orgn. for Polit. Action; S.Dak. Consumers League; mem. bd. dirs, Black Hills Consumers League; Elks. Outstanding Young Dem. for S.Dak, 61. Rel: Unitarian. Legal Res: 2216 Cerro Court, Rapid City, S.Dak. 57701. Mailing Add: P.O. Box 589, Rapid City, S.Dak. 57701.

KANE, ANGELINE BETTY D
V.Chmn, Chemung Co. Dem. Party, N.Y.
b. Virgil, N.Y, 1/25/26; d. Arthur Raymond Hutchings and Pearl Maynard H; m. 11/16/46 to Thomas Francis Kane; c. Mary Theresa and Thomas Francis. Educ: De Forest's Sch. Electronics, Electronics Technician, 44; Elmira Col, 66. Polit. & Govt. Pos: Committeewoman, Big Flats Dem. Party, N.Y, 57-68; secy, Young Dem. Club, co-chmn, Big Flats Dem. Club, v.chmn, Big Flats Dem. Cmt, prog. chmn, Chemung Co. Dem. Woman's Club, chmn, various Dem. campaign hq, del. or alternate del, N.Y. Dem. State Conv. and Dem. nominee for Chemung Co. Clerk, town clerk and justice of the peace, Big Flats, 57-69; secy, Chemung Co. Dem. Party, 62-66, v.chmn, 69-, secy, Elmira Dem. Party, 64-66. Bus. & Prof. Pos: Electronics technician, Eclipse Machinery, Elmira, 44-45; assembler, Remington Rand, 45-47; accounts receivable office clerk, S.F. Iszards, 49-51; dining room hostess, Mark Twain Hotel, 51-53; bookkeeper and office mgr, Chem. Co. Fed. Employ. FCU, 63-; real estate saleswoman, E.E. Wood, 65-68. Publ: Quarterly article, 'From the President's Pen', N.Y. State Post Office Clerk, 65-. Mem: Woman's Auxiliary to United Fedn. of Postal Clerks (N.Y. State Pres, 65-69); Chemung Co. Dem. Womans Club. Rel: Catholic. Mailing Add: 107 Grove St, Elmira, N.Y. 14905.

KANE, DAVID RONALD D
Ark. State Rep.
b. Okmulgee, Okla, 2/17/34; s. David William Kane and Clara Thionnett K; m. 6/8/57 to Judith Tiderman; c. Kathy, Mark and Darby. Educ: Kans. Univ, B.S. in Bus, 56; Phillips 66 scholarship; Phi Kappa Psi; Alpha Kappa Psi. Polit. & Govt. Pos: Ark. State Rep, Pulaski-Perry Co, 69- Bus. & Prof. Pos: Sales trainee, sr. sales rep. and supplies and sch. mgr, IBM Corp, Little Rock, Ark, 56-64; v.pres. and dir. of agencies, Fifth Largest Ark. Life Ins. Co, 64-67; sr. partner, Kane-Ferrill & Assocs, 67-; regional dir, Financial Serv. Corp. of Am, 68-; pres. and bd. chmn, Evast Funding Int. Mem: Prin, Nat. Asn. Securities Dealers; Nat. Asn. Life Underwriters; Nat. Soc. State Legislators; Jaycees (past pres, Little Rock Chap); mem. bd, Easter Seals; C. of C. Grateful Orgn. Plaque, U.S. Jaycees, 63. Rel: Episcopal; Vestryman, St. Mark's Episcopal Church, 65-67. Legal Res: 321 Fairfax, Little Rock, Ark. 72205. Mailing Add: 306 First National Bank Bldg, Little Rock, Ark. 72201.

KANE, F. JAMES JR. D
b. Buffalo, N.Y, 9/26/35; m. to Barbara Leavers; c. Elizabeth and Laurie. Educ: Canisius Col, B.S, 57; Notre Dame Law Sch, LL.B, 60. Polit. & Govt. Pos: N.Y. State Assemblyman, 64-66. Bus. & Prof. Pos: Attorney, law firm of Diebold and Millonzi. Mem: N.Y. State and Erie Bar Asns; Notre Dame Law Asn.(dir); Marshall Club; Dem. Lawyers Club; Cath. Lawyers Guild. Rel: Catholic. Mailing Add: 98 Argonne Dr, Kenmore, N.Y. 14217.

KANE, IRVING EDWARD D
Mayor, Lynn, Mass.
b. Lynn, Mass, 5/2/30; m. to Mary Judith Hameline; c. Katherine Hines. Educ: Boston Col. and Law Sch. Polit. & Govt. Pos: Asst. registrar of probate, Essex Co, Mass, 56-66; councilor-at-lg, Lynn City Coun, 62-65; mayor, Lynn, 66- Bus. & Prof. Pos: Practicing Attorney, self-employed, 54- Mil. Serv: Entered as Pvt, Marine Corps, 54, released as Cpl, 56, after serv. in Legal Off. Mem: Pres, Lynn Catholic Charities; dir, Lynn Econ. Opportunity; dir, Lynn Civic Music; founder, The Magic Lantern Players; Ancient Order of Hibernians. Rel: Roman Catholic. Mailing Add: 123 Range Ave, Lynn, Mass. 01904.

KANE, KATHARINE D. D
b. Indianapolis, Ind, 4/12/35; d. Joseph Johnston Daniels and Katharine Holliday D; m. 9/21/57 to Louis I. Kane; c. Elizabeth Holliday, Jennifer Johnston and Joseph Daniels. Educ: Smith Col, B.A, 56; Phi Beta Kappa. Polit. & Govt. Pos: Research asst, White House, 56 and U.S. Dept. State, 57; Mass. State Rep, Third Suffolk Dist, 65-69; mayor's spec. asst. for cult. affairs and dir, Summerthing, Boston, 68- Mem: Pres, League of Women Voters, Boston, 61-64. Mailing Add: 10 Chestnut St, Boston, Mass. 02108.

KANE, WALTER J. D
b. Providence, R.I, 5/31/28; m. to Ruth M. Educ: Bryant Col, B.S, 50. Polit. & Govt. Pos: Former chmn, Smithfield Dem. Town Cmt, R.I; R.I. State Sen, 55-66, Dep. Majority Leader, R.I. State Senate, 61-66. Bus. & Prof. Pos: Self-employed. Mil. Serv: Army. Mailing Add: 932 Greenville Ave, Greenville, R.I. 02828. (1967)

KANE, WILLIAM B. R
Mem, Ill. Rep. State Cent. Cmt.
b. Chicago, Ill, 12/31/12; s. William Joseph Kane and Florence Meyers K; m. 3/20/40 to Ruth B. Schultz; c. Sharon. Educ: DePaul Univ. Col. of Law; Delta Theta Phi. Polit. & Govt. Pos: Police magistrate, Harvey, Ill, 47-59, mayor, 59-63; mem, Thornton Twp. High Sch. and Jr. Col. Bd. Educ, 50-59, pres, 54-59; mem, Ill. Cmn. Higher Educ, 57-59; dep. chmn, Cook Co. Cent. Cmt, 62-64; del, Rep. Nat. Conv, 64 & 68; tax collector, Thornton Twp, 65-; mem, Fourth Cong. Dist, Ill. State Rep. State Cent. Cmt, mem. exec. bd, Rep. State Cent. Cmt. and Cook Co. Cent. Cmt. and Rep. committeeman, Thornton Twp, Cook Co, currently. Bus. & Prof. Pos: Attorney-at-law. Mem: Pres, Tax Collector's Asn. Ill; mem. exec. bd. Twp. Officials Asn, Ill; v.pres, Munic. League, Ill; AF&AM; Scottish Rite; Valley of Chicago; Shrine. Rel: Christian Scientist. Mailing Add: 26 E. 150th St, Harvey, Ill. 60426.

KANTER, SAMUEL A. R
Asst. Attorney Gen, Ill.
b. Dubuque, Iowa, 9/3/05; s. Louis Kanter and Celia Cohn K; m. 11/5/64 to A.Dee. Educ: DePaul Univ, LL.B, 27. Polit. & Govt. Pos: Asst. city prosecutor, Chicago, Ill, 29-31; referee, Dept. of Revenue, 42-49; Rep. committeeman, 23rd Ward, Chicago, 46-64; asst. attorney gen, Ill, 52- Mem: Chicago and Am. Bar Asns. Rel: Jewish. Mailing Add: 5401 S. Oak Park, Chicago, Ill. 60638.

KAPENSTEIN, IRA D
b. New York, N.Y, 2/12/36; s. Joseph Kapenstein (deceased) and Alice Askern K; m. 6/10/56 to Betty Ann Kunik; c. Joel Eli, David Jay and James Marshall. Educ: Univ. Iowa, B.A, 56; Omicron Delta Kappa; Sigma Delta Chi; Alpha Epsilon Pi. Polit. & Govt. Pos: Spec. asst. to the Postmaster Gen, U.S, 63-68; asst. to Nat. Dir, Orgn, Robert F. Kennedy for Pres. Campaign, Wash. Hq, 68; exec. asst. to Dem. Nat. Chmn, Dem. Nat. Cmt, Wash, D.C, 68-69. Bus. & Prof. Pos: Reporter and Wash. correspondent, Milwaukee J, Milwaukee, Wis. and Wash, D.C, 56-63; exec. asst. to Pres. McDonnell & Co, Inc, N.Y.C. and mem. bd. dirs, McDonnell Fund, Inc, 69- Mem: Nat. Press Club; Milwaukee Press Club; Wash. Chap, Sigma Delta Chi; B'nai B'rith; Univ. Iowa Alumni Asn. Postmaster Gen. Benjamin Franklin Award, 65; William A. Jump Mem. Found. Meritorious Award for Pub. Admin, 68. Rel: Jewish. Legal Res: 140 Roxen Rd, Rockville Centre, N.Y. 11570. Mailing Add: McDonnell & Co, Inc, 120 Broadway, New York, N.Y. 10005.

KAPLAN, JEROME D
Pres, Third Dist. New Dem. Coalition, Pa.
b. Jersey City, N.J, 3/17/26; s. Julius Kaplan and Leah Levy K; m. 9/6/53 to Edith Jaffy; c. Paul Louis. Educ: Temple Univ, B.S; Univ. Mich, J.D; Tau Epsilon Rho. Polit. & Govt. Pos: Pres, Cent. Phila. Reform Dem, Pa, 66; del, Dem. Nat. Conv, 68; chmn, Third Cong. Dist. McCarthy for Pres, 68; chmn. exec. cmt, Am. Dem. Action, Phila, Pa. and mem. nat. bd. dirs, currently; pres, Third Dist. New Dem. Coalition, 68- Bus. & Prof. Pos: Internal revenue agent, U.S. Treas, Dept, 53-55. Mil. Serv: Pvt, Army, 44-45, with serv. in Inf, ETO, 45; Combat Inf. Badge. Publ: 'Buy, Sell Agreements,' Ins. Mag. Mem: Phila. and Am. Bar Asns; Am.Jewish Cong; Am. Civil Liberties Union; Nat. Cmt. for Sane Nuclear Policy; Urban League; Citizens Cmt. Pub. Educ. Rel: Jewish. Legal Res: 2042 Pine St, Philadelphia, Pa. 19103. Mailing Add: 15th Floor, 226 S. 16th, Philadelphia, Pa. 19103.

KAPLAN, NATHAN JOSEPH D
b. Chicago, Ill, 6/29/10; s. David Kaplan and Eva Erenberg K; m. 11/23/39 to Anne Vogel; c. Herbert, Frances and Barry. Educ: Chicago Law Sch, LL.B, 34; Tau Sigma Omicron. Polit. & Govt. Pos: Alderman, 40th Ward, Chicago, Ill; Ill. State Rep, 13th Dist, 57-63; assoc. judge, Circuit Court of Cook Co, Ill; v.chmn, Ill. Cmn. on Aging, 59-69. Bus. & Prof. Pos: Attorney-at-law, 35-; pres, Lakeview Construction Co, 58-, Skokie Valley Manor, 62- Mem: Ill, Am. and Chicago Bar Asns; Decalogue Soc. of Lawyers; Judicature Soc; Shrine; Mason; B'nai B'rith; North River Cmn; Peterson Park Improv. Asn. Rel: Jewish. Legal Res: 3434 W. Glenlake Ave, Chicago, Ill. 60645. Mailing Add: Civic Center, Chicago, Ill. 60602.

KAPLAN, STANLEY NORRIS D
b. Cleveland, Ohio, 4/23/26; s. Joseph S. Kaplan and Tylie Menitoff K; m. 3/15/64 to Harriet Jane Atlass; c. Leslie Ann and Susan. Educ: Univ. Mo; Univ. Miami, N.Y. Univ, B.A. & M.A; Harvard Bus. Sch; Phi Beta Kappa. Polit. & Govt. Pos: Mem. steering cmt, Mecklenburg Co. Dem. Party, N.C; chmn, Spec. Mecklenburg Co. Elec. Cmt; campaign mgr, Lt. Gov. N.C; del, Dem. Nat. Conv, 68. Bus. & Prof. Pos: V.Pres. in charge of sales, Balaban Stas, 58-60; exec. v.pres, Mars Broadcasting, 60-63; exec. v.pres, WMEX Radio, Boston, 63-65; pres, WAYS Radio, Charlotte, 65- Mil. Serv: Entered as Pvt, Army, 43, released in 45, after serv. in 11th Armored Div, ETO, 43-45; Purple Heart with Cluster; Silver Star. Mem: Nat. Asn. Broadcasters; South. Polit. Educ. Action Cmt.(treas); Rating Serv. Cmt.(chmn, Radio Advert. Bur); Rotary; Am. Legion; bd. dirs, Boys Town; Carolinas' Carrousel (pres). Rel: Jewish. Legal Res: 1333 Queens Rd, Charlotte, N.C. 28214. Mailing Add: 400 Radio Rd, Charlotte, N.C. 28214.

KAPLINSKI, HENRY STANISLAUS R
b. Chicago, Ill, 8/4/17; s. Florian Kaplinski and Emily Przekop K; div. Educ: Roosevelt Univ, B.A, 51; Univ. Ariz, B.S, 53. Polit. & Govt. Pos: Nominee, U.S. Rep, Ill, 68. Bus. & Prof. Pos: Proofreader, Chicago Tribune, 56-; sports ed, Polish Daily Zgoda, Chicago, 66- Mil. Serv: Entered as A/S, Naval Res, 39, released as SC-1/C, 45, Good Conduct Medal; Am. Defense Serv. Medal with Fleet Clasp; Am. Campaign Medal; Asiatic-Pac. Campaign Medal with Silver Star; World War II Victory Medal; Philippine Liberation Ribbon with two Bronze Stars; Navy Unit Commendation. Mem: Polish Nat. Alliance; ITU. Mailing Add: 2420 N. Kedzie Blvd, Chicago, Ill. 60647.

KAPLOWITZ, PAUL D
b. Atlantic City, N.J, 4/22/06; s. Morris Kaplowitz and Dora Pollack K; m. 1/24/38 to Dora Berkman; c. Morris. Educ: Am. Univ, LL.B, 28. Polit. & Govt. Pos: Asst. gen. counsel, U.S. Tariff Cmn, 43-50, gen. counsel, 50-64, chmn, 61-67; adv. to U.S. del, Second Meeting UN Prep. Cmt, Int. Conf. Trade and Employ, Geneva, Switz, 47, participant, Contractive Parties to Gen. Agreement Tariffs and Trade Meeting, Torquay, Eng, 51; tariff consult, Ways and Means Cmt, U.S. House of Rep, 65- Rel: Jewish. Mailing Add: 5135 Linnean Ave. N.W, Washington, D.C. 20008.

KAPTIK, ALEXANDER, JR. R
b. Philadelphia, Pa, 4/3/39; s. Alexander Kaptik, Sr. and Mary Demanchyk K; m. 6/22/63 to Margaret M. Lineman. Educ: Abraham Lincoln High Sch, grad, 57. Polit. & Govt. Pos: Tax Analyst, State of Pa, 64-; Rep. Cand, U.S. House Rep, 68; Rep. chmn, N.E. Pa. 55th Ward, currently; mem, Tax Equalization Bd, currently. Bus. & Prof. Pos: Pres, Numismatic Co, 64- Mil. Serv: Army Spec. Serv, 59-61, Pvt, serv. in 14th Armored Cavalry, Fulda, Germany. Rel: Baptist. Mailing Add: 6259 Mulbery St, Philadelphia, Pa. 19135.

KARABIAN, WALTER JOHN D
Calif. State Assemblyman
b. Fresno, Calif. 3/14/38; s. John J. Karabian and Gladys Mae Shishmanian K; single. Educ: Univ. South. Calif, B.A, 60, LL.B, 63 and M.S, 65; Blue Key; Phi Alpha Sigma; Pi Alpha Theta; Theta Chi. Polit. & Govt. Pos: Dep. dist. attorney, Los Angeles Co, Calif, 65-67; Calif. State Assemblyman, 45th Dist, 67- Publ: Baker vs. Carr, Univ. South. Calif. Sch. Law, 64; 'California's Implied Consent Statute,' Loyola Univ. Law Rev; 'The Legality or Illegality of Wiretapping,' Pac. Law J. Mem: State Bar of Calif; Am. Bar Asn; bd. dirs, Calif. Pediatric Center. Rel: Presbyterian. Mailing Add: Garfield Bank Bldg, 231 W. Garvey, Monterey Park, Calif. 91754.

KARBER, JAMES WINFIELD D
b. Elizabethtown, Ill, 7/8/14; s. James Fred Karber and Myrtle Tyer K; m. August, 1935 to Irma Cox; c. Karen Sue (Mrs. Purvis). Educ: Univ. Ill, A.B, 34; LL.B, 36. Polit. Pos: Mem, Ill. State Dem. Cent. Cmt, 43-46. Govt. Pos: Chmn, Ill. Commerce Cmn, 61-69; Ill. State Rep, 46-50; state attorney, Gallatin Co, Ill, 36-40. Bus. & Prof. Pos: Pres, Nat. Asn. of R.R. & Utilities Cmnrs, 67-68; pres, Gallatin Co. State Bank, 47-53, Gallatin Co. Abstract and Title Co, 39-47 and Ill. Title Asn, 44-45. Publn: 'Looking Forward in Regulation,' Pub. Utilities Fortnightly, 64; 'Regulatory Philosophy—A Regulator Speaks,' Financial Analysts Journal, 65; 'Some Observations Concerning Fair Value,' Public Utility Survey Investment Dealers Digest, 66. Mem: Pres, Midwest Asn. of R.R. and Utilities Cmnrs, 64-65; Great Lakes and Nat. Asns. of R.R. and Utilities Cmnrs; Ill. Bar Asn; Shrine, Mason (32°); Farm Bureau; Nat. Popcorn Farmers Day, Inc. Rel: General Baptist. Mailing Add: Box 298, Ridgway, Ill. 62979.

KAREY, JOSEPH NORMAN R
Chmn, Baltimore Co. Rep. Cent. Cmt, Md.
b. Baltimore, Md, 4/1/32; s. Joseph P. Karcauskas and Margaret E. Kraft K; m. 9/29/56 to Mary Patricia Fuchs; c. Mary Abigail, J. Alexander and Amy E. Educ: Loyolla Col, B.S. in Bus. Admin; N.Y. Univ, M.B.A; Univ. Md. Law Sch, B.LL. Polit. & Govt. Pos: Chmn, Baltimore Co. Rep. Cent. Cmt, 67-; alternate del, Rep. Nat. Conv, 68. Mil. Serv: Entered as Seaman, Navy, 56, released as Seaman 3/C, 58. Mem: Baltimore City, Md. and Am. Bar Asns; Oriole Advocates, Inc; Sports Reporters Asn. Legal Res: 3624 Lochearn, Baltimore, Md. 21207. Mailing Add: 1515 Washington Blvd, Baltimore, Md. 21230.

KARNIS, THEODORE HENRY R
N.H. State Rep.
b. Ft. Bragg, Calif, 11/9/11; married. Educ: Univ. Conn. Polit. & Govt. Pos: New Ipswich fire chief and dep. warden, State N.H. Forest Fire Serv; N.H. State Rep, 61-, mem, Claims and Aeronaut. Cmt, N.H. House Rep, 61, 63 & 65, clerk, 63 & 65, mem, Transportation Cmt, 67; del, Constitutional Conv, 64. Bus. & Prof. Pos: Dir, Mason Village Savings Bank; owner, gas station. Mem: F&AM; past pres, N.H. Fire Chiefs; New Ipswich Athletic Asn; N.H. Farm Bur; Bethel Lodge No. 24; N.H. Consistory S.P.R.S.(32°); Grange (4°); past pres, Hillsborough Co. Forest Fire Wardens; v.pres, Int. Asn. Fire Chiefs; N.E. Asn. Fire Chiefs; Souhegan Valley Radio League; S.W. N.H. Mutual Aid Fire Syst; legis. cmt, N.H. Fire Chiefs Club, Hillsborough Co. Forest Fire Wardens Asn. and N.H. Fedn. Forest Fire Asns; pres, Fire Mutual Aid Asns. of N.H; AAONMS. Rel: Protestant. Mailing Add: Box 122, New Ipswich, N.H. 03071. (1967)

KAROUB, JAMES H. D
Mich. State Rep.
b. 6/16/29; c. James M, Alex J, Stephen J. and David C. Educ: Highland Park Jr. Col; Mich. State Univ. Polit. & Govt. Pos: Former mem, Police and Fire Civil Serv. Cmn; Mich. State Rep, 62-64, 65- Bus. & Prof. Pos: Owner, Peerless Sales Co. Mem: Metrop. Club; Shrine; Fraternal Order of Police and Firefighters; Highland Park P.O.A; Bd. of Commerce. Rel: Protestant. Mailing Add: 13724 Woodward, Highland Park, Mich. 48203.

KARPINSKI, HELEN BERNICE D
Pres, Federated Dem. Women of Ohio
b. Cleveland, Ohio, 10/7/99; d. John Olszewski and Anna Grabowski O; m. 8/27/24 to John J. Karpinski, wid; c. Gloria Joy (Mrs. Battisti), Mercedes (Mrs. Spotts) and Diane Joan. Polit. & Govt. Pos: Dem. ward leader and precinct committeeman, Ward 21, Ohio, 38-50; del, Dem. Nat. Conv, 40, 64 & 68; pres, Women's Cosmopolitan Dem. League, 42-50; mem, Ohio Dem. State Exec. Cmt, 42-50; dep. clerk, Jury Cmn. Common Pleas Court, Cuyahoga Co, 45-59; pres, Cleveland Civil Serv. Cmn, 59-68; Dem. precinct committeeman, Ward 29 S, 65-; former first v.pres, prog. chmn. and recording secy, Federated Dem. Women of Ohio, pres, currently; mem, Bd. of Tax Rev, Cuyahoga Co, 69- Mem: Polish Women's Alliance of Am; Alliance of Poles; Am. Polish Women's Club of Gr. Cleveland; Catholic Ladies of Columbia; Cleveland Cultural Garden Fedn; Women's Cosmopolitan Dem. League; Polish Legion of Am. Vet. Auxiliary; Fedn. Dem. Women of Ohio. Rel: Catholic. Mailing Add: 2897 Ludlow Rd, Cleveland, Ohio 44120.

KARREL, OSCAR D
Chmn, Redding-Georgetown Dem. Town Cmt, Conn.
b. Boston, Mass, 6/23/05; m. 8/4/34 to Frances Whipple; c. John Whipple. Educ: Northeast. Univ. Law Sch, LL.B, 31. Polit. & Govt. Pos: Chmn, Redding-Georgetown Dem. Town Cmt, Conn, 67- Bus. & Prof. Pos: Buyer, Lord & Taylor, N.Y, 34-68; mkt. rep, Assoc. Dry Goods, 68- Mil. Serv: Entered as Pvt, Army, 43, released as Capt, 46, after serv. in Off. Qm. Gen, Wash, D.C. Rel: Jewish. Mailing Add: R.F.D. 3, West Redding, Conn. 06896.

KARSON, MARC D
b. Brooklyn, N.Y, 2/8/20; s. Martin Karson and Sally Friedman; div; c. Clara Lucy, Keir Thomas, Michael Andrew and David Scott. Educ: Am. Univ, B.S, 46; London Sch. Econ. & Polit. Sci, Ph.D, Polit. Sci, 49. Polit. & Govt. Pos: Dem. cand, U.S. House Rep, 14th Cong. Dist, Ill, 68; precinct committeeman, Dem. Party, Lisle Twp, 68-69; mem. exec. bd, Dupage Co. Dem. Orgn, 68-69. Bus. & Prof. Pos: Assoc. prof. polit. sci, South. Ill. Univ, 56-60; nat. educ. dir, Amalgamated Clothing Workers Am, 60-65; prof. polit. sci, North Cent. Col, 65- Mil. Serv: Entered as Aviation Cadet, Air Force, 41, released as Flight Officer, 45, after serv. in ETO, 43. Publ: American Labor Unions and Politics, 1900-1918, South. Ill. Univ. Press, 58; 'Civil Rights and the White Community,' New Politics, summer, 64; 'The AFL and the Negro Worker 1894-1949,' In: The Negro and American Labor Movement, Doubleday, 68. Rel: Unitarian. Legal Res: 25 729 N. Williams Rd, Warrenville, Ill. 60555. Mailing Add: R.R. 1, Box 11, Warrenville, Ill. 60555.

KARST, ARTHUR E. D
b. Orlando, Fla, 4/5/14; m. to Kathryn Williams; c. Arthur E, Jr, Jacelyn, Janice and Sharon. Educ: Univ. Fla; Phi Kappa Tau. Polit. & Govt. Pos: Former Fla. State Rep. Bus. & Prof. Pos: Citrus grower and grove mgt. Mem: C. of C; Indian Chiefs; past pres, Jaycees; Taxpayers Asn. Citrus Mutual; Indian River Citrus League; state dir. and v.pres, Farm Bur; Agr. Coun; Agr. Tax Coun; past pres, Citrus Prod. Mgr; Univ. Fla. Alumni Asn; Hort. Soc; Vero Beach Country Club; Vero Beach, Riomar Bay, Pelican and Buccaneer Yacht Clubs. Rel: Methodist; Mem, Off. Bd. Mailing Add: 2311 Victory Blvd, Vero Beach, Fla. 32960. (1967)

KARST, CHARLES EDWARD
Mayor, Alexandria, La.
b. New Orleans, La, 9/18/31; s. Dr. Charles Karst, Jr. and Ethel Drouin K; m. 12/27/65 to Judith Ward Steinman. Educ: Tulane Univ, B.A. in Polit. Sci, 52; Loyola Univ, J.D, 65. Polit. & Govt. Pos: Mayor, Alexandria, La, 69- Bus. & Prof. Pos: Attorney-at-law, 65- Mil. Serv: 2nd Lt, Air Force, 52, with serv. in Korea, 53; Maj, Air Force Res, currently. Mem: Alexandria, La. and Am. Bar Asns; Am. Trial Lawyers Asn; Lions Int; Moose; Am. Legion; VFW; C. of C; Rapides Wildlife Asn; Aircraft Owners and Pilot's Asn. Rel: Catholic. Legal Res: 2236 Jackson St, Alexandria, La. 71301. Mailing Add: City Hall, Alexandria, La. 71301.

KARSTEN, FRANK M. D
b. St. Louis, Mo, 1/7/13; m. to Opal Osborn; c. LaVerne and Frank, Jr. Educ: Nat. Univ, D.C, LL.B. Polit. & Govt. Pos: Cong. secy. to late U.S. Rep. John Cochran, 34-46; U.S. Rep, Mo, 46-68. Mem: D.C. Bar. Rel: Episcopal. Mailing Add: 2521 University St, St. Louis, Mo. 63107. (1967)

KARSTEN, HERBERT H. R
N.H. State Rep.
b. New York City, 3/1/06; married; c. two. Educ: Albany, N.Y, Bus. Col. Polit. & Govt. Pos: Selectman; N.H. State Rep, 61-67 & 69- Bus. & Prof. Pos: Motel Bus; Karsten Dairies. Mem: F&AM; C. of C. Rel: Protestant. Mailing Add: Holderness, N.H. 03245.

KARTH, JOSEPH E. DFL
U.S. Rep, Minn.
b. New Brighton, Minn, 8/26/22; m. to Charlotte Nordgren; c. three sons. Educ: Univ. Nebr. Sch. Eng. Polit. & Govt. Pos: Minn. State Rep, 50-58; U.S. Rep, Minn, 58-; del, Dem. Nat. Conv, 68. Bus. & Prof. Pos: Formerly with, Minn. Mining & Mfg. Co; former Int. Rep, OCAW-AFL-CIO, ten years. Mil. Serv: Army, serv. in ETO. Mem: VFW; Am. Legion; Indianhead Coun. Boy Scouts. Outstanding Legislator, 58th Spec. Session, Minn. State House of Rep. Rel: Presbyterian. Legal Res: St. Paul, Minn. Mailing Add: 4678 Leslie Ave. S.E, Washington, D.C. 20031.

KASER, LEONARD H. R
N.J. State Assemblyman
b. Franklinville, N.J, 10/9/31; s. Henry L. Kaser and Julia Butenewicz K; m. 5/2/53 to Nancy Turner; c. Nancy Ellyn, Richard S. and Steven F. Educ: LaSalle Col, B.S; Georgetown Univ. Law Sch, J.D; Delta Theta Phi. Polit. & Govt. Pos: Committeeman, Monroe Twp. Rep. Party, N.J, 63-69, exec. cmt. chmn, 65-67; N.J. State Assemblyman, 68- Bus. & Prof. Pos: Attorney, Kaser & Ginsburg, Williamstown, N.J, 57- Mem: Gloucester Co. Bar Asn; Workmen's Compensation Asn. N.J; K. of C; Kiwanis; Monroe Twp. Rep. Club. Rel: Catholic. Legal Res: 126 Pine St, Williamstown, N.J. 08094. Mailing Add: P.O. Box 175, Williamstown, N.J. 08094.

KASHIWA, SHIRO R
Asst. Attorney Gen. for Land & Natural Resources, Dept. of Justice
Mailing Add: Dept. of Justice, Constitution Ave. & Tenth St. N.W, Washington, D.C. 20530.

KASTENMEIER, ROBERT WILLIAM D
U.S. Rep, Wis.
b. Beaver Dam, Wis, 1/24/24; s. Leo Henry Kastenmeier and Lucille Powers K; m. 6/27/52 to Dorothy Chambers; c. William, Andrew and Edward. Educ: Carleton Col, Army Specialized Training Prog, 43-44; Univ. Wis, LL.B, 52; Phi Alpha Delta. Polit. & Govt. Pos: Br. off. dir, Claims Serv, War Dept, Philippine Islands, 46-48; chmn, Jefferson Co. Dem. Party, Wis, 53-56; mem, Dem. Cent. Cmt, Wis, 55-56; justice of peace, Dodge and Jefferson Co, 56-59; del, Dem. Nat. Conv, 56, 64 & 68, mem. credentials cmt, 64; U.S. Rep, Wis, 59- Mil. Serv: Entered as Pvt, Army, 43, released as 1st Lt, 46, after serv. in Hq. Claims Serv, Armed Forces, West. Pac. Publ: Vietnam Hearings: Voices From the Grass Roots, Artcraft Press, 65; 'CBR: Pentagon Boobytrap,' The Progressive, 3/60; 'Pacem in Terris,' Continum, 63. Mem: Secy, Watertown Bar Asn, 53-54; v.chmn, Jefferson Co. Bar Asn, 57-58. Legal Res: 300 N. Water St, Watertown, Wis. 53094. Mailing Add: 2232 House Office Bldg, Washington, D.C. 20515.

KASTRUP, HARRY FREDERICK D
b. Russell Co, Kans, 2/28/02; s. George Frederick Kastrup and Emma Buhrle K; 1st m. to Anna Sigrid Nelson; wid; 2nd m. 4/3/48 to Mary Alice Gale; c. Joanne Marie (Mrs. Franz). Educ: St. Joseph Law Sch, LL.B, 34; Sigma Delta Kappa. Polit. & Govt. Pos: Dir, Fed. Transient Prog, 34-36; attorney in charge of Legal Aid Soc, Div. Polk Co. Social Welfare, Iowa, 36-37; treas, Dem. State Hq, 38-41; city attorney, Perry, 56-60; former chmn, Dallas Co. Dem. Cent. Cmt. Bus. & Prof. Pos: Mem, Bd. Dirs, Morton Truck Lines, Inc, Credit Bureau of West Central Iowa, Inc, West Central Collectors, Inc, Mid-Iowa Collectors, Inc. and Kastrup-McCauley Building, Inc; pres, Industrial Savings & Loan Bank, Topeka, Kans, 29-32. Mil. Serv: Entered as Pvt, Army, 42, released as Cpl, 43; spec. agent, Mil. Intel, 41-42; subsequently field dir, Am. Red Cross, ETO. Mem: Iowa State and Fed. Bar Asns; Soc. Am. Acct; Am. Trial Lawyers' Asn; Am. Legion; Elks; Kiwanis; Shrine. Rel: Christian. Legal Res: 1709 Willis Ave, Perry, Iowa 50220. Mailing Add: 1313 Second St, Perry, Iowa 50220.

KATO, JAMES H. D
V.Chmn, State Cent. Cmt, Dem. Party of Hawaii
b. Wailulu Maui, Hawaii, 7/26/24; s. Michitaro Kato and Toku Matsubara K; m. 6/21/52 to Shizuko Ochiai; c. Kelvin H. and Carlton E. Educ: Univ. Hawaii, B.Ed, 50, grad. study, 51; Phi Delta Kappa. Polit. & Govt. Pos: Chmn, Jefferson-Jackson Day Dinner, Hawaii Co. Dem. Party, Hawaii, 62; mem, Hawaii Co. Cmt, Dem. Party of Hawaii, 62-, chmn, 63-; v.chmn, Dist. Dem. Party, 69-; v.chmn, State Cent. Cmt, Dem. Party of Hawaii, currently. Mil. Serv: Entered Army, 43, released, 46, after serv. in 442 Inf. Regt. Combat Team, ETO, 44-45; Am. Campaign, Europe-African-Middle East and Asiatic-Pac. Serv. Medals; Distinguished Unit Badge; Good Conduct and Victory Medals. Mem: Dir, Big Island Teachers FCU; Hilo Teachers Asn; Nat. and Hawaii Educ. Asns; Lions; PTA. Mailing Add: 231-C W. Lanikaula St, Hilo, Hawaii 96720. (1967)

KATUS, THOMAS MICHAEL D
b. McIntosh, S.Dak, 2/13/40; s. Elwyn D. Katus and Marjorie Thompson K; m. 9/5/64 to Mariette A. Pellitier; c. Karen and David. Educ: Univ. Wis-Milwaukee, B.S, 65; Univ. Calif, Los Angeles, 65-66. Polit. & Govt. Pos: Alternate del, Dem. Nat. Conv, 68. Bus. & Prof. Pos: Dir. Africa Training, Univ. Wis-Milwaukee, 67; pres, Vol. Training Specialists Inc, 67- Mil. Serv: Entered as Pvt, Nat. Guard, 58, released as SP-4, 64, after serving in Combat Engrs. Publ: Congressional-Executive Relations, Univ. Wis-Milwaukee, 65. Legal Res: Box 156, McIntosh, S.Dak. 57641. Mailing Add: 1411 Underwood St. N.W, Washington, D.C. 20014.

KATZ, A. MARTIN D
b. Victoria, B.C, Can, 6/18/16; s. Joseph Katz and Lottie Pozar K; m. to Dorothy Zweig; c. Michael, Jody, Richard and Ronald. Educ: Ind. Univ. Sch. of Law, LL.B, 41. Polit. & Govt. Pos: Judge, City Court, Gary, Ind, 56-63; Mayor, Gary, 64-67; cmnr, Lake Criminal Court, 68- Mem: Ind. and Gary Bar Asns; B'nai B'rith; Moose; Optimist; Elks. Rel: Jewish. Legal Res: 631 Lincoln, Gary, Ind. 46402. Mailing Add: 504 Broadway, Gary, Ind. 46402.

KATZ, BENNETT DAVID R
Maine State Sen.
b. Springfield, Mass, 10/7/18; s. Samuel J. Katz and Frances Wolk K; m. 7/2/43 to Edith H. Colmes; c. Joyce E. and Roger J. Educ: Tufts Col, A.B, 40; Alpha Epsilon Pi. Polit. & Govt. Pos: Councilman, Augusta City Coun, Maine, 54-56; chmn, Maine Rep. First Cong. Dist. Cmt, 62-64, v.chmn, 66-; mem, Gov. Air Serv. Adv. Cmt, 62-; Maine State Rep, 63-66; chmn, Augusta Rep. City Cmt, Maine, 64-66; mem, Maine Transportation Cmn, 65-67; mem, Kennebec Co. Rep. Cmt, Maine, 66-; mem, Maine Cmn. on Rehabilitation Needs, 66-69, v.chmn, 69-; Maine State Sen, 67-, Senate Majority Floor Leader, 67-, chmn. interim legis. cmt. on Pub. Educ. Eval, 69-; mem, Maine Sch. Bldg. Authority, 69-; Maine Rep. to Educ. Cmn. of States, 69- Bus. & Prof. Pos: Treas, Dow & Stubling, Portland, Maine, 58-; pres, Nicolson & Ryan, Augusta, 66-; dir, Maine Retail Jewelers Asn, 66- Mil. Serv: Entered as Flying Cadet, Army Air Corps, 40, released as Major, 45, after serv. in 1st Pursuit Group, Air Corps Ferry Command, 1st Troop Carrier Command, Mil. Air Transport Serv; Air Medal; Pearl Harbor Ribbon; Am, Asiatic-Pac. and ETO Ribbons. Mem: Shtrine; Kiwanis; Am. Legion; B'nai B'rith. Rel: Jewish. Mailing Add: 27 Westwood Rd, Augusta, Maine 04330.

KATZ, HAROLD A. D
Ill. State Rep.
b. Shelbyville, Tenn, 11/2/21; s. Maurice W. Katz and Evelyn Cohen K; m. 7/25/45 to Ethel Mae Lewison; c. Alan M, Barbara R, Julia L. and Joel A. Educ: Vanderbilt Univ, B.A, 43; Univ. Chicago, J.D, 48, M.A. in Econ, 58; bd. ed, Univ. Chicago Law Rev. Polit. & Govt. Pos: Spec. legal consult, Gov. Ill, 61-63; master-in-chancery, Circuit Court, Cook Co, Ill, 63-67; Ill. State Rep, 65-, chmn, Cmn. on the Orgn. of the Gen. Assembly, Ill. House Rep, 65- Bus. & Prof. Pos: Attorney, Katz & Friedman, Chicago, Ill, 48-; lectr, Univ. Chicago, Univ. Col, 59-64. Publ: Labor Law: Cases, Materials & Comments (with C. Gregory), Michie Casebook Corp, 48; 'Liability of Automobile Manufacturers for Unsafe Design of Passenger Cars,' Harvard Law Rev, 10/56; 'Make Your Opinion Count.,' Reader's Digest, 12/68. Mem: Am. Polit. Sci. Asn; Am. Bar Asn; Int. Soc. for Labor Law and Soc. Legis;(U.S. chmn, 61-67); Am. Trial Lawyers' Asn. Recipient of Best Legislator Award, Independent Voters of Ill, 24th & 75th Gen. Assembly, 66 & 68; Citation for Meritorious Serv, President's Cmt. on Employ. of the Handicapped, 67. Rel: Jewish. Legal Res: 1180 Terrace Court, Glencoe, Ill. 60022. Mailing Add: 7 S. Dearborn St, Chicago, Ill. 60603.

KATZENBACH, NICHOLAS de BELLEVILLE D
b. Phila, Pa, 1/17/22; s. Edward Lawrence Katzenbach and Marie L. Hilson K; m. to Lydia King Phelps Stokes; c. Christopher Wolcott, John Strong Miner, Maria Louise Hilson and Anne de Belleville. Educ: Princeton Univ, B.A; Yale Law Sch, LL.B; Rhodes scholar, Balliol Col, Oxford Univ, 47-49. Polit. & Govt. Pos: With Off. of Gen. Counsel, Air Force, 50; Asst. U.S. Attorney Gen, 61-62, Dep. U.S. Attorney Gen, 62-64, U.S. Attorney Gen, 65-66; Under Secy. of State, 66-69. Bus. & Prof. Pos: Assoc. prof, Yale Univ. Law Sch; prof. of int. law, Univ. Chicago, 56-60; v.pres. and gen. counsel, Int. Bus. Machines Corp, 69- Mil. Serv: Air Force, 1st Lt, 41-45; Air Medal with three clusters. Publ: Political Foundations of International Law (with Morton A. Kaplan), 61. Mem: N.J. and Conn. Bar Ford Found. fel, 60-61. Rel: Episcopal. Mailing Add: International Business Machines Corp, Armonk, N.Y. 10504.

KAUFMAN, EUGENE S. D
b. Manitowoc, Wis, 9/28/22. Educ: Elgin Watchmakers Col, 48. Polit. & Govt. Pos: Mem, Co. Bd. Supvr, Wis, 6 years; Wis. State Assemblyman, 62-66. Bus. & Prof. Pos: Former installer, Dial Phone Syst; retail jeweler. Mil. Serv: World War II Vet, Army. Mem: Holy Name Soc; K. of C; Am. Legion; DAV; Amvets; Eagles; Co. Fish and Game Protective Asn; Dep. Sheriffs Asn; Wis. Retail Jewelers Asn. Mailing Add: 918 S. 13th St, Manitowoc, Wis. 54220. (1967)

KAUFMAN, GERALD D
Pa. State Rep.
b. Pittsburgh, Pa, 6/14/32; s. Samuel Kaufman and Sara Phillips K; m. 9/2/56 to Carol Benjamin; c. Ann Phillips and James Benjamin. Educ: Yale Univ, B.A, 54; Columbia Univ. Law Sch, LL.B, 57. Polit. & Govt. Pos: Pa. State Rep, 66-; mem, Pa. Bd. Welfare, currently. Bus. & Prof. Pos: Lawyer, Kaufman & Kaufman, 58- Mil. Serv: Entered as Pvt, Army, 57, released as SP-5, 63, after serv. in Res. Publ: 'Towards a Smaller House,' Nat. Munic. League Reporter, 4/68. Mem: Am, Pa. and Allegheny Co. Bar Asns; v.pres, Jewish Family & Children's Serv; Am. Civil Liberties Union (mem. state bd). Leadership Award, Pa. Asn. Retarded Children; Spec. Award, United Ment. Health Serv. of Allegheny Co. Rel: Jewish. Mailing Add: 5612 Maple Heights Court, Pittsburgh, Pa. 15232.

KAUFMAN, PAUL JOSEPH D
b. Charleston, W.Va, 3/16/20; s. Sydney Joseph Kaufman and Sylvia Rose Miller K; m. 5/31/51 to Rose Jean Levinson; c. Tod Joseph, Timothy Michael and Steven Miles. Educ: W.Va. Univ, A.B, 42; Univ. Va. Law Sch, LL.B, 48; Pi Lambda Phi; Sphinx. Polit. & Govt. Pos: Mem, Charleston Police Civil Serv. Cmn, W.Va, 54-56; pres, Young Dem. Club, Kanawha Co, W.Va, 56-60; W.Va. State Sen, 60-68, mem, Commun. Develop. Bd. Dirs, 67-; del, Dem. Nat. Conv, 68. Bus. & Prof. Pos: Gen. law practice, 48- Mil. Serv: Entered as A/S, Coast Guard, 42, released as Lt, 46, after serv. in Pac. Theater and ETO. Publ: 'The State We're In,' Am. Legislator, winter 65; 'Fewer Checks, More Balance,' Nat. Civic Rev, 3/66. Mem: Am, W.Va. State and Kanawha Co. Bar Asns; bd. gov, Charleston Art Gallery, 63-65 & 66-; Legal Aid Soc. (founder and mem. bd. dirs, 51-); bd. dirs, Coun. South. Mt, 69-; chmn, Pub. Affairs Conf. of W.Va, 68-; trustee, W.Va. Fund, 69- Rel: Reform Jewish. Legal Res: 410 Sheridan Circle, Charleston, W.Va. 25314. Mailing Add: 300 Union Bldg, Charleston, W.Va. 25301.

KAUFMAN, SAMUEL R
b. St. Paul, Minn, 2/14/21; s. Samuel Kaufman and Anna O. Larson K; m. 8/19/45 to Helen B. Motzka; c. James, George, Frank and Randall. Educ: Univ. of Idaho, B.A, 42, LL.B, 48; Blue Key; Kappa Sigma. Polit. & Govt. Pos: Idaho State Rep, Ada Co, 56-60; mem, Idaho Rep. Coun. of State Govt, 59-60; precinct committeeman, Rep. Party, Ada Co, 62-66; Idaho State Sen, Dist. 15, 66-68. Bus. & Prof. Pos: Attorney-at-law. Mil. Serv: Entered as Pfc, Marine Corps, 42, released as 1st Lt, 45, after serv. in 1st Bn, 7th Marines, 1st Div, S.Pac, 43-45; Bronze Star. Mem: Am. and Idaho State Bar Asns; Boise Bar Asn.(treas, 50, pres, 53); Am. Trial Lawyers Asn; Mason; Elks; Am. Legion. Mailing Add: 720 Wyndemere Dr, Boise, Idaho 83702.

KAUFMAN, VERNON D
b. Frankfurt, Germany, 4/3/17; s. Leopold Kaufman and Isabella Gideon K; m. 4/4/49 to Hanne Lotte Wertheimer; c. Lucy, Roger and Jeffrey. Polit. & Govt. Pos: Mem, Dem. State Cent. Cmt, Calif, 65; mem, Motor Vehicle Pollution Control Bd, 65-; spec. asst. to Mayor, San Francisco, 68-, chmn, Mayor's Official Host Cmt, 68- Bus. & Prof. Pos: Owner, Vernon Kaufman Co, 46- and Kaufman Develop. Co, 64-; pres, Safe-Cut Inc, 65- Mil. Serv: Entered as Pvt, Army, 41, released as Capt, 47; Army Commendation Ribbon. Mem: Lions; Elks; Concordia-Argonaut; Am. Legion; Asn. of the U.S. Army. Rel: Jewish. Legal Res: 25 Presidio Terrace, San Francisco, Calif. 94118. Mailing Add: 973 Market St, San Francisco, Calif. 94103.

KAUFMANN, ALOYS P. R
b. St. Louis, Mo, 12/23/02; s. John Kaufmann and Sophia Woehr K; m. to Margaret C. Uding; c. Michael A. Educ; Benton Law Sch. Polit. & Govt. Pos: Pres, Bd. of Aldermen, St. Louis, Mo, 41-43, mayor, 43-49. Mem: St. Louis and Am. Bar Asns; Lawyers Asn; several civic clubs. Rel: Catholic. Mailing Add: 705 Olive St, St. Louis, Mo. 63101.

KAUPER, THOMAS E. R
Dep. Asst. Attorney Gen, Dept. of Justice
Mailing Add: Dept. of Justice, Constitution Ave. & Tenth St. N.W, Washington, D.C. 20530.

KAVANAGH, THOMAS MATTHEW D
Assoc. Justice, Mich. Supreme Court
b. Carson City, Mich, 8/4/09; s. Thomas Kavanagh and Margaret Barrett K; m. 10/27/30 to Agnes C. Miller; c. Doris Jeanne (Mrs. Closser), Donna Joan (Mrs. Baker), Patricia Ann (Mrs. Kean) and Kathleen (Mrs. Zipperer). Educ: Univ. Detroit Sch. Law, LL.B, 32. Polit. & Govt. Pos: First chmn, Great Lakes Cmn, Mich; attorney gen, 55-57; Justice, Mich. Supreme Court, 58-64, Chief Justice, 64-67, Assoc. Justice, currently. Mem: State Bar of Mich; Am. Bar Asn; Cmt. on Post-Conviction Remedies, Conf. of Chief Justices; exec. bd, Nat. Conf. on Bail and Criminal Justice; former state dep, K. of C; Lions; City Club of Lansing. Rel: Roman Catholic. Mailing Add: Michigan Supreme Court, Lansing, Mich. 48903.

KAVULICH, STEPHEN JAMES D
b. Taylor, Pa, 9/14/18; s. John Kavulich and Elizabeth Popcun K; m. 4/2/45 to Anne V. Darlak; c. Stephen J. J. Educ: Univ. Scranton, Pa, 3 yrs. Polit. Pos: Tax Collector, 58- Bus. & Prof. Pos: Retail Merchant, 37-; mem. adv. bd, Taylor Branch, Third Nat. Bank & Trust Co. Mem: First v.pres, Pa. Slovak Catholic Union; past pres, Lions Club, Taylor, Pa; past pres, Am. Slovak Soc. Lackawanna & Susquehanna Counties; K. of C. (4°), Coun. 280, Scranton, Pa. Rel: Roman Catholic. Legal Res: 135 Oak St, Taylor, Pa. 18517. Mailing Add: 401 S. Main St, Taylor, Pa. 18517.

KAY, BUDDY D
Mo. State Rep.
b. St. Louis, Mo, 12/12/14. Educ: Mo. Bus. Sch. Polit. & Govt. Pos: Mo. State Rep, 60- Bus. & Prof. Pos: Prfnl. orchestra leader; pres, Kay & Co; real estate and ins. Mil. Serv: World War II. Mem: Good Hope Lodge 218; past pres, Revelers; Mason; Scottish Rite; ALHAMBRA Grotto; Moolah Temple. Rel: Baptist. Mailing Add: 2639 Keokuk St, St. Louis, Mo. 63118. (1967)

KAY, PETER R
Ariz. State Rep.
b. N.Y.C, 2/18/24; s. E.M. Kay and S.V. K; m. 2/20/49 to Miriam Spitalny; c. Karen and Dianne. Educ: Univ. N.C, A.B, 44; Stanford Univ, 43-44; Southwest Univ, LL.B, 49. Polit. & Govt. Pos: Mem. and precinct capt, Ariz. Rep. State Cent. Cmt, 52-69; Ariz. State Rep, 69- Bus. & Prof. Pos: Casualty claims adjuster, Ariz. Adjust. Agency, 52-69. Mil. Serv: Entered as Pvt, Army, 43, released as T/5, 46, after serv. in Signal Corps Cryptography, China-Burma-India Theatre, 45-46. Mem: Former pres, Ariz. Claimsmen's Asn. Mailing Add: 5002 Calle Redonda, Phoenix, Ariz. 85018.

KAY, THOMAS
City Mgr, Flint, Mich.
b. Detroit, Mich, 11/25/24; s. Frederick Thomas Kay and Elizabeth Josephine K; m. 9/24/49 to Rose Helen Smith; c. Mary Jane, Frederick, Sharon, Patricia and Colleen. Educ: Mich. State Univ, B.A, 48. Polit. & Govt. Pos: Mem, Cent. Budget Cmt, Mich; chmn, Flint Transportation Authority; asst. to city mgr, Flint, Mich, 53-57, dep. city mgr, 57-62, city mgr, 63- Bus. & Prof. Pos: Newspaper reporter, 49-53. Mil. Serv: Marine Corps Res, 50-51 and 42-45. Mem: Flint Red Feather Fund; Int. City Mgrs. Asn. Named Outstanding Young Man of Year, Flint Jr. C. of C, 58. Legal Res: 3221 Yale St, Flint, Mich. 48503. Mailing Add: 1101 S. Saginaw St, Flint, Mich. 48503.

KAY, THOMAS OLIVER R
b. Anderson, S.C. 9/29/29; s. Thomas Crayton Kay and Gertrude Whitworth K; m. 11/1/66 to Bette Hutto Weathers; c. Dallon H, Bruce T. and George M. Educ: Furman Univ, A.B, 50; Blue Key; Hand and Torch. Polit. & Govt. Pos: Admin. asst. to U.S. Rep. John H. Buchanan, Ala, 66- Bus. & Prof. Pos: Mem. relig. educ. staff, First Baptist Churches, Cochran, Ga, 54-58 and Washington, Ga, 58-65; agent, New York Life Ins. Agency, Atlanta, Ga, 65-66. Mem: Mason; Kiwanis; Capitol Hill Club; Poets; Bull Elephants. Rel: Methodist. Mailing Add: 1121 Arlington Blvd, Tyler,1003, Arlington, Va. 22209.

KAYE, ALLEN E. R
Mem, Rep. Cong. Adv. Cmt, N.Y.
b. N.Y.C, 7/9/39; s. Sol Kaye and Kate Zegarek K; single. Educ: Queen's Col, B.A. cum laude, 61; Columbia Law Sch, LL.B, 64; N.Y. Univ. Law Sch, LL.M, 66; Dean's List; Pi Sigma Alpha; Phi Beta Kappa; Phi Alpha Delta; Phi Epsilon Pi. Polit. & Govt. Pos: V.pres, Eighth Assembly Dist. Young Rep. Club, N.Y, 60-61; v.pres, Queen's Col. Young Rep. Club, 61; student asst. to chief asst. U.S. attorney Vincent T. McCarthy, East. Dist, summer 63; campaign coordinator for Rep. Seymour Halpern, 64; mem, Rep. Cong. Adv. Cmt, 64-; committeeman, Queen's Co. Rep. Party, 27th Assembly Dist, 65-; secy, New Yorkers for Ed Brooke, 66; Queen's Co. campaign coordinator, N.Y. State Young Rep. Asn, 66; chmn, Membership and Publicity Cmts, N.Queen's Young Rep. Club, 66-; chmn, Publicity Cmt, 27th Assembly Dist. Regular Rep. Club, 66- Bus. & Prof. Pos: Law clerk, Harry H. Rains, Esquire, 65; attorney, Guggenheimer & Untermyer, 65-; vol. researcher in labor for U.S. Sen. Jacob K. Javits, 66. Mem: N.Y. State and Am. Bar Asns; Acad. of Polit. Sci; N.Y. and N.Queen's Young Rep. Clubs; v.pres, John V. Lindsay Young Rep. Club. Rel: Jewish. Legal Res: 150-47 Horace Harding Expressway, Flushing, N.Y. 11300. Mailing Add: 80 Pine St, New York, N.Y. 10005. (1967)

KAYLOR, OMER THOMAS, JR. R
Chmn, State Rep. Cent. Cmt, Washington Co, Md.
b. Hagerstown, Md, 7/14/23; s. Omer Thomas Kaylor and Mabel Slagen K; m. 8/23/47 to Jean Haskin Johnston; c. Omer T, III, Laura H, Gwen S, Mark J. and John M. Educ: Washington and Lee Univ, B.S, 45 and LL.B, 49; Phi Beta Kappa; Phi Alpha Delta; Omicron Delta Kappa; Phi Kappa Psi. Polit. & Govt. Pos: Md. State Del, 51-54; state's attorney, Washington Co, Md, 55-58;

chmn, State Rep. Cent. Cmt, Washington Co, currently. Mil. Serv: Entered as A/S, Navy 43, released as Lt.(jg), 46, after serv. in Pac. Theatre. Mem: Am, Md. and Co. Bar Asns; Am. Judicature Soc; Am. Legion; Exchange Club; Salvation Army Bd; VFW; dir. and past pres, United Fund; YMCA Bd. Rel: United Church of Christ. Mailing Add: 940 The Terrace, Hagerstown, Md. 21740.

KAZEN, ABRAHAM D
U.S. Rep, Tex.
b. 1919; m. to Consuelo. Educ: Cumberland Univ, Tenn; Univ. of Tex, LL.B. Polit. & Govt. Pos: Tex. State Rep, 47-53; Tex. State Sen, 53-66; U.S. Rep, Tex, 67- Bus. & Prof. Pos: Attorney-at-law. Mil. Serv: Army Air Corps. Mem: Am. Legion; K. of C; bd. of dir, Laredo Int. Fair and Expos, Inc. Rel: Catholic. Legal Res: 2301 Fremont, Laredo, Tex. 78040. Mailing Add: Room 1514, Longworth House Office Bldg, Washington, D.C. 20515.

KEADLE, HAYGOOD D
b. Barnesville, Ga, 2/9/18; s. Homer L. Keadle and Neva Haygood K; m. 6/30/39 to Grace Newberry; c. Patsy Grace, Haygood Jr, Timothy Allen. Educ: Gordon Mil. Col, 37. Polit. & Govt. Pos: Ga. State Rep, 61-64. Bus. & Prof. Pos: Hardware merchant. Mil. Serv: Army, 1st Lt, 42-44. Mem: Mason; Scottish Rite; Shrine; past pres, Kiwanis; trustee, Gordon Mil. Col, 50- Rel: Primitive Baptist. Mailing Add: Barnesville, Ga. 30204. (1967)

KEADY, GEORGE CREGAN, JR. R
Mem, Longmeadow Rep. Town Cmt, Mass.
b. Brooklyn, N.Y, 6/16/24; s. George C. Keady and Marie V. Lussier K; m. 9/2/50 to Patricia Drake; c. Margaret D, Marie E, George C, III, Catherine A. and Kathleen V. Educ: Fordham Univ, 41-43, B.S, 49; Univ. Kans, 43-44; Columbia Univ, J.D, 50; Phi Delta Phi. Polit. & Govt. Pos: Pres, Springfield Young Men's Rep. Club, Mass, 52-54; mem, Longmeadow Rep. Town Cmt, 52-, v.chmn, 58-62; pub. adminstr, Hampden Co, 56-; alternate del, Rep. Nat. Conv, 60, del, 64; selectman, Town of Longmeadow, 58-67, chmn, 60, 63 & 66, moderator, 67- Bus. & Prof. Pos: Lectr, West. New Eng. Col. Law Sch, 53-; pres, Child Guid. Clin. of Springfield, 62-64; asst. treas, Wesson Maternity Hosp, 63-; pres, Hampden Dist. Ment. Health Clin, 65- Mil. Serv: Entered as Pvt, Army, 43, released as 1st Sgt, 46, after serv. in 42nd Div, ETO, 45-46; Bronze Star; ETO Campaign Ribbon. Mem: Pres, Hampden Co. Bar Asn, 65-67; Mass. and Am. Bar Asns; Mass. Rep. Club; Mass. Conveyancers Asn; Am. Legion; Longmeadow Men's Club; Colony Club. Rel: Roman Catholic. Mailing Add: 238 Longmeadow St, Longmeadow, Mass. 01106.

KEALY, ROBERT LOUIS D
b. St. Paul, Minn, 5/5/16; s. Peter Kealy and Emma Leopold K; m. 6/20/50 to Molly Abbott; c. Erin, Jared, Abby, Megan, Molly and Peter. Educ: Univ. Chicago, J.D, 49; Univ. Wis, M.A, 69. Polit. & Govt. Pos: Attorney, U.S. Dept. Agr, 49-66; alternate del, Dem. Nat. Conv, 68. Mil. Serv: Entered as Pvt, Army, 42, released as S/Sgt, 45, after serv. in Tenth Army, Cent. Pac. and Far East Theatres, 42-45; Army Res, 49-, Lt. Col. Mem: Ill. and Wis. Bar. Rel: Unitarian. Mailing Add: 34012 Valley Rd, Oconomowoc, Wis. 53066.

KEANE, FRANCIS MICHAEL D
Mass. State Rep.
b. Natick, Mass, 4/8/33; s. Michael F. Keane (deceased) and Clara A. K.(deceased); m. Apr. 1965 to Phyllis Ann; c. Stacy Ann and Michael Francis. Educ: Boston Col, 52-54 & 56-58; Portia Law Sch, LL.B, 68. Polit. & Govt. Pos: Mass. State Rep, 40th Middlesex Dist, 69- Mil. Serv: Entered as Pfc, Army, 54, released as Sgt, 56, after serv. in 82nd Paratroops; Paratrooper Wings. Mem: Elks; Kiwanis. Rel: Catholic. Mailing Add: 169 Cottage St, Natick, Mass. 01760.

KEANE, JACK D
b. St. Louis, Mo, 7/31/27; m. 5/20/50 to Mary Jane Welte; c. Karen Ann, John Michael, Kelly Kathleen, Timothy Patrick. Educ: St. Louis Univ. Polit. & Govt. Pos: Mo. State Rep, 64-66. Bus. & Prof. Pos: V.pres, Shamrock Chem. Co; fireman, 6 years; prof. baseball player; union rep, AFL-CIO, 10 years. Mil. Serv: Army, 46-48. Mem: Hibernian; Kiwanis; Webster Groves Sunday Morning Club. Rel: Catholic. Mailing Add: 7648 Grant Haven Dr, Affton, Mo. 63123. (1967)

KEANE, MICHAEL J. D
b. Manchester, N.H, 1/17/96; married; c. two. Educ: Manchester schs. Polit. & Govt. Pos: N.H. State Rep, -67; Mem, N.H. State Fish & Game Comm; Bd. of Mayor & Alderman from Ward 6 Manchester. Bus. & Prof. Pos: Retired. Mil. Serv: U.S. Army, WW I. Mem: Am. Legion; E. Manchester Fish & Game Club; Goffstown Fish Game Club. Rel: Catholic. Mailing Add: 55 Cedar Dr, Manchester, N.H. 03103. (1967)

KEARNEY, JOHN PETERS D
b. Buffalo, N.Y, 6/7/40; s. Norman Loyola Kearney and Dorothy Peters K; m. 12/23/68 to Carol Jean Walker; c. Roberta Jean, Anthony Allen, Brian Leigh, Jeffrey Reynald and David Bennett. Educ: St. Benedict's Col, B.A, 62; Univ. Mich, M.A, 63; Univ. Wis, Ph.D, 68. Polit. & Govt. Pos: Chmn, McCarthy for Pres, Superior, Wis, 68; alternate del, Dem. Nat. Conv, 68. Bus. & Prof. Pos: Asst. prof, Wis. State Univ, Superior, 67-68; asst. prof, Seattle Univ, Wash, 68- Mem: Am. Asn. Univ. Prof; Modern Lang. Asn. Mailing Add: 1714 E. Prospect, Seattle, Wash. 98102.

KEARNEY, JOSEPH MATTHEW D
Mass. State Rep.
b. Providence, R.I, 2/23/27; s. Clarence Byron Kearney and Anna L. Murray K; m. 10/1/55 to Mary M. Wallace; c. Joseph M, Jr, Marianne, Karen Marie and Stephan Paul. Educ: Staley Col, B.A; Newman Club. Polit. & Govt. Pos: Mass. State Rep, currently. Bus. & Prof. Pos: Carrier, U.S. Post Off, 50-60. Mil. Serv: Entered as Seaman 2/C, Navy, 45, released as Radioman Striker, 46; Honor Man; Am. Theater of War Ribbon. Mem: Am. Legion; Eagles. Rel: Catholic. Mailing Add: 40 Austin St, Hyde Park, Mass. 02136. (1967)

KEARNS, CARROLL D. R
b. Youngstown, Ohio, 5/7/00; s. Patrick Henry Kearns and Ida May Carroll K; m. 8/30/33 to Nora Mary Lynch. Educ: Chicago Musical Col, B.M, M.M. and D.Mus; Westminster Col, B.S; Univ. Pittsburgh, M.Ed; Phi Mu Alpha. Polit. & Govt. Pos: U.S. Rep, 28th and 24th Dists, Pa, 47-63, ranking mem, House Cmt. Educ. and Labor and mem, D. C. Cmt; mem, D.C. Stadium and Cultural Cmn. Bus. & Prof. Pos: Asst. dir. spec. schs, Chicago, Ill, 26-29; theater dir, 29-31; head of music dept, Greenville Pub. Schs, Pa, 31-38 and Slippery Rock State Teachers Col, 38-41; supt. of schs, Farrell, 41-45; v.pres, Shenango Metalcraft Co, Pa, 63-67, pres, 67- Mil. Serv: Student Army Training Corps, 18. Publ: Miscellaneous mag. articles. Mem: Mason; Blue Lodge; Consistory; Shrine; Elks; Moose; K. of P; Grange; Cong. Country Club, Wash, D.C; Iroquois Boating and Fishing Club. Rel: Lutheran. Mailing Add: R.D. 1, Conneaut Lake, Pa. 16316.

KEARNS, HENRY R
Pres. and Chmn, Export-Import Bank of the U.S.
b. Salt Lake City, Utah, 4/30/11; s. Henry A. Kearns and Mary Orilla Robbins K; m. 10/31/38 to Marjorie Harriett Prescott; c. Patricia (Mrs. Clabaugh), Henry Timothy, Mary (Mrs. David Rohe) and Michael Prescott. Educ: Univ. Utah, 29-30. Hon. D.B.A, Woodbury Col, 60. Polit. & Govt. Pos: Mem, Hoover Cmn. Task Force on Intel. Activities, 55-56; mem, Nat. Coun. of Consult, Small Bus. Admin, 55-60; chmn, Cmt. on Export Expansion, 57-60, U.S. Govt. Rep, Gen. Agreement on Tariffs and Trade, Int. Union of Off. Travel Orgns, Int. Air Transport Asn. and Pac. Area Travel Asn; Asst. Secy. of Commerce for Int. Affairs, 57-60; exec. mem, Nat. Exec. Reserve Corps, 61-; mem, Los Angeles Dist. Attorney's Adv. Coun, 64-69; pres. and chmn, Export-Import Bank of the U.S, 69- Publ: Various articles on int. affairs. Mem: Am. Soc. of Int. Exec; Licensing Exec. Soc, Inc; San Gabriel Country Club, Pasadena, Calif; The George Town Club, Wash, D.C; Lotos Club of N.Y; Carmelita Lodge, Pasadena, Calif; Overland Club of Pasadena; pres, U.S. Jr. C. of C, 45-46; dir, Citizens Cmt. for the Hoover Reports, 55-58; pres, Pasadena Tournament of Roses Asn, 66-67. Rel: Episcopal. Mailing Add: 4903 Rockwood Pkwy. N.W, Washington, D.C. 20016.

KEARNS, TOM D
b. Somerville, Mass, 11/26/19; m. to Helen Meekins K; c. Thomas N. Jr, Clifton, Kerry Ellen, Edith. Educ: Univ. of Miami; Iron Arrow Award; Lambda Chi Alpha. Polit. & Gov. Pos: Fla. State Rep, 64-66. Bus. & Prof. Pos: Pres, transit-mix concrete and concrete block. Mil. Serv: Navy, 41. Mem: K. of C; Elks; Am. Legion; Cmt. of 100; Broward Mfrs. Asn; Navy League. Rel: St. Gregory's Catholic Church. Mailing Add: 3140 Pembroke Rd, (P.O. Box 3657), W. Hollywood, Fla. 33023. (1967)

KEAS, JACQUELINE B. R
Women's V.Chmn. North. Div, Rep. State Cent. Cmt, Calif.
b. Buchanan, Mich, 8/22/24; d. Benedict Bilotti and Frances Roti B; m. 11/8/52 to William O. Keas, Jr; c. William O, III and Stephanie. Educ: Vogue Sch. Merchandising, Chicago, Ill, 1 year. Polit. & Govt. Pos: Pres, Suburban Rep. Women, Sacramento, Calif, 61-63; campaign and precinct chmn, Calif. Rep. Women, North. Calif, 63-67; v. chmn, Co. Rep. Cent. Cmt, 64-68; women's v.chmn, North. div, Rep. State Cent. Cmt, 65-; youth activities state bd. chmn, Calif. Rep. Women, 66-67; second v.pres, Rep. Women of Calif, 68; elector, Richard M. Nixon for Pres, 68; alternate del, Rep. Nat. Conv, 68. Bus. & Prof. Pos: Millinery buyer, 44-50; ready to wear buyer children's clothes, Jackson, Mich, 50-52; exec. secy. for lawyer and real estate broker, Jackson, Mich, 52-54. Mem: Calif. PTA; Calif. Rep. Women of Sacramento; Am. River Col. Patrons. Calif. Hon. Life Membership, Calif. Cong. PTA. Rel: Episcopal. Mailing Add: 4340 Figwood Way, Sacramento, Calif. 95825.

KEASLER, WILLIAM HENRY R
Secy. and Treas, Gallatin Co. Rep. Cent. Cmt, Ill.
b. Omaha, Ill, 5/17/20; s. Samuel R. Keasler and Grace Hall K; m. 7/3/42 to Wanda Faulkner; c. Pamela (Mrs. Edward Metten) and Mike. Educ: Ridgway High Sch. Polit. & Govt. Pos: Rep. precinct committeeman, Omaha, Ill, 58-; twp. supvr, 64-; secy. and treas, Gallatin Co.Rep. Cent. Cmt, 66- Mil. Serv: Army, 42, released as Cpl, 45, after serv. in 28th Div, ETO, 44-45; Personal Citation. Mem: VFW. Mailing Add: Omaha, Ill. 62871.

KEATING, EDGAR J. D
Mo. State Sen.
b. Chicago, Ill, 3/28/89; m. 6/10/18 to Hazel Murray; c. Four. Educ: Kansas City Law, 17. Polit. & Govt. Pos: Mo. State Rep, 30-38; Mo. State Sen, 48- Bus. & Prof. Pos: Lawyer. Mem: K. of C; St. Vincent de Paul; Holy Name; Am. and Mo. Bar Asns; Kans. City Bar; Am. Judicature Soc; Elks; Hillcrest Country Club. Rel: Catholic. Mailing Add: 314 Norton, Kansas City, Mo. 64124. (1967)

KEATING, EDWARD MICHAEL
b. N.Y.C, 4/17/25; s. George Thomas Keating and Harriet Martin K; m. 9/14/47 to Helen Beatrice English; c. Michael, Karen, Stephen, Mary Melissa and Katherine Ann. Educ: Stanford Univ, A.B, 48, LL.B, 50. Bus. Pos: Ed. and publisher, Ramparts Mag. Mil. Serv: Naval Res, 43-46. Recipient Brotherhood Award, Peninsula Coun. B'nai B'rith, 64. Mailing Add: 54 Rosewood Dr, Atherton, Calif. 94025. (1967)

KEATING, KENNETH B. R
U.S. Ambassador to India
b. Lima, N.Y, 5/18/00; s. Thomas Mosgrove Keating and Louise Barnard K; m. 4/11/28 to Louise DePuy, wid; c. Judith (Mrs. James E. Howe). Educ: Genesee Wesleyan Sem, 11-15; Univ. Rochester, A.B. 19; Harvard, LL.B, 23; Delta Upsilon; Phi Beta Kappa. Hon. LL.D, Univ. Rochester, 54 and Harvard. Polit. & Govt. Pos: U.S. Cong. Del. to Coun. of Europe, Interparliamentary Union, Wash, 53, Vienna, 54, Helsinki, 55, Bangkok, 56 and London, 57; U.S. Rep, N.Y, 46-58; del, Intergovt. Cmt, European Migration Conf, 56-57; U.S. Sen, N.Y, 58-64; judge, Court of Appeals, N.Y, 65-69; U.S. Ambassador to India, 69- Bus. & Prof. Pos: Assoc, Harris, Beach, Keating, Wilcox, Dale & Linowitz, Attorneys, Rochester, N.Y, 23-46 & 65, Royall, Koegel & Rogers, New York, 65- Mil. Serv: From Sgt. to Brig. Gen, Army, World War II; Legion of Merit with Oak Leaf Cluster; Am, European and Asiatic Theatre Ribbons with 3 Battle Stars; Order of the Brit. Empire. Mem: Am. Legion; VFW; ROA; Am, N.Y. State, N.Y.C. and Monroe Co. Bar Asns; Mason (33°); Moose; Elks; Eagles; Univ, Rochester, Brook, Sky and New York Clubs. Rel: Presbyterian. Legal Res: 3500 Elmwood Ave, Rochester, N.Y. 14610. Mailing Add: U.S. Embassy, New Delhi, India.

KEATING, RICHARD MICHAEL D
Chmn, Wayne Co. Dem. Exec. and Cent. Cmts, Ohio
b. Cleveland, Ohio, 7/22/26; s. John Thomas Keating and Elizabeth Lillian Walsh K; m. 7/31/54 to Martha Marie Franko; c. Louise Walsh and John Thomas. Educ: Cleveland Marshal Law Sch, LL.B. magna cum laude, 51; Delta Theta Phi. Polit. & Govt. Pos: Chmn, Wayne Co. Dem. Exec. and Cent. Cmt, Ohio, 64-; mem, Wayne Co. Bd. Elec, 66-; del, Dem. Nat. Conv, 68. Mil. Serv: Entered as A/S, Navy, 44, released as Electrician 2/C, 46, after serv. in Pac. Theater. Mem: Elks; Moose; K. of C; Am. Legion. Rel: Catholic. Legal Res: 889 Northview Dr, Wooster, Ohio 44691. Mailing Add: 141 E. Liberty, Wooster, Ohio 44691.

KEATINGE, RICHARD HARTE D
b. San Francisco, Calif, 12/4/19; m. 4/20/44 to Betty West; c. Richard West, Daniel Wilson and Anne Elizabeth. Educ: Univ. Calif, A.B. in Econ, 39; Harvard Univ, M.A. in Econ, 41; Georgetown Univ. Law Sch, LL.B, 44; Phi Beta Kappa; mem, bd. of eds, Georgetown Law Jour; admitted to D.C. Bar, 44, N.Y. Bar, 45, Calif. Bar, 47 and U.S. Supreme Court, 64. Polit. & Govt. Pos: Del, Dem. Nat. Conv, 52 & 64; trustee, Dem. Assocs, Inc, 58-, chmn, 67-; mem, Calif. Law Rev. Cmn, 61-68, v.chmn, 63-65, chmn, 65-67; Spec. Asst. Attorney Gen, Calif, 64-68; pub. mem, Admin. Conf. of the U.S, 68- Bus. & Prof. Pos: Pvt. law practice, N.Y.C, 44-45, Wash, D.C, 45-47 and Los Angeles, 47-; sr. partner, Keatinge & Sterling, 48-; dir, KRATOS and Armstrong Nurseries, Inc, Los Angeles. Mem: Fel, Am. Bar Found; Am. Law Inst; Am. Bar Asn.(nat. secy. jr. bar conf, 59-60, admin. law sect, coun. mem, 61-64 & 65-69, chmn, 67-68, mem. spec. cmt. housing and urban develop. law, 68-); State Bar of Calif; Los Angeles Co. Bar Asn.(del, Conf. of State Bar Del, 66 & 67, chmn, taxation sect, 66-67); Inter-Am. Bar Asn; Int. Bar Asn; Am. Judicature Soc; Nat. Planning Asn.(nat. coun, 56-); Am. Arbit. Asn.(mem. nat. panel arbitrators, 50-); trustee, Coro Found, 62-; mem, Los Angeles Athletic Club; Balboa Bay Club; Racquet Club; Harvard Club of South. Calif. Rel: Episcopal. Legal Res: 1160 Virginia Rd, San Marino, Calif. 91108. Mailing Add: 458 S. Spring St, Los Angeles, Calif. 90013.

KEATON, CLARIS EDMOND D
Chmn, Brown Co. Dem. Party, Ind.
b. Brown Co, Ind, 7/10/08; s. Roy Miller Keaton and Lena Richardson K; m. 4/2/33 to Laura Edith Mathis; c. William Roy, Phillip Ray and Linda Kay. Polit. & Govt. Pos: Assessor, Brown Co. Hwy. Dept, Dept. of Co. Govt, Ind, 48-58, supt, 58-61; chmn, Brown Co. Dem. Party, 52- Mem: Asn. of Ind. Officials, Inc; F&AM; Eastern Star; Scottish Rite; Lions; Farm Bur; Auctioneers. Rel: Christian Church. Mailing Add: R.R. 2, Nashville, Ind. 47448.

KEATON, HARRY JOSEPH R
Mem, Calif. Rep. State Cent. Cmt.
b. Prague, Czech, 6/8/25; s. Fred G. Keaton and Nina Ordner K; m. 12/21/52 to Minto E. Hannus; c. Elizabeth, Deborah, Janette and Juliana. Educ: San Francisco City Col, 47-48; Univ. of Calif, Berkeley, B.A. in econ, 50, Sch. of Law, LL.B, 53; Phi Beta Kappa; revising ed, Calif. Law Rev, 52-53; Order of the Coif; Phi Alpha Delta. Polit. & Govt. Pos: Participant, Rep. Polit. Campaigns, including those for Eisenhower and Nixon, 60, 62 & 68; gen. counsel, Young Rep. of Calif, 60-61, nat. committeeman, 61-62 and pres, 62-63; mem, Calif. Rep. State Cent. Cmt, 61-, mem. exec. cmt. and chmn. labor cmt, 61-64; founding mem, Calif. Rep. League, past exec. v.pres, South. Calif. v.pres. for legal affairs, 68; v.pres, Los Angeles Co. Rep. Assembly, 64; treas, Calif. Lawyers for Nixon-Agnew, 68. Bus. & Prof. Pos: Partner, Rutan & Tucker, Attorneys, Los Angeles and Santa Ana, Calif, currently; lectr, labor law, Univ. of South. Calif, 62-66. Publ: Author, articles on labor law and other legal subjects, 62-66. Mem: Sponsor, Atlantic Coun. of the U.S, Inc; Los Angeles World Affairs Coun; Atlantic Asn. of Young Polit. Leaders (Am. del. to meetings in Bonn, 63, Oxford, 65 and Paris, 65, treas. and mem. exec. cmt. 63-65); Orange Co. Bar Asn; Los Angeles Co. Bar Asn.(del, state bar conf, 7 years, chmn, lawyer reference and legal aid cmt, 68-69, bd. of trustees, 69-); Am. Bar Asn.(mem, co. and state bar cmts. and cmts. of labor law sect); Los Angeles Dist. Attorneys Adv. Coun, 65-; Town Hall; Los Angeles Athletic Club; Anti-Defamation League West. Regional Adv. Bd.(chmn. civil rights cmt, mem. exec. cmt); past mem, Commun. Rels. Cmt. of the Jewish Fedn-Coun. of Gr. Los Angeles; bd. of dirs, Los Angeles Neighborhood Legal Serv. Soc. Rel: Jewish. Mailing Add: 10638 Ashton Ave, Los Angeles, Calif. 90024.

KEE, C.G. R
b. Barnes Count, N.Dak, 6/30/06; married; c. 7. Polit. & Govt. Pos: N.Dak. State Sen, 55-61; N.Dak. State Rep, 41. Bus. & Prof. Pos: Farmer; auto implement dealer. Mil. Serv: WW II. Mem: Masons; Knights Templar; Shrine. Rel: Presbyterian. Mailing Add: Ellendale, N.Dak. 58436. (1967)

KEE, ELIZABETH D
m. to John Kee (deceased); c. James, Frances. Polit. & Govt. Pos: U.S. Rep, W.Va, 82nd and 88th Cong, mem, Cmt. Vet. Affairs and Interior and Insular Affairs. Bus. & Prof. Pos: Author weekly column, W.Va. papers and weekly radio and TV progs, W.Va. networks; author of articles on real estate. Mem: Am. Newspaper Women's Club; Cong. Club; Bluefield Country Club. Rel: Catholic. Mailing Add: 105 Oakhurst Ave, Bluefield, W.Va. 24701.

KEE, JAMES D
U.S. Rep, W.Va.
b. Bluefield, W.Va, 5/15/17; s. John Kee and Elizabeth K; m. to Helen Lee Chapman; c. Three daughters. Educ: Southeast. Univ. Law Sch; Sch. of For. Serv, Georgetown Univ. Polit. & Govt. Pos: Career for. serv. staff officer, U.S. State Dept; asst. to clerk of U.S. House of Rep, 4 years; housing adv, U.S. Housing Authority; admin. asst. to U.S. Rep. Elizabeth Kee, 53-65; chmn, State Soc. Participation Cmt, Kennedy-Johnson Inaugural Cmt, W.Va, 61; U.S. Rep. W.Va, 65- Mil. Serv: Army Air Force. Mem: Wash. Coal Club; Elks; hon. v.pres, Dem. Club of D.C; past pres, Greenbriar Mil. Sch. Alumni Asn; past pres, Conf. of State Soc; Am. Legion. W.Va. Son of the Year, 62; W.Virginian of the Year, 64. Rel: Episcopal. Legal Res: 105 Oakhurst, Bluefield, W.Va. 24701. Mailing Add: 215 Cannon House Office Bldg, Washington, D.C. 20515.

KEEFE, JAMES EDWARD D
Wash. State Sen.
b. N.Y.C, 1908; m. to Eileen; c. Two. Educ: Gonzaga High Sch. Polit. & Govt. Pos: Wash. State Sen, currently. Bus. & Prof. Pos: Sales mgr. Mem: Elks. Mailing Add: 412 N. Glass Ave, Spokane, Wash. 99205. (1967)

KEEFE, JAMES THOMAS D
b. Lowell, Mass, 9/5/29; s. Thomas Keefe and Josephine Manning K; m. 12/27/52 to Janet Mansfield; c. Joseph, Quentin, Paul, Thomas, James, Jr, Anne, Maura and Patrick. Educ: Keith Acad; Merrimack Col. Polit. & Govt. Pos: Pres, Merrimack Col. Young Dem, 51-52; chmn, Rockingham Co. Dem. Cmt, N.H, 60-64; admin. asst. to U.S. Sen. McIntyre, N.H, 62-68; mem. exec. cmt, N.H. State Dem. Cmt, 63-64; Dem. nominee, U.S. Rep, First Cong. Dist, N.H, 68; state dir, Fed. Housing Admin, 68- Bus. & Prof. Pos: Gen. mgr, Dunfey Agency, Inc, Hampton, N.H, 54-64. Mem: Nat. Capital Dem. Club. Rel: Catholic. Mailing Add: 75 Steinmetz Dr, Manchester, N.H. 03104.

KEEFE, JOHN B. R
Minn. State Rep.
b. Chicago, Ill, 5/28/28; s. John L. Keefe and Aurlia Gagnon K; m. 11/3/53 to Rosemary A. Campion; c. John, Jr, Lynn, Stephen and Lisa. Educ: Macalester Col, 49-51; Univ. Minn, B.A, 53; William Mitchell Col. Law, LL.B, 58; Alpha Tau Omega. Polit. & Govt. Pos: Munic. judge, Hopkins, Minn, 62-63, mem, Park and Recreation Cmn, 64-66; Minn. State Rep, Dist. 29 B, 67- Mil. Serv: Pfc, Army, 46-47, serv. in Seventh Cavalry, Japan. Mem: Co. and State Bar Asns; Lions Club; Elks; K. of C; Citizens League; Am. Judiciary Soc; Interlocken Country Club. Rel: Catholic. Legal Res: 201 Oakwood Rd, Hopkins, Minn. 55343.

KEEFE, ROBERT JOSEPH D
b. Huntington, Ind, 5/29/34; s. Francis J. Keefe and Helen Teusch K; m. to Sheila M; c. Scot T, Michael J, Erin M, Kevin S, Dirk P. and Christopher F. Educ: Marquette Univ, B.S, 56; Sigma Delta Chi; Alpha Phi Omega. Polit. & Govt. Pos: Admin. asst. to U.S. Rep. J. Edward Roush, 60-62; admin. asst. to U.S. Sen. Birch Bayh, Ind, 63- Bus. & Prof. Pos: Copywriter, Louis E. Wade Advert, 56; sales & promotion mgr, WANE-TV, 57-60. Rel: Catholic. Legal Res: 962 N. Guilford St, Huntington, Ind. 46750. Mailing Add: 100 W. Linden St, Alexandria, Va. 22301.

KEEFE, RUTH ELEANOR D
Mem, Hamilton Co. Dem. Exec. Cmt, Ohio
b. Cincinnati, Ohio, 7/17/24; d. William A.A. Castellini and Ruth McGregor C; m. 9/27/47 to Judge John W. Keefe; c. John M, Thomas W, Daniel McGregor, Kevin Lausche, Ruth S. and Lelia M. Educ: Univ. Cincinnati, B.A. with high honors, 46; Alpha Lambda Delta; Guidon; Mortar Bd; Theta Phi Alpha. Polit. & Govt. Pos: Mem. bd, Hamilton Co. Women's Dem. Club, Ohio, 57-59; del, Dem. Nat. Conv, 64; campaign mgr. for Dem. Judicial Cand, 63, 65 & 66; chmn, women's div, Hamilton Co. Dem. Party, 64-66, precinct exec, 66-; mem, Hamilton Co. Dem. Exec. and Steering Cmts, Ohio, 66-; v.chmn, Fourth Ward, Cincinnati, Hamilton Co. Dem. Orgn, 68-69. Bus. & Prof. Pos: Chmn. pub. rels, Youth Employ. Serv, 61- Mem: V.pres. exec. cmt, trustee and past treas, Citizens' Cmt. on Youth, Cincinnati, Ohio; St. Mary Hosp. Guild; Our Lady of Mercy Hosp. Guild; Mothers of Twins Club. Rel: Roman Catholic. Mailing Add: 3662 Kendall Ave, Cincinnati, Ohio 45208.

KEEFE, WILLIAM F. D
b. Portsmouth, N.H, 4/16/11; married; c. One; three grandchildren. Educ: Portsmouth. Polit. & Govt. Pos: Clerk, Portsmouth del, N.H; registr, Voters-at-Lg; ward clerk; mem, City Coun; N.H. State Rep, 59-69. Bus. & Prof. Pos: Real estate broker. Mem: K. of C; Moose; Holy Name Soc. Rel: Catholic. Mailing Add: 80 Concord Way, Portsmouth, N.H. 03801. (1967)

KEEGAN, BETTY ANN SOUTHWICK D
North. Dist. Chairwoman, Women's Div, Dem. State Cent. Cmt, Ill.
b. Springfield, Ill, 1/23/20; d. Harry Holmes Southwick, M.D. and Benita Brown S; m. 6/24/42 to Thomas Arthur Keegan; c. Anne Brunk, Elizabeth Talbot and Thomas Southwick. Educ: Rockford Col, B.A, 41; Univ. Wis, grad. study. Polit. & Govt. Pos: Dem. chairwoman, Winnebago Co, Ill, 44-46; mem, Ill. Cmn. on Children and Youth, 49-53; Dem. state cent. committeewoman, 16th Cong. Dist, Ill, 62-64; nat. committeewoman, Young Dem. of Ill; pub. mem, Ill. Elec. Laws Cmn, 63-; north. dist. chairwoman, women's div, Dem. State Cent. Cmt, 64-; del-at-lg, Dem. Nat. Conv, 64 & 68, mem. cmt. on permanent orgn, 64 and rules cmt, 68. Mem: League of Women Voters; Jr. League of Rockford. Rel: Congregational. Mailing Add: 1210 National Ave, Rockford, Ill. 61103.

KEEGAN, JOHN FRANCIS D
b. Chicago, Ill, 5/1/31; s. Frank H. Keegan and Muriel Janisch K; m. 6/15/57 to Rosemary Cuny; c. Timothy J. and Colleen M. Educ: LaSalle Inst, Mo, 49-53. Polit. & Govt. Pos: Alternate del, Dem. Nat. Conv, 68; dir, Dem. for Democracy, Miramar, Fla, mem, North Dade Dem, North Miami Beach and adv. to State Treas. and Ins. Cmnr, currently. Bus. & Prof. Pos: State agent, U.S. Underwriters of Ga. and v.pres, Am. Maritime Serv. Agency, Inc, currently. Mem: Fla. Shrimp Asn.(pres, 67-68); Southeast. Fisheries Asn;(mem. ins. cmt); Gulf & Caribbean Fisheries Inst; Am. Soc. Int. Execs; Propeller Club U.S; Elks; Navy League; Cath. Order Foresters; Greater Miami C. of C. Rel: Catholic. Mailing Add: 1779 N.E. 174th St, North Miami Beach, Fla. 33162.

KEEGAN, JOSEPH M. D
b. Passaic, N.J, 2/27/22. Educ: Holy Cross Col, B.A; John Marshall Law Sch, LL.B. Polit. & Govt. Pos: Secy. to Cmnr. of Revenue and Finance, Passaic, N.J, secy. to Mayor; former N.J. State Sen. Bus. & Prof. Pos: Attorney. Mem: Am. Legion; DAV; Marine Corps League; Friendly Sons of St. Patrick. Mailing Add: 165 Prospect St, Passaic, N.J. 07055. (1967)

KEEGAN, WILLIAM TOOMEY D
Chmn, Washington Co. Dem. Party, Maine
b. Weymouth, Mass, 8/10/20; s. Charles J. Keegan and Agnes Louise Toomey K; m. 2/27/41 to Carolyn Alley; c. Agnes Bonnie Lee (Mrs. William Miliken); grandchildren, Melanie, Maryellen and Carol Michele. Educ: Weymouth High, 34-38; Int. Correspondence Sch, 66-69. Polit. & Govt. Pos: Chmn, Jonesport Dem. Town Cmt, Maine, 60-; chmn, Wash. Co. Dem. Party, 66-; selectman, Jonesport, Maine, 67-68; mem, Washington Co. Adv. Cmt, 68- Bus. & Prof. Pos: Carpenter, Consolidated Construction, 57-59; carpenter-welder, Petit

Kiewit Co, 59-66; supvr, N.E. Peat Moss Inc, 66- Mil. Serv: Entered as Pvt, 43, released 46, after serv. in 101st MP, Fifth Army, ETO, 44-46; ETO Ribbon; Good Conduct Medal. Mem: Jonesport C. of C; Wash. Co. C. of C; Am. Legion. Rel: Catholic. Mailing Add: 95 Main St, Jonesport, Maine. 04649.

KEEL, JOHN PEYTON D
Chmn, Jackson Co. Dem. Cent. Cmt, Ark.
b. Pine Bluff, Ark, 1/11/05; s. John Hardee Keel and Gertrude Tucker K; m. 3/5/30 to Gladys Spencer; c. Mary Katherine, Gertrude, Patsy, Joan, John Edward and Franklin. Educ: Newport High Sch, grad. Polit. & Govt. Pos: Mem, Jackson Co. Dem. Cent. Cmt, Ark, 28- Rel: Methodist. Mailing Add: Route 4, Newport, Ark. 72112.

KEEL, WILLIAM ARNOLD, JR. D
b. Louisville, Ky, 10/10/24; s. William Arnold Keel and Birdie Viola Durham K; m. 10/27/49 to Jean Harmon; c. William Baker. Educ: Carson-Newman Col, 1 year; Univ. Tenn, B.S. in Bus. Admin; Phi Beta Phi; Journalism Club; Orange and White. Polit. & Govt. Pos: Asst. to dep. chmn. for pub. affairs, Dem. Nat. Cmt, 62-63, White House liaison for dept. of pub. affairs, 63, research dir. and ed. of The Dem, 63-64; spec. asst. to adminstr, U.S. Small Bus. Admin, 64-65; admin. asst. to U.S. Rep. Joe L. Evins, Tenn, 65- Bus. & Prof. Pos: Govt. and polit. writer, Nashville Tennessean, 52-62. Mil. Serv: Entered as A/S, Navy, 43, released as Pharm. Mate, 2/C, 46, after serv. in Sixth Marine Corps Naval Hosp, U.S. and Pac. Theatre, 45-46; Victory Medal, Asiatic-Pac. Medal, Am. Theatre Medal. Mem: Burro Club; Cong. Secy's Club; Tenn. State Soc; Univ. Tenn. Alumni Asn. Rel: Baptist. Legal Res: Smithville, Tenn. 37166. Mailing Add: 8418 Stonewall Dr, Vienna, Va. 22180.

KEELE, HAROLD O. D
b. Dysart, Iowa, 6/11/11; s. Peter Keele and Emma Fillgraf K; m. 8/7/37 to Louise Hutchison; c. Karen (Mrs. Madden) and James. Educ: Cornell Col, B.A; State Univ. Iowa, J.D; Gamma Eta Gamma; pres, Sr. Law Class; Alpha Chi Epsilon. Polit. & Govt. Pos: Mayor, West Liberty, Iowa, 46-56; alternate del, Dem. Nat. Conv, 60 & 64. Mil. Serv: Entered as Lt.(jg), Navy, 44, released as Lt. Mem: Pres, Muscatine Co. Bar Asn, 43-44; Iowa and Am. Bar Asns; Mason, Consistory, Shriner; C. of C; Rotary. Rel: Methodist. Legal Res: 201 W. Maxon Ave, West Liberty, Iowa 52776. Mailing Add: 104 E. Third St, West Liberty, Iowa 53776.

KEELER, VIRGINIA LEE D
V.Chmn, Dutchess Co. Dem. Cmt, N.Y.
b. White Plains, N.Y, 10/17/30; d. Wilbur Elwood Miles, Jr. and Elizabeth Mary Woods M; m. 8/27/49 to Howard Stewart Keeler; c. Scott Howard, Robin Elizabeth, Michael William, J. Stuart and twins, Kerry Michael and Kelly Ann. Educ: Dutchess Commun. Col, various courses. Polit. & Govt. Pos: Town committeewoman, Wappingers Falls, N.Y, 65-69; v.chmn, Wappingers Dem. Club, 66-68 and Wappingers Dem. Cmt, 68-69; recording secy, Dutchess Co. Women's Dem. Club, 67-69, chmn. of nominating cmt, 69-; v.chmn, Citizens for Robert Kennedy, 68; v.chmn, Dutchess Co. Dem. Cmt, 68- Mem: Town chmn, Commun. Chest, 67; past bd. mem. and ed. of paper, League of Women Voters of Poughkeepsie; past bd. mem, White Plains Women's Club and Jr. Auxiliary of the White Plains Hosp. Rel: Unitarian; chmn. of Denominational Affairs, Unitarian Church. Mailing Add: Spook Hill Rd, Wappingers Falls, N.Y. 12590.

KEENA, THOMAS EUGENE JOSEPH D
b. Hartford, Conn, 7/3/20; s. Michael Thomas Keena and Mary Agnes Sleeth K; m. 10/8/49 to Gloria E. Maguire; c. Paris. Educ: Yale Univ, B.A; Univ. Paris, cert. Polit. & Govt. Pos: Admin. asst, U.S. Rep. E.Q. Daddario, Conn, 59- Bus. & Prof. Pos: Mem. staff, Hartford Courant, 41-58. Mil. Serv: Entered as Pvt, Army, 42, released as Lt. Col, 62, after serv. in 43rd Inf. Div, NATO ETO; Army Res, Lt. Col.(Ret). Rel: Catholic. Mailing Add: 4019 Veazey St. N.W, Washington, D.C. 20016.

KEENAN, EDWARD JOHN R
N.Y. State Assemblyman
b. New York, N.Y, 12/7/27; s. Thomas J. Keenan and Julia B. Saunders K; m. 12/6/54 to Erika C. Athing; c. Denise, Edward, Michele, John, Yvonne and James. Educ: N.Y. State Inst, 47-48. Polit. & Govt. Pos: Mayor, Ogdensburg, N.Y, 62-66; N.Y. State Assemblyman, St. Lawrence Co, 67- Bus. & Prof. Pos: Pres, Ogdensburg Commerce & Navigation, Keenan Shipping, Sea Bulk Corp. and Potsdam Dew Drop Up Corp. Mil. Serv: Merchant Marines, 44-45; re-entered serv. as Ens, Navy, 53, released as Lt, 57, after serv. in Mil. Sea Transporation Serv. Off; Bremerhaven; Lt, Res; European-Am. Defense Medal; Korean Medal; Atlantic-Pac. Victory Medal. Mem: VFW; Am. Legion; Rotary; Navy League; Naval Res. Officers' Asn. City Man of the Year Award, 62 and State Man of the Year Award, 63, Jr. C. of C. Rel: Roman Catholic. Legal Res: 502 Ford St, Ogdensburg, N.Y. 13669. Mailing Add: 228 Franklin St, Ogdensburg, N.Y. 13669.

KEENAN, FRANCIS JOYCE R
b. Dover, N.H, 1/19/24; s. Thomas H. Keenan and Mary E. Winslow K; m. 4/14/56 to Joan M. Swenson; c. Thomas Winslow and Alan Joyce Christopher. Educ: Univ. Notre Dame; Harvard Univ. Grad. Sch. Arts and Scis; Econ. Round Table, Notre Dame. Polit. & Govt. Pos: Admin. Asst. to U.S. Rep. Florence P. Dwyer, 12th Dist, N.J, 58-; legis. asst. to Sen. John Sherman Cooper, Ky, 56-57; campaign coordinator for U.S. Rep. Perkins Bass, N.H, 54; asst. chief clerk, Cmt. on Interstate and For. Commerce, U.S. Senate, 51-53; staff mem, Select Cmt. on Small Bus, U.S. Senate, 50; asst. campaign mgr. for Sen. Charles W. Tobey, N.H, 50. Bus. & Prof. Pos: Legis Ed, Am. Aviation Publns, 55-56; rep, Louis de Rochemont-Cinerama, Wash, 53-56; correspondent, Commonweal Magazine, Wash, 53-55. Mil. Serv: Entered as A/S, Navy, 43, released as Lt.(jg), 46, after service in Pacific Area; Atlantic Campaign, Asiatic-Pac. Campaign, Philippines and China Occupational Ribbons. Mem: Am. Polit. Sci. Asn; Notre Dame Club of Wash; adv. cmt, Rep. for Progress; Am. Montessori Soc; past pres, Capitol Hill Montessori Sch, Inc. Rel: Roman Catholic. Legal Res: 39 Hough St, Dover, N.H. 03820. Mailing Add: 115 Sixth St. S.E, Washington, D.C. 20003. (1967)

KEENAN, MADELYN CAHILL D
V.Chmn, Vt. State Dem. Cmt.
b. Island Pond, Vt, 12/8/12; d. John T. Cahill and Kathryn McNamara C; m. 5/28/38 to Roland Edmund Keenan; c. Kathleen (Mrs. Camisa) and Maureen Carol. Educ: Champlain Col, 31. Polit. & Govt. Pos: Mem, Dem. City Cmt, Vt, 48, treas, 50; committeewoman, Vt. State Dem. Cmt, 54, v.chmn, 58-; mem, Franklin Co. Dem. Cmt, 56; historian, Dem. State Women's Club, 65. Bus. & Prof. Pos: Adv. bd. mem, Fanny Allen Sch. of Practical Nurses, 56- Mem: Autonoe Club; Cath. Daughters Am; Am. Legion Auxiliary. Rel: Catholic. Mailing Add: 112 Lincoln Ave, St. Albans, Vt. 05478. (1967)

KEENAN, PAUL A, JR. D
Mem, Ga. Dem. Exec. Cmt.
b. Albany, Ga, 11/15/20; s. Paul A. Keenan and Mattie Wilkerson K; m. to Lucile Dennison; c. Jere W, William P, Alexander S. and David L. Educ: Baylor Sch, 38; Emory Univ, B.Ph, 42, J.D, 47; Omicron Delta Kappa. Polit. & Govt. Pos: Mem, Ga. Dem. Exec. Cmt, 62-; mem, Ga. Waterways Cmn. and chmn, Dougherty Co. Cmn, 65- Bus. & Prof. Pos: Partner, Watson, Keenan, Spence and Lowe, Attorneys, 48-; pres, Keenan Auto Parts Co, 62- Mil. Serv: Entered as Pvt, Army, 43, released as 2nd Lt, Inf, 46. Mem: Am. Legion. Rel: Episcopal. Legal Res, 3303 Old Dawson Rd, Albany, Ga. 31701. Mailing Add: P.O. Box 347, Albany, Ga. 31702.

KEENAN, ROBERT P. D
Kans. State Rep.
b. Great Bend, Kans, 12/30/22; s. Patrick L. Keenan and Mary Hall K; m. 9/9/61 to Dorothy B. Burnette; c. Robert P, II, Gregory C. and Rodney R. Educ: Ft. Hays, Kans. State Col, B.S. in Bus. Admin, 45; Univ. Kans, J.D, 49; Phi Delta Phi; Seventh Cavalry; Tau Kappa Epsilon; Newman Club. Polit. & Govt. Pos: Kans. State Rep, Dist. 108, 67-, Dem. caucus chmn, Kans. House of Rep, 69-; pres, Kans. Dem. Club, 69-; v.pres, Kans. Dem. Vet. Club, 69- Bus. & Prof. Pos: Attorney, self-employed, 49-56; partner, Law Firm of Keenan & Keenan, 56-66. Mil. Serv: Entered as Seaman, Navy, 43, released as Lt.(jg), 46, after serv. as Exec. Officer, USS Dobler, Atlantic and USS Crosley, Pac, 44-46; European and Asiatic Theater Ribbons. Mem: Past pres, Barton Co. Bar Asn; Kans. and Southwest Kans. Bar Asns; exalted ruler, Elks Lodge 1127; v.pres. and bd. mem, Great Bend Kiwanis Club; post advocate, VFW 3111; past pres, Great Bend Jr. C. of C. Rel: Catholic. Legal Res: 2511 Broadway, Great Bend, Kans. 67530. Mailing Add: P.O. Drawer 459, Great Bend, Kans. 67530.

KEENAN, THOMAS LE ROY D
b. Buffalo, N.Y, 7/7/28; s. William Stephen Keenan, Sr. and Catherine Lang K; m. 7/7/66 to Marilyn T. Mahoney; c. Carolyn Mary and Joseph Thomas. Educ: Univ. Buffalo Law Sch, 51-52; Univ. Buffalo, Millard Fillmore Col, 52-53; Univ. Mich, A.B, 54; Univ. Mich. Sch. of Soc. Work, M.S.W, 64; N.Y. Vet. Scholarship, 52; N.Y. Dept. of Soc. Serv. Scholarship, 62. Polit. & Govt. Pos: Charter mem, Young Dem. of West. N.Y, 52; chmn, 21st Ward Young Dem. for Adlai Stevenson, Buffalo, N.Y, 52; mem, Human Rels Cmn, Battle Creek, Mich, 66-68; del, Mich. State Dem. Conv, 68; Dem. cand. for U.S. Rep, Third Cong. Dist, Mich, 68; rep. of poor, Calhoun Commun. Action Agency, 68-; chmn, Third Cong. Dist. State Dem. Conv, 69. Bus. & Prof. Pos: Sr. caseworker, Erie Co. Dept. of Soc. Serv, Buffalo, N.Y, 59-62; unit supvr, Multi-Prob. Unit, Niagara Co. Dept. of Soc. Serv, Niagara Falls, 63; field rep, N.Y. Dept. of Soc. Serv, Buffalo, Rochester and N.Y.C, 64-66; dir, Calhoun Co. Dept. of Soc. Serv, Battle Creek, Mich, 66-68; dir, Pub. Housing Soc. Serv. Prog, Neighborhood Serv. Orgn, Detroit, 69- Mil. Serv: Entered as Pvt, Army, 46, released as Cpl, 48, after serv. in 702nd Counter Intel. Corps Detachment, U.S. Air Forces in Europe, 47-48. Publ: 'The Impact of Financing on Social Services at the Federal, State and Local Levels of Government,' Univ. Mich. Sch. of Soc. Work, 64. Mem: Exec. cmt, Southwest. Mich. Chap, Nat. Asn. of Soc. Workers, 67-68; del, Mich. Soc. Work Coun, 67-68; Am. Pub. Welfare Asn; Nat. Asn. of Housing and Redevelop. Off; Am. Civil Liberties Union; Bellmen and Waiters Club of Battle Creek, Rel: Roman Catholic. Mailing Add: 117 Chestnut St, Battle Creek, Mich. 49017.

KEENAN, WILLIAM Q. D
b. Cleveland, Ohio, 4/27/21; s. Joseph B. Keenan and Charlotte Quigley K; m. 8/20/50 to Mary Ann Lizars; c. Christopher David, Gregory Paul, Leslie, Geoffrey Michael and Joel. Educ: Georgetown Univ, A.B, 47; Harvard Law Sch, LL.B, 49. Polit. & Govt. Pos: Law clerk, Chief Judge George S. Sweeney, U.S. Dist. Court, Mass, 49-50; mem, Wallingford Dem. Town Cmt, Conn, 54-55; pres, Young Dem, Wallingford, 54-56; mem, Bd. of Finance, Wallingford, 55-58, chmn, 58-59; committeeman, Westchester Co. Dem. Party, N.Y, 62-65; research cmn. exec. cmt, White Plains Dem. City Cmt, 64-65; mem, Bd. of Educ, White Plains, 65-; mem. del. assembly, Coalition for Dem. Alternative, N.Y, 67-68; mem. exec. cmt, Concerned Dem. of Westchester, 67-68, v.chmn, Concerned Dem. of White Plains, 67-68; del, Dem. Nat. Conv, 68. Bus. & Prof. Pos: Commerce counsel, New Haven R.R, Conn, 50-60; gen. solicitor, REA Express, N.Y.C, 60-68; partner, Arsham & Keenan, 68- Mil. Serv: Entered as Pvt, Air Force, 42, released as 2nd Lt, 46, after serv. in Mil. Intel. and Army Airways Commun. Serv, ETO, 44-45; Three ETO Battle Stars. Publ: 'Assertive Administrative Agency Report,' Interstate Commerce Cmn. Practitioners J, 58. Mem: Asn. of the Bar of City of N.Y.(past chmn, Admin. Law Cmt); Interstate Commerce Cmn. Practitioners Asn; White Plains, N.Y. Bar Asn. Rel: Roman Catholic. Legal Res: 62 Greenridge Ave, White Plains, N.Y. 10605. Mailing Add: 233 Broadway, New York, N.Y. 10007.

KEENE, BERNARD D
Ky. State Rep.
b. Bardstown, Ky, 1926. Polit. & Govt. Pos: Ky. State Rep, currently. Bus. & Prof. Pos: Farmer. Mil. Serv: World War II and Korean War. Mem: Farm Bur; past treas, Nat. Farmers Orgn; Grand Knight, K. of C, 64-65; C. of C. Rel: Catholic. Mailing Add: Bardstown, Ky. 40004. (1967)

KEENEY, PHYLLIS MOTTRAM R
N.H. State Rep.
b. Hartford, Conn, 12/10/25; d. Frank Edward Mottram and Gracie Burroughs M; m. 6/15/46 to Dr Norwood Henry Keeney, Jr; c. Norwood Henry, III. Educ: Pa. State Univ, B.A, 46; Columbia Univ. Sch. of Libr. Serv, M.S, 52; Phi Sigma Iota. Polit. & Govt. Pos: Libr. messenger, N.H. Constitutional Conv, 64; N.H. State Rep, 67-, mem, Interim. Cmt. on Medicaid, 67-68 and v.chmn, Legis. Rev. Cmt, 69-, N.H. State House of Rep. Bus. & Prof. Pos: Asst. in acquisitions, Trinity Col. Libr, Conn, 47-48; reference asst, Pub. Libr, Bangor, Maine, 48-50; cataloguer, Brown Univ, 50-51; for. law cata-

loguer and asst. to dept. head, Harvard Univ. Law Libr, 52-57; cataloguer, Regina Libr, Rivier Col, Nashua, N.H, 67- Publ: Individual poems. Mem: Nashua League of Women Voters (past pres); Hudson Fortnightly Club (past pres); founding mem, Hudson Hist. Soc; charter mem, Nashua Br, Am. Asn. of Univ. Women; Order of Women Legislators. Amateur Painter and Poet. Rel: Episcopal. Mailing Add: Wason Rd, Hudson, N.H. 03051.

KEESE, WILLIAM BREWER R
Exec. Dir, El Paso Co. Rep. Cent. Cmt, Colo.
b. Millburn, N.J, 12/16/10; s. Franklin Hawxhurst Keese and Marguerite Mills K; m. 5/14/37 to Courtenay Baylor Illg; c. Marguerite (Mrs. John Robert Ferrari) and Henry Baylor. Educ: Cornell Univ, B.S, 32; Sigma Nu. Polit. & Govt. Pos: Exec. dir, El Paso Co. Rep. Cent. Cmt, Colo, 68- Mil. Serv: Entered as 2nd Lt, Army Air Force, 32, released as Maj. Gen, 67; Distinguished Serv. Medal; Silver Star; Distinguished Flying Cross with One Oak Leaf Cluster; Air Medal with Three Oak Leaf Clusters; Legion of Honor; Chevalier and Croix de Guerre, France. Mem: Daedalians. Rel: Presbyterian. Mailing Add: 1700 Stardust Dr, Colorado Springs, Colo. 80906.

KEETER, ALBERT McKINLEY R
Chmn, Murray Co. Rep. Party, Ga.
b. Sweetwater, Tenn, 5/8/20; s. Lewis Ross Keeter and Annie Catherine Sluder K; div; c. Kim, Kara and William Ross. Educ: Dalton Pub. Sch, 31-37; completed high sch in U.S. Army under G.I. Bill of Rights. Polit. & Govt. Pos: Mem. adv. cmt, Murray Co, Rep. Party, Ga, 56-57, first v.chmn, 58-62, chmn, 62- Bus. & Prof. Pos: Owner and mgr, Peggy Ann Grill, 46-48, Kin's Restaurant, 48- Mil. Serv: Entered as Pvt, Army, Sixth Calvary, 36-37; 1st Lt, Ga. Nat. Guard, 40-43; Pvt. 1/C, Army 395th Div, 43-45; Purple Heart; Good Conduct Medal; Presidential Award; Combat Inf. Citation. Mem: Am. and Ga. Restaurant Asns; Am. Express Credit Corp; Dixie Hwy. Asn; Murray Co. Tourism Asn; Shrine; Scottish Rite; York Rite; Mason; Am. Legion; VFW; DAV. Capt, Provost Guard, Crown of Honor and Serv. Award Plaque for Crippled Childrens' Hosp. Rel: Baptist. Legal Res: 709 S. Third Ave, Chatsworth, Ga. 30705. Mailing Add: P.O. Box C, Chatsworth, Ga. 30705.

KEETH, GERALDINE AUDREY R
Committeewoman Fla. Rep. State Cmt.
b. Chicago, Ill, 6/13/26; d. Charles Arthur Rollberg and Frances Sorenson R; m. 8/27/49 to Allan Francis Keeth; c. William Don, Robert Allan and Elizabeth Ann. Educ: William Woods Col, AA, 46; Rosary Col, 47-49; Rollins Col, BGS, 69. Polit. & Govt. Pos: Committeewoman, Seminole Co. Rep. Cmt, 66-, Committeewoman, Fla. Rep. State Cmt, 66-; alternate del, Rep. Nat. Conv, 68; Admin. asst. to Fla. State Rep. L.V. Wood, 69- Bus. & Prof. Pos: Teacher, Seminole Co. Assoc. for Retarded, 62-64; Office Mgr, Keeth Heating and Air Conditioning, 64-67; Teacher, Seminole Co. Bd. of Pub. Instr, 67- Mem: Lake Mary Woman's Club; Seminole Co. Asn. for Retarded; Am. Red Cross (past mem. bd). Rel: Presbyterian. Mailing Add: 205 Crystal View South, Sanford, Fla. 32771.

KEHE, LUVERN WILLIAM R
Iowa State Rep.
b. Waterloo, Iowa, 12/2/09; s. Henry W. Kehe and Louise Steege K; m. 11/3/37 to Dorothy Stoneburner; c. L. William and David Oliver. Educ: Univ. Iowa, B.S, 31; Tau Beta Pi; Theta Tau. Polit. & Govt. Pos: Iowa State Rep, 69- Bus. & Prof. Pos: Civilian engr, Corps of Engrs, 31-40; owner, Kehe Construction Co, Waverly, 46-; owner, Cedar Valley Eng. Co, 46- Mil. Serv: Entered as Capt, Army, 40, released as Col, 46, after serving as Engr. on Construction, Northwest Serv. Command & Manhattan Dist; Army Res, 46-52. Mem: Iowa Eng. Soc; Nat. Soc. Prfnl. Engrs; Assoc. Gen. Contractors Am; Elks; Am. Legion; VFW; Amvets; Farm Bur; C. of C. Rel: Lutheran. Mailing Add: 303 Third Ave. N.E, Waverly, Iowa 50677.

KEHOE, EDWARD FRANKLIN D
b. Rutland, Vt, 4/4/17; m. to Pauline I. Gregory; c. Four daughters. Educ: Rutland High Schs. Polit. & Govt. Pos: Selectman, Vt, 52-55; town mgr, Castleton, 55-65; pres, Rutland Coun. Develop. Asn, 64; Vt. State Rep, 65-67. Bus. & Prof. Pos: Pres, Castleton Indust. Mil. Serv: Cpl, Army, 44-47. Mem: Lions; Am. Legion; DAV; Elks. Rel: Catholic. Mailing Add: Castleton, Vt. 05735. (1967)

KEHOE, JOHN THOMAS D
b. Kansas City, Mo, 8/24/30; s. Thomas Charles Kehoe and Faye Nellie McFarland K; m. to Mary Magee; c. Caroline. Educ: Rockhurst Col, Kansas City, Mo, B.S, 51; Univ. Mich, M.A, 58; Georgetown Univ, 52-53; Pi Kappa Delta; Col. Varsity Debate Team. Polit. & Govt. Pos: Asst. city mgr, Hayward, Calif, 58-60; admin. asst, Rep. Miller, Calif, 60-68. Mil. Serv: Pvt. to 2nd Lt, U.S. Army Counter Intel. Corps, 53-56; UN Ribbons; Good Conduct Medal; Nat. Defense Medal. Mem: Am. Polit. Sci. Asn; Am. Soc. Pub. Admin; Int. City Mgrs. Asn; Am. Legion; past pres, Hayward Jr. C. of C; Am. Fed. Govt. Employee Union Local 65; Cong. Secys. Club; S.Alameda Co, Calif. Young Dem; past pres, Burros Club. Publ: 'Labor Unions In Municipal Government,' read before Nat. Conv. Am. Soc. for Pub. Admin. Rel: Roman Catholic. Legal Res: Hayward, Calif. 94541. Mailing Add: 6137 Leesburg Pike, Falls Church, Va. 22046. (1967)

KEHRES, RAYMOND C. D
Mich. State Rep.
b. Monroe, Mich, 6/2/15; m. 1941 to Eleanor M. Payment; c. Judith Ann and Robert W. Educ: High Sch, grad. Polit. & Govt. Pos: Former chmn, Dem. Co. Cmt, Mich; Mich. State Rep, 64- Bus. & Prof. Pos: Welding foreman. Mil. Serv: Army, S/Sgt, 41-45. Mem: K. of C; Moose; DAV; Detroit Beach Boat Club; E.Side Bus. Men's Asn. Rel: Catholic. Mailing Add: 536 St. Marys St, Monroe, Mich. 48161. (1967)

KEIER, RICHARD FREDERICK R
Treas, Mich. Fedn. of Young Rep.
b. Toledo, Ohio, 11/5/39; s. Frederick Henry Keier and Lazetta Meister K; m. 8/17/68 to Karen Sue Rowland. Educ: Wittenberg Univ, B.S, 61; Am. Col. Life Underwriters, CLU, 69; Phi Gamma Delta. Polit. & Govt. Pos: Rep. precinct del, Mich, 62-64; del, Nat. Young Rep. Conv, 67 & 69; treas, Oakland Co. Young Rep, Mich, 66, chmn, 67; treas, Mich. Fedn. of Young Rep, 68-; mem, 18th Cong. Rep. Exec. Cmt, Mich, 69. Bus. & Prof. Pos: Ins. agent, Prudential Ins. Co. of Am, 62- Mem: South Oakland Life Underwriters Asn.(Nat. Quality Awards, 66-69); Detroit Grad. Chap, Phi Gamma Delta (pres, 67, secy, 68-69); Wittenberg Univ. Alumni for Southeast. Mich (pres, 64-68). Sen Robert P. Griffin Award for Outstanding Young Rep. Man in Michigan, 67-68. Rel: Lutheran. Mailing Add: 2722 Crooks Rd, Royal Oak, Mich. 48073.

KEIL, A(RMIN) T(HEODORE) R
Mem, N.Mex. Rep. State Cent. Cmt.
b. New York, N.Y, 5/14/30; s. Ernest A. Keil and Gertrude Novich K; m. 8/15/59 to Lois Moses; c. Rebecca Susan, David Seth and Jonathen Matthew. Educ: Univ. Conn, 48-50; George Wash. Univ, A.A, 50, B.S, 52; Northwest. Univ, M.D, 56; Tau Epsilon Phi; Gate and Key Soc. Polit. & Govt. Pos: Chmn, Colfax Co. Rep. Party, N.Mex, 66-69; mem, N.Mex. Rep. State Cent. Cmt, 66-; mem, State Adv. Hosp. Coun, 68- Bus. & Prof. Pos: Self-employed physician, 62- Mil. Serv: Lt, Med. Corps, Naval Res, 57-59, serv. in Naval Air Sta, S. Weymouth, Mass, Res, 59-68. Mem: Am. Med. Asn; N.Mex. Med. Soc; Am. Col. of Physicians; Am. Soc. of Internal Med; Rotary. Mailing Add: McFarland Rd, Raton, N.Mex. 87740.

KEIL, CHARLES K. D
b. Wilmington, Del, 9/14/33; s. Leo Keil and Helene Kornhauser K; m. 6/19/55 to Barbara Pearl Silverman; c. Lea and Mark. Educ: Univ. Pa. Wharton Sch, B.S. in Econ, 55, Law Sch, LL.B, 61; Sigma Alpha Mu. Polit. & Govt. Pos: Admin. asst. to the Gov, Del, 63-65; Del. State Rep, 64-67; trustee, Del. Dept. of Ment. Health, 67-68, v.chmn, 68-; mem, Del. Constitutional Rev. Cmn, 68-, mem, Gov. Task Force on Exec. Reorgn, 69- Bus. & Prof. Pos: Attorney-at-Law, 61- Mil. Serv: Entered as 2nd Lt, Air Force, 57, released as 1st Lt, 59, after serv. in 379th Bombardment Wing, Strategic Air Command, 57-58; Capt, Air Force Res, 59-68. Mem: Am, Del. and New Castle Co. Bar Asns; Am. Trial Lawyers Asn; B'nai B'rith; AF&AM; Jewish War Vets; YMCA. Rel: Jewish. Mailing Add: 502 W. 38th St, Wilmington, Del. 19802.

KEIL, NORMA FERN D
Dem. Nat. Committeewoman, Mont.
b. Speed, Kans, 9/27/06; d. Edgar A. Elliott and Mary Etta George E; m. 5/18/28 to John Keil, wid; c. Edgar R, Daniel D. and Stephen M. Educ: Kans. State Teachers Col, 27. Polit. & Govt. Pos: Dem. precinct committeewoman, Mont, 50-64; v.chmn, Mont. State Dem. Women, 55-58, pres, 58-61; Dem. state committeewoman, 58-64; v.chmn, Mont. State Dem. Cent. Cmt, 62-65; chmn, Dem. Women's Conf, 66; del, Dem. Nat. Conv, 68; Dem. Nat. Committeewoman, Mont, 68- Bus. & Prof. Pos: Sch. teacher, 24-28; pres, Pondera Action Coun, 68- Mem: Eastern Star; Farmers Educ. & Coop. Union (v.chmn); dir, Home Talent Plays, Ledger Commun. Club. Rel: Presbyterian; Elder, 65- Mailing Add: Ledger, Mont. 59456.

KEILBAR, MONA MARY R
Chmn, Ways and Means Cmt, Calif. Fedn. Rep. Women, North. Div.
b. Honaker, Va, 3/10/15; d. John Randolph Hubbard and Amanda Hess H; m. 1/16/45 to Leland C. Keilbar, Jr. Educ: Bus. course, Honaker, 33; Tenn. Sch. Beauty Culture, Dipl, 41; Oakland Sch. Real Estate, 68. Polit. & Govt. Pos: V.pres. and auditor, Rep. Womens Club of Alameda, Calif, 65, pres, 66, v.pres. and chmn. progs, 67, mem. bd. dirs, 69; mem, Alameda Co. Coord. Coun, 66-, treas, 69-; secy. and treas, Pres. Coun. of Alameda Co, 67; mem. bd. dirs, Alameda Rep. Assembly, 67 & 68, treas, 69; chmn. ways and means cmt, Calif. Fedn. Rep. Women, North. Div, 68-; unit dir, Alameda Co. Coord. Rep. Assembly, 69; mem, Calif. Rep. State Cent. Cmt, 69- Bus. & Prof. Pos: Merchandiser, various stores, Va, 30's; mgr. and buyer for commissary, Flatrock Coal Co, Honaker, 36; cosmetologist, Roxies, 41-42; inspector, Aluminum Co. of Am, Marysville, Tenn, 41-42; photographer, Dorlan Studio, San Bernardino, Calif, 43-44; merchandiser, Darrahas Pharm, 43-44; merchandiser, Cochran cosmetic line, I Magnin & Co, San Francisco, 44-46; owner and mgr, Moderne Salon of Beauty, 46-64. Mem: Home Owners Asn; Rep. Womens Club; Nat. Fedn. Rep. Women; Calif. Hist. Soc; Ikebana Int. Rel: Protestant. Mailing Add: 629 Pond Isle, Alameda, Calif. 94501.

KEISTER, ROBERTA ELAINE D
Committeewoman, Seventh Dist. Dem. Party, Iowa
b. Bayard, Iowa, 3/7/34; d. Delbert Hugh Ford and Lillian Kinnick F; m. 6/15/52 to William Karl Keister, II; c. Ellen Jeanette and W. Karl. Educ: Coon Rapids Pub. High Sch, grad. salutatorian, 52; Falk Sch. Photog, Maryville, Mo, 57. Polit. & Govt. Pos: Pres, Carroll Co. Dem. Women's Club, 63-64; dist. secy. and off. mgr, Seventh Cong. Dist. Dem. Party Off, 65-66; committeewoman, Seventh Cong. Dist. Dem. Party, Iowa, 67-; del. and mem. nat. credentials cmt, Dem. Nat. Conv, 68; mem, Iowa Dem. State Cent. Cmt, currently. Bus. & Prof. Pos: Mgr. and photographer, Bill's Portrait Studio, Coon Rapids, Iowa, 56-65; dist. secy and off. mgr, Iowa State Rep. John Hansen, Council Bluffs, 65-66; pub. rels, E.L. Nogg Fruit Co, Omaha, Nebr, 67 & 68; area mgr, Fine Arts Sterling Silver Co, Omaha, Nebr. and Iowa, 68-; pres, Council Bluffs Women's Div. C. of C, 68- Mem: League Women Voters (budget chmn); PEO (recording secy); Friends of Music Concert Series (v.pres); Council Bluffs-Omaha Symphony Guild; Council Bluffs C. of C. Women's Div. (pres, 68-). Rel. Lutheran. Mailing Add: 1235 Wedgewood Dr, Council Bluffs, Iowa 51501.

KEITH, A. M. 'SANDY' DFL
m. to Marion Sanford; c. Ian and Douglas. Educ: Amherst Col, B.A, magna cum laude, 50; Yale, LL.B, 53; Phi Beta Kappa. Polit. & Govt. Pos: Minn. State Sen, 59-63, Asst. Minority Leader, Minn. State Senate, 61; Lt. Gov, Minn, 62-64. Bus. & Prof. Pos: Assoc. legal counsel, Mayo Clin, 55-60; law practice, 60- Mil. Serv: Marine Corps, 1st Lt, 53-55. Mailing Add: 1104 Sixth St. S.W, Rochester, Minn. 55901.

KEITH, FREDERICK R. R
b. Wilmington, N.C. 12/25/00; s. Benjamin Franklin Keith and Lillie Rulfs K; m. 11/24/27 to Grace Butler; c. Fred. R, Jr, Mary A. and Thomas J. Educ: Campbell Col, 17-18; N.C. State Col, 19-20; Auburn Univ, B.S, 22; Exec. Prog, Univ. N.C, 54; Tau Kappa Epsilon. Polit. & Govt. Pos: Mem, Robeson Co. Rep. Exec. Cmt, N.C. at present, and chmn, 24-54; Rep. cand. for N.C. State Treas, 60, for N.C. Cmnr. Agr, 56, for U.S. Rep, 48, for N.C. State Sen, 44 and for N.C. State Rep, 40; mem, N.C. Cmt. of Farmers Home Admin, 58-60; del, Rep. Nat. Conv, 60 and 48; chmn, Rep. 7th Cong. Dist, 56;

chmn, N.C. Agr. Stabilization Cmt. and N.C. Drought Cmt, U.S. Dept. Agr, 54; mem, State Munic. Rels. Cmt, 51-53; former mayor and cmnr. of St. Pauls and past state dir, Rep. Exec. Cmt. Bus. & Prof. Pos: Chmn, St. Pauls Guaranty Savings & Loan, 63-; dir, Guaranty Savings & Loan Co. and St. Pauls First Union Nat. Bank; pres, Keith Hardware & Furniture Co, Inc, St. Pauls Drug Co, Inc, St. Pauls Bldg. & Loan Asn. and Keith Farm and Land Co. Mil. Serv: Pvt, Army, 18-19. Mem: Pres, Lumberton Bd. Realtors, 60; N.C. and Nat. Asns. of Real Estate Bd, Inc; Am. Inst. Banking; pres, Robeson Co. Munic. Asn, 51; chmn, Robeson Co. Rural Fire Asn, 50-56; trustee and mem, exec. cmt, Campbell Col; Robeson Co. Exec. Club; Rotary; Mason; Shriner; Lumberton Country Club; Am. Legion; Farm Bur. Rel: Baptist. Legal Res: 2100 N. Elm St, Lumberton, N.C. 28358. Mailing Add: Keith Realty Co, Inc, St. Pauls, N.C. 28384.

KEITH, HASTINGS R
U.S. Rep, Mass.
b. Brockton, Mass, 11/22/15; s. Roger Keith (deceased) and Carolyn Hastings K; m. 8/31/43 to Louise Harriman; c. Helen H.(Mrs. A.M. Brink, Jr), Carolyn L. Educ: Univ. Vt, B.S, 38; grad. study Harvard Univ; grad, Command and Gen. Staff Sch; Sigma Phi. Polit. & Govt. Pos: Mass. State Sen, 52-56; U.S. Rep, Mass, 59-, mem, Interstate and For. Commerce Cmt, Merchant Marine and Fisheries Cmt, U.S. House of Rep, mem. Policy Cmt, 62-64; alternate del, Rep. Nat. Conv, 68. Bus. & Prof. Pos: C.L.U. Mgt. training course, Equitable Life of U.S, 38, agent, 38-40, asst. mgr, Boston Agency, 46-52; incorporator, People's Savings Bank; partner, Roger Keith and Sons, gen. ins, Brockton, Mass. Mil. Serv: Mass. Nat. Guard, 40-42; Army, Lt. Col, G-3, 42-45, Col, Res. Mem: Aircraft Owners and Pilots Asn; Am. Legion; VFW; Elks; Mason; Capitol Hill Club; Cong. Country Club; Univ. Club. Rel: Congregational. Legal Res: 91 River St, West Bridgewater, Mass. 02324. Mailing Add: House Office Bldg, Washington, D.C. 20515.

KEITH, LEON R
Wyo. State Rep.
b. Desdemona, Tex, 1/16/24; m. to Virginia; c. 4. Educ: Univ. of Wyo. Polit. & Govt. Pos: Wyo State Rep, currently. Bus. & Prof. Pos: Rancher. Mil. Serv: Vet. World War II. Mem: Farm Bur; Grange; Wyo. Stock Growers Asn; Mason. Rel: Methodist. Mailing Add: Kaycee, Wyo. 82639.

KEITH, THOMAS JOSEPH R
Chmn, Robeson Co. Rep. Party, N.C.
b. Lumberton, N.C, 5/31/41; s. Frederick Rulfs Keith and Grace Butler K; single. Educ: N.C. State Univ, 59-61; Campbell Col, B.S, 64. Polit. & Govt. Pos: Secy-treas, N.C. State Col. Rep. Party, 60, v.chmn, 61; organizer and v.chmn, Campbell Col. Rep. Party, 63; alternate del, Rep. Nat. Conv, 64; finance chmn, Robeson Co. Rep. Party, N.C, 64, mem. exec. cmt, 64-, chmn, 68-; secy-treas, Seventh Cong. Dist. Rep. Party, 66-; mem. credentials cmt, N.C. Rep. Party, 68. Bus. & Prof. Pos: Asst. mgr, Keith Farm Co, 64-; secy-treas, Keith Realty Co, Inc, 65- Mem: Cand, Am. Inst. of Real Estate Appraisers; Lumberton Bd. of Realtors (pres, 68); dir, Robeson Co. Farm Bur; Campbell Col. Alumni Chap; Elks (Esteemed Leading Knight, Lumberton Lodge); New River Grape Growers Asn; Lumberton Jaycees; St. Pauls C. of C; Pine Crest Country Club, Lumberton. Rel: Baptist. Mailing Add: 2100 N. Elm St, Lumberton, N.C. 28358.

KEITH, WAYNE R
Iowa State Sen.
b. Burt, Iowa, 5/24/08; s. Lynn Wood Keith and Claire Dalton K; m. 9/19/29 to Doris M. Brown; c. Jane (Mrs. Jack McMullen), Edgar W, Mary (Mrs. David Yeoman) and Margaret (Mrs. Terry Heald). Educ: Algona Pub. Sch, 12 years. Polit. & Govt. Pos: Dir, Sch. Bd, Iowa, 55-64; dir, Civil Defense, 67-68; Iowa State Sen, 69- Mem: Kossuth Co. Hist. Soc; Mason; Shrine; Rotary; Farm Bur. Master Swine Producers award; Master Farmer award; Rotary Commun. Serv. award. Rel: Baptist. Mailing Add: R.R. 2, Algona, Iowa 50511.

KELCHNER, GEORGE CURRY R
b. Altoona, Pa, 7/8/42; s. William Curry Kelchner and Jane Berkowitz K; single. Educ: Pa. State Univ, B.S, 64; Delta Chi. Polit. & Govt. Pos: Del, Rep. Nat. Conv, 64; trainee, Commonwealth of Pa, 64-65, admin. officer, 65- Bus. & Prof. Pos: V.pres, Curry Canan & Co, Inc, 64- Mem: Int. City Mgr. Asn; Am. Bus. Club, Altoona; Harrisburg Jr. C. of C; Pa. Young Rep; Pa. C. of C. Rel: Presbyterian. Mailing Add: 513 27th Ave, Apt. 5, Altoona, Pa. 16601.

KELEHER, LEO D. D
b. Danbury, Iowa, 7/3/05; m. 1927 to Marie Hansen; c. Nine. Educ: St. Patricks High Sch. Polit. & Govt. Pos: Iowa State Rep, 66-67. Bus. & Prof. Pos: Real estate. Mem: Eagles; Moose. Rel: Catholic. Mailing Add: 1221 Douglas, Sioux City, Iowa 51105. (1967)

KELLAM, JAMES ROBERT R
b. New Castle, Ind, 1/5/25; s. Chester Armacost Kellam and Berna Dena Mercer K; m. 1/18/58 to Josephine E. Adams; c. Mark Bryon and Marie Denise. Educ: Ind. Univ, B.S. in Bus, 50, LL.B, 52; Phi Eta Sigma; Delta Theta Phi. Polit. & Govt. Pos: Probation officer, Henry Circuit Court, Ind, 57-62; prosecuting attorney, 53rd Judicial Circuit, 63-; chmn, Henry Co. Rep. Cent. Cmt, 64-68. Mil. Serv: Entered as Pvt, Air Force, 43, released as Sgt, 46. Mem: Ind. Bar Asn; Elks; F&AM; Ind. Correctional Asn; Ind. State Juvenile Officers Asn. Rel: Disciples of Christ. Mailing Add: R.R. 2, New Castle, Ind. 47362.

KELLAM, SIDNEY SEVERN D
b. Princess Anne, Va, 7/6/03; s. Abel E. Kellam and Clara O. Eaton K; m. 1/21/33 to Odie A. Butt; c. Jane B. and Elizabeth. Educ: High Sch. Polit. & Govt. Pos: Treas, Princess Anne Co, Va, 31-50; chmn, Va. Dept. Conserv. and Develop, 50-53; chmn. bd, Tidewater Va. Develop. Coun; dir, United Commun. Fund; mem, Chesapeake Ferry Dist. Cmn; chmn, First Dist. Dem. Cmt; former mem, Dem. Nat. Cmt; del, Dem. Nat. Conv, 68. Bus. & Prof. Pos: Partner, Kellam-Eaton Ins. Co, Va. Beach, 30-; secy-treas, Sea Realty Corp, Beach Land, Inc, Thunderbird Motor Lodge, Holliday Sands Motel, Fremac Corp. and Sir Walter Hotel; pres, Va. Beach Pub. Co; dir. and mem. exec. cmt, Allied Security Life Ins. Co, Charlotte, N.C; chmn. bd. dirs, Bank of Va. Beach; chmn. bd. dirs, Bank of Princess Anne; mem. bd. dirs, Va. Beach Fed. Savings & Loan Asn. Mem: Bd. trustees, Blackstone Col; Mason; Shrine; Rotary; Princess Anne Country Club; Cape Henry Club, Va. Beach; Commonwealth Club, Richmond. Rel: Methodist. Mailing Add: 510 Cavalier Dr, Virginia Beach, Va. 23451. (1967)

KELLAM, WILLIAM PAGE D
b. Princess Anne Co, Va, 11/20/14; m. to Josephine Wiley. Educ: Norfolk Bus. Col. Polit. & Govt. Pos: Mem, Va. Beach Dem. Cmt, Va; Va. State Del, 64-66; Va. State Sen, 66-68. Bus. & Prof. Pos: Ins. and real estate. Mil. Serv: Army, Capt, Airborne Inf. Mem: Past pres, Kiwanis; past pres, Ruritan; Elks; past State Comdr, Am. Legion; Bay Harbour Yacht Country Club; Fraternal Order of Police; bd. dirs, Va. State C. of C; dir, Va. Beach Real Estate Bd; Va. Asn. of Ins. Agents. Rel: Presbyterian. Mailing Add: 3111 Pacific Ave, P.O. Box 777, Virginia Beach, Va. 23451. (1967)

KELLAR, CHARLES L. D
Mem, Clark Co. Dem. Cent. Cmt, Nev.
b. Barbados, W.I, 6/11/09; s. James Kellar and Lowrencha Smith K; m. 9/3/60 to Cornelia Street; c. Charles L, Jr. and Michael. Educ: City Col. N.Y, B.S. and M.S, 33; St. John's Univ, LL.B, 41; Omega Psi Phi. Polit. & Govt. Pos: Soc. investr, Dept. Welfare, N.Y, 34-36; probation officer, Domestic Rels. Court, 37-40; probation officer, Kings Co. Court, 40-42; chmn, U.S. Draft Bd. 205, N.Y, 46; del, Dem. Nat. Conv, 68; mem, Clark Co. Dem. Cent. Cmt, Nev, 68- Bus. & Prof. Pos: Practicing attorney, N.Y, 42-; mem, Dept. of Immigration & Appeals, Dept. of Justice, 45; practicing attorney, Nev, 65-; mem, U.S. Court of Appeals for various circuits, 66, U.S. Tax Court and U.S. Supreme Court, 68. Mem: Am, Nat, Clark Co, N.Y. State and Kings Co. Bar Asns; Am. Trial Lawyers Asn; Brooklyn-L.I. Lawyers Asn; Boys Club of Clark Co; NAACP (pres, Las Vegas Br, currently); Int. Elks. Legal Achievement Award, 67, Award of Merit, 60-65, Outstanding Achievement Award, 69, Thalheimer Award awarded to Las Vegas Br, 68, Br. also received Noah Griffin Award, NAACP, 68. Rel: Episcopal. Legal Res: 1133 Comstock Dr, Las Vegas, Nev. 89106. Mailing Add: 1042 W. Owens Ave, Las Vegas, Nev. 89106.

KELLEHER, FRANK HENRY D
b. Marlboro, Mass, 4/4/11; s. Frank F. Kelleher and Hannah Mulcahy K. (both deceased); m. 6/23/45 to Congetta J. Leone. Educ: Bentley Col, grad. in acct, 33; Bentley Col. Assocs. Polit. & Govt. Pos: Mem, Marlboro Sch. Cmt, Mass, 38-46, chmn, 58-60; prin. assessor, Marlboro, 53-58; mayor, Marlboro, 58-60; chmn, City of Marlboro Dem. Cmt, 59-66; alternate del, Dem. Nat. Conv, 64. Bus. & Prof. Pos: Pres, Kelleher Ins. Agency, Inc, 38-; dir, First Nat. Bank, 65- Mil. Serv: Entered as Pvt, Air Force, 42, released as S/Sgt, 45, after serv. in 321st Bomb Group, ETO, 43-44; Presidential Unit Citation; ETO Ribbon with Battle Stars; Rome-Arno-Balkans-Italian-African and Tunision Theater Ribbons. Mem: Pres, Eagles, 58-64; exec. cmt, Am. Legion, 47; VFW; DAV; Hibernians; K. of C; Cath. Order of Foresters; Moose; C. of C. Rel: Roman Catholic. Mailing Add: 72 Hillcrest Rd, Marlboro, Mass. 01752.

KELLEHER, HERBERT DAVID D
b. Camden, N.J, 3/12/31; s. Harry Aloysius Kelleher and Ruth Moore K; m. 9/9/55 to Joan Negley; c. Julia Gage, John Michael, Ruth Moore and David Negley. Educ: Wesleyan Univ, A.B, 53; N.Y. Univ. Sch. of Law, Root-Tilden Scholar and LL.B, 56; Skull and Serpent; Phi Delta Phi. Polit. & Govt. Pos: Law secy, Supreme Court of N.J, 56-59; coordinator, Connally for Gov. Campaign, Tex, 62, 64 & 66; del, Dem. Nat. Conv, 64 & 68; co-chmn, Lawyers for Waggoner Carr, Bexar Co, Tex, 66. Bus. & Prof. Pos: Assoc, Lum, Bianno and Tompkins, 59-61; partner, Matthews, Nowlin, Macfarlane and Barrett, 61-66. Mem: Bars of N.J. and Tex; Am, Tex. and San Antonio Bar Asns; pres, Traveler's Aid Soc, San Antonio, chmn, Educ. Cmt, San Antonio C. of C; San Antonio Country Club. Rel: Episcopal. Legal Res: 144 Thelma Dr, San Antonio, Tex. 78212. Mailing Add: 1500 Alamo National Bldg, San Antonio, Tex. 78205. (1967)

KELLEHER, NEIL WILLIAM R
N.Y. State Assemblyman
b. Troy, N.Y, 5/9/23; s. Cornelius James Kelleher and Helen Fleming K; m. 6/9/46 to June Elizabeth Frank; c. Timothy, Neil and Tracy. Educ: Lansingburgh High Sch, 4 years. Polit. & Govt. Pos: City alderman, Troy, N.Y, 53-59, mayor, 60-63; N.Y. State Assemblyman, 67- Mil. Serv: Entered as Seaman, Navy, 42, released as PO , 45, after serv. in Destroyer Unit, Pac, 42-45. Mem: DAV; Am. Legion; VFW; Navy Petty Officers. Rel: Catholic. Mailing Add: 406 Sixth Ave, Troy, N.Y. 12182.

KELLEHER, ROBERT LEE D
b. Oak Park, Ill, 3/30/23; s. Leo Francis Kelleher and Mary Carlson K. (deceased); m. 9/16/48 to Geraldine DeBacker; c. Robert L, Jr, Gerrie, David P, Mary Adele, Richard V. and Dennis M. Educ: Mt. Carmel Col, Ont, Can, Ph.B, 45; Cath. Univ. Am, J.D, 50, M.A, 56. Polit. & Govt. Pos: Exec. Secy, Yellowstone Co. Dem. Cent. Cmt, Mont, 56-57; Dem. nominee for Cong. Mont. Second Dist, 68. Bus. & Prof. Pos: Attorney, anti-subversive sect, criminal div, Justice Dept, 51-52. Mil. Serv: Lt. Col, Intel. Off, Army Res, 69-; grad, U.S. Army Command & Gen. Staff Col, 69. Mem: Am. and Mont, Trial Lawyers Asns; Mont. and Yellowstone Co. Bar Asns; Defense Res. Inst; ROA (pres. Mont. Dept. and past pres, Billings Chap). Rel: Roman Catholic. Legal Res: 4020 Rimrock Rd, Billings, Mont. 59102. Mailing Add: 1343 Grand Ave, Billings, Mont. 59102.

KELLEHER, THOMAS D
b. Providence, R.I, 1/4/23; m. to Mary Frances. Educ: Providence Col; Boston Univ. Law, 1948. Polit. Pos: R.I. State Rep, 55-66; Probate Judge Solicitor in Smithfield; Chmn, Cmt. on Juvenile Delinquency, 1961; Govt. Task Force Ment. Health, 1963; Dep. Majority Leader, 1965. Bus. & Prof. Pos: Lawyer. Mil. Serv: WW II, USN; Capt, ROA. Mailing Add: 72 Hilltop Ave, Providence, R.I. 02908. (1967)

KELLER, CHARLES F. D
Ill. State Rep.
b. Effingham, Ill, 1/22/39; s. Lolami Keller and Thelma Bushue K; m. 2/24/62 to Nome Hardiek; c. Charles and Kiedrah. Educ: Univ. Tulsa, 61;

Tau Kappa Epsilon. Polit. & Govt. Pos: Ill. State Rep, Springfield, 69- Bus. & Prof. Pos: Pres, Keller Develop. Corp, 62; mgr, Ramada Inn, Effingham, Ill, 63- Mem: Elks; K. of C; Kiwanis; C. of C; Moose. Rel: Catholic. Mailing Add: 800 W. Fayette, Effingham, Ill. 62401.

KELLER, DONALD MONROE R
Mem, Needham Rep. Town Cmt, Mass.
b. Tuscaloosa, Ala, 2/4/33; s. Dr. Allen Dudley Keller and Marion Monroe K; m. 6/4/55 to Jo Ann Duval; c. Patricia Ann, Donald Monroe, Jr. and Joseph Bourey. Educ: Dartmouth Col, A.B, 54, Amos Tuck Sch. of Bus. Admin, M.B.A, 55; Alpha Theta. Polit. & Govt. Pos: Mem, Needham Rep. Town Cmt, Mass, 64-, chmn, 67-69. Bus. & Prof. Pos: Mgr. mgt. serv, Touche Ross Bailey & Smart, Boston and Detroit, 58-68; investment analyst, Keystone Custodian Funds, Boston, 68- Mil. Serv: Entered as Ens, Navy, 55, released as Lt.(jg), 58, after serv. in U.S.S. New and Comphiblant Staff, Atlantic Fleet, 56-58. Mem: Am. Inst. of CPA; Mass. Soc. of CPA; Nat. Asn. of Acct; Ft. Hill Club; Needham Pool & Racquet Club; Needham Rep. Club. Rel: Protestant. Mailing Add: 55 Nichols Rd, Needham, Mass. 02192.

KELLER, EMMA KNAUSS R
b. N.Dak. 2/12/01; d. Daniel Joseph Knauss and Margaret Gringham K; wid; c. Louis Edward, Robert Daniel and George Albert. Polit. & Govt. Pos: Secy, Rep. Womens Club, Corona, Calif, 65, pres, 66 & 68; del, Nat. Conv. Rep. Women, 67; Calif. hostess, Rep. Nat. Conv, 68; membership chmn, Riverside Co. Rep. Party, 69- Bus. & Prof. Pos: Owner and buyer, furniture bus, Corona, Calif, 28-68. Mem: Women's Improv. Club Corona (past pres); Jr. High Sch. PTA and Soroptimist Club of Corona (past pres); chmn, Grey Ladies. Rel: Methodist. Legal Res: 2600 Garretson Ave, Corona, Calif. 91720. Mailing Add: P.O. Box 417, Corona, Calif. 91720.

KELLER, FRANK L. D
b. Mitchell, S.Dak, 5/1/24; s. Edmund C. Keller and Lillian Brunner K; c. Patricia Lee, Cindy Lou, Francine Lynn, Mary Lisa and Robert Lance. Educ: Seattle Univ, B.S, 57. Polit. & Govt. Pos: V.chmn, Kitsap Co. Dem. Cent. Cmt, Wash, 59-64, Sixth Dist. Cong. Dem. Orgn, 59-64 and West. States Dem. Conf; chmn, Wash. State Dem. Cmt, 62-67; state campaign coordinator, Robert F. Kennedy Orgn, 68; aide, Sen. Warren G. Magnuson Campaign, 68. Bus. & Prof. Pos: Trustee, Teamsters Local 672, 59-; sales mgr, Glaser Beverage Co, 68- Mil. Serv: Entered Navy, 42, released as Shipfitter 3/C, 44, after serv. in Pac. and European Theatres. Mem: Elks; Eagles; VFW; Am. Legion; Teamsters Union. Rel: Catholic. Mailing Add: 5427 37th Ave. S.W, Seattle, Wash. 98126.

KELLER, JOHN L. D
b. Harrodsburg, Ky, 5/12/19; s. John Keller and Viola Cole K; m. 9/7/47 to Patricia Clarke; c. Mary Wendelle, John Clarke, Michael, David, Gregory, Patrick and Christopher. Educ: Univ. Ky; Phi Kappa Tau; Pershing Rifles; Scabbard & Blade. Polit. & Govt. Pos: City attorney, Harrodsburg, Ky, 66; del, Dem. Conv, 63. Bus. & Prof. Pos: Dir, Mercer Co. Nat. Bank, 50- Mil. Serv: Entered as 2nd Lt, Air Force, 43, released as Capt, 46, after serv. in Pac; Am. Defense and Air Medal; Pac. Theater Ribbon. Mem: Jr. C. of C; Toastmasters; Am. Legion. Rel: Catholic. Mailing Add: Louisville Rd Harrodsburg, Ky. 40330. (1967)

KELLER, LEONARD R
b. Chicago, Ill; s. Charles L. Keller and Pauline K; single. Educ: Univ. Wis, 28-32; Metrop. Sch. Music, D.Mus. Polit. Pos: State Campaign Chmn. for Scranton, Fla, 64. Bus. & Prof. Pos: Pres, Miami Beach Bd. of Realtors, 64-66; pres, Leonard Keller Realty, 54-66; pres. and founder, Metrop. Sch. of Music, Chicago, Ill, 45-51; producer, musical show for the war effort, Marching With Johnny. Mem: Pres, Rep. Club of Miami Beach, 58-66; past pres, Exchange Club and Exec. Club, Miami Beach; Elks; Eagles; Am. Fedn. of Musicians, 26-66. Rel: Christian Science. Legal Res: 1369 N. Venetian Way, San Marco Island, Miami, Fla. 33139. Mailing Add: 4301 W. Flagler St, Miami, Fla. 33134. (1967)

KELLER, MARVIN V. R
Pa. State Sen.
b. Langhorne, Pa, 9/19/06; s. Walter H. Keller and Bertha V. K; m. to Dorothy M. Hickman; c. two. Educ: Rider Col. Polit. & Govt. Pos: Treas, Newton Borough Sch. Dist, Pa; elect. registr, Wills, 43; Pa. State Rep, 48-58; Pa. State Sen, 58-; del, Rep. Nat. Conv, 64 and Constitutional Conv. of Pa, 67-68. Bus. & Prof. Pos: Bldg. contractor; dir, Langhorne Fed. Savings and Loan Asn. Mem: Newton Exchange Club(past pres); Mason; Consistory. Rel: Methodist. Mailing Add: Century House South, 303 W. State St, Doylestown, Pa. 18901.

KELLER, MILLETT FREDERICK R
b. Libby, Mont, 12/31/15; s. Frederick Herbert Keller and Maude Millett K; m. 10/28/38 to Mary A. Robischon; c. Millett F, Jr, Jeffrey T, Judith Ann, Jeanne Marie and Janet F. Educ: Univ. Calif, Berkeley, A.B, 36; Omega Delta. Polit. & Govt. Pos: Rep. precinct committeeman, Mont, 52-56; chmn, State Welfare Bd, 52-60; co. chmn, Rep. Party, 56-58; Mont. State Rep, 61-64; chmn, Mont. State Rep. Cmt, 66-69; mem, Medicaid Adv. Bd, State Welfare, 66-; mem, Rep. Nat. Cmt, Mont, 66-69. Mem: Am. and Mont. Optometric Asns; Optometric Exten. Prog; Am. Optometric Found; pres, Mont. Optometric Asn, 43 and Great Falls Kiwanis Club, 42; Elks; Kiwanis; Farm Bur. Rel: Catholic. Mailing Add: 3101 Fourth Ave. N, Great Falls, Mont. 59401.

KELLERMAN, ELIZABETH ROUNTREE R
Rep. Nat. Committeewoman, Hawaii
b. High Point, N.C, 9/1/06; d. Jame Braswell Rountree and Elizabeth Rebecca Anderson R; m. 10/8/40 to George Horace Kellerman; c. George Rountree and James Phillips. Educ: Sweet Briar Col. B.A. 26; Columbia Univ. Law Sch, LL.B, 33. Polit. & Govt. Pos: Attorney, Reconstruct. Finance Corp, 33-34; attorney, Fed. Emergency Admin, Pub. Works, 34-38; del, Hawaii Constitutional Conv, 50; co. committeewoman, Oahu Co. Rep. Cmt, 54-55; Rep. Nat. Committeewoman, Hawaii, 63-; mem. exec. cmt, Rep. Nat. Cmt, 64-69; del, Rep. Nat. Conv, 64, alternate del, 68; mem, Hawaii Coun. Crime and Delinquency. Bus. & Prof. Pos: Trustee, Hawaii Pac. Col, 67- Mem: We, The Woman of Hawaii; Am. Asn. Univ. Women; World Brotherhood; Hawaii Found. for Am. Freedoms; Honolulu Br, Nat. League Am. Pen Women. Rel: Episcopal. Mailing Add: 104 Wailupe Circle, Honolulu, Hawaii 96821.

KELLEY, CHARLES P. D
b. Providence, R.I, 12/7/02; m. to Helen. Educ: Bryant Col, B.A, 24; Brown Univ, exten. courses; Providence Col; Dale Carnegie Cert; Dom. Comb. Entr-N.E. Solid Fuels Sch. Polit. & Govt. Pos: Mem. adv. bd, R.I. Fuel Cmn, 39-; R.I. State Rep, 64-68. Bus. & Prof. Pos: CPA; gen. mgr. and treas, Easter Fuel Co. Mem: Nat. Soc. Pub. Acct; Hibernians; Providence Lodge; Elks; K. of C; New Eng. Town Criers; Lions; Nat. Asn. Pub. Acct; R.I. Pub. Acct. Asn; Sons of St. Patrick; Order of Police Lodge; R.I. Fuel Dealers Asn; Ind. Oilmen's Asn; Tidewater Oil Co. Distributors Asn. Mailing Add: 58 Fisk Ave, Providence, R.I. 02905. (1967)

KELLEY, DONALD E. R
Justice, Colo. Supreme Court
b. McCook, Nebr, 1/29/08; s. Charles W. Kelley and Elsie Aston K; m. 6/21/30 to Georgia Pyne; c. John Michael and Donald Pyne. Educ: Kearney Mil. Acad; Univ. Nebr; Phi Delta Phi; Delta Upsilon. Polit. & Govt. Pos: Asst. attorney gen, Nebr, 39-41; attorney, Red Willow Co, 42-44; U.S. Dist. Attorney, Colo, 53-59; attorney, Denver City and Co, 59-61; Colo. State Sen, 63-67; Justice, Colo. Supreme Court, 67- Bus. & Prof. Pos: Gen. practice of law, McCook, Nebr, 30-38 & 42-45; mem, law firm of Kelley, Inman, Flynn & Coffee, Denver, Colo, 62-67. Mem: Exec. cmt, Colo. div, Am. Cancer Soc; bd. gov, Colo. Bar Asn; bd. trustees, Denver Bar Asn; pres, Denver chap, Fed. Bar Asn, 56; Nebr. and Am. Bar Asns; Nat. Asn. of Munic. Law Officers (regional v.pres, 59-61); Am. Judicature Soc; Denver Law Club. Rel: Episcopal. Mailing Add: 3144 S. Columbia St, Denver, Colo. 80210.

KELLEY, FRANK R
Ariz. State Rep.
b. 1923. Polit. & Govt. Pos: Former aide to former U.S. Sen. Frank Carlson, Kans; Ariz. State Rep, 65- Bus. & Prof. Pos: Former newspaper ed; pub. rels. dir, Good Samaritan Hosp, Phoenix. Mailing Add: 5009 E. Sheridan, Phoenix, Ariz. 85008. (1967)

KELLEY, FRANK J. D
Attorney Gen, Mich.
b. Detroit, Mich, 12/31/24; s. Frank E. Kelley and Grace Spears K; m. 6/30/45 to Josephine Palmisano; c. Karen Anne, Frank E, II and Jane Frances. Educ: Univ. Detroit Sch. of Commerce and Finance, 48, Law Sch, J.D, 51; v.pres, Student Body; Moot Court; Law Journal; Alpha Kappa Psi; Gamma Eta Gamma. Polit. & Govt. Pos: Pub. adminstr, Alpena Co, Mich, 56, mem, Bd. of Supvrs, 58-61; city attorney, Alpena, 58-61; Attorney Gen, Mich, 62-; chmn, Mich. Munic. Finance Cmn, chmn, Corp. Tax Appeal Bd. and mem, State Admin. Bd, Judges and State Employees Retirement Systs. and Judicial Conf. of Mich, currently; del, Dem. Nat. Conv, 68. Bus. & Prof. Pos: Attorney, Detroit until 54 and Alpena, 54-61; instr. real estate law, Univ. Mich. Exten. Serv. and econ, Alpena Community Col. Mem: 26th Judicial Bar Asn.(past pres); Am. and Mich. State Bar Asns; Nat. Asn. Attorneys Gen. (mem. bd. dirs, pres, 67-); chmn, Midwest Regional Conf. of Attorneys Gen; dir. and pres, Northeast Mich. Child Guid. Clin; former dir. and pres, Northeast Mich. Cath. Family Serv; charter officer and dir, Alpena Co. United Fund; pres, Community Serv. Coun; K. of C.(Advocate of Coun. 529). Admitted to practice before U.S. Supreme Court. Rel: Roman Catholic. Legal Res: 4267 Mar-Moor Dr, Lansing, Mich. 48917. Mailing Add: The Capitol Bldg, Lansing, Mich. 48933.

KELLEY, GLEN E. D
b. Crossett, Ark, 11/30/31; s. John E. Kelley and Claudell Rodgers K; m. 8/30/52 to Lou Ann Hiland; c. Steve, Minta, Walter, Caroline and Kathleen. Educ: Ouachita Baptist Univ, B.A, 54; Univ. Ark, M.Ed, 60, Ed.D, 62; Phi Delta Kappa; Kappa Delta Pi. Polit. & Govt. Pos: Ark. State Rep, Dist. 35, 67-69. Mil. Serv: Entered as 2nd Lt, Army, 55, released as 1st Lt, 56, after serv. in 27th Inf, Hawaii; Maj, Army Res. Mem: Ark. and Nat. Educ. Asns; Nat. Asn. for Higher Educ; Lions Int. Rel: Baptist. Mailing Add: 309 Hardin, Arkadelphia, Ark. 71923. (1967)

KELLEY, JOAN GUND D
Alternate Mem, Mich. Dem. State Cent. Cmt.
b. Lockport, Ill, 12/19/16; d. John Walter and Elizabeth Gund W; div; c. Vesta Elizabeth (Mrs. Svenson) and Michael Kiernan. Educ: Rockford Col; Univ. Chicago. Polit. & Govt. Pos: Staff rep. for U.S. Sen. Philip A. Hart, 64-; alternate mem, Mich. Dem. State Cent. Cmt, currently. Bus. & Prof. Pos: Editorial, Legal Chronicle, 52-64. Mem: Bus. & Prfnl. Women; Highland Park Caucus Club; Trade Union Leadership Coun. Rel: Roman Catholic. Mailing Add: 44 Pilgrim, Highland Park, Mich. 48203. (1967)

KELLEY, JOSEPH JOHN, JR. R
Secy. of the Commonwealth, Pa.
b. Phila, Pa, 5/31/14; s. Joseph John Kelley and Kathryne M. Hookey K; m. 6/11/49 to Eleanor Eileen Dougan; c. Roger D, Janet E. and Heather A.(deceased). Educ: LaSalle Col, B.S, 37; Univ. Pa. Law Sch, 37-39; Temple Univ. Law Sch, J.D, 41; Phi Alpha Delta. Polit. & Govt. Pos: Law clerk, Judge James G. McGranery, U.S. Dist. Court, Phila, Pa, 46-47; exec. secy, Gov. Raymond P. Shafer, Pa, 67; secy. of the Commonwealth, Pa, 68- Bus. & Prof. Pos: Attorney-at-law, Phila, 47-53; mem. faculty, Valley Forge Mil. Acad. Jr. Col, 47-48 & 52-53; mem. faculty, Drexel Inst. Tech, 52-53; dir. legis. bur, Pa. State C. of C, 53-66. Mil. Serv: Entered as Ens, Navy, 41, released as Lt. Comdr, 46, after serv. in Intel; Res, Lt. Comdr.(Ret). Publ: Numerous articles; former ed, Pa. State C. of C. Legis. Bul. Mem: Am. and Pa. Bar Asns; U.S. Naval Inst; Am. Legion. George Wash. Honor Medals, Freedoms Found, 53 & 57. Rel: Protestant. Mailing Add: 15 N. 27th St, Camp Hill, Pa. 17011.

KELLEY, OSCAR LYTLE D
b. Palestine, Tex, 5/2/03; s. W. Oscar Kelley and Etta McCracken K; m. 7/2/32 to Marie Oliver; c. Carolyn, Kathleen, Chris and Phil. Educ: Abilene Christian Col, B.A, 30; Univ. of Tex, Grad. Study; Blue Key. Polit. & Govt. Pos: Chmn, Dickens Co. Dem. Party, Tex, 54-66; alderman, City of Spur, Tex, 59-61; del, State Dem. Conv, 56, 52, and 48; chmn, Dickens Co. Sch. Bd, 48-54. Prof. Pos: Co. sch. supt, Dickens Co, Tex, 39-47. Mil. Serv: Chmn, Selective Serv. Bd, 40-44. Publn: 'Rural Libraries,' Tex. Outlook, 42. Mem: Tex. State Teacher Asn; Boy Scouts; 4-H Club adv, 60-; past. pres, secy, Spur Rotary Club. Rel: Church of Christ. Legal Res: 814 W. Third St, Spur, Tex. 79370. Mailing Add: Box 686, Spur, Tex. 79370. (1967)

KELLEY, PRESCOTT C. D
b. Derby, Vt, 7/7/21; m. to Lillian Turowski; c. Three sons and two daughters. Educ: Derby Acad. Polit. & Govt. Pos: Vt. State Rep, 65-67. Bus. & Prof. Pos: Owner, restaurant and motor court. Mem: Rotary; Elks; Mason. Rel: Protestant. Mailing Add: Derby Line, Derby, Vt. 05829. (1967)

KELLEY, RALPH HOUSTON D
Mayor, Chattanooga, Tenn.
b. Chattanooga, Tenn, 9/23/28; s. Glenn Blair Kelley and Louise Hobson K; m. to Barbara Fahl; c. Laura, Ellen Kay and Karen Lynn. Educ: Univ. Chattanooga, B.A; Vanderbilt Univ, LL.B, 54; Blue Key; Lambda Chi Alpha; Delta Theta Phi. Polit. & Govt. Pos: Page, U.S. Cong, 41, spec. page to Speaker Rayburn; pres, Young Dem. Club, Tenn, 56; asst. attorney gen, Hamilton Co; Tenn. State Rep, 58; mayor, Chattanooga, 63- Bus. & Prof. Pos: Attorney, Kelley & DiRisio. Mil. Serv: Army Air Corps, 46-49. Mem: V.pres. and state dir, Chattanooga Jr. C. of C; chmn, Americanism Cmt. of the Exchange Club; chmn, Crime Prevention Week, several years; Commodore, Chattanooga Boating Club, 61; pres, Lambda Chi Alpha Alumni Asn; Am. Judicature Soc; Chattanooga, Tenn. and Am. Bar Asns; C. of C; Mountain City Club. Legal Res: 18 S. Sweetbriar, Chattanooga, Tenn. 37411. Mailing Add: Office of the Mayor, Chattanooga, Tenn. 39411. (1967)

KELLEY, ROGER T. R
Asst. Secy. of Defense for Manpower and Reserve Affairs, Dept. of Defense
b. Milwaukee, Wis, 1/14/19; married; c. Mary Ellen, Timothy, Roger, Peter, Stephen and Paul. Educ: Col. of The Holy Cross, B.S, 41; Harvard Grad. Sch. of Bus. Admin, grad, 42. Polit. & Govt. Pos: Asst. Secy. of Defense for Manpower and Reserve Affairs, Dept. of Defense, 69- Bus. & Prof. Pos: Employee, Caterpillar Tractor Co, Peoria, Ill, 46-54, labor rels. mgr, 54-63, dir. of educ. and training, 62-64 and v.pres. for personnel and pub. affairs, 64-69. Mil. Serv: Entered Navy, 42, released as Lt, 46, after serv. aboard a minesweeper in Atlantic Theatre and in command of a coastal transport in Southwest Pac. Theatre. Mem: V.pres, Caterpillar Found; trustee, Lakeview Center Arts and Sci; dir, Ill. C. of C; Cath. High Schs. Bd. of Peoria. Mailing Add: Dept. of Defense, Pentagon, Washington, D.C. 20301.

KELLIHER, WALTER JAMES D
Mayor, Malden, Mass.
b. Malden, Mass, 2/9/13; s. Hugh Cornelius Kelliher and Catherine Meaney K; m. 10/10/42 to Agnes Mary Lynch; c. Nancy Kathleen. Educ: Northeast. Univ, LL.B, 40. Polit. & Govt. Pos: Mem, Malden Sch. Cmt, Mass, 52-55, chmn, 54; mayor, Malden, 58-59 & 62-; del-at-lg, Dem. Nat. Conv, 64; mem, City Dem. Cmt, 64-; State Dem. Committeeman, Fourth Middlesex Dist, 64- Mil. Serv: Entered as Yeoman 3/C, Navy, 42, released as Lt.(jg), 46, after serv. in Staff, Comdr. Naval Forces, ETO, 43-45; Victory Medal; Am. Theater and ETO Ribbons; Lt.(sg)(Ret), Naval Res. Mem: Mass. Trial Lawyers Asn; First Dist. Middlesex, Mass. and Fed. Bar Asns; K. of C; Elks; Hibernians; Eagles; Kiwanis; Moose; Am. Legion; VFW. Rel: Roman Catholic. Mailing Add: 99 Woodland Rd, Malden, Mass. 02148. (1967)

KELLIS, JAMES GEORGE D
Chmn, Fairfield Dem. Town Cmt, Conn.
b. Greece, 7/6/17; s. George John Kellis and Marina Loizos K; m. 9/8/42 to Sophie John Mourges; c. John George and Michael J. Educ: Georgetown Univ, B.A, 47, M.A, 53, Ph.D, 63. Polit. & Govt. Pos: Cmnr, Redevelop. Cmn, Fairfield, Conn, 63-66; v.chmn, Housatonic Commun. Col. Coun, 65-; chmn, Fairfield Improv. Cmn, 66-67; chmn, Fairfield Dem. Town Cmt, 67- Bus. & Prof. Pos: Adj. prof. polit. sci, Univ. Detroit, 56-61, dir. opers. res, Sikorsky Aircraft, United Aircraft Corp, 61-; lectr. polit. sci, Fairfield Univ, 62- Mil. Serv: Entered as Pvt, Army, 36, released as Col, Air Force, 60, after serv. in Third Air Force, Off. Strategic Serv, Cent. Intel. Agency, NATO, Joint Chief Staff and Dept. Air Force; Legion of Merit with Cluster; Bronze Star; Purple Heart. Mem: Am. Polit. Sci. Asn; Am. Econ. Asn; Air Force Asn. Rel: Eastern Orthodox. Mailing Add: 175 Godfrey Rd, Fairfield, Conn. 06430.

KELLNER, DOROTHY DELL D
V.Chmn, Cheyenne Co. Dem. Party, Kans.
b. Giddings, Tex, 10/7/38; d. Alfred Albert Schroeder and Ruth Olga Vahrenkamp S; m. 6/11/61 to Elmer N. Kellner; c. Virginia Belle and Nathan Karl. Educ: Lutheran Concordia Col, 57-59; Concordia Teachers Col, 59-60. Polit. & Govt. Pos: V.chmn, Cheyenne Co. Dem. Party, Kans, 68- Mem: Cheyenne-Rawlins Asn. for Retarded Children; PTA; Lutheran Women's Missionary League (Christian growth chmn, Zone 13, Kans. Dist, 67-69); secy-treas, St. Francis Camp, Gideon Auxiliary, 67- Rel: Lutheran. Legal Res: 302 E. Spencer, St. Francis, Kans. 67756. Mailing Add: P.O. Box 871, St. Francis, Kans. 67756.

KELLOFF, GEORGE D
Chmn, Rio Grande Co. Dem. Party, Colo.
b. Segundo, Colo, 2/22/21; s. Najib Kelloff and Susan Bacash K; m. 6/4/50 to Edna Mae Cunico; c. Susan Reñee and George Karl. Educ: Trinidad Jr. Col, A.A; Adams State Col, B.A; Phi Beta Kappa. Polit. & Govt. Pos: City councilman, Aguilar, Colo, 47-49; committeeman, Rio Grande Co, 65-68; chmn, Rio Grande Co. Dem. Party, 69- Bus. & Prof. Pos: Pres, Kelloff Enterprises, Inc, 64- Mil. Serv: Entered as A/S, Navy, 42, released as Chief Yeoman, 46, after serving in Asiatic & Pac. Theatres, 42-46. Mem: VFW; Am. Legion; Ment. Health Clin; past pres, C. of C; Co. Zoning Bd. Rel: Catholic. Mailing Add: R.R. 2, Two Miles West, Monte Vista, Colo. 81144.

KELLOGG, KENNETH T. R
b. Rutland, Vt, 1/11/98; m. to Thelma H. Morse; c. Two sons and one daughter. Polit. & Govt. Pos: Former Town Justice of the Peace, Vt; Vt. State Rep, 63-69. Bus. & Prof. Pos: Dairy and poultry farmer; retired. Mem: Mason; Farm Bur; dir, Rutland Milk Prod. Assoc. Rel: Protestant. Mailing Add: R.F.D. 1, Rutland, Vt. 05701. (1967)

KELLY, ALBERTA METCALF D
b. Nichols, Iowa, d. Berton L. Metcalf and Ina Lee Hankins M; married. Educ: Univ. Iowa, B.A. and M.A, 36; Alpha Xi Delta; Lambda Theta; Univ. Chorus. Polit. & Govt. Pos: Dem. precinct committeewoman, Pike Twp, Iowa, currently; former v.chmn. and First Dist. committeewoman, Muscatine Co. Dem. Party; Dem. Nat. Committeewoman, Iowa, 53-68; del, Dem. Nat. Conv, 68. Bus. & Prof. Pos: Former high sch. teacher; instr, Univ. Iowa, 57-58. Mem: Eastern Star; mem. bd, Iowa Center for Educ. in Polit, Univ. Iowa. Rel: Christian Church. Mailing Add: Box 176, Nichols, Iowa 52766.

KELLY, ANITA PALERMO D
Pa. State Rep.
b. Long Island, N.Y; d. Peter Palermo and Beatrice P; wid. Educ: Pub. and parochial high schs, Long Island, N.Y. Polit. & Govt. Pos: Chmn. credential cmt, Women's Dem. Club, Phila, Pa; mem, 34th Ward Dem. Exec. Cmt; Pa. State Rep, 63- Mem: Bd. gov, Am. Cmt. on Italian Migration. Mailing Add: 6113 Master St, Philadelphia, Pa. 19151. (1967)

KELLY, ARTHUR JOHN D
Treas, West Haven Dem. Town Cmt, Conn.
b. West Haven, Conn, 9/9/22; s. Joseph F. Kelly and Catherine McDermott K; m. 10/16/48 to Mary Jane Mansfield; c. Michael John, Mary Jane, Marcella Jean and Arthur John, Jr. Educ: West Haven High Sch, Conn, grad. Polit. & Govt. Pos: Mem, Develop. Cmn, West Haven, Conn, 52-54, chmn, Bd. of Park Cmn, 54-60, second selectman, 58-59, Redevelop. Cmnr, 59-61 and Police Cmnr, 68-; mem, West Haven Dem. Town Cmt, 53-, dist. chmn, 53-59 and treas, 65-; del, Conn. State Dem. Conv, 58-68; alternate del, Dem. Nat. Conv, 68. Bus. & Prof. Pos: Pres, Joseph F. Kelly Co, Inc, Gen. Contractors, 52- Mil. Serv: Pvt, Army, 44-45, serv. in 102nd Inf. Unit. Mem: V.pres, Conn. Chap, Asn. Gen. Contractors, 56-57, pres, 57-58 and bd. dirs, 59-68; pres, New Haven Gen. Contractors Asn, 58-60; bd. trustees, Conn. Bldg. Trades Welfare & Ins. Fund, 68-; chmn, Conn. Bricklayers Pension Fund, 56-; bd. trustees, Conn. Laborers Pension Fund, 59-; chmn, Conn. Laborers Welfare Fund; K. of C; Elks; Knights of St. Patrick; Racebrook Country Club. Elk of the Year Award for Commun. Serv, 58; Boy Scouts Award for Youth Serv, 58; Gold Bat Award, West Haven Twi-Light Baseball League, 64; Jimmy Fund Award for Youth Serv, 68; Knights of St. Patrick Commun. Serv. Award, 68. Rel: Catholic. Mailing Add: 137 Main St, West Haven, Conn. 06516.

KELLY, AUDREY R. R
m. to Melvin Kelly; c. John, Larry, Kathleen, Paul, David. Educ: Cornell Law Sch. Polit. & Govt. Pos: Del, Rep. Nat. Conv, 56; Rep. statewide cand, Sec. Int. Affairs, 62; Pa. Ins. Cmnr, 63-67; Rep. State Cmt, 10 yrs; pos. held with Pa. Coun. of Rep. Women; pres, Susquehanna Co. Coun; statewide polit. activities; chmn, Finance Chmn, Cong. Chmn; secy, Susquehanna Co. Rep. Cmt; secy, Susquehanna Young Rep; Chmn, Pa. Del. to Nat. Rep. Women's Conf; mem, platform Cmt. NRWC, 58 & 62; mem, Gov. Cmt. on Status of Women. Bus. & Prof. Pos: Attorney-at-law. Mem: Red Cross; Bus. & Prfnl. Women's Club; Altar Rosary Soc; Pa. Ment. Health Asn. Rel: Catholic. Mailing Add: 50 S. Main St, Montrose, Pa. 18801.

KELLY, BOBBY D. D
b. Anderson, S.C, 8/17/28; s. Joseph D. Kelly and Thelma Adams K; m. 2/17/51 to Lula A. Watkins. Educ: L.B.C. High Sch, 46. Polit. & Govt. Pos: S.C. State Rep, -66. Bus. & Prof. Pos: Ins. agent, St. Farm Ins. Co. Mil. Serv: Navy, 47-48. Mem: Pres, L.B.C. Lions. Mailing Add: Box 217 Clearwater, S.C. 29822. (1967)

KELLY, CHARLES HENRY D
b. Davenport, Iowa, 8/13/21; s. Glenn Dunn Kelly and Edna Timmons K; m. 6/1/44 to Geraldine Grace Allen; c. Timmons Allen, John Charles, James Dunn and Thomas George. Educ: St. Ambrose Col, 46-48; Drake Univ. Law Sch, 48-49; LaSalle Exten. Law Sch, 64-; LaSalle Prfnl. Soc. Polit. Pos: Alternate del, Dem. Nat. Conv, 64 and del, 60; chmn, Farmers for Sen. Paul H. Douglas, 58; pres, Young Dem. of Piatt Co, 56. Mil. Serv: Entered as Coxswain, Coast Guard Res, 42, released as Boatswain 2/C, 46, after serv. in 7th Fleet, Security 9th Naval Dist, Pac. Theater; Pac. Theater Ribbon. Publn: United Nations World Food Bank Plan, Rep. Printing, 59, Farmers Consumers General Welfare Plan, 59 and United Nations Control Disarmament Plan, 61. Mem: Am. Legion; Nat. Farmer's Union; Farm Bureau; former mem. U.S. Power Sq; U.S. Coast Guard Auxiliary. Rel: Presbyterian. Mailing Add: 1124 North State St, Monticello, Ill. 61856. (1967)

KELLY, DANIEL M. D
b. Manhattan, N.Y, 2/6/15. Educ: Manhattan Col, B.B.A. cum laude, 36; N.Y. Law Sch, LL.B, 39; Brooklyn Law Sch, D.J.S, 53. Polit. & Govt. Pos: Vol, Speakers Bur, War Savings Bond Staff, U.S. Treas. Dept; asst. to cmnr, Dept. Invest, N.Y.C; mem, N.Y. Young Dem; past chmn, Dem. Co. Cmt; mem. adv. bd, Riverside Dem; N.Y. State Assemblyman, 50-68. Bus. & Prof. Pos: Attorney; guest lectr. law and govt, N.Y.C. Cols. Mil. Serv: Army, 42-46, Anti-air-craft Intel, Pac. Theatre. Mem: N.Y. City and Am. Bar Asns; N.Y. Co. Lawyers Asn; Cath. Lawyers Guild; K. of C; Hibernians; C.W.V; VFW; Am. Legion; Riverside Chap, A.V.C; Am. Irish Hist. Soc. Rel: Catholic. Mailing Add: 924 West End Ave, New York, N.Y. 10025. (1967)

KELLY, DEE J. D
b. Bonham, Tex, 3/7/29; s. Dee C. Kelly and Era Lee Jones K; m. 12/30/54 to Janice Lynn LeBlanc; c. Cynthia Lynn, Dee J, Jr. and Craig LeBlanc. Educ: Tex. Christian Univ, B.A; George Wash. Univ, LL.B; Delta Theta Phi. Polit. & Govt. Pos: Asst. to U.S. Rep. Sam Rayburn, Tex, 49-51 & 53-54; legal exam, Oil and Gas Div. of R.R. Cmn. of Tex, Austin, 55-56; mem. bd. of dirs, Tex. Turnpike Authority, 67-; mem. bd. of regents, State Sr. Cols, Tex, 69- Bus. & Prof. Pos: Attorney, Cantey, Hanger, Gooch, Cravens & Scarborough, 56-58; gen. counsel, Moncrief Oil Interests, 58-64; pvt. law practice, Ft. Worth, 64-; mem. bd. dirs, Tom Brown Drilling Co, Midland; chmn. bd, Bank of N.Tex, Hurst. Mil. Serv: Entered as 2nd Lt, Air Force, 51, released as 1st Lt, Hq. Air Force, 53. Mem: Charter mem, Tex. Bar Found; Am, Tex. and Ft. Worth-Tarrant Co. Bar Asns; trustee, Sam Rayburn Libr. and Found, Bonham, Tex; Shady Oaks, River Crest and Ft. Worth Clubs, Ft. Worth; Citadel Club, Austin; Dallas Club. Rel: Protestant. Legal Res: 1315 Hillcrest, Ft. Worth, Tex. 76107. Mailing Add: 1113 Fort Worth National Bank Bldg, Ft. Worth, Tex. 76102.

KELLY, DORCAS BURNUMN R
b. Pawnee Co, Okla, 5/27; d. Thaddeus Ramey Tracy and Martha Elizabeth Stecker T; m. 4/16/22 to Albert Kelly, wid, 46; c. Albert Charles, Levan, Tracy, Allison A. and Royce; ten grandchildren. Educ: Cent. Col; Univ. Mich; Tulsa Sch. Nursing, grad, RN. Polit. & Govt. Pos: Registr, Vital Statist,

Tulsa, Okla, 20-21; committeewoman, Okla. State Rep. Cmt, 50-52, v.chmn, 56-59; hon. v.pres, Rep. Nat. Conv, 52, del. and mem, Rules Cmt, 64, alternate del, 68; Rep. nat. committeewoman, Okla, 60-68. Bus. & Prof. Pos: Founder and operator, Bristow Gen. Hosp, 21-22; pres, Kelly Bros, Bus. Trust, 55-; dir, Am. Nat. Bank, Bristow, 59- Mem: Bus. & Prfnl. Women's Club; Rotary Ann's; dir, Bristow United Fund; Bristow Planning Cmn; Bristow Beautification Cmt; Bristow Country Club; Tulsa Town Hall. Rel: Presbyterian. Mailing Add: 119 E. 12th St, Box 1199, Bristow, Okla. 74010. (1967)

KELLY, ED J. D
b. Flemingsburg, Ky, 1904. Educ: St. Mary's Col; Univ. Wis. Polit. & Govt. Pos: Former mayor, Flemingsburg, Ky, 8 years; mem, Ky. Conserv. Coun; mem, Nat. Cmt. Support of Pub. Schs; Ky. State Sen, 56-68. Bus. & Prof. Pos: Farm supplies and fuel distributor. Mem: Farm Bur; Sportsman Club; Mammoth Cave Nat. Asn; Ky. Hist. Soc; past pres. and mem. bd. dirs, C. of C. Rel: Catholic. Mailing Add: 209 Stockwell Ave, Flemingsburg, Ky. 41041. (1967)

KELLY, EDNA F(LANNERY) D
b. East Hampton, N.Y, 8/20/06; d. Patrick J. Flannery and Mary Ellen F; m. to Edward L. Kelly, wid; c. William E, II and Maura Patricia; grandchildren, Edward, William, Robert, Richard, Ellen, Elizabeth Ann, Elaine Mary Kelly and Michael Bruce. Educ: Hunter Col, B.A, 28. Polit. & Govt. Pos: Assoc. research dir, Dem. Party, in N.Y. State Legis. 43, chief research dir, 44-49; del, 18th Gen. Assembly, UN; Dem. Nat. Committeewoman, N.Y; mem. exec. cmt, Kings Co. Dem. Party, 44-; U.S. Rep, N.Y, 49-67; del, Dem. Nat. Conv, 68. Mailing Add: 1247 Carroll St, Brooklyn, N.Y. 11213. (1967)

KELLY, EDWARD FLORIAN D
b. Logansport, Ind, 3/7/33; s. Sylvester Kelly and Germaine K; single. Educ: Univ. Notre Dame, A.B, 55; Univ. Wis, J.D, 63. Polit. & Govt. Pos: Asst. U.S. Attorney, Indianapolis, Ind, 64-68; Dem. nominee, U.S. Rep, 68; minority counsel, Ind. State Senate, 69. Mil. Serv: Entered as Ens, Navy, 57, released as Lt, 60, after serv. in Panama and Wash. D.C; Lt. Comdr, Navy Res. Mailing Add: 220 South St, West Lafayette, Ind. 47906.

KELLY, FRANCES FLOYD R
Mem, Madison Co. Rep. Exec. Cmt, Ala.
b. Phenix City, Ala, 6/25/40; d. Dr. Cyril Franklin Floyd and Loette McGinty F; m. 12/16/60 to Joshua Oscar Kelly, Jr; c. Joshua O, III and Matthew Russell. Educ: Auburn Univ, 3 years; Delta Zeta. Polit. & Govt. Pos: Asst. campaign dir, Martin-for-Gov, Madison Co, Ala, 66; del, Rep. State Conv, 66 & 68; del, Nat. and Ala. Fedn. Rep. Women's Convs, 67; pres, Liberty Fedn. Rep. Women, 67-68; del, Rep. Nat. Conv, 68; coordinator, TAR Nixon Campaigners, 68; mem. campaign staff, Weir-for-Judge, Madison Co, 68, mem, Hooper-for-Sen. Campaign, 68. Mem: Grace Club Auxiliary; Red Cross Vol; Ala. Cowbelles Asn. Rel: Methodist. Mailing Add: Route 3, Box 807, Huntsville, Ala. 35806.

KELLY, HENRY WILLIAM D
Chmn, East. Cong. Dist. Dem. Non-Partisan League, N.Dak.
b. Webster, N.Dak, 7/7/26; s. Henry E. Kelly and Anna O'Brien K; m. 1/8/49 to Georgette Assad; c. Sean William, Gregory Shannon, Colleen and Dennis Kevin. Educ: Univ. Minn, Minneapolis, B.A. in Journalism, 49; Graphic Arts Inst. of Minneapolis, Cert. in Typography and Advert. Layout, 50; Sigma Delta Chi. Polit. & Govt. Pos: Precinct committeeman, Park River Third Ward, N.Dak, 60-; treas, N.Dak. Dem. Non-Partisan League, 62-63; chmn, Walsh Co. Dem. Non-Partisan League, 62-66; chmn, 16th Dist. Dem. Non-Partisan League, Walsh Co, 66-; chmn, Region Five of N.Dak. Dem. Non-Partisan League, 67-69; mem, State Campaign Finance Cmt, 68; chmn, Northeast Conf. of N.Dak. Dem. Non-Partisan League, 68-; chmn, East. Cong. Dist, N.Dak. Dem. Non-Partisan League, 68-; mem, State Century Club Cmt, 69- Bus. & Prof. Pos: Managing ed. and co-publisher, Walsh Co. Press, Inc, Park River, 56- Mil. Serv: Entered as A/S, Navy, 44, released as Signalman 3/C PO, 46, after serv. in Pac. Theatre, Occup. of Japan, 45-46. Mem: VFW; Am. Legion; K. of C; hon. mem, Future Farmers of Am. Rel: Catholic. Legal Res: 215 Park Ave, Park River, N.Dak. 58270. Mailing Add: Box 49, Park River, N.Dak. 58270.

KELLY, JAMES ANTHONY, JR. D
Mass. State Sen.
b. Worcester, Mass, 5/11/26; s. James Anthony Kelly and Florence Adams K; m. 7/3/48 to Elisabeth M. Allen; c. James, Thomas, Michael, Robert, Paul, Jean and Maureen. Educ: Becker Jr. Col, Worcester, Mass, 46-47; Clark Univ, B.B.A, 50. Polit. & Govt. Pos: Mem, sch. cmt, Leicester, Mass, 48-51; Mass. State Rep, 58-64; Mass. State Sen, Fourth Dist, 64- Bus. & Prof. Pos: Owner, James A. Kelly CPA, Leicester, Mass, 50-69. Mil. Serv: Entered as A/S, Navy, 44, released as Aer M 2/C, 46, after serv. in Weather Dept, Asiatic-Pac. Theatre, 45-46; Good Conduct Medal; Am. Theatre Medal; World War II Victory Medal; Asiatic-Pac. Theatre Medal. Publ: 'Home Rule,' Selectman's Mag, 67; 'Computer Law,' Boston Bar, 68. Mem: Am. Inst. of Certified Pub. Acct; Mass. Asn. of Certified Pub. Acct; Am. Acct. Asn; VFW; Am. Legion; Amvets, Mass; Elks; Eagles; Century Sportsmens Club, Auburn; K. of C. Citation, Mass. Dept. of Polish Am. Veterans. Rel: Catholic. Legal Res: Stafford St, Oxford, Mass. 01540. Mailing Add: Stafford St, Rochdale, Mass. 01542.

KELLY, JAMES H. D
b. 1920; m. to Charlotte Mulligan; c. Anne, James Jr, Cheryl, Edward and Charlotte. Educ: Northeastern Univ. Polit. & Govt. Pos: Cand, Mass. State Auditor. Bus. & Prof. Pos: Ins. broker. Mil. Serv: Marine Corps, World War II, Iwo Jima. Mem: Am. Legion, DAV; Holy Name Soc; Carondelet Fathers Club; Ignation Club. 1967 Legal Res: 372 Arbor Lane, Boston, Mass. No mailing address available. (1967)

KELLY, JAMES P. R
Mo. State Sen.
b. Pleasant Hill, Ill, 3/11/11; married; c. Linda. Educ: Kemper Mil. Sch; Univ. Mo, B.S, 33. Polit. & Govt. Pos: Former Young Rep. Nat. Committeeman; Mo. State Sen, 54-; mem, Rep. State Cmt, 56; alternate del, Rep. Nat. Conv, 60. Bus. & Prof. Pos: Farmer; sales and advert. rep. Mil. Serv: Army Air Force, World War II. Mem: Mason; Elks; Am. Legion; VFW; pres, Kemper Mil. Sch. Rel: Methodist. Mailing Add: 302 Center St, Boonville, Mo. 65233.

KELLY, JOHN BARNES R
b. West Liberty, Ohio, 8/29/25; s. John Davis Kelly and Ruth Barnes K; m. 6/5/53 to Joan Louise Pearson; c. John Pearson, Patricia Joan, Mary Margaret and Kathryn Ann. Educ: Ohio State Univ, 46-51, B.S. & LL.B; Phi Alpha Delta; Sigma Nu. Polit. & Govt. Pos: Prosecuting attorney, Logan Co, Ohio, 53-56; chmn, Logan Co. Rep. Cent. Cmt, 56-69. Mil. Serv: Entered as Cadet, Air Force, 43, released as 2nd Lt, 46. Mem: Mason; Shrine. Rel: Episcopal. Mailing Add: 1108 Knowlton Rd, Bellefontaine, Ohio 43311.

KELLY, JOHN BRENDEN, JR. D
Chmn, Non-Partisan Register and Vote Cmt. of Phila, Pa.
b. Philadelphia, Pa, 5/24/27; s. John B. Kelly and Margaret Major K; m. 3/4/54 to Mary Freeman; c. Ann F, Susan E, Maura G, Elizabeth B, John B, III and Margaret C. Educ: Univ. Pa, A.B. in Econ, 50; Kappa Sigma; Varsity Club; rowing team. Polit. & Govt. Pos: Chmn, Non-Partisan Register and Vote Cmt. of Phila, Pa, currently. Bus. & Prof. Pos: Pres, John B. Kelly, Inc, 60-; mem. bd. dirs, Lincoln Nat. Bank. Mil. Serv: Seaman, Naval Res, 45-46; Ens, Naval Res, 51-53, serv. on destroyer, Atlantic and Mediterranean Fleets; Lt.(jg), Naval Res, 52-66. Mem: Bricklayers Union; Employing Bricklayers Asn. of Del. Co; pres, Phila. Athletic Club, 62-69; Vesper Boat Club; Phila. Country Club; Bala Golf Club; chmn, Phila. Bi-Centennial Cmt; Mayor's Sports Adv. Coun; v.pres, Phila. Philanthropies; chmn, Phila. Youth Fitness Cmt; v.chmn, Police Athletic League; Young Pres. Orgn; Urban Club; Catholic Charities; Freedom Found; Gr. Phila. Olympic Cmt; Nat. Conf. Christians and Jews; Small Bus. Admin; Amateur Athletic Union; Nat. Asn. Amateur Oarsmen; Phila. Olympians; U.S. Rowing Soc; Phila. Swimming Dirs. Soc. Winner, U.S. Olympic Team Single Sculls, 48-56 and Double Sculls, 60; European, Swiss and Belgium Singles Champion, 49; Mex. Singles Champion, 53; Pan Am. Games Singles Champion, 55 and Doubles Champion, 59; Phila. Singles Champion, ten times, U.S, 8 times and U.S. schoolboy, 2 times; Sullivan Award, Outstanding Amateur Athelete in U.S, Amateur Atheletic Union, 47; won, Pa. State Apprentice Bricklaying Championship, 53; Man of Year Award, Cath. War Vet, 56; Young Man of Achievement Award, Golden Slipper Square Club, 57; Outstanding Young Man of the Year Award, Pa. Jr. C. of C, 60 & 61; Am. Heritage Found. Award, 60 & 64; Phila Zionist Award, 64; Brotherhood Award, Jewish War Vet, 66. Rel: Roman Catholic. Legal Res: Plaza Apts, 28G, 18th & Parkway, Philadelphia, Pa. 19103. Mailing Add: 1720 Cherry St, Philadelphia, Pa. 19103.

KELLY, JOHN HENRY D
Treas, W.Va.
b. Kanawha Co, W.Va, 2/5/22; s. Lewis H. Kelly and Rebecca Morrow K, both deceased; m. 2/25/49 to Theodocia Romaine Hardin; c. Karen. Educ: Morris Harvey Col, B.S, 49; Int. Acct. Soc. of Chicago. Polit. & Govt. Pos: Dir. of finance, W.Va. Dept. of Agr, 48-60; treas, W.Va, 61-; alternate del, Dem. Nat. Conv, 68. Mil. Serv: Entered as Seaman 1/C, Navy, 42, released as Machinist's Mate 1/C, 45. Mem: Past pres, Charleston Optimists and Charleston Jr. C. of C; VFW; Moose; Odd Fellows; Kanawha Valley Acct. Soc. Rel: Baptist. Mailing Add: 1527 Dogwood Rd, Charleston, W.Va. 25314.

KELLY, JOHN MARTIN D
b. Chelsea, Mass, 10/1/14; s. James B.A. Kelly and Elizabeth B.A. Ford K; m. 12/29/38 to Esther Elizabeth Ladenburg; c. Joseph James, Patricia Elizabeth, Mary Ann and John Michael. Educ: N.Mex. Sch. of Mines, B.S. in Mining eng, 36 and petroleum engr, 39. Hon. D.Sc, N.Mex. Inst. Mining and Tech, 63. Polit. & Govt. Pos: Mem. and exec. dir, N.Mex. Oil Conserv. Cmn, 41-45; dir, N.Mex. Bur. of Mines and Mineral Resources, 41-45; State Geologist, N.Mex, 41-45; coordinator of mines in N.Mex, War Prod. Bd, 41-45; mem, Nat. Coun. of Petroleum Regulatory Authorities under the Petroleum Admin. for War, 41-45; consult. and mineral adv, N.Mex. State Land Off, 45-61; Asst. Secy. of the Interior for mineral resources, U.S. Dept. of the Interior, 61-65; U.S. del, Energy and Petroleum Cmts, Orgn. for Econ. Coop. and Develop, Paris, France, 61-65, mem, adv. cmt. to UN del, Petroleum Cmt, 65-; U.S. del, NATO Petroleum Planning Cmt, Paris, France, 61-65; chmn, U.S. del, Second Petroleum Conf. on Asia and the Far East, Econ. Cmn. for Asia and the Far East, UN, Teheran, Iran, 62 and Third Petroleum Conf. on Asia and the Far East, Tokyo, Japan, 65; mem, Nat. Petroleum Coun, 65-; consult. to Secy of the Interior, 65- Bus. & Prof. Pos: Mining engr, Rosedale Gold Mines, 36; mine chemist, Am. Metal Co, 36-37; petroleum engr, Lea Contractors Co, 37-41; registered prfnl. engr, N.Mex, 38-; petroleum consult, 45-61 & 65-; pres, Elk Oil Co, 45-61; dir, Yucca Water Co, 45-61. Mem: N.Mex. Bd. of Educ. Finance; adv. bd, Small Bus. Admin; Am. Inst. Mining Engrs; Am. Asn. of Petroleum Geologists; Am. Asn. of Petroleum Landmen; Am. Inst. of Prfnl. Geologists; fel, Geol. Soc. of Am. and Am. Asn. for the Adv. of Sci; Mining and Metallurgical Soc. of Am; Am. Petroleum Inst. (25 Year Club); Independent Petroleum Asn. of Am; N.Mex. Oil and Gas Asn. (dir); Rocky Mt. Geol. Soc; N.Mex. Mining Asn; N.Mex. Landmen's Asn; Mining Club, N.Y.C; Am. Farm Bur; Elks; K. of C. Rel: Roman Catholic; Knight Comdr, Holy Sepulchre, Knight of St. Gregory. Legal Res: Box 310, Roswell, N.Mex. 88201. Mailing Add: 1001 Connecticut Ave. N.W, Suite 625, Washington, D.C. 20036.

KELLY, JOSEPH I. D
b. San Francisco, Calif, 3/11/30; s. Dennis Peter Kelly and Mary Twohig K; m. 1/24/57 to Cynthia Arden Brown; c. Kathleen Ann, Joseph I, Carol Eileen, Patricia Layne and Cynthia Marie. Educ: Univ. San Francisco, B.S, 52; Univ. Calif. Hastings Col. Law, LL.B, 58. Polit. & Govt. Pos: Mem, Calif. Dem. State Cent. Cmt, 60-68; cmnr, San Francisco Pub. Utilities Cmn; alternate del, Dem. Nat. Conv, 64 & 68. Mil. Serv: Entered as Pvt, Army, 52, released as Cpl, 55, after serv. in Army Security Agency, Korea, 53-54. Mem: Calif. State and San Francisco Bars; Barristers' Club; San Francisco Lawyers Club; exec. cmt, Univ. of San Francisco Alumni Asn; exec. cmt, St. Ignatius High Sch. Alumni Asn; Hastings Col. Law Alumni Asn; Veterans Polit. Coun; K. of C. Rel: Roman Catholic. Legal Res: 460 Magellan Ave, San Francisco, Calif. 94116. Mailing Add: 1255 Post St, San Francisco, Calif. 94109. (1967)

KELLY, MARY PRUDENCE D
b. Springfield, Ky; d. John William Kelly (deceased) and Sara Simms K.(deceased). Polit. & Govt. Pos: Secy, Ky. Dept. of Hwy, 36-44; secy, Ky. State Senate, 44; former admin. asst. to former U.S. Rep. Frank Chelf, Ky. Rel: Catholic. Legal Res: Springfield, Ky. 40069. Mailing Add: 1 Scott Circle N.W, Washington, D.C. 20036.

KELLY, MILTON GUDMUNDUR R
N.Dak. State Sen.
b. Milton, N.Dak, 10/2/95; s. Fred Joseph Kelly and Karitas Grimson K; m. 4/27/18 to Sybil Baker; c. Fred Baker, Milton Wallace, Elizabeth Jane (Mrs. McErlane), Caryl Anne (Mrs. Reslock) and Sybil Marguerite (Mrs. Knudson). Educ: Univ. of N.Dak, 16-18; Alpha Tau Omega. Polit. & Govt. Pos: Rep. precinct committeeman, Devils Lake, N.Dak; mem, Ramsey Co. Rep. Cmt; N.Dak. State Sen, Dist. 15, 67-; mem, N.Dak. Research Cmt. Subcmts. on Natural Resources, 68 and Polit. Subdiv, N.Dak. State Senate. Bus. & Prof. Pos: Pres, Farmers Mill & Elevator Asn, 19-66. Mil. Serv: Entered as Pvt, Army, 18, released as Cpl, 19, after serv. in E. Co, 313 Eng, 88th Div, France. Mem: Elks (past state pres); C. of C.(past pres, Devils Lake Chap); Mason; Am. Legion (past dept. comdr); VFW; Vet. of World War I; Int. Vet. Rel: Episcopal. Mailing Add: Apt. Nine, Town's Edge Apt, Route 2, Devils Lake, N.Dak. 58301.

KELLY, PHYLLIS MATHEIS R
Asst. Chmn, Erie Co. Rep. Cmt, N.Y.
b. Buffalo, N.Y, 5/7/21; d. Charles William Matheis and Florence Schlegel M; m. 9/7/46 to James Edward Kelly; c. James E, III, Maureen, Colleen and Kathleen. Educ: Univ. Buffalo, B.A, 42; Phi Beta Kappa; Cap and Gown; Theta Chi; Pres, Panhellenic Council. Polit. & Govt. Pos: Exec. secy, Citizens for Eisenhower, Erie Co, N.Y, 51-52; co-chmn, Erie Co. Citizens for Rockefeller, 58; founder, 20 Rep. Women's Clubs, Erie Co, 61-; asst. chmn, Erie Co. Rep. Cmt, 61-; mem, N.Y. State Rep. Platform Cmt, 66; coordinator, Eighth Judicial Dist. Women for Nixon-Agnew, 68; chmn, Erie Co. Women for Nixon-Agnew, 68; v.chmn, N.Y. State Citizens for Javits, 68. Bus. & Prof. Pos: Ed, Bell Aircraft News, Bell Aircraft Corp, N.Y, 43-45. Mem: Women's Exec. (pres); Buffalo Philharmonic; Zonta Club Amherst; Erie Co. Fedn. Women's Rep. Clubs (pres); N.Y. State Fedn. Women's Rep. Clubs (past v.pres); Univ. Buffalo Alumnae Asn.(past pres). Erie Co. Rep. Woman of the Year, 65. Rel: Roman Catholic. Mailing Add: 1 Ellicott Square, Buffalo, N.Y. 14203.

KELLY, ROBERT F. R
N.Y. State Assemblyman
b. Brooklyn, N.Y, 5/25/17; m. to Ethel Hall. Educ: St. Johns Sch. of Commerce; St. Johns Law Sch. Polit. & Govt. Pos: Pres, Ninth Assembly Dist. Rep. Club, N.Y; N.Y. State Assemblyman, 60- Bus. & Prof. Pos: Attorney. Mem: K. of C; past pres, Bay Ridge Lawyers Asn; dir, Bay Ridge Real Estate Bd; Lawyers Club of Brooklyn; Men's Club of Bay Ridge; 86th St. Bd. of Trade; Dyker Heights Civic Asn. Mailing Add: 226 76th St, Brooklyn, N.Y. 11209. (1967)

KELLY, ROY R. D
b. Macon, Ga, 4/26/24; s. Roy R. Kelly, Sr. and Althea Jordan K; m. 12/20/46 to Nancy R. Banks; c. Roy Robinson III, John Banks, Paul Hunt. Educ: N. Ga. Col, 43; Univ. of Ga, B.S.A, 47. Polit. & Govt. Pos: Ga. State Rep, 59-66; Ga. State Sen, 57-58; State Dem. Exec. Cmt, 60. Bus. & Prof. Pos: Banker; farmer; ginner; warehouseman; bd. of dirs, Jasper Co. Develop. Corp, 59-62; v.pres, Citizens Bank of Shady Dale, Ga; secy-treas, Banks-Kelly Co, Inc. Mil. Serv: Air Force, S/Sgt; awarded six battle stars. Mem: Bd. of dirs, Jasper Co. C. of C, 59-62; pres. Jasper Co. Farm Bur. Rel: Presbyterian. Mailing Add: Monticello, Ga. 31064. (1967)

KELLY, STUART STACY D
b. 3/4/13; s. George Washington Kelly and Harriett Stacy K; m. 5/3/47 to Marguerite Sampson; c. Vicki Mariena and Maurice Stacy. Polit. & Govt. Pos: Chmn, Spencer Co. Dem. Party, Ky, until 69. Mailing Add: Route 3, Taylorsville, Ky. 40071.

KELLY, WILLIAM F, JR. D
N.J. State Sen.
b. Jersey City, N.J, 7/20/11; s. William F. Kelly, Sr. and Anne Morgan K; m. to Catherine Gallagher; c. Mary Ann, Kathleen, Jeanne, Winifred, William F, III, Margaret and Patricia Elizabeth Educ: Seton Hall Univ; Fordham Univ. Law Sch. Polit. & Govt. Pos: Munic. court magistrate, N.J, 49-51; sheriff, Hudson Co, 51-54; pres, N.J. State Civil Serv. Cmn, 54-57; N.J. State Sen, 57- Bus. & Prof. Pos: Former attorney, Law Firm of Milton, McNulty and Angelli; attorney, Law Firm of Wall, Walsh, Kelly and Whipple, 48- Mil. Serv: Army, CID agent, Southwest Pac, 3 years. Mem: Hudson Co. and State Bar Asns; St. Aedans' Holy Name Soc; CID Agents Asn; past dir, Commun. Chest Dr. Rel: Catholic. Mailing Add: 595 Newark Ave, Jersey City, N.J. 07306. (1967)

KELLY, WILLIAM JAMES D
Chmn, Sandusky Co. Dem. Party, Ohio
b. Somerset, Ohio, 9/1/24; s. Paul Edward Kelly and Geneive Litizinger K; m. 6/28/47 to Mary Ann Snider; c. Mary Kathleen, Carol Ann, Colleen Marie and John Francis. Educ: Holy Trinity High Sch, grad; Ohio State Univ; Int. Correspondence Schs, grad. Polit. & Govt. Pos: Pres, Sandusky Co. Young Dem, Ohio, 1 year; mem. Bd. Elec, Sandusky Co, 1 year; del, Dem. Nat. Conv, 68; chmn, Sandusky Co. Dem. Party, 68- Mil. Serv: Entered as PO 1/C, Navy, 42-46 on USS Yorktown, Pac. Theatre; Good Conduct Medal; Pac. Theatre, 7 Stars; Presidential Unit Citation. Mem: Am. Legion; VFW; AFL-CIO; Plumbers and Steamfitters Union; Fremont Yacht Club; Cath. Men's Club. Rel: Catholic. Mailing Add: 908 N. Fifth St, Fremont, Ohio 43420.

KELLY, WILLIAM THOMAS R
Chmn, Pulaski Co. Rep. Cmt, Ark.
b. Little Rock, Ark, 11/6/19; s. W.J. Kelly and Bertha Dehmer K; m. 9/1/41 to Lucille Elizabeth Metrailer; c. W.T, Jr, Carolyn Jane (Mrs. O'Connor), Cornelia Marie, Paul Dehmer, Lucille Elizabeth, Kathleen Rose, Margaret Mary, Christine Louise, Marie Patrice, Francis Matthew, John Kevin, Joseph Lee, Brian Anthony and Michael Edward. Educ: St. Louis Univ; Ark. Law Sch, LL.B; Phi Sigma Eta. Polit. & Govt. Pos: Chmn, Pulaski Co. Elec. Cmn, Gov. Coun. Human Resources and Pulaski Co. Rep. Cmt, Ark, currently. Bus. & Prof. Pos: Treas, Ark. Coun. Human Rels, currently. Mil. Serv: Entered as Pvt, Army, 43, released as S/Sgt, 46, after serv. in Signal Intel, China-Burma-India Theatre. Mem: Ark. Bar Asn; Million-Dollar Roundtable, 67-68. Rel: Catholic. Legal Res: 5423 Maryland, Little Rock, Ark. 72204. Mailing Add: 401 Commercial Nat. Bank, Little Rock, Ark. 72201.

KELMEL, DOROTHY ELLEN R
Chmn, Caldwell Co. Rep. Cent. Cmt, Mo.
b. Hamilton, Mo, 5/31/20; d. Wallace Power Craig and Eva Francis Manning C; m. 12/30/41 to Laurence Otto Kelmel; c. Sharrie Ann (Mrs. Frederick S. Grant), Launnie Lee and Chris Craig. Educ: Univ. Kansas City, Mo, 39-40. Polit. & Govt. Pos: Twp. committeewoman, Rep. Party, Hamilton, Mo, 64-; chmn, Caldwell Co. Rep. Cent. Cmt, 68- Bus. & Prof. Pos: Private secy, Schick Elec. Shaver Corp, Kansas City, Mo, 40-41; clerk-typist, Puget Sound Navy Yard, Bremerton, Wash, 44-45. Mem: Caldwell Co. Fedn. Rep. Women; Am. Legion Auxiliary; 40 et 8; Womens Progressive Farmers Asn. Mo; PTA; Band Mothers Penny Sch; Sacred Heart Altar Soc; Legion of Mary; Diocesan Coun. Cath. Women. Rel: Catholic. Mailing Add: 204 E. Berry St, Hamilton, Mo. 64644.

KELSCH, WILLIAM CHARLES R
N.Dak. State Rep.
b. Bismarck, N.Dak, 9/2/32; s. Clemens F. Kelsch and Mary Roche K; m. 8/16/54 to Joan E. Wise; c. Steven W, Thomas D, Mary Elizabeth and Jean Catherine. Educ: St. John's Univ, Minn, B.A, 53; Univ. N.Dak, J.D, 56; Order of the Coif. Polit. & Govt. Pos: States attorney, Morton Co, N.Dak, 59-67; N.Dak. State Rep, Dist. 34, 67-; mem, N.Dak. Law Enforcement Coun, 67-; state chmn, Romney for Pres, 68. Bus. & Prof. Pos: Attorney-at-law, Kelsch, Scanlon & Kelsch, Mandan, N.Dak, 56-59; attorney-at-law, 67- Mem: Am. and N.Dak. State Bar Asns; N.Dak. States Attorney's Asn; Rotary Int; K. of C; Elks. Rel: Catholic. Legal Res: 738 Custer Dr, Mandan, N.Dak. 58554. Mailing Add: 100 W. Main, Mandan, N.Dak. 58554.

KELSEY, JAMES R. R
b. Portland, Maine, 6/24/99; married; c. one. Educ: Union Col. Polit. & Govt. Pos: N.H. State Rep, -67; Town Budget Cmt; Zoning Bd. of Adjust; Auditor Cemetery Trustee; former Town Selectman; Sch. Bd. Bus. & Prof. Pos: Retired Civil Engr. Mem: Fellow Am. Soc. of Civil Engrs. Rel: Protestant. Mailing Add: Rt. No. 1, Durham, N.H. 03824. (1967)

KELSEY, JOHN T. D
Mich. State Rep.
b. Hamtramck, Mich, 12/22/21; m. 11/24/45 to Anne Ambrowski; c. John Charles, Christine and Mark Anthony. Educ: Detroit Col. of Law, 1½ years. Polit. & Govt. Pos: Twp. trustee, Mich, 51-53; justice of the peace, Warren Twp, 53-58; munic. judge, Warren, 58-61; del, Constitutional Conv, 61-62; Mich. State Rep, 64- Bus. & Prof. Pos: Real estate salesman. Mil. Serv: Army, 42-45. Mem: United Dem. of Warren; K. of C; DAV; Polish Century Club; Exchange Club. Rel: Roman Catholic. Mailing Add: 8435 Westminster, Warren, Mich. 48089.

KELTON, WINIFRED WILLENA R
b. Swanton, Vt, 8/18/00; d. Henry Preston Sweet and Mary Rebecca Niles S; wid; c. Joan Winifred (Mrs. Lake), Merle Wilfred, Carl Edwin and Hollon Alfred. Educ: Bellows Falls High Sch, 15-17. Polit. & Govt. Pos: Vt. State Rep, 55-67. Mem: Bellows Falls Women's Club; Home Demonstration Group; Odd Fellows Auxiliary. Rel: Methodist; mem, WSCS; Supt, Sunday Sch. Mailing Add: Box 75, Grafton, Vt. 05146.

KELTY, JOHN EDWARD D
Vt. State Rep.
b. Boston, Mass, 8/12/98; m. to Irene Bourassa; c. One daughter. Educ: Pub. Schs, Westwood, Mass. Polit. & Govt. Pos: Alderman, Winooski, Vt, 33-34 & 38-40, mayor, 34-38; Vt. State Rep, 59-65; chmn, Bd. Listers; Vt. L.B. No. 4; Govt. appeal agent; chmn, City Planning Cmn. and Assessor; Vt. State Sen, 65-66; del, Dem. Nat. Conv, 68; Vt. State Rep, 69- Bus. & Prof. Pos: With Am. Woolen Co, 30 years; restaurant operator, 11 years; retired. Mil. Serv: Co. G, Vt. Nat. Guard and Co. K, 103rd Inf, 26th Div, World War I, stationed in France, 17-19. Mem: Elks; K. of C; VFW. Rel: Catholic. Mailing Add: 239 Weaver St, Winooksi, Vt, 05404.

KEMP, FRANK ALEXANDER, JR. R
Colo. State Sen.
b. Denver, Colo, 5/10/21; s. Frank A. Kemp and Estelle Kyle K; m. 6/16/51 to Pauline Wilson; c. Frank A, III and John Hovey. Educ: Yale Univ, B.A, 42; Delta Kappa Epsilon; Skull and Bones. Polit. & Govt. Pos: Colo. State Rep, Denver Co, 52-54 & 62-66. Bus. & Prof. Pos: Dir, Great West. Sugar Co, 66. Mil. Serv: Entered as Officer Candidate, Marine Corps, 41, released as Capt, 47, after serv. in First Marine Raider Bn. & 1st Bn, Fourth Marines, Pac, 42-45; Silver Star; 2 Bronze Stars; Soldier's Medal; 2 Purple Hearts. Mem: Am. Soc. of Farm & Ranch Mgrs. and Rural Appraisers (dir); Denver Area Coun, Boy Scouts; dir, Denver Boys Club; Metrop. Coun. Commun. Serv; Vis. Nurse Asn. Rel: Episcopal. Mailing Add: 149 High St, Denver, Colo. 80218.

KEMP, ROBERT WATSON D
S.C. State Rep.
b. Sylvania, Ga, 3/3/22; s. R. W. Kemp and Norma Harley K; m. 4/15/48 to Virginia Beard. Educ: Univ. of S.C, LL.B, 49. Polit. & Govt. Pos: Mem, Va. Bd. Bamberg; S.C. State Rep, 63- Bus. & Prof. Pos: Spec. agent, Fed. Bur. Invest, 49-56; lawyer, Kearse, Kemp and Rhoad. Mil. Serv: Marine Corps, 42-46. Mailing Add: Bamberg, S.C. 29003. (1967)

KEMPTER, PAUL E. D
b. Bellevue, Iowa, 3/18/10; m. 8/11/34 to Edna Schuster; c. Mary Patricia and Mary Jeanne. Educ: Notre Dame Univ, BA, LLB. Polit. Pos: Iowa State Rep, 66; Dep. Collector Internal Revenue, Des Moines, Cedar Rapids. Bus. & Prof. Pos: Lawyer. Mil. Serv: Korea and WWII. Mem: Iowa and Wyo. Bar; K. of C, Past Comdr, Am. Legion. Rel: Catholic. Mailing Add: Route 2, Bellevue, Iowa 52031. (1967)

KENCHELIAN, KARNEY K. R
Mem, Calif. Rep. State Cent. Cmt.
b. Fresno, Calif, 6/22/17; s. Leon Kenchelian and Helen Choagian K; m. 3/2/46 to Geraldine E. Earp; c. Helene E, Christine A, Mary L. and Mark L. Educ: Stanford Univ, B.A, 40; El Chadro Club. Polit. & Govt. Pos: Mem, Calif. Rep. State Cent. Cmt, 65-; mem. bd. educ, Napa Unified Sch. Dist, 67- Bus. & Prof. Pos: Div. mgr, North. Div, Pac. Tel, 62- Mil. Serv: Entered as Pvt, Army, 42, released as 1st Lt, 46. Mem: Native Sons Golden West; Elks; Rotary; Silverado Country Club. Rel: Catholic. Legal Res: 1196 Ross Circle, Napa, Calif. 94558. Mailing Add: 2438 Jefferson St, Napa, Calif. 94558.

KENDALL, DON ROBERT R
Chmn, Rep. State Cmt, Md.
b. Seymour, Ind, 4/21/26; s. Will Marion Kendall and Kathryne Holman K; m. 7/4/51 to Barbara Marion Berry; c. Kathryn Ann, William Wayne, Don Robert, Jr. and Geoffrey Grisby. Educ: Harvard Col, A.B, 49; Am. Univ, 53-55. Polit. & Govt. Pos: Admin. asst. to U.S. Rep. William G. Bray, Ind, 51-66; pres, Montgomery Co. Young Rep. Club, Md, 60; asst. chief sgt-at-arms for Radio and TV, Rep. Nat. Conv, 60; pres, Md. Fedn. Young Rep, 61-63; temporary chmn, Md. Rep. Conv, 62 & 66; chmn, Montgomery Co. Rep. Cent. Cmt. 62-66; U.S. del, Conf. Young Polit. Leaders of NATO Nations, Bonn, 63; v.chmn, Md. State Rep. Cent. Cmt, 66-69; exec. dir, Rep. Nat. Cmt, 66-69; dep. chief of staff, Platform Cmt, Rep. Nat. Conv, 68; Chmn, Rep. State Cmt, Md, 69- Mil. Serv: Entered Army Air Force, 44, released as Pfc, 46, after serv. in Air Transport Command. Mem: Am. Polit. Sci. Asn; Capitol Hill Club; Am. Legion. Cong. Staff Fel, 66. Rel: United Church of Christ. Mailing Add: 7506 Maple Ave, Chevy Chase, Md. 20015.

KENDALL, JAMES ALLEN R
Chmn, Midland Co. Rep. Cmt, Mich.
b. Midland, Mich, 4/19/27; s. Harold St. Clair Kendall and Freda Spetz K; m. 4/6/57 to Mary Ranney; c. Anne, Charles and Peter. Educ: Albion Col, A.B, 50; Univ. Mich, LL.B, 52; Phi Delta Phi; Phi Mu Alpha; Delta Tau Delta; Barristers. Polit. & Govt. Pos: Pres, Midland Co. Young Rep, Mich, 54; finance chmn, Midland Co. Rep. Cmt, 56-59, chmn, 65- Bus. & Prof. Pos: Pres, Midland Music Found, 63-64; counsel, Saginaw Valley Col, currently; partner, Currie & Kendall, Attorneys, 65- Mil. Serv: Entered as Seaman, Navy, 45, released as PO 3/C, 46. Mem: Pres, Midland Co. Bar Asn, 61; State Bar of Mich; Am. Bar Asn; Rotary Int; Midland Country Club; former bd. mem, Midland Art Asn; Midland Symphony Orchestra Asn. Rel: Presbyterian; Trustee, Memorial Presbyterian Church, Midland, 62- Mailing Add: 3716 Valley Dr, Midland, Mich. 48640. (1967)

KENDALL, ORIN PARKER D
Mont. State Rep.
b. Williams, Iowa, 4/30/04; s. Oliver Perry Kendall and Nellie Parker K; m. 12/28/27 to Ivy Agnes Reeder; c. Willene (Mrs. William Smith), JoAnne (Mrs. Johnson), Patricia (Mrs. Melvine Eldridge), Glenda (Mrs. James Farlan) and Orin G. Educ: East. Wash. Col. Educ, 2 years; Univ. of Mont, 1 year. Polit. & Govt. Pos: Treas, Sanders Co, Mont, 43-47 and sch. supt, 47-49; Mayor, Thompson Falls, 61-; Mont. State Rep, Mineral-Sanders Co, 69- Mem: Mason; Order of Eastern Star; Grange (present Mont. State master, Patrons of Husbandry). Rel: Protestant. Legal Res: 205 Gallatin, Thompson, Falls, Mont. 59873. Mailing Add: P.O. Box 563, Thompson Falls, Mont. 59873.

KENDALL, WILLIAM T. R
b. Newark, N.J, 5/8/21; s. Harry W. Kendall and Jane Bell K; m. 3/3/45 to Doris M. Czernicki; c. Paul W. and Jonathan P. Educ: Rutgers Univ, A.B, 49; Columbia, M.A, 51; Harvard Univ; Cong. Staff fel, 65-66; Phi Beta Kappa; Sigma Xi; Phi Lambda Upsilon. Polit. & Govt. Pos: Pres, Morris Co. Young Rep, N.J, 53-54; campaign mgr, U.S. Rep. Frelinghuysen, 54, 56 & 58; co. Rep. committeeman and precinct leader, Florham Park, 56-59; chmn. southeast dist, Morris Co. Rep. Cmt, 58-59; spec. asst. to chmn, Rep. Cong. Campaign Cmt, 62-64; admin. asst. to U.S. Rep. Peter H.B. Frelinghuysen, N.J; mem. staff, platform cmt, Rep. Nat. Conv, 68. Bus. & Prof. Pos: Research chemist, Allied Chem. Corp, 50-59. Mil. Serv: Entered as Pvt, Army, 43, released as S/Sgt, 46, after serv. in Fourth Army of U.S; Am. Theater Ribbon; Victory and Good Conduct Medals. Mem: Am. Chemical Soc; Am. Legion; Capitol Hill Club; Harvard Faculty Club; Florham Park Rep. Club; Ripon Soc. U.S. patent for purification of acetone, 52. Rel: Episcopal. Legal Res: 96 Hillcrest Ave, Morristown, N.J. 07960. Mailing Add: 7606 Geranium St, Bethesda, Md. 20034.

KENDIG, A. EDWARD D
Wyo. State Sen.
b. Burns, Wyo, 6/28/25; single. Educ: Univ. Colo, B.S; Harvard Law Sch, LL.B; Beta Gamma Sigma; Beta Theta Pi. Polit. & Govt. Pos: Sch. trustee, Sch. Dist. Nine, Wheatland, Wyo, 59-67; Wyo. State Sen, 63- Bus. & Prof. Pos: Banker-lawyer. Mil. Serv: Entered as Pvt, Army, 43, released as Sgt. 1/C, 46, after serv. in 506th M.P. Bn, ETO, 44-45. Mem: Wyo. Bankers Asn.(past pres); Lions; Am. Legion; VFW. Rel: Presbyterian. Mailing Add: 301 Tenth St, Wheatland, Wyo. 82201.

KENDRICK, CHARLES RICHARD R
b. Denver, Colo, 4/22/14; s. Leslie Ray Kendrick and Eda Burkhalter K; m. 1/4/41 to Cecily Jansen; c. Charles R, Jr, Clinton J. and Katherine E. Educ: Princeton Univ, A.B, 35; Campus Club. Polit. & Govt. Pos: Mgr. of Gen. Serv, City & Co. of Denver, Colo, 63-67; admin. asst. U.S. Sen. Peter H. Dominick, Colo, 67- Bus. & Prof. Pos: V.pres, Kendrick-Bellamy Co, 35-63; pres, Gladstone Investment Co, 46- Mil. Serv: Entered as Pvt, Army, 43, released as 1st Lt, 46, after serv. in 313th Troop Carrier Group, Ninth Air Force, ETO, 44-45. Rel: Presbyterian. Legal Res: 111 Gilpin St, Denver, Colo. 80218. Mailing Add: 810 Albany Ave, Alexandria, Va. 22302.

KENDRICK, EDWARD STOREY D
b. Fulton Co, Ga, 5/31/24; s. Edward S. Kendrick and Lillian Johnson K; m. 10/11/46 to Martha Anna Wiman; c. Daniel Frederick; David Edward; Gary Lee; Randy Thomas; Anna Ruth. Educ: Baylor Col, A.B, 48; Emory Univ, 56. Polit. & Govt. Pos: Ga. State Sen, 63-66. Bus. & Prof. Pos: Teacher, Fulton Co, 50-51; dir. of spec. servs, Cobb Co. and Marietta pub. schs. Mil. Serv: WWII. Mem: Pres, Marietta Civitan Club, 62; pres. GEA Audio Visual Affil, 52. Rel: Presbyterian. Mailing Add: Bells Ferry Rd, Marietta, Ga. 30060. (1967)

KENDRICK, FRANK JENNESS DFL
Dist. Rep, Seventh Dist. Dem-Farmer-Labor Exec. Cmt, Minn.
b. Ft. Wayne, Ind, 10/18/28; s. Frank Jenness Kendrick and Dorothy Gray Whatmough K; m. 3/17/56 to Betty June Grant; c. Ellen Barclay, Elizabeth Jenness, Grant Jenness and Emily Gray. Educ: Grinnell Col, B.A, 50; Univ. Chicago, M.A, 56, Ph.D, 62; Int. Rels. Club; Students for Dem. Action. Polit. & Govt. Pos: Cmnr. dist. chmn, Clay Co. Dem-Farmer-Labor Party, Minn, 65-67; Dem-Farmer-Labor cand, Minn. State Senate, 66; chmn, Clay Co. Dem-Farmer-Labor Party, 67-69; mem, Minn. Dem-Farmer-Labor Cent. Cmt, 67-69; dist. rep, Seventh Dist. Dem-Farmer-Labor Exec. Cmt, 68- Bus. & Prof. Pos: Asst. prof. govt, Wofford Col, 58-60; vis. instr. hist. and polit. sci, Evansville Col, 61-62; asst. prof. polit. sci, Drury Col, 62-63; assoc. prof. polit. sci, Moorhead State Col, 63-69. Mil. Serv: Entered as Pvt, Army, 51, released as Pfc, 53, after serv. in Army Hosp, Far East Command, 52-53; Korean Serv. Medal; UN Serv. Medal. Publ: 'A Non-Partisan Election in Minnesota,' J. Minn. Acad. Sci, 67; 'The United States and the International Protection of Human Rights,' N.Dak. Quart, spring 68; 'Student Power,' Minn. Teacher, winter 69. Mem: Am. Polit. Sci. Asn; Minn. Acad. Sci; Am. Asn. Univ. Prof; Midwest Conf. Polit. Scientists; Mo. Polit. Sci; Am. Civil Liberties Union. Rel: Protestant. Mailing Add: 1212 11th St. S, Moorhead, Minn. 56560.

KENDZIORSKI, CASIMIR D
Wis. State Sen.
b. Poland, 12/3/98. Educ: High Sch. in Poland, Evening Courses in Milwaukee. Polit. & Govt. Pos: Wis. State Assemblyman, 46-49; Wis. State Sen, 49-; v.pres. local union. Bus. & Prof. Pos: Real estate broker, 28-30; machinist and qual. control inspector, 30- Mem: Active in Civic and Labor Activities. Mailing Add: 2025 S. 14th St, Milwaukee, Wis. 53204. (1967)

KENKEL, GERHARD H. R
Committeeman, Ark. State Rep. Party
b. Chicago, Ill, 11/3/93; s. Fredick P. Kenkel and Elenor Von Kamptz K; m. 8/8/17 to Rose H. Scholl; c. Elizabet K, Robert, Mary Bell and Kitty Lou. Educ: Univ. Mo, Agr. Dept, Columbia, Mo. Polit. & Govt. Pos: Committeeman, Ark. State Rep. Party, currently; chmn, Monroe Co. Rep. Party, 36-66, committeeman, 66-; chmn, Monroe Co. Agr. Soil Conserv. Cmt, 40-46. Bus. & Prof. Pos: Dir, Ark. Cotton Growers Asn, 24-30 and Mid-South Cotton Growers, 30-32. Mem: Farm Bur.(secy, Monroe Co. Farm Bur, 45-48, dir, 52-67); nat. trustee, Cath. Knight of Am. Fraternal Asn, 55-63; pres, Ark. Fraternal Cong, 64; Exalted Ruler, Elks Lodge 1252, 51-52. Rel: Catholic. Mailing Add: R.R. 1, Box 125, Brinkley, Ark. 72021.

KENNAN, GEORGE FROST
b. Milwaukee, Wis, 2/16/04; m. 9/11/31 to Annelise Soerenson; c. Grace, Joan E, Christopher and Wendy. Educ: Princeton Univ, A.B, 25. Hon. LL.D, Yale Univ, and Dartmouth Col, 50, Colgate Univ, 51, Univ. Notre Dame, 53, Kenyon Col, 54, New Sch. Soc. Res, 55, Univ. Mich. and Northwest. Univ, 57, Brandeis Univ, 58 and Univ. Wis. and Harvard Univ, 63; D.C.L, Oxford Univ. and fel, All Souls Col, 69. Polit. & Govt. Pos: U.S. For. Serv; V.consul, Hamburg, 27 and Tallinn, 28, third secy, Riga, Kovno and Tallinn, 29; lang officer, Berlin, 29; third secy, Riga, 31; accompanied Ambassador Bullitt to Moscow, 33; third secy, Moscow, 34; second secy. and consul, Vienna, 35; second secy, Moscow, 35 and Praha, 38; consul, Prague, 39; second secy, Berlin, 39 and first secy, 40; counsr. of legation, Lisbon, 42; dep. dir. for foreign affairs, Nat. War Col, Wash, D.C, 46; mem. policy planning staff, Dept. of State, 47, dept. counsr. and chief long-range adv. to Secy. of State, 49; Ambassador to U.S.S.R, 52 and Yugoslavia, 61-63. Bus. & Prof. Pos: Stafford Little lectr, Princeton Univ, 54; George Eastman vis. prof, Oxford Univ, 57-58; permanent prof, sch. of hist. studies, Inst. for Adv. Studies, 56- Publ: Russia Leaves the War, Atheneum, 56 (Bancroft Prize, 56, Nat. Book Award, Francis Parkman Prize and Pulitzer Prize, 57); Memoirs 1925-1950, 67 (Pulitzer Prize in Biog. and Nat. Book Award, 68) and Democracy and The Student Left, 68, Atlantic, Little Brown; From Prague After Munich: Diplomatic Papers 1938-1940, Princeton Univ, 68. Mem: Nat. Inst. Arts and Letters (pres, 65-68); Am. Acad. Arts and Letters (pres, 68-). Mailing Add: Institute for Advanced Study, Princeton, N.J. 08540.

KENNEALLY, GEORGE VINCENT, JR. D
Mass. State Sen.
b. Boston, Mass, 12/29/29; s. George Vincent Kenneally and Claire A. Hart K; m. 4/19/54 to Carole A. O'Leary; c. Denise T, Patrice C, George V, III, Kevin G. and Michael F. Educ: Northeast. Univ, A.A; Suffolk Law Sch, LL.B. Polit. & Govt. Pos: Mass. State Rep, 56-62; Mass. State Sen, 62-; del, Dem. Nat. Conv, 64 & 68; del, Mass. State Dem. Conv, 66. Bus. & Prof. Pos: Attorney, 57- Mil. Serv: Entered as Airman Apprentice, Navy, 48, released as Airman, 51. Mem: Amvets; Am. Legion; K. of C. Rel: Roman Catholic. Mailing Add: 4 Blackwell St, Boston, Mass. 02122.

KENNEDY, CAROLYN BURTON R
b. St. Louis, Mo, 5/1/23; d. Clinton Burton Abrams and Hilda Fruth A; m. 8/14/43 to James Patrick Kennedy; c. Michael, Peter, Barbara, John and Susan. Educ: Nat. Park Sem; Conn. Col. for Women. Polit. & Govt. Pos: Secy, Mo. Rep. State Cmt, 62-64; alternate del, Rep. Nat. Conv, 64; committeeman, St. Louis Co. Rep. Cmt, 64-69. Publ: Mo. Rep. Handbook, 65. Mem: Mo. Hist. Soc. Rel: Episcopal. Mailing Add: 911 Lay Rd, St. Louis, Mo. 63124. (1967)

KENNEDY, CARROLL HENRY D
Miss. State Rep.
b. Puckett, Miss, 6/2/02; married. Polit. & Govt. Pos: Miss. State Rep, 56-60 & 68-; Brandon bd. alderman, 8 years. Bus. & Prof. Pos: Farmer; motor truck and hardware dealer. Mem: Mason; Farm Bur. Rel: Baptist. Mailing Add: P.O. Box 82, Brandon, Miss. 39042. (1967)

KENNEDY, DAVID BOYD R
Wyo. State Rep.
b. Ann Arbor, Mich, 9/2/33; s. James Alexander Kennedy and Elizabeth Earhart K; m. 10/31/64 to Sally Martin Pyne. Educ: McGill Univ, 51-52; Univ.

Mich, 52-54; Ind. Univ, A.B, 58; Yale Univ, 61-62; Univ. Mich, LL.B, 63. Polit. & Govt. Pos: Wyo. State Rep, 67- Bus. & Prof. Pos: Partner, Burgess, Kennedy & Davis, Sheridan, Wyo, 63- Mil. Serv: Entered as Pvt, E-1, Army, 54, released as SP-5, E-5, 57. Mem: Wyo. State, Mich. State and Am. Bar Asns; Farm Bur; Wyo. Stock Growers Asn; C. of C.(v.pres, Sheridan Co. Chap); Elks; Rotary. Mailing Add: P.O. Box 276, Dayton, Wyo. 82836.

KENNEDY, DAVID J. R
Maine State Rep.
b. Milbridge, Maine, 2/11/07; s. David J. Kennedy and Lillian Grant K; m. 3/5/39 to Dorothy Wallace; c. Jane, George, Bruce and Ralph. Polit. & Govt. Pos: Maine State Rep, 59-, speaker, Maine House Rep, 63-; del, Rep. Nat. Conv, 68. Bus. & Prof. Pos: Pharmacist. Mil. Serv: Navy, 44-46. Mem: Maine Pharm. Asn; Mason; Shrine. Mailing Add: 59 Bridge St, Milbridge, Maine 04658. (1967)

KENNEDY, DAVID MATTHEW R
Secy. of Treas.
b. Randolph, Utah, 7/21/05; s. George Kennedy and Katherine Johnson K. (deceased); m. Lenora Bingham; c. Marilyn (Mrs. Verl L. Taylor), Barbara (Mrs. Carol Law), Carol Joyce (Mrs. Jack Whittle) and Patricia Lenore (Mrs. Lewis Campbell). Educ: Weber Col, B.A, 28; George Wash. Univ, M.A, 35, LL.B, 37; Rutgers Univ. Stonier Grad. Sch. of Banking, grad, 39. Hon. LL.D, Brigham Young, Roosevelt and Geroge Wash. Univs; L.H.D, Lake Forest Col. Polit. & Govt. Pos: Tech. asst, div. of bank opers, asst. chief of govt. security sect, div. of research and statist. and asst. to chmn. of bd, Bd. of Gov, Fed. Reserve Syst, 30-46; spec. asst. to Secy. of Treas. George M. Humphrey, 53-54; Secy. of Treas, 69- Bus. & Prof. Pos: Bond Dept, Continental Ill. Nat. Bank and Trust Co, Chicago, 46-51, v.pres, 51 & 54-56, dir. and pres, 56-59, chmn. bd. of dirs. and chief exec. officer, 59-69; publisher, Chicago Mag. Mem: Chmn, Mayor's Cmt. for Econ. and Cultural Develop, Chicago; chmn, New Chicago Found; dir, Chicago Found. for Cultural Develop; exec. cmt. chmn, Citizens Bond Cmt. for Greater Chicago; trustee, Presby-St. Lukes Hosp, over ten years; Fed. Adv. Cmt. on Financial Assets; Nat. Pub. Adv. Cmt. on Regional Econ. Develop; Fed. Adv. Coun. of Fed. Reserve Syst; chmn, Cmn. on Budgetary Concepts, 67; trustee, Univ. Chicago and George Wash. Univ; chmn. exec. cmt, develop. coun, Brigham Young Univ; mem, bd. of assocs, DePaul Univ; mem, citizens cmt, Univ. Ill; Old Elm Club, Chicago. Rel: Latter-day Saint; First Councilor, Chicago Stake Presidency and Bishop, Wash, D.C. Legal Res: Northfield, Ill. Mailing Add: Dept. of the Treasury, Washington, D.C. 20220.

KENNEDY, DON WILLIAM D
Mo. State Rep.
b. Schell City, Mo, 10/16/25; m. to Audrey Lois Tohtz; c. Julianne, Jennifer, Roger Quin and Priscilla. Educ: Southwest Baptist Col; Univ. Mo, A.A, LL.B. Polit. & Govt. Pos: Prosecuting attorney, Vernon Co, Mo, 49-53; asst. attorney gen, Mo, 53-54; mayor, Nevada, Mo, 58; mem, Mo. State Banking Bd, 61-64; Mo. State Rep, 64- Bus. & Prof. Pos: Lawyer. Mem: Mason. Rel: Southern Baptist. Mailing Add: 612 W. Cherry, Nevada, Mo. 64772. (1967)

KENNEDY, DONALD PATRICK R
Committeeman, Erie Co. Rep. Party, Pa.
b. Erie, Pa, 11/29/11; s. John C. Kennedy and Helen Kitzer K; m. 1/20/33 to Treva J. Kenyon; c. Patrick K, Robert T, Susan M, John D, James E. and Dennis M. Educ: Correspondence courses in eng. Polit. & Govt. Pos: Committeeman, Erie Co. Rep. Party, Pa, 56-; del, Rep. Nat. Conv, 24th Dist, Pa, 64. Bus. & Prof. Pos: Consult. Engr, pvt. practice, 50- Mem: Nat. Soc. Prfnl. Engrs.(past pres, Erie Chap); Univ. Club; Maennerchor Club. Licensed engr. in N.Y, Pa. and Ohio. Rel: Christian. Mailing Add: 441 W. 31st St, Erie, Pa. 16508.

KENNEDY, EARL R
Second V.Chmn, Mich. Rep. State Cent. Cmt.
b. Jersey City, N.J, 3/16/17; m. to Jessie M. Educ: Morehouse Col, B.S; Wayne State Univ; Univ. Mich. Exten. Sch. Polit. & Govt. Pos: Mem, Citizens for Bob Griffin, Con-Con Petition Cmt, Don Leonard for Gov. Cmt, Cogo Citizens Cmt, Lafayette Park Rep, Romney Vols. and Bagwell Boosters; Commun. Col. Cand; cand, U.S. House of Rep, Mich, 58; nominee, Mich. State Legis; chmn, Citizens for Eisenhower, First Cong. Dist; mem, Mich. Rep. State Cent. Cmt, second v.chmn, currently. Bus. & Prof. Pos: Real estate broker, Torch Realty Co; dir, Kennedy Travel Agency and Bahamas Develop. Co. Mil. Air Force, World War II. Mem: Higher Educ. Opportunities Cmt; Am. Legion; DAV; Amvets; Mason (32°); Shrine; Am. Fedn. of State, Co. and Munic. Employees; Trade Union Leadership Coun; NAACP; Nat. Sanitarians Asn; Gr. Detroit Bd. of Commerce; adv. bd, Clairmont-West Grand Blvd; Civic Improv. Asn; Booker T. Wash. Bus. Asn; YMCA; Kiwanis; Alpha Phi Alpha; Mich. Partners of Alliance; Mich. Selective Bd, Wayne Co. Rel: Episcopal. Mailing Add: 9334 Woodward Ave, Detroit, Mich. 48202.

KENNEDY, EDWARD MOORE D
Asst. Majority Leader, U.S. Senate
b. Boston, Mass, 2/22/32; s. Joseph Patrick Kennedy and Rose Fitzgerald K; m. 11/29/58 to Virginia Joan Bennett; c. Kara Ann, Edward Moore and Patrick Joseph. Educ: Harvard, B.A, 54; Univ. Va, LL.B, 59. Polit. & Govt. Pos: Asst. dist. attorney, Suffolk Co, Mass, 61-62; U.S. Sen, Mass, 62-, Asst. Majority Leader, U.S. Senate, 69-; del, Dem. Nat. Conv, 68. Bus. & Prof. Pos: Lawyer. Mem: Pres, Joseph P. Kennedy, Jr. Found, 61-; adv. bd, Emmanuel Col; bd. trustees, Boston Univ, Lahey Clin, Boston, Boston Symphony, John F. Kennedy Center for Performing Arts, Wash, D.C, Children's Hosp. Med. Center, Boston, Mus. of Sci, Boston, and John F. Kennedy Libr; bd. visitors, Fletcher Sch. Mil. Serv: Enlisted as Pvt-1, Army, 51, released as Pfc, 53, after serv. in France, 52-53; Decorated Order of Merit, Italy. Publ: Decisions For a Decade, Doubleday, 68. Selected as One of Ten Outstanding Young Men of 67 by U.S. Jr. C. of C; Humanitarian Award from United Hebrew Immigrant Aid Soc. Serv; Citations for Meritorious Serv. from U.S. Cmt. for Refugees and Am. Immigration and Citizenship Coun. Rel: Catholic. Legal Res: 3 Charles River Square, Boston, Mass. 02114. Mailing Add: Senate Office Building, Washington, D.C. 20510.

KENNEDY, EUGENE FREDERICK R
Councilman, City and Co. of Honolulu, Hawaii
b. Honolulu, Hawaii, 7/22/13; s. E. Eugene Kennedy and Lucille Spencer K; m. to Eva A. Lum; c. Frederick Francis, Evagene Frances, Patricia Lucille, Eugene Allen, Kathleen Virginia and Margaret Ann. Educ: St. Louis Col, Honolulu, Grad, 31. Polit. & Govt. Pos: Councilman and supvr, City and Co. of Honolulu, Hawaii, 57-58, chmn, Bd. of Parks and Recreation, 59-60. Bus. & Prof. Pos: Pres, Royal State Nat. Ins. Co, Eugene F. Kennedy Real Estate, Inc, Eugene F. Kennedy Invest, Inc. and mgr, Eugene F. Kennedy Co, currently. Mem: C. of C; Lions. Rel: Catholic. Mailing Add: 4436 Sierra Dr, Honolulu, Hawaii 96816. (1967)

KENNEDY, FRANCIS X. D
b. North Adams, Mass, 12/6/15; m. to Mary L. Lombardi. Educ: Pub. sch, Warwick, R.I. Polit. & Govt. Pos: R.I. State Rep, 59-68; West Warwick Dem. Town Cmt. Bus. & Prof. Pos: Salesman. Mil. Serv: Navy, World War II. Mem: C. of C; Am. Legion; 40 et 8; Crompton Vet. Orgn; Phenix Sportsmen's Club; Elks; West Warwick Country Club; Hibernians; Holy Name St. Mary's Church; del, United Irish Coun. Rel: Catholic. Mailing Add: 38 Lexington Ave, West Warwick, R.I. 02893. (1967)

KENNEDY, FRANK WILLIAM R
Mem, Tenn. State Rep. Exec. Cmt.
b. Enid, Okla, 6/15/32; s. William Herbert Kennedy and Hazel Muriel Banfield K; m. 4/20/54 to Marjorie Kate Buck; c. Anita Jean and Linda Marie. Educ: Univ. Ariz, B.S. in Bus, 55; Am. Inst. For. Trade, B.F.T, 56; Phi Delta Theta. Polit. & Govt. Pos: Rep. Precinct worker, Bedford Co, Tenn, 64; chmn, Bedford Co. Rep. Orgn, 66-69; pres, Bedford Co. Young Rep, 67; mem, Sixth Dist. Rep. Cong. Cmt, 68-; mem, Tenn. State Rep. Exec. Cmt, 68- Bus. & Prof. Pos: V.pres, South. Rendering Co, Shelbyville, 60- Mem: Boy Scouts (v.pres. Bedford Dist. and mem. exec. cmt, Mid. Tenn. Dist). Rel: Presbyterian. Mailing Add: Rt. 5, Riverbend Rd, Shelbyville, Tenn. 37160.

KENNEDY, FRED J. R
b. Foster, R.I, 2/3/96; m. to Ruth Steere. Educ: Pub. sch, Foster, R.I. Polit. & Govt. Pos: R.I. State Rep, 63-68. Bus. & Prof. Pos: Retired, Quonset Point, N.A.S, 20 years. Mil. Serv: Army, Sgt, 17-19, serv. in 82nd Div, 319th F.A. in AEF, Grad. Saumur Artil. Officer Training Sch, Saumur, France, 19. Mem: RSM; Moosup Valley Grange (past master); Kent Co. Pomona Grange; R.I. State Grange; Am. Legion; Eastern Star; RAM; AF&AM (past master, Ionic Lodge). Mailing Add: Moosup Valley Rd, Foster, R.I. 02825. (1967)

KENNEDY, GENE V. D
Iowa State Rep.
b. Le Mars, Iowa, 10/28/27; s. Eugene M. Kennedy and Lillian Banks K; m. 5/21/52 to Dorothy E. Sell; c. Candace, Michael, Mary, Teresa, Patrick, Dianna, Maurreen and Edward. Educ: Loras Col, B.A, 48. Polit. & Govt. Pos: Iowa State Rep, 69- Bus. & Prof. Pos: Patrolman, Iowa Hwy. Patrol, 50-54; ins. adjustor, Crocker Claims, Omaha, Nebr, 54-67; pres, Kennedy & Co, Dubuque, 67- Mem: Prfnl. Adjustors Syst. Am; K. of C; Foresters; Optimists; Dubuque Area C. of C; 1752 Club of Iowa; YMCA. Rel: Catholic. Mailing Add: Route 1, J.F.K. Rd, Dubuque, Iowa 52001.

KENNEDY, GOLDIE L. D
Mem, Calif. Dem. State Cent. Cmt.
b. Novinger, Mo, 2/18/05; d. William Burris Lilly and Edna May Harris L; m. 6/12/27 to Eugene V. Kennedy; c. Neil E. Educ: Kirksville State Teachers Col, 21-24; Univ. South. Calif, 24. Polit. & Govt. Pos: Secy, Calif. Dem. State Cent. Cmt, 50-54, v.chmn, 54-56, state chmn. women's div, 56-58, mem, currently; asst. secy, Dem. Nat. Conv, 52, mem. fund raising cmt. and credential cmt, 56, chmn, nat. del. hostess cmt, 60, originator of Golden Girls, 60; state women's chmn, Stevenson for Pres. Campaign, 56; nat. chmn. and originator 'hole in the sole,' pin campaign for Adlai Stevenson, 56; state women's chmn, Lt. Gov. Glenn N. Anderson Campaign, 58; creator of slogan and silver broom 'sweep the state in 58' for State Dem. Party Campaigns, 58; asst. coordinator, Calif. Disaster Off, 59-62; mem, Lyndon Johnson Del, 68; Ventura Co. campaign coordinator, Hubert Humphrey, 68; mem, Ventura Co. Dem. Cent. Cmt, currently. Bus. & Prof. Pos: Prin, Bardadale Elem. Sch, Fillmore, Calif, 43-53; exec. dir, Fiesta De La Marina, City of Ventura, Calif, 67 & 68. Rel: Protestant. Mailing Add: 575 Via Cielito, Ventura, Calif. 93003.

KENNEDY, H. FRANCIS R
Pa. State Rep.
b. Admans Twp, Pa, 7/7/18; s. Harold P. Kennedy and Melverna Truver K; m. to Martha Everett; c. four. Educ; Mars High Sch. Polit. & Govt. Pos: Mem, sch. bd, Butler, Pa, 42-56, pres, 6 years; Pa. State Rep, 62- Bus. & Prof. Pos: Dairy Farmer; Purebred Cattle Bus. Mem: Exec. Cmt, Butler Co. Agr. Exten. Asn; Royal, Pomona, State Grange; Dir, Butler Farm Show, 11 years; Butler 4-H; Dir, Secy, D.H.I.A; Dir, V.Pres, 9 years, Country Belle Farmers Coop; Treas, Pa. Purebred Dairy Cattle Asn; Nat. B.S. Cattle Asn; Pa. State Asn; Brown Swiss Cattle Asn, hon. dir; Vol. Fire Co; Butler Co. and Pa. Farmers Asn; Mason; Consistory; AAONMS. Rel: Presbyterian. Mailing Add: Royal Oak Rd, R.D. 6, Butler, Pa. 16001.

KENNEDY, J. C. D
Chmn, Okla. Dem. Party
Mailing Add: Security Bank Bldg, Lawton, Okla. 73501.

KENNEDY, JAMES NORMAN D
b. Brighton, Vt, 1/18/22; single. Educ: McGill Univ, B.A, 42, D.D.S, 50; Princeton Univ; N.Y. Univ. Polit. & Govt. Pos: Vt. State Rep, 59 & 61; secy, Civil & Mil. Affairs, 63; Exec. Clerk Liaison Gov, 64; mem, Brighton Sch. Bd; Vt. State Sen, 65-66; past chmn, Essex Co. Dem. Party; chmn, Vt. Soc. Welfare Bd, 66-67; postmaster, Island Pond, 67- Bus. & Prof. Pos: Dentist. Mil. Serv: Army, World War II, 3 years as Inf. Officer; Korean War, 2 years as Dent. Officer. Mem: Am. Dent. Asn; Vt. Dent. Soc; K. of C; Civil War Centennial; Brighton Bd. of Trade. Rel: Catholic. Mailing Add: Birch St, Island Pond, Vt. 05846.

KENNEDY, JEWEL R
Mo. State Rep.
b. Liberal, Mo, 2/7/10; d. Harry O. Baker and Velma Russell B; m. 9/20/31 to Dean Sabin Kennedy; c. Sharon (Mrs. Ronald K. Ward, Jr) and Larry Dean. Educ: Manual High Sch, Kansas City, Mo, grad, 27. Polit. & Govt. Pos: Rep.

committeewoman, Brooking Township, Mo, 64-66; Rep. v.chmn, Fourth Cong. Dist, 64-66; Mo. State Rep, 66-; del. and mem. platform cmt, Rep. Nat. Conv, 68. Mem: St. Matthews Women's Auxiliary (pres, 62); PTA (former officer); Am. Red Cross; C. of C. Rel: Episcopal. Mailing Add: 6111 Harris, Raytown, Mo. 64133.

KENNEDY, JOHN LLOYD D
b. Holly Springs, Miss, 3/24/31; s. John Lee Kennedy and Elizabeth Rittelmeyer K; m. 8/19/53 to Alma McAlexander; c. Helen Elizabeth, Sylvia Ann, John Marshall and Patricia Mosal. Educ: Miss. State Univ, 49-50; U.S. Naval Acad, 50-53; Univ. Miss, 53, Sch. of Commerce, B.A, 56, Sch. of Law, LL.B, 59; U.S. Army Eng. Sch, Ft. Belvoir, Va, with honors, 54; San Francisco State Col, 54-55; Marina Adult Speech Sch, with honors, 54-55; Phi Delta Phi; Phi Kappa Theta. Polit. & Govt. Pos: Miss. State Rep, Marshall Co, 60-64; del, Dem. Nat. Conv, 68. Mil. Serv: Entered as Pvt, Army, 54, released as Cpl, 55, after serv. in Sixth Army, 54-55. Mem: Miss. Educ. Asn; Marshall Co. Teacher Asn; Miss. Bar Asn; Marshall Co. Bar Asn.(pres); founder and dir, Citizens Conf. for Stronger Marriage Laws; Am. Legion; Farm Bur; Miss. Forestry Asn; Miss. State Alumni Asn; Univ. Miss. Alumni Asn; Colonel's Club of Miss. State; chmn, Marshall Co. Ment. Health Drive; Phi Delta Phi; Pub. Speakers Bur. Runnerup, Miss. Man of the Year, 57; nominee, Miss. Outstanding Serv. Award in the Field of Govt, 58. Rel: Catholic. Legal Res: 320 Chulahoma Ave, Holly Springs, Miss. 38635. Mailing Add: P.O. Box 668, Holly Springs, Miss. 38635.

KENNEDY, JOSEPH EVERETT D
Ga. State Sen.
b. Claxton, Ga, 10/8/30; s. Jesse Gordon Kennedy and Nannie Byrd DuPree K; m. 12/25/53 to Lalah Jane; c. Debra, Cliff and Adam. Educ: Claxton High Sch, Ga, grad, 47; Ga. Mil. Col, Bus, 49. Polit. & Govt. Pos: Ga. State Sen, 67- Bus. & Prof. Pos: Self-employed accountant, currently. Mil. Serv: Entered as Pvt, Army, 50, released as Capt, 53, after serv. in 8th U.S. Army, Korea, 52-53; Bronze Star Medal; United Nations Ribbon; Korean Serv. Medal with two Battle Stars. Mem: Rotary; Am. Legion; VFW; Scottish Rite; Mason (32°); Shrine (pres, Claxton Club). Outstanding Young Man of Year, Claxton Jaycees, 62. Rel: Baptist; Chmn. Bd. Deacons, First Baptist Church. Legal Res: 206 New Drive, Claxton, Ga. 30417. Mailing Add: Box 246, Claxton, Ga. 30417.

KENNEDY, KEITH K. D
b. Center Point, Iowa, 6/27/19; s. William Norman Kennedy and Mary Edith Taylor K; m.6/28/40 to Mina Wright; c. Vicki and Paula. Educ: Coe Col. Polit. Pos: Iowa State Rep, 1966; Town Coun; Sch. Bd. Bus. & Prof. Pos: Agency Supvr, Bankers Mutual Life Ins. Co. Mem: Masonic; Eastern Star; All Sports Booster Club; Secy, Cedar Valley Coon Hunters Asn. Rel: Christian Church. Mailing Add: Center Point, Iowa. 52213. (1967)

KENNEDY, LELAND J. D
Ill. State Rep.
b. Alton, Ill, 12/3/08; m. to Mary E. Cain; c. Patrick and Maureen. Educ: Alton pub. and parochial schs. Polit. & Govt. Pos: Mem, Alton City Coun, 41; Ill. State Rep, 65th, 66th, 67th, 68th, 73rd, 75th and 76th Gen. Assemblies; del, Dem. Nat. Conv, 68. Bus. & Prof. Pos: Operating eng. Mil. Serv: World War II. Mem: K. of C.(4°). Rel: Catholic. Mailing Add: 926 Washington Ave, Alton, Ill. 62002.

KENNEDY, MICHAEL KELLY D
Iowa State Rep.
b. New Hampton, Iowa, 10/30/39; s. William J. Kennedy and Eileen Kelly K; m. 8/14/65 to Linda Weiss. Educ: Univ. Notre Dame, B.A, 61; Univ. Iowa Law Sch, J.D, 68; Phi Delta Phi. Polit. & Govt. Pos: Iowa State Rep, 69- Bus. & Prof. Pos: Basketball coach and athletic dir, Newman High Sch, Mason City, 62-65; attorney, Kennedy & Kennedy, 68- Publ: 'Law Review Comment,' Iowa Law Rev, 66. Mem: Am. and Iowa Bar Asns; New Hampton C. of C, Country Club and Quarterback Club; K. of C. Rel: Roman Catholic. Mailing Add: 525 W. Spring, New Hampton, Iowa 50659.

KENNEDY, NELSON D. D
Polit. & Govt. Pos: Former Ind. State Rep. Bus. & Prof. Pos: Ins. agent. Mil. Serv: Army. Mem: Eagles; Young Dem. Rel: Methodist. 1967 Legal Res: Crawford, Ind. No mailing address available. (1967)

KENNEDY, RICHARD LEE D
Ore. State Rep.
b. Seattle, Wash, 3/17/32; s. George F. Kennedy and Frances Huse K; m. 7/24/55 to Barbara Joann Kennedy K; c. Steven Douglas, Shannon Karol and Matthew Sean. Educ: Univ. Ore, B.S, 57; Pi Sigma Alpha. Polit. & Govt. Pos: Reading Clerk, Ore. State House of Rep, 61; Ore. State Rep, Lane Co, 63-, exec. secy, Interim Cmt. on Urban Problems, Ore. State House of Rep, 61-63; del, Dem. Nat. Conv, 64 & 68. Bus. & Prof. Pos: Teacher Am. govt. and hist, Ore, 58-60; owner, Northwest Ballot Box, 63- Mil. Serv: Entered as A/S, Navy, 52, released as PO 3/C, 54; Good Conduct and Korean Serv. Medals. Publ: Metropolitan and Urban Problems in Oregon, State of Ore, 63. Mem: C. of C; Asn. Ore. Indust. Rel: Protestant. Legal Res: 761 E. 20th, Eugene, Ore. 97405. Mailing Add: 119 E. Broadway, Suite 210, Eugene, Ore. 97501.

KENNEDY, WALTER LAWRENCE R
Vt. State Rep.
b. Chelsea, Vt, 5/10/20; m. to Phyllis I. Playful; c. 2 sons, 1 daughter. Educ: High Sch, Chelsea. Polit. & Govt. Pos: Chmn, Town Selectmen; overseer of the poor; Vt. State Rep, 61-, v.chmn. bank and corp. cmt, Vt. State House of Rep, 63, chmn, hwy. traffic cmt, 65, chmn. hwy. cmt, 66-67 & 69-, Majority Leader, 69- Bus. & Prof. Pos: Auto dealer. Mil. Serv: Cpl, Army Air Force, World War II, 43-46. Mem: Mason; Am. Legion; AAONMS; RAM; St. Aldemar Commandery; Mt. Sinai Temple. Rel: Congregational. Mailing Add: Box 158, Chelsea, Vt. 05038.

KENNEDY, WALTER P. R
Minority Pair Clerk, U.S. House of Rep.
s. Thomas Kennedy and Mary McElvogue K; m. to Ana Louise Bou; c. Walter P, Jr, Ana Louise, Thomas Francis, Dennis Michael, Stella Marie, Kevin and Kathleen. Educ: Paterson State Teachers Col; Seton Hall Univ, B.S, 46; John Marshall Col. Law, LL.B, 48; Columbia Univ; Georgetown Univ. Polit. & Govt. Pos: Admin. asst. to U.S. Rep. Canfield, 48-60; Minority Pair Clerk, U.S. House of Rep, currently. Legal Res: Paterson, N.J. Mailing Add: 9804 Parkwood Dr, Bethesda, Md. 20014.

KENNEY, BURTON R
Chmn, Provincetown Town Rep. Cmt, Mass.
b. Sanford, Maine, 4/3/10; s. Reginald Cleveland Kenney and Mary Lydia Kaye K; m. 4/4/32 to Florence Volton; c. Joan M. (Mrs. Tremblay). Educ: Sanford High Sch, 16-28. Polit. & Govt. Pos: Chmn, Provincetown Town Rep. Cmt, Mass, 62- Bus. & Prof. Pos: Acct, Metrop. Life Ins. Co, Plymouth, Mass, 50- Mem: Past Master, King Hiram's Lodge AF&AM, Provincetown; past pres, Cape Cod Shrine Club; Mass. Consistory, Boston; AAONMS, Boston. Rel: Protestant. Mailing Add: 8 Pleasant St, Provincetown, Mass. 02657.

KENNEY, DANIEL JOSEPH R
b. Boston, Mass, 11/29/19; s. George Thomas Kenney and Grace Gibbons K; m. 6/23/45 to E. Mary Guthrie; c. Daniel J, Mary E, Stephen M, Robert E, William F. and Nancy L. Educ: Boston Col, 37-38; Millikin Univ, 39-40; Boston Col. Law Sch, LL.B, 46-49. Polit. & Govt. Pos: Chmn, Belmont Rep. Town Cmt, Mass, 64-; chmn, Belmont Housing Authority, Mass, 65-66. Bus. & Prof. Pos: Lawyer, 49- Mil. Serv: Entered as Pvt, Army, 42, released as Maj, 46, after serv. in 412th Fighter Squadron, 373rd Fighter Group, Ninth Air Force, ETO, 44-45; Distinguished Flying Cross; Air Medal with 12 Oak Leaf Clusters; Army Commendation Ribbon; Air Force Commendation Ribbon; European-African-Middle East. Campaign Medal with Five Battle Stars; Belgian Fourragere; World War II Victory Medal; Air Force Res. Medal; Col, Air Force Res, 61- Mem: Mass. and Fed. Bar Asns; assoc. mem, Am. Museum of Nat. Hist; VFW (past comdr, Waverley Post 1272); Am. Legion; K. of C. Rel: Catholic. Mailing Add: 29 Myrtle St, Belmont, Mass. 02178. (1967)

KENNEY, EDWARD BECKHAM R
b. Augusta, Ga. 12/1/29; s. Robert Edward Kenney and Betty Beckham K; m. 10/20/58 to Erica Grete Grossman; c. Robert E, II, Susan Lynn and twins, Alison Leigh and Beth Marie. Educ: Presby. Col, A.B, 50; Blue Key; Int. Rels. Club. Polit. & Govt. Pos: Exec. asst. to U.S. Sen. Strom Thurmond, S.C, 61-67 and admin. asst, 67-69; prfnl. staff mem, Senate Preparedness Investigating Subcmt, 69- Bus. & Prof. Pos: City ed, Aiken Standard and Rev, Aiken, S.C, 50-51 and news ed, 54-61; bur. chief, Sims News Bur, Wash, D.C, 61. Mil. Serv: Entered as 2nd Lt, Army, 50, released as 1st Lt, 54, after serv. as Platoon Leader, Bn. S-2, Regt. Asst. S-3, Korea, 52-53; Maj, Army Res, currently; Bronze Star for Valor with Oak Leaf Cluster; Purple Heart; Combat Infantryman Badge; UN and Korean Serv. Medals; Three Battle Stars. Mem: Jaycees; Am. Legion; Senate Staff Club; Cong. Secretaries Club; Senate Press Asn. Distinguished Commun. Serv. Awards from Jaycees, Am. Legion and VFW; Gold P Award, Presby. Col. Rel: Episcopal. Mailing Add: 6826 Nashville Rd, Lanham, Md. 20801.

KENNEY, EDWARD WILLIAM D
b. Boston, Mass, 10/13/13; s. William J. Kenney and Julia Fay K; m. 5/7/53 to Maxine Swineford; c. Paul Richard. Educ: Holy Cross Col, Ph.B, 35; Boston Col. Law Sch, 36-38; Boston Univ. Grad. Sch. Bus, 38-39; Northeast. Univ, 42. Polit. & Govt. Pos: Field auditor, U.S. Treas. Dept, Boston, Mass, 35-40; exec. secy, Indust. Develop. Cmn, N.Y, 61-62; del, Dem. Nat. Conv, 68. Bus. & Prof. Pos: Asst. br. oper. mgr, Am. Optical Co, 41-47; economist, UN, 48-50; dir. research and educ, Int. Woodworkers of Am, AFL-CIO, 51-58; asst. dir. employee rels, U.S. Brewers Found, 58-60; dir, employee rels, Am. Hotel Asn, 60-65; staff and prog. adminstr, Educ. Systs. Div, Litton Industs, Inc, 65- Mem: Am. Econ. Asn; Am. Adult Educ. Asn; Am. Personnel & Guid. Asn; Am. Arbit. Asn; Am. Voc. Asn; Am. Mgt. Asn; Indust. Rels. Research Asn; State, Co. and Munic. Employees Union; IBT; Culinary, Restaurant and Bartenders Union. Rel: Catholic. Mailing Add: 2170 36th Ave, San Francisco, Calif. 94116.

KENNEY, VIRGINIA BANNING R
Mem-at-lg, Exec. Cmt, Nat. Fedn. Rep. Women
b. Evanston, Ill, 12/6/22; d. Thomas Allen Banning and Margery Ames B; m. 2/12/44 to Frank D. Kenney; c. Claudia Anne, Pamela Jane (Mrs. Voetberg), Sarah Deming and Stuart Deming. Educ: Univ. Chicago, Ph.B, 45; Wyvern Club. Polit. & Govt. Pos: Co-chmn, Citizens for Eisenhower, Chicago, Ill, 52 & 56; co-chmn, Cook Co. Young Rep. Orgn, 56-57; secy, Ill. Rep. Citizens League, 60-62; 1st v.pres, Ill. Fedn. Rep. Women, 62-64, pres, 64-68, mem-at-lg, exec. cmt, 68-; alternate del-at-lg, Rep. Nat. Conv, 68. Bus. & Prof. Pos: Supvr, sch. food serv, Springfield, Ill, 67- Mem: Nat. Conf. Christians and Jews; Int. Platform Soc; Int. Oceanographic Found. Award for Serv. With the Atomic Energy Cmn, Manhatten Proj. Rel: Unitarian. Mailing Add: Route 2, Box 179A, Barrington, Ill. 60010.

KENNICK, JOSEPH M. D
Calif. State Sen.
b. Saginaw, Mich, 9/25/05; m. 5/5/27 to Ruth Wood; c. Joan Ruth (Mrs. Scott) and David Michael. Educ: Southwest. Univ. Law Sch; Univ. South. Calif. Sch. Govt. Polit. & Govt. Pos: Past pres, Nat. Conf. Juvenile Agencies; supvr, Dept. Soc. Welfare and Juvenile Bur, Long Beach, Calif, 34-58; attorney gen, Citizen Crime Cmn; Calif. State Assemblyman, 58-66; Calif. State Sen, 67- Bus. & Prof. Pos: Soc. worker. Mem: Mason; Elks; Moose; hon. mem, Long Beach Optimists; life mem, PTA. Legal Res: 2375 Eucalyptus Ave, Long Beach, Calif. 90806. Mailing Add: 110 Pine Ave, Suite 606, Long Beach, Calif. 90802. (1967)

KENNY, EUGENE PATRICK R
b. Jersey City, N.J, 2/15/15; s. Michael J. Kenny and Margaret Sheridan; single. Educ: St. Peter's Col, N.J, 33-35; Fordham Univ. Sch. of Law, LL.B, 38. Polit. & Govt. Pos: Asst. prosecutor, Hudson Co, N.J, 55-58; Dep. Attorney Gen, N.J, 58; Rep. cand. for Cong, 13th Dist, 62; del, Rep. Nat. Conv, 64; Rep. cand. for N.J. State Sen, 68. Bus. & Prof. Pos: Lawyer, Jersey City, N.J, 46- Mem: Hudson Co. Bar Asn; Am. Trial Lawyers Asn; Friendly Sons of St. Patrick of Hudson Co.(past pres); Sierra Club of Hudson Co.(past pres). Rel: Roman Catholic. Mailing Add: 51 Bidwell Ave, Jersey City, N.J. 07305.

KENNY, FREDERICK LEO D
b. 1904. Educ: Dean Acad; Lowell Tech. Inst. Polit. & Govt. Pos: Formerly Mass. State Rep; chmn, Uxbridge Indust. Cmn; Uxbridge selectman. Bus. & Prof. Pos: Ret. supt, Bachhmann Uxbridge Worsted Co. Mailing Add: 8 Susan Pkwy, Uxbridge, Mass. 01569. (1967)

KENOYER, KENNETH DALE D
Committeeman, Calif. Dem. State Cent. Cmt.
b. Kimball, Nebr, 9/18/25; s. Asa Vern Kenoyer and Jennie O'Neal K; m. 12/22/49 to Beverly J. Swinford; c. Kent B. Educ: San Jose State Col, 48-50; Am. Col. of Life Underwriters, 58-63; Studies in European Polit, Cabrillo Col, 65; Kappa Xi. Polit. & Govt. Pos: Committeeman, Calif. Dem. State Cent. Cmt, 64-; committeeman, Santa Cruz Co. Dem. Cent. Cmt, 64- Bus. & Prof. Pos: Pres, Santa Cruz Co. Life Underwriters, 65-67, legis. chmn, 67-69, pres-elec. dir, "Miss Santa Cruz Co. Pageant," 67-69, nat. committeeman, currently. Mil. Serv: Entered as Seaman 2/C, Navy, 44, released as PO 3/C, 46, after serv. in S.Pac. Task Force 58, 44-46; S.Pac. Ribbon; Am. Theater Ribbon; Philippine Liberation Medal, Okinawa with one Star. Mem: Nat. Life Underwriters Asn; Calif. Asn. Life Underwriters; Santa Cruz Life Underwriters Asn. Charter Pres. Award, Nat. Life Underwriters Asn; Miss Calif. Pageant Dir. Award; various sales achievement awards. Rel: Protestant. Legal Res: 5317 Scotts Valley Dr, Santa Cruz, Calif. 95060. Mailing Add: 5268 Scotts Valley Dr, Santa Cruz, Calif. 95060.

KENT, JAMES CALVIN R
Mem, Hanover Co. Rep. Cmt, Va.
b. Baltimore, Md, 4/30/20; s. Durward Harding Kent and Bruna Hilda Smith K; m. 1/8/48 to Gene Stiles; c. James Calvin, Jr. and Christopher Harding. Educ: Randolph-Macon Col, 40-45; Univ. Richmond, law and bus, 46-51; Smith-Deal Massey Col. Law, 49-51; Commons Club. Polit. & Govt. Pos: Co-chmn, Hanover Co. Rep. Cmt, Va, 64-65, mem, 66- Bus. & Prof. Pos: Attorney-at-Law, 51-; dir. on bd. of ten corps. Mil. Serv: Entered as Pvt, Army Air Force, 41, released as Sgt, 45, after serv. in ETO, 42-45; European-African and Middle East. Serv. Ribbons with 5 Battle Stars; 2 Distinguished Unit Citations. Mem: Va. State Bar; Am. Legion; Ruritans; Moose. Rel: Episcopal. Mailing Add: Box 654, Ashland, Va. 23005.

KENT, ROGER D
b. Chicago, Ill, 6/8/06; s. William Kent and Elizabeth Thacher K; m. 8/26/30 to Alice Cooke; c. Clarence C, Mary (Mrs. Schardt) and Alice (Mrs. Stephens). Educ: Thacher Sch; Yale Col. and Law Sch. Polit. & Govt. Pos: Alternate del, Dem. Nat. Conv, 48, del, 56, 60 & 64, v.chmn, 60; gen. counsel, Defense Dept, 52-53; v.chmn. and chmn, Calif. Dem. State Cent. Cmt, 54-65, mem, Postmaster Gen. Stamp Adv. Cmt, 61-68; mem, Int. N.Pac. Fisheries Cmt, 64-68. Mil. Serv: Entered as Lt, Naval Res, 42, released as Lt. Comdr, 45; Silver Star; 2 Presidential Unit Citations; Pac. Area Campaign Ribbons. Mem: Am. Calif. and San Francisco Bar Asns; pres, Yale Law Sch. Asn, North. Calif, 60-62. Rel: Protestant. Legal Res: 200 Woodland Rd, Kentfield, Calif. 94904. Mailing Add: 155 Montgomery St, San Francisco, Calif. 94104.

KENYON, ARNOLD OAKLEY R
Chmn, Union Co. Rep. Cent. Cmt, Iowa
b. Ord, Nebr, 6/29/26; s. Arnold Oakley Kenyon and Mabel Schollar K; m. 1/21/51 to Joy Jeannette Lawrence; c. Arnold O, III, Gregory L, Timothy R. and Cynthia J. Educ: Grinnell Col, 43-44; Central Col, 44-45; Univ. of Notre Dame, 45-46; Drake Univ, summer of 49; Univ. of Iowa Law Sch, LL.B, 50; Gamma Eta Gamma. Polit. & Govt. Pos: Precinct chmn, Rep. Party, Iowa, 58-66; chmn, Union Co. Rep. Cent. Cmt, currently. Mil. Serv: Entered as Seaman 3/C, Navy, 44, released as Ens, 47, after serv. in V-12 and NROTC, U.S.S. Rodman (DMS-21). Mem: Pres, Union Co. Bar Asn, 65; Elks; Am. Legion; Rotary. Rel: Methodist. Mailing Add: 124 N. Elm, Creston, Iowa 50801.

KENYON, CECIL CLARK R
b. Riegelsville, Pa; d. John Wilson Clark and Emma Virginia Hudnut C; m. to Raymond Grant Kenyon (deceased); c. Grant Hudnut, David Vreeland and Clark Justus. Educ: Occidental Col, B.A; Univ. Calif. and Univ. South. Calif, grad. courses. Polit. & Govt. Pos: Mem. exec. cmt, Calif. State Rep. Cent. Cmt; mem. and former v.pres, Nat. Fedn. Rep. Women; state women's finance chmn, Gov. Campaign, 66; del, Rep. Nat. Conv, three times. Award for Outstanding Work as Vol. Leader in Calif. Politics, Calif. State Legis. Rel: Christian. Mailing Add: 2805 Carlaris Rd, San Marino, Calif. 91108. (1967)

KENYON, KYLE R
Wis. State Assemblyman
b. Wyeville, Wis. Educ: Univ. Wis. Law Sch, LL.B, 52. Polit. & Govt. Pos: Wis. State Assemblyman, 56-; co. vets. serv. officer. Bus. & Prof. Pos: Attorney. Mil. Serv: Army, 43-46. Mailing Add: 1007 Superior Ave, Tomah, Wis. 54660. (1967)

KENYON, TRACY EDMUND, JR. R
b. Bennington, Vt, 1/28/36. Educ: Rittners Sch, Boston, Mass. Polit. & Govt. Pos: Vt. State Rep, 61-66; chmn, Shaftsbury Rep. Town Cmt; mem, Bennington Co. Rep. Cmt. Bus. & Prof. Pos: Floral Designer. Mil. Serv: Army Res, Sgt. Mem: Elks; Vt. Young Rep. Club. Rel: Baptist. Mailing Add: Bennington, Vt. 05201. (1967)

KEOGH, BROOKS JAMES R
Chmn, McKenzie Co. Rep. Party, N.Dak.
b. Williston, N.Dak, 8/4/14; s. Frank Patrick Keogh and Elizabeth Carney K; m. 1/4/44 to Kathleen Hyland; c. Frank P, Kathleen and Mary Elizabeth. Educ: St. John's Univ, Minn, 33-35; Univ. of N.Dak, 35-37; Col. of St. Thomas, Minn, B.A, 38; Neuman Club; Kappa Sigma. Polit. & Govt. Pos: Precinct committeeman, McKenzie Co. Rep. Party, Berg Twp, N.Dak, 54-, chmn, McKenzie Co, 63-; del, Rep. Nat. Conv, 60; chmn, Goldwater for Pres. Club, N.Dak, 60 and committeeman, 64. Bus. & Prof. Pos: Dir, Nodak Mutual Ins. Co, 58-64 and Northwest Bell Tel. Co, 64- Mil. Serv: Pfc, Marines, 43. Mem: N.Dak. Stockmen's Asn.(pres, 53-56); Am. Nat. Cattlemen's Asn.(pres, 64-65); N.Dak. Farm Bur.(past dir); Elks; K. of C; Newcomen. Soc; Reform Club, London, Eng. Rel: Catholic. Mailing Add: Keene, N.Dak. 58847. (1967)

KEOGH, EUGENE JAMES D
b. Brooklyn, N.Y, 8/30/07; s. James Preston Keogh and Elizabeth Kehoe K; m. 6/10/49 to Virginia Fogarty; c. Susan (Mrs. Louis Benedict Clarke) and E. Preston. Educ: N.Y. Univ. Sch. Commerce, B.C.S, 27; Fordham Univ. Sch. Law, LL.B, 30. Polit. & Govt. Pos: N.Y. State Assemblyman, 35-36; U.S. Rep, N.Y, 37-67; dir, N.Y. World's Fair Corp, 64-65; chmn, Franklin Delano Roosevelt Mem. Cmn, currently. Bus. & Prof. Pos: Lawyer, Halpin, Keogh & St. John, dir, City Title Ins. Co, trustee and counsel, East N.Y. Saving Bank and dir, Athlone Industs, Inc, currently; dir, Am. Chemosol Corp. Mem: Brooklyn, N.Y. State, Am. and Fed. Bar Asns; Asn. of the Bar of the City of N.Y; Bar Asn. of D.C. Rel: Catholic. Legal Res: 333 E. 57th St, New York, N.Y. Mailing Add: 630 Fifth Ave, New York, N.Y. 10020.

KEOHANE, PAUL J. D
b. Boston, Mass, 10/28/32; s. Paul Keohane and Margaret Mahoney K; m. 7/1/60 to Suzanne Marie Seymour; c. Sean Paul and Jennifer. Educ: Boston Univ, B.S. in Bus. Admin, 55; South. Methodist Univ, LL.B, 63; Phi Delta Phi. Polit. & Govt. Pos: Treas, Fremont Co. Young Dem, 65 and pres, 66; chmn, Fremont Co. Dem. Party, Colo, 66-68. Bus. & Prof. Pos: Private practice, Canon City, Colo, 65-66. Mil. Serv: Entered as 2nd Lt, Army, 55, released as 1st Lt, 57, after serv. in Inf. Mem: Elks; Am, Colo. and 11th Judicial Dist. Bar Asns; Jr. C. of C. Rel: Catholic. Legal Res: 918 N. 15th, Canon City, Colo. 81212. Mailing Add: 105 N. Seventh, Canon City, Colo. 81212. (1967)

KEOWN, WOODROW N. D
Mem, Ark. State Dem. Cent. Cmt.
b. Aliceville, Ala, 1/6/20; s. William C. Keown and Janie Hughes K; m. 6/14/47 to Mable Louise Daniels; c. Barbara J, Phillis A, Woodrow, Jr, James E, Ronald L, Avis C. and Karen J. Educ: Payne Col, 41; Stillman Col, 41-42; Philander Smith Col, 52-54. Polit. & Govt. Pos: Mem, Pulaski Co. Dem. Cmt, Ark, 66-68; del, Dem. Nat. Conv, 68; mem, Ark. State Dem. Cent. Cmt, 68-; Justice of the Peace, Little Rock, Ark, 69- Bus. & Prof. Pos: Staff mgr, Universal Life Ins. Co, currently. Mil. Serv: Entered as Pvt, Army, 42, released as S/Sgt, 46, after serv. in 654 Qm. Gas Supply Co, European Theatre, 44-46, Sgt. 1/C, Korean Conflict, 51-53; Good Conduct Medal; 3 Battle Stars; Unit Commendation. Mem: VFW. Rel: Methodist. Mailing Add: Route 2, Box 659, Little Rock, Ark. 72206.

KEPPLER, ERNEST C. R
Wis. State Sen.
b. Sheboygan, Wis, 4/5/18. Educ: Univ. of Wis, B.S, 49, LL.B, 50. Polit. & Govt. Pos: Sheboygan Alderman, Wis, 41-45 & 51-53; Wis. State Assemblyman, 43-45; Asst. Dist. Attorney, Sheboygan, 53-54; city and co. civil defense dir, 56-61; Wis. State Sen, 60-, Majority Leader, Wis. State Senate, 69- Bus. & Prof. Pos: Former factory worker, truck driver and bookkeeper; attorney; real estate broker. Mil. Serv: Army, World War II and Korean Conflict. Mem: Boy Scouts; civic, vet, fraternal and prfnl. orgn. Silver Beaver Award, Boy Scouts. Mailing Add: 909 New York Ave, Sheboygan, Wis. 53082.

KERNAGHAN, MAE W. R
Pa. State Rep.
b. Phila, Pa; d. Arthur C. Winter and Elizabeth Benchert W; m. to Frank J. Kernaghan; c. one son. Polit. & Govt. Pos: Mem, Young Rep, 8 years; state committeewoman, Delaware Co, Pa; alternate del, Rep. Nat. Conv, 44; mem, Delaware Co. Recreation Bd; Pa. State Rep, 56-, Rep. Caucus chmn, 66- Bus. & Prof. Pos: Salvation Army Maintenance Campaign Officer in Delaware Co, 10 years and P.R. Dir, Salvation Army, Delaware Co, 2 years. Mem: Pres, Yeadon Pub. Libr; Bus. & Prfnl. Women Club (dist. chmn); bd. dir, Camp Sunshine for underprivileged children; pres, Delaware Co. Park and Recreation Bd; Am. Legion Auxiliary; Women's Club of Yeadon (past pres); Women's Rep. Club of Delaware Co. Mailing Add: 912 Myra Ave, Yeadon, Pa. 19050.

KERNER, OTTO D
b. Chicago, Ill, 8/15/08; s. Otto Kerner and Rose Barbara Chemlik K; m. 10/20/34 to Helena Cermak; c. Tony and Helena. Educ: Brown Univ, B.A, 30; Trinity Col, Cambridge Univ, 30-31; Northwest. Univ. Law Sch, J.D, 34; Phi Delta Phi; Alpha Delta Phi. Hon. LL.D, Brown, Northwest. and South. Ill. Univs. and St. Procopius, Quincy and McKendree Col; L.H.D, Lincoln Col; D.P.A, Culver-Stockton Col; also hon. degrees from Ill. Inst. Tech, Bradley Univ. and Chicago-Kent Col. Law. Polit. & Govt. Pos: U.S. Attorney, North. Dist, Ill, 47-54; judge, Cook Co, 54-60; gov, Ill, 61-68; chmn, President's Adv. Cmn. on Civil Disorders, 67-68; U.S. Circuit Judge, U.S. Court of Appeals, Seventh Circuit, 68- Mil. Serv: Entered as Pvt, Ill. Nat. Guard, 34; transferred to Army as Maj, 42, released as Lt. Col. after serv. in 33rd Inf. Div, 34th Artil, 9th Inf. Div. and 32nd Inf. Div, Pac. Theater; Maj. Gen, Ill. Nat. Guard, Ret, 54. Mem: Fed, Am, Chicago and Ill. State Bar Asns; Chicago 7th Circuit Bar; W.Suburban Bar; Bohemian Lawyers' Asn; Law Club; Legal Club; Mason (33°); Shrine; v.pres, Chicago Area Coun, Boy Scouts and John Howard Asn; dir, Adult Educ. Coun. of Gr. Chicago; dir, Chicago Commons Asn, Chicago Coun. on For. Rels. and Ment. Health Asn. of Gr. Chicago. Rel: Presbyterian. Legal Res: 233 E. Walton Place, Chicago, Ill. 60611. Mailing Add: 219 S. Dearborn St, Chicago, Ill. 60604.

KERR, BAILEY FURMAN R
Mem, Calif. Rep. State Cent. Cmt.
b. Okla, 7/16/06; s. Charles Randolph Kerr and Mary Pybas K; m. 2/11/25 to Darline Craig; c. Bailey F, Jr. Educ: Manzanola High Sch, Colo, 12 years. Polit. & Govt. Pos: Cmnr, Whittier City Planning Cmn, Calif, 64-; mem, Calif. Rep. State Cent. Cmt, 69- Bus. & Prof. Pos: Pvt. secy, Colo. Fuel & Iron Co, Pueblo, Colo, 27-33; prin. clerk, asst. regional acct, regional fiscal inspector and dep. regional fiscal agent, U.S. Forest Serv, Atlanta, Ga. and Albuquerque, N.Mex, 33-47; off. mgr, F.R. Yates Construction Co, South Gate, Calif, 48-54; controller, John D. Lusk & Son, Whittier, Calif, 55-60; dir. of pub. rels, Suburban Water Syst, La Puente, Calif, 61- Mem: Calif. Water Asn; Southland Water Cmt; pres, Whittier Area Rose Float Asn; C. of C.(dir, Whittier Chap. and mem, La Puente, La Mirada and West Covina Chap). Cmt. Chmn-of-the-Year Award, La Puente C. of C, two times. Rel: Episcopal. Mailing Add: 16203 E. Honnington, Whittier, Calif. 90603.

KERR, GORDON E. R
b. Brookport, Ill, 2/13/12; m. to Lorraine Land; c. Carolyn Sue. Educ: Brookport Pub. Sch. Polit. & Govt. Pos: Ill. State Rep, 4 terms; Massac Co. Cmnr, Ill, 3 years; pres, Bd. of Educ, 30 years; former mem, Brookport City Coun; Ill. State Sen, 58-64; exec. secy, President's Adv. Bd. on Water Pollu-

tion, Dept. of Interior, Wash, D.C, 69- Bus. & Prof. Pos: Farmer; v.pres, Nat. Bank. Mem: Am. Legion (Past Comdr); Elks; Masons; VFW; Lions. Rel: Church of Christ. Mailing Add: RFD 1, Brookport, Ill. 62910.

KERR, JOHN H, JR. R
Chmn, Ky. State Rep. Cent. Cmt.
b. Lexington, Ky, 10/9/21; s. J. Hervey Kerr and Elizabeth Latham K; m. 5/17/47 to Mary LaBach; c. John H. III, Mary Shepherd and Bettie LaBach. Educ: Univ. Ky, B.S, 43; Omicron Delta Kappa; Beta Gamma Sigma; Phi Mu Alpha; Pershing Rifles; Scabbard and Blade. Polit. & Govt. Pos: Mem, State Police Merit Bd, Ky, 50-52; precinct committeeman, Fayette Co. Rep. Party, 52-; co. cmnr, Fayette Co, 53-57; co. chmn, Fayette Co. Rep. Campaign, 54, 56 & 60; asst. state chmn, Ky. Rep. Campaign, 62, 64, 66 & 67 and chmn, 68; city cmnr, Lexington, 63-65; del, Rep. Nat. Conv, 68; chmn, Ky. State Rep. Cent. Cmt, 68- Bus. & Prof. Pos: State secy-treas, Funeral Dir. Asn. of Ky, Inc, 50-; partner, Kerr Bros. Funeral Home, 60- Mil. Serv: Entered as Pvt, Army, 43, released as 1st Lt, 45, after serving in 28th Inf. Div, ETO, 44-45; Purple Heart. Mem: Am. Legion; Mason. Named Outstanding Young Man by Lexington Jaycees, 53 and one of three Outstanding Young Men of Ky. by Jaycees, 54. Rel: Christian Church. Legal Res: 124 S. Ashland Ave, Lexington, Ky. 40502. Mailing Add: 463 E. Main St, Lexington, Ky. 40507.

KERR, ROBERT MABRY R
b. Newell, Ala, 10/10/21; s. Joseph Kerr and Alma Thompson K; m. 12/24/44 to Wilma Stevens; c. Alyce Cheryl, Robert Mabry, Jr. and Alan Logan. Polit. & Govt. Pos: Dir, Randolph Co. Goldwater Orgn, 64; orgn. dir, Randolph Co. Rep. Party, Ala, 66, chmn, 67; Rep. nominee, U.S. Rep, Ala, 68. Bus. & Prof. Pos: CPO, Career Navy, 41-62; farmer, 62- Mil. Serv: Entered as A/S, Navy, 41, released as Master Chief Personalman, 62, after serv. in many stas. and ships, all oceans and continents, 41-62; Presidential Unit Citation; Good Conduct Medal with Seven Awards; Am. Defense Serv. Medal; Asiatic, Pac. Theater Medal; Am. Theater Medal; World War II Victory Medal; Korean War Serv. Medal. Publ: Aircraft Maintenance Procedures, U.S. Navy Bur. Aeronaut, 48. Mem: Cattleman's Asn; Moose. Rel: Protestant. Mailing Add: P.O. Box 291, Wedowee, Ala. 36278.

KERR, ROBERT SAMUEL, JR. D
b. Ada, Okla, 10/25/26; s. Robert Samuel Kerr and Grayce Breene K; m. 1/23/49 to LaMoyne Cody; c. Robert S, III, Sharon L, Cody T, William R. and Valerie Kay. Educ: Univ. Okla, A.B, 51, LL.B, 55; Phi Delta Theta; Phi Alpha Delta. Polit. & Govt. Pos: Del, Dem. Nat. Conv, 68. Bus. & Prof. Pos: Assoc, Kerr, Conn & Davis, 55-60, partner, 60-63; partner, Kerr, Davis, Roberts, Irvine & Burbage, Attorneys-at-Law, 63- Mil. Serv: Cadet, Merchant Marines and Naval Res, 45-47; 1st Lt, Army, 51-53, serv. in 999th Field Artil. Bn, Korea. Mem: Am. and Okla. Bar Asns; Am. Judicature Soc; Okla. City C. of C; President's Air Quality Adv. Bd. Rel: Methodist. Legal Res: 7205 Nichols Rd, Oklahoma City, Okla. 73120. Mailing Add: 1500 Kermac Bldg, Oklahoma City, Okla. 73102.

KERR, WILLIAM GRAYCEN D
b. Okla. Co, Okla, 10/18/37; s. Robert Samuel Kerr and Grayce Breene K; m. 8/4/56 to Joffa Gemar; c. David Kenworthy, Joffa, Kavar and Mara. Educ: Univ. Okla, B.A, 59, LL.B, 62; Phi Delta Theta; Phi Alpha Delta. Polit. & Govt. Pos: Chmn, Dem. State Cent. Cmt, Okla, 67-69; del, Dem. Nat. Conv. and chmn, Okla. Del, 68; chmn, Youth Adv. Coun, Dem. Nat. Cmt, 68. Bus. & Prof. Pos: Dir, Farmers & Merchants Bank & Trust Co. of Tulsa, Okla, 63-; dir, Penn Sq. Nat. Bank, Oklahoma City, 65-; chmn. bd, Citizens Bank of Ada, 66-; attorney, Kerr, Davis, Irvine & Burbage, 67-; chmn. bd, Pub. Leasing Co, 69- Mem: Bd. Mgt, Okla. City Cent. Br. YMCA; hon. trustee, Nat. Cystic Fibrosis Research Found; trustee, Kerr Found; trustee, Nat. Cowboy Hall of Fame and West. Heritage Cent. Rel: Methodist. Legal Res: 2414 Smoking Oak, Norman, Okla. 73069. Mailing Add: 1510 Kermac Bldg, Oklahoma City, Okla. 73102.

KERSHAW, JOSEPH LANG D
Fla. State Rep.
b. Live Oak, Fla, 6/27/11; s. Albert Julius Kershaw and Theresa Lang K; m. 7/18/41 to Mamie Newton; c. Joseph L, Jr. Educ: Fla. Agr. & Mech. Univ, A.B, 35, M.Ed, 55; Kappa Alpha Psi. Polit. & Govt. Pos: Mem, Mayor's Cmt. on Civil Disobedience; mem, Miami Econ. Adv. Cmt; Fla. State Rep, 68-. Mem: Classroom Teachers Dade Co; Nat. Educ. Asn; Fla. Educ. Asn; South. Polit. Sci. Asn; Nat. Track Coaches Asn; K. of C.(4°); Holy Name Soc. Rel: Catholic. Legal Res: 2539 N.W. 46th St, Miami, Fla. 33142. Mailing Add: 286 Holland Bldg. Tallahassee, Fla. 32304.

KERTZ, HAROLD ALLAN R
Mem. Exec. Adv. Cmt, D.C. Rep. Cmt.
b. Allentown, Pa, 12/2/06; s. Christian John Kertz and Elizabeth Rudy K; m. 5/1/44 to Genevieve Hastings; c. Robert Allan. Educ: Georgetown Col; Georgetown Univ. Law Center, LL.B, 28; Columbus Univ, LL.M, 32; Sigma Nu Phi. Polit. & Govt. Pos: Precinct chmn, Rep. Party, Wash, D.C, 48, 52, 56 & 60; v.chmn, D.C. Pub. Serv. Cmn, 57-62; mem, D.C. Rep. cmt, 60-, mem. finance cmt, 62- and mem. exec. adv. cmt, 64-; chmn, Oper. Legal Eagle, 64; v.chmn, D.C. Del, Rep. Nat. Conv, 68. Bus. & Prof. Pos: Asst. trust officer, Nat. Metrop. Bank, Wash, D.C, 31-40; partner, Roberts & McInnis, 40-54; partner, Mercier, Kertz & Sanders, 54-57; legal contrib. ed, Trusts and Estates and dir, Henlopen Hotel Corp, Chem-Met Co, O'Donnell's Sea Grill, Inc, R.E. Darling, Inc, Nat. Litho Co, James R. Dunlop, Inc. and D&P Prod, Inc, currently. Mem: Interstate Commerce Cmn. Practitioners Asn; Fed. Commun. Bar Asn; Fed, Am. and D.C. Bar Asns; Kiwanis; Capitol Hill Club; Columbia Country Club; Univ. Club; Nat. Press Club; Farmington Country Club. Rel: Episcopal. Legal Res: 2500 Virginia Ave. N.W, Washington, D.C. 20037. Mailing Add: 910 17th St. N.W, Washington, D.C. 20006.

KERVICK, JOHN A. D
State Treas, N.J.
b. Elizabeth, N.J, 5/6/06; m. to Catherine B. Burke; c. Mrs. William J. Corbet, Mrs. Robert J. Arrix, Mrs. Frank H. Connelly, Jr, Margaret and Mary. Educ: Fordham Univ, B.A, 27; Mercer Beasley Sch. of Law, 31. Polit. & Govt. Pos: Asst. regional dir. and regional dir, Fed. Pub. Housing Admin, 44-53; former dir, Elizabeth Authority, N.J; state treas, N.J, 58- Mem: Chmn. bd, Nat. Housing Conf. Mailing Add: 102 Fairfield Dr, Short Hills, N.J. 07078.

KESLER, JOHN A. D
Ind. State Rep.
b. Marshall, Ill; s. Hal H. Kesler and Clara Hurst K; m. 5/13/48 to Maxine Weaver; c. Nicki Lynn, Bradley Weaver and John A, II. Educ: Ind. State Univ, A.B, 48, Ind. Univ. Sch. Law, J.D, 51. Polit. & Govt. Pos: Chief dep. prosecutor, Vigo Co, Ind, 54-58; Ind. State Rep, Vigo and Sullivan Co, 69- Bus. & Prof. Pos: Attorney-at-law, 51- Mil. Serv: Entered as Pvt, Army, 43, released as S/Sgt, 46, after serv. in Signal Corps, S.Pac-Philippines, 44-46; Good Conduct Ribbon with Four Bronze Battle Stars. Mem: Am, Ind, Ill. and Terre Haute Bar Asns; Am. Trial Lawyers Asn; Am. Legion; Elks; Optimists (past pres); life mem. and past pres, Jaycees; Nat. Asn. State Legislators. Local Good Govt. Award; Outstanding Freshman Orator, 96th Ind. Gen. Assembly, 69. Rel: Methodist. Mailing Add: R.R. 1, Box 178, West Terre Haute, Ind. 47885.

KESSELRING, LEO JOHN Conservative Party, N.Y.
Regional V.Chmn, Conservative Party, N.Y.
b. Rochester, N.Y, 5/13/33; s. Clarence Charles Kesselring and Mary Mahoney K; m. 9/17/60 to Patricia Jean Dyer; c. Susan Elizabeth and Stephen Lee. Educ: St. John Fisher Col, B.A. in Acct. cum laude, 55; St. John's Univ. Sch. Law, LL.B, 58; Phi Delta Phi; mem. ed. staff, St. John's Law Rev. and Cath. Lawyer Mag, 56-58. Polit. & Govt. Pos: Research asst, U.S. Attorney's Off, U.S. Dept. Justice, 56-57; mem. legal staff, Joint Cmt. Legis. Practices and Procedures, N.Y. State Legis, 58-59; Monroe Co. committeeman, Conservative Party, N.Y, 62-68, mem. exec. cmt, 62-68 and chmn, 65-68; regional v.chmn. and mem, State Exec. Cmt, Conservative Party, N.Y, 68- Bus. & Prof. Pos: Lectr. real estate law, Rochester Inst. Tech, 59-65, bus. law, Rochester Bus. Inst, 60-61; attorney, Burns, Suter & Doyle, Rochester, 61- Mil. Serv: Entered as Recruit E-1, Army, 59, released as Spec. 4/C, 65, after serv. in 727th Ordnance Bn, 27th Armored Div, N.Y. Nat. Guard. Publ: 'The Attorneys Duties of Disclosure,' St. John's Law Rev, 57, 'The Supreme Court, The Smith Act, and the 'Clear and Present Danger' Test,' 57. Mem: Monroe Co, N.Y. State and Independent Bar Asns; Sertoma Club. Rel: Roman Catholic. Legal Res: 333 Thayer Rd, Fairport, N.Y. 14450. Mailing Add: 529 Times Square Bldg, Rochester, N.Y. 14614.

KESSINGER, EDWARD L. R
b. Osawatomie, Kans, 2/9/18; s. Jesse Harrison Kessinger and Grace Johnson K; m. 6/12/38 to Mona Elaine; c. Karl Kurt, Kristin Elaine, Lisa Kim, Judy Lee and Jan Henderson. Educ: Univ. Wichita, A.B, 42. Polit. & Govt. Pos: Kans. State Rep, 61-64 & 67-68, mem, legis. coun, Kans. State House of Rep, 63-64. Bus. & Prof. Pos: Ed. & publisher, Craig Leader, Mo, 48-50 and Junction City Rep, Kans, 50-; publisher, Ogden Sun, 64- and Wakefield Sun, Kans, 66- Mil. Serv: Entered as Ens, Navy, 44, released as Lt.(jg), 46, after serv. in U.S.S. Guam, Pac; Am, Asiatic-Pac. Ribbons; Victory, Philippine Liberation and Korean Occup. Medals. Mem: Cent. Kans. Press Asn.(pres, 66-67); Nat. Newspaper Asn; Kans. Press Asn; Geary Co. Fish & Game Asn; Am. Legion; VFW; Mason (32°); Shrine; Shrine Legion of Honor; Rotary; C. of C; Family YMCA; United Fund Bd; Asn. U.S. Army. Rel: Presbyterian. Mailing Add: 237 W. Vine, Junction City, Kans. 66441.

KESSINGER, JAMES EDWARD D
b. South Charleston, W.Va, 9/13/37; s. L.C. Kessinger and Marcel H. Thacker K; m. 12/21/59 to Jacqueline Lyon; c. James E. Jr. Educ: W.Va. Univ, B.A, 60; LL.B, 63; Kappa Alpha; Phi Alpha Delta. Polit. & Govt. Pos: W.Va. State Del, 64-66; mem, Young Dem. Bus. & Prof. Pos: Lawyer. Mem: Civitan Club; Kanawha Bar Asn; W.Va. Bar; C. of C; Kanawha Co. Employ. for Youth. Rel: Baptist. Mailing Add: 95 Main St, St. Albans, W.Va. 25177. (1967)

KESSLER, FREDERICK PHILIP D
Wis. State Assemblyman.
b. Milwaukee, Wis, 1/11/40; s. Frederick P. Kessler and Marie Schroeder K; m. 9/10/66 to Joan Fowler. Educ: Univ. Wis, B.S, 62, LL.B, 66; Theta Delta Chi. Polit. & Govt. Pos: Chmn, Wauwatosa Dem. Club, Wis, 59; chmn, State Youth for Kennedy Club, 60; Wis. State Assemblyman, 60-61 & 64- Bus. & Prof. Pos: Attorney at Law, 66- Mem: Wis, Milwaukee and Milwaukee Jr. Bar Asns; Am. Civil Liberties Union (mem. bd. dirs, Milwaukee chap, 69-); Lutheran Human Rels. Asn. of Wis.(state chmn, 69-); Cmn. on Family Life, South Wis. Dist. of Lutheran Church, Mo. Synod, 68-69. Rel: Lutheran-Mo. Synod. Mailing Add: 2719 W. Juneau, Milwaukee, Wis. 53208.

KESSLER, HARRY A. R
b. Danville, Pa, 8/20/02; s. John P. Kessler and Theresa Smith K; m. to Mary Mildred Schultz; c. four. Educ: Danville High Sch. Polit. & Govt. Pos: Pa. State Rep; Former Invest. Dept. of Revenue, Pa, 26 years. Bus. & Prof. Pos: Cost clerk office mgr. Mem: Elks; Moose; Goodwill Fire Co; Six Co. Firemans Asn. Rel: Lutheran. Mailing Add: 36 Ash St, Danville, Pa. 17821.

KESTER, BETTYE JEAN D
Secy-Treas, Crowley Co. Dem. Party, Colo.
b. Colorado Springs, Colo, 3/12/29; d. Fred Leroy Bunch and Florence O'Halloran B; m. 1/5/47 to Bill Denley Kester; c. Constance Lee, Kathryn Jean and Bill Denley, II. Educ: Calhan High Sch, 9 years. Polit. & Govt. Pos: Committeewoman, Lincoln Co. Dem. Party, Colo, 52-60; committeewoman, Crowley Co. Dem. Party, 62-65, secy-treas, 66-; elec. judge, Crowley Co, 62-69. Mem: Altar and Rosary Soc; Dem. Club. Rel: Roman Catholic. Legal Res: 417 Otero Ave, Ordway, Colo. 81063. Mailing Add: P.O. Box 57, Ordway, Colo. 81063.

KESTER, JOHN BARTON R
Secy, Darke Co. Rep. Cent. Cmt, Ohio
b. Greenville, Ohio, 4/29/24; s. John Barton Kester and Ella Mae Stoner K; m. 5/16/52 to Joan May Forward; c. Rebbecca Joan and Cheryl Lynn. Educ: Ohio North. Univ. Polit. & Govt. Pos: Secy, Darke Co. Rep. Cent. Cmt, Ohio, 64-, committeeman, 68- Bus. & Prof. Pos: Pres, Kesco Prod. Co, 48- Mil. Serv: Entered as Pvt, Army, 43, released as Sgt. 45, after serv. in Ninth Div, ETO, 45. Legal Res: Park Ave, Greenville, Ohio 45331.

KESTER, STANLEY R. R
Pa. State Rep.
b. Wilkes-Barre, Pa, 5/21/29; s. Russell Kester and Geraldine Heffrom K;

m. to Rebecca M. MaNulty; c. Four. Polit. & Govt. Pos: Mem. exec. bd, Chester Twp. Rep. Orgn, 59-; justice peace, 59-; Delaware Co. tax assessor, 63-64; Rep. Committeeman; Pa. State Rep, 64- Bus. & Prof. Pos: Mem. staff, Sun Oil Co. Refineries. Mil. Serv: Army, World War II and Korean War. Rel: Catholic. Mailing Add: 2417 Green St, Feltonville, Chester, Pa. 19013. (1967)

KESTNER, DOLORES MERVILLE R
Mem, Tenn. Rep. State Exec. Cmt.
b. Nashville, Tenn, 1/8/27; d. Oscar Hamilton Merville and Katherine Hardcastle M; m. 9/29/45 to James Vell Kestner; c. Jamie (Mrs. DuRard) and Joel Merville. Educ: Cohn High Sch, grad. Polit. & Govt. Pos: Pres, Davidson Co. Rep. Women's Club, Tenn, 59-60; del, Co, Dist. and State Rep. Conv, 60 & 68; Rep. Elec. Cmnr, Williamson Co, 60-; alternate del, Rep. Nat. Conv, 68; mem, Tenn. Rep. State Exec. Cmt, Sixth Cong. Dist, 68- Bus. & Prof. Pos: Curator, Carter House, Asn. for Preservation of Tenn. Antiq, 67-69. Mem: Williamson Co. Rep. Women's Club; Williamson Co. Hist. Soc. Rel: Methodist. Mailing Add: Route 7, Franklin, Tenn. 37064.

KETCHAM, DOUGLAS THEODORE, SR. R
Chmn, Sixth Dist. Rep. Cmt, Minn.
b. Rice Lake, Wis, 5/16/16; s. Theodore S. Ketcham and Matie Redmond K; m. 6/12/41 to Geraldine Ann Newcomb; c. Douglas T, Jr, Nancy Ann (Mrs. Schroer) and Pamela Martha. Educ: Minn. Sch. Bus, Minneapolis, 35-36; Univ. Minn, night sch. Polit. & Govt. Pos: Secy, Renville Co. Rep. Party, Minn, 58-60, v.chmn, 60-62, chmn, 62-67; chmn, Sixth Dist. Rep. Cmt, 67-; del. Rep. Nat. Conv, 68. Bus. & Prof. Pos: Owner, D.T. Ketcham Co, Fuel Co. in Minneapolis, 36-38; salesman and later plant supt, Am. Excelsior Corp, 38-46; partner, Ketcham Farm Supply, Olivia, 46-55; salesman, Ramy Seed Co, Mankato, 55-68; salesman, Peterson Seed Co, Savage, 68- Publ: Your Collie, training book, donated to Collie Club of Minn, 46. Mem: Mason (past master); Kiwanis (past pres); PTA (past pres); Eastern Star (past patron). Rel: United Methodist. Mailing Add: 306 E. DePue Ave, Olivia, Minn. 56277.

KETCHUM, WILLIAM MATTHEW R
Calif. State Assemblyman
b. Los Angeles, Calif, 9/2/21; s. Robert Milton Ketchum and Charmian Richards K; m. 7/11/42 to Lola Marie Heegaard; c. Robert Milton and Margaret Kathleen. Educ: Colo. Sch. of Mines, 39; Univ. South. Calif, 40-41; Alpha Kappa Psi; Kappa Alpha. Polit. & Govt. Pos: Mem, Rep. State Cent. Cmt, Calif, 64-66; Calif. State Assemblyman, 29th Dist, 67-; alternate del, Rep. Nat. Conv, 68. Bus. & Prof. Pos: Owner-operator, West. Auto Dealer Store, 46-50; sales, Mell O. Haldeman Corp, 53-55; sales, Republic Van Lines, 55-57; owner, Dairy Farm, 57-59; owner-operator, Farview Farms, 59- Mil. Serv: Entered as 2nd Lt, Army, 42, released as 1st Lt, 46, after serv. in 77th Inf. Div, Pac. Theater, recalled as Capt, 50, released as Maj, 53, after serv. in 441st Counter Intel. Corps, Korean War and Japan; Bronze Star; Purple Heart; Am. Theater Ribbon; Asiatic Pac. Medal with 3 Battle Stars; Combat Inf. Badge; Philippine Liberation and Korean Serv. Medals. Mem: Farm Bur; Calif. Farm Bur. Fedn. Rel: Episcopal. Legal Res: Route 1, Box 40, Paso Robles, Calif. 93446. Mailing Add: 668 N St. Sacramento, Calif. 95814.

KEY, GLEN R. D
b. Chandler, Okla, 11/17/16; s. Samuel D. Key and Cloe Bridge K; m. 6/16/38 to Martha Marie George; c. Anita Jean (Mrs. Snapp), Kathryn E. (Mrs. Jordan) and Phillip R. Educ: Hills Bus. Univ, Okla. City, 34-36. Polit. & Govt. Pos: Coordinator of activities, Gen. Elec. Campaign, State Dem. Hq, Oklahoma City, Okla, 52; chmn, Lincoln Co. Dem. Cent. Cmt, 53-54; secy-treas, Okla. Turnpike Authority, 53-55, mem, 61-62; chmn, Murray Co. Dem. Cent. Cmt, 59. Mil. Serv: Entered as Pvt, Army, 45, released as Sgt, 45. Mem: Am. Bankers Asn; Okla. Bankers Asn; AF&AM, Scottish Rite; Consistory; Am. Legion. Rel: Christian Church. Mailing Add: 8 W. Vinita, Sulphur, Okla. 73086.

KEYES, ORVAL ANDREW R
Nebr. State Sen.
b. Springfield, Nebr, 10/31/13; s. Robert H. Keyes and Mary E. Martenson K; m. 8/7/39 to Lois E. Gottsch; c. Gloria (Mrs. Sass), Jodine (Mrs. Osborn), Jerry, Mary Jean, Cheryl (Mrs. Smith), Kimberly K, Glenda G. and Brenda B. Educ: Springfield High Sch, Nebr, 26-30. Polit. & Govt. Pos: Nebr. State Sen, 69- Bus. & Prof. Pos: Operating engr, packing house indust, 15 years; journeyman machinist, Douglas Aircraft Co. Inc. Mem: AFL-CIO. Rel: Methodist. Mailing Add: R.R. 3, Papillion, Nebr. 68046.

KEYES, THOMAS J, JR. D
b. Waterbury, Conn, 9/2/26; s. Thomas J. Keyes, Sr. and Anna Valaitis K; single. Educ: Post Jr. Col. of Commerce, 44; St. Lawrence Univ, 46-47; Sigma Pi. Polit. & Govt. Pos: Secy, Vet. Admin, U.S. Dept. Labor, Wage Stabilization Bd. and Fed. Commun. Cmn, 46-54; exec. secy. to U.S. Rep. Arnold Olsen, Mont, 61-62; admin. asst. to U.S. Rep. John C. Mackie, Mont, 65-66 and U.S. Rep. Mario Biaggi, N.Y, 69-; legis. asst. to U.S. Rep. Joshua Eilberg, Pa, 67-68. Bus. & Prof. Pos: Legis. secy, AFGE, AFL-CIO, Wash, D.C, 58-59 and IAFF, AFL-CIO, 59-60; legis. asst, Bldg. and Construction Trades Dept, AFL-CIO, 63-65 and UAW, Wash, D.C, 65-66. Mil. Serv: Naval Res, Active, World War II. Mem: Off. and Prfnl. Employees Int. Union, AFL-CIO; Cong. Secy. Club; Nat. Capitol Dem. Club. Rel: Catholic. Legal Res: Waterbury, Conn. 06702. Mailing Add: Longworth House Office Bldg, Washington, D.C. 20515.

KEYS, JOHN GRANT D
V.Chmn, Lorain Co. Dem. Exec. Cmt, Ohio
b. Barnesville, Ohio, 6/15/17; s. James Ambrose Keys and Bertha Kathryn Glasow K; m. 12/27/44 to Mary Catherine Meany; c. Corinne (Mrs. Kent Dawson), Mary Michele, Michael Brian, Patrick Grant, John Robert, Kelly Ellen, Thomas James, Timothy Grant, Anthony Regan, Kathleen Mary, James Gerald and Colleen Margaret. Educ: Ohio Univ, A.B, cum laude, 60; Omicron Delta Kappa. Polit. & Govt. Pos: Mayor, Elyria, Ohio, 54-59; Dem. Precinct Committeeman, Elyria, 54-; del, Dem. Nat. Conv, 56, 64 & 68; Ohio Dist. Dem. Committeeman, 13th Cong. Dist, 56-; v.chmn, Lorain Co. Dem. Exec. Cmt, 56-; mem, Lorain Co. Bd. Elec, 57-59; Ohio Dir. Hwy. Safety, 59-63; treas, Lorain Co, 63-; v.chmn, Ohio Dem. Cent. and Exec. Cmt, 68- Bus. & Prof. Pos: V.pres, Elyria Bldg. Co, Inc, 60-; mem, exec. cmt, Pioneer Fed. Savings & Loan, 62- Mil. Serv: Entered as Pvt, Air Force, 42, released as 1st Lt, 46, after serv. as pilot, ETO; Victory Medal. Mem: Ohio Archaeol. Soc.(treas); Lorian Co. Archaeol. Soc.(pres); Am. Legion; life mem. Amvets; Northeast. Ohio Heart Asn.(v.pres); Lorain Co. Chap. Heart Asn.(pres). Outstanding Serv. Award, VFW; Distinguished Serv. Award, Ohio Univ. Alumni; Outstanding Commun. Serv, Elyria Vet. Coun; Cath. Man of the Year, Holy Name Soc; Distinguished Serv. Award, Eagles; Distinguished Leadership Award, State and Prov. Safety Coordinators; Distinguished Leadership, Heart Asn. Rel: Catholic. Mailing Add: 409 Washington Ave, Elyria, Ohio 44035.

KEYSERLING, MARY DUBLIN D
Mem. Bd. of Gov, Women's Nat. Dem. Club, Wash, D.C.
b. N.Y.C, 5/25/10; d. Dr. Louis I. Dublin and Augusta Salik D; m. 10/4/40 to Leon H. Keyserling. Educ: Barnard Col, 30; London Sch. Econ, 31-32; Columbia Univ, 32-33; Phi Beta Kappa. LL.D, Bryant Col, 65; L.H.D, Woman's Med. Col. Pa, 68. Polit. & Govt. Pos: Positions in Fed. Serv, 41-46; chief spec. progs. div, U.S. Dept. of Commerce, 46-49, chief int. econ. anal. div, 50-53; first v.pres, Woman's Nat. Dem. Club, Wash, D.C, 61-63, pres, 63-64, mem. bd. of gov, 69-; dir. woman's bur, U.S. Dept. of Labor, 64-69. Bus. & Prof. Pos: Staff mem, Cmt. Costs of Med. Care, 30 and State Charities Aid Asn, 31; teacher of econ, Sarah Lawrence Col, 33-38; exec. dir, Nat. Consumers League, 38-40; assoc. dir, Conf. on Econ. Progress, 53-64. Publ: Author, numerous articles and pamphlets on econ. subjects. Mem: Am. Econ. Asn; mem. bd, Nat. Consumers League, Nat. Fedn. of Settlements and Neighborhood Centers, Henry St. Settlement and Friendship House; trustee, Nat. Assembly Social Policy and Develop. Freedom Award, Roosevelt Univ, 47; Achievement Award, Zeta Phi Beta, 66; Woman Behind the Woman Award, 69. Mailing Add: 2908 Albemarle St. N.W, Washington, D.C. 20008.

KEYSTON, DAVID HILL R
b. San Mateo, Calif, 8/2/25; s. George Noel Keyston and Hazel Elander K; m. 12/16/51 to Dolly Dee Janisch; c. David Lawson, Douglas Arthur and Dee Ann. Educ: Univ. Minn, B.S, 45; Stanford Univ, M.S. in Bus. Admin, 48; Phi Kappa Sigma. Polit. & Govt. Pos: Mem, San Mateo Co. Rep. Cent. Cmt; assoc. mem, Calif. State Rep. Cent. Cmt; dir-at-lg, Calif. Rep. Assembly; chmn, United Rep. Calif. Mid-Peninsula Unit; founding mem, Citizens for Constructive Action. Bus. & Prof. Pos: Exec. V.Pres, Anza Pacific Corp; partner, Keyston & Co; dir. and treas, Keyston Bros. Mil. Serv: Lt, Naval Res, World War II and Korean War. Mem: Exec. cmt, Govt. Research Coun. San Mateo Co; San Mateo Co. Develop. Asn; Rotary. Rel: Christian Science. Legal Res: 1452 Floribunda Ave, Burlingame, Calif. 94010. Mailing Add: 1310 Bayshore Highway, Suite 25, Burlingame, Calif. 94010.

KEZON, PETER PAUL D
Mem, 14th Ward Dem. Orgn, Chicago, Ill.
b. Scarbro, W.Va, 2/19/06; s. Joseph Kezon and Mary Jarosz K; m. 4/21/57 to Ann M. Glista; c. Peter P, Jr, Martina Marie, Susan Carol, Joseph Peter and Angela Marie. Educ: Lindblom High Sch, 19-21. Polit. & Govt. Pos: Mem, 14th Dem. Orgn, Chicago, Ill, 30-; auditor, Pub. Accounts, State of Ill, 33-37; head storekeeper, Chicago, 37-41; baliff, Munic. Court, 41-43; del, Dem. Nat. Conv, 56, 60, 64 & 68. Bus. & Prof. Pos: Chmn. bd, Supreme Savings and Loan Asn, Chicago, Ill, 29-; chief clerk, W.W. Person, Receiver, 32-33; pres-dir, Vacek & Co, Inc, 41- and Kezon Currency Exchange, 48-; secy-dir, Pete Kezon, Inc, 61- Mil. Serv: Entered as Pvt, Army, 43, released as Cpl, 45, after serv. in Hq. Fifth Serv. Command. Mem: Pres. Coun, St. Ignatius High Sch; Back of Yards Bus. Businessmen Asn; K. of C; Polish Nat. Allience; Polish Roman Catholic Union; Polish Highlanders; J.J. Zientek Post 419; Polish Legion Am. Vet. Rel: Roman Catholic. Legal Res: 10456 S. Lawndale Ave, Chicago, Ill. 60655. Mailing Add: 1751-1755 W. 47th St, Chicago, Ill. 60609.

KHACHADOORIAN, GREGORY BENJAMIN R
Mass. State Rep.
b. South Boston, Mass, 7/8/28; s. Peniamin Khachadoorian and Yeranig Sulujian K; m. 5/23/59 to Mary Teresa Morey. Educ: Boston Univ. Sch. Law and Col. of Bus. Admin; Perkins Sch. for the Blind, Watertown, Mass. Polit. & Govt. Pos: Mem, Arlington Young Rep. Club and Rep. Town Cmt, Mass; Mass. State Rep, 59-; mem, Mass. Cmn. for the Blind Adv. Bd, 62- and Mass. Voc. Rehab. Planning Cmn, 66-67. Mem: Mass, Boston, Cambridge and Middlesex Co. Bar Asns; Mass. Bar; Boston Univ. Law Sch. Alumni Asn; Perkins Sch. for the Blind Asn; Lions; Arlington Boys' Club Assocs; AF&AM; Eastern Star; Scottish Rite; Valley of Boston; Shrine. Admitted to practice before U.S. Supreme Court, U.S. Court of Appeals and U.S. Dist. Court. Rel: Armenian Apostolic. Mailing Add: 154 Highland Ave, Arlington, Mass. 02174.

KIBBEY, JACK ROBINSON R
Commonwealth Attorney, 20th Judicial Dist. of Ky.
b. Grayson, Ky, 12/29/18; s. Delbert Valley Kibbey and Susie Helen Robinson K; m. 12/29/39 to Ruby Perry; c. Mary Sue (Mrs. Robert Stovall) and Linda Faye. Educ: Morehead State Univ. Teaching Cert, 39; Jefferson Sch. of Law, Louisville, Ky, LL.B, 49. Polit. & Govt. Pos: City attorney, Vanceburg, Ky, 53-57; commonwealth attorney, 20th Judicial Dist. of Ky, 58- Mil. Serv: Entered as Pvt, Army, 44, released as First Sgt, 46. Mem: Lions; Farm Bur; Am. Legion. Rel: Protestant. Mailing Add: P.O. Box 36, Vanceburg, Ky. 41179.

KIBBIE, JOHN P. D
b. Palo Alto Co, Iowa, 7/14/29; m. 1958 to Alice Austin; c. Luanne, Jackie, Patrick John, James and Margaret Helen. Educ: Silver Lake High Sch, 47. Polit. & Govt. Pos: Iowa State Rep, two terms; Dem. co. chmn, 10 years; Iowa State Sen, 66-68; del, Dem. Nat. Conv, 68. Bus. & Prof. Pos: Farmer. Mil. Serv: Tank Comdr, Army, Korea. Mem: K. of C; Am. Legion; Farmers Union; Nat. Farmers Orgn. Outstanding Young Man of Am, 65; C.Y.O. Adult Leadership Award, 67. Rel: Catholic. Mailing Add: R.F.D. 2, Box 520, Emmetsburg, Iowa 50536.

KIBBIE, RICHARD PATRICK D
Chmn, Palo Alto Co. Dem. Cent. Cmt, Iowa
b. Ayrshire, Iowa, 9/3/33; s. Joseph Emmet Kibbie and Gertrude McCarugy K; single. Educ: Ayrshire Consol. High Sch, 4 years, dipl. Polit. & Govt. Pos: Chmn, Palo Alto Co. Dem. Cent. Cmt, Iowa, 66- Mil. Serv: Entered as

Pvt, Army, 54, released as Sp-4/C, 56, after serv. in Transportation Corps, Arctic Group, Greenland, as high speed radio operator, 55-56. Mem: Emmetsburg Iowa Country Club. Rel: Catholic. Mailing Add: Route 1, Curlew, Iowa 50527.

KICKBUSH, ROBERT JAMES R
b. Cattaraugus, N.Y, 5/21/24; s. Leonard H. Kickbush (deceased) and Rena Boberg K; m. 6/30/47 to Jeanette Heber; c. Charlene, Brian, Rogene, Brent, Bruce, Lorene and Janene. Educ: Valparaiso Univ, B.A, 50; Univ. of Buffalo, M.B.A, 55. Polit. & Govt. Pos: Town Justice, Otto, N.Y, 51-58; v.chmn, Cattaraugus Co. Rep. Party, 66-68; civil serv. cmnr, Cattaraugus Co, 68-; legis. aide, N.Y. State Assembly, 68- Bus. & Prof. Pos: Purchasing agent and traffic mgr, U.S. Plywood Corp, E.P. Div, 50-; dir, Tri Co. Hosp, Gowanda, N.Y, 68- Mil. Serv: Entered as Seaman, Navy, 42, released as YNSl, 46, after serv. in Seabees, Pac. Theatre, 44-46; Navy Res, 46-54, with serv. in Off. of Chief of Naval Opers, Pentagon, 51-52. Mem: Am. Legion; Magistrates' Asn. Rel: Lutheran. Legal Res: 113 Main St, Otto, N.Y. 14766. Mailing Add: Box 55, Otto, N.Y. 14766.

KIDD, D. THOMAS R
b. Laramie, Wyo, 2/1/34; m. to Sally; c. Two. Educ: Dartmouth Col; Univ. Wyo, B.A, LL.B. Polit. & Govt. Pos: House attorney, 61; State Rep, until 67. Bus. & Prof. Pos: Lawyer. Mem: Wyo. State Bar Asn; ABA; Natrona Co. Bar Asn; Kiwanis. Rel: Episcopalian. Mailing Add: 3321 Carol Dr, Casper, Wyo. 82601. (1967)

KIDD, PAUL H. D
b. Glenville, W.Va, 3/12/07; s. Lelia Johnson and Sen. R.F. Kidd (deceased); m. 6/1/32 to Marie Tinney; c. Paul Eakle, Shirley Marie (Mrs. Robert White). Educ: Glenville State Col; W.Va. Univ. Col. of Law. Polit. & Govt. Pos: W.Va. State Del, 36-38, 46-50 & 54-66; mem, Dem. State Exec. Cmt, 36-40; dep. state securities cmnr, 52-54; dep. cmnr, forfeited and delinquent lands. Bus. & Prof. Pos: Lawyer. Mem: Am. and W.Va. Bar Asns; Rotary. Rel: Methodist. Mailing Add: Glenville, W.Va. 26351. (1967)

KIDO, MITSUYUKI D
b. Keahua, Maui, Hawaii, 9/7/06; s. KiuKichi Kido and Masue Tsuchiyama K; m. 12/23/38 to Shigeko Eguchi; c. Lynette. Educ: Univ. Hawaii, B.A, 28, M.Ed, 38; Phi Beta Kappa, Phi Kappa Phi; Pi Gamma Mu. Polit. & Govt. Pos: Hawaii Territorial Rep, 46-52; supvr, City and Co. Honolulu, 52-56; Hawaii Territorial Sen, 56-59; Hawaii State Sen, 62-66; del, Dem. Nat. Conv, 68. Bus. & Prof. Pos: V.chmn. bd, Cent. Pac. Bank, Honolulu, 52-; dir, Aloha Airlines, Inc, 58-; chmn. bd, K. Yamada Distributors, Inc, 64-; pres, Universal Am. Export Corp, 65- Mem: Hon. mem, 442 Vets. Club. Rel: Protestant. Legal Res: 404 N. Kuakini St, Honolulu, Hawaii 96817. Mailing Add: 33 S. King St, Honolulu, Hawaii 96813. (1967)

KIDWELL, ALLEN V. D
b. Kingston, Tenn, 2/19/32; s. Allen V. Kidwell and Annie Young K; m. 4/4/52 to Virginia Hannah; c. Karen Kay. Educ: Univ. Tenn, B.S, 56 and LL.B, 59; Phi Kappa Phi; Phi Delta Phi. Polit. & Govt. Pos: Mem, Tenn. Cmn. of Inter-Govt. Corp, Dem. Exec. Cmt, Coun. State Govt. and Tenn. Legis. Coun; del, Constitutional Conv, Tenn, 59; Tenn. State Rep, 61-68; city judge, Oak Ridge, 65- Bus. & Prof. Pos: Attorney-at-Law, 59- Mem: Anderson Co, Tenn. and Am. Bar Asns; C. of C.(dir, Oak Ridge Chap, 64-); Oak Ridge Boys Club (dir, 65-); Elks; Am. Legion; Amvets; Eagles; Oak Ridge Country Club. Rel: Presbyterian. Mailing Add: 101 E. Tennessee Ave, Oak Ridge, Tenn. 37830. (1967)

KIDWELL, ALVIN D
b. Oldham, Ky, 11/27/93; s. Thomas S. Kidwell and Nannie Butler; m. 6/23/34 to Josephine Graham. Polit. & Govt. Pos: Ky. State Sen, 42-65. Bus. & Prof. Pos: Nurseryman, Willadean Nursery, 29- and Dews Nursery, 23- Mil. Serv: Entered as Pvt, Army, 18, released as Sgt, 19. Mem: Mason; Am. Legion. Rel: Methodist. Mailing Add: Sparta, Ky. 41086. (1967)

KIDWELL, THOMAS McKINLEY D
b. Augusta, Kans, 9/10/20; s. Joseph McKinley Kidwell and Frances Thomas K; m. to Betty Jean Thompson, wid; c. Diana Jean and Kimberlyn Kay. Educ: St. Johns Col, Winfield, Kans, 36-40. Polit. & Govt. Pos: Kans. State Rep, 69th Dist, 65-66. Bus. & Prof. Pos: Owner and operator, Consolidated Freightways Inc, 55-65 and Kidwell Trucking Serv, 65- Mem: Moose; Eagles. Rel: Lutheran. 1967 Legal Res: Wichita, Kans. No mailing address available. (1967)

KIDWELL, WAYNE LE ROY R
Idaho State Sen.
b. Council, Idaho, 6/15/38; s. John A. Kidwell and Estelle Irene Konkle K; m. 7/25/62 to Shari Lynn; c. Dale E. and Vaughn W. Educ: Univ. Idaho, B.S, 60, LL.B, 64; Sigma Chi; Delta Sigma Rho; Phi Alpha Delta; Bench and Bar; Sr. Honor Court. Polit. & Govt. Pos: Chmn, Univ. Idaho Young Rep, 63; research asst. for U.S. Sen. Len Jordan, 63; prosecuting attorney, Ada Co, 66-68; Idaho State Sen, 69-, chmn. local govt. and taxation cmt, 69- Bus. & Prof. Pos: Lawyer, 64-66. Mil. Serv: Entered as 2nd Lt, Army, 60, released as 1st Lt, 61, after serv. in Mil. Police Corps, Korea, 13 months. Publ: Prosecuting Attorney's Form Book, 67. Mem: Idaho State, Fourth Judicial and Am. Bar Asns; Idaho Peace Officers Asn; Am. Trial Lawyers Asn; mem. faculty, Univ. Idaho Exten. Prog; Idaho Prosecuting Attorney's Asn; U.S. Fed. Dist. Court; Nation Dist. Attorney's Asn; Am. Judicature Soc; Mason; adv, Boise Col. Criminology Cmt; Scottish Rite; Shrine; Nat. adv. bd, Col. Young Rep. Outstanding Young Man, Jr. C. of C. Award, 67. Rel: Methodist. Legal Res: 1902 Empire Way, Boise, Idaho 83705. Mailing Add: P.O. Box 519, Boise, Idaho 83701.

KIEFER, ALFRED W. D
b. Jersey City, N.J, 1/5/12; m. to Carolyn Zaeh; c. Barbara. Educ: Columbia Col, 28-30; John Marshall Col. of Law, LL.B. cum laude, 33. Polit. & Govt. Pos: Former borough attorney, Little Ferry, Little Ferry Bd. of Educ. and Hasbrouck Heights Bd. of Educ; N.J. State Sen, 66-67. Bus. & Prof. Pos: Sr. mem, Kiefer, Bollermann and Durkin Law Firm; dir. and treas, Nat. Beryllia Corp. Mem: C. of C.(former pres, Hackensack Chap); pres, South Bergen Hosp; gen. counsel, N.J. Synod of Lutheran Churches of Am; past pres, Bergen Co. Coun. of Churches; trustee and pres, N.J. Coun. of Churches; mem. study cmt. for Bergen Co. Col. Mailing Add: 303 Washington Place, Hasbrouck Heights, N.J. 07604.

KIEFER, EDGAR L. R
State Committeeman, Fla. Rep. Party
b. Newark, N.J, 5/25/92; s. Carl J.J. Kiefer and Lina Ziegler K; m. 12/6/46 to Carolyn Isabella Fletcher. Educ: Clason Point Mil. Acad. Polit. & Govt. Pos: Asst. to chmn, Pinellas Co. Rep. Party, Fla, 58-61; chmn, Pinellas Co. Rep. Exec. Cmt, 61-; del, Rep. Nat. Conv, 68; state committeeman, Fla. Rep. Party, 68- Bus. & Prof. Pos: Actor and singer, shows and vaudeville, 20-30; mgr, theatrical co, 30-41; regional rep, Pepsi-Cola Co, N.Y.C, 42-58. Cited as Mr. Republican by elected officials for work during 1968 Rep. Campaign. Rel: Presbyterian. Legal Res: 4525 Hyacinth Way, South St. Petersburg, Fla. 33705. Mailing Add: Pinellas County Republican Executive Cmt, P.O. Box 7384, St. Petersburg, Fla. 33734.

KIERNAN, JAMES HENRY D
b. Providence, R.I, 9/1/84. Educ: Univ. R.I, LL.D, hon, 63. Polit. & Govt. Pos: Majority leader, R.I. State House of Reps, 41-67, mem, 15-67; mem, Gov. Fiscal Adv. Coun, 50; chmn, 6th Ward Dem. Club; mem, Dem. State Cmt; Dem. Exec. Cmt; Dem. Nat. Cmt, 60-64; v.chmn, R.I. Del. to Dem. Nat. Conv, 48. Bus. & Prof. Pos: Attorney; official starter, U.S. Trotting Asn, R.I. Mem: ABA; R.I. Bar Asn; pres, Friendly Sons of St. Patrick, 42; K. of C; Aerie; Eagle; AOH; Sons of Irish Kings; R.I. Driving Club; VFW; R.I. Police Chief's Asn, hon. mem. Rel: Catholic. Mailing Add: 122 Beaufort St, Providence, R.I. 02908. (1967)

KIILSHOLM, KARL ERIK R
b. Algona, Iowa, 10/13/24; s. Viggo Kiilsholm and Camilla Wendner K; m. 6/17/50 to Fidelia Evelyn Skow; c. Bonita, Edward and Timothy. Educ: Teachers Col. in Denmark, 50. Polit. & Govt. Pos: Precinct, chmn, Rep. Party, Algona, Iowa, 65-66; Iowa State Rep, 67-68. Mem: Farm Bur; Toastmasters Int. Rel: Presbyterian. Mailing Add: R.R. 2, Box 232, Algona, Iowa 50511. (1967)

KILBURN, CLARENCE EVANS R
b. Malone, N.Y, 4/13/93; s. Frederick Douglas Kilburn and Clara Barry K; m. 8/16/17 to Anne Elizabeth Crooks; c. James Crooks, Katharine (Mrs. Bullard) and William Barry. Educ: Cornell Univ, B.A, 16; St. Lawrence Univ, hon. LL.B, 58; Psi Upsilon. Polit. & Govt. Pos: U.S. Rep, N.Y, 40-65. Bus. & Prof. Pos: Pres, Kirk-Maher Ice Cream Co, Malone, N.Y, 21-26; managing dir, Gen. Ice Cream Corp, 26-30; pres, Peoples Trust Co, Malone, 30-55; v.pres, North. N.Y. Trust Co, 55-58. Mil. Serv: Entered as 1st Lt, Army, 17, released as Capt, 18. Mem: Mason; Elks; Am. Legion; VFW. Rel: Methodist. Mailing Add: 59 Milwaukee St, Malone, N.Y. 12953.

KILBURY, CHARLES DEBRIEL D
State Committeeman, Wash. State Dem. Party.
b. Yakima, Wash, 2/2/19; s. George William Kilbury and Rosa Hawthorne K; m. 6/27/44 to Florence delGrosso; c. Brian Michael, Kathleen and Dennis Patrick. Educ: Yakima Valley Jr. Col. Polit. & Govt. Pos: Mem, Planning Cmn, Pasco, Wash, 56-60; Dem. precinct committeeman, Precinct 5, 56-; mem, Gov. Bd. for Employ. of Offenders, 58-62; councilman Pasco, 60-64; chmn, Franklin Co. Dem. Cent. Cmt, 62-68, exec. secy, 68-; Presidential elector, 64; chmn, Fourth Cong. Dist. Dem. Coun, 64-69, exec. secy, 69-; chmn, Franklin Co. Dem. Club, 68-69; state committeeman, Wash. State Dem. Party, 68- Bus. & Prof. Pos: Yardmaster, North. Pac. Rwy. Co, 51-65; ins. agent, Farmers Ins, 54-65; ins. broker, Kilbury Ins, 66- Mil. Serv: Entered as Seaman, 40, released as Master Merchant Marine, 46; Lt. Comdr, Merchant Marine, 46- Mem: Charter mem. and past pres, Pasco Exchange Club; BRT (legis. rep, Lodge 667); United Transportation Union (chmn. consol. cmt, 69-); Rwy. Labor Coun.(founder, pres. and pres. emer); trustee, Benton-Franklin Cent. Labor Coun; bd. dirs, Lincoln Terr. Housing Proj. Legal Res: 1840 W. Margaret, Pasco, Wash. 99301. Mailing Add: Box 2482 Tri Cities, Wash. 99302.

KILCHER, YULE F. D
b. Laufen, Switzerland, 3/9/13; s. Edwin Kilcher and Lina Alter K; m. 7/23/41 to Ruth Helen Weber; c. Mairiis, Wurtila, Fay, Attila Kuno, Sunrise, Edwin Otto, Stella and Catkin. Educ: Univ. Berlin, 32-33; Univ. Berne, 33-34; Univ. Grenoble, B.A, 35. Polit. Pos: Alaska State Sen, 63-67; del, Alaska Constitutional Conv, 55-56. Bus. & Prof. Pos: Pres, Totem Builders, Inc, 66. Publn: Carpathian Culture,' Aftenposten, Norway, 38; TV Color Short, Pioneer Family, on series, It's a Small World. Mem: 55 Club; dir, Fox River Cattlemen's Asn. and pres, 62. 50 Kilometer Champion, Swiss Academic Races, 35. Rel: Unitarian. Legal Res: McNeil Canyon, Homer, Alaska 99603. Mailing Add: Box 353, Homer, Alaska 99603. (1967)

KILDAHL, ERLING OLIVER R
b. Whitehall, Wis, 7/25/28; s. Einar Kildahl and Olga Foss K. (deceased); m. 6/5/54 to Margrete Elaine Christianson; c. Daniel Nash and Heidi Christine. Educ: First Cavalry Div. Clerk Typist Sch, Japan; Northwest Schs, Correspondence Course in TV-Radio Repair, Portland, Ore. Polit. & Govt. Pos: Chmn, Houston Co. Rep. Party, Minn, 65-68. Mil. Serv: Entered as Pvt, Army, 49, released as S/Sgt, 53, after serv. in Japan, 49-53 and as clerk typist for Army Air Force Courier Serv, D.C, 53. Mem: Mason; Houston Co. Farm Bur.(bd. dirs); Minn. Farm Bur; Am. Legion. Rel: Lutheran; Mem. Bd. Educ, Cross of Christ Lutheran Church of Houston. Mailing Add: R.R. 1, Houston, Minn, 55943. (1967)

KILDEE, DALE E. D
Mich. State Rep.
b. Flint, Mich, 9/16/29; m. 2/27/65 to Gayle Heyn. Educ: Sacred Heart Sem, B.A; Univ. Detroit, teacher's cert; Univ. Mich, M.A; grad. studies in hist. and polit. sci. under a Rotary Found. Fel. at the Univ. Peshawar, Pakistan; Phi Delta Kappa. Polit. & Govt. Pos: Mich. State Rep, 64-, mem, Appropriations Cmt, chmn, Sub-Cmt. on Pub. Safety & Defense and mem, Intergovt. Coop. Cmn, currently; del, Dem. Nat. Conv, 68. Bus. & Prof. Pos: Teacher. Mem: Optimists; Urban League; K. of C; Am. Fedn. of Teachers. Rel: Catholic. Mailing Add: 2317 E. Court St, Flint, Mich. 48503.

KILEY, DANIEL PATRICK, JR. D
Mayor, Lawrence, Mass.
b. Lawrence, Mass, 3/8/24; s. Daniel Patrick Kiley and Margaret Monahan K; m. 4/4/43 to Marcia Elizabeth Peterson; c. Daniel Patrick, III, Thomas M, Ellen, Marcia E, Mark P. and Robert P. Educ: Univ. N.H, 42-43 & 46-47; Boston Col. Law Sch, LL.B, 49; Sigma Beta. Polit. & Govt. Pos: Asst. Attorney Gen, Mass, 59-63; mayor, Lawrence, 66-; del, Dem. Nat. Conv, 68. Mil. Serv: Entered as Pvt, Army, 43, released, 46, after serv. in Combat Engrs. 78th Div, European Theatre, 44-46. Mem: Mass. and Fed. Bar Asns; Univ. N.H. and Boston Col. Alumni; Boston Col. Law Club; Am. Legion; VFW. Rel: Catholic. Legal Res: 635 Haverhill St, Lawrence, Mass. 01840. Mailing Add: 200 Common St, Lawrence, Mass. 01840.

KILEY, RICHARD B. D
R.I. State Rep.
b. Pawtucket, R.I; m. to Ann T. Educ: Providence Col, 1959. Polit. & Govt. Pos: R.I. State Rep, 64- Bus. & Prof. Pos: V.pres, Daniel P. Kiley Inc. Mil. Serv: Army Res, Six years CID. Mailing Add: 517 Pleasant St, Pawtucket, R.I. 02860. (1967)

KILFOY, FRED F. D
b. Muskogee, Okla, 7/22/11; m. to Helen; c. five. Educ: 1 year col; pres, High Sch. 4H. Polit. & Govt. Pos: Former Wyo. State Rep. and Riverton City Councilman. Bus. & Prof. Pos: Gen. contractor; motel owner. Mem: Mason; Shrine; Rel: Baptist. Mailing Add: 119 W. Main St, Riverton, Wyo. 82501. (1967)

KILGARLIN, WILLIAM WAYNE D
b. Houston, Tex, 11/29/32; s. William Kilgarlin and Juanita Lawther K; m. 12/28/63 to Margaret Rose Kruppa. Educ: Univ. Houston, B.S; Univ. Tex, LL.B; Phi Theta Kappa. Polit. & Govt. Pos: Chmn, Harris Co. Dem. Party, 62-66; pres, Young Dem. Clubs of Tex, 59-61; Tex. State Rep, 58-60. Mil. Serv: Entered as 2nd Lt, Army, 55, released as 1st Lt. Mem: Park Place Lodge 1172, AF&AM; Tex. Bill of Rights Found. Rel: Methodist. Legal Res: 305 Glenwood Dr, Houston, Tex. 77007. Mailing Add: 500 State Nat. Bldg, Houston, Tex. 77002. (1967)

KILGORE, JOE MADISON D
b. Brown Co, Tex, 12/10/18; s. William H. Kilgore and Myrtle Armstrong K; m. 7/28/45 to Jane Redman; c. Mark, Shannon, Dean and William. Educ: Westmoorland Col, San Antonio, Tex, 35-36; Univ. Tex, 36-37, 38-41 and 45-46; Delta Theta Phi. Polit. & Govt. Pos: Tex. State Rep, 47-55; del, Tex. Dem. State Conv, 47-66; U.S. Rep, 15th Dist, Tex, 55-65; del, Dem. Nat. Conv, 56, 60 & 68; chmn, Water Adv. Panel, Tex. Water Develop. Bd, 65-66. Bus. & Prof. Pos: Partner, McGinnis, Lochridge, Kilgore, Byfield, Hunter & Wilson, 65-; dir, Tex. State Bank, Austin, 66-; mem. bd. dir, First State Bank & Trust Co, Mission, 66-; mem, Nat. Pollution Control Found, Inc; mem, Coun. Admin. Conf. U.S; bd. regent, Univ. Tex. Syst. Mil. Serv: Entered as Aviation Cadet, Army Air Corps, 41, released as Maj, 45, after serv. in Ninth Bomber Command, Mediterranean Theater, 42-43; Silver Star; Distinguished Flying Cross, Air Medal with two Oak Leaf Clusters; Commendation Medal with Oak Leaf Cluster; Am. Defense Serv. Medal; Am. Theater Campaign Medal with four Bronze Serv. Stars; World War II Victory Medal; Maj. Gen, Air Force Res, currently. Mem: Am, Tex. and Travis Co. Bar Asns; dir, Austin C. of C, 67-; bd. trustees, United Fund, Austin, 67- Rel: Methodist. Legal Res: 3311 River Rd, Austin, Tex. 78703. Mailing Add: 1030 Brown Bldg, Austin, Tex. 78701.

KILHAM, DIXIE DONALD D
b. Pittsburgh, Pa. 3/5/20; s. Richard D. Kilham and Edna Merryman K; div; c. Dianna. Educ: Baltimore City Col, 4 years; Duke Univ, 2 years; Univ. Md. Sch. of Law, LL.B. and J.D, 49. Polit. & Govt. Pos: Mem, W.Va. Arts and Humanities Coun, 67-; alternate del, Dem. Nat. Conv, 68; chmn, Jefferson Co. Humphrey for Pres, W.Va, 68; mem. exec. cmt. and bd. dirs, Partners for the Alliance, Alliance for Progress Sister State Prog, W.Va. and Espirito Santo, Brazil, 68- Bus. & Prof. Pos: Attorney-at-law, Baltimore, Md, 49-65; pres, Hilltop Theatre Sch. of Arts, 54-63; owner-mgr, Hilltop House Hotel-Restaurant, Coffee Mill Restaurant, Coach House Gifts and John Brown Wax Mus, Harpers Ferry, W.Va, 55- Mil. Serv: Entered as Pvt, Army Air Force, 43, released as Sgt, 46; Good Conduct Medal; Am. Theatre Ribbon; World War II Victory Medal. Mem: Jefferson Co. C. of C.(bd. dirs); W.Va. Restaurant Asn.(bd. dirs). Rel: Episcopal. Mailing Add: Hilltop House, Ridge St, Harpers Ferry, W.Va. 25425.

KILLAM, ANNE LORETTA D
Committeewoman, Colo. State Dem. Cent. Cmt.
b. Columbus, Ohio, 8/10/28; d. Walter James Schirtzinger and Loretta Stine S; m. 11/19/49 to John George Killam; c. Mary, John Richard, Robert G. and Annette Marie. Educ: Ohio State Univ, 1 year. Polit. & Govt. Pos: Committeewoman, Adams Co. Dem. Cmt, Colo, 62-; dist. capt, Westminster area, 64-66; committeewoman, Colo. State Dem. Cent. Cmt, 64-; dist. capt, Sherrelwood area, 66-68; asst. mgr, Westminster Dem. Hq. Orgn, 67; treas, Jane Jefferson Dem. Club, 69- Bus. & Prof. Pos: Supvr, Nationwide Ins. Co, 47-50. Mem: PTA; Beta Sigma Phi. Rel: Catholic. Mailing Add: 7961 Valley View Dr, Denver, Colo. 80221.

KILLEY, RALPH ALLEN R
Chmn, Warren Co. Rep. Party, Ill.
b. Ill, 3/7/08; s. Phillip Isaac Killey and Alice Winebright K; m. 5/27/32 to Frances Brent; c. Barbara, Lester, William and Frank. Educ: High Sch. and Brown's Bus. Col. Polit. & Govt. Pos: Farmer coordinator, Goldwater Campaign, Ill, 64; mem. platform cmt, Ill. Rep. Conv, 66; del, Rep. Nat. Conv, 68; chmn, Warren Co. Rep. Party, currently. Bus. & Prof. Pos: Farmer. Mem: Farm Bur; Shrine; Monmouth Col. Asn. Rel: Methodist. Mailing Add: Route 4, Monmouth, Ill. 61462. (1967)

KILLIAN, ROBERT KENNETH D
Attorney General, Conn.
b. Hartford, Conn, 9/15/19; s. Edward Francis Killian and Annie Nemser K; m. 12/7/42 to Mildred Evelyn Farnan; c. Robert Kenneth, Jr. and Cynthia Elaine. Educ: Union Col, N.Y, B.A, 42; Univ. Conn, LL.B, 48; Pres, Student Coun. and Student Body; Beta Theta Pi. Polit. & Govt. Pos: Asst. corp. counsel, Hartford, Conn, 51-54; chmn, Hartford Dem. town cmt, 63-67; attorney general, Conn, 67- Bus. & Prof. Pos: Law partner, Gould, Killian & Krechevsky, Hartford, 48- Mil. Serv: Entered as Pvt, Army, 42, released as 1st Lt, 46, after serv. in Inf, Pac. Theatre, 43-46; Purple Heart. Mem: Am. Judicature Soc; Am. Trial Lawyers Soc; Am, Conn. and Hartford Co. Bar Asns; chmn. Conn. Cmt, Nat. Jewish Hosp. & Research Center, Denver, 68-; trustee, Hartford Div, Conn. Cancer Soc, 59-; mem. bd. dir, Hartford Legal Aid Soc, 67- Man of the Year, Columbus Day Cmt, 67. Rel: Roman Catholic. Legal Res: 234 Terry Rd, Hartford, Conn. 06105. Mailing Add: 37 Lewis St, Hartford, Conn. 06103.

KILLIAN, WILLIAM RUSSELL D
b. Gadsden, Ala, 11/15/20; s. Paul Killian and Nell Russell K; m. 1/12/45 to Peggy Ruth Harper; c. William Russell, Jr, Robert Paul, Nell Marie. Educ: Grad. Glynn Acad, 39; Univ. Ga, LL.B, 43; Sigma Chi. Polit. & Govt. Pos: Judge of Munic. Court, Brunswick, Ga, 52-53; Ga. State Rep, 55-64; U.S. Cmnr, Brunswick Div. of the U.S. Dist. Court for South. Dist. of Ga, 58-59. Bus. & Prof. Pos: Attorney. Mil. Serv: Army, ETO. Mem: Brunswick Bar Asn.(pres, 58-59); Am. Legion; Elks. Rel: Presbyterian. Mailing Add: Brunswick, Ga. 31520.

KILPATRICK, BISHOP ROBBINS D
Ohio State Sen.
b. Warren, Ohio, 12/10/06; s. William Bishop Kilpatrick and Dorothy Robbins K; m. 12/10/44 to Dorla Trask Taylor. Polit. & Govt. Pos: Ohio State Rep, 35-67; dep. collector, Internal Revenue Dept, 45-49; Ohio State Sen, 67- Bus. & Prof. Pos: Tax consult, 49- Mil. Serv: Entered as Pfc, Army Res, 41, released in 43, after serv. as Civilian Pilot Training Instr. Mem: Silver Wings; Ox-5; Elks; SAR. Rel: Christian Church. Mailing Add: 195 Oak Knoll Ave. N.E, Warren, Ohio 44483.

KILPATRICK, KENNETH D
b. Forest Park, Ga, 11/5/33; s. George Madison Kilpatrick and Mary Mitchell K; m. 12/18/58 to Martha Blaney; c. Scott Ethan and Lee Madison. Educ: Ga. State Col, B.B.A, 54; Univ. Ga. Sch. Law, LL.B, 56; Blue Key; Phi Alpha Delta. Polit. & Govt. Pos: Former Ga. State Sen, 44th Dist. Bus. & Prof. Pos: City attorney, Lake City, Ga, 62- and Forest Park, Ga, 64- Mil. Serv: Entered as A/S, Naval Res, 56, released as Lt.(jg), 59, after serv. in West. Pac. Mem: Clayton Co, Ga. and Am. Bar Asns; Kiwanis. Rel: Episcopal. Legal Res: 102 N. Cheryl Dr, Morrow, Ga. 30260. Mailing Add: 134 W. Mill St, Jonesboro, Ga. 30236. (1967)

KILPATRICK, RUFUS UNDERWOOD D
Tex. State Rep.
b. Beaumont, Tex, 3/17/16; s. Rufus Frank Kilpatrick and Annie Ruth Williams K; m. 3/23/46 to Ruby Pearl Nappier; c. Rufus Underwood, Jr, Emery Dale, William Gerard, Ruby Dianne and Bradford Lee. Polit. & Govt. Pos: Tex. State Rep, 55- Bus. & Prof. Pos: Owner, Kilpatrick's Transfer & Storage Co, 37- and Kilpatrick's Pallet Mfg. Co, 60-; pres, Kilpatrick's Bonded Warehouse Inc, 60- Mil. Serv: Entered as Pvt, Army, 44, released as Pfc, 46; Am. and Asiatic Pac. Theater Ribbons; Victory Medal. Mem: Tex. Motor Transportation Asn; Southwest Warehouseman's Asn; Bus. & Prfnl. Men's Club; Am. Legion; VFW; 40 et 8; Elks; Optimists; Gulf Coast Rod Reel and Gun Club. Rel: Church of Christ. Mailing Add: 260 E. Circuit Dr, Beaumont, Tex. 77706.

KILVER, WAYNE M. D
Chmn, Scott Co. Dem. Orgn, Ill.
b. Winchester, Ill, 4/14/28; s. Clifford R. Kilver and Helen L. Massey K; m. 6/26/66 to Phyllis G. Strawn. Educ: Winchester High Sch, 46. Polit. & Govt. Pos: Chmn, Scott Co. Dem. Orgn, Ill, 59- Mil. Serv: Entered as Pvt, Army, 51, released as Sgt, 53, after serv. in Signal Corps, Korea; Good Conduct Medal; Korean Medal. Mem: Odd Fellows; Mason; Shrine; Consistory; Am. Legion; Farm Bur; Elks. Rel: Methodist. Mailing Add: R.R. 1, Winchester, Ill. 62694. (1967)

KIM, JOHN EN SUK R
b. Honolulu, Hawaii, 9/15/21; s. Won Sam Kim and Myung Soon Park K; m. 9/6/47 to Edith Leong; c. Beverly S.B. and Barbara Ann. Educ: Pearl Harbor Apprentice Sch, Journeyman, 4 years; Univ. Hawaii, Bus, 2 years. Polit. & Govt. Pos: Rep. precinct pres, 62-66; Rep. State Conv. chmn, 64; Rep. dist. chmn, 66-68; alternate del, Rep. Nat. Conv, 68. Bus. & Prof. Pos: Supvr, Pearl Harbor Naval Shipyard, 40-59; gen. mgr. and owner, United Delivery Serv, 59-62; pub. rel. asst, AmFac, Inc, 62-69. Mil. Serv: Entered as Pvt, Army, 45, released as S/Sgt, 47, after serv. in Counter Intel. Corps, Hawaii and Korea. Rel: Episcopal. Mailing Add: 1410 Kohou St, Honolulu, Hawaii 96817.

KIMBALL, EDWARD W. R
b. Haverhill; m. to Elizabeth J. Benner; c. four. Educ: Burdett Col; Col. of Bus. Admin, Boston Univ, B.S. Polit. & Govt. Pos: Sch. Cmt, 51-; former mem. High Sch. Bldg. Cmt. and Recreation Cmn; former pres. of Young Men's Bus. Coun; former pres. Commun. Coun. of Gr. Haverhill; mem. and secy, Haverhill Dist, Ins. Workers Int. Union, AFL-CIO. Bus. & Prof. Pos: Life ins. agent, John Hancock Mutual Life Ins. Co. Mil. Serv: Navy, WWII. Mem: John Greenleaf Whittier PTA; chmn, YMCA Jr. Football League, 64. Mailing Add: 24 Seventeenth Ave, Haverhill, Mass. 01830. (1967)

KIMBALL, HAYFORD T. R
N.H. State Rep.
b. Chester, N.H, 11/30/93; married; c. two. Educ: Pinkerton Acad, Derry, N.H. Polit. & Govt. Pos: Mem, Town Govt. Study Cmt; Rockingham Co. Court House Construction Cmt; Derry Rep. Club; N.H. State Rep, 59- Bus. & Prof. Pos: Bd. dirs, Derry Coop. Bank; pres, Derry Develop. Corp. Mem: Nufield, State and Nat. Granges; Odd Fellows; Kiwanis; Barbershoppers; Chester Rod & Gun Club; State Grange Tax Cmt. Mailing Add: 13 Clark St, Derry, N.H. 03038. (1967)

KIMBRELL, J.P.
Tenn. State Rep.
b. West Point, Tenn, 5/3/95; married. Polit. & Govt. Pos: Tenn. State Rep, 24th Floterial Dist, currently. Mailing Add: Route 1, Westpoint, Tenn. 38486.

KIMBROUGH, LORRAINE M. D
b. Ft. Worth, Tex, 7/25/21; s. Richard Bland Mumford and Sallie Eva Hudson M; m. 12/23/43 to Calvin Rayburn; c. Calvin Rayburn, Richard Earl. Educ: Brantley Draughon Bus. Col, Ft. Worth. Polit. & Govt. Pos: Secy, Rep. Ray Roberts; clerk, Speaker Rayburn, 47-62. Legal Res: Sherman, Tex. 79605. Mailing Add: 5305 Seventh St, S. Arlington, Va. 22204. (1967)

KIME, ALLAN G. R
S.Dak. State Rep.
b. Kennedy, Nebr, 12/5/99; married; c. one daughter. Polit. & Govt. Pos: Former supvr, Gregory Co. Soil Conserv. Dist; dir, Sch. Bd, 10 years; precinct assessor, 8 years; S.Dak. State Rep, 58- Bus. & Prof. Pos: Rancher. Mem: Dir, Gregory Co. Livestock Improv. Asn; dir, S.Dak. Feeder Cattle Asn; AF&AM 148, Burke, Oriental Consistory, Yankton, El Riad Shrine. Rel: Presbyterian. Mailing Add: Burke, S.Dak. 57523.

KIME, F. WILLARD R
b. Hartford, Mich, 4/9/98; s. George W. Kime and Arminta Graff K; m. 1/21/17 to Jennie B. Hope. Educ: Univ. Wash, 1 year; Ore. State Col, E.E, 24; Kalamazoo Col, B.S, 30; Emanuel Col, B.D, 40; Mich. State Univ, Ph.D, 58. Polit. & Govt. Pos: V.chmn, Kalamazoo Co. Dem. Party, Mich, 33-35; chief auditor, Mich. State Hwy. Dept, 34-42; U.S. Govt. acct. and investr, 42-45, postmaster, 46-53; city clerk, Bangor, Mich, 48-50, v.chmn, Charter Cmn, 66, mem, City Planning Cmn, 66-68; mem, State Bd. of Alcoholism, 59-61; chmn, Van Buren Co. Dem. Party, 66-67. Bus. & Prof. Pos: Secy-treas, D'Arcy Spring Corp, Kalamazoo, Mich, 25-34; engr. and acct, Bangor, 46-50; Congregational minister, 50-65. Mil. Serv: Entered as Pvt, Army, 17, released as Lt, 19, after serv. in Seventh and 20th Field Artil, Eng. and France, 18-19; Distinguished Serv. Cross. Mem: Mich. Eng. Soc; Nat. Asn. Cost Acct; Nat. Asn. Hwy. Acct.(pres); VFW (nat. Comdr); Am. Legion; Mason (32°); Shrine; K.T; Kiwanis Int. Hon. degrees, VFW. Rel: Congregational. Mailing Add: 116 Randolph St, Bangor, Mich. 49013.

KIMMELL, CURTIS VOLLMER D
Mem, State Finance Cmt, Dem. Party, Ind.
b. Vincennes, Ind, 12/20/15; s. Joseph Woodman Kimmell and Cora Vollmer K; m. 9/2/39 to Dorothy Jane Funk; c. Kathryn Jane, Joseph W, II and Deborah Ann. Educ: Va. Mil. Inst, 33-34; Ind. Univ, LL.B, 34-39; Delta Upsilon. Polit. & Govt. Pos: Precinct committeeman, Dem. Party, 39-53; mem, Knox Co. Finance Cmt, Dem. Party, Ind, 46- and State Finance Cmt, 60-; state treas, Young Dem. and pres, Seventh Dist, 47-49; dep. prosecutor, Knox Co, 47-49; City attorney, Vincennes, 48-52 & 60-64; chmn, Dem. Seventh Cong. Dist, 49-52. Mil. Serv: Entered as A/S, Navy, 39, released as Lt.(sg), 45, after serv. in Am. and Pac. Theaters. Mem: Jr. C. of C.(pres,40); Knox Co. Bar Asn.(pres, 48); Elks (Exalted Ruler, 50-51); Shrine; Moose; Eagles; VFW; 40 et 8; Am. Legion; Corpus Lex; Indianapolis Athletic Club; Indianapolis Press Club; Antelope Club; Columbia Club, Indianapolis. Rel: Methodist. Mailing Add: 112 N. Seventh St, Vincennes, Ind. 47591.

KIMMITT, JOSEPH STANLEY D
Secy. for Majority, U.S. Senate
b. Lewistown, Mont, 4/5/18; m. 3/18/47 to Eunice L. Wegener; c. Robert M, Kathleen A, Joseph H, Thomas P, Mark T, Mary P. and Judy J. Educ: Utah State Univ, B.S, 60; George Washington Univ; Phi Sigma Kappa. Polit. & Govt. Pos: Admin. asst. to Majority Leader, U.S. Senate, Secy. for majority, U.S. Senate, 66- Mil. Serv: Entered as Pvt, Army, 41, released as Col, 66; Silver Star; Legion of Merit; Bronze Star with 3 Oak Leaf Clusters. Mem: Elks; K. of C. Awarded Order of Mennelik II for Valor, Ethiopia. Rel: Catholic. Legal Res: Great Falls, Mont. 59401. Mailing Add: 6004 Copley Lane, McLean, Va. 22101.

KIMMONS, JAMES ROYCE R
Chmn, Appling Co. Rep. Party, Ga.
b. Surrency, Ga, 4/1/32; s. Jacob Felix Kimmons and Lennie Bell Carter K; m. 10/23/60 to Margaret Joanne Bowser; c. Helen Suzzanne and Michael Royce. Educ: Univ. Ga, Waycross Center, 2 years. Polit. & Govt. Pos: City councilman, Surrency, Ga, 59-60; justice of the peace, 65-69; chmn, Appling Co. Rep. Party, currently. Bus. & Prof. Pos: Self-Employed. Mil. Serv: Entered as Pvt, Army, 55, released as E-4, after serv. in Tenth Div. Artillery Med. Detachment, Seventh Army, Germany, 55-56; SP-4, Army Res, 56-63. Mem: Moose; VFW; Kiwanis; Am. Farm Bur. Rel: Missionary Baptist. Mailing Add: P.O. Box 155, Surrency, Ga. 31563.

KIMURA, ROBERT YUTAKA D
Hawaii State Rep.
b. Honolulu, Hawaii, 8/12/24; s. Toraki Kimura and Shitsu Matsumori K; m. 11/2/57 to Elsie Kim; c. Robert, Jr, Kimberly, Arnold and Pamela. Educ: Univ. Hawaii, B.A, 48; Northwest. Univ. Sch. of Law, J.D, 51. Polit. & Govt. Pos: Milk cmnr, State Dept. Agr, Hawaii, 67-68; Hawaii State Rep, 68- Bus. & Prof. Pos: Instr. bus. law, Univ. Hawaii, 53-60; attorney-at-law, 53- Mil. Serv: Entered as Pvt, Army, 43, released as S/Sgt, 45, after serv. in Hq. Tenth Army, Asiatic-Pac. Theater, 44-45; Res, 45-67, Maj; Dept. Army Commendation Medal. Mem: Hawaii Bar Asn; Mil. Intel. Vet. Club Hawaii; Pauoa Commun. Asn. Rel: Protestant. Legal Res: 240 Puiwa Rd, Honolulu, Hawaii 96817. Mailing Add: Suite 446, Merchandise Mart Bldg, 184 S. Hotel St, Honolulu, Hawaii 96813.

KINALLY, NATHAN J. D
b. Chicago, Ill, 6/18/11; m. to Celeste Condon K; c. three daughters. Educ: U. of Chicago; Kent Col. of Law, Chicago. Polit. & Gov. Pos: Ill. State Sen, 3 terms; Ill. State Rep; Asst. States Attorney Cook Co, 17 years; Enforcement Dir. for Ill. U.S. Off. of Price Stabilization, 51-52. Bus. & Prof. Pos: Lawyer. Mil. Serv: U.S. Navy, W.W. II, Lt. Mem: K. of C. Rel: Roman Catholic. Mailing Add: 7234 S. Paxton Ave, Chicago, Ill. 60649 or 1 N. LaSalle St, Chicago Ill. 60602. (1967)

KINCAID, DONALD R. R
N.C. State Rep.
b. Lenoir, N.C, 6/2/36; s. Hugh Theodore Kincaid and Myrtle McCall K; m. 6/30/56 to Syretha Weatherford; c. Donald, Jr. and Lisa Anette. Educ: Appalachian State Teachers Col, B.S, 59. Polit. & Govt. Pos: N.C. State Rep, 67- Mil. Serv: Entered as Pvt, N.C. Nat. Guard, 53, released as E-5, 62. Mem: N.C. Educ. Asn, 60-64; Lenoir Lions Club. Rel: Baptist. Mailing Add: R.R. 6, Box 246, Lenoir, N.C. 28645.

KINCAID, HUGH ARTHUR D
W.Va. State Del.
b. Point Pleasant, W.Va, 2/2/11; s. Arthur O. Kincaid and Anna Jane Hunter K; m. 10/18/41 to Emma Lou Kittle; c. Hugh A, Jr, Catherine Ann (Mrs. Jack R. Blacka), Carroll Barte (Mrs. Charles F. Twiss), Charles M. and Jefferson C. Educ: Marshall Univ; Cincinnati Col. of Embalming. Polit. & Govt. Pos: Former mem, Cabell Co. Dem. Exec. Cmt, W.Va; W.Va. State Del, 54-56 & 58- Bus. & Prof. Pos: Mortician. Mem: Mason; Odd Fellows; Elks; Big Green Club; exec. cmt, YMCA; E. Huntington Civic Club; W. Huntington Commercial Club; Huntington C. of C; past pres, Huntington Jr. C. of C. Rel: Methodist. Mailing Add: 1544 5th Ave, Huntington, W.Va. 25701.

KINCER, RUPERT NEAL R
b. Wytheville, Va, 5/7/09; s. Wythe Gleaves Kincer and Bertie S. Riggle K; m. 10/12/29 to Louise E. Shupe; c. Reba Elizabeth (Mrs. W.M. Jennings, Jr.), Gary Rupert (deceased) and William Barton. Educ: Emory & Henry Col, 28-29; Hermesian Lit. Soc. Polit. & Govt. Pos: Va. State Del, Wythe Co, 64-66; mem, Wytheville Town Coun, 45-46. Bus. & Prof. Pos: Ins. Agent, 57-63; farmer, 46-57; owner & operator, R.N. Kincer Feed & Farm Supply & Transfer Co, 30-54. Rel: Methodist. Mailing Add: 615 N. 8th St, Wytheville, Va. 24382. (1967)

KINCHEN, LONNIE LEE D
Chmn, Dunklin Co. Dem. Cmt, Mo.
b. Hollywood, Mo, 3/5/31; s. Sidney O. Kinchen and Hattie Buck K; m. 6/9/51 to Jean Branum; c. Steven, Scott and Sarah. Educ: Tulane Univ; Mo. Univ; Ark. State Col; Beta Gamma Sigma; Delta Sigma Phi. Polit. & Govt. Pos: Chmn. bd, Clay Twp, Mo, 58-66; mem, Dunklin Co. Dem. Cmt, 56-66, chmn, 62-66 and currently. Bus. & Prof. Pos: Partner, Branum-Kinchen Farms, 56-66; cashier, Bank of Kennett, 66. Mil. Serv: Entered as 2nd Lt, Army, 53, released as 1st Lt, 55, after serv. in 94th Field Artil. Group, Ft. Sill, Okla. Mem: Mason; Am. Legion Post 362; Farmers & Merchants Club; Farm Bur; Mo. Cotton Prod. Asn; Am. Soybean Asn; Mo. Soc. of Rural Appraisers. Student Achievement Award, Wall St. J. Rel: Protestant. Legal Res: Box 52, Hornersville, Mo. 63855. Mailing Add: Box 311, Kennett, Mo. 63857. (1967)

KINDER, LON CLARK, SR. R
W.Va. State Del.
b. Hurricane, W.Va, 9/21/14; s. Ambrose Ethelbert Kinder (deceased) and Hester Taylor K; m. 1/21/37 to Lillian Virginia Copley; c. Lon Clark, Jr, Joyce Ann (Mrs. Ronald G. Cox) and John Timothy. Educ: Marshall Col. Polit. & Govt. Pos: W.Va. State Del, 67- Bus. & Prof. Pos: Field rep, Kanawha Valley Baptist Asn, 46 Churches; co-owner, The Book Mart, Montgomery, W.Va. Mem: PTA (past pres, Lincoln Elem. Sch); adult leader, Kanawha Boys Co, 10 years; Boy Scouts (leader, 10 years). Rel: Baptist; Trustee, Calvary Baptist Church, Charleston. Legal Res: 306 W. Lee St, Charleston, W.Va. 25302. Mailing Add: P.O. Box 528, Charleston, W.Va. 25322. (1967)

KINDLE, HERBERT R
Finance chmn, Okla. State Rep. Party
b. Proctor, Okla; s. E.W. Kindle and Floy McCollum K; single. Educ: Northeast. State Col, B.S, 50, M.A. in Educ, 57. Polit. & Govt. Pos: Coordinator, George Lange for Cong, Second Dist, Okla, 64; Goldwater worker, 64; del, Rep. State Conv, 64-69; chmn, Adair Co. Rep. Cent. Cmt, 65-67; Nixon coordinator, Adair Co, 68; State committeeman and finance chmn, Okla. Rep. Party, 66- Bus. & Prof. Pos: Teacher, Kans, 53-56; with Ohio Oil Co, Tulsa, 57-59; farmer, Proctor, 59- Mil. Serv: Entered as Pvt, Army, 50, released as Sgt, 52, after serv. in Hq, Second Armored Div, European Command, Germany, 51-52. Mem: Mason; Am. Legion; VFW. Mailing Add: Proctor, Okla. 74457.

KING, BILL B. R
Chmn, Lipscomb Co. Rep. Party, Tex.
b. Canadian, Tex, 9/5/42; s. Jack Richard King and Lois Carol Bryant K; m. 11/30/62 to Denny Eldridge; c. Jan. Educ: Tex. Tech. Univ, B.S. in Agr, 66; Block & Bridle Club; Tex. Tech Rodeo Club; Future Farmers of Am. Polit. & Govt. Pos: Chmn, Lipscomb Co. Rep. Party, Tex, 68- Bus. & Prof. Pos: Self employed breeder of Hereford cattle. Rel: Baptist. Mailing Add: Route 3, Canadian, Tex. 79014.

KING, BRUCE D
Polit. & Govt. Pos: Co. cmnr, N.Mex, 54-58; N.Mex. State Rep, 59-68, Speaker, N.Mex. House of Rep, 62-68; legis. mem, Bd. Finance, N.Mex, 61-62; chmn. N.Mex. Dem. Party, 66-67; pres, N.Mex. Constitutional Conv, currently. Bus. & Prof. Pos: Rancher; livestock feeder. Mil. Serv: World War II. Mem: Exec. cmt, Nat. Conf. of Legis. Leaders, 62-68; West. Coun. of State Govt, 62-68; chmn, N.Mex. Hwy. Users Conf, 68-69; N.Mex. Farm and Livestock Bur.(bd. dirs); N.Mex. Cattle Growers Asn; N.Mex. Soil and Water Conserv.(v.pres); North. N.Mex. Fair Asn.(chmn); N.Mex. LPG Asn.(bd. mem); N.Mex. Wild Life and Conserv. Asn; N.Mex. Amigos; Elks; Am. Legion; VFW. Rel: Protestant. Mailing Add: Stanley, N.Mex. 87056.

KING, BRYON ROY D
b. Malden, Mo, 8/29/00; m. 1924 to Maud Ezell; c. Peggy, Jo, Freda, Roger. Educ: Dunklin Co. Pub. Schs. Polit. & Govt. Pos: Mo. State Rep, 65-66; Assoc. Judge First Dist, Dunklin Co, 59-65; mem. bd. of educ, Malden Sch. Dist, 51-56; Bd. of Pub. Works, Malden, 52-65, chmn. of bd, 59-65. Bus. & Prof. Pos: Dir. of Malden Savings & Loan Co. Mem: Past pres. Malden Lions Club. Rel: Methodist. Mailing Add: 303 N. Marion, Malden, Mo. 63863. (1967)

KING, CARLETON JAMES R
U.S. Rep, N.Y.
b. Saratoga Springs, N.Y, 6/15/04; m. to Constance M. Roddy; c. Lt. Comdr. Carleton J, Jr, Navy and Mrs. James A. Murphy, Jr. Educ: Union Univ,

LL.B, 26. Polit. & Govt. Pos: Acting city judge, Saratoga Springs, N.Y, 36-41; Asst. Dist. Attorney, Saratoga Co, 42-50, Dist. Attorney, 50-60; U.S. Rep, N.Y, 60- Bus. & Prof. Pos: Lawyer, King, Duval & Murphy. Mem: State Bar Asn; Saratoga Co. Bar Asn.(pres, 59-60); N.Y. State Dist. Attorney's Asn. (pres, 55). Legal Res: 444 Broadway, Saratoga Springs, N.Y. 12866. Mailing Add: 560 N St. S.W, Apt. N604, Washington, D.C. 20024.

KING, CECIL R. D

b. Youngstown, Ft. Niagara, N.Y, 1/13/98; married; c. one. Educ: Pub. schs, Los Angeles. Polit. & Govt. Pos: Chmn, Calif. Cong. Del, Calif. State Legis, 32-42; U.S. Rep, Calif, 42-68, ranking mem, House Ways and Means Cmt; mem, Joint Cmt. on Internal Revenue Taxation and Joint Cmt. on Reduction of Nonessential Expenditures; House Rep, U.S. Common Mkt. Negotiating Team; cong. adv, UN Conf. for Trade and Develop. Bus. & Prof. Pos: Businessman. Mailing Add: 8704 Tenth Ave, Inglewood, Calif. 90305. (1967)

KING, CHARLES JAMES R

Fla. State Rep.

b. Atlanta, Ga, 2/3/25; s. Lewis Reed King and Mary Green K. m. 5/27/50 to Lydia V. Schuster; c. Janet Helen, Annette Laura, James Reed and Elaine Heidi. Educ: Univ. Miami, J.D, 55; Delta Theta Phi. Polit. & Govt. Pos: Munic. prosecutor, Oakland Park, Fla, 65-66; judge, Oakland Park, 66; Fla. State Rep, 89th Dist, 67- Bus. & Prof. Pos: Trust officer, Broward Nat. Bank, 55-57; attorney-at-law, Charles J. King, Ft. Lauderdale, Fla, 57- Mil. Serv: Entered as Pvt, Marine Corps, 42, released as S/Sgt, 46, after serv. in Third Marine Air Wing, Pac. Theatre, 44-45; Re-entered as Sgt, Army, 48, released as 1st Lt, 52, after serv. in Second Armored Cavalry Regt, European Theatre, 49-50. Mem: Fla. Bar; Broward Co. Bar Asn; Air Force Asn. Rel: Baptist. Legal Res: 621 N.W. 66th Ave, Plantation, Fla. 33313. Mailing Add: 3041 E. Commercial Blvd, Ft. Lauderdale, Fla. 33308.

KING, CHET D

b. Doty, Wash, 1901; m. to Ella Mae; c. Three daughters. Educ: High Sch. Polit. & Govt. Pos: Wash. State Rep, until 66. Bus. & Prof. Pos: Boom man. Mil. Serv: Navy, 3 years. Mem: Eagles; Elks; Grange; Int. Woodworkers Union; Int. Fishermen's Union. Mailing Add: 435 Seventh St, Raymond, Wash. 98577. (1967)

KING, CLARENCE LEROY, JR. D

Chmn, Saline Co. Dem. Party, Kans.

b. Salina, Kans, 4/5/32; s. Clarence Leroy King and Margaret Swift K; m. 8/18/51 to Doris I. Altman; c. Jeff and Joni. Educ: Kans. Wesleyan Univ, A.B 54; Washburn Univ, LL.B, 57; Beta Tau Omega; Phi Alpha Delta. Polit. & Govt. Pos: Dem. precinct committeeman, Kans; pres, Saline Co. Young Dem; mem, Leadership Conf, Denver, Colo, 60; chmn, Saline Co. Dem. Party, 66-; mem, Century Club; del, Dem. Nat. Conv, 68; mem, Gov. Cmn. Criminal Admin, 69. Bus. & Prof. Pos: Partner, Law Firm of King & Stokes, Salina. Mem: Am. Bar Asn; Kans. Bar Asn.(medico-legal, unauthorized practice and reorgn. cmts); Northwest Kans. Bar Asn.(exec. cmt, 61); Saline Co. Bar Asn. (pub. rels, ins. and bench and bar cmts); Kans. Young Lawyers (v.pres, 59, pres, 64); Am. and Kans. Trial Lawyers Asns; Defense Research Inst; Am. Jr. Bar Conf, Miami, 59; trustee, Saline Co. Libr; Exchange Club (pres, 60); C. of C; Kans. Wesleyan Univ. Alumni Asn.(pres, 59-60); Kans. Col. Off. Asn. (bd. dirs, 59-60); bd. dirs, Children's Spec. Educ. Center, chmn, 66-67; chmn. bd, Cent. Kans. Ment. Health Center, 64-65; YMCA (Secy, youth cmt); life mem, PTA (pres, Grace Stewart Chap, 66-67); Adult Chap. Fellowship Christian Athletics; Big Brothers of Salina (organizer and hon. mem. bd. dirs); originator, Peace Officer of the Year Award; active in juvenile projs. through Court and Salina Police Dept; originated juvenile delinquency maps for Salina Police Dept; organizer and moderator of juvenile panels for local info. purposes; nominating and joint cmts. for planning, Univ. Methodist Church and Kans. Wesleyan Univ. Outstanding Young Man of Salina, 61; Outstanding Young Alumnus, Kans. Wesleyan Univ, 65. Rel: Methodist; Past teacher, mem. Off. Bd. and mem. Christian Social Concerns, Finance and Long Range Planning Cmns. Mailing Add: 2037 Leland Way, Salina, Kans. 67401.

KING, DAVID S. D

U.S. Ambassador to Malagasy Repub. and Mauritius.

b. Salt Lake City, Utah, 6/20/17; s. Sen. William H. King (deceased); married; c. eight. Educ: Univ. Utah, B.A, 37; Georgetown Univ. Sch. of Law, LL.B. Polit. & Govt. Pos: Law clerk, Judge Harold Stephens of U.S. Court of Appeals for D.C; counsel, Utah State Tax Cmn, 43-45; U.S. Rep, Utah, 58-66; U.S. Ambassador, to Malagasy Repub, 67- and Mauritius, 68- Bus. & Prof. Pos: Lawyer; instr. of commercial law, 10 years. Rel: Latter-day Saint; Missionary, Gt. Brit, 2 years; Asst. Gen. Supt. Mutual Improv. Asn. for Latter-day Saints. Mailing Add: 9614 Dewmar Lane, Kensington, Md. 20795.

KING, DONALD R. D

Tenn. State Cmnr. of Revenue

b. Marshall Co, Tenn, 10/3/27; s. Guy King and Willie Emma More K; m. to Joanne Kay Smith; c. Donna and three sons. Educ: Univ. of Tenn. Jr. Col, Martin, Tenn; Univ. of Tenn, Knoxville; licensed pub. acct. Polit. & Govt. Pos: Jr. auditor, Off. Comptroller of Treas, Tenn; budget and syst. analyst, dir. of local finance, dir. co. audits and asst. to comptroller, 50-63; Tenn. State Cmn. Revenue, 63- Mil. Serv: Navy. Mem: Munic. Finance Officers Asn; Nat. Tax Asn; Am. Legion; VFW; Rel: Church of Christ. 1967 Legal Res: Nashville, Tenn. No mailing address available. (1967)

KING, EDGAR A. R

Conn. State Rep.

b. McLean, Ill, 11/20/23; s. Edgar O. King and Nellie M. Swearingen K; m. 12/19/49 to Marjorie Dwyer; c. Marjorie E, John M, Robert D. and Kathryn. Educ: Ill. Wesleyan Univ, Ph.B, 49; Univ. Conn. Sch. Law, LL.B; Theta Chi. Polit. & Govt. Pos: Town councilman, Farmington, Conn, 61-65; Conn. State Rep, Farmington, 67- Bus. & Prof. Pos: Attorney, Phoenix of Hartford Group, 55-68; attorney, Travelers Ins. Co, 68- Mil. Serv: Entered as Recruit, Navy, 41, released as Machinists Mate 2/C, 45, after serv. in ETO, 42-44. Rel: Episcopal. Mailing Add: 11 Ledgewood Dr, Farmington, Conn. 06032.

KING, ETHYL BELL R

Chmn, Rep. Cmt. Worth Co, Mo.

b. Near Oxford, Mo, 7/13/03; d. Oliver Roberts and Eva Miller R; m. Dec. 1923 to Harlan F. King; c. Oliver Fredrick and Keith Samuel. Educ: Worth High Sch, 2 years; Grant City High Sch, grad, 22. Polit. & Govt. Pos: Mem, Rep. Cmt. of Worth Co, Mo, 44-, chmn, currently. Bus. & Prof. Pos: Nurse aide, Mo. Methodist Hosp, St. Joseph, Mo, ten years. Mem: Eastern Star; leader, 4-H Club, 10 years. Rel: Christian. Mailing Add: Parnell, Mo. 64475.

KING, FREDERICK JENKS R

Chmn, West Feliciana Parish Rep. Exec. Cmt, La.

b. East Cleveland, Ohio, 2/18/11; s. Herbert Doan King and Lillian Jenks K; m. 4/15/42 to Augusta Walmsley; c. Semmes W, Frederick J, Carolyn D. and Katharine H. Educ: Yale Univ, B.A, 33; Delta Kappa Epsilon. Polit. & Govt. Pos: Mem, West Feliciana Parish Rep. State Cent. Cmt, La, 52-68; chmn, West Feliciana Parish Rep. Exec. Cmt, 66-; Judge, West Feliciana Parish, 68- Bus. & Prof. Pos: Auditor, Cent. Nat. Bank, Cleveland, Ohio, 33-35; broker, Prescott Co, Cleveland, Ohio, 35-49; asst. v.pres, La. Nat. Bank, Baton Rouge, La, 53- Mil. Serv: Entered as 2nd Lt, Army Res, 33, released as Lt. Col, 46, after serv. as Dep. A-1, Hq. West. Tech. Training Command, Denver, Colo, 42-46; Col. Air Force Res, 42- Mem: Am. Bankers' Asn; The Felicianians; Baton Rouge C. of C; Nat. Rifle Asn; Am. Legion; Air Force Asn. Rel: Episcopal. Mailing Add: P.O. Box 2, Bains, La. 70713.

KING, J. D. R

Chmn, Douglas Co. Rep. Cent. Cmt, Kans.

b. Batesville, Ark, 9/5/19; s. Rev. T. J. D. King and Roxy Kemp K; m. 7/22/41 to Flora Rae Keesee; c. Jama E.(Mrs. Larry Vanek) and Cora Jane (Mrs. Robert Misner). Educ: Ark. Col, 39-40. Polit. & Govt. Pos: Chmn, Douglas Co. Rep. Cent. Cmt, Kans, 58- Mil. Serv: Entered as Pvt, Army, 42, released as 1st Lt, 45, after serv. in 28th Inf. Div. ETO; Good Conduct Medal; Purple Heart. Mem: Officer Sch, Ft. Benning, Ga; Elks; Am. Legion; 40 et 8; Rotary (past pres); Lawrence C. of C.(past v.pres); chmn, United Fund Drive. Rel: Protestant. Mailing Add: 844 Broadview Dr, Lawrence, Kans. 66044.

KING, JAMES SAVERY R

V.Chmn, Jefferson Parish Rep. Exec. Cmt, La.

b. Cleveland, Ohio, 1/31/29; s. John Savery King and Margaret Andrews K; m. 1/3/51 to Joan Lois Merrin; c. Wendy Ann, Jill Andrews and Kent Savery. Educ: Univ. Fla, 2 years. Polit. & Govt. Pos: Chmn, Jefferson Parish Rep. Action Counc, 66-; del, Rep. Nat. Conv, 68; v.chmn, Jefferson Parish Rep. Exec. Cmt, 68- Mailing Add: 1105 Moss Lane, New Orleans, La. 70123.

KING, JENNINGS GRAHAM D

b. Durham, N.C, 7/11/08; s. Thomas Wesley King and Bessie Odom K; m. 6/5/43 to Vertie Doretha Prince; c. Jennings Graham, Jr, Carolyn Elizabeth. Educ: Duke Univ, B.A, 29, Law Sch, 28-30; Phi Beta Kappa; Omicron Delta Kappa; Tau Kappa Alpha; Sigma Upsilon. Polit. & Govt. Pos: City attorney, Laurinburg, N.C; N.C. State Rep, 36-38; N.C. State Sen, 61-66. Bus. & Prof. Pos: Lawyer. Mil. Serv: Army, 42-45. Mem: 16th Dist Bar Asn; N.C. State Bar; Am. Bar Asn; 13th Dist. Bar (pres, 36-37); mem, State Bar Coun, 49-52. Rel: Methodist. Mailing Add: Laurinburg, N.C. 28352. (1967)

KING, JOAN MERRIN R

State V.Chmn, La. Rep. Party

b. Tampa, Fla, 2/24/30; d. Joe Knox Merrin and Lois Burnett M; m. 1/3/51 to James Savery King; c. Wendy Ann, Carol Merrin (deceased), Jill Andrews and Kent Savery. Educ: Fla. State Univ, 2 years; Delta Delta Delta. Polit. & Govt. Pos: Young Rep, 52; Rep. ward leader, Jefferson Parish, 64, v.chmn, 65; charter pres, Jefferson Parish Rep. Women's Federated Club, 65, campaign activities chmn, 66, chmn. affiliated clubs, Jefferson Parish Rep. Club, 65, 66, 67, mem. co. chmn, 67; worker, Kenner campaign and Limes for Cong, 66; research chmn, Jefferson Parish Rep. Polit. Action Coun, 67; first v.pres, La. Fedn. of Rep. Women's Club, 67; del, Rep. Women's Conv, Wash, D.C; v.chmn, Metro. Finance Cmt; state coordinator, Citizens for Nixon-Agnew Clubs, 68; presidential elector, La, 68; state v.chmn, La. Rep. Party, 68- Mem: First v.pres, Moss Woods Civic Asn; Gr. New Orleans C. of C. Auxiliary; Jefferson Parish Civic Coun. Rep; Jefferson Cmt. for Better Schs; Hazel Park PTA; Riverdale High Sch. PTA; Jr. DAR (Spirit '76 Chap). Rel: Episcopal. Mailing Add: 1105 Moss Lane, New Orleans, La. 70123.

KING, JOHN W. D

b. Manchester, N.H, 10/10/18; s. Michael J. King and Anna Lydon K; m. to Anna McLaughlin. Educ: Harvard Col, B.A; Columbia Univ, M.A. in Pub. Law; Columbia Univ. Law Sch, LL.B; Phi Delta Phi. Hon. LL.D, Columbia Univ, St. Anselm's Col. and Univ. N.H; hon. M.A, Dartmouth Col; hon. Dr. Civil Laws, New England Col; hon. Dr. Pub. Admin, Franklin Pierce Col. and Suffolk Univ. Polit. & Govt. Pos: N.H. State Rep, 56-62, former mem, Ballot Law Cmn, Manchester Charter Revision Cmn. and House Appropriations and Rules Cmts. and Minority Leader, 59-62, N.H. State House of Rep; Gov, N.H, 62-68; del, Dem. Nat. Conv, 68. Bus. & Prof. Pos: Sr. partner, King, Nixon, Christy and Tessier, Manchester, N.H, currently; mem, teaching staff, St. Anselm's Col. Mem: Am. and N.Y. State Bar Asns; N.H. Bar Asn.(ed, Bar J); Bar Asn. City of N.Y; dir, Am. Judicature Soc; K. of C; Elks; Eagles; Moose; Turn Verein; Manchester Press Club; Canadien Club (state co-chmn, New Eng. Regional Cmn). Rel: Roman Catholic. Mailing Add: Connemara Farm, Kennedy Hill Rd, R.D. 1, Goffstown, N.H. 03045.

KING, KENNETH L R

Chmn, Jackson Co. Rep. Party, Minn.

b. Austin, Minn, 1/13/19; s. Benjamin A. King and Clara Quast K; m. 8/12/47 to Lee O. Thornton; c. Bradley Alan, Nancy Lee and Robert Scott. Educ: Austin High Sch. Polit. & Govt. Pos: Chmn, Jackson Co. Rep. Party, Minn, 64- Bus. & Prof. Pos: Cattle Buyer, Geo. A. Hormel Co, 36- Mil. Serv: Entered as Pvt, Air Force, 41, released as 2nd Lt, 45. Mem: C. of C; Lions. Rel: Methodist. Mailing Add: 805 Frost Ave, Jackson, Minn. 56143. (1967)

KING, LESLIE HENRY R

b. Los Angeles, Calif, 3/28/23; s. Leslie Lynch King and Margaret Atwood K; m. 8/14/43 to Virginia Hester Hodges; c. Pamela Virginia (Mrs. A. Hubert Smith, Jr), Kyra Leslie (Mrs. Gary Patton Wyatt), Leslie Henry, Jr. and Craig Hodges. Educ: Lincoln High Sch, Nebr, 36-39; Kemper Mil. Acad, Booneville, Mo, 39-40 & 41. Polit. & Govt. Pos: Chmn, Putnam Co. Rep. Party, Tenn, 64-68; alternate del, Nat. Rep. Conv, 68. Bus. & Prof. Pos: Owner and operator, King Auto Parts, Cookeville, Tenn, 48-68; owner, Goodyear Tire Center, 68- Mem: Mason; Shrine; Cookville Optimist Club (Lt. Gov. of Zone 7, Tenn. Dist. Optimist Int, 2 years); Co. Voting Cmn; C. of C; Tenn. Rep. Capitol Club. Rel: United Methodist. Mailing Add: 1256 E. Eighth St, Cookeville, Tenn. 38501.

KING, MARJORIE PITTER D

b. Seattle, Wash, 3/8/21; d. Edward Alexander Pitter and Marjorie Allen P; m. 6/17/45 to John Thomas King; c. Walter Joseph and Edward Allen. Educ: Univ. Wash, Seattle; Howard Univ, Wash, D.C; City Col, N.Y.C; past pres, Alpha Omicron; Delta Sigma Theta. Polit. & Govt. Pos: Pres, Metrop. Dem. Womens Club, Wash, 59-63; v.chmn, 37th Dist. Dem. Precinct Orgn, 58-60, chmn, 60-64; v.chmn, King Co. Dem. Cent. Cmt, 60-67; nominating chmn. and state finance chmn, State Fedn. Dem. Womens Clubs, 61-62, state treas, 63-64 and orgn. chmn, 66-68; organizer, State Tenn-Age Dem, Wash. State Cent. Cmt, 66; mem, Credentials Cmt, Dem. Nat. Conv, 64, del, 68; Wash. State Rep, 65-67, former mem, Joint Interim Cmt. on Educ. and Cmt. of Urban Govt, Wash. State House of Rep; state chmn, operation support, Wash. State Dem. Cmt, 67-; pres, Ann T. O'Donnell Metrop. Dem. Women, 68-; pres, Seventh Cong. Dist. Fedn. Dem. Womens Clubs, 69- Bus. & Prof. Pos: Clerk, Adj. Gen. Off, War Dept, 42-43; indust. engr, Univ. Labs, 44; accts. receivable clerk in charge-clerk, IV Seattle Eng. Dept, 51-56; self-employed tax consult, letter shop, M & M Serv. Shop, 47- Mem: Prog. chmn, Legis. Cmt. Bus. & Prfnl. Women, 62-65; bd. mem, YMCA; bd. mem, Urban League; NAACP; E.Madison Commercial Club; 3 M Urban Renewal; Voter Action Cmt; Cub Scout Den Mother, 5½ years; Citizen's Cmts, PTA, Sch. Levy; Commun. Concert Asn; Wash. State Women's Civil Rights Cmt; Nat. Coun. of Negro Women; Booker T. Washington Am. Legion Auxiliary; bd, Lutheran Family & Child Serv, Wash. Rel: Lutheran. Mailing Add: 1627 25th Ave, Seattle, Wash. 98122.

KING, MARY LOIS R

Dep. Pres, Tex. Fedn. of Rep. Women

b. Breckenridge, Tex, 7/6/24; d. John C. Ward and Mabel Daniel W; m. 6/11/48 to Gordon R. King; c. Gordon R, III, John C. and David M. Educ: Hockaday Jr. Col, 42-43; South. Methodist Univ, B.M, 45; Univ. of Colo, Boulder, 45; Delta Delta Delta. Polit. & Govt. Pos: Rep. campaign hq. chmn, McLennan Co, Tex, 62, 63 and 64, 'get-out-the-vote' chmn, 64; del, Rep. State Conv, 64, 66, 68 and Rep. Nat. Conv, 68; v.chmn, McLennan Co. Rep. Party, 66; key Rep, Tex, 66; pres, McLennan Co. Rep. Women, 67; dep. pres, Tex. Fedn. of Rep. Women, 68- Mem: Serv. League; Am. Asn. of Univ. Women; PTA. One of Ten Outstanding Rep. Women of Tex, 67. Rel: Methodist. Mailing Add: 4516 Thunder Rd, Dallas, Tex. 75234.

KING, PETER COTTERILL R

Adminstr, Southwest. Power Admin, Dept. of Interior

b. White Plains, N.Y, 8/23/30; s. Robert Cotterill King and Ruth McKeown K; m. 6/28/58 to Nancy English; c. Margot E. and Philip M. Educ: U.S. Mil. Acad, West Point, N.Y, B.S, 52; Univ. Pa, M.B.A, 58; Harvard, Mgt. Seminar, cert, 68. Polit. & Govt. Pos: Councilman, Lawton, Okla, 68-69; adminstr, Southwest. Power Admin, Dept. of Interior, 69- Bus. & Prof. Pos: Systs. engr, Research Center, Int. Bus. Machines Corp, Yorktown Heights, N.Y, 58-62; v.pres, Security Bank & Trust Co, Lawton, Okla, 62-69; pres, Security Broadcasting Corp, Lawton, 64-69. Mil. Serv: Entered as 2nd Lt, Army, 52, released as 1st Lt, 56, after serv. in 350th Inf. Regt, Austrian Theatre, 52-55; Maj, Army Res, 66; Nat. Defense and Reserve Officers Serv. Medal; Army of Occupation Medal; Expert Inf. Badge; Parachutist Badge. Mem: U.S. C. of C; Nat. Asn. of Mfrs; Okla. Bankers Asn. Rel: Episcopal. Mailing Add: 1120 E. 24th Place, Tulsa, Okla. 74114.

KING, PHILIP E. D

Ky. State Rep.

b. 1929. Educ: Georgetown Col; Univ. of Ky; Univ. of Cincinnati Col. of Law, LL.B. Polit. & Govt. Pos: Ky. State Rep, currently. Bus. & Prof. Pos: Attorney-at-law. Mil. Serv: Army. Mem: Kenton Co. and Ky. Bar Asns; Taylor Mill Lions Club; Brotherhood of R.R. Trainmen. Rel: Baptist. Mailing Add: 15 W. Southern Ave, Covington, Ky. 41015.

KING, R. EDWIN D

b. Vicksburg, Miss, 9/20/36; s. Ralph E. King and Julia Tucker K; m. 7/3/60 to Jeannette Sylvester; c. Lillian and Margaret. Educ: Millsaps Col, B.A, 58; Boston Univ. Sch. Theol, B.D, 61, S.T.M, 63; Harvard Divinity Sch, spec. study, 66. Polit. & Govt. Pos: Founding mem, Miss. Freedom Dem. Party and Freedom Vote cand. for Lt. Gov, 63, nat. committeeman and mem. state exec. cmt, 64-68; del, Dem. Nat. Conv, 64 & 68; mem. state exec. cmt, Miss. Loyal Dem, 68. Bus. & Prof. Pos: Minister, United Methodist Church, 61-; chaplain, mem. faculty and dean of students, Tougaloo Col, 63-67; educ. prog. dir. delta ministry, Nat. Coun. Churches, Greenville, 67- Mem: Nat. Cmt. for a Sane Nuclear Policy; Fel. of Reconcilliation; Clergy and Lawmen United Against War in Vietnam. Jailed over ten times for civil rights work in Ala. and Miss; Merrill fel, Harvard Divinity Sch, 66; J.F. Kennedy Freedom Award, Cath. Coun. on Civil Liberties, 65. Rel: Methodist. Mailing Add: 1314 Calhoun St, New Orleans, La. 70118.

KING, R. J, JR. R

Mo. State Rep.

b. St. Clair, Mo, 9/28/13; m. 4/16/34 to Cecelia LaPee; c. John P, P. Timothy, R. Jerrard, Cecelia M. and Kevin L. Educ: Univ. Mo. Polit. & Govt. Pos: Pres, Young Rep. Club Franklin Co, Mo, 34-39; dir, Rep. State Campaign, 46, pres, Mo. Asn. Rep, 48; Mo. State Rep, 58-; Majority Floor Leader, 64th Gen. Assembly; del, Rep. Nat. Conv, 68. Bus. & Prof. Pos: Ins. broker; pres. Galena Abstract Co. Mem: Prfnl. and Businessmen's Club of the Hill; bd. trustees, St. Benedict's Col, Atchison, Kans. Rel: Roman Catholic. Mailing Add: 816 S. Hanley, St. Louis, Mo. 63105. (1967)

KING, RAYMOND E, JR. D

Mem, N.C. Dem. Exec. Cmt.

b. Monticello, Fla, 12/30/23; s. Raymond E. King and Viola Clark K; m. 3/3/44 to Sara Jean Agnew; c. Sara Anne and Raymond E, III. Educ: Abraham Baldwin Col, grad; Univ. Ga, B.S; Demothenian Literary Soc; Univ. Ga. Debate Team and Club. Polit. & Govt. Pos: Precinct chmn, Mecklenburg Co. Dem. Party, N.C. and chmn, 61-64; mem, Charlotte-Mecklenburg Intergovt. Task Force Cmt. and Charlotte Redevelop. Cmn, 65-; mem, N.C. Dem. Exec. Cmt, currently. Mil. Serv: Entered as Pvt, Army, 44, released as Sgt, 46, after serv. in Austria; 3 ETO Campaign Ribbons. Mem: Nat. Asn. of Life Underwriters (v.pres); N.C. Asn. of Life Underwriters (v.pres, 63, pres, 64, secy-treas, 68-69); Chartered Life Underwriters Soc.(pres, Charlotte Chap, 61); N.C. Health Underwriters Asn.(mem. bd. dirs); Ala. Health Underwriters Asn.(pres, 57); Gen. Agents and Mgrs. Conf; N.C. Gen. Agents and Mgrs. Asn.(pres, 62); Int. Asn. of Health Underwriters; Rotary; Dem. Men's Club; N.C. Heart Asn; Charlotte Sales and Mkt. Execs. Club; Charlotte Execs. Club; London Dinner Club; Charlotte City Club; Mason; Scottish Rite; Shrine; Red Fez Club; Am. Legion; Navy League; VFW. Several life ins. articles in nat. publ; former athletic coach. Rel: Presbyterian. Legal Res: 4015 Arbor Way, Charlotte, N.C. 28211. Mailing Add: 1373 E. Morehead St, Charlotte, N.C. 28204.

KING, RAYMOND LAMPREY R

Finance Chmn, Ogemaw Co. Rep. Party, Mich.

b. Braintree, Mass, 9/1/29; s. Samuel Winslow King and Doris Lamprey K; m. 1/6/51 to Jean Ellen Peters; c. Deborah Rae, David Winslow and Kathryn Mae. Educ: Univ. Maine, B.A, 52; Boston Univ. Sch. Law, LL.B, 57; class pres, Boston Univ. Sch. Law, 57; Theta Chi; Univ. of Maine Men's Senate. Polit. & Govt. Pos: Rep. precinct del, Pontiac, Mich, 58-60; statutory mem, Oakland City Rep. Cmt, Mich, 59-60; mem. finance staff, Oakland Co. Rep. Cmt, 60; del, Mich. Constitutional Conv, 60-61; prosecuting attorney, Ogemaw Co, Mich, 62-68; finance chmn, Ogemaw Co. Rep. Party, 62-; mem, Mich. Rep. State Cent. Cmt, Tenth Dist, 63-64; chmn, Tenth Cong. Dist. Rep. Cmt, 64-68; city attorney, West Branch, Mich, 64-68; del, Rep. Nat. Conv, 68; probate judge, Ogemaw Co, Mich, 68- Bus. & Prof. Pos: Mgt. trainee and merchandising mgr, Sears Roebuck & Co, Bangor, Maine, 52-54; supvr. purchasing admin, Ford Motor Co, Dearborn, Mich, 57-60. Mil. Serv: Entered as Sgt, Air Force, 51, released as S/Sgt, 52, after serv. in 132nd Fighter-Interceptor Squadron, East. Air Defense Command; Air Force Res, inactive, 1st Lt. Mem: Am. Bar Asn; Am. Judicature Soc; Mich. Bar Asn.(chmn. Tenth dist. character and fitness cmt); Kiwanis (past pres, West Branch Chap); West Branch Country Club (past pres); Am. Law Students Asn.(v.pres). Recipient of Ford Motor Co. Award for Outstanding Commun. Serv, 59. Rel: Protestant. Legal Res: 321 Sidney St, West Branch, Mich. 48661. Mailing Add: P.O. Box 165, West Branch, Mich. 48661.

KING, RICHARD ARTHUR D

Wash. State Rep.

b. Ritzville, Wash, 8/30/34; s. George Stanford King and Elsie O'Donnell K; m. 3/19/55 to Mary Evelyn Butler; c. Douglas Ritchie, Diana Marie, Shawn O'Donnell and Sherry Elaine. Educ: Univ. Wash, B.A, 56, M.A, 58; Delta Sigma Rho; Acacia. Polit. & Govt. Pos: V.pres, Young Dem. of Wash, 59-61, pres, 61-63; chmn, Snohomish Co. Young Citizens for Kennedy-Johnson, 60; chmn, Snohomish Co. Cent. Dem. Club, 60-62; v.pres, Second Cong. Dist. Dem. Coun, 64; Wash. State Rep, 65- Mem: Phi Rho Pi (nat. v.pres, 60-61 & 66-67); Nat. and Wash. Educ. Asns; Am. Asn. of Univ. Profs; Speech Asn. of Am; West. and Wash. Speech Asns; Am. Fedn. of Teachers; v.pres, Everett Fedn. of Teachers (v.pres, 62-64); Eagles. Rel: Unitarian. Mailing Add: 309 77th Place, S.W, Everett, Wash. 98201.

KING, ROBERT THOMAS R

Auditor Acct, Vt.

b. Jericho, Vt, 3/15/17; s. Perley Joseph King and Alice Kirby K; single. Educ: Burlington Bus. Col, 37-38; Col. William and Mary, A.B, 50. Polit. & Govt. Pos: Auditor, Inc. Sch. Dist, Vt. and Underhill-Jericho Water Dist; state auditor, Vt, 50-63, dep. auditor of acct, 63-69, auditor of acct, 69- Bus. & Prof. Pos: Clerk, Haigh Lumber Co, Burlington, Vt, 38-41; waybill tracer, Seaboard Air Line R.R, Portsmouth, Va, 41-42 & 46. Mil. Serv: Entered as Pvt, Army, 42, released as Warrant Officer (jg), 46, after serv. in Adj. Gen. Corps, India-Burma Theater from 43-46; Asiatic-Pac. Serv, Am. Serv, World War II Victory and Good Conduct Medals. Mem: Munic. Finance Officers Asn. U.S. and Can; past pres. and dir, N.Eng. States and Munic. Finance Officers Asn; Nat. Asn. State Auditors, Comptrollers and Treas; moderator, Mt. Mansfield Union Sch. Dist, Underhill Graded Sch. Dist. and Jericho-Underhill Water Dist; treas. and clerk, Cemetery Asn; comdr, adj. and chaplain, Am. Legion Post 22; chief, Underhill-Jericho Fire Dept; Mason. Rel: Congregational. Legal Res: Jericho, Vt. 05465. Mailing Add: Montpelier, Vt. 05602.

KING, SELBY R

b. Preston, Mo, 11/23/11; m. 2/10/39 to Elizabeth Ruth Harris; c. Elizabeth Ann. Educ: Mo. State Col, Springfield, Mo, B.S, Educ. Polit. & Govt. Pos: State Rep, 64-66. Bus. & Prof. Pos: Prin, Wheatland, Hermitage, Weaubleau, Dadeville and Cross Timbers High Schs, 55-64; auto bus, 47-55; supt. Preston High Sch, 41-46; Rural and Preston grade schs. Rel: Methodist. Mailing Add: Preston, Mo. 65732. (1967)

KING, SEMMES WALMSLEY R

Mem, La. Rep. State Cent. Cmt.

b. New Orleans, La, 11/6/43; s. Frederick Jenks King and Augusta Walmsley K; single. Educ: Riverside Mil. Acad, Gainsville, Ga, grad, 61; La. State Univ, 61; Tulane Univ, 64; La Salle Law Sch, 66- Polit. & Govt. Pos: Mem, Action Coun. Bd. Dirs, West. Feliciana Parish, La, 66-68; chmn, Rep. Exec. Cmt. West Feliciana Parish, 66-68; chmn, West. Feliciana Parish, Rep. Party La, 68-, secy, exec. cmt, 68-, mem-at-lg, 68-; official, Polit. Action Coun, Rep. Party, La, 68-, chmn. West Feliciana Parish Rep. Polit. Action Coun, 68-; constable, Parish of West Feliciana, 68-; mem, La. Rep. State Cent. Cmt, 11th Rep. Dist, 68- Bus. & Prof. Pos: Dir, Delta Tugs Ltd, Nassau and New Orleans, 69-, Richardson King Indust, New Orleans, 69- and Alfa Enterprises, Inc, 69- Mil. Serv: Entered as Pvt, Marines, 61, released as Pvt, 63, after serv. in Marine Aviation Detachment, Naval Air Station, Millington, Tenn, 62-63. Mem: La. Peace Officer Asn; La. Justice of the Peace and Constables Asn.(Justices of the Peace Educ. Cmt.); West Feliciana Parish Justice of the Peace and Constable Asn; Cmt. Pro-Am. For. Policy; sustaining mem, Rep. Nat. Cmt; La. Coun. Music and Performing Arts; La. Rep. Asn; Young Men's Bus. Club Gr. New Orleans; Jeunesse d'Orleans; Air Force Asn; West Feliciana Parish Develop. Asn. Aide de Camp on staff of Rep. John R. Rarick. Mailing Add: P.O. Box 2, Bains, La. 70713.

KING, SPENCER M.

U.S. Ambassador to Guyana

b. San Juan, P.R, 8/11/17; s. Amos J. King and Cora S. Morison K; m.

11/19/66 to Josephine Montes Smith. Educ: Yale Univ, B.A, 40; Sch. For. Serv, Georgetown Univ, summer 40; Civil Affairs Training Sch, Univ. Mich, 44-45; Univ. Chicago, 51; Nat. War Col, grad, 58. Polit. & Govt. Pos: Mem, For. Serv, 45-; third secy. and v.consul, La Paz, Bolivia, 46-48; assigned to Dept. of State, 48-51; first secy. and consul, Prague, Czechoslovakia, 51-54; chief, E.European Br, Voice of Am, 54-55; spec. asst. to the Asst. Secy. of State for Inter-Am. Affairs, 55-57; for. serv. inspector, 58-62; dep. chief of mission and consul gen, Quito, Ecuador, 62, Santo Domingo, Dominican Repub, 62-64; dep. inspector gen, Dept. of State, 64-69; U.S. Ambassador to Guyana, 69- Mil. Serv: Entered Army, 41, released as Maj, 46, after serv. in Pac. Theatre of Opers. Mem: Am. Soc. of Int. Law; Alpha Sigma Phi; Cum Laude Soc; Canon and Castle; Yale Club, N.Y.C. and Wash; Manor Country Club, Rockville, Md; Univ. Club, Wash. Legal Res: 21 Pearl St, Belfast, Maine 04915. Mailing Add: U.S. Embassy, Georgetown, Guyana.

KING, STAFFORD R
Married; c. two. Educ: Univ. Minn; St. Paul Col. of Law. Polit. & Govt. Pos: State auditor, Minn, 30-69. Bus. & Prof. Pos: Co. sch. teacher; State Forestry Serv. Mil. Serv: Mexican Border War; World War I; World War II; Air Intel, Pac. Command, World War II. Mem: Mason (Past State Grand Master). Rel: Methodist; bd. mem, Cleveland Ave. Methodist Church, St. Paul. Mailing Add: 1919 Stanford Ave, St. Paul, Minn. 55105.

KING, TOM COBB, JR. R
Mem. Exec. Cmt, Calhoun Co. Rep. Cmt, Ala.
b. Gadsden, Ala, 11/30/15; s. Tom Cobb King and Sadie Belle Cox K; m. 1/24/42 to Joan Taylor; c. Thomas, Wendy, Clifton, Joanne and Nancy. Educ: Univ. Va, B.S, 38, M.D, 41; Phi Beta Kappa; Alpha Tau Omega; Tilka; German Club; Calconon Club. Polit. & Govt. Pos: Mem. exec. cmt, 52- and chmn, Calhoun Co. Rep. Cmt, Ala, 66-67. Bus. & Prof. Pos: Pvt. med. practice, 49-; pres, S.G. & O, Inc, 65-66. Mil. Serv: Entered as 1st Lt, Army, 42, released as Major, 45, after serv. in 559th F.A. Bn, ETO; ETO Medal with 5 Battle Stars; Bronze Star. Mem: Fel, Am. Col. of Surgeons; fel, Am. Col. Obstetricians and Gynecologist; Ala. Med. Asn; Co. Med. Soc; Ala. Asn. of Obstetricians and Gynecologists; South Cent. Obstetricians and Gynecologists Soc; J. Marion Sims Soc; Rotary; Anniston Country Club; Birmingham Sailing Club. Rel: Episcopal. Mailing Add: 543 Hillyer High Rd, Anniston, Ala. 36201.

KING, WILLIAM HAMPTON D
State Auditor Pub. Accts, Miss.
b. Heidelberg, Miss, 10/1/09; s. William Elisha King and Sarah Covington K; m. 7/6/34 to Eldridge Douglas Banks; c. Carolyn (Mrs. Andrew) and Sarah Kathryn (Mrs. Kay). Educ: Hinds Jr. Col, 25-28; YMCA Grad. Sch, 30-34; Univ. Miss, B.A, 39. Polit. & Govt. Pos: Field staff auditor, State Dept. of Audit, Jackson, Miss, 53-56, asst. dir, 56-62, dir, 62-63, state auditor pub. accts, 64- Bus. & Prof. Pos: Cannery mgr, Cumberland Coop, Crossville, Tenn, 37-39; faculty mem, Clarke Jr. Col, Newton, Miss, 39-40; chief transportation sect, Ord. Training Center & Plant, Flora, Miss, 41-44; acct, Woods Builders Supply Co, Jackson, Miss, 45-47; acct-in-charge, Scott Bldg. Supply Corp, Cleveland, Miss, 47-52; CPA, self-employed, Cleveland, 52-53. Mem: Miss. Soc. CPA; Am. Inst. CPA; Am. Acct. Asn; Nat. Asn. State Auditors, Comptrollers & Treas.(treas); F&AM; Optimist (pres, Jackson Optimist 69-); Optimist Int; Knife and Fork Club. Rel: United Methodist. Legal Res: 404 Colonial Circle, Jackson, Miss. 39211. Mailing Add: P.O. Box 1060, Jackson, Miss. 39205.

KING, WILLIAM THEODORE R
Mem, Calif. Rep. State Cent. Cmt.
b. Detroit, Mich, 2/3/33; s. Erle E. Wright and Helen Louise Colvin W; m. 6/13/54 to Joan C. Hutchon; c. Jonatha Helen, Patrice Marie and William Theodore II. Educ: Principia Col, B.A. cum laude, 54; Harvard Univ, LL.B, 57. Polit. & Govt. Pos: Chmn, Californians for Reagan, 66; state speakers chmn, Kuchel for Sen, 68; South. Calif. chmn, Citizens for Nixon, 68; spec. gifts chmn, United Rep. Finance Cmt, Los Angeles Co, 68; campaign chmn, Alphonzo Bell for Mayor Cmt, 69; co-chmn, Thomas Bradley for Mayor Cmt, 69; field rep. for Congressman Alphonzo Bell, currently; mem, Calif. Rep. State Cent. Cmt, currently. Bus. & Prof. Pos: Partner, Law Off, Lindstrom, Robison, Lovell & King, mem. Alumni Exec. Cmt, Principia Col. and trustee, Clairbourn Sch. currently. Mem: Am. Bar Asn.(real property, probate and trust sect); Los Angeles Co. Bar Asn.(exec. cmt, Los Angeles probate and trust cmt); Calif. State Bar Asn; Am. Judicature Soc; Town Hall; Jr. C. of C; World Affairs Coun; Calif. Club. Rel: Christian Science. Legal Res: 15534 Nalin Place, Los Angeles, Calif. 90024. Mailing Add: 615 S. Flower St, Suite 808, Los Angeles, Calif. 90024.

KING, WOODROW WILSON D
b. Rock Falls, Ill, 7/1/13; s. David Ira King and Maude E. Huff K; m. 8/5/36 to Loraine Oltman; c. Woodrow W, David O. and Jay P. Educ: Wash. and Lee Univ, 31 & 32. Polit. & Govt. Pos: Mem, Gov. Kerner and Shapiro's Agr. Adv. Cmt, 61-68; mem, Gov. Kerner's State Revenue Adv. Cmt, 62-66; mem, President Kennedy's Cmt. Beef Imports, 63; mem, Secy. Agr. Nat. Beef Indust. Cmt, 63-67 and Nat. Feed Grain & Wheat Cmt, 63-69; Ill. State chmn, Rural Am. for Johnson-Humphrey, 64; mem. livestock and nutrit. seminar, Int. Trade Fair, Milan, Italy, 64; mem, President Johnson's Nat. Cmn. Rural Poverty, 66-67; Ill. state chmn, Farmers for Humphrey-Muskie, 68; del, Dem. Nat. Conv, 68. Bus. & Prof. Pos: Pres, Kinglore Farms, Inc, currently. Mem: Charter mem. Rock Falls Rotary Club (past pres); Chicago Land Angus Asn.(pres, 52-54); Ill. State Angus Asn.(pres, 62-63). Nat. Skelly Award, Agr. Rel: Methodist. Mailing Add: Kinglore Farms Inc, RFD 2, Rock Falls, Ill. 61071.

KING, ZOLA M. D
Pres, Mo. Fedn. of Womens Dem. Clubs
b. Kirksville, Mo, 6/13/21; d. Charles William Perry (deceased) and Lizzie Belle Brown P; m. 4/8/49 to Fred Douglas King; c. Sherri Lee (Mrs. Ewing), Deborah Ann, Douglas Deon and Janine Marie. Educ: High sch. Polit. & Govt. Pos: Ward leader, Cong. of Dem. Clubs, 61-, pres, Womens Auxiliary, 62-63; committeewoman, Blue Twp, Mo, 66-68; mem, Fourth Cong. Dist. Dem. State Cmt, 66-68; first v.pres, Fourth Cong. Dist. of Federated Womens Clubs, 67-69, pres, 69-; pres, Mo. Fedn. of Womens Dem. Clubs, 67-; del-at-lg, Dem. Nat. Conv, 68. Publ: Speeches and ed, State and Local Newspapers, 62- Mem: VFW Auxiliary; Optimist; solicitor, Am. Cancer Fund and Polio Fund, 62, 64 & 65. Rel: Baptist. Mailing Add: 1402 N. Pearl Dr, Independence, Mo. 64050.

KINGMAN, WILLIAM SALEM R
State Committeeman, N.Y. Rep. Party
b. Norwich, N.Y, 9/16/06; s. Frederick William Kingman and Grace Morse K; m. 6/22/27 to Gladys Seely; c. Jane S.(Mrs. Joris F. Kenyon) and William Seely. Educ: Pace Col, 25-27. Polit. & Govt. Pos: Chmn. finance cmt, Chenango Co. Rep. Cmt, N.Y, 58-64; Rep, Chenango Co. Rep. Judicial Cmt, 59; state committeeman, N.Y. Rep. Party, 60-; Rep. alderman, Ward 2, Norwich, 60-63; del, Rep. Nat. Conv, 68; nat. chmn. commun, Vol. for Nixon-Agnew, 68. Bus. & Prof. Pos: Methods acct, N.Y. Tel. Co, Albany, 27-36; br. mgr, C.I.T. Corp, Binghamton, 36-41; treas, Ludlow Motor Co, Inc, 41-42, asst. to pres, v.pres. and treas, 46-48; exec. v.pres. and currently chmn. bd, Chenango & Unadellalel Corp, 48-; pres, C & U Commun. Corp, 67-, chmn. bd, currently; v.pres. govt. rels, Continental Tel. Corp, Wash, D.C, 68-; dir, Nat. Bank & Trust Co, Norwich, N.Y. and Preferred Mutual Ins. Co, New Berlin, currently. Mil. Serv: Entered as 1st Lt, Air Force, 42, released as Maj, 46, after serv. in 15th Air Force, ETO, 44-45. Publ: Author of articles in Telephony, Pub. Utilities Fortnightly and Investment Dealers Digest. Mem: U.S. Independent Tel. Asn.(pres. and dir); N.Y. State Tel. Asn.(dir); Mason; Shrine; Capitol Hill Club; Elks; Army and Navy Club; Am. Legion. Rel: Episcopal. Legal Res: Corner Plymouth and Fuller Rds, Norwich, N.Y. 13815. Mailing Add: Suite I-340, Sheraton Park Hotel, Washington, D.C. 20008.

KINGSBERY, JOHN RUSSELL R
b. Akron, Colo, 7/20/22; s. Everette George Kingsbery and Ora Nell Moore K; m. 1/3/59 to Frances Marie Duhame; c. Karen, Peter, Guy, Spencer, Ken, Robert and Douglas. Educ: Grinnell Col, 39-40; U.S. Naval Acad, 41-42; Univ. Tex, B.B.A; Delta Sigma Chi; Pi Kappa Alpha. Polit. & Govt. Pos: Mem. Exec. Cmt, Travis Co. Rep. Party, Tex, 62-65, finance chmn, 63-64 and chmn, Goldwater Cmt, 64; del, Rep. Nat. Conv, 64; mem, City of Austin Bd. of Tax Equalization, 65-66; finance chmn. and campaign chmn, Tenth Cong. Dist. Race, 68; dist. dir, Dist. 16, Tower Senate Club, 68-69; mem, Cmt. Higher Educ, Tex, 69. Bus. & Prof. Pos: Pres, Southwest Rep. Corp, 63-; chmn. bd, Featherlite Corp, 63- Mil. Serv: Entered as Pvt, Air Force, 43, released as 2nd Lt, 45, after serv. in Training and Instructing, 43-45 and B 25's and Helicoptors, 45. Publ: Ed. Writer, Austin Am. Statesman, 63-64. Mem: Bd. dirs, Laguna Gloria Art Mus, Austin; charter mem, Gr. Austin Asn; Toastmaster Int; dir, Austin Boys Clubs Am, 68-69; dir, Austin Arts Coun, 69; dir, bd. dirs, Austin C. of C, 69. Rel: Episcopal. Legal Res: 3709 Eastledge Dr, Austin, Tex. 78731. Mailing Add: P.O. Box 6220, Austin, Tex. 78702.

KINGSFORD, LEONARD O. R
Chmn, Caribou Co. Rep. Cent. Cmt, Idaho
b. Grace, Idaho, 5/22/18; s. Robert Kingsford and Martha Mildred Ormond K; m. 6/3/42 to Helen Bernice Erickson; c. Eric. L. and Edward. Educ: Univ. Idaho, B.S. in Bus, 41, LL.B, 48; Phi Alpha Delta. Polit. & Govt. Pos: Prosecuting attorney, Madison Co, Idaho, 49-50; precinct committeeman, Madison Co, 52-56, Bannock Co, 58-59 and Caribou Co, 62-; chmn, Caribou Co. Rep. Cent. Cmt, 66- Mil. Serv: Entered as 2nd Lt, Army, 41, released as 1st Lt, 46, after serv. in various units, Am. and European Theaters, 41-46; Maj, Fin. Dept, Army (Hon. Res), 65- Mem: Am. and Idaho Bar Asns; Am. Judicature Soc; Am. Land Title Asn; Idaho Land Title Asn.(pres, 65); pres, Soda Springs C. of C, 66; Lions. Rel: Latter-day Saint. Legal Res: 110 MacArthur Ave, Soda Springs, Idaho 83276. Mailing Add: P.O. Box 915, Soda Springs, Idaho 83276.

KINGSTON, GEORGE J, JR. D
b. Northfield, Vt, 7/23/24; m. to Beverly Pine; c. three sons and three daughters. Educ: St. Michael's High Sch; New Eng. Inst. of Embalming. Polit. & Govt. Pos: Vt. State Rep, 63-68. Bus. & Prof. Pos: Merchant; real estate broker. Mil. Serv: S/Sgt, Army Med, 43-45. Mem: Am. Legion; Elks; Cath. Order of Foresters; State Bd. of Ment. Health; trustee, Northfield Trust Co; co-chmn, Northfield Indust. Cmt. Rel: Catholic. Mailing Add: 5 Prospect St, Northfield, Vt. 05663. (1967)

KINGSTON, JOHN EARL R
Majority Leader, N.Y. State Assembly
b. Niagara Falls, N.Y, 12/11/25; s. Paul E. Kingston and Georgia Dickson K; m. 4/16/55 to Margaret Smith; c. Henry and Kathleen. Educ: Williams Col, A.B, 48; N.Y. Univ. Law Sch, LL.B, 50. Polit. & Govt. Pos: N.Y. State Assemblyman, Nassau Co, 17th Dist, 59-, minority whip, N.Y. State Assembly, 67 & 68, majority leader, 69-; alternate del, Rep. Nat Conv, 68. Bus. & Prof. Pos: Attorney, 51- Mil. Serv: Entered as A/S, Navy, 44, released as Seaman 2/C, 46, after serv. in Am. Theatre. Mem: Past pres, Westbury Rep. Club; past pres. and chmn. bd, Nassau Co. Jaycees; F&AM; Elks; bd. dirs, Family Serv. Asn. of Nassau Co. Distinguished Serv. Award and Americanism Award, Nassau Co. Am. Legion and VFW. Rel: Episcopal. Legal Res: 97 Ward St, Westbury, N.Y. 11590. Mailing Add: 290 Old Country Rd, Mineola, N.Y. 11501.

KINK, DICK J. D
Wash. State Rep.
b. Bellingham, Wash, 1921; wid; c. one daughter. Educ: W. Wash. State Col. Polit. & Govt. Pos: Wash. State Rep, currently. Bus. & Prof. Pos: Capt, Commercial Fisherman and fish buyer, Alaska Packers Asn. Mil. Serv: Navy. Mem: VFW; Am. Legion; K. of C; Purse Seine Vessel Owners Marketing Asn.(dir). Rel: Catholic. Mailing Add: 1124 15th St, Bellingham, Wash. 98225. (1967)

KINKEAD, CECIL CALVERT D
Chmn, Unicoi Co. Dem. Party, Tenn.
b. Waycross, Tenn, 10/21/11; s. Robert David Kinkead and Winnie Alice Wilson K; m. 6/29/47 to Betty Alice Lane; c. Lane Cecile, Emily Alice and Lizbeth Sue. Educ: High Sch. Polit. & Govt. Pos: Chmn, Unicoi Co. Dem. Party, Tenn, 62- Mil. Serv: Entered as Pvt, Army, 42, released as 1st Lt, 43, after serv. in Artil. Bn, Am. Theater; Am. Theater Ribbon; Victory Medal. Mem: Am. Legion; VFW; Elks. Rel: Protestant. Legal Res: Jonesboro Rd, Erwin, Tenn. 37650. Mailing Add: P.O. Box 147, Erwin, Tenn. 37650. (1967)

KINKEAD, SHELBY C. D
b. Lexington, Ky, 1913. Educ: Univ. Ky, B.S. Polit. & Govt. Pos: City cmnr, Lexington, Ky, 54-56, mayor, 56-60; Ky. State Sen, 64-68. Bus. & Prof. Pos: Businessman; farmer. Mil. Serv: Navy. Rel: Episcopal. Mailing Add: 254 S. Ashland Ave, Lexington, Ky. 40502. (1967)

KINLER, GLADYS VERONICA R
Rep. State Cent. Committeewoman, La.
b. La, 1/13/09; d. Felix Brown and Helena Brulet B; m. 9/24/29 to Emile Joseph Kinler; c. Marlene (Mrs. Daspit) and Elton. Educ: Esplanade High Sch, 2 years; Shaw Bus. Sch, 1 year. Polit. & Govt. Pos: Chmn. hq, Goldwater Campaign, La, 64; Rep. leader, Seventh Ward, St. Tammany Parish, 64-; chmn. Rep. Parish Polit. Action Coun, 65-68; mem-at-lg, St. Tammany Rep. Exec. Cmt, 65-; Rep. committeewoman, 12th Representative Dist, 67-; rep. committeewoman, 25th Sen. Dist, 67-; Rep. State Cent. Committeewoman, 67- Mem: Served as pres, secy. and bd. mem, Lacombe Youth Center, 49-; publicity chmn, St. Tammany Parish Fair Asn; pres. adv, Bayou Womens Rep. Club; PTA; pres, Lacombe Home Demonstration Club, 65-68; charter mem, Bayou Lacombe Garden Club. Rel: Catholic. Mailing Add: Route 1, Box 118, Lacombe, La. 70445.

KINNAMAN, ELMER D. D
Wyo. State Sen.
b. Rawlins, Wyo, 4/6/02; wid; c. two. Educ: High Sch. Polit. & Govt. Pos: Dem. state committeeman, Carbon Co, Wyo, 20 years; Wyo. State Rep, 14 years, Wyo. State Sen, currently; del, Dem. Nat. Conv, 68. Bus. & Prof. Pos: Pres, Kinnaman Supply Co, Rawlins; v.pres, Automotive Parts, Casper; Auto Parts Inc, Sheridan. Mem: Shrine; Elks; VFW; Am. Legion; Lions. Rel: Protestant. Mailing Add: 320 8th St, Rawlins, Wyo. 82301.

KINNAMAN, THEODORE DWIGHT D
Chmn, Wis. New Dem. Coalition
b. Evanston, Ill, 11/19/28; s. Theodore James Kinnaman and Mamie Carolyn Robinson K; m. 8/7/53 to Janice Marilyn Herrington; c. Jacqueline Ann, Kathleen Joyce and Theodore James. Educ: Northwest. Univ, B.Mus.Ed, 50 and M.Mus, 57; Univ. Iowa, summers 61, 66 & 69; Pi Kappa Lambda. Polit. & Govt. Pos: Co-chmn, Janesville Citizens for McCarthy, Wis, 68; alternate del, Dem. Nat. Conv, 68; mem. nat. steering cmt, New Dem. Coalition, 69-; chmn, Wis. New Dem. Coalition, 69- Bus. & Prof. Pos: Chmn. music dept, Univ. Wis, Rock Co. Campus, 66- Mem: Music Educators Nat. Conf; Nat. Cmt. for Sane Nuclear Policy; Am. Civil Liberties Union. Rel: Protestant. Mailing Add: 1213 Columbus Circle, Janesville, Wis. 53545.

KINNEALLY, JAMES JOSEPH D
Chmn, Union Co. Dem. Cmt, N.J.
b. Rahway, N.J, 1/18/03; s. William H. Kinneally and Mary Crahan K; m. 9/22/25 to Gertrude A. Marvel; c. Mary D. (Mrs. Cahill), Gertrude A. (Mrs. Robison), James J, Jr, Kathleen K. (Mrs. Phillips), Barbara R. (Mrs. Husbands), William T, Doris A. and Georgene A. Polit. & Govt. Pos: Dir. revenue and finance, Rahway, N.J, 8 years, city treas, 37-42, secy, Bd. Water Cmnrs, 42-; chmn, Rahway Dem. City Cmt, 34-55; del, Dem. Nat. Conv, 68; chmn, Union Co. Dem. Cmt, N.J, currently. Mem: Munic. Finance Officers Asn; Elks; Eagles; K. of C.(4°). Rel: Roman Catholic. Mailing Add: 680 Seminary Ave, Rahway, N.J. 07065. (1967)

KINNEY, CLARKE D
b. Memphis, Tenn, 7/22/24; s. Kenneth Hays Kinney and Ruby Baird K; m. 4/27/68 to Fonda Lou Baker; c. Katherine K.(Mrs. Smith), Karen Jane and Clarke Kenneth. Educ: Memphis State Univ, B.S. in Econ, 62; Northwest. Univ, Financial Pub. Rels, 63-64. Polit. & Govt. Pos: Mem, City Coun, Hughes, Ark, 57-59; Ark. State Rep, 59-66, mem, Ark. Legis. Coun, 63-64. Bus. & Prof. Pos: Mgr, K.H. Kinney & Sons, 46-60; zone mgr, Investors Diversified Serv, 60-62; dir. pub. rels, Planters Bank and Trust Co, 62-65; v.pres, Union Mgt. Corp, 65-66; info. officer, Int. Bank Reconstruction & Develop, 66-; agency supvr, Union Life Ins. Co, Little Rock, Ark, 69- Mil. Serv: Entered as Pvt, Army, 43, released as 1st Lt, 46, after serv. in 539th Engr. Pontoon Bridge Co, Corps of Engrs, Far East Command, Okinawa Engr. Dist, 51; Good Conduct Medal. Mem: AAONMS; Little Rock Racquet Club; Red Gum Lodge 696; Razorback Club; Am. Legion; Exec. and Prfnl. Hall of Fame. Hobbies: Swimming and tennis. Rel: Methodist. Legal Res: 6616 Waverly Dr, Little Rock, Ark. 72202. Mailling Add: Union Life Annex, Little Rock, Ark. 72203.

KINNEY, DAVID B. D
b. Auburn, N.Y, 1/11/21; s. William Cady Kinney and Bernice Bowen K; m. 8/23/43 to Jean Eleanor Wilson; c. Jonathan C, Andrea J. and David H. Educ: Alma Col, B.A, 43; George Wash. Univ. Law Sch, J.D, 51. Polit. & Govt. Pos: Mem. electoral bd, Arlington, Va, 55; Co. Judge, Arlington Co, 56-58; Dem. cand. for U.S. Rep, Tenth Dist, Va, 68; alternate del, Dem. Nat. Conv, 68. Bus. & Prof. Pos: Analyst, Nat. Security Agency, 43-52; sr. partner, Attorney's Kinney, Smith & Barham, Arlington, Va. 52-; dir. and gen. counsel, Commonwealth Nat. Bank, 66-; spec. counsel, Arlington Co. Med. Soc. Mem: Va. Trial Lawyers Asn; North Va. Trial Lawyers Asn.(pres-elect); Arlington Co, Va, Va. State and Am. Bar Asns; AF&AM; RAM; Cmt. of 100, Arlington Co; Kiwanis; Young Leadership Coun, Dem. Nat. Cmt. Rel: Presbyterian. Legal Res: 3636 N. 38th St, Arlington, Va. 22207. Mailing Add: 2007 N. 15th St, Arlington, Va. 22216.

KINNEY, ROXIE W. R
V.chmn, Muskegon Co. Rep. Party, Mich.
b. Carrollton, Miss, 1/23/36; d. Eli Eugene Wiltshire and Katherine Broome W; m. 9/1/57 to Lowell Duayne Kinney; c. Kathy, Rebecca and Stephen. Educ: Memphis Bus. Sch, 54; Phyllis Bell Modeling Sch, 56. Polit. & Govt. Pos: Del, Muskegon Co. Rep. Conv, Mich, 66-68; del, Mich. State Conv, 68; v.chmn, Muskegon Co. Rep. Party, 69- Bus. & Prof. Pos: Clerical staff, Network traffic, Voice of Am, Wash. D.C, 55-58; radio traffic mgr, WJIM Radio, Lansing, Mich, 60-63; instr, charm class, Muskegon Commun. Col, 66-67. Rel: Baptist. Mailing Add: 600 W. Hile Rd, Muskegon, Mich. 49441.

KINNEY, WILLIAM B. R
b. Denver, Colo, 12/1/23; married; c. Three. Polit. & Govt. Pos: Cand, Colo. House of Rep, 60, 62 & 66. Bus. & Prof. Pos: Machine mech. for Gardner-Denver Co. Mem: Past pres. and charter mem, Rep. Toastmaster Club; Steelworkers Union. Mailing Add: 9821 Highways 6 and 85, Henderson, Colo. 80640.

KINNIE, KENNETH IVAN R
Chmn, Sedgwick Co. Rep. Cent. Cmt, Colo.
b. Julesburg, Colo, 4/28/23; s. Ernest H. Kinnie and Ruth Smith K; m. 4/28/42 to Lucille H. Fox; c. Kenneth Joe, Dennis Craig and Ernest LeRoy. Educ: Colo. Univ, 1 year. Polit. & Govt. Pos: Chmn, Sedgwick Co. Rep. Cent. Cmt, Colo, 65- Bus. & Prof. Pos: Farmer and rancher, 46-; v.pres, Hodges-Kinnie Grain Co, 58- Mil. Serv; Entered as A/S, Navy, 42, released as PO 3/C, 44. Mem: Jaycees; Farm Bur; Wheat Growers Asn. Rel: Methodist. Mailing Add: Box 25, R.R, Julesburg, Colo. 80737.

KINSELLA, GEORGE BRENDAN D
b. Hartford, Conn, 3/10/27; s. George Francis Kinsella (deceased) and Dorothea Mooney K; m. 11/26/55 to Patricia Keen; c. William Brenda, George, Richard Daniel, Ann Elizabeth and Stephen. Educ: Univ. Hartford; Univ. Conn. Polit. & Govt. Pos: Councilman, Hartford, Conn, 61-65, mayor, 65-67. Mil. Serv: Navy, World War II. Rel: Catholic. Legal Res: 230 Grandview Terr, Hartford, Conn. 06114. Mailing Add: 550 Main St, Hartford, Conn. 06103. (1967)

KINSOLVING, CHARLES McILVAINE, JR. D
First V.Chmn, N.Y. Co. Dem. Exec. Cmt.
b. N.Y.C, 1/27/27; s. Charles McIlvaine Kinsolving and Florence Natalie Hogg K; m. 7/13/63 to Coral May Eaton. Educ: Univ. Pa, A.B, 49; grad. work at Harvard, Columbia and N.Y. Univs. and the Sorbonne; Phi Beta Kappa; Delta Psi. Polit. & Govt. Pos: Mem. exec. cmt, secy. and treas, Lexington Dem. Club, 52-58; mem. city and state bd, Am. for Dem. Action, 54-; pres, Murray Hill Dem. Club, 58-61; mem. and secy, Cmt. for a Better N.Y, 60-64; dist. leader, 62nd Assembly Dist, Part D, 61-; secy. and mem. exec. cmt, Cmt. for Dem. Voters, 59-66; v.chmn, N.Y. Co. Dem. Exec. Cmt, 62-67, first v.chmn, 67-; co-chmn, Cmt. to Keep N.Y. Habitable, 63-66; mem, Direct Primary Cmt, 65-; del, Dem. Nat. Conv, 68. Bus. & Prof. Pos: Stockholder rels. rep, Am. Tel. & Tel. Co, N.Y.C, 51; research analyst, Young & Rubicam Advert. Agency, 51-53; assoc. mgr. media research, McCann-Erickson Advert. Agency, 53-58; mgr. plans develop, Nat. Broadcasting Co, 58-60; v.pres. mkt. planning, Bur. of Advert, Am. Newspaper Publishers Asn, 60- Mil. Serv: Entered as Pvt, Army, 45, released as S/Sgt, 46, after serv. in Army Ground Forces, Continental U.S, 45-46. Publ: 'The Little Old Lady from Keokuk (and Other Traveler Types),' ASTA Travel News, 10-11/66; 'What is Your Image and Who Cares? (Savings Banks Forum),' U.S. Investor, 2/3/69. Mem: Am. Mkt. Asn; Union Club; Metrop. Squash Racquets Asn; Am. Legion; India-Am. League; NAACP; Am. Civil Liberties Union; Citizens Union; Nat. Urban League; U.S. UN Asn. Rel: Episcopal. Mailing Add: 441 Park Ave. S, New York, N.Y. 10016.

KINTNER, ROBERT EDMONDS
b. Stroudsburg, Pa, 9/12/09; m. 3/9/40 to Jean Rodney; c. Susan, Michael and Jeffry. Educ: Swarthmore Col, B.A, 31. Polit. & Govt. Pos: Spec. Asst. to President of U.S, 66-67. Bus. & Prof. Pos: Reporter, New York Herald Tribune, 33-35, Wash. bur, 33-37; partner, Joseph Alsop and Robert Kintner, Wash. columnists, 37-41; pres, Am. Broadcasting Co, Inc, 50; exec. v.pres, Nat. Broadcasting Co, 57-58, pres, 58-66, chmn. and chief exec. officer, 66. Mil. Serv: Lt. Col, Army; exec. War Dept. Bur. of Pub. Rels, Wash. Publ: Washington White Paper: Men Around the President (w. Joseph Alsop). Recipient Keynote Award, Nat. Asn. Radio and TV Broadcasters. Mailing Add: 2727 Q St. N.W, Washington, D.C. 20007. (1967)

KIPLEY, EDWARD LORENZ, SR. R
Ill. State Rep.
b. Riverdale, Ill, 1/5/15; s. Edward Andrew Kipley and Mary Clark K; m. 11/18/38 to Dorothy Katherine Schroll; c. Edward L, Jr, Janet Ann (Mrs. Napoli) and Peggy. Educ: Northwest. Eve. Sch. Commerce. Polit. & Govt. Pos: Mem, zoning bd. appeals, Riverdale, Ill, 51-55, bd. trustees, 55-57 and mayor, 57-67; Ill. State Rep, 69- Bus. & Prof. Pos: Asst. credit mgr, Acme Steel Co, 39-62; credit mgr, Acme Steel Co, Interlake Steel Corp, 62-66; gen. credit mgr, Interlake Steel Corp, 66- Mem: Bd. dirs, Chicago-Midwest Credit Mgt. Asn; C. of C. Rel: Roman Catholic. Mailing Add: 323 W. 145th Place, Riverdale, Ill. 60627.

KIPP, REX, JR. D
b. 1935. Educ: N.Mex. State Univ; Tex. West. Col. Polit. & Govt. Pos: N.Mex. State Rep, 61-66. Bus. & Prof. Pos: Rancher. Mil. Serv: Army, 2 years. Mem: Masons; Elks. Rel: Methodist. Mailing Add: P.O. Box 704, Lordsburg, N.Mex. 88045. (1967)

KIPPING, GREGORY AUGUST D
Chmn, Monroe Co. Dem. Cent. Cmt, Ill.
b. Valmeyer, Ill, 1/10/29; s. August C. Kipping and Margaret Mathews K; m. 12/28/48 to Betty Vee Limestall; c. Terrence, Jenelle, Kimberely and Jeffrey. Polit. & Govt. Pos: Chmn, Monroe Co. Dem. Cent. Cmt, Ill, 56-; dep. sheriff, Monroe Co, 58-62; chmn, 56th Sen. Dist. and 57th Rep. Dist, 66. Mil. Serv: Entered as Pvt, Air Force, 47, released as Sgt, 50. Mem: Waterloo Optimist; Waterloo Sportsmen Club (pres, 2 years); Marystown Sportsmen Club; K. of C. Rel: Catholic. Mailing Add: R.R. 2, Waterloo, Ill. 62298. (1967)

KIPPING, ROBERT KIRTLEY R
Chmn, Carroll Co. Rep. Exec. Cmt, Ky.
b. Carrollton, Ky, 3/11/09; s. Oscar Gier Kipping and Mabel Kirtley K; m. 6/5/45 to Bulah Baker Butler; c. Karlene Kirtley. Educ: Wis. State Univ, Superior, summer sch; Univ. Ky, A.B; Sigma Chi; K Club. Polit. & Govt. Pos: Dep. Ky. State Fire Marshal, 47-49; elec. cmnr, Carroll Co, 49-55; chmn, Carroll Co. Rep. Exec. Cmt, 56- Bus. & Prof. Pos: Licensed funeral dir, Ky, 38-; pres, Scenic Rwys, Inc, 56- and Park Lanes, Inc, 63- Mil. Serv: Entered as Pvt, Army, 42, released as Capt, 46, after serv. in Mil. Police Corps, Am. Theater; Am. Theater Ribbon; Victory Medal; Expert Marksmanship Badge. Mem: F&AM; Kiwanis. Right tackle, Univ. Ky. Football Team, 29-32. Rel: Baptist. Legal Res: 716 Highland Ave, Carrollton, Ky. 41008. Mailing Add: Box 55, Carrollton, Ky. 41008. (1967)

KIRBY, EDWARD PAUL R
Cmnr, Plymouth Co, Mass.
b. Whitman, Mass, 1/10/28; s. Frank A. Kirby and Mabel K. Linn; m. 10/26/57 to Mary Alice Mraz; c. Matthew Paul, Jane DeChantal and Thomas More. Educ: Holy Cross Col, A.B, 49; Boston Col. Law Sch, J.D, 52. Polit. & Govt. Pos: Mass. State Rep, 61-66; cmnr, Plymouth Co, Mass, 69- Bus. & Prof. Pos: Private practice law, 56- Mil. Serv: Entered as Pvt, Army, 52, released as 1st Lt, 55, after serv. in Judge Adv. Gen. Corps, 53-55; Capt. (Ret). Mem: Mass. Bar Asn. Rel: Roman Catholic. Mailing Add: 379 Harvard St, Whitman, Mass. 02382.

KIRBY, JAMES RUSSELL D
N.C. State Sen.
b. Wilson Co, N.C, 2/17/22; s. Sanford Kirby; Cora Scott K; m. 12/19/46 to Rebekah Fulghum; c. James Russell II, David Fulghum, Jane Darden. Educ: Univ. N.C, B.S, 43; Univ. N.C. Law Sch, LL.B, 48. Polit. & Govt. Pos: Del, Dem. Nat. Conv, 64; former chmn, Traffic Code Cmn; N.C. State Sen, 63-, speaker, Ban Cmn, 65, trustee, State Educ. Asst. Authority, 66-69 and chmn, Cmt. on Higher Educ. and mem, N.C. Bd. Higher Educ, 69-, N.C. State Senate. Bus. & Prof. Pos: Lawyer. Mil. Serv: Sgt, Army, 43-45. Mem: Mason; Elks; Rotary. Rel: Methodist. Mailing Add: 1711 Brentwood Circle, Wilson, N.C. 27893.

KIRBY, PATRICK GEORGE R
b. Providence, R.I, 1/25/34; s. George L. Kirby and Ann Sullivan K; m. 10/15/59 to Patricia Gray; c. Patrick George, Jr, Michael Colm and Owen Hugh. Educ: Providence Col, A.B. in Econ, 55. Polit. & Govt. Pos: Trustee, pub. libr, Newport, R.I, 60-, mem, sch. cmt, 61-; secy, Pub. Libr. Bldg. Cmt, 66-; R.I. State Rep, 99th Dist, 67-69. Bus. & Prof. Pos: Secy, Kirby, Inc, Newport, R.I, 58- Mil. Serv: Entered as 2nd Lt, Marine Corps, 55, released as 1st Lt, 58, after serv. in Third Marine Div, FMF, 56-57 and Force Troops, Atlantic, 57-58; Capt, Commanding Officer, Ninth 105mm Howitzer Battery, Marine Corps, Res, 58- Mem: C. of C.(cmt. mem, Newport Co. Chap, 64-66, v.pres, 63-64); Rotary; K. of C; Capt, Newport Artil. Co, R.I. Militia. Rel: Roman Catholic. Mailing Add: 31 Clarke St, Newport, R.I. 02840. (1967)

KIRBY, PETER R
Mem, Calif. Rep. State Cent. Cmt.
b. Washington, D.C, 11/7/28; s. Thomas Kirby and Marguerite McKinley K; single. Educ: Univ. of Pa, B.Archit, 51; Univ. of Calif, Berkeley, M.A, 55; Tau Sigma Delta; Delta Kappa Epsilon. Polit. & Govt. Pos: Mem. bd. of dir, San Francisco Young Rep, 57-64, v.pres, 60, pres, 61; mem, San Francisco Rep. Cent. Cmt, 60-68; mem, Calif. Rep. State Cent. Cmt, 64- Bus. & Prof. Pos: Job capt, Leo A. Daly & Assocs, 55-62; proj. mgr, John Carl Warnecke & Assocs, 62-64; exec. architect, Kump, Masten & Hurd, 64-66; proj. mgr, Wurster, Bernardi & Emmons, 67-68; dir. of San Francisco off, Wm. L. Pererra & Assocs, 68- Mil. Serv: Entered as Ens, Navy, 51, released as Lt.(jg), 54, after serv. in Mobile Construction Bn. 6, Atlantic; Comdr, Naval Res, 66; Nat. Defense Ribbon; Armed Forces Res. Ribbon. Mem: Am. Inst. of Architects; Commonwealth Club of Calif; Naval Order of the U.S; Navy League. Rel: Episcopal. Mailing Add: 3952 19th St, San Francisco, Calif. 94114.

KIRBY, VINCENT JOHN D
Chmn, Madison Co. Dem. Cent. Cmt, Nebr.
b. Hadar, Nebr, 8/26/27; s. Raymond William Kirby and Margaret Risse K; m. 5/12/51 to Bernadine Timpe; c. Michael, Marian, Rebecca, Stephanie, Regina, Kelly, Rose Marie and Maureen. Educ: Creighton Univ, LL.B, 57. Polit. & Govt. Pos: Co. attorney, Madison Co, Nebr, 57-63; chmn, Madison Co. Dem. Cent. Cmt, 58- Bus. & Prof. Pos: Partner, McFadden & Kirby, 59- Mil. Serv: Entered as Pvt, Army, 50, released as Sgt, 52. Mem: Am, Nebr. and Madison Co. Bar Asns; 9th Judicial Dist. Bar Asn; Greater Creighton Univ. Convocation; Elks; Lions; Country Club; Livestock Feeders Asn; K. of C. Admitted to practice in U.S. Supreme Court. Rel: Catholic. Legal Res: Battle Creek, Nebr. 68715. Mailing Add: P.O. Box 308, Norfolk, Nebr. 68701.

KIRCHER, MARTIN A. D
Md. State Del.
b. Baltimore, Md, 6/25/30; married. Educ: Baltimore City Col; Ohio State Univ; Syracuse Univ; Univ. of Baltimore; Univ. of Baltimore Sch. of Law, LL.B, 58. Polit. & Govt. Pos: Md. State Del, 63-, chmn, Judiciary Cmt, Md. State House of Del, 69- Bus. & Prof. Pos: Attorney-at-law. Mil. Serv: Air Force, 51-55. Mem: Am. and Md. Bar Asns; Loch Raven Improv. Asn; Alhambra; K. of C. Mailing Add: 6000 Hillen Rd, Baltimore, Md. 21212.

KIRCHNER, WILLIAM G. Non-Partisan
Minn. State Sen.
b. Iowa, 1916; married; c. Four. Educ: Morningside Col, B.A; Harvard Grad. Sch. of Bus, M.B.A. Polit. & Govt. Pos: Minnesota State Rep; Minn. State Sen, currently. Bus. & Prof. Pos: Banker. Mil. Serv: Navy, 44-46, Pac. Mem: Officer and cmt. mem. several banker's trade asns; commun. group; trustee, Morningside Col; Boy Scouts of Am; Girl Scouts; YMCA. Rel: Methodist. Mailing Add: 6830 Newton Ave. S, Richfield, Minn. 55423.

KIRK, CLAUDE ROY, JR. R
Gov, Fla.
b. San Bernardino, Calif, 1/7/26; s. Claude Roy Kirk and Sarah McLure K; m. 2/18/67 to Erika Mattfeld; c. Sarah Stokes, Katherine Gilmer, Franklin, William, Adriana and Claudia. Educ: Emory Univ; Duke Univ, B.S, 45; Univ. Ala, Law, 49; Sigma Alpha Epsilon. Polit. & Govt. Pos: Gov, Fla, 67-; del, Rep. Nat. Conv, 68. Bus. & Prof. Pos: Salesman, ins. and bldg. supplies, 49; v.chmn, Am. Heritage Life Ins. Co, 54; partner, Hayden, Stone, Inc, 60; founder, Kirk Investment Co, 64. Mil. Serv: Entered as 2nd Lt, Marine Corps, 43, released as 1st Lt, 46, reenterd, 50 and released, 52, after serv. in Korean Conflict; Air Medal. Mem: Financial Analysts Soc; trustee, Episcopal Church Found; Saints and Sinners; 21 Club, N.Y.C. Rel: Episcopal. Mailing Add: The Capitol, Tallahassee, Fla. 32304

KIRK, GLADYS R
Wash. State Rep.
b. Colorado; m. to Douglas G. Kirk; c. two sons. Educ: Bus. Col. Polit. & Govt. Pos: Wash. State Rep, currently. Mem: Bus. & Prfnl. Women; Am. Legion Auxiliary (past pres. assembly); Gov. Coun. on Aging. Mailing Add: 1236 Bigelow N, Seattle, Wash. 98109. (1967)

KIRK, JOHN FRANCIS, JR. R
Del. State Rep.
b. Wilmington, Del, 6/15/31; s. John Francis Kirk and Mary I. Moody K; m. 12/12/53 to Margaret F. Nickle; c. John F, III, David Keith and Cynthia Sue. Educ: Goldey Col, 49-50. Polit. & Govt. Pos: Bd. mem, Gunning Bedford Sch. Dist, Del, 65-66, pres, sch. bd, 66-69; v.pres, interim sch. bd, Gunning Bedford-New Castle Dist, 69-, bd. mem, 69-; Del. State Rep, 69-; mem, New Castle Co. Rep. Exec. Cmt, 69- Mil. Serv: Entered as Pvt, Army, 51, released as Cpl, 53, after serv. in 7774th Signal Bn, ETO, 52-53; European Occup. Medal. Mem: Del. Sch. Bd. Asn; Lions Int; Grange. Rel: Catholic. Legal Res: 522 St. Georges Rd, Delaware City, Del. 19706. Mailing Add: State House of Representatives, Dover, Del. 19901.

KIRK, PHILLIP JAMES, JR. R
State Chmn, N.C. Young Rep.
b. Salisbury, N.C, 11/24/44; s. Phillip James Kirk and Geneva Bostian K; m. 6/11/66 to Carolyn Viola Parks. Educ: Catawba Col, A.B, 67. Polit. & Govt. Pos: Pres, East Rowan TAR, 63; state pres, N.C. TAR, 64, adv, 65; publicity chmn, N.C. Young GOP Exec. Cmt, 66, publ. chmn, 66-68 and ed, Tarheel YR, 66-68; adv, East Rowan Teen Age GOP, 67-; pub. rels. dir, Earl Ruth for Cong, 68; sr. party chmn, Rowan Co. Rep, 68-; treas, N.C. Young Rep, 69, state chmn, 69- Bus. & Prof. Pos: Reporter, Salisbury Eve. Post, N.C, 63-67; teacher, Knox Jr. High Sch, Salisbury, 67- Mem: N.C. Educ. Asn; Nat. Educ. Asn; Salisbury Classroom Teachers; Nat. Asn. of Sportswriters and Sportscasters; Optimists (past pres, v.pres. and mem. bd. dirs, Salisbury Optimist Club). N.C. Teen Age Rep. of Year, 63; N.C. Young Rep. of Year, 67; First Runner-up, Nat. Male Young Rep. of Year, 67; Rookie of Year, Salisbury Optimist Club. Rel: First United Church of Christ. Mailing Add: Route 5, Box 238, Salisbury, N.C. 28144.

KIRK, POLLY R
Secy, Kans. Rep. State Cmt.
b. Sumner, Mo, 12/17/19; d. John L. Brown (deceased) and May Leathem B. (deceased); m. 8/30/41 to Orlin H. Kirk, Jr; c. Linda A. and Kevin D. Educ: Cent. Bus. Col, Kansas City, Mo, grad, 39. Polit. & Govt. Pos: Secy, Mo. State Soc. Security Cmn, 39-43; v.chmn, Overland Park Rep. City Cmt, Kans, 60-68; precinct committeewoman, Johnson Co. Rep. Cent. Cmt, 60-, secy, 61-64; mem, Rep. Gubernatorial Campaign Cmts. for John Anderson, 62, Paul Wunsch, 64, William Avery, 66 and Richard Harman, 68; v.pres, Overland Park Women's Rep. Club, 63-64, pres, 64-65; chmn, Kans. State Bd. of Rev, 63-66; women's campaign chmn, U.S. Sen. James B. Pearson, Kans, 66; asst. to U.S. Sen. James B. Pearson, Kans, 67-; Johnson Co. chmn, Kans. Day Club, 68-; sustaining mem, Rep. Nat. Cmt. Bus. & Prof. Pos: Secy, Lord Mfg. Co, Burbank, Calif, 43-45. Mem: Libr. chmn, Overland Park PTA; group leader, Campfire Girls; den mother, Overland Park Coun. Boy Scouts; pres, Kans. State Univ. Alpha Chi Omega Mother's Club; Kans. Fedn. of Rep. Women; C. of C; Kans. Rep. Five-Score Club; Citizens Adv. Cmt. on Sports for Johnson Co. Commun. Col. Distinguished Jayhawker Award, 64. Rel: Methodist. Legal Res: 8710 Eby Dr, Overland Park, Kans. 66212. Mailing Add: 5410 W. 58th Terr, Mission, Kans. 66205.

KIRKENDALL, MARY MARGARET R
Secy, Jackson Co. Rep. Cent. Cmt, Ohio
b. Oak Hill, Ohio, 7/5/17; d. David Newton Davis and Annetta Evans D; m. 6/10/45 to Rothbe H. Kirkendall; c. LeAnne (Mrs. Kamber) and Jerry. Educ: Ohio State Univ, summer 38-42; Rio Grande Col, B.S. in Educ, 60; Alpha Sigma Tau; Dramatics Club; Womens Athletic Asn. Polit. & Govt. Pos: Rep. Cent. Committeeman, Madison Twp, Oak Hill, Ohio, 55-; secy, Jackson Co. Rep. Cent. Cmt, 60- Bus. & Prof. Pos: Teacher, Moriah Rural Sch, Oak Hill, Ohio, 37-38; first and second grade teacher, Higby Sch, Chillicothe, 38-41; third grade teacher, Cent. Sch, Oak Hill, 41-45; clerk-typist, Ord, Ft. Hood, Tex, 45-46; fifth grade teacher, Oak View Sch, Oak Hill, Ohio, 55- Mem: Jackson Co. Teachers Asn; Ohio Educ. Asn. Rel: Protestant. Mailing Add: Route 4, Box 216, Oak Hill, Ohio 45656.

KIRKLAND, ALMA WALSH R
V.Chmn, Young Rep. Nat. Fedn.
b. N.Y.C, 7/22/34; d. Donald E. Walsh and Edith de Bretteville W; m. 6/18/54 to E.R. Kirkland; c. Bonnie and Craig. Educ: Univ. Miami; Capitol Hill Club. Polit. & Govt. Pos: First v.pres, S.C. Fedn. of Rep. Women, 63-64, state rev. chmn, 64-65; del, Rep. Nat. Conv. and mem, Permanent Orgn. Cmt, 64; secy, Horry Co. Rep. Party, S.C, 64-66; v.chmn, Young Rep. Nat. Fedn, 67-, former co-dir, Region IV, nat. committeewoman, S.C, 69- Mem: Women's Nat. Rep. Club. Rel: Unitarian. Mailing Add: 26 Glebe St, Charleston, S.C. 29401.

KIRKLAND, HOGAN EMIL D
b. Glennville, Ga, 12/23/06; s. James Ellis Kirkland and Minerva Bacon K; m. 5/24/28 to Winnie Bryant Howard; c. Hal Howard. Educ: Glennville High Sch; attended Univ. of Ga, 27. Polit. & Govt. Pos: Ga. State Rep, 61-64. Bus. & Prof. Pos: Farmer. Mem: Mason; Shriner. Rel: Methodist. Mailing Add: Glennville, Ga. 30428. (1967)

KIRKPATRICK, BRUCE WILBUR R
Chmn, Lyon Co. Rep. Cmt, Minn.
b. Mountain Lake, Minn, 4/4/22; s. Virgil LeRoy Kirkpatrick and Nita Lange K; m. 8/17/47 to Marcella Maxine Kemnitz; c. Linda Sue, Candace Lee and Peter Owen. Educ: Univ. Minn. Col. Pharm, B.S, 49; Kappa Psi. Polit. & Govt. Pos: Alderman-at-lg, Tracy City Coun, Minn, 58-63; v.chmn, Lyon Co. Rep. Cmt, 63-65, chmn, 65-; mem, Minn. State Rep. Cent. Cmt, 65-; mem, Tracy Charter Cmn, 67- Bus. & Prof. Pos: Owner and mgr, Kirkpatrick Drug, Tracy, 49-64, pres. and mgr, 64-67; self-employed pharmacist, 67- Mil. Serv: Entered as Pvt, Army, 43, released as Tech. 4th grade, 46, after serv. in Med. Detachment, 16th Inf, First Inf. Div, ETO, 44-46; Good Conduct Medal; Combat Med. Badge; Bronze Star Medal. Mem: Minn. Pharmaceutical Asn; Nat. Asn. Retail Druggists; C. of C; AF&AM; Am. Legion; Southwest. Minn. State Col. Alumni Asn. Rel: Lutheran. Mailing Add: 713 Second East St, Tracy, Minn. 56175.

KIRKPATRICK, EVRON MAURICE D
b. Benton Co, Ind, 8/15/11; m. to Jeane Jordan; c. Douglas, John and Stuart. Educ: Univ. Ill, B.A, 32 and A.M, 33; Yale Univ, Ph.D, 39; Phi Beta Kappa; Pi Sigma Alpha. Polit. & Govt. Pos: Asst. research dir, research and anal. br, Off. of Strategic Serv, 45; with Dept. of State, 46-54; exec. dir, Am. Polit. Sci. Asn, 54- Bus. & Prof. Pos: Instr, Univ. Minn, 35-39, asst. prof, 39-43, assoc. prof, 43-48, prof, 48; ed. adv. polit. sci, Henry Holt & Co, 52-; pres, Opers. and Policy Research, Inc, 56- Publ: Auth, The People, Politics and the Politician, 41; co-auth, Running the Country, 46 and Elections—USA, 56; plus others. Mem: Bd. of trustees, Inst. for Am. Univs; Citizenship Clearing House; Helen Dwight Reid Found; coun. and exec. cmt, Int. Polit. Sci. Asn; Nat. Arbit. Asn.(bd. arbitrators, 43-47); ed. adv. bd, Who's Who in Am. Politics, 67 & 69. Legal Res: 6812 Granby St, Bethesda, Md. 20034. Mailing Add: 1527 New Hampshire Ave. N.W, Washington, D.C. 20036.

KIRKPATRICK, JAMES C. D
Secy. of State, Mo.
b. Braymer, Mo, 6/15/05; s. Ray N. Kirkpatrick and Lena L. Rea K; m. 8/18/27 to Jessamine Elizabeth Young; c. Don; grandchildren, Larry and Dee Anne. Educ: Cent. Mo. State Col, Warrensburg, Mo; Sch. of Journalism, Univ. of Mo. Polit. & Govt. Pos: Formerly admin. asst. to Gov; mem, Gov. Cmt. on Commerce and Indust. Develop; dir, Missourians for Progress, 62; Secy. of State, Mo, 64- Bus. & Prof. Pos: Publisher, Windsor Rev; former ed, Warrensburg Daily Star Jour, Jefferson City Post-Tribune and Capital News. Mem: Mo. Press Asn.(past pres); Cent. Mo. Press Asn; Dem. Ed. of Mo; C. of C.(former pres, Warrensburg, Windsor Chap); Jefferson City Rotary Club (first v.pres); Windsor Lions Club (pres); mem. bd. regents, Cent. Mo. State Col, 10 years, as pres. bd, 12 years; mem. bd, Mo. 4-H. Found. Mo. Acad. Squires, 68; Mo. Good Rds. and Sts. Honor Award, 68; Medalists for distinguished serv. to journalism, Mo. Sch. Journalism, 69. Rel: Methodist. Mailing Add: Jefferson City, Mo. 65101.

KIRKPATRICK, WILLIAM HUNTINGTON R
b. Easton, Pa, 10/2/85; s. Hon. William S. Kirkpatrick and Elizabeth H. Jones K; m. 5/17/13 to Mary Stewart Wells; c. William S. and Miles. Educ: Lafayette Col, A.B, 05, LL.D, 44; Student Law Dept, Univ. of Pa, 05-06, LL.M, 37. Polit. & Govt. Pos: U.S. Rep, Pa, 21-23; U.S. Dist. Judge, East. Dist, Pa, 27-58, Sr. Dist. Judge, 58-; trustee, Lafayette Col, 33-61, emer. trustee, currently. Mil. Serv: Lt. Col, Judge Adv. Gen. Dept. and mem, Bd. of Rev. of Courts Martial, World War I. Rel: Presbyterian. Mailing Add: Route 1, Box 166, Harwood, Md. 20776.

KIRSCH, CHARLES EDWARD R
Chmn, Mich. State Rep. Finance Cmt.
b. Sturgis, Mich, 9/21/27; s. Guy Waldo Kirsch and Flora Callender K; m. 6/22/57 to Barbara Jean Carls; Kathleen Lynn, Lauri Beth, Amy Judith, Charles Douglas and Martha Ann. Educ: De Pauw Univ, 46-48; West. Mich. Univ, 49-50; Lambda Chi Alpha. Polit. & Govt. Pos: City finance chmn, Rep. Party, Sturgis, Mich, 59; finance chmn, Rep. Party, St. Joseph Co, 60; chmn, Mich. State Rep. Finance Cmt, 67-; del, Rep. Nat. Conv, 68. Bus. & Prof. Pos: Sales trainee, Kirsch Co, Sturgis, Mich, 49, asst. sales mgr, 52-55, sales mgr, 55-57, exec. v.pres, mkt, 57-60, exec. v.pres, 60-65, pres, 65- Mil. Serv: Navy, 45-46. Mem: Elks; F&AM; K.T; Shrine; AAONMS; Scottish Rite; Rotary; Klinger Lake Country Club; Macatawa Bay Yacht Club; Chicago Yacht Club. Rel: Presbyterian. Legal Res: 1108 S. Lakeview, Sturgis, Mich. 49091. Mailing Add: c/o Kirsch Co, 309 N. Prospect, Sturgis, Mich. 49091.

KIRSCH, MORRIS R
b. Brooklyn, N.Y, 10/4/06; s. Hyman Kirsch; m. 11/13/27 to Bertha Cohen; c. Leon Robert, David Allan and Sara Joyce (Mrs. Lampert). Polit. & Govt. Pos: Mem, War Finance Prog, Nat. War Fund; dep. sector comdr, air raid wardens, Dept. Civilian Defense; commodity chmn, Gasoline Dept. and mem, Price Control Panel, Off. Price Admin; mem, Nat. and 10th Assembly Dist. Rep. Clubs; mayor, Williamsburg, N.Y; mem, East. Dist, U.S. Cmnr. of Jurors, 66- Bus. & Prof. Pos: Chmn, Beverage Indust. Drive, United Serv. Orgn, World War II; dir, Kings Co. Lafayette Trust Co; mem. adv. bd, Mfrs. Hanover Trust Co; chmn. of bd, Kirsch Beverages, Inc. and NO.CAL Corp, 68- Mem: Membership chmn, N.Y. State, Nat. Soft Drink Asn; dir. and past pres, N.Y. State Bottlers of Carbonated Beverages and Metrop. Soft Drink Bd. of Trade; mem. distribution cmt, Nat. Asn. of Mfrs; v.pres. and chmn. pub. rels, Brooklyn C. of C; pres. coun, Am. Inst. of Mgt; Brooklyn Club; Knights of the Round Table; dir. and past pres, Williamsburg Kiwanis; dir, Unity Club of Brooklyn and Knights Before Xmas; Temple Club; Williamsburg Luncheon Club; Elks; Shrine; Pilgrim Lodge; dir, Harvest Lodge, B'nai B'rith; Rotary; Sales Exec. Club of N.Y; Excelsior Club; Gov. Club; dir, United Jewish Appeal; chmn. bd, Brooklyn Unit; and trustee, N.Y. Br, Am. Cancer Soc; pres, Isaac Albert Research Inst, 54-59, hon. pres, 59; Kings Co. chmn, Historic State Cmn, Hudson-Champlain Celebration, 59; treas, Brooklyn Philharmonia; dir, Brooklyn Col. Hillel Found; v.pres, Youth United; dir, Jewish Hosp. of Brooklyn; pres. and dir, Kingsbrook Med. Center; dir. and v.pres, Pride of Judea Children's Serv; dir. and secy, Williamsburg YMHA and YWHA; adv. bd, Parent Educ. Prog; dir, Indust. Home for the Blind; life mem, Brownsville Boy's Club; past pres, Men's Adv. Coun, Williamsburg Settlement House; dir. and v.chmn. of bd, Am. Red Cross; Mayor's Cmt. for Better Housing; panel mem, Am. Arbit. Asn; Mayor's Cmt. to Keep N.Y. Clean; John Cashmore Mem. Cmt; N.Y. World's Fair 1964 Corp; pres, N.Y. League of Locality Mayors; bd. of visitors, Brooklyn State Hosp; dir, Gr. N.Y. Histadrut Coun; adv. bd, Gr. N.Y. Safety Coun; Brooklyn Commun. Dist. Planning Bd. 8; nat. trustee and dir. Kings Co, Nat. Conf. of Christians & Jews; drive chmn, Travelers Aid, YMCA, N.Y. Coun, Boy Scouts, United Hosp. Fund, Gr. N.Y. Fund, Am. Cancer Soc; United Serv. Orgn, Joint Defense Appeal, Hebrew Immigrant Aid Soc, United Jewish Appeal, Am. Red Cross, Salvation Army, Anti-Defamation League, Nat. Found. of Infantile Paralysis, Fedn. of Jewish Philanthropies and N.Y. Heart Asn; hon. chmn, Sister Kenny Found; Honor Legion, N.Y.C. Police Dept. Williamsburg Settlement Gold Medal Award, 61; State of Israel Historic Award; Founder's Award, Isaac Albert Research Inst, 54; Israel's Bar Mitzvah Award, 64; Ky. Col, 57; Adm, N.C. Navy, 62; Men's Club Honoree, Vis. Nurse Asn, 66; Citizens Award Kings Co. Med. Asn, 66; N.Y. State Mason of the Year, 67; Serv. Award, Flatbush C. of C, 67; Brooklyn Hall of Fame, 67; Distinguished Serv. Award, Histadrut, 68; Brooklyn Man of the Year, Israel Bond Drive, 68; United Jewish Appeal, 68. Rel: Jewish; Trustee, Union Temple of Brooklyn. Legal Res: 135 Eastern Parkway, Brooklyn, N.Y. 11238. Mailing Add: 921 Flushing Ave, Brooklyn, N.Y. 11206.

KIRSCH, NATHAN S. D
b. N.Y.C, 10/2/18; s. Benjamin Kirsch and Rebecca Leitner K; m. 7/15/38 to Anne Rizack; c. Daniel E. and George B. Educ: City Col. New York, B.S, 39, M.A, 41; Sch. Law, N.Y. Univ, LL.B, 64. Polit. & Govt. Pos: Chmn, Minority Study Group, Mayor's Adv. Cmt, 58-; munic. prosecutor, Hackensack, N.J, 66-67 & 69-; del, Dem. Nat. Conv, 68; chmn, Bergen Co. Dem. Coalition, 68-69; chmn, Dem. Coalition Party, 13th Assembly Dist, Bergen Co, 69. Bus. & Prof. Pos: Pres, Roses, Indescribable, 55- Mil. Serv: Entered as Pvt, Army, 44, released as Army Student, 45, after serv. in Army Specialized Training Prog, Japanese Lang. Study, Univ. Chicago. Mem: Am, N.J. and Bergen Co. Bar Asns; Nat. Dry Goods Retail Asn; chmn, Tenants Asn, Bergen Mall Shopping Center, 58-59; chmn, Merchants Div. Commun. Chest, 59. Rel: Hebrew. Legal Res: 429 Heath Place, Hackensack, N.J. 07601. Mailing Add: 25 E. Salem St, Hackensack, N.J. 07601.

KIRTLEY, DONALD RAY R
b. Cleburne, Tex, 7/26/38; s. Ott G. Batts (stepfather) and Odell Davis B; m. 2/5/60 to Sharon Curtis; c. Gregory F. and Melissa L. Educ: Boston Univ, 62; Univ. Md, B.S, 61; Sigma Delta Chi; Kappa Alpha Mu; Alpha Tau Omega. Polit. & Govt. Pos: Admin. asst. to U.S. Rep. William V. Roth, Del, 66-69. Bus. & Prof. Pos: Pub. rels, E.I. DuPont Co, Wilmington, Del, 65-66; pub. affairs officer, Hercules, Inc, 69- Mil. Serv: Entered as 2nd Lt, Air Force, 61, released as Capt, 65, after serv. in U.S. Mil. Assistance Command, Vietnam, Pac. Air Forces, 63-64; Cert. of Merit, Vietnam; Southeast Asia Expeditionary Forces Medal. Mem: Sigma Delta Chi; Air Force Asn; Bull Elephants; VFW. Rel: Protestant. Mailing Add: 22 Drummond Dr, Wilmington, Del. 19808.

KIRTLEY, JAMES MARION D
b. Crawfordsville, Ind, 7/23/10; s. William Raymond Kirtley and Laurel S. Miller K; m. 2/14/43 to Lee A. Black; c. David James, Samuel William and Raymond Marion. Educ: Wabash Col, A.B, 32; Ind. Univ. Sch. of Med, M.D, 36; Pi Delta Epsilon; Blue Key; Kappa Sigma; Nu Sigma Nu. Polit. & Govt. Pos: Councilman-at-lg, Crawfordsville Common Coun, Ind, 55-62; Joint Sen, Ind. Gen. Assembly, 63-66; chmn, Gov. Cmn. on the Handicapped, 68- Mil. Serv: Entered as 1st Lt, Army, 40, released as Lt. Col, 45, after serv. as Fourth Inf. Div. Regimental Surgeon, 22nd Inf, Med. Corps, ETO Theater, 44-45; Col, Med. Corps, Army Res, currently; Bronze Star with Two Oak Leaf Clusters & V Device; Medical Badge; Presidential Unit Citation; ETO Ribbon with Invasion Arrowhead and Five Battle Stars; American Defense Ribbon; American Theater Ribbon; Occupation of Germany; Army Reserve Medal; Belgian Fourragere. Mem: Montgomery Co. Med. Soc. (pres, 55 & 69); F&AM; York Rite; Scottish Rite; Murat Shrine; Kiwanis; Am. Legion; VFW. Rel: Disciples of Christ. Legal Res: 615 Thornwood Rd, Crawfordsville, Ind. 47933. Mailing Add: P.O. Box 506, Crawfordsville, Ind. 47933.

KIRTLEY, LOUISE GASSER D
b. Owensboro, Ky; d. Joseph Valentine Gasser and Elizabeth Neicam G; m. to W.W. Kirtley, wid; c. Elisabeth Anne (Mrs. Jacobs), Wesley W. and Robert Milton. Educ: Smith Col, A.B. cum laude; Univ. Louisville Law Sch, LL.B. Polit. & Govt. Pos: Ky. State Rep, 62-65; city attorney, Owensboro, 58-60 and city judge, 45-52; v.chmn, Ky. Cmn. on Status of Women; Publn: Article on legis. Mem: Am. and Ky. Bar Asns; v.pres, Daviess Co. Bar Asn, 62-64; Nat. Asn. Women Lawyers; pres, Ky. Div, Am. Asn. Univ. Women, 64-66; chmn, Ky. Women Lawyers, 62-66; treas, Daviess Co. Libr. Cmt, 58-; pres, Owensboro Bus. & Prfnl. Women's Club, 59-60, Owensboro Estates Coun, 62-63 and Owensboro Am. Legion Auxiliary, 42. Rel: Presbyterian. Legal Res: 1924 Lexington Ave, Owensboro, Ky. 42301. Mailing Add: Masonic Bldg, Owensboro, Ky. 42301. (1967)

KIRVIN, JOHN F. D
b. Easthampton, Mass, 10/7/26; m. to Jean Reisinger; c. three. Educ: Mass. and Schenectady schs. Polit. & Govt. Pos: Minority leader, Schenectady Co. Bd. of Supvrs, N.Y, 2 years; councilman, Rotterdam, 55-57; supvr, 57-64 & 68-69; N.Y. State Assemblyman, 64-66. Bus. & Prof. Pos: Ins. broker; secy. treas, Cervera, Feldman and Kirvin, Inc. Mem: Kiwanis; Rotterdam Bus. Men's Asn; Four Chaplains War Mem. Cmt; hon. life mem, Rotterdam Vol. Fire Asn. Mailing Add: 1213 Fort Hunter Rd, Rotterdam, N.Y. 12303.

KIRWAN, MICHAEL JOSEPH D
U.S. Rep, Ohio
b. Wilkes-Barre, Pa, 12/2/86; s. John Kirwan and Mary Duddy K; m. 9/15/20 to Alice Kane; c. John Joseph, Michael Joseph and Mary Alice. Polit. & Govt. Pos: Asst. chmn, V.I. and Guam Off. Territories; mem, Youngstown City Coun, Ohio, 32-36; U.S. Rep, Ohio, 37-, chmn, Dem. Nat. Cong. Cmt, 68- Mil. Serv: Army, AEF, 64th Artil, 17-19. Mem: Adv. cmt, Who's Who in Am. Polit, 67 & 69; Am. Legion; VFW. Legal Res: Youngstown, Ohio. Mailing Add: Room 2470 Rayburn House Bldg, Washington, D.C. 20515.

KIRWIN, ARTHUR ROBERT D
b. Albany, N.Y, 8/3/06; s. James A. Kirwin and Sarah A. Herkenham K; m. 8/11/34 to Arlene L. Dwyer; c. Arthur R, Jr, John D, Peter D. and Christine (Mrs. Robert J. Krackeler). Educ: Russell Sage Col, eve. div, 1 year. Polit. & Govt. Pos: Off. court reporter, City Court of Albany, N.Y, 32-34, Co. Court of Albany, 34-44 and N.Y. State Supreme Court, Third Judicial Dist, 44-59; del, N.Y. State Dem. Conv, 44, 48, 52, 54, 60 & 64; consultation clerk, N.Y. State Supreme Court, Appellate Div, Third Judicial Dept, 59-; secy, Albany Co. Dem. Cmt, 66; alternate del, Dem. Nat. Conv, 68. Mem: N.Y. State Shorthand Reporters Asn.(past mem. exec. cmt); Cert. Shorthand Reporter, State of N.Y; Nat. Shorthand Reporters Asn; Elks; K. of C. Rel: Roman Catholic; Past trustee, St. Teresa of Avila Roman Cath. Church. Legal Res: 1 Ichabod Lane, Albany, N.Y. 12211. Mailing Add: Supreme Court, Appellate Division, Third Dept, County Court House, Albany, N.Y. 12207.

KISER, ROGER CLINTON D
b. Yadkin Twp, N.C, 8/30/94; s. Edwin Kiser; Amy Florence Butner; m. 8/14/26 to Gertrude Margaret Bedell; c. Mrs. Philip J. Crutchfield and

Edwin Marten. Educ: Guilford Col; Univ. N.C; Teachers Col, Columbia Univ; Appalachian State Teachers Col. Polit. & Govt. Pos: N.C. State Rep, 49-68. Bus. & Prof. Pos: Teacher; farmer. Mem: Mason; Legionnaire. Rel: Christian Church. Mailing Add: Vance St, Laurinburg, N.C. 28352. (1967)

KISNER, IGNATIUS 'ICKIE' D
V.Chmn, Stafford Co. Dem. Party, Kans.
b. Hays, Kans, 8/18/25; s. Ignatz Kisner and Kathrine Gabel K; m. 9/12/48 to Jo Ann Dobbs; c. Bobby Duane, Karla Rea and Kristi Lynn. Educ: Dodge City High Sch, Kans. Polit. & Govt. Pos: V.chmn, Stafford Co. Dem. Party, 69- Bus. & Prof. Pos: Purchasing agent, Truck-Trailer Supply Co, Inc, 54-61; owner, Ickie Kisner & Assocs, Stafford, 61- Mil. Serv: Entered as Seaman, Navy, 43, released as CSG 2, 46 and Korea, 50-52. Mem: Independent Agents Asn; Life Underwriters Asn; C. of C; Optimists; Wheat Growers Asn. Legal Res: 328 N. Keystone, Stafford, Kans. 67578. Mailing Add: P.O. Box 27, Stafford, Kans. 67578.

KISSACK, JOHN WALTER D
Mem, Dem. State Exec. Cmt, Nebr.
b. Flint, Mich, 8/6/29; s. Elmer Richard Kissack and Marie Pfeffer K; m. 8/23/55 to Marjorie Ann Monasmith; c. Susan Marie, John Walter, Jr, Kathleen Diane, Barbara Lynn and Diana Michelle. Educ: Univ. Colo, B.S. in Bus. Admin, 51; Alpha Kappa Psi; Kappa Kappa Psi; treas, Independent Students Asn, 50-51; Newman Club; Viking Club. Polit. & Govt. Pos: Del, Dem. State Conv, Nebr, 52, 56, 58, 60, 64, 66 & 68; former Dem. precinct capt. and del, Scotts Bluff Co. Dem. Cent. Cmt, chmn. orgn. cmt, 58-60, v.chmn, 60-62 and chmn, 62-; mem, Nat. Adv. Coun, Small Bus. Admin, 63-67; mem, Sixth Dist. Supreme Court Nominating Cmn, 62-; mem, 48th Dist. State Dem. Exec. Cmt. and committeeman, 48th Dist. State Dem. Cent. Cmt, 66- Bus. & Prof. Pos: Partner, Elmer R. Kissack Co, 51-, sales mgr, 59-63, gen. mgr, 63- and owner, 67- Mil. Serv: Entered as Recruit, Navy, 51, released as Seaman 1/C, 51. Mem: Nat. Off. Prod. Asn; Nat. Off. Machine Dealers Asn; Lions Int; K. of C; C. of C. Rel: Catholic. Mailing Add: 1805 Q St, Gering, Nebr. 69341.

KISSE, DAN R
b. 12/25/08; married; c. Seven. Educ: Pub. Schs. Polit. & Govt. Pos: N.Dak. State Sen, 59-66; Dunn Co. FHA Bd. mem, 3 terms. Bus. & Prof. Pos: Farmer, rancher; Consol. Tel. Co. Mem: Farm Bur; PTA (pres, Dist. Five, 3 years); chmn. bd, St. Luke's Nursing Home, Dickinson, until 69; dir. bd, Sunset Home, Bowman, 3 years, chmn, 69- Rel: Lutheran. Mailing Add: Halliday, N.Dak. 58636.

KISSINGER, HENRY ALFRED
Asst. to the President for Nat. Security Affairs
b. Fuerth, Germany, 5/27/23; s. Louis Kissinger and Paula Stern K; div; c. Elizabeth and David. Educ: City Col, N.Y.C, 41-43; Harvard Univ, A.B, 50, M.A, 52, Ph.D, 54. Polit. & Govt. Pos: Consult. to various Govt. agencies including, Weapons Syst. Evan. Group of the Joint Chiefs of Staff, Nat. Security Coun, U.S. Arms Control and Disarmament Agency and State Dept, 59-68; Asst. to the President for Nat. Security Affairs, 69- Bus. & Prof. Pos: Dir. study on nuclear weapons and for. policy, Coun. on For. Rels, N.Y, 55-56; dir. spec. study proj, Rockefeller Bros. Fund, 56-58; assoc. dir, Center for Int. Affairs, dir, Harvard Int. Seminar, dir, Nat. Security Studies Prog. and assoc. prof, Harvard Univ, 58-68. Mil. Serv: Army, 84th Inf. Div, 970th Counter Intel. Corp, 43-46, Capt, Mil. Intel, Res, 46-59. Publ: Nuclear Weapons and Foreign Policy, 57 and The Necessity for Choice: Prospects of American Foreign Policy, 61, Harper & Bros; The Troubled Partnership: A Reappraisal of the Atlantic Alliance, McGraw Hill, 65. Mem: Phi Beta Kappa; Century Club, N.Y.C; Cosmos Club, Wash, D.C; Fed. City Club; Asn. of U.S. Army; Am. Acad. Arts & Sci, Boston. Citation by Overseas Press Club for Nuclear Weapons and Foreign Policy, 58; Woodrow Wilson Prize for best book in fields of govt, polit. and int. affairs, 58; Guggenheim Fel, 65-66; Harvard Nat. Scholarship; Harvard Fel; Harvard Detur; Rockefeller Found. Fel for Polit. Theory. Legal Res: Cambridge, Mass. Mailing Add: The White House, Washington, D.C. 20500.

KISSINGER, JOSEPH GRIFFIN R
Mem. Cand. Selection Cmt, Hamilton Co. Rep. Party, Tenn.
b. Chattanooga, Tenn, 9/4/26; s. Joseph Floyd Kissinger and Lavada Willingham K; m. 3/20/49 to Betty Jo Robinson; c. Sherry, Marcella and Millicent. Educ: Univ. Chattanooga, B.S, 52. Polit. & Govt. Pos: Tenn. State Rep, 65-68; mem. cand. selection cmt, Hamilton Co. Rep. Party, 69- Bus. & Prof. Pos: V.pres, Chattanooga Dry Cleaner Asn, 54, pres, 55. Mil. Serv: Entered as Pvt, Army, 45, released as T/5, 46, re-entered as 2nd Lt, 52, released 53, after serv. in Italy, 45-46 and Korea, 53. Mem: Mason; Lions. Rel: Presbyterian. Mailing Add: 4300 Highwood Dr, Chattanooga, Tenn. 37415.

KISTLER, GUY A. R
Pa. State Rep.
b. Nanticoke, Pa, 11/15/10; s. Wilbur A. Kistler and Blance Nash K; m. to Beatrice Davis Jenkins; c. three. Educ: Plymouth Twp. High Sch; Newberry-Murphy Schs. of Merchandising, Mgt, and Investment Control. Polit. & Govt. Pos: Former v.chmn, Finance Cmt. Cumberland Co. Rep. Orgn, Pa; past pres, Coun. of Borough, Camp Hill; Pa. State Rep, 61-, chmn, Cmt. Elec. and Apportionment, v.chmn, Cmt. Game and Fisheries, mem, Higher Educ. Cmt. and Cmt. Ways and Means, Pub. Health and Welfare, Joint State Govt. Cmn. Task Force on Conserv, Historic Sites, and Optimum Use of State Col. Facilities and mem. bd. Pa. Higher Educ. Asst. Agency and chmn, Cmt. on Appeals, Pa. State House of Rep. Bus. & Prof. Pos: Former mgr. dept. stores; former exec. v.pres, Sucuritext, Inc; owner, Puritan Brookwood Co. and Puritan Sales Co. Mem: Engrs. Soc. Pa; F&AM; Harrisburg Consistory; AAONMS; Harrisburg Hunters & Anglers; Carlisle Fish and Game Club. Rel: Methodist; bd. mem, Grace Methodist Church. Mailing Add: 2327 Harvard Ave, Camp Hill, Pa. 17011.

KITCHEL, DENISON R
b. Bronxville, N.Y, 3/1/08; s. William Lloyd Kitchel and Grace Wheeler K; m. 4/22/41 to Naomi Margaret Douglas; c. James Douglas and Harvey Denison. Educ: Yale, B.A, 30; Harvard, LL.B, 33; Psi Upsilon; Scroll & Key. Polit. & Govt. Pos: Rep. precinct committeeman, Ariz, 56-68; employer del, Tripartite tech. meeting on mines, Int. Labor Orgn, Geneva, 57; gen. counsel, Ariz. State Rep. Cmt, 57-63; chmn, Platform Cmt, Ariz. State Rep. Conv, 58 & 60; mem. adv. panel, Revision of Labor-Mgt. Rels. Laws, U.S. Senate Cmt. on Labor & Pub. Welfare, 59-60; alternate del, Rep. Nat. Conv, 60, del, 64; gen. dir, Rep. Presidential Campaign and Goldwater for Pres. Cmt, 64; mem, Task Force on Functions of Fed, State and Local Govt, Rep. Coord. Cmt, 65- Bus. & Prof. Pos: Assoc, Ellinwood & Ross, 34-38; partner, Evans, Kitchel & Jenckes, 38- Mil. Serv: Entered as 1st Lt, Army Air Force, 42, released as Lt. Col, 45, after serv. in Hq. 8th Air Force as sr. intel. officer, combined oper. planning cmt, USAAF-RAF, ETO, 42-44, as spec. intel. officer, Hq. 20th Air Force, D.C, 44-45, and as chief, anal. sect, 45; ETO and Am. Theater Campaign Ribbons. Publ: Too Grave A Risk—The Connally Amendment Issue, William Morrow & Co, 63. Mem: Am. Bar Asn; Am. Judicature Soc; Am. Inst. of Mining, Metallurgical & Petrol. Engrs; pres, Free Soc. Asn. Rel: Episcopal. Mailing Add: 2912 E. Sherran Lane, Phoenix, Ariz. 85016.

KITCHEL, DOUGLAS BINNEY R
Vt. State Sen.
b. Old Greenwich, Conn, 3/1/15; m. to Sybil Beck; c. Three sons and one daughter. Educ: Fessenden Sch; Phillips Acad; Harvard Col, B.A, 38. Polit. & Govt. Pos: Vt. State Sen, 65-; alternate del, Rep. Nat. Conv, 68. Bus. & Prof. Pos: Dairyman, farmer. Mem: Conn. River Watershed Coun; Fairbanks Mus. of Natural Sci; St. Johnsbury C. of C; New England Coun; Blue Shield; Water Resources Bd. Rel: Congregational. Mailing Add: Passumpsic, Vt. 05861. (1967)

KITCHENER, RUTH MAE R
Chmn, Wilmington Rep. Town Cmt, Mass.
b. Orr's Island, Maine, 12/13/07; d. Charles Agustus Coffin and Ella MacKeil C; m. 6/13/31 to Albert Edward Kitchener; c. Loraine Ruth (Mrs. James Martin Jones) and Albert Edward, Jr. Educ: Morse High Sch. Polit. & Govt. Pos: Secy, Wilmington Rep. Town Cmt, Mass, 50-64, finance chmn, 59-64, chmn, 64-; del, Mass. Rep. State Conv, 50-; del, Nat. Fedn. Rep. Women, 67. Mem: Mass. Rep. Club; Mass. Fedn. Rep. Women; Wilmington Women's Club; Women's Soc. Christian Serv, Methodist Church (pres); 4-H; Salvation Army (chmn); Red Cross; Cub Scouts; Rainbow Girls. Rel: Methodist. Mailing Add: 116 Aldrich Rd, Wilmington, Mass. 01887.

KITCHIN, ALVIN PAUL D
b. Scotland Neck, N.C, 9/13/08; s. Alvin Paul Kitchin and Carrie Lawrence K; m. 10/13/34 to Dora Bennett Little; c. A. Paul, Jr. and Henry Little. Educ: Oak Ridge Mil. Inst; Wake Forest Col. Polit. & Govt. Pos: Mem, Fed. Bur. of Invest, 33-45; U.S. Rep, N.C, 57-63; counsel, U.S. Sen. Judiciary Subcmt, 63 & 64; Bus. & Prof. Pos: Attorney-at-Law, 30-33, 65- Mem: Scottish Rite; Mason (32°); Rotary; Moose. Rel: Southern Baptist. Legal Res: Country Club Rd, Wadesboro, N.C. 28170. Mailing Add: Box 394, Wadesboro, N.C. 28170.

KITNER, ARTHUR J. R
Iowa State Rep.
b. Tama Co, Iowa, 3/10/19; s. Isiah Jess Kitner and Jennie Kluver K; m. 6/1/47 to Maxyne Taylor; c. John, Cody, Rita, Judy and Paul. Educ: Gladbrook High Sch, Iowa. Polit. & Govt. Pos: Iowa State Rep, 67- Bus. & Prof. Pos: Farmer; chief, Police Force, Independence, Iowa, 64-66. Mil. Serv: Entered as Pvt, Army, 41, released as 2nd Lt, 45, after serv. in 1st Army, ETO, 42-45; Legion's Merit; Soldier's Medal. Mem: N.E. Iowa Police Officers; Am. Legion; VFW; Farm Bur; Lions. Rel: Methodist. Mailing Add: 712 Seventh St. N.E, Independence, Iowa 50644.

KITTREDGE, ENID SUZANNE R
Chmn, West Bridgewater Rep. Town Cmt, Mass.
b. Des Moines, Iowa, 4/30/32; d. Dr. Louis Edgar Hutt and Charlotte Egbert H; m. Jan. 1952 to Wallace Randall Kittredge; c. Randall Grant and Christopher Forrest. Educ: Univ. Md, B.S, 55; Gamma Phi Beta; Gymkana Troupe. Polit. & Govt. Pos: Chmn, Brockton Rep. City Cmt, Ward II, Mass, 63-64; co-chmn, Citizens for Goldwater Hq, 64; mem-at-lg, Norwell and South Shore Women's Rep. Club, 66; del, Mass. Rep. State Conv, 66; secy, West Bridgewater Rep. Town Cmt, 66-67, chmn, 68-; corresponding secy, Tri-Town Women's Rep. Club, 66-67, recording secy, 67- Bus. & Prof. Pos: Girls phys. educ. dir, Childrens' Center, Laurel, Md, 55-56; girls' phys. educ. and girls sports dir, S.Jr. High Sch, Brockton, Mass, 58-59, elem. phys. educ. supvr, Attleboro Pub. Schs, 59-61; girls phys. educ. and sports dir, Rockland High Sch, 61-63, Taunton High Sch, 66-68 and Henry Lord Jr. High Sch, Fall River, 68-69. Mem: Am. Asn. Health, Phys. Educ. and Recreation; Cranberry Players; Tri-Town Women's Rep. Club; Mutual Improvement Asn. Rel: Latter-day Saint. Mailing Add: 6 Plain St, West Bridgewater, Mass. 02379.

KIVEN, ARLINE RUTH D
b. New York, N.Y, 3/1/16; d. William Francis Ruth and Ruth Wilkinson R; m. 4/28/40 to Nathan J. Kiven, M.D, wid; c. Ruth (Mrs. Bowden) and Charles Wilkinson. Educ: Rhode Island Col, Ed.B, 59; Brown Univ, M.A, 65; Kappa Delta Pi. Polit. & Govt. Pos: R.I. State Rep, 60-66. Bus. & Prof. Pos: Dir. grad. placement, Brown Univ, 63-64; teacher, Providence Sch. Dept, 64-65; instr, R.I. Jr. Col, 66- Mem: R.I. Col. Found; League of Women Voters; Coun. of Commun. Serv; Adv. Cmt. on the Aged; Spec. Cmn. Studying the Entire Field of Educ. in R.I. Rel: Unitarian. Mailing Add: 111 Waterman St, Providence, R.I. 02906. (1967)

KIVIMAKI, ELMER NORMAN DFL
b. Iron, Minn, 4/11/22; s. Konsta Kivimaki and Aini Paananen K; m. 2/2/46 to Lora Mae Laukkonen; c. Sharen Mae. Educ: Eveleth Jr. Col, 40; Mil. Intel. Training Center, 43. Polit. & Govt. Pos: Del, State Dem-Farmer-Labor Conv, Minn, 58, 60, 62 & 64; chmn, Citizens Cmt. for Dem-Farmer-Labor, 61-64; dir, Nat. Pub. Adv. Bd. to ARA, 63-64; chmn, 62nd Legis. Dist, 63-65; del, Dem. Nat. Conv, 64; mem. exec. bd, St. Louis Co. Econ. Opportunity Agency, 65- Bus. & Prof. Pos: Dist. Mgr, Mutual Ins. Co, St. Paul, 50-; instr, Life Underwriters Training Coun, 59-62. Mil. Serv: Entered as Pvt, Army, 42, released as S/Sgt, 65; served as spec. agent, 223rd Counter Intel. Corps, ETO; 3 Battle Stars; Good Conduct Medal; European Theater Ribbon. Publ: Sales articles, in company's sales bull. Mem: Life Underwriters Asn; VFW; Am Legion; Elks; Moose. Rel: Unitarian. Mailing Add: 311 Sixth Ave. N, Virginia, Minn. 55792.

KIZER, BERNICE L. D
Ark. State Rep.
b. Fort Smith, Ark, 8/14/15; d. Ernest C. Lichty and Opal Culler L; m. 10/2/60 to Harlan D. Kizer; c. Dr. James Mayne Parker, Jr, Shirley Kathrine Parker (Mrs. Wilhite) and Karolyn Kay Parker (Mrs. Sparkman). Educ: Stephens Col; Univ. Ark, LL.B, 46; Delta Delta Delta. Polit. & Govt. Pos: Ark. State Rep, Sebastian and Crawford Co. 3, 61-, chmn, Labor Cmt, mem, Ark. Legis. Coun. and Joint Budget Cmt, Ark. State House of Rep. Rel: Episcopal. Mailing Add: 221 May, Fort Smith, Ark. 72901.

KIZER, MARSHALL FORCE D
Ind. State Sen.
b. Plymouth, Ind, 2/13/07; s. Ethan Allen Kizer and Paulina Harverstraw K; m. 5/9/36 to Lucille Jane Erwin; c. John Erwin, Carolyn Paulina (Mrs. McClure) and Elizabeth Ann. Educ: Univ. Notre Dame, LL.B, 30. Polit. & Govt. Pos: Del, Ind. State Dem. Conv, 34-68; co. attorney, Marshall Co, Ind, 35-36; prosecuting attorney, 72nd Judicial Circuit, 37-41; alternate del, Dem. Nat. Conv, 48, del, 52, 56, 60 & 64; chmn, Marshall Co. Dem. Party, 46-52; chmn, Third Dist. Dem. Party, 52-66; Ind. State Sen, 56-64 & 68-; mem, Constitutional Rev. Cmn, 68- Bus. & Prof. Pos: V.pres, Ind. Trial Lawyers Asn, 68. Mem: Marshall Co. Bar Asn; Am. Judicature Soc; Ind. Trial Lawyers Asn; Mason; Shrine; Kiwanis Club; Farmers Union; Plymouth Country Club. Rel: Episcopal. Mailing Add: R.R. 5, Plymouth, Ind. 46563.

KJAR, ALBERT A. D
b. Lexington, Nebr, 5/9/90; m. 1/4/50 to Marian Voss; c. Albert W. Educ: Univ. Nebr. Agr. Sch. Polit. & Govt. Pos: Mayor, Lexington, Nebr, 2 terms, city councilman; chmn, Dawson Co. Dem. Cent. Cmt; mem, Dri Platte Valley Pub. Power and Irrigation Dist, 7 years, pres, 5 years; dir, Dawson Co. Pub. Power Dist, 15 years, pres. of bd, 14 years; past pres, Nebr. State Irrigation Asn; past pres, Nebr. Reclamation Asn; Nebr. State Sen, 61-69. Bus. & Prof. Pos: Pres, Kjar Hay and Grain Co; farm operator. Mem: Rotary Int.(dist. gov); K. of C.(state dep); Dawson Co. Farm Bur.(dir). Rel: Roman Catholic. Legal Res: 1403 Grant St, Lexington, Nebr. 68850. Mailing Add: 101 S. Washington St, Lexington, Nebr. 68850.

KLAS, JOHN HALL D
Chmn, Utah State Dem. Cmt.
b. Beaver Dam, Wis, 9/24/17; s. John Charles Klas and Helen Hall K; div; c. Mary Lynn (Mrs. H.F. Nelson, Jr). Educ: State Univ. of Iowa, B.S; Alpha Gamma Rho. Polit. & Govt. Pos: Chmn, Voting Dist 43 and Legis. Dist. 5, Salt Lake Co. Dem. Party, Utah; chmn, Utah State Dem. Cmt, 68- Bus. & Prof. Pos: V.pres, Continental Bank & Trust Co. Mil. Serv: Col.(Ret), Army, 40-45. ETO: Bronze Star for Valor; Purple Heart with Cluster. Rel: Unitarian. Mailing Add: 40 South Ninth East, Salt Lake City, Utah 84102.

KLASSEN, E. T. R
Dep. Postmaster Gen.
b. Hillsboro, Kans, 11/6/08; s. John A. Klassen and Mary Petker K; m. to Marie Callahan; c. Joan M.(Mrs. Schroeder) (deceased). Educ: Harvard Bus. Sch. Polit. & Govt. Pos: Dep. Postmaster Gen, 69- Bus. & Prof. Pos: With, Am. Can Co, 25-69, gen. mgr, indust. rels, 55-58, v.pres, indust. rels, 58-61, v.pres and gen. mgr, Canco Div, 62-64, exec. v.pres, div. operations, 64, exec. v.pres, corporate operations, 64-65, pres, 65-68, dir, 64-69; bus. consult, 68-69. Mem: Chmn. bd, Inst. for Collective Bargaining & Group Rels; chmn. bd, Post Grad. Inst. of Osteopathic Med. & Surg; Elks. Rel: Methodist. Legal Res: Reed Bridge Rd, Conway, Mass. 01341. Mailing Add: Watergate Apts. West, Washington, D.C. 20037.

KLATTENHOFF, WILLIAM JOHN R
b. Taylor, Tex, 2/25/99; s. M. F. Klattenhoff and Lina Pfluger K; m. 5/20/22 to Chloe Fowler; c. William J, Jr. Polit. & Govt. Pos: Mem, Tex. State Rep. Exec. Cmt, 28th Senatorial Dist, 60-66. Mil. Serv: A/S, Navy, 1918. Mem: Rotary. Rel: Lutheran. Legal Res: 850 W. Crosby, Slaton, Tex. 79364. Mailing Add: Box 234, Slaton, Tex. 79364. (1967)

KLAUS, ARTHUR CARL R
Capt, 29th Precinct, Chicago, Ill.
b. Chicago, Ill, 6/19/25; s. Edmund Klaus and Olga Heine K; m. 6/26/49 to Helen Jarzemski; c. Christine and Gregory. Polit. & Govt. Pos: Capt, 29th Precinct, 35th Ward, Chicago, Ill, 62-; alternate del, Rep. Nat. Conv, 64. Mil. Serv: Entered as A/S, Navy, 42, released as Signalman 1/C, 45, after serv. in Pac. Fleet. Rel: Roman Catholic. Mailing Add: 2935 N. Kildare Ave, Chicago, Ill. 60641. (1967)

KLAUS, WALTER KLOEPPING R
Minn. State Rep.
b. Empire, Minn, 4/19/12; s. George Henry Klaus and Wilhelmina Kloepping K; m. 1/13/68 to Virginia Taylor; c. Caroline. Educ: Hamline Univ, B.A, 34; Univ. Minn, grad. work; Pi Kappa Delta; Kappa Phi Sigma; Kappa Gamma Chi. Polit. & Govt. Pos: Treas, Young Rep. League of Minn, 46-48; chmn, Dakota Co. Rep. Cmt, 48-56; Minn. State Rep, 57-; chmn, Second Cong. Dist. Rep. Cmt, 58-62. Bus. & Prof. Pos: Dir, State Bank of Hampton, Minn, 57- Mem: Farm Bur; Ayrshire Breeders Asn. Rel: United Methodist. Mailing Add: 302 Fourth, Farmington, Minn. 55024.

KLAUS, WILLIAM J. R
Chmn, Sharkey Co. Rep. Party, Miss.
b. Vicksburg, Miss, 2/1/07; s. Edward Klaus and Gussie Haas K; m. 2/18/32 to Sadye Grundfest. Educ: Wash. Univ, 2 years; Zeta Beta Tau. Polit. & Govt. Pos: Mem, bd. aldermen, Cary, Miss, 45-69; chmn, Sharkey Co. Soil Conserv. Cmt, to 69; mem. co. and dist. bd, Sharkey Co. Elected Rep. committeeman; chmn, Sharkey Co. Rep. Party, 69- Bus. & Prof. Pos: Secy, Grundfest and Klaus Gin Co, 35-63; pres, Evanna Plantation, 46-; pres, Sabill Plantation Inc, 47- Mil. Serv: Entered as Pvt, Army Air Force, 42, released as Sgt, 45, after serv. in 27th Bn. Unit, Eighth Air Force and 853rd Bomber Squadron, 491st Bomber Group, ETO, 43-45; Unit Citation; Bronze Star; EMATO Medal. Mem: Miss. Econ. Coun; 4-H; Rotary (pres. Rollingfork Club, 55); Boy Scouts (Andrew Jackson Coun); Delta Coun.(pres, 68); Am. Soy Bean Asn; Miss. Pork Prod. Asn; Miss. Cattlemens Asn; Patio Club; Adm. Club; Sharkey Co. Country Club (bd. dirs, 67-); Rivertown Club; VFW. Various farm awards. Rel: Jewish. Mailing Add: Cary, Miss. 39054.

KLAVER, SAM R
Nebr. State Sen.
b. Romania, 10/16/01; m. 12/21/24 to Ann Roitstein; c. one son. Educ: Omaha Univ; Creighton Law Sch, LL.B. Polit. & Govt. Pos: Clerk, Co. Treas. Off, Co. Assessors Off, City Appeal Bd. and City Attorney's Off, Nebr; Nebr. State Sen, 39- Bus. & Prof. Pos: Attorney; newspaper publisher. Mem: Past pres, Mid-City Businessmen's Asn; Douglas Co. Voters League (past pres); Odd Fellows; Elks; K. of P; Pearl Harbor Lodge of War Dads (pres); B'nai B'rith. Rel: Hebrew. Mailing Add: 702 S. 22nd St, Omaha, Nebr. 68102.

KLEBANOFF, HOWARD MICHAEL D
Conn. State Rep.
b. New Haven, Conn, 5/17/37; s. Max Edward Klebanoff and Sayre Witten K; m. 6/14/59 to Sandra Fleischner; c. Marcie Lynne, Amy Beth and Betsy Jill. Educ: Yale Univ, B.A, 59; Univ. Conn, LL.B, 62; Phi Gamma Delta. Polit. & Govt. Pos: Dem. Cmt. Mem, 24th Dist, Conn, 63-64 and Dem. Co-Capt, 64-68; Justice of the Peace, 67-69 and 69-71; cmnr, Human Rels. Cmt, Hartford, Conn, 67-70; Conn. State Rep, Ninth Assembly Dist, 69- Bus. & Prof. Pos: Attorney, U.S. Dept. Labor, Wash, D.C, 62-63; attorney, Ritter & Berman, Conn, 63-67 and partner, 67-69; attorney and partner, Novick, Klebanoff & Ellis, 69-; dir. and asst. secy, Conn. Housing Investment Fund, Inc, 67- Mem: Nat. Soc. State Legislators; Am, Conn. and Hartford Co. Bar Asns; past pres. and dir, Blue Hills Civic Asn; dir, Hartford Chap, NAACP; Gr. Hartford Commun. Coun; commun. rels. cmt, Hartford Jewish Fedn; Urban Relig. Coalition. Rel: Jewish. Legal Res: 127 Ridgefield St, Hartford, Conn. 06112. Mailing Add: 410 Asylum St, Hartford, Conn. 06103.

KLECZKA, GERALD DANIEL D
Wis. State Assemblyman
b. Milwaukee, Wis, 11/26/43; s. Harry J. Kleczka and Agnes P. Dusza K; m. 6/1/69 to Carole L. Roberts. Educ: Univ. Wis-Milwaukee, 1 year. Polit. & Govt. Pos: Dem. Conv. del, 14th Ward Dem. Unit, 64, 65 & 68; co. coun. rep, Milwaukee Co, 65-68; Wis. State Assemblyman, 14th Dist, 69- Bus. & Prof. Pos: Acct, Northwest. Nat. Ins. Co, currently. Mil. Serv: Entered as Airman Basic, Wis. Air Nat. Guard, 62, released as Sgt, 68, after serv. in 128th Tactical Dispensary, 128th Air Refueling Squadron; Sgt, Wis. Air Nat. Guard Res. Mem: Wilson Park Adv. Asn; S.Side Bus. Club; St. Joseph's Athletic Asn; Elks; Don Bosco Alumni Asn; Polish Nat. Alliance; pres, St. Helen's Holy Name Soc. Rel: Catholic. Mailing Add: 3427 S. Ninth Place, Milwaukee, Wis. 53215.

KLEFSTAD, GILBERT E. D
b. Felch, Mich, 5/20/19; s. Ole S. Kelfstad; Anna R. K; m. 12/31/45 to Julia J. Chapin; c. Faye Ann; Gilbert Eugene; Kaye Lorraine. Educ: Felch High Sch; Elec. Commun. Sch, Wash, D.C. Polit. & Govt. Pos: Iowa State Sen -66; Iowa State Rep, 59th Gen. Assembly. Bus. & Prof. Pos: Electrician. Mil. Serv: Navy, 40-47, USS Lexington CVII, Lost in Battle of Coral Sea. Mem: Am. Legion; VFW; T J High Sch. Band Parents; Masons, Coun. Bluffs; Excelsior 259; Star Chap. 247; Commandery Abu-Bekr Shrine, Sioux City; pres, Coun. Bluffs Labor Union. Rel: Lutheran. Mailing Add: 315 N. 19th St, Council Bluffs, Iowa. 51501. (1967)

KLEI, LOUIS WILLIAM R
Treas, 17th Cong. Dist. Rep. Cmt, Mich.
b. Detroit, Mich, 3/25/26; s. Louis T. Klei and Edna M. Lobenstein K; m. 7/23/49 to Shirley Rundorff; c. Karen Kay and Katherine Sussanne. Educ: Lawrence Inst. Tech, B.S. Archit. Eng, 50; Phi Kappa Upsilon; hon. mention, Nat. Garden Apt. Design Competition, 49; outstanding sr. award, dept. archit, Lawrence Inst. Tech, 50. Polit. & Govt. Pos: Precinct del, 17th Cong. Dist. Rep. Cmt, Mich, 62-, campaign mgr, 63, mem. statutory bd, 63-, chmn. cmt, 63-66, treas, 69-; del, Mich. State Rep. Conv, 62-; mem, State Bldg. Cmn, 64-; del, Rep. Nat. Conv, 68. Bus. & Prof. Pos: Archit. engr, Bery and Knapp, Archit, 50-52 and George J. Bery, Archit, 52-54; partner, Bery-Klei and Assocs, Archit, 54- Mil. Serv: Entered as Pvt, Marine Corps, 43, released as Cpl, 47, after serv. in 26th Marines, 5th Div. and 8th Marines, 2nd Div, Pac. Theater, 44-47; Pac. Theater ribbon with star; Presidential Unit Citation with star; Victory Medal. Mem: Am. Legion; Kiwanis Int; Northwest Rep. Club, Northwest Civic Fedn. Rel: Lutheran. Mailing Add: 18264 Winston, Detroit, Mich. 48219.

KLEIN, AARON EDWARD D
Chmn, Ulster Co. Dem. Cmt, N.Y.
b. New York, N.Y, 5/19/12; s. Simon Klein and Julia Horowitz K; m. 5/8/40 to Florence Propp; c. Louis M, Phyllis E. and Brenda C. Educ: Brooklyn Law Sch, LL.B, 35; New York Univ, Postgrad. Study, 46-47. Polit. & Govt. Pos: City judge, Kingston, N.Y, 58-62; chmn, Kingston City Dem. Cmt, 61-63; chmn, Ulster Co. Dem. Cmt, 63-; corp. counsel, Kingston, currently. Bus. & Prof. Pos: Partner, Schick & Klein, Esqs, 57- Mem: Am. Trial Lawyers Asn; Ulster Co. and N.Y. State Bar Asns; N.Y. Magistrates Asn; Ulster Co. Magistrates Asn; B'nai B'rith; DUSO Shomrim Soc; F&AM; Elks. Rel: Jewish. Legal Res: 60 W. Chestnut St, Kingston, N.Y. 12401. Mailing Add: 259 Fair St, Kingston, N.Y. 12401. (1967)

KLEIN, BEN D
Colo. State Rep.
b. Denver, Colo, 11/5/26. Polit. & Govt. Pos: Former precinct committeeman; Colo. State Rep, currently. Bus. & Prof. Pos: Lawyer. Legal Res: 1597 Zenobia St, Denver, Colo. 80204. Mailing Add: 2709 Security Life Bldg, Denver, Colo. 80202. (1967)

KLEIN, CARL LOUIS R
Asst. secy. Water Qual. and Research, Dept. Interior.
b. Butternut, Wis, 5/17/17; s. John T. Klein, Sr. and Elise Wichman K; m. 10/23/41 to Emma Muriel North; c. Karen E. and Carl L, Jr. Educ: Cent. YMCA Col, B.A, Hist. and Polit. Sci, 39; DePaul Univ, J.D, 42; Delta Theta Phi. Polit. & Govt. Pos: Ill. State Rep, 65-69; acting ward committeeman, 15th Ward, Chicago, 64-68, ward committeeman, 68-69; chmn, Water Pollution and Water Resources Cmn, 65-69; asst. secy. water qual. and research, Dept. Interior, 69- Bus. & Prof. Pos: Attorney at law, 46-69. Mil. Serv: Entered as Pvt, Army, 43, released as 1st Lt, 46, after serv. in Counter Intel. Corps. Publ: Reports of Water Pollution and Resources Cmn. of State of Ill. Mem: Ill. State and Chicago Bar Asns; Kiwanis Club; C. of C; Am.

Legion. Legislator of the Year Ill, Izaak Walton League, 67. Rel: Lutheran. Legal Res: 6428 S. Francisco Ave, Chicago, Ill. 60620. Mailing Add: Dept. of Interior, Room 4154, Washington, D.C. 20240.

KLEIN, DOROTHEA ELIZABETH D
V.Chmn, Shawnee Co. Dem. Cent. Cmt, Kans.
b. Topeka, Kans, 1/9/10; d. George A. Klein and Elizabeth Glanzer K; single. Educ: Kans. State Univ, B.S. and M.S. in phys. chem. Polit. & Govt. Pos: Precinct committeewoman, Dem. Party, Kans, 56-66, capt, Ward Four, 60-65; secy, Dist. Two Dem. Cmt, 63-66; v.chmn, Shawnee Co. Dem. Cent. Cmt, Kans, 66-; alternate del, Dem. Nat. Conv, 68; pres, Kans. Bd. of Hearing Aid Exam, 68- Bus. & Prof. Pos: Chief chemist, Lab, Weldon Spring Ord, 40-44; works lab. supvr, Atomic Energy Cmn, K-25, Oak Ridge, Tenn, 44-48; owner and mgr, Audiphone Co, Topeka, Kans, 49-66; partner, Petty-Klein Co, St. Louis, Mo, 57-66. Mem: Am. Chem. Soc; Am. Inst. of Chem. Engrs; Univ. Womens Club; Mathematics Soc; past pres, Kans. Hearing Aid Dealers; Nat. Hearing Aid Soc; Nat. Coun. Hearing Aid Dealers; Pilot Club Int; Inter-Club Coun; C. of C; former mem, State Civil Defense and State Atomic Energy Adv. Coun. Rel: Lutheran. Mailing Add: 304 Fillmore, Topeka, Kans. 66606.

KLEIN, EDITH MILLER R
Idaho State Sen.
b. Wallace, Idaho, 8/4/15; d. Fred L.B. Miller and Edith Gallup M; m. 7/11/49 to Sandor S. Klein. Educ: Univ. Idaho, B.S. in Bus, 35; Wash. State Univ, grad. teaching fel, 35-36; George Wash. Univ, LL.B, 46, LL.M, 54; Kappa Beta Pi. Polit. & Govt. Pos: Interviewer, Idaho State Employ Serv, 40-41; personnel specialist, War Dept, D.C, 43-46; judge, Munic. Court, Boise, Idaho, 47-49; Idaho State Rep, 49-50 & 65-68, chmn, judiciary cmt, Idaho House of Rep; attorney, Fed. Commun. Cmn, D.C, 53-54 and Fed. Housing Admin, N.Y.C, 55-56; chmn, Idaho Gov. Cmn. on Status of Women, 65-; Idaho State Sen. and chmn, Senate Health and Welfare Cmt, 69- Bus. & Prof. Pos: Teacher, Grangeville High Sch, 37-38; private practice of law, 47-53; Lawyer, Langroise, Clark & Sullivan, Boise, Idaho, 57- Mem: Fed, Am. and Idaho Bar Asns; Am. Asn. Univ. Women (v.pres, Boise Br, 47-49); Boise Altrusa (pres, 51-52); Ada Co. Rep. Women's Club (pres, 59-61); DAR; League of Women Voters; Bus. & Prfnl. Women's Club; pres, Idaho State Conf. on Soc. Work, 49-50; Boise Toastmistress Club (pres, 61); Idaho Ment. Health Asn; Boise Art Asn. Admitted to practice of law before U.S. Supreme Court, D.C, 46 and Idaho, 47. Rel: Congregational. Legal Res: 1732 War Springs Ave, Boise, Idaho 83702. Mailing Add: P.O. Box 475, Boise, Idaho 83701.

KLEIN, H. BERYL D
b. Aliquippa, Pa, 3/11/28; s. Adolph Klein and Gizella Karp K; m. to Mildred Lubovsky; c. Lloyd, Roberta and Arnold. Educ: Univ. Pittsburgh, B.Sc, 49; Duquesne Univ. Sch. of Law, J.D, 57. Polit. & Govt. Pos: Inst. Dist. Solicitor, 60-62; Pa. State Rep, 60-66; legal and research counsel to Minority Leader, Pa. State Senate, 67- Bus. & Prof. Pos: Attorney. Mil. Serv: Army, Korean Conflict, 50-52. Mem: Beaver Co, Pa, and Am. Bar Asns. Admitted to practice Beaver Co. Court, Pa. Appellate Courts and West. Dist. Court, Pittsburgh. Mailing Add: 2009 Main St, Aliquippa, Pa. 15001.

KLEIN, HENRY R
Chmn, St. Lucie Co. Rep. Exec. Cmt, Fla.
b. Brooklyn, N.Y, 2/5/05; s. Wilhelm Carl Klein and Marie Anna Muller K; m. 5/23/53 to Louise Mae Kelly. Polit. & Govt. Pos: Chmn, St. Lucie Co. Rep. Exec. Cmt, Fla, currently. Bus. & Prof. Pos: Plumbing, heating and bldg. contractor, 25-35; Lt, N.Y.C. Fire Dept, 35-55; plumbing and heating contractor, Henry Klein & Bros, 55-65; real estate salesman, Laura B. Hancock, Realtor, 65- Mem: St. Lucie Co. Tax-Payers Asn.(secy-treas); St. Lucie Co. Rep. Club; fire cmnr, St. Lucie Co-Ft. Pierce Fire Control Bd. Rel: Methodist. Mailing Add: 1003 Flood Rd, Ft. Pierce, Fla. 33450.

KLEIN, HERBERT CHARLES D
b. Newark, N.J, 6/24/30; s. Alfred Klein and Fae Sackin K; m. 8/3/52 to Jacqueline Krieger; c. Roger M. and Cynthia N. Educ: Rutgers Univ, B.A, 50; Harvard Univ. Law Sch, LL.B, 53; N.Y. Univ, LL.M, 59; Tau Kappa Alpha; Tau Delta Phi. Polit. & Govt. Pos: Mem, Passaic Co. Dem. Cmt, N.J, 58-63; pres, Clifton Dem. Club, 60-67; counsel, Passaic Co. Park Cmn, 62-68; cand. for freeholder, Passaic Co, 67; alternate del, Dem. Nat. Conv, 68; Passaic Co. campaign mgr. for Gov. Robert Meyner, 69. Bus. & Prof. Pos: Assoc, Budd, Larner & Kent, Law Firm, Newark, 56-60; partner, Krieger & Klein, Passaic, 61-; trustee, First Real Estate Investment Trust of N.J, Hackensack, 61- Mil. Serv: Entered as 2nd Lt, Air Force, 54, released as 1st Lt, 56, after serv. in Air Material Command, Los Angeles Air Procurement Dist, 54-56. Mem: Passaic Co. and N.J. Bar Asns; B'nai B'rith; Am. Jewish Cmt; Jewish War Vet; YMHA; Nat. Jew. Welfare Bd; Anti-Defamation League; Harvard Law Sch. Asn; Clifton Mental Health Center. Rel: Jewish. Mailing Add: 34 Lenox Ave, Clifton, N.J. 07012.

KLEIN, HERBERT GEORGE R
Dir. of Commun. for the Exec. Br.
b. Los Angeles, Calif, 4/1/18; s. George J. Klein; m. 11/1/41 to Marjorie Galbraith; c. Joanne (Mrs. Robert Mayne) and Patricia (Mrs. Thomas Howell). Educ: Univ. South. Calif, A.B. in Journalism, 40; Sigma Delta Chi. Polit. & Govt. Pos: Press secy. to Richard M. Nixon for cong. campaigns, 48 & 50, vice presidential campaigns, 52 & 56, presidential campaign, 60 and gubernatorial campaign, 62; press secy. and spec. asst. to Vice President Richard M. Nixon, 56-60; chmn, bd. of trustees, Rep. Assocs. of San Diego Co; mgr. for commun, Nixon for President Cmt, 68; Dir. of Commun. for the Exec. Br, 69- Bus. & Prof. Pos: Reporter, Iron Age Mag, 40; news ed, Alhambra Post-Advocate, 40-50; editorial page ed, San Diego Union, 52-56, exec. ed, 56-59, ed, 59-68. Mil. Serv: Entered as Ens, Navy, 42, released as Comdr, 46. Mem: Hon. mem, Alhambra Rotary Club; bd. of dirs, Kiwanis; bd. of dirs, Am. Red Cross; Am. Legion. Rel: Presbyterian; mem, Nat. Coun, Presbyterian Church and Center. Legal Res: La Jolla, Calif. Mailing Add: White House, Washington, D.C. 20500.

KLEIN, JAMES TACKETT R
Iowa State Rep.
b. Alton, Iowa, 7/31/37; s. Edsko Gerald Klein and Myrtle Tackett K; m. 8/12/60 to Barbara Mae Calsbeek; c. Barbara Hope and James Robert. Educ: Buena Vista Col. B.A, 61. Polit. & Govt. Pos: Chmn, Young Rep. of Buena Vista Col, 60-61; mem, Gov. Amish Study Cmt, 67; Iowa State Rep, Winnebago and Worth Co, 67-, chmn, Appropriations Cmt. on Natural Resources, Iowa State House of Rep, 69-; mem, Gov. Bldg. Code Study Cmt, 68-69; chmn, Third Cong. Dist. State Rep. Legislators, 68-; mem, Iowa Crime Cmn. Bus. & Prof. Pos: Prod. coordinator, Minneapolis-Honeywell, 63-64; sr. prod. planner and analyst, Deluxe Prod. Corp, 64-66; exec. dir, Lake Mills C. of C, 69- Mil. Serv: Entered as Pvt, Army, 61, released as Sgt, 63; Good Conduct Award. Mem: Mason; Lions Int; v.chmn, Iowa Easter Seal Soc. Rel: Methodist. Mailing Add: 901 S. Grant St, Lake Mills, Iowa 50450.

KLEIN, MARGAREE SELMA D
b. St. Louis, Mo, 11/1/20; d. Morris Bornstein and Clara Blumenthal B; m. 10/4/42 to Dudley Maurice Klein; c. Larry Michael. Educ: Cincinnati Conservatory of Music, 38-39; Juilliard Sch. of Music, 39-41. Polit. & Govt. Pos: Dem. committeewoman, Creve Coeur Twp, Mo, 56-64; v.chmn, Second Cong. Dist. Dem. Party, 58-60; mem, Mo. Dem. State Cmt, 58-64; del, Dem. Nat. Conv, 60 & 64; University City Rep. to St. Louis Co. Munic. League, Mo, 66-68; polit. speech writer, Dem. Primary, 68. Bus. & Prof. Pos: Newspaper columnist, St. Louis Co. Watchman-Advocate, 65-69; ed. writer, Lin Broadcasting Co, St. Louis, Mo, 67-69. Publ: 'How to Take Part in Politics,' Creve Coeur Twp. Dem. Club, 60; 'The Role of Women in Politics,' Wash. Univ. Free Lance Mag, 9/63. Mem: Chmn, Cleaner Air Cmt; Valley Press Club, Los Angeles, Calif; Pub. Rels. Round Table. Winner, Nat. Award for Best Educ. Air Pollution Prog. Mailing Add: 4540 Hazeltine, Sherman Oaks, Calif. 91403.

KLEIN, WILLIAM C. D
b. Oak Park, Ill, 1921; m. to Phyllis K; c. Two. Educ: Wash. State Univ; Univ. Wash. Sch. Law, Sigma Alpha Epsilon; Delta Theta Phi. Polit. & Govt. Pos: Mem, Wash. Tax Adv. Coun; city attorney; Asst. Attorney Gen, Wash; chmn, Wash. State Constitutional Adv. Coun; former Wash. State Rep; mem, Bonniville Power Admin. Adv. Cmt, currently; del, Dem. Nat. Conv, 68. Bus. & Prof. Pos: Lawyer. Mil. Serv: Army. Mem: Clark Co. Bar Asn.(past pres). Mailing Add: 601 E. McLoughlin Blvd, Vancouver, Wash. 98663.

KLEINBAUM, JACK Liberal
Minn. State Rep.
b. 1917; married; c. John, Richard, James and Jeff. Educ: N. High Sch, Minneapolis. Polit. & Govt. Pos: Mem, Citizens Adv. Cmt; with Housing and Redevelop. Authority; mem, City Coun, 60-64; Minn. State Rep, 67- Bus. & Prof. Pos: Owner and mgr, Jack's Outlet. Mil. Serv: Navy, Forman in Tacoma Shipyards. Mem: Elks; Eagles; Moose; Mason; Sertoma; bd. of dirs, Cath. Charities; exec. bd, Red Cross; disaster chmn, Stearns Co. Red Cross; Shrine. Sertoman of the Year, 64. Rel: Jewish. Mailing Add: 1100 N. 23rd Ave, St. Cloud, Minn. 56301.

KLEINDIENST, RICHARD GORDON R
Dep. Attorney Gen, Dept. of Justice.
b. Winslow, Ariz, 8/5/23; s. Alfred R. Kleindienst and Gladys Love K.(deceased); m. 9/3/48 to Margaret Dunbar; c. Alfred Dunbar, Wallace Heath, Anne Lucile and Carolyn Love. Educ: Univ. Ariz, 41-42; Harvard Univ, A.B. magna cum laude, 47, Law Sch, LL.B, 50; Phi Beta Kappa; Sigma Alpha Epsilon. Polit. & Govt. Pos: Ariz. State Rep, 53-54; chmn, Airz. Young Rep. League, 55; chmn, Rep. State Cmt, Ariz, 56-63; mem, Rep. Nat. Cmt, 56-63, gen. counsel, 68; nominee for Gov. of Ariz, 64; nat. dir. of field opers, Goldwater for Pres. Cmt, 64 and Nixon for Pres. Cmt, 68; del, Rep. Nat. Conv, 60 & 64; Dep. Attorney Gen, Dept. of Justice, 69- Bus. & Prof. Pos: Law Clerk, Ropes & Grey, Boston, Mass, 49-50; assoc. and partner, Jennings, Strouss, Salmon & Trask, Phoenix, Ariz, 50-57; sr. partner, Shimmel, Hill, Kleindienst & Bishop, 58-69. Mil. Serv: Entered as Pvt, Army, 42, released as 1st Lt, 45, after serv. as Navigator, 15th Air Force, Italy; ETO Ribbon. Mem: State Bar of Ariz; Am. Bar Asn; Am. Legion; VFW; Urban League; Good Will Industs; Ariz. and Am. Heart Asns; Phoenix Day Nursery; Phoenix and Off. Econ. Opportunity Small Bus. Develop; Phoenix Thunderbirds; Ariz. Univ, Army-Navy Country and George Town Clubs. Rel: Episcopal; Lay Reader, Past Warden and Vestryman, Trinity Episcopal Cathedral and All Saints Episcopal Church; former mem. exec. coun, Ariz. Diocese, Episcopal Church. Legal Res: Phoenix, Ariz. Mailing Add: Room 4111, Dept. of Justice, Washington, D.C. 20530.

KLEINER, A. ROBERT D
Chmn, Kent Co. Dem. Cmt, Mich.
b. Grand Rapids, Mich, 12/2/16; s. Anthony Kleiner and Lillian Lubetsky K; m. 12/11/43 to Dorothy Jane Kettring; c. Nancy Elizabeth. Educ: Univ. Mich, A.B, 38, Law Sch, LL.B, 41. Polit. & Govt. Pos: Chmn, Fifth Cong. Dist. Dem. Orgn, Mich, 59-61; secy, Kent Co. Dem. Cmt, 60-68, chmn, 68-; mem, Cmn. on Legis Apportionment, 63-66; del, Dem. Nat. Conv, 64 & 68. Bus. & Prof. Pos: Attorney in pvt. practice. Mil. Serv: Entered as Pvt, Army Ord. Dept, 43, released as 1st Lt, 46, after serv. in Off. Chief of Ord, Detroit, 44-46. Mem: Am, Mich. and Grand Rapids Bar Asns. Mailing Add: 1134 Idema Dr. S.E, Grand Rapids, Mich. 49506.

KLEINER, ROBERT I. D
City Councilman, Long Beach, N.Y.
b. 4/20/10; s. Max Kleiner and Rose Kastenbaum K; m. 4/14/35 to Claire Roth; c. Jo Ann. Educ: City Col, N.Y; N.Y. Univ. Law Sch. Polit. & Govt. Pos: Co. committeeman, Sixth Elec. Dist, N.Y, 50-58; counsel, Long Beach Pub. Libr, 51-58; acting city judge, Long Beach, 59-61; former exec. chmn, Long Beach Zone Dem. Cmt; city councilman, Long Beach, currently, former pres, City Coun. Bus. & Prof. Pos: Attorney, self-employed, 37- Mil. Serv: Entered as Pvt, Army, 43, released as S/Sgt, 46, after serv. in 15th Cavalry Reconnaissance, ETO; 4 Major Campaign Ribbons. Mem: Past comdr, Am. Legion Victor Murtha Post; past pres, Long Beach Lions; past chancellor, K. of P; Jewish War Vet; Elks; Moose; trustee, Long Beach Hosp, Temple Israel and Hebrew Acad; chmn. of many philanthropic drives. Rel: Hebrew. Mailing Add: 271 Laurelton Blvd, Long Beach, N.Y. 11561.

KLEINKORT, CHARLES B. R
Ind. State Sen.
b. Beckemeyer, Ill, 11/3/19; s. Henry F. Kleinkort and Anna Bross K; m. 11/3/45 to Kathryn Adair Ade; c. Karl Ade and Donald Bross. Educ: Tex. A&M Univ, 1 year; Univ. Ariz, 2 years; Sigma Chi. Polit. & Govt. Pos:

Ind. State Sen, Newton, Jasper and Porter Counties, 68- Bus. & Prof. Pos: Farmer, Brook, Ind, 47- Mil. Serv: Entered as Pvt, Marine Corps, 42, released as Comdr. Warrant Off, 46, after serv. in First Marines, S. Pac, 43-44. Publ:'George Ade,' Sigma Chi Fraternity, 64. Mem: Am. Legion; Lions; Newton Co. Historical Soc; Brook Civic Club; Dir. George Ade Mem. Asn; Marine Corps Reserve Officers Asn. Rel: United Methodist. Legal Res: Hazelden Farm, Brook, Ind. 47922.

KLEMPNOW, PAUL L. J. D
Mem, Saginaw Co. Dem. Exec. Cmt, Mich.
b. Saginaw, Mich, Aug. 1936; s. John Klempnow and Josephine Donohue K; m. June 1966 to Nancy Dorian; c. Jefferson Austin. Educ: U.S. Mil. Acad, B.S, 58; Univ. Mich. Law Sch, 62-64. Polit. & Govt. Pos: Precinct del, Dem. Party, Ann Arbor, Mich, 63-65; del, Mich. State Dem. Conv, 63-69; treas, Saginaw Co. Dem. Cmt, Mich, 66-68; mem. steering cmt, Eighth Dist. Dem. Cmt, Saginaw, 66-68; alternate del, Dem. Nat. Conv, 68; mem, Saginaw Co. Dem. Exec. Cmt, 68- Bus. & Prof. Pos: Salesman, Morgan Real Estate and Charles Cook, Realtor, 64-68; broker, Clover Realty Co, Saginaw, Mich, 68- Mil. Serv: Entered as 2nd Lt, Army, 58, released as Capt, 62, after serving in 4th Armored Div, Europe, 60-62. Mem: Nat. Educ. Asn; Boy Scouts, Order of Arrow; YMCA; NAACP; K. of C. Mailing Add: 7366 Cole Rd, Saginaw, Mich. 48601.

KLEPPE, THOMAS S. R
U.S. Rep, N.Dak.
b. Kintyre, N.Dak, 7/1/19; m. to Glendora Loew; c. Janis (Mrs. Jerry G. Cunningham), Thomas Stewart, Jane and Jill. Educ: Valley City State Teachers Col, 37. Polit. & Govt. Pos: Mem. subcmt. on local govt, Intergovt. Rels. Cmn; Mayor, Bismarck, N.Dak, 50-54; U.S. Rep, N.Dak, 66- Bus. & Prof. Pos: Asst. mgr. and helper, Farmers Co, Kintyre, 37-41; clerk and asst. cashier, Dakota Nat. Bank, Bismarck and Stock Growers Bank, Napoleon, 41-42; v.pres. and treas, Gold Seal Co, Bismarck, 48-58, pres. and treas, 58-64; dir, J.M. Dain & Co, Inc, Minneapolis, Minn, 65-66. Mil. Serv: Army, WO (jg), Finance Dept. attached to Air Corps, 42-46. Mem: Lions; Am. Legion; Elks; Minneapolis Athletic Club; pres. and chmn. Slope Lutheran Homes, Inc. Outstanding Young Man Award, Jaycees, 50. Rel: Lutheran; Chmn. Cmts, Trinity Lutheran Church. Legal Res: 233 Divide Ave, Bismarck, N.Dak. 58501. Mailing Add: 9609 Hillridge Dr, Kensington, Md. 20795.

KLEPPER, CARL J. R
Chmn, Huntington Co. Rep. Party, Ind.
b. Ft. Wayne, Ind, 7/20/09; s. William A. Klepper and Ceclia R. Hergenroether K; m. 11/20/29 to Rose Marie Smith; c. Carla Rose (Mrs. Thomas Hebein), Jean Ann (Mrs. Michael McNamara) and James L. Educ: Purdue Univ, 1 year. Polit. & Govt. Pos: Chmn, Huntington Co. Rep. Party, Ind, 64- Bus. & Prof. Pos: V.pres, Cloverleaf Creameries, Huntington, Ind, 45-55; pres, Luick Dairy, Ice Cream and Wis. Creameries, Milwaukee, Wis, 49-55; pres, Hydrox Corp, Chicago, Ill, 55-57; pres, Robert A. Johnson Co, Milwaukee, Wis, 57-59. Mem: Rotary (dist. gov); Milwaukee Athletic Club; Wis. Club; Univ. Club; Boy Scouts (Area Coun). Rel: Roman Catholic. Mailing Add: R.R. 9, P.O. Box 916, Huntington, Ind. 46750.

KLICKSTEIN, DAVID D
b. Malden, Mass. 8/4/26; s. Alec Klickstein (deceased) and Anna Block K; m. 1953 to Elfriede W.M. Neumann; c. Alexis Heidi. Educ: Mass. State Col, 43; Amherst Col, 43; Trinity Col, B.A, 47; Boston Univ. Law Sch, 47-49; New Eng. Sch. Law, LL.B. & J.D, 51; mgr. and catcher, Trinity Col. baseball team; mgr, soccer team, left halfback; Undefeated Heavyweight Boxer; Heavyweight Wrestler; Track-Two Miler; pres, Non-Fraternity Neutrals; bus. and advert. mgr, Trinity Tripod, Newspaper. Polit. & Govt. Pos: Dem. cand, Co. attorney, Maine, 56 & 58; chmn. cmt. for enrolling new Dem. registrants and converts, Sagadahoc Co. Dem. Party, 56-64; mem, Bath City Dem. Cmt, 56-69; Committeeman, Sagadahoc Co. Dem. Cmt, 59-60; Disclosure cmnr, Sagadahoc Co, 59-; Dem. cand, Co. Judge of Probate, 60; Dem. cand, Maine State Rep, 62 & 64; complaint justice, Sixth Dist. Court, Sagadahoc Co, 65-; alternate del, Dem. Nat. Conv, 68. Bus. & Prof. Pos: Attorney-at-law, Maine; pres, Qualitas Specialty Corp, Wilmington, Del, 67-69, Amalgamated Leather Co, Inc, Wilmington, 67-69, Qualitas Mgt. Corp, Maine, 68-69, Nibblers, 69 and Regimental Stripe, 69. Mil. Serv: Volunteered as Aviation Cadet, Army Air Force, 44, released as Cpl, 46, after serv. in 134th AACS, ETO, 45-46; Good Conduct Medal; Europe-Africa-Middle East. Campaign Medal; German Occup. Medal. Mem: Sagadahoc Co. Bar Asn; Elks; Am. Legion (post comdr, 55-56, Brunswick Legis. Rep, Dept. Maine, 57-58); B'nai B'rith (past pres). Rel: Hebrew. Legal Res: 1135 Washington St, Bath, Maine 04503. Mailing Add: 220 Maine St, Brunswick, Maine 04011.

KLINDT, HERBERT JAMES R
Mont. State Sen.
b. Sheridan, Wyo, 12/18/01; s. James Klindt and Amelia Keefauver K; m. 2/10/32 to Clara Gore. Educ: Univ. Ill, B.S, 25; Wittenburg Col; Anubis. Polit. & Govt. Pos: Mont. State Sen, 67- Bus. & Prof. Pos: Athletic dir, Rocky Mt. Col, 31-; personnel dir, Elastic Stop Nut, 42-43; dir. labor rels, Woods Bros, 43-44 and Pac. Car Foundry, 45. Mem: Am. Asn. Univ. Prof; life mem, Mont. Coaches Asn; Lions Int; Nat. Asn. Intercol. Athletics; Hilands Golf Club; life mem, Midland Round Table. Award of Merit, Nat. Asn. Intercol. Athletics. Rel: Methodist. Mailing Add: 402 Alderson, Billings, Mont. 59102.

KLINE, ALLEN J. D
Chmn, Bowman Co. N.Dak.Dem-Non-Partisan League.
b. Scranton, N.Dak, 9/19/28; s. Harry A. Kline and Lucy M. Jolivette K; m. 10/16/54 to Ruth E. Snow; c. Nicole Kay, Colleen Marie, Bradley Allen, Lea Patrice and Brian Dwight. Educ: Scranton Pub. High Sch, grad, 46. Polit. & Govt. Pos: Precinct committeeman, Bowman Co. N.Dak. Dem-Non-Partisan League, 58-66, v.chmn, 60-62, chmn, 62- Bus. & Prof. Pos: Farmer. Mem: K. of C.(3°), past grand knight, St. Isidoro Coun. 4553. Rel: Catholic. Mailing Add: R.R. 3, Bowman, N.Dak. 58623. (1967)

KLINE, BOYD HOWARD R
Mem, Rep. State Finance Cmt, Pa.
b. Orange Twp, Col Co, Pa, 5/28/03; s. Eppy Wadsworth Kline and Harriet L. Mellick K; 2nd m. 9/20/51 to Virginia Hughes; c. Jean (Mrs. Lamon) and Robert O. Polit. & Govt. Pos: Chmn, Schneebeli for Cong. Campaign, Pa, 60; chmn, Nixon Campaign Cmt. of Columbia Co, 60 & 68; mem, Columbia Co. Rep. Exec. Cmt, 60-; chmn, Columbia Co. Rep. Finance Cmt, 63-; del, Rep. Nat. Conv, 64; mem, Rep. State Finance Cmt, 68- Bus. & Prof. Pos: Owner, Boyd H. Kline Construction Co, 27-; pres, Boyd H. Kline Corp, 47-; dir, Bloomsburg Hosp, 50-57; pres, Boyd H. Kline Assocs, Inc, 67-; dir, Cosmopolitan Investors Funding Co, Trans Imp. Enterprises and Gibraltar Life Ins. Co, 68- Mem: President's Club; Am. Inst. Mgt; Assoc. Builders & Contractors of Am; contrib, Taft Mem, Wash, D.C, Eisenhower Libr, Nat. Cong. Rep. Cmt. and Karl Mundt Libr; donor, Columbia Co. Rep. Cmt, Pa. Rep. Cmt. and Nat. GOP Cmt; Elks; Moose, Eagles, Pa. Rep. Century Club; Rep. Capitol Hill Club; RN Assocs; Camp Develop. & Nom. Cmts. of Penn's Woods Girl Scout Coun; sustaining mem, Boy Scouts, Girl Scouts and Rep. Nat. Party Club; charter mem, Heart Fund 500 Club; hon. citizen, Boys Town of Am. Rel: Lutheran. Legal Res: R.D. 2, Columbia County, Orangeville, Pa. 17859. Mailing Add: Old Berwick Rd, Bloomsburg, Pa. 17815.

KLINE, DAVID LOUIS D
b. Ashville, N.C, 7/25/35; s. Rabbi Alexander S. Kline and Eleanore Spitz K; m. 8/15/65 to Barbara Jane Furth; c. Auram Joseph. Educ: Brandeis Univ, B.A, 57; Hebrew Union Col, M.A.H.L. and Rabbinic Ordination, 62; Columbia Univ, 63-66. Polit. & Govt. Pos: Del, Dem. Nat. Conv, 68. Bus. & Prof. Pos: Rabbi, Riverdale Temple, N.Y, 66-67 and Temple Menorah, Little Neck, 67- Publ: 'At the Democratic Convention,' Jewish Spectator, 11/68. Mem: N.Y. Bd. Rabbis; Cent. Conf. Am. Rabbis; L.I. Asn. Reform Rabbis; chmn, Little Neck-Douglaston Ministerial Asn. Rel: Jewish. Mailing Add: 15-72 217 St, Bayside, N.Y. 11360.

KLINE, ERNEST P. D
Pa. State Sen.
b. Allentown, Pa, 6/20/29; s. Allen J. Kline and Elna Natali K; m. to Josephine Recupero; c. seven. Educ: Rostraver High Sch. Polit. & Govt. Pos: Mem, Beaver Falls City Coun, Pa, 56-59; Workman's Compensation Referee, 61-63; Pa. State Sen, 64-, Minority Leader, Pa. State Senate, 67-; del, Dem. Nat. Conv, 68. Bus. & Prof. Pos: Radio newsman. Rel: Catholic. Mailing Add: 2209 Seventh Ave, Beaver Falls, Pa. 15010.

KLINE, HELEN M. D
b. Hartford, Conn, 9/21/13; d. Henry Manewitz and Lena Lifland M; m. 9/4/39 to Morris Kline; c. Elizabeth (Mrs. Jonathan Landers), Judith and Douglas. Educ: N.Y. Univ, B.A, 39; Phi Beta Kappa. Polit. & Govt. Pos: Del, Dem. Nat. Conv, 68, del-at-lg, Kings Co. Dem. Coalition, Brooklyn, N.Y, 68- Bus. & Prof. Pos: Substitute teacher, high sch. math, N.Y.C; free-lance French translator. Rel: Jewish. Mailing Add: 1024 E. 26th St, Brooklyn, N.Y. 11210.

KLINE, MORGAN MARSHALL R
Chmn, Bloomfield Rep. Town Cmt, Conn.
b. Springfield, Mass, 5/6/22; s. Abraham Alfred Kline and Rachel Caplan K; m. 9/8/46 to Frances Schulman; c. Jeffrey Lewis and Jonathan Andrew. Educ: Univ. Conn, B.S, 48, Sch. Law, LL.B, 51; Phi Sigma Delta. Polit. & Govt. Pos: Justice of the peace, Hartford, Conn, 52-58, Bloomfield, 65-; chmn, Bloomfield Rep. Town Cmt, 67- Bus. & Prof. Pos: Partner, Stoner, Gross and Kline, Attorneys, Hartford, Conn, 51- Mil. Serv: Entered as Pvt, Army, 43, released as T/Sgt, 46, after serv. in Seventh Cavalry Reconnaissance Troop, Seventh Inf. Div, Asiatic-Pac, 43-46; Res, Lt. Col.(Ret). Mem: Am, Conn. State and Hartford Co. Bar Asns; AF&AM; AASR (32°); Consistory; AAONMS; Am. Cancer Soc.(chmn. Conn. Div. Exec. Cmt); dir, Combined Health Appeal Gr. Hartford. Rel: Jewish. Mailing Add: 10 Old Orchard Rd, Bloomfield, Conn. 06002.

KLINE, PAUL ARTHUR R
b. Mahanoy City, Pa, 10/29/19; s. William Kline and Ellen Eckler K; m. 10/6/56 to Freeda M. Swartz; c. Richard A, Betsy J.(Mrs. Husson) and Gretchen Ellen. Educ: Univ. Maine, 46-49; George Wash. Univ, B.A, 51. Polit. & Govt. Pos: Clerk, U.S. Rep. Frank Fellows, Maine, 49-52; legis. asst. to U.S. Rep. Clifford G. McIntire, Maine, 53-64; research specialist, House Republican Conf, 65-66; legis. asst. to U.S. Rep. Catherine May, Wash, 66-67; admin. asst. to U.S. Rep. George A. Goodling, 19th Dist, Pa, 67- Mil. Serv: Entered as Pfc, Army Air Force, 42, released as Cpl, 45, after serv. in 589th Air Force Bn, ETO, 45; Good Conduct Medal; ETO Medal. Rel: Protestant. Mailing Add: 1505 Vivian Place, Silver Spring, Md. 20902.

KLINEMAN, ALAN I. D
Educ: Phi Delta Phi; Pi Lambda Phi. Polit. & Govt. Pos: Ind. State Sen, -66; supvr, Criminal Court Div. 2; prosecuting attorney, Marion Cty, 59-63. Bus. & Prof. Pos: Partner, Klineman & Rose, attorneys at law. Mem: Indianapolis and Ind. State Bar Asns. Rel: Hebrew. Mailing Add: 1122 Circle Tower, Indianapolis, Ind. 46204. (1967)

KLINGBIEL, RAY I. R
Justice, Ill. Supreme Court
b. Moline, Ill, 3/2/01; s. Henry F. Klingbiel and Minnie Lebbert K; m. 10/5/26 to Julia Stone; c. Donna (Mrs. Simpson) and Tom. Educ: Univ. Ill, Champaign-Urbana, LL.B; Hon. LL.D, Univ. Ill, Chicago Kent Col. Law and Chicago Kent Univ. Polit. & Govt. Pos: Justice of Peace, East Moline, Ill, 25-29, city attorney, 29-39, mayor, 39-45; Judge of the Circuit Court, Rock Island County, 45-53; justice, Ill. Supreme Court, 53-, chief justice, 56-57, permanent chief justice, 64-67. Publ: Observe the Law-Key to Order, Justice, Freedom, Chi Daily Law Bul, 4/65; Landmark Opinions: Molitor v. Kaneland Commun. Unit Dist. 302 (18 Ill 2d 11 and 24 Ill 2d 467); Wolfson v. Avery 6 Ill 2d 78; Peo v. Speck, 41 Ill 2d 177. Mem: Am, Ill. and Rock Island Co. Bar Asns; Am. Judicature Soc; hon. Mason (33°); Univ. Club. of Chicago; Short Hills Country Club; Rock Island Arsenal Country Club; Rotary; hon. mem, Moline-Silvis Asn. of C. of C. Rel: Protestant. Legal Res: 4801 Coaltown Rd, Moline, Ill. 61265. Mailing Add: 1610 8th St, East Moline, Ill. 61244.

KLINK, LESLIE C. R
Iowa State Sen.
b. Littleport, Iowa, 8/11/26; s. LeRoy J. Klink and Irma M. K; single. Educ: Iowa State Univ, 3 years. Polit. & Govt. Pos: Iowa State Sen, 69- Mil. Serv: Entered as Pvt, Army, 53, released 54, after serv. in 624 Transportation Co,

Korea. Mem: Am. Nat. Cattleman's Asn; Am. Angus Asn; Iowa Beef Producer's; Mason; Shrine; Am. Legion. Rel: Protestant. Legal Res: Brown Hotel, Des Moines, Iowa. Mailing Add: Elkader, Iowa 52043.

KLINKEL, THOMAS EDWARD D
b. Sioux Falls, S.Dak, 10/5/46; s. Vernon Arthur Klinkel (deceased) and Norma Lucille Jensen K; single. Educ: S.Dak. State Univ, B.S, 68; Univ. Americas, Mexico, M.A, 70; Phi Kappa Phi; Pi Kappa Delta; Pi Gamma Mu; Blue Key; Student Govt. Bd. of Control; Toastmasters; Rotary Found. grad. fel; finalist, Rhodes Scholar Competition, 68. Polit. & Govt. Pos: Pres, Young Dem, S.Dak. State Univ, 67-68; S.Dak. co-chmn, Students for Kennedy, 68; del, Dem. Nat. Conv, 68; political intern, off. of U.S. Sen. George McGovern, S.Dak, 68, area coordinator, Sen. campaign of George McGovern, 68. Mil. Serv: Commissioned as 2nd Lt, Army, ROTC, 68; Army Res, 69-; Distinguished Mil. Student; Distinguished Mil. Grad; Legion of Valor Award, 67; Asn. of U.S. Army Award for Outstanding Leadership and Scholarship, 68. Mem: De Molay (Local Master Coun, State Master Coun, S.Dak. and Chevalier); Mason. 40 trophies and awards for debate, oratory and extemporaneous speaking. Rel: Methodist. Mailing Add: 518 20th Ave, Brookings, S.Dak. 57006.

KLOEB, FRANK LeBLOND D
b. Celina, Ohio; 6/16/90; s. Charles A. Kloeb and Emma LeBlond K; m. 9/2/30 to Florence Root; c. Carol LeBlond. Educ: Ohio State Univ, 08-09; Ohio State Univ. and Univ. Wis, law study, 15-17; Univ. Toledo, hon. LL.D; Sigma Alpha Epsilon; Phi Delta Phi. Polit. & Govt. Pos: Prosecuting attorney, Mercer Co, Ohio, 21-24; U.S. Rep, Ohio, 33-37; U.S. Dist. Judge, 37-64; sr. dist. judge, U.S. Dist. Court, N.Dist, Ohio, 64- Bus. & Prof. Pos: Began law practice in Celina, Ohio, 19; mem, Loree & Kloeb, 21. Mil. Serv: Navy, Ens. Mem: Am. and Ohio Bar Asns; Am. Legion; K. of C. Rel: Catholic. Legal Res: 3156 Kylemore Rd, Toledo, Ohio 43606. Mailing Add: U.S. District Court, Federal Bldg, Toledo, Ohio 45504.

KLOET, ALVIN ROBERT R
Chmn, Sheboygan Co. Rep. Party, Wis.
b. Kenosha, Wis, 2/25/32; s. Adrian Kloet and Grace Burman K; m. 9/4/53 to La Vonne K. Dykstra; c. Jeffrey Allan. Educ: Calvin Col, A.B; Univ. Wis, LL.B. Polit. & Govt. Pos: Asst. dist. attorney, Sheboygan Co, Wis, 62-66; chmn, Sheboygan Co. Rep. Party, currently. Mil. Serv: Entered as Pvt, Army, 53, released as Cpl, 55, after serv. in Scarwaf, Far East; Good Conduct Medal; Far East and Korean Campaign Ribbons. Mem: Sheboygan Co. and Wis. State Bar Asns. Rel: Christian Reformed. Mailing Add: 602 N. Sixth St, Sheboygan, Wis. 53081. (1967)

KLONOSKI, FRANK J. D
Chmn, Naugatuck Town Dem. Cmt, Conn.
b. Naugatuck, Conn, 3/13/07; s. Frank M. Klonoski and Martha Jursyn K; m. 8/13/28 to Lily Elizabeth McDonnell; c. Karyl, Frank and Sandra. Educ: Alliance, A.B.S, 27. Polit. & Govt. Pos: Chmn, Naugatuck Town Dem. Cmt, Conn, 58-, Zoning Bd. Appeals, 60-64, Citizens Action Cmt, 61-62 and Indust. Develop. Cmt, 62-63. Bus. & Prof. Pos: Maintenance Supvr, UniRoyal U.S. Rubber Co, 32- Mem: Am. Inst. Plant Engrs; Am. Soc. Lubrication Engrs; Elks; Polish Falcons; Am. Brass Country Club; St. Francis Holy Name Soc; Naugatuck Volunteer Fire Dept. Rel: Roman Catholic. Mailing Add: 19 Fern St, Naugatuck, Conn. 06770. (1967)

KLUCZYNSKI, JOHN CARL D
U.S. Rep, Ill.
b. Chicago, Ill, 2/15/96; s. Thomas Kluczynski and Mary Zulawski K; m. 11/15/39 to Stephanie Estelle Polowy. Polit. & Govt. Pos: Ill. State Rep, 32-48; Ill. State Sen, 48-49; U.S. Rep, Ill, 50- Bus. & Prof. Pos: Owner and operator, Syrena Restaurant & Caterers, Chicago, Ill. Mil. Serv: Entered as Pvt, Eighth Field Artil, 18, released as A Waggoner, 19. Mem: Am. Legion; VFW; Army and Navy Club; Admirals Club; City Club of Chicago; C. of C; Chicago Motor Club; Polish Commercial Club; Polish Legion of Am. Vets; Polish Nat. Alliance; Polish Roman Cath. Union; Polish Dem. Clubs; Irish Fel. Club; Travelers Club and others. Rel: Roman Catholic. Legal Res: 2450 W. 55th St, Chicago, Ill. 60609. Mailing Add: 4270 S. Archer Ave, Chicago, Ill. 60616.

KLUENDER, AL R
b. Paullina, Iowa, 1/10/25; s. Albert Kluender (deceased) and Louise Mueller K; m. 1/29/44 to Betty Loraine Onnen; c. Douglas and Allan. Educ: Phoenix Col. Polit. & Govt. Pos: Ariz. State Rep, 65-68, mem, Hwy. and State Fact Finding Cmt, Ariz. House Rep, 66-68, v.chmn, House Educ. Cmt, 65-66, chmn, 67-68. Bus. & Prof. Pos: V.pres, Ariz. Gasoline Retailers Asn, 61, pres, 62; pres, Maryvale Merchants Asn, 66- Mem: Kiwanis Int; Kiwanis (v.pres, Phoenix Chap, 64); charter mem, Trunk'n Tusk Club; Antique Automobile Club Am; Int. Asn. of Machinists, AFL, 43-52. Rel: Lutheran; Mem, Church Coun, 63-66. Mailing Add: 5702 W. Indianola, Phoenix, Ariz. 85031. (1967)

KLUEVER, LESTER LUVERNE R
Iowa State Rep.
b. Atlantic, Iowa, 2/29/20; s. Emil C. Kluever and Louise A. Lilienthal K; m. 5/10/47 to Gwyn H. Hughes; c. Lora L, Chris L, Dan L. and Jerri L. Educ: Creighton Univ; Univ. of Iowa, B.Sc, 47 and J.D, 50; Phi Delta Phi; Delta Sigma Pi; Sigma Nu. Polit. & Govt. Pos: Co. attorney, Cass Co, Iowa, 52-56; Iowa State Rep, Cass Co, 57-, speaker pro tempore, Iowa House of Rep, 67-69. Mil. Serv: Entered as Cadet, Army Air Force, 41, released as Capt, 46, after serv. in 92nd Bomb Group, 8th Air Force, ETO, 43; Prisoner of War, Stalag Luft III, Sagan, Germany, 43-45; Purple Heart; ETO Ribbon. Mem: Am, Iowa State and Southwest Iowa Bar Asns; pres, Cass Co. Bar Asn, 65-66; Am. Asn. of Trial Lawyers; Am. Judicature Soc; Iowa Acad. of Trial Lawyers; life mem, State Hist. Soc; Univ. of Iowa Alumni Assoc; Univ. of Iowa Dad's Asn; YMCA; Mason; Shrine; Elks; Rotary; Cass Co. Soil Conserv. Dist. Asn; Am. Legion; VFW; Amvets; Farm Bur; C. of C; Cass Co. Game Conserv. Club. Rel: Presbyterian. Mailing Add: 309 W. 14th St, Atlantic, Iowa 50022.

KLUNK, FRED G. D
Chmn, Adams Co. Dem. Cmt, Pa.
b. Centennial, Pa, 7/30/10; s. Edward G. Klunk (deceased) and Rose Gebhart K; m. 6/26/33 to Florence Elizabeth Rinehart; c. Sylvia, James,Warren, Rosalie, Wayne, Fred R. and Christine. Educ: Bus. Col. Polit. & Govt. Pos: Mem, City Coun, New Oxford, Pa, 3 terms and pres, 2 terms; dir, Bur. of Liquid Fuels Tax, Pa. Dept. Revenue; dep. secy, Dept. of Property and Supplies; exec. secy, State Retirement Bd; mem, Adams Co. Dem. Cmt, 33-, chmn, 43-; mem, State Dem. Cmt, 38-41. Bus. & Prof. Pos: Asst. Dir, Bur. of Securities & Deposits, State Treas. Dept; mfr. of Bakery Prods. Mem: K. of C.(4°); Elks; Moose; Eagles; Lions; Munic. Finance Officers, U.S. and Can. Rel: Catholic. Mailing Add: 15 N. Peter St, New Oxford, Pa. 17350. (1967)

KNAGGS, JOHN RYAN R
b. Cotulla, Tex, 5/24/34; s. Albert Urban Knaggs and Samantha Murphy K; m. 2/17/62 to Joan Wright; c. Lisa, Ryan and Barton. Educ: Univ. Tex, B.A; Sigma Delta Chi. Polit. & Govt. Pos: Pub. Rel. dir, Rep. Party of Tex, 63-67. Bus. & Prof. Pos: Correspondent, United Press Int, 62-63; partner, Collins-Knaggs & Assoc, Austin, Tex, 67- Mil. Serv: Entered as Pvt, Army Res, 57, released as S/Sgt, 63. Mem: Tex. Pub. Rels. Asn; Austin Advert. Club. Rel: Methodist. Legal Res: 3703 Hillbrook Dr, Austin, Tex. 78731. Mailing Add: 1905 N. Lamar, Suite 208, Austin, Tex. 78705.

KNAPP, G. ED(WARD) R
Ga. State Rep.
b. Ypsilanti, Mich, 3/22/16; s. Jay (N) Knapp and Clara Norwood K; m. 8/15/45 to Mary Elizabeth Scott; c. Nancy L, Henry Scott and Gregory Lee. Educ: East. Mich. Univ, 34-36; Univ. Mich, B.S.F, 40; Mich. Forestry Club. Polit. & Govt. Pos: Ga. State Rep, Dist, 81, Post 2, 66-; Bibb Co. Rep, Mid. Ga. Recreation Cmn, 68-; chmn, Bibb Co. Forestry Bd, Ga, 68- Mil. Serv: Pilot Instr. and ATC Pilot, Air Force Res, 42-44. Mem: Soc. of Am. Foresters (chmn, Southeast. Sect, 68); Forest Farmers Asn; Am. and Ga. Forestry Asns; Mem: Pres, Macon Farmers Club, 59; Rotary. Rel: Baptist. Legal Res: 661 Forest Hill Rd, Macon Ga. 31204. Mailing Add: 4435 Pio Nono Ave, Macon, Ga. 31206.

KNAPP, V. K. R
W.Va. State Sen.
b. Buffalo, W.Va, 12/19/13; s. A.L. Knapp and Ora Forbus K; m. 6/3/37 to Lillian Louise Mitchell; c. Melissa Jane. Educ: W.Va. Inst. of Tech, A.B; W.Va. Univ, LL.B. Polit. & Govt. Pos: Former town attorney, Huntington and Bancroft, W.Va; prosecuting attorney, Putnam Co, 53-60; W.Va. State Sen, 62- Bus. & Prof. Pos: Lawyer. Mil. Serv: World War II. Mem: Putnam Co. and W.Va. Bar Asns; Am. Legion. Rel: Baptist. Mailing Add: 167 Midland Trail, Hurricane, W.Va. 25526. (1967)

KNAPP, WALTER LEE, JR. D
Tex. State Rep.
b. Jacksonville, Tex, 10/24/30; s. Walter Lee Knapp, Sr. and Lottie L. Russell K; m. 12/28/68 to Nancy Kay Sappington; c. Sheri Lynn and Dustin Lee Knapp and stepchildren, Debbie Lynn and Elizabeth Ann Houghton. Educ: Univ. Tex, B.A. in Govt, 52, LL.B, 59; Delta Theta Phi; hon. Lambda Chi Alpha. Polit. & Govt. Pos: City attorney, Amarillo, Tex, 59, first asst. dist. attorney, 59-61; Tex. State Rep, 62-; mem, Gov. Cmn. of 500 on Tex. Water. Bus. & Prof. Pos: Lawyer, self-employed, 61- Mil. Serv: Entered as 2nd Lt, Army, 52, released as 1st Lt, 54, after serv. in 25th Inf. Div, Korea, 53-54; Capt, Res, 61; Nat. Defense Serv. Medal; Korean Serv. Medal with Two Campaign Stars. Mem: Tex. and Amarillo Bar Asns; Am. Bus. Club; Moose. Distinguished Serv. Award, Tex. Bar Asn, 65 & 67; Oustanding Serv. Award, VFW, 67. Rel: Methodist. Mailing Add: 621 W. Eighth, Amarillo, Tex. 79101.

KNAUFT, MILFORD ROY, JR. R
Mem, Calif. Rep. State Cent. Cmt.
b. St. Paul, Minn, 8/26/18; s. Milford Roy Knauft and Marie Simonet K; m. 1/18/46 to Doris Bovee; c. Robert Lee, Nancy Louise and Sally Ann. Educ: Univ. Calif, Los Angeles, 4 years; Sigma Nu; Scabbard & Blade. Polit. & Govt. Pos: Dir, Yorba Linda Co. Water Dist, 65-; sch. bd. mem, Placentia Unified Sch. Dist, 67-; mem, Calif. Rep. State Cent. Cmt, currently. Bus. & Prof. Pos: Off. mgr, Hollywood Wholesale Paper Corp, Calif, 46-50, gen. mgr. and treas, 50-61; retired. Mil. Serv: Entered as 2nd Lt, Army Air Force, 43, released as 1st Lt, 45, after serv. in 96th Bomb Group, Eighth Air Force, ETO, 44-45; Air Medal; 3 Oak Leaf Clusters; Distinguished Flying Cross. Mem: Rotary Club; life mem, PTA. Rel: Presbyterian. Mailing Add: 5682 Orchard Dr, Yorba Linda, Calif. 92686.

KNAUR, RAYMOND MOWRY R
Mayor, Williamsport, Pa.
b. Williamsport, Pa, 8/9/17; s. Christian Mowry Knaur; m. 3/21/51 to Helen Mary Tyler; c. Richard M, Marcella A. and Mowry S. Educ: Dickenson Seminary, 34-36; Pa. State Univ, 37. Polit. & Govt. Pos: Mayor, Williamsport, Pa; mem, Rep. League and Young Men's Rep. Club. Bus. & Prof. Pos: Pres, Eureka Paper Box Co, 47-55, chmn. bd, 56-; v.pres, Eureka Sales Co, 52-55, pres, 55-66, chmn. bd, 56- Mil. Serv: Entered as Pvt, Army, 43, released as S/Sgt, 46, after serv. in China Burma India Theater, 44-46; Burma Campaign, Kwalin and S.Pac. Asiatic Ribbons. Mem: Folding Paper Box Asn. of Am; Blue Lodge, Consistory, Shrine, Grotto; Elks; Moose; Am. Legion; Int. Rotary. Rel: Lutheran. Mailing Add: 601 Orchard Place, Williamsport, Pa. 17701. (1967)

KNEECE, ROBERT EDWARD D
S.C. State Rep.
b. Columbia, S.C, 12/20/33; s. Otis Salter Kneece and Elise Blackmon K; m. 6/1/57 to Margaret Ann Medders; c. Melanie Carol, Melinda Kyle, Robert Edward, Jr, Richard Otis, Rexford Patrick and Margaret Ann. Educ: Univ. S.C, LL.B, 58; Sigma Chi. Polit. & Govt. Pos: Pres, Richland Co. Young Dem, S.C, 61; pres, S.C. Young Dem, 60-62; S.C. State Rep, 67-, second v.chmn, Judiciary Cmt, S.C. State House of Rep, currently. Bus. & Prof. Pos: Attorney at Law, 58- Mem: Mason, Shrine; C. of C. Rel: Lutheran. Mailing Add: 4110 Parkman Dr, Columbia, S.C. 29206.

KNEEN, RICHARD A. R
V.Chmn, Hillsdale Co. Rep. Party, Mich.
b. Hillsdale, Mich, 3/19/38; m. 8/20/60; c. Kurtis R. and Scott E. Educ: Cornell Univ, B.M.E. and M.B.A. Polit. & Govt. Pos: V.chmn, Hillsdale Co.

Rep. Party and chmn, Hillsdale City Park Cmn, currently. Bus. & Prof. Pos: Materials mgr, Simpson Industs, Litchfield, Mich. Mem: Pi Tau Sigma; Psi Upsilon. Rel: Presbyterian. Legal Res: 119 Orchard Ridge, Hillsdale, Mich. 49242. Mailing Add: Simpson Industries, 917 S. Anderson Rd, Litchfield, Mich. 49252.

KNEIP, RICHARD FRANCIS D
S.Dak. State Sen.
b. Tyler, Minn, 1/7/33; s. Frank J. Kneip and Bernice D. Peterson K; m. to Nancy Lou Pankey; c. Kevin, Keith, Paul, Kent, Kurt, Philip and Patrick. Polit. & Govt. Pos: S.Dak. State Sen, McCook, Hanson and Sanborn Co, 64-, Minority Leader, S.Dak. State Sen, 67-; mem. exec. bd, Legis Research Coun. and mem. 13 Man Constitutional Rev. Cmn, currently. Bus. & Prof. Pos: Mem, Diocesen Sch. Bd, Cath. Diocese of Sioux Falls, S.Dak, 67- Mil. Serv: Entered as Pvt, Air Force, 51, released as S/Sgt, 55; German Occup. Medal. Mem: Am. Legion. Rel: Catholic. Mailing Add: 300 E. Lincoln, Salem, S.Dak. 57058.

KNICELY, CARROLL FRANKLIN D
b. Staunton, Va, 12/8/28; s. Bernard Clyde Knicely, Sr. and Violet Phillips K; m. 2/4/48 to Evelyn Virginia Furr; c. Evie Kaye, Brenda Sue; Beverly Carol, Carroll, Jr. and Daryl Wayne. Educ: Augusta Mil. Acad, grad. Polit. & Govt. Pos: Postmaster, Glasgow, Ky, 65-; chmn, Barren Co. Recreational Cmn, 63-65; committeeman, Barren Co. Dem. Cmt, 61-65; del, Ky. 2nd Cong. Dist, Dem. Nat. Conv, 64 and from Ky. 4th Cong. Dist, 60; mem, Mayor's Adv. Cmt, Glasgow, Ky, 62-64; mem, Ky. Gov. Adv. Cmn. on Higher Educ, 61-64; committeeman, Waynesboro City Dem. Cmt, Va, 54-57. Bus. & Prof. Pos: Treas, Glasgow Pub. Corp, Ky, 65- and pres, 57-65; pres, Campbellsville Pub. Corp, and Glasgow Loan Co. and secy-treas, Scottsville Welfare Lenders, 65-; chmn. bd. of dirs, Sun Pub. Co, Pineville and dir, First Financial Life Ins. Co, Bowling Green, Ky, 63-; pres, Associated Publns, Inc, Glasgow, 62- Mem: Nat. dir, Travelers Protective Asn. of Am; Mason (32°), Shriner; Rotarian; Nat. Ed. Asn; Nat. League of Postmasters; Nat. Asn. of Postmasters of U.S. Rel: Baptist. Mailing Add: 908 S. Green St, Glasgow, Ky. 42141 (1967)

KNIEVEL, ANTON JOHN, III R
b. Butte, Mont, 8/26/25; s. Anton John Knievel, Jr. and Eunice Churchill K; div; c. Cindy Ann. Educ: Wash. State Univ; pres, Alpha Chapter, Nat. Collegiate Radio Guild; secy, Theta Chi. Polit. & Govt. Pos: Admin. Asst. to U.S. Rep. Catherine May, Wash, 59- Bus. & Prof. Pos: Announcer, Radio Sta. KXRO, Aberdeen, 48-51; chief announcer, Radio Sta. KWSC, Wash. State Univ, 51; news dir, Cascade Broadcasting Co, Yakima, Wash, 51-58. Mil. Serv: Entered as A/S, Naval Res, 43, released as Radioman 2/C, 46, after serv. in Pac; Am. Area Campaign Medal; Victory Medal; Philippine Liberation Medal with 1 Star; Asiatic-Pac. Area Campaign Medal with 5 Stars; Presidential Unit Citation. Mem: Yakima Co. Men's Rep. Club; Cong. Secretaries Club; Bull Elephants Club. Rel: Episcopal. Legal Res: Yakima, Wash. Mailing Add: 2332 Rayburn House Office Bldg, Washington, D.C. 20515.

KNIGHT, A. J. D
Chmn, Imperial Co. Dem. Cent. Cmt, Calif.
b. Holtville, Calif, 12/10/27; s. Grover Cleveland Knight and Mary E. Ethridge K; m. 8/3/52 to Helen L. Sever; c. T. Craig, Nancie L. and Lester C. Educ: Holtville High Sch, grad, 45. Polit. & Govt. Pos: Pres, El Centro Dem. Club, Calif, 60-61; v.pres, Bus. & Prfnl. Dem, 62-63 and pres, 64-65; chmn, Imperial Co. Dem. Cent. Cmt, 67- Bus. & Prof. Pos: Barber, AJ's Barber Shop, Calif, 52- Mil. Serv: Entered as Seaman 3/C, Navy, 45, released as Seaman 1/C, 46, after serv. in 7th Fleet, S.Pac. Theatre, 45-46. Rel: Episcopal. Legal Res: 745 Tangerine Dr, El Centro, Calif. 92243. Mailing Add: 300 S. Imperial, Suite 1, El Centro, Calif. 92243.

KNIGHT, ALICE D. TIRRELL R
N.H. State Rep.
b. Manchester, N.H, 7/14/03; d. Nathan Arthur Tirrell and Clara Stiles T; m. 11/16/52 to Norman Knight. Educ: Univ. N.H, B.A, 25; grad. study at Univ. N.H, Univ. Mass. and Boston Univ. Polit. & Govt. Pos: Women's coordinator, Goffstown Rep. Club, N.H; mem. budget cmt, Goffstown, 66-; N.H. State Rep, 67- Bus. & Prof. Pos: Prin, Bartlett Sch, Goffstown, N.H, 32-35; home lighting specialist, Pub. Serv. Co, N.H, 35-39; teacher merchandising, Mt. Ida Jr. Col, 39-45; home serv. dir, Boyd Corp, 45-47; dist. home economist, Frigidaire Sales Corp, New Eng, 48-64. Mem: Am. Women in Radio & TV; Nat. Home Fashion League; Am. Home Econ. Asn; Soroptimist Int; League of Women Voters; Eastern Star; White Shrine; N.H. Coun. on World Affairs; Nat. Grange; DAR; Bus. & Prfnl. Women; pres, Hillsborough Co. North Cancer Soc; bd. dirs, N.H. Cancer Soc; treas, Nat. Order Women Legislators. Rel: Congregational. Mailing Add: Addison Rd, R.D. 2, Goffstown, N.H. 03045.

KNIGHT, DURELL WARTHEN, JR. D
b. Dexter, Ga, 11/24/21; s. D. W. Knight and Sybil Haskins K; m. 4/14/46 to Minnie Virginia Ward; c. Durell Warthen Knight III, John Ward. Educ: Dublin High Sch; Mid. Ga. Col; Mich. State Col. Polit. & Govt. Pos: Ga. State Rep, 61-64; Mayor, Dexter, 59-62; City Coun. of Dexter, 46-47. Bus. & Prof. Pos: Ins; farmer; gen. farm supplies. Mil. Serv: Air Force, WW II, 43-45, S/Sgt; 11 Combat Stars; 2 Presidential Unit Citations. Mem: Elks; Lions; Masons; VFW. Rel: Baptist. Mailing Add: Dexter, Ga. 31019. (1967)

KNIGHT, EVELYN DELORIS D
Treas, Calif. Dem. State Cent. Cmt.
b. Mobile, Ala, 12/19/33; d. Clarence Knight and Odell Deal K; single. Educ: St. Louis Univ, B.S, 55, M.S.W, 60; Univ. South. Calif, 65; Univ. Calif, Berkley, 66-67. Polit. & Govt. Pos: Secy, Eastside Dem. Orgn, Calif, 64-65; treas, 32nd Cong. Dist. Coun, 63-65; mem. bd, Citizens Urban Renewal Adv. Bd, 66-67; mem. and treas, Calif. Dem. State Cent. Cmt, 68- Bus. & Prof. Pos: Classroom teacher, Archdioces of St. Louis, 55-58; child welfare supvr, City of St. Louis, 58-62; family agency supvr, Cath. Welfare Bur, 62-66; commun. orgn. prog. develop. dir, Contra Costa Co. Commun. Serv, 66-67; sr. soc. scientist, Westinghouse Elec. Corp, 67-68, dir. field serv, 68-; assoc. dir. Protestant Commun. Serv, currently; past time instr, Calif. State Col. Long Beach, currently. Mem: Nat. Asn. Soc. Workers; Acad. Cert. Soc. Worker-Nat. Conf. Soc. Welfare; Int. Orgn. Commun. Develop; Nat. Asn. Afro-Am. Educators; Inst. Training and Prog. Develop. Rel: Roman Catholic. Mailing Add: 2535 Cota Ave, Long Beach, Calif. 90810.

KNIGHT, GOODWIN S. R
Mem, Calif. Rep. State Cent. Cmt.
b. Provo, Utah, 12/9/96; s. Jesse Knight and Lillie J. Milner K; m. 1954 to Virginia Carlson; c. Marilyn (Mrs. E. Eaton) and Carolyn (Mrs. C. Weedman). Educ: Stanford Univ, A.B, 19. Polit. & Govt. Pos: Judge, Los Angeles Co. Superior Court, Calif, 35-46; Lt. Gov, Calif, 46-53, Gov, 53-59; mem, Calif. Rep. State Cent. Cmt, currently. Bus. & Prof. Pos: Former owner-operator, Elephant Eagle Mines, Soleoao, Calif; lawyer, 21-35 & 46-53. Mil. Serv: Comdr, Navy, 18-19; Star of Ital. Solidarity; Grand Cross Order Star, Ethiopia; Royal Order of Phoenix, Greece. Publ: Good's Budget of Boy's Stories, 10. Mem: Calif. State Bar Asn; VFW; Am. Legion; Mason; Shrine; Scots; K. of P; Moose; Eagles; Elks; 100F; Ahepa; Jonathan; Wilshire Country, Bel Air, Del Paso Country and Sutter Clubs. Rel: Protestant. Mailing Add: 540 S. Aroen Blvd, Los Angeles, Calif. 90005. (1967)

KNIGHT, HAROLD LAVERNE R
Iowa State Rep.
b. Ames, Iowa, 2/10/11; s. Charles Dakota Knight and Mary Orda Craven K; m. 4/7/35 to Fern Beatrice Bennett; c. Dean LaVerne, Kent Lloyd and Ray Lee. Educ: Iowa State Univ, B.S.A, 37; Theta Chi. Polit. & Govt. Pos: Iowa State Rep, Humboldt and Pocahontas Co, 67- Bus. & Prof. Pos: Dairy bacteriologist, Anderson-Erickson Dairy, 38-; pres, Knights Cottage Cheese, 50-64; dir, First Nat. Bank, 52- Mem: DeMolay Legion of Honor; Knights Comdr, Court of Honor; Red Cross of Constantine; Royal Order of Scotland; Mason (32°); York Rite; Grand Lodge of Iowa (Grand Treas); C. of C.(pres, Humboldt Chapter, 57). Rel: Methodist. Mailing Add: 708 Fifth Ave, Humboldt, Iowa 50548.

KNIGHT, HARRY FRANK D
Cmnr, City of Key West, Fla.
b. Key West, Fla, 10/3/22; s. Jefferson Hunt Knight, Sr. and Mereline Florence Biaza K; m. 3/17/44 to Ramona C. Lopez; c. Harry F. Knight, Jr. Educ: Univ. Fla, 39-40. Polit. & Govt. Pos: Chmn, Monroe Co. Dem. Exec. Cmt, Fla, 58-; cmnr, City of Key West, Fla, 59- Bus. & Prof. Pos: Transmission Dept, Am. Tel.& Tel. Co, 45. Mil. Serv: Entered as Cadet, Army Air Corps, 42, released as Sgt, 45, after serv. in Cent. Flying Training Command. Mem: Past Exalted Ruler, Key West Elks Lodge; Shrine; Key West Lions Club; S.P.E.B.S.Q.S.A; Navy League; Jr. C. of C; past pres, C. of C. Mil. Affairs Cmt; Key West Country Club. Hobbies: Golf. Rel: Episcopal. Mailing Add: 3615 Ave. E, Key West, Fla. 33040. (1967)

KNIGHT, JAMES EDWARD R
Chmn, Dallam Co. Rep. Exec. Cmt, Tex.
b. Electra, Tex, 12/4/20; s. James Meadow Knight and Kathryn Love K; m. 5/6/51 to Elizabeth Stell Johnson; c. J. Barry. Educ: Texas A&M Univ, 38-39; Tarleton Col, 39-40, 40-41; Univ. of Tex, 45-46; Delta Tau Delta. Polit. & Govt. Pos: V.chmn, Dallam Co. Rep. Exec. Cmt, Tex, 63, chmn, 64- Mil. Serv: Entered as Flying Cadet, Air Force, 41, released as Capt, 46; Lt. Col, 9913th Air Res. Squadron, West. Training Command, Air Force Res, retired 69; Commendation, Air Res. and Am. Campaign Medals. Mem: Mason; Scottish Rite; Shrine; Farm Bur. Rel: Christian. Mailing Add: 1006 Keeler Ave, Dalhart, Tex. 79022.

KNIGHT, JOHN ELLSWORTH R
Nebr. State Sen.
b. Lincoln, Nebr, 5/14/25; s. George Alexander Knight and Helen Gruver K; m. 5/25/46 to Ruth Irene Bintz; c. Kristine Louise, Mary Jo, Barbara Jean and Jan Elizabeth. Educ: Nebr. Wesleyan Univ, A.B, 47; Univ. Nebr; Garrett Seminary, 54; Psi Chi; Phi Delta Kappa; Pi Gamma Mu; Blue Key; Theta Chi; all conf. back, Nebr. Col. Conf. Polit. & Govt. Pos: Nebr. State Sen, 26th Dist, 65-; del, Nebr. State Rep. Cent. Cmt, 26th Dist, 66- Bus. & Prof. Pos: V.Pres, Citizens State Bank; pres, Gates-Knight Ins. Agency; minister, Methodist & United Church of Christ; dir. of educ, Reformatory for Men; teacher and coach, Louisville High Sch, Nebr; pres, Packers Nat. Bank, Omaha, 68- Mil. Serv: Entered as A/S, Navy, 43, released as Aviation Cadet, 45. Mem: Nebr. Bankers Asn; Lincoln Asn. Ins. Agents; Mason; Eastern Star; Am. Legion; Kiwanis. Rel: United Church of Christ. Legal Res: 5400 Garland, Lincoln, Nebr. 68504. Mailing Add: 2500 North 48th, Lincoln, Nebr. 68504.

KNIGHT, JOHN STEVERSON 'STEVE' D
Ga. State Sen.
b. Columbus, Ga, 8/11/22; s. Enoch Jacques Knight and Alta Ethel Steverson K; m. 8/18/52 to Jane Dillard; c. John Steverson, Jr, Leslie Dillard, William Coley and Robert Dillard. Educ: The Citadel, B.A, 43; Univ. Ga. Sch. Law, LL.B, 50; Phi Delta Phi; Phi Delta Theta. Polit. & Govt. Pos: Cmnr, Muscogee Co. Cmn, Ga, 53-57, chmn, 56-; mem, Gov. Staff, 59; cmnr, Columbus City Cmn, 60-66; mayor, Columbus, 62-63; Ga. State Sen, currently. Bus. & Prof. Pos: Attorney-at-law, 50-; chmn. bd. dirs, Opelika Scrap Material Co, pres, E.J. Knight Scrap Material Co, Inc. and v.pres, E.J. Knight Brokerage Corp, 60- Mil. Serv: Entered as Pvt, Army, 42, released as Capt, 46; Bronze Star; Ryukuyus Campaign Ribbon. Mem: Jr. C. of C.(past pres, past dist. pres. and int. v.pres, int. sen. and mem, U.S. exec. cmt); Columbus C. of C; Ga. C. of C.(past mem. bd. dirs); United Givers Campaign (chmn, 54); past mem. bd. dirs, YMCA, Girls Club, Boy Scouts, Ga. Heart Asn. and Columbus Area Tuberc. Asn; Ga-Ala. Coun. Boy Scouts, past pres; Nat. Boy Scout Coun; bd. dirs, Jr. Achievement; bd. dirs, and past pres, Columbus Little Theater; bd. dirs, Broadway Theater League; exec. cmt, Ga. Crippled Children's Asn; W. Ga. chmn, March of Dimes, 62; Columbus Auxiliary Police; bd. dirs, Ment. Health; Exec. Club; bd. dirs, Echo Day Center, Inc. and bd. trustees, Springer Opera House. Selected Outstanding Young Man of Year in Columbus and One of Five Outstanding Young Men in State of Ga, 54. Rel: Methodist; Former treas. and mem. official bd, St. Paul Methodist Church; mem. choir. Legal Res: 2518 Country Club Rd, Columbus, Ga. 31906. Mailing Add: P.O. Box 1271, Columbus, Ga. 31902.

KNIGHT, RIDGWAY BREWSTER
U.S. Ambassador to Portugal
b. Paris, France, 6/12/11; m. to Colette Lalier; c. Five. Educ: Univ. Paris,

B.S, 28 and Ph.B, 29; Harvard Bus. Sch, M.B.A, 31. Polit. & Govt. Pos: Career officer, U.S. Dept. of State For. Serv, 41-43 & 45-; v.consul, Casablanca, Algiers, 41-43; spec. asst. to ambassador, Paris, 45-49; dep. dir. NATO Affairs, 50-51; dir. West. European Affairs, 52-53; U.S. asst, High Cmnr. for Germany, Berlin, 54-55; polit. adv. to Gen. Gruenther and Norstad at SHAPE, Paris, 55-57; minister-counsr, Karachi, 57-59; consul gen, Syria, 60-61; U.S. Ambassador to Syria, 61-65, Belgium 65-69 and Portugal, 69- Bus. & Prof. Pos: Bus. exec, 31-41. Mil. Serv: Maj, Army, 43-45; Salerno, Anzio and S. France landings. State Dept. Superior Serv. Award for Serv. in Syria, 65. Legal Res: c/o George W. Knight, 120 E. 81st St, New York, N.Y. 10028. Mailing Add: U.S. Embassy, Lisbon, Portugal.

KNIGHT, THOMAS A. D
b. Charleston, W.Va, 10/15/33; s. Frank A. Knight (deceased) and Orpha Regina Thomas K; m. 8/20/55 to Margaret A. Fitzpatrick; c. Thomas Jr, John Anthony, Brian Francis, Stephen Roy and Theresa Lynn. Educ: Ohio Univ, A.B. Polit. & Govt. Pos: W.Va. State Del, 64-66; del, Dem. Nat. Conv, 68. Bus. & Prof. Pos: Newspaper reporter. Mil. Serv: Navy, 55-57. Mem: Charleston Press Club. Rel: Catholic. Mailing Add: 501 Superior Ave, Charleston, W.Va. 25303. (1967)

KNIGHT, V. LANE R
Mem, Calif. Rep. State Cent. Cmt.
b. Melbourne, Mo, 8/4/12; s. William J. Knight and Harriet Mae Harrison K; m. 3/18/50 to Vivian Sharp; c. Oren, Merrily (Mrs. Skinnell), Susie and Robin. Educ: La Salle Exten. Univ, LL.B, 57. Polit. & Govt. Pos: Rep. nominee, Calif. State Senate, 32nd Dist, 66; mem, Calif. Rep. State Cent. Cmt, 66- Bus. & Prof. Pos: Attorney-at-law, 60- Mil. Serv: 1st Lt, Civil Air Patrol. Mem: Orange Co. Bar Asn; State Bar of Calif; Kiwanis. Rel: Protestant. Mailing Add: 9291 Graham Circle, Cypress, Calif. 90630.

KNIGHT, WILLIAM D. D
b. Ray City, Ga, 3/2/34; s. E.M. Knight and Ezena Daniel K; m. 8/6/60 to Jane Frances Stallings; c. Edna Elizabeth and William D, Jr. Educ: Valdosta State Col, B.S, 55; Univ. Ga, J.D, 58; Phi Delta Phi; Kappa Alpha. Polit. & Govt. Pos: City councilman, Ray City, Ga, 59-60; Ga. State Rep, 61-66. Bus. & Prof. Pos: Attorney; farmer. Mil. Serv: Ga. Nat. Guard. Mem: Alapaha Bar Asn.(pres); State Bar of Ga; Am. Bar Asn; Order of Gridiron Soc; Sons of Confederate Vets; New Lois Commun. Club.(pres, 68-69); Berrien Co. Civic Club (pres, 67-). Legal Res: R.F.D. 2, Nashville, Ga. 31639. Mailing Add: P.O. Box 647, Nashville, Ga. 31639.

KNIGHT, WILLIAM NOEL R
Chmn, Seventh Cong. Dist. Exec. Rep. Cmt, La.
b. Oakdale, Allen Parish, La, 8/5/35; s. Norris Knight (deceased) and Jessie Watkins K; m. 11/11/61 to Donna Kay Bendily; c. Nolan Roy, Stacey Lynn, Jodi Layne and Jill Watkins. Educ: La. State Univ, B.S, 59, LL.B. and J.D, 59; Kappa Sigma; Gamma Eta Gamma. Polit. & Govt. Pos: Chmn, Jennings Munic. Exec. Rep. Cmt, La. and Jefferson Davis Parish Exec. Rep. Cmt, 66-; mem, Rep. State Cent. Cmt, 66; del, Rep. Nat. Conv, 68; chmn, Seventh Cong. Dist. Exec. Rep. Cmt, 68- Bus. & Prof. Pos: Secy-treas, Jefferson Davis Parish Bar Asn, 64- Mem: La. Trial Lawyers Asn.(mem, bd. gov, 67-68); Am. Trial Lawyers Asn; Am. Judicature Soc; La. State Univ. Law Sch. Alumni Asn; Lions (past pres. Jennings Lion Club); Jennings Asn. of Commerce; Boy Scouts; Jennings Golf Club; Jefferson Davis Parish Country Club. Rel: United Methodist. Legal Res: 610 Plaquemine St, Jennings, La. 70546. Mailing Add: P.O. Drawer 542, Jennings, La. 70546.

KNOBEL, ARTHUR ROBERT 'BOB' R
b. Casper, Wyo, 7/22/23; s. Kenneth B. Knobel and Alice E. Coy K; m. 6/26/43 to Jeannette Lois Klien; m. 7/6/68 to Joanne Redman; c. Jacqueline Jeannette (Mrs. Clapp) and Dianne Lee. Polit. & Govt. Pos: Chmn. and mem. of many local Rep. functions, 50-; Rep. precinct committeeman, Fremont and Natrona Co, intermittently, 52-; chmn, Fremont Co. Rep. Cent. Cmt, 62-64; alternate del, Rep. Nat. Conv, 64. Mil. Serv: Entered as Aviation Cadet, Army Air Force, 42; released as 1st Lt, 46, after serv. as B29 Pilot; Capt, Hon. Air Force Res, 58. Mem: Wyo. Real Estate Bd. Realtors Washington Cmt; Wyo. Asn. Realtors,(mem, bd. dirs, 57-62, pres, 61); Fremont Co. Bd. Realtors (pres, 59); Wyo. HiWay 26 Asn.(pres, 55); Am. Legion; Elks; Kiwanis; Sertoma; C. of C; Riverton Country Club. Mailing Add: Box 1344, Riverton, Wyo. 82501.

KNOBLAUCH, REUBEN A. D
Wash. State Sen.
b. Sumner, Wash, 1914; single. Educ: Sumner High Sch. Polit. & Govt. Pos: Wash. State Rep, 47-53; Wash. State Sen, 53- Bus. & Prof. Pos: Retired farmer. Mil. Serv: World War II. Mem: VFW; Am. Legion; Kiwanis; Grange. Mailing Add: P.O. Box 306, Sumner, Wash. 98390.

KNOLES, THOMAS M, JR. D
Ariz. State Sen.
m. to Eleanor Greenlaw; c. Charles (deceased), Bob, Marshall and Thomas III. Polit. & Govt. Pos: Mem. sch. bd, Flagstaff, Ariz, 9 years; Ariz. State Rep, 56-62; Ariz. State Sen, 62- Mem: Rotary, past pres; Pow Wow Cmt; Ariz. Acad; Townjacks. Mailing Add: Box 189, Flagstaff, Ariz. 86001. (1967)

KNOPKE, RAY C. D
Fla. State Sen.
b. Chicago, Ill, 12/13/13; m. to Virginia Lacy K; c. Susan, Keenan and Ray, Jr. Educ: Ohio State Univ; St. Petersburg Jr. Col. Polit. & Govt. Pos: Mayor, Temple Terrace, Fla, 14 years; city councilman; Fla. State Rep, 63-66; Fla. State Sen, currently. Bus. & Prof. Pos: Pres, Garden of Memories, Inc. Mil. Serv: Air Force, 3 years. Mem: Dir, several cemetery orgns; Mason; Shrine; Elks; Lions; dir, Temple Terrace C. of C; Tampa Jaycees; State C. of C; Cmt. of 100; Am. Legion; VFW. Rel: Presbyterian; Deacon. Mailing Add: 4207 E. Lake Ave, Tampa, Fla. 33610. (1967)

KNOREK, LEE J. D
Chmn, Wood Co. Dem. Exec. Cmt, Ohio.
b. Rossford, Ohio, 7/14/21; S. Michael Knorek and Katherine Paczyna K; m. 11/8/47 to Margaret B. Hrabovsky; c. Kristine Cuprys. Educ: Univ. Detroit, 2 years; DeSales Col, 2 years; Sigma Alpha Epsilon; Ohio Mu. Polit. & Govt. Pos: Mem, Dem. Precinct Cmt, Rossford, Ohio, 55-; chmn, Wood Co. Dem. Exec. Cmt, 59-; pres, Rossford City Coun, 60-62; mem, Bd. of Elec, Bowling Green, 62-; del, Dem. Nat. Conv, 68. Bus. & Prof. Pos: Mgr. New York Knicks, Madison Sq. Garden, 46-50, Tuck Tape, N.Y, 50-52; Ohio Mgr, Schenley Distillers, 52-69. Mil. Serv: Entered as Seaman, Navy, 43, released as Lt, Naval Res, 46, after serv. in Underwater Demolition Team 12, Pac. Theatre; Unit Citation. Mem: Ohio Distillers Asn; Election Officials Trustee, Ohio; Eagles; K. of C; Am. Legion (Comdr); VFW; Polish Nat. Alliance; Moose; Legion of Moose. Rel: Roman Catholic. Mailing Add: 1 Riverside Dr, Rossford, Ohio 43460.

KNORR, MARTIN J. R
N.Y. State Sen.
b. Kings Co, N.Y, 1/31/06; s. Martin G. Knorr and Wilhelmine Rappold K; m. 10/10/38 to Pauline Richardson; c. Clement Richardson, Constance Bradford and Prudence Ellis. Educ: Dartmouth Col, grad, 27; Brooklyn Law Sch. of St. Lawrence Univ, LL.B; Phi Delta Phi. Polit. & Govt. Pos: Mem. exec. cmt, Queens Co. Rep. Party, N.Y, 44-; asst. attorney gen, N.Y. Attorney General's Off, 45-47; law asst, Surrogate's Court, Queens Co, N.Y, 47-49; alternate del, Rep. Nat. Conv, 52, 60 & 68; N.Y. State Assemblyman, Third Dist, 53-54; secy. to munic. court judge, Fourth Munic. Court Dist, 55-59; Estates Tax attorney for Queens Co, N.Y. State Dept. of Taxation and Finance, 59-64; mem, N.Y. Rep. State Cmt, 64-; law secy. to Albert H. Buschmann, N.Y. State Supreme Court, Queens Co, 65; N.Y. State Sen, 12th Dist, 66- Bus. & Prof. Pos: Attorney-at-law, 34- Mem: Queens Co. Bar Asn; Blackstone Club of Ridgewood; pres, Assoc. Civic Orgn. of Ridgewood, Glendale, Maspeth and Middle Village, 42-; Yale Rep. Club (past pres). Outstanding Commun. Serv. Award, Am. Legion Post 104, Queens Co, 64. Rel: Lutheran. Legal Res: 61-46 Palmetto St, Ridgewood, Queens Co, N.Y. 11227. Mailing Add: 901 Seneca Ave, Ridgewood, Queens Co, N.Y. 11227.

KNOTT, JAMES W. R
Chmn, Meade Co. Rep. Exec. Cmt, Ky.
b. Rhodelia, Ky, 12/12/18; s. L.F. Knott and Lilly D. K; m. 5/5/42 to Mary Ethel Mattingly; c. Brenda Jean, Lois Ann (Mrs. Wooldridge), Nancy, Kaye, James Ronald, William Gary and Mark Anthony. Educ: Univ. Ky, 1 year. Polit. & Govt. Pos: Mem, Meade Co. Purgation Bd, Ky, 50-65, Bd. Educ, 52-65; chmn, Meade Co. Rep. Exec. Cmt, 68- Bus. & Prof. Pos: Owner and operator, James W. Knott Supply and James W. Knott Farms, 39- Mem: K. of C; Moose; Farm Bur; Nat. Farm Orgn. Rel: Roman Catholic. Mailing Add: Rhodelia, Ky. 40161.

KNOTT, LAWSON B, JR. D
b. Wendell, N.C, 4/6/12; s. Lawson Beasley Knott and Julia Marsh K; m. 1/18/41 to Marian Corry Lunt; c. Marcia Elaine and Gregory Lawson. Educ: Duke Univ, A.B, 33; student, Wake Forest Col. and George Wash. Univ. Law Schs; Nat. Univ, LL.B, 41. Polit. & Govt. Pos: Admin. and legal pos. relating to real property progs, Depts. of Agr. and Army, 35-56; asst. cmnr. acquisition and disposal, Pub. Bldgs. Serv, 56-59, dep. cmnr, 59-61; dep. adminstr, Gen. Serv. Admin, 61-64, acting adminstr, 64-65, adminstr, 65-69. Bus. & Prof. Pos: Pres, Lawson Knott Assocs, Inc, D.C, 69- Mil. Serv: Entered as 1st Lt, Army, released as Capt; Lt. Col.(Ret), Army Res. Mem: Va, D.C. and U.S. Supreme Court Bars. Rel: Methodist. Mailing Add: 1712 N. Highland St, Arlington, Va. 22201.

KNOTT, WALTER R
b. San Bernardino, Calif; s. Elgin Charles Knott and Virginia Dougherty K; m. 6/3/11 to Cordelia Hornaday; c. Russell, Virginia (Mrs. Reafsnyder), Rachel Elizabeth (Mrs. Oliphant) and Marion (Mrs. Anderson). Educ: High Sch. Polit. & Govt. Pos: Former mem, Orange Co. Cent. Cmt, Calif; del, Rep. Nat. Conv, 68. Bus. & Prof. Pos: Self-employed, 20- Mem: Farm Bur; Nat. Asn. of Mfgs; U.S. and Calif. C. of C. Rel: Methodist. Mailing Add: 8281 Beach Blvd, Buena Park, Calif. 90620. (1967)

KNOTTS, EUGENE A. D
b. Parkersburg, W.Va, 9/21/29; s. Simon A. Knotts and Ethel Marshall K; m. 8/6/49 to Dortha Russell; c. Jeffrey, Sharon and Joyce. Educ: Parkersburg Pub. Schs. Polit. & Govt. Pos: Pres, Young Dem. Club of Wood Co, W.Va, 62, v.pres, 63; W.Va. State Del, 64-66; co. assessor, Wood Co, 68- Bus. & Prof. Pos: Pres, Knotts Inc, currently. Mem: V.pres, Criss Sch. PTA; former treas, Park Sch. PTA; leader, Little League and Boy Scouts; C. of C. Rel: Methodist. Mailing Add: 2705 Harrison Ave, Parkersburg, W. Va. 26101.

KNOUS, ROBERT LEE D
b. Ouray, Colo, 11/1/17; s. William Lee Knous and Marie Grabow K; m. 9/26/42 to Elizabeth Austin; c. Robert Lee, Jr, William Austin, Jack Melville and Twins, Kathleen and Kristine. Educ: Univ. Colo, B.A; Univ. Denver, LL.B; Phi Epsilon Phi; Delta Tau Delta. Polit. & Govt. Pos: Lt. Gov. Colo, 58-66; nominee, Gov. of Colo, 66; Colo. State Sen, 52-56; chmn, Colo. Cmn. on Aging, 54-56; secy, Gov. of Colo, 48-51. Bus. & Prof. Pos: Lawyer, 48- Mil. Serv: Entered as Lt.(jg), Navy, 41, released as Lt. Comdr, 46. Rel: Episcopal. Mailing Add: 1745 Locust St, Denver, Colo. 80220. (1967)

KNOWLAND, WILLIAM FIFE R
b. Alameda, Calif, 6/29/08; s. Joseph Russell Knowland and Ellie Fife K; m. 12/31/26 to Helen Davis Herrick; c. Emelyn (Mrs. Jewett), Joseph W. and Helen E. (Mrs. McKeen). Polit. & Govt. Pos: Calif. State Assemblyman, 33-35; Calif. State Sen, 35-39; mem, Rep. Nat. Cmt, 38; mem, U.S. Del, 11th Session UN Gen. Assembly; chmn, Rep. Exec. Cmt, 41-42; U.S. Sen, Calif, 45-58, Majority Leader, U.S. Sen, 53-54, Minority Leader, 55-58; mem, Goldwater Campaign Cmt, 64; del, Rep. Nat. Conv, 68. Bus. & Prof. Pos: Pres, Tribune Pub. Co; ed. and publisher, Oakland Tribune; pres, Franklin Investment Co. and Tribune Bldg. Co. Mil. Serv: Army, 42-45. Mem: Zeta Psi; Sigma Delta Chi; U.S. C. of C.(west. v.pres. and dir); Mason; Shrine; Scottish Rite (33°); Native Sons of the Golden West; Eagles; Moose; Elks; Bohemian Club, San Francisco; Athenian-Nile Club. Rel: Methodist. Legal Res: 100 Guilford Rd, Piedmont, Calif. 94611. Mailing Add: Tribune Bldg, Oakland, Calif. 94612.

KNOWLES, ROBERT PIERCE R
Pres. Pro Tempore, Wis. State Senate
b. River Falls, Wis, 2/25/16; s. Warren P. Knowles and Anna Deneen K; m.

8/23/41 to Madeline Lucille Ullrich; c. Barbara (Mrs. Nelson), Robert P, Jr, Warren Patrick and Terence C. Educ: Wis. State Univ, River Falls, B.S, 38. Polit. & Govt. Pos: Wis. State Sen, Tenth Dist, 54-, Majority Leader, Wis. State Senate, 63-67; asst. housing chmn, Rep. Nat. Conv, 60, exec. secy. arrangements cmt, 64 & 68. Bus. & Prof. Pos: Dir, Bank of New Richmond, Bank of Clear Lake and Bank of Centuria, Wis, 64- Mil. Serv: Entered as Aviation Cadet, Army Air Force, 41, released as Capt, 45, after serv. in 44th Bomb Group, Eighth Air Force, ETO, 44-45; Air Medal with 4 Oak Leaf Clusters; Presidential Citation; Distinguished Flying Cross. Mem: Bd. trustee, Wis. State Univ. Found; adv. cmt, Engleton Inst. of Polit, Rutgers Univ; pres, Nat. Conf. State Legis. Leaders, 65; Elks; VFW; Am. Legion. Mailing Add: 335 E. First St, New Richmond, Wis. 54017.

KNOWLES, WARREN P. R
Gov, Wis.
b. River Falls, Wis, 8/19/08; s. Warren P. Knowles and Anna Deneen K; m. 4/17/43 to Dorothy Guidry; div. Educ: Carleton Col, B.A, 30; Univ. Wis. Law Sch, LL.B, 33. Hon. LL.D, Northland Col, Marquette Univ, Ripon Col. and Lakeland Col; L.H.D, Carroll Col. Polit. & Govt. Pos: Mem, St. Croix Co. Bd, Wis, 35-40; Wis. State Sen, Tenth Dist, 40-55, Rep. Floor Leader, Wis. State Sen, 43-53, mem, Judicial Coun, 51-53, auth. and sponsor of bill creating Legis. Coun. and first chmn, auth, 1949 act creating State Bldg. Cmn. and authorizing long-range state bldg. prog. and auth. of laws creating Hosp. Surv. and Construction Act, Aeronautics Cmn. and various aviation measures; del, Rep. Nat. Conv, 48, 56, 60, 64 & 68; Lt. Gov, Wis, 55-59 & 61-63, Gov, 64- Bus. & Prof. Pos: Lawyer, Doar and Knowles, New Richmond, Wis, 33- Mil. Serv: Entered as Lt.(jg), Navy, 42, released as Lt, 46, after serv. in Aleutians, Normandy and South. France; Aleutians, ETO and Mediterranean Campaign Ribbons. Mem: Am. and St. Croix-Pierce Co. Bar Asns; Wis. Acad. Sci, Arts and Letters; Int. Asn. Ins. Counsel; co-chmn, Upper Great Lakes Regional Planning Cmn; chmn, Midwest. Gov. Conf; Am. Legion; Eagles; VFW; Navy Club of the U.S; Sons of Union Vet. of the Civil War; Wis. Alumni Asn.(pres, 52-53). Distinguished Serv. Award, Milwaukee Tech. Col; Outstanding Pub. Serv. Award, St. John's Mil. Acad; Outstanding Contributions to Educ. Award, Wis. PTA; Alumni Achievement Award, Carleton Col; Award for Distinguished Serv. in Promotion of Traffic Safety, Wis. Fedn. of Women's Clubs; Spec. Award for Great Achievements in the Field of Conserv, Wis. Wildlife Fedn; Presidential Citation for Leadership in Field of Pub. Health and Pub. Welfare, State Med. Soc. of Wis; Communications Achievement Award, Milwaukee Advert. Club; Distinguished Serv. Award, Wis. Alumni Club. of Milwaukee. Rel: Protestant. Legal Res: 251 W. Second St, New Richmond, Wis. 54017. Mailing Add: 99 Cambridge Rd, Madison, Wis. 53704.

KNOWLTON, DANIEL DAVID R
Chmn, Guernsey Co. Rep. Cmt, Ohio
b. Crooksville, Ohio, 5/2/24; s. Daniel David Knowlton and Letha Langfried K; m. 8/14/48 to Barbara Pfaadt; c. Karen and D. David. Educ: Ohio State Univ, 45-48; Ohio North. Univ, LL.B, 51; Phi Kappa Psi; Phi Delta Theta. Polit. & Govt. Pos: Chmn, Guernsey Co. Rep. Cmt, Ohio, currently; city solicitor, Cambridge, Ohio, 52-58; treas, Guernsey Co. Rep. Exec. Cmt, 54-66. Mil. Serv: Entered as Pvt, Air Force, 42, released as 2nd Lt, Pilot, 45, after serv. in ETO Theater, 44-45; Air Medal; ETO Ribbon. Mem: Ohio State Bar Asn; pres, Guernsey Co. Bar Asn, 59-60; Elks. Rel: Episcopal. Mailing Add: 1290 Edgeworth, Cambridge, Ohio 43725. (1967)

KNOWLTON, FRANKLIN WHITESIDES R
Utah State Rep.
b. Layton, Utah, 11/12/22; s. Franklin Richards Knowlton and Mary Edwina Whitesides K; m. 10/14/51 to Lillian Joy Plannette; c. Franklin Reynolds, Janice, Kevin Franklin, Ethan Franklin, Jacob Franklin and Maggie Joy. Educ: Univ. Utah, 1/4 year; Weber Col, 1/4 year. Polit. & Govt. Pos: Utah State Rep, Dist. 48, 67- Mil. Serv: Entered as Pvt, Army, 43, released as 1st Lt, 46, after serv. in Seventh and 20th Air Force, China-Burma-India, Pac. Theatre. Rel: Latter-day Saint. Legal Res: Willow Creek Rd, Layton, Utah 84041. Mailing Add: Box 426, Layton, Utah 84041.

KNOWLTON, WILLARD BURR R
N.J. State Sen.
b. Plainfield, N.J, 7/20/16; s. Walter Edward Knowlton and Edith Groff K; m. 8/23/40 to Marjorie Merritt; c. Thomas Merritt and Nancy Barnes. Educ: Bowdoin Col, A.B. with honors in hist, 39; Columbia Univ. Sch. of Law, J.D, 49; Psi Upsilon; Englewood Club. Polit. & Govt. Pos: Spec. asst. to Attorney Gen, N.J, 50-52; mem. borough coun, Tenafly, N.J, 51-61, mem. planning bd, 54-58, mayor, 61-63 and borough prosecutor, 67-68; spec. counsel to the Dep. Attorney Gen. in Charge of the Prosecutor's Off, Bergen Co, 52-54; counsel, Bd. of Educ, Demarest, 53-56; spec. counsel, Bd. of Educ, Alpine, 58-59; asst. co. counsel, Bergen Co, 61-63; N.J. State Sen, 13th Dist, Bergen Co, 68-, chmn, Senate Joint Cmt. on Passed Bills, mem, Cmts. on Air and Water Pollution and Pub. Health, Appropriations, Co. and Munic. Govt, Fed. and Interstate Rels, Labor Rels. and State Govt. Mil. Serv: Entered as Ens, Naval Res, 42, released as Lt.(sg), 46, after serv. in ETO and S. Atlantic; Area Ribbons, Two with Battle Stars. Nat. Soc. of State Legislators; Am. and N.J. Bar Asns; Am. Legion; chmn, Tenafly Commun. Chest, 50. Rel: Episcopal. Mailing Add: 10 Glenwood Rd, Tenafly, N.J. 07670.

KNOX, JAMES WILLIAM D
b. Emsworth, Pittsburgh, Pa, 5/4/19; m. 3/17/53 to Valerie O. Weber; c. Jennie Lynn, Christopher John and Ronald James. Educ: Univ. Pittsburgh, B.A. in Polit. Sci. and Econ; Phi Sigma Alpha; Order of Artus. Polit. & Govt. Pos: Controller, Allegheny Co, Pa, 48-68; exec. dir, Allegheny Co. Housing Authority, 68- Mil. Serv: Navy. Publ: 'The Ol' Double Trouble' 55. Mem: YMCA (mem. and v.pres. bd. dirs, North Boroughs Chap); chmn, Million Dollar Fund Drive for Addition to Bellevue Suburban Gen. Hosp, 57; pres. bd. dirs, Suburban Gen. Hosp; pres. bd. dirs, Coun. of Churches, Gr. Pittsburgh Area; chmn, Cultural and Educ. Exchange Found, Univ. Pittsburgh; Gaelic Arts Soc, Am. Legion; VFW; Mil. Order of World Wars; Mason; Syria Temple. Rel: Lutheran. Mailing Add: 106 Redbird Point, Emsworth, Pittsburgh, Pa. 15202.

KNOX, JOHN THERYLL D
Calif. State Assemblyman
b. Reno, Nev, 9/30/24; s. Ernest B. Knox and Jean Monat K; m. 12/27/49 to Margaret Jean Henderson; c. John Henderson, Charlotte Marie and Mary Lucretia. Educ: Occidental Col, A.B, 49; Hastings Col. of Law, J.D, 52; Sigma Alpha Epsilon; Phi Delta Phi. Polit. & Govt. Pos: Mem, Contra Costa Co. Dem. Cent. Cmt, Calif, 55-69; mem. exec. bd, Calif. State Dem. Cent. Cmt, 60-; Calif. State Assemblyman, 11th Dist, 60-, chmn, Calif. State Assembly Local Govt. Cmt, 62-, chmn, Joint Legis. Cmts. on Open Space and on Bay Area Regional Orgn, 67-; mem, Little Hoover Cmt, Calif, 62-66; mem, President's Adv. Cmt. on Real Estate, 64- Mil. Serv: Entered as Pvt, Army, 43, released as Sgt, 45, after serv. in 1469th Air Force Base Unit, Nome, Alaska; Asiatic-Pac. Theatre Ribbon. Mem: Calif. Local Bar Asns; secy, Richmond Bar Asn, 60; pres, Richmond Jr. C. of C, 58; F&AM; Elks; Eagles; Moose; Lions. Rel: Protestant. Legal Res: 229 Bishop Ave, Richmond, Calif. 94801. Mailing Add: 12730 San Pablo Ave, Richmond, Calif. 94805.

KNOX, KATHARINE McCOOK R
b. Washington, D.C; d. Anson G. McCook and Hettie Beatty M; wid. of Hugh Smith Knox; c. Kathleen (Mrs. Richard Austin Smith) and two grandchildren, Richard Austin, Jr. and Roderick Sheldon. Educ: Miss Spence's Sch, N.Y.C, diploma, 08. Polit. & Govt. Pos: Prog. chmn, League of Rep. Women, D.C, 59-61; del, Nat. Fedn. Rep. Women, 60; alternate del, Rep. Nat. Conv, 60, del. and mem, Credentials Cmt, 64; v.chmn, Rep. Cmt, D.C. and mem, Forward Looking Rep, Cmt, currently. Publ: The Sharples: Their Portraits of George Washington and His Contemporaries, 30; Adams-Clement Portraits and Their Painters; Healy's Lincoln; Surprise Personalities in Georgetown, D.C; and others. Mem: Reference worker and trustee, Frick Art Reference Libr; donor and coun. mem, Corcoran Gallery of Art; chmn, art exhibitions, Wash, D.C; Colony Club of N.Y; Chevy Chase Club; City Tavern Asn; bd. gov. and art and lit. cmt, Capitol Hill Club; Sulgrave Club; Boosters. Recipient Medal of Merit, Corcoran Gallery of Art, 66, Medal of Honor, Lincoln Sesquicentennial Cmn, 60 and Meritorious Pub. Serv. Award, Rep. Cmt. of Wash, D.C, 60. Rel: Presbyterian. Mailing Add: 3259 N St. N.W, Washington, D.C. 20007.

KNOX, PATTI D
V.Chmn, Mich. Dem. State Cent. Cmt.
b. Detroit, Mich, 8/18/25; d. Dedrick F. Stearns and Amelia V. Seanor S; m. 11/27/46 to Robert D. Knox; c. John. Educ: Mich. State Univ, 46-48. Polit. & Govt. Pos: V.chmn, Mich. Dem. State Cent. Cmt, 67-; pres, Mich. Fedn. of Dem. Women, 67-; del, Dem. Nat. Conv, 68; mem, Polit. Reform Cmn, Detroit, 69-; mem, McGovern Cmn. on Party Structure and Del. Selection, Wash, D.C, 69-; secy, Dem. Mid-W. Conf, 69- Bus. & Prof. Pos: Mem, personnel dept, Mfrs. Bank, 45 and Ford Motor Co, 49-54. Mem: Trade Union Leadership Coun; Mich. Educ. Found; NAACP; League of Women Voters. Rel: Protestant. Legal Res: 17597 Oak Dr, Detroit, Mich. 48221. Mailing Add: 1535 E. Lafayette, Detroit, Mich. 48207.

KNOX, VICTOR A. R
b. Chippewa Co, Mich, 1/13/99; m. to Bertha V. Byers; c. William D. Polit. & Govt. Pos: U.S. Rep, Mich, 83rd-88th Cong; Mich State Rep, 37-52, speaker, 47-52; Supvr, Soo Twp, 6 yrs, Treas, 2 yrs; Coun. State Govt; State Planning Cmn; State Crime Cmn. Bus. & Prof. Pos: Retail heating and plumbing bus; rep, Lake Shore Engr. Co, East. Upper Peninsula, Mich, 46; farmer, retired, 43; mgr, Chippewa Co. Farm Bur, 43-46. Mem: Grange; Mason; Elk; K. of P; Lions; Soo Locks Centennial Cmn. Rel: Presbyterian. Mailing Add: Sault Ste. Marie, Mich. 49783. (1967)

KNOX, WAYNE N. D
Colo. State Rep.
b. Denver, Colo, 6/30/27. Polit. & Govt. Pos: Colo. State Rep, 61-62, 65- Bus. & Prof. Pos: Sch. teacher. Mem: Denver Young Dem.(former pres); Colo. Fedn. Teachers (pres, currently). Mailing Add: 1373 W. Gill Place, Denver, Colo. 80223.

KNUDSEN, D. L. 'IKE' D
Mont. State Rep.
b. Malta, Mont, 7/5/30; s. George Victor Knudsen and Mary Bibeau K; m. 6/2/52 to Mary Ann Shores; c. Earline Maryann, Donald George, Vicki Rae and Lloyd Robert. Educ: North. Mont. Col, B.S, 63; Tau Kappa; Circle K. Polit. & Govt. Pos: City councilman, Glasgow, Mont, 67-; Mont. State Rep, Dist 5-B, Valley and Daniels Co, 69-; mem, Valley Co. Dem. Cent. Cmt, Mont, currently. Bus. & Prof. Pos: Elem. teacher, Prairie Union and South Wagner Schs, South Phillips Co, 50-54; rancher, 54-57; dept. mgr, Sears, Lewiston, 58-60; math. instr, Glasgow, Mont, 63- Mem: Glasgow Educ. Asn; Mont. Educ. Asn.(charter mem, Big Sky Legis. Univ); Nat. Educ. Asn.(life mem); Nat. Coun. Math. Teachers; Elks; Eagles; Toastmasters; Kiwanis; Farmers Union; Valley Co. Hist. Soc; Coast Guard Auxiliary. Rel: Congregational. Mailing Add: 65 Aberdeen, Glasgow, Mont. 59230.

KNUDSEN, EUGENE PETER DFL
b. Kingsbury Co, S.Dak, 3/10/15; s. Alfred M. Knudsen and Anna Steffensen K; m. 12/31/36 to Violet E. Dahl (deceased) and m. 5/23/64 to Virginia C. Neal; c. Marvis (Mrs. William Hallberg), Audrey (Mrs. Terrance Thompson), Norman, Melvin, Wayne, Carol Lynn, Larry and Darlene; stepchildren, Bruce, Kenneth, Margaret and Joyce Neal. Educ: Kandiyohi Pub. Schs. Polit. & Govt. Pos: Co. chmn, Dem-Farmer-Labor Party, 50-54; Minn. State Rep, 54-62; secy, State Legis. Bldg. Cmn, 59-60, chmn, 61-62; chmn, Welfare Cmt, 59-61; Minn. State Sen, 62-66. Bus. & Prof. Pos: Chmn, Kandiyohi Sch. Bd, 46-54; dir, Kandiyohi Farmers Union Elevator, 47-60; rural chmn, March of Dimes, 50-54; rural chmn, Cancer Fund, 66; farmer and breeder, Registered Holstein Cattle; dir, Holstein Bd. Mem: 4-H Leader of Club; trustee, treas. and pres, Lutheran Brotherhood. Recipient, W.G. Shelly Award for Superior Achievement in Agr, 50. Rel: Lutheran; President of the Congregation. Mailing Add: R.R. 1, Kandiyohi, Minn. 56251.

KNUDSEN, HENRY, I D
S.Dak. State Rep.
b. Morris, Ill, 6/12/99; m. 1932 to Naoimi Eddy; c. Muriel, David, Mary Ann, Alice Ruth, Emily Gail and John. Educ: N.Dak. State Col, 2 years. Polit. & Govt. Pos: Twp. supvr, S.Dak, 10 years; sch. bd. clerk, 20 years; S.Dak. State Sen, 54-61; S.Dak. State Rep, currently. Bus. & Prof. Pos: Pres, Roberts Co. Fed. Land Bank Asn, 14 years; dir, Farmer Creamery and Locker, 8 years; dir, Roberts Co. Crop Improv. Asn, 10 years; pres, Nat. Farm Loan Asn,

Roberts Co, 12 years; pres, Victor Coop Elevator, 17 years; farmer and feeder. Mem: Mason Lodge 212, AF&AM; Easter Star 164. Rel: Lutheran; Deacon, Brandvold Lutheran Church. Mailing Add: New Effington, S.Dak. 57255. (1967)

KNUDSEN, MILO R
b. Glenville, Minn, 4/30/01; married; c. 1. Educ: N.Dak. State Univ. of Agr. and Appl. Sci. Polit. & Govt. Pos: N.Dak. State Rep, 55-66. Bus. & Prof. Pos: Druggist. Mem: Masons; Shriners; Lions. Mailing Add: Edgeley, N.Dak. 58433. (1967)

KNUDSON, HARVEY BORNEMANN R
Judge, N.Dak. Supreme Court
b. Finley, N.Dak, 6/26/03; s. Enoch Bornemann Knudson and Josephine Emelia Hanson K; m. 6/17/33 to Pearl Irene Pederson; c. Harvey B, Jr, Duane A, Marion J.(Mrs. Rud) and Kay E.(Mrs. Jacobs). Educ: Univ. N.Dak. Law Sch; Phi Alpha Delta. Polit. & Govt. Pos: Sch. treas, Finley, N.Dak, 34-38; N.Dak. State Rep, 37-38; mem, Traill Co. War Bd, 42-46; N.Dak. State Sen, 51-58; alderman, City Coun, Mayville, 42-48, city attorney, 58-65; judge, N.Dak. Supreme Court, 65- Mem: Am. and N.Dak. State Bar Asns; First Dist. Bar Asn.(pres, 51-53); Mayville State Col. Found, 61-65; chmn, Traill Co. Savings Bond Cmt, 44-65; Mason; Shrine; Eagles; Farm Bur; Execs. Club; Lions; Apple Creek Country Club. Rel: Lutheran. Legal Res: Mayville, N.Dak. 58257. Mailing Add: 2124 Second St, North, Bismarck, N.Dak. 58501.

KNUDSON, KENNETH R
N.Dak. State Rep.
b. Taylor, N.Dak, 11/9/27; s. Knute Knudson and Evaline Hendrickson K; single. Educ: St. Olaf Col, B.A, 48. Polit. & Govt. Pos: Precinct committeeman, Stark Co. and Dist. 38 Rep. Party, N.Dak, 62-; exec. committeeman, Dist. 38 Rep. Party, 67-; N.Dak. State Rep, Dist, 38, 67-, v.chmn, House Educ. Cmt. and mem, LRC Cmt. on Educ, N.Dak. House of Rep, 67- Bus. & Prof. Pos: Prin, Taylor High Sch, N.Dak, 64-69. Mil. Serv: Entered as Pvt, E-1, Army, 50, released as Cpl, E-4, 52, after serv. in 40th Inf. Div, Korean Conflict; Army Occup. Medal; UN Serv. Medal; Korean Serv. Medal. Mem: N.Dak. Educ: Asn; Nat. Coun. for Soc. Studies; N.Dak. Farm Bur; VFW; Am. Legion. Rel: Lutheran. Mailing Add: Box 264, Taylor, N.Dak. 58656.

KNUDSON, LOYD G. R
S.Dak. State Rep.
b. Mound City, S.Dak, 3/6/10; m. to Leona Falde; c. Robert, Gary, Tom, Joy. Educ: Univ. of S.Dak. Polit. & Govt. Pos: Former supt. schs. Dewey Co; Corson Co. Rep. chmn; clerk, Sch. Bd. and Twp. Bd; S.Dak. State Rep, currently. Bus. & Prof. Pos: Rancher and farmer. Mem: Crop Improv. Asn. (chmn); Agr. Stabilization & Conserv. Serv. Cmt; Livestock Asn; chmn, Commun. Hosp; Mason; Shrine; Commercial Club. Rel: Lutheran. Mailing Add: McLaughlin, S.Dak. 57642.

KNUEPFER, JACK TARRANT R
Ill. State Sen.
b. Chicago, Ill, 11/16/20; s. Claude A. Knuepfer and Ella Tarrant K; m. to Virginia Maurer; c. Paul, Claude, Mark, Barbara and Suellyn. Educ: Carleton Col, 39-40; Univ. Chicago, M.B.A, 47; Phi Kappa Sigma. Polit. & Govt. Pos: Alderman, Elmhurst, Ill, 54-58; precinct committeeman, Rep. Cmt, 61-; Ill. State Rep, 65-67; Ill. State Sen, 67- Mil. Serv: Entered as Pvt, Army, 42, released as 1st Lt, 46, after serv. in African and European Theaters. Mem: Dir, Nat. Metal Trades Asn. 58-, Ill. Mfg. Costs Asn. and Nat. Safety Coun. Small Bus. Cmt, 54-58. Rel: Presbyterian. Mailing Add: 901 Washington, Elmhurst, Ill. 60126.

KNUPPEL, SHIRLEY LaVAUNE R
Mem, Calif. Rep. State Cent. Cmt.
b. Clinton, Iowa, 11/3/24; d. Gerald Bertram Smith and Hazel Berger S; m. 1/8/44 to Wesley Franklin Knuppel; c. Kay, Lee and Neil. Educ: James Millikin Univ; Indees. Polit. & Govt. Pos: Rep. precinct capt, Lakewood, Calif, 64-66; Ways and Means Chmn, Long Beach G.O.P. Jr. Rep. Women, 65; assoc. mem, Calif. Rep. State Cent. Cmt, 66-68, mem, 69- Bus. & Prof. Pos: Secy-treas, Guild of Prfnl. Musicians, Los Angeles, Calif, 59-68. Mem: Eastern Star, Rock Falls, Ill; Fullerton Federated Rep. Women. Hon. life mem, Calif. Cong. of Parents and Teachers Inc. Rel: Protestant. Mailing add: 1653 Sunset Lane, Fullerton, Calif. 92633.

KNUTSON, HOWARD ARTHUR R
Minn. State Rep.
b. Grand Forks, N.Dak, 5/16/29; s. Arthur K. Knutson and Ella Kamplin K; m. 8/2/58 to Jerroldine Margo Sundby; c. David Lee, Douglas Arthur, Eric, Amy Lynn and Annette. Educ: Wabash Col, 47-49; Luther Col, A.B, 51; William Mitchell Col. of Law, LL.B, 59; Delta Theta Phi. Polit. & Govt. Pos: Chmn, Burnsville Indust. Planning Cmn, Minn, 64-66; Minn. State Rep, Dist. 12B, North. Dak. Co, 67- Bus. & Prof. Pos: Partner, Bergman, Knutson, Street & Ulmen, Attorneys-at-law, Minneapolis, Minn. Mil. Serv: Entered as Pvt, Army, 51, released as Cpl, 53, after serv. in Signal Corps, ETO, 52-53. Mem: Hennepin Co, Minn. State and Am. Bar Asns; Optimist; Open Door Soc. Rel: Lutheran. Mailing Add: 1907 Woods Lane, Burnsville, Minn. 55378.

KNUTSON, TERRENCE ANDREW DFL
b. Minneapolis, Minn, 12/2/39; s. Andrew Knutson and Coya Gjesdal K; m. 7/1/61 to Barbara Lois LaJambe; c. Jacqueline Lee. Educ: Luther Col, Iowa, 57-58; Concordia Col, Minn, 58; Bemidji State Col, Minn, B.S, 65; Univ. Minn, grad. study, 65; Campus Players, Luther Col; Footlight Guild and Eng. Club, Bemidji State Col. Polit. Pos: Co. Del, Dem. Farmer Labor Party, 64-66; del, Dem. Nat. Conv, 64. Govt. Pos: Employment Officer, U.S. Dept. of Labor, 61- Mem: Minn. Educ. Asn, mem. local prog. cmt, 65-66; Minn. Speech Asn; Nat. and Minn. Coun. of Teachers of Eng; Farmers Union; Elks; Rotary. Attended Nat. Convs, 64, 60, 56 and 52; active participation in Dist. and State Campaigns, 52-64. Rel: Lutheran. Mailing Add: 3935 Bryant Ave. S, Minneapolis, Minn. 55409. (1967)

KOBALINSKI, STEPHEN A. D
b. Boston, Mass, 11/19/03; m. to Blanch H.K. Educ: Boston Col, A.B. and M.S. Polit. & Govt. Pos: Mem, Hiring Code Cmn, Pension Cmn. and Tiverton Planning Bd, R.I; R.I. State Sen, 64-66; town clerk, Tiverton, 68-; chmn, Tiverton Dem. Town Cmt, 67-69; town clerk, Tiverton, currently. Bus. & Prof. Pos: Retired sonar engr. Mem: R.I. Asn. of City and Town Clerks; C. of C. (dir, Tiverton Chap); Holy Name Soc; Rotary. Rel: Catholic. Mailing Add: 86 Fir Ave, Tiverton, R.I. 02878.

KOBAYASHI, BERT TAKAAKI D
Assoc. Justice, Supreme Court of Hawaii
b. Honolulu, Hawaii, 7/8/16; s. Zengoro Kobayashi and Kiyo Yamasaki K; m. 11/25/38 to Victoria Tsuchiya; c. Bert Takaaki, Josephine Leilani, Victoria Puanani and Lincoln Kalani. Educ: Gettysburg Col, A.B, 38, LL.D, 66; Harvard Univ, LL.B, 43. Polit. & Govt. Pos: Law clerk to Attorney Gen, Hawaii, 45; dep. city and co. attorney, Honolulu, 46; dep. pub. prosecutor, Honolulu, 47-48; magistrate, Waialua Court, Oahu, 52-59; mem, Gov. Cmt. on Sex Offenders, 59-60; Attorney Gen, Hawaii, 62-69; assoc. justice, Supreme Court, Hawaii, 69- Bus. & Prof. Pos: Pvt. practice of law, Honolulu, 48-62; former dir, Island Venetian Blind Co, Aluminum Prod. of Hawaii, Toma Contractor, Inc. and Hardwood Furnishings, Ltd. Mem: Hawaii Subversive Activities Cmt, 58-; Bar Asn. of Hawaii (pres, 59); YMCA (mem. bd, Nuuanu Chap, 52-53). Mailing Add: 4738 Analii St, Honolulu, Hawaii 96821.

KOCH, EDGAR JURGEN R
Iowa State Rep.
b. Charter Oak, Iowa, 10/11/25; s. Edgar Henry Koch and Martha C. Ackelbein K.(deceased); m. 2/23/47 to Darlene M. Miller; c. Diana L.(Mrs. Michael Havenstrite), Robert A, LuAnn R, Karla K, Gerald L. and Lisa C.(deceased). Educ: Univ. S.Dak. Law Sch, 48-49; Morningside Col, B.S. in Econ. and Finance, 49; Delta Theta Phi. Polit. & Govt. Pos: Iowa State Rep, 67- Bus. & Prof. Pos: Income tax consult, 50-; ins. salesman, 50-; real estate salesman, 54-; golf course construction consult, 64- Mil. Serv: Entered as A/S, Navy, 43, released as Radioman 2/C, 46, after serv. in Battleship U.S.S. N.C. and Destroyer U.S.S. Gatling, Third and Fifth Fleets, Pac. Theater, 43-45, Comdr, Res, 67-, Commanding Officer, Naval Res. Group Command, Sioux City, Iowa, currently; Asiatic Pac. Theater Medal with Nine Engagement Stars; Philippine Liberation Medal with One Engagement Star; Naval Res. Medal; Navy Occup. Serv. Medal; Philippine Repub. Presidential Unit Citation; Armed Forces Res. Medal; Commendation for Serv. in personnel assignments during flood work. Mem: Life Underwriters Asn; Shrine (Abu Bekr Wrecking Crew); Mason; Consistory; Scottish Rite; Nat. Sojourners Heroes of '76; Siouxland Sq. and Compass Club; Sertoma; Am. Legion; two terms mem, Ninth Naval Dist. Naval Reserve Policy Bd. Rel: Lutheran. Mailing Add: 2325 Douglas St, Sioux City, Iowa 51104.

KOCH, EDWARD HERMAN D
Secy, Clinton Co. Dem. Cent. Cmt, Ill.
b. Trenton, Ill, 10/19/36; s. Herman Albert Koch and Frances Dressler K; m. 6/6/64 to Karen Patrica Kuhfuss; c. Devin Edward and Caroline Suzanne. Educ: McKendree Col, 54-56; Ill. State Univ, B.S, 59, M.S, 64. Polit. & Govt. Pos: Dem. precinct committeeman, Trenton, Ill, 66-; secy, Clinton Co. Dem. Cent. Cmt, 68- Bus. & Prof. Pos: Teacher, Dept. of Army, Frankfurt, Germany, 61-63; teacher, Dept. of Defense, Upper Heyford, Eng, 64-65; partner, Koch Candy Co, Trenton, Ill, 65- Mem: Nat. and Ill. Asns. of Tobacco Distributors; C. of C. Rel: United Church of Christ. Mailing Add: 222 N. Washington, Trenton, Ill. 62293.

KOCH, EDWARD IRVING D
U.S. Rep, N.Y.
b. New York, N.Y, 12/12/24; s. Louis Koch and Joyce Silpe K.(deceased); single. Educ: City Col. of N.Y, 41-43; N.Y. Univ, LL.B, 48; Omega Chi. Polit. & Govt. Pos: Dem. Dist. Leader, Greenwich Village, N.Y, 63-65; city councilman, New York City, 67-68; U.S. Rep, 17th Dist, N.Y, 69- Bus. & Prof. Pos: Former partner, Koch, Lankenau, Schwartz & Kovner, 63-68. Mil. Serv: Entered as Pvt, Army, 43, released as Sgt, 46, after serv. in U.S. Inf, ETO, 44-46; 2 battle stars. Mem: N.Y. Co. Lawyers; Village Independent Dem; Am. Civil Liberties Union. Mailing Add: 14 Washington Place, New York, N.Y. 10003.

KOCH, HENRY FERD R
Idaho State Rep.
b. Hammett, Idaho, 2/27/13; s. Henry Ferdinand Koch and Amy S. Krauth K; m. 5/4/35 to Marjorie Talboy; c. Ronald, Roger, Cheryl (Mrs. Zollman), Deanne M. and Lynne E. Educ: Univ. Idaho, B.S.E.E, 34; Sigma Tau; Scabbard and Blade; Blue Key; Silver Lance; Sigma Nu. Polit. & Govt. Pos: Chmn, Idaho State Elec. Bd, 49-63; chmn, Idaho State Pub. Works License Bd, 56-; mem, Boise City Coun, Idaho, 58-67, pres, 65-67; Idaho State Rep, 62-, chmn. state affairs cmt, Idaho House of Rep, 66-, chmn. local govt. cmt, 68-, chmn. interim tax study cmt, 68-, mem, Idaho Legis. Coun, 67-; pres, Idaho Asn. of Cities, 66-67. Bus. & Prof. Pos: Mem. exec. cmt, Boise Indust. Found, 66- Mil. Serv: Entered as 1st Lt, Army Res, 41, released as Lt. Col, 46, after serv. in 314th Inf, 79th Inf. Div, ETO, 44-45, Lt. Col, Inactive Res; Purple Heart; Silver Star; Combat Inf. Badge; Croix de Guerre Unit Citation; two Presidential Unit Citations. Mem: Chmn, Snake River Elec. Asn, 56; research cmt, Nat. Elec. Contractors Asn.(gov, 58); C. of C.(dir, 66); Scottish Rite; Mason; Rotary; Elks; Am. Legion; Knife & Fork; Idaho Asn. for Retarded Children. Distinguished Citizen, Idaho Daily Statesman. Rel: Methodist. Mailing Add: 257 Circleway Dr, Boise, Idaho 83702.

KOCH, JAMES H. D
N.Mex. State Rep.
b. Santa Fe, N.Mex, 6/4/35; s. Ferdinand A. Koch and Kathleen Long K; m. 8/28/60 to Nene Ackerman; c. Amy. Educ: Univ. N.Mex, B.A, 58; Kappa Sigma; Lettermen's Club; Head Dormitory Counsr. Polit. & Govt. Pos: Precinct chmn. Dem. Party; chmn, State Dem. Conv. Cmt; temporary chmn, Santa Fe Co. Dem. Party, N.Mex, twice; N.Mex. State Rep, Dist. 3, 69- Bus. & Prof. Pos: V.pres, Santa Fe Elec. Laundry, currently. Mil. Serv: Entered as Pfc, Marine Corps, 57, released as Sgt. E4, 63, after serv. in Res. Unit, N. Mex. Mem: Am. Inst. Laundries; bd. dirs, C. of C; bd. assocs, St. John's Col; v.pres, Boys' Club; chmn, U.S. Olympic Cmt; Jaycees (past pres, Santa Fe Club); past chmn, March of Dimes; bd. dirs, United Fund. Jaycee Distinguished Serv. Award. Rel: Episcopal, Treas, Church of the Holy Faith. Legal Res: 1453 Don Gaspar, Santa Fe, N.Mex. 87501. Mailing Add: P.O. Box 1926, Santa Fe, N.Mex. 87501.

KOCH, LESTER DONALD R
Chmn, Tazewell Co. Rep. Cent. Cmt, Ill.
b. Tremont, Ill, 10/20/19; s. Silas A. Koch and Nora Luft K; m. 9/24/44 to Barbara Pflederer; c. Joyce Kay and Michael Silas. Educ: High Sch. Polit. & Govt. Pos: Rep. committeeman, Rep. Party, Ill, 56-58, precinct committeeman, 56-66, sen. committeeman, 66; trustee, Tremont, Ill, 57-63, mayor, 63-66; chmn, Tazewell Co. Rep. Cent. Cmt. and Rep. committeeman, 46th Dist, currently. Bus. & Prof. Pos: Agr. fieldman, Libby McNeil and Libby, 61-66, agr. supvr, 66. Mil. Serv: Entered as Pvt, Air Force, 41, released as Sgt, 45, after serv. in ETO; European-African-Middle Eastern Theater Ribbon with 1 Silver and 2 Bronze Battle Stars; 4 Overseas Serv. Bars; 1 Serv. Stripe; Good Conduct Medal; 82nd Group Distinguished Unit Badge with 2 Bronze Oak Leaf Clusters. Mem: Eagles; Am. Legion; VFW; Tremont Commun. Men's Club; Tazewell Co. Mayors Asn; Tazewell Co. Young Rep; Methodist Men's Club. Rel: Methodist. Legal Res: 309 W. South St, Tremont, Ill. 61568. Mailing Add: Box 104, Tremont, Ill. 61568.

KOCHTITZKY, ROBERT BOONE D
Secy, Hinds Co. Dem. Exec. Cmt, Miss.
b. Little Rock, Ark, 7/24/28; s. John S. Kochtitzky and Lucy Carr K; m. 7/23/66 to Catherine Haggerty; c. Christopher Shawn. Educ: Millsaps Coll, 45-47; Miss. State Univ, B.S, 50; South. Methodist Univ. Perkins Sch. Theol, B.D, 62; Blue Key; Kappa Sigma. Polit. & Govt. Pos: Secy, Hinds Co. Dem. Exec. Cmt, Miss, 68- Mil. Serv: Entered as Airman, Air Force, 50, released as Cpl, 51 after serv. in Pub. Info. Off. Rel: United Methodist. Legal Res: 1628 Wilhurst, Jackson, Miss. 39205. Mailing Add: Box 5031, Jackson, Miss. 39216.

KOEBBE, LAWRENCE EDWIN D
Mayor, Hardin, Mont.
b. Hardin, Mont, 1/25/24; s. Jacob A. Koebbe and Amelia Sticka K; m. 10/18/47 to Margaret Mary McNally. Polit. & Govt. Pos: City councilman, Hardin, Mont, 59-63; chmn, Big Horn Co. Dem. Cent. Cmt, 62-; mayor, Hardin, Mont, 63- Mil. Serv: Entered as Pvt, Army, 44, released as Sgt, 46, after serv. in 172nd Mil. Police Co, Asian Theater, 45-46; Meritorious Unit Award, Asiatic Pac. Serv, Good Conduct and Victory Medals. Mem: Elks; K. of C. Rel: Roman Catholic. Mailing Add: 16 Cody Ave, Hardin, Mont. 59034. (1967)

KOEHLER, RICHARD NORMAN D
Chmn, Butler Co. Dem. Exec. Cmt, Ohio
b. Hamilton, Ohio, 7/9/26; s. Harry J. Koehler and Grace Heistermann K; m. 6/14/46 to Elva M. Schell; c. Paula, Richard N, II and Claudia. Educ: Oberlin Col, 1 year; Miami Univ, A.B; Chase Col. Law, LL.B. Polit. & Govt. Pos: Chmn, Butler Co. Dem. Exec. Cmt, Ohio, 68- Mil. Serv: Naval Res, 44-45, A/S, serv. in Naval aviation. Rel: Protestant. Mailing Add: 748 Main St, Hamilton, Ohio 45013.

KOEHN, EMIL ALVIN R
Mem, Turner Co. Rep. Cent. Cmt, S.Dak.
b. Hillside, S.Dak, 6/16/16; s. William A. Koehn and Martha Wenzel K; m. 1/20/41 to Doris Louise Benning; c. Stephen C, Thomas K. and Margaret Ann. Educ: Univ. S.Dak, B.A, 38; Delta Sigma Phi. Polit. & Govt. Pos: Chmn, Parker Bd. of Educ, S.Dak, 57-62; Rep. state cent. committeeman, 59-66; v.chmn, S.Dak. State Bd. of Educ, 60-66, pres, 68-69; finance chmn, Turner Co. Rep. Party, 61-66; chmn, Turner Co. Rep. Cent. Cmt, 66-68, mem, 68- Bus. & Prof. Pos: Owner, Koehn's Dept. Store, 38-66; mem. bd. dirs, Mom & Dad's Inc, Sioux Falls, S.Dak, 60-, pres, 60-61 & 69- Mil. Serv: Entered as 2nd Lt, Army Air Force, 41, released as Maj, 46. Mem: Area v.pres, Nat. Asn. State Bds. of Educ, 64-66, treas, 66-67, v.pres, 67-68, pres-elect, 68-69, pres, 69-; AF&AM;(past master, Parker Lodge 30); Parker Shrine Club (past pres); Oriental Consistory; Mason (32°); mem, Divan El Riad Shrine, 64-66; Lions (past pres, Parker Club); Am. Legion; Par Mar Country Club (mem. bd. dirs); Westward Ho Country Club. Rel: Presbyterian. Mailing Add: P.O. Box 278, Parker, S.Dak. 57053.

KOELLA, ERNEST, JR. R
b. Blount Co, Tenn, 2/18/18; m. 2/11/42 to Jean M; c. Karol, Ernest and Lisa. Educ: McCallie Sch, Chattanooga, Tenn, 36; N.C. State Sch. of Textiles, B.S. in Textiles, 40. Polit. & Govt. Pos: Pres, Blount Co. Young Rep. Club, Tenn, 48; mem, Blount Co. Rep. Exec. Cmt, 48-50, v.chmn, 50-54, chmn, 60-66; former Rep. Nat. Committeeman, Tenn. Bus. & Prof. Pos: Rockford Mfg. Co. Mem: Bd. dirs, Blount Co. C. of C; Rockford Masonic League. Rel: Presbyterian. Mailing Add: Rockford, Tenn. 37853. (1967)

KOEPPEL, WILLARD MAURICE R
Sheriff, Peoria Co, Ill.
b. Peoria, Ill, 7/12/15; s. William Sebastian Koeppel and Antionette Wolf K; m. 5/9/36 to Dorothy Minnick; c. Philip Willard, George William, James Maurice and William Edward. Educ: Northwest. Univ, 36-40; Univ. Louisville, 41-42. Polit. & Govt. Pos: Dir, Narcotics Control, Iowa, 62; chief of detectives, Peoria, Ill, 64; sheriff, Peoria Co, 66-; del, Rep. Nat. Conv, 68. Mem: Nat. Sheriff's Asn.(trustee, youth farm); Tri-Co. Juvenile Officers Asn; Ill. Sheriff's Asn; Ill. Juvenile Officers Asn; Ill. Police & Fire & Comnrs; Elks; Kiwanis; K. of C. Good Govt. Award, U.S. C. of C, 52; Child Safety Award, Travelers Protective Asn. Rel: Roman Catholic. Mailing Add: 2607 W. Manor Pkwy, Peoria, Ill. 61604.

KOETHER, HERBERT FRANKLIN R
b. Detroit, Mich. 8/8/13; s. Bernard Gustave Koether and Mary Bowerman K; m. 3/7/47 to Sarah Louise Jones; c. Frederick Gustave, James Hutington, Philip Hathaway, Sarah Louise and stepson, Douglas Jefferson Arnot. Educ: Univ. Ariz; George Wash. Univ; Alpha Kappa Psi. Polit. & Govt. Pos: Treas, Arapahoe Co. Rep. Cent. Cmt, Colo, 62; mem, Colo. State Rep. Cent. Cmt. and chmn, Rep. Presidential Campaign Cmt, 64. Bus. & Prof. Pos: Priorities officer, Minerals Bur, War Prod. Bd, D.C, 41-42; regional mgr, Apex Elec. Mfg. Co, Cleveland, Ohio, 46-49; Chicago regional mgr, refrigerator dept, Crosley Div, AVCO Mfg. Co, 49-51, mgr. refrigerator dept, 51-52; pres, Koether-Cox Co, 56-66 and Over-Lowe Co, Inc, Denver, Colo, 65-66. Mil. Serv: Entered as Pvt, Army Air Force, 42, released as 1st Lt, after serv. in Materiel Command, 46; Award of Merit. Mem: Adv. Bd, Mt. States Salvation Army. Rel: Episcopal. Mailing Add: 29 Martin Lane, Englewood, Colo. 80110.

KOEZE, ELLA DEMMINK R
b. Grand Rapids, Mich, 7/25/05; d. Henry John Demmink and Alida Elizabeth Hesselink D; m. 7/29/33 to Albert J. Koeze; c. Dr. Thomas H, A. Scott, David S, Robert P. and Marybeth. Educ: Davenport Col, 24-25. Polit. & Govt. Pos: V.chmn, Kent Co. Rep. Cmt, Mich, 44-50; mem, Mich. Rep. State Cent. Cmt, 47-51, v.chmn, 57-61; del. or alternate del, Rep. Nat. Conv, 52-; mem. bd, Rep. Nat. Fedn, 53-57; pres, Mich. Rep. Women's Fedn, 53-57; mem, Rep. Nat. Cmt, Mich, 60-69, mem. exec. cmt, Rep. Nat. Cmt, 62-69. Bus. & Prof. Pos: Secy-treas, Koeze Mfg. Co, Grand Rapids, Mich, 33- Mem: Charter mem. Grand Rapids Women's Rep. Club; Mary A. Welsh Guild; Blodgett Mem. Hosp; Wyoming, Mich. People to People Orgn; Hist. & Cult. Soc; Bus. & Prfnl. Women's Club, Grand Rapids. Rel: Christian Reformed Church. Mailing Add: 2036 Radcliffe S.E, Grand Rapids, Mich. 49506.

KOFMAN, ABRAHAM D
b. Brockton, Mass, 1/26/03; s. Edward Kofman and Rachael Leah Hurwitz K; m. 5/4/24 to Sara Fay Feldman; c. Morton, Stephen and Kenneth. Educ: High Sch. Polit. & Govt. Pos: V.chmn, Calif. State Hwy. Cmn; del, Dem. Nat. Conv, 64. Bus. & Prof. Pos: Publisher, News Observer, Inc, 39-; chmn, bd, Calif. Financial Corp, 57-62. Mem: Shrine, Mason (32°); B'nai B'rith; Elks; Eagles; hon. mem, Jr. C. of C; Presidents Club. Rel: Jewish. Mailing Add: 633 Water View Isle, Alameda, Calif. 94501. (1967)

KOGA, GEORGE M. D
Councilman, City and Co. of Honolulu, Hawaii
b. Honolulu, Hawaii, 3/19/28; s. Kiuta Koga and Michie Eguchi K; m. 11/28/58 to Ruth Kiyoko Kamuri; c. Suzanne. Educ: Univ. of Hawaii, B.A, 50; Georgetown Univ, LL.B, 56. Polit. & Govt. Pos: Hawaii State Rep, 59-64; councilman, City and Co. of Honolulu, Hawaii, 65-, v.chmn. and floor leader, City Coun, 69- Bus. & Prof. Pos: Gen. counsel, Legal Aid Soc. of Hawaii, 57-58; secy, Bar Asn. of Hawaii, 58; instr. bus. law, Chaminade Col, 61-62. Mil. Serv: Entered as 2nd Lt, Army, 51, released as 1st Lt, 53. Legal Res: 1254 Center St, Honolulu, Hawaii 96816. Mailing Add: 195 S. King St, Honolulu, Hawaii 96813.

KOGOVSEK, JOHN J. D
Mem, Colo. Dem. State Cent. Cmt.
b. Pueblo, Colo, 7/16/46; s. Frank L. Kogovsek and Mary Blatnick K; single. Educ: South. Colo. State Col, B.A, 68; Pi Delta Phi. Polit. & Govt. Pos: Mem, Pueblo Co. Dem. Cent. Cmt, Colo, 68-; mem, Colo. Dem. State Cent. Cmt, 68- Bus. & Prof. Pos: Teacher hist. and French, Seton High Sch, 68- Mem: Pres, Slovan Lodge, West. Slovanic Asn. Rel: Roman Catholic. Mailing Add: 2024 Pine St, Pueblo, Colo. 81004.

KOGOVSEK, RAY P. D
Colo. State Rep.
b. Pueblo, Colo, 8/19/41; s. Frank L. Kogovsek and Mary Blatnick K; m. 6/27/64 to Eulice A. Kroschel; c. Lisa Marie and Toni Rae. Educ: Pueblo Jr. Col, A.A, 62; Adams State Col, B.A. in Bus, 64; Iota Xi. Polit. & Govt. Pos: Chief Dep. co. clerk, Pueblo Co, Colo, 66-; Colo. State Rep, 69- Mem: Data Processing Mgr. Asn; Am. Fedn. of Musicians, Local 69. Rel: Catholic. Mailing Add: 1627 Horseshoe Dr, Pueblo, Colo. 81001.

KOHLER, FOY DAVID Independent
Consult, Dept. of State
b. Oakwood, Ohio, 2/15/08; s. Leander David Kohler and Myrtle McClure K; m. 8/7/35 to Phyllis Penn. Educ: Ohio State Univ, B.S, 31; Phi Beta Kappa; Delta Upsilon; Beta Gamma Sigma. Hon. L.H.D, Ohio State Univ, 62; LL.D, Univ. Toledo, 64, Findlay Col, 67 and Univ. Akron, 67. Polit. & Govt. Pos: Career officer, U.S. Dept. of State For. Serv, 31-, consol, Windsor, Ont, Can, 32, Bucharest, 33-36 and Athens, 36-38; third secy, Cairo, 41; attended, Nat. War Col, 46; counsr, Moscow, 47-49; mem. staff, Int. Broadcasting Serv; dir, Voice of Am, 49-52; mem, Policy Planning Staff, Dept. State, 52-53; counsr, Ankara, 53-55; mem, ICA Eval. Team, 56-58; Dep. Asst. Secy. of State for European Affairs, 58-59, asst. secy, 59-62; U.S. Ambassador to U.S.S.R, 62-66; Dep. Under Secy. of State for Polit. Affairs, 66-67; consult, Dept. of State, 68- Bus. & Prof. Pos: Bank teller, 24-27; prof. int. studies, Cent. Adv. Int. Studies, Univ. Miami, 68- Publ: The Problems We Face: An Introductory Comment,' Annals Am. Acad. Polit. & Soc. Sci, 11/68. Mem: Coun. For. Rels: Am. Acad. Polit. & Soc. Sci; Wash. Inst. For. Affairs; Am. For. Serv. Asn; Tequesta Country Club; Faculty Club, Univ. Miami. Superior Serv. Award, Dept. State, 52; Distinguished Honor Award, 66; Rockefeller Pub. Serv. Award, 67. Rel: Methodist. Legal Res: 215 Golf Club Circle, Village of Tequesta, Jupiter, Fla. 33458. Mailing Add: P.O. Box 8123, University of Miami, Coral Galbes, Fla. 33124.

KOHLER, WALTER JODOK, JR. R
b. Sheboygan, Wis, 4/4/04; s. Walter Jodok Kohler and Charlotte Schroeder K; m. 11/8/48 to Charlotte McAleer; c. Terry Jodok and Charlotte Nicolette. Educ: Yale, Ph.B, 25. Hon. LL.D, Beloit Col. and Northland Col; Hon. Litt.D, Ripon Col; Hon. L.H.D, Lakeland Col. Polit. & Govt. Pos: Chmn, Wis. Del, Rep. Nat. Conv, 48 & 56; Gov, Wis, 50-57. Bus. & Prof. Pos: Secy, Kohler Co, 37-47; chmn. and pres, The Vollrath Co, 47- Mil. Serv: Entered as Lt, Naval Res, 42, released as Lt. Comdr, 45, after serv. in Solomon Islands and Fast Carrier Task Force of Third and Fifth Fleets, West. Pac. Area, 43-45; Am. Theater Medal; Pac. Theater Medal with 5 Stars; Philippine Liberation Medal with 2 Stars; Bronze Star; Presidential Unit Citation; Victory Medal. Mem: Chmn, bd. dirs, Am. Cancer Soc, 53-59. Legal Res: Windway, Kohler, Wis. 53044. Mailing Add: Box 611, Sheboygan, Wis. 53081.

KOHNEN, RALPH BERNARD, JR. R
b. Cincinnati, Ohio, 10/22/35; s. Ralph Bernard Kohnen and Helen Rose Hillenbrand K; m. 8/20/60 to Nancy Marie Stone; c. Ralph William, Allen Stone, Nancy Marie, Jr. and Daniel. Educ: Georgetown Univ. Col. Arts and Sci, A.B, 57; Univ. Cincinnati Col. Law, LL.B, 60; Phi Alpha Delta. Polit. & Govt. Pos: Ohio State Rep, 63-67; city councilman, Cincinnati, 67- Bus. & Prof. Pos: Assoc, Waite, Schindel, Bayless & Schneider, Law Firm, 61-65, partner, 66- Mil. Serv: Pfc, Army, 60-61. Mem: Cincinnati, Ohio State and Am. Bar Asns; C. of C; bd. trustees, Ment. Health Asn, Commun. Ment. Health and Mental Retardation Bd, Resident Home for Ment. Retarded and Assoc. for Blind; Ohio Crime Cmn. Rel: Catholic. Legal Res: 2959 Wold Ave, Cincinnati, Ohio 45206. Mailing Add: 1318 Central Trust Tower, Cincinnati, Ohio 45202.

KOIVISTO, CLIFFORD DANIEL R
Chmn, Gogebic Co. Rep. Party, Mich.
b. Ironwood, Mich, 10/19/47; s. Clifford Elmer Koivisto and Dorothy Elizebeth Mattila K; single. Educ: Gogebic Commun. Col, A.A. in Polit. Sci, 67; North. Mich. Univ, B.S. in Polit. Sci, 69; Circle K; Young Rep. Polit. & Govt. Pos: Chmn, Wright for Rep. Cmt, 110th Dist, Mich, 66 & 68; chmn, Ruppe for Cong. Cmt, Gogebic Co, 66 & 68; del, Mich. Rep. Conv, 67, 68 & 69; mem, Gogebic Co. Rep. Exec. Cmt, Mich, 67-69; pres, North. Mich. Univ. Young Rep, 67-69; chmn, Upper Peninsula Youth for Nixon, 11th Cong. Dist, Mich, 68; chmn, Gogebic Co. Rep. Party, 69- Bus. & Prof. Pos: Salesman, Santini Distributing Co, 67-69; teacher, Ontonagon Area Schs, Mich, 69- Mem: Mich. and Nat. Educ. Asns; Gogebic Range Beagle Club; Kiwanis; North. Mich. Univ. Young Rep; Gogebic Co. Rep. Men's Club; Aurora Athletic Club; Norrie Amateur Sports Club. Outstanding Sr. Student, Polit. Sci. Dept, North. Mich. Univ. Rel: Lutheran; Mo. Synod. Mailing Add: 417 Van Buskirk Rd, Ironwood, Mich. 49938.

KOK, PETER R
Mich. State Rep.
b. Grand Rapids, Mich, 10/24/19; married; c. three. Educ: Calvin Col, A.B. Polit. & Govt. Pos: Mich. State Rep, 64- Bus. & Prof. Pos: Realtor. Mil. Serv: Capt, Air Force, four years. Rel: Christian Reformed Church. Mailing Add: 1920 Philadelphia, S.E, Grand Rapids, Mich. 49506. (1967)

KOLB, EUGENE J. D
Chmn, Gratiot Co. Dem. Party, Mich.
b. Germany, 2/3/17; s. Eugene Kolb and Martha Knupfer K; m. 1/2/44 to Marion F. Sindlinger; c. Karen E. and Edward L. Educ: City Col, New York, B.A, 61; City Univ. N.Y, M.A, 63; Yale Univ, Ph.D, 66; Phi Beta Kappa. Polit. & Govt. Pos: Del, Dem. Nat. Conv, 68; chmn, Gratiot Co. Dem. Party, Mich, 68-; chmn, Permanent Platform and Resolutions Cmt, Mich. Dem. Party, 68-; mem, Mich. Dem. Party Polit. Reform Cmn, 69-; chmn, Mich. Dem. Party Cmt. on Nat. Party Reform, 69- Bus. & Prof. Pos; Prof. polit. sci, Alma Col, 65- Mil. Serv: Entered as Pvt, Army, 42, released as Lt. Col, 63, after serv. in Mil. Intel, Europe, Far East; Bronze Star Medal; two Commendation Medals. Mem: Am. Polit. Sci. Asn. Rel: Episcopal. Mailing Add: 435 Yale Ave, Alma, Mich. 48801.

KOLB, JAMES D
Chmn, Crenshaw Co. Dem. Party, Ala.
b. Luverne, Ala, 12/24/98; s. Graham Kolb and Lizzie Bradley K; m. to Willie Byrd; c. Maxine K.(Mrs. Sanders), Yvonne (Mrs. Brackett), Anna (Mrs. Williams), James Jr. and Maurice. Educ: Antioch Grammar Sch. Polit. & Govt. Pos: Chmn, Crenshaw Co. Dem. Party, Ala, 54-; alternate del, Dem. Nat. Conv, 68. Rel: Church of Christ. Mailing Add: Route 2, Box 90, Luverne, Ala. 36049.

KOLB, JAMES MONROE, SR. D
Chmn, Johnson Co. Dem. Cent. Cmt, Ark.
b. Clarksville, Ark, 12/14/04; s. James Silas Kolb, M.D, and Mollie Virginia Clark K; m. 4/17/30 to Reba Lois Garner; c. James Monroe, Jr, M.D. and Martha Jane (Mrs. James Richard Callaway). Educ: Col. of Ozarks, A.B, 25; Univ. Ark. Sch. of Med, M.D, 30; pres, Sr. Class, Col. Ozarks, 24-25; pres, Earle Literary Soc; Debating Team; Football Letterman; house mgr, Phi Ro Sigma, 3 years; pres, Square & Compass. Polit. & Govt. Pos: Coroner, Johnson Co, Ark, 35; secy, Elec. Cmn, Johnson Co, 46-49; del, State Dem. Conv, 46-; chmn, Johnson Co. Dem. Cent. Cmt, 46-; del, Dem. Nat. Conv, 64. Bus. & Prof. Pos: Mem. bd. trustees, Col. Ozarks, 35-56; chmn, Clarksville Airport Cmn, Ark; chief of staff, Clarksville Hosp. Mil. Serv: Entered as Capt, Army Air Force, 43, released as Maj, 45, after serv. as Flight Surgeon, Med. Dept, Cent. States Training Command. Publ: Numerous med. articles. Mem: Am. Med. Asn.(Ark. Med. Soc. del, 55-69, mem. coun. on constitution and bylaws, House of Del, v.chmn. of coun, 68-); Ark. Med. Soc.(mem. coun, 50-, chmn, 58-59, pres, 59-60); Am. Acad. Gen. Practice (pres. Ark. Chap, 53-54, Ark. Chap. del, Cong. of Del, 54-64); Am. Soc. Abdominal Surgeons; Lions (pres, Clarksville Chap, 35, 41 & 47); Col. Ozarks Alumni Asn.(pres, 34); Ark. Livestock Asn; Ark. and Am. Herford Asn; Farm Bur; Scottish Rite; York Rite; Mason; Shrine; Am. Legion; C. of C. Hobbies: Hunting, camping and carpentry. Legal Res: 121 Rogers St, Clarksville, Ark. 72830. Mailing Add: Box 380, Clarksville, Ark. 72830.

KOLETSKY, JOSEPH QUINT R
Chmn, Waterford Rep. Town Cmt, Conn.
b. New Haven, Conn, 2/28/38; s. Joseph Koletsky and Mary Quirk K; m. 12/29/62 to Ann McGrail; c. Mary Elizabeth and Joann. Educ: Fairfield Col. Prep. Sch, 51-55; Yale Col, B.A, 59; Yale Law Sch, LL.B, 62; Delta Kappa Epsilon. Polit. & Govt. Pos: Chmn, Waterford Rep. Town Cmt, Conn, 66-; mem, Waterford Bd. Educ, 69- Bus. & Prof. Pos: Partner, attorney, Copp, Brenneman and Tighe, New London, Conn, 66- Mil. Serv: Entered as Lt.(jg), Naval Res, 62, released as Lt, 66, after serv. as law specialist; Res, Judge Adv. Gen. Corps, Lt. Comdr. Rel: Roman Catholic. Legal Res: 9 Quinley Way, Waterford, Conn. 06385. Mailing Add: 302 State St, New London, Conn. 06320.

KOLKMAN, LAWRENCE RICK D
b. Webster, S.Dak, 7/13/46; s. Lawrence Henry Kolkman and Clara Kuernevig K; m. 5/31/69 to Karen Kay Bucks. Educ: Augustana Col, B.A, 68; Chi Sigma Kappa. Polit. & Govt. Pos: Chmn, Augustana Students for Kennedy, 68; organizer, Augustana Young Dem, 68; campaign mgr, Kermit Sande, Cand. for Cmnr. of Sch. and Pub. Lands, 68; alternate del, Dem. Nat. Conv, 68. Bus. & Prof. Pos: Soc. sci. instr, Wood High Sch, Wood, S.Dak, 68-69, Centerville Mid. Sch, 69- Mem: S.Dak. Educ. Asn; PTA. Rel: American Lutheran. Mailing Add: Centerville, S.Dak. 57014.

KOLNACKI, CATHERINE FAHEY
b. Washington, D.C, 8/22/25; d. James Thomas Fahey and Elizabeth Bowan F; m. 6/11/54 to Francis A. Kolnacki. Educ: Dunbarton Col, B.A, 47. Polit. & Govt. Pos: Chief clerk, Joint Cmt. on Reduction of Fed. Expenditures, U.S. Cong, 47- Rel: Catholic. Legal Res: 5125 Baltimore Ave, Montgomery Co, Md. Mailing Add: 5125 Baltimore Ave, Washington, D.C. 20016.

KOLSKI, EDWIN THOMAS R
b. Chicago, Ill, 9/5/11; s. Theodore Kolski and Cecilia Altman K; m. 10/1/38 to Charlotte Olivia Dickow; c. James, Gerald and Philip. Educ: Notre Dame Univ, A.B, 32. Polit. & Govt. Pos: Rep. ward committeeman, 32nd Ward, Ill, 48-; del, Rep. Nat. Conv, 52 & 60. Bus. & Prof. Pos: Ins. broker, 44-; pres, Evergreen Bowl, Inc, 56- Mem: Notre Dame Alumni Club; Chicago Notre Dame Club; Lions; Chicago Press Club; Polish Nat. Alliance; Eagles Am. Sports Club; Bowling Proprietors Asn. Rel: Roman Catholic. Mailing Add: 1627 N. Maplewood Ave, Chicago, Ill. 60647.

KOLSTAD, ALLEN C. R
Mont. State Rep.
b. Chester, Mont, 12/24/31; s. Henry B. Kolstad and Mabel Webb K; m. 9/2/51 to Iva Matteson; c. Cedric A, Chris A, Cheryl D. and Corrine F. Educ: Concordia Col, Moorhead, Minn, 2 years; Alpha Epsilon Sigma. Polit. & Govt. Pos: Precinct committeeman, 62-66; chmn, Liberty Co. Rep. Party, 67-68; del, Rep. Nat. Conv, 68; Mont. State Rep, Dist. 19, 69- Mem: Concordia Col. Alumni Asn.(past mem. bd. dirs); mem. bd. dirs, Lutheran Home of the Good Shepherd, Havre, Mont; Mason (past Master); Shrine; past state dir, J.C's; mem. bd. dirs, Chester J.C's; past pres, Havre Conf. of Am. Lutheran Churchmen. Outstanding Young Farmer Award, 65; one of Outstanding Young Men of Am, 66. Rel: Lutheran; past pres, St. Olaf Lutheran Church. Legal Res: Chester, Mont. 59522. Mailing Add: Ledger, Mont. 59456.

KOLTER, JOSEPH PAUL D
Pa. State Rep.
b. McDonald, Ohio, 9/3/26; s. Stephen Kolter and Frances Shuster K; m. 2/9/49 to Dorothy Marie Gray; c. Joseph P, Jr, James S, David M. and Julie Ann. Educ: Geneva Col, B.S.B.A, 50. Polit. & Govt. Pos: Treas, Beaver Co. Dem. Cmt, 54-56; committeeman, Dem. Party, Beaver Co, 54-67; councilman, New Brighton, Pa, 62-66; mem, Civil Serv. Cmn, 63-67; Pa. State Rep, 14th Legis. Dist, 68- Bus. & Prof. Pos: Cashier, St. Joseph Lead Co, Monaca, Pa, 64-67; owner and operator, New Brighton Roller Drome, 67-69. Mil. Serv: Entered as Pvt, Air Force, 45, released as Cpl, 46. Mem: Nat. Asn. Acct; Am. Legion; Eagles; Optimist Int. Beaver Valley. Mailing Add: 2185 Mercer Rd, New Brighton, Pa. 15066.

KONDELIK, EVELYN M. D
b. Helena, Mont, 6/25/37; d. Basil O. Gavin and Paulina Geiger G; m. 4/8/61 to Emil John Kondelik; c. Douglas Orin, Joseph LeRoy, Andrew John and Maureen Ann. Educ: High Sch. Polit. & Govt. Pos: Dem. precinct committeewoman, Mont, 63; chmn, McCone Co. Dem. Cent. Cmt, 64-67; v.pres, McCone Co. Dem. Club, 64-66. Bus. & Prof. Pos: Secy. to Dawson Co. Attorney, Glendive, Mont, 58-61. Mil. Serv: Entered as Pvt, Women's Army Corps, 55, released as SP-4, 58, after serv. in Fifth Army Finance and Acct. Off, Fifth Army Hq, Chicago, Ill, 55-57 and Med. Supply Control Agency, Maison Forte, Orleans Area Command, France, 57-58; Airman 2/C, Air Force Res, 58-61; Good Conduct Medal. Mem: Women of the Moose; Mont. Farmers Union; McCone Co. Home Demonstration Club. Rel: Catholic. Mailing Add: R.R, Circle, Mont. 59215. (1967)

KONDO, RONALD YONEO D
Hawaii State Rep.
b. Lahaina, Maui, Hawaii, 2/18/32; s. Sango Kondo and Etsu Takita K; m. 8/4/56 to Janice Takako Honda; c. Diane, Ronald Jr. and Janine. Educ: Univ. Hawaii, B.S, 57. Polit. & Govt. Pos: Mem, Hawaii State Bd. of Paroles and Pardons, 66-68; dir, Maui Young Dem, 66-69; Hawaii State Rep, 68- Bus. & Prof. Pos: Pres, West Maui Bus. & Prof. Asn, 65-66 & 67-68, dir, 66-67 & 68- Mil. Serv: Entered as Pvt, Army, 51, released as Sgt, 54, after serv. in Far East Command, Korea and Japan, 52-54. Mem: Jaycees; West Maui Vet. Club. Rel: Methodist. Mailing Add: 252 Lahainaluna Rd, Lahaina, Maui, Hawaii 96761.

KONE, SAM L, JR. R
Chmn, Zavala Co. Rep. Party, Tex.
b. San Antonio, Tex, 5/18/25; s. Sam L. Kone and Justine McKay K; m. 12/28/60 to Billie Deane Pearce, wid; c. Edwin G. Peters, Jr. Educ: Tex. Agr. and Mech. Col, 46-47; Tex. Agr. and Indust. Col, 48-49. Polit. & Govt. Pos: Co-chmn, Citizens Asn. Serv. All Am; chmn, Zavala Co. Rep. Party, Tex, 68- Mil. Serv: Entered as Pvt, Air Corps, 43, released as T-5, 46, after serv. in Aviation Eng. Unit, Okinawa and Ie Shima, 45-46. Mem: Crystal City C. of C.(pres, 66-67). Rel: Methodist. Legal Res: La Pryor, Tex. 78872. Mailing Add: P.O. Box 175, Crystal City, Tex. 78839.

KONRADY, BERNARD WENDELL D
Ind. State Sen.
b. Gary, Ind, 8/30/15; s. Andrew S. Konrady and Julia Galik K; m. 2/4/40 to Dorine Caviness; c. Lynne (deceased), Veronica, Bernard, Jr, Jeffrey and Dorine Gail. Educ: Ind. Univ, B.S; Theta Chi. Polit. & Govt. Pos: Precinct committeeman, Dem. Party, Gary, Ind, 58-68; Ind. State Sen, 69- Mem: Oil Heat Inst.(pres, Gary, Ind, 54-); Calumet Petroleum Asn; Ind. Independent Petroleum Asn; Teamsters Local 142; Ind. Univ. Varsity Club; Ind. Univ. Alumni Asn; K. of C; Moose; Fraternal Order of Police; C. of C; Slovak Club. Rel: Catholic. Mailing Add: 524 Cleveland, Gary, Ind. 46404.

KONRADY, EMERY L. D
Polit. & Govt. Pos: Ind. State Sen, -66. Bus. & Prof. Pos: Pres, Konrady Brothers Corp, distrib. fuel. Mil. Serv: Air Force. Mem: VFW; Am. Legion; Canadian Legion; Optimists Club; K. of C; Elks; Eagles; Fraternal Order of Police Asn. Rel: Roman Catholic. Mailing Add: 640 Roosevelt St, Gary, Ind. 46404. (1967)

KOOKER, MARGARETTE FRALEY SPARVER R
b. Harrisburg, Pa, 4/10/96; d. William J. Sparver and Rose Fraley S; m. 9/11/19 to Howard Kooker, jr; c. Frances Elaine (Mrs. Harvey D. Groff) and one granddaughter, Marcia Nina. Educ: Harrisburgh High Sch, 14; Latin, sci. and bus. courses. Polit. & Govt. Pos: Former committeewoman, Third Ward Rep. Party, Quakertown, Pa; former pres. and organizer, North Pa. Coun. Rep. Women, dir. and mem. exec. bd, currently; former pres. and secy, Buck Co. Coun. Rep. Women, hon. pres. and mem. exec. bd, currently; Pa. State

Rep, 54-66, former mem, Joint State Govt. Chmn. on Retirement, Cmn. Task Force on Historic Sites, Adv. Coun. Study on Cigarettes to Minors, Gov. Hosp. Study Cmn. and State and Local Welfare Cmn. and chmn, Pub. Health and Welfare Cmt, Pa. State House of Rep; Gov. rep, White House Conf. on Aging, 63-64. Mem: Eastern Star; legis. chmn. and past. pres, Am. Legion Auxiliary and Quakertown Women's Club; hon. mem, Soroptimist Int. Club; Adult Welfare Adv. Cmt; hon. pres, Upper Bucks Activity Center of Bucks Co. Asn. Retired Citizens; past dir, Am. Red Cross; Richland Grange; Quakertown Commun. Hosp. Auxiliary. Received Outstanding Serv. in Pub. Rels, Soroptimist Int. Club of Quakertown, 63; Outstanding Woman in Field of Pub. Affairs, Quakertown Bus. & Prfnl. Club, 57; was first woman elected to Young Rep. Hall of Fame, Pa, 59. Rel: Lutheran. Mailing Add, Fifth and Park Ave, Quakertown, Pa. 18951.

KOONCE, SARAH ADA D
b. Norton, Va, 10/23/22; d. David P. Nickels and Nelly Cox N; m. Feb, 1944 to George S. Koonce; c. Charlotte Maria, Sarah Jane, Rebecca Eileen and Georgiana. Educ: George Wash. Univ. Polit. & Govt. Pos: Clerk assignment off, Prince George's Co. Circuit Court, Md, 60-64, assignment cmnr, 64-; Md. State Del, Prince George's Co, 62-66. Bus. & Prof. Pos: Resident mgr, Deer Park Hts. Housing Develop, 55-60. Rel: Baptist. Mailing Add: 5401 Wheeler Rd, Oxon Hill, Md. 20021. (1967)

KOONS, JAMES L. D
Chmn, Noble Co. Dem. Party, Ind.
b. Avilla, Ind, 6/1/15; s. William E. Koons and Cecilia Ley K; m. 8/23/56 to Dorothy Mae Finney; c. James William. Educ: Avilla High Sch. Polit. & Govt. Pos: Chmn, Noble Co. Dem. Party, Ind, 41-; chmn, Fourth Dist. Dem. Party, 48-65; alternate del, Dem. Nat. Conv, 68. Bus. & Prof. Pos: Owner and operator of food mkt, 41- Mem: Ind. Soc; Avilla C. of C.(pres, 69); Elks (Past Exalted Ruler); Moose; K. of C.(3° and 4°). Young Dem. of Ind. Rel: Catholic. Legal Res: 120 Baum St, Avilla, Ind. 46710. Mailing Add: Main St, Avilla, Ind. 46710.

KOONTZ, ELIZABETH DUNCAN D
Dir, Women's Bur, U.S. Dept. of Labor
b. Salisbury, N.C, 6/3/19; d. Samuel Edward Duncan and Lena Jordan D; m. 11/26/47 to Harry Lee Koontz. Educ: Livingstone Col, A.B, 38; Atlanta Univ, M.A, 41; Columbia Univ. and Ind. Univ, grad. study; hon. mem, Zeta Phi Beta. Hon. L.H.D, Livingstone Col, 67 and Coppin State Col, 69; Pd.D, Pac. Univ, 69 and Bryant Col, 69; Litt.D, Atlanta Univ, 69; Ed.D, Howard Univ, 69; LL.D, Am. Univ, Wash, D.C, 69; H.H.D, East. Mich. Univ, 69; Sc.D. in Ed, Northeast. Univ, 69. Polit. & Govt. Pos: Mem, Gov. Cmn. on the Status of Women, N.C, 62; mem, President's Adv. Coun. on Educ. of Disadvantaged Children, 65-68; U.S. Del, UN Cmn. on the Status of Women, 69-; dir. women's bur, U.S. Dept. of Labor, 69- Bus. & Prof. Pos: Pub. sch. teacher, N.C, 38-68. Mem: Salisbury Teachers Asn; N.C. Asn. of Classroom Teachers (pres, 58-62); Nat. Educ. Asn.(pres, Asn. of Classroom Teachers, 65-66, nat. v.pres, 67-68, nat. pres, 68-69); Rowan Co. Negro Civic League, 48; Youth Cmn. of Rowan Co, 55-57. Distinguished Alumni Medallion for Achievement, Livingstone Col; Distinguished Teacher Award, Civitan Club of Salisbury; Distinguished Citizenship Award, N.C. Dist. W, of Civitan Int. Rel: Episcopal. Legal Res: 418 S. Caldwell St, Salisbury, N.C. 28144. Mailing Add: 1830 16th St. N.W, Washington, D.C. 20009.

KOONTZ, JOHN D
Secy. of State, Nev.
b. Goldfield, Nev, 10/19/06; s. Louis K. Koontz and Ada May Halstead K; m. 4/20/40 to Margaret E. Bennett. Polit. & Govt. Pos: Auditor and recorder, Esmeralda Co, Nev, 35-42; Chief Dep. Supt. of Banks and Chief Dep. State Auditor, 43-46; Secy. of State, Nev, currently. Mil. Serv: Army, 43. Publ: Political History of Nevada, State of Nev, 59, revised ed, 65. Mem: Elks; Lions; Eagles. Rel: Methodist. Legal Res: 302 E. John St, Carson City, Nev. 89701. Mailing Add: P.O. Box 309, Carson City, Nev. 89701.

KOONTZ, ROBERT J. R
b. 1935. Educ: Univ. Idaho, B.A, 57, LL.B, 63. Polit. & Govt. Pos: Idaho State Rep, 67-69; former del. Nat. and State Rep. Conv; former mem, Ada City Young Rep. Bus. & Prof. Pos: Attorney, Elam, Burke, Jeppesen and Evans. Mailing Add: 940 Argyll, Boise, Idaho 83702. (1967)

KOORY, EDWARD FREDRICK, JR. R
Ariz. State Rep.
b. El Paso, Tex, 3/9/40; s. Edward Fredrick Koory and Mary Lee Abdou K; m. 5/27/61 to Jessica Dorothea Thomas; c. Deborah Lee and Edward Fredrick, Ill. Educ: Ariz. State Univ, B.A, 61; Blue Key; Kappa Delta Pi. Polit. & Govt. Pos: Rep. precinct committeeman, Ariz, 66-; Ariz. State Rep, Dist. 8-0, 67- Mil. Serv: Entered as 2nd Lt, Marine Corps, 61, released as 1st Lt, 64; 1st Lt, Marine Corps Res, 64- Mem: Rotary; Toastmasters; C. of C; bd. dirs, United Fund. Rel: Conservative Baptist. Mailing Add: 5753 West Morten, Glendale, Ariz. 85301. (1967)

KOPECKY, BERNIE D. D
S.Dak. State Rep.
b. Highmore, S.Dak; s. Ernest Kopecky and Ida Berreth K; m. 6/11/54 to Helen Vetch; c. Vicky, Sandra, Kathleen and Gregory. Educ: Westport High Sch, 4 years. Polit. & Govt. Pos: Dep. sheriff, Brown Co, S.Dak, 54-60, sheriff, 60-66; del, Dem. Nat. Conv, 68; S.Dak. State Rep, 69- Bus. & Prof. Pos: Salesman, Leisen Realty Co, 66-68; v.pres, 69- Mil. Serv: Entered as Pvt, Marine Corps, 51, released as Cpl, 53, after serv. in First Marine Div, Korean Conflict, 51-52; Three Purple Hearts. Mem: Elks; Moose; Am. Legion; 40 et 8; Nat. Sheriff's Asn; S.Dak. Sheriff and Peace Officers Asn; Hub City Riders Club; Quarter Horse Asn. Rel: Catholic. Mailing Add: 405 N. Congress, Aberdeen, S.Dak. 57401.

KOPEIKIN, LEONARD I.
City Councilman, Santa Barbara, Calif.
b. Brooklyn, N.Y, 1/9/31; s. Harry Kopeikin and Bessie Belford K; m. 3/25/51 to Judith M. Kraus; c. Hal Stephen, Marc Stuart, Brian Neil and Jill Fawn. Educ: City Col. New York; Tau Beta Pi; Pi Tau Sigma. Polit. & Govt. Pos: City councilman, Santa Barbara, Calif, 65- Bus. & Prof. Pos: Engr, Greer Hydraul, Inc, 52-54; engr, Strategic Syst. Analysis, G.E. Tempo, 54-55, mem. prfnl. staff, 58-63, mgr, 63- Mil. Serv: Entered as Officer Cand, Navy, 55, released as Lt.(jg), 58, after serv. in Naval Air Spec. Weapons Facility. Publ: Numerous Technical Papers and Reports. Mem: Am. Inst. Aeronaut. & Astronaut. Mailing Add: 650 Island View Dr, Santa Barbara, Calif. 93105. (1967)

KOPEL, GERALD L. D
b. Md, 6/16/28; married; c. two. Polit. & Govt. Pos: Spec. Asst. Attorney Gen. for Legis. Drafting, Colo, 59-61; Colo. State Rep, 65-67. Bus. & Prof. Pos: Lawyer. Mem: Chmn, Bar Asn. Bankruptcy Cmt, 62-65 and Park Hill Action Cmt, 68-69. Mailing Add: 1755 Glencoe, Denver, Colo. 80220.

KOPP, DONALD LEE D
W.Va. State Del.
b. Clarksburg, W.Va, 5/23/35; s. Francis Kopp and Jenny Wilkinson K; m. 8/21/55 to Beverley Ann Wyckoff; c. Donald Lee II and Jenny Le. Educ: Clarksburg Pub. Schs. Polit. & Govt. Pos: W.Va. State Del, 64- Bus. & Prof. Pos: Indust. glass worker. Mem: Elks; Moose; former v.pres. Rolland Local 6; del. to Harrison Co. Fedn. of Labor. Rel: Methodist. Mailing Add: 1631 W. Pike St, Clarksburg, W.Va. 26301. (1967)

KOPP, JOHN GLENWRIGHT R
Chmn, Charlton Co. Rep. Exec. Cmt, Ga.
b. Augusta, Ga, 3/18/23; s. Charles Heartter Kopp and Maurine Parks K. (deceased); m. 4/8/67 to Jewell Mizell; c. Joseph Harper. Educ: Norman Col, 40-42; Col. William & Mary, 43; Mercer Univ, A.B, 46, LL.B, 49; Kappa Sigma. Polit. & Govt. Pos: Mem, Ware Co. Rep. Exec. Cmt, Ga, 58-67; chmn, Charlton Co. Rep. Exec. Cmt, 67-; gen. counsel, Eighth Cong. Rep. Cmt, 68- Bus. & Prof. Pos: Secy. and dir, United Fed. S&L Assoc, Ga, 63- Mil. Serv: Entered as Pvt, Army, 43, released as Sgt, 45, after serv. in 95th Inf. Div, Europe-Africa-Middle East, 44-45; Bronze Star; Purple Heart; Combat Medics Badge; Good Conduct Ribbon; Europe-Africa-Middle East Ribbon with 3 stars. Mem: Am. and Ga. Bar Asns; Waycross Bar Asn.(past pres); Elks; Lion (past pres); Okefenokee Golf Club (past pres). Rel: Baptist. Legal Res: 708 Martin St, Folkston, Ga. 31537. Mailing Add: Box 356, Folkston, Ga. 31537.

KOPP, W. BREWSTER R
b. Rochester, N.Y, 11/4/25; s. Frederick J. Kopp and Bernice C. Woodworth K; m. 6/18/49 to Ruth S. Philpotts; c. Bradford B, Jeffrey B. and Alexander B. Educ: Harvard Col, A.B, 47, Harvard Bus. Sch, M.B.A, 49. Polit. & Govt. Pos: Asst. Secy. of the Army for Financial Mgt, 65-67; consult, Dept. Defense, 67-69. Bus. & Prof. Pos: Financial analyst, Fitch Investors Serv, 46-47, Wertheim & Co, 49-50 and Standard Oil Co. of Ohio, 51-53; various financial positions, including div. comptroller and corp. mgr. of financial planning and budgets, Am. Can. Co, 54-65; sr. v.pres, First Nat. Bank of Boston, Mass, 67-69; v.pres. finance and admin, Digital Equip. Corp, Maynard, 69- Mem: Financial Execs. Inst; Am. Inst. Banking; Harvard Bus. Sch. Asn. of Boston (dir); Harvard Club of Boston; Norfolk Country Club; Boy Scouts (dir, Cambridge Coun. and Boston Coun); Asn. of U.S. Army; C. of C. Rel: Protestant. Legal Res: Winchester Rd, Norfolk, Conn. 06058. Mailing Add: 134 Coolidge Hill, Cambridge, Mass. 02138.

KOPP, W. ROY R
b. Platteville, Wis, 3/17/05; s. Arthur W. Kopp and Emily Hutton K; m. 8/4/32 to Frances L. Webb; c. Sally (Mrs. Frederick A. More). Educ: Univ. Wis, Ph.B, 26, LL.B, 28; Sigma Alpha Epsilon; Phi Delta Phi. Polit. & Govt. Pos: Chmn. bd. trustees, Platteville Munic. Hosp, Wis, 54-57; former chmn, Grant Co. Rep. Party, 10 years; chmn, Third Cong. Dist. Rep. Party until 67; former mem. bd. regents, Wis. State Cols; pres. bd. regents, Wis. State Univs, currently; mem, Coord. Coun. for Higher Educ. and Higher Educ. Aids Bd, Wis, currently. Mem: Am. and Grant Co. Bar Asns; Wis. State Bar Asn. (mem. bd. gov, 44-47); Kiwanis. Rel: Congregational. Legal Res: 250 Southwest Rd, Platteville, Wis. 53818. Mailing Add: Kopp, McKichan & Geyer, First National Bank Bldg, Platteville, Wis. 53818.

KOPPERL, GEORGE D. R
N.H. State Rep.
b. Orange, N.J, 3/17/30; married; c. two. Educ: Princeton Univ, B.S. and M.S. in Eng. Polit. & Govt. Pos: N.H. State Rep. Mil. Serv: Coast Guard Res. Rel: Protestant. Mailing Add: Morrill Rd, Canterbury, N.H. 03224.

KOPPLE, ROBERT D
b. N.Y.C, 11/26/10; s. Morris David Kopple and Florence Lipshutz K; m. 7/22/44 to Dorothy Stuhlbarg; c. Ann Howard and Nancy Dunn. Educ: N.Y. Univ, B.A, 32, J.D, 34. Polit. & Govt. Pos: Mem, Nassau Co. Dem. Cmt, 46-51; Dem. cand, N.Y. State Sen, Nassau Co, 50; spec. adv. to Mayor N.Y.C. for Tercentenary Celebration, 59-60; mem, N.Y. Am. Revolution Bicentennial Cmn, currently. Bus. & Prof. Pos: Admitted to N.Y. Bar 34; practice of law, N.Y.C, 34-39; gen. mgr, Columbia Aircraft Prod, Somerville, N.J, 39-42; partner, Kopple & Pine, 46-53; exec. v.pres, Midtown Realty Owners Asn; Inc, N.Y.C, 53-; trustee, Bldg. Serv. Welfare Fund, 53-; pres, Exitolite Corp, Quick Response Serv. Inc. and exec. v.pres, Owners Cmt. on Elec. Rates, 54-; trustee, Bldg. Serv. Pension Fund, 58-; organizer and first exec. v.pres, N.Y. World's Fair Corp, 58-60; partner, Kopple & Scham, 62-; exec. dir, Cmt. for Reasonable World Trade Center, 64-; pres, Ready Alarm Inc, currently. Mil. Serv: Signal C, Army, 42-46. Mem: Little Neck Bay Power Squadron (comdr); U.S. Power Squadrons (rear comdr, nat. pub. rels. officer); Am. Soc. Mil. Engrs; N.Y. State Bar Asn; Real Estate Bd. N.Y; Mutual Admiration Soc. N.Y. (pres); Tau Delta Phi; Sands Point Bath and Tennis Luncheon Club; Rockefeller Center Luncheon Club. Legal Res: 17 Greenway, Roslyn, N.Y. 11576. Mailing Add: 450 Seventh Ave, New York, N.Y. 10001.

KOPYCINSKI, STEPHEN JOSEPH D
Councilman-at-Large, Jersey City, N.J.
b. Jersey City, N.J, 8/18/12; s. Anthony Kopycinski and Albina Czachorowski K; m. 6/10/36 to Helen V. Blonski; c. Stephen R, John A. and Aleta M. Educ: Dickinson Evening High Sch. Polit. & Govt. Pos: Chief clerk, Hudson Co. Registers Off, 33-66; councilman-at-lg, Jersey City, N.J, 65- Mem: Nat. dir.

of the Asn. Sons of Poland; 2nd v.pres, N.J. Fraternal Cong; exec. v.pres, Gen. Pulaski Mem. Cmt, N.Y. Grand Marshal, 1947 Pulaski Parade. Rel: Roman Catholic. Mailing Add: 169 Fourth St, Jersey City, N.J. 07302. (1967)

KORDJA, BETTY McNAMARA D
d. John McNamara and Elizabeth Layden McN; m. to Raymond Kordja; c. Raymond, Jr. Polit. & Govt. Pos: Trustee, O'Byrne Women's Dem. Club, N.J; co. committeewoman, Eighth Ward Dem. Party, Paterson; N.J. State Assemblywoman, 58-69; del, Dem. Nat. Conv, 68. Bus. & Prof. Pos: Former teacher; asst. buyer; receptionist, Mayor's Office, Paterson, N.J, 56-57. Mailing Add: 85 Mary St, Paterson, N.J. 07503. (1967)

KORDUS, ROBERT PAUL D
b. Milwaukee, Wis, 8/1/39; s. Benedict M. Kordus and Marie Czaja K; m. 11/24/60 to Caroll R. Swiatek; c. Robert P, Peter J, Karen T. and Jan M. Educ: Milwaukee Inst. Tech, A.Sc, 59. Polit. & Govt. Pos: Mem, 14th Ward Dem. Party, Wis; Wis. State Assemblyman, 65-67; alderman, 14th Ward, Milwaukee, 68- Mem: Nat. Asn. Accts; Wilson Park Adv. Asn; S.Side Businessmen's Club; counsr, Boy Scout Merit Badge; Fathers & Sons Club; bd. dirs, St. Joseph's Home for Children Asn; Polish Roman Cath. Union; St. Helen Holy Name Soc; Our Lady Queen of Peace Holy Name Soc; Polish Nat. Alliance, Milwaukee Soc; Pulaski; Alumni Asn; Fourth of July Asn; Century Club. Rel: Roman Catholic. Mailing Add: 3457 S. 25th St, Milwaukee, Wis. 53215.

KOREN, HENRY LLOYD THORNELL
b. Princeton, N.J, 3/13/11; s. William Koran and Adelaide Louise Tornell K; m. 8/30/41 to Ely Virginia Cain; c. Henry Lloyd Thornell, Anne Copeland Beale. Educ: Princeton, B.A. cum laude, 33. Polit. & Govt. Pos: With Cent. Intel Agency, 47-48; second secy, Port-au-Prince, 48-51 and Bern, Switz, 51-52; on leave to Dept. Army, 53-58; exec. asst, White House, 56-58; counselor, Manila, Philippines, 58-61; dir. off, N.E. Asian Affairs, Dept. of State, 61 and S.E. Asian Affairs, 62-64; Ambassador to Rep. of the Congo, 64-66; asst. dep. ambassador, Am. Embassy, Saigon, Vietnam, 66-67, dep. for CORDS III, Marine Amphibious Forces, Danang, Vietnam, 67-69. Bus. & Prof. Pos: With Ward Banking Co, 33-35 and Bank of N.Y, 36-40. Mil. Serv: Col, Army For. Affairs, 40-46. Mem: Chevy Chase Club; Army Navy Country Club. Mailing Add: 4707 Reservoir Rd. N.W, Washington, D.C. 20007. (1967)

KORESKI, DONALD EUGENE D
b. Yakima, Wash, 4/17/17; s. Francis E. Koreski and Josephine A. Eschbach K; m. 12/30/39 to Oleta A. Selna; c. Mary Janis, Robert and David. Educ: Univ. San Francisco, 37-38; Univ. Calif, 39-40. Polit. & Govt. Pos: Sunnyvale Planning Cmnr, Calif, 57-61; mem, Sunnyvale City Coun; v.mayor, Sunnyvale, 66-67, mayor, 67-68, city councilman, 69- Mem: Lions. Rel: Catholic. Legal Res: 510 S. Murphy Ave, Sunnyvale, Calif. 94086. Mailing Add: P.O. Box 796, Sunnyvale, Calif. 94088.

KORN, CHARLES A. D
b. Wapello, Iowa, 5/4/16; s. John A. Korn; m. 2/1/48 to Dorothy C. Clausen. Educ: Iowa State Univ, B.S, Agronomy, 1947. Polit. Pos: Iowa State Rep, 1966. Bus. & Prof. Pos: Farmer; Eight years U.S. Soil Conserv. Serv. Mil. Serv: U.S. Navy, WWII, Pac. Mem: Kiwanis Club; Farmers Union. Rel: Lutheran. Mailing Add: RFD Box 13, Logan, Iowa 51546. (1967)

KORNEGAY, HORACE ROBINSON D
b. Asheville, N.C, 3/12/24; s. Marvin Earl Kornegay and Blanche Person Robinson K; m. to Annie Ben Beale; c. Horace Robinson Jr, Kathryn Elder and Martha Beale. Educ: Wake Forest Col, B.S, LL.B; Phi Delta Phi; Omicron Delta Kappa; Alpha Sigma Phi. Polit. & Govt. Pos: Prosecuting attorney, 12th Dist, N.C, 54-60; U.S. Rep, N.C, 60-69. Bus. & Prof. Pos: Lawyer. Mil. Serv: U.S. Army, 43-46; Combat Inf. Badge; Purple Heart; Bronze Star; 2 Campaign Stars. Mem: Greensboro, N.C, Am. Bar Asns; Am. Judicature Soc; Fed. Bar Asn; Am. Legion; VFW; Amvets; Hon. Mem, British Legion; N.C. Soc, SAR; Masonic Order, Scottish Rite; Shrine; Bd. of Visitors Wake Forest Law Sch. Licensed to Practice Law in N.C, Supreme Court, N.C, U.S. Supreme Court. Rel: Methodist; former mem. off. bd, West Market St. Methodist Church. Mailing Add: 1201 Grayland St, Greensboro, N.C. 27403.

KORNEGAY, JESSE DEXTER D
State Treas, N.Mex.
b. Centreville, Ala, 9/15/17; s. Jesse D. Kornegay and Georgia Pierson K; m. 11/7/48 to Lucille B. Walters; c. Ronald, Christopher, Kathryn and Patricia. Educ: Hueytown High, Ala, 32-35. Polit. & Govt. Pos: Mem, Santa Fe Co. Cmn, N.Mex, 54-58; chief, State Tax Cmn, 63-68; state treas, 68- Mem: Int. Asn. Assessing Officers; Mason. Rel: Episcopal. Legal Res: 1908 Conejo Dr, Santa Fe, N.Mex. 87501. Mailing Add: Box 608, Santa Fe, N.Mex. 87501.

KORNICK, MICHAEL D
Secy, Mahoning Co. Dem. Party, Ohio
b. Vanderbilt, Pa, 5/8/05; s. John Kornick and Mary Olenick K; m. 10/5/54 to Margaret Leitch Gorby; stepchildren: Kathryn Corinne Gorby and Carolyn Joyce (Mrs. William Little). Educ: Sherwin Cody Sch. Eng, 25; Youngstown YMCA Col, 26-27. Polit. & Govt. Pos: Dem. precinct committeeman, Mahoning Co. Dem. Party, Ohio, 34-69, secy, 50-; twp. trustee, Coitsville, Ohio, 36-39, chmn, 37-38; mem, Mahoning Co. Dem. Cent. and Exec. Cmt, 40-; dep. clerk of courts, Mahoning Co, 43-69; mem, Campbell Sch. Bd, 48-55, chmn, 53 & 55; campaign mgr, speaker and speech writer for various Dem. cand, including, Joseph Vrabel, former Mayor of Campbell. Bus. & Prof. Pos: Ins. agent, Firemen's Ins. Co, Newark, N. J, 36-68; real estate broker, 36-43; ed, Campbell News-J, 44; owner, Campbell Florists, 42-69. Publ: 'Short Sketch on Helen Gibson,' Films in Rev, 1/68; 'Hollywood Trip thru Movieland,' 2/69 and 'Biography on Charles Ray,' Film Classic Collector, 69; plus others. Mem: Secy, Baseball Town U.S.A. Oldtimers, 63-69. Known historian on early movies and baseball and as such speak at various banquets and meetings; Vaudeville performer, singer and character actor. Rel: Byzantine Catholic. Mailing Add: 241 Gordon Ave, Campbell, Ohio 44405.

KORNICK, NICHOLAS D
Treas, Fayette Co, Pa.
b. Vanderbilt, Pa, 12/15/12; s. John Kornick and Katherine Bodnovich K; m. to Margaret Duke; c. two. Educ: Pa. State Exten. Polit. & Govt. Pos: Pa. State Rep, 50-67; Justice of Peace; Committeeman; Chmn, Dem. Party, Uniontown; treas, Fayette Co, 68- Bus. & Prof. Pos: Safety engr; scale inspector, Pa. Mem: Publicity chmn, Fayette Co. Crippled Children; Am.(Russky) Soc. Club; Pres, Big Ten Baseball League, Fayette, Washington, Greene Co, 46-; Uniontown Slovak Club; Connellsville Slovak Club; Tower Hill Vol. Fire Co. Rel: Catholic. Mailing Add: 37 S. Pennsylvania Ave, Uniontown, Pa. 15401.

KOROLOGOS, TOM CHRIS R
b. Salt Lake City, Utah, 4/6/33; s. Chris T. Korologos and Irene Kolendrianos K; m. 6/16/60 to Carolyn Joy Goff; c. Ann and Philip Chris. Educ: Univ. Utah, B.A, 55; Columbia Univ, Grantland Rice Mem. fel, 57, Pulitzer traveling fel. and M.S, 58; Sigma Delta Chi; Kappa Tau Alpha. Polit. & Govt. Pos: Press secy. to U.S. Sen. Wallace Bennett, 62-65, admin. asst, 65- Bus. & Prof. Pos: Reporter, Salt Lake Tribune, 50-60 and New York Herald Tribune, 58; account exec, David W. Evans & Assocs, Salt Lake City, Utah, 60-62. Mil. Serv: Entered as 2nd Lt, Air Force, 56, released as 1st Lt, 57, after serv. in 825th Air Div, Strategic Air Command, Little Rock Air Force Base, Ark; Capt, Air Force Res. Mem: U.S. Senate Press Secy. Asn; Asn. Admin. Assts. to U.S. Senators; Ahepa. Rel: Greek Orthodox, Legal Res: 536 E. Fourth South, Salt Lake City, Utah 84111. Mailing Add: 8222 Smithfield Ave, Springfield, Va. 22150.

KORPELA, ERNEST JOHN D
Wis. State Assemblyman
b. Wakefield, Mich, 12/19/36; s. Waino Korpela and Hilda Ronn K; m. 7/30/60 to Janice Marie Blair; c. Jodi, Cynthia and Eric. Educ: Allan Hancock Col, 55-56; Wis. State Univ, B.S, 59; M.Ed, 63. Polit. & Govt. Pos: Dist. admin, St. Croix Sch. Dist. 1, Solon Springs, Wis, 63-66; supt. of schs, Washburn City Schs, 66-69; Wis. State Assemblyman, 69- Bus. & Prof. Pos: Teacher, Elmendorf Air Force Base Schs, Anchorage, Alaska, 59-60 and Eau Claire Pub. Schs, 60-62; ed-publisher, Washburn Times, 69- Publ: Memories of Corn Crib, Christian Sci. Monitor. Mem: Phi Delta Kappa; Wis. Asn. of Sch. Dist. Adminstr; Wis. and Nat. Educ. Asns; Am. Asn. of Sch. Adminstr; Lions Int. Rel: Lutheran. Mailing Add: 633 E. Third, Washburn, Wis. 54891.

KORRELL, RITA MAY R
V.chmn, Cheyenne Co. Rep. Cent. Cmt, Colo.
b. First View, Colo, 5/3/28; d. William Sherman Alderson and Urtle Gay Webb A; m. 3/22/48 to Gordon LeRoy Korrell; c. Charlotte Ann and Michael James. Educ: Kit Carson High Sch, grad. Polit. & Govt. Pos: Pres, Cheyenne Co. Rep. Women's Club, Colo, 66-68; v.chmn, Cheyenne Co. Rep. Cent. Cmt, 69-; committeewoman, Cheyenne Wells Precinct Three Rep. Party, 69- Bus. & Prof. Pos: Dep. co. clerk, Cheyenne Co, Cheyenne Wells, Colo, 65- Mem: VFW Auxiliary (pres, William A. Kimmel Post 9700, 51-); Eastern Star (Worthy Matron Cheyenne Wells Chap. 110, 67-68). Rel: Methodist. Legal Res: 50 W. Fourth St. N, Cheyenne Wells, Colo. 80810. Mailing Add: P.O. Box 518, Cheyenne Wells, Colo. 80810.

KORTH, FRED D
b. Yorktown, Tex, 9/9/09; s. Fritz R.J. Korth and Eleanor Marie Stark K; div; c. Nina Marie, Fritz-Alan and Vera Sansom. Educ: Univ. Tex, A.B, 32; George Wash. Univ, LL.B, 35; Phi Delta Phi; Sigma Phi Epsilon. Hon. LL.D, George Wash. Univ, 60. Polit. & Govt. Pos: Dep. counsr, Dept. of Army, 51-52, Asst. Secy. of Army, 52-53, consult. to Secy. Army, 53-60; Secy. of Navy, 62-63. Bus. & Prof. Pos: Law practice, Ft. Worth, Tex, 35-62; partner, Wallace and Korth, 48-51; exec. v.pres, Continental Nat. Bank, Ft. Worth, 53-59, pres, 59-61; treas, Ft. Worth Air Terminal Corp, 53-60; mem. bd. dirs, Panama Canal Co, 61-64; Lawyer, Korth and Korth, Wash, D.C. 64-; mem. bd. dirs, Fischbach & Moore, Am. Air Filter Co. and Southwest Nat. Bank, El Paso, Tex. Mil. Serv: Lt. Col, Air Transport Command, Army, 42-46. Mem: Tex. Atomic Energy Cmn; pres, United Fund, Ft. Worth, Tarrant Co, 57-58; dir, Tex. and Southwest. Expos. and Fat Stock Show, Ft. Worth, 53-63, treas, 60-61; Am. and Tex. Bar Asns; Am. Law Inst; Am. Judicature Soc; Am. and Tex. Bankers Asns; Nat. Planning Asn.(mem. nat. coun); Tex. and Southwest. Cattleraiser's Asn.(treas); Ft. Worth, Army-Navy, Int. and Georgetown Clubs. Exceptional Civilian Serv. Award, Dept. of Army, 53. Mailing Add: Barr Bldg, Farragut Square, Washington, D.C. 20006.

KORUNA, STEVEN D
b. Chicago, Ill, 2/21/12; s. Stephan Koruna and Anna Benda K; m. 9/18/37 to Alice Anne Marsik; c. Alice Joy (Mrs. Reinertson) and Stephen John. Educ: Chicago Bus. Col, grad. Polit. & Govt. Pos: Dem. precinct committeeman, 15th Precinct, Du Page Co, 54-69; mem, exec. cmt, Du Page Co. Dem. Party, 60-69; inheritance tax inspector, Ill. State Treasury Dept, 62-64; inspector, Ill. State Athletic Cmn, 64-66; chmn, Downers Grove Twp. Dem. Party, 66-; mutual clerk, Ill. Racing Cmn, 67 & 68; village trustee, Westmont, 69- Bus. & Prof. Pos: Truck driver, E.A. Keller, La Grange, Ill, 51-69. Rel: Lutheran. Mailing Add: 420 N. Wilmette Ave, Westmont, Ill. 60559.

KORY, DELORES NEVADA R
Mem, Rep. State Cent. Cmt, Mich.
b. Chicago, Ill, 3/30/28; d. Ernest Raymond Olsen and Genevieve Goldman O; m. 3/30/52 to Don E. Kory; c. Deanna and Donna. Educ: Univ. Mich, B.A, 50; Wayne State Univ, currently; Pi Sigma Alpha. Polit. & Govt. Pos: V.chmn, 19th Dist. Rep. Party, Mich, 64-66; chmn, 19th Dist. Rep. Party Wayne Co, 66-68; del, Rep. Nat. Conv, 68; mem, Rep. State Cent. Cmt, 19th Cong. Dist, 69- Mailing Add: 25721 Deborah, Detroit, Mich. 48239.

KOSAKOWSKI, CHESTER G. D
b. Baltimore, Md, 7/6/15; married. Educ: Univ. of Md. Sch. of Pharm, 37. Polit. & Gov. Pos: Md. State Del, 39-51, 59-67. Mailing Add: 635 S. Lakewood Ave, Baltimore, Md. 21224. (1967)

KOSCO, JOHN C. R
Chmn, Elk Co. Rep. Cmt, Pa.
b. Dubois, Pa, 9/20/32; s. Joseph B. Kosco and Julia Reagle K; m. 6/16/56 to Mary Mullaney; c. Thomas, Ellen, Mary Patricia, Maurus and Anne. Educ: Univ. of Notre Dame, B.S, 54; Princeton Univ, M.S, 56; Pa. State Univ, Ph.D, 58; Sigma Xi; ASM. Polit. & Govt. Pos: Borough chmn, St. Marys Rep. Party, Pa, 62-64; chmn, Elk Co. Rep. Cmt, 64- Bus. & Prof. Pos: Research metallurgist, Stackpole Carbon Co, 58-65, dir. metallurgical research, 65-66, chief engr, 66- Publ: 'Detergency During Infiltration in Powder Metal,' 15th

Annual Metal Powder Indust. Fedn. Meeting, N.Y, 59; 'Development of Composites by Liquid Phase Techniques,' Am. Soc. for Metals, 65; 'Contact Materials,' Electrotechnology, 66. Mem: Am. Soc. for Metals; Am. Chem. Soc; Am. Inst. of Mining & Metall. Engrs; Am. Powder Metal Inst. Rel: Roman Catholic. Legal Res: 571 Charles St, St. Marys, Pa. 15857. Mailing Add: Stackpole Carbon Co, St. Marys, Pa. 15857.

KOSEK, ERNEST R
Iowa State Sen.
b. Cedar Rapids, Iowa, 3/13/07; s. Charles K. Kosek and Anna Hradecky K; m. 6/14/33 to Vlasta V. Vondracek; c. Ann J. (Mrs. Kincaide), Karen V. (Mrs. Nelson) and Ernest George. Educ: Coe Col; Univ. Iowa, B.S. in Commercial Eng; Alpha Kappa Psi. Polit. & Govt. Pos: Mem, Linn Co. Bd. Educ. and Sch. Bd, Cedar Rapids, Iowa, 38-43; Iowa State Rep, 47-59; Iowa State Sen, 67- Bus. & Prof. Pos: Sole proprietor, Ernest Kosek & Co, 34-66; dir, Hotel Roosevelt, Iowa Bus. Investment, Iowa Fund, Inc. and Pioneer Ins. Co. Mil. Serv: Commissioned 31, Army Engrs, entered Army Air Corps as Flying Cadet, March Field, Calif; reentered as Lt, Navy, 43-46, serv. as Asst. Disbursing Officer for 3rd Naval Dist. Disbursing Off, N.Y. Mem: Bd. Dir, Nat. Ment. Health Asn; past. pres, Iowa Asn. for Ment. Health; Iowa Investment Bankers Asn. (past pres); Mason (32°); Shrine; Am. Legion; West. Bohemian Fraternal Asn; Elks; Kiwanis; Odd Fellows; I Men's Club; Sokols; Farm Bur; C. of C. Rel: Presbyterian. Legal Res: 340 27th St. Drive S.W, Cedar Rapids, Iowa 52403. Mailing Add: 501 Merchants National Bank Bldg, Cedar Rapids, Iowa 52401.

KOSLOSKE, JOHN T. R
b. Sauk Rapids, Minn, 12/19/07; s. John Kosloske, Sr. and Minnie Radomski K; m. 9/1/36 to Marcella A. Brunce. Polit. & Govt. Pos: Justice of the Peace, Sauk Rapids, Minn, 28-48; Minn. State Rep, 49-54; Mayor, Sauk Rapids, 66-67; bd. mem, Tri-County Action Programs, Inc, currently. Mem: Sauk Rapids Sportsman Club; Brotherhood Railway Carman of Am, Local 812. Minn. Amateur baseball hall of fame. Rel: Lutheran. Mailing Add: 320 N. Broadway, Sauk Rapids, Minn. 56379.

KOSLOSKY, JANIS MARVIN R
Alaska State Sen.
b. Muskogee, Okla, 7/17/09; s. Issac Koslosky and Lena Schindelman K; m. 5/12/65; c. Susan Diane, Linda Ann and Janis M, Jr. Educ: Univ. Wash, 3½ years; Sigma Alpha Mu. Polit. & Govt. Pos: City councilman, Palmer, Alaska, 54-57, Matanuska Susitna Borough chmn, 64-66; Alaska State Sen, Dist. D, 67- Bus. & Prof. Pos: Secy-treas, Koslosky's Dept. Store, Inc, Palmer, Alaska, 35-, Hub Clothing Co, Inc, Anchorage, 35-, Hub Men's Wear, Inc, Northern Lights, 35- and Koslosky's Men's Shop, Inc, Anchorage, 35- Mil. Serv: Entered as Pvt, 42, released as Sgt, 45, after serv. in Qm. Detachment, Alaska, Asiatic and Pac. Theatres, 42-45. Mem: Past Exalted Ruler, Elks; VFW; Am. Legion; 40 et 8. Mailing Add: Box I, Palmer, Alaska 99645.

KOSS, ESTHER ELIZABETH D
b. Detroit, Mich, 4/18/23; d. John Celeskey and Pauline Mudloff C; m. 7/2/43 to Harold Albert Koss; c. Harold John and Linda Ann. Polit. & Govt. Pos: Del, Precinct 212, 17th Cong. Dist, Mich, 60-, del, State and Co. Conv, 62-69, membership chmn, 63-66, treas, 64-68, mem, exec. bd, 64-, off. mgr, 66; alternate del, Dem. Nat. Conv, 64, del, 68; mem, Mich. State Cmt. for Permanent Orgn, 62-69; acct. clerk II, Wayne Co. Rd. Cmn, 67- Bus. & Prof. Pos: Asst. off. supvr, Metrop. Life Ins. Co, 41-49; acct, Redford Rambler, 58-66. Mem: Bus. & Prfnl. Women's Club (recording secy; del, State Conv, 68-69); Local 101, Am. Fedn. State Co. Munic. Employees (del, Int. Conv, 68); Wayne Co. Rd. Employees Asn; VFW Auxiliary; St. Scholastica Altar Soc. Rel: Catholic. Mailing Add: 19140 Margareta, Detroit, Mich. 48219.

KOSSOI, MILTON R
Chmn, Dighton Twp. Rep. Cmt, Mass.
b. Fall River, Mass, 11/3/15; s. Peter Kossoi and Alice Silvers K; single. Polit. & Govt. Pos: Mem, Mass. Rep. Club; chmn, Dighton Planning Bd, 57-60; dir, Fifth Bristol Representative Coun, 60-, treas, 64-; chmn, Dighton Twp. Rep. Cmt, 60-; secy, Bristol Co. Rep. Club, 64- Bus. & Prof. Pos: Orgn. sales & detail, Stanley Oil Co. Mem: Former Scoutmaster, Boy Scouts, Inst. Rep, Committeeman and Neighborhood Cmnr, at present; Moose; Elks; past pres, Dighton Lions Club; AF&AM; Middlesex Club; former clerk, Southeast. Mass. Regional Planning Dist. Rel: Jewish. Legal Res: 225 Main St, Dighton, Mass. 02715. Mailing Add: P.O. Box 1, Dighton, Mass. 02715.

KOSTEL, GEORGE JAMES D
Va. State Del.
b. Clifton Forge, Va, 10/30/27; m. to Helen Harriet Elite. Educ: Hampden-Sydney Col, B.A; Wash. and Lee Univ, LL.B, Omicron Delta Kappa; Pi Kappa Alpha. Polit. & Govt. Pos: Va. State Del, 63- Bus. & Prof. Pos: Lawyer; Dir, First Nat. Bank of Clifton Forge; First Fed. Savings & Loan Asn. of Clifton Forge. Mil. Serv: Marines, 51-53. Mem: Va. Bar Asn; Lions; Elks; Mason; Cliftondale Country Club. Rel: Episcopal. Mailing Add: 732 Palace Blvd, Clifton Forge, Va. 24422. (1967)

KOSTER, HAROLD R. R
Colo. State Rep.
b. Yonkers, N.Y, 5/14/93; s. Frederick M. Koster and Henrietta Breithack K; m. 1940 to Mary Kelso; c. F. Wallace and Frances (Mrs. Byford). Educ: Mt. Hermon Col, Eng. Polit. & Govt. Pos: Col. State Rep, Dist. 59, 67-; chmn, Housing Authority, Game and Fish and Gov. Coun. Unemployment Ins. Bus. & Prof. Pos: Ins. counsr, Camp Hale. Mil. Serv: Army, 17-19, France. Mem: State Insurors and Consumer Finance Co. of Colo; cmt. chmn, Colo. Mining Asn; Rotary (past dist. gov, Colo. Club); Elks; State and Nat. Cmt. on Sr. Citizens Prob; chmn, Boy Scouts; chmn, Salida Gold Club; comdr, Am. Legion; life mem, DAV; chmn. cmt, VFW; pres, C. of C; pres. and officer of all civic units. Rel: Episcopal. Mailing Add: P.O. Box 868, Salida, Colo. 81201.

KOSTER, RICHARD M. D
Dem. Nat. Committeeman, C.Z.
b. Brooklyn, N.Y, 3/1/34; s. Harry Koster and Lily Silverstein K; m. 7/18/59 to Otilia Tejeira; c. Ricardo and Lily. Educ: Yale Col, B.A, 55; N.Y. Univ, M.A, 62. Polit. & Govt. Pos: Del, Dem. Nat. Conv, 64 & 68; Dem. Nat. Committeeman, C.Z, 66- Bus. & Prof. Pos: Instr, Nat. Univ. Panama, 60-61; correspondant, Copley News Serv, San Diego, Calif, 64-66; assoc. dir. and lectr. Eng, Fla. State Univ, C.Z. Br, 64- Mil. Serv: Army, Counter Intel. Corps, South. Command, 56-59. Publ: Contrib, The New Republic. Legal Res: Calle 47, No. 9, Panama, Republic of Panama. Mailing Add: Box 930, Albrook, Canal Zone 09825.

KOSTOPULOS, NICK PETER D
b. Portsmouth, Va, 11/12/16; s. Peter Nicholas Kostopulos and Lilly Dufexis; m. 3/26/51 to Madeline Anagnos; c. Nicholas P, Jr. and Dianne. Educ: Woodrow Wilson High Sch, Portsmouth, Va, grad, 33. Polit. & Govt. Pos: Asst. to U.S. Sen. Estes Kefauver in Kefauver for Pres. Campaign, 52 & 56; asst. to U.S. Sen. Hubert H. Humphrey in Johnson-Humphrey Campaign, 64-65; consult, Off. of Econ. Opportunity, 65-68; asst. to Vice President Hubert H. Humphrey, 68 and Humphrey for Pres, Dem. Nat. Cmt, 68; spec. asst. to U.S. Sen. Fred R. Harris, Okla, chmn, Dem. Nat. Cmt, 69- Bus. & Prof. Pos: Owner, Monroe Restaurant, Portsmouth, Va, 41-50; registered rep, Investors Diversified Serv, Norfolk, 50-53; sole proprietor, Consolidated Investment Serv, 53- and Saxony Motel, Virginia Beach, 58- Mem: Mason; Ahepa. Rel: Greek Orthodox. Mailing Add: 2109 Atlantic Ave, Virginia Beach, Va. 23451.

KOSTRON, FRANK E. D
Mo. State Rep.
b. St. Louis, Mo, 4/6/16; m. 10/31/42 to Margaret D. Namentcavage; c. One daughter. Educ: McKinley High Sch. Polit. & Govt. Pos: Mo. State Rep, 50- Bus. & Prof. Pos: Brewery worker. Mil. Serv: Navy, 34-38, 41-45, S.Pac. Mem: VFW; Am. Legion. Rel: Protestant. Mailing Add: 2812 Texas St, St. Louis, Mo. 63118. (1967)

KOTHMANN, GLENN HAROLD D
b. San Antonio, Tex, 5/30/28; s. Wilkes John Kothmann and Lilly Mertz K. Educ: Tex. A&M, B.S, 50. Polit. & Govt. Pos: Tex. State Rep. until 67. Mil. Serv: Lt. Col, Army Res. Rel: Methodist. Mailing Add: 4610 Sea Breeze, San Antonio, Tex. 78220.

KOTTIS, JOHN GREGORY R
Chmn, Uxbridge Rep. Town Cmt, Mass.
b. Epirus, Greece, 8/9/25; s. Angelo Gregory Kottis and Mary D. Tashulas K; m. 12/30/56 to Mary George Patrinos; c. Van J, Chrys A, George B. and Carl J. Educ: Brown Univ; Boston Univ. Sch. Law; Delta Pi Phi; Brown Debating Club. Polit. & Govt. Pos: Field secy, Mass. Rep. State Cmt, 52; selectman, Uxbridge, Mass, 53-59; chmn, Uxbridge Rep. Town Cmt, currently. Mil. Serv: Entered as Pvt, Army, 43, released as Sgt, 46, after serv. in Combat Engrs; Am, European and German Theater Ribbons with 2 Battle Stars. Publ: Articles published on constitutional law in Christian econ, 63-64. Mem: Mass. and Worcester Co. Bar Asns; VFW; DAV; Am. Legion; Lions (dep. dist. gov, Mass. Dist. 33A); Eagles; Mason (32°). Rel: Greek Orthodox. Legal Res: 29 Henry St, Uxbridge, Mass. 01569. Mailing Add: 10 South Main St, Uxbridge, Mass. 01569.

KOTTLER, JOSEPH D
b. Brooklyn, N.Y, 12/29/10; m. to Florence Magezis; c. Harry, Jonathan and Debbie (Mrs. Bernard Grobman); grandchildren, Sharyn and Laurie. Educ: City Col. of N.Y, B.A, 31; Brooklyn Law Sch, LL.B, 34. Polit. & Govt. Pos: Past chmn, Local Sch. Bd, 38, NYC Bd. Educ; dir, Roosevelt Dem. Club; asst. dist. attorney, Kings Co, 56-58, dep. chief, Rackets Bur, 56-58; N.Y. State Assemblyman, 58-68. Bus. & Prof. Pos: Attorney. Mem: Dir, Zionist Dist. of Boro Park; Am. Jewish Cong; March of Dimes; chmn, Boy Scouts Finance Dr; Infants Home of Brooklyn; YMHA of Boro Park; F&AM. Rel: Jewish; Trustee, Temple Emanu -El, Boro Park. Mailing Add: 310 Beverly Rd, Brooklyn, N.Y. 11218. (1967)

KOUNS, SINCLAIR BERT D
b. Shreveport, La, 12/25/26; s. Bert Kouns and Bert Sinclair K; m. 6/17/55 to Jeri Thompson; c. Leigh Lane, Lauren Elizabeth, Sinclair B, Jr. and Merrill Thompson. Educ: La. State Univ, B.A, 51; Kappa Alpha. Polit. & Govt. Pos: Mem. police jury, Caddo Parish, La, 68; del, Dem. Nat. Conv, 68. Bus. & Prof. Pos: Pres, Kouns & Walke, Inc, Consolidated Container Co. and Scott's Fried Chicken, 69-; dir, Pioneer Bank & Trust, 69- Mil. Serv: Entered as Pvt, Army, 45, released as S/Sgt, 47, after serv. in Inf-Spec. Serv, U.S.,45-47. Mem: Shreveport Asn. of Ins. Agents; Life Underwriters; pres, Sales & Mkt. Exec; C. of C. (dir, Shreveport Chap); Shreveport Country Club; Shreveport Petroleum Club; Pierremont Oaks Tennis Club; East Ridge Country Club; pres, Shreveport Sports Found; pres, Parents League; pres, Holiday in Dixie; King of Cotillion. Young Man of the Year. Rel: Methodist; Chmn, Cmn. on Educ, First Methodist Church. Legal Res: 6112 Creswell Rd, Shreveport, La. 71106. Mailing Add: 1200 Mid South Tower, Shreveport, La. 70102.

KOVACH, ALEXANDER CHARLES D
Chmn, Chester Co. Dem. Cmt, Pa.
b. Phoenixville, Pa, 12/24/26; s. Alexander Kovach and Emma Nagy K; m. 8/7/48 to Elsie Angeline Colatosti; c. Alexander Charles, James Joseph, Carol and Jeffrey Allan. Educ: High Sch. Polit. & Govt. Pos: Councilman, Phoenixville Borough Coun, Pa, 56-, pres, 66-; chmn, Chester Co. Dem. Cmt, 64- Mem: Hungarian Club; Polish Club; Italian Club; West End Fire Co; Friendship Fire Co; Kimberton Fish and Game Asn; St. Gabriel's Lodge; recording secy, USW, Local 2322. Rel: Hungarian Reformed, United Church of Christ. Mailing Add: 976 Cherry St, Phoenixville, Pa. 19460. (1967)

KOWALSKI, FRANK D
b. Meriden, Conn, 10/18/07; s. Frank Kowalski and Mary Miller K; m. 10/20/31 to Helene Amelia Bober; c. Carol Helene (Mrs. R.F. Reidy, Jr) and Barry F. Educ: U.S. Mil. Acad, B.S, 30; Mass. Inst. Tech, M.S, 37; Columbia Univ, Int. Rels, 45-46. Polit. & Govt. Pos: U.S. Rep, Conn, 59-63; mem, Subversive Activities Control Bd, 63- Mil. Serv: Entered as Pvt, Army, 25, released as Cpl, 26; Cadet, Mil. Acad, 26-30; reentered as 2nd Lt. released as Col, Army, 30-58, after serv. in ETO, U.S. and Europe, 44-45 and Supreme Comdr. Allied Powers, Japan, 48-52, Col.(Ret), 58; Legion of Merit with Oak Leaf Cluster; Bronze Star; Commendation Ribbons; Am, European, Korean and Other Ribbons. Publ: 'Stifling Embrace of the Staff,' Army Mag, 56; 'Delegate Don't Deputize,' Army Mgt; 'GI Slaves,' Reader's Digest, 60.

Mem: Am. Mgt. Asn; Am. Legion; VFW. Have 6 U.S. Patents. Rel: Catholic. Legal Res: 65 Harvard St, New Britain, Conn. 06051. Mailing Add: 7204 Regent Dr, Alexandria, Va. 22307.

KOWALYSHYN, RUSSELL D
Pa. State Rep.
b. Northampton, Pa, 9/16/18; s. Steven Kowalyshyn and Anna Kuzyk K. Educ: Leigh Univ, B.A; Columbia Univ, M.A; Dickinson Sch. of Law, LL.B; Phi Beta Kappa. Polit. & Govt. Pos: Asst. district attorney, Northampton Co, Pa, 56-63; mem, Northampton Area Sch. Bd, 60-65; solicitor, Moore Twp, Northampton Borough; Pa. State Rep, 64- Bus. & Prof. Pos: Lawyer. Mil. Serv: Entered Army, 42, released as Capt, 46. Mem: Northampton Co. and Am. Bar Asns. Admitted to practice before, Pa. Supreme and Superior Courts. Rel: Catholic. Mailing Add: 1929 Lauback Ave, Northampton, Pa. 18067. (1967)

KRABACH, RICHARD LOWELL R
Dir. of Finance, State of Ohio
b. Wapakoneta, Ohio, 5/25/13; s. Joseph A. Krabach and Eleanor C. Tebben K; m. 9/10/40 to Henrietta Pete; c. Joseph A, II, Kathryn Ann and Constance. Educ: Xavier Univ, B.S.C; Ohio North. Univ, LL.B; Phi Alpha Delta. Polit. & Govt. Pos: Chmn, Allen Co. Rep. Orgn, Ohio, 50-56; mem, Ohio Rep. Cent. and Exec. Cmt, 54-46; U.S. Comptroller, V.I, 55-58; chmn. bd. rev, Bur. Unemploy. Compensation, Ohio, 58-64; dir. finance, Ohio, 63-; del-at-lg, Rep. Nat. Conv, 64, alternate del, 68; city mgr, Cincinnati, Ohio, 69- Bus. & Prof. Pos: Supvr. of Budgets, Westinghouse, Lima, Ohio, 42-47; attorney, Lima, Ohio, 47- Mem: Am. and Ohio State Bar Asns; past pres, United Fund, Commun. Chest and Jr. C. of C. Rel: Catholic. Legal Res: 417 S. Kenilworth, Lima, Ohio 45805. Mailing Add: City Hall, 1800 Central Ave, Cincinnati, Ohio 45202. (1967)

KRABBE, LOUIS AUGUST D
Committeeman, Ill. Dem. Cent. Cmt.
b. Thornton, Ill, 10/22/93; s. Charles John Krabbe and Mary Wendte K; wid; c. Wayne and Avanelle (Mrs. Spitz). Educ: High sch, 1 year; Union Christian Col, Merom, Ind, grad, Bus. Course. Polit. & Govt. Pos: Chmn, Effingham Co. Dem. Party, Ill, 33-54; Dem. precinct committeeman, Bishop Twp, 33-67, Dem. supvr, 43-67; mem, Co. Bd. of Rev, 65-; committeeman, Ill. Dem. Cent. Cmt, 66- Bus. & Prof. Pos: Owner and operator of gen. store, Dieterich, Ill, 16-59. Mem: Twp. chmn, Red Cross and Salvation Army; solicitor, Cancer Drive and Hosp. Bldg. Fund; Elks, Effingham, Ill. Rel: Lutheran. Mailing Add: Park and Section St, Dieterich, Ill. 62424.

KRADEL, JOHN F. D
b. 12/8/31; s. Joseph C. Kradel and Sarah F. Goodhart K; m. to Nancy Park; c. six. Educ: Univ. of Pittsburgh, B.A; Dickinson Sch. of Law, LL.B; Sarah Mellon Scaife scholarship; Pitcairn-Crabbe Christian Educ. scholarship. Polit. & Govt. Pos: Mem. exec. cmt, Westmoreland Co. Young Dem; mem, Seward Borough Coun, Ligonier Valley Sch. Dist; mem, Bd. of Fairfield Twp. Supvr; solicitor, Ligonier Twp. Bd. Supvrs; Pa. State Rep, 64-67. Bus. Prof. Pos: Attorney. Mil. Serv: Korean Mil. Adv. Group, 53-55, Capt, Army Res. Mem: Westmoreland Co. Bar Asn; Pa. Supreme and Superior Courts; U.S. Dist. Court. Legal Res: 416 N. St. Clair St, Ligonier, Pa. 15658. Mailing Add: 209 E. Main St, Ligonier, Pa. 15658.

KRAEMER, JAMES S. R
Pres, Calif. Rep. Assembly
b. San Francisco, Calif, 2/8/19; s. Sanford J. Kraemer (deceased) and Cora Saroni K; m. 12/11/41 to Helen Bjork; c. James Sanford, Allan Lage and Susan Jean. Educ: San Francisco Jr. Col, A.A, 38; Univ. Calif. Exten, Cert. in Real Estate, 48. Polit. & Govt. Pos: Mem. fund raising cmt, Goldwater for Pres. Campaign, 63-64; pres, Oakland Rep. Assembly, 64 & 69; dir. Seventh Cong. Dist, Calif. Rep. Assembly, 65-67, v.pres, 67-68, pres, 69-; mem. finance cmt, Alameda Co. Reagan Campaign, 66; registrn. chmn, Don Mulford Campaign, 66-68; registrn. chmn, 16th Assembly Dist. Rep. Party, 66-68; mem, Calif. Rep. State Cent. Cmt, 66-69; v.pres, Alameda Co. Coord. Rep. Assembly, 67; treas, Lincoln Club of Alameda Co, 67-69; Alameda Co. chmn, Rafferty for U.S. Senate Campaign, 68. Bus. & Prof. Pos: Realtor and ins. broker; partner, Kraemer & Kraemer, currently. Mil. Serv: Entered as Pvt, Army Air Force, 42, released as T/Sgt, 46, after serv. in Army Airways Commun. Syst, ETO, 44-46. Mem: Real Estate Cert. Inst; Oakland Real Estate Bd; Calif. Real Estate Asn; Nat. Asn. Real Estate Brokers; F&AM; Scottish Rite; Shrine; Oakland High Twelve Club (past pres); Piedmont High Sch. Dad's Club (past pres); Boy Scouts (exec. bd, Piedmont Coun); exec. bd, Goodwill Industs, Inc. Rel: Protestant; Trustee and mem. bd, Piedmont Commun. Church. Legal Res: 124 Nova Dr, Piedmont, Calif. 94610. Mailing Add: 2914 Telegraph Ave, Oakland, Calif. 94609.

KRAF, HARRY D
N.Y. State Assemblyman
b. New York, N.Y; m. to Lee Rosenfeld; c. Elaine and Michael. Educ: Fordham Law Sch, LL.B. Polit. & Govt. Pos: Supvr, Local Cong. Dist. Census, 40; former v.pres, Monroe Dem. Club; former N.Y. State Sen; N.Y. State Assemblyman, 69- Bus. & Prof. Pos: Lawyer. Mil. Serv: Mem, Local Draft Bd. 75, World War II; Cong. Serv. Medal. Mem: Bronx Co. Bar Asn; Jewish Center of Univ. Heights; Nat. Conf. of Jews and Christians; Tau Epsilon Phi; Mid-Bronx Commun. Coun; secy, W. Bronx Jewish Commun. Coun; Bronx Lodge, Elks; dir, Bronx Div, Hebrew Home for the Aged; dir, Claremont Center, Inc; Urban League; B'nai B'rith; dir, Bronx Ment. Health Soc. Rel: Jewish; trustee, Congregational Hope of Israel. Mailing Add: 711 Walton Ave, Bronx, N.Y. 10451. (1967)

KRAFT, RALPH GLENN R
b. Chicago, Ill, 4/1/27; s. Alvin Adolph Kraft and Rosa Kubat K; m. 6/17/50 to Virginia Ann Roberts; c. Deborah Ann, Barbara Jean, Richard Ralph, Carol Joan and Heather Rose. Educ: Univ. Ill, B.S. in Eng, 49, M.S. in Eng, 53; Tau Beta Pi; Sigma Tau; Keramos; Student Br, Am. Ceramic Soc. Polit. & Govt. Pos: Zone leader, Rep. Party, Wis, 58-60; v.chmn, Bayside Rep. Club, 60-62; chmn, North Shore Rep. Club, 62-64; chmn, Ninth Cong. Dist. Rep. Party, 65-69; alternate del, Rep. Nat. Conv, 68. Bus. & Prof. Pos: Ceramic engr, Argonne Nat. Lab, 50-53; develop. engr, Allen-Bradley Co, 53-55, proj. engr. and dept. head, 55- Mil. Serv: Entered as Pvt, Army, 45, released as S/Sgt, 47, after serv. in ETO; Victory Medal; Occupation Medal. Mem: Lions; Am. Ceramic Soc; Univ. of Ill. Alumni Asn. Rel: Methodist. Mailing Add: 458 W. Ellsworth Lane, Milwaukee, Wis. 53217. (1967)

KRAMER, A. LUDLOW, III R
Secy. of State, Wash.
b. New York, N.Y, 6/10/32; s. A. Ludlow Kramer, II and Mary Delafield Bowes K; m. 10/16/55 to Patricia Ann Klos; c. Mary Delafield, William Ludlow, Ann Livingston and John Leighton. Educ: Univ. Md. Overseas; Am. Inst. Banking. Polit. & Govt. Pos: City councilman, Seattle, Wash, 62-64; Secy. of State, Wash, 65-; chmn, Gov. Adv. Coun. on Urban Affairs and Cmn. on Causes and Prev. of Civil Disorder, currently; del, Rep. Nat. Conv, 68. Bus. & Prof. Pos: With investment off, Seattle Trust and Savings, Wash, 55-61; acting dir. of Spec. Events, Seattle Worlds Fair, 62. Mil. Serv: Entered as Pvt, Air Force, 52, released as Sgt, 55, after serv. in 440th Fighter Interceptor Squadron, Europe-Africa. Mem: Lions Int; Elks; Jaycees; Bd. Dirs, Olympia Campfire Girls; Adv. Bd, St. Peter Hosp, Olympia. Selected one of nations outstanding young men of 1964, U.S. Jaycees; one of 3 outstanding young men, 1965, Wash. State Jaycees. Rel: Episcopal. Legal Res: Seattle, Wash. Mailing Add: Legislative Building, Olympia, Wash. 98501.

KRAMER, ALBERT A. D
Mich. State Rep.
b. Mt. Clemens, 10/15/23; m. 1952 to Sedell Ilene Gould; c. Maxine Fran, Matthew Loren, Rhonda Ann. Educ: Wayne State Univ, LL.B, 49. Polit. & Govt. Pos: Chmn, Oakland Co. Div. Jefferson-Jackson Day Dinner, 61; del, Dem. State Conv, 61-64; Dem. nominee for Mich. State Rep, 62; former mem, Oakland Co. Dem. Exec. Cmt. and 18th Cong. Dist. Dem. Exec. Cmt; Mich. State Rep, 64- Bus. & Prof. Pos: Attorney-at-law. Mil. Serv: Army, World War II. Mem: Sustaining mem, Boy Scouts; Oakland Co. Citizens League; Wayne State Univ. Alumni Asn; Workmen's Compensation Sect, State Bar Mich; various fraternal and veteran's orgn. Rel: Jewish. Mailing Add: 23651 Radclift, Oak Park, Mich. 48237. (1967)

KRAMER, EDWARD G. Independent
Married; c. seven. Educ: Univ. Minn. Sch. of Agr. Polit. & Govt. Pos: Clerk, Quincy Town Bd, Minn, 9 years. Bus. & Prof. Pos: Farmer. Mem: Secy, Olmstead Co. Twp. Officers Asn; Nat. Farmers Orgn.(state secy); First Dist. Nat. Farmers Orgn (pres); Moose; Whitewater Valley Sportsman's Club; Minn. Farm Mgrs. Asn; Minn. Crop Improv. Asn; Minn. and Am. Soybean Asns. Outstanding Young Farmer, St. Charles Jaycees, 61 and Rochester Jaycees, 69; second runner-up in State Outstanding Young Farmer Competition, 69. Rel: Catholic. Mailing Add: R.R. 3, Box 35, St. Charles, Minn. 55972.

KRAMER, SIDNEY S. R
Ind. State Sen.
b. New York, 2/29/12; s. J.H. Kramer and Jennie K; m. 2/10/35 to Tresa; c. Larry Richard, Linda Sue and Pamela Kay. Educ: Evansville Col; Sigma Alpha Mu. Polit. & Govt. Pos: Chmn, Eighth Cong. Dist. Gov. Youth Coun, 58 & 69; del, Ind. Rep. State Conv, 60, mem. platform cmt, 67; precinct v.committeeman, 66; Ind. State Sen, 67- Bus. & Prof. Pos: Pres, Sidney's Uniform Co, currently. Mem: Hon. mem. branch 377 N.A.L.C; finance chmn, Civil Defense, 62; chmn. clothing div, Red Cross Disaster Cmt, 63-69; pres, Commun. Coun, 63-65; v.chmn, Regional Ment. Health, 64-67; Elks; Optimist; C. of C; Dads Club; YMCA; Key Mens Christian Orgn; Humane Soc. Citizen of Month Award, Evansville Future Orgn; Honor Citation, Dale Carnegie Asn; Legis. Award, Citizens for Educ. Freedom, 67; Citizen of Week Award, WJPS, 68. Legal Res: 1424 Brookside Dr, Evansville, Ind. 47714. Mailing Add: 200 Main St, Evansville, Ind. 47708.

KRAMPE, BERNARD J. D
Polit. & Govt. Pos: Ind. State Sen, 62-66; precinct committeeman, 58-62; pres, 8th Dist. Young Dems, 59-61; DuBois Co. Young Dems, 57-59. Bus. & Prof. Pos: Gen. mgr, Educ. Inst. Mil. Serv: Army Air Force. Mem: Ferdinand Jaycees; K. of C; Wabash Valley Asn; assoc. mem, Fraternal Order of Police. Rel: Catholic. Mailing Add: Ferdinand, Ind. 47532. (1967)

KRANZLER, RICHARD MARTIN D
Mem, Colo. State Dem. Cent. Cmt.
b. Farmingdale, N.Y, 3/5/31; s. Charles Kranzler and Eva Pines K; m. 4/29/56 to Dorothy Ruth Finger; c. David Ian, Jean Ann and Susan Jane. Educ: Hofstra Univ, B.S, 54; Denver Univ. Col. Law, LL.B, 58; Delta Tau; Phi Delta Phi. Polit. & Govt. Pos: Dist. capt, Jefferson Co. Dem. Party, 62-69; mem. exec. cmt, Arvada Dem. Club, 67-; chmn, Jefferson Co. Citizens for Humphrey, 68; mem, Colo. State Dem. Cent. Cmt, 69- Bus. & Prof. Pos: Attorney, 58-64; partner-attorney, Brenman, Ciancio, Rossman & Baum, 64- Mil. Serv: Entered as Pvt, Army, Released as Sp 4, 56, after serv. in sch. Troops. Mem: Colo, Denver and Adams Co. Bar Asns; Am. and Colo. Trial Lawyers Asns; Am. Arbit. Asn; Am. Jewish Cmt. Rel: Jewish. Mailing Add: 4095 Dudley St, Wheatridge, Colo. 80033.

KRASNOW, MILDRED D
b. Yonkers, N.Y, 4/15/15; d. Louis Hillel Blumberg and Henrietta Paseltiner B; m. 5/26/40 to George Kransow; c. John Lee. Educ: Columbia Univ. Sch. of Bus, B.S, Teachers Col, M.A. Polit. & Govt. Pos: Pres, Dem. Club of Closter and munic. chmn, Closter Dem. Cmt, N.J, 58-60 & 63-64; pres, Dem. Women of Bergen Co, 59-64; v.chmn, Nominating Cmt, Bergen Co. Dem. Cmt, 59, chmn, 63-65, asst. v.chmn, Bergen Co. Dem. Cmt, 65-66; del, Dem. Nat. Conv, 64; cmnr, Legalized Games of Chance Control Cmn, N.J, 66-; mem. prfnl. adv. cmt, Bergen Co. Health & Welfare Coun. Bus. & Prof. Pos: Copewriter and time-buyer for radio and asst. to dir, United Serv. Orgn, formerly; exec. adminstr. and pub. rels. consult, Harold G. Jaffer & Co, 45-48; pub. rels. consult, Mildred Kransow and Assocs, 58-; exec. dir, Bergen Co. Center on Aging, 66- Mem: Nat. Coun. on the Aging; Geront. Soc; N.J. Adult Educ. Asn; N.J. Pub. Health Asn; bd. dirs, Closter Nature Center; League of Women Voters; Am. Asn. of Univ. Women; Women's Auxiliary, Pascack Valley Hosp; Dem. Women of Bergen Co. Woman of Achievement Award, Bus. and Prfnl. Women's Club, 68. Rel: Hebrew. Mailing Add: 761 Old Closter Dock Rd, Closter, N.J. 07624.

KRAUS, ELMER J. R
Chmn, Hancock Co. Rep. Cent. Cmt, Ill.
b. Nauvoo, Ill, 11/26/17; s. John A. Kraus and Minnie M. Bruegger K; m. 4/20/40 to Adeline Dorothy Kaiser; c. Daniel, Cathy, David, Jon and Deborah. Educ: Local schs. Polit. & Govt. Pos: Mem, Tourism Adv. Cmn, Dept. of Bus. & Econ. Develop, State of Ill, 65-, mem, Gov. Adv. Coun, 69; Rep. precinct committeeman, 66; chmn, Hancock Co. Regional Planning Cmn, 66-; chmn, Hancock Co. Rep. Cent. Cmt, 68- Mem: Ill. Hotel and Motel Asn.(pres, 64-65, chmn. bd, 65-); Elks; K. of C. Rel: Catholic. Mailing Add: Nauvoo, Ill. 62354.

KRAUS, WILLIAM McCULLOCH R
b. Marshfield, Wis, 3/5/26; s. Melvin Hugo Kraus and Lynette McCulloch K; m. 12/20/47 to Edith Davidson; c. Nancy, Sally and Marcia. Educ: Univ. Minn, B.S, 46; Univ. Wis, LL.B, 49; Phi Delta Phi. Polit. & Govt. Pos: Dist. chmn, Knowles in 64 Cmt; state chmn, Knowles for Gov. Cmt, 66 & 68; mem, Rep. Statutory Cmt, 66-; state v.chmn, Wis. Nixon for Pres. Cmt, 67-68 and Leonard for Sen. Cmt, 68; alternate del, Rep. Nat. Conv, 68. Bus. & Prof. Pos: Various pos, Sentry Ins, Stevens Point, Wis, 49-63, pres, 63- Mil. Serv: Entered as A/S, Navy, 44, released as Ens, 46, after serv. in several V-12 progs. and some minor sea duty, 44-46. Rel: Presbyterian. Mailing Add: 321 Sunrise Ave, Stevens Point, Wis. 54481.

KRAUTKRAMER, RAY GEORGE D
Chmn, Calumet Co. Dem. Party, Wis.
b. Marathon, Wis, 8/29/08; s. Frank Krautkramer and Mary Clare K; m. 10/7/40 to Margaret Schnitzer. Educ: Marathon High Sch, grad. Polit. & Govt. Pos: Chmn, Calumet Co. Dem. Party, Wis, 68- Bus. & Prof. Pos: Salesman, Elm Tree Bakery, 31-41; owner, Gen. Store, 41- Mem: K. of C; C. of C. Rel: Catholic. Mailing Add: 215 Eighth St, Hilbert, Wis. 54129.

KRAWCHECK, LEONARD D
S.C. State Rep.
b. Charleston, S.C, 1/20/41; s. Jack Krawcheck and Esther Bielsky K; m. 6/8/62 to Towning Tyler; c. Kenneth Charles, Sallie Lee, Jonathan Tyler and Elizabeth Towning. Educ: Duke Univ, 58-60; Col. of Charleston, B.S, 62; Tulane Univ. Sch. Law, LL.B, 65. Polit. & Govt. Pos: S.C. State Rep, 66- Mem: Elks; Alumni exec. cmt, Col. of Charleston; chmn, Charleston Co. Muscular Dystrophy Drive, 66. Legal Res: 3 Colonial St, Charleston, S.C. 29402. Mailing Add: P.O. Drawer 1018, Charleston, S.C. 29402.

KREAMER, ROBERT McDONALD R
Iowa State Rep.
b. Sioux City, Iowa, 1/5/41; s. Floyd W. Kreamer and Helen E. McDonald K; m. 12/20/64 to Charlotte Anne Hooker; c. Todd Allan. Educ: Univ. Iowa, B.A, 63; Univ. Iowa Law Sch, J.D, 66; Phi Kappa Psi; Phi Delta Phi. Polit. & Govt. Pos: Iowa State Rep, 69- Bus. & Prof. Pos: Attorney, Gamble, Reipe, Martin & Webster, Des Moines, Iowa, 66-69; trust officer, First Fed. State Bank, 69- Mem: Polk Co, Iowa State and Am. Bar Asns; YMCA; Big Bros. Am; Young Rep. of Iowa; Westminister United Presby. Church Men's Club. Rel: Presbyterian. Mailing Add: 4705 Beavercrest Dr, Des Moines, Iowa 50310.

KREBS, PAUL J. D
b. N.Y.C, 1/26/12; m. to Peggy Thompson. Educ: High sch. Polit. & Govt. Pos: U.S.Rep, N.J, 64-69; mem, Exec. Cmt. Essex Co. Dem. Cmt. Bus. & Prof. Pos: Shop steward, secy, dir. Polit. Action Regional Area 9, UAW. Mailing Add: 156 W. Hobart Gap Rd, Livingston, N.J. 07039. (1967)

KRECHEVSKY, ROBERT LEON D
Councilman, West Hartford Town Coun, Conn.
b. Hartford, Conn, 8/11/22; s. Morris Krechevsky and Anna Levine K; m. 10/16/55 to Phyllis Joan Swirin; c. Curtis, Mara, Hallie and Kira. Educ: Yale Univ, B.A, 43; Univ. Conn. Sch. of Law, LL.B, 48. Polit. & Govt. Pos: Councilman, West Hartford Town Coun, Conn, 61-; dep. mayor, West Hartford, 67- Bus. & Prof. Pos: Lectr. in Law, Univ. Conn. Sch. of Law, 55-; partner, Gould, Killian & Krechevsky, Hartford, Conn, currently. Mil. Serv: Entered as Pvt, Air Force, 43, released as Sgt, 46. Mem: Am, Conn. State and Hartford Co. Bar Asns. Rel: Jewish. Mailing Add: 22 Highwood Rd, West Hartford, Conn. 06117.

KREEGER, GEORGE H. D
Ga. State Rep.
b. Atlanta, Ga, 7/6/41; s. George W. Kreeger; single. Educ: Univ. of Ga, B.S. Ed, 63 and J.D, 66; Sigma Pi; Phi Delta Phi. Polit. & Govt. Pos: Ga. State Rep, 69- Bus. & Prof. Pos: Partner, Law Firm, Tate & Kreeger, Marietta, Ga. Mil. Serv: S/Sgt, Ga. Air Nat. Guard. Mem: Optimist Int; Jaycees; Am. Legion. Rel: Methodist. Mailing Add: 1281 Love St, Smyrna, Ga. 30080.

KREIN, REINHOLD D
b. Leola, S.Dak, 1/15/12; s. Eward Krein and Paulina Martel K; m. 11/29/32 to Florence Margarette Galster; c. Larry E, Lilas (Mrs. Duane Skoglund) and Harlan R. Polit. & Govt. Pos: Co. cmnr, McPherson Co, S.Dak, 52-68; chmn, McPherson Co. Dem. Party, 58-68. Mem: Mason; Scottish Rite; Shrine; Eastern Star. Rel: Methodist. Mailing Add: Leola, S.Dak. 57456.

KREMER, MAURICE A. R
Nebr. State Sen.
b. Milford, Nebr, 8/31/07; m. 5/12/32 to Alice M. Troyer; c. Kenneth D, Robert M, Ardys Ann (Mrs. Rozhart), Beth Lorraine. Educ: Farm Operators Col. of Agr, Lincoln, Nebr. Polit. & Govt. Pos: Nebr. State Sen, 62-; mem. and pres, Aurora Sch. Bd; Hamilton Co. Exten. Bd; chmn, Hamilton Co. Irrigation Bd. Bus. & Prof. Pos: Farmer; partner, Farmade Inc, Aurora, Nebr. Mem: Chaplain, Gideons; bd. of dir, State Dairymen's Asn; Aurora C. of C; state pres, Gideons Int. Mailing Add: 1415 Seventh St, Aurora, Nebr. 68818. (1967)

KRENIK, GEORGE B. Conservative
Minn. State Rep.
b. LeSuer Co, Minn, 4/23/09; married; c. Three. Educ: Pub. Schs. Polit. & Govt. Pos: Mem, Cordova Town Bd, Minn, 43-58; Minn. State Rep, 58- Bus. & Prof. Pos: Farmer. Mem: Prod. and Mkt. Admin. and Agr. Stabilization Conserv. Cmt. Mailing Add: Route 2, LeCenter, Minn. 56057.

KRENIK, LAURIS D. R
V.chmn, Second Cong. Dist. Rep. Cmt, Minn.
b. Madison Lake, Minn, 5/13/32; s. Delford L. Krenik and Adeline Fahning K; m. 6/26/54 to Nancy Helen Hanson; c. Kristine, Karla and Michael. Educ: Univ. Minn, B.S; Farm House. Polit. & Govt. Pos: Chmn, Le Seur Co. Rep. Cmt, Minn, 63-67; mem, Rep. State Cent. Cmt, 63-67; mem, Second Cong. Dist. Rep. Cmt, 63-, v.chmn, 67- Bus. & Prof. Pos: Mem. bd. dirs, Immanuel-St. Joseph's Hosp, Mankato, Minn, 69- Mil. Serv: Entered as 2nd Lt, Air Force, 54, released as 1st Lt, 57, after serv. in 58th Fighter Interceptor Squadron, Air Defense Command; Capt, Air Force Res. Mem: Farm Bur.(pres, Le Seur Co. Chap, 60-62); Farm Serv. Coop.(v.pres); Minn. Valley Agr-Bus. Asn. Outstanding Young Farmer, Jaycees, 64. Rel: Lutheran; Mem, Church Coun. Mailing Add: R.R. 1, Madison Lake, Minn. 56063.

KREPS, LESLIE RAY D
b. Powell, Wyo, 10/9/24; s. Ray R. Kreps and Mae Folsom K; m. 3/26/46 to Betty Sheehan; c. Katherine, Barbara and David. Educ: Nebr. Wesleyan Univ, B.A, 47; Harvard Univ, A.M, 49; Northwest. Univ, Ph.D, 57; Pi Kappa Delta; Pi Gamma Mu; Phi Kappa Tau. Polit. & Govt. Pos: Admin. Asst, U.S. Sen. Fred R. Harris, Okla, 66-69; staff dir, Subcmt. on Govt. Research, Sen. Govt. Opers. Cmt, 69- Bus. & Prof. Pos: Educ. missionary, Methodist Bd. of Missions, Tokyo, Japan, 50-55; prof. and head, speech dept, Okla. State Univ, 57-66. Mil. Serv: Entered as A/S, Navy, 43, released as Ens, 46, after serv. in Naval Lang. Sch, Stillwater, Okla; resigned as Lt.(jg), Naval Res, 64. Publ: 'The Image of Japan in the Speaking of U.S. Congressmen,' Doctoral Dissertation, 57; 'A Forensic Program for Land Grant Institutions,' The Forensic, 60. Mem: Speech Asn. of Am; Cent. States Speech Asn; Okla. Speech Asn. Rel: Methodist. Legal Res: Stillwater, Okla. 74074. Mailing Add: 1812 Great Falls St, McLean, Va. 22101.

KRET, DAVID B. R
Ariz. State Sen.
b. Philadelphia, Pa, 6/8/27; s. Maxwell Kret and Esther Rosenblatt K; m. 6/28/53 to Estelle S.Schwartz; c. Dorothy, Martin, Steven, Deborah, Bernard and Carol. Educ: Mass. Inst. Tech, B.S, 50; Newark Col. of Eng, M.S, 54; N.Y. Univ. spec. engr. courses; Alexander Hamilton Inst, correspondence courses; Mass. Inst. Tech, Intercollegiate Debate Team. Polit. & Govt. Pos: Mem, Maricopa Co. Rep. Cent. Cmt. and Ariz. State Rep. Cent. Cmt, 60-; precinct committeeman, Rep. Party, 60-; Ariz. State Rep, 61-66; Ariz. State Sen, 66- Bus. & Prof. Pos: Asst. prof. elec. eng, Pa. Mil. Col, 51-52; develop. engr, A.B. Dumont Labs, 52-54; standards engr, Radio Corp. Am, 54-57; mgr, product planning, Motorola, 57-61, consult. engr, 61-64, staff engr. and prin. integrated circuit engr, 64- Mil. Serv: Entered as Seaman, Navy, 44, released as Radio Technician, 46, after serv. on Destroyer Escorts. Publ: Tranducers—A Compilation, A.B. DuMont, 53; 'Integrated Circuit Eng' I.C.E, 65. Mem: Inst. Elec. and Electronics Eng; trustee, Elks 2148, Scottsdale, Ariz. Registered Prfnl Engr, State of Ariz. Rel: Jewish. Mailing Add: 2420 N. 73rd St, Scottsdale, Ariz. 85257.

KRETSCHMAR, BRUCE E. R
b. Venturia, N.Dak, 12/26/16; s. Otto B. Kretschmar and Florence Wiedmann K; m. 2/14/47 to Helen A. Zidzik; c. Susan Ann, Marian, John W. and David B. Educ: Univ. N.Dak; Univ. Wash, LL.B. Polit. & Govt. Pos: States attorney, McIntosh Co, N.Dak, 47-; precinct committeeman, Rep. Party, currently, former co. chmn; former committeeman, N.Dak. State Rep. Cent. Cmt. Mil. Serv: Entered as Yeoman 3/C, Navy, 42, released as Lt.(jg), 46, after serv. in Amphibious Forces, Pac, 46; South Pac. Campaign Ribbons. Mem: Pres, Third Judicial Bar Asn; exec. cmt, N.Dak. Bar Asn; N.Dak. Centennial Cmn, Greater N.Dak. Asn, 61; zone chmn, Dist. 5 N.E. and past pres, Lions; Am. Legion; C. of C. Rel: Lutheran. Mailing Add: P.O. Box 36, Ashley, N.Dak. 58413.

KRETCHMER, JEROME D
N.Y. State Assemblyman
b. Bronx, N.Y, 9/15/34; s. Charles Kretchmer and Mollie Denerstein K; m. 1/30/60 to Dorothy Steinfeld; c. Stephanie Lisa, Andrea Gail and Laurence Adam. Educ: N.Y. Univ, B.A, 55; Columbia Law Sch, LL.B, 58; Perstare et Praestare, N.Y. Univ. Polit. & Govt. Pos: Leader, 68th Assembly Dist. Dem. Party, N.Y, 61-62; N.Y. State Assemblyman, 65th Dist, 63- Bus. & Prof. Pos: Attorney and partner, Olshan, Grundman, Frome and Kretchmer, currently. Mem: N.Y. State Bar Asn; Ansonia Independent Dem; Am. Civil Liberties Union; Lincoln Sq. Commun. Coun; NAACP; Am. for Dem. Action; Columbia Law Sch. Alumni Asn; N.Y. Univ. Alumni Asn. Rel: Jewish. Legal Res: 28 W. 69th St, New York, N.Y. 10023. Mailing Add: 90 Park Ave, New York, N.Y. 10016.

KRIEGER, HAROLD G. R
Minn. State Sen.
b. New Ulm, Minn, 10/3/26; s. Henry F. Krieger and Hertha Radke K; m. 12/22/50 to M. Pauline Mattson; c. Scott, Lisa, Harold and Jean. Educ: Macalester Col, B.A. summa cum laude, 50; St. Paul Col. Law, LL.B, 55; Delta Theta Phi; Pi Kappa Delta. Polit. & Govt. Pos: Finance chmn, Olmsted Co. Rep. Party, Minn, 61-62; Minn. State Sen, Fourth Legis. Dist, 62- Mil. Serv: Entered as S 2/C, Navy, 44, released as PO 3/C, 46, after serv. in U.S.S. Maloy, Atlantic Theater. Mem: Am. and Minn. State Bar Asns; Am. Trial Lawyers Asn; Elks; Mason; Am. Legion; Sertoma; state bd, Minn. Soc. Crippled Children & Adults; Gamehaven Coun, Boy Scouts. Rel: Presbyterian; bd. trustees, First Presbyterian Church. Mailing Add: 811 Seventh Ave. S.W, Rochester, Minn. 55901.

KRIEGER, HARVEY S. D
b. Erie, Pa, 6/16/29; s. Harry Krieger and Bertha Adelman K; m. 7/12/53 to Betty Barbara Gordon; c. Mellanie Beth, Glen Ross, Dean Andrew and Lisa Robin. Educ: Univ. Calif, Los Angeles, A.B. in polit. sci, 50; Harvard Law Sch, LL.B, 53; Phi Sigma Delta. Polit. & Govt. Pos: Councilman, West Covina, Calif, 64-, v.mayor, 65-66, mayor until 68; chmn, E. San Gabriel Valley Planning Cmt, 65- Mil. Serv: Entered as 2nd Lt, Air Force, 53, released as 1st Lt, 55, after serv. in Strategic Air Command. Mem: Am. and Citrus Bar Asns; Am. Judicature Soc; Harvard Law Sch. Asn; Exchange Club; Elks. Rel: Jewish. Mailing Add: 1326 Hollencrest Dr, West Covina, Calif. 91790. (1967)

KRIEKARD, HAROLD EDWARD R
Chmn, Alger Co. Rep. Party, Mich.
b. Kalamazoo, Mich, 10/31/12; s. Edward C. Kriekard and Nellie Gideon K; m. 9/10/38 to Marjorie Frances Wilson; c. Thomas E, John A. and Daniel J. Educ: Kalamazoo Col, B.A; Inst. of Paper Chem, 1 year; Sigma Rho Sigma; K Club. Polit. & Govt. Pos: Chmn, Alger Co. Rep. Party, Mich, 69- Bus. & Prof. Pos: Planning and materials supt, Kimberly-Clark, Niagara, Wis, 53-63, mgr. and packaging specialist, Neenah, 63-65 and mgr. admin. serv, Munising,Mich, 66- Mem: Rotary; Boy Scouts (coun. pres, 64-65). Rel: Episcopal. Mailing Add: Sand Point Rd, Munising, Mich. 49862.

KRIER, RAYMOND VALENTINE D
Mem, Ill. Dem. State Cent. Cmt.
s. Martin Krier 'Scotty' and Elizabeth Nusbaum K; m. to Virginia Hogan; c. Scott, Thomas, Dennis and Rickey. Educ: High Sch. Polit. & Govt. Pos: Trustee, Skokie, Ill, 55-61; committeeman, Niles Twp. Dem. Orgn, 66-; del, Dem. Nat. Conv, 68; mem, Ill. Dem. State Cent. Cmt, 69- Bus. & Prof. Pos: Former dir, Skokie Credit Union; partner, Krier Brothers Realtors and Ins. Mem: Past pres, Niles Twp. Real Estate Bd; Skokie Athletic Asn; K. of C; Moose; C. of C; Kiwanis. Guest of Honor, Israel Bond Tribute Banquet, 12/14/65. Rel: Catholic. Mailing Add: 5341 George St, Skokie, Ill. 60076. (1967)

KRIM, ARTHUR B. D
b. N.Y.C, 4/4/10; m. 12/7/58 to Mathilde Galland; c. Daphna. Educ: Columbia Col, B.A, Law Sch, LL.B. Polit. & Govt. Pos: Chmn, Dem. Nat. Finance Cmt, 66-68; del, Dem. Nat. Conv, 68; spec. consult. to the President of the U.S. 68-69. Bus. & Prof. Pos: Partner, Phillips, Nizer, Benjamin, Krim and Ballon, 32-; pres, United Artists Corp, 51-69, chmn. of bd, 69- Mil. Serv: Entered as 1st Lt, Army, 42; released as Lt. Col, 45. Legal Res: 33 E. 69th St, New York, N.Y. 10021. Mailing Add: 729 Seventh Ave, New York, N.Y. 10019.

KRNACIK, JOHN, JR. D
Membership Secy, 14th Dist. Dem. Party, Mich.
b. Arnold, Pa, 5/30/36; s. John Krnacik and Ann Rywak K; m. 8/27/60 to Mildred Helen Bauman; c. Michael John. Educ: Duquesne Univ, B.A. cum laude, 58, M.A, 61; Univ. Mich, Ph.D, 68. Polit. & Govt. Pos: Membership secy, 14th Dist. Dem. Party, Mich, 67-; alternate del, Dem. Nat. Conv, 68; mem, Wayne Co. Dem. Cmt, 69- Bus. & Prof. Pos: Reporter, New Kensington Daily Dispatch, Pa, 56-60; instr. Eng, Univ. Detroit, 60-62; Wayne State Univ, 64-68, asst. prof, 68-69; chmn. dept. commun, Macomb Co. Community Col, Mt. Clemens, Mich, 69- Publ: 'Thomas Jefferson's Interest in Italian Life, Language, and Art,' Ky. For. Lang. Quart, 66. Mem: Mod. Lang. Asn. Am; Am. Fedn. Teachers. Civilian Citation, Detroit Police Dept, 66. Rel: Roman Catholic. Mailing Add: 12735 Alcoy St, Detroit, Mich. 48205.

KROCK, EDWARD D
b. Old Boylston, Mass, 4/19/12; s. Max Krock and Rose Shain K; m. 7/30/37 to Miriam Alpert; c. Richard Alan and Nancy Ruth. Educ: Pub. sch. Polit. & Govt. Pos: Alternate del, Dem. Nat. Conv, 56, 60 & 64. Bus. & Prof. Pos: Founder, pres. and treas, Edward Krock Industs, 49-; spec. consult. to Small Bus. Asn. Mem: B'nai B'rith. Recipient, Free Enterprise Asn. Award. Rel: Jewish. Mailing Add: Rockinghorse Farm, Brookfield, Mass. 02146.

KROEGER, NADINE CLARA D
V.Chmn, Trego Co. Dem. Party, Kans.
b. Hays, Kans, 4/3/24; d. Pete A. Burbach and Minnie Tilton B; m. 5/1/64 to Lawrence Kroeger; c. Patricia (Mrs. Gerald Schremner), Terry, Randall, Lonnie and Jacquelyn Claycamp, Douglas and Gary Kroeger. Educ: Ft. Hays Kans. State Coll, two years; YWCA. Polit. & Govt. Pos: Co. assessor, Trego Co, Kans, 62-69; v.chmn, Trego Co. Dem. Party, 66- Bus. & Prof. Pos: Owner retail gas bus, Kans, 44-64; nurses aide, Trego Lake Mem. Hosp, 64-69. Publ: 'Epsilon Sigma Alpha Sorority,' Wichita Eagle-Beacon Paper, Kans, 69; articles in West. Kans. World. Mem: Rebeka (past Noble Grand); Epsilon Sigma Alpha (past pres); chmn, Trego Co. Tuberc. Asn; past leader, Girl Scouts and Cub Scouts. Rel: Lutheran; past pres, ladies orgn. Mailing Add: 121 S. Sixth, Wa Keeney, Kans. 67672.

KROEHLER, FRANKLIN P. Non-Partisan
b. Henderson, Minn, 1897; married; c. Four. Polit. & Govt. Pos: Minn. State Sen, 54-66; chmn, Co. Bd. of Supvrs. of Soil Conserv; clerk, local Sch. Bd, 21 years. Bus. & Prof. Pos: Retired farmer; secy, Star Creamery Asn, 20 years. Mem: Pres, Minn. Territorial Pioneers; Co. pres, Hist. Soc. Mailing Add: Henderson, Minn, 56044. (1967)

KROG, DONALD RICHARD D
b. Gannvalley, S.Dak, 4/14/22; s. Eaner Krog and Esther Farrington K; m. 8/2/42 to Pearl Opal Tereldal; c. Charlene (Mrs. Von Eye), Lydell, Gayle and Twila. Educ: Wessington Springs High Sch, 4 years. Polit. & Govt. Pos: Chmn, Buffalo Co. Dem. Party, S.Dak, 64-68. Bus. & Prof. Pos: Farmer-rancher, 44- Rel: Lutheran. Mailing Add: Gannvalley, S.Dak. 57341.

KROGSENG, DAVID NEIL R
b. Duluth, Minn, 6/16/36; s. Peter Torlaf Krogseng and Esther Stormoen K; m. 6/22/58 to Joan Johnson; c. Pamela Diane and Julianne Joan. Educ: Univ. Minn, B.A. in polit. sci. and hist, 58, Grad. Sch; Phoenix Soc; Grey Friars Soc; Order of the Gopher. Polit. & Govt. Pos: Admin. Asst. to Congressman Clark MacGregor, Minn, 65-; asst. dir. research, Rep. Nat. Cmt, 64-65; dir. research, William E. Miller Vice Presidential Campaign, 64 and Minn. Rep. Party, 58-64. Publn: State Polit. Research Manual, Rep. Nat. Cmt, 65. Mem: U.S. Capitol and Minnesota Hist. Soc; Minn. Alumni Asn; Rep. Workshop Minn. Rel: Lutheran. Mailing Add: 4507 Saul Rd, Kensington, Md. 20795. (1967)

KROHN, DOROTHY J. R
b. Monmouth Beach, N.J, 3/20/15; d. Reuben Johnson and Alice Kittell J; m. 5/26/42 to Norris F. Krohn; c. Norris F. II, Jeffrey O. and Patrick B. Educ: State Col, Montclair, N.J, B.A, 35. Polit. & Govt. Pos: First v.chmn, Rep. Party, Wis, 59-67; del, Rep. Nat. Conv, 60, alternate del, 64; chmn, Midwest & Rocky Mt. Rep. V.Chmn; v.chmn, Winnebago Co. Rep. Party, Wis; pres, Winnebago Fedn. Rep. Women. Mem: Salvation Army Adv. Bd, Oshkosh, 50-, chmn, 69-; 20th Century Womens Club (pres, 50-52); Am. Asn. Univ. Women (pres, 48-50); Col. Women's Club; Am. Legion Auxiliary. Rel: Presbyterian. Mailing Add: 1222 Washington Ave, Oshkosh, Wis. 54901.

KROHN, FRANKLIN BERNARD D
Committeeman, Erie Co. Dem. Cmt, N.Y.
b. Erie, Pa, 7/1/33; s. Lewis H. Krohn (deceased) and Marian Post K; wid; c. Robert Alan, Debra Janis and Lynette Beth. Educ: Bryant & Stratton Bus. Inst, N.Y, 52-54 & 56-58; Univ. Md, 55-56; State Univ. N.Y, Buffalo, 67-69. Polit. & Govt. Pos: Committeeman, Erie Co. Dem. Cmt, N.Y, 61-; admin. asst. to town Dem. chmn, Tonawanda Dem. Cmt, 63-, secy, 66-68, zone chmn, 68-; del, Dem. State Conv, 66; alternate del, Dem. Nat. Conv, 68. Bus. & Prof. Pos: Owner, Select Home Utilities Co, 56- Mil. Serv: Entered as Pvt, Army, 54, released as SP-3, 56, after serv. in 2000th S.U, Second Army Hq, Inspector Gen. Sect, Ft. George G. Meade, Md, 54-56; Nat. Defense Serv. Medal; Good Conduct Medal. Mem: B'nai B'rith; life mem, Amvets; life mem, N.Y. State PTA; Brighton Elem. Sch. PTA; Four Gallon Club; Am. Red Cross (bd. dirs, Kenmore-Tonawanda Br); Temple Beth El; Anti-Defamation League (regional bd); Kennedy Dem. Club; Truman Dem. Club. Man of Year Award, B'nai B'rith, 60; Dem. Serv. Award, Tonawanda Dem. Cmt, 62; hon. mem, Town Dem. Chairman's Asn. Rel: Hebrew. Mailing Add: 120 Fries Rd, Tonawanda, N.Y. 14150.

KROHN, HELEN JOSEPHINE D
Chmn, St. Clair Co. Dem. Cmt, Mich.
b. Traverse City, Mich, 10/10/14; d. Napoleon Joseph Pelky and Julia Mary Perrault P; m. 10/2/34 to George Frederick Krohn; c. Frederic William, David Lee and Terry George. Educ: St. Francis High Sch; Sodality of the Blessed Virgin Mary. Polit. & Govt. Pos: V.chmn, St. Clair Co. Dem. Cmt, Mich, 59-60, chmn, 60-; del, mem. steering cmt. and secy. Mich. Del, Dem. Nat. Conv, 64; mem, Bd. Canvassers, Port Huron Area Sch. Dist; del, and v.chmn. or secy, ten Dem. State Conv. Bus. & Prof. Pos: Confidential clerk, Chrysler Corp, 47-49, group leader, 49-53. Mem: Sparlingville Women's Orgn; League of Cath. Women. Rel: Roman Catholic. Mailing Add: 3596 Sunset Lane, Port Huron, Mich. 48060. (1967)

KROMBERG, JEROME I. D
Mem, Nebr. Dem. State Cent. Cmt.
b. N.Y.C, 12/11/27; m. 6/17/50 to June Brown; c. Patricia, Jeffery, Norman and Russell. Educ: Northwest. Univ, grad, 50. Polit. & Govt. Pos: Mem, Nebr. Dem. State Cent. Cmt, 66-; del, Dem. Nat. Conv, 68; treas, Lancaster Co. Dem. Party, 68- Mil. Serv: Navy, 44-46. Rel: Unitarian. Mailing Add: 7301 Holdrege St, Lincoln, Nebr. 68505.

KRONICK, RUSSELL D
Chmn, Sacramento Co. Dem. Cent. Cmt, Calif.
b. Pittsfield, Mass, 10/11/21; s. Edward Kronick and Fanny Levy K; m. 8/29/48 to Alice Eisenberg; c. Stephen and Janice. Educ: Boston Univ, 41-42; Syracuse Univ, B.S. in Bus. Admin, 46-48. Polit. & Govt. Pos: Secy, N.Adams Recreation Cmn, Mass, 56-58; mem, Calif. State Dem. Cent. Cmt, 62-; v.chmn, Sacramento Co. Dem. Cent. Cmt, Calif, 62-65, chmn, 65- Mil. Serv: Pvt, Army, 42. Mem: Mason. Rel: Hebrew. Mailing Add: 2032 Ione St, Sacramento, Calif. 95825. (1967)

KROTZ, VIRLA ROPER R
Mem. Exec. Cmt, Calif. Rep. State Cent. Cmt.
b. Ashland, Ore, 3/23/05; d. Frederick L. Roper and Rosetta Chapman R; m. 10/12/29 to Donald P. Krotz; c. Douglas Roper. Educ: Univ. Calif, B.S, 26; Beta Gamma Sigma; Phi Chi Theta; Phi Mu. Polit. & Govt. Pos: Pres, North. Calif. Fedn. of Rep. Women, 60-63; alternate del, Rep. Nat. Conv, 60 & 68, del, 64; mem. exec. cmt, Calif. Rep. State Cent. Cmt, 60-, dep. precinct chmn, 65-66; v.pres, Calif. Fedn. of Rep. Women, 63-65, pres, 66-68; mem, Calif. State Bd. of Educ, 68- Mem: Bd. of Dirs, Mt. Diablo Therapy Center and Orinda Libr; secy-treas, Nat. Asn. of State Bds. of Educ, 68-69. Rel: Congregational. Mailing Add: 44 Monte Vista Rd, Orinda, Calif. 94563.

KROUSE, MORRIS J. D
b. Overbrook, Kans, 2/20/15; s. Marcus Wittenberg Krouse and Emma Louise Lint K; m. 7/4/40 to Flossie W. Nicewander. Educ: Topeka Bus. Col, dipl, 32; Northwest. Univ, 43-44; For. Serv. Sch, 44; Naval Intel. Sch, 44; Wichita Univ, 47-48; Delta Sigma Pi. Polit. & Govt. Pos: Mem. staff, Soil Conserv. Serv, Wash, 15 years; enforcement rep, Dept. Labor; chief. admin. div, Vet. Admin. Regional Off, Kans, 45-51; chmn, Kans. Vet. Cmn, 57-61 & 68-; del, Dem. Nat. Conv, 68. Bus. & Prof. Pos: Owner, White Motor Co. Distributorship, Springdale, Ark; pres, Wichita White Truck Sales, Inc; pres, Wichita Truck Lease & Finance, currently. Mil. Serv: Entered as Sp-1, Navy, 42, released as Chief Specialist, 45, after serv. in Naval Intel, Chicago Dist. Off, Kans. City Zone Off. and Naval Mission in Vienna and Mobile Intel. Unit, North Africa, Italy and Austria. Mem: Wichita C. of C.(dir, v.chmn, rd. & hwy. cmt); Ambassador Club; Jr. Achievement Wichita (dir, fund campaign dir); North Wichtia YMCA (dir, team capt, Capital Fund Drive); chmn, United Fund Drive for Automobile and Truck Dealers; Wichita Coun. Commun. Develop.(chmn. exec. cmt, v.chmn. finance and admin. cmt); Ark Valley Hwy. Asn.(v.chmn. bd); Elks; Lions; Kans. C. of C; Mason; Consistory; Shrine; Am. Legion; Kans. Motor Carriers Asn; Nat. Motor Car Dealers Asn; Wichita Club; Mil. Order Cootie; VFW (post athletic dir, 3 years, dist. athletic dir, 2 years, state athletic dir, 3 years, chmn. bldg. cmt, formerly post jr. v.comdr, sr. v.comdr. and comdr, state jr. v.comdr, presently). Rel: Presbyterian. Legal Res: 2605 Glen Oaks Dr, Wichita, Kans. 67201. Mailing Add: P.O. Box 1003, Wichita, Kans. 67201.

KROUT, HOMER LEE R
b. David, W.Va, 9/2/17; s. Curtis H. Krout and Nora Blanche Alderton K; m. 3/14/48 to Doris Langman; c. John C, David A. and Robert K. Educ: Univ. Ala, B.S, 51; Phi Eta Sigma; Beta Gamma Sigma; Omicron Delta Kappa; Pi Kappa Phi. Polit. & Govt. Pos: Mem. campaign cmt. for U.S. Rep, Joel T. Broyhill, Va, 52-, admin. asst, 54-; cmt. chmn. and cmt. mem. various positions, Arlington Co. Rep. Party and Tenth Dist. Rep. Party, 52-; mem. campaign cmt. for various co. bd. cand, 6 years; chmn. rules cmt, Co. Mass Meeting, 67 & 69; co-chmn. party plans cmt, Arlington Rep. Party, 68-69; mem. rules cmt, Va. Rep. State Conv, 68 & 69. Bus. & Prof. Pos: Purchas-

ing agent, M.T. Broyhill & Sons, Realtors, Arlington, Va, 51, subcontracts asst, 52, personnel officer, 53, off. mgr, 54. Mil. Serv: Entered as Airman, Royal Can. Air Force, 41, released as Cpl, 43, after serv. in Royal Air Force Bomber Squadron, Eng; transferred to U.S. Air Force, as Sgt, released as Warrant Officer, 45. Mem: Optimist; VFW; PTA (pres, v.pres, Co. Coun); Lyon Village Civic Asn; YMCA (bd. dirs, adv. bd, scout official). Distinguished Serv. Award, Tenth Dist. Chap. Va. DAV, 64. Rel: Baptist. Mailing Add: 1605 N. Johnson St, Arlington, Va. 22201.

KRUCK, WARREN J. D
Iowa State Sen.
b. Sioux City, Iowa, 6/1/21; s. Albert J. Kruck; m. 11/10/46 to Kathryn Ann Smith; c. Stephen Warren, Karen Pamela and Deborah Kay. Educ: Boone High Sch. and Jr. Col. Polit. & Govt. Pos: Iowa State Sen, 64-; mem, Small Bus. Admin. Adv. Coun. for Iowa. Bus. & Prof. Pos: Owner, Kruck Plumbing & Heating Co. Mech. Contractors. Mil. Serv: Navy Pilot, World War II, 10 years serv; Navy Cross and Distinguished Flying Cross. Mem: Nat. Asn. Mech. Contractors; Boone Co. Civil Defense; YMCA (pres. bd. dirs, 60-65); pres. merged bd. YMCA-YWCA, 65-; Kiwanis (pres, 64); Boone Golf & Country Club (dir); C. of C;(dir. and past chmn, Boone Indust. Develop. Cmt); Am. Legion; VFW. First Dem. Sen. in Boone Co. Hist. Rel: Lutheran; Trustee, Trinity Lutheran Church. Mailing Add: P.O. Box 189, Boone, Iowa 50036.

KRUEGER, CARL EDMUND R
b. Sturgeon Bay, Wis, 8/21/34; s. Edmund C. Krueger and Lilla Luethge K; m. 12/28/63 to Elizabeth M. Ballo; c. Karin K. Educ: High Sch, Wis. Polit. & Govt. Pos: Chmn, Door Co. Young Rep. Cmt, Wis, 59-63; chmn, Door Co. Rep. Orgn, 65-69. Mil. Serv: Entered as Pvt, Army, 54, released as Pfc, 56; Korean War Medal; Good Conduct Medal. Mem: Jaycees. Rel: Lutheran. Mailing Add: R.R. 1, Sturgeon Bay, Wis. 54235. (1967)

KRUEGER, CLIFF W. R
Hawaii State Rep.
b. Chicago, Ill, 5/14/29; s. Walter Henry Otto Krueger and Alice Haun K; m. 8/11/51 to Caryl Waller; c. Claire Waller, Chris Walter, Carrie Wendy and Cameron Walaka. Educ: Northwest. Univ, B.S. in Econ, 50; Univ. Chicago. Polit. & Govt. Pos: Hawaii State Rep, 17th Dist, currently. Bus. & Prof. Pos: Lectr. for Nat. and State Conv, U.S. and Can; founder and dean, Real Estate Inst. of Hawaii; instr, Real Estate Inst. of Chicago and Univ. Ind; past off. mgr, Island Homes Realtors; past pres, The Homefinders, Inc; dir, pres. and founder, Island Fed. Savings & Loan Asn. Publ: Sales books and records, McGraw-Hill. Mem: State gov, Nat. League of Insured Savings Asns; Fed. Charter Cmt, U.S. Savings & Loan League; Nat. Asn. Real Estate Bd; Honolulu Bd. Realtors; Savings and Loan League, Hawaii, Calif. and Wash; Savings and Loan Found; Bus. League for Sound Govt; Hawaii Employers Coun; Better Bus. Bur; Int. Union Bldg. Socs. and Savings and Loan Asns; Am. Savings and Loan Inst; Inter-Am. Savings and Loan Union; Credit Bur. of Hawaii; Oahu Grand Jury, 64; budget cmt, Hawaii Visitors Bur; chmn, Mayor's Selection Panel for Employee-of-Year Award; cmts, Honolulu C. of C; dist. rep. and Aloha Coun. Finance Cmt, Boy Scouts; former scoutmaster; bd. dirs, Camp Fire Girls of Am; bd, Kahala Sch. PTA; Rep. Party of Hawaii; former mem, Rotary; Young Presidents Orgn. of Am. Received Outstanding Young Man of Year Award, Jaycees, 59 and Distinguished Serv. Award, 64. Rel: Christian Science. Legal Res: 4433 Kahala Ave, Honolulu, Hawaii 96815. Mailing Add: P.O. Box 2521, Honolulu, Hawaii 96804.

KRUEGER, CLIFFORD W. R
Wis. State Sen.
b. Madison, Wis, 6/24/18. Educ: Merrill Commercial Col. Polit. & Govt. Pos: Former alderman, Merrill, Wis; Wis. State Sen, 46-54 & 56- Bus. & Prof. Pos: Sales Mgr. Mailing Add: 122 N. State St, Merrill, Wis. 54452. (1967)

KRUEGER, CULP D
b. Riesel, Tex, 6/8/13; s. Louis Adolph Krueger and Minnie Lee Culp K; m. 11/29/36 to Evelyn Smidt; c. Cay. Educ: Univ. Tex; Houston Night Law Sch; Radio & Journalism Clubs. Polit. & Govt. Pos: Mem, Tex. State Dem. Exec. Cmt, 52-56; Tex. State Sen, 15th Dist, 56-67, Pres Pro-Tempore, Tex. State Sen, 62; regional coordinator for Johnson and adv. man for Kennedy-Johnson, 60; Acting Lt. Gov, Tex, 62, Acting Gov, 62; regional coordinator for 8 states, Johnson-Humphrey Campaign, 64; former chmn. pollution, Multiple Use Study Tex. Waters. Bus. & Prof. Pos: Dist. supvr, Tex. Unemploy. Cmn, 37-41; partner, Smidt-Krueger Motors, 46-54; pres, Radio Sta. KULP, 46-68; publisher, El Campo Leader-Sooboda News, 55-68; pres, Culp Krueger Real Estate, Inc. and partner, Black Jak Farms currently. Mil. Serv: Entered as Pvt, Army, 43, released as 1st Lt, 46, after serv. in Cavalry, Pac. Theater; 4 Battle Stars. Mem: Sigma Delta Chi; Am. Legion; VFW; Elks; Boy Scouts (Eagle Scout, 32). Rel: Catholic. Mailing Add: 908 Georgia St, El Campo, Tex. 77437.

KRUEGER, ROBERT WILLIAM R
Mem, Calif. Rep. State Cent. Cmt.
b. Phila, Pa, 11/16/16; s. Robert Henry Krueger and Frieda Lehmann K; m. 7/26/41 to Marjorie Evelyn Jones; c. Arlene R.(Mrs. Reher) and Diane L. Educ: Univ. Calif, Los Angeles, A.B, 37, M.A, 38, Ph.D. in Physics, 42; Phi Delta Kappa; Mason. Polit. & Govt. Pos: Head, various Rep. precinct orgn, Calif. Rep. Assemblys and cong. campaign cmts, 49-69; pres, 60th Dist. Calif. Rep. Assembly, 50-52; area chmn, 59th Dist. Rep. Precinct Orgn, 51-61; mem, 59th Dist. Rep. Cent. Cmt, 56-61, chmn, 58-61; chmn, 59th Dist. Rep. Coord. Coun, 58-61; pres, 59th Dist. Calif. Rep. Assembly, 58-61; campaign chmn, Robert S. Stevens for 60th Assembly, 62; mem, Calif. Rep. State Cent. Cmt, 62-; campaign chmn, Paul Priolo for 60th Assembly, 66; mem, Rep. Assocs. and Rep. Nat. Assembly, 68- Bus. & Prof. Pos: Research physicist, Douglas Aircraft, 42-46; asst. chief missiles div, Rand Corp, Los Angeles, 46-53; pres, Planning Research Corp, 54- Mem: Am. Phys. Soc; Opers. Research Soc. Am; Inst. Mgt. Sci; Los Angeles C. of C; Calif. State C. of C; UCLA Found. Rel: Protestant. Mailing Add: 1016 Moraga Dr, Los Angeles, Calif. 90049.

KRUEGER, VERNON H. R
Chmn, Webster Co. Rep. Orgn, Nebr.
b. Blue Hill, Nebr, 7/26/23; s. Hugo Krueger and Johanna Vanboening K; m. 6/5/45 to Marcylene A. Rasser; c. Janice (Mrs. K. Budde) and Tom R. Educ: Kearney State Col, 2 years; Washburn Univ, 1 semester; Okla. State Univ, 1 semester. Polit. & Govt. Pos: Precinct committeeman, Webster Co. Rep. Orgn, Nebr, 52-58, secy, 58-66, chmn, 68- Bus. & Prof. Pos: Dir. and secy, Farmers Union Gas & Oil, 52-61; dir. and chmn, Farmers Union Coop, 58-64, Agri-Serv. Inc, 60-64; dir, Cent. Voc. Col, 67-69. Mil. Serv: Entered as A/S, Navy, 42, released as AETM/2, 45, after serv. in VB 7, Pac. Theatre. Mem: VFW; Am. Legion; Lions. Rel: Lutheran. Mailing Add: Box 346, Red Cloud, Nebr. 68970.

KRUEGER, YVONNE R
Chmn, Osborne Co. Rep. Cent. Cmt, Kans.
b. Luray, Kans, 6/24/11; d. Clyde S. Paschal and Martha Blanche Robinson P; m. 8/28/29 to Harold Roy Krueger; c. Roy Rand, Thomas Henry, Marilyn (Mrs. Bob Chesney), Cynthia, Pamela (Mrs. Gary Miller) and Sylvia (Mrs. Ken Havner). Educ: Luray High Sch, grad, 29. Polit. & Govt. Pos: Committeewoman, Rep. Party, 46-69; dir, Natoma Bd. of Educ, 54-57, treas, 60-63; del, Rep. Nat. Conv, 60; Natoma rep, Co. Sch. Unification Bd, 64-65; v.chmn, Osborne Co. Rep. Cent. Cmt, Kans, 52-68, chmn 66- Mem: Eastern Star (Worthy Matron, 54); Mother Adv, Order of Rainbow for Girls, 64; Self Culture Club (pres, 66-69); Grand Cross of Colors; Harmony Study Club. Rel: United Methodist. Mailing Add: Natoma, Kans. 67651.

KRUG, ANDREW JOSEPH D
b. Baltimore, Md, 1/24/25; s. Andrew Clarence Krug and Emma Torrence K; m. 6/17/50 to Jeanne F. Steffy; c. Karen J, Andrew C, Barbara A, Mary C, Jane F. and Paul J. Educ: St. Bonaventure Univ, A.B, 46; Univ. of Md. Sch. of Law; Columbus Univ, LL.B, 55. Polit. & Govt. Pos: Justice of the Peace, Md, 59-62; Md. State Del, Third Dist, Baltimore City, 62-66; mem, Gov. Study Cmn. for Workmen's Compensation, 64-68. Bus. & Prof. Pos: Ins. adjustor, Liberty Mutual Ins. Co, 47-49 and Hartford Accident & Indemnity Co, 49-52; asst. claims mgr, Ins. Co. of N.Am, 52-58; lawyer, Firm of Berman & Berman, 58-64 and Firm of Dickerson, Nice, Sohol and Horn, 64- Mem: Va. Bar, 54; Md. Bar, 56; U.S. Dist. Court for Dist. of Md, 58; Bar. Asn. of Baltimore City; Citizens Planning & Housing Asn. of Baltimore City; K. of C; United Christian Citizens Inc; Christian Family Movement; St. Vincent De Paul Soc. Rel: Roman Catholic. Legal Res: 6129 N. Charles St, Baltimore, Md. 21212. Mailing Add: 1704 Court Square Bldg, Baltimore, Md. 21202.

KRUGER, ALICE L. R
b. Omaha, Nebr, 3/19/31; d. Paul Sierk Kruger and Beatrice Colburn K; single. Educ: Univ. Nebr, B.Ed, 52; Univ. Omaha, 56; Co-ed Counsrs; Dormitory Counsr. Polit. & Govt. Pos: Secy, U.S. Rep. Dave Martin, 61-65, exec. secy, 65-68. Bus. & Prof. Pos: Teacher Soc. studies, Whiting, Kans, 52-53, Gordon, Nebr, 53-54 and Plattsmouth, 54-57; div. mgr, Cornhusker Motor Club, AAA, 57-60. Mem: Bd. of Gov, Nebr. Soc. of Wash, 63-66; regional dir, Conf. of State Socs, 66-67; Rep. Women of Capitol Hill; Cong. Secys. Club; Am. Asn. of Univ. Women; Lincoln Co. Rep. Women; Eastern Star. Rel: Presbyterian. Mailing Add: Fort Calhoun, Nebr. 68023. (1967)

KRUGER, JOHN W. R
Chmn, Pulaski Co. Rep. Party, Ind.
b. Winamac, Ind, 8/6/13; s. Will K. Kruger and Letitia K; m. 11/20/41 to Marceil F. Owen; c. Katherine (Mrs. Kiesling). Educ: Winamac High Sch, grad, 31. Polit. & Govt. Pos: Bd. trustees, Winamac, Ind, 55-63, Co. Cmnr, Pulaski Co, 63-; chmn, Pulaski Co. Rep. Party, 63- Mil. Serv: S/Sgt, Army, 42, released, 45, after serv. in 24th Air Service Command, S.Pac, 43-45. Mem: Amvets; Shrine; Am. Legion; Mason; VFW; Scottish Rite. Rel: Presbyterian. Mailing Add: 308 S. Riverside Dr, Winamac, Ind. 46996.

KRUGER, SYLVIA MORGAN D
b. Oakes, N.Dak, 10/30/30; d. George Michael Morgan and Caroline Erickson M; m. 7/20/55 to Eugene Albert Kruger; c. Kristin Marlene and Hallie Eugenia. Educ: Northwest. Univ, B.S. and M.A; Zeta Phi Eta; Alpha Omicron Pi; Edgewater Drama Club scholarship for jr. year at Northwest. Univ. Sch. of Speech and Isabel Lovedale scholarship for grad. work. Polit. & Govt. Pos: Precinct committeewoman, Dist. 24, N.Dak. Dem. Party, 67-69; del, Dem. Nat. Conv, 68; secy, N.Dak. Concerned Dem, 68; mem, McCarthy for Pres. Adv. Cmt, Dist. 24, 68; mem, N.Dak. Adv. Cmt, Dist. 24, 69. Bus. & Prof. Pos: High sch. teacher, Dundee, Ill, 52-53; teaching asst, Northwest. Univ, 53-54; high sch. teacher, Santa Maria, Calif, 54-55 and Oslo, Minn, 55-56; instr, N.Dak. State Univ, 56-61; instr. humanities, Moorhead State Col, 62- Mem: Am. Asn. Univ. Prof; Inter-faculty Orgn, Minn. State Col. Syst; Moorhead State Col. Faculty Asn; N.Dak. Citizens Against the ABM. Rel: Unitarian. Mailing Add: 1315 S. Ninth, Fargo, N.Dak. 58102.

KRUGLER, ARNOLD FRANK R
Chmn, Seward Co. Rep. Cent. Cmt, Nebr.
b. Chicago, Ill, 8/14/33; s. William Krugler and Florence Erber K; m. 6/1/57 to Margaret Edna Grewe; c. Kathryn and Karl. Educ: Valparaiso Univ, B.A; Concordia Theol. Sem, Dipl; Lutheran Sch. Theol, Chicago, S.T.M; Alpha Phi Omega. Polit. & Govt. Pos: Faculty adv, Concordia Teachers Col. Young Rep, Nebr, 64-68; del, Nebr. State Rep. Conv, 64, 66 & 68; chmn, Seward Co. Rep. Steering Cmt, Nebr, 65-68; chmn, Seward Co. Citizens and Nebr. Teachers for Curtis, 66; chmn, Seward Co. Rep. Cent. Cmt, 68- Bus. & Prof. Pos: Cost auditor, U.S. Air Force, Chicago, Ill, 55; educator, Concordia Teachers Col, Seward, Nebr, 61- Publ: 'Civil Rights,' Lutheran Educ, 4/67. Rel: Lutheran. Mailing Add: 514 N. First St, Seward, Nebr. 68434.

KRULL, JACOB EDWARD D
b. Sibley, Iowa, 1/13/09; s. Jacob Sebastin Krull and Lina Poppen K; m. 6/6/32 to Katherine DeBerg; c. Darlene Jean (Mrs. Norman Olson), Kay Irene, Mary Ann (Mrs. William S. Ricker), Darrell Lee and Jacob James. Educ: Munger Public Sch, 8 years; Nat. Rural Coop. Mgt. Inst. grad. Polit. & Govt. Pos: Mem, Munger Sch. Bd, 32-36; mem, Foley Sch. Bd, 38-56; S.Dak. State Rep, Codington, Co, 60-62; chmn, Codington Co. Dem. Party, S.Dak, 64-68. Bus. & Prof. Pos: Agent, Farmers Union Ins, Watertown, S.Dak, 60- Mem: Watertown Coop. Elevator Bd; Codington-Clark Elec.(past pres, 41-); East River Elec. Bd, 64-; Lions; Farmers Union. Rel: Congregational; mem, church bd, 58-67. Mailing Add: Route 3, Watertown, S.Dak. 57201.

KRUMME, JAMES LEON R
Chmn, Cobb Co. Rep. Cmt, Ga.
Educ: Univ. of Okla, B.S. in Chem. Eng, 56. Polit. & Govt. Pos: Chmn, Cobb Co. Rep. Cmt, Ga, currently; dir, Seventh Dist. Cong. Dist. Rep. Party; mem, Ga. Rep. State Cmt; chmn, Cobb Co. Rep. Exec. Cmt; past chmn, Cobb Co. Rep. Asn. Bus. & Prof. Pos: Research and develop. and sales engr, Alcoa, 56-61, dist. sales mgr. in southeast, chem. and pigments,61-64; pres, Vinings Chem. Co, Ga, 64- Mil. Serv: Air Force, 2 years. Mem: Tech. Inst. of Pulp and Paper Inst. and Salesmans Soc. to Dixie Pulp and Paper Mills; C. of C; past chmn, Vinings Heights Civic Club. Mailing Add: 110 Shady Lane, Smyrna, Ga. 30080.

KRUMME, ROY ARCHIBALD D
b. St. Joseph, Mo, 8/28/92; s. John William Krumme and Dora Ellen McBride K; wid; m. 3/11/66 to Ruth Margaret Phillips; c. Margaret (Mrs. James Whitcomb), Rachel (Mrs. Ralph T. McMillen), Roy Harlan, George William and Jefferson Bryan. Educ: Elementary schs, Okla. and Mo. Polit. & Govt. Pos: Rural mail carrier, 13-18; fourth class postmaster, 24-40; mem. draft bd, Creek Co, Okla, 41-61; del, Dem. Nat. Conv, 68. Bus. & Prof. Pos: Dir, Commun. State Bank, Bristow, Okla, 30-; dir, Am. Gen. Ins. Co. Okla, 31-; pres, Ill. Refining Co, Okla, 45-; dir. and former pres, East Cent. Okla. Elec. Coop, 49- Mem: Mason; Lions; Farmers Union Okla; hon. mem. 4-H Club. Mr. Democrat of Creek Co, Creek Co. Conv, 69. Rel: Southern Baptist. Legal Res: 409 W. 11th St, Bristow, Okla. 74010. Mailing Add: P.O. Box 749, Bristow, Okal. 74010.

KRUPA, JOHN GEORGE D
Chmn, Lake Co. Dem. Cent. Cmt, Ind.
b. East Chicago, Ind, 7/21/16; s. John Krupa and Edith Zuby K; m. 3/31/48 to Lee Ann Jacobs; c. Kathleen Louise, Marilyn Ann and Sandra Lee. Educ: Ind. Univ. Exten. Polit. & Govt. Pos: Chief dep. clerk, Lake Co, Ind, 48-63; chmn, Lake Co. Dem. Cent. Cmt, 62-; clerk, Lake Circuit Court, Ind, 64-; sustaining mem, Nat. Dem. Party. Mil. Serv: Entered as Pvt, Air Force, 44, released as Cpl, 46. Mem: Ind. Asn. Co. Clerks (state pres, 67-); Elks; Am. Legion. Rel: Roman Catholic. Legal Res: 5611 Northcote Ave, East Chicago, Ind. 46312. Mailing Add: P.O. Box 123, Crown Point, Ind. 46307.

KRUPSAK, MARY ANNE D
N.Y. State Assemblyman
b. Schenectady, N.Y, 3/26/32; d. Ambrose M. Krupsak and Mary Regina Wytrwal K; m. 6/30/69 to Edwin Margolis. Educ: Univ. Rochester, B.A. in Hist; Boston Univ, M.S. in Pub. Commun; Univ. Chicago Law Sch, J.D, 62; Theta Eta; Marsiens. Polit. & Govt. Pos: Prog. and legis. aide to former Gov. W. Averell Harriman, N.Y, 55-58; admin. asst. to Rep. Samuel S. Stratton, 59; asst. counsel to pres. protempore of N.Y. Senate, 65-66; asst. counsel to speaker of Assembly, 65-68; N.Y. State Assemblyman, 104th Assembly Dist, 68- Mem: N.Y. State Bar; N.Y. State and Montgomery Co. Bar Asns; Bar of the City of New York; state chmn, annual legis. conf, N.Y. State Bus. & Prfnl. Women's Club, 69, legis. chmn, Amsterdam; Emblem Club. Rel: Roman Catholic. Mailing Add: Shaper Ave. Exten, Canajoharie, N.Y. 13317.

KRUSE, DEAN VERL R
Ind. State Sen.
b. Auburn, Ind, 9/21/41; s. Russell W. Kruse and Luella Boger K; m. 6/26/60 to Carol Ann Yoder; c. Mitchell Dean. Educ: LaSalle Law Sch. Polit. & Govt. Pos: Organizer, DeKalb Co. TAR, Ind; del, State Rep. Conv, 60, 62 & 64; caucus chmn, Rep. Nat. Conv, 62 & 64 and del, 64; mem, State Rep. Policy Cmt, 66-67; mem, Electoral Col, 68; Rep. precinct committeeman, currently; chmn, DeKalb Co. Rep. Cmt, currently; Ind. State Sen, currently. Bus. & Prof. Pos: Mem. bd, Wabash Life Ins. Co. Mem: V.pres, Northeast. Ind. Realtors Asn, 66 and Ind. Auctioneers Asn, 66-67; Columbia Club; Indianapolis; Ind. Farm Bur; Ind. Asn. Elected Officers; Ind. Soc. Chicago; Press Club; C. of C. Rel: Church of God. Mailing Add: R.R. 2, Auburn, Ind. 46706.

KRUSE, EDWARD H, JR.
b. Fort Wayne, Ind, 10/22/18; s. Edward H. Kruse and Geneva Maxwell K; m. 3/3/45 to Joan Ley; c. 7. Educ: Ind. Univ, LL.B, 42; Butler Univ; Beta Theta Pi. Polit. & Govt. Pos: Judge, Allen Superior Court, Fort Wayne, Ind. 52; U.S. Rep, 49-50. Bus. & Prof. Pos: Pres, Kruse, O'Connor & Ling, Inc, Consulting Actuarial Firm. Mil. Serv: Entered as A/S, Navy, 42, released as Lt.(sg), after serv. in PT Boats, Solomon Islands; Secy. of Navy Commendation; Bronze Star; Pac. and Am. Theater Ribbons. Mem: Cmt. on Taxation, Am. Bar Asn; trustee, Nova Univ. of Technology. Rel: Catholic. Legal Res: Rt. 1, 5700 Holatee Trail, Fort Lauderdale, Fla. 33314. Mailing Add: 1415 Sunrise Blvd, Fort Lauderdale, Fla. 33304.

KRUSE, MILDRED THOMAS D
b. San Luis Obispo Co, Calif, 11/11/18; d. Brenard Jefferson Thomas and Mildred Lemen T; div; c. Rae (Mrs. Porter) and Thomas Edward. Polit. & Govt. Pos: Mem. exec. bd, Washoe Co. Dem. Women's Club, Nev, 58-66, pres, 60-62; del, Dem. Nat. Conv, 60 & 64, mem, Credentials Cmt, 60; mem. exec. bd, Washoe Co. Dem. Cent. Cmt, 60-66; in charge, Washoe Co. Gov. Sawyer's Campaign, 62; secy, Nev. State Dem. Cent. Cmt, 62-64; pres, West. Co. Dem. Women's Club, 63-65; Dem. nat. committeewoman, Nev, 64-69. Mem: Reno Bd. Realtors; Women's Realtors Coun; Reno Chap, Bus. & Prfnl. Women; Nev. Chap. 13, Eastern Star. Named Outstanding Young Dem. Woman, State of Nev, 55. Rel: Lutheran. Mailing Add: 480 E. Plumb Lane, Reno, Nev. 89502. (1967)

KUBERT, CAROLYNNE FRANCES D
V.Chmn, Wayne Co. Dem. Cmt, Mich.
b. Detroit, Mich, 8/8/24; d. Sylvester A. Mauer and Laura F. Wells M; m. 7/23/49 to Clifford Gerald Kubert; c. Jonathan. Educ: Marygrove Col, B.A, 46; Univ. Detroit, M.A. in Polit. Sci, 63, Ford Found. and Robert Taft Inst. Polit. Sci. Scholarships; grad. study, Wayne State Univ. and Univ. Mich; Richard Club. Polit. & Govt. Pos: Precinct del, Dem. Party, Mich, 54-60; v.chmn, First Cong. Dist. Dem. Party, 56-61; v.chmn, Wayne Co. Dem. Cmt, 61- Bus. & Prof. Pos: Saleswoman, J.L. Hudson Co, Mich, 42-46; secy, Briggs Mfg. Co, summers, 42, 43 & 44; teacher social studies, Detroit Pub. Schs, 46-, head dept, Longfellow Jr. High, Detroit, 67-; ins. rep, Security Ins. Group, U.S. Fidelity and Guaranty Co, 59- Mem: Am. Asn. of Univ. Women; Detroit Fedn. Teachers; Orgn. Detroit Women Sch. Adminstr; Orgn. Adminstrs. and Supvr; PTA; Citizens for Schs; Citizens for Educ. Rel: Roman Catholic. Mailing Add: 20223 Carrie, Detroit, Mich. 48234.

KUBIAK, DAN D
Tex. State Rep.
b. Reagan, Tex, 3/19/38; s. John T. Kubiak and Connie Snider K; m. 12/23/67 to Zana Bassler. Educ: Blinn Col, A.A, 59; Univ. Tex, Austin, B.B.A, 62; Midwest. Univ, M.Ed, 68; Phi Beta Kappa; pres. of 16 college organizations. Polit. & Govt. Pos: Dem. precinct chmn, Milam Co, Tex, 65-67; secy, Milam Co. Dem. Party, 67-68; pres, Dem. of Tex, 68-69; Tex. State Rep, Dist. 27, 69- Publ: Americans All, Taylor, 65; Ten Tall Texans, Naylor, 67; 'We, The Americans,' Tex. Educ. Asn, 66. Mem: Tex. State Teachers Asn.(v.pres, 63-64, treas, 64-65, pres, 67-68); Nat. Educ. Asn; pres, Authors of Tex. Asn, 68-69; Lions. Teacher of the year award, 66-67; Author of the Year Award, 67; Outstanding Young Man, 67. Rel: Catholic. Legal Res: 2004 Murray St, Rockdale, Tex. 76567. Mailing Add: Box 272, Rockdale, Tex. 76567.

KUCERA, ROBERT C. R
b. Minn, 4/7/25. Educ: Col. of St. Thomas, B.A, 48; St. Paul Col. of Law, B.S.L, 50, LL.B, 52. Polit. & Govt. Pos: Minn. State Rep, 58-69. Mil. Serv: Army Air Corps, 43-46. Mailing Add: Northfield, Minn. 55057. (1967)

KUCHEL, THOMAS H. R
b. Anaheim, Calif, 8/15/10; s. Henry Kuchel (deceased) and Lutetia Bailey K; m. to Betty Mellethin; c. Karen (Mrs. Delman W. Smith). Educ: Univ. South. Calif, LL.B, 35; Phi Delta Phi; Phi Kappa Phi; Phi Kappa Psi. Hon. LL.D, Univ. South. Calif, Chapman Col, Univ. of Pac, Univ. Santa Clara, Tufts Univ; Hon. L.H.D, Univ. Judaism, Hoyt Fellow, Jonathan Edwards Col, Yale Univ. Polit. & Govt. Pos: Calif. State Assemblyman, 36-39; chmn, Rep. State Cent. Cmt, Calif, 40; Calif. State Sen, 40-43; state controller, Calif, 46-52; U.S. Sen, Calif, 53-69, mem, Pub. Land Law Rev. Cmn, U.S. Rep, Pres. Inaugurations, Mex, del, Interparliamentary Conf. NATO, 56-58, 60, 62, 64, del, Interparliamentary Union, 60, 64 & 66, asst. Rep. Leader, Ranking Minority Mem, Interior and Insular Affairs Cmt, v.chmn, Select Sen. Cmt. on Nat. Water Resources and mem, Appropriations Cmt, U.S. Senate. Bus. & Prof. Pos: Practicing attorney, 35-46. Mem: Calif. State Bar; Native Sons of the Golden West; Am. Legion; Mason; Elks. Rel: Episcopal. Mailing Add: 315 S. Claudina St, Anaheim, Calif. 92805. (1967)

KUEHN, DUANE ARTHUR R
N.Dak. State Rep.
b. Elgin, N.Dak, 7/4/28; s. Daniel J. Kuehn (deceased) and Ottilie Weiss K; m. 3/18/51 to Dorothy Delores Tietz; c. David, Douglas and Brian. Educ: Bismarck, N.Dak. Jr. Col, 48-49. Polit. & Govt. Pos: N.Dak. State Rep, 67- Elec. serviceman, Mont-Dakota Utilities, Bismarck, N.Dak, 46-52, elec. serv. foreman, Mandan, N.Dak, 54-63, elec. and gas serv. foreman, 63-68, asst. safety dir, Bismarck, N.Dak, 68- Mil. Serv: Entered as Pvt, Army, 52, released as Sgt. 1/C, 54, after serv. in 45th Div, Artil; Korea, 52-53; Commendation Ribbon with Metal Pendant. Mem: N.Dak. Soc. Safety Engrs; Lions; Am. Legion. Jaycee Outstanding Young Man Award. Rel: Lutheran. Mailing Add: 708 First Ave. N.E, Mandan, N.Dak. 58554.

KUEHNLE, JAMES PAUL R
Wash. State Rep.
b. Dubuque, Iowa, 12/2/23; s. Louis Frederick Kuehnle and Weltha Groom K; m. 9/9/45 to Georgia Micka; c. Kristine Joyce and Jeanette Lee. Educ: Ore. State Univ, B.S, 46. Polit. & Govt. Pos: Mem, Spokane Co. Rep. Cent. Cmt, Wash, 66-68; precinct committeeman, Spokane Co, 66-69; Wash. State Rep, Fourth Dist, 69- Bus. & Prof. Pos: Pres, Leader Lumber & Hardware, Inc, Spokane, 54-68, Holiday Pools, Inc, 60- Mil. Serv: Pvt, Army Res, 43. Mem: Codes and Standards Cmt, Nat. Swimming Pool Inst; bd. of approval, Jacuzzi Bros, Inc; Kiwanis; C. of C; Elks; Mason; Aircraft Owners & Pilots Asn; Wash. State Law Enforcement Asn. Hon. Life Mem, PTA. Rel: Protestant. Mailing Add: E 12415 Trent, Spokane, Wash. 99216.

KUHLE, DONALD LEWIS D
Secy, Christian Co. Dem. Party, Ill.
b. Assumption, Ill, 7/24/12; s. Lewis Kuhle and Freda K; m. 3/3/34 to Edwina Kuhle; c. Dona Kent and Mark. Polit. & Govt. Pos: Precinct committeeman, Dem. Party, Assumption, Ill; mem, sch. bd, 20 years; secy, Christian Co. Dem. Party, currently. Bus. & Prof. Pos: Farmer; Int. Harvester Dealer, Assumption, and Taylorville, Ill; Ford Dealer, Assumption, Ill. Soy Bean Award; Agr. Honor Award. Rel: Presbyterian. Mailing Add: R.R.1, Assumption, Ill. 62510.

KUHN, BRENDA D
Committeewoman, York Co. Dem. Cmt, Maine
b. New York, N.Y, 6/13/11; d. Walter Francis Kuhn 'Walt' and Vera Spier K; single. Educ: Freinds Sem, 30; training by parents in estate mg. of Walt Kuhn, 30-49. Polit. & Govt. Pos: Committeewoman, York Co. Dem. Cmt, Maine, 66-; mem, Art Cmn, State Maine, 67-; alternate del, Dem. Nat. Conv, 68; hon. dep. sheriff, York Co. Sheriff Dept, 69. Bus. & Prof. Pos: Asst. mgr, Estate of Walt Kuhn, 49-50, mgr, 56-61; mgr, Estate of Vera Kuhn, 61-66; founder, Cape Neddick Park, 65, Founder, Kuhnhouse, 67; pres. and caretaker, Kuhn Mem. Corp, 68- Mil. Serv: Air raid warden, Greenwich Village, N.Y.C, 42-45. Mem: Life mem, Univ. Calif. Los Angeles Art Coun, Munson-Williams-Proctor Inst, Wilderness Soc, Mus. Fine Arts Boston, Portsmouth Hist. Soc, Am. Fedn. Arts; Maine Audubon Soc, Nat. Audubon Soc, Mark Twain Mem, Smithsonian Soc. Assoc, Tombstone Restoration Cmn, Am. Forestry Asn, Art Inst. Chicago, Nordica Mem. Asn, Portland Mus. Art, Cincinnati Art Mus, Brick Store Mus, Metrop. Mus. Art and Am. Mus. Natural Hist; mem. Arch. Am. Art; Nat. Wildlife Fedn; Old Gaol Mus; Natural Resources Coun; Soc. Preservation Hist. Landmarks York Co; Maine Dem. State Cmt. 500 Club; League of Women Voters Kittery York; York Women's Club; Woman's League of York Maine; Copley Soc. Boston. Citizenship Award, York, Maine VFW, 67; Conserv. Award, York Fish and Game Asn, 67; Citizen of the Year, York C. of C; 68; Appreciation Serv, York Dist. Boy Scouts, 68; Lifetime Appreciation Mem, York Art Asn, 68. Rel: Society of Friends. Mailing Add: Cape Neddick Park, Cape Neddick, Maine 03902.

KUHN, JAMES CRAIGHEAD, JR. D
City Councilman, Pittsburgh, Pa.
b. Wilkinsburg, Pa, 4/18/21; s. James Craighead Kuhn and Marion Albert Steigerwalt K; m. 9/28/42 to Mary Regina Jacob; c. Mary Alisoun (Mrs. L.J. Witting), James Craighead, III, Andrew Charles, David Rittenhouse and Thomas Murray. Educ: Dartmouth Col, A.B. cum laude, 42; Univ. Pittsburgh Sch. of Law, LL.B, 48; Order of the Coif. Polit. & Govt. Pos: City Councilman, Pittsburgh, Pa, currently. Bus. & Prof. Pos: Partner, Wilner, Wilner & Kuhn, 52-; bd. mem, Urban Redevelop. Authority of Pittsburgh, Pa. and trustee, Buhl Planetarium & Inst. of Popular Sci, 60-; trustee, Carnegie Inst. Libr. of Pittsburgh, 61- Mil. Serv: Entered as Ens, Naval Res, 42, released as Lt. Comdr, 46, after serv. in Mediterranean and Philippines, 43-46; Commendation Ribbon; Philippine Liberation Medal; ETO and Am. and Pac. Theater Ribbons. Publ: Co-ed, Public Health Laws of City of Pittsburgh, Univ. of Pittsburgh, 51. Mem: Allegheny Co, Pa. and Am. Bar Asns. Rel: Presbyterian. Legal Res: 1175 Murray Hill Ave, Pittsburgh, Pa. 15217. Mailing Add: City-County Bldg, Pittsburgh, Pa. 15219.

KUHNEN, RICHARD F. R
Chmn, Broome Co. Rep. Cmt, N.Y.
b. Binghamton, N.Y, 4/8/17; s. Joseph F. Kuhnen and Anna Cuffe K; m. 11/30/46 to Constance Andersen; c. Cynthia, Frederick and Richard. Educ: Manhattan Col, B.B.A, 38; St. John's Univ, LL.B, 42. Polit. & Govt. Pos: City Chmn, Rep. Party, Binghamton, N.Y, 59-61; mem, N.Y. State Rep. Exec. Cmt; chmn, Broome Co. Rep. Cmt, currently. del, Rep. Nat. Conv, 64 & 68 and N.Y. Constitutional Conv, 67. Mil. Serv: U.S. Coast Guard, 42-45. Rel: Roman Catholic. Legal Res: 11 Avon Rd, Binghamton, N.Y. 13905. Mailing Add: Marine Midland Bldg, Binghamton, N.Y. 13901.

KULL, ROBERT R. D
b. Curtis, Nebr, 1918; m. to Bernita K. Educ: Univ. of Colo, B.A, Journalism, cum laude. Polit. & Govt. Pos: Wash. State Rep, until 66; del, Dem. Nat. Conv, 68. Bus. & Prof. Pos: Radio farm dir; writer. Mil. Serv: Navy Warrant Officer. Mem: Elks. 1967 Legal Res: Yakima, Wash. No mailing address available. (1967)

KUNDE, KENNETH D
b. 7/24/16. Educ: Oshkosh State Col; Univ. Wis. Exten. Div. Polit. & Govt. Pos: Cand. for U.S. Rep, Wis, 48 & 50; chmn, Dem. Co. Cmt, 57; v.chmn, Sixth Dist. Dem. Party, Wis, 60; Wis. State Assemblyman, 62-69. Bus. & Prof. Pos: Former credit and sales mgr; formerly in pub. rels; bus. mgr, currently. Mil. Serv: Army, 41-45; Wis. Nat. Guard. Mem: Amvets (state comdr, 48 & 56, state legis. dir, 49-51); v.pres, Wis. Vet. Coun. Mailing Add: 2831 S. Tenth St, Sheboygan, Wis. 53081. (1967)

KUNDERT, ALICE E. R
State Auditor, S.Dak.
b. Java, S.Dak, 7/23/20; d. Otto J. Kundert and Maria Rieger K; single. Educ: North. State Teachers Col, Teacher's Cert; correspondence, off-campus and summer schs. Polit. & Govt. Pos: Dep. supt. of schs, Campbell Co, S.Dak, 54, co. clerk of courts, 55-60, co. register of deeds, 61-68; secy-treas, Campbell Co. Rep. Party, 62-64, finance chmn, 62-68, v.chmn, 64-69; presidential elector, Rep. Party, S.Dak, 64; mem, S.Dak, State Rep. Adv. Cmt, 65-67; town treas, Mound City, 65-68; adv. Campbell Co. TAR, 66-69; mem, State Local Study Cmn, 68-; state auditor, 69- Bus. & Prof. Pos: Teacher, Campbell Co, S.Dak, 39-43 & 49-54; from clerk to mgr. & buyer, dept. store and dress shop, Calif, 43-48. Publ: Compiler and ed, Mound City Anniversary History Book, 59 and Macra Na Tuaite Book, Int. Leaders Training Lab, Ireland, 63; auth, History of the County of Campbell, 60. Mem: Leader and co. proj. leader, 4-H; chief supvr, Ground Observer Corp; secy, Gr. Campbell Co. Asn; organizor and leader, Mound City Craft and Recreation Club; bd. mem. and past chmn, acting chmn. and v.chmn, Black Hills Leaders Lab; exec. secy, citizen's responsibility cmt, Int. Leaders Training Lab, Ireland, 63; adv, Campbell Co. TAR Club. Rel: Congregational. Legal Res: Mound City, S.Dak. 57646. Mailing Add: 407 N. Van Buren, Pierre, S.Dak. 57501.

KUNKEL, JOHN CRAIN R
b. Harrisburg, Pa, 7/21/98; s. John Christian Kunkel and Louisa Sergeant K; m. 10/11/47 to Katherine Smoot; stepchildren; W. Minster Kunkel, Mrs. Hasbrouck S. Wright and Mrs. Kenneth R. Stark, Jr. Educ: Yale Univ; Harvard Law Sch. Polit. & Govt. Pos: Former cmnr, Dauphin Co. Bd. Cmnrs, Pa; U.S. Rep, Pa, 39-50 and 61-66. Bus. & Prof. Pos: With Harrisburg Nat. Bank and Trust Co. Mil. Serv: Pvt, Army. Mem: Bd. dirs, Harrisburg Pub. Libr; pres, Boys Club of Harrisburg, 3 years; Family and Children's Serv; YMCA; Am. Legion; Odd Fellows. Bridge; Nat. Championship, Mens Pairs, 35; many regional sect. championships, 50-61; 317 Master Points. Mailing Add: 102 Wiconisco St, Harrisburg, Pa. 17110.

KUNZE, EMMA LOUISE R
Committeeman, Ill. Rep. Cent. Cmt.
b. Red Bud, Ill, 2/2/11; d. Herman C. Becker and Elizabeth M. Rabe B; m. 8/17/32 to Elmer George Kunze; c. Barbara (Mrs. Fred Falkner). Educ: Waterloo High Sch, Ill, grad, 28. Polit. & Govt. Pos: Rep. precinct committeeman, York Twp, DuPage Co, Ill, 54-; committeeman, 37th Representative Dist, Ill. Rep. Cent. Cmt, 66- Mem: Elmhurst Rep. Woman's Club (pres, 58-62); Du Page Co. Fedn. of Women's Rep. Clubs (pres, 62-66); York Dames (pres, 1 year); Elmhurst Woman's Club; Elmhurst Hosp. Guild (prog. chmn, 2 years). Rel: Presbyterian. Mailing Add: 551 Berkley, Elmhurst, Ill. 60126.

KUNZIG, ROBERT LOWE R
Adminstr, Gen. Serv. Admin.
b. Phila, Pa, 10/31/18; s. Robert Weiss Kunzig and Hilda Lowe K; married; c. Kim and Robert, Jr. Educ: Univ. Pa, B.A, 39, LL.B, 42; Phi Beta Kappa; Phi Sigma Kappa; Pi Gamma Mu. Polit. & Govt. Pos: Chmn, Phila. Young Rep, 48-50; Dep. Attorney Gen, Pa. 48-53; state chmn, Young Rep. of Pa, 51-52; mem, Pa. Young Rep. Hall of Fame; counsel, U.S. Cong. Cmt, 53-54; exec. dir, U.S. Civil Aeronaut. Bd, 55-58; dir, Nat. Rep. Truth Squad, 56, 60 & 68; mem, U.S. For. Claims Settlement Cmn, 58-61; Rep. cand. for Attorney Gen, Minn, 62; campaign mgr, U.S. Sen. Hugh Scott, Pa, 64, Dist. Attorney Campaign, 65 and Rep. Gubernatorial Campaign 66; exec. dir, Gen. State Authority, Pa. 67-69; adminstr, Gen. Serv. Admin, Wash, D.C, 69- Bus. & Prof. Pos: Attorney, Clark, Ladner, Fortenbaugh & Young, 48-; v.pres, E.G. Clinton Co, 61-62; lectr. and polit. speaker. Mil. Serv: Entered as 2nd Lt, Army, released as Capt, after serv. in Provost Marshal Gen. Off; co-prosecutor of Buchenwald Concentration Camp Case, 47; two Army Commendation Ribbons. Publ: Articles in Look Mag. and American Mag. Mem: Phila, Pa, Minn. and Am. Bar Asns; Union League of Phila; Mask & Wig of Phila. Two Distinguished Serv. to Govt. Awards, Civil Aeronaut. Bd. Rel: Episcopal. Legal Res: Philadelphia, Pa. Mailing Add: Wheat Row, Harbour Square, 1315 Fourth St. S.W, Washington, D.C. 20024.

KUPFERMAN, THEODORE R. R
Justice, Supreme Court of N.Y.
b. N.Y.C, 5/12/20; m. to Dorothee Hering (deceased); c. Theodore R, Jr. and Stephanie. Educ: City Col. New York, B.S; Columbia Univ. Law Sch, LL.B, Kent Scholar; ed, Law Rev; Phi Beta Kappa. Polit. & Govt. Pos: Law secy. to presiding justice, appellate div, Supreme Court First Dept, 48-49; chmn. bd, N.Y. Young Rep. Club, 49-50; counsel and legis. asst. to minority leader, N.Y.C. Coun, 58-62; councilman, N.Y.C, 62-66; U.S. Rep, N.Y, 66-69; justice, Sureme Court of N.Y, 69- Bus. & Prof. Pos: Mem. legal dept, Nat. Broadcasting Co, 51-53; gen. counsel, Cinerama Prod. Corp, 53-58; adj. prof. law, N.Y. Law Sch, 59-64; counsel, Battle, Fowler, Stokes & Kheel, 67-69. Mem: Pres, Fed. Bar Asn. N.Y, N.J, Conn, 54-56, chmn. bd, 56-60; former chmn, Patent, Copyright and Trademark Rels. Cmt, Sect. of Int. and Comp. Law, Am. Bar Asn. and former ed, Bul. of Int. and Comp. Law; ed, Family Legal Adv; bd. trustees and pres, Consular Law Soc; panel of arbitrators, Am. Arbit. Asn; former chmn, Youth Serv. Cmt. and mem. bd, YMCA; pres, City Club, N.Y.C, 56-58. Mailing Add: 140 E. 72nd St, New York, N.Y. 10021.

KUPKA, GEORGE D
b. S. Prarie, Wash, 1912; single. Educ: High Sch. Polit. & Govt. Pos: Former Wash. State Sen; Wash. State Rep, 4 terms. Bus. & Prof. Pos: Jewelry Bus. Mil. Serv: Navy. Mem: Elks; Eagles. Mailing Add: 1316 S. Eighth, Tacoma, Wash. 98405. (1967)

KURFESS, CHARLES FREDERICK R
Ohio State Rep.
b. Wood Co, Ohio, 2/1/30; s. John F. Kurfess and Margaret Zingg K; m. 6/2/56 to Helyn T. Rudolph; c. Todd Frederick, Ann Libbe and Laura Helyn. Educ: Bowling Green State Univ, B.A, 51; Ohio State Univ, LL.B, 57; Voelker fel, Wayne Univ, 51-52; Omicron Delta Kappa; Pi Sigma Alpha; Phi Kappa Tau; Phi Delta Phi. Polit. & Govt. Pos: Ohio State Rep, Wood Co, 57-, Speaker, Ohio State House of Rep, 67-; mem, Wood Co. Rep. Cent. and Exec. Cmts, 64-; del, Rep. Nat. Conv, 68. Bus. & Prof. Pos: Attorney-at-law, 58- Mil. Serv: Entered as Pvt, Army, 52, released as Cpl, 54, after serv. in Counter Intel. Corps, Far East, 53-54. Mem: Wood Co, Ohio State, Northwest Ohio and Am. Bar Asns; C. of C; Wood Co. Farm Bur. Fedn; Bowling Green State Univ. Alumni Asn. Outstanding Young Man of Bowling Green, Ohio and area, 65. Mailing Add: 9449 Reitz Rd, R.R. 1, Perrysburg, Ohio 43551.

KURKE, ELEANOR BERGAN R
State Committeewoman, Rep. State Cmt. of Fla.
b. Williston, N.Dak, 6/24/21; d. Thomas Alfred Bergan and Ada Claire Brownson B; m. 3/16/42 to John Matthew Kurke; c. Susan (Mrs. Larry G. Heine), John Matthew, Jr, William Jeffrey, Lance Brownson and Benjamin Thomas. Educ: N.Dak. State Univ, 2 years; Gamma Phi Beta. Polit. & Govt. Pos: Pres, Women's Rep. Club of Gr. Naples, Fla, 66-; alternate del, Rep. Nat. Conv, 68; chmn, Nixon for President, Collier Co, Fla, 68; state committeewoman, Rep. State Cmt. of Fla, 68- Mem: Soc. of Mayflower Descendants; Daughters of the Am. Colonists; DAR; Nat. and Fla. Fedn. of Rep. Women; Ment. Health Asn. Rel: Catholic. Mailing Add: 570 Palm Circle W, Naples, Fla. 33940.

KURMEL, EDWARD A. D
b. New York, 6/10/12; s. John Kurmel and Sophia Terpilowski K; m. 4/23/38 to Josephine Harsche; c. Geraldine. Educ: St. John Univ, 30-34. Polit. & Govt. Pos: N.Y. State Assemblyman until 67; alternate del, Dem. Nat. Conv, 68. Bus. & Prof. Pos: V.censor, Polish Nat. Alliance of Brooklyn, 54-62, pres, 62- Rel: Catholic. Legal Res: 54 Russell St, Brooklyn, N.Y. 11222. Mailing Add: 180 Driggs Ave, Brooklyn, N.Y. 11222.

KURTH, RICHARD AUGUSTIN R
b. Sommerville, Mass, 4/22/89; married. Educ: Boston Eng. High Sch; scholarships to Royal Conservatory of Music, Leipzig and Stern Conservatory, Berlin. Polit. & Govt. Pos: N.H. State Rep, until 67. Bus. & Prof. Pos: Retired. Mil. Serv: U.S. Army, retired; WWI; WWII Commendation Ribbon and pendant, Meritorious Serv. WWII. Mem: Charter and life mem, Nat. Soc. State Legislators; life mem, Zetland Lodge, AF&AM, Boston; Mass. Consistory; Eastern Star; White Shrine of Jerusalem; Winnepesaukee Shrine Club; Disabled Officers Asn; Mil. Order of For. Wars; U.S. Nat. Grange; Commissioned Officers Open Mess; Bsn. Naval Shipyard; Asn. Musicians Asn. local 9 AF of M, CIO, (life mem.); Nat. Retired Teachers Asn; Bektash Temple Shrine AAONMS Concord, N.H. Rel: Protestant. Mailing Add: North Sandwich, N.H. 03259. (1967)

KURTZ, ROBERT M, JR. R
Mem, Pa. Rep. State Exec. Cmt.
m. to Katharine Buckingham; c. Michael and David. Educ: Univ. of Redlands, B.S, 56; Pa. State Univ. Polit. & Govt. Pos: Del, Rep. Nat. Conv, 64; mem, Pa. Rep. State Cmt, 66- and Pa. Rep. State Exec. Cmt, currently. Bus. & Prof. Pos: V.pres, Kurtz Bros. Mil. Serv: Entered as Pvt, Army, 56, released as Cpl, 58. Rel: Presbyterian. Mailing Add: 214 Charles Rd, Clearfield, Pa. 16830.

KURY, FRANKLIN L. D
Pa. State Rep.
b. Sunbury, Pa, 10/15/36; s. Barney Kury (deceased) and Helen Witkowski K; m. 9/14/63 to Elizabeth Heazlett. Educ: Trinity Col, Hartford, Conn, A.B, 58; Univ. Pa. Law Sch, LL.B, 61; Phi Beta Kappa; Pi Kappa Alpha. Polit. & Govt. Pos: Staff asst. to Gov. George M. Leader Off, 58; state co-chmn, Pa. Students for Kennedy-Johnson, 60; legal asst. and Dep. Attorney Gen, Pa. Dept. of Justice, 61-62; exec. asst. to U.S. Rep. George M. Rhodes, 62, field

rep, 63-66; secy, Sunbury Dem. Cmt, Pa, 64-; committeeman, Northumberland Co. Dem. Cmt, Pa, 64-; Pa. State Rep, 108th Dist, 66- Mil. Serv: Entered as Pvt. E-1, Army, 62, released as Pvt. E-2, 63; 1st Lt, Army Res. Publ: 'Crisis in Law of Presidential Succession,' Pa. Bar Asn. Quart, 3/65. Mem: Am. and Northumberland Co. Bar Asns; Pa. Bar Asn.(chmn. cmt. on pres. disability and v.pres. vacancy, 65-). Rel: Presbyterian. Legal Res: 124 Market St, Sunbury, Pa. 17801. Mailing Add: 216 Market St, Sunbury, Pa. 17801.

KUSHNIR, MARY CONSTANCE D
Mem, Colo. Dem. State Cent. Cmt.
b. Beaver Falls, Pa, 6/16/08; d. Abraam Isaac Fistell and Ella Pitler F; m. 10/25/43 to Jacob J. Kushnir; c. Deborah Lee. Educ: Univ. Denver, 25-28; Pueblo Jr. Col, 1 year; South. Colo. State Col, spec. course; West. State Col, spec. courses; Adams State Col, spec. courses. Polit. & Govt. Pos: Secy, Young Dem, Pueblo, Colo, 59-60; del, Young Dem. Conv, 4 times; Dem. precinct v.chmn, 12 years; mem, Colo. Dem. State Cent. Cmt, currently. Bus. & Prof. Pos: Field secy, Am. Med. Center, Denver, Colo, 35-61, Children's Asthmatic Research Inst, 61-62. Mem: Muscular Dystrophy Asn. of Am.(publicity chmn, Pueblo Chap, 6 years); Prairie Belle Baton Corp. of Pueblo (pres, 68-69). Cert. of Merit, Muscular Dystrophy; Cert. of Merit, Am. Cancer Soc. Rel: Jewish. Mailing Add: 818 Albany, Pueblo, Colo. 81003.

KUSIBAB, THAD I. D
Ill. State Sen.
b. Chicago, Ill, 1/19/10; m. to Jeanette Pyrek K; c. Melvin P. and Gilbert J. Educ: DePaul Univ. Polit. & Govt. Pos: Secy, 26th Ward Dem. Orgn, Ill, 44-; Ill. State Sen, 62- Bus. & Prof. Pos: Treas, Joseph T. Beran Ins. Co. Mem: K. of C; Polish Nat. Alliance; Polish Roman Cath. Union; Local 130, U.A. Rel: Catholic. Mailing Add: 2043 Augusta Blvd, Chicago, Ill. 60622. (1967)

KUTHY, EUGENE WENDEL D
Chmn, 18th Cong. Dist. Dem. Cmt, Mich.
b. Dearborn, Mich, 12/17/30; s. Wendell Kuthy and Elizabeth R. Silagyi K; m. 8/30/52 to Jacqueline Ruth Getoor; c. Douglas Eugene, James Alan, Thomas Jay and Robin Jacqueline. Educ: Univ. Mich, A.B, 54; Detroit Col. Law, J.D, 64; Druids; Delta Theta Phi. Polit. & Govt. Pos: Precinct del, Royal Oak Dem. Party, Mich, 62-; registr. dir, Oakland Co. Dem. Cmt, 64, finance dir, 65-66; del, Dem. Nat. Conv, 64 & 68; v.chmn, 18th Cong. Dist. Dem. Cmt, 64-65, chmn, 65- Bus. & Prof. Pos: Mem. faculty, Univ. Mich. Bus. Admin. Col, Dearborn, 61-; partner, Renfrew & Edberg, 64-; v.pres, Am. Acad. Transportation, 66- Mil. Serv: Entered as A/S, Navy, 54, released as Lt.(jg), 58, after serv. in Off. Chief Naval Opers, D.C, 55-58; Comdr, Naval Res. Security Group Div. 9-6, Detroit. Mem: Am, Oakland Co. and Mich. State Bar Asns; Am. Judicature Soc. Rel: Protestant. Mailing Add: 4595 Valleyview Dr, Orchard Lake, Mich. 48033.

KUTZ, ROBERT BOYNE R
b. San Francisco, Calif, 1/12/22; s. Charles Conyngham Kutz and Mildred Boyne K; m. 9/17/66 to Marguerite Ellis; c. Robert Wade, Katherine Elizabeth, William Pillsbury, James Charles, Ted James, Julie Ann and Roy Ellis. Educ: Univ. Calif, Berkeley, 39-42; Hastings Col. of Law, J.D, 48; founding mem, Thurston Soc, Hastings Col. of Law; Chi Phi. Polit. & Govt. Pos: Mem, Butte Co. Rep. Cent. Cmt, Calif, 58-61; Butte Co. primary and gen. elections chmn, Reagan for Gov, 66; Butte Co. chmn, Friends of Gov. Reagan, 67-; mem, New Car Dealers Policy and Appeals Bd, State of Calif, 68, pres, 69-; alternate del, Rep. Nat. Conv, 68. Bus. & Prof. Pos: Assoc, Law Offices of Duard F. Geis, Willows, Calif, 49; attorney, Law Offices of Robert B. Kutz, Chico, Calif, 49-54 & 58-; partner, Ware and Kutz, Attorneys at Law, 54-58. Mil. Serv: Entered as Seaman 1/C, Navy, 42, released as Sp.(C) 2/C, 46, after serv. in Dist. Intel. Office and Classification Centers, Continental U.S; Naval Res, 51-58, Lt.(jg). Mem: State Bar of Calif; Butte Co. Bar Asn.(pres, 66-67); Am. Judicature Soc; Rotary; Elks; Commonwealth Club of Calif; Soc. of Calif. Pioneers; Am. Legion; Colusi Hist. Soc. Rel: Protestant. Legal Res: 2619 Burnap Ave, Chico, Calif. 95926. Mailing Add: P.O. Box 3297, Chico, Calif. 95926.

KUYKENDALL, DAN HEFLIN R
U.S. Rep, Tenn.
b. Cherokee, Tex, 7/9/24; s. Tom Groves Kuykendall and Sarah Johnson K; m. 7/6/51 to Jacqueline Meyer; c. Dan Heflin, Jr, John Meyer, Kathleen Virginia and Jacqueline Kay. Educ: Tex. A&M Col, B.S, 47. Polit. & Govt. Pos: U.S. Rep, Tenn, 67-; del, Rep. Nat. Conv, 68. Bus. & Prof. Pos: Management, Procter & Gamble Co, 47-64; agent, Equitable Life Assurance Soc, 64- Mil. Serv: Lt, Air Force, 42-45, serv. as B-29 Pilot. Mem: Mil. Order World Wars. Rel: Methodist. Legal Res: 395 N. Graham, Apt. 7, Memphis, Tenn. 38117. Mailing Add: 7902 Greentree Rd, Bethesda, Md. 20034.

KUYKENDALL, JEROME KENNETH R
Chmn, Indian Claims Cmn.
b. Pomeroy, Wash, 12/8/07; s. Elgin Victor Kuykendall and Margaret Scully K; m. 8/10/36 to Jane Brehm; c. Gretchen Anne (Mrs. Jones) and Penny Jane (Mrs. Engle); m. 2nd to Helen Douglas Dickinson. Educ: Univ. Wash, Seattle, J.D, 32; Phi Delta Phi; Phi Delta Theta; Oval Club. Polit. & Govt. Pos: Asst. Attorney Gen, Wash, 41-44 & 46; chmn, Pub. Serv. Cmn, Wash, 51-53; chmn, Fed. Power Cmn, 53-61; chmn, Indian Claims Cmn, 67- Bus. & Prof. Pos: Lawyer, Seattle, Wash, 32-41, Pebbles and Kuykendall, Olympia, Wash, 47-51 and Shanley, Fisher & Kuykendall, Wash, D.C, 62-67. Mil. Serv: Entered as Lt.(jg), Naval Res, 44, released as Lt, 46. Mem: Wash. State, D.C, Am. and Fed. Bar Asns; Army and Navy Club; Capitol Hill Club, Wash. D.C. Rel: Unitarian. Mailing Add: 2700 N. Oakland St, Arlington, Va. 22207.

KUYKENDALL, RUFUS CALVIN R
b. Indianapolis, Ind, 9/24/03; s. John H. Kuykendall and Anna B. Jackson K; m. 4/1/39 to Clemmie Ethel Ransom. Educ: Ind. Univ, A.B, 27; Sch. Law, LL.B, 42; Kappa Alpha Psi; Sigma Pi Phi. Polit. & Govt. Pos: Organizer, Young Negro Rep, Ind, 24; worker, Young Negro Marion Co. Groups for Hoover, 28; organizer and asst. dir, Young Negro Rep. Clubs, 30; asst. to State Chmn, Rep. State Cent. Cmt, 36 & 46; mem, State Platform Cmt, 43-50; dep. prosecutor, 43-52; co-chmn, Seventh Ward Marion Co. Rep. Cmt, 52; asst. city attorney, 52-55; mem, U.S. Cmn. for UNESCO, 54-55; asst. staff dir, Legal Staff, U.S. Cmt. on Civil Rights, 59-60; city councilman; Criminal Court pub. defender, 64; judge, Marion Superior Court, currently. Bus. & Prof. Pos: Legal Adv, Frederick Douglas Rep. Club, 65. Publ: Negro at Indiana, The Vagabond, 27. Mem: Marion Co. Bar Asn.(pres, 62-66); Kappa Alphi Psi (state legal adv, 62-66); first v.pres, Citizens Forum, Inc, 64-65; Sigma Pi Psi (secy, currently); Indianapolis, Ind. State, Nat. and Am. Bar Asns; Juvenile Aid Div. Adv. Cmt; C. of C; Fedn. of Assoc. Clubs, Inc; Commun. Serv. Coun; Family Serv. & Legal Aid Soc; Ind. Soc. for Prev. of Blindness; Nat. Negro Rep. Assembly; Indianapolis Urban League. Indianapolis Recorder Newspaper Honor Roll, 55; NAACP Man of the Year, 57; C. Francis Stratford Award, Nat. Bar Asn, 63; Outstanding Kappa of the Year, Kappa Alpha Psi, 63. Rel: African Methodist Episcopal. Legal Res: 2202 North Capitol Ave, Indianapolis, Ind. 46208. Mailing Add: Marion County Superior Court Room 6, Room W-542 City-County Bldg, Indianapolis, Ind. 46204.

KVAALEN, OSCAR SEIGEL R
Mont. State Rep.
b. Lambert, Mont, 1/1/21; s. Ostien Sonderson Kvaalen and Esther Armston K; m. 3/5/60 to Ruth C. Johnson; c. Jon Seigel and Elizabeth Esther. Educ: Concordia Col, B.A, 43. Polit. & Govt. Pos: Conservationist, U.S. Soil Conserv. Serv, 49-52; field agent, State Land Dept, Mont, 53-55; Mont. State Rep, 59-64 & 67-, chmn, Educ. Cmt, Mont. State House of Rep, 61 & 63. Mil. Serv: Entered as Midshipman, Naval Res, 43, released as Lt.(jg), 46, after serv. in Amphibious Forces, Pac. Fleet; Am. Theater and Pac. Theater Ribbons with 2 Stars. Mem: VFW; Farm Bur. Rel: Lutheran. Mailing Add: Lambert, Mont. 59243. (1967)

KVAM, ADOLPH Conservative
Minn. State Rep.
b. Willmar, Minn; s. Andrew Kvam; m. to Doris Holm; c. David, Gregory, Kristin and Karen. Educ: Univ. of Minn, B.B.A. Polit. & Govt. Pos: Minn. State Rep, 67-; mem, Gov. Adv. Cmn. on Sch. Aids Formula; treas, Litchfield Sch. Bd. Mil. Serv: World War II; China and India. Mailing Add: 25 W. Lockerbie, Litchfield, Minn. 55355.

KWITOWSKI, WALTER ANTHONY D
Treas, Erie Co. Dem. Party, Pa.
b. Erie, Pa, 8/13/24; s. Walter Kwitowski and Pearl Kinecki K; m. 11/27/52 to Jeannette Marie Gorny; c. Walter Andrew, Mark Anthony and Christine Marie. Educ: Gannon Col, 3 years; Univ. Miami, 1 year. Polit. & Govt. Pos: Second Ward Chmn, Erie Dem. Party, Pa, 50-52; chmn, Erie Young Dem, 51; personnel dir, Erie, 66-; treas, Erie Co. Dem. Party, 66-; alternate del, Dem. Nat. Conv, 68. Bus. & Prof. Pos: Real estate agent, Hurle Real Estate, 51-54; mgr, Erie Press Club, 54-55; investr, Commonwealth Pa. Dept. Pub. Instr, 55-61. Mil. Serv: Entered as Pvt, Army, 43, released as Pfc, 46, after serv. in Seventh Div. Mem: Northwest. Pa. Personnel Asn; Phila. Chap, Pub. Personnel Asn. Rel: Roman Catholic. Mailing Add: 542 E. 12th St, Erie, Pa. 16503.

KYER, HARRY FRANKLIN R
Chmn, Braxton Co. Rep. Party, W.Va.
b. Gassaway, W.Va, 5/15/24; s. Henry Earl Kyer and Emma Lockard K; m. 9/13/48 to Mary Louise Brady; c. Ben L. Educ: Bowling Green Bus. Univ, B.S. in Acct, 53. Polit. & Govt. Pos: Mem. Town Coun, Gassaway, W.Va, 67-69; chmn, Braxton Co. Rep. Party, 67- Bus. & Prof. Pos: Owner and operator of independent ins. agency. Mil. Serv: Entered as Seaman, Navy, 43, released as PO 1/C, 46, after serv. aboard U.S.S. Ranger, ETO and U.S.S. Wasp, Pac. Theatre, 44-45; Unit Citation; Good Conduct Medal; ETO Award; Battle Stars. Mem: Lions; VFW. Rel: United Methodist. Mailing Add: 500 Braxton St, Gassaway, W.Va. 26624.

KYES, ERNEST G. R
s. Lester Kyes; m. to Della Jacques; c. Gayton, Dennis, Dana, Dianna and Jeffrey. Polit. & Govt. Pos: Maine State Rep, 67-69. Bus. & Prof. Pos: Operator, Kyes Motel. Mil. Serv: Marine Corps, World War II. Mem: VFW; Am. Legion; Rotary; Eagles; Tourist Hospitality; K. of C; Sports Boosters; past pres, C. of C; Dir, Maine Motel Asn, 5 years, v.pres, 1 year. Recognized for Outstanding Contribution to Maine Hospitality, 64. Mailing Add: 217 W. Front St, Skowhegan, Maine 04976. (1967)

KYHL, VERNON H. R
Iowa State Sen.
b. LaPlata, Mo, 7/30/08; s. Christian Kyhl and Dorothea K; m. 1936 to Alice Manning (deceased); c. Curtis, Jerry (Mrs. Jerry Amosson), Kenneth, Rebecca and Kevin. Educ: State Col. Iowa. Polit. & Govt. Pos: Former chmn, Butler Co. Rep. Party, Iowa; pres, Parkersburg Sch. Bd, 12 years; Iowa State Sen, 66 and currently. Bus. & Prof. Pos: Owner, automobile bus; owner, Farmech Mfg. & Sales Co; treas, Waterloo Register Co, Cedar Falls, Iowa; pres, Farm & Home Supply Co, Marshalltown; co-owner, Butler Co. Farm. Mem: Past pres, Parkersburg Rotary Club; past pres, Commercial Club; Elks. Mailing Add: State Capitol, E. Tenth & Grand Ave, Des Moines, Iowa 53019. (1967)

KYL, JOHN H. R
U.S. Rep, Iowa
b. Wisner, Nebr, 5/9/19; s. John George Kyl and Johanna Boonstra K; m. 5/16/41 to Arlene Griffith; c. Jon, Jannene, Jayne. Educ: Nebr. State Teachers Col, Wayne, A.B; Univ. of Nebr, M.A; Univ. of Nebr. and Drake Univ, Des Moines, grad. work. Polit. & Govt. Pos: U.S. Rep, Iowa, 59-64 & 66-; mem, Pub. Land Law Rev. Cmn. and Outdoor Recreation Resources Rev. Cmn; mem, Lewis and Clark Trail Cmn. Bus. & Prof. Pos: Hist. teacher; coach, faculty mem. of col, Wayne, Nebr; C. of C. mgr; farmer; dir, news and spec. events, KTVO, Ottumwa, Iowa; TV newscaster, 57-59. Rel: Presbyterian. Legal Res: 208 W. North St, Bloomfield, Iowa 52537. Mailing Add: 1026 Longworth House Office Bldg, Washington, D.C. 20515.

KYLE, CHARLES CLAYTON 'CASEY' R
City Councilman, Santa Maria, Calif.
b. Whitehall, Mont, 2/27/23; s. Charles Larabee Kyle and Marguerite Pearl Stephens K; m. 12/26/53 to Carmen Marie Bahr; c. Candy Ann, Colleen Denise and Casey Jon. Educ: Santa Barbara Bus. Col, 48. Polit. & Govt. Pos: City councilman, Santa Maria, Calif, 56-64 & 69, mayor, 60-64; mem, Santa Bar-

bara Co. Cong. Mayors, 60-64; chmn. channel div, League of Calif. Cities, 63; mem, LAFCO, Santa Barbara Co, 64; mem, Calif. Rep. State Cent. Cmt, 69- Bus. & Prof. Pos: Co-owner, secy. and treas, Kyle Roofing Co, Inc, 55-68; life underwriter, N.Y. Life Ins. Co, 68- Mil. Serv: Entered as A/S, Navy, 43, released as Gunners Mate 3/C, 46, after serv. in Armed Guard, Pac. Theatre, 43-46; Six Ribbons. Mem: Santa Maria Contractors Asn; Roofing Contractors Asn; Nat. Asn. Life Underwriters; Kiwanis (past pres, 60); Mason; Scottish Rite (secy); Shrine; Santa Maria Shrine Club (past pres, 65); Legion of Honor; Elks; Health Planning Asn. South. Calif. Jr. C. of C. Distinguished Serv. Award, 60. Rel: Christian Church of N.Am. Mailing Add: 231 N. Palisade Dr, Santa Maria, Calif. 93454.

KYLE, JOHN WILLIAM R
W.Va. State Del.
b. Cressmont, W.Va, 6/29/12; s. John Riley Kyle and Elizabeth Krantz K; m. 5/9/37 to Rebecca Mae Hanshaw; c. Margaret (Mrs. Campbell) and Kenton (deceased). Educ: Fairmont State Col, A.B; Epsilon Pi Tau. Polit. & Govt. Pos: W.Va. State Del, 69- Bus. & Prof. Pos: W.Va. mine foreman, 40; Am. Baptist clergyman, 50-64; pub. sch. teacher, Clay Co. Schs, 64- Mem: Am. and W.Va. Indust. Arts Asns; hon. mem, Future Farmers of Am. Rel: Baptist. Mailing Add: Box 195, Clay, W.Va. 25043.

KYLE, MARCUS AURELIUS R
b. Bennington, Okla, 12/13/23; s. Don Thomas Kyle and Irene Corbett K; m. 10/29/49 to Carmen Lucila Perez; c. Alan Glenn. Educ: Univ. of Denver. Polit. & Govt. Pos: Treas, Dist. 15 and chmn, Precinct 221, Harris Co, Tex, 56-58; membership chmn, Dade Co. Rep. Exec. Cmt, Fla, 60 & 62, chmn, 62 & 66. Bus. & Prof. Pos: Part-time bus driver, Univ. of Denver, 47-48; mechanic's helper, Pan Am. Airways, 46, traffic suprv, 48-52; asst. dir. of stations, Trans-Tex. Airways, 52-58; supvr. tech. publ, Nat. Airlines, Inc, Miami, Fla, 58-68, dir. off. serv, 68- Mil. Serv: Entered as A/S, Coast Guard, 42, released as Radarman 2/C, 45, after serv. in Amphibious Forces; Am. and Asiatic-Pac. Theater Campaign Ribbons; Philippine Liberation Medal with Two Battle Stars. Mem: Past dist. comdr, 12th Dist. of La, VFW. Rel: Presbyterian; Elder. Mailing Add: 925 Majorca, Coral Gables, Fla. 33134.

KYLE, SAMUEL WILLIAM 'BILL' R
Chmn, Clark Co. Rep. Cmt, S.Dak.
b. Redfield, S.Dak, 4/12/25; s. William Cassidy Kyle and Frances Hewitt K; m. 6/7/64 to Norma Suzanne Lyons; c. Tracey, Carrie and Christopher. Educ: Clark High Sch, 4 years. Polit. & Govt. Pos: Chmn, Clark Co. Rep. Cmt, S.Dak, 63-; dir, S.Dak. State Agency Surplus Property, 69. Bus. & Prof. Pos: Mgr, Kyles Hardware, Clark, 48- Mil. Serv: Entered as A/S, Navy, 43, released as Pharmacist's Mate 3/C, 45, after serv. in Naval Hosp, Fleet Air Wing 13, Pac. Theater, 43-45. Mem: Mason; Shrine; Am. Legion. Rel: Congregational. Mailing Add: 210 N. Cloud, Clark, S.Dak. 57225.

KYNES, JAMES W. D
b. Marianna, Fla, 8/31/28; s. James Walter Kynes and Grace Rowell K; m. 7/1/50 to Marjorie A. Hiatt; c. James H, William L, John F. Educ: Univ. of Fla, B.S, 50, LL.B, 55; Kappa Alpha; Phi Delta Phi. Polit. & Govt. Pos: Mem, Fla. Revenue Cmn, Fla. Budget Cmn, Fla. Pardon Bd, Fla. Judiciary Coun. and bd. educ, Fla. Securities Cmn; Coord. Fla. Dem. Cand, 60; exec. asst. to Gov, 60-63; del, Dem. Nat. Conv, 64, alternate del, 68; attorney gen, Fla, 64-66. Mil. Serv: 1st Lt, Air Force, 51-53. Mem: Nat. Asn. Attorneys Gen; chmn, trustees, Cent. Fla. Jr. Col, 57-61; Univ. Fla. Corp; Univ. Fla. Alumni Asn; Kiwanis; Blue Key. Rel: Methodist. Mailing Add: P.O. Box 9128, Tampa, Fla. 33604. (1967)

KYROS, PETER NICHOLAS D
U.S. Rep, Maine
b. Portland, Maine, 7/11/25; s. Nicholas Kyros and Anna Poulos K; m. 9/28/47 to Alice Williams; c. Peter N, Jr. and Joanne Carol. Educ: Mass. Inst. Tech; U.S. Naval Acad, B.S, 47; Harvard Law Sch, LL.B, 57. Polit. & Govt. Pos: Attorney, Maine Pub. Utilities Cmn, 57-60; chmn, First Dist. Dem. Cmt, Maine, 62-64; chmn, Maine State Dem. Cmt, 64-66; U.S. Rep, Maine, 67-; del, Dem. Nat. Conv, 68. Mil. Serv: Entered as Midshipman, Navy, 45, released as Lt, 53, after serv. in Naval Supply Corps. Mem: Am. and Maine Bar Asns; Am. and Maine Trial Lawyers Asn; Maine Hist. Soc; AF&AM; Am. Legion. Rel: Greek Orthodox. Legal Res: 76 Pearl St, Portland, Maine 04111. Mailing Add: 327 Cannon House Office Bldg, Washington, D.C. 20515.

L

LABERGE, ROMEO LOUIS D
Maine State Rep.
b. Auburn, Maine, 12/8/89; s. Laurent Laberge and Annie Beaudette L; m. 6/8/36 to Dorila Smith; c. Romeo Jr. and Norman. Polit. & Govt. Pos: Maine State Rep, 65-66 & 69- Bus. & Prof. Pos: Owner of Supermarket, Laberge Bros, Auburn, Maine, 10-60. Mil. Serv: Army, 17-18, Pvt, serv. in 305th Machine Gun Batallion, France, 17-18. Mem: Life mem, Am. Legion; VFW; K. of C; Credit Union; Award for 10 year Serv. Award, Credit Union. Rel: Roman Catholic. Mailing Add: 55 Broad St, Auburn, Maine 04210.

LABORDE, PAULIN JOSEPH, JR. D
La. State Rep.
b. Marksville, La, 10/10/39; s. Paulin Joseph Laborde and Addie Rose Bordelon L; m. 6/4/60 to Gayle Marcotte; c. P.J, III, Jeanne M, David C. and Ann M. Educ: Univ. Southwest. La, B.A, 60; Tulane Univ. Law Sch, J.D, 63; Blue Key; Circle K; Phi Alpha Delta. Polit. & Govt. Pos: Del, Dem. Nat. Conv, 68; La. State Rep, 68- Mem: Am. Bar Asn; La. State Bar Asn.(house of del, 67); Avoyelles Parish Bar Asn.(pres, 65). Rel: Catholic. Legal Res: Coulee des Grues Rd, Marksville, La. 71351. Mailing Add: 226 E. Mark St, Marksville, La. 71351.

LABOUISSE, CAROLYN GAY D
Mem, La. State Dem. Cent. Cmt.
b. Plaquemine, La, 11/15/14; d. U.S. Sen. Edward James Gay (deceased) and Gladys Fenner G; m. 3/19/38 to Frank Monroe Labouisse; c. Frank Monroe, Jr. and Anne Gay (Mrs. William Dean). Educ: Smith Col, 32-33; Newcomb Col, Tulane Univ, 33-34. Polit. & Govt. Pos: Pres, Independent Women's Orgn, 53-56; mem, League of Women Voters of New Orleans, 53-; mem, New Orleans Park and Pkwy. Cmn, 54-62; chmn, La. Voting Laws Asn, 56-59; mem. and current v.pres, S.La. Dem. Women's Club, 56-; mem. staff of U.S. Rep. Hale Boggs, La, 62-63; mem, La. State Dem. Cent. Cmt, from 27th Dist, Wards 10 and 11, Orleans Parish, 64-; chmn, Coun. for Housing and Commun. Develop, 67-; del, Dem. Nat. Conv, 68. Rel: Episcopal. Mailing Add: 1211 Philip St, New Orleans, La. 70130.

LaBROSSE, FRANCIS DFL
Minn. State Sen.
b. Duluth, Minn, 1908; married; c. two. Educ: Duluth Schs. Polit. & Govt. Pos: Minn. State Sen, 64-; Minn. State Rep, 16 years. Mil. Serv: Navy. Mem: VFW; Am. Legion; Elks; Moose; Eagles; Musicians Union, AFL-CIO, 30 years. Mailing Add: 3138 Restormel St, Duluth, Minn. 55806. (1967)

LACEY, (WILLIAM) CHARLES R
S. Dak. State Rep.
b. Minnehaha Co, S. Dak, 3/25/07; s. William Gregory Lacey and Christina Kurtzhals L; m. to Nellie Gembarouski; c. Greg, Catherine, Patrick H, Cynthia and Margaret. Educ: Columbus Col; Univ. S. Dak, LL.B; Phi Delta Phi. Polit. & Govt. Pos: S. Dak. State Rep, 44- Bus. & Prof. Pos: Lawyer. Mem: State Bar, S. Dak; Kiwanis; Elks; SAR; C. of C; Am. Bar Asn. Citation of Merit, Muscular Dystrophy Asns. of Am, Inc, 69. Rel: Catholic. Mailing Add: 1004 E. 35th St, Sioux Falls, S.Dak. 57105.

LaCHAPELLE, FRANCIS JOSEPH D
R.I. State Sen.
b. Natick, R.I, 9/26/13; m. to Yvonne Raboin. Educ: LaSalle Acad, 31. Polit. & Govt. Pos: R.I. State Sen, 55- Bus. & Prof. Pos: Bus. operator; U.T.C. Mil. Serv: Navy. Mem: Pres, West Warwick Little League; West Warwick Babe Ruth League; P.V. Softball League; former pres, Kent Co. Basketball League; chmn, St. James Alumni Basketball Tournament; P.V. March of Dimes Sports; Elks; Frontenac Club; Phenix Sportsman Club; Skin Divers Club. Pawtucket Valley C.Y.O. Man of the Year, 54. Mailing Add: 1441 Main St, West Warwick, R.I. 02893. (1967)

LACKEY, J. M. D
Chmn, Alexander Co. Dem. Exec. Cmt, N.C.
b. Alexander Co, N.C, 3/29/16; s. Chalmers A. Lackey and Pearl Price L; m. 6/18/42 to Hazel Elizabeth Barnes; c. Lynne and Joy. Educ: N.C. State Col, Raleigh. Polit. & Govt. Pos: Chmn, Alexander Co. Dem. Exec. Cmt, N.C, currently. Mil. Serv: Entered as Pvt, Army, 43, released as S/Sgt, 45, after serv. in Inf, ETO. Mem: Mason; Farm Bur; C. of C; Grange; N.C. State Bd. of Health; Am. Legion. Rel: Presbyterian. Mailing Add: Rt. 2, Hiddenite, N.C. 28636.

LA CORTE, NICHOLAS ST. JOHN R
N.J. State Sen.
b. Elizabeth, N.J, 3/8/18. Educ: Cornell Univ, B.A; Rutgers Law Sch, LL.B. Polit. & Govt. Pos: Former mem. bd. trustees, Libr. Bd, Cranford, N.J; former mem. Bd. Health and Planning Bd, former asst. prosecutor, Union Co, former mayor, Cranford; mem. gov. body, Cranford, 57-63; former counsel, Borough Mountainside; former N.J. State Assemblyman; N.J. State Sen, 69- Bus. & Prof. Pos: Attorney. Mem: Past Grand Knight Elizabeth Coun. 253 K. of C; Lions; past counsel, East. Union Co. Jaycees. Mailing Add: 143 E. Jersey St, Elizabeth, N.J. 07201. (1967)

LADD, KENNETH RICHARD R
Mem, Calif. Rep. State Cent. Cmt.
b. Newton, Kans, 2/17/22; s. Harley C. Ladd and Lena M. Schmahl L; m. 5/28/44 to Nancy Jean Hogue. Educ: Stockton Col, 46. Polit. & Govt. Pos: Mem, San Joaquin Rep. Cent. Cmt, Calif, 52-69, v.chmn, 56-66, chmn, 66-69; mem, Calif. Rep. State Cent. Cmt, 69- Bus. & Prof. Pos: Real estate salesman, 46-58; real estate broker, 58-64; owner and pres, Sims & Grupe, Stockton, Calif, 64- Mil. Serv: Entered as Pvt, Army, 41, released as 1st Lt, Air Force, 45; Silver Star with Oak Leaf Cluster; Distinguished Flying Cross; Air Medal with Clusters; S.W. Pac. Campaign Ribbon. Mem: Am. Legion; VFW; past pres, Stockton Bd. of Realtors; Calif. Real Estate Asn; past pres, San Joaquin Co. Econ. Develop. Asn; Soc. Res. Appraisors; Lions; Commonwealth Club of Calif. Rel: Methodist. Legal Res: 1128 Lincoln Rd, Stockton, Calif. 95207. Mailing Add: P.O. Box 1888, Stockton, Calif. 95201.

LADEAU, CHRISTINE BURBANK R
b. Marshfield, Vt, 8/3/19; m. to Alden M. Ladeau (deceased). Educ: St. Johnsbury Acad; Santa Ana Jr. Col; Univ. of Vt; Johnson Teachers Col, 38-39. Polit. & Govt. Pos: Vt. State Rep, 63-66. Bus. & Prof. Pos: Teacher; sch. dir, 54- Rel: Methodist. Mailing Add: Plainfield, Vt. 05667. (1967)

LADEAU, GEORGE ARTHUR, JR. R
Chmn, Chicopee City Rep. Cmt, Mass.
b. Chicopee, Mass, 8/18/28; s. George Arthur Ladeau and Blanche Dauphinais L; m. 10/11/50 to Anna Lamanna; c. George, III, Kenneth and Jolene. Educ: Springfield Col, B.S, 55; Westfield State Col, M.E, 64. Polit. & Govt. Pos: Chmn, Chicopee City Rep. Cmt, Mass, 62-; cmnr. of health, Chicopee, 65-, mem. Bd. of Health, currently; mem. adv. bd, Holyoke Commun. Col, currently. Bus. & Prof. Pos: Teacher of biol. sci. Mil. Serv: Entered as Pvt, Marine Corps, 46, released as Cpl, 51, after serv. in First and Second Marine Div, Korea; Purple Heart; Korean Serv, UN, Victory and Japanese Occup. Medals. Mem: Mass. Pub. Health Asn; Elks; Am. Legion. Rel: Catholic. Mailing Add: 49 Ducharme Ave, Chicopee, Mass. 01013.

LADNER, HEBER AUSTIN D
Secy. of State, Miss.
b. Pearl River City, Miss, 10/4/02; m. to Daisy Bowles; c. Two. Educ: Millsaps Col, B.S, 29; Duke Univ, M.A, 38. Polit. & Govt. Pos: Miss. State Rep, 36-40; secy, State Budget Cmn, 40-42; clerk, Miss. House of Rep, 42-48; Secy. of State, Miss, 48- Bus. & Prof. Pos: Farmer; teacher. Publ: James Kimball Vardaman in Mississippi Politics, 38. Rel: Baptist. Mailing Add: State Capitol, Jackson, Miss. 39205.

LADNER, HIRAM GRIFFIN D
b. Gulfport, Miss, 1/7/18; married. Educ: Phi Kappa Psi. Polit. & Govt. Pos: Former Miss. State Rep. Bus. & Prof. Pos: Attorney and ins. agent.

Mem: Miss. Bar Asn; Mason (32°); C. of C; Pine Hill Golf & Country Club; Am. Legion; Boy Scout Coun; Ripley Football Booster Club. Rel: Presbyterian. Mailing Add: 120 Jefferson St, Ripley, Miss. 38663. (1967)

LADY, ELAINE R
Md. State Del.
b. Montrose, Colo; d. John Wesley Staggers and Ruth Elizabeth Warner S; m. 1/4/35 to Harold Wendell Lady; c. Donald Staggers and Diana (Mrs. Dougan). Educ: Univ. Miami; Univ. Philippines; Seoul Cent. Univ, hon. LL.D; Kappa Kappa Gamma. Polit. & Govt. Pos: V.chmn, Fedn. Rep. Women Md, 47-48; mem. and v.chmn, Montgomery Co. Bd. Appeals, 63-66; Md. State Del, 67- Bus. & Prof. Pos: Daily columnist, Tribune, Pocatello, Idaho, 46-47. Mem: Health and Welfare Coun, Montgomery Co. Rel: Protestant. Mailing Add: 4101 Bradley Lane, Chevy Chase, Md. 20015.

LaFAUCI, THOMAS V. D
b. Astoria, L.I. City, N.Y; m. to Florence Zinna. Educ: St. John's Univ. and Sch. of Law. Polit. & Govt. Pos: N.Y. State Assemblyman, 52-69; v.pres, Regular Dem. Club; past pres, Astoria, L.I. City Health Coun. Bus. & Prof. Pos: Lawyer, 43- Mil. Serv: Field Artil, World War II. Mem: N.Y. State Bar Asn; Queens Co. Bar Asn; L.I. City Lawyers; Columbia Lawyers Asn; Queens Co. Criminal Bar Asn; past v.comdr, Maj. James McKenna Post, Am. Legion; past v.pres, Mt. Carmel Holy Name Soc. of Astoria; judge-advocate, Richard J. Kenny Post, CWV; Lincoln Coun, K. of C; Lions of Astoria; Queensboro Welfare Center; Queensboro Elks; Commodore Barry Assembly 4th Degree; Italian Charities and Welfare Center of Queens; St. John's Alumni Asn; Phi Delta Phi; Corp. Vincent Marzano Garrison and Queens Co. Army and Navy Unions, USA; dir, Astoria Child Care Center and Steinway Vets. Asn. Mailing Add: 32-21 Broadway, Long Island City, N.Y. 11106. (1967)

LaFAVE, REUBEN R
Wis. State Sen.
b. Oconto, Wis. Educ: Wis. Pub. Schs; R.R. Auditors Sch. Polit. & Govt. Pos: Wis. State Assemblyman, 37-51; former mem, Co. Bd; former pres, Northeast. Wis. Conserv. Coun; former chmn, Sportsmen's Conserv. Cong; Wis. State Sen, 57- Bus. & Prof. Pos: Real estate broker. Mil. Serv: Coast Guard. Outstanding Achievement in Conservation Field Award, Mil. Sen, 53; Mr. Conservation, Wis. Conserv. Club 256, 60. Mailing Add: La Veaux Rd, Route 1, Oconto, Wis. 54153. (1967)

LA FOLLETTE, BRONSON CUTTING D
b. Washington, D.C, 2/2/36; s. Robert Marion La Follette, Jr. and Rachel Young L; m. 9/7/57 to Lynn Denison Godwin; c. Deborah Case and Robert Marion, IV. Educ: Univ. Wis, B.A, 58, LL.B, 60; Phi Delta Phi; Phi Gamma Delta. Polit. & Govt. Pos: Asst. U.S. Attorney, West. Dist, Wis, 62-64; Attorney Gen, Wis, 65-69; nominee, Gov, Wis, 68; del, Dem. Nat. Conv, 68. Bus. & Prof. Pos: Private practice of law, La Follette, Sinykin, Doyle, Anderson & Davis, 60-62. Mem: State Bar of Wis; Milwaukee, Dane Co, Fed. and Am. Bar Asns; Am. Judicature Soc; Atlantic Union; Jr. C. of C. Mem: President's Consumer Adv. Coun; grantee, Am. Specialists Abroad Prog, U.S. State Dept. Legal Res: 733 Lakewood Blvd, Village of Maple Bluff, Madison, Wis. 53704. (1967)

LaFOND, ALPHONSE A. D
b. Hooksett, N.H, 2/15/94; widower; c. seven. Educ: Hooksett schs. Polit. & Govt. Pos: N.H. State Rep, -67. Bus. & Prof. Pos: Retired Master Printer; Check List Supvr, 10 yrs. Mem: K. of C; Pinnacle Fish & Game Club; Hooksett Indust. Adv. Coun. Rel: Catholic. Mailing Add: 5 Highland St, Hooksett, N.H. 03106. (1967)

LAFORE, JOHN ARMAND, JR. R
b. Bala, Pa, 5/25/05; s. John Armand Lafore and Anne Francis Shearer L; m. 9/27/33 to Margaret Dexter Read. Educ: Swarthmore Col, 23-25; Univ. Pa, 25-26. Polit. & Govt. Pos: U.S. Rep, Pa, 57-61; Gen. Assembly, Pa, 50-57. Bus. & Prof. Pos: V.pres. finance Day & Zimmermann, Inc, 65-; pres, Kellett Aircraft Corp, 61-64; pres, Cent. City Chevrolet Co, Phila, 32-57; Phila. Zone Planning Asn, 50-53. Mil. Serv: Naval Res, Lt. Comdr, 42-45. Mem: Pres, Nat. Skeet Shooting Asn, 46-47; Navy League, U.S; Clubs: Union League (Phila.); Merion Cricket (Haverford, Pa.); Phila. Country (Gladwyne, Pa.); Rolling Rock (Ligioner, Pa.). Mailing Add: 511 Avonwood Rd, Haverford, Pa. 19041. (1967)

LaFRANCE, AUGUST P. D
Secy. of State, R.I.
b. Fall River, Mass, 12/15/09; s. Peter P. LaFrance and Anna Vaillancourt L; m. 2/14/42 to Virginia L. Graveline; c. Joyce L.(Mrs. Andrew P. Tormey) and Cynthia A;(Mrs. Charles J. Luty, Jr). Educ: Pawtucket High Sch. Polit. & Govt. Pos: Past hon. pres, Young Dem. of R.I; mem. exec. bd, Young Dem. of Pawtucket; former mem. exec. cmt, Pawtucket Dem. City Cmt; former chmn, Fifth Ward Dem. Cmt. of Pawtucket; R.I. State Rep, 39-58, chmn. House Cmt. on Corp, 55-58 and House Dem. Steering Cmt, 57-58; mem, Cmt. on Rules & Order; chmn, Dem. State Conv, 58, 62, 64 & 68, secy, 60 & 66; Secy. of State, R.I, 59-; Presidential Elector and del, Dem. Nat. Conv, 60, 64 & 68; del, and permanent secy, R.I. Constitutional Conv, 64. Bus. & Prof. Pos: Pres, LaFrance-Dunn Agency, Inc, Real Estate and Ins. Mem: R.I. Realty Brokers Asn; Nat. Asn. of Realtors; Pawtucket Bd. of Realtors; Pawtucket C. of C; Nat. Asn. of Independent Ins. Agents; Nat. Soc. State Legislators; Int. Inst. Munic. Clerks; Nat. Asn. Secy. of State (former v.pres, pres, 69-); life mem, Elks; moose; K. of C; Le Foyer; Fedn. Francaise; R.I. Hist. Soc. Chevalier de l'Order National du Merite, 65; Hon. Citizen of Wash, 61 and Tenn, 69; Hon. Ky. Col, 61. Rel: Catholic. Legal Res: 58 Felsmere Ave, Pawtucket, R.I. 02861. Mailing Add: Room 219, State House, Providence, R.I. 02902.

LAFRENIERE, BERTHA R
b. Bolton, Vt, 1/28/08; m. to Leo Lafreniere; c. Two sons, two daughters. Educ: Richmond High Sch. Polit. & Govt. Pos: Vt. State Rep, 61-66; former health officer and libr. cmnr; former asst. town clerk. Bus. & Prof. Pos: Housewife; clerical work; sch. dir. Mem: Farm Bur; Co. Fish & Game; Beacon Light Grange No. 557. Rel: Catholic. Mailing Add: RFD 1, Waterbury, Vt. 05676. (1967)

LAGOMARSINO, ROBERT JOHN R
Calif. State Sen.
b. Ventura, Calif. 9/4/26; s. Emilio J. Lagomarsino and Marjorie Gates L; m. 11/10/60 to Norma Jean Mabrey; c. Karen, Dexter and Dana. Educ: Univ. Calif, Santa Barbara, B.A, 50; Univ. Santa Clara, LL.B, 53; Alpha Sigma Nu; Delta Sigma Phi. Polit. & Govt. Pos: Mayor and city councilman, Ojai, Calif, 58-61; Calif. State Sen, 24th Sen. Dist, Ventura Co, 61-; del, Rep. Nat. Conv, 68. Mil. Serv: Entered as A/S, Navy, 44, released as Pharmacist Mate 2/C, 46, after serv. in U.S. and Pac. Theatre. Mem: Elks; Eagles; Moose; Am. Legion; Rotary. One of California's 5 Outstanding Young Men, Calif. Jr. C. of C, 61. Rel: Catholic. Legal Res: 1137 Gridley Rd, Ojai, Calif. Mailing Add: 305 Central Building, 21 S. California St, Ventura, Calif. 93001.

LAGONEGRO, EDWARD THOMAS D
Mayor, Elmira, N.Y.
b. Elmira, N.Y, 4/29/21; s. Harry J. Lagonegro and Katherine S. Stapleton L; m. 4/10/48 to Marion L. Swain; c. Laurene M, Ellen T, Katherine M, Harry J. and Edward P. Educ: Syracuse Univ. Col. of Forestry, B.S, 43; Pi Kappa Alpha. Polit. & Govt. Pos: Mayor, Elmira, N.Y, 62-63, 64-65 and 68-; alternate del, Dem. Nat. Conv, 68. Bus. & Prof. Pos: Pres, N.Y. State Asn. of Tobacco Distributors, 61-62; pres, Nat. Asn. Tobacco Distributors, 67-69. Mil. Serv: Entered as Pvt, Air Force Signal Corps, 43, released as T/5, 46, after serv. in Pac, 43-46. Publ: Many articles in trade publications, Tobacco J. and Tobacco Leaf. Mem: Pres, Econ. Opportunity Prog. of Chemung Co; treas, Arctic League, Inc; treas, Dunn Field Corp; budget cmt, Commun. Chest; bd. mem, YMCA; pres, Elmira-Corning Area, Syracuse Univ. Alumni Asn; Chemung Co. Health Planning Cmt; Chemung Co. Human Rels. Cmt; Area-Manpower Coordinating Cmt; bd. dirs, Asn. of Commerce; trustee, Robert Packer Hosp; NAACP; Elks; Eagles; Moose; Holy Name Soc; K. of C; Rotary; Am. Legion; Ital. Am. Vet. Club; Elmira City Club; Elmira Country Club; Syracuse Univ. Varsity Club. Named Outstanding Young Exec. in the Wholesale Tobacco Trade, 60; Nat. Asn. Tobacco Distributors Cert. of Recognition, 60; Commun. Builder, C. of C, 66. Rel: Roman Catholic. Mailing Add: 800 W. Water St, Elmira, N.Y. 14905.

LAHAYE, JAMES S. D
b. Ville Platte, La, 7/11/12; s. Dominique Lahaye and Ollie Thompson L; m. 5/10/42 to Lois Ethel Armentrout; c. Judi Ann, John William, Donald James and Deborah Lois. Educ: High Sch; Col, 2 years; Correspondence Course in Bus. Admin. Polit. & Govt. Pos: Justice of the Peace, El Paso Co, Colo, 51-54, committeeman, Precinct 71, El Paso Co, 60-66; Colo. State Rep, 65-67; acting postmaster, Green Mt. Falls, 67- Mem: Master Mason; Past Patron, Eastern Star. Rel: Protestant. Mailing Add: P.O. Box 204, Green Mountain Falls, Colo. 80819.

LAHEY, DANIEL FRANCIS D
Mayor, Jacksonville, Ill.
b. Jacksonville, Ill, 6/19/29; s. Leo Thomas Lahey and Mary Burke L; m. 7/27/53 to Helen Elizabeth Abbott; c. Terrance Danel, Sheryl Ann, Jerry Kay, Gary Dennis, Lawrence Thomas and Carey Philip. Educ: Routt Col, grad, 47; Brown's Bus. Col, grad, 49. Polit. & Govt. Pos: Dem. precinct committeeman, Jacksonville, Ill, 64; pres, Morgan Co. Young Dem, 67; chmn, Morgan Co. Dem. Party, 68; mayor, Jacksonville, 69- Bus. & Prof. Pos: Farmer, 53-; compliance officer, Ill, 66-69. Mil. Serv: Entered as Pvt, Army, 51, released as Cpl, 53. Mem: Amvets; Am. Legion; Am. Bus. Club; K. of C; Elks; Moose; Eagles; Routt Boosters; C. of C. Rel: Catholic. Mailing Add: 415 E. Douglas Ave, Jacksonville, Ill. 62650.

LAIRD, H. V. R
Chmn, Walthall Co. Rep. Party, Miss.
b. Bassfield, Miss, 5/26/13; s. Earl D. Laird and Ether Broom L; m. 12/9/30 to Jessie Leu Hathorn; c. Darroh H, Dalton, Kenneth D, Duel and Daphne. Educ: Bassfield High, Bassfield, Miss. Polit. & Govt. Pos: Chmn, Walthall Co. Rep. Party, Miss, 63- Bus. & Prof. Pos: Owner and mgr, Laird Motor Co, 49- and Laird Garage and Serv. Sta. Rel: Baptist. Legal Res: Route 2, Tylertown, Miss. 39667. Mailing Add: P.O. Box 287, Tylertown, Miss. 39667.

LAIRD, MELVIN ROBERT R
Secy. of Defense
b. 9/1/22; s. Melvin Robert Laird and Helen Connor L; m. 10/15/45 to Barbara Masters; c. John Osborne, Alison and David Malcolm. Educ: Carleton Col, B.A. Polit. & Govt. Pos: Wis. State Sen, 46-52, chmn, Senate Vet. Affairs Cmt. and mem, Labor and Mgt, Joint Finance and Legis. Procedure Cmts, chmn, Wis. Legis. Coun; del, Rep. Nat. Conv, 48-68, mem, platform cmt, 52 & 56, v.chmn, 60 and chmn, 64; chmn, Wis. State Rep. Conv, 54 & 60; U.S. Rep, Seventh Dist, Wis, 53-69, mem, House Agr. Cmt, 55-57, mem, Appropriations Cmt. and Defense and Labor, Health, Educ. and Welfare Subcmts, chmn, Joint House-Senate Cmt. on Rep. Policy, 60, chmn, House Rep. Conf, U.S. House of Rep, 65-69; mem. U.S. Del, WHO, 59, 63 & 65; mem, Rep. Coord. Cmt, 64-; Secy. of Defense, 69- Mil. Serv: Entered Navy, 42-46, serv. in Third Fleet, Pac. Theater; Purple Heart. Publ: A House Divided: America's Strategy Gap, Henry Regnery Co, 62; ed, The Conservative Papers, 64 and Republican Papers, 68, Doubleday and Co. Mem: Am. Legion; 40 et 8; VFW; DAV; Mil. Order of Purple Heart; F&AM; United Commercial Travelers; Elks. 15th Annual Albert Lasker Med. Research Award; Man of Year Awards, Am. Cancer Soc, Nat. Asn. Ment. Health, Nat. Research Found. to Prevent Blindness and Am. Asn. Med. Cols. and Univs, 60; selected Outstanding Young Man in Wis. for Govt. Serv, Jr. C. of C, 57. Rel: Presbyterian; Elder, First Presbyterian Church, Marshfield, Wis. Legal Res: 207 S. Cherry St, Marshfield, Wis. 54449. Mailing Add: The Pentagon, Washington, D.C. 20301.

LAISE, CAROL
U.S. Ambassador to Nepal
b. Winchester, W.Va, 11/14/17; m. to Ellsworth Bunker. Educ: Am. Univ, B.A, 38 and M.A, 40. Polit. & Govt. Pos: Mem, Civil Serv. Cmn, 41-46; UNRRA, London, 46-47; career officer, U.S. Dept. of State Foreign Service, 48-; State Dept. Officer on Int. Orgn. Affairs, 48-55; consul and first secy, New Delhi, 56-61; Sr. Seminar on For. Affairs, 61-62; dep. dir, Near East. and S.Asian Affairs, 62-65; dir, Off. of S.Asian Affairs, 65-66; U.S. Ambas-

sador to Nepal, 66- Superior Accomplishment Award, 45; Commendable Serv. Award, 60; Fed. Woman's Award, 65. Legal Res: Washington, D.C. Mailing Add: U.S. Embassy, Kathmandu, Nepal.

LAITE, WILLIAM E, JR. D
b. Tampa, Fla, 8/19/32; s. William Edward Laite and Frances Regener L; m. 8/07/53 to Marilyn McCoy Meeks; c. William Edward III, Jennifer Lynn, Katherine Frances and Kelly Marilyn. Educ: Univ. Ga, B.S, 54; Sigma Alpha Epsilon. Polit. & Govt. Pos: Ga. State Rep, 63-69. Bus. & Prof. Pos: Owner, Exterminating bus; entomologist. Mem: Elk; Moose. Rel: Methodist. Mailing Add: 2948 Crestline Dr, Macon, Ga. 31204. (1967)

LAKE, JAMES HOWARD R
Mem, Calif. Rep. State Cent. Cmt.
b. Fresno, Calif, 8/16/37; s. Howard Benton Lake and Maryetta McPherson L; m. 10/21/67 to Kathryn Elaine Heimforth; c. James Charles, Michael Benton and Garrett Douglas. Educ: Bakersfield Col, A.A, 57; Univ. Calif, Los Angeles, B.S, 59; Pi Rho Phi; Alpha Gamma Sigma; William H. Danforth Fel; Circle K Int. Polit. & Govt. Pos: Clerk and trustee, Delano Union Sch. Dist, Calif, 64-66; dist. rep. to Bob Mathias, U.S. Rep, 18th Dist, Calif, 67-; mem, Calif. Rep. State Cent. Cmt, 69- Mem: Pres, Delano Businessmen's Asn, 62-63; dir, Delano Dist. C. of C, 62-64; dir, Kiwanis, Delano, 64; pres, Delano Harvest Holidays, Inc, 63; Mason; Commonwealth Club Calif. Rel: Christian Science. Mailing Add: 3000 Sunset Ave, Bakersfield, Calif. 93304.

LAKE, MARTIN R
Ind. State Rep.
b. Sweetser, Ind, 2/5/39; s. Lora Paul Lake and Hazel Downey L; m. 8/13/60 to Sondra Kay Ancil; c. Martin, II and John William, III. Educ: Purdue Univ, B.S. in Econ, 61; Ind. Univ. Law Sch, grad. study; Scabbard and Blade; Sigma Delta Chi; Alpha Gamma Rho; Gimlets. Polit. & Govt. Pos: Trustee, town bd, Swayzee, Ind, 61-62; Ind. State Rep, 66- Bus. & Prof. Pos: Managing ed, Swayzee Press, 61-64, publisher, 64- Mil. Serv: Entered as 2nd Lt, Army, 62, released as 1st Lt, 64; Capt, Army Res, 67. Publ: The Speedkings, Lake Publ. Co, 61. Mem: Reserve Officers Asn; Nat. Soc. State Legislators; F&AM; Lions; Columbia Club. Ind. 4-H Safety Winner and Ind. 4-H Dairy Judging Champion, 55. Rel: Methodist. Mailing Add: 212 S. Washington St, Swayzee, Ind. 46986.

LAKE, ROBERT CAMPBELL, JR. D
S.C. State Sen.
b. Whitmire, S.C, 12/27/25; s. Robert Campbell Lake, Sr. and Susan Howze L; m. 7/5/55 to Carolyn Young Gray; c. Sarah Linda, Robert C, III and Samuel Young. Educ: Univ. S.C, 43-47, Law Sch, LL.B, 49; Blue Key; Pi Kappa Phi. Polit. & Govt. Pos: Pres, Newberry Co. Dem. Conv, 52-64; del, S.C. Dem. State Conv, 54-66; city attorney, Whitmire, S.C, 55-; attorney, Newberry Co, 60-68; secy, Nursing Home Cmn, S.C, 63-; del, Dem. Nat. Conv, 64; mem, S. C. Study Cmn. on Higher Educ, 65-66; S.C. State Sen, Laurens, Newberry and Union Co, 68- Bus. & Prof. Pos: Pres, Whitmire Jr. C. of C, 52; attorney, State Bldg. & Loan Asn, 55-; pres, Newberry Co. Bar Asn, 62; v.chmn, Whitmire United Fund, 66-67 & 68; dir, State Bank & Trust Co, Whitmire, 66-; chmn, Newberry Co. Develop. Bd, 67 & 68. Mil. Serv: Entered as Pvt, Army, 44, released as Pfc, 45, after serv. in Spec. Serv; Good Conduct Medal. Mem: Am, S.C. State and Newberry Co. Bar Asns; S.C. Trial Lawyers Asn; High Priest and Prophet, Hejaz Shrine Temple; Union Elks Lodge 1321; finance officer, Am. Legion Post 70; Newberry and Mid-Carolina Country Clubs; Greenville City and Palmetto Clubs. Rel: Presbyterian; Deacon, Presby. Church of Whitmire. Legal Res: 101 N. Church St, Whitmire, S.C. 29178. Mailing Add: P.O. Box 51, Whitmire, S.C. 29178.

LAKE, WALTER THOMAS D
S.C. State Rep.
b. Newberry, S.C, 7/6/23; s. Edwin Orlando Lake and Bessie Nichols L; m. 6/26/55 to Annelle Ruff; c. Susan Annelle and Walter Thomas, Jr. Educ: Newberry Col, B.S, 45; Univ. of S.C. Sch. of Law, LL.B, 49. Polit. & Govt. Pos: S.C. State Rep, 49-52 and 69-, mem, Judiciary Cmt, S.C. House of Rep, 69-; mem, S.C. Educ. Finance Cmn, 59; mem, S.C. Indust. Cmn, 60-64. Mem: Newberry Co. Bar Asn.(pres, 69); S.C. State Bar Asn; S.C. Trial Lawyers' Asn; Newberry Co. Hist. Cmn, 64-; Moose; Newberry Col. Indian Club. Rel: Lutheran. Mailing Add: 1215 Friend St, Newberry, S.C. 29108.

LALIBERTE, HENRY E. D
R.I. State Sen.
b. Providence, R.I, 5/24/19. Educ: Providence Col; Boston Univ, LL.B, 50. Polit. & Govt. Pos: Councilman, Providence, R.I, 55-65; R.I. State Sen, 64- Bus. & Prof. Pos: Attorney. Mil. Serv: Army Air Force, World War II, 42-45, Pac; Bronze Star Medal. Mailing Add: 42 Chambers St, Providence, R.I. 02907. (1967)

LAMA, ALFRED A. D
N.Y. State Assemblyman
married; c. One. Educ: City Col; Cooper Union. Polit. & Govt. Pos: N.Y. State Assemblyman, 42-; past chmn, 73rd Precinct, Off. Civil Defense, Kings Co. Bus. & Prof. Pos: Architect, sr. mem, firm of Lama, Proskauer and Prober, Architects. Mem: Pres, Brooklyn Soc. of Architects; secy, N.Y. Soc. of Architects, 39-; Am. Inst. of Architects; Elks; pres, Ocean Hill Civic Asn; pres, United Welfare League of Brownsville and Ocean Hill; dir, Brownsville Boys Club and Youth Serv. League. Mailing Add: 9029 Kings Hwy, Brooklyn, N.Y. 11212. (1967)

LaMARCA, RUSSELL J. D
Pa. State Rep.
b. Reading, Pa, 12/17/28; s. Harry LaMarca and Mary Genova L; m. to Elizabeth Keiper; c. One. Educ: Univ. Pittsburgh Col, B.A; Univ. Pittsburgh Sch. of Law, LL.B; Sigma Alpha Epsilon; Phi Alpha Theta; Phi Alpha Delta. Polit. & Govt. Pos: Solicitor, Reading Redevelop. Authority, Pa, 61-64; Pa. State Rep, 64- Bus. & Prof. Pos: Attorney. Mil. Serv: Sgt, Marine Corps, Korean Conflict. Mem: Amalgamated Clothing Workers. Admitted to practice, Pa. Supreme and Superior Courts, U.S. Fed. Dist. Court, U.S. Court of Appeals. Mailing Add: 45 S. Carroll St, Reading, Pa. 19602. (1967)

LAMB, CECIL PORT R
Colo. State Rep.
s. Silas S. Lamb and Anna Melissa Legg L; m. 3/4/16 to Josephine Menard Girardot; c. Anna Belle Chesney, Betty Jo Chesney and Dorothy Drake. Educ: Colo. State Univ, D.V.M. Polit. & Govt. Pos: Colo. State Rep, Morgan Co, 53- Mil. Serv: Entered as 2nd Lt, Vet. Med. Corps, 16, released as 1st Lt, 17. Mem: Mason; C. of C; Am. Legion; Vet. Med. Soc. Colo. State Univ. Alumni Award, 66. Rel: Methodist. Mailing Add: 509 Clayton, Brush, Colo. 80723.

LAMB, EDWARD D
Mem, State Dem. Exec. Cmt, Ohio
b. Toledo, Ohio, 4/23/02; s. Clarence M. Lamb and Mary Gross L; m. 6/21/31 to Prudence Hutchinson; c. Edward Hutchinson and Prudence Priscilla (Mrs. Guyton). Educ: Dartmouth Col, N.H; Harvard Law Sch; West. Reserve Law Sch. Hon. L.H.D, Wilberforce Univ; LL.D, Gannon Col. Polit. & Govt. Pos: Mem, State Dem. Exec. Cmt, Ohio, currently; del-at-lg, Dem. Nat. Conv, 64. Publ: The Planned Economy of Soviet Russia, 34; No Lamb for Slaughter, 64. Mem: Overseas Press Club; Nat. Press Club; Am. Bar Asn. Rel: Episcopal. Mailing Add: 600 Edward Lamb Bldg, Toledo, Ohio 43604.

LAMB, FRANK T. D
Mayor, Rochester, N.Y.
b. Rochester, N.Y, 8/24/22; s. Frederick D. Lamb and Gertrude C. Thompson L; m. 8/17/46 to Janet Sage; c. Patricia Ellen, Gary Thompson, Douglas Paul and David Jeffrey. Educ: Duke Univ, B.S. in polit. sci, 48; Univ. Rochester and Springfield Col, grad. courses in Sociology. Polit. & Govt. Pos: Councilman-at-lg, City Coun, Rochester, N.Y, 57, 61 & 65, v.mayor, 62-63, mayor, 64-; del, N.Y. State Constitutional Conv, 67; mem, Nat. League of Cities, v.chmn, Cmt. on Munic. Govt. and Admin; mem, U.S. Conf. of Mayors; v.pres. and dir, Town Affil. Asn. of U.S; del, Dem. Nat. Conv, 68; pres, N.Y. State Conf. of Mayors, 69. Bus. & Prof. Pos: Dir, People to People, Inc; past mem. dir, Rochester YMCA; dir, Colonial Oil & Gas Co. Mil. Serv: Navy and Coast Guard, 46. Mem: Past pres, Rochester and Monroe Co. Chap, Duke Univ. Alumni Asn; former chmn, West N.Y, Duke Univ. Loyalty Fund; spec. cmt. mem, Constitutional Conv; Am. Soc. for Pub. Admin; Am. Acad. Polit. & Soc. Sci; Mason; Lalla Rookh Grotto, Damascus Temple, Consistory, Royal Order of Jesters; Moose; Rochester-Monroe Co. life mem, Sigma Chi; hon. chmn, Rochester Conv. Bur. Rel: Presbyterian; Deacon and trustee, Westminister Presby. Church, former pres, Church Couples Club. Mailing Add: 62 Genesee Park Blvd, Rochester, N.Y. 14611.

LAMB, GERALD A. D
Treas, Conn.
b. Elizabeth City, N.C, 8/25/24; s. Thomas Richard Lamb and Addie Louise Shannon L; m. 8/5/50 to Verna Grier; c. Genero Elaine. Educ: Kerpel Sch. Dental Tech, N.Y.C. 46-48. Polit. & Govt. Pos: Secy, Conn. State Fedn. of Negro Dem. Clubs; mem, State Banking Cmn, State Bond Cmn, Expressway Bond Cmn, Gov. Finance Adv. Cmt. and Rental Housing Bond Cmt; mem, Waterbury Bd. of Park Cmnrs, 59-62; alderman, Waterbury Bd. of Aldermen, 59-62; treas, Conn, 63-; dir, St. Mary's Hosp, Waterbury, Conn. Hosp. Planning Asn, Conn. Blue Cross and Conn. Pub. Deposit Protection Cmt, currently; mem, President's Consumer Adv. Coun, currently; del, Dem. Nat. Conv, 68. Bus. & Prof. Pos: V.pres. and secy, Waterbury Dental Labs, 48-62 and Meadow Homes, Inc, 60- Mil. Serv: Entered as A/S, Coast Guard, 42, released as PO 1/C, 46, after serv. in European and Pac. Theaters; Good Conduct Medal. Mem: Nat. Asn. State Auditors, Comptrollers and Treasurers; Negro Bus. and Prfnl. Men's Asn; Goodwill Lodge of Elks; NAACP; exec. coun, Episcopal Diocese, Conn; Conn. Fedn. of Negro Dem. Clubs; dir. and past pres, Pearl St. Neighborhood House; dir, Waterbury United Fund; dir, Waterbury Red Cross. Lovejoy Award, Int. Elks, 63; ambassador to Venezuela to represent the U.S. at Inaugural of Dr. Leoni as President, 64. Rel: Episcopal. Mailing Add: 95 Fleetwood Dr, Waterbury, Conn. 06706.

LAMB, HAROLD EDWARD R
Exec. Dir, Nev. Rep. State Cent. Cmt.
b. Reno, Nev, 8/26/36; s. Max Edward Lamb and Adelaide Merialdo L; m. 8/13/59 to Nancy Mary Lewis; c. Kendall Marie and Gaelen Michael. Educ: Univ. Nev, $3\frac{1}{2}$ years. Polit. & Govt. Pos: Pres, Ormsby Co. Young Rep. Club, 65-66; chmn, Ormsby Co. Rep. Cent. Cmt, 66-69; exec. dir, Nev. Rep. State Cent. Cmt, 69- Mem: Dir, Carson City C. of C, 63-66; pres, Carson City YMCA, 66-67. Rel: Catholic. Mailing Add: 1321 W. Fourth St, Carson City, Nev. 89701.

LAMB, JERRY ALLEN R
Ind. State Rep.
b. Tell City, Ind, 11/29/34; s. Coleman Lamb and Irene Howe L; m. 12/21/56 to Marilyn Seybold; c. Lori Ann, Jerry Allen, Jr. and Scott Bradley. Educ: Reitz High Sch, grad, 52; Univ. Evansville. Polit. & Govt. Pos: Precinct committeeman, Vanderburgh Co, Scott Twp, Ind, 67-69; mem, Interim Study Cmt. on Higher Educ, 69; Ind. State Rep, Vanderburgh Co, 69- Bus. & Prof. Pos: Pres, Burch & Lamb Inc, 59-69; pres, Lamb Investment Corp, 63-69; secy-treas, Kauai Corp, 67-69. Mem: Am. Inst. Plant Engrs; Assoc. Gen. Contractors of Am; Mason; Scottish Rite; Shrine; Evansville Country Club; Evansville Kennel Club; Elks; Fraternal Order Police; Nat. Soc. State Legislators; trustee, Lower Ohio Valley Carpenters Welfare & Pension Funds. Rel: Protestant. Mailing Add: 11801 Darmstadt Rd, Evansville, Ind. 47711.

LAMB, OLIVER BURNELL D
Cmnr, Daggett Co, Utah
b. Rock Springs, Wyo, 9/23/38; s. Archie Marcell Lamb and Berniece Schofield L; m. 12/14/67 to Carolyn Sue Mann; c. Bernie, Todd, Ruby, Lee and Marcell. Educ: Manila High Sch, Utah, grad. Polit. & Govt. Pos: Councilman, Manila, Utah, 63-65; chmn, Daggett Co. Dem. Party, 64-67, cmnr, Daggett Co, 69-; del, Dem. State Conv, 67. Rel: Latter-day Saint. Mailing Add: Box 387, Manila, Utah 84046.

LAMB, THOMAS F. D
Pa. State Sen.
b. Pittsburgh, Pa, 10/22/22; s. James J. Lamb and Agnes B. Dunne L; m. 10/5/57 to Barbara Joyce; c. Thomas, Jr, James, Michael and Barbara.

Educ: Duquesne Univ, B.A, 48 and LL.B, 52. Polit. & Govt. Pos: Pa. State Rep, 58-66; Pa. State Sen, 66- Bus. & Prof. Pos: Attorney, Allegheny Co. Bar Asn, 53- Mil. Serv: Entered as A/S, Navy, 42, released as Lt.(jg), 46, after serv. in Pac. Theater. Mem: Am. Legion; VFW; K. of C; Knights of Equity. Rel: Roman Catholic. Mailing Add: 905 Gladys Ave, Pittsburgh, Pa. 15216.

LAMBERT, AARON COLUS 'BUTCH' D
Miss. State Rep.
b. Holcut, Miss, 2/27/23; s. Alvin Grady Lambert and Gertrude Jourdan L; m. 1/3/42 to Ida Yvonne Gilliland; c. Butch, Jr, Vicki, Scott and Amy. Educ: Univ. Mo, B.S.P.E. Polit. & Govt. Pos: Miss. State Rep, 60-64 & 68- Bus. & Prof. Pos: Athletic dir, Itawamba Jr. Col, 49-52; field agent, Miss. State Tax Cmn, 52-56; personnel mgr, Rockwell Mfg. Co, 56- Mil. Serv: Entered as A/S, Navy, 43, released as 1/C PO, 45, after serv. in Great Lakes Naval Training Center. Mem: Soc. Adv. Mgt; Tupelo Indust. Club (past pres. and past dir); Mason; Shrine; Touchdowner; Southeast. Conf. Football Referee; Southeast. Conf. Basketball Referee. Officiate, Sugar Bowl Football Game, Gator Bowl Football Game, three NCAA Basketball Tournaments and Sugar Bowl Basketball Tourney. Rel: Church of Christ. Mailing Add: 1007 Hoover St, Tupelo, Miss. 38801.

LAMBERT, EZEKIEL ROY D
Ga. State Rep.
b. Madison, Ga, 6/18/25; s. Ezekiel R. Lambert and Lula Bowers L; m. 5/16/54 to Christine Davis; c. Leigh and Anne. Educ: Tulane Univ; Univ. Ga, B.B.A, LL.B; Phi Delta Theta. Polit. & Govt. Pos: Ga. State Sen, 55-56 & 61-62; Ga. State Rep, 63- Bus. & Prof. Pos: Attorney. Mil. Serv: QM 3/C, Navy, 43-46. Mem: Kiwanis; Am. Legion; VFW. Rel: Methodist. Mailing Add: 431 N. Main St, Madison, Ga. 30650. (1967)

LAMBERT, J. KENTON R
W.Va. State Sen.
b. Parsons, W.Va, 8/28/10; s. J. Herman Lambert and Bess Kalar L; m. 1/11/36 to Laura Vere Orr; c. James K, II, Amanda Lee, Anthony Orr and Rex Kevin. Educ: W.Va. Univ, B.A, 34; Tau Kappa Epsilon. Polit. & Govt. Pos: City councilman, Parsons, W.Va, 46-48; W.Va. State Sen, 62- Bus. & Prof. Pos: Teacher and athletic coach, Parsons High Sch, W.Va, 34-43; pres, Parsons Motor Sales, 46-49, Lambert Chevrolet Co, 49- and Parsons Handle Factory, 60-; v.pres, Valley Acceptance Co, 63- Mil. Serv: Entered as Lt.(jg), Navy, 43, released as Lt, 46, after serv. in Small Craft, Pac. Theater, 43-46; Ret. Res. Mem: Nat. Auto Dealers Asn. and W.Va. Auto Dealers Asns; mem. long range develop. cmt, Davis Elkins Col; Gov. Study Cmn. on Voc. Rehab; Mason; Shrine; Kiwanis (past gov, W.Va, Dist); Ruritan Nat; Farm Bur; Izaak Walton League; Am. Legion (past post comdr. and mem, W.Va. Dept. Americanism Cmt); VFW; Elks; Boy Scouts (v.pres, Cent. Area Coun, 69). Silver Beaver Award, Boy Scouts. Ky. Col; Outstanding Civic Leader Award; Community Leader of Am. Award, 68. Rel: Presbyterian; Elder and moderator, Greenbrier Presbytery. Mailing Add: 201 River Ave, Parsons, W.Va. 26287.

LAMBERT, JOEL WILLIAM D
b. Sampson Co, N.C; s. William H. Lambert and Estella Pope L; m. 12/13/41 to Reba Livingston; c. Joel W, Jr, Phillip L, Pharis H. Educ: Appalachian State Col, 38; New Eng. Aircraft Sch, 42. Polit. & Govt. Pos: N.C. State Rep, 63-66. Bus. & Prof. Pos: Barber; rental bus. Mil. Serv: USAF, 42-45, S/Sgt. Mem: Asn. Master Barbers & Beaut. of Am; United Commer. Travelers. Rel: First Presbyterian Church; Chmn, Bd. Deacons, 62-64; Elder, 65-67. Mailing Add: 111 S. Betty St, Spring Lake, N.C. 28390. (1967)

LAMBERT, WILLIAM CHESLEY R
Chmn, Shenandoah Co. Rep. Cmt, Va.
b. Edinburg, Va, 12/28/14; s. William Franklin Lambert and Mary Lottie Painter L; m. 1/11/36 to Evelyn Pauline Eckard; c. Jerry Franklin, Wayne Allen and Bonnie Jo. Educ: Nat. Bus. Col, Roanoke, Va, 32; Massanutten Mil. Acad, Woodstock, 32-33. Polit. & Govt. Pos: Va. State Del, 48-49; mem, Woodstock Town Coun, Va, 54-58; finance chmn, Shenandoah Co. Rep. Cmt, 67, chmn, 68- Bus. & Prof. Pos: Owner and operator, Lambert's Poultry Co, 39-50, Valley Alleys, 50-52 and private real estate and farm opers, 50- Mem: Lions; bd. dirs, Shenandoah Co. Mem. Hosp; chmn, Chenandoah Co. March of Dimes. Selected Citizen of the Week by Shenandoah Herald, Woodstock, Va. Rel: United Methodist. Mailing Add: Route I, Box 139-B, Woodstock, Va. 22664.

LAMBETH, THOMAS WILLIS D
b. Clayton, N.C, 1/8/35; s. Mark Thomas Lambeth and Ina Henrietta Willis L; m. 7/18/64 to Donna Brooks Irving; c. Donna Catherine, Mark Hunter and Thomas Richard. Educ: Univ. N.C, A.B. in Hist, 57, grad. work in Hist, 57-58; Phi Alpha Theta; Order of the Golden Fleece; Order of the Grail; Order of the Old Well; Amphoterothen Soc. Polit. & Govt. Pos: Asst. to the Chmn, N.C. Dem. Exec. Cmt, Fall Campaign 60; admin. asst. to the Gov. N.C, 61-65; mem. bd. dirs, Guilford Co. Young Dem, 68-; exec. asst. to Rep. Richardson Preyer, 69-; trustee, Univ. N.C, 69- Bus. & Prof. Pos: Dir, Univ. N.C, Chapel Hill Student Union, 57-58; reporter and copy ed, Winston-Salem Journal, 59; admin. assoc, Smith Richardson Found, Greensboro, 65-69. Mil. Serv: Entered as Pvt, Army Reserve, 58, released as Sgt, 65, after serv. in 805th Military Police Corps. Mem: Bd. of dirs, PATH Sch, Greensboro; Nat. Repertory Theatre (bd. dirs, N.C. Chap); bd. trustees, Ruth Z. Fleishman Found; Nat. Cmt. for Support of Pub. Schs. Rel: Methodist. Legal Res: Box 13182, Greensboro, N.C. 27805. Mailing Add: 3809 Forest Grove Dr, Annandale, Va. 22003.

LAMBORN, CLIFTON C. R
Iowa State Sen.
b. Bellevue, Iowa, 1/17/19; s. Chas. E. Lamborn and Inez Montgomery L; m. 12/4/42 to Marshalline Davis; c. Janet Anne. Polit. & Govt. Pos: Iowa State Sen, currently, chmn, Senate Transportation Cmt, 69- Mil. Serv: Entered as Pvt, Army, 41, released as M/Sgt, 46, after serv. in 1023rd Engr. Treadway Bridge Co, European and Pac. Theaters; Victory Medal; Am. Theater Ribbon; European-African-Middle East. Theater Ribbon; Asiatic-Pac. Theater Ribbon. Mem: Lions; Farm Bur. Rel: Methodist. Mailing Add: 207 S. Vermont, Maquoketa, Iowa 52060.

LAMBOURN, ROBERT C. R
b. Ocheyedan, Iowa, 3/8/23; s. Clarence W. Lambourn and Millie E. L; m. 8/3/45 to Wanda Faye Johnson; c. Robert V, Roger E, Rebecca L. and Martha Jo. Educ: N.Dak. State Col, B.S. in Animal Husbandry; Alpha Gamma Rho. Polit. & Govt. Pos: Co. chmn, Beerman for Congress, 60 & 62; Justice of the Peace, Fremont, Nebr, 60-; co. chmn, Rep. Party, 64-66; co. chmn, Citizens for Curtis, 66; del. to three Rep. State Conv; mem. & v.pres, Fremont Bd. of Educ, 68- Bus. & Prof. Pos: Mgr, Hog Buying Dept, George A. Hormel & Co, 48- Mil. Serv: Entered as Pvt, Army Inf, 42, released as 1st Lt, Army Air Force, 46, after serv. in 15th Air Force, Italy; Air Medal with 4 Clusters; Distinguished Flying Cross. Mem: All Masonic Orgns; Elks; Izaac Walton League; Country Club. Athletics; Col. Football. Rel: Lutheran; Pres. of Congregation. Mailing Add: Route 1, Fremont, Nebr. 68025.

LAMBROS, NICK GEORGE D
b. Ada, Ohio, 7/11/26; s. George N. Lambros and Evangeline Paulakos L; m. 4/24/55 to Anna Pappas; c. Georgia, Vangela and Michael. Educ: Emory Law Sch, Atlanta, LL.B; Phi Alpha Delta. Polit. & Govt. Pos: Former Ga. State Rep. Bus. & Prof. Pos: Partner, Kanes, Benator & Lambros, Attorneys-at-Law, 59- Mem: Mason; Civitan; C. of C; Piedmont-Cheshire Bus. Mens Asn. Rel: Greek Orthodox. Mailing Add: 1032 Wildwood Rd. N.E, Atlanta, Ga. 30306. (1967)

LAMBROS, THERESA 'TERRY' R
Mem, Calif. Rep. State Cent. Cmt.
b. Los Angeles, Calif, 3/25/33; d. Joseph Ugliano and Louise Saviano U; m. 6/29/57 to Paul A. Lambros; c. Robert Paul, Ralph Anthony and Richard Joseph. Educ: Los Angeles City Col, A.A, 53, Los Angeles State Col, B.A, 55; Univ. South. Calif, grad. work; Delta Beta Sigma. Polit. & Govt. Pos: Chmn. for Max Rafferty, South Gate, Calif, 61, co-chmn. for Joe Shell, 61; area chmn. for Sen. Barry Goldwater, 38th, 52nd and 55th Assembly Dist, 64; co-chmn. for Floyde Wakefield, 52nd Assembly Dist, 66; area co-chmn. for Max Rafferty, 38th and 52nd Assembly Dist, 68; mem, Calif. Rep. State Cent. Cmt, 69- Bus. & Prof. Pos: Teacher, Los Angeles City Schs, 55- Mem: Asn. Classroom Teachers of Los Angeles; Calif. Teachers Asn. Rel: Catholic. Mailing Add: 9407 Dorothy Ave, South Gate, Calif. 90280.

LaMERE, ALBERT J. D
Ind. State Sen.
b. Gary, Ind, 3/27/25; s. Joseph A. LaMere and Eileen Hendron L; m. 8/16/47 to Dorothy M. Trapp; c. Norene, Eileen, Kathleen, Jeanne Ann, Mary Ann, Mary Therese, Dorothy and Pierre. Educ: Univ. Notre Dame, B.S. cum laude, 48; Northwest. Univ, M.B.A, 56. Polit. & Govt. Pos: Del, Ind. Dem. State Conv, 60-68; committeeman, First Precinct, Munster, Ind, 60-64; chmn, Munster Dem. Precinct Orgn, 62-64; co-chmn, Lake Co. Oper. Support for Presidential Elec, 64; Ind. State Sen, Lake Co, 67- Bus. & Prof. Pos: Exec, Ill. Bell Tel. Co, 48-; instr, Evening Div, St. Joseph's Col, East Chicago, Ind, 56-58. Mil. Serv: Entered as Aviation Cadet, Air Force, serv. as Bomber Pilot 2½ years, active duty World War II and 8½ years Reserve duty, released as Capt. Mem: Am. Bus. Writers Asn; v.pres, Ind. Fedn. of Citizens for Educ. Freedom, 65-67; Am. Legion; K. of C; Vets. in Politics. Rel: Catholic. Mailing Add: 7827 Hohman, Munster, Ind. 46321.

LAMKIN, EUGENE HENRY, JR. 'NED' R
Ind. State Rep.
b. Owensboro, Ky, 2/23/35; s. Eugene Henry Lamkin and Nancy Elizabeth Davidson L; m. 8/24/68 to Martha Savanah Dampf. Educ: De Pauw Univ, B.A, 56; Ind. Univ. Sch. Med, M.D, 60; internship, Phila. Gen. Hosp, 60-61; residency in int. med, Ind. Univ. Med. Center, 61-62 and 64-65; Phi Eta Sigma; Phi Beta Kappa; Delta Omicron Chi; Alpha Omega Alpha; Beta Theta Pi; Nu Sigma Nu; nat. v.pres, Student Am. Med. Asn, 59-60. Polit. & Govt. Pos: V.pres, Marion Co. Young Rep, 66-67; Ind. State Rep, Marion Co, 66-, chmn, Marion Co. del, Ind. State House of Rep, 69. Bus. & Prof. Pos: Private practice, internal med. and endocrinology, Campbell, Gabovitch, Lamkin and Tavel, 66-; pres, Reference & Index Serv, Inc, 66-; instr. med, Ind. Univ. Med. Center, 66-; mem. teaching faculty, Methodist Hosp. of Indianapolis, 66-; mem, bd. of dirs, Kennedy Mem. Christian Home, 69- Mil. Serv: Capt, Army, 62-64, serv. in 1st Corps Artil, Korea, 62-63 and Ft. Hamilton Dispensary, Brooklyn, N.Y, 63-64. Mem: Marion Co, Ind. and Am. Med. Asns; Mason; Jr. C. of C.(former mem, bd. of dirs); Indianapolis Ski Club (former mem, bd. of dirs). Rel: Christian; Deacon, Northwood Christian Church. Legal Res: 4443 Jamestown Court, Indianapolis, Ind. 46226. Mailing Add: 1815 N. Capitol 505, Indianapolis, Ind. 46202.

LAMM, RICHARD D. D
Colo. State Rep.
b. Madison, Wis, 8/3/35; married; c. Scott Hunter. Polit. & Govt. Pos: Past pres, Denver Young Dem; v.pres, Colo. Young Dem; mem, Mayor's South Platte River Cmt; Colo. State Rep, currently. Bus. & Prof. Pos: Attorney-at-law; CPA. Mil. Serv: 1st Lt, Army Res. Mailing Add: 2500 S. Logan, Denver, Colo. 80202.

LAMONTAGNE, LAURIER D
N.H. State Sen.
b. Berlin, N.H, 3/6/17; married; c. Six. Educ: St. Patrick Sch. Polit. & Govt. Pos: N.H. State Sen, 55-, Minority Floor Leader, N.H. Senate; Mayor, Berlin, N.H, 58-62. Bus. & Prof. Pos: Operator, Lamontagne's Express. Mil. Serv: Navy, World War II. Mem: Past Dep. Comdr, DAV; chmn, Nat. Finance Cmt; Nat. Legis. Officer, DAV and VFW; Am. Legion; Elks; Eagles; pres, Tri-State Truck Owners Asn, Inc; Snowshoe Club; Joliette Hist. Soc; past pres, N.H. Vets. Asn. Rel: Catholic. Mailing Add: Box 509, Berlin, N.H. 03570.

LA MORA, JUDY LYNNE R
Mem, Colo. Rep. State Cent. Cmt.
b. San Antonio, Tex. 3/23/39; d. Timothy E. Gristy and Clovis Mooring Hills G; m. 11/10/60 to Donald E. La Mora; c. Leigh Suzanne and Grant Donald. Educ: Tex. Tech. Col, 56-60; Kappa Alpha Theta. Polit. & Govt. Pos: Mem. publ. cmt, Dominick for Sen, El Paso Co, Colo, 62 & 68; Rep. precinct committeewoman, Precinct 16, El Paso Co, 62; first v.pres, Pikes Peak Rep. Women's Roundtable, 64-68; pub. rels. chmn, Colo. Fedn. Rep. Women, 65-

67; publicity chmn, El Paso Co. Rep. Cent. Cmt, 66; publicity for Colo. Third Rep. Cong. Dist, 66; mem. exec. cmt, Colo. Fedn. Rep. Women, 67-69; mem. publicity cmt, Bradley for Cong, 68; mem, Gov. Cmn. on Status of Women, 68-; mem, Colo. State Rep. Cent. Cmt, 69- Bus. & Prof. Pos: Proofreader, Lubbock, Tex. Avalanche-J, 59-60; reporter, Colo. Springs Gazette Tel, 60; lectr. pub. rels, 64- Rel: Christian Church of N.Am. Mailing Add: 2909 Chelton Rd, Colorado Springs, Colo. 80909.

LAMPORT, PAUL H. R
City Councilman, Los Angeles, Calif.
b. Los Angeles, Calif, 2/3/07; s. William L. Lamport and Frances Weiner L; m. Dec, 1945 to Ruth G. Gidlow; c. Stanley William. Educ: College courses from U.S. Armed Forces Inst. and Chapman Law Sch. Polit. & Govt. Pos: City councilman, 13th Dist, Los Angeles, Calif, 65-, chmn, Bldg. and Safety Cmt, v.chmn, State, Co. and Fed. Affairs Cmt. and mem, Finance Cmt; chmn, Mayor's Econ. Develop. Bd. Bus. & Prof. Pos: Property developer and owner; gen. contractor; restaurant owner; dir, Metrop. Bank, Hollywood. Mil. Serv: Entered as Pvt, Army, 42, released as 1st Lt, 44, after serv. in Combat Engrs, ETO; former mem, Army Res; ETO Ribbon with eight Battle Stars. Mem: Bldg. Contractors Asn; dir, Hollywood C. of C. and Los Angeles Jr. C. of C; pres, Hollywood Homeowners Asn; past pres, Los Angeles Hq. City Develop. Asn; Elks; Past Commodore, Long Beach Yacht Club; pres, Regatta Asn. Rel: Jewish. Legal Res: 2000 3/4 La Brea Terr, Los Angeles, Calif. 90046. Mailing Add: City Hall, Los Angeles, Calif. 90012. (1967)

LAMPSON, ELBERT WELLINGTON R
Ohio State Rep.
b. Jefferson, Ohio, 5/17/04; s. Edward Chester Lampson and Pearle Evans L; m. 10/22/32 to Doris Durey; c. John. Educ: Miami Univ, A.B, 27; Delta Tau Delta. Polit. & Govt. Pos: Mem, Co. Bd. of Elec, 44-45; Ohio State Rep, currently. Bus. & Prof. Pos: Pres, Ohio Fair Mgr. Asn, 48 and Buckeye Press Asn, 50; trustee, Ohio Newspaper Asn, currently. Mem: Great Lake Cmn; Mason; Elks; Grange; Farm Bur. Rel: Episcopal. Mailing Add: 126 W. Jefferson St, Jefferson, Ohio 44047.

LAMSON, ELIZABETH JOSEPHINE R
V.Chmn, Prowers Co. Rep. Cent. Cmt, Colo.
b. Wiley, Colo, 12/1/08; d. William Harve Blosser and Lela Tweedie B; m. 2/10/40 to Don Carlos Lamson; wid. Educ: Colo. State Col. Educ, life cert, 28. Polit. & Govt. Pos: Committeewoman, Prowers Co. Rep. Cent. Cmt, Colo, 59-69, v.chmn, 65- Bus. & Prof. Pos: Teacher, Prowers Co. Schs, Colo, 28-40; farm mgr, Wiley, 53- Mem: Farm Bur; Colo. Cattlemens Asn; Southeast Colo. Cowbelles; Wiley Woman's Club. Rel: United Methodist. Mailing Add: Wiley, Colo. 81092.

LAMSON, FRED I. R
Mass. State Sen.
b. Stonington, Maine, 12/11/10; s. Fred Irvin Lamson and Florence Noyes L; m. 5/19/31 to Glenys Davis L; c. Fred I, Jr. Educ: Everett High Sch. Polit. & Govt. Pos: Councilman, Malden, Mass, 40-41, alderman, 42-43, mayor, 48-57; Mass. State Rep, 45-48; pres, Mass. Mayors Asn, 52; Mass. State Sen, 53-; chmn, Malden City Rep. Cmt, 65-; del, Rep. Nat. Conv, 68. Bus. & Prof. Pos: Pres, Lamson & Davis Inc, Malden, Mass, 48-58. Mem: Elks; Moose; Odd Fellows; Grange; Kiwanis; Munic. Employees Union; B'nai B'rith; United Amvets; Mass. Mayors Asn. Rel: Protestant. Mailing Add: 36 Dodge St, Malden, Mass. 02148.

LANAGHEN, CAROL LOVE R
Bonus Mem, Colo. State Rep. Cent. Cmt.
b. Ringgold, La, 3/31/32; d. Harmon Eli Davenport and Edith Davis D; m. 12/29/55 to Francis Edward Lanaghen; c. David Kyle, Steven Grigware and Carol Ann. Educ: Tex. State Col. for Women, B.S, 52; Sigma Alpha Iota; Adelphian Club. Polit. & Govt. Pos: Committeewoman, Arapahoe Co. Rep. Party, Colo, 62-, area leader, 68; chmn. orgn. cmt. for sch. bond elec, Sch. Dist. Six, 69; bonus mem, Colo. State Rep. Cent. Cmt, 69- Bus. & Prof. Pos: Music teacher, Port Arthur, Tex. Sch. Syst, 52-54; music teacher, Cody, Wyo. Sch. Syst, 55. Mem: Tex. and Wyo. Educ. Asns. Rel: Episcopal. Mailing Add: 555 W. Caley Circle, Littleton, Colo. 80120.

LANCASTER, GLEN R
Chmn, Adams Co. Rep. Cent. Cmt, Colo.
b. Bennett, Colo, 7/23/30; s. Alvin Leroy Lancaster and Marion Sutherland L; m. 5/25/47 to Margie Ann Beck; c. Cliff Boyd, Richard Loyd and Peggy Sue. Educ: Bennett High Sch. Polit. & Govt. Pos: Justice of the Peace, Colo, 56-58; Rep. committeeman, 56-60; pub. trustee, Adams Co, 63-67; chmn, Adams Co. Rep. Cent. Cmt, currently; dir, Colo. Rep. Chmn. Asn, 66- Bus. & Prof. Pos: Self-employed restaurant bus, 49-62. Mem: Bd. of dirs, Brighton Kiwanis. Rel: Presbyterian. Mailing Add: 131 W. Egbert, Brighton, Colo. 80601. (1967)

LANCASTER, HOWELL D
Fla. State Rep.
b. Eugene, Fla, 7/31/11; m. to Virginia Deen; c. Linda, Margaret and Howell Eugene. Educ: Univ. of Fla. Polit. & Govt. Pos: Former mayor, Trenton, Fla; Fla. State Rep, 48- Bus. & Prof. Pos: Petroleum prod. jobber; farmer; cattleman. Mem: Past pres, Rotary Club; Trenton PTA. Rel: Baptist. Mailing Add: P.O. Box 66, Trenton, Fla. 32693. (1967)

LANCASTER, ROBERT SAMUEL R
b. Floyd, Va, 7/9/09; s. Robert Tazwell Lancaster and Rachel Elma Barnard L; m. 6/21/31 to Ernestine Desporte; c. Evelyn Rachel (Mrs. David Tyrrell) and Ulysse (Mrs. A. P. Butler). Educ: Hampden-Sydney Col, B.A, 29; Univ. of the South, M.A, 34; Andrew Jackson Univ. Sch. Law, 36-38; Univ. Mich, Ph.D, 52; Phi Beta Kappa; Chi Phi; Sigma Upsilon; Tau Kappa Alpha; Blue Key; Pi Gamma Mu; Pi Sigma Alpha. Polit. & Govt. Pos: Campaign mgr. for Sen. Howard Baker, middle Tenn. area, 66; alternate del, Rep. Nat. Conv, 68. Bus. & Prof. Pos: Instr, Gulf Coast Mil. Acad, Gulfport, Miss, 29-31; instr, Sewanee Mil. Acad, Tenn, 31-38; attorney-at-law, Pulaski, Va, 38-41; commandant of cadets, Sewanee Mil. Acad, 41-43, instr, 46-49; asst. prof. polit. sci, Univ. of the South, 49-53, assoc. prof, 53-55, prof, 55-, dean of men, 53-57, dean of Col. of Arts and Sci, 57-69; Fulbright lectr, Col. Arts and Sci, Baghdad, Iraq, 55-56 and Seoul Nat. Univ, Korea, 64-65. Mil. Serv: Entered as Lt.(jg), Navy 43, released as Lt, 46, after serv. in Air Combat Intel. Publ: Co-auth, An Introduction to American Government, Stackpole, 54; contrib. to Sewanee Rev. and Vanderbilt Law Rev. Mem: Am. and South. Polit. Sci. Asns; Va. and Tenn. State Bar Asns; Sewanee Civic Asn; EQB Faculty Club. Rel: Episcopal. Mailing Add: University Sta, Sewanee, Tenn. 37375.

LANCIONE, A. G. D
Minority Leader, Ohio House of Rep.
b. Cementon, Pa, 2/12/07; s. John Baptist Lancione and Elizabeth Del Guzzo L; m. 11/19/31 to June Davies Morford; c. John, Bernard and Richard. Educ: Ohio State Univ, A.B, 27, J.D, 29; Alpha Phi Delta. Polit. & Govt. Pos: Asst. prosecuting attorney, Belmont Co, Ohio, 36-44; Ohio State Rep, 47-, Majority Leader, Ohio State House of Rep, 49-51, former Speaker-Pro-Tem, Minority Leader, 61-; nat. committeeman, Young Dem. of Ohio, 48-49; chmn, Taxation Cmn, 59-61; v.chmn, Ohio Legis. Serv. Cmn, 65-66 & 69-70; alternate del, Dem. Nat. Conv, 68. Bus. & Prof. Pos: Dir. and v.pres, Farmers and Merchants Nat. Bank. Mil. Serv: Cand. in Officer Training Sch. Mem: Ohio Acad. Trial Lawyers (mem. bd. gov, 65-66); Belmont Co. Bar Asn.(pres, 44 & 68-69, v.pres, 66); Ohio State and Am. Bar Asns; Am. Judicature Soc; Pub. Affairs Cmn; Ohio Bankers Asn; Fraternal Order of Police Assocs. of Bellaire (pres, 66); C. of C; Kiwanis; Elks; Eagles; Moose; Foresters; DAV; life mem, Am. Legion and Sons of Italy. Rel: Episcopal. Legal Res: 3765 Tallman Ave, Bellaire, Ohio 43906. Mailing Add: 204 Farmers and Merchants Bank Bldg, Bellaire, Ohio 43906.

LANCIONE, NELSON D
b. Bellaire, Ohio, 7/10/21; s. John B. Lancione (deceased); m. 2/12/48 to Tillie L. Lapitsky; c. Nelson William, Robert Michael and David. Educ: Ohio State Univ, B.S, 41, J.D, 43; Alpha Phi Delta; Phi Delta Phi; Inter-Fraternity Pres. Coun. Polit. & Govt. Pos: With Off. Gen. Counsel, U.S. Treas. Dept, 43-49, U.S. Treas. rep, 45-47, acting treas. attache, Am. Embassy, Manila, Philippines, 46-47, asst. attorney gen, Ohio, 49-50; pres, Ohio League of Young Dem. Clubs, 54-55; chmn, Speakers Bur, Ohio Dem. Hq, 56; v-pres, Young Dem. Clubs of Am, 56-57, pres, 57-58; del, Dem. Nat. Conv, 56, 60, 64 & 68; del, Atlantic Conf. Polit. Youth Leaders, 58; spec. counsel for Attorney Gen, Ohio, 58-62; del, Atlantic Cong, 59; mem. and chmn. finance cmt, Franklin Co. Dem. Exec. Cmt, Ohio, 68-69. Bus. & Prof. Pos: Attorney-at-law, self-employed, 51-; secy. and gen. counsel, N.Am. Equitable Life Assurance Co, 59- Publ: Preliminary Study of Certain Financial Laws and Institutions: Denmark, 9/44 and Albania, 11/44; 'The Ohio Agents—General Motors Fight on Agents Licensing,' Rough Notes, 1/53. Mem: Am. Judicature Soc; Am, Int. Am. and Ohio State Bar Asns; Ohio Acad. of Trial Lawyers; Am. Trial Lawyers Asn; Columbus Bar Asn; Am. Soc. Int. Law; life mem, Moose; Ohio State Univ. Asn; Brookside Golf and Country Club; Guild Athletic Club; Columbus Area C. of C; Franklin Co. Mental Health Asn; Int. Platform Asn; Wayfarers Club; hon. fel, Harry S Truman Libr. Inst. Rel: Methodist. Legal Res: 3838 Walhaven Rd, Columbus, Ohio 43221. Mailing Add: 42 E. Gay St, Suite 1312, Columbus, Ohio. 43215.

LAND, HENRY WILLIAM D
Chmn, Orange Co. Dem. Exec. Cmt, Fla.
b. Plant City, Fla, 7/3/13; s. Bennett Land and Josephine Schneider L; m. 8/19/35 to Abby Josephine Simpson; c. Sara Josephine (Mrs. Payson N. Sullivan), Mary Catherine (Mrs. James W. Hooten, Jr.), Henry William, II, David Bennett, Albion Winslow and Thomas Milton. Educ: Univ. Fla, B.S. in agr, 33; Phi Kappa Phi; Alpha Zeta; Scabbard & Blade; Lambda Chi Alpha; elected to Student Honor Court. Polit. & Govt. Pos: Mem. bd, Orange Co. Cmnr, Fla, 41-42; precinct committeeman, and mem, Orange Co. Dem. Exec. Cmt, chmn, currently; Fla. State Rep, Orange Co, 52-57 & 62-69; alternate del, Dem. Nat. Conv, 64. Bus. & Prof. Pos: Pres. and gen. mgr, Consumers Lumber and Veneer Co, Apopka, Fla, 35-38; dir, State Bank of Apopka, 47-, v.chmn. bd, 66; dir, Plymouth Citrus Growers Asn. and Plymouth Citrus Prods. Coop, 56- Mil. Serv: Entered as 1st Lt, Army, 42, released as Maj, 45, after serv. in 559th Field Artil. Bn, Eighth Corps, ETO; Bronze Star Medal. Mem: Rotary; Elks; Moose; Farm Bur; Nat. Asn. Real Estate Bd; Mil. Order of World Wars; Am. Legion; VFW. Rel: Episcopal. Mailing Add: Route 2, Box 582, Apopka, Fla. 32703. (1967)

LAND, W.R, JR. D
b. Hamlet, N.C, 10/26/16; s. W.R. Land and May LeGrand L; m. 11/22/40 to Ruth Sykes; c. W.R. Land, III and Vance S. Educ: Mars Hill Col, 34-35; Clemson Col, 36-37. Polit. & Govt. Pos: Mem. bd. cmnrs, Richmond Co, N.C, 58-62; N.C. State Rep, 63-66. Bus. & Prof. Pos: Farming and timber bus; truck and tractor dealer, Int. Harvester. Mil. Serv: ROTC, Clemson Col, 36-37. Mem: Moose; Benedict Club; Nite Lighter Club; Richmond Co. Country Club; Hamlet Gun Club. Rel: Presbyterian; Deacon and pres. Howell Bible Class, 59. Mailing Add: Bauersfeld St, Hamlet, N.C. 28345.

LANDERS, WILLIAM LYTLE 'JUG' D
Mem, Tenn. State Dem. Exec. Cmt.
b. Shelbyville, Tenn, 4/9/26; s. W.A. Landers (deceased) and Elaine Taylor Ingle L; m. 6/1/52 to Jean Wiggs; c. Ben and John. Educ: Mid. Tenn. State Univ, B.S, 50; Vanderbilt Univ. Law Sch, 50; Phi Delta Theta. Polit. & Govt. Pos: Secy. and clerk, Off. of U.S. Sen. K.D. McKellar, 51-52; del, Tenn. Ltd. Constitutional Conv, 59 & 65; mem, State Libr. & Arch. Cmn, Tenn, 63-; Bedford Co. co-chmn. Johnson-Humphrey Ticket, 64 and Humphrey-Muskie Ticket, 68; secy, Bedford Co. Dem. Primary Bd, Tenn, 66-; mem, Tenn. State Dem. Exec. Cmt, Fourth Cong. Dist, 66-; del, Dem. Nat. Conv, 68. Bus. & Prof. Pos: Civil Serv. job, Wash. D.C, 53-54; ins. agent, Tullahoma, Tenn, 55-59; owner, Lytle Landers Agency, Shelbyville, 59- Mil. Serv: Entered as Pvt, Marines, 45, released as Pfc, 46, after serv. in Sixth Marine Div, 15th Marines, Pac. Theatre, China, 45-46. Mem: Chmn, Bedford Co. Insurers, 67; Am. Legion (past adj. and finance officer); VFW; Rotary; C. of C; past chmn, City Sch. Bd; past chmn, Bedford Co. Libr. Bd; v.pres, Mid. Tenn. State Univ. Alumni Asn; mem, Mid. Tenn. State Univ. Found. Our Stake in Better Govt. Award, Shelbyville Jaycees, 65. Rel: Christian Church of N.Am; deacon, First Christian Church. Legal Res: 114 Burrum Dr, Shelbyville, Tenn. 37160. Mailing Add: P.O. Box 617, Shelbyville, Tenn. 37160.

LANDGRAF, VERNON H. R
b. Cape Girardeau, Mo, 10/4/24; s. L. H. Landgraf and Hilda Gerler L; m. 7/3/52 to Mary Victoria Williams; c. Mark Thomas, Luke Turner, Jeffrey

Franklin and John Paul. Educ: South East Mo. State Col, 1942 & 46-48; Los Angeles City Col, 44; Webster Society. Polit. & Govt. Pos: Mem, Mo. State Finance Cmt, 67-68; Rep. nominee, U.S. Rep, Mo, 68. Bus. & Prof. Pos: V.pres, L.H. Landgraf Lumber Co, Inc, 50-69; pres, Landgraf Real Estate & Develop. Corp, 58-69; mem. exec. bd, Cape Supply Co, 62-68; Pres, SLR Promotion Co, Inc, 63-69; Treas, Rental Land, Inc, 66-69; v.pres, West Side Improv. Co., Inc, 66-69. Mil. Serv: Entered as Pvt, Army, 43, released as S/Sgt, 46, after serv. in 548th Field Artillery Bn, ETO, 44-46. Mem: Southwest. Lumbermen's Asn; VFW; Am. Legion; C. of C.(pres); Lions (pres); Jaycees (pres). State Distinguished Serv. Award, Jaycees. Rel: Lutheran, Mo. Synod. Mailing Add: 2551 Meadow Lane, Cape Girardeau, Mo. 63701.

LANDGREBE, EARL FREDERICK R
U.S. Rep, Ind.
b. Valparaiso, Ind, 1/21/16; s. Edward William Landgrebe and Benna Marie Broderman L; m. 7/12/36 to Helen Lucile Field; c. Ronald and Roger. Educ: Wheeler High Sch, 4 years. Polit. & Govt. Pos: Ind. State Sen, 59-68; U.S. Rep, Ind, 69- Bus. & Prof. Pos: Pres, Landgrebe Motor Transport, Inc, 43-; dir, First Fed. Savings & Loan, 57-; pres, Landgrebe and Son, 67- Mem: Rotary; C. of C. Rel: Lutheran. Legal Res: R.R. 2, Valparaiso, Ind. 46383. Mailing Add: Coronet Apts, 200 C St. S.E, Washington, D.C. 20003.

LANDIS, FREDERICK R
b. Logansport, Ind, 1/17/12; s. Frederick Landis, Sr. and Bessie Baker L; m. 7/4/45 to Joyce Stevenson; c. Diana, Frederick, III, Susan, Gillian and Kenesaw Mountain, III. Educ: Wabash Col, Ind; Ind. Univ, A.B, Law Sch, LL.B; Phi Delta Phi; Delta Tau Delta. Polit. & Govt. Pos: Prosecuting attorney, 29th Judicial Circuit, Ind, 38-40; Ind. State Rep, 50-52; Ind. State Sen, 52-55; judge, Supreme Court of Ind, 55-65; judge, U.S. Customs Court, 65- Mil. Serv: Enlisted in Navy, 42, released as Lt, 46, after serv. in ETO. Mem: Chmn, Ind. Judges Retirement Fund, 65; Cass Co. Bar Asn.(pres, 48-51; Fed. and Ind. Bar Asns; Am. Judicature Soc; Indianapolis Press Club; hon. mem, Nat. Lawyers Club, Wash, D.C; Am. Legion; VFW; Columbia Club. Rel: Protestant. Mailing Add: 1 Federal Plaza, New York, N.Y. 10007.

LANDOLT, ALLAN FRANCIS R
Chmn, Cass Co. Rep. Cent. Cmt, Ill.
b. Litchfield, Ill, 6/20/25; s. Harold F. Landolt and Anna M. Talley L; m. 6/9/49 to Joan Adel Burns; c. Mary Theresa, Kathleen Ann, Allan Joseph, Maura Jane, Mark William, Renee Louise and Matthew Girard. Educ: Univ. Notre Dame, B.A. in Bus. Admin, 50. Polit. & Govt. Pos: Chmn, Cass Co. Rep. Cent. Cmt, Ill, 66- Bus. & Prof. Pos: Mgr, Am. Investment Co. of Ill, 51-54; supvr, Liberty Loan Corp, St. Louis, Mo, 54-58; v.pres. and loan officer, Northtown Bank, Decatur, Ill, 58-61; pres. and owner, Cass Consumers Serv, Inc, Virginia, Ill, 61- Mil. Serv: Entered as Aviation Cadet, Navy, 43, released as Lt.(jg), 50, after serv. in Naval Air Transport Serv, Hawaii and Aleutions, 45-46. Mem: K. of C; Kiwanis; Am. Legion; Elks. Rel: Roman Catholic. Mailing Add: 333 E. Union, Virginia, Ill. 62691.

LANDOLT, GENE D
Chmn, Calloway Co. Dem. Party, Ky.
b. Bonne Terre, Mo, 12/21/31; s. Harold Landolt and Loretta Horn L; m. 6/12/54 to Lochie Faye Hart; c. George David, Deborah Jene and Lore Broach. Educ: Univ. Mo, B.S, 54; Phi Kappa Psi. Polit. & Govt. Pos: Escort for President Truman's visit of West. Ky, Calloway Co. Young Dem, Ky, 62, v.pres, 64; prog. chmn. for gubernatorial cand, 63; del, Dem. Nat. Conv, 64; chmn, Calloway Co. Dem. Party, 64- Bus. & Prof. Pos: Head basketball coach, Renick High Sch, 53-54; instr. and asst. basketball coach, Murray State Univ, Ky, 56-57; teller, Bank of Murray, 57-58, asst. v.pres, 58-; owner, Gene Landolt Ins. Agency, 67-; pres, Hartland, Inc, 68- Mil. Serv: Entered as 2nd Lt, Army, 54, released as 1st Lt, 56, after serv. in 3420th Serv. Unit, 3rd Army. Mem: Ky. Bankers Installment Loan Asn; chmn, Educ. Asn. and Ky. Bankers Asn; C. of C; Jr. C. of C; Civitan Club; Murray Civic Improv. Asn. Co-capt, Univ. Mo. basketball team, 52-53; life mem, Univ. Mo. M Club for Varsity Athletics. Rel: Disciples of Christ. Legal Res: 1318 Wells Blvd, Murray, Ky. 42071. Mailing Add: Box 428, Murray, Ky. 42071.

LANDON, ALFRED M. R
b. West Middlesex, Pa. 9/9/87; s. John M. Landon and Anne Mossman L; m. 1/19/15 to Margaret Fleming (deceased); c. Margaret Anne; m. 1/15/30 to Theo Cobb; c. Nancy Josephine and John Cobb. Educ: Univ. Kans, LL.B, 08; Phi Gamma Delta; Phi Delta Phi. Hon. LL.D, Washburn Col, 33, Marietta Col, 34, and Boston Univ, 39; hon. L.H.D, Kans. State Univ, 68. Polit. & Govt. Pos: Chmn, Kans. Rep. State Cent. Cmt, 28; Gov, Kans, 33-37; cand. for President, 36; mem, Pan Am. Conf, Lima, Peru, 38; del-at-lg, Rep. Nat. Conv, 40, 44 & 48. Bus. & Prof. Pos: Bookkeeper; oil producer, 12-; radio broadcasting stas, 50- Mem: Odd Fellows; Elks; Am. Legion; Mason; hon. mem, Blue Key, 69. Rel: Methodist. Legal Res: Prospect Hills, Topeka, Kans. 66606. Mailing Add: 1001 Fillmore St, Topeka, Kans. 66604.

LANDON, ALICE CONANT R
b. New Haven, Vt, 9/23/94; m. to Carroll Hoyt Landon, wid; c. Two daughters. Educ: Beeman Acad, 11; Tilton Sem, 12; Emerson Col, 15. Polit. & Govt. Pos: Mem, New Eng. and Vt. Co. and State Rep. Cmts; former Vt. State Rep. Bus. & Prof. Pos: Farmer; breeder of Holstein-Friesian cattle. Mem: Ladies Aid; PTA; DAR; Nat. League, Am. Penswomen; Rowland Robinson Mem. Asn; Garden Club; Farm Bur; Vt. Dairymen's Wives & Daughters Asn; Holstein-Friesian Asn. of Am. Rel: Congregational. Mailing Add: Elmwood Farms, New Haven, Vt. 05472. (1967)

LANDRENEAU, J. VERNON D
b. Ville Platte, La, 5/8/16; s. Leo Oswald Landreneau and Lula Chenevert L; m. 8/30/36 to Maxie Adele Plauche; c. Maxine L.(Mrs. Juneau), Bonnie L. (Mrs. Plauche), Karen L.(Mrs. Firmin), Joey and Celeste. Educ: Univ. of Southwest. La, B.A; La. State Univ, M.Ed; Phi Delta Kappa. Polit. & Govt. Pos: La. State Rep, Avoyelles Parish, 64-69. Bus. & Prof. Pos: Teacher and coach, Plaucheville High Sch, La, 39-64, prin, 64- Mil. Serv: Entered as Pvt, Army, 43, released as Lt, 52. Mem: Am. Legion; La. Teachers Asn; Avoyelles Teachers Asn; Pub. Affairs Res. Coun; Avoyelles Prin. Asn; K. of C. Rel: Catholic. Mailing Add: Plaucheville, La. 71362.

LANDRETH, JOSEPH FRANKLIN R
Chmn, Dade Co. Rep. Cent. Cmt, Mo.
b. Aldrich, Mo, 12/25/07; s. Lola Montez Landreth and Winnie Edge L; m. 8/6/38 to Mabel Dorothy Burros. Educ: Southwest Mo. State Col, B.S, 33; Country Life Club. Polit. & Govt. Pos: Chmn, Dade Co. Rep. Cent. Cmt, Mo, 64- Bus. & Prof. Pos: Soc. sci, phys. educ. and sci. instr, pub. schs, Southwest Mo, 30-42; sr. aircraft inspector, U.S. Navy, 42-46; mgr. and owner, Landreth Supermkt, Greenfield, Mo, 46-68; gen agent, Mod. Security Life Ins, Springfield, Mo, 69- Mem: C. of C; Odd Fellows; Lions; Farm Bur. Hon. Chap. Farmer, Future Farmers of Am. Rel: Baptist. Mailing Add: 728 Crestview, Greenfield, Mo. 65661.

LANDRUM, PHILLIP MITCHELL D
U.S. Rep, Ga.
b. Martin, Ga, 9/10/07; s. Phillip Davis Landrum and Blanche Mitchell L; m. 7/30/33 to Laura Brown; c. Phillip Mitchell and Susan. Educ: Piedmont Col, 39; Atlanta Law Sch, LL.B, 41; Mercer Univ; La. State Univ. Polit. & Govt. Pos: Asst. attorney gen, Ga, 46-47; exec. secy. to Gov, Ga, 47-48; U.S. Rep, Ga, 53-, co-auth,Landrum-Griffith Bill, U.S. Cong, 59. Bus. & Prof. Pos: High sch. athletic dir. and coach, Bowman, Ga, 32-35 and Nelson, Ga, 35-37; supt. pub. schs, Nelson, 37-41; attorney-at-law, Jasper, 49- Mil. Serv: Army Air Force, 42-45. Mem: Ga. Bar Asn; Am. Legion; VFW; Mason; Elks. Rel: Baptist. Legal Res: Jasper, Ga. Mailing Add: 2308 Rayburn House Office Bldg, Washington, D.C. 20515.

LANDSMAN, ALBERT MICHAEL D
Treas, Nev. Dem. Party
b. Kiev, Russia, 6/21/07; s. Phillip Landsman and Sarah Becker L; m. 6/15/52 to Mary E. Karsh; c. Sally R.(Mrs. Gutkin). Educ: Chicago and Harrison High Sch. Polit. & Govt. Pos: Trustee and receiver, Bankruptcy Court, 56-; treas, Nev. Dem. Party, 59-; chmn, Dem. Exec. Cmt, 60-62; mem, Nev. Constables Asn, 60-; mem, adv. cmt, Small Bus. Asn, 62-66; cmnr, State of Nev. Cmt. on Equal Rights, 63-65; del, Dem. Nat. Conv, 64 & 68; receiver and forclosurer, Fed. Housing Admin. Apt. Forclosures, 64-, contracting agent, Fed. Housing Admin, 65-; v.chmn, Clark Co. Housing Authority, 65- Bus. & Prof. Pos: Owner, Towne & Country Interiors, 53-; part owner, Craig Rd. Speedway, 65- Mil. Serv: CPO, Navy, 43-45 & 50-51, serv. in Seabees, Pac. Theatre and Korea, Seabees, Naval Res, 51-58; Expert Rifleman Medal; Overseas Duty Medal; Good Conduct Medal; One Star. Mem: Mason; Shrine. Rel: Jewish. Legal Res: 2112 Santa Ynez, Las Vegas, Nev. 89105. Mailing Add: 701 E. Stewart, Las Vegas, Nev. 89101.

LANE, ARCHIE TRAVERS, SR. D
b. Perquimans Co, N.C, 9/26/00; s. Thomas C. Lane and Minnie Copeland L; m. Aug, 24 to Sallie Perry McNider; c. Archie T, Jr. Educ: Eastman Bus. Col. Polit. & Govt. Pos: N.C. State Rep, 61-66; Bd. Co. Cmnrs, 37-42, 49-58, Chmn, 8 yrs. Bus. & Prof. Pos: Farmer; bus. man; Mgr, Dir, Chmn. Bd. of Dirs, Albemarle Elec. Mem. Corp; Exec. Bd, Tar Heel Elec. Asn, V.Pres. Mem: Farm Bur, Pres, 42-47; N.C. Elec. Coop; Chmn, Bear Swamp Drain Comm, 40-; Dist. Health Bd; Past Chmn. Exec. Bd, Dist. TB Asn; Exec. Bd, Boy Scouts; Perquimans No. 106 AF&AM, Master, 45-46; Lions, Pres, 44, Dist. Dep. Dir, 45. Misc: Church Clerk. Rel: Baptist; Deacon. Mailing Add: Hertford, N.C. 27944. (1967)

LANE, CASWELL P. D
b. Mt. Sterling, Ky, 7/14/21; s. Ratliff Horace Lane and Anna Caswell Prewitt L; m. 9/1/47 to Sara Jeanette Leegan; c. Prewitt, Richard and Bill. Educ: Univ. Ky, A.B, 43, LL.B, 48; Phi Delta Phi; Kappa Alpha Order. Polit. & Govt. Pos: Judge, Montgomery Co. Court; city police judge, Mt. Sterling, Ky, 53-61. Mem: Rotary; Mt. Sterling C. of C. Rel: Disciples of Christ. Mailing Add: 321 W. Main, Mt. Sterling, Ky. 40353. (1967)

LANE, CLARENCE D. R
N.Y. State Assemblyman
b. Ashland, N.Y, 3/17/22; s. Eli Lane and Nora Dolan L; m. to Eleanor Thompson; c. Jeffry, Claudia, Roger and Kenneth. Educ: Ithaca Col, B.S, deans list, 3rd in class; Columbia Univ. Polit. & Govt. Pos: Organizer and first pres, Windham Rep. Club; budget officer, Greene Co. Bd. Supvrs; former supvr, Windham; co. supvr, 57-62; N.Y. State Assemblyman, 62- Bus. & Prof. Pos: Former sch. teacher; resort owner and mgr; dir, Windham Water Co. Mil. Serv: Lt, Marine Corps. Mem: Mason; Boy Scouts; Farm Bur. Rel: Methodist; trustee, Windham Methodist Church. Mailing Add: Windham, N.Y. 12496.

LANE, DAVID CAMPBELL R
Fla. State Sen.
b. Medford, Mass, 6/17/27; s. Thomas Edward Lane and Jean Mathilda Campbell L; m. 6/6/58 to Benita Johnson; c. Benjamin Johnson, Brett Mullikin, Helen Lucinda and David Campbell, Jr. Educ: Univ. Tenn. and Harvard Univ; Okla. A&M Col, B.S, 47; Univ. Tenn. Med. Sch, M.D, 51; Univ. Wis. Med. Sch, D.A.B, 57; Phi Epsilon Psi; Omicron Delta Kappa; Alpha Omega Alpha; Sigma Chi; Phi Chi. Polit. & Govt. Pos: Fla. State Sen, 67-, mem, Fla. State Senate Cmts. of Health and Welfare, Educ, Rules and Calendar, Select Cmt. on Gubernatorial Suspension, Select Cmt. on Tuberc. Hosp. and Spec. Select Cmt. on Univ. Fla. Med. Sch, chmn, Welfare Cmt, Legis. Coun, Fla. State Senate, 67-69; mem, Electoral Col, 68; mem, Hosp. Serv. for Indigent Adv. Bd, State of Fla, 69- Mil. Serv: Entered as Seaman, 1/C, Naval Res, 44, released as Comdr, 64, after serv. in Asiatic-Pac. Theatre, 44-46; Comdr.(Ret), Naval Res; Maj.(Ret), Army Res; Asiatic-Pac. Theatre; Philippine Liberation Ribbon; Am. Theatre; Victory Medal. Mem: Fel, Am. Col. of Surgeons, 68-; fel, Int. Col. of Surgeons, 61-; Ft. Lauderdale Surg. Soc; Harvey Cushing Soc; South. Neurosurg. Soc; Am. Asn. of Neurological Surgeons; Cong. of Neurological Surgeons; Int. Cong. of Neurological Surgeons; Fla. Neurosurg. Soc; Carribean Neurosurg. Soc; Pan-Am. Med. Asn; Broward Co. Med. Asn.(exec. cmt, 69-); Fla. Med. Asn.(House of Del, 67-); Am. Med. Asn; Lauderdale Yacht Club (bd. gov); Sigma Chi Alumni Asn; Ft. Lauderdale C. of C; Navy League Coun; bd. dirs, Rep. Citizen's Cmt; bd. dirs, Ft. Lauderdale Mus. of Arts; Ft. Lauderdale Hist. Soc; Friends of the Libr; Cmt. for Aid to Handicapped; United Cerebral Palsy Bd; YMCA; Ment. Health Asn; Int. Oceanographic Asn; Nat. Rehabilitation Asn; Fla. Asn. for Retarded Children; Fla. Fedn. of Blind; Jr. Achievement;

Boy's Club. One of Five Outstanding Young Men in Fla, Jaycees; Outstanding Sen. in Cmt, Fla. Senate, 69. Rel: Episcopal. Legal Res: 1233 N. Rio Vista Blvd, Ft. Lauderdale, Fla. 33301. Mailing Add: 500 S.E. 17th St, Ft. Lauderdale, Fla. 33316.

LANE, DAVID JUDSON R
Chmn, Essex Rep. Town Cmt, Mass.
b. Rockport, Mass, 7/6/27; s. Roy H. Lane and Clara C. Clark L; m. 10/6/51 to Claire A. Beckmann; c. Heather Lea and Judson Arthur. Educ: Harvard Col, A.B, 48. Polit. & Govt. Pos: Dist. coordinator, Brooke for Attorney Gen, Mass, 64; chmn, Essex Rep. Town Cmt, 65-; town moderator, Essex, 66-; dist. coordinator, Brooke for Sen, 66; cmnr, Spec. Cmn. on Automobile Ins, 68- Bus. & Prof. Pos: Exec. v.pres, Hastings-Tapley Ins. Agency, 66- Mil. Serv: Entered as Seaman 1/C, Navy, 45, released as ETM 3/C, 46. Mem: Soc. Chartered Property & Casualty Underwriters (pres, Boston Chap, 65-66); Mass. Asn. Independent Ins. Agents and Brokers (pres). Mailing Add: John Wise Ave, Essex, Mass. 01929.

LANE, EDWARD E. D
Va. State Del.
b. Richmond, Va, 1/28/24; m. to Jean Wiltshire. Educ: Va. Polytech. Inst; Univ. Richmond Law Sch, LL.B. Polit. & Govt. Pos: Va. State Del, 54-, chmn, Welfare Cmt, mem, Gov. Budget Adv. Cmt. and House Appropriations Cmt, Va. State House of Del. Bus. & Prof. Pos: Lawyer. Mil. Serv: World War II Pilot. Mem: Co-chmn, Va. Coun. on Educ. TV; Country Club of Virginia; past pres, R.E. Lee Boy Scouts; chmn, Jefferson Jackson Day Dinner, 57. Distinguished Serv. Award, Jr. C. of C, 52. Rel: Episcopal; former vestryman. Mailing Add: 6301 Ridgeway Rd, Richmond, Va. 23229. (1967)

LANE, GARLAND D
Mich. State Sen.
b. Flint, Mich, 3/28/19; s. Dewey W. Lane and Bessie Irene Baker L; m. 7/25/41 to Dolores M. Comeau; c. Garland, Jr; five grandchildren. Educ: Flint Cent. High Sch, grad, 37. Polit. & Govt. Pos: Mich. State Sen, 29th Dist, 48-, mem, Appropriations Cmt, 53-, mem, Fiscal Agency Cmt, Legis. Coun. and Senate Cmt. on Cmts; mem, Mich. Cmn. on Interstate Coop, bd. mgrs, Coun. State Govts. and exec. cmt, Nat. Legis. Conf. Bus. & Prof. Pos: Owner and ins. agent, Garland Lane Agency, Inc, Flint, 51- Mil. Serv: Entered as Pvt, Army, 41, released as S/Sgt, 46, after serv. in ETO; Purple Heart. Mem: Mich. Ins. Asn; DAV; VFW; Am. Legion; 125th Inf. Asn. of World War II; Order of the Purple Heart. Rel: Lutheran. Mailing Add: 3162 Flushing Rd, Suite 23, Flint, Mich. 48504.

LANE, JANET ISABEL R
b. Columbus, Ohio, 1/12/22; d. Herbert Charles Bowers and Anna Laura Chambers B; m. 2/20/42 to Raymond Paul Lane; c. Shirley Rae (Mrs. Larry Alspaugh, Jr) and Dennis Ray. Educ: Columbus Comptometer Sch, grad, 40. Polit. & Govt. Pos: Dep, Clerk of Courts, Logan Co, 60-63, clerk, 69-; dep. registr, Bellefontaine, Ohio, 66-69. Bus. & Prof. Pos: Payroll clerk, Timken Roller Bearing, Columbus, Ohio, 40-42; secy, Union Implement Co, Marysville, Ohio, 63-64; off. worker, John Deere Implement, West Mansfield, Ohio, 64-65. Mem: Rep. Women's Orgn; Starlight Circle of Kings Daughters. Rel: Methodist. Mailing Add: E. State St, West Mansfield, Ohio 43358.

LANE, JIM E. D
Okla. State Sen.
b. Broken Bow, Okla, 5/5/34; s. Clarence Henery Lane and Vivian Wood L; m. 9/25/54 to Nancy Griggs; c. Steven Bradley, Clarence Thomas, James Edwin, Jr, Cynthia Joy and Joe Glenn. Educ: East. Okla. A&M Col, 55. Polit. & Govt. Pos: Okla. State Rep, First Dist; Okla. State Sen, Dist. 5, currently. Bus. & Prof. Pos: Serv. mgr, Lane Motor Co, 56-57; owner, Jim Lane Ford Sales, 66; partner, J&J Cattle Co. and pres, McCurtain Leasing Co, currently; owner, Frontier Motors, Broken Bow, Okla, 68- Mem: Okla. and Nat. Auto Dealers Asn; Okla. Cattlemen's Asn; Mason; Jaycees. Designated by For. Policy Asn. as one of the 500 Men under 35 Most Likely to Effect the Future Foreign Policy of U.S, 68; Outstanding Dealer Award, Okla. Auto Dealers Asn, 68. Rel: Presbyterian. Legal Res: Route 3, Box 51C, Idabel, Okla. 74745. Mailing Add: 10 N.E. First, Idabel, Okla. 74745.

LANE, PERRY M. D
b. Dallas Co, Mo, 9/24/30; m. 5/31/53 to Beulah M. Jackson; c. Terry A. and Lisa D. Educ: Buffalo High Sch. Polit. & Govt. Pos: Dep. collector, Buffalo Off, State Dept. of Revenue, 54-62; Mo. State Rep, 64-66; presiding judge, Dallas Co. Court, currently. Bus. & Prof. Pos: Farmer. Mil. Serv: Navy, 48-52, Atlantic and Pac. Theatres. Mem: Amvets; DAV. Rel: Baptist. Mailing Add: RFD 3, Box 182, Buffalo, Mo. 65622.

LANE, THOMAS J. D
Mem, Mass. Exec. Coun.
b. Lawrence, Mass, 7/6/98; m. to Jane R. Murphy. Educ: Suffolk Law Sch; Hon. B.S. in Pub. Admin, Suffolk Univ. Polit. & Govt. Pos: Mass. State Rep, 27-38; Mass. State Sen, 39-41; U.S. Rep, Mass, 41-61, chmn. subcmt. 2, Judiciary Cmt, U.S. House of Rep; mem, Gov. Coun, Fifth Dist, 64; mem, Mass. Exec. Coun, currently. Bus. & Prof. Pos: Attorney. Mil. Serv: Vet. of World War I. Mem: Am. Legion; Elks; Hiberians; K. of C; World War I Vets. of U.S. Sponsor of G.I. Bill. of Rights, U.S. House of Rep; Hon, Ital-Am. Vets. Rel: Catholic. Mailing Add: 92 Abbott St. Lawrence, Mass. 01843.

LANE, W. JONES D
Ga. State Rep.
b. Statesboro, Ga, 6/23/20; s. Emory Spree Lane and Mary Jones L; m. 6/08/41 to Susie May Franklin; c. William Jones Jr, Gloria Suzan, Robert Emory and Mary Ann. Educ: Univ. of Ga, 2 years. Polit. & Govt. Pos: Ga. State Rep, 61- Bus. & Prof. Pos: Gen. contractor. Mem: Rotary (dir, 62); Elks. Rel: Primitive Baptist. Mailing Add: 111 Donaldson St, Statesboro, Ga. 30458. (1967)

LANE, WILLIAM J. D
Pa. State Sen.
b. Brownsville, Pa. 2/7/05; s. J. William Lane and Alice Mary Pursglove L; m. to Audrey Louise Horton; c. One. Educ: Univ. of Pittsburgh, B.S; Delta Tau Delta. Hon. D.H.L, Univ. of Pittsburgh. Polit. & Govt. Pos: Pa. State Rep, 42-45; Pa. State Sen, 45-, Majority Whip, 61, Minority Whip, 63 & 65, Asst. Minority Leader, currently; mem, exec. cmt, Joint State Govt. Cmt; mem, Pa. Aeronaut. Cmn, 61- Bus. & Prof. Pos: Real estate and ins. broker. Mem: Chmn, Wash.Co. Orgn. Retarded Children; F&AM; Scottish Rite; Gourgas Lodge of Perfection, 14; Pa. Coun, Prin. of Jerusalem (16°); Pittsburgh Chap, Rose Cruix (18°); Pa. Consistory; S.P.R.S; Syria Temple (32°); AAONMS; Elks; hon. mem, Monongahela Valley Chap, Demolay. Mailing Add: R.D. 2, Box 455, Brownsville, Pa. 15417.

LANEY, DAN FOSTER, JR. D
S.C. State Rep.
b. Bishopville, S.C, 6/13/31; s. Dan F. Laney and Mary Olive Anderson L; m. 4/10/52 to Adville C. Baskin; c. Dan F, III, Marion E, James E. and Alan N. Educ: The Citadel, 48-52; Univ. S.C, LL.B, 54; Magister, Phi Delta Phi. Polit. & Govt. Pos: S.C. State Rep, 61- Bus. & Prof. Pos: Lawyer; pres. and mem. bd. dirs, Peoples Bank of Bishopville, S.C. Mil. Serv: 1st Lt, Air Force, Judge Adv. Gen. Dept, 55-57; Staff Judge Adv. of 52nd Fighter Group and 35th Air Div. Mem: C. of C; Farm Bur; past pres, Jaycees and Lions; pres, Bishopville Little League; hon. coun, Wig & Robe. Young Man of Year, 64; BNA Award. Rel: Baptist: Deacon and Sunday Sch. Teacher, First Baptist Church. Mailing Add: 119 Ridge St, Bishopville, S.C. 29010.

LANEY, JAMES ARCH D
b. Blackstone, Va, 5/19/26; s. Benjamin Ward Laney and Alline Nelson L; m. 9/11/48 to Rachel Flowe; c. Michael Nelson and Debra Alline. Educ: Univ. N.C, Chapel Hill, 1 year; Wingate Jr. Col, 2 years; Delta Psi Omega. Polit. & Govt. Pos: Union Co. chmn, Sanford for Gov, N.C, 60; mem. bd. dir, Young Dem. Club, High Point, N.C, 61-62; campaign mgr, Scott for Lt. Gov, 63; chmn, precinct orgn. cmt, Dem. Party, High Point, 63-65; mem, N.C. Scott Key Man Cmt, 68; second v.chmn, exec. cmt, Caldwell Co. Dem. Party, 68; Caldwell Co. mgr, Scott for Gov, 68; del, Dem. Nat. Conv, 68; Mayor-Pro-Tem, Rhodhiss, 68- Bus. & Prof. Pos: Gen. mgr. and v.pres, Radio Sta. WMAP, Monroe, N.C, 50-61; sales mgr. and v.pres, Radio Sta. WNOS, High Point, 61-65; gen. mgr, Radio Sta. WVGT, Mt. Dora, Fla, 65-66; gen. mgr. and secy. treas, Radio Sta. WKJK, Granite Falls, 66-69; dir, dept. of pub. affairs, N.C. State Hwy. Cmn, 69- Mil. Serv: Entered as A/S, Navy, 43, released as Seaman 1/C, 46, after serv. in Task Force 92, Destroyer No. 655, N.Pac, Aleutians, 44-46; Good Conduct and Pac. Theatre Ribbons; Meritorious Serv. Ribbon with One Star. Publ: 'Union Suits Me,' bi-weekly column in the Monroe J, N.C, 56-61; 'The Pace Lap,' weekly column in the Mt. Dora Topic, Fla, 65-66. Mem: N.C. and Nat. Asn. Broadcasters; South. Motorsports Writers Asn; Mt. Dora, Fla. and Monroe, High Point, Lenoir and Hickory, N.C, C. of C; Jr. C. of C; Civitan; Optimists (pres, Monroe Club, 56 and High Point Club, 62, v.pres, Hickory Club, 67); Ruratan; Elks; Toastmasters; Am. Legion; VFW; Monroe Little Theatre; Hickory, N.C. Human Rels. Cmt; first pres, West. Piedmont Coun. of Govt, 68. Young Man of Year, Monroe, N.C, 55; First Place United Press Int. Radio Ed. for N.C, 63; Awards for Best Performances in Little Theatre, Monroe, N.C. and Mt. Dora, Fla. Rel: Methodist; Sunday sch. teacher and mem. official bd, First United Methodist Church, Granite Falls, N.C. Mailing Add: 3203 Childers St, Raleigh, N.C. 27609.

LANG, JOHN ERNEST D
Chmn, Pottawatomie Co. Dem. Cmt, Kans.
b. Arkansas City, Kans, 12/27/36; s. Ernest R. Lang and Ruth Evans L; m. 11/27/59 to Joleen Charlotte Jilka; c. Jill Kay and Jeffrey Ray. Educ: Univ. Kans, A.B, 58; Washburn Univ, LL.B, 62; Kappa Alpha Mu; Phi Alpha Delta. Polit. & Govt. Pos: Ed, Kans. Young Dem. Newsletter, 57-58; v.pres, Univ. Kans. Young Dem, 57-58; legal aide, Kans. Corp. Cmn, 58-59; pres, Washburn Univ. Young Dem, 59-60; tax exam, State Dept. of Revenue, 59-60; state collegiate chmn, Kans. Young Dem. Clubs, 60-61; chmn, Pottawatomie Co. Dem. Cmt, Kans, 64-; co. attorney, Pottawatomie Co, 67-; chmn, Wamego Housing Authority, 67-; trustee, Wamego City Hosp, 68-; mem, Gov. Cmt. on Criminal Admin, 68- Bus. & Prof. Pos: Practicing attorney, 61- Mil. Serv: Sgt. E-5, Army Res, 58-64. Mem: Kans. State Bar Asn; Nat. Dist. Attorneys Asn; Kans. Peace Officers Asn; Lions (pres, Wamego Club); C. of C.(pres, Wamego Chap); secy, City Coun. of Churches, Wamego; AF&AM; AAONMS; Consistory; Elks. Rel: Methodist. Mailing Add: 614 Spruce, Wamego, Kans. 66547.

LANG, PHILIP DAVID D
Ore. State Rep.
b. Portland, Ore, 12/16/29; s. Henry W. Lang and Vera M. Kern L; m. 5/29/52 to Marcia Jean Smith; c. Philip D, III. Educ: Lewis & Clark Col, Portland, Ore, 54; Northwest. Col. Law, 56; Theta Chi. Polit. & Govt. Pos: Admin. asst. to mayor, Portland, Ore, 56-58; mem, Multnomah Co. Dem. Cent. Cmt, 56-; del, Ore. Dem. State Conv, 60-66; Ore. State Rep. 61- Bus. & Prof. Pos: State police officer, Ore, 53-55; adjuster, Glen Falls Ins. Co, 55-56 and Ore. Auto Ins. Co, 59-61; asst. mgr, N.Pac. Ins. Co, 61-63, mgr. and asst. v.pres, 63- Mil. Serv: Entered as Pvt, Air Force, 47, released as Sgt, 50, after serv. in Air Force Intel, Far East and Japan; Occupation Medal. Mem: Mason; DeMolay Legion of Honor; VFW; City Club of Portland; Ore. Ins. Underwriters Asn. Rel: Methodist. Mailing Add: 7330 S.E. 42nd Ave, Portland, Ore. 97206.

LANG, WILTON EARL, JR. D
b. Pitt Co, N.C, 2/29/12; s. Wilton Earl Lang and Lillie Yelverton L; m. 12/17/38 to Margaret Davis; c. Earlene Davis. Educ: N.C. State Univ, B.S, 36. Polit. & Govt. Pos: Cmnr, Town of Walstonburg, N.C, 41-51; mem, N.C. State Dem. Exec. Cmt, 48-52; mem, Greene Co. Dem. Exec. Cmt, 48-56; del, Dem. Nat. Conv, 64. Bus. & Prof. Pos: Owner and mgr, W.E. Lang, Jr. Ins. Agency, 38-; owner and mgr, W.E. Lang, Jr. Gen. Merchandise, 43-61; mem, adv. bd, Home Fed. Savings and Loan Asn. and Wachovia Bank and Trust Co, 64- Mem: Lions; sponsoring cmt, Walstonburg 4-H Club and Local Boy Scouts of Am. Hobbies: Boating and fishing. Rel: Disciples of Christ. Legal Res: N. Wilson St, Walstonburg, N.C. 27888. Mailing Add: Box 175, Walstonburg, N.C. 27888.

LANGAN, JOSEPH NICHOLAS D
City Cmnr, Mobile, Ala.
b. Mobile, Ala, 3/11/12; s. David Damasus Langan and Teresa C. McAleer L; m. 1/19/43 to Maude Adele Holcombe. Educ: Spring Hill Col, B.S, 51, hon. LL.D; Sigma Nu; Phi Kappa Theta. Polit. & Govt. Pos: Ala. State Rep, 39-43;

dir, Selective Serv, Ala, 47-48; mem, State Bd. of Educ, 47-49; Ala. State Sen, 47-51; co. cmnr, Mobile Co, Ala, 51; city cmnr. and mayor, Mobile, 53-; alternate del, Dem. Nat. Conv, 68. Bus. & Prof. Pos: Attorney, Mobile, Ala, 35-53; secy, treas. and dir, Spring Hill Ins. Co, 63-69, Badger Ins. Agency, 67-69. Mil. Serv: Entered as Pvt, Nat. Guard, 31, released as Brig. Gen, 65, after serv. in C.G. 31st Inf. 'Dixie' Div, Pac. Theatre, 40-45, Maj. Gen.(Ret); Bronze Star Medal with Oak Leaf Cluster; Am. Defense & Pac. Theatre Medal; Philippine Liberation Medal; Korean Serv. Medal; Ala. Distinguished Serv. Medal. Mem: Bar Asn, Mobile, Ala; Am. Legion; VFW; Exchange Club; WOW. Knight of St. Gregory. Rel: Roman Catholic. Legal Res: 758 St. Michael St, Mobile, Ala. 36602. Mailing Add: 267 Houston St, Mobile, Ala. 36606.

LANGDON, JIM CALHOUN D
b. Stephenville, Tex, 12/14/14; s. George Muncie Langdon and Blanche Oates L; m. 6/1/43 to Jean Eleanor Steadman; c. Jim, Jr, Joe, John, Jerry and Julie. Educ: John Tarleton Col; Univ. Tex. Sch. of Law, LL.B, 40; Friars; Tex. Cowboys; Exec. Coun, Texas-X. Polit. & Govt. Pos: Cmnr, Tex. R.R. Cmn, 63-; chief justice, 8th Court of Civil Appeals, 59-63; judge, 112th Judicial Dist, 54-59; v.pres, McCamey Independent Sch. Dist, 48-50; spec. agent, Fed. Bur. of Invest, 40-43. Bus. & Prof. Pos: Chmn, Legal Cmt, Interstate Oil Compact, 64-; practice of law, McCamey, Tex, 46-54. Mil. Serv: Entered as Ensign, Naval Res, 43, released as Lt.(jg), 46, after serv. in Pac; Am, South Atlantic, Pac. and Okinawa Campaign Ribbons. Publ: Numerous articles on oil, gas and transportation. Mem: Am, El Paso and Trans-Tex. Bar Asns; v.chmn, mineral law sect, Tex. Bar Asn. and exec. cmt, judicial sect, 56-57; charter mem, Tex. Bar Found; Lions. Rel: Methodist. Legal Res: El Paso Co, Tex. Mailing Add: 5828 Trailridge Dr, Austin, Tex. 78731.

LANGE, ELMER F. R
Iowa State Sen.
b. Sac City, Iowa, 4/13/17; m. 6/16/46 to Beth Thomas; c. Mary Beth and Martha Jane. Educ: Iowa State Univ; Drake Univ. Polit. & Govt. Pos: Former Iowa State Rep; Iowa State Sen, currently. Bus. & Prof. Pos: Dairy Prod. Corp. exec; dir. and past. pres, Iowa Ice Cream Mfrs. Asn; dir, Second Savings Bank and Union State Bank, Winterset, Iowa. Mil. Serv: World War II, Prisoner of War, Germany; Army Res. Mem: Am. Legion; DAV; VFW; Amvets; Reserve Officers Asn; Ex-Prisoners of War; Kiwanis; Shrine; Mason (Past Master). Rel: Presbyterian; Elder. Mailing Add: 1010 Hillcrest, Sac City, Iowa 50583.

LANGE, ERNEST J. D
Chmn, Valley Co. Dem. Cmt, Nebr.
b. Ord, Nebr, 1/21/00; s. George H. Lange and Augusta M. Bremer L; m. 5/28/21 to Esther Marie Bredthauer; c. Vesta L.(Mrs. Huffman), Eldon E, David G, Wilma J.(Mrs. Loseke), Geralding E.(Mrs. Don Uden) and Carol E. (Mrs. David Uden). Polit. & Govt. Pos: Chmn, Valley Co. Dem. Cmt, Nebr, 66-; pres, Rural Fire Dist. and Rural Sch. Dist; alternate del, Dem. Nat. Conv, 68. Bus. & Prof. Pos: Farmer, irrigator and livestock feeder. Mem: Nat. Farmers Orgn; Lions. Rel: Lutheran. Mailing Add: R.R. 3, Ord, Nebr. 68862.

LANGE, MARTHA LUND R
Mem. Exec. Bd, Wis. Rep. Party
b. Hammond, Ind, 9/24/02; d. Erick Lund and Belle Jenks L; m. to Harold Kelso (deceased); m. 12/21/40 to Rudolph Fritsch Lange; c. George Kelso and Louise Esther. Educ: Purdue Univ; Ind. State Teachers Col, Muncie and Terra Haute. Polit. & Govt. Pos: Del, Wis. State Rep. Conv, 58-, chmn, Credentials Cmt, 63 and mem, Resolutions Cmt, twice; First Dist. chmn. and Walworth Co. pres, Fedn. of Rep. Women, 60-64; v.chmn, Walworth Co. Rep. Party, 60-64; participant, Annual Spring Conf. Rep. Women, D.C, 60-66; state chmn, Pyramid Nat. Fund Raising Proj, Women's Div, Rep. Party, 61-62; pres, Wis. Fedn. Rep. Women and mem, Nat. Bd. Dirs, Fedn. Rep. Women, 63-67, participant, Nat. Bd. Dirs. Conf, Phoenix, Ariz, 63, Louisville, Ky, 64, N.Y.C, 65 and Colorado Springs, 66; mem, State Exec. Bd, Wis. Rep. Party, 63- Mem: Former first v.regent, Daughters of Am. Colonists, state chaplain, 62-65 and state regent, 67-70; state chmn, resolutions cmt. and state second v.regent, DAR, state chaplain, 61-64 and regent, John Melchert Vanderpool Chap, 59-63; Am. Legion Auxiliary Unit, 95; pres, Clippers Investment Club; Walworth Co. Hist. Club; organizer and sr. pres, Philemon Baldwin Chap, Children of Am. Revolution; bd. mem, Music by the Lake; pres, Monday Club, 56-58 and Delavan Theater Guild, 45-47. 4 Gold Awards, John Melchert Vanderpool Chap, DAR, 59-63. Rel: Episcopal. Mailing Add: 115 Vine St, Delavan, Wis. 53115.

LANGE, MICHAEL BAKER D
b. Tiffin, Ohio, 7/18/35; s. Gilmore Henry Lange and Ruth Baker L; m. 8/20/60 to Susanne Gerhardstein; c. John, Mary, Ann, Jean and Michelle. Educ: Univ. Detroit, Ph.B, 58; Univ. Detroit Law Sch, LL.B. cum laude, 61; N.Y. Univ, LL.M, 62; Debating Soc; St. Francis Club; Law J. Polit. & Govt. Pos: Del, Rep. State Conv, 64-66 & 68; asst. city solicitor, Tiffin, Ohio, 64-; chmn, Seneca Co. Dem. Cent. Cmt, 66-69. Publ: 'Bootstrap Financing,' Tax Law Rev, 63. Mem: Cmt. on corp, Am. Bar Asn; sub-cmt. closed corp, Ohio State Bar Asn; Seneca Co. Bar Asn.(secy, 63-65, treas, 65-66); pres, Tiffin United Commercial Travelers and Tiffin Jr. C. of C. Taxation Award for Outstanding Student. Rel: Catholic. Legal Res: 194 Coe St, Tiffin, Ohio 44883. Mailing Add: 55 E. Perry St, Tiffin, Ohio 44883.

LANGE, WALTER HENRY D
b. Seymour, Ind, 1/27/13; s. August Frank Lange and Emma Meyer; single. Educ: Ind. Univ, B.A, 48, M.A, 52; Phi Beta Kappa. Polit. Pos: Research and Publn. Coordinator, Ind. State Dem. Cent. Cmt, 63-65; alternate del, Dem. Nat. Conv, 64; hq. chmn, Jackson Co. Dem. Cent. Cmt, 54, 40 and 38; treas, Jackson Co. Young Dem, 39-40. Govt. Pos: Records storage adminstr, Ind. State Govt, 66-; specifications writer, Dept. of Admin, Ind, 65, supvr, records mgt, 63; asst. to Admin. Asst. to Gov, 62; supvr, Next-of-Kin Section, Ind. State Bonus Div, 52-53 and 49-51. Bus. & Prof. Pos: Librarian, Atterbury Job Corps Training Center, Ind, 65-66; book selection librarian, Ind. State Library, 48-49; asst. to Librarian, Ind. Hist. Soc. Library, 48. Mil. Serv: Entered as Pvt, Army, 43, released as Sgt, 45, after serv. in 984th Signal Serv. Co, Signal Corps, European-African-Middle East. Theater, 43-45; European-African-Middle East. Ribbon with 2 Bronze Stars; Good Conduct and Victory Medals; Meritorious Unit Award. Publn: 'Fauxdauphinomanie,' The Ind. Quarterly for Bookmen, 1/47; 'The Lost Dauphin,' Am. Heritage, 50; 'The Wandering Corpse of John Wilkes Booth,' Am. Heritage, 52. Mem: Am. Hist. Asn; Ind. Hist. Soc; Soc. for French Hist. Studies; Manuscript Soc; Am. Legion; VFW. Collector of manuscripts and books concerning Louis XVII of France. Rel: Lutheran. Mailing Add: 424 North Park St, Seymour, Ind. 47274. (1967)

LANGEN, CHARLES EDWARD D
Second V.chmn, King Co. Dem. Cent. Cmt, Wash.
b. Boston, Mass, 4/28/30; s. John Henry Langen Sr. and Catherine Louise Mahoney L; m. 10/2/54 to Ruth Rosalee Burns; c. Rita Marie, Susan Elaine, Rachael Annette, Charles Edward, Jr, Mary Margaret and Bernadette Clair. Educ: Olympic Jr. Col, 1 year; St. John's Univ, Minn, one semester; Seattle Univ, B.A, 58. Polit. & Govt. Pos: Dem. Precinct committeeman, King Co, Wash, 61-; chmn, 35th Legis. Dist. Dem. Party, 67-68; alternate del, Dem. Nat. Conv, 68; second v.chmn, King Co. Dem. Cent. Cmt, 68- Bus. & Prof. Pos: Computing syst. analyst, Boeing Co, 55- Mil. Serv: Entered as Pvt, Army Med. Corps, 48, released as Pfc, 49, re-entered 50, released as Cpl, 53, serv. in 72nd Tank Bn, Second Inf. Div, Korea, 51, and Germany, 52-53; Combat Med. Badge; Distinguished Unit Citation; Korean Serv. Medal with 5 Campaign Stars; Korean Distinguished Unit Citation; Good Conduct Medal; European Occup. Medal; UN Serv. Medal. Mem: Urban League; Seattle Cath. Interracial Coun. Rel: Roman Catholic. Mailing Add: 1636 S. 136th St, Seattle, Wash. 98168.

LANGEN, ODIN R
U.S. Rep, Minn.
b. Minneapolis, Minn, 1/5/13; s. Joe Langen and Selma Almquist L; m. 12/23/28 to Lillian Clauson; c. Wayne, Lynden and Lois. Educ: Dunwoody Inst, 2 years. Polit. & Govt. Pos: Chmn. and cmt. mem, Prod. and Mkt. Admin, Kittson Co, Minn, 46-50; chmn, sch. bd, Kennedy, Minn. and mem, Red River Town Bd, 47-50; Minn. State Rep, 50-58; U.S. Rep, Minn, 58-; del, Rep. Nat. Conv, 68. Bus. & Prof. Pos: Farmer, 35- Mem: Mason; Lions; past chmn, Red River Farmers Club; Farm Bur; Lutheran Churchmen; 4-H Club; C-400 Club. Rel: Lutheran. Legal Res: Kennedy, Minn. 56733. Mailing Add: Rayburn House Office Bldg, Washington, D.C. 20515.

LANGLAND, WALTER V. R
b. 9/16/27; married; c. Two. Educ: Luther Col. Polit. & Govt. Pos: Precinct committeeman; mem, Decorah Sch. Bd, Iowa; Iowa State Rep, 67-69. Bus. & Prof. Pos: Former teacher; crop and dairy farmer. Mem: Past pres, Winneshiek Co. Farm Bur; bd. mem, N.E. Iowa Farm Serv. Rel: Lutheran. Legal Res: Iowa. Mailing Add: Route 1, Spring Grove, Minn. 55974.

LANGLEY, LAWRENCE DESALES D
Mem, Arlington Dem. Exec. Cmt, Va.
b. Washington, D.C, 11/5/05; s. Andrew DeSales Langley and Pearl E. L; m. June 1934 to Elise Foster; c. Richard Lawrence. Educ: George Wash. Univ, 24. Polit. & Govt. Pos: Mem, Arlington Dem. Exec. Cmt, Va, 50-, treas, 57-61; del, Dem. State Conv, 52, 56, 60, 64 & 68; del, Dem. Nat. Conv, 60, 64 & 68; co-chmn. precinct orgn, Arlington Co, J. Lindsey Almond Campaign for Gov, 57, Alburtis Harrison, Jr, 61 and Mills Godwin, 65; chmn. precinct orgn, late Harry F. Byrd, Sr. Campaign for U.S. Senate, 64 and Harry F. Byrd, Jr, 66; mem. adv. cmt, Tenth Cong. Dist. of Va. for Kennedy-Johnson Presidential Campaign, 60, Johnson-Humphrey, 64 and Humphrey-Muskie, 68; mem, Cmt. Strip Mining and Hwy. Construction Practices, Va. Adv. Legis. Coun, 64-65, Cmt. Surface Mining other than Coal, 66-67; cmt. clerk, Va. Gen. Assembly, currently. Bus. & Prof. Pos: Time clerk, Chesapeake and Potomac Tel. Co. of Va, 25-26, stock clerk, 26-30, installer, 30-44; co. repairman, 44-54, analyst, 54-66. Mem: Soc. Va; Lyon Village Citizens Asn; CWA; Pioneers of Am; founder, Old Dominion Baseball League, 35, pres, 35-45. Rel: Episcopal. Mailing Add: 1612 North Edgewood St, Arlington, Va. 22201.

LANGLEY, WALTER B. R
N.Y. State Sen.
b. Amsterdam, N.Y, 4/7/21; s. Walter B. Langley and Anna Mae McCaffrey L; m. 5/23/64 to Harriet Shaughnessy. Educ: Niagara Univ, B.B.A, 43; N.Y. Univ. Sch. Law, J.D, 50, LL.M, Taxation, 52. Polit. & Govt. Pos: Spec. asst. to Attorney Gen, Tax Div, Dept. of Justice, Wash, D.C, 53-58; N.Y. State Sen, 40th Dist, currently. Bus. & Prof. Pos: Law partner, Langley & Kinnum, Albany, N.Y, 60- Mil. Serv: Entered as Cpl, Army, 43, released as 1st Lt, 46, after serv. in 407th Inf, 102nd Div, ETO, 44-46. Mem: Am. and N.Y. State Bar Asns; Asn. of the Bar of the City of N.Y; Am. Legion; VFW; Ancient Order of Hibernians. Rel: Roman Catholic. Mailing Add: 225 Jay St, Albany, N.Y. 11210.

LANHAM, F. WAYNE D
B. Harrison Co, W.Va, 3/17/09; s. James E. Lanham and Mary Daisy Webb L; m. 8/2/34 to Elizabeth Ruth Hustead; c. James Wayne, Cindy Beth, John Mark. Educ: W.Va. Bus. Col. Polit. & Govt. Pos: W.Va. State Del, 64-66; retired state policeman, 35-64. Bus. & Prof. Pos: Auto salesman. Mem: Mason; Elks; Lions. Rel: Methodist. Mailing Add: St. Marys, Pleasants Co, W.Va. 26170. (1967)

LANHAM, JOHN CALHOUN D
Hawaii State Sen.
b. Summerton, S.C, 12/6/24; s. Frederick Lanham and Sue Cantey L; m. 6/21/19 to Annie Leimomi Naylor; c. Joanne Marie, Patrice Ann, Robert Cantey and Catherine Helen. Educ: Univ. S.C. Law Sch, LL.B, 49. Polit. & Govt. Pos: Pres, Hawaii Young Dem, 59; Hawaii State Rep, 59-66; Hawaii State Sen, 66- Bus. & Prof. Pos: Ins. adjuster, Home Ins. Co, Territory Hawaii, 56; attorney, 56- Mil. Serv: Entered as Recruit, Army Air Force, 44, released as Sgt, 45, after serv. in Judge Adv. Gen. Corps, China, Burma and India, 44-46; re-entered as 1st Lt, 51, released as Capt, 56, after serv. in Judge Adv. Gen. Corps, Korea, 51-52; Air Medal; Three Bronze Battle Stars; Good Conduct Medal. Mem: Hawaii and Am. Bar Asns; Am. Judicature Soc; Kiwanis. Rel: Catholic. Legal Res: 95-311 Alo Place, Wahiawa, Hawaii 96786. Mailing Add: 531 Avocado St, Wahiawa, Hawaii 96786.

LANIGAN, CHARLES THOMAS R
Chmn, N.Y. Rep. State Cmt.
b. Rome, N.Y, 2/3/25; s. Charles T. Lanigan; m. 1/29/49 to Barbara Gifford;

c. Charles T, III, Mary Kay, Valerie, Catherine and Julie. Educ: Colgate Univ, B.A, 49; Delta Kappa Epsilon. Polit. & Govt. Pos: Mayor, Rome, N.Y, 60-62; mem. exec. cmt, Oneida Co. Rep. Cmt, 63-66; dir, N.Y. State Off. Planning Coord, 67-69; chmn, N.Y. Rep. State Cmt, 69-; mem, Rep. Nat. Cmt, 69- Bus. & Prof. Pos: Sales prom. mgr. indust. prod, Revere Copper & Brass, Rome Mfg. Co. Div, 55-59; mem. bd. dirs, Homestead Savings & Loan Asn, Utica, 65- Mil. Serv: Entered as A/S, Navy, 43, released as FC 3/C, 46, after serv. in U.S.S. Aegir, Atlantic and Pac. Theaters, 44-46. Mem: Am. Soc. Pub. Admin; Pres. Asn, Am. Mgt. Asn; Rome C. of C.(exec. secy, 53-55). Young Man of the Year Award, Rome Jr. C. of C. Rel: Roman Catholic. Legal Res: 11 Coventry Rd, Glenmont, N.Y. 12077. Mailing Add: 315 State St, Albany, N.Y. 12210.

LANIGAN, JOHN J. R
Ill. State Sen.
b. Chicago, Ill, 2/9/35; s. John J. Lanigan and Nellie Sullivan L; m. 5/4/63 to Joanne L. Rogozinski; c. John J, Jr. and Mary L. Educ: DePaul Univ, B.Sc, 59. Polit. & Govt. Pos: Pres, 13th Ward Rep. Orgn, Chicago, Ill, 63; Ill. State Sen, 12th Dist, 65-67, 27th Dist, 67-, mem, Pension Laws Cmn, 65-, chmn, Computer & Data Processing Study Cmn, 65-67, chmn, Ment. Health Fund Adv. Cmt, 67-69, chmn, Pensions Cmt, 67- and mem, Legis. Audit Cmt, Ill. State Senate. Bus. & Prof. Pos: Jr. auditor, F.W. LaFrentz & Co, 59-61; sr. auditor, Lybrand, Ross Bros. & Montgomery, 61-67; audit mgr, Warren W. Wilson CPA, 67- Mil. Serv: Entered as Airman 3/C, Air Force Nat. Guard, 53, released as S/Sgt, 59, after serv. in 126th Fighter Interceptor Wing. Mem: Nat. Soc. State Legis. Rel: Roman Catholic. Legal Res: 7204 S. Talman Ave, Chicago, Ill. 60629. Mailing Add: 505 N. La Salle St, Chicago, Ill. 60610.

LANKFORD, RICHARD ESTEP D
b. Wilmington, Del, 7/22/14; s. Floyd Lankford and Sarah Tillard Estep L; m. 6/8/39 to Mary Elizabeth Allen; c. Sallie Estep and Richard Estep, Jr. Educ: Univ. Va, B.S, 37; Univ. Mo, LL.B, 40; Kappa Sigma; Skull & Keys. Polit. Pos: U.S. Rep, Md, 55-65; Md. State Del, 48-64. Govt. Pos: Cmnr, Md. Dept. of Chesapeake Bay Affairs, 66- Bus. & Prof. Pos: Private Practice of Law, 40-55. Mil. Serv: Entered as Ens, Naval Res, 42, released as Lt, 46, after serv. in U.S. and European Theaters. Mem: Anne Arundel Co. and Md. State Bar Asns; Annapolis Yacht Club; Annapolitan Club; New Providence Club. Rel: Episcopal. Mailing Add: Richard's Gift, R.F.D. 3, Annapolis, Md. 21403. (1967)

LANKFORD, THOMAS J. R
b. Sandborn, Ind, 12/5/26; s. Thomas Calvin Lankford and Susie E. Berryman L; m. 4/14/56 to Patricia Ann Fulmer; c. Thomas Todd and Patricia Kim. Educ: Vincennes Univ, A.S. in Eng, 46; Evansville Col, B.S. in Bus. Admin, 50; Georgetown Law Sch, 53-54; life mem, Acacia. Polit. & Govt. Pos: Rep. precinct committeeman and ward chmn, Ind, 48-52; Rep. cand. for auditor, Knox Co, 50; exec. asst. to U.S. Rep. William G. Bray, 51-52; Majority Clerk, U.S. House of Rep, 53, Minority Clerk, 54-; del, Rep. Nat. Conv, 56, alternate del, 60, 64 & 68. Bus. & Prof. Pos: Admin. asst, William A. Atkins Enterprises, 53. Mil. Serv: Entered as A/S, Navy, 44, released as PO 2/C, 46, after serv. in Supply, Ammunition Depot, Hawthorne, Nev. Mem: Lions; Elks; Mason; Shrine; Am. Legion; 40 et 8; Bull Elephants; Congressional Secretaries Club; Columbia Club Indianapolis; Congressional Country Club; Ky. Col; Capitol Hill Club (mem. bd. gov). Deans list in college. Rel: Methodist; trustee Potomac United Methodist Church. Legal Res: Box 231, Sandborn, Ind. 47578. Mailing Add: 9209 Farnsworth Dr, Potomac, Md. 20854.

LANKLER, ALEXANDER MacDONALD R
b. Wilkes-Barre, Pa, 6/30/28; s. Ralph Conover Lankler and Helen MacDonald L; m. 10/13/51 to Celeste Baldwin Skeen; c. Melissa M. and Lesley L. Educ: Hamilton Col, B.A, 48; Cornell Law Sch, LL.B, 51; Cornell Law Quart; Phi Kappa Phi; Sigma Phi. Polit. & Govt. Pos: Founder and pres, Younger Rep. Clubs Am, 44; pres, Jr. Rep. N.Y. State, 46; pres, Jr. Rep. Am, 48; dir. youth activities, N.Y. Rep. State Cmt, 49-50, Dir. N.Y. State Registrn. Vote, 60; law asst, Gov. Thomas E. Dewey, 54; asst. to Sen. Irving M. Ives, 56; asst. to asst. secy. treas, David Kendall, 57; adminstr. spec. asst, Gen. Serv. Admin, 57-59; dep. mgr, Nelson A. Rockefeller Reelection Campaign, 62 and Campaign for Pres, 63-64 & 68; finance chmn, Md. State Rep. Cmt, 67-68, counsel to state chmn, 69- Bus. & Prof. Pos: Assoc, Chapman, Bryson, Walsh & O'Connell, N.Y.C. and Wash, D.C, 53-56; partner, Chapman, Walsh, O'Connell, Hawkins, Delafield & Wood, 59-64; private practice of law, Wash, D.C, 64-67; sr. partner, Lankler & Crolius, 67- Mil. Serv: Entered as Ens, Coast Guard Res, 51, released as Lt.(jg), 53, after serv. at Hq, Wash, D.C. Mem: Asn. of Bar of City of N.Y; N.Y. State Bar Asn; Metrop. Club; Montgomery Co. Men's Rep. Club; Nat. Press Club; Sigma Phi Soc; Union League Club; West Montgomery Citizens Asn; Fed. City Club. Distinguished Serv. Medal, Gen. Serv. Admin, 59; Am. Heritage Found Award, 61. Rel: Presbyterian. Legal Res: Red Barn Lane, Potomac, Md. 20854. Mailing Add: 3526 K St. N.W, Washington, D.C. 20007.

LANNING, CHARLES D. R
Chmn, Washoe Co. Rep. Cent. Cmt, Nev.
b. Paonia, Colo, 4/1/20; s. Charles W. Lanning and Reva Smelser L; m. 4/20/52 to Regina O'Kane; c. Susan, Douglas and William. Educ: Univ. Denver, B.A, 41; Univ. Colo. Med. Sch, M.D, 60; Alpha Omega Alpha; Sigma Alpha Epsilon; Nu Sigma Nu. Polit. & Govt. Pos: Chmn, Washoe Co. Rep. Cent. Cmt, Nev, 66-; del, Rep. Nat. Conv, 68; chmn, Gov. Adv. Cmt, 68-69. Bus. & Prof. Pos: Ophthalmologist, 50- Mil. Serv: Entered as Cadet, Army Air Force, 42, released as Capt, 46, after serv. in Fourth Fighter Group, ETO, 42-45; ETO Medal; 4 Battle Stars; Presidential Unit Citation. Publ: Orbital Cellulitis, Proc. of Children's Hosp, Wash, D.C, 54. Mem: Am, Nev. State and Washoe Co. Med. Asns; Reno Surg. Soc; Pac. Coast Oto-Ophthalmologic Soc; San Francisco Ophthalmologic Round Table; Asn. U.S. Army. Rel: Protestant. Mailing Add: 3355 W. Plumb Lane, Reno, Nev. 89502.

LANTAFF, WILLIAM C. 'BILL' D
b. Buffalo, N.Y, 7/31/13; s. Walter R. Lantaff and Charmaine Brooks L; m. 5/11/38 to Betty Wilcox; c. W. Courtland, Kent, Cathy. Educ: Univ. of Fla, A.B, 34, LL.B, 36. Polit. & Govt. Pos: U.S. Rep, Fla, 51-55; del. Dem. Nat. Conv, 56,60; Fla. Legis, 46-50; pres, Dade Co. Young Dems, 47-48; city judge, Miami Beach, 38. Bus. & Prof. Pos: Lawyer, Walton, Lantaff, Schroeder, Carson & Wahl, Miami, Fla. law practice, 45-; 36-41; dir. City Nat. Bank of Miami. Mil. Serv: 1st Lt, Fla. Nat. Guard, 41; serv. with Gen. Staff Corps; discharged to res. as Lt. Col, 45; asst. Chief of Staff G/2, 51st Inf. Div, Fla. Nat. Guard, 45-50; Col, M.I. Div, Dept. Army, 50- Mem: Am. Legion; Mil. Order of World Wars; Am, Fla, Dade Co. Bar Asns; Miami Beach Jr. C. of C. (pres, 38), Miami-Dade Co; Phi Alpha Delta; Phi Kappa Tau; Mason (Shriner, Jester); Clubs: Metrop. (Wash.); Lions, Miami (Gov, 64). V.pres, Orange Bowl Cmt, 65 and pres, 67-68; pres. Dade Co. Commun. Chest, 57, chmn. dr, 55-56; elected 1 of 5 outstanding citizens Fla. by C. of C, 48. Legal Res: 990 Hunting Lodge Dr, Miami Springs, Fla. 33166. Mailing Add: DuPont Bldg, Miami, Fla. 33131. (1967)

LANTERMAN, FRANK D. R
Calif. State Assemblyman
b. Los Angeles, Calif, 11/4/01; single. Educ: Univ. South. Calif. Col. of Music; Pi Kappa Lambda. Polit. & Govt. Pos: Mem, Los Angeles Rep. Cent. Cmt, Calif, 38-50; Calif. State Assemblyman, 50-; del, Rep. Nat. Conv, 68. Bus. & Prof. Pos: Land Developer. Mem: Kiwanis; C. of C; Red Cross; life mem, Musicians Local 47, AFL. Rel: Congregational. Mailing Add: 106-A S. Los Robles, Pasadena, Calif. 91101. (1967)

LANTING, WILLIAM JOHN R
Speaker, Idaho House of Rep.
b. Twin Falls, Idaho, 3/18/18; s. John Lanting and Grace Visser L; m. 11/20/40 to Marguerite Lillian Caudle; c. James William, Arthur John, Patricia Grace and Robert Joseph. Polit. & Govt. Pos: Trustee, Filer Sch. Dist, Idaho, 52-61; Idaho State Rep, Twin Falls Co, 59-, majority leader, Idaho House of Rep, 63-67, speaker, 67-; mem. exec. bd, West. Conv. of Coun. State Govt, 62-, chmn, Water Probs. Cmt, 64-65 and Human Resources Cmt, 65-, v.pres, 66-68, pres, 68-; mem, Idaho Legis. Coun, 63-, co-chmn, 65-; mem. bd. mgrs, Coun. State Govts, 66-; v.chmn, Nat. Coun. State Govt, 69- Bus. & Prof. Pos: Farmer and stockraiser, 40- Mem: Farm Bur; Grange; Idaho Cattlemen's Asn; past dir, Twin Falls C. of C. Rel: Presbyterian. Legal Res: Hollister, Idaho. Mailing Add: Route 1, Twin Falls, Idaho 83301.

LANTZ, BETTY L. R
d. Peter Lantz and Margaret Smith L. Polit. & Govt. Pos: Admin. asst. to U.S. Rep. Leon H. Gavin, Pa, 43-63 and U.S. Rep. Albert W. Johnson, Pa, 63-67; exec. asst, United Citizens for Nixon-Agnew, 68; asst, 1969 Inaugural Cmt, 68-69. Mem: Capitol Hill Club; Rep. Women of Capitol Hill. Mailing Add: 2400 S. Glebe Rd, Arlington, Va. 22206.

LANTZ, MARIE D
b. Philippi, W.Va; d. Charles Leonard Lantz and Delta Burner L. Educ: Davis & Elkins Col, W.Va. Polit. & Govt. Pos: Admin. asst, U.S. Sen. Jennings Randolph, W.Va, currently. Legal Res: Elkins, W.Va. 26241. Mailing Add: 3900 Tunlaw Rd. N.W. Washington, D.C. 20007.

LaPAN, JAMES EDWARD D
b. Champlain, N.Y, 5/11/24; m. to Edna Petotte; c. four. Educ: Union Col; Wash. and Jefferson Col; Univ. of Nancy, France; Albany Law Sch. Polit. & Govt. Pos: N.Y. State Assemblyman, 64-66; Franklin Co. Bd. of Supvrs, 55-57; Planning Bd, Saranac Lake; Adult Educ. Com, Saranac Lake Cent. Sch. Bus. & Prof. Pos: Lawyer, firm of McCormick and LaPan. Mil. Serv: U.S. Army, Inf, 3 yrs, wounded in Germany. Mem: N.Y. State Bar Asn; past pres, Franklin Co. Bar Asn; v.pres, Dir, Gen. Hosp. of Saranac Lake; Am. Legion Post 447; K. of C. Coun. 599; Elks Lodge 1508; VFW. Mailing Add: 71 Riverside Dr, Saranac Lake, N.Y. 12983. (1967)

LAPAR, WILLIAM EDWARD R
Ind. State Rep.
b. Greenville, Mich, 5/26/20; s. Paul Lapar and Anna Palas L; m. 3/15/47 to Betty L. Chamness; c. Carol Sue and Paula Ann. Educ: Lincoln Chiropractic Col, D.C, 49. Polit. & Govt. Pos: City councilman, Winchester, Ind, 64-68; chmn, Randolph Co. Rep. Party; Ind. State Rep, Wayne and Randolph Co, 69- Bus. & Prof. Pos: Dr. of chiropractic, 49-69. Mil. Serv: Entered as Pvt, Army, 41, released as T/Sgt, 45, after serv. in 477th Engrs, Southwest Pac, 41-45; Presidential Unit Citation; Three Bronze Campaign Stars; Good Conduct Medal. Mem: Ind. State and Mich. State Chiropractic Asns; Nat. Asn. of Legislators; Am. Chiropractic Asn; Am. Legion; Int. Gideons Inc.(past pres, Randolph Co. Chap); Kiwanis Int.(past lt. gov); U.S. Coast Guard Auxiliary. Recipient of Kiwanis New Club Bldg. Award; Ind. Fire Fighters Legis. Award. Rel: Congregational. Legal Res: 611 Lawn St, Winchester, Ind. 47394. Mailing Add: 131 N. Meridian St, Winchester, Ind. 47394.

LAPER, OSCAR A. R
Wis. State Assemblyman
b. Green Lake Co, Wis, 7/13/15; s. Oscar H. Laper and Gertrude Doherty L; m. 5/20/39 to Lois M. Luck; c. Myrna. Educ: Northwest. Col, Watertown, Wis, grad. of commercial dept, 36. Polit. & Govt. Pos: Town treas, Twp. of Excelsior, Wis, 49-51, town chmn, 51-; supvr, Dist. 11, Sauk Co, 51-; v.chmn, Sauk Co. Bd, 64-; Wis. State Assemblyman, Sauk Co, 67- Bus. & Prof. Pos: Dir, Nat. Asn. Soil & Water Conserv. Dist, 56-60, area v.pres, 60-64; treas, Wis. Asn. Soil & Water Conserv. Dist, 58-60, pres, 60-64, secy, 65- Am. Motors Conserv. Award, 62. Rel: Lutheran. Mailing Add: Rock Springs, Wis. 53961.

LAPHAM, HARRY HOUSTON, JR. R
Chmn, Thurston Co. Rep. Cent. Cmt, Wash.
b. Ocala Fla, 1/6/07; s. Harry Houston Lapham and Ethel B. Mark L; m. 12/18/51 to Grace Ellen Read. Educ: Univ. of Fla, 24-28; Alpha Kappa Psi; Scabbard & Blade; Sigma Lambda Tau. Polit. & Govt. Pos: Treas, Thurston Co. Rep. Cent. Cmt, 64-65, chmn, 65-; asst. sgt. at arms, Wash. House Rep, 67-; Del, Rep. Nat. Conv, 68. Mil. Serv: Entered as Pvt, Army, 43, retired as Maj, 63, after serv. in Far East Command, Japan, 47-51, U.S. Commun. Zone, France, 54-57 and 8th Army-U.N.C. Korea, 60-61; Bronze Star; Army Commendation Medal. Mem: Olympia Lions Club (past pres); VFW; Salvation Army Advisory Bd.(past chmn). Thurston Co. Distinguished Serv. Award, 68. Rel: United Church of Christ. Mailing Add: Route 3, Box 525, Olympia, Wash. 98501.

LAPIDES, JULIAN LEE D
Md. State Sen.
b. Baltimore, Md, 9/17/31; s. Solomon M. Lapides and Doris Racusin L; m. 3/15/64 to Linda Zeva Fishman. Educ: Towson State Col, B.S, 54; Univ. Md. Sch. of Law, LL.B, 61; Kappa Delta Pi, pres, Towson Chap, 53-54. Polit. & Govt. Pos: Pres, Mt. Royal Dem. Club; Md. State Del, Second Dist, Baltimore City, 63-67; Md. State Sen, 67-; mem, Legis. Coun. Md, 69- Bus. & Prof. Pos: Teacher sci, High sch, 56-60; attorney-at-law, 60- Mil. Serv: Entered as Pvt, Army, 54, released as E-4 Spec. 3rd, 56, after serv. in 2nd Inf. Bn. Combat Team, Iceland Defense Force, 55-56; Good Conduct Medal. Mem: The Peale Mus; Baltimore Mus. of Art; bd. mem, Baltimore Heritage; bd. mem. and v.pres, Md. Kidney Found; trustee, Md. Environ. Trust; Senate Rep, Md. Arts Coun; Hist. Annapolis; Citizens Adv. Bd, Alcoholism Clinic of Baltimore; founder and chmn, Baltimore Beautification Cmt. Mailing Add: 1528 Bolton St, Baltimore, Md. 21217.

LAPIDUS, I. RICHARD D
b. Brooklyn, N.Y, 4/7/35; s. George Lapidus and May Goldstein L; m. 2/28/59 to Leah Kahan Blumberg; c. Louise Diana and Lenora Michelle. Educ: Univ. Chicago, A.B, 55, B.S, 56, M.S, 57; Columbia Univ, Ph.D, 63. Polit. & Govt. Pos: Chmn, Teaneck Dem. Coun, N.J, 66-67; chmn, Bergen Co. Dem. Coun, 67-68; mem. exec. bd, N.J. Dem. Coun, 67-68; mem. exec. bd, Bergen Co. and N.J. Vol. for McCarthy, 68; del, Dem. Nat. Conv, 68; trustee, Teaneck Polit. Assembly, 68-; chmn, Dem. Coalition of Bergen Co, 69- Bus. & Prof. Pos: Teaching asst, N.Y. Univ, 56, Univ. Chicago, 56-57 and Columbia Univ, 57-59; lectr, City Col. New York, 59-61; research asst, Columbia Univ, 61-63, research assoc, 63; asst. prof, Stevens Inst. Tech, 63-68, assoc. prof, 68- Publ: Approximately 15 articles on physics in prfnl. journals, since 60. Mem: Sigma Xi; Am. Phys. Soc; Ital. Phys. Soc; Am. Asn. Adv. Sci; Am. Asn. Physics Teachers; Am. Asn. Univ. Prof; Fedn. Am. Scientists; Teaneck Fair Housing Cmt.(chmn, 66-67); Teaneck Citizen for Pub. Schs. Ford Found. scholar, 51-55; Univ. Chicago scholar, 55-56; NASA faculty fel, 66; Stevens Inst. Tech. research grants, 65 & 68. Mailing Add: 1273 W. Laurelton Pkwy, Teaneck, N.J. 07666.

LaPLANTE, BRYAN FRANKLIN R
Assoc. Cmnr, Fed. Water Pollution Control Admin, Dept. of Interior
b. Mine LaMotte, Mo, 10/20/15; s. Charles Marion LaPlante and Alma Rickman L; m. 4/26/41 to Helen Friedlinda Sonnleitner. Educ: Jefferson Col, 35-36; Wash. Univ, 34-38; Indust. Lenders Tech. Inst, 40-42. Polit. & Govt. Pos: Dir. security opers, asst. gen. mgr. and legis. liaison, U.S. Atomic Energy Cmn, D.C, 47-58; dep. staff dir, U.S. Senate Rep. Policy Cmt, 61-69; assoc. cmnr, Fed. Water Pollution Control Admin, Dept. of Interior, 69- Bus. & Prof. Pos: Client rep, Joyce & Fisher Assocs, 58-60; dir, Wash, D.C. 46, after serv. as Intel. Officer, Manhattan Eng. Dist, D.C. and N.Y, 44-46; Res. Officer, Mil. Intel, 47-50. Mem: Nat. secy, mem. exec. cmt. and secy. D.C. Chap, Am. Nuclear Soc; Am. Ordnance Asn; Army Navy Country Club; Men of Holy Cross; Army and Navy Town Club; Nat. Defense Post, Am. Legion; John Carroll Soc. Rel: Catholic. Mailing Add: 4601 Orleans Place, Alexandria, Va. 22304.

LaPLANTE, ROLAND HENRY D
N.H. State Rep.
b. Nashua, N.H, 7/27/33; s. Edward P. LaPlante and Juliette Theriault L; m. 1/3/58 to Sally A. Higgins; c. Denise, Ronald, Lawrence and Michele. Educ: Nashua High Sch, N.H; Cambridge Sch, Mass; Gardner State Hosp. Sch. Practical Nursing. Polit. & Govt. Pos: V.chmn, Ward 3 Dem. Orgn, Nashua, N.H; N.H. State Rep, 65-66 and currently. Mil. Serv: Entered as S.R, Navy, 51, released as Hospitalman, 54, after serv. in Korea; UN Serv. Award; Nat. Defense Serv. Ribbon. Mem: Am. Legion; Loyal Club of Nashua; RCIA, AFL-CIO. Rel: Roman Catholic. Mailing Add: 70 Chandler St, Nashua, N.H. 03060. (1967)

LaPLUME, LORETTA GRACIELLA D
State Committeewoman, Vt. Dem. Party
b. Bury, Que, Can, 11/14/20; d. Joseph Louis Cyr and Roseanna Filiau C; m. 5/27/47 to Rosaire Stanislaus LaPlume; c. Gerard, Yvan, Yvette, Rachel, Guy, Cyril and Andre. Educ: Newport High Sch, grad, 40. Polit. & Govt. Pos: Secy, Dem. Town Cmt, Vt, 65; State Committeewoman, Vt. Dem. Party, 67- Rel: Catholic. Mailing Add: Star Route, Westfield, Vt. 05874.

LAPOINTE, AGNES R. R
V.Chmn, R.I. Rep. State Cent. Cmt.
b. Providence, R.I, 10/29/29; d. William Robidoux and Eugenie Dionne R (deceased); m. 3/28/48 to Charles William Lapointe, Jr; c. William Charles, Shirley-Ann and Stephen Michael. Educ: Warwick and Providence Sch. Syst. Polit. & Govt. Pos: Mem, Coventry Town Rep. Cmt, R.I, 61-; mem, Rep. Women's Club Coventry, 61-; mem, Housing Authority, Coventry, 67-; mem. exec. bd, Fedn. Rep. Women, 68; v.chmn, R.I. Rep. State Cent. Cmt, 69- Rel: Catholic. Mailing Add: 26 Grant Dr, Coventry, R.I. 02816.

LAPOINTE, FRANCIS CHARLES D
Mass. State Rep.
b. Chicopee, Mass, 1/13/39; s. Francis Joseph Lapointe and Edna Vandal L; m. 6/6/64 to Adele Evelyn Ruel; c. David Ruel and Audrie Caron. Educ: State Col. Westfield, B.S, 62; State Col. Westfield and Univ. Mass, 62-64, M.Ed, 64; fel, Col. Holy Cross, Univ. Calif, Los Angeles and N.Y. Univ. Polit. & Govt. Pos: Mass. State Rep, Third Hampden Dist, 69- Bus. & Prof. Pos: Instr, Chicopee High Sch, Mass, 62-64, Huntington Sch, San Marino, Calif, 64-65 and Van Sickle Sch, Springfield, Mass, 65-68. Publ: Monthly newspaper column for the Holyoke Daily Transcript, Holyoke, Mass. Mem: AFL-CIO; Am. Fedn. Teachers; Soc. State Legislators; Jaycees; K. of C. Distinguished Serv. Award, U.S. Jaycees, 66. Rel: Catholic. Mailing Add: 49 Prospect St, Chicopee, Mass. 01013.

LaPORTE, ALFRED O. R
Secy, Mich. State Rep. Cent. Cmt.
b. Pinconning, Mich, 9/8 /20; s. Oscar J. LaPorte and Virginia Jasman L; m. 6/23/45 to Geraldyne M. Whyte; c. JoAnn and Daniel. Educ: St. Michael High Sch, Pinconning. Polit. & Govt. Pos: Chmn, Arenac Co. Rep. Party, Mich, 58-66; chmn, Tenth Dist. Rep. Party, 60-65; mem, Mich. Apportionment Cmn, 63; del, Rep. Nat. Conv, 64 & 68; secy, Mich. State Rep. Cent. Cmt, 65-, mem, 66- Bus. & Prof. Pos: Owner, LaPorte Beverage, 46-49; owner, LaPorte Agency, 49- Mil. Serv: Entered as Pvt, Marine Corps, 42, released as Cpl, 45, after serv. in Tank Bn, S.Pac; S.Pac. Campaign Medal and three Battle Stars. Mem: Fund. dir, Arenac Co. Red Cross and co. chmn. for 5 years; Standish Develop. Corp; past membership chmn, dir, v.pres. and pres, Standish C. of C; cmnr. and finance chmn, Standish Girl Scouts; mem. coun, Standish Boy Scouts; organizer and past v.pres, pres. and lt. gov, Standish Kiwanis; organizer, 1st secy, and past pres, Standish Bowling Asn. Rel: Catholic. Mailing Add: 206 N. Court St, Standish, Mich. 48658. (1967)

LAPPIN, WILLIAM J. D
R.I. State Rep.
b. Scotland, 1/24/21; m. to Kathleen. Educ: In Ireland. Polit. & Govt. Pos: Mem, Burrillville Dem. Town Coun, R.I, 60-62; R.I. State Rep, 63- Bus. & Prof. Pos: Salesman. Mil. Serv: Royal Air Force, 4½ years, China, Burma, India. Mailing Add: 21 Mill St, Oakland, R.I. 02858. (1967)

LaRAIA, JOSEPH J. D
b. Quincy, Mass. Educ: Boston Col, B.S; Ford Motor Inst, bus. mgt. cert. Polit. & Govt. Pos: City Coun, 60-65; Young Dems. of Quincy; Chmn, Quincy Develop. Commis, 63-64. Bus. & Prof: Off. Manag, Drake's Bakeries, Div. of Borden Corp. Mem: J. Quincy Adams Club; Amvets; Quincy K. of C. Coun; Quincy Sons of Italy Lodge; Am. Legion; Elks; Jaycees. Mailing Add: 54 Grogan Ave, Quincy, Mass. 02169. (1967)

LAREY, BETHEL BRYAN R
Cmnr. of Revenue, Ark.
b. Texarkana, Ark, 11/15/33; s. Bert Bethel Larey and Mayno Britt L; m. 8/22/54 to Emma Lee Tomlinson 'Lucy'; c. Keith and David. Educ: Henderson State Col, B.S.E, 57; Vanderbilt Univ. Law Sch, LL.B, 59; Delta Theta Phi. Polit. & Govt. Pos: Chmn, Ark. Revenue Bldg. Cmn, 67-; chmn, Ark. Reciprocity Cmn, 67-; secy, Ark. Racing Cmn, 67-; Cmnr, Revenue, Ark, 67- Bus. & Prof. Pos: Secy, Miller Co. Bar, Texarkana, Ark, 63-65; Cmt. of 100, Texarkana C. of C, 66. Mil. Serv: Entered as 1st Lt, Air Force, 60, released as Capt, 63, after serv. in Judge Adv. Gen. Corps, Hq. 3500 Pilot Training Wing, Reese AFB, Tex, 60-63; Maj, Air Force Res; Presidential Unit Citation. Mem: Ark. Bar Asn; Lions; Southwest. Little Jaycees Outstanding Young Man of the Year Award, 68. Rel: Methodist. Legal Res: 2600 Locust, Texarkana, Ark. 75501. Mailing Add: Ark. Revenue Dept, Little Rock, Ark. 72202.

LARGENT, FLOURNOY LEONARD, JR. D
Va. State Del.
b. Cumberland, Md, 12/29/16; s. Flournoy Leonard Largent and Ethyl Riley L; m. 8/24/40 to Anne Russell; c. Anne L.(Mrs. Kennedy) and Gay Durbin. Educ: Lynchburg Col, 33-34; Univ. Va, LL.B, 38. Polit. & Govt. Pos: Spec. agent, Fed. Bur. of Invest, 40-42; munic. judge, Winchester, Va, 42-43, mem, common coun, 52-56, mem, Sch. bd, 56-60; Va. State Del, 68- Bus. & Prof. Pos: Counsel, Winchester-Frederich Indust. Develop. Corp, 56- Mil. Serv: Entered as Ens, Navy, 42, released as Lt, 46, after serv. in Air Combat Intel, Atlantic and Pacific Theatres, 43-46; Unit Citation. Mem: Va. and Am. Bar Asns; Winchester Bar Asn.(pres, 62); Elks; VFW; Moose; Am. Legion; pres, Winchester Jaycees, 48, Winchester Rotary Club, 54 and Shenandoah Apple Blossom Festival, 57-58. Rel: Presbyterian. Legal Res: 630 Tennyson Ave, Winchester, Va. 22601. Mailing Add: P.O. Box 444, Winchester, Va. 22601.

LARK, HENRY W. R
Mem, Pa. Rep. State Exec. Cmt.
b. Shamokin, Pa, 5/16/05; s. H. Wilson Lark and Grace Aucker L; m. 10/2/26 to Isabel Witmer; c. Isabel. Educ: Franklin and Marshall Col, A.B, 26; Phi Kappa Psi. Polit. & Govt. Pos: Chmn, Northumberland Co. Rep. Cmt, 39-; mem, Pa. Rep. State Exec. Cmt, 41-; del, Rep. Nat. Conv, 48, 52, 56 & 64, secy. of del, 56; chmn, Pa. Rep. State Primary Campaign Cmt, 56. Bus. & Prof. Pos: Dir, Ashland Coal and Coke, W.Va. and Ashland Mining Corp; treas, Harmon Mining Corp, Grundy, Va; v.pres, Sovereign Pocahontas Co, Bluefield, W.Va, Filmore Construction Co, Edwardsville, Pa. and Sovereign Coal Corp, Jamboree, Ky; pres, Indust. Coal Sales Co, Tremont, Pa. and Gateway Apt. Assocs, Wilkesbarre; dir, Majestic Collieries Co, Majestic, Ky. Mem: Trustee, Franklin and Marshall Col. and Muncy Valley Hosp; Union League of Phila; Nat. Rep. Club, N.Y; Pottsville Club; Mason (32°); Shrine; Shrine Country Club; Elks; Moose. Rel: United Church of Christ. Legal Res: Apple Hill Farm, Dewart, Pa. 17730. Mailing Add: Sixth & Market St, Sunbury, Pa. 17801.

LARKIN, CHARLES ARTHUR R
S.Dak. State Rep.
b. Grand Forks, N.Dak, 8/21/21; s. Charles A. Larkin and Evalyn Erd L; m. 2/3/43 to Shirley Jeanne Walton; c. Leslie Ann (Mrs. Schranz), Charles A, III and John W. Educ: Univ. N.Dak, B.S, 42; Phi Beta Psi; Sigma Chi. Polit. & Govt. Pos: Mem. sch. bd, Dist. 65, Clark, S.Dak, 10 years and chmn, 2 years; S.Dak. State Rep, 20th Dist, 67- Bus. & Prof. Pos: Dir, Nat. Potato Coun, 15 years; dir. & past pres, S.Dak. Potato Growers Asn. Mil. Serv: Entered as Cpl, Air Force, 43, released as Capt, 46. Mem: Elks; Am. Legion; Izaak Walton League. Rel: Catholic. Mailing Add: 310 S. Commercial, Clark, S.Dak. 57225.

LARKINS, CHARLES HAYMORE, JR. D
N.C. State Sen.
b. Kinston, N.C, 10/3/30; s. Charles H. Larkins and Margaret Hamilton L; m. 5/19/51 to Ann Marie Flowers; c. Charles H, III. Educ: Wake Forest Col, B.B.A, 52; law sch, one-half year; Kappa Alpha. Polit. & Govt. Pos: N.C. State Sen, 68- Bus. & Prof. Pos: Bd. dir, Childrens Home Soc. of N.C, 64-65. Mil. Serv: Entered as CTSN, Navy, 53, released 64, after serv. in Naval Security Sta, Wash, D.C, 53-54. Mem: Bd. dir, N.C. Merchants Asn; Elks; Kinston C. of C.(v.pres, 65-68). Rel: Baptist. Legal Res: 1200 Sweet Briar, Kinston, N.C. 28501. Mailing Add: P.O. Drawer 3029, Kinston, N.C. 28501.

LARKINS, JOHN DAVIS, JR. D
b. Morristown, Tenn, 6/8/09; s. John D. Larkins and Emma Cooper L; m. 3/15/30 to Pauline Murrill; c. Emma Sue (Mrs. D. H. Loftin) and Polly (Mrs. J.H. Bearden). Educ: Wake Forest Col, B.A, 29; Belin Univ, LL.D, 57; Phi

Alpha Delta. Polit. & Govt. Pos: N.C. State Sen, 36-44 & 48-54; del-at-lg, Dem. Nat. Conv, 40, 44, 48, 56 & 60; chmn, Gov. Adv. Budget Cmn, N.C, 51-53; secy, N.C. Dem. Exec. Cmt, 52-54, chmn, 54-59; mem, Dem. Nat. Cmt, 58-60; U.S. Dist. Judge, East. Dist, N.C, currently. Bus. & Prof. Pos: Law practice; secy. Larkins Stores, Inc; dir. Life Ins. Co. of N.C. Mil. Serv: Pvt, Army, 45. Mem: Am. N.C. Bar Asn; N.C. Bar, Inc; dir, nat. bd. dirs. and v.chmn, Am. Cancer Soc; trustee Univ. N.C. Baptist Hosp; Am. Legion; 40 et 8; WOW; Mason; Elk; Moose. Distinguished Serv. Award, Am. Cancer Soc. Rel: Baptist; Deacon. Legal Res: Trenton, N.C. 28585. Mailing Add: c/o Federal Bldg, Trenton, N.C. 28585.

LAROCHE, LEO D
N.H. State Rep.
b. Can, 11/3/99; s. Joseph Laroche and Caroline Tessier L; m. 6/27/27 to Leonille Gobeil; c. Maurice, Roger, Lucille (Mrs. Howard) and Rachel (Mrs. Downe). Educ: Schs. in Can. Polit. & Govt. Pos: N.H. State Rep, currently. Bus. & Prof. Pos: Grocer. Mem: Elks; K. of C.(4°). Rel: Catholic. Mailing Add: 663 Central St, Franklin, N.H. 03235.

LA ROCHE, ULYSSES D
b. W. Warwick, R.I, 7/31/08. Educ: R.I. Sch. of Design. Polit. & Govt. Pos: R.I. State Rep, 47-66. Bus. & Prof. Pos: Sign painter; ice bus. Mil. Serv: Army, 42-45. Mem: Club Frontenac; Am. Legion; Amvets; Phenix Sportsman Club. Mailing Add: 9 Terrence Ct, West Warwick, R.I. 02893. (1967)

LARRIMORE, W. GARRETT D
b. Annapolis, Md, 7/19/22; married. Educ: Univ. of Md, Univ. of Md. Law Sch, LL.B, 49. Polit. & Govt. Pos: Md. State Del, 59-67; Del, Dem. State Conv, 54, 58; 1st Dist. Dem. Club; S. Anne Arundel Co. Dem. Club. Bus. & Prof. Pos: Lawyer. Mil. Serv: Army Air Force, 43-46. Mem: Md. and Anne Arundel Co. Bar Asns; past V.Pres, Md. Jaycees; Annapolis Yacht Club; S. Anne Arundel Lions. Mailing Add: Route 3, Box 290, Edgewater, Md. 21037. (1967)

LARSEN, JOHN H. D
b. Dodgeville, Wis, 1/12/38; s. J. Harlan Larsen and Harriet Loeffler L; single. Educ: Univ. Wis, B.A, 60. Polit. & Govt. Pos: Secy, Green Co. Dem. Party, Wis, 58-59; chmn, Iowa Co. Dem. Party, 65-66; field dir, Dem. Party, Wis, 66-68; home secy, U.S. Sen. William Proxmire, 68- Bus. & Prof. Pos: Teacher, Mineral Point Pub. Schs, 61-63, elem. prin, 63-65, bus. mgr, 65-66. Rel: Unitarian. Mailing Add: 1203F MacArthur Rd, Madison, Wis. 53714.

LARSEN, JOHN J. R
Committeeman, Wash. State Rep. Party
b. Centralia, Wash, 7/20/23; s. John J. Larsen and Elise Nelson L; m. 9/1/51 to Clare C. Moshofsky; c. John J, Jr, Karen Ann, Gregory and Robert. Educ: Univ. Wash, B.S.M.E, 50; Newman Club. Polit. & Govt. Pos: V.chmn, Cowlitz Co. Rep. Party, Wash, 62-64, chmn, 64-66 & 68; committeeman, Wash. State Rep. Party, 67 & 68-; del, Rep. Nat. Conv, 68. Bus. & Prof. Pos: Plant maintenance supt, Reynolds Metals Co, Longview, Wash, 54-56, plant engr, 56- Mil. Serv: Entered as Pvt, Army Air Force, 42, released as Capt, 45, after serv. in 20th Air Force, China-Burma-India and Pac. Theatres, 44-45; Air Medal; Distinguished Flying Cross. Mem: Am. Soc. Mech. Engrs; C. of C; Elks. Rel: Catholic. Mailing Add: 959 21st Ave, Longview, Wash. 98632.

LARSEN, RICHARD F. R
Lt. Gov, N.Dak.
Mailing Add: State Capitol, Bismarck, N.Dak. 58501.

LARSEN, SHARP McCOY D
b. Spring City, Utah, 3/17/02; s. John H. Larsen and Eliza Jane Behunin L; m. 6/2/23 to Clara Rebecca Andersen; c. Ralph S. and Helen (Mrs. Roland Wyatt). Educ: Henagers Sch. of Bus, Salt Lake City, Utah. Polit. & Govt. Pos: Chief acct, Transportation, Union Pac. R.R, 23-38; off. mgr, Salt Lake Co. Hosp, Utah, 40-45; right-of-way engr, Utah State Dept. of Hwy, 46-48; auditor, Salt Lake City Auditor's Off, 49-50; Co. Treas, Salt Lake Co, 51-60; State Treas, Utah, 61-64, State Auditor, 65-69; exec. dir, Utah Liquor Control Cmn, 69- Mem: Elks Lodge 85, Salt Lake City; Sons of Utah Pioneers; Utah State Asn. of Co. Off; Nat. Asn. of State Auditors, Comptrollers & Treas; past pres, Nat. Asn. of Co. Treas. and Finance Off. of the U.S. and Can, 58-59. Rel: Latter-day Saint. Legal Res: 351 Westminster Ave, Salt Lake City, Utah 84115. Mailing Add: 1625 S. Eighth W, Salt Lake City, Utah 84114.

LARSON, A. WILLIAM D
b. Brooklyn, N.Y, 10/18/20; s. Carl Arthur Larson and Florence Williams Larson Grandeman; m. 12/27/41 to Barbara Slawson; c. Brooke (Mrs. Lawrence Shute), David Bradford, Kim and Jodie. Educ: Dartmouth Col, B.A, 41; Syracuse Univ, J.D, 48; Phi Delta Theta; Phi Delta Phi. Polit. & Govt. Pos: Mem, Bd. of Educ, Union Free Sch. Dist. Five, Levittown, N.Y, 50-53; del, Dem. Nat. Conv, 68; mem, Advisory Cmt, N.Y. State Joint Legislative Cmt. on Problems of Pub. Health, Medicare, Medicaid and Compulsory Health and Hosp. Ins, 68- Bus. & Prof. Pos: Counsel, Kemper Ins, N.Y.C, 49-53; v.pres, Martin E. Segal Co, 53-60; pres. and dir, Woodward and Fondiller, Inc, 60-; v.pres. and dir, Stony Brook Foundation, Stony Brook, 68- Mil. Serv: Entered as Pfc, Marine Corps Res, 39, released as Capt, 46, after serv. in 1st Marine Div. and U.S.S. Portland, S. Pac, 42-45; Col. (Ret), Marine Corps Res, 63. Publ: 'The Actuarial Treatment of Corporate Exposures' Am. Management Assoc, 62; 'Can Health Care Costs Be Contained?' Insurance Mag, 63; 'The Government's Role in Insurance Marketing' Best's Insurance News, 67. Mem: N.Y. Bar; Nassau Co, N.Y. State and Am. Bar Asns; Am. Acad. of Polit. and Soc. Sci; Am. Mgt. Asn; Ins. Soc. of N.Y; Marine Corps Res. Officer's Asn; ROA; United Nations Advisory Cmt. of Unitarian-Universalist Asn; Int. Soc. for Rehabilitation of Disabled; Coun. of African-Am. Inst; Freedom House; Am. Civil Liberties Union; Am. for Dem. Action; VFW; 1st Marine Div. Asn; pres, Nassau Co. Asn. for the Help of Retarded Children, 54; mem. and acting chmn, Coun. State Univ. N.Y. at Stonybrook, 58; chmn, Nassau Co. Exec. Cmt. Handicapped, 64. District Five Educ. Asn. and Nassau Co. Asn. for the Help of Retarded Children Awards. Rel: Unitarian-Universalist. Mailing Add: 2526 Harrison Ave, Baldwin, N.Y. 11510.

LARSON, ALMA R
Secy. of State, S.Dak.
b. Vivian, S.Dak, 5/21/32. Educ: Opportunities Inst. of Denver. Polit. & Govt. Pos: Secy. of State, S.Dak, 64- Mem: Am. Legion Auxiliary Bus. & Prfnl. Women's Club; past v.chmn, S.Dak. Young Rep. League; chmn, L.B.H. Asn. Rel: Lutheran. Legal Res: Vivian, S.Dak. 57576. Mailing Add: State Capitol, Pierre, S.Dak. 57501. (1967)

LARSON, CALVIN RUBEN R
Minn. State Rep.
b. Glyndon, Minn, 8/10/30; s. Clarence Alfred Larson and Pearl Krogen L; m. 8/28/55 to Loretta Oline Pederson; c. Laura Ann and Peter Allen. Educ: Concordia Col, Moorhead, Minn, B.A, 52; Alpha Epsilon Sigma; Int. Rels. Club. Polit. & Govt. Pos: Precinct chmn, Ottertail Co. Rep. Party, 62, ward chmn, 63, city chmn, 64; Minn. State Rep, currently. Bus. & Prof. Pos: Field adjuster, Universal C.I.T. Credit Corp, 56, collection mgr, 57, credit mgr, 58, br. mgr, 59; spec. rep, Bus. Men's Assurance Co, 60- Mil. Serv: Entered as A/S, Navy, 52, released as PO 2/C, 56; Korean Serv. Medal; Good Conduct Medal. Mem: Rotary; Am. Legion; Nat. Asn. of Life Underwriter's; C. of C; bd. of dirs, Fergus Falls Jr. Hockey Asn; Concordia Col. C-400 Club Steering Cmt; pres, United Fund Bd, 65 and drive chmn, 64. Received Fergus Falls Jaycee Distinguished Serv. Award, 64. Rel: American Lutheran Church; Chmn. of Church Planning Cmn. Bd. Mailing Add: 322 E. Cherry, Fergus Falls, Minn. 56537. (1967)

LARSON, CLARENCE EDWARD R
Cmnr, Atomic Energy Cmn.
b. Cloquet, Minn, 9/20/09; s. Louis L. Larson and Caroline Ullman L; m. 4/27/57 to Jane R. Warren; c. Robert E, E. Lawrence and Lance S. Educ: Univ. Minn, B.S, 32; Univ. Calif, Berkeley, Ph.D, 37; Phi Lambda Epsilon; Sigma Xi; Tau Beta Pi. Polit. & Govt. Pos: Mem, Gov. Cmt. on Sci. & Tech, Tenn, 68-69; cmnr, Atomic Energy Cmn, 69- Bus. & Prof. Pos: Chmn. chem. dept, Col. of the Pac, 38-42; dir. research & develop, Electromagnetic Plant, Oak Ridge, Tenn, 43-47, supt, 47-49; dir, Oak Ridge Nat. Lab, 50-55; v.pres. research, Union Carbide Corp, N.Y, 56-61, pres. nuclear div, 61-69. Mem: Am. Chem. Soc; Am. Nuclear Soc; Soc. Exp. Biol. & Med; Cosmos Club; Rotary. Distinguished Mgt. Award, Soc. for Adv. of Mgt. Rel: Protestant. Legal Res: 6514 Bradley Ave, Bethesda, Md. 20034. Mailing Add: Atomic Energy Cmn, Washington, D.C. 20545.

LARSON, DOROTHY M. D
Committeewoman, Idaho State Dem. Cent. Cmt.
b. Potlatch, Idaho, 4/5/17; d. Lars Lande and Nickolene Soholt L; m. 9/21/40 to Phillip C. Larson; c. Judy, Dennis and Gary. Educ: Lewiston Normal Sch, Lewiston, Idaho. Polit. & Govt. Pos: V.chmn, Idaho State Dem. Cent. Cmt, 62-64, chmn, 64-66, committeewoman, 66- Rel: Lutheran. Mailing Add: Potlatch, Idaho 83855. (1967)

LARSON, ELDON C. D
V.Chmn, 25th Dist. Dem. Party, N.Dak.
b. Fargo, N.Dak, 8/22/30; s. Clifford Larson and Isabel Tolstad L; m. 11/24/56 to Catherine Crogan; c. Susan, Cheryl, Jean and Janice. Educ: State Sch. of Sci, Wahpeton, N.Dak, 2 years. Polit. & Govt. Pos: Dwight Twp. clerk, N.Dak, 57-69; Dwight church trustee, 58-68; N.Dak. State Rep, 65-67; v.chmn, 25th Dist. Dem. Party, N.Dak, 69- Mem: Mason; Elks; PTA; Brotherhood; Toastmasters. Richland Co. Outstanding Young Farmer, 63. Rel: Lutheran. Mailing Add: Route 1, Wahpeton, N.Dak. 58075.

LARSON, GUY FREDERICK R
N.Dak. State Sen.
b. Bismarck, N.Dak, 1/6/12; s. John L. Larson and Bertha Von Schwartz L; m. 10/31/42 to Margaret Forister; c. Frederick Guy and Lynda Peggy. Educ: Luther Col, 29-32; Concordia Col, Moorhead, Minn, B.A, 33; Grad. Study, Northwest. Univ, summers 38 & 39, Univ. Idaho, summers 41 & 42. Polit. & Govt. Pos: Mem, Bismarck Bd. of Educ, N.Dak, 48-57; mem. bd, Bismarck Jr. Col, 48-; N.Dak. State Rep, 53-57; N.Dak. State Sen, 32nd Legis. Dist, 57-, mem, Legis. Research Coun, 67-69. Bus. & Prof. Pos: Teacher, Concordia Col, Moorhead, Minn, 33-34, Bismarck Sch. Syst, 34-45; owner, Guy Larson Music Co, 45-, Electronic Center, 53-56 and Hardware Co, 56-66. Mem: Honorary life membership, Elks; Mason; Scottish Rite; Shrine; Rotary (past pres); Dakota Zoological Soc; secy, Mo. Slope Irrigation Asn; dir, N.Dak. Water Users Asn; mem. bd, St. Vincents Home; United Commercial Travelers. N.Dak. Educator of the Year, 58; Nation Award of Merit, Brand Names Found, 60; Rural Leadership Award, 67. Rel: Presbyterian. Legal Res: 2205 Ave. F East, Bismarck, N.Dak. 58501. Mailing Add: 307 E. Main, Bismarck, N.Dak. 58501.

LARSON, HARVEY CASPER R
Chmn, 32nd Dist. Rep. Party, N.Dak.
b. Bismarck, N.Dak, 5/26/22; s. Andrew Nels Larson and Helen Satter L; m. 7/23/43 to Roberta Jean Burman; c. Bonnie Rae (Mrs. John Warren Lee). Polit. & Govt. Pos: Precinct committeeman, Burleigh Co. Rep. Party, N.Dak, 61-, treas, 62-63, chmn, 63-; chmn, 32nd Dist. Rep. Party, 63-; state campaign chmn, N.Dak. Rep. Party, 66-67, treas, 66-68, mem. state exec. cmt, 67-68, mem. state cmt, 67-; del, Rep. Nat. Conv, 68. Bus. & Prof. Pos: Pressman, Commercial Printing Co, 46-55, mgr, 55-68, owner-mgr, 68- Mil. Serv: Entered as Pvt, Army, 42, released as Cpl, 46, after serv. in Med. Corps, S.Pac. Theater, 44-46. Mem: Am. Legion (Past Comdr, Bismarck Post); Mason (Past Master, Bismarck Lodge); Rotary. Rel: Protestant. Mailing Add: 2217 Ave. E East, Bismarck, N.Dak. 58501.

LARSON, LEONARD ROBERT R
Chmn, Banner Co. Rep. Cent. Cmt, Nebr.
b. Kimball, Nebr, 11/4/29; both parents deceased; m. 6/21/53 to Agnes Marie Grissinger; c. Susan Ann and Eric Robert. Educ: Univ. Nebr, Lincoln, 49; Univ. Denver, 50-52. Polit. & Govt. Pos: Chmn, Banner Co. Rep. Cent. Cmt, Nebr, 66-; secy-treas, Banner Co. Rural Fire Dist. Bd. Dir, 69. Mil. Serv: Entered as E-1, Army, 52, released as Cpl, 54, after serv. in 226 OBD, Korea, 54; Nat. Defense Serv, Korean Serv, UN Serv. and Good Conduct Medals. Mem: K. of P; Am. Legion; Am. Farm Bur. Fedn; Alliance, Nebr. Consistory. Rel: Methodist. Mailing Add: Route 1, Box 11, Harrisburg, Nebr. 69345.

LARSON, LeROY MELVIN R
N.Dak. State Rep.
b. Grand Forks, N.Dak, 3/16/21; s. Adolph Larson and Edith Steele L; m.

6/15/47 to Donna D. Olson; c. Gary, Janine, Rodney, Roger and Pamela. Educ: Northwest Sch. Agr, 3 years. Polit. & Govt. Pos: N.Dak. State Rep, 21st Dist, 68- Mil. Serv: Entered as Pvt, Marines, 42, released as Cpl, 45, after serv. in Third Marines, Ninth Regt, S.Pac, 43-45; Purple Heart. Mem: Am. Legion; VFW; DAV; Lions; Elks; West Fargo C. of C.(pres, 67); pres, Commercial Club, Condo, 55. Rel: Lutheran. Mailing Add: 519 Fourth Ave, W, West Fargo, N.Dak. 58078.

LARSON, LESTER GEORGE D
N.Dak. State Sen.
b. Nelson Co, N.Dak, 12/26/14; s. Ole B. Larson and Gunhild Shjervem L; m. 11/17/34 to Clara Knutson; c. Janet Yvonne. Polit. & Govt. Pos: Former mem. bd, Brocket Twp, N.Dak; N.Dak. State Rep, 56-63; N.Dak. State Sen, 65- Bus. & Prof. Pos: Former sch. dir; mem, Farmers Union Oil Co; pres, Equity Elevator and Trading Co. Mem: Crop Improv. Asn. Rel: Lutheran; Clerk and Treas. Mailing Add: Brocket, N.Dak. 58321.

LARSON, LEVERN ORVILLE DFL
b. Kasson, Minn, 1/8/19; s. Edward Alexander Larson and Caroline Severson L; m. 6/21/41 to Wava Jean Francis; c. Clinton, Lorraine (Mrs. Roger Merideth) and Karen (Mrs. Lewis). Educ: Kasson High Sch, Minn, 2 years. Polit. & Govt. Pos: Treas, Dodge Co. Dem-Farmer-Labor Party, Minn, 60-66, Kasson Village Precinct chmn, 64-, co. chmn, 66-68; alderman, Kasson Village Coun, 65- Mem: Eagles; Minn. and Dodge Co. Farmers Union; dir, Dodge Co. Fair Bd, 61- Perfect Attendance Action Officer Award for Ten Consecutive Years, Kasson Local, Dodge Co. Farmers Union. Rel: Lutheran. Mailing Add: 107 Fourth Ave. N.W, Kasson, Minn. 55944.

LARSON, LEW W. Conservative
Minn. State Sen.
b. Preble Twp, Minn, 1911; married; c. Two sons and one daughter. Educ: Univ. Minn. Polit. & Govt. Pos: Cmnr, Fillmore Co, Minn, 53-59; Minn. State Sen, 58- Bus. & Prof. Pos: Breeder registered livestock; farmer. Mem: Mason; pres, State Asn. Co. Cmnr, 57. Mailing Add: Mabel, Minn. 55954.

LARSON, MARGARET ANN R
Rep. Nat. Committeewoman, Guam
b. Omaha, Nebr, 3/15/28; d. Micheal Calnicean and Matilda Johnson C; div. Educ: Omaha N. High, grad, 45; Univ. Omaha, 1 year; Nat. Honor Soc. Polit. & Govt. Pos: Exec. secy, Rep. Party, Guam, 67; Rep. Nat. Committeewoman, Guam, 68-; exec. asst. to Gov, 69- Bus. & Prof. Pos: Mem, Credit dept, Standard Oil Co, Omaha, 46-54; exec. secy, G.W. Martin Co, Grand Island Nebr, 57-60; off. mgr, secy-treas, Bob Souders Pontiac, Sioux City, Iowa, 61-65; office mgr, Maro Watch Co, Agana, Guam, 66-67, secy-treas. and gen. mgr, 67- Mem: Pres, Guam Bus. & Prfnl. Women's Club; secy, Guam Women's Club; dir, Guam Press Asn; dir, Guam Tuberc. Asn; Red Cross Bd; Guam Mem. Hosp. Vol. Asn. Rel: Lutheran. Legal Res: 13 Casa de Flores, Agana, Guam 96910. Mailing Add: P.O. Box CV, Agana, Guam 96910.

LARSON, MARGARET BRUNSDALE R
Chmn, 20th Legis. Dist. Rep. Party, N.Dak.
b. Minneapolis, Minn, 8/27/25; d. Norman Brunsdale and Carrie Lajord B; m. 10/8/55 to Edson Germain Larson. Educ: Wellesley Col, B.A, 47. Polit. & Govt. Pos: Secy. to chmn, Rep. Nat. Finance Cmt, 53-55; chmn, Traill Co. Rep. Party, N.Dak, 62-66; del. and mem, rules cmt, Rep. Nat. Conv, 64; chmn, 20th Legis. Dist. Rep. Party, N.Dak, 66- Mem: Farm Bur. Rel: Lutheran. Mailing Add: Mayville, N.Dak. 58257.

LARSON, MILDRED D
Dem. Nat. Committeewoman, Ariz.
m. to Henry R. Larson. Educ: Lasalle Exten. Univ. Polit. & Govt. Pos: Superior Court reporter; asst. supt. of schs; secy. to mgr. of Navy Yard, Pearl Harbor; secy. to U.S. Sen. and majority leader Ernest W. McFarland; former secy, West. States Dem. Conf. and chmn, 67-69; mem, Defense Adv. Cmt. on Women in Mil. Serv; del. and mem. platform cmt, Dem. Nat. Conv, 64 & 68, co-chmn. rules cmt, 64; Dem. Nat. Committeewoman, Ariz, 65- Bus. & Prof. Pos: Law librn; spec. serv, KTVK-TV, Channel 3 presently. Mem: State regent, DAR; Phoenix Musical Theatre Guild; Phoenix Symphony Guild; Daughters of the Nile; Phoenix PTA; bd. dirs, Ariz. Mus; Jr. Womans Club. Mailing Add: 4701 N. 24th St, Phoenix, Ariz. 85016.

LARSON, NORMAN J.
b. Borup, Minn, 12/26/02; married; c. One son. Educ: St. Olaf Col; Univ. Mich. Polit. & Govt. Pos: Minn. State Sen, 39-69, pres. pro tempore, Minn. State Senate, 61. Bus. & Prof. Pos: Sch. teacher. Mil. Serv: World War II. Mailing Add: Box 186, Ada, Minn. 56510.

LARSON, RICHARD ROSEN R
Ill. State Sen.
b. Galesburg, Ill, 10/11/07; s. G.V. Larson and Emma Rosen L; m. 8/8/42 to Lucy Davis; c. Sarah A. and Samuel F. Educ: Lombard Col, B.A, 29; Knox Col, B.A, 33; Pi Kappa Delta; Pi Gamma Mu; Phi Delta Theta. Polit. & Govt. Pos: Ill. State Rep, 43rd Dist, 53-57; Ill. State Sen, 57th Dist, 57-67 and 42nd Dist, 67- Mil. Serv: Entered as Pvt, Air Force, 42, released as T/Sgt, 45, after serv. in 309th Bomb Group, Am. Theater. Mem: Elks; Am. Legion; 40 et 8; Odd Fellows; Rebekah; John Ericsson League of Ill; Rep. Vet. League. Rel: Methodist. Mailing Add: 694 Bateman St, Galesburg,

LaRUE, FRED R
b. Athens, Tex, 10/11/28; m. 9/12/53 to Joyce; c. Grace, Ike, Fred, Jr, Patricia, Leslie and Stephen. Educ: Univ. Okla, B.S. in geol, 51. Polit. & Govt. Pos: Former Rep. Nat. Committeeman, Miss; former mem, exec. cmt, Rep. Nat. Cmt; former exec. committeeman, Rep. Nat. Finance Cmt; alternate del, Rep. Nat. Conv, 68. Bus. & Prof. Pos: Pres, Larco Drilling Corp. Rel: Methodist. Mailing Add: P.O. Box 2599, Jackson, Miss. 39207. (1967)

LASER, WILLIAM CHARLES D
b. Mansfield, Ohio, 11/7/19; s. Clifton Charles Laser and Margaret Flaharty L; m. 7/12/41 to Eleanor Ruth Boock; c. Douglas William. Educ: Lewis Motel Training Sch, grad, 65. Polit. & Govt. Pos: V.pres, Richland Co. Young Dem, Ohio, 46-48; v.chmn, Richland Co. Dem. Exec. Cmt, 55-58; v.chmn, Richland Co. Dem. Cent. Cmt, 58-62, chmn, 62-66; serv. safety dir, City Admin, Mansfield, 62. Bus. & Prof. Pos: V.pres, Ohio Asn. Real Estate Bd, 52-53; pres, Mansfield Bd. Realtors, 55-56. Mil. Serv: Entered as Pvt, Army, 42, released as Sgt, 46. Mem: Nat. Inst. Real Estate Brokers; Nat. Asn. Real Estate Bd; pres, Past Presidents Club, 63-64; Lewis Hotel Training Sch. Alumni Asn; Am. Legion; Mason; Alladin Shrine Temple; Kiwanis; YMCA. Rel: Lutheran. Legal Res: 632 Courtright Blvd, Mansfield, Ohio 44907. Mailing Add: 901 S. Main St, Mansfield, Ohio 44907.

LASH, CARL D. R
Educ: Otterbein Col; Zeta Phi. Polit. & Govt. Pos: Ind. State Rep, 66. Bus. & Prof. Pos: Exec. dir, Wernle Childs' Home. Mil. Serv: Naval Air Corps. Mem: Past pres, Ind. Asn. Child Care Asns; Wayne Coun, Retarded Children; Optimist Club; Elks; Richmond Comm. of 100; Ind. Conf. Soc. Workers. Rel: Lutheran. 1967 Legal Res: Richmond, Ind. No mailing address available. (1967)

LASHER, MICHAEL ALBERT, JR. 'MIKE' R
b. Louisville, Ky, 8/17/32; s. Michael A. Lasher and Esther Speckner L; single. Educ: Univ. of Louisville, B.A, 53, LL.B, 55; Phi Alph Delta. Polit. & Govt. Pos: Attorney, Nat. Labor Rels. Bd, 59-63; U.S. Cmnr, U.S.Dist. Court for Dist. of Ariz, 64-65; precinct committeeman, Rep. Party, Globe, 64-; chmn, Gila Co. Rep. Party, 65-67. Bus. & Prof. Pos: Assoc, Morris & Malott, 63- Mil. Serv: Entered as 2nd Lt, Judge Adv, Air Force, 55, released as 1st Lt, 57, after serv. in Strategic Air Command, Malmstrom Air Force Base, Mont. Mem: Am, Ky. and Gila Co. Bar Asns; State Bar of Ariz; v.pres, Rotary Club, Globe; mem, bd. of dirs, Globe C. of C. Rel: Catholic. Legal Res: 10 Wesson Rd, Globe, Ariz. 85501. Mailing Add: P.O. Box 351, Globe, Ariz. 85501. (1967)

LASHLEY, F. J, JR. R
Chmn, Cottom Co. Rep. Party, Okla.
b. Tulsa, Okla, 6/9/33; s. Floyd Johnson Lashley and Hattie Lu Trammell L; m. 12/2/61 to Barbara Ann MacDonald; c. Douglas Trammell. Educ: Okla. State Univ, 2 years; Tulsa Univ, B.S, 56; Univ. Okla. Sch. Med, M.D, 60; Sigma Chi. Polit. & Govt. Pos: Chmn, Cotton Co. Rep. Party, Okla, 67- Mem: Am. Med. Asn; Okla. State Med. Soc; Rotary; C. of C. Rel: Methodist. Legal Res: 112 W. Wash, Walters, Okla. 73572. Mailing Add: 223 S. Broadway, Walters, Okla. 73572.

LASKEY, NORMA JEAN R
Exec. V.Chmn, Wayne Co. Rep. Cmt, Mich.
b. Ludington, Mich, 9/15/30; d. Walter Hutchison and Ida E. Knaebe H; m. 10/15/52 to Stephen M. Laskey. Educ: Wayne Univ, 49-50; Nat. Young Rep. Leadership Sch, Wash, D.C, grad, 63. Polit. & Govt. Pos: Chmn, Wayne Co. Young Rep. Cmt, Mich, 62-64; mem, Olympic Exec. Cmt, 63; committeewoman from Mich, Nat. Young Rep, 63-65, mem, exec. bd, 65; mem, Orgn. of Young Am. for North-Atlantic Treaty, 66; co-ordinator, Griffin for U.S. Sen, 66; v.chmn, Wayne Co. Rep. Cmt, 66-68, exec. v.chmn, 68-; Rep. nominee, Wayne Co. Charter Cmn, 68; del, Seven Mich. Rep. Conv. Bus. & Prof. Pos: Mem, speakers bur, Repub. Steel Corp, 69. Publ: 'Mandatory Jail Sentences for Serious Crime Offenders,' 11/68, 'Inauguration of President Nixon,' 1/69 and 'The Argument for A.B.M,' 5/69, East-Side Newspapers. Mem: Pub. conduct cmt, Mich. C. of C; area co-ordinator, Muscular Dystrophy. Miss Young Rep. of Mich, 62; Outstanding Young Rep. Woman in the U.S, 63. Rel: Lutheran. Mailing Add: 6164 Guilford Ave, Detroit, Mich. 48224.

LASKIN, LEE B. R
N.J. State Assemblyman
b. Atlantic City, N.J, 6/30/36; s. Howard M. Laskin (deceased) and Ruth Braer L; m. 1/31/60 to Andrea Solomon; c. Shari Lynn and Howard (deceased). Educ: American Univ, $1\frac{1}{2}$ years; Temple Univ, 1 year; Rutgers Col. of Law, LL.B, 61; J.D, 69. Polit. & Govt. Pos: Asst. city solicitor, Camden, N.J, 62-63; asst. U.S. Attorney, N.J, 64-66; N.J. Assemblyman, 67-; zoning bd. solicitor, Berlin, 68 and munic. attorney, 69; sch. bd. mem, Kellman Acad, Cherry Hill, 68- Bus. & Prof. Pos: Attorney-at-law, 62-66; partner, Rudd, Laskin & Madden, 66- Mil. Serv: Entered as Pvt, Marine Corps Res, 57, released as Cpl, after serv. in 68th Spec. Inf; Fourth Dist. Marine Res. Winner of Technique of Mil. Instr; Third Place Winner, U.S. Competition; Outstanding Recruit at Parris Island. Mem: Am, N.J. and Camden Co. Bar Asns; Lions; South Camden YMCA (bd. mgt); Jewish Family Serv. Bd; Camden City Lodge, Brith Sholom. Rel: Jewish. Mailing Add: 3010 Clinton St, Camden, N.J. 08105.

LASSITER, CHARLIE D
Ky. State Rep.
b. 1920. Educ: Murray State Col. Polit. & Govt. Pos: Ky. State Rep, 62- Bus. & Prof. Pos: Sch. prin. Mil. Serv: Air Force. Mem: Mason; Eastern Star; Am. Legion; WOW. Rel: Methodist. Mailing Add: 507 Chestnut St, Murray, Ky. 42071. (1967)

LASSITER, ROBERT L. D
b. Jackson, N.C, 10/19/20; married. Polit. & Govt. Pos: Former Miss. State Rep. Bus. & Prof. Pos: Farmer; carpenter. Rel: Baptist; Deacon. Mailing Add: Route 2, Richton, Miss. 39476. (1967)

LASTRA-GONZALEZ, CARLOS JUAN
b. Ponce, P.R, 8/4/19; s. Francisco Lastra Carrasquillo and Margarita Gonzalez L; m. to Idalla de Leon; c. Amir, Sarai, Juan C, Daniel and David. Educ: Univ. P.R, B.A. magna cum laude, 54; Harvard Univ, M.A, 56 and Ph.D, 61. Polit. & Govt. Pos: Secy. of Commerce, P.R, 61-64 and Secy. of State, 64-68. Bus. & Prof. Pos: Off. mgr, Hosp. Supply Co, San Juan, P.R, 38-43; acct. with Julio Rodriguez, 47-48; head acct, Procter and Gamble, 48-49; instr, Univ. P.R, 56-57; chancellor, Inter-Am. Univ. of P.R. Mem: Am. Statist. Asn; Am. Econ. Asn; P.R. Econ. and Statist. Asn; Nat. Asn. Accts. Recipient, Gold Medal Econ, Univ. P.R, 54. Legal Res: Urb. Riverside, San Germán, P.R. 00753. Mailing Add: Inter-American University, San Germán, P.R. 00753. (1967)

LATER, CHESTER J. R
b. Hartford, Conn, 8/5/25; s. Charles William Later and Anne Levin L; m. 8/18/63 to Leah Wolpin; c. Stephen F. and David A. Educ: Trinity Col, B.A, 49; Harvard Law Sch, LL.B, 52; Bacon Law Club; Chancery Club. Polit. & Govt.

Pos: Mem, Wethersfield Rep. Party, Conn, 58-, publicity chmn, 64-68; Conn. State Rep, Wethersfield, 61-67, chmn, Liquor Control Cmt, 62-67; town attorney, Wethersfield, 64-66; chmn, Wethersfield Charter Rev. Cmn, 69. Mil. Serv: Entered as Pvt, Army, 43, released as Pfc, 46, after serv. in 1st Inf. Div, ETO, 44; Purple Heart; Good Conduct Medal; ETO and Am. Theater Ribbons. Mem: Am, Conn. and Inter-Am. Bar Asns; Nat. Soc. of State Legislators; Am. Trial Lawyers Asn; Mason; Elks; Civitan Club; Wethersfield Businessmen's & Civic Asn; Harvard Club of North. Conn; C. of C. Rel: Judaism. Mailing Add: 484 Coppermill Rd, Wethersfield, Conn. 06109.

LATHAM, JAMES C. D
b. Baltimore, Md, 5/19/18; married. Educ: Johns Hopkins Univ. Polit. & Govt. Pos: Md. State Del, 55-67; Chmn, East. Shore Del, 59-61 sessions; Easton City Coun, 50-54; Easton Planning and Zoning Cmt, 50-54; Chief of Opers, Talbot Co. Civil Defense; past Pres, Talbot Co. Real Estate Bd. Bus. & Prof. Pos: Real estate broker. Mil. Serv: Marines, 34-38. Mem: C. of C; past dist. dep, Elks; K. of C; past pres, Easton Lions; Talbot Co. Country Club; Isaak Walton League. Mailing Add: Box 53, RFD 4, Easton, Md. 21601. (1967)

LATHEN, BERNICE A. D
Mem, Calif. Dem. State Cent. Cmt.
b. Kansas City, Mo, 8/23/18; d. Edmond E. Anderson and Alice Moore A; m. 8/18/57 to Stanley Lathen, Sr; c. Joann (Mrs. Ron G. Messer) and Christina O'Dell; stepchildren: Stanley, Jr, Donald and Robert Lathen. Educ: East High Sch, Kansas City, Mo, dipl, 35. Polit. & Govt. Pos: V.pres, Solano Co. Dem. Club, Calif, 57 and secy, 58 & 59; v.pres. and charter mem, Vallejo Dem. Club, Calif, 61 & 62 and pres, 63 & 64; Vallejo Women Chmn. to elect Lt. Gov. Glenn M. Anderson, 62 and re-elect Rep. Robert L. Leggett, 64; v.pres, Fedn. of Solano Co. Dem, 63-64 and pres, 65-66; secy-treas, Fourth Cong. Dist. Dem. Coun, 63 & 64 & 66-69; Solano Co. Women Chmn, Alan Cranston for Senate Campaign, 64 and re-elect Lt. Gov. Glenn M. Anderson, 66; mem, Calif. Dem. State Cent. Cmt, 64-; chmn, Solano Co. Women's Asn. of North. Calif, 65; Vallejo Women Chmn, Pearce Young for State Senate Campaign, 66; Solano Co. Women Chmn, Alan Cranstan for U.S. Sen. Campaign, 68. Bus. & Prof. Pos: Off. mgr, Plumbers-Steamfitters Local 343, 15 years. Publ: Columnist, Solano-Napa Labor J, 3 years. Mem: Eastern Star; Daughters of the Nile; Shrine; N.Bay Bus. and Prfnl. Women; Office Workers Local 86 (past pres); Women of Moose. Rel: Presbyterian. Mailing Add: 1327 Louisiana St, Vallejo, Calif. 94590.

LATHEROW, CLIFFORD BRANDON R
Ill. State Sen.
b. La Harpe, Ill, 12/4/15; s. George Alexander Latherow and Gail Miller L; m. 6/26/40 to Betty Jane Hungate; c. Linda Lou, Donald Brice and Jerry Allen. Educ: West. Ill. Univ, B.Ed, 37. Polit. & Govt. Pos: Supvr, Twp, Ill, 51-65; Ill. State Sen, 58th Dist, 65- Bus. & Prof. Pos: Coach and teacher, High Sch, 37-43. Mil. Serv: Entered as Ens, Navy, 43, released as Lt, 46, after serv. in Am, Atlantic, Pac. and Asiatic Theaters. Mem: Ill. Police Asn; Mason (32°); Shrine; Farm Bur; Am. Legion; VFW. Rel: Presbyterian. Mailing Add: Route 3, Carthage, Ill. 62321.

LATHROP, CLARENCE GEORGE R
b. Bristol, Vt, 8/28/99; s. William Noah Lathrop and Louina Cora Hall L; m. 9/20/21 to Eleizabeth May Doner; c. Claire Clarence and Noah William. Polit. & Govt. Pos: Selectman, Vt, 38-41; Justice of the Peace; Vt. State Rep, 59-66, mem. cmts, Hwy. and Bridges, Gen. Cmt, and Conservation and Develop. Cmt. and worked for approval to connect McClough Turnpike to State Route 116, Vt. State House of Rep; Vt. State Sen, 67-68, clerk, State and Court Expenses Cmt. and Fish and Game Cmt. and mem. Hwy. and Bridges Cmt. and worked for policy approval for future construction of access hwys. for bus, schs, hosp. and recreation areas, Vt. State Senate. Bus. & Prof. Pos: Owner and mgr. dairy farm, 29-39 and lumber bus, 31-44; census reporter, Agr. Dept, Boston, 29-40; overseer forestry, Addison Co, LaSalle Col, 31-34. Mem: Past pres, PTA; Int. Platform Asn; C. of C; Farm Bur; Grange; Recreation Club. Legal Res: 19 Maple St, Bristol, Vt. 05443. Mailing Add: P.O. Box 533, Bristol, Vt. 05443.

LATOUR, JOHN H. D
N.H. State Rep.
b. Nashua, N.H, 5/14/10; married; c. Two. Educ: Nashua Schs. Polit. & Govt. Pos: N.H. State Rep, 57- Bus. & Prof. Pos: Agent and owner, Ins. Agency. Mem: K. of C.(4°); Elks; Holy Name Soc; N.H. Asn. Ins. Agts; Nashua Fire & Casualty Underwriters. Rel: Catholic. Mailing Add: 40 Dexter St, Nashua, N.H. 03060. (1967)

LATSON, WILLIAM ROY R
b. Cleveland, Ohio, 2/5/22; s. William Latson and Lucette Linget L; m. 7/1/44 to Marjorie V; c. Ann (Mrs. Frost) and William R. Leslie. Educ: Ohio State Univ. Polit. & Govt. Pos: Former chmn, Exec. Cmt, Rep. Orgn, Fla. Bus. & Prof. Pos: Paint sales rep. Mil. Serv: Pvt, Air Force, 42-45, serv. in 100th Bomb Group, Eng; Purple Heart. Mem: K. of C. Rel: Catholic. Mailing Add: 2121 Carmen Ave, Dade City, Fla. 33525. (1967)

LATTA, CLIFFORD B. D
Ky. State Sen.
b. Prestonsburg, Ky, 12/8/28; s. Clifford B. Latta and Olga H. May L; m. 5/19/69 to Ann Roberts; c. Robert A, Clifford B, III and James P. and Audrey Kay (Mrs. Hudson). Educ: Wash. and Lee Univ, B.A, 50; Univ. Ky. Law Sch, LL.B, 54; Sigma Nu; Phi Delta Phi. Polit. & Govt. Pos: City Attorney, Prestonsburg, Ky, 64-68; Ky. State Sen, 29th Dist, 68- Mem: Jaycees, Kiwanis; C. of C. Rel: Baptist. Legal Res: 33 N. Arnold Ave, Prestonsburg, Ky. 41653. Mailing Add: Box 550, Court St, Prestonsburg, Ky. 41653.

LATTA, DELBERT L. R
U.S. Rep, Ohio
b. Weston, Ohio, 3/5/20; m. to Rose Mary Kiene; c. Rose Ellen and Robert Edward. Educ: Ohio North. Univ, A.B. and LL.B. Polit. & Govt. Pos: Ohio State Sen, 3 terms; U.S. Rep, Ohio, 59-; del, Rep. Nat. Conv, 68. Rel: Church of Christ. Legal Res: Bowling Green, Ohio 43402. Mailing Add: Room 2423 House Office Bldg, Washington, D.C. 20515.

LATZ, ROBERT DFL
b. Minneapolis, Minn, 7/15/30; s. Rubin Latz and Rose Arnove L; m. 8/6/61 to Carolyn Spater; c. Ronald Steven, Martin Edward and Michael David. Educ: Univ. Minn, B.S.L, 52; Univ. Minn. Law Sch, LL.B, 54; Delta Sigma Rho; Sigma Alpha Mu. Polit. & Govt. Pos: Mem, Minn. Dem-Farmer-Labor State Cent. Cmt, 52; asst. attorney gen, Minn, 55-58; Minn. State Rep, 39th Dist, 58-66; del, Dem. Nat. Conv, 60 & 64; chmn, Dem-Farmer-Labor State Conv, 63 & 64; cand, Attorney Gen, Minn, 66. Bus. & Prof. Pos: Partner, Sachs, Latz & Kirshbaum, 60-; mem, Nat. Panel of Arbitrators, Am. Arbit. Asn, 67- Mil. Serv: Entered as Seaman Recruit, Naval Air Res, 48, released as S/A, 52. Publ: Co-author, 'The Minnesota and National Relations Act-A Substantive and Procedural Comparison,' Univ. Minn. Law Rev, 54. Mem: Minn. and Hennepin Co. Bar Asns; bd, Minneapolis Urban Coalition; B'nai B'rith and other civic and human rels. orgns. Rel: Jewish. Legal Res: 6850 Harold Ave, Minneapolis, Minn. 55427. Mailing Add: 848 Roanoke Bldg, Minneapolis, Minn. 55402.

LATZ, WILLIAM S. R
Ind. State Rep.
b. 1922. Educ: Wash. and Lee Univ. Polit. & Govt. Pos: Mem, Bd. of Zoning Appeals and Tax Adjust. Bd, Ind; pres, Co. Coun; Ind. State Rep, 67- Bus. & Prof. Pos: Consultant. Mailing Add: 614 Ft. Wayne Bank Bldg, Ft. Wayne, Ind. 46802.

LAUB, WILLIAM MURRAY R
Rep. Nat. Committeeman, Nev.
b. Corregidor, Philippines, 7/20/24; both parents deceased; m. 7/26/47 to Mary McDonald; c. William, Jr, Andrew, Mary, John and David. Educ: Univ. Calif, Los Angeles; Univ. Calif, Berkeley, B.S, 47. Polit. & Govt. Pos: Chmn, Clark Co. Rep. Cent. Cmt, Nev, 64-; Rep. Nat. Committeeman, Nev, currently; del, Rep. Nat. Conv, 68. Bus. & Prof. Pos: Exec. v.pres. and various capacities, Southwest Gas Corp, 48-64, pres, 64-; law practice, Los Angeles, 51-55. Mil. Serv: Lt.(jg), Navy, 42-46, serv. in Pac. Rel: Methodist. Mailing Add: 1000 Rancho Circle, Las Vegas, Nev. 89107.

LAUCK, MARIE THERESA D
b. Indianapolis, Ind; d. Anthony P. Lauck and Marie E. Habig L; single. Educ: St. Mary-of-the-Woods Col, B.A, 34; Butler Univ, M.A, 47; Ind. Univ. Sch. of Law, J.D, 55; Sigma Tau Delta; Kappa Gamma Pi. Polit. & Govt. Pos: Probation officer, Marion Co. Munic. Court, Ind, 35-48; civilian instr, Adj. Gen. Sch, U.S. Army, 51-55; secy. to House Attorneys and legislators, 51-59; cand. for Ind. State Rep, 56 & 62; Ind. State Rep, 59-60; Ind. State Sen, 64-69, mem, Ind. Legis. Adv. Coun, 67-68. Bus. & Prof. Pos: Attorney-at-Law, Indianapolis, Ind. Publ: Free Lance articles in such magazines as Catholic Digest, School Journals and Extension Mag. Mem: Del. from Ind, Nat. Asn. of Women Lawyers, 65-; pres, Ind. Asn. of Women Lawyers, currently, secy, 63-64; St. Thomas More Soc. of Lawyers, secy, 63-64; gov. Ind. Chap, Int. Fedn. of Cath. Alumnae, 38-40; chmn. Ind. Chap, Legion of Decency, 34-; Hospitality Cmt, Indianapolis Bar Asn, 64; Ind. Bar Asn; Ind. and Indianapolis Women Lawyers Asns. Admitted to practice law before U.S. Supreme Court and U.S. Dist. Court, Ind. Rel: Catholic. Mailing Add: 323 Peoples Bank Bldg, Indianapolis, Ind. 46204.

LAUDADIO, JOHN F. D
Pa. State Rep.
b. Penn, Pa, 12/26/16; s. Frank Laudadio and Marie Dreistadt L; m. 6/8/40 to Pearl E. Ferrara; c. John F, Jr. Educ: Carnegie Inst. Tech, cert, 44. Polit. & Govt. Pos: Former mem, Westmoreland Co. Recreation and Park Cmn, former chmn, Park Develop; Pa. State Rep, 63-, v.chmn, House Fisheries Cmt, Pa. House of Rep. Mem: Pres, Pa. Fedn. Sportsmen's Clubs and past pres, Southwest. Div; past pres, Westmoreland Co. Sportsmen's League; officer, Penn Rod and Gun Club, 38-; chmn, United Cerebral Palsy, West. Pa; exec. bd, Local 601, IUE, AFL-CIO. Cert. of Merit, Isaac Walton League, 65; 1st State Award as Legis. Conservationist of Year, 65; Nat. Award as Legis. Conservationist of Year, Nat. Wildlife Fedn. and Sears Roebuck Conserv. Found, 65. Rel: Catholic. Mailing Add: 925 S. Jefferson St, Jeannette, Pa. 15644. (1967)

LAUFENBURGER, ROGER ALLYN D
Minn. State Sen.
b. Stockton, Minn, 9/5/21; s. Ray Morse Laufenburger and Rosa Marie Hoppe L; m. 3/25/47 to Selma Louise Nesbit; c. Carolyn Jean, Bruce Allyn, Kay Ann and Dawn Marie. Educ: Winona Pub. Schs, Minn. Polit. & Govt. Pos: Justice of the peace, Minn, 54-56; Lewiston Village councilman, 57-63; Minn. State Sen, Winona Co, 63-67 and currently, secy, Dem-Farmer-Labor Lib. Caucus, Minn. State Senate, 65-67. Mem: Pres, Lewiston Bus. Asn, 56 and Lions Club, 61; Mason, Winona Shrine Club, Osman Temple, St. Paul; Winona Athletic Club, Elks and Eagles; Redmen's Club; United Commercial Travelers. Named Winona Co. Centennial Sports Champion, 58 and Regional Baseball Cmnr, 59-64. Rel: Presbyterian. Mailing Add: Box 6, Lewiston, Minn. 55952. (1967)

LAUGHLIN, EVERETT E. R
Ill. State Sen.
b. 9/2/15; m. to Lucille Schauer; c. Nancy, Ton and Jim. Educ: Cornell Col, A.B, 37; Univ. Ill. Col. of Law, LL.B, 39. Polit. & Govt. Pos: Pres, Bd. of Educ, Freeport Pub. Schs, Ill, 48-52; states attorney of Stephenson Co, 52-56; Ill. State Sen, 60- Bus. & Prof. Pos: Lawyer, Laughlin and Laughlin. Mem: Mason; Am. Legion; Amvets; Stephenson Co, Ill. State and Am. Bar Asns. Rel: Methodist. Mailing Add: 1563 Parkside Court, Freeport, Ill. 61032.

LAUGHLIN, GLORIA B. R
Chairwoman, Sixth Dist. Rep. Party, Minn.
b. Gibbon, Minn; d. John W. Boock and Willa Naegali B; m. to Joseph C. Laughlin; c. Kathleen (Mrs. Robert Pauly), John and James. Educ: Univ. Minn, Minneapolis, B.S, 36; Zeta Phi Eta; Pi Beta Phi. Polit. & Govt. Pos: Chairwoman, Sixth Dist. Rep. Party, Minn, 67-; del, Rep. Nat. Conv, 68. Mem: League of Women Voters; Am. Asn. Univ. Women. Rel: Episcopal. Mailing Add: 53 Highbanks, St. Cloud, Minn. 56301.

LAUGHLIN, LAWRENCE ROY D
b. Quebec City, Can, 8/1/16; s. Francis Patrick Laughlin and Lillian Roy L; m. 5/31/41 to Janet Tighe; c. Peter Michael and Julie Ann. Educ: Dartmouth Col, 34-37; Museum Sch. Fine Arts, Boston, Mass, 38; Northeast. Univ, evenings, 48; Sigma Phi Epsilon. Polit. Pos: Campaign Dir, Edward M. Kennedy for Senate, 64, campaign dir. of orgn. and scheduling, 62; North Middlesex City secy, John F. Kennedy for President, 60; local secy, John F. Kennedy for Senate, 58 and 52. Govt. Pos: Regional Dir, Small Bus. Admin, Boston, Mass, 66-; exec. asst. to U.S. Sen. Edward M. Kennedy, 62-66. Bus. & Prof. Pos: Ins. Underwriter & Sales, Cushing & Lyons, Boston, Mass, 62; ins. broker, self-employed, Chelmsford, 58-62; ins. underwriter, Fire & Inland Marine, Traders Mechanics Ins. Co, Lowell, 47-58; special agent, N.Y. Life Ins. Co, 46-47 and 38-42. Mil. Serv: Entered as Pvt, Army, 42, released as Capt, 46, after serv. in 203rd Antiaircraft Artil. Bn, 7th Armored Div, ETO; Bronze Star; ETO Ribbon with 5 Battle Stars; Capt.(Ret), Army Res, at present. Mem: Trustee, Lowell Tech. Inst. and Research Found; treas. and dir, Lowell Art Asn; C. of C; former mem, Rotary; Vesper Country Club; past pres, Holy Name Soc, St. Mary's Church. Rel: Roman Catholic. Mailing Add: 7 Housatonic Ave, Chelmsford, Mass. 01824. (1967)

LAUGHLIN, MICHAEL LUKENS D
S.C. State Sen.
b. Aiken, S.C. 3/20/44; s. Thomas I. Laughlin and Louise Bailey L; single. Educ: Univ. Va, B.S, 66; Sigma Phi. Polit. & Govt. Pos: S.C. State Sen, 69- Bus. & Prof. Pos: V.pres. and treas, Horizon Aviation, Inc, Charlottesville, Va, 65-; pres. and chmn. bd, Eagle Aviation, Inc, Aiken, S.C, 67-; dir. S.C. Nat. Bank, 68-; pres. and chmn. bd, V.I.P. Indust, Inc, Columbia, 68-; pres, Coosaw River Develop. Co, Aiken. Mem: Rotary; Civil Air Patrol; Farm Bur; dir, C. of C; Nat. Coun, Boy Scouts; Aircraft Owners and Pilots Asn; commodore, Fishers Island Yacht Club. Rel: Episcopal. Legal Res: 330 Kershaw St, S.E, Aiken, S.C. 29801. Mailing Add: P.O. Box 921, Aiken, S.C. 29801.

LAURICELLA, SAL A. R
b. Italy, 11/10/31; s. Luigi Lauricella and Michelina Lombardo L; m. 11/4/60 to Nancey E. Williams; c. Dina Marie, Julie Ann and Stacy Rae. Educ: Quinnipiac Col, 53-54; Wayne State Univ, B.S, 57. Polit. & Govt. Pos: Publicity chmn, Rep. Nationalities Coun, 66-68; alternate del, Rep. Nat. Conv, 68; pres, Rep. State Nationalities Coun, 68-; dir, Nationalities Div. for State of Mich, 68- Bus. & Prof. Pos: Underwriting supvr, Gen. Accident Group, 56-58; pres, Wolverine Agency Inc, 58- Mil. Serv: Entered as Pvt, Army, 49, released as S/Sgt, 52, after serv. in 7964 Hq. Group, La Rochelle, France, 50-52. Mem: Mich. Ins. Agent's Asn; chmn, 1965 Columbus Day Cmt. Mailing Add: 301 Kerby Rd, Grosse Pointe Farms, Mich. 48236.

LAURINO, ANTHONY C. D
Alderman, Chicago, Ill.
b. Chicago, Ill, 7/27/10; s. Vito Laurino and Angelina Monelli L; m. 3/11/36 to Marie Bateman; c. William, Marie and Margaret. Educ: De Paul Univ, 2 years; County Club; Cath. Youth Orgn; pres, Sheet Boys Club; pres, Paulist A. Club. Polit. & Govt. Pos: Secy. to Philip A. Shaprio, Alderman, Chicago, Ill, alderman, currently. Mem: K. of C(4°); Holy Name Soc; Moose; Volturno Lodge; Sacred Hearts Sem. Cath. Youth Orgn; Clenza Richeganzn Soc; Villa Scalabrini chmn, Cancer Soc; Boy and Girl Scouts. Rel: Catholic. Legal Res: 4938 N. Kenneth Ave, Chicago, Ill. 60645. Mailing Add: Chicago City Council, Room 208, Chicago, Ill. 60602.

LAUSCHE, FRANK J. D
b. Cleveland, Ohio, 11/14/95; m. 1928 to Jane Sheal. Educ: John Marshall Law Sch, LL.B; Delta Theta Phi; Phi Sigma Kappa; Omicron Delta Kappa. Hon. LL.D, John Marshall Law Sch, Kenyon Col, Denison Univ, Ohio Wesleyan Univ, Miami Univ, Ashland Col, Defiance Col, Wash. and Jefferson Col, Oberlin Col, West. Reserve Univ, Ohio Univ, Akron Univ, Marietta Col. and Le Moyne Col; Dr. of Pub. Serv, Rio Grande Col; Dr. of Commun. Sci, Tiffin Bus. Col. Polit. & Govt. Pos: Judge, Munic. Court, Cleveland, Ohio, 32-37; judge, Common Pleas Court, 37-41; mayor, Cleveland, 41-44; Gov, Ohio, 45-46 & 49-56; U.S. Sen, Ohio, 56-68. Centennial Award, Northwest. Univ; Vet. Award, Joint Vet. Cmt. of Cuyahoga, 58; Good Citizen Medal, SAR; Cert. of Merit, Am. Vet. World War II. Legal Res: Cleveland, Ohio. Mailing Add: 6916 Marbury Rd, Bethesda, Md. 20034. (1967)

LAUTENSCHLAGER, LESTER N. D
b. Berthold, N.Dak, 6/7/04; married; c. 9. Educ: State Teachers Col, Minot. Polit. & Govt. Pos: N.Dak. State Sen, 59-66; Sch. Bd. Bus. & Prof. Pos: Farmer; Secy. Treas, Farmers Union Oil Co. Mem: Farmers Union. Mailing Add: Berthold, N.Dak. 58718. (1967)

LAUTERBACH, WILBUR H. R
Ill. State Rep.
b. Bartonville, Ill, 7/15/13; s. Henry E. Lauterbach and Clara A. H. L; m. to Mary; c. Wayland and Allyn. Educ: Chicago Tech. Col. Polit. & Govt. Pos: Mayor, Bartonville, 16 years; pres, Bartonville Bd. of Educ, 2 years; mem, Bartonville Bd. of Trustees, 2 years; fire chief, Bartonville Vol. Fire Dept, 2 years, asst. chief, 12 years; chmn, Peoria Co. Housing Authority, 18 years; pres, Peoria Tazewell Crippled Children's Center, 2 years; del, Rep. Nat. Conv, 56; Ill. State Rep, 67- Bus. & Prof. Pos: Pres, W.H. Lauterbach Home Builders Center, Inc; pres, Commun. Enterprises, Inc; mem. bd. of dirs, Madison Park Bank, Peoria; chmn, Wil-Mar Knoll and W. Mead Subdivs. Mem: Nat. Asn. of Retail Lumber Dealers; Int. Asn. of City Mgrs; Int. Asn. of Fire Chiefs. Peoria Jr. C. of C. Good Govt. Award. Rel: Lutheran. Mailing Add: 3 Holly, Lauterdale Subdivision, Bartonville, Ill. 61607.

LAVALLÉE, GASTON HAROLD R
Chmn, Woonsocket Rep. City Cmt, R.I.
b. Woonsocket, R.I, 1/13/16; s. Frank Lavallée and Palmyre Lamoureux L; m. 6/27/36 to Lillian Blais; c. Claudette (Mrs. La France), Jacqueline (Mrs. Rogeski) and Therese. Educ: R.I. State Col. Exten, Eng. Sci. and Mgt. Polit. & Govt. Pos: Chmn, Woonsocket Rep. City Cmt, R.I, 32- Bus. & Prof. Pos: Employ. mgr, Owens Corning Fiberglass, 40-46; gen. contractor, 46- Mem: Club Marquette. Exceptional Serv. Award, Civil Air Patrol; Award, Auxiliary of the U.S. Air Force, 56. Rel: Catholic. Mailing Add: 580 Front St, Woonsocket, R.I. 02895.

LAVENDER, ROBERT EUGENE R
Justice, Okla. Supreme Court
b. Muskogee, Okla, 7/19/26; s. Harold James Lavender and Vergene Martin L; m. 12/22/45 to Maxine Knight; c. Linda (Mrs. Dean Courter), Robert K, Debra Lucille and William J. Educ: Univ. Tulsa, Pre-Law, 46-49; Univ. Tulsa Sch. of Law, LL.B, 53. Polit. & Govt. Pos: Asst. city attorney, Tulsa, Okla, 54-55; mem. sch. bd, Catoosa Independent Dist. Two, Rogers Co, 58-65; city attorney, Catoosa, 62-65; Justice, Okla. Supreme Court, 65- Bus. & Prof. Pos: Private practice law, Tulsa, Okla, 55-60 and Claremore, 61-65; mem. law firm, Bassmann, Gordon, Mayberry & Lavender, 62-65. Mil. Serv: Entered as A/S, Navy Res, 44, released as Seaman 1/C, 46, after serv. in Armed Guard, Okinawa Campaign, S.Pac, 45; Battle Ribbons. Publ: Author, various opinions as mem. of Okla. Supreme Court, since 65. Mem: Okla. Bar Asn; Am. Bar; Am. Judicature Soc; Okla. Judicial Conf; AF&AM; Am. Legion; hon. mem, Phi Alpha Delta. Rel: Methodist. Legal Res: 1020 N. Lynn Lane Rd, Tulsa, Okla. 74138. Mailing Add: 2910 Kerry Lane, Oklahoma City, Okla. 73120.

LAVENDER, ROBERT M. R
Chmn, Navarro Co. Rep. Party, Tex.
b. Santa Anna, Tex, 3/14/06; s. Thomas Headlee Lavender and Martha Crum L; m. 6/29/29 to Lucile Eliot. Educ: Univ. Tex, Austin. Polit. & Govt. Pos: Precinct chmn, Corsicana, Tex, 50-66; chmn, Navarro Co. Rep. Party, Tex, 66- Bus. & Prof. Pos: Rancher, Navarro Co, Tex, 30-; airport mgr, Beaumont, Tex, 32-40. Mil. Serv: Entered as 1st Lt, Army, 40, released as Maj, 45, after serv. in Ord. Dept, Tex. & Ga. Mem: Bd. dirs, Corsicana C. of C, and chmn, water cmt; bd. dirs, Lions Club; v.chmn, Cmnr. Corsicana Housing Authority; bd. dirs, First Nat. Bank, Dawson, Tex. Rel: Methodist; Bd. Stewards, First Methodist Church, Corsicana, Tex. Mailing Add: 1901 Sycamore, Corsicana, Tex. 75110.

LaVERDURE, BETTY D
b. Belcourt, N.Dak, 6/2/30; d. Albert Wilkie and Elizabeth Allard W; m. 8/17/51 to Andrew R. LaVerdure; c. Andrea, Andrew, Julienne, Betsy, Napoleon, Adrienne and Lee Peltier (foster daughter). Educ: High Sch, Turtle Mt, N.Dak, 4 years; various law inst. relating to Indian law. Polit. & Govt. Pos: Chief judge, Turtle Mt. Band of Chippewa Indians, N.Dak, 62-; del, Dem. Nat. Conv, 68; v.pres, Nat. Am. Indian Court. Bus. & Prof. Pos: Secy, Arrow Inc, Wash, D.C, 69. Mem: Nat. Am. Indian Court Judges Asn. Recipient of First Incentive Award through Bur. of Indian Affairs to Indian Judge for New Indian Law and Order Code; Gov. of N.Dak. Award for Outstanding Contribution in Correctional Rehabilitation Cmt. Rel: Catholic. Mailing Add: Box F, Belcourt, N.Dak. 58316.

LAVERNE, THOMAS R
N.Y. State Sen.
b. Rochester, N.Y; married; c. Four daughters. Educ: N.Y. State Teachers Col, Albany, B.A, 39; Cornell Law Sch, LL.B, 48. Polit. & Govt. Pos: N.Y. State Sen, 60- Bus. & Prof. Pos: Partner, Laverne, Sortino and Noto, Attorneys. Mil. Serv: Army, wounded in combat, ETO; Purple Heart; Combat Inf. Badge. Mem: Monroe Co, N.Y. and Am. Bar Asns; past comdr, Monroe Co. VFW; Am. Legion; DAV; past pres, Italian Civil League of Rochester; nat. dir. and gen. counsel, Circus Saints and Sinners; Kiwanis; Elks; Moose; dir, Irondequoit Athletic Asn; chmn, Irondequoit Pop Warner League; Ad, Cornell and Rochester Clubs; CYO; CMA. Mailing Add: 711 Executive Office Bldg, 36 Main St. W, Rochester, N.Y. 14614.

LAVERTY, IRENE C. R
b. Burlington, Iowa, 6/18/21; d. Rollen R. Upton and Mamie P. Distlehorst U; m. 6/9/46 to Charles O. Laverty; c. Becky and David. Educ: Burlington Col. of Commerce. Polit. & Govt. Pos: Pres, Warren Co. Rep. Women, Iowa, 54-56; Rep. committeewoman, Lincoln Twp, 54-60; v.chmn, Fifth Cong. Dist. Rep. Party, 56-62; v.chmn, Iowa State Rep. Cent. Cmt, 60-66; secy, Midwest-Rocky Mt. Vice Chairmen's Asn, 61-66. Bus. & Prof. Pos: Secy, Young People's Dept, Iowa Farm Bur, 44-46; clerk, 54th Gen. Assembly, 51-52. Mem: PEO; PTA; Iowa Heart Asn. Rel: Methodist. Mailing Add: R.R. 4, Box 198, Indianola, Iowa 50125.

LAVERY, VINCENT JOSEPH D
Mem, Merced Co. Dem. Cent. Cmt, Calif.
b. Dublin, Ireland, 1/21/36; s. Philip Lavery and Carmel O'Connor L; single. Educ: Merced Jr. Col, Calif, A.A, 67; Fresno State Col, B.Sc. in Polit. Sci, 70. Polit. & Govt. Pos: Mem, Merced Assoc. Dem, Calif, 66-; Merced Co. chmn, Citizens for Robert F. Kennedy, 67-68, Citizens for Cranston, Citizens for Sisk and Citizens for Hubert H. Humphrey, 68; del, Dem. Nat. Conv, 68; mem, Merced Co. Dem. Cent. Coun, 68- Bus. & Prof. Pos: Dance promoter, Univ. of Prod, 65- Mil. Serv: Entered as Pvt, Army, 56, released as Cpl, 59, after serv. in 82nd Airborne Div, Ft. Bragg, N.C; Parachutist Badge; Good Conduct Medal. Mem: NAACP; Am. Legion; Holy Name Soc. Rel: Catholic. Mailing Add: 1830 I St, Merced, Calif. 95340.

LAVERY, WILLIAM JAMES D
Conn. State Rep.
b. Bridgeport, Conn, 3/26/38; s. William James Lavery and Helen Keniley L; m. 5/11/68 to Flora Vigliotti. Educ: Fairfield Univ, A.B; Fordham Univ. Law Sch, LL.B. Polit. & Govt. Pos: Alderman, Bridgeport, Conn, 63-67; Conn. State Rep, 67-, chmn, House Pub. Health and Safety Coun, Conn. House Rep, 69-71. Bus. & Prof. Pos: Attorney, Ehrsam, Flonigan & Lavery (Partner), currently; attorney, Bridgeport Housing Authority, currently. Mil. Serv: Army Res, 60-61, Sp-4, serv. in Third Army, active duty 15 months. Mem: Bridgeport and Conn. Bar Asns; Elks; K. of C; budget bd, United Fund; bd. dirs, Hall Neighborhood House; bd. dirs, Bridgeport Ment. Health Coun. Rel: Roman Catholic. Mailing Add: 84 Ashley St, Bridgeport, Conn. 06610.

LaVIGNE, FRANCIS C. D
Committeeman, St. Lawrence Co. Dem. Cmt, N.Y.
b. Ogdensburg, N.Y, 10/20/28; s. Frank E. LaVigne and Mary E. Fraser L; m. 12/28/53 to Mary Ellen Deserre; c. Anne E, Jane F, Mary Patricia, Cecily, Bryan Joseph, Christopher J, Robert L, Peter D. and Mark F. Educ: Cath. Univ. Am, Wash, D.C, B.A, 50; Albany Law Sch, LL.B, 58; Alpha Phi Omega. Polit. & Govt. Pos: Committeeman, St. Lawrence Co. Dem. Cmt, N.Y, 59-, chmn, 62-68; town justice, Massena, 62-; del, Dem. Nat. Conv, 64. Mil.

Serv: Entered as Airman, Air Force, 51, released as 1st Lt, 56, after serv. in Strategic Air Command, 53-56; Maj, Air Force Res. Mem: Am, N.Y. State and St. Lawrence Co. Bar Asns; Am. Trial Lawyers Asn; K. of C. Rel: Roman Catholic. Mailing Add: 128 Allen St, Massena, N.Y. 13662.

LAW, ARTHUR J. D
Mich. State Rep.
b. Poteau, Okla, 1/12/06; married; c. Phyllis Elaine, Charles Edward, Marilyn Francis and Juanita Marie. Educ: Univ. Ill, 2 years. Polit. & Govt. Pos: Labor rep, Off. Price Admin. and War Prod. Bd; mayor, Pontiac, Mich, 6 years, city cmnr, 12 years; Mich. State Rep, 58- Bus. & Prof. Pos: Grocer. Mem: F&AM; AASR; Valley of Detroit Moslem Temple of Detroit. Rel: Protestant. Mailing Add: 27 Miami St, Pontiac, Mich. 48053. (1967)

LAW, JAMES L. R
Chmn, Sixth Dist. Rep. Party, Tenn.
b. Westmoreland, Tenn, 1/1/26; s. Henry Clay Law and Gracie Freeman L; m. 7/22/44 to Eunice Dorris; c. Larry C. and Dorris E.(Mrs. Mikeal Tully). Educ: High Sch. Polit. & Govt. Pos: Chmn, Sumner Co. Rep. Party, Tenn; mem, Westmoreland City Coun; chmn, Sixth Dist. Rep. Party, 68- Bus. & Prof. Pos: Pres, L&B Lumber Co, Inc, 53- Rel: Methodist. Mailing Add: Box 443, Westmoreland, Tenn. 37186.

LAW, ROBERT DALE R
Ill. State Rep.
b. Freeport, Ill, 6/12/22; s. Dale Franklin Law and Johanna Sophie Entmeier L; single. Educ: Univ. Ill, B.S, 50; Univ. Wis, LL.B, 54. Polit. & Govt. Pos: Secy, Stephenson Co. Rep. Cent. Cmt, Ill, 57-59, chmn, 63-; Asst. Attorney Gen, Ill, 58-59; chief asst. to State's Attorney, Stephenson Co, 59-; Rep. del, Nat. Electoral Col, 60; Rep. Sen. committeeman, 61-63; mem. exec. cmt, Ill. Co. Chmn. Asn, 61-; Rep. Representative committeeman, 63-65. Bus. & Prof. Pos: Mem, Miami Investment, 63; owner, Robert D. Law, Attorney, 65. Mil. Serv: Entered as Pvt, Army, 43, released as Pfc, 46, after serv. in C Co, 329th Regt, 83rd Inf. Div, ETO, 44-45; Combat Inf. Badge; European Campaign Ribbons; Purple Heart; Army Occup. Medal. Mem: Am. Acad. Polit. & Soc. Sci; Am. and Ill. Bar Asns; Stephenson Co. Bar Asn.(treas, 59); Univ. Ill. and Wis. Alumni Asns; Elks; Lions; Germania Soc; Freeport Country Club; 83rd Inf. Div. Asn; Am. Legion; Amvets. Rel: Methodist. Mailing Add: Box 65, Cedarville, Ill. 61013.

LAW, ROBERT EUGENE R
Chmn, Blount Co. Rep. Party, Tenn.
b. Maryville, Tenn, 6/21/15; s. John Abner Law and Mary Susannah Walker L; m. 4/27/40 to Bessie Lou Ratledge. Educ: Maryville Col, B.A, 39. Polit. & Govt. Pos: Chmn, Tenth Dist. Blount Co. Rep. Party, Tenn; chmn, Blount Co. Rep. Party, 64- Bus. & Prof. Pos: Qual. coordinator, Aluminum Co. Am, 41- Mil. Serv: Entered as Pvt, Army, 42, released as 1st Lt, 46, after serv. in Transportation Corps, ETO, 45-46, Capt, Army Res.(Ret); Good Conduct Medal. Mem: Kiwanis. Rel: Presbyterian. Mailing Add: Route 10, Maryville, Tenn. 37801.

LAWLER, JOSEPH JOHN D
b. Jessup, Pa, 1/12/01; s. John J. Lawler and Bridget Langan L; m. 10/30/28 to Mary R. Flanagan. Educ: Catholic Univ, LL.B, 22; St. Thomas Col, A.B, 24. Polit. & Govt. Pos: Chief, Enforcement Div, Pub. Utility Cmn, Pa, 37-42; chief, Inheritance Tax Div, Auditor Gen. Off, 44-45; asst. postmaster gen, 45-52; dist. dir, Internal Revenue Serv, 52-54; secy. of hwy, 55-57; chmn, Pa. Turnpike Cmn, 57-66; del, Dem. Nat. Conv, 68. Bus. & Prof. Pos: Teacher and coach, all sports, Jessup High Sch, Pa, 24-35; dir. athletics, Mt. St. Marys Col, 35-37. Mil. Serv: Army, 42-44. Rel: Catholic. Mailing Add: 225 Bridge St, Jessup, Pa. 18434. (1967)

LAWLER, VIOLET M. D
Vice Chairwoman, Laramie Co. Dem. Cent. Cmt, Wyo.
b. Lawrence, Kans, 7/16/97; d. Wallace Edward Newman and Lou Arnette N; m. 7/8/46 to Joseph P. Lawler. Educ: Stamford Col, 13-16; Univ. Tex, Austin, 17-20. Polit. & Govt. Pos: Precinct committeewoman, Laramie Co. Dem. Cent. Cmt, Wyo, 58-64, dist. capt, 62-64, co. treas, 63-66, mem, State Finance Cmt, 63-, vice chairwoman, 68-, ed, newsletter, 69; del. and mem, Credentials Cmt, Dem. Nat. Conv, 64 & 68; Wyo. chmn, Women's Nat. Dem. Conf, 68. Bus. & Prof. Pos: Buyer, Nat. Furs & Fashion, 50-60; owner and mgr, Holiday Motel, 51-69. Mem: Am. Bus. Women Asn.(past pres, Cheyenne Chap. and past regional dir); Laramie Co. Chap, Nat. Found. on Polio (past secy); Cheyenne Drove (past pres); Benevolent Patriotic Order of Does. Certificate of Appreciation, March of Dimes; Nat. Citation, Am. Bus. Women's Asn. Rel: Episcopal. Mailing Add: 1507 W. Lincolnway, Cheyenne, Wyo. 82001.

LAWLESS, KIRBY GORDON, JR. R
b. Birmingham, Ala, 8/12/24; s. Kirby Gordon Lawless and Ethel May Black L; m. 4/13/51 to Dora May Busbee; c. Kirby Gordon, III, Madelene and Marc. Educ: Auburn Univ, B.A, 48; Emory Univ, LL.B, 51; pres, Phi Alpha Delta; Legal Aide Soc. of Atlanta; Kappa Sigma; Case Club. Polit. & Govt. Pos: Attorney, Gen. Counsel, Civil Aeronaut. Admin, 51-53; chmn, Young Rep. Club, Tuscaloosa, Ala, 56-60; secy, Young Rep. Fedn. of Ala, 58-62; alternate del, Rep. Nat. Conv, 60 & 64; v.chmn, Co. Rep. Cmt. of Tuscaloosa, 60-64; mem, Ala. State Rep. Exec. Cmt, 62-; mem, Zoning Bd. of Appeals, Tuscaloosa, 64-; chmn, Rep. finance cmt, Fifth Cong. Dist, Ala, 69- Bus. & Prof. Pos: Credit mgr, Southeast. Tool & Die Co, 53-55; v.pres. and gen. mgr, Phifer Wire Prod, Inc, 55-66, pres, 68-; dir, Aluminum Siding Asn, 68- Mil. Serv: Entered as Aviation Cadet, Navy, 42, released as Lt, 46, after serv. in Naval Training Command, Corpus Christi, Tex; Lt, Naval Res, 46-66; Am. Theater Ribbon; Reserve Medal. Publ: 'Commerce Clause,' Emory Univ. Law Rev, 51. Mem: Aircraft Owners and Pilots Asn; Ala. Regional Export Expansion Coun; dir, Tuscaloosa C. of C; Ga. Bar Asn; chmn, Tuscaloosa Appeals Rev. Bd; v.chmn, Am. Soc. of Precision Nailmakers; dir, Screen Mfrs. Asn; chmn, nail cmt, Aluminum Asn, 69; bd. mem, Tuscaloosa Acad, 67-; adv. mem, AISEC, Univ. Ala, 67-; chmn, prod. prom, Wire Weavers Asn, 65-, mem, adv. cmt, 68-; chmn, Mfrs. Forum, Tuscaloosa, 62-64; first v.pres, Kiwanis, 65; Indian Hills Country Club; Navy League. Rel: Methodist; Mem, Bd. of Stewards. Mailing Add: 1228 Claymont Dr, Tuscaloosa, Ala. 35401.

LAWLOR, DANIEL F. D
b. Scott Co, Iowa, 1/31/19; s. John Lawlor and Mary L; m. to Myrlyn Kerr; c. Daniel P, Maria P. Educ: Bennett High Sch. Polit. & Govt. Pos: Iowa State Rep, until 66. Bus. & Prof. Pos: Technician, Alum. Co. of Am. Mil. Serv: U.S. Air Force, WWII, Ground Instr. Mem: Am. Legion; Exec. Bd. Local 1379, IBEW; Past Pres, LeClaire Civic Club. Rel: Catholic. Mailing Add: 2nd and Chestnut, Le Claire, Iowa. 52753. (1967)

LAWRENCE, GEORGE ROLAND R
Vt. State Rep.
b. Albany, Vt, 5/8/09; m. to Ruth E. Anderson; c. One son and two daughters. Educ: Craftsbury Acad; Burlington Bus. Col. Polit. & Govt. Pos: Town committeeman, Agr. Stabilization & Conserv. Cmt; mem, nomination cmt, Exten. Serv. Adv. Bd; sch. dir, 30 & 57-59; selectman, 40-52 & 49-51; town auditor, 47-48; Vt. State Rep, 65- Bus. & Prof. Pos: Farmer; trustee, Craftsbury Acad. Mem: Maple Valley Grange. Rel: Methodist. Mailing Add: Star Route, Albany, Vt. 05820. (1967)

LAWRENCE, H. BEMIS R
Mem, Jefferson Co. Rep. Exec. Cmt, Ky.
b. Tompkinsville, Ky, 12/1/14; s. Hebron Lawrence and Mabel M. Bemis L; m. 10/6/38 to Mildred Elizabeth Ward; c. Anne Marie (Mrs. Braxton B. Townsend, Jr.) and William Ward. Educ: West. Ky. Univ, A.B, 36; Jefferson Sch. of Law, Univ. of Louisville, LL.B, 39; Sigma Delta Kappa. Polit. & Govt. Pos: Spec. agent, Fed. Bur. of Invest, 40-46, admin. asst. to J. Edgar Hoover, 3 years; secy-counsr, Ky. State Real Estate Cmn, 46-57; cmnr, Jefferson Co. Ky, 61-; Rep. nominee for Lt. Gov, 63; pres, Lincoln Club of Ky, 64-67; co-campaign chmn. for local and statewide cand, Louisville and Jefferson Co, 67; alternate del, Rep. Nat. Conv, 68; mem, R.N. Assocs, currently; mem, Jefferson Co. Rep. Exec. Cmt, currently. Mem: Soc. of Former Spec. Agents of the Fed. Bur. of Invest.(nat. pres, 67-68); Louisville Bar Asn.(pres, 68); Am. Bar Asn.(House of Del, 68-); Nat. Conf. of Lawyers and Realtors; Shrine; Royal Order of Jesters. Bd. of Regents of West. Ky. Univ. Named a New Ten Story Boys Dormitory in Honor of his Serv. on Behalf of that Univ. Rel: Christian; Mem. Bd. of Deacons, First Christian Church. Legal Res: 1616 Gardiner Lane, Louisville, Ky. 40205. Mailing Add: 1129 Kentucky Home Life Bldg, Louisville, Ky. 40202.

LAWRENCE, M. LARRY D
b. Chicago, Ill, 8/16/26; s. Sidney A. Lawrence and Tillie P. Astor L; m. 6/26/49 to Geraldine Elinor Polland; c. Robert Scott, Leslie Anne and Andrea Sue. Educ: Univ. Ariz, B.A, 47; Zeta Beta Tau. Polit. & Govt. Pos: Mem, Point Loma Dem. Club, 54-69; alternate del, Dem. Nat. Conv, 60, del, 64 & 68; chmn. and finance chmn, Van Deerlin for Cong, 61-66; finance cmt. mem, Mills for Assembly, 62-64 and Brown for Gov, 62-66; caucus chmn. and v.chmn, San Diego Co. Dem. Cent. Cmt, 62-66, finance chmn, 63-66; v.chmn, finance cmt, Calif. Dem. State Cent. Cmt, 63-66; San Diego Co. chmn, No on 14 Cmt, 64; finance cmt. chmn, Coates for Assembly, 64; mem, President's Club, 64-67; charter mem, Golden Bear Club, 65-67; mem, Mills for Senate Cmt, 66; chmn, San Diego Co. Voter Registrn. Proj, 66; co-chmn, state campaign, Gordon for Secy. of State, 66; San Diego Co. finance chmn. and exec. cmt. mem, nat. finance cmt, McCarthy for Pres. Campaign, 68. Mil. Serv: Entered as Duty Officer (jg), Maritime Serv, 44, released as Duty Officer, 45, after serv. in Gulf and Pac. Theatres. Mem: Pres, Youth Home Builders, 53-54; Calif. Hotel and Motel Asn; South. Calif. Restaurant Asn; Calif. Laundry and Linen Supply Asn; polit. affairs chmn, Coronado Realty Bd, 68-69; San Diego and Coronado C. of C; Calif. State Cmn. on Tourism and Visitor Serv; San Diego Conv. and Visitors Bur; v.pres, United Jewish Fedn. of San Diego, 54-64; San Diego chmn, United Jewish Appeal, 58-61; pres, San Diego Commun. Serv. Orgn, 61-62; bd. trustees, San Diego Citizens United, 65-67; San Diego campaign dir, United Commun. Serv, 65-67; v.pres, Loma Portal Civic Club, 65-67; campaign cabinet, Tri-Hosp. Dr, 65-68; B'nai B'rith; Guardians of San Diego; sustaining mem, San Diego YMCA; bd. dir, Citizens United, 66-67; chmn, Coronado United Crusade, 67; Navy League; San Diego Taxpayers Asn; int. visitors cmt. and fel. cmt, Coronado Rotary Club, 68, prog. cmt, club publicity and bul. cmt. and Buyer-seller rels. cmt, 69; dir, world affairs coun, San Diego State Col, 68-69; task force cmt. on housing, Urban Coalition, 68-69; assoc. mem, U.S. Naval Inst. Rel: Jewish. Legal Res: 3626 Alcott St, San Diego, Calif. 92106. Mailing Add: 1500 Orange Ave, Coronado, Calif. 92118.

LAWS, DONALD BOYD D
Secy, Shelby Co. Dem. Cmt, Ohio
b. Sidney, Ohio, 9/30/41; s. Ancil Matt Laws and Mae Swain L; m. 12/12/59 to Alice Faye Zimpfer; c. Timothy Scott and Bryan Keith. Educ: Anna Local School, Ohio, 12 years. Polit. & Govt. Pos: Councilman-at-lg, Sidney, Ohio, 65-67; Sheriff, Shelby Co, 68-; committeeman, Shelby Co. Dem. Cent. Cmt, 68-; secy, Shelby Co. Dem. Cmt, 69- Mil. Serv: Entered as Airman Basic, Air Force, 59, released as Airman 1/C, 63, after serv. in Strategic Air Command, 16th Air Force, Sevilla, Spain, 62-63; Air Force Commendation Medal; Good Conduct Award; Longevity Award. Mem: Am. Legion; Nat. and Buckeye State Sheriff's Asns; Elks; Eagles; Ohio Dem. Club; Kiwanis; YMCA; Am. Fedn. Police; Honorary Mem, Disabled Am. Vet; hon. mem, Ohio Twp. Trustees and Clerks Asn; Shelby Co. Dem. Club. Rel: Lutheran. Mailing Add: 202 South Main, Sidney, Ohio 45365.

LAWS, WILLIAM CHARLES R
b. Philadelphia, Pa, 6/8/08; s. Charles Laws and Esther V. Golding L; m. 11/16/29 to Verna R. Keim; c. Jacquelyn, Ronald, William, Jr. and Marilyn. Polit. & Govt. Pos: Dir. accts. and finance, Reading, Pa. Bus. & Prof. Pos: Sales consult, J.P. Gordon Co, 24-33, territory sales mgr, 33-39; div. sales mgr, Dunlop Tire & Rubber Corp, 39-51; owner, Garage, 51-66; sales coun. and bus. analyst, currently. Mem: United Commun. Serv; Econ. Opportunity Coun; YMCA; past pres. and chaplain, Am. Bus. Club; Elks. Rel: Evangelical United Brethren. Mailing Add: 320 McClellan St, Brookline, Reading, Pa. 19602.

LAWSON, GEORGE R
b. Canada, 9/27/97; m. to Bertha L. True; c. 1 son, 1 daughter. Educ: Newport High Sch; Vail Agr. Sch. Polit. & Govt. Pos: Vt. State Sen, 63-66; Vt. State Rep, 55-63; selectman, 25 years; sch. dir; past mem, Orleans Co. Tax Bd. of Appeals. Bus. & Prof. Pos: Farmer; Ins; auditor, overseer of poor.

Mem: Grange; Farm Bur; North. Farms; Chmn, State Grange Exec. Comm; 4-H Camp Adv. Comm; Dir, Cook Fire Ins. Asn. of Vt. Rel: Methodist. Mailing Add: Coventry, Vt. 05825. (1967)

LAWSON, JAMES BYRUM D
b. Cross Keys, S.C, 2/4/97; s. Wylie L. Lawson and Mary Cooper L; m. 9/20/21 to Lucille Jeter; c. J.B, Jr.(deceased), Elizabeth (Mrs. Copeland), Martha (Mrs. Taylor) and Nancy Wilma (Mrs. Sloan). Educ: Cross Keys Sch, 07-16; Correspondence Course, 19-20. Polit. & Govt. Pos: S.C. State Rep, 43-48 & 51-54; S.C. State Sen, 55-58 and 63-64; del, State and Nat. Dem. Conv, 56, 60 & 64. Bus. & Prof. Pos: Retired merchant and farmer. Mil. Serv: 18-19. Mailing Add: Sandy Springs, S.C. 29677.

LAWSON, MURRAY CARTER R
Iowa State Rep.
b. Fargo, N.Dak, 9/7/23; s. Millard Christian Lawson and Joyce Berkin L; m. 10/3/59 to Jean Kathleen Cady; c. Mark Charles and Julia Louise. Educ: Grinnell Col, B.A, 48; Friars Club. Polit. & Govt. Pos: Co-chmn, Mason City Planning and Zoning Cmn, Iowa, 66-69; Iowa State Rep, Cerro Gordo Co, 68- Bus. & Prof. Pos: Mgr. refrigeration div, Maytag Co, Newton, Iowa, 49-57; pres, Klipto Printing & Off. Supply, Mason City, 57- Mil. Serv: Entered as Aviation Cadet, Navy, 43, released as Ens, 46, after serv. in Navy Air Corps, Am. Theater; Lt.(jg), Naval Res, 51. Mem: Rotary; Mason; Shrine; Elks. Rel: Episcopal. Mailing Add: 671 E. State, Mason City, Iowa 50401.

LAWSON, PAUL M. D
Pa. State Rep.
b. Franklin, Pa, 1/29/14; m. to Alma Carter; c. One. Educ: Hampton Univ; Pa. State Univ. exten. course on arbitration. Polit. & Govt. Pos: Pa. State Rep, 60- Bus. & Prof. Pos: UAW-AFL-CIO Int. Trustee. Mil. Serv: World War II. Mem: VFW. Rel: Catholic. Mailing Add: 5425 Sansom St, Philadelphia, Pa. 19139. (1967)

LAWSON, WILLIAM VINTON, JR. R
Tenn. State Rep.
b. Omaha, Nebr, 9/3/31; s. William Vinton Lawson (deceased) and Elva Erickson,L; m. 6/18/55 to Mary Carolyn Townes; c. Mary Lucian, William Vinton, III and Carolyn Townes. Educ: Tex. A&M Univ, 49-50; Southwestern at Memphis, 50-54; Sigma Alpha Epsilon (chap. pres, 54). Polit. & Govt. Pos: Tenn. State Rep, Shelby Co, Dist. 9, 68- Bus. & Prof. Pos: Field rep, Gen. Motors Acceptance Corp, Tupelo, Miss. and Memphis, Tenn, 54-56; agent, Nat. Life Ins. Co. of Vt, Memphis, Tenn, 56-63; spec. agent, Northwest. Mutual Life Ins. Co, 63- Mil. Serv: Entered as Pvt, Army Res, 51, released as Cpl, 57, after serv. in various units of active Reserve. Mem: Memphis Asn. of Nat. Asn. of Life Underwriters (secy, 66-67, treas. and membership chmn, 67-68); Memphis Chap, Am. Soc. of Chartered Life Underwriters (received Designation, 64); Univ. Club. of Memphis. Received Nat. Membership Award, Nat. Asn. Life Underwriters as Membership Chmn. of Memphis Asn, 68. Rel: Episcopal. Legal Res: 19 S. Ashlawn Rd, Memphis, Tenn. 38112. Mailing Add: 1420 Union Ave, Apt. 517, Memphis, Tenn. 38104.

LAWTHER, ROBERT M. R
Mayor, Lakewood, Ohio
b. McKeesport, Pa, 5/23/27; s. LeRoy Lawther and Martha Helen Morledge L; m. 10/28/53 to Jo Anne Evelyn Paxton. Educ: Col. of Wooster, B.A, 50; West. Reserve Univ, Sch. of Law, LL.B, 53; Delta Sigma Rho; Pi Sigma Alpha; Phi Alpha Delta. Polit. & Govt. Pos: Precinct committeeman, Co. Rep. Orgn, Ohio, 55-59; mem, Lakewood City Planning Cmn, 56-57; mem, Lakewood City Coun, 57-63, pres. 62-63; mem, Cuyahoga Co. Rep. Exec. Cmn, 64-; Mayor, Lakewood, Ohio, 64-; pres, Cuyahoga Co. Mayors and City Mgrs. Asn, 68- Bus. & Prof. Pos: Practice of law, 53- Mil. Serv: Seaman 1/C, Navy, 44-46. Mem: Cleveland and Ohio Bar Asns. Rel: Protestant. Mailing Add: 17904 Lake Rd, Lakewood, Ohio 44107.

LAWTON, MARION R. R
b. Garnett, S.C, 3/5/18; s. Brewton Sams Lawton and Marian Smith L; m. 2/15/47 to Margaret Dell Leech; c. Marion R, Jr, Margaret Doris and Brewton Wallace. Educ: Clemson Univ, B.S, 40; Blue Key; Tiger Brotherhood. Polit. & Govt. Pos: Precinct chmn, Estill Rep. Party, S.C, 64; chmn, Hampton Co. Rep. Party, 65-69; del, Rep. Nat. Conv, 68. Bus. & Prof. Pos: Partner, Walker & Lawton Lumber Co, 50; owner, Estill Feed Milling Co, 50; owner, M.R. Lawton Poultry Farms, 65; pres, Patrick Henry Acad. Mil. Serv: Entered as 2nd Lt, Army, 40, released as Maj, 46, after serv. in Inf, Attached to Philippine Army, Bataan Bn. Comdr, 42-43; prisoner of war, 42-45; Bronze Star; Purple Heart; Distinguished Unit Citation with 3 Clusters. Mem: Lions; Am. Legion; Clemson Univ. Alumni Asn.(nat. dir, 54-55); v.pres, Coastal Empire Coun, Boy Scouts, 60-62, mem. exec. bd, 62-64, mem-at-lg, 65-66. Silver Beaver Award, Boy Scouts, 57. Rel: Presbyterian; Elder. Mailing Add: Lawton Ave, Estill, S.C. 29918.

LAXALT, PAUL R
Gov. of Nev.
b. Reno, Nev, 8/2/22; s. Dominique Laxalt and Theresa Alpetche L; m. 6/23/46 to Jackalyn Ross; c. Gail, Sheila, John, Michelle, Kevin and Kathleen. Educ: Santa Clara Univ, 40-43; Univ. Denver, B.S, LL.B, 49. Polit. & Govt. Pos: Dist. Attorney, Ormsby Co, Nev, 51-54; City Attorney, Carson City, 54-55; Lt. Gov, Nev, 62-67, Gov, 67-; del, Rep. Nat. Conv, 68. Bus. & Prof. Pos: Lawyer; partner, Firm of Laxalt, Ross & Laxalt, 54-62; practice, Carson City, Nev. Mem: Am. Bar Asn; Am. Legion; VFW; Eagles. Mailing Add: Governor's Mansion, Carson City, Nev. 89701.

LAXSON, JOHN H. R
Chmn, Dimmit Co. Rep. Party, Tex.
b. Atascosa Co, Tex, 7/13/86; s. John Laxson and Georgia Titsworth L; m. 6/16/30 to Dorothy McNallie; c. Gaye (Mrs. C.W. Turner), Kaye (Mrs. C.J. Hall), June (Mrs. Hubert Lynch), Bay Clifton, Wilma (Mrs. Paul Hodge), Nellie V.(Mrs. Rowill Jones), Johnanna (Mrs. E.J. Bowers) and J.H. Polit. & Govt. Pos: Chmn, Dimmit Co. Rep. Party, Tex, 60-; sgt-at-arms, Rep. Nat. Conv, 68. Bus. & Prof. Pos: Travelling salesman, San Antonio Grocery; rancher, 10-60; citrus farmer, 64-69. Mem: Odd Fellows; Rotary; Lions; Farm Bur. Rel: Church of Christ. Mailing Add: Carrizo Springs, Tex. 78834.

LAYNE, HERBERT CLAYTON R
b. Daus, Tenn, 9/3/13; s. John Abner Layne and Martha Emma Hackworth L; m. 8/17/40 to Ora Irene Sanders; c. Donald Clayton, Miriam Louise, Tommy Levoy, Glenda Sue and Reba Sharon. Educ: Col, 2 years. Polit. & Govt. Pos: Elec. cmnr, Sequatchie Co, Tenn, 48- Bus. & Prof. Pos: Real estate; sch. teacher, 9 years, grocery store owner, 10 years; surveyor, 25 years. Mil. Serv: Pvt, Army, 45. Freedoms Found. Award as a Sch. Teacher. Rel: Baptist. Mailing Add: Box 563, Dunlap, Tenn. 37327.

LAYNE, WILLIAM HENRY R
Chmn, Rowan Co. Rep. Party, Ky.
b. Paintsville, Ky; s. James Trimble Layne and Flora May Wheatley L; m. 9/22/31 to Francis Elizabeth McKinney; c. William Joseph. Educ: Univ. Ky, 30-31; Morehead State Univ, 3 years; Delta Tau Delta. Polit. & Govt. Pos: Mem, Rowan Co. Sch. Bd, Ky, 34-44; mayor, Morehead, Ky, 46-; chmn, Rowan Co. Rep. Party, 62-; Rep. v.chmn, Seventh Cong. Dist, 67- Bus. & Prof. Pos: Clothing merchant, 48- Mem: Pres, Morehead C. of C, 69; past pres, Ky. Munic. League, 60-61; past comdr, Morehead F&AM, 68; Shrine. Distinguished faculty award, Morehead State Univ. Alumni. Rel: Methodist. Legal Res: 112 Wilson Ave, Morehead, Ky. 40351. Mailing Add: 110 Main, Morehead, Ky. 40351.

LAYSON, JEFFERSON VIMONT, JR. R
Chmn, Bourbon Co. Rep. Exec. Cmt, Ky.
b. Lexington, Ky, 3/21/38; s. Jefferson Vimont Layson and Ruth Womack L; m. 8/22/59 to Carol Ann Baumgardner; c. Jeff, III and Stephen. Educ: Denison Univ, A.B, 60; Univ. Ky, LL.B, 63; Kappa Sigma; Phi Delta Phi. Polit. & Govt. Pos: Chmn, Bourbon Co. Rep. Exec. Cmt, Ky, 64-; hearing officer, Ky. Workmen's Compensation Bd, 68- Publ: 'Finance Company as a Holder in Due Course,' Univ. Ky. Law J, 62. Mem: Bourbon Co, Fayette Co. and Ky. Bar Asns; Lions; Farm Bur; Paris-Bourbon Co. C. of C.(dir). Rel: Presbyterian. Mailing Add: 3038 Lynnwood Dr, Paris, Ky. 40361.

LAZARECK, ISADORE LUKE D
Mem. N.Dak. Dem. Non-Partisan League State Exec. Cmt.
b. Winnipeg, Manitoba, Can, 11/13/15; s. Jacob Lazareck and Emma Zelbovitz L; m. 9/8/49 to Sibil Marjorie Marcoe; c. Ruth Karen, Jack, Allen, Mira, Maxine and Leslie. Educ: Univ. Manitoba, M.D, 40. Polit. & Govt. Pos: Chmn, Ramsey Co. Dem. Party, N.Dak, 62-68; finance chmn, State Century Club, 65-; del, Dem. Nat. Conv, 68; mem, N.Dak. Dem. Non-Partisan League State Exec. Cmt, 69- Bus. & Prof. Pos: Medical practitioner, 40- Mil. Serv: Entered as Lt, Can. Army Med. Corp, 42, released as Capt, 45, after serv. in ETO, 42-44; Sicilian-Italian Campaign Medal. Mem: Am. Med. Asn; N.Dak. Obstetrics and Gynecology Asn; Dist. Med. Asn; VFW; Am. Legion; Mason (32°); Shrine; dir, Devils Lake C. of C; pres, Lake Region Curling Club; Lake Region Jr. Col. Bd. Rel: Jewish. Legal Res: 1032 Fifth St, Devils Lake, N.Dak. 58301. Mailing Add: 411 Fourth Ave, Devils Lake, N.Dak. 58301.

LAZZIO, THOMAS R
b. Paterson, N.J, 7/29/11; s. Salvatore Lazzio and Caterina L; m. 6/19/38 to Theresa C. Mandata. Educ: Rutgers Univ. Polit. Pos: N.J. State Assemblyman, 52-57; mem, Vets. Reemployment Rights Cmt. and Civil Rights Cmt; cmnr, Paterson Bd. of Educ, N.J; one of thirty original mems, White House Conf. on Educ, Eisenhower Admin. Bus. & Prof. Pos: Field serv. rep, Wright Aero Div, Curtiss Wright Corp, civilian adviser on engines attached to airforce with 9th Bomb Group B-29, Tinian and Saipan, 2nd World War. Publn: Free Trade Unions Method of Combating Communist Unions in Italy, State Dept, 54; Labor & Cooperative Movement's Influence of Government of Scandinavian Countries, State Dept, 54. Mem: Serv. rep, T.O.P. Dept, UAW, pres, Local 300, 52-63, financial secy, 50-52, treas, 48-50. All State Pitcher & Quarterback, Central High Sch, Paterson, N.J; Interstate Jr. Iceskating Champion, N.Y. & N.J. Rel: Catholic. Mailing Add: 25 Doremus St, Paterson, N.J. 07522. (1967)

LEACH, CHARLES PARMLEY, SR. R
Chmn, Clarion Co. Rep. Orgn, Pa.
b. New Bethlehem, Pa, 9/27/11; s. George Washington Leach and Ursula Dawes Parmley L; m. 4/30/36 to Clare Louise Skinner; c. Charles Parmley, Jr, Cara L.(Mrs. Thornley) and Hamilton Skinner. Educ: Bucknell Univ, 29-31. Polit. & Govt. Pos: Councilman, New Bethlehem Borough, Pa, 42-58, pres, 48-58; mem, Pa. State Rep. Finance Cmt, 54-; mem, Pa. State Rep. Exec. Cmt, 62-; sch. dir, New Bethlehem, 62-; chmn, Clarion Co. Rep. Orgn, 64- Bus. & Prof. Pos: Secy, Joe F. Sherman Co, 46-; dir, H.E. Brosius Co, Inc, 54-; pres, Bruin Drilling Corp, 60-; dir, Hawthorne Mfg. Co; pres, Charles P. Leach Agency, Inc, 67- Mem: Eagles; Moose; N.B.A.D. Corp; Elks; dir, C. of C; exec. cmt. of Region III, Boy Scouts of Am. Rel: Presbyterian. Legal Res: 533 Penn, New Bethlehem, Pa. 16242. Mailing Add: Broad, New Bethlehem, Pa. 16242.

LEADER, GEORGE MICHAEL D
b. York, Pa, 1/17/18; s. Guy Alvin Leader and Beulah Boyer L; m. 9/17/39 to Mary Jane Strickler; c. George Michael, Frederick, Jane Ellen and David. Educ: York Collegiate Inst, 34-35; Gettysburg Col, 36-38; Univ. Pa, B.S, 39. Polit. & Govt. Pos: Pa. State Sen, 50-54; Gov, Pa, 55-59; del, Dem. Nat. Conv, 68. Bus. & Prof. Pos: Chmn. of bd, Better Govt. Assoc, Inc; pres, Commonwealth Indust, Inc; pres, Paradise Mutual Ins. Co; mem. of bd. and v.pres, Capitol Prod. Corp; mem. of bd, Colonial Metals Corp. Mem: Bd, Am. Cancer Soc; Temple Univ, Pa. Ment. Health Found, Lincoln Univ. and Harcum Jr. Col. Legal Res: 1010 Black Rock Rd, Gladwyne, Pa. 19035. Mailing Add: Bryn Mawr Mall, Bryn Mawr, Pa. 19010.

LEAFSTEDT, WENDELL EDWARD R
S.Dak. State Sen.
b. Alcester, S.Dak, 9/9/03; s. Edward Leafstedt and Jennie Nilson L; m. to Marguerite Peterson; c. James and Stuart. Educ: High sch; Block and Bridle Club, S.Dak. State Univ. Polit. & Govt. Pos: S.Dak. State Sen, currently. Bus. & Prof. Pos: Farmer and stock grower, currently. Mem: Mason. Rel: Baptist. Mailing Add: Alcester, S.Dak. 57001.

LEAGUE, JAMES CHRISTOPHER D
b. Spartanburg, S.C, 12/14/03; s. Berry League and Florence Bolt L; m. 4/12/34 to Rosabelle Flemming. Educ: Hickory Tavern High Sch, 22. Polit. &

Govt. Pos: S.C. State Rep, 66. Bus. & Prof. Pos: Sales and divisional mgr, Carolina Vend-A-Matic Co; farmer; Irving Trust Co, N.Y.C, 29-31; cmn. agent and jobber gasoline and oil, 32-42; salesman, 48-, Naco Farm Supply, South. Fertilizer Co. Mil. Serv: Marine Corps, 23-26; 42-44. Rel: A.R.P. Church; elder. Mailing Add: Ora, S.C. 29371. (1967)

LEAHY, ELIZABETH CLARE D
b. Conneaut, Ohio, 4/12/11; d. John Gilbert Kelley and Mary Shannon K; m. 2/8/37 to James Clarence Leahy; c. James Patrick, Daniel Edward, Susan Elizabeth (Mrs. Aller), Timothy Joseph, Colleen Marie, Shannon Rosanne, Theresa Louise (Mrs. Kline) and Mary Catherine. Educ: St. Mary's High Sch, Conneaut, Ohio, 4 years. Polit. & Govt. Pos: Dem. precinct worker, Ashtabula Co, Ohio, 34-37, Seneca Co, various times from 40-69; committeeman, Dem. Cent. Cmt, 57 & 58-69; v.pres, Dem. Women of Seneca Co, 57-59, pres, 59-63, prog. chmn, 60-69; secy, Seneca Co. Dem. Exec. and Cent. Cmts, 59-69. Mem: Emblem Club; from cmt. mem. to leader to neighborhood chmn. to Coun. Pub. Rels. chmn. to city pres, Nat. Girl Scouts; Federated Dem. Women of Ohio; Daughters of Isabella; St. Mary's Altar Soc; St. Francis Guild. Nat. Girl Scout Thank You Award. Rel: Roman Catholic. Mailing Add: 275 W. Market St, Tiffin, Ohio 44883.

LEAKE, JOHN GREY D
V.Chmn, Harrisonburg Dem. Party, Va.
b. Harrisonburg, Va, 5/26/24; s. Ellis William Leake and Keziah Lloyd L; m. 10/22/54 to Rosalie Miller Kite; c. Anne Elizabeth and John Grey, Jr. Educ: Harrisonburg High Sch, Grad, 43. Polit. & Govt. Pos: Mem, Harrisonburg Dem. Party, Va, 53-, v.chmn, 63-; del, Va. Dem. State Conv, 53-; Dem. chmn, Ward II, Precinct 3, Harrisonburg, 57-; del, Dem. Nat. Conv, 68. Bus. & Prof. Pos: Desk Sgt, Harrisonburg Police Dept, Va, 45-63; license agent, Harrisonburg License Agency, 63; warrant justice, Dayton, Va, 65- Mil. Serv: Entered as Pvt, Army, 43, released as Cpl, after serv. in 35th Inf. Div, ETO, 44-45; recalled, 50-51, serv, in Korea; Bronze Star. Mem: Harrisonburg Lions Club (past pres); Elks (secy, 14 years); United Commercial Travelers. Rel: Presbyterian; Bd. Deacons, First Presbyterian Church, Harrisonburg. Mailing Add: 541 Maryland Ave, Harrisonburg, Va. 22801.

LEAKE, PAUL RAYMOND D
b. Dixon, Calif, 8/26/90; s. Edward E. Leake and Cecelia Snyder L; m. 10/6/14 to Aileen McFadden; c. Kenneth, Robert and Paula (Mrs. J.L. Porter). Educ: Univ. of Santa Clara, A.B, 12. Polit. & Govt. Pos: Collector of customs, Port of San Francisco, Calif, 39-52; mem, Calif. State Bd. of Equalization, 52- Bus. & Prof. Pos: Ed. and publisher, Woodland Daily Dem, 26- Mem: Calif. Newspaper Publishers Asn. (past pres); San Francisco Olympic Club. Rel: Catholic. Legal Res: 911 First St, Woodland, Calif. 95695. Mailing Add: State Board of Equalization, Box 1799, Sacramento, Calif. 95808.

LeaMOND, FREDERICK JULIAN D
S.C. State Rep.
b. Charleston, S.C, 3/5/05; s. Frederick Julian LeaMond and Marie Wing L; m. 2/16/26 to Catherine Frances Dowling; c. Frederick Julian, Jr, Harold Joseph, Catherine Ann, John Eugene and Jean Marie. Polit. & Govt. Pos: S.C. State Rep, 54-; consult. sea and airlift matters, House Cmt. on Armed Servs, U.S. Congress, 61-64. Bus. & Prof. Pos: Pres. and treas, Allied Paper Co, Charleston and Dangerous Materials Disposal Co, v.pres, Regis Milk Co. and dir, Cooper River Savings & Loan Asn, currently. Mil. Serv: Entered as Fireman 3/C, Navy, 26, retired as Capt, 51, after serv. as Commanding Officer of various types of Navy ships, all theaters; Bronze Star Medal with Combat V; Navy Commendation with Combat V; Naval Res. Medal with Star; Am. Defense Ribbon with Star; Am, ETO, African and Asiatic-Pac. Ribbons; Victory Medal; Expert Pistol and Expert Rifle Medals; Command-at-Sea Insignia. Mem: Mason (Past Master); Shrine; Rotary; Country Club; Propeller Club; Elks. Coach, U.S. Navy Boxing Team. Rel: Episcopal. Mailing Add: 165 St. Margaret St, Charleston, S.C. 29403.

LEARY, HILARY ASHBURN D
b. Old Trap, N.C, 8/23/12; s. Hilary Needham Leary and Carrie Ferebee L; m. 1/2/32 to Mary Wilson; c. Iris (Mrs. Curtis Perry). Educ: Univ. N.C, 28-32. Polit. & Govt. Pos: Constable and dep. sheriff, Camden, N.C, 34-36; exec. chmn, Camden Dem. Party, 59-66; campaign mgr. for Gov. Terry Sanford, 60, Lt. Gov. Bob Scott, 64 and N.C. State Sen. Everette Jordan, 66, Camden Co; magistrate, 66- Bus. & Prof. Pos: Farmer and produce dealer, 32-62; security chief, Hayes Int, Weeksville, N.C, 62-65; security guard, N.C. Ports Authority, 65-66. Mem: WOW; Farm Bur; Mason; Ruritan. Rel: Baptist. Mailing Add: Camden, N.C. 27921.

LEARY, JEREMIAH R. D
R.I. State Sen.
b. Hartford, Conn, 11/25/40; s. Richard B. Leary and Mary Sullivan L; m. 8/15/67 to Lisa Donohue; c. Richard B. and John Philip. Educ: Col. Holy Cross, A.B, 62; Univ. Va, LL.B, 65; Phi Alpha Delta. Polit. & Govt. Pos: R.I. State Sen, 69- Bus. & Prof. Pos: Attorney-at-law, 66- Mil. Serv: Lt, Naval Res, 67- Mem: Newport Co. Bar Asn; K. of C; Lions. Rel: Roman Catholic. Mailing Add: 68 Narragansett Ave, Tiverton, R.I. 02878.

LEARY, WILLIAM CORNELIUS D
Conn. State Rep.
b. Hartford, Conn, 8/4/38; s. Elmer Gerald Leary and Wilhelmina Driscoll L; single. Educ: Providence Col, A.B, 60; Univ. Conn. Sch. Law, LL.B, 65. Polit. & Govt. Pos: Mem, Windsor Locks Dem. Town Cmt, Conn; mem, Seventh Sen. Dist. Orgn; secy, Citizens Charter Study Cmt, 61; chmn, Windsor Locks Police Cmn, 63-65; chmn, Citizens' Adv. Cmt, 66; Conn. State Rep, currently. Bus. & Prof. Pos: Partner, Alfano, Bumster & Leary, 68- Mil. Serv: Conn. Air Nat. Guard. Mem: Am, Conn. and Hartford Co. Bar Asns; K. of C; Lions. Rel: Roman Catholic. Mailing Add: 60 Suffield St, Windsor Locks, Conn. 06096.

LEASE, M. HARRY, JR. D
b. Plainfield, Ind, 8/15/27; s. Martin Harry Lease and Beatrice Irene Krebs L; m. 9/6/69 to Jeanne Marie Lachance. Educ: Ind. Univ, Bloomington, B.A, 53, M.A, 55, Ph.D, 61; Pi Sigma Alpha. Polit. & Govt. Pos: Del, Dem-Farmer-Labor Co, Cong. Dist. and State Conv, Minn, 62 & 68; Dem. precinct chmn, Duluth, 62-69; chmn, 61st Legis. Dist, 64-65; city chmn, Dem-Farmer-Labor Party, 65-67; del, Dem. Nat. Conv, 68. Bus. & Prof. Pos: Instr, Univ. Miami, 55-56; assoc. prof. polit. sci. and asst. dean, grad. sch, Univ. Minn, Duluth, 57- Mem: Am. Polit. Sci. Asn; Midwest Polit. Sci. Asn; Am. Asn. Univ. Prof. Nat. Center for Educ. in Polit. fel, West. States Dem. Conf, 62-63. Mailing Add: Dept. of Political Science, University of Minnesota Graduate School, Duluth, Minn. 55812.

LEASURE, KENNETH SAY R
N.Y. State Assemblyman
b. Beaver, Pa, 5/31/23; s. Clyde Wilson Leasure and Florence Say L; m. 12/16/43 to Mary Kathryn Goehring. Educ: Univ. Mich, A.B, 48 and LL.B, 49. Polit. & Govt. Pos: Campaign chmn, Rep. Party, Endicott, N.Y, 59; mem, West Union Rep, 59-61, chmn. exec. cmt, 66; del, N.Y. Rep. Conv, 66; N.Y. State Assemblyman, 123rd Dist, 67- Mil. Serv: Entered as Aviation Cadet, Army Air Force, 42, released as 1st Lt, 45, after serv. as Aerial Navigator, 485th Bomb Group, N.Africa, Italy, S.France, 44; Silver Star; Air Medal with 3 Clusters; Purple Heart; Presidential Unit Citation; European-African-Middle East. Ribbons with 6 Battle Stars; 1st Lt, Army Air Force Res, 45-55. Mem: Broome Co. Bar Asn. (dir, 58-60); N.Y. State Bar Asn; Kiwanis (pres, Endicott Club, 65); C. of C. (v.pres, 63-64); Broome Co. C. of C; VFW; Am. Legion; Binghamton Country Club. Rel: Presbyterian; Elder, First Presbyterian Church, Endicott, N.Y; v.pres. bd. trustees, Susquehanna Presbytery. Legal Res: 500 Marcella St, Endicott, N.Y. 13760. Mailing Add: Professional Bldg, 101 Jefferson Ave, Endicott, N.Y. 13760.

LEATHERMAN, CLARENCE EDWIN D
N.C. State Rep.
b. Bessemer City, N.C, 7/2/25; s. E.Y. Leatherman and Essie Pendleton L; m. 4/5/52 to Charlesanna Walker; c. Celia Ann, Rhonda Kay and Lamont E. Educ: Gardner-Webb Col, 41-42; Appalachian State Teachers Col, 46-47; Univ. of Tenn, Col. of Law, LL.B, 49. Polit. & Govt. Pos: Del, Young Dem. Nat. Conv, 56; mem, Lincoln Co. Young Dem. Club, 56-58, secy, 57-60; state parliamentarian, Young Dem. Club, 58; N.C. State Rep, 61- Bus. & Prof. Pos: Lawyer. Mil. Serv: Navy, RM3C (LC), 44-46. Mem: N.C. and Am. Bar Asns; N.C. State Bar; 27th Judicial Bar Asn; K. of P. Rel: Baptist. Mailing Add: 307 N. Roberts Ave, Lincolnton, N.C. 28092.

LEATHERMAN, JEFFERSON FRANKLIN R
Mem, Calif. Rep. State Cent. Cmt.
b. Tucson, Ariz, 5/3/43; s. John Dan Leatherman and Parthene Jesse Stockton L; m. 11/4/61 to Jill Melinda LaDue. Educ: San Diego State Col, 1 year; San Diego City Col, 3 years; Calif. Young Rep. Col. Fedn. Polit. & Govt. Pos: Worker, San Diego Co. Rep. Precinct Orgn, Calif, 64-67, capt, 66-67, registrn. coordinator, 67; mem, Calif. Rep. State Cent. Cmt, 69- Bus. & Prof. Pos: Field rep, Guardian Ins. Co, San Diego, 66; independent ins. agent, 67; Rep. co. coordinator, 68; mkt. consult, Mgt. Clearing, Inc, Phoenix, Ariz, 69- Mil. Serv: Entered as AR, Navy, 60, released as Hospitalman 3/C, 66, after serv. in Haval Hosp, San Diego and U.S.S. Oriskany; Nat. Defense Medal; Vietnam Serv. Ribbon. Publ: Several manuals for use by Rep. Precinct Orgn. in San Diego Co. Rel: Protestant. Legal Res: 1315 Somermont Dr Dr, El Cajon, Calif. 92020. Mailing Add: 4429 N. 44th St, Phoenix, Ariz. 85018.

LEAVEL, WILLARD HAYDEN D
Mem, Colo. Dem. State Cent. Cmt.
b. Columbia, Mo, 7/28/27; s. Willard Hayden Leavel and Beatrice Temmen L; single. Educ: Univ. Denver, BA & MA, 48-53; Univ. Wash-Seattle, Ph.D, 53-60; Phi Beta Kappa, Omicron Delta Kappa, Phi Sigma Alpha, Acacia. Polit. & Govt. Pos: Campaign mgr, Wes Uhlman, Wash. House Rep, 58 & 60; mem, King Co. Dem. Exec. Cmt, 59-60; campaign mgr, Mark Hogan for Colo. House Rep, 64 & Lt. Gov, 66; chmn, Dem. Cmt. on Reapportionment, 65; mem, Denver Co. Dem. Cent. Cmt, 65-, capt-at-lg, 65-; mem, Colo. Dem. State Cent. Cmt, 67-; chmn, Cmt. to Elect a Dem. Legis, 68. Bus. & Prof. Pos: Instr, Univ. Wash, 58-60; asst. prof, Wis. State Col, Eau Claire, 60-62; assoc. prof, Univ. Denver, 62- Mil. Serv: Entered as Pvt, Air Force, 46, released as Cpl, 47. Publ: Campaign, Prentice-Hall, 60. Mem: Am. Asn. Univ. Prof; West. Polit. Sci. Asn. Mailing Add: 2037 S. Milwaukee, Denver, Colo. 80210.

LEAVITT, DIXIE L. R
Utah State Sen.
b. St. George, Utah, 8/27/29; s. Vincen E. Leavitt and Erma Leavitt L; m. 6/30/49 to Anne Okerlund; c. Michael O, Dane O, Mark O, Eric O. and David O. Educ: Col. of Southern Utah, grad; Utah State Univ, grad. Polit. & Govt. Pos: Utah State Rep, 63-65; Utah State Sen, 65- Bus. & Prof. Pos: Pres, Dixie Leavitt Ins. Agency, 55- Mem: Kiwanis. Rel: Latter-day Saint. Mailing Add: 393 S. 700 West, Cedar City, Utah 84720. (1967)

LEAVITT, JAMES F. R
N.H. State Rep.
b. North Hampton, N.H, 11/28/90; married; c. one son. Educ: North Hampton Pub. Schs; Hampton High Sch. Polit. & Govt. Pos: Past moderator, auditor and mem, Zoning Bd, North Hampton; treas, Winnacunnet High Sch; N.H. State Rep, currently. Mem: F&AM (Past Master, St. Johns Lodge No. 1, Portsmouth, N.H); all Scottish Rite Bodies. Rel: Congregational. Mailing Add: 261 Atlantic Ave, North Hampton, N.H. 03862.

LEAVITT, LEVI DUDLEY R
Vt. State Rep.
b. East Barnard, Vt, 3/23/98; m. to Josephine E. Moore; c. Three sons and four daughters. Educ: S. Royalton High Sch; U.V.M. Polit. & Govt. Pos: Town lister, 27 years; chmn, Rep. Town Cmt; Vt. State Rep, 59- Bus. & Prof. Pos: Real estate & ins. broker. Mil. Serv: AEF 102nd Machine Gun Batt, 17-19. Mem: East Barnard Grange; F&AM. Rel: Methodist. Mailing Add: South Royalton, Vt. 05068. (1967)

LEBAMOFF, IVAN A. D
Chmn, Allen Co. Dem. Party, Ind.
b. Fort Wayne, Ind, 7/20/32; s. Argire V. Lebamoff and Helen Katsandonoff L; m. 6/9/63 to Katherine Stephanoff; c. Damian I. and Jordan I. Educ: Ind. Univ, A.B, 54; Ind. Univ. Law Sch, J.D, 57; Phi Alpha Theta; Phi Delta Phi. Polit. & Govt. Pos: U.S. Cmnr, North. Dist. of Ind, 62; del, Dem. Nat. Conv, 68; chmn, Allen Co. Dem. Party, Ind, 68- Bus. & Prof. Pos: Partner,

Lebamoff & Ver Wiebe, Ft. Wayne, Ind, 68- Mil. Serv: Entered as Airman Basic, Air Force, 58, released as A/1C, 64, after serv. in Air Guard, France, 62-63. Mem: Ind. and Am. Bar Asns; Mason. Rel; Eastern Orthodox. Legal Res: 205 E. Packard, Fort Wayne, Ind. 46806. Mailing Add: 1310 Anthony Wayne Bank Bldg., Fort Wayne, Ind. 46802.

LEBENBOM, DAVID D
Chmn, Wayne Co. Dem. Cmt, Mich.
b. N.Y.C, 7/7/25; s. Morris Lebenbom and Lena Jacobowitz L; m. 5/30/57 to Elaine C. Friedman; c. Miriam, Sallie, Matthew and Michael. Educ: Wayne State Univ; Columbia Law Sch. Polit. & Govt. Pos: Attorney, Mich. State Racing Cmn, 53-56; chmn, Wayne Co. Dem. Cmt, 60-; chmn, State Bd. of Canvassers, 61-64, mem, 64- Mil. Serv: Entered as Pvt, Air Force, 43, released as Sgt, 66, after serv. in ETO; ETO Medal with Battle Star. Mem: V.chmn, Mich. Bar Asn. Cmt. on Equal Opportunities; Standard City Club; Econ. Club of Detroit; Mason (32°); Law Rev. Cmt, Mich, 66- Rel: Jewish. Legal Res: 3529 Sherbourne Rd, Detroit, Mich. 48221. Mailing Add: 2118 Guardian Bldg, Detroit, Mich. 48226. (1967)

LEBLANC, CHARLES JOHN R
Mem, Rep. State Cent. Cmt, La.
b. Plattenville, La, 7/15/98; s. Ernest T. Leblanc and Alice Fremin L; single. Educ: St. James High Sch. Polit. & Govt. Pos: Mem, Rep. State Cent. Cmt, La, 56-; W. Baton Rouge Parish Dir, U.S. Census, 60. Publ: 'Poetry,' Am. Poets and Songwriter, 49; 'Poetry,' Talent, Songwriters and Poets, 47. Mem: Am. Soc, Composers, Authors, Publishers; Boy's Town. Rel: Pentacostal. Legal Res: 470 Michigan Ave, Port Allen, La. 70767. Mailing Add: Box 443, Port Allen, La. 70767.

LEBLANC, J. LOUIS D
Mass. State Rep.
b. New Bedford, Mass, 1/6/40; s. Joseph Ernest Leblanc and Loretta Pontbriand L; m. 6/4/66 to Claudette Mary Lucy Gautreau; c. Michelle C. and Marc A. Educ: Southeast. Mass. Tech. Inst, B.S. in Bus. Admin, 62; Portia Law Sch, LL.B, 66; Delta Kappa Phi. Polit. & Govt. Pos: City councillor, New Bedford, Mass, 62-65; Mass. State Rep, 65- Mem: Mass. Legislators Asn; K. of C. Youngest man ever elected to public office in history of New Bedford. Rel: Roman Catholic. Mailing Add: 3735 Acushnet Ave, New Bedford, Mass. 02745.

LeBLANC, J. LUKE D
La. State Rep.
b. Abbeville, La, 1/30/23; s. Odeon LeBlanc and Cecile Lormand L; m. 7/11/43 to Ruth Trahan; c. Glenn W. and Jerry L. Educ: Lafayette High Sch. Polit. & Govt. Pos: Mem, Lafayette Parish Police Jury, La, 56-64; chmn, Lafayette City Dem. Exec. Cmt, 60-64; La. State Rep, 64- Bus. & Prof. Pos: Barber, Lafayette, La, 47-64; real estate broker, 64- Mil. Serv: Entered as Pvt, Army, 43, released as Sgt, 45, after serv. in Corps of Engrs, Normandy, North. France, Rhineland; Good Conduct Medal; Europe-Africa-Middle East Theatre Medal. Mem: Am. Legion; WOW; U.S.L. Century Club; Labor Local Union. Rel: Catholic. Mailing Add: 151 S. Acadian Dr, Lafayette, La. 70505.

LeBLANC, JOHN DENNIS D
b. Delcambre, La, 5/18/09; s. Joseph A. LeBlanc and Nelia L; m. 12/26/36 to Claire Landry; c. Phyllis, Patrick C. and John Dennis, Jr. Educ: La. State Univ, B.A. in educ; Tau Kappa Nu; Phi Delta Kappa. Polit. & Govt. Pos: City clerk, Delcambre, La, 45-63; mem, Iberia Parish Sch. Bd, 51-66; chmn, Iberia Parish Dem. Exec. Cmt, 54-68; mem, Port Cmn, Delcambre, 59- Bus. & Prof. Pos: Operator of cattle farm; high sch. teacher, asst. prin. and basketball coach, Iberia Parish Sch, 40-58, adult educ. supvr, 58- Mem: La. Sugar Cane Festival Asn; WOW, secy, La. 532, 15 years; YMBC; La, Iberia Parish and Nat. Educ. Asns; bd. dirs, S.W. La. Livestock Asn; La. Cattlemen's Asn; Delcambre Shrimp Festival Asn; pres, Adult Educ. Asn. for La. Named Mr. Woodman, 58. Rel: Catholic. Mailing Add: 206 Bourque St, Delcambre, La. 70528. (1967)

LeBOUTILLIER, PHILIP, JR. R
Mem, Ohio Rep. Finance Cmt.
b. N.Y.C, 2/24/16; s. Philip LeBoutillier and Gertrude H. Tifft L; m. 7/13/40 to Felia Ford; c. Philip Grandin, George Ford and Ford. Educ: Princeton Univ, A.B. cum laude, 38. Polit. & Govt. Pos: Dep. Asst. Secy of Defense for Supply and Logistics, 59-60; mem, Ohio Rep. Finance Cmt. and co-chmn, Lucas Co. Rep. Finance Cmt, currently. Bus. & Prof. Pos: Pres, Ottawa River Paper Co, 48-58; v.pres, Mead Containers, Inc, 58; chmn. and pres, Hixon-Peterson Lumber Co, 58-60; gen. partner, Collin, Norton & Co, 61-64; v.pres, Clark Dodge & Co, Inc, 64- Mil. Serv: Entered as Ens, Navy, 42, released as Comdr, 45, after serv. in N.Atlantic Patrol, Caribbean, Normandy, Philippines and Iwo Jima; Silver Star; Secy. of Defense Meritorious Serv. Award Medal. Mem: Dir, Boys' Clubs of Am; trustee, Boys' Clubs of Toledo; Exec. Cmt, Commun. Improv. Corp, Toledo. Rel: Episcopal. Legal Res: 29407 E. River Rd, Perrysburg, Ohio 43551. Mailing Add: 506 Madison Ave, Toledo, Ohio 43604.

LECH, CHESTER D
b. Central Falls, R.I, 7/19/14; m. to Emily E. Cassola. Educ: Joseph Jenks Jr. High Sch. Polit. & Govt. Pos: Mem, Central Falls City Coun, 2 terms; R.I. State Rep, 59-69. Bus. & Prof. Pos: Clerk. Mil. Serv: Navy, $7\frac{1}{2}$ years, Gunners Mate 2/C, Am, Pac. Theaters; Korean War, 1 year. Mem: Elks; Am. Legion; Polish-Am. VFW; Polish Cong. of Am; Pulaski Mutual Aid Soc; Polish-Am. Citizens Club. Mailing Add: 120 Summit St, Central Falls, R.I. 02863. (1967)

LECHOWICZ, THADDEUS STANLEY D
Ill. State Rep.
b. Chicago, Ill, 12/20/38; s. Frank Lechowicz and Rose Loboda L; m. 9/12/64 to Suzanne N. Keiler; c. Edward John. Educ: Wright Jr. Col, Chicago, Ill, A.A, 58; N. Park Col, B.A, 60; De Paul Univ, 1 year; Delta Sigma Pi; Newman Club; bd. dirs, W.N.P.C; Kiwanis; Commerce Club, De Paul Univ. Polit. & Govt. Pos: 35th ward rep, Young Dem. of Cook Co. and Ill, 60-68; 35th ward bd. dirs, Regular Dem. Orgn, Ill, 60-69; w. area chmn, Young Dem. of Cook Co, 62-63, Eighth Cong. Dist. chmn, 66; Cook Co. regional dir, Young Dem. of Ill, 65-67, second v.pres, 68; Ill. State Rep, 15th Dist, 69-, mem, Appropriations and Munic. Cmts, Ill. House of Rep, 69- Bus. & Prof. Pos: Dir. data processing, Ill. Toll Hwy. Cmn, 65, asst. dir. finance, 66-68; sr. syst. analyst, Cook Co, 69- Mil. Serv: 1st Lt, Army Res, 68; Outstanding Trainee of the Cycle, Ft. Leonard Wood, Mo. Mem: Data Processing Mgt. Asn; Am. Mgt. Asn; finance cmt, Int. Bridge Tunnel & Turnpike Asn, 67-68; K. of C; Holy Name Soc; Amvets; Polish Nat. Alliance; Chicago Soc; founder and past pres, Lockwood Improvement Asn. Outstanding Young Dem, State of Ill, 69. Rel: Catholic. Mailing Add: 5058 W. Altgeld St, Chicago, Ill. 60639.

LECKMAN, HENRY T. D
Mayor, Coalinga, Calif.
b. Pasadena, Calif, 8/24/24; s. Henry Theodore Leckman and Louise Arnold L; m. 8/4/56 to Barbara Kent Mattox; c. Susan Ann, Helene Katherine and Patricia Leigh. Educ: Stanford Univ, B.A, 46; Hastings Col. of Law, J.D, 50; Alpha Delta Phi. Polit. & Govt. Pos: Mem, Fresno Co. Dem. Cmt, Calif, 56-64; councilman, Coalinga, Calif, 62-66 and mayor, 68-; mem, Calif. Dem. State Cent. Cmt, 66- Mil. Serv: Entered as Seaman, Navy, 42, released as Lt, 46, after serv. in Pac. Theatre, 44-46 and re-entered as Lt, 50-52, serv. in Korea. Mem: Calif. State Bar; Am. Bar Asn; Elks; Am. Legion. Rel: Episcopal. Legal Res: 1512 Coalinga St, Coalinga, Calif. 93210. Mailing Add: 135 E. Elm Ave, Coalinga, Calif. 93210.

LECLERC, CHARLES J. D
N.H. State Rep.
b. Manchester, N.H, 7/10/12; married; c. Four. Educ: Manchester Schs. Polit. & Govt. Pos: Clerk, Old Age Laws Study Cmt, N.H, 46; N.H. State Rep, currently, former chmn, Manchester Del, N.H. State House of Rep. Bus. & Prof. Pos: Diemaker. Mem: Pres, Diemaker Local 136 AFL, 50-52. Rel: Catholic. Mailing Add: 275 Somerville St, Manchester, N.H. 03103. (1967)

LeCOMPTE, KARL MILES R
b. Corydon, Iowa, 5/25/87; s. Charles Francis LeCompte and Hannah Miles L; m. 8/10/27 to Dorothy Tye. Educ: Univ. Iowa, B.A, 09; Sigma Delta Chi; Sigma Delta Kappa; Phi Theta Pi. Polit. & Govt. Pos: Iowa State Sen, 16-20; U.S. Rep, Iowa, 38-58. Bus. & Prof. Pos: Publisher, Corydon Times-Rep. Mil. Serv: Army, 18. Mem: Iowa Hist. Soc; Mason; Elk; K. of P. Mailing Add: Corydon, Iowa 50060.

LE CONTE, DOROTHY TEAGAR D
Mem, Exec. Cmt, Calif. Dem. State Cent. Cmt.
b. St. Louis, Mo; d. J. Staley Teagar and Mary Louie Van Sant T; m. to Joseph Le Conte; c. Joseph, Jr. and John. Educ: Univ. Calif, Berkeley, A.B; Univ. Calif, Los Angeles, M.A, 65, doctoral cand, currently; Falk fel; Prytanean; Pi Kappa Alpha; Delta Delta Delta. Polit. & Govt. Pos: Alternate del, Dem. Nat. Conv, 48; secy, Kern Co. Dem. Cent. Cmt, Calif, 48-52; mem, Calif. Dem. State Cent. Cmt, 48-54, 60-62 & 68-, mem. exec. cmt, 50-54 & 68-, co-chmn, 28th Cong. Dist, 68-; chmn, North. Calif. Women for Stevenson, 52; field rep. for Congressman Harlan Hagen, 53-54; mgr, 46th Assembly Dist. Dem. Campaign, 60; South. Calif. coordinator, Mosk for Attorney Gen, 62; women's chmn, S.Bay Cmt. for Salinger for U.S. Senate, 64; state v.chmn, Dem. Vol. of Calif, 67-; del, Dem. Nat. Conv, 68. Bus. & Prof. Pos: Prof. polit. sci, Calif. State Col. at Long Beach, 68- Mem: Am. Polit. Sci. Asn; Nat. Coun. Soc. Studies; League Women Voters; Am. Asn. Univ. Women (past br. pres. and state officer); UN Asn; Rolling Hills Commun. Asn.(past pres); Palos Verdes Peninsula Friends of Libr; Am. Field Serv; life mem, PTA. Rel: United Church of Christ. Mailing Add: 8 Hackamore Rd, Rolling Hills, Calif. 90274.

LeCRAW, JULIAN R
First V.Chmn, Fulton Co. Rep. Party, Ga.
b. Atlanta, Ga, 5/21/30; s. Roy LeCraw and Julia Adams L; m. 8/8/52 to Joanne Sue DeLany; c. Suzanne Alice, Ellen Elaine and Julian, Jr. Educ: Ga. Inst. of Tech, B.S. in indust. mgt, 52; Woodrow Wilson Col. of Law, LL.B, 58; Chi Phi. Polit. & Govt. Pos: Alternate del, Rep. Nat. Conv, 64; first v.chmn, Fulton Co. Rep. Party, Ga, 64- Mil. Serv: Entered as Ens, Navy, 52, released as Lt.(jg), 55, after serv. in Amphibious Forces in Atlantic; Lt, Naval Res, 60-; Korean Serv. Medal. Mem: Capital City Club; Commerce Club; mem, Chair Pvt. Enterprise, Ga. State Col; pres, Atlanta Country Club Estates. Multi-Engine and Instrument Rated Pilot. Rel: Presbyterian. Mailing Add: 3445 Wood Valley Rd. N.W, Atlanta, Ga. 30327. (1967)

LECY, RAYMOND OSCAR R
Mem, Wood Co. Rep. Exec. Cmt, Wis.
b. Chicago, Ill, 6/25/27; s. Curtis M. Lecy and Marie Vetrano L; m. 6/12/48 to Lorraine Kreuser; c. Vicki, Teresa, Joni, Ray, Jr, Gary and Lori. Educ: Wis. State Univ, B.E, 52; Univ. Wis, Madison, M.S, 60. Polit. & Govt. Pos: Young Rep. chmn, Wis. State Univ, 51; co-chmn, State Young Rep. for Taft, 51-52; state treas, Wis. Fedn. of Young Rep, 51-52, first v.chmn, 53-54, publicity dir, 55; secy, Wood Co. Rep. Party, 54-59, v.chmn, 60-66, chmn, 67-68; secy, Seventh Cong. Sr. Rep. Dist, 56-60; Rep. precinct committeeman, Grand Rapids, 60-69; mem, Wood Co. Rep. Exec. Cmt, 69- Bus. & Prof. Pos: Prin, Woodside Sch, Wis. Rapids, Wis, 60-69. Mil. Serv: Entered as A/S, Navy, 45, released as Yeoman 3/C, 46, after serv. at Naval Air Sta, Pac. Sta. Command, 45-46; Unit Commendation. Mem: Phi Delta Kappa; Wis. Educ. Asn; Wis. Elem. Prin. Asn; pres, Wood Co. Educ. Asn, 59-60; secy, Wis. Rapids Prin. Asn, 67-68; Elks. Rel: Catholic. Mailing Add: 3751 Seventh St. S, Wisconsin Rapids, Wis. 54494.

LEDBETTER, CALVIN REVILLE, JR. D
Ark. State Rep.
b. Little Rock, Ark, 4/29/29; s. Calvin Reville Ledbetter and Virginia Campbell L; m. 7/26/53 to Mary Brown Williams; c. Grainger, Jeffrey and Snow. Educ: Princeton Univ, B.A, 51; Univ. Ark. Law Sch, LL.B, 54; Northwest. Univ, Ph.D, 60; Phi Alpha Theta; Blue Key; Phi Delta Theta; Sigma Alpha Epsilon; Student Sen, Univ. Ark. Polit. & Govt. Pos: Chmn, Pulaski Co. Community Action Prog, Ark, 65; mem. exec. cmt, Young Dem. of Ark, 65-66; Ark. State Rep, 67-; del, Dem. Nat. Conv, 68; mem, Citizens Adv. Cmt. to City Govt, Little Rock, Ark, 69- Bus. & Prof. Pos: Mem. bd. trustees, Philander Smith Col, Ark, 63-68; bd. dir, Health and Welfare Coun. of Pulaski Co, 65-68; mem. Ark, Adv. Coun. of Pub. Elem. and Sec. Educ, 69- Mil. Serv: Entered as 1st Lt, Army, 55-57, after serv. in Judge Adv. Gen. Corps, Hq. U.S. Army Europe, Heidelberg, Germany, 55-57, Capt, Army Res, 57-59.

Publ: Annulment by Parents Minors Above Statutory Marriage Age, fall 53 and Property-Recognition of Rights in Ideas, Schemes, and Plans, spring 54, Ark. Law Rev. Mem: Am. Acad. Polit. & Soc. Sci; Am. Polit. Sci. Asn; Nat. Soc. of State Legislators; Am, Ark. and Pulaski Co. Bar Asns; South. Polit. Sci. Asn; Ark. Acad. Sci; Ark. Hist. Asn; Ark. Educ. Asn.(first v.pres, dept. higher educ, 63); Rotary. Educator of the Year, 68. Rel: Presbyterian; Deacon, 63-66; Elder, 69- Mailing Add: 3230 Ozark, Little Rock, Ark. 72205.

LEDBETTER, JOEL YOWELL D
Ark. State Rep.
b. Little Rock, Ark, 2/19/11; s. Calvin Reville Ledbetter and Snow Yowell L; m. 2/2/37 to Julia Katharine Bond; c. Virginia, Joel, Jr. and Julia. Educ: Wash. Univ, B.S.B.A, 33; Phi Delta Theta. Polit. & Govt. Pos: Ark. State Rep, 49-, chmn, Legis Coun, Ark. House of Rep, 63-65. Bus. & Prof. Pos: Asst. mgr, Hewled Mfg. Co, 33-35; salesman, Williams and Rosen Ins, 35-46; v.pres, Boyle Realty Co, 46-66. Mil. Serv: Entered as 1st Lt, Army Air Force, 40, released as Lt. Col, 45, after serv. in Air Transport Command, U.S, India-Burma-China, 41-45; Lt. Col.(Ret), Air Force Res, 55; Bronze Star, Am, Pac, Asian and ETO Ribbons; Presidential Citation; Chinese Medal of Serv. Mem: Rotary; C. of C; Am. Legion; VFW. Mo. Valley Swimming Champion Freestyle Dash, 30-32. Rel: Presbyterian. Legal Res: 4610 Crestwood Dr, Little Rock, Ark. 72207. Mailing Add: Boyle Bldg, Little Rock, Ark. 72201.

LEDDY, JOHN M. D
b. Chicago, Ill, 6/29/14; m. to Louise Crawford; c. Thomas Byron Crawford. Educ: Georgetown Univ, B.S. For. Serv, 41. Polit. & Govt. Pos: Mem. staff, Pan Am. Union, 37-41; econ, financial and soc. policy adv, State Dept, 41-57; spec. asst. to Under Secy. of State, 57-61; Asst. Secy. of the Treas. for Int. Affairs, 61-62; U.S. Ambassador to Orgn. for Econ. Coop. and Develop, Paris, 62-65; Asst. Secy. of State for European Affairs, 65-69. Mailing Add: 1619 Brookside Rd, McLean, Va. 22101.

LEDERER, WILLIAM J. D
b. Philadelphia, Pa, 12/14/24; s. Miles W. Lederer and Susan Scullin L. Educ: LaSalle Col, A.B; Temple Univ. Law Sch, LL.B; Alpha Epsilon; Tau Epsilon Rho. Polit. & Govt. Pos: Judge Advocate; pres, Young Dem, Phila, Pa, 53; mem, Dem. Co. Cmt, 54-, former Sgt. at Arms; chmn, Dem. Vet. Cmt; gen. coun, Registr. of Wills; first dep. secy. of rev. to Judge Gerald Gleason; spec. dep. attorney gen; legis. asst. to Dem. Minority Leader; chmn, Phila. Vet. Cmn, 57-64, former Vet. Cmnr, Pa. State Rep, 64-68; mem, Legis. Task Force on State Taxes, 68. Mem: Phila. and Am. Bar Asns; Am. Trial Lawyers' Soc; John F. Kennedy Club Phila.(chmn. and founder). Mailing Add: 1237 Shackamaxon St, Philadelphia, Pa. 19125.

LEDERMAN, JACK SHERER D
State Treas, Nebr. Dem. Party
b. Lincoln, Nebr, 10/3/13; s. Morris Lederman and Jennie Epstien L; m. 5/31/38 to Helyn Shryer; c. Joel, Judith Ann and Brenda Sue. Polit. & Govt. Pos: Co. supvr, Buffalo Co, Nebr, 62-66; state treas, Nebr. Dem. Party, 65- Bus. & Prof. Pos: Chmn, hosp. adv. bd, Good Samaritan Hosp, 60. Mem: Bd. of trustees, Kearney Elks Lodge 984; bd. of dirs, Kearney Lions Club, 62; Kearney Country Club; Kearney C. of C. Rel: Hebrew. Legal Res: 3314 Fifth Ave, Kearney, Nebr. 68847. Mailing Add: P.O. Box 37, Kearney, Nebr. 68847.

LEDGER, LOVETT LEWIS D
b. Florence, Tex, 12/11/09; s. Logan Ledger and Francis Lewis L; m. 2/12/34 to Lea Roy Thompson; c. Marky and Leslie. Educ: Daniel Baker Col, B.S. in Educ, 36. Polit. & Govt. Pos: Pres, Copperas Cove Sch. Bd, Tex, 53-69; alternate del, Dem. Nat. Conv, 68; Dem. precinct chmn, Coryell Co, 69- Bus. & Prof. Pos: Owner-mgr, Ledger Furniture Co, 50-69; dir, Cove State Bank, 59-69; dir, Southwest Assoc. Furniture Buyers, Inc, 63-69. Mem: Committeeman, cmt. of 10, Tex. Asn. of Sch. Bd, 62-69; Mason; C. of C; Toastmaster Club. Citation of Merit, Copperas Cove VFW Ladies Auxiliary; Man of the Year, 58; Cert. of Serv, Copperas Cove PTA; Award of Merit, Retail Furniture Asn. of Tex. Rel: Methodist. Legal Res: 402 Urbantke Lane, Copperas Cove, Tex. 76522. Mailing Add: 104 E. Ave. D, Copperas Cove, Tex. 76522.

LEDMAN, ELDON DALE R
Chmn, Cass. Co. Rep. Cmt, Mich.
b. Viroqua, Wis, 6/17/12; m. 8/26/40 to Jean K. Gwilt. Educ: Univ. Wis, B.A; Delta Kappa Epsilon. Polit. & Govt. Pos: Chmn, Cass Co. Rep. Cmt, Mich, 67-; mem, Mich. State Rep. Cent. Cmt, currently. Bus. & Prof. Pos: Mfg. rep. Mem: Elks; Nat. 'W' Club. Legal Res: R.R. 5, Dowagiac, Mich. 49047. Mailing Add: P.O. Box 141, Dowagiac, Mich. 49047.

LEE, ADRIAN GORDON D
Chmn, Adams Co. Dem. Exec. Cmt, Miss.
b. Pinola, Miss, 8/3/29; married; c. Charmaine, Adrian, Jr. and Carolyn. Polit. & Govt. Pos: Miss. State Rep, Adams Co, 64-68; chmn, Adams Co. Dem. Conv, 68; chmn, Adams Co. Dem. Exec. Cmt, 68- Bus. & Prof. Pos: Businessman and farmer. Mem: Farm Bur; RAM; F&AM; Shrine; Pilots Int. Asn. Rel: Baptist. Mailing Add: 101 Woodville Dr, Natchez, Miss. 39120.

LEE, ALBERT
Auditor Gen, Mich.
b. Detroit, Mich, 12/15/10; m. to Delphine Baron; c. Helaine Sharon and Marc. Educ: Walsh Inst. of Acct. and Bus. Admin, grad, 42; Detroit Inst. of Tech; Beta Alpha Psi. Polit. & Govt. Pos: Auditor for contract termination div, U.S. Army Ord, 40-45; spec. consult. to former Auditors Gen. Frank S. Szymanski, Otis M. Smith and Billie S. Farnum; secy-treas, Mich. State Bd. of Acct, 59-63; v.chmn, Gov. Williams and Gov. Swainson Spec. Task Force on State Probs, 59-63; Auditor Gen, Mich, currently. Bus. & Prof. Pos: Pub. acct, 45-; founder and sr. partner, Albert Lee & Co, Detroit, 50-65. Mem: Am. Inst. of CPA; Mich. Asn. of CPA; Nat. Asn. of Acct; Am. Acct. Asn; Mason (32°); Crisis Club of Detroit. Mailing Add: Office of the Auditor, 567 Hollister Bldg, 108 W. Allegan, Lansing, Mich. 49033.

LEE, ALBERT RAY, JR. R
Chmn, Third Dist. Rep. Party, Miss.
b. Memphis. Tenn, 11/11/33; s. Albert Ray Lee and Nona Gillham L; m. 5/27/55 to Elisabeth Butler; c. Ray, III, Gay, Ammy, Ben and Jason. Educ: Southwest Miss. Jr. Col, 52-53; Univ. of South. Miss, B.S, 56; Univ. of Miss. Med. Sch, M.D, 63; Nu Sigma Nu. Polit. & Govt. Pos: Third Dist. Rep. Party, Miss, 67- Mem: Am. and Miss. State Med. Asns; Am. Acad. of Gen. Practice; Kiwanis (pres, Pearl Club, 66); C. of C.(pres, Liberty Chap, 69); Mason; Lions. Rel: Baptist. Mailing Add: Liberty, Miss. 39645.

LEE, ARTHUR T. R
b. Newport, R.I, 10/26/12; m. to Ann M. Brownell. Educ: De La Salle Acad; R.I. Col. of Educ, De La Salle Fathers Club, Alumni Asn. Polit. & Govt. Pos: Mem, Middletown Town Coun, R.I, 2 terms; R.I. State Rep, 59-68, Dep. Minority House Leader, 63-68. Bus. & Prof. Pos: R.I. State Police, 20 years; head, Plant Fire, Safety and Security, Raytheon Co. Mem: Lions; Elks; K. of C; Fraternal Order of Police; Harvard Asn. Police Sci. Mailing Add: 40 Dudley Ave. N, Middletown, R.I. 02840. (1967)

LEE, BILL H. R
b. Earth, Tex, 3/2/30; s. William Carrol Lee and Venona McNiell L; m. 3/2/56 to Pauline Marian Cummins; c. Lorena Lynette, Bonnie Jean and Julie Ann. Educ: Tex. Tech. Col, 48; Baylor Univ, B.A, 52; Univ. of Tex. Med. Br, M.D, 56; Nat. Biol. Hon. Soc; Taurus Soc; Phi Chi. Polit. & Govt. Pos: City health officer, Tex. State Dept. of Health, 62; precinct chmn, Castro Co. Rep. Party, Tex, 62, chmn, 63-68. Mem: Am. Chem. Soc; Am. Med. Asn; Tex. Med. Asn.(del. to conv, 63-64); secy, Tierra Blanca Med. Soc, 63; v.pres, C. of C, 65; Lions; Farm Bur. Rel: Episcopal. Legal Res: 706 Maple, Dimmitt, Tex. 79027. Mailing Add: Box 1038, Dimmitt, Tex. 79027. (1967)

LEE, BILLY JOE D
b. Arm, Miss, 3/14/29; married. Polit. & Govt. Pos: Miss. State Rep, 62-68. Bus. & Prof. Pos: Farmer; cattleman; merchant. Mem: Mason; Farm Bur; C. of C; Jaycees. Rel: Baptist. Mailing Add: Route 1, Box 190A, Silver Creek, Miss. 39663. (1967)

LEE, BLAIR, III D
Secy. of State, Md.
Mailing Add: State House, Annapolis, Md. 21404.

LEE, CATHERINE PATRICIA R
V.Chmn, Kent Co. Rep. Exec. Cmt, Mich.
b. Canonsburg, Pa, 6/13/25; d. Ruel Otis Redinger and Catherine M. Collins R; m. 7/8/50 to Albert Benjamin Lee; c. A. Scott, Mary Catherine and Mark Jorgenson. Educ: Miami Univ, B.A, 50; Alpha Omicron Pi. Polit. & Govt. Pos: Rep. precinct committeewoman, Broward Co, Fla, 63-64; v.chmn, Broward Co. Rep. Exec. Cmt, 64; acting chmn, Broward Co. Rep. Party, 65; Rep. precinct del, Kent Co, Mich, 68; v.chmn, Kent Co. Rep. Exec. Cmt, 69- Bus. & Prof. Pos: V.pres, Financial Investment Research & Develop. Co, 66- Mem: Delphian Soc; pres, Grand Rapids Civic Theatre Guild; Sigmas of Sigma Chi; Woman's City Club; Alpha Omicron Pi Alumni; Breadboard Guild of Blodgett Hosp; Cascade Country Club; Grand Rapids Yacht Club; Peninsular Club; Kent Co. Women's Rep. Club; South Kent Women's Rep. Club; Arthur Vandenburg Rep. Bus. and Prfnl. Women's Club. Rel: Roman Catholic. Mailing Add: 2150 Robinson Rd. S.E, East Grand Rapids, Mich. 49506.

LEE, CHARLES MARKS R
b. N.Y.C, 4/21/14; s. David Lee and Theresa Marks L; m. 8/2/42 to Anita Karpen. Educ: City Col. New York; Brooklyn Law Sch. of St. Lawrence Univ. Polit. & Govt. Pos: Asst. U.S. Attorney, South. Dist, N.Y, 53-55; Spec. Asst. Attorney-Gen, N.Y, 56-57; mem. exec. cmt, Bronx Co. Rep. Cmt, 61-66; counsel to Bronx Borough Pres, 62; N.Y. State Rep. Committeeman, 62-66; cmnr, Dept. Mkts, N.Y.C, 66-68; dir, N.Y.C. Firearms Control Bd, 68- Mil. Serv: Entered as Pvt, Army, 42, released as Pfc, 46, after serv. in 69th Inf. Div, ETO; Bronze Star; Presidential Citation; Med. Inf. Combat Badge; Good Conduct Medal; ETO Medal with 4 Battle Stars. Mem: Fed. Bar Asns. of N.Y, N.J. and Conn; Bronx Co. and N.Y. State Bar Asns; N.Y. State Plaintiffs' Trial Lawyers' Asn; Elks; B'nai B'rith; Am. Legion; Jewish War Vets; 69th Inf. Div. Asn. Rel: Hebrew. Mailing Add: 2155 Paulding Ave, New York, N.Y. 10462.

LEE, CLYDE D
b. McCellan Township, Ill, 2/6/09; m. to Bernice Rough L; c. Virginia Ann, John Edward. Educ: Mt. Vernon Township High Sch, 28. Polit. & Govt. Pos: Ill. State Rep, until 66; Ill. State Sen, 40; Ill. State Rep, 38-40; City Treas, Jefferson City, 34; City Treas, Mt. Vernon, 33; Ill. Legis. Coun; Sch. Problems Cmt. Bus. & Prof. Pos: Ins. Bus. Mil. Serv: U.S. Marine Corps, 43-45. Mailing Add: 818 Pace Ave, Mt. Vernon, Ill. 62864. (1967)

LEE, D. R. 'JACK' D
b. Shivers, Miss, 1/12/23; s. Dallas R. Lee and Willie Leona Manchester L; m. 7/19/44 to Montel Elizabeth Erickson; c. Marlene Fern (Mrs. Davidson), Douglas Arwell, Katrine Montel, Darrell Alfred and Kristeen Lanay. Educ: Spring Arbor Col, 41-43; Greenville Col, B.A, 49; Miss. Col, M.Ed, 65; Northwest. State Col, 66; Kappa Delta Pi. Polit. & Govt. Pos: Chmn. and mem, LaSalle Parish Dem. Exec. Cmt, La, 60-68; mem, Welfare Bd, 60-, chmn, 64- Bus. & Prof. Pos: Credit mgr, Billups Petroleum Co, 49-50; salesman and agent, Standard Oil Co, 50-57; mem, Parish and State Teachers Asns, 57-; supvr, LaSalle Parish Schs, 66-; v.pres. and mem, Eighth Dist. Supvr. Asn. and mem, State Supvr. Asn, 66- Mil. Serv: Pvt, Army, 46, serv. in 181st Signal Corp, Tex. and La. Mem: Lions; Cenla Agr. Asn; La. Teachers Asn. Rel: Free Methodist. Legal Res: Route 1, Box 54, Olla, La. 71465. Mailing Add: P.O. Box 915, Jena, La. 71342.

LEE, FRANCES MARRON R
Rep. Nat. Committeewoman, N.Mex.
b. Albuquerque, N.Mex; m. to Floyd Willard Lee; c. Harry F. and Harriet F. Educ: Notre Dame Col, Belmont, Calif; Univ. Calif, Berkeley, grad. Polit. & Govt. Pos: Mem, bd. regents, Univ. N.Mex, 12 years; chmn, bd. of educ. and Grants Munic. Consolidated Schs, 7 years; app. by President Eisenhower as permanent U.S. Del. to Inter-Am. Cmn. of Women, 52-60, Ninth Assembly, Asuncion, Paraguay, Sept, 52, Tenth Inter-Am. Conf, Caracas, Venezuela, Tenth Assembly, San Juan, P.R. and pres. of the Assembly, Eleventh Assembly, Dominican Repub. and v.pres. of the Assembly and 13th Assembly, Pan-Am. Union, June 57; Rep. Nat. Committeewoman, N.Mex, 57- Bus. & Prof.

Pos: Valencia Co. Pub. Sch. Mem: Past dist. pres, Delta Delta Delta; first pres, N.Mex. Schs. Study Coun; Nat. Citizen's Coun; Delta Kappa Gamma; Bus. & Prfnl. Women; life mem, Am. Asn. Univ. Women; pres, Chaparrel Coun, Girl Scouts. Received honors in recognition of work with 4-H Clubs and Brotherhood Award, Nat. Conf. of Christians and Jews. Mailing Add: San Mateo, N.Mex. 87050.

LEE, GROVER B. D
b. DuPont, Ga, 11/12/98; s. Columbus Colquitt Lee and Dorcas Lancaster L; m. 11/05/22 to Doris Register; c. Grover Columbus, Doris Christine and Stella Ann. Educ: Grad, DuPont High Sch. Polit. & Govt. Pos: Mem, Clinch Co. Bd. of Co. Cmnrs, 47-; mem, Clinch Co. Hosp. Authority, 55-64; Ga. State Rep, 61-66. Bus. & Prof. Pos: Contractor; farmer; pres, Lee Eng. & Construction Co. Mem: Mason. Rel: Baptist; Deacon. Mailing Add: Box 86, DuPont, Ga. 31630.

LEE, H. REX D
Cmnr, Fed. Commun. Cmn.
b. Rigby, Idaho, 4/8/10; s. Hyrum Lee and Eliza Farnsworth L; m. 5/29/37 to Lillian Carlson; c. Lillian Sherry, Dixie Joanne (Mrs. Born), Linda Louise (Mrs. Irvine), Duane Rex and Mark Carlson. Educ: Univ. Idaho, B.S. in Agr. Econ, 36. Hon. LL.D, Univ. Idaho, 64. Polit. & Govt. Pos: Economist, Dept. of Agr, Moscow, Idaho, 36-37; exten. agent, Univ. Idaho, 37-38; economist, Bur. of Agr. Econ, Dept. of Agr, Berkeley, Calif, 38-42; asst. to dir. and chief, Relocation Div. and Evacuee Property Div, War Relocation Authority, Wash, D.C, 42-46; asst. dir, Off. of Territories, Dept. of Interior, 46-50, assoc. and dept. cmnr, Bur. of Indian Affairs, 50-61; Gov, Am. Samoa, 61-67; asst. admin, Agency Int. Develop, 67-68; Cmnr, Fed. Commun. Cmn, 68- Mem: The Fed. City Club, Wash, D.C. Rel: Protestant. Legal Res: 4740 Connecticut Ave. N.W, Washington, D.C. 20008. Mailing Add: Federal Communications Commission, Washington, D.C. 20554.

LEE, JACK ORBAN R
b. St. Louis, Mo, 12/13/29; s. Orban Aubrey Lee and Wanda Church L; m. 10/22/55 to Shirley Rose Siefker; c. Lori Denise and Daryl Wayne. Educ: Wash. Univ, 49. Polit. & Govt. Pos: Mo. State Rep, 48th Dist, 67-69. Mem: Past Master, Univ. Lodge 649, AF&AM. Rel: Methodist. Mailing Add: 11011 Ridge Forest Dr, St. Louis, Mo. 63126. (1967)

LEE, JAMIE FLETCHER D
b. Bennettsville, S.C, 5/10/30; s. James T. Lee, Jr. and Louise Fletcher L; m. 12/3/54 to Mary Weatherly Breeden. Educ: Univ. of S.C, B.S, 57, Law Sch, LL.B, 59. Polit. & Govt. Pos: S.C. State Rep, 63-66. Bus. & Prof. Pos: Lawyer; bd. dirs, United Fund of Marlboro Co, Inc. Mil. Serv: Army, 48-53, Com. Inf, Parachutist, 504th Airbrn. Inf. Regt, 82nd Airbrn. Div; Res. Officer, JAG, Res, Myrtle Beach A.F.B. Mem: Trustee, VFW, Post 6120; Jaycees; Am. Legion; S.C. and Co. Bar Asns; Ment. Health Asn; Bennettsville Sch. Area Bd. of Trustees, 67. Rel: First Methodist Church. Mailing Add: Box 22, Bennettsville, S.C. 29512. (1967)

LEE, JOHN DAVID 'J.D.' D
b. Tellico Plains, Tenn, 5/3/29; s. Clement Ernest Lee and Emma Hunt L; m. 4/18/61 to Sarah Craig Swively; c. John D, II, David and Allison E. Educ: John B. Stetson Univ, 48; E. Tenn. State Univ, B.S, 51; Univ. Tenn, LL.B, 54; Phi Delta Phi; Omicron Delta Kappa. Polit. & Govt. Pos: Del, Tenn. Constitutional Conv, 53; secy, Monroe Co. Elec. Cmn, Tenn, 53; chmn, Monroe Co. Dem. Exec. Cmt, Tenn, 53-54; clerk and master, Monroe Chancery Court, 54-59; secy, Tenn. Conserv. Cmn, 63-66; del, Dem. Nat. Conv, 64. Mil. Serv: Entered as Pvt, Army, 46, released as Cpl, 47, after serv. in 174th Mil. Police Co, 11th Air Force, Ft. Richardson, Alaska; Naval Res, 49-51; Air Force Res, 1st Lt, 51-57. Publ: 'Wrongful Death,' Tenn. Bar J, 11/65. Mem: Monroe Co. Bar Asn.(pres, 63); Am, Tenn. and Knoxville Bar Asns; bd. gov, Mich, Ohio, Ky. and Tenn, Am. Trial Lawyers Asns; bd. dirs, Tenn. Trial Lawyers Asn; Nat. Lawyer's Club; Seldon Soc; Am. Judicature Soc; N.Y. State Asn. Trial Lawyers; Nat. Asn. Claimant's Counsel of Tenn.(pres,59); Mason; Shrine; Am. Legion; Optimists. Lectr, Nat. Bar groups and law schs. on successful trial techniques. Rel: Baptist. Legal Res: Oak Grove Rd, Madisonville, Tenn. 37354. Mailing Add: Box 566, Madisonville, Tenn. 37354.

LEE, JOHN M. R
Wyo. State Sen.
b. Rock Springs, Wyo, 11/16/22; s. E.H. Norton Lee and Mary Bryant L; m. 2/10/44 to Jerry Riley; c. Kathryn Jean, Amy Frances, John M, Jr, Mary Ann, Abby Jane and Casey Thomas. Educ: Univ. Wyo, 1 year; Colo. Sch. of Mines, 1 year. Polit. & Govt. Pos: Cmnr, Wyo. Commerce and Indust. Cmn, 51-55; finance chmn, Sweetwater Co. Rep. Party, 52-64; Wyo. State Sen, 69- Mem: Mason; Shrine; Elks; pres, Rock Springs C. of C, 50-51 and Hwy. 30 Travel Asn, 50-51. Rel: Episcopal. Mailing Add: 710 A St, Rock Springs, Wyo. 82901.

LEE, JOSEPH BRACKEN
Mayor, Salt Lake City, Utah
b. Price, Utah, 1/7/99; s. Arthur J. Lee and Ida May Leiter L; m. 2/23/28 to Margaret Draper; c. Helen Virginia, James Bracken, Margaret Jon and Richard Lewis. Educ: High Sch. grad. Polit. & Govt. Pos: Mayor, Price, Utah, 36-47; Gov. of Utah, 49-57; Mayor, Salt Lake City, 59- Mil. Serv: Entered as Sgt, Army, 17, released as 2nd Lt, 19; Officer, Reserve Corps, 19-29. Mem: Charter mem, Elks; Mason, Shrine (33°); pres, Utah Munic. League, 39-40. Rel: Protestant. Class B Trapshooting Title in State Amateur Trapshooting Asn. single matches, 50; Tom McCoy Award for outstanding munic. officer, Utah Munic. League, 67. Legal Res: 2031 Laird Dr, Salt Lake City, Utah 84108. Mailing Add: Room 211, City and County Bldg, Salt Lake City, Utah 84114.

LEE, KENNETH B. R
Pa. State Rep.
b. Nauvoo, Pa, 1/23/22; s. Edward Lee and Evelyn Evans L; m. to Marjorie Cole; c. Susanne, Scott, Cole, Laura and Kenneth. Polit. & Govt. Pos: Pa. State Rep, 56-, Majority Leader, Pa. State House of Rep, 63-65, Minority Leader, 65-; alternate del, Rep. Nat. Conv, 68. Bus. & Prof. Pos: Attorney, Dushore, Pa; bd. dirs, 1st Nat. Bank of Dushore, Muncy Valley Hosp. Mailing Add: 1 Lakewood Ave, Eagles Mere, Pa. 17731. (1967)

LEE, KENNETH K. L. D
Hawaii State Rep.
b. Honolulu, Hawaii, 3/13/27; m. to Peggy Y.M; c. Marion K.Y, Sandra K.O, Kenyon H.T, Kendall H.C. and Debra. Educ: Univ. of Hawaii, B.B.A; Pi Sigma Epsilon. Polit. & Govt. Pos: Hawaii State Rep, 68- Bus. & Prof. Pos: Insurance Agent and acct. Mil. Serv: Entered as Pvt, Army, 45, released as Sgt, 47. Rel: Protestant. Mailing Add: 516-B Hiram Lane, Honolulu, Hawaii 96817.

LEE, L. J. DFL
Minn. State Rep.
b. Pope Co, Minn, 1907; married; c. Two. Polit. & Govt. Pos: Minn. State Rep, 60-; del, Dem. Nat. Conv, 68. Rel: Lutheran. Mailing Add: 508 Geary Ave, Bagley, Minn. 56621. (1967)

LEE, LAWRENCE J. D
Mo. State Sen.
b. St. Louis, Mo, 11/4/32; s. Patrick W. Lee and Ruth Rose Allaway L; m. 1/28/56 to Joan Margaret Steube; c. Daniel, Karen, Lawrence, Jr, Mark and Joan. Educ: St. Louis Univ. Sch. of Commerce and Finance, B.S.C, 54, Sch. of Law, LL.B, 56. Polit. & Govt. Pos: Prosecuting attorney, St. Louis, Mo, 64-66; Mo. State Sen, Third Dist, 66- Bus. & Prof. Pos: Practicing attorney, 56- Mem: Bar Asn. of Metrop. St. Louis; Mo. and Am. Bar Asns; Lawyers Asn. Meritorious Pub. Serv. Award, St. Louis Globe Dem, 68. Rel: Catholic. Legal Res: 9 Arundel Place, St. Louis, Mo. 63105. Mailing Add: 506 Olive St, St. Louis, Mo. 63101.

LEE, LENA KING D
Md. State Del.
b. Creighton, Pa, 7/14/11; d. Samuel S. King and Lula Gully K; wid. Educ: Morgan State Col, B.S, 39; N.Y. Univ, M.A, 47; Univ. Md, J.D, 51; Lambda Kappa Mu; Sigma Gamma Rho. Polit. & Govt. Pos: Mem, Mayor's Redevelop. Cmn, 55; mem, Mayor's Mfrs. Tax Cmt, 56; mem, Urban Renewal and Housing Cmn, 56-62; pres, Womens Dem. Auxiliary, Inc, 58-; mem, Adv. Coun. on Higher Educ, 64; mem, Mayor's Adv. Cmt. on Housing and Zoning, 65; Md. State Del, currently. Bus. & Prof. Pos: Teacher, Baltimore City Schs, 31-38, adminstr. and prin, 38-64; lawyer, 52-; owner and mgr, Biddle Theater, 59- Publ: Newspaper articles. Mem: Bar Asn. of Baltimore; Nat. Asn. of Parliamentarians; Women's Bar Asn. of Md; Int. Platform Asn; Monumental Bar Asn; AFL-CIO Teachers Union; Eastern Star; pres, Md. League of Women's Clubs. Founder, Herbert M. Frisby Hist. Soc. Rel: Methodist. Mailing Add: 1818 Madison Ave, Baltimore, Md. 21217.

LEE, LINDA K. R
b. Hartford, Conn, 2/22/40; d. Malcolm H. Lee and Josephine Potter L; single. Educ: Smith Col, A.B. summa cum laude, 61; George Wash. Law Sch, LL.B, 64; Columbia Univ. Sch. of Int. Affairs, 67-68; Phi Beta Kappa; Order of the Coif, Larner Medal, 64; pres, Smith Col. House of Rep; ed-in-chief, George Wash. Law Rev, 63-64. Polit. & Govt. Pos: Asst. to Conn. Secy. of State, summers, 56 & 57; pres, Smith Col. Young Rep. Club, 58-60; research asst. for Sen. Wm. A. Purtell, summer, 58 and Rep. State Cmt, Hartford, Conn, summer 60; asst. Conn. State Auditors Off, summer, 59; mem, Steering Cmt, Col. Youth for Nixon-Lodge, 60; clerk, Libr. of Cong, 61; asst. to Sen. Prescott Bush, 62; law clerk, U.S. Cmn. on Civil Rights, 62-63; legis. asst. to U.S. Rep. F. Bradford Morse, Mass, 63-64 and admin. asst, 64-69; dir. of research and commun, Morse for Cong. Cmt, Lowell, Mass, 64, 66 & 68; exec. asst. del. off, Rockefeller for President Cmt, 68. Bus. & Prof. Pos: Research asst, Nat. Planning Asn, fall, 61; research asst. to Arnold S. Trebach, Esquire, winter, 61-62; Attorney at law, Off. of Henry L. Diamond, 69- Publ: European Council on Human Rights, 6/63 and Congressional Conflict of Interest, 6/64, George Wash. Law Rev. Mem: D.C. and Fed. Bar Asns; Inter-Am. Bar Asn; Am. Soc. Int. Law; Ripon Soc.(mem, nat. gov. bd. exec. cmt, D.C. Chap); Smith Col. Club of Wash, D.C. and Hartford, Conn. Am. Polit. Sci. Asn. Cong. Staff fel, 67. Legal Res: 15 Old Pepperidge Lane, Wethersfield, Conn. 06109. Mailing Add: 2713 P St. N.W, Washington, D.C. 20007.

LEE, NOBLE W. R
b. Buffalo, N.Y; m. to Gertrude Smith; c. Four. Educ: Univ. of Wis; Harvard, A.B, 20; John Marshall Law J.D, 23. Polit. & Govt. Pos: Spec. asst. attorney gen, Ill, 28; pres, S. Park Improv. Asn, 38-43; former Ill. State Rep. Bus. & Prof. Pos: Lawyer. Mil. Serv: Army, World War I. Mem: City Club (secy, 25-30); Am. Legion; VFW; Am, Ill. State and Chicago Bar Asns; Am. Law Inst; Am. Judicature Soc; Kiwanis. Mailing Add: 5541 S. Woodlawn Ave, Chicago, Ill. 60637. (1967)

LEE, PAUL D
b. Ludlow, Miss, 2/14/10; married. Polit. & Govt. Pos: Former Miss. State Rep. Bus. & Prof. Pos: Motel operator. Mem: Mason; Rotary (past pres); dir, Leake Co. C. of C; VFW. Rel: Baptist. Mailing Add: 405 Van Buren St, Box 247, Carthage, Miss. 39051. (1967)

LEE, RICHARD CHARLES D
b. New Haven, Conn, 3/12/16; s. Frederick Lee and Mary Connolly L; m. 4/16/48 to Ellen Griffin; c. Sarah Anne, David Richard and Tara Elizabeth. Educ: Hillhouse High Sch, 30-34; Yale Univ, Hon. M.A, 61, Rollins Col, Hon. LL.D, 68 and St. Lawrence Univ, 69. Polit. & Govt. Pos: Alderman, New Haven, Conn, 39-47; mayor, New Haven, 54-69. Bus. & Prof. Pos: Ed. staff, New Haven J-Courier, 35-40; dir, Yale Univ. News Bur, 43-54. Mil. Serv: Army, 42-43, Pvt. Mem: New Haven Jr. C. of C.(pres); U.S. Conf. Mayors (pres, 62-63, exec. cmt, 63-); Nat. League Cities (adv. coun, 65); Urban Renewal (past chmn); President's Adv. Cmn. Intergovt. Rels.(chmn. adv. cmt. urban probs, 65-, dem. adv. coun, 58-); Knights St. Patrick; K. of C.(4°); hon. mem, Am. Inst. Architects; Rotary. LaGuardia Mem. Award. Rel: Catholic. Mailing Add: 255 McKinley Ave, New Haven, Conn. 06515.

LEE, RICHARD ERNEST R
b. Jefferson, Iowa, 12/26/26; s. Ernest E. Lee and Ruby E. Robbins L; m. 9/13/49 to Mary Louise Lichty; c. Deanna, Barbara, Clayton and Richard F. Educ: Drake Univ, LL.B, 52; Phi Alpha Delta. Polit. & Govt. Pos: Attorney, Hamilton Co, Iowa, 65-66; Iowa State Rep, Hamilton Co, 67-69. Mil. Serv: En-

tered as Fireman 2/C, Navy, 42, released as Fireman 1/C, 46; Asian Theater Ribbon. Mem: Am. Legion; Mason; Elks. Rel: Protestant. Mailing Add: R.R. 2, Webster City, Iowa 50595. (1967)

LEE, ROBERT E, JR. D
Ga. State Sen.
b. Fitzgerald, Ga, 2/09/14; s. Robert E. Lee and Mary Wasserman L; m. 6/12/40 to Mary Alice Manley; c. Rita M, Mary Linda; Robert E, III. Educ: Mercer Univ, A.B, 35; Alpha Tau Omega. Polit. & Govt. Pos: Mem, State Personnel Bd, Ga, 58-62, chmn, 61; Ga. State Sen, 47th Dist, 63- Bus. & Prof. Pos: Gen. Ins. Mil. Serv: Navy, 42-45. Mem: Elks; pres, Elberton Rotary, 62-63; dir, Elbert Co. C. of C, 56-58, 60-62 & 63-64; pres, Ga. Athletic Coaches Asn, 41-42; Lt. Pres, N.Ga. Football Asn, 37-38. Rel: Methodist; chmn. bd. trustees, 59-63. Mailing Add: Box 548, Elberton, Ga. 30635.

LEE, ROBERT EMMET R
Cmnr, Fed. Commun. Cmn.
b. Chicago, Ill, 3/31/12; s. Patrick J. Lee and Delia Ryan L; m. 2/30/36 to Wilma Rector; c. Robert E, Michael B. and Patricia (Mrs. Martin Fisher). Educ: De Paul Univ. Col. of Commerce & Law. Polit. & Govt. Pos: Spec. agent, Fed. Bur. Invest, 38-53; staff dir, Appropriations Cmt, U.S. House of Rep, 46-53; cmnr, Fed. Commun. Cmn, 53- Bus. & Prof. Pos: Chmn, Govt. Indust. Cmt. for Full Develop. of All Channel Broadcasting and Govt. Indust. Cmt. for Educ. Broadcasting. Mem: Inst. Elec. & Electronics Engrs; Capital Hill Club; Cong. Country Club. Rel: Roman Catholic. Mailing Add: 3147 Westover Dr. S.E, Washington, D.C. 20020.

LEE, ROBERT M. R
Polit. & Govt. Pos: N.Mex. State Sen, -66. Bus. & Prof. Pos: Rancher; bd. dir, N.Mex. Cattle Growers Asn. Mil. Serv: Marine Corps, Lt. Mem: Pres. N.Mex. Horse Breeders Asn. Mailing Add: Horse Springs, N.Mex. 87822. (1967)

LEE, ROBERT REID R
Mem, Calif. Rep. State Cent. Cmt.
b. Ft. Gibbon, Alaska, 7/9/07; s. Joel Robert Lee and Gertrude Louise Hughes L; m. 6/25/38 to Gwendolyn Jones; c. David Robert. Educ: Univ. of Calif, Berkeley, B.A. with honors. Polit. & Govt. Pos: Appraising officer, U.S. Treas. Dept, 35-56; v.pres, Berkeley Rep. Assembly, 68-69; mem, Calif. Rep. State Cent. Cmt, 69- Bus. & Prof. Pos: Appraiser of art, 56- Mil. Serv: Entered as 1st Lt, Army, 42, released as Maj, 46, after serv. in Gen. Staff, Wash, D.C; Maj.(Ret), Army Res. Publ: 'Mount Willing,' Sewanee Rev, 32; 'Rivets,' Adventure, 34. Mem: Am. Acad. of Polit. and Soc. Sci; Am. Legion; Berkeley Citizens United; life mem, Commonwealth Club. Rel: Protestant. Mailing Add: 1224 Campus Dr, Berkeley, Calif. 94708.

LEE, RONALD BARRY D
Asst. Postmaster Gen.
b. N.Y.C, 5/26/32; s. Kermit James Lee and Lillian Bryant Jackson L; m. 11/18/60 to Joyce Juanita Thomas; c. Dean Eric; stepson, Gregory Carter Anderson. Educ: Springfield Col, 49-50; U.S. Mil. Acad, B.S, 54; Univ. Md, Sukiran, Okinawa, 57-59; Defense Lang. Inst, Monterrey, Calif, Viet Namese, grad. with distinction, 62; Syracuse Univ, M.B.A, 64; Am. Univ, Ph.D. cand, 65-; Beta Gamma Sigma; Alpha Phi Alpha. Hon. LL.D, West. New Eng. Col, 69. Polit. & Govt. Pos: White House Fel, White House and Post Off. Dept, 65-66; dir, Planning and Systs. Anal, U.S. Post Off. Dept, 66-68, Asst. Postmaster Gen, 69- Bus. & Prof. Pos: Prof, Asst. Provost, Dir, Cent. for Urban Affairs and Dir, Equal Opportunity Progs, Mich. State Univ, 68-69; chmn. of adv. cmt, Afro-Am. Heritage Libr. MDI Publishers, Wayne, Pa, currently. Mil. Serv: Entered as 2nd Lt, Army, 54, released as Maj, 67, after serv. in Signal Corps, Armored and Inf. Units throughout World including Adv. Duty in Viet Nam, 62-63; Maj, Army Res, 67-; Nat. Defense Serv. Medal with Oak Leaf Cluster; AEF Medal; Army Commendation Medal with Oak Leaf Cluster; Viet Nam Campaign Medal; Parachutist Badge. Publ: 'Washington: Fable and Fact,' Mich. Bus. Rev, 5/67; 'Needed: A Managerial Monroe Doctrine,' Personnel Admin, 2-3/68; 'Postal Service Today and Tomorrow: Solving the Problems of the Next Decade,' Vital Speeches of the Day, 12/68; plus six others. Mem: Asn. of Syracuse Army Comptrollers; Am. Soc. for Pub. Admin; White House Fels. Asn.(past pres); Am. Acad. of Polit. and Soc. Sci; fel, Nat. Acad. of Pub. Admin; Asn. of W.Point Grad; Md. Suburban Fair Housing. Arthur Flemming Award as one of the ten most outstanding young men in the fed. serv, 67; Outstanding Civilian Serv. Medal, Dept. of the Army, 68. Rel: Protestant. Mailing Add: 8213 Burning Tree Rd, Bethesda, Md. 20034.

LEE, THEODORE ROBERT 'TED' R
V.Chmn, Albany Co. Rep. Cent. Cmt, Wyo.
b. Hilliard, Fla, 8/29/23; s. Elmer E. Lee and Carrie Franston L; m. 8/24/48 to Jacquelyn Anderson; c. Wayne, Greg, Scott and Mark. Educ: Univ. Wyo, grad, 64. Polit. & Govt. Pos: Rep. precinct capt, Wyo, 55-67; v.chmn, Albany Co. Rep. Cent. Cmt, 67-; alternate del, Rep. Nat. Conv, 68. Bus. & Prof. Pos: Hwy. patrolman, Wyo, 55-59, probation and parole officer, 59- Mil. Serv: Entered as Pvt, Army, 45, released as Sgt, 47, after serv. as paratrooper, 82nd Airborne Div, Germany, ETO; Army Res, 47-50; Paratrooper Wings; ETO Ribbon; Good Conduct Ribbon. Publ: 'Conditional Release Procedures,' Wyo. Law Enforcement Mag, 66. Mem: Wyo. Law Enforcement and Peace Officer's Asn; Probation, Parole and Corrections Asn; Mason (Deacon, Lodge No. 3, Laramie, Wyo); Toastmaster's Club (past area gov, Laramie, Wyo); Odd Fellows; Univ. Wyo. Alumni Asn. Mem, Honor Guard for Gen. Dwight D. Eisenhower, Frankfurt, Germany, 46; Capt, football team. Rel: United Methodist. Mailing Add: 719 Hancock St, Laramie, Wyo. 82070.

LEE, THOMAS J. 'TOM' D
b. Canton, China, 9/25/23; s. Fook Sune Lee and Lui Shee L; m. 12/21/45 to May Land Wong; c. Robert Thomas, Richard Henry and Linda Louise. Educ: St. Mary's Univ, Tex, B.B.A. in acct; St. Mary's Law Sch, Tex, LL.B; Kappa Pi Sigma. Polit. & Govt. Pos: Asst. dist. attorney and admin. chief, Bexar Co, Tex, 63-64; Tex. State Rep, 68th Dist, Place 3, 64-69. Bus. & Prof. Pos: Attorney-at-Law, 60- Mil. Serv: Entered as S/A, Navy, 42, released as Lt.(jg), 46, after serv. in Pac. Theater; also served in Korean Conflict; Comdr, Naval Res, 42-; Naval Res, Navy Occupation, Nat. Defense Serv, China Serv, Am. Campaign, Asiatic-Pac. Campaign and Victory Medals. Mem: San Antonio Bar Asn; State Bar of Tex; League of United Latin Am. Citizens; Chinese Am. Optimist Club; Am. Legion. Rel: Baptist. Legal Res: 1607 W. Ashby Place, San Antonio, Tex. 78201. Mailing Add: 1616 Tower Life Bldg, San Antonio, Tex. 78205. (1967)

LEE, TOM R
N.Mex. State Sen.
b. China Spring, Gallup, N.Mex, 2/14/20; s. Tom Lee and Mary Brown L; m. 7/14/47 to Emma Rose Casuse; c. Sylvia Ann, Willa Ann (deceased), Clarence Claude, Randolph Juan, Cherie Ophelia, Wendell Winright and Erecka Elvina. Educ: Tohatchi Boarding Sch, N.Mex, 8 years. Polit. & Govt. Pos: Commun. leader, Navajo Land, N.Mex, currently; mem. sch. bd, Bur. Indian Affairs Indian Sch, 60-66; N.Mex. State Sen, Dist. 3, McKinley Co, 66- Bus. & Prof. Pos: Owner and operator, Twin Lakes Trading Post, N.Mex, 52- Mil. Serv: Entered as Pvt, Army, 41, released Cpl, 46, after serv. in 200th and 515th Coast Artil. Antiaircraft, Am. ex-prisioner of War, Japan, 42-45; Am. Defense Medal with One Bronze Serv. Star; Asiatic Pac. Theater Medal with One Bronze Serv. Star; Philippine Defense Ribbon with One Bronze Serv. Star; Good Conduct Medal; Distinguished Unit Badge with Two Oak Leaf Clusters; Victory Medal; Philippine Liberation Ribbon. Mem: VFW; N.Mex. Cattle Grower's Asn; Bataan Vet. Orgn.(bd. dirs, Navajo Chap, 58-64); Am. Defenders of Bataan & Corregidor, Inc.(chap. pres, 54-62). Rel: Penticostal Full Gospel. Mailing Add: Twin Lakes Trading Post, Gallup, N.Mex. 87301.

LEE, WANDA KAREN R
V.Chmn, Beadle Co. Rep. Party, S.Dak.
b. Gregory, S.Dak, 8/4/34; d. Walter K. Johnson and Harriet Aldrich J; m. 2/1/58 to Myrth O. Lee, Jr; c. Mark, Karen and Todd. Educ: S.Dak. State Univ, 52-54. Polit. & Govt. Pos: Secy. to Sen. Karl Mundt, S.Dak, 56-58; secy, Civil Serv, State Asn, Huron, S.Dak, 58; v.chmn, Beadle Co. Rep. Party, 66-; del, Rep. Nat. Conv, 68. Rel: Lutheran. Mailing Add: 438 Jefferson Blvd. S.E, Huron, S.Dak. 57350.

LEE, WILLIAM ELLSWORTH R
Tex. State Rep.
b. Houston, Tex, 12/21/40; s. Donald A. Lee and Dorothy Greer L; single. Educ: Wash. and Lee Univ, B.S. in commerce, 62; Univ. Houston Law Sch, LL.B, 66; Delta Tau Delta; Student Bar Asn.(pres, 65). Polit. & Govt. Pos: Tex. State Rep, Dist. 22, Place 2, 69- Bus. & Prof. Pos: Attorney, Helm Jones & Pletcher, Houston, 66-67; Attorney, Wandel and Bousquet, 68- Mem: Phi Alpha Delta (pres. Hichman chap, 65). Rel: Episcopal. Mailing Add: 1903 Olympia, Houston, Tex. 77019.

LEE, WILLIAM J. 'BILL' D
Ga. State Rep.
b. Forest Park, Ga, 12/15/25; s. Colie Rufus Lee and Velma Haynie L; m. 8/20/49 to Mary Mathews. Educ: Atlanta Law Sch, LL.B, 60. Polit. & Govt. Pos: Ga. State Rep, 59- Bus. & Prof. Pos: South. Railway Co, 42- Mil. Serv: Navy, 44-46. Mem: Kiwanis; Mason; Jr. and Sr. C. of C; Moose. Rel: Baptist. Mailing Add: 5325 Hillside Dr, Forest Park, Ga. 30050.

LEE, WILLIAM SPENCER D
Ga. State Rep.
b. Angelus, S.C, 7/08/15; s. John Emsley Lee and Mayme McDaniel L; m. 9/08/40 to Willie Bess Gassett; c. William Spencer IV, Rebecca and David Carl. Educ: Mid. Ga. Jr. Col, 34; Univ. of Ga, LL.B, 38; Phi Delta Theta. Polit. & Govt. Pos: Spec. agent, Fed. Bur. of Invest, 41-56; Chief of Police, 56-58; Ga. State Rep, 63- Bus. & Prof. Pos: Attorney-at-law, Fort Valley, 38-41 and Albany, 58- Mem: Am. Bar Asn; Am. Judicature Soc; Albany Bar Asn.(pres, 68-69); Elk; pres, Albany Jr. High PTA, 56-57; v.pres, Kiwanis, 61; adv. bd, Salvation Army, 62; chmn, O & E Cmn, Cent. Dist, Albany Boy Scouts, 61-62. Rel: Baptist; Deacons Adv. Bd, 63. Legal Res: 1215 Baker Ave, Albany, Ga. 31705. Mailing Add: Royal Bldg, Albany, Ga. 31701.

LEECH, ROBINSON R
b. Brooklyn, N.Y, 1/24/17; s. Robinson Leech; m. 8/17/45 to Elisabeth Barnes; c. Robinson, Jr and Rosalind. Educ: Williams Col, 40; Sigma Phi Soc; charter mem, Nat. Soc. State Legis. Polit. & Govt. Pos: Chmn, Salisbury Rep. Town Cmt; pres, Salisbury Young Rep. Club; finance chmn, Litchfield Co. Rep. Orgn; Conn. State Rep. until 67. Bus. & Prof. Pos: Overseas air freight and passenger traffic mgr, Pan Am. Airways, 41-44; farm mgr; master hist. and dir. admissions, Salisbury Sch; pres. and owner, Robinson Leech Realtors, 62- Mil. Serv: Lt.(jg), Navy, 44-46. Mem: Past pres, Housatonic Psychiat. Center; bd, Salisbury Welfare Asn; Lakeville Hose Co; past. pres. and founder, Opinions Unlimited; Williams Club of N.Y; Nat. Asn. of Real Estate Bds; Litchfield Co. Real Estate Bd; Litchfield Co. Univ. Club; Int. Platform Asn; Mason. Rel: Congregational. Mailing Add: Main St, Salisbury, Conn. 06068.

LEEDOM, JOHN NESBETT R
Mem Rep. State Exec. Cmt, Tex.
b. Dallas, Tex, 7/27/21; s. Floyd H. Leedom and Gladys D. Nesbett L; m. 3/17/56 to Betty Lee Harvey; c. Joanne, Judy, Linda and John, Jr. Educ: Rice Univ, B.S. in Elec. Eng, 43; Tau Beta Pi. Polit. & Govt. Pos: Pres, Dallas Co. Rep. Men's Club, Tex, 61-62; chmn, Dallas Co. Rep. Exec. Cmt, 62-66; mem, Rep. State Exec. Cmt, Tex, 67-; Bus. & Prof. Pos: Pres, N.Tex. Chap, Nat. Electronic Distributors Asn, 61; chmn, Mid-Tex. Chap, Young Pres. Orgn, 63, nat. dir, currently. Mil. Serv: Entered as Ens, Navy, 44, released as Lt.(jg), 45, after serv. in Naval Res. Lab, Wash, D.C, 44-45. Mem: Inst. Elec. & Electronics Engrs; Rotary Int. Rel: Grace Bible Church. Mailing Add: 11012 Westmere Circle, Dallas, Tex. 75230.

LEEDS, ISABELLE R. D
Committeewoman, R.I. Dem. State Cmt.
b. N.Y.C, 12/6/26; d. Louis Russek and Rose Bauman R; m. 10/19/47 to Marshall P. Leeds; c. David Russek and Amy Beth. Educ: Wellesley Col, B.A, 47. Polit. & Govt. Pos: Spec. asst. to U.S. Sen. Claiborne Pell, 61-; mem, R.I. Adv. Cmt. to U.S. Civil Rights Cmn, 62-; alternate del, Dem. Nat. Conv, 64, del, 68; chmn, Dem. Representative Dist. Cmt, 66-68; committeewoman, R.I. Dem. State Cmt, 68- Rel: Jewish. Mailing Add: 252 Freeman Pkwy, Providence, R.I. 02903.

LEEDY, JAMES K. R
Ohio State Sen.
b. Shreve, Ohio, 1924; m. to Juanita; c. Four. Educ: Muskingum Col; Ohio North. Univ. Col. of Law, LL.B, 49. Polit. & Govt. Pos: Wayne Co. Prosecutor, Ohio, 53-66; Ohio State Sen, 67- Mil. Serv: World War II. Mem: Bd. of dirs, Ohio Prosecuting Attorneys Asn; pres, Wayne Co. Bar Asn, 63. Wooster Jaycees Outstanding Young Man of the Year, 57. Mailing Add: 1500 Christman Run Blvd, Wooster, Ohio 44691.

LEET, LOUIS R
b. Devils Lake, N.Dak, 12/24/90; s. Ole Leet and Margaret Fladland L; m. 11/27/16 to Carrie Johnson; c. Margaret (Mrs. Glenn Oleson) and James O; m. 11/27/58 to Julia Omdahl. Educ: N.Dak. State Univ, Farm Husbandry, 10-13. Polit. & Govt. Pos: N.Dak. State Rep, Ramsey Co, 43-66, mem, Legis. Res. Cmt. and chmn, Rep. Faction, N.Dak. State House of Rep, 47-55. Bus. & Prof. Pos: Farmer. Mil. Serv: Pvt, Nat. Guard, 14-15. Mem: Farm Bur; Mason. Rel: Presbyterian; Elder, 17 years. Mailing Add: 792 A Via Los Altos, Laguna Hills, Calif. 92653.

LeFEVER, ROSE ISABEL R
V.Chmn, Ulster Co. Rep. Cmt, N.Y.
b. Walton, N.Y, 8/22/23; d. Cecil Edward Feltman and Mary Cordelia Budine F; m. 8/23/41 to Raymond Freer LeFever; c. Mary Jane (Mrs. John Thomas Welsek), Frederick Spencer; grandchildren, Dawn Marie and Jeffery Raymond Welsek. Educ: Walton High Sch, grad, 41. Polit. & Govt. Pos: Sch. tax collector, Creek Locks Dist, N.Y, 50-58; corresponding secy, Ulster Co. Women's Rep. Club, 57-58, first v.pres, 59, pres, 59-61; v.chmn, Ulster Co. Rep. Cmt, 60-, receptionist, 69; dir, Third Judicial Dist, N.Y. State Fedn. of Rep. Women, 61-62, treas, 64-65. Bus. & Prof. Pos: Dept. mgr, J.J. Newberry, 44; owner and mgr, Volocta Farm Gift Shoppe, 49-55. Mem: 4-H (leader, Ulster Co. Asn, 55-58, judge for dress rev, 60-69); Ulster Co. Women's Rep. Club, Rosendale Libr. Asn; N.Y. State Fedn. of Rep. Women; Hist. Asn; Nat. Fedn. of Rep. Women; Ladies Auxiliary of Bloomington Fire Compound; Boy Scouts (Rip Van Winkle Coun). Rel: Protestant. Mailing Add: Box 115, Bloomington, N.Y. 12411.

LeFEVRE, CHARLES FREDERIC R
b. Northville, S.Dak, 6/3/31; s. H.G. LeFevre and Dacotah Brenkle L; m. 6/8/57 to Gwen Stemsrud; c. Camille and Lee. Educ: S.Dak. State Univ, B.S, 56, M.S, 58; Alpha Zeta. Polit. & Govt. Pos: Chmn, Jackson Co. Rep. Party, Wis, 65-69. Bus. & Prof. Pos: Asst. nutritionist, Int. Milling Co, 58-60; nutritionist, Springfield Milling Corp, 60-63; v.pres. and nutritionist, H.H. Van Gordon & Sons, 63-67; pres, Vet. Indorsed Prod, Inc, 67-69. Mil. Serv: Entered as Pvt, Army, 52, released as Cpl, 54, after serv. in Vet. Corp, Camp Chaffee, Ark. Publ: 'Cellulose Digestion Invitro and Invivo,' J. Animal Sci, 8/60. Mem: Am. Dairy Sci. Asn; Am. Soc. of Animal Sci; Mason. Rel: Lutheran. Mailing Add: 522 Van Buren St, Black River Falls, Wis. 54615.

LEFEVRE, WALTER (DOC) D
b. Marion, N.C, 1918; m. Polit. & Govt. Pos: Alaska State Rep, 64-66; Fairbanks City Coun. Bus. & Prof. Pos: Optometrist. Mem: Kiwanis; Elks; Mason. Mailing Add: P.O. Box 1954, Fairbanks, Alaska. 99701. (1967)

LEFKOWITZ, LOUIS J. R
State Attorney Gen, N.Y.
b. N.Y.C, 7/3/04; m. to Helen Schwimmer; c. Joan (Mrs. Harold Feinbloom) and Stephen; grandchildren, David and Stephen Ellis Feinbloom. Educ: Fordham Univ. Sch. of Law, LL.B, 25. Polit. & Govt. Pos: Chmn, Law Cmt, N.Y. Rep. Co. Cmt, N.Y; counsel, N.Y. Rep. State Cmt; research counsel to Speaker of N.Y. State Assembly; del, N.Y. State Rep. Conv; N.Y. State Assemblyman, 28-30; judge, Munic. Court of N.Y.C, 35; dep. tax cmnr, 43-44; counsel, Joint Legis. Cmt. on Elec. Laws, 53-54; justice, City Court of N.Y, 54; del, Rep. Nat. Conv, 56, 60, 64 & 68; State Attorney Gen, N.Y, 57- Bus. & Prof. Pos: Lawyer. Mem: Gen. chmn, U.J.A, 59; v.chmn, lawyers div, U.J.A. and Fedn. of Jewish Philanthropies; chmn, gen. cmt. of Gr. N.Y. Coord. Cmt. on Released Time of Jews, Protestants and Catholics; bd. of councillors, Florence Crittenton League; campaign chmn, City of Hope Nat. Med. Center; chmn, N.Y. State Employees Unit, Gr. N.Y. Fund; hon. dir, Manhattan Chap. of Free Nurses Inst; adv. coun, Grad. Sch. of Educ, Yeshiva Univ; Albany Soc; Nat. Post of Am. Friends of the Hebrew Univ; Manhattan Club; Grand St. Boys Asn; K. of P; B'nai B'rith; Boys Club Alumni; Salvation Army Asn; N.Y. State Bar Asn; Asn. of Bar of N.Y.C; N.Y. Co. Lawyers Asn; Fed. Bar Asn. of N.Y, N.J. and Conn; Asn. of Lawyers of the Criminal Courts of Manhattan. Legal Res: 80 Center St, New York, N.Y. 10013. Mailing Add: c/o State Capitol, Albany, N.Y. 12224. (1967)

LEGARE, ALLEN T. JR.
b. Charleston, S.C, 7/22/15; s. T. Allen Legare and Lilly Mikell L; m. to Virginia Irene Green; c. Virginia Green, Sarah Mikell, Irene Green, Edward Thomas. Educ: Univ. S.C, A.B, 38. Polit. & Govt. Pos: S.C. State Sen, 53-64; S.C. State Rep, 47-48, 51-66. Bus. & Prof. Pos: Lawyer. Mil. Serv: WWII. Mailing Add: Box 578, Charleston, S.C. 29402. (1967)

LEGATE, A. B. VIRKLER R
b. Watertown, N.Y, 5/6/24; s. Alexis Whitney Legate and Gladys Virkler L; m. 10/19/45 to Mary Virginia Cook; c. Lauren Cook and Kelly Elizabeth. Educ: Stetson Univ, B.S, 50; Sigma Alpha Epsilon. Polit. & Govt. Pos: Press asst. to U.S. Rep. William C. Cramer, Fla, 61-62; admin. asst. to U.S. Rep. Bradford Morse, Mass, 62; asst. to U.S. Rep. Robert C. McEwen, N.Y, 65-69. Bus. & Prof. Pos: Dir. pub. rels, N.Y, New Haven and Hartford R.R, 54-56; exec. asst. to pres, Boston and Maine R.R, 56-61; sr. analyst, Real Estate Research Corp, 63-65. Mil. Serv: Entered as A/S, Navy, 42, released as PO 3/C, 46, after serv. in Amphibian Corps. and Third Fleet, Pac; Philippine Liberation Medal; Pac. Theater Ribbon; Good Conduct Medal. Mem: Am. Mgt. Asn; Ancient & Hon. Artil. Co; Pub. Rels. Soc. of Am; AF&AM; Am. Legion. Rel: Episcopal. Mailing Add: 3418 Executive Ave, Falls Church, Va. 22042. (1967)

LEGG, LOUIS E, JR. R
Chmn, Sixth Cong. Dist. Rep. Cmt, Mich.
b. Coldwater, Mich, 1/21/28; s. Louis E. Legg and Dorothy A. Wood L; m. 6/21/53 to Joan Mary Touhy Donkin; c. Louis, III and Thomas Charles. Educ: Mich. State Univ, B.S, 50; Blue Key; Pi Kappa Delta; Beta Theta Pi; Excalibur. Polit. & Govt. Pos: Chmn, Meridian Twp. Rep. Cmt, Mich, 60-62; chmn, Ingham Co. Rep. Cmt, 62-65; del, Rep. Nat. Conv, 64; chmn, Sixth Cong. Dist. Rep. Cmt, Mich, 64-; mem, Mich. State Bldg. Cmn, 67- Bus. & Prof. Pos: Home builder, Battle Creek, Mich, 50-52; pres, Lansing Lumber Co, 52-, Pageant Homes, Inc, 56-, Home Assistance Corp, and Marion Lumber & Supply, Ind, 69- Mil. Serv: Entered as 2nd Lt, Army Res, 50, released as Capt, 60. Mem: Dir, Lansing Metro Develop. Authority; Nat. Retail Lumber Dealers Asn; Contractors & Suppliers Asn.(v.pres); C. of C.(dir, Gr. Lansing Chap. and pres, 69-); YMCA (v.pres. Lansing Chap. and pres, 68, dir, Parkwood Chap); City Club.of Lansing; Romney Inaugural Cmt, 63 & 65. Rel: Protestant. Mailing Add: 4361 Wausau Rd, Okemos, Mich. 48864.

LEGGETT, ROBERT LOUIS D
U.S. Rep, Calif.
b. Richmond, Calif, 7/26/26; m. to Barbara Burnett; c. Diana, Jeanne and Rob. Educ: Univ. Calif, B.A. in Polit. Sci, 47 and Boalt Hall Sch. Jurisp, LL.B, 50. Polit. & Govt. Pos: Calif. State Assemblyman, 61-62; U.S. Rep, Calif, 62-, mem, Armed Serv. Cmt, U.S. House of Rep; alternate del, Dem. Nat. Conv, 68. Bus. & Prof. Pos: Lawyer; sr. partner, Leggett, Gianola, Dacey and Harrison. Mil. Serv: Navy Air Corps, 2 years. Mem: Kiwanis; Elks; Redmen; Sons of Italy; Am. Legion; 20-30 Int. Legal Res: Vallejo, Calif. 94590. Mailing Add: 3606 Pinetree Terr, Falls Church, Va. 22041.

LeGRESLEY, ROSCOE EDWARD D
Chmn, Idaho Co. Dem. Cent. Cmt, Idaho
b. Emporia, Kans, 2/26/15; s. James Robert LeGresley and Cora Stewart L; m. 2/13/32 to Geneva Louise Timmons; c. Jacqulyn Anne (Mrs. Haight), Pierre James, Janice Lorraine (Mrs. Howell), Nigel Leon, and foster son, Kenneth Herbert Saunders. Polit. & Govt. Pos: Chmn, Idaho Co. Dem. Cent. Cmt, Idaho, 68- Bus. & Prof. Pos: Writer & Photographer, 38 years. Rel: Methodist. Mailing Add: Box 275, Kooskia, Idaho 83539.

LEGRID, GLORIA JEAN R
Dist. Chmn, N. Dak. Rep. Party
b. Tappen, N.Dak, 9/28/29; d. Fred William Buck and Jennie Montgomery B; m. 8/31/52 to Donald Allen Legrid; c. Keith, Carol and Jennifer. Educ: Jamestown Col, 47-49; St. Cloud Hosp. Sch. of Med. Tech, Med. Technician; Alpha Zeta. Polit. & Govt. Pos: Campaign chmn, Co. Rep. Party, N.Dak, 56-66; nat. committeewoman, N.Dak. Young Rep, 61-63; Rep. precinct committeeman, Jamestown, 64-69; dist. chmn. and mem. exec. cmt, N.Dak. Rep. Party, 66- Rel: Lutheran. Mailing Add: 224 15th Ave. N.E, Jamestown, N.Dak. 58401.

LEHMAN, ED R
Ill. State Rep.
b. East St. Louis, 3/1/07; m. to Mildred Hankins L. Educ: High Sch, East St. Louis. Polit. & Govt. Pos: Mem, C. of C; Ill. State Rep, currently. Bus. & Prof. Pos: Sheet metal bus. Mem: AF&AM; Moose; Eagles; Exchange Club; Elks. Rel: Lutheran. Mailing Add: 519 N. 38th St, East St. Louis, Ill. 62205. (1967)

LEHMAN, EDITH ALBAN R
Mem, Calif. Rep. State Cent. Cmt.
b. Walla Walla, Wash, 7/23/03; d. Herbert Alban Cunningham and Ada Allen Henraid C; m. 6/12/22 to M. Lewis Lehman; c. Robert Alban and Anthony Lewis. Educ: Annie Wright Episcopal Sem, B.A; Univ. Wash; Delta Delta Delta. Univs. of Edinburough and Frankfort, hon. degrees in polit. sci. Polit. & Govt. Pos: Chmn. and mem. exec. cmt, 63rd Assembly Dist, Los Angeles Rep. Cent. Cmt, Calif, 48-49 and 15th Cong. Dist, 49-56; chmn, Women's Div, Calif. Rep. State Cent. Cmt, 50-52, mem. exec. cmt, 6 years and platform cmt, 50-; v.chmn, Rep. West. States Conf, 50-52; organizer and pres, Crenshaw Rep. Women, 50-55; del, Rep. Nat. Conv, 52 & 64; mem, U.S. Del, Geneva Conf, 56 & 57; mem, state and nat. speakers bur, Rep. Party; mem, Nixon Cmn. and local and nat. finance cmts. Publ: Book of Poems, privately publ, 50-; polit. articles, seven Calif. and Wash. papers; feature articles, Scripps-Howard, Seattle & Tacoma Times. Mem: DAR, past v.regent, Cabrillo Chap; Daughter of Runnymede; First Families of Va; Balboa Bay and Shadow Mt. Clubs; Los Angeles Athletic Club; Wilshire Rep. Women's Club. Spec. Award, Pope Pius, 56. Rel: Episcopal. Mailing Add: 314 S. Rimpau Blvd, Los Angeles, Calif. 90005.

LEHMAN, JESSE E, JR. R
b. Chicago, Ill, 8/4/23; s. Jesse E. Lehman and Agnes Erikson L; m. 6/28/47 to Jean R. Phillips; c. Elizabeth A, Jesse E, III, Nancy C. and Helen P. Educ: Knox Col, A.B, 47; Phi Gamma Delta. Polit. & Govt. Pos: Chmn, Nixon-Lodge Vol, 60; pres, Rep. Workshop, Schaumburg Twp, Ill, 60-61; mem, Cook Co. Rep. Cent. Cmt, 61-66; Rep. Presidential elector and alternate del, Rep. Nat. Conv, 13th Cong. Dist, 64; chmn, Citizens for Nixon-Agnew, Wheeling Twp, 68. Bus. & Prof. Pos: Acct. exec, Cunningham & Walsh, Inc, Chicago, 58-63, Tatham-Laird & Kudner, Inc, 63-66 and Young & Rubicam, Inc, 66-67; acct. supvr, Don Kemper Co, Inc, 67-69 and Rink Wells & Assocs, 69- Mil. Serv: Pvt, Army, 43-44, serv. in 66th Inf. Div. Rel: Protestant. Mailing Add: 635 S. Pine Ave, Arlington Heights, Ill. 60005.

LEHNHAUSEN, ROBERT JOSEPH R
b. Peoria, Ill, 9/11/19; s. Frank W. Lehnhausen and Florence Clark L; m. 6/23/45 to Elizabeth Ann Waugh; c. Mary Jo, Phillip, Ann, Thomas, Kathleen, Steven and David. Polit. & Govt. Pos: Councilman, Peoria, Ill, 53-55 & 57-61; cmnr, Greater Peoria Airport Authority, 55-57; alderman, Peoria City Coun, 61-65; Mayor, Peoria, 65-69. Bus. & Prof. Pos: Mem, bd. dir, Peoria Asn. of Commerce, Ill, 54-57; treas, 57-58; mem, bd. dir, Sheridan Village State Bank, 54-; mem, bd. dir, First Fed. Savings and Loan Asn, 68- Mil. Serv: Entered as Pvt, Army, 41, released as Lt. Col, 46, after serv. in Army Air Corps, Eighth Air Force, 44th Bomb Group, Eng. and Africa, 43-45; Distinguished Flying Cross, with two Oak Leaf Clusters; Air Medal with three Oak Leaf Clusters; Purple Heart with Oak Leaf Cluster; Soldiers Medal; Am. Defense Ribbon; European-African Theatre Ribbon with nine Campaign Clusters; Presidential Unit Citation with two Oak Leaf Clusters; French Croix de Guerre with Bronze Palm; Lt. Col, Air Force Res, 46- Mem: Officer, dir, Peoria Jaycees, 47-53. Rel: Roman Catholic. Mailing Add: 407 Fulton St, Peoria, Ill. 61602.

LEHR, STANFORD BUD R
Pa. State Rep.
b. York, Pa, 5/13/12; s. John Alexander Lehr and Mable Meisenhelder L; m. 3/7/37 to Naomi Jane Huson; c. Stanford Terry and John Frederich. Educ: North York High Sch, grad. Polit. & Govt. Pos: Pa. State Rep, 95th Dist, 69- Bus. & Prof. Pos: Merchant, Lehr's Food Mkt, 47-67. Mem: Elks; Exchange Club; York Co. Meat Dealers Asn; Am. Fedn. of Musicians. Rel: Lutheran. Mailing Add: 1511 W. Market St, York, Pa. 17404.

LEHRKIND, CARL, JR. R
Mont. State Sen.
b. Bozeman, Mont, 9/10/06; s. Carl Lehrkind and Helen Hancock L; m. 9/8/37 to Margaret Virginia Thompson; c. Carl, III, Harry Tom and Robert Hancock. Educ: Mont. State Univ, 24-25; Univ. Mont, 26-29; Phi Delta Theta. Polit. & Govt. Pos: Mem, dist. sch. bd, 37-41; Mont. State Rep, 37-41 & 45-47; mem, high sch. bd, 47-55; Mont. State Sen, 49-51 & 57-; mem. Mont. State Welfare Bd, 53-59. Bus. & Prof. Pos: Mgr. and owner, Coca Cola Bottling Co, Bozeman, 31- Mil. Serv: Marine Res, 29-35. Mem: Elks; Eagles; Shrine. Rel: Episcopal. Mailing Add: 1013 E. Olive, Bozeman, Mont. 59715.

LEHTONEN, ALFRED JOHN R
Adminstr, Interstate Land Sales Registrn, Dept. of Housing and Urban Develop.
b. Bergenfield, N.J, 10/10/30; s. John E. Lehtonen and Eva Raitanen L; m. 6/26/54 to Lucille Elotta Fisher; c. Alfred John, II. Educ: Rutgers Univ, B.A, 52; Univ. Tex. Law Sch, LL.B, 59; Alpha Sigma Phi; Delta Theta Phi. Polit. & Govt. Pos: City attorney, Rollingwood, Tex, 65-69, city councilman and mayor pro-tem, 67-69; adminstr, Interstate Land Sales Registrn, Dept. of Housing and Urban Develop, 69- Bus. & Prof. Pos: Attorney-at-law, Austin, Tex, 59-69. Mil. Serv: Entered as 2nd Lt, Air Force, 52, released as 1st Lt, 54, after serv. as Post Exchange Officer. Mem: Travis Co. Bar Asn; State Bar of Tex; Delta Theta Phi Alumni; Gr. Austin Asn; Scottish Rite; Mason (32°); Shrine; Eastern Star. Rel: Lutheran. Mailing Add: 2411 Babcock Rd, Vienna, Va. 22180.

LEIBHAN, JOE B. R
N.Dak. State Rep.
b. Berwick, N.Dak, 7/26/25; s. Alex Leibhan and Lucy L; m. 10/10/51 to Berenice Ann Leier. Educ: Esmond Pub. Sch. Dist, 12 years. Polit. & Govt. Pos: City Alderman, Esmond, N.Dak, 51-; Qm, Benson Co. VFW Post 4251, 51-; N.Dak. State Rep, 12th Dist, 67-, State and Fed. Govt. Cmt, N.Dak. House Rep, 67-68, mem, Cmt. Educ, State Educ. Research Cmt. and Vet. Affairs Cmt, 69- Bus. & Prof. Pos: Secy. and treas, Commun. Recreational Center, Inc, 62- Mil. Serv: Entered as Pvt, Army, 43, released as M/Sgt, 46, after serv. in 204th Ord. and 164th N.Dak. Nat. Guard, Asian-Pac. Theatre, 44-46; Good Conduct Medal; Infantry Combat Badge; S.Philippine Liberation Medal with One Bronze Serv. Star; Army Occupation Meal, Japan; Victory Medal. Mem: VFW; Am. Legion; Eagles; Sprotsmen Club; Nat. Farmers; Farm Bur; K. of C. Lifetime mem, VFW. Rel: Catholic. Mailing Add: Box 8, Esmond, N.Dak. 58332.

LEICHTER, FRANZ S. D
N.Y. State Assemblyman
b. Vienna, Austria, 8/19/30; s. Otto Leichter and Katherine Pick L; m. 7/3/58 to Nina Williams. Educ: Swarthmore Col, B.A, 52; Harvard Law Sch, LL.B, 57. Polit. & Govt. Pos: Dem. dist. leader, 69th Assembly Dist, Manhattan, N.Y, 61-69; v.chmn, N.Y. Co. Dem. Exec. Cmt, 62-63; del, N.Y. State Dem. Conv, 62, 64 & 66 and Dem. Nat. Conv, 64; N.Y. State Assemblyman, 69th Assembly Dist, 69- Bus. & Prof. Pos: Attorney, Robbins, Galton & Bondi. Mil. Serv: Entered as Pvt, Army, 53, released as Cpl, 55, after serv. in Far East. Mem: N.Y.C. Bar Asn; Harvard Law Sch. Asn; Am. Civil Liberties Union; NAACP. Rel: Jewish. Legal Res: 250 W. 104th St, New York, N.Y. 10025. Mailing Add: 21 E. 40th St, New York, N.Y. 10016.

LEIGHTY, RONALD A. D
b. Aberdeen, S.Dak, 8/27/30; s. C. Harland Leighty and Elizabeth Schmaltz L; m. 11/26/55 to Marlene J; c. LeAnn. Educ: North. State Col, B.S, 58. Polit. & Govt. Pos: S.Dak. State Rep, Brown Co, 63-67; pres, Brown Co. Young Dem. and regional dir, S.Dak. Young Dem, 62-63. Bus. & Prof. Pos: Life Underwriter, Brookings Int. Life, 61-66; bus. mgr, State Training Sch, 60-61; motor truck salesman, Int. Harvester, 58-60. Mil. Serv: Entered as Basic Airman, Air Force, 50, released as Airman 1/C, 54, after serv. in ETO, 51-54. Mem: Hole-In-One Club; Elks; Am. Legion. Rel: Catholic. 1967 Legal Res: Aberdeen, S.Dak. No mailing address available. (1967)

LEIMBACK, HARRY EDWARD D
Wyo. State Sen.
b. Joliet, Mont, 10/5/25; s. Claude Leimback and Bessie Duffy L; m. 4/3/48 to Melda L. Christiansen; c. Thomas, Patrick and Linda. Educ: Casper Col, A.A, 48; Univ. Wyo, J.D, 51. Polit. & Govt. Pos: Munic. judge, Casper, Wyo, 51-53; co. and prosecuting attorney, Natrona Co, 58-66; Wyo. State Sen, 67- Bus. & Prof. Pos: Practicing attorney, Casper, Wyo, 51- Mil. Serv: Entered as A/S, Navy, 43, released as Radioman 3/C, 46, after serv. aboard ship in S.Pac, 44-46. Mem: Am. and Wyo. Bar Asns; Rotary; Elks; Eagles. Rel: Lutheran. Mailing Add: 1108 W. 25th, Casper, Wyo. 82601.

LEINBERRY, WILBUR STANLEY R
Mem, Calif. Rep. State Cent. Cmt.
b. Philadelphia, Pa, 9/12/28; s. Wilbur Leinberry and Joanna McLaughlin L; m. 4/15/61 to Gaye Lee Davison. Educ: Tufts Univ. Col. Eng, B.S.M.E, 50. Polit. & Govt. Pos: Assoc. mem, Calif. Rep. State Cent. Cmt, 66-67, mem, 68- Bus. & Prof. Pos: Assoc. Engr, design, Lockheed Aircraft, Burbank, Calif, 53-54; design engr, asst. chief engr, Vinson Eng. & Mfg, Van Nuys, 54-57; sr. aerospace design specialist, Sterer Eng. & Mfg, Los Angeles, 58- Mil. Serv: Entered as Ensign, Navy, 50, released as Lt.(jg), 53, after serv. in Naval Forces, Far E. and N. Korea, 51-53; Presidential Unit Citation with Star; World War II Victory Medal; Navy Occupation Medal; China Serv. Medal; Korean Serv. Medal with two Bronze Stars; Korean Presidential Unit Citation; UN Serv. Medal. Mem: Am. Soc. of Mech. Engrs; San Fernando Valley Bus. and Prfnl. Asn; pres, Studio City-Sherman Oaks Young Rep, 67-68. Merit Award, Studio City-Sherman Oaks Young Rep, 65 & 67; Nat. Award for Campaign and Pub. Rels, Young Rep. Nat. Fedn, 67-69; Club. of the Year Award, Los Angeles Co. Young Rep, 68. Rel: Protestant. Mailing Add: 11527 Doña Dolores Pl, Studio City, Calif. 91604.

LEINER, HENRY ROBERT R
Chmn, Camden Co. Rep. Party, N.J.
b. N.Y.C, 2/11/16; s. Leo Martin Leiner and Magadalena Reindel L; m. 7/23/38 to Grace Loretta Dobbs; c. Grace Loretta (Mrs. McKiernan), Sharon (Mrs. Bianchi), Robert Henry and JoAnn Henrietta (Mrs. Burgess). Educ: Camden Cath. High Sch, N.J, grad; night sch, writing and journalism, 2 years. Polit. & Govt. Pos: Pres, 11th Ward Rep. Club, Camden, N.J, 51-52; Rep. co. committeeman, 64-69; chmn, Camden Co. Rep. Party, 66-; alternate del, Rep. Nat. Conv, 68; pres, Camden Co. Park Cmn, 69. Bus. & Prof. Pos: V.pres. and dir. book sales, Curtis Circulation Co, N.Y.C, currently. Mem: 25 Year Club of Independent Distributors of Newspapers & Mag; League to Aid Retarded Children (former chmn, nursery sch. bd, Camden Co, N.J.); PTA; Cherry Hill Twp. Assembly; Cmt. of 100, Cherry Hill Rep. Club. Rel: Catholic. Mailing Add: 157 Valley Run Dr, Cherry Hill, N.J. 08034.

LEININGER, THEODORE E. R
Chmn, Fulton Co. Rep. Exec. Cmt, Ohio
b. Archbold, Ohio, 2/8/02; s. Simon Leininger and Christina Herrmann L; m. 3/15/20 to Mearle E. Dailey; c. Doris (Mrs. John Ely), Leroy, Florence (Mrs. Clifford Ziegler), Dorothy (Mrs. Bob Meehan), Laureta (Mrs. Richard Stonebreaker), Claire, Jane (Mrs. Darrel Knisely) and Marilyn (Mrs. Joseph Sarnac). Educ: Tedrow Spec. Dist. Sch, Ohio, 8 years. Polit. & Govt. Pos: Clerk, sch. bd, Gorham Twp, Ohio, 36-37; mem, Fulton Co. Rep. Cent. Cmt, 42-; crew leader, Fulton Co. Agr. Census, 59 & 60; on Fed. Jury, Toledo, Ohio, 64 & 67; chmn, Fulton Co. Rep. Exec. Cmt, 68- Mem: Dir. and treas, Fulton Co. Agr. Soc, 53-; co-chmn, Fulton Co. Heart Drive, 66-67; mem, Twp. and State Trustees Asn; Fulton Co. Farm Bur; Lions; hon. mem, Gorham Twp. Sch. Future Farmers of Am. Rel: Evangelical Lutheran. Mailing Add: Route 1, Fayette, Ohio 43521.

LEININGER, WILLIAM H, JR. R
b. Loup City, Nebr, 1921; m. to Fran Fordik; c. three. Educ: Univ. of Nebr. Mil. Serv: WW II, U.S.M.C; Korean War, U.S.M.C. Mem: Am. Legion, Comdr; Comdr, Flathead Post No. 7; Chmn, United Vets. Coun, Flathead Co; Scoutmaster, No. 76; Zone Chmn, Red Cross. Mailing Add: Kalispell, Mont. 59901. (1967)

LEISCHNER, ELLIS EDWARD D
Chmn, Piatt Co. Dem. Party, Ill.
b. DeLand, Ill, 8/31/14; s. William Edward Leischner and Winnie G. Ellis L; m. 12/31/41 to Henrietta E. Weber; c. Judith Anita, Charles Edward, Robert Ellis and Connie Joe. Educ: DeLand Twp. High Sch. Polit. & Govt. Pos: Town Clerk, DeLand, Ill, 50-58, Mayor, 6 years; enforcement officer, Ill. Commerce Cmn, 61-69; chmn, Piatt Co. Dem. Party, currently. Bus. & Prof. Pos: Asst. Mgr, S.S. Kresge Co, 36-40; owner, Bud's Grocery, 46-47; partner, D & L Co, 47-62; with, Roosevelt Nat. Life Ins. Co, 66- Mil. Serv: Entered as Pvt, Army, 41, released as 1st Lt, 45, after serv. in Tenth Armored Div, ETO, 44-45; Purple Heart; Bronze Star. Mem: Mason; Consistory; Shrine; Am. Legion; Farmers Union. Rel: Methodist. Mailing Add: DeLand, Ill. 61839.

LEISETH, ROBERT VERNON R
Minn. State Sen.
b. Peever, S.Dak, 4/29/28; s. Soren Henry Leiseth and Bertha Jordahl L; m. 8/4/57 to Marilyn Kathleen Johnson; c. Bruce Robert, Jon Robert and Kristi Kay. Educ: N.Dak. State Univ, 53-54; Concordia Col, B.A. in Bus. Admin, 56; Sch. of Banking, Univ. Wis, grad, 66. Polit. & Govt. Pos: Secy, Becker Co. Rep. Cmt, Minn, 62-63, chmn, 63-66; Minn. State Sen, 65th Dist, 67- Mil. Serv: Entered as Sgt, Army, 50, released as Sgt. 1/C, 52, after serv. in Heavy Mortar Co, 196th Regt, Alaskan Theater; Good Conduct Medal; Nat. Defense Medal; 1st Lt.(Ret), Army Res, 63. Mem: V.pres, Minn-Dak. Conf. NABAC, 60, pres, 61; dir, Detroit Lakes Rotary, 63-64, v.pres, 66-67, pres, 67-68; dist. dir, Minn. Bankers Asn, 64-66; Am. Legion; C. of C; C-400 Club, Concordia Col, Moorhead, Minn; Farm Bur. Rel: Lutheran. Mailing Add: R.R. 3, Detroit Lakes, Minn. 56501.

LEISSNER, MARTIN WILLIAM, JR. R
Chmn, Brazos Co. Rep. Party, Tex.
b. Houston, Tex, 9/7/32; s. Martin William Leissner, Sr. (mother deceased); m. 6/17/61 to Helen Francis Dedeke; c. Donna Lynn. Educ: Tex. A&M Univ, B.B.A, 55. Polit. & Govt. Pos: Campaign worker for Barry Goldwater, Brazos Co, Tex, 64; chmn, Brazos Co. Rep. Party, 66- Mil. Serv: Entered as 2nd Lt, Army, 55, released as 1st Lt, 57, after serv. in Transportation Corps, Korea, 55-57. Mem: Brazos Co. A&M Club; Brazos Co. A&M Quarterback Club; C. of C. Rel: First Christian Church of N.Am. Mailing Add: 3804 Kelli Lane, Bryan, Tex. 77801.

LEITCHER, ELIZABETH S. R
Mem, Calif. Rep. State Cent. Cmt.
b. Grand Rapids, Mich, 10/21/16; d. Joseph Thomas Sullivan and Lillie Kelk S; m. 7/4/48 to Robert D. Leitcher; c. Stefani (Mrs. Ortman), Kathleen and Michael. Educ: San Jose State Col, 33-36; Heald's Bus. Col, San Jose, Calif, 37. Polit. & Govt. Pos: Pres, Rep. Women's Club, Federated, San Luis Obispo, Calif, 64 & 65; co. campaign chmn. for Calif. State Senators Vernon L. Sturgeon and Donald Grunsky, 66; mem, Calif. Rep. State Cent. Cmt, 66-; alternate del, Rep. Nat. Conv, 68; v.pres, Region III, Cent. Div, Calif. Fedn. Rep. Women's Clubs, 68-69; secy, San Luis Obispo Co. Rep. Cent. Cmt, 69. Mem: Past pres, Children's Home Soc. of Calif; San Luis Obispo Co. Hist. Soc; San Luis Obispo Antique Car Club; Art Asn; Econ. Opportunities Cmn; Hon. Life Membership, PTA. Rel: Protestant. Mailing Add: 642 Monterey St, San Luis Obispo, Calif. 93401.

LEITHMAN, JOHN KENNETH D
La. State Rep.
b. New Orleans, La, 7/24/30; s. John William Leithman and Annabel Poche L; m. 6/12/54 to Joan Cynthia Tillotson; c. Lauren Maria. Educ: Loyola Univ. of the South, B.S. and distinguished mil. grad, 52; Sigma Alpha Kappa. Polit. & Govt. Pos: Mem, Sch. Bd, Jefferson Parish, La, 64-68; La. State Rep, 68-

Bus. & Prof. Pos: V.Pres, Hartwig Moss Ins. Agency, New Orleans, 54-64; owner and pres, Leithman & Assoc. Inc, Ins. Agency, 64- Mil. Serv: Entered as 2nd Lt, Army, 52, released as 1st Lt, 54, after serv. in Mil. Police, Korea, 53-54; Korean Theatre Decoration. Mem: Nat. and La. Asns. Ins. Agents; New Orleans Ins. Exchange; Lions; Lafitte Yacht Club; David Crockett Fire Co; Knights of Columbus (4°); Gould Volunteer Fire Co; St. Anthony Church Men's Club; New Orleans Track & Field Officials Asn; Sugar Bowl Track Official; American Red Cross; Rotary. Outstanding Citizenship Award, West Bank Rotary; Outstanding Citizens Award, West Bank Lions. Rel: Catholic. Mailing Add: 50 Smithway Dr, Gretna, La. 70053.

LeKANDER, GILBERT R
Chmn, William Co. Rep. Party, Va.
b. Butte, Mont, 6/1/18; m. 3/10/43 to Carol Foster; c. Adele Ann and John Foster. Educ: Mont. Univ, B.A; Sigma Delta Chi; Sigma Alpha Epsilon. Polit. & Govt. Pos: Admin. asst. to U.S. Rep. Frank T. Bow, Ohio, 45-; chmn, William Co. Rep. Party, Va, currently. Bus. & Prof. Pos: Gen. ed. work, Assoc. Press, 40-41. Mil. Serv: Entered as Pvt, Army Air Force, released as Capt, after serv. in N.Africa and China-Burma-India, 42-46; Distinguished Flying Cross; Air Medal. Mailing Add: Box 299, R.R. 3, Manassas, Va. 22110. (1967)

LELAND, ALFRED E. R
Wash. State Rep.
b. St. Marie, Idaho, 1921; single. Educ: Univ. of Wash; Spec. Course, Boeing Sch. Aeronaut, Oakland, Calif. Polit. & Govt. Pos: Mayor, Kirkland, Wash, 6 years; mem, Wash. State Good Rd. Asn; mem, C. of C; Wash. State Rep, currently. Bus. & Prof. Pos: Real Estate. Mil. Serv: Army Air Force. Mem: Elks; Sons of Norway. Mailing Add: Box 715, Redmond, Wash. 98052. (1967)

LEMBO, ARMAND E. D
b. Newark, N.J, 8/31/26. Educ: Univ. of Ill, B.S. Polit. & Govt. Pos: Dir. of inspections, Newark; former agent, Fed. Bur of Narcotics; spec. investr, Port of N.Y. Waterfront Cmn; co. committeeman, N. Ward Dem. chmn, Newark; del, Dem. Nat. Conv, 64, alternate del, 68; former N.J. State Assemblyman. Bus. & Prof. Pos: Asst. football coach, Villanova Col; teacher. Mil. Serv: Army, World War II. Mem: Moose. Mailing Add:329 Grafton, Newark, N.J. 07104.

LEMIRE, GEORGE D
N.H. State Rep.
b. Berlin, N.H, 11/12/29; married; c. Seven. Educ: Berlin pub. schs. Polit. & Govt. Pos: N.H. State Rep, currently. Bus. & Prof. Pos: Papermaker. Rel: Catholic. Mailing Add: 786 Hillside Ave, Berlin, N.H. 03570. (1967)

LEMKE, HERMAN G. P. D
Chmn, Honolulu City Coun, Hawaii
b. Honolulu, Hawaii, 5/17/17; s. Herman G. Lemke and Adele Robinson L; m. 1/3/42 to Florence Chalmers; c. Marlene, David, Michael, Adele and Herman, Jr. Educ: Santa Clara Univ, Ph.B, 39. Polit. & Govt. Pos: Chmn, Territorial Civil Serv, Hawaii, 48-53; mem, bd. supvr, City and Co. of Honolulu, 55-60, councilman, 61-; chmn, Honolulu City Coun, 65- Bus. & Prof. Pos: Mem. staff, Dept. of Internal Revenue, 40-43; pub. acct, 43-57; partner, Herman Lemke, CPA, 57-61; partner, Lemke & Co, CPA's, 61- Mem: Dir, Hawaii Soc. of CPA; off, Hawaiian Civic Club; dir. and chmn, educ. cmt, Jr. C. of C; chmn, Commun. Betterment Cmt; Off. Precinct Club, Dem. Party. Tree-shell collection used for research purposes by Bishop Museum. Rel: Catholic. Legal Res: 919 Noio St, Honolulu, Hawaii 96816. Mailing Add: City Council, Room 307, Honolulu, Hawaii 96813. (1967)

LEMKUIL, LINDA LEE R
Committeewoman, Colo. Rep. State Cent. Cmt.
b. Norton, Kans, 12/30/41; d. Francis Alton Switzer and Eulala Pearl Poage S; m. 9/22/62 to Dirk Lemkuil; c. Matthew Karl and Daniel Jake. Educ: Parks Sch. of Bus, 60; Adams State Col, 61-62; Pi Kappa Beta. Polit. & Govt. Pos: Committeewoman, Colo. Rep. State Cent. Cmt, 66-; chmn, Sen. Dist. Rep. Party and House Dist. Rep. Party, 67-68; secy, Adams Co. Young Rep, 67-69, v.chmn, 69-; Rep. cand, U.S. House Rep, 68; pub. notary, 69- Rel: Baptist. Mailing Add: 7014 Elati, Denver, Colo. 80221.

LEMLEY, BILL L. D
Ala. State Rep.
b. Birmingham, Ala, 3/28/25; s. Geo. Leonard Lemley and Velma Tolbert L; m. 7/28/46 to Billie Smith; c. Cindy and William. Educ: Gupton-Jones Col. of Mortuary Sci, D.M.S, 51; Pi Sigma Eta. Polit. & Govt. Pos: Mem, Sch. Bd, Oneonta City Schs, Ala, 53-56; coroner, Blount Co, 58-66; Ala State Rep, currently. Bus. & Prof. Pos: Pres, Lemley Funeral Chapel, Inc, 52- Mil. Serv: Entered as Seaman 2/C, Navy, 43, released as AMM 3/C, 46, after serv. in S.Pac, 44-46. Mem: Ala. and Nat. Funeral Dirs. Asns; Mason; Shrine; VFW; Am. Legion; Rotary; Jaycee; C. of C. Rel: Baptist. Legal Res: Old Birmingham Hwy, Oneonta, Ala. 35121. Mailing Add: P.O. Box 456, Oneonta, Ala. 35121.

LEMME, JOHN HEWETT 'JACK'
b. Duluth, Minn, 3/21/25; s. Oscar Lemme and Elsie Hewett L; m. 8/2/52 to Jean Antoinette Hedahl; c. Linda Lee, Steven William, Mark John and Kathryn Ann. Educ: Univ. Minn, B.S.L, 05 and LL.B, 52. Polit. & Govt. Pos: Former Minn. State Rep, Dist. 53A. Bus. & Prof. Pos: Pres. and gen. mgr, Little Falls Broadcasting Co, 52-; v.pres. and chmn. bd, Crestline Prod, Inc, 63-66; mem, bd. dir, Minn. Power and Light Co, 66- Mil. Serv: Entered as A/S, Navy, 43, released as Qm. 1/C, 46, after serv. in Pac. and S.W. Pac. Theatres, 44-46. Mem: Bd. of dir, Nat. Asn. of Broadcasters; co-chmn, Finance Cmt, Future of Broadcasting in Am. Cmt; bd. of dir, Minn. Broadcasters Asn; Mason; Lions; past pres, Little Falls C. of C; pres, Little Falls Int. Club. Rel: Episcopal. Mailing Add: 1101 Mississippi Blvd, Little Falls, Minn. 56345. (1967)

LEMMON, RAY ALLEN D
Tex. State Rep.
b. Houston, Tex, 4/6/26; s. Rufus Claude Lemmon and Kate Mitcham L; m. 4/22/50 to Elizabeth Ann Davidson; c. Patricia Ann, Ray Allen, II, Lorraine Leigh, David Mitcham and Paula Ann. Educ: Univ. Houston, B.S, 55; Frontiersman Asn. Polit. & Govt. Pos: Tex. State Rep, Dist. 24, 69- Bus. & Prof. Pos: Owner, Ray Lemmon Ins, Houston, Tex, currently. Mil. Serv: Entered as Pvt, Marines, 44, released as Cpl, 46, after serv. in First Marine Air Wing, S. Pac, 44-45; Victory Medal. Mem: Houston, Tex. and Nat. Asns. of Ins. Agents; AF&AM; Amvets; Toastmasters Int; YMCA Indianguides; Boy Scouts (committeeman); Eastern Star. Rel: Unitarian. Legal Res: 11101 Elback, Houston, Tex. 77035. Mailing Add: 3100 Richmond Ave, Suite 300, Houston, Tex. 77006.

LEMMON, WILLARD LINCOLN D
Va. State Del.
b. Marion, Va, 9/30/24; s. Frank Tremaine Lemmon and Alexina Lincoln L; m. 2/14/46 to Rosa Kevan Rogerson; c. Alexina (Mrs. Curtis Copenhaver) and Elizabeth (Mrs. Lynn Sayers). Educ: Davidson Col, 1 year; Univ. Va, 6 months; Beta Theta Pi. Polit. & Govt. Pos: Va. State Del, 68- Bus. & Prof. Pos: Pres, Lemmon Transport Co, Inc, 46, Lemmon Investment Corp, 50 and Consolidated Real Estate Corp, 56; dir, Va. Commonwealth Life Ins. Co, 68. Mil. Serv: Entered as Pvt, Army, 43, released as Sgt, 45, after serv. in Co. I, 309th Inf, ETO, 44-45; Purple Heart; Bronze Star; Combat Inf. Medal; Theatre Ribbons. Mem: Chmn, bd. of trustees, Mary Baldwin Col; v.pres, Smyth Co. Commun. Hosp; Kiwanis; Am. Legion; VFW. Chosen outstanding young man, State of Va, 56. Rel: Presbyterian. Legal Res: Ridgeway Rd, Marion, Va. 24354. Mailing Add: 1424 N. Main St, Marion, Va. 24354.

LEMON, THOS. L. D
Chmn, Monroe Co. Dem. Cent. Cmt, Ind.
b. Bloomington, Ind, 8/8/14; s. Thomas Mack Lemon and Mary Figg L; m. 6/19/58 to Elizabeth Watkins; c. T. Ridley, S. Timothy, Rebecca, Kathryn, James and Tracey. Educ: Bloomington High Sch, dipl. Polit. & Govt. Pos: Mayor and judge, Bloomington, Ind, 48-52, mayor, 56-60 & 60-62; city mgr, Sanford, Fla, 52-54; dep. dir, U.S. Post Office Dept, Cincinnati, Ohio, 62-63; del, State Dem. Conv, 68; del, Dem. Nat. Conv, 68; chmn, Monroe Co. Dem. Cent. Cmt, 66- Bus. & Prof. Pos: Pres, Cantol Wax Prod. Co, 33-52 and Thos. L. Lemon & Assoc. Inc, 54-69; v.pres, Russel, Schubert, Hamilton & Assoc, 68-69; exec. dir, Home Owners Mutual Equity, Inc, 69. Mem: Ind. State Steam Pollution Bd, 61-62; Ind. Baptist Homes and Hospitals, 64-65; Am. Water Works Asn; Int. City Mgr. Asn; Am. Munic. Asn; Nat. and Ind. Munic. Leagues; U.S. Conf. of Mayors; Int. Union of Local Authorities; Am. Ord. Asn; Am. Pub. Works Asn; C. of C; Jr. C. of C; Ky. Col; bd. dirs, YMCA; chmn, Monroe Co. Heart Fund; bd. dirs, United Fund; Ind. Econ. Coun; Co. Bd. of Review; bd, Salvation Army; Wabash Valley Asn; Lake Monroe Asn. Rel: Baptist. Mailing Add: 2727 N. Dunn Rd, Bloomington, Ind. 47401.

LEMUCCHI, TIMOTHY JON D
b. Bakersfield, Calif, 5/5/37; s. Louis Lemucchi and Leah Williams L; div; c. Lisa Amelia. Educ: Stanford Univ, B.A. & M.A; Georgetown Law Sch, J.D, 65; Univ. Mex, 67; Univ. de las Americas, 68; Zeta Psi. Polit. & Govt. Pos: Mem. staff, U.S. Sen. Clair Engle, Calif, 61-63; mem. staff, Dem. Nat. Cmt, Wash, D.C, 64-65; consult, Calif. State Legis, 66; Dem. nominee, Calif. State Legis, 68- Bus. & Prof. Pos: Lawyer, Chain & Younger, 67- Mil. Serv: Seaman, Naval Res, 54-62. Mailing Add: 2700 Alta Vista, Bakersfield, Calif. 93305.

LENA, SAM D
Ariz. State Sen.
b. Evergreen, La, 1/23/21; s. Sam Lena and Mamie Dolce L; m. 3/29/51 to Gloria O. Gabusi; c. Sam, Jr, Kathrine and John. Educ: Thomas Jefferson High Sch, Pt. Arthur, Tex, grad, 39. Polit. & Govt. Pos: Ariz. State Rep, Dist. 16, Pima Co, 65-66, Dist. 7C, 67-68; Ariz. State Sen, Dist. 7C, 69- Bus. & Prof. Pos: Foreman, Sheet Metal Dept, Davis Monthan Air Force Base, 43-46; self-employed retailer, 47-52 & 55-; salesman, Coca Cola Bottling Co, 52-55. Mem: Bd. dirs, Retail Licensed Beverage Asn; adv. bd, Ariz. Asn. for Retarded Children; Elks; K. of C; S. Tucson Lions; Pueblo Optimist Club. Rel: Roman Catholic. Mailing Add: 2331 E. Beverly Dr, Tucson, Ariz. 85719.

LENARD, HENRY M. D
Ill. State Rep.
b. Chicago, Ill, 9/23/03. Educ: Tilden Tech. High Sch. Polit. & Govt. Pos: Court bailiff, Ill, 55-; Ill. State Rep, currently. Mem: K. of C; St. Jude Police League; Ill. Police Asn; St. Michael's Boys Club; Eagles; South Chicago Aerie No. 1358; Polish Nat. Alliance No. 94; Polish Falcons. Rel: Catholic. Mailing Add: 8111 S. Colfax St, Chicago, Ill. 60617. (1967)

LENCH, RONALD G. D
b. Bridgeport, Conn, 1/7/33; s. Morris Lench, Bessie Marcus L; m. to Susan Mark; c. One. Educ: Pa. State Univ; Univ. Pittsburgh Sch. Law, LL.B. Polit. & Govt. Pos: Chmn, Beaver Co. Citizens for Clark and Dilworth, Pa; solicitor, Beaver Falls Area Sch. Dist, Borough of Big Beaver; solicitor, Beaver Co. Planning Zoning Cmt, 59-63; Beaver Falls city solicitor, 60-61; pres, Beaver Young Dem, 62; asst. D.CA, Beaver Co, 62-64; Beaver Falls Dem. City chmn, 63-64; Pa. State Rep, 64-68; del, Dem. Nat. Conv, 68. Bus. & Prof. Pos: Lawyer. Mil. Serv: Army Res. Mem: Am. Trial Lawyers Asn; Beaver Co. and Pa. Bar Asns. Mailing Add: 533 Blackhawk Rd, Beaver Falls, Pa. 15010. (1967)

LENDE, RUSSELL MELVIN R
Chmn, Clatsop Co. Rep. Cent. Cmt, Ore.
b. Sandstone, Minn, 11/13/37; s. Melvin Oluf Lende and Myrtle Elizebeth Adams L; m. 12/5/59 to Patricia Kay Goldmund; c. Russell Melvin, Jr. and Johnny Adam. Educ: Pac. Univ, B.Sc, 59, O.D, 60; Omega Epsilon Phi. Polit. & Govt. Pos: V.chmn, Young Rep, 64, chmn, 65; legis. chmn, Grange and Optom. Socs, 66-; chmn, Clatsop Co. Rep. Cent. Cmt, Ore, 68- Publ: Practice management article, J. Am. Optom. Asn, 4/65. Mem: Secy-treas, Ore. Optom. Asn, 67-69; Grange (mem. various cmts); Rotary (past treas, secy. and v.pres, currently pres, 69-); Seaside Police Reserve (Capt, Lt. and Sgt); Sch. Bd, 67-72. Awarded first place in driving competition and knowledge of driving laws in West Linn and Ore. City High Sch. student competition, 54 & 55. Legal Res: Hamlet Route, Seaside, Ore. 97138. Mailing Add: 10-A N. Holladay Dr, Seaside, Ore. 97138.

LENHART, THOMAS B. D
b. Vancouver, B.C, 8/26/10; s. Frank A. Lenhart and Irene Clemens L; m. 1934 to Rachel E. Educ: Grants Pass High Sch, Ore, grad, 27; U.S. Naval Acad, 30-31; Naval Supply Sch, Harvard Grad. Sch. Bus. Admin, 44. Polit. & Govt. Pos: Dem. cand, U.S. House Rep, 35th Dist, Calif, 66 & 68. Bus. & Prof. Pos: Owned and operated Arrow Laundry and Cleaners, 55-63. Mil. Serv: Marine Corps, 28; aide in formation and enlistee in Marine Corps Res. Bn, 39, entered active duty Marines, 40, commissioned 2nd Lt, 42, retired as Maj, 59, after serv. as instr, Marine Corps Sch. of Qm. Admin, 42-43, S.Pac. Theatre, 44 and Korea, 53-54; Bronze Star with Combat V; Navy Commendation Medal with Combat V; Presidential Unit Citation; Navy Unit Citation; Korean Presidential Unit Citation. Mem: Retail Clerks Union (pres, Portland Chap, 37-39). Mailing Add: 13881 Dall Lane, Santa Ana, Calif. 92705.

LENHOFF, BERNARD R
Chmn, North Adams Rep. City Cmt, Mass.
b. North Adams, Mass, 10/4/19; s. Jacob Lenhoff and Fanny Snyder L; m. 12/28/41 to Lillian Giuffre; c. Marsha, John and Arlene. Educ: Suffolk Univ. Law Sch, LL.B, 41. Polit. & Govt. Pos: Mem, North Adams Rep. City Cmt, Mass, 52-; pub. adminstr, Berkshire Co, 55-; mem, North Adams Sch. Cmt, 56-60; chmn, North Berkshire Regional Voc. Planning Cmt, 58-59 and North Berkshire Voc. Regional Dist. Sch. Cmt, 59-63; city solicitor, North Adams, 62-67. Mil. Serv: Entered as Pvt, Army Air Force, 42, released as Sgt, 45. Mem: Mass. and Berkshire Co. Bar Asns; Mass. Trial Lawyers Asn; City Solicitors & Town Counsel Asn. Rel: Jewish. Legal Res: 229 Church St, North Adams, Mass. 02147. Mailing Add: 57 Main St, North Adams, Mass. 01247.

LENKER, WILLIAM FRED R
Chmn, Minnehaha Co. Rep. Cent. Cmt, S.Dak.
b. Colome, S.Dak, 3/22/23; s. Carle B. Lenker and Madeline Flint L; m. 6/27/52 to Mary Ann Boyce; c. Linda, Laura, Timothy, Arthur and William. Educ: Univ. Minn, Bus. Admin, 49; Sigma Alpha Epsilon. Polit. & Govt. Pos: Del, State Cent. Conv, 64 & 66; chmn, Minnehaha Co. Rep. Cent. Cmt, S.Dak, 66- Bus. & Prof. Pos: Pres, Lenker, Nugen & Williams Agency, 55; pres, Lenker-Wheeler Realty, 66. Mil. Serv: Entered as Cadet, Army Air Corps, 42, released as 1st Lt, 46, after serv. in 305 Bomb Group, Eighth Air Corps, ETO, 45-46; Air Medal; European Theatre Ribbon. Mem: Chmn, Nat. Rehabilitation Cmn, Am. Legion (past state comdr, S.Dak); chmn, Gov. Vet. Cmn; Lions; Shrine; VFW; Elks; Mason; chmn, Mil. Affairs Cmt, C. of C.; Boys Club (past pres); Minnehaha Country Club; Navy League. Rel: Episcopal. Mailing Add: 1408 South Kiwanis, Sioux Falls, S.Dak. 57105.

LENNON, ALTON ASA D
U.S. Rep, N.C.
b. Wilmington, N.C, 8/17/06; m. to Karine Welch; c. Mrs. Lewis R. Frost, III and Alton Yates. Educ: Wake Forest Col. Polit. & Govt. Pos: N.C. State Sen, 47 & 51; judge, New Hanover Co. Recorders Court; U.S. Sen, N.C, 53-54; U.S. Rep, N.C, 57- Bus. & Prof. Pos: Lawyer. Mailing Add: 306 Colonial Dr, Wilmington, N.C. 28401.

LENNON, ARTHUR THOMAS R
Committeeman, Ill. Rep. Cent. Cmt.
b. Joliet, Ill, 8/11/23; s. Arthur A. Lennon and Irene Haughton L; m. 5/5/51 to Jean Canty; c. Dinah J, Elizabeth A, Arthur C. and John H. Educ: Univ. Ill, B.S, 48, J.D, 49; Sachem; Sigma Alpha Epsilon; Phi Alpha Delta. Polit. & Govt. Pos: Attorney, Joliet Bd. Local Improv, Ill, 55-67; Rep. precinct committeeman, Joliet, 62-69; attorney, Joliet Plan Cmn, 64-67; committeeman, Ill. Rep. Cent. Cmt, 66-; asst. states attorney, Will Co, 68-69. Bus. & Prof. Pos: Attorney-partner, Murphy Timm & Lennon; mem. faculty, Ill. Inst. Continuing Legal Educ, currently. Mil. Serv: Entered as Pvt, Army, 42, released as 1st Lt, 45, after serv. in Air Corps, Europe; 44-45; Col, Air Force Res; Distinguished Flying Cross; World War II Victory Medal; Nat. Defense Medal; Res. Medal; 7 Air Medals and 3 Battle Stars. Mem: Am, Ill. State and Will Co. Bar Asns; Am. Judicature Soc; Cath. Lawyers Guild; Am. Legion; Union League Club Chicago; Elks; Kiwanis; ROA; Air Force Asn; K. of C; Farm Bur. Outstanding Rep. Precinct Committeeman, 62. Rel: Catholic. Legal Res: 1405 Mayfield Ave, Joliet, Ill. 60435. Mailing Add: 5 E. Van Buren St, Joliet, Ill. 60431.

LENNON, ROBERT LAWRENCE D
Miss. State Rep.
b. N.Y.C, 3/13/33; s. Thomas A. Lennon and Helen Paul Breckenridge L; m. 7/11/59 to Mary Rush; c. Robbie, Dana, Julie, Rush and Stacey. Educ: Univ. South. Miss, B.S, 59; Univ. Miss, LL.B. and JD; Alpha Tau Omega; Interfraternity Coun. (pres). Polit. & Govt. Pos: Miss. State Rep, currently. Bus. & Prof. Pos: Attorney-at-law. Mil. Serv: Entered as Pfc, Army, 53, released as Cpl, 55, after serv. in Combat Command Bn, 1st Army Div. Mem: Phi Delta Phi; Am, Jr. and Miss. Bar Asns; Kiwanis; C. of C; Jr. C. of C; Red Cross; United Giver's Fund; March of Dimes (chmn). Rel: Baptist. Legal Res: 528 South 28th Ave, Hattiesburg, Miss. 39401. Mailing Add: P.O. Box 1254, Hattiesburg, Miss. 39401.

LENT, BERKELEY D
Ore. State Sen.
b. Los Angeles, Calif, 9/22/21; s. Oscar Paul Lent and Lucile Berkeley L; m. 12/27/68 to Joan Kay Burnett; c. Patricia Lee, Deirdre Jan (Mrs. Paris), Eric Berkeley and Terry Ann. Educ: Reed Inst, Portland, Ore, 41-42 & 46-47; Occidental Col, 44-45; Willamette Univ. Col. Law, J.D, 50. Polit. & Govt. Pos: Ore. State Rep, 57-59 & 63-67; Ore. State Sen, 67-, Majority Leader, Ore. State Senate, currently. Bus. & Prof. Pos: Assoc. ed, Willamette Law J, Willamette Univ. Col. Law, 50; attorney, Bonneville Power Admin, Portland, 50-53; partner, Peterson, Pozzi & Lent, 57-59, Peterson & Lent, 59-62, Peterson, Lent & Paulson, 62-64, Lent, York & Paulson, 64-67 and Lent, York, Paulson & Bullock, 67- Mil. Serv: Entered as A/S, Navy, 42, released as Signalman 2/C, 45, after serv. in Armed Guard, Pac. Fleet, 42-45; Theatre Ribbons. Publ: 'Compensability of Non-Occupational Disease,' Willamette Law J, Vol. 1, No. 24. Mem: Am, Ore. State and Multnomah Co. Bar Asns; Am. Judicature Soc; Am. Trial Lawyers Asn; VFW; Elks. Legal Res: 12710 S.E. Madison St, Portland, Ore. 97233. Mailing Add: 410 Labor Center, Portland, Ore. 97201.

LENT, NORMAN F. R
N.Y. State Sen.
b. East Rockaway, N.Y, 1931; s. Norman F. Lent; m. to Nancy; c. Norman, III, Barbara Anne and Thomas Benjamin. Educ: Hofstra Col, grad, 52; Cornell Law Sch, grad, 57. Polit. & Govt. Pos: Former assoc. police justice, East Rockaway, N.Y; pres, Lynbrook Chap, Nassau Co. Rep. Recruits, 60; confidential law secy. to Supreme Court Justice Thomas P. Farley, 61-63; N.Y. State Sen, Nassau Co, 63-, chmn, Joint Legis. Cmt, on Pub. Health and Senate Cmt. on Health, mem, Joint Legis. Cmts. on Munic. Tort Liability and Matrimonial and Family Laws and Senate Cmts. on Judiciary, Corp, Pub. Serv. and Affairs of Villages; sponsor, Lent-Van Cott Bill to bar mandatory transportation sch. children. Bus. & Prof. Pos: Law partner, Hill, Lent & Troescher, N.Y, 57-; mem, East Rockaway Bd. Trade. Mil. Serv: Entered as Seaman Recruit, Naval Res, 50, graduated Officers Candidate Sch, 52, 2 yrs. active duty, Korean War; Lt, Naval Res, at present. Mem: Nassau Co. and N.Y. State Magistrates Asns; Am. and Nassau Co. Bar Asns; former chmn, Am. Cancer Crusade and East Rockaway Crusade and sectional chmn, S. Shore Crusade; mem-at-lg, S. Cent. Dist, Nassau Co. Boy Scouts; Elks; Am. Legion; Hofstra Col. and Cornell Law Sch. Alumni Asns. Mailing Add: 48 Plymouth Rd, East Rockaway, N.Y. 11518.

LENTO, THOMAS JOSEPH R
b. Chicago, Ill, 3/7/29; s. Frank Lento and Concetta Vite L; m. 5/2/52 to Marian Bogacz; c. Marilyn, Joanne, Rose Ann, Concetta, Thomas Joseph, II and Joseph Henry. Educ: Loyola Univ, B.S, 56; Cent. YMCA Col, Cert. of Real Estate. Polit. & Govt. Pos: Cand, U.S. Rep, Ill, 68; pres, 25th Ward Rep. Orgn, currently; legis. asst. to Ill. State Rep. Peter C. Granata, currently. Bus. & Prof. Pos: Owner and operator, Thomas J. Lento Realty Co, Chicago, Ill, 52-; real estate consult. and appraiser, 1st Nat. Bank of Schiller Park, 64- and Parkway Bank, Harwood Heights, 68-; v.pres. and dir, Parkway Towers Ins. Agency, 69- Mem: Moose; Order of Sons of Italy of Am; West Side Commun. Cmt. Rel: Roman Catholic. Mailing Add: 747 S. Western Ave, Chicago, Ill. 60612.

LENTOL, EDWARD S. D
N.Y. State Sen.
b. Brooklyn, N.Y, 12/26/09; s. Joseph Lentol and Rose Beato L; m. 12/15/35 to Matilda A. Postis; c. Edward, Jr, Joseph and Gilbert. Educ: St. John's, N.Y, LL.B, 32. Polit. & Govt. Pos: N.Y. State Assemblyman, [illegible]9-62; N.Y. State Sen, 63- Bus. & Prof. Pos: Attorney, 34-; secy. and gen. counsr, Transworld Life Ins. Co, N.Y.C, 67- Mem: Kings Co. Criminal Bar Asn; Sons of Italy; K. of C. Rel: Catholic. Legal Res: 152 Russell St, Brooklyn, N.Y. 11222. Mailing Add: 44 Court St, Brooklyn, N.Y. 11201.

LENTZ, EARL LEROY, JR. R
Chmn, Clinton Co. Rep. Cmt, Pa.
b. Sunbury, Pa, 8/31/24; s. Earl Leroy Lentz and Hilda Getz L; m. 5/29/48 to Dorothy Marie Schrock; c. William David and Beth Ann. Educ: Pa. State Univ, B.S. in Chem. Eng, 47; Lincoln Chiropractic Col, D.C, 50; Phi Lambda Upsilon; Tau Beta Pi; Delta Tau Alpha. Polit. & Govt. Pos: Pres, Lock Haven Sch. Bd, Pa, 58-; v.chmn, Clinton Co. Rep. Cmt, Pa, 61-63, chmn, 63-; mem, State Bd. Chiropractic Exams, 65. Mil. Serv: Entered as A/S, Navy, 44, released as Electronics Technician 2/C, 46, after serv. in Commun. Unit 624, Pac. Theater. Mem: Pa. Chiropractic Soc; Am. Chiropractic Asn; Masonic Bodies; Elks; Am. Legion. Hobbies: Skiing; sailing; golf; tennis. Rel: Evangelical United Brethren. Mailing Add: 113 E. Church St, Lock Haven, Pa. 17745.

LENTZ, WILLIAM B. R
Pa. State Sen.
b. Millersburg, Pa, 5/14/20; s. Charles W. Lentz and Minnie Reigle L; m. to Ruth J. Wiest; c. three. Educ: Berrysburg High Sch; U.S. Armed Forces Inst. Polit. & Govt. Pos: Mem, Millersburg Borough Coun, Pa, 6 years; mem, Dauphin Co. Planning Cmn, 63-64; mem, Dauphin Indust. Develop. Cmn; Pa. State Sen, 15th Dist, 64- Bus. & Prof. Pos: Real estate broker. Mil. Serv: S/Sgt, Army, 41-45. Mem: Am. Legion; VFW; Dauphin-Perry Co. Tuberc. Asn; Rotary Club, Susquehanna Lodge 364; Mason. Mailing Add: R.F.D. 1, Millersburg, Pa. 17061.

LENZI, STEPHEN E. R
b. New Haven, Conn, 10/29/13; s. Joseph Lenzi and Adeline Civitello L; m. 8/30/43 to Helen M. Garguilo; c. Joseph L. and Linda Lee. Educ: Col. of William & Mary, B.A. in Govt, 41; Omicron Delta Kappa; pres, Sigma Rho; 13 Club; Varsity Club. Polit. & Govt. Pos: Conn. State Rep, 61-66. Bus. & Prof. Pos: Asst. football coach, Yale Univ, 47-52; secy-treas, Thompson-Lenzi Agency, Inc, 55-; dir. & v.pres, Bank & Trust Co, North Branford, Conn, 61- Mil. Serv: Entered as Ens, Navy, 43, released as Lt.(jg), 46, after serv. in Naval Ammunition Depot, Phila, Pa. and Atlantic Theater. Mem: Shoreline, Conn. and Nat. Bd. of Realtors; dir, New Haven Rehabilitation Center; Elks; Lions; New Haven Boys Club Alumni Asn; Nutmeg Athletic Club; Melebus Club; N.H. Chap, Nat. Found. and Football Hall of Fame; past chmn, March of Dimes and North Branford Heart Fund and Recreation Cmn. Lettered in football, Col. of William & Mary; N.E. Scout for Buffalo Bills, Am. Football League. Rel: Roman Catholic. Mailing Add: Twin Lakes Rd, North Branford, Conn. 06471.

LEON, CLAIRE JENSEN D
State Committeewoman, Wyo. Dem. Party
b. Kensal, N.Dak, 1/20/32; d. Clarence Loyal Jensen and Lillian Hovland J; m. 3/27/57 to Maurice Leon Jr; c. Jennifer and Margo. Educ: Concordia Col, Moorhead, Minn, 49-51; Univ. Colo, B.A, 54; Univ. Women's Club, Univ. Colo. Polit. & Govt. Pos: Mem, press credentials cmt, Dem. Nat. Conv, 68; pres, Sheridan Co. Dem. Women's Club, Wyo, 68-69; state committeewoman, Wyo. Dem. Party, 68- Bus. & Prof. Pos: Teacher, elem. sch, Rocky Ford, Colo, 54-55. Mem: Sheridan Fine Arts Club; Story Garden Club. Rel: Protestant. Mailing Add: Box 368, Story, Wyo. 82842.

LEON, JOHN F. D
b. Chicago, Ill, 3/9/10; married; c. John Jr. Educ: Chicago pub. schs. Polit. & Govt. Pos: Ill. State Rep, -66; former pres. now secy. 36th Ward Dem. Org. Mem: St. Philomena Holy Name Soc; K. of C; City Club, Chicago. Rel: Catholic. Mailing Add: 1811 N. Tripp Ave, Chicago, Ill. 60639. (1967)

LEON, MAURICE 'MIKE' D
b. Manhattan, N.Y, 7/10/24; s. Maurice Leon and Frances Webster Goodrich L; m. 3/27/57 to Claire Lillian Jensen; c. Claire Jennifer and Margo Lael. Educ: Yale Univ, B.A, 47, Grad. Sch, M.A, 49; Phi Beta Kappa; Honors in Sociol. Polit. & Govt. Pos: Ed, The Spokesman, Wyo. Dem. Voice, 63-; precinct committeeman, Story Dem. Party, 64-; mem, adv. coun, Wyo. Small Bus. Admin, 67-68; del-at-lg, Dem. Nat. Conv, 68; mem, permanent platform cmt, Dem. Party of Wyo, 68- Bus. & Prof. Pos: Photographer-reporter, Casper, Wyo, newspapers, 50-52; free lance photographer-journalist, 50-56; ed. and publisher, Wyo. Mag, 56-58; free lance writer, 58-63. Mil. Serv: Pvt, Army. Mailing Add: Box 368, Story, Wyo. 82842.

LEONARD, CHARLES LEE D
b. Beverly, W.Va, 4/16/20; s. Fred Lee Leonard and Mary Clary Buckey L; m. 12/18/43 to Elaine Miller; c. Charles L, Samuel Bradbury and William Parker. Educ: W.Va. Univ, A.B, 41 and B.S, 42; Temple Univ, M.D, 43; Phi Chi. Polit. & Govt. Pos: Del, Dem. Nat. Conv, 64. Bus. & Prof. Pos: Dir, W.Va. Med. Polit. Action Cmt, 64-66; mem. coun, W.Va. State Med. Asn, 62-66; pres, Barbour-Randolph-Tucker Med. Soc, 50. Mil. Serv: Lt.(jg), Navy, 43-45. Mem: Admiral of Cherry River Navy; Am. Med. Polit. Action Cmt; Elks; VFW; Am. Legion; 40 et 8. Rel: Catholic. Legal Res: Kerens Hill, Elkins, W.Va. 26241. Mailing Add: P.O. Box 848, Elkins, W.Va. 26241. (1967)

LEONARD, GERALD H. D
Ga. State Rep.
b. Chatsworth, Ga, 3/12/22; s. Francis C. Leonard Sr. and Annie Groaks L; m. 9/04/53 to Joan Chastain; c. Gerald Thomas, Cheryl Ann, Jennifer Jane, Michael William. Educ: Murray Co. High Sch, 41. Polit. & Govt. Pos: Tax cmnr, Ga, 46-60; Ga. State Rep, 63- Bus. & Prof. Pos: Ins. agent, 60-62. Mil. Serv: Air Force, 42-45; Cpl. Mem: Mason; pres, Chatsworth Lions; pres, Murray Co. Saddle Club. Rel: Methodist. Mailing Add: Box 291, Chatsworth, Ga. 30705. (1967)

LEONARD, HERBERT LEE R
Chmn, Lafayette Parish Rep. Exec. Cmt, La.
b. Morgan City, La, 6/20/31; s. Byron Peter Leonard and Jeanne Braud L; m. 1/30/55 to Audrey Gary; c. Bannie Lynn, Keitha Ann, Byron Madison, Patrick Olivier, Peter Justin and Rachel. Educ: Southwest. La. Inst; La. State Univ, B.A, 53 and LL.B, 55; Phi Delta Phi; Sigma Nu. Polit. & Govt. Pos: Past parish chmn, O'Hearne Senate Race, Lyons Gubernatorial Race and Goldwater Nat. Race; chmn, Lafayette Parish Rep. Exec. Cmt, La. and Lafayette Parish Polit. Cmt, currently. Bus. & Prof. Pos: Mem. law firm, Voorhies, Labbe, Fontenot, Leonard & McGlasson. Mil. Serv: Entered as 2nd Lt, Air Force, released as 1st Lt, 57; 1st Lt, Air Force Res. Mem: La. State and Am. Bar Asns; Maritime Law Asn. Rel: Catholic. Legal Res: 2020 E. Pine St, Lafayette, La. 70501. Mailing Add: P.O. Box 3527, Lafayette, La. 70501.

LEONARD, JERRIS R
Asst. Attorney Gen. for Civil Rights, Dept. of Justice
b. Chicago, Ill, 1/17/31; s. Jerris Gilbert Leonard and Jean Marie Reville L; m. 8/22/53 to Mariellen Catherine Mathie; c. Mary Alice, John Edward, Francis Xavier, Jerris Gilbert, Kathleen Ann and Daniel Joseph. Educ: Marquette Univ, B.S. in Bus. Admin, 52, J.D, 55; Alpha Sigma Nu; Sigma Nu Phi; Delta Sigma Pi. Polit. & Govt. Pos: Mem, Wis. Young Rep. Party, 49-66 and Wis. Rep. Party, 49-; Wis. State Assemblyman, 57-61; Wis. State Sen, 61-69, majority leader, Wis. State Senate, 67-69; Rep. nominee for U.S. Senator, Wis; Asst. Attorney Gen. for Civil Rights, Dept. of Justice, 69- Bus. & Prof. Pos: Attorney-at-law, 55-64; attorney, Michael, Best and Friedrich, 64-69. Mem: Am, Wis, Wilwaukee, Fed. and Nat. Bar Asns. Rel: Roman Catholic. Legal Res: Milwaukee, Wis. Mailing Add: Civil Rights Div, Dept. of Justice, Washington, D.C. 20530.

LEONARD, JOE ELDON R
Chmn, Faulkner Co. Rep. Cmt, Ark.
b. Damascus, Ark, 1/31/22; s. Joe Sevier Leonard and Elizebeth Graham L; m. 11/20/46 to Wilma Douglas; c. Beth (Mrs. Parish), Joe D, Timmy and Bobby. Educ: State Col. Ark, 41. Polit. & Govt. Pos: Mem, Faulkner Co. Rep. Cmt, 52-, chmn, 62- Bus. & Prof. Pos: Owner, Leonard Construction Co. Legal Res: Damascus, Ark. 72039.

LEONARD, LOUIS D
b. Belgium, 4/22/80; s. Julius Leonard and Catherine Legot L; m. to Margaret B. McClennan (deceased); c. eleven. Polit. & Govt. Pos: Pa. State Rep, 40-44, 48-64. Bus. & Prof. Pos: Retired Steelworker, 22 yrs; Int. Secy-treas, Amalgamated Asn. of Iron, Steel and Tin Workers of N. Am, 19-42. Mem: Moose; Elks; Eagles. Mailing Add: 1217 Strahley Place, Pittsburgh, Pa. 15220. (1967)

LEONARD, MACK R
b. Minter City, Miss, 6/19/19; s. Coleridge Leonard and Martha Givins L; m. 8/9/41 to Rachel Sweet; c. Emma Ruth and Elbert Tucker. Educ: Nat. Trade Sch, Memphis, Tenn, 1 year; Palmer Inst. of Creative Writing, Calif, 2 years. Polit. & Govt. Pos: Track clerk and recorder of deeds, Cook Co, Ill, 59-60; license examiner for Secy. of State, Ill, 60-62; dep. sheriff, Cook Co, 62-69; Rep. committeeman, Second Ward, 68- Bus. & Prof. Pos: Owner, Mack's Restaurant, Chicago, 67-68. Mil. Serv: Entered as Pvt, Army, 41, released as Pvt, 45, after serv. in 578th Heavy Field Artil. Div, ETO, 44-45; European-African-Middle East. Ribbon with Five Bronze Stars; Am. Theater Ribbon; Good Conduct Medal; World War II Victory Medal; Normandy; North. France, Ardennes, Rhineland and Cent. Europe Medals. Mem: UAW; Urban League; NAACP; Mason. Serv. Award, Second Ward Regular Rep. Orgn, 63. Rel: Protestant. Mailing Add: 555 E. 33rd Place, Chicago, Ill. 60616.

LEONARD, RICHARD WILSON D
N.H. State Sen.
b. Nashua, N.H, 8/6/19; s. Thomas J. Leonard and Cecelia M. Cone L; m. 12/30/50 to Andrea Desmond; c. Janet E. Educ: Univ. Va, B.S, 41, LL.B, 47. Polit. & Govt. Pos: Dem. Cand. to Cong, 48; del, Dem. Nat. Conv, 60 & 64; mem, Sch. Bd, Nashua, N.H, 63-; N.H. State Rep, 65-67; N.H. State Sen, 67- Bus. & Prof. Pos: Partner, Leonard, Leonard & Prolman, 48- Mil. Serv: Entered serv. as Cadet, Army Air Corps, 41, released as Capt, 45, after serv. in 451st Bomb Squadron, ETO; reentered serv. as Capt, Air Force, 50, released as Maj, 53, after serv. in 136th Tactical Fighter Wing, Korea; reentered as Lt. Col, Air Force, 61, released as Lt. Col, 62, after serv. in 102nd Tactical Fighter Wing, Europe; Distinguished Flying Cross; Air Medal with 15 Oak Leaf Clusters; Army and Air Force Commendation Medals; ETO Ribbon with 6 Battle Stars; Korean Medal with 3 Battle Stars; Japanese Occupation Medal; Distinguished Unit Citation. Mem: N.H. and Am. Bar Asns; Elks; Am. Legion; U.S. Air Force Res. U.S. Air Force Command Pilot. Rel: Catholic. Legal Res: 7 Farmington Rd, Nashua, N.H. 03060. Mailing Add: Box 615, Nashua, N.H. 03060.

LEONARD, RODNEY EDWIN D
b. Eureka, Kans, 12/7/29; s. Clarence Eugene Leonard and Muriel Barnard L; m. 6/13/55 to Elizabeth Karin Berg; c. Karin Frances, Jane Elizabeth and John Arthur. Educ: Kans. State Col, B.S, 51; Univ. Minn, Minneapolis, 53-55; Kappa Tau Epsilon; Sigma Delta Chi. Polit. & Govt. Pos: Press asst, Gov. of Minn, 58-61; asst. to secy, Consumer and Mkt. Serv, U.S. Dept. Agr, 61-66, dep. asst. secy, 66- Bus. & Prof. Pos: Reporter, Minneapolis Star & Tribune, 55-56; pub. rels. dir, Minn. Mining & Mfg. Co, 56-58. Mil. Serv: Army, 51-53, Cpl; Combat Inf. Badge; Korean Theater Ribbon. Mem: Nat. Press Club. Rel: Presbyterian. Mailing Add: 5710 Kingswood Rd, Bethesda, Md. 20014.

LEONARD, WILL ERNEST, JR. D
Cmnr, U.S. Tariff Cmn.
b. Shreveport, La, 1/18/35; s. Will Ernest Leonard and Nellie Kenner L; m. 2/23/57 to Peggy Crosby; c. Will Ernest, III, Sherry Elizabeth and Robert Scott. Educ: Tulane Univ, B.A, 56; Tulane Univ. Law Sch, LL.B, 58; Harvard Univ, LL.M, 66; Phi Beta Kappa; Omicron Delta Kappa. Polit. & Govt. Pos: Legis. asst. to U.S. Sen. Russell B. Long, La, 60-65; prfnl. staff mem, Senate Finance Cmt, 66-68; cmnr, U.S. Tariff Cmn, 68- Mem: Bars of U.S. Supreme Court, State of La. and D.C. Cong. Staff Fel. Rel: Roman Catholic. Legal Res: 6012 Camphor St, Metairie, La. 70003. Mailing Add: 3717 Fordham Rd. N.W, Washington, D.C. 20016.

LEONARDSON, ELMER CHARLES R
b. Small, Idaho, 11/21/18; s. Carl F. Leonardson and Leah Thomas L; m. 3/14/39 to Anne B. Larsen; c. Michael C, Patric K, Terry C. and Vicki A. Educ: Henninger's Bus. Col. Polit. & Govt. Pos: Idaho State Rep, Clark Co, 65-67; chmn, 6th Dist. Trustee Asn, 61-62 and Clark Co. Sch. Bd, 53-62; chmn, Clark Co. Rep. Cmt, Idaho, 55-59 and precinct chmn, 53-55. Mem: Pres, Dubois Lions Club; zone chmn, Lions Clubs; pres, C. of C; pres, Clark Co. Cmn. Credit Union; scout master and chmn. of Scout Coun; Clark Co. PTA; Idaho Food Retailers Asn. Rel: Baptist. Mailing Add: P.O. Box 6, Dubois, Idaho 83423. (1967)

LEONHART, WILLIAM
U.S. Ambassador to Yugoslavia
b. Parkersburg, W.Va, 8/1/19; s. Harry Kempton Leonhart and Rae Corinne Kahn L; m. 9/20/44 to Florence Lydia Sloan; c. Deborah and Victoria. Educ: W.Va. Univ, A.B, 39; Princeton Univ, M.A, 41, Ph.D, 43. Polit. & Govt. Pos: Economist, Off. of Coordinator, Inter-Am. Affairs, 41-43; econ. analyst, For. Serv. Auxiliary, Am. Embassy, Buenos Aires, Argentina, 43-46; third secy. and v.consul, Belgrade, Yugoslavia, 46-49; second secy. and v.consul, Rome, Italy, 49-50; second secy. and consul, Saigon, Phnom Penh and Vientiane, Indo China, 50-51; first secy. and consul, Tokyo, 52-54; mem, policy planning staff, Dept. of State, 55-57; Dept. of State alternate rep, Planning Bd. Nat. Security Coun, 56-57; Dept. of State rep, Imperial Defense Col, London, Eng, 58; counselor with rank of minister, Am. Embassy, Tokyo, Japan, 59-62; first U.S. Ambassador to Tanganyika, 62-64; U.S. Ambassador to United Repub. of Tanganyika and Zanzibar, 64 and United Repub. of Tanzania, 64-65; detailed White House, 66, spec. asst. to the President, 67-68; spec. asst. to the President-Elect's For. Policy Liaison Rep, 68-69; U.S. Ambassador to Yugoslavia, 69- Bus. & Prof. Pos: Mem. faculty, dept. of polit, Princeton Univ, 39-40. Mil. Serv: Army. Mem: Phi Beta Kappa; Delta Sigma Rho. Legal Res: 2618 30th St. N.W, Washington, D.C. 20008. Mailing Add: U.S. Embassy, Belgrade, Yugoslavia.

LEONOUDAKIS, STEPHAN CONSTANTINE D
b. Carbonado, Wash, 8/10/24; s. Constantine Leonoudakis and Katherine Tsurunakis L; m. 7/29/47 to Rosemary Rita Elms; c. Stephan John, Catherine Rita, Timothy Kevin, Jon Brenden and Kristi. Educ: Univ. San Francisco, LL.B, 50; Phi Alpha Delta. Polit. & Govt. Pos: Dir, Golden Gate Bridge and Hwy. Dist, San Francisco, Calif, 62-; mem, Calif. Dem. State Cent. Cmt, 63; mem, Bay Area Transportation Study Cmn, Berkeley, 67-68; mem, San Francisco-Marion Water Transportation Study Cmn, 68-69. Bus. & Prof. Pos: Attorney-at-law, Leonoudakis, Foran & McCarthy, 51- Mil. Serv: Entered as Pvt, Air Force, 42, released as S/Sgt, 45, after serv. in S.Pac. Theatre, 44-45; Distinguished Flying Cross; Air Medal with Four Oak Leaf Clusters. Mem: Am, Calif. and San Francisco Bar Asns; Am. Legion; Commonwealth Club of San Francisco; League to Save Lake Tahoe. Rel: Greek Orthodox. Mailing Add: 145 Ulloa St, San Francisco, Calif. 94127.

LEOPOLD, ARTHUR FREDRIC D
Councilman, Beverly Hills, Calif.
b. Woodmere, N.Y, 11/10/19; s. Arthur Siegbert Leopold and Mildred Felicia Weiner L; div; c. Georgene, Dorian, Fredric and Theresa. Educ: Dartmouth Col, A.B, 41; Columbia Univ. Sch. of Law, LL.B, 48; Phi Beta Kappa. Polit. & Govt. Pos: Councilman, Beverly Hills, Calif, 64-, mayor, 67-68; v.chmn, Dem. State Finance Cmt, Calif, 66; v.chmn, Los Angeles Co. Mayors' Asn, 68; del, Dem. Nat. Conv, 68. Bus. & Prof. Pos: Partner, Youngman, Hungate & Leopold, 54- Mil. Serv: Entered as A/S, Navy, 42, released as Lt, 46, after serv. as Bomb Disposal Officer, Southwest and West. Pac. Areas, 43-45; 5 Battle Stars. Mem: Los Angeles and Beverly Hills Bar Asns. Mailing Add: 1901 Building, Suite 1530, Century City, Los Angeles, Calif. 90067.

LEOPOLD, WILLIAM WOLF R
b. Rensselaer, Ind, 12/23/28; s. Glenn H. Leopold and Pauline Wolf L; single. Educ: Ind. Univ. Polit. & Govt. Pos: Chmn, Second Dist. Young Rep, Ind, 56-66; asst. to permanent chmn, Rep. Nat. Conv, 60, del, 64; Young Rep. nat. committeeman, 60-66; former treas, Second Dist. Halleck for Cong. Cmt; former treas, Second Dist. Rep. Cent. Cmt. Bus. & Prof. Pos: Pres, Home

Finance Co, Inc, 69- Mil. Serv: Entered as Pvt, Army, 52, released as Sgt, 54. Mem: Mason (32°); Shrine. Rel: Jewish. Mailing Add: 304 Home Ave, Rensselaer, Ind. 47978.

LePORE, RALPH FRANK D
b. Wheeling, W.Va, 3/2/13; s. Frank LePore and Katheryn Callandra L; m. 5/27/39 to Florence Becker Rockabrand; c. Frank August and Stephen Ralph. Educ: Elliott's Bus. Sch, 35-39; Inst. Appl. Sci, Chicago, Ill, 41; Fed. Bur. Invest. Nat. Acad, D.C, 41. Polit. & Govt. Pos: Clerk, Recreation Dept, Wheeling, W.Va, 33-36; clerk of police court, Wheeling Police Dept, 36-41; spec. agent, Fed. Bur. Invest, 41-48; chief dep. sheriff, Ohio Co, 49-53, spec. investr, Sheriff's Off, 57-61; chmn, W.Va. Racing Cmn, 53-57; compliance officer, U.S. Dept. of Labor, 61-64; alternate del-at-lg, Dem. Nat. Conv, 64 & 68; chmn, Italian Div, W.Va. All Am. Coun; Sheriff and Treas, Ohio Co, 69- Bus. & Prof. Pos: V.pres, Int. Research Consults, 56-60; owner and operator, Ralph F. LePore Assocs, 64-66; v.pres, Intel. Serv, Inc, 64- Mem: Soc. Former Spec. Agents of Fed. Bur. of Invest; Am. Soc. for Indust. Security; Fed. Bur. Invest. Nat. Police Acad; Nat. Sheriff's Asn; Fraternal Order of Police; Pa. Police Chief's Asn; TWA Ambassador; Half Million Miler, United Airlines; Am. Red Cross; Crippled Children's Fund; Am. Legion Golden Gloves Boxing Tournament; Wheeling Soap Box Derby; Commun. Fund; Envoy Club and Variety Club, Pittsburgh, Pa; pres, Amen Corner, Pittsburgh, Order Paul Revere Patriots, Mass. Hon. Ky. Col. Rel: Roman Catholic. Mailing Add: 22 Hamilton Ave, Wheeling, W.Va. 26003.

LEPPARD, EDWARD MELVER D
b. Chesterfield, S.C, 11/5/24; s. James Ernest Leppard Sr. and Anne Owens L; m. to Virginia Emory. Educ: Univ. S.C, A.B, 44; LL.B, 49. Polit. & Govt. Pos: S.C. State Sen, 63-66; S.C. State Rep, 61-62. Mil. Serv: Navy. Mem: Kappa Sigma; Legion; Masons; Civitan Club; Cheraw Moose. Rel: Baptist. Mailing Add: Box 190, Chesterfield, S.C, 29709. (1967)

LEPPERT, GEORGE D
b. Kansas City Mo, 7/17/24; s. George Alva Leppert and Leah Oleve L; m. 1/16/61 to Helen Robinson; c. Elizabeth Ann Wood and Ralph R. Liddle. Educ: Harris Jr. Col, 41-43; Univ. Wis, Madison, B.S, 47; Ill. Inst. Tech, Ph.D, 54; Tau Beta Pi; Pi Mu Epsilon. Polit. & Govt. Pos: Dem. cong. nominee, Tenth Dist, Calif, 66; mem, Calif. Dem. State Cent. Cmt, 66-68; pres, Palo Alto-Stanford Dem. Club, 67; del, Dem. Nat. Conv, 68. Bus. & Prof. Pos: Mech. engr, Monsanto Chem. Co, St. Louis, 47-49, Dayton, 53-54; instr, Wash. Univ, 49-50; mech. engr, Argonne Nat. Lab, Chicago, 50-53; prof. mech. eng, Stanford Univ, 54-69; prof. and chmn. dept, Clarkson Col, 69- Mil. Serv: Entered as A/S, Navy, 43, released as Lt.(jg), 46, after serv. in Submarine Serv, Southwest Pac. Theatre, 45-46. Publ: Numerous articles on heat transfer, especially for nuclear reactors. Mem: Am. Soc. Mech. Engrs; Am. Nuclear Soc; Am. Inst. Aeronaut. and Astronaut; Am. Soc. for Eng. Educ; Am. Asn. Univ. Prof; Sigma Xi; Am. Friends Serv. Cmt.(chmn, peace educ. cmt, North. Calif, 67-68); Coun. for a Livable World. Am. Soc. Mech. Engrs. Postgrad. Student Award, 53. Mailing Add: Route 1, Potsdam, N.Y. 13676.

LERANDEAU, WILFRED P. D
b. Quincy, Mass; married; c. two sons. Educ: Marlborough & Keene Pub. Schs. Polit. & Govt. Pos: N.H. State Rep, - 67. Bus. & Prof. Pos: Retired. Mil. Serv: WW I. Mem: Am. Legion. Mailing Add: RFD 1, Marlborough, N.H. 03455. (1967)

LERCH, ORVILLE HARFORD R
Alternate Fed. Co-Chmn, Appalachia Regional Cmn.
b. Pittsburgh, Pa, 4/16/35; s. Quay Lerch and Hazel Harford L.(deceased); m. 11/12/66 to Lucinda John Abernethy; c. Scott Abernethy and Matthew Harford. Educ: Pa. State Univ, B.S. in Wood Utilization. Polit. & Govt. Pos: Campaign staff aide to Raymond P. Shafer, Gov. of Pa, sr. staff aide, 65-67; co. campaign mgr. for Congressman Albert W. Johnson; former dir-at-lg, Young Rep. Pa; past chmn, Young Rep, Clarion Co; dir. coal land improv. fund, Dept. Mines and Mineral Industs, 67-68; dep. chmn, Rep. State Cmt, Pa, 68-69; alternate fed. co-chmn, Appalachia Regional Cmn, 69- Bus. & Prof. Pos: Indust. tech. area salesman, Sherwin Williams, Co, Chicago, Ill, 57-60; math. instr, Clarion Area Schs, 60-65. Mil. Serv: Pvt, Army, 57-64. Mem: Forest Prod. Research Soc; Clarion Area Educ. Asn.(cmt. chmn, pres); Grange; charter mem, Clarion Jaycees; Clarion Co. Heart Asn.(past chmn). Rel: Protestant. Legal Res: R.D. 1, Sligo, Pa. 16255. Mailing Add: 5621 Newington Rd, Bethesda, Md. 20016.

LEREW, THEODORE D
b. 8/10/25; married; c. Tamyra, Patricia, Nancy, Susan and Joell. Educ: High Sch. Polit. & Govt. Pos: Co. cmnr, 4 years; twp. clerk, 8 years; S.Dak. State Rep, 64-66. Mil. Serv: Army. Mem: Legion. Rel: Methodist. Mailing Add: Faulkton, S.Dak. 57438.

LERMAN, PHILIP E. D
Chmn, Fifth Cong. Dist. Dem. Party, Wis.
b. Milwaukee, Wis, 5/17/19; s. Benjamin Lerman and Rose Holzman L; m. 3/23/44 to Anne Louise Levy; c. Richard M, Elizabeth A. and David M. Educ: Univ. Wis. Polit. & Govt. Pos: Mem, exec. cmt, Milwaukee Co. Dem. Party, Wis, 61-67; mem, Gov. Cmn. on Human Rights, 62-64; chmn, Third Ward Dem. Party, 62-65; mem, Wis. Dem. State Cent. Cmt, 65-67; pres, Wis. State Bd. of Vocational, Tech. and Adult Educ, 65-67; mem, Coord. Cmt. for Higher Educ, 65-; mem, Wis. Adv. Coun, U.S. Cmn. on Civil Rights, 65-; chmn, Fifth Cong. Dist. Dem. Party, currently. Mil. Serv: Entered as Pvt, Army, 42, released as Sgt, 45, after serv. in Tenth Mt. Div, Italy; Bronze Star Medal; Apennine-Po Valley and North. Italy Campaign Ribbons. Mem: Secy, Wis. Independent Tire Dealers Asn, 59-62; B'nai B'rith; Nat. Tire Dealers & Retreaders Asn; Urban League; Am. Civil Liberties Union. Rel: Jewish. Mailing Add: 2645 N. Summit Ave, Milwaukee, Wis. 53211. (1967)

LERNER, LOUIS A. D
b. Chicago, Ill, 6/12/35; s. Leo A. Lerner and Deana Duskin L; m. 7/22/57 to Susan Winchester; c. Lucy. Educ: Univ. Chicago, A.B, 54; Roskilde Col, Denmark, 58; Roosevelt Univ, B.A, 60. Polit. & Govt. Pos: Exec. dir, Students for Stevenson, 52; bd. mem, Students for Dem. Action, 53; organizer, Re-elec. Mayor Richard J. Daley, Chicago, Ill, 67; dir, Chicago Pub. Libr, Ill, 67-; alternate del, Dem. Nat. Conv, 68. Bus. & Prof. Pos: Correspondent, Accredited Home Newspapers Am, Copenhagen, Denmark, 56-58; exec. v.pres, Lerner Home Newspapers, Chicago, 61-69 and publisher, 69- Mil. Serv: Sgt. E 6, Army Res, 54-61. Publ: 'News and News Values in the Danish Press,' Scandinavian Seminars, 57. Mem: Sigma Delta Chi; Headline Club; Cmt. for Free and Competitive Press; Chicago Cmt. Ill. Sesquicentennial; Statewide Citizens Cmt, Ill. for Air and Water Pollution Abatement; chmn, Spec. Chicago Park Dist. Cmt. on Bldg. Rehabilitation; Chicago Press Club; bd. dirs, Bank of Niles, Ill; dir, Chicago Better Bus. Bur; dir, Cert. Audit of Circulations, Inc, N.Y; citizens bd, Cath. Interracial Coun; Am. Acad. Polit. & Soc. Sci; bd. gov, City Club Chicago. Legal Res: 442 W. Wellington, Chicago, Ill. 60657. Mailing Add: 7519 N. Ashland Ave, Chicago, Ill. 60626.

LESAGE, ROMEO R. D
N.H. State Rep.
b. Nashua, N.H, 4/29/02; s. John B. Lesage and Emelia Descherus L; wid; c. Gloria (Mrs. Plourde), Lucille (Mrs. Dobrowolski) and Claudette (Mrs. Calutte). Educ: St. Francis Sch; Broden Sacred Heart Sch. Polit. & Govt. Pos: N.H. State Rep, currently. Bus. & Prof. Pos: Meat and grocery bus, 48 years. Rel: Roman Catholic. Mailing Add: 9 Tolles St, Nashua, N.H. 03060.

LESHER, HERBERT A. R
Del. State Rep.
b. Northumberland, Pa, 3/12/15; s. Harold V. Lesher and Elizabeth Mertz L; m. 7/12/41 to Lois Marion Hopewell; c. Elizabeth Ann, Clifford A, James H, John C, Helen I. and H. Daniel. Educ: Bucknell Univ, B.S.Ch.E, 39; Pi Mu Epsilon. Polit. & Govt. Pos: Chmn, Rep. Fund Dr, 65; alternate del, State Rep. Conv; Del. State Rep, 67-, chmn, Joint House and Senate Finance Cmt, chmn, Appropriations Cmt. and mem, Pub. Bldgs. and Lands Cmt, Del. House of Rep. Bus. & Prof. Pos: Tech. consult, film dept, E.I. du Pont de Nemours & Co, Inc. Mem: Claymont PTA (past pres. and v.pres); Claymont Band Boosters (past pres); Claymont Sports Boosters (past pres); Bucknell Univ. Alumni Asn.(past pres, Wilmington Chap); YMCA (past co-chmn, Brandywine Br. Membership Dr); Brandywine Heights Civic Asn.(past pres). Rel: Methodist; mem. bd. trustees, Atonement Methodist Church. Mailing Add: 1120 Harvey Rd, Claymont, Del. 19703.

LESHY, JOHN D
m. 1/12/40 to Dolores Kind; c. John David, Mary Katherine (Mrs. Kelly) and Dolores D. Educ: Ohio State Univ, B.S, 38. Polit. & Govt. Pos: Mem, Peebles Sch. Bd, Ohio, 61-69, pres, 65. Bus. & Prof. Pos: Pres. and gen. mgr, Haas Lumber Co, 58-; pres, McHenry Supply Co, 58- Mil. Serv: Entered as Pvt, Army, 45, released as Pfc, 46, after serv. in Inf. Mem: Lions; Mason; Shrine; Am. Legion. Rel: Protestant. Legal Res: 193 N. Main St, Peebles, Ohio 45660. Mailing Add: 41 Elm St, Peebles, Ohio 45660.

LESINSKI, T. JOHN
b. Detroit, Mich, 4/28/25; s. John Lesinski and Frances Falinski L; m. 2/5/49 to Carol Jeanne Siegel; c. Susan Lynne, Mary Frances, Patricia Anne, Kevin John, Steven Mark, Thomas John. Educ: Univ. Detroit, 45-47, J.D, 50; Delta Theta Phi; Upsilon Delta Sigma. Polit. & Govt. Pos: Mich. State Rep, 51-60; Lt. Gov, Mich, 60-64; chief Judge, Mich. Court of Appeals, 65- Mil. Serv: Entered as A/S, Nat. Maritime Serv, 44, released as Radio Warrant Officer, 45, after serv. in Pac-India-Atlantic Theaters, 44-45. Mem: Inst. of Judicial Admin; Nat. Judicature Soc; Am. Bar Asn; Nat. Conf. of Appellate Judges (dir. and secy); State Bar of Mich; Nat. Advocates; Detroit Advocates; Hamtramck Bar Asn; K. of C; Polish Nat. Alliance; Crisis Club. Rel: Catholic. Legal Res: 18664 Birchcrest, Detroit, Mich. 48221. Mailing Add: Ninth Floor, First Federal Bldg, Detroit, Mich. 48226.

LESLIE, JACQUES ROBERT D
b. Washington Co, Pa, 7/18/08; m. to Aleen Wetstein; c. Jacques, Jr. and Diane (Mrs. Huffman). Educ: Univ. Pittsburgh and Law Sch. Polit. & Govt. Pos: Mem. finance cmt, Dem. Nat. Conv, 60 and Dem. State Cmts; alternate del, Dem. Nat. Cmt, 64; former dir, Metrop. Transit Authority; judge, Beverly Hills Judicial Dist, 64-65. Bus. & Prof. Pos: Resident counsel, RKO Radio Motion Picture Co, 41-45; mem. bd. dirs, Greenway Productions, Inc, currently; sr. partner, Law Firm of Leslie, Rubin & Teplin, currently. Mem: Los Angeles Co, Beverly Hills and Am. Bar Asns; State Bar of Calif; Am. Adjudicature Soc; Dist. Attorney Adv. Coun; Speaker's Bur; Beverly Hills Improv. Asn; charter mem, Golden Bear Club; President's Club; founder, Music Center of Los Angeles for the Performing Arts; Beverly Hills Tennis Club. Mailing Add: 124 Lasky Dr, Beverly Hills, Calif. 90212.

LESNIAK, BEN, JR. D
Educ: Ind. Univ; Worsham Col. Mortuary Sci. Polit. & Govt. Pos: Ind. State Rep, -66. Bus. & Prof. Pos: Ins. agent; funeral dir. Mem: E. Chicago Real Estate Bd; Young Dems. Rel: Catholic. Mailing Add: 4819 Wegg Ave, East Chicago, Ind. 46312. (1967)

LESNIAK, RICHARD JOHN D
Ind. State Rep.
b. East Chicago, Ind, 3/29/39; s. Benjamin J. Lesniak, Sr. and Helen Gajda L; m. 8/17/63 to Janice Kmiecik; c. Linda, Karen and Richard. Educ: Wabash Col, A.B, 61; Ind. Univ. Law Sch, Bloomington, LL.B, 64; Phi Delta Theta. Polit. & Govt. Pos: Ind. State Rep, Lake Co, 69- Bus. & Prof. Pos: Escrow officer, Lake Co. Title Co, Crown Point, Ind, 64-; trial dep, Lake Co. Prosecutor's Off, 65-68; attorney-at-law, Given, Dawson & Cappas, East Chicago, Ind, 68- Mem: Ind. and East Chicago Bar Asns; Lake Co. Young Lawyers Asn. Rel: Roman Catholic. Legal Res: 1205 Beacon St, East Chicago, Ind. 46312. Mailing Add: 4846 Indianapolis Blvd, East Chicago, Ind, 46312.

LESSEG, WALTER AUGUST R
b. Brussels, Ill, 3/2/96; s. Fred George Lesseg and Lena Schulze L; m. 3/9/18 to D. Anna Fredrickson; c. George F, Sibyl, Walter A, Allegra, Darwin C. and Avala. Educ: Gem Bus. Col, grad. Polit. & Govt. Pos: Precinct committeeman, Calhoun Co. Rep. Cent. Cmt, Ill, 46-, former chmn. Bus. & Prof. Pos: Rural teacher, Pub. Sch, 15-42; farmer and fruit grower, 20-62; sch. treas, Ill, 38-52. Mil. Serv: Hosp. Corpsman 2/C, Navy, 17. Mem: Comdr, World War I Barracks; Farm Bur. Rel: Lutheran. Mailing Add: Brussels, Ill. 60213.

LESTER, HELEN MacDONALD R
b. Boston, Mass, 2/6/03; d. William MacDonald and Mary Murray M; m. 10/19/29 to Joseph W. Lester; c. Mary Louise (Mrs. Clark), Joseph W, Jr. and Daniel B. Educ: Mt. Holyoke Col, A.B, 23; Simmons Col, M.S, 24. Polit. & Govt. Pos: Conn. State Rep, 57-67; mem, Platform Cmt, Conn. Rep. Party, 62; third v.pres, Conn. Coun. of Rep. Women, 62-; chmn, Primary Law Coun, Cmn. to Revise Elec. Laws, 63; alternate del, Rep. Nat. Conv, 64; mem, Litchfield Rep. Town Cmt, Conn, 64-68. Bus. & Prof. Pos: Personnel dir, Eards' Dept. Store, Charlotte, N.C, 24-25; employee, Training Dept, Jordan Marsh Co, Boston, Mass, 25-28, Gimbels, N.Y.C, 28-29. Rel: Congregational. Mailing Add: South St, Litchfield, Conn. 06759. (1967)

LESTER, HORACE BAXTER D
Miss. State Rep.
b. Quitman Co, Miss, 9/5/19; s. Simon Edward Lester and Willie Reid L; m. 5/12/42 to Dora Essie Sanford; c. Horace B, Jr. and Thomas S. Educ: Int. Correspondence Course in Eng; Scabbard and Blade. Polit. & Govt. Pos: Miss. State Rep, Hinds Co, currently. Bus. & Prof. Pos: Engr, 46-48; field civil engr, 48-50; chief engr, supv. construction of sewer and water systs, 50-51; private practice, 51-54; consult. engr, 55- Mil. Serv: Entered as Pvt, Army, 42, released as Capt, 46, after serv. in Pac. Theater; Lt. Col, Army Res, currently; Am. and Pac. Theater Ribbons; Philippine Liberation and Reserve Medals; Victory Medal with 2 Overseas Serv. Bars. Mem: Fel, Am. Soc. Civil Engrs; Nat. and Miss. Soc. Prfnl. Engrs; Miss. Econ. Coun; Am. Water Works Asn; Miss. Sewage and Indust. Wastes Asn; Rivers and Harbors Asn. of Miss; Am. Soc. of Planning Off; Soil Conserv. Soc. Am; Int. Platform Asn; W.Cent. Miss. Waterway Cmn; ROA; Rotary; C. of C. Rel: Baptist. Mailing Add: 1350 Eastover Dr, Jackson, Miss. 39211.

LESTER, JAMES LUTHER D
Chmn, Richmond Co. Dem. Exec. Cmt, Ga.
b. Augusta, Ga, 1/12/32; s. William McMorris Lester and Elizabeth Miles L; m. 1/18/58 to Gwendolyn Gleason; c. James L, Jr. and Frank G. Educ: The Citadel, A.B; Univ. Ga, LL.B; Sigma Chi. Polit. & Govt. Pos: Pres, Young Dem. Richmond Co, Ga, 64-66; chmn, Richmond Co. Dem. Exec. Cmt, 66- Mil. Serv: Entered as 2nd Lt, Army, 52, released as Capt, 59, after serv. in 81st Inf. Div, Korea, 53-54. Mem: Am. and Ga. Bar Asns; Kiwanis; Am. Legion. Rel: Methodist. Legal Res: 3205 Wheeler Rd, Augusta, Ga. 30904. Mailing Add: First Federal Savings Bldg, Augusta, Ga. 30902.

LETCHER, ISABELLE SCOTT R
V.chmn, Ottawa Co. Rep. Party, Okla.
b. Wilkes-Barre, Pa, 7/10/08; d. Frank L. Scott and Jean Fraser Menzies S; m. 10/14/33 to Dr. Charles Wesley Letcher; c. Charles Scott, John Henry, Frank Scott and William Frederick. Educ: Wyo. Sem, Pa, 2½ years; Wilson Col, 1½ years. Polit. & Govt. Pos: Precinct chmn, Miami, Okla, 50; pres, Rep. Women's Club, 54-56 & 65-69; dist. committeewoman, Ottawa Co, 67-68; alternate del, Rep. Nat. Conv, 68; v.chmn, Ottawa Co. Rep. Party, 68- Mem: Letters and Arts; Garden Club; Rep. Women's Club; Lioness Club. Rel: Presbyterian. Mailing Add: 1525 Lincoln Blvd, Miami, Okla. 74354.

LETSEN, ROYDEN A. D
b. Brooklyn, N.Y, 6/24/18; m. to Agnes Macis. Educ: Wharton Sch. of Finance and Commerce, Univ. of Pa, B.S; N.Y. Univ, M.B.A; N.Y. Law Sch, LL.B. Polit. & Govt. Pos: N.Y. State Sen, 64-67; formerly Yonkers Planning Bd. Bus. & Prof. Pos: Lawyer. Mil. Serv: Lt. Col, JAG, Army Res. Mem: Yonkers Lawyers Asn; LaRabida Coun, K. of C; past comdr, Alan F. Waite Post 299, Am. Legion; past chmn, Cent. Cmt. of War Vets. Orgns; past pres, E. Yonkers Rotary; past pres, adv. bd. CYO; past pres, Yonkers Chap, UN Asn; Res. Officers Asn; counsel, Lithuanian Citizens Club; bd, United Givers Funds St. Mary's Post, CWV; Yonkers Elks 707. Rel: Church of Christ the King. Mailing Add: 135 Holls Terr. N, Yonkers, N.Y. 10701. (1967)

LEUTHOLD, LOUISE POSPISIL R
b. Lost Springs, Kans, 3/29/09; d. John Joseph Pospisil and Josephine Navratt P; m. 5/27/33 to Albert Edward Leuthold; c. Kenneth Duane, Eddie Bert, Betty Louise (Mrs. Waddell) and Stephen Bruce. Educ: Eastern Mont. Col. Educ, 27-28; Deaconess Hosp, nurse training, 26-27. Polit. & Govt. Pos: Judge and clerk, Sch. and State Elec. Bd, 32-40; staff mem, J. H. Leuthold for Gov. Club, 40; organizer, Laurel Tel. Campaign to elect Sen. Ecton, Representative D'Ewart and Hon. J. Hugo Aronson, 46-54; asst. secy, Leuthold Sect. State Rep. Club, 60; asst, Hon. Donald Nutter and Gov. Tim Babcock, 60-68; chmn, Gov. Inaugural Ball Decorations Cmt, 64-65; membership chmn, Lewis and Clark Co. Rep. Women's Club, 64-69, pres, 65, campaign activities chmn, 66-69; precinct committeewoman, Lincoln Day Dinner Cmt, 65-68; hq. chmn, Lewis and Clark Rep. Cent. Cmt, 66, acting chmn, 68, v.chmn, 66-69; co. chmn, Betty Guffey for Secy. State Rep. Club, 68; alternate del, Rep. Nat. Conv, 68. Mem: Eastern Star; Rainbow Girls (Past Mother Adv); Laurel and Helena Women's Club; bd. mem, Deaconess Home Children; Deaconess Home Auxiliary. Rel: Methodist. Mailing Add: Box 116, Columbus, Mont. 59109.

LeVANDER, HAROLD R
Gov, Minn.
b. Swede Home, Nebr, 10/10/10; s. Peter Magni LeVander and Laura La Vene L; m. 9/15/38 to Iantha Powrie; c. Harold, Jean and Diane. Educ: Gustavus Adolphus Col, B.A, 32 and LL.D; Univ. Minn, LL.B, 35; Pi Kappa Delta; Gamma Eta Gamma. Polit. & Govt. Pos: Asst. co. attorney, Dakota Co, Minn, 35-39; Gov, Minn, 67-; del, Rep. Nat. Conv, 68. Bus. & Prof. Pos: Pres, United Fed. Savings & Loan Asn; prof. speech, Macalester Col; attorney-at-law, St. Paul, 39-67. Mem: Secy, Nat. Lutheran Coun; Am. and Minn. Bar Asns; St. Paul C. of C; St. Paul Athletic Club. Mailing Add: 2323 Thompson Ave, St. Paul, Minn. 55118.

LeVASSEUR, EDWARD J. D
b. Fall River, Mass, 5/27/20; married. Educ: Fall River Pub. Sch. Polit. & Govt. Pos: N.H. State Rep, -67. Bus. & Prof. Pos: Realtor insurer. Mil. Serv: U.S. Army; N.H. State Guard, 2nd Lt. Mem: Queen City Bd. Realtors; Multiple Listing Serv; Lions; K. of C; Am. Legion. Rel: Catholic. Mailing Add: 8 Pinard St, Manchester, N.H. 03102. (1967)

LEVEE, MICHAEL CHARLES, JR. D
Financial Chmn, South. Calif. State Dem. Cent. Cmt.
b. Los Angeles, Calif, 9/22/20; s. Michael Charles Levee, Sr. and Roze Hirschkowitz L; m. 6/5/48 to Margaret Fisher; c. Margaret Catherine and Victoria. Educ: Stanford Univ, A.B, 42. Polit. & Govt. Pos: Dem. TV adv. for Gov. Edmund G. 'Pat' Brown, Calif, 62 & 66, Sen. Clair Engel, 62 and Hon. Jesse Unruh, 68; del, Dem. Nat. Conv, 68; financial chmn, South. Calif. State Dem. Cent. Cmt, 69- Mailing Add: 715 N. Canon Dr, Beverly Hills, Calif. 90210.

LEVER, ASBURY FRANCIS, JR. D
b. Washington, D.C, 11/9/18; s. Asbury Francis Lever and Lucile Butler L; m. 9/26/42 to Martha Yates Monteith; c. Ann Butler, Asbury Francis, III and George Edward. Educ: The Citadel, B.A, 39; Univ. S.C, LL.B, 42; Sigma Alpha Epsilon; Phi Delta Phi. Polit. & Govt. Pos: Del, S.C. State Dem. Conv, 44-68; S.C. State Rep, 46-50, chmn, Lexington Co. Dem. Party, S.C, 50-67; del, Dem. Nat. Conv, 56, alternate del, 60, 64 & 68; Gov. appointee, Cmt. to Investigate Small Loans, 65. Mem: Am, S.C. and Lexington Co. Bar Asns; Am. Judicature Soc; Mason; Lexington Co. Farm Bur. Rel: Methodist. Legal Res: Harmon St, Lexington, S.C. 29072. Mailing Add: 136 E. Main St, Lexington, S.C. 29072.

LEVERICH, JAMES EARL R
b. Angelo, Wis. Educ: Madison Col, Univ. of Wis, Agr. Polit. & Govt. Pos: Mem, Co. Bd, Wis; town chmn; town clerk; sch. clerk; Wis. State Sen, 34-38 & 42-66. Bus. & Prof. Pos: Dairy farmer and fruit grower; farm leader; former bank v.pres; pres, Coop Creamery Asn; pres, Livestock Shipping Asn. Mem: Various state-wide agr. and dairy cmts. Mailing Add: Route 4, Sparta, Wis. 54656. (1967)

LEVERING, ROBERT W. D
b. Knox Co, Ohio, 10/3/14; m. to Eileen Rosemary Burdick; c. Roberta Carmen and Usher Lloyd. Educ: Denison Univ, A.B, 36; George Wash. Univ. Law Sch, LL.B, 40; Tau Kappa Alpha. Polit. & Govt. Pos: Mem, U.S. War Dept, Philippines, 41; asst. to Ohio Attorney Gen, 49-50; U.S. Rep, Ohio, 59-60; Dem. cand. for U.S. Rep, Ohio, 68. Bus. & Prof. Pos: Lawyer, Mt. Vernon, Ohio and cattleman, Fredericktown, Ohio. Mil. Serv: Civilian vol. in defense of Bataan, World War II; survived Death March and 3½ years in prisoner of war camps; Maj, Judge Adv. Gen. Dept, Army Res. Publ: Horror Trek. Mem: Past pres, Knox Co. Bar Asn. and Mt. Vernon Kiwanis; judge advocate, Am. Defenders of Bataan and Corregidor; Mason (32°); Shrine; Buckeye and Am. Polled Hereford Asns; Farm Bur; Dan Emmett Grange; Mt. Vernon Sons of Vet. Fife and Drum Corps. Recipient Distinguished Alumni Award for Excellence in Pub. Speaking, Tau Kappa Alpha, 63. Rel: Presbyterian. Mailing Add: R.F.D. 2, Fredericktown, Ohio 44627.

LEVESQUE, EMILIEN A. D
Minority Floor Leader, Maine House of Rep.
Polit. & Govt. Pos: Chmn, Madawaska Town Dem. Cmt, Maine, 55-67; Maine State Rep, 61-, mem, Educ. Cmt, Maine House of Rep, 61-, Majority Floor Leader, chmn, Labor Cmt. and mem, Legis. Research Cmt, 65-66, Minority Floor Leader, 67- Bus. & Prof. Pos: Asst. supt. mech. maintenance. Mailing Add: 58 Mountain View, Madawaska, Maine 04756. (1967)

LEVESQUE, FREFFLE GEORGE D
b. Nashua, N.H, 8/3/96; s. Joseph M. Levesque and Clara April L; m. 10/15/66 to Lena Doyle Dupray; c. Dr. J. Gerard, Paul L, Mrs. Estelle Richard and Mrs. Leonard Boucher. Polit. & Govt. Pos: N.H. State Rep, 65-66. Bus. & Prof. Pos: Shoe worker and edge trimmer, W. H. and J. F. McAlwain. Mem: Treas, Moose, 5 years; highest degree Pilgrim. Rel: Catholic. Mailing Add: 2 Haines, Nashua, N.H. 03060.

LEVESQUE, THOMAS HUGHES D
b. Portsmouth, R.I, 4/8/19; m. to Anna Doyle; c. 4 sons, 1 daughter. Educ: Providence Col; Boston Col. Law. Polit. & Govt. Pos: Town solicitor, Portsmouth, R.I, 59-; R.I. State Sen, 61-66; del, Dem. Nat. Conv, 68. Bus. & Prof. Pos: Lawyer. Mil. Serv: Army, World War II. Mailing Add: 136 W. Main St, Middletown, R.I. 02840. (1967)

LEVEY, BARRY R
Ohio State Rep.
b. 1931. Educ: Univ. Mich; Ohio State Univ. Col. Law; Northwest. Univ. Col. Law. Polit. & Govt. Pos: Ohio State Rep, 63-, chmn, Judiciary Cmt, Ohio State House of Rep, 69- Bus. & Prof. Pos: Attorney; partner, Levey & Levey law firm. Mailing Add: First National Bank Bldg, Middletown, Ohio 45042.

LEVEY, NITA B. R
V.Chmn, Ionia Co. Rep. Exec. Cmt, Mich.
b. Lansing, Mich, 2/3/24; d. Clifford H. Williams and Beulah Sellers W; m. 1/29/61 to Lawrence Harold Levey; c. Lynne (Mrs. Francis Sim). Educ: Everett High Sch, Lansing, Mich. Polit. & Govt. Pos: V.chmn, Ionia Co. Rep. Exec. Cmt, Mich, 69- Mem: Ionia Commun. Theatre; Ionia Co. Coun. of Commun. Serv; Ionia State Hosp. Women's Vol. Guild. Rel: Protestant. Mailing Add: 619 Townsend St, Ionia, Mich. 48846.

LEVIN, BERNARD D
Va. State Del.
b. Portsmouth, Va, 11/3/21; m. to Carla B. deCreny. Educ: Wash. & Lee Univ, B.S, 42. Polit. & Govt. Pos: Va. State Del, 62-; del, Dem. Nat. Conv, 68. Bus. & Prof. Pos: Lawyer. Mil. Serv: Naval Res, 4½ years. Mem: Am, Va, Norfolk and Portsmouth Bar Asns; Va. Trail Lawyers Asn; pres, Sertoma Club; Norfolk Consistory; pres, Wash. & Lee Alumni, Inc; pres, United Cerebral Palsy Asn, Norfolk; Bd. Tidewater Sonic Hearing-Impaired Children; Omicron Delta Kappa. Rel: Jewish. Mailing Add: 133 Grayson, Portsmouth, Va. 23707. (1967)

LEVIN, GEORGE DANIEL D
b. Sturgis, S.Dak, 7/4/21; s. Daniel Oscar Levin and Dorothy Frazee L; m. 6/14/43 to Laura K. Butler; c. Lauren, Dennis and Sheryl. Polit. & Govt. Pos: Del, Dem. Nat. Conv, 68. Mem: Bd, S.Dak. Farmers Union, 66-; chmn. bd, S.Dak. Div, Independent Stockgrowers of Am, 68- Rel: Protestant. Mailing Add: Hereford, S.Dak. 57743.

LEVIN, SANDER M. D
Mich. State Sen.
b. Detroit, Mich, 9/6/31; m. 1957 to Victoria Schlafer; c. Jennifer, Andrew, Madeleine and Matthew. Educ: Univ. Chicago, B.A; Columbia Univ, M.A; Harvard Law Sch, LL.B. Polit. & Govt. Pos: Dem. chmn, Oakland Co, Mich, 61-64; Oakland Co. Bd. of Supvrs, 3 terms; Mich. State Sen, 64-, minority leader, 69-; chmn, Mich. Dem. Party, 67-68. Bus. & Prof. Pos: Attorney-at-Law. Mem: Oakland Co. Bar Asn. Mailing Add: 1922 Edgewood Blvd, Berkley, Mich. 48072.

LEVINE, BARRY S. D
b. Brooklyn, N.Y, 3/30/46; s. Morris Carl Levine and Ray Hodos L; single. Educ: L.I. Univ, B.A. in Hist, 66; Univ. Md. Grad. Sch; Georgetown Univ. Law Sch; Phi Alpha Theta. Polit. & Govt. Pos: Student activities coordinator, Johnson-Humphrey-Kennedy Campaign, Brooklyn, N.Y, 64; mem, state exec. cmt, N.Y. State Col. Young Dem, 64-65, N.Y.C. regional coordinator, 65-66; v.pres, L.I. Univ. Young Dem, 64-66; col. coordinator, Dem. Mayoralty Campaign, N.Y.C, 65; del, U.S. Youth Coun, 65-67; treas, Col. Young Dem. Clubs of Am, 65-67; mem. exec. cmt, Kings Co. Young Dem, 66-68; admin. asst. to the City Adminstr. and Dep. City Clerk, Takoma Park, Md, 68- Publ: 'Good Business v. Equal Justice,' Georgetown Univ. Law Quarterly, 66. Mem: Am. Polit. Sci. Asn; Law Student Div, Am. Bar Asn; Am. Soc. for Pub. Admin. Recipient of internship from Metropolitan N.Y. Center for Education in Politics, 65-66. Rel: Jewish. Legal Res: 1516 E. 15th St, Brooklyn, N.Y. 11230. Mailing Add: 7710 Maple Ave, Takoma Park, Md. 20012.

LEVINE, JOSEPH SAMUEL D
b. Brooklyn, N.Y, 8/24/32; s. Irving Levine and Yvette Kleinfeld L; m. 1/14/60 to Harriet M. Medney; c. Peter Mark and Burton Alan. Educ: Cornell Univ, B.A, 54; N.Y. Univ. Sch. Law, LL.B, 59. Polit. & Govt. Pos: Asst. counsel, Judicial Inquiry, Supreme Court, 59-60; rackets investigator, Dist. Attorney's Off, Kings Co, N.Y, 60-62, asst. dist. attorney, 62-65; secy. to Hon. Thomas R. Jones, Civil Court, N.Y.C, 65-66; former N.Y. State Assemblyman, 51st Dist, Kings Co. Mil. Serv: Entered as 2nd Lt, Army, 54, released as 1st Lt, 56, after serv. in Co. D, 67th Tank Bn, Second Armored Div, ETO, 59. Mem: Brooklyn and N.Y. State Bar Asns; past pres. and present chmn, exec. cmt, Kings Co. Young Dem. Club, Inc; secy, N.Y. State Young Dem; adv. cmt, assocs. div, President's Club; jr. cmt, Nat. Dem. Club; Flatbush Jewish Center; Munic. Lodge, B'nai B'rith; Brooklyn Lawyers' Club; Fedn. of Jewish Philanthropies. Rel: Jewish. Mailing Add: 110 Canton Ave, Brooklyn, N.Y. 11218. (1967)

LEVINE, PHILIP MICHAEL R
Chmn, Putnam Co. Rep. Party, N.Y.
b. New York, N.Y, 8/14/06; s. Julius Levine and Mary Wolk L; m. 11/7/48 to Hilda Koenigsberg; c. Judith Irene. Educ: N.Y. Univ, 2 yrs; St. John's Law Sch, 2 yrs; basketball team. Polit. & Govt. Pos: Town chmn, Rep. Party, 60, co-chmn, 64; alternate del, Rep. Nat. Conv, 64; chmn, Putnam Co. Rep. Party, N.Y, 64- Bus. & Prof. Pos: Pres, Leesons Clothes, Inc. and J. Levine Sons Corp. Mil. Serv: Entered as Pvt, Army, 42, released as Sgt, 45, after serv. in Mil. Police Command; Good Conduct Medal. Mem: Vets. Asn; Zionist; Clothing Mfrs. Asn; K. of P; Mahopac Civic Asn. Rel: Jewish. Legal Res: N. Lake Blvd, Mahopac, N.Y. 10541. Mailing Add: 2 Harrison Place, Brooklyn, N.Y. 11206.

LEVINE, SOLOMON D
b. Queens, N.Y, 5/13/21; s. William Levine and Lillian Snitovsky L; m. 12/26/44 to Herta Borkum; c. Mark David. Educ: Queens Col, 39-41; N.Y. Univ, B.S, 47, M.A, 50; Dead End Boys, Queens Col. Polit. & Govt. Pos: Alternate del, Dem. Nat. Conv, 68; del, New Dem. Coalition, Queens, N.Y, 68 & 69; mem, bd. dir, Adlai E. Stevenson Club, Forest Hills, 69. Bus. & Prof. Pos: Teacher indust. arts, Bd. of Educ, N.Y.C, 48- Mil. Serv: Entered as Pvt, Army Air Force, 42, released as S/Sgt, 45, after serv. in 845th Bomb Squadron, Eighth Air Force, 43-45; Normandy, Rhineland, North. France and Air Offensive Europe Battle Stars; Am. Campaign Medal; Europe-Africa-Middle East Serv. Medal; Victory Medal; Good Conduct Medal. Publ: 'A.P.R. Program for Teachers and Supervisors' Indust. Arts and Vocational Educ, 6/62. Mem: Indust. Arts Teachers Guild; v.pres, United Fedn. of Teachers, AFL-CIO; del, N.Y.C. Cent. Labor Coun. Albert Lee Smallheiser Citation. Rel: Hebrew. Mailing Add: 150-15 72nd Rd, Flushing, N.Y. 11367.

LEVITAS, ELLIOTT HARRIS D
Ga. State Rep.
b. Atlanta, Ga, 12/26/30; s. Louis Joseph Levitas and Ida Goldstein L; m. 6/8/55 to Barbara Claire Hillman; c. Karen Eve, Susan Debra and Kevin Noah. Educ: Emory Univ, B.A, 52 and Law Sch, LL.B, 56; Oxford Univ, Rhodes Scholar, 52, B.A, 54 and M.A, 58; Phi Delta Phi; Phi Beta Kappa; Omicron Delta Kappa. Polit. & Govt. Pos: Chmn, Ga. Gov. Spec. Cmt. on Legis. Constitutional Coord. and del, Dem. Nat. Conv, 64; Ga. State Rep, Dist. 77, 66- Bus. & Prof. Pos: Partner, Arnall, Golden & Gregory, 55- Mil. Serv: Entered as Lt, Air Force, 55, released as Capt, 62, after serv. as Judge Adv, Air Force, 56-58. Mem: Atlanta and Am. Bar Asns; Lawyers Club of Atlanta; Commerce Club of Atlanta; Emory Univ. Alumni Asn; Emory Law Alumni Asn.(pres, 66). Rel: Jewish. Legal Res: 1352 Jody Lane. N.E, Atlanta, Ga. 30329. Mailing Add: 1000 Fulton Federal Bldg, Atlanta, Ga. 30303.

LEVITT, ARTHUR D
Comptroller, State of N.Y.
b. Brooklyn, N.Y, 6/28/00; s. Israel A. Levitt and Rose Daniels L; m. 6/30/29 to Dorothy M. Wolff; c. Arthur, Jr. Educ: Columbia Univ, A.B, 21, LL.B, 24; Phi Sigma Delta. Polit. & Govt. Pos: Pres, bd. of educ, N.Y, 52-55; Comptroller, N.Y, 55-; chmn, Dem. State Conv, 65; del, Dem. Nat. Conv, 68. Bus. & Prof. Pos: Partner, Gates, Levitt & Nottlins, Attorneys, 46-55. Mil. Serv: Pvt, Inf, World War I, reentered as Capt, Judge Adv. Gen. Corps, Army, 46, released as Col, 46, after serv. in Judge Adv. Div, 1st Army, Transportation Corps; Legion of Merit; World War I and II Victory Medals; Army Commendation, ETO and African Theater Ribbons; Col, Army Res, 66- Mem: Mason (33°); Shrine; K. of P; Odd Fellows; Nat. Dem. Club; Am. Legion; VFW; Jewish War Vets. Rel: Hebrew. Mailing Add: 203 E. 72nd St, New York, N.Y. 10021.

LEVITT, ROBERT ELWOOD R
Ohio State Rep.
b. Los Angeles, Calif, 11/1/26; s. George L. Levitt and Clara Olston L; m. 2/14/48 to Barbara Ann Toot; c. John, Thomas and Susan. Educ: St. Ambrose Col, 44-45; Northwest. Univ, B.S, 47; West. Reserve Univ, LL.B, 53; Phi Gamma Delta; Phi Delta Phi. Polit. & Govt. Pos: Spec. counsel to Ohio Attorney Gen, 56-58; asst. solicitor, Canton, Ohio, 56-59, councilman, 60-63; Ohio State Rep, 63-, Majority Floor Leader, Ohio State House of Rep, 69- Bus. & Prof. Pos: Attorney, Day, Ketterer, Raley, Wright & Rybolt, 60- Mil. Serv: Entered as A/S, Navy, 44, released as Ens, 46. Mem: Am. Legion; Stark Co. and Ohio Bar Asns; trustee, Ment. Health Asn; bd, YMCA Boys Br; Brookside Country Club; Atwood Yacht Club. Rel: Presbyterian. Legal Res: 252 23rd St. N.W, Canton, Ohio 44709. Mailing Add: 800 Cleve-Tusc. Bldg, Canton, Ohio 44702.

LEVY, EUGENE R
N.Y. State Assemblyman
b. Brooklyn, N.Y, 12/1/26; s. Jack Levy and Helen Gerber L; m. 10/29/50 to Geraldine Elaine Schack; c. Felicia and William. Educ: N.Y. Univ, 44. Polit. & Govt. Pos: V.pres, W. Ramapo Rep. Club, Suffern, N.Y, 63; dep. dir, Rockland Co. Civil Defense, 63; Councilman, Ramapo, 64-68; N.Y. State Assemblyman, 94th Assembly Dist, 69- Bus. & Prof. Pos: Pres, Plaza Restaurant Inc, Spring Valley, N.Y. Mil. Serv: Entered as HA 2/C, Navy Med. Corps, 44, released PhM 3/C, 46. Mem: F&AM (past Master, Athelstane Lodge); Rotary (bd. dirs, Spring Valley Club); Masters and Wardens Asn. (past pres); B'nai B'rith; K. of P; Am. Legion; Jewish War Vet; charter mem, Spring Valley Museum; Rockland Co. Young Mens Hebrew Asn.(bd. dirs); Am. Parkinson Disease Asn.(hon. pres, Rockland Co. Chap); adv. bd, Rockland State Hosp. Guild. Friend of the Handicapped, Rockland Co. Exceptional Child Parent Teachers Asn, 69; Man of the Year Award, Spring Valley Jr. C. of C, 69. Rel: Jewish. Mailing Add: 2 East Place, Suffern, N.Y, 10901.

LEVY, GERALD D
b. Des Moines, Iowa, 12/26/22; s. Lewis Levy and Belle Cohen L; m. 9/20/58 to Cynthia Gorrell; c. Sally, Lisa, Ruth and David. Educ: Univ. of Mich, B.B.S, 46; Drake Univ, LL.B, 62; Phi Alpha Delta. Polit. & Govt. Pos: Del, Dem. Nat. Conv, 68. Mil. Serv: Entered as A/S, Navy, 42, released as Ens, 59, after serv. in World War II, 42-45. Mem: Iowa State Bar Asn; Am. Inst. of C.P.A's; Am. Asn. of Attorney-C.P.A's (bd. mem, 68); Mason; Shrine. Rel: Jewish. Legal Res: 2508 Meadow Lane, West Des Moines, Iowa 50265. Mailing Add: 909 Bankers Trust Bldg, Des Moines, Iowa 50309.

LEVY, HARRY CHARLES D
Treas, Nev. State Dem. Cent. Cmt.
b. Batavia, N.Y, 9/12/10; s. Max Levy and Esther Holtzer L; m. 6/3/28 to Jeanne Sklar; c. Alvin M. and Elaine L.(Mrs. Turk). Educ: Los Angeles High Sch, grad, 27. Polit. & Govt. Pos: Chmn, Clark Co. Juvenile Bd, Nev, 51-67; chmn, Las Vegas Housing Authority, 51; mem. bd. dirs, Nat. Housing Conf, 58-; mem, Clark Co. Dem. Cent. Cmt, 59-; cmnr, Nev. State Tax Cmn, 59-61; cmnr, Las Vegas, Nev, 61-65; mem, Small Bus. Adv. Cmt, 63-65; treas, Nev. State Dem. Cent. Cmt, 66-; chmn, Civilian-Mil. Coun, S. Nev, 67-; del, Dem. Nat. Conv, 68. Bus. & Prof. Pos: Treas, Transwest. Life Ins. Co, Reno, 58-64; dir, Nev. Title Ins. Co, 60-65; treas, Nev. Savings & Loan, 61-66; dir, Nev. State Bank, Las Vegas, 61-65; dir, Nev. Nat. Bank, Reno, 66- Mem: Mason; Scottish Rite; Shrine; Elks; Kiwanis; C. of C; B'nai B'rith. (pres, Las Vegas Lodge). Variety Club Humanitarian Heart Award, 55; City of Hope Man of Year Award, 62; Jewish War Vet. Commun. Serv. Award, 66; Anti-Defamation League Man of Year Award, 62; B'nai B'rith Man of Year, 58. Rel: Jewish; pres, Temple Beth Sholom, 54-55. Mailing Add: 1700 Rexford Dr, Las Vegas, Nev. 89105.

LEWELLEN, HOMER WILLIAM D
b. Iuka, Ill, 9/10/05; s. William Harvey Lewellen and Ida Alice Luttrell L; m. 4/21/40 to Bernice Wyman; c. Margaret Delaine (Mrs. John Timko, Jr) and Diana Gail. Educ: Iuka Schs. Polit. & Govt. Pos: Guard, Ill. State Farm, Vandalia, Ill, 35-38; treas, Marion Co, 38-42, sheriff, 42-46, supvr. of assessments, 59-; automobile license investr, Secy. of State's Off, 46-53, drivers license exam, 67-; chmn, Marion Co. Dem. Party, 46-48; del, Dem. Nat. Conv, 64. Mem: Secy, Co. Treasurers' Asn, Ill, 38-42; Ill. Sheriff's Asn; Farm Bur; Elks; United Commercial Travelers. Rel: Presbyterian. Legal Res: Marion County Courthouse, Salem, Ill. 62881. Mailing Add: R.R. 4, Hawthorne Rd, Salem, Ill. 62881.

LEWINTER, MURRAY D
b. Bronx, N.Y. Educ: CCNY, B.B.A; N.Y. Law Sch, LL.B. Polit. & Govt. Pos: N.Y. State Assemblyman, 60-66; former secy. to Judge Vincent Trimarco, Bronx Munic. Court; v.pres, Jackson Dem. Club. Bus. & Prof. Pos: Accountant. Mem: VFW; Jewish War Vets; NAACP; Fed. of Jewish Philanthropies; E. Bronx Commun. Coun; Forest Neighborhood House; U. J. A; Neighborhood Asn. of E. Bronx; Youth Coun. of E. Bronx. Rel: Jewish. Mailing Add: 1510 Crotana Park E, Bronx, N.Y. 14060. (1967)

LEWIS, BRIAN JOHN R
Wash. State Sen.
b. Clacton-on-Sea, Essex, Eng, 9/8/29; s. Randal John Lewis and Marjorie Pauline Chaston L; m. 8/20/55 to Elaine Cecilia Pfister; c. Randal John, II, Geoffrey David, Matthew Frank, Jennifer Elaine and Jason Daniel. Educ: Univ. Durham, Scholar, 48, B.Sc. Civil Eng, 51, Grad. Cert. Pub. Health Eng, 51; Univ. Del, fel, 52-53; Univ. Calif, Los Angeles, M.S, Traffic and Transportation Eng, 54. Polit. & Govt. Pos: Mem, Gov. Expenditures Adv. Coun, 59-61, author sect. relating to Dept. Hwy. and Toll Bridge Authority; mem, Citizens Port Cmt, Seattle, 60; mem, Citizens Adv. Cmt. Joint Cmt. Urban Area Govt, 61-62; mem, Mayor's Cmt. Rapid Transit, 61-62; mem, Adv. Cmt. King Co. Develop, 63; chmn, 48th Dist. Cmt, Dan Evans for Govt. Cmt, 63-64, mem, King Co. Cmt, 64; mem, Bd. Adjustment, Bellevue, 63-66, v.chmn, 64; alternate del, Rep. State Conv, 64; del, King Co. Rep. Conv, 64; chmn, Gov. Birthday Party, Statewide Fund Raising Campaign, 65; mem. organizing group and pres, Puget Sound Suburban Hwy. Coun, 65-; Wash. State Rep, 41st Dist, 67-69, mem. cmts. on transportation, local govt, natural resources, ins. and financial insts, Wash. House Rep, chmn, Subcmt. Rapid Transit, mem, Legis. Joint Cmt. Hwy, 67-, chmn, Subcmt. Hovercraft and

Hydrofoils; West. Wash. campaign coordinator, United Citizens for Nixon-Agnew, 68; chmn, Eastside Area Campaign Cmt, Decision Cmt. Forward Thrust, 68; Wash. State Sen, 69-; mem. subcmt, rapid transit and develop. Seattle CBD, Munic. League Seattle and King Co; mem, Utilities Cmt, Garbage Subcmt. and Co. Opers. Cmt. Bus. & Prof. Pos: Lectr. pub. health engr, Univ. Durham, 51-52; research asst. traffic safety and traffic signalization anal. proj, Inst. Transportation and Traffic Engr, Univ. Calif, Los Angeles, 53-54; jr. civil engr, South. Calif. Edison Co, Los Angeles, 54-55; prin. asst, W.O. Wagner, Consult. Engrs, Pasadena, 55-56; civil engr, Skidmore, Owings and Merrill, Archit. and Engrs, San Francisco, 56-57; proj. engr, Porter, Urquhart, McCreary & O'Brien, Consult. Engrs, San Francisco and Seattle, Wash, 57-60; assoc. and proj. engr, Whipple, Murphy, Pearson and Assocs, Consult. Engrs. Palo Alto and Seattle, 60-61; pres, Lewis-Redford-Engrs, Inc, Consult. Engrs, Bellevue, Wash, 61-; pres, Hubbell and Waller Eng. Corp, 68- Mem: Am. Soc. Civil Engrs.(secy, Seattle sect, 62, mem. commun. proj. cmt, 63-65, chmn, 63, chmn, transportation tech. div, 65-); Inst. Traffic Engrs; Hwy. Res. Bd, Nat. Acad. Sci; Am. Pub. Works Asn; Planning Asn. Wash; Am. Soc. Planning Off; Consult. Eng. Coun. Wash.(v.pres, 68, pres, 69-); San Francisco Engr. Speakers Club (pres, 57); Rainier Club; Wash. Athletic Club; Bellevue Rotary Club; Izaak Walton League; Jr. C. of C.(pres, Seattle, 60, v.pres, Wash. State, 62, int. dir, Wash. State, 62, state chmn. govt. affairs, 63); Lake Wash. Good Rd. Asn.(mem. spec. action cmt, 62-); Bellevue C. of C.(chmn. planning subcmt. new bus. and indust. cmt, dir, 65-66, chmn. new bus. and indust); mem. fund raising adv. cmt, Wash. State Heart Asn, 65-67, chmn, King Co. Campaign, 66; mem. bd. dirs, Overlake Mem. Hosp, 68-; YMCA (campaign cmt. Eastside Bldg. Fund, 68); Wash. State Oceanographic Cmn; Young Men's Rep. Club King Co; King Co. Young Rep. Rel: Latter-day Saint; Elder. Mailing Add: 1804 127th Ave. S.E, Bellevue, Wash. 98004.

LEWIS, CHARLES WILLIAM 'BILL' R
Ariz. State Rep.
b. Warwick, N.Y, 4/7/26; s. Charles William Lewis and Oleta Fuller L; m. 6/22/47 to Pearl Louise Pomeroy; c. Charles Alan, Gary Steven and Donn William. Educ: Tusculum Col, A.B, 47. Polit. & Govt. Pos: Ariz. State Rep, 69- Bus. & Prof. Pos: Free lance author and photographer, 47-; prog. dir, KRIZ Radio, Phoenix, 51-53; assoc. ed, Ariz. Farmer/Ranchman mag, 53-55; chief of info. and educ, Ariz. Game and Fish Dept, 55-64; sports writer and announcer, KTAR AM & TV, Phoenix, 64-68; registered rep, Financial Progs, Inc, 68- Mil. Serv: Entered as A/S, Navy, 44, released as Sonarman 3/C, 45, after serv. in Fleet Sonar Sch, U.S, 44-45. Publ: Over 300 articles published in West. Outdoors, Outdoor Life, Phoenix, Wildlife-Sportsman, Ariz; Ariz. Hwys, Wildlife Views, Saturday Evening Post and others. Mem: Outdoor Writers Asn. of Am; Ariz. Outdoor Writers; Phoenix Press Box Asn.(past pres); Phoenix Press Club; Am. Asn. Conserv. Educ; Elks (trustee); F&AM; Ariz. Sportsmasters Rod & Gun Club; Phoenix Forward Cmt; Phoenix Civitan Club (past pres). Rel: Methodist; Mem. Choir, Brooks United Methodist Church, Phoenix. Mailing Add: 4426 N. 63rd Ave, Phoenix, Ariz. 85033.

LEWIS, DAVID JOHN R
b. Coalton, Ohio, 12/22/83; s. John Michael Lewis and Martha Williams L; m. 6/7/28 to Ethel Grace Trout; c. John T, Robert E, Linton D, Donald L. and David G. Polit. & Govt. Pos: Treas, Perry Co, Iowa, 24-28; div. chief, Dept. Indust. Rels, Ohio, 30-32; auditor, Dept. of Taxation, 35-45; Ohio State Rep, 51-56. Bus. & Prof. Pos: Pres, Davis & Lewis Coal Co, Inc, 18-24; land agent, Sunnyhill & Peabody Coal Co, 46-65. Mem: Nat. Asn. of Power Engrs; Craftsman's Coun. Engrs; Mason, Chap, Coun, Commandry, Shrine Aladdin Temple, Zavi Shrine Club; Elks; Lions; Perry Co. Farm Bur. Man of the Month, Nat. Asn. of Power Engrs, 6/60. Rel: Methodist. Mailing Add: 418 Mill St, New Lexington, Ohio 43764.

LEWIS, DEAN D
b. East Prairie, Mo, 12/30/33; s. Alex Lewis and Lillian Schilling L; single. Educ: Doniphan High Sch, Mo. Polit. & Govt. Pos: Campaign mgr. for John Reynolds for Gov, 62-64; v.chmn, Outagamie Co. Dem. Party, Wis, 63-64; del, Dem. Nat. Conv, 64; dist. coordinator, U.S. Sen. William Proxmire, Wis. Mil. Serv: Navy, 51-58; Un Serv. Ribbon; Korean Occupation Ribbon with 2 Battle Stars; Syngman Rhee Citation. Mem: Bd. dir, Appleton Optimist Club Int. Rel: Church of Christ. Legal Res: 524 N. Morrison St, Appleton, Wis. 54911. Mailing Add: 114 N.Oneida St, Appleton, Wis. 54911.

LEWIS, E. BROOKS D
b. Abbeville, Ga, 2/18/12; s. Erasmus Hughes Lewis and Martha Brooks L; m. 6/21/42 to Klonnie Eloise Wren; c. Martha Eloise. Educ: Mid. Ga. Col. Polit. & Govt. Pos: Ga. State Rep, 10/25/61-66; Gordon City Coun, 10 yrs; Mayor, City of Gordon, 10 yrs; Dem. Exec. Committeemen, 16 yrs. Bus. & Prof. Pos: Oil distributor. Mem: 240 F&AM Masonic Lodge; Scottish Rite; Al Schoh Temple; W.O.W; Moose. Rel: Baptist. Mailing Add: Box 296, Gordon, Ga. 31031. (1967)

LEWIS, EDWARD BARKER R
Maine State Rep.
b. Bristol, Maine, 5/13/04; s. William M. Lewis and Flora Palmer L; m. 7/2/27 to Gladys Dearing; c. Virginia Ann. Educ: Gorham State Col, 24; Boston Univ, B.S, Educ. Polit. & Govt. Pos: Chmn, Bristol Sch. Cmt, Maine, 52-57; chmn. bd. selectmen, Bristol, Maine, 63-69, chmn. park cmn, 64-65; Main State Rep, 65-; mem, Co. Rep. Cmt, 68-69. Bus. & Prof. Pos: Teacher, Milton, Mass. Pub. Schs, 27-48; owner and operator, Ed. Lewis Guest House and Cottages, 48- Mem: Mason (32°); Lions; Eastern Star. Rel: Congregational. Mailing Add: Pemaquid Beach, Maine 04559.

LEWIS, ERNEST CROSBY D
Chmn, S.C. Dem. Party
b. Winnsboro, S.C, 3/4/34; s. Ernest Vann Lewis and Nell Brooks L; m. 8/7/55 to Emily Judith Williams; c. Lisa LaVell and Allyson Lee. Educ: Univ. S.C, Columbia, 52-55; Univ. S.C. Sch. Law, LL.B, 58; Phi Alpha Delta; Block C Club. Polit. & Govt. Pos: S.C. State Rep, 61-64, chmn, Mil, Pub. & Munic. Affairs Cmt, S.C. State House of Rep, mem. & v.chmn, Joint House and Sen. Standing Cmt. on Educ. Against Communism, 62-64: mem. bd. trustees, S.C. Med. Col. of Charleston, 62-64; mem. bd. visitors, The Citadel, 62-64; mem. & v.chmn, S.C. State Bd. Educ, 65-69; del, Dem. Nat. Conv, 68; chmn, S.C. Dem. Party, 68- Bus. & Prof. Pos: Partner, Law Firm of Lewis, Cobb & Lewis, 58-; dir, Riverland Develop. Corp, currently; dir, Taylor Properties, Inc, 68- Mil. Serv: Entered as Pvt, Army, 52, released as Capt, 64, after serv. in 12th Judge Advocate Gen. Corp, Third Army, 58-64. Mem: Richland Co, S.C. and Am. Bar Asns; Mason (32°); Sons of the Confederacy; Shrine; Forest Lake Country Club; Carolina Soc; YMCA. Eagle Scout; v.pres. and pres, S.C. Law Student Bd; vice justice and justice, Phi Alpha Delta. Rel: Methodist. Legal Res: 1544 Heatherwood Rd, Columbia, S.C. 29205. Mailing Add: 1711 Gervais St, Columbia, S.C. 29201.

LEWIS, GEOFFREY W.
U.S. Ambassador to Cent. African Repub.
b. Brookline, Mass, 5/20/10; m. to Elizabeth Locke; c. Geoffrey W, Jr. and Mrs. Robin Herbert. Educ: Harvard Univ, B.A, 32; Trinity Col; Cambridge Univ. Polit. & Govt. Pos: Staff mem, Cabinet Cmt. on Palestine and Related Probs, London, 46; career officer, U.S. Dept. of State For. Serv, 46-; for. affairs specialist, 46-49; acting asst. chief, Div. of German Econ. Affairs, 49-50; dep. dir, Bur. of German Affairs, 50-54; Nat. War Col, 55-56; first secy. and counsr, Karachi, 56-58; first secy, USRO, Paris, 58-61; dep. chief of mission, Amman, 61-65; U.S. Ambassador to Mauritania, 65-69 and Cent. African Repub, 69- Bus. & Prof. Pos: Asst. dean and asst. hist. instr, Harvard, 33-37; headmaster, private sch, 39-40. Mil. Serv: Lt. Col, Army, 41-46. Mailing Add: U.S. Dept. of State Foreign Service, Washington, D.C. 20521. (1967)

LEWIS, GERALD D
Fla. State Rep.
b. Alabama. Educ: Harvard Univ; Harvard Law Sch. Polit. & Govt. Pos: Exec. v.pres, Young Dem. Club of Dade Co, Fla; Fla. State Rep, 67- Bus. & Prof. Pos: Attorney. Mil. Serv: Commanding Officer of a spec. forces detachment, Fla. Nat. Guard. Parachutist, Jumpmaster. Mailing Add: 719 City National Bank Building, 25 W. Flagler St, Miami, Fla. 33130. (1967)

LEWIS, HAROLD V. D
married; c. Kathy and David. Educ: Ore. Col. of Educ, B.A, 38; Ore. State Univ, B.S, 47. Polit. & Govt. Pos: Ore. State Rep, 65-68. Bus. & Prof. Pos: Ins. underwriter; former teacher and F.F.A. instr; mgr, Yamhill Co. Fair, 56-65. Mil. Serv: Navy. Mem: Former pres, McMinnville Rotary and Dayton Lions; former chmn, United Good Neighbors. Rel: Methodist; Finance chmn. and trustee. Mailing Add: 1147 S. Davis St, McMinnville, Ore. 97128. (1967)

LEWIS, HARRY B. R
Wash. State Sen.
b. Pittsburgh, Pa, 1927; married; c. three. Educ: Univ. Wash. Polit. & Govt. Pos: Wash. State Sen, currently; Wash. State Rep, 2 terms. Bus. & Prof. Pos: Owner, Hyak Co. Mil. Serv: Army. Mem: Soc. Am. Foresters, Elks; Phi Delta Theta; Am. Legion. Mailing Add: 2019 Clairmont Circle, Olympia, Wash. 98501. (1967)

LEWIS, JAMES E. D
Ky. State Sen.
b. Wurtland, 7/22/25; s. Elva Virgil Lewis, Sr. and Lucille Vanhorn L; m. 7/10/46 to Mynea Edith Ferguson; c. Karen Lynn, Sharon Ann and Mark Edward. Educ: Morehead State Univ, 2 years; Louisville Sch. Mortuary Sci, 1 year. Polit. & Govt. Pos: Coroner, Elliott Co, Ky, 52-66; Ky. State Sen, 18th Sen. Dist, 66-; del, Dem. Nat. Conv, 68. Bus. & Prof. Pos: Chmn, Elliott Co. Develop. Asn; mem. bd. dirs, Grayson RECC. Mem: Mason; York Rite; Shrine. Rel: Protestant. Mailing Add: Main St, Sandy Hook, Ky. 41171.

LEWIS, JOHN HENRY D
Chmn, Lewis Co. Dem. Cent. Cmt, Mo.
b. Bowling Green, Mo, 4/15/19; s. P.L. Lewis and Nellie Marie Inlow L; m. 6/7/42 to Virginia A. Payne; c. Nancy M. and Steve M. Educ: Bowling Green High Sch, Mo, dipl, 37. Polit. & Govt. Pos: Treas, Lewis Co. Dem. Cent. Cmt, Mo, 50-60, chmn, 60- Bus. & Prof. Pos: Operator, serv. sta. and restaurant, 46-; distributor, Staab Battery, 62- Mil. Serv: Entered as Pvt, Air Force, 43, released as T/Sgt, 45, after serv. in Army Air Corp, ETO, 43-45. Mem: Mason; Quincy Coin Club; Co. Sport Club; Am. Legion; pres, Ewing Fire Dept; bd. mem, Ewing Water Dept; local Civil Defense. Rel: Protestant. Mailing Add: Box 226, Ewing, Mo. 63440.

LEWIS, JOHN M. R
Ind. State Rep.
b. Seymour, Ind, 1/28/13; s. John M. Lewis and Emma Crabb L; m. 6/3/39 to Josephine M. Deputy; c. John M, IV and Fred D. Educ: Hanover Col, A.B, 32; Ind. Law Sch, LL.B, 39; Beta Theta Pi. Polit. & Govt. Pos: Rep. co. chmn, Ind, 40-41; prosecuting attorney, Jackson Co, 46-52; judge, Circuit Court, Ind, 53-64; Ind. State Rep, currently. Bus. & Prof. Pos: Attorney, self-employed, 39-; city attorney, Seymour, Ind, 66- Mil. Serv: Entered as Pvt, Army, 43, released as 1st Lt, 46, after serv. in Pac. Theater, 18 months; Lt. Col, Army Res, currently; Bronze Star; Commendation Ribbon; Asiatic-Pac. Theater Ribbon with 2 Stars; Victory Medal; Japan Occup. Ribbon. Mem: Ind. and Am. Bar Asns; Am. Trial Lawyers Asn; Elks; Am. Legion; VFW; C. of C. Rel: Baptist. Legal Res: 207 Emerson, Seymour, Ind. 47274. Mailing Add: P.O. Box 1, Seymour, Ind. 47274.

LEWIS, JOHN W, JR. R
b. Marshall, Ill, 9/6/05; m. to Mahala Forsythe; c. Joan (Mrs. Ingram), Janice (Mrs. Marsh); three grandchildren. Educ: Univ. of Ill. Polit. & Govt. Pos: Ill. State Rep, 9 terms & 62-68; Ill. State Sen, 2 years; dir, Ill. Dept. of Agr, 69- Bus. & Prof. Pos: Farmer, livestock dealer, auctioneer. Mem: Mason; Consistory; Shrine; K. of P; DOKK; Elks; Moose; Delta Upsilon; Lions; C. of C; Clark Co. Farm Bur. Rel: Congregational. Mailing Add: R.R. 2, Marshall, Ill. 62441.

LEWIS, LORRAINE D
Committeewoman, Union Co. Dem. Cmt, N.J.
b. N.Y.C, 5/8/26; d. Sol Strauss and Grace Goldberg S; m. 3/23/46 to Philip L. Lewis; c. Donald and Hal. Educ: Hunter Col, B.A, 46; Pi Alpha Tau. Polit.

& Govt. Pos: Committeewoman, Union Co. Dem. Cmt, N.J, 54-; mem, Union Co. Bd. of Ment. Health, 3 years; alternate del, Dem. Nat. Conv, 68; del-at-lg, N.J. New Dem. Coalition, 69. Bus. & Prof. Pos: Travel consult, Fischer Bros. Travel Bur, Irvington, N.J, 62- Mem: PTA (past pres, Springfield Chap). Rel: Jewish. Mailing Add: 385 Milltown Rd, Springfield, N.J. 07081.

LEWIS, ORME, JR. R
Dep. Asst. Secy. for Pub. Land Mgt, Dept. of the Interior
b. Phoenix, Ariz, 4/26/35; s. Orme Lewis and Barbara Smith L; m. 10/17/64 to Elizabeth Bruening; c. Orme Joseph. Educ: Univ. Ariz, B.S, 58; Alpha Kappa Psi; Sigma Nu. Polit. & Govt. Pos: Rep. precinct committeeman, Phoenix, Ariz, 60-62 & 66-68; mem, Ariz. Rep. State Cmt, 66-68; Ariz. State Sen, Maricopa Co, 66-69, majority whip, chmn. finance and revenue cmt, and mem, Legis. Coun, Ariz. State Senate; v.chmn, Ariz. Legis. Campaign Cmt, 68-69; Dep. Asst. Secy. for Pub. Land Mgt, Dept. of the Interior, 69- Mem: Ariz. Real Estate Bd; treas, Ariz. Club; Phoenix Press Club; Art Museum; Men's Art Coun; Paradise Valley Country Club; Ariz. Educ. Planning and Coord. Coun. Rel: Episcopal. Legal Res: 2200 N. Central Ave, Phoenix, Ariz. 85004. Mailing Add: 3522 N. Third, Arlington, Va. 22201.

LEWIS, PRESTON BROOKS D
Ga. State Rep.
b. Augusta, Ga, 5/2/30; s. Preston Brooks Lewis and Clifford McElmurray L; m. 9/10/53 to Katherine D. Hill; c. Preston B, III, Clifford Ellis, Julian Carlton and Katherine Virginia. Educ: Univ. Ga, B.B.A, 55, LL.B, 58; Phi Kappa Alpha; Phi Delta Phi. Polit. & Govt. Pos: Secy-treas, Burke Co. Dem. Exec. Cmt, Ga, 60-; Ga. State Rep, 50th Dist, 61- solicitor, City Court of Waynesboro, 63-64. Bus. & Prof. Pos: Attorney-at-Law, Lewis & Lewis, 58- Mil. Serv: Seaman, Navy, 48-49; entered Army, 51, released as 1st Lt, 53, after serv. in 45th Inf. Div, Korea; Capt, Army Res; Bronze Star. Mem: Mason; Shrine; Rotary; Am. Legion; VFW; Ga. Farm Bur. Rel: Methodist. Legal Res: Forrest Dr, Waynesboro, Ga. 30830. Mailing Add: Box 88, Waynesboro, Ga. 30830.

LEWIS, RALPH T. R
R.I. State Sen.
b. Concord, N.H, 1/15/00. Educ: Bryant and Brown Univ. Extension. Polit. Pos: R.I. State Sen, 55-61 & 63- Bus. & Prof. Pos: Engr. Mil. Serv: Navy World War I. Mem: Am. Legion, past pres; St. Johns Commandery; Scottish Rite 32; Palestine Shrine; Salvation Army; Kent Co. chmn, Muscular Dystrophy; assoc. Fraternal Order Police. Mailing Add: 139 Gould Ave, Warwick, R.I. 02888. (1967)

LEWIS, ROBERT M. R
b. Bethlehem, N.H, 1/16/98; married; c. one adopted son. Educ: Dartmouth Col; Duke Univ. Polit. & Govt. Pos: N.H. State Rep, 63-67; former Chmn, Lebanon Budget Cmn; former Chmn, Lebanon Planning Bd; former mem, Lebanon Coun; former mem, State Personnel Cmn. Bus. & Prof. Pos: Retired laundry & drycleaning plant owner. Mil. Serv: U.S. Army, WW I. Mem: Past Cmdr, Am. Legion; Lebanon Rotary. Rel: Protestant. Mailing Add: 9 Kimball St, Lebanon, N.H. 03766. (1967)

LEWIS, ROGER KEITH D
b. N.Y.C, 8/17/23; s. Harry Clay Donecker and Kretchen D; m. Sept, 1946 to Julia Louise Kobman; c. Cheryl and Neal. Educ: Univ. Ariz, B.A, 52; Phi Beta Kappa. Polit. & Govt. Pos: Admin. asst, U.S. Rep. Morris Udall, Ariz, 61- Bus. & Prof. Pos: Reporter, Ariz. Repub, Phoenix, 52-60; copy desk, Tucson Daily Citizen, 60-61. Mil. Serv: Entered as Pvt, Army, 43, released as S/Sgt, 46, after serv. in Signal Corps, Iran. Rel: Protestant. Mailing Add: Route 1, Round Hill, Va. 22141.

LEWIS, STACY LEE D
b. Fayetteville, N.C, 11/3/00; s. William LaFayette Lewis and Carrie Jane Taylor L; m. 6/7/31 to Florine Sellars Humble. Educ: Campbell's Col, Buie's Creek, N.C, 18. Polit. Pos: Del, Presidential Nomination Conv, Atlantic City, 65. Mem: Past commodore and mem, Cambridge Yacht Club, Inc; past trustee, Elks 1272; past dir, Cambridge Rotary Club; Moose. Yachting-U.S. Power Squadron Cert. Seamanship. Rel: Methodist. Legal Res: 312 Glenburn Ave, Cambridge, Md. 21613. Mailing Add: P.O. Box 143, Cambridge, Md. 21613. (1967)

LEWIS, WALTER WOODWARD D
b. Winnsboro, S.C, 5/10/09; s. Thomas Walter Lewis and Mary Ellen Street L; m. 6/19/35 to Florrie Jane Bethea; c. Jane Bethea (Mrs. John McNair Turner), Thomas Woodward (deceased) and Ellen Street (Mrs. Richard Fletcher). Educ: Univ. S.C, B.S. in commerce, 31; Delta Sigma Pi; Caroliniana Soc. Polit. & Govt. Pos: Clerk of circuit court, Fairfield Co, S.C, 33-64, judge of probate court, 39; chmn, Fairfield Co. Dem. Exec. Cmt, 56-67; state tax cmnr, S.C. Tax Cmn, 64-67; cmnr, S.C. Alcoholic Beverage Control Cmn, Columbia, 67-69, chmn, 69- Bus. & Prof. Pos: Owner and operator, Adgerlan Plantation, Winnsboro, S.C, 43- Mem: Pres, Fairfield Co. Hist. Soc, 66-68; pres, S.C. State Asn. of Clerks and Registers of Mesna Conveyances, 58-59; chmn, Fairfield Co. Chap, Nat. Found. for Infantile Paralysis, 50-63 and 64-65; Policy Cmt, Southeast. Asn. of Tax Adminstrs, 65-66; mem, Nat. Conf. of State Liquor Adminstr, 67-; Masonic Lodge 11 F&AM; Rotary; Nat. Tax Asn; life mem, Am. Bible Soc; hon. mem, S.C. Asn. of Clerks & Registers; S.C. and Am. Rose Societies; Alumni Asn. Univ. S.C; Mt. Zion Soc. Rosarian and grower of exhibition type roses. Rel: Methodist. Mailing Add: Route 2, Adgerlan, Winnsboro, S.C. 29180.

LEWIS, WILLIAM HUGH R
Chmn, Putnam Co. Rep. Party, Ga.
b. Lincolnton, Ga, 1/15/17; s. George A. Lewis and Thersie Grant L; m. 6/2/39 to Lola Brown; c. Linda Joyce (Mrs. Jerry Garden) and Donna Lee (Mrs. David Sanders). Educ: Washington High Sch, grad, 35. Polit. & Govt. Pos: Chmn, Jasper Co. Rep. Party, Ga, 60-65; area chmn, Jasper-Putnam Co. Rep. Party, 65-66; chmn, Putnam Co. Rep. Party, 69- Mem: Worshipful Master, Masonic Lodge 200, Walton. Rel: Baptist; Deacon and Sunday Sch. Teacher. Mailing Add: Box 102, Shady Dale, Ga. 31085.

LEWISON, BERNARD R
Wis. State Assemblyman
b. Viroqua, Wis, 2/7/02. Educ: Lawrence Col, 21-22. Polit. & Govt. Pos: Mem. bd, Vernon Co, Wis; city alderman, Viroqua, mayor, 43-48; Wis. State Assemblyman, 54- Bus. & Prof. Pos: Tobacco buyer; real estate broker, dir, savings and loan asn; operator, automobile agency and body shop. Mailing Add: 11 S. Washington Heights, Viroqua, Wis. 54665.

LIAS, THOMAS LEE R
Dep. Spec. Asst. to President
b. Akron, Iowa, 9/27/34; s. Earl Lias and Bess Stoutenburg L; m. 12/28/58 to Sharon Garrison; c. Lisa. Educ: State Univ. Iowa, B.A, 56. Polit. & Govt. Pos: Campaign dir, assoc. ed, Newsletter and asst. to exec. dir, Nat. Rep. Cong. Cmt, 59-69; dep. spec. asst. to President, 69- Mem: Capitol Hill Club. Rel: Methodist. Legal Res: Akron, Iowa. 51001. Mailing Add: 215 E St, S.E, Washington, D.C. 20003.

LIBONATI, ROLAND VICTOR D
Treas, First Ward Dem. Orgn, Chicago, Ill.
b. Chicago, Ill, 12/29/00; s. Ernest M. Libonati and Fiore Pellitteri L; m. 12/29/42 to Jeannette K. Van Hanxleden; c. Michael E. Educ: Univ. Mich; Northwest. Univ. Law Sch. Polit. & Govt. Pos: Ill. State Rep, 30-34 & 40-42; Ill. State Sen, 42-57; U.S. Rep, Ill, 57-64; mem, Nat. Dem. Club; treas, First Ward Dem. Orgn, Chicago, currently. Mil. Serv: Lt, Army, 18, serv. in Inf, 86th Div, 9th Machine Gun Group. Mem: Justinian Soc; Chicago and Am. Bar Asns; Moose; Fed. Post, Am. Legion; Elliodore Libonati World War I Barracks; Voiture 220, 40 et 8; Past Comdrs. Club; Italo-Am. Union; Italo-Am. Civic Cmt; v.chmn, State Legis. Cmn, Am. Legion, Dept. of Ill. Sponsor and builder, Am. Boys Camp for Indigent Children, Coloma, Wis. Rel: Roman Catholic. Legal Res: 909 S. Loomis St, Chicago, Ill. 60607. Mailing Add: Room 1301, 134 N. La Salle St, Chicago, Ill. 60602.

LICHT, FRANK D
Gov, R.I.
b. Providence, R.I, 3/3/16; s. Jacob Licht and Rose Kassed L; m. 6/16/46 to Dorothy Shirlee Krauss; c. Beth Ellen, Carol Ann and Judith Joan. Educ: Brown Univ, A.B, 38; Harvard Law Sch, LL.B, 41; Phi Beta Kappa. Polit. & Govt. Pos: R.I. State Sen, 49-56; assoc. Justice, R.I. Superior Court, 56-68; Gov, R.I, 69- Bus. & Prof. Pos: Law partner, Letts & Quinn, Providence, R.I, 43-56. Publ: Co-author, 'Trial Judges' Code,' Mass. Law Quart, 6/65. Mem: Am. and R.I. Bar Asns; founding mem, Providence Human Rels. Cmn; chmn, Chapin Hosp. Cmn; chmn, R.I. Coun. Conf. of Christians and Jews; trustee and mem. bd. dirs, Butler Hosp. Recipient of Lehman Award for R.I, 65; Man of the Year, R.I. Mag. of Providence Sunday J, 69. Rel: Jewish. Legal Res: 640 Elmgrove Ave, Providence, R.I. 02906. Mailing Add: Executive Chamber, State House, Providence, R.I. 02903.

LICHTENFELD, SAMUEL D
b. Berwyn, Pa, 11/17/05; s. Karl Lichtenfeld and Anna Schiller L; m. 6/24/34 to Sylvia Landau. Educ: Univ. Pa, B.S. in Econ, 27 and LL.B, 30. Polit. & Govt. Pos: Chmn, Chester Co. Dem. Cmt, 48-58 & 60-62; del, Dem. Nat. Conv, 52; Spec. Attorney Gen, Pa, 59-60; judge, Court of Common Pleas, Chester Co, 60; pres, Chester Co. Indust. Develop. Authority, 69- Mil. Serv: Army, Pvt, 43-44, serv. in Inf. Mem: Chester Co. Bar Asn.(mem. nomination cmt, 61-63, pres, 69); Pa. Bar Asn.(mem. constitutional rev. cmt, 60-61); Am. Bar Asn; Am. Trial Lawyers Asn; Am. Judicature Soc; Mason; Lions; Elks; Am. Legion. Rel: Hebrew. Mailing Add: 71 Crestline Rd, Strafford, Wayne, Pa. 19087.

LICHTMAN, SIDNEY ALFRED D
N.Y. State Assemblyman
b. Pittston, Pa, 5/20/22; s. Harry Lichtman and Elizabeth Niman L; m. to Beverly Waltzer; c. Jay and Steven. Educ: N.Y. Univ, B.S, 46; St. Johns Law Sch, LL.B, 48; Sigma Tau Epsilon. Polit. & Govt. Pos: Counsel, N.Y.C. Housing Authority, 52-56, N.Y. State Banking Dept, 58-59; asst. dist. attorney, Kings Co. Dist. Attorney's Off, N.Y, 59-69; N.Y. State Assemblyman, 44th Assembly Dist, Kings Co, 69- Bus. & Prof. Pos: Mem, law firm, Hervey, Legum and Lichtman, Brooklyn, N.Y, 69- Mil. Serv: Entered as Pvt, Army, 41, released as Pfc, 44, after serv. in U.S. Infantry, African, Sicilian and Italian Theatres; Serv. Ribbons; Battle Stars. Mem: Brooklyn Bar Asn; Brooklyn Lawyers Club; Kings Co. Criminal Bar Asn; Nat. and State Dist. Attorneys Asns; past pres, Jewish Communal Center of Flatbush; Speakers Bur; Fedn. Jewish Philanthropies; United Jewish Appeal; dist. cmnr, Boy Scouts. Rel: Hebrew. Legal Res: 1094 E. 18th St, Brooklyn, N.Y. 11230. Mailing Add: 16 Court St, Brooklyn, N.Y. 11201.

LICKAR, JOHN IVAN D
b. Krain, Yugoslavia, 11/15/01; s. John Lickar, Sr. and Mary Stular L; m. 10/23/43 to Antiona Ulcar; c. John, Jr, Edward, Evelyn, Tonie, Kenneth, Joe, Bob, Wilima, Dorthy, Hildereth, Danny and Diane. Educ: Mich. Col. Mines, 26. Polit. & Govt. Pos: Precinct committeeman and mem. exec. bd, Clark Co. Dem. Party, Wash, 58-66; del, Wash. Dem. State Conv, 60-, mem, Resolutions and Agr. Cmts, Dem. Platform Cmt, 60; del, Dem. Nat. Conv, 64; treas, Clark Co. Dem. Club and Third Cong. Dist. Dem. Party; mem. exec. cmt, Clark Co. Dem. Cent. Cmt; del, Wash. Dem. Cent. Cmt. Bus. & Prof. Pos: Master farmer, Ill, 1930's; dairy farmer, Wash, currently. Mem: Grange (7°); C. of C; La Center Wheel Club; Cmt. on Rural Area Expansion & Develop, Wash. State Dairy Fedn; treas, Fifth Ave. Dem. Club. Rel: Lutheran. Mailing Add: Rt. 1, Box 653, Ridgefield, Wash. 98642.

LICKLE, WILLIAM CAUFFIEL R
b. Wilmington, Del, 8/2/29; s. Charles Harold Lickle and Hazel Cauffiel L; m. 11/24/50 to Renee Carpenter Kitchell; c. Sydney Cauffiel, Garrison duPont, Ashley Morgan and Kemble Carpenter. Educ: Univ. of Va, B.A, 51, Law Sch, LL.B, 53; Kappa Alpha; Phi Alpha Delta. Polit. & Govt. Pos: Finance chmn, Vol. for Nixon, Del, 60; coordinator, Del. for Goldwater, 64; New Castle Co. Airport Cmnr, 64-67; treas. and mem. finance cmt, Del. Rep. Party, 64-68. Bus. & Prof. Pos: Former chmn, Registrar & Transfer Co, N.Y.C; pres. and dir, Laird, Bissell & Meeds, Inc, currently. Mem: Am. and Va. Bar Asns; treas. and dir, Blue Cross of Del, 63-68; treas. and dir, Boys Club of Wilmington, Del, 63-69; dir. and treas, Wilmington Med. Center; dir, Del. Soc. of Crippled Children; Wilmington Club; Wilmington Country Club; Vicmead Hunt Club. Rel: Episcopal. Mailing Add: Box 3793, Greenville, Del. 19807.

LIEB, HELEN BOWMAN R
b. Knoxville, Tenn, 11/28/06; d. William Henry Bowman; Mary Walters B; m. 6/15/33 to Joseph Patrick Lieb; c. Joseph Patrick. Educ: Univ. Richmond, B.A, 30; pvt. tutoring in music. Polit. & Govt. Pos: Mem, Rep. Nat. Cmt. for Fla, 52-56; del. at large, Rep. Nat. Conv, 52; Rep. State Finance Cmt, 52; Rep. State Exec. Cmt, 36-54; mem, Young Rep. Nat. Cmt. for Fla, 36-40. Bus. & Prof. Pos: High Sch. teacher, 30-33. Mem: Nat. Adv. Cmt, Diabetes Found, Inc; Am. Asn. of Univ. Women; Friday Morning Music Club; League of Women Voters; Nat. Fdn. of Women's Rep. Club; Women's Nat. Rep. Club. Rel: Baptist. Mailing Add: 2007 Bayshore Blvd, Tampa, Fla. 33606. (1967)

LIEBERMANN, SHIRLEY CORRELL R
Chmn, Northampton Co. Rep. Cmt, Pa.
b. Easton, Pa, 10/3/17; d. Paul Correll, M.D. and Bertha Ingham C; m. 10/3/53 to James Ward Liebermann. Educ: Hartridge Sch. & Knox Sch. Polit. & Govt. Pos: Committeewoman, Pa. Rep. State Cmt, 58-66; v.chmn, Northampton Co. Rep. Cmt, 66, chmn, 66- Bus. & Prof. Pos: Saleswoman with several real estate agencies, 46-53; chief inheritance tax appraiser, Dept. of Revenue, Pa, 63- Mem: Past pres, v.pres. and currently mem. bd. of dir, Easton Children's Home. Rel: Presbyterian. Mailing Add: 7 Lehn's Court, Easton, Pa. 18042.

LIEBLONG, WARREN GEORGE R
b. Greenbriar, Ark, 7/2/22; s. William Anderson Lieblong (deceased) and Carrie May L; m. 6/30/46 to Mary Louise Austin; c. Warren G, Jr, Marcia Carrie and Daniel Austin. Educ: Ark. State Teachers Col, B.S.E; Northwest. Univ, M.A; Phi Sigma Epsilon; Alpha Psi Omega. Polit. & Govt. Pos: Mem, Jefferson Co. Rep. Cmt, Ark, 52-67, chmn, 61-62; del, Rep. Nat. Conv. and originator & chmn, Draft Rockefeller for Gov. Cmt, 64; Rep. cand, U.S. Cong, Fourth Dist, 62. Bus. & Prof. Pos: Supts. of Schs, Humphrey, Ark, 51-53; sales rep, Josten's, 53-64; councilor, Little Rock Sch. Bd, 64-65; state mgr, Cattlemen's Life Ins. Co, 65- Mil. Serv: Entered as Pvt, Army, 42, released as 2nd Lt, 46, after serv. in Signal Corps, Allied Experimental Sta. Mem: Am. Legion; Mason; Methodist Men; organizer, Humphrey Men's Civic Club; adv. bd, Arrowhead Lake Estates, Hot Springs, Ark. Most valuable student, Northwest. Univ; planned and supervised construction of WNUR radio Sta. Rel: Methodist; Mem, official bd. of finance chmn, Hawley Methodist Church. 1967 Legal Res: Pine Bluff, Ark. No mailing address available. (1967)

LIEBMAN, LAWRENCE MAURICE D
Cmnr, Bd. of Harbor Cmnrs, Conn.
b. New Haven, Conn, 9/13/30; s. Meyer Liebman and Anna Knosen L; m. 12/23/63 to Sorel Rossinoff; c. Norry J. and Eric J. Educ: Univ. Conn, B.S, 52; Boston Univ. Law Sch, LL.B, 55; Tau Epsilon Phi. Polit. & Govt. Pos: Alderman, New Haven, Conn, 59-61 & 63-65; cmnr, Bd. of Harbor Cmnrs, New Haven Harbor, 63- Bus. & Prof. Pos: Partner, Gamm, Liebman & Rashba, Attorneys, 56-66; asst. prof. law, Quinnipiac Col, 65-66. Mil. Serv: Navy, 56. Mem: Am, Mass, Conn. and New Haven Co. Bar Asns; Am. Trial Lawyers Asn; Oaklane Country Club; Probus Club. Golf Club Champion, 65. Rel: Jewish. Mailing Add: Tumblebrook Rd, Woodbridge, Conn. 06525.

LIEBOWITZ, SIMON J. D
b. Brooklyn, N.Y; married; c. Three. Educ: City Col. New York; Brooklyn Law Sch, cum laude, 26; Philonomic Coun. Polit. & Govt. Pos: Pres, 22nd Assembly Dist. Dem. Club of Brooklyn; N.Y. State Sen, 59-68; judge of the civil court, currently. Bus. & Prof. Pos: Attorney-at-law. Mem: Brooklyn Bar Asn; Iota Theta; N.Y. State Bar Asn; N.Y.Co. Lawyers Asn; past chmn, E. N.Y. Area of Red Cross and Boy Scouts; Past noble Grand of Abraham Lincoln Lodge 456, Odd Fellows; past pres, E. N.Y. Lodge, B'nai B'rith; legal adv, Knickerbocker Lodge 510, K. of P; hon. chmn, Fed. of Jewish Philanthropies of E. N.Y; bd. E. N.Y. Youth and Adult Center. Rel: Past pres. hon. pres, Temple Sinai, Brooklyn. Mailing Add: 156 Sunnyside Ave, Brooklyn, N.Y. 11207.

LIEDERMAN, DAVID SAMUEL D
Mass. State Rep.
b. Malden, Mass, 4/26/35; s. Harry Liederman and Pauline Kaplan L; m. 6/8/56 to Toby Newman; c. Wendy, Keith and Larry. Educ: Univ. Mass, Amherst, B.A, 57; Springfield, Col, Mass, M.Ed, 58; Univ. Pittsburgh, M.S.W, 62; Alpha Epsilon Pi. Polit. & Govt. Pos: Mass. State Rep, 17th Middlesex Dist, 69- Bus. & Prof. Pos: Asst. dir, Roxbury Fedn. Neighborhood Centers, Boston, Mass, 64-66; dir. of relocation, United South End Settlements, 66-68; asst. prof. social work, Boston Univ, 68- Mil. Serv: E-3, Army Res, 54-62. Mem: Nat. Asn. Social Workers; Acad. Cert. Social Workers; Nat. Asn. Housing & Redevelop. Officials; Lions; B'nai B'rith; YMCA. Rel: Jewish. Mailing Add: 69 Tremont, Malden, Mass. 02148.

LIFSET, HARVEY MERVIN D-Liberal
b. Schenectady, N.Y, 3/6/16; s. Abram Lifset and Rose Barish L; m. 5/3/42 to Violet Leah Rubin; c. Marc J. and Reid J. Educ: Union Col, A.B, 37; Albany Law Sch, LL.B, 40; Justinian Soc; Phi Sigma Delta. Polit. & Govt. Pos: N.Y. State Assemblyman, 57-68, chmn, Ways and Means Cmt, N.Y. State Assembly, 66-68. Mil. Serv: Entered as Pvt, Army, 41, released as Maj, 46, after serv. in 82nd Airborne Div, ETO, 43-45; Col, Army Res, 65; Army Commendation Medal; Bronze Star; Am. Theater Ribbon; ETO Ribbon with 6 Battle Stars and Bronze Arrow Head; Victory Medal; Pre-Pearl Harbor Ribbon; Army Res. Ribbon with 2 Clusters. Mem: N.Y. and Albany Co. Bar Asns; Mason; B'nai B'rith; ROA; Elks; Lions; Am. Legion. Rel: Jewish. Legal Res: 380 Albany-Shaker Rd, Loudonville, N.Y. 12211. Mailing Add: 90 State St, Albany, N.Y. 12207.

LIGARDE, HONORE D
Tex. State Rep.
b. Laredo, Tex, 4/11/20; s. Amedee Ligarde and Sara Saenz L; m. 8/30/42 to Betty Jo Neel; c. Janelle Alise. Educ: Tex. A&M Univ; Univ. Tex; Phi Alpha Delta. Polit. & Govt. Pos: Co. chmn, Dem. Exec. Cmt, Tex, 56-60; committeeman, Tex. Dem. State Exec. Cmt, 21st Sen. Dist, 60-64; Tex. State Rep, 69th Dist, 62- Mil. Serv: Entered as Aviation Cadet, Air Force, 41, released as Capt, 45, after serv. in 321st Bomb Group, 12th Air Force; Air Medal with Nine Oak Leaf Clusters; Presidential Unit Citation. Mem: Past dir. and active officer, Laredo C. of C, Kiwanis, Cancer Soc, Commun. Chest, USO Serv. Center, Boys' Club, Heart Asn. and Laredo Chap. Tex. Mfg. Asn; Am. Legion Post 59, Lulac Coun. 12, Vets. Land Bd. Cmt. for Webb Co. Rel: Catholic. Legal Res: 3500 Bartlett, Laredo, Tex. 78040. Mailing Add: P.O. Drawer 1359, Laredo, Tex. 78040. (1967)

LIGHT, CATHERINE D
Mem. Exec. Bd, Mich. Dem. State Cent. Cmt.
b. Manhattan, N.Y, 11/29/06; d. Joseph Arleo and Madeline La Rocca A; wid; c. Rosanne and Richard Allan. Educ: N.Y. Univ, 3 years. Polit. & Govt. Pos: Co-founder Detroit Chap, Vol. for Stevenson, Mich, 52; mem. policy and exec. cmt, 17th Cong. Dist. Dem. Orgn, 54-; mgr, Secy. of State Off, 55-; mem, Mich. Dem. State Cent. Cmt, 58-, mem. exec. bd, currently; del, Dem. Nat. Conv, 60, 64 & 68. Bus. & Prof. Pos: Clerk, Abraham & Straus, Brooklyn, N.Y, 22-25, mgr. childrens books, 30-36; bookstore mgr, 25-27; mgr. bookstore, Lit Bros. Dept. Store, 27-30. Rel: Catholic. Mailing Add: 718 Great Oaks Blvd, Rochester, Mich. 48063.

LIGHT, ELEANOR M. D
Chmn, Sanilac Co. Dem. Exec. Cmt, Mich.
b. Hartland, Mich, 7/16/19; d. Charles Berchman Gannon and Kathryn Bergin G; m. 6/24/39 to Frank J. Light; c. Patrick, Daniel, Jeannette and Lauretta. Educ: Hartland High Sch, 37. Polit. & Govt. Pos: Del, Sanilac Co. Dem. Conv, Mich. and Dem. State Conv, 50-65; secy, Dist. Sch. Bd, 59-67; mem, Mich. Dem. State Cmt, 63-65; alternate del, Dem. Nat. Conv, 64; v.chmn, Sanilac Co. Dem. Exec. Cmt, 65-67 and chmn, 67-; mem. of bd, Off. of Econ. Opportunity Thumb Area, 65-69; chmn, Thumb Area Econ. Opportunity Cmn. Bd. of Dirs, 67-69; mem, Eighth Dist. Dem. Cent. Cmt, 69. Mem: Farmers Union; pres, St. Joseph Altar Soc, 3 two year terms; treas, DCCW, 60-62 and bd. mem; McKenzie Mem. Hosp. Auxiliary, 67-69. Rel: Catholic. Mailing Add: 310 Snover Rd, Sandusky, Mich. 48471.

LIGHT, FRANCES H. R
b. Appalachia, Va, 5/10/23; d. Joel C. Haun (deceased) and Myrtle M. Hurd H. (deceased); wid; c. Jennifer Kay and Gwendolyn Sue. Educ: Middletown Bus. Col, 41-42. Polit. & Govt. Pos: Mem, Sullivan Co. Rep. Womens Orgn, Tenn, 60-; exec. secy. to U.S. Rep. James H. Quillen, Tenn, 63-; mem, Rep. Womens Club of Capitol Hill, 68- Mem: Kingsport Altrusa Club; asst. treas, Tenn. State Soc; VFW Auxiliary; Girl Scouts (past leader); mem, bd, Hire the Handicapped, State of Tenn. Rel: Baptist. Legal Res: 234 Hammond Ave, Kingsport, Tenn. 37660. Mailing Add: 5021 Seminary Rd, Alexandria, Va. 22311.

LIGHT, WILLIAM JASPER D
Chmn, Morton Co. Dem. Cent. Cmt, Kans.
b. Rolla, Kans, 9/25/23; s. William Clarence Light and Zula Tartar L; m. 8/18/46 to Geneva Mardelle Cullison; c. Nancy Delle, Peggy Ann, David C, William C, II, Linda Gail and Ellen Jean. Educ: High Sch. Polit. & Govt. Pos: Chmn, Morton Co. Dem Cent. Cmt, Kans, 56-64 & currently; mem. sch. bd, Rolla, 58-61, mayor, 58-62; Kans. State Rep, 65-66. Bus. & Prof. Pos: Pres, Rolla Coop. Asn, Kans, 58-60 and Southwest Kans. Bd. of Realtors, 63. Mil. Serv: Entered as Pvt, Marine Corps, 42, released as Cpl, 46, after serv. in S.Pac, 44-45; Good Conduct Medal. Mem: Am. Legion. Rel: Baptist. Mailing Add: Box 166, Rolla, Kans. 67954. (1967)

LIGHTSEY, HUGH TUTEN D
S.C. State Rep.
b. Brunson, S.C, 5/3/25; s. John Herman Lightsey and Addie T. Educ: Citadel, B.S, 50. Polit. & Govt. Pos: Chmn, Hampton Co. Dem. Exec. Cmt, S.C. and S.C. State Rep, currently. Bus. & Prof. Pos: Farmer and businessman. Mil. Serv: Navy, World War II. Mem: Shrine; Mason; Rotary; Eastern Star; Watermelon Growers Dist. Asn; exec. cmt, Bank Dir; exec. bd, Tuberc. Asn; Am. Legion; 40 et 8; Elks. Rel: Baptist. Mailing Add: Brunson, S.C. 29911. (1967)

LIGHTSEY, WILLIAM MARION D
Va. State Del.
b. Fairfax, S.C, 2/8/11; m. to Eleanor Marie Weiler. Educ: Citadel, Charleston, S.C. Polit. & Govt. Pos: Va. State Del, 66- Bus. & Prof. Pos: Park adminstr. Mem: Masons; PTA; Nat. Wildlife Fed; Nat. Cmt. for Support Pub. Schs. Rel: Lutheran. Mailing Add: 231 N. Evergreen St, Arlington, Va. 22203. (1967)

LIKES, HENRY L. D
b. Sayre, Okla, 8/29/13; s. William Ed Likes and Mary Ann Loveless L; m. Jan. 1935 to Billie Geraldine Tackett; c. Jerry, Buddy and David. Educ: High Sch, Grad. Polit. & Govt. Pos: Exec. reservist, Okla. Dept. Labor, currently; del, Dem. Nat. Conv, 68. Bus. & Prof. Pos: Secy-treas, Okla. State AFL-CIO, 64-68, pres, 68-; pres, State Pipetrades, currently; financial secy, Plumbers Local 351, currently. Mil. Serv: Navy, World War II. Mem: Mason; VFW; Am. Legion. Legal Res: 704 Edmond, Muskogee, Okla. 74401. Mailing Add: 111 N.E. 26th St, Oklahoma City, Okla. 73105.

LILES, WOODIE A. D
b. Andalusia, Ala, 3/19/22; m. to Helen Pasquarelli L; c. Cheryl Marie; Andrew Jay. Educ: Augusta Jr. Col; Univ. of Fla, LL.B, 53; Phi Delta Phi; Kappa Alpha; Fla. Blue Key; Pres. of Student Body. Polit. & Gov. Pos: Fla. State Rep, 58-66; Asst. Co. Attorney of Hillsborough Co; City Attorney of Zephyrhills; past Pres, Young Dem. of Fla. Bus. & Prof. Pos: Lawyer. Mil. Serv: Army Inf; Purple Heart. Mem: past Pres, E. Hillsborough Co. C. of C. Rel: Bd. of Stewards, Methodist church. Mailing Add: P.O. Box 551, Plant City, Fla. 33566. (1967)

LILJEDAHL, GEORGE H. D
b. 5/8/04; m. 7/8/35 to Genevieve Forster. Educ: Iowa State Univ, B.S; Univ. Iowa and Iowa State Univ. grad. work. Polit. & Govt. Pos: McCook Co. Bd. Educ, S.Dak, 56-65; S.Dak. State Rep, 59-60, 65-66 & 67-68. Bus. & Prof. Pos: Teacher and supt. of schs; farmer, currently. Mem: Phi Kappa Tau; Nat. Educ. Asn; McCook Co. Livestock Improv. Asn; treas, McCook Co. Crop Improv. Asn. Rel: Lutheran. Mailing Add: Salem, S.Dak. 57058.

LILJEGREN, DOROTHY JEAN R
Chairwoman, Third Dist. Rep. Party, Minn.
b. Benson, Minn, 2/21/30; d. Nelbert Monson and Mary Shigley M; m. 3/19/49 to M. Peter Liljegren; c. Susan, Thomas and Jeanne. Educ: Univ.

Minn, 1 year. Polit. & Govt. Pos: Chairwoman, Eden Prairie, Minn, 64-67; chairwoman, Third Dist. Rep. Party, Minn, 67-; alternate del, Rep. Nat. Conv, 68. Rel: Lutheran. Mailing Add: 15801 Cedar Ridge Rd, Eden Prairie, Minn. 55343.

LILL, RAYMOND JOSEPH D
N.Y. State Assemblyman
b. Rochester, N.Y, 7/26/13; s. Harry Peter Lill and Viola Kleisle L; m. 10/1/38 to Marion C. Fichtner; c. Donald Raymond. Educ: St. Joseph's High Sch, 27-28; Eastman Kodak Courses, 45-49. Polit. & Govt. Pos: Mem, Dem. Co. Cmt, 34-; city councilman, Rochester, N.Y, 62-67; N.Y. State Assemblyman, 67- Bus. & Prof. Pos: Mgr, Moser Studio, 29-43; foreman, Eastman Kodak, 43-69. Mem: C. of C; Moose; Liederkranz Club; Rochester Turners; Steuben Soc; Kodak Foreman Club. Rel: Catholic. Mailing Add: 31 Wolfert Terr, Rochester, N.Y. 14621.

LILLARD, ROBERT EMMITT D
Pres, Davidson Co. Dem. League, Tenn.
b. Nashville, Tenn, 3/23/07; s. John Walter Lillard and Virginia Allen L; m. 1/23/28 to Hallie Moore; c. Gladys, Sandra and Robert Walter. Educ: Biggins Commercial Col; Kent Col. of Law; Omega Psi Phi. Polit. & Govt. Pos: City councilman, Nashville, Tenn, 51-; mem, Bd. of Paroles and Pardons, Tenn, 65-; exec. secy, Tenn. Fedn. of Dem. Leagues; pres, Davidson Co. Dem. League, currently; mem, President's Cmt. on Civil Rights Under Law; del, Dem. Nat. Conv, 68. Mem: World Peace Through Law, Am. & Tenn. Bar Asns; Atomic Attack Cmt, Am. Bar Asn; Exec. Cmt, Nat. Bar Asn; former pres, J.C. Napier's Lawyers Asn; Libr. Asn; Am. Judicature Soc; Prince Hall (32°) F&AM; Pride of Tenn. Lodge, Elks, Col. in Antlered Guard; AFL. Rel: Methodist. Legal Res: 1062 Second Ave. S, Nashville, Tenn. Mailing Add: 1031 Stahlman Bldg, Nashville, Tenn. 37201.

LILLEHAUGEN, C. ARNOLD R
N.Dak. State Rep.
b. Brocket, N.Dak, 11/13/21; s. Micheal T. Lillehaugen and Marie Moe L; m. 6/23/46 to Lorayne T. Keck; c. Meredith June (Mrs. Dale Washburn), Mark Arnold and Paige Marie. Educ: Park River Agr. Sch, 1 year. Polit. & Govt. Pos: Rep. precinct committeeman, Perth Twp, N.Dak, 57-66, twp. clerk, 57-; N.Dak. State Rep, 17th Dist, 67-, mem. state and fed. govt. cmt, N.Dak. House of Rep, 67 & 69, mem. judiciary cmt, 67, mem. nat. resources cmt, 67 & 69, mem. agr. cmt, 69. Mem: Farmers Union; Nat. Farmers Orgn; Elks. Rel: Am. Lutheran. Mailing Add: Brocket, N.Dak. 58321.

LILLEY, DANIEL T. D
N.C. State Rep.
b. Martin Co, N.C, 8/15/20; s. Alfred T. Lilley (deceased) and Ethel G. Gurkin L.(deceased); m. 7/7/44 to Imojene P. Hites; c. Eileen Carol and Daniel T, Jr. Educ: Spartan Sch. Aeronautics, Tulsa, Okla, dipl; CLU, Am. Col. Life Underwriters. Polit. & Govt. Pos: Cmnr, Lenoir Co, N.C, 64-68; N.C. State Rep, 68- Bus. & Prof. Pos: Airport mgr, Stallings Field, Kinston, N.C, 49-50; salesman, The Penn Mutual Life Ins. Co, 50- Mil. Serv: Entered as Pvt, Army Air Corps, 39, released as M/Sgt, 45, after serv. in 24th Fighter Squadron, Panama, 39-43; Maj, Air Force Res, 43-69; group comdr, N.C. Wing, Civil Air Patrol, Lt. Col. Mem: East. N.C. Chap. Chartered Life Underwriters; Lenoir Co. Life Underwriters Asn; Rotary Int; Am. Legion; Old Time Assay Cmnrs. Soc. Distinguished Serv. Awards, U.S. C. of C, 54 and Kinston C. of C, 63. Rel: Disciples of Christ; Lay Minister, Cove City Christian Church, N.C. Legal Res: 1805 Sedgefield Dr, Kinston, N.C. 28501. Mailing Add: P.O. Box 824, Kinston, N.C. 28501.

LILLEY, JOHN ROBERT, II R
b. Worcester, Mass, 3/18/27; s. Russell L. Lilley and Cecile L. Belisle L; m. 8/8/53 to Nathalie V. Roche; c. Russell L. and Barbara M. Educ: Clark Univ. Polit. & Govt. Pos: Former mem. and chmn, Paxton Rep. Town Cmt, Mass. Mil. Serv: Entered as Pvt, Marine Corps, 46, released from active duty as Sgt, re-entered as 2nd Lt, 51, released to inactive duty as 1st Lt, after serv. in Korea; Lt. Col, Marine Corps Res, currently; Silver Star; Purple Heart; Korean Serv. Medal with three Stars; Presidential Unit Citation; Korean Presidential Unit Citation; Nat. Defense Medal; UN Medal. Mem: V.pres, Indust. Mgt. Club; Marine Corps League; Am. Legion; AF&AM. Rel: Unitarian. Mailing Add: American Legion Post 306, Paxton, Mass. 01612. (1967)

LILLEY, TOM R
Dir, Export-Import Bank of the U.S.
b. Bluefield, W.Va, 8/13/12; s. Charles Ellis Lilley and Minnie Holland L; m. 12/27/36 to Nancy Clegg; c. Anne (Mrs. Hammond), Cynthia (Mrs. Mazer) and Susan. Educ: Harvard Col, A.B, 34, Bus. Sch, M.B.A, 36; Phi Beta Kappa; Delta Upsilon. Polit. & Govt. Pos: Mem, Nat. Export Expansion Coun, 61-64; dir, Export-Import Bank of the U.S, 65- Bus. & Prof. Pos: Mem, indust. dept, Lehman Bros, N.Y.C, 36-40; mem. staff, Burlington Mills, Greensboro, N.C, 41-42; assoc. prof. and asst. dir. of research, Harvard Bus. Sch, 42-48; mem. controller's off, prod. planning mgr, Ford div, asst. gen. mgr, int. div. and v.pres, int. staff, Ford Motor Co, Dearborn, Mich, 48-65. Mem: Past dir, Nat. Foreign Trade Coun; former trustee, U.S. Coun, Int. C. of C. Rel: Presbyterian. Mailing Add: 1522 34th St, N.W, Washington, D.C. 20007.

LILLIE, ARLINE WHIPPLE R
Mem, Calif. Rep. State Cent. Cmt.
b. San Francisco, Calif, 2/19/10; d. George Lewis Whipple and Ida Sylvania Bell W; m. 4/21/34 to Wilbur C. Lillie; c. Diana (Mrs. Seely) (deceased). Educ: Univ. Pac, 2½ years; Delta Delta Delta. Polit. & Govt. Pos: Legis. chmn, Stockton Rep. Women's Club, Calif, 65 & 66, pres, 67 & 68; alternate mem, Calif. Rep. State Cent. Cmt, 67 & 68, mem, 69-; mgr. staff hq, VanDyken for Cong, 30th Dist, 68; mem, Calif. Rep. Assembly, 68 & 69; alternate mem, San Joaquin Co. Rep. Cent. Cmt, 69; mem. hosp. adv. bd, Calif. Dept. Pub. Health, 69; dir. pub. rels, Calif. Fedn. Rep. Women, Cent. Div, 69, corresponding Secy, 70- Mem: Red Cross Auxiliary; March of Dimes. Rel: Protestant. Mailing Add: 1335 N. Baker St, Stockton, Calif. 95203.

LIMPER, WILLIAM D
b. Phila, Pa, 1/27/99; s. William Limper and Anna Sickles L; m. to Clara McCartney; c. one son. Educ: Pub. Schs. Polit. & Govt. Pos: Pa. State Rep, 48-64-67; mem, 19th Ward Dem. Exec. Comm, 30- Bus. & Prof. Pos: Printing bus. Mem: Lighthouse Boys Club. Mailing Add: 169 W. Huntingdon St, Phila, Pa. 19133. (1967)

LINCOLN, EMMA ETHEL R
Chmn, New London Rep. City Cmt, Conn.
b. East Lyme, Conn, 1/20/14; d. Daniel Higgins and Mary Emma Holmes Higgins Lincoln (both deceased); single. Educ: Northfield Sch. for Girls, Mass; Williams Mem. Inst, New London, Conn. Polit. & Govt. Pos: Pres, New London Rep. Women's Club, Conn, 53-54, pres, First Ward, 57-58; secy, New London Rep. City Cmt, 55-66, chmn, 66-; Justice of Peace, 60-; alternate del, Rep. Nat. Conv, 68. Bus. & Prof. Pos: Owner, Lincoln Auto Serv, 40-; pres. and treas, Lincoln Center Inc, 63- Mem: Bus. & Prfnl. Women's Club; Dale Carnegie Alumnae Asn; Girls Serv. Orgn. of YMCA; Alumnae Orgn. of Northfield and Williams Mem. Inst; chmn. of bd, YWCA in New London, 67-69; v.chmn. bd, New London Red Cross Chap, 68 & 69; chmn. bd, New London Middlesex Counties Chap, Nat. Multiple Sclerosis Soc, 68 & 69; Rebekah (Noble Grand); chmn. of night vol. in coffee shop, Lawrence Mem. Hosp; Southeast. C. of C; New London Country Club; Osprey Beach Club; Capital Hill Club; Lawrence Mem. Hosp. and Norwich State Hosp. Women's Auxiliaries; vol. worker, Am. Cancer Soc, 64-, United Fund in S.E. Conn, 69- and 4-H Club Capital Funds Drive. First person and only woman to break ground for bldg. in New London's Redevelop, 64. Rel: Baptist. Legal Res: 16 Glenwood Place, New London, Conn. 06320. Mailing Add: P.O. Box 869, New London, Conn. 06320.

LINCOLN, GEORGE A. R
Dir, Off. of Emergency Preparedness
b. Harbor Beach, Mich, 7/20/04; s. Burr B. Lincoln and Esther Hoare L; m. 8/19/36 to Frederica Bellamy; c. Frederica Esther, Daniel Bellamy, Joyce LeFevre and Lorna Harriet. Educ: Univ. Wichita, 24-25; U.S. Mil. Acad, B.S, 29; Rhodes Scholar, Madgalen Col, Oxford Univ, 29-32; Oxford Univ, B.A. and M.A, 38. Hon. LL.D, Univ. Pittsburgh, 68. Polit. & Govt. Pos: Former chief, Strategy and Policy Group, World War II Opers. Div, head of plans for Gen. Marshall and later for Gen. Eisenhower; former chief, Control and Planning Br, G-4 Hq, Serv. of Supply, ETO; former head, Army Orientation Prog; mil. adv. to the Secy. of State, Paris Peace Conf, 46; dep. to the Under Secy. of the Army, 48-49; Dept. of Defense rep, Interdepartmental Cmt. Drafting First Mutual Security Prog, 51; defense adv. to U.S. Rep, Temporary Coun. Cmt, NATO, 51-52; mem, U.S. NATO Del, Rome and Lisbon, 51-52; spec. asst. to the Secy. of Defense, 51-53; coordinator, President's Cmt. to Study the Mil. Assistance Prog, Draper Cmt, 58-59; consult, U.S. Arms Control and Disarmament Agency, 61-65; mem, President's Adv. Panel, Nat. Acad. of For. Affairs, 62; spec. adv. to the adminstr, Agency for Int. Develop, 64-65; dir. Off. of Emergency Preparedness, Wash, D.C, 69- Bus. & Prof. Pos: Former prof. soc. sci. and former head dept, U.S. Mil. Acad; former consult, Woodrow Wilson Sch. of Int. and Pub. Affairs, Princeton Univ; panelist, Gaither and Rockefeller Reports, 57-58; mem. vis. cmt, Hist. Dept, Harvard Univ, 62-68; mem. adv. bd, Inter-Am. Defense Col, currently. Mil. Serv: Entered as 2nd Lt, Army, 29, released as Brig. Gen, 69, after serv. in 36th Regt, Combat Engrs, Corps of Engrs; Legion of Merit with Oak Leaf Cluster, 43; Distinguished Serv. Medal, 45; Hon. Comdr, Order of the Brit. Empire, 45; Distinguished Serv. Medal with Oak Leaf Cluster, 69. Publ: Collaborator, Economics of National Security, Prentice Hall, 50, rev. ed, 54, International Politics, 54 and Dynamics of International Politics, 62, rev. ed, 67, MacMillan. Mem: Coun. on For. Rels; Inst. for Strategic Studies; Soc. of Am. Mil. Engrs; Asn. of Am. Rhodes Scholars; Army and Navy Club; Denver Country Club. Rel: Protestant. Legal Res: Harbor Beach, Mich. 48441. Mailing Add: 2828 Albemarle St. N.W, Washington, D.C. 20008.

LINCOLN, JACK D. R
Chmn, Mineral Co. Rep. Cent. Cmt, Mont.
b. Sandpoint, Idaho, 9/8/39; s. Gary L. Lincoln and Marie Carlson L; m. 6/9/62 to Marguerite D. Doyle; c. Jon Grant, David Ladd and Katharine Maureen. Educ: Univ. Mont, B.A. in Bus. Admin. cum laude, 61; Alpha Kappa Psi; Sigma Alpha Epsilon. Polit. & Govt. Pos: Chmn, Mineral Co. Rep. Cent. Cmt, Mont, 64- Bus. & Prof. Pos: Secy-treas, Lincolns Silver, Inc, 61; owner and mgr, St. Regis Gift Shop, 61-66; Dir. and pres, Mineral Ins. and Develop, Inc, currently; Mem: Elks; Lions (2nd v.pres. and charter mem); Mineral Co. Sportsmen's Club, Superior, Mont. Rel: Methodist. Mailing Add: Box 252, St. Regis, Mont. 59866.

LINCOLN, RAY WILLIAM R
Idaho State Rep.
b. Filer, Idaho, 11/11/15; s. William A. Lincoln and Lennie Daniels L; m. 8/8/38 to Ida May Gillenwater; c. Stephen, David, Lance, Kathleen and Linda. Educ: Univ. Idaho, B.S. in Agr; Sigma Alpha Epsilon; Press Club; bus. mgr, sch. paper; Scabbard & Blade. Polit. & Govt. Pos: Pres, State Adv. Bd, Bur. Land Mgt, 62-66; Idaho State Rep, 64- Bus. & Prof. Pos: Pres, Idaho Wool Growers, 61-64. Mil. Serv: Entered as 2nd Lt, Army, 40, released as 1st Lt, 42. Mem: Elks; Kiwanis; Mason. Rel: Methodist. Mailing Add: 546 Sunrise Blvd, Twin Falls, Idaho 83301. (1967)

LIND, ALDEN E. D
b. Duluth, Minn, 3/24/35; s. John Lind and Iona Hill L; m. 8/24/59 to Ora Jane Cone. Educ: Reed Col, B.A, 60; Univ. Ore, Ph.D, 66; Predoctoral and postdoctoral fels. Polit. & Govt. Pos: Chmn, Lake Co. Dem-Farmer-Labor Party, Minn, 56-57; v.pres, Gr. Portland Young Dem, Ore, 58-59; mem, various Dem. campaigns and local Dem. party activities, 60-68; state coordinator, N.C. Citizens for McCarthy, 68; del, Dem. Nat. Conv, 68. Bus. & Prof. Pos: Prof. polit. sci, Univ. N.C, Chapel Hill, 65- Mem: Am. Polit. Sci. Asn; South. Polit. Sci. Asn; Am. Asn. Univ. Prof. Legal Res: 410 Whitehead Circle, Chapel Hill, N.C. 27514. Mailing Add: Political Science Dept, University of North Carolina, Chapel Hill, N.C. 27514.

LIND, JAMES FRANCIS D
b. York, Pa, 10/17/00; s. William E. Lind and Alice K. Shanabrough L; m. 6/22/22 to Grace Elizabeth Stahl; c. James R. Educ: Pa. State Univ. Exten, 25. Polit. & Govt. Pos: U.S. Rep, Pa, 49-52; co. controller, York Co, Pa, 54- Mil. Serv: Sgt, Army, 17-20, Lt. Col, 41-46 and 53; Col.(Ret), Army Res, 60. Aisne, Champagne-Marne, Aisne-Marne and Meuse Argonne Medals; Army of Occup. Medal; Rhineland, ETO and Africa-Middle East Serv. Medals; Am.

Defense and Serv. Medals; Victory Medal; Nat. Defense Serv. Medal. Mem: F&AM; Consistory (32°), Shrine; Am. Legion. Rel: Lutheran. Mailing Add: 141 N. Keesey St, York, Pa. 17402.

LINDAHL, BRUCE DFL
Minn. State Rep.
b. Brookings, S.Dak, 1919; s. John O. Lindahl and Edna Bushnell L; m. 12/20/46 to Constance Fuller; c. Laurie, Mary and Marcia. Polit. & Govt. Pos: Minn. State Rep, 64- Bus. & Prof. Pos: Sci. and math. teacher. Mil. Serv: Air Force. Mem: St. Paul Fedn. Teachers (mem. exec. bd). Mailing Add: 1551 E. Iowa Ave, St. Paul, Minn. 55106.

LINDBERG, CLIFFORD L. R
b. Jamestown, N.Dak, 2/14/15; married; c. Three. Educ: N.Dak. State Univ. of Agr. and Applied Sci. Polit. & Govt. Pos: N.Dak. State Rep, 51-66. Bus. & Prof. Pos: Contractor. Mem: Am. Legion; Elks; Mason. Mailing Add: Jamestown, N.Dak. 58401. (1967)

LINDBERG, GEORGE W. R
Ill. State Rep.
b. Crystal Lake, Ill, 6/21/32; s. Dr. Alger V. Lindberg and Rilla Wakem L; m. 6/20/64 to Linda Merlo; c. Karen Dawn and Kirsten Ann. Educ: Northwest. Univ, B.S, 54; Northwest. Sch. of Law, J.D, 57; Phi Delta Phi. Polit. & Govt. Pos: Ill. State Rep, 32nd Dist, 67-, chmn, Spec. House Cmt. to Investigate Ill. Judiciary, 69- Bus. & Prof. Pos: V.pres, John E. Reid and Assocs, Chicago, 55-68; assoc, Franz, Franz, Wardell and Lindberg, Crystal Lake, Ill, 68- Mem: Ill. State Bar Asn; Ill. Chiefs of Police Asn; Spec. Agents Asn; Am. Polygraph Asn; Am. Acad. Forensic Sci; Nat. Dist. Attorneys Asn; Am. Judicature Soc; Ill. Crime Investigating Cmn; Judicial Adv. Coun; Lions. Outstanding Legislator Award. Rel: Episcopal. Mailing Add: 356 Maplewood Lane, Crystal Lake, Ill. 60014.

LINDBLOM, RITA D
Treas, Mont. Dem. Women's Club
b. Wahpeton, N.Dak, 5/17/29; d. Arthur M. Forman and Hazel Miller F; m. 5/29/49 to Chester W. Lindblom; c. Karen and Bradley. Educ: N.Dak. State Sch. Sci, 4 quarters. Polit. & Govt. Pos: Secy, Sheridan Co. Dem. Cent. Cmt, Mont, 58-61, v.chmn, 64-68, precinct committeewoman, 66-, state committeewoman, 67-; treas, Mont. Dem. Women's Club, 67-; del, Dem. Nat. Conv, 68; asst. bill clerk, Mont. State Sen, 69. Bus. & Prof. Pos: Linotype operator, Plentywood Herald, 48-49 & 61-68; off. secy, Fed. Crop Ins. Corp, 58-61; liquor store vendor, 69- Mem: Int. Toastmistress; VFW Ladies Auxiliary; Nat. Farm Orgn; Nat. Farmers Union; co. and state Mont. Dem. Women's Club (officer). Outstanding State Pres. Award, Nat. VFW Auxiliary, 63-64. Rel: Lutheran. Mailing Add: Outlook, Mont. 59252.

LINDBLOOM, HAROLD SETH D
Mem. Cand. Cmt, Boulder Co. Dem. Party, Colo.
b. Holdrege, Nebr, 6/7/06; s. Albert John Lindbloom and Mabel Hallgren L; m. 12/31/35 to Pauline Funk; c. Betty Rae and Elise Anne. Educ: Colo. State Col, A.B; Univ. Denver, M.A; Phi Delta Kappa. Polit. & Govt. Pos: Committeeman, Boulder Co. Dem. Party, Colo, 46-56, co-chmn, 65 and mem. cand. cmt, currently; co-chmn, Colo. Dem. State Finance Cmt, 58-60. Bus. & Prof. Pos: Northwest rep, Scott, Foresman & Co, 30-34, Colo-Wyo. rep, 35-42 & 45- Mil. Serv: Entered as Pvt, Army, 42, released as Capt, 45, after serv. in Manila Harbor; S.Pac. and Philippines Ribbons; Victory Medal with Four Battle Stars. Publ: Co-author, Colorado Citizen, Old West Publ. Co, Denver. Mem: Pres, Colo-Wyo. Bookmen's Asn, 48-49; Am. Legion; Am. Civil Liberties Union; corresponding mem, Denver Westerners. Rel: Unitarian. Mailing Add: 1950 Dartmouth, Boulder, Colo. 80302.

LINDE, FREDRICK ADOLPHUS R
Kans. State Rep.
b. St. Louis, Mo, 5/6/14; s. William Linde and Elisabeth Niemoeller L; m. 3/6/43 to Frances Page Medairy; c. Elisabeth (Mrs. L.P. Jeter) and Barbara. Educ: Wash. Univ, A.B, 36, M.S, 37; Sigma Xi. Polit. & Govt. Pos: Mem. subcmt, St. Louis Health Dept, Mo, 48-52; precinct committeeman, Sedgwick Co. Rep. Cent. Cmt, Kans, 62-64; Kans. State Rep, 67-; del, Kans. State Rep. Conv, 68; bd. dirs, Kans. Paraguay Partnership, 68- Bus. & Prof. Pos: Supvr, Monsanto Chem. Co, St. Louis, Mo, 38-52; supt, Pittsburgh Coke & Chem. Co, Pittsburgh, Pa, 52-55; chem. engr, Vulcan Materials Co, Wichita, Kans, 55- Mem: Am. Inst. Chem. Engrs; Kans. Acad. Sci.(mem. coun). Rel: Episcopal. Mailing Add: 6008 Grace Lane, Wichita, Kans. 67208.

LINDE, HANS ARTHUR D
b. Berlin, Germany, 4/15/24; s. Bruno C. Linde and Luise Rosenhain L; m. 8/13/45 to Helen Tucker; c. Lisa and David Tucker. Educ: Reed Col, B.A, 47; Univ. Calif, Berkeley, J.D, 50; Phi Beta Kappa; Order of the Coif. Polit. & Govt. Pos: Law clerk to Assoc. Justice Wm. O. Douglas, U.S. Supreme Court, 50-51; attorney, Off. Legal Adv, State Dept. and U.S. Mission to UN Gen. Assembly, 51-53; legis. asst. to U.S. Sen. Richard L. Neuberger, 55-58; mem, Ore. Constitutional Revision Cmn, 61-62; consult, Arms Control and Disarmament Agency, 62-65; alternate del, Dem. Nat. Conv, 64. Bus. & Prof. Pos: Assoc. prof, law, Univ. Ore, 59-64, prof, 64-; vis. prof, Univ. Calif, Berkeley, 64-65; Fulbright lectr, Univ. Freiburg, Germany, 67-68. Mil. Serv: Entered as Pvt, Army, 43, released as Pfc, 46, after serv. in 414th Armored Field Artil. Bn, ETO, 45. Publ: 'Constitutional Rights in the Public Sector,' Wash. Law Rev, 65; numerous articles in other law journals. Mailing Add: 1858 University St, Eugene, Ore. 97403.

LINDEKUGEL, FRED R
b. Jefferson Co; m. to Vera Marie; c. six. Educ: Columbus Col; Gen. Beadle State Teachers Col, Madison. Polit. & Govt. Pos: Pub. utilities cmnr, S.Dak, 42, 48-68; mem, Rates of Pub. Utilities Cmt, Nat. Asn. of R.R. Utilities Cmnr, 45-; pres, Midwest Asn. of R.R. and Utilities Cmnr, 59-60; mem, State Motor Patrol, 6 years; pres, NW Weights Measures Asn, 2 terms. Bus. & Prof. Pos: Petroleum salesman, 6 years and mem. of staff, 4 years. 1967 Legal Res: Madison, S.Dak. No mailing address available. (1967)

LINDENMEYER, PAUL ANDREW R
Chmn, Douglas Co. Rep. Cent. Cmt, Ill.
b. Pawnee City, Nebr, 2/25/05; s. Theodore Andrew Lindenmeyer and Daisy Ware L; m. May, 1931 to Marlene A. Hawver; c. D.W. and Patricia (Mrs. John Benison). Educ: Univ. Mo, M.A. and B.J, 27; Sigma Delta Chi; Kappa Tau Alpha; MDS. Polit. & Govt. Pos: Precinct committeeman, Arcola Twp, Ill, 50-66; Rep. committeeman, 48th Dist; chmn, Douglas Co. Rep. Cent. Cmt, currently; del, Dem. Nat. Conv, 68. Bus. & Prof. Pos: Ed, Custer Co. Chief, Broken Bow, Nebr, 28-29 and Regional News, Lake Geneva, Wis, 29-31; city ed, Record-Herald, 32-36, ed. and publisher, 36-57; ed. and publisher, Broom & Broom Corn News, Arcola, 40- Mem: Mason; Elks; Moose; Arcola C. of C; U.S. C. of C. Has done considerable work on legislation pertaining to the broom and allied industries in Wash, and obtained passage of two major bills. Rel: Christian Church. Legal Res: 252 S. Pine St, Arcola, Ill. 61910. Mailing Add: P.O. Box 523, Arcola, Ill. 61910.

LINDER, A. JAMES D
b. Hamburg, Ark, 7/23/21; s. Allen Jefferson Linder and Fannie Grey Moseley L; m. 4/22/43 to June Evelyn Thach; c. Jo Evelyn and Carolyn Jeanne. Educ: Univ. Ark. Law Sch, Little Rock, LL.B, 46. Polit. & Govt. Pos: City attorney, Hamburg, Ark, 46-60; dep. prosecuting attorney, Tenth Dist, 47-50, prosecuting attorney, 51-60; munic. judge, Hamburg, 61-62; del, Dem. Nat. Conv, 68. Bus. & Prof. Pos: Practicing attorney, Hamburg, 46-62; gen. counsel, first v.pres. and secy-treas, Nat. Investors Life Ins. Co, Little Rock, 61- Mil. Serv: Entered as Pvt, Army, 42, released as Sgt, 46, after serv. in Hq. Eighth Serv. Command, 42-46. Mem: Mason; Shrine; Am. Legion; Rotary. Rel: Baptist. Legal Res: 214 E. Jackson Ave, Hamburg, Ark. 71676. Mailing Add: 3224 Shenandoah Valley Dr, Little Rock, Ark. 72776.

LINDER, HAROLD FRANCIS
b. Brooklyn, N.Y, 9/13/00; s. Dr. William Linder and Florence Strauss L; m. 10/5/30 to Bertha Rubin; c. Prudence (Mrs. Daniel Steiner) and Susan. Educ: Columbia Univ, 17-19. Polit. & Govt. Pos: Dep. Asst. Secy. of State for Econ. Affairs, 51, Asst. Secy, 52-53; pres. and chmn, Export-Import Bank, Wash, D.C, 61-68; U.S. Ambassador to Canada, 68-69. Bus. & Prof. Pos: Mfg. bus, 19-25; partner, Cornell, Linder & Co, 25-33 and Carl M. Loeb, Rhoades & Co, 33-38; pres, Gen. Am. Investors Co, Inc, 48-56; chmn. of bd. and trustee, Inst. for Adv. Studies, Princeton, N.J, 69- Mil. Serv: Comdr, Naval Res, 42-45. Mem: Hon. trustee, Inst. Int. Educ; trustee, Inst. for Philos. Research, Chicago; v.chmn, Am. Joint Distribution Cmt, 38-41; For. Policy Asn; Coun. For. Rels; Cosmos, Fed. City and Int. Clubs, Wash, D.C; Recess and Sky Clubs, N.Y.C. Mailing Add: 1901 24th St. N.W, Washington, D.C. 20008.

LINDERMAN, DALE D
N.Dak. State Rep.
b. Wells Co, N.Dak, 3/20/24; s. George W. Linderman and Christine Valer L; m. 9/1/46 to Jean Harriet Hanson; c. Kent Dale, Georgia Gail, Monica Jean, Roxanne Marie and Nadine Jo. Educ: Carrington, N.Dak. High Sch. Polit. & Govt. Pos: N.Dak. State Rep, Dist. 13, 63-66 and 68- Mem: Farmers Union; Nat. Farmers Orgn. Rel: United Church of Christ. Mailing Add: Route 2, Carrington, N.Dak, 58421.

LINDGREN, DONALD ARTHUR D
Mem, Calif. Dem. State Cent. Cmt.
b. Racine, Wis, 4/17/32; s. Arthur Edmond Lindgren and Dorothy Palmer L; m. 9/13/58 to Vilma Lopour; c. Leslie Ann and Allison Leigh. Educ: Univ. Wis, Madison, B.B.A, 57, M.B.A, 59, Ph.D, 68, Int. Bus. Mach. fel, summer 59; Nat. Asn. of Purchasing Agents fel; Alpha Kappa Psi; Kappa Sigma. Polit. & Govt. Pos: Pres, Arizona Dem. Coun, 64-64; Dem. cand. for U.S. Rep, 36th Dist, Calif, 68; mem, Downtown Dem, Calif, 68-; mem, Calif. Dem. State Cent. Cmt, 68-; mem, United Dem, 69- Bus. & Prof. Pos: Statist. analyst, Gen. Motor-Cent. Foundry Div, 57-58; asst. prof. mkt, Ariz. State Univ, 62-65; assoc. prof. mkt. and chmn. dept, San Diego State Col, 65-; pres, Lindgren Research Assocs, 68- Mil. Serv: Entered as Pvt, Army, 53, released as Pfc, 55, after serv. in Army Intel, Seattle, Wash. and Okinawa; Defense Medal. Mem: Am. Mkt. Asn; Asn. Calif. State Col. Prof.(state secy); Mkt. and Sale Execs; Am. Asn. of Univ. Prof; Dem. clubs and orgn. Outstanding Prof, Sch. of Bus, San Diego State Col, 69. Rel: Methodist. Mailing Add: 11054 Dutton Dr, La Mesa, Calif. 92041.

LINDH, PATRICIA SULLIVAN R
Secy-Treas, E.Baton Rouge Parish Rep. Exec. Cmt, La.
b. Toledo, Ohio, 10/2/28; d. Lawrence W. Sullivan and Lillian Devlin S; m. 11/12/55 to H. Robert Lindh, Jr; c. Sheila, Deborah and Robert L. Educ: Trinity Col, Wash, D.C, B.A, 50. Polit. & Govt. Pos: V.pres, E.Baton Rouge Parish Women's Rep. Club, 66-67, pres, 67-69; revisions chmn, La. Fedn. Rep. Women, 67-68, mem-at-large exec. cmt, 69-; mem, E.Baton Rouge Parish Polit. Action Coun, 67-; secy-treas, E.Baton Rouge Parish Rep. Exec. Cmt, 67-; alternate del, Rep. Nat. Conv, 68. Mem: Jr. League of Baton Rouge; mem. govt. cmt, Goals for Baton Rouge Prog. mem. bd. and exec. cmt, La. Arts and Sci. Center; mem. bd, Baton Rouge Symphony Asn. Rel: Roman Catholic. Mailing Add: 3731 S. Lakeshore Dr, Baton Rouge, La. 70808.

LINDHOLM, FRANCES MARION R
Mem, Calif. Rep. State Cent. Cmt.
b. Minneapolis, Minn, 10/19/18; d. Jens M. Svendsen and Marie Fladeland S; m. 5/1/38 to Edward Lindholm, Jr, wid; c. George Edward, Rex Ruben, Mark James and Michael Thomas. Educ: Washburn High Sch, Minneapolis, Minn, grad; Univ. Minn, 2 years. Polit. & Govt. Pos: Mem, Ways and Means Cmt, Reseda Rep. Women's Club, Fed, Calif, 64-65, Membership Cmt, 65-66, Publicity Cmt, 67-69 and pres, 69-; secy, W.Valley 64th Calif. Rep. Assembly, 65-67; campaign off. mgr, Calif. State Sen. Lou Cusanovich, 23rd Sen. Dist, 66, Calif. Assemblyman Patrick McGee, 64th Assembly Dist, 68; mem, Calif. Rep. State Cent. Cmt, 66-68 & 69- Bus. & Prof. Pos: Exec. Secy, Save Am. Movies, Hollywood, Calif, 62-68, Scenic and Title Artists, 62-69. Mem: Friends of Taxco; Sister City Div, Canoga Park C. of C; bd. dirs, Canoga Park Civic Asn. Rel: Lutheran. Mailing Add: 20846 Runnymede St, Canoga Park, Calif. 91306.

LINDHORST, AMBROSE H. R
Mem, Ohio Rep. State Exec. Cmt.
b. Cincinnati, Ohio, 7/27/13; s. Harry Lindhorst and Elizabeth Evers L; m. 6/13/43 to Betty Bush; c. Claudia. Educ: Xavier Univ; Univ. of Cincinnati; Chase Col. of Law. Polit. & Govt. Pos: Former chmn, Hamilton Co.

Rep. Exec. Cmt, Ohio; mem, Ohio Rep. State Exec. Cmt, currently; del, Rep. Nat. Conv, 68. Bus. & Prof. Pos: Law Partner, Lindhorst & Dreidame, Attorneys; dir, Southern Ohio Bank, Buckeye Savings Asn, First Ohio Savings Asn, Cincinnati Royals and Cincinnati Gardens; mem, bd. trustees, Good Samaritan Hospital and Victor Transit Corp. Mem: Cincinnati, Ohio and Am. Bar Asns; Am. Col. Trial Lawyers; Am. Judicature Soc. Rel: Catholic. Legal Res: 1044 Roodwood Dr, Cincinnati, Ohio 45208. Mailing Add: 1200 American Bldg, Cincinnati, Ohio 45202.

LINDJORD, HAAKON
Asst. Dir, Off. of Emergency Preparedness
b. Kristiansand, Norway, 7/10/15; s. Jacob H. Lindjord and Jorgine Haugland L; m. 12/21/45 to Nancy Lancaster; c. Jon Douglas, Bonnie Williams, Leigh Jorgine and Richard Charles. Educ: Univ. Wash, A.B. in Econ. and Bus. summa cum laude, 41; Princeton Univ, M.A. in Int. Rels, 50, Ph.D. in Polit. Sci, 51; Naval War Col, 61-62; Phi Beta Kappa; Beta Gamma Sigma. Polit. & Govt. Pos: In charge of policy planning tasks for the Mid.E. and Africa areas, Army Gen. Staff, Pentagon, 58-61; mem. staff, Off. of the Dep. Asst. Secy. for Politico-Mil. Affairs, U.S. Dept. of State, 63-66; from div. chief to dir, Policy Planning Staff, Off. of the Asst. Secy. of Defense for Int. Security Affairs, Pentagon, 66-68; prfnl. staff mem, Senate Sub-Cmt. on Nat. Security and Int. Opers, 68-69; spec. asst. for planning, Off. of Emergency Preparedness, 69, asst. dir, 69- Mil. Serv: Entered as 2nd Lt, Army, 41, retired as Col, 68, after serv. in Intel. Div, Supreme Hq, Allied Expeditionary Forces, ETO, 44-45, Berlin, 45-47, NATO Hq, Norway, 51-54 and Korea, 57-58; Legion of Merit with Two Oak Leaf Clusters; Army Commendation Medal; French Croix de Guerre; Belgian Croix de Guerre. Mem: Asn. of Princeton Grad. Alumni; Asn. of the U.S. Army; Princeton Club of Wash. Procter fel. for high scholarship, Princeton, 50; Superior Honor Award, U.S. Dept. of State, 66. Rel: Protestant. Legal Res: 9740 Eighth Ave. N.W, Seattle, Wash. 98107. Mailing Add: 1643 Wrightson Dr, McLean, Va. 22101.

LINDLEY, JOHN WILLIAM R
Chmn, Orange Co. Rep. Cent. Cmt, Ind.
b. Paoli, Ind, 8/25/20; s. Harry V. Lindley and Dana F. L; m. 11/2/47 to Sara E. Tegarden; c. John H, Candace Anne and Mike T. Educ: High Sch; Ind. Univ. Exten. Courses. Polit. & Govt. Pos: Pres, bd. trustees, Orleans, Ind, 54-58, mem, 58-62; finance chmn. and treas, Orange Co. Rep. Cent. Cmt, 64-65, chmn, 65- Bus. & Prof. Pos: Serv. mgr, Dictaphone Corp, 42-46; grocery bus, 47- Mem: Mason; Elks; Kiwanis; C. of C; Farm Bur. Sagamore of the Wabash. Rel: Christian. Mailing Add: 365 W. Vincennes St, Orleans, Ind. 47452.

LINDROOS, LaVANNE M. R
Chmn, Marquette Co. Rep. Party, Mich.
b. Mitchell, S.Dak; d. Ole T. Martinson and Ida Fiedler M; m. 9/9/51 to Emert W. Lindroos; c. Susan and William. Educ: High sch. Polit. & Govt. Pos: V.chmn, Marquette Co. Rep. Party, Mich, 58-68, chmn, 69-; mem, Mich. Rep. State Cent. Cmt, 61-63; mem, 11th Dist. Rep. Exec. Cmt, 64-66; del, Rep. Nat. Conv, 68- Mem: Ishpeming Women's Civic League (pres, 69-); Beta Sigma Phi. Rel: Lutheran. Mailing Add: 751 Mather Ave, Ishpeming, Mich. 49849.

LINDSAY, JOHN CHARLES D
S.C. State Sen.
b. Bennettsville, S.C, 4/18/27; s. Roos Moore Lindsay, Sr. and Louise Crosland Bair; m. 6/15/49 to Frances Maxine. Educ: Univ. S.C, LL.B, 51. Polit. & Govt. Pos: S.C. State Rep, 53-62; S.C. State Sen, 63- Bus. & Prof. Pos: lawyer; dir, McColl State Bank; v.pres, McColl Investors, Inc. Mil. Serv: Marine Corps, 44-46, serv. in A Co, 1st Bn, 21st Regt, Third Marine Div. Mem: Bd. dirs, Jaycees; Red Cross Charity Fund; VFW; Am. Legion; Mason; Alpha Tau Omega; Phi Delta Phi; Wig and Robe Honor Soc. Mailing Add: Box 250, Bennettsville, S.C. 29512. (1967)

LINDSAY, JOHN VLIET R
Mayor, New York, N.Y.
b. N.Y.C, 11/24/21; s. George Nelson Lindsay and Eleanor Vliet L; m. 6/18/49 to Mary Harrison; c. Katherine, Margaret, Anne and John Vliet. Educ: Yale Univ, B.A, 44, LL.B, 48. Polit. & Govt. Pos: Exec. asst. to U.S. Attorney Gen, 55-57; U.S. Rep, N.Y, 59-65; Mayor, N.Y.C, 65-; del, Rep. Nat. Conv, 68. Bus. & Prof. Pos: Counsel, Law Firm of Webster, Sheffield, Fleishman, Hitchcock and Chrystie, 65-; bd. of dirs, Freedom House. Mil. Serv: Lt, Naval Res, 43-46. Mem: Asn. of Bar of City of New York; Am. and N.Y. Bar Asns. Rel: Episcopal. Mailing Add: City Hall, New York, N.Y. 10007. (1967)

LINDSAY, ROBERT GOODALL D
Chmn, Richmond Co. Dem. Cmt, N.Y.
b. Glasgow, Scotland, 10/28/97; s. William Ross Lindsay and Mary Kane L; wid; c. Robert Arthur. Educ: Bus. Col. Polit. & Govt. Pos: Secy. to Boro pres, Richmond, 33; U.S. marshal, 38; mem, N.Y.C. Coun, currently; mem, N.Y. Dem. State Cmt, 62-; chmn, Richmond Co. Dem. Cmt, 62- Bus. & Prof. Pos: Pres, Giffords Seafood Inc, 40- Mem: K. of C. Rel: Catholic. Mailing Add: 891 Forest Ave, Staten Island, N.Y. 10310. (1967)

LINDSETH, JON A. R
Finance Chmn, 54th Legis. Dist. Rep. Party, Ohio
b. Cleveland, Ohio, 6/20/34; s. Elmer L. Lindseth and Anne Fluckey L; m. 11/12/55 to Virginia MacDonald; c. Andrew, Steven, Karen and Peter. Educ: Cornell Univ, B.M.E, 57; Beta Theta Pi. Polit. & Govt. Pos: Rep. committeeman, Fourth Ward, Waynesboro, Va, 60-66; mem, Va. State Rep. Cent. Cmt. and treas, Rep. Party of Va, 61-66; mem, Seventh Cong. Dist. Rep. Cmt. and chmn, Finance Cmt, Va, 63-66; mem, Va. Rep. Finance Cmt, 63-66; alternate del, Rep. Nat. Conv, 64; v.chmn. bd. trustees, Waynesboro Pub. Libr, 64-66; finance chmn, 54th Legis. Dist. Rep. Party, Ohio, 66-; finance chmn, Taft for Mayor of Cleveland Cmt, 67. Bus. & Prof. Pos: Sales specialist, Gen. Elec. Co, 59-65; mgr. of mkt, TRW, Inc, 66- Mil. Serv: Entered as Ens, Navy, 57, released as Lt.(jg), 59; Lt. Comdr, Naval Res, 59-66. Mem: Union Club; Cleveland Country Club. Rel: Protestant. Mailing Add: 2827 Scarborough Rd, Cleveland Heights, Ohio 44118.

LINDSEY, JACK B. R
Mem, Calif. Rep. State Cent. Cmt.
b. Taft, Calif, 11/20/25; m. 1/24/48 to Jean Catherine O'Brien; c. Daniel Lee and David Allan. Educ: Univ. Calif, Berkeley, B.A.S. in Elec. Eng, 46; Stanford Univ, M.B.A, 50; Harvard Bus. Sch, Navy Supply Corps Sch, Cert, 46; Phi Gamma Delta; Golden Bear; Calif. Club. Polit. & Govt. Pos: Mem. policy and doctrine cmt, Los Angeles Rep. Cent. Cmt, Calif, 64; assoc. mem, Calif. Rep. State Cent. Cmt, 64-66, mem, 66-; legis. secy. to Gov. Reagan, 67; chmn, Favorite Son Cmt, 68; alternate del, Rep. Nat. Conv, 68; Rep. cand. for Cong, 27th Cong. Dist, 69. Bus. & Prof. Pos: Mkt. mgr, Carnation Co, Los Angeles, 50-59; asst. to pres, Microdot, Inc, South Pasadena, 59-62; pres, Lindsey-Westwood Assocs, Los Angeles, 62-; v.pres. and dir, Early Calif. Indust, 64-; pres, Data-Pol, Inc. and pres. and publisher, The Press, Portland, Ore, 69- Mil. Serv: Inducted, Naval Res, 44, released as Lt.(jg) SC, 47, after serv. on U.S.S. Harwood, Seventh Fleet, China-Korean and S.Pac. Theaters, 46-47; Am. and China Theater Ribbons; Korean, World War II Victory and Asiatic Pac. Medals. Mem: Inst. Electronic & Elec. Engrs; Am. Asn. Adv. Sci; Am. Ord. Asn; Air Force Res; Navy League; Mason. Legion of Honor, DeMolay. Rel: Christian Science. Legal Res: 24450 Malibu Rd, Malibu, Calif. 90265. Mailing Add: 1100 Glendon Ave, Los Angeles, Calif. 90024.

LINDSEY, JORDAN D
b. Corning Ark, 4/2/08; s. Sterling Price Lindsey and Anna Jordan L; m. 4/6/31 to Gracia Lorene Day; c. Anna Louise (Mrs. Ledbetter), Jordan Day and Dayle Price. Educ: Ark. State Col. Polit. & Govt. Pos: Treas, Cass Co. Dem. Cmt, Mo, 56-64; mayor, Harrisonville. Bus. & Prof. Pos: Pres, Allen Bank and Trust Co, 53-66; exec. v.pres, Cabool State Bank, 34-52. Mem: Mason; Shriners; dir, Harrisonville Kiwanis and Harrisonville Develop. Co; dir. and treas, C. of C; treas, Jr. Baseball Asn, Cass Co. soc. for Crippled Children & Adults and Salvation Army Welfare Fund. Rel: Methodist. Mailing Add: 401 Stella Rd, Harrisonville, Mo. 64701. (1967)

LINDSEY, WALLACE HENRY, III 'PAT' D
Ala. State Sen.
b. Meridian, Miss, 3/17/36; s. Wallace Henry Lindsey, Jr. and Mary Lula Christopher L; m. 3/30/67 to Patsy Hurtt; c. Lori. Educ: Univ. Ala, B.S. in geol, 58; Univ. Ala. Sch. of Law, LL.B, 62; Sigma Chi. Polit. & Govt. Pos: Ala. State Sen, 18th Sen. Dist, 66- Bus. & Prof. Pos: Attorney, Town of Butler and Choctaw Co, currently. Mil. Serv: Entered as 2nd Lt, Army, 58, released as 1st Lt, 60, after serv. as Capt. Commanding A Co, 156 M.P. Bn, Ala. Nat. Guard, 63- Mem: Pres, Choctaw Co, Univ. of Ala. Alumni Asn; v.pres, Choctaw Co. C. of C. Rel: Methodist. Mailing Add: 126 S. Mulberry, Butler, Ala. 36904.

LINDSTROM, ERNEST A. R
Minn. State Rep.
b. Marion, N.Dak, 8/25/31; s. Carl Lindstrom (deceased) and Mabel S. Brox L; m. to Jeanne E. Turnquist; c. Monica Jeanne, Mark Ernest, Eric John and Paul Alan. Educ: Concordia Col, Moorhead, Minn; Univ. N.Dak, B.S.C, 53; CPA, Univ. Minn, 54, LL.B, 57; Beta Alpha Psi; Phi Delta Phi; Sigma Alpha Epsilon. Polit. & Govt. Pos: Spec. munic. judge, Richfield, Minn, 62-64; Minn. State Rep, Dist. 28A, currently. Bus. & Prof. Pos: Attorney and CPA, private practice. Publ: Several case notes and one note, Minn. Law Rev, 56-57. Mem: Minn, Am. and Hennepin Co. Bar Asns. Rel: Lutheran. Mailing Add: 7501 Humboldt Ave. S, Minneapolis, Minn. 55423.

LINDSTROM, JACK LEWIS IRVIN D
Okla. State Rep.
b. Los Angeles, Calif, 2/5/24; s. William John Lindstrom and Elizabeth Ann Dahlman L; div; c. Margo Ann. Educ: South. Ore. Col; Univ. P.R; Cameron Col; Univ. Omaha, B.G.E, 59. Polit. & Govt. Pos: Okla. State Rep, 68- Bus. & Prof. Pos: Pres, Lawton Finance Corp, Lawton, Okla, 66- Mil. Serv: SC 3/C, Navy, 43-49, served on U.S.S. Otus; Maj, Army, 49-66, served at U.S. Army Artillery and Missile Center, Ft. Sill, Okla; Am. Theater Medal; Asiatic-Pac. Medal; Most Noble Order of the Crown of Thailand; Korean Presidential Unit Citation; Bronze Star; Victory, Occup, Nat. Defense Serv, Korean Serv, Armed Forces Res, Philippine Liberation, Philippine Independence and UN Serv. Medals. Mem: Southwest. Okla. Life Underwriters; ROA; Kiwanis. Rel: Quaker. Mailing Add: 1810 N. Sheridan Rd, Lawton, Okla. 73501.

LINEBERGER, LAWRENCE M. D
Chmn, Owyhee Co. Dem. Party, Idaho
b. St. Louis, Mo, 11/16/15; s. Ira H. Lineberger and Vera McCaul L; m. 5/7/60 to Menna Bruns; c. Alfred. Educ: Univ. Idaho, B.S. in Bus. Polit. & Govt. Pos: Dem. precinct committeeman, Idaho, 51-56; chmn, Owyhee Co. Dem. Party, 56- Mem: Elks; AF&AM; Scottish Rite; Shrine. Mailing Add: Route 1, Box 55, Homedale, Idaho 83628.

LING, ROGER D. R
Chmn, Minidoka Co. Rep. Cent. Cmt, Idaho
b. Rupert, Idaho, 11/5/33; s. Merin V. Ling and Delphia E. Rogers R; m. 5/26/61 to Judy E. Jones; c. Dawn Catherine, Melissa Ann, Robert Clay and Timothy Darren. Educ: Idaho State Univ, B.S. in Acct, 61; Willamette Univ, LL.B, 64; Phi Delta Phi. Polit. & Govt. Pos: Dep. prosecuting attorney, Minidoka Co, Idaho, 64-66; chmn, Minidoka Co. Rep. Cent. Cmt, 67- Bus. & Prof. Pos: Legal counsel, Minidoka Irrigation Dist, Rupert, Idaho, 64-69; dir, Columbia Plateau Resources Coun, Inc, Spokane, Wash, 66-69; legal counsel, A & B Irrigation Dist, Rupert, Idaho, 69- Mil. Serv: Entered as Pvt, Army, 64, released as SP-4, 66, after serv. in 496th AAA Bn, 20th Group, Fifth Army, 65-66; Good Conduct Medal. Mem: Idaho State and Fifth Judicial Bar Asns; Rotary; C. of C; Elks; Rupert Country Club. Rel: Methodist. Legal Res: R.R, Rupert, Idaho 83350. Mailing Add: P.O. Box 623, Rupert, Idaho 83350.

LINGENFELTER, CORNELIUS WILSON R
Nev. State Assemblyman
b. Fonda, N.Y, 8/22/31; s. Cornelius Thomas Lingenfelter and Eleanor Barker L; m. 7/12/52 to Laura May Saver; c. Brad Leo, Patricia Virginia, Julie Ann and Jay Cornelius. Educ: Univ. Nev, B.S, 52, grad. work in econ; Theta Chi. Polit. & Govt. Pos: Nev. State Assemblyman, Washoe Co, 68- Bus. & Prof. Pos: Owner, Lingenfelter Realty and Ins, Reno, Nev, 56- Mil. Serv: Entered as A-3/C. Air Force, 52, released as S/Sgt, 56, after serv. in 30th

Weather Squadron, Fifth Air Force, 53-54; T/Sgt, Air Force Res, 60; Good Conduct Medal; UN Ribbon. Mem: Nat. Asn. Real Estate Bd; Farm Bur; Grange; Toastmasters Int. Key Man of the Year, Jr. C. of C, 60; Outstanding Realtor in Civic Work, Reno Bd. Realtors, 68. Rel: Protestant. Mailing Add: 20975 David Dr, Reno, Nev. 89502.

LINK, ARTHUR A. D
N.Dak. State Rep.
b. Alexander, N.Dak, 5/24/14; married; c. six. Educ: N.Dak. State Univ. Agr. and Applied Sci. Polit. & Govt. Pos: N.Dak. State Rep, 47-; mem, sch, co. welfare and twp. bds. Bus. & Prof. Pos: Farmer. Mailing Add: Alexander, N.Dak. 58831. (1967)

LINK, JOSEPH, JR. D
b. Cincinnati, Ohio, 11/6/13; s. Joseph Link, Sr. and Baroness Magdalena von Strobl L; m. 12/17/60 to Margaret Closterman Schott; stepchildren, Walter E. Schott, Jr. and Margo S. (Mrs. Homan). Educ: Xavier Univ, Cincinnati, Ohio, Ph.B. magna cum laude, 35; Univ. Cincinnati, M.Ed. in bus. educ, 40, D.Ed, 60; Phi Delta Kappa; Phi Kappa. Polit. & Govt. Pos: Pub. affairs attache, asst. to Am. Ambassador, Korea, 51-52; trustee, City Retirement Syst. and Dunham Hosp. and mem. parole bd, Cincinnati, Ohio. Bus. & Prof. Pos: Adminstr, Ft. Scott Summer Camps, 37-60; prof. of econ. and bus. admin, Xavier Univ, Cincinnati, 45-; dir, Radio TV Dept, Col. Conserv. of Cincinnati, 54-60; v.pres, Vernon Manor Hotel, Cincinnati and Swan Creek Lumber Co, Toledo, 60- Mil. Serv: Entered as Pvt, Army, 43, released as Maj, SS, 46, after serv. as Admin. Officer and Off. Info. Coord, Stars and Stripes, ETO, Faculty, Army Info. and Educ, Staff Sch, UN Paris, France; Agent, Counter Intel. Corps, Columbus, Ohio; ETO Ribbon; Good Conduct Medal; Commendation Ribbon; Maj, SS Army Res. Publ: Ed, Econ. Section, Lincoln Library of Essential Information Encyclopedia, Rev. Editions. Mem: Torch Club; President's Club, White House; Xavier Univ. Alumni Asn; Univ. Cincinnati Alumni Asn; Ohio Hist. Soc; K. of C. (4°); Newman Found, Univ. Cincinnati. Rel: Roman Catholic. Mailing Add: 5475 Salem Rd, Cincinnati, Ohio 45230.

LINKE, EDWIN HENRY R
Chmn, Grand Co. Rep. Party, Colo.
b. Granby, Colo, 4/14/92; s. Emil Linke and Sophie Weil L; m. 2/23/30 to Susie Winifred Ellis; c. Alta Ruth (Mrs. Jack Orr) and Edwin Henry, Jr, 'Eddie'. Educ: Barnes Bus. Col, Denver, 13. Polit. & Govt. Pos: Rep. committeeman, Precinct Two, Granby, Colo, 36-66; chmn, Grand Co. Rep. Party, 66- Bus. & Prof. Pos: Ranch owner and operator, Ed Linke Ranch, Granby, 19-56, Retired, 56. Mil. Serv: Entered as Pvt, Army, 17, released as Horse Shoer, 19, after serv. in 89th Div. and Mil. Police, A.E.F, Marseilles, France, 18-19. Mem: Mason; Am. Legion; VFW; Colo. Cattlemen's Asn; Grand Co. Pioneers. Rel: Protestant. Mailing Add: Box 306, Granby, Colo. 80446.

LINKOUS, T. CECIL D
Chmn, Warren Co. Dem. Exec. Cmt, Ohio
b. Stillwater, Ky, 3/12/20; s. Otis B. Linkous and Margaret Cecil L; m. 10/24/42 to Dorothy Welch; c. Diana R, Steven A, Jennifer and Jeffrey B. Educ: Lebanon High Sch, grad, 39. Polit. & Govt. Pos: Co. cmnr, Warren Co, Ohio, 59-62; precinct committeeman, Dem. Party, Mich; chmn, Warren Co. Dem. Exec. Cmt, Ohio, 68- Bus. & Prof. Pos: Ins. Agent, 50- Mil. Serv: Entered as Pvt, Army, 42, released as Cp., 43, after serv. in 14th Armored Div. Mem: Am. Legion; Dem. Club. Rel: Protestant. Mailing Add: 2633 Dayton Rd, Lebanon, Ohio 45036.

LINKS, KARL HENRY R
b. Marlboro, Conn, 4/30/97; s. Jacob A. Links and Louise Wyss L; m. 10/1/21 to Louise A. Tufvander; c. Beatrice Louise and Robert Karl. Educ: High Sch; Int. Correspondence Sch. Polit. & Govt. Pos: Former chmn, Hebron Bd. of Assessors, Conn; zoning agent, Hebron; Conn. State Rep. until 67. Bus. & Prof. Pos: V.chmn, Conn. Wholesale Milk Producers Asn, 36-48. Mil. Serv: Entered as A/S, Navy, 17, released as Electrician 3/C, 19, after serv. in Atlantic Fleet. Rel: Protestant. Legal Res: West St, Hebron, Conn. 06248. Mailing Add: R.F.D. 1, Hebron, Conn. 06248.

LINN, BERNARD R
Cmnr, Sch. and Pub. Lands, S.Dak.
b. Pine Ridge Indian Reservation at Potato Creek, Washabaugh Co, S.Dak, 2/18/98; m. 1924 to Marie Kinney; c. Joann (Mrs. Ellis), Jeanne (Mrs. Kelley), James (deceased), Jerilyn (Mrs. Lappat) and John. Educ: Dakota Wesleyan Univ. Polit. & Govt. Pos: Supt. Schs, Meade Co, S.Dak, 25-37; field auditor, S.Dak. Div. of Taxation, 37-40; asst. cmnr, Sch. and Pub. Lands, S.Dak, 40-48, cmnr, 48-; S.Dak. chmn. and pres. S.Dak. Chap, Cmn. on Interstate Coop, 51-55. Bus. & Prof. Pos: Teacher rural schs. in Meade and Perkins Counties. Mem: Pres, S.Dak. Educ. Asn, 36; pres, West. States Land Cmnr. Asn, 36, 56 & 69. Mailing Add: 118 E. Prospect, Pierre, S.Dak. 57501.

LINOWITZ, SOL MYRON D
b. Trenton, N.J, 12/7/13; s. Joseph Linowitz and Rose Oglenskye L; m. 9/3/39 to Evelyn Zimmerman; c. Anne, June, Jan and Ronni. Educ: Hamilton Col, A.B, 35; Cornell Univ, LL.B, 38; Phi Beta Kappa; Phi Kappa Phi; Order of the Coif. Polit. & Govt. Pos: Asst. gen. counsel, Off. Price Admin, Wash, D.C, 42-44; former U.S. Ambassador, Orgn. Am. States; U.S. Rep, Inter-Am. Cmn. of Alliance for Progress, 66- Bus. & Prof. Pos: Partner, Sutherland, Linowitz & Williams, 46-58; firm, Harris, Beach, Keating, Wilcox, Dale & Linowitz, Rochester, N.Y, 58-66; chmn. bd. and chmn. exec. cmt, Gen. Counsel, Xerox Corp; dir, Rank Orgn, Ltd, Fuji Xerox, Ltd, Japan, Security Trust Co, Vet. Broadcasting Co, Inc, Superba Cravats, Inc. and Rank Xerox Ltd, London; chmn, State Dept. Adv. Cmt. on Int. Orgn. Mil. Serv: Lt.(sg), Naval Res, 44-46. Mem: Trustee, Rochester Savings Bank; dir, United Jewish Welfare Fund; bd, JFK Center for Performing Arts Bd, Hamilton Col. and Am. Jewish Cmt; trustee and mem. exec. cmt, Univ. Rochester; bd. mgr, Eastman Sch. Music; co-chmn, Organizing Cmt, Int. Exec. Serv. Corp; Am. Asn. for UN (pres, N.Y. State); Rochester Asn. for UN (pres, 52); pres, Rochester C. of C, 58-66; Am. and N.Y. Bar Asns; v.pres, Rochester Bar Asn; Univ. Club. Rel: Jewish. Mailing Add: 5 S. Fitzhugh St, Rochester, N.Y. 14614.

LINSKY, MARTIN A. R
Mass. State Rep.
b. Boston, Mass, 8/28/40; s. Harold M. Linsky and Ruth Doran L; m. 12/10/64 to Helen Strieder; c. Alison. Educ: Williams Col, B.A, 61; Harvard Law Sch, LL.B, 64. Polit. & Govt. Pos: Mem. research staff of Sen. Leverett Saltonstall of Mass, 60; mem, Town Meeting, Brookline, 64-; mem, Brookline Rep. Town Cmt, 64-; legis. and research asst. to Lt. Gov. of Mass, 65-66; asst. attorney general, Commonwealth of Mass, 67; Mass. State Rep, 13th Norfolk Dist, 67-; alternate del, Rep. Nat. Conv, 68. Bus. & Prof. Pos: Instr, Fed-State Rels, Northeast. Univ, Boston, 66- Publ: 'From the Harvard Lampoon to Foggy Bottom,' Ripon Forum, 2/69. Mem: Mass. and Boston Bar Asns; Mass. Legislators Asn; Nat. Asn. of State Legislators; exec. bd, Ripon Soc, 66-; World Affairs Coun. of Boston; New Eng. Regional Bd, Anti-Defamation League of B'nai B'rith; Jewish Voc. Serv. of Greater Boston; Brookline Coun. for Planning and Renewal; Mass. Voc. Rehabilitation Planning Cmn; Brookline Ment. Health Asn. Selected as one of the ten Outstanding Young Men of the Year, Greater Boston Jr. C. of C, 68; Citation for Outstanding Achievement in Pub. Serv, Bryant and Stratton Sch, Boston, 68. Rel: Jewish. Mailing Add: 10 Abbottsford Rd, Brookline, Mass. 02146.

LINTON, SAMUEL CLIFTON, JR. D
b. Riverside, Md, 8/21/23; s. Samuel C. Linton and Emily Marbury L; m. 6/10/44 to Jane Bradford Blake; c. Jane Keithley, Ellen Marbury, Carol Bradford, Samuel Clifton, III and Nancy Grafflin. Polit. & Govt. Pos: Md. State Del, 58-66. Mil. Serv: Entered as Pvt, Army Air Force, 43, released as S/Sgt, 46, after serv. in 8th Air Force 305th Bomb Group, 364th Squadron, ETO, 44-46; Am, European and N.African Theater Ribbons; Presidential Unit Citation with 2 Clusters. Mem: Farm Bur; VFW. Rel: Protestant. Mailing Add: Holly Springs Rd, Nanjemoy, Md. 20662.

LIPIN, ALFRED JEROME D
Md. State Del.
b. Anne Arundel Co, Md; married; c. Mary Lou, Nancy Lee, Jack and Laura. Educ: Univ. of Baltimore. Polit. & Govt. Pos: Md. State Del, Dist. 6-A, Anne Arundel Co, currently, mem, spec. joint legis. coun. exec. cmt. on an in-depth study of Md. sales, use and admission taxes, 68, chmn. legis. subcmt. of Md. Airport Study, 69-70. Mil. Serv: Participated in five European campaigns during World War II; Silver Star. Mem: North Arundel Hosp. Asn. (former two term pres); organized, Glen Burnie First Nat. Guard Unit; C. of C. (founder and three term pres, Glen Burnie Chap); Civitan Int; VFW; Am. Legion; Elks. Mailing Add: 502 Second Ave. S.W, Glen Burnie, Md. 21061.

LIPP, JOHN L. D
Polit. & Govt. Pos: Ind. State Rep, -66. Bus. & Prof. Pos: Electrician, Gen. Motors. Mil. Serv: WWII and Korean Conflict. Mem: Kokomo; Am. Legion; VFW; Elks; UAW. Rel: Methodist. Mailing Add: 409 Hemlock Dr, Frankfort, Ind. 46041. (1967)

LIPPINCOTT, C. LYDON R
b. Denver, Colo, 5/16/03; s. Charles Clarence Lippincott and Ida May Lydon L; m. 8/18/41 to Clare L. Alden; c. Dr. C. Laurence. Educ: Univ. Colo. Polit. & Govt. Pos: Treas, San Bernardino Co. Rep. Cent. Cmt, Calif, 64-65, former chmn. Bus. & Prof. Pos: Owner, Lippincott's Camera Center, 39-59. Mem: Mason; Al Malaikah Shrine; San Bernardino Shrine Club; secy. and past pres, Uptown Exchange Club; past pres, Orange Empire Dog Club; past pres, Club Canofilo de Baja Calif; past pres, San Bernardino Pictorial Soc. Photography and Dogs. Rel: Episcopal. Mailing Add: 23842 Windmill Lane, Laguna Niguel, Calif. 92677.

LIPPITT, FREDERICK R
R.I. State Rep.
b. Wash, D.C, 12/29/16. Educ: Yale Univ, B.A, 39; Yale Law Sch, LL.B, 46. Polit. & Govt. Pos: R.I. State Rep, 61-; del, Rep. Nat. Conv, 68. Bus. & Prof. Pos: Lawyer. Mil. Serv: Army, World War II. Mailing Add: 1109 Hospital Trust Building, Providence, R.I. 02903. (1967)

LIPPMAN, GEORGE JENNINGS R
Chmn, Holyoke City Rep. Cmt, Mass.
b. Holyoke, Mass, 11/1/14; s. George Garfield Lippman and Lucy Shaw L; m. 3/1/42 to Barbara Jeanne Messmer; c. John M. and Jeanne L. Educ: Univ. Mass. and Am. Int. Col, exten. courses. Polit. & Govt. Pos: Chmn, Holyoke City Rep. Cmt, Mass, 62-; v.chmn, Bd. of Pub. Works Cmn, Holyoke, 68-; cmnr, Mass. State Recreational Tramway Authority, 69- Bus. & Prof. Pos: Formerly mem, Holyoke Draft Bd. 71, Mass; personnel dir, Am. Writing Paper Corp, 40-45; salesman, Am. Type Founders, 45-60; v.pres, Whitbeck Printing Co, 60-62; owner, Lippman Litho Machinery Co, 62- Mem: Lions; Melha Shrine Temple. Rel: Congregational. Legal Res: 4 Irving St, Holyoke, Mass. 01040. Mailing Add: 94 Commercial St, Holyoke, Mass. 01040.

LIPPOLD, DONALD L. R
Iowa State Rep.
b. Oswego, Ill, 1/22/15; s. Theodore William Lippold and Mabel Johnson L; m. 7/8/50 to Helen Gottshalk Ericksen; c. Kathryn Gae, Cynthia Kay, Erik William and Thomas William. Educ: Stout State Univ, B.S, 47; M.S, 48. Polit. & Govt. Pos: Mayor, Castle Hill, Iowa, 59-60; v.pres, Waterloo Planning Cmn, Waterloo, Iowa, 60-; mem, Black Hawk Co. Metrop. Planning Cmn, 64-; secy, 64-67; Iowa State Rep, Fifth Sub Dist, Black Hawk Co, 69- Bus. & Prof. Pos: Supvr, All-Steel Equip. Co, Aurora, Ill, 37-42; teacher, Milwauke Pub. Schs, Wis, 48-51; dir. indust. and adult educ, Waterloo Pub. Schs, Iowa, 51-65; dir. voc. & tech. educ, Hawkeye Inst. of Tech, 65- Mil. Serv: Entered as Pvt, Army, 42, released as Maj, 62, after serv. in Inf, 44th & 33rd Div, Southwest Pac. Theater, 42-46 and mil. govt, 46-62; Combat Infantryman Badge; Bronze Star; Am. Theater Ribbon; AP Theater Ribbon with Two Battle Stars; World War II Victory Medal; Philippine Liberation Ribbon with One Battle Star. Publ: 'Business Education Day,' Sch. Shop, 58; 'Exploratory Programs In Industrial Arts,' Indust. Arts and Voc. Educ, 60; 'Adult Education In Iowa,' Midland Schs, 66; plus 1 other. Mem: Am. Voc. Asn; Nat. Educ. Asn; Iowa State Educ. Asn; Nat. Asn. of Pub. Sch. Adult Educators; Iowa Voc. Asn; Iowa Adult Educ. Asn; Kiwanis; Am. Legion; UN; Waterloo Tech. Soc; Phi Delta Kappa; United Serv. of Black Hawk Co; Boy Scouts; Girl Scouts. Rel: Congregational. Mailing Add: 140 Faber, Waterloo, Iowa 50701.

LIPS, EVAN EDWIN R
N.Dak. State Sen.
b. Bismarck, N.Dak, 10/17/18; s. William Edwin Lips and Margaret

Griffith L; m. 8/3/46 to Elsa M. Kavonius; c. Evan William, Deborah Jane and Erik George. Educ: Univ. N.Dak, B.S, 41; Blue Key; Alpha Tau Omega. Polit. & Govt. Pos: Precinct committeeman, Rep. Party, N.Dak, 50; dist. chmn, Rep. Party, 50-54; Mayor, Bismarck, 54-66; S.Dak. State Sen, Dist. 32, 60- Bus. & Prof. Pos: Pres, Murphy Ins, Inc, 52- and Dakota Fire Ins. Co, 57-; dir, First Nat. Bank, 61-, Bismarck Bldg. and Loan Asn, 62- and Provident Life Ins. Co, 67- Mil. Serv: Entered as Pfc, Marine Corps, 41, released as Maj, 46, after serv. in Third Marine Div, Pac. Theater, Staff Officer, 43-45; Col.(Ret), Marine Corps Res; Presidential Unit Citation; Legion of Merit; Bronze Star. Mem: N.Dak. Asn. of Ins. Agents; Nat. Asn. of Independent Ins. Agents; United Commercial Travelers; Am. Legion; VFW; C. of C; Elks; Eagles; Mason; Shrine. Boss-of-the-Year Award and Distinguished Serv. Award, Jaycees; Distinguished Serv. Award, Eagles. Rel: Lutheran. Mailing Add: 203 W. Owens Ave, Bismarck, N.Dak. 58501.

LIPSCOMB, GLENARD P. R
U.S. Rep, Calif.
b. Jackson, Mich, 8/19/15; m. 9 /4/36 to Virginia Sognalian L; c. Diane Marie (Mrs. Louis Grasso),and Joyce Elaine (Mrs. Robert Murrell). Educ: USC; Woodbury Col. Polit. & Govt. Pos: Calif. State Rep, 47-52; U.S. Rep, Calif, 53- Bus. & Prof. Pos: Pub. acct. Mil. Serv: Army. Mem: Kiwanis; Elks; Mason; Am. Legion; Soc. Calif. Acct; Nat. Soc. of Pub. Accts. Rel: Baptist. Mailing Add: 704 Lindaropa Park, Alhambra, Calif. 91801. (1967)

LIPSCOMB, JAMES WALTON, III D
b. Jackson, Miss, 12/7/35; s. Dr. James Walton Lipscomb, Jr.(deceased) and Anne Dubard L; single. Educ: Millsaps Col, B.S, 56; Miss. State Univ, B.S, 58; Omicron Delta Kappa; Alpha Epsilon Delta; Lambda Chi Alpha. Polit. & Govt. Pos: Alternate del, Dem. Nat. Conv, 68. Bus. & Prof. Pos: Jr. acct, Dick D. Quin and Co, Jackson, Miss, 58-60; supvr, Peat, Marwick, Mitchell & Co, 61-66; asst. controller, Duke Univ, 66-68; controller, Miss. Hosp. and Med. Serv, Jackson, 68; audit and syst. mgr, Millsaps Col, 69- Mil. Serv: Entered as Sgt, Army Nat. Guard, 61, released as Sgt, 62, after serv. in 134th Surg. Hosp, Ft. Polk, La. Mem: Miss. Soc. of CPA; N.C. Asn. of CPA; Am. Inst. of CPA; bd. dirs. and treas, Laymen's Overseas Serv, Inc; bd. dir, Bethlehem Center and Hinds Co. Proj. Head Start. Rel: Methodist. Mailing Add: 911 Belhaven St, Jackson, Miss. 39202.

LIPSCOMB, MARK G, JR. D
Wis. State Assemblyman
b. Milwaukee, Wis, 9/1/35. Educ: Marquette Univ, B.S, 57, LL.B, 64. Polit. & Govt. Pos: Wis. State Assemblyman, 64- Bus. & Prof. Pos: Former postal clerk; attorney-at-law. Mil. Serv: Marine Corps, 57-60; Ready Res, Marine Corps Res. Mem: Marquette Univ. 'M' Club; Holy Name Soc; St. Vincent de Paul Soc; AFL-CIO United Fedn. of Postal Clerks; Mem. Bar Asns. Mailing Add: 5349 N. Dexter Ave, Milwaukee, Wis. 53209.

LIPSCOMB, WILLIE G, JR. R
Chmn, 13th Cong. Dist. Rep. Party, Mich.
b. Knoxville, Tenn, 3/4/43; s. Willie G. Lipscomb, Sr. and Minnie Collins L; single. Educ: Univ. of Md, exten. Athens, Greece, 62-64; Wayne State Univ, 66-; Kappa Alpha Psi. Polit. & Govt. Pos: Precinct del, 13th Cong. Dist. Rep. Party, Mich, 68-, dist. chmn, 69- Bus. & Prof. Pos: Teacher, Detroit Pub. Schs, 69; counsr, Wayne State Univ, 69. Mil. Serv: Entered as E-1, Air Force, 61, released as E-4, 66, after serv. in 7206 Air Force Dispensory; good conduct award; longevity award. Rel: Protestant. Legal Res: 643 McDougall, Detroit, Mich. 48207. Mailing Add: 4620 Woodward, Detroit, Mich. 48201.

LIPSKY, JOAN R
Iowa State Rep.
b. 1919; m. to Abbott Lipsky; c. Ann, John and Abbott, Jr. Educ: Northwest. Univ, B.A; Univ. of Iowa Grad. Sch, 1 year. Polit. & Govt. Pos: Iowa State Rep, 67- Bus. & Prof. Pos: Housewife. Mailing Add: State Capital, E. Tenth & Grand Ave, Des Moines, Iowa 50319.

LIS, JOHN B. D
N.Y. State Assemblyman
b. Buffalo, N.Y, 5/28/15; m. to Edna Jarosz; c. Joyce, John and Joseph. Educ: Fosdick-Masten Park High Sch. Polit. & Govt. Pos: Mem, Erie Co. Bd. of Supvrs, 49-53; pres, Fifth Assembly Dem. Club; N.Y. State Assemblyman, 54-; alternate del, Dem. Nat. Conv, 68. Bus. & Prof. Pos: Salesman. Mem: Am. Legion; VFW; Amvets; CWV; Prfnl. Businessmans Asn; K. of C; First Friday Club; Fillmore Peckham and E. Lovejoy Citizens and Taxpayers Asns; Jay-Cee Harmony Club; Roman's Civic and Soc. Club; Moniuszko Singing Soc; Adam Mickiewixz Dramatic Club; Chopins Singing Soc; Stans Civic and Soc. Club; Buch's Soc. and Athletic Club; dist. cmt, Boy Scouts; Holy Name Soc; pres, Precious Blood Holy Name Soc. Rel: Choir Chmn, pres. of Allied Soc, Precious Blood Church. Mailing Add: 117 Thomas St, Buffalo, N.Y. 14206. (1967)

LISCO, ARCHIE L. D
b. Barrineau Park, Fla, 12/4/24; s. Ora L. Lisco and Mary Barlow L; m. 2/1/46 to Dorothea Alice Burns; c. Archie Lee, Thomas J, Larry A. and John F. Educ: Univ. Colo. Polit. & Govt. Pos: Colo. State Rep, 65-67; dist. chmn, Dem. Party, 53-, precinct committeeman, 52-, adv. to State Chmn, 63-64. Mil. Serv: Entered as Seaman 2/C, Navy, 42, released as Radioman 1/C, 46, after serv. with 3rd Fleet, Pac; 4 Battle Stars; Asiatic-Pac. Campaign Ribbon. Mem: Optimist Club; Denver Dem. Club. Rel: Catholic. Mailing Add: 1860 S. Wyandot St, Denver, Colo. 80223. (1967)

LISK, DAVID KENNETH R
b. Rome, N.Y, 11/26/28; s. Maynard Carlton Lisk and Rose Brooks L; m. 6/27/53 to Jean Hebard; c. Timothy David, Thomas Alan and Robert Kenneth. Educ: Univ. Rochester. Polit. Pos: Chmn, Roanoke Rep. Party, 64-65; state finance chmn, 6th Dist. Rep. Party, 63-64; pres. and nat. committeeman, Young Rep. Club of Va, 54-60. Bus. Pos: Assoc. exec. dir, Easter Seal Soc, Va, currently. Mil. Serv: Entered as Cadet, Air Force and released as 1st Lt, 50, also Res. Capt, Air Force, 3565th Training Squadron Instr, 50; Good Conduct Medal; Purple Heart; Am. Victory Award. Mem: Dir, Civitan Club, 66; maj, Roanoke Civilian Police, 65-; pres, PTA, 65-66; dir, Miss Va. Pageant, 64, 65 and 66; campaign dir, Roanoke Va. Heart Asn, 65-66; Jr. C. of C; Roanoke C. of C; Fraternal Order of Police; Moose; Human Rels. Coun, Roanoke Develop. Cmt, Roanoke City Coun. Named Jaycee of Month three times and received Key Man Award, 63-64. Rel: Episcopal; Vestryman, Lay Leader and Dir. Christian Educ, St. Elizabeth Episcopal Church. Mailing Add: 908 Carrington Ave. S.W, Roanoke, Va. 24015.

LISLE, HENRY L. D
b. Butler, Mo, 10/1/13; m. 3/31/39 to Theresa Crispin; c. Susan, William Henry. Educ: Univ. Mo, LL.B. Polit. & Govt. Pos: Magistrate, Probate Judge, Barton Co, 66-; Mo. State Rep, 64-66; alderman, Lamar City Coun, 58-62. Bus. & Prof. Pos: Lawyer; formerly Travelers Ins. Co; FBI; Frank Horton Co. Mem: Soc. Former Spec. Agents. Rel: Presbyterian. Mailing Add: 208 W. Second, Lamar, Mo. 64759. (1967)

LISLE, VERN R
Iowa State Sen.
b. Clarinda, Iowa, 10/1/06; m. to Dorthy Schwimmer; c. Edwin S. and Charles V, Jr. Educ: Univ. Mich, Civil Engr, B.S, 28. Polit. & Govt. Pos: Mem, Clarinda Sch. Bd, Iowa; Iowa State Sen, currently. Bus. & Prof. Pos: Pres, Lisle Mfg. Co, 36- Mem: Mason. Rel: Methodist. Mailing Add: State Capitol, E. Tenth & Grand Ave, Des Moines, Iowa 50319. (1967)

LISS, SOLOMON D
b. Baltimore, Md, 3/6/15; s. Louis Liss and Sophia Caplan L; m. 6/10/63 to Florence Frahm; c. Linda (Mrs. Hirshberg), Debra (Mrs. Tyrangiel), Jeffrey and stepchildren, Steve Gilden and Marcia (Mrs. Kaplan). Educ: Univ. Baltimore, LL.B, 37; Sigma Alpha Omicron; Phi Delta Tau. Polit. & Govt. Pos: Police magistrate, Md, 42-46; mem, City Coun, Baltimore, 58-63; adv. metrop. affairs to Mayor, Baltimore, 63-64; chmn, Pub. Serv. Cmn. Md, 64-; Judge, Supreme Bench, Baltimore, 68- Publ: 'Ground Rent System of Maryland,' 8/37 and 'Tax Sales in Maryland,' 8/37, Daily Record of Baltimore; Baltimore's Biggest Birghday, Baltimore Asn. of Commerce, 7/59. Mem: Am, Md. and Baltimore Bar Asns; Trial Lawyers Asn; Mason (32°), Scottish Rite; B'nai B'rith; Zionist Orgn. of Am; Advert. Club. Toastmaster for numerous charity functions. Rel: Jewish. Legal Res: 3207 Fallstaff Rd, Baltimore, Md. 21215. Mailing Add: Court House, Baltimore, Md. 21202.

LITCHMAN, MARK, JR. D
Wash. State Rep.
b. Seattle, Wash, 1925; married; c. three. Educ: Univ. Wash, B.A, LL.B. Polit. & Govt. Pos: Wash. State Rep, currently. Bus. & Prof. Pos: Lawyer. Mil. Serv: Naval Officer; Legal Res, 13th Dist. Mem: Kiwanis; Elks; Am. Legion; DAV; Jewish War Vet; PTA. Mailing Add: 13706 Second N.E, Seattle, Wash. 98125. (1967)

LITTEN, CHARLES WARNER R
N.Dak. State Sen.
b. Kansas City, Mo, 11/28/14; s. Charles William Litten and Kathleen Warner L; m. 6/28/41 to Mary Elizabeth Baillie; c. Jean (Mrs. Rosenow), Kathleen (Mrs. McConahey), Charles Warner and Mary Ruth. Educ: N.Dak. State Univ, B.S, 36; Blue Key; Alpha Phi Omega; Gamma Tau Sigma; Scabbard and Blade; Sigma Alpha Epsilon. Polit. & Govt. Pos: Mem, bd. of educ, Fargo, N.Dak, 48-54, libr, bd, 49-51; civilian aide to the secy. of the army, State of N.Dak, 48-53; N.Dak. State Sen, 67- Bus. & Prof. Pos: Salesman and cashier, N.W. Bell Tel. Co, N.Dak, 36-41; bus. mgr, Fargo Clin, 46- Mil. Serv: Entered as Pvt, Army, 42, released as Capt, 46, after serv. in Fifth Inf, 71st Div, ETO, Europe-Africa-Middle East, 45-46; Combat Inf. Badge; Europe-Africa-Middle East Medal with 2 Bronze Stars; Am. Theatre Medal; Victory Medal. Mem: Am. Col. of Clin. Mgr; pres, Med. Group Mgt. Asn; N.Dak. Asn. of Clin. Adminstr; Am. Legion; VFW; Elks; Mason; Shrine; Rotary; YMCA; Red River Valley Fair Asn; N.Dak. Sch. of Relig; Fargo Indust. Develop. Corp; C. of C; N.Cent. Educ. TV, Inc. Alumni Achievement Award, N.Dak. State Univ; Jr. C. of C. Distinguished Serv. Award; Cosmopolitan Club Distinguished Serv. Award. Rel: Presbyterian. Mailing Add: 1122 S. Ninth St, Fargo, N.Dak. 58102.

LITTLE, CARL O. R
b. Saginaw, Mich, 9/17/99; married; c. Roger C. and Marilyn (Mrs. James Z. McClune). Educ: Walton Sch. of Commerce; Am. Exten. Univ. Polit. & Govt. Pos: Dep. co. treas, Saginaw Co, Mich, 4 years, treas, 26 years; Mich. State Rep, 60-68. Bus. & Prof. Pos: Retired. Mem: Past pres. and past secy-treas, Mich. Asn. of Co. Treas; Mason; Bay City Consistory A.A.S.R, Shrine; Odd Fellows; served on United Fund drives and active in Boy Scouts and Red Cross. Rel: Methodist. Mailing Add: 5355 Glenfield Dr, Saginaw, Mich. 48603.

LITTLE, CHRISTOPHER MARK D
b. Tazewell, Va, 3/11/41; s. Haskin Vincent Little and Janet Kessinger L; m. 12/27/63 to Elizabeth Silver; c. Timothy Mark. Educ: Yale Univ, B.A, 63; Harvard Law Sch, 63-64; Tex. Law Sch, LL.B, 66. Polit. & Govt. Pos: Admin. Asst. to U.S. Rep. Bob Eckhardt, Tex, 68- Bus. & Prof. Pos: Assoc, Covington & Burling, 66-68. Rel: Episcopal. Legal Res: 312 W. 31st, Houston, Tex. 77018. Mailing Add: 909 Enderby Dr, Alexandria, Va. 22302.

LITTLE, DAVID R
Rep. Nat. Committeeman, Idaho
b. Emmett, Idaho, 1/31/18; s. Andrew Little and Agnes Sproat L; m. 9/9/41 to Geraldine Laidlaw; c. James A, Judith Ann 'Judy' and Bradley Jay. Educ: Univ. Idaho, B.S.Ed, 41; Sigma Chi. Polit. & Govt. Pos: Finance chmn, Idaho Rep. Party, 51-53, co.chmn, 65-67; Rep. Nat. Committeeman, Idaho, 68- Mem: Idaho Wool Growers Am.(pres, 49-52); Nat. Wool Growers Asn.(v.pres, 56-58); Idaho Cattleman Asn.(dir, 67-); Idaho Livestock Prod. Credit Union (v.pres, 64-); South. Idaho Timber Protective Asn.(pres, 67-); Elks. Legal Res: E. Fourth, Emmett, Idaho 83617. Mailing Add: 210 Main, Box 68, Emmett, Idaho 83617.

LITTLE, DOROTHY LYNN 'DOT' D
Committeewoman, Madison Co. Dem. Exec. Cmt, Ala.
b. Jasper, Ala, 12/6/28; d. Cleveland Posey and Celestie Long P; m. 2/10/51 to Cecil Scott Little; c. Scott, Chris and Davie. Educ: Judson Col, Marion,

Ala, 48-49. Polit. & Govt. Pos: Treas, Madison Co. Young Dem, Ala, 64-68; pub. rels. dir, Madison Co. Dem. Women, 66, pres, 67, adv, 68-69; del-at-lg, Dem. Nat. Conv, 68; nominee for elector, Dem. Nat. Party, 68; committee-woman, Madison Co. Dem. Exec. Cmt, 68- Mem: Garden Clubs; Drake-Garth Women's Club; Valley Recreational Club; v.pres, Grissom PTA; mem. bd. dirs, Harris Home for Children. Rel: Baptist. Mailing Add: 1013 Toney Dr, S.E, Huntsville, Ala. 35802.

LITTLE, DUANE EWING D
Nat. Committeeman, Young Dem. Clubs of Idaho
b. Kellogg, Idaho, 7/2/37; s. Ewing Henry Little and Elizabeth Sala L; single. Educ: Univ. Idaho, B.S. in bus. admin, 61. Polit. & Govt. Pos: V.pres, Univ. Idaho Young Dem, 60-61; pres, Shoshone Co. Young Dem, Idaho, 61-62 & 64-66; asst. dir, Shoshone Co. Civil Defense, 64-; exec. bd. mem, Shoshone Co. Dem. Cent. Cmt, 64-; treas, Young Dem. Clubs of Idaho, 64-66, Nat. Committeeman, 66-; chmn, West. States Conf, Young Dem. Clubs of Am, 68. Bus. & Prof. Pos: Secy-treas, Jackass Ski Bowl Asn, Inc, 64-; partner in charge, Turnbow, Maisel, Little & Assocs, 65-; v.pres, R-G Mining Co, 66-; partner, Silver Develop. Co, 67-; secy, Silver Aurora Mining Co, Inc, 67-; v.pres, Silver Ramona Mining Co, Inc, 67-; pres, Silver Horizon Mining Co, Inc, 67-; pres, Silver Chalice Mining Co, Inc, 67-; consult, McKim-Kiser Co, 68- Mem: Jaycees; Am. Chem Soc; Citizenship Clearing House. Among the first 12 chosen for the Peace Corps' first project. Rel: Congregational. Mailing Add: 211 W. Elder St, Kellogg, Idaho 83837.

LITTLE, ERICK PAUL R
Chmn, Wilson Co. Rep. Party, N.C.
b. Wilson, N.C, 1/19/33; s. Lee Roy Little and Rosa Burress L; m. 3/23/57 to Betty Lou Amerson; c. Angela Donel. Educ: Atlantic Christian Col, 2 years; Coyne Elec. Inst, 1 year. Polit. & Govt. Pos: Precinct del, Wilson Co. Rep. Party, N.C, 68, chmn, 69-; chmn, Second Dist. Rep. Party, N.C. Bus. & Prof. Pos: Estimator, Watson Elec. Construction Co, 57-60; supt, Dickerson, Inc, 60-64 and Jones Bros. & Co, 64- Mil. Serv: Entered as Pvt, Army Airborne, 51, released as Sgt. 1/C, 64, after serv. in Second Inf. Div, Korea, 62-64; Korean Serv. Medal with Two Bronze SUC Stars; UN SUC Medal; Nat. Defense SUC Medal with Two Overseas Bars; Parachute Badge; Combat Inf. Badge. Mem: Am. Legion; VFW; Moose; secy, Jaycees; Toastmasters (past pres); pres, Wilson Childrens Zoo. Chosen Toastmaster of the year. Rel: Free Will Baptist. Mailing Add: 703 Grove St, Wilson, N.C. 27893.

LITTLE, HENRY MARTIN D
b. Pittsburgh, Pa, 2/14/06; s. Henry J. Little and Daisy Martin L; m. 4/17/42 to Mary Virginia Kilmer. Educ: Davis-Elkins Col, 31; Univ. Md, 31-32; Chi Beta Phi; TVC Soc. Club. Polit. & Govt. Pos: Mem, Martinsburg City Dem. Exec. Cmt, W.Va, 56-; mem, Berkeley Co. Dem. Exec. Cmt, 58-69, chmn, 65-69; councilman, Martinsburg, 59-63. Bus. & Prof. Pos: Realtor, Martinsburg, W.Va, 33-43; supvr, Fairchild Aircraft Corp, Hagerstown, Md, 45-63; Victor Prod. Corp, 64- Mil. Serv: Entered as Pvt, Army, 43, released as T/Sgt, 45; Breast Order of Cloud and Banner. Mem: Am. Legion; Elks (past Exalted Ruler, Martinsburg, W.Va); past pres, Past Exalted Rulers Asn, W.Va, dist. Dep. Grand Exalted Ruler, 68-69. Elk of the Year, 63-64. Rel: Roman Catholic. Mailing Add: 1306 W. Race St, Martinsburg, W.Va. 25401.

LITTLE, MADGE CRAM D
Chmn, Kane Co. Dem. Party, Utah
b. Kanab, Utah, 7/26/00; d. John Smith Cram and Fannie Bunting C; m. 6/25/20 to Lester Findlay Little; c. John K, Lorna (Mrs. L.G. Cottam), Larry L, Caroline (Mrs. L.S. Lippencott) and Clara B. (Mrs. Johe E. Grams). Polit. & Govt. Pos: Mem, Utah State Dem. Cent. Cmt, 40-66; co-chmn, Kane Co. Dem. Party, 40-62, chmn, 69-; mem, State Adv. Coun. Deaf & Blind Sch, 46-50; del, Dem. Nat. Conv, 48, 56, 64 & 68; mem, State Dem. Platform Cmt, 64; mem, Utah State Fair Bd, 65-; mem, Utah Bd. of Expositions, 67- Bus. & Prof. Pos: Mem. bd. of dirs, Finance Co, 65-66. Mem: Nat. Cmt. for Support of Pub. Schs; co. chmn, Am. Red Cross; Bus. & Prfnl. Women's Club; Woman's Civic Club & Literary League; Farmers Union; Int. Platform Asn; Kanab Coord. Coun; 100 Club. Distinguished Serv. Award, World War II Minute Woman, 45. Rel: Unitarian. Mailing Add: 69 E. First South, Kanab, Utah 84741.

LITTLE, SUE LOHMILLER R
Mem, Ohio State Cent. and Exec. Cmt.
b. Cleveland, Ohio, 2/16/15; d. Calvin Arthur Lohmiller and Elizabeth Turner Klinefelter L; m. to Bascom Little; wid. Educ: Vassar Col, 32-34. Polit. & Govt. Pos: Mem, Ohio State Cent. and Exec. Cmt, 22nd Dist, 54- Mem: Jr. League of Cleveland; Citizens League of Cleveland. Rel: Episcopal. Mailing Add: 2065 Lyndway Rd, Cleveland, Ohio 44121.

LITTLE, TANDY DUNCAN, JR. R
Finance chmn, Ala. State Rep. Exec. Cmt.
b. Montgomery, Ala, 7/22/21; s. Tandy Duncan Little, Sr. and Julia Holladay L; m. 5/22/43 to Virginia Ruth Blair; c. Linda, Tandy Duncan, III, Donald Blair and Ann Holladay. Educ: Auburn Univ, B.E.E, 43; Eta Kappa Nu; Tau Kappa Epsilon. Polit. & Govt. Pos: Ala. State Rep, 62-66; finance chmn, Ala. State Rep. Exec. Cmt, 67-; chmn, Cent. Ala. Regional Planning Cmn, 67- Bus. & Prof. Pos: Partner, T.D. Little Elec. Co, 55- Mil. Serv: Entered as Pvt, Army, 43, released as 1st Lt, 46, after serv. in 756th Field Artil. Bn, Pac. Theater, 45-46. Mem: Nat. Elec. Contractors Asn.(pres, Cent. Ala. Chap, 59-67). Rel: Presbyterian. Mailing Add: 683 Cloverdale Rd, Montgomery, Ala. 36106.

LITTLE, THOMAS LAWRENCE R
Del. State Rep.
b. Pottsville, Pa. 1/23/36; s. Patrick Francis Little and Ann Dewey L; m. 9/9/61 to Kay Gaglione; c. Ann Catherine, Patrick Francis and Kelly Marie. Educ: Bloomsburg State Col, B.S.Ed, 62; v.pres, Vet. Asn. Polit. & Govt. Pos: Elec. dist. chmn, Brandywine Hundred, Del, 66-67; v.pres, Brandywine Hundred Young Rep, 66-67, dir, New Castle Co. Young Rep, 67-69; treas, Del. Young Rep, 67-69, nat. committeeman, 69-; Del. State Rep, 68-; treas, Nat. Fedn. Young Rep, 69- Bus. & Prof. Pos: Dir. and coach, Sunbury YMCA; 62-64; teacher and coach, A.I. du Pont Sch. Dist, 64-66; mgr, Financial Progs, Inc, 66-68; v.pres. and gen. mgr. invest. div, Evans & Assoc, Inc, 69- Mil. Serv: Entered as Pvt, Marine, 54, released as Sgt, 58, after serv. in Second Marine Div, Parris Island Recruit Training Co; Good Conduct Medal; Nat. Defense Medal; European Occupation Medal. Mailing Add: 16 York Rd, Wilmington, Del. 19803.

LITTLEFIELD, THOMAS C. R
b. New Shoreham, 1/27/07; m. to Esther T. Educ: Pub. Sch, New Shoreham. Polit. & Govt. Pos: R.I. State Sen, 63-66; chmn, New Shoreham Twp. Rep. Cmt, currently. Bus. & Prof. Pos: Pyrofax gas distributor and appliance dealer. Mailing Add: Box 579, Block Island, R.I. 02807. (1967)

LITTLEJOHN, TALMADGE D. D
b. Blue Springs, Miss, 10/18/35; married. Polit. & Govt. Pos: Miss. State Rep, 60-64; Miss. State Sen, 64-68. Bus. & Prof. Pos: Lawyer. Mem: Phi Alpha Delta; Union Co. Miss. Resource Develop. Comm; Union Co, Miss, Am. Bar; dir, Union Co. and Miss. Asns. for Retarded Children; Miss. Forestry Asn. Rel: Baptist. Mailing Add: New Hwy. 15 S, P.O. Box 833, New Albany, Miss. 38652. (1967)

LITTLER, RICHARD L. R
Chmn, Chase Co. Rep. Party, Kans.
b. Cottonwood Falls, Kans, 10/25/30; s. Clyde F. Littler and Kathryn Tipton L; m. 3/4/51 to Ora Lou Drinkwater; c. Kathryn Maree and David Eugene. Educ: Kans. State Teachers Col, 49-50; Phi Delta Chi. Polit. & Govt. Pos: Chmn, Chase Co. Rep. Party, Kans, 68- Bus. & Prof. Pos: Pres, Mark Cattle Co, Strong City, Kans, 66. Mil. Serv: Entered as Pvt, Army, 51, released as Sgt. 1/C, 53, after serv. in 25th Inf. Div, Artil, Korea, 52-53; Korean and UN Ribbons; Good Conduct Medal. Mem: Am. Legion; VFW. Rel: Presbyterian. Mailing Add: Route 1, Cottonwood Falls, Kans. 66845.

LIVANOS, PETER E, JR. R
b. Oakland, Calif, 10/24/37; s. Peter E. Livanos and Helen Beeson L; m. 8/19/61 to Gayle Laura Jones; c. Peter E, III and Michael Thomas. Educ: Univ. of Calif, Berkeley, B.A, 59; Hastings Col. of Law, J.D, 62; Chi Psi; Phi Alpha Delta. Polit. & Govt. Pos: Dir, Castro Valley Rep. Assembly, Calif, 67-69; mem, Calif. Rep. State Cent. Cmt, 69. Bus. & Prof. Pos: Dep. dist. attorney, Kern Co, Calif, 64-65; partner, Raymond, Keon & Livanos, Bakersfield, Calif, 65-66; attorney-at-law, Law Off. of Peter Livanos, Castro Valley, Calif, 66- Mil. Serv: Entered as Lt, Army, 59, released as Capt, 69, after serv. in Seattle Indust. Security Field Off, 62-64. Mem: Alameda Co. and South. Alameda Co. Bar Asns; Barristers Club of Alameda Co. (dir, 67, v.pres, 68 and treas, 69); C. of C.(pres, Castro Valley Chap, 69); dir, Castro Valley Boys Club, 67-; Lions; F&AM. Cert. of Excellence in Corp. Law, Hastings Col. of Law, 62; Citizen of the Day, Kabel, Bay Area, 67; Man of the Year, Castro Valley, 68. Rel: Protestant. Mailing Add: 5717 Coldwater Dr, Castro Valley, Calif. 94546.

LIVELY, ROBBIE J. D
b. Clinton, Ky, 2/6/90; d. George Washington Johnson and Susan Jordan J; wid; c. Arnette L. (Mrs. Walters) and Garland L. Educ: Ouachita Col, Bus. Sch, grad; Univ. Ark. Law Sch, 2 years. Polit. & Govt. Pos: Payroll clerk, Farmers Union Neighborhood Youth Corps, 65-; pres, Women Mem. Ark. Dem. Party, 63-66; Ark. State Chmn, Women Dem. for Johnson-Humphrey Campaign, 64; del, Nat. Dem. Conv, 64; auditor, finance dept, Nat. Dem. Cmt, John F. Kennedy Campaign, D.C. and Inaugural Cmt, 60; secy, chief disbursing officer then auditor, Bur. Internal Revenue, 33-60; asst. jour. clerk, Ark. House of Rep, 33; law secy, 21-33; clerk, Ark. State Senate, 21; secy, State Hwy. Cmn. and Adv. Bd, 15-21. Mem, Charter mem, Soroptimist Int. and Life mem, treas. and Bd. mem; Women's Social Serv. Club; Charter mem, Women's C. of C. and past pres; past pres. UDC, Little Rock Chap; past pres, Nat. Fedn. of Fed. Employees; Bd. mem, Woman's City Club; Little Rock Bus. and Prfnl. Women's Club; Little Rock Federated Clubs; Pub. Welfare Forum; Ark. Art Center; Little Rock City Beautiful Cmn. Attended White House Conf. on Beautification, 65. Rel: Presbyterian; past pres, Bus. Womens Circle and mem, Covenanter Sunday Sch. Class. Mailing Add: 2700 Flakewood, Little Rock, Ark. 72207. (1967)

LIVERANCE, IRMA MILDE R
b. Cleveland, Ohio, 7/18/05; d. Paul H. Milde and Clara Schweitzer M; m. 3/7/40 to Howard J. Liverance; c. Bert H. and Howard H. Educ: Univ. Wis, A.B; Alpha Phi. Polit. & Govt. Pos: Dir, Women's Finance, Oakland Co, Mich, 55-58, chmn, 59-61; del. and mem, Rules and Resolutions Cmt, Rep. Nat. Conv, 64; chmn, Gov. Status of Women Cmn, Mich, 67-68. Bus. & Prof. Pos: Exec. secy, League of Women Voters, Cuyahoga Co, Ohio, 35-38. Mem: Nat. Farm and Garden; League Women Voters. Rel: Protestant. Mailing Add: Tubac, Ariz. 85640.

LIVERMORE, PUTNAM R
V.Chmn, Calif. Rep. State Cent. Cmt.
b. San Francisco, Calif, 5/29/22; s. Norman Banks Livermore and Caroline Sealy L; single. Educ: Univ. Calif, A.B, 46, Law Sch, LL.B, 49; pres, Berkeley Chap, Alpha Delta Phi, 43; Big C. Soc; Golden Bear; Winged Helmet; Skull and Keys. Polit. & Govt. Pos: Elec. day chmn, San Francisco, Calif, 59-60; chmn, Rep. Precinct Orgn, 61-62; v.chmn, San Francisco Co. Rep. Cent. Cmt, 63-64, former chmn; v.chmn, Calif. Rep. State Cent. Cmt, currently. Mil. Serv: Entered as Pvt, Marines, 42, released as Capt, 58, after serv. in Pac. Theater, 44-45; Iwo Jima, Okinawa, Philippines, Formosa Straits Campaign Ribbons. Publ: Law rev. article in Calif. Law Rev, 49. Mem: State Bar of Calif; Am. and San Francisco Bar Asns; Am. Judicature Soc; bd. dir, Barrister's Club, San Francisco, 52-54 and Legal Aid Soc, 53-57; dir, Calif. Hist. Soc; asst. secy, Nature Conserv; founder and dir, Conserv. Law Soc. of Am. and San Francisco Bay Conserv. Fund. Mem, Univ. Calif. crew which won the West. U.S. Championship, 43. Rel: Episcopal. Mailing Add: 111 Sutter St, 12th Floor, San Francisco, Calif. 94104.

LIVINGSTON, DELILA ELIZABETH 'DEE' R
b. Kalix, Sweden, 1/2/05; d. Oscar Wickstrom and Davida Larson W; m. 1/18/30 to Lester Lewis Livingston. Educ: High sch, Sweden, grad. Polit. & Govt. Pos: Precinct committeewoman, Clallam Co. Rep. Cent. Cmt, Wash, 52-, v.chmn, 60-64, mem. exec. bd, 60-69, mem, Rep. Club Port Angeles, 52-69; mem, Sequim Rep. Club 62-69; state committeewoman, Clallam Co. Rep.

Party, 64-69; alternate del, Rep. Nat. Conv, 68. Mem: VFW Auxiliary; Fleet Reserve Asn. Auxiliary. Rel: Lutheran. Mailing Add: Route 5, Box 816, Port Angeles, Wash. 98362.

LIVINGSTON, JAMES EDWIN D

Chief Justice, Supreme Court of Ala.

b. Notasulga, Ala, 3/17/92; s. James Cooper Livingston and Stella Elizabeth Burks L; m. to Marie Wise (deceased); c. Willard Wise and Edwin Burks. Educ: Ala. Polytech. Inst, Auburn Univ, 2 years; Univ. Ala, LL.B, 18; Phi Delta Phi; Phi Gamma Delta. Polit. & Govt. Pos: Assoc. Justice, Supreme Court of Ala, 40-51, Chief Justice, 51- Bus. & Prof. Pos: Law partner, Livingston & Smith, 19-20, Livingston, Smith and Livingston, 22-25 and Livingston and Livingston, 25-40; part-time instr. law, Univ. Ala, 22-40. Mil. Serv: Pfc, Army, Artil. Officers' Training Camp, Camp Zachary Taylor, Louisville, Ky, 18. Mem: Ala. State Bar; Am. Bar Asn; Conf. of Chief Justices (chmn, 62-63); Mason; Elks; K. of P; Sons of Confederate Vet; Am. Legion. Plaque in appreciation of helpfulness to Sch. Law, Univ. Ala, Farrah Order of Jurisp, 69. Rel: Methodist. Legal Res: Tuscaloosa, Ala. 35401. Mailing Add: P.O. Box 218, Supreme Court of Alabama, Montgomery, Ala. 36101.

LLOYD, DAISY RILEY D

b. Laurence, Kans, d. Isaac Riley and Nettie Henrie R; m. 1/17/59 to Frank P. Lloyd, M.D; c. Shelly P, Riley P, Frank P, Jr. and Karen Anne. Educ: Howard Univ, B.A, 47-50. Govt. Pos: Ind. State Rep, 65-66; res. asst, Legis. Ref. Serv, Sr. Spec. Sect, Library of Cong, 46-50. Mem: Jack & Jill, Inc; Gay Northeasterners; Am. Civil Liberties Union; League of Women Voters; life mem, NAACP. Rel: Roman Catholic. Mailing Add: 4210 N. Illinois St, Indianapolis, Ind. 46208. (1967)

LLOYD, JACQUELINE VAUGHAN D

Mem, Calif. Dem. State Cent. Cmt.

b. Covina, Calif, 7/3/26; d. John Paul Vaughan and Winona Parrish V; m. 11/27/48 to James Fredrick Lloyd; c. Brian Patrick. Educ: Pomona Col, 43-45; Stanford Univ, B.A, 47; Tulane Univ, 52; A&I, 59. Polit. & Govt. Pos: Secy, Covina Dem. Club, 66-68; mem, Calif. Dem. State Cent. Cmt, 68- Bus. & Prof. Pos: Partner-acct. exec. Lloyds Pub. Rels, 66- Publ: 'Navy Wives Go To Sea,' U.S. Lady, 54; Women's World (weekly-column), Guantanamo Gazett, 62-63. Mem: Assoc. mem, Covina Valley Realty Bd; Pomona Col. Alumni Asn; Stanford Univ. Alumni Asn; Covina C. of C. Rel: Protestant. Mailing Add: 3240 Whitebirch Dr, West Covina, Calif. 91790.

LLOYD, JAMES FREDRICK D

City Councilman, West Covina, Calif.

b. Helena, Mont, 9/27/22; s. Robert E. Lloyd and Maria Lunders L; m. 11/27/48 to Jacqueline Vaughan; c. Brian. Educ: Univ. Ore, 2 years; Stanford Univ, B.A. in Polit. Sci, 58; U.S. Naval Post Grad. Sch, 58; Univ. South. Calif, M.A, 66; Pi Sigma Alpha; Kappa Sigma. Polit. & Govt. Pos: Mem, Los Angeles Co. Dem. Cent. Cmt, 66-68; mem, Calif. Dem. State Cent. Cmt, 68; city councilman, West Covina, Calif, 68- Bus. & Prof. Pos: Dir. pub. rels, Aerojet Gen. South Calif. Plants, 63-64; owner & exec. dir, Lloyds Pub. Rels, 66-; bd. of dirs, Cable Air Flight Contractors and Nat. Shopping Centers, 69. Mil. Serv: Entered as Seaman 2/C, Navy, 42, released as Lt. Comdr, 63, after serv. in Naval Aviation, S.Pac, Korea and Guantanamo Bay, Cuba, 42-63; Asiatic Pac. Theater, World War II, Occup, Philippine Liberation, Nat. Defense, Cold War and Expert Pistol & Rifle Naval Unit Commendations. Mem: Bd. dirs, Friends of Ontario Int. Airport; pub. relations cmt, Los Angeles Int. Airport; West Covina C. of C; Covina C. of C; Hollywood Coun, Navy League. Rel: Protestant. Legal Res: 3204 Whitebirch Dr, West Covina, Calif. 91790. Mailing Add: 3104 E. Garvey Ave, West Covina, Calif. 91790.

LLOYD, O. WINFIELD D

b. Falling Waters, W.Va, 1/23/10; s. Francis M. Lloyd and Blanche Virginia Emerson L; m. to Mable Marguerite Lemaster; c. Anita L.(Mrs. Wright), Judith Virginia Mable (Mrs. Henderson) and Winfield Scott. Educ: High sch. Polit. & Govt. Pos: Committeeman, Falling Waters Dem. Cmt, W. Va, 36-; safety inspector, State Rd. Cmn, 40-43; chmn, Berkeley Co. Dem. Cent. Cmt, 62-67; state inspector, Shenandoah Downs Race Track, 63 & 64. Bus. & Prof. Pos: Owner and operator, Gen. Merchandise Store, 43-58; realtor, 60-66. Mem: Nat. Geog. Soc; Jefferson Co. and Berkeley Co. Hist. Soc; Issac Walton League; Marlowe Ruritans; Berkeley Co. Women's Dem. Club; Berkeley Co. Young Dem. Club; Berkeley Co. Dem. Exec. Cmt. Rel: Methodist. Mailing Add: Falling Waters, W.Va. 25419. (1967)

LLOYD, SHERMAN PARKINSON R

U.S. Rep, Utah

b. St. Anthony, Idaho, 1/11/14; s. Charles Edward Lloyd and Lucy Parkinson L; m. 9/25/35 to Edith Ann Gunn; c. Sherman G, Kathryn (Mrs. Sharp), Diane (Mrs. McMaster) and Elizabeth Ann. Educ: Utah State Univ, B.S; George Wash. Univ. Law Sch, LL.B. Polit. & Govt. Pos: Utah State Sen, 55-62, pres, Utah State Sen, 59-61, mem, Legis. Coun, 57-61 and chmn, 59-61, Utah rep. on Bd. of Mgrs, Coun. State Govts, Rep. Majority and Minority Leader, chmn, Judiciary, Sifting and Salary Cmts, Standing Cmt. on Bus. and Commerce, Labor Cmt, Nat. Legis Cmt, Joint Rep. Caucus Cmt. on Labor Legis. and Appropriations Subcmt. for State Bldgs; del, Rep. Nat. Conv. and cand, U.S. Rep, Utah, 60; U.S. Rep, Utah, 63-64 & 67-, mem, Cmt. on Banking and Currency and Subcmts. on Bank Supv. and Ins, Int. Trade and Int. Finance, U.S. House of Rep, mem, For. Affairs Cmt, 69- Bus. & Prof. Pos: Exec. mgr. and gen. counsel, Utah Retail Grocers Asn, 40-64; vis. lectr. polit. sci, Univ. Utah, 65; founder and mem. exec. cmt, Beehive State Bank. Mem: Utha State Bar Asn; C. of C.(mem. bd. gov, Salt Lake Chap); chmn, March of Dimes; Kiwanis (dir, Salt Lake Club); state chmn, Nat. Libr. Week, 66. Rel: Latter-day Saint. Legal Res: 1467 Arlington Dr, Salt Lake City, Utah 84103. Mailing Add: 1116 Longworth House Office Bldg, Washington, D.C. 20515.

LLOYD, THOMAS REESE R

Mem, Ohio Rep. State Cent. Cmt.

b. Cambridge, Ohio, 1/5/20; s. John Russell Lloyd and Margaret Patterson L; m. 8/26/62 to Doris Irene Alloway. Educ: Muskingum Col, A.B, 44; Ohio State Univ. Col. of Eng, 41-44; Duke Univ. Sch. of Law, LL.B, 47; Delta Tau Delta; Phi Delta Phi. Polit. & Govt. Pos: del, Rep. State Conv, Ohio, 48-64; chmn, Guernsey Co. Rep. Cent. and Exec. Cmts, 48-68; asst. attorney gen, Ohio, 51-55 and spec. counsel to Attorney Gen, 55-58 & 63-; chmn, Ohio State Racing Cmn, 55-60; mem, Guernsey Co. Bd. of Elec, 59-; del, Rep. Nat. Conv, 60; mem, Ohio Rep. State Cent. and Exec. Cmts, 60-64 & 68-; v.pres, Guernsey Regional Planning Cmn, 62- Bus. & Prof. Pos: Civil engr, N.Y. Cent. R.R, 43-44; attorney-at-law, Cambridge, Ohio, 47-; acting adminstr, Cambridge Commun. Hosp, 63-64. Mem: Guernsey Co, Ohio State and Am. Bar Asns. Admitted to practice before Supreme Court of Ohio, Supreme Court of U.S, U.S. Court of Appeals and U.S. Dist. Court. Rel: Presbyterian. Legal Res: 1350 Edgeworth Ave, Cambridge, Ohio 43725. Mailing Add: P.O. Box. 705, Cambridge, Ohio 43725. (1967)

LOBLE, LESTER HENRY, II D

Mont. State Rep.

b. Helena, Mont, 11/14/41; s. Henry Loble and Grayce Eckhardt L; m. 3/8/68 to Arlene Joyce Blewett. Educ: Stanford Univ, A.B, 63; Univ. Mont. Law Sch, J.D, 66; Leaphart Scholar, 64-65; Kappa Alpha. Polit. & Govt. Pos: Attorney-adv, U.S. Dept. Interior, 66-67; Mont. State Rep, Dist. 21, 68-; mem, Helena City-Lewis and Clark Co. Health Bd, 69- Bus. & Prof. Pos: Partner, Loble, Picotte and Loble, Helena, 67- Mem: Am, Mont, First Dist. and Fed. Bar Asns; Lions; Eagles; Jaycees; C. of C; United Givers (chmn). Outstanding Freshman Legislator, 71st Mont. Legis. Assembly, 69. Mailing Add: 1001 Billings, Helena, Mont. 59601.

LOCHER, RALPH SIDNEY D

b. Moreni, Romania, 7/24/15; s. Ephriam Locher and Natalie Voigt L; m. 6/18/39 to Eleanor Worthington; c. Virginia L. Educ: Univ. Dayton, 32; Bluffton Col, B.A, 36; West.Reserve Univ, LL.B, 39; admitted to Ohio Bar, 39. Polit. & Govt. Pos: Secy, Indust. Cmn, Ohio, 45; legal counsel to Gov, Ohio, 46; secy. to Gov, 49-53; law dir, Cleveland, 53-62; Mayor, Cleveland, 62-67; judge, Court of Common Pleas, Cuyahoga Co, currently. Bus. & Prof. Pos: Bd. mgr, Cent. Bank. Mem: Am, Ohio, Cleveland and Cuyahoga Co. Bar Asns; Citizens League of Cleveland; YMCA (mem. bd. dirs). Legal Res: 13714 Ardoon Ave, Cleveland, Ohio 44120. Mailing Add: Cuyahoga County Court House, Lakeside Ave, Cleveland, Ohio 44113.

LOCKAMY, JOHN NATHAN D

b. Sampson Co. N.C, 8/21/27; s. William Lischer Lockamy and Dora Patience Pope L; m. 9/2/50 to Jean Evelyn Strickland; c. John Nathan, Jr. Educ: High Sch, grad, 44. Polit. & Govt. Pos: Dem. precinct chmn, Belvoir Precinct, Sampson Co, N.C, 58-; commun. committeeman, U.S. Dept. Agr, Belvoir Precinct, Sampson Co, 63-66, v.chmn, 66-; mem, N.C. Agr. Stabilization and Conservation Serv. State Training Center, Raleigh, 68; mem. bd. dirs, N.C. Asn. Farmer Elected Committeeman, 67-; southeast area dir, Nat. Asn. Farmer Elected Committeeman, 67-; del, Dem. Nat. Conv, 68; chmn, Sampson Co. Dem. Finance Cmt, 68-; asst. cmnr, N.C. Dept. Motor Vehicles, 69- Bus. & Prof. Pos: Farmer, Clinton, N.C, 44-; owner and operator, Farm Supplies, 46-; v.chmn, Farmers' Dehydration, Inc, 67- Mil. Serv: Merchant Marine, 45-46; N.C. Nat. Guard, 50-52, Sgt. Mem: Mason; Shrine; Sudan Temple; Sudan Temple Oriental Band; Asn. Shrine Oriental Bands; Lakewood Country Club; N.C. Asn. Farmer Elected Committeeman; Sampson Co. Asn. Retarded Children; Nat. Farmers' Orgn; Methodist Men's Club. Cert. of Appreciation, N.C. Dem. Exec. Cmt, 66. Rel: Methodist. Mailing Add: Route 1, Clinton, N.C. 28328.

LOCKARD, JOSEPH FRANCIS D

b. Pittsburgh, Pa, 8/1/13; s. Joseph Aloysius Lockard and Mary Harkey L; m. 12/20/50 to Ruth Klein; c. Joseph Franklin and David Lee. Educ: Pa. State Univ, A.B. in journalism, 35; Harvard Univ, grad. work in pub. admin, 45-46; Temple Univ, 67-; Pi Delta Epsilon; Phi Kappa. Polit. & Govt. Pos: Proj. dir, West. Pa, Nat. Youth Admin, 38-42; committeeman, 41st Ward Dem. Cmt, Pa, 53-67; admin. asst. to Phila. Dem. City Chmn, 54-67; dep. controller, Phila, 58-59; committeeman, 65th Ward Dem. Cmt, 65-67. Bus. & Prof. Pos: Pres, Serv. Trades Inst, 47-51 and Shoes, Inc, 50-57. Mil. Serv: Entered as Pvt, Army Air Force, 42, released as S/Sgt, 45, after serv. in Hq, 438th Troop Carrier Group, 1st Allied Airborne Army, ETO; Distinguished Unit Badge; Normandy, North. France, Rome-Arno, South. France, Ardennes, Rhineland and Cent. Europe Campaign Ribbons. Mem: Pa. State Alumni Asn; Am. Polit. Sci. Asn. Mailing Add: 226 W. Willow Grove Ave. Philadelphia, Pa. 19118.

LOCKE, BARRY M. R

Spec. Asst. to Secy. of Transportation.

b. Boston, Mass, 12/21/30; s. Arthur Leo Locke and Lillian Mahler L; m. 10/22/58 to Ann Boggio; c. Vanessa, Alison and Valeria. Educ: Boston Univ, B.S, 53. Polit. & Govt. Pos: Chief adminstr. and press secy. to Gov. Keyser, Vt, 61-63; New Eng. pub. info. officer, U.S. Internal Revenue Serv, Boston, Mass, 63-64; chief press secy. to Gov. John A. Volpe, Mass, 64-68; spec. asst. to Secy. of Transportation John A. Volpe, Dept. of Transportation, Wash, 69- Bus. & Prof. Pos: Ed, Three Rivers, Mich, Daily Newspaper, 56-57; guest lectr, Boston Univ. Sch. of Pub. Commun, currently. Mil. Serv: Entered as Pvt, Army, 53, released as Sgt. 1/C, 55. Mem: Bd. dir, Boston Univ. Sch. of Pub. Commun. Alumni, 68-69; Emerson Col. Develop. Adv. Coun; Publicity Club of Boston; pub. rels. cmt, Winterfest, 67; Cmt. for Christian A. Herter Endowment, Brandeis Univ. Cert. of Merit for distinguished serv. as staff correspondent, United Press Int. News and Vt. State Bur. Mgr. Mailing Add: 11821 Milbern Dr, Potomac, Md. 20854.

LOCKE, DAVID HENRY R

Mass. State Sen.

b. Boston, Mass, 8/4/27; s. Allen W. Locke and Florence Elizabeth Henry L; m. 2/19/52 to Barbara Blood; c. David Byron, Jeffrey Allen, Jennifer, Amy Beth and John Adam. Educ: Harvard Univ, A.B, 51; Harvard Law Sch, LL.B, 54. Polit. & Govt. Pos: Mem, Wellesley Town Meeting, Mass, 49-69; mem, Wellesely Rep. Town Cmt, 52-69; selectman, Wellesley, 59-62; Mass. State Rep, 60-68; Mass. State Sen, Norfolk-Middlesex Dist, 69- Bus. & Prof. Pos: Spec. asst. dist. attorney, Norfolk Co, Mass, 56-57; attorney, Jameson, Locke & Fullerton, Wellesley. Mil. Serv: Entered as Pvt, Marines, 45, released as Pfc, 46. Mem: Am, Mass, and Boston Bar Asns; pres, Norfolk Co. Bar Asn. (secy, 64-68, v.pres, 68-69); Trial Lawyer's Asn. Rel: Roman Catholic. Legal Res: 15 Ordway Rd, Wellesley Hills, Mass. 02181. Mailing Add: 8 Grove St, Wellesley, Mass. 02181.

LOCKE, EUGENE MURPHY

b. Dallas, Tex, 1/6/18; m. to Adele Neely; c. Aimee Marie, John Patrick and Thomas Neely. Educ: Univ. Tex, B.A, 37; Yale Univ, LL.B, 40. Polit. &

Govt. Pos: Mem. legal staff, Off. of Price Admin, 41-42; chmn, Tex. Dem. State Exec. Cmt, 63; del, Dem. Nat. Conv, 64; campaign mgr, Connally for Gov, Tex, 62; U.S. Ambassador to Pakistan, 66-67; Dep. Ambassador to Vietnam, 67-68. Bus. & Prof. Pos: Attorney, Dallas, 40-41; sr. partner, Locke, Purnell, Boren, Laney & Neely, Attorneys, 45- Mil. Serv: Navy, Pac. Theatre, 42-45. Mem: Chmn. of bd, Sr. Citizens Found. of Dallas; dir, Sam Rayburn Found; dir. and past pres, Tex. Independent Producers and Royalty Asn; dir, Mid-Continent Oil and Gas Asn; Am, Tex. and Dallas Bar Asns; Yale Law Sch. Alumni Asn.(former v.pres. and mem. exec. cmt); Phi Beta Kappa; Order of the Coif; Phi Delta Theta. Legal Res: 3805 McFarlin Blvd, Dallas, Tex. 75205. Mailing Add: 3600 Republic Bank Tower, Dallas, Tex. 75201.

LOCKE, MRS. EUGENE MURPHY D
b. Comanche, Tex, 11/11/19; d. Eugene Gentry Neely and Nell Orand N; m. 10/27/41 to Eugene Murphy Locke; c. Aimee Marie, John Patrick and Thomas Neely. Educ: Univ. Tex, B.A, 40; Phi Beta Kappa; Pi Beta Phi; Sigma Delta Pi; Phi Eta Sigma; Pi Lambda Theta; Alpha Lambda Delta. Polit. & Govt. Pos: Tex. state chmn, Womens Activities for Gov. John Connally, 64; mem. exec. cmt, Dem. Nat. Cmt, 64, Dem. Nat. Committeewoman, Tex, 64-67. Mem: Chmn, Dallas Ment. Health Asn, 64; hospitality bd, Metrop. Opera, Dallas, 62-; bd. dirs, Jr. League of Dallas; Jr. Assembly; trustee, Timberlawn Found; exec. cmt, Gr. Dallas Coun. Churches; Daughters of Rep. of Tex; Dallas Woman's, Dallas Garden and Dallas Country Clubs. Rel: Episcopal. Mailing Add: 3805 McFarlin Blvd, Dallas, Tex. 75205.

LOCKE, HUGH ALLEN JR. D
b. Birmingham, Ala, 4/3/24; s. Hugh Allen Locke and Mabel Lillian Plosser L; single. Educ: Birmingham-South. Col, 47; Birmingham-South. Law, 47-50. Polit. & Govt. Pos: Ala. State Rep, 49-67; chmn, Anti-subversive Activities Comm. for Ala. Bus. & Prof. Pos: Lawyer. Mil. Serv: Army. Mem: Am. Legion; pres. Jefferson Co. Coun. Legion Posts; DAV; Exchange Club; Knights of Pythias; Eagles; State Judge Advocate of Am. Legion. Rel: Methodist. Mailing Add: 952 Conroy Rd, Birmingham, Ala. 35222.

LOCKE, NINA SPENCER R
Mem, Orange Co. Rep. Exec. Cmt, Fla.
b. N.Y.C, 11/13/29; d. Charles Burr Spencer and Marjorie Thorp S; m. 5/6/50 to James Locke; c. Marjorie Vivian, Diana Stoddard and John. Polit. & Govt. Pos: Vol. chmn, Young Rep, 62; precinct coordinator, Gurney for Cong, 62 & 64; mem, Winter Park Draft Goldwater Cmt, 63; mem, Orange Co. Rep. Exec. Cmt, Fla, 63-, precinct educ. chmn, 64-65; mem, Exec. Cmt, Winter Park Citizens for Goldwater and co-chmn, 11th Dist. Citizens for Goldwater, 64; del, Rep. Nat. Conv, 64; chmn, Orange Co. MORE Prog, 64; Fla. State Rep. committeewoman, Orange Co, 64-66; asst. to chmn. and precinct dir, Orange Co. Kirk for Gov. Cmt, 66; precinct dir, Ken Plante for Sen, 66. Mem: Orlando Women's Rep. Club; charter mem, Cent. Fla. Rep. Club; Youth Center; Women's Cmt. Fla. Symphony; Gala Guild. Rel: Presbyterian. Mailing Add: 1508 Park Ave. N, Winter Park, Fla. 32789.

LOCKER, DALE LE ROY D
b. Sidney, Ohio, 11/2/29; s. Claude Locker and Ada Allen L; m. 7/5/50; to LaDonna Mae Limbert; c. LaDonna Kae, Dale LeRoy, II, Louis Randolph, Alan Jay, Eric Justin and Aaron Frazier. Educ: Bowling Green State Univ, B.S. in ed, 53; Ohio Northern Univ, 60; Ohio Univ, 62. Polit. Pos: Ohio State Rep, Shelby Co, 65-67. Bus. & Prof. Pos: Guid. dir, Jackson Center Pub. Sch, 59-; music instr, Huntsville Pub. Sch, 55-58 and Melmore Pub. Sch, 54. Mem: Life mem, Nat. Ed. Asn, Music Educators Nat. Conf. and Ohio Music Ed. Asn; Ohio Ed. Asn; Kiwanis; Moose; Civic Asn. Rel: Methodist. Mailing Add: Box 356, Anna, Ohio 45302. (1967)

LOCKHART, RICHARD SPENCE R
N.H. State Rep.
b. Belmont, Mass, 6/21/27; s. Hubert Winfield Lockhart and Emily Buckout L; m. 9/4/54 to Joan Heselton; c. William Lawson and R. Spence. Educ: Univ. Maine, B.A, 50; Beta Theta Pi. Polit. & Govt. Pos: Sch. bd. mem, New Castle, N.H, 63-; bd. mem, New Castle Recreation & Conserv. Cmn, 65-; chmn, New Castle Rep. Cmt, 67-68; N.H. State Rep, 69- Bus. & Prof. Pos: Salesman, Von-Olker, Snell Paper Co, 50-52; East. supvr, Joseph Dixon Crucible Co, 53-56; publisher's rep, D.C. Heath & Co, 56-69; bus. adminstr, Portsmouth Mental Health Clinic, 69- Mil. Serv: Entered as A/S, Coast Guard, 45, released as Fireman 1/C, 46, after serv. in U.S.S. Charlotte and Potomac, Am. and European Theaters, 45-46; seaman 1/C, Navy, 50-52, with serv. in U.S.S. New Jersey, Korea, 50-52; Am. and European Theater, Good Conduct and Japanese Occup. Ribbons; Korea Campaign Ribbon With One Star. Mem: Prfnl. Bookmen of Am; New Eng. Educ. Salesmen's Asn; dir, Kittery Point Yacht Club; Portsmouth Yacht Club. Rel: Congregational. Legal Res: Wild Rose Lane, New Castle, N.H. 03854. Mailing Add: Box 245, New Castle, N.H. 03854.

LOCKLIN, JACK G. D
Mem, Ky. State Dem. Cent. Exec. Cmt.
b. Monroe, Ga, 4/15/03; s. William Clarence Locklin and Daisy Griffeth L; m. 8/21/26 to Reatha Webb. Educ: Ga. Sch. of Tech, 21-23; Sigma Alpha Epsilon. Polit. & Govt. Pos: Dist. engr, Ky. Dept. Hwy, 23-36; mem, Ky. State Dem. Cent. Exec. Cmt, 60-; chmn, Whitley Co. Dem. Cmt, Ky, 60-; city judge, Williamsburg, Ky, 63- Bus. & Prof. Pos: Consult, Eng. Gen, Ky, 36-46; owner, Williamsburg Supply Co, 46-60; partner, Personal Finance Co, Whitley City, 60-64; mgr. and partner, City Loan Co, Williamsburg, 60-; partner, Burnside Loan Co, 64- Mem: Prfnl. Engrs. of Ky; Mason; Shrine; Elks. Mailing Add: Box 383, Williamsburg, Ky. 40769.

LOCKLIN, ROBERT RIVES D
b. Monroeville, Ala, 5/20/29; s. Anderson J. Locklin and Irene Elizabeth Moore L; m. 1/29/50 to Betty Jean Huffstutler; c. Jeanie and Eleanor. Educ: Univ. Ala, B.A, 50, LL.B, 52; Delta Kappa Epsilon. Polit. & Govt. Pos: Mem, Ala. State Bd. of Educ, 55-61; v.pres, Young Dem. of Ala, 56; gen. counsel, U.S. Senate Select Cmt. on Small Bus, 61-67; admin. asst. to Sen. John Sparkman, Ala, 67-; del, Dem. Nat. Conv, 68. Bus. & Prof. Pos: Partner, Law Firm of Hamilton, Denniston, Butler & Riddick, Mobile, Ala, 55-61. Mil. Serv: Entered as 2nd Lt, Air Force, 53, released as 1st Lt, 55, after serv. in Judge Adv. Gen. Dept, 53-55. Mem: Ala. & Am. Bar Asns; Admin. Asst. Asn; Int. Trade Club, Mobile, Ala; Nat. Capital Dem. Club, Wash, D.C; Ala. State Soc. of Wash, D.C.(pres, 68). Rel: Methodist. Legal Res: Mobile, Ala. Mailing Add: 3203 New Senate Office Bldg, Washington, D.C. 20510.

LOCKWOOD, EMIL R
Mich. State Sen.
b. Ottawa, Ill, 9/23/19; s. Henry Clare Lockwood and Mabel Archard L; m. 3/23/52 to Mariella Coffey; c. Eric, Lori and Lorette. Educ: Kemper Mil. Sch, A.A, 39; Univ. Mich, B.A, 41, M.B.A, 47; Phi Delta Theta. Polit. & Govt. Pos: Supvr, Gratiot Co, Mich, 59-61; mem, sch. bd, St. Louis, 59-62; Mich. State Sen, 63-; del, Rep. Nat. Conv, 68. Mil. Serv: Entered as Ens, Navy, 42, released as Lt.(sg), 46, after serv. in Amphibious Forces, Pac. Theater, 42-46; 7 Major Invasion Ribbons; Pac. Theater Ribbon. Mem: Am. Inst. of CPA's; Mich. Asn. of CPA's; VFW; Am. Legion; Elks; Saginaw Club. Rel: Episcopal. Mailing Add: 106 Surrey Rd, St. Louis, Mich. 48880.

LOCKWOOD, JANE BIGGERS R
b. Toledo, Ohio, 8/12/20; d. John David Biggers and Mary Kelsey B; m. 7/6/42 to Corwin Rees Lockwood, Jr; c. Corwin Rees, III. Educ: Garland Jr. Col, Boston, Mass, 39-41; King-Smith Studio Sch, Wash, D.C, 41-42. Polit. & Govt. Pos: Mem, Rep. Nat. Finance Cmt, 48-54, vol. absentee voters bur, 48-59; mem. and mem. bd, D.C. League Rep. Women's Club, 48-62; vol, Sen. J. Glenn Beall Sr. Campaign, 52, Eisenhower-Nixon Campaign, 52 & 56, Rep. DeWitt S. Hyde Campaign, 54 and Sen. John Marshall Butler Campaign, 56; asst. Rep. chmn, Precinct 7-7, Montgomery Co, Md, 58, chmn, 59-63; patron, Montgomery Co, 59-69; mem, Nixon-Lodge Campaign Cmt, Montgomery Co, 60; committee mem, Rep. Charles M. Mathias Jr. Campaign, 60 & 62; vol, Montgomery Co. Rep. Hq, 61-67; women's v.chmn, Montgomery Co. Rep. Cent. Cmt, 63-69; committee mem, Goldwater-Miller Campaign, 64; campaign mgr, Edward J. Clarke for House Del, 66; mem, Constitutional Conv. Nominating Cmt, 67; del, Rep. Nat. Conv, 68; co-chmn, Nixon-Agnew Cmt. Montgomery Co, 68; chmn, Women for Nixon-Agnew Montgomery Co, 68; v.chmn. hospitality cmt, Nixon-Agnew Inaugural, 68-69; co-chmn, Invitation Cmt. for the Reception for Vice President Elect and Mrs. Agnew, Inaugural Cmt, 68-69. Mem: Rock Creek Women's Rep. Club (former mem. bd). Rel: Methodist. Mailing Add: 10500 Rockville Pike, Apt. 1702, Rockville, Md. 20852.

LOCKWOOD, LORNA E. D
V.Chief Justice, Ariz. Supreme Court
b. Douglas, Ariz, 3/24/03; d. Alfred Collins Lockwood and Maude Lincoln L; single. Educ: Univ. Ariz, A.B, 23, J.D, 25; Pi Kappa Phi; Chi Omega. Polit. & Govt. Pos: Ariz. State Rep, 39-42 & 47-48; price attorney, Dist. of Ariz, U.S. Off. of Price Admin, 42-44; asst. attorney gen, Ariz, 48-50; judge, Maricopa Co, 51-60; justice, Ariz. Supreme Court, 61-, v.chief justice, 64-65 & 69-, chief justice, 65-66. Bus. & Prof. Pos: Mem. firm, Lockwood and Savage, Phoenix, Ariz, 39-41; Cox, Lockwood and Lockwood, 44-48. Mem: State Bar of Ariz; Maricopa Co. and Am. Bar Asns; Am. Law Inst; Inst. of Judicial Admin; Nat. Asn. of Women Lawyers; Am. Judicature Soc; Phoenix Bus. and Prfnl. Women's Club; Eastern Star; Soroptimist Club; Ariz. Judges Asn; Plus 60 Personnel; Am. Asn. of Univ. Women; Gov. Cmn. on Status of Women. Medallion of Merit and Alumni Achievement Award, Univ. Ariz; Outstanding Woman in the Field of Law, Who's Who of Am. Women; Ariz. Award for Women of Achievement, Asn. for Women's Active Return to Educ; Woman of Achievement Award, Am. Asn. of Univ. Women, Phoenix Br; Humanitarian Award, South. Pac. Coast Region of Hadassah; Woman of Distinction Citation, Pac. Region Soroptimist Fedn. of the Am; Prfn. Woman of the Year, State Fedn. of Bus. and Prfnl. Women's Clubs; Award of Merit in Pioneering Delinquency Control Inst. of Ariz, Ariz. Conf. on Crime and Delinquency Prevention and Control. Rel: Congregational. Legal Res: 1146 W. MacKenzie Dr, Phoenix, Ariz. 85013. Mailing Add: Arizona Supreme Court, State Capitol Bldg, Phoenix, Ariz. 85007.

LODESTRO, RICHARD L. R
b. Illinois, 8/20/36; s. Leonard LoDestro. Educ: U. Chicago, 60; Northern Ill. U, 61, grad. study in admin, Ill. State U. Bus. & Prof. Pos: Instr, Chicago Pub. Sch. Mil. Serv: U.S. Army, 54-56. Mem: Leyden Township Young Rep; Leyden reg. Rep. Orgn; Chicago Teachers Union; Charter Mem, Y's Mens Club; YMCA; Garfield Lodge No. 685, AF & AM, Chicago; Medinah Temple; AAONMS; U. Ill. Alumini Asn; State Normal U. Alumini Asn. Mailing Add: 1940 N. 75th Court, Elmwood Park, Ill. 60635. (1967)

LODGE, GEORGE CABOT R
b. Boston, Mass. 7/7/27; s. Henry Cabot Lodge and Emily Sears L; m. 4/23/49 to Nancy Kunhardt; c. Nancy Kunhardt, Emily Sears, Dorothy Meserve, Henry Cabot, George Cabot and David. Educ: Harvard Col, A.B. cum laude, 50. Polit. & Govt. Pos: Dir. of info, Dept. of Labor, 54-58; Asst. Secy. for Int. Affairs, 58-61. Bus. & Prof. Pos: Reporter, Boston Herald, 50-54; lectr, Harvard Bus. Sch, 63-68, assoc. prof, 68- Mil. Serv: Seaman 1/C, Navy, 45-46; Ens, Naval Res, 46-50. Publ: Spearheads of Democracy, Harper & Row, 62. Mem: Coun. on For. Rels; UN Asn. of the U.S; Asn. Harvard Alumni. Rel: Protestant. Mailing Add: 275 Hale St, Beverly, Mass. 01915.

LODGE, HENRY CABOT R
b. Nahant, Mass, 7/5/02; s. George Cabot Lodge and Elizabeth Davis L; m. 7/1/26 to Emily Sears; c. George Cabot and Henry Sears. Educ: Harvard Col, A.B, 24. Hon. degrees from Northeast, Clark, Norwich, Laval, Bishop's, Boston, Harvard, N.Y, Fordham, Lehigh, Columbia and Princeton Univs; Franklin and Marshall, Hamilton, Williams, Union, Boston and Adelphi Cols; Univs. of N.H, Pa, Notre Dame and Mass; Rensselaer Polytech. Inst. Polit. & Govt. Pos: Mass. State Rep, 33-37; U.S. Sen, Mass, 36-46, mem, for. rels. cmt, U.S. Senate; chmn. resolutions cmt, Rep. Nat. Conv, 48; campaign mgr, Effort to Secure Rep. Pres. Nomination for Gen. Eisenhower, 52; U.S. rep, UN and mem, President Eisenhower's Cabinet, 53-60; Rep. nominee for V Pres. of U.S, 60; dir. gen, Atlantic Inst, 61-63; U.S. Ambassador, Viet-Nam, 63-64 & 65-67; Ambassador-at-lg, 67-68; Ambassador, Germany, 68-69; Personal Rep. of the President of the U.S, Paris Meetings on Viet-Nam, 69- Mil. Serv: Entered as Pvt, Army Res, 25, released as Lt. Col, 45, after serv. in Second Armored Div, Fourth Corps, Sixth Army Group, World War II; Maj. Gen, Army Res; ETO Ribbon with Five Battle Stars; Legion of Merit; Bronze Star; French Legion d'Honneur and Croix de Guerre with Palm; Brit. Mid.E. Citation; Bronze Star Citation. Sylvanus Thayer Medal, West Point;

VFW Gold Medal for Distinguished Serv; cited by six vet. orgns. for work in bringing about release of U.S. prisoners held in Korea; Theodore Roosevelt Asn. Medal; Chevalier, Order of Polonia Restituta; Humane Order of African Redemption, Liberia; Grand Cross of Merit, Sovereign Order of Malta; Grand Cross, Nat. Order, Repub. of Viet-Nam. Legal Res: 275 Hale St, Beverly, Mass. 01915. Mailing Add: American Embassy, APO San Francisco, Calif. 96243.

LODGE, JOHN DAVIS R
U.S. Ambassador to Argentina
b. Washington, D.C; s. George Cabot Lodge and Matilda E.F. Davis L; m. to Francesca Braggiotti; c. Lily and Beatrice; 5 grandchildren. Educ: Harvard, B.A, 25 and LL.D, 29; Ecole de Droit, Paris; Phi Beta Kappa. Hon. LL.D, Trinity Col, Middlebury Col. and Hobart and William Smith Cols; D.Sc, Worcester Polytech. Inst; L.H.D, Fairfield Univ. Polit. & Govt. Pos: U.S. Rep, Fourth Dist, Conn, 47-51, mem, For. Affairs Cmt, U.S. House of Rep; Gov, Conn, 51-55; chmn, New Eng. Gov. Conf, 2 terms; chmn, New Eng. Cmt. for Peaceful Uses of Atomic Energy; spec. ambassador for President Eisenhower to Panama, Costa Rica and P.R, 53; U.S. Ambassador to Spain, 55-61; del. and asst. floor leader, Conn. Constitutional Conv, 65; U.S. Ambassador to Argentina, 69- Bus. & Prof. Pos: Attorney, Cravath, de Gersdorff, Swaine & Wood, N.Y.C; actor, motion pictures and theatre; attorney-at-law. Mil. Serv: Navy, World War II; Capt, Naval Res; Croix de Guerre with Palm; Chevalier, French Legion of Honor. Mem: Am. Legion; VFW; ROA; Navy League; hon. mem, Nat. Order of Polish Legion of Am. Vet, Sons of Italy and Trinacria and Faetana Socs; Conn. State Grange (7°); Harvard Club, N.Y.C; Nat. Press Club; Dacor Club, Wash, D.C; nat. pres, Jr. Achievement, 63-64; chmn, Cmt. for the For. Policy Research Inst. of Univ. Pa; Rep. Task Force on For. Policy; chmn, Cmt. to End Aid to the Soviet Enemy. Degree of Grand Officer of the Order of Merit of the Repub. of Italy, 53; Grand Cross of the Noble Order of Charles III, highest Spanish Civilian Decoration, and Gold Medal of Madrid, 62; Order of Polonia Restituta, highest Civilian Decoration of Polish Govt-in-Exile, 6 . Legal Res: 129 Easton Rd, Westport, Conn. 06880. Mailing Add: American Embassy, Buenos Aires, Argentina.

LODWICK, SEELEY G. R
Iowa State Sen.
b. Evanston, Ill, 10/19/20; s. William G. Lodwick and Florence Seeley L; m. 1945 to Helen Barbre; c. Barbara, Margery and Helen. Educ: Iowa State Univ, 38. Polit. & Govt. Pos: Mem, Rep. Resolution State Cmt, Iowa, 60 & 68; chmn, Lee Co. Zoning Cmn; v.pres, Upper Miss. Flood Control Asn; past mem, Govt. Cmt. for Agr. Prod. Utilization; Iowa State Sen, currently, Pres Pro Tempore, Iowa State Senate, currently, mem. platform cmt, Iowa Republicans, 68. Bus. & Prof. Pos: Farm Mgr; secy-treas, Fox Farm Supply Corp. Mil. Serv: Marine Corps, World War II. Mem: Am. Soc. of Farm Mgrs. and Rural Appraisers; Iowa Asn. for Farm Mgrs. and Rural Appraisers: past v.pres, Agr. Ammonia Inst; Am. Soy Bean Asn.(v.pres); trustee, Iowa Wesleyan Col; Rotary (past pres); Masons; Am. Legion; C. of C. Rel: Presbyterian; Elder. Mailing Add: Box 208, Wever, Iowa 52658.

LOEB, HENRY, III
Mayor, Memphis, Tenn.
b. Memphis, Tenn, 12/9/20; s. William L. Loeb and Ethel L; m. 4/7/51 to Mary Letitia Gregg; c. Henry, Tom and Elizabeth. Educ: Phillip Andover Acad, grad, 39; Brown Univ, B.A, 43. Polit. & Govt. Pos: With Memphis Park Cmn, Tenn, 50-56; cmnr. pub. works, Memphis, 56-60, mayor, currently. Bus. & Prof. Pos: Commentator, WHBQ-TV; pres, Loeb's Laundry-Cleaner, 63-66. Mil. Serv: Naval Res, World War II. Mem: Am. Legion (past comdr); Delta Kappa Epsilon. Recipient, Pub. Personnel Award, President Kennedy, 63. Mailing Add: 365 Colonial Rd, Memphis, Tenn. 38117.

LOEB, JOHN LANGELOTH, JR. R
Mem, New York Co. Rep. Finance Cmt, N.Y.
b. N.Y.C, 5/2/30; s. John Langeloth Loeb and Frances Lehman L; single; c. Alexandra. Educ: Harvard Col, B.A. cum laude, 52, Harvard Bus. Sch, M.A, 54. Polit. & Govt. Pos: Mem, Various Cmts. during elections of Louis Lefkowitz, Paul Fino, John Gilhooley, John Lindsay, Jacob Javits, Kenneth Keating and Nelson Rockefeller; alternate del, Rep. Nat. Conv, 64; chmn, Citizens Cmt. for a Greater N.Y.C, 65; hon. finance chmn, Cong. Campaign of Theodore Kupferman, 66; mem. adv. coun, Joint Legis. Cmt. on Matrimonial and Family Laws, N.Y, 66; trustee and mem. exec. cmt, Rep. Citizens Cmt. of the U.S; spec. asst. to Gov. Nelson A. Rockefeller for air pollution; mem, New York Co. Rep. Finance Cmt, N.Y, currently. Bus. & Prof. Pos: Mem, mgt. cmt, various positions, Loeb, Rhoades & Co, 55-59, partner, 59-; chmn. of bd. and mem. exec. cmt, Holly Sugar Corp, Colorado Springs, Colo; dir, Int. Housing Capital Corp, N.Y.C, Am. Star Ins. Co, San Francisco and Denver & Rio Grande West. R.R. Co, Denver; dir. and mem. finance cmt, Metro-Goldwyn-Mayer Inc, N.Y.C; dir, Societe Financiere pour les Industries du Tourisme, Paris, France; mem, N.Y. Cocoa Exchange, N.Y. Cotton Exchange and Phila-Baltimore-Wash, D.C. Stock Exchange; dir, Vis. Nurse Serv, N.Y; mem, Int. Coun, Mus. Modern Art; trustee, Mus. of N.Y.C, mem, fine arts vis. cmt, Bd. Overseers, Harvard; trustee, Montefiore Hosp. and Med. Sch; bd. of dirs, Int. Rescue Cmt, Am. Field Serv. Mil. Serv: Entered as 2nd Lt, Air Force, 54, released as 1st Lt, 56. Mem: N.Y.C. C. of C; France-Am. Soc; SAR; Pilgrims of U.S; City Midday, Recess, Harvard (N.Y.C) and St. James, London, Eng) Clubs; Century Country Club (White Plains, N.Y.); N.Y. Young Rep. Club. Rel: Jewish. Legal Res: 237 E. 61st St, New York, N.Y. 10021. Mailing Add: 42 Wall St, New York, N.Y. 10005.

LOEN, VERNON CARROLL R
b. Howard, S.Dak, 10/18/31; s. Lauris Loen and Selina Edith Langorgen L; m. to Raemalee J. Anderson; c. Douglas Todd, Vance Stephen and Jeffrey Scott. Educ: S.Dak. State Col, B.S, 53. Polit. & Govt. Pos: Asst. to U.S. Sen. Case, 58-61; admin. asst. to U.S. Rep. Reifel, S.Dak, 62-68, U.S. Rep. Quie, Minn, 68- Bus. & Prof. Pos: Writer, Sioux Falls Argus-Leader, 54-58. Mem: Past pres. and past v.pres, S.Dak. State Soc. of Wash; Cong. Secretaries Club. Rel: Lutheran. Legal Res: Sioux Falls, S.Dak. Mailing Add: 5201 Bangor Dr, Kensington, Md. 20795. (1967)

LOESCH, HARRISON R
Asst. Secy. for Pub. Land Mgt, Dept. of the Interior
m. to Louise Mills; c. Jeffrey. Educ: Colo. Col, B.A; Yale Univ, LL.B; Denver Univ. Law Sch. Polit. & Govt. Pos: Former consult, Bur. of Land Mgt, Nat. Park Serv, Bur. of Reclamation and Geol. Surv, Dept. of the Interior, Asst. Secy. for Pub. Land Mgt, 69- Bus. & Prof. Pos: Attorney-at-law, Loesch, Kreidler and Durham, Montrose, Colo, 61- Mil. Serv: Entered Army, released as Maj, 45, after serv. in ETO. Mem: Past pres, Colo. Bar Asn. Mailing Add: Dept. of the Interior, C St. between 18th & 19th St. N.W, Washington, D.C. 20240.

LOESER, ANNETTE BAKER D
Dem. Nat. Committeewoman, Fla.
b. N.Y.C, 11/30/23; m. to Bernhardt Loeser; c. Robert Warren Baker II. Educ: Hunter Col; Principia Col; Univ. South. Calif. Polit. & Govt. Pos: Del, Dem. Nat. Conv, 64 & 68; Dem. Nat. Committeewoman, Fla, 64- Bus. & Prof. Pos: Secy-treas, Precision Tool Inc; dir, Koscot Inter-planetary, Inc, currently. Mem: Clearwater Women's Club; Fine Arts Soc; Bus. & Prfnl. Women's Club; Dem. Women's Club; Dem. Women's Club of Fla.(pres, 62); Carlouel Yacht Club; Am. Legion Auxiliary; VFW Auxiliary; Lions Auxiliary; YWCA; Girl Scouts; PTA; League of Women Voters; Nat. Soc. of Arts & Letters; Nat. Fedn. of Women's Clubs. Mailing Add: 1001 Eldorado Dr, Clearwater, Fla. 33515.
Mem: Fed, Am, D.C, Minn. and Hennepin Co. Bar Asns; Am. Judicature Soc; Am. Asn. for the Adv. of Sci; Am. Acad. of Polit. and Soc. Sci. Outstanding Achievement Award of the Regents of Univ. of Minn, 68. Rel: Unitarian. Mailing Add: 5669 Bent Branch Rd, Washington, D.C. 20016.

LOEVINGER, LEE D
b. St. Paul, Minn, 4/24/13; s. Gustavus Loevinger and Millie Strouse L; m. 3/4/50 to Ruth E. Howe; c. Barbara Lee, Eric Howe and Peter Howe. Educ: Univ. Minn, B.A. summa cum laude, 33, Sch. Law, LL.B, 36; Phi Beta Kappa; Sigma Xi; Delta Sigma Rho; Sigma Delta Chi; Phi Delta Gamma; Tau Kappa Alpha; Alpha Epsilon Rho. Polit. & Govt. Pos: Regional attorney and attorney, Nat. Labor Rels. Bd, 37-41; attorney, Antitrust Div, Dept. of Justice, 41-46; spec. counsel, U.S. Senate Small Bus, Cmt, 51-52; chmn, Minn. Atomic Develop. Probs. Cmt, 57-59; assoc. justice, Supreme Court of Minn, 60-61; asst. attorney gen. in charge of Antitrust Div, Dept. of Justice, 61-63; cmnr, Fed. Commun. Cmn, 63-68. Bus. & Prof. Pos: Partner in law firm, Larson, Loevinger, Lindquist, Freeman & Fraser, Minneapolis, Minn, 46-60; counsel, Hogan & Hartson, Wash, D.C, 68-; v.pres, Craig-Hallum, Inc, Minneapolis, 68-; chmn. of bd, Atoka, Inc, Olney, Tex, 68- Mil. Serv: Entered as Lt.(jg), Navy, 42, released as Lt. Comdr, 46, after serv. in Amphibious Force, N.Y. Port Dir. Off. and U.S. Naval Transportation Corps, ETO and Am. Theater; Lt. Comdr.(Ret), Naval Res; ETO Ribbon with 1 Battle Star; Am. Theater Ribbon; Victory Ribbon. Publ: The Law of Free Enterprise, Funk & Wagnalls, 49; 'An Introduction to Legal Logic,' Ind. Law J, 52; 'Regulation and Competition as Alternatives,' Antitrust Bul, 65; plus more than 75 other articles.

LOFASO, GERALD FRANCIS D
La. State Rep.
b. Houma, La, 9/4/31; s. Frank J. Lofaso and Hilda Dumez L; m. 12/28/57 to Dolores Greely; c. Lee Patrick, Mary Pamela, Michael Francis, John Andrew and Matthew Thomas. Educ: F.T. Nicholls Jr. Col, Thibodaux, La, 48-50; La. State Univ, B.S. and LL.B, 54; Theta Xi. Polit. & Govt. Pos: Asst. dist. attorney, 17th Judicial Dist, La, 61-63; La. State Rep, Ninth Dist, Terrebonne Parish, 68- Mil. Serv: Entered as Pvt, Army, 54, released as Cpl, 56, after serv. in Army Audit Agency, European Theatre. Mem: Terrebonne, La. and Am. Bar Asns; K. of C. Rel: Catholic. Mailing Add: 504 Funderburk Ave, Houma, La. 70360.

LOFTUS, JOSEPH ANTHONY R
Spec. Asst. to the Secy. of Labor for Commun.
b. Scranton, Pa, 6/1/07; s. George J. Loftus and Bridget Duffy L; m. 7/13/56 to Mary Frances Schoeps Mann; c. JoAnne (Mrs. Thomas O. Young) and Marianne (Mrs. John B. Cumming). Educ: Scranton Univ, A.B, 28; Columbia Univ, M.S, 31; Harvard Univ, Stark Fel, 60-61. Polit. & Govt. Pos: Spec. asst. to the Secy. of Labor for Commun, Dept. of Labor, 69- Bus. & Prof. Pos: Correspondent, N.Y. Times, Wash, D.C, 44-69. Mem: Fed. City Club; Nat. Press Club. Rel: Unitarian. Mailing Add: 3327 Legation St. N.W, Washington, D.C. 20015.

LOGAN, BARD A. American Party
State Chmn, American Party of Tex.
b. Hancock Co, Ind, 4/4/12; s. Ralph Gates Logan and Carrie Lucille Jackson L; m. 5/24/36 to Mary Ann Miller; c. John Frederick, B. Arnold and Andrew Brandt. Educ: Ind. Univ, A.B, 35; Phi Beta Pi; Kappa Delta Rho. Polit. & Govt. Pos: Co-founder, Constitution Party, 50, state chmn, 60-62; cand. for U.S. Senate, Constitution Party, 58 & 60; state chmn, Conservative Party of Tex, 63-68; state chmn, American Party of Tex, 68- Bus. & Prof. Pos: Bacteriologist, Eli Lilly & Co, 35-40; sales rep, Winthrop Chem. Co, 40-49; owner and mgr, The Criss Cross Serv, 49- Mil. Serv: Entered as 1st Lt, Army, 42, released as Capt, 46, after serv. in Med. Corps, 35th Gen. Hosp, 33rd Gen. Hosp, Hq. Camp Swift, Tex. and 193rd Gen. Hosp, ETO, 44-45; ETO Ribbon with 1 Battle Star; Am. Defense Medal. Mem: VFW; Am. Legion; DAV; SAR. Rel: Protestant. Mailing Add: 4519 Rimrock, San Antonio, Tex. 78228.

LOGAN, BENJAMIN CICERO, SR. R
b. Ellijay, Ga, 8/10/89; s. John A. Logan and Rebecca Bramlett L; m. 12/02/06 to Nola Dover; c. Charlie, Ernest H, Leola (Mrs. Tankersley), Louise (Mrs. Holt), B.C. Jr, Clay, Bessie (Mrs. Ravan), Frankie (Mrs. Garland). Educ: Attended Gilmer Co. Schs. Polit. & Govt. Pos: Ga. State Rep, 63-66; mayor, City of Ellijay; co. cmnr. of Rds. and Rev, 47-58. Bus. & Prof. Pos: Retired merchant. Rel: Baptist. Mailing Add: Ellijay, Ga. 30540. (1967)

LOGAN, CECILIA M. D
Single. Polit. & Govt. Pos: Ind. State Rep, -66; former secy, Ind. State Dem. Women; v.pres, JFK 10th Ward Dem. Club; Ward v.chmn, mbs; Marion Co. Dem. Womens Club; State Fedn. Dem.Women. Bus. & Prof. Pos: Acct; former secy. Mem: Civic Theatre; Riley Toastmistress Club. Rel: Catholic. Mailing Add: 1616 Sturm Ave, Indianapolis, Ind. 46201. (1967)

LOGAN, FRANCES D. D
b. Chicago, Ill, 12/24/99; d. William F. Dummer and Ethel S. D; m. 8/4/30 to S. Rae Logan; c. Francis Dummer, Katharine (Mrs. Herbert Tugendhat). Educ: Univ. Wis, B.A, 21; N.Y. Sch. Soc. Work, M.S.W, 26. Polit. & Govt. Pos: Co-dir, Chicago Civil Defense and Coun. Agencies Vol. Off, 42-43; Dem. Cong. Committeewoman, First Dist, Mont, 56-58; Dem. Nat. Committee-woman, Mont, 60-67. Bus. & Prof. Pos: Teacher, 21-24; psychiat. soc. worker, 25-26; dir, dept. educ. counsel, Winnetka Pub. Sch, 26-30. Mem: Co-founder and exec. secy, Cmt. for Paradise Dam. Mailing Add: Charlo, Mont. 59824.

LOGAN, IRENE ELIZABETH R
Mem. Exec. Cmt, Rep. State Cent. Cmt, Mich.
b. Granite City, Ill, 10/31/12; d. Harry Cole Rae and Jennie Hutton R; m. 8/15/52 to Kenneth John Logan. Educ: Bus. sch. in St. Louis, Mo. Polit. & Govt. Pos: Mem. Exec. Cmt, Rep. State Cent. Cmt, Mich, 64-; del, Rep. Nat. Conv, 68. Bus. & Prof. Pos: Legal secy, Logan & Huchla, 47- Mem: River Rouge Womens Club; v.pres, Bus. & Prfnl. Womens Club. Rel: Presbyterian. Mailing Add: 74 Chestnut, River Rouge, Mich. 48218. (1967)

LOGAN, JAMES DUVAL R
b. Paris, France, 4/27/20; s. Frank Berryman Logan and Germaine Duval L; m. 4/10/47 to Mary Quinn Cobb; c. Moira J, Angela G, J. Patrick and Kate T. Educ: Kenyon Col, A.B, 42; Harvard Law Sch, 46-47; Delta Tau Delta. Polit. & Govt. Pos: Exec. asst. to U.S. Rep. Edward G. Biester, Jr, Eighth Dist, Pa, 67; alternate del, Rep. Nat. Conv, 68; dep. exec. dir, Gen. State Authority of Pa, 68, exec. dir, 69- Bus. & Prof. Pos: Prod. mgr, Time, Inc, 47-52; v.pres, Pittsburgh Conduit Co, 52-63; pres, Robroy, Inc, 63-67. Mil. Serv: Entered as Ens, Naval Res, 42, released as Lt.(sg), 46, after serv. in Destroyer, Pac. Theatre, 43-46; Bronze Star Medal. Mem: Metrop. Club N.Y; Capitol Hill Club Wash, D.C. Rel: Roman Catholic. Legal Res: 1207 Evergreen Rd, Morrisville, Pa. 19067. Mailing Add: c/o General State Authority, 18th and Herr Sts, Harrisburg, Pa. 17120.

LOGEMANN, KENNETH LAVERN R
Chmn, Worth Co. Rep. Cent. Cmt, Iowa
b. Albert Lea, Minn, 7/11/37; s. J. Barney Logemann and Martha Aurdal L; m. 5/26/62 to Rebecca Lynn Buenneke; c. Rhonda Lamar and Renae Lynette. Educ: Iowa State Univ, 2 years; Friley Hall. Polit. & Govt. Pos: Chmn, Worth Co. Young Rep, Iowa, 62; chmn, Worth Co. Rep. Cent. Cmt, 66-; adv, Northwood-Kensett TAR, 67- Bus. & Prof. Pos: Farmer, 60; salesman, Trojan Seed Co, 67; pres, Worth Co. Farm Bur, 69. Mil. Serv: Cpl, Army, 58-60; Spec. Presidential Security Unit, 58-60; Good Conduct Medal; White House Serv. Cert. Mem: Iowa Farm Bur; Albert Lea, Minn. Saddle Club; Northwood Jr. C. of C; Agr. Study Cmt, N. Iowa Area Develop-Nine Co, 67-; state resolutions cmt, Iowa State Farm Bur, 69-; Pork Producers Asn; Am. Soybean Asn; Soil Conserv. Serv. 4-H Meritorious Serv. Award. Rel: Lutheran. Mailing Add: R.R. 2, Northwood, Iowa 50459.

LOGGINS, JOSEPH E. D
b. Trion, Ga, 9/17/28; s. James Wheeler Loggins and Addie Williams L; m. 4/10/65 to Helen Joyce Howell. Educ: Univ. Ga, 47-50; Woodrow Wilson Col. Law, LL.B. and LL.M; pres, Sr. Class; Beta Club. Polit. & Govt. Pos: Ga. State Sen, 63-66; Ga. State Rep, 59-62; Del, Dem. Nat. Conv, 66 and 60; dir, Civil Defense, Chattooga Co, 58-59. Bus. & Prof. Pos: Pres, Lookout Mt. Bar Asn, 66. Mem: F&AM; Elks; People to People Orgn. Rel: Baptist. Legal Res: Apple Blossom Lane, Summerville, Ga. 30747. Mailing Add: W. Washington St, Summerville, Ga. 30747. (1967)

LOGUE, DANIELS CHARLES R
Co-Chmn, Yolo Co. Rep. Cent. Cmt, Calif.
b. Clairton, Pa, 9/15/23; s. Lester B. Logue and Bertha Farrell L; m. 4/23/48 to Kate Carrington Connor; c. Kate Connor, Susan Farrell and Daniels Russell. Educ: Univ. N.C, B.S. in Geol, 50; Sigma Nu. Polit. & Govt. Pos: Rep. precinct chmn; co-chmn, Rep. Cmt. for Goldwater, 64; del, Rep. Nat. Conv, 64; co-chmn, Yolo Co. Rep. Cent. Cmt, Calif, 65- Bus. & Prof. Pos: Owner, Dan Logue Assocs, Realtor and Ins. Broker. Mil. Serv: Entered as Pvt, Army, 43, released as Pfc, 46, after serv. in European and S.Pac. Theaters, 44-45; Battle Stars. Mem: Nat. Real Estate Asn; Nat. Ins. Agent Asn; Elks; Odd Fellows; Am. Legion; YMCA. Football player for the Univ. N.C, 46-49, participant in Sugar Bowl Games, 47 and 50 and Cotton Bowl Game, 49. Rel: Episcopal. Mailing Add: Route 2, Box 605, Woodland, Calif. 95695.

LOHR, CHARLES E. D
W.Va. State Del.
b. Moundsville, W.Va, 4/30/16; s. Charles Lohr and Florence Guthrie L; m. 7/19/39 to Mary Elizabeth Crumpecker; c. Charles E, II and Mary Elizabeth. Educ: W.Va, B.A, Bus. Admin. Polit. & Govt. Pos: W.Va. State Del, 60- Bus. & Prof. Pos: Drug store owner. Mem: Elks; Moose; Red Men; Mercer Angler Club; Triangle Club; Mercer Coon Hunters Club; Gideons; and Kiwanis. Rel: Methodist. Mailing Add: Route 1, Princeton, W.Va. 24740. (1967)

LOHREY, CARL N. R
Mem. Exec. Cmt, Montgomery Co. Rep. Party, Ohio
b. Dayton, Ohio, 7/2/13; s. Louis W. Lohrey and Elisabeth Stauffer L; m. 12/28/40 to Betty Stafford; c. Robert S. and Barbara L. (Mrs. David C. Banker). Educ: Univ. Cincinnati, Com. Eng, 41; Pi Kappa Alpha. Polit. & Govt. Pos: Mem. exec. cmt, Montgomery Co. Rep. Party, Ohio, 60-, Harrison Twp. committeeman, 68-; alternate del, Rep. Nat. Conv, 68. Bus. & Prof. Pos: Registered prfnl. engr, Ohio. Mem: Dayton Soc. Prfnl. Engrs.(pres, 50); trustee, Ohio Soc. Prfnl. Engrs, 51-54; trustee. bd. gov, Engr. Club Dayton, 68-69; Am. Soc. Metals; Montgomery Co. Rep. Men's Club; Harrison Twp. Rep. Club; mem. all Dayton Cmt, Lions Club of Dayton; YMCA. Rel: Congregational. Mailing Add: 23 Deshler Place, Dayton, Ohio 45405.

LOHREY, MARYANN (MRS. FRED H.) R
Campaign Coordinator, Dutchess Co. Rep. Cmt, N.Y.
b. Scranton, Pa, 10/14/32; d. James Paul Morrissey and Hildegarde Margaret Barnes M; 2nd m. 9/29/62 to Fred H. Lohrey; c. Pamela Anne Johnstone, Sarah Margaret Johnstone and Eric Christian. Educ: Indiana Univ, Bloomington, 1 year; Univ. of Buffalo, B.S, 55; Sigma Kappa. Polit. & Govt. Pos: Coun. mem, N.Y. State Fedn. of Women's Rep. Clubs, 65-; campaign coordinator, Dutchess Co. Rep. Cmt, 65-; personal rep, Congressman Hamilton Fish, Jr. and mem. strategy cmt. to elect Ham Fish to Congr; charter mem, Dutchess Co. Mosquito Control Cmt, 66-; first pres, Dutchess Co. Fedn. of Women's Rep. Clubs, 68-; mem, Dutchess Co. Rep. Exec. Cmt, currently. Mem: Mem, bd. dirs, Hudson Valley Philharmonic Soc; mem, Poughkeepsie Tennis Club; mem, Poughkeepsie Women's Rep. Club. Rel: Catholic. Mailing Add: 46 Skyview Dr, Poughkeepsie, N.Y. 12603.

LOISELLE, ANDREW J. D
R.I. State Sen.
b. Pawtucket, R.I, 7/29/22. Educ: E. High PS; Pawtucket PS. Polit. & Govt. Pos: R.I. State Sen, currently. Bus. & Prof. Pos: Owner, Loiselle Bakery. Mil. Serv: Sgt, Army, 3 years. Mem: Adv. cmt, Ment. Retardation; past pres, R.I. Bakers, Inc. Mailing Add: 37 Arland Dr, Pawtucket, R.I. 02860. (1967)

LOIZEAUX, M. SUZANNE R
Secy, N.H. Rep. State Cmt.
b. Boston, Mass, 9/3/05; s. J.J. Loizeaux and Margaret Sanderson L; single. Educ: Abbot Acad, Andover, Mass, 25-26; Simmons Col. Grad. Sch, 27. Polit. & Govt. Pos: N.H. State Rep, 49, 53, 55 & 59; N.H. State Sen, 51-52; v.chmn, N.H. Rep. State Cmt, 67-68, secy, 69- Bus. & Prof. Pos: Ed. and publisher, Plymouth Record, newspaper, 30-43; realtor, N.H. Colonials, 45- Mem: Lakes Region Bd. Realtors; N.H. State Bd. Realtors; Nat. Realtors Bd; State chmn, N.H. Heart Fund, 69; Asquamchumauke Chap, DAR; Pemigewasset Women's Club; N.H. Hist. Soc; Twin Valleys Women's Rep. Club; N.H. Heart Asn.(regional coun. Lakes Region Asn, dir). Rel: Congregational; Bd. Trustees. Mailing Add: Dave Gibson Farm, R.F.D. 2, Plymouth, N.H. 03264.

LOKEY, HAMILTON
b. Atlanta, Ga, 8/30/10; s. Hugh Montgomery Lokey and Rebecca Crawford Hamilton L; m. 7/18/44 to Muriel Ann Mattson; c. Hamilton, Jr, William Mattson, Fletcher, Ann Montgomery and Rebecca Hazel. Educ: Univ. Ga, A.B, 31, LL.B, 33; Phi Beta Kappa; Phi Kappa Phi; Phi Delta Phi; Sigma Alpha Epsilon; Sphinx and Gridiron Honor Socs. Polit. & Govt. Pos: Ga. State Rep, Fulton Co, 53-56; chmn, Fulton Co. Dem. Party, Ga, 64-65. Bus. & Prof. Pos: Practicing attorney, 33-; mem, Lokey and Bowden, 39- Mil. Serv: Entered as Lt.(jg), Naval Res, 42, released as Lt. Comdr, 45, after serv. in Pac. Theater; Comdr, Korean Conflict, 50-51; Comdr, Naval Res; Pac. Theater Medal with Seven Battle Stars; Am. Defense and Victory Medals; Presidential Unit Citation; Philippine Liberation Medal with Two Battle Stars; Philippine Repub. Presidential Unit Citation; Korean Conflict Ribbon. Mem: Mason; Am. Legion. Rel: Episcopal. Legal Res: 737 Woodward Way, Atlanta, Ga. 30327. Mailing Add: 2610 First National Bank Bldg, Atlanta, Ga. 30303.

LOKEY, LEONARD N. D
b. Thomson, Ga, 2/26/06; s. George W. Lokey and Julia Culpepper L; m. 10/01/35 to Martha Brown; c. Leonard Nunally, Jr, Martha Brown, Julia Kathryn (Mrs. Palmer), grandchildren: E.H. Palmer, III, Ben Malone Palmer, A.L. Pate, III, Leonard N. Lokey, III, Augustus Thorpe Lokey. Educ: Bingham Mil. Inst. Polit. & Govt. Pos: Ga. State Rep, 57-64, 47-50. Bus. & Prof. Pos: Wood Box & Lumber Mfg. Mem: Mason; Shriner; Kiwanis, Pres, 45-46; Lt. Gov, 8th Dist. Ga. Kiwanis, 47. Rel: Baptist. Mailing Add: Thomson, Ga. 30824. (1967)

LOLAS, ALEXANDER D
Mass. State Rep.
b. 1932; single. Educ: Monson Acad; Am. Int. Col, Springfield, Mass. Polit. & Govt. Pos: Redistricting chmn, Hampden Co, Mass, 63; former chmn, Monson Dem. Town Cmt; Mass. State Rep, currently. Mil. Serv: Korean conflict. Mem: Am. Legion; VFW. Mailing Add: Upper Palmer Rd, Monson, Mass. 01057. (1967)

LOLLEY, WILMER RAY D
Ala. State Sen.
b. Goodman, Ala, 10/16/24; s. Andrew B. Lolley and Flora B. Miller L; m. 5/21/44 to Florence Eugenia Lindsey; c. Jane Ray and Jennifer Jill. Educ: Coffee Co. Schs. Polit. & Govt. Pos: Mem, Enterprise City Coun, Ala; Ala. State Sen, 63- Bus. & Prof. Pos: Real estate, ins, construction. Mil. Serv: Army. Mem: Mason. Rel: Methodist. Mailing Add: 121 N. Main St, Enterprise, Ala, 36330.

LOMAS, ANNA COCHRANE R
b. Monroe, Iowa, 6/25/96; d. William Cochrane and Myrtle Murphy C; m. 12/27/17 to Malcolm DeWitt Lomas; c. Mary Josephine (Mrs. Bruce Van Druff), Louise (Mrs. James Bastron) and Margaret (Mrs. Jack Brandt). Educ: Univ. of Iowa, 14-16; Delta Gamma. Polit. & Govt. Pos: Mem, Iowa Rep. State Cmt, 44-52; mem, Rep. Nat. Cmt. for Iowa, 52-64; del, Rep. Nat. Conv, 52, 56, 60 & 64; mem. adv. cmt, White House Conf. on Aging; mem, Gov. Cmn. on Aging. Mem: Iowa Hist. Soc; PEO; Eastern Star. Rel: Methodist. Mailing Add: 805 Prospect St, Red Oak, Iowa 51566.

LOMAX, WILLIAM ALEXANDER D
Chmn, Grenada Co. Dem. Exec. Cmt, Miss.
b. Greenwood, Miss, 4/10/07; s. Clifton Lamar Lomax and Annie Fay Dubard L; m. 6/1/35 to Marguerite M. Swanson. Educ: Emory Univ, 23-25; Univ. Miss, LL.B, 28, B.A, 29; Phi Delta Phi; Sigma Upsilon; Delta Psi; Moaks. Polit. & Govt. Pos: Mem. and chmn, various Off. Price Admin. orgns, World War II; mem. and chmn, Grenada Co. Draft Bd, Miss, $17\frac{1}{2}$ years; mem. and ticket cmnr, Grenada Co. Elec. Cmn, 43-56 & 60-; chmn, Grenada Co. Dem. Exec. Cmt, 45- Mem: Ill. and Miss. Bar Asns. Rel: Methodist. Mailing Add: 861 Line St, Grenada, Miss. 38901. (1967)

LOMBARD, JAMES A. D
b. Ft. Plain, N.Y, 3/4/22; m. to Marfisa; c. five. Educ: U.S. Merchant Marine Acad; Russell Sage Col. Polit. & Govt. Pos: N.Y. State Assemblyman, 64-67; former alderman, city of Troy. Bus. & Prof. Pos: Automobile dealer. Mil. Serv: Merchant Marine; U.S. Naval Res. Mem: Troy Lodge of Elks; Emerald Club; St. Paul's Holy Name Soc; Am. Rifle Asn; dir, Campfire Girls. Mailing Add: 2263 Burdett Ave, Troy, N.Y. 12180. (1967)

LOMBARD, JAMES MANUEL R
b. London, Eng, 6/11/38; s. Laurence Manuel Lombard and Cornelia McLanahan Curtis L; m. Jan. 1970 to Susan Sweet. Educ: Colo. Col, 57-58; Har-

vard Col, A.B, 61; Varsity Club. Polit. & Govt. Pos: Campaign asst, Re-elec. of U.S. Sen. Leverett Saltonstall, Mass, 60; campaign dir, Coun. for Constitutional Reform, 63; asst. campaign mgr, Re-elec. of Attorney Gen. Edward Brooke, 64; del, Mass. Rep. Conv, 64, mem. platform cmt, 66; admin. and legal asst. to Mass. Dept. of Attorney Gen, 64-66; mem, Town Meeting, Dedham, 64-, mem, recreation cmn, 68-; secy-treas, Boston Arena Authority, 65-; campaign mgr, J. Buckley for State Auditor Cmt, 66; del-at-lg, Mass. Rep. Issues Conv, 67; cand. for Norfolk Co. Cmnr, 68. Bus. & Prof. Pos: Asst. gen. alumni secy, Harvard Univ, 67-69; asst. dir. admissions, Harvard Col, 69- Mil. Serv: Pvt, Army Res, 62, currently 1st Lt. Mem: Bd. dir, Boston Coun. for Int. Visitors; corp. mem, Dynamic Action Residence Enterprise, Boston; Am. Legion. Rel: Protestant. Legal Res: Westfield St, Dedham, Mass. 02026. Mailing Add: Westfield St, Needham, Mass. 02192.

LOMBARDI, ANGELA FUNAI R
Mem, Calif. Rep. State Cent. Cmt.
b. Barga, Tuscany, Italy, 3/20/98; d. Alessandro Funai and Maria Cocchini F; m. 6/21/24 to Louis Lombardi; c. Marta (Mrs. Lawson M. Brown), Sandra (Mrs. Frederick Farrell), Nalda (Mrs. Charles J. Staff, Jr.), Louis Lombardi, Jr. and Adria (Mrs. Don Tresca). Educ: Boston Univ, A.B, 20, A.M, 22; Harvard, 23; Gamma Phi Beta. Polit. & Govt. Pos: Mem, Calif. Rep. Women's Fedn, 40-, Los Angeles Co. Pres, 58-60, state v.pres, 63-66, state pres, 68-69; mem, Calif. Rep. State Cent. Cmt, 48-; assembly-precinct dir, Rep. Party, Calif, 50-54; del, Rep. Nat. Conv, 68. Bus. & Prof. Pos: Teacher, Mass. & Calif. Mem: Am. Asn. Univ. Women; Women's Civic League of Glendale; Glendale Symphony Bd; Glendale Beautiful. Los Angeles Rep. Assocs. Serv. Award; Press Woman of the Year, Glendale News, 68; Commendation from City of Pomona. Rel: Congregational. Mailing Add: 1945 W. Mountain St, Glendale, Calif. 91201.

LOMBARDI, TARKY JAMES, JR. R
N.Y. State Sen.
b. Syracuse, N.Y, 9/2/29; s. Tarky Lombardi and Jenny Cerio L; m. 9/20/58 to Marianne Edgcomb; c. Tarky, III, Jennine, Marianne and Michael. Educ: Syracuse Univ, B.S, 51; Syracuse Univ. Col. of Law, LL.B, 54. Polit. & Govt. Pos: Rep. dist. councilman, Syracuse, N.Y, 60-63, councilman-at-lg, 64-65; N.Y. State Sen, Onondaga-Madison Co, 66, 46th Dist, Onondaga-Cortland Co, 67- Mil. Serv: Entered as Pvt, Army, 55, released as SP-3 (T), 57, after serv. in Battery C, 505 AA Missile Bn. Mem: Am, N.Y. State and Onondaga Co. Bar Asns. N.Y. State Jr. C. of C. Distinguished Serv. Award, 60. Rel: Catholic. Legal Res: 99 Burlingame Rd, Syracuse, N.Y. 13203. Mailing Add: 723 Hiawatha Blvd, W, Syracuse, N.Y. 13201.

LOMEN, MARY ELIZABETH R
Secy, Alaska Rep. State Cent. Cmt.
b. Seattle, Wash, 7/20/19; d. Elmer G. Shipman and Elizabeth Kirkham S; m. 5/9/42 to Alfred J. Lomen; c. Gilbert J, Julie Ann and James W. Educ: Stephens Col, 37-38; Univ. Wash, B.A, 41, 43-44; Pi Beta Phi. Polit. & Govt. Pos: Pres, Fairbanks Rep. Women's Club, Alaska, 59; mem. and chmn, Cent. Dist. Rep. Cmt, 60-66; secy, Alaska Rep. State Cent. Cmt, 66- Mem: Girl Scouts Bd; Garden Clubs; exec. bd, United Good Neighbors (drive chmn, 57); cmnr, West. Interstate Cmt. for Higher Educ. Rel: Protestant. Mailing Add: 202 Slater Dr, Fairbanks, Alaska 99701.

LOMENZO, JOHN P. R
N.Y. Secy. of State
b. Rochester, N.Y; m. to Dorothy Hampson; c. Jacqueline Ann, John Jr, Nancy Jane, Daniel W. and Susan Marie. Educ: Niagara Univ; Univ. of Fordham Sch. of Law, LL.B, 39; Univ. of Michigan. Hon. LL.D, Union Col, 65. Polit. & Govt. Pos: City court judge, Rochester, N.Y, 55-61; judge and chief judge, Monroe Co. Court, 61-63; Secy. of State, N.Y, 63-; del, Rep. Nat. Conv, 68. Bus. & Prof. Pos: Trial attorney; former mem. faculty, Am. Inst. of Banking, Niagara Univ. and Rochester Inst. Tech; mem. law faculty, St. John Fisher Col, on leave. Mil. Serv: Entered as Pvt, Army, commissioned 1st Lt, 43, released 45, after serv. in Judge Adv. Gen. Dept, Army Judge; Citation from Commanding Gen. of Army Serv. Force. Mem: Bd, former counsel, CYO; trustee, Holy Angels Home; N.Y. State Asn. for Retarded Children; adv, Boy Scouts; past v.pres, Rochester Bar Asn; N.Y. State Bar Asn; Am. Fedn. of Bar Asns; Am. Judicature Soc; Judge Adv. Gen. Dept. Asn; dir, Park Ave. Hosp, Rochester; bd. Salvation Army; former bd. mem, Coun. of Soc. Agencies; Prfnl. Men's Club; Businessmen's Asn; C. of C; Am. Legion; Am. Turnverein; Rochester Club; Elks; K. of C; Moose; hon. mem, Rochester Firefighters' Benevolent Asn; N.Y. State Firefighters' Asn; Locust Club; Rosewood Club of Rochester Police Dept. Monroe Co. Citizen of the Year Award, Citizens Club of Rochester, 61. Rel: Our Lady of Lourdes Church. Mailing Add: 1889 Highland Ave, Rochester, N.Y. 14618. (1967)

LONABAUGH, E. E. R
Wyo. State Rep.
b. San Diego, Calif, 2/24/23; s. Alger W. Lonabaugh and Marion Bailey L; div; m. 12/20/67 to Jean Nelson; c. William Marr, Ellsworth E, Carol W. and Jason A. Educ: Univ. Colo, 41-43, 45-47, 48-50 and J.D, 50; Univ. Wyo, 47-48; Sigma Chi; Phi Delta Phi; Potter Law Club. Polit. & Govt. Pos: Wyo. State Rep, 55-57 & 67-; city attorney, Sheridan, Wyo, 57; cmnr, Nat. Conf. Cmnrs. on Uniform Laws, 63-; chmn, Sheridan Co. Rep. Cent. Cmt, 65-67. Mil. Serv: Entered as Pvt, Army, 42, released as S/Sgt, 45, after serv. in 104th Inf. Regt, ETO, 44-45; Bronze Star; France and Rhineland Campaign Ribbons. Mem: Am. Bar Asn; Judiciary Bar Asn.(secy, Real Property Probate and Trust Law); State Bars of Tex. and Wyo; Sheridan Co. Bar (pres, 61-62); Elks; Mason; Scottish Rite; Shrine; K.T; DAV; C. of C; Rotary; Am. Legion; Jr. C. of C;(v.pres, Sheridan Co. Chap, 54, pres, 55). Rel: Episcopal. Legal Res: 854 Lewis St, Sheridan, Wyo. 82801. Mailing Add: P.O. Box 685, Sheridan, Wyo. 82801.

LONDERHOLM, ROBERT CARL R
b. Kansas City, Mo, 7/5/31; s. Carl Walter Londerholm and Ruth M. Jones L; m. 4/5/53 to Beverly Blakesley; c. Robert Carl, David Blakesley, Stephen Frank and Katherine Alice. Educ: Univ. of Kans, B.A, 53, LL.B, 55; Sigma Phi Epsilon; Phi Delta Phi. Polit. & Govt. Pos: Asst. Attorney Gen, Kans, 57-61, Attorney Gen, 65-69; gen. counsel, Kans. Dept. of Revenue, 61-63; admin. asst. to the Gov, 63-64. Bus. & Prof. Pos: Assoc, Blackmar, Swanson, Midgeley, Jones & Eager, Kans. City, Mo, 55-57. Mil. Serv: Maj, Air Force. Mem: Am. and Kans. Bar Asns. Mailing Add: Box 2, Olathe, Kans. 66061.

LONDON, MAYLON KERMIT D
Ga. State Sen.
b. Cornelia, Ga, 11/16/39; s. Thomas Leonard London and Viola Barrett L; m. 6/17/67 to Bobbie Jo Berrong; c. Lea Lange. Educ: Univ. Ga, B.S.A.E. & LL.B, 57-63; Blue Key; Gridiron Soc; Demosthenian Lit. Soc; Student Coun; Campus Leader, 61-62; X-Club. Polit. & Govt. Pos: Ga. State Sen, 50th Dist, 67-; Gov. Hon. Staff, Ga, 67- Bus. & Prof. Pos: City attorney, Helen, Ga, 66-; city attorney, Cleveland, 66-; attorney for White Co. Bd. Educ, 67-69; co. attorney, White Co, 68-69. Mil. Serv: Entered as E-2, Army, 63, released as E-6, 68, after serv. in Third Army; Most Outstanding Soldier, Ft. Knox, Ky. for period of June through Aug, 63. Mem: State Bar of Ga; Northeast. Bar Asn; Mason; Kiwanis; Am. Legion; Farm Bur; Upper Chattahoochee Soil and Water Conserv. Dist; Elks; C. of C.(pres, White Co. C. of C, 67). Rel: Baptist. Legal Res: Underwood St, Cleveland, Ga. 30528. Mailing Add: Box 325, Cleveland, Ga. 30528.

LONDRIGAN, JAMES T. D
Ill. State Rep.
b. Springfield, Ill, 2/23/25; s. James Edward Londrigan and Sophia Albright L; m. 4/22/50 to Marilyn Jeanne Brust; c. Linda, Janet, Timothy, Lisa and Mary Jeanne. Educ: Univ. Ill, 43, 45-47; Kent Col. Law, J.D, 49. Polit. & Govt. Pos: Hearing officer, State Ill, 50-53; pres, Young Dem. Ill, 60-62, nat. committeeman, 63-65; city attorney, Springfield, 61-63; technical legal advisor, State of Ill, 63-69; Ill. State Rep, 69- Mil. Serv: Entered as Pvt, Army, 43, released as Pfc, 45, after serv. in 75th Inf. Div, ETO, 44-45; Two Purple Hearts. Mem: Ill. State and Sangamon Co. Bar Asns; DAV; K. of C; VFW; Am. Legion; Am. Bus. Club; Aid to Retarded Children; Ill. Pub. Health Asn. Rel: Catholic. Mailing Add: 2019 Briarcliff, Springfield, Ill. 62704.

LONG, BETTY JANE D
Miss. State Rep.
b. Electric Mills, Miss, 5/5/28; single. Polit. & Govt. Pos: Miss. State Rep, 56- Bus. & Prof. Pos: Lawyer. Mem: Am. Asn. Univ. Women; Miss. Farm Bur; Pilot Club; Bus. & Prfnl. Womens Club; Salvation Army Bd; Cerebral Palsy Bd. Rel: Presbyterian. Mailing Add: 2219 49th Ave, Meridian, Miss. 39301. (1967)

LONG, BLANCHE R. D
Dem. Nat. Committeewoman, La.
b. Covington, La, 12/17/04; d. Robert Harrison Revere and Beulah Talley R; m. 8/17/32 to Gov. Earl Kemp Long (deceased). Educ: Tulane Univ. Polit. & Govt. Pos: Dem. Nat. Committeewoman, La, 60-; del, Dem. Nat. Conv, 68. Bus. & Prof. Pos: Mem, La. Tax Cmn, 64- Mem: V.pres. bd, La. Arts and Sci. Centre; Ment. Health Cmn. Rel: Methodist. Mailing Add: 7449 Boyce Dr, Baton Rouge, La. 70809.

LONG, CAROL D. R
b. Preble Co, Ohio, 9/16/15; s. William Henry Long and India Rice L; m. Oct, 1937 to Beryl Mollard; c. Don C. and Robert A. Educ: Ohio State Univ, B.S, 37. Polit. & Govt. Pos: Ohio State Rep, 55-67; asst. auditor, Ohio, 67-68, dep. auditor, 68- Bus. & Prof. Pos: Pub. sch. teacher, Ohio, 37-44; owner and operator, Long's Music Store, 48- Mil. Serv: Entered as Pvt, Army, 44, released as 1st Lt, 46, after serv. in 350th Inf, Italy; Capt.(Ret), Army Res. Mem: Mason; Lions; Am. Legion; Farm Bur. Rel: Methodist. Legal Res: 336 Lafayette Ave, Urbana, Ohio 43078. Mailing Add: 237 N. Main St, Urbana, Ohio 43078.

LONG, CAROLE ANN. See BEAUCHAMP, CAROLE ANN.

LONG, CLARENCE DICKINSON, JR. D
U.S. Rep, Md.
b. South Bend, Ind, 12/11/08; s. Clarence Dickinson Long and Gertrude Cooper L; m. 12/20/37 to Susanna E. Larter; c. Clarence D, III and Susanna Elizabeth (Mrs. Philip Moore). Educ: Wash. & Jefferson Col, A.B, 32, A.M, 33; Princeton Univ, A.M, 35, Ph.D, 38; Phi Beta Kappa; Alpha Tau Omega. Polit. & Govt. Pos: Mem, research staff, Nat. Bur. of Econ. Research, 46-56; assoc. task force dir, First Hoover Cmn, 49; sr. staff mem, President's Coun. of Econ. Adv, 53-54 & 56-57; acting chmn, Md. State Dem. Cent. Cmt, 61-62; U.S. Rep, Second Dist, Md, 63-; del, Dem. Nat. Conv, 68. Bus. & Prof. Pos: Instr, Wesleyan Univ, 36-40, assoc. prof, 41-45; assoc. prof, Johns Hopkins Univ, 46-47, prof, 47-62. Mil. Serv: Entered as Lt.(jg), Naval Res, 43, released as Lt, 46, after serv. in Bur. of Ships. Publ: Building Cycles and the Theory of Investment, 40, The Labor Force Under Changing Income and Employment, 58 and Wages and Earnings in the United States, 1860-1960, 60, Princeton Univ. Press. Mem: Fel, Am. Asn. for Adv. of Sci; Am. Legion; L'Hirondelle Club, Ruxton, Md; 14 W. Hamilton St. Club, Baltimore, Md. Rel: Presbyterian. Mailing Add: Boyce Ave, Ruxton, Md. 21204.

LONG, EDWARD V. D
b. Lincoln Co, Mo, 7/18/08; m. to Florence Secor; c. Ann L.(Mrs. Miller). Educ: Culver-Stockton Col; Univ. Mo. Polit. & Govt. Pos: Prosecuting attorney, Pike Co, Mo, 37; pres, Pike Co. Young Dem. Club, 40-44; attorney, Bowling Green, 41-45; Mo. State Sen, 45, Majority Floor Leader, Mo. State Senate, Pres. Pro Tem, 68th Gen. Assembly; Lt. Gov, Mo, 56-60; U.S. Sen, Mo, 60-68; del, Dem. Nat. Conv, 68. Bus. & Prof. Pos: Attorney; admitted to Mo. Bar, 36. Mem: Pike Co, Mo. and Fed. Bar Asns; Rotary Int.(dist. gov, 42 & 43) dir, 50-52); AF&AM; Consistory; Mason (33°); Moolah Temple, RAM, Ascalon Commandery; Eastern Star; Odd Fellows; Elks; SAR. Rel: Baptist. Mailing Add: Bowling Green, Mo. 63334.

LONG, GEORGE JAMES R
b. Louisville, Ky, 11/9/23; s. George J. Long and Corinė McKenna L; single. Educ: Univ. of Louisville and Sch. of Law. Polit. & Govt. Pos: Past mem, Louisville and Jefferson Co. Rep. Exec. Cmt, Ky; past chmn, bd. dir, Young Rep. Club of Ky; charter mem, past pres, v.pres, treas. and prog. chmn, Young Rep. Clubs of Louisville and Jefferson Co; elector, Third Cong. Dist, 60; trial cmnr, Jefferson Co. Quarterly Court, Louisville, 61-; former co-chmn, B Dist, Jefferson Co. Rep. Party; v.chmn, Regional Crime Coun. Bus. & Prof. Pos: Attorney-at-law, private practice, 52- Mil. Serv: Entered as Pvt, Air Force, 43, released as Maj; ETO Ribbon; Maj, Judge Adv. Gen. Dept, Air Force Res. and Ky. Air Nat. Guard, presently. Mem: Bd. dirs, Lawyer Pilots Bar Asn; Am, Ky, Louisville and Fed. Bar Asns; Am. Judica-

ture Soc; Lions; Ky. Air Nat. Guard Aero Club; Flying Farmers; Aircraft Owners and Pilots Asn. Rel: Catholic. Legal Res: 8501 Bardstown Rd, Fern Creek, Ky. 40291. Mailing Add: 408 Louisville Trust Bldg, Louisville, Ky. 40202.

LONG, GILLIS WILLIAM D
b. Winnfield, La, 5/4/23; s. Floyd H. Long and Birdie Shumake L; m. 6/21/47 to Mary Catherine Small; c. George Harrison and Janis Catherine. Educ: La. State Univ, B.A, 49, J.D, 51; Omicron Delta Kappa; Delta Kappa Epsilon. Polit. & Govt. Pos: Legal counsel, Select Cmt. on Small Bus, U.S. Sen, 51-53; chief legal counsel, Spec. Cmt. on Campaign Expenditures (elecs), U.S. House of Rep, 52, 56, 58 & 60; assoc. counsel, Adv. Cmt. on Rules, Dem. Nat. Cmt, 54-55; U.S. Rep, La, 63-65; del, Dem. Nat. Conv, 64; asst. dir, Off. Econ. Opportunity, Exec. Off. of the President, 64-66; mem, Spec. Cmt. on Hist. Preservation and Spec. Cmt. on Urban Growth, currently. Mil. Serv: Capt, Army Inf, World War II, ETO Ribbon; Bronze Star; Purple Heart. Mem: Am, La. and Alexandria Bar Asns; VFW; Am. Legion; Lions. Extensive travel in Europe. Rel: Baptist. Mailing Add: P.O. Box 1727, Alexandria, La. 71301.

LONG, HILDA SHEETS D
Dem. Nat. Committeewoman, W.Va.
m. to Edward H. Long (deceased); c. Berridge (Mrs. Noel Copen). Educ: Marshall Univ, 25. Polit. & Govt. Pos: Mem, Gov. Adv. Cmt. on Ment. Health and Gov. Adv. Cmt. of Employ. Security Coun; Dem. Nat. Committeewoman, W.Va, currently. Bus. & Prof. Pos: Exec. v.pres. and treas, Huntington Publ. Co, 59-63, pres, 63-; publisher, Huntington Advertiser, 60-; asst. secy, Radio Sta. WJR, Inc, 61-64. Mem: Nat. bd. adv, Nat. Asn. for Retarded Children; adv. coun, W.Va. Dept. of Employ. Security; v.pres, Marshall Univ. Alumni Bd, 60-63; dir, United Commun. Serv, 62; bd. dirs, Stella Fuller Settlement, 58-67; bd. dirs, Huntington Chap, Am. Red Cross and Cabell Huntington Horse Show; Inst. Newspaper Controllers and Finance Officers; Jr. League of Huntington; Huntington Advert. Club; Am. Inst. of Mgt; Colonial Dames of Am; DAR; Delta Zeta; Huntington Garden Club; Woman's Club; Assoc. Press; Monitoring Factfinding Cmt, Southwest. Commun. Action Coun, Inc; pres. adv. cmt. on bus. admin, Marshall Univ. Legal Res: 2020 Wilshire Blvd, Huntington, W.Va. 25701. Mailing Add: 946 Fifth Ave, Huntington, W.Va. 25720.

LONG, JIMMY DALE D
La. State Rep.
b. Winnfield, La, 10/6/31; s. Ruben Ray Long and Ruby Smith L; m. 12/19/53 to Dorothy Griffin; c. Jimmy D, Jr. Educ: Northwest. State Col, 1 year. Polit. & Govt. Pos: La. State Rep, 37th Dist, 68- Bus. & Prof. Pos: Owner, Dixie Food Store, Natchitoches, La, 59-, Dixie Creme, 66- and Zesto of Natchitoches, 68- Mil. Serv: Entered as A/S, Navy, 48, released as CS-2, 54, after serv. in Atlantic A or C, Pacific Fleet. Mem: Mason; VFW; Kiwanis; C. of C. Outstanding Young Man, Natchitoches Parish, 64. Rel: Baptist. Legal Res: Route 2, Natchitoches, La. 71457. Mailing Add: 1232 Texas St, Natchitoches, La. 71457.

LONG, JOHN D, III D
S.C. State Sen.
b. Union, S.C, 2/20/30; s. John D. Long and Mary Baker L; m. 3/10/56 to Patricia Ann Willard; c. Lou Ann, Mary Jane, John William and Stephen Willard. Educ: Univ. S.C, A.B, 51, LL.B, 53. Polit. & Govt. Pos: Chief Page, S.C. House of Rep, 53; co. solicitor, Union Co, S.C, 61-64; S.C. State Sen, Dist. 5, Union Co, 66- Bus. & Prof. Pos: Lawyer, currently. Mil. Serv: Enlisted man, 101st Airborne Div, Army, 2 years, Maj, Judge Adv. Gen. Corps, Army Res, currently. Mem: Elks; Shriner; Hejaz Temple; Mason (32°). Pres, Student Body, Union High Sch, 46-47. Mailing Add: Box 266, Union, S.C. 29379.

LONG, JOHN FLETCHER D
b. Statesville, N.C, 8/19/03; s. Henry F. Long and Carrie Allison L; m. to Mary DeNeale McKenzie (deceased); c. John F, Jr, Allison DeNeale (Mrs. Hughes) and Mary DeNeale (Mrs. Gilbert). Educ: Va. Mil. Inst, 2 years; N.C. State Univ, B.S; Kappa Sigma. Polit. & Govt. Pos: Mem, Iredell Co. Bd. Cmnr, N.C, 30, chmn, 32-58; chmn, Iredell Co. Dem. Party Orgn, 34-68. Mil. Serv: Entered as Pvt, N.C. Nat. Guard, 29, released as 1st Lt, 39. Mem: Farm Bur. Rel: Presbyterian. Mailing Add: Route 1, Statesville, N.C. 28677.

LONG, JOHN JOSEPH D
Mass. State Rep.
b. Fall River, Mass, 12/10/27; s. William F. Long, Sr. and Susanna G. Daley L; m. 5/30/51 to Clare Patricia Coogan; c. John Patrick, Susanne Marie, Terence, Stephen, James Joseph and Annemarie. Educ: B.M.C. Durfee High Sch, grad; Boston Univ. Col. Bus. Admin, 1 year. Polit. & Govt. Pos: Mass. State Rep, 57-; del, Dem. Nat. Conv, 68. Bus. & Prof. Pos: Ins. broker, Long & Parent Ins. Agency Inc, 52-, real estate broker, Long & Parent Realty, 52- Mil. Serv: Entered as Pvt, Army, 46, released as Sgt, 48, after serv. in 63rd Inf. Regt, Korea. Mem: Mass. Legislators Asn; Fall River Realtors; Gr. Fall River Ins. Agents Asn; DAV; Elks; K. of C. Rel: Roman Catholic. Mailing Add: 109 Barre St, Fall River, Mass. 02723.

LONG, JOSEPH J, SR. D
Md. State Del.
b. Delmar, Md, July, 1921; married. Educ: Paynter Bus. Sch. Polit. & Govt. Pos: Pres, Young Dem. Club of Wicomico Co, Md, 60-61; mem, Salisbury Dem. Cmt; mem, Salisbury City Coun; Md. State Del, 63- Bus. & Prof. Pos: Electrician. Mil. Serv: Air Force, 42-46. Mem: Moose; Am. Legion; E. Side Men's Club; Farm Bur. Mailing Add: 204 White St, Salisbury, Md. 21801. (1967)

LONG, MACON MELVILLE D
Va. State Sen.
b. Rappahannock Co, Va, 4/2/85; m. to Charlotte Tompkins. Educ: Univ. Richmond, B.L. Polit. & Govt. Pos: Former chmn, Va. Adv. Legis. Coun. and mem, Judicial Coun; del, Dem. Nat. Conv, 40, 48 & 56; Va. State Rep, 40-42; Va. State Sen, 44- Bus. & Prof. Pos: Attorney-at-law. Mem: Am. Bar Asn; former pres, Wise Co. Bar Asn; former pres, Va. State Bar; former v.pres, Va. State Bar Asn; trustee, Univ. Richmond. Rel: Baptist. Mailing Add: P.O. Box 188, St. Paul, Va. 24283.

LONG, ROBERT CHARLES BIGGY D
b. Westover, Md, 5/15/19; married. Educ: Beacom Bus. Col. Polit. & Gov. Pos: Md. State Del, 59-67; Pres, Bd. of Co. Cmnrs, Somerset Co, 54-58. Bus. & Prof. Pos: Farmer; canner; merchant. Mil. Serv: Navy, 42-45. Mem: Farm Bur; Tri-State Packers' Asn; Elks; past Pres, Princess Anne Lions; Am. Legion; VFW. Mailing Add: Westover, Md. 21871. (1967)

LONG, RUSSELL B. D
U.S. Sen, La.
b. Shreveport, La, 11/3/18; s. Huey P. Long and Rose McConnell L. Educ: La. State Univ, B.A, 41 and LL.B, 42; Delta Kappa Epsilon; Omicron Delta Kappa; Order of Coif; Tau Kappa Alpha; Phi Delta Phi. Polit. & Govt. Pos: U.S. Sen, La, 48-, chmn, Finance Cmt, U.S. Senate, 66-; del, Dem. Nat. Conv, 68. Bus. & Prof. Pos: Attorney; admitted to La. Bar, 42. Mil. Serv: Lt, Naval Res, 42-45. Mem: Lions; Elks; Am. Legion. Legal Res: Baton Rouge, La. Mailing Add: 217 Senate Office Bldg, Washington D.C. 20710.

LONG, SPEEDY O. D
U.S. Rep, La.
b. Tullos, La, 6/16/28; s. Felix F. Long and Verda Pendarvis L; m. to Florence Marie Theriot; c. Felix Paul and David Theriot. Educ: Northeast Jr. Col, 50; Northwest. State Col, B.A, 51; La. State Univ. Law Sch, J.D, 59. Polit. & Govt. Pos: La. State Sen, 56-64; U.S. Rep, La, 64- Mil. Serv: Navy, 46-48 & 51-53. Mem: La. Bar Asn; Am. Bar Asn. of La; Am. Legion; Mason (32°); Shrine; Jena and La. Jr. C. of C; hon. chap. farmer, LaSalle Parish Future Farmers of Am. Rel: Baptist. Legal Res: Jena, La. 71342. Mailing Add: 419 Cannon House Office Bldg, Washington, D.C. 20515.

LONG, VERNE EVERETT R
Minn. State Rep.
b. Pipestone, Minn, 9/24/25; s. Samuel Everett Long and Florence Dingler L; m. 3/21/48 to Wilma Dean Watts; c. Judith Anne, Kathryn Jo and James Douglas. Polit. & Govt. Pos: Sch. bd. mem, Pipestone Twp, Minn, 54-62, Twp. supvr, 58-62; pres, Twp. Officer's Asn, 62; Minn. State Rep, 63-; co-chmn, Pipestone Co. Rural Area Develop, 64- Mem: Kiwanis; pres, Pipestone Co. Hist. Soc, 64-68; Farm Bur; Pipestone Co. Asn. for Retarded Children; Cmt. on Aging; Mason; Hi-Way 23 Asn; pres, Southwest. Minn. Legislators. Amateur Photographer. Rel: Methodist. Mailing Add: R.R. 1, Box 307, Pipestone, Minn. 56164.

LONG, WILLIAM C, JR. R
Kans. State Rep.
b. Wichita, Kans, 4/2/29; s. William C. Long and Bethene Florence L; m. 8/16/56 to Carol V. Drouhard; c. Mary Beth, John C, James J, Nathan and Anne. Polit. & Govt. Pos: Kans. State Rep, 105th Dist. Mem: Kans. Oil Men's Asn; C. of C.(pres, 63-64); pres, United Fund, 66-67; Elks; K. of C; Lions; Farm Bur. Rel: Catholic. Mailing Add: 406 College Ave, Harper, Kans. 67058.

LONG, WINONA RUTH D
b. Ft. Thompson, S.Dak, 12/7/32; d. Benjamin Harrison Thompson and Ruth May Walton T; m. 7/18/51 to Dallas H. Long; c. Michelle Annette and Bernard Neil. Educ: South. State Teachers Col, Springfield, S.Dak, 50-51. Polit. & Govt. Pos: Secy-treas, Turner Co. Dem. Party, S.Dak, 62-63, chairwoman, 63-68; del, Dem. Nat. Conv, 64. Bus. & Prof. Pos: Elem. rural sch. teacher, 51-52; secy-treas, Lower Brule Tribal Coun, 64-66. Mem: Nat. Cong. of Am. Indians; United Sioux Tribe of S.Dak. Rel: American Lutheran. Mailing Add: R.R. 2, Box 22, Viborg, S.Dak, 57070. (1967)

LONGAKER, DANIEL NORMAN, JR. D
b. Philadelphia, Pa, 8/30/09; s. D. Norman Longaker and Alice Mary Coggins L; m. 5/30/35 to Louise Pond; c. Daniel N, III and David Prosser. Educ: Univ. Ore, B.S, 32; Chi Psi. Polit. & Govt. Pos: Chmn, Berkeley Dem. Caucus, Calif, 60-62; pres, Alameda Co. Dem, 62-64; mem. steering and exec. cmts, Calif. State Dem. Cent. Cmt, 62-68; asst. chief, Div. Labor Law Enforcement, 63-68; chmn, Alameda Co. Dem. Cent. Cmt, 62-68; dir, off. employ. standards, U.S. Dept. Labor, Wash, D.C, 68- Rel: Unitarian. Legal Res: 1156 Josephine St, Berkeley, Calif. 94707. Mailing Add: 2100 Connecticut Ave. N.W, Apt. 408, Washington, D.C. 20008.

LONGLEY, BENJAMIN LEHMANN R
Tenn. State Rep.
b. La Grange, Ga, 8/7/30; s. Julian McLauren Longley, Sr. and Mary Bowen Robertson L; m. 10/26/57 to Anne Elizabeth Hayes; c. Mary Elizabeth and Amy Lauren. Educ: Vanderbilt Univ, B.A, 51; Pi Kappa Alpha. Polit. & Govt. Pos: Secy, Tenn. Young Rep, 63-65; staff mem, U.S. Rep. W.E. Brock, Tenn, 63-65; dist. chmn, Third Cong. Dist, Tenn. Rep. Party, 65-; Tenn. State Rep, 66-; alternate del, Rep. Nat. Conv, 68. Bus. & Prof. Pos: Credit mgr, Hardwick Stove Co, 54-61, controller, 62-66; agent, Mutual Benefit Life Ins. Co, 61-62; agent, Provident Life Ins. Co, 66- Mil. Serv: Entered as Pvt, Army, 51, released as Sgt, 54. Mem: Million Dollar Round Table; Nat. Asn. of Life Underwriters; Am. Legion; Elks; Toastmasters. Rel: Methodist. Legal Res: 3635 Westview Dr. N.E, Cleveland, Tenn. 37311. Mailing Add: P.O. Box 211, Cleveland, Tenn. 37311.

LONGLEY, IRIS HULL R
Chmn, Mercer Co. Rep. Cent. Cmt, Ohio
b. Ft. Recovery, Ohio, 5/18/04; d. John J. Hull and Nelle Lipps H; m. 6/22/35 to John Hyler Longley; c. Sharon Nelle. Educ: Ohio State Univ, B.S, in Educ, 27; Ball State Univ, M.A, 58; Pi Lambda Theta; Delta Kappa Gamma; Alpha Sigma Alpha; Delta Theta Tau. Polit. & Govt. Pos: Precinct committeewoman, Rep. Party, Ohio, 50-; chairwoman, Mercer Co. Rep. Party, 54-62; chmn, Mercer Co. Rep. Cent. and Exec. Cmts, 54-; mem, Mercer Co. Elec. Bd, 56-; mem, Ohio Rep. State Cmt, 58-62; mem, Ohio Rep. State Cent. Cmt, currently. Bus. & Prof. Pos: Teacher, social studies, Logan Sr. High Sch, Ohio, 27-35 and Portland Sr. High Sch, Ind, 52- Mem: Nat. Asn. of Social Studies Teachers; Nat. Educ. Asn; Ind. Classroom Teachers Asn; Twentieth Century Club; pres, Ft. Recovery Hist. Soc; Ohio Hist. Soc. Rel: United Church of Christ. Mailing Add: 401 S. Wayne St, Ft. Recovery, Ohio 45846. (1967)

LONGMIRE, GEORGE R
N.Dak. State Sen.
b. LaFollette, Tenn, 8/2/15; married; c. Two. Educ: Lincoln Mem. Univ; Univ. of N.Dak; George Wash. Univ. Polit. & Govt. Pos: Former states attorney, Grand Forks Co, N.Dak; former chmn, N.Dak. Rep. Party; N.Dak. State Sen, 57- Bus. & Prof. Pos: Lawyer. Mailing Add: 24 N. Fourth St, Grand Forks, N.Dak. 58201.

LONGORIA, RAUL L. D
Tex. State Rep.
b. Grulla, Tex, 2/22/21; s. Andres Longoria and Enriqueta L; m. 9/9/47 to Martha Earlene Moorman; c. Samuel Glenn, Janiece Maxene, Roy Alan and twins, Martha Elaine and Cecilia Joyce. Educ: Univ. Tex, B.B.A, and LL.B, 52. Polit. & Govt. Pos: Tex. State Rep, Dist. 38, Place 1, 61-63, Dist. 37-F, 65-67 and Dist. 49, Place 1, 67- Bus. & Prof. Pos: Attorney-at-law, 52-53 & 64-; assoc, Hartley & Latimore, Attorneys, 53-55; asst. dist. attorney, Hidalgo Co, Tex, 55-57; assoc, Longoria & Evins, Attorneys, 57-64. Mil. Serv: Entered as Pvt, Air Force, 42, released as Sgt, 46, after serv. in ETO. Mem: Lions Int; Am. Legion; Tex. and Hidalgo Co. Bar Asns; Tex. Asn. of Plaintiff's Attorneys. Rel: Catholic. Legal Res: 106 S. Esperanza, Pharr, Tex. 78577. Mailing Add: P.O. Box 182, Edinburg, Tex. 78539.

LONGSTREET, VICTOR MENDELL D
b. Louisville, Ky, 1/1/07; s. Joseph Emens Longstreet and Allan McKinley L; m. 8/9/30 to Mary Margaret Landry; c. Katherine Allan (Mrs. Goett). Educ: Harvard Col, B.S, 30; Phi Beta Kappa. Polit. & Govt. Pos: Sr. economist, Fed. Reserve, Bd, 40-43; assoc. chief div. of econ. develop, State Dept, 45-48; dep. U.S. sr. rep, NATO Finance Cmt, 50-51; dep. dir. off. of trade & finance, Econ. Coop. Admin, Paris, 51-52; Asst. Secy, Dept. of Navy, 62-65. Bus. & Prof. Pos: V.pres, Fed. Reserve Bank of St. Louis, 53-57; dir. of mgt. research, Schering Corp, 57-62; assoc. dir, Int. Mgt. Group of Boston, Mass. and exec. assoc, Dunlap & Assocs, Darien, Conn, 66-; dir, Baldt Corp, 69- Mil. Serv: Entered as Capt, Army Air Corps, 43, released as Lt. Col, 45; Navy Meritorious Citation. Publ: Financial Control in Multi-National Companies, Financial Execs. Research Found, N.Y.C, 69. Mem: Am. Econ. Asn; Coun. on For. Rels; Army Navy Club; Harvard Club of Boston. Rel: Non-Denominational. Legal Res: Depot Rd, Truro, Mass. 02666.

LONGSWORTH, JOHN ROBERT R
b. Sherrodsville, Ohio, 7/29/39; s. William Saviors Longsworth and Mary Miskimen L; single. Educ: Baldwin-Wallace Col, B.S, 61; Rutgers Univ, M.S, 63; Alpha Sigma Phi. Polit. & Govt. Pos: Ohio State Sen, 30th Dist, 66-68. Bus. & Prof. Pos: Math teacher, Steubenville High Sch, Ohio, 65. Mem: Jr. C. of C. Rel: Methodist. Mailing Add: 1347 E. State St, Salem, Ohio 44460. (1967)

LONSDALE, HOWARD C. R
Mem, Calif. Rep. State Cent. Cmt.
b. Berlin, Germany, 9/26/33; s. Henry G. Lonsdale, M.D. and Hilda Wentzel L; m. 6/7/66 to Ramona Mae Dieterle; c. Henry, Lauren and Elizabeth. Educ: Princeton Univ, A.B, 55; Univ. Ark. Sch. of Med, M.D, 60; Cloister Inn, Princeton Univ. Polit. & Govt. Pos: Chmn, Solano Co. Comprehensive Health Planning Coun, Calif, 68-; chmn, Solano Co. Young Rep, 69; assoc. mem, Solano Co. Rep. Cent. Cmt, 69; mem, Calif. Rep. State Cent. Cmt, 69- Physician, private practice of ear, nose and throat, 66-69. Mil. Serv: Capt, Air Force, 64-66, serv. in Travis Hosp, Travis Air Force Base, Calif; Mil. Serv. Medal. Mem: Solano Co, Calif. and Am. Med. Socs; Am. Asn. for Adv. of Sci; Calif. Speech & Hearing Soc; dir, Bay Area Comprehensive Health Planning Coun; dir, Calif. Med. Soc. Polit. Action Cmt; bd. dirs, Kiwanis, United Crusade, Boy Scouts and pres, Vallejo Symphony. Man of the Year, Vallejo, Calif, 68. Rel: Episcopal. Legal Res: 7C St, Vallejo, Calif. 94590. Mailing Add: 600 Marin St, Vallejo, Calif. 94590.

LOO, FRANK W. C. D
b. Honolulu, Hawaii, 11/20/22; s. Man Kwong Loo and Ngo Wong L; m. 11/24/55 to Florence K.O. Tong; c. Frank Martin, Claire Terese, John Francis, Brian and Lianne. Educ: Yale Univ. Law Sch, LL.B; Ohio Univ, B.A; U.S. Merchant Marine Acad, B.S; Univ. Hawaii; Pearl Harbor Naval Shipyard Apprentice Sch, machinist; St. Louis. Col. Polit. & Govt. Pos: 13th Dist. chmn, Oahu Co. Dem. Cmt, Hawaii, 54, finance chmn, 55; senate attorney, Hawaii Territorial Legis, 57; mem, Territorial Civil Serv. Cmn, 57-58; Hawaii State Rep, 59-66; alternate del, Dem. Nat. Conv, 60; state del, Golden Anniversary White House Conf. on Children and Youth, 60, Nat. Legis. Conf, 62, and Conf. of Cmnr. on Uniform State Laws, 63; mem, adv. bd, U.S. Merchant Marine Acad, 65-; pres, Fifth Precinct, 12th Rep. Dist. Dem. Party, 66- Bus. & Prof. Pos: Mem, mgt. cmt, Foremost Finance Co, Inc, 62-; ed, Probate Law Digest, Sullivan's Probate Dir. and Nat. Asn. Probate and Bank Attorneys, 63-65; ed, Banking and Commercial Law Digest, Rand McNally List of Bank Recommended Attorneys, 66-; pres, Aloha Loans and Mortgage Corp, Hawaii, 66- Mil. Serv: Entered as Cadet-Midshipman, Naval Res, 44, released as Ens, 47, after serv. in U.S. Merchant Marine Acad. Publ: 'Many Challenges Confront the Legal Profession,' U.S. Jr. C. of C. Mag, 57; 'Political Life of the Chinese in Hawaii,' Honolulu Advertiser and 50th Anniversary Book, Chinese C. of C, Hawaii. Mem: Am. and Hawaii Bar Asns; Am. Trial Lawyers Asn; co-chmn, World Trade and Commerce Cmt, Commercial Law League Am, 65-, exec. coun, West. Regional Mem. Asn, 66-; Lions; Toastmasters. Selected Outstanding Young Man of Honolulu, 55; 1 of 10 Outstanding Young Men of Am, 65; Outstanding Alumnus, U.S. Merchant Marine Acad; 4.0 Grade Point Average Scholastic Award, Ohio Univ. Rel: Catholic. Mailing Add: 2271-B Liliha St, Honolulu, Hawaii 96817. (1967)

LOO, GEORGE WING TAT D
Hawaii State Rep.
b. Honolulu, Hawaii, 12/28/30; s. Man Kwong Loo and Ngo Wong L; single. Educ: Univ. Hawaii, B.S. in Civil Eng, 52; Univ. Mich. Law Sch, LL.B, 57. Polit. & Govt. Pos: Patent exam, U.S. Patent Off, 56-60; res. asst, Judiciary Cmt, Hawaii State House of Rep, 62, majority attorney, 63 & 64; Hawaii State Rep, 13th Dist, 64-; del, Constitutional Conv, 68. Bus. & Prof. Pos: Attorney and patent lawyer, 60- Mil. Serv: Entered as 2nd Lt, Army, 52, released, 54, after serv. in Pac; Korean Serv, UN and Nat. Defense Ribbons. Mem: Am, Hawaii and Fed. Bar Asns; Patent Off. Soc; Am. Patent Law Asn; Univ. Hawaii and Univ. Mich. Alumni Asns. Rel: Episcopal. Mailing Add: 1203 Palama St, Honolulu, Hawaii 96817.

LOOBY, JOSEPH LAWRENCE D
Wis. State Assemblyman
b. Eau Claire, Wis, 11/24/17; s. Thomas E. Looby and Anna Sippel L; m. 7/12/42 to Myrtle Irene Brettingen; c. Judith Ann (Mrs. John Ruhe); Kathleen Jo, Cheyrl Marie, Kevin Thomas, Karen Lea, Brian Timothy and Constance Sue. Educ: St. Patricks High Sch, Eau Claire, Wis, grad. Polit. & Govt. Pos: Mem, State Exec. Bd, Wis. AFL-CIO, Milwaukee, 62-; Mem, Eau Claire City Coun, 64-68; mem, Eau Claire Co. Bd, 64-; Wis. state assemblyman, Eau Claire First Dist, 69- Bus. & Prof. Pos: Secy-treas, URW Lodge 19, 61-69. Mil. Serv: Entered as Pvt, Army, 43, released as Pfc, 46, after serv. in Tenth Mt. Div, Europe and Mid.E, 44-46. Rel: Catholic. Mailing Add: 1156 E. Madison St, Eau Claire, Wis. 54701.

LOOKADOO, J. HUGH D
Ark. State Sen.
b. Arkadelphia, Ark, 8/17/25; s. Jonathan Houston Lookadoo and Caldonia Daniel L; m. 8/17/51 to Valarie Collins; c. Jonathan Houston, III, Laurie and Lizabeth. Educ: Univ. Ark, B.A, 48, Ark. Law Sch, LL.B, 51; Sigma Chi. Polit. & Govt. Pos: Dep. prosecuting attorney, Clark Co, Ark, 51-54; Ark. State Rep, 59-62; Ark. State Sen, Sixth Dist, 67-; mem-at-lg, Legis. Coun, 67-68, alternate mem, 69-70; alternate mem, Legis. Joint Audit, 67-70. Bus. & Prof. Pos: Partner, Lookadoo, Gooch and Lookadoo, Attorneys, 51- Mem: Am, Southwest Ark, Ark. and Clark Co. Bar Asns; past pres, Am. Trial Lawyers Asn; Ark. Trial Lawyers Asn; Am. Judicature Soc; Mason; Lions. Rel: Methodist. Legal Res: 1612 Phillips St, Arkadelphia, Ark. 71923. Mailing Add: P.O. Box 357, Arkadelphia, Ark. 71923.

LOOKINLAND, PAUL RUSSELL R
Mem, Calif. Rep. State Cent. Cmt.
b. San Pedro, Calif, 6/17/34; s. Orrin Paul Lookinland and Madeline Tait L; m. 6/13/58 to Karen Ruth McKinney; c. Terese Lee, Michael Paul and Eric Todd. Educ: Los Angeles Harbor Col, A.A, 54; Brigham Young Univ, B.S, 56; Long Beach State Col, M.A, 63. Polit. & Govt. Pos: Mem, Los Angeles Rep. Cent. Cmt, Calif, 66-; Rep. cand, 68th Dist, Calif. State Assembly, 68; mem, Calif. Rep. State Cent. Cmt, 69- Bus. & Prof. Pos: Teacher, Orem High Sch, Utah, 59-60; Los Angeles City Sch. Dist, Calif, 60-67, audio-visual consult, 67, registrar, 67-69. Mil. Serv: Pvt, Marine Corps Res, 58-62. Rel: Latter-Day Saint. Mailing Add: 1417 N. Cabrillo Ave, San Pedro, Calif. 90731.

LOOMIS, HENRY Independent
Dep. Dir, U.S. Info. Agency
b. Tuxedo Park, N.Y, 4/19/19; s. Alfred Lee Loomis and Ellen Holman Farnsworth L; m. 5/18/46 to Mary Paul Macleod; c. Henry Stimson, Mary Paul, Lucy Farnsworth and Gordon Macleod. Educ: Harvard, A.B, 41; Univ. Calif, Berkeley, 46-47. Polit. & Govt. Pos: Asst. to chmn, Research & Develop. Bd, Dept. Defense, 50-51; consult, Psychol. Strategy Bd, 51-52; staff asst, President's Cmt. on Info, 53; chief, Off. of Research and Intel, U.S. Info. Agency, Wash, D.C, 54-57, dir, Voice of Am, 58-65, dep. dir, U.S. Info. Agency, 69-; staff dir. to spec. asst. to President for Sci. and Tech, 57-58; dep. U.S. Cmnr. of Educ, Dept. Health, Educ. and Welfare, 65-66. Bus. & Prof. Pos: Mem, Staff, Radiation Lab, Univ. Calif, 45-47; asst. to pres, Mass. Inst. of Tech, 47-50; partner, St. Vincents Island Co, 66-68. Mil. Serv: Entered as Ens, Navy, 40, released as Lt. Comdr, 45, after serv. on Staff, Comdr-in-Chief, Pac. Theatre; Bronze Star and Air Medal. Mem: Coun. on For. Rels, Inc; Wash. Inst. of For. Affairs; Chevy Chase and Metrop. Clubs, Middleburg Hunt Club; Cruising Club of Am; Myopia Hunt Club; Manchester Yacht Club. Rockefeller Pub. Serv. Award in For. Affairs and Distinguished Serv. Award, U.S. Info. Agency, 63. Rel: Episcopal. Legal Res: Trough Hill Farm, Middleburg, Va. 22117. Mailing Add: U.S. Information Agency, Washington, D.C. 20547.

LOOMIS, SAMUEL R. R
b. Huron, S.Dak, 2/22/93; s. William Henry Loomis and Florence Weller L; m. 7/1/23 to Winnifred Alice Silloway; c. Winona Ruth (deceased). Educ: Univ. Vt, 25; Univ. Nebr, summers and eve; Union Col, Nebr, 19-21; Gem City Bus. Col, M. of Acct, 16. Polit. & Govt. Pos: Mayor, College View, Lincoln, Nebr, 29; Vt. State Rep, 53-63; Vt. State Sen, Lamoille Co, 63-68. Bus. & Prof. Pos: Head, commercial dept, College View High, Lincoln, Nebr, 22-30; secy-treas, Bolivian Mission of Seventh-day Adventists, La Paz, 30-36; trustee, North. New Eng. Conf. of Seventh-day Adventists and Park View Hosp, Brunswick, Maine, 55-60. Mil. Serv: Entered as Pvt, Army, 18, released as Sgt, 19. Mem: Am. Legion; Farm Bur. Rel: Seventh-day Adventist. Mailing Add: R.R. 1, Hyde Park, Vt. 05655.

LOONEY, JAMES CULLEN D
b. Kossuth, Miss, 5/18/03; s. James Owen Looney and Virginia Dean L; m. 6/15/33 to Margaret Montgomery; c. Margaret (Mrs. McAllen), D'Ette and Cullen R. Educ: George Peabody Col, 19-21; Vanderbilt Univ, B.A, 24, LL.B, 26; Pi Kappa Alpha. Polit. & Govt. Pos: Chmn, Hidalgo Co. Dem. Exec. Cmt, Tex, 32-40 & 54-68; co. judge, Hidalgo Co, 41-46; mem, Tex. Citrus Cmn, 49-51; mem, Tex. Cmn. on Higher Educ, 63-65; mem, Coord. Bd, Tex. Col. and Univ. Syst, 65; del, Dem. Nat. Conv, 68. Bus. & Prof. Pos: Regent, Pan Am. Col, 52-58; corp. dir, First Nat. Bank, Mercedes and La Feria, Tex, Security State Bank, Pharr, First State Bank & Trust Co, Border Bank, Hidalgo, Edinburg, Tropical Savings & Loan Asn, Harlingen, Valley Transit Co, Inc, Valley Bus. Co, Inc, R K & L Co, Valley Garage Co, Valley Bus Serv. Co, Valley Bus Equip. Co, Valley Express Co, Pan Am. Motor Coaches, Harbenito Broadcasting Co, Radio Corp. and Realty Corp, Cent. Valley Ready Mix Concrete Co, San Juan, Leon Land & Cattle Co, Ft. Stockton, Leon Water Enterprises, Ft. Stockton, Grande Invest. Co, Mercedes, Hillcrest Mem. Park, Edinburg, Triple City Lumber Co, Pharr, Vackar Lumber & Supply Co, Edinburg, B & P Bridge Co. of Weslaco, VICO, Inc, Edinburg, Hidalgo Mortgage Co, Atlantic Oil Corp, Edinburg Commun. Hotel, Inc, Joe Daniel Tire Co, Pharr, KUNO Radio, Inc, Corpus Christi, RA JO Sales Co, Inc, La Feria, KIFN Radio, Inc. and Phoenix, Ariz; trustee, Edinburg Improv. Asn, Tex, Ashley McAllen Trust, Melanie McAllen Trust and Looney Found.

Mem: Am, Tex. and Hidalgo Co. Bar Asns; pres, Edinburg Kiwanis, 34, Edinburg C. of C, 36, Rio Grande Valley C. of C, 59 and Hidalgo Co. Health Bd, 47-48; AF&AM; K.T; AAONMS; RAM; R&SM; McAllen Country Club; Edinburg Country Club; Tropicana Club. Rel: Episcopal. Legal Res: Casa Cul-Mar-Dee, Edinburg, Tex. 78539. Mailing Add: P.O. Box 390, Edinburg, Tex. 78539.

LOOP, JAMES WHITCOMB D
W.Va. State Del.
b. Morristown, Tenn, 3/12/00; s. James Willis Loop and Dora Noe L; m. 3/9/24 to Marguerite McCracken. Educ: W.Va. Inst. Tech, B.S, 45; Marshall Univ, M.A, 51; Epsilon Pi Tau; Kappa Delta Pi. Polit. & Govt. Pos: W.Va. State Del, 47-56, 65-66 & 69- Bus. & Prof. Pos: Teacher, Charleston High Sch, W.Va, 27-60; gen. secy, Scottish Rite Bodies, Charleston, W.Va, 60- Publ: Printing for the Beginning Pupil, privately publ, 36, 39, 44, 46, 48 and 56. Mem: Charleston Typographical Union; Mason; York Rite Mason; AASR (33°); Shrine; Royal Order of Scotland; Civitan Club. Rel: Methodist. Mailing Add: 1410-A Jackson St, Charleston, W.Va. 25301.

LOOPER, MAXINE MOODY D
Co-chmn, LeFlore Co. Dem. Cent. Cmt, Okla.
b. Blakely, Ga, 10/21/26; d. Sam Moody and Mary Myrtle Hobby M; m. 12/12/48 to Dr. Omer Joe Looper; c. Mary Ivylyn, Felda Kathryn and John Franklin. Educ: Tift Col, B.S.H.E. cum laude, 47; Univ. Okla, M.S.H.E, 49; Omicron Nu; Sigma Xi; Delta Sigma Chi; Alpha Sigma Chi. Polit. & Govt. Pos: Pres, LeFlore Co. Young Dem, Okla, 59-60, secy, 64-65 and pres, 65-66; v.pres, Okla. Young Dem. Club, 61-62, third dist. co-chmn, 62-63; co-chmn, LeFlore Co. Dem. Cent. Cmt, 67-; del, Dem. Nat. Conv, 68. Bus. & Prof. Pos: Teacher, Blakely-Union High Sch, 47-48; res. fel, Univ. Ga, 49-50; eng. technician, West. Elec. Co, Winston-Salem, N.C, 51-52. Publ: The Effect of the Addition of Powdered Skim Milk and Ground Eggshell to Certain Foods, Univ. Okla, 49; Ways of Adding Calcium to the Diet, Acad. Sci, 49. Mem: Fedn. Women's Clubs; Heavener Women's Club; Epsilon Sigma Alpha Int; Nat. Asn. Ment. Health; NAACP. Rel: Baptist. Mailing Add: 205 W. Fourth St, Heavener, Okla. 74937.

LOORAM, MATTHEW
U.S. Ambassador, Repub. of Dahomey
b. New York, N.Y, 3/26/21; s. Matthew Looram and Constance Peabody L; m. 9/18/43 to Bettina de Rothschild; c. Bettina and Peter. Educ: Harvard Col, B.A, 43. Polit. & Govt. Pos: For. serv. officer, U.S. State Dept, 48-; Third and second secy, Rome, 48-52; second secy, Paris, 52-55; European Bur, U.S. State Dept, 55-59; U.S. Consul, Ethiopia, 59-62; African Bur, U.S. State Dept, 63-69; U.S. Ambassador, Repub. of Dahomey, 69- Mil. Serv: Entered as Pvt, Army, 43, released as Capt, 46, after serv. in 13th ABN Div. and 88th Inf. Div, ETO. Mem: Metrop. Club, Wash, D.C. Rel: Protestant. Legal Res: 1308 29th St. N.W, Washington, D.C. 20007. Mailing Add: U.S. Embassy, Cotonov, Dahomey.

LOPEZ, EDWARD JOSEPH D
N.Mex. State Rep.
b. Cincinnati, Ohio, 5/3/38; s. Joseph Francis Lopez and Norma Brunton L; m. 6/21/58 to Rozella Melinda Lucero; c. Melinda L, Edward J, Jr. and Elizabeth A. Educ: Univ. New Mexico, 56 & 57. Polit. & Govt. Pos: Supvr. traffic div, N.Mex. State Police, 59-62; Dem. precinct chmn, Precinct 17, Santa Fe Co, 62-64; mem, Santa Fe Co. Dem. Cent. Cmt, 62-64; admin. officer oil and gas units div, N.Mex. State Land Off, 62-68; mem, Santa Fe Co, Dem. Exec. Cmt, 69; N.Mex. State Rep, Santa Fe Co, Dist. Two, 69- Bus. & Prof. Pos: Landman, Bokum Corp, 68- Mem: Elks; N.Mex. State Employees Credit Union (chmn. bd); Jr. C. of C; YMCA (bd. dirs); Univ. N.Mex. Alumni Assoc. Rel: Roman Catholic. Mailing Add: 216 Sereno Dr, Santa Fe, N.Mex. 87501.

LOPEZ, HILTON L. R
b. Arroyo, P.R, 12/30/43; s. Hilton L. López and Stella Peña L; single. Educ: Univ. Md, 1 year; Univ. P.R, 3 years; Phi Eta Mu. Polit. & Govt. Pos: V.pres. and founder, Action for Statehood, P.R, 64-66; treas, P.R. Statehood Rep. Party, 68-69. Bus. & Prof. Pos: V.pres, First Conventional Investment, Inc, 65-67; pres, Empresas López, Inc, 66-; Caparra Gardens Highland Develop. Corp, 66-; H.P, Inc, 68-; Morovis Develop. Corp, 68- Mem: Caparra Country Club; Club Nautico. Rel: Roman Catholic. Legal Res: Caribbean Towers, No. 914, Santurce, P.R. 00907. Mailing Add: Box 13332, Santurce, P.R. 00907.

LOPEZ, JUNIO R
N.Mex. State Sen.
b. Las Animas, Colo, 8/12/24; s. Eleuterio Lopez and Josephine Blea L; m. 5/26/52 to Anne Romero; c. Paula Maye, Alonzo Arthur, David Mario, Viola June and Roxanne. Educ: Las Vegas High Sch, N.Mex. Polit. & Govt. Pos: Mem, N.Mex. Rep. State Exec. Cmt, 56-62; mayor, Las Vegas, 58-62; mem. sch. bd, Las Vegas, 58-64; chmn, San Miguel Co. Rep. Party, 59-63; N.Mex. State Sen, 66-; state chmn, Viva Nixon Cmt, 68- Bus. & Prof. Pos: Owner, Wholesale Automotive, 52-; Clothing and Hardware Store, 56-; owner and publisher, Alpha News, 65-68; owner, Las Vegas Drilling Co, 66-; Bakery and Floral Stores, 69- Mil. Serv: Entered as Pvt, Army, released as Pfc, after serv. in ETO. Publ: 101 poems in Eng. and Spanish; plays, short stories and novel in Eng. Mem: Am. Legion; VFW; Elks; C. of C. All Am. City Award given to Las Vegas during first term as mayor. Legal Res: 714 South Pacific, Las Vegas, N.Mex. 87701. Mailing Add: P.O. Box 1718, Las Vegas, N.Mex. 87701.

LOPEZ, SOTO DANNY New Progressive, P.R.
Rep, P.R. House of Rep.
b. Utuado, P.R, 3/13/41; s. Pablo López Vera and Mariana Soto de L; m. 10/2/64 to Merilyn Pujals; c. Danny and Merilyn. Educ: Univ. P.R, B.B.A, 65. Polit. & Govt. Pos: Pres, Third Precinct Young Rep, P.R, 56-60; v.pres, San Juan Young Rep, 60-64; v.pres, P.R. Young Rep, 64-67; Rep. Third Precinct, P.R. House of Rep, 69- Bus. & Prof. Pos: Loan rep, Chase Manhattan Bank, 64-65; owner, Bargain Center, Inc, 65-69. Citation for Meritorious Serv, Am. Legion. Rel: Catholic. Mailing Add: Inmaculada 419, Monteflores, Santurce, P.R. 00915.

LORD, LILIAS MONTGOMERY R
Pres, Rep. Women of Pa.
b. Phila, Pa, 9/1/08; d. William Morgan Montgomery and Elizabeth Leewright M; m. 2/19/30 to John Whitaker Lord, Jr; c. John Whitaker, III. Educ: Stevens Sch; 27; Univ. of Pa, 31; Dale Carnegie Course, 47; Woodmere Art Gallery, 60-61. Polit. & Govt. Pos: Pres, Rep. Women of Pa, 46-54 & 63-; chmn, Women's Spec. Events Cmt, Rep. Nat. Conv, 48; mem, bd. dirs and v.chmn, membership exten. cmt, Nat. Fedn. Rep. Women, 53-54; mem, bd. dirs, Pa. Coun. Rep. Women, 53-54 & 65-, first state chmn, Teenage Groups, 64-65; chmn, First Ladies Group, Southeast. Dist, Rep. Finance Cmt. Pa, 54; mem, Nat. Coun, Women's Nat. Rep. Club, N.Y, 64-; mem, Woman's Adv. Cmt. to Rep. Nat. Committeewoman, 65-; mem, Legis. Steering Cmt, World Affairs Coun, Phila, 66-; mem, Policy Cmt, Phila. Rep. Cent. Campaign Cmt, 66-; mem, Mayors Cmt. for Law Day, U.S.A, 66-69; alternate del, Rep. Nat. Conv, 68; mem, Phila. Bd. of Assistance, 68-; mem, Citizens' Cmt. for New Court House, 68- Mem: Women's Exec. Cmt, Hero Scholarship Fund; adv. bd, Asn. Del. Valley Art Centers; regent, Thomas Leiper Chap, DAR, 57-60, v.chmn, State Cmt. for Americanism, 65; chmn, Ladies Presidential Campaign Cmt, Union League Phila; Phila. Fedn. Womens' Clubs; French Soc. Phila; Civic Opera Co. Phila; Eastern Star; Huguenot Soc. Pa; Daughters of Am. Colonists; Sons and Daughters of Pilgrims; Daughters Colonial Wars; adv. bd, Salvation Army and Women's Div, March of Dimes; Am. Cancer Soc; Arthritis and Rheumatism Found; chmn. Women's Div, Red Cross, 49; Emergency Aid Pa; Holland Relief Fund; Variety Club; Sister Kenney; chmn, Hannah Penn Friends, St. Christophers Hosp; adv. mem, Nat. Leadership Coun, Nat. Cmt. for Children and Youth; bd. mem, Phila. Asn. Retarded Children; Alumnae Group Alpha Omicron Pi, Univ. Pa; pres, Stevens Sch. Alumnae, 48-49; Girl Scouts; Center City Resident's Asn; v.chmn, nat. cmt, DAR Serv. for Vet-Patients, 68-; Ladies Luncheon Cmt, Union League of Phila, 69; Judge of Miss Torch, United Fund (Bell Tel. Co), 68. Legion of Honor Award, Chapel of Four Chaplains, 66; White Orchid, registered in Eng, Named Lilias M. Lord, 69. Rel: Episcopal. Legal Res: 211 W. Tulpehocken St, Philadelphia, Pa. 19144. Mailing Add: 250 S. 16th St, Philadelphia, Pa. 19102.

LORGE, GERALD D. R
Wis. State Sen.
b. Bear Creek, Wis, 7/9/22; s. Joseph J. Lorge and Anna Marie Petersen L; m. 4/15/57 to Christina C. Ziegler; c. Robert, William and Anna Marie. Educ: Marquette Univ. Law Sch, LL.B, 52 and J.D, 68. Polit. & Govt. Pos: Wis. State Assemblyman, 50-54; Wis. State Sen, 54- Bus. & Prof. Pos: Attorney-at-law. Mil. Serv: T/Sgt, Marine Corps, 42-46. Mem: Moose; K. of C; Bear Creek and Outagamie Conserv. Clubs; Am. Legion; Outagamie and Wis. Bar Asns. Rel: Catholic. Legal Res: 147 Lorge Bldg, Bear Creek, Wis. 54922. Mailing Add: P.O. Box 147, Bear Creek, Wis. 54922.

LORING, DR. MURRAY D
Representative, Va. State Cent. Dem. Cmt.
b. New York, N.Y, 9/1/17; s. Philip Murray and Rose M; m. 3/15/45 to Mildred Rogers; c. Arthur S, Trudy and Sandra Ellen. Educ: Brooklyn Col, B.A; Cornell Univ; Middlesex Univ, D.V.M; Marshall-Wythe Sch. of Law, Col. William & Mary, J.D, 68. Polit. & Govt. Pos: Del, Dem. Nat. Conv, 63; chmn, Johnson-Humphrey Campaign, 63, Gov. Godwin Campaign, 64 and Senator William B. Spong Campaign, 66; chmn, Williamsburg-James City Co; supvr. and mem, Planning Cmt, James City Co, 64-; representative, Va. State Cent. Dem. Cmt, currently. Bus. & Prof. Pos: Pres, C. of C, 63; mem, Williamsburg-James City Merger Cmt, 63; mem, Welfare Bd, 64-; General practice of law, Williamsburg, Va, currently. Mil. Serv: Army Veterinary Corps, 44-46. Publ: Liability of Cat Scratch, Int. Cat Fancy, 68; Liability, Kennel Mgt, 68. Mem: Am. and Va. State Vet. Med. Asns; Va, Am. and Williamsburg Bar Asns; Ruritan; AF&AM. Assoc. ed, Kennel Mgt. Mag. Legal Res: 104 Willow Dr, Williamsburg, Va. 23185. Mailing Add: Drawer 280, Williamsburg, Va. 23185.

LOSCH, JOHN CHARLES R
Mass. State Rep.
b. Boston, Mass, 3/23/32; s. Paul Kenneth Losch and Helen Rorex L. (deceased); m. 1/20/68 to Lydia Ann Bachorowski. Educ: Hamilton Col, 51-54; Lambda Chi Alpha. Polit. & Govt. Pos: Chmn, Indust. Cmn, Holliston, Mass, 64-66, mem, Zoning Study Cmn, 65-, mem, Bd. of Selectmen, 67-, chmn, 69-; Mass. State Rep, 41st Middlesex Dist, 69- Bus. & Prof. Pos: Owner, John C. Losch & Co, 55- Publ: Ser. of 14 articles, 'Clockmaker's Notebook,' Bul, Nat. Asn. Watch and Clock Collectors, 8/64-12/67. Mem: Fel, Nat. Asn. Watch and Clock Collectors, Inc; Mason. Mailing Add: 2345 Washington St, Holliston, Mass. 01746.

LOSER, JOSEPH CARLTON D
b. Nashville, Tenn, 10/1/92; s. Henry J. Loser and Willie May McConnico L; m. 1/25/15 to Pearl Dean Gupton; c. Mrs. Paul Storey, Mrs. Don Gass and Judge Joe C, Jr. Educ: Cumberland Univ, LL.B, 23; Sigma Alpha Epsilon; Colemere Club. Polit. & Govt. Pos: Secy. to mayor, Nashville, Tenn, 17-20; asst. city attorney, Nashville, 23-29; asst. attorney, Tenth Judicial Dist, Tenn, 29-34, dist. attorney, 34-56; del, Dem. Nat. Conv, 44, 52 & 60; U.S. Rep, Tenn, 56-62; former Dem. Presidential Elector, committeeman, Davidson Co. Dem. Cmt. and committeeman and secy, Tenn. State Dem. Cmt. Mil. Serv: Coast Guard Res, 44. Mem: Pres, Nashville Bar Asn, 53; v.pres, Tenn. Bar Asn; Mason, K.T, KCCH (32°), Shrine; D. of A; Kiwanis; Int. Typographical Union. Rel: Baptist. Mailing Add: 4008 Newman Place, Nashville, Tenn. 37204.

LOTT, CHESTER TRENT
b. Grenada, Miss, 10/9/41; s. Chester Paul Lott and Iona Watson L; m. 12/27/64 to Patricia Elizabeth Thompson; c. Chester Trent, Jr. Educ: Univ. Miss, B.P.A. and J.D; George Washington Univ, currently; Phi Alpha Delta; Sigma Nu. Polit. & Govt. Pos: Admin. Asst. to U.S. Rep. William M. Colmer, Miss, 68- Bus. & Prof. Pos: Field Rep, Univ. Miss, 63-65, Law Alumni Secy, 66-67; Private Practice, Bryan & Gordon, Attorneys, Pascagoula, Miss, 67-68. Mem: Jackson Co, Miss. and Am. Bar Asns; Jaycees. Rel: Baptist. Legal Res: 1106-12th St, Pascagoula, Miss. 39567. Mailing Add: 732 Sixth St. S.W, Apt. 206, Washington, D.C. 20024.

LOTTERHOS, FREDERICK JACOB, JR. D
Miss. State Rep.
b. Jackson, Miss, 9/30/29; s. Frederick Jacob Lotterhos and Margaret Gor-

don Green L; m. 12/20/52 to Mary Evelyn Hand; c. Frederick Jacob, III, Mary Melonee and David Hand. Educ: Univ. Miss, B.A, 50; Univ. Va, LL.B, 56; Scabbard & Blade; Kappa Alpha Order. Polit. & Govt. Pos: Miss. State Rep, 30th Dist, Hinds Co, 68- Mil. Serv: Entered as 2nd Lt, Air Force, 53, released as 1st Lt, 55, after serv. in 463rd Troop Carrier Wing, Ardmore, Okla, 53-55. Publ: 'Supreme Court Practice,' Miss. Law J, 59. Mem: Hinds Co. and Miss. Bar Asns; Miss. Hist. Soc; C. of C; Kiwanis; River Hills Club. Rel: Episcopal. Legal Res: 242 Chippewa Circle, Jackson, Miss. 39211. Mailing Add: 236 E. Capitol St, Jackson, Miss. 39201.

LOTTO, MYRON PETER R
Wis. State Sen.
b. Green Bay, Wis, 4/7/25; m. 6/1/46 to Margaret Hutjens; c. Michael, Nancy, Cynthia, Diane, Mary Louise, Bernard and Denis. Educ: St. Norbert Col, 42. Polit. & Govt. Pos: Town clerk, DePere, Wis, 49-55, town chmn, 55-67; co. supvr, Brown Co, 55-; chmn, Brown Co. Bd, 63-68; Wis. State Sen, 69- Bus. & Prof. Pos: Farmer, 43- Mem: Holy Name Soc; K. of C; Jaycees. Outstanding Farmer of Brown Co, Jaycees, 1957. Rel: Catholic. Legal Res: Route 3, Green Bay, Wis. 54301. Mailing Add: Senate Chambers, State Capitol, Madison, Wis. 53702.

LOUGHLIN, JOHN JOSEPH D
Ind. State Rep.
b. South Bend, Ind, 7/14/26; s. William H. Loughlin and Burnadette Martin L; m. 12/19/58 to Margaret Barrie Snyder; c. Margaret Joann, Neil William and Carol Joann. Educ: Ind. Univ, Bloomington, M.S; Phi Delta Kappa; Phi Kappa Tau. Polit. & Govt. Pos: Ind. State Rep, 69- Bus. & Prof. Pos: Teacher, South Bend, Ind. Mil. Serv: Seaman 1/C, Navy, with serv. in Seabees, Pac, 2 years; Am, Pac. and Victory Medals. Mem: Nat. Educ. Asn; Nat. Coun. of Teachers of Math; Phi Delta Kappa. Rel: Presbyterian. Mailing Add: 1228 E. Wayne N, South Bend, Ind. 46615.

LOUGHRAN, FRANCIS J. D
b. Joliet, Ill, 11/19/97; m. to Marie Dwyer L; c. four, six grandchildren. Educ: DePaul U, Law, 22. Polit. & Gov. Pos: Ill. State Rep, -66; Past Spec. Asst. State Attorney of Will Co; Dem. State Cent. Cmt, 14 years. Bus. & Prof. Pos: Lawyer. Mil. Serv: U.S. Army, W.W. I. Mem: Am. Legion; Will Co. Bar; Eagles; Old Timers Baseball Asn; Holy Name Soc; Parish Chr; High Sch. Expansion Prog. Rel: Catholic. Mailing Add: 1220 Sterling Ave, Joliet, Ill. 60432. (1967)

LOUKAS, JAMES PETER D
Ill. State Sen.
b. Chicago, Ill, 12/25/16; s. Peter Loukas and Katina Grachis L; m. 11/14/43 to Helen Kokinis; c. Maralyne. Educ: Wright Jr. Col, 36-38; Chicago Kent Col. Law, 38-41; Northwest. Univ, 51. Polit. & Govt. Pos: Field auditor, Ill. Dept. Revenue; zone dep. collector, Bur. Internal Revenue; mem, 47th Ward Dem. Orgn, Ill, 38-; Ill. State Rep, 57-67, floor leader on all revenue matters, Ill. State House of Rep, 60-67, chmn, Conflict of Interest Laws Study Cmn, officer, Legis. Audit Cmn, v.chmn, Standing House Revenue Cmt. and mem, Govt. Revenue Study Cmn; Ill. State Sen, currently. Bus. & Prof. Pos: Acct, Chicago, Ill. Mem: C. of C; Int. Soc. Tax Consult; Nat. Soc. Pub. Acct; Independent Acct. Asn. Ill; Ahepa; River Park Athletic Asn; Moose; Mason; Shrine; City Club Chicago. Rel: Greek Orthodox. Mailing Add: 2612 W. Farragut Ave, Chicago, Ill. 60625.

LOUNSBERRY, RICHARD C. R
b. Lounsberry, N.Y, 2/21/16; s. Stephen M. Lounsberry; m. 10/21/39 to Mabel O'Donnell; c. four. Educ: Cornell Univ, B.A, 37, LL.B, 40. Polit. & Govt. Pos: N.Y. State Assemblyman, 52-66; Asst. Dist. Attorney, Tioga Co, 49-52; Tioga Co. Rep. Cmt. Bus. & Prof. Pos: Lawyer; past asst. to v.pres. of personnel, Remington Rand, Johnson City, 42-44. Mil. Serv: Ens, Naval Res, 44, 18 months. Mem: Past pres, Tioga Co. Bar Asn; N.Y. State Bar Asn; past Exalted Ruler, Owego Lodge of Elks 1039; past comdr, Tioga Post 401, Am. Legion; Owego Lodge, 1595, Moose; Friendship Lodge 153, F&AM; Voiture 1283, 40 et 8; Tioga Co. Sportsmen's Asn; dir, Owego Boys Club. Rel: St. Paul's Episcopal Church, Owego. Mailing Add: 329 Main St, Owego, N.Y. 13827. (1967)

LOUNSBURY, JAMES WILLIAM D
b. Springfield, Mass, 7/24/16; m. to Frances Janiszewski; c. One son. Educ: High Sch, Pittsfield, Mass; Bershire Bus. Col, Pittsfield, Mass. Polit. & Govt. Pos: Vt. State Rep, 59-68. Bus. & Prof. Pos: Storekeeper. Mil. Serv: Chief Purser, Merchant Marine. Mailing Add: North Pownal, Vt. 05260. (1967)

LOUNSBURY, ROBERT HASTINGS D
b. New York, N.Y, 6/15/21; s. Orlando Hastings Lounsbury and Elsa Cook L; div; c. Robert Hastings, Jr. and Anne Cornell. Educ: Princeton Univ. Woodrow Wilson Sch. Pub. and Int. Affairs, A.B. cum laude, 43; Yale Univ. Law Sch, LL.B, 49; Harvard Univ. Grad. Sch. Bus, Adv. Mgt. Prog, 60; Phi Beta Kappa; Order of the Coif; Colonial Club; Corby Court. Polit. & Govt. Pos: Asst, Off. of Dir, Cent. Intel. Agency, 51-52; mem. sr. staff, President's Cmt. on Int. Info. Activities, 53; former mem, N.Y. Dem. Co. Cmt; exec. dir, Nat. Businessmen for Harriman, 56; del, N.Y. Co. Dem. Judicial Conf, 57 & 66; mem, Lehman, French, vanden-Heuvel and Akers Campaigns for Cong, 17th Dist, N.Y; mem. finance cmt, Lehman for U.S. Sen; secy, businessmen's div, Citizens for Harriman and Hogan, 58; mem, Planning Cmt. and witness, N.Y. Civil Rights Conf, 60; mem. steering cmt, Dem. Forum, 60-; former mem, Lexington Dem. Club; dinner sponsor, Cmt. for Dem. Voters; sponsor, Phoenix Reform Dem. Club; v.chmn. finance cmt, N.Y. State Dem. Cmt, 60-64, co-chmn, campaign finance cmt, 64; alternate del-at-lg, Dem. Nat. Conv, 64; co-chmn, N.Y. Co. Citizens for Johnson-Humphrey-Kennedy, 64; asst. campaign mgr, Ryan for Mayor, 65; mem, Chelsea Reform Dem. Club; mem. adv. coun, Murray Hill Citizens, Conf. Dem. Students and N.Y. Young Dem. Club; campaign chmn, Robert J. Schwartz for Cong, 65-66; chmn, polit. action cmt, N.Y. State Bd, Am. for Dem. Action, 65-66 & 68- and mem, Nat. Bd, 66; mem, Commun. Planning Bd. 6, N.Y.C, 67-68; mem, Nat. Businessmen for Humphrey-Muskie and finance co-chmn, N.Y. Citizens for Kennedy Campaign, 68. Bus. & Prof. Pos: Asst. instr. Spanish, Yale Univ, 46-49, law, Yale Law Sch, 48-49; assoc. attorney, Cravath, Swaine and Moore, 49-50 & 53-56; dir, Intercontinent Finance Corp, 55-61 and Hambro Automotive Corp, 57-63; counsel, Gen. Prod. Div. and asst. counsel, Data Processing Div, Int. Bus. Mach. Corp. and gen. counsel and asst. secy, subsidiary, Serv. Bur. Corp, 56-60; gen. counsel, Kennecott Copper Corp, N.Y.C, 60-67; v.pres and gen. counsel, Eltra Corp, 67- Mil. Serv: Entered as Pvt, Army, 42, released as 1st Lt, 46, after serv. in Inf; recalled 49-50, serv. in Korea. Mem: Am. and N.Y. State Bar Asns; Asn. Bar City N.Y; Am. Judicature Soc; speaker for seminars, Practising Law Inst; former chmn. and current v.chmn, Nat. Businessmen's Coun; chmn. adv. bd, Center for Occup. Ment. Health, Cornell Univ. Med. Sch; life mem, Acad. Polit. Sci; chmn, N.Y. State Opera Soc, Inc; int. sponsors cmt, Norman Thomas Endowment; U.S. cmt, Inter-Am. Asn. for Freedom and Democracy; Princeton Club; Penn Plaza Club. Rel: Unitarian; chmn, N.Y.C. Cmt. of Sustaining Friends. Legal Res: 61 Jane St, New York, N.Y. 10014. Mailing Add: 2 Pennsylvania Plaza, New York, N.Y. 10001.

LOUPEE, EVA CELESTIA R
b. Lenawee Co, Mich, 3/15/94; d. Gustavus Adolphus Wagner and Lois Ann Whaley W; m. 7/26/14 to William B. Templeton, wid. 4/23/39; 11/24/52 to Sherman L. Loupee, M.D; c. John Earl, Herbert Wagner and William Burch Templeton. Educ: Lenawee Normal Col, Teacher's Cert, 13; Detroit Bus. Col, 43. Polit. Pos: Chmn, Cass Co. Rep. Party, Mich, 62-67; v.chmn, 58-62; membership chmn, Cass Co. Rep. Women's Club, 60-64, v.pres, 57-58; state Rep. cent. committeewoman, 4th Cong. Dist, 59-61. Bus. & Prof. Pos: Mem, Dowagiac City Library Bd, Mich, 59-65; bus. mgrs. off, Detroit Bd. of Educ, 41-52; special educ. teacher, 39-41; grade teacher, 13-14. Mem: Eastern Star; White Shrine of Jeruselem; Amaranth. Rel: Federated Church of Dowagiac; mem, exec. bd, 5 yrs, pres, Women's Fel, 4 yrs. Mailing Add: 108 Orchard St, Dowagiac, Mich. 49047. (1967)

LOURIE, ISADORE E. D
S.C. State Rep.
b. St. George, S.C, 8/4/32; s. Louis Lourie and Ann Friedman L; m. 11/29/59 to Susan Reiner; c. Lance, Joel and Neal. Educ: Univ. S.C, LL.B, 56; pres. student body, 53; Blue Key; Phi Epsilon Pi. Polit. & Govt. Pos: S.C. State Rep, 65- Bus. & Prof. Pos: Attorney-at-law. Mem: Am, State and Local Bar Asns; Am. and State Trial Lawyers Asn; pres, S.C. Jaycees, 59-60; Civitan Club; B'nai B'rith. Named Young Man of the Year, Columbia, S.C, 60. Rel: Jewish. Mailing Add: 3152 Pine Belt Rd, Columbia, S.C. 29201.

LOURIGAN, JOSEPH D
Wis. State Sen.
b. Kenosha, Wis, 3/19/01. Educ: Kenosha Bus. Col. Polit. & Govt. Pos: Mem, City Coun, Kenosha, Wis, 47, 49 & 54; Wis. State Assemblyman, 51-55; Wis. State Sen, 64- Bus. & Prof. Pos: Auto worker. Mem: Auto Workers Local (secy, 43-44, pres, 45-47). Mailing Add: 3604 19th Ave, Kenosha, Wis. 53140. (1967)

LOUX, RICHARD CHARLES 'PETE' D
Kans. State Rep.
b. Ottawa, Kans, 4/2/29; s. John Peter Loux and Zelma Sutherland L; m. 10/7/48 to Opal Lee Hill; c. Chrysa Jeanne, Marilyn Lee, Joan Lorraine, Judy Janel, Mary Jane, Paula Jean and Richard Lawrence. Educ: Wichita State Univ, B.A, 51. Polit. & Govt. Pos: Kans. State Rep, 83rd Dist, 65-, Dem. Leader, Kans. State House of Rep, 69- Bus. & Prof. Pos: Pres, Wichita Estate Planning Coun, 66-67 and Wichita CPA, 64-65. Mem: Kiwanis; Am. Inst. CPA; Nat. Asn. Acct; Toastmasters Int. Rel: Catholic. Legal Res: 237 S. Custer, Wichita, Kans. 67213. Mailing Add: 435 N. Main, Wichita, Kans. 67202.

LOVE, CLARENCE CHESTER D
Kans. State Rep.
b. Weir City, Kans, 2/24/22; s. Arthur James Love and Frances Frey L; m. 5/11/41 to Travestine Myers; c. Marva (Mrs. John Roberson), Cheryl (Mrs. Nelson Thompson), Travestine (Mrs. Clarence Moore), Terri Lynn and Clarence Jr. Educ: Kans. State Teachers Col, 2 years. Polit. & Govt. Pos: Kans. State Rep, 67- Bus. & Prof. Pos: Owner, dry cleaners, 46-60. Mil. Serv: Entered as Pvt, Army, 44, released as S/Sgt, 45, after serv. in Qm, Pac, 44-45. Mem: Mason; Cleaners Union 12; Orient Consistory. Rel: Methodist. Mailing Add: 2853 Parkview, Kansas City, Kans. 66104.

LOVE, CLYDE B. D
Mem, Calif. Dem. State Cent. Cmt.
b. Tupelo, Miss, 11/2/21; s. Thomas L. Love and Mont Stockard L; m. 2/25/46 to Phyllis Jean Briney; c. Jack Daniel and Russell Alan. Polit. & Govt. Pos: Mem, Calif. Dem. State Cent. Cmt, 68- Bus. & Prof. Pos: Partner, Mineral King Broadcasters and Rebfin of Calif; v.pres, Cent. Calif. Musicast, Nickabob Sales Co; pres, Pac. Coin Machine Distributors. Mil. Serv: Entered as SF 3/C, Navy, Seabees, 43, released as SF 2/C, 45, after serv. in 105th Bn, Pac. Theatre, 44-45. Mem: Bd. dirs, Calif. Music Merchants Asn, Mt. Whitney Area Boy Scouts and Tulare Co. March of Dimes; Visalia Moose; C. of C; Elks; Music Operators of Am; Kiwanis. Rel: Protestant. Mailing Add: 933 W. Iris St, Visalia, Calif. 93277.

LOVE, HUGH J. D
b. Beersheba Community, 9/21/95; s. Hugh S. Love and Sara Hughes L; m. 5/24/28 to Winnie Ethel Brown. Polit. & Govt. Pos: S.C. State Rep, 35-36 & 55-67. Bus. & Prof. Pos: Farmer; notary pub; merchant; secy, treas. and gen. mgr, Clover Gin & Feed Co, Inc. Mil. Serv: World War I, 18-19; spec. duty with Mil. Police. Mem: Past comdr, Clover Post 38 Am. Legion; Master Mason. Rel: Presbyterian; Elder. Mailing Add: Clover, S.C. 29710.

LOVE, JAMES PERCY D
b. McAdams, Miss, 7/12/02; married. Polit. & Govt. Pos: Miss. State Rep, 56-68. Bus. & Prof. Pos: Planter and cattleman. Mem: ODK; Nat. Cotton Producers Inst; Delta Coun; Farm Bur; Miss. Livestock Asn; Nat. Livestock Asn; Miss. Hereford Asn; Am. Hereford Asn. Rel: Baptist. Mailing Add: Tchula, Miss. 39169. (1967)

LOVE, JIMMY LEWIS D
N.C. State Rep.
b. Sanford, N.C, 12/21/34; s. James Alonzo Love and Willie Brannon L; m. 11/9/57 to Etta Brown Howard; c. Joni Brown, Jimmy L, Jr. and Melody

Campbell. Educ: Univ. N.C, A.B, 53, LL.B, 60. Polit. & Govt. Pos: Pres, Lee Co. Young Dem. Club, N.C, 58; solicitor, Lee Co. Criminal Court, 61-66; N.C. State Rep, 66- Bus. & Prof. Pos: Law clerk to Chief Justice, N.C. Supreme Court, 60661. Mil. Serv: 2nd Lt, Air Force, 57-58; serv. in 464th Combat Support Group, Pope Air Force Base, N.C, Judge Advocate Gen, 61-; Capt, Air Force Res, 61- Mem: Am. and N.C. Bar Asns; N.C. State Bar; Mason; Rotary. All-state baseball. Rel: Baptist. Legal Res: Route 5, Sanford, N.C. 27330. Mailing Add: P.O. Box 309, Sanford, N.C. 27330.

LOVE, JOHN ARTHUR R
Gov, Colo.
b. Gibson City, Ill, 11/29/16; s. Arthur C. Love and Mildred Shaver L; m. 10/23/42 to Ann Daniels; c. Dan, Andy and Becky. Educ: Univ. of Denver, B.A, 38 and Law Sch, LL.B, 41; Omicron Delta Kappa; Sigma Phi Epsilon. Hon. LL.D, Colo. Col, Colo. Sch. Mines and Univ. Denver. Polit. & Govt. Pos: Pres, El Paso Co. Young Rep, Colo, 47-48; former mem, Colo. Rep. Cent. Cmt. and El Paso Co. Rep. Exec. Cmt; chmn, Nat. Gov. Cmt. State Planning; former mem, Rep. Coord. Coun; Gov, Colo, 62-; chmn, Rep. Gov. Conf, 66- Bus. & Prof. Pos: Practice of law. Mil. Serv: Pilot, Navy, World War II, serv. with Black Cat Sq, S.Pac; Distinguished Flying Cross; Air Medal with several clusters. Mem: Colo. and Am. Bar Asns; pres, Colo. Springs C. of C, 54; Rotary; Am. Legion; plus many other prfnl. and civic orgn. Selected Colo. Man of the Year, United Press Int. for 3 years. Rel: Congregational. Mailing Add: Capitol Bldg, Denver, Colo. 80203.

LOVE, JOHN CLARK D
Chmn, Attala Co. Dem. Party, Miss.
b. Tchula, Miss, 9/19/07; married. Polit. & Govt. Pos: Mayor, Kosciusko, Miss; Miss. State Sen, 56-64 & 66-68; chmn, Attala Co. Dem. Party, currently. Bus. & Prof. Pos: Lawyer. Mem: Mason; Shrine; Sigma Phi Epsilon; Rotary; Rod and Gun Club; Kosciusko Water and Light Cmn; Kosciusko Country Club; Ole' Miss. Alumni Asn; Farm Bur; Kosciusko Golf Club; Kosciusko-Attala Co. C. of C; pres, Attala Bar Asn; State Bar Asn. Rel: Methodist. Mailing Add: Box 527, Kosciusko, Miss. 39090. (1967)

LOVE, LUCILLE A. R
R.I. State Rep.
b. Fall River, Mass, 6/28/22; m. to M. Fred Love. Educ: J.F. Wilbur High Sch, 40. Polit. & Govt. Pos: Mem, R.I. Rep. State Cent. Cmt; mem, Little Compton Rep. Town Cmt; R.I. State Rep, 63- Bus. & Prof. Pos: Housewife and tel. operator. Mailing Add: Potterville Rd, Little Compton, R.I. 02837. (1967)

LOVE, RODNEY MARVIN D
b. Dayton, Ohio, 7/18/08; s. Robert M. Love and Sallie Ray Schenck L. (both deceased); m. 12/29/34 to Margaret Sullivan; c. Nancy (Mrs. Cleaves) and Robert S. Educ: Ohio State Univ, A.B, 30; Univ. Dayton, LL.B, 33; Mich. Law Sch, summer sch. for lawyers, 61; Delta Chi. Polit. & Govt. Pos: Chief dep, Probate Court, Montgomery Co, Ohio, 41-45, probate judge, 45-59; U.S. Rep, Third Dist, Ohio and mem, House Armed Serv. Cmt, 65-66; judge, Common Pleas Court of Montgomery Co, 69- Bus. & Prof. Pos: Partner, Smith & Schnacke, Dayton. Publ: 'Hospitalized or Committed,' Pub. Welfare Mag, 50; 'Transfer of Decedents' Estates,' Practising Law Inst. of Ohio State Bar Asn, 50. Mem: Sect. mem, Real Property, Probate & Trust Law, Am. Bar Asn; pres, Dayton Bar Asn, 62-63; exec. cmt, exec. liaison mem, Probate & Trust Law & Family Law Cmts, Ohio State Bar Asn; The Dayton Lawyers Club; Miami Valley Lodge 660, Scottish Rite (32°); exec. cmt. and bd. dirs, Ment. Health Asn, Montgomery Co, Ohio; exec. cmt. and bd. dirs. and hon. serv. award, Ohio Ment. Health Asn, Inc; bd. dir, Adult Psychiat. Clin; pres, Ohio Soldiers and Sailors Orphans Home, 62-63 and bd. trustees, 60-63; past pres. and past gov, Sertoma Club; mem. corporate bd. trustees, Dayton Auto Club; chmn, freedom agenda prog, League of Women Voters, 54-55; coun, Retarded Children, Montgomery Co; Dayton Coun. World Affairs; Gem. City Dem. Club; past chmn, Speaker's Bur, past co-chmn, Campaign Cmt, World Fixers; comdr, Civilian Defense Corps, Van Buren Twp. Rel: Presbyterian. Mailing Add: 209 E. Dorothy Lane, Dayton, Ohio 45419.

LOVE, RONALD L. R
b. Clarksburg, W.Va, 7/28/36; s. John Wesley Love and Louise Isner L; m. 5/22/65 to Patricia Delbrook; c. Wendy Allyn. Educ: George Washington Univ, 54-56; West Virginia Univ, A.B. and LL.B; Iota Sigma Alpha. Polit. & Govt. Pos: Del-at-lg, Rep. Nat. Conv, 68; del, Rep. State Conv, W.Va, 68; committeeman, W.Va. Rep. State Finance Cmt, 68. Bus. & Prof. Pos: Stockbroker, Bache & Co, Parkersburg, W.Va, 62- Mil. Serv: Entered as Pfc, Army Res, 61. Mem: W.Va. State, Monongolia and Harrison Co. Bar Asns; W.Va. Law School Asn; Parkersburg Country Club; Jaycees; C. of C. Rel: Episcopal. Mailing Add: 23 Valley View Dr, Vienna, W.Va. 26101.

LOVE, SAMUEL DAVID D
b. York, Ala, 12/4/46; s. David Brown Love and Bessie Dial L; div; c. Alicia Elizabeth. Educ: Marion Mil. Inst, 64-65; Miss. State Univ, 65-69; Pi Delta Epsilon. Polit. & Govt. Pos: Alternate del, Dem. Nat. Conv, 68; nat. committeeman, Miss. Young Dem, 68- Publ: 'Mississippi Speaker Ban,' New South, 7/69. Legal Res: 200 Fellowship St, Starkville, Miss. 39759. Mailing Add: Box 585, State College, Miss. 39762.

LOVELESS, HERSCHEL CELLEL D
b. Hedrick, Iowa, 5/5/11; s. Mace Loveless and Sophia Gearing L; m. 10/1/33 to Amelia Rebecca Howard; c. Alan Kay and Sandi Ann (Mrs. Yates). Educ: High Sch; hon, Phi Theta Pi; assoc. mem, Eng. Soc. Polit. & Govt. Pos: Supt, Street Dept, Ottumwa, Iowa, 47, Mayor, 49-53; mem. legis. cmt, Iowa League of Munic, 51, chmn. first class cities group, 52; del-at-lg, Dem. Nat. Conv, 52, 56, 60 & 64; Gov, Iowa, 57-61; chmn. states cmt, Mo. Basin Inter-Agency Cmn, 59; mem. exec. coun, Gov. Conf, 59; chmn, Nat. Adv. Cmt. on Agr, Dem. Nat. Cmt, 59-60; nat. chmn, Farmers for Kennedy & Johnson and chmn, Iowa Del. and rules cmt, 60; mem, Renegotiation Bd, 61-69. Bus. & Prof. Pos: With Chicago, Milwaukee, St. Paul and Pac. R.R, 27-39, 44-47 & 48; power plant operator, John Morrell & Co, 39-44; owner and operator, Gen. Munic. Supplies, 54-56; v.pres, Chromalloy Am. Corp, 69- Mem: Platform Asn; past mem, Rwy. Clerks, AFL-CIO; Lions; Elks; Eagles; mem-at-lg, Boy Scouts, holder of Silver Beaver Award. Rel: Methodist. Legal Res: 1952 Gladstone St, Ottumwa, Iowa 52501. Mailing Add: 7523 17th St. N.W, Washington, D.C. 20012.

LOVELL, PAUL DEAN D
V.Chmn, Kankakee Co. Dem. Cmt, Ill.
b. Kankakee, Ill, 3/16/31; s. Francis Lovell and Elizabeth Wagner L; m. 4/28/51 to Norma Carroll; c. Linda Beth, Christine Ann, Karen Jean and Patrick Dean. Educ: Int. Correspondence Sch, 50-51; Gen. Motors Inst. Tech, 55. Polit. & Govt. Pos: Civil Defense dir, Bradley, Ill, 65-67; Dem. precinct committeeman, Precinct 2, Bourbonnais Twp, Ill, 65-; assessor, Bourbonnais Twp, 65-; mem, sch. bd, Bishop McNamara High Sch, Kankakee, 67-68; v.chmn, Kankakee Co. Dem. Cmt, 67- Bus. & Prof. Pos: Staff adjustor, Motors Ins. Corp, Kankakee, Ill, 55-; partner, N.L.S. Realty, 67-; pres, Olsten Corp. of Kankakee, 68- Mem: Nat. Asn. of Assessing Off; Nat. Asn. of Real Estate Brokers; Kankakee Co. Bd. of Realtors; Lions; K. of C; Local 11 Bldg. Serv. Employees. Rel: Catholic. Mailing Add: 532 Park Ave, Bradley, Ill. 60615.

LOVENHEIM, DAVID A. R
b. Hackensack, N.J, 10/1/42; s. Earl P. Lovenheim and Belle Yampolski L; m. 8/1/65 to Robert Levine. Educ: Brown Univ, B.A, 64; George Wash. Univ, J.D, 67; Tower Club; Phi Delta Phi. Polit. & Govt. Pos: Legis. aide to U.S. Rep. Frank Horton, N.Y, 65-67, admin. asst, 67-, mem, Cong. Staff Task Force, Human Investment Act, 66. Publ: Berlin: A Tale of Two Cities,' Brown Daily Herald Suppl, 63, 'Birmingham in Crisis,' (series), Brown Daily Herald, Providence Evening Bul. Mem: Bull Elephants; Cong. Secy. Club; CRONY; George Wash. Law Asn. Rel: Jewish. Legal Res: 90 Georgian Court Rd, Rochester, N.Y. 14610. Mailing Add: 4839 Yorktown Blvd, Arlington, Va. 22207.

LOVERIDGE, DELLA LISONBEE D
Utah State Rep.
b. Monroe, Utah, 8/9/04; d. Lorenzo Lisonbee and Sarah Petersen L; m. 9/18/21 to Elmo S. Loveridge; c. Max Elmo. Educ: Brigham Young Univ; L.D.S. Bus. Col. Polit. & Govt. Pos: Utah State Rep, Utah Co, 43-47, Salt Lake Co, 59-, Minority Whip, Utah House Rep, Minority Floor Leader; mem. adv. coun, State Welfare Cmn, 45-48, 60-63 & 67-69; mem. and del, State Cent. Cmt, 10 years; pres. and organizer, State Fed. Dem. Women's Clubs, 58-62; chairlady, Utah Co. Dem. Party; co-chmn, Legis. Dist. and Sen. Dist. Dem. Party; mem, Utah Co. Dem. Cent. Cmt. and State Platform, Credentials and Resolutions Cmts; mem, State Cmt. Aging and del, Nat. White House Conf. on Aging, 59-63, mem, Legis. Coun, 60-63 & 67-69; del, President Kennedy's Cmn. Ment. Retardation, West. Regional Conf. Commun, Population Dilemma and Family Planning Conf. West. States, West States Leaders Conf. and Nat. Legis. Leaders Conf; mem, Gov. Cmt. Handicapped Children; mem, State Rehabilitation Cmt. for Blind; faculty, 13 West. States Commun. Serv. Conf. Voc. Rehabilitation. Bus. & Prof. Pos: Owner and operator two apt. houses, 34-69 and sch. of beauty culture, 47-50; instr, Adv. Hair Design, 50-56. Mem: State and Nat. Order Women Legislators, nat. parliamentarian; Bus. & Prfnl. Women's Club, 29-69; Lady Lions; Women's State Legis. Coun; Salt Lake Coun. Women; pres, Utah Beauticians Asn; Daughters of Utah Pioneers. Named Mother of the Year, South Salt Lake; Outstanding Bus. Women, 57, Bus. & Prfnl. Women's Club. Rel: Latter-day Saint. Mailing Add: 2336 S. Third E, Salt Lake City, Utah 84115.

LOVETT, ROBERT ABERCROMBIE D
b. Huntsville, Tex, 9/14/95; s. Robert Scott Lovett and Lavinia Chilton L; m. 4/19/19 to Adele Quartley Brown; c. Evelyn, Robert Scott II. Educ: Yale, B.A, 18; Harvard, 19-20; Harvard Grad. Schs, 19-21. LL.D, Amherst Col, Brown Univ, Columbia Univ, Harvard Univ, L.I. Univ, Princeton Univ, Sam Houston State Teachers Col. and Williams Col; hon. M.A. and LL.D, Yale. Polit. & Govt. Pos: Spec. asst. to Secy. of War, 40-41, Asst. Secy. of War for Air, 41-45; Undersecy. of State, 47-49; Dep. Secy. Defense, 50-51; Secy. of Defense, 51-53; consult. to President Kennedy, 61-63. Bus. & Prof. Pos: Clerk, Nat. Bank of Commerce, N.Y.C, 21; gen. partner, Brown Bros, Harriman & Co, 26-; dir. and mem, exec. cmt, Union Pac. R.R. and subsidiary transportation co; dir, Union Pac. Corp, N.Y. Investment Cmt, Royal-Globe Ins. Co; dir. and mem, finance cmt, CBS, Inc; dir, Freeport Sulphur Co; trustee, Carnegie Inst, Wash; life mem. corp, Mass. Inst. Tech. Mil. Serv: Entered as A/S, Navy, 17, released as Lt. Comdr, 18; Distinguished Serv. Medal; Grand Cross Order Leopold II, Belgium; Presidential Medal of Freedom. Mem: Century Asn; Yale, Creek, Metrop. and Links Clubs. Mailing Add: Locust Valley, Long Island, N.Y. 11560.

LOVETT, WELLS THOMAS D
Owensboro, Ky, 12/6/23; s. Joe Thomas Lovett and Laurine Wells L; m. 4/12/53 to Mary Whitfield McKinley; c. John T, Howard W. and James W. Educ: Murray State Univ, 40-41; Univ. Ky, 41-42; Ohio State Univ, B.S. in Bus. Educ, 43; Univ. Mich. Law Sch, J.D, 49; Phi Delta Phi; Sigma Alpha Epsilon. Polit. & Govt. Pos: Mem, Ky. Pub. Serv. Cmn, 63-68, chmn, 68; alternate del, Dem. Nat. Conv, 68. Bus. & Prof. Pos: Partner, Lovett and Kusch, Attorneys-at-law, Owensboro, 50-; pres, Citizens Security Life Ins. Co, 68- Mil. Serv: Entered as A/S, Navy, 43, released as Lt.(jg), 46, after serv. in Amphibious Forces, West. Pac. and Japanese Theaters, 44-46. Mem: Am. Bar Asn. Rel: United Methodist. Legal Res: 2829 Eastern Pkwy, Owensboro, Ky. 42301. Mailing Add: 208 W. Third St, Owensboro, Ky. 42301.

LOVITT, CRAIG EDWARD D
Committeeman, Ill. State Dem. Cent. Cmt.
b. Terre Haute, Ill, 2/18/32; s. John Preston Lovitt and Mildred Pence L; single. Educ: Knox Col, B.A, 54; Univ. of Va, M.A, 59; Phi Beta Kappa; Delta Sigma Rho; Alpha Delta. Polit. & Govt. Pos: Chmn, Knox Col. Students for Stevenson, Ill, 52; chmn, Knox Co. Citizens for Sen. Douglas, 54; precinct committeeman, Knox Co. Dem. Cent. Cmt, 60-, chmn, 64-; admin. asst. to U.S. Rep. Gale Schisler, Ill, 65-66; asst. to Gov. Otto Kerner, Ill, 67-68; committeeman, 19th Cong. Dist, Ill. State Dem. Cent. Cmt, 67-; asst. to Gov. Samuel Shapiro, Ill, 68-69; admin. asst. to Lt. Gov. Paul Simon, Ill, 69- Bus. & Prof. Pos: Admissions counsr, Knox Col, 56-57; admin. asst. to Dir. of Soviet Bloc For. Econ. Rels. Proj, Univ. of Va, 57-59; assoc. dir. and dir. of pub. rels, Knox Col, 59-64. Publ: 'Soviet Foreign Economic Policy in

Yugoslavia,' Swiss Rev. of World Affairs, 59; 'Yugoslavia and the Soviet Union,' Pakistan Horizon, 59; 'State Practices to Coordinate Applications for Federal Aid Grants at the State Level,' Proceedings of 1968 Conference on State Aspects of Federal Aid Programs, Ill. Cmn. on Intergovt. Coop. Mem: Am. Col. Pub. Rels. Asn; Am. Soc. Pub. Admin; Lions. Rel: Unitarian. Mailing Add: 364 Day St, Galesburg, Ill. 61401.

LOW, DANIEL TIEN KEE R
b. Honolulu, Oahu, Hawaii, 9/19/98; s. Louis Sam Low (deceased) and Lucy Kyau Tai Fong Wong L; m. 6/25/29 to Katherine Hoon Seu Young; c. Mildred H.O. (Mrs. Dwight McGraw) and Donald H.C. Educ: Univ. Hawaii, B.S. Polit. & Govt. Pos: Alternate del, Rep. Nat. Conv, 68. Bus. & Prof. Pos: Cadastral engr, Co. of Maui, Hawaii, retired. Mil. Serv: Cpl, Student Army Training Corps, 18. Mem: Am. Legion Post No. 8, Maui, Hawaii and Post No. 11, Honolulu, Hawaii; Hawaiian Govt. Employees Asn; Maui Hist. Soc. Rel: Protestant. Legal Res: 324 Oluloa Dr, Wailuku, Maui, Hawaii 96793. Mailing Add: P.O. Box 962, Wailuku, Maui, Hawaii 96793.

LOW, FLETCHER R
b. Essex, Mass, 4/7/93; s. George Percy Low and Elizabeth Burnham L; wid; c. Nancy E. and Joanne (Mrs. Donald W. Publicover). Educ: Dartmouth Col, B.S, 15; Columbia Univ, M.A, 17, Ph.D, 27; Sigma Xi; Kappa Kappa Kappa. Polit. & Govt. Pos: Mem, sch. bd, Hanover, N.H, 41-50; selectman, Bd. Selectmen, Hanover, 50-64; N.H. State Rep, 61-67; VISTA vol, 66-67. Bus. & Prof. Pos: Instr. chem, Dartmouth Col, 17-24, asst. prof, 24-34 and prof, 34-60. Mem: Pres, N.H. Munic. Asn, 56 and N.H. State Assessors Asn, 53; Am. Chem. Soc; Am. Asn. Univ. Prof. Prfnl. baseball, 15-19. Rel: Congregational. Mailing Add: Hanover, N.H. 03755.

LOW, NORMAN C, JR. D
Chmn, Pickens Co. Dem. Exec. Cmt, Ga.
b. Talking Rock, Ga, 12/16/25; s. Norman C. Low, Sr. and Jewell Bunch L; m. 4/29/56 to Helen Hobson; c. Michael C, Holly Lynn and Joe C. Educ: N.Ga. Col, 1½ years. Polit. & Govt. Pos: Chmn, Pickens Co. Dem. Exec. Cmt, Ga, 67- Bus. & Prof. Pos: Owner, N.C. Low Gen. Merchandise, 50-; mgr, N.C. Low Pulpwood Co, 52- Mil. Serv: Entered as Pvt, Marines, 44, released as Sgt, 46, after serv. in Second Marine Air Wing, Pac. Theater, 45-46. Mem: Mason; Farm Bur; Ga. Forestry Asn; Am. Pulpwood Asn. Rel: Baptist. Mailing Add: P.O. Box 5, Talking Rock, Ga. 30175.

LOW, ROBERT A. Dem-Liberal
Councilman, N.Y.C.
b. Scarsdale, N.Y, 6/6/19; s. Clarence Low and Madeleine Mayer L; m. 1/31/52 to Frances D. Levison; c. Allen Robert and Roger Morton. Educ: Stanford Univ, B.A, 41; George Washington Univ. Law Sch, LL.B, 54; Phi Beta Kappa; Sigma Delta Chi. Polit. & Govt. Pos: Legis. asst. to Sen. Herbert N. Lehman, 50; exec. secy. to Rep. Henry M. Jackson, 51; spec. asst. to legal advisor, U.S. Dept. State, 52-54; asst. campaign mgr, Wagner for Senate, 56; asst. to Mayor Robert F. Wagner, 59-61; asst. to Dem. Nat. Chmn, 60; councilman, N.Y.C, 61-; co-chmn, Platform Cmt, N.Y. State Dem. Cmt, 62-66. Bus. & Prof. Pos: Advert. mgr, Saturday Review, 45-50. Mil. Serv: Entered as Midshipman, Naval Res, 41, released as Lt. Comdr, 45, after serv. in Pac; Am. and Pac. Theater Ribbons with 9 Battle Stars; Philippines and Victory Medals. Publ: 'Unconventional Conventions,' Saturday Rev, 60; various book reviews. Mem: VFW; Amvets Cmt; B'nai B'rith; Am. Jewish Cmt; Citizens for Clean Air, Inc; East Harlem Civic Asn; Yorkville C. of C. Nat. Boys Indoor Tennis Champion, singles & doubles, 33; Nat. Interscholastic Tennis, singles & doubles, 36. Rel: Jewish. Mailing Add: 527 E. 84th St, New York, N.Y. 10028.

LOW, THEODORE F. R
R.I. State Rep.
b. Providence, R.I, 3/31/27; s. Isador S. Low and Cecile Siden L; m. 10/21/60 to D. Kay Hohenthaner; c. Sara Beth and Emily Lauren. Educ: Brown Univ, B.A, 49; Ohio State Sch. of Bus, 54; Pi Lambda Phi; pres. of class, 49. Polit. & Govt. Pos: R.I. State Rep, Fourth Dist, Providence, 65-; mem, Rep. Second Ward Cmn, Providence, 65-; chmn, Rep. Party of Providence, currently; mem, R.I. State Rep. Cent. Cmt, currently. Bus. & Prof. Pos: Pres, Kinsley Burner & Machine Co, 58-62; pres. and chmn. bd, Sims Corp, 58- Mil. Serv: Entered as Pvt, Army, 44, released as Capt, 52; served in 43rd Inf. and other divs, 8th Army, 44-47, Pac. Theater, 47 and Korean Theater, 50-52; Pac. Theater, Am. Theater and Victory Ribbons; Korean Conflict Ribbon with 3 Battle Stars; UN and Unit Commendation Medals. Mem: Univ. Club; Saunderstown Yacht Club; Twenty Hundred Club; bd. dirs, Brown Club of R.I; R.I. Sch. of Design Mus; Nat. Soc. of State Legis; pres, Moses Brown Sch. Alumni Asn. and mem. bd. trustees; trustee, World Affiars Coun; Providence C. of C; Pawtucket C. of C; v.pres, Jewish Orphanage of R.I; bd. dirs, Planned Parenthood of R.I. Yachting. Rel: Jewish. Mailing Add: 95 Blackstone Blvd, Providence, R.I. 02906.

LOWANCE, CARTER OLIN D
b. Greenville, W.Va, 12/3/10; s. William Franklin Lowance and Dora Gibson L; m. 6/14/33 to Sarah Elizabeth Austin. Educ: Roanoke Col, A.B, 31; Blue Key. Polit. & Govt. Pos: Exec. asst. to Gov, Va, 47-58 & 62-; Alternate del, Dem. Nat. Conv, 48, 56 & 64; asst. pres, Med. Col. of Va, 58-62; State Comnr. of Admin, 66- Bus. & Prof. Pos: Reporter and ed, Roanoke Times, Va, 31-36; staff writer, Assoc. Press, 36-47; dir, N.Am. Assurance Soc. of Va, 62- Mil. Serv: Entered as Pvt, Army, 42, released as 2nd Lt, 45, after serv. in Counterintel. Corps, ETO, 44-45; Lt.Col.(Ret), Va. Army Nat. Guard; Presidential Unit Citation; Normandy, North. France, Ardennes, Rhineland and Cent. Europe Campaign Ribbons; direct cmn. in France. Publ: 'The Governor of Virginia,' Univ. Va. News Letter, 2/60. Mem: Torch; Nat. Guard Asn. of the U.S; charter mem, 82nd Airborne Div. Asn. Va. Distinguished Serv. Medal, 68. Rel: Episcopal. Mailing Add: 1120 West Ave, Richmond, Va. 23220.

LOWANCE, FRANKLIN E. R
City Councilman, Santa Barbara, Calif.
b. Monroe Co, W.Va, 12/29/07; s. William Franklin Lowance and Dora Hill Gibson L; m. 6/12/30 to Thelma Duane Beckham; c. William Franklin. Educ: Roanoke Col, B.S, 27; Duke Univ, A.M, 31 and Ph.D, 35; Sigma Xi. Polit. & Govt. Pos: City councilman, Santa Barbara, Calif, 65- Bus. & Prof. Pos: Prof, physics, Ga. Inst. of Tech, 42-50; assoc. tech. dir, Naval Ord. Test Sta, 53-55; v.pres, Westinghouse Air Brake Corp, 55-58; v.pres, Crosley Div, Avco Corp, 58-60; pres, Adv. Tech. Corp, 60-63. Publ: Engineering Organization, Riverside Press, 61; 'Magnetic Effects in Metals,' Phys. Rev, 35; Operations Research, Case Inst, 55. Mem: Nat. Soc. Prfnl. Engrs; fel, Am. Soc. Civil Engrs; Railway Soc. of Pittsburgh; Am. Ord. Asn; Am. Phys. Soc; La Cumbre Country Club; Edgeworth Club; Channel City Club; bd. of dirs, City Col. Adv. Coun. and pres, 64-65. Rel: Presbyterian. Mailing Add: 41 Tierra Cielo, Santa Barbara, Calif. 93105.

LOWDEN, ELMER WILLIS D
Conn. State Rep.
b. Stamford, Conn, 7/19/10; s. Amos Elmer Lowden and Alice Fairchild L; m. 8/4/33 to Edna Irene Kristiansen; c. Lynn M, Scott R. and Laureen S. Educ: N.Y. Univ, 28-30. Polit. & Govt. Pos: Mem, Stamford Dem. City Cmt, Conn, 50-66 and chmn, 62-64; mem, Bd. of Tax Rev, Stamford, 55-57 and Zoning Bd, 62-64; Justice of Peace, 56-66; Conn. State Rep, 67- Bus. & Prof. Pos: Title exam, Cummings & Lockwood, Attorneys, 30-45 and chief of title sect, 45-66. Mem: The Roasters Lampoon Club. Rel: Methodist. Mailing Add: 60 Fairview Ave, Stamford, Conn. 06902. (1967)

LOWE, ALLEN JAMES R
b. Glen Flora, Tex, 3/8/08; s. Martin Frank Lowe and Lula Amos L; m. to DeNage Kleespies; c. Allen James, Jr. Polit. & Govt. Pos: Del, Rep. Nat. Conv, 68. Bus. & Prof. Pos: Asst. mgr, Palmer House, Chicago, Ill, 35-36; sales mgr. and resident mgr, Pick-Carter Hotel, 36-38, managing dir, 40-60; gen. mgr, Rowe Hotel, Grand Rapids, Mich, 36-40; pres. and gen. mgr, Sheraton-Cleveland Hotel, Cleveland, Ohio, 60- Mem: Canterbury Country Club; Cleveland Athletic Club; Mid-Day Club; City Club; Shrine Luncheon Club; Kiwanis; Touchdown Club; Ohio Soc. of N.Y. Mailing Add: Sheraton-Cleveland Hotel, Public Square, Cleveland, Ohio 44101. (1967)

LOWE, AYLMER LYNN R
b. Garland, Ark, 3/6/36; s. Jessie Luther Lowe and Ruth McKinley L; m. 7/8/56 to Nedria Jean Bledsoe; c. Evelyn Ruth, Michael Lynn and Martha Elizabeth. Educ: Univ. Ark, B.S.A.E, 59. Polit. & Govt. Pos: Mem, Garland Sch. Bd, Ark, 60-67; mem, Miller Co. Rep. Cmt, 64-66; chmn, Fourth Dist. Rep. Cmt, 64-66; mem, Ark. Rep. Exec. Cmt, 64-69; Rep. cand, U.S. Rep, Ark, 66; del, Rep. Nat. Conv, 68; treas, Ark. State Rep. Party, 68-69; mem, Miller Co. Levee Bd, 68-; mem, McKinney Bayou Drainage Bd, 68-; mem, Ark. State Agr. Stabilization & Conserv. Serv. Cmt, 69- Mem: Farm Bur; Ark. Cattlemans Asn. Rel: Lutheran; Mo. Synod. Mailing Add: Route 4, Box 481, Texarkana, Ark. 75501.

LOWE, DAVID WILLIAM D
Mem, Calif. Dem. State Cent. Cmt.
b. La Crosse, Wis, 2/15/35; s. John Van der veer Lowe and Carla Grotefend L; m. 6/6/64 to Patricia Rose Bradley; c. David Bradley and Pamela Elisabeth. Educ: Univ. Calif, Berkeley, A.A. & A.B, LL.B. & J.D, 61; Charles Mills Galey fel, 58-59; Tau Kappa Epsilon; Gavel & Quill; Calif. Club; Order of the Golden Bear. Polit. & Govt. Pos: Attorney, Housing & Home Finance Agency, 61-62; dep. dist. attorney, Alameda Co, Calif, 62-65 and Solano Co, Calif, 65-67; mem, Calif. Dem. State Cent. Cmt, 68-; secy, Solano Co. Dem. Cent. Cmt, 68- Bus. & Prof. Pos: Assoc, Dobbins, Weir & Thompson, Vacaville, Calif, 67- Mil. Serv: Entered as Pvt. E-1, Army, 53, released as Pfc, 55, after serv. in Second Armoured Div, Hq, Bad Kreuznach, Germany, 53-55; Nat. Defense, Army of Occup. and Good Conduct Medals. Mem: Phi Delta Phi; Alameda Co. Lawyers Club; Alameda Co. Dem. Lawyers Club; Calif. State Bar; Solano Co. Bar Asn; Am. and Calif. Trial Lawyers Asns; Am. Judicature Soc; Commonwealth Club of Calif; Vacaville C. of C; Rotary. Legal Res: 536 W. Deodara St, Vacaville, Calif. 95688. Mailing Add: 500 Main St, Vacaville, Calif. 95688.

LOWE, DOROTHY ERMINIE R
Rep. Chmn, Precinct 165, Harris Co, Tex.
b. Alvarado, Tex, 4/27/08; d. J. Stone Rives and Annie Williams R; m. 9/29/28 to Emilus Preston Lowe; c. Sara (Mrs. Bolieu). Educ: Lon Morris Col, A.A, 26; Univ. Houston, B.S, 48, M.Ed, 51; Kappa Delta Pi. Polit. & Govt. Pos: Del. to Co. and State Rep. Conv, 62 & 64; East Harris Co. campaign mgr. for Bill Hayes for Lt. Gov, 62 and for Congressman, 64; mem. from Precinct 165, Fund Raising and Tel. Cmts, 62-; Del, Rep. Nat. Conv, 64; mem, Vacancy Cmt, Harris Co. Rep. Party, 64-; Rep. chmn, Precinct 165, Harris Co, Tex, 64- Bus. & Prof. Pos: Teacher, Burnet Independent Sch. Dist, Tex, 26-27, London Independent Sch. Dist, Tex, 27-28; Lometa Independent Sch. Dist, 29-30; hist. teacher, Goose Creek Independent Sch. Dist, 46-66. Mem: Baytown Educ. Asn; Tex. State Teachers Asn; Tex. Classroom Teachers Asn; Rep. Women's Club. Rel: Church of Christ. Mailing Add: 502-A, Catter Dr, Austin, Tex. 79704.

LOWE, HERBERT JULIAN D
b. Buffalo, Ala, 3/24/23; m. to Dorthy Ramona Green; c. 2. Educ: Woodland High Sch. Polit. & Govt. Pos: Ala. State Sen, 62-66. Bus. & Prof. Pos: Dodge auto dealer. Mil. Serv: U.S. Maritime Serv. Mem: Kiwanis; Quarterback Club. Rel: Methodist. Mailing Add: P.O. Box 592, Roanoke, Ala. 36274. (1967)

LOWE, HERMAN JOSEPH 'MONDAY' D
b. Chamberlin, La, 7/25/23; s. Shelby Bernard Lowe, Sr. and Maude Petite L; m. 11/23/47 to Bessie Peavy; c. Laurie Elizabeth, Elizabeth Rema, Linda Kathryn and Letitia Anne. Educ: La. State Univ, B.S; Beta Alpha Psi. Polit. & Govt. Pos: Asst. secy-treas, West Baton Rouge Parish, La, 54-64; City Clerk, Port Allen, 56-64; treas, West Baton Rouge Parish Commun. Center Cmn, 56-64; former La. State Rep, West Baton Rouge Parish. Bus. & Prof. Pos: Mem, exec. bd, La. Laundry and Cleaners Asn, 64-; mem, bd. dir, West Baton Rouge Parish Bank, 66- Mil. Serv: Entered as Seaman, Navy, 43, released as Torpedoman 2/C, 46, after serv. in Field Torpedo Unit 21; Am. Theater and Asiatic-Pac. Campaign Ribbons. Mem: Treas, Baton Rouge Chap, La. CPA's, 60, v.pres, 61, pres, 62; exec. bd, La. Soc. of CPA's, 66-67; Am. Inst. of CPA's; past pres, Holy Family Sch. Boosters Club; Port Allen Rotary Club; West Baton Rouge Parish Farm Bur. Rel: Roman Catholic. Legal Res: 568 Ave. C, Port Allen, La. 70767. Mailing Add: 313 S. Jefferson Ave, Port Allen, La. 70767. (1967)

LOWE, HERMUS W. D
b. Delmar, Del, 7/12/14; married. Educ: Delmar pub. schs. Polit. & Gov. Pos: Md. State Del, 63-67; formerly, Wicomico Co. Bd. of Co. Cmnrs; Wicomico Co. Planning and Zoning Cmn; Salisbury Planning and Zoning Cmn; Wicomico Co. Sch. Bldg. Cmt. Bus. & Prof. Pos: Real estate appraiser; owner, oper, drive-in restaurant. Mil. Serv: Navy. Mem: Elks; Moose; Am. Legion; VFW; Exchange Club. Mailing Add: 1301 Woodland Rd, Salisbury, Md. 21801. (1967)

LOWE, JAY R. D
Chmn, Legis. Dist. 26, Dem. Party, Idaho
b. Franklin, Idaho, 12/18/26; s. Acel Lowe and Ramona Richards L; m. 8/3/51 to Pauline Ray; c. Cris, Paula, Richard, Kathy and Roger. Educ: Idaho State Univ; Brigham Young Univ. Polit. & Govt. Pos: Chmn, Legis. Dist. 26, Dem. Party, Idaho, 66- Mil. Serv: Entered as Pvt, Army, 45, released as Pfc, 47. Rel: Latter-day Saint. Mailing Add: Moore, Idaho 83255. (1967)

LOWE, JERE B. R
Chmn, Poinsett Co. Rep. Party, Ark.
b. Fulton, Ky, 6/30/29; s. Kellie R. Lowe and Nelle Graves L; m. 12/20/58 to Gertrude Nidermaier; c. Derek Bates and Brendon Slemp. Educ: Univ. Louisville, 47-48; Okla. Baptist Univ, 48-49; Univ. Tenn, D.D.S, 60; Delta Sigma Delta. Polit. & Govt. Pos: Chmn, Poinsett Co. Rep. Party, Ark, 66-; judicial appointments adv. to Gov. and mem, Citizens Adv. Cmt. to Gov, Ark, 67-; chmn, Northeast Ark. Co. Rep. Chairmen, 69- Bus. & Prof. Pos: Dental health consult, Ark. Pub. Health Dept, 61- Mil. Serv: Entered as Pvt, Air Force, 50, released as S/Sgt, 54, after serv. at Laon-Couvron Air Force Base Hosp, France, 52-54. Mem: Am. and Ark. State Dental Asns; Northeast Ark. Dental Soc.(exec. coun, 66-); Ark. Soc. of Dentistry for Children (exec. coun, 64-69); Mason; Am. Legion; Farm Bur; Rotary; exec. bd, Northeast Ark. Coun, Boy Scouts. Rel: Methodist; Mem. off. bd, First Methodist Church, Harrisburg, Ark. Legal Res: 405 Brooks St, Harrisburg, Ark. 72432. Mailing Add: P.O. Box 587, Harrisburg, Ark. 72432.

LOWE, KENNETH C.
N.Dak. State Sen.
b. Bemidji, Minn, 2/13/04; married: c. four. Polit. & Govt. Pos: Mem, city coun, 9 years. State Elec. Bd, 9 years and former N.Dak. State Rep; mem, Educ. Cmn. of the States; N.Dak. State Sen, currently. Bus. & Prof. Pos: Motion Picture Projectionist. Mem: Mason; Shrine; Elks; bd. dirs. representing N.Dak, Merchant Marine Asn, Inc, Kings Point, N.Y. Rel: Lutheran. Mailing Add: 718 N. Fifth St, Grand Forks, N.Dak. 58201.

LOWE, RALPH GEORGE D
Dem. Precinct Committeeman, Concord Twp, Louisa Co, Iowa
b. Letts, Iowa, 1/27/94; s. George B. Lowe and Alice Wagner L; m. 5/29/15 to Laura May Shellabarger; c. G. Ralph, Jr. and Dean H.(deceased). Educ: High sch. Polit. & Govt. Pos: Del, Dem. Nat. Conv, 40 & 44, sgt-at-arms, 48, mem, Harriman Cmt, 52, alternate del, 56 & 60, del-at-lg, 64; Dem. Precinct committeeman, Concord Twp, Louisa Co, Iowa, 42-; chmn, Louisa Co. Dem. Party, 51-62. Mem: Mason; DeMolay; Scottish Rite (32°); Shrine; Elks; Farmers Union. Rel: Methodist. Mailing Add: Letts, Iowa 52754. (1967)

LOWE, THOMAS HUNTER D
Speaker, Md. House of Del.
b. McDaniel, Md, Jan, 1928; s. Denton Scott Lowe and Louise Price L; m. 1/30/53 to Jane Bradley; c. John Vincent. Educ: Towson Jr. Col, A.A, 50; Wash. Col, A.B. cum laude, 52; Univ. Md. Law Sch, LL.B, 56; Omicron Delta Kappa;Kappa Alpha (pres). Polit. & Govt. Pos: Law clerk, Supreme Court, 54-55; mem. Dept. of Legis. Reference, Md. House of Del, 55-56, Md. State Del, 57-, chmn, House Judiciary Cmt, 61-69, majority leader, 67-69, speaker, 69-; gen. counsel, Dem. Party, 67-; alternate del, Dem. Nat. Conv, 68. Bus. & Prof. Pos: Attorney-at-law, 56-, St. Michaels, 58-, Penn Cent. R.R, 68-; gen. counsel, Dem. Party Md. Mil. Serv: Marine Corps, 45-46. Mem: Talbot Co, Md. State and Am. Bar Asns; fel, Md. Bar Found; Md. Farm Bur; Elks Lodge, Easton 1622; Easton Lions Club; Talbot Retriever Club; Am. Legion; Miles River Yacht Club; VFW; Talbot Rod & Gun Club; Easton Jr. C. of C; Talbot Football, Inc. Rel: Protestant. Legal Res: Wittman, Md. 21676. Mailing Add: 225 Stewart Bldg, Easton, Md. 21601.

LOWE, WILLARD D
Educ: Ind. Cent. Col, B.S; Butler Univ. Polit. & Govt. Pos: Ind. State Rep, -66. Bus. & Prof. Pos: Retired teacher; operator, laundromat. Mem: Past master, Mason; OES, past patron; Kiwanis, past pres and Lt. Gov. Rel: Baptist. Mailing Add: Westport, Ind. 47283. (1967)

LOWELL, HARRIETTE MARY R
Second V.Chmn, Livingston Co. Rep. Cmt, N.Y.
b. Dalton, N.Y, 10/31/16; d. Walter Lawrence Kelley and Mildred G.A. White K; m. 7/2/38 to Francis William Lowell; c. Terry Kelley, Nancy Sue and Bradley Walter. Educ: Sch. of Commerce, Rochester, N.Y, 34-35. Polit. & Govt. Pos: Active in getting out the vote, N.Y, 34-62; pres, Livingston Co. Rep. Women's Club, N.Y, 62; del, Rep. State Conv, 62 and alternate del, 66; secy. to finance chmn, Livingston Co. Rep. Party, 62; head, Austin Crevin Erwin Campaign, 62; mem, Livingston Co. Rep. Cmt, 10 years, second v.chmn, 68-; mem, Rep. Assembly Cmt, 69; mem, Rep. Cmts, James Emery for Assemblyman and Barber Conable. Bus. & Prof. Pos: Bookkeeper and bus. mgr, Dalton Tel. Corp, 39-60; mem. staff, Div. Unemploy. Ins, 60-64; secy, State Univ. N.Y, 64- Mem: PTA (pres, Dalton Chap); Eastern Star; chmn, March of Dimes; chmn, Heart and Cancer Drives. Rel: Methodist. Mailing Add: 10052 Fair St, Dalton, N.Y. 14836.

LOWELL, JAMES BELDEN, JR. R
Conn. State Rep.
b. Hartford Conn; s. James B. Lowell and Ruth E. Wheeler L; m. 6/19/51 to Barbara R. Elston; c. James B, III, Mark E, Jennifer and L. Jeffrey. Educ: Dartmouth Col, B.A, 51; Theta Chi. Polit. & Govt. Pos: Conn. State Rep, 61- Bus. & Prof. Pos: Independent ins. agent in partnership with J.B. Lowell & Son, 55-68; secy-treas, Kenney, Webber & Lowell, Inc, 69. Mil. Serv: Entered as Pvt, Army, 52, released as 2nd Lt, 53, after serv. in Artil. Officer Cand. Sch, 44th and 40th Inf. Div, Korea, 53; Maj, Army Res, 66- Mem: Mason; Grange; state dir, Conn. Asn. Independent Ins. Agents, 66- Rel: Protestant. Mailing Add: 8 Spring St, Collinsville, Conn. 06022.

LOWELL, STANLEY H. D
b. N.Y.C, 4/13/19; s. Isidore Lowenbraun and Mildred Cohen L; m. 3/29/47 to Vivian Abrams; c. Jeffrey, Darcy and Lauri. Educ: City Col, New York, B.S.S, 39; Harvard Law Sch, LL.B, 42; Lock and Key. Polit. & Govt. Pos: Asst. U.S. attorney, South Dist, N.Y, 43-47; asst. to Pres. Borough of Manhattan, 50-53; exec. asst. to the Mayor, N.Y.C, 54-57, dep. mayor, 58; campaign exec, Robert F. Wagner for Sen, 56 and Robert F. Wagner for Mayor, 57-61; del, N.Y. Dem. State Conv; chmn, N.Y.C. Cmn. on Human Rights, 60-65; del, Dem. Nat. Conv, 60, 64 & 68; campaign mgr, Paul R. Screvane for Mayor, 65; campaign dir, Robert F. Wagner, Dem. Primary for Mayor, 69; mem. exec. cmt, N.Y. Dem. State Cmt, 61-69; v.chmn, N.Y. Dem. State Adv. Coun, 69. Bus. & Prof. Pos: Partner, Lowenbraun & Lowell, 47-52, Corcoran, Kostelanetz, Gladstone & Lowell, 58-64 and Gladstone & Lowell, 65- Mem: Asn. of the Bar of the City of New York; N.Y. State Bar Asn; N.Y. Co. Lawyers Asn; Citizens Cmt. for Children; bd. trustees, Harvard Law Sch. Asn. of N.Y; v.pres, City Col. Alumni Asn; v.pres, Nat. Am. Jewish Cong; co-pres, Manhattan Br, NAACP; bd. mem, Urban League. Medal of City of New York, 65. Rel: Jewish. Legal Res, 173 Riverside Dr, New York, N.Y. 10024. Mailing Add: 99 Park Ave, New York, N.Y. 10016.

LOWENSTEIN, ALLARD K. D
U.S. Rep, N.Y.
b. Newark, N.J, 1/16/29; m. Jennifer Lyman; c. Frank Graham and Thomas Kennedy. Educ: Univ. N.C, B.A, 49; Yale, LL.B, 54. Polit. & Govt. Pos: Spec. asst, Sen. Frank Porter Graham, N.C, 49; for. policy asst, Sen. Hubert H. Humphrey, Minn, 59; alternate del, Dem. Nat. Conv, 60, del, 68; U.S. Rep, N.Y, 68- Bus. & Prof. Pos: Mem. faculty, Stanford Univ, N.C. State Univ. and City Col. of N.Y. Mil. Serv: Enlisted man, Army, 54-56. Publ: Brutal Mandate, Macmillan Co, 62. Legal Res: Long Beach, N.Y. 11561. Mailing Add: 1410 Longworth House Office Bldg, Washington, D.C. 20515.

LOWERY, PHILIP E. D
b. Grove Springs, Mo, 2/22/32; married; c. Two. Polit. & Govt. Pos: Dist. co-capt, Dem. Party, Colo; probation officer, Juvenile Court, 56-61, referee, 61-62; former Colo. State Rep. Bus. & Prof. Pos: Lawyer. Mailing Add: 130 Monaco Pkwy, Denver, Colo. 80211. (1967)

LOWERY, THOMAS JOHN, JR. D
b. Syracuse, N.Y, 9/4/29; s. Thomas John Lowery and Gladys Helen Thurston L; m. 11/15/53 to Mary Frances Boynton; c. Maureen, Deborah and Martha. Educ: Lemoyne Col, B.S, 51; Syracuse Univ. Col. of Law, LL.B. and J.D, 53; Phi Beta Phi; Alpha Phi Omega. Polit. & Govt. Pos: Treas, Onondaga Co. Dem. Cmt, N.Y, 66-68; cmnr, N.Y. State Lottery, 67-; N.Y. Coordinator, Robert F. Kennedy for Pres, 68; alternate del, Dem. Nat. Conv, 68. Bus. & Prof. Pos: Partner, Lowery & Mancuso, Attorneys-at-law, Syracuse, N.Y, 53-; pres, Syracuse Sand & Gravel Co, 61-63; treas, Onondaga Ready Mix Inc, 62-63, Consumer Ready Mix Inc, 62-63; dir, Metrop. Bank of Syracuse, 65- Mil. Serv: Entered as Pvt, Army Res, 52, released as Sgt. 1/C, 60, after serv. in 1209th ARASU, Syracuse, N.Y. Mem: Onondaga Co, N.Y. State and Am. Bar Asns; Upstate Trial Lawyers Asn; Gr. Syracuse C. of C; Am. Cancer Soc.(dir); Leiderkranz Club; Cavalry Club; pres, Assocs. Lemoyne Col. Rel: Roman Catholic. Legal Res: 5092 Bradbury Dr, Syracuse, N.Y. 13215. Mailing Add: Suite 304, Warren Bldg, 499 S. Warren St, Syracuse, N.Y. 13202.

LOWMAN, R. L. R
b. Bethlehem, Pa, 3/23/17; s. R. L. Lowman and Verne Morris L; m. Aug, 1948 to Mary Colvin; c. Danny and Libby. Educ: W.Va. Univ, B.S; Baltimore Col. Dent. Surgery, Univ. of Mo. Polit. & Govt. Pos: Chmn, Upshur Co. Rep. Exec. Cmt, 62-66 and mem, 56-60. Mil. Serv: Entered as Pvt, Army, 42, released as Sgt, 46, after serv. in 30th Engrs, Pac. Theater; European and Asiatic Pac. Theaters Ribbon. Mem: Elks; VFW. Rel: Presbyterian. Mailing Add: Riley Heights, Buckhannon, W.Va. 26201. (1967)

LOWMAN, ZELVIN DON R
Nev. State Assemblyman
b. McCune, Kans, 9/8/21; s. James Martin Lowman and Mary Bonner L; m. 10/24/43 to Mary Bethena Hemphill; c. Freda (Mrs. Douglas Farr), James Fredrick, William Martin and Elizabeth June. Educ: West. State Col, Colo, A.B, 43; Univ. South. Calif, 46-47. Polit. & Govt. Pos: Personnel tech, San Diego, Calif, 46-47 and Los Angeles, Calif, 47-50; Nev. State Assemblyman, Dist. 4, 67-, Majority Floor Leader, 69, mem, Legis. Cmn, Cmt. on Judiciary and Cmt. on Pub. Resources; mem, Cent. Cmt, Nev. Rep. Party. Bus. & Prof. Pos: Personnel dir, South. Nev. Power Co, 54-57; commercial mgr, Nev. Power Co, 57-63, dir. pub. rels, 63- Mil. Serv: Entered as A/S, Navy, 43, released as Lt.(jg), 46, after serv. in Asiatic-Pac. Area and in Korea, 50-54; Capt, Naval Res, 64; Navy Unit Commendation; Armed Forces and Naval Res. Ribbons; Asiatic-Pac. Theater Ribbon with 4 Stars; Am. Theater and Nat. Serv. Ribbons; Philippines Liberation Ribbon with 2 Stars; Victory Medal. Mem: Pres, Boulder Dam Area Boy Scouts; Vigil hon. mem, Nebagamon Lodge, Order of Arrow, Silver Beaver Award winner; cmt. chmn, Girl Scouts; pres, Kiwanis of Uptown Las Vegas; Fed. Employers of Nev, Elec. League of South. Nev, and South. Nev. Alumni Club of West. State Col; chmn, Las Vegas City Solicitation Rev. Bd. of Educ. Cmt, Las Vegas C. of C; Nev. Cmt. on Employment of Physically Handicapped; Civil Serv. Bd. of Las Vegas; Nev. Mining Asn; dir, United Fund of Clark Co, Better Bus. Bur. of South. Nev. and Federated Employers; dir, South. Nev. Chap, Nat. Conf. of Christians & Jews; Las Vegas Press Club; Fraternal Order of Police Assocs; Navy League of U.S; ROA; Int. Platform Asn. Served as Skipper, Nat. Presbyterian Mariners, 61-62; named Kiwanian of Year, Las Vegas, 63 and presented with Heart Award of Variety Tent 39, 64; winner, George Washington Hon. Medal of Freedom Found, 62; life mem, West Charleston PTA, 60; Outstanding Freshman Assemblyman, Kiwanis Club of Uptown Las Vegas, 67; Meritorious Serv. Award, Clark Co. Classroom Teachers Asn, Elem. Prin. Asn. and Sec. Prin. Asn, 67; Service to Mankind Award, N. Los Angeles Dist. Sertoma Int, 69. Rel: Presbyterian; Ruling elder and chmn, Christian Educ. Cmn, Westminster United Presbyterian Church. Mailing Add: 1246 Cashman Dr, Las Vegas, Nev. 89102.

LOWNEY, JERRY, JR. D
b. Butte, Mont, 7/7/39; s. Jerry Lowney, Sr. and Rita Mahoney L; single. Educ: St. Anthony Novitiate, Angola, Ind, 57-58; Our Lady of Carey Unit, Dayton Univ, 58-59; Carroll Col, 60; Home Ins. Co. Multi-Line Training Sch, N.Y.C, 67. Polit. & Govt. Pos: Clerk, Silver Bow Co. Surveyor's Off, Mont, 59-60; pres, Silver Bow Co. Young Dem, 60-61, Lewis & Clark Co. Young Dem, 61-63; dep. clerk, Supreme Court, 61-63; state pres, Young Dem. Clubs of Mont, 62-64, nat. committeeman, 64-66; dep. chmn, bd. of regional dirs, Young Dem. Clubs of Am, 65-66; spec. asst. to pres, 66-68; co-chmn, Vol. for Kennedy, Los Angeles, Calif, 68; adv, Alliance for Progressive Dem. Action, San Diego, 68-69. Bus. & Prof. Pos: Part time reporter, United Press Int, 62; property mgr, Prudential Servs, 63; ins. agent, Prudential Ins. Co, 63-64, Norby & Watson, 64-66 and Home Ins. Co, Calif, 66-68; spec. agent, Aetna Ins. Co, San Diego, 68-69, Raleigh, N.C, 69- Publ: 'JFK . . . and a Legacy,' Cordett Mag, 1/64. Mem: Ins. Club of Raleigh, N.C; K. of C; teacher, Confraternity of Christian Doctrine. Chosen One of Ten Outstanding Young Dem. in Am, 65. Rel: Catholic. Mailing Add: 531 N. Blount, Apt. 205, Raleigh, N.C. 27604.

LOWREY, ROBERT SIDNEY, SR. D
b. Rome, Ga, 9/30/11; s. Robert Sidney Lowrey and Edna Cowan L; m. 8/30/32 to Nell Ellenburg; c. Bob, Shirley, Sammy, Penny, Darrill. Educ: Model High Sch. Polit. & Govt. Pos: Mem. bd, Floyd Co. Rd. and Revenue, Ga, 49-57; Ga. State Rep, 59-66. Bus. & Prof. Pos: Farmer. Rel: Methodist. Mailing Add: R.F.D. 7, Rome, Ga. 30161. (1967)

LOWRY, BENJAMIN JAMES R
b. Louisville, Ga, 2/11/91; s. Benjamin Lowry, Sr. and Margaret Evans L; m. 7/17/12 to Evelyn Solomon; c. Alfonso L, Benjamin III and Leonard W. Educ: Yale Univ, A.B, 20; N.Y. Univ, M.A, 38; Kappa Beta Sigma. Hon. D.D, Morehouse Col. and Va. Sem. Polit. & Govt. Pos: City chaplain, Brooklyn, N.Y, 65-; trustee, Brooklyn Pub. Libr, 67-; alternate del, Rep. Nat. Conv, 68. Bus. & Prof. Pos: Minister, Zion Baptist Church, N.Y, 21-; pres, L.I. Baptist Conv, 68- Mem: Mason (32°, Grand Chaplain N.Y. State F.A.M). Rel: Missionary Baptist. Mailing Add: 1363 President St, Brooklyn, N.Y. 11213.

LOWRY, SAMUEL EARLE D
Chmn, Oconee Co. Dem. Party, S.C.
b. Seneca, S.C, 10/10/10; s. Earle Westmoreland Lowry and Roxie Duncan L; m. 11/27/45 to Fayetta Alexander; c. Brenda (Mrs. Cromer); Sandra Lou and Lydia Kaye. Educ: Clemson Univ, B.S. in Elec. Eng. Polit. & Govt. Pos: Mem, Oconee Co. Sch. Bd, S.C, 60-68, chmn, 62-68; dir, S.C. Sch. Bd. Asn, 62-68; chmn, Oconee Co. Centennial Cmn, 68; alternate del, Dem. Nat. Conv, 68; chmn, Oconee Co. Dem. Party, S.C, 68- Bus. & Prof. Pos: Teacher, Oconee Schs, Seneca, S.C, 33; clerk, Texaco Oil Dist. Plant, 33-41; distributor, Texaco Oil, Loris, 46-53 and Seneca, 53-; dir, Oconee Savings & Loan Asn, 59- Mil. Serv: Entered as 2nd Lt, Army, 42, released as Maj, 46, after serv. in 1447 Intel. Corps Unit, Ft. Benning, Ga, Lt. Col, Army Res, Retired; Commendation Medal; Victory Medal; Meritorious Serv. Unit Award; 4th Serv. Command Cert. of Commendation. Mem: Am. Legion; Farm Bur. Rel: Baptist; Deacon, Seneca Baptist Church. Mailing Add: Route 5, Seneca, S.C. 29678.

LOWTHER, GERALD HALBERT D
Treas, Mo. State Dem. Party
b. Slagle, La, 2/18/24; s. Fred B. Lowther and Beatrice Velma Halbert L; m. 11/2/46 to Patti Jean Byers; c. Teresa, Craig, Natalie and Lisa. Educ: Pepperdine Col, A.B, 48; Univ. Mo, LL.B, 51; Beachcombers; Phi Delta Phi. Polit. & Govt. Pos: Mem, Mo. Savings & Loan Cmt, 64-68; mem, Mo. Sen. Redistricting Cmt, 65; del, Dem. Nat. Conv. and mem. rules cmt, 68; mem, Mo. Indust. Develop. Cmt, 68-; treas, Mo. State Dem. Party, 68- Bus. & Prof. Pos: Sr. partner, Miller, Fairman, Sanford, Carr & Lowther, 51-; bd. dirs, Modern Am. Life Ins. Co, Am. Investors Life Ins. Co, Founders Am. Investment Co, First City Bank and Am. Nat. Bank, currently. Mil. Serv: Entered as Pvt, Army, 46, released as Sgt, 47, after serv. in Signal Corp. Publ: Pleading Res Ipsa Loquitur, 63 and Defense of Products Liability Cases, 67, Mo. Bar J. Mem: Int. Asn. of Ins. Counsel; Mo. and Am. Bar Asns; Law-Sci. Acad.(lectr); Kiwanis (past pres); bd. dir, Burge Hosp; dir, C. of C; dir, Ozark Christian Counseling Serv. Rel: Protestant. Mailing Add: 2540 S. Luster, Springfield, Mo. 65804.

LOZIER, MARY JONES D
Pres, Fedn. Women's Dem. Clubs of Mo.
b. Centralia, Mo, 8/7/67; d. Dr. T. H. Jones and Maude Hall J; m. to Judge Lue Carruthers Lozier. Educ: Christian Col; Medallion Club. Polit. & Govt. Pos: Pres, local Dem. club and Round Table Club; del, Dem. Nat. Conv, 48, 52 & 64; mem, Mo. Coun. of Arts, 66-; past dist. secy, treas, and pres, Fedn. Women's Dem. Clubs of Mo, pres, currently. Mem: Past regent, Daughters of Am. Colonists; past pres, Am. Legion Auxiliary; past chapeau, 40 et 8. Rel: Christian. Mailing Add: Rosemary Heights, Moberly, Mo. 65270. (1967)

LUBNAU, THOMAS E. R
Chmn, Campbell Co. Rep. Party, Wyo.
b. Grosse Pointe, Mich, 10/23/31; s. Oscar E. Lubnau and Mary Ruth Ryan L; m. 9/2/56 to Cynthia L'Vere Kirkland; c. Thomas Edwin II, Kathryn Lee and Robert Douglas. Educ: Casper Col, A.A, 52; Univ. Wyoming, B.A, 57, J.D, 60; Sigma Chi. Polit. & Govt. Pos: Police Judge, Gillette, Wyo, 61-; Chmn, Campbell Co. Rep. Party, 63-; dist. bar cmnr, Fourth Judicial Dist, 64-66; mem. Bd. Dirs, Campbell Co. Grade Schs, 65-67; Alternate Del, Rep. Nat. Conv, 68. Mil. Serv: Entered as Pvt, Army, 54, released as Cpl, 56, after serv. in 6th Inf; Nat. Defense Serv. Award; Good Conduct Medal. Publ: 'The Spouse Is A Stranger to the Deed,' 59 and Incorporating Non-Testamentary Documents Into a Will,' 60, Wyoming Law Journal. Mem: Campbell Co, Wyo. and Am. Bar Asns; Am. Judicature Soc; Wyo. Mining Asn; Asn. Petroleum Landmen; Rotary; Odd Fellows; Elks; C. of C.(bd. dirs, Campbell Co. Branch, 63 & 64). Rel: Protestant. Mailing Add: P.O. Box 1028, Gillette, Wyo. 82716.

LUCAS, ALLEN THURMAN D
b. Chandlerville, Ill, 7/20/17; s. Allen Thurman Lucas and Josephine Sarff L; m. Jan. 1943 to Marcella Wetterer; c. Allen Thurman. Educ: Univ. Ill, B.A, 40; Northwest. Univ. Law Sch, 46; DePaul Univ. Col. Law, J.D, 48; Phi Delta Theta. Polit. & Govt. Pos: Dep. collector, U.S. Treasury Dept, 41-42; tech. adv, Ill. State Fire Marshal, 50-54; Ill. State Rep, 54-68. Bus. & Prof. Pos: Attorney-at-Law, Lucas and Lucas, 48- Mil. Serv: Entered as Lt, Navy, 42, released as Lt. Comdr, 45, after serv. in Atlantic and Pac. Theatres. Mem: Mason; Elks; Am. Legion; VFW. Rel: Protestant. Mailing Add: 2216 Whittier Ave, Springfield, Ill. 62704. (1967)

LUCAS, ANDY DELERRIAN D
b. Denver, Colo, 3/5/30; s. Rio G. Lucas and Rose Hershokwizt L; m. 7/23/50 to Carol L. Ciancio; c. Andrea Dee, Doreen Louise, Denise Marie and David Gordon. Educ: Lamar Jr. Col; Univ. Colo; Denver Univ. Polit. & Govt. Pos: Co. judge, Colo, 54-58; Colo. State Rep, 58-64; Colo. State Sen, 64-68. Bus. & Prof. Pos: Pres, Andy Lucas Realty Co, 56- Mil. Serv: Pvt, Nat. Guard, 48-50. Mem: Mason; Elks. Rel: Methodist. Mailing Add: 7550 Meade Way, Westminster, Colo. 80030. (1967)

LUCAS, ETHEL VIOLET D
Secy-Treas, Exec. Cmt, Ohio Dem. Party
b. Linton, Ind, 10/15/13; d. Desire Cuvelier and Minnie Barnett C; m. 4/26/31 to Robert Elmo Lucas; c. Patricia Lee and Leslie Louise (Mrs. Neumann). Educ: Linton High Sch. Polit. & Govt. Pos: Rural mail carrier, Ohio, 45-60; pres, Fulton Co. Bd. of Elec, 48-; precinct committeewoman, Dem. Party, 50-; postmaster, Wauseon, 52-53; alternate del, Dem. Nat. Conv, 60, 64 & 68; pres, Ohio State Elec. Off, 66; secy-treas, exec. cmt, Ohio Dem. Party, currently. Mem: Eastern Star; State Bd. of Elec. Off; Bus. & Prfnl. Women's Club; Elks Ladies. Rel: Congregational; mem, Church Choir. Mailing Add: 311 S. Fulton St, Wauseon, Ohio 43567.

LUCAS, GERALD PATRICK D
b. Oklahoma City, Okla, Nov. 1933; s. L.A. Lucas; m. 6/14/58 to Mary Dell Miller; c. Scott, Craig, Tod, Kent, Mark and Maura. Educ: Creighton Univ, D.D.S, 57. Polit. & Govt. Pos: Alternate del, Dem. Nat. Conv, 68. Mem: Am. Dent. Asn; Okla. Dent. Asn; Xi Psi Phi; co-chmn, Coun. for 1989; chmn, Forum Contemporary Thought, 59-63; mem, Okla. for Indian Opportunity; Urban Action Found; Capital Improv. Prog. Eval. Cmt; Mummers Theatre; Okla. City Symphony; Okla. Art Center; Contemporary Arts Found; Lyric Theatre; mem. bd. dirs, Okla. City C. of C; chmn. screening cmt. proj. & policies, C. of C, 68; mem. bd. dirs, Commun. of John XXIII. Legal Res: 12813 Twisted Oak Rd, Oklahoma City, Okla. 73120. Mailing Add: 509 N.W. 11th, Oklahoma City, Okla. 73103.

LUCAS, JAMES P. R
Mont. State Rep.
b. Worland, Wyo, 4/7/27; s. Peter James Lucas and Helen Adolph L; 2nd m. 7/10/65 to Carol Jean Dunstan; c. Leslie; c. by 1st m. James Peter, II and Mark Clinton. Educ: Univ. of Mont, B.A. in Bus. Admin, 50, B.A. and LL.B, 51; Phi Delta Phi; Alpha Kappa Psi; Sigma Nu; Univ. Bus. Mgr, 49. Polit. & Govt. Pos: Mem, Mont. Rep. Cent. Cmt, 52-56; co. attorney, Custer Co, Mont, 53-62; del, Rep. Nat. Conv, 56, alternate del, 68; Mont. State Rep, 63-, Minority Leader, Mont. House of Rep, 63-66, Majority Leader, 67-69, Speaker, 69-; mem, Mont. Centennial Cmn, 64-66, Mont. Space Coun, 64-66 and Mont. Cmt. on Aging, 65-66. Bus. & Prof. Pos: Chmn, Custer Co. Jr. Col. Bd, 53-66; mem, Univ. Coun. of 50, 64-66, bd. of visitors, Mont. Law Sch, 64-66 and bd. trustee, Univ. Mont. Found, 66-; instr, Mont. Realtors Asn, 69-70. Mil. Serv: Entered as Pvt, Army, 44, released as Technician 4/C, 46. Mem: Am. and Mont. Trial Lawyers Asn; Nat. Soc. State Legislators; Kiwanis; Toastmasters; Elks; Eagles; Mason; Al Bedoo Shrine; Am. Legion; C. of C. Rel: Protestant. Mailing Add: 500 S. Strevell, Miles City, Mont. 59301.

LUCAS, LLOYD M. R
R.I. State Rep.
b. Lafayette, R.I, 11/8/05; m. to Laura I. Educ: North Kingstown Schs. Polit. & Govt. Pos: Mem, R.I. Town Coun, 18 years, pres, 9 years; R.I. State Rep, 59- Bus. & Prof. Pos: Retail sales, bldg. supplies. Mem: Grange; AF&AM. Mailing Add: 366 Tower Hill Rd, North Kingstown, R.I. 02852.

LUCAS, MARY LOUISA D
b. Marion, Va, 8/2/36; d. Benjamin Lucas and Mary Rosa Gibson. Educ: Mary Wash. Col; Pan-Am. Sch. Polit. & Govt. Pos: Admin. Asst. to U.S. Rep. John J. Flynt, Jr, Ga, currently. Bus. & Prof. Pos: Exec. secy, Fulton Nat. Bank of Atlanta, 57-62. Mem: Asbury Mem. Methodist Church; Am. Shetland Pony Club; Am. Horse Show Asn; Midwest Hockney Soc. Rel: Methodist. 1967 Legal Res: Griffin, Ga. No mailing address available. (1967)

LUCAS, MAXWELL DAVIS, JR. D
b. Memphis, Tenn, 10/27/36; s. Maxwell Davis Lucas and Ruth Plyler L; m; c. Katherine and Davis. Educ: Vanderbilt Univ, B.A, 58 and LL.B, 60; Kappa Alpha Order. Polit. & Govt. Pos: Tenn. State Rep, 66-68. Bus. & Prof. Pos: Attorney, Kirkpatrick & Lucas. Mem: Memphis, Shelby Co, Tenn. and Am. Bar Asns. Rel: Episcopal. Legal Res: 5332 Colony Lane, Memphis, Tenn. 38117. Mailing Add: 2005 First National Bank, Memphis, Tenn. 38103.

LUCAS, OPAL M. R
b. Laurel Co, Ky, 15/23/05; d. James B. McCowan and Emma Hurley M; m. to Fred V. Lucas; c. Fred V, II, James R. Educ: East. State Col, Richmond, Ky. Polit. & Govt. Pos: Ky. presidential campaign chmn, 56; mem, Rep. Nat. Cmt, 57-67. Bus. & Prof. Pos: Teacher, pub. schs, 34-44; partner, Lucas Motor Co, London, Ky, 45- Mem: Dir, Ky. Fed. Women's Clubs. Named Outstanding Alumnae of Year, Sue Bennett Col, 53; Ky. Col, 54. Rel: Christian. Mailing Add: 207 W. Seventh St, London, Ky. 40741. (1967)

LUCAS, SCOTT WIKE D
b. Cass Co, Ill, 2/19/92; s. William D. Lucas and Sarah Catherine Underbrink L; m. Jan, 1923 to Edith Biggs; c. Scott W, Jr. Educ: Ill. Wesleyan Univ, LL.B, 14; Phi Alpha Delta. Hon. LL.D, Ill. Wesleyan Univ, John Marshall Law Sch. and West. Md. Col. Polit. Pos: Del, Dem. Nat. Conv, 40-64 and 32; chmn, Midwest. Regional Hq, Dem. Nat. Cmt. for Campaign to re-elect Franklin D. Roosevelt, 40. Govt. Pos: Majority Leader, U.S. Senate, 49-50, U.S. Sen, Ill, 39-50; U.S. Rep, Ill, 35-39; chmn, Ill. State Tax Cmn, 33-35; state attorney, Mason Co, 20-26. Bus. & Prof. Pos: Mem. Bd. Dirs,

State Loan and Finance Corp. and Wash. Mutual Investors Fund, at present; attorney at law, 14- Mil. Serv: Entered as Pvt, Army, 18, released as Lt, 18, after serv. at Fortress Monroe, Va; Officers' Res. Corps, 18-34, then Judge Adv. Gen. with rank of Col, Ill. Nat. Guard. Mem: Am, Ill. and D.C. Bar Asns; pres, Burning Tree Club, Bethesda; Comdr, Dept. Ill, Am. Legion, 26, selected Nat. Judge Adv, Am. Legion at Paris Conv, 27 and 4 terms thereafter. Played prfnl. baseball, 3-I League, 3 yrs; won 3 letters, baseball, basketball and football, Ill. Wesleyan Univ. Rel: Baptist. Legal Res: 314 W. Main St, Havana, Ill. 62644. Mailing Add: 1028 Connecticut Ave, N.W, Washington, D.C. 20036. (1967)

LUCAS, WALTER CLYDE D
Chmn, Randolph Co. Dem. Exec. Cmt, N.C.
b. Union Twp, Randolph Co, N.C, 6/24/05; s. Walter Ransdale Lucas and Mary Elizabeth Davil L; m. 12/22/29 to Pearlie Jane Moore; c. Joyce (Mrs. Jerry G. Ward) and Janet (Mrs. David L. Graves). Polit. & Govt. Pos: Chmn, Randolph Co. Bd. of Cmnrs, N.C, 37-42; Mayor, Asheboro, 45-49; chmn, Randolph Co. Dem. Exec. Cmt, 44-48 & 66- Bus. & Prof. Pos: Pres, Asheboro C. of C, 42. Mem: Mason (32°); Elks; WOW; Kiwanis (pres, Asheboro Club, 42); Asheboro Shrine Club (pres, 47 & 65); pres, Asheboro Mem. Found, 46. Rel: Baptist. Legal Res: Highland Court, Asheboro, N.C. 27203. Mailing Add: P.O. Box 1107, Asheboro, N.C. 27203.

LUCE, CLARE BOOTHE R
b. New York, N.Y, d. William F. Boothe and Ann Snyder B; m. 11/23/35 to Henry R. Luce. Educ: The Castle, Tarrytown, N.Y, 17-19. Hon. Litt.D, Colby Col, Fordham Univ, Mundelein Col. and Seton Hall Univ; hon. LL.D, Temple Univ, Creighton Univ. and Georgetown Univ; hon. D.F.A, St. John's Univ, N.Y, 64. Polit. & Govt. Pos: U.S. Rep, Conn, 43-47; U.S. Ambassador to Italy, 53-57. Bus. & Prof. Pos: Assoc. ed, Vogue, 30; managing ed, Vanity Fair, 33-34; newspaper columnist, 34; playwright, 35-; consult, Encyclop. Britannica. Publ: Stuffed Shirts, 33; Europe in the Spring, 40; Abide with Me, 37; collected and edited Saints for Now, 52; ed. column, 'Without Portfolio,' McCall's Mag, 60-67. Grand Cross of the Order of Merit of the Ital. Repub, 56; Dame of Malta, Rome, 56; plus numerous other awards. Rel: Roman Catholic. Mailing Add: Honolulu, Hawaii 96815.

LUCE, GORDON C. R
Mem. Exec. Cmt, Calif. Rep. State Cent. Cmt.
b. San Diego, Calif. 11/21/25; s. Edgar A. Luce and Carma C. Coppard L; m. 9/3/55 to Karon Turnbow; c. Randall, Kelly and Andrew. Educ: Stanford Univ, B.A, 50 and M.B.A, 52; Am. Savings & Loan Sch, grad; Chi Psi. Polit. & Govt. Pos: Chmn, Point Loma Nixon for Gov. Campaign, 62; treas. and spec. events chmn, Goldwater Campaign for President, 64; alternate del, Rep. Nat. Conv, 64, del. and whip, Calif. Favorite Son Del, 68; chmn, San Diego Co. Repl Assocs, 64; chmn. and trustee, Rep. Assocs, 66-67; chmn, San Diego Co. Reagan for Gov. Cmt, 66; mem. exec. cmt, Calif. Rep. State Cent. Cmt, 69-; exec. dir. bus. and transportation, State of Calif, currently. Bus. & Prof. Pos: Pres, Am. Savings and Loan Inst, 59. Mil. Serv: Entered as Pvt, Army, 44, released as Cpl, 46, after serv. in 97th Inf. Div, Europe and Japan, 44-46; Bronze Star; Combat Inf. Badge; European Operation Medal with 2 Battle Stars. Mem: Pres, San Diego Downtown Asn, 65, Univ. Club, 64 and Stanford Club, 64; Savings Inst. Mkt. Soc. of Am; dir, San Diego Symphony and Combined Arts of San Diego. Rel: Episcopal. Legal Res: 1700 La Playa Way, Sacramento, Calif. 95825. Mailing Add: P.O. Box 1139, Sacramento, Calif. 95805.

LUCE, WILLIAM GARRETT D
Chmn, McMullen Co. Dem. Exec. Cmt, Tex.
b. Crockett, Tex, 1/1/01; s. A.P. Luce and Vina Graham L; m. 4/18/22 to Buna Cathleen Crawford; c. Eris (Mrs. J.R. White), Billy Jack, W.G, Jr. and Bobbie (Mrs. Douglas Miller). Educ: Sam Houston State Col, B.S. Polit. & Govt. Pos: Secy, McMullen Co. Rural High Sch. Bd, Tex, 45-54; mem. bd, Nueces River Reclamation and Conserv, 50-54; chmn, McMullen Co. Dem. Exec. Cmt, 52- Bus. & Prof. Pos: Owner-operator, W.G. Luce Gen. Merchandise, 45-66. Mem: Sam Houston Ex-Students Asn; AF&AM; Lions; Farm Bur. Rel: Baptist; Chmn, Bd. of Deacons, Tilden Baptist Church. Mailing Add: P.O. Box 257, Tilden, Tex. 78072. (1967)

LUCEY, PATRICK JOSEPH D
b. LaCrosse, Wis, 3/21/18; s. Gregory Charles Lucey and Ella Young McNamara L; m. 11/14/51 to Jean Vlasis; c. Paul, Laurie and David. Educ: Univ. Wis, 46. Polit. & Govt. Pos: Wis. State Assemblyman, 49-50; state chmn, Proxmire Senate Campaign, 57; state chmn, Dem. Party, 57-63; Lt. Gov, Wis, 65-66. Mil. Serv: Entered as Pfc, 41, released as Capt, 45. Mailing Add: 1015 Farwell Court, Madison, Wis. 53704. (1967)

LUCKEN, JOHN HENRY R
Iowa State Sen.
b. Akron, Iowa, 2/6/96; s. Gerhard Lucken and Caroline Beerman L; m. 12/17/17 to CeCelia Margerette Woll; c. Lucile (Mrs. Fox), Donald Wayne, Robert Edward, Frank Evan and Ronald Gene. Educ: Westmar Col, bus. course, 15. Polit. & Govt. Pos: Dir. and chmn, Twp. Sch. Bd, Iowa, 25-48; Iowa State Rep, 47-60; Iowa State Sen, 60- Bus. & Prof. Pos: Dir. and pres, Plymouth Coop. Oil Co, 26-47 and Woodbury & Plymouth Farm Loan Asn, 31-48. Mil. Serv: Entered as Pvt, Army, 18, released as Pfc, 19, after serv. in 19th Mil. Police, 19th Div. Mem: Mason; Consistory, KCCH, Shrine; Am. Legion; Lions Int; Farm Bur; World War I Barracks; Izaak Walton League. Rel: Presbyterian; Elder. Mailing Add: 531 Central Ave. S.W, Le Mars, Iowa 51031.

LUCKEY, MARY ELLEN D
V.Chmn, Brule Co. Dem. Party, S.Dak.
b. White Lake, S.Dak, 9/16/26; d. Claude G. Mahoney and Anna Rowan M; div; c. Mark Patrick, Mary Jean and Anne E. Educ: White Lake High Sch, S.Dak, 4 years. Polit. & Govt. Pos: Mem, Civil Aeronautics Authority, Kodiak, Alaska, 44-47; mem, Atomic Energy Cmn, Richland Wash, 52-53; dep. co. treas, Brule Co, S.Dak, 57-60 and auditor, 61-; v.chmn, Brule Co. Dem. Party, 62-66 & 68- and chmn, 66-68. Bus. & Prof. Pos: Teller, Bank of Kimball, S.Dak, 56-57. Mem: S.Dak. Asn. Co. Officials. Rel: Catholic. Mailing Add: Box 203, Kimball, S.Dak. 57355.

LUCKHART, ELTON WAGNER R
Chmn, Mahoning Co. Rep. Cent. and Exec. Cmts, Ohio
b. Tylersburg, Pa, 3/26/10; s. John Webster Luckhart and Harriet Wagner L; m. 4/25/64 to Elaine Cossler; c. Leland Richard, Robert Allen and Shirley. Educ: Univ. Ala, B.S. in Educ, 32; Univ. Colo, M.A. in Eng. Lit, 38; Youngstown Univ, LL.B, 47; Phi Delta Kappa; Kappa Delta Pi; Psi Chi. Polit. & Govt. Pos: Pres, Mahoning Co. Young Rep, Ohio, 48-50; asst. city law dir, Youngstown, Ohio, 48-54; off, Rep. Nat. Conv, 52, del, 64 & 68; pres, McKinley Club of Niles, 55; asst. prosecutor, Mahoning Co, 56-58; mem, Mahoning Co. Bd. of Elecs, 58-62; chmn, Mahoning Co. Rep. Cent. and Exec. Cmts. and mem, Ohio State Cent. and Exec. Cmts, 65-66. Bus. & Prof. Pos: Supv. prin, West Middlesex Schs, Pa, 42-45; instr, Youngstown Univ, 48-54; sr. partner, Luckhart, Mamaw, Morrisroe, Zellers and Robinson, 58-; dir, Falcon Foundry Corp, 65- Mem: Ohio State, Mahoning Co. and Trumbull Co. Bar Asns; Elks; Eagles; Moose; Odd Fellows; Optimist; C. of C. Rel: Unitarian. Legal Res: 2705 Normandy Dr, Youngstown, Ohio 44511. Mailing Add: 305 Legal Arts Centre, Youngstown, Ohio 44503.

LUCKINA, HOWARD JOSEPH D
R.I. State Sen.
b. Pittsfield, Mass, 4/29/04; s. Joseph J. Luckina and Lillian Hyatt L; m. 6/10/31 to Madeline Bragg; c. Stuart Howard. Educ: Palmer Sch. of Chiropractic, Iowa. Polit. & Govt. Pos: Mem, North Smithfield Dem. Cmt, R.I, 58; R.I. State Sen, 59- Mem: Elks; R.I. Chiropractic Soc. Rel: Episcopal. Mailing Add: 28 Homestead Ave, North Smithfield, R.I. 02895. (1967)

LUCKING, WILLIAM ALFRED, JR. R
Chmn, 13th Cong. Dist. Rep. Cmt, Calif.
b. Detroit, Mich, 6/10/17; s. William Alfred Lucking, Sr. and Catherine Eustis L; m. Lavon Carsner; c. Helen L. (Mrs. Paul Fredell), William A, III, Caroline E, Ruth C, Terry L. Eicher, J. Scott Eicher and Barbara J. Eicher. Educ: Dartmouth Col, A.B, 40; Univ. Mich. Law Sch, J.D, 49; Phi Gamma Delta. Polit. & Govt. Pos: Mem, Ventura Co. Rep. Cent. Cmt, Calif, 50-68, chmn, 54-58; mem, Calif. Rep. State Cent. Cmt, 52-; mem, Calif. Rep. Assembly, 52-; mem, 13th Cong. Dist. Rep. Cmt, Calif, 52-, chmn, 60-; del, Rep. Nat. Conv, 60; mem, Calif. Recreational Trails Cmt, 68- Bus. & Prof. Pos: Dir, Chicago Duluth & Georgian Bay Transit Co, 46-55 & 60-; partner, Johnston, Lucking & Bertelsen Attorneys, 50-; dir, Intex Oil Co, 60, Ojai Orange Asn, 69. Mil. Serv: Entered as A/S, Naval Res, 40, released as Lt. Comdr, 46, after serv. in Destroyers, Pac. Fleet, Asiatic Theatre, 41-46; Comdr.(ret), Naval Res; Bronze Star; Gold Star in lieu of Second Bronze Star with 'V's; Naval Res. Medal; Navy Unit Commendation. Mem: Calif. State and Ventura Co. Bars; Am. Bar Asn; trustee, Ojai Valley Sch. and Ojai Youth Tennis Found; Ventura Yacht Club; Ventura Co. Taxpayers Asn;(dir, treas); Ventura Co. Farm Bur; Santa Barbara Museum of Art; Ventura Co. Sheriff's Posse; Calif. Cattlemens Asn. Rel: Protestant. Legal Res: Old Matilija Rd, Ojai, Calif. 93023. Mailing Add: P.O. Drawer, Ventura, Calif. 93001.

LUDDEN, BARBARA ANN HARRISON R
b. Washington, D.C, 11/6/32; d. William Henry Harrison and Lois Magee H; m. 12/28/57 to James Gregory Ludden. Educ: U.S. Dept. Agr. Grad. Sch, 50-51; Am. Univ, 51-52. Polit. & Govt. Pos: Conf. asst. to dir, Off. Econ. Opportunity, 69-; admin. asst. to U.S. Rep. Donald Rumsfeld, Ill, 63-69; personal and polit. secy. to U.S. Rep. Marguerite Stitt Church, 54-63; mem, U.S. Del. to UN, 61; mem, Citizens Cmt. on Fair Labor Standards, 57 and U.S. Atomic Energy Cmn, Reactor Develop. Div, 50-54. Mem: Cong. Secretaries Club; Immaculate Conception Acad. Alumnae; D.C. Young Rep. Rel: Roman Catholic. Mailing Add: 8512 Stable Dr, Alexandria, Va. 22308.

LUDDY, WILLIAM F. D
Chmn, Westchester Co. Dem. Party, N.Y.
b. Cambridge, N.Y, 10/23/10; s. Thomas W. Luddy and Mary Kane L; m. 3/11/40 to Virginia M. O'Neil; c. Thomas W, Brian A, David F, James N. and Jean M. Educ: Cambridge High Sch. Polit. & Govt. Pos: Del, Dem. Nat. Conv, 48, 54, 56, 60, 64 & 68; state committeeman, N.Y, 41-; chmn, Westchester Co. Dem. Party, currently. Mailing Add: 48 Mamaroneck Ave, White Plains, N.Y. 10601.

LUDLAM, LILLIAN J. R
Secy, Conn. Rep. State Cent. Cmt.
b. N.Y.C, 11/1/18; m. 6/22/46 to Richard Price Ludlam. Educ: Rider Col; New Sch. for Soc. Research. Polit. & Govt. Pos: Pres, New Hartford Women's Rep. Club, Conn, 54; pres, Litchfield Co. Women's Rep. Club, 56-62; committeewoman, Conn. State Rep. Cent. Cmt, 60-64 & 66-, secy, 64-, secy. and bd. mem, Pub. Rels. Cmt, 65-; chmn, Liason Cmt, Rep. Coun, 63; v.pres, Sixth Cong. Dist. W. Rep. Party, presently. Bus. & Prof. Pos: Asst. bus. mgr, Electronics Mag, McGraw-Hill Publ. Co, N.Y, 38-44; admin. asst, Lord and Taylor, 44-45; advert. and publicity dir, Monitor Equip. Corp, 45-48; morning radio prog, Sta. WTOR, 53-55; acct. exec, B.R. Martin Assocs, Ill, 57-; v.pres, Village Lumber and Oil, Conn, 60-; publisher, Foothills Trader, New Hartford, Conn, 64- Mem: Dir, former chmn. and v.chmn, New Hartford Commun. Club; Conn. State Fedn. Women's Clubs; v.pres, Winsted Area Commun. Chest. Rel: Congregational; Mem, Stewardship Cmt. Mailing Add: Town Hill, New Hartford, Conn. 06057.

LUDWIG, DONALD JOSEPH R
b. N.Y.C, 7/5/30; s. Frederick Joseph Ludwig and Beatrice Stenson L; m. 7/4/58 to Lois Belle Whitmer; c. Valerie Ardith, Diane Marcella, Allison June and Frederick Donald. Educ: Col. of The City of N.Y, B.A, 53; Georgetown Univ. Law Sch, 2 years; Theodore Roosevelt Sch. Journalism, grad; Hist. Soc; Am. Soc. Mil. Engrs; Delta Kappa Epsilon; Newman Club. Polit. & Govt. Pos: Area chmn, Rep. Presidential Campaigns, N.J, 60, 64 & 68; Rep. dist. committeeman and Rep. munic. chmn, Berkeley Heights, N.J, 65-; del, Rep. Nat. Conv, 68. Bus. & Prof. Pos: Buyer trainee, J.C. Penney Co, Inc, N.Y.C, 58-62 and merchandise buyer, 63- Mil. Serv: Entered as 2nd Lt, Army, 53, released as Capt, 62, after serv. in Inf. and Army Intel, Alaska, 57-58; Commendation Award; Nat. Serv. Defense Award; Res. Officers Award; Expert Infantryman, Am. Soc. Mil. Engrs. Medal. Mem: K. of C; Elks. Rel: Roman Catholic. Mailing Add: 24 Timber Dr, Berkeley Heights, N.J. 07922.

LUDWIG, JOSEPH LAFE R
b. Grand Forks, N.Dak, 6/12/09; s. Arthur Leroy Ludwig and Rosella Labine L; m. 2/14/46 to Jeanne C. Casenave. Educ: Univ. of N.Dak, B.A,

31 and B.S, 33; Rush Med. Col, Univ. of Chicago, M.D, 36; Blue Key; Phi Delta Theta; Phi Rho Sigma. Polit. & Govt. Pos: Mem, Citizens Adv. Cmt, Calif. Legis, 56-57; alternate del, Rep. Nat. Conv, 60, del, 64. Mil. Serv: Entered as Lt, Naval Res, 42, released as Lt. Comdr, 46, after serv. in Pac. Mem: Coun. on Legis, Am. Med. Asn, 51-62, Coun. Med. Serv, 55-63, Calif. del, 51-66; Calif. and Los Angeles Co. Med. Asns; Los Angeles Country Club; Eldorado Country Club. Rel: Roman Catholic. Legal Res: 220 S. Spalding Dr, Beverly Hills, Calif. 90212. Mailing Add: 3731 Stocker St, Los Angeles, Calif. 90008.

LUECK, HENRY LONGLEY D
b. Holton, Kans, 1/18/13; s. Charles D. Lueck and Bertha M. Longley L; m. 11/4/45 to Alice Hess. Educ: Univ. Kans, two years; Kappa Sigma. Polit. & Govt. Pos: Pres, Kans. Washington Day Club, 46; chmn, Jackson Co. Dem. Cmt, 46-; pres, Kans. Dem. Vet. Club, 48; chmn, Second Cong. Dist. Dem. Party, 50-66; mem, Kans. Grain Adv. Cmn, 68- Mil. Serv: Entered as Pvt, Army, 41, released as T/Sgt, 45, after serv. in Co. B, 103rd Inf, 43rd Div, Pac. Theater; Purple Heart with Oak Leaf Cluster. Mem: Dir, Nat. Grain and Feed Dealers Asn, 64- and Kans. Grain and Feed Dealers Asn, 65-; Rotary; Am. Legion; VFW. Rel: Methodist. Mailing Add: Netawaka, Kans. 66516.

LUEDTKE, ROLAND ALFRED R
Nebr. State Sen.
b. Lincoln, Nebr, 1/4/24; s. Alfred C. Luedtke and Caroline Senne L; m. 12/1/51 to Helen Dorothy Snyder; c. Larry O. and David A. Educ: Univ. Nebr, B.S, 49; Col. Law, Univ. Nebr, LL.B, 51; Delta Theta Phi. Polit. & Govt. Pos: Treas, Lancaster Co. Young Rep, Nebr, 46-47; treas, Nebr. Young Rep, 53-54; Dep. Secy. of State, Nebr, 53-59; jr. pres, Founders Day, Rep. Orgn, 58; chmn, Lancaster Co. Rep. Party, 62-64; Nebr. State Sen, 28th Legis. Dist, 67- Bus. & Prof. Pos: Partner, Law Firm of Kier & Luedtke, 62- Mil. Serv: Entered as Pvt, Army, 43, released as Pfc, 45, after serv. in 26th Inf. Div. and Ninth Air Force, ETO, 44-45; Bronze Star Medal; Purple Heart; Combat Inf. Badge; France and Rhineland Campaign Ribbons. Publ: 'Nebraska Corporation Law, a Statutory Jungle,' Nebr. Law Rev, 5/57. Mem: Am, Nebr. State and Lincoln Bar Asns; Am. Judicature Soc; Lutheran Lawyers Asn; Am. Legion; DAV; Gateway Sertoma Club; Lutheran Laymen's League. Rel: Lutheran, Missouri Synod. Legal Res: 327 Park Vista, Lincoln, Nebr. 68510. Mailing Add: 303 Executive Bldg, Lincoln, Nebr. 68508.

LUETKEMEYER, JOHN ALEXANDER D
State Treas, Md.
b. Cleveland, Ohio, 2/12/10; s. Gustave William Luetkemeyer and Julia Lueke L; m. 6/16/39 to Anne Austin McLanahan; c. Jean Scott and twins, John Alexander and Anne Austin. Educ: Harvard Univ, A.B, 33. Polit. & Govt. Pos: State Treas, Md, 63- Bus. & Prof. Pos: Pres. and dir, Equitable Trust Co, Baltimore, 61-, chmn. bd, 67-; dir, Savings Bank, Baltimore; Ramsay Scarlett & Co; Baltimore Stevedoring Co; Johnson Motor Lines, Charlotte, N.C. Mem: Harvard Club; Elkridge Club; Bachelors Cotillon, Baltimore; trustee, Calvert Sch, Goucher Col, Church Home and Hosp, Sheppard Pratt Hosp. Mailing Add: 6 Cotswold Rd, Baltimore, Md. 21210.

LUFFMAN, DON RAMON D
b. Tazewell, Va, 5/26/28; s. Walter Quay Luffman and Edna Myers L; m. 12/31/48 to Rachel Ann Henley; c. Nancy Elizabeth, James Henley and Linda Lee. Educ: Univ. of Va, B.S, 51; Beta Gamma Sigma; Jefferson Soc. Polit. & Govt. Pos: Campaign mgr. for John F. Kennedy, 14th Cong. Dist, Ohio, 60; campaign mgr. for Mayor Erickson, Akron Dem. Party, 61 & 63; chmn, Akron Planning Cmn, 62-66; v.chmn, Summit Co. Dem. Exec. Cmt, 62-68; campaign mgr. for President Johnson, 14th Cong. Dist, 64; del, Dem. Nat. Conv, 64; state campaign mgr, John Glenn for Senate Cmt, 64; mem. adv. coun, Small Bus. Admin, 64-66. Bus. & Prof. Pos: Pres, Brimfield Farms, Inc, 64-66 and Tri-Co. TV Corp, 65-66. Mil. Serv: Entered as Pvt, Army, 45, released as Lt, 48. Mem: Mason (32°); Shrine; Optimist Int; Fairlawn Country Club; Silver Lake Country Club; Akron City Club. Rel: Presbyterian; Elder. Legal Res: 96 N. Revere Rd, Akron, Ohio 44313. Mailing Add: 450 E. Exchange St, Akron, Ohio 44304.

LUFTIG, RITA SHEILA D
Secy, Co. Dem. Cent. Cmt, Calif.
b. Union City, N.J, 6/23/27; d. Samuel Stillman and Eleanor Sophie Drapkin S; m. 6/22/47 to Murry Luftig; c. Vicki Ann, Mitchell Louis, Andrea Gail and Laura Rae. Educ: Univ. Calif. at Los Angeles; Phrateres. Polit. & Govt. Pos: Mem, State Cent. Cmt, Calif, 6 years; v.pres, Calif. Dem. Coun; former treas, Co. Dem. Cent. Cmt, secy, currently. Bus. & Prof. Pos: Govt. teacher, San Diego Unified Sch. Dist, 69. Mem: League of Women Voters; Hadassah. Rel: Jewish. Mailing Add: 5730 Bounty St, San Diego, Calif. 92120.

LUGAR, RICHARD GREEN R
Mayor, Indianapolis, Ind.
b. Indianapolis, Ind, 4/4/32; s. Marvin L. Lugar and Bertha Green L; m. 9/8/56 to Charlene Smeltzer; c. Mark, Robert, John and David. Educ: Denison Univ, B.A, 54; Oxford Univ, B.A. & M.A, 56; Phi Beta Kappa; Omicron Delta Kappa; Blue Key; Pi Delta Epsilon; Pi Sigma Alpha; Beta Theta Pi. Polit. & Govt. Pos: Mem, Bd. of Sch. Cmnr, Indianapolis, Ind, 64-67; del, Ind. State Rep. Conv, 64 & 68; del, Rep. Nat. Conv. and mem, Platform Cmt, 68; Mayor, Indianapolis, Ind, 68-; mem, Adv. Cmn. on Intergovt. Rels, 69- Bus. & Prof. Pos: V.pres. and treas, Thomas L. Green & Co. Inc, 60-; treas, Lugar Stock Farm, Inc, 60- Mil. Serv: Entered as Seaman, 2/C, Navy, 57, released as Lt.(jg), 60, after serv. on Staff of Chief of Naval Opers, Pentagon, 58-60. Mem: U.S. Dept. Commerce Regional Export Expansion Coun; Rotary; Indianapolis Urban League; Ind. Farm Bur. Outstanding Young Man, Indianapolis, 66; One of Five Outstanding Young Men, Ind, Jr. C. of C, 66. Rel: Methodist. Legal Res: 3200 Highwoods Court, Indianapolis, Ind. 46222. Mailing Add: 2501 City-County Bldg, Indianapolis, Ind. 46204.

LUGER, CHARLES R
Pa. State Rep.
b. New York, N.Y, 3/23/22; s. Sigmund Luger and Gertrude Zwicker L; m. 11/21/43 to Anne Kay Kurland; c. Lisa Barbara, Michael Ian and Elliot Barry Kurland. Educ: Temple Univ. Eve. Sch. Polit. & Govt. Pos: V.chmn, Policy Bd. Statewide Planning Proj. for Voc. Rehab. Serv, 66- and Scranton Sch. Bldg. Authority; Pa. State Rep, 112th Dist, 67- Bus. & Prof. Pos: Pres, Luger Wire Mfg. Corp. Mil. Serv: Entered as Pvt, Army Air Force, 42, released as S/Sgt, 45, after serv. in Base Serv. Sq, 385th Air Serv. Group, Fifth Air Force, South. Philippines, Luzon Ie Shima and Japan, 45-46; Good Conduct Medal; Am. Campaign Medal; Philippine Liberation Ribbon with 1 Bronze Star; World War II Victory Medal; Asiatic Pac. Campaign Medal with 2 Bronze Stars. Mem: Pres, United Cerebral Palsy of Lackawanna Co, Scranton Jewish Commun. Cent, Amos Lodge of B'nai B'rith and East Scranton Little League; C. of C; Optimists (mem. bd. gov); dir, Jewish Fed, Temple Israel, Pinemore Camp, Am. Red Cross and Allied Serv. for Handicapped; chmn, B'nai B'rith Youth Orgn; team capt, Keystone Jr. Col. Bldg. Drive; Mayor's Citizen Cmt. on Transportation; adv. cmt, Scranton Indust. Develop. Authority; nat. coun, Joint Distribution Cmt; bldg. cmt, Allied Serv. for Handicapped; pres. bd, Univ. Scranton and United Cerebral Palsy of Pa; Elks; Progressive Cent; Purple Club; Jewish War Vets; YMCA; Everhart Mus. Asn; adv. bd, Salvation Army. Received Employer Merit Award for Hiring Handicapped; Man of Year Award for Commun Serv, fel. Club, Jr. C. of C. and Sr. Serv. Award, Jewish Commun. Cent. Rel: Jewish. Legal Res: 319 Wheeler Ave, Scranton, Pa. 18510. Mailing Add: 1625 Nay Aug Ave, Scranton, Pa. 18509.

LUICK, A. W. R
N.Dak. State Sen.
b. Hampton, Iowa, 11/8/91; married; c. Six. Polit. & Govt. Pos: N.Dak. State Rep, 45-49; N.Dak. State Sen, 51- Bus. & Prof. Pos: Retired farmer; v.pres, People's State Bank of Fairmount, N.Dak; pres, bd. dirs, Wahpeton Fed. Land Bank Asn. Mem: Farm Bur; Elks. Mailing Add: Fairmount, N.Dak. 58030.

LUJAN, FRANCISCO GUERRERO D
Sen, Guam Legis.
b. Agana, Guam, 5/2/04; s. Jesus Santos Lujan and Dolores San Agustin Guerrero L; wid; m. 7/3/57 to Lydia Mafnas Bernardo; c. Frank, Doris (Mrs. Antonio Balajadia), Rufo, Victor, James, David and Julia (Mrs. Joseph Torres). Educ: Univ. Hawaii, 46; Lasalle Exten. Univ, 47-52. Polit. & Govt. Pos: Sch. prin, Agana, Guam, 24-46; assemblyman, Guam Assembly, 35-36; judge, Police Court, 47-60; Sen, Guam Legis, 63-, mem. judiciary cmt, 63-64 & 65-66, chmn. 65-, v.chmn, judiciary cmt, 69-, mem. rules cmt, 65. Bus. & Prof. Pos: Notary Pub. Guam, 30-40. Mem: Judicial Coun. Guam; Guam Bar Asn. Rel: Roman Catholic. Legal Res: Chalan Pago, Agana, Guam 96910. Mailing Add: P.O. Box 1279, Agana, Guam 96910.

LUJAN, JIM D
Single. Polit. & Govt. Pos: N.Mex. State Rep, 61-68. Bus. & Prof. Pos: Funeral dir. Mem: Elk; La. Union Protective; Eagle; GI Forum. Rel: Catholic. 1967 Legal Res: Santa Fe, N.Mex. No mailing address available. (1967)

LUJAN, MANUEL, JR. R
U.S. Rep, N.Mex.
b. San Ildefonso, N.Mex, 5/12/28; s. Manuel Lujan and Lorenzita Romero L; m. 11/8/48 to Jean Couchman; c. Terra, James, Barbara and Jeff. Educ: Col. Santa Fe, B.A, 50. Polit. & Govt. Pos: Former v.chmn, N.Mex. State Rep. Party; U.S. Rep, N.Mex, First Dist, 69- Bus. & Prof. Pos: Partner in ins. bus, currently. Mem: Adv, Nat. Spanish-Speaking Businessmen's Asn; past pres, Santa Fe Commun. Coun; Coronado Kiwanis, St. Michael's Col. Alumni Asn. and N.Mex. Independent Ins. Agents Asn; Past Grand Knight, K. of C; Elks; Eagles. Commendation from Coronado Kiwanis for Effectiveness in Helping United Fund; Outstanding Alumnus, Col. of Santa Fe. Rel: Catholic. Legal Res: 1209 California N.E, Albuquerque, N.Mex. 87110. Mailing Add: 1317 Longworth Bldg, Washington, D.C. 20515.

LUKE, CLARENCE D. D
b. Scott City, Kans, 4/16/16; s. W. D. Luke and Mary E. Cheney L; m. 4/1/39 to Mary K. Flood; c. Ashley D, Linda Kay, Jessie Louise, and Diane Marie. Educ: High Sch. Polit. & Govt. Pos: Dem. Precinct Committeeman, Kans, 54-; campaign chmn, Breeding for Cong, 56-62; Co. Chmn, Dem. Party, 64-68. Rel: Methodist. Legal Res: 1105 College, Scott City, Kans. 67871. Mailing Add: Box 601, Scott City, Kans. 67871

LUKE, VIRGINIA PAVELKA D
b. Aberdeen, S.Dak, 12/26/45; d. Robert H. Pavelka and Phyllis Reese P; m. 8/15/69 to Hugh J. Luke. Educ: Am. Univ, B.A, 68, grad. studies, 68-; Pi Sigma Alpha; Phi Mu. Polit. & Govt. Pos: Del-at-lg, Dem. Nat. Conv, 68. Rel: Presbyterian. Mailing Add: 4640 Bryan Circle, Lincoln, Nebr. 68506.

LUKENS, DONALD E. R
U.S. Rep, Ohio
b. Harveysburg, Ohio, 2/11/31; s. William A. Lukens and Edith Greene L; single. Educ: Ohio State Univ, B.Sc. in Criminology, 54; Delta Chi; Alpha Phi Omega; Arnold Air Soc; Scabbard & Blade; Student Coun. on Relig. Affairs; Student Coun, Mil. Coun; Univ. 4-H; Univ. Grange; Ohio Union Bd; May Week; Homecoming Week; Greek Week. Polit. & Govt. Pos: Minority Counsel, U.S. House of Rep. Rules Cmt, 61-63; mem, D.C. Rep. Cent. Cmt, 62-63; pres, D.C. Young Rep, 62-63; chmn, bd. of dirs, Young Rep. Nat. Leadership Training Inst, 63-65; mem, exec. cmt, and nat. chmn, Young Rep. Nat. Fedn, 63-65; mem, Butler Co. Rep. Exec. Cmt, Ohio, 66-; U.S. Rep, Ohio, 66-, mem, House Post Off. and Civil Serv. Cmt. and House Sci. and Astronautics Cmt, U.S. House of Rep, currently. Bus. & Prof. Pos: Mgt. Consult, 65-66. Mil. Serv: Entered as 2nd Lt, Air Force, 54, released as Capt, 60, after serv. in Off. of Spec. Invest, 56-60; Capt, Air Force Res, 66- Mem: Mason; Shrine; Ahepa; Toastmasters; Jaycees; Heart Asn; Proj. Hope; YMCA; Middletown Civic Asn. Rel: Quaker. Legal Res: Middletown, Ohio 45042. Mailing Add: 1338 Longworth Bldg, Washington, D.C. 20515.

LUM, TENNYSON KUM WING R
Hawaii State Rep.
b. Honolulu, Hawaii, 2/28/41; s. Chock Ki Lum and Esther Low L; c. Deborah Ann, Tennyson, Jr. and Alison Pualani. Educ: Univ. Hawaii, B.Ed, 63; Tu Chiang Sheh. Polit. & Govt. Pos: Hawaii State Rep, 66-; del, Hawaii State Constitutional Conv, 68. Bus. & Prof. Pos: Teacher, State of Hawaii, 63-64; sales mgr, Aetna Life & Casualty, 64-66, sales rep, 66-; sales agent, Tropic Shores Realty, 67- Mem: Honolulu Asn. of Life Underwriters; Honolulu Bd. of Realtors; Bus. League for Sound Govt; exec. cmt, March of Dimes; dir, YMCA; dir, John Howard Soc; Waialae-Kahala Jaycees; Iolani Alumni Asn; Univ. Ha-

waii Alumni Asn; Waialae Nui Ridge Commun. Asn; dir, Cmt. on Addiction; asst. coach, Roosevelt High Sch. Rel: Episcopal. Legal Res: 1941 Alaeloa St, Honolulu, Hawaii 96821. Mailing Add: State Capitol, Honolulu, Hawaii 96813.

LUND, RHODA S. R
Rep. Nat. Committeewoman, Minn.
b. Butternut Valley, Minn; d. Andrew O. Berge and Thalia Sunde B; m. 12/25/29 to Russell Thomas Lund; c. Russell T, Jr. and Mrs. Robert Row. Educ: St. Olaf Col, B.A, 26. Polit. & Govt. Pos: Chairwoman, Third Dist. Rep. Party, Minn, 51-52; chairwoman, State Rep. Party, 53-54; mem, Defense Adv. Cmt. on Women in the Serv, 58-61; pres, Rep. Workshop of Minn, 59-60; del, Rep. Nat. Conv, 56, 64 & 68; alternate del, 60, mem, Platform and Arrangements Cmts, 64 & 68; Rep. Nat. Committeewoman, Minn, 60-; mem, Minn. Adv. Cmt, U.S. Cmn. on Civil Rights, 64- Mem: Minn. Coun. Delinquency and Crime; bd. mem, Correctional Serv. Minn. and Minneapolis Boys Club Women's Auxiliary. Rel: Lutheran. Mailing Add: 4814 Lakeview Dr, Minneapolis, Minn. 55424.

LUNDBERG, LOIS ANN R
35th Assembly Dist. Chmn, Orange Co. Rep. Cent. Cmt, Calif.
b. Tulsa, Okla, 9/21/28; d. John T. McQuay and Anna M. Patterson M; m. 9/30/54 to Ted W. Lundberg; c. Linda Ann and Sharon Lynn. Educ: Long Beach City Col, 1 year. Polit. & Govt. Pos: Mem. bd. dir, La Habra Rep. Women, Calif, 61-62 and currently, secy, 63, pres, 64-65; area chmn, Orange Co. Rep. Precinct Orgn, 61-65, div. chmn, 65, precinct capt, 65-; 35th Assembly Dist. chmn, Orange Co. Rep. Cent. Cmt, 65-, assoc. mem, 68-; mem, Calif. Rep. State Cent. Cmt, 67- Bus. & Prof. Pos: Bus. off. rep, Pac. Tel. Co, 50-57, serv. observer, 57-60, bus. off. supvr, 60-65. Mem: United Rep. of Calif. Orange Co. Rep. Award for Outstanding Serv, 67; Gov. Reagan Award as One of the Top Ten Polit. Precinct Chmn. in Calif, 68. Rel: Lutheran. Mailing Add: 1341 Carmela Lane, La Habra, Calif. 90631.

LUNDBERG, MELVIN EDWARD R
b. Woods Cross, Utah, 4/13/04; s. Alfred A. Lundberg and Margaret Southworth L; m. 6/15/26 to Reva Rowe. Educ: Univ. Utah, B.S, in Eng, 30. Polit. & Govt. Pos: Mem, Nev. State Planning Bd, 47-56; mem, Columbia Interstate Compact Cmt, 51-58 chmn, Gov. Sch. Surv. Cmt, 53-57; chmn, Nev. Del. to White House Conf. on Educ, 55; chmn, Elko Co. Rep. Cent. Cmt, 56-64; mem, Nev. State Parole Bd, 57-; del, Rep. Nat. Conv, 60, alternate del, 64 & 68; Finance chmn, Nev. State Rep. Party; Rep. Nat. Committeeman and mem, Rep. Nat. Finance Committee, Nev, 64-68; chmn, Nev. State Coun. on Educ. and mem, Nat. Citizens' Coun. Better Schs; mem, Gov. Cmt. on Educ, 65; mem, Citizens' Conf. on Nev. Courts, 68. Bus. & Prof. Pos: Secy. and gen. mgr, Uintah Power & Light Co, 32-39; asst. mgr. and dir, Nev. Power Co, 40-53, v.pres. and gen. mgr, 53-61, v.pres, dir. and div. mgr, 61-; dir, Elio Broadcasting Co, 48-; dir, Transwest. Life Ins. Co, 58-67. Mem: Nev. Soc. Prfnl. Engrs; Nev. Taxpayers Asn.(pres. and dir); hon. life mem, Nev. Cong. of Parents and Teachers; Elks (past Exalted Ruler, hon. life mem. and Dist. Dep. Grand Exalted Ruler, 59-60); C. of C.(dir. and past pres, Elko Chap); Lions (past pres, Elko Club). Rel: Latter-day Saint. Legal Res: 720 Rahas Rd, Apt. 10, Elko, Nev. 89801. Mailing Add: 542 Commercial St, Elko, Nev. 89801.

LUNDERVILLE, HOWARD P. R
Vt. State Rep.
b. Williston, Vt, 8/18/23; single. Educ: Burlington High Sch. Polit. & Govt. Pos: High bailiff, Essex Junction, Vt, 51-53, acting chief of police, 56; acting chief of police, South Burlington, Vt, 59-60, first constable, tax collector and dep. sheriff, 43-, fire chief, 49-, fire warden, 59- and cemetery cmnr, 50-; Vt. State Rep, 53-57 & 63- Bus. & Prof. Pos: Farmer, part-time. Mem: K. of C; Grange; Holy Name Soc. Rel: Catholic. Mailing Add: Williston, Vt. 05495. (1967)

LUNDGREN, CONRAD F. 'CON' R
Mont. State Rep.
m. to Jean McConochie; c. Gail and Robert. Educ: Mont. Col. of Mineral Sci. and Tech, Sch. of Mines. Polit. & Govt. Pos: Mem, Bd. of Trustees, Columbia Falls Dist. Six; Mont. State Rep, currently. Bus. & Prof. Pos: Partner, W. Glacier Mercantile. Mil. Serv: World War II. Mailing Add: 844 Woodland, Kalispell, Mont. 59901. (1967)

LUNDQUIST, CLARENCE THEODORE D
b. Chicago, Ill, 1/3/09; s. Frank Lundquist and Bessie Larson L; m. 7/9/38 to Edith Margaret Otte; c. Donna Fey. Educ: Univ. of Ill, B.S, 32; Northwestern Univ, grad. sch, 32-35; Georgetown Law Sch, LL.B, 44; 2nd prize High Scholarship, Sr. Year Law Sch. Polit. & Govt. Pos: Various fed. govt. pos, 35-55; dep. adminstr, wage and hour and pub. contracts div, U.S. Dept. of Labor, 55-57, adminstr, 58-69. Bus. & Prof. Pos: With Ill. Bell Tel. Co, Chicago, 29-30; attorney-arbitrator, 69- Mil. Serv: Entered as 2nd Lt, Army, 42, released as Lt. Col, 46, after serv. in Intel. Activities; Army Commendation Ribbon; Lt. Col.(Ret), Army Res. Mem: D.C. Bar; Nat. Press Club; Am. Legion. Rel: Protestant. Legal Res: Illinois. Mailing Add: 4822 Tilden St. N.W, Washington, D.C. 20016.

LUNDQUIST, ELDON F. R
Ind. State Sen.
Polit. & Govt. Pos: Mem, bd. trustees, Ind. Voc. Tech. Col; mem, Elkhart Bd. Parks and Recreation, 51-55; secy, Sch. Bd. Trustees, 55-60; Ind. State Rep, 61-64; Ind. State Sen, currently. Bus. & Prof. Pos: Lectr, Grad. Sch. Banking, Univ. Wis; v.pres. and pub. rels. dir, St. Joseph Valley Bank, 61-64. Mem: Ind. Bankers Asn; Educ. Found. Comm; Elks; City Club, Elcona Country Club. Rel: Methodist. Mailing Add: 600 E. Boulevard, Elkhart, Ind. 46514. (1967)

LUNDY, RAYFIELD R
b. Calif, 7/30/16; s. John P. Lundy and Martha Walker L; m. 9/22/42 to Maxene Lorena Thomas; c. Rayfield, Jr, Keith Roger, Marsha Darlene, Laurel Theresa, William L. and Marnetta Lynette. Educ: Howard Univ, 34-39, Law Sch, 39-42; Southwest. Univ. Law Sch, 46-48; Univ. South. Calif, 48-52, Law Sch, 52-56; Kappa Sigma Debating Soc; Kappa Alpha Psi. Polit. & Govt. Pos: Mem. and pres. bd. trustees, Los Angeles Co. Sch. Bd, Calif, 51-54; mem, Los Angeles Co. Rep. Cent. Cmt, 52-69; mem, Calif. Rep. State Cent. Cmt, 54-69, mem. exec. cmt, 69; Rep. nominee, U.S. Rep, Calif, 62, 64 & 68; mem, Calif. State Bd. Pharm, 69- Mil. Serv: Entered as Pvt, Army Transportation Corps, 42, released as M/Sgt, 46, after serv. in First Ave. Cantonment, Seattle, Wash, New Orleans Army Air Base and Camp Lee, Va, 42-46; Good Conduct and Expert Rifleman Medals. Mem: Am. Bar Asn; Am. Judicature Soc; Calif. State Bar; U.S. Supreme Court; Criminal Courts Bar Asn.(founder); Compton Lawyers Asn; Southeast Dist. Bar Asn; Langston Law Club; Bd. of Immigration Appeals; Tax Court U.S; Compton Bar Asn.(bd. dirs, 56-60); Am. Legion; Compton Human Rels. Coun; Boys Club; YMCA; Boy Scouts; PTA; Centennial High Sch. Boosters Club (founder). Compton Civic Merit Award, Club Ideal. Rel: Methodist. Legal Res: 1816 E. 122nd St, Los Angeles, Calif. 90059. Mailing Add: 527 W. Compton Blvd, Compton, Calif. 90220.

LUNGREN, JOHN HOWARD R
Chmn, Milwaukee Co. Rep. Party, Wis.
b. Chicago, Ill, 2/11/25; s. Charles Howard Lungren and Edna Edwards L; m. 12/12/53 to Joan Jolidon; c. John Eric and Matthew Christopher. Educ: Beloit Col, B.A, 48; Marquette Univ, J.D, 52; Sigma Alpha Epsilon. Polit. & Govt. Pos: Rep. ward committeeman, Waunatosa, Wis, 62-; del, Rep. State Conv, 62-67; chmn. statutory cmt, Milwaukee Co. Rep. Party, 64-67, chmn, 67-; justice of the peace, Waunatosa, Wis, 64-68; campaign mgr, cong. campaigns, 64-; mem, state exec. cmt, Rep. Party, Wis, 67-; alternate del, Rep. Nat. Conv, 68. Bus. & Prof. Pos: Attorney, Standard Oil Co, Ind, 53-54; corporate counsel, Clark Oil & Refining Corp, 54-64; asst. gen. counsel and asst. secy, A.O. Smith Corp, 64- Mil Serv: Entered as Seaman, Navy, 43, released as M.M. 3/C, 46, after serv. in 112th N.C.B, Pac. Theatre, 44-46; Combat Theatre Medal. Mem: Milwaukee, Wis. and Am. Bar Asns; Am. Legion; F&AM. Rel: Congregational. Mailing Add: 124 N. 85th St, Waunatosa, Wis. 53226.

LUNSTAD, ERNEST S. D
b. Simpson, Mont, 1916; s.Christian Clinton Lunstad and Caroline Koch L; m. to Betty Aadsen; c. Steve, Craig, Lance and Joel. Educ: Attended Schs, Simpson, Mont, Crosby, N.Dak, Opheim, Mont. Polit. & Govt. Pos: Former Sch. Bd. Mem, 9th Sch. Dist. Bus. & Prof. Pos: A.E. Mercer, 35; Eastside Grange. Mem: Carpenters Local 911, 35-; Scandinavian Fraternity, past pres; former dir, Immanuel Lutheran Home. Rel: Lutheran; Treas, Bethany Lutheran Church. 1967 Legal Res: Kalispell, Mont. No mailing address available. (1967)

LUNTE, CHARLES DAVID R
Chmn, Twin Falls Co. Rep. Party, Idaho
b. Pocatello, Idaho, 5/27/16; s. W. E. Lunte and LuLu Sechler L; m. 5/29/37 to Ruth Nelson; c. James W. Educ: Idaho State Col. Polit. & Govt. Pos: Precinct committeeman, Twin Falls Co. Rep. Party, Idaho, 56-66, chmn, currently; del, Rep. Nat. Conv, 68. Bus. & Prof. Pos: Pres. and gen. mgr, WEFCO, Inc, 58-; dir, Wilma's, Inc, 63- Mem: AF&AM, El Korah Shrine; Kiwanis; C. of C. Jr. C. of C. DSA Award. Rel: Christian. Mailing Add: R.R. 1, Buhl, Idaho 83316. (1967)

LUPTON, JOHN MATHER R
Conn. State Sen.
b. Mattituck, N.Y, 3/1/17; s. Robert Mather Lupton and Virginia C. Craven L; m. 4/13/40 to Mavis Wort; c. Nan (Mrs. Charles Dietrich), Penelope (Mrs. Douglas Given), John M, III, Josiah E. and Deborah. Educ: Univ. Minn, 36-37. Polit. & Govt. Pos: Chmn, Conn. State Young Rep, 53-54; chmn, Weston Town Rep. Cmt, Conn, 55-56; Conn. State Rep, 56-60; exec. dir, Conn. Rep. Citizens Cmt, 63-66; Conn. State Sen, currently. Bus. & Prof. Pos: Pres, John Mather Lupton Co, Inc, N.Y.C, 44-62; exec. secy, Choate Sch. Found, Inc; dir, Hamar Laser Co, Inc. Mem: Alpha Delta Sigma; Mason. Rel: Congregational. Mailing Add: Norfield Rd, Weston, Conn. 06880.

LUPTON, WALTER JONES D
b. Scranton, N.C, 1/9/06; s. Silas S. Lupton and Georgia Ann Robinson L; m. 3/7/36 to Margaret T. Fisher; c. Richard. Educ: Univ. N.C, 24-27; Univ. N.C. Law Sch, one year. Polit. & Govt. Pos: Asst. emergency loan supvr, N.C; chmn, Hyde Co. Dem. Party, 54-56; co. acct; N.C. State Rep, 63-66. Bus. & Prof. Pos: Farmer. Mem: Farmer Home Admin, Hyde Co, 56-58; master, Mason, 42-64, secy, several years. Rel: Methodist. Mailing Add: Swan Quarter, N.C. 27885. (1967)

LURVEY, MILDRED EDWINA R
Mem, Mass. State Rep. Cmt.
b. Rochester, N.H, 7/6/27; d. Richard Edward Stebbins and Sarah Elizabeth Dopheny S; m. 5/12/50 to Robert Joseph Lurvey. Educ: Colby Jr. Col, 43-45; Univ. N.H, A.B, 47. Polit. & Govt. Pos: Finance chmn, Groton Rep. Town Cmt, Mass, 64-66, chmn, 66-; mem, Mass. Rep. State Cmt, 68- Mem: Groton Womans Club (past pres); Mass. State Federated Womens Clubs (dir, currently); Nat. Early Am. Glass Club (pres, currently). Rel: Protestant. Mailing Add: 24 Blossom Lane, Groton, Mass. 01450.

LUSK, GEORGIA LEE D
b. Eddy, N.Mex, 5/12/93; d. George W. Witt and Mary Isabel Gilreath W; wid; c. Virgil Witt, Morgan Dolph and Thomas Eugene. Educ: Silver City Normal, grad, 14; Colo. State Teachers Col; Highland Univ, 28-29; Delta Kappa Gamma. Polit. & Govt. Pos: State supt, N.Mex. Pub. Schs, 55-58; mem, War Claims Cmn, 49-53; U.S. Rep, N.Mex, 47-48; state supt, N.Mex. Sch. Syst, 43-46 and 31-34; supt. schs, Lea Co, 25-28; teacher, Jr. High Sch, 22-23 and Elem. Schs, 14-15 and 21-23. Mem: Admin. Women of N.Mex; N.Mex. Educ. Asn; Nat. Educ. Asn; Future Farmers of Am; Am. Legion Auxiliary; Co. Home Dem. Clubs; N.Mex. Fedn. Womans Clubs. Rel: Methodist. Mailing Add: 663 Washington, Santa Fe, N.Mex. 87501. (1967)

LUSK, HALL S. D
b. Washington, D.C, 9/21/83; s. Charles Stoner Lusk and Florence Speake L; m. 9/30/14 to Sara Catherine Emmons; c. Polly Carpenter (Mrs. Lloyd Appleman); Catherine Holmead, Margaret Addison (Mrs. Edgar Framm), Mary Emmons (Mrs. Glenn Meade) and Jeanne Van Wyck (Mrs. Donald Fox). Educ: Georgetown Univ, B.A, 04, LL.B, 07, hon. LL.D, 54; Univ. Portland, hon. LL.D, 41; Delta Chi; Delta Theta Phi. Polit. & Govt. Pos: Secy. to Chief Justice Shepard, Court of Appeals, D.C, 06-09; asst. U.S. Attorney, Dist. of Ore, 18-20; circuit judge, Multnomah Co, 30-37; app. to court, 37, elected to

court, 34, 44, 50 & 56, chief justice, 49-52; U.S. Sen, Ore, 60; judge pro tem, Supreme Court of Ore, 61-67. Bus. & Prof. Pos: Former instr. corp. law, N.W. Col. Law, Portland; attorney-at-law, Portland, 10-12; assoc, Dolph, Mallory, Simon and Gearin, 12-18; partner, Emmons, Lusk and Bynon, Attorneys, 20-30. Mem: Am. and Ore. State Bar Asns; Univ. Club; Multnomah Athletic Club; Arlington Club. Rel: Catholic. Mailing Add: 1780 Fairmont Ave. S, Salem, Ore. 97302.

LUSK, RAYMOND FRANCIS R

b. Lima, Ohi, 9/9/17; s. Raymond F. Lusk and Martha Van Cleave L; m. 10/14/44 to Betty Jane McAdams; c. Linda, Nancy and Cindy. Educ: Northwest. Sch. of Commerce, Lima Ohio, grad, 47. Polit. & Govt. Pos: Secy, Putnam Co. Rep. Exec. Cmt, Ohio; mem, Putnam Co. Rep. Cent. Cmt; Ohio State Rep, 63-67; chmn, Putnam Co. Regional Planning Cmn. and secy, Putnam Co. Bd. Ment. Retardation. Bus. & Prod. Pos: Farm owner; gen. supvr, Equity Dairy Stores, Inc, 47-58; Bus. Promotion Rep, West Ohio Gas Co, 58- Mil. Serv: Entered as Pvt, Marine Corps, 41, released as Master T/Sgt, 45, after serv. in Marine Air Group 21, Southwest Pac; South. Solomans, New Georgia and Bougainville Campaign Ribbons. Mem: Am. Gas Asn; Mason (32°); K. T; Am. Legion; VFW; Lions; Grange. Rel: United Church of Christ. Mailing Add: 620 W. Sycamore, Columbus Grove, Ohio 45830.

LUSSIER, ARTHUR EDGAR D

Mayor, Woonsocket, R.I.

b. Woonsocket, R.I, 3/23/19; s. Joseph Lussier and Laurie L; m. 6/21/41 to Constance L. Vachon; c. Donald E, Paulette A. and A. Andrew. Educ: Univ. R.I. Exten. course, Pub. Rels. Mgt. Polit. & Govt. Pos: Secy, Woonsocket Dem. Cmt, R.I; councilman, Woonsocket, 53-65, mayor, 65- Bus. & Prof. Pos: Foreman, Gauge Div, Taft-Peirce Mfg. Co, 46-57, sales and serv. engr, 57-65. Mil. Serv: Entered as A/S, Navy, 43, released as Aviation Ordinance Man 2/C, 46; Am. Theater Medal; World War II Medal. Mem: Lions; Club Marquette; C. of C; Am. Legion; Pawtucket Country Club; Int. Rep. Munic. Explorer Post, Boy Scouts. Rel: Roman Catholic. Legal Res: 72 Ave. B, Woonsocket, R.I. 02895. Mailing Add: City Hall, Main St, Woonsocket, R.I. 02895.

LUSTIG, WAYNE R

Chmn, Second Cong. Dist. Rep. Cmt, Va.

b. White Plains, N.Y, 12/19/34; s. Joseph Lustig and Cecelia Blau L; m. 6/16/57 to Elaine Bohorad; c. Tracy Allison, Charles Barnet and Heidi Anne. Educ: Univ. Pa, B.A, 56; Univ. Va. Sch. Law, LL.B, 59; Delta Sigma Rho; Sigma Alpha Mu. Polit. & Govt. Pos: Mem, City of Norfolk Rep. Cmt, Va, 61-; mem, Va. State Rep. Cent. Cmt, 63-; chmn, Second Cong. Dist. Rep. Cmt, Va, 63-; Rep. cand, U.S. Rep, Second Dist, Va, 64; Rep. cand, Va. State Sen, Norfolk, 67; chmn, Whitehurst for Cong. Campaign Cmt, 68; del, Rep. Nat. Conv, 68; mem, Va. State Rep. Exec. Cmt, 68- Bus. & Prof. Pos: Bd. dirs, Commun. Rels. Coun, 66-69; v.pres. and bd. mem, Jewish Family Serv, 69. Mil. Serv: Entered as Pvt, Army Res, 59, released as 1st Lt, 67, after serv. in Judge Adv. Gen. Corps. Mem: Am. Judicature Soc; Am. and Va. State Bar Asns; Va. Trial Lawyers Asn; Norfolk-Portsmouth Bar Asn.(chmn. young lawyers sect. and mem. exec. cmt, 68-69); United Jewish Fedn. Bd; bd. dir, Norfolk Jr. C. of C, 63-67; AF&AM; B'nai B'rith; RAM; Norfolk Sports Club; Lafayette Yacht Club; Harbor Club. First Place, Va. State Speak-Up Jaycee Award, 60. Rel: Jewish. Legal Res: 6813 Meadowlawn Dr, Norfolk, Va. 23510. Mailing Add: 1340 Virginia National Bank Bldg, Norfolk, Va. 23518.

LUTHER, ERNEST M. D

b. Hooper, Nebr, 2/16/97; s. Edward M. Luther and Augusta Alfs L; m. 9/6/21 to Marguerite Cullamore; c. Ernest H, Clark E, Clyde L. and Dorothy J. Educ: Hooper High Sch, Nebr, grad, 13; Mosher Lampman Bus. Col, Omaha, 14. Polit. & Govt. Pos: Employee, U.S. Dept. of Agr, Farm Programs, 33-48; del, Dem. Nat. Conv, 60 & 68. Bus. & Prof. Pos: Self-employed farmer, cattle feeder and buyer, 20- Mil. Serv: Pvt, Ambulance Unit, Army, 18. Mem: Mason; Am. Legion; 40 et 8; Ak-sar-ben. Rel: Protestant. Mailing Add: 4615 California St, Omaha, Nebr. 68132.

LUTTY, PAUL F. D

Pa. State Rep.

b. Pittsburgh, Pa, 6/30/17; s. William Lutty and Victoria Huneck L; m. to Rita Herold; c. Paul, Jr. Educ: St. Michael Parochial Sch; South High Sch. Polit. & Govt. Pos: Dem. committeeman and secy. of 17th Ward Orgn, Pa, 42-50; Pa. State Rep, 50- Bus. & Prof. Pos: Paper hanging contractor, 36-39. Mem: Former del, Pittsburgh Cent. Labor Union; pres, Local 233, Joint Coun. of Teamsters; bd, Hill Top YMCA; Elks; Moose. Mailing Add: 1101 E. Warrington Ave, Pittsburgh, Pa. 15210.

LUTZ, HARRY FRANCIS R

Kans. State Rep.

b. Wallace, Kans, 3/6/05; s. Ward Henry Lutz and Mary L. Buchanan L; m. 4/14/36 to Jean Dexter; c. Helen (Mrs. Bullock) and Ward A. Educ: Kans. State Univ, Manhattan, B.S. in Rural Commerce, 25; Sigma Nu. Polit. & Govt. Pos: Mayor, Sharon Springs, Kans, 37-40, city councilman, 41-42; cmnr, Kans. Forestry, Fish & Game Cmn, Pratt, Kans, 41-49, asst. dir, 49-55; Kans. State Rep, 63- Bus. & Prof. Pos: Owner, ed. and publisher of weekly newspaper, West. Times, Sharon Springs, Kans, 34-49; exec. v.pres, Peoples State Bank, 55- Mem: Kans. Multistate Tax Compact; Farm Bur; Kans. Livestock Asn; Mason; Shrine; Elks; Rotary; C. of C. Rel: Methodist. Mailing Add: Sharon Springs, Kans. 67758.

LUUKINEN, (ROBERTA) JEANNE R

Secy, Rep. State Cent. Cmt, Minn.

b. Webster City, Iowa, 3/31/26; s. Roy Jesse Lee and Lila Weedman L; m. 2/23/47 to Rudolph Terho Luukinen; c. Lynn and Kay. Educ: Stephens Col, A.A, 46; Alpha Epsilon Rho; Delta Chi Delta. Polit. & Govt. Pos: Secy, Rep. State Cent. Cmt, Minn, 69- Bus. & Prof. Pos: Continuity writer, KICD, Spencer, Iowa, 47 and Heinrich Advert, Peoria, Ill, 52-54; continuity writer & women's dir, WIRL, Peoria, Ill, 56; traffic mgr, WDSM Radio/TV, Duluth, Minn, 60; writer/public rel, H.E. Westmoreland, Inc, Duluth, Minn, 66- Mem: Twin Ports Press Club; Women's Asn. of the Duluth Symphony; Duluth Contract Bridge League; Duluth Women's Rep. Club; Northland Chap, Am. Red Cross. Rel: Presbyterian. Legal Res: 1816 Vermilion Rd, Duluth, Minn. 55803. Mailing Add: H.E. Westmoreland, Inc, 1 E. First St, Duluth, Minn. 55802.

LYKENS, RONALD EVERETT R

Chmn, Pittsylvania Co. Rep. Cmt, Va.

b. Sommerville, Mass, 9/23/37; s. Walter Everett Lykens and Phyllis Hayes L; m. 1/19/57 to Joanne Ross; c. Margit Sue, Richard Everett and Brent Ross. Educ: Univ. Toledo, 2 years; Univ. Va, Patrick Henry Col, 2 years. Polit. & Govt. Pos: V.pres, Danville Young Rep, Va, 66, pres, 67; cand. for Va. State Del, 67; chmn, City of Danville and Pittsylvania Co. Rep. Cmt, 68- Bus. & Prof. Pos: Supvr, acct. dept, Gulf Oil Corp, Toledo, Ohio, 55-58; dept. mgr, J.C. Penney's, 58-61; store mgr, Spiegel's, Pittsburgh, Pa, 62-64; mkt. rep, Am. Oil Co, Danville, Va, 64- Mil. Serv: Entered as Seaman Recruit, Naval Res, 54, released as YN2, 62, after serv. in Surface Div, 4-6 (D). Mem: Jaycees; Toastmasters; bd. adv, Danville Soc. Serv. Bur. Rel: Lutheran. Mailing Add: 520 Granville Dr, Danville, Va. 24541.

LYMAN, CURTIS LEE R

Chmn, Orleans Co. Rep. Cmt, N.Y.

b. Albion, N.Y, 4/5/26; s. William Chester Lyman, Sr. and Laura Lee L; m. 9/11/48 to Evelyn M. Lake; c. Curtis, Jr, Nathan M. and James G. Educ: Hiram Col, A.B, 48; Cornell Law Sch, LL.B, 51; Pi Kappa Delta; Ball and Chain; Phi Alpha Delta. Polit. & Govt. Pos: Research asst, Joint Legis. Cmt. Water Resources Planning, 58-61; trustee, Albion, N.Y, 62-66; v.chmn, Orleans Co. Rep. Cmt, 65-67, chmn, 67-; asst. counsel, Joint Legis. Cmt. Court Reorgn, 66-67; assoc. counsel, Joint Legis. Cmt. Problems Ment. Handicapped, 68-69; del. and alternate del, Eighth Judicial Dist. Conv, various times. Bus. & Prof. Pos: Mem. Panel arbiters, Am. Arbit. Asn, 57-; attorney, Marine Midland Trust Co. West. N.Y, Albion Off, 60- Mil. Serv: Entered as E-1, Army, 43, released as Sgt, 46, after serv. in Coast Artil. Command, Panama Canal Defense, 45-46; recalled 51-61, Capt, Artil, Am. Theatre, 51-52; Good Conduct Medal; Am. Theatre Ribbon; World War II Victory Medal; Korean Serv. Medal. Publ: 'History of the Orleans County Courthouse,' N.Y. State Bar Asn, 59. Mem: Orleans Co. Bar Asn.(secy, v.pres. and pres); Monroe Co, N.Y. State and Am. Bar Asns; Bar of the Supreme Court U.S; F&AM; Am. Legion; Albion Sportsmen's Club; Cobblestone Soc; NAACP; Orleans Co. Exten. Serv; Am. Red Cross; Gov. Club; Town Club Albion. Leonard H. Milliman Coop. Award, 51. Rel: Presbyterian; Past Ruling Elder, First Presbyterian Church Albion. Legal Res: 231 N. Main St, Albion, N.Y. 14411. Mailing Add: 51 N. Main St, Albion, N.Y. 14411.

LYMAN, FRANK D

Ill. State Rep.

b. Chicago, Ill, 1/20/17; married. Educ: Loyola Acad; DePaul Univ. Polit. & Govt. Pos: Committeeman, 48th Ward, Chicago, Ill, 48; Asst. State Treas, Ill, 50-51; asst. co. treas, 55; Ill. State Rep, 58- Bus. & Prof. Pos: Ins. bus. Mil. Serv: 108th Observation Squadron, Ill. Nat. Guard, 40; Army Air Force, 41-45. Mem: Ill. Athletic Club; Am. Legion; Uptown Lions Club; Uptown Chicago Cmn; DePaul Alumni Asn. Mailing Add: 5000 Marine Dr, Chicago, Ill. 60640. (1967)

LYNAM, MARSHALL L. D

b. Bishop, Tex, 11/27/24; s. Elbert L. Lynam and May Pierson L; m. 7/3/49 to Eddie Ann Forrest; c. Marsha Ann, Charles Lee and Sharon Kaye. Educ: Tex. Col. Arts & Indust. Polit. & Govt. Pos: Admin. asst. to U.S. Rep. Jim Wright, Tex, 62- Bus. & Prof. Pos: Reporter, Ft. Worth Star-Telegram. Mil. Serv: Entered as Pvt, Army Air Force, 43, released as S/Sgt, 45, after serv. as Gunner on B-17 with 15th Air Force in Italy and 97th Bomb Group, 44-45. Rel: Protestant. Legal Res: 1005 Sharondale, Ft. Worth, Tex. 76115. Mailing Add: 6423 Lee Hwy, Arlington, Va. 22205.

LYNBOURGH, WILLIAM B. D

b. Manchester, N.H, 11/14/14; married; c. two. Educ: Univ. of N.H. Polit. & Govt. Pos: N.H. State Rep. until 67; acting postmaster, Center Strafford, N.H, 67- Bus. & Prof. Pos: Poultry farmer; physical educ. dir. Mem: Grange; Civil Defense Dir. Rel: Protestant. Mailing Add: Center Strafford, N.H. 03815.

LYNCH, ALICE CLARKE R

Exec. Secy, Third Dist. Re. Cmt, Va.

b. Dinwiddie Co, Va, 5/28/30; d. Berkley Zacheus Clarke and Alice Hovey C; m. 9/2/49 to Robert Lee Lynch; c. Charles Patrick, Michael Clarke, Van Linden and Berkley Allen. Educ: Westhampton Col, B.A, 50. Polit. & Govt. Pos: Secy, Young Rep. Fedn. of Va, 51-53; committeewoman, Richmond Rep. Cmt, 51-69; secy, Third Dist. Rep. Cmt, 52-56, exec. secy, 64-; treas, Rep. Women's Club, 52-57, pres, 63-65; del, Rep. Nat. Conv, 68; chmn, Bd. of Housing & Hygiene, 66- Mem: Pres, Mary Mumford PTA; v.pres, Colonial Place Garden Club. Rel: Baptist. Mailing Add: 4701 Stuart Ave, Richmond, Va. 23226.

LYNCH, DANIEL CORNELOUS D

Chmn, Douglas Co. Dem. Party, Nebr.

b. Omaha, Nebr, 8/9/29; s. Phillip C. Lynch, Sr. and Minnie E. Lyck L; m. 7/1/50 to Elva Jane Haskins; c. Debbra Ann, Julia Mea, Marrianne Margret, Daniel Cornelous, Jr. and Maureen Kay. Educ: Univ. Omaha, 49; Loras Col, 47-48; Univ. Trade School, Kansas City, Mo, grad, 50. Polit. & Govt. Pos: Pres, Douglas Co. Young Dem, Nebr, 54-55; pres, Nebr. Young Dem, 56-57; chmn, Douglas Co. Dem. Party, 60-; secy-treas, Nebr. Asn. Co. Officials, 67, v.pres, 68, pres, 69-; del. and chmn, Nebr. del, Dem. Nat. Conv, 68; mem. bd. dirs, Nat. Asn. Co. Officers, Wash, D.C, 68- Bus. & Prof. Pos: Pres, Phil C. Lynch Plumbing & Heating Co. Omaha, Nebr, 59-; bd. dirs, United Plumbing & Heating Supply Co, 63-67; pres, Lynch Bros. Invest. Co, 65- Mil. Serv: Entered as E-3, Army, 53, released as Acting Sgt, 55, after serv. in 74th AFA, Landshut, Germany, 53-55; Good Conduct Medal; European Theatre Ribbon; Unit Citation. Publ: Miscellaneous articles for state association in Nebr, 66-; 'Strengthening County Government in America,' Nat. Asn. Mag, 68; 'Partisan Politics and Reality,' Sun Papers, 69. Mem: Omaha Plumbing, Heating and Cooling Contractors Asn.(pres, 62); Nebr. Plumbing, Heating and Cooling Contractors Asn.(pres, 63, bd. dirs, 63-67); Nat. Plumbing Heating and Cooling Contractors Asn; Am. Soc. Sanitary Eng; Notre Dame Acad. Bd. Educ; Cath. Youth Orgn.(bd. dirs); Eagles; Ancient Order Hibernians; Florence Men's Club; N.Omaha Commercial Club; C. of C; Q Street Merchants; Athletic, Field and Birchwood Clubs. Outstanding Young Man, Omaha, 62; Best Actor Awards, Kingmarle Theatre; N. Omaha Commercial Awards, C. of C. Awards. Rel: Catholic. Mailing Add: 8115 N. 37th St, Omaha, Nebr. 68112.

LYNCH, DANIEL FRANCIS D
Chmn, Colo. Dem. State Cent. Cmt.
b. Los Angeles, Calif. 12/30/30; s. Frank Joseph Lynch, Jr. and Grace Sutherland L; m. 2/14/58 to Suzanne Harvey; c. Ann Sutherland, Daniel F, Jr, Eleanor Harvey and John Carroll. Educ: Univ. Colo, B.A, 52; Univ. Colo. Law Sch, 55-56; Georgetown Univ. Law Center, LL.B, 59. Polit. & Govt. Pos: Legis. asst. to Sen. John A. Carroll, 57-60; counsel, Colo. Real Estate Cmn, 60-61; regent, Univ. Colo, 65-; chmn, Colo. Dem. State Cent. Cmt, 69- Bus. & Prof. Pos: Partner, Lynch, MacIntosh & Lynch, Law firm, Denver, 61- Mil. Serv: Entered as 2nd Lt, Marine Corps, 52, released as 1st Lt, 55, after serv. in First and Third Eng. Bn, Korea, Japan, Camp Pendleton, Calif. and Quantico, Va. Mem: Am, Colo. and Denver Bar Asns; Am. G.I. Forum. Rel: Roman Catholic. Legal Res: 1750 Ivy St, Denver, Colo. 80220. Mailing Add: 1712 Sherman St, Denver, Colo. 80203.

LYNCH, FRANCIS J. D
Committeeman, Ill. Dem. Cent. Cmt.
b. Oak Park, Ill, 3/13/21; s. Patrick Columbus Lynch and Mary Casey L; m. 12/27/47 to Susan Babson Alling; c. Laura Stanwood, Sarah Gibbons, David Patrick, Daniel Alexander and Austin Canavan. Educ: Univ. Chicago, B.A, 46; Chicago Kent Col. of Law, LL.B, 50; Delta Kappa Epsilon. Polit. & Govt. Pos: Dem. committeeman, Rich Twp, Cook Co, Ill, 54-; Dem. State Cent. Committeeman, Fourth Cong. Dist, Ill, 62-; hearing officer, Ill. Dept. of Financial Insts, 63-68; alternate del, Dem. Nat. Conv, 68. Bus. & Prof. Pos: Secy, Indust. Cmn. Cmt, Chicago Bar Asn, 62-63, chmn, 63-65. Mil. Serv: Entered as Pvt, Army, 42, released as S/Sgt, 65, after serv. in 19th Inf. Regt, 24th Inf. Div, South West Pac. Theater, 64-65; Purple Heart with Cluster; South West Pac. Theater Ribbon. Mem: Ill. State and Chicago Bar Asns; Fedn. of Ins. Counsel; Workman's Compensation Lawyer's Asn. of Chicago; Chicago Civil War Round Table; Ill. State Hist. Soc; Chicago Urban League. Rel: Roman Catholic. Legal Res: 104 Warwick St, Park Forest, Ill. 60466. Mailing Add: 39 S. La Salle St, Chicago, Ill. 60603.

LYNCH, FRANK J. R
Pa. State Rep.
b. Phila, Pa, 11/6/22; s. Daniel J. Lynch and Elizabeth Fox L; m. 11/19/55 to Eleanor Marie King; c. Daniel J, Edward A, James F. and Dennis A. Educ: LaSalle Col; Temple Univ. Law Sch, LL.B, 52. Polit. & Govt. Pos: Pa. State Rep, 164th Dist, currently. Mil. Serv: Entered as Pvt, Army, 43, released as 1st Sgt, 46, after serv. in Ord. Dept, Asiatic-Pac. Theater; Asiatic-Pac. Campaign Medal; Good Conduct Medal; World War II Victory Medal; Am. Campaign Medal. Mem: Dir, Del. Co. Bar Asn, 63-64 and secy, 61; Pa. Bar Asn; St. Thomas More Soc; LaSalle Col. Alumni Asn; Temple Univ. Law Alumni; Am. Legion; dir, Upper Darby Forum; Phila. Mus. of Art. Rel: Roman Catholic. Legal Res: 620 Shadeland Ave, Drexel Hill, Pa. 19026. Mailing Add: Law Bldg, Ludlow St. & Copley Rd, Upper Darby, Pa. 19082.

LYNCH, IDA W. R
V.Chmn, Orleans Co. Rep. Cmt, N.Y.
Educ: Univ. Rochester, A.B. Polit. & Govt. Pos: Elec. cmnr, Orleans Co, N.Y, currently; v.chmn, Orleans Co. Rep. Cmt, currently. Mailing Add: Waterport, N.Y. 14571.

LYNCH, JAMES H. D
Chmn, Caroline Co. Dem. Cent. Cmt, Md.
b. Ridgely, Md, 11/20/19; s. Calvin D. Lynch and Lotela Golt L; m. 3/17/69 to Mary B. Long; c. Carol (Mrs. Eugene Dempsey); James H, Jr. and Robert T. Educ: Goldey Bus. Col, 2 years. Polit, & Govt. Pos: Mayor, Ridgely, Md, 50-53; mem. state Dem. Cent. Cmt, Md, 60-; chmn, Caroline Co. Dem. Cent. Cmt, 64- Bus. & Prof. Pos: Pres, Lynch Oil Co, 55-; pres, Lynch Grain & Feed Inc, 60- Mil. Serv: Entered as Pvt, Army, 43, released as S/Sgt, 46, after serv. in 82nd Airborne Div, ETO, 44-46; Belgian Citation; Holland Citation; Good Conduct Medal. Mem: Lions (dep. dist. gov); VFW; Am. Legion; secy, Caroline Co. Country Club. Rel: Catholic. Mailing Add: 101 Sunrise Ave, Ridgely, Md. 21660.

LYNCH, JAMES L. D
b. Bancroft, Iowa, 12/5/36; m. 1963 to Marilyn; c. Lisa, Lana and Amy. Educ: Mason City Jr. Col; State Univ. of Iowa, B.A; Northeast Mo. State Teachers Col, grad. work. Polit. Pos: Dir, Lien Div, State Tax Cmn, Iowa, at present; Iowa State Rep, 66. Bus. & Prof. Pos: High sch. teacher; co-owner, LaFollete Label Serv. 1967 Legal Res: 904 W. Third, Indianola, Iowa. No mailing address available. (1967)

LYNCH, JEREMIAH C, JR. D
b. Newport, R.I, 11/30/28; m. to Carol M. L. Educ: Providence Col, 51; Harvard Univ. Law Sch, LL.B, 54. Polit. & Govt. Pos: Mem, Newport City Coun, R.I, 60-61; R.I. State Rep, 61-66. Bus. & Prof. Pos: Lawyer. Mil. Serv: Army, 55-57. Mem: Advocate K. of C; pres, Hibernians. Rel: Catholic. Mailing Add: 2 Rose St, Newport, R.I. 02840. (1967)

LYNCH, JIM C. R
Chmn, Lake Co. Rep. Cent. Cmt, Ore.
b. Lakeview, Ore, 2/2/36; s. Con Lynch and Mary Barry L; single. Educ: Univ. Ore; Ore. Sch. Law; Phi Beta Kappa; Alpha Tau Omega; Phi Delta Phi. Polit. & Govt. Pos: Chmn, Lake Co. Rep. Cent. Cmt, Ore, 66- Bus. & Prof. Pos: Partner, Conn & Lynch, Ore, 64- Mil. Serv: Entered as 1st Lt, Army, 62, released as Capt, 63, after serv. in Mil. Dist. of Wash. Mem: Elks; K. of C; Lions; C. of C; Ore. and Am. Bar Asns. Winner of Koyl Cup and Paul Patterson Mem. Scholarship. Rel: Roman Catholic. Mailing Add: P.O. Box 424, Lakeview, Ore. 97630.

LYNCH, JOHN A. D
N.J. State Sen.
b. New Brunswick, N.J, 3/10/08; s. John T. Lynch and Margaret Corrigan L; m. to Evelyn Rooney; c. Barbara, John, Bill, Mary-Lynn and Gerry. Educ: Fordham Univ, LL.B. Polit. & Govt. Pos: Clerk to late Supreme Court Justice Peter F. Daly; mem, Middlesex Co. Bd. of Elec, N.J; Prosecutor of the Pleas of Middlesex Co; magistrate, New Brunswick, 6 years, former dir. of Parks and Pub. Property, former dir. of Revenue and Finance, former dir. of Pub. Affairs and former acting dir. of Pub. Safety, mem. Bd. of City Cmnrs. and Mayor, 4 years; N.J. State Sen, 55-, Pres, N.J. State Senate, 66. Bus. & Prof. Pos: Trial lawyer. Mem: Past pres, Middlesex Co. Bar Asn. Mailing Add: 217 New York Ave, New Brunswick, N.J. 08901. (1967)

LYNCH, JOHN PHILIP D
R.I. State Rep.
b. Pawtucket, R.I, 6/24/34; s. William J. Lynch, Sr. and Anna Collins L.(deceased); m. 5/5/62 to Eleanor Anne Fry; c. Mary Ellen, Therese Marie and Daniel Patrick. Educ: Am. Col, Univ. Louvain, 4 years; Providence Col, A.B, 61. Polit. & Govt. Pos: R.I. State Rep, 69- Bus. & Prof. Pos: Partner, William J. Lynch & Sons, Pawtucket, R.I, 61-69. Mem: Treas, Blackstone Valley Asn. of Fire and Casualty Agents; legis. cmt, New Eng. Agents Mutual Asn; fire prev. cmt, Blackstone Valley C. of C; R.I. Asn. of Independent Ins. Agents; K. of C.(past Grand Knight, Delaney Coun, 57, past dist. dep, State of R.I); pres, St. Michael's Holy Name Soc; pres, Our Lady of Providence Alumni Asn. Rel: Roman Catholic. Mailing Add: 10 Meadow View Dr, Esmond, R.I. 02917.

LYNCH, JOHN WILLIAM D
b. Athens, Ohio, 5/27/98; s. Edward Albert Lynch and Anna Call L; wid; c. Patricia, Jean, JoAnn, Rosemary, John W, Jr. and Edward M. Educ: Cambridge Col, Ohio, grad. Polit. & Govt. Pos: Mem, Tulare Co. Dem. Cent. Cmt, 56-58; mem, Second Dist, Calif. State Bd. of Equalization, 59-, v.chmn, 59-65, chmn, 69- Bus. & Prof. Pos: Employee, major oil companies, 25 years; dep. collector, internal revenue agent and mem. racket squad, Bur. Internal Revenue, 11 years; tax consult. and pub. acct, Tulare, Calif, 56- Mil. Serv: Pvt, Army, 17-19, serv. in Princess Patricia's Can. Light Inf, France; British and Can. Victory Medals; Mil. Medal. Mem: Commonwealth Club; E. Clampus Vitus; Am. Legion; Moose; Elks; life mem, DAV; past pres, Tulare Lions; Nat. Tax Asn; exec. cmt. and past pres, Nat. Asn. Tax Adminstr; bd. trustees and past chmn, Fedn. Tax Adminstr; pres, West. States Asn. Tax Adminstr. Rel: Roman Catholic. Legal Res: 270 N. Yosemite, Fresno, Calif. 93701. Mailing Add: P.O. Box 2246, Fresno, Calif. 93720.

LYNCH, MARJORIE W. R
Wash. State Rep.
b. London, Eng; m. to E. Donald Lynch; c. Three. Educ: In England. Polit. & Govt. Pos: Wash. State Rep, currently. Bus. & Prof. Pos: Homemaker. Mil. Serv: Women's Auxiliary Air Force, Royal Air Force; Am. Red Cross. Mem: Bus. & Prfnl. Women; Zonta; League Women Voters. Mailing Add: 802 Pickens Rd, Yakima, Wash. 98902. (1967)

LYNCH, NEIL JOSEPH D
Mont. State Sen.
b. Butte, Mont, 9/18/34; s. of Mr. & Mrs. Earl J. Lynch; m. to F. Charlotte; c. Kimberly Elaine, Anne Marie, Neil Joseph, Marcella Florence and Kelly Elizabeth. Educ: Santa Clara Univ, 52-53; Mont. State Univ, B.S.Mech.Eng, 57; Columbus Law Sch, LL.B, 60. Polit. & Govt. Pos: Patent exam, U.S. Patent Off, 57-60; asst. attorney gen, Mont, 63-64; committeeman, Silver Bow Co. Dem. Cmt, 66-68; Mont. State Sen, 69- Bus. & Prof. Pos: Engr, Mont. Power Co, 60-63; Attorney-at-law, Genzberger, Genzberger & Lynch, Butte, Mont, 64- Mem: Am. Soc. Mech. Engr; Am, Mont. and Silver Bow Bar Asns; pres, Silver Bow Co. Dem. Club, 64-68; mem, Butte Exchange Club; dir, Butte Indust. Develop. Corp, 66-; secy, Park N Shop Inc, 66-; cmt. chmn, Butte C. of C, 67; dir, Mont. Tech. Boosters Club, 67; pres, Mont. State Univ. Alumni Asn, 67; dir, Promote Active Commun. Effort, 67-69; chmn, Am. Red Cross, 68; chmn, Butte U.S. Olympic Cmt, 68; secy, Butte Youth Corp, 68-; pres, Mont. Soc. Crippled Children, 68- Admitted to practice before Mont. Supreme Court, U.S. Dist. Court, U.S. Supreme Court and Interstate Commerce Cmn; Outstanding Young Men of Am. Award, 69. Mailing Add: 3561 Hartford, Butte, Mont. 59701.

LYNCH, RICHARD H. R
b. St. Paul, Minn, 11/11/85; married. Polit. & Govt. Pos: Auditor, Divide Co, N.Dak, 18-35; N.Dak. State Sen, 43-49; mem, Legis. Research Cmt, 47-55; N.Dak. State Rep, 51-57. Bus. & Prof. Pos: Farmer. Mailing Add: Crosby, N.Dak. 58730. (1967)

LYNCH, RICHARD J. D
b. Milwaukee, Wis, 6/11/21. Educ: West Allis Pub. Schs. Polit. & Govt. Pos: Mem, West Allis Dem. Unit, Wis; Wis. State Assemblyman, 62-68. Bus. & Prof. Pos: Former life ins. agent, R.R. fireman and machine operator; dep. sheriff, Milwaukee, Wis. Mil. Serv: Army, 42-45. Mailing Add: 824 S. 120th St, West Allis, Wis. 53214. (1967)

LYNCH, THOMAS CONNOR D
Attorney Gen. of Calif.
b. San Francisco, Calif, 5/20/04; s. Patrick Lynch and Mary O'Connor L; m. 1/23/32 to Virginia Lee Summers; c. Michael Summers and Kevin Conor. Educ: Univ. Santa Clara; grad, Univ. San Francisco; Phi Alpha Delta. Polit. & Govt. Pos: Former asst. U.S. attorney and former dist. attorney, San Francisco, Calif; North. Calif. chmn, Campaigns for Gov. Edmund G. Brown, 58 & 62, John F. Kennedy, 60 and Lyndon B. Johnson, 64; mem, President's Nat. Crime Cmn; del, Dem. Nat. Conv, 60 & 64; Attorney Gen, Calif, 64-; mem, Calif. Dem. State Cent. Cmt, currently; mem, President's Cmn. on Obscenity and Pornography, 68-; mem. adv. bd, Nat. Crime Info. Center, 69- Mem: Am. Law Inst. Adv. Cmt. on Model Code of Pre-Arraignment Procedure Proj; Am. Col. Trial Lawyers; Native Sons of Calif. Rel: Roman Catholic. Mailing Add: 98 Clarendon Ave, San Francisco, Calif. 94114.

LYNG, RICHARD R
Asst. Secy, U.S. Dept. Agr.
b. San Francisco, Calif, 6/29/18; s. Ed. J. Lyng and Sarah McGrath L; m. 6/25/44 to Bethyl Ball; c. Jeanette (Mrs. Robinson) and Marilyn. Educ: Univ. Notre Dame, Ph.B. Polit. & Govt. Pos: Dir, Calif. Dept. of Agr, 68-69; Asst. Secy, U.S. Dept. Agr, 69- Bus. & Prof. Pos: Pres, Ed J. Lyng Co, Inc, Modesto, Calif, 49-67. Mil. Serv: Entered as Pvt, Army, 42, released as 2nd Lt, 45, after serv. in S. Pac. Theater, 42-44. Rel: Roman Catholic. Legal Res: 2102 College, Modesto, Calif. 95350. Mailing Add: 4100 Cathedral N.W, Washington, D.C. 20016.

LYON, CARL VERNON R
Dep. Adminstr, Fed. R.R. Admin, Dept. of Transportation
b. Clarksburg, W.Va, 1/20/25; s. Vernon Arthur Lyon and Bess Frush L; m. 12/28/49 to Willa Wethered; c. David H, Thomas C, J. Michael, Jonathan E. and Daniel P. Educ: W.Va. Wesleyan Col, A.B, 49; Am. Univ, Wash. D.C, M.A, 51; George Wash. Univ, LL.B, 59; Phoenix Club. Polit. & Govt. Pos: Precinct capt, Springfield Rep. Party, Va, 61-64, area chmn, 62-65; mem, Fairfax Co. Rep. Cmt, 62-69; chmn, Parris for Supvr. Cmt, Fairfax Co, 63; del, Va. Rep. State Conv. and Tenth Cong. Dist. Rep. Conv, 64, 66 & 68; mem, Fairfax Co. Sch. Bd, 64-68; chmn, Fairfax Co. Rep. Conv, 65, 67 & 68; chmn, Parris for Bd. Chmn, Fairfax Co, 67; dep. adminstr, Fed. R.R. Admin, Dept. of Transportation, 69- Mil. Serv: Entered as A/S, Navy, 43, released as Radioman 1/C, 46, after serv. in Seventh Fleet Amphibious Corps, S.Pac. Theatre, 44-46; Am. and Pac. Theatre Medals; Philippine Theatre Medal with Five Battle Stars. Publ: A Survey of the Freight Car Shortage in the United States, Am. Univ, 51; 'The Inherent Advantages of Railroads and How They Can Best Be Protected,' Off. Proc. of N.Y. R.R. Club, Inc, 3/17/55; 'Lobbying, Liberty, and the Legislative Process: An Appraisal of the Proposed Legislative Activities Disclosure Act,' George Wash. Law Rev, 3/58. Mem: Pub. Utility Law Sect, Am. Bar Asn; Nat. Defense Transportation Asn; Interstate Commerce Cmn. Practitioners' Asn.(chmn, D.C. Chap. and Cmt. on Legis, 68-69); Va. State Bar Asn; Traffic Club of Wash, D.C; Country Club of Fairfax; Hillbrook Citizens Asn, Annandale. Rel: Methodist. Mailing Add: 6816 Cherry Lane, Annandale, Va. 22003.

LYON, CECIL BURTON
b. N.Y, 1903; m. 1933 to Elizabeth S. Grew; c. Two. Educ: Harvard Univ, B.A. Polit. & Govt. Pos: Career officer, U.S. Dept. of State For. Serv, 30-; v.consul, Havana, Cuba, 31 and Hong Kong, 32; third secy, Tokyo, 33 and Peiping, China, 33-38; third and second secy, Santiago, Chile, 38-42; with Dept. of State, 42-44; first secy, Cairo, 44-46; spec. asst. to Asst. Secy. of State for Polit. Affairs, 47-48; counsr, Warsaw, Poland, 48-50; Nat. War Col, 50-51; dir, Off. of High Cmnr. for Germany, Berlin, 51-54; dir, Bur. of German Affairs, State Dept, 54-55; Dep. Asst. Secy. of State for Inter-Am. Affairs, 55-56; U.S. Ambassador to Chile, 56-58; U.S. Minister, France, 58-64; U.S. Ambassador to Ceylon, 64-68. Bus. & Prof. Pos: Investment banking firm, N.Y, 27-30. Legal Res: Hancock, N.H. Mailing Add: c/o U.S. Dept. of State Foreign Service, Washington, D.C. 20521. (1967)

LYON, N. F. 'RED' R
b. Perkins Co, S.Dak, 3/21/15; s. Vivian Dake Lyon and Lulu Long L; m. 7/13/36 to Margaret Tidball; c. Laska L.(Mrs. Schoenfelder), James N, Lu Anne (Mrs. Jordan), Vivan W, Norman F, Barbara E. and Ralph M. Polit. & Govt. Pos: S.Dak. State Sen, 65-66; S.Dak. State Rep, First Dist, 67-68. Mem: Mason; Shrine. Rel: Presbyterian. Mailing Add: Meadow, S.Dak. 57644. (1967)

LYON, ROBERT PAUL D
b. Sasakwa, Okla, 7/20/21; s. Charlie N. Lyon (deceased) and Lula Mae Cargill L.(deceased); m. 11/12/41 to Jannie Louise Akin; c. Richard Danny and Lonnie David. Educ: E. Cent. State Col, B.S, 51; Okla. Univ, M.S, 56. Polit. & Govt. Pos: Chmn, Seminole Co. Dem. Party, Okla, 68-69; Dem. precinct chmn, 69- Mil. Serv: Entered as Pvt, Air Force, 42, released as Cpl, 45. Mem: Okla. and Nat. Educ. Asns; Asn. of Sch. Adminstrs; pres, Seminole Co. Teachers Asn, 67; pres, Seminole Co. Schoolmasters, 69; Lions; Am. Legion; Am. Red Cross. Rel: Baptist. Mailing Add: Route 1, Seminole, Okla. 74868.

LYONS, CHARLTON HAVARD, SR. R
b. Melville, La, 9/3/94; s. Ernest John Lyons and Joyce Bentley Havard J; m. 8/17/17 to Marjorie Hall; c. Charlton Havard, Jr. and Hall McCord. Educ: La. State Univ; Tulane Univ; Kappa Alpha; Phi Delta Phi. Polit. & Govt. Pos: Rep. cong. cand, 62; chmn, Rep. State Cent. Cmt, La, 63-68; gubernatorial cand, 64; mem, Rep. Nat. Cmt, La, 64-68; former chmn, Bd. Elec. Supvr, Caddo Parish; del, Rep. Nat. Conv, 68. Bus. & Prof. Pos: Law practice, Winnfield, La, 18-21 and Shreveport, 21-30; dir, La. Bank and Trust Co; partner, Lyons Petroleum, Shreveport. Mil. Serv: Pvt, Army, 17-18. Mem: Shreveport Bar Asn; Independent Petroleum Asn. Am.(dir, mem. exec. cmt. and past pres); Am. Petroleum Inst.(dir); dir, Coun. for Better La; Farm Bur; Am. Legion; F&AM; Shreveport and U.S. C. of C; Rotary Int; past pres. and dir, Shreveport-Bossier Found; Gen. Mid-Continent Oil and Gas Asn. (past pres. asn. and La-Ark. Div); Children's Serv. Bur. and Commun. Fund Shreveport and Caddo Parish; Nat. Asn. Mfrs.(past dir); dir, Pub. Affairs Res. Coun; former mem. bd. trustees, Centenary Col. and hon. life mem. and former chmn, Gr. Centenary Col. Prog; former mem, Nat. Petroleum Coun. Medallion Award, Shreveport Commun. Chest, 53; Award for Civic Serv, Optimists, 59; selected Mr. Conservative of 1965, Americanism Forum Shreveport. Rel: Episcopal; former vestryman, St. Marks Episcopal Church. Legal Res: 6336 Querbes Dr, Shreveport, La. 71106. Mailing Add: 1500 Beck Bldg, Shreveport, La. 71101.

LYONS, IDA RITA D
b. Boston, Mass, 10/12/15; d. Ross A. Maloof and Deebe Dow M; m. 5/3/40 to James Francis Lyons. Polit. & Govt. Pos: Founder, Quincy Women's Club, Mass; first v.pres, Mass. Fedn. Women's Clubs; mem, Quincy Dem. Cmt, 51-64, treas, 51-58; v.chmn, Mass. State Dem. Cmt, 52-64; Mass. State Dem. Committeewoman, 52-68; del, State Dem. Conv, 54-66; del-at-lg, Dem. Nat. Conv, 56, 64 & 68, secy. of del, 56, mem, Credentials Cmt, 64; exec. secy. to Attorney Gen. E.J. McCormack, 58-63; presidential elector, 60 & 64; asst. dir, Mass. Dept. of Commerce and Develop, 63- Mem: VFW Auxiliary. Rel: Catholic. Mailing Add: 21 Shellton Rd, Quincy, Mass. 02169.

LYONS, JOHN A. D
R.I. State Rep.
b. Fall River, Mass, 10/4/66; m. to Phoebe M. Educ: Providence Col. Polit. & Govt. Pos: R.I. State Rep, 63- Bus. & Prof. Pos: Publisher, self employed. Mem: Lions; K. of C; Holy Name; Yacht Club Tiverton. Rel: Catholic. Mailing Add: 60 Summit Ave, Tiverton, R.I. 02878. (1967)

LYONS, ROBERT EMMET D
b. Wagner, S.Dak, 12/29/09; s. William F. Lyons and Katherine Cosgrove L; m. 10/5/35, wid; m. 5/15/53 to C. Alice Bickford; c. John C. Educ: High School, grad, 1929. Polit. & Govt. Pos: Dem. Twp. Committeeman, S.Dak, 49-; del, Dem. Nat. Conv, 68; agr. chmn, S.Dak. Dem. Party, 68-; zone capt, various counties, S.Dak, 69- Bus. & Prof. Pos: Farmer, 34- Mem: K. of C; Rotary; Farmers Union; Nat. Farmers Orgn. Rel: Catholic. Mailing Add: Route 1, Wagner, S.Dak. 57380.

LYONS, THOMAS G. D
b. Chicago, Ill, 5/24/31; s. Thomas Vincent Lyons and Marian Daniels L; m. 8/9/58 to Ruth Tobin; c. Mary Alexandra, Francis Xavier, Thomas V. and Rachel Ann. Educ: Xavier and Loyola Univs; Loyola Univ. Law Sch; Blue Key; Alpha Sigma Nu; Pi Alpha Lambda. Polit. & Govt. Pos: Precinct capt, 38th Ward Regular Dem. Orgn, Chicago, Ill, 59; mem. bd. dirs, 45th Ward Regular Dem. Orgn, 61 and ward committeeman, 68-; Ill. State Sen, 64; v.chmn, Ill. Constitution Study Cmn, 65 and chmn, 67. Bus. & Prof. Pos: Attorney-at-law, 57, Cook Co. Assessor's Off, 58 and O'Keefe, O'Brien, Hanson, Ashendon & Assocs, 64-; asst. attorney gen, State of Ill, 61-64. Mil. Serv: Entered as 2nd Lt, Army, 54, released as 1st Lt, 56, after serv. in Third Inf. Div, Z.I; Army Res, 56-62, Capt. Publ: 'The Revenue Article,' Ill. Bar Record, 66. Mem: Chicago and Ill. State Bar Asns; Ill. Police Asn; Chicago Patrolmen's Asn; K. of C.(4°); Amvets; Moose; Lions; mem. adv. bd, New Horizons Center. Selected Best New Mem. Ill. Senate, 65; Chosen Outstanding Young Mem. of Ill. Legis, Rutgers Univ, 66. Rel: Catholic. Legal Res: 6457 N. Hiawatha Ave, Chicago, Ill. 60646. Mailing Add: 38 S. Dearborn St, Chicago, Ill. 60603.

LYONS, WILLIAM 'BILL' D
Ill. State Sen.
b. Eagarville, Ill, 1/27/20; m. 1938 to Edith Hamilton; c. Francis William, Michael Charles, Carolyn Jean, Diana Marie and David Alan. Educ: Gillespie Commun. High Sch. Polit. & Govt. Pos: V.chmn, Macoupin Co. Young Dem, Ill, 2 years, chmn, 2 years; Dem. precinct committeeman, 40; alderman, Gillespie, 40; Ill. State Rep, 3 terms; Ill. State Sen, currently. Bus. & Prof. Pos: Owner, supply store. Mem: K. of C; Eagles; Moose; Progressive Miners Local Number 1; Steel Workers. Rel: Catholic. Mailing Add: 501 E. Elm St, Gillespie, Ill. 62033.

LYONS, WILLIAM JOSEPH, JR. R
Conn. State Rep.
b. Norwalk, Conn, 7/16/21; s. William J. Lyons and Mary Byrnes L; m. 1/6/52 to Patricia Ann Russell; c. Michael, Barbara, Timothy, Edward, and Susan. Educ: Univ. Notre Dame, Architec. Polit. & Govt. Pos: Dist. cmnr, Norwalk, Conn, currently; Conn. State Rep, 69- Bus. & Prof. Pos: Exec. v.pres, William J. Lyons Construction Co, Inc, Norwalk, Conn. Mil. Serv: Entered as Pvt, Army, 42, released as Lt, 45, after serv. in 4th A.D, ETO; Combat Inf. Badge; Presidential Citation. Mailing Add: Raymond Lane, East Norwalk, Conn. 06855.

LYTAL, LAKE HENRY D
Chmn, Palm Beach Co. Dem. Cmt, Fla.
b. St. Martinville, La, 8/26/06; s. James True Lytal and Pauline Fleming L; m. 5/29/34 to Ruth Best; c. Lake Henry Jr. and Lynn (Mrs. Donald Fountain). Educ: Loyola Univ, 28-30; Univ. Fla, 31; Cumberland Law Col, LL.B, 32; Blue Key. Polit. & Govt. Pos: Mem, Bd. of Co. Cmnrs, Palm Beach County, Fla, 42-66; chmn, Palm Beach Co. Dem. Cmt, currently. Bus. & Prof. Pos: Bus. consult, Self-employed, 66- Mem: Pres, Fla. Asn. of Co. Cmnrs; Jr. C. of C; Kiwanis; Elks. Good Government Award, Jaycees, Exchange Club and Civitan. Rel: Catholic. Mailing Add: 7200 W. Lake Dr, West Palm Beach, Fla. 33406.

M

MAACK, HERBERT R. R
b. Batavia, N.Y, 5/23/24; s. Hermann E. Maack and Blanche Ripperger M; m. 6/28/47 to Adeline Longaker; c. Deborah, Nancy and Susan. Educ: Lehigh Univ, B.S. in bus. admin, 49; Alpha Chi Rho. Polit. & Govt. Pos: Dir, Pottstown Sch. Bd, 52-56; Pa. State Rep. until 68. Mil. Serv: Entered as Pvt, Army, released as 1st Lt, after serv. in 401st Combat Engrs, 2nd Corp. Mem: Philadelphia Asn. of Metal Finishers; Am. Electroplaters Soc; Rotary; Am. Legion. Rel: Episcopal. Mailing Add: Briar Lane, Pottstown, Pa. 19464.

MAAG, JAMES S. R
Kans. State Rep.
b. Ottawa, Kans, 11/24/39; s. L.W. Maag and Mildred Scoville M; m. 6/20/64 to Kathleen Covert; c. Laura Denise and Jared Scoville. Educ: Washburn Univ, B.A, 61; Univ. Kans, M.A, 64; Sagamore; Alpha Delta. Polit. & Govt. Pos: Kans. State Rep, 119th Dist, 69- Bus. & Prof. Pos: Instr, Dodge City Commun. Jr. Col, 64-69. Mem: Kans. Hist. Teachers Asn; Kans. State Teachers Asn; Kans. Asn. of Pub. Commun. Jr. Cols. Rel: Methodist. Mailing Add: 2207 Fifth, Dodge City, Kans. 67801.

MABRY, MALCOLM H, JR. R
Miss. State Rep.
b. Dublin, Miss, 6/28/33; single. Polit. & Govt. Pos: Miss. State Rep, currently. Bus. & Prof. Pos: Farmer, currently. Mem: Farm Bur. Rel: Methodist. Mailing Add: Dublin, Miss. 38739.

McADAMS, HERBERT HALL D
b. Jonesboro, Ark, 6/6/15; s. Dr. Herbert Hall McAdams and Stella Mae Patrick M; m. 4/3/38 to Ruth Noyes; c. Judith Ann (Mrs. DeRoeck), Sandra Gail (Mrs. Connor), Herbert Hall, III and Penny Marguerite. Educ: Northwest. Univ, B.S, 37; Harvard Law Sch, 37-38; Loyola Univ, Ill, 38-39; Univ. Ark, LL.B. with honors, 40; Sigma Nu (pres). Polit. & Govt. Pos: Secy, Craighead Co. Dem. Cent. Cmt, Ark, 41-60; mem. credentials cmt, Dem. Nat. Conv, 64; mem, Ark. Indust. Develop. Cmn, 65-, chmn, 67-; del. and mem. platform cmt, Dem. Nat. Conv, 68. Bus. & Prof. Pos: Chmn. and pres, Citizens Bank, Jonesboro, Ark, 59-; dir, Ark. La. Gas Co, Shreveport, La, 64-, Ins. and Bank Stock Fund, Inc, 65- and Union Fund, Inc, 66- Mil. Serv: Entered as Ens, Navy, 43, released as Lt.(jg), 46, after serv. in U.S.S. Gamble, Pac. Theater; Purple Heart, Iwo Jima; Presidential Citation. Mem: Am. and Ark. Banker's Asns; Am. and Ark. Bar Asns; Craighead Co. Bar Asn.(pres, 52); Little Rock Country Club; Top of the Rock Club; Little Rock Club; Tenn. Club, Memphis; Summit Club, Memphis, Tenn; Jonesboro Country Club; Am.

Legion; VFW; Farm Bur. Rel: Presbyterian. Legal Res: 1420 Elmwood Place, Jonesboro, Ark. 72401. Mailing Add: Citizens Bank, Jonesboro, Ark. 72401.

McAFEE, GARLAND E. R
b. Clifton, Tenn, 8/29/12; s. Wilbert McAfee and Birdie Mayberry M; single. Educ: Metropolis Commun. High Sch, 4 years. Polit. & Govt. Pos: Rep. precinct committeeman, Precinct 1, Ill, 54-69; field transportation supvr, 64-; alderman, First Ward, Metropolis, 65. Bus. & Prof. Pos: Merchant, furniture dealer, 47-69. Mil. Serv: Entered as Pvt, Army, 43, released as S/Sgt, 45, after serv. in 777th Field Artil. Bn, ETO, 44-45; Certificate of Merit. Mem: Grand Master, Odd Fellows, Ill, Wis. and Mo. Rel: Protestant. Legal Res: 1016 Vienna St, Metropolis, Ill. 62960. Mailing Add: 219 W. Seventh St, Metropolis, Ill. 62960.

McAFEE, LILIAN FOOTE R
Third V.Pres, Ga. Fedn. of Rep. Women
b. Chicago, Ill, 8/27/11; d. Lyle Milton Foote and Mae Speitel F; m. 10/1/34 to William Fort McAfee, Jr, wid; c. Linda (Mrs. William F. Halford) and William Fort McAfee, III. Educ: Ward-Belmont Col, Nashville, Tenn, 1 year. Polit. & Govt. Pos: Pres, Albany Rep. Women, Ga, 66-68; v.chmn, Dougherty Co. Rep, 66-68; mem, Ga. Rep. Cent. Cmt, 66, 68 & 69; del, Rep. Nat. Conv. and mem. platform cmt, 68; dist. dir, Second Dist. Rep. Women, Ga, 68; third v.pres, Ga. Fedn. of Rep. Women, 68- Albany Woman of the Year, 52; Albany Rep. Woman of the Year, 68; Ga. State Rep. Woman of the Year, 69. Rel: Methodist. Mailing Add: 2103 Nottingham Way, Albany, Ga. 31705.

McALEAR, ALLEN LEE D
Chmn, Gallatin Co. Dem. Cent. Cmt, Mont.
b. Havre, Mont, 3/25/28; s. J.H. McAlear and Annastasia Lee M; div. Educ: Univ. Nev, 48; Univ. Ore, 49-50; Univ. Mont, LL.B, 53; Phi Delta Phi; Pi Kappa Alpha. Polit. & Govt. Pos: Chmn, Gallatin Co. Dem. Cent. Cmt, Mont, 66- Bus. & Prof. Pos: Alumnus counsr, Mont. State Pi Kappa Alpha, 63-; ed, Mont. Trial Lawyers, 66- Mil. Serv: Entered as Pfc, Marines, 46, released 48, after serv. in Hawthorne Guard Co. Mem: Elks; Eagles; Lions (pres, Bridger, Mont. Club, 55). Rel: Methodist. Legal Res: Bear Canyon, Bozeman, Mont. 59715. Mailing Add: First Bank Bldg, Bozeman, Mont. 59715.

McALHANY, JOSEPH CARLISLE D
b. Reevesville, S.C, 6/7/15; s. John H. McAlhany and Mattie Bryant M; m. 4/19/38 to Juanita A. Murray; c. Joseph Carlisle Jr, Johnny. Educ: St. George High Sch, 32. Polit. & Govt. Pos: S.C. State Rep, 61-68. Bus. & Prof. Pos: Businessman; pres, First Nat. Bank of St. George; farm machinery & fertilizer dealer; ginner & buyer of cotton, cotton seed; owner, J.C. McAlhany Implement Co. and McAlhany's Ginnery. Mem: St. George Civitan Club; v.chmn, St. George Develop. Bd; v.chmn, Dorchester Soil Conserv. Dist; chmn, St. George Rural Develop. Bd. Rel: Baptist; Deacon, Reevesville Baptist Church. Mailing Add: Reevesville, S.C. 29471. (1967)

McALISTER, ROBERT BEATON D
b. N.Y.C, 10/5/32; s. Richard Charles McAlister and Martha Weisenbarger M; m. 7/13/57 to Sonya Douglas; c. Michael Richard, Peter Douglas and Betsy Anne. Educ: Kenyon Col, A.B, 54; Univ. of Mich, J.D, 57; Beta Theta Pi; Phi Delta Phi. Polit. & Govt. Pos: Alternate del-at-lg, Dem. Nat. Conv, 68; chmn, Ohio Elec. Day Legal Serv. Cmt, Ohio Dem. Party and Dem. Nat. Cmt, 68; chmn, Ohio Party Struct. and del, Selection Cmt, 69; chmn, Ohio Elec. Reform Cmt, Ohio Dem. Party, 68-69. Bus. & Prof. Pos: Attorney, Alexander, Ebinger, Holschuh & Fisher, Columbus, Ohio, 57-69. Mil. Serv: Entered as Airman Basic, Air Nat. Guard, 57, released as A/2C, 63, after serv. in Ohio Air Nat. Guard. Mem: Columbus, Ohio State and Am. Bar Asns; Downtown Coun. of Churches; bd. dirs, Metrop. Area Church Bd. Rel: Episcopal. Legal Res: 137 S. Virginia Lee Rd, Columbus, Ohio 43209. Mailing Add: 17 S. High St, Columbus, Ohio 43215.

McALISTER, THOMAS BUELL R
Chmn, Franklin Co. Rep. Cmt, Ala.
b. Russellville, Ala, 12/10/22; s. Charlie Edward McAlister and Gertrude Steele M; m. 2/27/47 to Dorothy Jackson; c. Thomas E. Educ: High sch. Polit. & Govt. Pos: Chmn, Russellville City Coun, Ala, 56-60; Rep. cand, Ala. State Rep, 66; chmn, Franklin Co. Rep. Cmt, currently. Bus. & Prof. Pos: Owner, Mac's Mkt, 46- Mil. Serv: Entered as Pvt, Army, 44, released as T-5, 46, after serv. in 2nd Div, ETO; 2 Battle Stars. Mem: VFW; Am. Legion. Rel: Methodist. Mailing Add: 815 Scott Ave. N.W, Russellville, Ala. 35653.

McALLEN, ROBERT ASHLEY D
Mem, State Dem. Exec. Cmt, Tex.
b. Brownsville, Tex, 10/1/34; s. Argyle Ashley McAllen and Margaret Huffaker M; m. 12/29/59 to Margaret Louise Looney; c. Cullen Ashley, Melanie Louise and Montgomery Argyle. Educ: Rice Univ, B.A. and B.S; La. State Univ. Grad. Sch. Banking, cert. Polit. & Govt. Pos: Alternate del, Dem. Nat. Conv, 68; precinct chmn, Dem. Party, Tex, currently; mem, State Dem. Exec. Cmt, currently; mem. bd, S.Tex. Rehabilitation Dist, currently. Bus. & Prof. Pos: Pres, Mid Valley State Bank, 65-; pres, Magic Valley Savings & Loan, 68- Mil. Serv: Entered as Pvt, Army, 64, released as SP-4, 65, after serv. in Nat. Guard. Mem: Rio Grande Valley Bankers Asn.(pres, 65); Rotary (pres); C. of C; Algodon Club (mem. bd); Boy Scouts (v.pres, Rio Grande Coun). Rel: Episcopal; Mem. Vestry, Trinity Church. Legal Res: 1113 W. Third, Weslaco, Tex. 78596. Mailing Add: P.O. Box 1015, Weslaco, Tex. 78596.

McALLISTER, LEWIS LESLIE, JR. R
b. Jackson, Miss, 9/25/32; s. Lewis Leslie McAllister and Annie Payne Lott M; m. 8/16/63 to Wanda Grant; c. Lewis L. McAllister, III. Educ: Ga. Tech, B.I.M, 54; Univ. Ala, M.B.A, 58; Omicron Delta Kappa; Kappa Alpha. Polit. & Govt. Pos: Miss. State Rep. and Minority Leader, Miss. House of Rep, 63-68. Mil. Serv: Entered as 2nd Lt, Army, 55, released as 1st Lt, 56, after serv. in Seventh Div, 15th Antiaircraft Bn, Korea. Mem: Am. Inst. CPA; Jaycees. Rel: Methodist. Mailing Add: 518 51st St, Meridian, Miss. 39301.

McALLISTER, WALTER W, SR.
Mayor, San Antonio, Tex.
b. San Antonio, Tex, 3/26/89; wid, c. Elizabeth (Mrs. O.J. Solcher, Jr), Walter W. Jr. and Gerald N; ten grandchildren, one great granddaughter. Educ: Univ. Tex, Austin, E.E, 10. Polit. & Govt. Pos: Trustee, City Water Bd, San Antonio, Tex, City Pub. Serv. Bd. and Police and Fire Pension Fund; mayor, San Antonio, 61-; hon. co-chmn, HemisFair. Bus. & Prof. Pos: Chmn. bd, San Antonio Savings Asn, 21-; dir, Mortgage Guaranty Ins. Corp, Milwaukee, Wis; dir, Kroehler Mfg. Co, Naperville, Ill; trustee, Southwest Research Inst. and Int. Union Bldg. Socs. & Savings Asns; dir, Educ. TV, Channel 9, KLRN, Austin. Mem: San Antonio Country Club; Argyle Club; Kiwanis; Scottish Rite (33°). Golden Deeds Award, Exchange Club San Antonio, 56; Outstanding Citizen Award, San Antonio Coun. Pres, 64; Golden Plate Award, Am. Acad. Achievement, 66. Legal Res: 103 Bushnell Place, San Antonio, Tex. 78212. Mailing Add: 111 Soledad St, San Antonio, Tex. 78205.

McALLISTER, WILLIAM MENZIES
Justice, Supreme Court of Ore.
b. Portland, Ore, 11/02/05; s. William James McAllister and Mary Menzies M; m. 6/04/32 to Jean Middleton; c. William Middleton and Kathryn Jean. Educ: Willamette Univ, LL.B, 28; admitted to Ore. Bar, 28; Wash. Bar, 29; Phi Delta Theta; Delta Theta Phi. Polit. & Govt. Pos: Ore. State Rep, 37-44, speaker, Ore. House of Rep, 43-44; Ore. State Sen, 49-50; justice, Supreme Court of Ore, 56-, chief justice, 59-66. Bus. & Prof. Pos: Attorney-at-law, Medford, Ore, 31-56. Mil. Serv: Maj, Army, 43-45. Mem: Am. Bar Asn. (coun. sect. judicial admin, 61-65, chmn, 68-69); Conf. of Chief Justices (chmn, 64-65); Ore. State Bar (bd. govs, 48-51; bd. bar exams, 53-56); Mason; Shrine; Arlington Club, Portland. Rel: Presbyterian. Legal Res: RFD 3, Box 681-11, Salem, Ore. 97302. Mailing Add: Supreme Court Bldg, Salem, Ore. 97310.

McALPIN EHRMAN T. D
Chmn, Simpson Co. Dem. Exec. Cmt, Miss.
b. Smith Co, Miss, 7/21/96; s. Lawrence M. McAlpin and Kiture Ware M; m. 9/14/16 to Emma Richardson; c. Mrs. B.B. Neely, Richard T. and Lawrence James. Educ: High sch. and col. Polit. & Govt. Pos: Chmn, Simpson Co. Dem. Exec. Cmt, 38- Bus. & Prof. Pos: Owner, McAlpin's Dept. Store, at present. Mem: Mason; Lions; C. of C. Rel: Missionary Baptist. Mailing Add: Magee, Miss. 39111.

McANENY, JOSEPH JOHN D
Pa. State Rep.
b. Johnstown, Pa, 7/20/24; s. Joseph M. McAneny and Agnes Keating M; m. 7/23/49 to Rebecca Claire Evans; c. Rebecca, Peter, Stephen, Thomas and Joseph. Educ: Univ. Nebr, B.S, 49, LL.B, 51; Phi Alpha Delta. Polit. & Govt. Pos: Mem, Johnstown Planning Cmn, Pa, 63-; Pa. State Rep, currently; alternate del, Dem. Nat. Conv, 68. Bus. & Prof. Pos: Pres, Pa. Claims Serv, 56-64; mgr, Manpower, Inc, 60-; owner, McAneny Ins. Agency, 65. Mil. Serv: Army, 43-46, serv. in 350th Inf, 88th Div, Italy; Combat Inf. Badge; Good Conduct and Victory Medals; European Campaign Ribbon. Mem: Past pres, Tri Co. Claim Men's Asn; Am. and Nebr. State Bar Asns; Elks; Am. Legion; CWV; Gr. Johnstown C. of C; Moose; North Fork Country Club. Rel: Catholic. Mailing Add: 182 Worth St, Johnstown, Pa. 15905.

McARDLE, WILLIAM THOMAS D
b. Pittsburgh, Pa, 5/26/43; s. William Thomas McArdle and Eleanor Borkoski M; m. 8/20/68 to Joanne Onofrey. Educ: Edinboro State Col, B.S, 65; Duquesne Univ, 65-67. Polit. & Govt. Pos: Del, Dem. Nat. Conv, 68. Bus. & Prof. Pos: Teacher, Pittsburgh, 65-69; agent, Fed. Bur. Invest, Kansas City, Kans, 69- Rel: Catholic. Legal Res: 2119 Wrights Way, Pittsburgh, Pa. 15203. Mailing Add: Apt. 3, Craigmont Apt, 9535 Melrose, Overland Park, Kans. 66214.

MacARTHUR, DOUGLAS, II
U.S. Ambassador to Iran
b. Bryn Mawr, Pa, 7/5/09; s. Capt. Arthur MacArthur, USN and Mary Hendry McCalla M; m. to Laura Barkley; c. Laura (Mrs. Goditiabois-Deacon). Educ: Yale Univ, B.A, 32. Polit. & Govt. Pos: Am. consulate, Vancouver, 35-36 and Naples, 36-38; mem. staff, Am. Embassy, Paris, 38-40 & 44-48, Vichy, 40-42; intern, Germany, 42-44; first secy. of embassy, Brussels, 48-49; chief, Div. West. European Affairs and dep. dir, Off. European Regional Affairs, 49-51; polit. adv. to Gen. Eisenhower at SHAPE, 51-52; counsr, Dept. of State, 53-56; U.S. Ambassador to Japan, 56-61 and Belgium, 61-65; Asst. Secy. for Cong. Rels, 65-67; U.S. Ambassador to Austria, 67-69 and Iran, 69- Mil. Serv: Lt, Army, 32-35. Mem: Bd. dirs, For. Serv. and Am. For. Serv. Asn. Coun. on For. Rels; Metrop. Club; Chevy Chase Club. Mailing Add: Dept. of State, Washington, D.C. 20521.

MACAULAY, JOSEPH HUGH R
b. De Soto, Wis, 5/28/24; s. Joseph A. Macaulay and Ruth French M; m. 8/27/60 to Patsy Parkin; c. Scott. Educ: George Wash. Univ, B.A, 62; Johns Hopkins Univ, 65; Am. Univ, 65-66; Cong. Staff fel, Am. Polit. Sci. Asn, 65; Pi Sigma Alpha. Polit. & Govt. Pos: Mem. staff, U.S. Rep. Henry J. Latham, Third Dist, N.Y, 47; admin. asst. to U.S. Rep. Charles B. Hoeven, 48-64 and Off. of U.S. Rep. Charlotte T. Reid, 15th Dist, Ill, 66- Mil. Serv: Navy, 45-46. Mem: Steering Cmt, Fed. Mgt. Conf, 66-68; Mason. Rel: Protestant. Mailing Add: 5712 Marengo Rd, Bethesda, Md. 20016.

McAULIFFE, JAMES S, JR. D
b. Washington, D.C, 3/24/31; married. Educ: Montgomery Jr. Col; Wash. Col. of Law, J.D, 54. Polit. & Gov. Pos: Asst. state's attorney, Montgomery Co, Md, 59-62; Md. State Del, 63-67. Bus. & Prof. Pos: Attorney-at-law. Mem: Exec. adv. cmt, Montgomery Co. Civic Fedn; Friendship Heights Citizens Asn. Mailing Add: 260 E. Jefferson St, Rockville, Md. 20850.

McAVOY, WALTER 'BABE' R
Ill. State Rep.
b. Chicago, Ill, 9/10/04; m. to Mary Egan; c. Patricia and Thomas J. Educ: Parochial, pub. schs. Polit. & Govt. Pos: Ill. State Rep, currently. Bus. & Prof. Pos: Real estate broker. Mem: Moose; Eagles; K. of C. Mailing Add: 6033 S. Richmond St, Chicago, Ill. 60629. (1967)

McBRAYER, W. TERRY D
Ky. State Rep.
b. Greenup, Ky, 9/1/37; s. Ward McBrayer and Ethel Brown M; m. 9/12/64

to Mary Ware; c. Sarah Randolph. Educ: Morehead State Univ, B.S; Univ. of Louisville Sch. of Law, LL.B. Polit. & Govt. Pos: Nat. committeeman, past secy-treas. and v.pres, Young Dem. of Ky. Club; mem, Ky. Port and River Develop. Cmn; mem, Gov. Cmn. on Educ, 66; Ky. State Rep, 76th Dist, 66-, Speaker Pro Tempore, Ky. House of Rep, 68-69; mem, Gov. Youth Adv. Cmn, 67; chmn. rules cmt, Ky. Dem. Conv, 68; del, Dem. Nat. Conv, 68. Bus. & Prof. Pos: Attorney-at-law. Mil. Serv: Army; Ky. Nat. Guard. Mem: Greenup, Boyd Co, Ky. and Am. Bar Asns; Am. Trial Lawyers Asn; past pres, v.pres. and dir, Greenup Lions; past v.pres. and dir, Greenup Jaycees; hon. life mem. and past dir, Morehead State Univ. Alumni Asn; past v.chmn, Greenup Co. United Fund; secy, Greenup Vol. Fire Dept; Greenup Co. Park Bd; Cmt. on Tourism and Recreation, Fivco Develop. Asn; counsel. and area adv, Greenup Co. Boy Scouts; Greenup Co. Develop. Asn; C. of C. Named Mr. Morehead, Morehead State Univ, 59, Outstanding Serv. Award, 66 and Outstanding Alumnus of 67; Serv. Award, Judge, Jefferson Co, 62; Presented Key to City, New Orleans, 62; Omicron Delta Kappa Award, Univ. of Louisville, 62; Award of Merit, Dept. of Natural Resources, 66; Duke of Paducah, 66; Outstanding Ky. Young Dem, 69. Rel: Christian Church; Deacon, Greenup Christian Church; Past Pres. Sunday Sch. Class; Teacher, Young Adults Class. Legal Res: 1208 Riverside Dr, Greenup, Ky. 41144. Mailing Add: Braden Bldg, Greenup, Ky. 41144.

McBRIDE, ANTHONY P. D
Mass. State Rep.
b. Adams, Mass, 8/28/32; s. Frank B. McBride and Geraldine Witt M; m. 7/27/57 to Ruth E. McLaughlin; c. Brian A, Peter F, Terrance K. and Julie A. Educ: Manhattan Col, B.S, 56; New Eng. Inst, 56-57. Polit. & Govt. Pos: Mem, North Berkshire Region Sch. Cmt, North Adams, Mass, 60-65; selectman, Adams, 65-68; Mass. State Rep, 69- Bus. & Prof. Pos: Partner, McBride Funeral Serv, 57-68. Mil. Serv: Entered as Pvt, Marines, 53, released as Cpl, 55, after serv. in FMF. Rel: Roman Catholic. Mailing Add: 10 Orchard St, Adams, Mass. 01220.

MacBRIDE, THOMAS JAMISON D
b. Sacramento, Calif, 3/25/14; s. Frank MacBride and Charlotte Kirtley Little M; m. 11/7/47 to Martha Harrold; c. Peter, Laurie, Thomas J, Jr. and David. Educ: Univ. Calif, Berkeley, A.B, 36, J.D, 40; Kappa Sigma; Phi Delta Phi. Polit. & Govt. Pos: Dep. attorney gen, Calif, 40-42; Calif. State Assemblyman, Sacramento Co, 55-60; judge, U.S. Dist. Court, East. Dist. of Calif, 61-67, chief judge, 67- Mil. Serv: Entered as Ens, Naval Res, 42, released as Lt, 46, after serv. in Naval Intel, Southwest Pac; Presidential Unit Citation; New Guinea, Philippines and Pac. Campaign Ribbons. Mem: Pres, Rotary, 66-67; Mason; Shrine; bd. trustees, Scottish Rite; KCCH; Am. Legion; bd. dirs, League to Save Lake Tahoe; hon. pres. Sacramento Chap, Am. Youth Hostels, Inc. Rel: Christian Science. Mailing Add: 1800 Rockwood Dr, Sacramento, Calif. 95825.

McBROOM, EDWARD R
Ill. State Sen.
b. Kankakee, Ill; s. Victor McBroom; m. to Eleanor Bowman; c. Victor. Educ: Univ. of Ill. Polit. & Govt. Pos: Former chmn, Kankakee Co. Rep. Cent. Cmt, Ill; Ill. State Rep, 62-64; Ill. State Sen, 66- Bus. & Prof. Pos: Automobile dealer. Mil. Serv: Navy. Mem: Am. Legion; Elks; Moose; Rotary; Medinah Temple. Rel: Methodist. Mailing Add: 1190 S. Eighth St, Kankakee, Ill. 60901. (1967)

McBRYDE, CHARLES MARION R
Chmn, Lee Co. Rep. Party, N.C.
b. Sanford, N.C, 8/26/18; s. Napoleon Douglas McBryde and Estella Spivey M; m. 6/30/44 to Lois Harrington; c. Martha M. (Mrs. Sealey), Frances Marion, Vicky Jane and Sarah Elizabeth. Educ: George Wash. Univ. Polit. & Govt. Pos: Chmn, Selective Serv. Bd, N.C, 48-; chmn, Lee Co. Rep. Party, N.C, currently. Mil. Serv: Entered as Pvt, Army, 36, released as 1st Lt, 44, after serv. in Inf, 1st Ranger Bn, Mediterranean Theater, Anzio, Italy, 44; Bronze Star; Purple Heart; ETO, Asiatic Pac. Theater Oper. and Am. Theater Oper. Medals; Good Conduct Medal; Combat Infantryman's Badge. Mem: Pres, Sanford Traffic Club, 65-66; past post comdr, Am. Legion; VFW; 40 et 8; past gov, Legion of Moose, past noble north Moose; Kiwanis. Rel: Protestant. Mailing Add: 633 Spring Lane, Sanford, N.C. 27330.

McBURNEY, JOHN FRANCIS, JR. D
R.I. State Sen.
b. Pawtucket, R.I, 2/26/25; m. to Ann Rivello. Educ: Providence Col, 48; Boston Col. Law Sch, 51. Polit. & Govt. Pos: R.I. State Sen, 59- Bus. & Prof. Pos: Attorney-at-law; elec. contractor. Mil. Serv: Army, World War II. Mailing Add: 15 Arlington St, Pawtucket, R.I. 02860. (1967)

McCABE, FRANCES H. D
R.I. State Rep.
b. Central Falls, R.I, 6/3/28; m. to Mary. Educ: LaSalle Acad, 46; Providence Col, A.B, 52. Polit. & Govt. Pos: R.I. State Rep, 55- Bus. & Prof. Pos: Proprietor, Pawtucket Driving Sch, Pawtucket, R.I. Mil. Serv: Navy, World War II. Mailing Add: 167 Dexter St, Pawtucket, R.I. 02860. (1967)

McCABE, JAMES L. D
b. Chicago, Ill, 7/11/31; s. LeRoy J. McCabe and Mary Fleming M; m. 9/20/58 to Mary Kathryn Sullivan; c. James, Ann, Carol, Robert, John and Jeanne. Educ: DePaul Univ, LL.B, 54; Phi Alpha Delta. Polit. & Govt. Pos: Asst. states attorney, Cook Co, Ill, 56 & 57; precinct capt, 37th Ward, Chicago Dem. Orgn, 56-64; pres, 37th Ward Young Dem, 58-60, mem, exec. bd, 58-62; mem, Young Dem. Exec. Cmt, 58-62; precinct capt, Wheeling Twp. Dem. Orgn, 62-67, committeeman, 67-; Dem. cand. for U.S. Rep, 13th Dist, Ill, 66; chief attorney, Dept. of Registrn. and Educ, Ill, 67-69; del, Dem. Nat. Conv, 68. Bus. & Prof. Pos: Partner, law firm of McCabe & Venit, Chicago, Ill, 57- Mil. Serv: Entered as Pfc, Army, 54, released as SP-3, 66, after serv. in Hq. Detachment, 35th Qm. Bn, Germany, 55-56; Good Conduct Medal; Marksmanship Medal; Occup. Forces Medal. Mem: Chicago and Northwest Suburban Bar Asns; Amvets; Elks; various church orgn. Rel: Roman Catholic. Mailing Add: 312 S. Ridge Ave, Arlington Heights, Ill. 60005.

McCABE, THOMAS BAYARD R
Rep. Nat. Committeeman, Pa.
b. Whaleyville, Md, 7/11/93; m. 2/28/24 to Jeannette L; c. Thomas B, Jr, Richard and James. Educ: Swarthmore Col, B.S, 15. Polit. & Govt. Pos: Dep, Lend-Lease Admin, 40-41; chmn. bd. gov, Fed. Reserve Syst, 49-51; Rep. Nat. Committeeman, Pa, currently; mem, Rep. Nat. Finance Cmt, currently. Bus. & Prof. Pos: Chmn. finance cmt, Scott Paper Co, currently. Rel: Presbyterian. Mailing Add: Scott Paper Co, Philadelphia, Pa. 19113.

McCAFFERY, DOROTHY KANE D
Committeewoman, Conn. State Dem. Cent. Cmt.
b. New York, N.Y, 8/1/16; d. Thomas F. Kane and Genevieve McCue K; m. to John K.M. McCaffery; c. Richard K.M, Peter G, Sean M. and Padraic. Educ: St. Joseph's Col. for Women, B.A. Polit. & Govt. Pos: Secy, Bd. of Dirs, Regional Educ. Concept Through United Effort, Conn; secy, Washington Planning Cmn, 55-59; chmn, Washington Town Dem. Party, 55-65; cmnr, Conn. State Bd. of Labor Rels, 55-; del, Dem. Nat. Conv, 56 & 60; dir, Conn. Fedn. of Dem. Women's Clubs, 58-62; 32nd Sen. Dist. committeewoman, Conn. State Dem. Cent. Cmt, 58-; mem, Gov. Dempsey's Clean Water Task Force, 65-66. Mem: League of Women Voters; Garden Club of Am. Rel: Catholic. Mailing Add: Kirby Corner, Washington, Conn. 06793.

McCAFFERY, JOSEPH JAMES, JR. D
b. Butte, Mont, 7/15/08; s. Joseph James McCaffery and Mary G. Riordan M; m. 9/15/34 to Helen-Marie Donahue; c. Lynn (Mrs. Ryan) and Judith (Mrs. Regan). Educ: Stanford Univ, B.A, 30; Mont. Univ, LL.B, 34; Phi Delta Phi; Delta Tau Delta. Polit. & Govt. Pos: Pres, Smith for President Club, Stanford Univ, 28 and Roosevelt for President Club, Mont. State Univ, 32; charter mem. and counsel, South Side Dem. Club, 34-60; attorney, Reconstruction Finance Corp, Mining Div, D.C, 36-36; spec. attorney, Mont, U.S. Dept. of Labor, 37; pres, Silver Bow Co. Young Dem, 37-39; counsel, Draft Bd, 40-47, mem, State Bd. of Appeals, Selective Serv. Syst, 50; chief dep. attorney, Silver Bow Bd. of Appeals, Selective Serv. Syst, 50; chief dep. attorney, Silver Bow Co, 45-46; spec. asst. to Attorney Gen, Mont, 49-58; state Dem. committeeman, Mont, 60-64; mem, Nat. Lawyers Cmt. for Johnson and Humphrey, 64; del, Dem. Nat. Conv, 64; mem, Mont. Fish and Game Cmn, 69- Bus. & Prof. Pos: Pres. and gen. counsel, Treasure State Life Ins. Co. and Treasure State Industs, Inc, 57-63; pres, Nat. Asn. of Life Companies, Inc, 61-63, assoc. gen. counsel, 63-; secy, Colonial Life & Casualty Co, 65-; secy-dir. and mem. exec. cmn, Seaboard Corp, Inc. and Seaboard Life Ins. Co. Mem: Law-Sci. Acad. of Am; Int. Acad. of Trial Lawyers; Am. Bar Asn; Mont. Bar Asn. (pres, 69); Butte Country Club; Mont. Club; pres, Butte Town Club, 61-63; Butte Exchange Club; Friendly Sons of St. Patrick; Idlewild Hunting Club; dir, Butte Commun. Chest; adv. bd, St. James Commun. Hosp. Sch. of Nursing; hon. mem, Indust. Col. of Armed Forces; chmn. bd, Little Theaters, 49-63; dir, Butte Develop. Asn; Early Birds Club, Spokane, Wash. Rel: Catholic. Legal Res: 106 Rampart Dr, Butte, Mont. 59701. Mailing Add: 27 W. Broadway, Butte, Mont. 59701.

McCAFFREE, MARY ELLEN R
Wash. State Rep.
b. El Dorado, Kans; m. to Kenneth; c. five. Educ: Kans. State Univ, B.A. Polit. & Govt. Pos: Wash. State Rep, currently. Bus. & Prof. Pos: Homemaker. Mailing Add: 5014 18th N.E, Seattle, Wash. 98105. (1967)

McCAIN, WILBUR TEAL D
Chmn, Grant Parish Dem. Cmt, La.
b. Colfax, La, 10/19/13; s. Clair Henry McCain and Minnie Gray M; m. 12/6/37 to Erin Purifoy Sandlin; c. Linnie (Mrs. Robert A. Lee), Emily (Mrs. Lynwood L. Vallee), Erin (Mrs. Charles C. Andrews), Laura, W. T, Jr, John Thomas, Catherine Beatrice, Wilmot Sandlin, Cora Elizabeth and Joseph Lemee, II. Educ: Northwest. State Col, B.A, 38; La. State Univ. Law Sch, LL.B, 43, J.D, 68; La. Law Rev; Moot Court Supreme Court Justice; Lambda Zeta. Polit. & Govt. Pos: La. State Rep, Grant Parish, 40-48; spec. asst. attorney gen, 62-; mem, 8th dist. La. State Hwy. Bd, 65-; Chmn, Grant Parish Dem. Cmt, Ward One, currently. Mem: Charter mem, La. State Bar Asn. (eighth dist. house of del, -67, bd. gov, eighth dist, 67-68); charter mem, La. Trial Lawyers Asn. (house of del, -67); Am, Grant-Winn Parish and Rapides Parish Bar Asns; Am. Trial Lawyers Asn; Am. Judicature Soc; Municipal Attorneys Asn; Boy Scouts (bd. execs, Choctaw Dist, Attakapas Coun). Outstanding Civic leader of Am, 67; Scroll from Cent. La. Mayor's Asn, Outstanding Hwy Bd. Mem, 67; Outstanding South. Civic Leader, 67. Rel: Catholic. Legal Res: 401 Second St, Colfax, La. 71417. Mailing Add: P.O. Box 595, 403 Second St, Colfax, La. 71417.

McCAIN, WILLIAM CLARENCE D
b. Dallas Co, Ala, 4/7/29; s. William Clarence McCain and Lennie Killingsworth Mc; m. 3/21/52 to Margaret Lee; c. Charles William, Margaret Lee, Susan Lynn, William Clarence, Jr. Educ: Univ. of Ala, B.S, 51; LL.B, 58. Polit. & Govt. Pos: Ala. State Sen, 63-66. Bus. & Prof. Pos: Lawyer. Rel: Baptist. Mailing Add: 803 First National Bldg, Tuscaloosa, Ala. 35403. (1967)

McCALEB, SAMMIE LEE R
b. Pinewood, Tenn, 7/4/11; s. John McCaleb and Mattie Haubson; m. 8/3/30 to Mattie Myatt; c. Rannic, Billy, Robert, Polly and Wayne. Educ: High Sch. Polit. & Govt. Pos: Chmn, Tenn. Agr. Soil Conserv. Cmt, 57-61; chmn, Hickman Co. Rep. Exec. Cmt, 66-67. Bus. & Prof. Pos: Farmer, 40 years and Cross Tie and Lumber bus, 25 years. Mem: Nat. Farm Bur. Rel: Church of Christ. Mailing Add: Bon Aqua, Tenn. 37025. (1967)

McCALL, ISODENE MARIE R
b. East Chicago, Ind, 2/2/16; d. John William O'Brien and Grace Edith Miner O; m. 11/26/38 to James Kennedy McCall; c. John Kennedy and Daniel Bogue. Educ: Flora Stone Mather Col, West. Reserve Univ, B.A, 38; Phi Kappa Zeta. Polit. & Govt. Pos: Pres, Lakewood Fedn. of Rep. Women, 54-55; first v.pres, Los Angeles Co. Fedn. of Rep. Women, 57-60, fourth v.pres, 65-66 and pres, 67-68; nationalities chmn, Calif. Fedn. of Rep. Women, 68-69; alternate del, Rep. Nat. Conv, 68. Mem: Bd. mem, Family Counseling Serv, Cleveland, Ohio, 38-41 and Long Beach, Calif, 51-57; pres, Mark Twain PTA, 56-57 and Wilson High Sch. PTA, 62-63; pres, Long Beach Auxiliary; pres, South. Calif. Symphony Asn, 63-64, mem, 65-66; founding secy, ENCORE; Long Beach Yacht Club; life mem. PTA. Award of Merit, Los Angeles Rep. Cent. Cmt. Rel: Episcopal. Mailing Add: 343 Bay Shore, Long Beach, Calif. 90803.

McCALL, JAMES KENNEDY R
Budget and Expenditures Chmn, Los Angeles Co. Rep. Cent. Cmt, Calif.
b. Cleveland, Ohio, 10/18/15; s. James Henderson McCall and Rachel Kennedy M; m. 11/26/38 to Isodene O'Brien; c. John Kennedy and Daniel Bogue. Educ: Case West. Reserve Univ, A.B, 38; Phi Kappa Psi. Polit. & Govt. Pos: Mem, Los Angeles Co. Rep. Cent. Cmt, Calif, 52- , budget and expenditures chmn, 66-; Mem, Long Beach Airport Cmn, 57-60 and Long Beach Marina Cmn, 60-65; chmn, 32nd Dist. Rep. Party, 64-67; mem, Long Beach Park Cmn, 65-, pres, 66-67. Bus. & Prof. Pos: Owner, J.K. McCall Co, Contractors, 60-; partner, Gardner & McCall, Contractors, 46-60. Mil. Serv: Entered as Ens, Navy Res, 44, released as Lt.(jg), 46, after serv. in Civil Engr. Corps, Pac. Theatre, 44-45; Theatre and Combat Area Awards. Mem: Dir, Long Beach Yacht Club; South. Calif. Tuna Club. Rel: Episcopal. Mailing Add: 343 Bay Shore Ave, Long Beach, Calif. 90803.

McCALL, JOHN ROBERT R
b. Rosman, N.C, 3/29/25; s. Rufus Sylvanus McCall and Idela Owens M; m. 10/23/48 to Esther Jean Holbrook; c. Barbara Jean, Kathryn Kayle and John Anthony. Educ: Brevard Bus. Col. Polit. & Govt. Pos: Former chmn, Tazewell Co. Rep. Cmt, Va. Mil. Serv: Entered as Pvt, Marines, 42, released as Pvt, 45, after serv. in Pac. Theater, 43-44; Pac. Theater Ribbon; Presidential Unit Citation. Mem: Treas, Lions, 63; AF&AM; exec. v.pres, Richlands Area C. of C; Eastern Star. Rel: Methodist. Mailing Add: 1421 Front St, Richlands, Va. 24641. (1967)

McCALL, TOM LAWSON R
Gov. of Oregon
b. Egypt, Mass, 3/22/13; s. Henry McCall and Dorothy Lawson M; m. 5/20/39 to Audrey Owen; c. Thomas, Jr. and Samuel. Educ: Univ. Ore, B.A, 36; Phi Delta Theta; Alpha Delta Sigma. Hon. LL.D, Linfield Col, 65. Polit. & Govt. Pos: Exec. asst. to Gov. McKay, Ore, 49-52; mem, Gov. Blue Ribbon Cmt. on Govt. Reorganization, 60; Secy. of State, Ore, 65-67; Gov. of Ore, 67-; mem, policy cmt, Rep. Gov. Asn; nat. chmn, Educ. Cmn. of the States, 69-; exec. secy, legis. Interim Cmts. on Welfare, Pub. Employees Retirement, Indian Affairs, Sex Offenses, Legis. Procedures; chmn, City of Portland Youth Cmn; mem, Gov. Cmts. on Indian Affairs, Air Pollution Abatement, Govt. Reorgn; pub. info. officer, Ore. Civil Defense Agency; mem, Cmt. on Race and Educ, Portland Sch. Dist. 1 and adv. cmt, Ore. Coun. on Crime and Delinquency; v.chmn, Ore. Coun. on Econ. Educ. Bus. & Prof. Pos: Polit. Analyst, KGW Radio and TV, Portland; founding partner, Goodrich, McCall & Snyder. Mil. Serv: Entered as Navy Combat Correspondent, 44, released as Specialist X 3/C, 46, after serv. in Pac. Mem: Bd. Overseers, Lewis and Clark Col; former pres, Ore. Asn. Crippled Children and Adults, Ore. Prison Asn, Press Club of Ore. and Portland Local of Am. TV and Radio Artists, AFL-CIO; former regional chmn, Nat. Conf. Christians and Jews; former secy, Portland Urban League; chmn, Ore. Crusade for Freedom; Nat. Coun. for Support of Pub. Schs; Ore. Hist. Soc.(mem. bd); bd. dirs, Delaunay Inst. Ment. Health, Salem Area Family Counseling Serv. and Ore. United Appeal, Portland; adv. bd, Multnomah Co. Sheriff's Off. and Salvation Army; exec. bd, Ore. Aerospace Educ. Coun; exec. cmt, Metrop. Interfaith Cmn. on Race; trustee, Indian Festival of Arts, Inc; Am. Legion. Best Educ. Forum Prog. Award, Ohio State Univ. Exhibit of Radio and TV, 53; Golden Beaver Award, Izaak Walton League, 59; Award for Outstanding Documentary in U.S, Sigma Delta Chi, 62; Brotherhood Award, Ore. Regional Conf. Christians and Jews, 64; Freedom's Found. Award for Weekly Radio Prog. Report to the People. Rel: Episcopal. Legal Res: 796 Winter N.E, Salem, Ore. 97301. Mailing Add: Office of the Governor, State Capitol, Salem, Ore. 97310.

MacCALLUM, DOUGLAS C. R
Chmn, Westchester Co. Rep. Cmt, N.Y.
b. N.Y.C, 7/10/02; s. Harry MacCallum and Agnes Curtis M; m. 3/10/25 to E. Claire Mersereau; c. Douglas C. Educ: New York Univ. Col, B.S, 25; New York Univ. Grad. Col, 1 year; Psi Upsilon. Polit. & Govt. Pos: Pres, Westchester Co. Young Rep, N.Y, 45-46; city councilman, White Plains, N.Y, 56-64; chmn, White Plains Rep. City Cmt, 62-69; mem, N.Y. State Rep. Cmt, 64-69, mem. exec. cmt, 69-; chmn, Westchester Co. Rep. Cmt, 68- Bus. & Prof. Pos: Resident mgr, G.H. Walker & Co, White Plains, N.Y, 57- Merit Award, White Plains C. of C. Rel: Methodist. Mailing Add: 44 N. Broadway, White Plains, N.Y. 10603.

McCALLUM, GEORGE R
b. Conrad, Mont, 7/8/19; s. Warren McCallum and Gwen Blackshaw M; m. 8/10/43 to Verdie Nadine Armstrong; c. Janice (Mrs. Johnson), Anita (Mrs. DeLong), Glenda (Mrs. Ueland) and Debra. Educ: Hot Springs High Sch, 33-37. Polit. & Govt. Pos: Chmn, Sanders Co. Rep. Cent. Cmt, Mont, 63-69. Bus. & Prof. Pos: Area supvr, J. Hofert Co, 60-69. Mem: Mason; Sch. Bd; Grange. Rel: Presbyterian. Mailing Add: Niarada, Mont. 59852.

McCALLUM, SHELBY D
Ky. State Rep.
b. 1918. Polit. & Govt. Pos: Ky. State Rep, 52-, Speaker, Ky. House of Rep, 64 & 66. Bus. & Prof. Pos: Radio broadcaster. Mil. Serv: Army, World War II. Mem: Rotary; Shrine. Rel: Methodist. Mailing Add: Box 7, Benton, Ky. 42025. (1967)

McCANDLESS, CLARENCE HEWITT R
b. Cottonwood Falls, Kans, 9/8/95; m. to Lois Wood; c. one son and one daughter. Educ: Col. of Emporia, B.A, 17; Kans. State Col, B.S, 21; Phi Kappa Phi; Sigma Tau. Hon. ScD, Col. Emporia, 67. Polit. & Govt. Pos: Vt. State Rep, 63-65; town auditor and moderator. Bus. & Prof. Pos: Prfnl. elec. engr, Retired. Mil. Serv: Topographical Sect, Fifth U.S. Engrs, Seventh Div, Puvenel Sector, France, 17-19. Mem: N.Y. Prfnl. Engrs; Nat. Grange; Tel. Pioneers. Rel: Presbyterian. Mailing Add: Chester, Vt. 05143.

McCANLESS, GEORGE FOLSOM D
Attorney Gen, Tenn.
b. Morristown, Tenn, 6/8/04; s. Michael C. McCanless and Nannie Louise Folsom M; m. 4/9/29 to Sarah Gaut Hardcastle; c. Sarah Hardcastle, George Folsom. Educ: Vanderbilt Univ, A.B, 26, LL.B, 28; Phi Kappa Sigma; Phi Delta Phi. Polit. & Govt. Pos: Chancellor, 13th Chancery Div. of Tenn, 37-38; cmnr, Finance and Taxation, 39-46; attorney Gen, 54-; mem, Tenn. Hist. Cmn, 61- Bus. & Prof. Pos: Pvt. practice, Morristown, Tenn, 28-37 & 46-54. Mem: Tenn. Hist. Soc.(pres, 59-61). Rel: Presbyterian. Mailing Add: Supreme Court Bldg, 401 Seventh Ave, Nashville, Tenn. 37219. (1967)

McCANN, CHARLES WILLIAM ALOYSIUS D
Ky. State Sen.
b. Louisville, Ky, 4/8/00; s. William Leonard McCann and Ella Hollihan M; m. 6/23/34 to Catherine Mary Riley. Educ: St. Xavier Col, B.S, 19; St. Xavier Alumni. Polit. & Govt. Pos: Ky. State Sen, 48-; secy, Dem. Caucus, Ky, 64- Bus. & Prof. Pos: Pres, McCann Chem. Co, 39-67, Mose Green Dem. Club, 45-50, Ky. State Health J, 55- and Ky. Sweepstakes Cmt, Inc, 64- Mem: Advert. Club of Louisville; C. of C; Beechmont and Iroquois Civic Clubs; K. of C.(4°); Knights of St. John; Pleasant Hill Estate Rd. Fund. Rel: Catholic. Mailing Add: 3519 Hillsboro Rd, St. Matthews, Ky. 40207.

McCANN, FRANCIS X. D
Mass. State Sen.
m. to Jacquelyn Doyle; c. Francis X, Jr, Susan Ellen, James Jude, Gregory and Gerald. Polit. & Govt. Pos: Mass. State Sen, 54- Mil. Serv: World War II. Mem: Am. Legion; VFW. Mailing Add: 19 Hutchinson St, Cambridge, Mass. 02138. (1967)

McCANN, JAMES A. D
b. Appleton, Wis, 3/7/24; s. John McCann and Mary Garvey M; m. 9/11/54 to Shirley A. Gerlach; c. Brian J, Timothy J, Maureen T, Kathleen M, Sharon L, and Michael J. Educ: Univ. Wis, B.B.A, 59. Polit. & Govt. Pos: Former Wis. State Assemblyman, 15th Dist. Bus. & Prof. Pos: Cost acct, Marathon Paper Corp, 49-55; owner and mgr, Real Estate and Ins. Agency, 60-65; CPA Off, 65- Mil. Serv: Entered as Pvt, Army, 42, released as M/Sgt, 46, re-entered 50, released 52, after serv. in 99th Inf. Div, 887th F.A. Bn, ETO; Three Battle Stars; Ardennes-Rhineland-Central Europe Campaign Ribbons; Presidential Unit Citation. Mem: K. of C.(4°); Eagles; Moose. Rel: Roman Catholic. Mailing Add: 3537 N. 95th St, Milwaukee, Wis. 53222. (1967)

McCARLEY, WILLIAM GEORGE D
Ala. State Sen.
b. Gadsden, Ala, 9/5/27; s. Ernest McCarley and Mamie Coe M; m. 12/19/51 to Helen May Hall; c. Gail Lee, Cheryl Lynn, Karen Anne, Robin Kaye and Robert Hall. Polit. & Govt. Pos: Ala. State Sen, 15th Dist, 67- Bus. & Prof. Pos: Salesman. Mil. Serv: Entered as A/S, Navy, 43, released as Chief Electronics Technician, 62, after serv. in various destroyers, shore duty as Recruit Co. Comdr. & Instr. Electronics Sch; Asiatic-Pac. Theater Ribbon; Victory, Philippine Liberation, Good Conduct, Nat. Defense, China Serv. and Occupation Medals; several Letters of Commendation. Mem: Mason; Lions Int; VFW; Am. Legion; Cattlemens Asn; Fleet Res. Asn; co-founder and mem. bd. of mgt, Prattville YMCA, Ala. Rel: Presbyterian. Mailing Add: 111 Melmar Dr, Prattville, Ala. 36067. (1967)

McCARNEY, ROBERT PATTERSON R
b. Churdan, Iowa, 1/28/12; s. Thomas D. McCarney and Rhoda Roberts M; m. 9/8/34 to Elizabeth Ann Huttner; c. Sharon E. (Mrs. Spaedy). Educ: Churdan High Sch, dipl. Polit. & Govt. Pos: Rep. cand. for gov, N.Dak, 68. Bus. & Prof. Pos: Pres. & owner, McCarney Ford Inc. and McCarney Credit Co. Mil. Serv: Entered as 1st Lt, Army, 42, released as Capt, 46 after serv. in 301st Armoured Regt, ETO, 43-46; Five Battle Stars; Good Conduct Medal. Mem: Elks; Eagles; Am. Legion; VFW; 40 et 8. Rel: Protestant. Mailing Add: 1244 Coulee Rd, Bismarck, N.Dak. 58501.

McCARTER, JOE T. D
Chmn, Legis Dist. 22 Dem. Party, Idaho
b. Gooding, Idaho, 5/30/30; s. William S. McCarter and Mattie Thorpe M; m. 2/21/58 to Mercedes A. Lolley; c. Kathleen L, William L and Joan L. Educ: Univ. of Idaho, 48-49. Polit. & Govt. Pos: Dem. Precinct committeeman, Camas Co, Idaho, 58-64; chmn, Canas Co. Dem. Party, 64-66; chmn, Legis. Dist. 22 Dem. Party, 66-, S. Cent. Idaho regional chmn, 67-; del, Dem. Nat. Conv, 68; coordinator for Hubert Humphrey , Second Cong. Dist, 68. Bus. & Prof. Pos: Secy-treas, McCarter Cattle Co. Inc, Corral, Idaho, 60- Mil. Serv: Entered ast Pvt, E-1, Army, 53, released as Cpl, E-4, 55, after serv. in MP Detachment, Ft. Lesley J. McNair, Mil. Dist. of Wash, 54-55; Good Conduct Medal. Mem: Idaho Cattlemen's Asn; Nat. Farmer's Orgn. Rel: Protestant. Mailing Add: Corral, Idaho 83322.

McCARTHY, EUGENE JOSEPH DFL
U.S. Sen, Minn.
b. Watkins, Minn, 3/29/16; s. Michael J. McCarthy and Anna Baden M; m. 6/25/45 to Abigail Quigley; c. Ellen Anne, Mary Abigail, Michael Benet and Margaret Alice. Educ: St. John's Univ, Minn, A.B, 35; Univ. Minn, M.A, 38. Hon. LL.D, St. Louis Univ. and Col. of St. Thomas. Polit. & Govt. Pos: Civilian tech. asst. in mil. intel, U.S. War Dept, 42-46; U.S. Rep, Minn, 49-59, mem, Cmts. on Post Off. and Civil Serv, Agr, Interior and Insular Affairs, Banking and Currency, and Ways and Means, U.S. House of Rep; cong. del. to int. conf, WHO, 58; del, NATO Parliamentarian's Conf, Paris, 56, 57 & 62; off. observer at Gen. Agreement on Trade and Tariffs, Geneva, 57 & 62; U.S. Sen, Minn, 59-, chmn, Sen. Spec. Cmt. on Unemploy. Probs, 59-60, mem, Dem. Steering Cmt, del, Dem. Nat. Conv, 68. Bus. & Prof. Pos: Teacher in pub. high schs. and pvt. cols, 10 years; acting head sociol. dept, Col. of St. Thomas until 48. Publ: Frontiers in American Democracy, World Publ. Co, 60; Dictionary of American Politics, Macmillan Co, 62; A Liberal Answer to the Conservative Challenge, Macfadden-Bartell, 64; plus others. Mem: Coun. on Relig. Freedom and Pub. Affairs, Nat. Conf. Christians and Jews; chmn, Franklin Delano Roosevelt Mem. Cmn, 67-; Bd. of Fed. Union, Inc. Rel: Roman Catholic. Legal Res: St. Paul, Minn. Mailing Add: U.S. Senate Office Bldg, Washington, D.C. 20510.

McCARTHY, FRANCIS J. R
Conn. State Rep.
b. N.Y.C, 8/8/18; s. Eugene McCarthy and Louise Wacker M; m. 1/19/41 to Barbara Cheney; c. Morrison and Melissa. Educ: Wesleyan Univ, A.B, 40; Yale Univ, LL.B, 47; Sigma Chi. Polit. & Govt. Pos: Mem, exec. cmt, Wethersfield Rep. Town Cmt, Conn; mem, Zoning Cmn, Wethersfield, 55-60, chmn, 58-59, councilman, 60-62, mayor and chmn. town coun, 62-66; U.S. Dist.

Court, Conn, 48; U.S. Court Appeals, 54; U.S. Supreme Court, 61; Conn. State Rep, 67- Bus. & Prof. Pos: Admitted to Conn. Bar, 47; mem, law dept, Travelers Ins. Co, Hartford, 47-, counsel, 63-; former instr. law, Univ. Conn. Law Sch; instr, Univ. Conn, 65- Mil. Serv: Navy, Lt. Comdr, 41-46. Publ: Various articles dealing with law. Mem: Conn. and Hartford Co. Bar Asns; Yale Law Sch. Asn; past pres, Friends of Wethersfield Libr; chmn, Kennedy Mem. Libr. Fund; Rotary; Hartford C. of C. Legal Res: 19 Coleman Rd, Wethersfield, Conn. 06109. Mailing Add: 700 Main St, Hartford, Conn. 06103.

McCARTHY, JAMES JOSEPH, JR. D
b. Derby, Conn, 4/22/27; s. James Joseph McCarthy and Marie Breault M; m. 12/29/51 to Claire Marguerite Duplese; c. James Joseph, III and Brian Gerard. Educ: Yale Univ, B.A, 48; Fordham Univ. Sch. of Law, LL.B, 51. Polit. Pos: Mem, Cmn. on Higher Educ, Conn, 64-; chmn, Young Dem. Conv, 62-; mem, Fed. and Intergovt. Cmn, 59-; bd. of mgrs, Coun. of State Govt, 63-65. Govt. Pos: Corp. counsel, Derby, Conn, 63-; Conn. State Sen. until 67; judge, Munic. Court, 56-58. Bus. & Prof. Pos: V.pres, Beacon Braids, Inc, Beacon Falls, Conn. and Attorney, 54- Mil. Serv: Seaman, Navy, 45-46, serv. in Am. Theater; entered Coast Guard as S/A, 51, released as Lt.(jg), 53, after serv. in N.Atlantic; Am. Theater Ribbon; Victory Medal; Am. Defense Medal; Lt. Comdr, Coast Guard Res, at present. Mem: Conn. Bar Asn; legis. cmt, Valley Bar Asn, 66; Past Exalted Ruler, Elks; Advocate, K. of C; Jr. C. of C; Am. Legion; Storm Engine Co; Yale Club of New Haven. Rel: Catholic. Mailing Add: 23 Cedric Ave, Derby, Conn. 06418. (1967)

McCARTHY, JOHN FRANCIS D
Mem, Bridgeport Dem. Town Cmt, Conn.
b. Bridgeport, Conn, 11/23/11; s. Timothy McCarthy and Julia Driscoll M; m. 6/29/40 to Florence Reilly; c. John F, Jr. Educ: Bridgeport Engr. Inst, 41-43, Evening Sch, 44-48. Polit. & Govt. Pos: Mem. and dist. chmn, Bridgeport Dem. Town Cmt, Conn, 37-; pres, Bridgeport Young Dem, 38-39; pres, Conn. State Young Dem, 40-46, nat. committeeman, 47-51; del, Dem. Nat. Conv, 44, alternate del, 48, 52, 56, 60, 64 & 68; dep. registr. voters, Bridgeport, 49-61, registr. voters, 61-; nat. treas, Young Dem. Clubs Am, 51-53. Mem: Fed. Bldg. & Loan Asn.(dir, 48-68),v.pres, 67-68); Home Bldg. & Loan Asn. (dir, 69); Neighborhood Orgn. Mentally Ill Children (dir, 66-); William Penn Fraternal Asn.(secy, 61-); Hibernians; K. of C.(3° and 4°); YMCA (bd. of mgt); Barnum Festival Soc.(pres, 66-67, bd. dirs, 60-); Bridgeport Little League (dir); Sr. City Baseball League (dir); Holy Name Soc; Commun. Chest and Coun.(dir, 67). Rel: Catholic; Trustee, St. George Roman Catholic Church. Mailing Add: 664 Atlantic St, Bridgeport, Conn. 06604.

McCARTHY, JOHN FRANCIS D
Mem, N.H. State Dem. Cmt.
b. Berlin, N.H, 9/18/40; s. John McCarthy and Helen Harriman M; single. Educ: Rensselaer Polytechnic Inst, B.C.E, 62; Univ. Calif, Berkeley, 65-66; Tau Beta Pi; Chi Epsilon. Polit. & Govt. Pos: Alternate del, Dem. Nat. Conv, 68; mem, N.H. State Dem. Cmt, 68- Mailing Add: 34 Main St, Cascade Gorham, N.H. 03581.

McCARTHY, JOHN G. R
N.Y. State Assemblyman
b. Long Island City, N.Y, 10/10/23; m. to Josephine Stanco; c. Seven boys and two girls. Educ: St. John's Univ. Sch. of Commerce, St. John's Univ. Sch. of Law. Polit. & Govt. Pos: N.Y. State Assemblyman, 62-; Huntington Sta. Rep. Club; Huntington Young Rep. Club. Bus. & Prof. Pos: Lawyer. Mil. Serv: Army, European and Pac. Theatres. Mem: Suffolk Co. Bar Asn; St. Hugh Holy Name Soc; VFW; Huntington Lawyers Club; Elks; bd, Suffolk Co. Chap, Am. Red Cross; past pres, bd, S. Huntington Kiwanis; Huntington C. of C. Rel: Catholic. Mailing Add: 8 Pinoak Court, Huntington Station, N.Y. 11746.

McCARTHY, JOHN V. D
Ohio State Representative
b. Youngstown, Ohio, 4/24/34; s. Justin H. McCarthy and Agnes M; m. 4/14/56 to Joan Lyden; c. Kathy, Joan, Mark, Sheila, Patric and Maureen. Educ: Youngstown Univ, 1 year. Polit. & Govt. Pos: City Councilman, Sixth Ward, Youngstown, Ohio, 64-67; Ohio State Rep, 81st Dist, 69- Bus. & Prof. Pos: Sales Mgr, Alum Fence Co. of America, 63- Mem: Elks; K. of C. Rel: Catholic. Mailing Add: 150 E. Lucius Ave, Youngstown, Ohio 44507.

McCARTHY, RICHARD DEAN D
U.S. Rep, N.Y.
b. Buffalo, N.Y, 9/24/27; m. 1957 to Gail E. Coughlin; c. Maura, Brendan, Dierdre, Dean and Barry. Educ: Canisius Col, B.A; Univ. of Buffalo; Cornell Univ; Harvard Univ. Polit. & Govt. Pos: U.S. Rep, N.Y, 64- Bus. & Prof. Pos: Former newsman, pub. rels. exec; dir, pub. rels, Nat. Gypsum Co, 56-64. Mil. Serv: Navy, 45-46; Army, 50-52. Mem: Cent. Park Asn; Buffalo Philharmonic Orch. Soc; Buffalo Area C. of C; Frontier Press Club; Buffalo & Erie Co. Hist Soc; Troop 1 Post, Am. Legion; Pres, Niagra Frontier Chap. Pub. Rels. Soc. of Am; past v.pres, Greater Buffalo Develop. Found. Rel: Catholic. Legal Res: N.Y. Mailing Add: 238 Cannon House Office Bldg, Washington, D.C. 20515.

McCARTHY, ROBERT W. D
Ill. State Sen.
b. 5/28/24; married; c. Douglas and Diane. Educ: Univ. Ill. Col. of Law. Polit. & Govt. Pos: Ill. State Rep. and v.chmn, Judiciary Cmt, Ill. House of Rep, formerly; Ill. State Sen, 60-, mem, Judiciary, Revenue, Elec. Exec. and Judicial Rev. Cmts; mem, Intergovt. Coop, Elec. Laws and Tort Liability Laws. Bus. & Prof. Pos: Attorney-at-law. Mil. Serv: World War II. Mem: Am. Bar Asn. Mailing Add: 260 N. Woodlawn Ave, Decatur, Ill. 62522.

McCARTHY, THOMAS CARRELL D
Mem, Exec. Bd, King Co. Dem. Cent. Cmt, Wash.
b. Ames, Iowa, 4/7/25; s. Carrell Cox McCarthy and Mary Gribbon M; m. 8/26/47 to Margaret Beall; c. Melissa and Becky. Educ: N.W. Mo. State Teachers Col, Maryville, 1 year; Iowa State Univ, B.S, 48; Univ. Iowa, J.D, 50; Phi Kappa Psi. Polit. & Govt. Pos: Dem. precinct committeeman, 54-59 & 68-; del, Co. and State Convs, 56 & 68; alternate del, Dem. Nat. Conv, 68; dist. coordinator, Wash. Dem. Coun, 68-69; mem. exec. bd, King Co. Dem. Cent. Cmt, 69- Bus. & Prof. Pos: Title exam, Wash. Title Ins. Co, Seattle, 50-53; asst. counsel, Fed. Nat. Mortgage Asn, 53; lawyer, Bellevue, 53-; cmnr, Bellevue Dist. Justice Court, 63- Mil. Serv: Entered as A/S, Navy, 43, released as Aviation Cadet, 45, after serv. in numerous training units in U.S. Mem: Wash. State and East King Co. Bar Asns. Mailing Add: 3111 98th N.E, Bellevue, Wash. 98004.

McCARTHY, WILLIAM AUGUSTUS R
b. Gloucester, Mass, 11/12/11; s. William Francis McCarthy and Lillian Astrom M; m. 4/18/53 to Mildred Nadeau; c. William J. and Janice Margaret. Educ: Wentworth Inst. Polit. & Govt. Pos: Chmn, Ward 8 Rep. City Cmt, Mass, 56-58; chmn, Gloucester Rep. City Cmt, 58-64; pres, Essex Club, 66-69; del, Rep. Nat. Conv, 68. Bus. & Prof. Pos: Pres. and treas, McCarthy Contracting Co, Inc, 46- Mil. Serv: Entered as Pvt, Army, 42, released as Maj, 1st Armored Div, ETO, 44-46; European-African-Middle-East. Serv. Medal; World War II Victory and Am. Serv. Medals; Bronze Star Medal; Meritorious Serv. Plaque. Mem: Lions; Am. Legion; VFW; Elks; Friends of the N. Shore Commun. Col; Soc. Am. Mil. Engrs; Rep. Club of Mass. Rel: Catholic. Legal Res: Hesperus Ave, Gloucester, Mass. 01930. Mailing Add: P.O. Box 42, Magnolia, Mass. 01930.

McCARTNEY, RALPH F. R
Majority Leader, Iowa House of Rep.
b. Charles City, Iowa; m. to Rhoda; c. Ralph, Julie and David. Educ: Iowa State Univ; Univ. Mich. Law Sch, J.D, 50. Polit. & Govt. Pos: Mem, Co. Rep. Resolutions Cmt; del, Co. and State Rep. Conv; Co. Finance Chmn, Rep. Party; Iowa State Rep, 67-, Majority Leader, Iowa House of Rep, 69- Bus. & Prof. Pos: Attorney-at-law. Mem: Past pres, Lions Club; Crippled Children's Soc; trustee, Salvation Army; C. of C; VFW; Am. Legion; Masons and Consistory; past pres, Floyd Co. Bar Asn; Am, Iowa, 12th Judicial Dist. Bar Asns. Rel: Congregational. Mailing Add: R.R. 4, Charles City, Iowa. 50616.

MacCARTY, COLLIN STEWART, JR. D
b. Rochester, Minn, 11/11/42; s. Collin Stewart MacCarty and Margery Deal M; m. 6/28/68 to Diane Mary Foster. Educ: Rochester Jr. Col, 60-63; Black Hills State Col, B.A, 65 and Ed.M, 69; Rodeo Club. Polit. & Govt. Pos: Regional dir, S.Dak. Young Dem, 64-65 and v.pres, 65; alternate del-at-lg, Dem. Nat. Conv, 68. Bus. & Prof. Pos: Instr. staff, polit. sci, Hiram Scott Col, Scottsbluff, Nebr, 67-68. Mil. Serv: Pvt, Army, 65-66, with serv. in Co. E, Third Brigade, Fifth Army, U.S; Sp-4/C, S.Dak. Nat. Guard, 66-69. Mem: Elks. Rel: Presbyterian. Mailing Add: Box 769, Homer, Alaska 99603.

McCARTY, DORIS MAXINE D
b. Barclay, Kans, 9/11/23; d. Clarence Samuel Richardson and Sylvia Evans R; m. 6/13/42 to Charles Leroy McCarty; c. Charles Samuel, Mary Elizabeth, Richard Leroy and John Wayne. Educ: Deming High Sch, N.Mex, grad. Polit. & Govt. Pos: Sheriff, Lordsburg, N.Mex, formerly, dep, currently. Bus. & Prof. Pos: Correspondent, El Paso Times, Herald Post and Lordsburg Liberal; co-ed, Lordsburg Liberal Newspaper, 60-64. Mem: Mgr-secy, Hidalgo Co. C. of C, 64-65; Eastern Star; Bus. & Prfnl. Women's Club; Woman's Soc. Christian Serv; Hidalgo Co. Farm and Livestock Bur; Heart Asn. Rel: Methodist. Mailing Add: 704 S. Shakespeare, Lordsburg, N.Mex. 88045.

McCARTY, FRANK JOHN R
Mem, Calif. Rep. State Cent. Cmt.
b. Chicago, Ill, 5/22/14; s. Eugene Burt McCarty and Goldie Burke M; m. 10/14/48 to Marion Delores Sadowski; c. Patricia Anne (Mrs. Stanley) and Dennis Keefe. Educ: Northwest. Univ, 1½ years. Polit. & Govt. Pos: Chmn, 49th Assembly Dist. Registrn. Cmt, Calif, 65-66; Rep. nominee, Calif. State Bd. of Equalization, Fourth Dist, 66; mem, Pomona Valley Rep. Coord. Coun, 66-67; mem, Calif. Rep. State Cent. Cmt, 24th Cong. Dist. Rep. Cent. Cmt, 35th Sen. Dist. Rep. Cent. Cmt. and 50th Assembly Dist. Rep. Cent. Cmt, 67- Bus. & Prof. Pos: Terminal mgr, Azusa Transfer Co, 52-56; terminal mgr, Doudel Transportation Co, 56-60; personnel and safety dir, Merrifield Trucking Co, 60-65; sales rep, Valley Copperstate Motor Lines, 65- Mil. Serv: Entered as Pvt, Army, 42, released as S/Sgt, 45, after serv. in 457 AAAW Bn, ETO, 42-45; Europe-Africa-Middle East Theatre Ribbon with One Silver and One Bronze Battle Star; Bronze Serv. Arrowhead; Purple Heart; Am. Defense Serv. Ribbon with For. Serv. Clasp; Normandy, South. France, Ardennes, Rhineland and Cent. Europe Battle Ribbons. Mem: Los Angeles and San Fernando Valley Transportation Clubs; Mason; PTA; past pres, Valley Copperstate employees Fed. Credit Union; dir, Home Owners Asn; Boy Scouts (former leader). Rel: Protestant. Mailing Add: 23536 Decorah Rd, Diamond Bar, Calif. 91766.

McCARTY, GLEN A. D
b. Reserve, N.Mex, 9/19/25; s. Florence Dude McCarty and Pearl Ward M; m. 12/10/49 to Caroline Ray; c. Glenna Carol, Shirley Jean and Richard Guy. Polit. & Govt. Pos: Former precinct chmn, Catron Co. Dem. Party, N.Mex, chmn, 63-68. Mil. Serv: Entered as Pvt, Army, 44, released as Cpl, 46. Mem: Elks; VFW. Rel: Presbyterian. Mailing Add: P.O. Box 227, Reserve, N.Mex. 87830. (1967)

McCARTY, GLENN D. Conservative
Minn. State Sen.
Married. Educ: Univ. Iowa, B.A. and J.D. Polit. & Govt. Pos: Minn. State Rep, 54-62; Minn. State Sen, 62-, mem, Legis. Interim Hwy. Cmn, 65- Bus. & Prof. Pos: Attorney-at-law. Mil. Serv: World War II. Mem: Am. Legion. Mailing Add: 2221 Humboldt Ave. S, Minneapolis, Minn. 55405.

McCARTY, JOHN MOORE D
b. Ft. Pierce, Fla, 11/23/15; s. Daniel Thomas McCarty and Frances Lardner Moore M; m. 7/16/41 to Martha Louise Fosgate; c. John Moore, Jr, Margaret Evelyn and Thomas Chester. Educ: Univ. of Fla, A.B. and LL.B, 41; pres, Student Body; Hall of Fame; Varsity Football, Basketball; Sigma Phi Epsilon; pres, Fla. Alpha Chap. Polit. & Govt. Pos: Munic. judge, City of Ft. Pierce, Fla, 47-51; circuit judge, Fla. Ninth Circuit, 57-59; Fla. State Sen, 12th Dist, 62-67; mem, Fla. Constitution Rev. Cmn, 65-66. Bus. & Prof. Pos: Fla. counsel, Sperry & Hutchinson Co. Mil. Serv: Entered as 1st Lt, Army, 42, released as Maj, C.O, 292nd Joint Assault Co, Pac, 46; Bronze Star Medal; Guam, Philippines, Okinawa and Japan Campaign Ribbons. Mem: Bd. of Gov, Fla. Bar, 63-69; pres, St. Lucie Co. Bar, 50, Ft. Pierce Mem. Hosp. and Ro-

tary Club, 48 and Ft. Pierce Jaycees, 47; Am. and Fla. Bar Asns; dir, Am. Judicature Soc; Ft. Pierce and Fla. C. of C; Scottish Rite; York Rite; Mason; K.T; Shrine; Royal Order of Jesters 88, Mahi Temple Miami; Am. Legion; VFW; Moose; Univ. Fla. Alumni Asn; bd. trustees, Univ. Fla. Law Center, 64-68. Rel: Episcopal. Legal Res: 2611 S. Indian River Dr, Fort Pierce, Fla. 33450. Mailing Add: Box 4412, Fort Pierce, Fla. 33450.

McCARTY, MACLYN, JR. D
Md. State Del.
b. Kenosha, Wis, 9/8/35; s. Maclyn McCarty and Anita Davies M; m. 6/6/56 to Sara Anna Renn; c. Debra Anita, Pamela Adele, Susan Michele and Kimberly Ivy. Educ: Johns Hopkins Univ, A.B, 57, M.A, 59 and Ph. D, 60; Sigma Xi. Polit. & Govt. Pos: Pres, Third Dist. Young Dem. Club, Md, 66-; Md. State Del, Second Dist, 67- Bus. & Prof. Pos: Asst. prof. chem eng, Johns Hopkins Univ, 60-67; research scientist, Research Inst. for Adv. Studies, 67- Publ: 'Collision Frequency of Molecules Excited by Monochromatic Light,' J. Chem. Phys. 42, 65; 'Highly Sensitive Electric Discharge Detector for Chromatographic Analysis,' Anal. Chem. 37, 65; 'Study of the Reaction of Electronically Excited Oxygen Molecules with Carbon Monoxide,' J. Chem. Phys. 45, 66. Mem: Am. Chem. Soc; Am. Phys. Soc; Am. Asn. for Adv. of Sci; Dem. Clubs. Rel: Protestant. Mailing Add: 2826 Maryland Ave, Baltimore, Md. 21218.

McCAUGHEY, ROBERT L. R
b. Aberdeen, S.Dak, 8/7/19; s. Lyle Robert McCaughey and Margaret Wells McC; m. 7/11/43 to Genevieve Mae Strauch; c. Karen Kay. Educ: North. State Teachers Col, Aberdeen, S.Dak, B.A, 37-41; Univ. of Minn, 38; Univ. of Miss, 43; Sigma Phi Epsilon. Polit. & Govt. Pos: Admin. asst, Sen. Karl Mundt, R-S.Dak, 45- Mil. Serv: Army, M/Sgt, 42-45. Mem: Elks; Masons; Am. Legion. Rel: Presbyterian. Legal Res: Aberdeen, S.Dak. 57401. Mailing Add: 2405 Gaither St. S.E, Washington, D.C. 20031. (1967)

McCAULEY, JOHN E. D
Mich. State Sen.
b. Delaware, Ohio, 4/28/24; married; c. Patrick Brian. Educ: Mich. State Univ; Wayne State Univ, LL.B. Polit. & Govt. Pos: Former chmn, Wayne Co. Bd. of Supvrs, Mich; del, Constitutional Conv; Mayor, Wyandotte, Mich, 4 years, councilman, 6 years; Mich. State Sen, 64- Bus. & Prof. Pos: Attorney-at-law. Mil. Serv: Army; Purple Heart. Mem: Am. Legion; VFW; Kiwanis; DAV; Eagles; Gr. Wyandotte Bd. of Commerce; Detroit and Mich. Bar Asns. Rel: Presbyterian. Mailing Add: 1605 23rd St, Wyandotte, Mich. 48192. (1967)

McCAULEY, MICHAEL SYLVESTER D
Chmn, Dubuque Co. Dem. Cent. Cmt, Iowa
b. Davenport, Iowa, 10/21/36; s. Michael Sylvester McCauley and Bernice Fautsch M; m. 5/2/64 to JoAnn Dingbaum; c. Patrick Michael. Educ: Loras Col, B.A, 58; State Univ. Iowa, LL.B, 62; Delta Sigma. Polit. & Govt. Pos: Dem. committeeman, First Precinct, Julien Twp, Iowa, 62-64; asst. co. attorney, Dubuque Co, 63-64, co. attorney, 67-; pres, Dubuque Co. Young Dem, 64; asst. attorney gen, State of Iowa, 65-66; chmn, Dubuque Co. Dem. Cent. Cmt, 67- Mem: Nat. Dist. Attorneys Asn; Iowa Co. Attorneys Asn; Am, Iowa and Dubuque Co. Bar Asns; K. of C; dir, Dubuque Jaycees, 64. Rel: Roman Catholic. Mailing Add: 648 S. Grandview, Dubuque, Iowa 52001.

McCAULEY, PHILIP W. R
b. Madison, Ind, 8/12/10; s. Roy Wilbert McCauley and Katherine Crawford M; m. 4/17/31 to Ida Laura Niesse; c. Donald L, Philip W, II, Susan (Mrs. Philetus S. Barber III) and Sarah (Mrs. Robert Heuel, Jr). Educ: St. Mary's Business Sch, grad, 26. Polit. & Govt. Pos: Pres, Jefferson Co. Welfare Dept, Ind, 62-; pres, Jefferson Co. Econ. Develop. Cmt, 67-; alternate del, Rep. Nat. Conv, 68. Bus. & Prof. Pos: Pres. The Madison Bank and Trust Co, Madison, Ind, 65-; Chmn. of the Bd, Rising Sun State Bank, 69- Mem: Ind. Bankers Asn(v.pres, 69); Mason; Shrine; Rotary Club (Pres, 68); Elks; Moose; Madison Country Club. Rel: Presbyterian. Legal Res: 739 W. Main St, Madison, Ind. 47250. Mailing Add: The Madison Bank and Trust Co, 213-215 E. Main St, Madison, Ind. 47250.

McCAY, THOMAS SCOTT R
b. Utica, Miss, 8/4/29; s. Gadi Lum McCay, Sr. and Mattie McLemore M; m. 1/21/58 to Bonnie Jean Barham; c. Marvin Barham, Elizabeth Kim and Thomas Scott, Jr. Educ: Miss. Col, B.S, 50; Univ. Miss. Sch. Med, cert, 51; Johns Hopkins Univ. Sch. Med, M.D, 53; Phi Chi. Polit. & Govt. Pos: Chmn, Humphreys Co. Rep. Party, Miss, formerly. Bus. & Prof. Pos: Radiologist, St. Dominic Hosp, Jackson, Miss, 68- Mil. Serv: Entered as Lt.(jg), Navy, 54, released as Lt, 57; Korean Campaign Ribbon. Mem: Cent. and Miss. State Med. Soc; Am. Med. Asn; Am. Col. Radiology; Miss. State Radiological Soc; Shady Oaks Country Club. Rel: Episcopal. Mailing Add: 303 Hester Dr, Clinton, Miss. 39056.

McCLAIN, EDWARD FERRELL D
b. Martinsburg, W.Va, 8/12/35; s. Russell Kenneth McClain and Faith Reynolds M; m. 3/21/64 to Mary Rosalind Moore; c. Russell Edward Moore and Matthew Leyton. Educ: W.Va. Univ, A.B, 61; South. Ill. Univ, M.A, 63, Ph.D, 69. Polit. & Govt. Pos: Chmn, McCarthy Campaign, Marathon Co, Wis, 68; del, Dem. Nat. Conv, 68. Bus. & Prof. Pos: Ed, Preston Co. News, Terra Alta, W.Va, 58-59; instr. philos, Hanover Col, 64-65; asst. prof. philos, Univ. Wis, Marathon Co. Campus, 65- Mil. Serv: Entered as Pvt, Army, 55, released as Cpl, 57, after serv. in Hq, Pac. Mem: Am. Asn. Univ. Prof; Am. Philos. Asn. Univ. Wis. Center Syst. Teacher of the Year Award, 67. Mailing Add: 408 S. Ninth Ave, Wausau, Wis. 54401.

McCLAIN, ELMO FRANCIS 'MAC' D
Ill. State Rep.
b. Kahoka, Mo, 8/4/17; s. Treo McClain and Marie Wall M; m. 12/26/45 to Margaret McIntire; c. Michael, Kevin, Kathy, Molly, Christopher, Mary and Anne. Educ: Quincy Col, Ill, B.A; West. Univ, M.S. Polit. & Govt. Pos: Ill. State Rep, 64- Bus. & Prof. Pos: Teacher of govt, Ill. High Sch, 48- Mil. Serv: Entered as Pvt, Army, 41, released as M/Sgt, 45, after serv. in ETO. Mem: K. of C; Am. Legion. Rel: Catholic. Mailing Add: 2049 Maine, Quincy, Ill. 62301. (1967)

McCLAIN, JOSEPH ADOLPHUS, JR. R
Fla. State Sen.
b. Ringgold, Ga, 5/1/03; s. Joseph A. McClain, Sr. and Robert Emily Jones M; m. 9/15/26 to Laura Elizabeth Burkett; c. Laura E. (Mrs. L. M. Anderson, Jr); Joseph A, III and David H. Educ: Mercer Univ, A.B, 25, LL.B, 24, LL.D, 41; Yale Univ. J.S.D, 29; Tulane Univ, LL.D, 44; Order of Coif; Pi Kappi Phi; Phi Alpha Delta. Polit. & Govt. Pos: U.S. Dept. Defense spec. counsel to UN Cmt. to Prepare Conv. for Int. Court Criminal Law, Geneva, 51; alternate del, Rep. Nat. Conv, 68; Fla. State Sen, Dist. 24, 67- Bus. & Prof. Pos: Dean law sch, Mercer Univ, 27-33, Univ. Louisville, 34-36, Wash. Univ, 36-42 and Duke Univ, 50-56; v.pres. and gen. counsel, Terminal R.R. Asn, St. Louis, Mo, 42-45; gen. counsel, Wabash R.R. Co, 45-50. Publ: Various articles in law journals. Mem: Am. Bar Asn; Am. Law Inst; Ga, Mo, N.C. and Fla. Bars; U.S. Supreme Court Bar; Mason (32°); Shrine. Rel: Baptist. Legal Res: 125 Baltic Circle, Tampa, Fla. 33606. Mailing Add: 615 Marine Bank Bldg, Tampa, Fla. 33602.

McCLAMROCK, MARGARET ELIZABETH R
Chmn, Grenada Co. Rep. Party, Miss.
b. Grenada, Miss, 1/20/30; d. Francis Allen Kincaid and Mamie Riley K; m. 6/16/48 to Marcus Neil McClamrock; c. Marcus Allen, Debra Frances, Margaret Gwen and Thomas Mike. Educ: Grenada Pub. Sch, 12 years; Miss. State Univ, 2 years. Polit. & Govt. Pos: Chmn, Grenada Co. Rep. Women, Phillips for Gov, Miss, 64 & 68; chmn, Grenada Co. Rep. Party, 67- Mem: Green Thumb Garden Club; Grenada Garden Club; Eastern Star; co-chmn, Grenada Cancer Soc. and residential chmn, Heart Drive. Rel: Presbyterian. Mailing Add: 29 Jones Rd, Grenada, Miss. 38901.

McCLAREN, HOWARD MAX D
Chmn, Milam Co. Dem. Exec. Cmt, Tex.
b. Cameron, Tex, 1/5/18; s. Sherwood Watson McClaren Sr. and Josephine Shafer S; m. 3/16/47 to Margie Lou Pratt; c. Mary Madeline and Melanie Jane. Educ: Baylor Univ, B.A; Symphony Club. Polit. & Govt. Pos: Dem. Elec. Mgr, Marlow Precinct, Tex, 48-50; chmn, Milam Co. Dem. Exec. Cmt, 51-; mem, Dem, Adv. Cmt, Tex, 52-56; mem, Good Govt. Adv. Cmt, 57-; chmn. Milam Co. Del, Tex. Dem. Conv, 60 & 68; mem, Tex. State Dem. Credentials Cmt, 68- Bus. & Prof. Pos: Asst. ed, Daily Midget Newspaper, 50-51, ed, weekly and daily ed, 51-52; prin, Ben Milam Sch, Cameron, 60-65; sch. coordinator, Milam Co, 65-68. Publ: Featured articles, Cameron Herald, weekly newspaper. Mem: Milam Co. Classroom Teachers Asn; Tex. State Teachers Asn.(v.pres, Milam Co. Unit, 58-59); Rotary; Cameron and Cent. Tex. Organ Club; C. of C; K. of P; Farmers Union; Farm Bur; Future Farmers Am; March of Dimes (chmn, Milam Co. Chap, 52-68, drive chmn, 58, 60 & 66); Cancer Drive Crusade (chmn, Milam Co, 68); PTA (life mem, Tex. Cong); Nat. Infantile Paralysis Found. Rel: Baptist. Legal Res: 1302 East 16th St, Cameron, Tex. 76520. Mailing Add: Box 8, Cameron, Tex. 76520.

McCLARY, JAMES DALY R
Treas, Idaho Rep. State Cent. Cmt.
b. Boise, Idaho, 7/19/17; s. Neil Hamacker McClary and Myrtle Daly M; m. 2/2/39 to Mary Jane Munger; c. Pamela and John. Educ: Boise Jr. Col, 34-36; Stanford Univ, B.A, 38. Polit. & Govt. Pos: Chmn, Idaho for Goldwater Cmt, 64; Idaho Coordinator for Goldwater, Rep. Nat. Cmt, 64; alternate del, Idaho State Rep. Conv, 64, Del, 66 & 68; treas, Idaho Rep. State Cent. Cmt, 64-; Presidential Elector, Idaho, 68. Bus. & Prof. Pos: Trustee, Boise State Col, 60-69. Mem: Fel. Am. Soc. Civil Engrs; Assoc. Gen. Contractors Am. (dir, 58- and exec. cmt, 61-); Consult. Constructors Coun. Am; Idaho Permanent Bldg. Fund Adv. Coun.(chmn, 64-); Elks; Hillcrest Country Club (pres, 67); DeMolay (Chevalier). Legion of Honor, DeMolay. Rel: Episcopal. Mailing Add: 4903 Roberts Rd, Boise, Idaho 83705.

McCLARY, MARY JANE R
Chmn, Ada Co. Rep. Cent. Cmt, Idaho
b. North Platte, Nebr, 12/26/15; d. William Horton Munger and Geraldine Bare M; m. 2/2/39 to James Daly McClary; c. Pamela Jane and John William. Educ: Univ. Nebr, B.Sc. in bus. admin, 37; Pi Beta Phi. Polit. & Govt. Pos: Precinct committeeman, Rep. Party, 58-; v.chmn, Ada Co. Rep. Cent. Cmt, Idaho, 62-64, chmn, 64- Mem: Bd. of dir, Boise United Fund; dir-chmn, Salvation Army; dir-chmn, adv. bd, Booth Mem. Hosp; dir, Music Week Bd; dir, Children's Home Soc, Idaho; DAR; Rep. Women's Fedn. Boise Woman of Year, 57. Rel: Episcopal. Mailing Add: 4903 Roberts Rd, Boise, Idaho 83705.

McCLATCHEY, DEVEREAUX FORE D
Ga. State Rep.
b. Marietta, Ga, 6/1/06; s. Devereaux Fore McClatchey and Leone Awtrey M; m. 7/12/30 to Dorothy Methvin; c. Eve L.(Mrs. Saunders) and Devereaux F, Jr. Educ: Emory Univ, B.Ph, 25; LL.B, 29; Phi Alpha Delta; Kappa Sigma. Polit. & Govt. Pos: Past pres, Atlanta Bd. Educ, Ga, 37-57; Ga. State Rep, Dist. 113, Fulton Co, currently. Bus. & Prof. Pos: Partner, Kilpatrick, Cody, Rogers, McClatchey & Regenstein, Attorneys. Mem: Pres, Atlanta Bar Asn, 51-52; past pres, Atlanta Civitan Club. Rel: Presbyterian. Mailing Add: 1045 Hurt Bldg, Atlanta, Ga. 30303.

McCLAUGHRY, JOHN R
Vt. State Rep.
b. Detroit, Mich, 9/15/37; s. Richard Thornton McClaughry and Marian Williams M; single. Educ: Miami Univ, A.B, 58; Columbia Univ, M.S, 60; Univ. Calif, Berkeley, M.A, 63; Phi Beta Kappa; Omicron Delta Kappa; Sigma Pi Sigma; Pi Mu Epsilon; Phi Eta Sigma; Alethenoi; Miami Independent Asn. Polit. & Govt. Pos: Dir. of research, Peterson Senate Campaign, Mich, 64; legis. aide to Sen. Winston Prouty, 65; dir. of research, Percy Senate Campaign, Ill, 66; spec. asst. to Sen. Charles Percy, 67; town moderator, Kirby, Vt, 67-; mem, Caledonia Co. Rep. Cmt, Vt, 67-; spec. asst. during campaign and transition period to Richard M. Nixon, 68; mem, Vt. Housing Cmn, 69; Vt. State Rep, 69- Bus. & Prof. Pos: Pres, McClaughry Assocs, Inc, Wash, D.C, 69- Mil. Serv: Marine Corps Res, 66-, Capt. Legal Res: Kirby, Vt. Mailing Add: P.O. Box 842, Lyndonville, Vt. 05851.

McCLEAREN, HARBER ADDISON R
b. Sango, Tenn, 2/19/21; s. Lloyd Edward McClearen and Annie Russell M; m. 6/28/46 to Margery Hovey; c. James Russell, Robert Frederick and

Anne Addison. Educ: Mid. Tenn. State Univ, 3 years; Univ. Tenn, B.S. in Educ, 42. Polit. & Govt. Pos: Pres, City of Aiken Rep. Club, S.C, 63-67; chmn, Aiken Co. Rep. Party, 66-68; del, Rep. Nat. Conv, 68. Mil. Serv: Entered as Pvt, Army, 42, released as Cpl, 46, after serv. in 979 Signal M.M. Co, ETO, 43-45. Rel: Episcopal. Mailing Add: 122 Dunbarton Circle, Aiken, S.C. 29801.

McCLEAVE, MILDRED ATWOOD R

b. Memphis, Tenn, 12/19/19; d. Carl Rivers Poston (deceased) and Ellen Winston P; m. to Ben Franklin McCleave, Jr; c. Ben F, III, Robert 'Bob' A, William 'Bill' S. and Bruce Poston. Educ: LeMoyne Col, B.A, 41; Denver Univ. Delta Phi Delta; Scribblers Forum; Pan-Am. Club; LeMoyne Players; Alpha Kappa Alpha; Tra-Co-Dram Drama Group. Polit. & Govt. Pos: Dist. Capt, Rep. Party, Denver, Colo, 60-; mem, Colo. State Rep. Cent. Cmt, 64-; mem, Denver Co. Patronage Cmt, 68- Bus. & Prof. Pos: Playground Dir, Memphis, Tenn. and Davenport, Iowa, 40-52; teacher, Memphis Pub. Schs, 41-53; teacher, Denver Pub. Schs, 58- Mem: Nat. and Colo. Educ. Asns; Denver Teachers' Club; Eastern Star; Coterie Literary Group; Jack and Jill of Am; YWCA; Northeast Denver Coordinating Coun; Episcopal Churchwomen; Girl Scouts (counsr). Rel: Episcopal. Mailing Add: 2236 High St, Denver, Colo. 80205.

McCLELLAN, JOHN L. D

U.S. Sen, Ark.

b. Sheridan, Ark, 2/25/96. Polit. & Govt. Pos: Prosecuting attorney, Seventh Judicial Dist, Ark, 26-30; mem, 74th and 75th Cong. from Sixth Cong. Dist; U.S. Sen, Ark, 43- Bus. & Prof. Pos: Lawyer. Mil. Serv: 1st Lt, A.S.S.C, World War I. Legal Res: Camden, Ark. 71701. Mailing Add: c/o Senate Office Building, Washington, D.C. 20510. (1967)

McCLELLAN, JOSEPH MARVIN R

S.C. Rep. State Exec. Cmt.

b. Girard, Ga, 5/23/23; s. Mack Marshall McClellan (deceased) and Emmie Elizabeth Holland (deceased); m. 7/22/49 to Virginia Elizabeth Young; c. Lynn Marie. Educ: Univ. S.C, A.B, Journalism, 46-50; Emory Univ. Law Sch, Atlanta, Ga, 56-58; Am. Univ. Law Sch, Wash. D.C, 62-64, J.D, 64; Phi Alpha Delta. Polit. & Govt. Pos: Pub. rels. dir, Ga. State Attorney Gen. Off, 56-58; admin. asst. to U.S. Rep. Prince H. Preston, Ga, 58-61; spec. asst. to U.S. Secy. Commerce and to Asst. Secy. Commerce, 61-62; spec. asst. pub. rels. and cong. rels, to adminstr, U.S. Bur. Pub. Rds, 62-63; spec. asst, Small Bus. Admin, 63-64; pub. rels. dir, S.C. Rep. Party Campaigns, 66; chmn, Greenwood Co. Rep. Party, S.C, 67-68; committeeman, S.C. Rep. State Exec. Cmt, 68- Bus. & Prof. Pos: Staff correspondent, United Press, Atlanta, Ga, 50-56. Mil. Serv: Entered as A/S, Navy, 43, released as AMM 2/C, 45, after serv. in Naval Air Stas, Fla. Mem: Am, S.C, Greenwood Co. and S.C. State Bar Asns; Sertoma; Am. Legion; Greenwood and S.C. Press Club. Rel: Southern Baptist; choir mem; mem. bd. trustees, Sunday Sch. Dept; supt, S.Main St. Baptist Church. Mailing Add: 117 Cothran Dr, Greenwood, S.C. 29646.

McCLELLAN, JOYCE NaVONNE R

V.Chmn, Walworth Co. Rep. Party, S.Dak.

b. Mobridge, S.Dak, 3/24/36; d. Alfred Bastian and Clara Baer B; m. 7/14/57 to Dr. Herbert Floyd McClellan, Jr; c. Lynnette NaVonne, Marc Herbert and Kymberly Ann. Educ: North. State Col, B.S. in Educ, cum laude, 57; Lutheran Students; Educ. Soc; Music Educ. Soc. Polit. & Govt. Pos: Block worker, Mobridge Rep. Party, S.Dak, 60-, zone leader, 64-; adv, Mobridge TAR, 67; v.chmn, Walworth Co. Rep. Party, 67- Bus. & Prof. Pos: Teacher, Richfield, Minn, 57-60. Mem: Minn, Nat. and Richfield Educ. Asns; Jaycettes (pres, S.Dak. Br, 66-67); Country Club; United Fund Bd.(secy); Thursday Afternoon Bowling League; Arts and Travels Study Club. Outstanding Young Woman Award; Outstanding Young Women of Am. Award; Outstanding Jaycette, twice. Rel: Lutheran. Mailing Add: 814 Third Ave. E, Mobridge, S.Dak. 57601.

McCLELLAN, THOMPSON D

b. West Point, Miss, 8/11/99; single. Educ: Sigma Chi. Polit. & Govt. Pos: Mayor, West Point, Miss, 46-53; former Miss. State Rep. Bus. & Prof. Pos: Attorney. Mem: Mason; Am. Legion; Newcomen Soc. in NA; chmn, bd. trustees, Carnegie Libr. Rel: Methodist. Mailing Add: Box 165, West Point, Miss. 39773. (1967)

McCLELLAND, RALPH, JR. D

b. Stone Mountain, Ga, 10/16/16; s. Ralph McClelland, Sr. and Marie McCurdy M; m. 12/27/41 to Marion Barber; c. James Ralph, III, Walter Barber, Dennis Marion. Educ: Davidson Col, A.B, 37; Atlanta Law Sch, LL.B, 41; Emory Univ. Law Sch, 46; Phi Delta Theta; Delta Theta Phi; Scabbard & Blade. Polit. & Govt. Pos: Ga. State Rep, 57-66. Bus. & Prof. Pos: Attorney. Mil. Serv: U.S. Army Res, World War II, 41-46, Lt. Col, Mil. Intel. Mem: Meninak Nat. Civic Club (v.pres, 60-61); Atlantic Athletic Club (bd. dirs, 57-60); Atlanta Bar Asn. (pres, 57-58); Gr. Atlanta Chap, ROA (pres, 56-57); Elks. Rel: Presbyterian; Former Elder now Deacon. Mailing Add: 2030 Fulton National Bank Bldg, Atlanta, Ga. 30303.

McCLENDON, BURWELL BEEMAN, JR. R

Mem, Miss. State Rep. Cent. Cmt.

b. Jackson, Miss, 12/24/30; s. Burwell Beeman McClendon and Mae Allred M; m. 3/29/53 to Grace Jean Gillespie; c. Marilyn Meek, Burwell Beeman, III and Barry Meek. Educ: Univ. Miss, B.A. with distinction and LL.B, 52; pres, Phi Delta Phi and Arnold Air Soc; Omicron Delta Kappa; Phi Eta Sigma; Pi Sigma Alpha; Pershing Rifles; Kappa Alpha Order. Polit. & Govt. Pos: Asst. dist. attorney, Hinds, Madison and Yazoo, Miss, 55-56; gen. counsel, Miss. Rep. Party, 56-; chmn, Miss. Young Rep. Fedn, 57-61; mem, exec. cmt, Nat. Young Rep. Fedn, 57-67, v.chmn, 63-65, gen. counsel, 65-67; chmn, Hinds Co. Rep. Exec. Cmt, 58-60; del, Rep. Nat. Conv, 60 & 64; chmn, Jackson Rep. Exec. Cmt, 61-64; mem, Miss. State Rep. Cent. Cmt, 62- Mil. Serv: Entered as 2nd Lt, Air Force, 52, released as 1st Lt, 54; Capt, Air Force Res. Mem: Hinds Co, Miss. State and Am. Bar Asns; fel, Miss. Bar Found, 63-; pres, Miss. Jr. Bar, 65-66, exec. cmt, 63-67; pres, Jackson Jr. Bar, 63-64, exec. cmt, 63-65; chmn, Miss. Law Inst, 62; trustee, Legal Aid, Inc, 57; Kiwanis; Kappa Alpha Alumni Asn; C. of C; Ole Miss Alumni Asn. Rel: Presbyterian. Legal Res: 4163 Dogwood Dr, Jackson, Miss. 39211. Mailing Add: 903 Deposit Guaranty Bank Bldg, Jackson, Miss. 39201.

McCLERKIN, HAYES CANDOR D

Speaker, Ark. House of Rep.

b. Texarkana, Ark, 12/16/31; s. Hayes Candor McClerkin and Orlean Maloney M; m. 8/30/58 to Lillian Riggs; c. Martha, Katherine and Lauren Hayes. Educ: Wash. & Lee Univ, B.S, 53; Univ. of Ark, LL.B, 59; Blue Key; Delta Theta Phi; Beta Theta Pi. Polit. & Govt. Pos: Ark. State Rep, Dist. 38, 61-, Speaker, Ark. House of Rep, 69- Mil. Serv: Entered as Seaman Recruit, Navy, 53, released as Lt, 56, after serv. in U.S.S. Chilton APA-38, Atlantic Fleet, 53-56; discharged Lt, Naval Res, 67; Naval Occup. Medal; Nat. Defense Medal. Mem: Miller Co, Ark. and Southwest Ark. Bar Asns; Lion (pres, Texarkana Club, 67-68); dir, Univ. of Ark. Alumni Bd; adv. bd, Salvation Army; Am. Legion; VFW. Rel: Presbyterian. Legal Res: 7 Colonial Dr, Texarkana, Ark. 75501. Mailing Add: 320 State First Nat. Bank Bldg, Texarkana, Ark. 75501.

McCLINTOCK, DARWIN GRAHAM D

Mem, Los Angeles Co. Dem. Cent. Cmt, Calif.

b. N.Y.C, 4/9/17; s. Darwin J. McClintock and Lillian Graham M; m. 2/14/43 to Vera Gull; c. Eve and Susan. Educ: Cooper Union Night Sch. Eng, 38-42; City Col. New York, B.E.E, 51. Polit. & Govt. Pos: Pres, Silver Spur Dem. Club, Palos Verdes, Calif, 61-63; treas, 28th Cong. Dist. Dem. Coun, 64-66, first v.pres, 67-69, second v.pres, 69; mem, Calif. Dem. State Cent. Cmt, 64-66 & 68-; mem, Los Angeles Co. Dem. Cent. Cmt, 64- Bus. & Prof. Pos: Instr. field training, Sperry Gyroscope Co, New York, 50-51; group head, Factory Training Sch, Hughes Aircraft Co, Culver City, Calif, 51-58; head, staff educ, TRW Systs, Redondo Beach, 58-66, head, tech. training, 66- Mil. Serv: Entered as Cpl, Army Signal Corps, 43, released as T/Sgt, 46, after serv. in Southwest Pac. Theater, 44-46. Mem: Nat. Soc. for Programmed Instr; Am. Soc. for Training & Develop; Inst. Elec. & Electronic Engrs; Am. Inst. Aeronaut. & Astronaut; Am. Soc. for Eng. Educ; Am. Vet. Cmt; Am. for Dem. Action. Rel: Unitarian. Mailing Add: 5262 Bluemound Rd, Rolling Hills Estates, Calif. 90274.

McCLINTON, CURTIS REALIOUS D

b. Brages, Okla, 3/20/13; s. Waymon McClinton and Agness Dade M; m. 6/15/37 to Mary Ella McGee; c. Curtis Realious, Jr. Educ: Langston Univ, B.S; Wichita State Univ, grad. study. Polit. & Govt. Pos: Precinct committeeman, Sedgwick Co. Dem. Cmt, Kans, 45-65; Kans. State Rep, 56-60; asst. ward supvr, Dem. Cent. Cmt, 57-60; presidential elector, Electoral Col, 59; mem, City of Wichita Coun. for Commun. Develop, 62-; Kans. State Sen, 65-68; del, Dem. Nat. Conv, 68. Bus. & Prof. Pos: Prin, pub. high sch, 38-40; owner, McClinton Mkt, 43-65 and McClinton Beauty Jobber, 50-66; real estate owner, 50-; mem, Nat. Asn. of Real Estate Brokers, 64-; v.pres. bd. dir, Wichita Area Credit Union, 66- Mem: Noble of the Mystic Shrine, Emith Temple 30, Wichita. Rel: Baptist. Mailing Add: 1201 E. 12th St, Wichita, Kans. 67214.

McCLORY, ROBERT R

U.S. Rep, Ill.

b. Riverside, Ill, 1/31/08; s. Frederick McClory and Catherine Reilly M; m. to Audrey B. Vasey (deceased); c. Beatrice (Mrs. Donald Etienne), Michael R. and Oliver S; m. 3/29/69 to Doris Hibbard. Educ: L'Institut Sillig, Vevey, Switzerland, 25-26 and 28-29; Dartmouth Col, 26-27; Chicago-Kent Col. Law, LL.B, 32; Psi Upsilon; Phi Delta Phi. Polit. & Govt. Pos: Ill. State Rep, 50-52; Ill. State Sen, 52-62; U.S. Rep, 12th Cong. Dist, 63-; participant, Am. Assembly, 64; mem. U.S. Del, Inter-Parliamentary Conf, 64-; participant, Ditchley Conf, London, 66; speaker, Nat. Rep. Cmt. and Nat. Rep. Cong. Cmt. Bus. & Prof. Pos: Sr. mem, McClory, Lonchar, Nordigian & Clark, Attorneys at Law, 51- Mem: Am, Ill. and Lake Co. Bar Asns; Chicago Law Club; Elks; Boy Scout Coun; Navy League; Lake Co. Civic League; C. of C. Rel: Christian Science. Legal Res: 340 Prospect Ave, Lake Bluff, Ill. 60044. Mailing Add: 426 Cannon House Office Bldg, Washington, D.C. 20515.

McCLOSKEY, MAXINE ELAINE D

b. Portland, Ore, 4/26/27; d. Leslie Z. Mugg and Lydia Sarajarvi M; m. 6/17/65 to J. Michael McCloskey; c. Claire Elaine Johnson, Laura Ann Johnson, James Leslie Johnson and Rosemary Ellen Johnson. Educ: Univ. Calif, Berkeley, A.A, 48; Portland State Col, B.S, 62; Reed Col, M.A. in Teaching, 63. Polit. & Govt. Pos: Secy. to U.S. Sen. Richard L. Neuberger, Portland, Ore, 55-56 & fall 59; secretarial asst, Maurine B. Neuberger for U.S. Sen. Campaign Off, Portland, 60; del, Ore. State Dem. Platform Conv, 60, 62 & 64; pres, Jane Jefferson Dem. Women's Club, Multnomah Co, 61-63; exec. secy, Scientists and Engrs. for Johnson and Humphrey, Ore. Br, 64; alternate del, Dem. Nat. Conv. and mem. platform cmt, 64; secy, Conservationists for Cohelan, fall, 68. Bus. & Prof. Pos: Intern teacher, Grant High Sch, Portland, 62-63; instr. sr. soc. studies, St. Helen's Hall, Portland, 63-64; instr. Am. hist, Portland State Col, 64-65; instr. Am. insts, Col. Marin, 65-66; instr, U.S. hist, Merritt Col, Oakland, Calif, 68-69. Publ: Wilderness and the Quality of Life (w. James P. Gilligan), Sierra Club, 69; 'Conservationists Face Their Challengers,' Calif. Garden, 10-11/66. Mem: Ore. Hist. Soc; Am. Hist. Asn; Sierra Club. Rel: Unitarian. Mailing Add: 93 Florada Ave, Piedmont, Calif. 94610.

McCLOSKEY, PAUL NORTON, JR. R

U.S. Rep, Calif.

b. San Bernardino, Calif, 9/29/27; s. Paul Norton McCloskey and Vera McNabb M; m. 8/6/49 to Caroline Wadsworth; c. Nancy, Peter, John and Kathleen. Educ: Stanford Univ, B.A, 50; Stanford Law Sch, LL.D, 53; Phi Delta Phi; Phi Delta Theta. Polit. & Govt. Pos: Dep. dist. attorney, Alameda Co, Calif, 53-54; co-chmn, Young Lawyers for Nixon-Lodge, 60; Palo Alto chmn, Tom Coakley for Attorney Gen, Calif, 62; chmn, Spencer Williams for Attorney Gen, Calif, 66; speaker, George Christopher for Gov. Campaign, 66; chmn, Critical Issues Conf, Calif. Rep. League, 67; U.S. Rep, Calif, 67-, mem, Cmts. on Govt. Opers. and Merchant Marine and Fisheries, mem, Subcmts. on Natural Resources, Merchant Marine, Fisheries and Wildlife Conserv, Conservation, and Maritime Educ. and Training, U.S. House of Rep. Bus. & Prof. Pos: Worked way through col. and law sch. holding various jobs such as laborer, hod carrier, garbage collector, athletic coach, semi-prfnl. baseball player and law librn; mem. law firm, Costello & Johnson, Palo Alto, Calif, 55-56; founding partner, McCloskey, Wilson, Mosher & Martin, Stanford, 56-67; lectr. on legal ethics, Santa Clara and Stanford Law Schs, 64-67; spec. counsel, Town of Woodside's Fight Against the Atomic Energy

Cmn. Power Lines to the Stanford Linear Accelerator, 65-67. Mil. Serv: Seaman 1/C, Navy, 45-47; 2nd Lt. Marine Corps, Korea, 50-52; Lt. Col, Marine Corps Res, currently; Navy Cross; Silver Star; Purple Heart. Publ: United States Constitution. Mem: Pres, Palo Alto Area Bar Asn, 60-61, Stanford Area Youth Plan, 60-66, Conf. of Barristers of State Bar of Calif, 61-62 and Palo Alto Fair Play Coun, 65-67; dir, Family Serv. Asn, 61-65; del, White House Conf. on Civil Rights, 63; Cmt. for Green Foothills, 63-67; Santa Clara Co. Bar Asn.(trustee, 65-67, mem. cmt. on legis. and the jour); counsel, Alpine Little League, 65-67; arbitrator, Am. Arbitration Asn, 66-67; Planning and Conserv. League for Legis. Action, 66-67; Sierra Club, 66-67. Named Young Man of the Year, Palo Alto Jr. C. of C, 61. Rel: Presbyterian. Legal Res: Portola Valley, Calif. Mailing Add: 1511 Longworth Bldg, Washington, D.C. 20515.

McCLOSKEY, ROBERT J.
Dep. Asst. Secy, Bur. of Pub. Affairs, Dept. of State
Legal Res: Pa. Mailing Add: Dept. of State, 2201 C St. N.W, Washington, D.C. 20520.

McCLUHAN, NEIL R. D
Committeeman, Iowa State Dem. Cent. Cmt.
b. Sioux City, Iowa, 5/14/23; s. John A. McCluhan and Adah Kelly M; m. 12/29/45 to Angela C. Camarda; c. Mary, Leah, Barbara, John, Kelly, Richard and Joan. Educ: Univ. Nebr, Lincoln, B.Sc. in Bus. Admin, 47; Creighton Univ, J.D, 50; Sigma Alpha Epsilon; Delta Theta Phi. Polit. & Govt. Pos: Asst. co. attorney, Woodbury Co, Iowa, 59; city attorney, Sioux City, 60-66; chmn, Woodbury Co. Dem. Cent. Cmt, 66-68; committeeman, Iowa State Dem. Cent. Cmt, Sixth Dist, 68- Mil. Serv: Entered as Aviation Cadet, Air Force, 43, released as 1st Lt, 45, after serv. in 448th Bomb Group, ETO, 45; Air Medal; Distinguished Flying Cross. Mem: Sioux City Bar Asn.(treas, 68, secy, 69); Gr. Sioux City Athletic Asn.(pres, 69); K. of C; Am. Legion; VFW; Elks. Rel: Catholic. Legal Res: 810 35th St, Sioux City, Iowa 51104. Mailing Add: 503 Toy National Bank Bldg, Sioux City, Iowa 51101.

McCLUNG, DAVID CHARLES D
Pres, Hawaii State Senate
b. Lansing, Mich, 9/22/26; s. John William McClung (deceased) and Daisy Knight M; m. 10/20/46 to Mildred Kim Tai Fong; c. Sharon Kim Nyuk. Educ: Univ. Mich, B.B.A, M.B.A. and LL.B; Beta Gamma Sigma; Phi Kappa Phi; Alpha Kappa Psi. Polit. & Govt. Pos: Rep, Territory of Hawaii, 58-59, Hawaii State Rep, 59-62; Hawaii State Sen, 67-, pres, Hawaii State Senate, 68-; del, Dem. Nat. Conv, 68; chmn, Dem. Party of Hawaii, 68- Bus. & Prof. Pos: Rep, Local Union, IBEW LU 1260, AFL-CIO, 56-58; exec. secy, Cent. Labor of Coun. of Honolulu, AFL-CIO, 58-60; attorney-at-law, private practice, 60- Mil. Serv: Entered as Seaman, Navy, 43, released as ARM 1/C, 46, after serv. in Pac. Mem: Hawaii Bar Asn; Am. Legion; IBEW, AFL-CIO; Honolulu Press Club; Propeller Club; 1399th Engr. Vet. Club; Int. Platform Asn; John Howard Asn. Legal Res: 3023 Pacific Heights Rd, Honolulu, Hawaii 96813. Mailing Add: Office of the Senate President, The Capitol, Honolulu, Hawaii 96813.

McCLURE, HAROLD MILTON R
Rep. Nat. Committeeman, Mich.
b. Mendon, Ohio, 1/13/21; s. Harold Milton McClure, Sr. and Eva Marie C. Stelzer M; m. 6/24/41 to Geraldine Adella Davis; c. Mary Kathleen (Mrs. James V. Addy), Marie Kristine (Mrs. Ronald L. Christensen), Elizabeth Karin and Robert Kevin. Educ: Ohio State Univ, 39-40; Mich. State Univ, 42; Univ. Ark. and Univ. Mo, 42-45; Phi Delta Theta. Polit. & Govt. Pos: Inaugural co-chmn, Mich. Rep. Party, 62, inaugural chmn, 64; co-chmn, Mich. Rep. State Finance Cmt, 65-67; finance chmn, Tenth Cong. Dist. Rep. Party, 65-67; co-chmn, Romney for Pres. Finance Cmt, 68; alternate del, Rep. Nat. Conv, 68; Rep. Nat. Committeeman, Mich, 68- Bus. & Prof. Pos: Owner and mgr, Alma Pipe & Supply, Mich, 38-39, Alma Drilling Co, 38-39, Allegan Pipe & Supply Co, 38-41 and McClure Drilling Co, 38-60; v.pres, Mercer Oil Co, 48-51, pres, 51-62; pres. and dir, McClure Oil Co, 50-; pres. and dir, Old Dutch Refining Co, Muskegon, 52-54, Wis. Petroleum Terminals Co, Milwaukee, Wis, 52-54, Mich. Tankers, Inc, 52-54 and Rex Petroleum Corp, Alma, Mich, 54-55; dir, N.Am. Drilling Co, Mt. Pleasant, 60-; pres. and dir, McClure, Inc, Alma, 60-; dir, Mich. Nat. Bank, Grand Rapids and Lansing, 64- Mil. Serv: Entered as Cadet, Air Force, 42, released as 2nd Lt, 45, after serv. in East. Flying Training Command Hq, Res, 45-60. Mem: Am. Petroleum Inst; Am. Asn. Oilwell Drilling Contractors; Interstate Oil Compact Cmn; Independent Petroleum Asn. Am; Mich. Oil and Gas Asn; Nat. Petroleum Coun; Nat. Stripper Well Asn; U.S. Exec. Reserves; Am. Gas Asn; trustee, Albion Col; C. of C; Alma Indust. Develop; Lions; Am. Legion; Crystal Downs Country Club; Crystal Lake Yacht Club; Shrine; Gratiot Commun. Hosp. Bd; Gr. Mich. Found; hon. mem, Jaycees; Mason; Mich. Dept. Econ. Expansion; Mich. State Univ. Alumni Asn. Develop. Fund (v.chmn); Otsego Ski Club; Peninsular Club; Pine River Country Club; Recess; West. Mich. Yachting Asn; Boy Scouts (Saginaw Bay Area Coun); Int. Christian Leadership; Mich. Conf. of the Methodist Church; Phi Delta Theta. Off. Emergency Planning Citation; Rep. Nat. Conv. Del. Mem. Rel: Methodist. Legal Res: 468 N. Luce Ave, Alma, Mich. 48801. Mailing Add: P.O. Box 147, Alma, Mich. 48801.

McCLURE, JAMES A. R
U.S. Rep, Idaho
b. Payette, Idaho, 12/27/24; s. W.R. McClure and Marie Freehafer M; m. 9/23/50 to Louise Miller; c. Marilyn, David and Kenneth. Educ: Univ. Idaho Col. of Law, LL.B, 50; Phi Alpha Delta; Sigma Nu. Polit. & Govt. Pos: Prosecuting attorney, Payette Co, Idaho, 51-56; city attorney, Payette, 53-66; Idaho State Sen, Payette Co, 60-67; secy-treas, Little Willow Irrigation Dist, 62-66; mem, Idaho Constitutional Rev. Cmn, 65-; U.S. Rep, Idaho, 67- Mil. Serv: Cadet, Navy, 42-45. Mem: Idaho State Bar Asn; Am. Judicature Soc; Nat. and Idaho Reclamation Asns; Am. Legion; Mason; Elks; Kiwanis. Rel: Methodist. Legal Res: 634 Hughes Dr, Payette, Idaho 83661. Mailing Add: Box 196, Payette, Idaho 83661. (1967)

McCOLGAN, EDWARD ANTHONY D
Mass. State Rep.
b. Florence, Mass, 3/20/32; s. Edward Anthony McColgan and Helen Hosford M; m. 9/17/55 to Mary Theresa Shaughnessy; c. Eileen, Sean, Maureen, Matthew, Bridget, Daniel and Michael. Educ: Springfield Col, B.S, 58; Univ. Conn, M.A, 60, grad. study, 60-64; Phi Alpha Theta. Polit. & Govt. Pos: City coun. Northampton, Mass, 66-68; Mass. State Rep, 69- Bus. & Prof. Pos: Teacher, Smith's Voc. High Sch, Northampton, Mass, 58-60; instr, Hampton Inst, Va, 60-62; asst. prof, Mass. State Col, Westfield, 62-69. Mil. Serv: Entered as Seaman, Navy, 48, released as Gunner's Mate 2, 52, after serv. on U.S.S. Batann, Pac. Theatre, 50-52. Mem: Am. Asn. Univ. Prof; Mass. Legislators Asn. Rel: Catholic. Mailing Add: 218 South St, Northampton, Mass. 01060.

McCOLL, JOHN ANGUS R
Mem, Calif. Rep. State Cent. Cmt.
b. San Diego, Calif, 6/22/28; s. William Frazer McColl and Esther Ann De Vries M; m. 12/31/58 to Sharon Lupton; c. Angus, William, Stuart and Theodore. Educ: Pomona Col, B.A, 50; Stanford Univ, M.B.A, 53; Zeta Psi. Polit. & Govt. Pos: Mem, Calif. Rep. State Cent. Cmt, 64-; chmn. bd. trustees, Rep. Assocs, San Diego, Calif, 69; mem, San Diego Co. Rep. Cent. Cmt, 69. Bus. & Prof. Pos: V.pres, Glore Forgan, William R. Staats, 63-68; resident mgr, Blyth & Co, Inc, 68- Mil. Serv: Entered as 2nd Lt, Army Res, 53, released as 1st Lt, 55, after serv. in Second Engr. Bn. Combat, Second Div, Eighth Army. Mem: Pres, San Diego YMCA, 69. Rel: Episcopal. Legal Res: 5942 Henley Dr, San Diego, Calif. 92120. Mailing Add: 530 B St, San Diego, Calif. 92101.

McCOLLEY, PEARCY L. D
Secy, Riverside Co. Dem. Cent. Cmt, Calif.
b. Nebo, Ill, 4/24/07; d. Noah L. Hamner and Pearl Walls H; m. 9/23/55 to Glenn Forrest McColley. Educ: Calif. Commercial Col, 26-28; Riverside City Col, self improv. courses; Univ. of Calif, Los Angeles. Polit. & Govt. Pos: Dem. precinct worker, Calif, 30-; mem, Calif. Dem. State Cent. Cmt, 62-; co-chmn. of Youth to Elect U.S. Rep. John V. Tunney, 38th Dist, Calif, 64; pres, Moreno Valley Dem. Club, 64-66; chmn, Dem. Campaign Hq, Sunnymead, 64-68; mem. polit. appointments cmt, Riverside Co. Dem. Cent. Cmt, 65-, secy, 65-; clerk, Moreno Valley Unified Sch. Dist. Bd. of Trustees, 69- Bus. & Prof. Pos: Clerk in charge of promotion and sale of war bonds, U.S. Army, Camp Haan, Calif, 42-48; personnel clerk, gen. contractor, Calif, 49-54; secy, Elem. Sch. Unified Sch. Dist, 54- Publ: Articles in Riverside Co. Educ. Off. Employees News Letter 62-64. Mem: Calif. Educ. Off. Employees; Riverside Co. Educ. Employees; life mem. Calif. Cong. of Parents and Teachers Inc; Auxiliary to U.S. Postal Supvr. Recipient of U.S. Treas. Dept. Distinguished Serv. Citation. Rel: Methodist. Legal Res: 24113 Eucalyptus Ave, Sunnymead, Calif. 92388. Mailing Add: P.O. Box 242, Sunnymead, Calif. 92388.

McCOLLOUGH, LUCILLE HANNA D
Mich. State Rep.
b. Huron Co, Mich, 12/30/05; d. William Hanna and Stella Stover H; m. 6/16/25 to Clarence Lindsay McCollough; c. Clarence, Jr, Marilyn (Mrs. Edwards) and Patrick H. Educ: West. Mich. Univ, grad, 23. Polit. & Govt. Pos: City councilman, Dearborn, Mich, 50-53; Mich. State Rep, 55- Bus. & Prof. Pos: Teacher, 23-24; private secy. to personnel mgr, Graham Paige Motors, several years; secy. stenographer, ins. and real estate off. Mem: Aviation Property Owners Asn; McDonald Sch. Mothers Club; Dearborn Fedn. Civic Asns; Women's Soc, Littiefield Blvd. United Presby. Church; Navy Mother's Club; Women of the Moose; Ladies Auxiliary, VFW; N.Am. Benefit Asn; League of Women Voters; YWCA; Women's Polit. Club Dearborn; Dearborn Dem. Club; Nat. Order Women Legislators; Citizens Traffic Safety Coun; Hist. Soc; Nat. Fedn. Bus. & Prfnl. Women. Several awards for perfect attendance in Mich. House Rep, 55-; Sr. Auto Worker Award, United Auto Worker Retired Workers, 64; Citation for Serv, Nat. Retired Teachers Asn. and Am. Asn. Retired Persons, 65; Bus. Woman of the Year, Mich. Fedn. Bus. & Prfnl. Women, 65 & 68; Cert. Appreciation, Vet. World War I, 66; Citation, VFW U.S, Dept. of Mich; Citation, Allied Vet. Coun. Dearborn, 66; Outstanding Health Serv. Award, Mich. State Med. Soc, 69. Rel: Presbyterian. Legal Res: 7517 Kentucky Ave, Dearborn, Mich. 48126. Mailing Add: Michigan State Capitol, House of Representatives, Lansing, Mich. 48901.

McCOLLUM, JOE D. R
b. Emerson, Ark, 6/1/18; s. Issac Newton McCollum and Daizy Paschel M; m. 8/23/44 to Ila Jean Hudson; c. Joe D, Jr. and William David. Educ: Univ. Ark, B.S.A, 39; Univ. Ill, 42; Alpha Gamma Rho; Alpha Zeta. Polit. & Govt. Pos: Precinct committeeman, Rep. Co. Cmt, Idaho, 52, chmn, 60; Rep. State Committeeman, Twin Falls Co, 64-66; secy, State Bd. of Educ, Bd. of Regents, Bd. of Trustees, 67- Bus. & Prof. Pos: Gen. mgr, Simplot Soilbuilders, J.R. Simplot Co, 46-66; dir, Pac. Northwest Fertilizer Asn, 47-66. Mil. Serv: Entered as Pvt, Army, 44, released as 1st Lt, 46, after serv. in Qm. Corps, Adak, Alaskan Command. Mem: C. of C; United Fund; Elks; Boy Scouts; Kiwanis; YMCA. Rel: Baptist. Mailing Add: Route 3, Twin Falls, Idaho 83301.

McCOLOUGH, CHARLES PETER D
b. Halifax, N.S, Can, 8/1/22; s. Reginald Walker McColough and Barbara Theresa Martin M; m. 4/25/53 to Mary Virginia White; c. Peter, Andrew, Virginia, Ian and Robert. Educ: Osgoode Hall Law Sch, Toronto, 45-46; Dalhousie Law Sch, LL.B, 47; Harvard Grad. Sch. Bus. Admin, M.B.A, 49. Polit. & Govt. Pos: Former chmn, Finance Cmt, Monroe Co. Dem. Party, N.Y; mem, Nat. Adv. Coun, Off. Econ. Opportunity, 66-67; mem, United Serv. Orgn, Inc, 66- Bus. & Prof. Pos: V.pres. in charge of sales, LeHigh Navigation Coal Co, Phila, Pa, 51-54; various positions, Xerox Corp, Rochester, N.Y, 54-60, v.pres. in charge of sales, 60-63, exec. v.pres. in charge of opers, 63-66, pres, 66-, chief exec. officer, 68-; dir, Rank Orgn. Ltd, London, Eng, and Fuji Xerox Co. Ltd, Tokyo, Japan. Mil. Serv: Naval Airman 2/C, Royal Navy, 44. Mem: Harvard Club of N.Y.C; City, Country and Genesee Valley Clubs; trustee, Univ. Rochester, Rochester Inst. of Tech, St. John Fisher Col. and Manhattanville Col. Pulse Man of the Year Award, 68. Rel: Roman Catholic. Mailing Add: Xerox Corporation, Stamford, Conn. 06904.

McCOMAS, ELIZABETH MAE VEITCH R
Vice-Chairwoman, N.Mex. Rep. Party
b. Mesilla, N.Mex, 6/17/29; d. Raymond J. Veitch and Erminda J. Fountain V; m. 6/4/52 to Dr. Robert Emmett McComas; c. Robert E, III, Timothy Stephen, Kathryn Elizabeth, Annemarie Minda, Mark Adrian, Rachael Erin and Johanna Magdalen. Educ: Hotel Dieu Sch. Nursing, R.N; St. Louis Univ. Sch. Nursing, 2 years. Polit. & Govt. Pos: Rep. precinct capt, Las Cruces, N.Mex, 61-64;

pres, Rep. Fedn. Woman's Orgn, 64-67; co. chairwoman, N.Mex, Rep. Party, 67-69 and v.chairwoman, 67-; del. and mem. platform cmt, Rep. Nat. Conv, 68. Mem: N.Mex. Nurses Asn.(prog. chmn, 65); bd. mem, Commun. Concert Asn; Elks; Rep. Federated Woman's Orgn; Am. Red Cross. Local Rep. Party awards for achievement. Rel: Catholic. Mailing Add: 1812 Apollo Dr, Las Cruces, N.Mex. 80081.

McCOMB, MARSHALL FRANCIS R
Assoc. Justice, Supreme Court of Calif.
b. Denver, Colo, 5/6/94; s. Harry McComb and Estelle Tradenick M; m. Educ: Stanford Univ, A.B, 17; Yale Univ. Sch. Law, LL.B. cum laude, 19; Delta Chi. Hon. LL.D, Loyola Univ, Calif. and Univ. San Fernando Valley Col. Law. Polit. & Govt. Pos: Judge, Superior Court, Los Angeles, Calif, 27-37; justice, Court of Appeal, Second Dist, Los Angeles, 37-56; assoc. justice, Supreme Court Calif, 56- Mem: Am, San Francisco, Los Angeles and Hollywood Bar Asns; Soc. Friendly Sons St. Patrick Los Angeles (past pres); Delta Theta Phi (past dean, Los Angeles Chap); Delta Chi; Sigma Kappa; U.S. Naval League; charter mem, Los Angeles Am. Legion; Elks (Past Exalted Ruler and Past Chief Justice Grand Forum); Calif. Club; Los Angeles Country Club; Los Angeles Athletic Club; Bohemian Club; Cuyamaca Club; Sutter Club. Legal Res: 215 So. Occidental Blvd, Los Angeles, Calif. 90057. Mailing Add: Room 4042, State Bldg, San Francisco, Calif. 94102.

McCOMB, THOMAS M. R
b. Los Angeles, Calif, 6/15/33; s. Thomas M. McComb and Dorothy Ann Long M; m. 7/12/58 to Nancy Jane Dickinson; c. Jane Ann, Thomas Jackson and Mary Frances. Educ: Univ. Colo, B.A, 55; Univ. Colo. Sch. of Law, LL.B, 57; Phi Epsilon Phi; Delta Upsilon. Polit. & Govt. Pos: Rep. precinct committeeman, Larimer Co, Colo, 63-; alternate del, Rep. Nat. Conv, 68. Bus. & Prof. Pos: Consult. actuary, 60- Mil. Serv: 1st Lt, Army, 59-60, with serv. in Fourth Inf. Div, Sixth Army. Mem: Assoc, Conf. of Actuaries in Pub. Practice; Rotary Int; Elks. Rel: Presbyterian. Legal Res: 1204 Teakwood Dr, Ft. Collins, Colo. 80521. Mailing Add: P.O. Box 48, Ft. Collins, Colo. 80521.

McCOMB, THOMAS V. R
Ind. State Rep.
b. Ft.Wayne, Ind, 10/19/36; s. John Hubert McComb and Margaret Edith Ridley M; m. 2/9/57 to Norma Jean Born; c. Bethany Ann, Kenneth Alan and Susan Marie. Educ: Ind. Univ, B.S, 59; Kappa Delta Rho. Polit. & Govt. Pos: Precinct committeeman, Rep. Party, Ind, 62-64; exec. v.pres, Ft. Wayne Conv. Bur, 63-64; Ind. State Rep, currently. Bus. & Prof. Pos: Owner, McComb Ins. Agency, 61- Mem: Independent Agents Asn. of Ind; Ind. Univ. Alumni Asn; Ind. Soc. of Chicago; Ft. Wayne Press Club; Nat. Soc. of State Legislators; bd. dirs, Lincoln Heritage Trail Found; past pres, Jaycees and Retarded Children's Soc; Mason; Scottish Rite; YMCA-Athletic Club; Columbia Club; Lions; Young Rep. Winner, Distinguished Serv. Award, Jaycees, 63. Rel: Protestant. Legal Res: 628 W. Oakdale Dr, Ft. Wayne, Ind. 46807. Mailing Add: 307 Strauss Bldg, Ft. Wayne, Ind. 46802.

McCOMBE, BOB D
b. Gt. Brit, 1902; married. Polit. & Govt. Pos: Alaska State Rep, 59-60, 63-66. Bus. & Prof. Pos: Lodge operator. Mem: Elks; Mason; Pioneers of Alaska; Yukon Order of Pioneers. Mailing Add: Chicken, Alaska. 99732. (1967)

McCONAUGHY, WALTER PATRICK
U.S. Ambassador to China
b. Montevallo, Ala, 9/11/08; m. to Dorothy Davis; c. Patricia and Mary Drucilla. Educ: Birmingham-South. Col, B.A, 28; Duke Univ. Polit. & Govt. Pos: Career officer, U.S. Dept. of State For. Serv, 30-; first and second secy, Tampico, 30-33, Kobe, Osaka, Taiwan and Nagasaki, 33-41, Peiping, 41-42, La Paz, 42-44 and Rio de Janeiro, 44-47; Nat. War Col, 47-48; consul, Shanghai, 48-50; consul gen, Hong Kong, 50-52; dir, Off. of Chinese Affairs, 52-57; U.S. Ambassador to Burma, 57-59 and Korea, 59-61; Asst. Secy. of State for Far East. Affairs, 61; spec. asst, Off. of Dep. Under Secy. of State for Admin, 61-62; U.S. Ambassador to Pakistan, 62-66 and China, 66- Bus. & Prof. Pos: High sch. teacher, 28-30; instr, Ala. Col, 29. State Dept. Commendable Serv. Award, 49. Mailing Add: American Embassy, Box 2, APO San Francisco 96363.

McCONKEY, GEORGE M, JR. R
b. Ann Arbor, Mich, 12/20/23; s. George M. McConkey and Eleanor Eberle M; m. to Helen Virginia Bolen; c. Virginia Kay and Judith Carolyn (Mrs. Frye). Educ: Colo. A&M, B.S. in Mech. Eng, 52. Polit. & Govt. Pos: Mem. steering cmt, Polk Co. Rep. Party of Fla, 61, chmn, Polk Co. Rep. Exec. Cmt, 62-66. Mil. Serv: Entered as Pvt, Army Air Corps, 43, released as 1st Lt, 45, after serv. in ETO, 44-45; Air Medal with 13 Oak Leaf Clusters; Presidential Unit Citation; North. France Campaign and Ardenne Ribbon. Mem: Am. Soc. Mech. Engrs; Am. Legion; Young Rep; Cosmopolitan. Rel: Protestant. Mailing Add: 18 Fairglen Dr, Titusville, Fla. 32780.

McCONNEL, A.B.
b. Woodstock, Ill; m. to Alice Bennett; c. Mrs. Jane Novak, A.B, Jr, Dr. David, Sarah Smith. Educ: Univ. of Ill. Polit. & Govt. Pos: Ill. State Rep, 68th 73rd Gen. Assemblies; McHenry Co. Bd. of Supvrs, chmn, 51-52; local sch. bd. Bus. & Prof. Pos: Real estate; farmer; Agr. Credit Asn. Mem: Dir, McHenry Co. Farm Bur. Bd; Masons; Shriner; Odd Fellows; Elks; Moose; Grange; C. of C. Rel: Congregational. Mailing Add: McConnell Rd, R.R. 2, Woodstock, Ill. 60098. (1967)

McCONNELL, DAVID MOFFATT D
b. Chester, S.C, 6/12/12; s. Harvey E. McConnell and Elizabeth Moffatt Simpson M; m. 12/31/56 to Ona Altman; c. David M, Jr, Lynn Torbit and Joseph Moore. Educ: Davidson Col, B.S. summa cum laude; Harvard Grad. Sch. Bus. Admin, Rumrill Award Scholar, 33 and 34; Harvard Law Sch; Georgetown Univ. Law Sch. and Grad. Law Sch, LL.M, 40, J.D, 68; Phi Beta Kappa. Polit. & Govt. Pos: Secy. and admin. asst. to U.S. Sen. James F. Byrnes, 36-38; counsel to U.S. Sen. Cmt. on Govt. Reorgn, 37-38; spec. counsel to U.S. Cmnr. Internal Revenue, 38-40; del, Dem. Nat. Conv, 48-68, mem. exec. cmt, Platform Cmt, 64 and mem. Platform Cmt. and Subcmt. on Drafting the Platform, 68; cmnr, N.C. Judicial Coun, 52-56; mem, N.C. Dem. Exec. Cmt. and chmn, N.C. Dem. Cmt. on Credentials and Appeals, 52-60; chmn. and secy, N.C. Bd. of Elec, 58-64; organizer and v.chmn, N.C. Businessmen's Cmt, Lyndon B. Johnson for President, 64; former chmn, Mecklenburg Co. Dem. Exec. Cmt, N.C; cmnr, N.C. Cmn. to Revise the Revenue Structure; U.S. Ambassador and Spec. Adv, UN Econ. and Soc. Coun, 68- Bus. & Prof. Pos: Attorney-at-law, Charlotte, N.C, 46-; v.pres. and gen. counsel, The Belk Dept. Stores; gen. counsel, The Leggett Dept. Stores; v.pres. and counsel, Red Bird Timber Corp; dir. and attorney, The Bank of Charlotte; pres, Providence Realty Holding Co. Mil. Serv: Entered as 1st Lt, Army, 40, released as Col, 46, after serv. in Inf, China and Burma, Chief Legis. Br, War Dept, Gen. Staff, G-1; Legion of Merit, Nat. Chinese Legion of Merit with Oak Leaf Cluster; Order of the Cloud and Banner; Am, European and Asiatic Pac. Campaign Ribbons with Battle Stars. Publ: 'Doctrine of Recoupment in Taxation,' Univ. Va. Law Rev. Mem: S.C, N.C, D.C. and U.S. Supreme Court Bars; Mason; Shrine; Scottish Rite; Am. Legion; 40 et 8; Tax Sect, Am. Bar Asn; Charlotte City Club; Charlotte Country Club; Univ. Club, Wash, D.C; Garden of the Gods Club, Colo. Springs, Colo; Kappa Alpha Order; Newcomen Soc; St. Andrews Soc. Rel: Presbyterian. Mailing Add: 920 Granville Rd, Charlotte, N.C. 28207.

McCONNELL, SAMUEL KERNS R
b. Eddystone, Pa, 4/6/01; s. Samuel K. McConnell and Clara A. Davis M; m. 10/17/25 to Helen C. Marple; c. Shirley. Educ: Univ. Pa, B.S. in econ, 23; Theta Xi. Polit. Pos: Chmn, Montgomery Co. Rep. Party, Pa, 54-57. Govt. Pos: U.S. Rep, Pa, 44-57. Bus. & Prof. Pos: Pres, Woodcock, Moyer, Fricke & French, Inc, 63-, v.pres, 61-63. Mem: Nat. V.Pres, United Cerebral Palsy Research & Educ. Found; nat. exec. dir, United Cerebral Palsy Asns, Inc, 57-61; past master, Franklin Lodge F&AM 135; Union League of Philadelphia; Univ. Club, D.C. Rel: Presbyterian. Mailing Add: 301 Hathaway Lane, Wynnewood, Pa. 19096. (1967)

McCORD, EUGENE WARREN D
b. Weston, W.Va, 2/3/21; s. Earl B. McCord and Golda Mary Groves M; m. to Jeanne Vivian Smith; c. Michael, David, John, Jennifer, Amy, Dan and Susanna. Educ: Kent State Univ, A.B, 43; Col. of City of N.Y, 43; Blue Key; Delta Epsilon. Polit. & Govt. Pos: Alternate del, Dem. Nat. Conv, 68. Bus. & Prof. Pos: Ed, Evening News-Banner, Bluffton, Ind, 46- Mil. Serv: Entered as Pvt, Army, 43, released as Cpl, 46, after serv. in 125th Evacuation Hosp, European Theatre, 45-46. Mem: Hoosier State Press Asn; Nat. Ed. Asn; United Press Int. Newspaper Eds. Asn(pres, 67-68); Kiwanis. Rel: Am. Baptist. Mailing Add: 504 W. Wiley Ave, Bluffton, Ind. 46714.

McCORKEL, FRANKLIN MYERS R
b. Dauphin Co, Pa, 8/10/20; s. Daniel B. McCorkel and Annie Myers M; m. to Jean C. Levens; c. Joel D. and Beth L. Educ: Syracuse Univ, 39-40; Franklin and Marshall Col, B.S. in Econ, 47. Polit. & Govt. Pos: Nominated for Lancaster Co. Controller, Pa; alternate del, Rep. Nat. Conv, 68. Bus. & Prof. Pos: Dist. mgr, New Holland Mfg. Div, 47-50; co-founder, Aggregates Equipment, Inc, 50, v.pres, 50-54, pres, 54- Mil. Serv: Entered as Pvt, Army, 42, released as Capt, 46, after serv. in Third Army, ETO, 44-46; Three Battle Stars. Mem: Trustee, Thaddeus Stevens Trade Sch; chmn, Upper Leacock Twp. Planning Cmn; Am. Legion; VFW; Lions (v.pres, Hamilton Club); Toastmasters (pres, Conestoga Chap); Speakers Bur. of Lancaster; Soc. for Adv. of Mgt.(former v.pres); Lancaster C. of C; F&AM; Harrisburg Consistory; Zembo Temple; Hershey Country Club. Rel: Presbyterian. Mailing Add: Beechdale Farm, R.D. 1, Bird-In-Hand, Pa. 17505.

McCORKLE, ZACK RESHESS D
Chmn, Taylor Co. Dem. Cmt, Ga.
b. Marion Co, Ga, 3/15/01; s. George Reshess McCorkle and Ada Hardridge M; m. 11/20/30 to Mary Cochran; c. Betty (Mrs. Allen) and Barbara (Mrs. Hartley). Polit. & Govt. Pos: Chmn, Taylor Co. Dem. Cmt, Ga, currently; mem, Draft Bd, 45- Rel: Primitive Baptist. Mailing Add: Butler, Ga. 31006. (1967)

McCORMACK, C. G. 'MIKE' D
Wash. State Sen.
b. Basil, Ohio, 12/14/21; s. Henry Arthur McCormack and Nancy Jane Jenkins M; m. 6/21/47 to Margaret Louise Higgins; c. Mark Alan, Steven Arthur and Timothy Arnold. Educ: Univ. Toledo, 39-43; Wash. State Univ, B.S, 48, M.S. in chem, 49; Alpha Chi Sigma; Sigma Chi; Polit. & Govt. Pos: Wash. State Rep, 56-61; Wash. State Sen, 16th Legis. Dist, 61- Bus. & Prof. Pos: Chemist and engr, Gen. Elec. Co, 50-66. Mil. Serv: Entered as Pvt, Army, 43, released as 1st Lt, 46, after serv. in Airborne Inf, European-Am. Publ: Washington State Taxation and Expenditure Patterns, 64. Mem: Am. Chem. Soc; Am. Legion; YMCA; Mason; Shrine. Mailing Add: 1314 Hains, Richland, Wash. 99352.

McCORMACK, EDWARD JOSEPH, JR. D
b. Boston, Mass, 8/29/23; s. Edward J. McCormack and Mary T. Coffey M; m. 10/19/46 to Emily Rupils; c. Edward Joseph, III and John W. Educ: Colby Col, 41-42; U.S. Naval Acad, B.S, 46; Boston Univ, LL.B, cum laude, 52. Polit. & Govt. Pos: Mem, Boston City Coun, Mass, 53-58, pres, 56; attorney gen, Mass, 58-63. Bus. & Prof. Pos: Admitted to Mass. Bar & practiced law, Boston, 52. Mil. Serv: Navy, 46-49. Mem: Chmn, Nat. Adv. Cmt, Cath. Coun. on Civil Liberties; Nat. Exec, Nat. Conf. of Christians and Jews. Rel: Catholic. Mailing Add: 19 Congress St, Boston, Mass. 02109.

McCORMACK, JOHN W. D
Speaker, U.S. House of Rep.
b. South Boston, Mass; m. to Harriet Joyce. Educ: Boston Pub. Schs. Hon. LL.D, Boston Univ, Holy Cross Col, Boston Col, Villanova Col, Tufts Col, Providence Col, Stonehill Col, Georgetown Univ, Cath. Univ. of Am, Suffolk Univ. and Staley Col. Polit. & Govt. Pos: Mem, Constitutional Conv, 17-18; Mass. State Rep, 20-22; Mass. State Sen, 23-26, Dem. Leader, Mass. State Senate, 24-26; U.S. Rep, Mass, 28-, Dem. Whip, U.S. House of Rep, 47-48 & 53-54, Majority Leader, 49-52 & 55-61, Speaker, 62- Mil. Serv: World War I. Mem: Order of Malta; K. of C. Peace Medal, Third Order of St. Francis; Knight Comdr, Order of St. Gregory the Great, with Star; Comdr, Legion of Honor, Repub. of Philippines; Bellarmine Medal, 57; Cardinal Gibbons Medal, 63; Comdr, Order of Duarte Sanches Y Mella, Dominican Repub; Grand Officer, Order Merito Della Republica, Italy; Titular De La

Cruz De Aloy Alfaro, Panama; Grand Comdr, Royal Order of Phoenix, with Star, Greece. Rel: Catholic. Legal Res: Boston, Mass. Mailing Add: H 204, U.S. House of Representatives, Washington, D.C. 20515. (1967)

McCORMICK, C. L. R
Ill. State Rep.
b. McCormick, Ill, 12/1/19; m. to Erma Lee Turner; c. Mike and Chris. Educ: Vienna Elem. and High Sch, Ill. Polit. & Govt. Pos: Former Rep. committeeman, Precinct One, Vienna, Ill; pres, Young Rep. of Johnson Co; co. clerk, Johnson Co, 50-58; Ill. State Rep, currently; chmn, Johnson Co. Rep. Party, currently; mem, Ill. Rep. State Cent. Cmt, currently. Bus. & Prof. Pos: Formerly restaurant and taxi bus; real estate; farming. Mil. Serv: Army, World War II. Mem: VFW; Am. Legion. Rel: Baptist. Mailing Add: Vienna, Ill. 62995. (1967)

McCORMICK, CHARLES F. D
Chmn, Franklin Co. Dem. Cmt, N.Y.
b. Chateaugay, N.Y, 4/5/06; s. John F. McCormick and Mary McCallum M; m. 8/14/50 to Isabel McCollester; c. Joan, Ann, Teresa, Michael and Kathleen. Educ: Chateaugay High Sch. and Chateaugay Teacher's Class; Clarkson Col. Tech. Polit. & Govt. Pos: Town supvr, Chateaugay, N.Y, 50-63; chmn, Franklin Co. Dem. Cmt, 63-; alternate del, Dem. Nat. Conv, 68. Bus. & Prof. Pos: Owner and operator, Dairy Farm, 42-66. Mem: K. of C; Elks. Rel: Catholic. Mailing Add: Chateaugay, N.Y. 12920.

McCORMICK, HAROLD CHARLES D
Iowa State Rep.
b. Manchester, Iowa, 10/10/10; s. Charles McCormick and Mary Powers M; m. 2/4/67 to Betty A. Primus; c. John P. and Julie (Mrs. O'Brien). Educ: Loras Col, 3 years. Polit. & Govt. Pos: Mem, city coun, Manchester, Iowa, 55-59; mem, city planning & zoning cmt, 63-68; Iowa State Rep, Delaware Co, 69- Mil. Serv: Army, 61, Pvt, Hq. and Hq. Co. Reception Center, Camp Dodge, Iowa; Good Conduct Medal. Mem: Am. Legion; K. of C; Lions; Co. Hist. Soc; Farm Bur; Fish & Game Club; C. of C. Rel: Roman Catholic. Mailing Add: 504 E. Butler St, Manchester, Iowa 52057.

McCORMICK, HAROLD L. R
Colo. State Rep.
b. Florence, Colo, 5/16/18; s. B.P. McCormick and Anna Hoffman M; m. 1/8/41 to Jeanne R. Rolfes; c. Brian, Carole and Ellen. Educ: Univ. Denver, B.S.C, 40; Omicron Delta Kappa; Beta Theta Pi. Polit. & Govt. Pos: Mem, Co. Rep. Cent. Cmt, 58; Colo. State Rep, Fremont, Custer and Saguache Co, 60- Mil. Serv: Entered as Pvt, Army Air Corps, 42, released as Capt, 46, after serv. in Second Air Div, ETO, 43-45; Col, Res, 45-68; Presidential Unit Citation; ETO Ribbon; Six Battle Stars. Mem: Canon City C. of C.(pres, 59); Mason; Am. Legion; VFW. Rel: Presbyterian. Mailing Add: 927 Greenwood, Canon City, Colo. 81212.

McCORMICK, HOPE R
Rep. Nat. Committeewoman, Ill.
b. New York, 7/9/19; d. Alexander Taylor Baldwin and Loise Bisbee B; m. 6/26/40 to Brooks McCormick; c. Martha (Mrs. William O. Hunt, Jr), Brooks, Jr, Mark and Abby. Educ: Ethel Walker Sch, Simsbury, Conn. Polit. & Govt. Pos: Ill. State Rep, 65-67; del, Rep. Nat. Conv, 68; Rep. nat. committeewoman, Ill, 68- Rel: Episcopal. Legal Res: St. James Farm, Butterfield and Winfield Rds, Warrenville, Ill. 60555. Mailing Add: 1530 N. State Pkwy, Chicago, Ill. 60610.

McCORMICK, JOHN E. D
Wis. State Assemblyman
b. Milwaukee, Wis, 5/20/24. Educ: Marquette Univ. Law Sch, LL.B, 51. Polit. & Govt. Pos: Wis. State Assemblyman, 60-; mem, 17th Ward Dem. Unit. Bus. & Prof. Pos: Attorney-at-law. Mil. Serv: Army Air Corps, 2½ years. Mem: Am. Legion; Bay View, Inc; Interorganization Coun, Bar Asn; Holy Name Soc; K. of C. Mailing Add: 2954 S. Wentworth Ave, Milwaukee, Wis. 53207. (1967)

McCORMICK, KEITH C. R
Ind. State Sen.
Polit. & Govt. Pos: Ind. State Sen, 63-; Boone Co. Rep. Finance chmn; del, Rep. State Conv. Bus. & Prof. Pos: Ins, real estate broker; chmn, Ind. Real Estate Cmn; v.pres, Ind. Real Estate Asn. Mil. Serv: Air Force. Mem: Local, state, nat. Real Estate Asns; Mason; Scottish Rite; Shrine; Elks; Am. Legion; Kiwanis; Lebanon C. of C; Lebanon Carnegie Libr. Bd. Rel: Presbyterian. Mailing Add: 1018 N. East St, Lebanon, Ind. 46052.

McCORMICK, ROBERT JOHN D
Controller, Cambria Co, Pa.
b. Barnesboro, Pa, 9/7/23; s. Robert John McCormick, Sr. (deceased) and Mary Mildred Sharbaugh M.(deceased); m. 4/28/56 to Anna Marie Byrnes; c. Michael Joseph, Marianne and Karen Marie. Educ: Univ. Pittsburgh, B.S. in bus. admin, 47. Polit. & Govt. Pos: Sch. dir, North. Cambria Joint schs. and Barnesboro Sch. Dist, Pa, 54-60; sealer, Weights and Measures, 58-64; mem, Exec. Cmt, Barnesboro Dem. Club, 58-65, pres, 61; Civil Defense dir, Cambria Co, 60-64; pres, Pa. Asn. Weights and Measure Inspectors, 63-64; del, Dem. Nat. Conv, 64; controller, Cambria Co, 64-; mem, Policy Cmt, Cambria Co. Dem. Cmt, currently; pres, Pa. State Asn. of Co. Controllers, 68-69. Bus. & Prof. Pos: Supt, McCormick Coal Co, 48-59. Mil. Serv: Entered as A/S, Navy, 43, released as Lt.(jg), Naval Res, 46, after serv. in Amphibious Force LCI(L) 814, Am-Asiatic-Pac. Theater, 44-46; Am-Asiatic-Pac. Theater Ribbon with 2 stars; Japan Occupation Forces Medal. Mem: Am. Legion; VFW; Lions (pres, Barnesboro Club, 68-69); Elks; Eagles; MossBarn Hunting and Fishing Club. PIAA Football Official. Rel: Catholic. Mailing Add: 1508 Park Ave, Barnesboro, Penn. 15714.

McCORMICK, ROBERT L. L. R
Dep. Asst. Secy. for Water Qual. and Research, Dept. of Interior
b. Wilkes-Barre, Pa, 12/24/17; s. Frank T. McCormick and Rose Marie Lynch M; m. 11/11/48 to Dorothy Mary Bragdon; c. Robert, Jr, Josephine, Peter, John Stewart, Dorothy Brigid and Anthony. Educ: Yale Univ, B.A, 40; Harvard Bus. Col; Fence Club. Polit. & Govt. Pos: Asst. to chmn, Cmn. on Orgn. of the Fed. Govt, 47-49; dir. of research, Rep. Nat. Cmt, 65-69; staff coordinator, Rep. Coord. Cmt, 65-69; Dep. Asst. Secy. for Water Qual. and Research, Dept. of Interior, 69- Bus. & Prof. Pos: Pres, McCormick Assocs, 55-65. Mil. Serv: Entered as Ens, Naval Res, released as Lt, after serv. in Off. of Secy, Mil. Govt. for Germany; several awards. One of Ten Outstanding Young Men of Year, U.S. Jr. Chamber of Commerce. Rel: Roman Catholic. Mailing Add: 7722 Georgetown Pike, McLean, Va. 22101.

McCORMICK, TABOT GREEN (T. G.) D
b. Forest, Miss, 6/6/99; married. Educ: Scott Cath. Alumni, Miss. State Univ. Polit. & Govt. Pos: Miss. State Sen, 60-68. Bus. & Prof. Pos: Wholesale automotive parts; farming. Mem: Mason; Am. Legion; S.E. Lackey Hosp. Corp. Rel: Baptist. Mailing Add: 526 Hillsboro St, Forest, Miss. 39074. (1967)

McCORMICK, W. L. 'BILL' D
b. Waukon, Iowa, 1925; m. to Jeri; c. Two daughters. Educ: High Sch. grad. Polit. & Govt. Pos: Former Wash. State Rep. Bus. & Prof. Pos: Indust. Rel. Consult, Columbia Lighting. Mil. Serv: Air Force, World War II. Mem: Eagles; Int. Footprint Asn; Am. Legion; Grange. Mailing Add: W. 3909 Lyons, Spokane, Wash. 99208. (1967)

McCORMICK, WILLIAM E. D
Ill. Dem. Cent. Cmt.
b. Ursa, Ill, 5/17/12; s. John Thomas McCormick and Clora Luella Murrah M; m. 6/6/52 to Barbara Louise Cutforth; c. Brent Alan, Karen Gail and Nancy Lynn. Educ: Western Univ, B.S, 38, M.S, 51; Univ. of Colo, summers, 52-55. Polit. & Govt. Pos: Dem. precinct committeeman, Ill, 55-; committeeman, Ill. Dem. Cent. Cmt, 60-; city councilman, Crystal Lake, 60- Bus. & Prof. Pos: Prin, grade sch, Ill, 34-38, high sch, 38-41; Inspector, Powder and High Explosives, Iowa Ordnance, 41-43; sci. teacher, 46- Mil. Serv: Entered as A/S, Navy, 43, released as 2/C ARTC, 45, after serv. in Electronic Experimental Unit, Patuxant River, Md, 44-45. Mem: Ill. and Nat. Educ. Asns; Ill. Chem.Teacher's Asn; Am. Legion; Moose; Farm Bur; Mason. Rel: Protestant. Mailing Add: 168 Peterson Pkwy, Crystal Lake, Ill. 60014.

McCORQUODALE, JOSEPH CHARLES, JR. D
Ala. State Rep.
b. Salitpa, Ala, 12/20/20; s. Joseph Charles McCorquodale and Winnie Lee Griffin; m. 1/17/42 to Mary E. McCrary; c. Joseph Charles III and Gaines Cowan. Educ: Marian Mil. Inst, 1 year; Univ. of Ala, 2 years; Lambda Chi Alpha. Polit. & Govt. Pos: Mem, Bd. of Trustees, Jackson Schs, Ala, 54-58; Ala. State Rep, 33rd Dist, 59- Bus. & Prof. Pos: Automobile dealer, Gen. Motors, Jackson, Ala, 50-53; owner, McCorquodale Agency Ins. and gen. agent for Piedmont Life of Atlanta, 63-; partner, Overstreet and McCorquodale Timber Dealers, 66- Mil. Serv: Entered as Pvt, Army Signal Corps, 42, released as 1st Lt, 46, after serv. in Air Corps 20th Bomb Group, Tinian Island, 43-46; Air Medal with 5 Oak Leaf Clusters. Mem: Life Underwriters of Ala; bd. of dirs, Clarke Washington Industs; trustee, Vanity Fair Found; State Bd. of Ment. Health; dir, Ala. Wild Life Fedn; VFW; Am. Legion; C. of C; Optimist. Gov. Award for Outstanding Legislator in Conserv, 62. Rel: Methodist; Mem, Bd. of Stewards, First Methodist of Jackson. Legal Res: Coffeeville Rd, Jackson, Ala. 36545. Mailing Add: P.O. Box 535, Jackson, Ala. 36545.

McCORT, WILLIAM R
b. New York, N.Y, 7/24/22; s. William McCort and Florence Station M; m. 9/23/60 to Doris May Rickard; c. Cheryl Lynn. Educ: Millville High Sch, N.J. Polit. & Govt. Pos: Former co. chmn, Rep. Party. Mil. Serv: Entered as Pvt, Army, 42, released as Cpl, 46, after serv. in Signal Corps, Pac. Mem: Soc. of Sales Exec; Univ. of Miami Leasing & Financing Soc. Mailing Add: 506 E. Ann St, Punta Gorda, Fla. 33950. (1967)

McCOURT, E. HANSFORD D
W.Va. State Sen.
b. Webster Springs, W.Va, 4/21/09; s. William L. McCourt and Maggie J. Lough M; m. 10/19/36 to Georgie Kidd; c. Maggie Jane and William Hansford. Educ: W.Va. Wesleyan Col, B.S; Alpha Sigma Phi. Polit. & Govt. Pos: W.Va. State Del, 53-55; W.Va. State Sen, 56- Bus. & Prof. Pos: Farmer. Mil. Serv: Army, 2nd Lt, 42-45. Mem: Mason; Shrine; Moose; Lions; Webster Co. Folklore Soc; Am. Legion. Conservationist for the Year, 66. Rel: Methodist. Mailing Add: Webster Springs, W.Va. 26288.

McCOURT, FRANK J. D
Md. State Sen.
b. New London, Conn, 9/17/35; s. Harry Frederick McCourt and Betty Lovett M; married. Educ: Fork Union Mil. Acad; Shepherd Col, W.Va; Univ. Baltimore, LL.B, 58. Polit. & Govt. Pos: Md. State Del, 63-66; Md. State Sen, 66-, mem, Econ. Affairs Cmt, Md. State Senate. Mem: Md. Bar Asn; pres, Center City Dem. and Young Dem. Club. Legal Res: Preston Apts, Baltimore, Md. 21202. Mailing Add: 1208 Munsey Blvd, Baltimore, Md. 21202.

McCOWEN, DEXTER R
b. 1938. Educ: East. Ky. State Col. Polit. & Govt. Pos: Ky. State Rep, 64-69; 2nd v.chmn, State Fedn. Young Rep; mem, State Bd. for Retarded Children. Bus. & Prof. Pos: Farmer. Mil. Serv: Army. Mem: Mason; Scottish Rite; Laurel Co. Found. for Mental Retardation. Mailing Add: East Bernstadt, Ky. 40729. (1967)

McCOWN, DAVID HENRY D
Chmn, Lawrence Co. Dem. Exec. Cmt, Ohio
b. Ironton, Ohio, 8/31/33; s. Henry A. McCown and Adrienne Tucker M; m. 8/8/55 to JoAnn Markins; c. Kevin and Derek. Educ: Miami Univ, B.S, 55; Univ. Mich. Law Sch, J.D, 60. Polit. & Govt. Pos: City solicitor, Ironton, Ohio, 61-67; chmn, Lawrence Co. Dem. Exec. Cmt, 63- Bus. & Prof. Pos: Attorney, Liberty Federal S & L, 64-; attorney, Crowe, McCown & McCown, 66- Mil. Serv: Entered as Ens, Navy, 55, released as Lt.(jg), 57, after serv. in Submarine Base, New London, Conn, 55-57. Mem: Am. and Ohio Bar Asns; Am. Trial Lawyers Asn; Jaycees; Elks. Rel: Presbyterian. Mailing Add: 1014 Pleasant St, Ironton, Ohio 45638.

McCOY, HOWARD WAYNE R
Mem, State Exec. Cmt, Rep. Party, Miss.
b. Vicksburg, Miss, 5/31/23; s. Howard Wayne McCoy and Gertrude Lassiter

M; m. 12/17/55 to Marcie Kellan; c. Howard Wayne, III. Educ: Univ. South. Calif, 46-47; Sigma Phi Epsilon. Polit. & Govt. Pos: Chmn, Warren Co. Rep. Party, Miss, 68-; mem, State Exec. Cmt, Miss. Rep. Party, 68- Bus. & Prof. Pos: Claims supvr, Ins. Co. of N.Am, Los Angeles, 63-67; securities and property mgr. Mil. Serv: Entered as Pvt, Air Nat. Guard, 43, released as M/Sgt, 61 after active serv. with 146th Air Transport Wing, ETO, 44-45; Air Force Commendation Medal; ETO Medal with 3 Stars. Mem: Optimist Int. Rel: Episcopal. Mailing Add: 720 Ft. Hill Dr, Vicksburg, Miss. 39180.

McCOY, RUFUS V, JR. R
Chmn, Dickenson Co. Rep. Party, Va.
b. Va, 10/25/30; s. Rufus V. McCoy and Dema Lou Alexandria M; m. 6/1/53 to Rose Mary Skeen; c. James Rufus 'Jamie.' Educ: Lincoln Mem. Univ, 47-51; Univ. of Va. Exten. Div, 54-55. Polit. & Govt. Pos: Chmn, Young Rep. Club, Va, 54-56 & 56-58; chmn, Dickenson Co. Rep. Party, 58-63 & 66- Bus. & Prof. Pos: Agent, Nationwide Ins, 60-; pres. and gen. mgr, Clintwood Chrysler-Plymouth Inc, 65- Mil. Serv: Entered as Pvt, Army, 51, released as Cpl, 53, after serv. in Korea, 52-53; President Truman and President Rhee Citations; 3 Battle Stars. Mem: VFW; Kiwanis; Bus. & Prfnl. Asn; United Commercial Travelers; Dickenson C. of C. Rel: Baptist. Mailing Add: Box 734, Clintwood, Va. 24228. (1967)

McCOY, RUFUS V, SR. R
Va. State Del.
b. Dickerson Co, Va, 10/29/01; m. to Dema L. Alexandria. Educ: Radford Teachers Col. Polit. & Govt. Pos: Mem. bd. supvr, Dickerson Co, 48-52; Va. State Del, 66- Bus. & Prof. Pos: Retired teacher. Mem: U.T.C; Local UMWA pres, 39-51. Rel: Baptist. Mailing Add: Route 1, Nora, Va. 24272.

McCOY, WILLIAM, JR. D
b. Franklin, W.Va, 5/14/21; s. William McCoy and Grace Hedrick M; m. 7/17/63 to Harriet Virginia Wright. Educ: Wash. and Lee Univ, A.B; W.Va. Univ, LL.B; Pi Kappa Alpha; Phi Alpha Delta. Polit. & Govt. Pos: W.Va. State Del, 52-66. Bus. & Prof. Pos: Lawyer; dir. Pendleton Co. Bank; publisher, Pendleton Times, W.Va. Mil. Serv: Vet. of World War II. Mem: S. Branch Valley and W.Va. Bar Asns; Lions; Am. Legion. Rel: Presbyterian. Mailing Add: Franklin, W.Va. 26807.

McCOY, WILLIAM, JR. D
Chmn, Multnomah Co. Dem. Cent. Cmt, Ore.
b. Indianola, Miss, 6/11/21; s. William McCoy and Lucy Lipscomb M; m. 2/28/51 to Gladys Sims; c. Krista, William, Paul, Mary, Cecilia, Peter and Martha. Educ: Univ. of Portland, B.A, 50. Polit. & Govt. Pos: Chmn, Multnomah Co. Dem. Cent. Cmt, Ore, 68-; alternate del, Dem. Nat. Conv, 68. Mil. Serv: Entered as Recruit, Navy, 42, released as Qm 3/C, 46 after serv. in N. Pac. Area. Rel: Catholic. Mailing Add: 6650 N. Amherst St, Portland, Ore. 97203.

McCRACKEN, JAMES ROY D
Ga. State Rep.
b. Avera, Ga, 12/26/03; s. John Wm. McCracken and Sabrina Rivers M; m. 3/27/37 to Rosa Kate Kirbo; c. Emily Jane (Mrs. Benjamin Franklin Wren, III) and William Robt; grandchildren: Benjamin Franklin Wren, IV. Educ: Mercer Univ, LL.B, 25. Polit. & Govt. Pos: Mayor, Avera, Ga, 33-34; chmn, Avera Sch. Bd, 33-56; Ga. State Rep, 37- Bus. & Prof. Pos: Attorney, began practice Louisville, 31; Mem, Harris, Chance & McCracken, Augusta. Mem: Mason; Elk; Shrine; WOW. Rel: Baptist. Mailing Add: 312 Broad St, Avera, Ga. 30803. (1967)

McCRACKEN, PAUL WINSTON R
Chmn, Coun. of Econ. Adv.
b. Richland, Iowa, 12/29/15; s. Sumner McCracken and Mary Coffin M; m. 5/27/42 to Emily Ruth Siler; c. Linda Jo and Paula Jeanne. Educ: William Penn Col, A.B; Harvard Univ, M.A. and Ph.D. in Econ. Hon. L.H.D, William Penn Col; LL.D, Albion Col. Polit. & Govt. Pos: Economist, U.S. Dept. of Commerce, 42-43; financial economist and dir. research, Fed. Reserve Bank of Minneapolis, Minn, 43-48; mem, Coun. of Econ. Adv, 56-59, chmn, 69-; mem, Task Force Reporting to President Kennedy on the Domestic Econ. Situation and the Balance of Payments, 61; mem, President's Cmn. on Budget Concepts, 67; delivered lect. and held conf. in West. Europe for U.S. Dept. State, Apr. and May 68. Bus. & Prof. Pos: Eng. teacher, Found. Sch, Berea Col, 37-40; assoc. prof, Sch. of Bus. Admin, Univ. Mich. 48-50, prof, Grad. Sch. of Bus. Admin, 50-65, Edmund Ezra Day Prof. bus. admin, 66-; lectr, Japan, summer 59, India, Dec. 63 and the Netherlands, Jan. 67; lectr, Seminar in Am. Studies, Doshisha Univ. and Univ. Kyoto, summer 65. Publ: 'Public Debt and Economic Stability,' Yale Rev, 6/51; 'The Role of The Council of Economic Advisers in Government,' Proc. Conf. on the Econ. Outlook, Univ. Mich, 59; 'Unemployment in an Expanding Economy—The Long View,' Mich. Bus. Rev, 7/64; plus others. Mem: Am. Econ. Asn; Am. Finance Asn; Am. Statist. Asn; Royal Econ. Soc; Cosmos Club, Wash, D.C; Harvard Club, N.Y. Civic Award, Alpha Kappa Psi, Miami Univ, 57; Distinguished Faculty Award, Univ. Mich, 59; Award of Merit, Alumni Asn, William Penn Col, 61. Rel: Presbyterian. Legal Res: 2564 Hawthorn St, Ann Arbor, Mich. 48104. Mailing Add: 5500 Prospect Place, Chevy Chase, Md. 20015.

McCRADY, BOB D
Chmn, Ellis Co. Dem. Party, Tex.
b. Waxahachie, Tex, 3/8/05; s. William James McCrady and Willie Ann M; m. 6/10/30 to Lois Goodlee; c. Yvonne (Mrs. Alcorn) and Charles. Educ: Weatherford Col, A.A, 26; Univ. Colo, 27; Univ. Ark, B.S, 32; South. Methodist Univ, M.A, 38; Psi Chi. Polit. & Govt. Pos: Supt. of schs, Red Oak Pub. Schs, Tex, 28-38 and 58-66; co. supt, Ellis Co. Pub. Schs, 38-47; chmn, Ellis Co. Dem. Party, 48- Bus. & Prof. Pos: Publisher, Waxahachie Daily Light, Tex, 47-49; dir. of instr, Waxahachie Pub. Schs, 49-54; rancher, 54-57. Mem: Tex. State Teachers Asn; Nat. Asn. Sch. Adminstr; Lions. Rel: Presbyterian. Mailing Add: Highway 35, P.O. Box 277, Waxahachie, Tex. 75165.

McCRAY, BILLY QUINCY D
Kans. State Rep.
b. Geary, Okla, 10/29/27; s. John J. McCray and Ivory B. Jessie M; m. 10/12/51 to Wyvette M. Williams; c. Frankie Leen, Anthony B, Melodie C. and Kent E. Educ: Langston Univ, 2 years; Colo. State Univ, 1 year. Polit. & Govt. Pos: Cmnr, Wichita Human Rels. Cmn, Kans, 61-64; mem, Mayors Adv. Cmt, Wichita, 64-65; Kans. State Rep, 67- Bus. & Prof. Pos: Owner, McCray's Enterprises, 67- Mil. Serv: Entered as Basic Airman, Air Force, 47, released as Airman 4/C, 51, after serv. in 332nd Fighter Wing Training Command, Nellis Air Force Base, Las Vegas, Nev, 49-51. Publ: 'A Tree By the Hiway' (poem), Bards & Poetry, 56. Mem: Langston Univ. Alumni Club of Wichita, Kans; Mason. Rel: African Methodist Episcopal. Mailing Add: 1532 N. Ash. St, Wichita, Kans. 67214.

McCREADY, CONNIE R
Ore. State Rep.
b. Pendleton, Ore, 8/21/21; d. Ed. F. Averill; m. 12/31/45 to Albert L. McCready; c. Molly, Martha and Nancy. Educ: Univ. Ore, degree in journalism. Polit. & Govt. Pos: Former Rep. precinct committeewoman; Ore. State Rep, 67-; alternate del, Rep. Nat. Conv, 68. Bus. & Prof. Pos: Former reporter, Coos Bay Times and The Oregonian; former ed, Sunday Oregonian's Home and Garden Mag. Publ: Co-auth with Peg Bracken, I Hate to Cook Book. Mem: Ore. Real Estate Bd. Mailing Add: 2407 N.E. 27th Ave, Portland, Ore. 97212. (1967)

McCREADY, ELLEN HAUSRATH R
Committeewoman, Tex. State Rep. Party
b. Cleveland, Ohio, 1/9/21; d. William Hausrath and Lucy Bandelow H; m. 6/9/45 to Robert Richard McCready; c. Karen Marie and Robert Mark. Educ: Kent State Univ, B.S. in Educ, 43; Alpha Psi Omega; Beta Gamma. Polit. & Govt. Pos: Alternate del, Rep. Nat. Conv, 68, committeewoman, Tex. State Rep. Party, 68- Rel: Lutheran. Mailing Add: 809 Wood River Rd, Dallas, Tex. 75232.

McCREARY, GERALD FREDRIC R
Chmn, Lake Co. Rep. Cent. Cmt, Ohio
b. Bedford, Pa, 10/29/14; s. Frank E. McCreary and Ada Miller M; m. 2/22/41 to Dorothy Ann Sanzobrino; c. Timothy Sean, Kevin Fitzgerald, Terrence Sean and Maureen Ann. Educ: Ohio Univ, 32-33. Polit. & Govt. Pos: Mem, Lake Co. Rep. Cent. Cmt, Ohio, 50, chmn, 64-; chmn, Willoughby Zoning Appeals Bd, 51-53; mem, Willoughby Planning Cmn, 54-55; councilman, Willoughby, 54-55; mem. and v.chmn, Lake Co. Planning Cmn, 56-64; mem, Lake Co. Rep. Exec. Cmt, 56- Bus. & Prof. Pos: Pres. and sales mgr, Hyke Rubber Co, 48-69; pres, Trump Plastics, Inc, 50-65. Mil. Serv: Entered as Pvt, Army, 41, released as Capt, 48, after serv. in 265th Engr. Combat Bn, Third Army, ETO, 44-45; Capt, Army Res, 45-52; Bronze Star; Am. Defense Ribbon; Europe-Africa-Middle East Theater Ribbon with Battle Stars for Rhineland and Cent. Europe Campaigns; Army of Occup. Ribbon. Mem: C. of C.(past pres, Willoughby Chap); DAV; Cleveland Chap, ROA. Rel: Roman Catholic. Mailing Add: 4683 Waldamere Ave, Willoughby, Ohio 44094.

McCREARY, RICHARD EDWARD, JR. R
Chmn, Fayette Co. Rep. Party, Tex.
b. Indianapolis, Ind, 1/7/17; s. Richard E. McCreary and Maude Clements M; m. 6/3/39 to Elizabeth Taggart; c. Jack Taggart. Educ: Wabash Col, 35-36; Ind. Univ, 37-38; Beta Theta Pi. Polit. & Govt. Pos: Chmn, Fayette Co. Rep. Party, Tex, 64- Bus. & Prof. Pos: Rancher. Mil. Serv: Baker 3/C, Navy, 43-45, with serv. in Supply Depot, Pac, 45. Mem: Am. and Tex. Angus Asns. Rel: Methodist. Mailing Add: Route 1, P.O. Box 290, Weimar, Tex. 78962.

McCREARY, ZORA A. R
b. Waukon, Iowa, 8/12/08; d. William E. Henderson and Lucy Washburn H; m. 8/27/27 to Elmer James McCreary; c. Lysbeth (Mrs. Robert J. Stephens), Marilyn (Mrs. Charles E. Simmons), James G. and Thomas A. Educ: High Sch. Polit. & Govt. Pos: Former secy. and parliamentarian, Rep. Women's Club, Okla; v.chmn, Cleveland Co. Rep. Cmt, 61-63, judge elec. bd, 62- and state committeewoman, 63-65; v.chmn, Fifth Dist. Rep. Party, 62-69; mem, Gov. Cmt. on Children and Youth, 63-; dep. ballot security officer, 64; taught election schs. in various counties in Okla, 64. Mem: Eastern Star; White Shrine. Rel: Christian Church. Mailing Add: 503 Rosedale, Norman, Okla. 73069. (1967)

McCREEDY, HARRY DUANE R
Chmn, Davis Co. Rep. Cent. Cmt, Iowa
b. Washington, Iowa, 11/21/22; s. Harry Duane McCreedy and Carrie Mae Evans M; m. 7/12/46 to Marilyn Tulare Morse; c. Barbara Anne, Harry David, Vicki Lynn, Leslie Tulare and Thomas Morse. Educ: Iowa State Univ, D.V.M, 45; Alpha Gamma Rho. Polit. & Govt. Pos: Chmn, Davis Co. Rep. Cent. Cmt, Iowa, 68- Mil. Serv: Entered as Pvt, Army Specialized Training, 43, released as Pfc, 44. Mem: Am. and Iowa Vet. Med. Asns; Mason; Rotary; Elks; Farm Bur. Rel: Episcopal. Mailing Add: Route 5, Bloomfield, Iowa 52537.

McCREESH, THOMAS P. D
Pa. State Sen.
b. Phila, Pa, 3/2/28; John J. McCreesh and Susan McCabe M; m. to Rita McTamney. Educ: St. Joseph Col, B.S. Polit. & Govt. Pos: Pa. State Sen, 58-; del, Dem. Nat. Conv, 60; mem, 27th Ward Dem. Cmt. Bus. & Prof. Pos: Real Estate; ins. broker. Mil. Serv: Army Counter-Intel. Corps, 51-53. Mem: Phila. Bd. of Realtors; W.Phila. Real Estate Bd; Pa. Bd. of Realtors; K. of C; Nat. Asn. Amateur Oarsmen; Armaugh Soc; W.Phila. C. of C; Phila, Harrisburg YMCA; Friendly Sons of St. Patrick; Right of Way Appraisers, Chap. 9, Pa. Mailing Add: 4043 Irving St, Philadelphia, Pa. 19104. (1967)

McCUBBIN, CARROL J. R
Mo. State Rep.
b. Bramley, Mo, 9/1/20; m. to Betty Gayle Gensert; c. Brenda, Becky, Gregory, Twyla, Beth, John Gale Atteberry, Paula and Winn Rowch. Educ: Cent. Mo. State Col; Univ. Mo; B.S, M.E. Polit. & Govt. Pos: Mo. State Rep, 64- Bus. & Prof. Pos: Educator; teacher; city, co. supt. of schs; poultry farmer; owner-operator of locker plant. Mil. Serv: Lt, Naval Res. Mem: Past master, Bramley Masonic Lodge. Rel: Baptist. Mailing Add: RFD 3, Eldon, Mo. 65026. (1967)

McCUE, AGNES LOUISE D
V.Chairlady, Wethersfield Dem. Town Cmt, Conn.
b. Windsor Locks, Conn, 11/9/05; d. Michael Joseph McCue and Mary

Manhire M; single. Educ: Morse Bus. Col; Hartford Secretarial Sch. Polit. & Govt. Pos: Secy, Wethersfield Dem. Town Cmt, Conn, 45-56, v.chairlady, 56-; pres, Wethersfield Dem. Women's Club, 49-51; secy, Hartford Co. Fedn. Women's Club, 63-; secy, Conn. Ninth Sen. Dist, 66; asst. secy, Dem. State Conv, 66. Rel: Roman Catholic. Mailing Add: 1 Center St, Wethersfield, Conn. 06109.

McCUE, EDWARD OVERTON, JR. D
b. Charlottesville, Va, 5/11/01; m. to Isabel Chamberlain Cochran. Educ: Univ. of Va, LL.B; Delta Tau Delta. Polit. & Govt. Pos: Former chmn, Va. Adv. Legis. Coun; Va. State Del, 34-48; Va. State Sen, 50-68. Bus. & Prof. Pos: Lawyer; businessman; ex-farmer. Mem: Elks; Mason; Moose; Redland Club; Farmington Country Club. Rel: Episcopal. Mailing Add: 412 E. Jefferson St, Charlottesville, Va. 22901.

McCUE, WARREN RICHARD D
b. Lakin, Kans, 5/25/38; s. G.L. McCue and Rosina Meyer M; m. 9/11/60 to Linda Vaneet Wilmeth; c. Tracy Lee. Educ: Colo. State Univ, B.S. in gen. agr, 61. Polit. & Govt. Pos: Chmn, Lincoln Co. Dem. Party, Colo, 63-67. Bus. & Prof. Pos: Farmer-Rancher, Colo, 61- Mem: Asst. master, Boy Scouts, 59-61; Lincoln Co. and Colo. State Cattlemen's Asns. Rel: Lutheran; Financial Secy, Immanual Lutheran Church. Mailing Add: Arriba, Colo. 80804. (1967)

McCUIN, GUY LUTHER D
b. Belvidere, Vt, 9/7/97; m. to Florence Martin; c. One son and two daughters. Educ: UVM, B.S, 23. Polit. & Govt. Pos: Selectman, Richford, Vt, 61-; Vt. State Rep, 61-69. Bus. & Prof. Pos: Former mgr, Atlas Plywood Corp, Retired. Mil. Serv: A/S, Navy, 18-19. Mem: Mason. Rel: Baptist. Mailing Add: 196 S. Main St, Richford, Vt. 05476. (1967)

McCUISTON, LLOYD CARLISLE, JR. D
Ark. State Rep.
b. Lucy, Tenn, 3/26/18; s. Lloyd Carlisle McCuiston and Myrtle Ola Potts M; m. 11/16/47 to Olivia Lucretia Graham; c. Diane Graham and Lloyd Carlisle, III. Educ: Univ. Ark, B.S.C.E, 41; Engr. Soc; Kappa Sigma. Polit. & Govt. Pos: Circuit Court Clerk, 49-58; Justice of Peace, 59-60; Ark. State Rep, 61- Bus. & Prof. Pos: Engr, U.S. Corps of Engrs, 40-41; farmer, 46-; v.pres, Russell Tractor Co, 63- Mil. Serv: Entered as Midshipman, Navy, 42, released as Lt.(sg), 46, after serv. in Construction Bn, Pac. Theatre, 44-45. Mem: Meadowbrook Country Club; Rotary; Am. Legion; VFW; Farm Bur. Rel: Baptist. Mailing Add: 1004 Avalon, West Memphis, Ark. 72301.

McCULLOCH, FRANK W. D
Chmn, Nat. Labor Rels. Bd.
b. Evanston, Ill, 9/30/05; s. Frank H. McCulloch and Catharine G. Waugh M; m. 4/2/37 to Edith F. Leverton; c. William H. and Frank H, II. Educ: Williams Col, B.A, 26; Harvard Law Sch, LL.B, 29; Phi Beta Kappa; Pi Delta Epsilon; Phi Gamma Delta. Hon. LL.D, Chicago Theol. Sem. and Olivet Col. Polit. & Govt. Pos: Former mem, Regional War Labor Bd, World War II; asst. to U.S. Sen. Paul Douglas, 49-61; chmn, Nat. Labor Rels. Bd, Wash, D.C, 61-; mem. and chmn, Civil Serv. Cmn. Adv. Cmt. on Hearing Exam, 62-69; mem. Am. del, Anglo-Am. Conf. on Admin. Law, 69. Bus. & Prof. Pos: Lawyer; indust. rels. secy, Coun. Soc. Action, Congregational-Christian Church, 35-46; dir. labor educ. div, Roosevelt Col, Chicago, 46-49. Mem: Chicago, Ill. State, Am. and Fed. Bar Asns. Rel: Congregational-Christian. Legal Res: 720 Ingelside Place, Evanston, Ill. 60202. Mailing Add: 3642 Upton St. N.W, Washington, D.C. 20008.

McCULLOCH, ROBERT WINSLOW D
Mem, Gunnison Co. Dem. Exec. Cmt, Colo.
b. Kansas City, Mo, 3/23/10; s. Albert Johnston McCulloch and Isabella Austin Winslow M; m. 7/13/33 to Margaret Elizabeth Young; c. Robert Charles, Margaret Marie (Mrs. Eastman) and Judith Anne (Mrs. Hessel). Educ: Albion Col, A.B, summa cum laude, 31; Univ. Mich, M.A, 32; Ph.D, 34; Delta Sigma Rho; Phi Kappa Phi; Phi Alpha Theta; Pi Gamma Mu; Pi Kappa Delta; Delta Tau Delta. Polit. & Govt. Pos: Mem, Gunnison Co. Dem. Finance Cmt, Colo, 52-56; chmn, Gunnison Co. Dem. Campaign, 58-62; committeeman, Precinct 1, Dem. Party, 58-63; Colo. State Sen, 62-65; Seventh Judicial Dist. rep, Colo. Dem. State Exec. Cmt; chmn, Gunnison Co. Dem. Cent. Cmt, Colo, 64-69; mem, Gunnison Co. Dem. Exec. Cmt, 69-; del, Dem. Nat. Conv, 68. Bus. & Prof. Pos: Instr, Univ. Tampa, 34-35; prof, Monmouth Col, 35-45 and Okla. State Univ, 45-47; prof, West. State Col, 47-, dir. grad. studies, 49-64. Publ: 'Parliamentary Control: Question Hour in England's House of Commons' Univ. Microfilms, Ann Arbor, Mich, 55; Inter-Institutional Cooperation: State Systems,' Coun. Grad. Schs, 12/64; 'Intergovernmental Relations as Seen by Public Officials,' Annals of Am. Acad. of Polit. & Soc. Sci, May, 65. Mem: Am. Asn. of Univ. Prof; Am. Polit. Sci. Asn; West. Serv. Award, West. Colo. Coun. of Boy Scouts, 57. Rel: Community Church. Legal Res: 500 N. Taylor St, Gunnison, Colo. 81230. Mailing Add: P.O. Box 945, Gunnison, Colo. 81230.

McCULLOCH, WILLIAM M. R
U.S. Rep, Ohio
b. Holmes Co, Ohio; m. 1925 to Mabel Harris; c. Nancy and Ann (Mrs. David Benson Carver); granddaughter, Elizabeth Wright Carver. Educ: Col. Wooster; Ohio State Univ. Col. Law, LL.B. Hon. LL.D, Ohio North. Univ. Polit. & Govt. Pos: Ohio State Rep, 5 terms, minority leader, Ohio House of Rep, 36-38, speaker, three terms; U.S. Rep, Fourth Dist, Ohio, 47-, ranking Rep. mem, House Cmt. on the Judiciary and mem. antitrust subcmt, mem, Joint Cmt. on Atomic Energy and Joint Cmt. on Immigration and Nationality Policy; mem, President's Cmn. on Causes and Prev. of Violence; v.chmn, Nat. Rep. Cong. Campaign Cmt; Cong. Rep. to Intergovt. Cmn. on European Migration, mem, President's Cmn. on Civil Disorders and Cmn. on Govt. Security, formerly. Bus. & Prof. Pos: Attorney-at-law. Mil. Serv: World War II. Mem: Bd. dirs, Piqua Nat. Bank and Trust Co. and Third Savings and Loan Co, Piqua; trustee, Piqua YMCA; Miami Co, Ohio State and Am. Bar Asns; Rotary; Am. Legion. Am. Polit. Sci. Asn. Cong. Distinguished Serv. Award; Distin-Alumni Award, Col. Wooster, Ohio; named Rep. of the Year, Harvard Univ. Young Rep. Club; Annual Watchdog of the Treas. Award, Nat. Asn. Businessmen, Inc. Legal Res: Piqua, Ohio. Mailing Add: 4100 Cathedral Ave. N.W, Washington, D.C. 20016.

McCULLOUGH, CALVIN R. D
Del. State Sen.
b. Wilmington, Del, 1912; m. to Charlotte Brown; c. Donall Lee, Robert W. and Joyce Kay. Educ: Boyd Bus. Sch. Polit. & Govt. Pos: State supvr, Sch. Bldgs. and Grounds, Del, 50-53; Del. State Rep, 52-56; Del. State Sen, 56-; del, Dem. Nat. Conv, 68. Bus. & Prof. Pos: Bldg. contractor. Mem: Mason; Moose; pres, Holloway Terrace Improv. Group. Rel: Baptist. Mailing Add: 605 Central Ave. at Holloway Terrace, New Castle, Del. 19720. (1967)

McCULLOUGH, GEORGE DEWEY R
Chmn, McIntosh Co. Rep. Party, Okla.
b. Gainsville, Mo, 9/29/99; s. Andrew Jackson McCullough and Surilda Webister M; m. 9/29/23 to Ola Lansford; c. Bobby Ruth (Mrs. Fred Shim) and Mary Jo (Mrs. Roger Foster). Educ: Northeast. State Col, B.A, 39; Okla. State Univ, M.S, 45. Polit. & Govt. Pos: Chmn, McIntosh Co. Rep. Party, Okla, 68- Bus. & Prof. Pos: Grade sch. prin, rural and consol. schs, 24-27; athletic coach, Checotah City Schs, 33-34, grade sch. prin, 33-45, high sch. prin, 45-64; retired. Mem: Okla. Educ. Asn; Odd Fellows (Past Grand Knight). Rel: Baptist. Mailing Add: 602 N.W. Fifth, Checotah, Okla. 74426.

McCULLOUGH, ROBERT EARL D
Chmn, Henry Co. Dem. Party, Iowa
b. Lancaster, Mo, 4/30/26; s. Earl McCullough and May Foglesong M; m. 11/12/54 to Mary Jane Dellinger; c. Steven, Jane and Judy. Educ: Kirksville State Teachers Col, M.A. Polit. & Govt. Pos: Chmn, Henry Co. Dem. Party, Iowa, 66-; mem, State Credentials Cmn, 68- Mil. Serv: Entered as A/S, Navy 44, released as 1 SC 3/C, 46, after serv. in Pac. Mem: Iowa State, Nat. and West. Educ. Asn; Masons; Am. Legion. Rel: Lutheran. Mailing Add: Swedesburg, Iowa 52652.

McCULLOUGH, ROLAND ALEXANDER
Dir, Export-Import Bank of the U.S.
b. Spartanburg, S.C, 11/29/17; s. Ashton Alexander McCullough and Mary Belle Cannon M; m. 9/8/40 to Birdie Brown West; c. Emily Alexandria, Mary Cecilia and Margaret Ann. Educ: Spartanburg Jr. Col, 35-37; Wofford Col, A.B, 39 and M.A, 42. Polit. & Govt. Pos: Research and press secy, Gov. James F. Byrnes, S.C, 51-54; admin. asst, U.S. Sen. Strom Thurmond, 55-57; mem, State Educ. Finance Cmn, 65-66; dir, Export-Import Bank of U.S, 69- Bus. & Prof. Pos: Sch. teacher and adminstr. hosp. investr. and bus. mgr, Spartanburg Co, S.C, 39-44; managing ed, Spartanburg Herald & Sunday Herald-J, 44-50; v.pres. and sr. v.pres, S.C. Nat. Bank, 57-69. Publ: Various by-line articles for Assoc. Press, 43-50; 'Byrnes Leads Educational Revolution,' wire serv. and numerous nat. newspapers, 54; 'Political Revolt in the South,' U.S. News and World Report, 5/56. Mem: Am. Soc. Newspaper Ed; Bank Mkt. and Pub. Rels. Asn; Advert. Club; Pub. Rels. Soc. of Am. Rel: Methodist. Mailing Add: 622 S. Lee St, Alexandria, Va. 22314.

McCULLOUGH, WILLIAM TODD D
Miss. State Rep.
b. Batesville, Miss, 10/28/03; married. Polit. & Govt. Pos: Miss. State Rep, 48- Bus. & Prof. Pos: Cotton buyer; merchant; druggist. Mem: Farm Bur; C. of C. Rel: Baptist; Bd. of Deacons, Sunday Sch. Teacher. Mailing Add: Box 82, Pope, Miss. 38658.

McCULLY, DEAN R
b. Marshall Co, Ill, 07; m. to Sarabeth Stoddard; c. 1 son, 3 daughters. Educ: Ill. Wesleyan; Univ. of Iowa Law Sch. Polit. & Govt. Pos: Former Ill. State Rep; Legis. Coun. Bus. & Prof. Pos: Farming; farm mgt; Chmn. Bd. Minonk State Bank. Mailing Add: Minonk, Ill. 61760. (1967)

McCUNE, JOHN W. D
Okla. State Rep.
b. 1905. Educ: Univ. Colo, B.A; Univ. of Mo. Law Sch, LL.B. Polit. & Govt. Pos: Former Asst. U.S. Dist. Attorney, Okla. and former asst. city attorney, Tulsa; Okla. State Rep, 59- Mem: Tulsa Co. and Okla. Bar Asns; C. of C; Mason. Mailing Add: 1011 S. Rockfield Ave, Tulsa, Okla. 74105. (1967)

McCURDY, M. JACQUELINE D
b. Baltimore, Md, 12/1/33; single. Educ: Hood Col, B.A, 55; Univ. Md. Sch. of Law, D.J, 58. Polit. & Govt. Pos: Mem, Baltimore Co. Dem. Clubs; Md. State Del, 64-67; asst. co. solicitor, Baltimore Co, 68-; admin. asst, Md. House of Del, 68- Bus. & Prof. Pos: Lawyer. Mem: Md. and Baltimore Co. Bar Asns; Phi Delta Delta; Soroptomist; YWCA (mem. adv. bd, North Area Chap). Outstanding Personality of the South, 67; Outstanding Young Woman of Am, 67. Mailing Add: 203 W. Chesapeake Ave, Towson, Md. 21204.

McCURN, NEAL PETERS D
b. Syracuse, N.Y, 4/6/26; s. Francis D. McCurn and Grace Peters M; m. 6/18/49 to Nancy Irving; c. Susan, Sharon, Carol, Nancy, Mary Pat and Neal, Jr. Educ: Syracuse Univ, A.B, 50, Col. of Law, LL.B, 52, J.D, 69; Beta Theta Pi; Phi Delta Phi. Polit. & Govt. Pos: Del, N.Y. State Constitutional Conv, 67; alt. del, Dem. Nat. Conv, 68. Bus. & Prof. Pos: Partner, Mackenzie, Smith, Lewis, Michel & Hughes, Law Firm, 59- Mil. Serv: Entered as Midshipman, Naval Res, released as Lt.(jg), 46. Mem: Onondaga Co. Bar Asn. (pres, 65(; Hiscock Legal Aid Soc.(pres, 66); March of Dimes (N.Y. State chmn, 67-69); Am. Red Cross (chap. chmn, 68-69). Rel: Catholic. Legal Res: 304 Summit Ave, Syracuse, N.Y. 13207. Mailing Add: 600 Onondaga Bank Bldg, Syracuse, N.Y. 13202.

McCUTCHEN, PLEASANT THEODORE 'PAT' D
b. Newman, Ga, 4/3/02; s. Pleasant Theodore McCutchen and Mai Close M; m. 12/30/30 to Irma Croker; P.T, Jr. and Samuel C. Educ: North Ga. Col, 21-23; Atlanta Law Sch, LL.B, 26; hon. mem, Gridiron Soc; Pi Kappa Alpha. Polit. & Govt. Pos: Hearing officer, Wage Stabilization Admin; clerk, Ga. State House of Rep, 43-46; del, Dem. Nat. Conv, 44 & 64; mem. and secy, State Constitution Revision Cmn, 44-45 & 62-63; exec. secy. to Gov, 46; secy-treas, State Bd. of Workmen's Compensation, 47-48; v.pres, Ninth Dist, Ga. Munic. Asn; attorney, Gilmer Co. and Ellijay, Ga, 58-; mem, State Budget Study Cmt, 61-62; Ga. State Rep, Gilmer Co, 61-62; mem, Ga. State Dem. Exec. Cmt, 63-66; mem, bd. of trustees, State Employees Retirement System, 63- Mem: Past pres, Blue Ridge Bar Asn; past pres. and zone

chmn, Ellijay Lions; Gilmer Sportsman Club; Quarterback Club; Commerce Club, Atlanta; dir, YMCA. Rel: Methodist. Legal Res: Blue Ridge Rd, Ellijay, Ga. 30540. Mailing Add: P.O. Box 433, Ellijay, Ga. 30540.

McCUTCHEON, ANDREW H, JR. D
b. Webster Springs, W.Va, 5/12/27; s. Andrew H. McCutcheon and Elsie Hamrick M; m. 1/26/52 to Charlotte Andrews; c. Sallie Baker. Educ: Univ. Tenn, 44; Emory Univ. and Ga. Inst. Tech, 45; Washington & Lee Univ, B.A, 48; Sigma Delta Chi; Sigma Chi. Polit. & Govt. Pos: Admin. asst. to U.S. Rep. J. Vaughan Gary, 60-64 and to U.S. Rep. David E. Satterfield, III, 65-67; specialist in cong. affairs, Off. Econ. Opportunity, 67-68; Dem. nominee for U.S. Rep, Eighth Dist, Va, 68. Bus. & Prof. Pos: Reporter, Richmond News Leader, Va, 49-60; community rels. mgr, Reynolds Metals Co, Richmond, currently. Mil. Serv: Aviation Cadet, Navy, 45-46; Army Res. Mem: South. Conf. Sports Writers Asn.(pres); Burro Club (secy); Am. Newspaper Guild, 49-60. Rel: Episcopal. Mailing Add: 1003 Francisco Rd, Richmond, Va. 23229.

McCUTCHEON, CHESTER M. R
b. Monroeville, Pa, 10/30/07; s. William Erwin McCutcheon and Margaret Myers M; m. 11/3/44 to Hellen S. Clawson; c. Ronald R, Rev. Brian L, Lynn Ellis, Mrs. William Rampley, Bruce A. and Curtis W. Educ: High Sch; various night schs. and correspondence courses. Polit. & Govt. Pos: Treas, Cobb Co. Rep. Asn, Ga, 61-62, chmn, 62-64; chmn, Cobb Co. Rep. Exec. Cmt, 64-69; co-chmn, Cobb Co. Callaway for Gov. Cmt, 66. Bus. & Prof. Pos: V.pres, Fulton Fed. Savings & Loan Asn, Atlanta, Ga, 48-; officer and dir, Southeast. Capital, Inc, Tuxedo Investment Co, Skyview Develop. Co. and Cherokee Enterprises, Investment Partnership. Publ: Various technical papers on savings and loan acct. Mem: Past pres, Nat. Soc. of Savings and Loan Controllers, 57-58. Rel: Presbyterian. Mailing Add: 96 Whitlock Ave, Marietta, Ga. 30060.

Mc CUTCHEON, JOHN T. D
Wash. State Sen.
b. Tacoma, Wash, 1892; m. to Tina; c. Three. Educ: Univ. of Wash; Ind. Univ. Law Sch, LL.B. Polit. & Govt. Pos: Wash. State Sen, currently; Wash. State Rep, one term. Bus. & Prof. Pos: Lawyer. Mem: Eagles; Grange. Mailing Add: P.O. Box 387, Steilacoom, Wash. 98388. (1967)

McCUTCHIN, PAT WINSTON R
Chmn, Hockley Co. Rep. Party, Tex.
b. Dallas, Tex, 1/20/42; s. Robert M. McCutchin and Verna Jones M; m. 9/2/61 to Nancy Padgett; c. Matthew P. Educ: Univ. Tex, Austin, B.B.A, 63; Alpha Delta Sigma; Alpha Epsilon Rho. Polit. & Govt. Pos: Chmn, Hockley Co. Rep. Party, Tex, 68- Mem: Lions; Jaycees. Rel: Episcopal. Legal Res: 103 Redwood, Levelland, Tex. 79336. Mailing Add: Box 131, Levelland, Tex. 79336.

McDADE, JOSEPH MICHAEL R
U.S. Rep, Pa.
b. Scranton, Pa, 9/29/31; s. John B. McDade and Genevieve Hayes M; m. 3/31/62 to Mary Theresa O'Brien; c. Joseph, Aileen, Deborah and Mark. Educ: Notre Dame Univ, B.A, 53; Univ. Pa. Sch. Law, LL.B, 56; James Wilson Law Club. Polit. & Govt. Pos: City solicitor, Scranton, Pa, 62; U.S. Rep, Tenth Cong. Dist, Pa, currently. Bus. & Prof. Pos: Attorney-at-law, Scranton, 57-66. Mem: Am, Pa. and Lackawanna Co. Bar Asns; C. of C; K. of C; Elks. Rel: Roman Catholic. Legal Res: 1645 N. Washington Ave, Scranton, Pa. 18509. Mailing Add: 4006 27th St. N, Arlington, Va. 22207.

McDANIEL, C. DEMPSEY R
N.C. State Rep.
b. High Point, N.C, 4/2/24; s. Carl McDaniel and Nellie Brown M; m. 11/17/52 to Gladys Bertha Keller; c. Patricia (Mrs. Gordon Cox), Donna (Mrs. Wayne Mullis), Dempsey O'Brien and Barry Wayne. Educ: Univ. Md, Far E. Div, Tokyo, Japan, B.A, 62; Winston-Salem State Univ, 62-63; Univ. N.C, Greensboro, M.Ed, 66. Polit. & Govt. Pos: Justice of the peace, Abbotts Creek Twp, Forsyth Co, N.C, 66-68; N.C. State Rep, 30th Dist, Forsyth Co, 68- Bus. & Prof. Pos: Secondary teacher, High Point City Sch. Syst, N.C, 65-67, guidance counselor, 67-; evening sch. instr, history, High Point Col, 67- Mil. Serv: Entered as Pvt, Army, 43, released as Sgt 1/C, 65, after serv. in 49th Fighter Group, Fifth Army Air Force, Ninth Inf. Div, Hq. Far East-UN Command, 43-65, (Ret), 65; Army Commendation Medal; Good Conduct Medal with Five Awards; Am. Campaign Medal; Asiatic-Pac. Campaign Medal with Eight Battle Stars; Victory Medal-World War II; Army of Occupation-World War II, Nat. Defense Medal with Two Awards; Philippine-Liberation with Two Battle Stars; Philippine Independence Ribbon; Congressional Unit Citation; Philippine Presidential Unit Citation; Army-Air Force Badge. Mem: Nat, N.C, High Point Educ. Asns; Classroom Teachers Asn; N.C. Personnel and Guidance Asn; N.C. Voc. Guidance Asn; N.C. Sch. Counselor's Asn; Nat. Rifle Asn.(life mem); N.C. Rifle & Pistol Asn; High Point Rod and Gun Club, Inc; Non-Commissioned Officers Asn. of U.S. Rel: Baptist. Mailing Add: Route 1, Box 402B, Kernersville, N.C. 27284.

McDANIEL, DONALD CONLEY R
b. Los Angeles, Calif, 4/2/32; s. Ivan Goodspeed McDaniel and Dorothy Katherine Belcher M; m. 7/31/54 to Marilyn Felicia Warnecke; c. Scott Conley and Margaret Lynn. Educ: Stanford Univ, A.B. cum laude in econ, 54; Univ. Calif, Los Angeles, LL.B, 61; Phi Delta Phi; Phi Delta Theta. Polit. & Govt. Pos: Mem, Los Angeles Co. Cent. Cmt, Calif, 62-; pres, Los Angeles Co. Young Rep, 64; del, Rep. Nat. Conv, 64; chmn, 60th Assembly Dist, Rep. Cent. Cmt, Calif, 64-66; gen. counsel, Calif. Young Rep, 65. Bus. & Prof. Pos: Attorney at Law, McDaniel & McDaniel, 61- Mil. Serv: Entered as 2nd Lt, Air Force, 54, released as 1st Lt, 57; Capt, Air Force Res. Rel: Protestant. Mailing Add: 839 Toyopa Dr, Pacific Palisades, Calif. 90272.

McDANIEL, ESTES CRUDEN D
Miss. State Rep.
b. Pontotoc, Miss, 6/28/09; s. Thomas L. McDaniel and Janie Inzer M; m. 6/30/51 to Grace B. Gary. Educ: Univ. of Okla, B.S, 31; Peabody Col, M.A, 41; Kappa Phi Kappa. Polit. & Govt. Pos: Miss. State Rep, Leflore & Sunflower Co, 64- Bus. & Prof. Pos: Farm owner and operator, currently; jr. high and high sch. supt, Morgan Co. Bd. of Educ, Decatur, Ala, 32-51. Mem: Miss. Cattlemans Asn; Miss. Angus Asn; Le Flore Co. Hunting & Fishing Asn; Delta Coun; Am. Angus Asn; Am. Soybean Asn; Lions; Eastern Star; Mason (32°); Shrine; charter mem, mem. bd. dirs, Nat. Soc. State Legislators and chmn, Miss. State Chap; WOW; Elks; Farm Bur. Rel: Presbyterian. Mailing Add: 301 E. Claiborne St, Greenwood, Miss. 38930.

McDANIEL, FRANCIS M, JR. D
b. Lantry, S.Dak, 3/25/23; single. Educ: Black Hills Commercial Col; Northrop Aeronaut. Inst. Polit. & Govt. Pos: S.Dak. State Rep, 62-66. Bus. & Prof. Pos: Sr. design engr, West. Electrochem. Co. and Am. Potash and Chem. Co, 51-58; auto dealer, 58- Rel: Catholic. Mailing Add: Lantry, S.Dak. 57636.

MacDANIEL, HAROLD KEMP D
b. Baltimore, Md, 6/3/21; s. Lawrence C. MacDaniel and Aidelaide J. Weissner M; m. 11/8/40 to Madeline E. Lietz; c. M. Elise (Mrs. Bill Cauthorn), Dyane (Mrs. Carson Fineham); Pamela L. and Kathleen A. Educ: Univ. Md, B.S. and B.A, Law Sch, LL.B, 51; Baltimore Col. Commerce, 44-46; Delta Theta Phi (dean); Law Class Pres; Dean Alumni. Polit. & Govt. Pos: Dist. leader, 13th Dist, Md, 49-67; mem, Patapsco Dem. Club, 51-67; mem. Baltimore Co. Young Dem, 56-61; Md. State Del, 58-66, mem, Judiciary cmt, Md. House Del, 58-66; mem. bd. trustees, Catonsville Commun. Col, 58-67, mem. bd. dirs, Baltimore Co. Gen. Hosp, 60-68; del, Dem. Nat. Conv, 64; circuit court judge, Baltimore Co, 66- Bus. & Prof. Pos: Legal adv, Halethorpe Commun. Asn, and Arbutus Vol. Fire Dept, 51-66; attorney, Seaboard Finance Co, 51-66, Rolling Rd. Golf Club, 57-66 and Wynnewood Improv. Asn, 56-66; law instr, Calvert Hall Coll, 52-56. Mil. Serv: Entered as Pfc, Army, 44, released as Sgt, 46, after serv. in 95th Div, ETO, 44-46; Marksman; battle decoration; wounded twice. Mem: Mason; Delta Theta Phi Alumnai; Hexagon Club; Nat. Trial Judges Asn; Exchange Club Catonsville; VFW; Am. Legion; Rolling Rd. Golf Club; Wynnewood Improv. Asn; Arbutus Commun; Halethorpe Improvement. Asn; York Rite. Rel: Methodist. Mailing Add: 5717 Oakland Rd, Baltimore, Md. 21227.

McDANIEL, JOE ANN D
b. Arcadia, Fla, 1/29/26; d. Obediah Oliver Walker and Maude Rhea W; m. 4/10/48 to Fred Atwood McDaniel, Jr; c. Sheryl Atwood. Educ: Brenau Col, Dramatic Cert, 46; Chushman Club; Tau Sigma; Study Coun; Phi Mu. Polit. & Govt. Pos: Elec. judge, West Kings Mountain, N.C, 52-60; del, N.C. Dem. State Conv, 60 & 64; first v.chmn, West Kings Mountain Dem. Precinct, 60-69; del, Dem. Nat. Conv, 64; first v.chmn, Cleveland Co. Dem. Party, 64-69; secy, Cleveland Co. Women's Dem. Club, 64-66, pres, 66- Bus. & Prof. Pos: Off. mgr, Assoc. Laundry Sales, Inc, 62-66. Mem: Past Worthy Matron, Order of the Eastern Star; past pres, Town and Country Garden Club; PTA; secy, Kings Mountain Baptist Church, 59-61. Hobbies: Art and Dramatics. Rel: Presbyterian. Mailing Add: 804 Williams St, Kings Mountain, N.C. 28086. (1967)

McDANIEL, MARLIN K. R
Ind. State Sen.
Educ: Purdue, B.S; Ind. Univ, LL.B; George Washington Univ. scholarship; Univ. Oslo, Norway. Polit. & Govt. Pos: Former Rep. Nat. Col. chmn; mem, Rep. State Platform Cmt, 64; chmn, Wayne Co. Rep. Party, Ind, 68-; Ind. State Sen, currently. Bus. & Prof. Pos: Attorney; former spec. agent, U.S. Counterintelligence. Mil. Serv: Officer, Ind. Nat. Guard. Mem: State and Co. Bar Asns; Mason; Scottish Rite; Eagles; Elks. Rel: Presbyterian. Mailing Add: 385 S. 32nd St, Richmond, Ind. 47374. (1967)

McDANIEL, WILLIAM COLLIN D
Chmn, Kleberg Co. Dem. Party, Tex.
b. Hemphill, Tex, 12/5/22; s. Collin Adrain McDaniel and Susan Smith M; m. 11/16/48 to Mattie Olene Evans; c. Vicki Lynn. Educ: Tex. A & I Univ, pre-law course, 2 years; Baylor Univ, J.D; Phi Alpha Delta. Polit. & Govt. Pos: Chmn, Kleberg Co. Dem. Party, Tex, currently; city attorney, Kingsville, currently. Bus. & Prof. Pos: Co-mgr, Kleberg Co. Abstract Co, Kingsville, Tex; Attorney-at-law and real estate broker. Mil. Serv: Entered as A/S, Navy, 40, released as 1/C PO, 46, after serv. in U.S.S. Savannah, S C 749, N. Atlantic and S. Pac. Theatres. Mem: Past dir, City Attorney's Asn. of Tex; pres, Kleberg-Kenedy Co. Bar Asn; chmn. of trustees and Past Exalted Ruler, Local Lodge, Elks; VFW; AF&AM; Scottish Rite; Shrine. Rel: Baptist. Legal Res: 1105 Lawndale, Kingsville, Tex. 78363. Mailing Add: P.O. Box 901, Kingsville, Tex. 78363.

McDAVID, MARION FOY D
b. Pelzer, S.C, 9/29/11; s. James Philip McDavid and Nora Dozier Foy M; m. 12/4/43 to Caroline Kelley Okey; c. Marion Foy, Jr. and William Okey. Educ: Davidson Col, A.B, 32; George Wash. Univ. Sch. of Law, LL.B, 40; Alpha Phi Epsilon; Sigma Alpha Epsilon. Polit. & Govt. Pos: Second v.pres, N.C. Dem. Club of Wash, D.C, 38-40; prin. claims examiner, Gen. Acct. Off, Wash, D.C, 40-42; City Judge, Harriman, Tenn, 51-55; former chmn, Roane Co. Dem. Exec. Cmt, Tenn; alternate del, Dem. Nat. Conv, 64. Mil. Serv: Entered as Pvt, Army, 42, released as Spec. Agent, Counter Intel. Corps, 45, after serv. in Mil. Intel. Div, Counter Intel. Corps, Fourth Serv. Command and Third Air Force, N.Am. Mem: Am. Bar Asn; pres, Roane Co. Bar Asn, 58-59; Bar Asn. of Tenn; Am. Legion; Emory Golf and Country Club. Rel: Baptist. Legal Res: Webster Pike, Harriman, Tenn. 37748. Mailing Add: P.O. Box 318, Harriman, Tenn. 37748.

McDERMOTT, EDWARD ALOYSIOUS D
b. Dubuque, Iowa, 6/28/20; s. Edward L. McDermott and Sarah Larkin M; m. 9/1/45 to Naola Spellman; c. Maureen, Edward, Aloysious, Charles Joseph and Daniel John. Educ: Loras Col, B.A, 39; Univ. Iowa, J.D, 42; Xavier Univ, hon. J.D, 62. Polit. & Govt. Pos: Del, Dem. Nat.Conv, 52, 60 & 64; mem, Iowa Dem. Cent. Cmt, 56-60; co-chmn, Iowans for Kennedy, 60; dep. dir, Off. of Emergency Planning, 61-62, dir, 62-65; mem, Nat. Security Coun; U.S. Rep. to Sr. Cmt. and other cmts, NATO, 62-65; chmn, President's Exec.Stockpile Cmt. and mem, President's Cmt. Employ. Handicapped, 62-65; Chmn, Nat. Civil Defense Adv. Coun, 62-65; mem, President's Cmt. on Manpower, 63-65; chmn, Cmt. on Assumptions for Non-Mil. Planning, 63-65; mem, Fed. Reconstruction and Develop. Cmn. of Alaska, 64-65; nat. coordinator, McGovern Campaign, 68. Bus. & Prof. Pos: Mem. legal dept, Travelers Ins. Co, Omaha, Nebr, 42-43; mem, legal dept, Montgomery Ward & Co, Chicago, 43-45; attorney, O'Connor, Thomas & O'Connor, 46-50; prof. bus. law and econ, Loras Col. and Clarke Col, Dubuque, Iowa; partner, O'Connor,

Thomas, McDermott & Wright, 51-61 and Hogan and Hartson, Wash, D.C, 65-; mem. bd. dirs, Am. Irish Found; bd. regents, Univ. Santa Clara; bd. adv, Indust. Col. of Armed Forces; bd. adv, Lynchburg Col. Mem: Fed, Iowa and D.C. Bar Asns; Am. Judicature Soc; Int. Asn. Ins. Counsels; Am. Asn. Ins. Affils; Nat. Lawyers, Nat. Capitol. Metrop, Int. and Cong. Country Clubs; 1925 F St. Club. Decorated Knight of Malta; Knight of Holy Sepulchre; Amvets Spec. Silver Helmet Award, 63. Legal Res, 5400 Albermarle St. N.W, Washington, D.C. 20016. Mailing Add: 815 Connecticut Ave, Washington, D.C. 20006.

McDERMOTT, FRANK X. R
Pres, N.J. State Senate
b. New York, N.Y, 10/15/24; s. Peter Joseph McDermott and Helen Gildea M; m. 1954 to Patricia Keogh; c. Colleen, Gregory, Marita, Matthew and Brendan. Educ: Columbia Col, B.A, 48, Law Sch, LL.B, 49; N.Y. Univ. Grad. Sch. of Pub. Admin, M.P.A, 53; N.Y. Univ, LL.M, 61; Phi Delta Phi. Polit. & Govt. Pos: N.J. State Assemblyman, 64-67, asst. majority leader, N.J. Gen. Assembly, 65, minority leader, 66; N.J. State Sen, 68-, majority leader, N.J. State Senate, 68, pres, 69- Bus. & Prof. Pos: Partner, Apruzzese & McDermott, 65- Publ: New Jersey Labor Laws, N.J. Mfrs. Asn, 57. Mem: N.J. and N.Y. Bars; Elks; Colonia Country Club. N.J. Del. to White House Conf. on Educ, 55. Rel: Roman Catholic. Mailing Add: 312 Massachusetts St, Westfield, N.J. 07090.

McDERMOTT, MICHAEL D
Ill. State Rep.
b. Chicago, Ill, 6/30/01; married. Educ: Northwest. Univ. Night Sch. Polit. & Govt. Pos: Ill. State Rep, currently; Dem. Ward committeeman, 13th Ward, Chicago, 50- Bus. & Prof. Pos: Chief Clerk, 50-; Clerk, Co. Clerks Off; secy, Chicago Park Dist. Mil. Serv: World War II, 438th Troop Carrier Command, ETO. Mem: K. of C; Am. Legion; Lions. Mailing Add: 6706 S. Wood St, Chicago, Ill. 60636. (1967)

McDERMOTT, RUSSELL WILLIAM R
b. Decatur, Ill, 6/19/05; s. Thomas Michael McDermott and Fleta Downing M; m. 4/25/31 to Cecelia McDermott; c. Martin Downing, R.C. 'Bo,' Kenneth Michael and Clune. Educ: Ind. Univ, A.B, 28; Delta Upsilon. Polit. & Govt. Pos: Chmn, local cmts. for Rep. cand; adv. to co. chmn; v.pres, U.S. Sen. Homer Capehart's Campaign, 56-62, mem, U.S. Sen. Capehart's Cmt. representing U.S. Govt. in Cent. Am. and S. Am, 57-60; Ind. State Finance Chmn, Scranton for President, 64; del, Rep. Nat. Conv, 64; chmn, Rep. State Almanac, 66; Ind. State Finance Chmn, Rockefeller for President, 68; off. host, reception for Ind. Gov. Elect and del. to Gov. Conf, Palm Springs, Calif, December 68, cmt. mem, Gov. Conf, December 69. Bus. & Prof. Pos: Assoc. mem, N.Y. Stock Exchange with Blythe, Fenner, Beane, Noyes and Co, 31-43; agency dir, Standard Life Ins. Co, 45-59, bus. consult, 65-; head, Bankers Life Ins. Co, 59-65; pres, Bankers Mortgage Co. and Bankers Growth, 60-65; mem, Million Dollar Round Table of Life Underwriters, 25 years. Mem: First state chmn, USO, 41, first state bond drive chmn, former regional chmn, mem, Nat. Bd, 67-68; hon. mem, Indianapolis Symphony Orchestra, dir, 15 years; chmn, Flanner House Negro Settlement Campaign, 41; dir, Nat. Asn. of Life Underwriters, 63-65; Indianapolis Asn. Life Underwriters; Highland Golf & Country Club; Indianapolis Athletic Club; Columbia Club; Racquet Club; O'Donnel Golf Club; organizer and exec. v.pres, Cmt. of 100, Benefit for Police and Firemen of Palm Springs, Calif, 69; Opera Guild; Ind. Soc. of Chicago; Contemporary Club. Rel: Catholic. Mailing Add: 4410 N. Penn, Indianapolis, Ind. 42605.

McDERMOTT, WILLIAM HENRY D
Ala. State Sen.
b. Mobile, Ala, 8/2/33; s. William Vincent McDermott and Jeanne Ledoux M; m. 8/13/60 to Catherine O'Brien; c. Michele Suzanne, Elizabeth, Annette, Jeanne and Mary. Educ: McGill Inst; Springhill Col; Univ. Ala, B.S, 54, LL.B, 58. Polit. & Govt. Pos: City attorney, Chickasaw, Ala, 61-; Ala. State Rep, 62-66; Ala. State Sen, 67- Bus. & Prof. Pos: Lawyer. Mil. Serv: Lt, Army, 55-56. Mem: K. of C. Rel: Catholic. Mailing Add: Box 2025, Mobile, Ala. 36601.

McDEVITT, BERNARD R
Ill. State Rep.
b. Chicago, Ill, 7/24/02; married; One son and three daughters. Educ: Loyola Univ, B.A; Chicago Kent Col. of Law. LL.B. Polit. & Govt. Pos: Ill. State Rep, currently. Bus. & Prof. Pos: Attorney-at-law; instr. of med. law, Stritch Sch. of Med. of Loyola Univ. Mem: Chicago, Ill. and Am. Bar Asns; Am. Judicature Soc; Asn. of Med. Cols; Admitted to law practice, Ill. Supreme Court, 10/15/25. Mailing Add: 21 N. Mason Ave, Chicago, Ill. 60644.

McDEVITT, CHARLES F. R
b. Pocatello, Idaho, 1/5/32; s. Bernard A. McDevitt and Margaret Hermann M; m. 8/14/54 to Virginia L. Heller; c. Eileen, Kathryn, Brian, Sheila, Terrence, Neal and Kendal. Educ: Idaho State Col, 49-50; Univ. Idaho, B.A, 55, LL.B, 56; pres, Associated Students, Univ. Idaho, 55-56; rep, 10 west. states, Nat. Debate Championship, West Point, N.Y, selected as 1 of 20 Outstanding Speakers. Polit. & Govt. Pos: Pres, Young Rep, Univ. of Idaho, 51; chmn, Ada Co. Young Rep, Idaho, 58-59; state chmn, Idaho Young Rep, 61; U.S. del, Young Polit. Leaders Conf, Bonn, Germany, 61; gen. counsel and mem. exec. cmt, Nat. Young Rep, 63; Idaho State Rep, Ada Co, 63-65; chmn, Rep. Legis. Dist. 18, 66-69. Bus. & Prof. Pos: Partner, Law Firm of Richards, Haga & Eberle, Boise, Idaho, 56-62; dir. admin. and gen. counsel, Boise Cascade Corp, 62-67, secy, 62-68, v.pres, 67-68; dir, Nat. Leadership Inst, 63; pres, Beck Industs, Inc, 68- Mil. Serv: Entered as Pvt, Army, 52, released as Sgt, 54. Mem: State dir, UN day, 59-62; Kiwanis; St. Adv, K. of C, 61; Am. Soc. Corp. Secretaries; Aspen Inst. for Humanistic Studies. Rel: Catholic. Legal Res: 309 Pondfield Rd, Bronxville, N.Y. 10708. Mailing Add: 25 W. 43rd, New York, N.Y. 10036.

McDIARMID, DOROTHY SHOEMAKER D
Va. State Del.
b. Waco, Tex, 10/22/07; d. Daniel N. Shoemaker and Frances Hartley S; m. to Hugh McDiarmid; c. Robert C. and Mary S. Educ: Swarthmore Col, A.B, 29; Delta Gamma. Polit. & Govt. Pos: Va. State Del, 60-62, 64- Bus. & Prof. Pos: Partner, McDiarmid Realty and Ins, 45-; v.pres, North. Va. Properties, Inc, 50-; mem. bd. mgr, Swarthmore Col, 64- Publ: Richmond Report, Fairfax Pub. Co, weekly column. Mem: Life mem, Va. Cong. PTA; pres, North. Va. Ment. Health Asn, 66-69; Va. Asn. for Ment. Health; Fairfax Hosp. Asn; Int. Student Serv. Coun; Metrop. Wash. Health and Welfare Coun; bd. trustees, Va. Coun. on Health and Med. Care; Bus. and Prfnl. Women's Club; League of Women Voters; Women's Nat. Dem. Club; Va. Tuberc. and Respiratory Diseases Asn; Fairfax Co. Bd, YWCA. Gardening, sailing. Rel: Quaker. Legal Res: 9950 Meadowlark Rd, Vienna, Va. 22180. Mailing Add: 390 Maple Ave. E, Vienna, Va. 22180.

MacDONALD, DONALD PAUL D
Dist. Capt, Colo. Dem. State Cent. Cmt.
b. Newport, R.I, 4/19/31; s. Bertram I. MacDonald and Pauline Toomey M; m. 12/28/59 to Diane Carroll; c. Theresa Carroll, Sheila Joan and D. Patrick. Educ: Providence Col, A.B, 52; Georgetown Univ, LL.B, 56, LL.M, 63; Phi Alpha Delta. Polit. & Govt. Pos: State coordinator, Sen. Carroll Senate Campaign, 62; dist. capt, Denver Co. Dem. Cent. Cmt, 66-; dist. capt, Colo. Dem. State Cent. Cmt, 66-; del-at-lg, Dem. Nat. Conv, 68; Denver chmn, Lynch Senate Campaign, 68; mem, Steering Cmt. for Humphrey, Colo, 68; chmn, Kennedy Campaign, Denver, 68. Bus. & Prof. Pos: Assoc, Law Firm, Smith & Pepper, Wash, D.C, 58-62; asst. U.S. attorney, Denver, Colo, 63-66; vis. lectr, Univ. Colo. Law Sch, 66-, dir, Legal Aid & Defender Prog, 67-69; partner, Law Firm, Carroll and MacDonald, 66- Mil. Serv: Entered as Pvt, Army, 52, released as Cpl, 54, after serv. in Spec. Serv, Ft. Dix, N.J, 52-54. Mem: Am. and Col. Bar Asns; Nat. Legal Aid and Defender Asn; Denver Bar Asn. (chmn, defense of indigents cmt); chmn, Metrop. Denver Chap, March of Dimes. Rel: Catholic. Mailing Add: 740 Fillmore St, Denver, Colo. 80206.

MacDONALD, ELMER R
Polit. & Govt. Pos: Ind. State Rep, until 66. Bus. & Prof. Pos: Pres. and gen. mgr, W. & W. Concrete, Inc, Roanoke. Mil. Serv: Corps of Engrs, Army. Mem: Scottish Rite; Home Lodge; Mizpah Temple; Elks; YMCA; Rotary; Optimists; Izaak Walton League; Assoc. Bldg. Contractors of Ft. Wayne; Ind. Gen. Contractors Asn; Ft. Wayne Asn. of Credit Mgt; Reserve Officers Asn; C. of C. Rel: Presbyterian. Mailing Add: 722 Pelham Dr, Ft. Wayne, Ind. 43805.

McDONALD, FRED N. D
b. Columbia, S.C, 10/5/23; s. R.E. McDonald and Agnes Smith Mc; m. 9/7/47 to Ruth Alford; c. Pamela Anne, Nancy Elizabeth, Margaret Rebecca. Educ: Univ. of Ala, 43; Furman Univ, B.A, 49; Univ. of S.C, LL.B, 50. Polit. & Govt. Pos: S. C. State Rep, 55-66. Bus. & Prof. Pos: Lawyer. Mil. Serv: WW II, USAF, pilot 450 Heavy Bombardment Gp, 15 AF, ETD. Rel: Buncombe Street Methodist Church. Mailing Add: 203 Lavinia Ave, Greenville, S.C, 29601. (1967)

McDONALD, GEORGE FRANCIS D
R.I. State Rep.
b. Providence, R.I, 3/28/35; s. George Francis McDonald, Sr. and Marguerite Murray M; m. 6/25/66 to Gloria Marie DiSandro. Educ: Providence Col, A.B, 62; Suffolk Univ. Law Sch, LL.B, 67. Polit. & Govt. Pos: Press secy, Dem. Gubernatorial Cmt, R.I, 64; R.I. State Rep, 69- Bus. & Prof. Pos: Reporter, The Providence J, R.I, 58-67; attorney-at-law, Beals, Sweeney & Jerue, 67. Mil. Serv: Entered as S/A, Navy, 53, released as CT 3/C, 56, after serv. in Security Group, Bremenhaven, Germany, 54-56; Good Conduct Medal; German Occupation Medal; Nat. Defense Medal. Publ: 'Legalized Gambling,' Rhode Islander Mag, 67. Mem: R.I. Bar Asn. (ed, annual); Am. Bar Asn; Am. Trial Lawyers Asn; Aurora Civic Asn. Award of Merit, New Eng. Assoc. Press Managing Ed. Conf. Rel: Roman Catholic. Legal Res: 58 Frankfort St, Cranston, R.I. 02920. Mailing Add: 188 Benefit St, Providence, R.I. 02903.

McDONALD, HEYWARD ELLIOTT D
b. Winnsboro, S.C, 9/27/25; s. J. Edwin McDonald and Lucy Pride Heyward M; m. 3/5/49 to Sylvia Jean Buck; c. Laurie, Linda and Mary Heyward. Educ: U.S. Naval Acad, B.S, 46; Univ. S.C. Law Sch, LL.B, Magna Cum Laude, 58; Kappa Alpha. Polit. & Govt. Pos: S.C. State Rep, 63-66; trustee, Richland Co. Sch. Dist. No. 1, currently. Bus. & Prof. Pos: Partner, Rogers, McDonald & Ross, Attorneys. Mil. Serv: Navy, 46-54; instr, Naval Acad; Korean Conflict, USS New Jersey, BB62. Mem: Am, S.C. and Richland Co. Bar Asns; Richland Sertoma; dir, State Easter Seal Soc. and S.C. Asn. of Sch. Bds. Rel: Presbyterian; Elder and Sunday Sch. Teacher, Shandon Presby. Church. Mailing Add: Box 58, Columbia, S.C. 29202.

MacDONALD, J. KENYON D
Calif. State Assemblyman
b. Pasadena, Calif, 6/15/16; s. John Forrest MacDonald and Lois Helen Warren M; wid; m. 5/30/68 to Leslie Bune Hodge; c. Stuart K, Stephen G. and Scott F. MacDonald, Judith H. (Mrs. Sinnott), Ann H. (Mrs. Hall) and John W. Hodge. Educ: Univ. South. Calif, B.S. in Bus. Admin, 39; Skull and Dagger; Sigma Sigma; Sigma Phi Epsilon. Polit. & Govt. Pos: Co. supvr, Ventura Co, Calif, 61-66; Calif. State Assemblyman, 67- Bus. & Prof. Pos: Fleet sales mgr, James E. Waters, Los Angeles, Calif, 46-50; truck tire mgr, Dodson Ltd, 52-54; pres. and gen. mgr, Ken MacDonald Chevrolet, Ojai, 55-60; pres, Ken MacDonald Inc, Ventura, 58-60. Mil. Serv: Entered as Storekeeper 3/C, Naval Res, 41, released as Lt. Comdr, 51, after serv. in Fleet Activities, Yokosuka, Japan, Destroyer Base, San Diego and Armed Guard, 41-46 & 51-52; Naval Res. Medal; World War II Campaign Medals; Campaign Medal for Korean War. Mem: Co. Supvr. Asn. Calif; South. Calif. Motor Car Dealers Asn; Nat. Auto Dealers Asn; Mason; Scottish Rite; Am. Legion; Rotary. Rel: Presbyterian. Legal Res: 505 Del Norte Rd, Ojai, Calif. 93023. Mailing Add: P.O. Box 92, Ojai, Calif. 93023.

McDONALD, JACK R
Mem, Rep. Nat. Cmt.
b. Glasgow, Scotland, 4/15/34; s. John R.H. McDonald and Dorcas Hutcheson M; m. 6/15/56 to Frances Willis; c. Frances Dunbar and John R.H, II. Educ: Emory Univ, B.B.A, 56; London Sch. of Econ, 57; Alpha Kappa Psi; Sigma Alpha Epsilon. Polit. & Govt. Pos: Mem, Tenn. Rep. State Cmt, 62-; region IV dir, Young Rep. Nat. Fedn, 63-65, treas, 65-67, chmn, 67-; del, Rep. Nat. Conv, 64 & 68; mem, Rep. Nat. Finance Cmt, 65-; mem, Rep. Nat. Cmt, 67- Bus. & Prof. Pos: V.pres, Green Acres of Am, Inc, presently. Mailing Add: 215 W. Brow Oval, Lookout Mountain, Tenn. 37350.

McDONALD, JACK H. R
U.S. Rep, Mich.
b. Detroit, Mich, 6/28/32; m. to Joyce Isbell; c. Michael and David. Educ: Wayne State Univ. Polit. & Govt. Pos: Former pres, Out-Co. Supvr. Asn, Mich; mem, Nat. Asn. of Co. Off; trustee, Metrop. Fund, Inc; mem, Nat. Parks and Recreation Asn, Supvr. Inter-Co. Cmt; bd. of dirs, Mich. Twp. Asn; census dir, U.S. Bur. of Census; Redford Twp. supvr; chmn, Wayne Co. Bd. of Supvr; U.S. Rep, Mich, 66-, mem, Pub. Works & Merchant Marine & Fisheries Cmts. & Rep. Task Force on Urban Affairs. Bus. & Prof. Pos: Self-employed, contracting bus. Young Man of the Year, Detroit Bd. of Commerce, 65; Young Man of the Year, Redford Jaycees, 64; Am. League Citizenship Award. Rel: Presbyterian. Legal Res: 28100 Grand River Ave, Farmington, Mich. 48024. Mailing Add: 9514 Neuse Way, Great Falls, Va. 22066.

McDONALD, JOHN ANGUS 'MACK' D
b. Pleasant Valley, Fla, 4/10/17; div; c. Johnny Wayne. Educ: Fla. State Univ, B.S, 57. Polit. & Govt. Pos: Fla. State Sen, 64-66. Bus. & Prof. Pos: Adminstr, Wash. Co. Hosp. Mil. Serv: Pvt, Army, 12 years; 2nd Lt, Res, Mem: Kiwanis (former pres); Delta Sigma Pi. Rel: Church of Christ. 1967 Legal Res: Chipley, Fla. No mailing address available. (1967)

McDONALD, JOHN CECIL R
Chmn, Iowa Rep. State Cent. Cmt.
b. Lorimor, Iowa, 2/19/24; s. Cecil F. McDonald and Mary Elsie Fletcher M; m. 5/8/43 to Barbara Joan Berry; c. Mary Elisabeth, Joan Frances and Jean Maurine. Educ: Simpson Col; South. Ill. Univ; Drake Univ. Law Sch, LL.B, 48, J.D, 68; Blackfriars; Alpha Psi Omega; Delta Theta Phi; Alpha Tau Omega. Polit. & Govt. Pos: Secy, bd. dirs, Dallas Center Commun. Fund, Iowa, 53-69; legal adv, Dallas Commun. Sch. Dist, 53-69; legal adv, Dallas Co. Bd. of Educ; chmn, Finance Cmt, Dallas Co. Rep. Cmt, 54-63, chmn, 63-68; co. attorney, Dallas Co, 58-62, asst. co. attorney, 63-69; city attorney, Dallas Center; del, Rep. Nat. Conv, 64; mem, Lincoln Club, 65-69; mem, Iowa Rep. State Cent. Cmt, 68-69, chmn, 69-; mem, Gov. Inaugural Cmt, 69; chmn, Seventh Cong. Dist. Rep. Cmt, currently. Bus. & Prof. Pos: Mem, bd. dirs, Dallas Center Promotions, Inc, 60-69 and Dallas Co. Develop. Co, Inc, 64-69. Mil. Serv: Entered as Aviation Cadet, Air Force, 42; Col, Air Forces Res, currently; Air Command & Staff Sch, 51; Nat. War Col, 69; Am. Campaign Medal; Asiatic-Pac. Campaign Medal; World War II Victory Medal; Air Force Longevity Serv. Award; Armed Air Forces Res. Medal. Mem: U.S. Supreme Court; U.S. Court of Mil. Appeals; Supreme Court of Iowa; bd. trustees, Dallas Co. Hosp; pres, Dallas Center Commercial Club and Dallas Co. Bar Asn; organizer and pres, Hillcrest Country Club; pres, Dallas Center Rotary; Mil. Affairs Cmt, Iowa State Bar Asn; bd. dirs. and secy, Center Bowl, 60; Mason (32°), Des Moines Consistory, Za Ga Zig Shrine; Rotary Int; Am. Bar Asn; Des Moines Club; trustee, Dallas Co. Hosp. Bd; bd. of educ; Dallas Commun. Sch. Dist; Farm Bur. Rel: Presbyterian. Legal Res: 1507 Vine St, Dallas Center, Iowa 50063. Mailing Add: 502 15th St, Dallas Center, Iowa 50063.

McDONALD, JOHN COOPER D
Minority Floor Leader, Ohio House of Rep.
b. Newark, Ohio, 11/12/36; s. George Jennings McDonald and Isabelle Cooper M; m. 6/5/59 to Mary Jane Jagger; c. Steven Jagger, Anne Cooper and Nancy Kendall. Educ: Denison Univ, A.B. with honors, 58; Ohio State Univ. Col, Law, J.D, 61; Omicron Delta Kappa; Order of the Coif; Tau Kappa Alpha; Pi Sigma Alpha; Phi Delta Theta; Phi Delta Phi. Polit. & Govt. Pos: Mem, Licking Co. Dem. Exec. Cmt, Ohio, 61-66, campaign chmn, 62; v.pres. and treas, Licking Co. Men's Dem. Club, 62-64; solicitor, Heath, Ohio, 62-65; dir, Licking Co. Young Dem. Club, 65-66; Ohio State Rep, 65-, Minority Floor Leader, Ohio House of Rep; mem, Ohio Dem. Exec. Cmt, 67-; del, Dem. Nat. Conv, 68. Bus. & Prof. Pos: Partner, McDonald, Robison, McDonald & Spahr, Attorneys, 61- Publ: 'Judicial Protection of Minority Voting Rights,' Ohio State Univ. Law Jour, 61. Mem: Am. and Ohio State Bar Asns; treas, Licking Co. Bar Asn; Jaycees; Licking Co. and Ohio State Hist. Socs; League of Ohio Sportsmen; scoutmaster, Boy Scouts, 61-66. Winner, Am. Col. of Trial Lawyers Nat. Moot Court Competition, 61; recipient, Newark Jaycees Distinguished Serv. Award, 64, 66 & 67; John F. Kennedy Pub. Serv. Award, 67; Named One of Ohio's Five Outstanding Young Men, Ohio Jaycees, 68; Recipient of Gov. Award for Advancement of Ohio, 68. Rel: Presbyterian. Legal Res: 695 Snowdon Dr, Newark, Ohio 43055. Mailing Add: 63 N. Third St, Newark, Ohio 43055.

McDONALD, JOHN KENNETH 'JACK' D
Mont. State Sen.
b. Anacond, Mont, 2/17/29; s. Lennie McDonald and Margaret Murphy M; m. 11/23/65 to Marilyn McCafferty; c. Deanna, Kenneth, Kelly, Laurel and stepchildren, Jeff and Wende. Educ: Mont. State Univ, B.A. Polit. & Govt. Pos: Mont. State Rep, 65-66; Mont. State Sen, 67- Bus. & Prof. Pos: Owner, cattle ranch, 14 years. Mem: Jaycees; Ment. Health Asn; Mont. Stockgrowers Asn; Foothills Livestock Asn; Sch. Bd. Rel: Catholic. Mailing Add: Belt, Mont. 59412.

McDONALD, JOSEPH FRANCIS, JR. D
b. Reno, Nev, 9/8/16; s. Joseph F. McDonald and Leola Lewis M; m. 2/3/46 to Mary Gene Christianson; c. Tori Bimbra, Sally Bails, Tracy and Joseph, III. Educ: Univ. Nev, B.A, 41; Am. Univ, LL.B, 53; Sigma Alpha Epsilon; Delta Theta Phi. Polit. & Govt. Pos: Staff, U.S. Sen. Patrick McCarran, 49-53; alternate del, Dem. Nat. Conv, 52, 56, 64 & 68; staff, U.S. Sen. Alan Bible, 58-60. Bus. & Prof. Pos: Attorney-at-law, Nev, 53-, D.C, 53- Rel: Catholic. Mailing Add: 1830 Palisade Dr, Reno, Nev. 89502.

McDONALD, JOSEPH PAUL R
Chmn, Greer Co. Rep. Cmt, Okla.
b. Mena, Ark, 6/25/14; s. Charles Augustus McDonald and Mary Gray Moore M; m. 1/28/34 to Opal Irene Hamilton; c. Maryanne (Mrs. Ernest Leo Fite) and one grandson, Kurt Leo. Educ: High sch; honor roll; student coun. Polit. & Govt. Pos: Mem, Okla. Rep. State Resolutions Cmt, 62-64; chmn, Sixth Cong. Dist. Rep. Cmt, 62-67; chmn, Greer Co. Rep. Cmt, 62-67 and currently; chmn, Okla. Rep. Cand. Recruitment Cmt, 63-64; mem, Okla. Agr. Prod. Research Fund, 63-66; Okla. mem, credentials cmt. and del, Rep. Nat. Conv, 64; mem, statement of principles cmt, Okla. Rep. State Conv, 64. Bus. & Prof. Pos: V.pres, Honor Bilt Feed Mills, Inc, Mangum, Okla, 49- Mil. Serv: Entered as Enlisted Res, Air Force, 41-44; student, Cent. Instr. Sch, Kelley Field, Tex, 41, then serv. as flying instr, Air Force, 31 months. Mem: Okla. asst. dir, Am. Radio Relay League; grand marshal, Masonic Grand Lodge of Okla, 65-66; Scottish Rite, Mason (32°); Am. Legion; Farm Bur; finance chmn, Girl Scouts; adv. bd, Rainbow Girls; Air Force Asn; adv. bd, Cameron Col. Served on speaker's bur. at state level; long-time master of ceremonies at Radio Conv. and Old Settlers' Reunion and Fiddlin Contests; gen. class amateur radio operator, W5CCV and mem. Storm Warning Net, Okla, which originated tornado warnings serv. now used throughout U.S. and recognized by Fed. Weather Bur. Rel: Methodist; Certified Lay-Speaker, Okla. Conf. of Methodist Church. Mailing Add: 129 E. Cleveland, Mangum, Okla. 73554. (1967)

McDONALD, LEON N, SR. D
b. Jasper, Fla, 1/15/16; m. to Anne West; c. Leon, Jr, Tommy and Marty. Polit. & Govt. Pos: Fla. State Rep, 60-68; mem, Live Oak City Coun, two 4 year terms. Bus. & Prof. Pos: Retail grocer. Mil. Serv: Navy. Mem: Former pres. bd, Suwannee C. of C, 2 years; Suwannee Co. Farm Bur; adv. bd, Advent Christian Home; Worshipful Master, Barrett Lodge 43, Mason, 54; Lions; former bd. mem, Suwannee Country Club; Am. Legion. Rel: Baptist; Sunday Sch. Supt, Deacon. Mailing Add: 409 Helvenston St, Live Oak, Fla. 32060. (1967)

McDONALD, MILFORD EDGAR D
S.C. State Sen.
b. Honeapath, S.C, 4/17/18; s. Calvin C. McDonald and Rosa Hinton M; m. 6/16/50 to Anne Harper Hall; c. Rose Marie and Eddie. Educ: Erskine Col, A.B, 43; Exten. Course in Human Rels, Univ. Buffalo, 49-50. Polit. & Govt. Pos: Secy. bd. trustees, Sch. Dist. 3, S.C, 52-57; v.chmn, Co. Bd. of Educ, 59-60; S.C. State Rep, 61-68; chmn, Co. Dem. Exec. Cmt, 62-66; S.C. State Sen, 68- Bus. & Prof. Pos: Cost acct, Riegel Mfg. Co, 43; teacher and prin, Iva High Sch, 43-48; personnel off. mgr, Jackson Mills. Mem: Co. Hosp. Asn; WOW (coun. cmdr); Lions; C. of C.(pres, 54); bd. dirs, co. chap, Am. Red Cross, 56-60; secy-treas, United Charities, 58-64. Rel: Baptist. Mailing Add: Box 8, Iva, S.C. 29655.

McDONALD, ROBERT FAUCETTE R
Mem, Scott Co. Rep. Exec. Cmt, Miss.
b. Conehatta, Miss, 12/23/12; s. Owen McDonald and Hattie Irene Woodward M; m. 11/11/38 to Annie Lucille May, wid; c. Willard, Elmer Dean, Rose Tjawan (Mrs. Dennis Waite), Linda Faye (Mrs. David Beard), Harold Owen, Mary Ann and Lucy Robert. Educ: Meridian Commercial Col, 2 years; Detroit Transmission Sch, Lansing, Mich, 1 month, 54. Polit. & Govt. Pos: Mem, Miss. State Rep. Exec. Cmt, 46-64; chmn, Scott Co. Rep. Party, Miss, 46-64; crew leader, Bur. of the Census, 55-56 & 59-60; Justice of the Peace, 56-60; mem, Scott Co. Rep. Exec. Cmt, 64- Bus. & Prof. Pos: Parts mgr, Forest Auto Parts, Miss, 46-54; owner and operator, Cattle Ranch, Forest, Miss, 48-68; shop foreman, Ross Motor Co, Pelagatchie, 54-56; owner and operator, Country Corner Grocery, Forest, 56-61; mem. staff, maintenance dept, Sunbeam Corp, Forest, 61-64. Mil. Serv: Entered Coast Guard, 43, released as A/S, 44. Mem: Mason; VFW; DAV; Farm Bur. Rel: Baptist. Mailing Add: Route 1, Box 245, Forest, Miss. 39074.

MacDONALD, ROBERT WILLIAM D
b. Boston, Mass, 4/4/16; s. William H. MacDonald and Margaret Monahan M; m. 9/26/53 to Barbara A. Peterson; c. Geoffrey, Heather, Toby and Juli. Educ: Suffolk Univ. Law Sch, J.D. cum laude, 53. Polit. & Govt. Pos: Town moderator, Bourne, Mass, 56-59; pub. adminstr, Barnstable Co, Mass, 58-63; asst. dist. attorney, South Dist. Mass, 60-64; cmnr. pub. safety, Commonwealth of Mass, 64-65; del, Dem. Nat. Conv, 68. Bus. & Prof. Pos: Attorney-at-law, 53- Mil. Serv: Entered as Pvt, Air Force, 41, released as Cpl, 45. Mem: Am. and Mass. Trial Lawyers Asns; Am. and Mass. Bar Asns; Ancient & Hon. Artil. Co; Elks. Rel: Catholic. Mailing Add: Old Main St, Sandwich, Mass. 02563.

McDONALD, ROMMIE GEAN D
Ark. State Rep.
b. Sheridan, Ark, 2/2/11; s. Monroe Newton McDonald and Eva Gean M; m. 8/2/41 to Nan Watson; c. Julie Watson and Terry Gean. Educ: Ark. Polytech, 2 years. Polit. & Govt. Pos: Co. and circuit clerk, Grant Co, Ark, 47-58; Ark. State Rep, Grant Co, 65-66, Position Five, Dist. 33, Grant and Jefferson Co, 67-, chmn. efficiency cmt, Ark. House of Rep, 69-, v.chmn. oil and gas cmt, 69-, mem. state agencies cmt. and revenue and taxation cmt, 69- Bus. & Prof. Pos: Owner and operator, McDonald Abstract Co, Sheridan, 54- Mil. Serv: Entered as Pvt, Air Force, 40, released as S/Sgt, 46, after serv. in Hq. and Hq. Squadron, 27th Bomber Group, Southeast Asia, Bataan, Philippine Islands, 41-46; Japanese prisoner of war, three years; several medals. Mem: Ark. Abstractors; Southeast Ark. E.O.D; Shrine; Rotary. Rel: Protestant. Legal Res: 310 W. High, Sheridan, Ark. 72150. Mailing Add: 108 E. Pine, Sheridan, Ark. 72150.

McDONALD, SID L. D
Ala. State Rep.
b. Springville, Ala, 5/18/38; s. Leighton D. McDonald and Marie Oliver M; m. 4/19/61 to Ann Burnham; c. Foster Oliver and Kelly Marie. Educ: Univ. Ala, B.S, 61; Phi Gamma Delta. Polit. & Govt. Pos: Ala. State Rep, Seventh Dist, 66- Bus. & Prof. Pos: Pres, Brindlee Mt. Tel. Co, Arab, Ala, 61- Rel: Methodist. Legal Res: 721 Sixth St. N.E, Arab, Ala. 35016. Mailing Add: Box 546, Arab, Ala. 35016.

McDONALD, THOMAS JAMES, JR. D
b. Dahlonega, Ga, 8/28/25; s. Thomas J. McDonald, Sr. and Ollie Anderson McD; m. 1/05/51 to Mildred Edwards; c. Cheryl Joyce, Jamie Lisa. Educ: Cleveland High Sch, 43. Polit. & Govt. Pos: Ga. State Rep, 61-64. Bus. & Prof. Pos: Salesman, 46- Mil. Serv: WW II, 43-Apr. 46. Mem: Mason; Elk; Kiwanis; Am. Legion; 40 et 8; VFW; Skitt Mt. Golf & Country Club. Rel: Baptist. Mailing Add: Cleveland, Ga. 30528. (1967)

McDONALD, TOM JOSEPH R
b. Fargo, N.Dak, 1/10/39; s. Freeman McDonald (deceased) and Fern Shannon M; m. 10/24/58 to Janet Smith; c. Terry, Tammy, Cheryl and Brian. Educ: N.Dak. State Univ, 2 years; Alpha Tau Omega. Polit. & Govt. Pos: For-

mer N.Dak. State Rep. Mem: Pres, Southwest Fargo Jaycees, 65-66; pub. rels. officer, N.Dak. State Jaycees, 66-67. Rel: Catholic. Mailing Add: 324 Cherry Court, West Fargo, N.Dak. 58078.

MacDONALD, TORBERT H. D
U.S. Rep, Mass.
b. Boston, Mass, 6/6/17; s. John G. MacDonald and Harriet Hart M; m. 6/44 to Phyllis Brooks; c. Torbert Hart, Laurie, Brian and Robin. Educ: Phillips Andover Acad; Harvard Univ, A.B, 40; LL.B, 46. Polit. & Govt. Pos: Trial attorney, New Eng. Nat. Labor Rels. Bd, 48-52; U.S. Rep, Mass, 55-; del, Dem. Nat. Conv, 68. Bus. & Prof. Pos: Legal asst. to Eric Johnston, Motion Picture Producers Asn, 46-47. Mil. Serv: Lt.(jg), USNR, 42-44; comdr, PT boat; decorated Silver Star; Presidential Citation. Mem: Fed, Mass. and Middlesex Bar Asns; All East. Selection Football, 39- Legal Res: 63 Appleton St, Malden, Mass. 02148. Mailing Add: 2448 Rayburn Bldg, Washington, D.C. 20515.

McDONALD, WALTER RALEIGH D
Cmnr, Ga. Pub. Serv. Cmn.
b. Augusta, Ga, 1/18/92; s. Alexander G. McDonald and Belzora Chambers M; m. Dec, 1932 to Estelle Carpenter; c. Walter R, Jr. and Martha (Mrs. Frank C. Griffin); Five grandchildren. Educ: Ga. Acad. for Blind; Overbrook Sch. for Blind, 10; Brown Col. Prep, 11; Univ. Ga, LL.B, 14; I.C.C. Practitioners; Gridiron Secret Soc; Old Warhorse Lawyers Club. Polit. & Govt. Pos: Ga. State Rep, 17-23; cmnr, Ga. Pub. Serv. Cmn, 23-; exec. secy. and dir, Freight Rate Sect, South. Gov. Conf, 30's-; mem, State Dem. Exec. Cmt, Ga; dir, Transportation and Utilities Sect. of State Civil Defense, Ga. and dir, Utilities Div, 42-46. Mem: Ga. Bar Asn; emer. pres, Ga. Fedn of Blind; v.pres, Ways and Means Cmt. for the Blind; chmn, DeKalb Educ. Found; Southeast. Asn. R.R. and Utilities Cmnrs.(pres); Nat. Asn. R.R. and Cmnrs.(chmn. cmt. on R.R. Probs. and subcmt. on asn. finance, former pres. Asn. and former chmn, Spec.War Cmt, World War II); Lions; Elks; K. of P. Rel: Baptist. Legal Res: Augusta, Ga. Mailing Add: 244 Washington St. S.W, Atlanta, Ga. 30334.

MACDONALD, WILLIAM D
Mem, Nev. State Dem. Cent. Cmt.
b. Los Angeles, Calif, 11/23/32; s. Maxwell Macdonald and Helen Margaret Langner M; m. 9/14/63 to Blanche Jean Trounday. Educ: Univ. of Nev, B.S. in Agr, 57; Wash. Col. of Law, LL.B, 63; Lambda Chi Alpha; Delta Theta Phi. Polit. & Govt. Pos: Del, Nev. State Dem. Conv, 54-; chmn. and alternate del, Dem. Nat. Conv, 56, del, 68; ranching rep, Nev. Indust. Cmt, 57-59; staff mem, U.S. Sen. Alan Bible, Wash, D.C, 60-63; lawyer and Asst. Dist. Attorney, Humboldt Co, Nev, 63-66, Dist. Attorney, 67-; Dep. Dist. Attorney, Lander Co, 64-66, acting Dist. Attorney, 66; chmn, Humboldt Co. Dem. Cent. Cmt, 64-66; mem, Nev. State Dem. Cent. Cmt, 64-, past chmn, 66-68. Bus. & Prof. Pos: Sportswriter, Nev. State Jour, Reno, 50-51 & 54-57; legal asst, Sierra Pac. Power Co, 63. Mil. Serv: Entered as Seaman 2/C, Navy, 52, released as PO 3/C, 53. Mem: K. of C; Elks; Nev. Taxpayers Asn; State Bar of Nev; Am. Bar Asn; dir, Humboldt Co. C. of C; Nev. Farm Bur; Sierra Nev. Sportswriters & Broadcasters Asn; exec. cmt, Univ. of Nev. Alumni Asn; Nev. State Cattle Asn; Las Vegas Press Club. Rel: Roman Catholic. Legal Res: One Vista Ave, Winnemucca, Nev. 89445. Mailing Add: Humboldt County Court House, Winnemucca, Nev. 89445.

McDONNELL, HOWARD ANDRE D
b. New Orleans, La, 6/13/09; married. Polit. & Govt. Pos: Miss. State Rep, 40-44; Miss. State Sen, 44-48, 52-56 & 64-69. Bus. & Prof. Pos: Attorney; criminologist; State Bd. of Bar Exam. Mem: Miss, Am. Bar Asn; Biloxi C. of C. Rel: Lutheran. Mailing Add: McDonnell Ave, Biloxi, Miss. 39531. (1967)

McDONOUGH, GEORGE GIBSON D
b. Brooklyn, N.Y, 11/1/32; s. Augustus McDonough (deceased) and Louise Gibson M; m. 10/6/56 to Carolyn Black; c. Carolyn Louise. Educ: Univ. Notre Dame, B.A, 54; Hunter Col, M.A, 62; Brooklyn Col, M.S, 67; Deans List; Scribes, Monogram Club. Polit. & Govt. Pos: Del, Dem. Nat. Conv, 68. Bus. & Prof. Pos: Col. counsr, Brooklyn Tech. High Sch, 61-; asst. prof, Eng, City Col, N.Y, 66- Mem: N.Y. City Asn. of Guid. Personnel; N.Y. City Asn. of Teachers of Eng; United Fedn. Col. Teachers; United Fedn. Teachers; Mensa. Rel: Roman Catholic. Mailing Add: 1475 E. 48th St, Brooklyn, N.Y. 11234.

McDONOUGH, GORDON LEO R
b. Buffalo, N.Y, 1/2/95; s. Sylvester Henry McDonough and Ellen Parker M; m. to Catherine Ann McNeil; c. Marie Louise (Mrs. Richard H. Miller), Lucile Elaine (Mrs. John F. Mannelly), Gordon L, Jr, Thomas C, James Q, Vincent S. and Paul M. Educ: Emporium High Sch, Pa. Polit. & Govt. Pos: Supvr, Los Angeles Co, Calif, 33-45; chmn, Los Angeles Co. Flood Control Dist. and Sanit. Dist; first chmn, Los Angeles Co. War Coun; U.S. Rep, Calif, 45-66, mem, House Banking and Currency Cmt, Merchant Marine and Fisheries Cmt, Subcmt. on Housing, Joint Cmt. on Defense Prod. and original mem, Sci. and Astronautics Cmt, U.S. House of Rep; U.S. del. to Interparliamentary Union. Bus. & Prof. Pos: Indust. engr, salesman and chemist with various companies, 11-33. Mem: Nat. Asn. Co. Officials; VFW (hon); exec. bd. Los Angeles Metrop. Area Coun. Boy Scouts. Received citation from Navy for aid in civilian recruiting, from U.S. Treas. for bond sales, from Am. Legion for meritorious serv. rendered to vets, from Cabrillo Assembly, K. of C, for leadership in civic affairs and humanitarian probs, from Cabrillo Chap, DAR, for serv. and accomplishments for protection of our Constitutional Republic. Rel: Catholic. Mailing Add: 4121 S. Bronson Ave, Los Angeles, Calif. 90008. (1967)

McDONOUGH, PETER J. R
N.J. State Assemblyman
b. Plainfield, N.J, 8/24/25; m. to Elizabeth Driscoll; c. Mary, Peter and Martha. Educ: St. Lawrence Univ. Polit. & Govt. Pos: Mem, Union Co. Welfare Bd. and Bd. Sch. Estimate, N.J; mem, Finance, Pub. Affairs, Admin. and Roads and Bridges Cmts; mem, Bd. Chosen Freedholders, 60-63; N.J. State Assemblyman, 63-, chmn, Educ. Cmt. and Cmn. to Study Child Labor Laws, mem, Pub. Safety, Defense and Vet. Affairs, Printed Bills, Rules and Order and Interstate Coop. Cmts, N.J. State Assembly, majority whip, 68-69; del, N.J. Constitutional Conv, 66. Bus. & Prof. Pos: V.pres, Plainfield Lumber & Supply Co; dir. and v.pres, J.S. Irving Co. and Auto Fleet Leasing Co; dir, Morris Plains Lumber & Coal Co. and Queen City Savings & Loan Asn; v.pres, All State Cablevision. Mil. Serv: Air Force, Japan and Pac. Theater, World War II. Mem: N.J. Lumber Dealers Asn; Union Co. Fuel Oil Dealers; Jr. C. of C; Kiwanis; VFW; Am. Legion; Nat. Rivers & Harbors Cong; C. of C; Hibernian Club; Boy Scouts; Cancer Fund; Elks; Crippled Kiddies Cmt; K. of C; Red Cross; March of Dimes; Heart Fund; High Sch. Boosters. Selected Young Man of Year, Jaycees, 58 and Man of Year, Plainfield Serv. Clubs, 60. Rel: Roman Catholic. Mailing Add: 925 Oakwood Place, Plainfield, N.J. 07060.

McDONOUGH, RAYMOND J. D
Md. State Del.
b. Glen Ridge, N.J, 11/14/21; married. Educ: George Wash. Univ, LL.B, 51. Polit. & Govt. Pos: Town attorney, Forest Heights, Md, 60-63; Md. State Del, 63- Mil. Serv: Army, 42-46. Mailing Add: 5410 Indian Head Highway, Oxon Hill, Md. 20021.

McDONOUGH, ROBERT PAUL D
b. Parkersburg, W.Va, 3/13/15; s. Patrick J. McDonough and Virginia Goff M; m. 12/26/41 to Martha Sinclair Smith; c. Sara Katherine and Robert Sinclair. Educ: Univ. Notre Dame, A.B, 36. Polit. & Govt. Pos: Chmn, W.Va. Dem. Exec. Cmt, 61-64; committeeman, Dem. Nat. Cmt, 64-65; dir, W.Va. Dept. Natural Resources, 65-66; Dem. campaign chmn. and alternate del, Dem. Nat. Conv, 68. Bus. & Prof. Pos: Pres, Park Press Inc, 46- Mil. Serv: Entered as Pvt, Infantry, 41, released as Capt, Corps Engrs, 45, after serv. in Seventh Army, ETO; Bronze Star. Mailing Add: 1124 Ann St, Parkersburg, W.Va. 26101.

MacDOUGAL, HARRY MARTIN R
Chmn, Essex Co. Rep. Cmt, N.Y.
b. Elizabethtown, N.Y, 8/12/83; s. Harry Martin MacDougal and Jennie Durand M; m. to Alice Dougan; wid. 56; c. Arline, Allister and Helen (Mrs. Richards). Educ: Elizabethtown High Sch; Albany Bus. Col. Polit. & Govt. Pos: Supvr, Elizabethtown, N.Y, 26-33; clerk, Essex Co, 33-65; chmn, Essex Co. Rep. Cmt, 56- Bus. & Prof. Pos: Past mercantile businessman, Elizabethtown, N.Y. Mem: Mason; Elks; Grange; Kiwanis. Rel: Congregational. Mailing Add: Elizabethtown, N.Y. 12932.

McDOUGAL, JEROME R. JR. D
b. Lynnbrook, N.Y, 2/2/28; m. to Rosa de Rosa; c. Jerome III, Linda Ann. Educ: Am. Inst. of Banking, Hofstra Col. Polit. & Govt. Pos: N.Y. State Assemblyman, 64-66. Bus. & Prof. Pos: Pres, Rupp Chevrolet Corp; former v.pres. of Dodge Agency in Freeport; former v.pres, Peninsula Nat. Bank of Cedarhurst. Mil. Serv: U.S. Army, Korean Conflict. Mem: Exec. bd, L.I. Better Bus. Bur; Northwest Civic Asn. of Freeport; S. Shore Chap. of Cancer Care; Cath. Interracial Coun; Nat. Conf. of Christians and Jews; Ancient Order of Hibernians; membership chmn, Sons of Italy; v.comdr, Cath. War Vets Holy Name Soc; past activities pres, Gr. New York, Long Island, and Westchester Auto Dealers Asn; Five Towns Family Serv. Asn; Five Towns Commun. Chest; Consumer Credit Cmt, Am. Bankers Asn; Installment Credit Cmt, N.Y. State Bankers Asn; treas, Lawrence-Cedarhurst Civil Defense Unit; pres. Holy Name Soc, St. Joachim's Church, Cedarhurst. Rel: Queen of the Most Holy Rosary Church, Roosevelt, L.I. Mailing Add: 134 N.Y. Ave, Freeport, N.Y. 11520. (1967)

McDOUGAL, MILTON R
Wis. State Assemblyman
b. Spruce, Wis, 7/21/17. Educ: High Sch. Polit. & Govt. Pos: Wis. State Assemblyman, 64-, v.chmn, Cmt. on Transportation and Joint Surv. Cmt. Retirement Systs, Wis. State Assembly. Bus. & Prof. Pos: Livestock bus, 35; owner and mgr, Dairy Farm. Mem: Sportsman's Club; REA; Elks; Mason (32°); Nat. Farm Orgn; Farmers Union; Grange. Mailing Add: 402 Chestnut St, Oconto Falls, Wis. 54154.

McDOUGALL, ROBERT DUNCAN R
Wash. State Sen.
b. Cashmere, Wash, 8/3/24; s. Ernest Barr McDougall and Martha Alice Umbarger M; m. 1/24/47 to Jacquelyn Horan; c. Douglas, Stuart and Scott. Educ: Wenatchee Valley Col, A.A; Wash. State Univ, B.A, 51; Sigma Delta Chi; Sigma Phi Epsilon. Polit. & Govt. Pos: Wash. State Rep, 60-68; Wash. State Sen, 68- Bus. & Prof. Pos: Sect. mgr, Horan Bros. Inc, 51-; owner, McDougall Orchards, 60-; pres, Skyline Orchards Inc, 66- Mil. Serv: Entered as A/S, Navy, 42, released as RM 1/C, 46, after serv. in Pacific Theatre, 45-46. Mem: Am. Legion; Elks; Grange; Washington-Oregon Canning Pear Asn; Wenatchee Golf and Country Club. Rel: Methodist. Mailing Add: Route 2, Box 2001, Wenatchee, Wash. 98801.

McDOW, JAMES THOMAS D
b. Roanoke, Ala, 5/11/20; s. J. R. McDow and Ruby Tyson M; m. 6/7/42 to Mildred Tipswood; c. James Thomas Jr, Richard Henry and Patricia Susan. Educ: Ga. Mil. Col; Auburn. Polit. & Govt. Pos: Ala. State Sen, until 66; Columbiana Housing Authority; City Coun; chmn, Water Bd; chmn, City Bd. of Sch. Tr. Bus. & Prof. Pos: Auto dealer. Mil. Serv: Navy. Mem: Mason; Shrine; moderator, Shelby Baptist Asn. Rel: Baptist; Sunday Sch. teacher. Mailing Add: Columbiana, Ala. 35051.

McDOWELL, HARRIS B, JR. D
b. Middletown, Del, 2/10/06; m. 1928 to Florence R. Neary; c. Kendall (Mrs. Ernest Wilson, Jr), Joan L.(Mrs. Arthur Connolly, Jr) and Harris, III. Educ: Beacon Bus. Col. Polit. & Govt. Pos: Mem, State Bd. Agr, Del, 37-40; Del. State Rep, 40-42; Del. State Sen, 42-46; chmn, New Castle Co. Dem. Cmt, 42-46; Secy. of State, Del, 49-53; mem, New Castle Zoning Cmn, 53-54; U.S. Rep, Del, 54-66; Dem. cand. for U.S. Rep, Del, 68. Bus. & Prof. Pos: Farmer; ins. and real estate. Rel: Presbyterian. Mailing Add: St. Ann's Church Rd, Middletown, Del. 19709. (1967)

McDOWELL, JOSEPH HAMPTON D
Mayor, Kansas City, Kans.
b. Belleville, Kans, 10/15/07; s. Joseph Hampton McDowell and Nellie P. Sandels M; m. 12/25/33 to Claudene Stone; c. Hampton. Educ: Kans. Univ; Debate Soc; Phi Alpha Delta. Polit. & Govt. Pos: Judge, City Court, Kansas

City, Kans, 36-40; attorney, Wyandotte Co, 40-42; Kans. State Sen, Fourth Dist, 48-64; mayor, Kansas City, 64-; del, Dem. Nat. Conv, 68. Mil. Serv: Entered as 1st Lt, Marine Corps, 43, released as Capt, 45, after serv. in Fleet Marine Force, Pac. Mem: Kans, Am. and Wyandotte Co. Bar Asns. Rel: Episcopal. Legal Res: 2100 Washington Blvd, Kansas City, Kans. 66102. Mailing Add: City Hall, Kansas City, Kans. 66101.

McDOWELL, MAY ROSS R
b. Buffalo, N.Y, 5/11/98; d. Elmer A. Ross and Susan Turner R; m. 8/29/38 to George Howard McDowell; c. George Ross (deceased). Educ: East Tenn. State Univ, 1½ years; East Tenn. Law Sch, LL.B; Kappa Delta. Hon. LL.D, Steed Col, 62. Polit. & Govt. Pos: Gen. chmn. or co-chmn, Lincoln Dinner, Johnson City, Tenn, 34-; co-chmn, Washington Co. Rep. Exec. Cmt, Tenn, 34-46; alternate del, Rep. Nat. Conv, 36 & 68; mem, State Rep. Exec. Cmt, 38-52; active in Rep. Workshop, several years; city cmnr, Johnson City, Tenn, 57-65, v.mayor, 2 years, mayor, 2 years, mem. city power bd, 2 years, mem. planning cmn, 2 years; representative, Inter-Am. Munic. Cong, Punta del Este, 62 and representative Sister City Affiliation, Ecuador, 63-; charter mem, Wash. Co. Fedn. Rep. Women, dir, 60-68; gen. chmn, Calvacade Stars Fund Raising Dinner, 68; patron, Wash. Co. Young Rep. Club and sponsor Tenn. Singing Rep. Bus. & Prof. Pos: Off. mgr. and corporate secy, Empire Chair Co, 21-34; lawyer, 35-43; v.pres. and secy, Johnson City Foundry & Machine Co, 46-69, pres. and treas, Johnson City Foundry & Machine Works, Inc, 69- Publ: History Patrick-Henry Families of Virginia, Inc, 56, rev. 66, History Johnson City Foundry & Machine Works, Inc, 68 and History Johnson City Business and Professional Women's Club, 69, locally published. Mem: Nat. Lawyers Club, D.C; Wash. Co, Tenn. and Am. Bar Asns; Nat. Asn. Women Lawyers; Am. Judicature Soc; Bus. & Prfnl. Women's Clubs; League Women Voters; Monday Club; Friends of Museum; Kappa Delta Alumnae Asn; C. of C; DAR; Colonial Dames of XVII Century; Daughters Colonial Wars; dir, Town Affiliation Asn. U.S; Johnson City Country Club. Cert. of Meritorious Serv, U.S. Dept. Labor, 63; Ky. Col, Gov. Ky, 64; First Distinguished Woman in Residence, Univ. Colo, 65; Woman of Year, Tenn. Fedn. Bus. & Prfnl. Women's Clubs, 66. Rel: Baptist. Legal Res: 426 Highland Ave, Johnson City, Tenn. 37601. Mailing Add: P.O. Box 359, Johnson City, Tenn. 37601.

McDOWELL, PATRICK GLENN, JR. D
b. East Spencer, N.C, 3/15/27; s. Patrick Glenn McDowell and Bertie Grubb M; m. 9/20/46 to Beulah Mae Hayes; c. Sherrie Diane, Patrick Glenn, III and Mona Lisa. Educ: San Jacinto Jr. Col, Deer Park, Tex. and Lee Jr. Col, Baytown, 1 year; Univ. Houston, 1 year. Polit. & Govt. Pos: City councilman, South Houston, Tex, 56-66; pres, Harris Co. Mayors & Councilmans Asn, Houston, 65-66; mem, Bd. of Dirs-Exec. Cmt, Off. Econ. Opportunity, 66-68; del, Tex. State Dem. Conv, 68; del, Dem. Nat. Conv, 68; mem, Bd. of Mgr, Harris Co. Hosp. Dist, Houston, Tex, 69- Bus. & Prof. Pos: Operator, Shell Oil Co, 52-63; co-owner, Rogers & McDowell Automotive, 63- Mil. Serv: Entered as A/S, Navy, 42, released as Motor Machinist Mate 1/C, 47, after serv. in Fleet, European-Africa-Middle East Theaters, 43-44; Am. Campaign Medal, European-Africa-Middle East Theatres; World War II Victory and Good Conduct Medals. Mem: Past pres, Methodist Men, 68-69; second v.pres, South Houston C. of C; post adj, South Houston VFW; AF&AM; past v.pres, South Houston Jr. C. of C; past pres, South Houston Optimist Club; Union Stewart, Local 4367, OCAWIU. Rel: Methodist. Mailing Add: 1303 Ave K, South Houston, Tex. 77587.

McDUNN, HENRY J. D
Chmn, Teton Co. Dem. Cent. Cmt, Mont.
b. Ft. Benton, Mont, 7/7/26; s. LeRoy Henry McDunn and Marie Qunell M; m. 3/31/51 to Eva Olson; c. Charlotte (Mrs. Goulet), Henry David, Richard, Ronald, John and Eva. Educ: High sch. Polit. & Govt. Pos: Secy, Dem. Club, Teton Co, Mont, 61; secy, Teton Co. Dem. Cent. Cmt, 63, chmn, 64- Bus. & Prof. Pos: Mgr, Stanford Coop. Asn, 48, F.U.G.T.A. Line Elevator, 51 and Dutton Coop Asn, 55- Mil. Serv: Entered as A/S, Navy, 44, released as OM 2, 47, after serv. in various Navy units, Pac. Theatre, 45-47. Rel: Catholic. Mailing Add: Dutton, Mont. 59433.

MACE, LEE F. D
b. Kanab, Utah, 9/5/26; s. Charles A. Mace and Blanche Hicks M; m. 5/7/54 to Shirley A. Maricle; c. Perry L, Charles A. and Debra A. Educ: Kanab High Sch, Utah, grad, 44; Army Air Force Tech. Sch, 6 months; Voc. Agr. Exten. Sch, 47-48; L.S. Symtronic TV Technician, 65; Utah State Voc. Educ. for Carpenter Foremen, 65. Polit. & Govt. Pos: Del, Uintah Co. Dem. Conv, 64, 65 & 68; del, Utah State Dem. Conv, 64, 65, 67 & 68; Dem. precinct chmn, Uintah Co, Utah, 65-; finance chmn, Uintah Co. Dem. Party, 66, chmn, 67-69; mem, Utah State Dem. Finance Cmt, 66; mem, Utah State Dem. Patronage Cmt, 67-69; del, Dem. Nat. Conv, 68; Uintah Co. campaign coordinator, Rampton for Gov. of Utah, 68. Bus. & Prof. Pos: Farmer and stock man, until 51; oil field driller, various West. States, 51-58; oil field sr. testing engr, Johnston Testers, Wyo, Colo. and Utah, 58-62; carpenter, Utah, 62- Mil. Serv: Entered as Pvt, Army Air Corps, 45, released as Sgt, 46, after serv. in 39th Fighter Squadron, 5th Air Force Japan; S/Sgt, Air Corps Res, 44-45 & 46-49; Asiatic Pac. Campaign Medal; World War II Victory Medal; Army of Occup. Medal. Mem: Trustee, Carpenters Local 2175, Vernal, Utah; Boy Scouts (adv. chmn); PTA. Rel: Latter-day Saint. Mailing Add: R.F.D. 1, Box 273A, Vernal, Utah 84078.

MACE, SHIRLEY A. D
b. Wayne, Nebr, 1/14/33; d. Seth A. Maricle and Lessie Mae Beaton M; m. 5/7/54 to Lee F. Mace; c. Perry L, Charles A. and Debra A. Educ: Greeley High Sch, Colo, grad. Polit. & Govt. Pos: Dem. precinct v.chmn, Maeser, Uintah Co, Utah, 64; census enumerator, Dept. of Agr, Uintah, 64; del, Uintah Co. Dem. Conv, 65 & 68; mgr, State Tax Cmn. Br. Off, Vernal, Utah, 65-; alternate del, Dem. Nat. Conv, 68. Bus. & Prof. Pos: Dept. supvr. and cashier, F.W. Woolworth, Greeley, Colo, 49-52; Mt. State Tel. Operator, 52-53; bookkeeper, Montgomery Wards, 58-59. Mem: VFW Auxiliary; DAV Auxiliary; Lazy Eye Clinic; Maeser Be Natural Club; Utah State Employees Asn; PTA. Rel: Latter-day Saint. Mailing Add: R.F.D. 1, Box 273A, Vernal, Utah 84078.

McEACHERN, PAUL D
City Coun, Portsmouth, N.H.
b. Portsmouth, N.H, 12/30/37; s. Archie D. McEachern and Ann T. Regan M; m. 9/15/62 to Donna Lucas; c. Claire, Alec and Duncan. Educ: Univ. of N.H, B.A, 63; Boston Univ. Sch. of Law, LL.B, 66. Polit. & Govt. Pos: N.H. State Rep, 63-65; del. Dem. Nat. Conv, 68; asst. mayor and city coun, Portsmouth, N.H, 68- Mil. Serv: Entered as Recruit, Navy, 56, released as GS-2, 60, after serv. in Guided Missiles, 56-60. Mem: Am. Bar Asn; Am. Trial Lawyers Asn. Rel: Catholic. Mailing Add: 50 Meadow Rd, Portsmouth, N.H. 03801.

McEACHERN, RAYMOND JOSEPH D
b. Portsmouth, N.H, 12/30/42; single. Educ: Univ. N.H. Polit. & Govt. Pos: N.H. State Rep, 65-66; del, Constitutional Conv; N.H. Young Dem; pres, Portsmouth Young Dem. Club. Rel: Catholic. Mailing Add: 70 Stark St, Portsmouth, N.H. 03801.

McELMURRAY, JEANNE FRANCES D
State Committeewoman, Dem. Exec. Cmt. Fla.
b. Junction City, Kans, 3/6/21; d. James Otto Delver and Elizabeth Stillie D; m. 7/8/44 to George Long McElmurray; c. Guy James Burnett and Peter Delver. Educ: Junction City High Sch, Kans, grad, 39. Polit. & Govt. Pos: Precinct committeewoman, Sarasota Co. Dem. Exec. Cmt, Fla, 60-, chmn, 66-67; pres, Sarasota Dem. Woman's Club, 64-65; v.pres, Seventh Cong. Dist. Dem. Woman's Club Fla, 65-66; pres, Cent. Sarasota Dem. Woman's Club, 65-67; v.chmn, Seventh Cong. Dist. Dem. Exec. Cmt. Fla, 66-; state committeewoman, Dem. Exec. Cmt. Fla, 66-; del, Dem. Nat. Conv, 68. Mem: Siesta Key C. of C; Sarasota Garden Club; Nat. League of Am. Pen Women; Sarasota Co. Civic League; Audubon Soc; Sarasota Community Serv. Club; Taxpayers Asn. of Siesta Key; Sarasota Co. Dem. Club; Eastern Star; Sarasota Mental Health Asn; Sarasota Bd. Realtors; Save Ours Bays Asn; Coun. on Epilepsy; Community Goals Coun; United Need. Community Leader of Am, 68; Only Hon. Life Mem, Cent. Sarasota Dem. Woman's Club; Beautification Cmt, State C. of C. Rel: Protestant. Mailing Add: 1661 Sunrise Lane, Sarasota, Fla. 33581.

McELROY, BERT R
b. Altus, Okla, 9/24/17; s. John W. McElroy and Tera Harrison McE; m. 8/20/39 to Nella Fae Colyar; c. Bert Colyar, Martha Jane and Meredith. Educ: Altus Jr. Col; Okla. Univ; Okla. Univ. Sch. Law, LL.B; N.Y. Univ, taxation study; Phi Delta Phi; Holmes Inn. Polit. & Govt. Pos: Pres, Tulsa Co. Young Rep, Okla, 47-48 and Tulsa Co. Rep. Minutemen, 51-52; chmn, Tulsa Co. Rep. Cmt, 52-54 & 65-67; Rep. State Committeeman, Tulsa Co, 54-62; del, Rep. Nat. Conv, 60; legal mem, Okla. State Ment. Health Bd, 64- Mil. Serv: Entered as Pvt, Army, 42, released as Capt, 46, after serv. in Inf. and Transportation Corps; recalled 50 and released 51, after serv. as Capt, 306th Logistical Command, Judge Adv. Gen. Corps; Army Commendation and Victory Medals; Am. Theater Ribbon. Mem: Chmn, Constitution and By-Laws Cmt, Tulsa Co. Bar Asn, 66, exec. cmt, 65-66 and chmn, Nominating Cmt, 65; Mason, Scottish Rite (32°), York Rite, Commandery; Okla. Bar Asn; Am. Judicature Soc; Appaloosa Horse Asn; Tex. and Southwest Cattlemen's Asn. Rel: Baptist; Deacon, chmn. of bd, First Baptist Church, Tulsa, Okla, 4 years. Mailing Add: 1382 E. 27th St, Tulsa, Okla. 74114. (1967)

McELROY, NEIL H. R
b. Berea, Ohio, 10/30/04; s. Malcolm Ross McElroy and Susan Harriet Hosler M; m. 6/29/29 to Mary Camilla Fry; c. Nancy Sue (Mrs. Folger), Barbara Ellen (Mrs. Dimling) and Malcolm Neil. Educ: Harvard Univ, A.B, 25. Polit. & Govt. Pos: Secy. of Defense, 57-59. Bus. & Prof. Pos: Chmn. of bd, Procter & Gamble Co, 59-; dir, Gen. Elec. Co; Chrysler Corp; Equitable Assurance Soc. U.S; trustee, Nat. Safety Coun; Atlantic Coun, U.S. Inc; chmn, Coun. Financial Aid to Educ; Nat. Coun. United Negro Col. Fund; Vis. Cmt. Harvard Center Int. Affairs; entered advert. dept, Procter & Gamble Co, 25, mgr. promotion dept, 29-40; mgr. advert. and promotion, 40-43, dir. and v.pres. in charge of advert, 43-46, v.pres. and gen. mgr, 46-48, pres, 48-57. Mem: Past mem. or exec. officer, several nat. citizens orgn. for educ. and commun. welfare; pres. bd. overseers, Harvard Univ, chmn. vis. cmt. grad. sch. of educ. and chmn. cmt. on univ. resources; Bohemian Club, San Francisco; Cincinnati Country Club; Harvard Club; Nat. Indust. Conf. Bd, Inc.(trustee, 53-57 & 60-64, v.chmn, 55-56, chmn, 57); chmn, White House Conf. on Educ, 54-55; Commonwealth Commercial Club, pres, 60-61; v.chmn, Tribute of a Grateful Nation Fund, Eisenhower Col, 69; Camargo Club; Queen City Club, Cincinnati; Links Club; 29 Club, N.Y.C; Chevy Chase Club, Wash, D.C; Bus. Coun; Cmt. for Corporate Support of Am. Univs. Legal Res: 3478 Vista Terr. Cincinnati, Ohio 45208. Mailing Add: 301 E. Sixth St, Cincinnati, Ohio 45202.

McELVEEN, GEORGE RAYMOND D
S.C. State Rep.
b. Sumter Co, S.C, 9/10/96; s. Robert Elliott McElveen and Mary Anne Skinner M; m. 6/25/24 to Susan V. Powers McElveen. Educ: Presby. Col, B.S, 18; Univ. S.C, LL.B, M.A, 21; Sigma Nu. Polit. & Govt. Pos: S.C. State Rep, 49- Bus. & Prof. Pos: Lawyer; farmer. Mil. Serv: Navy, World War I. Mem: Palmetto Club; Exec. Club; Forest Lake Club. Mailing Add: 1525 Wyndham Rd, Columbia, S.C. 29205. (1967)

McELWAIN, CALVIN LEWIS D
Mem, Calif. Dem. State Cent. Cmt.
b. Lewistown, Pa, 4/25/29; s. Herbert Clifford McElwain and Mildred Guthridge M; m. 7/21/49 to Juneita May Nelle 'Nita'; c. Mickey Stephen, Bradford Allen, Daira Lee, Eric Dane, Erin Jo and Jason Cowan. Educ: Chaffey Jr. Col, part time 1 year. Polit. & Govt. Pos: Legis. rep, Subdist. two, USW, Nev. and South. Calif, 67-69; mem, exec. cmt, West End Dem. Club, Upland, 68-69; mem, Calif. Dem. State Cent. Cmt, 68- Mil. Serv: Entered as Pvt, Army, 46, released as Pfc, 48, after serv. in First Cavalry Div, Pac. Theatre, Japan. Mem: Mason; Elks; Scottish Rite Bodies; Am. Legion; Shrine. Rel: Baptist. Mailing Add: 2658 Mountain Ave, Upland, Calif. 91786.

McELWAIN, S. MARION D
Dir, State's Speakers Bur, Colo. Dem. Party
b. Chicago, Ill, 5/28/32; d. Herbert Holm and Mary Eleanor Stevenson H; m. 12/30/50 to William H. McElwain; c. Mary K, Martin William and Donna Marie. Educ: Univ. Colo, 59-63. Polit. & Govt. Pos: Committeewoman, Boulder Co. Dem. Party, Colo, 61-; treas, Dem. Women Boulder Co, 65-67 and pres, 67-68; mem, Boulder Co. Dem. Exec. Cmt, 68; dir, state speaker's bur, Colo. Dem. Party, 68-; mem, Colo. State Dem. Cent. Cmt, 69; cand. for

state v.chmn, Colo. Dem. Party, 69. Bus. & Prof. Pos: Acct, Ball Bros. Research, Boulder, 64-66; bookkeeper, Pruett Press, 66-69. Mem: Int. Toastmistress Clubs; League Women Voters; Jane Jefferson Club of Denver. Rel: Catholic. Mailing Add: 4450 Chippewa Dr, Boulder, Colo. 80303.

McESSY, EARL F. R
Wis. State Assemblyman
b. Fond du Lac Co, Wis, 2/12/13. Educ: Marquette Univ, B.S, 39. Polit. & Govt. Pos: Wis. State Assemblyman, 56-; undersheriff; traffic officer. Bus. & Prof. Pos: Real estate broker; formerly purchasing agent; factory laborer. Mil. Serv: Navy, 42-46; S. Pac, 7 Battle Stars; 3 Spec. Citations. Mem: Elks Youth Activity Cmt, 58-61; chmn. Red Cross Chap, 57-58; pres. local PTA, 53-55; v.pres. Cent. Educ. Coun, 53-55. Mailing Add: 361 Forest Ave, Fond du Lac, Wis. 54934. (1967)

McEVOY, JOHN THOMAS D
b. Council Bluffs, Iowa, 4/9/37. Educ: Creighton Univ. Law Sch, LL.B, 64; Georgetown Univ. Law Cent, LL.M. Polit. & Govt. Pos: Asst. to the Gen. Counsel, Dept. of the Army, 62-64; staff asst. to spec. asst. to the Secy. of Defense, 65; legis. asst. to U.S. Sen. Joseph D. Tydings, Md, 66-68; staff dir, Senate Cmt. on D.C, 69- Mil. Serv: Entered as 1st Lt, Army, 61, released as Capt, 64, after serv. in Judge Adv. Gen. Corps. Mailing Add: Room 6222, New Senate Office Bldg, Washington, D.C. 20510.

McEWEN, ROBERT CAMERON R
U.S. Rep, N.Y.
b. Ogdensburg, N.Y, 1/5/20; m. to Anita Sharples; c. Nancy and Mary. Educ: Univ. of Vt; Wharton Sch. of Finance, Univ. of Pa; Albany Law Sch. Polit. & Govt. Pos: N.Y. State Sen, 54-64; U.S. Rep, N.Y, 64- Mil. Serv: Sgt, Air Force, World War II. Mem: Am. Legion; VFW; Mason; Elks. Legal Res: RFD 2, Ogdensburg, N.Y. 13669. Mailing Add: House Office Bldg, Washington, D.C. 20515. (1967)

McFADDEN, ROBERT HOLLAND R
b. St. Johnsbury, Vt, 12/18/37; s. Charles Wesley McFadden and Miriam Holland M; m. 11/7/59 to Annettli Apollonia Helen Baumann; c. Justin and Maia. Educ: Park Col, B.A, 59; Duke Univ, M.A, 66. Polit. & Govt. Pos: Admin. asst. to U.S. Rep. Charles E. Chamberlain, Mich, 65- Mailing Add: 3509 T St. N.W, Washington, D.C. 20007.

McFADDEN, ROBERT LAWRENCE D
S.C. State Rep.
b. Camden, S.C, 8/25/29; s. Lawrence Walker McFadden and Eunice Long M; m. 9/24/60 to Martha Anne Stewart; c. Robert Lawrence, Jr. and Sarah Anne. Educ: Duke Univ, B.A, 51, LL.B, 54; Delta Theta Phi. Polit. & Govt. Pos: S.C. State Rep, 61- Bus. & Prof. Pos: Lawyer, Gettys, McFadde & Wilkerson, currently. Mil. Serv: Army, 54-56. Mem: Elks; York City Hist. Soc; Kiwanis; former Cubmaster. 1960 Rock Hill DSA Award. Rel: Presbyterian; Deacon. Mailing Add: 949 Beverly Dr, Rock Hill, S.C. 29730.

McFADDEN, WILMOT CURNOW D
Committeewoman, Wyo. State Dem. Cent. Cmt.
b. Lead, S.Dak, 10/30/19; d. William Curnow and Ingeborg Christianson C; m. K. Hamm, div; m. 3/21/65 to John McFadden; c. Christina Hamm. Educ: S.Dak. State Col, Brookings; Univ. Minn. Polit. & Govt. Pos: Committeewoman, Sweetwater Co, Wyo. State Dem. Cent. Cmt, 50-; pres, Sweetwater Co. Dem. Woman's Club, 52-54; del, Dem. Nat. Conv, 56 & 64; vice chairwoman, Wyo. State Dem. Party, 63-64; del, State Dem. Conv, 68; mem, Wyo. Adv. Bd, Fed. Cmn. on Civil Rights, 69- Publ: Compiler, Handbook for Wyoming Library Trustees. Mem: Fed. Womans' Clubs; Am. Libr. Asn; Am. Legion Auxiliary; Does; Women's Dem. Club; Dist. 4 Sch. Bd, 66-71, clerk-secy, 69-; Wyo. rep, Mt. Plains Libr. Asn, 66-, chmn, Pub. Libr. Sect, 68-; West. Wyo. Commun. Col. Coun, 65-69; mem. from Wyo, Am. Libr. Asn. Coun, 61-65; mem, Arch. and Hist. Bd, Wyo. State Libr, 59-65 & 67; chmn, Wyo. Libr. Trustee Asn. to Am. Libr. Trustee Asn, 59-63; secy, Mt. Plains Libr. Asn, 59; pres, Wyo. Libr. Asn, 58; exec. dir. for Wyo, Nat. Libr. Week, 69. Rel: Congregational. Mailing Add: 28 Cedar, Rock Springs, Wyo. 82901.

McFADIN, RICHARD E. (GENE) D
b. Kans. City, Mo, 1925; m. 1947 to Marjorie Ann Nelson; c. Debra Lynn, Tina Lee, Tracy Ann, Cynthia Gene. Educ: Park Col; Univ. of Kans. City, B.A, LL.B; Phi Delta Phi. Polit. & Govt. Pos: Mo. State Rep, 62-66; prosecuting attorney, Clay Co, 58-62. Bus. & Prof. Pos: Lawyer, McFadin and Spooner; prin, Henrietta High Sch; Tr. off, City Nat. Bank, Kans. City, Mo. Mil. Serv: Army. Mem: Pres. N. Kans. City Jr. C. of C; dir. N. Kans. City Kiwanis. Rel: Methodist. Mailing Add: 5409 N. Cypress, Kansas City, Mo. 64119. (1967)

McFADYEN, NEILL LAUCHLIN D
N.C. State Rep.
b. Hoke Co, N.C, 9/19/11; m. 6/12/37 to Mary Virginia McLean; c. Neill Jr, Virginia Purcell, William McLean and John Currie. Educ: Davidson Col, 33. Polit. & Govt. Pos: Cmnr, Raeford, N.C, 41-43, mayor, 43-47; mem, Hoke Co. Bd. Educ, 49-, chmn, 55-60; N.C. State Rep, 61- Bus. & Prof. Pos: Farming; real estate. Rel: Presbyterian; Deacon, 40-49, Elder, 49- Mailing Add: 111 Highland St, Raeford, N.C. 28376. (1967)

McFALL, DAVID MERRILL D
b. Indianapolis, Ind, 5/18/31; s. The Rev. Merrill B. McFall and Mary Elizabeth Glossbrenner M; m. 10/5/51 to Patricia Louise Marlin; c. Valerie Kay, David Marc, Robert Neil, Marlin Keith and Cristopher Merrill. Educ: Ind. Univ, 48-51; Ind. Col. Mortuary Sci, Embalmer, 52. Polit. & Govt. Pos: Campaign mgr, Hamilton for Cong, 64-66 & 68; admin. asst. to U.S. Rep. Lee H. Hamilton, Ind, 65- Bus. & Prof. Pos: Embalmer and funeral dir, V. L. Poindexter and Day Funeral Homes, 52-54; salesman, Sun Life Assurance Co. of Can, 54-55; claim agent, N.Y. Cent. R.R, 55-61; field claim rep, State Farm Mutual Ins. Co, 61-64; pres, McFall Claims Serv, 64-65. Mil. Serv: Entered as Recruit E-1, Ind. Nat. Guard, 50, released as 1st Sgt, 56, after serv. in Hq. & Hq. Battery, 38th Div. Artil, Inf; Unit Commendation, 55. Publ: 'Aspects of Crossing Accident Investigation,' The Bul. & The Chronicle, Asn. Am. R.R. & Nat. Asn. Railway Trial Counsel, 2/61. Mem: Cong. Secretaries Club; Burro Club; Capitol Hill, Ind. & 9th Dist. Young Dem; Ind. Soc; Elks; Rotary Int; committeeman, Explorer Post 29 and chmn, Orgn. and Exten, Hoosier Hills Coun, Boy Scouts of Am. Rel: United Methodist. Mailing Add: 1011 Gaiser Dr, Seymour, Ind. 47274.

McFALL, JOHN J. D
U.S. Rep, Calif.
b. Buffalo, N.Y, 2/20/18; m. to Evelyn Anklam M; c. Joseph, Alicia and Sarah. Educ: Modesto Jr. Col, 36; Univ. Calif, A.B, 38; LL.B, 41. Polit. & Govt. Pos: Mayor, Manteca, Calif, 48-50; Calif. State Assemblyman, 51-56; U.S. Rep, Calif, 56- Bus. & Prof. Pos: Lawyer, 46- Mil. Serv: S/Sgt, Intel. Corps, 42-46. Mem: Calif. Bar Asn; Odd Fellows; Shrine; Mason; Scottish Rite; Eagles; Lions; Grange; Am. Legion. Legal Res: 316 W. N St, Manteca, Calif. 95336. Mailing Add: 2445 Rayburn Bldg, Washington, D.C. 20515. (1967)

McFARLAND, ERNEST WILLIAM D
Justice, Ariz. Supreme Court
b. Earlsboro, Okla, 10/9/94; s. William Thomas McFarland and Kesiah Smith M; m. to Edna Eveland; c. Jewell (Mrs. Delbert Lewis). Educ: E.Cent. State Teachers Col, Ada, Okla, 13-14; Univ. Okla, A.B, 17; Stanford Univ, J.D, 21 and A.M, 22; Univ. Ariz, LL.D, 50. Polit. & Govt. Pos: Co. Attorney, Pinal Co, Ariz, 24-30; Judge of Superior Court, Pinal Co, 35-41; U.S. Sen, Ariz, 41-53, Majority Leader, U.S. Senate, 51-53; Gov, Ariz, 55-59; chmn. Ariz. del, Dem. Nat. Conv, 64; Justice, Ariz. Supreme Court, 65- Bus. & Prof. Pos: Pres, Ariz. TV. Co, Phoenix, 55- Mil. Serv: Seaman, Navy, World War I; Lt. Comdr, Navy, World War II. Mem: Am. Legion; Mason; Shrine, Jester; K. of P; Elks; Odd Fellows; State, Pinal Co. and Maricopa Co. Bar Asns; Am. Judicature Soc. Rel: Methodist. Legal Res: Florence, Ariz. 85232. Mailing Add: 306 W. Royal Palms, Phoenix, Ariz. 85021.

McFARLAND, JAMES THOMAS R
N.Y. State Assemblyman
b. Buffalo, N.Y, 3/13/30; s. Ralph J. McFarland and Collette Roy M; m. 8/16/58 to Geraldine T. Walsh; c. Katherine, Susan, James T, Jr. and Lynne. Educ: Canisius Col, B.S, 51; Univ. of Buffalo Law Sch, LL.B, 54, J.D, 68; Gold Key Club. Polit. & Govt. Pos: Counsel, N.Y. Assembly Health Cmt, Joint Legis. Cmt. on Housing and Urban Develop, 64; N.Y. State Assemblyman, 66-, chmn, Assembly Minority Subcmt. on Medicaid Law of N.Y, N.Y. State Assembly, chmn, Ways and Means Subcmt. in Fields of Soc. Serv. and Health, and Joint Legis. Cmt. on Commerce, Econ. Develop, Tourism and Motor Boats, 69- Bus. & Prof. Pos: Attorney, Buffalo, N.Y, 54- Mil. Serv: Entered as Pvt, Army, 54, released as SP-3, 56, after serv. in C.I.C, G-2, Fourth Army Hq, Fourth Army Area, Ft. Sam Houston, Tex; Good Conduct and Sharpshooter Medals. Mem: Erie Co. and N.Y. State Bar Asns; Erie Co. Trial Lawyers Asn; Jay Cee; Ken-Ton Rep. Club; K. of C. Portrait of the Year Award, Ken-Ton Young, Rep. Couples Club, 68; Citizen of the Year Award, Ken-Ton Jaycees, 69. Rel: Catholic. Mailing Add: 21 Grosvenor Rd, Tonawanda, N.Y. 14223.

McFARLAND, MARY ANN R
Mem, Calif. Rep. State Cent. Cmt.
b. Detroit, Mich, 6/5/39; d. Joseph Orlando Ciampichini and Anne Korpak C; m. 9/3/64 to Archie Alexander McFarland; c. Linda and Gary. Educ: St. Bernard's High Sch, Detroit, Mich, grad. Polit. & Govt. Pos: Admin. asst, Los Angeles Co. Rep. Cent. Cmt, Calif, 67-68; hq. chmn, Rep. Assembly cand, 65th Dist, 68; alternate, 65th Assembly Dist. Rep. Cent. Cmt, 68-; mem, Calif. Rep. State Cent. Cmt, 69- Bus. & Prof. Pos: Private secy, H.W. Rickel & Co, Detroit, Mich, 55-60; free lance secy, 60-64. Rel: Protestant. Mailing Add: 11121 Cedar Ave, Inglewood, Calif. 90304.

MacFARLANE, JOHN DEE D
Colo. State Sen.
b. Pueblo, Colo, 10/4/33; s. John Lincoln MacFarlane and Estamae Lewis M; m. 12/28/62 to Janet Gertmenian; c. Jennifer, John L. and Andrew Galt. Educ: Harvard Col, A.B. cum laude, 55; Stanford Law Sch, LL.B, 62; Stanford Law Rev; Harvard Band. Polit. & Govt. Pos: Mgt, analyst, Air Staff, U.S. Air Force, 55-57; Dep. Dist. Attorney, Pueblo Co, Colo, 62-64; v.pres, Pueblo Co. Young Dem, 63-64; dist. dir, Colo. Young Dem, 63-65; Colo. State Rep, 64-68; Colo. State Sen, 68- Bus. & Prof. Pos: Attorney, 65- Mil. Serv: Entered as Pvt, Army, 57, released as Pfc, 59, after serv. in Signal Corps, ETO, 58. Publ: Comment: Shareholder Suits, 60-61 and Comment: Securities Act Pledges, 60-61, Stanford Law Rev. Mem: Pueblo Co, Colo. and Am. Bar Asns. Legal Res: 2109 Seventh Ave, Pueblo, Colo. 81003. Mailing Add: P.O. Box 777, Pueblo, Colo. 81002.

MACFARLANE, M. JAMES D
b. Hooper, Utah, 7/7/21; s. John Menzies Macfarlane and Nora Parker M; m. 8/16/49 to Marilyn Petty; c. Sheri Lynn, Geri Ann, John P. and Janene. Educ: Brigham Young Univ, B.S, 47; Univ. Utah, M.S, 59; Phi Delta Kappa. Polit. & Govt. Pos: Utah State Rep, 60-67 and chmn, Revenue and Taxation Cmt, 61 and 65; mem, Utah Legis. Coun, 65- Bus. & Prof. Pos: Elem. sch. prin, Jordan Sch. Dist, 59-, co-dir, Jordan Dist. Merit Study, 56-59 and teacher, Health and Phys. Educ, 47-56. Mil. Serv: Entered as Pvt, Army Air Corps, 42, released as 1st Lt, 45; Distinguished Flying Cross; Air Medal with 3 Oak Leaf Clusters; ETO Campaign Ribbon with 2 Battle Stars; Maj, Air Force Res, at present. Mem: Nat. Educ. Asn; pres, Utah Educ. Asn, 57-58 and Jordan Educ. Asn, 55-56; chmn, Nat. Cmn. on Safety Educ, 64-65; pres, Midvale Kiwanis Club, 64. Rel: Latter-day Saint. Mailing Add: 567 Coolidge St, Midvale, Utah 84047. (1967)

McFARLANE, WILLIAM D. D
b. Greenwood, Ark, 7/17/94; s. Robert William McFarlane and Maggie Harris M; m. 12/23/23 to Alma Carl, wid. 4/6/38; m. 6/2/45 to Inez Bishop; c. Mary, William D, Jr, Betty Ann, Barbara Frances and Robert Carl. Educ: Univ. Ark, A.B, 19; Chicago-Kent Col. Law, LL.B, 21, J.D, 69; Tau Kappa Alpha; Delta Chi. Polit. & Govt. Pos: Tex. State Rep, 23-27; Tex. State Sen, 27-31; U.S. Rep, Tex, 33-39; spec. asst. to Attorney Gen, 39-44; dir, Surplus Property Small War Plants Corp, 45-46; trial attorney, U.S. Dept. of Justice, 46-66. Bus. & Prof. Pos: Owner, Co. Store, 14-18. Mil. Serv: Entered as Pvt, Army, 18, released as 2nd Lt, 18, after serv. in 87th Div, Camp Pike, Ark. Mem: Fed, Tex. State and Young Co. Bar Asns; Mason (32°); Shrine; Am. Legion. Mem. 'A' Club, Univ. Ark. Rel: Methodist. Legal Res: Graham, Tex. 76046. Mailing Add: 6327 West. Ave. N.W, Washington, D.C. 20015.

McFERN, GENEVIEVE P. R
V.Chmn, St. Clair Co. Rep. Party, Mich.
b. Detroit, Mich, 9/11/00; m. 4/4/31 to Leon E. McFern; c. Leigh S.(deceased). Educ: Univ. Sch. of Music, Ann Arbor, Mich. Polit. & Govt. Pos: Del, Co. and State Rep. Conv; v.chmn, St. Clair Co. Rep. Party, Mich, currently. Bus. & Prof. Pos: Music teacher, Detroit Pub. Schs, 15 years; housewife. Mem: River Dist. Hosp. Bd. of St. Clair; Commun. Chest, March of Dimes, Cancer Fund and Easter Seal Drives. Mailing Add: 4419 Clarke Dr, St. Clair, Mich. 48079.

McFETRIDGE, WILLIAM LANE D
Cmnr. and V.Pres, Chicago Park Dist.
b. Chicago, Ill, 11/28/93; s. William Francis McFetridge and Wilhelmina Quesse M; m. 10/20/23 to Barbara Quesse; c. Dorothy (Mrs. Theodore Krueger). Educ: Hon. LL.D, St. Josephs Col, Rensselaer, Ind; Daniel H. Burnham Award, Roosevelt Univ; Hon. Fel, Bar Ilan Univ, Israel. Polit. & Govt. Pos: Mem. bd, Ill. Mediation and Conciliation Dept, 29-49; dir. salvage, Chicago Metrop. Area, 42-45; one of five rep. to ask establishment of UN Hq. in Chicago, London, 45; cmnr. and v.pres, Chicago Park Dist; chmn, Citizens Cmt. for Cleaner Chicago; mem, Chicago Police Bd, Pub. Bldgs. Cmn, R.R. Terminals Authority, Hosp. Planning Bd, Cmn. for Sr. Citizens and Cmt. on Econ. and Cultural Develop; del, Dem. Nat. Conv, 68. Bus. & Prof. Pos: V.pres, Bldg. Serv. Employees Int. Union, 26-40, gen. pres, 40-60; pres, Bldg. Serv. Employees Union Local 46, 27-48; pres, Chicago Flat Janitors Union Local 1, 37-; v.pres, Ill. State Fedn. Labor, 39-50; pres, Marina City Bldg. Corp; bd. dirs, Marina City Bank. Mem: Lay Bd, Northwest. Univ, DePaul Univ. and Loyola Univ; assoc. dir, Gr. N. Mich. Ave. Asn; bd. dirs, Chicago Urban League; Chicago Area Coun, Boy Scouts; Am. Heart Asn; Nat. Conf. Christians and Jews; Parents Asn. for Cerebral Palsy Children; Israel Bond Cmt. Award of Merit, U.S. Dept. of Labor, 60. Rel: Protestant. Legal Res: 300 North State St, Chicago, Ill. 60610. Mailing Add: 318 West Randolph St, Chicago, Ill. 60606. (1967)

McGAH, JOSEPH PATRICK D
Ill. State Rep.
b. Chicago, Ill, 2/22/22; s. William J. McGah and Kathrine Conlin M; m. 6/18/49 to Barbara Tighe; c. Barbara, Joseph, Jr, Mary and James. Educ: Holy Cross, A.B, 43; Loyola Law Sch, Chicago, J.D, 48. Polit. & Govt. Pos: Village clerk, Berkeley, Ill, 52-53, police magistrate, 53-61; justice of the peace, Proviso Twp, 61-64; magistrate, Circuit Court, Cook Co, 64-65; Ill. State Rep, currently. Mil. Serv: Entered as Pvt, Army, 43, released as Pfc, 46, after serv. in Anti-Tank Co, 291st Inf, 75th Div, ETO; 3 Battle Stars. Mem: Chicago Bar Asn; West Suburban Asn; Berkeley Post, Am. Legion; Hillside Post, Am. Legion; Moose 777; VFW, Austin Post. Rel: Roman Catholic. Mailing Add: 5904 Huron, Berkeley, Ill. 60613. (1967)

McGANN, PATRICK J, JR. D
b. Teaneck, N.J, 5/17/27; s. Patrick J. McGann and Ethel Schneider M; m. 9/22/51 to Bernadette E. Tyndall; c. Patrick, III, Maura, Michael, Deirdre and Meghan. Educ: Fordham Col; Fordham Univ. Sch. of Law. Polit. & Govt. Pos: V.pres, N.J. State Constitutional Conv, 66, N.J. State Assemblyman, 64-65. Prof. Pos: Partner, law firm of Reussille, Cornwell, Mausner, Carotenuto & McGann, 59-; Borough attorney, Borough of Keansburg and Borough of Sea Bright, at present, Borough of Red Bank, 64-65 and Borough of Union Beach, 60-65; attorney, Matawan Twp. Munic. Utilities Authority, at present; N.J. State Dep. Attorney Gen, 62-63. Mil. Serv: Entered as Seaman 1/C, Navy, 45, released as PO 1/C, 46, after serv. in USNAS; Corpus Christi, Tex: re-entered serv. as 2nd Lt, Army, 51, released as 1st Lt, 53, after serv. in AA&GM Sch, Ft. Bliss, Tex: Victory Medal. Mem: Am, N.J. State and Monmouth Co. Bar Asns; pres, Monmouth Co. Fedn. of Holy Name Socs; former v.pres, Young Dem. Club. of N.J. Rel: Roman Catholic. Legal Res: 9 Woodland Dr, Lincroft, N.J. 07738. Mailing Add: 34 Broad St, Red Bank, N.J. 07701. (1967)

McGAUGHEY, NOEL DOUGLAS D
b. Tylertown, Miss, 10/8/16; married. Polit. & Govt. Pos: Former Miss. State Rep. Bus. & Prof. Pos: Mgr. Sunflower Food Store. Mem: Mason; Am. Legion; PTA. Rel: Baptist. Mailing Add: Route 2, Prentiss, Miss. 39474. (1967)

McGAW, ROBERT WALTER D
b. Rockford, Ill, 4/9/23; s. James L. McGaw and Loren M. Lynch M; m. 6/23/46 to Peggy A. Schindler; c. Marlis Jean, Roberta Sue and Raymond William. Educ: North. Ill. Univ, B.S, 50, M.S, 66; Univ. Ill; Wash. Univ; Kappa Delta Pi. Polit. & Govt. Pos: Dem. precinct committeeman, Ill, 50-; alderman, Rockford, Ill, 55-63; cand. for Lt. Gov, 60; co. chmn, Dem. Party, 62-64; del, Dem. Nat. Conv, 68. Bus. & Prof. Pos: Teacher, High Sch, 50-68; prin, Rock Cut Teacher Training Sch, 68. Mil. Serv: Entered as Pvt, Army, 42, released as Sgt, 46, after serving in 90mm Gun Bn; ETO, 44-46; 4 battle ribbons. Mem: VFW; Mason (32°); Moose. Rel: Presbyterian. Mailing Add: 2016 E. State St, Rockford, Ill. 61108.

McGEACHY, NEILL HECTOR, JR. D
Pres. Pro-Tem. and Majority Leader, N.C. State Senate
b. Fayetteville, N.C, 8/8/17; s. Neill Hector McGeachy and Kate McArthur McGeachy; m. 10/21/51 to Mildred Satterfield Kelly. Educ: Davidson Col, B.S, 38; Univ. N.C. Law Sch, LL.B, 41, Omicron Delta Kappa; Kappa Sigma. Polit. & Govt. Pos: N.C. State Sen, 61-62, 65-66, 67-68 & 69-, Pres. Pro-Tem. and Majority Leader, N.C. State Senate, 69-, chmn, State Legis. Serv. Cmn. and co-chmn, State Legis. Research Cmn, 69-; mem, Reorgn. State Govt. Cmt. and State Cmn. on Selection of Bd. of Educ, 61-63. Bus. & Prof. Pos: Attorney-at-law, McGeachy, Pope & Reid, 41-; dir, South. Nat. Bank and Mid-South Ins. Co, 65-69. Mil. Serv: Entered as 2nd Lt, Army, 41, released as Capt, 45 after serv. in 121st Inf. Regt, Eighth Inf. Div, ETO, 41-45; Bronze Star; Combat Infantryman's Badge; Four Campaign Stars. Mem: Pres, Cumberland Co. Bar Asn, 65-66; bd. visitors, St. Andrews Presby. Col, 67-; Am. Judicature Soc; Am. Bar Asn; Kiwanis; York Rite Mason; Scottish Rite Mason; Shrine. Rel: Presbyterian. Legal Res: 2011 Winterlochen Rd, Fayetteville, N.C. 28305. Mailing Add: P.O. Drawer 1358, Fayetteville, N.C. 28302.

McGEE, GALE WILLIAM D
U.S. Sen, Wyo.
b. Lincoln, Nebr, 3/17/15; s. Garton W. McGee and Frances McCoy M; m. 6/11/39 to Loraine Baker; c. David Wyant, Robert Merrill, Mary Gale and Lori Ann. Educ: Nebr. State Teachers' Col, B.A, 36; Univ. Colo, M.A, 39; Univ. Chicago, Ph.D, 47. Hon. LL.D, Univ. Wyo, East. Ky. Univ, Am. Univ, Seton Hall Univ. and Allegheny Col. Polit. & Govt. Pos: U.S. Sen, Wyo, 58-, mem, Senate Commerce Cmt, 59-66, Senate Appropriations Cmt, 59-, Senate Banking and Currency Cmt, 67-68 and Senate For. Rels. Cmt, 69-, chmn, Senate Post Off. and Civil Serv. Cmt, 69-; del, Dem. Nat. Conv, 60, 64 & 68. Bus. & Prof. Pos: Prof. Am. hist, Crofton, Nebr. High Sch, 36-37, Kearney, Nebr. High Sch, 37-40, Nebr. Wesleyan Univ, 40-43, Iowa State, 43-44, Univ. Notre Dame, 44-45, Univ. Chicago, 45-46 and Univ. Wyo, 46- Publ: The Responsibilities of World Power, Nat. Press, Inc, 68. Mem: Am. Asn. Univ. Prof; Am. Hist. Asn; Miss. Valley Hist. Asn; Am. Asn. for the UN; Coun. on For. Rels; Izaak Walton League; Eagles. Rel: Presbyterian. Legal Res: Laramie, Wyo. Mailing Add: 7205 Marbury Rd, Bethesda, Md. 20034.

McGEE, JOSEPH HALSTEAD, JR. D
b. Charleston, S.C, 4/6/29; s. Joseph H. McGee and Madeleine Stoney Mc; m. 6/25/60 to Evelyn Brabbam Moore; c. two daughters. Educ: Wash. & Lee Univ, B.A, 50, LL.B, 52; Phi Delta Phi. Polit. & Govt. Pos: S.C. State Rep, 63-69. Bus. & Prof. Pos: Lawyer, Moore, Mouzon, McGee; exec. bd, Coastal Carolina Coun, Boy Scouts. Mil. Serv: Navy, 52-56; Lt, Naval Res. Mem: Dir, Kiwanis; dir, Charleston U.S.O; Omicron Delta Kappa; Coastal Carolina Coun, Boy Scouts. Rel: Presbyterian; Bd. of Deacon, Second Presbyterian Church of Charleston. Mailing Add: 2-A Ladson St, Charleston, S.C. 29401. (1967)

McGEE, PATRICK D'ARCY R
Calif. State Assemblyman
b. Osceola, Ontario, Can, 3/5/16; s. Michael Thomas McGee and Anna Dillon M; m. to Eleanor Cornehl; c. Thomas D'Arcy. Educ: Univ. Notre Dame; Portland Univ; Harvard Law Sch. Polit. & Govt. Pos: Calif. State Assemblyman, 50-57 & 67-; mem. city coun, Los Angeles, Calif, 57-61. Mil. Serv: Entered Royal Can. Air Force and U.S. Navy, released as Lt. Comdr; Brit. Distinguished Flying Cross. Rel: Roman Catholic. Legal Res: 17304 Sherman Way, Van Nuys, Calif. 91406. Mailing Add: 6355 Tapanga Canyon, Woodland Hills, Calif. 91364. (1967)

McGEE, THOMAS W. D
Mass. State Rep.
b. Lynn, Mass; s. Thomas McGee and Mary O'Shea M; m. to Ann Sorrenti; c. Four. Educ: Boston Univ, LL.B, 53. Polit. & Govt. Pos: Mem, Ward Five City Coun, Mass; pres, City Coun, 58-69; del, Dem. Nat. Conv, 68; Mass. State Rep, currently, Majority Leader, Mass. House Rep, 69- Bus. & Prof. Pos: Ins; former U.S. Dept. of Labor employee. Mil. Serv: World War II, S.Pac. Mem: Am. Legion; Amvets; DAV. Mailing Add: 9 Pine Rd, Lynn, Mass. 01904.

McGEE, WILLIAM SEARS D
Assoc. Justice, Supreme Court of Tex.
b. Houston, Tex, 9/29/17; s. James Butler McGee (deceased) and Alice Sears M; m. 3/8/41 to Mary Beth Peterson; c. James Sears, Mary Gray (Mrs. Nelson), Claire (Mrs. Sher), Alice, George Sears and Erwin Smith. Educ: Rice Univ, 35-37; Univ. Tex, Austin, LL.B, 40; Phi Delta Theta. Polit. & Govt. Pos: Co. judge, Harris Co, Tex, 48-54, judge, 151st Dist. Court, 54-55, judge, 55th Dist. Court, 58-68; assoc. justice, Supreme Court, Tex, 69- Mil. Serv: Entered as Ens, Naval Res, 43, released as Lt, 46, after serv. in D.E. 363, Pac. Theatre, 44-45. Mem: Houston and Am. Bar Asns; State Bar Tex.(dir, 57-59); Am. Judicature Soc; AF&AM; Scottish Rite; Sons of Hermann; SPJST Lodge; Shrine. Rel: Episcopal. Mailing Add: 2300 Quarry, Austin, Tex. 78703.

McGHEE, FLORA DEVAUGHAN D
b. Marengo Co, Ala, 8/10/24; d. Rev. Frank Scott Devaughan and Ida Glover D; m. 1/9/40 to Herschel H. McGhee, Sr; c. Herschel, Jr, Franklin D, Christopher, Ida D.(Mrs. Parker), Floreida and Charles. Educ: Sunlight Sch. of Beauty Culture, Mobile, Ala, cosmetologist, 48; Grace Downs Sch. for Models, N.Y.C, prfnl. model instr, 58; John Robert Powers Charm Sch, N.Y.C, 58; Univ. Ala, interior decorator, 68. Polit. & Govt. Pos: Second v.chmn, Dem. Women Activity Cmt, Birmingham, Ala, 67-69, prog. chmn, 68-69; recording secy, Dem. Women's Club, 68-; alternate del, Dem. Women's Club Conv; standing del, Jefferson Co. Dem. Coun, Ala, 66-69; chmn. voter registrn, North. Sect, Birmingham, Ala, 67; membership chmn, Northside Br. NAACP, Birmingham, Ala, 67-68; alternate del, Dem. Nat. Conv, 68; prog. cmt. chmn, Fountain Heights Civic League, Birmingham, 69. Bus. & Prof. Pos: Supvr, Flora McGhee Charm and Modeling Sch, Birmingham, Ala, 60-, instr. supvr, 68-; pres, Women's Auxiliary of Daniel Payne Col, 68- Mem: Modeling Asn. of Am; Eastern Star; treas, Progressive Ladies Soc. Club. Pi Lambda Sigma, Daniel Payne Col. Hon. Soc; Zetas for Christian Women; Maceo Jennings Award for serv. beyond the call of duty in instr. charm and modeling; Vol. Serv, YWCA. Rel: African Methodist Episcopal. Mailing Add: 1614 11th Ave. N, Birmingham, Ala. 35204.

McGHEE, GEORGE CREWS
b. Waco, Tex, 3/10/12; s. George Summers McGhee and Magnolia Spruce M; m. 11/24/38 to Cecilia Jeanne DeGolyer; c. Marcia Spruce, George DeGolyer, Dorothy Hart, Michael Anthony, Cecilia Goodrich and Valerie Foster. Educ: South. Methodist Univ, 28, D.C.L, 53; Univ. Okla, B.S, 33; Oxford Univ, Rhodes scholar and D.Phil, 37; Univ. London, 37; Phi Beta Kappa; Sigma Xi. Hon. LL.D, Tulane Univ, 57 and Univ. Maryland; hon. fel, Queen's Col, Oxford. Polit. & Govt. Pos: Coordinator aid to Greece and Turkey, Dept. of State, 47-49; asst. secy. of state, Near East, S.Asian and African Affairs, 49-51; sr. adv, N.Atlantic Treaty Coun, Ottawa, 51; ambassador and chief, Am. Mission for Aid to Turkey, 51-53; consult, Nat. Security Coun. and Cmt. Int. Econ. Growth, 58; mem, President's Cmn. to Study U.S. Mil. Asst. Prog, 58-59; dir, Cmt. for Econ. Develop, 57-61; chmn, Policy Planning Coun. and counsr, Dept. of State, 61; Under Secy. of State for Polit. Affairs, 61-63; Ambassador to Fed. Repub. of Germany, 63-68; Ambassador-at-lg, 68-69; spec. asst. to the chmn, Urban Coalition, 69-; chmn, Bus. Coun. for Int. Understanding, 69-; mem, Gov. Cmn. for Econ. Develop. and Conserv, Va, 69- Bus. & Prof. Pos: Registered engr, Tex; oil geologist, 30-40; owner, McGhee Prod. Co, 40-; mem. bd, Mobil Oil Corp, 69- Mil. Serv: Naval Res: 43-45; Legion of Merit; Asiatic Ribbon with 3 battle stars. Mem: Trustee or dir, Duke Univ, 62, For. Serv. Educ. Found. and Sch. for Adv. Studies, Johns Hopkins Univ, 47-, Vassar Col, 59-63, Fed. City Coun, 58-61, Southwest. Le-

gal Found, 57-61, Brookings Inst, 54-61 and Robert Col, Istanbul, 53-61; mem. bd, Aspen Inst. Humanistic Studies, 56-, South. Methodist Univ. and Near East Found, 56- and Mid. East Inst, 53-58; bd. trustees, Thessalonica Agr. and Indust. Inst, 49-; mem. vis. cmt, Mid. East. Studies and Summer Sch, Harvard Univ, 54-61; adv. coun. dept. oriental lang. and lit, Princeton Univ, 49-61; int. cmt, YMCA, 49-61; sponsor, Atlantic Inst, 54-60; Am. Asn. Petrol. Geol; Soc. Exp. Geophys; Am. Inst. Mining, Metall. & Petrol. Engrs; Rotary; Metrop, Chevy Chase, Brook and Century Asn. Clubs. Legal Res: Farmers' Delight, Middleburg, Va. 22117. Mailing Add: 2808 N St. N.W, Washington, D.C. 20007.

McGHEE, MILTON LORENZO D
City Councilman, Sacramento, Calif.
b. Atlanta, Ga, 2/18/32; s. Milton Aaron McGhee and Jackie Lucille Logan M; m. 6/23/56 to Jean Ollivette Young; c. Milton Emerson, George Kenneth and Karen Ollivette. Educ: Clark Col, A.B, 53; Howard Univ, LL.B, 58; Univ. Calif, Berkeley, LL.M, 60; Alpha Phi Alpha. Polit. & Govt. Pos: Law clerk on Attorney Gen. Honor Law Grad. Prog, Attorney Gen. U.S, 58-59; legis. intern on Calif. Assembly and Ford Found. Legis, Internship Prog, Calif. Assembly, Sacramento, Calif, 60-61; city councilman, Sacramento, 68- Bus. & Prof. Pos: Attorney, Colley & McGhee, 61- Mil. Serv: Entered Army, 53, released, 55, after serv. in Army Med. Serv. Corps; Soldier of the Month, Brooke Army Med. Center, Ft. Sam Houston, Tex, Apr. 55. Publ: Co-auth, The House I Live In, A Study in Fair Housing, 59 & Law in Transition, 62; The California and Washington Fair Housing Cases, Cornell Law Rev; plus others. Mem: Am. Bar Asn; Calif. Trial Lawyers Asn; Am. Judicature Soc; bd. dirs, Womens Civic Improv. Club; NAACP (pres, Sacramento Chap, 67); bd. dirs, KVIE Educ. TV, Capital City Lawyers Club, Sacramento Chap, Big Bros. Am, Sacramento Metrop. C. of C. and Sacramento Chap, Urban League. Admitted to practice before the U.S. Supreme Court, U.S. Court of Appeals, Wash, D.C, Ninth Circuit Court, U.S. Dist. Courts of Calif. and Wash, D.C. and State Supreme Court of Calif. Named Young Man of the Year by Sacramento Jr. C. of C, 67, distinguished serv. award, 68. Rel: Protestant; Deacon, Parkside Community Church. Legal Res: 6131 Fordham Way, Sacramento, Calif. 95831. Mailing Add: 1810 S St, Sacramento, Calif. 95814.

McGILL, DONALD S. D
Iowa State Sen.
b. Grandview, Iowa, 7/20/06; s. James Franklin McGill and Elisa Gromer M; m. 6/6/34 to Merna D. Irvine; c. James Irvine. Educ: Parsons Col, B.S, 32; Iowa Univ, grad. work, 36; Alpha Kappa Chi. Polit. & Govt. Pos: Chmn, Lucas Co. Agr. Stabilization and Conserv. Serv, Iowa, 61-62; mem, Farmers Home Admin. Cmt, Lucas & Wayne Co, 62-63; Iowa State Sen, Third Dist, currently. Bus. & Prof. Pos: Sch. supt, State of Iowa, 30-49 and Logan Co, Colo, 49-58. Mem: Mason. Rel: Methodist. Mailing Add: Melrose, Iowa 52569.

McGILL, DUANE S. R
Kans. State Rep.
b. Grandview, Iowa, 4/25/22; s. Jesse D. McGill and Faith Stineman M; m. 5/20/54 to Wanda Crowe; c. Pamela Jo and Scott Duane. Educ: Southwest. Col, B.A, 51; Univ. Kans, M.A, 52. Polit. & Govt. Pos: Kans. State Rep, 61-65 & 67-; mem, Cmt. on Interstate Coop, Kans, 63-64; del, Rep. Nat. Conv, 64. Bus. & Prof. Pos: Pres, Rapids Amusements, Inc, 59-61; mem. bd. dirs, Tom-Kat, Inc, 65- Mil. Serv: Entered as Pvt, Army, 41, released as 1st Sgt, 45, after serv. in Seventh Inf. Div, Pac, 43-45; Am. Defense Serv, Good Conduct and Asiatic Pac. Campaign Medals; Philippines Liberation Ribbon with two Bronze Stars; Mem: Bd. of Dirs, Kans. Restaurant Asn, 59-, Kans. Girl Scout Coun, 63-64, Local C. of C, 61-63; Am. Legion; VFW; Elks. Rel: Methodist. Mailing Add: 1313 E. 12th, Winfield, Kans. 67156. (1967)

McGILL, SAM P. D
Ga. State Sen.
b. Hartwell, Ga, 8/30/14; s. Adolphus Cecil McGill and Lillian Norman M; m. 9/22/35 to Florence Clary; c. Sam Clary and Kathryn (Mrs. Jackson). Educ: South Ga. State Col, grad. Polit. & Govt. Pos: Councilman, City of Wash, Ga, 44-54; Ga. State Sen, 50th Dist, 59-60, 24th Dist, 65- Bus. & Prof. Pos: Partner, McGill Truck & Tractor Co, 39- and Wilkes Co. Stock Yard, 50-; pres, Saluda Co. Stock Yard, Inc, 57-; partner, Thomson Stock Yard, 63- Mem: Wash. Lions Club (past pres); C. of C.(pres); Ga. Farm Equip. Asn.(past pres); Ga. Stock Yard Asn.(pres); Ga. Automobile Dealer's Asn. (dir). Rel: Baptist. Legal Res: Tignall Rd, Washington, Ga. 30673. Mailing Add: P.O. Box 520, Washington, Ga. 30673.

McGILLICUDDY, LILLIAN GRACE R
Rep. Nat. Committeewoman, Ark.
b. Chicago, Ill, 5/12/93; d. Gustave Flumey and Louise Peters F; m. 1916 to Shelby M. Boorhem; c. Shelby (deceased) and William; m. 1/22/38 to Frank McGillicuddy (deceased). Educ: Chicago Teachers Col, 10-12. Polit. & Govt. Pos: V.chmn, Ark. State Rep. Cmt, 40-64; del, Rep. Nat. Conv, 40, 44, 52, 64 & 68; chmn, Hot Spring Co. Cmt, Ark, 42-48; chmn, Am. Red Cross, Hot Springs, 42-48; pres, Malvern Rep. Womens' Club, 46-48; pres, Pulaski Co. Rep. Womens' Club, Little Rock, 48-60; co-chmn, State Eisenhower Campaign, 52; Rep. Nat. Committeewoman, Ark, 64-; del, Rep. Nat. Conv, 68. Publ: Auth. of column in Winthrop Rockefeller Campaigner, 63-64; contributor, Ark. Outlook, 65- Mem: Nat. Soc. Arts and Letters (pres, 62-64); Nat. League of Am. Pen Women (mem. bd, 68-70); Ark. Fedn. Rep. Women; Ark. Art Center; Fine Arts Club. Award for grad. with highest scholastic average, Chicago Teachers Col. Rel: Episcopal. Mailing Add: 463 Rivercliff Apts, Little Rock, Ark. 72202.

MacGILLIVRAY, W. DONALD R
Calif. State Assemblyman
b. Los Angeles, Calif, 8/13/19; m. to Mary Eloise Dunham; c. Sandra and Jock. Educ: Los Angeles City Col; Santa Barbara State Col. Polit. & Govt. Pos: Councilman, Santa Barbara, Calif, 47-51, airport cmnr, 57-61 and mayor, 63-67; Calif. State Assemblyman, currently. Bus. & Prof. Pos: Gen. contractor, 46-63. Mil. Serv: Entered as Aviation Cadet, Navy, 41, released as Lt. Comdr.(Ret), 47. Mem: Am. Legion; Amvets; Eagles; Moose; Mason. Rel: Protestant. Mailing Add: 3326 Braemar Rd, Santa Barbara, Calif. 93105. (1967)

McGINLEY, DONALD F. D
b. Keystone, Nebr, 6/30/20; m. 12/27/47 to Evaleen Mueller; c. One daughter. Educ: Univ. Notre Dame, A.B, 42; Georgetown Univ, LL.B, 49. Polit. & Govt. Pos: Nebr. State Sen, 55-57 & 63-64; U.S. Rep, Nebr, 58-60; del, Dem. Nat. Conv, 68. Bus. & Prof. Pos: Lawyer; livestock farmer; reporter, copy ed, The Register, Denver, Colo, 45-46. Mil. Serv: Army Air Force, 42-45. Mem: Elks; Am. Legion; VFW; K. of C; Ogallala C. of C.(secy, 51, pres, 52). Rel: Catholic. Mailing Add: 401 E. A, Ogallala, Nebr. 69153.

McGINLEY, PAUL MARTIN D
b. Lebanon, Ind, 9/17/07; s. James McGinley and Delia King McG; m. 8/23/47 to Rosemary Sherrill; c. Martin P, John E. and Patricia Ann. Educ: Butler Univ, 28-29; Univ. Ala, 31; Delta Tau Delta. Polit. & Govt. Pos: Adminstr, Fed. Works Admin, 33-42; registrn. off, Vet. Admin, 46-51; chmn, Boone Co. Dem. Cent. Cmt, Ind, 56-68; chmn, Sixth Dist. Dem. Party, 64-68; postmaster, Lebanon, 68- Bus. & Prof. Pos: Men's Wear Merchant, 51-58; Gen. Ins, 59- Mil. Serv: Entered as Pvt, Army, 42, released as M/Sgt, 45, after serv. in Signal Corp in European & N.African Theaters; Bronze Star. Mem: Elks; Am. Legion; VFW. Rel: Catholic. Mailing Add: 218 Esplanade, Lebanon, Ind. 46052.

McGINNIS, BERNARD B. D
b. Genessee, Pa, 12/178; s. Bryan McGinnis and Ellen Moran M; m. to Hildegarde M. Krieger. Educ: Cornell Univ, B.A. Polit. & Govt. Pos: Pa. State Sen, 34-67; asst. co. solicitor, Allegheny Co; U.S. Attny. west. dist. Pa; del. to Dem. Nat. Conv, 32, 40; chmn, Allegheny Co. Dem. Comm, 39-; appraiser of customs, Port of Pittsburg, Pa. Bus. & Prof. Pos: Attorney. Mem: Bar of Allegheny Co; mem, Supreme Court of U.S. and Pa. Mailing Add: 1213 Arch St, Pittsburg, Pa. 15212. (1967)

McGINNIS, EDWARD FRANCIS R
b. Chicago, Ill, 4/10/97; s. Frank P. McGinnis and Ellen Sutton M; m. 5/30/31 to Wilma Fay Hargrove. Educ: Chicago Col. of Commerce. Polit. & Govt. Pos: Sgt-at-arms, U.S. Senate, 47-48; chief sgt-at-arms, Rep. Nat. Conv, 60, 1st sgt-at-arms, 64 and del, 68; former mem, Rep. State Cmt, D.C; chmn. organizing cmt, Vet. for Nixon; nat. co-chmn, Vet. for Nixon-Agnew, 68; chmn. vet. cmt, 1969 Inaugural. Bus. & Prof. Pos: Invest banker, Chicago, Ill, 27-42; v.pres. and dir, Montgomery Fed. Savings & Loan Asn; nat. dir. pub. rels, Am. Legion, 49-54; v.pres, Seagram Distillers, 54-66. Mil. Serv: Entered as Pvt, Army Air Corps, 17, released after serv. as Aerial Machine Gunner, World War I, 19; re-entered as Lt, Naval Res, 42, serv. in China-Burma-India, released as Comdr, OSS, 46; also serv. as observer for Navy in Korea; Africa, China-Burma-India and Philippines Service Ribbons. Mem: Am. Legion; VFW; Amvets; CWV; K. of C; Knight of Malta; Knight Holy Sepulchre; Army & Navy Club; founder and bd. dir, Capitol Hill Club. Appointed to Am. Battle Monuments Cmt. by Presidents Eisenhower and Johnson. Rel: Roman Catholic. Mailing Add: 4201 Cathedral Ave, Washington, D.C. 20016.

McGINTY, VERNON CHARLES R
Ky. State Sen.
b. Kimball, S.Dak, 6/19/15; s. Charles McGinty and Salome Senneff M; m. 8/2/41 to Lucille A. Stickell; c. Gary Charles. Educ: Univ. of Ill, B.S. in acct, 41; Alpha Kappa Psi. Polit. & Govt. Pos: Ky. State Sen, 62-, Rep. caucas chmn, Ky. State Senate, 66-; mem, Legis. Res. Cmn, Ky. Gen. Assembly, 66- Bus. & Prof. Pos: Financial mgr, Gen. Elec. Co, 41- Mil. Serv: Entered as Pvt, Army, 43, released as 2nd Lt, 46, after serv. in Korea Occup. Forces, 45-46. Mem: Mason. Rel: Methodist. Mailing Add: 403 Kingston Ave, Louisville, Ky. 40214.

McGLAMERY, WILEY A. D
b. Hayesville, N.C, 8/18/09; s. Ben A. McGlamery and Ida Bell Herbert M; m. 5/18/28 to Ora M. Killian; c. Wiley Dan. Educ: Cecils Bus. Col. Polit. & Govt. Pos: N.C. State Rep, 63-69. Bus. & Prof. Pos: Dairy, poultry farmer; farm supply store; interest Ford dealership; dir, Citizens Bank & Trust Co; past dir, local R.C.A. Corp. Mil. Serv: Res. Rel: Methodist; Dist. Steward. Mailing Add: Hayesville, N.C. 28904. (1967)

McGLENNON, JOHN AUSTIN SHAW R
Mass. State Rep.
b. Newton, Mass, 8/10/35; s. John Austin Shaw McGlennon, Jr. and Helen Bridges M; m. 10/3/59 to Mary Jane Bullard; c. Jane Alling and Lindsay Shaw. Educ: Bowdoin Col, B.A, 57; Psi Upsilon. Polit. & Govt. Pos: Field coordinator, Mass. Rep. State Cmt, 64; secy. to Gov. John A. Volpe, 65-66; Mass. State Rep, 67- Bus. & Prof. Pos: Group rep, Aetna Life Ins. Co, 57-62; sales mgr, Aid Inc, Concord, Mass, 63. Mil. Serv: 2nd Lt, 57-58; Yankee Div, Mass; Capt, Reserves, at present. Mem: Mason; Concord Country Club. Rel: Congregational. Mailing Add: Lowell Rd, Concord, Mass. 01742. (1967)

McGLINCHEY, HERBERT J. D
Pa. State Sen.
b. Phila, Pa, 11/7/04. Educ: Pub. and parochial schs, Phila. Polit. & Govt. Pos: Supvr. inspection, East. Dist, Pa. Dept. Labor and Indust, 35-37; U.S. Rep, Pa, 79th U.S. Cong; mem, Tax Equalization Bd, 56-63; Pa. State Sen, 64-; alternate del, Dem. Nat. Conv, 68. Bus. & Prof. Pos: Pres, Mfgs. Sales & Equip. Co; pres, Bd. of Mercantile Appraisers of Phila, 37-44. Mailing Add: 4714 N. Front St, Philadelphia, Pa. 19120.

McGLINN, FRANK C. P. R
b. Philadelphia, Pa, 11/19/14; s. Dr. John A. McGlinn and Emma F. Potts M; m. 9/9/42 to Louise C. Lea; c. Marion (Mrs. Myron E. Lockwood, Jr), Alice Ashton, Louise Steuart and Ann Croasdale. Educ: Univ. N.C., A.B, 37; Univ. Pa, LL.B, 40; Phi Beta Kappa; Delta Kappa Epsilon; Sharswood Law Club. Polit. & Govt. Pos: Exec. secy, Rep. Finance Cmt, Pa, 40-53, chmn, 63-65; alternate del, Rep. Nat. Conv, 40, alternate del-at-lg, 52, del-at-lg, 64 & 68; chmn, Pa. Fedn. of Young Rep. Clubs, 48-50; v.chmn, Nat. Young Rep. Fedn, 51-53; mem. exec. cmt, Pa. State Rep, Cmt, 48-50 & 63-; v.chmn, Rep. Nat. Finance Cmt, 65-68. Bus. & Prof. Pos: Marine counsel, Reliance Ins. Co, 40-42; assoc, Pepper, Hamilton & Sheetz, Attorneys, 46-53; v.pres. and asst. to pres, Al Paul Lefton Co, Inc, Advert, 53-58; sr. v.pres, Fidelity Bank, Phila, Pa, 58- Mil. Serv: Entered as Ens, Naval Res, 42, released as Lt, 46, after

serv. in Mediterranean and Pac, 43-45; Purple Heart; Am. and Asiatic Theaters and ETO Ribbons; Anzio, S. France and Japan Campaign Ribbons. Mem: Union League, Philadelphia; life trustee, Free Libr. of Phila; Phila. Bar Asn; trustee, Temple Univ; hon. chmn, Nat. Conf. of Christians and Jews; pres, World Affairs Coun; Pub. Rels. Soc. Am; K. of M. Rel: Roman Catholic. Legal Res: 729 Millbrook Lane, Haverford, Pa. 19041. Mailing Add: 135 S. Broad St, Philadelphia, Pa. 19109.

McGLOON, THOMAS ARTHUR D
Minority Leader, Ill. State Senate
b. Chicago, Ill, 12/18/11; s. James C. McGloon and Mary A. Wiley M; c. Marianne. Educ: DePaul Univ. Law Sch, LL.B, 35. Polit. & Govt. Pos: Former asst. pub. defender, Chicago, Ill. and asst. state's attorney, Cook Co; Ill. State Sen, 58-, Minority Leader, Ill. State Senate, 65-; del, Dem. Nat. Conv, 68. Bus. & Prof. Pos: Lawyer. Mil. Serv: Lt, Naval Res, 42-45, serv. in Second and Third Marine Div, S.Pac; Two Presidential Unit Citations; Letter of Commendation from Commanding Gen. Gravesby Erskine. Mem: Chicago Bar Asn; Phi Alpha Delta; Am. Legion; Amvets; Elks; Stewart Club. Rel: Roman Catholic. Legal Res: 5964 W. Adams Blvd, Chicago, Ill. 60644. Mailing Add: 1 N. LaSalle St, Chicago, Ill. 60602.

McGOFF, JOHN PETER R
b. Pittsburgh, Pa, 6/29/24; s. Peter Frank McGoff and Sarah Robinson M; m. 8/21/54 to Margaret Ewert; c. Susan Ellen, Thomas James and David Scott. Educ: Mich. State Univ, B.A. & M.A. Polit. & Govt. Pos: Mem, Gov. Blue Ribbon Cmt. on Higher Educ, Mich, 62-65 and Bd. of Control, North. Mich. Univ, 64-; chmn, Ingham Co. Rep. Cmt, Mich, 65-69. Bus. & Prof. Pos: Dir, Off. Campus Projects, Mich. State Univ, 50-59; pres, Panay Corp, 59- Mil. Serv: Entered as Pvt, Army, 43, released as Cpl, 46, after serv. in N.Africa, Middle East and European Theaters; recommissioned, 2nd Lt, 50; African, Middle Eastern and European Theater Ribbons with 8 Battle Stars and 3 Arrowheads. Mem: Rotary; Navy League; Sigma Delta Chi; NAACP; Nat. Asn. Broadcasters. Rel: Methodist. Mailing Add: Route 2, Box 182A, Williamston, Mich. 48895. (1967)

McGOLDRICK, PAUL J. R
Chmn, Littleton Rep. Town Cmt, N.H.
b. Boston, Mass, 3/8/35; s. Charles C. McGoldrick, Sr. and Elizabeth Proulx M; m. 10/10/64 to Stephanie Eaton; c. Michael. Educ: Bowdoin Col, B.A, 57; Harvard Bus. Sch, M.B.A, 59; Psi Upsilon. Polit. & Govt. Pos: Chmn, Littleton Rep. Town Cmt, N.H, 66-; Grafton-Coos Co. chmn, Peterson for Gov, 68. Bus. & Prof. Pos: Dist. plant supt, N.E. Tel. Co, 61-66; life ins. agent, State Mutual Life, 66- Mem: Nat. Asn. Life Underwriters; Life Underwriters Polit. Action Cmt; Rotary Int. Mailing Add: Box 478, Littleton, N.H. 03561.

McGOUGH, KENT B. R
Treas, Ohio State Rep. Cent. & Exec. Cmt.
b. Harrod, Ohio, 7/20/17; s. John M. McGough and Mae Brown M; m. 8/25/40 to Wilda Mae Teter; c. Sandra, Debra, Cynthia and John. Educ: Miami Univ, Oxford, Ohio, B.A, 39; Sigma Nu. Polit. & Govt. Pos: Precinct committeeman, Allen Co. Rep. Party, Ohio, 50-; chmn, Rep. Exec. Cmt, Allen Co, 52-; mem, State Rep. Cent. Cmt, Fourth Cong. Dist, 56-; alternate del, Rep. Nat. Conv, 64, del, 68; treas, Ohio State Rep. Cent. and Exec. Cmt, 68- Bus. & Prof. Pos: Partner, McGough Ins. Agency, Lima, Ohio, 46-; v.pres. & treas, Kay-Bee Corp, 60- Mil. Serv: Entered as Pvt, Army, 45, released as M/Sgt, 46, after serv. in Departmental Hq, Alaskan Theatre, 45-46. Mem: Am. Inst. for Property and Liability Underwriters, Inc; Mason; life mem, Jr. Chamber of Commerce; life mem, Optimist Int. Rel: United Methodist. Mailing Add: 450 S. Rosedale Ave, Lima, Ohio 45805.

McGOVERN, FRANCES D
b. Akron, Ohio, 4/18/27; d. Bernard F. McGovern and Pauline Menegay; single. Educ: Univ. Akron, A.B, 48; West. Reserve Univ, LL.B, 49; Pi Kappa Delta; Phi Delta Delta; Kappa Kappa Gamma. Polit. & Govt. Pos: Ohio State Rep, 55-60, chmn, Judiciary Cmt, Ohio Gen. Assembly, 59; mem, Ohio Judicial Coun, 59; mem. and chmn, Ohio Pub. Utilities Cmn, 60-63; del, Dem. Nat. Conv, 60 & 64; mem. adv. coun. on employ. security, U.S. Dept. of Labor, 62-68. Bus. & Prof. Pos: Attorney, Motz, Morris, Wilson & Quine, 49-60, Quine, Infield and McGovern, 63-65 and Ohio Edison Co, 65- Mem: Am, Ohio State and Akron Bar Asns; past mem. exec. cmt, Nat. Asn. Regulatory Utility Cmns; mem. bd, Ohio Citizens Coun. for Health & Welfare; Ohio Planning Conf, Summit Co. United Community Coun, Summit Co. Ment. Hyg. Clin, Summit Co. Ment. Health & Retardation Bd, Portage Path Ment. Health Center and YWCA; C. of C; Jr. League of Akron; League of Women Voters; various Dem. orgn. Outstanding House Mem. Award, 59; Dem. Woman of the Year Award, Ohio, 60; Nat. Award, Kappa Kappa Gamma, 61; Akron Beacon J. Woman of Distinction Award, 68; United Fund Outstanding Citizen Award, 69. Rel: Catholic. Mailing Add: 550 Woodside Dr, Akron, Ohio 44303.

McGOVERN, GEORGE D
U.S. Sen, S.Dak.
b. Avon, S.Dak, 7/19/22; s. Joseph C. McGovern and Frances McLean M; m. 10/31/43 to Eleanor Faye Stegeberg; c. Ann, Steven, Susan, Mary and Teresa. Educ: Dakota Wesleyan Univ, B.A, 46; Northwest. Univ, M.A, 49 and Ph.D, 53. Polit. & Govt. Pos: Exec. secy, S.Dak. Dem. Party, 54-57; U.S. Rep, First Dist, S.Dak, 57-61; dir, Food for Peace Prog, 61-62; spec. asst. to President Kennedy; U.S. Sen, S.Dak, 63-; Presidential cand, 68. Mil. Serv: Entered as Air Cadet, Army Air Force, 43, released as 1st Lt, 45, after serv. in ETO; Distinguished Flying Cross; Air Medal with Oak Leaf Clusters. Publ: War Against Want, Walker & Co, N.Y.C, 64; Agricultural Thought in the 20th Century, Bobbs-Merrill & Co, 66; A Time of War/A Time of Peace, Random House, 68. Mem: Kiwanis; Am. Legion; VFW; Mason. Rel: Methodist. Legal Res: 103 E. Third, Mitchell, S.Dak, 57301. Mailing Add: 362 Old Senate Office Bldg, Washington, D.C. 20510.

McGOVERN, TERRY PATRICK D
Conn. State Rep.
b. Bridgeport, Conn, 6/24/39; s. John Joseph McGovern, Jr.(deceased) and Marie Lesko M; m. 9/7/68 to Toni Ann Derose. Educ: Quinnipiac Col, 57-58; Univ. of Bridgeport, 58-61; South. Conn. State Col, 62-69. Polit. & Govt. Pos: Conn. State Rep, 67- Bus. & Prof. Pos: Supvr, Lycoming Div, Avco Corp, 62-; sales rep, Hamilton Mgt. Corp, 69- Mil. Serv: Entered as E-1, Army Res, 61, released as Pvt, E-2, 67, after serv. in 158th Transportation Corps; Sharpshooter. Rel: Roman Catholic. Mailing Add: 73 Birdsey St, Bridgeport, Conn. 06610.

McGOWAN, EDGAR LEON D
Secy-Treas, Dem. Party of S.C.
b. Conway, S.C, 6/1/20; s. Edgar Leon McGowan and Sarah Frances Mishoe M; m. Apr. 1941 to Mildred Gene Parris; c. Edgar Linden. Educ: Univ. S.C, B.S, 47, M.S, 50, LL.B, 57; Beta Alpha Psi; Delta Sigma Pi. Polit. & Govt. Pos: City judge, Forest Acres, S.C, 63-65, councilman, 65-; secy, Richland Co. Dem. Party, 66-; secy-treas, Dem. Party of S.C, 66-; del, Dem. Nat. Conv, 68. Bus. & Prof. Pos: Instr, Univ. S.C, 46-50, asst. prof, 50-57 and assoc. prof, 58-; pub. acct, Columbia, S.C, 47-50, CPA, 50-57; attorney-at-law, 57- Mil. Serv: Entered as Pvt, Army, 41, released as Sgt, 45, after serv. in 3104 Signal Unit, ETO, 44-45; Good Conduct Medal; European Theatre with Normandy, North. France and Rhineland Battle Stars; Am. Theatre of Opers. Ribbons; World War II Victory Medal. Mem: Am, S.C. and Richland Co. Bar Asns; Am. Acct. Asn; Palmetto Club; Lions; A&FM; Consistory; Shrine. Rel: Methodist. Legal Res: 5067 Hillside Rd, Columbia, S.C. 29206. Mailing Add: 1500 Washington St, Columbia, S.C. 29201.

McGOWAN, EDWIN A. R
b. Plymouth, Ind, 4/16/09; m. to Elsie Weitendorf; c. Edwin A, Jr, Margaret M. and William L. Educ: De Paul Univ. Col. of Law, LL.B. Polit. & Govt. Pos: Former Ill. State Rep; Thornton Twp. Regular Rep. Orgn. Bus. & Prof. Pos: Lawyer. Mem: Lodge 1242, Elks; Harvey Asn. of Commerce and Indust; Harvey-Calumet Bar Asn. Mailing Add: 21 W. 150th St, Harvey, Ill. 60426. (1967)

McGOWAN, JOSEPH E. D
Polit. & Govt. Pos: Precinct committeeman; former Howard Co. Dem. chmn; dep. assessor and off. mgr, city owned utility; co. recorder, 46, 50; Ind. State Rep, -66. Bus. & Prof. Pos: Ins. agent; real estate broker. Mil. Serv: Army. Mem: Am. Legion; Eagles; Elks; Fraternal Order of Police; K. of C. Rel: Catholic. Mailing Add: 1008 Mulberry St, Kokomo, Ind. 46901. (1967)

McGOWAN, LEO PATRICK D
Committeeman, R.I. Dem. Party
b. Providence, R.I, 7/16/05; s. Owen Joseph McGowan and Nora McCauley M; m. 8/1/32 to Doris L. Richards; c. Maureen (Mrs. Hodgkinson) and Dianne (Mrs. Lynch). Educ: Georgetown Univ, B.S.F.S, 27; Boston Col. Law Sch, J.D. Polit. & Govt. Pos: Dem. town chmn, Barrington, R.I, 51-67; del, Dem. Nat. Conv, 56, 58, 60 and alternate del, 64 & 68; committeeman, R.I. Dem. party, currently. Bus. & Prof. Pos: Pub. defender, R.I, 61-66. Publ: 'Procedures in Criminal Law,' R.I. Bar J. Mem: R.I. and Am. Bar Asns; Past Exalted Ruler Elks; past Advocate, K. of C. Rel: Roman Catholic. Legal Res: 51 Middle Hwy, Barrington, R.I. 02806. Mailing Add: 1412 Industrial Bank Bldg, Providence, R.I. 02903.

McGOWAN, MARTIN JAMES, JR. DFL
b. Appleton, Minn, 10/28/20; s. Martin James McGowan and Olga W. Vieg M; m. 7/3/43 to Elizabeth Jane Nolan; c. Martin J, III, Vincent L, Brendan T, Daniel P, Kevin F, Maureen E, Margaret E, Sean T. and Michael J. Educ: Univ. Notre Dame, 38-41; Univ. of Mo, B.A, in hist. and polit. sci, 43; Tau Kappa Epsilon; Sigma Delta Chi. Polit. & Govt. Pos: Secy, Swift Co. Dem-Farmer-Labor Party, Minn, 46-65; Minn. State Rep, 23rd Dist, 59-67, secy, Minority Caucus, Minn. State House of Rep, 62-66; secy, Sixth Dist, Dem-Farmer-Labor Party, 62-64. Bus. & Prof. Pos: Ed. and publisher, Appleton Press, 43-65 and Swift Co. News, Benson, Minn, 60-62; proj. coordinator, Twin City Area ETV Corp, St. Paul, 65- Mem: K. of C.(3° and 4°); bd. of dirs, Minn. Press Club and Minn. Newspaper Asn; Kiwanis. Amateur Radio Operator, Station WØUGV. Rel: Roman Catholic. Mailing Add: 1437 Frankson Ave, St. Paul, Minn. 55108.

McGOWAN, MARY ELIZABETH D
Ohio State Rep.
b. Akron, Ohio, 5/25/85; d. James McGowan and Ellen Sweeney M; single. Educ: St. Vincents Cath. Sch; Bus. Col, Akron. Polit. & Govt. Pos: Official court reporter, Summit Co. Probate Court, Ohio, 40-60; Dem. State Cent. committeewoman, 14th Dist, Ohio, 38-; in charge Akron Off, Dept. of Liquor Control; Dem. Nat. Committeewoman, Ohio, 52-56; Ohio State Rep, 14th Dist, 62-, former asst. secy, Liquor Control Cmt. and mem, Educ. and Financial Insts. Cmts. Mem: Hon. life mem, Ohio Fed. Dem. Women; organizer, Akron Womens Dem. Club; Fed. Dem. Women of Summit Co.(campaign chmn); Adv. Coun. of Civic Unity; Mothers March, chmn, March of Dimes, Greater Summit Co, 67 & 68; Hibernians (past recording secy. and pres, Mark Heffernan Div, Akron); Cath. Daughters of Am. Dem. Woman of the Year, 65. Rel: Catholic. Mailing Add: 1018 Copley Rd, Akron, Ohio 44320.

McGOWEN, FAISON WELLS D
b. Kenansville, N.C, 7/20/03; s. Thomas James McGowen and Julia Robert Stokes M; m. 7/8/32 to Pearl Cynthia Canady. Educ: James Sprunt Inst; Grove Inst; King's Bus. Col; Inst. of Govt, Univ. N.C, Chapel Hill. Polit. & Govt. Pos: Dep. sheriff and treas, Duplin Co, N.C, 24-29, acct. and tax supvr, 29-68; chmn, Duplin Co. Dem. Exec. Cmt, 29 years; co. chmn, Civil Defense, World War II; secy, N.C. Cmt. for Study Pub. Sch. Finance, 57-58; mem. bd. cmnrs, Neuse River Planning and Develop. Cmn, 67-70; mem.bd. trustees, James Sprunt Inst, 67-75; former secy, Duplin Gen. Hosp. Bd. Trustees and emer. trustee, 69- Mem: Mem-at-lg, JOUAM (past coun, Warsaw Coun); Nat. Asn. of Co. Treasurers and Finance Officers; Duplin Co. Indust. and Agr. Coun; N.C. Asn. of Co. Accts.(past pres); life mem, N.C. Asn. of Assessing Officers (past pres); Int. Asn. of Assessing Officers (state chmn, 51); secy, Liberty Hall Hist. Cmn; secy, Hosp. Bldg. Cmt; Boy Scouts; Red Cross; WOW; Mason (past Master, St. John's Lodge 13); Eastern Star (Past Patron); Rotary (past pres Warsaw Club); moderator, East. Baptist Asn, 13 years. Scholarship medal, James Sprunt Inst, 18; Serv. Award, Grand Lodge, AF&AM, N.C, 57; Serv. Award, N.C. Asn. of Co. Cmnrs, 62, Outstanding Co. Off. Award, 63; cert. of Serv, State Asn. of Co. Accts, 65; Serv. Award, State Dem. Exec. Cmt, N.C, 65; Serv. and Leadership Award, N.C. Asn. Accts, 67. Mailing Add: Box 158, Kenansville, N.C. 28349.

McGRATH, THOMAS CHARLES, JR. D
Treas, N.J. Dem. State Cmt.
b. Philadelphia, Pa, 4/22/27; s. Thomas Charles McGrath and Helen Glacken M; m. 3/3/62 to Elizabeth Butler. Educ: Univ. Notre Dame, 44-45; U.S. Naval Acad, B.S, 50; Univ. Pa. Law Sch, LL.B, 57. Polit. & Govt. Pos: Dep. attorney gen, N.J, 63; U.S. Rep, Second Dist, N.J, 64-66; gen. counsel, U.S. Dept. of Housing and Urban Develop, 67-69; treas, N.J. Dem. State Cmt, 69- Bus. & Prof. Pos: Attorney, Dechert, Price & Rhoads, 57-63. Mil. Serv: Enlisted ranks, World War II; Atlantic and Pac. Fleets, 50-54; serv. in USS Missouri, Korean Conflict; Lt, Naval Res; 5 Battle Stars. Mem: Am, N.J, and Pa. Bar Asns. Admitted to practice before Supreme Courts of U.S, N.J. and Pa. Rel: Blessed Sacrament Church, Margate. Mailing Add: 110 S. Kenyon Ave, Margate, N.J. 08402.

McGRAW, ANDREW J. D
Pa. State Rep.
b. Sturgeon, Pa, 3/9/38; s. Peter McGraw and Bridget Taggart M; m. 6/30/56 to Elaine J. Matthews; c. Andrew, Mark, Maureen, Michael and Melissa. Educ: Univ. Pittsburgh, 62-66. Polit. & Govt. Pos: Pa. State Rep, 67- Rel: Catholic. Mailing Add: 306C, Oak Ridge Rd, R.D. 2, McDonald, Pa. 15057.

McGRAW, ANN R. R
Committeewoman, St. Louis Co. Rep. Cent. Cmt, Mo.
b. Boston, Mass, 11/26/30; d. Leon Russell Harvey and Flora Gillespie Douglas H; m. to Thomas E. McGraw; c. Lee Ann, James Russell and Elizabeth Ann. Educ: Univ. of Vt, 48-51. Polit. & Govt. Pos: Precinct committeewoman, Gravois Twp. Rep. Org, 62-64; del, Rep. State Conv, Mo, 64 & 68; committeewoman, St. Louis Co. Rep. Cent. Cmt, 64-; v.chmn, Second Cong. Dist. Rep. Party, 66-68; del, Nat. Fedn. Rep. Women Conv, 67 and Rep. Nat. Conv, 68. Mem: DAR. Rel: Presbyterian. Mailing Add: 330 S. Maple Ave, Webster Groves, Mo. 63119.

McGRAW, JOSEPH ROBERT, JR. R
Okla. State Sen.
b. Tulsa, Okla, 11/19/32; s. Joseph Robert McGraw and Kathryn Ittner McGraw; m. 6/6/66 to Deana Sanditen; stepchildren, Michael Cohen and Tab Cohen. Educ: B.A. in Govt, Univ. Notre Dame, 55; Univ. Tulsa, LL.B, 59. Polit. & Govt. Pos: Dist. dir, Tulsa Co. Rep. Party, 57-59; legal counsel, Okla. Young Rep, 57-61; Okla. State Rep, 64-66; Okla. State Sen, 67-; mem, Okla. Young Rep. and Rep. State Cmt. Mem: Okla. Bar Asn; Tulsa Co. Bar Asn.(mem. legis. cmt, 66-69); Tulsa Real Estate Bd.(mem. legis. and housing cmts, 66-69, mem, Making Am. beautiful cmt, 68-69); Nat. Coun. Crime & Delinquency; South. Coun. of State Govt; Nat. Soc. State Legis; C. of C.(mem. legis. cmt, Tulsa Chap, 66-69, mem. indust. develop. cmt, 69); Okla. Gov. Club; Notre Dame Found; Notre Dame Alumni Asn; Kiwanis Int; Civic Music Asn; YMCA; Broadway Theater League; Little Theatre; Hurricane Club; Commun. Chest. Rel: Roman Catholic. Legal Res: 1747 S. College Ave, Tulsa, Okla. 74104. Mailing Add: Suite N, 3314 E. 51st St, Tulsa, Okla. 74135.

McGRAW, WARREN RANDOLPH D
W.Va. State Del.
b. Mullens, W.Va, 5/10/39; s. Darrell V. McGraw and Julia Zekany M; m. 8/20/61 to Peggy Ann Shufflebarger; s. Warren Randolph, II and Helen Suzanne. Educ: Morris Harvey Col, A.B. in Polit. Sci, Hist. and Econ, 60; W.Va. Univ. Grad. Sch, 60; Wake Forest Univ, LL.B; Pi Kappa Delta; Phi Alpha Delta. Polit. & Govt. Pos: Trial attorney, U.S. Dept. Justice, Wash, D.C, 64-65; W.Va. State Del, Wyo. Co, 68- Mem: Am. Soc. Composers, Authors and Publishers; Jaycees. First prize for Copyright Law. Rel: Methodist. Mailing Add: 101 Locust, Pineville, W.Va. 24874.

MacGREGOR, CLARK R
U.S. Rep, Minn.
b. Minneapolis, Minn, 7/12/22; s. William E. MacGregor and Edith Clark M; m. to Barbara Porter Spicer; c. Susan, Laurie and Eleanor. Educ: Dartmouth Col. on acad. scholarship, A.B, 44, with honors; Univ. of Minn, LL.B, 48. Polit. & Govt. Pos: U.S. Rep, Minn, 60-; del, Rep. Nat. Conv, 64 & 68. Bus. & Prof. Pos: Lawyer, practicing trial lawyer, 48-60, partner in King & MacGregor. Mil. Serv: Army; commissioned directly in the field in Burma while serv. with Off. Strategic Serv. Mem: Am. Legion; VFW. Rel: Presbyterian. Legal Res: Plymouth, Minn. Mailing Add: 2834 Foxhall Rd, N.W, Washington, D.C. 20007.

McGREGOR, GEORGE R. J. D
b. Troy, N.Y, 4/26/07; m. to Edith Rubyor; c. five sons and two daughters. Educ: Athens Sch. of Commerce; Albany Col. of Pharm; Union Univ. Polit. & Govt. Pos: Vt. State Sen, 61-66; Police Cmnr; Off St. Parking Cmnr; Advisory Cmn, Civil Defense, 50. Bus. & Prof. Pos: Pharmacist; Tr. of UVM; Rutland Railway Study Cmn; Vt. State Bd. of Pharm. Mem: Elks; Ethan Allan Club; Burlington Cnty. Club; Nat. Asn. of Retail Druggists; Am. Pharmaceutical Asn; 4th Degree, K. of C; Chittenden Co. Druggists Asn; Vt. State Pharmaceutical Asn; Vt. Heart Asn. Rel: Catholic. 1967 Legal Res: 129 N. Prospect St, Burlington, Vt. No mailing address available. (1967)

McGREGOR, JACK EDWIN R
Pa. State Sen.
b. Kitanning, Pa, 9/22/34; s. Russell A. McGregor and Leah Hampton M; m. to Carol Dangerfield; c. Nancy, Douglas, Elisabeth and Heather. Educ: Yale Univ, B.S, 56; Univ. Pittsburgh Sch. of Law, LL.B, 62; Order of the Coif; Delta Kappa Epsilon; Skull and Bones. Polit. & Govt. Pos: Pa. State Sen, 62-; del, Rep. Nat. Conv, 64. Bus. & Prof. Pos: Assoc, Reed, Smith, Shaw & McClay, Attorneys, 62-68. Mil. Serv: Entered as 2nd Lt, Marine Corps, 56, released as 1st Lt, 59; Capt, Marine Res, 63. Mem: Legis. cmt, Allegheny Co. Bar Asn; pres. and dir, Hockey Club of Pittsburgh; West. Pa. Conservancy; State sect. chmn, United Fund Campaigns, 63 & 64; trustee, West. Pa. Sch. for the Deaf and Point Park Col; Citizens Adv. Cmt. for Juvenile Court. Selected as One of the Outstanding Young Men in Am, U.S. Jr. C. of C, 64. Rel: Presbyterian. Mailing Add: 136 W. Swissvale Ave, Edgewood, Pittsburgh, Pa. 15218.

McGREGOR, NANCY ROHWER R
V.Chmn, Wash. Rep. State Cent. Cmt.
b. Spokane, Wash, 4/9/30; d. Frederick H. Rohwer and Annabelle Howard R; m. 4/24/54 to William McGregor; c. DeEtte and Alyson. Educ: Univ. Mex, 50-51; Vassar Col, B.A, 52; Stanford Univ, 53-54. Polit. & Govt. Pos: Rep. precinct committeewoman, Precinct 50, Whitman Co, Wash, 64-; committeewoman, Wash. Rep. State Cent. Cmt, 64-68, v.chmn, 68-, mem, exec. bd, 69-; mem. exec. bd, Whitman Co. Rep. Cent. Cmt, 64-68 and Whitman Co. Rep. Women's Clubs, 64-68; credentials chmn, State Rep. Conv, 66; del. and mem, Nat. Platform Cmt, Rep. Nat. Conv, 68; adv. to exec. bd, Wash. State Fedn. of Rep. Women, 69; secy, Nat. State V.Chmn. Asn, 69. Mem: Exec. bd, Epton Soc. for the Retarded, 66-67; secy. and mem. bd. of dirs, Champagne Charities, Spokane, Wash; East. Wash. Hist. Soc; Wash. State Wheat Growers Asn. Rel: Episcopal. Mailing Add: Hooper, Wash. 99333.

McGREW, FINLEY R
b. Fairfield, Iowa, 3/6/08; s. Harry L. McGrew and Rose Culbertson M; m. 4/6/35 to Harriet G. Leonard; c. Jane (Mrs. Robert Cram) and David F. Educ: Ohio Wesleyan Univ, A.B, 31; Sigma Phi Epsilon. Polit. & Govt. Pos: Admin. asst. to U.S. Rep. John N. Erlenborn, Ill, 65- Bus. & Prof. Pos: Assoc. ed, Press Publ, Elmhurst, Ill, 46-61, ed, 61-62; ed, Glen Ellyn News and Wheaton Leader, Glen Ellyn, 62-65. Mil. Serv: Specialist 1/C, Navy, 42-45. Mem: Nat. Ed. Asn; Ill. Press Asn; AF&AM. Rel: Methodist. Legal Res: 386 S. Kenilworth Ave, Elmhurst, Ill. 60126. Mailing Add: 4501 Arlington Blvd, Apt. 210, Arlington, Va. 22203.

McGREW, LESLIE FRANK R
Secy, Van Wert Co. Rep. Cent. & Exec. Cmt, Ohio
b. Cincinnati, Ohio, 6/8/99; s. Charles Livingston and Mamie Steinmetz L; m. 8/30/22 to Mildred Dixie Fulton; c. Elizabeth Jean (Mrs. Otis Coon), Virginia Edythe (Mrs. Forest Gribler) and Mildred Janet (Mrs. William Pheanis). Educ: Woodward High Sch, Cincinnati, Ohio. Polit. & Govt. Pos: Councilman at large, Van Wert, Ohio, 48-49; Secy, Van Wert Co. Rep. Cent. & Exec. Cmt, 64-; mem, elec. bd, Van Wert Co, 68- Bus. & Prof. Pos: Traffic mgr, Glenn L. Martin Co, Cleveland, Ohio, 20-29; chief of stores & traffic mgr, Great Lakes Aircraft Co, 29-32; purchasing and sales mgr, Dunson Supply, Van Wert, Ohio, 32-39; coordinator material control and purchasing agent, Continental Can Co, 39-64. Mil. Serv: Entered as Pvt, Marines, 18, released as Cpl, 20, after serv. in Third Regt, 44th Co, Dominican Repub, 18-20; Good Conduct Medal. Mem: Mason; Methodist Men's Club; adv, DeMolay; Am. Legion; Eastern Star; pres, off. bd. trustees, finance chmn. and treas, Ohio Higher Educ. Asn. Rel: Methodist. Mailing Add: 628 N. Market St, Van Wert, Ohio 45891.

McGUIRE, DAVID KELTY D
Mem, Union Co. Dem. Exec. Cmt, N.J.
b. Pittsburgh, Pa, 12/18/34; s. Paul J. McGuire and Dorothy Power M; m. 12/27/65 to Meredith Anne Black; c. Daniel Cronin. Educ: St. Vincent Col (Pa), B.S, 57; Univ. Pittsburgh, Ph.D, 64. Polit. & Govt. Pos: Mem, Union Co. Dem. Exec. Cmt, N.J, 68-; del, Dem. Nat. Conv, 68; chmn, Union Co. New Dem. Coalition, 68-69. Bus. & Prof. Pos: Research fel, Brookhaven Nat. Lab, 64-65; asst. prof. chem, Rider Col, 65-67; assoc. prof, Upsala Col, 67- Publ: 'Relative Basicities of Nitriles, Acetone, and Water,' 67: 1810 and 'Comparison of Polarographic Half-Wave Potentials,' 67: 1814, J. Phys. Chem; 'Polarographic Studies in Dimethysulphone,' J. Inorg. & Nuclear Chem, 28: 2659. Mem: Am. Chem. Soc; Sigma Xi; N.J. Sci. Teacher's Asn; N.J. Asn. Laymen; Union Dem. Club. Rel: Catholic. Mailing Add: 802 Lafayette Ave, Union, N.J. 07083.

McGUIRE, E. PERKINS R
b. Boston, Mass, 10/22/04; s. Clarence W. McGuire and Evelyn Slattery M; m. 10/5/29; to Katerineh Ward. Educ: Lowell Textile Inst, B.T.E. and D.Sc. Polit. & Govt. Pos: Asst. Secy. of Defense, 57-61; mem, Wash. D.C. Rep. Cmt. and v.chmn. finance cmt, 62-; chmn, D.C. Nixon Cmt, 67-68; chmn, D.C. Del. to Rep. Nat. Conv, 68; exec. v.chmn, Inauguration Cmt, 69. Bus. & Prof. Pos: Dir, Burlington Industs, Bunker Ramo Corp, Logetronics Corp. and South. Air Transport Co, currently. Mil. Serv: Entered as Lt, Navy, 42, released as Comdr; Legion of Merit; Defense Pub. Serv. Medal. Rel: Catholic. Legal Res: 2420 Tracy Place N.W, Washington, D.C. 20003. Mailing Add: 800 17th St. N.W, Washington, D.C. 20006.

McGUIRE, HENRY M. D
b. Lawrence, Mass, 1922; s. Patrick McGuire and Celanire Demers M. (deceased); m. to Theresa Retelle; c. nine. Educ: Marist Col, Poughkeepsie, N.Y. Polit. & Govt. Pos: Lawrence Fire Dept, 16 years; Res. firefighter 48, permanent in 61, Lt, 64; Ward 5 Dem. City Cmt. Mil. Serv: WW II Merchant Marine. Mailing Add: 137 Oxford St, Lawrence, Mass. 01841. (1967)

McGUIRE, JOHN ANDREW D
b. Wallingford, Conn, 2/28/06; s. John Joseph McGuire and Katherine Agnes Barry M; m. 7/6/36 to Dorothy May Martin; c. John Martin and Lois Ann (Mrs. Dillon). Educ: Dartmouth Col; Lambda Chi Alpha. Polit. & Govt. Pos: Town clerk, Wallingford, Conn, 34-49; chmn, Conn. State Dem. Cent. Cmt, 46; U.S. Rep, Conn, 49-52; Mayor, Wallingford, 56-58; Conn. State Rep, 60-62. Bus. & Prof. Pos: Owner, John A. McGuire, Ins-Real Estate-Travel Agency, 38- Mem: Pres, Conn. Town Clerks Asn, 40-46; Elks; K. of C.(4°); John Barry Assembly; Red Men. Sponsor, McGuire Fair Trade Act. Rel: Roman Catholic. Mailing Add: 221 N. Main St, Wallingford, Conn. 06492.

McGUIRE, JOHN MICHAEL D
b. Parkersburg, W.Va, 3/17/44; s. Charles Braden McGuire and Virginia Dare Woodyard M; single. Educ. W.Va. Univ, A.B, 66, M.A, 67; Univ. of Minn, 68-69; Phi Alpha Theta. Polit. & Govt. Pos: Del, Dem. Nat. Conv, 68; del. contact staff, Sen. Eugene McCarthy for Pres. Cmt, 68. Rel: Protestant. Mailing Add: 1610 Dewey St, Parkersburg, W.Va. 26101.

McGUIRE, JOSEPH EDWARD D
b. Worcester, Mass, 11/30/27; s. Joseph A. McGuire and Julia Kenney M; m. 6/17/67 to Sheila Nelson. Educ: Georgetown Univ, B.S, 48; U.S. Maritime Acad, N.Y, 1 year; Georgetown Univ. Sch. Law, LL.B. and J.D; Delta Theta Phi. Polit. & Govt. Pos: Mem, Worcester Area Rent Control Bd, Mass, 53-55; Master in Chancery, Worcester, 53-59; cmnr, Mass. Indust. Accident Bd, Boston, 59-65; mem. exec. cmt, Int. Asn. of Indust. Accident Bd. & Cmns, 63, chmn. legis. cmt, 65; Dem. nominee for Lt. Gov. of Mass, 66; del, Dem. Nat.

Conv, 68. Bus. & Prof. Pos: Attorney-at-law, 53- Mil. Serv: Entered as A/S, Naval Res, 46, released as Lt. Comdr, 66, after serv. in Naval Intel. Res. Unit, 1-1-2, Worcester, Mass, 52-66, Retired. Mem: Am, Mass. and Worcester Co. Bar Asns; K. of C; Naval Res. Asn; Dem. City Cmt. Outstanding Young Man Award of Worcester, Jr. C. of C, 60. Rel: Catholic. Legal Res: 12 Schussler Rd, Worcester, Mass. 01609. Mailing Add: 340 Main St, Worcester, Mass. 01608.

McGUIRE, MARIE COLLINS D
b. Washington, D.C, 12/1/04; d. Lewis Franklin Collins and Mary Agnes Fitzpatrick C; wid. Educ: George Wash. Univ, 22-29; Univ. Tex, 41-42; Univ. Houston, 44-48; Theta Sigma Phi; Kappa Delta. Polit. & Govt. Pos: Asst. exec. dir, Houston Housing Authority, Tex, 41-49; exec. dir, San Antonio Housing Authority, 49-61; cmnr, Pub. Housing Admin, 61-66; former acting dep. asst. secy, Dept. of Housing and Urban Develop, asst. for probs. of the elderly and handicapped, Renewal Housing Assistance Admin, currently. Publ: Housing for the Elderly, San Antonio Housing Authority, 57-59; Increasing the Span of Independent Living, Nat. Inst. Ment. Health, 60; pamphlets, speeches, papers, Pub. Housing Admin. Mem: Nat. Asn. Housing & Redevelop. Off; Nat. Housing Center; Nat. Coun. on Aging; Nat. Geriatric Asn; Am. Newspaper Women's Club; Zonta Int; Nat. Dem. Women's Club. Rel: Catholic. Legal Res: San Antonio, Tex. Mailing Add: 1727 Massachusetts Ave. N.W, Washington, D.C. 20036.

McGUIRE, MICHAEL E. DFL
b. Sibley Co, Minn, 6/5/25; married; c. five. Educ: Col. of St. Thomas, B.A; Univ. Minn. Law Sch, LL.B. Polit. & Govt. Pos: Minn. State Rep, 55-57; Minn. State Sen, 58-66. Bus. & Prof. Pos: Lawyer. Mil. Serv: World War II, Combat Inf. Mailing Add: Montgomery, Minn. 56069.

McGUIRK, HARRY J. D
Md. State Sen.
b. Baltimore, Md, 11/7/23; married. Educ: Univ. of Md, Cornell Univ. Polit. & Govt. Pos: Mem, Rent Adv. Bd, Baltimore, Md, 51-, chmn, 52-53; mem, Zoning Cmn, 58-; Md. State Del, 60-67; Md. State Sen, 67-; del, Dem. Nat. Conv, 68. Bus. & Prof. Pos: Mfr. wood prod. Mil. Serv: Navy, 42-46. Mem: Former Exalted Ruler, Baltimore Lodge 7, Elks; Former Comdr, Welbrook Post 118 Am. Legion. Mailing Add: 310 Long Island Ave, Baltimore, Md. 21229. (1967)

MACH, JOSEPH V. D
b. Petersburg, Va, 3/5/21; married. Educ: Va. parochial and pub. schs. Polit. & Govt. Pos: Pres, First Bohemian Dem. Club, Seventh Ward; Md. State Del, 51-59; chmn, Baltimore City Del, 53-; Md. State Sen, 59-67; city councilman, Baltimore, 68- Bus. & Prof. Pos: Businessman. Mil. Serv: Navy, 44-46, Asiatic-Pac. Theatre. Mem: Chmn. of bd, Czech-Am. Civic Asn; exec. dir, Mary Dobkin Childrens Fund; Am. Legion; VFW. Mailing Add: 2300 Ashland Ave, Baltimore, Md. 21202.

MACHEN, HERVEY GILBERT, JR. D
b. Washington, D.C, 10/14/16; s. Hervey Gilbert Machen and Helen Middleton M; m. 5/3/41 to Marian Kathryn Davis; c. William L, Hervey G, III, Susan H. (Mrs. Gill), Judith A. and Theodore D. Educ: Southeast. Univ, Wash, D.C, LL.B, 39 and LL.M, 41; Sigma Delta Kappa; Delta Sigma Phi. Polit. & Govt. Pos: Asst. state's attorney, Prince George's Co, Md, 47-51; city attorney, Cheverly, 47-57, Hyattsville, 50-57; Md. State Del, 55-64; U.S. Rep, Md, 65-69; del, Dem. Nat. Conv, 68. Bus. & Prof. Pos: Attorney-at-law, 40-64; dir, Md. Home Title Co, 54-, Citizen's Bank of Md, 61-; partner, Machen & Brooks, Attorneys, 64- Mil. Serv: Enlisted in Coast Artil, Army, 41, released as Capt, 46, after serv. in Qm. Gen. Off, Wash. D.C. and Spec. Detachment, European Theater, 44-45; European Campaign Ribbon with 2 Battle Stars. Mem: Md. and Am. Bar Asns; past pres, Kiwanis Club; Am. Legion; Almas Temple Shrine; Mt. Hermon Lodge; Moose; past pres, Hyattsville Prfnl. & Businessmen's Asn; Prince George's Co. C. of C. Rel: Episcopal. Legal Res: 4107 Hamilton St, Hyattsville, Md. 20781. Mailing Add: 4328 Farragut St, Hyattsville, Md. 20781.

McHENRY, DONALD FRANCHOT
Spec. Asst. to the Counsr, Dept. of State
b. St. Louis, Mo, 10/13/36; s. Limas McHenry and Dora Brooks M; m. 8/8/62 to Mary Elizabeth Williamson; c. Michael Stephen, Christina Ann and Elizabeth Ann. Educ: Ill. State Univ, B.S, 57; South. Ill. Univ, M.S, 59; Georgetown Univ, 59-62; Pi Sigma Alpha; Pi Kappa Delta; Tau Kappa Alpha; Alpha Delta. Polit. & Govt. Pos: Officer-in-charge, Dependent Areas Sect, Off. of UN Polit. Affairs, Dept. of State, Wash, D.C, 65-69, spec. asst. to the counsr, dept, 69- Bus. & Prof. Pos: Instr. Eng, Howard Univ, 59-62, dir. debate, 61-62; adv, U.S. Del. to the UN Trusteeship Coun, 64, 65, 67 & 68, alternate U.S. rep, 67; adv, U.S. Del. to the 21st UN Gen. Assembly and UN Spec. Cmt. on Colonialism, 66; alternate U.S. rep, UN Seminar on Apartheid and Racial Discrimination, 67; mem, U.S. Del, UN Int. Conf. on Human Rights, 68. Mem: Am. Polit. Sci. Asn; Panel on Self-Determination, Am. Soc. Int. Law. Superior Honor Award, Dept. of State, 66. Rel: Unitarian. Legal Res: 922 Millet St, East St. Louis, Ill. 62201. Mailing Add: 7512 16th St. N.W, Washington, D.C. 20012.

McHENRY, GAIL PITTS D
b. Winston-Salem, N.C, 11/25/48; d. Louis Porter McHenry, Sr.(deceased) and Eleanor Pitts M; single. Educ: Ind. Univ, Bloomington, sociol, 66-; Delta Sigma Theta, Inc. Polit. & Govt. Pos: Del, Dem. Nat. Conv, 68; mem. adv. cmt, Citizens for Hubert Humphrey, 68. Bus. & Prof. Pos: Undergrad. adv. coun. of exec. bd, Delta Sigma Theta, Inc, 69. Mem: Afro-Afro-Am. Student Asn; Ind. Univ. Young Dem. Club. Mille Award, Mademoiselle Mag, 68. Rel: Methodist. Mailing Add: Route 2, Russellville Rd, Hopkinsville, Ky. 42240.

MACHROWICZ, THADDEUS MICHAEL D
b. Gostyn, Poland, 8/21/99; s. Boniface Machrowicz and Frances Werbel M; m. 6/5/35 to Sophia Jara M; c. Tod and Don. Educ: Student, Alliance Col, Pa, 16; Univ. of Chicago, 17; DePaul Univ, 21; Detroit Col. Law, LL.B, 24. Polit. & Govt. Pos: Pub. mem, War Labor Bd; mem, Am. Tech. Adv. Bd. to Poland, 20-21; City Attorney, Hamtramck, Mich, 34-36, munic. judge, 42-50; legal dir, Mich. Pub. Utilities Cmn, 38; U.S. Rep, Mich, 51-61; U.S. Dist. Judge, East. Dist, Mich, 61- Bus. & Prof. Pos: Law practice, Detroit, 24-34. Mil. Serv: Entered as Pvt, Polish Army, 17, released as 1st Lt, after serv. in Infantry, France and Poland, 17-20; Polonia Restitusa. Mem: Nat. Advocates Asn; Polish Am. Cong; Am. Legion; Polish Nat. Alliance; Mich. and Detroit Bar Asns; K. of C. Rel: Roman Catholic. Mailing Add: 149 S. Cranbrook Cross Rd, Birmingham, Mich. 48010.

McHUGH, DOROTHY BARBREE R
Rep. Nat. Committeewoman, N.Y.
b. Oakland, Calif; d. Joseph Barbree and Nellie Snowden B; m. 12/4/57 to Keith S. McHugh; c. Michael B; Harry. Educ: Univ. of Calif; Sigma Kappa. Polit. & Govt. Pos: Rep. campaign mgr, N.Y.C. Mayoral Race, 61 and N.Y. Gubernatorial Race, 62 & 66; mem. adv. bd, N.Y.C. Rep. Women, 63-; Rep. Nat. Committeewoman, N.Y, 63-; del, Rep. Nat. Conv, 68. Mem: Pres, Assistance League, Glendale, Calif, 40-41; dir, Women's Auxiliary Inst. Phys. Med. & Rehab, 59-; Asn. Homemaker Serv, 61-62. Mailing Add: 10 Gracie Sq, New York, N.Y. 10028. (1967)

McILVAIN, BILL D. R
Wyo. State Rep.
b. Alma, Okla, 8/28/32; s. Tommy O. McIlvain and Birtie Chaudion M; m. 8/16/55 to Ila M. Anderson; c. Lavonda, Sandra, Larry and Mark. Educ: John Brown Univ, B.S.S.E, 57; Univ. Wyo, 58; State Teachers Col, Greeley, Colo, summers 58-60. Polit. & Govt. Pos: Wyo. State Rep, 69- Bus. & Prof. Pos: Mem. staff, Summer Inst. Ling, Peru. Mem: Gov. Educ. Cmn, 63-64; pres, Cheyenne Classroom Teachers Asn. 64-65; pres, Cheyenne Educ. Asn, 69-; life mem, Nat. and Wyo. Educ. Asns; Farm Bur. Teacher of the Year, Cheyenne. Rel: Baptist. Mailing Add: 1109 Cactus Hill Rd, Cheyenne, Wyo. 82001.

McILVAINE, ROBINSON
U.S. Ambassador to Repub. of Kenya
b. Downington, Pa, 7/17/13; m. to Alice W. Nicholson M; c. Stevenson, Mia Carol, Ian and Katherine. Educ: Harvard Univ, B.A, 35, grad. work, 35-36. Polit. & Govt. Pos: Off. of Asst. Secy. for Pub. Affairs, 53; chmn, U.S. Sect. of Caribbean Cmn, 53-56; Dep. Asst. Secy. of State for Pub. Affairs, 54-56; Dep. Chief of Mission at Lisbon and Leopoldville; Ambassador to Dahoney; coordinator, Nat. Interdept. Seminar, 64; head, Congo Working Group of State Dept, 64; spec. asst, Off. of Ambassador-at-lg. Harriman, 65-66; co-dir, five W.African Nations, State Dept, 66; U.S. Ambassador to Guinea, 66-69; Repub. of Kenya, 69- Mil. Serv: Comdr, Navy. Mailing Add: U.S. Embassy, Nairobi, Kenya.

McINERNEY, JOHN S. R
Md. State Del.
b. Washington, D.C, 3/13/29; married. Educ: Devitt Prep; Am. Univ, B.S, 58; Wash. Col. of Law, LL.B, 60. Polit. & Govt. Pos: Md. State Del, 63- Mil. Serv: Marine Corps, Korea. Mailing Add: 101 S. Washington St, Rockville, Md. 20850. (1967)

McINERNEY, THOMAS J. D
b. Yonkers, N.Y, 6/12/24; single. Educ: Pace Col, degree in bus. admin; Columbia Univ; City Col. New York. Polit. & Govt. Pos: N.Y. State Assemblyman, 64-69; mem, First Ward Dem. Club. Bus. & Prof. Pos: Owner of a hearing aid sales and serv. bus, Yonkers. Mil. Serv: Vet, World War II. Mem: Dir, Yonkers Br, Nat. Conf. of Christians and Jews; dir, Yonkers Commun. Planning Coun; adv. bd, Yonkers C.Y.O; former mem, bldg. cmt, Yonkers Girl Scouts; Lud-Dale Youth Activities, past pres; Holy Name Soc; St. Mary's Alumni; CWV; Lions; Elks; K. of C; Am. Legion. Honors: Presidential Award of Honor from Jr. C. of C. for establishment of hearing aid prog. for underprivileged children in conjunction with Bd. of Educ; CYO's Award for Outstanding Serv. to the Co. Youth Prog, 63; Outstanding Sports Personality of Yonkers for work with Athletics and Youth Activities, 56; Cert. of Merit from Vet. Admin. for Outstanding Vol. Work With Paralyzed Vets, 55. Rel: Catholic. Mailing Add: 106 Morris St, Yonkers, N.Y. 10705. (1967)

McINNES, THERESA R
Mem, Calif. Rep. State Cent. Cmt.
b. Norderney, W.Germany, 7/11/33; d. Heinrich Theodor Pleines and Therese Rass P; m. 2/14/59 to John Donald McInnes; c. Stewart and Andrew. Educ: Educated In Germany. Polit. & Govt. Pos: Assoc. mem, Sacramento Co. Rep. Cent. Cmt, Calif, 67, mem, 68-, mem. exec. cmt, 68, permanent voting alternate for Secy. of State Frank M. Jordan, 69; first v.pres, Rep. Women's Club Sacramento, Federated, 67, pres, 68 & 69; assoc. mem, Calif. Rep. State Cent. Cmt, 67-68, mem, 69-; mem. bd. dirs, Sacramento Rep. Fund, 69-Sacramento Rep. Fund Award, 68. Rel: Protestant. Mailing Add: 4339 Sierra Madre Dr, Sacramento, Calif. 95825.

McINTIRE, CLIFFORD GUY R
b. Perham, Maine, 5/4/08; s. Frank Charles McIntire and Velma Lee Smith M; m. 9/11/31 to Wilda Autice Holts; c. Patrice (Mrs. Malcolm Andrews) and Blynn C. Educ: Univ. Maine, B.S. in agronomy, 30; Phi Kappa Phi; Alpha Zeta; Phi Sigma; Alpha Gamma Rho. Hon. M.S, Maine Maritime Acad; hon. LL.D, Univ. Maine and Bowdoin Col. Polit. & Govt. Pos: Regional mgr, fieldman and appraiser, Farm Credit Admin, Springfield, Mass, 33-47; U.S. Rep, Third Cong. Dist, Maine, 51-62, Second Cong. Dist, 62-64. Bus. & Prof. Pos: Farm owner and operator, 31-51; asst. mgr, Maine Potato Growers, Inc, 47-51; dir, Natural Resources Dept, Am. Farm Bur. Fedn, 65. Mem: F&AM; Shrine; Elks; Rotary; Am. Farm Bur. Fedn; Cong. Country Club; Capital Hill Club. Author of McIntire-Stennis Forestry Research Act; Outstanding farmer of Maine, Univ. of Maine, 51. Rel: Baptist. Legal Res: Perham, Maine. 04766. Mailing Add: 3 N. Seminary Ave, Park Ridge, Ill. 60068.

Mc INTIRE, JOHN ELMER D
b. Caribou, Maine, 4/10/11; s. Percy Everett Mc Intire and Margaret Farren M; m. May, 1934 to Thelma Leone Buchanan; c. John Farren, David Llewellyn and Marcia Leone. Polit. Pos: Chmn, Montcalm Co. Dem. Party, Mich, 64-67; secy, 10th Dist. of Mich. Dem, 64-66. Govt. Pos: Supvr. in charge of 1960 Census, Census Dept, Montcalm Co, Mich, 60. Mem: Pres, Music Boosters Club, Lakeview, Mich; v.pres, Lakeview High Sch. PTA; Boy Scout master of Greenville and Charlotte, Mich. Rel: Congregational. Mailing Add: RFD 1, Coral, Mich. 48388. (1967)

McINTIRE, POPE BARROW D
Mem, Ga. State Dem. Exec. Cmt.
b. Savannah, Ga, 10/7/24; s. Francis P. McIntire and Lucy Barrow M; m. 7/7/45 to Palmour Holmes; c. Palmour Holmes and Sarah Ellen. Educ: Swarthmore Col, 41-43; Univ. Ga, LL.B, 47; Phi Beta Kappa; Phi Delta Theta. Polit. & Govt. Pos: Mem, Fulton Co. Court Study Cmt, Ga, 61-63; v.chmn, State Constitution Rev. Cmn, 62-64; co-chmn, Johnson-Humphrey Campaign in Ga, 64; chmn, City Tax Study Cmt, 64-; mem, Ga. State Dem. Exec. Cmt, currently. Mil. Serv: Entered as Aviation Cadet, Army Air Force, 43, released as Lt, 45, after serv. in Eighth Air Force 388th Bomb Group (H), ETO, 45. Mem: State Bar of Ga.(mem. bd. gov, 63-); Lawyers Club of Atlanta (pres, 61); Am. and Atlanta Bar Asns. Rel: Episcopal. Legal Res: 40 the Prado N.E, Atlanta, Ga. 30309. Mailing Add: 434 Trust Co. of Ga. Bldg, Atlanta, Ga. 30303.

McINTOSH, ANNE MAGWOOD R
b. Rumney, N.H; d. William Magwood and Nellie Girdler M; m. 12/17/38 to Colin Hugh McIntosh. Educ: N.H. Univ, B.S, 28; N.Y. Univ, grad. study in educ, 32; Phi Mu; Col. Debating Soc. Polit. & Govt. Pos: Pres, Mt. Vernon Women's Rep. Club, Va, 59 & 65; Tenth Dist. chmn, Rep. Women and mem, Tenth Dist. Rep. Cmt, 60-61; mem, Fairfax Co. Rep. Cmt, 60-62 & 65-68; prog. chmn, Va. Fedn. of Rep. Women, 62-63; del-at-lg. from Va. and mem. credentials cmt, Rep. Nat. Conv, 64; co-chmn, Tenth Dist. Women for Goldwater, 64; mem, Rep. Campaign Orgn. Cmt, Palm Beach Co, Fla, 68-69. Bus. & Prof. Pos: Eng. Teacher, jr.high sch, New Britain, Conn, 29-33, high sch, Willimantic, Conn, 34-35 and jr. high sch, Malden, Mass, 36-38. Mem: Past mem, North. Va. Alumnae Chap. of Phi Mu and Thomas Lee Chap, DAR; chmn, Mt. Vernon area, United Givers Fund, 57; Mt. Vernon chmn, Nat. Symphony Sustaining Fund, 62; vice-regent, Palm Beach Chap, DAR, 68-69; Phi Mu Alumnae Asn. of Fla. Rel: Episcopal. Mailing Add: 2840 S. County Rd, Palm Beach, Fla. 33480.

McINTOSH, CARL DANIEL R
Chmn, McLennan Co. Rep. Party, Tex.
b. Brownwood, Tex, 5/17/27; s. Carl Daniel McIntosh and Blanche McKinley Eaton M; m. 9/1/48 to Janis Faye Hicks; c. Carl Daniel, III, Donald Edward, Dewitt Hicks, Joel Eaton and Mary Lou. Educ: Tex. Agr. and Mech. Univ, B.S, 50. Polit. & Govt. Pos: Chmn, McLennan Co. Rep. Party, Tex, 68- Bus. & Prof. Pos: Pres, Oasis Water Co, Waco and San Benito, Tex, 53-, Oasis Lawn Sprinkler Co, 63-, Waco Brick Mfg. Co, Waco, 65- and Star Finance Corp, 67- Mil. Serv: Entered as A/S, Naval Res, 45, released as Coxswain, 46, after serv. in Naval Training Center, San Diego, Calif; Lt. Col, Army Res, 493rd Engr. Group, Dallas, Tex; Am. Defense Medal; Army Res. Medal; Army Occupation Medal; ETO Medal. Mem: Tex. Soc. of Prfnl. Engrs; Rotary, Waco. Rel: Methodist. Mailing Add: 4824 Pecan Terrace, Waco, Tex. 76710.

McINTOSH, JAMES DAVID D
Chmn, W. Carroll Parish Dem. Exec. Cmt, La.
b. Rayville, La, 8/21/16; s. John R. McIntosh and Edna Brown; m. 7/18/48 to Kate White; c. James D, Jr. and Mary Kate. Educ: La. State Univ, B.A. and J.D, 33-39. Polit. & Govt. Pos: Asst. dist. attorney, Fifth Judicial Dist, La, 48-50; chmn, W. Carroll Parish Dem. Exec. Cmt, currently. Bus. & Prof. Pos: Partner, Law Firm McIntosh, Hester, Gilfoil & Fox, Oak Grove and Lake Providence, La, currently. Mil. Serv: Entered as Pvt, released as 1st Lt, after serv. in Counter Intel. Corps, ETO, 42-46. Mem; La. State and Am. Bar Asns; Am. Trial Lawyers Asn; Lions; VFW; Am. Legion. Rel: Methodist. Legal Res: McIntosh St, Oak Grove, La. 71263. Mailing Add: Box 207, Oak Grove, La. 71263.

McINTURFF, CARL EMANUEL R
Rep. Mem, Tenn. State Bd. of Elec.
b. Erwin, Tenn, 10/29/98; s. Robert Nathaniel McInturff and Ida Timberlake; m. 11/20/21 to Ada Conley; c. Robert N. and Joe G. Educ: Unicoi Co. High Sch. Polit. & Govt. Pos: Justice of the peace, Unicoi Co, Tenn, 30-34, sheriff, 34-40 & 42-46; Tenn. State Rep, 42-44 & 48-50; del, Rep. Nat. Conv, 52 & 64; Rep. mem, Tenn. State Bd. of Elec, 65- Bus. & Prof. Pos: Chmn. bd, Rutherford Freight Lines Inc, 46- Mem: BRT; Southeast. Dairy Asn; Mason; Shrine; Eastern Star. Rel: Protestant. Mailing Add: 101 Clinchfield Ave, Erwin, Tenn. 37650. (1967)

McINTYRE, ALEX, JR. R
Ky. State Rep.
b. 1919. Educ: Maryville Col. Polit. & Govt. Pos: Mem. sch. bd, Hazard, Ky; Ky. State Rep, 64- Bus. & Prof. Pos: Wholesale grocer. Mil. Serv: Army, World War II; Silver Star; Purple Heart; Combat Inf. Badge. Mem: Past pres, Hazard Rotary; past post comdr, dist. comdr, Am. Legion; Hazard Jaycees. Rel: Presbyterian. Mailing Add: Hazard, Ky. 41701.

McINTYRE, JOHN JOSEPH D
Justice, Wyo. Supreme Court
b. Dewey Co, Okla, 12/17/04; s. Frank P. McIntyre and Orah Jarvis M; m. 7/31/38 to Ferm Gillilan M; c. J. Joseph, Donald N, Ruth (Mrs. Norris W. Miller), Darel D and John F. Educ: Univ. Colo, LL.B, 28. Polit. & Govt. Pos: Co. and prosecuting attorney, Converse Co, Wyo, 33-36; spec. attorney, Dept. of Justice, 36-38; assoc. attorney, Solicitor's Off, Dept. of Agr, 38; U.S. Rep, Wyo, 41-43, dep. attorney gen, 43-44, auditor, 46; Justice, Wyo. Supreme Court, 60- Bus. & Prof. Pos: Attorney, Glenrock, Wyo, 29-31, Douglas, 31-41. Mil. Serv: Wyo. Nat. Guard, 35-41; served with Field Artil, Army; decorated Croix de Guerre. Mailing Add: Supreme Court Bldg, Cheyenne, Wyo, 82001.

McINTYRE, N. J. 'BUD' R
b. Gypsum, Kans, 5/28/18; married; c. seven; three grandchildren. Educ: Jefferson Sch. Law, Louisville, Ky. Polit. & Govt. Pos: Former Colo. State Rep; Rep. Finance Drives; mem. speaker's bur, Senate Campaign, 62. Bus. & Prof. Pos: Bus. personnel consult. Mil. Serv: Army (Ret), 59. Mailing Add: 5471 E. Tennessee Ave, Denver, Colo. 80222. (1967)

McINTYRE, SCOTT, JR. R
Iowa State Rep.
b. Cedar Rapids, Iowa, 1933; married; c. Kent and Kaye. Educ: Univ. Iowa, B.A; Univ. Pa, M.B.A; Phi Beta Kappa. Polit. & Govt. Pos: Iowa State Rep, 67- Bus. & Prof. Pos: Pres, United Life Ins. Co; exec. v.pres, United Fire and Casualty Co. Mailing Add: 4271 Fox Meadow Dr. S.E, Cedar Rapids, Iowa 52403. (1967)

McINTYRE, THOMAS JAMES D
U.S. Sen, N.H.
b. Laconia, N.H, 2/20/15; m. to Myrtle Ann Clement; c. Martha Grey. Educ: Dartmouth Col, 37; Boston Univ. Law Sch, 40. Polit. & Govt. Pos: Mayor, Laconia, N.H, 49-51, city solicitor, 53; Cand, U.S. Rep, N.H, 54; del, Dem. Nat. Conv, 56 & 68; chmn, Laconia Dem. City Cmt. and Belknap Co. Dem. Cmt; N.H. State Sen, 62-67; U.S. Sen, N.H, currently. Bus. & Prof. Pos: Hon. pres. bd. trustees, Taylor Home for Aged, 54-62. Mil. Serv: Army, 42-46, serv. in 376th Inf, 94th Div, Third Army; Maj.(Ret); Combat Inf. Badge; Bronze Star; Oak Leaf Cluster; four battle stars. Mem: Belknap Co. Bar Asn. (pres, 61-63); Fed. Bar Asn; N.H. Bar Asn; Kiwanis; K. of C; VFW; Am. Legion; CWV; Grange. Legal Res: 45 Roundbay Rd, Laconia, N.H. 03246. Mailing Add: 1001 Wilson Blvd, Arlington, Va. 22209. (1967).

MacIVER, DALE DFL
b. Superior, Wis, 4/13/23; s. Ernest D. MacIver and Elsie Swanson M; single. Educ: Univ. Minn. Sch. Bus. Admin, B.B.A, 47, Law Sch, LL.B, 50; Phi Delta Phi. Polit. & Govt. Pos: Asst. city attorney, Duluth, Minn, 51-54; asst. attorney gen, Minn, 55 & 62; cmnr. of aeronaut, State of Minn, 56-61; admin. asst. to U.S. Rep. Don Fraser, 63- Mil. Serv: Entered as A/S, Navy, 43, released as Lt.(jg), 46; Atlantic and Pac. Theatre Ribbons. Mem: Am. and Fed. Bar Asns. Rel: Presbyterian. Legal Res: 5613 W. Eighth St, Duluth, Minn. 55807. Mailing Add: 1001 Third St. S.W, Washington, D.C. 20024.

McIVER, EDGAR WILSON R
Committeeman, Ill. Rep. Cent. Cmt.
b. Roodhouse, Ill, 6/30/15; s. Harold Anson McIver and Virginia Wilson M; m. 12/25/35 to Leona Ryan; c. Harold A, John T. and Mary Christine (Mrs. Rust). Educ: Roodhouse High Sch, Ill, grad, 33. Polit. & Govt. Pos: Precinct committeeman, First Precinct, Roodhouse, Ill, 36-42; committeeman, Ill. Rep. Cent. Cmt, 15th Dist, 62-; dir, 20th Cong. Dist. Rep. Adv. Coun, Ill, 62-; mem, Nat. Rep. Cong. Adv. Cmt, 62-; Green Co. dir, U.S. Rep. Paul Findley's Vol. for Findley, 62- Mem: AF&AM, Roodhouse, Ill; Kiwanis Int; United Transportation Union. Cong. Cert. of Recognition. Rel: Baptist. Mailing Add: 120 E. Clay St, Roodhouse, Ill. 62082.

MacIVER, JOHN KENNETH R
b. Milwaukee, Wis, 3/22/31; s. Wallace MacIver and Elizabeth MacRae M; m. 9/4/54 to Margaret Jean Vail; c. Douglas Bruce, Carolyn Vail, Kenneth Dunkin and Laura Elizabeth. Educ: Univ. Wis, B.S, 53, LL.B, 55; Phi Kappa Psi; Phi Delta Theta; Phi Delta Phi. Polit. & Govt. Pos: Urban coordinator, Knowles for Gov. Cmt, 64 & 66, v.chmn, 68; chmn, Wis. Nixon for Pres. Cmt, 67-68; v.chmn, Leonard for U.S. Sen. Cmt, 68; del, Rep. Nat. Conv, 68. Mem: Wis. Bar Asn.(chmn. labor law sect. and chmn. antitrust cmt. of bus. law sect); Nat. Coun. Alcoholism (v.pres, mem. bd. and exec. cmt); Wis. Coun. Econ. Develop.(mem. bd); Milwaukee Co. Youth Opportunities Bd. Community Serv. award, Milwaukee Coun. on Alcoholism. Rel: Methodist. Mailing Add: 5486 N. Lake Dr, Milwaukee, Wis. 53217.

McIVOR, JAMES CHRISTOPHER R
Chmn, Bedford Co. Rep. Party, Va.
b. Forest, Va, 3/14/33; s. Malcolm Earl McIvor and Cornelia Overstreet M; m. 7/18/64 to Leigh Ann Cowan; c. Tracy Lynn and Elizabeth Allen. Educ: Lynchburg Col, B.A, Univ. Richmond, LL.B; McNeil Law Soc, Univ. Richmond Law Sch. Polit. & Govt. Pos: Chmn, Bedford Co. Rep. Party, Va, 64- Mil. Serv: Entered as Pvt, Army, 54, released as SP-3, 56, after serv. in 176th Signal Corps, ETO. Rel: Methodist. Mailing Add: 1235 Windsor Dr, Bedford, Va. 24523.

MACK, BARRON BAYLES D
Exec. Committeeman, York Co. Dem. Party, S.C.
b. Ft. Mill, S.C, 9/19/34; s. William Bayles Mack and Elizabeth Mills M; m. 2/9/57 to Joanne Arnold; c. Barron Bayles, Jr. and Frances Elizabeth. Educ: Davidson Col, B.S, 56; Wash. & Lee Univ, LL.B, 60; Sigma Phi Epsilon; Phi Delta Phi. Polit. & Govt. Pos: Exec. Committeeman, York Co. Dem. Party, S.C, 60-; admin. asst. to Congressman Tom S. Gettys, 64-65, home secy, 65; del, Dem. Nat. Conv, 68. Bus. & Prof. Pos: Partner, Mack & Mack, Attorneys at law, 60-; pres, Ft. Mill Credit Bur. Inc, 61-, Dollars & Sense Investment Co. Inc, 63- and Key Investment Corp, 66- Mil. Serv: Entered as 2nd Lt, Army, 56, released as Capt, 68, after serv. in Judge Adv. Gen. Corps. Mem: York Co. and S.C. Bar Asns; Am. and S.C. Trial Lawyers Asns; C. of C; Lions; Ft. Mill Yellow Jacket Club; Am. Legion; Elks; York Co. Tuberc. Asn; SAR; S.C. Soc. of Metrop. Wash, Cong. Secy. Club; United Fund; York Co. Cancer Asn. Distinguished Serv. Award and Outstanding Young Man of the Year, Ft. Mill Jr. C. of C. Rel: Presbyterian; pres. of men and deacon, Unity Presbyterian Church. Legal Res: 217 Banks St, Ft. Mill, S.C. 29715. Mailing Add: P.O. Box 128, Ft. Mill, S.C. 29715.

MACK, PETER FRANCIS JR. D
b. Carlinville, Ill, 11/1/16; s. Peter F. Mack and Catherine Kelly M; m. to Romona North; c. Mona Catherine and Romona Melanie. Educ: Blackburn Col; St. Louis Univ; aviation courses at Springfield Jr. Col, Springfield Aviation Sch. Polit. & Govt. Pos: U.S. Rep, Ill, 49-63; del, Dem. Nat. Conv, 68. Bus. & Prof. Pos: Sponsor, Mack Educ. Tours; commercial pilot; pilot, Friendship Flame, flight in interest of peace; asst. to pres, South. Rwy. Syst, 63- Mil. Serv: Aviator, Naval Air Force, 4 years; Comdr, Res; Air Trophy, 52. Rel: Catholic. Mailing Add: 1524 South Grand W, Springfield, Ill. 62703.

MACK, WALTER R. R
b. Orford, N.H, 5/11/09; married. Educ: Orford. Polit. & Govt. Pos: Overseer of the Poor; former Police Chief; selectman and health officer; N.H. State Rep. until 67. Bus. & Prof. Pos: Bldg. contractor. Mem: Grange; Mason. Rel: Protestant. Mailing Add: Orford, N.H. 03777.

McKAY, CHARLES WATSON, JR. D
b. Ashland, Ala, 4/29/21; s. Charles Watson McKay and Bessie Birchfield McK; m. 8/20/42 to Ann F. McGee; c. Travis G, Margaret R, Martha J.

and Polly A. Educ: Univ. Ala, B.A, 43, LL.B, 46; Pi Kappa Alpha; Phi Delta Phi. Polit. & Govt. Pos: Adminstr, Civil Serv. Bd, Sylacauga, Ala, 52-58, city attorney, 52-; Ala. State Rep, 55-59; mem, Dem. Nat. Cmt, Ala, 56-60; mem. exec. cmt, Ala. Dem. Cmt, 63-69. Bus. & Prof. Pos: Law practice, Sylacauga, 46- Mil. Serv: 1st Lt, Air Force, 43-46; Air Medal with 2 Oak Leaf Clusters, 5 Battle Stars. Mem: Am. and Ala. Bar Asns; Sylacauga C. of C; Scabbard & Blade; Sylacauga Exchange. Legal Res: Primrose Path, Sylacauga, Ala. 35150. Mailing Add: First Federal Bldg, Sylacauga, Ala. 35150. (1967)

McKAY, J. CURTIS R
Chmn, Ozaukee Co. Rep. Party
b. Chicago, Ill, 10/10/26; s. John L. McKay and Theodora Bennett M; m. 9/25/65 to Ruth L. Cary; c. Thomas E, Joan E, Janet L, Kimberly C, Shane D. and Holly. Educ: Grinnell Col, Grinnell, Iowa, B.A, 51; Northwest. Law Sch, J.D, 57; Sigma Delta Chi; Phi Delta Phi. Polit. & Govt. Pos: Wis. State Assemblyman, 60-69, Majority Floor Leader, Wis. State Assembly, 67-69; mem, Nat. Legis. Leaders Conf, 63-68; mem. exec. cmt, Legis. Conf, 65-67; Statutory chmn, Wis. State Rep. Party, 68-70; co. chmn, Ozaukee Co. Rep. Party, 68- Mem: Am, Ill. and Wis. Bar Asns; former mem. bd. dir, Lawyer-Pilots Asn; Farm Bur; Int. Platform Asn; Am. Judicature Soc; Airplane Owners and Pilots Asn; Nat. Legis. Leaders Conf. Rel: Protestant. Legal Res: 534 N. Washington Ave, Cedarburg, Wis. 53012. Mailing Add: 10305 Sherman Rd, Cedarburg, Wis. 53012.

MACKAY, JAMES ARMSTRONG D
b. Fairfield, Ala, 6/25/19; s. Edward George Mackay and Beulah Mason M; m. 9/20/42 to Mary Caroline Lee M; c. Kathleen Elizabeth and James Edward. Educ: Emory Univ, A.B, 40, LL.B, 47; Kappa Alpha; Phi Delta Phi; Omicron Delta Kappa; Alumni Trustee; Pres, Alumni Asn, Emory Univ, 56-57. Polit. & Govt. Pos: Ga. State Rep, 51-52 & 55-64; pres, Fulton and DeKalb Co. Family Serv. Soc, 53-56; U.S. Rep, Ga, 64-67; Dem. cand. for U.S. Rep, Ga, 68. Bus. & Prof. Pos: Attorney. Mil. Serv: Coast Guard Res, Lt; Bronze Star Medal. Mem: Stone Mountain Circuit and Am. Bar Asns; Civitan; State Bd, Ga. State YMCA. Rel: Methodist; Steward. Mailing Add: 500 First National Bank Bldg, 315 W. Ponce de Leon, Decatur, Ga. 30030.

McKAY, KELSEY B. R
Mem, Miss. State Rep. Exec. Cmt.
b. Ft. Wayne, Ind, 11/4/24; s. James M. McKay and Alida Kelsey Babcock M; m. 12/19/53 to Martha Wagner; c. John and Mary. Educ: Wabash Col, B.A, 49; Univ. Fla, M.A, 51. Polit. & Govt. Pos: Chmn, Pike Co. Rep. Party, Miss; mem, Miss. State Rep. Finance Cmt; mem, Miss. State Rep. Exec. Cmt, currently. Mil. Serv: Entered as Pvt, Army, 43, released as 1st Lt, 46, after serv. in Pac. Theater. Rel: Presbyterian. Mailing Add: 316 Hickory, McComb, Miss. 39648.

McKAY, KOLN GUNN D
b. Ogden, Utah, 2/23/25; s. James Gunn McKay and Elizabeth C. Peterson M; m. 5/5/50 to Donna Biesinger; c. Gunn Biesinger, Mavis, Marl Biesinger, Kolene, Carla, Ruston Biesinger, Chad Biesinger and Ruth. Educ: Weber State Col, grad; Utah State Univ, grad. Polit. & Govt. Pos: Utah State Rep. and mem, Utah Legis. Coun, 65-67; admin. asst. to Gov, Utah, 68- Mil. Serv: Entered as A/S, Coast Guard, released as 3/C PO, after serv. in 12th Naval Dist. Mem: Am. Legion; Meat Packers Union; Sons of Utah Pioneers. Rel: Latter-day Saint. Mailing Add: 141 S. 7600 E, Huntsville, Utah 84317.

McKAY, MARTHA CLAMPITT D
b. Winchester, Mass, 5/16/20; d. Robert Hamilton Clampitt and Cornelia Morrison C; m. 7/11/41 to Herbert Stacy McKay; c. Alexander Stacy, Brian McNeil and Anna Katherine. Euuc: Univ. N.C. Chapel Hill, B.A. in Econ, 41; Alpha Delta Pi. Polit. & Govt. Pos: Precinct committeeman, Dem. Party, N.C, 50-60; secy, Precinct Dem. Cmt, 50-60; mem, Sixth Cong. Dist. Legis. Cmt, 60-62; mem, N.C. Dem. Exec. Cmt, 60-64; mem, Dem. Nat. Cmt, 60-64, mem. exec. cmt, 62-64; consult, Off. Inspection, Off. Econ. Opportunity, 65- Bus. & Prof. Pos: Mem, Comptrollers Staff, N.C. Shipbuilders, 42-45; self employed, Acct. & Food Serv. Bus, 52-65; asst. to exec. dir, N.C. Fund, 66-67; dir. spec. proj, N.C. Manpower Develop. Corp, 67-68; field exec, US R&D Corp, N.Y, 68- Mem: Nat. Citizen's Cmt. Commun. Rels; Gov. Sanford's Good Neighbor Coun, 64-65; Chapel Hill Country Club; N.C. Coun. Human Resl.(bd. dirs); N.C. Consumers Coun.(bd. dirs). Rel: Presbyterian. Mailing Add: 406 Westwood Dr, Chapel Hill, N.C. 27514.

McKAY, MARTHA WAGNER R
V.Chmn, Pike Co. Rep. Party, Miss.
b. Indianapolis, Ind, 12/2/28; d. Eldo I. Wagner and Mary Blacklidge W; m. 12/19/53 to Kelsey B. McKay; c. John Wagner and Mary. Educ: Butler Univ, B.S, 51; Kappa Alpha Theta. Polit. & Govt. Pos: Del, Miss. Rep. State Conv, 60, 64 & 68; pres, Pike Co. Rep. Women's Club, 61-65; del. and mem. rules cmt, Rep. Nat. Conv, 64; del, Nat. Fedn. of Rep. Women Biennial Conv, 64, 67 & 69; v.chmn, Pike Co. Rep. Party, Miss, 64-67 & 69-; Americanism chmn, Miss. Fedn. of Rep. Women, 65-67, pres, 67-69 and 2nd v.pres, 69-; mem, Miss. Rep. Cent. Cmt, 67-69; mem. bd. of dirs, Nat. Fedn. of Rep. Women, 67-69. Mem: Past pres. and life mem, McComb Jr. Auxiliary; past regional dir, Nat. Asn. of Jr. Auxiliaries; charter pres, McComb Garden Club; exec. bd, Otken PTA; mem. temporary bd. of dirs. and charter mem, Southwest Miss. Gen. Hosp. Auxiliary. Escorted Vice Presidental Nominee William Miller to the Platform at 1964 Rep. Nat. Conv. Rel: Presbyterian. Mailing Add: 316 Hickory, McComb, Miss. 39648.

MACKAY, WILLIAM RAYNOR R
Mont. State Sen.
b. Tenafly, N.J, 11/12/11; s. Malcolm S. Mackay and Helen Raynor M; m. 1/8/37 to Joyce Selleck Childs; c. Julia Childs (Mrs. Snell), Helen (Mrs. Kampfe) and William R, Jr. Educ: Williams Col, 35; Kappa Alpha. Polit. & Govt. Pos: Mont. State Rep, 51-53; Mont. State Sen, Dist. 13, 53-; chmn, Mont. Rep. State Cent. Cmt, 54-56; mem, Mont. Legis. Coun, 57-63, chmn, 61-63, chmn, Mont. Legis. Audit Cmt, 67-69, mem, 69- Bus. & Prof. Pos: Pres, Lazy E.L. Ranch Corp, 34-; secy, Foothills Co, 55- Mem: Mason; Elks; Shrine; Mont. Club; pres, Mont. Stockgrowers Asn, 67-69; Mont. Farm Bur. Rel: Congregational. Mailing Add: Lazy E. L. Ranch, Roscoe, Mont. 59071.

McKEE, DOUGLAS ARTHUR R
Mem, Calif. Rep. State Cent. Cmt.
b. Lincoln, Nebr, 7/13/40; s. Donald Hugh McKee and Harriett Smith M; m. 5/17/69 to Sheila Kay Crosier. Educ: Calif. State Col, Los Angeles, B.S, 62; Univ. Calif. Sch. Law, Los Angeles, J.D, 65; Phi Alpha Delta. Polit. & Govt. Pos: Mem, 61st Assembly Dist. Rep. Cent. Cmt, Los Angeles Co. Rep. Cent. Cmt. and Calif. Rep. State Cent. Cmt, 68-; dep. dist. attorney, Los Angeles Co, Calif; mem, Culver City Sch. Bd, 69- Mil. Serv: Entered as Pvt, Nat. Guard, 65, currently Capt, Judge Adv. Gen. Corps. Mem: Am. and Los Angeles Co. Bar Asns; Calif. State Bar; Criminal Courts Bar, Los Angeles Co. Rel: Methodist. Mailing Add: 4114 Duquesne, Apt. 2, Culver City, Calif. 90230.

McKEE, JOHN HENRY R
b. Bemidji, Minn, 11/10/09; s. Henry N. McKee and Christine Strum M; m. 9/4/34 to Norma Lee Babcock; c. Mary C. (Mrs. Anderson) and John B. Educ: Bemidji State Col, 29-30; Univ. N.Dak, 30-31; Univ. Minn, 35-36; Sigma Alpha Epsilon. Polit. Pos: Minn. State Sen, 55-67, Minn. State Rep, 51-53. Bus. & Prof. Pos: V.pres, Bemidji Saving & Loan Asn, 51-; owner & mgr, Caravan Motel, 50- and McKee Funeral Home, 41-; field dir, Nat. Aeronaut. Asn, 45-46. Mem: Elks; Rotary; Mason (32°); Shrine. Rel: Presbyterian. Mailing Add: 1002 Bemidji Ave, Bemidji, Minn. 56601.

McKEE, RICHARD NEWCOMBE R
b. New Castle, Pa, 2/25/27; s. Frederick Wick McKee and Rebekah Reis M; m. 6/20/55 to Mary Eleanor Shoaff; c. Dana Louise, Eleanor Leslie, Jared Reis and Douglas Newcombe. Educ: Dartmouth Col, A.B, 50; Univ. of Mich. Law Sch, LL.B, 54; Beta Theta Pi; Phi Alpha Delta. Polit. & Govt. Pos: Treas, Lawrence Co. Rep. Cmt, Pa, 55, chmn, 58-60 & 64-66, finance chmn, 60-64; co. chmn, Citizens for Eisenhower, 56. Mil. Serv: Entered as A/S, Navy, 45, released as Seaman 1/C, 46. Mem: YMCA; Newcastle Country Club; Lawrence Club. Rel: Episcopal. Mailing Add: 51 Valhalla Dr, New Castle, Pa. 16101.

McKEE, WILLIAM F.
b. Va, 10/17/06; m. to Gertrude S; c. Christopher Fulton and William St. John. Educ: U.S. Mil. Acad, B.S, 29; Coast Artil. Sch, grad. reg. course, 36. Polit. & Govt. Pos: Asst. v.chief of staff, Air Force, 47, v.comdr, Air Material Command, Wright Patterson Air Force Base, Ohio, 53, comdr, Air Force Logistics Command, 61-62, v.chief of staff, Air Force, 62-64; asst. adminstr. mgt. develop, NASA, 64-65; adminstr, Fed. Aviation Admin, 64-68. Bus. & Prof. Pos: Pres, Schriener & McKee Assocs, Inc, Arlington, Va, 68- Mil. Serv: Army, 29-61, Gen.(Ret); Distinguished Serv. Medal with 2 Oak Leaf Clusters. Mailing Add: 2410 S. Lynn St, Arlington, Va. 22202.

McKEEVER, PATRICK JAMES D
b. Lennox, S.Dak, 5/5/36; s. George L. McKeever and Maye MacIvenna M; m. 4/8/67 to Juanita M. McAtee; c. Patrick J, Jr. and Christin M. Educ: Creighton Univ, Omaha, B.A, 60; Univ. S.Dak, LL.B, 60. Polit. & Govt. Pos: Legal adv. for Lyman Co. Sch. Bd. and mem, Lyman Co. Sanity Bd, S.Dak, 61-62; Lyman Co. State's Attorney, Dem. Party, 61-62; S.Dak. State Rep. until 66. Bus. & Prof. Pos: State Rep. for Sen. George McGovern; partner, Jones & McKeever, Attorneys, Presho, S.Dak, 62-66. Mem: State Bar of S.Dak; Am. Bar Asn; K. of C; Jaycees. Rel: Catholic. Mailing Add: Box 727, Mitchell, S.Dak. 57301.

McKEITHEN, JOHN JULIAN D
Gov, La.
b. Grayson, La, 5/28/18; s. Jesse Japheth McKeithen and Agnes Eglin M; m. 6/14/42 to Marjorie H. Funderburk; c. Jay, Fox, Rebecca, Melissa, Pamela and Jeneva. Polit. & Govt. Pos: La. State Rep, 48-52; mem, La. Pub. Serv. Cmn, 54-62; Gov, La, 64-; del, Dem. Nat. Conv, 68. Mil. Serv: Army, Inf, 1st Lt. Mem: Am. Legion; VFW; La. Farm Bur; Delta Coun. Rel: Methodist. Mailing Add: Governor's Mansion, Baton Rouge, La. 70804.

McKELDIN, THEODORE R. R
b. Baltimore, Md, 11/20/00; s. James A. McKeldin and Dora Grief M; m. 10/17/24 to Honolulu Manzer; c. Theodore R, Jr. and Clara (Mrs. Ziegler). Educ: Univ. Md. Sch. of Law, LL.B, 24; Johns Hopkins Univ, post grad. study in econ; Omicron Delta Kappa; Sigma Phi Epsilon; Order of the Coif. Polit. & Govt. Pos: Mayor, Baltimore, Md, 43-47 & 63-67; former mem, Nat. Immigration and Naturalization; gov, Md, 51-59; del, Rep. Nat. Conv, 52; chmn, Rep. Nat. Cmt, Md, 52-60; Bus. & Prof. Pos: Attorney-at-law, Baltimore, Md, 31-43, 47-51 & 59-63; mem. bd, Reistertown Fed. Savings and Loan Asn, Md; former mem. faculty, Univ. Baltimore Law Sch, Baltimore Col. Commerce, Baltimore Inst. and Forest Park Eve. High Sch. Publ: Co-auth, The Art of Eloquence, 52; auth, Washington Bowed, 56; No Mean City, 64. Mem: Nat. and South. Gov. Conf. Sydney Hollander Found. Award; 5 Freedoms Found. Awards; Int. Youth's Distinguished Serv. Citation, Int. Soc. Christian Endeavor; Histadrut Award; Man of Year, Advert. Club Baltimore, 53; Citation, Nat. Conf. Christians and Jews, 53; Annual Award, Nat. Fedn. Jewish Men's Club, 54; Citation, Mass. Cmt. Catholics, Protestants and Jews; DeMolay Legion of Honor Medal; Am-Israel Friendship Award, Mizrachi Women's Orgn; Grand Comdr. of Order of Phoenix, King of Greece; Grand Comdr. and Grand Band of Star of Africa, Pres. of Liberia; fel, Brandeis Univ. and has teaching fel. named in his honor; numerous hon. degrees. Rel: Episcopal. Legal Res: 103 Goodale Rd, Baltimore, Md. 21212. Mailing Add: City Hall, Baltimore, Md. 21202. (1967)

MACKELL, THOMAS JAMES D
Dist. Attorney, Queens Co, N.Y.
b. New York, N.Y, 7/19/14; s. Peter Francis Mackell and Mary Keating M; m. 9/8/39 to Dorothea Lang; c. Thomas J, Jr, Patricia Ann (Mrs. Robertson) and Terrence Peter. Educ: City Col. of New York, B.S. in Soc. Sci, 38; St. John's Univ. Law Sch, J.D, 42. Polit. & Govt. Pos: N.Y. State Sen, 55-66; del, Dem. State Conv, 58, 62 & 66 and Dem. Nat. Conv, 60, 64 & 68. Mem: Am, N.Y. State and Queens Co. Bar Asns; Asn. of The Bar of City of N.Y; Queens Co. Criminal Bar; Elks; K. of C; Ahepa; Lions; Nat. Conv. Christians and Jews; NAACP; Am. Civil Liberties Union; Emerald Asn. Rel: Roman Catholic. Legal Res: 300 Arleigh Rd, Douglaston, N.Y. 11363. Mailing Add: 125-01 Queens Blvd, Kew Gardens, N.Y. 11415.

McKEMIE, HENRY GRADY D
b. Zetto, Ga, 11/20/95; s. William Johnstone McKemie and Gertrude Arnold McK; m. 12/01/15 to Jennie Claude Hammack; c. William Frank, Merle, Kate, Henry Grady Jr. Educ: Locust Grove Inst. Polit. & Govt. Pos: Ga. State Rep, 63-64, 59-60; Clay Co. Bd. Cmnrs, 42-60. Bus. & Prof. Pos: Farmer. Rel: Methodist. Mailing Add: Coleman, Ga. 31736. (1967)

MACKEN, JAMES LEE R
b. Alliance, Nebr, 2/17/29; s. Ervin John Macken and Julia McCann M; m. 12/28/54 to Iris V. Killday; c. Stephen, Julia, Anne, James and Laura. Educ: Casper Col, 46-48; Creighton Univ, 48-49; Creighton Univ. Sch. of Law, LL.B, 52; Phi Theta Kappa; Phi Alpha Delta. Polit. & Govt. Pos: Co. attorney, Morrill Co, Nebr, 59-69; pres. bd. educ, Bridgeport Sch. Dist, 64-67 and mem. educ. serv. unit, 66-69; chmn, Morrill Co. Rep. Cent. Cmt, 64-65, secy, 68-69; co. judge, Scottsbluff Co, 69- Mil. Serv: Entered as 2nd Lt, Army, 52, released as 1st Lt, 55. Mem: Lions Int; Am. Legion; K. of C. Rel: Roman Catholic. Legal Res: 1209 R St, Bridgeport, Nebr. 69336. Mailing Add: 2017 Fourth Ave, Scottsbluff, Nebr. 69361.

MacKENDRICK, DONALD ANTHONY D
Mem, Mesa Co. Dem. Exec. Cmt, Colo.
b. Hotchkiss, Colo, 11/8/25; s. Richard P. MacKendrick and Isabelle Johan Kuester M; single. Educ: Colo. State Univ, B.S, 50; Univ. Colo, M.A, 53; Lancers; Pacemaker; Pi Delta Epsilon; Ind. Students Asn. Polit. & Govt. Pos: Secy, Mesa Co. Dem. Cent. Cmt, Colo, 61-67, chmn, 67-69; mem, Mesa Co. Libr. Bd, 67-; mem, Colo. State Dem. Reorgn. Cmt, currently; mem, Mesa Co. Dem. Exec. Cmt, 69- Bus. & Prof. Pos: Teacher, Delta Co. Pub. Schs, 50-55; instr. hist, Mesa Co. Jr. Col, 55- Mil. Serv: Entered as Pvt, Army, 44, released as S/Sgt, 46, after serving in 90th Mil. Govt. Co, Army of Occupation, Japan, 45-46; Good Conduct Medal; Pac. Theatre Ribbon. Mem: Am. Asn. Univ. Prof; Orgn. Am. Historians; Colo. Hist. Soc; VFW. Rel: Roman Catholic. Mailing Add: 117 Red Mesa Heights, Grand Junction, Colo. 81501.

McKENNA, ARTHUR JAMES D
Mass. State Rep.
b. Springfield, Mass, 11/29/14; s. Jeremiah Francis McKenna and Elizabeth Mary Moriarty M; m. 4/19/38 to Rita Gladys Chapedelaine; c. Arthur, Jr, Patricia, Ann Maria and John Paul. Educ: Cathedral High Sch. Polit. & Govt. Pos: City alderman, Springfield, Mass, 54-62; Mass. State Rep, Tenth Dist, 63-; mem, Mass. State Dem. Cmt, 64-66. Bus. & Prof. Pos: Mgr. of Yankee Div, 51-55. Mil. Serv: Seaman 1/C, Navy, 45. Mem: Am. Legion; CIO Local 206; Am. Bosch Inc. Rel: Roman Catholic. Mailing Add: 652 Chestnut St, Springfield, Mass. 01107.

McKENNA, ELLANORE LOUISE D
V.Chmn, La Plata Co. Dem. Party, Colo.
b. Denver, Colo, 6/23/25; d. Hammond Mathews and Edna Mitchell M; m. 8/8/49 to Robert Ludwig McKenna; c. Marc Edward, Nancy Louise, Edna Elizabeth-Marie and Madeline Eileen (deceased). Educ: Colo. Woman's Col, A.A, 45; Univ. Colo, B.A, 48; Phi Theta Kappa; Beta Phi Gamma; Chi Omega. Polit. & Govt. Pos: Mem. and v.chmn, Colo. State Bd. for Voc. Educ, 57-63; mem. state exec. cmt, Golden Anniversary White House Conf. on Children and Youth, 59-60; mem. exec. cmt. and past pres. of bd, Southwest Colo. Ment. Health Center, Inc, 60-69; Dem. precinct committeewoman, Precinct 5, La Plata Co, 62-69; mem. of bd. and v.chmn, San Juan Basin Pub. Health Unit, 63-; v.chmn, La Plata Co. Dem. Party, 69- Bus. & Prof. Pos: City ed, Durango News, 48-49. Mem: PEO; Durango Reading Club; Durango League of Women Voters (former pres). State Am. Asn. Univ. Women scholarship to attend Vassar Inst. of Family and Commun. Living, Vassar Col, June-July, 55. Rel: Catholic. Legal Res: 1623 Forest Ave, Durango, Colo. 81301. Mailing Add: P.O. Box 888, Durango, Colo. 81301.

McKENNA, PATRICK E. R
Polit. & Govt. Pos: Mem, Ward 22 Rep. Cmt; mem, Rep. State Cmt. Pre-Primary Conv, 66; nominee, Mass. State Senate, 68. Bus. & Prof. Pos: Prfnl. Engr; gen. mgr, Stahleker Steel Corp. Mem: Am. Asn. for Adv. of Science; Am. Soc. for Metals; Metrop. Chap. Mass. Soc. of Prfnl. Engr.(pres, 69); Dir. Chmn, Sports Coun, Cambridge YMCA. Hon. Award, Cambridge YMCA, 1966. Mailing Add: Perthshire Rd, Brighton, Mass. 02135.

McKENNEY, HAROLD CHARLES D
Chmn, McHenry Co. Dem. Cent. Cmt, Ill.
b. Detroit, Mich, 2/12/31; s. Harold C. McKenney, Sr. and Joan Bolinger M; m. 8/11/62, div; m. 10/5/68 to Merry Ann Carlson; c. Bruce, Jannon, Susan, David, Diane, Philip. Educ: Wash. Univ; Univ. Ill, Champaign, LL.B, 58; Kappa Alpha; Phi Alpha Delta. Polit. & Govt. Pos: Asst. states attorney, Winnebago Co, Ill, 59-60; Asst. Attorney Gen, Ill, 62-69; mem, McHenry Co. Bd. Sch. Trustees, 66-; precinct committeeman, Dem. Party, Ill, 66-; chmn, McHenry Co. Dem. Cent. Cmt, 66- Mil. Serv: Entered as Pvt, Army, 53, released as Pfc, 55. Mem: McHenry Co. Bar Asn. Rel: Catholic. Legal Res: 441 Warwick Lane, Crystal Lake, Ill. 60014. Mailing Add: 88 Grant St, Crystal Lake, Ill. 66014.

MacKENZIE, BERNICE K. D
b. Canton, Ohio, 2/23/05; d. Claude J. Keplinger and Besse Buckwalter K; m. to Robert E. MacKenzie; wid. Educ: Mt. Holyoke Col, 22-24; Akron Law Sch, 28-31. Polit. & Govt. Pos: Ohio State Rep, Stark Co, 41-42 & 59-66; councilman-at-lg, Canton City Coun, Ohio, 56-58; del-at-lg, Dem. Nat. Conv, 64; mem, Dem. Nat. Platform Cmt, 64. Mil. Serv: Entered as Officer Candidate, WAAC, 42, released as Maj, 45, after serv. in Mil. Dist. of Washington, 43-45; Legion of Merit. Mem: Stark Co. Bar Asn; past pres, Canton Bus. and Prfnl. Women's Club; former trustee, Canton YWCA, Gr. Canton United Fund and Stark Co. Ment. Health Asn; dir, Ohio Citizens Coun. for Health and Welfare, Stark Wilderness, Inc. and Ohio Soc. for Prev. of Blindness; League of Women Voters; Canton Urban League; Canton Audubon Soc; Stark Co. Humane Soc; v.pres, Canton Family Serv. Soc; mem. and secy, Stark Co. Commun. Ment. Health and Retardation Bd; mem. and treas, Stark Wilderness Center; adv. bd, Salvation Army of Canton. Rel: Presbyterian. Mailing Add: 403 32nd St. N.W, Canton, Ohio 44709.

McKENZIE, EARL EUGENE R
Chmn, Scioto Co. Rep. Exec. Cmt, Ohio
b. Lucasville, Ohio, 10/9/16; s. Earl McKenzie and Margaret Fullerton M; m. 4/25/39 to Janice Joan Jones; c. Betty Joan (Mrs. David T. Jenkins) and Ronald Eugene. Educ: Ohio Univ, B.S. in Educ, 38; Marshall Univ, M.A. in Sch. Admin, 63; Kappa Delta Pi. Polit. & Govt. Pos: Secy, Scioto Co. Rep. Exec. Cmt, Ohio, 54-63, chmn, 63-; mem, Scioto Co. Rep. Cent. Cmt, 54-; mem, bd. of elec, Scioto Co. Representative of Secy. of State, 63-. Bus. & Prof. Pos: Teacher and coach, Rush Twp. Schs, McDermott, Ohio, 38-41; teacher, coach and athletic dir, Valley Local Schs, Lucasville, Ohio, 41-50, teacher, 50-62; dist. mgr, Fed. Mutual Ins. Co, 50-57; prin, Wash. Local Schs, West Portsmouth, Ohio, 62-65, supt, 65- Mil. Serv: Entered as Pvt, Army, 45, released as Sgt, 46, after serv. in Hq, BTS, Ft. Lewis, Wash, 45-46; Victory Medal. Mem: Ohio Sch. Bd. Asn; Ohio Educ. Asn; Ohio Asn. of Sch. Adminstrs; Nat. Educ. Asn; Am. Asn. of Sch. Adminstrs; Ohio Asn. of Elec. Offs; Am. Legion; Elks; Lucasville Civic Serv. Club. Rel: Methodist. Legal Res: Broad St, Lucasville, Ohio 45648. Mailing Add: P.O. Box 686, Lucasville, Ohio 45648.

McKENZIE, FRANK R
S.Dak. State Rep.
b. Spencer, Nebr, 6/26/11; m. to Florence Lang; c. Joan, Wayne. Educ: Bus. Col. Polit. & Govt. Pos: Former mem. Twp. Bd, Winner, S.Dak. and Sch. Bd; former assessor; S.Dak. State Rep, 60- Bus. & Prof. Pos: Wheat farmer. Mem: Mason; K.T; RAM; Eastern Star; past Master AF&AM; past pres, Rosebud Shrine; Isaak Walton League. Rel: Episcopal. Mailing Add: Winner, S.Dak. 57580. (1967)

MACKENZIE, HUGH MAXWELL R
First Selectman, Waterford, Conn.
b. Waterford, Conn, 10/31/24; s. Hugh MacKenzie and Nettie Edwards M; 5/17/58 to Mary Carol Hoffmeyer; c. Hugh M, Jr, Kate and Molly. Educ: Univ. Conn, B.S, 51; Alpha Zeta. Polit. & Govt. Pos: Conn. State Rep, 53-57 & 61-67; pres, 20th Dist. Shoestring Rep. Club, 59-61; mem. bd. selectmen, Waterford, Conn, 57-63, first selectman, 63-; chmn, Waterford Rep. Town Cmt, 64-65. Mem: Grange; Farm Bur. Mailing Add: 317 Rope Ferry Rd, Waterford, Conn. 06385. (1967)

MacKENZIE, MALCOLM KERR R
b. Gaylord, Minn, 4/3/26; s. Claude H. MacKenzie and Ruth Jean Wheelock M; m. 6/24/50 to Donna M. Tauer; c. Kyle, Charles and Bruce. Educ: Univ. Minn; Delta Theta Phi. Polit. & Govt. Pos: Co. attorney, Nicollet Co, Minn, 55-66; Congressman's spec. rep. on Minn. State Rep. Cent. Cmt, 58-63; secy, Second Cong. Dist. Rep. Cmt, 59-63; chmn, State Rep. Constitutional Cmt, 61-62; chmn, Nicollet Co. Rep. Cmt, 63-66. Mil. Serv: Entered as Pvt, Army Air Force, 44, released as Pfc, 45, after serv. in Am; Am. Theater Ribbon. Mem: Past pres, Ninth Dist. Bar Asn; past dist. gov, Lions Int; v.pres, St. Peter C. of C; Am. Legion; v.pres, Minn. Valley Area Coun, Boy Scouts; Mason; Minn. Farm Bur. SPAN Scholarship for Foreign Study, 48. Rel: Presbyterian. Mailing Add: 848 Lower Johnson Circle, St. Peter, Minn. 56082.

Mac KENZIE, MARY ANN D
m. to Donald G. MacKenzie; c. Kirk Lyle Francis, Erik Joseph. Educ: Alfred Univ; Univ. of Miami, BS 46; LL.B, 57; Kappa Beta Pi. Pol. & Govt. Pos: Fla. State Rep, 63-66. Bus. & Prof. Pos: Attorney; Formerly sch. teacher and business exec, real estate. Mem: Dade Co. Juvenile Coun; Dade Co. Cmt. on Children and Youth; Legal Adv, Dade Youth Coun; Bd. of Dir. and former Gen. Counsel; S. Fla. Chapter Nat. Hemophilia Foundation; Gov's Cmt. for Employ. of the Handicapped; Altrusa Int. Inc; Dade Bus. and Prof. Woman's Club; Dem. Womens Club of Dade Co, pres. 64-65; Bd. of Dirs, Med. Research and Health Servs. Foundation; Variety Children's Hosp. Devel. Fund, Area chm. 63; Mothers March of Dimes, Area chm, 63; United Fund of Dade Co, Dist. chm, 62; Dade, Fla, and Am. Bar Asns; Miami-Dade C. of C; Fla. Asn. of Women Lawyers; Key Biscayne Women's Club; Iham Ladies Club; Coral Gables High PTA. Who's Who of Am. Women. Rel: Episcopal. Mailing Add: 720 S. Mashta Drive, Key Biscayne, Fla. 33149. (1967)

McKENZIE, RODERICK TULLOCH R
Ore. State Rep.
b. Walnut Creek, Calif, 4/11/19; s. Robert George McKenzie, Sr. and Lucile Sorenson M; m. Feb, 1946 to Grace Enid Goucher; c. Roderick A. and David K. Educ: Ore. State Univ, B.S, 41; Alpha Zeta; Theta Chi. Polit. & Govt. Pos: Ore. State Rep, 17th Dist, 53-57 and 67- Bus. & Prof. Pos: Pres, Curry Co. Livestock Cmt, 51-52; mem, State Brucellosis Cmt, 57-61; dir, Coos Forest Patrol, 59- Mil. Serv: Entered as Pvt, Marine Corps, 41, released as Platoon Sgt, 46; Purple Heart; Letter of Commendation. Mem: Elks; Mason (32°), Scottish Rite; Grange; Am. Legion; Coos and Curry Co. Livestock Asn. Rel: Presbyterian. Mailing Add: Cape Blanco Rd, Sixes, Ore. 97476. (1967)

MacKENZIE, RONALD CONRAD R
Mass. State Sen.
b. Waltham, Mass, 5/3/34; s. Gordon Sidebotham (stepfather) and Area Freeman S; m. 6/28/58 to Janet Lee Proctor; c. Jody and Scott. Educ: Dartmouth Col, A.B, 56; Phi Gamma Delta. Polit. & Govt. Pos: Mem, Burlington Rep. Town Cmt, 62-; Mass. State Sen, 66-; del, Rep. Nat. Conv, 68. Mil. Serv: Entered as 2nd Lt, Army, 56, released as 1st Lt, 58, after serv. in 325th AAA Bn, Air Defense Command, 56-58. Mem: Mass. and Nat. Legis. Asns; Boston Life Underwriters Asn; Elks; Rotary; Jaycees; Coun. of Human Rels; Jr. Chamber Int. Senate. Named one of four outstanding young men in Mass. and one of three outstanding young men in New Eng, 68. Rel: Protestant. Mailing Add: 18 Spruce Hill Rd, Burlington, Mass. 01803.

McKENZIE, WILLIAM IRVING D
Treas, Douglas Co. Dem. Cent. Cmt, Wash.
b. Westhope, N.Dak, 5/15/04; s. Thomas McKenzie and Catherine McNeill M; m. 8/18/42 to Dorthy Rinn; c. Thomas C, James H. and Kathleen A. Educ: Daybreak Sch, West Hope, N.Dak. Polit. & Govt. Pos: Precinct committeeman, 58-; v.chmn, Douglas Co. Dem. Cent. Cmt, 60-62, treas, 62-64 & 66-, chmn, 64-66. Mil. Serv: Entered as C.E.M, Navy, 42, released as C.E.M.P.A, 45, after serv. in 40th & 76th Construction Bn, Pac. Theater; Pac. and Asiatic Theater Ribbons; Presidential Unit Citation. Mem: Odd Fellows; IBEW;

Mason; adv, DeMolay. Rel: Presbyterian. Legal Res: Route 3, Box 3276, Wenatchee, Wash. 98801. Mailing Add: P.O. Box 0146, East Wenatchee, Wash. 98801.

McKEON, JOHN LUKE D
Mont. State Sen.
b. Anaconda, Mont, 10/6/25; s. Michael McKeon and Eleanor McMahon M; m. 8/10/45 to Dixie Eklund; c. Michael John, Mary Michele, Timothy Willis and John Luke, Jr. Educ: Univ. Mont, LL.B, 51. Polit. & Govt. Pos: Trustee sch. bd, Deer Lodge Co, Mont, 51 & 62; asst. attorney gen, Mont, 51-53; co. attorney, Deer Lodge Co, 57-59; Mont. State Sen, 61-63 & 67-; del, Dem. Nat. Conv, 68. Mil. Serv: Entered as A/S, Navy, 43, released as Seaman 1/C, after serv. in Coast Guard, N.Pac. Mem: Mont. 3rd Judicial Dist. Bar Asn; Mont. and Am. Bar Asns; VFW; DAV; Am. Legion; Elks; Ancient Order of Hibernians. Rel: Roman Catholic. Legal Res: 316 E. Seventh St, Anaconda, Mont. 59711. Mailing Add: 124 Oak St, Anaconda, Mont. 59711. (1967)

MACKEY, EARL SEAY D
b. Cape Girardeau, Mo, 12/16/37; s. C. C. Mackey and Gracia Seay M; m. 8/29/59 to Karen Mahan; c. Christopher. Educ: Univ. Mo, B.A, 59 and LL.B, 62; Mo. Law Review; Phi Gamma Delta. Polit. & Govt. Pos: Legis. asst. to U.S. Sen. Stuart Symington, 62-64; former mem, Cape Co. Young Dem, Mo; Mo. State Rep, 67-69. Bus. & Prof. Pos: Attorney, MFA Ins, 62; practicing attorney, currently. Mil. Serv: Entered as Pvt, Army Res, 55, released as Sgt, 63. Publ: 'Resignation From the Bar Under Charges,' Mo. Law Review, 58, '1st Amendment Restraints on Congressional Inquiries,' 59. Mem: Mo. and Cape Girardeau Co. Bars; Jr. C. of C. Rel: Methodist. Mailing Add: 445 Marie, Cape Girardeau, Mo. 63701. (1967)

MACKEY, MALCOLM H. D
Mem, Calif. Dem. State Cent. Cmt.
b. Hoboken, N.J, 7/20/29; s. William G. Mackey and Winifred Walker Hamilton M; m. 9/1/62 to Sharon Scovill; c. Michael M; Educ: N.Y. Univ, A.B, 51; Southwest. Law Sch, LL.B. & J.D, 58; Univ. South. Calif, 58-59; Sigma Lambda Sigma. Polit. & Govt. Pos: Mem, Los Angeles Co. Dem. Cent. Cmt, Calif, 65-66; chmn, 54th Dist. Dem. Party, 66-68; pres, Glen Eagle Park Dem. Club, 67-69; mem, Calif. Dem. State Cent. Cmt, 68- Bus. & Prof. Pos: Sales rep, Tidewater Oil Co, Calif, 51-54 and Richifed Oil Co, 54-55; ins. adjuster, All State Ins. Co, 55-56; attorney-at-law, 59- Mil. Serv: Entered as Pvt, Marine Corps, 46, released as Cpl, 48, after serv. in Tank Corps, E.Coast and Mediterranean Areas, 46-48; Cpl, Marine Corps Res, 49-50; Navy Good Conduct and World War II Victory Medals; Navy Occup. Medal, Mediterranean Area. Mem: Am, Glendale and Los Angeles Co. Bar Asns; Lawyers Club of Los Angeles; Mason; Mexican Am. Polit. Asn; Sons of Italy; Foot Printers; N.Y. Univ. Alumni Asn. Rel: Presbyterian. Legal Res: 5351 Vincent Ave, Los Angeles, Calif. 90041. Mailing Add: 215 W. Fifth St, Los Angeles, Calif. 90043.

MACKEY, OSCAR POWELL D
Miss. State Rep.
b. Memphis, Tenn, 8/13/38; s. Oscar Powell Mackey, Jr. and Lucy Clyde Wallace M; single. Educ: Univ. Miss, B.B.A, LL.B. and J.D; Alpha Phi Omega; Delta Kappa Epsilon. Polit. & Govt. Pos: Miss. State Rep, 14th Dist, Yalobusha and Tallahatchie Co, 68- Bus. & Prof. Pos: Attorney-at-law, Water Valley, Miss, 63- Mem: Am, Miss. State, Yalobusha Co. and Water Valley Bar Asns; Am. Judicature Soc; Am. Soc. State Legislators; Jaycees; C. of C; Rotary; Sportsman's Club. Rel: Presbyterian. Legal Res: 1015 Main St, Water Valley, Miss. 38965. Mailing Add: P.O. Box 588, Water Valley, Miss. 38965.

MACKEY, RALPH EARLE R
b. Everett, Wash, 6/17/30; s. Earle M. Mackey and Laura L. Johnson M; m. 9/11/54 to Maurine Emily Gerards; c. Kevin, David and Jeffrey. Educ: Univ. of Puget Sound, B.A. in Bus, 54; Sigma Chi. Polit. & Govt. Pos: Rep. Precinct Committeeman, Wash, 60-63; Snohomish Co. Chmn, 62-64; chmn, Snohomish Co. Rep. Cent. Cmt, 62-66; cmnr, Wash. State Parks and Recreation Cmn, 67- Bus. & Prof. Pos: Mem. Bd, Fireplace Asn. of Am, 69- Mem: Everett Elks; Everett Yacht Club; Salvation Army; Boy Scouts; Mountaineers; Am. Alpine Club; Everett Mountain Rescue Unit. Snohomish Co. Man of the Year Award in Sports, 63; Climbed Mt. McKinley, Alaska, Mt. Aconcagua, Argentina and Mt. Kilimanjaro, Africa. Rel: Presbyterian. Mailing Add: 4611 Westview Dr, Everett, Wash. 98201.

McKIBBEN, JADIE CLIFFORD D
Chmn, Polk Co. Dem. Exec. Cmt, Ga.
b. Polk Co, Ga, 12/11/99; s. James William McKibben and Sara Winkles; m. 10/7/23 to Paschal Lovvorn; c. Aline and Helen. Educ: High sch. grad. Polit. & Govt. Pos: Chmn, Polk Co. Dem. Exec. Cmt, Ga, currently. Bus. & Prof. Pos: Shoe repairman, 28-65. Mem: Mason. Rel: Baptist. Mailing Add: 133 Cobb St, Cedartown, Ga. 30125.

MACKIE, JOHN C. D
b. Toronto, Ont, Can, 6/1/20; s. Robert Mackie and Isabella Homer M; m. 12/1/43 to Kathleen Flood; c. Anne, Margaret and Lora. Educ: Lawrence Inst. of Tech; Mich. State Univ, B.S. in civil eng, 42 and Hon. LL.D, 65; Tau Beta Pi; Sigma Alpha Epsilon. Polit. & Govt. Pos: Hwy. cmnr, Mich. Hwy. Dept, 57-65; U.S. Rep, Mich, 65-67. Mil. Serv: Entered as Air Force Cadet, Army Air Force, 42, released as 1st Lt, 45, after serv. in Air Transport Command, Cent. Pac, 43-45; Bronze Star. Mem: Am. Asn. of State Hwy. Officials; Mich. Soc. of Planning Officials; Mich. Eng. Soc; Soc. of Mich. Registered Land Surveyors; Mich. Soc. of Prfnl. Engrs; Flint Lodge 490 F&AM, Elf Kurafeh Shrine; Nat. Farm Orgn. Rel: Unitarian. 1967 Legal Res: Flint, Mich. No mailing address available. (1967)

MACKIE, JOHN GOLDEN R
b. Warren, Pa, 6/14/20; s. Donald W. Mackie and Harriet Golden M; m. 12/31/47 to Susan Hunter Grymes; c. John, Jr, Meredith, Kristen, Troye and Peter. Educ: Univ. Colo, B.A, 43 and LL.B, 48; Phi Delta Phi; Phi Epsilon Phi. Polit. & Govt. Pos: Rep. precinct committeeman, Colo, 49; Colo. State Rep, Dist. 42, Boulder Co, 53-67, Majority Floor Leader, Colo. Assembly-House, 63-65, Minority Floor Leader, 65-66; del, Rep. Nat. Conv, 54; charter del, Longmont Charter Conv, 60; mem, Cmn. for Higher Educ, Colo, 65-67; cmnr, West. Interstate Compact for Higher Educ, 65- Bus. & Prof. Pos: Lawyer, 48-; secy-treas, Longmont Indust. Bank, Colo, 58-; v.pres, Atlas Bradford Co, Houston, Tex, 63- Mil. Serv: Entered as Pvt, Army, 43, released as 1st Lt, 45, after serv. in 28th Inf. Div, ETO; Combat Inf. Badge; Europe-Africa-Middle East Medal with Five Bronze Stars. Mem: Past pres, Boulder Co. Bar Asn; Colo. Bar Asn; Shrine; Mason; Elks; Am. Legion; Rotary; Boulder Fair Bd. Rel: Episcopal. Legal Res: 948 Collyer St, Longmont, Colo. 80501. Mailing Add: Box 765, Longmont, Colo. 80501. (1967)

MACKIE, WILLIAM O. D
b. Mt. Ayer, Iowa, 4/3/98; m. 6/20/20 to Mabel Harlan; c. Maxine (Mrs. Farrar) and William E. Educ: Northeast Mo. State Teachers Col. Polit. & Govt. Pos: Adair Co. Dem. Chmn, Mo, 4 years; Mo. State Rep, 56; Mo. State Sen, 58-66. Bus. & Prof. Pos: Wholesale grocer. Mil. Serv: Army. Mem: Loyal Order Moose; Mason; Shrine. Rel: Christian Church. Mailing Add: 1606 S. Downing, Kirksville, Mo. 63508.

McKILLEN, JEAN BARBARA R
Cmnr, Calif. Rep. State Cent. Cmt.
b. Chicago, Ill, June 11; d. James Arcus and Ethel Agate A; m. 8/14/32 to Bruce Abbott McKillen; c. Zelma Ethelyn (Mrs. Turner). Educ: Private tutoring, ballerina. Polit. & Govt. Pos: Held all pos. up to supvr. in filter stations, Bakersfield, Los Angeles and Oakland, 6th Army, Calif, 41-44; organizer and secy, Eden Area Rep. Club, Calif. Rep. Assembly, 52-59; Parliamentarian, Chabot Rep. Women's Federated Club, 66-68; cmnr, Calif. Rep. State Cent. Cmt, 68-; del, State and Nat. Rep. Conv; coordinator and hq. mgr. of numerous rep. cand. Mem: Calif. Federated Women's Clubs; Castro Valley C. of C; Castro Valley Womens' Club, Federated; Am. Legion Auxiliary; Chabot Rep. Club; Organaires Club; East Bay Cooperative Libraries (cmnr); Livermore Valley Hist. Soc; Georgetown Divide Rep. Women; Nat. Grange (Patron of Husbandry); Marshall Grange. Castro Valley C. of C. Award for a civic proj; eleven Dist. Awards, Calif. Federated Women's Clubs. Rel: Protestant. Mailing Add: Box 291, Georgetown, Calif. 95634.

McKIM, ADELE W. R
V.Chmn, Bergen Co. Rep. Cmt, N.J.
b. Little Falls, N.J, 9/27/14; d. James J. Marley and A. Adele W. Maass M; m. 8/7/37 to Thomas McKim; c. Bonita Dorothy (Mrs. Courtney John Dow) and Thomas Craigie. Educ: Paterson Cent. High Sch, 28-32; N.Y. Sch. Modeling, 34-35. Polit. & Govt. Pos: Chmn, Midland Park Rep. Co. Cmt, 53-, munic. chmn, 59-; secy. and v.pres, United Rep. Club, Midland Park, 59-60; chmn. dist. 12, Bergen Co. Rep. Cmt, 59, v.chmn, 67-, registrn. chmn, 68-69; pres, Midland Park Rep. Women Inc, 60-62, secy, 64-66; secy, Bergen Co. Women's Rep. Club, 63-67, mem. bd. trustees, 67-; mem, Bergen Co. Rep. Policy Cmt, 67-; chmn, Women for Nixon, Bergen Co, 68; mem. finance cmt, N.J. Fedn. Rep. Women, 69. Bus. & Prof. Pos: Treas, Midland Park Libr. Bd. of Trustees, 59- Mem: Ladies Auxiliary VFW (pres, 66-67); Am. Legion Auxiliary; Daughters of Scotia (past chief daughter); Eastern Star; Libr. Guild, Midland Park; Midland Park Br. Valley Hosp. Auxiliary; Midland Park Christians Concerns Cmt. Rel: Protestant. Mailing Add: 251 Park Ave, Midland Park, N.J. 07432.

McKIM, GEORGE WILLIAM R
Finance Chmn, N.Mex. Rep. Party
b. Clearwater, Nebr, July 3; s. Lisbon Clarence 'Posy' McKim and Elizabeth Anderson M; m. 8/27/36 to Della Harnish; c. Barbara Jeanine. Educ: Wayne State Teachers Col, 21-25; Delta Sigma Rho; Tau Kappa Alpha. Polit. & Govt. Pos: Chmn, Bernalillo Co. Rep. Party, N.Mex, 55-58; Rep. cand, U.S. Rep, N.Mex, 58; finance chmn, N.Mex. Rep. Party, 58-63 & 67- Mil. Serv: Entered as A/S, Navy, 26, released as Radioman 3/C, 29, after serv. aboard U.S.S. Omaha. Mem: Nat. Asn. Mutual Ins. Agents (nat. dir, 57-58, N.Mex. v.pres, 58-61, N.Mex. dir, 67-); Albuquerque Bd. Realtors (dir, 57-59 & 69-); Mason; Elks; Albuquerque Petroleum Club; Toastmasters Int.(past pres, past dist. gov, past int. dir); C. of C; Sertoma (past pres, past dir. bd, Albuquerque Br); Commun. Chest (past mem. bd. dirs); N.Mex. Hist. Soc.(treas, past five years); mem. and secy, N.Mex. Real Estate Licensing Cmt. Rel: Methodist; Treas, First United Methodist Church, 53- Mailing Add: 1406 Harvard N.E, Albuquerque, N.Mex. 87106.

McKINLEY, IRA BLAKELY R
Chmn, House Dist. 11, Rep. Orgn, Alaska
b. Detroit, Mich, 9/28/34; s. Dr. Lee L. McKinley and Doris Blakely M; m. 6/10/61 to Pauline Joan Oeser; c. Ira Blakely, Jr, Robert Paul and Susan Lee. Educ: Univ. Alaska, B.Ed, 58; Univ. Mo, Kansas City Dent. Sch, D.D.S, 66; Omicron Kappa Upsilon; Xi Psi Phi. Polit. & Govt. Pos: Rep. precinct committeeman, Chugiak Area, Alaska, 58-60; del, Rep. State Conv, Alaska, 60; state pres, Alaska Young Rep, 60-61; Rep. precinct committeeman, Third Ward, Kansas City, Mo, 64; dist. chmn, Kodiak Area Rep. Party, Alaska, 67-; chmn, House Dist. 11 Rep. Orgn, 67-; del, S.Cent. Dist. Rep. Conv, 68. Bus. & Prof. Pos: Teacher, Chugiak, Alaska, 58-60, Anchorage, 60-61 and Kansas City, Kans, 61-62; dentist, Anchorage, Alaska, 66 and Kodiak, 66- Mil. Serv: 2nd Lt, Army Chem. Corps, 59; Army Nat. Guard, 59-66, 1st Lt. Mem: Am. Dent. Asn; Alaska Dent. Soc; Kenai-Kodiak Dent. Soc.(secy-treas, 69); Asn. Am. Dentists; Mason; C. of C, Kodiak Area (chmn, Airport Cmt. to obtain joint use of Navy airfield); Rotary; Univ. Alaska Alumni Asn; Alaska Cancer Soc; Alaska Heart Asn; Shrine; Navy League. Rel: Church of God. Legal Res: Tenth and Simeonoff, Kodiak, Alaska 99615. Mailing Add: Box 573, Kodiak, Alaska 99615.

McKINLEY, WILLIAM EDWARD 'BILL' D
Miss. State Sen.
b. Mize, Miss, 1/3/31; s. William Wallace McKinley and Hazel Marie Stringer M; m. 7/24/55 to Willa Joy White; c. William Bruce, Karl Dibrell and Kathleen Marie. Educ: Millsaps Col, B.A. in Econ; Jackson Sch. of Law, LL.B; Kappa Sigma; Sigma Delta Kappa. Polit. & Govt. Pos: Miss. State Rep, 64-68; Miss. State Sen, 68- Bus. & Prof. Pos: Attorney, Jackson, Miss, 58- Mil. Serv: Entered as Corp, Army, 50, released as Sgt, 1/C, 52; after serv. in 155th Inf, N.Am. Command, 50-52; Expert Infantryman Badge. Mem: Am, Hinds Co. and Miss. State Bar Asns; Am. Judicature Soc; Mason; Shrine; Civitan; Am. Legion; Moose; Boys Club Alumni Asn. Outstanding Young Man of Jackson, Miss. Rel: Methodist. Mailing Add: 2073 Shady Lane Dr, Jackson, Miss. 39204.

McKINNEY, FRANK EDWARD D

b. Indianapolis, Ind, 6/16/04; s. Roscoe Anthony McKinney and Anna Moss M; m. 11/24/32 to Margaret K. Warner; c. Claire Marie (Mrs. James C. Clark), Robert Warner, Frank E, Jr. and M. Kathleen. Educ: Ind. Univ. Exten. Div; LaSalle Inst. Acct; Beta Gamma Sigma; Sigma Alpha Epsilon. Hon. LL.D, Loretto Col. Polit. & Govt. Pos: Treas, Indianapolis Dem. City Cmt, Ind, 28-32; treas, Marion Co. Dem. Cent. Cmt, 32-34; treas, Marion Co, 35-39; Ind. sub-treas, Dem. Nat. Cmt, 36; v.chmn, Dem. Nat. Finance Cmt, 40; treas, Ind. Dem. State Cent. Cmt, 48-51; chmn, Dem. Nat. Cmt, 51-52. Bus. & Prof. Pos: Chmn. of bd. and pres, Fidelity Bank & Trust Co, 35-59; chmn. of bd, Am. Fletcher Nat. Bank and Trust Co, 59-68; chmn. of bd, Am. Fletcher Corp, 69-; dir, dir, Ind. Bell Tel. Co, Indianapolis Power and Light Co, Nat. Homes Corp, Shorewood Corp. and U.S. Corrugated Fibre Box Co, currently; dir. and treas, Blue Shield Mutual Med. Ins, Inc, currently. Mil. Serv: Entered as Maj, Army, 42, released as Col, 45, after serv. in Advance Payment and Loan Br, Fiscal Div, 42-45 and asst. dir. of Contract Settlement, Wash, D.C, 45. Mem: Dir, Ind. Univ. Found; dir, Cent. Ind. Coun, Boy Scouts of Am; dir, Indianapolis Hosp. Develop. Asn; Nat. Adv. Cmt. on Banking Policies and Practices; chmn. of bd, Winona Mem. Found; Ind. Law Enforcement Training Bd; treas, Civic Center Donors, Inc; Hoosier for Vet. Employ. Cmt; hon. chmn. of bd, Indians, Inc; trustee, St. Joseph's Col; dir, United Fund; Am. Legion; pres, Hundred Club of Indianapolis, Inc; Indianapolis Athletic Club; Columbia Club; Highland Golf and Country Club; Indian Creek Country Club; Meridian Hills Country Club; Old Baldy Club; Univ. Club; K. of M. Rel: Roman Catholic. Legal Res: 300 Willow Spring Rd, Indianapolis, Ind. 46240. Mailing Add: 111 Monument Circle, Indianapolis, Ind. 46204.

McKINNEY, HELEN MATHEWS R

Idaho State Rep.

b. Idaho Falls, Idaho, 10/30/17; d. Eugene W. Mathews and Hilda Johnson M; m. 7/27/40 to Jack W. McKinney; c. John S. Educ: Univ. Utah; Univ. Idaho; Alpha Chi Omega. Polit. & Govt. Pos: Past secy. and committeewoman, Idaho Rep. Cent. Cmt; mem, Gov. Status of Women's Cmn, Idaho; Idaho State Rep, Dist. 20-A, Lemhi, Anl and Custer Counties, 65-, mem. adv. bd, Challis Nat. Forest, Rep. Caucus secy. and v.chmn, Appropriations Cmt, Idaho House of Rep, currently. Bus. & Prof. Pos: Educator, jr. high sch, 40-55. Mem: Bus. and Prfnl. Women's Club; Int. Toast Mistress; Nat. Educ. Asn; v.pres, N. Idaho C. of C; dir, E. Idaho C. of C; exec. bd, Univ. Idaho Alumni Asn; Outstanding Citizen's Award, 65; Woman of the Year, 66. Rel: Episcopal. Mailing Add: Box 457, Salmon, Idaho 83467.

McKINNEY, JAMES GROVER R

Assoc. Mem, Calif. Rep. State Cent. Cmt.

b. San Francisco, Calif, 10/30/45; s. Byron Curtis McKinney and Doris O'Reilly M; single. Educ: San Diego State Col, B.A, 68; Pi Kappa Delta; Tau Kappa Epsilon; Men's Glee Club. Polit. & Govt. Pos: Mem, Calif. Rep. Assembly, 64-; del, Calif. Young Rep. Conv, 65-69; assoc. mem, Calif. Rep. State Cent. Cmt, 65-; pres, San Diego State Col. Young Rep, 66; pres, Calif. Young Rep. Col. Fedn, 67-68; assoc. mem, San Diego Co. Rep. Cent. Cmt, 67-68; v.pres, San Diego Co. Young Rep, 67-69; del, Young Rep. Nat. Conv. and Col. Rep. Nat. Conv, 67 & 69; campaign mgr, Bill Ayers for Assembly, 77th Dist, 68; chmn, West. Area Fedn, Col. Rep. Nat. Cmt, 68- Bus. & Prof. Pos: Sports ed, Star-News, Chula Vista, Calif, 63; instr, San Diego State Col, summers 66 & 67; asst. prof, Calif. West. Univ, 69- Publ: 'Desert Awakening', Phoenix Mag, San Diego State Col, 8/64. Mem: Nat. City Jr. C. of C; San Diego State Col. Circle K Club. Second Place, oratory, Nat. Forensic League Tournament, 63; Second Place, Pi Kappa Delta West. Debate Tournament, 66; First Place, extemporaneous speaking, Pac. Southwest Collegiate Forensic Asn. Championships, 66 & 67. Rel: Evangelical Presbyterian. Mailing Add: 120 Valva Ave, National City, Calif. 92050.

McKINNEY, JOSEPH EVANS D

V.chmn, Md. Dem. State Cent. Cmt.

b. Elkton, Md, 5/21/13; s. Joseph B. McKinney and Bertha Payne M; m. 5/1/41 to Janet C. Deibert; c. Robert A. and James C. Educ: Johns Hopkins, 35-37. Polit. & Govt. Pos: Eng. aide, U.S. Corps of Engrs, 37-44; pres, Cecil Co. Young Dem, Md, 50-52; chmn, Cecil Co. Dem. State Cent. Cmt, Md. and co-chmn, East. Shore Dem. Cmt, Md, 58-66; del, Md. Dem. State Conv, 64; hon. secy. Md. del. and del, Dem. Nat. Conv, 64; v.chmn, Md. Dem. State Cent. Cmt, 68- Bus. & Prof. Pos: Admin. clerk, E.I. du Pont de Nemours & Co, Inc, 44- Mem: Assoc, Singerly Fire Co; past pres, Elkton Rotary Club; secy, Kiwanis Club of Elkton. Rel: Methodist. Mailing Add: 405 Park Circle, Elkton, Md. 21921.

McKINNEY, LLOYD R

Ky. State Rep.

b. Foxtown, Ky, 5/23/22; s. Bill McKinney and Allie Rea Isaacs M; m. 1/23/50 to Ruby Rose; c. Judy and Patty Jo. Educ: East. Ky. Univ, B.S, 55. Polit. & Govt. Pos: Dist. committeeman, Rep. Party of Ky, 50-67; secy. and treas, Jackson Co. Rep. Party, 52-63; Ky. State Rep, 68- Mil. Serv: Entered as Pvt, Air Force, 42, released as Sgt, 45, after serv. in GOI Bombardment, ETO; Good Conduct Ribbon; European-African-Middle East. Serv. Medal with Six Bronze Stars; Two Overseas Serv. Bars. Mem: R.H. Johnson Post 945 (master, two years); Farm Bur; Ky. and Nat. Educ. Asns; VFW; pres, Jackson Co. Teachers Asn; Honorable Order of Ky. Colonels. Mailing Add: Route 1, Box 388, McKee, Ky. 40447.

McKINNEY, ROBERT D

b. Shattuck, Okla, 8/28/10; s. Edwin S. McKinney and Eva Moody M; m. 4/30/43 to Louise Trigg; c. Robin. Educ: Univ. Okla, A.B, 32; Univ. N.Mex, LL.D, 64; Phi Beta Kappa; Phi Gamma Delta. Polit. & Govt. Pos: Chmn, N.Mex. Econ. Develop. Cmn. and Water Resources Develop. Bd, 49-51; Asst. Secy. of Interior, 51-52; chmn, Panel to Report to Cong. on The Impact of the Peaceful Uses of Atomic Energy, 55-56; permanent U.S. Rep. to Int. Atomic Energy Agency, Vienna, 57-58; dir, Rev. of the Int. Atomic Policies and Progs. of the U.S, for Joint Cmt. on Atomic Energy, U.S. Cong, 59-60; U.S. Ambassador, Switz, 61-63; exec. officer, Presidential Task Force on Int. Investments, 63-64; U.S. Rep, Int. Centre for Settlement of Investment Disputes, Wash, D.C, 67-; chmn, Presidential Indust-Govt. Spec. Task Force on Travel, 68; del, Dem. Nat. Conv, 68. Bus. & Prof. Pos: Publisher, The Santa Fe New Mexican; chmn, The New Mexican, Inc. and affiliated co; dir, Copper Range Co, Surveyor Fund, Inc, Martin Marietta Corp. and Trans World Airlines, Inc; pres, Robert Moody Found; mem. adv. coun, Southwest Center for Adv. Studies, Dallas. Mil. Serv: Entered as Lt.(jg), Navy, 42, released as Lt, 45. Publ: The Scientific Foundation for European Integration, 59; On Increasing the Effectiveness of Western Science and Technology, 59; The Red Challenge to Technological Renewal, 60. Mem: Dir, For. Policy Asn; Am. Soc. of Newspaper Ed; Coun. For. Rels; Chevy Chase Club; F Street Club; Metrop. Club, Wash, D.C; Brook Club; Century Club; Links Club; Univ. Club, N.Y.C. Rel: Christian Church of N.Am. Legal Res: Route 1, Box 172, Santa Fe, N.Mex. 87501. Mailing Add: P.O. Box 1705, Santa Fe, N.Mex. 87501.

McKINNEY, ROBERT HURLEY D

b. Indianapolis, Ind, 11/7/25; s. E. Kirk McKinney and Irene Hurley M; m. 11/28/51 to Arlene Allsopp; c. Robert Carlton, Marni Frances, Kevin Kirk, Kent Allsopp and Lisa Carol. Educ: U.S. Naval Acad, B.S, 46; Ind. Univ. Law Sch, J.D, 51; Phi Delta Phi. Polit. & Govt. Pos: Del, Ind. State Dem. Conv, 54, 56, 60, 64 & 68; chmn, Ind. Dem. Party, Kennedy for Pres. Campaign, 60; del, Dem. Nat. Conv, 68. Bus. & Prof. Pos: Chmn, First Fed. Savings of Indianapolis, 61-; pres, Jefferson Corp. & Subsidiaries, 61-; partner, Bose, Buchanan, McKinney & Evans, Law Firm, 63- Mil. Serv: Entered as Midn, Navy, 43, released as Lt. Comdr, 53, after serv. in Pac. Theatre, 46-49 & 51-53, Lt. Comdr, Naval Res; Pac. Theatre Awards. Publ: Law Review articles. Mem: Am. Bar Asn; dir, Ind. State Bar Asn; Asn. Life Ins. Counsel; dir, Boy Scouts; dir, Univ. Club. Rel: Catholic. Legal Res: 7770 N. Pennsylvania St, Indianapolis, Ind. 46240. Mailing Add: 1100 First Federal Bldg, Indianapolis, Ind. 46204.

McKINNEY, STEWART BRETT R

Minority Leader, Conn. House of Rep.

b. Pittsburg, Pa, 1/30/31; s. James Polk McKinney and Clare Brett M; m. 10/4/54 to Lucie Bedford Cunningham; c. Stewart Brett, Jr, Lucie Bedford, Jean Curry, Elizabeth Cunningham and John Polk. Educ: Princeton Univ, Class of 53; Yale Univ, A.B, 58. Polit. & Govt. Pos: Conn. State Rep, 67-, minority leader, 69- Bus. & Prof. Pos: Pres, C.M.F. Tires Inc. Mil. Serv: Entered as Pvt, Air Force, 51, released as Sgt, 55, after serv. in U.S. Mem: Am. Red Cross (past pres, Fairfield chap); Greater Bridgeport Symphony Orchestra (past pres); dir, Bridgeport Child Guid. Clin; dir, Rehabilitation Center of East. Fairfield Co; Rotary (v.pres, Fairfield club); Yale Club (v.pres); Bridgeport C. of C.(dir). Rel: Episcopal; mem. of vestry, St. Timothy's Church. Legal Res: 4480 Congress St, Fairfield, Conn. 06430. Mailing Add: P.O. Box 543, Fairfield, Conn. 06430.

McKINNON, CLINTON D. D

b. Dallas, Tex, 2/5/06; s. John C. McKinnon and Tennie Clifdel Hawkins M; m. 10/15/32 to Lucille Virginia McVey; c. Dan Clinton, Michael and Connie. Educ: Univ. of Redlands, B.A, 30; Univ. of Geneva, Switz, post grad. work, 30. Hon. D.H.L, Univ. Redlands, 68. Polit. & Govt. Pos: U.S. Rep, Calif, 49-52; v.chmn, Calif. Dem. State Cent. Cmt, 52-54; mem, Gov. Bus. Adv. Coun; Disaster Gov. of Calif; chmn, Indust. Develop. Cmn, San Diego, 64-; pres, San Diego Urban Coalition, 69. Bus. & Prof. Pos: Reporter, ed. and adv. mgr, various South. Calif. newspapers, 31-35; pres. and gen. mgr, Valley News Corp, 35-43; establisher, San Fernando Valley Times, 35, Los Angeles Aircraft Times, 40, Long Beach Shipyard Times, 41 and San Diego Daily J, 44, ed, publisher and owner, 46-48; pres, ed. and publisher, McKinnon Publ, San Diego, 45-48; owner, radio sta. KSDJ, Columbia affiliate, San Diego, 45-48; co-owner, Coronado J, 53-; pres, N.Shores Publ. Co, San Diego, 53-; ed. and publisher, Los Angeles Daily News, 54; pres. and gen. mgr, Alvarado TV Co, Inc, KVOA-TV, Tuscon and KOAT-TV, Albuquerque, 55-63; pres, Sentinel Savings and Loan Asn, 63-68; pres, San Diego Transit Corp, 67- Mem: Rotary; Cuyamaca. Mailing Add: 2724 Garnet Ave, San Diego, Calif. 92109.

MacKINNON, GEORGE EDWARD R

b. St. Paul, Minn, 4/22/06; s. James Alexander MacKinnon and Cora Asselstine M; m. 8/20/38 to Elizabeth Valentine Davis; c. Catharine A, James D. and Leonard D. Educ: Univ. Colo, 23-24; Univ. Minn, 24-29; Phi Delta Phi; Delta Tau Delta; M Club. Polit. & Govt. Pos: Minn. State Rep, 29th Dist, 35-42; U.S. Rep, Third Dist, Minn, 47-48; U.S. Attorney, Dist. of Minn, 53-58; Rep. nominee for Gov, Minn, 58; spec. asst. to U.S. Attorney Gen, Dept. of Justice, 60; judge, U.S. Court of Appeals, D.C. Circuit, 69- Bus & Prof. Pos: Asst. to counsel, Investors Syndicate, 29-42; gen. counsel and v.pres, Investors Mutual, Inc, 61-69. Mil. Serv: Entered as Lt.(jg), Naval Res, 42, released as Comdr, 46, after serv. in East. Sea Frontier; cited for meritorious serv. by Comdr. Air Force, U.S. Atlantic Fleet. Publ: Author, Old Age Assistance Act, 36, Minn. Reorganization Act and State Civil Service Act, 39. Mem: Am. and Minn. Bar Asns; Am. Judicature Soc; Mason; Scottish Rite; Minneapolis Club; Wayzata Country Club. Football, 25-27, track, 26-28, basketball, 27. Rel: Episcopal. Mailing Add: U.S. Court of Appeals, Washington, D.C. 20001.

McKINNON, TALMADGE D

b. Pearson, Ga, 11/04/19; s. Grover McKennon and Mary Howell McK; m. 4/27/40 to Laura Highsmith; c. Bobby Eugene, Jerry Roger, Janice Pruella, Barry Craig. Educ: Pearson High Sch, 38. Polit. & Govt. Pos: Ga. State Sen. (7th dist.), 63-66; Chmn, Sch. Bd. of Willachoochee High Sch, 54-56. Bus. & Prof. Pos: Farmer. Mil. Serv: WW II, 1/17/45-10/30/46; Victory Ribbon, Asiatic Pacific Campaign Ribbon, Philippine Liberation Ribbon, 3 Overseas Bars, Army of Occupation Ribbon. Rel: Methodist; Chmn. Bd. Stewards, 59-60; Sunday Sch. Supt, 60-61. Mailing Add: Willacoochee, Ga. 31650. (1967)

McKISSICK, FLOYD BIXLER

b. Asheville, N.C, 3/9/22; s. Ernest Boyce McKissick and Magnolia Ester Thompson M; m. 9/1/42 to Evelyn Williams; c. Joycelyn D, Andree Y, Floyd Bixler and Stephanie. Educ: Morehouse Col, 49; Univ. N.C, A.B, 51, LL.B, 52; Alpha Phi Alpha. Polit. & Govt. Pos: Counsel, Cong. Racial Equality, 60-, nat. dir, 66- Bus. & Prof. Pos: Lawyer, McKissick & Burt, Durham, N.C; lectr. and pub. speaker on race rels. Mem: Nat. and Southeast. Bar Asns; N.C. Col. Alumni Asn; Amvets; Elks. March on Wash, 63; Ike Smalls Civil Rights Award, NAACP, 62; Conf. Award for Civil Rights, African Methodist Episcopal Church, 64. Legal Res: 1123 N. Roxboro St, Durham, N.C. 27701. Mailing Add: 213 1/3 W. Main St, Durham, N.C. 27701. (1967)

McKISSICK, HOWARD FRANK, JR. R
Speaker, Nev. State Assembly.
b. Reno, Nev, 5/5/27; s. Howard F. McKissick, Sr. and Frankie Porter M. (deceased); m. 10/3/65 to Dorothy June Tutt; c. Blair, twins Bruce and Pam, John, Patty and Molly. Educ: Univ. Nev, B.S, 50; Hastings Col. Law, Univ. Calif, J.D, 53; Phi Kappa Phi; Order of the Coif; Sigma Nu; Phi Delta Phi; Fleishmann Scholarship, 47-50, Wilson Scholarship, 53; Thurston Soc; student body pres, 52-53; Hastings Law Rev, 52-53. Polit. & Govt. Pos: Legis. bill drafter, Nev. State Legis, 55; Nev. State Assemblyman, 57-, minority floor leader, 59, speaker of the assembly, 69-; mem. Nev. Rep. State Cent. Cmt; currently. Mil. Serv: Navy, 45-46, Seaman 1/C, Serv. in Amphibian Forces, S.Pac, 45-46; recalled 2nd Lt, Air Force, 50, serv. Camp Stoneman, Calif. Publ: 'New Laws of Interest to Nevada Lawyers,' Nev. State Bar J, spring 59, 61, 63, 67 & 69; 'Demonstrative Evidence in Criminal Cases,' 69 and 'The New Gun Control Law' 69, Am. Trial Lawyers Asn; plus others. Mem: Calif, Nev, Washoe Co. and Am. Bar Asns; Am. Trial Lawyers Asn.(state committeeman, 58-59, v.chmn. for state affairs, legis. sect); Nev. Trial Lawyers Asn.(co-founder and secy, 65-69); North. Nev. Trial Lawyers Asn.(pres, 69-); Am. Judicature Soc; Admitted to Supreme Courts U.S, Calif. and Nev; Ski Reno (exec. cmt, 68-69); Nat. Asn. State Legis. Leaders (charter mem); C. of C. Registrant, John Appleman's Prfnl. Trial Lawyers Seminar, Urbana, Ill, 69. Rel: Protestant. Legal Res: 905 Manzanita Lane, Reno, Nev. 89504. Mailing Add: Suite 1104, 1 E. First St, Reno, Nev. 89501.

McKNEALLY, MARTIN B. R
U.S. Rep, N.Y.
b. Newburgh, N.Y, 12/31/15; s. George F. McKneally and Ellen Leahy M; single. Educ: Holy Cross Col, A.B, 36; Fordham Univ. Law Sch, LL.B, 39. Polit. & Govt. Pos: Confidential secy, N.Y. State Supreme Court Justice; pres. bd. educ, Newburgh, N.Y; mem, N.Y. State Defense Coun, 60-68; coun, N.Y. State Cmn. on World's Fair; spec. coun. to Lt. Gov, N.Y. State, 60-68; U.S. Rep, N.Y, 69- Mil. Serv: Army, 41, Maj, ETO and Pac. Theatre; Decorated by France and Belgium. Mem: Am. Legion (former state and nat. comdr); hon. Rotarian; state pres, March of Dime, 5 years. Rel: Roman Catholic. Legal Res: 329 First St, Newburgh, N.Y. 12550. Mailing Add: 1534 Longworth House Office Bldg, Washington, D.C. 20515.

McKNIGHT, ED M. R
N.C. State Rep.
b. Dallas, N.C, 6/21/08; s. Samuel W. McKnight and Bessie V. Mc; m. to Dorothy Mae Essex; c. Keith Jay, Martha Gayle, Don B, Mrs. D.M. Matthews Jr. Educ: Am. Inst. of Banking, 32-35. Polit. & Govt. Pos: N.C. State Rep, 63- Bus. & Prof. Pos: Pres, Edmac Inc. Mil. Serv: Sgt, Marine Corps, 24-32. Mem: Am. Welding Soc; Nat. Welding Supply Asn. Rel: Calvary Moravian Church. Mailing Add: Route 2, Keithgayle Dr, Clemmons, N.C. 27012.

McKNIGHT, HENRY T.
Minn. State Sen.
b. Minneapolis, Minn, 1913; m; c. five. Educ: Minneapolis Univ; Yale Univ, B.A. Polit. & Govt. Pos: Mem, Nat. Agr. Adv. Cmn, 52-60; former chmn, Minn. Natural Resources Coun; Minn. State Sen, 62- Bus. & Prof. Pos: Dir, Am. Forestry Asn. Mil. Serv: Navy, 41-45; Bronze Star. Mailing Add: 24 Carver's Green at Hazeltine, Chaska, Minn. 55318. (1967)

McKOWN, C. H. D
W.Va. State Sen.
b. Ripley, W.Va, 10/10/07; s. John G. McKown and Charlotte Staats M; m. to Mary Sinclair; c. Charles Henry, Jr. Educ: Marshall Univ, A.B; Univ. of Cincinnati; Phi Delta Kappa; Kappa Alpha. Polit. & Govt. Pos: W.Va. State Sen, 40-52 & 58-; v.chmn, Wayne Co. Dem. Exec. Cmt; mem, W.Va. State Dem. Exec. Cmt; W.Va. mem. adv. cmt, South. Coun. of State Govt, 61-; mem, Educ. Cmn. of States, 67-; mem, Gov. Bd, Coun. of State Govt, 68- Bus. & Prof. Pos: Sales rep; former athletic dir, Marshall Univ; former prin, Wayne Co. High Sch; chmn, Wayne Co. Chap. Nat. Found; dir, Guaranty Nat. Bank, Huntington, Wayne Co. News, Wayne and Applachiane Life Ins. Co, Huntington. Mem: Elks; Mason; Shrine; Am. Bus. Club; C. of C. Rel: Methodist. Mailing Add: 127 Roanoke Circle, Wayne, W.Va. 25570.

McKOWN, GEORGE WASHINGTON D
b. Gaffney, S.C, 7/10/06; s. Edward L. McKown and Bessie Lancaster M; m. 10/18/25 to Delia Gettys. Educ: Shelby High Sch, 24. Polit. & Govt. Pos: S.C. State Rep, 35-36; mem, Seventh Circuit State Hwy. Cmn, 36-39; S.C. State Sen, 39-42 & 47-67. Bus. & Prof. Pos: Farmer. Mailing Add: RFD 2, Gaffney, S.C. 29346. (1967)

MacLAFFERTY, JAMES WATSON R
b. Cedar Rapids, Iowa, 8/1/05; s. William Smith MacLafferty and Eva Maude Watson; m. 6/19/28 to Maurine Roberts Stonebraker; c. Paul Stonebraker and Mary Alice (Mrs. Johnson). Educ: Coe Col, B.S, 26; Command and Gen. Staff Col, Ft. Leavenworth, 44; Indust. Col. of Armed Forces, Emergency Mgt. of the Nat. Econ, 52; Scabbard and Blade; Pi Delta Epsilon; Sigma Delta Chi; Phi Kappa Tau. Polit. & Govt. Pos: Mem, Hickenlooper for Senate Club, Iowa, 48; mem, Co. Rep. Adv. Cmt, 58-62; block worker, Rep. Precinct Orgn, 60-; co-chmn, Bottum for Senate Club, 62; S.Dak. State Rep. Cent. Committeeman from Minnehaha Co, 62-66; alternate del, Rep. Nat. Conv, 64; mem, S.Dak. State Bd. of Mil. Affairs, 66- Bus. & Prof. Pos: Dist. commercial supvr, N.W. Bell Tel. Co, 31-33, sales engr, 33-37, mgr, Council Bluffs Exchange, 37-42, Nebr-S.Dak. rate engr, 46-57, S.Dak. commercial engr, 57-68, commercial supvr, independent co. rels. and tariffs, 67- Mil. Serv: Entered as 1st Lt, Army, 42, released as Maj, 46, re-entered as Maj, 51, released as Lt. Col, 52, serv. in Signal Corps, Off. Chief Signal Officer and Asiatic Pac. Theater; Lt. Col.(Ret), Army Signal Corps Res, 65. Army Commendation, Army Res, Victory and Am. Theater Medals; Asiatic-Pac. Medal with 2 Stars; Philippine Medal for Mil. Merit; Philippine Liberation Medal with 1 Star; Korean War Serv. Medal. Publ: The MacLafferty Family in the United States, 63; 'The Other Fellow's Shoes,' Telephony, 30. Mem: Res. Officers' Asn; Am. Legion; VFW; AF&AM, K.T, Consistory, Shrine, High Twelve; Kiwanis; Rotary (pres, Sioux Falls-West Club, 69-70); S.Dak. State Bd. of Mil. Affairs. Rel: Presbyterian; Elder. Legal Res: 4 Riverview Heights, Sioux Falls, S.Dak. 57105. Mailing Add: Northwest Bell Telephone Company, 132 S.Dak, Sioux Falls, S.Dak. 57101.

McLAIN, EUGENE MILTON D
Ala. State Rep.
b. Clay Co, Ala, 2/14/31; s. Eugene Milton McLain (deceased) and Sarah Louise Leftwich M; m. 8/23/53 to Jerrie Phillips; c. David Scott and Caroline. Educ: Auburn Univ, B.S, 53; Cambridge Univ, 53-54; Univ. Ala, LL.B, 59; Omicron Delta Kappa; Blue Key; Gamma Sigma Delta; Alpha Zeta; Scabbard and Blade; Bench and Bar Legal Honor Soc. Polit. & Govt. Pos: Ala. State Rep, currently. Mil. Serv: Entered as 2nd Lt, Air Force, 53, released as 1st Lt, 56; Capt, Air Force Res. Mem: Madison Co, Ala. and Am. Bar Asns; chmn, Young Lawyers Section, Ala. Bar Asn, 64-65, mem, grievance cmt, 64-66, fed. legis. cmt, Young Lawyers Conf, 66-67, award & achievement cmt, 66-67; Jaycees; past pres, Huntsville Civic Clubs Coun; dir, Better Bus. Bus; YMCA; Salvation Army Adv. Bd. Rel: Baptist. Legal Res: 4101 Piedmont Dr. S.E, Huntsville, Ala. 35802. Mailing Add: P.O. Box 2005, Huntsville, Ala. 35804.

McLAM, DONALD CLIFFORD R
b. Topsham, Vt, 3/24/10; m. to Helen Jackson; c. one son and one daughter. Educ: Bradford Acad. Polit. & Govt. Pos: Vt. State Rep, 61-67; former v.chmn, Rep. Town Cmt; former chmn, Rep. Co. Cmt. Bus. & Prof. Pos: Dealer in lumber, hardware, bldg. materials; sch. dir, Corinth, 42-51. Mem: Blue Lodge; Mason; Shrine; Eastern Star; Men's Club; Friendship Club of Church. Rel: Congregational. Mailing Add: Bradford, Vt. 05033. (1967)

McLAREN, RICHARD WELLINGTON R
Asst. Attorney Gen. of the U.S.
b. Chicago, Ill, 4/21/18; s. Grover C. McLaren and Nita Waggoner M; m. 9/20/41 to Edith Gillett; c. Patricia M.(Mrs. MacDonald), Richard W, Jr, Sandra and James G. Educ: Yale Col, B.A, 39; Yale Law Sch, LL.B, 42; Phi Beta Kappa. Polit. & Govt. Pos: Asst. Attorney Gen. of the U.S, 69- Bus. & Prof. Pos: Assoc. lawyer, Reavis & McGrath, N.Y.C, 46-49; partner, Chadwell, Keck, Kayser, Ruggles & McLaren, Chicago, Ill, 50-69. Mil. Serv: Entered as Pvt, Air Force, 42, released as Capt, 46, after serv. in Air Transport Command, U.S. Mem: Am, Fed, Ill. and Chicago Bar Asns. Legal Res: 801 Central St, Evanston, Ill. 60201. Mailing Add: 4840 Glenbrook Rd. N.W, Washington, D.C. 20016.

McLAUGHLIN, CHARLES F. D
b. Lincoln, Nebr, 6/19/87; s. William McLaughlin and Mary Ann Cavanaugh M; m. 6/19/20 to Margaret Bruce; c. Edward Bruce and Mary Elizabeth (Mrs. Edmund Wellington, Jr). Educ: Univ. Nebr, B.A, 08; Columbia Univ, LL.B, 10; Phi Delta Theta; Phi Delta Phi. Polit. & Govt. Pos: Master in Chancery, Fed. Court, 16-17; del, Nebr. State Constitutional Conv, 19-20; U.S. Rep, Nebr, 35-43; mem, Am-Mex. Claims Cmn, 43-47; Judge, U.S. Dist. Court, D.C, 49- Bus. & Prof. Pos: Lawyer, Omaha, Nebr, 10. Mil. Serv: Army, Europe, 17-19; Capt. Field Artil; Maj, Res. Rel: Catholic. Mailing Add: 2101 Connecticut Ave. N.W, Washington, D.C. 20008. (1967)

McLAUGHLIN, JAMES JOSEPH R
Chmn, Pierce Co. Rep. Party, Wis.
b. North Adams, Mich, 4/6/11; s. James Leonard McLaughlin and Etta Bury M; m. 9/18/32 to Margaret Nash (deceased); m. 7/20/57 to Mary Ullman; c. Susan Jean (Mrs. Zuleger) and Nona Jane (Mrs. Lewis). Educ: East. Mich. Univ, A.B, 33; Univ. Mich, A.M, 36, Ed.D, 53; Kappa Delta Pi; Phi Delta Kappa; Alpha Tau Delta. Polit. & Govt. Pos: Asst. to chmn, Third Dist. Rep. Party, Wis; secy, Pierce Co. Rep. Party, 58-65, 65-; hon. asst. sgt. at arms, Rep. Nat. Conv, 68; mem, Miss. River Planning Cmn, 68- Bus. & Prof. Pos: Teacher, Mich. High Schs, 33-39; dir, Student Union, Cent. Mich, Univ, 39-41; instr, Ford Airplane Sch, Mich, 42-44; supvr, Brazilian Air Ministry Mech. Sch, Sao Paulo, 44-46; prof. math. and dean, Wis. State Univ, River Falls, 47-69, dir. instnl. studies, 69- Mem: Wis. State Univ. Faculties (past pres); Wis. Asn. Collegiate Registrs. and Admissions Officers (past pres); trustee, Corp. of Am. Col. Testing Prog, 69- and Wis. rep; founder River Falls United Fund; Lions. Rel: Methodist. Legal Res: Route 1, Box 117, River Falls, Wis. 54022. Mailing Add: Wisconsin State University, River Falls, Wis. 54022.

McLAUGHLIN, JAMES ROBERT D
b. St. Louis, Mo, 1/3/02; s. James Robert McLaughlin and Agnes Hegney M; m. 6/10/22 to Gladys Perry; c. Mary Elizabeth (Mrs. Sehr), James John and Stephen Michael. Educ: St. Louis Univ, 2 years. Polit. & Govt. Pos: Mem. of staff, Secy. of State, Ill, 35-44; downstate liquor cmnr, 44-52; asst. clerk of appellate court, Fourth Dist, 4 years; clerk of appellate court, 52-58 & 62-68; nominee, Secy. of State, 60; del, Dem. Nat. Conv, 68; clerk of appellate court, Fifth Dist, 68- Mem: K. of C (4°); Moose; Elks; secy, Mt. Vernon Air Port Authority, 52-62. Honored for contributions to life, family and state, Ill. House Rep, 69. Rel: Catholic. Mailing Add: Ashley Rd, Mt. Vernon, Ill. 62864.

McLAUGHLIN, JOHN A. D
b. Newark, N.J, 10/31/34. Educ: Seton Hall Univ, B.A, 56; LL.B, 65. Polit. & Govt. Pos: Mem, Dem. Co. Cmt, 58-60; chmn, Kearny Youth for Kennedy, 60; mem, Kearny Tantagua Dem. Club; chmn, Kearny Young Citizens for Johnson and Humphrey, 64; former N.J. State Assemblyman. Bus. & Prof. Pos: Teacher of soc. studies, St. Cecilia High Sch, Kearny, 57-64. Mem: Bd. of trustees, Kearny Free Pub. Libr, 60-, pres. of bd, 63-67; Advance Gifts chmn, W. Hudson Div. United Appeals, 63; del, White House Conf. on Children and Youth, 60; adv. to Essex Co. Teenage Coun. of Catholic Youth, 59-; pres, Nat. Coun. of Catholic Youth, 57-59; chmn, Newark Archdiocesan CYO, 57-59; Kearny Shade Tree Cmn, 58-60; N.J. and Hudson Co. Bar Asns; N.J. Educ. Asn; St. Stephen Holy Name Soc, Kearney. Rel: Catholic. Mailing Add: 315 Elm St, Kearny, N.J. 07032.

McLAUGHLIN, JOHN JAMES D
Mayor, Great Falls, Mont.
b. Butte, Mont, 9/17/09; s. John McLaughlin, Sr. and Kathryn Isabel McCormick M; m. Oct. 1935 to Mary Grahek; c. Patricia, Kathleen, Jack and Phil. Educ: Univ, Mont; LaSalle Exten. Course, Higher Acct. and Traffic Mgt; Alpha Tau Omega. Polit. & Govt. Pos: Chmn, Cascade Co. Dem. Cent. Cmt, Mont, 62-64; Dem. mem, Mont. Liquor Control Bd, 63-66; mayor, Great Falls, 67-; del, Dem. Nat. Conv, 68; first v-pres, Mont. League of Cities and Towns; 68-69; mem, Gov. Crime Control Cmn; mem, U.S. Conf. Mayors. Bus. &

Prof. Pos: Employee, Firestone Tire and Rubber Co, Billings, early 30's; mgr, Empire Motors, late 30's; employee, A.B. Cobb of Home Oil & Refining Co, Great Falls, 41; mgr, Home Oil Truck Fleet, World War II; co-owner, Synder Truck and Parts and S&M Blacktoppers, 45-54; builder, owner and operator, Gen. Truck & Tractor Co, 54-65; dealer, GMC Trucks and Dorsey Trailers, 14 years. Mem: Elks; K. of C; United Commercial Travellers; C. of C; v-chmn, Mont. Hwy. Users Conf; Nat. Defense Transportation Asn. (co-organizer, Mont. Chap). Rel: Catholic. Mailing Add: 2425 Fourth Ave. S, Great Falls, Mont. 59401.

McLAUGHLIN, MAURICE 'MAC' D
Fla. State Sen.
b. Crestview, Fla, 6/10/24; m. to Katrina Sibley; c. Margaret Elaine, Lynne Marie and Cynthia Anne. Educ: Auburn Univ; Nashville Col. of Mortuary Sci. Polit. & Govt. Pos: Mem, Ft. Walton Beach Indust. Bd, Fla; Ft. Walton Beach City councilman; Fla. State Rep, 62-64; Fla. State Sen, 64- Bus. & Prof. Pos: Mortician. Mil. Serv: Merchant Marine, World War II. Mem: Elks (former Exalted Ruler, Ft. Walton Lodge 1795); Bowlegs Festival Asn.(former pres); Ft. Walton Yacht Club; C. of C; Choctawhatchee Quarterback Club. Outstanding Young Man of the Year Award, Ft. Walton Beach Jaycees, 62. Rel: Methodist. Mailing Add: P.O. Box 957, Ft. Walton Beach, Fla. 32548.

McLAUGHLIN, ROBERT FRANCIS D
b. Mountain Home, Idaho, 7/11/20; s. Daniel McLaughlin and Mary Ryan M; m. 6/5/46 to Patricia O'Connell; c. James Daniel, John Patrick, Michael Robert, Mary Kathleen and Elizabeth Ann. Educ: Univ. Idaho, B.S, 48, LL.B, 50; Practicing Law Inst, Carnegie Scholarship, 56; Blue Key; Phi Alpha Delta. Polit. & Govt. Pos: City attorney, Glenns Ferry, Idaho, 50-52 & 58-66; prosecuting attorney, Elmore Co, 50-60; chmn, Elmore Co. Dem. Cmt, 54-58; secy, State Platform Conv, 54, chmn, 58; del, Dem. Nat. Conv, 56 & 64; State Dem. Committeeman, Idaho, 58-60 & 64-66; Dem. precinct committeeman, 60-66; city attorney, Mountain Home, 60-66. Bus. & Prof. Pos: Chmn, Magistrate's Manual Cmt, Idaho, 56-58. Mil. Serv: Entered as S/Sgt, Army, 40, released as Capt, 46, after serv. in 298th Inf, 24th Div, Pac. Theater, 42-45; Am. Defense Medal; Distinguished Unit Citation; Combat Infantry Badge; 5 Campaign Stars; 1 Spear Head. Publ: Idaho Magistrate's Manual, Idaho Dept. of Law Enforcement, 56. Mem: Idaho Bar Asn; Am. Trial Lawyers Asn.(pres, Idaho Chap, 68-69); Int. Platform Asn; Idaho Prosecuting Attorneys Asn.(secy, 52-56, pres, 58-60); Univ. Idaho Law Sch. Alumni Asn.(pres, 62-65); Am. Legion; VFW; K. of C.(4°); Cooties; 40 et 8. Admitted to practice before U.S. Supreme Court, 57. Rel: Catholic. Legal Res: 1120 N. Eighth East St, Mountain Home, Idaho 83647. Mailing Add: 159 N. Third East St, Mountain Home, Idaho 83647.

McLAUGHLIN, WILLIAM FRANCIS R
Chmn, Mich. State Rep. Cent. Cmt.
b. Syracuse, N.Y, 10/10/32; s. Edward Joseph McLaughlin and Rosalind Couch M; m. 10/29/60 to Janet Ann Lemaster; c. Michael, Patrick, Timothy and Sean. Educ: Lemoyne Col, 50-51; Univ. Detroit, 51-56. Polit. & Govt. Pos: Rep, cand. for Mich. State Legis, 62; mem, Macomb Co. Bd. of Canvassers, 63-64; chmn, Macomb Co. Rep. Cmt. 63-65; mem, Mich. State Fair Authority, 64; del, Rep. Nat. Conv, 64, alternate del, 68; entertainment chmn, Mich. Inaugural, 65; v.chmn, Mich. State Rep. Cent. Cmt, 65-69, chmn, 69-; campaign coordinator, State Rep. Campaign, 66 & 68; co-chmn, Govt. Day-Mich. Week, 69; mem, Rep. Nat. Cmt, 69- Bus. & Prof. Pos: Publicity and advert. dir, Cinerama Music Hall, 56-65. Rel: Roman Catholic. Mailing Add: 592 Reed, Northville, Mich. 48167.

McLAUGHLIN, WILLIAM J, III R
b. Phila, Pa, 6/27/28; s. William J. McLaughlin Jr. and Edith T. Jones M. Educ: William Penn Charter Sch; Amherst Col, B.A; Univ. Pa. Law Sch, LL.B. Polit. & Govt. Pos: Law clerk, Court of Common Pleas 5, Pa, 55-57; pres, Valley Green Young Rep, 59-60; financial secy, Germantown Rep. Club; mem, 59th Ward Rep. Exec. Cmt. of Phila; attorney exam, Pa. Bur. of Sales and Use Tax, 63-65; Pa. State Sen, 65-67; del, Rep. Nat. Conv, 68. Bus. & Prof. Pos: Attorney-at-law; bd. mgr, Grandon Inst. Mil. Serv: Cpl, 273rd Inf. Regt, 69th Inf. Div, 53-55; Citation of Achievement & Merit. Mem: Phila, Pa. and Am. Bar Asns; Corp. Friends Hosp; Speakers' Bur; United Fund; Phila-Amherst Alumni Asn; Amherst Col. Alumni Coun; Mt. Airy Lions. Mailing Add: 321 E. Mt. Airy Ave, Phila, Pa. 19119.

MacLAURY, BRUCE K. R
Dep. Under Secy. for Monetary Affairs, Treas. Dept.
b. Chappaqua, N.Y, 1932; m. to Virginia Doris Naef; c. John Kenneth and David Bruce. Educ: Princeton Univ, A.B, 53; Harvard, M.A. in Econ, 58 and Ph.D, 61. Polit. & Govt. Pos: Consult. in int. finance, Orgn. for Econ. Coop. and Develop. in Paris, 62-63; Dep. Under Secy. for Monetary Affairs, Treas. Dept, 69- Bus. & Prof. Pos: Economist, For. Research Div, Fed. Reserve Bank of New York, 58-62, mgr, for. dept, 63-65, asst. v.pres, for. dept, 65-68, v.pres, for. dept, 68-69. Mil. Serv: Lt, Artil, Army, 54-56. Legal Res: N.J. Mailing Add: Treasury Dept, 15th and Pennsylvania Ave, Washington, D.C. 20220.

McLAY, JAMES B. D
b. Cripple Creek, Colo, 5/3/98; s. James McLay and Margaret Swords M; m. 8/26/41 to Era B. Harrison. Educ: Univ. Ariz. Polit. & Govt. Pos: Clerk of Superior Court, Yuma Co, 51-; chmn, Yuma Co. Dem. Party, Ariz, 64-69. Mil. Serv: Pfc, Army, 18. Mem: Elks; Eagles; Am. Legion; K. of C. Rel: Catholic. Mailing Add: 879 First St, Yuma, Ariz. 85364. (1967)

McLEAN, DICKSON, JR. D
b. Lumberton, N.C, 6/20/27; s. J. Dickson McLean and Katherine Sartor M; m. 8/20/60 to Jane Savage; c. J. Dickson, IV and Robert Savage. Educ: The Citadel, 44-45; Univ. N.C, A.B, 49, Univ. N.C. Law Sch, J.D, 52; Phi Beta Kappa; Order of the Coif; Phi Gamma Delta. Polit. & Govt. Pos: Chmn, Robeson Co. Dem. Exec. Cmt, N.C, 58-68; Co. Attorney, Robeson Co, 59-; del, Dem. Nat. Conv, 68. Bus. & Prof. Pos: Pres, Robeson Co. Bar Asn, 59-60; pres. and trustee, Southeast. Gen. Hosp, 62-63; dir, South. Nat. Bank, 56- Mil. Serv: Navy, 45-46. Mem: Am. and N.C. Bar Asns; Robeson Co. Bar Asn.(pres, 58-59); 16th Judicial Bar Asn.(v.pres, 68-); Am. Legion. Rel: Presbyterian. Legal Res: 404 W. 35th St, Lumberton, N.C. 28358. Mailing Add: Drawer 1087, Lumberton, N.C. 28358.

MacLEAN, HECTOR D
N.C. State Sen.
b. Baltimore, Md, 9/15/20; s. Angus Wilton MacLean and Margaret French M; m. 12/18/44 to Lyl Warwick; c. Lyl Billings. Educ: Davidson Col, 41; Univ. N.C. Sch. Law, 48; Phi Delta Phi; Omicron Delta Kappa; Sigma Alpha Epsilon. Polit. & Govt. Pos: Mayor, Lumberton, N.C, 48-52; N.C. State Sen, Robeson Co, 61- Bus. & Prof. Pos: Pres, Lumberton Implement Co, N.C, 48; pres, South. Nat. Bank, 55-; pres, Va. and Carolina South. R.R. Co, currently. Mil. Serv: Entered as Lt, Army, 42, released as Capt, 46, after serv. in ETO; Bronze Star. Mem: Am. and N.C. Bar Asns; VFW; Am. Legion. Rel: Presbyterian. Legal Res: 2101 Elm St, Lumberton, N.C. 28358. Mailing Add: P.O. Box 1489, Lumberton, N.C. 28358.

McLEAN, JOSEPH WOODFEN D
s. Joseph Clayton McLean and Vera Babb M; m. 10/2/48 to Dawn Poston; c. Joseph W, Jr. Polit. & Govt. Pos: Admin. asst, Rep. E. Jones, D-Tenn. Mil. Serv: Navy, 36-40; Army, 41-46. Mem: Am. Legion; VFW. Rel: Church of Christ. Legal Res: Route 1, Alamo, Tenn. 38001. Mailing Add: 4701 Kenmore Ave, Alexandria, Va. 22304.

MACLEAN, MALCOLM RODERICK D
b. Easthampton, L.I, N.Y, 9/14/19; s. Malcolm Roderich Maclean and Emily Mariott Helm M; m. 11/13/48 to Frances Ravenel Grimball; c. Frances Delancey and John Helm. Educ: Yale Univ, A.B, 41; Harvard Law Sch, LL.B, 48; Phi Beta Kappa; Delta Kappa Epsilon. Polit. & Govt. Pos: Mayor, Savannah, Ga, 60-66, mayor pro tem, 57-60 and asst. city attorney, 55-57. Bus. & Prof. Pos: Partner, Connerat & Dunn et al, Attorneys at Law, 48- Mil. Serv: Entered as Ens, Naval Res, 41, released as Lt. Comdr, 46, after serv. in Convoy Escort Duty, N.Atlantic, reentered 50, released as Comdr, 52, after serv. in Bur. of Personnel, Wash, D.C, Korean Action; Bronze Star; Navy Commendation Ribbon; Pre-Pearl Harbor, Am. and European Campaign Ribbons. Publn: Declaratory Judgments, Ga. Bar Jour, 52; C.S.S. Atlanta, Ga. Historical, 56; Reapportionment, Ga. Bar Jour, 65. Mem: Bd. of Gov, State Bar of Ga; Ga. Waterways Cmn; Pub. Officials Adv. Coun. to OEO; Am. Legion; Elks; Mason; Scottish Rite, Shrine. Rel: Episcopal; Chancellor Episcopal Diocese of Ga. Legal Res: 412 E. 45th St, Savannah, Ga. 31405. Mailing Add: P.O. Box 1038, Savannah, Ga. 31202. (1967)

McLEAN, RICHARD CAMERON D
b. Denver, Colo, 11/6/31; s. Leslie Robert McLean and Alberta Payne M. m. 5/28/55 to Carolyn Lee Lindseth; c. Scott Cameron and Joan Carolyn. Educ: Stanford Univ, B.A, 54; Univ. Colo, LL.B, 58; Phi Alpha Delta; Alpha Sigma Phi. Polit. & Govt. Pos: Law clerk, Tenth Circuit, U.S. Court of Appeals, 58; Dem. precinct committeeman, Colo, 60-65; mem, Dem. Exec. Cmt, Boulder, Colo, 63-65; chmn, Boulder Co. Dem. Cent. Cmt, 65-66; chmn, Boulder Co. Dem. for McCarthy, 68. Bus. & Prof. Pos: Lawyer, Sheldon, Nordmark & Boyer, 59-69. Mil. Serv: Entered as 2nd Lt, Army, 55, released as 1st Lt, 57, after serv. in Post Q.M, Ft. Carson, Fifth Army, 56. Mem: Am, Colo, Denver and Boulder Bar Asns; Law Club of Denver; Boulder Dem. Men's Club; Int. Asn. Ins. Counsel. Amateur Astronomer. Rel: Congregational. Mailing Add: 2345 Kohler Dr, Boulder, Colo. 80302.

MacLEAN, WILLIAM Q, JR. D
Mass. State Rep.
b. New Bedford, Mass, 11/4/34; s. William Q. MacLean and Charlotte L. Hillman M; m. 11/24/56 to Martha M. George; c. Douglas Louis, Kim Marie and Laureen Jean. Educ: Univ. Mass. Polit. & Govt. Pos: Mem, Fairhaven Sch. Cmt, Mass, 59-60; Mass. State Rep, currently. Bus. & Prof. Pos: MacLean's Seafood, 60-66; Cornish & Co, Gen. Ins, 66- Mem: Moose; Lions. Rel: Episcopal. Mailing Add: 60 Lafayette St, Fairhaven, Mass. 02719.

McLEMORE, CARL RAY R
Chmn, Lawrence Co. Rep. Party, Ala.
b. Moulton, Ala, 3/1/22; s. Robert Emmett McLemore and Estie Sparks M; m. 4/6/52 to Jeffie Cowart; c. Carla Susan, Stephen Ray and Lee Jeffrey. Educ: Samford Univ, B.S, 54. Polit. & Govt. Pos: Chmn, Lawrence Co. Rep. Party, Ala, 67- Bus. & Prof. Pos: Pharmacist, York's Pharm, Birmingham, 52-53; pharmacist, Moulton Drug Co, 53-57; pharmacist and owner, The Drug Shop, 57- Mil. Serv: Army. Mem: Ala. Pharmaceutical Asn; Nat. Asn. Retail Druggists; Registered Pharmacist, Ala. State Bd. of Pharm; Mason; VFW; Boy Scouts; Am. Legion; C. of C; Ala. Cattlemen's Asn. Mailing Add: 101 Main S.E, Moulton, Ala. 35650.

McLENDON, JAMES ANDREW D
Ill. State rep.
b. Washington, Ga, 5/7/06; s. Toombs McLendon and Fannie Willis M; m. 12/20/43 to Elnora Davis. Educ: Fisk Univ, A.B; Northwest. Univ. Sch. of Law, J.D; Alpha Phi Alpha; Frogs Club. Polit. & Govt. Pos: Master in Chancery, Chicago, Ill; Ill. State Rep, currently. Mil. Serv: Entered as Pvt, Army, 41, released as Maj, 46, after serv. in Off. of Judge Advocate Gen; Lt. Col. (ret), Army Res: Army Commendation Medal. Mem: Chicago, Ill. State, Am. and Cook Co. Bar Asns. Rel: Protestant. Legal Res: 1015 E. Hyde Park Blvd, Chicago, Ill. 60615. Mailing Add: 100 N. LaSalle St, Chicago, Ill. 60602.

McLENDON, JAMES MALCOLM D
S.C. State Rep.
b. Marion, S.C, 12/20/09; s. James Madison McLendon and Virginia Lupo M; m. 4/15/44 to Edna Miles; c. Kennerly and Virginia. Educ: Univ. S.C, LL.B, 35. Polit. & Govt. Pos: S.C. State Rep, 55-56, 61-66 and currently. Bus. & Prof. Pos: Lawyer. Mil. Serv: Naval Res. Armed Guard Div, 42-45; Lt. Naval Res. Mailing Add: Box 1034, Marion, S.C. 29571. (1967)

McLENDON, LENNOX POLK, JR. D
b. Durham, N.C, 2/2/21; s. Lennox Polk McLendon and Mary Lilly Aycock M; m. 12/29/45 to Mary L. Inabnet; c. Lennox P, III, Christopher B, Brantley Aycock and Mary Inabnet. Educ: Univ. N.C, A.B, 42; Univ. N.C. Law Sch, LL.B, 48; Phi Delta Phi; Sigma Alpha Epsilon; N.C. Law Rev, 46-48. Polit. & Govt. Pos: Former pres, Guilford Co. Young Dem. Club, N.C; mem, Greensboro Bd. Educ, 60; N.C. State Sen, 63-69. Bus. & Prof. Pos: Attorney. Mil. Serv: Lt, Air Force, 42-45; serv. in 389th Bomb Group; Maj, Air Force Res, 58-; Distinguished Flying Cross. Mem: N.C. Bar Asn; Am. Bar Asn;

pres, Greensboro Commun. Coun, 2 terms; mem. bd. dirs, Greensboro C. of C, 63-64. Rel: Presbyterian; chmn. bd, Deacons. Mailing Add: 201 Kimberly Dr, Greensboro, N.C. 27408. (1967)

McLEOD, DANIEL R. D
Attorney Gen, S.C.
b. Sumter, S.C, 10/6/13; s. Daniel Melvin McLead and Bertie Estelle Guyton M; m. to Virginia Hart. Educ: Wofford Col; Univ. of S.C, LL.B, 48. Polit. & Govt. Pos: Asst. Attorney Gen, S.C, 50-59, Attorney Gen, 59- Mil. Serv: Navy, 40-45. Mem: S.C, Richland Co. and Am. Bar Asns; S.C. Archives Coun. Rel: Methodist; Mem. Off. Bd, Washington Street Methodist Church. Mailing Add: 4511 Landgrave Rd, Columbia, S.C. 29206.

MacLEOD, KENNETH PARKER R
Pres, Maine State Senate
b. Skowhegan, Maine, 2/14/23; s. George Clifford MacLeod and Mabel McLaughlin M; m. 1/26/51 to Priscilla A. Ayer; c. Kenneth P, Jr, Pamela Lee, Kathy Jean, Scott A, Barry C. and Audrey A. Educ: Univ. Maine, B.A, 47. Polit. & Govt. Pos: Mem. city coun, Brewer, Maine, 55-56, sch. bd, 58-63; Maine State Rep, 63-64; nominee, U.S. Rep, Maine, 64; Maine State Sen, currently, pres, Maine State Senate, 69- Bus. & Prof. Pos: Dist. sales, Proctor & Gamble, 47-49; life ins. agent, Nat. Life of Vt, 49-69. Mil. Serv: Aviation Cadet, Army Air Corps, 42-45, and 1st Lt, Air Force, 51-52, serv. in 51st Fighter Interceptor Wing and 311th Fighter Bomber Wing, China-Burma-India, World War II and Korea; Air Medal; UN Ribbon with 3 Battle Stars; Asiatic Pac. Theater Ribbon with 3 Battle Stars. Mem: Past pres, East. Maine Life Underwriters Asn; Maine Chap, Chartered Life Underwriters; Am. Soc. of Chartered Life Underwriters; Mason; Scottish Rite; Shrine; Am. Legion. Rel: Protestant. Mailing Add: 203 Parkway N, Brewer, Maine 04412.

McLEOD, L. DONALD Conservative
Educ: Lewiston, Minn. High Sch. grad. Polit. & Govt. Pos: Minn. State Rep, 65-66 and 56-62. Bus. & Prof. Pos: Farmer; dir, v.pres, Camera Art, Inc. Mem: Treas, Farmers Commun. Park Bd; Masons, Shriner. Rel: Presbyterian. Mailing Add: Lewiston, Minn. 55952. (1967)

McLEOD, WILLIAM JAMES D
S.C. State Rep.
b. Timmonsville, S.C, 3/24/19; s. William Rogers McLeod and Ellen Byrd M; m. 4/24/48 to Sara A. Carmichael; c. William J, Jr. and Martha A. Educ: Furman Univ, 36-39; Univ. S.C, LL.B, 42; Omicron Delta Kappa; Kappa Alpha; Phi Delta Phi. Polit. & Govt. Pos: City recorder, Dillon, S.C, 53-61; mem, co. bd. educ, Dillon Co, 61-63; mem. and treas, Dunbar Mem. Libr, Dillon, 63-; S.C. State Rep, Dillon Co, 66- Mil. Serv: Entered as Pfc, Marine Corp, 42, released as Capt, 46, after serv. in Pac. Theatre, 43-46; S.C. Nat. Guard, 49-, Lt. Col; Am. Defense and Am. Theater Medals; Asiatic Pac. Theatre Ribbon with Two Battle Stars; Victory Medal; Army of Occup; Res. Medal. Mem: Dillon Co. and S.C. Bar Asns; Am. Judicature Soc; S.C. Nat. Guard Asn.(pres, 62-63); Lions; Am. Legion; VFW; C. of C; Dillon Co. Farm Bur. Rel: Methodist. Mailing Add: 600 E. Jackson St, Dillon, S.C. 29536.

McLEON, ADDISON M. D
N.J. State Assemblyman
b. Harnett Co, N.C, 6/17/21; m. to Louise Williams; c. three. Educ: Lincoln Univ, B.A, 49; Cortez W. Peters Sch. of Bus. completed course in bus. admin, 51. Polit. & Govt. Pos: N.J. State Assemblyman, Dist. 12-A, currently; housing mgr, Jersey City Housing Authority; mem, Jersey City Bd. of Educ. Bus. & Prof. Pos: Broker, Murl Realty Co. Mil. Serv: Air Force, Personnel Sgt. Maj, 44-46. Mailing Add: 135 Clerk St, Jersey City, N.J. 07305.

McLIN, CLARENCE JOSEF, JR. D
Ohio State Rep.
s. Clarence Josef McLin and Rubie Thomas M; div; c. Rhine Lana, Sherrie and Clarence Josef, III. Educ: Va. Union Univ; Cincinnati Sch. of Embalming, grad. Polit. & Govt. Pos: Ohio State Rep, 88th Dist, currently; v.chm, Montgomery Co. Dem. Exec. Cmt; chmn, Dem. Voters League; del, Dem. Nat. Conv, 68. Mil. Serv: Entered as Pvt, Army, 42, released as Pfc, 44; Good Conduct Medal; ETO Medal. Mem: VFW; Int. Elks; Am. Legion; Montgomery Co. Agr. Soc; v.pres, Buckeye State Funeral Dir. Asn. One of the first elected Dem. leaders. Mailing Add: 1130 Germantown St, Dayton, Ohio 45408.

McLOONE, PHILIP JOSEPH D
Exec. Treas, Miss. Dem. Party
b. Brooklyn, N.Y, 5/13/21; s. Philip McLoone and Mary Ferry M; single. Educ: Epiphany Col, 37-41; Cath. Univ, Wash, D.C; St. Joseph Sem, Wash, D.C, 41-47. Polit. & Govt. Pos: Del, Miss. Loyalist Conv, 68; exec. treas, Miss. Dem. Party, 68- Bus. & Prof. Pos: Asst. pastor, New Orleans, La, Pass Christian, Miss, St. Joseph, La, Beaumont, Tex, N.A.L.M. and Wash, D.C; pastor, St. Joseph, Glenarden, Md, St. Philip, New Orleans, La. and Our Mother of Mercy, Pass Christian, Miss, currently. Mem: Pass Christian Progressive Civic League. Rel: Roman Catholic. Legal Res: 224 E. Railroad Ave, Pass Christian, Miss. 39571. Mailing Add: P.O. Box 162, Pass Christian, Miss. 39571.

McLOUGHLIN, JAMES PATRICK D
Asst. Majority Leader, Conn. House of Rep.
b. Bridgeport, Conn, 10/15/29; s. Terence P. McLoughlin and Elizabeth Gill; m. 8/19/61 to Diane Jean Danko; c. Terence John and Megan Anne. Educ: St. Mary's Univ, Baltimore, Md, A.B, 51; Fairfield Univ, M.A, 52; Univ. Conn. Sch. Law, Hartford, LL.B, 59. Polit. & Govt. Pos: Alderman, Common Coun, Bridgeport, Conn, 59-63; Conn. State Rep, 132nd Assembly Dist, 63-, Asst. Majority Leader, Conn. House of Rep, 69-; counsel, Bridgeport Charter Rev. Cmn, 68. Bus. & Prof. Pos: Partner, Plotkin, McLoughlin & Milwe, Attorneys, Bridgeport, Conn, 59- Mil. Serv: Entered as Seaman Recruit, Navy, 52, released as Lt, 56, after serv. in U.S.S. Leyte C.V.S. 32 and U.S.S. Lookout YAGR-2, Atlantic Fleet; Korean Defense Medal; Good Conduct Award. Mem: Conn. and Bridgeport Bar Asns; Ancient Order of Hibernians; Elks; K. of C; Am. Legion; C. of C; Sacred Heart Univ. Assocs; bd. of commun. dirs, Conn. Educ. TV; chmn. bd. of dirs, Conn. Student Loan Found; Gov. Joint Exec-Legis. Econ. Coun; Nat. Legis. Coun. Rel: Roman Catholic. Legal Res: 1045 Briarwood Ave, Bridgeport, Conn. 06604. Mailing Add: 285 Golden Hill St, Bridgeport, Conn. 06604.

McLOSKEY, ROBERT T. R
b. Monmouth, Ill, 6/26/07; s. John A. McLoskey and Lillian Shawler M; m. 6/15/29 to Elizabeth Dickson; c. Robert D, Anne (Mrs. Romine), Margaret Gail (Mrs. McNitt) and Mary Alice (Mrs. Toal). Educ: Monmouth Col, B.S, 28; Theta Chi. Polit. & Govt. Pos: Mem. bd, Co. Tax Rev, Ill, 36-40; mem. bd. gov, Ill. Young Rep, 40-44; field supvr, Ill. Dept. of Health, 41-48; alternate del, Rep. Nat. Conv, 44 & 48; mem, Co. Bd. of Supvr, 48-50; co. chmn, Rep. Party, 50-60; Majority Whip, Ill. Gen. Assembly, 50-62; U.S. Rep, Ill, 62-64. Bus. & Prof. Pos: Asst. to pres, Bank, 29-32; funeral dir, Lugg & Holliday, 36-50; farm mgt, self-employed, 58-; consult, self-employed, for Ill. Coun. for Branch Banking and Ill. Tobacco Distributors, 65- Mem: Elks; Low Twelve Club; RAM; Farm Bur; C. of C; Prime Beef Asn; Monmouth Assocs; Gibson Woods Golf Club; Col. Bd. Dirs, Col. Athletic Bd; past pres, Lettermans Club. Rel: Methodist. Mailing Add: R.R. 2, Lake Warren, Monmouth, Ill. 61462.

McLUCAS, JOHN L. R
Under Secy. of the Air Force
b. Fayetteville, N.C, 8/22/20; m. to Patricia Knapp; c. Pamela, Susan, John and Roderick. Educ: Davidson Col, B.Sc, 41; Tulane Univ, M.Sc. in Physics, 43; Pa. State Univ, Ph.D. in Physics, 50. Polit. & Govt. Pos: Active in civic affairs in Pa. and Mass; Dep. Dir. of Defense Research and Eng, Tactical Warfare Progs, Dept. of Defense, 62-64; Asst. Secy. Gen. for Sci. Affairs, NATO Hq, Paris, France, 64-66; Under Secy. of the Air Force, 69- Bus. & Prof. Pos: Co-founder or founder, several small businesses; v.pres. and tech. dir, Haller, Raymond and Brown, Inc, State College, Pa, 50-57; pres, HRB-Singer, Inc, 58-62; pres. and chief exec. officer, Mitre Corp, Bedford, Mass. and McLean, Va, 66-69. Mil. Serv: Officer, Navy, 43-46. Publ: Author of numerous scientific articles. Mem: Fel. Inst. of Elec. and Electronic Engrs; Young Pres. Orgn; Nat. Acad. of Eng; Am. Phys. Soc; Am. Inst. of Aeronaut. and Astronaut; Opers. Research Soc. of Am; Sigma Pi Sigma; Sigma Xi. Received Distinguished Pub. Serv. Award, Dept. of Defense, 64. Mailing Add: Dept. of the Air Force, Room 4 E 886, The Pentagon, Washington, D.C. 20330.

McMAHON, CARLYLE C. D
b. Stowe, Vt, 4/29/11; m. to Diana Salvas. Educ: Norwich Univ, B.S, 32. Polit. & Govt. Pos: Vt. State Rep, 65-67. Bus. & Prof. Pos: Semi-retired; Pres, Miles, McMahon & Co, Inc; acct. dept, Lake Champlain Trans. Co. Mil. Serv: U.S. Cavalry Res, 1st Lt. Mem: Mystic Lodge; F&AM; exec. secy, pres, Stowe Rotary Club. Rel: Congregational. Mailing Add: Stowe, Vt. 05642. (1967)

McMAHON, CHARLES T. D
b. Newton, Mass, 1/10/32; married; c. five. Educ: Univ. of Md; Merrimack Col; Lowell Inst. Polit. & Govt. Pos: N.H. State Rep, -67; Rockingham Co. Dem. Comm; Chmn, Salem Sch. Bd. Bus. & Prof. Pos: Real estate broker; mech. engr. Mil. Serv: U.S.A.F. Mem: Recreational Comm; Budget Comm; past pres, Jr. C. of C; K. of C. Mailing Add: Main St, Salem, N.H. 03079. (1967)

McMAHON, JAMES ROBERT, JR. D
b. Hartford, Conn, 10/31/29; s. James R. McMahon and Marion Edna Ryan M; m. 6/14/52 to Theresa Marie Prusko; c. James Robert, III, William Joseph, Mary Theresa, John Thomas and Christine. Educ: Suffolk Univ, B.S. in bus. admin; Suffolk Law Sch; Wig and Robe Soc. Polit. & Govt. Pos: Chmn, Dem. Town Cmt, Bourne, Mass, 56-64 & 68-69; chmn, Barnstable Co. Dem. Cmt, 57-58; Mass. State Rep, Third Barnstable Dist, 65-66; mem, Finance Cmt, Bourne, 65-66, overseer, pub. welfare, 68, selectman and assessor, 68- Rel: Catholic. Mailing Add: 25 Canal View Rd, Buzzards Bay, Mass. 02532.

McMAHON, JOHN J. SR. D
Del. State Rep.
b. 1913. Educ: St. Paul's; Salesianum; Goldey Beacom. Polit. & Govt. Pos: Del. State Rep, currently; life mem, 11th Ward Dem. Legion; support officer, Family Court. Bus. & Prof. Pos: Fireman, 20 years; letter carrier; off. worker. Mem: Fraternal Order of Firemen; Police and Fire Holy Name Soc; Salesianum Alumni; St. Eliz. Athletic Asn; Labor Lyceum. Mailing Add: 1714 Maple St, Wilmington, Del. 19806. (1967)

McMAHON, JOSEPH PATRICK D
Asst. Secy. of State, Ill.
b. Chicago, Ill, 9/11/21; s. Patrick Joseph McMahon and Margaret Whalen M; m. 8/12/50 to Rosemarie Kelly; c. Joseph, Jr, Timothy, Anita, Brian, Kevin and Neil. Eudc: John Carroll Univ, B.S.C, 43; Loyola Univ, B.S.C, 47. Polit. & Govt. Pos: Past pres. and past nat. committeeman, Young Dem. Ill; clerk, Circuit Court, Cook Co, 60-64; Asst. Secy. State, Ill, 64- Bus. & Prof. Pos: owner, Joseph P. McMahon Floral Co, 52-; mem. bd. dirs, Garfield Ridge State Bank, 64- Mil. Serv: Entered as Pvt, Army, 43, released as Capt, 46; Bronze Star with Oak Leaf Cluster; Purple Heart. Mem: VFW; Amvets; Elks; Am. Legion; Chicago Asn. of Commerce & Indust. Rel: Roman Catholic. Mailing Add: 9424 S. Hoyne Ave, Chicago, Ill. 60620.

McMANUS, DONALD FRANCIS D
Exec. Committeeman, Broome Co. Dem. Cmt, N.Y.
b. Binghamton, N.Y, 12/23/17; s. David F. McManus and Agnes McCabe M; m. 4/10/58 to Ruth M. Spalt; c. Edward F, Kevin J. and Maureen A. Educ: Georgetown Univ, B.S.S, 40; Union Univ, Albany Law Sch, LL.B, 47. Polit. & Govt. Pos: V.chmn, Binghamton Housing Authority, N.Y, 50-52, counsel, 52-; chmn, Dem. City Cmt, Binghamton, 57; chmn, Broome Co. Dem. Cmt, 57-63, exec. committeeman, 57-; chmn, Sixth Judicial Dist. Conv, 58-65; del, Dem. State Conv, 58-66; del, Dem. Nat. Conv, 60, alternate del, 64; judge, City Court, 64; counsel, Binghamton Urban Renewal Agency, 64-66; Dem. cand. for Justice, Supreme Court, Sixth Judicial Dist, 66. Mil. Serv: Entered as Pvt, Army, 42, released as 1st Lt, 45; Asiatic-Pac. Campaign Ribbon; Am. Campaign Ribbon. Mem: Am, N.Y. and Broome Co. Bar Asns; chmn, Adv. Bd,

Catholic Charities, Broome Co, 60-63; dist. dep, K. of C, 57. Rel: Roman Catholic. Legal Res: 11 Edgebrooke Rd, Binghamton, N.Y. 13903. Mailing Add: 801 Press Bldg, Binghamton, N.Y. 13901.

McMANUS, EDWARD JOSEPH D
b. Keokuk, Iowa, 2/9/20; s. Edward W. McManus and Kathleen O'Connor M; m. to Sally Hassett; c. David P, Edward W, John N, Thomas J. and Dennis Q. Educ: St. Ambrose Col, Iowa, 36-38; Univ. of Iowa, B.A, 40, Col. of Law, J.D, 42; Beta Theta Pi; Phi Delta Phi. Polit. & Govt. Pos: City attorney, Keokuk, Iowa, 46-55; Iowa State Sen, 55-59; Lt. Gov, Iowa, 59-61; Chief Judge, U.S. Dist. Court, North. Dist. Iowa, 62- Mil. Serv: Entered as Seaman 2/C, Navy, 42, released as Lt, Naval Res, 46. Mem: Order of Coif; Am. and Iowa State Bar Asns. Rel: Catholic. Legal Res: 2135 Country Club Pkwy. S.E, Cedar Rapids, Iowa 52403. Mailing Add: P.O. Box 5005, Cedar Rapids, Iowa 52407.

McMANUS, LEWIS NICHOLS D
W.Va. State Del.
b. Beckley, W.Va, 9/8/29; s. Joab L. McManus and Mattie Ferguson M; single. Educ: Beckley Col; Morris Harvey Col, B.A. magna cum laude, 56. Polit. & Govt. Pos: W.Va. House of Del, 64-, chmn, Finance Cmt, W.Va. House of Del, 69- Bus. & Prof. Pos: Gen. ins. bus. Mem: W.Va. Asn. Realtors; W.Va. Hist. Drama Asn.(mem. bd. dirs, 67-); Raleigh Co. Commun. Action Asn.(mem. bd. dirs, 68-); C. of C; Am. Bowling Cong; Beckley Bowling Asn.(pres, 64-); Elks; Moose; AF&AM. Rel: Presbyterian. Legal Res: 114 King St, Beckley, W.Va. 25801. Mailing Add: P.O. Box 1818, Beckley, W.Va. 25801.

McMASTER, ANDREW R
b. St. Paul, Nebr, 8/9/96; wid; c. One. Polit. & Govt. Pos: Wyo State Rep; State Bd. of Agr; State Sch. Bd; Coun of State Govt; State Sen -67. Bus. & Prof. Pos: Rancher, Banker. Mem: Elks; Farm Bur; Wyo. Stock Growers Asn; Am. Legion; VFW. Rel: Catholic. Mailing Add: Van Tassell, Wyo. 82242. (1967)

McMASTER, FITZ-JOHN CREIGHTON D
Chmn, Fairfield Co. Dem. Party, S.C.
b. Winnsboro, S.C, 6/13/29; s. Spencer Rice McMaster and Mary Frances Williford M; m. 4/23/55 to Anne Ashe Edmunds; c. Sally Anne, William Spencer and Esther Ashe. Educ: Duke Univ, A.B, 51; Omicron Delta Kappa; Kappa Alpha Order. Polit. & Govt. Pos: City cmnr, Winnsboro, S.C, 58-64; chmn, Fairfield Co. Dem. Party, 67- Bus. & Prof. Pos: Mgr, Winnsboro Petroleum Co, 53-69. Mil. Serv: Entered as 2nd Lt, Marines, 51, released as 1st Lt, 53, after serv. in First Marine Div, Fleet Marine Forces, Pac, 52-53. Mem: Rotary; U.S. Jaycees; C. of C. Rel: Methodist. Mailing Add: 406 W. High St, Winnsboro, S.C. 29180.

McMATH, GEORGE NOTTINGHAM D
Va. State Del.
b. Onley, Va, 8/28/32; m. to Emma Allen Harlan; c. Two daughters. Educ: Randolph-Macon Acad; Univ. Va, B.A; Am. Univ, M.A. Polit. & Govt. Pos: Va. State Del, 63-; Chincoteague-Assateague Bridge and Beach Author. Bus. & Prof. Pos: Pres. East. Shore News, Inc; pres, Va. Press Asn; pres, East. Shore Indust. Develop. Corp; bd. of dirs, Farmers and Merchants Nat. Bank. Mil. Serv: Army, 54-56. Mem: Delmarva Adv. Coun; Va. Outdoor Recreation Study Cmn; Exec. Cmt. Ment. Health Study Cmn; Randolph-Macon Acad. Alumni Asn. pres; Va. Jr. C. of C.(pres, 64-65); former pres. East. Shore Yacht and Country Club. Named Virginia's Most Outstanding Young Man, 65. Rel: Methodist. Mailing Add: Onley, Va. 23418.

McMATH, SIDNEY S. D
b. Magnolia, Ark, 6/14/12; s. Hal Pierce McMath and Nettie Sanders M; m. to Ann Phillips; c. Sandy, Phillip, Bruce and twins, Melissa and Patricia. Educ: Pub. Schs. of Hot Springs, Ark, 12 years; Univ. Ark; Univ. Ark Law Sch, 36; Blue Key; Sigma Alpha Epsilon. Polit. & Govt. Pos: Prosecuting attorney, 18thJudicial Dist. of Ark; Gov. of Ark, 48-51; nat. chmn, Water Resources Conserv. & Develop. Cmn; chmn, Interstate Oil Compact Cmn; Ark. State chmn, Humphrey-Muskie for President Campaign, 68; del, Dem. Nat. Conv, 68. Mil. Serv: Marines, serving in Southwest Pac. in World War II, 40-46, Maj. Gen, Marine Corps Res, 46-66; Silver Star; Legion of Merit. Mem: Former mem. bd. gov, Law Sci. Acad. and Am. Trial Lawyers Asn; fel, Int. Acad. of Trial Lawyers; fel, Int. Soc. of Barristers; VFW; Amvets; Am Legion; Mason. One of 12 Outstanding Young Men of Am. selected by Jr. C. of C, 49. Rel: Methodist. Legal Res: 711 W. Third St, Little Rock, Ark. 72201. Mailing Add: 22 E. Palisades Dr, Little Rock, Ark. 72207.

McMEEKIN, NORMAN A. R
N.H. State Rep.
b. Newbury, Vt, 10/8/91; married; c. One son. Educ: Woodsville Schs. Polit. & Govt. Pos: N.H. State Rep, 43-47, 51-53, 57-59 & 63-, Speaker, N.H. House of Rep, 54, Majority Leader, 57; N.H. State Sen, 49, 55 & 61, Majority Floor Leader, N.H. State Senate, 55. Bus. & Prof. Pos: Mem. staff, factory br, Fletchers Milford Paint Works. Mem: Am. Legion; Brotherhood Locomotive Engrs. Rel: Methodist. Mailing Add: 2 School St, Woodsville, N.H. 03785. (1967)

McMILLAN, ARCHIBALD ALEXANDER D
N.C. State Rep.
b. Raleigh, N.C, 1/28/20; s. Robert Leroy McMillan and Mary Lee Swan M; m. 1/23/54 to Carol Montgomery Street; c. Carol, Julia, Amanda, Alexandra and Archibald Alexander, Jr. Educ: Wake Forest Col, A.B, 41; Pres, Sr. Class, 41; studied law under Claude Love, Asheville, N.C; Omicron Delta Kappa; Kappa Alpha. Polit. & Govt. Pos: N.C. State Rep, 61- Mil. Serv: Marine Corps, 41-46, Capt. Mem: N.C, Wake Co. Bar Asns; Am. Legion. Rel: Baptist. Mailing Add: 3309 Felton Place, Raleigh, N.C. 27609.

McMILLAN, BROCKWAY R
b. Minneapolis, Minn, 3/30/15; s. Franklin R. McMillan and Luvena L. Brockway M; m. 9/2/42 to Audrey Wishard; c. Sarah Linn (Mrs. D.J. Yim), Douglas Wishard and Gordon Brockway. Educ: Mass. Inst. Tech, B.S, 36, Ph.D, 39. Polit. & Govt. Pos: Bd. Ed, Summit, N.J, 58-61; Asst. Secy. Research and Develop, Air Force, 61-63, Under Secy, 63-65. Bus. & Prof. Pos: Proctor fel. and H.B. Fine instr, Princeton, 39-40; staff mem, Bell Telephone Labs, 46-59, dir. mil. research, 59-61, exec. dir. mil. research, 65-69, v.pres. mil. develop, 69- Mil. Serv: Naval Res, 42-45. Mem: Soc. Indust. and Appl. Math; Am. Math. Soc; Math. Asn. of Am; Inst. Math. Statist; Am. Asn. for Adv. of Sci; Inst. of Radio Engrs. Mailing Add: 6 Hawthorne Place, Summit, N.J. 07901.

McMILLAN, CLARA GOODING D
b. Brunson, S.C, 8/17/94; d. William James Gooding and Mary Webb G; m. 12/14/16 to Thomas Sanders McMillan, wid; c. Thomas S, Jr, James C, William Gooding, Edward Webb and Robert Hampton. Educ: Confederate Col; Flora McDonald Col. Polit. & Govt. Pos: U.S. Rep, S.C, 39-42; with Off. of Govt. Reports, 42; info. specialist, Off. of War Info, 42-45; legis. asst, U.S. Dept. of State, 45-57. Bus. & Prof. Pos: Teacher, S.C. Pub. Sch, 15-16. Rel: Presbyterian. Mailing Add: 2402 Hagood Ave, Barnwell, S.C. 29812.

McMILLAN, DAVID E. D
b. Coleville, Wash, 1897; m. to Mary; c. two daughters. Educ: Univ. Wash. Polit. & Govt. Pos: Former Wash. State Sen. Bus. & Prof. Pos: Farmer; cattleman. Mil. Serv: World War II Mem: Am. Legion; Elks; Mason. Mailing Add: Route 3, Coleville, Wash. 99114. (1967)

McMILLAN, GAINES D
b. Washington, D.C, 7/13/08; married. Educ: Donaldson Sch; Gilman Sch; Univ. of Va. Polit. & Gov. Pos: Md. State Del, 63-67. Bus. & Prof. Pos: Treas. of Ins. Agency. Mil. Serv: Navy. Mem: Baltimore C. of C; Md. Ins. Agents Asn; Md. Chap, Univ. of Va. Alumni Asn; Kappa Alpha; Soc. of the Cincinnati in Md; Bd. of Govs. and Pres, Md. Club; Bachelors Cotillon; Green Spring Valley Hunt Club. Mailing Add: 4401 Roland Ave, Apt. 115, Baltimore, Md. 21210.

McMILLAN, HARRY R
b. Nebr, 10/24/07; m. to Gertrude; c. Three. Educ: Univ. Wyo, BS. Polit. & Govt. Pos: Wyo. State Rep. until 67. Bus. & Prof. Pos: Mgr, Grain and Feed Elevator. Mem: Mason; Lions; C. of C. Rel: Methodist. Mailing Add: 111 W. Park, Riverton, Wyo. 82501.

McMILLAN, HELEN E. DFL
Minn. State Rep.
b. Ortonville, Minn, 1909; Married. Educ: Univ. Minn. Polit. & Govt. Pos: Former state pres, League of Women Voters; secy, Gov. Human Rights Cmn; Minn. State Rep, 62- Bus. & Prof. Pos: Housewife; bd. of dir, Mower Co. Red Cross. Mem: V.pres, United Coun. of Church Women. Rel: Presbyterian. Mailing Add: 1230 Second Dr. N.E, Austin, Minn. 55912.

McMILLAN, JOHN L. D
U.S. Rep, S.C.
s. M. L. McMillan and Mary Alice Keith M. Educ: Univ. N.C; S.C. Univ. Law Sch; All-State Col. Football Team, 4 years; All-South, 1 year and All Time Star Football Team, S.C. Polit. & Govt. Pos: U.S. Rep, S.C, 39-; U.S. Rep, Interparliamentary Union, London, 60 and Tokyo, 61; chmn, Dist. Cmt; dean, S.C. Cong. Del. Mem: Mason; 40 et 8; F. Sexton Am. Legion Post. Rel: Baptist. Legal Res: Florence, S.C. 29501. Mailing Add: 4740 34th St. N, Arlington, Va. 22207. (1967)

McMILLAN, LESTER A. D
b. Wis, 9/19/99; m. 1926 to Alta Rae King; c. Byron; granddaughter Julie Ann. Educ: Northwest. Univ; Univ. of South. Calif, LL.B; Delta Theta Phi. Polit. & Govt. Pos: Exec. officer Div. of Fish and Game, Calif, 39-40; Calif. State Assemblyman, 42-69; del, Dem. Nat. Conv, 68. Bus. & Prof. Pos: Lawyer. Mil. Serv: Army, 17-19. Mem: Am. Legion; VFW. Mailing Add: 2771 Forrester Dr, Los Angeles, Calif. 90064. (1967)

McMILLAN, ROSCOE DRAKE, JR. D
N.C. State Rep.
b. Red Springs, N.C, 6/11/13; s. Roscoe Drake McMillan and Gertrude Anne Garrison M; m. 7/9/37 to Eleanor Webb Powe; c. Roscoe Drake III and Anne Eleanor. Educ: Univ. of N.C, B.S, 34; Pi Kappa Alpha. Polit. & Govt. Pos: N.C. State Rep, 61- Bus. & Prof. Pos: Farm machinery & auto dealer; dir, Red Springs Fed. Savings & Loan Asn; dir, N.C. Auto Dealers Asn; dir, First Union Nat. Bank; teacher, Univ. of N.C. Mil. Serv: Capt, Naval Res, 42-45. Mem: Mason; Am. Legion (Comdr, 49); VFW; 40 et 8; Red Springs Rotary (pres, 48); pres, Red Springs C. of C, 61; pres, Univ. of N.C. Robeson Co. Alumni Asn, 60; past dir, Robeson Co. Chap. Red Cross. Rel: Presbyterian; teacher, Presbyterian Home, High Point, N.C; Cmnr. to Gen. Assembly of Presbyterian Church, U.S, 52-53; Moderator, Fayetteville Presbytery, 56. Mailing Add: Box 352, Red Springs, N.C. 28377. (1967)

McMILLIN, M. JUNE D
Mem, Kans. State Dem. Exec. Cmt.
b. Butler, Mo, 2/7/21; d. L. Lloyd Gaines and Ethel Coonrod G; m. 10/12/40 to Eugene S. McMillin, wid; c. Carol J. (Mrs. Walker) (wid) and Daniel A. Educ: Univ. Kans, 1 year; Alpha Delta Pi. Polit. & Govt. Pos: Receptionist, Congressman Newell A. George, Wash, D.C, 58-60; pres, Douglas Co. Dem. Women's Club, Kans, 60-62; v.chmn, Douglas Co. Dem. Party, 66-; precinct committeewoman, Lawrence Dem. Party, Kans, 66-; secy, Third Dist, Fedn. Dem. Women's Clubs, 66-; publicity chmn, Kans. Fedn. Dem. Women's Clubs, 67-; del, Dem. Nat. Conv, 68; Dem. v.chmn, Third Dist, 68-; mem, Kans. State Dem. Exec. Cmt, 68- Bus. & Prof. Pos: Advert. and receptionist, Sta. KLWN, Lawrence, 61-62; mgr and buyer, Kirsten's, 62-66; mgr. and buyer, The Alley Shop, 66- Mem: Beta Sigma Phi; Alpha Delta Pi Alumni, Am. Legion Auxiliary; Dem. Women's Clubs; Kans. Dem. Century Club; Lawrence C. of C. Rel: Protestant. Mailing Add: 2328 Murphy Dr, Lawrence, Kans. 66044.

McMULLEN, DANIEL G. JR. D
b. Clearwater, Fla, 12/18/34. Educ: St. Petersburg Jr. Col; Clemson Col. Polit. Pos: Fla. State Rep, 64-66; Campaign Mgr. for Doyle Conner. Bus. & Prof. Pos: Real Estate and Ins. Mil. Serv: 8 Years in Active Res. Mem: Ahepa. Rel: Methodist. Mailing Add: R.F.D. Box 330, Clearwater, Fla. 33515. (1967)

McMULLEN, MARY LOUISE D
Committeewoman, Tex. State Dem. Exec. Cmt.
b. Santa Anna, Tex, 10/23/31; d. Harry Brooks Baker, Sr. and Louise Martha

Mills B; m. 8/22/52 to James Abney McMullen, III; c. Wade Hampton and Kay Louise. Educ: Univ. Tex, Austin, 49-52; Delta Delta Delta. Polit. & Govt. Pos: Committeewoman, Tex. State Dem. Exec. Cmt, 67-; Chmn. Voter Registrn. Sub-cmt. and v-chmn. Woman's Orgn. Sub-cmt; alternate del, Dem. Nat. Conv, 68. Mem: Ft. Worth Lawyers Wives Club (past pres); Delta Delta Delta House Corp, Tex. Christian Univ. past-pres; Delta Delta Delta Alumnae Asn. Ft. Worth (pres); Jr. Woman's Club; Ft. Worth Opera Guild; Ft. Worth Ballet Guild; Ft. Worth Boys Choir Guild; All Saints Hosp. Auxiliary; Barnaby Club. Rel: Episcopal. Mailing Add: 3017 Simondale Dr, Ft. Worth, Tex. 76109.

McMULLIN, JOHN BOYD D
b. Essex, Mo, 6/27/03; s. Elam B. McMullin and Addie Gertrude Swan M; m. 9/14/25 to Melissa Effie Kearbey; c. John Boyd, Jr. Educ: Essex High Sch; Blackstone Law, 27-29. Polit. & Govt. Pos: Mo. State Rep, 62-66. Bus. & Prof. Pos: Agent, Poplar Bluff, 48-; Mo. Pac. Rail, agent, telegrapher, 42; Mem: R.R. Telegraphers (gen. cmt. div, 31, dist. chmn, Mo. div); AF&AM; Scottish Rite; John W. Calhoun Mem. Class (v.pres); Kiwanis; Ozark Assoc. Club; S.E. Mo. Sportsmens Asn; Poplar Bluff Industs.(former v.pres); Poplar Bluff C. of C.(bd. dir). Citation, President H. S Truman for activities in sale of war bonds, World War II, 45; Honored by Kiwanis Int. for serv. to City, Co. and State. Rel: Presbyterian; Bd. Trustees, Men's Coun. Mailing Add: RFD 2, Box 382, Poplar Bluff, Mo. 63901.

McMURRAN, LEWIS ARCHER, JR. D
Va. State Del.
b. Newport News, Va, 4/11/14; m. to Edith Margaret Lea; c. Lewis Archer III and Edith Lea. Educ: Wash. and Lee Univ. Polit. & Govt. Pos: Va. State Del, 48-; del, Dem. Nat. Conv, 48-68; mem, Dem. Nat. Platform Cmt, 60-68; Cmnr, Peninsula Port Auth. of Va; chmn, Va. Independence Bicentennial Cmn; chmn, State Air Pollution Control Bd; past pres, Young Dem. Clubs of Va. Bus. & Prof. Pos: Secy-treas. and dir, Citizens Rapid Transit Co; secy. and dir, Bank of Warwick; dir, Va. Commonwealth Bankshares Corp. Mil. Serv: Naval Res, World War II, Lt. Comdr; Bronze Star (Combat V) ; Navy Commendation Medal. Mem: Past pres, dir, Peninsula C. of C; v.chmn, Peninsula Indust. Cmn; chmn, Jamestown Found; chmn, Jamestown Corp; trustee, War Mem. Mus. of Va; Order First Families Va.(pres). Officer, Order of the British Empire. Rel: Presbyterian. Legal Res: 1109 Riverside Dr, Newport News, Va. 23606. Mailing Add: First and Merchants Bldg, 2600 Washington Ave, Newport News, Va. 23607.

McMURRAY, JOHN ODELL R
b. Oakley, Idaho, 5/20/03; s. John A. McMurray and Louise Dahlquist M; m. 8/31/43 to Virginia Hume; c. Michael Kay and John Patrick. Educ: Univ. Idaho, B.A, 27; Blue Key; Theta Nu Epsilon; Beta Theta Pi. Polit. & Govt. Pos: Mem, Idaho State Rep. Finance Cmt, 45-55; finance chmn, Ada Co. Rep. Party, 56-60, Precinct committeeman, 56-61; chmn, Idaho Rep. Cent. Cmt, 61-69; del, Rep. Nat. Conv, 64, alternate del, 68. Bus. & Prof. Pos: V.pres, McMurray Land and Livestock Co, 40-66; v.pres. and partner, Stein-McMurray Ins. Agency, 43-66; mem, State Adv. Cmt-Small Bus. Admin, 56-60. Mem: Elks; Arid Club; Hillcrest Country Club. Rel: Latter-day Saint. Mailing Add: 1207 Happy Dr, Boise, Idaho 83704. (1967)

McNAIR, CLARISSA WALTON R
V.Chmn, Third Cong. Dist. Rep. Party, Miss.
b. St. Davids, Pa, 9/5/10; d. Thomas England Walton and Georgia Winifred Bonnell W; div; c. Stirling Sharp, Jr, Thomas Walton, David Crawford, Clarissa and Patricia. Educ: Ogontz Jr. Col, B.A, 29; Univ. Redlands, 27-28; Pa. Acad. Fine Arts, 29-30. Polit. & Govt. Pos: Alternate del, Hinds Co. Rep. State Conv, 60; women workers recruiter, Hinds Co. Nixon Presidential Campaign, 60; v.pres. and prog. chmn, Hinds Co. Rep. Women's Club, 63-65; area precinct cmmn, Rep. Party, Hinds Co, 64, 65 & 66; v.chmn, Third Cong. Dist. Rep. Party, Miss, 65-; co-chmn. and canvass chmn, Hinds Co. Rubel Phillips Gubernatorial Campaign, 67; v.chmn, State Fund Raising Dinner, 67; alternate del-at-lg. and chmn. Arrangements Cmt, Rep. Nat. Conv, 68; area chmn, Women for Nixon, 68. Bus. & Prof. Pos: Vol. instr. art class, Miss. State Hosp, Whitfield, 67 & 68. Mem: Jackson Symphony Orchestra (past mem. string sect); Jr. League Jackson; Jackson Yacht Club; YMCA (bd. dirs, 67-). Rel: Episcopal. Mailing Add: 403 Turtle Creek Dr, Route 3, Brandon, Miss. 39042.

McNAIR, ROBERT EVANDER D
Gov, S.C.
b. Cades, S.C, 12/14/23; s. Daniel Evander McNair and Claudia Crawford M; m. 5/30/44 to Josephine Robinson; c. Robert E, Jr, Robin Lee, Corinne Calhoun and Claudia Crawford. Educ: Univ. of S.C, A.B, 47 and LL.B, 48. Hon. LL.D, Univ. of S.C, 67. Polit. & Govt. Pos: S.C. State Rep, Allendale Co, 50-60; Lt. Gov, S.C, 62; chmn, Nat. Conf. of Lt. Gov, 65-66; Gov, S.C, 65-; chmn, South. Regional Educ. Bd, 67-68; del, Dem. Nat. Conv, 68; chmn, Educ. Cmn. of the States, 68-; chmn, South. Gov. Conf, 68-; chmn, Nat. Dem. Gov. Conf, 68-; chmn, educ. cmt, Nat. Gov. Conf; mem, transportation cmt, Fed-State Rels. Cmt, Nat. Gov. Conf; mem, Cmt. Assessing Progress of Educ; mem, Nat. Cmt. for Support of Pub. Schs. Bus. & Prof. Pos: Attorney, McNair & Lawton, Allendale Co, S.C. Mil. Serv: Lt.(jg), Naval Res, 42-46, 22 months with 7th Amphibious Forces, Pac. Theater. Mem: Interim Planning & Steering Cmt; Compact for Educ, 65; Lions; Am. Legion; Farm Bur; Kappa Sigma Kappa; Blue Key; Mason; Shrine. Rel: Baptist. Legal Res: Allendale, S.C. Mailing Add: P.O. Box 450, Columbia, S.C. 29201.

MacNAIR, ROBERT WYNN R
Chmn, 64th Dist. Rep. Cent. Cmt, Calif.
b. Hemet, Calif, 6/14/28; s. Robert Leslie MacNair and Helen Tanner M; m. 8/6/50 to Beverly Anne Miller; c. Anne Jennifer, Robert Wynn II, Alexander Cameron, Andrew Houston, Leslie Jeanne, Hugh Raymond and Dana Meredith-Educ: Occidental Col, B.A, 50; Phi Gamma Delta. Polit. & Govt. Pos: Pres, 64th Dist. Calif. Rep. Assembly Club, 60-61; treas, 64th Dist. Rep. Cent. Cmt, 60-62, chmn, 62-64, 68-; v.chmn, 22nd Cong. Dist. Rep. Cent. Cmt, 62-64, chmn, 64-66; mem, Calif. Rep. State Cent. Cmt, 62-66, 68-70; chmn, Speakers Bur, Los Angeles Co. Rep. Cent. Cmt, 69. Bus. & Prof. Pos: Asst. v.pres, Coast Fed. Savings & Loan Asn, Los Angeles, Calif, 52-69; dir, v.pres. and treas, Cardinal Investment Co, 69- Mil. Serv: Entered as Cpl, Army, 50, released 52, after serv. in 40th Inf. Div, Sixth Army, Calif. Nat. Guard, 50-52. Mem: San Fernando Valley Bus. and Prfnl. Asn; research cmt, Los Angeles C. of C; assoc. mem, Bldg. Ind. Asn; assoc. mem, Soc. Real Estate Appraisers; past pres, Coast Toasters Toastmasters Club; Free Enterprise Speakers Bur. Mailing Add: 7349 Darby Place, Reseda, Calif. 91335.

McNALLY, EDWARD WILLIAM D
Pa. State Sen.
b. Pittsburg, Pa, 1/2/00; s. Edward McNally and Margaret Madigan M; m. 10/2/26 to Clara Hoffman; c. Sally (Mrs. Anderson). Educ: Carnegie Tech, 3 years; Duffs Iron City Col, 1 year. Polit. & Govt. Pos: Pa. State Rep, 61-; mem, Pa. Hwy. Cmn. and chmn, Hwy. Cmt, 65-66. Bus. & Prof. Pos: Pres. and treas, McNally Tire & Rubber Co, 45-66; pres, Johnstown Hockey Co, 58-59. Mem: Bd. dir, Kiwanis Club, 53-55; mem. bd, Cambria Co. Recreation, 58-66; K. of C; Elks; Moose. Rel: Roman Catholic. Mailing Add: 1646 Colonial St, Johnstown, Pa. 15905. (1967)

McNALLY, JAMES M. D
b. Sioux City, Iowa, 10/23/34; s. John Edward McNally and Mary Loretta Mc; m. 6/6/64 to Mary Elizabeth Davis. Educ: Univ. of S. Dak, LLB. Polit. & Govt. Pos: Iowa State Sen, -66; Asst. U.S. Dist. Attorney, 62-64. Bus. & Prof. Pos: Attorney. Rel: Catholic. Mailing Add: 3100 Giles St, West Des Moines, Iowa 50265. (1967)

McNAMARA, JOHN R. D
b. Helena, Mont, 9/30/13; s. John R. McNamara and Kathryn N. Flavin M; m. 3/22/42 to Mary Ann Cooney; c. Elizabeth A. (Mrs. War) and Susan K. (Mrs. Phillips). Educ: Helena High Sch; Bus. Col, grad. Polit. & Govt. Pos: Mont. State Rep, 65-67; postmaster, Helena, Mont, 67- Mil. Serv: Entered as Pvt, Army, 42, released as Maj, 66. Mem: Pres, Helena Asn. Life Underwriters, 58-59; comdr, Lewis & Clark Post 2, Am. Legion, 57-58; K. of C; Eagles; Mont. Club. Rel: Catholic. Mailing Add: 916 Stuart St, Helena, Mont. 59601.

McNAMARA, KEITH R
Ohio State Rep.
b. 1928; married; c. Four. Educ: Amherst, B.A; Ohio State Univ. Law Sch, J.D. Polit. & Govt. Pos: Ohio State Rep, 61- Bus. & Prof. Pos: Attorney-at-law. Mem: Prof. Ethics Cmn, Ohio State Bar Asn; Big Brothers; Boy Scouts; Conserv. League. Rel: Presbyterian. Mailing Add: 225 S. Drexel, Columbus, Ohio 43209.

McNAMARA, NELL GUY D
Ky. State Rep.
Educ: Morehead Col; West. State Col; East. State Col, A.B, B.S; Univ. Ky. Polit. & Govt. Pos: Ky. State Rep, 64- Bus. & Prof. Pos: Teacher and Adminstr; nurse's aid. Mem: Pres. Am. Legion Auxiliary 22; city chmn. Jr. Red Cross; city chmn. Womans Div. Civil Defense; Garden Club; YWCA; Womens Club of Cent. Ky; Farm Bur; Student Loan Funds Chmn; Mary Chiles Hosp; State Pub. Chmn. Girls State. Mailing Add: RFD 4, Mt. Sterling, Ky. 40354. (1967)

McNAMARA, WALTER LYNN D
b. Newhall, Iowa, 1932; single. Educ: State Univ. Iowa, B.S.C, 57; Univ. Iowa Col. of Law, 61. Polit. & Govt. Pos: Former Iowa State Rep. Bus. & Prof. Pos: Attorney. Mem: Linn Co, Iowa and Am. Bar Asns; Am. Judicature Soc; Rotary Int; Harmony Hawks Barber Shop Chorus. Rel: Catholic. Mailing Add: 1544 Second Ave. N.E, Cedar Rapids, Iowa 52401.

McNEAL, THEODORE D. D
Mo. State Sen.
b. Helena, Kans, 11/5/05; m. 8/25/50 to Virgie Louise Foreman; c. Phillip W, Theodore D. Jr, Betty Louise (Mrs. Wheeler), Catherine (Mrs. Fisher). Polit. & Govt. Pos: Mem, Joint Interim Cmt. on Govt. Problems of St. Louis City and St. Louis Co, Mo, 61-62 and Cmt. on Workmen's Compensation and Discrimination Against the Aged, 63-64; Mo. State Sen, 65- Bus. & Prof. Pos: Mem, Nat. Staff Sleeping Car Porters Union, 37-, pres, 50- St. Louis Globe Dem. award Most Effective First Term Sen. in 71st Gen. Assembly; awards from St. Louis Argus, New Citizen, St. Louis Civil Liberties Cmn, NAACP, Urban League, Frontiers Int, Nat. Asn. of Col. Women and St. Louis Fedn. of Musicians for work in Gen. Assembly. Mailing Add: 4772 Palm St, St. Louis, Mo. 63115. (1967)

McNEALY, ROBERT J. (BOB) D
b. Nebr, 1907; married; c. 5. Polit. & Govt. Pos: Alaska State Sen, 59-66; pres. of Sen, 64-; Alaska Terr. Rep, 55-57; del. Const. Conv; U.S. Cmnr; U.S. Attorney. Bus. & Prof. Pos: Attorney, 37 years. Mem: Elks. Mailing Add: P.O. Box 1912, Fairbanks, Alaska 99701. (1967)

McNEELY, JAMES MICHAEL D
Chmn, Mich. Dem. State Cent. Cmt.
b. Detroit, Mich, 5/11/30; s. Edward McNeely and Mary L. Sullivan M; m. 2/19/55 to Marialyce LaRock; c. Mary Jo, Michael, Tim, Tom, Beth, Patti and Christopher. Educ: St. Norbert Col, B.A, 55; Wayne State Univ, M.A, 60. Polit. & Govt. Pos: Dep. chmn, Oakland Co. Dem. Cmt, Mich, 62-65; dep. chmn, Mich. Dem. State Cent. Cmt, 68-69, chmn, 69-; chmn, 1968 Mich. Register & Voter Cmt, 68. Bus. & Prof. Pos: Pub. rels, WBAY-TV, Green Bay, Wis, 53-55; teacher, Farmington Pub. Schs, Farmington, Mich, 55-62. Mil. Serv: Entered as Pvt, Army Inf, 51, released as S/Sgt, 53, after serv. in 40th Inf. Div, Korea 52-53; Commendation Medal; Combat Inf. Medal; Sygmund Rhee Unit Citation; Presidential Unit Citation. Mem: Mich. Educ. Asn.(regional exec. secy, 56-60); exec. dir, Oakland Co. Cmn. on Econ. Opportunity, 65-68; Polit. Sci. Asn; Nat. Educ. Asn; NAACP. Rel: Catholic. Legal Res: 5190 Wardcliff Dr, East Lansing, Mich. 48823. Mailing Add: 900 W. Michigan Ave, John F. Kennedy House, Lansing, Mich. 48915.

McNEELY, MATTHEW D
Mich. State Rep.
b. Millen, Ga, 5/11/20; s. Whaley McNeely and Nina Norton M; m; c. Carl, Roy, Christopher, Clotelle, Camille and Cynthia. Educ: Highland Park Jr. Col; Lansing Commun. Col, winter, 66. Polit. & Govt. Pos: Pres, 18th and 20th Wards, Dem. Club, Mich; v.chmn, 16th Cong. Dist. Orgn, Detroit, 6 years; mem, Detroit Bd. Educ. Adv. Cmt. Schs; Mich. State Rep, 64-, assoc. speaker, Mich. House Rep, 69, mem. Educ, Soc. Serv. & Corrections Cmt.

and v.chmn, City Corp, Tourist and Legis. Coun. Bus. & Prof. Pos: Consult, Mich. State Bd. Escheats; educ. dir, Local 306, UAW, 4 years. Mem: Boy Scouts; NAACP; Mich. Partners Alliance (bd. dirs). Rel: Baptist; Mem. Sustaining Membership Cmt. Mailing Add: 3556 S. Bassett St, Detroit, Mich. 48217.

McNEIL, HIRAM A. D
State Rep, Colo.
Polit. & Govt. Pos: Colo. State Rep, 54- Mailing Add: Box 284, RFD 4, Montrose, Colo. 81401. (1967)

McNEIL, JEAN McINTYRE R
Mem, Calif. Rep. State Cent. Cmt.
b. West Kilbride, Ayrshire, Scotland, 6/7/11; d. John McIntyre and Jean Cook M; m. 8/1/38 to John Edmund McNeil. Educ: Ardrossan Acad, grad; Gateside Hosp, Greenock, Scotland, nurses training, 3 years. Polit. & Govt. Pos: Mem, Calif. Rep. State Cent. Cmt, 67-; adv, Watsonville Youth for Talcott (U.S. Rep, 12th Dist, Calif), currently; mem, U.S. Rep. Burt Talcott's Cong. Cmt, 12th Dist, currently. Bus. & Prof. Pos: Mem. staff, Gateside Hosp, Greenock, Scotland, 18 months; staff nurse, Mearnskirk Glasgow Corp. Hosp, formerly; pvt. duty nursing, 34-36; nurse and tutor, Mr. George Dickinson's Home, Three Gables, York, Eng, 36-38; owner and operator, McNeil Nursing Home, Watsonville, Calif, 50-62. Mem: Santa Cruz Co. Farm Bur, Women's Div; Rebekah; Watsonville Women's Club; Lady Elks; campaign and precinct chmn, Pajaro Valley Fedn. of Rep. Women (past pres. and v.pres), Watsonville, Calif. Rel: Protestant. Mailing Add: 21 St. Francis Dr, Watsonville, Calif. 95076.

McNEILL, WELTON R. D
Chmn, Okmulgee Co. Dem. Party, Okla.
b. Ada, Okla, 5/20/17; s. R.H. McNeill and Ethel Townsend M; m. 3/16/40 to Helen M. Sallis; c. Randy. Educ: High Sch, grad, 35. Polit. & Govt. Pos: Chmn, Okmulgee Co. Dem. Party, Okla, 64- Mil. Serv: Pvt, Army, 33-36, Nat. Guard, 43-46, Sgt. Mem: United Glass and Ceramic Workers of N. America, AFL-CIO-CLC. Rel: Methodist. Mailing Add: 1016 W. Tenth, Okmulgee, Okla. 74447.

McNEMAR, GEORGIA ARLONE R
Prog. Planning Chmn, Nat. Fedn. of Rep. Women
b. Portsmouth, Va, 7/31/33; d. John Holland McNemar and Georgia Cartwright M; single. Educ: Norfolk Div, William and Mary; Va. Polytech. Inst, A.A, 52; Wake Forest Col, B.S, 54, Wake Forest Col. Sch. of Law, LL.B, 56; Phi Alpha Delta; Pi Kappa Delta. Polit. & Govt. Pos: Magistrate, Charlotte Twp, Mecklenburg Co, N.C, 58-60; ed, NCYR News, N.C. Young Rep. Fedn, 59-60, gen. counsel, 60-62; mem, Second Dist. Rep. Cmt, 63-65; Second Dist. rep, Young Rep. Fedn, Va, 63-65; alternate del, Rep. Nat. Conv, 64; hq. coordinator, Rep. Campaign Cmt, Second Cong. Dist, 64; librarian, Div. Educ. and Training, Rep. Nat. Cmt, 65-67; prog. planning chmn, Nat. Fedn. of Rep. Women, 68- Bus. & Prof. Pos: Attorney-at-law, 56-69. Publ: Editing and Revision, GOP Leader's Manual, Ed. Press, Hyattsville, Md, 66. Mem: N.C. State and Va. State Bar Asns; Eastern Star; North. Va. Club; Int. Toastmistress Club. Mailing Add: 415 New Jersey Ave. S.E, Washington, D.C. 20003.

McNICHOLS, STEPHEN L. R. D
Dem. Nat. Committeeman, Colo.
b. Denver, Colo, 3/17/14; s. William H. McNichols and Cassie F. Warner M; m. 6/27/42 to Marjory Roberta Hart; c. Stephen L. R, Robert M, William H, Mary Elizabeth and Marjory. Educ: Regis Col, Ph.B, 36; Cath. Univ, LL.B, 39. Polit. & Govt. Pos: Agent, Fed. Bur. Invest, 40; dep. dist. attorney, Denver, Colo, 41; from spec. asst. to Attorney Gen, U.S. Dept. Justice, 46-48; Colo. State Sen, 49-54; Lt. Gov, Colo, 54-56; Gov, Colo, 56-63; chmn, Nat. Gov. Conf, 59-60 & 60-61; Dem. Nat. Committeeman, Colo, currently; nominee, U.S. Sen, Colo, 68; del, Dem. Nat. Conv, 68. Bus. & Prof. Pos: Attorney, Denver, Colo, 48- Mil. Serv: Lt. Comdr, Navy, 41-46; Bronze Star. Mem: Am. Bar Asn; Am. Legion; VFW; Elks; Moose; K. of C; Dem. Club of Denver. Mailing Add: 400 Hilton Office Bldg, Denver, Colo. 80202.

McNULTY, CLIFFORD ALLEN R
Fla. State Rep.
b. Palm Bay, Fla, 12/25/30; s. Chester Hugh McNulty and Jennie Larson M; m. 3/16/63 to Mary Louise Legge; c. Keith Alan, Cathryn Colleen, David Kevin and Mary Kay. Educ: Univ. of Fla, B.S.B.A, 56. Polit. & Govt. Pos: Fla. State Rep, 67- Mil. Serv: Entered as Seaman Recruit, Coast Guard, 51, released as SK-2, 54. Mem: Shrine. Rel: Methodist. Legal Res: 3301 Avenida Del Sol, West Melbourne, Fla. 32901. Mailing Add: P.O. Box 247, Melbourne, Fla. 32901.

McNULTY, JOHN F. D
b. Crisfield, Md, 5/29/96; married. Educ: Univ. of Md; grad, St. Charles Col, Cape Charles, Va. Polit. & Gov. Pos: Md. State Del, 63-67; 47-55, 59-62; Md. State Sen, 62-63; State Tobacco Inspector, 55-59. Bus. & Prof. Pos: former State Serv. Officer, Md. Vets. Cmn. Mil. Serv: Navy, Lt. Comdr, 17-19; Capt, 42-45. Mem: Pres, Md. State Fireman's Asn, 40; State Comdr, Am. Legion, 34-35. Mailing Add: 207 S. Hammond's Ferry Rd, Linthicurn Heights, Md. 21090. (1967)

MACOMBER, WILLIAM BUTTS, JR. R
Asst. Secy. for Cong. Rels, Dept. of State
b. Rochester, N.Y, 3/28/21; s. William Butts Macomber and Elizabeth Currie Ranlet M. Educ: Yale, A.B, 43, M.A, 47; Harvard, LL.B, 49; Univ. of Chicago, M.A, 51. Polit. & Govt. Pos: Rep. committeeman, Rochester, N.Y, 46-51; with, Cent. Intel. Agency, 51-53; spec. asst. to spec. asst. to secy. for intel, U.S. Dept. State, 53-54; admin. asst. to Sen. John S. Cooper, 54; spec. asst. to Undersecy. of State Herbert Hoover, Jr, 55, spec. asst. to Secy. of State John F. Dulles, 55-57; Asst. Secy. of State for Cong. Rels, 57-62 and 67-, ambassador to Jordan, 61-64, asst. adminstr, Agency for Int. Develop, 64-67. Bus. & Prof. Pos: Lectr, govt, Boston Univ, 47-49. Mil. Serv: Marine Corps, 43-46. Mem: Capitol Hill Club. Rel: Episcopal. Legal Res: 5 Buckingham St, Rochester, N.Y. 14607. Mailing Add: Dept. of State, Washington, D.C. 20520.

McPARLAND, LELAND S. D
Wis. State Sen.
b. Thorp, Wis, 12/18/96. Educ: Oshkosh State Col, 2 years; Marquette Univ, LL.B. Polit. & Govt. Pos: Wis. State Assemblyman, 41-55; chmn, Milwaukee Co. Dem. Organizing Cmt, 52-53; Wis. State Sen, 55- Bus. & Prof. Pos: Teacher, 20-27; attorney, 27- Mil. Serv: Navy, 17-18. Mailing Add: 4757 S. Packard Ave, Cudahy, Wis. 53321. (1967)

McPARTLIN, ROBERT F. D
Ill. State Rep.
b. Chicago, Ill, 11/2/26; m. to Geraldine Cronin; c. nine. Educ: St. Ignatius High Sch; Campion High Sch, Prairie du Chien, Wis. Polit. & Govt. Pos: Ill. State Rep, currently. Mil. Serv: Marine Corps, 43-46. Mem: Ted Knusman Amvets, Post Number 13; K. of C; Int. Munic. Signal Asn; IBEW. Mailing Add: 1104 N. Lockwood Ave, Chicago, Ill. 60651.

MACPHERSON, GORDON LEROY R
Ore. State Rep.
b. McMinville, Ore, 11/30/36; s. Adam Macpherson and Louise Powers M; m. 12/19/59 to Jannette Marie Wooden. Educ: Willamette Univ, B.S. in Law, 59, J.D, 61; Sigma Chi; Phi Delta Phi. Polit. & Govt. Pos: Lincoln Co. Chmn, Tom McCall Polit. Campaigns, 64 & 68; mem, Exec. Bd. Legis. Interim Cmt. to Study and Suggest Improvements to Ore. Legis, 67-68; Ore. State Rep, Lincoln Co, 69- Bus. & Prof. Pos: Organizer, dir, secy. and legal counsel for Lincoln Develop. Co; chmn, Lincoln Co. Sch. Dist. Budget Cmt, Lincoln Co. Juvenile Adv. Coun. Mil. Serv: Entered as Pvt, Nat. Guard, 54, released as Sgt, Artil. Battery. Mem: Ore. State Bar Asn.(mem, Grievance Cmt); Lincoln Co. Bar Asn.(pres); Am. Bar Asn; Lions Int; Elks (chmn, Toledo Lodge Youth Scholarship and Leadership Cmt); AFL-CIO; C. of C, Toledo; Ore. State Pub. Port Authorities Asn.(dir); Clean Rivers Asn. Yachats-Waldport Classroom Teachers Asn. Hon. Citizen for Educ, 66. Rel: Methodist. Mailing Add: Box 205, Waldport, Ore. 97394.

McPHERSON, HARRY CUMMINGS, JR. D
b. Tyler, Tex, 8/22/29; s. Harry Cummings McPherson and Nan Hight M; m. 8/30/52 to Clayton Read; c. Courtenay and Peter. Educ: Univ. of the South, B.A, 49; Columbia Univ, 49-50; Univ. of Tex. Law Sch, LL.B, 56; Blue Key; Phi Alpha Delta; Sigma Alpha Epsilon. Hon. D.Civil Laws, Univ. of the South, 65. Polit. & Govt. Pos: Gen. counsel, Senate Dem. Policy Cmt, 60-63; dep. Under Secy. of the Army, Int. Affairs, 63-64; asst. Secy. of State, Educ. and Cultural Affairs, 64-65; spec. asst. to the President, 65-66, spec. counsel to the President, 66-69. Bus. & Prof. Pos: Mem. law firm, Verner, Liipfert, Bernhard and McPherson, Wash, D.C, 69- Mil. Serv: Entered as Pvt, Air Force, 50, released as 2nd Lt, 53, after serv. in Tactical Air Command, 52-53 and Hq, Europe, 53; Army Distinguished Civilian Serv. Award, 64. Mem: Tex. and D.C. Bar Asns. Arthur S. Flemming Award, One of Ten Outstanding Young Men in Govt, 67. Rel: Episcopal. Mailing Add: 30 W. Irving St, Chevy Chase, Md. 20015.

McPHERSON, MICHAEL CLAUDE D
b. St. Louis, Mo, 11/1/31; s. Earl C. McPherson and Daisy L. Bell M; m. 3/2/55 to Edna L. Hill; c. Tracy Ann. Educ: Stowe Jr. Col, 49-52; Rutgers Univ, B.S, 54; Alpha Phi Alpha. Polit. & Govt. Pos: Admin. asst. to U.S. Rep. William L. Clay, Mo, 69- Bus. & Prof. Pos: Cartographer, Aeronaut. Chart & Info. Center, St. Louis, Mo, 55-62; ins. consult, Mutual of N.Y, 62-69. Rel: Catholic. Legal Res: 4642 Newberry Terr, St. Louis, Mo. 63113. Mailing Add: 430 M St. S.W, Washington, D.C. 20024.

McPHERSON, THOMAS ALLEN D
b. Bement, Ill, 4/26/35; s. A. T. McPherson and Doris Luttrell M; m. 5/18/57 to Virginia Lee Scott; c. Scott and Dirk. Educ: Stetson Univ. Polit. & Govt. Pos: Former Fla. State Rep, Broward Co; Mayor, Cooper City, 63-65. Bus. & Prof. Pos: Owner, Happy Cackle Egg Ranch, 59. Mil. Serv: Entered as 2nd Lt, Army, 58, released as 1st Lt, 59. Mem: Elks; Jaycees; Kiwanis. Rel: Methodist. Mailing Add: 9011 S.W. 49th St, Cooper City, Fla. 33165. (1967)

McPHERSON, WILLIAM HAUHUTH R
b. Bremerton, Wash, 5/16/22; s. James Gunn McPherson and Hertha Hauhuth M; m. 6/16/51 to Donnalie Wiggins; c. Jon Lindsey, Jeanne Ann and Wendy Lou. Educ: Shanghai Am. Sch, China, grad, 40; Stanford Univ, A.B. in econ. and hist, 48, LL.B, 51; Phi Alpha Delta. Polit. & Govt. Pos: V.pres, Calif. Rep. Assembly, 57-58; mem, Solano Co. Rep. Cent. Cmt, 52-, chmn, 54-56 & 64-66; mem, Calif. State Rep. Cent. Cmt, 54-66. Bus. & Prof. Pos: Instr, Continuing Educ. of Bar, Univ. Calif; chmn, Solano Col. Site Selection Cmt, Calif, 66; pres, Vallejo Merchants and Property Owners Asn, 68-69; mem. bd. of gov, Calif. Maritime Acad, 68- Mil. Serv: Entered as Pvt, Army, 43, released as Capt, after serv. in ETO; Bronze Star with Oak Leaf Cluster; Combat Inf. Badge, Commendation Medal. Mem: Am. and Calif. State Bar Asns; Solano Co. Bar Asn.(pres, 68); Am. Trial Lawyers Asn; Commonwealth Club of San Francisco; dir, N.Bay United Crusade, 56-64; pres, Napa-Solano Co. Girl Scout Coun, 60-63; pres, Fairfield-Suisun Rotary, 56; dir, Fairfield-Suisun C. of C, 60-65; Vallejo C. of C; Elks; Legal Res: 139 Toyon Dr, Vallejo, Calif. 94590. Mailing Add: P.O. Box 96, Fairfield, Calif. 94533.

McQUADE, FRANK JOSEPH, JR. D
Md. State Del.
b. Baltimore, Md, 5/28/10; s. Frank J. McQuade and Marie Mavers M; single. Educ: Strayers Bus. Col, 2 years; McCoy Col. Polit. & Govt. Pos: Chmn, Baltimore Third Dist. Dem. Cent. Cmt, Md, 66-; Regional v.chmn, Md. Dem. State Cent. Cmt, 66-; Md. State Del, 66- Bus. & Prof. Pos: Real estate broker, 49- Mem: Kiwanis; Hibernian Soc; Hamilton Dem. Club. Rel: Catholic. Mailing Add: 3017 E. Glenmore Ave, Baltimore, Md. 21214.

McQUILKIN, FORD LINCOLN R
Chmn, Columbiana Co. Rep. Cent. and Exec. Cmt, Ohio
b. Homeworth, Ohio, 2/12/11; s. James Robert McQuilkin and Dora L. Pickens M; m. 5/27/38 to Mildred A Thomas; c. Philip Ford. Educ: Alliance Bus. Col, Cert. bus. admin, 33. Polit. & Govt. Pos: Mem, Columbiana Co. Rep. Cent. Cmt, Ohio, 52-69, mem, exec. cmt, 58-69; v.chmn, Columbiana Co. Rep. Cent. and Exec. Cmt, 62-68, chmn, 68-; mem. bd. elec, Columbiana Co,

68- Bus. & Prof. Pos: Owner, McQuilkin Lumber Co, Homeworth, Ohio, 48- Mil. Serv: Entered as Pvt, Air Force, 42, released as S/Sgt, 45, after serv. in 49th Bomb Wing Squadron, 15th Air Force, Ital-N.Africa, 44-45. Mem: F&AM (past master, Lodge 499); RAM; RSM; K.T; Eastern Star (past patron, charter organizing officer and life mem, Homeworth Eastern Star 552); Am. Legion (past comdr. and life mem, Geo. D. Worth Post); Homeworth Lions Club (charter mem. and past pres); founder and life mem, West. Columbiana Co. Hist. Soc.(pres, 64-); SAR. Rel: Presbyterian. Legal Res: Winchester Dr, Homeworth, Ohio, 44634. Mailing Add: P.O. Box 162, Homeworth, Ohio 44634.

McQUILKIN, MARGARET R
Chmn, Clebourne Co. Rep. Party, Ark.
b. Wynne, Ark, 7/6/08; d. John Elmer Grover and Alla Cathey G; m. to William Robert McQuilkin, wid. Polit. & Govt. Pos: Chmn, Clebourne Co. Rep. Party, Ark, 68- Mem: Tumbling Shoals Sr. Home Extension Serv; World War I Auxiliary, Heber Spring. Rel: United Methodist. Mailing Add: Tumbling Shoals, Ark. 72581.

McQUONE, GARY HARDING R
b. DuBois, Pa, 10/27/38; s. Irvin William McQuone and Ruth Harding M; m. 8/26/61 to Beverly Titus; c. Shelly Jean and Shannon Corin. Educ: St. Joseph's Col, Pa, 57-59; Thiel Col, B.A, 61; Univ. Va. Law Sch, LL.B, 64; Lambda Chi Alpha; Phi Alpha Delta. Polit. & Govt. Pos: Chmn, Elk Co. Young Rep, Pa, 64-66; mem. state cmt, Pa. Young Rep, 64-68; mem. adv. cmt, Elk Co. Rep. Cmt, 64-68; mem. exec. cmt, Pa. Youth for Shaffer, 66; mgr, Edwards for Cong. Cmt, 68; del, Rep. Nat. Conv, 68. Mem: Allegheny Co, Pa. and Am. Bar Asns; Elks. Mailing Add: 450 Maple Lane, Sewickley, Pa. 15143.

MACRAE, CLARA DELLE R
b. New Albany, Miss, 8/25/22; d. David Earl Craft and Frances Lindsey C; m. 10/14/61 to Douglas F. Macrae; c. Douglas F, Jr. Educ: High Sch. and Strayer Bus. Col, D.C. Polit. & Govt. Pos: Admin. asst. to U.S. Sen. George H. Bender, 46-56; exec. secy. to U.S. Rep. Arch A. Moore, Jr, 57-69; admin. asst. to U.S. Rep. Wilmer D. Mizell, 69- Mem: Eastern Star; Bus. and Prfnl. Women's Club; Rep. Women of Capitol Hill. Rel: Methodist. Legal Res: 3676 Rawnsdale Rd, Shaker Heights, Ohio 44120. Mailing Add: 714 N. Lincoln St, Arlington, Va. 22201.

McRAE, DOROTHY A. R
Dep. State Treas, Colo.
b. Iowa Falls, Iowa, 1/12/01; d. Ernest K. Jackson and Margaret Pierce J; div. Educ: Huff's Bus. Col, Kansas City, Mo, secretarial course. Polit. & Govt. Pos: Admin. asst. to late Sen. Eugene D. Millikin, Colo, 42-56; dep. state treas, Colo, 67-; alternate del, Rep. Nat. Conv, 68. Bus. & Prof. Pos: Secy, Kinney-Coastal Oil Co, 57-60, D.A. Shale, Inc, Denver, Colo, 60-66. Mem: V.chmn, Colo. Cmn. on Status of Women, 64-65; Int. Asn. of Personnel Women; past pres, U.S. Senate Secy. Asn; Zonta Club of Denver; Bus. & Prof. Woman's Club of Denver; Colo. Safety Asn; Denver C. of C; hon. mem. Alpha Iota. Woman of the Year, Am. Bus. Women's Asn, 58. Rel: Protestant. Mailing Add: 1200 Humboldt St, Apt. 304, Denver, Colo. 80218.

McRAE, JOHN HECTOR D
b. Ewen, Mich, 3/19/25; s. Hector McRae and Helen Richard M; m. 2/2/57 to Betty Ann Kenna; c. Bruce John, Therese Catherine, Maureen Elizabeth and John Donald. Educ: Mich. State Univ, B.A, 49; Georgetown Univ, LL.B, 52; Delta Theta Phi. Polit. Pos: Chmn, Spokane Co. Dem. Cent. Cmt, Wash, 62-66; del, Dem. Nat. Conv, 64; alternate del, 56, 52 and 48; del, Wash. State Dem. Conv, 64, 60 and 58; pres, Men's Dem. Club of Spokane, 62. Bus. & Prof. Pos: Lawyer, self employed, Spokane, Wash, 57-; assoc, Cashatt & Williams, 54-57; adjuster, Northwest. Mutual Ins. Co, Seattle, 53-54; assoc, Joseph M. Donnelly, Lawyer, Houghton, Mich, 52-53. Mil. Serv: Entered as Pvt, Army, 43, released as Cpl, 45, after serv. in Battery B, 229th Field Artillery Bn, 28th Inf. Div, ETO; Rhineland, Central Europe and Ardennes Campaign Ribbons; Good Conduct Medal; 2nd Lt, Inactive Res. Mem: Am, Mich. State, Wash. State and Spokane Co. Bar Asns; past Grand Knight,K. of C. (3°), K. of C. (4°); Elks; Spokane Club; Spokane Sailing Club; treas, English Speaking Union; Spokane Hist. Soc. Rel: Roman Catholic. Mailing Add: S. 1217 Wall St, Spokane, Wash. 99204. (1967)

McRAE, RAY A. R
b. Plainville, Ill, 11/14/10; s. Clifford McRae and Viola P. Wagy M; m. 10/13/49 to Elizabeth Lenora Higham. Educ: Univ. of Wis, 29-33; Alpha Tau Omega. Polit. & Govt. Pos: Spec. asst. to U.S. Sen. Charles H. Percy, Ill, currently. Mil. Serv: Army, Pvt, ETO, 42-45. Mem: Mason; Elks; Am. Legion; Ill. Nat. Press Asn. Mailing Add: 262 G St. S.W, Washington, D.C. 20024.

McRAE, WILLIAM ALLAN JR. D
b. Marianna, Fla, 9/25/09; s. William Allen McRae and Mary Parker McR; m. 8/29/42 to Aline Virginia Dearing McR; c. Aline Virginia, William Allan III, Dearing. Educ: Univ. of Fla, A.B, 32, J.D, 33; Rhodes Scholar Christ Ch, Oxford Univ. (Eng.), 33, B.A. in Jurisp, 35, B. Litt, 36, M.A, 46; Phi Beta Kappa; Order of the Coif; Fla. Blue Key; Phi Kappa Phi; Phi Delta Phi; Omicron Delta Kappa; past Pres, Alpha Tau Omega. Polit. & Gov. Pos: U.S. Judge Middle Dist. of Fla, 61-; mem, Fla. Constitution Adv. Cmt; Sr. Consult, AEC, Wash, 46; trustee, Univ. of Fla, Jacksonville Univ, Univ. of Fla. Law Center Asn; endowment Corp, Univ. of Fla. Law Rev, 46-49. Bus. & Prof. Pos: Lawyer, mem. firm, Holland, Bevis, McRae & Smith, 46-61; Prof. Law; Univ. of Fla, 40-41; with Giles G. Patterson, 38-40; with Knight, Adair, Cooper & Osborne, 36-38. Mil. Serv: Army Air Force, 42-45, Col; Decorated Legion of Merit. Mem: Fellow Am. Col. Trial Lawyers; Am. and Fed. Bar Asn; Am. Law Inst; Selden Soc; past Pres, Bd. Govs, Judical Coun. of Fla. Bar; bd. Dir, Am. Judicature Soc; past Pres, Univ. of Fla. Alumni Asn; Fla. Yacht Club; Rotary. Legal Res: Jacksonville, Fla. Mailing Add: U.S. Dist. Court, P.O. Box 4070, Jacksonville, Fla. 33001. (1967)

McREYNOLDS, ELIZABETH SANFORD R
V.Chmn, Idaho State Rep. Cent. Cmt.
b. Reno, Nev, 1/15/30; d. John Sanford and Myrtle Helen Brooks S; m. 8/19/50 to Lauren Hall McReynolds, Jr; c. Anne, Mary, James, Margaret and Graham. Educ: Univ. Ore, B.A, 50; Pi Lambda Theta. Polit. & Govt. Pos: V.chmn, Gooding Co. Rep. Cent. Cmt, Idaho, 58-60, precinct committeeman, 58-61, secy, 60-61; precinct committeeman, Shoshone Co. Rep. Cent. Cmt, 62-69, state committeewoman, 64-66; pres, West Shoshone Rep. Women, 63-65, exec. dir, 65-69; chmn, First Dist, Idaho Fedn. Rep. Women, 64-66; v.chmn, Idaho State Rep. Cent. Cmt, 65-; mem, Idaho Coun. for Hosp. Construction, 69. Bus. & Prof. Pos: Teacher, Codornices Sch, Albany, Calif, 50-53; piano teacher, Kellogg, Idaho, 62-; kindergarten teacher, A.A.U.W. Kindergarten, 67; teacher, Sch. Dist. 391, 69- Mem: Calif. and Nat. Educ. Asns; PEO. Mailing Add: 518 Second St, Kellogg, Idaho 83837.

McREYNOLDS, LEAH NIELSEN R
b. Salem, Va, 11/18/44; d. Leonidas Nielsen McReynolds and Beatrice Morris M; single. Educ: Roanoke College, B.A, 66; XI Theta Chi; Phi Mu; Young Rep; Women's Athletic Asn. Polit. & Govt. Pos: Asst. to the legis. asst, U.S. Rep. Larry Winn, Kans, 67- and personal secy, 69; secy. to William E. Casselman, Dep. Spec. Asst. to the President for Cong. Rels, 69- Rel: Lutheran. Legal Res; 341 Pennsylvania Ave, Salem, Va. 24153. Mailing Add: 4901 Seminary Rd, Alexandria, Va. 22311.

McRITCHIE, THOMAS PARKE D
Chmn, Ottawa Co. Dem. Party, Ohio
b. Port Clinton, Ohio, 4/11/25; s. David Kenneth McRitchie and Leah Darlison M; m. 10/23/48 to Janice E. Bartlebaugh; c. Thomas Park. Educ: Univ. Toledo, 4 years. Polit. & Govt. Pos: Chmn, Ottawa Co. Dem. Party, Ohio, currently. Bus. & Prof. Pos: Sales mgr. and owner, Quikstir, Inc. Rel: Episcopal. Mailing Add: 222 Washington St, Port Clinton, Ohio 43452.

McSPADDEN, CLEM ROGERS D
Okla. State Sen.
b. Bushyhead, Okla, 11/9/25; s. Herbert T. McSpadden and Madalyn Palmer M; m. 2/11/62 to Donna Marie Casity; c. Barton Casity. Educ: Univ. Tex, B.A; Redlands Univ; Okla. State Univ, degree in animal husbandry. Polit. & Govt. Pos: Okla. State Sen, 54-, Asst. Floor Leader, Okla. State Senate, 61 & 63, Pres. pro-tempore, 65-67, chmn, Appropriations and Budget Cmt, 68-69; del, Dem. Nat. Conv, 68. Bus. & Prof. Pos: Owner, Cattle Ranch, Northeast. Okla; nat. TV sportscaster for world wide rodeos; rodeo announcer; v.pres. and dir, Cattlemen's Life Ins. Co, Oklahoma City, 61-; contract dir, Rodeo Cowboy's Asn, 63-; reai estate and property developer; gen. mgr, Nat. Finals Rodeo, Oklahoma City. Mil. Serv: Navy V-12. Rel: Methodist. Legal Res: R.R. 3, Box 588, Claremore, Okla. 74017. Mailing Add: State Senate, State Capitol, Oklahoma City, Okla. 73105.

McSPEDON, THOMAS G. D
Chmn, Yonkers Dem. City Cmt, N.Y.
b. Yonkers, N.Y, 1/29/18; s. Frank D. McSpedon and Catherine Carroll M; m. 7/16/44 to Alice Gorman; c. Thomas J. Educ: U.S. Army Schs, Evening Adult Educ. Classes. Polit. & Govt. Pos: Committeeman, Westchester Co. Dem. Cmt, N.Y, 40-; mem, Bd. Supvr, Westchester Co, 54-66, Dem. minority leader, 60-61 & 64-65; Dem. cand, N.Y. State Assembly, 62; committeeman, N.Y. State Dem. Cmt, 64-67; Dem. cand, Mayor, Yonkers, 65; alternate del, Dem. Nat. Conv, 64 & 68; chmn, Yonkers Dem. City Cmt, 67- Bus. & Prof. Pos: Various bldg. and construction trades; supvr. maintenance and dir, Munic. Housing Authority, 60; secy, Job Develop. Corp.Yonkers, currently; sales promotion, Co. Asphalt Inc, currently. Mil. Serv: Entered as Pvt, Army, 43, released as T/Sgt, 46, after serv. in Artil. and Transportation Corps, Am. and ETO,43-45; Am. Theatre Ribbon; European Theatre Ribbon; Good Conduct Medal. Mem: Int. Brotherhood of Elec. Workers; Am. Legion; VFW; UN Asn; Elks K. of C.(3° and 4°); Family Serv. Soc; Holy Name Soc; Century Club; Yonkers League Retarded Children; Chippewa Club; N.Yonkers Boys Club; Capuchin Auxiliary; Friendly Sons St. Patrick; C. of C; Track and Field Coun; March of Dimes, Heart Fund. Distinguished Serv. Award Westchester Co; Citation Meritorious Serv, Am. Legion. Rel: Roman Catholic. Mailing Add: 48 Emmett Place, Yonkers, N.Y. 10703.

McSWEAN, ROBERT HORACE D
Chmn, Henry Co. Dem. Exec. Cmt, Ala.
b. Ozark, Ala, 12/4/15; s. Robert Lee McSwean and Octavia Dillard M; m. 12/25/38 to Leslie Holland; c. Robert Lee. Educ: Dale Co. High Sch, Ozark, Ala. Polit. & Govt. Pos: Mayor, Abbeville, Ala, 48-56; chmn, Henry Co. Dem. Exec. Cmt, currently. Bus. & Prof. Pos: Owner-mgr, McSweans Mens Store, 34-69, McSweans Casual Corner, 64-69. Mil. Serv: Entered as Pvt, Army, 42, released as S/Sgt, 46, after serv. in 3520th Ordnance Co, Ryukus Group, Pac. Theatre, 45-46. Mem: C. of C.(pres, 4 years); Lions (past pres); Am. Legion; Nat. Rivers & Harbors Cong; Tri-River Develop. Asn.(pres, 2 years). Man of the Year Award, City of Abbeville, 52. Rel: Baptist. Mailing Add: Briarhill Rd, Abbeville, Ala. 36310.

McSWEEN, DONALD M. D
Tenn. Cmnr. of Conserv.
b. Newport, Tenn, 5/18/15; s. Judge W. D. McSween and Rowena Jones M; m. 1938 to Louise Valentine. Educ: Univ. Tenn; Cumberland Univ. Sch. of Law; Sigma Alpha Epsilon. Polit. & Govt. Pos: Mem, Cmn. Employ. Security, Tenn, 53; v.pres, Interstate Conf. Employ. Security Agencies, 56; Tenn. Cmnr. of Conserv, 63- Mil. Serv: Army Signal Corps, World War II. Mem: Tenn. and Am. Bar Asns; life mem. Int. Asn. Personnel Employ. Security; Am. Legion (State Judge Adv, 46, State Comdr, 47); Mason (32°); Scottish Rite; K.T; Shrine; Elks; 40 et 8. Outstanding Young Man of the Year, Tenn. Jr. C. of C, 46. Rel: Presbyterian. Mailing Add: Carson Springs Rd, Newport, Tenn. 37821. (1967)

McSWEEN, HAROLD BARNETT D
b. Alexandria, La, 7/19/26; s. John Howard McSween and Velma Barnett M; m. 12/21/48 to Sally Foster; c. John Charles, Robert Douglas, Elizabeth and Sally Foster. Educ: La. State Univ, LL.B, 50; Sigma Alpha Epsilon. Polit. Pos: Nominee, Presidential Elector from La, Dem. Party, 64; del, Dem. Nat. Conv, 60. Govt. Pos: U.S. Rep, 8th Dist, La, 59-63; mem, La. State Bd. of Educ, 58 and 57; mem, Rapides Parish Sch. Bd, La, 56 and 55. Bus. & Prof. Pos: Partner, McSween and McSween, Attorneys, 50-; pres, Rapides Savings and Loan Asn, 65- Mil. Serv: Entered as Midshipman, U.S. Maritime Serv, 44, released as Purser, 46, after serv. in Pac. and Atlantic Oceans. Mem: Am. and La. State Bar Asns; Acad. of Polit. Sci; Kiwanis. Rel: Methodist. Legal Res: Grove Lane, Alexandria, La. 71301. Mailing Add: P.O. Box 1908, Alexandria, La. 71301. (1967)

McSWEENEY, JOHN D
b. Wooster, Ohio, 12/19/90; s. John McSweeney and Ada Jane Mullins M; m. 7/9/24 to Abby Conway Schaefer. Educ: Wooster Col, Ph.D, 12; Trinity Col, Dublin, Ireland, 19; Inns of Court, London, Eng, 20; Phi Gamma Delta. Polit. & Govt. Pos: Pres, Wooster City Coun, Ohio, 14-15; mem, Wooster Sch. Bd. and Civil Defense Bd; asst. to Michael D. Salle as Price Stabilizer in charge of Ohio Sale of U.S. Defense Bonds; U.S. Rep, 16th Dist, Ohio, 22-28 & 48-50, Rep-at-lg, 36-38; dir, Pub. Welfare, Ohio, 31-35; del, Dem. Nat. Conv, 68. Mil. Serv: Entered as Pvt, Army, 17, released as Capt, 18, after serv. in France and Belgium; re-entered as Maj, World War II, released as Lt. Col, after serv. in Africa, Sicily and Italy; Citation Gen. Pershing; Legion of Merit; Purple Heart with 2 Clusters; Order of Malta; Medal from Pope Pius XII; Order of St. George; Order of St. Hubert; Italian Red Cross Medal; Commendatore of the Crown of Italy. Publ: Articles on Forest, Ohio Forest Magazine. Mem: Founding mem, Am. Legion; VFW; DAV; Ohio Grange; Izaak Walton League; life mem, Ohio and U.S. Forestry Asns; Wash. Fire & Police Asn; Wayne Co. Bar Asn; Univ. Club of Cleveland; Cong. Club of Wooster Col. Achievement Awards from Wooster Col. and Kent Univ. Rel: Episcopal. Mailing Add: 531 Market, Wooster, Ohio 44691.

McSWEENEY, JOHN MORGAN
U.S. Ambassador to Bulgaria
b. Boston, Mass, 6/9/16; m. to Henrica Moorman; c. Brian and Dennis. Educ: Brown Univ, A.B, 38; Cornell Univ, 46. Polit. & Govt. Pos: Career officer, U.S. Dept. of State For. Serv, 40-44 & 46-; v.consul, Montreal, 40-41; admin. and econ. officer, Lagos, 41-42, Accra, 42-43, Cairo, 43-44, Moscow and Vladivostok, 46-48; officer in charge of Soviet affairs, Off. of E. European Affairs, 48-49; counsr. for polit. affairs, Moscow, 51-53; with Nat. War Col, 53-54; sr. polit. adv, U.S. Mission to UN, 54-55; spec. liaison officer, Comdr-in-chief of Allied Forces, South. Europe, 56-58; dep. dir. and dir, Off. of Soviet Union Affairs, 59-61; dep. chief of mission, Moscow, 61-63; polit. adv. to Comdr-in-chief, Strategic Air Command, 63-64; dep. chief of mission, Brussels, 64-66; U.S. Minister to Bulgaria, 66-67, U.S. Ambassador, 67- Mil. Serv: Navy, 44-46. Mailing Add: U.S. Embassy, Sofia, Bulgaria.

McVANEY, BEATRICE D
Del, Calif. Dem. State Cent. Cmt.
b. Friend, Nebr, 12/7/95; d. James Leo McVaney and Elizabeth Ahern M; single. Educ: Kearney State Col, A.B, 22; Univ. Calif, M.A, 34. Polit. & Govt. Pos: Del, Calif. Dem. State Cent. Cmt, 34-36 & 68-; alternate del, Dem. Nat. Conv, 48. Bus. & Prof. Pos: Teacher, Buffalo Co, Nebr, 13; high sch. teacher, Thedford, 19-21, Farnum, 21-22, Wheatland, Wyo, 22-24 and Lewiston, Mont, 24-29; elem. sch. teacher, Berkeley, Calif, 29-58; parochial sch. teacher, N.Y.C, Wash, D.C. and Oakland and Berkeley, Calif, 58-64. Mem: Nat. Teachers Asn; Am. Fedn. Teachers. Rel: Catholic. Mailing Add: 1679 Addison, Berkeley, Calif. 94703.

McVEIGH, RICHARD LAWRENCE D
Alaska State Rep.
b. Spalding, Nebr, 6/12/33; s. Arthur Stanley McVeigh and Alberta Miles McVeigh Clarke; m. 3/28/59 to Carolyn Best; c. David Lawrence, Katherine Lewis and Steven Lawrence. Educ: Univ. of Alaska, 1 year; Univ. of Notre Dame, B.A, 55; Georgetown Univ Law Sch, LL.B, 62. Polit. & Govt. Pos: Asst. attorney gen, Alaska, 62-63; Alaska asst. dist. attorney, Anchorage, 63; U.S. Attorney for Alaska, 64-68; Alaska State Rep, 69- Bus. & Prof. Pos: Pvt. law practice, 64, 68- Mil. Serv: Entered as 2nd Lt, Air Force, 55, released as 1st Lt, 59, after serv. in Strategic Air Command, 55-59. Mem: Elks; Pioneers of Alaska. Rel: Roman Catholic. Legal Res: 4809 Nottingham Way, Anchorage, Alaska 99503. Mailing Add: 507 E St, Suite 204, Anchorage, Alaska 99501.

McVEY, CAROLINE MARIE D
Mem, State Dem. Cent. Cmt, Calif.
b. Philadelphia, Pa, 9/27/20; d. Sebastian Philip Ziemann and Margaret Stoudt Z; m. 3/9/35 to Leon Steely McVey; c. Robert Leon, Kathryn Carol (Mrs. Henley) and John William. Educ: Univ. Calif, Los Angeles, 43-44; San Diego State Col, 53-54. Polit. & Govt. Pos: Campaign coordinator, James R. Mills for Senate, 66; exec. secy, San Diego Co. Dem. Cent. Cmt, Calif, 67-; mem, State Dem. Cent. Cmt, Calif, 68- Mem: Calif. Press Women; Nat. Press Women; Chula Vista Dem. Club; League Dem. Women; hon. life mem, PTA. Nat. Serv. Award, Camp Fire Girls, Inc. Rel: Roman Catholic. Legal Res: 437 Moss St, Chula Vista, Calif. 92011. Mailing Add: Suite 238, U.S. Grant Hotel, San Diego, Calif. 92101.

McVEY, LAUDER TULLY R
Chmn, Lowndes Co. Rep. Party, Ga.
b. Vancouver, B.C, 6/7/24; s. James Lelin McVey and Belle Hukill Dilg M; m. 11/26/46 to Clara Elizabeth Chason; c. Lauder Tully, Jr. and Scott Douglas. Educ: Fla. State Univ, 2 years; Univ. of Fla, B.I.E, 53. Polit. & Govt. Pos: Chmn, Lowndes Co. Rep. Party, Ga, 68- Bus. & Prof. Pos: Design engr, Food Machinery & Chem. Corp, Lakeland, Fla, 53-55; indust. engr, and asst. supt. of power, Owens-Ill, Valdosta, Ga, 55- Mil. Serv: Entered as Pvt, Army Air Force, 43, released as Cpl, 46, after serv. in Detached Serv, 11th Air Force, Alaska, 43-46. Rel: Baptist. Mailing Add: 2314 N. Toombs St, Valdosta, Ga. 31601.

McVEY, WALTER LEWIS, JR. R
b. Independence, Kans, 2/19/22; s. Walter Lewis McVey and Nona Inge M; 2nd m. 4/3/64 to Velma Graham; c. by 1st m. Walter L, III and David Ayers. Educ: Univ. Kans, A.B, 47, LL.B, 48, J.D, 68. Polit. & Govt. Pos: Kans. State Rep, 49-52; Judge, Independence, Kans, 52-56; Kans. State Sen, 57-61; U.S. Rep, Third Dist, Kans, 61-63; exec. dir, Fulton Co. Rep. Party, Ga, 64-65. Bus. & Prof. Pos: Attorney-at-Law, Independence, Kans, 48-61; consult, Melpar, Inc, 63-64; staff counsel, Ga. Munic. Asn, Atlanta, Ga, 65-66; sr. consult, McVey Consult. Assocs, Atlanta, 66-; faculty mem. polit. sci, Ga. State Col. and DeKalb Col, 68- Mil. Serv: Entered as Pvt, Army Air Force, 43, released as S/Sgt, 46. Publ: A Federal-Aids Manual for Municipalities, Ga. Power Co, 66. Mem: Am, Ga. State and Kans. State Bar Asns; Am. Legion; Elks; pres, Kans. Day Club. Nat. speaker, Assoc. Clubs, Inc; photographer with contributions to various publ. Rel: Methodist. Legal Res: 712 E. Paces Ferry Rd, Atlanta, Ga. 30305. Mailing Add: P.O. Box 18505, Atlanta, Ga. 30326.

McVICKER, ROY HARRISON D
b. Edgewater, Colo, 2/20/24; s. Rev. Roy H. McVicker, Sr; m. to Harriett Runge; c. Bill, Theresa and Lisa. Educ: Denver Univ; Columbia Col; Columbia Law Sch. Polit. Pos: U.S. Rep, Colo, 65-67; Colo. State Sen, 56-64. Govt. Pos: Dir, Bi-Nat. Develop, Agency for Int. Develop, Dept. of State, 67- Bus. & Prof. Pos: Lawyer, Wheat Ridge, Colo, 53- Rel: Methodist. Legal Res: 14405 Foothill Dr, Golden, Colo. 80401. Mailing Add: 4485 Wadsworth Blvd, Wheat Ridge, Colo. 80033.

McWHERTER, NED R. D
Tenn. State Rep.
b. Dresden, Tenn, 10/15/30; s. Harmon R. McWherter and Lucille Smith M; div; c. Mickial R. and Mary Lina Coppee (stepdaughter). Educ: Dresden High Sch, grad. Polit. & Govt. Pos: Tenn. State Rep, 68- Bus. & Prof. Pos: Self employed. Mil. Serv: Entered as Pvt, Army Nat. Guard, 47, released as Maj, 69. Rel: Methodist. Mailing Add: Cedar St, Dresden, Tenn. 38225.

McWHORTER, WILLIAM HUGH D
b. Buckhead, Ga, 7/03/94; s. John Welby McWhorter and Eva Zuber McW; m. 6/06/14 to Edina Lee Fenwick; c. William Hugh, Jr. (deceased), Virginia Lee (Mrs. Freeman), Dorothy Jane (Mrs. Altman). Educ: Oconee Co. Schs. Polit. & Govt. Pos: Ga. State Sen, (43rd dist.) 63-66; (34th dist.), 61-62; Ga. State Rep, 12/45-60. Bus. & Prof. Pos: Printing & Pub. Bus; DeKalb New Era, 22-1/01/64. Mil. Serv: USN prior to WW I, 11-14. Mem: Pres, Ga. Press Asn, 51-52. Rel: Baptist; Deacon, 8 yrs. 1st Baptist Church; Chmn. of Bd, 4 yrs. Mailing Add: Decatur, Ga. 31930. (1967)

McWILLIAMS, JOHN CECIL D
Chmn, La Fayette Co. Dem. Party, Wis.
b. New Diggings, Wis, 1/4/17; s. Michael James McWilliams and Emma Jane Sullivan M; m. 11/7/42 to Mary Eileen Gille; c. John Michael, Linda K, Daniel P, Timothy G, Vickie L. and Julie Ann. Educ: New Diggings High Sch, grad, 34. Polit. & Govt. Pos: Chmn, New Diggings Town Dem. Party, Wis, 55-67; mem, Bd. La Fayette Co, 55-; various cmts. such as agr, fair bd, bonds and salaries, health, ment. health, welfare and chmn. bldg. cmt, Co. Nursing Home, 62; pres, La Fayette Co. Fair Bd; pres, Wis Asn. Fairs, 67-68. Bus. & Prof. Pos: Mem, Civilian Conserv. Corps, 34-35. Mem: F.H.A. (committeeman); K. of C. (Past Grand Knight). Rel: Catholic. Mailing Add: Route 1, Shullsburg, Wis. 53586.

McWILLIAMS, WILLIAM JAMES D
Chmn, Anne Arundel Co. Dem. Cmt, Md.
b. Hudson, N.Y, 2/28/04; s. William F. McWilliams and Mary C. Ryan M; m. 10/5/40 to Nancy Butler Leighton; c. Ann Garrett, William James, John Michael, Mary Howard, Hugh Leighton, Carla Wilcox, Patricia Foster, Stephen, Francis and Bernard II. Educ: Loyola Col, A.B, 26, Univ. of Md, LL.B, 30; Phi Kappa Sigma. Polit. & Govt. Pos: City counsr, Annapolis, Md, 35-37; chmn, Selective Serv. Bd, 42-47; secy. of state, Md, 43-45; assoc. judge, Fifth Judicial Circuit, Md, 46-48; mem, Standing Cmt. on Rules of Practice and Procedure, Court of Appeals, 45-61; mem, Case Cmn, 49; mem, Miles Cmn, 53; mem, Joint Cmn. on Potomac River, 58; chmn, Anne Arundel Co. Dem. Cmt, currently; assoc. judge, Court of Appeals, Md, 65- Bus. & Prof. Pos: Sr. partner, McWilliams, Evans & Melvin, 48-65; dir, Chesapeake & Potomac Tel. Co. of Md, 58-68; pres, Anne Arundel Gen. Hosp. Mil. Serv: Sgt, 104th Obs. Squadron, 1st Inv, Md. Nat. Guard, 24-27; Capt, 110th F.A, Md. Nat. Guard, 27-33; 58th Brigade Staff, 33-35. Publ: Chap. and Code of the City of Annapolis, 35. Mem: Am. and Anne Arundel Co. Bar Asns; past pres, Md. Bar Asn; Am. Judicature Soc; Am. Col. Trial Lawyers; Md. Hist. Soc; South. Md. Soc; Hamilton St, Rule Day Round Table, Baltimore; Annapolis Yacht and New Providence Clubs. Rel: Catholic. Legal Res: 61 Franklin St, Annapolis, Md. 21401. Mailing Add: 212 Duke of Gloucester St, Annapolis, Md. 21401.

MACY, JOHN WILLIAMS, JR. D
b. Chicago, Ill, 4/6/17; s. John Williams Macy and Juliette Shaw M; m. 2/12/44 to Joyce Hagen; c. Thomas L, Mary D, Susan B. and Richard H. Educ: Wesleyan Univ, B.A, 38; Am. Univ, 38-39; Phi Beta Kappa. Hon. LL.D, Cornell Col, 63, Colgate Univ, 65, Allegheny Col, 65, East. Ky. Co, 66, Dartmouth Col, 66, Univ. of Del, 67, Wesleyan Univ, 67, Ind. State Univ, 68, Ithaca Col, 69 and St. John's Univ, 69. Polit. & Govt. Pos: Asst. dir, Civilian Personnel, War Dept, Wash, D.C, 40-43 & 46-47; dir. of personnel and orgn, Santa Fe Opers. Off, Atomic Energy Cmn, Los Alamos, N.Mex, 47-51; spec. asst. to Under Secy. of Army, Wash, D.C, 51-53; exec. dir, U.S. Civil Serv. Cmn, 53-58, chmn, 61-69. Bus. & Prof. Pos: Exec. v.pres, Wesleyan Univ, 58-61; pres, Corp. for Pub. Broadcasting, Wash, D.C, 69- Mil. Serv: Entered as Pvt, Air Force, 43, released as Capt, 47, after serv. in U.S. and Pac. Theaters. Mem: Am. Soc. for Pub. Admin; Soc. for Adv. of Mgt; Pub. Personnel Asn; Soc. for Personnel Admin. Presidential Medal of Freedom, 69. Rel: Episcopal. Legal Res: 291 Washington Terr, Middletown, Conn. 06457. Mailing Add: 1127 Langley Lane, McLean, Va. 22101.

MACY, RICHARD JAMES D
b. Saranac Lake, N.Y, 6/2/30; s. James Edward Macy and Gertrude Tredeau M; m. 9/1/56 to Emily Ann Sedlecek; c. Anne Louise, Patricia Lynn and Mark Edward. Educ: Univ. Wyo, B.S, 55, J.D, 58; Sigma Chi. Polit. & Govt. Pos: City attorney, Sundance, Wyo, 62-64, Hulett, 62-; chmn, Crook Co. Dem. Cent. Cmt, 64-67; chmn, Sch. Dist. 1, Sundance, 66-; chmn, Crook Co. Recreation Bd, 66- Bus. & Prof. Pos: Cmnr, Wyo. Bar Asn, 64-67. Mil. Serv: Entered as A/C, Navy, 50, released as Yeoman 2/C, 54, after serv. in Pac. Amphibious Fleet, Korean Theater; Korean Ribbons with six battle stars. Mem: Am. Bar Asn; trustee, Wyo. Alumni Asn; Elks; Am. Legion; Farm Bur. Rel: Catholic. Mailing Add: Box 515, Sundance, Wyo. 82729.

MADDEN, HARRY C. D
b. Union City, Iowa, 12/4/09; s. Mr. and Mrs. Charles Madden; m. 3/10/28 to Helen Short; c. Dale William; grandchildren, Richard Dale and Robert Allen. Educ: Kent High Sch, 1927. Polit. Pos: Iowa State Rep, 66; Rural Sch. Bd, Union City. Bus. & Prof. Pos: Farming and Livestock Feeding. Mem: Masons, Past Master since 1955. Rel: Christian Church. Mailing Add: R.F.D, Kent, Iowa 50850. (1967)

MADDEN, JOHN THOMAS D
b. Glen Dale, W.Va, 7/13/32; s. Francis C. Madden and Elizabeth Bowen M; m. 7/11/53 to Donna Ann Jones; c. John Thomas, Ronald Craig, Helen Eliza-

beth and Patrick Brian. Educ: Lafayette Col, A.B; W.Va. Univ. Col. of Law, LL.B; Delta Tau Delta. Polit. & Govt. Pos: W.Va. State Del, 64-66; city attorney, Glen Dale and McMechen. Bus. & Prof. Pos: Lawyer. Mem: Moose; Elks; pres, Upper Ohio Valley G.S. Coun, Inc; former pres, Marshall Co. Jaycees. Rel: Episcopal. Mailing Add: Moundsville, W.Va. 26041.

MADDEN, MARY ANN D
Chmn, Wahkiakum Co. Dem. Party, Wash.
b. Minneapolis, Minn, 2/16/17; d. Leon Pilon, Jr. (deceased) and Maria Fisette P; m. 7/3/36 to Howard LaMonte Madden; c. Howard Leon, Mary Catherine (Mrs. Harper), Elizabeth Louise (Mrs. Johnson), Margaret Diane (Mrs. Alston), Penelope Ann (Mrs. Weathers) and Patrick E. Educ: St. Margaret's Acad, Minneapolis, Minn. Polit. & Govt. Pos: Chmn, Wahkiakum Co. Dem. Party, Wash, 60- Mem: Skamokawa Mentor Club, Wash. State Fedn. of Womens Clubs. Rel: Catholic; Teacher, Fourth Grade, Confraternity of Christian Doctrine. Mailing Add: Box 162, Skamokawa, Wash. 98647. (1967)

MADDEN, RAY J. D
U.S. Rep, Ind.
b. Waseca, Minn. Educ: Creighton Univ, LL.B. Polit. & Govt. Pos: Munic. judge, Omaha, Nebr; city comptroller, Gary, Ind, 35-38; treas, Lake Co, 38-42; U.S. Rep, Ind, currently; del, Dem. Nat. Conv, 68. Bus. & Prof. Pos: Attorney. Mil. Serv: World War I. Mem: Am. Legion. Legal Res: Gary, Ind. Mailing Add: 100 Maryland Ave. N.E, Washington, D.C. 20002.

MADDEN, ROBERT BRUCE D
Kans. State Rep.
b. Norfolk, Va, 11/22/44; s. Bruce B. Madden and Helen Bradshaw M; single. Educ: Ventura Jr. Col, 63-64; Rockhurst Col, 64-65. Polit. & Govt. Pos: Precinct committeeman, Dem. Party, Kans, 66-; Kans. State Rep, 85th Dist, 67- Bus. & Prof. Pos: Restaurant Bus. Owner. Mil. Serv: Entered as Pvt, Army, 67, serv. in 2/503rd ABN Inf, 173rd Airborne, Bde, Vietnam; Bronze Star; Air Medal; Vietnamese Serv. Medal; Vietnam Campaign Ribbon; Nat. Defense Medal. Mem: VFW; Am. Legion; Elks. Rel: Catholic. Legal Res: 2602 S. Fern, Wichita, Kans. 67217. Mailing Add: 1st Lt. Robert B. Madden 05355812, D-Co 2/503rd (ABN) Inf, 173rd Airborne Bde, Vietnam, APO San Francisco 96250.

MADDOX, CHARLES M. R
Educ: Purdue Univ; Delta Tau Delta. Polit. & Govt. Pos: Ind. State Sen, 59-66, previously 47-57; state hwy. cmn, 57-58; Rep. Caucus chmn, 65. Bus. & Prof. Pos: Farmer; dir, Lafayette Nat. Bank; dir, Remington Ins. Co; pres, Benton Cty. Seed Co. Mil. Serv: WWII. Mem: Scottish Rite; Am. Legion; Farm Bus; Purdue Univ. Agr. Alumni. Rel: M.E. Church. Mailing Add: R.R. 1, Otterbein, Ind. 47970. (1967)

MADDOX, HENRY D
Ky. State Rep.
b. 1906. Educ: Murray State Col. Polit. & Govt. Pos: Ky. State Rep, 62- Bus. & Prof. Pos: Farmer, currently. Mem: Mason; dir, Farmers Bank, Rel: Christian Church; Deacon. Mailing Add: Route 4, Hickman, Ky. 42050. (1967)

MADDOX, LESTER G. D
Gov, Ga.
b. Atlanta, Ga, 9/30/15; s. Dean G. Maddox and Flonnie M; m. 1936 to Virginia Cox; c. Linda, Lester, Jr, Virginia Louise and Larry. Educ: Col. equivalent correspondence course. Polit. & Govt. Pos: Gov. of Ga, 67- Bus. & Prof. Pos: Real estate, grocery, restaurant, furniture store. Mem: Mason; Moose; Travelers' Protective Asn; JOUAM; Buckhead 50 Club; hon. mem, Ga. Sheriffs' Asn, Peace Officers' Asn. and Justices of Peace and Constables' Asn; pres, Westgate Merchants Asn. Rel: Baptist. Mailing Add: 391 W. Paces Ferry Rd, N.W, Atlanta, Ga. 30305.

MADDUX, DON STEWART D
Ohio State Rep.
b. Lancaster, Fairfield Co, Ohio, 3/23/40; s. Robert Wilson Maddux and Donna L. Potter M; single. Educ: Wittenburg Univ, B.S. in Educ, 62; Ohio North. Law Sch, 65-66; Ohio State Univ. Grad. Sch, currently; Varsity W Club, Wittenburg Univ, won two varsity letters in track, in wrestling and in diving, three varsity letters in football. Polit. & Govt. Pos: Ohio State Rep, 25th Dist, 69- Bus. & Prof. Pos: Lifeguard, Miller Pool, Lancaster, Ohio, 56-59, mgr, 60; asst. mgr. and swimming and diving coach, Tiki Swim Club, 61; lifeguard, Glen Echo Swim Club, Glen Echo, Md, 62; mem. staff, YMCA, Springfield, Ohio, 62; teacher of health and Am. hist. and softball coach, Alice Deal Jr. High Sch, Wash, D.C, 62-65 & 66; with Recreation Dept, Columbus, Ohio, 66; teacher of Am. hist, diving coach and jr. class adv, Lancaster High Sch, Lancaster, Ohio, 67- Mem: Lions; Jaycees. Rel: Presbyterian. Mailing Add: 111 W. Mulberry St, Lancaster, Ohio 43130.

MADDUX, JOHN JARED D
b. Buffalo Valley, Tenn, 7/20/11; s. Solon Maddux and Daisy Jared M; m. 1935 to Mary Virginia Lane M; c. three. Educ: Tenn. Tech, B.S, 34; E. Tenn. Law Sch, LL.B, 39; grad. work toward Master's degree, Northwest. U. Polit. & Gov. Pos: Tenn. State Sen, 63-67; Speaker of Sen. and Lt. Gov, 53, 55, 57; Comptroller of Treas, 45-48; Asst. Chief Clerk, and Chief Clerk, Tenn. State House of Reps, 43-44. Mil. Serv: Navy. Mem: Am. Legion, Past Cmdr, Dept. of Tenn, 58; Past Pres, Tenn. Jaycees; Lions; 40 et 8; Masons; Shrine; U.S. and Tenn. Bar Asns. Rel: Methodist. Mailing Add: 201 Whitson Bldg, Cookeville, Tenn. 38501. (1967)

MADESON, MARVIN LOUIS D
b. New York, N.Y, 7/8/25; s. Morris Madeson and Ann Levine M; m. 8/19/49 to Phyllis Katherine Barnett; c. Marianne, Frances and Julia. Educ: Brooklyn Col, B.A, 47; N.Y. Univ. Sch. of Law, J.D. cum laude, 50; Phi Delta Phi. Polit. & Govt. Pos: Del, Dem. Nat. Conv, 68; chmn, McCarthy for Pres. Campaign, Mo, 68; committeeman, Hadley Twp. Dem. Club, St. Louis Co, 68-; chmn, New Dem. Coalition of Metropolitan St. Louis, 68- Bus. & Prof. Pos: Attorney, Office of Price Stabilization, Wash, D.C, 51-53; Supvr. sales, First Investors Corp, N.Y.C, 53-56; Divisional Dir, Heritage Securities, 56-58; v.pres, Empire Planning Corp, 58-60; treas, ITT Aetna Corp, St. Louis, Mo, 60-68. Mil. Serv: Entered as Pvt, Air Force, 43, released as Sgt, 46, after serv. in Army Airways Communications Syst, S.Atlantic Theatre, 44-46; Good Conduct Medal; S.Atlantic Theatre Ribbon. Mem: N.Y. State and District of Columbia Bar Asns; Univ. City Civic Asn. (former chmn); Univ. City Plan Cmn.(former v.chmn). Rel: Jewish. Mailing Add: 751 Radcliffe Ave, St. Louis, Mo. 63130.

MADIGAN, ALBERT E. R
b. Burlington, Pa; s. George A. Madigan and Emma Campbell M; m. to Ada Allen; c. 2 daughters, 1 son. Polit. & Govt. Pos: Pa. State Sen, 52-67; Pa. State Rep, 42-52. Bus. & Prof. Pos: Owns and operates dairy farm. Mem: Past master, Bradford Co. Pomona Grange; past mem, exec. and legis. coms. of Pa. State Grange; Former mem, Bradford Co. Sch. Bd; Union Lodge F&AM; pres, Pa. State Asn. of Artificial Breeding Coops, N.E. Pa. Artificial Breeding Coops; exec. comm, State Coun. of Farm Orgs; Trustee, Pa. State Univ. Mailing Add: R.D. 3, Towanda, Pa. 18848. (1967)

MADISON, EDWARD P. R
Chmn, Kankakee Co. Rep. Cent. Cmt, Ill.
b. Clifton, Ill, 5/6/03; s. Knute P. Madison and Lena Rasmussen M; m. 8/11/24 to Irene Des Lauriers; c. Joyce Marie. Educ: Kankakee High Sch. Polit. & Govt. Pos: City collector, Kankakee, Ill, 34-40, mayor, 53-61; mem, secy. and pres, Bd. Dirs, Kankakee Pub. Schs, 36-53; coroner, Kankakee Co, 40-48; chmn, Kankakee Co. Rep. Cent. Cmt, currently. Mem: Kankakee Co. Real Estate Asn; Life Underwriters Asn; Rotary; Elks; v.pres, Rainbow Coun, Boy Scouts; United Travelers Asn; exec. cmt, Rep. Co. Chmn. Asn, Ill. Rel: Methodist. Legal Res: 1005 S. Lincoln Ave, Kankakee, Ill. 60901. Mailing Add: 401 Volkmann Bldg, Kankakee, Ill. 60901.

MADSEN, ALFRED JAMES D
b. Provo, Utah, 12/24/05; s. Charles Alfred Madsen and Roxie Ann Garner M; m. 6/21/31 to Verda Pauline Carter; c. Preston Alfred, Mary Moana, Pauline, Roxie Ann and Katheryn. Educ: Univ. Ill, spec. exten. training; Student Body Pres. Polit. & Govt. Pos: Utah State Rep. until 67; mem, Jr. Dem. Orgn. and Alpine Sch. Bd. Bus. & Prof. Pos: Dir, Soil Conserv. Serv; mem, Utah Lake Water Cmn. Mem: Pres, Utah Lake Farmers Asn; pres. and secy, Utah Co. Farm Bureau. Selected as Farmer of the Year, 65, FHA. Rel: Latter-day Saint. Mailing Add: R.F.D. 1, Box 352, Provo, Utah 84601. (1967)

MADSEN, PETER EDGAR R
Wyo. State Sen.
b. Alta, Iowa, 9/23/05; s. Christian Madsen and Christina Peterson M; m. 6/1/32 to Alice Fraser; c. Barbara (Mrs. Rogers) and Karen. Educ: Colo. State Univ, D.V.M, 31; Alpha Tau Omega. Polit. & Govt. Pos: Wyo. State Rep, 57-61; Wyo. State Sen, 61-, v.pres, Wyo. State Senate, 66-69, Majority Floor Leader, 69- Bus. & Prof. Pos: Pres, Whitney Trust, 65- Mil. Serv: Entered as 1st Lt, Army, 42, released as Maj, 46, after serv. in Material Command with Air Corps. Mem: Am. Vet. Med. Asn; Wyo. Vet. Med. Asn. (pres, 49); bd. dirs, Wyo. Taxpayers Asn, 68-; Mason; Shrine; Royal Order of Jesters; Rotary; Am. Legion; Farm Bur. College football. Rel: First Baptist. Mailing Add: 1760 Martin Ave, Sheridan, Wyo. 82801.

MADURO, JOHN LAWRENCE D
Pres, V.I. Legis.
b. St. Thomas, V.I, 7/1/21; s. Joseph L. Maduro and Azalia Sille M; m. 8/19/49 to Claudia W. Huyghue; c. Juanito, Winthrop and Janice Mabel. Educ: Hampton Inst, 41-43; N.Y. Univ, B.S, 48; Nat. Univ. Sch. Law, LL.B, 54. Polit. & Govt. Pos: Sen, V.I. Legis, 58-, pres, 69-; del, Dem. Nat. Conv, 68; Bus. & Prof. Pos: Attorney-at-Law, Birch, Maduro, PeJangh & Parrelly, 55- Mil. Serv: Entered as Pvt, Army, 43, released as M/Sgt, 46, after serv. in 13th Hu Pon Br, N. Africa, Italy, France and Germany, 43-46; Good Conduct Medals; Theatre Ribbons. Mem: V.I, Supreme Court and Am. Bar Asns; Am. Legion. Rel: Roman Catholic. Mailing Add: Prindcesse Gach 25, St. Thomas, V.I. 00801.

MAESTAS, CIRILIO DANIEL D
b. 1934. Educ: A.B; 42 hours grad. work at N.Mex. Highlands Univ. Polit. & Govt. Pos: N.Mex. State Sen, 61-66; Cty. clerk, Mora Cty. Bus. & Prof. Pos: Elem. teacher. Mil. Serv: Army, two years, Korea and Japan. Mem: Am. Legion; VFW; NMEA. Rel: Presbyterian. Mailing Add: P.O. Box 37, Holman, N.Mex. 87723. (1967)

MAGAW, ELDEN SAMUEL D
b. Downs, Kans, 1/24/06; s. James Willis Magaw and Ella Uglow M; m. 6/29/33 to Mildred Holloway. Educ: Kans. State Univ, 24-27; Univ. of Okla, A.B, 28 and LL.B, 31; Georgetown Univ, S.J.D, 39; Acacia; Phi Alpha Delta; Supreme Justice, 64-66. Polit. & Govt. Pos: Dem. cand. for Burgess of Lansdowne, Pa, 49; Dem. cand. for Pa. State Sen. from Delaware Co, 60; solicitor to co. controller, Delaware Co, 61; alternate del-at-lg, Dem. Nat. Conv, 64. Bus. & Prof. Pos: Private practice of law, Oklahoma City, Okla, 31-33; prof. law, Temple Univ, 33-, asst. dean, 47-; vis. prof, N.Y. Univ. Law Sch, 58. Mem: Am, Pa, Delaware Co. and Okla. Bar Asns; pres, Kiwanis Club of Phila, 56; Benjamin Franklin Consistory, Phila; past pres, High Twelve Club of Phila; Phila. Art Alliance; asst. secy, Goodwill Industs. of Phila. and Vicinity, 68-; v.chmn, Bd. of Trustees, Methodist Home for the Aged in Phila, 67- Rel: Methodist. Mailing Add: 92 E. Greenwood Ave, Lansdowne, Pa. 19050.

MAGEE, DOUGLAS McARTHUR R
b. Magee, Miss, 1/22/42; s. Walter Whaley Magee and Eva Ainsworth M; m. 11/26/64 to Jan Walker; c. Deborah. Educ: Univ. South. Miss, B.S. eng, 63; Univ. Miss. Sch. Law, 63-65, J.D, 67; George Wash. Sch. Law, 65-66; pres, Senior Class, Univ. South. Miss, 63 & pres, Freshman Law Class, 64; Scabbard & Blade; Omicron Delta Kappa; Phi Kappa Tau. Polit. Pos: Admin. asst. to U.S. Rep. Prentiss Walker, 4th Dist, Miss, 65-66; campaign mgr, Prentiss Walker, 64; chmn, Univ. Miss. Young Rep, 63. Mil. Serv: Capt, Judge Adv. Gen. C, U.S.A, 67- Mem: Phi Delta Phi. Rel: Baptist. Legal Res: Mize, Miss. 39116. Mailing Add: 2334 Sumac Dr, Augusta, Ga. 30906.

MAGEE, ROBERT R
b. Oak Park, Ill, 5/19/12; s. Delbert Elmer Magee and Mathilda Parnell M; m. 3/25/38 to Mary Jane Branstrom; c. Barbara (Mrs. Kemble), Susan and

James R. Educ: Carleton Col, B.A; Delian Soc; C Club. Polit. & Govt. Pos: Mem, War Rationing Bd, Newaygo Co, Mich, 40-41; co. del. chmn, Mich. Rep. Conv, 62, 64, 66 & 68; chmn, Newaygo Co. Rep. Party, 62-68; founding dir, Off. of Econ. Opportunity, Newaygo Co, 66-68. Bus. & Prof. Pos: Ford Mercury dealer, Magee Motor Sales, Fremont, Mich, 37-64, v.pres, 48; pres, Fremont Indust. Develop. Corp, 63-66; dir, Old State Bank, 64-; pres, Fremont Found, 67- Mil. Serv: Entered as 1st Lt, Army, 42, released as Capt, 45, after serv. in Ord. Div, U.S. Mem: Rotary; Ramshorn Country Club; pres, J. Andrew and Mattie A. Gerber Mem. Fund, 67- Rel: Protestant. Legal Res: 338 E. Main St, Fremont, Mich. 49412. Mailing Add: Box 230, Fremont, Mich. 49412.

MAGERS, WILLIAM L. R
Mayor, Cadiz, Ohio
b. Cambridge, Ohio, 10/13/24; s. Harry M. Magers and Rose M. Tigue M; m. 8/22/46 to Wanda E. Paden; c. Jeffrey W, Jody L. and Jason L. Polit. & Govt. Pos: Pres, Harrison Co. Law Enforcement Officers Orgn, Ohio, 58-59; mem, Harrison Co. Rep. Cent. Cmt, 58-, chmn, 62-; chmn, Harrison Co. Rep. Exec. Cmt, 62-; coun. mem, Cadiz, 62-64, mayor, 64-; alternate del, Rep. Nat. Conv, 64; chmn, Harrison Co. Planning Cmt. and Harrison Commun. Health Center, 64- Mil. Serv: Entered as Pvt, Army, 43, released as Sgt, 45, after serv. in Hq. Co, 324 Inf, 44th Div, ETO, 44-45; Purple Heart; Bronze Star; Combat Inf. Medal; ETO Ribbon with Three Battle Stars; Good Conduct Medal. Mem: F&AM, Cambridge; AASR (32°); Am. Legion, Cadiz. Rel: Methodist. Legal Res: 408 Park Ave, Cadiz, Ohio 43907. Mailing Add: P.O. Box 72, Cadiz, Ohio 43907.

MAGGARD, JACK SAMUEL D
Chmn, Leslie Co. Dem. Exec. Cmt, Ky.
b. Hyden, Ky, 7/9/32; s. Claude Maggard and Evelyn Morgan M; m. 12/24/59 to Eva Caldwell; c. Roderick Claude, Bige Colin, Jack Samuel, II and Michele. Educ: Univ. Ky, A.B, 53; Cmt. of 240. Polit. & Govt. Pos: Co. campaign chmn, Kennedy-Johnson, 60, Breathitt for Gov, 63, Johnson-Humphrey, 64; del, Ky. Dem. State Conv, 60, chmn. co. del, 64 & 68; mem, Leslie Co. Bd. Elec. Cmnrs, Ky, 60-63; chmn, Leslie Co. Dem. Exec. Cmt, Ky, 60-; campaign chmn, Humphrey-Muskie, 68. Bus. & Prof. Pos: Teacher-coach, Leslie Co. Schs, 53-61; dir. pupil personnel, 61-63, and vis. teacher, 63-; guid. counsr, Leslie Co. Adult Educ, 65-; partner, Maggards Dept. Store, Hyden, Ky, 65-; ed. asst. Leslie Co. Independent, 69- Mil. Serv: Entered as Pvt, Army, 55, released as Specialist in Communications, 57, after serv. in Hq. Third Reconnaissance Bn, Third Inf. Div, U.S. Mem: Leslie Co, Upper Ky. River, Ky. and Nat. Educ. Asns; Univ. Ky. Alumni Asn. Rel: Presbyterian. Mailing Add: Hyden, Ky. 41749.

MAGGIACOMO, EDWARD LOUIS D
R.I. State Rep.
b. Providence, R.I, 7/2/36; s. Giuseppe Maggiacomo and Giulia Cicerone M; m. 6/24/61 to Ingeborg Leers; c. Susanne E, Edward L, Jr, Michael A. and Stephen F. Educ: Providence Col, B.S, 58; Georgetown Univ. of Law, LL.B, 64. Polit. & Govt. Pos: Mem, Personnel Appeals Bd, Cranston, R.I, 64-65; town solicitor, Smithfield, 66; trustee, Cranston Pub. Libr, 67-; R.I. State Rep, Dist. 24, 67- Mil. Serv: Entered as 2nd Lt, Army, 59, released as 1st Lt, 61, after serv. in Mil. Intel, ETO. Mem. R.I. Bar Asn. Rel: Catholic. Legal Res: 32 Belcrest Rd, Cranston, R.I. 02920. Mailing Add: 1560 Cranston St. Cranston, R.I. 02920.

MAGILL, JOE EDWARD R
b. Wheat, Tenn, 7/3/29; s. Charles Robert Magill and Cynthia Ann Freels M; m. 3/19/54 to Mary Elizabeth Farmer; c. Elizabeth Ann, Michael Edward and Angela Renee. Educ: Carson Newman Col, B.A; Univ. of Tenn, LL.B; Alpha Psi Omega. Polit. & Govt. Pos: Chmn, Anderson Co. Rep. Party, Tenn, 63-66; judge, Anderson Co, 66. Mem: Anderson Co. Bar Asn, 56. Rel: Baptist. Mailing Add: Route 5, Clinton, Tenn. 37716.

MAGIN, WILBUR WRIGHT D
b. Taylorsville, Md, 6/25/09; s. George Washington Magin and Florence Wright M; m. 3/31/38 to Gladys Marian Snead. Polit. & Govt. Pos: Md. State Del, 59-66; committing magistrate, Carroll Co, 46-50. Bus. & Prof. Pos: Vice-pres. and dir, Woodbine Nat. Bank, 58-66; field agt, Modern Woodmen of Am, Inc, 57-66; owned and operated gen. store, 45-58. Mem: Mason, Shrine; Farm Bureau. Rel: Methodist. Mailing Add: Route 6, Westminster, Md. 21157. (1967)

MAGNANI, MAURO Conservative, N.Y.
Chmn, Kings Co. Conservative, N.Y.
b. Phila, Pa, 1/3/29; s. Orazio Magnani and Nella Del Debbio M; m. 11/28/53 to Ernesta Merlini; c. Stephen, Lisa and Andrew. Educ: N.Y. Univ, 47-49; Brooklyn Col, 49-50; N.Y.C. Commun. Col, A.A. in Appl. Sci, 65. Polit. & Govt. Pos: Chmn, Kings Co. Conservative, N.Y, currently. Mil. Serv: Entered as Pvt, Army, 51, released as Cpl, 53, after serv. in 23rd Ord. Corps, Trust Command, Trieste, Italy, 52-53. Mem: Dyker Heights Civic Asn; Ital-Am. Brotherhood. Rel: Roman Catholic. Mailing Add: 243 95th St, Brooklyn, N.Y. 11209. (1967)

MAGNESS, JAMES M. D
Dem. Nat. Committeeman, S.Dak.
b. Ute, Iowa, 6/27/90; m. to Mabel Magness; c. One. Educ: High sch. Polit. & Govt. Pos: S.Dak. State Sen, 33; chmn, S.Dak. State Dem. Party, 56-62; Dem. nat. committeeman, S.Dak, 66-; del, Dem. Nat. Conv, 68. Bus. & Prof. Pos: Livestock auctioneer. Mem: Civic and Commerce; Elks; livestock orgn. Rel: Presbyterian. Mailing Add: 303 Fifth St, Miller, S.Dak. 57362. (1967)

MAGNUSON, DONALD HAMMER D
b. Freeman, Wash, 3/7/11; s. Ellis William Magnuson and Ida Hammer M; div; c. Craig, Terry Lynn (Mrs. Cairns), Joel Ellis, Mary Elizabeth and Erik George. Educ: Spokane Univ, 26-28; Univ. Wash, A.B, 31; Theta Xi. Polit. & Govt. Pos: U.S. Rep, Wash, 83rd-87th Cong; spec. asst, U.S. Dept. Interior, 63-69, consult, 69- Bus. & Prof. Pos: Reporter, Daily Olympian, Olympia, Wash, 34-41 and Seattle Times, 41-52. Mem: Am. Newspaper Guild. Rel: Presbyterian. Legal Res: Box 11, Dockton, Wash. 98018. Mailing Add: 101 N. Carolina Ave. S.E, Washington, D.C. 20003.

MAGNUSON, PAUL A. R
Chmn, Dakota Co. Rep. Party, Minn.
b. Carthage, S.Dak, 2/9/37; s. Arthur Magnuson and Emma Elleda Paulson M; m. 12/21/59 to Sharon Schultz; c. Kevin Matthew and Kara Elizabeth. Educ: Gustavus Adolphus Col, B.A, 1959; William Mitchell Col. of Law, LL.B, 63; Alpha Kappa Psi; Phi Alpha; Delta Theta Phi. Polit. & Govt. Pos: Precinct chmn, Rep. Party, South St. Paul, Minn, 65; chmn, Dakota Co. Young Rep. League, 66; chmn, First Dist. Young Rep. League, 66; assoc. campaign mgr, LeVander for Gov, 66; Nat. committeeman, Minn. Young Rep. League, 67, state chmn, 67; chmn, Dakota Co. Rep. Party, 67- Bus. & Prof. Pos: Pres, Gustavus Adolphus Col. Alumni Bd, 64- Mem: Am, Minn. State and Dakota Co. Bar Asns; Am. Judicature Asn; First Judicial Dist. Bar Asn; Am. Trial Lawyers Asn; South St. Paul Kiwanis Club (dir, 66-); Jaycees; C. of C. Rel: Lutheran. Mailing Add: 521 Napolean Circle, South St. Paul, Minn. 55075.

MAGNUSON, WARREN G. D
U.S. Sen, Wash.
b. Moorhead, Minn, 4/12/05; s. William G. Magnuson and Emma Carolina Anderson M; m. 10/4/64 to Jermaine Elliott Peralta. Educ: Univ. Wash, LL.B, 29; Gonzaga Univ, LL.D, 61; Theta Chi; Burning Tree. Polit. & Govt. Pos: Prosecuting Attorney, King Co, Wash, 31-33; Wash. State Rep, 33-34; U.S. Rep, Wash, 36-44; U.S. Sen, Wash, 44-; del, Dem. Nat. Conv, 68. Mil. Serv: Lt. Comdr, Navy, 40-41, serv. in Pac; Lt. Comdr, Naval Res. Mem: Adv. Cmt, Who's Who in Am. Polit, 67 & 69; Elks; Eagles; Am. Legion; VFW; Amvets; Sons of Norway; Wash. Athletic Club; City Club. Rel: Lutheran. Legal Res: 5103 Columbia Dr, Seattle, Wash. 98104. Mailing Add: 127 Senate Office Bldg, Washington, D.C. 20510.

MAGNUSSON, CYRUS E. Independent
b. Minneapolis, Minn, 10/2/04; s. Martin Magnusson and Elnora Thompson M; m. 8/30/30 to Mabel Irene Egeberg; c. Robert, Charles, John and Paul. Educ: Univ. Minn, B.S. and M.A. Polit. & Govt. Pos: Mayor, Two Harbors, Minn, 49-55; exec. secy. to Gov. Orville L. Freeman, 55-59; State Ins. Cmnr, Minn, 59-67. Bus. & Prof. Pos: Teacher and coach, Two Harbors High Sch, Minn, 30-55; chmn. of bd, Commun. Health Center, Two Harbors, 44-51. Mem: Pres, State Coaches Asn, 48-49; Minn. Fedn. of Teachers (v.pres, 52-55); Nat. Asn. of Ins. Cmnr.(pres, 64-65); Mason; Moose. Rel: Lutheran. Mailing Add: 7100 Chicago Ave, Minneapolis, Minn. 55423.

MAGNUSSON, KINGDON B. R
Chmn, Ninth Rep. Legis. Dist, N.Dak.
b. Wolford, N.Dak, 5/7/05; s. Walter L. Magnusson and Hannah Burger M; m. 12/28/41 to Olga Lillion Erickson; c. Keith C. and James R. Educ: Univ. N.Dak, B.S. in commerce, 27. Polit. & Govt. Pos: Mayor, Rolette, N.Dak, 66-; chmn, Ninth Rep. Legis. Dist, 67-; co. cmnr, Rolette Co, 69- Bus. & Prof. Pos: Auditor, Red Owl Stores, Inc, Minneapolis, 29-42, store mgr, Rolla, N.Dak, 45-47; self-employed, Rolette, 47-66; rep, Hamilton Mgt. Co, Denver, Colo, 66- Mil. Serv: Entered as Pvt, Army, 42, released as Technician-5, 45, after serv. in 163rd Engr. Combat Bn, ETO, 43-45. Mem: Elks; Am. Legion; VFW. Rel: Presbyterian. Mailing Add: Rolette, N.Dak. 58366.

MAGUIRE, JOHN N. D
b. Wilmington, Del, 9/19/14; married. Educ: Univ. of Va; Univ. of Md, LL.B, 40. Polit. & Govt. Pos: Md. State Del, 55-67; chmn, Baltimore Co. Dem. State Cent. Cmt, 62-63; Trial Magistrates' Cmn, 59; Ice Milk Cmn; Govs. Cmn. to Study Sentencing in Criminal Cases; Govs. Cmn. to Study Reapportionment of the Gen. Assembly; Banking Laws Study Cmn; Trial Magistrate, Essex, 49-55. Mil. Serv: Counterintelligence Corps, 42-45. Mem: Bd. of dirs. and former pres, Essex-Middle River C. of C; Md. and Baltimore Co. Bar Asns; Trial Magistrates' Asn; Mil. Intel. Asn; Nat. Intel. Asn; Moose; former pres, Middle River Rotary Club; K. of C; Cath. War Vets; Univ. of Md. Alumni Asn; Univ. of Va. Alumni Asn. Rel: Catholic. Mailing Add: 14 Murray Hill Circle, Baltimore, Md, 21212. (1967)

MAGUIRE, RICHARD D
b. Boston, Mass, 4/9/14; s. William C. Maguire and Mary Alice O'Connell M; m. 7/6/42 to Marian Grady; c. James, Maeve, Tara, Richard, William. Educ: Phillip Exeter Acad, 32; Harvard Univ, A.B, LL.B, 39. Polit. & Govt. Pos: Mem White House staff, 61-62; treas, Dem. Nat. Cmt, 62-65. Bus. & Prof. Pos: Law practice, Boston, Mass, 39-41, 46-60; Maguire & Tucker, Wash. D.C, 65- Legal Res: 8921 Durham Dr, Potomac, Md. 20854. Mailing Add: 2000 L St. N.W, Washington, D.C. 20036.

MAGUIRE, ROBERT CHARLES D
Mayor, Lowell, Mass.
b. Lowell, Mass; s. Joseph Henry Maguire and Margaret McDonough M; m. 5/8/55 to Helen Melancon; c. Michael, Lynn, Patricia and Robert. Educ: Providence, Col, 45-47. Polit. & Govt. Pos: Mem, Bd. of Appeals, Lowell, Mass, 64-65, mem, City Coun, 66-68, mayor, 68-, chmn, Sch. Cmt, 68-, Rep. nominee, U.S. Rep, Mass, 68. Bus. & Prof. Pos: Field acct, treas. dept, N.E. Power Serv. Co, 55- Mil. Serv: Entered as Pvt, Army, 50, released as Cpl, 52, after serv. in Signal Corps, Germany, 51-52. Mem: K. of C; Jr. C. of C; Elks; Am. Legion. Man of the Year, Lowell Jr. C. of C, 67. Rel: Roman Catholic. Mailing Add: 348 Wilder St, Lowell, Mass. 01851.

MAGUIRE, WILLIAM JAMES D
Chmn, Haverhill Dem. City Cmt, Mass.
b. Haverhill, Mass, 9/23/07; s. William A. Maguire and Alfonsa C. Ryan M; m. 10/12/31 to Mary E. Delaney; c. William J, Jr, Katherine E. (Mrs. Thomas Greene) and Richard P. Educ: St. James High Sch, grad, 24. Polit. & Govt. Pos: Del, Mass. Dem. State Conv, 34, 36 & 58; chmn, Haverhill Dem. City Cmt, Mass, 38-42 & 56-; mem, Merrimack Valley Sewerage Bd, 48-54; del, Dem. Nat. Conv, 48, 52, 56, 60 and del-at-lg, 68; mem. adv. bd, North. Essex. Commun. Col, 64-69. Bus. & Prof. Pos: Treas. and gen. mgr, William A. Maguire Co, Inc, 41- Mem: Nat. and New Eng. Pest Control Asns; Men of Merrimack (past pres); K. of C.(4°, Past Faithful Navigator); Cath-Jewish Dialogues, Inc.(second v.pres). Rel: Roman Catholic. Mailing Add: 8 Harding Ave, Haverhill, Mass. 01830.

MAHADY, PAUL W. D
Pa. State Sen.
b. Latrobe, Pa, 11/19/08; s. James J. Mahady and Katharine O'Neill M; m. to

Janet Matlock; c. Two. Educ: Harvard Col, A.B; Harvard Univ. Law Sch, LL.B; Ames Competition; Sayre Law Club; McReynolds Law Club. Polit. & Govt. Pos: Pa. State Sen, 58- Bus. & Prof. Pos: Practiced law before the Westmoreland Co. Courts, Pa. Superior and Supreme Courts, Fed. Dist. Court and U.S. Supreme Court; author and ed; dir-secy, Newcomer Prod. Inc, Westmoreland Fed. Savings and Loan Asn. and Latrobe Broadcasters, Inc. Mil. Serv: Lt. Col, Army, 41-46; Legion of Merit; Army Commendation Ribbon with Oak Leaf Clusters. Mem: Former chmn. adv. bd, Salvation Army Int; Lions Int.(int. dir. and solicitor to int. bd); city chmn, Heart Fund; dir, Cerebral Palsy; Am. Legion; Am. Asn. of Univ. Prof; Pa. and Westmoreland Co. Bar Asns; Fayette-Westmoreland Boy Scouts Coun; Harvard Club; Officers Club of Army and Navy in N.Y.C; Qm. Procurement Assocs; Am. Acad. of Polit. & Soc. Sci; adv. bd, St. Vincent Col; adv. cmt, Pa. State Univ, New Kensington and Univ. Pittsburgh, Greensburg; Pa. Local Govt. Cmn; Pa. Hist. and Mus. Cmn; Pa. Coun. Aged; bd. dirs, Pa. Higher Educ. Assistance Agency and Pa. Planning Cmn. Mailing Add: 824 Walnut St, Latrobe, Pa. 15650.

MAHAFFEY, AUDLEY F. R
Wash. State Rep.
b. Pawnee, Okla, 1899; married; c. Three sons. Educ: Univ. Wash. Polit. & Govt. Pos: Wash. State Rep, currently. Bus. & Prof. Pos: Educator. Mil. Serv: Navy. Mem: Mason. Mailing Add: 5241 16th St. N.E, Seattle, Wash. 98105. (1967)

MAHALAK, EDWARD E. D
Mich. State Rep.
b. Wyandotte, Mich, 9/25/21; married; c. Gregory and Denise. Educ: Wayne State Univ; Detroit Col. of Law. Polit. & Govt. Pos: Justice of the Peace, Mich, 3 consecutive 4 year terms beginning in 55; Mich. State Rep, 64- Mil. Serv: Air Force, World War II. Mem: Ushers Club; VFW; Polish Legion of Am. Vet. Post 7. Rel: Catholic. Mailing Add: 10154 Marian, Romulus, Mich. 48174. (1967)

MAHAN, BRUCE E. D
b. Near Bedford, Iowa, 11/25/90; s. Thomas Shelton Mahan and Luvira Titus M; m. 4/22/14 to Edna Rohret; c. Louis F. and Thomas P. Educ: State Univ. of Iowa, B.A, M.A, and Ph.D. Polit. & Govt. Pos: Supt. of Schs, Cascade, Iowa, 4 years; Iowa State Rep, 62-66. Bus. & Prof. Pos: Mem. staff, State Univ. of Iowa, 23-61, long time mem, bd. in control of athletics and bd. of trustees, Sch. of Relig, dir. and dean, exten. div, 32 years, emer. prof. and emer. dean, 61-; asst. prin, Iowa City High Sch, 5 years. Mem: Assoc. ed, State Hist. Soc, 6 years, Triangle; Rotary; K. of C. Author of Books, Articles and Pageants on Iowa Hist. Rel: Catholic. Mailing Add: 319 Koser Ave, Iowa City, Iowa 52240.

MAHAN, DAUSWELL ROGERS, JR. R
Chmn, Whitfield Co. Rep. Party, Ga.
b. Chattanooga, Tenn, 10/3/26; s. Dauswell Rogers Mahan, Sr. and Minnie Ford M; m. 10/7/50 to June Ann Cooley; c. Deborah Jean, Stephen Cooley and Mark Rogers. Educ: Univ. of Chattanooga, B.B.A, 50; Univ. of Tenn. Col. of Med, M.D, 63; Alpha Phi Omega. Polit. & Govt. Pos: Chmn, Whitfield Co. Rep. Party, Ga, 66 & 68-; chmn, Seventh Dist. Rep. Party, 67. Mil. Serv: Entered as A/S, Navy, 43, released as PO 2/C AP, 47, after serv. in U.S. Pac. Fleet Air Force, 43-47; entered as Ens, Naval Res, 52, released as Lt.(jg), 53, after serv. in U.S. Atlantic Fleet Asiatic Pac. Theatre, Lt. Comdr. (Ret), Naval Res; Victory and European Occup. World War II Medals; Nat. Defense and Armed Forces Res. Ribbons. Mem: Am. Med. Asn; Mason; Elks. Rel: Methodist. Legal Res: 1503 Beverly Dr, Dalton, Ga. 30720. Mailing Add: 1219 Memorial Dr, Dalton, Ga. 30720.

MAHAN, JOHN WILLIAM D
Chmn, Subversive Activities Control Bd.
b. Missoula, Mont, 6/24/23; s. John W. Mahan and Iola Morgan M; m. 8/4/43 to Shirley Tuohy; c. Kim, Shelley, Bartley and John William, III. Educ: St. Marys, 42; Carroll Col, 45-46; Univ. Mont, LL.B, 49; Sigma Alpha Epsilon. Polit. & Govt. Pos: Spec. Asst. Attorney Gen, Mont, 52-56; nat. chmn, Vet. for Kennedy and Johnson, 59-60, Vet. for Johnson and Humphrey, 63-64; chmn, Subversive Activities Control Bd, 66- Mil. Serv: Entered as 2nd Lt, Navy, 43, released as Maj, Marine Corps, after serv. in Pac. Mem: Am. and Mont. Bar Asns; Nat. Comdr, VFW, 58-59; Am. Legion; DAV; Mason (32°); Shrine; Navy League. Rel: Episcopal. Legal Res: 620 Madison Ave, Helena, Mont. 59601. Mailing Add: 4746 N. Dittmar Dr, Arlington, Va. 22207.

MAHANEY, JOHN DANIEL D
Conn. State Rep.
b. Waterbury, Conn, 2/18/29; s. Daniel J. Mahaney and Marie Lawlor M; m. 8/22/53 to Ellen C. McNaney; c. D.J, Beth, Meg and John. Educ: Fairfield Univ, B.S.S. in Hist. and Govt, 52; Univ. Conn. Sch. Law, LL.B, 57. Polit. & Govt. Pos: Justice of the Peace, Waterbury, Conn, 6 years; asst. corp. counsel, Waterbury, 60-65; Conn. State Rep, 92nd Dist, currently. Mil. Serv: Entered as Seaman, Naval Res, 47, released as Seaman 1/C, 52. Mem: Am. and Conn. State Bar Asns; Elks; Hibernians. Rel: Catholic. Mailing Add: 15 Gayfield Rd, Waterbury, Conn. 06706. (1967)

MAHANY, ROWLAND B. R
Chmn, Crawford Co. Rep. Cmt, Pa.
b. Jersey City, N.J, 11/2/04; s. Walter R. Mahany and Rebecca Baldwin M; m. to Mabel E. Crouch; c. one. Educ: Alleghany Col, A.B; Dickinson Law Sch, LL.B. Polit. & Govt. Pos: City chmn, Titusville Rep. Party, Pa; city solicitor, Titusville, Pa, 36-56; Pa. State Rep, 42-44; Pa. State Sen, 46-67, Majority Leader, Pa. State Senate, 53-58; chmn, Crawford Co. Rep. Cmt, 68- Bus. & Prof. Pos: Lawyer; mem, Crawford Co, Pa. Superior and Supreme and U.S. Courts; dir, Pa. Bank & Trust Co; dir, Titusville Dairy Co. Mem: Dir, Titusville C. of C; Rotary; Elks; Mason. Mailing Add: 213 W. Spruce St, Titusville, Pa. 16354.

MAHE, HENRY EDWARD, JR. 'EDDIE' R
Field Dir, Nat. Rep. Cong. Cmt.
b. Pueblo, Colo, 8/12/36; s. Henry Edward Mahe and Guernadine Boston M; m. 9/28/62 to Frances Ogden Harvey; c. Sharon Kay, Theresa Ann, William, Kathy and Debra Lee. Educ: Univ. Denver, B.S.B.A, 58; Lambda Chi Alpha. Polit. & Govt. Pos: Chmn, N.Mex. Young Rep. State Conv, 65, v.pres, N.Mex. Young Rep, 65-66; mem, Cent, Exec. and Finance Cmts, Bernalillo Co. Rep. Party, N.Mex, 65-66, exec. secy, 66; mem, Cent. Cmt, Rep. Party of N.Mex, 65-67, exec. dir, 67-69; field dir, Nat. Rep. Cong. Cmt, 69- Bus. & Prof. Pos: Salesman, Weagley Real Estate Agency, Albuquerque, 63-66. Mil. Serv: Army, 1 month. Mem: N.Mex. Asn. Real Estate Brokers; Elks. Young Rep. Man of Year, Bernalillo Co. and N.Mex, 66. Rel: Protestant. Mailing Add: 3912 Pitt, N.E, Albuquerque, N.Mex. 87111.

MAHER, JAMES C. D
R.I. State Sen.
b. Burrillville, R.I, 4/10/13; m. to Averill M. Educ: Burrillville Schs. Polit. & Govt. Pos: Mem, Dem. Town Cmt, R.I, chief, Glendale Fire Dept, 39-; mem, Burrillville Bd. of Estimate, 47-63; R.I. State Rep, 59-63; R.I. State Sen, 63- Bus. & Prof. Pos: Sales mgr. Mem: Lions; Fire Chiefs Club of R.I; New Eng. Asn. of Fire Chiefs; Wallum Lake Rod and Gun Club; North R.I. Firemen's League. Mailing Add: Box 188, Glendale, R.I. 02826.

MAHON, DONALD DUPHORNE R
b. Albia, Iowa, 6/19/09; s. Francis E. Mahon and Alma Duphorne M; m. to A. Charlene Gaffney; c. Colleen Marie, Michael Donald and Casey Dee. Educ: Albia High Sch, Iowa, grad; correspondence and night schs. Polit. & Govt. Pos: Labor mem, Fed. Meat Packing Cmn; labor rep, Nat. War Labor Bd; Rep. precinct committeeman and mem. exec. cmt, Polk Co. Rep. Cent. Cmt, Iowa, 16 years; del, co. and state Rep. conv; mem, Ideas for a Better Iowa Cmt, 66; nominee, U.S. Rep, Fifth Dist, Iowa, 66 & 68. Rel: Lutheran. Mailing Add: 1201 E. Court Ave, Des Moines, Iowa 50316.

MAHON, GEORGE HERMAN D
U.S. Rep, Tex.
b. near Haynesville, La, 9/22/00; s. John Kirkpatrick Mahon and Lola Willis Brown M; m. 12/21/23 to Helen Stevenson; c. Daphne (Mrs. Duncan W. Holt, Jr). Educ: Simmons Univ, Abilene, Tex, B.A, 24; Univ. Tex, Austin; Univ. Minn, LL.B, 25; Phi Delta Phi; Delta Theta Phi. Polit. & Govt. Pos: Co. attorney, Mitchell Co, Tex, 26; dist. attorney, Thirty-Second Judicial Dist, 27-32; U.S. Rep, Tex, 35- Bus. & Prof. Pos: Attorney-at-Law, Colorado City, Tex, 25. Mem: Am. Bar Asn; Regent, Smithsonian Inst; Mason; Lions; Kiwanis; Rotary. Am. Polit. Sci. Asn. Cong. Distinguished Serv. Award, 63; George Wash. Award, Am. Good Govt. Soc, 69. Rel: Methodist. Legal Res: P.O. Box 1555, Lubbock, Tex. 79401. Mailing Add: Rayburn House Office Building, Wash, D.C. 20515.

MAHONEY, EUGENE HENRY D
Majority Floor Leader, Mont. State Senate
b. Anaconda, Mont, 4/1/14; s. Michael P. Mahoney and Anna O'Leary M; m. 1/11/46 to Gertrude J. Lord; c. Joy Mary (Mrs. Halterman) and Michael R. Educ: Mont. Sch. of Mines, 1 year; Washburn Col, Ph.D; Univ. of Mont, LL.B, 38; Sigma Nu; Phi Kappa Delta. Polit. & Govt. Pos: Co. Attorney, Sanders Co, Mont, 49-53; Mont. State Rep, Sanders Co, 53-59, Majority Floor Leader, Mont. House Rep, 55 and Speaker of House 57; city attorney, Thompson Falls, Mont, 53-68; Mont. State Sen, 59-, Pres. Pro tempore, 65 and Majority Floor Leader, 67- Bus. & Prof. Pos: Attorney, 38-41 & 47-; dep. regional dir, War Assets Admin, 46-47. Mil. Serv: Entered as Pvt, Army Air Force, 41, released as Maj, 45, after serv. in Eighth Air Force, ETO, 43-46; European Theatre, Am. Defense and Bronze Star Victory Medals. Mem: West. Mont. and Mont. Bar Asns; VFW (past dept. comdr); Lions (pres, Thompson Falls Club); Thompson Falls Rod & Gun Club (pres); VFW (comdr, John Robb Post 2896); Am. Legion (comdr, Post 44); Elks. Rel: Catholic. Mailing Add: P.O. Box 38, Thompson Falls, Mont. 59873.

MAHONEY, EUGENE T. R
Nebr. State Sen.
b. Chicago, Ill, 3/27/28; single. Educ: Univ. Omaha. Polit. & Govt. Pos: Nebr. State Sen, 61-; former Admin. Asst. of Congressman Glenn Cunningham. Bus. & Prof. Pos: Dir. of Commercial Savings Asn; Pub. Rels-Customer Rels. Mil. Serv: Officer in U.S. Army Res. Corps. Mem: Bd. of Dirs, St. Vincent De Paul Stores, St. John's Sem. Asn, O. St. Merchants, Nat. Conf. Christians and Jews and Citizens for Decent Lit; Soc. Settlement House Cmt, UCCS; K. of C; Eagles; S.Omaha Merchants and Professional-men's Asn; Better Omaha Club; Eagle Scout; Chmn, Boy Scouts S.Dist; cmt, Douglas City Hosp. Expansion; Ed, K. of C. Newspaper. Rel: Catholic; St. Stanislaus Parish and Holy Name Soc. Mailing Add: 4956 S. 41st St, Omaha, Nebr. 68107. (1967)

MAHONEY, FRANCIS JAMES D
Conn. State Rep.
b. Manchester, Conn, 5/12/14; s. John Frank Mahoney and Ruth Stonebridge M; m. 9/12/40 to Lucille Murphey; c. Nancy (Mrs. Mark Mooney) and Susan (Mrs. Robert Broniell). Educ: Manchester High Sch, Conn, 4 years. Polit. & Govt. Pos: Mem. bd. dirs, Manchester, Conn, 56-69, mayor, 62-66; mem, Conn. River Valley Flood Control Cmn, 64-; Conn. State Rep, 69- Mem: Campbell Coun, K. of C; Elks; Manchester Brit. Am. Club. Plaques for contributions to K. of C. and Manchester, Conn. Rel: Catholic. Mailing Add: 19 Hamlin St, Manchester, Conn. 06040.

MAHONEY, FRANCIS XAVIER D
b. Peabody, Mass, 3/21/22; s. Joseph R. Mahoney and Lucy H. Hahesy M; m. 12/2/44 to Ruth Lambert; c. Michael. Educ: Boston Col, A.B, 43; Northwest. Univ. Sch. of Law, J.D, 48; Phi Alpha. Polit. & Govt. Pos: Dem. precinct committeeman, 17th Precinct, Stephenson Co, Ill. and v.chmn, Stephenson Co. Dem. Cent. Cmt, 64; Ill. State Rep, Freeport, 65-66; former mem, Constitution Study Cmn, Ill. Mil. Serv: Entered Navy, 43, released as ETM 2/C, 46, after serv. in Amphibious Forces, Atlantic; Victory Medal and Atlantic Theater Ribbon. Mem: Ill, Wis. and Stephenson Co. Bar Asns; Am. Legion; VFW; Moose; Elks; Germania; K. of C. Rel: Roman Catholic. Legal Res: 707 E. Garden St, Freeport, Ill. 61032. Mailing Add: 214 W. Stephenson St, Freeport, Ill. 61032.

MAHONEY, GEORGE P. D
b. Baltimore, Md, 12/16/01; s. William D. Mahoney and Matilda Cook M; m. 11/24/27 to Abagal Catherine O'Donnell; c. Perry Abigal (Mrs. D. Rossi), George Perry. Polit. & Govt. Pos: Dem. Cand. for Md. Gov, 50, 54, 62, 66; Md. Sen. Dem. Cand, 52, 56, 58; Del. Dem. Nat. Conv, 52, 56, 60, 64. Bus. &

Prof. Pos: Owner, Mahoney Bros. Engr. & Const. Co, Inc, 23-; Pres, Mahoney Asphalt Co, Inc, Mahoney Equip. Co, Inc; real estate developer; owner, dairy & grain farms. Mem: Am. Soc. C.E; Md. Asn. Engrs; Soc. Am. Mil. Engrs; Balt. Asn. Comm; Ancient Order of Hibernians; Soc. Friendly Sons St. Patrick; Elk; Moose. Misc: Inventor, nerve detector to identify nerved horses; established receiving barn mobile lab for testing doped horses. Mailing Add: Prospect Farm, Owings Mills, Md. 21117. (1967)

MAHONEY, J. DANIEL Conservative, N.Y.
State Chmn, Conservative Party, N.Y.
b. Orange, N.J, 9/7/31; s. Daniel Vincent Mahoney and Louisa Dunbar M; m. 10/22/55 to Kathleen Mary O'Doherty; c. J. Daniel, Jr, Kieran Vincent, Francis Kirk, Mary Louisa and Eileen Ann. Educ: St. Bonaventure Univ, B.A, magna cum laude, 52; Columbia Univ. Law Sch, Kent Scholar and LL.B, 55; Phi Alpha Delta. Polit. & Govt. Pos: State v.chmn, Conservative Party, N.Y, 62, state chmn, 62- Bus. & Prof. Pos: Assoc, Simpson, Thacher & Bartlett, 58-62; assoc, Wormser, Koch, Kiely & Alessandroni, 65-66, partner, 66- Mil. Serv: Entered as A/S, Coast Guard, 55, released as Lt.(jg), 58. Publ: Action Speaks Louder—The Story of the New York Conservative Party, Arlington House, 67; various articles & book reviews for B.N.A, Am. Bar Asn. Jour, Columbia Law Review, Nat. Review and Modern Age. Mem: Am. and N.Y. State Bar Asns. Rel: Roman Catholic. Legal Res: 82 Brookfield Rd, Mt. Vernon, N.Y. 10552. Mailing Add: 444 Madison Ave, New York, N.Y. 10022.

MAHONEY, JOHN F, JR. D
Chmn, Fulton Co. Dem. Cmt, N.Y.
b. Gloversville, N.Y, 11/2/23; s. John F. Mahoney and Genevieve Hine M; m. 1/17/52 to Ann Van Arnam; c. Elizabeth, Monica, John, III, Patrick, Paul, Stephen, Bridget and David. Educ: Georgetown Univ, B.S.S; N.Y. Univ. Grad. Sch. of Polit. Sci, 1 year. Polit. & Govt. Pos: Chmn, Fulton Co. Dem. Cmt, N.Y, 65-; elec. cmnr, Fulton Co, 65- Bus. & Prof. Pos: Pres, Alma Leather Co, Inc, 58. Mil. Serv: Entered as Pvt, Army, 43, released as Sgt, 45, after serv. in 386th AAA Bn, ETO, 43-45. Mem: K. of C; Red Men; Eccentric Club; Cath. War Vet; VFW; Concordia Club. Rel: Roman Catholic. Mailing Add: 133 First Ave, Gloversville, N.Y. 12078.

MAHONEY, JOHN FRANCIS D
b. Syracuse, N.Y, 4/30/38; s. Richard Thomas Mahoney and Marion Gorman M; single. Educ: LeMoyne Col, B.S, 59; Cath. Univ. Grad. Sch, 2 years; pres, Polit. Sci. Acad; Boiled Moose Club. Polit. & Govt. Pos: Research asst, U.S. Dept. of the Interior, 59-61; staff asst. to U.S. Rep. Bob Casey, Tex, 61-62 and Dem. Cong. Campaign Cmt, 62-65; admin. asst. to U.S. Rep. James M. Hanley, N.Y, 65- Mem: Burro Club; Cong. Secy. Club; Nat. Capital Dem. Club; LeMoyne Col. Alumni Asn; Ancient Order of Hibernians. Rel: Roman Catholic. Mailing Add: 1900 S. Eads St, Arlington, Va. 22202.

MAHONEY, MARGARET ANNETTE D
b. Cleveland, Ohio, 7/12/96; d. Timothy Mahoney and Catherine Malloy M; single. Educ: Cleveland-Marshall Law Sch, LL.B, 29; Kappa Beta Pi. Polit. & Govt. Pos: Ohio State Rep, 39-43; Ohio State Sen, 43-51, Pres. Pro Tem and Majority Leader, Ohio State Senate, 49-51; presidential elector, Dem. Party, 48; Dir. Indust. Rels, Gov. Cabinet, Ohio, 51-57 & 59-63; mem, Cleveland Civil Serv. Cmt, 57-59; del, Dem. Nat. Conv, 56, 60 & 64. Mem: Cleveland Bus. & Prfnl. Women's Club; Cleveland and Cuyahoga Co. Bar Asns; Women Lawyers Asn; Order of Women Legislators; Citizens League of Cleveland. Rel: Roman Catholic. Mailing Add: 2623 Kingston Rd, Cleveland Heights, Ohio 44118.

MAHONEY, ROBERT D. D
Mich. State Rep.
b. Duluth, Minn, 10/16/21; m. 11/29/41 to Jennie Kubinger; c. Gary, Roberta, Rosemary, Dennis, Colleen, Joseph, Mark, Michael, William and Robert. Educ: Detroit Northwest. High Sch. Polit. & Govt. Pos: Mich. State Rep, 54- Bus. & Prof. Pos: Salesman. Mem: V.pres, Blind Serv. Center; Moose; Detroit Fedn. of Blind. Rel: Catholic. Mailing Add: 19971 Dresden, Detroit, Mich. 48205. (1967)

MAHONEY, THOMAS RANDOLPH D
Ore. State Sen.
b. Anaconda, Mont, 9/18/96; s. Thomas Francis Mahoney and Mary Randolph M; m. to Zella Campbell; c. Eileen and Thomas Collins. Educ: Parochial and Pub. Schs; Northwestern Col. of Law; Christian Bros. Col. Polit. & Govt. Pos: Mem. Cmn. Rev. Ore. Constitution and State Cmt. Americanization; chmn. Ore. del, Dem. Nat. Conv, 44 & 48, del, 52 & 60; Circuit Judge Pro Tempore, 54; Ore. State Sen, currently, chmn. cmt. judiciary, Ore. State Senate; mem, Judicial Coun. Ore, 65-68. Mil. Serv: Enlisted in Navy, 17, released as Cpl, Army, 19, after serv. in 12th Inf. Mem: State Bar; Am. Bar Asn; Am. Legion; Elks. Rel: Catholic. Legal Res: 257 S.W. Marconi Ave, Portland, Ore. 97201. Mailing Add: 510 Oregon Bank Bldg, Portland, Ore. 97204.

MAHONEY, WILLIAM PATRICK, JR. D
b. Prescott, Ariz, 11/27/16; s. William Patrick Mahoney and Alice Fitzgerald M; m. 5/16/46 to Alice Doyle; c. William Patrick, III, Gladys S, Richard D, Mary Alice, Eileen, Lawrence V, J. Emmett, Noel F. and Sheila P. Educ: Univ. Notre Dame, A.B, 39, LL.B, 40; hon. J.D, St. Norbert's Col, 64. Polit. & Govt. Pos: Asst. attorney gen, Ariz, 46-48; Dist. Attorney, Maricopa Co, 53-57; U.S. Ambassador, Ghana, W. Africa, 62-65; fed. aid coordinator, Maricopa Co, Ariz, 66-68; mem, Nat. Adv. Cmt. to Legal Serv. Program, Off. of Econ. Opportunity, 67-; del, Dem. Nat. Conv, 68. Bus. & Prof. Pos: Bd. of dirs, GRAMCO Int, Nassau, Bahamas, 66 and Greater Ariz. Savings & Loan Asn, Phoenix, Ariz, 67- Mil. Serv: Entered as Ens, U.S. Navy, 42, released as Lt.(sg), 45, as Trial Judge Adv. War Crimes Cases, Pac. Ocean. Publ: 'Nkrumah in Retrospect,' Rev. Polit, 4/68; and numerous other articles in professional and scholarly publications. Mem: Am. Soc. Int. Law; Am. Judicature Soc; panel arbitrators, Am. Arbit. Asn; Supreme Court U.S, and Ariz. Bar Asns; Maricopa Co. Bar Asn.(secy); Am. Acad. Polit. & Soc. Sci; Newcomen Soc. N.Am; Notre Dame Law Asn; Law Soc. Ariz. State Univ; LEAP; Nat. Conf. Christians and Jews; Phoenix Symphony Asn; Maricopa Co. Commun. Action Agency; dir, Good Shepherd Sch. Girls; bd. regents, Phoenix Cath. High Schs; Phoenix Urban League; Ariz. Club; Notre Dame Alumni Asn. (nat. pres, 62). Rel: Catholic. Mailing Add: 6248 N. Seventh Ave, Phoenix, Ariz. 85013.

MaHOOD, CECIL HEBER R
Chmn, Sandisfield Rep. Town Cmt, Mass.
b. Marathon, Iowa, 8/23/00; s. Herbert William Langmore MaHood and Jean Gibson M; m. 1/6/28 to Mayme Revere Cudd; c. James Herbert. Educ: Morningside Acad. and Morningside Col, A.B, 22; Teachers Col, Columbia Univ, A.M, 35; N.Y. Univ, 35-40; Phi Sigma; Tau Kappa Epsilon; Philomathean Soc. Polit. & Govt. Pos: Campaign mgr, Co. Sheriff, Sioux City, Iowa, 22; press secy, U.S. Sen. D.W. Stewart, 26-27; mem, Bd. Appeals, Sandisfield, Mass, 63-65, selectman, 65-67; del, Mass. Rep. State Conv, 67; del, Berkshire Co. Rep. Asn, 67-; chmn, Sandisfield Rep. Town Cmt, 68- Bus. & Prof. Pos: Reporter, Sioux City Tribune, Iowa, 22-26; mgr, Wash, D.C. News Agency, 26-27; teacher, Stevens Prep. Sch, Hoboken, N.J, 27-29; mem. training squad, R.H. Macy, 30-33; teacher and asst. prin, high schs, L.I, 33-45, prin, 45-47; local correspondent Berkshire Eagle, Mass, 68- Mil. Serv: Entered as Pvt, Army, 18, released as Sgt. 1/C, 19, after serv. in Amb. Co, 21, Fourth Div, ETO, 18-19; Campaign Ribbons. Publ: Auth, Washington Column in Weekly Iowa Newspapers, 26-27. Mem: Am. Legion; Grange; Mason. Nat. War Fund Campaign Citation, 43; Cert. Appreciation from Presidents, F.D. Roosevelt, Dwight D. Eisenhower, John F. Kennedy and Harry S Truman; Cong. Selective Serv. Medal. Rel: Episcopal. Legal Res: Montville-to-Beech Plain Rd, Sandisfield, Mass. 01255. Mailing Add: P.O. Box 140, Otis, Mass. 01253.

MAHOWALD, ROBERT A. Conservative
b. Breckenridge, Minn, 1924; Married; c. Five. Educ: St. John's Univ; Univ. Minn; grad, U.S. Mil. Acad. at W. Point. Polit. & Govt. Pos: Minn. State Rep, -66. Bus. & Prof. Pos: Partner in gen. ins. agency. Mil. Serv: WWII and Korean Conflict vet; Silver Star; Bronze Star; Purple Heart; Inf. Officer in Korean Conflict; presently Lt. Col. in Minn. Nat. Guard. Mailing Add: 1540 6th Ave, N, St. Cloud, Minn. 56301. (1967)

MAHOWALD, ROBERT E. D
Ind. State Sen.
Polit. & Govt. Pos: Mem, Mayor's Traffic and Safety Cmt, South Bend, Ind, 64; Ind. State Sen, currently. Bus. & Prof. Pos: Pres, Mahowald's, Inc, retail luggage and leather goods store; v.pres, Leatherfoam, Inc, distrubutor of custom vinyl prod. Mem: Toastmasters; Jaycees; Moose; C. of C. Rel: Catholic. Mailing Add: 234 S. Michigan St, South Bend, Ind. 46601. (1967)

MAIER, HENRY W. D
Mayor, Milwaukee, Wis.
b. Dayton, Ohio, 2/7/18; s. Charles Maier, Jr. and Marie L. Kniseley M; m. 6/25/41 to Mary Ann Monaghan; c. Melinda Ann (Mrs. Carlisle), Melanie Marie. Educ: Univ. Wis, B.A, 40 and M.A, 64. Polit. & Govt. Pos: Wis. State Sen, 50-60, Minority Leader, Wis. State Senate, 53, 55, 57 & 59; Mayor, Milwaukee, 60-; mem. adv. bd, U.S. Conf. Mayors; past pres, Nat. League of Cities. Mil. Serv: Naval Res, World War II, Lt.(sg). Mailing Add: City Hall, Milwaukee, Wis. 53202.

MAIERS, JERALD EDWARD D
b. Waterloo, Iowa, 12/21/40; s. Walter N. Maiers and Claire Manahan M; m. 6/12/65 to Mary Ann Milewski; c. Charity Lee and Martin John. Educ: Loras Col, B.S, 62; North. Iowa Univ, 62-63; Marquette Univ, M.A, 66; Creighton Univ, 66-67; Omaha Univ, 67; Univ. Wis-Milwaukee, 67-69; Alpha Phi Omega. Polit. & Govt. Pos: Dem. primary cong. cand, Wis, 68; alternate del, Dem. Nat. Conv, 68. Bus. & Prof. Pos: Physics teacher, Columbus High Sch, Waterloo, Iowa, 63-64; instr. theol. Creighton Univ, 65-67; chmn. dept. relig. studies, Dominican Col, 67- Mem: Soc. Sci. Stud. Relig; Am. Sociol. Asn. Rel: Catholic. Mailing Add: 3723 Astoria Dr, Racine, Wis. 53402.

MAILE, FRANCIS A. D
b. Phoenixville, Pa, 11/19/19; s. Joseph Maile and Ellen Lawlor M; m. 11/10/62 to Marguerite Rose Kappus; c. Michael and Shawn. Educ: St. Ann's Parochial Sch, 10 years. Polit. & Govt. Pos: Alternate del, Dem. Nat. Conv, 68. Bus. & Prof. Pos: Dir, polit. dept, URW, AFL-CIO, Akron, Ohio, 62- Mil. Serv: Entered as Pvt, Army, 40, released as Sgt, 45, after serv. in U.S. Ranger Dept. and 80th Inf. Div, ETO, 43-45; Bronze Star; various serv. ribbons. Rel: Catholic. Legal Res: 476 E. Hopocan, Barberton, Ohio 44203. Mailing Add: 87 S. High, Akron, Ohio 44308.

MAILER, NORMAN KINGSLEY D
b. Long Branch, N.J, 1/31/23; s. Isaac Barnett Mailer and Fanny Schneider M; m. to Beverley Rentz Bentley; c. Susan, Danielle, Elizabeth, Kate, Michael and Stephen. Educ: Harvard, B.S, 43. Polit. & Govt. Pos: Cand, Dem. primary for mayor, N.Y.C, 69. Mil. Serv: Army, 44-46, Field Artil. and Cavalry, 112th RCT, Pac. Theater. Publ: The Naked and the Dead, 48; The Armies of the Night and Miami and the Siege of Chicago, World, 68. Nat. Book Award and Pulitzer Prize, 69. Rel: Jewish. Mailing Add: c/o Rembar, 19 W. 44th St, New York, N.Y. 10036.

MAILLIARD, WILLIAM SOMERS R
U.S. Rep, Calif.
b. Belvedere, Calif, 6/10/17; s. John Ward Mailliard, Jr. and Kate Peterson M; m. 7/10/57 to Millicent Fox; c. William Somers, Jr, Antoinette, Henry Ward, Kristina, Julia Ward, Josephine Fox and Victoria Leigh. Educ: Yale Univ, B.A, 39. Polit. & Govt. Pos: Asst. to dir, Calif. Youth Authority, 47; secy. to Gov. Earl Warren, 49-51; U.S. Rep, Sixth Dist, Calif, 53- Bus. & Prof. Pos: Asst. to dir, Am. Trust Co, San Francisco, 40-41 & 46 and Calif. Acad. Sci, 51-52. Mil. Serv: Entered as Ens, Naval Res, 39, released as Lt. Comdr, 46, after serv. as Asst. Naval Attache, U.S. Embassy, London, Eng, 39-40; Bur. of Naval Personnel, 41-42 and Flag Lt. & Aide to Vice Adm. D.E. Barbey, Seventh Amphibious Force, 43-46; Bronze and Silver Stars; Legion of Merit; Naval Reserve, Asiatic-Pac. Campaign, China Serv, Am. Defense Serv, Armed Forces Reserve, Am. Campaign, Navy Occup. Serv. and Philippine Liberation Ribbons; Victory Medal; Order of Yun Hui; Rear Admiral, Naval Res, 66. Mem: Am. Soc. of the Order of St. John; Bd. of Trustees, The Jr. Statesman Found; Propeller Club of U.S; Bay Area Trustee, United Seamen's Serv; Am. Legion; Marine Mem. Asn; Mil. Order of Carabao; U.S. Navy League; VFW; Capitol Hill Club.of Wash, D.C; Pac. Union Club of San Francisco; Presidio Golf Club of San Francisco; Family Club of San Francisco; Fed. City Club of Wash. Rel: Episcopal. Legal Res: 3375 Jackson St, San Francisco, Calif. 94118. Mailing Add: 2336 Rayburn Bldg, House of Representatives, Washington, D.C. 20515.

MAIN, FRANKLIN SMITH D
Chmn, Decatur Co. Dem. Cent. Cmt, Iowa.
b. Mt. Ayr, Iowa, 11/3/16; s. Lewis Cass Main and Clara Smith M; m. 3/21/37 to Donna Louise Burchett; c. Nancy (Mrs. Furman) and Stewart. Educ: Mt. Ayr High Sch. Polit. & Govt. Pos: Iowa State Rep, Decatur Co, 57-63; Iowa State Sen, Fourth Sen. Dist, 63-69; chmn, Decatur Co. Dem. Cent. Cmt, 67- Bus. & Prof. Pos: Farmer. Rel: Baptist. Mailing Add: Lamoni, Iowa 50140.

MAIZLISH, LEONARD MURRAY D
Mem, Calif. State Dem. Cent. Cmt.
b. Lynn, Mass, 2/7/32; s. Sam Maizlish and Ida M; m. 6/13/54 to Sondra Tobin; c. Greg and Bryan. Educ: Univ. Calif, Los Angeles, A.A, 53; Stanford Univ, A.B, 53, LL.B, 55; Order of the Coif; Tau Epsilon Phi. Polit. & Govt. Pos: Research consult, Calif. Law Rev. Cmn, 55 and Attorney Gen. of Calif, 56; Dem. nominee, Calif. State Assembly, 57th Dist, 68; Presidential elector, Dem. Party, 68; del, Dem. Nat. Conv, 68; mem. platform cmt, Calif. Dem. Conv, 68; mem, Los Angeles Co. Dem. Cent. Cmt, Calif, 68-; mem, Calif. State Dem. Cent. Cmt, 68- Bus. & Prof. Pos: Law clerk, U.S. Circuit Judge Stanley N. Barnes, 56-57; asst. resident counsel, Columbia Broadcasting Syst, 57-59; attorney, private practice, 59- Mem: State Bar Calif; Beverly Hills Bar Asn; Thalians. Rel: Jewish. Legal Res: 5142 Allentown Place, Woodland Hills, Calif. 91364. Mailing Add: 9441 Wilshire Blvd, Beverly Hills, Calif. 90212.

MAJEWSKI, CHESTER P. D
b. Chicago, Ill, 3/9/28; s. Bruno Majewski and Anna Lesniak M; single. Educ: Northwest. Univ, B.S, 52, J.D, 56; Phi Alpha Delta; Advocate Soc; Deru Honor Soc. Polit. & Govt. Pos: Asst. pub. defender, Cook Co, Ill, 61-69; Ill. State Rep, 63-67; chmn, Ill. Automation & Tech. Progress Cmn; del, Dem. Nat. Conv, 68; trustee, Metrop. Sanit. Dist. of Gr. Chicago, 68- Mil. Serv: Enlisted in the Army, 46, released as Sgt, 48, after serv. in 25th Inf. Div, Far East Command. Mem: Ill. Bar Asn; Trial Attorneys Asn; Advocate Soc; Ill. Young Dem; New Horizons Center for Mentally Retarded Children; Amvets; Phi Alpha Delta; CWV; Polish Legion of Am. War Vet; Chicago Soc. of Polish Nat. Alliance; 38th Ward Dem. Orgn; K. of C (4°); Polish Roman Catholic Union; Polish Nat. Alliance; Polish Alma Mater; Moose; VFW; Lions; Int. Kiwanis. Elected outstanding Ill. Young Dem. of 1964 at state conv; award for contrib. to govt; citations for outstanding meritorious serv. to vet. in Ill, DAV; Am. Legion, VFW and Amvets award from citizens of northwest community of Chicago for outstanding legis. record; 97 commendation letters from civic orgn. Rel: Roman Catholic. Legal Res: 3906 N. Oketo Ave, Chicago, Ill. 60634. Mailing Add: 7357 W. Addison St, Chicago, Ill. 60634.

MAJHANOVICH, STEVE D
Wyo. State Rep.
b. Rock Springs, Wyo, 1/20/26; s. Bob Majhanovich and Mary Ivankovich M; m. 7/3/48 to Caroline Shipley Wilde; c. Carole Ann. Educ: Col. of St. Thomas 43-45. Polit. & Govt. Pos: City councilman, Rock Springs, Wyo, 50-58; Wyo. State Rep, 65- Mil. Serv: Entered as A/S, Navy, 43, released as Ens, 46, after serv. in Amphibious Assault Group, Philippine Islands, 45-46; Philippine Campaign Ribbon. Mem: Elks; Southwest. Wyo. Jr. Col. Adv. Bd; Exchange Club; Sweetwater Co. Conserv. Asn; C. of C. Rel: Catholic. Mailing Add: 1412 Clark St, Rock Springs, Wyo. 82901.

MAJORS, DAMON D
b. 1915. Polit. & Govt. Pos: Ky. State Rep, 50-54 & 62-68. Bus. & Prof. Pos: Freight Line Owner and Operator. Mil. Serv: Army, World War II. Mem: Dir, Grayson City Mem. Hosp; secy-treas, Pine Knob Lake, Inc; v.pres, Grayson City C. of C. Rel: Christian. Mailing Add: Caneyville, Ky. 42721. (1967)

MAJORS, JOE INMAN D
Tenn. State Rep.
b. Lunchburg, Tenn, 12/25/36; s. Shirley Inman Majors and John Elizabeth Bobo M; m. 6/18/60 to Nancy Sue Winton; c. Robert Inman and William Franklin. Educ: Univ. Ala, 55-56; Fla. State Univ, B.S, 61; Vanderbilt Univ, LL.B, 65; Phi Delta Theta. Polit. & Govt. Pos: City attorney, Tullahoma, Tenn, 65-68; Tenn. State Rep, 14th Dist, 69- Mem: Tenn. Bar Asn; Coffee Co. Bar Asn. (secy, 68-); Rotary; C. of C. Rel: Methodist. Mailing Add: 509 West Side Heights Dr, Tullahoma, Tenn. 37388.

MAJURE, IRBY WILMOT D
b. Walnut Grove, Miss, 9/12/99; married. Polit. & Govt. Pos: Former Miss. State Rep. Bus. & Prof. Pos: Stock farmer; ins. agent. Mem: Mason; Farm Bur. Rel: Methodist; Methodist Men's Club. Mailing Add: Route 3, Union, Miss. 39365. (1967)

MAKRIS, HARRY PETER D
Exec. Dir, N.H. Dem. Party.
b. Nashua, N.H, 12/24/25; s. Nicholas D. Makris and Fannie Tsintsiras M; div; c. Alexis and Deborah. Educ: Univ. N.H, B.S, 49; Kappa Sigma; Mask and Dagger Club; Interfraternity Coun. Polit. & Govt. Pos: N.H. State Rep, Ward 5, 65-66; alternate del, Dem. Nat. Conv, 68; exec. dir, N.H. Dem. Party, 68- Mil. Serv: Entered as A/S, Navy, 43, released as QM 2/C, 46, after serv. in Pac. Fleet, Southwest Pac, 44-46. Mem: Int. Kiwanis; Am. Legion; Elks. Rel: Greek Orthodox. Mailing Add: 25 Vine St, Nashua, N.H. 03060.

MALADY, REGIS ROWLAND D
Pa. State Rep.
b. Elizabeth, Pa, 2/9/17; s. James C. Malady and Laura Kistler M; m. 8/25/41 to Virginia Sullivan; c. Regis R, Jr, Linda M, James Kevin, Virginia Ann, John Francis, Mary Beth, Neil Patrick and Michael Roderick. Educ: Pa. State Exten, 36-38; Allegheny Tech. Inst, Electronic and Instrument Eng, 60-62. Polit. & Govt. Pos: Borough councilman, Elizabeth, Pa, 62-65, mayor, Elizabeth, 66-; exec. committeeman, Asn. Mayors of Boroughs of Pa, 66-68, fed. legis. rep, 67-, v.pres, 68-; exec. committeeman, Allegheny Co. Borough Mayors, 68-; chmn, Elizabeth Dem. Party, 69-; Pa. State Rep, 39th Legis. Dist, Allegheny Co, 69- Bus. & Prof. Pos: Shipping clerk, Miss. Glass Co, Floreffe, 36-37; wire and cable inspector, Copperweld Steel Co, Glassport, 37-49, electronic instrument repairman, 49-53, instrument engr, 53- Mem: Sr. mem, Instrument Soc. Am; Inst. Certification of Eng. Technicians; charter mem, Am. Soc. Cert. Eng. Technicians (sr. cert); Lions Int; Moose; Owls; Polish Nat. Alliance; Elizabeth, Blaine Hill and Forward Vol. Firemen; West. Pa. Firemens Asn; Anglers Club Clairton; Am. Ord. Asn; Nat. Soc. State Legislators; Boy Scouts (dist. v.chmn, Yohogania Area Coun). Rel: Catholic. Mailing Add: 709 Seventh Ave, Elizabeth, Pa. 15037.

MALEK, FREDERIC VINCENT R
Dep. Under Secy, Dept. Health, Educ. and Welfare
b. Oak Park, Ill, 12/22/36; s. Frederic William Malek and Martha Smickilas M; m. 8/5/61 to Marlene McArthur; c. Frederic and Michelle. Educ: U.S. Mil. Acad, B.S.E, 59; Harvard Grad. Sch. Bus. Admin, M.B.A. with honors, 64. Polit. & Govt. Pos: Mem, Calif. Rep. State Cent. Cmt, 66-67; former mem, exec. cmt, Los Angeles Co. Rep. Precinct Orgn; dep. under secy, Dept. Health, Educ. and Welfare, 69- Bus. & Prof. Pos: Mkt. planner, Swissair, Zurich, Switz, 63; mgt. consult, McKinsey & Co, Los Angeles, Calif, 64-67; chmn. and co-chief, exec. officer, Triangle Corp, Orangeburg, S.C, 67-69; adj. prof, Univ. S.C. Mil. Serv: Entered as 2nd Lt, Army, 59, released as 1st Lt, 62, after serv. as Counter Guerilla Warfare Adv, Vietnam, 60-61; Armed Forces Expeditionary Medal; Ranger Award; Airborne Grad. Publ: 'Building Profits Through Facilities Planning,' Factory; 'Assessment of Management Quality,' Bus. Horizons; 'An Analytical Approach to Merger Negotiations,' Harvard Bus. Rev. Mem: Am. Mgt. Asn; first v.pres. and dir, Harvard Club of South. Calif; chmn. membership cmt, Univ. Club of Los Angeles; indust. develop. cmt, Los Angeles C. of C. Rel: Episcopal. Legal Res: 917 Windsor Dr, Los Angeles, Calif. Mailing Add: 6709 Lupine Lane, McLean, Va. 22101.

MALEY, WALTER F. D
b. Des Moines, Iowa, 10/19/28; s. Irene Maley; m. to Elizabeth J. Theiler; c. Four children. Educ: Rockhurst Col, B.A. and Drake Univ, LL.B. Polit. Pos: Iowa State Rep, 1966; Justice of the Peace, Valley Twp, Polk City, 60-64. Bus. & Prof. Pos: Lawyer. Mil. Serv: Korean Conflict and WWII Vet. Mem: Jr. C. of C; C. of C; K. of C; Polk City Bar Asn; Iowa Bar Asn; Am. Bar Asn; Elks; Moose. Rel: Sacred Heart Catholic Church. Mailing Add: 201 5th St, Des Moines, Iowa 50309. (1967)

MALIN, MARJORIE CLAIRE D
Mem, Ark. State Dem. Cent. Cmt.
b. Augusta, Ark, 6/21/28; d. William E. Malin, Sr. and Lura Elizabeth Thomason M; single. Educ: Ward-Belmont Jr. Col, Nashville, Tenn, grad, 46; Univ. Ark, B.S, 48; Ind. Univ, Bloomington, M.A. in Zool, 51; Chi Alpha; Chem. Club, Univ. Ark; Sigma Sigma Sigma; Nat. Sci. Found. grant, Desert Biol. Inst. for Col. Prof, Ariz. State Univ, summer 60. Polit. & Govt. Pos: Pres, Woodruff Co. Young Dem. Club, Ark, 65-66; v.pres, Ark. State Young Dem. Club, 66, acting pres, 66-67; mem, Ark. State Dem. Cent. Cmt, 66-; del. and mem. platform cmt, Dem. Nat.Conv, 68. Bus. & Prof. Pos: Sci. teacher, Augusta High Sch, Ark, 51-55; mgr, Lura Theatre, Augusta, 51-69; asst. prof. biol, State Col. of Ark, Conway, 57-64; sci. teacher, Cotton Plant High Sch, 68-69. Mem: Am. Inst. of Biol. Sci; Bus. & Prfnl. Women's Club (pres, 66-67); Ark. Educ. Asn; Ark. Theatre Owners (bd. dirs, 63-); Nat. Asn. of Theatre Owners of Ark-Miss-Tenn.(bd. dirs, 62-); Woodruff Co. Teachers Asn.(corresponding secy, 68-69). Showman of the Year, Nat. Asn. of Theatre Owners of Ark-Miss-Tenn. Orgn, 65; Awarded Plaque, State Conv. of Young Dem. Club, 69; hon. lifetime mem, Ark. Young Dem. Club. Rel: Methodist. Mailing Add: 109 N. Third, Augusta, Ark. 72006.

MALINZAK, FRANK LEONARD D
Co. Cmnr, Fayette Co, Pa.
b. Fredericktown, Pa, 11/29/25; s. Joseph A. Malinzak and Sophia E. Pepson M; m. 4/26/45 to Garnet Louise Whetsel; c. Judith Marlana, Sandra Louise and Dale Leonard. Polit. & Govt. Pos: Pa. State Rep, 65-66; co.cmnr, Fayette Co, Pa, 68- Bus. & Prof. Pos: Owner, Malinzak Gas & Oil Co, 52- Mil. Serv: Entered as Seaman, Maritime Serv. and Merchant Marine, 44, released as Chief Radio Officer, 46; Atlantic, Mediterranean and Far East Theater Ribbons. Mem: Uniontown C. of C; Am. Slovak Union Jednota; Pa. Econ. League. Rel: Catholic. Mailing Add: P.O. Box 53, Oliver, Pa. 15472.

MALKUS, FREDERICK C. D
Md. State Sen.
b. Baltimore, Md, 7/1/13; married. Educ: West. Md. Col, A.B, 34; Univ. of Md, LL.B, 38. Polit. & Govt. Pos: Md. State Del, 47-51; Md. State Sen, 51- Mil. Serv: Army. Mem: Md. Bar. Mailing Add: Spring St, Cambridge, Md. 21613. (1967)

MALLARY, RICHARD WALKER R
Vt. State Sen.
b. Springfield, Mass, 2/21/29; s. R. De Witt Mallary and Gertrude Robinson M; m. 12/10/55 to Mary Harper Coxe; c. Richard Walker, Jr, Anne Campbell, Elizabeth Harper and Sarah Roberts. Educ: Dartmouth Col, A.B, 49; Phi Beta Kappa. Polit. & Govt. Pos: Selectman and chmn. bd, Fairlee, Vt, 51-53; mem, Fairlee Rep. Town Cmt, 52-, chmn, 56-58; alternate del, Rep. Nat. Conv, 56, del, 68; Vt. State Rep, 61-69, chmn, Appropriations Cmt, Vt. House of Rep, 63-65, Speaker, 66-69; trustee and treas, Vt. State Col, 62-65; mem. and v.chmn, Vt. Constitutional Rev. Cmt, 68-; Vt. State Sen, 69- Mem: Trustee, East. States Expos, 56-; Orange Co. Farm Bur.(v.pres, 55-56); New Eng. Holstein Friesian Asn.(dir, 54-56); Vt. Holstein Asn.(pres, 54-56); Vt. Farm Bur. Mailing Add: Mallary Farm, Bradford, Vt. 05053.

MALLOY, BOYD EDWARD D
Mem, Calif. Dem. State Cent. Cmt.
b. Detroit, Mich, 11/30/37; s. James Earl Malloy (deceased) and Bernadette Campbell M; single. Educ: San Diego State Col, B.A, 62; Blue Key; OCEOTL; pres, Delta Kappa Chap, Pi Kappa Alpha; student body pres, San Diego State Col, 61-62 and grad. rep, student coun, 62-63. Polit. & Govt. Pos: Exec. secy, Calif. State Senate Subcmt. on Legis. Representation, 62; nominee, 38th senate dist, Calif, 66-; mem, San Diego Co. and Calif. Dem. State Cent. Cmts, 66- Bus. & Prof. Pos: Elem. teacher, Los Angeles City Schs, currently. Mil. Serv; Entered as E-1, Army, 57, released as E-3, 59, after serv. in Fourth Engr. Bn, Sixth Army, 57-59; Good Conduct Medal. Mem: Asn. of Classroom Teachers of Los Angeles. Named outstanding sr. in student govt, San Diego State Col, 61-62. Rel: Unitarian. Mailing Add: 9082 Harness Dr, Spring Valley, Calif. 92077.

MALLOY, JAMES EDWARD D
Cmnr, Motor Vehicle Dept, Montpelier, Vt.
b. Boston, Mass, 3/23/14; s. James E. Malloy Sr. and Lousia Johnson M; m. to Ruth E. Tims; c. James E, Jr, David M, Richard A, Michael J, Patarica A. and Daniel P. Educ: St. Michael's Schs, Montpelier, Vt; Montpelier Sem; State Traffic Mgt. Course, N.Y. Univ; law student in Attorney's Off, 35-43. Polit. & Govt. Pos: Mem, Hwy. Patrol, Vt, 35-47; former inspector, Motor Vehicle Dept, Montpelier, cmnr, currently; alderman, St. Albans, 58-60, mayor, 60-62; Governor's rep. to Dept. of Transportation. Bus. & Prof. Pos: Mgr, United Bag Corp, Vt, 47-65. Mem: Exec. reservist, U.S. Dept. Commerce; Am. Asn. Motor Vehicle Adminstrs; pres, East. Conf. of Motor Vehicle Adminstrs; K. of C; Elks; Int. and New Eng. Asns. Chiefs of Police; Nat. Hwy. Safety Adv. Cmt; Gov. Cmn. on Crime Control and Prev; former mem, Off. of Price Stabilization Adv. Cmt, D.C. and Vt. Passenger Tramway Bd. Rel: Catholic. Mailing Add: 106 Bank St, St. Albans, Vt. 05478.

MALLOY, LEAH BLOCK R
b. York, Pa, 1/31/34; d. Harry Aaron Block and Edith Miller B; m. 8/19/55 to Raymond James Malloy; c. Karen L, Raymond C, Kirk D. and Karel E. Educ: George Wash. Univ, B.A, 55; Phi Beta Kappa; Delta Sigma Rho. Polit. & Govt. Pos: Secy. to U.S. Rep. William C. Cramer, 55, U.S. Rep. Alphonzo Bell, 61; alternate del, Rep. Nat. Conv, 64; pres, Hillsborough Women's Rep. Club, Fla; former v.chmn, Hillsborough Co. Rep. Exec. Cmt, 66-68. Mem: Corresponding secy, Am. Bus. Women's Asn, 66. Rel: Jewish. Mailing Add: 459 W. Davis Blvd, Tampa, Fla. 33606. (1967)

MALMBERG, STEVEN ROBERT D
Chmn, Chippewa Co. Dem. Party, Mich.
b. Pontiac, Mich, 11/3/42; s. Hans Reino Malmberg (deceased) and Joanne D. Zack Malmberg Soine; single. Educ: Gogebic Commun. Col, 61-63; North. Mich. Univ, B.A, 66; Phi Alpha; Phi Kappa Tau. Polit. & Govt. Pos: Supvr-cmnr, Chippewa Co, Mich, 69-; mem, hist. cmn, City of Sault Ste. Marie, 69-; mem, Chippewa Co. Bd. of Health, 69-; chmn, Welfare Bd. of Supvr, Chippewa Co, 69-; chmn, Chippewa Co. Dem. Party, 69- Bus. & Prof. Pos: Instr, Pub. Schs, Sault Ste. Marie, Mich, 66-, Lake Superior State Col, 67- and U.S. Air Force, Kincheloe Air Force Base, 68- Publ: Ed, On the Streets Where We Live, 68 and La Portage: A Walk Down Water Street, 69, Le Sault De Sainte Marie, Inc; auth, 'Creativity in the Classroom,' Mich. Asn. of Sch. Bd. J, 4/68; plus others. Mem: Sault Ste. Marie, Mich. and Nat. Educ. Asns; Elks; Lions Int; Sault Ste. Marie and Mich. Jaycees; bd, Ontonagon and Chippewa Co. Hist. Soc; bd, United Fund; Mich. State Hist. Soc; bd, East. Upper Peninsula Ment. Health; bd. Chippewa Co. Humane Soc; Le Sault De Sainte Marie Historic Sites, Inc. Outstanding Young Educator Award, East. Upper Peninsula of Mich, 69; named one of Top Ten Young Educators in State of Mich. by Mich. Jaycees, 69. Rel: Lutheran. Mailing Add: 916 Augusta St, Sault Ste. Marie, Mich. 49783.

MALONE, DAN RICHARD D
Ala. State Rep.
b. Milledgeville, Ga, 5/31/38; s. Howard Russell Malone and Eloise Mayo M. (deceased); single. Educ: Univ. Ala, B.S, 59; Omicron Delta Kappa; Druids; Pi Kappa Phi. Polit. & Govt. Pos: Ala. State Rep, Etowah Co, currently. Mil. Serv: 2nd Lt, Army, 59-60; 1st Lt, Army Res, 66. Mem: Mason. Rel: Methodist. Mailing Add: 149 Dortch Dr, Gadsden, Ala. 35901. (1967)

MALONE, J. EDWARD D
Md. State Del.
b. Baltimore, Md, 11/25/27; s. William James Malone, Sr. and Rosemary Sullivan M; m. 8/18/56 to Margaret Daniels; c. James E, Jr, Peggy Ann, Daniel Sullivan and Patrick Shawn. Educ: St. Charles' Col, 2 years; St. Mary's Univ, 1 year. Polit. & Govt. Pos: Del, Md. State Dem. Conv, 64; Md. State Del, 67- Bus. & Prof. Pos: Clerk, West. Md. Railway Co, 47-55, eng. inspector, 55-59, supvr. track, 59-67, eng. asst, 67-69; asst. mgr, Indust. Develop. and Real Estate, 69- Mil. Serv: Entered as Recruit, Army, 50, released as Sgt, 52, after serv. in 70th AAA, Baltimore and Wash. Areas, 50-52. Mem: Elks; Optimist Club; Am. Legion; Eng. Consul; Woodlawn and Patapsco Dem. Clubs; Arbutus Commun. Asn; Arbutus Vol. Fire Dept; Gay Oaks Improv. Asn; Old Timers' Baseball Asn; K. of C; Consolidated Dem. Club. Rel: Roman Catholic. Mailing Add: 5536 Oakland Rd, Baltimore, Md. 21227.

MALONE, JUDSON PERRY R
b. Sugar Valley, Ga, 3/5/17; s. Thomas Watson Malone and Zoa Dacus M; m. 6/4/39 to Annie Lorene Parramore; c. Barbara Lee, Anne Lorene, Judson Perry, Jr. and Evelyn Rebecca. Educ: Abraham Baldwin Agr. Col. Polit. & Govt. Pos: Chmn, Brooks Co. Rep. Party, Ga, 64-66; mayor, Barwick, 64-66; mem, Ga. State Rep. Cmt, 66-68; first v.chmn, Thomas Co. Rep. Party, Ga, 66-68. Mil. Serv: Entered as Recruit, Navy, 43, released as Radioman 2/C, P.T. Fleet, Pac, 45. Mem: Barwick C. of C; Amvets; Farm Bur; Thomasville-Thomas Co. C. of C. Bd. Rel: Methodist. Mailing Add: P.O. Box 237, Barwick, Ga. 31720. (1967)

MALONEY, ANNA D
Ind. State Rep.
Educ: Univ. Chicago, B.S; Ind. Univ, M.S. Polit. & Govt. Pos: del, White House Conf. on Youth and Educ, 50; U.S. del, World Conf. on Educ, Geneva, Switz, 53; Ind. State Rep, 61- Bus. & Prof. Pos: Retired teacher. Mem: Am. Fedn. Teachers (nat. v.pres); exec. bd, Nat. Arthritis and Rheumatism Found; Am. Asn. of Univ. Women. Mailing Add: 131 E. Fifth Ave, Gary, Ind. 46402.

MALONEY, JAMES A. D
Attorney Gen, N.Mex.
Mailing Add: State Capitol, Santa Fe, N.Mex. 87501.

MALONEY, JAMES E. D
b. Bondurant, Iowa, 9/26/38; s. Dan Maloney and Alice Tilton M; m. Sept. 1964 to Sharon Kay Morrow; c. Maureen Susan, Daniel Mark, Kathyrn Marie and Elizabeth Ann. Educ: Marquette Univ, B.S. in bus. admin, 61. Polit. & Govt. Pos: Iowa State Rep, Polk Co, 67-69; auditor, Polk Co, 69- Bus. & Prof. Pos: Group rep, Bankers Life Co, Des Moines, 63-65, spec. agent, 65- Mil. Serv: Entered as Pvt. E-1, Army, 61, released as 2nd Lt, 63; Cmn. through Inf. Officer Cand. Sch; Airborne and Ranger Qualified; 2nd Lt, Army Res, currently. Mem: K. of C; Toastmasters; John F. Kennedy Club; New Frontier Club. Rel: Roman Catholic. Mailing Add: 3401 S.E. Fourth, Des Moines, Iowa 50315.

MALONEY, MICHAEL JOSEPH R
Majority Whip, Ohio State Senate
b. Covington, Ky, 1/31/29; s. Michael J. Maloney and Sara E. Fisher M; m. 7/28/57 to Mary Catherine Bollman; c. Timothy M, Thomas N, Richard P, Patrick J. and Bridget M. Educ: Xavier Univ, B.S, magna cum laude, 61. Polit. & Govt. Pos: Asst. to chmn, Hamilton Co. Rep. Cent. Cmt, Ohio, 62-; Ohio State Sen, 64-, Majority Whip, Ohio State Senate, currently. Bus. & Prof. Pos: Gen. assignment reporter, Cincinnati Enquirer, Columbus, Ohio 48-56, polit. reporter, 56-61 and chief bur, 61-62. Mil. Serv: Entered as Pvt, Air Force, 50, released as T/Sgt, 54, after serv. in Far East Air Logistic Forces; Korean Theater, 52-54; Korean Theater, UN Forces and Good Conduct Ribbons. Mem: Am. Polit. Sci. Asn; Xavier Univ. Alumni Asn; K. of C. Cong. fel, Am. Polit. Sci. Asn, 86th Cong. Rel: Roman Catholic. Legal Res: 8560 Gwilada Dr, Cincinnati, Ohio 45236. Mailing Add: State Capitol Bldg, Columbus, Ohio 43215.

MALONEY, THOMAS M. D
Chmn, Whitman Co. Dem. Cmt, Wash.
b. Raymond, Wash, 2/18/31; s. Peter Maloney and May Jacobson M; m. 12/10/60 to Donna J. MacCallum; c. William T, Carol D. and Joseph R. Educ: Wash. State Univ, B.A, 56; Phi Delta Kappa; Epsilon Pi Tau. Polit. & Govt. Pos: Dem. Precinct committeeman, Whitman Co, Wash, 63-66; committeeman, State Dem. Party, Wash, 65-66; State chmn, Dollars for Dem, 65-66; chmn, Whitman Co. Dem. Party, Wash, 66- Bus. & Prof. Pos: Wood Technologist, Wash. State Univ, 56- Publ: Ed, Proceedings of First WSU Particleboard Symposium, 67 and Proceedings of Second WSU Particleboard Symposium, 68, Wash. State Univ; 'Effect of Production Variables on Particleboards of Planer Shavings,' Forest Products J, 58. Mem: Forest Products Research Soc; Soc. of Wood Sci. and Tech, Northwest Wood Products Clinic; Elks: Kiwanis; Int. Order of Hoo-Hoo. Mailing Add: 116 Fountain, Pullman, Wash. 99163.

MALOOMIAN, SARKIS D
N.H. State Rep.
b. Armenia, 12/15/06; married; c. Two. Educ: Bus. sch. Polit. & Govt. Pos: Mem, N.H. State Adv. Cmt. Kennedy for President; former city councilman, Somersworth, N.H; ward committeeman, Rep. Party, N.H; N.H. State Rep, 55- Bus. & Prof. Pos: Shoe store operator. Mem: Lions; Eagles; chmn, Boy Scouts drives; former pres, Little League; v.pres, Merchants Asn; local civic and commun. groups. Rel: Gregorian. Mailing Add: 8 Emery St, Somersworth, N.H. 03878. (1967)

MALOON, JAMES HAROLD D
b. Union City, Ohio, 6/22/26; s. Charles Elias Maloon and Bertha Creviston M; m. 1/1/48 to Frances Louise Trick; c. Sharon (Mrs. Marsh), Craig James, Elizabeth Margaret and Douglas C.T. Educ: Univ. Miss, 45-46; Miami Univ, B.A, 48; Ind. Univ. M.A, 49, Ph.D, 52. Polit. & Govt. Pos: Dir. finance, State of Ohio, 59-63; del, Dem. Nat. Conv, 60 & 68; consult. higher educ, White House Conf, 64; consult. higher educ, U.S. Cmt. Educ, 64; consult. econ. develop, Govt. Pakistan, 64-65. Bus. & Prof. Pos: Exec. v.pres, Reston, Va, Inc, 63; pres, J.H. Maloon Assocs, 65-67; v.pres, Columbia Gas Syst, Inc, 67- Mil. Serv: Entered as A/S, Navy, 44, released as Midn, 46, after serving in Officers Training, 45-46. Mem: Am. Econ. Asn; Nat. Tax Asn; Am. Asn. for Adv. of Pub. Admin. Legal Res: 6050 Olentangy River Rd, R.R. 4, Delaware, Ohio 43015. Mailing Add: 120 E. 41st St, New York, N.Y. 10017.

MALOON, WAYNE ALLEN D
Mem. Exec. Cmt, Darke Co. Dem. Party, Ohio.
b. Union City, Ohio, 5/7/21; s. Charles E. Maloon and Bertha L. Creviston M; m. 8/5/39 to Neva M. Kochersperger; c. Trisha C. Educ: Banking Schs, Kent State and Ohio Univs. Polit. & Govt. Pos: Mayor, Union City, Ohio, 50-57; Ohio State Rep, Darke Co, 59-60; alternate del, Dem. Nat. Conv, 68; mem. Exec. Cmt, Darke Co. Dem. Party, Ohio, 68- Bus. & Prof. Pos: Adjuster, Hub City Finance Co, Union City, Ind, 50-61; cashier, Citizens Bank Co, Ansonia, Ohio, 61- Mil. Serv: Entered as Pvt, Army Air Force, 43, released as Cpl, 45. Mem: Mason; Scottish Rite; Kiwanis; Grange. Rel: Protestant. Mailing Add: 224 Delaware Ave, Greenville, Ohio 45331.

MAMMENGA, GENE DFL
Minn. State Sen.
b. Oregon, Ill, 1/14/31; s. Frank Mammenga and Geneva Steffa M; m. 8/24/52 to Ruth Sampe; c. Melora and Sharon. Educ: St. Cloud State Col, B.S, 53; Univ. Minn, M.A, 58. Polit. & Govt. Pos: Minn. State Sen, 64th Dist, 67-; alternate del, Dem. Nat. Conv, 68. Bus. & Prof. Pos: Asst. prof. hist, Bemidji State Col, 61- Mil. Serv: Entered as Pvt, Army, 53, released as Cpl, 55, after serv. in 70th Ord, South. France, 54-55. Rel: Methodist. Mailing Add: 2319 Birchmont Dr, Bemidji, Minn. 56601. (1967)

MAN, BARBARA SMITH R
b. El Paso, Tex, 12/14/18; d. Reed Joel Smith and Eva Janet Hunter S; m. 9/27/41 to John Clark Man, Jr; c. Randolph Jay and Larry Clark. Educ: Baylor Univ, 36-40; Colo. Univ; DAP. Polit. & Govt. Pos: Precinct chmn, Wichita Co. Rep. Party, Tex, 58-60, v.chmn, 60-61; del, Rep. Nat. Conv, 60 & 64; pres, Tex. Fedn. Rep. Women, 61-63; former Rep. nat. committeewoman, Tex. Mem: Past dir, Baylor Univ. Ex-Students Asn; Coun. of Instnl. Develop, Baylor Univ. Mailing Add: 2000 Avondale, Wichita Falls, Tex. 76707. (1967)

MANASCO, CARTER D
b. Townley, Ala, 1/3/02; s. John Claude Manasco and Dora Letitia Beaty M; m. 8/1/42 to Mae Emma Guyton (deceased); c. two. Educ: Howard Col, 20-22; Univ. of Ala, LL.B, 27. Polit. & Govt. Pos: Ala. State Rep, 30-34; mem, Hoover Cmn; U S. Rep, Ala, 41-49. Bus. & Prof. Pos: Lawyer; pub. rels. Mem: Ala. Bar Asn; Mason; Lions. Mailing Add: 5932 Chesterbrook Rd, McLean, Va. 22101.

MANATOS, MIKE N. D
b. Gunn, Wyo, 8/30/14; s. Nicholas Manatos and Anna Anezakis M; m. 7/3/38 to Dorothy Varanakis; c. Ann (Mrs. George Hatsis), Andrew and

Kathleen. Educ: Strayer's Col; George Wash. Univ. Polit. & Govt. Pos: Admin. aide to U.S. Sen. H.H. Schwartz, Wyo, 38-44 and U.S. Sen. Joseph C. O'Mahoney, Wyo, 44-53; admin. asst. to U.S. Sen. Lester C. Hunt, Wyo, 53-54 and Sen. Joseph C. O'Mahoney, Wyo, 54-64; admin. asst. to the President of the U.S, 61-69; del, Dem. Nat. Conv, 68. Bus. & Prof. Pos: Assoc. dir. govt. affairs, Procter and Gamble Mfg. Co, D.C, 69- Rel: Greek Orthodox. Legal Res: 118 M St, Rock Springs, Wyo. 82901. Mailing Add: 5341 Nevada Ave. N.W, Washington, D.C. 20015.

MANATT, CHARLES TAYLOR D
b. Chicago, Ill, 6/9/36; s. William Price Manatt and Lucille Taylor M; m. 12/29/57 to Kathleen Klinkefus; c. Michele Anne, Timothy Taylor and Daniel Charles. Educ: Iowa State Univ, B.S, 58; George Wash. Univ. Law Sch, J.D, 62. Polit. & Govt. Pos: Nat. committeeman, Iowa Young Dem, 58-59; chmn, Nat. Col. Young Dem, 59-61; exec. secy, Young Dem. of Am, 61-62; chmn, Young Citizens for Johnson, Humphrey South. Calif, 64 and Cranston, Van Nuys, Calif, 68; mem, Calif. Dem. Adv. Cmt, 67-68; Dem. Elector Nominee, 68; mem, Calif. Dem. State Cent. Cmt, 68-69. Bus. & Prof. Pos: Lawyer, O'Melveny & Myers, Los Angeles, Calif, 62-63, Wyman, Finell & Rothman, 63-64 and Manatt & Phelps, Van Nuys, 64- Mil. Serv: 2nd Lt, Army, 59, with serv. in Qm. Corps; Capt, Judge Adv. Gen. Dept, Army Res; Distinguished Serv. Medal. Mem: Treas, San Fernando Valley Bar Asn; corp. cmt, Calif. Bar Asn; adv. cmt, Calif. Banking Law; C. of C.(dir, Van Nuys Chap). Outstanding Serv. Award, Young Dem. of Am. Rel: Methodist. Mailing Add: 6842 Van Nuys Blvd, Suite 517, Van Nuys, Calif. 91405.

MANATT, FRANK BENTLEY D
Ark. State Rep.
b. Blytheville, Ark, 8/4/33; s. Sam Logan Manatt, Sr. and Nettie Klein Elliott M; m. 10/16/55 to Patsy L. Simpson; c. Frank Bentley, Jr, Christina Klein and Nicholas Anthony. Educ: Univ. Iowa, 51-53; Univ. Ark, B.S.B.A, 56; Sigma Alpha Epsilon. Polit. & Govt. Pos: Ark. State Rep, Sixth Dist, 66- Bus. & Prof. Pos: Mem. bd. dirs, Corning Bank, 53-60, exec. v.pres, 60- Mil. Serv: Entered as 2nd Lt, Army, 57, released as 1st Lt, 65. Mem: Exec. coun, Ark. Bankers' Asn; Am. Legion; C. of C; Farm Bur; Am. Inst. of Mgt; past pres, Corning Sch. Bd. Rel: Baptist. Mailing Add: Creason Rd, Corning, Ark. 72422.

MANBECK, CLARENCE F. R
Pa. State Sen.
b. Bethel, Pa, 9/21/08; s. Webster Manbeck and Salome Yeich M; m. to Eve Pyse; c. Aletta and Barbara. Educ: Pub. Schs. Polit. & Govt. Pos: Former mem, Sch. Bd, Fredericksburg, Pa; mem. exec. cmt, Lebanon Co. Rep. Cmt; Pa. State Rep, 60-67; Pa. State Sen, 67- Bus. & Prof. Pos: Farmer; dir, First Nat. Bank of Fredericksburg. Mem: Dir, C. of C; dir, Commun. Chest; int. counsr, Lions; bd. mgr, Good Samaritan Hosp. Rel: Lutheran. Mailing Add: R.D. 1, Fredericksburg, Pa. 17026. (1967)

MANCHESTER, JOHN C. R
b. Corchester, Mass, 3/6/11; married; c. Three. Educ: Dartmouth Col; Theta Delta Chi. Polit. & Govt. Pos: Mem, Town Finance Cmt, Hanover, N.H, former mem, Sch. Bd; former N.H. State Rep. Bus. & Prof. Pos: Garage owner. Mem: Rotary. Rel: Protestant. Mailing Add: 3 Dana Rd, Hanover, N.H. 03755. (1967)

MANCINI, JOSEPH A. R
Chmn, Hardee Co. Rep. Cmt, Fla.
b. New Britain, Conn, 4/9/18; s. Anthony Mancini and Margarite Totire M; m. 11/20/50 to Marjorie Louise Howard; c. Joseph A, Jr, John Daniel and Richard A. Educ: Edison Col; Miami Inst. Food Tech. Polit. & Govt. Pos: Co-chmn, Kirk for Gov. Cmt, Fla; chmn, Hardee Co. Rep. Cmt, currently. Bus. & Prof. Pos: Pres, The Mancini Packing Co, 48-; organizer, 1st Nat. Bank, Wauchula, Fla, 60, chmn. bd. dirs, 66-; pres, J. & R. Fruit Harvesters, 61- Mil. Serv: Entered as Pfc, Marine Corps, 43, released as Capt, Marine Corps Res, 58, after serv. in Fleet Marine Force, Pac. Mem: Inst. Food Technologists; Elks. Legal Res: 705 W. Main St, Wauchula, Fla. 33873. Mailing Add: P.O. Box 395, Wauchula, Fla. 33873. (1967)

MANCINI, SALVATORE D
Chmn, North Providence Dem. Town Cmt, R.I.
b. Cranston, R.I, 7/31/19; s. Vincent Mancini and Josephine Maggiacomo M; single. Educ: Cranston High Sch. Polit. & Govt. Pos: Mem, Town Coun, North Providence, R.I, 64, mem, Town Cmt, 66; chmn, North Providence Dem. Town Cmt, 66-; mem, R.I. State Dem. Exec. Cmt, 67- Bus. & Prof. Pos: Pres, Barbara Realty, 45-60, Ace Hardware Co, 48-, Oakwood Homes, 57- and Tri-Town Liquor, 66- Mil. Serv: Entered as Pvt, Army, 41, released as Pfc, 42, after serv. in Coastal Artil. Mem: Centredale Businessmen's Asn; Centredale Workingmen's Club; Lions; North Providence Boosters Club; K. of C; United Commercial Travelers; North Providence Columbus Club; Cent. Credit Union; Amvets. R.I. Recreation Dirs. Award. Rel: Roman Catholic. Mailing Add: 1989½ Smith St, North Providence, R.I. 02911.

MANDEL, MARVIN D
Gov, Md.
b. Baltimore, Md, 4/19/20; married. Educ: Univ. of Md; Johns Hopkins Univ; Univ. of Md. Law Sch, LL.B, 42. Polit. & Govt. Pos: Justice of the Peace, Baltimore, Md, 51; mem, Dem. State Cent. Cmt, 51; mem, Gov. Cmn. on Munic. Court for Baltimore; Md. State Del, 52-69, Acting Speaker, 63, Speaker, 64-69; del, Dem. Nat. Conv, 68; Gov. Md, 69- Mil. Serv: Army, 42-44. Mem: Am, Md. and Baltimore Bar Asns; Am. Legion; Jewish War Vet. Rel: Jewish. Legal Res: 2900 W. Strathmore Ave, Baltimore, Md. 21209. Mailing Add: State House, Annapolis, Md. 21404.

MANDELBAUM, DAVID M. D
b. Newark, N.J, 12/13/35; s. Philip Mandelbaum and Ella Baum M; m. 8/25/64 to Karen Krupnick; c. Richard Barry. Educ: Princeton Univ, A.B, 57; Harvard Law Sch, LL.B, 60. Polit. & Govt. Pos: N.J. State Assemblyman, 62-67. Bus. & Prof. Pos: Attorney, Mandelbaum & Mandelbaum, Esq, 60- Rel: Hebrew. Legal Res: 467 Valley St, Maplewood, N.J. Mailing Add: 17 Academy St, Newark, N.J. 07102. (1967)

MANDERS, ADRIAN J. D
b. Wrightstown, Wis, 4/17/12. Educ: Univ. Wis, 61. Polit. & Govt. Pos: Chmn, Eighth Ward Dem. Unit, Wis, 58-59; mem, Milwaukee Co. Dem. Exec. Bd, 59-60; Chief Sgt-at-Arms, Wis. State Dem. Conv, 59-60; Wis. State Assemblyman, 60-69. Bus. & Prof. Pos: Former sheet metal mechanic; real estate broker. Mem: S. 16th St. Muskego Ave. Businessmen's Asn; S.Div. St. Civic Asn; Sheet Metal Workers Union; Holy Name Soc. Cited at 58 Dem. Conv. for Outstanding Pub. Rels. and Recruiting; Awarded Mr. Dem. Title, 59; main author of Bill that took Bingo and Sweepstakes out of stores and taverns in Wis. Mailing Add: 1406 S. 36th St, Milwaukee, Wis. 53215. (1967)

MANDIGO, MELVIN HARVEY R
Vt. State Rep.
b. Moretown, Vt, 7/16/13; s. Arthur A. Mandigo and Louella Harvey M; m. 4/1/34 to Enid Wakeman. Educ: Dartmouth Col, 31-33; Univ. Vt, B.S, 37; Alpha Zeta; Kappa Phi Kappa. Polit. & Govt. Pos: Tax assessor, Glover, Vt, 52-60; Vt. State Rep, Dist. 28, 66 & 69-; moderator, Glover Town Meeting, 66-; chmn, Orleans Co. Rep. Party, 68-; mem, Vt. Rep. State Cmt, 68-; sch. dir, Glover Town Sch. Dist, 69- Bus. & Prof. Pos: Instr. in voc. agr, Thayer High Sch, Winchester, N.H, 37-41 and Barton Acad, Vt, 42-46; farm mgt. and operation, 46-48; Instnl-on-Farm vet. instr, Orleans High Sch, Vt, 48-60; distributor-inseminator, Curtiss Breeding Serv, 53- Mem: Orleans Co. Farm Bur.(secy, 50-57, pres, 57-59). Rel: Protestant. Mailing Add: Glover, Vt. 05839.

MANERI, DOROTHY B. R
b. Albany, N.Y, 11/29/20; d. Joseph Louis Berkowitz and Anna Abelowitz B; m. 2/16/52 to Charles S. Maneri. Educ: N.Y. State Col. for Teachers, Albany, A.B, 41. Polit. & Govt. Pos: Stenographer, N.Y. State Dept. of Health, Albany, 42-43, sr. stenographer, 46-55; secy. to N.Y. State Assemblyman Hyman E. Mintz, 57; exec. secy. to N.Y. State Assemblyman Edward J. Amann, 59-64; pres, Mr. & Mrs. GOP Club, Guilderland, 63 & 64; Rep. town committeewoman, Guilderland, 63 & 64; treas, Rep. Women of the Legis, 64; v.pres, Rep. Women's Club, Guilderland, 64; exec. secy. and off. mgr. to U.S. Rep. Barber B. Conable, Jr, N.Y, 65-; mem, Rep. Women of Capitol Hill, currently. Bus. & Prof. Pos: High sch. teacher, 45-46. Mem: Pres, McKownville-Westmere PTA; Guilderland Cent. Schs, 62; secy. and exec. cmt. mem, McKownville Improvement Asn, Albany, 60-64; corresponding secy, Tantallon Citizens Asn, 69- Rel: Jewish. Legal Res: Maryland. Mailing Add: 12205 Braemer Circle, Washington, D.C. 20022.

MANGANO, GUY JAMES D
b. Brooklyn, N.Y, 1/14/30; m. to Anne De Marco; c. James Vincent II; Guy James II. Educ: Poly Prep. Sch; Carson-Long Mil. Acad; Fordham Univ; St. John's Univ. Law Sch, grad. 55. Polit. & Govt. Pos: Judge, Family Court, State of N.Y, at present; N.Y. State Sen, 62-66; N.Y. State Assemblyman, 58-62; asst. coun, Joint Legis. Cmt. on Offensive and Obscene Material, 55-58; City Clerk's Off, N.Y.C, 51-52; also currently dist. capt. of the 8th Assembly Dist. Kings Co; mem, United Mazzini Dem. Club, 86th A.D. Bus. & Prof. Pos: Lawyer, firm of Hauptman & Mangano, Brooklyn, N.Y. Mem: Legal adv, Columbia Asn. of the Dept. of Sanitation of the City of N.Y; Boy Scouts Adv. Coun. for Kings Co; Brooklyn Bar Asn; Lawyers Club of Brooklyn; Gowanus Settlement; St. Paul's Coun; K. of C; Lions Club. Rel: Our Lady of Peace Roman Catholic Church. Mailing Add: 202 Seeley St, Brooklyn, N.Y. 11218. (1967)

MANGANO, JAMES V. D
b. Brooklyn, N.Y, 11/21/05; s. Gaetano Mangano and Virginia Verdoliva M; m. 9/26/28 to Rose Mancaruso; c. Guy James. Educ: State Univ. N.Y; Syracuse Univ, pub. serv. training. Polit. & Govt. Pos: N.Y. State Assemblyman, 35-37; sheriff, Kings Co, N.Y, 38-41; secy. to Supreme Court Justices E. Ivan Ruberstein, 42-50, Charles E. Murphy, 51-53 and Anthony J. DiGiovanna, 53-54; admin. dir. and gen. clerk, Supreme Court, Kings Co, 54-; del, N.Y. State Dem. Conv. and Dem. Nat. Conv; del, Judicial Conv; Dem. State Committeeman, 53rd Assembly Dist, Kings Co; mem, Dem. Exec. Cmt. of Kings Co; United Mazzini Dem. Club of 53rd Assembly Dist, Kings Co; chmn, Brooklyn del, N.Y. State Constitutional Conv, 67; del, Dem. Nat. Conv, 68. Mil. Serv: Capt, N.Y. State Nat. Guard, 14th Regt. Publ: Articles for The Barrister published by Brooklyn Bar Asn. and other periodicals. Mem: N.Y State Sheriffs' Asn; Columbian Asn. of Civil Serv. Employees; Elks; chmn. bd. dirs, Gowanus Settlement; dir, Liberty Savings & Loan Asn; S. Brooklyn Youth Prog; mem. and officer, Citizens' Cmt; Boy Scouts; Navy Yard YMCA; Gr. N.Y. Fund; United Hosp. Fund; Big Brother Movement; Cath. Charities and Cath. Youth Orgn; Holy Name Soc; Am. Red Cross; Brooklyn Cancer Cmt; Salvation Army; Cerebral Palsy; Lions; Navy Yard Club; Seaman's Inst; Heart Fund; Police Athletic League; PTA; Gowanus Commun. Center; Our Lady of Peace Youth Centers; March of Dimes; dir, Swedish Hosp. VFW Plaque for Aid to Disabled Vet; Citations from Noah Cohen Lodge 335, Brith Sholom, Columbia Asn. of Civil Serv. Employees of Dept. of Sanit, N.Y.C, Civil Serv. Employees Asn. of City of N.Y, St. Francis Prep. Sch, Filipino Am. and Soc. of Old Brooklynites; Citation and Plaque, Grand Coun. of Columbia Asn. of Civil Serv. Employees of City of N.Y; Performance Serv. Citation, Brooklyn Trial Lawyers Asn; Civic Serv. Award, Columbia Asn. of N.Y.C. Transit Authority; Star of Solidarity, Repub. of Italy; Amerigo Vespucci Award, Fedn. Ital. Am. Dem. Orgn, N.Y, 63; Spec. Citation for Outstanding Civic Leadership, Freedoms Found. at Valley Forge, 64; Americanism Award, Kings Co. Coun. of Jewish War Vet; Cited as Israel Bond Drive dinner given in honor of James V. Mangano, 66. Rel: Roman Catholic. Mailing Add: 664 Union St, Brooklyn, N.Y. 11215.

MANGUM, JOHN KNIGHT R
b. Provo, Utah, 2/11/30; s. Willis Lester Mangum and Jennie Knight M; m. 10/12/51 to Alice Wilkinson; c. John K, Jr, Geoffrey W, Michael P. and Melissa. Educ: Brigham Young Univ, B.S, 52; Univ. Calif. Law Sch, LL.B, 55; Order of the Coif; Revising Ed, Calif. Law Rev; Phi Kappa Phi; Gold Bricker Social Unit; Phi Alpha Delta. Polit. & Govt. Pos: Spec. legal counsel, Salt Lake Co. Grand Jury, Utah, 65; former voting dist. chmn, and mem. membership selection cmt, Salt Lake Co. Rep. Party; former mem, State and Co. Rep. Cent. Cmts; former secy, Utah State Rep. Exec. Cmt. Bus. & Prof. Pos: Law lectr, various Utah State Bar Insts. Mem: Am. Bar Asn.(Sect. on Taxation); Utah State Bar Asn.(chmn, Investigating Cmt); Salt Lake Co. Bar Asn; Salt Lake City Jr. C. of C.(v.pres, dir. and legal counsel); Utah Jr. C. of C.(legal

counsel). Rel: Latter-day Saint. Legal Res: 4085 Cumberland Dr, Salt Lake City, Utah 84117. Mailing Add: 315 E. Second South, Salt Lake City, Utah 84111. (1967)

MANGUM, TOM GIBSON D
S.C. State Rep.
b. Chesterfield, S.C, 1/23/16; s. Inglis Parks Mangum and Sara Funderburk M; m. to Louise Clyburn. Educ: Univ. S.C, 33-34; Wingate Jr. Col, 34-35. Polit. & Govt. Pos: S.C. State Rep, 55-58 & 61- Bus. & Prof. Pos: Merchant; farmer; real estate. Mil. Serv: Army Air Force, 45. Mailing Add: Main St, Lancaster, S.C. 29720. (1967)

MANIBOG, G. MONTY D
Committeeman, Calif. Dem. State Cent. Cmt.
b. Manila, Philippines, 2/14/30; s. Gonzalo Manibog and Adela Montilla M; m. 6/1/54 to Jean Gingerich; c. G. Monty, Jr, Adela Lisa, Ricardo Luis, Marina Lana and Dean Carlo. Educ: Univ. of the Philippines, B.A, 52; Loyola Univ. Sch. of Law, J.D, 60; Van Norman Univ. Col. of Law, LL.M. and LL.D, 69; Phi Alpha Delta. Polit. & Govt. Pos: Mem. adv. cmt, Calif. State Sen. Alfred Song, 68-; committeeman, Calif. Dem. State Cent. Cmt, 68- Bus. & Prof. Pos: Sr. partner, Manibog, Tso & Dresselhaus, Attorneys, Los Angeles, Calif, 61- Mil. Serv: Entered as Pvt, Army, 54, released as Specialist 3/C, 56, after serv. in Psychol. Warfare Sect, Tokyo, Japan, 54-56; Capt, Judge Adv. Corps, Army Res; Spec. Commendation for Outstanding Serv, Psychol. Warfare Sect, 56. Publ: Weekly series, Point of Law, Philippine News, San Francisco, Calif, 67-68. Mem: Am. and Los Angeles Co. Bar Asns; pres, Monterey Park Beautiful, Inc. Rel: Catholic. Legal Res: 489 Van Buren Dr, Monterey Park, Calif. 91754. Mailing Add: 1725 Beverly Blvd, Los Angeles, Calif. 90026.

MANIS, JAMES EDWARD R
Mem, Calif. Rep. State Cent. Cmt.
b. Indianapolis, Ind, 8/12/26; s. Chester G. Manis and Bertha F. Comely M; m. 6/27/48 to Charlotta Jean Flora; c. Eric Wayne, Elaine Louise and Neil Craig. Educ: Ind. State Univ, 1 year; Wharton Sch. of Finance and Commerce, Univ. Pa, B.S. in Econ, 47; Alpha Phi Omega. Polit. & Govt. Pos: Precinct worker, Westminster Rep. Party, Calif, 64; del, United Rep. of Calif. State Conv, 66-69; unit chmn, United Rep. of Calif, Westminster, 67, chmn, 69th Assembly Dist, 68; chmn. city victory squad, Rep. Hq, Westminster, 68; campaign co-chmn, Rep. Cand. for 69th Assembly Dist, 68; conv. chmn, United Rep. of Calif, Area 14, 68; mem, Calif. Rep. State Cent. Cmt, 69- Bus. & Prof. Pos: Exec. trainee, Int. Harvester Co, Indianapolis, Ind, 47-50, div. acct, Chicago, Ill, 50-52 and supvr. of syst. and procedures, Indianapolis, Ind, 54-59; staff asst, controllers off, Space Tech. Labs, Los Angeles, Calif, 59-61; mkt. rep, Magnavox Research Labs, Torrance, 61-64; staff asst. to chief qual. engr, McDonnell Douglas Astronautics Co, Huntington Beach, 65- Mil. Serv: Entered as A/S, Navy, 44, released as Lt.(jg) SC, 54, after serv. in supply and finance, 44-46; recalled 52-54; Am. Theater Victory Medal, World War II. Mem: Am. Soc. Qual. Control; Nat. Mgt. Asn; Syst. and Procedures Asn. Rel: Methodist. Mailing Add: 5091 Dartmouth Ave, Westminster, Calif. 92683.

MANKIEWICZ, DON MARTIN D
V.Chmn, Nassau Co. Dem. Cmt, N.Y.
b. Berlin, Germany, 1/20/22; s. Herman J. Mankiewicz and Sara Aaronson M; m. 3/26/46 to Ilene Korsen; c. Jane and John Herman. Educ: Columbia Sch. Law, 41-42; Columbia Col, B.A, 42. Polit. & Govt. Pos: Del. or alternate, numerous N.Y. State Dem. Conv; mem. campaign staff, Herbert Lehman for Sen, 50, Stevenson for Pres, 52 & 56 and Robert F. Kennedy for Sen, 64; v.chmn, Nassau Co. Dem. Cmt, 53-; campaign mgr, Nassau Co. Dem. Party, 58; alternate del, Dem. Nat. Conv, 60, del, 68; del-at-lg, N.Y. Constitutional Conv, 67. Bus. & Prof. Pos: Reporter, New Yorker Mag, 46-48; freelance writer, novels, plays, mag. articles, motion pictures, radio, TV and short stories, 47- Mil. Serv: Entered as Pvt, Army, 42, released as S/Sgt, 46, after serv. in Intel. and Counter-Intel, ETO, 44-46; ETO Ribbon; Two Battle Stars. Publ: See How They Run, A.A. Knopf, 50; Trial, Harper Bros, 55; It Only Hurts a Minute, Putnam, 67. Mem: Nat. Acad. TV Arts and Sci.(bd. gov); Authors League; Dramatists Guild; Writers Guild of Am, E. Harper Prize for novel Trial, 55; nominated for Motion Picture Acad. Award for I Want To Live, 59; nominated for TV Acad. Award for Ironside, 68. Mailing Add: 20 Split Oak Dr, East Norwich, N.Y. 11732.

MANKIN, JACK HERMAN D
b. Terre Haute, Ind, 7/20/21; s. Joseph Paul Mankin and Hyla Lakin M; m. 12/23/43 to Betsy Cane; c. John William and Catherine Ann. Educ: Ind. State Univ, B.S, 43; Univ. Chicago Law Sch, J.D, 48; Alpha Delta Phi. Polit. & Govt. Pos: Pres, Young Dem. of Ind, 51-53; Chief Dep. Prosecuting Attorney, Vigo Co, 53-55 & 59-60; Ind. State Sen, 60-68, former pres. pro tem, Ind. State Senate. Mil. Serv: Entered as Midn, Navy, 43, released as Lt.(jg), 46, after serv. in Southwest Pac, 44-45; Five Battle Stars. Mem: Am. Legion; VFW; Elks. Rel: Presbyterian. Mailing Add: 2636 N. 10th St, Terre Haute, Ind. 47801. (1967)

MANKUS, LOUIS A. D
b. Chicago, Ill, 8/26/24; single. Educ: Univ. of Wyo, B.S, LL.B. Polit. & Govt. Pos: Wyo. State Rep, 65-67; Munic. and Juvenile Judge; Dep. City Attorney; Staff of Sen. Joseph C. O'Mahoney & Sen. Lester C. Hunt. Bus. & Prof. Pos: Attorney. Mem: Am. Legion; VFW; Bar Asn. Rel: Catholic. 1967 Legal Res: 819 1/2 W. 18th St, Cheyenne, Wyo. No mailing address available. (1967)

MANLEY, ART D
Idaho State Sen.
b. Coeur d' Alene, Idaho, 1/22/16; s. Roy A. Manley and Gurie Braaten M; m. 7/19/41 to Margaret Swan; c. Victor, Mary Carol and James. Educ: Univ. Idaho, B.A. in Polit. Sci, 38, M.A. in Polit. Sci, 40. Polit. & Govt. Pos: Case worker and co. supv, Idaho Dept. of Pub. Assistance, 39-46; with U.S. Civil Serv. Cmn, Wash, D.C, 40-41; Idaho State Rep, Kootenai Co, 64-66; Idaho State Sen, Dist. 2, 66- Bus. & Prof. Pos: Off. mgr. and acct, Boundary Farmers Supply, Inc, 48, Co-op Supply, Inc, 48-51 and Van's Creamery, Inc, 51-65; mgr. real estate dept, Thomas Agency, 65- Mil. Serv: Entered as Pvt, Army, 43, released as Tech. 3/C, 45, after serv. in Southwest Pac, 44-45; New Guinea, South. Philippines and Luzon Campaign Ribbons; Good Conduct Medal; Victory Medal; Asiatic-Pac. Serv. Medal; Philippine Liberation Medal with 1 Bronze Star; Bronze Star. Mem: Eagles; VFW; state pres, Idaho Wildlife Fedn, 66. Rel: Baptist. Mailing Add: 1109 11th St, Coeur d' Alene, Idaho 83814.

MANLEY, BRUCE R
N.Y. State Assemblyman
b. Reading, Pa, 1/16/21; s. Addis B. Manley and Adeline Childs M; m. 11/29/40 to Nancy Clifford; c. Susan (Mrs. Verry). Educ: State Univ. N.Y. at Fredonia; St. Lawrence Univ; Albany Law Sch. Polit. & Govt. Pos: Justice of the Peace, Pomfret, N.Y; N.Y. State Assemblyman, 55-; del, New York State Constitutional Conv, 67; mem, New York State Tax Cmn, currently. Mil. Serv: Served with 106th Inf. Div. overseas in World War II. Mem: VFW; Am. Legion; Elks; Rotary. Rel: Protestant Episcopal. Legal Res: 40 Curtis Place, Fredonia, N.Y. 14063. Mailing Add: 226-227 Russo Bldg, Fredonia, N.Y. 14063.

MANLEY, RICHARD SHANNON D
Ala. State Rep.
b. Birmingham, Ala, 6/23/32; s. Richard Sabine Manley (deceased) and Alice Hughes M.(deceased); m. 8/23/53 to Lillian Grace Cardwell; c. Richard Shannon, Jr. and Alyce Hughes. Educ: Univ. Ala, B.S, 53 and LL.B, 58; Phi Delta Phi; Delta Chi. Polit. & Govt. Pos: Secy, Demopolis City Planning Cmn, Ala, 60-68; Ala. State Rep, Dist. 27, 66-, mem, Spec. Cmt. Intergovt. Coop, Ala. House Rep, 69-; chmn, Demopolis City Bd. Educ, 69-; dir, Marengo Co. Ment. Health Asn, 68-; v.pres. and dir, W. Ala. Regional Develop. Coun, 69. Bus. & Prof. Pos: Attorney-at-law, 58-; mem, bd. dirs, New Southland Nat. Ins. Co, 69- Mil. Serv: Entered as Pvt, Marine Corps, 54, released as 1st Lt, 56, after serv. in G-2 Sect, Second Marine Air Wing, Continental U.S, 54-56; Maj, Marine Corps Res; Nat. Defense Serv. Ribbon; Marine Res. Medal. Mem: Ala. State, 17th Judicial Circuit and Am. Bar Asns; Am. Trial Lawyers Asn; Commercial Law League of Am; Am. Judicature Soc; Rotary; C. of C; Univ. Ala. Nat. Alumni Asn; Marengo Co. Hist. Asn; Marine Corps Res. Officers Asn; Demopolis and Indian Hills Country Clubs; The Club; Demopolis Athletic Club. Rel: Methodist. Legal Res: 1501 Country Club Dr. S.W, Demopolis, Ala. 36732. Mailing Add: P.O. Box 338, Demopolis, Ala. 36732.

MANN, C. HARRISON, JR. D
Va. State Del.
b. Mobile, Ala, 1/15/08; m. to Frances Hart. Educ: Univ. Va, LL.B. Polit. & Govt. Pos: Dir, State Educ. Assistance Authority, Va; Va. State Del, 54- Bus. & Prof. Pos: Lawyer; publisher. Mil. Serv: Marines; Capt, Va. State Guard. Mem: Marine Corps Res. Officers Asn; Arlington, Loudoun, Clarke and Va. Hist. Soc; Renaissance Soc; Nat. Trust for Hist. Preservation; Raven Soc; C. of C; Exchequer Club; Nat. Press Club; Am. Legion; Izaak Walton League; dir. Children's Home Soc. of Va; trustee, Longwood Col. Found; chmn, Bd. of Control, North. Va. Col, 57-61; adv. cmt, George Mason Col. Rel: Episcopal. Mailing Add: 1818 S. Arlington Ridge Rd, Arlington, Va. 22202.

MANN, CHARLES W. R
Mass. State Rep.
b. Pittsfield, Mass, 4/27/35; s. Howard Gorden Mann and Marion L. Cummings M; m. 6/7/58 to Jacqueline E. Storm; c. Deborah, Karen and Jennifer. Educ: Northeast. Univ, 3 years. Polit. & Govt. Pos: Mem, sch. cmt, Hanson, Mass, 63-67; Mass. State Rep, 67-; chmn, Hanson Rep. Town Cmt, 68-69. Bus. & Prof. Pos: Sales mgr. and food broker, F.N. McClure of Mass, Inc, 58-66; real estate broker, 68- Mil. Serv: Entered as Pvt, Army, 55, released as Cpl, 56. Mem: Mass. Legislators Asn; Boston Press Club; Kiwanis; Elks; Hanson Athletic Asn; Whitman-Hanson Citizens Scholarship Found. Rel: Episcopal. Mailing Add: 801 Winter St, Hanson, Mass. 02341.

MANN, DAULTON, JR. R
b. San Francisco, Calif, 6/25/21; married; c. Two sons and one daughter. Educ: Yale Univ, B.A, 44. Polit. & Govt. Pos: Former town auditor, town clerk and town treas, Peru, Vt, town moderator; Vt. State Rep, 59-67. Bus. & Prof. Pos: Investor. Mil. Serv: Navy, 42-46, Lt, Naval Res, 46-56. Rel: Episcopal. Mailing Add: Peru, Vt. 05152. (1967)

MANN, ELVA DON R
b. Dunnegan, Mo, 5/13/13; m. 4/22/40 to Eva Grant; c. Clyde Rex, Grant Boyd. Educ: Dunnegan Pub. Schs. Polit. & Govt. Pos: Mo. State Rep, 58-66; Polk City committeeman, 6 years. Bus. & Prof. Pos: Farming. Mem: Masons. Rel: Christian Church. Mailing Add: RFD 2, Aldrich, Mo. 65601.

MANN, FLETCHER CULLEN R
Attorney, S.C. Rep. Party
b. Pittsboro, N.C, 9/21/21; s. Fletcher C. Mann and Bertie Outlaw M; m. 3/11/44 to Blanche Poole; c. Sharon (Mrs. Joe Piper), Fletcher C, Jr. and William P. Educ: Univ. N.C, Chapel Hill, A.B, 42, LL.B, 48; Phi Alpha Delta. Polit. & Govt. Pos: Del, S.C. Rep. State Conv, 64, 66 & 68; chmn, Greenville Co. Rep. Conv, S.C, 66 & 68; attorney, S.C. Rep. Party, 66-; chmn, S.C. Lawyers for Nixon-Agnew, 68; chmn, City of Greenville Rep. Conv, S.C, 69. Bus. & Prof. Pos: Partner, Leatherwood, Walker, Todd & Mann, Attorneys, Greenville, S.C, 48- Mil. Serv: Entered as Ens, Navy, 43, released as Lt, 45, after serv. in ETO; ETO Theater Ribbon and Battle Star. Mem: Greenville Co, S.C. and Am. Bar Asns; Int. Asn. Ins. Counsel; Am. Judicature Soc; Asn. Ins. Attorneys. U.S. C. of C.(Govt. Opers. & Expenditures Cmt); Am. Red Cross (Southeast. Area Adv. Coun). Rel: Episcopal. Legal Res: 110 Rock Creek Dr, Greenville, S.C. 29605. Mailing Add: P.O. Box 2248, Greenville, S.C. 29601.

MANN, GEORGE D
Minn. State Rep.
b. Heron Lake, Minn, 3/26/18; s. Chas. Mann and Carrie M; m. 12/22/39 to Alice May Benson. Educ: Jackson Co. Pub. Schs, 32. Polit. & Govt. Pos: Minn. State Rep, 58-; mem, Nat. Bd. of Rural Am. for Johnson and Humphrey, 64. Bus. & Prof. Pos: Farmer, 30 years; former mem, USDA Nat. Corn Cmt; pres, Windom Coop. Elevator; dir, Farmers Union G.T.A; leader, U.S.A. People to People del. to Europe and Soviet Union, 67. Mem: Mason; Shrine; Nat. Farmers Orgn; Farmers Union. Rel: Methodist; Trustee, Windom Methodist Church. Mailing Add: Windom, Minn. 56101.

MANN, JAMES ROBERT D
U.S. Rep, S.C.
b. Greenville, S.C, 4/27/20; s. Alfred Cleo Mann and Nina Mae Griffin M; m. 1/15/45 to Virginia Thomason Brunson; c. James Robert, Jr, David Brunson, William Walker and Virginia Brunson. Educ: The Citadel, B.A, 41; Univ. of S.C, LL.B, 47; Phi Beta Kappa; Omicron Delta Kappa; The Citadel Hon. Soc; Wig and Robe. Polit. & Govt. Pos: S.C. State Rep, Greenville Co, 49-52; solicitor, 13th judicial circuit, S.C, 53-63; exec. committeeman, S.C. State Dem. Party, Greenville Co, 64-66; U.S. Rep, Fourth Dist, S.C, 69-. Bus. & Prof. Pos: Sr. partner, Mann & Mann Attorneys, 56-63, Mann, Foster, Johnston & Ashmore Attorneys, 63-68 and Mann, Foster, Ashmore & Brissey Attorneys, Greenville, S.C, 69-; dir, Palmetto State Life Ins. Co. Columbia, S.C, 57-; dir, Southeast. Injection Molding Co, Greenville, S.C, 61-; pres, Gr. Greenville C. of C, 65. Mil. Serv: Entered as 2nd Lt, Army, 41, released as Lt. Col, 46, after serv. in 82nd AAA Group, Panama Canal Dept, 41-45; Col, Army Res. Publ: 'The Writ of Prohibition,' Selden Soc. Yearbook, (Univ. of S.C. Law Quart), 47. Mem: Greenville Co, State of S.C. and Am. Bar Asns; Am. Judicature Soc; Shrine; A.F.M; Am. Legion; WOW; Kiwanis; Elks; Travelers Protective Asn; ROA; VFW (S.C. Dept Comdr, 51-52). Rel: Baptist. Legal Res: 118 W. Mountain View Ave, Greenville, S.C. 29609. Mailing Add: 1109 Longworth House Off. Bldg, Washington, D.C. 20515.

MANN, MARCUS D
Chmn, Magoffin Co. Dem. Exec. Cmt, Ky.
b. Salyersville, Ky, 4/20/13; s. Solomon L. Mann and Bess Arnett M; m. 5/5/49 to Prudence Arnett. Educ: Lees Jr. Col; East. State Teachers Col; Univ. of Ky, LL.B, 49; Phi Alpha Delta. Polit. & Govt. Pos: City attorney, Salyersville, Ky; chmn, Magoffin Co. Dem. Exec. Cmt, 65-; co. attorney, Magoffin Co, 69-. Mil. Serv: Carpenters Mate 2/C, Navy, 43-45, served in Sea Bees, Pac. Mem: Am. and Ky. Bar Asns; Am. Legion; Soil Conserv. Serv. Rel: Presbyterian. Mailing Add: Salyersville, Ky. 41465.

MANN, MAURICE
Asst. Dir, Bur. of the Budget
b. Peabody, Mass, 2/22/29; s. Abram S. Mann and Jennie Goldberg M; m. 9/6/53 to Betty M. Melnick; c. Deborah Ellen and Pamela Sue. Educ: Northeast. Univ, B.A, 51; Boston Univ, M.A, 52; Syracuse Univ, Ph.D, 55. Polit. & Govt. Pos: Asst. dir, Bur. of the Budget, 69-. Bus. & Prof. Pos: Asst. prof. econ, Ohio Wesleyan Univ, 55-58; financial economist, Bur. of Old-Age and Survivors Ins, Baltimore, Md, 58-60; v.pres. and gen. economist, Fed. Reserve Bank of Cleveland, 60-69. Publ: 'How Does Monetary Policy Affect the Economy, Fed. Reserve Bul, 10/68. Mem: Am. Econ. Asn; Am. Finance Asn; Nat. Asn. of Bus. Economists; Am. Statistical Asn; Nat. Economists Club; dir, Ohio Coun. in Econ. Educ; dir, Appalachian Finance Asn; Nat. Alumni Coun. and The Academy, Northeast. Univ. Ford Found. Fel, 56. Rel: Jewish. Mailing Add: 7017 Tilden Lane, Rockville, Md. 20852.

MANN, ROBERT E. D
Ill. State Rep.
b. Hyde Park-Kenwood, Ill; m. to Sylvia Romagnoli; c. Stephen and Stuart. Educ: Univ. Ill, grad, 50; Univ. Chicago, M.B.A. and J.D. Polit. & Govt. Pos: Legis. asst. to U.S. Sen. Marshall Korshak; Ill. State Rep, currently. Bus. & Prof. Pos: Taught in Sch. of Bus, Univ. Chicago; assoc, Chicago Jury Proj; partner, Law Firm of Mann and Rifken. Mil. Serv: Army, two years. Mem: Past pres, Chicago Lodge B'nai B'rith; chmn, Coun. Commun. Rels; Century Club; YMCA; bd. dirs, KAM Temple Men's Club; Urban League; Hyde Park Bus. and Prfnl. Asn. Mailing Add: 5339 S. Harper, Chicago, Ill. 60615. (1967)

MANN, ROBERT T. R
b. Tarpon Springs, Fla, 6/5/24; m. to Elizabeth Brown; c. Robert Trask, Jr. and Margaret Elizabeth. Educ: Univ. Fla, B.S.B.A, 46, LL.B, 51; George Wash. Univ, M.A, 48; Harvard Univ, LL.M, 53; Yale, LL.M, 68; assoc. ed, Fla. Alligator; ed-in-chief, Fla. Law Rev. Polit. & Govt. Pos: Fla. State Rep, 56-68; judge, Second Dist. Court of Appeal, Fla, 68-. Mil. Serv: Army, World War II, India, Burma, Ceylon. Mem: Dist. Lay Leader of the Methodist Church, Tampa Dist, 56-66. Rel: Methodist. Legal Res: Lake Weeks, Seffner, Fla. 33584. Mailing Add: P.O. Box 327, Lakeland, Fla. 33802.

MANN, RONALD M. R
b. Provo, Utah, 5/14/33; s. Oscar W. Mann and Ruby Anderson M; m. to Renate I. Trumpp; c. Rodney W, Yvonne R. and Heide R. Educ: Brigham Young Univ, B.S, 60. Polit. & Govt. Pos: Mem, Stinson Cmt, Seventh Cong. Dist, Wash, 62-64; mem, King Co. Rep. Exec. Bd, 62-64 & 66-68; regional chmn, 47th Legis. Dist. Rep. Party, 62, chmn, 62-64 & 66-68; del, Rep. Nat. Conv, 64; mem, Munn for Cong. Exec. Cmt, Wash, 66. Bus. & Prof. Pos: Mkt. analyst, Boeing Co, 60666. Mil. Serv: Entered as Airman Basic, Air Force, 52, released as S/Sgt, 56, after serv. in 6900th Security Wing, Security Serv. Rel: Latter-day Saint. Mailing Add: 3209 Tenth Place N, Renton, Wash. 98055. (1967)

MANN, THEODORE D. R
Mass. State Rep.
b. Boston, Mass; married; c. five. Educ: Boston Univ; Boston Col. Polit. & Govt. Pos: Mass. State Rep, currently, mem, Ins, Mil. Affairs and Low Income Housing Cmts, Mass. House of Rep; alderman, Newton, Mass; former chmn, Franchise and Licenses Cmt, mem, Urban Renewal, Pub. Bldgs, Educ, Ward Lines and Munic. Parking Cmts; mem, Mass. Bd. of Elevator Regulations, 2 terms; mem, Adv. Consumers Coun; mem, Spec. Cmt. of Mass. Legis. to Investigate M.D.C, Logan Airport and Solid Waste Disposal. Bus. & Prof. Pos: Chmn, Strauss-Mann Ins. Assocs, Inc. and Strauss-Mann Life Ins. Assocs, Inc; v.pres, Gotham Finance Co; dir, Ft. Hill Ins. Agency, Inc; dir. and chmn. ins. cmt, Garden City Trust Co; licensed ins. advisor. Mil. Serv: Navy, World War II; Seven Battle Stars; Unit Citation. Mem: Adult advisor, Newton Youth Coun; past mem. adv. coun, Recreation Dept. of Brookline; bd. of trustees, New Eng. Hosp. for Women, Parker Hill Med. Center; pres. and treas, Mass. Cancer Detection Center; chmn, Red Feather Drive and Heart Drive Ins. Team, Newton; Kiwanis Int.(New Eng. Chmn, Boys and Girls Work Cmt, pres, Roxbury Club); Combined Jewish Philanthropies (bd. of trustees); pres, Newton Rep. Club; develop. bd, Univ. Hosp; past dir, Exec. Coun. of Ins. Brokers of Mass; Am. Legion; Canopy Club; Jewish War Vet. of U.S; AF&AM; Big Brother Asn; Oak Hill Park Asn; Oak Hill Improv. Asn; B'nai B'rith; VFW. Distinguished Serv. Award, Kiwanis; Advocate Carnation; Award in Recognition of Dedicated Serv, Combined Jewish Philanthropies. Mailing Add: 21 Littlefield Rd, Newton Centre, Mass. 02159.

MANN, THOMAS CLIFTON Independent
b. Laredo, Tex, 11/11/12, s. Thomas Cullee Mann and Ida Mae Moore M; m. 12/7/33 to Nancy Milling Aynesworth; c. Clifton Aynesworth. Educ: Baylor Univ, A.B. and LL.B, 34. Hon. LL.D, Baylor Univ, Rollins Col, Notre Dame Univ, Drexel Inst. of Tech. and DePauw Univ. Polit. & Govt. Pos: For. Serv. Officer, 42-66; Ambassador, El Salvador, 55-57, Mexico, 61-64; Asst. Secy. of State for Econ. Affairs, 57-61, Under Secy. of State for Econ. Affairs, 65-67; Asst. Secy. State for Inter-Am. Affairs, 64-65. Bus. & Prof. Pos: Attorney-at-law, Laredo, 34-42; pres, Automobile Mfrs. Asn, Inc, 67-. Mem: Metrop. Club, Wash, D.C. Rel: Baptist. Legal Res: Laredo, Tex. 78040. Mailing Add: 4355 Lowell St. N.W, Washington, D.C. 20016.

MANN, VIRGINIA H. R
Chmn, Rep. Party, Mont.
b. Missoula, Mont, 6/6/17; d. Lawrence L. Howland and Elizabeth Miller H; m. 12/31/38 to Orville H. Mann; c. Charles O. Educ: Butte Commercial Col, 34-35. Polit. & Govt. Pos: Treas, Missoula Co. Rep. Club, Mont, 60-62; mem, State Bd. of Health, Helena, 61-, chmn, 68-; v.chmn, Babcock for Gov. Club, 64, west. dist. coordinator, Babcock for Sen. Club, 66; state v.chmn, Rep. State Cent. Cmt, Mont, 67-69, state chmn, 69-; del, Rep. Nat. Conv, 68. Bus. & Prof. Pos: Legal secy, Missoula, Mont, 35-40; co-owner, abstract of title bus, 40-43; with Bur. of Bus. Res, Ind. Univ, Bloomington, 44-45; legal secy, Smith, Boone & Karlberg, Missoula, 57-64; secy-treas. and dir, Union Construction Co, 61-. Mem: Mont. Rep. $50 Club; Lady Lions. Rel: Congregational. Mailing Add: P.O. Box 945, Missoula, Mont. 59801.

MANN, DR. WILLIAM C. R
Ky. State Sen.
b. 1908. Educ: Palmer Col, Davenport, Iowa, grad. Polit. & Govt. Pos: Ky. State Rep, 42 & 54; Ky. State Sen, 62-; chmn, Cumberland Co. Rep. Party, Ky, 68-. Bus. & Prof. Pos: Chiropractor; farmer. Mem: Mason; Farm Bur; Eastern Star. Mailing Add: Burkesville, Ky. 42717. (1967)

MANNA, MARIO JOSEPH R
Mem, Conn. State Rep. Cent. Cmt.
b. Middletown, Conn, 3/23/15; s. Antonio Manna and Angelina Baraiola M; single. Educ: Bentley Col. of Acct. and Finance, Mass; Kappa Pi Alpha. Polit. & Govt. Pos: Dist. chmn, Second Dist. Rep. Cmt, Conn, 55-65; city treas, Bristol, 59-63; town chmn, Rep. Town Cmt, 65-66; 31st Sen. Dist. mem, Conn. State Rep. Cmt, currently. Bus. & Prof. Pos: Secy, A.M. Lederer and Assocs, 62-; v.pres, Vizvary Corp, 65-. Mil. Serv: Entered as Pvt, Army, 42, released as Capt, 46, after serv. in N.African Div, Air Transport Cmn; reentered serv. as Capt, Air Force, 51, released, 52, after serv. with Auditor Gen. in Europe; Good Conduct and Reserve Medals; ETO and Am. Theater Ribbons; Bronze Medal. Mem: Past Comdr, Seicheprey Post 2, Am. Legion; Elks; K. of C; charter mem, Air Force Asn. Rel: Roman Catholic. Mailing Add: 377 Pine St, Apt. 1, Forestville, Conn. 06010.

MANNING, ALFRED GEORGE D
N.H. State Rep.
b. Portland, Maine, 4/12/99; married; c. Two sons. Educ: Portland, Maine High Sch. Polit. & Govt. Pos: N.H. State Rep, currently. Bus. & Prof. Pos: Retired clerical supvr, Can. Nat. Railways. Mil. Serv: Army, AEF, 17-19. Mem: Past post comdr, Am. Legion; past state dep, K. of C. Rel: Catholic. Mailing Add: 32 State St, Groveton, N.H. 03582. (1967)

MANNING, DAVE MARTIN D
Mont. State Sen.
b. Chippewa Falls, Wis, 2/28/97; s. David Jaction Manning and Amelia Hogan M; m. 12/20/20 to Ruth Ann Clark; c. Shirley (Mrs. Mouat), Vivian (Mrs. LaSalle) and David (deceased). Educ: Univ. of Mont. Polit. & Govt. Pos: Mont. State Rep, 33-41, Speaker, Mont. House of Rep, 39-40; Mont. State Sen, 41-; del, Dem. Nat. Conv, 68. Bus. & Prof. Pos: Gen. contractor, Dave M. Manning Construction Co, 29-69. Rel: Catholic. Mailing Add: Hysham, Mont. 59038.

MANNING, DONALD J. D
Mass. State Representative
b. Waltham, Mass, 6/23/29; s. George Manning and Mary Roach M; m. 1/30/54 to Pauline Elizabeth Kondrup; c. Cheryl Ann, Robbin Theresa and Donna Jeanne. Educ: Boston Col, B.S. in Economics, 1958; Portia Law Sch, L.L.B, 66; Chess Club. Polit. & Govt. Pos: City Coun, Waltham City Coun, Mass, 58-; Mass. State Representative, 11th Middlesex Dist, 61-. Bus. & Prof. Pos: Salesman, Door & Window Co, Waltham, 58-61; Attorney, 67-. Mil. Serv: Entered as Pvt, Army, 51, released as Acting Cpl, 53 after serv. in Signal Corps. Mem: Moose. Rel: Catholic. Mailing Add: 45 Wellington St, Waltham, Mass. 02154.

MANNING, ETHEL LEONARD D
Mem: La. Dem. State Cent. Cmt.
b. Kenosha, Wis, 11/9/23; d. William Charles Leonard and Alma Frieda Koch L; m. 11/25/40 to Frank Wilson Manning, Sr; c. Frank Wilson, Jr, Carol (Mrs. E.A. Petzing), Mary Belle (Mrs. Peter Joseph Early), Dale Virginia, Robert William and David Michael. Educ: Spencer Bus. Col, grad. Polit. & Govt. Pos: Secy, U.S. Rep. Hale Boggs, La, 62-; mem, La. Dem. State Cent. Cmt, 62-; del, Dem. Nat. Conv, 68. Bus. & Prof. Pos: Secy-treas. and gen. mgr, Manning Shrimp Lure Co, 47-50; v.pres, Manning Moon Ball Co, 57-69. Mem: Speakers bur, United Fund, New Orleans, La, 59-; mem. bd, Sophie Gumble Home Guild, 68-; chmn. bd, Apple Tree Sch, 68-. Rel: Catholic. Mailing Add: 4321 Perrier St, New Orleans, La. 70115.

MANNING, KARL RAYMOND D
b. St. Johnsbury, Vt, 9/20/96; s. Martin Henry Manning and Alice Tinker M; m. 6/12/30 to Madelyn Churchill; c. Malcolm Monroe. Educ: Lamiolle Cent. Acad; Univ. Vt; Carnegie Inst. of Tech. Polit. Pos: Justice of Peace and mem, town cmt, Vt, 64-; Vt. state rep, 62-64. Mil. Serv: Entered as Pvt,

Army, 17, released as Cpl, 19, after service in Signal Corps, 16th Radio Develop; Cpl, Marine Corps Res, 42. Mem: Am. Legion; Vet. World War I. Rel: Universalist. Mailing Add: R.F.D. 1, Morrisville, Vt. 05661. (1967)

MANNING, M. JOSEPH D
Mass. State Rep.
b. Milton, Mass, 9/23/24; s. M. Joseph Manning and Mary E. Chisolm M; m. 4/25/65 to Audrey L. Hawkins; c. M. Joseph, Jr. Educ: Milton High Sch, Mass, grad, 42; Bentley Col. Acct. & Finance, Boston, grad, 51. Polit. & Govt. Pos: Mem, Town Meeting, Milton, Mass, 46-, Bd. of Park Cmnrs, 50-59, Dem. Town Cmt, 50- and Bd. Assessors, 57-; notary pub, Commonwealth of Mass, 61-; Mass. State Rep, 67- Bus. & Prof. Pos: Training admin, Mass. Dept. Labor & Industs, 47-, presently on leave of absence. Mil. Serv: Entered as Pvt, Marine Corps, 43, released as T/Sgt, 46, after serv. in Marine Bombing Squadron 443-MAG 61, First Marine Air Wing, S.Pac. Theatre, 44-45; Asiatic Pac. Campaign Medal; World War II Medal; Presidential Unit Citation. Mem: Int. Assessor's Asn; Asn. Mass. Assessors (past pres); Am. Legion; Carlson Raiders (Marine); K. of C; Amvets; Elks; Mass. Legislators Asn; First Marine Div. Asn; Mass. Dem. State Cmt. Rel: Catholic. Mailing Add: 583 Adams St, Milton, Mass. 02186.

MANNING, MADELYN C. D
b. Craftsbury, Vt, 6/16/12; married. Polit. & Govt. Pos: Vt. State Rep, 65-67. Bus. & Prof. Pos: Housewife. Mem: Am. Legion Auxiliary. Rel: Methodist. Mailing Add: R.F.D. 1, Morrisville, Vt. 05661. (1967)

MANNING, MARGARET R. R
Del. State Sen.
b. 1918; m. to Robert N. Educ: Conn. Col, B.A. Polit. & Govt. Pos: Del. State Rep, 2 terms; Del. State Sen, currently. Mailing Add: 605 Greenbank Rd, Wilmington, Del. 19808. (1967)

MANNS, PAUL W. D
Va. State Sen.
b. Traverse City, Mich, 6/18/10; m. to Emma Nunnally. Educ: William and Mary Exten, Richmond, Va. Polit. & Govt. Pos: Va. State Del, 52; Va. State Sen, 66- Bus. & Prof. Pos: Newspaper ed. and publisher; funeral dir. Mem: Ruritans; Mason; South. Regional Ed. Bd.(legis. adv. coun. and past chmn); Va. Press Asn.(exec. cmt. and past pres). Rel: Methodist. Mailing Add: Bowling Green, Va. 22427. (1967)

MANRIQUEZ, CAROL HUANTE D
Mem, Calif. Dem. State Cent. Cmt.
b. Los Angeles, Calif, 3/19/30; d. Joe O. Huante and Jessie Vergara H; m. 1/8/49 to Gil Moreno Manriquez; c. Gilbert Charles, Jr. and Maria Lisa. Educ: Univ. High Sch, Westwood, Calif, grad, 48. Polit. & Govt. Pos: Mem, Calif. Dem. State Cent. Cmt, 68- Mem: Mexican Am. Polit. Asn, San Fernando; Latin Am. Civic Asn; Rotary (Womens Div); League United Latin Am. Citizens Nat. Orgn; C. of C. Rel: Catholic. Mailing Add: 10012 Memory Park Ave, Sepulveda, Calif. 91343.

MANROSE, DOROTHY JEAN D
Chmn, Atchison Co. Dem. Cent. Cmt, Mo.
b. Rock Port, Mo, 5/6/23; d. Preston Robert Burke and Billie B. Ruddell B; m. 3/26/48 to Donald Rex Manrose; c. Cheryl Jean and Lu Ann. Polit. & Govt. Pos: Treas, Atchison Co. Dem. Cent. Cmt, Mo, 57-58 & 59-60, v.chmn, 61-62, chmn, 63-; mem, State Cmt. of Mo. Sixth Cong. Dist, 65- Bus. & Prof. Pos: Office mgr, Allen Ford Sales, Rock Port, Mo, 64- Rel: Methodist. Mailing Add: 201 W. Second, Rock Port, Mo. 64482.

MANSFIELD, EDWARD WILSON D
b. Bridgeport, Conn, 1/21/14; s. Edward W. Mansfield and Francis Bliss M; m. 11/21/41 to Maryan Brainard. Educ: Yale, B.S, 36. Polit. & Govt. Pos: Town Meeting Rep, Fairfield, Conn, 59-67; mem, Gr. Bridgeport Regional Planning Agency, 61-64; mem. Charter Rev. Cmt, 66-67; Conn. State Rep, 142nd Dist, 67-68. Rel: Episcopal. Mailing Add: 31 Woodland Rd, Fairfield, Conn. 06430.

MANSFIELD, MICHAEL J. D
Majority Leader, U.S. Senate
b. N.Y.C, 3/16/03; m. 1931 to Maureen Hayes; c. Anne. Educ: Mont. Sch. Mines, 27-28; Univ. Mont, A.B, 33, M.A, 34; Univ. Calif, Los Angeles, 35-37. Hon. LL.D, Univ. Mont, Mich. State Univ, Gonzaga Univ, Col. of Great Falls, Carroll Col, Stonehill Col, Clarke Univ, St. Mary Col. and Univ. Maine. Polit. & Govt. Pos: U.S. Rep, Mont, 43-53; U.S. Sen, Mont, 53-, Dem. Whip, U.S. Senate, 57, Majority Leader, 61-; del, Dem. Nat. Conv, 68. Bus. & Prof. Pos: Miner and mining engr, 22-30; prof. Latin Am. and Far East. Hist, Univ. Mont, 33-42. Mil. Serv: S-2/C, Navy, 18-19; Pvt, Army, 19-20; Pfc, Marine Corps, 20-22. Legal Res: Missoula, Mont. Mailing Add: Room 133, Old Senate Office Bldg, Washington, D.C. 20510.

MANSI, NICHOLAS ANTHONY D
Chmn, Warren Dem. Party, R.I.
b. Providence, R.I, 12/15/30; s. Louis Mansi and Felicia Petrucci M; m. 8/27/55 to Anna Cotoia; c. Sheila Ann, Nicholas A, Deborah Joyce and Stephen John. Educ: Boston Univ, A.B, 61; R.I. Col, M.A, 67; Boston Univ. Novice Debating Team; Newman Club. Polit. & Govt. Pos: Chmn, Warren Dem. Party, R.I, 67-; mem, Legislative Cmn. Studying the Feasibility of Regulating Correspondence Schs. in R.I, R.I. Gen. Assembly, 68-69. Bus. & Prof. Pos: Salesman, Bristol Co. Bus. Machines, R.I, 57-61; Eng. and Soc. Studies Teacher, Voc. Tech. Sch, R.I, Providence, 61-67; guid. counsr, Portsmouth High Sch, 67- Mil. Serv: Entered as A/S, Navy, 50, released as Radarman 2/C, 54, after serv. in U.S.S. Atka, U.S.S. Waccamaw and U.S.S. Allagash, Atlantic Serv. Fleet Command; Good Conduct Ribbon; Korean Campaign Ribbon. Mem: R.I. and Nat. Educ. Asns; Am. and R.I. Personnel and Guid. Asns: Italian Am. War Vet.(post comdr); chmn. Float Sect, Bristol Fourth July Cmt; K. of C; Warren Rod and Gun Club; Touisset Fire Co. Rel: Catholic. Mailing Add: 111 A Touisset Rd, Warren, R.I. 02885.

MANTEY, CARL F. R
Chmn, Tuscola Co. Rep. Cmt, Mich.
b. Fairgrove Twp, Tuscola Co, Mich, 9/21/02; s. Rudolph R. Mantey and Bertha Ecklemann M; m. 6/10/25 to Bernice J. Campbell; c. Helen (Mrs. Wm. Young), Carol (Mrs. Norbert Jankowski) and Gretchen (Mrs. Alex Amstutz). Educ: Ferris Inst, 20-21. Polit. & Govt. Pos: Chmn, Tuscola Co. Rep. Cmt, Mich, 64-; del, Rep. Nat. Conv, 68. Bus. & Prof. Pos: Operator, Laundry and Dry Cleaning Plant, currently. Mem: Pres. & secy, Exchange Club and Rotary of Caro; secy, Caro Develop. Corp. Rel: Protestant. Legal Res: 229 Quinn Ave, Caro, Mich. 48723. Mailing Add: 141 S. Almer St, Caro, Mich. 48723.

MANTHEY, CHARLES EDWIN R
Treas, Rep. Citizens Cmt. Broward Co, Fla.
b. Akron, Ohio, 12/24/22; s. Edwin Louis Manthey and Mary Gledhill M; m. 12/6/52 to Catherine Livingston McKeever; c. Cheryl, Valarie, Mary, Robert, Catherine and Edward. Educ: West. Reserve Univ, 40-43; George Wash. Univ. Sch. of Med, M.D, 46; Delta Tau Delta. Polit. & Govt. Pos: Chmn, Broward Co. Physicians for Goldwater, Fla, 64; alternate del, Rep. Nat. Conv, 64; health officer, City of Oakland Park, Fla, 65-69; finance chmn, Broward Co, Gurney for Sen, 68; treas, Rep. Citizens Cmt. Broward Co, 68- Mil. Serv: Entered as Pfc, Army, 43, released as Capt, 49, after serv. in Army Med. Corps, ETO, 47-49; Good Conduct Medal. Mem: Iowa Soc. Anesthesiologists (secy-treas, 57-58, pres, 59); Am, Fla. and Broward Co. Med. Asns; Coral Ridge Yacht Club; Navy league of U.S. Rel: Catholic. Mailing Add: 1800 N.E. 43rd Court, Oakland Park, Fla. 33308.

MANTLE, C. LEE R
Chmn, Lake Co. Rep. Exec. Cmt, Ohio
b. Painesville, Ohio, 11/26/11; s. Hermon Lee Mantle and Elizabeth Herring M; m. 8/1/36 to Helen Curtiss; c. Nancy (Mrs. Glascoe) and Charles Curtiss. Educ: Oberlin Col, 30-32; Ohio State Univ, B.A, 35; Alpha Gamma Sigma. Polit. & Govt. Pos: Mem, Painesville Twp. Bd. of Educ, Ohio, 48-56; mem, Lake Co. Bd. of Educ, 52-56 & 62-, pres, 65-; Ohio State Rep, Lake Co, Ohio, 55 & 56; Ohio State Sen, 24th-26th Dist, N.E. Ohio, 57 & 58; committeeman, Ohio State Rep. Cent. Cmt, 11th Dist, 62-64; chmn, Lake Co. Rep. Exec. Cmt, Ohio, 62-; del, Rep. Nat. Conv, 68. Bus. & Prof. Pos: Instr, Lakeland Commun. Col, 68. Mem: Lake Co. Bd. of Realtors (pres, 66, secy-treas, 69); Ohio Asn. of Real Estate Bd.(state trustee, 67 & 68, chmn. membership cmt, 67); Nat. Asn. of Real Estate Bd; Soc. of Real Estate Appraisers; C. of C; Lake Co. Farm Bur. Fedn.(pres, 61 & 62) Lake Co. Hist. Soc; Mason; Shrine; Elks; Kiwanis. Realtor of the Year, Lake Co. Bd. Realtors, 68. Rel: Congregational. Legal Res: 188 Mantle Rd, Painesville, Ohio 44077. Mailing Add: P.O. Box 699, Painesville, Ohio 44077.

MANZANARES, ALFONSO B. R
b. San Pablo, Colo, 7/18/11; s. Celestino Manzanares and Senaida Roybal M; m. 6/10/46 to Edith Vialpando; c. Wayne and Veronica. Educ: Adams State Col, B.A, 52. Polit. & Govt. Pos: Undersheriff, 45-46; co. assessor, Costilla Co, Colo, 46-48; chmn, Costilla Co. Rep. Cent. Cmt, 60-68, secy, 68-69. Bus. & Prof. Pos: Teacher, Centennial R-1, 51-69. Mil. Serv: Pvt, Army, 42-45, serv. in 807th Tank Destroyers Bn, U.S. Mem: Centennial and Colo. Educ. Asns; K. of C; Sociedad Protección Mutua; Am. Legion. Rel: Catholic. Mailing Add: Box 326, San Pablo, Colo. 81153.

MANZI, ALBERT PAUL R
b. Worcester, Mass, 6/10/11; s. Luciano A. Manzi and Lucia A. Ungaro M; m. 6/25/55 to Juliette Irene Messier. Educ: Holy Cross Col, 30-33. Polit. & Govt. Pos: Mem, Bd. of Appeal, Worcester, Mass, 40-44; bd. of trustee, Worcester State Hosp, 42-49; pres, Young Mens Rep. Club, 47-49, v.chmn, Worcester Rep. City Cmt, 58-62; cmnr, Mass. Turnpike Authority, 67-; del, Rep. Nat. Conv, 68. Bus. & Prof. Pos: Owner, L.A. Manzi Inc, Worcester. Mil. Serv: Entered as Pvt, Army, 42, released as Capt, 46, after serv. in Off. QM. Gen; recalled 50-52. Mem: Int. Bridge, Tunnel and Turnpike Asn. Inc; Am. Road Builders' Asn; K. of C; Sons of Italy; Am. Legion; Ital-Am. War Veteran. Rel: Catholic. Mailing Add: 315 Pleasant St, Paxton, Mass. 01612.

MAPELLI, ROLAND LAWRENCE D
b. Denver, Colo, 6/10/22; s. Herman Mapelli and Della Borelli M; m. 4/5/42 to Neoma Robinson; c. Terralyn and Geraldine. Educ: Regis Col, 2 years. Polit. & Govt. Pos: Chmn, Denver Off-St. Parking Cmn, Colo; mem, Gov. 100-Man Local Affairs Cmn; state finance chmn, Dem. Party; mem, Denver City Coun, 55-59; Colo. State Rep, 61-62; Colo. State Sen, 62-66. Bus. & Prof. Pos: Co-owner and operator, Mapelli Bros. Co. Ranch; chmn. bd, Mapelli Bros. Co, 67-, Denver Union Stockyards Co, 69- Mil. Serv: Entered as Pvt, Air Force, 42, released as Warrant Officer, 46, after serv. in 8th Air Force, ETO, 44; Normandy, North. France and Rhineland Campaign Ribbons; 2nd Lt, Air Force Res, until 55. Mem: Adv. bd, Ft. Logan Ment. Health Center; adv. bd, St. Anthony's Hosp; bd. of ambassadors, Loretto Heights Col; bd, N. Denver Civic Asn; div. chmn, 1962 Mile High United Fund. Recipient of the Knute Rockne Award for outstanding civic achievement, 61. Rel: Roman Catholic. Legal Res: 3131 E. Alameda, Denver, Colo. 80209. Mailing Add: P.O. Box 5103, Terminal Annex, Denver, Colo. 80217.

MAPLE, BARBARA D. R
Mem: Calif. Rep. State Cent. Cmt.
b. San Diego, Calif. 9/18/15; d. Hubert L. Dawson and Lillian J. Crutcher D. m. 6/29/39 to Earl Woods Maple; c. Thomas Hadley, Earl Christopher, Robert C, Timothy J, and Melanie E. Educ: Fullerton Jr. Col, 33-35; Whittier Col, B.A, 37; Athenian Soc. Polit. & Govt. Pos: Mem, Calif. Rep. State Cent. Cmt, 66-; first v-pres, Whittier Area Rep. Womens Club, 68-69. Bus. & Prof. Pos: Teacher, El Monte Sch. Dist, 37-41. Mem: Spastic Childrens League; Nat. Charity League; Whittier Hist. Cmt; Rep. Women's Club Federated. Rel: Protestant. Mailing Add: 15070 La Cuarta, Whittier, Calif. 90605.

MAPOLES, CLAYTON W. D
b. Laurel Hills, Fla, 5/23/14; m. to Hazel Byrd; c. Harris B, Nelda (Mrs. Thompson), Clayton W, Jr. and Carolyn Ann. Polit. & Govt. Pos: Mem, Santa Rosa Grand Jury Cmn, Fla; div. dir, Game and Fresh Water Fish Cmn, 53-54; Fla. State Sen, 60-67. Bus. & Prof. Pos: Organizer and former v.pres, Bank of Jay; former owner and publisher, Okaloosa Messenger, Crestview, Okaloosa Beaches News, Ft. Walton, Milton Gazette and Tri-Co. Gazette, Jay; owner, radio Stas. WEBY, Milton and WBLO, Evergreen, Ala. Mem: Kiwanis; Navy League; Quarterback Club; Band Asn. Rel: Baptist. Mailing Add: Box 588, Milton, Fla. 32570. (1967)

MARAGOS, SAMUEL C. D
Ill. State Rep.
b. Sioux City, Iowa, 8/19/22; s. Constantine T. Maragos and Irene Maragos; m. 5/28/50 to Cleo Mavrick; c. Dean, Thomas, James and George. Educ: Univ. of Chicago, A.B, 43; John Marshall Law Sch, J.D, 48; Delta Theta Pi. Polit. & Govt. Pos: Hearing officer, Bd. of Tax Appeals, Cook Co, Ill, 55-56; hearing referee, Dept. of Revenue, Ill, 61-66; Ill. State Rep, 30th Dist, 69- Bus. & Prof. Pos: S. law partner, Maragos, Richter, Russell & Gardner, Chicago, Ill, 48- Mil. Serv: Entered as Pvt, Army, 43, released as 2nd Lt, 46, after serv. in various dept. of the Army; Hon. Res, 53. Mem: Chicago and Ill. State Bar Asns; Chicago Coun. of For. Rels; Nat. Soc. of State Legis; South Chicago Bar Asn.(past pres); Am. Legion (past comdr, Post 493); South Chicago C. of C.(past pres); Kiwanis; Medinah Shrine (past Comdr, Englewood Commandry 59); Chicago Area Coun. of Boy Scouts (mem, exec. bd); Calumet Dist. of Boy Scouts (past chmn). Silver Beaver Award, Chicago Area Coun. of Boy Scouts. Rel: Greek Orthodox. Mailing Add: 9207 S. Yates Ave, Chicago, Ill. 60617.

MARAZITI, JOSEPH J. R
N.J. State Sen.
b. Boonton, N.J, 15/6/12; m. to Eileen Hopkins; c. Joseph J, Jr, Charles, Eileen, Margaret, Mary Ellen (Mrs. Baldwin), Katherine and Maria. Educ: Fordham Univ. Pre-Law Sch; Fordham Univ. Law Sch; N.J. Law Sch, LL.B. Polit. & Govt. Pos: Legis. legal adv. to Morris Co. Bd. of Chosen Freeholders, N.J, 52-55; chmn, Boonton Charter Cmn. Study Group; Town Police Judge, Boonton; first asst. prosecutor, Morris Co; N.J. State Assemblyman, 58-69, mem, Insts, Pub. Health and Welfare Cmt, mem, Joint Legis. Appropriations Cmt, Law Rev. and Legis. Serv. Cmn. and Uniform Commercial Code Cmn, N.J. Gen. Assembly; alternate del, Rep. Nat. Conv, 68; N.J. State Sen, 69- Bus. & Prof. Pos: Munic. attorney. Mem: N.J. Bar Asn; U.S. Supreme Court; K. of C. Selected Legislator of the Year, State Asn. of Freeholders, 62; recipient of Educ. Award, 66. Legal Res: 414 Dixon Ave, Boonton, N.J. 07005. Mailing Add: 117 Cornelia St, Boonton, N.J. 07005. (1967)

MARBURY, CHARLES CLAGETT D
Judge, Court of Appeals, Md.
b. Upper Marlboro, Md, 11/2/99; s. Alexander Marshall Marbury and Lucy Clagett Berry M; m. 4/18/27 to Kathryn Worthington Lancaster; c. Priscilla (Mrs. William Fitts Ryan). Educ: Johns Hopkins Univ, A.B, 22; Georgetown Univ, Law Sch, LL.B, 25; Alpha Delta Phi. Polit. & Govt. Pos: Md. State Del, 30, 34; Md. State Sen, 38-41; Judge, Seventh Judicial Circuit of Md, 41-60; Judge, Court of Appeals, Md, 60- Bus. & Prof. Pos: Attorney-at-law, Md. and D.C, 25-41. Mil. Serv: Pvt, Md. Nat. Guard, 17-19, released after serv. in Battery D, 110th Field Artil. 29th Div, AEF, France. Mem: Prince George's Co, Md. State and Am. Bar Asns; Am. Legion; VFW; AF&AM; Soc. of the Cincinnati of Md; Lords of the Md. Manors; Soc. of the Lees of Va. Cert. of 25 years of serv. as Chmn, Selective Serv. Bd. No. 56, Md. Rel: Episcopal. Legal Res: Upper Marlboro, Md. 20870. Mailing Add: P.O. Box 58, Upper Marlboro, Md. 20870.

MARBUT, GARY RAYMOND R
Mont. State Rep.
b. Denver, Colo, 2/28/27; s. George C. Marbut and Charlotte B. Reed M; m. 1/1/53 to Edith Tupper True; c. Michael, Stephen, Debra and Randall. Educ: Univ. Denver, 49-51; Univ. Mont, 51-53; Pi Gamma Mu. Polit. & Govt. Pos: Elem. sch. trustee, Missoula Co, Mont, 53-57; Mont. State Rep, 67- Bus. & Prof. Pos: Pres, Grant Creek Ranch Corp, 57- Mem: V.pres, Mont. Asn. for Retarded Children, Inc, 69-; finance chmn, Missoula Crippled Children's Center, Inc, 69-; Sierra Club; Elks; Lions; Mont. Farm Bur; Mont. Stockgrowers Asn. Rel: Episcopal. Mailing Add: Route 2, Grant Creek, Missoula, Mont. 59801.

MARCANO, HIPOLITO Popular Dem, P.R.
Majority Leader, P.R. Senate
b. Humacao, P.R, 8/13/13; s. Miguel Marcano and Josefa Ortiz M; div; c. David and Hipolito, Jr. Educ: Inter-Am. Univ. of P.R, A.B, 37; Univ. P.R. Law Sch, LL.B, 40. Hon. LL.D, Inter-Am. Univ. of P.R, 63. Polit. & Govt. Pos: Legal counsel, Dept. of Labor of P.R, 42-43; mem, Cent. Cmt, Popular Dem. Party, 56-60 & 64-; Sen, P.R. Senate, 56-, Majority Leader, 69- Bus. & Prof. Pos: Gen. counsel, P.R. Fedn. of Labor, AFL-CIO, 43-; dean, Inter-Am. Univ. of P.R. Law Sch, 60-; secy. bd. of dirs, Labor Bank of P.R, 62- Mem: Am, Inter-Am. and Fed. Bar Asns; Int. Acad. of Law and Sci; Am. Acad. of Soc. Sci; P.R. Acad. of Polit. Sci; Inter-Am. Univ. Alumni Asn; Univ. P.R. Alumni Asn; Mason (33°); grand master, P.R. Masons, 55-69; past pres, Inter-Am. Masonic Conf; mem, Grand Masters Conf. of N.Am; Masonic Serv. Asn; Shrine; Scottish Rite; Eastern Star; Royal Order of Scotland; Cigarmakers Int. Union, AFL-CIO; Int. Soc. Develop; Elks. Rel: United Church of Christ. Legal Res: 804 Ponce de León Ave, Stop 12, Santurce, P.R. 00907. Mailing Add: Box 1648, San Juan, P.R. 00903.

MARCANTEL, BERNARD NORMAN D
Dist. Attorney, 31st Judicial Dist. of La.
b. Oberlin, La, 7/14/23; s. Emile Marcantel and Florence Reed M; m. 6/23/46 to Martha T. deGravelles; c. David, Peter, Nancy and Gregory. Educ: Univ. of Southwest. La, B.S, 46; Univ. of Chicago, J.D, 49; Tulane Univ, LL.B, 50; Phi Kappa Phi; Blue Key. Polit. & Govt. Pos: Dist. Attorney, 31st Judicial Dist. of La, 53- Mil. Serv: Entered as Pvt, Army, 43, released as Cpl, 46, after serv, in 273rd Inf. 69th Div, ETO. Mem: La. Dist. Attorneys Asn; La. and Am. Bar Asns; Elks; Am. Legion; VFW; Boy Scouts; K. of C. Rel: Roman Catholic. Legal Res: 1331 N. Cutting Ave, Jennings, La. 70546. Mailing Add: P.O. Box 488, Jennings, La. 70546.

MARCEL, CLEVELAND JOSEPH, SR. D
La. State Rep.
b. Houma, La, 11/13/20; s. Gilbert G. Marcel and Zulama Brunet M; m. 8/5/40 to Laura LeCompte; c. Cleveland J. Jr, and Carolyn (Mrs. Boudreaux), Michael J, Deborah (Mrs. Duplechin), Denise, Jennie, Linette, Mary and Gina. Educ: Loyola Univ. of the S, J.D, 43; Nicholls State Col, 55-56; St. Thomas More Law Club. Polit. & Govt. Pos: La. State Rep, ninth Dist, Terrebonne Parish, 64-; S.La. Tidewater Levee Dist. Mem, Terrebonne and Lafourche Parishes, 68-; reapportion committeeman, Terrebonne Parish, 69. Bus. & Prof. Pos: Secy, Gold Crest Cleaners, Inc, 63-; pres, G. G. Marcel & Sons, Inc, 66-; v.pres, Goodearth, Inc, 66-; secy, Chauvin Cleaners, Inc, 67- Mil. Serv: Entered as A/S, Navy Seabees, 43, released as Chief PO, 45, after serv. in Advanced Base Construction Depot, Pac. Theatre, 43-45. Mem: Terrebonne and La. Bar Asns; Am. Legion; VFW; K. of C. Rel: Roman Catholic. Legal Res: 1758 Acadian Dr, Houma, La. 70360. Mailing Add: P.O. Box 10098, Houma, La. 70360.

MARCH, KATHLEEN OLSEN R
b. Eureka, S.Dak, 7/17/20; d. Gerner Arthur Olsen and Irene Gerdes Treick O; m. 4/14/41 to George L. March; c. Mary (Mrs. A.J. Robell). Educ: Univ. of S.Dak, B.S. in Ed, 41; Kappa Alpha Theta. Polit. & Govt. Pos: Mem-at-large, st. bd, Nat. Fedn. of Rep. Women; Clay Co. chmn, Women for Nixon, 68; alternate del, Rep. Nat. Conv, 68; Rep. precinct committeewoman, cent. ward, Clay Co, S.Dak, 68- Mem: Kappa Alpha Theta Alumni Club; PEO; Eastern Star; Clay Co. Hist. Soc. Rel: United Church of Christ. Mailing Add: Park Lane, Vermillion, S.Dak. 57069.

MARCHAM, JOHN D
Committeeman, Tompkins Co. Dem. Cmt, N.Y.
b. Ithaca, N.Y, 10/30/27; s. Frederick G. Marcham and Mary Cecelia Deacon M; m. 6/12/51 to Jane Margaret Haskins; c. David, Bruce and Sarah. Educ: Cornell Univ, A.B, 50; Watermargin House; Outstanding Senior, Cornell Univ, 50. Polit. & Govt. Pos: Committeeman, Tompkins Co. Dem. Cmt, N.Y, 60-, second ward chmn, 66; chmn, Tompkins Co. Dem. for McCarthy, 67-68; mem, exec. cmt, N.Y. State Coalition for Dem. Alternative, 68; del, Dem. Nat. Conv, 68; supvr, Tompkins Co, Ithaca, 68- Bus. & Prof. Pos: Reporter, Life Mag, N.Y.C, 50-52; publisher, Glastonbury Citizen, Conn, 52-53; city ed, Ithaca J, N.Y, 55-60; ed, Cornell Alumni News, Ithaca, N.Y, 61-64 & 67-; dir. univ. rels, Cornell Univ, 64-67. Mil. Serv: Entered as Pvt, Army, 46, released as Sgt, 47, after serv. in Daily Pacifician (newspaper), U.S. Armed Forces West. Pac, 46-47. Mem: Nat. Press Photographers Asn; Am. Alumni Coun; Am. Col. Pub. Rels. Asn. Time-Life-Sports Illustrated Mag. Improv. Award, 63; Silver Beaver Award, Louis Agassiz Fuertes Coun, Boy Scouts, 69. Rel: Congregational. Mailing Add: 414 E. Buffalo St, Ithaca, N.Y. 14850.

MARCHANT, BEATRICE ALVARETTA D
Utah State Rep.
b. Koosharem, Sevier Co, Utah, 12/27/03; d. Frands Peter Peterson and Anna Christine Pearson P; m. 12/19/23 to Stephen Casper Marchant; wid; c. LeGrande, George, Maurice, Lucy (Mrs. Robert Butters), Wanda (Mrs. Paul Rosander), Elva (Mrs. Richard Barnes), Joan (Mrs. Charles Braunersrither), Renée (Mrs. Roger Rampton), Richard, Lois (Mrs. Lindsay Steele), Stephen Roger, Marva Beth (Mrs. Roger Davis), Herbert Byron, Karen (Mrs. Ross Derbidge) and Frands Dwight. Educ: Univ. Utah, teachers cert, 21. Polit. & Govt. Pos: Pres, Women's Dem. Study Group, First Ward, Salt Lake City, Utah, 49 & 50; secy, Salt Lake Co. Dem. Party, 52-53; v.chmn, Voting Dist. 10 Dem. Party, Salt Lake Co, 52-69; v.chmn, Fourth Legis. Dist. Dem. Party, Salt Lake City, 60-64; mem, Salt Lake Co. Dem. Exec. Cmt, 60-66; pres, Women's Dem. Club, Fourth Legis. Dist. Salt Lake City, 62-66; v.chmn, Third Legis. Dist. Dem. Party, Salt Lake City, 64-66; Utah State Rep, Dist. 3, 69- Bus. & Prof. Pos: Teacher, North Summit Sch. Dist, Coalville, Utah 21-22; Sevier Sch. Dist, Redmond, 22-23; South Summit Sch. Dist, Peoa, 23-24; teacher-librn, Highland Park Sch, Salt Lake City, 53-54; McKinley Sch, 54-55; mem. staff microfilming photo copy dept, Salt Lake Co. Recorder's Off, 58-62, universal microfilming, 63-67; foster grandparent, Sch. for Sensory Impaired, Primary Childrens Hosp, 67-68. Mem: Utah Libr. Asn; Utah Educ. Asn; Utah PTA; Ladies Auxiliary, VFW; Women's Legis. Coun. Rel: Latter-day Saint. Mailing Add: 415 Williams Ave, Salt Lake City, Utah 84111.

MARCHI, JOHN JOSEPH R
N.Y. State Sen.
b. Staten Island, N.Y, 5/20/21; s. Louis B. Marchi and Alina Girardello M; m. 11/14/48 to Maria Luisa Davini; c. Joan Mary and Aline Grace. Educ: Manhattan Col, B.A, 42; St. John's Univ. Sch. of Law, LL.B, 49; Brooklyn Law Sch, J.S.D, 52; Epsilon Sigma Pi. Polit. & Govt. Pos: N.Y. State Sen, currently, counsel, N.Y. State Senate and Joint Legis. Cmt. on Natural Resources, 53-54, chmn, Senate Cmt. on N.Y.C, mem. exec. cmt. for Coun. State Govt. and chmn, Joint Legis. Cmt. for Interstate Coop; alternate del, Rep. Nat. Conv, 68. Mil. Serv: Entered Coast Guard, 42, combat serv. in Am, Pac. and Asiatic Theaters; released to active res. in 46, Comdr, at present. Mem: Am. and Richmond Co. Bar Asns; Am. Judicature Soc; Am. Legion; VFW; N.Y.C. Coun. on Econ. Educ. Rel: Catholic. Mailing Add: 79 Nixon Ave, Staten Island, N.Y. 10304.

MARCOTTE, RONALD J. D
N.H. State Sen.
b. Berwick, Maine, 3/26/37; single. Educ: Somersworth High Sch. Polit. & Govt. Pos: N.H. State Rep, Dist. 5, 67-68; N.H. State Sen, 20th Dist, 69- Bus. & Prof. Pos: Bartender. Mil. Serv: Navy, 4 years. Mem: N.H. State Senate Asn; CWV; Lions. Rel: Catholic; Mem, Holy Name Soc, St. Jean Baptiste. Legal Res: Howe's Rd, Rollinsford, N.H. 03869. Mailing Add: P.O. Box 279, Dover, N.H. 03820.

MARCOTTE, ROLAND LOUIS D
b. Lewiston, Maine, 3/25/18; s. Jean B. Marcotte and Regina Deshaiès M; m. 6/20/42 to Eileen F. Hopkins; c. Roland L, Jr, Mary Elizabeth and Brian M. Educ: Lewiston High Sch, 4 years. Polit. & Govt. Pos: Alderman, Lewiston, Maine, 49-50, mayor, 53, 54 & 64; del, Dem. Nat. Conv, 68. Bus. & Prof. Pos: Salesman, Standard Brands, Inc, Cambridge, Mass, 39, 40 & 46; installer, New Eng. Tel. & Tel. Co, Lewiston, Maine, 47-48; salesman, sales mgr. and gen. mgr, Puritan Chevrolet, Inc, Lewiston, 49-59; dealer, Marcotte Chevrolet, Inc, Auburn, 60- Mil. Serv: Entered as Pvt, Army, 41, released as 1st Lt, 45, after serv. in East. Flying Training Command, as a Flying Liaison Officer, French Pilot Training Prog, 43-45; Good Conduct and French Flying Medals; French Pilot Wings. Mem: Am. Legion; Kiwanis; Elks; trustee, Cent. Maine Gen. Hosp; C. of C. Rel: Roman Catholic. Legal Res: 276 Stevens Mills Rd, Auburn, Maine 04210. Mailing Add: P.O. Box 286, Auburn, Maine 04210.

MARCOUX, HECTOR T. D
b. Jacksonville, Vt, 11/1/05; m. to Frances McDowell McGibney; c. six sons and four daughters. Educ: Albany Bus. Col. Polit. & Govt. Pos: Vt.

State Sen, 55-59, 63-65; Vt. State Rep, 49, 51; deputy sheriff; sch. treas, Underhill, Inc; treas, Underhill-Jerisho Fire Dept. Bus. & Prof. Pos: State mgr, Melrose Distillers Co. Mem: chm, Social Welfare Bd; Elks; Ethan Allen Club. Rel: Catholic. 1967 Legal Res: 9 Birch St, S. Burlington, Vt. No mailing address available. (1967)

MARCOUX, KATHREN EVELYN D
Dem. Precinct Co-Chmn, Okeene, Okla.
b. Thomas, Okla, 9/26/19; d. William Carl Campbell and Maud Hooper C; m. 5/22/43 to Bennett Joseph Marcoux. Polit. & Govt. Pos: Dem. precinct co-chmn, Okeene, Okla, 60- Rel: Baptist. Legal Res: 115 West E, Okeene, Okla. 73763. Mailing Add: Box 384, Okeene, Okla. 73763. (1967)

MARCUS, EDWARD LEONARD D
Majority Leader, Conn. State Senate
b. Brooklyn, N.Y, 6/14/27; s. Isaac Horatio Marcus and Dorothy Kirschstein M; m. 9/18/48 to Phyllis Betzes; c. Shelley and Susan. Educ: Yale Univ, B.A, 47; Yale Law Sch, LL.B, 50; football, basketball, baseball and wrestling. Polit. & Govt. Pos: Mem, New Haven Bd. Aldermen, Conn, 51-56; Conn. State Sen, 58-, Majority Leader, Conn. State Senate, currently; chmn, Conn. Cmn. Inter-Govt. Rels; mem, Bd. Mgr, Coun. of State Govt, former v.chmn, chmn, 67-68; chmn, Cmn. Investigating Conn. Zoning Laws; chmn, Northeast. Conf. of States; chmn, Cmn. to Investigate Uninsured Motorists; del, Dem. Nat. Conv, 67-68. Bus. & Prof. Pos: Dir, New Haven Commun. Coun, 66-; dir, Second Nat. Bank of New Haven, Atlantic Franchise Corp. and Connsurance Corp, 69- Mem: Am. Juridical Soc; New Haven Co, State and Am. Bar Asns; Yale Club, New Haven; Woodbridge Country Club; New Haven Racquet Club. Holder, Doubles Title, Tennis, New Haven; Finalist, State Doubles Tennis Tournament, 64-67; Winner, State Doubles Tennis Tournament, 68. Rel: Jewish. Legal Res: 135 Westwood Rd, New Haven, Conn. 06515. Mailing Add: 38 Trumbull St, New Haven, Conn. 06510.

MARCY, ORRIN JAY D
Chmn, Sheridan Co. Dem. Party, Nebr.
b. Hay Springs, Nebr, 7/15/16; s. Orrin Jay Marcy and Nelle Johansen M; m. 8/18/40 to Gladys Irene Lambert; c. Douglas Clark and Dennis Dean. Educ: Univ. Nebr, Lincoln, B.S, 39; Kans. State Univ, M.S, 41; Block and Bridle Club; Phalanx; Alpha Gamma Rho. Polit. & Govt. Pos: Pres, Co. Exten. Bd, Nebr, 46-50; secy, Local Sch. Dist. 74, 46-60; Dem. precinct committeeman, East Mirage, 64-68; chmn, Sheridan Co. Dem. Party, Nebr, 68- Bus. & Prof. Pos: Instr, Univ. Maine, 40-42; rancher, Sheriden Co, Nebr, 46- Mil. Serv: Entered as 2nd Lt, Army Res, 39, released as 1st Lt, 46, after serv. in Field Artil, continental U.S. Spec. Instr. & Sch. Troops, 42-46, Hon. Res, 46-50. Mem: Am. and Nebr. Angus Asns; Nebr. Stock Growers; Nebr. Wheat Growers; Mason; Am. Legion; Hay Springs C. of C. Rel: Methodist. Mailing Add: Hay Springs, Nebr. 69347.

MARDEN, ROBERT ALLEN R
Rep. Nat. Committeeman, Maine
b. Waterville, Maine, 1/4/27; s. Harold Chesterfield Marden and Dorothy Harlow M; m. 6/14/49 to Shirley Irene Marshall; c. Sharon I, Robert M, Holly and Eric. Educ: Colby Col, 46-48; Boston Univ. Sch. of Law, LL.B, 51. Polit. & Govt. Pos: Mem. city coun, Waterville, Maine, 51-52; asst. co. attorney, Kennebec Co, 53-55, co. attorney, 55-59; Maine State Sen, 60-62, pres, Maine State Senate, 62-64; del, Rep. Nat. Conv, 64, alternate del, 68; mem, Maine Constitutional Cmn, Gov. Adv. Bd. on Ment. Health and Air Transportation; Rep. Nat. Committeeman, Maine, currently. Bus. & Prof. Pos: Admitted to Supreme Court of Maine, 51; assoc, Joly & Marden, Attorneys, 51-63; partner, Marden, Dubord, Bernier, Chandler & Ayoob, Attorneys, 64. Mil. Serv: Naval Air Force, 45-46; Lt. Col, Civil Air Patrol. Mem: Unauthorized Practice Cmt, Am. Bar Asn; exec. cmt, Maine State Bar Asn; pres. and trustee, Thayer Hosp; trustee, Waterville Savings Bank; dir, Sugarloaf Mt. Corp. Rel: Methodist. Legal Res: 51 Roosevelt Ave, Waterville, Maine 04901. Mailing Add: 44 Elm St, Waterville, Maine. 04901.

MARDESICH, AUGUST P. D
Wash. State Sen.
b. San Pedro, Calif, 1920; m. to Rosemary M; c. Five. Educ: Univ. Wash. Law Sch. Polit. & Govt. Pos: Wash. State Rep, 50-61; Wash. State Sen, currently. Bus. & Prof. Pos: Attorney; commercial fisherman. Mem: Elks; VFW; Am. Legion. Mailing Add: 4712 Mermont Dr, Everett, Wash. 98202. (1967)

MARDIAN, ROBERT CHARLES R
Gen. Counsel, Dept. of Health, Educ. and Welfare
b. Pasadena, Calif, 10/23/23; s. Samuel Mardian and Akabe Lukerian M; m. 4/14/46 to Dorothy Drusilla Denniss; c. Robert Charles, Jr, William Denniss and Blair Anthony. Educ: Pasadena Jr. Col, 39-41; Santa Barbara State Col, 41-43; Univ. South. Calif, J.D, 49; Phi Alpha Delta; Order of the Coif. Polit. & Govt. Pos: Mem, Pasadena Bd. of Educ, Calif, 55-57, pres, 57; mem, Jr. High Sch. Dist. and Jr. Col. Dist, Calif, 55-57; west. field dir, Rep. Nat. Cmt, 64; mem, Los Angeles Co. Rep. Cent. Cmt, 64-69 and v.chmn, 66-69; mem, Calif. Rep. State Cent. Cmt, 64-69; chmn. state adv. cmt, Reagan for Gov, 66; west. regional dir, Nixon for Pres. Cmt, 68; mem, Presidential Transition Cmt, Wash, D.C, 68-69; gen. counsel, Dept. of Health, Educ. and Welfare, 69- Bus. & Prof. Pos: Lawyer, Poole & Mardian, Pasadena, Calif, 49-51 and Boyle, Atwill, Mardian & Stearns, 51-62; v.pres. and gen. counsel, Wasco Financial Corp, 62-69. Mil. Serv: Entered as A/S V-7, Navy, 42, released as Lt.(jg), 46, after serv. as Commanding Officer, U.S.S. PC 818, Asiatic-Pac. Theatre, 44-46; World War II Victory Medal; Am. and Asiatic-Pac. Theatre Medals. Publ: 'What is Commerce,' 49, 'When is Commerce Interstate,' 49 and other legal articles, 47-49, Univ. South. Calif. Law Rev. Mem: State Bar of Calif; Am, D.C, Fed. and Los Angeles Co. Bar Asns; Anandale Golf Club; Overland Club. Distinguished Serv. Award, U.S. C. of C, 56. Rel: Protestant. Legal Res: 360 Camino San Clemente, San Clemente, Calif. 92672. Mailing Add: 1062 Rector Lane, McLean, Va. 22101.

MAREK, FRANK A. R
b. Chicago, Ill; m. to Phyllis Blazek M. Educ: Ph. G, U. of Ill. Col. of Pharm. Polit. & Gov. Pos: Ill. State Rep, 8 terms; elected mem. of Sch. Dist. No. 99, served as Secy. Bus. & Prof. Pos: Registr. Pharmacist. Mil. Serv: W.W. II, U.S. Navy. Mem: Dir, St. Mary's Youth Cent, Cicero; Am. Legion; Elks; Moose; U. of Ill. Alumni Asn; Cmdr, Polish Legion of Amvets. Mailing Add: 5434 W. 31st St, Cicero, Ill. 60650. (1967)

MAREK, RICHARD JOHN D
V.Chmn, Mich. Young Dem.
b. Grand Rapids, Mich, 12/29/46; s. Norbert Charles Marek and Doris Boss M; single. Educ: Grand Valley State Col, B.A, 69. Polit. & Govt. Pos: Pres, Grand Valley Col. Young Dem, 65-68; del, Mich. State Dem. Conv, 67-69; regional coordinator, Mich. Young Dem, 67-68, v.pres, 69-; mem, Kent Co. Dem. Exec. Cmt, 67-69; precinct del, Kent Co. Dem. Party, 68-; admin. asst, Kent Co. Dem. Cmt, 68; alternate del, Dem. Nat. Conv, 68; chmn, Kent Co. Young Dem, 69- Bus. & Prof. Pos: Clerk, Grand Valley Col. Libr, 65-69; in charge of billing, Gen. Tech. Serv, Grand Rapids, Mich, 69- Rel: Roman Catholic. Mailing Add: 328 Valley N.W, Grand Rapids, Mich. 49504.

MARES, JOHN KIETH R
b. Bear Creek, Wis, 10/31/24; s. George P. Mares and Hildegard Schindel M; m. 6/27/53 to Jean Lachelt; c. Deborah. Polit. & Govt. Pos: Former chmn, Waushara Co. Rep. Club, Wis. Mil. Serv: Entered as Pvt, Army, 42, released as T/Sgt, 45, after serv. in ETO; Purple Heart; ETO Medal with four stars. Mem: Jaycees. Hobby: Bowling. Rel: Catholic. Mailing Add: Box 271, Wautoma, Wis. 54982. (1967)

MARESCA, OREST V. D
b. New York, N.Y; s. Michael V. Maresca and Vincentini Durso M. Educ: St. Johns Univ, B.S; N.Y. Law Sch, LL.B. Polit. & Govt. Pos: Probation officer, N.Y.C. Magistrates Court, 46-47; asst. U.S. Attorney, Dept. of Justice, 47-50; N.Y. State Assemblyman, formerly, chmn, City of N.Y, Rules, Judiciary, Ins. and Excise Cmts; judge, Civil Court, N.Y.C, currently. Bus. & Prof. Pos: Lawyer; N.Y. State Bar; also admitted to practice: U.S. Dist. Court for the South. Dist, U.S. Court of Appeals, U.S. Supreme Court. Mil. Serv: Army, 42-46. Mem: Fed. Bar Asn; Dist. Attorney's Asn. of the State of N.Y; Cath. Lawyers Guild; Child Welfare Cmt; Am. Legion; chmn, Americanism and Constitution Cmt; dir, Inter-Faith Movement, Inc; K. of C; Elks Lodge 1; Grand Street Boys Asn; and many other civic and rel. asns. Rel: Catholic. Mailing Add: 111 Centre St, New York, N.Y. 10013.

MARETT, DAN THOMPSON D
S.C. State Rep.
b. Madison, S.C, 3/26/15; s. C.D. Marett and Nettie Thompson M; m. 3/4/36 to Mary Mayben; c. C. Don, Philip Guy, Dan Thompson, Jr. and Tweetie. Educ: Clemson Univ, 32-33; Draughon's Bus. Col, 1 year. Polit. & Govt. Pos: S.C. State Rep, 67-, 2nd v.chmn, Agr. and Conserv. Cmt, S.C. House of Rep, 67-69, mem, Juvenile Cmt, 69- Bus. & Prof. Pos: Pres, S.C. Florist Asn, 51, South. Retail Florist Asn, 52, Southeast. Florist Asn, 60 and Anderson Merchants Asn, 60-61; dist. rep, Florist's Transworld Delivery Asn, 60-61. Mem: Hejaz Temple; pres, Red Fez Shrine Club; Elks; pres, Anderson Lions Club, A&FM; S.C. Angus Asn; S.C. Farm Bureau; Pendleton Farmers Soc; C. of C. Rel: Baptist. Legal Res: Route 2, Pendleton, S.C. 29760. Mailing Add: 110 W. River St, Anderson, S.C. 29621.

MARGETTS, JOSEPHINE SHARON R
N.J. State Assemblyman
b. Marysville, Pa; d. Samuel A. Sharon and Mae Jones S; m. 7/18/35 to Walter T. Margetts, Jr; c. Sharon (Mrs. Richard Doremus), Susan Meredith (Mrs. Charles Connell), Cynthia (Mrs. Charles Robinson) and Walter T, III. Educ: Columbia Univ; Drew Univ; Rutgers Univ. Polit. & Govt. Pos: V.pres, Morris Co. Women's Rep. Club, N.J; mem, Nat. Rep. Club; pres, N.J. Fedn. Rep. Women; mem, N.J. Rep. Finance Cmt; mem. exec. cmt, N.J. State Rep. Cmt, currently; N.J. State Committeewoman; mem, Gov. Cmt. on Higher Educ; N.J. State Assemblyman, currently. Bus. & Prof. Pos: Owner, Sharon Orchards, Newport, Pa. Mem: Morristown and Passaic Valley Garden Clubs; officer, Summit-Morris-Somerset Women's Cmt. for the N.J. Symphony; trustee, Morristown Memorial Hosp, N.J. Camp for Blind Children, Inc. and Frost Valley Asn, YMCA. Only woman member of N.J. State Legis. Rel: Episcopal. Mailing Add: Holly Hill Farm, Blue Mill Rd, New Vernon, N.J. 07976.

MARGETTS, WALTER T, JR. R
m. 7/18/35 to Josephine Sharon; c. Sharon (Mrs. Richard Doremus), Cynthia (Mrs. Charles Robinson), Walter T, III and Susan Meredith (Mrs. Charles Connell). Educ: Am. Inst. Banking, grad; N.Y. Univ; St. Lawrence Univ, LL.B. and LL.M; Columbia Univ; Alpha Chi Epsilon; Delta Theta Phi. Hon. LL.D, Fairleigh Dickinson Univ, 53. Polit. & Govt. Pos: Mem, Nat. War Labor Bd, until 45; chmn, N.J. State Bd. Mediation, 45-49; treas, N.J, 49-54; former mem, Cmt. Interstate Coop; former chmn, N.J. Cmn. Inter-Govt. Rels; former chmn. and treas, N.J. Rep. Finance Cmt. Bus. & Prof. Pos: Employee, Brooklyn Trust Co, 23-29; assoc, Beekman, Bogue and Clark, 29-35; partner, law firm of Bainton, McNaughton and Douglas, N.Y.C; owner and operator, two farms, N.J. and Pa; trustee, Margetts Found, Laytham Found. and Little Ben Found; pres. and dir, Hudson & Manhattan Corp; dir, numerous other co; chmn. bd. and pres, Bright Star Industs, 52-; counsel, Forstmann Woolen Co, 54-; chmn. bd, Laytham Foundry, Inc, 56, v.chmn, currently. Mem: Fel, Fairleigh Dickinson Univ; div. chmn, Seton Hall Univ. Founders' Fund; former trustee, Rutgers Univ; former pres. and trustee, Passaic Collegiate Sch; adv. bd, All Souls' Hosp, Morristown; gov, Passaic Gen. Hosp; chmn. and trustee, N.J. Camp for Blind Children, Inc; Am. Arbitration Asn; former pres. and dir, N.J. Taxpayer's Asn; pres. and dir, N.J. Foundrymen's Asn; dir, Morris Co. Bridle Path Asn; trustee, State Soc. of Battleship New Jersey; pres. and trustee, Frost Valley Asn: YMCA; F&AM; life mem, Scottish Rite and AAONMS; life mem, Elks, St. Andrew's Soc. and Downtown Athletic Club; hon. life mem, Patrolmen's Benevolent Asn; Spring Valley Hunt Asn; Nat. Press Club; Capitol Hill Club; Metrop. Club; Essex Club; Morristown Club; Somerset Hills Country Club; trustee, Educ. Assistance Fund of Morris Co. Rel: Episcopal; Former vestryman, St. John's Episcopal Church. Legal Res: Holly Hill Farm, Blue Mill Rd, New Vernon, N.J. 07976. Mailing Add: Laytham Foundry, Inc, 899 Market St, Paterson, N.J. 07513.

MARGIOTTA, JOSEPH MICHAEL R
N.Y. State Assemblyman
b. Brooklyn, N.Y, 6/6/27; s. Michael D. Margiotta and Angela Lamanna M; m.

7/7/56 to Dorothy Crean; c. Michael and Carol Lynn. Educ: Hofstra Univ, B.A, 50; Brooklyn Law Sch, LL.B, 55; Crown and Lance, Hofstra Univ. Polit. & Govt. Pos: Committeeman, 62nd Elec. Dist, Uniondale, N.Y, 55; pres, Uniondale Rep. Club, 58; legis. counsel, N.Y. State Sen. Edward J. Speno, 59; counsel, Joint Legis. Cmt. on Hwy. Safety and Motor Vehicles, 60-64; exec. committeeman, Uniondale, L.I. Exec. Area, 62; legis. consult, Nassau Co. Bd, of Supvr, 65; N.Y. State Assemblyman, 12th Dist, 65-, v.chmn, Joint Legis. Cmt. on Educ, mem, Assembly Ways and Means Cmt. and Cmt. on Local Govt; dep. chmn, Hempstead Town Rep. Cmt, 66, chmn, 67; del, Rep. Nat. Conv, 68; chmn, Nassau Co. Rep. Cmt, N.Y, 68- Bus. & Prof. Pos: Attorney, Margiotta, Planders & Ricigliano, 53- Mil. Serv: Entered as A/S, Navy, 45, released as Yeoman 3/C, 46, after serv. aboard various ships; Asiatic-Pac. Victory Medal. Mem: Nassau Co. Bar Asn; Nassau Co. Hist. Soc; former trustee, Hofstra Univ; past pres. and bd. chmn, Hofstra's Alumni Asn; founder and past chmn, Uniondale Library Bd; former Comdr, Uniondale VFW Post; former chmn, Boy Scouts; Hempstead Elks; Uniondale Kiwanis; K. of C. Outstanding Alumnus, Hofstra's Alumni Asn, 66; Grass Roots Award, Nassau Press Asn; Columbian of the Year, 69. Rel: Catholic. Mailing Add: 844 Bedford Court, Uniondale, N.Y. 11553.

MARIANI, PETER P. R
b. New London, Conn, 8/1/15; m. 1941 to Alida M. Dufresne; c. Peter Jr, Ralph, Paul, Lenore, Alane, Alida and Evelyn Blance. Educ: Univ. Ala, B.A, 37; M.A, 38. Polit. & Govt. Pos: Burgess, Borough Groton, Conn, 50-56; former chmn, Groton Rep. Town Cmt; Conn. State Sen, 56-67, Asst. Minority Leader, 59-60 and Minority Leader, 61-67, Conn. State House of Rep; Rep. cand. for U.S. Rep, Conn, 68. Bus. & Prof. Pos: Elec. and hardware construction and supply indust. Mem: Dir. of New London Fed. Savings and Loan Asn; Conn. Bank and Trust Co, Groton Br; Winthrop Bank and Trust Co, New London bd. of trustees of Lawrence Mem. Assoc. Hosps, New London; Mitchell Col, New London; U.S. Cmn. on Civil Rights, Conn. Adv. Coun. Rel: Trustee, Sacred Heart Parish, Groton, Conn, active in Parish Develop. Prog. Mailing Add: 127 Tyler Ave, Groton, Conn. 06340. (1967)

MARINE, JOSEPH E. D
b. N.Y, N.Y, 12/19/05; m. to Josephine Del Genio; c. Dolores, Edward. Educ: N.Y. City Col; N.Y. Univ; N.Y. Univ. Sch. for Pub. Admin; Pace Inst. of Accountancy and Law. Polit. & Govt. Pos: N.Y. State Sen, 60-66; Exec. Asst. to Lt. Gov. George De Luca, 55-59; Admin. Asst. to Comptroller of the City of N.Y, 51-55; Torts Examiner, Bur. of Law and Adjustment, Comptroller's Off. of the City of N.Y; currently: Trustee, Siwanoy Dem. Orgn, 11th Assembly Dist, Bronx Co; Chmn, Joint Legis. Cmt. on Alcoholic Beverage Control Law. Bus. & Prof. Pos: V.Pres. and Comptroller, Hallen Construction Co, Inc; Off. and Ticket Mgr, N.Y. Yankees baseball club, 46-51. Mem: Past Pres, Columbia Asn. of Comptroller's Off; Secy, Bronx Chap, ACIM; NAACP, Williamsburg Br; Exec. Mem, Youth Coun, P.A.L; Nat.Conf. of Christians and Jews; Columbus Alliance; ESCA Club; E. Bronx. Hemophilia Guild; Bronx Lodge 871, Elks; Mary, Queen of Peach Coun, K. of C; N.E. Bronx Lodge 2091; Sons of Italy. Rel: Catholic. Mailing Add: 2071 Joel Place, Oceanside, N.Y. 11572. (1967)

MARINEAU, WILLIAM THOMAS R
b. Mason, Wis, 12/17/95; s. Ferdinand Marineau (deceased) and Octavia Dubois M. (deceased); m. 6/9/27 to Sophia Marie Kambistch; c. William Pierre and Arlen Jacque. Educ: Pub. high schs, Sandpoint, Idaho; 12 years; Sigma Delta Chi. Polit. & Govt. Pos: Idaho State Rep, Clearwater Co, 27-30; committeeman, Clearwater Co. Rep. Party; committeeman, Idaho State Rep. Party; mayor, Elk River; justice of the peace; mem, Bonneville Power Admin. Cmt; del, Rep. Nat. Conv, 68. Bus. & Prof. Pos: Publisher, Elk River News, 19-32; gen. mgr, Moscow News-Rev, 32-67; publisher, The Daily Idahonian, 67-; dir, Gen. Tel. Co. of the Northwest. Mil. Serv: Entered as Musician, Navy, 18, released as First Musician, 19, after serv. in U.S.S. St. Louis, Atlantic, 18-19. Mem: Elks; Am. Legion (nat. exec. committeeman from Idaho, 4 years, former State of Idaho Grande Chef DeGare and former state Sgt. at Arms); Kiwanis; hon. mem. Univ. Idaho Alumni Asn; Idaho State C. of C; Moscow C. of C.(pres, 2 terms). Hon. Serv. Award Plaque and prin. bldg. named William T. Marineau Bldg, Gen. Tel. Co. of the Northwest; Idaho State Ed-Publisher Plaque; Plaque Moscow C. of C. Rel: Catholic. Mailing Add: 611 E. Third St, Moscow, Idaho 83843.

MARINO, ANTHONY V. R
s. John V. Marino; m. to Frances Massa; c. John, Paula, Anthony Jr, Ralph, Cathy. Polit. & Govt. Pos: Town Meeting Mem; app. to a second term on Winthrop Housing Authority. Bus. & Prof. Pos: V. Pres. in charge of field opers. for Mari & Sons Flooring Co, Somerville. Mil. Serv: WW II vet, Army. Mem: Bldg. Trades Union; Don Orione Home Adv. Bd; Boston Bus. & Prof. Men's Lodge, 2030; Sons of Italy; Winthrop Lodge 2057, Sons of Italy; Kiwanis; Amvets Post 48; Winthrop Yacht Club; K of C, Coun. 162. Mailing Add: 33 Winthrop Shore Dr, Winthrop, Mass. 02152. (1967)

MARINO, RALPH JOHN R
N.Y. State Sen.
b. Rochester, N.Y, 1/2/28; s. James Marino and Antoinette Saraceno M; m. 3/15/55 to Ethel Bernstein; c. Judith, James and Robert. Educ: Syracuse Univ, B.A, 51; Fordham Univ. Law Sch, LL.B, 54. Polit. & Govt. Pos: Councilman, Oyster Bay Town Bd, N.Y, 66-68, majority leader, 67-68; Rep. committeeman, East Norwich, 58-; exec. leader, East Norwich-Brookville Rep. Party, 67-; N.Y. State Sen, Third Dist, 69- Bus. & Prof. Pos: Attorney, Zipper, Marino & Cronin, 55-59; attorney, Marino & Bernstein, 61- Mil. Serv: Entered as Pvt, Army, 46, released as Tech. 5/C, 47, after serv. in Med. Corps; Victory Medal. Mem: Nassau Bar Asn; Elks; Lions; C. of C; Sons of Italy. Rel: Catholic. Mailing Add: 3 Lea Court, Muttontown, Syosset, N.Y. 11791.

MARION, J. HARDIN D
b. Charlotte, N.C, 11/7/34; s. John Hardin Marion, Jr. and Beatrice Van Wie M; m. 6/21/58 to Patricia Hamm; c. David H, Michael S. and Laura E. Educ: Wash. & Lee Univ, B.A, 55, Law Sch, LL.B, 58; Phi Beta Kappa; Omicron Delta Kappa; Order of the Coif; Phi Gamma Delta. Polit. & Govt. Pos: Chmn, Young Lawyers for Kennedy-Johnson, Md, 60; asst. U.S. Attorney, Dist. of Md, 61-63; exec. dir, Joseph D. Tydings for U.S. Sen, Md, 64; campaign staff dir, Md. Dem. Campaign Cmt, 64; admin. asst. to U.S. Sen. Joseph D. Tydings, Md, 65-67; pres, City Co. Dem. Club, Baltimore, 65-67; del, State Constitutional Conv, 67-68; exec. dir, Md. Citizens for Proposed Constitution, 68; pres, Baltimore Co. Fourth Dist, Forum Four, 68-69; treas, Md. Salute to Sen. Joseph D. Tydings, 69. Mil. Serv: Entered as Pvt, Army, 58, released as 1st Lt, 64, after serv. in Md. Army Nat. Guard, Ft. Knox and Ft. Jackson. Mem: Am, Md. State, and Baltimore City Bar Asns; Jr. Bar Asn. Baltimore City; Am. Judicature Soc; Young Dem; bd. govs, Rodgers Forge Commun. Asn, 68-; exec. cmt, Rodgers Forge Elem. Sch. PTA, 68-; second v.pres, Baltimore Co. Coun, PTA, 69-; bd. dirs, Citizens Planning and Housing Asn, 60-63. Rel: Presbyterian; bd. Deacons, Brown Mem. Presbyterian Church, chmn, 68-69. Mailing Add: 7217 Lanark Rd, Baltimore, Md. 21212.

MARION, JOHN LEONARD D
Chmn, 39th Dist. Dem. Non-Partisan League, N.Dak.
b. Alta Vista, Iowa, 11/7/21; s. John Marion and Mary Elizabeth Clancy M; m. 7/14/45 to Bernice Ione White; c. James Leonard, Kathleen Marie, Theresa Anne, Elizabeth Alice, Thomas Edward and William John. Educ: Hettinger High Sch, N.Dak, dipl; Nat. Hon. Soc. Polit. & Govt. Pos: Chmn, Adams Co. Dem. Party, N.Dak, 66-68; city councilman, Hettinger, N.Dak, 68-; chmn, 39th Dist. Dem. Non-Partisan League, 68- Bus. & Prof. Pos: Partner, construction co, 46-69; pres, Hettinger C. of C, 58-59. Mil. Serv: Entered as Pvt, Army, 43, released as Tech. 3rd Grade, 45, after serv. in 3103 Signal Serv. Bn, ETO, 43-45; Good Conduct Medal; Marksman; Meritorious Serv. Award; Four Battle Stars. Mem: K. of C; C. of C; Eagles; Am. Legion; VFW; Toastmasters. Received speakers trophies in Toastmasters. Rel: Catholic. Mailing Add: Hettinger, N.Dak. 58639.

MARIONNEAUX, JOHN ESPER, JR. D
La. State Rep.
b. Plaquemine, La, 10/27/28; s. John Esper Marionneaux and Mary Alice Gravois M; m. 4/15/51 to Betty Clay Hebert; c. John Esper, Stephen Hebert, Paul David, Timothy Charles and Melonie Ann. Educ: Univ. Southwest. La, B.S, 49; Alpha Sigma Kappa. Polit. & Govt. Pos: Alderman, Krotz Springs, La, 56-60 & 64-66; La. State Rep, Tenth Dist, 68- Bus. & Prof. Pos: Sales mgr, Esper Marionneaux Lumber Co, 50- Mem: Nat. Hardwood Lumber Asn; South. Hardwood Producers; Southwest. Hardwood Mfrs; Pointe Coupee Cattlemens Asn; Pointe Coupee Parish Farm Bur; K. of C; Elks; Lions. Rel: Catholic. Mailing Add: P.O. Box 8, Livonia, La. 70755.

MARK, NORMAN LEROY R
b. Yuba City, Calif, 10/28/33; s. Wesley Steel Mark and Lottie Kratz M; m. 6/22/57 to Carolyn Cooper; c. Diane and Virginia. Educ: Univ. Calif. at Berkeley, A.B, 55; Phi Beta Kappa. Polit. Pos: Treas, Young Rep. of Calif, 66-67, asst. treas, 65-66; chmn, Sutter Co, 64-65. Bus. & Prof. Pos: Acct, Harry M. Straine and Co, 66-; off. mgr, Gillett-Harris-Duranceau & Assoc, 63-66; off. mgr, Young Construc. Co, 62-63. Mil. Serv: Entered as Pvt, Army, 56, released as Sgt, 58, after serv. in Security Agency Training Center, 1st Army, 56-59. Mailing Add: 3277 Rosemont Dr, Sacramento, Calif. 95826. (1967)

MARKEL, J. OGDEN D
b. New Orleans, La, 8/18/98; s. Jules W. Markel and Ada Dillon M; m. 10/27/26 to Helena Lieberman; c. Barbara Lee, Jules and twins, Louise and Joyce. Polit. & Govt. Pos: City Councilman, Santa Ana, Calif, 54-58 & 65-69. Bus. & Prof. Pos: Gen. contractor, 36- Mem: Lions; K. of C; Holy Name Soc; Toastmasters; S. Main Improvement Asn. Beni Morenti Gold Medal by Pope John 23rd. Rel: Catholic. Legal Res: 1814 S. Parton St, Santa Ana, Calif. 92707. Mailing Add: P.O. Box 2012, Santa Ana, Calif. 92707.

MARKERT, LOUIS A. D
Ill. State Rep.
b. Mt. Sterling, Ill, 12/15/27; s. Louis F. Markert and Corrinne Borden Kircher M; m. 2/22/49 to Barbara J. Anderson; c. Anne E, Daniel L, Jane L. and Mary Kay. Educ: St. Mary's Acad, 4 years. Polit. & Govt. Pos: Chmn, Brown Co. Dem. Cmt, Ill, 63-; secy, 20th Cong. Dist. Dem. Orgn, currently; Ill. State Rep, 69- Bus. & Prof. Pos: Self-employed in Agr. Mem: Elks; K. of C; Farm Bur. Rel: Catholic. Mailing Add: R.R. 1, Mt. Sterling, Ill. 62353.

MARKEY, DAVID JOHN, III R
b. Frederick, Md; s. David John Markey, Jr. (deceased) and Mary Alice Moberly M; single. Educ: West. Maryland Col, B.S, 63; Univ. Maryland, Law Sch, LLB, 67; Delta Pi Alpha. Polit. & Govt. Pos: Law clerk, Judge Edward Northrop, Fed. Dist. Court, 65; law clerk, Judge Stewart Dag, Third Judicial Circuit, Md, 65-67; asst. legis. officer, Gov. Spiro T. Agnew, 67-69; admin. asst, U.S. Rep. J. Glenn Beall, Jr, 69- Mil. Serv: Entered as Pvt, Army, 58, released as Pfc, 68 after serv. in Signal Corp. Mem: Am. and Md. State Bar Asns. Rel: Protestant. Legal Res: 201 Grove Blvd, Frederick, Md. 21701. Mailing Add: 8318 Donnell Pl. 4D, Forestville, Md. 20028.

MARKHAM, ALLAN WHITLOCK D
b. Charlottesville, Va, 3/5/31; s. Edwin Carlyle 'Jerry' Markham and Janet Whitlock M; div; c. Janet Leigh, Diane Carter, David Allan and Jerri Elizabeth. Educ: Univ. of Colo, 49-51; Univ. of N.C, A.B, 54 and J.D, 61; Order of the Coif; Sigma Chi; Phi Alpha Delta. Polit. & Govt. Pos: Asst. dir, Inst. of Govt, 61-66; dir, div. of inst. eval. and accreditation, N.C. Dept. of Commun. Cols, 66-68; admin. asst. to U.S. Rep. Nick Galifianakis, Fourth Dist, N.C, 69- Mil. Serv: Entered as Aviation Mid, Navy, 52, released as Comdr, 68, after serv. in Korea, 52-53, Japan, 54-58 and Viet Nam, 68; Comdr, Naval Air Res; PTO; Korean Serv. Medal; UN Medal; Nat. Defense Serv. Medal; China Serv. Medal; Expert Rifle and Pistol; three Air Medals. Publ: Public Education Organization in North Carolina, 65, County Government in North Carolina, 66 and Public School Transportation in North Carolina, 66, Univ. of N.C. Mem: N.C. State Bar; N.C. and Am. Bar Asns; Nat. Asn. on Legal Probs. in Educ; Nat. Asn. of Co. Off; N.C. Dem. Club of Wash; Cong. Secy. Club. Rel: Protestant. Legal Res: P.O. Box 341, Chapel Hill, N.C. 27514. Mailing Add: 922 N. Carolina Ave. S.E, Washington, D.C. 20003.

MARKHAM, CHARLES BUCHANAN R
Dep. Asst. Secy. for Metrop. Develop, Dept. of Housing and Urban Develop.
b. Durham, N.C, 9/15/26; s. Charles Blackwell Markham and Sadie Hackney

M; single. Educ: Duke Univ, A.B, 45; Univ. N.C. Law Sch, Chapel Hill, 45-46; George Wash. Univ. Law Sch, LL.B, 51; Phi Beta Kappa; Omicron Delta Kappa; Phi Delta Theta. Polit. & Govt. Pos: Dir. publicity and research, Young Dem. Clubs of Am, 48-49, exec. secy, 49-50; research analyst, Dem. Sen. Campaign Cmt, 50-51; spec. attorney, Internal Revenue Serv, Wash, D.C. and N.Y.C, 52-60; dir. of research, Equal Employ. Opportunity Cmn, Wash, D.C, 65-68; mem, Legal Research for Vote Fraud Task Force, Nat. Lawyers Cmt. for Nixon-Agnew, 68; Dep. Asst. Secy. for Metrop. Develop, Dept. of Housing and Urban Develop, 69- Bus. & Prof. Pos: Ed-in-chief, Duke Chronicle, Duke Univ, 44-45; reporter, Durham Sun, N.C, 45; asst. state ed. and ed. writer, Charlotte News, 47-48; assoc, Battle, Fowler, Stokes & Kheel, N.Y.C, 60-65. Publ: Ed, Jobs, Men and Machines: The Problems of Automation, Frederick A. Praeger, Inc, 64 and Equal Employment Opportunity Report No. 1, Equal Employ. Opportunity Cmn, 3 vols, 69. Mem: Am. Bar Asn; Asn. of the Bar of the City of N.Y. Admitted to practice before U.S. Supreme Court and the Bars of N.Y. and D.C. Rel: Protestant Episcopal. Legal Res: 102 E. 22nd St, New York, N.Y. 10010. Mailing Add: 824 New Hampshire Ave. N.W, Washington, D.C. 20037.

MARKHAM, HARLEY BRUCE, SR. R
b. Longmont, Colo, 12/21/04; s. Charles Robert Markham and Effie Evans M; m. 8/27/29 to Ruth McCormick; c. H. Bruce. Educ: Colo. State Univ; A Club; Scabbard and Blade; Sigma Phi Epsilon. Polit. & Govt. Pos: Mem. exec. cmt, Idaho State Rep. Cent. Cmt, 58; chmn, Idaho State Rep. Finance Cmt, 59-68; mem, Rep. Nat. Cmt, 59-68. Bus. & Prof. Pos: Chmn. bd, Markham Advert. Co, Inc, 45-; mem. exec. cmt, Outdoor Advert, Inc, 47-63; pres. and chmn. bd, Outdoor Advert. Asn. of Am, 56-60. Mil. Serv: Entered as 1st Lt, Army, 42, released as Maj, 45, after serv. in Field Artil, ETO; Bronze Star. Mem: Pocatello C. of C.(pres, 50); Mason; Elks; Am. Legion; VFW. Golf and fishing. Rel: Methodist. Mailing Add: 204 S. 14th, Pocatello, Idaho 83201.

MARKHAM, W. ALLEN D
b. Cincinnati, Ohio, 1/29/11; m. to Alice Armstrong; c. Thomas A, Charles R, Martha Ann, Mary Jane, Edward and Tina. Educ: Roanoke Col. Polit. & Govt. Pos: Fla. State Rep, 58-66. Bus. & Prof. Pos: Dir, Okeechobee Co. Bank and United Capital Corp, West Palm Beach, Fla; vegetable and fruit canner, farmer and cattleman. Mem: State and U.S. C. of C; Former Dir, Okeechobee C. of C; Okeechobee Co. Welfare Bd; U. S. Savings Bond Chmn; Dir, Fla. Fruit and Vegetable Asn; Fla. Vegetable Canners Asn, pres. 58-60; Dir, Nat. Canners Asn; Former pres. Nat. Tomato Coun; 64 Conv. Chmn, Fla Fruit and Vegetable Asn; Boy Scouts, former pres; Gulf Stream Coun; chmn, Section Five, Nat. Coun, 58-60; Masons; Shrine; Eastern Star, former Patron; Odd Fellows, former Noble Grand; Rotary Club, ,former pres; Boat Club; Bedford Co. Country Club; Capital City Country Club; Okeechobee Country Club; PTA. Honors: Cert. of Appreciation in the form of Resolution of Commendation from Fla. Nurserymen & Growers Asn, 63. Rel: Baptist (former Sunday Sch. Teacher). Mailing Add: P.O.Box 428, Okeechobee, Fla. 33472. (1967)

MARKHAM, WILLIAM EDWIN R
Ore. State Rep.
b. Chehalis, Wash, 10/9/22; s. John Howard Markham and Grace Young M; m. 9/25/43 to Jean Eddins; c. Lt. William E, Jr, Michael J. and Patrick A. Educ: Univ. Wash, Bus, 46; Delta Chi. Polit. & Govt. Pos: Mem. Bd, Riddle Sch. Dist. 70, Ore, 60-68; mem. Bd, Umpqua Col, 64-69; Ore. State Rep, Douglas Co, 69- Bus. & Prof. Pos: Owner, Markham Lumber Co, Riddle, 47- Mil. Serv: Army Air Force, 42, released as Lt, 45 after serv. in 398 Bomb Group, Eighth Air Force, Europe, as a Bomber Pilot; Air Medal with Clusters. Mem: Farm Bureau; Am. Legion; VFW; Elks; Mason; Shrine; Lions. Rel: Episcopal. Legal Res: Route 1, Glenbrook Loop Rd, Riddle, Ore. 97469. Mailing Add: P.O. Box 285, Riddle, Ore. 97469.

MARKLE, JOHN, JR. R
Mem. Finance Cmt, Chester Co. Rep. Party, Pa.
b. Allentown, Pa, July 1931; s. John Markle, II; m. to Mary B. McLean; c. Ellen, John, III, Patricia, Stephen and Mary. Educ: Yale Univ, B.A, 53; Harvard Law Sch, LL.B, 58; Delta Psi. Polit. & Govt. Pos: Committeeman, Willistown Twp. Rep. Cmt, Pa, 61-69; dist. adminstr, Pa. Young Rep, 62-64, mem. exec. cmt. and gen. counsel, 64-68; chmn, Chester Co. Young Rep, 63-64; mem. finance cmt, Chester Co. Rep. Party, 66-; del, Rep. Nat. Conv, 68. Bus. & Prof. Pos: Assoc, Drinker, Biddle & Reath, 58-64, partner, 64- Mil. Serv: Entered as 2nd Lt, Marine Corps, 53, released as 1st Lt, 55, after serv. in Ninth and Fifth Regt, Japan and Korea, 54-55, Lt. Col, Res, 55-69; UN, Korean and Nat. Defense Medals. Mem: Phila, Pa. and Am. Bar Asns; Indust. Rels. Asn; Indust. Rels. Research Asn; Am. Arbit. Asn.(nat. panel); Merion Cricket Club; Union League of Phila; Yale Club of Phila. Waynesborough Country Club; Childrens Aid Soc. Pa. Outstanding Young Rep. in Pa, 66-68. Rel: Episcopal. Legal Res: 23 Andrews Rd, Malvern, Pa. 19355. Mailing Add: 1100 Philadelphia Nat. Bank Bldg, Philadelphia, Pa. 19107.

MARKLEY, MARIAN E. R
b. Treichlers, Pa; d. Edgar E. Hall and Bertie Berlin H; m. to Franklin H. Markley. Educ: Northampton High Sch. Polit. & Govt. Pos: Mem, Rep. Co. Cmt, Pa, 12 years; secy. to Majority Leader, Pa. House of Rep, 43-45, admin. asst. to Speaker, 47; Pa. State Rep, 50-68. Bus. & Prof. Pos: Off. mgr. in private indust, 15 years. Mem: Lehigh Co. Coun. of Rep. Women; Allentown Quota Club; Bus. and Prfnl. Women of Emmaus and Macungie; Pomona and State Grange; pres, Lehigh Valley Guid. Clin; State Bd. of Pub. Welfare; mem. bd, Am. Cancer Soc; trustee, Lehigh Valley-Del. Valley Cystic Fibrosis Found. Distinguished Daughter of Pa. Award, 57. Mailing Add: R.D. 1, Macungie, Pa. 18062. (1967)

MARKMAN, SHERWIN J. D
b. Des Moines, Iowa, 1/19/29; s. Morris Markman and Dorothy Caspe M; m. 8/26/51 to Marilyn Louise Gates; c. Stephen Madison, Nicole Mari and Stacy Lynn. Educ: State Univ. of Iowa, B.A, 49; Yale Univ, LL.B, 52; Phi Beta Kappa; Omicron Delta Kappa; Delta Sigma Rho. Polit. & Govt. Pos: State exec. dir, Iowa Citizens for Stevenson, 56; del, Dem. Nat. Conv, 56, 60 & 64; state chmn,Iowa Citizens for Hughes, 64; chmn, Des Moines Planning & Zoning Cmn, 57-65; dep. dir. cong. liaison, Agency for Int. Develop, Dept. of State, 65-66; asst. to the President, U.S, 66-68. Mem: Exec. cmt, Polk Co. Bar Asn, 63-65; Am. Bar Asn; commun. serv. chmn, Gr. Des Moines C. of C, 63-64; Nat. Capitol Dem. Club; Wakonda Club. Rel: Jewish. Legal Res: Des Moines, Iowa. Mailing Add: 8100 Hamilton Spring Rd, Bethesda, Md. 20034. (1967)

MARKOVITZ, HARRY R
b. McKeesport, 3/7/17; s. Samuel M. Markovitz and Helen Fishman M; m. to Rose M. Bergstein; c. two. Educ: Univ. of Pittsburgh, B.S; Univ. of Pittsburgh Law Sch, LL.B. Polit. & Govt. Pos: Pa. State Rep, 64-67. Bus. & Prof. Pos: Attorney, admitted to practice before the Allengheny Co. Bar and the U.S. Supreme Court. Mil. Serv: WW II; Capt. in USAAF, Navigation Off, B-29 Bomber Group. Mem: United Jewish Fed; past Dept. Comdr, Pa. Jewish War Vets; Nat. exec. com. of the Jewish War Vets of the U.S., 10 yrs; Bd. of Dir, Nat. Jewish War Vets' Mem. Shrine; past comdr. Post 577, Am. Legion; past dep. Comdr, 35th Dist. of the Am. Legion of Pa; past pres, B'nai Brith Lodge 1821; bd. of the Pittsburgh JCRC; Masons; Squirrel Hill Bd. of Trade. Rel: Jewish. Mailing Add: 5635 Melvin St, Pittsburgh, Pa. 15217. (1967)

MARKS, CHARLES HARDAWAY D
Va. State Del.
b. Hopewell, Va, 1/31/21; m. to Archie Davis Andrews H. Educ: Wake Forest Col, B.A; Duke Univ; Univ. Va. Law Sch; Delta Sigma Phi; Delta Theta Phi. Polit. & Govt. Pos: Del, Dem. Nat. Conv, 60; Va. State Del, 62- Bus. & Prof. Pos: Lawyer. Mil. Serv: Capt, Marines, 42-46, wounded on Iwo Jima. Mem: Farm Bur; exec. cmt, Robert E. Lee Boy Scouts; VFW; Am. Legion; Moose; Sons of Confederate Vet; Young Dem; Am, Va. State and Hopewell Bar Asns; past pres. and past chmn, Hopewell Commun. Chest and Red Cross; past pres, Hopewell United Givers Fund. Rel: Baptist. Mailing Add: Perry Bldg, 1000 River Dr, Hopewell, Va. 23860.

MARKS, DORRIS DOTY R
b. Waupun, Wis, 12/10/92; d. David Putman Doty and Fannie Conant D; m. 5/9/19 to Melvin Charles Marks; c. David Walter, Judith Alita (Mrs. Gatzke) and Geraldine Frances (Mrs. Tatham). Educ: Milwaukee State Normal, grad; Marquette Univ. Night Sch. and Milwaukee Voc. Sch, courses in advert. and art, 6 years; Delta Omicron; Thalia. Polit. & Govt. Pos: Former secy. and committeewoman, Montgomery Co. Rep. Party, Ark. Publ: Stories, series and feature articles in Milwaukee J. and assoc. papers. Rel: Methodist. Mailing Add: Caddo Gap, Ark. 71935.

MARKS, GORDON SUTTON D
Miss. State Rep.
b. Jackson, Miss, 7/11/28; married. Educ: Millsaps Col, B.S; Northwest. Univ, M.S; Pi Kappa Alpha; Pi Alpha Mu. Polit. & Govt. Pos: Miss. State Rep, 60- Bus. & Prof. Pos: Advert. agency exec. Mem: Jackson C. of C; Miss. Mfrs. Asn; MEC; Kiwanis. Rel: First Christian Church. Mailing Add: Box 1757, Jackson, Hinds County, Miss. 39205.

MARKS, HOWARD R. R
b. Sebree, Ky, 9/18/02; s. Arch D. Marks and Lillie Mae Wiley M; m. 1924 to Ona Poole, wid, 1936; m. 1943 to Allyne Melton; c. John W, Howard R, Jr, Burrel T, Roberta A, Ronald E. and Rachel J. Educ: High sch. Polit. & Govt. Pos: Co. hwy. foreman, Ky. State Hwy. Dept, 45-47 and currently; past chmn, Webster Co. Rep. Exec. Cmt, Ky. Bus. & Prof. Pos: Clerk and route salesman, Standard Oil Co, 50- Mem: WOW. Rel: General Baptist. Mailing Add: Route 2, Dixon, Ky. 42409.

MARKS, JEROME WALTER D
b. New York, N.Y, 6/22/15; s. Harry L. Marks and Pearl Kanowitt M; m. 1951 to Patricia Graham; c. Lorna and Gael. Educ: St. Johns Univ; Brooklyn Law Sch. Polit. & Govt. Pos: N.Y. State Assemblyman, 63-68; judge, Civil Court, N.Y.C, 69- Mil. Serv: Entered as Pvt, Air Force, 42, released as 1st Lt, after serv. in N.Africa. Mem: N.Y. Co. Lawyers; Am. Legion; VFW. Rel: Jewish. Mailing Add: 115 E. Ninth St, New York, N.Y. 10003.

MARKS, LEONARD HAROLD D
b. Pittsburgh, Pa; s. Samuel Marks and Ida Lewine M; m. 6/3/48 to Dorothy Ames; c. Stephen Ames and Robert Evan. Educ: Univ. Pittsburgh, B.A, 35, LL.B, 38; Omicron Delta Kappa; Sigma Delta Chi; Phi Beta Kappa. Polit. & Govt. Pos: Asst. to gen. counsel, Fed. Commun. Cmn, 42-46; del, Int. Broadcast Conf, Mexico City, 48; del, N. Am. Regional Broadcast Conf, Montreal, 49; State Dept. lectr, adminstr. and consult. law, India, 58 and Pakistan, Afghanistan-Iran, Turkey, 61; mem, U.S. Del, Int. Telecommun. Conf, Geneva, 59 & 63; head, U.S. Info. Agency, 65-68; ambassador-chmn, Int. Conf. on Commun. Satellites, 68-69. Bus. & Prof. Pos: Prof. law, Univ. Pittsburgh Law Sch, 38-42; prof. law, Nat. Univ, 43-55; partner, Cohn and Marks, Attorneys-at-law, 46-65 & 69- Mem: Am, D.C, Fed. Commun.(past pres, 59-60), Allegheny Co, Inter-Am. and Int. Bar Asns; Order of Coif; Cosmos, Fed. City, Nat. Press, Nat. Lawyers and Broadcasters (pres, 57-59) Clubs. Legal Res: 2833 McGill Terr. N.W, Washington, D.C. 20008. Mailing Add: 1920 L St. N.W, Washington, D.C. 20036.

MARKS, MILTON R
Calif. State Sen.
b. San Francisco, Calif, 7/22/20; m. 8/14/55 to Carolene Wachenheimer; c. Carol, Milton and Edward David. Educ: Stanford Univ, A.B; San Francisco Law Sch, LL.B. Polit. & Govt. Pos: Calif. State Assemblyman, 58-66; Calif. State Sen, Ninth Sen. Dist, 67- Bus. & Prof. Pos: Former Judge, Munic. Court. Mil. Serv: Army; combat in Philippines; occup. forces in Japan. Mem: VFW; Am. Legion; Press and Union League Club of San Francisco; Lions; dir, Calif. League for the Handicapped, Inc; trustee, Lincoln Univ. and Spanish-Speaking Citizens Found; adv. bd, South of Market Boys, Inc. Legal Res: 55 Jordan Ave, San Francisco, Calif. 94118. Mailing Add: Room 2070 State Capitol, Sacramento, Calif. 95814.

MARKS, ROBERT D
b. Chicago, Ill, 9/26/16; m. to Jeanne Mooren; c. Joel Alan and Joan Barbara. Educ: Univ. of Chicago; Northwest. Univ. Law Sch, 40; former nat. pres, Tau Epsilon Rho. Polit. & Govt. Pos: Former chmn, Evanston Cmt. of the City Mgr; Ill. State Rep; chmn, Cook Co. Zoning Bd. Appeals, currently. Bus. & Prof. Pos: Lawyer, admitted to Ill. Bar, 40; mem. faculty, Northwest.

Univ. Sch. Law, 49-60. Mem: Chicago and Fed. Bar Asns; Evanston Human Rel. Coun; Dem. Club Evanston; Evanston Reg. Dem. Orgn; Beth Emet Synagogue Bd. Trustees. Pub. Serv. Award, Tau Epislon Rho; Best Legislator Award; Brotherhood Award; Press Award as Outstanding Orator, Ill. House Rep. Mailing Add: 420 Ashland Ave, Evanston, Ill. 60202.

MARKS, ROBERT L. R
Mont. State Representative
b. Helena, Mont, 1/11/32; s. Merle Milton Marks and Evelyn Rutherford M; m. 6/3/51 to Barbara Myles; c. Robert David, Beverly Jean, Gary Douglas, Steven Michael, Richard Daniel and Christian Jay. Educ: Mont. State Univ, 1 year; Univ. Mont, 1 year. Polit. & Govt. Pos: Mem. Clancy Sch. Bd, Mont, 53-61; mem, Jefferson Co. High Sch. Bd, 63- Mont. State Rep, Dist. 16, 69- Bus. & Prof. Pos: Chmn, Helena Nat. Forest Cattleman's Adv. Bd, 62- Mem: Montana Stock Growers Asn; Mason; Scottish Rite. Rel: Methodist.. Mailing Add: Clancy, Mont. 59634.

MARKUN, PATRICIA MALONEY D
b. Chisholm, Minn, 8/24/24; d. Andrew Michael Maloney and Helen Ryan M; m. 6/14/48 to David J. Markun; c. Sybil Ann, Paul Addam, Meredith Helen and David J, Jr. Educ: Univ. Minn, B.A, magna cum laude, 45; Theta Sigma Phi; Zeta Phi Eta. Polit. & Govt. Pos: Mem, C.Z. Regional Dem. Party, 62-68; Dem. nat. committeewoman, C.Z, 64-68. Bus. & Prof. Pos: Pub. rels. dir, Minneapolis Inst. of Arts, 46-48, Hotel Nicollet, Minneapolis, 48; author of children's books, 56- Publ: The Secret of El Baru, 57; The First Book of the Panama Canal, 57; The First Book of Central America and Panama, 62. Mem: League of Am. Authors; Nat. League of Am. Pen Women; C.Z. Col. Club. Rel: Catholic. Legal Res: 626 Cascadas Rd, Balboa Heights, C.Z. Mailing Add: Box 393, Balboa Heights, C.Z. (1967)

MARLATT, RALPH HIERS R
b. Peru, Ind, 7/20/08; s. Norval Gourland Marlatt and Genevieve Smith M. m. 8/1/36 to Kathleen Stella Mahoney; c. Ralph Jerome. Educ: Univ. Mich, 26-27. Polit. & Govt. Pos: Ed. writer, Off. Secy. of Defense, 51-52; admin. asst. to U.S. Rep, Walter H. Judd, Minn, 52-55, David Dennison, Ohio, 56-58, Henry O. Talle, Iowa, 58-59, Bruce Alger, Fifth Dist, Tex, 59-65, James D. Martin, Seventh Dist, Ala, 65-67 and to Dan Kuykendall, Ninth Dist, Tenn, 67-; research asst. to U.S. Rep, Oliver Bolton, Ohio, 55-56. Bus. & Prof. Pos: Ed. and writer, Mich. weekly newspapers, 27-44; ed, Sanger Herald, Calif, 44-49. Mem: Cong. Secretaries Club; Men. of St. John's Col. High Sch; Men of St. Anthony High Sch; Kiwanis; Capitol Hill Club. Rel: Catholic. Mailing Add: 7401 New Hampshire Ave, Apt. 1114, Hyattsville, Md. 20783.

MARLER, FRED WILLIAM, JR. R
Calif. State Sen.
b. Auburn, Calif, 4/6/32; s. Fred William Marler and Hazel Scott M; m. 6/18/55 to Irene Elaine Carlson; c. Eric Scott and Aaron Mitchell. Educ: Univ. Calif, Berkeley, A.B, 54, Sch. of Law, 59; Phi Delta Phi. Polit. & Govt. Pos: Calif. State Sen, Fifth Sen. Dist, 65-66 and Second Sen. Dist, 67- Bus. & Prof. Pos: Attorney-at-law, 60- Mil. Serv: Entered as 2nd Lt, Air Force, 54, released as 1st Lt, 56, after serv. in Hq. 15th Air Force, Strategic Air Command. Mem: Elks, F&AM; Rotary; Calif. State and Shasta-Trinity Co. Bar Asns. Rel: Protestant. Legal Res: 1352 Norman Dr, Redding, Calif. 96001. Mailing Add: P.O. Box 2297, Redding, Calif. 96001.

MARLIN, DON LEE ROY D
b. Peru, Nebr, 7/15/18; s. Jess B. Marlin and Lettie Marie Bachleor M; m. 5/6/42 to Jacqueline A. Doogan; c. Christopher Jess and Brock Allen. Educ: West. State Col, Gunnison, Colo, grad, 41; Kappa Sigma; Kappa Delta Mu. Polit. & Govt. Pos: Del. and mem, Mich. Dem. State Cent. Cmt, 58-59; supvr, Howard Twp, Mich, 58-; chmn, Cass Co. Dem. Party, 67-68. Bus. & Prof. Pos: Owner-mgr, Marlin Village, 54- Mil. Serv: Entered as Pvt, Army Air Force, 41, released as S/Sgt, 45, after serv. in Seventh Air Force S.Pac. Theatre, 42-45; Purple Heart; Good Conduct Medal; Am. Theatre Medal; Pac. Theatre Medal. Mem: Mason; Shrine; Elks; Am. Legion; Toastmasters; Howard Twp. Lions; past pres, Cass Co. Chap, Mich. Twp. Asn. Most Outstanding Football Lineman, Pac. Area. Rel: Episcopal. Mailing Add: 2995 Detroit Rd, Niles, Mich. 49120.

MAROOTIAN, SIMON D
Mem, Calif. Dem. State Cent. Cmt.
b. Fresno, Calif, 8/31/23; s. Marginus Marootian and Anna Kalalian M; m. 12/6/52 to Irene DeVan; c. Marcus and Robyn Ann. Educ: Fresno State Col, 41-43; Hastings Col. of Law, Univ. Calif, LL.B. and J.D, 48; Sigma Nu Phi. Polit. & Govt. Pos: Mem, Fresno Co. Dem. Cent. Cmt, Calif, 60-62 & 66-68, chmn, 66-68; mem, Calif. Dem. State Cent. Cmt, 66-; co-chmn, Humphrey for Pres, Fresno Co, Calif. and Cranston for Sen, 68. Bus. & Prof. Pos: Attorney at Law, 49- Mil. Serv: Entered as Pvt, Air Force, 43, released as 2nd Lt, 45, after serv. in Army Air Corps, Pac-Asiatic Theatre, 1 year; Asiatic-Pac. Combat Medal; Philippine-Pac. Combat Medal. Mem: Dir, Fresno Co. Bar Asn; Elks; Am. Legion; Fed. Raisin Adv. Bd. Rel: Armenian Apostolic. Legal Res: 6347 S. Clovis Ave, Fowler, Calif. Mailing Add: 907 Del Webb Center, Fresno, Calif. 93721.

MARQUARDT, LEWIS R. D
S.Dak. State Rep.
b. Jamestown, N.Dak. 11/7/36; s. George R. Marquardt and Lucille Grimes M; m. 7/12/59 to Judith A. Woods; c. Kathryn, Mark, David, Steven and Gregory. Educ: Colo. State Col, M.FA, 65; Minot State Col. Polit. & Govt. Pos: S.Dak. State Rep, Day Co, 69- Bus. & Prof. Pos: Dir, instrumental music, Webster Pub. Schs, 63- Mil. Serv: Entered as Pvt. E-1, Army, 58, released as Specialist 5, 61, after serv. in Army Security Agency, Germany, 60-61. Mem: Nat. Educ. Asn; Nat. Band Asn; Phi Mu Alpha. Rel: Roman Catholic. Mailing Add: 445 W. Eighth Ave, Webster, S.Dak. 57274.

MARQUIS, NORMAN J. F. D
Maine State Rep.
b. Lewiston, Maine, 10/23/30; s. Norman H. Marquis and Jeannette Poudrier M; m. 7/19/58 to Patricia Ann Hopkins; c. Jacqueline Jeanne, David Dean and Peter Francis. Educ: Bradley Univ, Cert; Cavalier Towne and Country Club; Montagnard Soc. Club. Polit. & Govt. Pos: Alderman, Lewiston, Maine, 66; Maine State Rep, 69- Bus. & Prof. Pos: Self employed, retail and wholesale, 60- Mil. Serv: Entered as Pvt, Air Force, 56, released as Airman 2/C, 60, after serv. in 316th A.D.V, Africa, Morocco, 58-60; Good Conduct Medal. Mem: Nat. Sporting Goods Asn; Jaycees. Outstanding Jaycee of the Year, 64. Rel: Roman Catholic. Mailing Add: 72 Riverside St, Lewiston, Maine 04240.

MARR, THOMAS MARSHALL D
Ala. State Rep.
b. Bowling Green, Ky, 3/28/32; s. Marshall Marr and Lenore Ferguson Marr Ackerman; m. 12/15/51 to Marion Jane Mullins; c. Thomas Marshall, Jr, Merri Lynn, James Bruce, Tara Jane and Gina Reneé. Educ: Marion Mil. Inst, Ala, A.S, 51; Univ. Ala, B.C.E, 54; Univ. Ala. Law Sch, LL.B, 57; Sigma Chi. Polit. & Govt. Pos: Spec. asst. attorney gen, Ala, 63; Ala. State Rep, Mobile Co, 66- Bus. & Prof. Pos: Gen. counsel, Palmer and Baker Eng. Co, Mobile, Ala, 57-58; attorney-partner, Tyson, Marr and Friedlander, 58-; chmn. bd. and pres, Deposit Nat. Bank of Mobile Co, Prichard, 66-68, mem. bd. dirs, 68- Mil. Serv: Entered as 2nd Lt, Army, 54, released in 55, after serv. in 308th Combat Engr. Group. Mem: Phi Alpha Delta; Ala. Trial Lawyers Asn; Am. Soc. Civil Engrs; Am, Ala. and Mobile Co. Bar Asns; Phi Kappa; Mobile Area C. of C; Shrine; Mobile Rescue Mission; Jaycees; Mason; Prichard C. of C. Rel: Baptist. Legal Res: 4059 Highpoint Dr. S, Mobile, Ala. 36609. Mailing Add: P.O. Box 1792, Mobile, Ala. 36601.

MARRA, AUGUST JAMES D
b. Albany, N.Y, 7/29/28; s. Salvatore Marra and Margaret Peters M; m. 6/24/50 to Mary Leslie Coelho; c. Anne Marie, Salvatore Arthur and Leslie Anne. Educ: Univ. Calif, Berkeley, B.A, 52; Phi Sigma Kappa; Big C Soc. Polit. & Govt. Pos: Del, Dem. Nat. Conv, 68. Bus. & Prof. Pos: Mgr, Pa. Mutual Life Ins. Co, Oakland, Calif, 53-60; v.pres, Bevit Enterprises, San Leandro, 60-; mgr, Phoenix Mutual Life Ins. Co, Oakland, 63-67; supt. of agencies, Voyager Life Ins. Co, 67-69; pres, Int. Funding Corp. of Am, 69- Mil. Serv: Entered in Navy, 46, released as Signalman 1/C, 48, after serv. in Submarine Serv. Mem: Million Dollar Round Table; Elks; E Clampus Vitus. Rel: Catholic. Legal Res: 4400 Ewing Rd, Castro Valley, Calif. 94546. Mailing Add: 235 W. MacArthur Blvd, Oakland, Calif. 94611.

MARRA, MARY ANN R
V.chmn, Clinton Co. Rep. Party, N.Y.
b. N.Y.C, 1/26/18; d. Peter Pepi and Penelope Cisco P; m. 6/17/44 to Robert Joseph Marra; c. Richard Anthony, Margaret Penelope and Thomas Vincent. Educ: Wadleigh High Sch, N.Y.C, 3 years. Polit. & Govt. Pos: Mem, Co. Cmt, Dist. 4, Champlain, 60; v.chmn, Clinton Co. Rep. Party, 66- Mem: Girl Scouts; Tri Co. Coun. for the Aged; Coun. on the Arts; North Country Golf Club; Coop. Exten; YWCA. Rel: Greek Orthodox. Mailing Add: 118 Maple St, Rouses Point, N.Y. 12979.

MARRIOTT, ALICE SHEETS R
V.Chmn, Rep. Nat. Cmt.
b. Salt Lake City, Utah, 10/19/07; d. Edwin Spencer Sheets and Alice Taylor S; m. 6/9/27 to John Willard Marriott; c. John Willard, Jr. and Richard Edwin. Educ: Univ. Utah, B.A, 27; Phi Kappa Phi; Chi Omega. Polit. & Govt. Pos: Asst. treas, D.C. League of Rep. Women, 55-57, v.pres, 57-59, campaign activities, 59-66, chmn, Ways and Means, 65-; mem, Rep. Nat. Cmt. for D.C, 59-; mem, D.C. Rep. Cmt, Exec. Cmt. and Sub Exec. Cmt, 59; treas, Rep. Nat. Conv, 64 & 68; mem, Rep. Coord. Cmt, 65; v.chmn. and mem. exec. cmt, Rep. Nat. Cmt, 65-; v.chmn, Inaugural Cmt, 69; chmn, Distinguished Ladies Reception Inaugural Cmt, 69. Bus. & Prof. Pos: Partner and co-founder, A&W Root Beer Stores, Wash, D.C, 27-29; v.pres. and mem. bd. dirs, Marriott-Hot Shoppes, Inc, 29- Mem: Nat. Adv. Coun. for Children and Youth, 65-; treas. and one of founders of Welcome to Wash. Int. Club, 59-66; mem, bd. dirs, Goodwill Indust. Guild, Arthritis and Rheumatism Asn. of Metrop. Wash. and Wash. Home Rules Cmt; Capital Speakers Club, 62-; Women's Nat. Rep. Club; Capitol Hill Club; The Wash. Club; Am. Newspaper Womens Club. Rel: Latter-day Saint. Mailing Add: 4500 Garfield St. N.W, Washington, D.C. 20007.

MARRIOTT, B. GLADYS D
Mo. State Rep.
b. Spearman, Tex, 1/3/22; d. Lew Ewing Armstrong and Bessie Gladys Irons A; m. 9/28/41 to Lloyd Harold Marriott; c. Marjorie Ann and Nancy Jane. Educ: High sch, Kansas City, Mo. Sch. Dist, grad. Polit. & Govt. Pos: Pres, North Blue Ridge Improvement Asn, 52; committeewoman, Jackson Co. Dem. Party, 61-67; v.chmn, Fourth Cong. Dist. Dem. Party, 63-65; v.pres, Jackson Co. Dem. Asn, 64; Mo. State Rep, 16th Dist, 67-; Dem. caucus secy, 75th Gen. Assembly, 69; pres, Women's East. Dem. Club, currently. Mem: C. of C; Eastern Star; music dir, Job's Daughter, Bethel 55; past pres, Fairview and Kans. City Coun, PTA. Rel: Christian. Mailing Add: 9001 Leeds Rd, Kansas City, Mo. 64129.

MARRIOTT, RICHARD HAROLD D
Mayor, Sacramento, Calif.
b. Ely, Nev, 2/7/18; s. Joseph Edmund Marriott and Anna Bernard M; m. 7/17/43 to Geraldine Thane; c. Richard, James, Anna Marie, Mary Beth, Martin and Christina. Educ: Univ. San Francisco, B.S, 40; Univ. Calif. Grad. Sch. Polit. & Govt. Pos: City councilman, Sacramento, Calif, 60-68, mayor, 68- Bus. & Prof. Pos: With bus. dept, Oroville Mercury, 45-47, Alameda Times Star, 47-50, Sacramento Union, 49-50, Cath. Herald, 50-54; ed-mgr, Sacramento Valley Union Labor Bul, 54-69. Mil. Serv: Marine Corps, OSC, 41-42. Mem: Pres, Calif. Labor Press Asn; bd. mem, Int. Labor Press Asn; bd. dirs, United Crusade; IBEW; Elks; Serra Club; Am. Red Cross; Univ. San Francisco and Univ. Calif. Alumni Asns. Rel: Catholic. Mailing Add: 2716 Tenth Ave, Sacramento, Calif. 95818.

MARRIOTT, VONCEILE JANIS D
b. Stanberry, Mo, 5/26/20; d. Charles Henry Myrick and Margot Scott M; m. 4/16/38 to Albert Reynold Marriott; c. Reynold Scott. Educ: Platte Col. of Commerce, 41-42; St. Joseph Jr. Col, 52-54; Univ. of Minn, 58; Univ. of Calif, 60; past. pres, Epsilon Alpha; Beta Sigma Phi. Polit. & Govt. Pos: Supvr. finance dept, U.S. Govt, Ft. Leavenworth, Kans, 44-46; chmn. UN Day, UN Cmt, St. Joseph, Mo, 62; alternate del-at-lg, Dem. Nat. Conv, 64; supvr, Buchanan & Clinton Co, U.S. Agr. Census, 64-65. Bus. & Prof. Pos: Mgr. retail sales, Anchor Serum Co, 46-57, sales conv. secy, 57-60; owner and mgr, Career Placement and Vonceile's Agency, 60-; dir, Manpower, Inc, St.

Joseph, 63-; representative to Wash, D.C, North Side Civic Club, 64; secy-treas, L&M Printing & Off. Supply, Inc, 64-65; owner and mgr, Exec. Exchange, 65-; real estate broker, 68-; mem. col. surv. cmt, N.W. Mo. State Col, 68; mem. adv. cmt, 69-; state chmn, Cert. Employ. Consult. in change of certification, 69- Mem: Nat. Personnel Assocs; Nat. Employ. Asn; Northwest Mo. Press Asn; St. Joseph Commun. Theater; certified employ. consult, Am. Inst. for Employ. Counseling; C. of C; North Side Civic Club; South Side Commerce Club; Moila Country Club; Metrop. Dinner Club; Dem. State-Club of Mo. Nat. Sales Award, Manpower, Inc, 65; Distinguished Serv. Award, UN Cmt, 62. Rel: Protestant; Second Evangelical Church, St. Joseph. Legal Res: 1709 Crescent Dr, St. Joseph, Mo. 64506. Mailing Add: 30 E. Hills Plaza, St. Joseph, Mo. 64506.

MARROW, GEORGE MEREDITH D
Chmn, Cheshire Co. Dem. Party, N.H.
b. Baltimore, Md, 8/17/11; s. George Peek Marrow and Laura Dickson Reynolds M; m. 4/26/35 to Louise Weber Remick; c. Clare (Mrs. E.R. Keller) and Ruth (Mrs. J.E. Joslin). Educ: Am. Inst. Banking, N.Y.C, Cert. in Investment Banking, 34. Polit. & Govt. Pos: Town auditor, Chesterfield, N.H, 59-, mem. planning bd, 67-; del, Dem. Nat. Conv, 68; chmn, Cheshire Co. Dem. Party, 68- Bus. & Prof. Pos: Auditor, Vt. Savings Bank, 47-54, treas, 54-56; partner, Boucher & Marrow, CPA, 56- Publ: 'A CPA's Recommended Minimum Audit Procedures,' Auditgram, 12/58. Mem: Nat. Asn. Bank Auditors and Comptrollers (pres, Vt. Conf, 49-50); Am. Inst. CPA (coun, 68-70); Vt. and N.H. CPA Soc; Mason (32°); F&AM; Lions. Rel: Episcopal. Mailing Add: Main St, Spofford, N.H. 03462.

MARSCHALK, JOHN DOUGLAS R
b. East Orange, N.J, 12/20/27; s. Henry Ernest Marschalk and Margaret Lee Coe M; m. 5/29/49 to Mary Elizabeth Shoemaker; c. Sandra Lee, Priscilla Ann, John Andrew and Barbara Sue. Educ: U.S. Coast Guard Acad; Univ. of Md; Boston Univ; George Washington Univ, B.A. in Govt. Polit. & Govt. Pos: Del, Md. State Conv, 58; precinct chmn, Montgomery Co. Rep. Orgn, 58-61; dir. educ, Baltimore Co. Rep. Orgn, 62-66; alternate del, Rep. Nat. Conv, 64; awards chmn. and dir, Md. Young Rep, 64-66; state campaign mgr, Md. Rep. Campaign Cmt, 66; registrn. chmn, Md. State Rep. Cent. Cmt, 66-67; co-chmn, Rep. Adv. Cmt, St. Louis Metrop. Area, 69- Bus. & Prof. Pos: Sales rep, Litton Automated Bus. Syst, 55-61, dist. mgr, 61- Publ: Chap. on Precinct Orgn, Maryland Young Republican Leadership Training Manual, 67. Mem: Past local pres. and nat. dir, Jaycees; speaker of year, Toastmasters Local Club, 59 & 60; Sales & Mkt. Exec. of Metrop. St. Louis; v.pres, Principia Dads Club. Winner of Salesman of Year Award, Silver Spring, Md, Jaycees, 58. Rel: Christian Science; Trustee, First Church of Christ, Scientist, Creve Coeur, Mo. Mailing Add: 920 Claymark Dr, St. Louis, Mo. 63131.

MARSH, BENJAMIN FRANKLIN R
b. Toledo, Ohio, 4/30/27; s. Lester Randall Marsh and Alice Smith M; m. 7/12/52 to Martha Flowers Kirkpatrick; c. Samuel Kirkpatrick and Elizabeth Randall. Educ: Ohio Wesleyan Univ, B.A, 50; George Wash. Univ, J.D, 54; Omicron Delta Kappa; Delta Sigma Rho; Theta Alpha Phi; Phi Delta Phi; Kappa Sigma. Polit. & Govt. Pos: Personnel officer, U.S. Atomic Energy Cmn, Wash, D.C, 50-54; admin. asst. to Legis. Serv. Cmn, Columbus, Ohio, 54-55; admin. asst. to Ray Bliss, Rep. State Chmn, 54-55; cand, Ohio State Rep, 56; cand, U.S. Rep, Ninth Dist, 68; asst. solicitor, Maumee, Ohio, 56-63, solicitor and prosecutor, 63-; pres, Lucas Co. Young Rep. Club, 57; mem, Lucas Co. Charter Cmn, Toledo, Ohio, 59-60; precinct committeeman, 59-; pres, Rep. Workshops of Ohio, Inc, 60-64; legal counsel and bd. mem, Nat. Coun. Rep. Workshops, 60-65; mem, Lucas Co. Rep. Exec. Cmt. and chmn, Maumee Rep. Cmt, Ohio, 60-; chmn, Lincoln Day Banquet, 62; alternate del, Rep. Nat. Conv, 64; v.chmn, Salute to Ray Bliss Dinner, 65; asst. attorney gen, Ohio, 69- Bus. & Prof. Pos: Partner, Law Firm of Doyle, Lewis & Warner, 55- Mil. Serv: Seaman 1/C, Navy, 45-46, serv. in Am. Theater. Mem: Am. and Ohio State Bar Asns; Toledo Bar Asn.(chmn, Inaugural Courts Cmt); Nat. Inst. Munic. Law Officers; Ohio Munic. League; Judges' Cmt. on Notaries Pub; Toledo Post, Am. Legion; Toledo Coun. on World Affairs; Cent. YMCA; Ind. Ave. YMCA; Toledo C. of C; Toledo Mus. of Art; Maumee Valley Hist. Soc; Maumee C. of C; Laurel Hill Swim and Tennis Club; Cmt. on Rels. with Toledo, Spain; former pres, Jr. C. of C; campaign chmn. and pres, Tuberc. Soc; Int. Platform Asn. Selected Outstanding Young Man of Toledo, 62. Rel: Presbyterian. Legal Res: 124 W. Harrison, Maumee, Ohio 43537. Mailing Add: 904 National Bank Bldg, Toledo, Ohio 43604.

MARSH, DANIEL G. D
Wash. State Rep.
b. Salem, Ore, 5/14/37; s. Gabriel J. Marsh and Anne Dooper M; m. 12/12/64 to Diane K. Spoklie; c. Douglas James. Educ: Willamette Univ, B.A, 59; Univ. Ore. Law Sch, LL.B, 62; Tau Kappa Alpha; Pi Gamma Mu; Phi Alpha Delta; Sigma Alpha Epsilon. Polit. & Govt. Pos: Wash. State Rep, 65- Bus. & Prof. Pos: Attorney, 63- Mil. Serv: Nat. Guard, 8 years. Mem: Clark Co, Wash. and Am. Bar Asns; Am. Trial Lawyers Asn; charter mem. Nat. Soc. State Legislators; Elks; Grange; Kiwanis. Legal Res: 207 Phoenix Way, Vancouver, Wash. 98661. Mailing Add: 1111 Broadway, Vancouver, Wash. 98660.

MARSH, FRANK R
Secy. of State, Nebr.
b. Norfolk, Nebr, 4/27/24; s. Frank Marsh and Delia Andrews M; m. 3/5/43 to Shirley Mac McVicker; c. Sherry Anne (Mrs. Tupper), Corwin Frank, Stephen Alan, Mitchell Edward, Dory Michael and Melissa Lou. Educ: Univ. Nebr, B.S.Ed, 50; Alpha Phi Omega. Polit. & Govt. Pos: Pres, Mayor's Cmt. for Int. Friendship; Chief Elec. Officer for State; Secy. of State, Nebr, 53- Bus. & Prof. Pos: Contractor, builder and businessman, self-employed, 46-52; part-time instr, Lincoln Pub. Schs, 50-52. Mil. Serv: Army, 43-46. Mem: Grad, Staff and Command Sch, Civil Defense Hq, Battle Creek; Grad, Nat. Parole Insts, 63 & 64; past pres, Nat. Asn. of Secretaries of State, 63; Nat. Livestock Brand Conf; Nat. Coun. on Crime and Delinquency; nat. bd. dirs, Nat. Coun. for Commun. Serv. to Int. Visitors, 69; Cent. States Corrections Asn; Nebr. Probation and Parole Asn; Nat. Asn. Real Estate License Law Off; Combined Orgn. of Police Serv; Lincoln Personnel Asn; Ak-Sar-Ben; Am. Legion; VFW; YMCA; Gateway Sertoma Club; Nebr. State Hist. Soc; Capital City Footprinters; Lincoln Gem and Mineral Club; Polemic Club. Rel: Methodist. Legal Res: 2701 S. 34th St, Lincoln, Nebr. 68506. Mailing Add: Capitol Bldg, Lincoln, Nebr. 68509.

MARSH, JOHN O. D
U.S. Rep, Va.
b. Winchester, Va, 8/7/26; m. to Glenn Ann Patterson M; c. John O, III, Rebecca Patterson and Scot Wayland. Educ: Wash. and Lee Univ, LL.B; Phi Kappa Psi; Phi Delta Phi; Omicron Delta Kappa. Polit. & Govt. Pos: U.S. Rep, Va, 62-, mem, Cmt. on Appropriations, U.S. House of Rep; former mem, Shenandoah Co. Sch. Bd, Va; town attorney of New Market; town judge, Strasburg. Bus. & Prof. Pos: Lawyer, mem. adv. cmt, The Papers of George Washington. Mil. Serv: Army, World War II, grad, Inf. Officers Cand. Sch; currently Lt. Col, Va. Nat. Guard; completed Airborne Mobility Parachute Course, 64 and Jumpmaster Sch, Ft. Benning, Ga, 69. Mem: Am. Revolution Bicentennial Cmn; Va. Jaycees; Am. Legion; VFW; Va. State Bar; Am. Bar Asn; Nat. Guard Asn. of the U.S; Va. Nat. Guard Asn; Mason. Designated Outstanding Young Man in Va, Va. Jaycees, 59; Awarded Distinguished Serv. Medal, Dept. of Va, Am. Legion. Rel: Presbyterian. Legal Res: Strasburg, Va. 22657. Mailing Add: U.S. House of Representatives, Washington, D.C. 20515.

MARSH, ROBERT T, SR. R
Chmn, Rutland Co. Rep. Cmt, Vt.
b. Boston, Mass, 12/17/20; s. Philip A. Marsh and Cora Miller M; m. 11/1/42 to Eleanor Hill; c. Robert T, Jr, William C. and Eleanor Ruth. Educ: Clark Univ, A.B, 42; Boston Univ, M.A, 47. Polit. & Govt. Pos: Mem, Bd. Selectman, Poultney, Vt, 61-64; chmn, Poultney Town Rep. Cmt, 64-66; justice of the peace, Poultney, 64-, chmn, Bd. Civil Authority, 66-; mem, State Rep. Cmt, 66-; chmn, Rutland Co. Rep. Cmt, 66- Bus. & Prof. Pos: Instr, Eng. Dept, Mass. Inst. Tech, 47-51; instr. Eng. Dept, Tufts Univ, 52-56; assoc. prof. Eng, Green Mt. Col, 56- Mil. Serv: Entered as Pfc, Marines Res, 42, released as Capt, 46, after serv. in First Marine Div. and V Corps Artil, Pac. Area, Guadalcanal, Guam & Tsingtao, China, 44-45, Inactive Res, 46-, Capt.(Ret). Publ: 'A Short Guide to Simplified Report Writing,' 1/56 and 'Basic Guide for Writing Progress Reports,' 4/65, Machine Design. Mem: Col. Eng. Asn; Mason (Past Master). Rel: Unitarian. Mailing Add: 13 Bentley Ave, Poultney, Vt. 05764.

MARSHA, HOWARD CLARENCE R
Chmn, Clinton Co. Rep. Cmt, N.Y.
b. Tupper Lake, N.Y, 11/17/93; s. Charles Marsha and Dora Payee M; m. 6/18/17 to Grace D. Sutton; c. Constance B. (Mrs. Grant). Educ: Univ. Buffalo, Ph.G, 17; Beta Phi Sigma. Polit. & Govt. Pos: Chmn, Clinton Co. Rep. Cmt, N.Y, 50-; election cmnr, Clinton Co, 50-; del, Rep. Nat. Conv, 60, alternate del, 64 & 68; pub. rels. staff of U.S. Rep. Carlton King, 61-64. Bus. & Prof. Pos: Pharmacist, 17-65. Mem: Pharmacy Alumni Asn, Buffalo; Prof. Off. Soc, N.Y.C; Mason; Elks. Mailing Add: 8 Union St, Peru, N.Y. 12972.

MARSHALL, CLIFFORD HOLMES D
Mass. State Rep.
b. Quincy, Mass, 12/14/37; s. Clifford Holmes Marshall (deceased) and Kathryn R. Engel M.(deceased); m. 2/18/61 to Louise Marie Caporale; c. Clifford Holmes, III, Michael Joseph, Paul Stephen and Christopher James. Educ: Quincy High Sch, Dipl, 56; Suffolk Univ, 69- Polit. & Govt. Pos: City coun, Quincy, Mass, 66-; Mass. State Rep, 69- Mil. Serv: Entered as Pvt, Marines, 58, released as Cpl, 62, after serv. in Naval Security Group; Good Conduct Medal; Outstanding Man Award, Parris Island, S.C; Awarded 3 Meritorious Masts for Outstanding Leadership and Performance. Mem: K. of C; Elks; U.S. Marine Corps League; Amvets; Ward Two Civic Asn; bd. dirs, Southeast. Chap, Mass. Heart Asn; Dem. Ward and City Cmts; Young Dem. Rel: Catholic. Mailing Add: 64 Edison St, Quincy, Mass. 02169.

MARSHALL, DENNIS H. D
b. Washington, D.C, 8/21/36; married. Educ: Prince George's Co. Pub. schs; Woodward Prep. Sch. Polit. & Govt. Pos: Md. State Del, 63-67; Queen Anne Dem. Club. Bus. & Prof. Pos: Ins. agent. Mem: Nat. Asn. of Life Ins. Underwriters; Crescent Cities Jaycees; K. of C. Rel: Catholic. 1967 Legal Res: Suitland, Md. No mailing address available. (1967)

MARSHALL, FREDERIC J. R
b. Allen Twp, Hillsdale Co, Mich, 3/1/03; m. 1925 to Berenece Helen Plum; c. Frederic J. and Wilhelmina. Educ: Quincy pub. schs. Polit. & Govt. Pos: Sheriff, Hillsdale Co, Mich, 38-48; Mich. State Rep, 50-68. Mem: Elks; Mason; Grange. Mailing Add: Allen, Mich. 49227. (1967)

MARSHALL, HOWARD W. R
Mayor, Beaver Falls, Pa.
b. New Galilee, Pa, Mar. 8; s. Samuel John Marshall and Nancy McKim M; m. 9/24/24 to Mary McMillen; c. James Hugh, Charles McMillen and John Curtis. Polit. & Govt. Pos: Committeeman, Beaver Co. Rep. Party, Pa, 63-; mayor, Beaver Falls, Pa, 66-; del, Rep. Nat. Conv, 68. Bus. & Prof. Pos: Supt, Babcock & Wilcox Tubular Prod, Beaver Falls, 55-57 and supt. cold drawn div, Wis, 57-61; consult, Works Mgr. Staff, Beaver Falls, 61-67; plant engr, United Hosp, New Brighton, 67- Mem: Rotary; Beaver Falls Turners; Salvation Army (adv. bd); Friends of Scouting; Mason. Rel: Presbyterian. Mailing Add: 915 11th St, Beaver Falls, Pa. 15010.

MARSHALL, JAMES JOHN R
b. Fall River, Mass, 4/15/30; s. John Marshall and Florence Carr M; m. 4/15/67 to Kathleen Seibert. Educ: Providence Col, B.S, 53; Columbia Univ. Sch. of Journalism, M.S, 54; ed. of col. newspaper, COWL; Student Congress; Dramatic Club. Polit. & Govt. Pos: Press secy, Gov. John H. Chafee, R.I, 63-67; campaign coordinator, Spec. Cong. Elec, First Dist, R.I, 67; pub. rels. dir, Rep. Gov. Asn, 67-69. Bus. & Prof. Pos: Newsman, Providence Journal-Bulletin, R.I, 54-55 & 57-60; pub. affairs dir, Citizens Cmt. for Postal Reform, 69-; pres, Pub. Affairs Consult. of Am, 69- Mil. Serv: Seaman, Navy, 55-57. Mem: Nat. Press Club, Wash, D.C; Wash. Chap, Pub. Rels. Soc. of Am; Univ. Club, R.I; Providence Col. Alumni Asn; Nat. Munic. League; bd. of dirs, Kingman Boys' Club. Rel: Roman Catholic. Legal Res: 26 Arnold St, Providence, R.I. 02906. Mailing Add: 4000 Tunlaw Rd. N.W, Washington, D.C. 20007.

MARSHALL, MARY AYDELOTTE D
Va. State Del.
b. Cook Co, Ill, 6/14/21; d. John Andrew Rice and Nell Aydelotte R; m. 3/3/44

to Roger Duryea Marshall; c. Nell, Jenny and Alice. Educ: Swarthmore Col, B.A. with highest honors, 42; Phi Beta Kappa. Polit. & Govt. Pos: Economists Dept. of Justice, 42-47; del, Dem. Nat. Conv, 60; chmn, Arlington Co. Dem. Cmt, 61-63; Va. State Del, 66- Mem: Va. Cmt. for Fair Representation; Va. Cmt. for the Pub. Schs; League of Women Voters; Am. Asn. of Univ. Women; Va. Ment. Health Asn; Arlington Beautification Cmt; United Church Women; State Libr. Bd. Rel: Congregational. Mailing Add: 2256 N. Wakefield St, Arlington, Va. 22207.

MARSHALL, RICHARD L. R
N.Y. State Assemblyman
b. Horseheads, N.Y, 8/21/17; s. Levi Marshall; m. to Jean Meiswinkel. Educ: Elmira Bus. Inst. Polit. & Govt. Pos: N.Y. State Assemblyman, 62-; trustee, acting mayor and budget officer, Village of Horseheads; Horseheads Planning Cmn. Bus. & Prof. Pos: Owner of Marshalls Feed Mill; dir, Horseheads Savings and Loan Asn; dir, Chemung Canal Trust Co, Elmira. Mem: Trustee, Horseheads Free Libr. Asn; dir, Chemung Co. Cmt. on Alcoholism; v.pres, Horseheads C. of C; former dir, Chemung Co. Commun. Chest; Rotary Club, former pres; Elmira Co. Club; Elmira City Club; Watkins Glen Yacht Club; S. Tier Flying Club; Horseheads Lodge 364; F&AM; Corning Consistory; Mason (32°); Kalurah Temple AAONMS, Binghamton, N.Y. Rel: Presbyterian; chmn. bd. of trustees. Mailing Add: Dr. C, Strathmont Park, Elmira, N.Y. 14905.

MARSHALL, RICHARD MILTON R
Mo. State Rep.
b. Mexico, Mo, 6/3/25; s. John Bryan Marshall and Verna Lowry; m. 6/8/48 to Floreine Garvin; c. Kent G, Richard M. and Todd R. Educ: Wash. Univ, A.B, 49, LL.B, 51. Polit. & Govt. Pos: Mo. State Rep, 43rd Dist, 67- Mil. Serv: Entered as Pvt, Army Air Corps, 43, released as Sgt, 45; also Served as PO 3/C, Navy, 48-52; Am. Theater Ribbon; Victory and Good Conduct Medals. Mem: Am. and St. Louis Bar Asns; chmn, pub. info. cmt, Mo. Bar Asn, 66-; chmn, pub. rels. cmt, St. Louis Co. Bar Asn, 65-; Mason. Rel: Christian Church. Mailing Add: 9206 Big Bend, Webster Groves, Mo. 63119.

MARSHALL, ROBERT DIXON, JR. R
Chmn, Bladen Co. Rep. Party, N.C.
b. Lumberton, N.C, 9/17/42; s. Robert Dixon Marshall and Alice Cross M; m. 7/9/66 to Katherine Farrar; c. Rebecca Katherine and Robert Dixon, III. Educ: Wingate Col, A.A, 64; Univ. of Ga; Lambda Chi Alpha. Polit. & Govt. Pos: Chmn, Bladen Co. Rep. Party, N.C, 66- Bus. & Prof. Pos: Advert. mgr, The Bladen J, Elizabethtown, N.C, 65-66; opers. officer, First Nat. Bank of East. N.C, 66- Mil. Serv: Entered as E-1, N.C. Nat. Guard, 63, released as E-3. Mem: Lions Int. Rel: Presbyterian. Mailing Add: P.O. Box 1142, Elizabethtown, N.C. 28337.

MARSHALL, THURGOOD
Assoc. Justice, U.S. Supreme Court
b. Baltimore, Md, 7/2/08; s. William Marshall and Norma A. Williams M; m. 12/17/55 to Cecilia S. Suyat; c. Thurgood and John. Educ: Lincoln Univ, A.B, 30; LL.D, 47; Howard Univ, LL.B, 33, LL.D, 54; Alpha Phi Alpha; hon. LL.D. from numerous Insts. Polit. & Govt. Pos: Civil rights cases argued include Tex. Primary Case, 44, Restrictive Covenant Cases, 48, Univ. Tex. and Okla. Cases, 50, visited Japan and Korea to investigate court martial cases involving Negro soldiers, 51, and sch. segregation cases, 52-53; rep, White House Conf. Youth and Children; consult, Constitutional Conf. on Kenya London, 60; U.S. Circuit Judge, 61-65; U.S. Solicitor Gen, 65-67; Assoc. Justice, U.S. Supreme Court, 67- Bus. & Prof. Pos: Attorney-at-law, Baltimore, 33-37; asst. spec. counsel, NAACP, 36-38, spec. counsel, 38-50, dir, Counsel Legal Defense and Educ. Fund, 40-61; mem, N.Y. State Cmn, Worlds Fair; mem. bd, John F. Kennedy Mem. Libr. Mem: Col. electors, Hall of Fame, N.Y. Univ; Nat. and Am. Bar Asns; N.Y.C. Co. Lawyers Asn; Mason (33°). Recipient, Spingarn Medal, 46; Living Hist. Award from Research Inst. Rel: Episcopal. Legal Res: Va. Mailing Add: Supreme Court of the U.S, Washington, D.C. 20543.

MARSHALL, WALTER HENRY D
Chief Clerk, Mont. House of Rep.
b. North Stonington, Conn, 1/25/21; s. Walter Henry Marshall and Ruby Ann Nicholes M; m. 1/25/47 to Doris Edna Marsolais. Educ: Univ. Denver, 50; Carroll Col, Helena, Mont, 51-53; Wash. State Col, B.A. in Speech, 54, grad. work, 54. Polit. & Govt. Pos: Mem, Census Bur, U.S. Dept. of Commerce, 49-50; asst. chief clerk, Mont. House of Rep, 49, 51 & 53, asst. sgt-at-arms, 55, pub. rels. clerk, 57 and chief clerk, 65-; asst. sgt-at-arms, Mont. State Senate, 59, 61, 63 & 67, secy, 69; past v.pres, Mont. Young Dem; mem, Vet. for Kennedy Nat. Cmt, 60, Vet. for Johnson Nat. Cmt, 64; mem, Mont. State Dem. Cent. Cmt, Radio and TV, 64; coordinator, Neighborhood Youth Corps, 66. Bus. & Prof. Pos: V.pres, New Placer Hotel; sales mgr, KBLL Radio-TV, 57-66; pres, Helena Unlimited, 62-; sales mgr, KCAP Radio, Mont, 66-; pres, Capital Rels. Consult, 69; info. educ. dir, Mont. State Indust. Accident Bd, 69. Mil. Serv: Entered as Pvt, 40, released as T/Sgt, 46, after serv. in 243rd Coast Artil, Am. Theater and ETO, 44; Presidential Citation; One Battle Star in ETO. Publ: The Major Campaigns of 1952 by Network Radio, Wash. State Univ. Press, 53. Mem: Past pres, Exchange Club; Eagles; Am. Educ. Theater Asn; Mont. Club; VFW (past Comdr, past nat. pub. rels. chmn, nat. legis. cmt. and Jr. Vice Comdr, Mont; mem. nat. voice of Democracy cmt, 69-, state comdr, Mont, 68-69, chmn, 20 State West. conf, 68-); State Educ. TV Cmt. Nat. 15 Kilometer Champion, Norwich, Conn, 1st NLC, 37; exec. producer, Old Brewery Theater, Helena, Mont. Rel: Protestant. Mailing Add: 931 Knight St, Helena, Mont. 59601.

MARSTALLER, LOUIS JOHN R
Maine State Rep.
b. Brunswick, Maine, 5/5/20; s. Ernest Frank Marstaller and Lelia Gatchell M; m. 3/28/48 to Clarabel Hadley; c. David Louis, Nancy Lou, Robert Ernest and Thomas Henry. Educ: Wentworth Inst, cert, 39; Earlham Col, A.B, 42. Polit. & Govt. Pos: Selectman, Freeport, Maine, 51-54; former mem, Sch. Bldg. Cmt; chmn, Rep. Town Cmt, 62-68; Maine State Rep, 69- Bus. & Prof. Pos: Mgr, motor court, Freeport, Maine, 45-; field secy, New Eng. Yearly Meeting of Friends, 57- Rel: Quaker. Mailing Add: R.F.D 3, Brunswick Rd, Freeport, Maine 04032.

MARTANO, FRANK LOUIS R
Mem, Kings Co. Rep. Cmt, N.Y.
b. Brooklyn, N.Y, 11/25/24; s. Joseph Martano and Josephine Forte M; m. 5/27/50 to Elizabeth A. DiDonna; c. Deborah and Diane. Educ: St. John's Univ, B.B.A, 50; Acct. Soc. Polit. & Govt. Pos: Rep. cand, U.S. House Rep, 68; mem, Kings Co. Rep. Cmt, 68- Bus. & Prof. Pos: Pub. acct, 51- Mil. Serv: Entered as Pvt, Army, 43, released as Sgt, 46, after serv. in 12th and First Armored Div, Europe-Africa-Middle East, 44-46; North. France, Cent. Europe, Ardennes and Rhineland Battle Stars; Europe-Africa-Middle East Serv. Medal; Good Conduct Medal; Am. Serv. Medal; World War II Victory Medal; Combat Inf. Badge. Mem: Empire State Asn. Pub. Acct.(past pres. Kings Co. Chap); Nat. Soc. Pub. Acct; Lions Int;(charter mem. and treas, Bergen Beach-Mill Basin Chap); Bergen Beach Civic Asn. (past pres, chmn. bd); Brooklyn Civic Coun.(bd. dirs); Joint Coun. for Commun. Betterment (first v.pres. and treas); 39th Assembly Dist. Regular Rep. Club (bd. dirs); St. Bernard's Holy Name Soc.(past officer). Rel: Catholic. Mailing Add: 2176 E. 72nd St, Brooklyn, N.Y. 11234.

MARTEL, LOUIS ISRAEL D
b. Manchester, N.H, 9/28/12; s. Louis-Euclide Martel and Marie-Georgienne Courchesne M; married; c. Four. Educ: Ecole St. Georges; Academie St. Augustin; St. Joseph High Sch, Manchester. Polit. & Govt. Pos: N.H. State Rep, 45-55 & 57-61; mem, N.H. State Legis. Coun, 53-54 & 63-64; del, N.H. Constitutional Conv, 56; del, Dem. Nat. Conv, 56, 60 & 64; N.H. State Sen. and Minority Leader, N.H. State Senate, 63-65. Bus. & Prof. Pos: Parliamentarian, 8 Co. Conf. of Carpenters, N.H; past v.pres. and legis. agent, N.H. State Fedn. of Labor; ward clerk, Local Union 625, United Brotherhood of Carpenters & Joiners of Am. AFL-CIO, 40-44, bus. rep. and financial secy-treas, del, Int. AFL-CIO Conv; founder, Cath. Press Serv, 43; pres, Franco-Am. Publ. Corp, Comitê de Vie Franco-Americaine and Manchester Indust. Coun; financial secy-treas, Manchester Cent. Labor Coun, AFL-CIO; founder and secy-treas, N.H. State Coun. of Carpenters. Mem: Pres. and Dist. Gov, Club Richelieu; past pres, Manchester Real Estate Bd. and Manchester Bldg. Trades Coun; founder, Manchester Labor-Mgt. Coun, 48; Asn. Canado-Amercaine; Manchester Hist. Soc; N.H. Hist. Soc; La Sociêtê Genealogique, Canadienna-Francaise; Third Order of St. Francis and League of the Divine Off; Zelateur des Annales de Notre-Dame du Cap; Nat. Conf. of State Legis. Leaders. Rel: Catholic; V.pres, Lique du Sacrê-Coeur of St. Georges Parish. Mailing Add: 102 Bridge St, Manchester, N.H. 03104. (1967)

MARTELL, ARLENE J. D
Vt. State Rep.
b. Milton, Vt, 6/19/26; d. Edward W. Jordan and Eva Messier J; m. 8/28/45 to Leonard J. Martell; c. Donna Ann (Mrs. Peacock), John, Steven, Gregory and Anthony. Educ: Milton High Sch, grad, 44. Polit. & Govt. Pos: Vt. State Rep, 69- Bus. & Prof. Pos: Homemaker, currently. Mem: Ga. Sch. Club; Farm Bur; Vt. Asn. for Children with Learning Disabilities; Kerbs Hospital Auxiliary. Rel: Catholic. Legal Res: Georgia, Vt. Mailing Add: R.F.D. 3, Fairfax, Vt, 05454.

MARTELL, KAY PATRICIA D
Pres, Saugus-Newhall Dem. Forum, Calif.
b. Montreal, Can; d. Edward Joseph Peter Nicholson and Mary Ellen Theresa Durnion N; m. 3/27/36 to Alphonse Martell; c. Nicka and Frankleen. Educ: Villa Maria, Montreal, grad; Academie St. Alfred, L'Epiphanie, Que. Polit. & Govt. Pos: Pres, Saugus-Newhall Dem. Forum, Calif, 66-; field rep, U.S. Rep. Everett G. Burkhalter; treas, Dem. State Cent. Cmt, South and orgn. chmn, Womens Div; mem, State Cmt. Exec. Bd, 4 years; State Cmt. Mem, 20 years; mem, 3 Dem. Del. Mem: Chmn, March of Dimes. Rel: Catholic. Mailing Add: 16301 Sierra Hwy, Saugus, Calif. 91350.

MARTENSON, DAVID LOUIS R
Chmn, Winnebago Co. Rep. Cent. Cmt, Ill.
b. Rockford, Ill, 11/20/34; s. Louis L. Martenson and Loretta L. Lind M; m. to Judith Ann Ehnen; c. Scott and Brian. Educ: Millikin Univ, B.A, 56; Univ. Chicago Law Sch, LL.D, 59; Tau Kappa Epsilon. Polit. & Govt. Pos: Pres, Millikin Univ. Young Rep. Club, 55; v.pres, Col. Orgn, Ill. State Young Rep, 56, pres, 58, mem. bd. dirs, 58-63; chmn, Winnebago Co. Rep. Cent. Cmt, Ill, 64- Bus. & Prof. Pos: Attorney, Anderson & Martenson. Mem: Winnebago Co, Ill. and Am. Bar Asns; Cosmopolitan Club; C. of C; Baltic Lodge; Univ. Club; Mauh-Nah-Tee-See Country Club. Chmn, March of Dimes Campaign, 64. Legal Res: 5720 Coachman Court, Rockford, Ill. 61111. Mailing Add: 401 W. State St, Rockford, Ill. 61101.

MARTHEN, ELSA W. R
b. Bridgeport, Conn, 10/5/20; d. James C. Jorgensen and Mary K. Schaufler J; m. 8/15/47 to George W. Marthen; c. James G. and Kristina K. Polit. & Govt. Pos: Pres, Nassau Co. Fedn. of Rep. Women, N.Y, 63-65, mem, 65-; v.chmn, Nassau Co. Rep. Cmt, 63-68; alternate del, Rep. Nat. Conv, 64. Mem: Past pres, Club of Nassau Co. Cancer Cmt, 65; Heart Fund Chmn. of Baldwin, 66; Eastern Star; past pres, Cent. Island Women's Rep. Club; past pres, immediate, Virginia M. Bacon Women's Rep. Club; Baldwin Rep. Club. Rel: Lutheran. Mailing Add: 755 Silver Lake Place, Baldwin, N.Y. 11510. (1967)

MARTI, DOUGLAS R
b. Matton, Ill, 2/21/34; s. Freeman R. Marti and Norma Suess M; m. 12/23/56 to Doris C. Crist; c. Kevin D. and Lydia S. Educ: Univ. Ill, B.S, 54, J.D, 68; Phi Kappa Phi; Phi Eta Sigma; Delta Theta Phi; Alpha Zeta. Polit. & Govt. Pos: Grad. asst, Agr. Law, 54-55; v.pres, Illini Young Rep. Club, 56, pres, 56-57; bill drafter, Legis. Reference Bur, 57; asst. state's attorney, Bond Co. Ill, 58; attorney, Off. of the Gen. Counsel, Dept. of Health, Educ. and Welfare, 58-61; asst. court adminstr, Ill. Supreme Court, 61-64; mem, Bd. of Gov, Sangamon Co. Young Rep. Club, 64; state's attorney, Bond Co, Ill, 64-68; chmn, Bond Co. Rep. Cent. Cmt, 66-68; alternate del, Rep. Nat. Conv, 68; mem, Parole and Pardon Bd, 69- Mil. Serv: 2nd Lt, Army, 57. Publ: Illinois Inheritance Laws, Wills and Joint Tenancy, Univ. of Ill. Col. of Agr, 6/55. Mem: Ill. State and Bond Co. Bar Asns; Am. Judicature Soc; Int. Platform Asn; Toastmasters. Rel: Baptist. Mailing Add: 812 E. Winter, Greenville, Ill. 62246.

MARTIN, BARON HAY, II D
b. Boston, Mass, 9/14/26; s. Baron Hay Martin and Margaret Jones M; married. Educ: Suffolk Univ, A.B, Law Sch, J.D; grad. fifth highest in class in law sch; awarded seven consecutive acad. scholarships; Alpha Phi Alpha. Hon. L.H.D, Saints Jr. Col, 69. Polit. & Govt. Pos: Dem. Ward Committeeman, 12th Suffolk Ward, Mass, 57-, del, Dem. State Conv, 60, 62, 64 & 66; alternate del, Dem. Nat. Conv, 68. Bus. & Prof. Pos: Trial attorney, Mass. Bay Transist Authority, 58; legal counsel, National Lee Corp, 66; legal counsel, AVCO Corp, Roxbury Div, 67; bd. dirs. and incorporator, Unity Bank & Trust, 68; trustee and dir, Mass. Ment. Health Center, 69. Mem: Admitted to practice Mass. Bar, Fed. Bar and U.S. Supreme Court; Am. Judicature Soc, Mass. Trial Lawyers Asn, Mass. and Boston Bar Asns; Acad. of Law and Sci; Mason (32°); Shrine; NAACP; Howard Univ. Club Boston. Outstanding achievement plaque, Alpha Phi Alpha Fraternity, Sigma Chap, 52, Politics and the Negro, 64. Rel: Congregational. Mailing Add: 14 Wabon St, Roxbury, Mass. 02121.

MARTIN, BLANCHE RUTH R
Committeewoman, Tex. State Ninth Sen. Dist. Rep. Party
b. St. Louis, Mo, 8/17/07; d. Richard E. Wachter and Blanche Reader W; m. 3/23/29 to Jack C.W. Martin; c. Joan (Mrs. McIntosh), Jacqueline (Mrs. Ryden) and Richard W. Educ: Soldan High Sch, Mo, grad. Polit. & Govt. Pos: V.chmn, Grayson Co. Rep. Party, Tex, 53-60, chmn, 60-66; committeewoman, Tex. State Ninth Sen. Dist, Rep. Party, 66- Rel: Presbyterian. Mailing Add: 1621 S. Austin, c/o La Villa Motel, Denison, Tex. 75020.

MARTIN, CAROL JEAN D
V.Chmn, Gunnison Co. Dem. Cent. Cmt, Colo.
b. Arvada, Colo, 11/26/38; d. William Eugene McKittrick and Marjorie Lucille Snow M; m. 3/25/57 to Eddie James Martin; c. Larry Dean. Educ: High sch. Polit. & Govt. Pos: Secy, Gunnison Co. Jane Jefferson Club, Colo, 64-66, first v.pres, 66-68 and pres, 68-; secy, Gunnison Co. assessor, 64-; state hist, State Fedn. of Jane Jefferson Dem. Clubs, 68-; v.chmn, Gunnison Co. Dem. Cent. Cmt, 69-; v.chmn, Seventh Judicial Dist. Dem. Orgn, 69-Bus. & Prof. Pos: Secy, Dr. Marvin L. Crawford, Steamboat Springs, Colo, 57-58; tel. operator, Mt. States Tel. and Tel, 59-63. Mem: Elks Ladies of Gunnison; Gunnison Co. chmn, Cystic Fibrosis Research Found. Nominated for outstanding young women of Am, 69. Rel: Protestant. Mailing Add: W. Tomichi Ave, Gunnison, Colo. 81230.

MARTIN, CELIA HARE D
b. Ishpeming, Mich, 10/4/14; d. Jeremiah Hare and Mary Ellen Sheridan H; wid; c. Rebecca Ellen. Educ: Col. of St. Scholastica, 2 years; Col. of St. Teresa, B.A, 32. Polit. & Govt. Pos: Admin. asst, U.S. Rep. Lloyd M. Bentsen, Jr, 48-55, U.S. Rep. Joe M. Kilgore, 55-65 and U.S. Rep. Eligio de la Garza, Tex, 65- Rel: Roman Catholic. Legal Res: 1102 Maple, McAllen, Tex. 78501. Mailing Add: 2500 Que. N.W, Washington, D.C. 20007.

MARTIN, CLARENCE DANIEL JR. D
b. Spokane, Wash, 10/23/16; s. Clarence Daniel Martin and Margaret H. Mulligan M; m. 4/9/44 to Charlotte Mary Yeoman M; c. Diana, Cary, Bradley. Educ: Harvard, B.S, 38; Univ. of Wash. Law Sch, 39. Polit. & Govt. Pos: Mem, Alaska Rail and Hwy. Cmn, 61-; Under Secy. Commerce for Transportation, 61-65; Dep. Chmn, Dem. Nat. Cmt, 60; Past Pres, Calif, also Santa Monica Bay Coun. Bus. & Prof. Pos: Retail auto and real estate bus, Calif. and Arizona, 50-; Panama Canal Corp, 61-; Wholesale hardware and raw materials bus, Seattle, 46-50; F.M. Martin Grain & Milling Co, Inc, Cheney, Wash, 39-41. Mil. Serv: Navy, Lt. Comdr, 41-46. Mem: Navy League; Rotarian. Mailing Add: 25 Oakmont Dr, Los Angeles, Calif. 90049. (1967)

MARTIN, CLARENCE E, JR. D
W.Va. State Sen.
b. Martinsburg, W.Va, 9/10/09; s. Clarence E. Martin and Agnes G. McKenna M; m. 6/6/42 to Catherine duB. Silver; c. Clarence E, III. Educ: Cath. Univ. of Am, A.B, 31, LL.B, 34, J.D. Polit. & Govt. Pos: Prosecuting attorney, Berkeley Co, W.Va, 41-49; W.Va. State Sen, 50-, Majority Leader, 53rd, 54th and 59th Legis. Bus. & Prof. Pos: Attorney-at-law. Mil. Serv: Navy, World War II. Mem: Moose; Elks; VFW; Am. Legion; fel, Am. Bar Found; Am. and W.Va. Bar Asns; Am. Law Inst; fel, Int. Asn. of Ins. Counsel; Am. Col. of Trial Lawyers; Am. Judicature Soc; pres, W.Va. State Bar, 54-55; pres, W.Va. Bar Asn, 60-61. Mailing Add: Martinsburg, W.Va. 25401.

MARTIN, CRAWFORD COLLINS D
Attorney Gen, Tex.
b. Hillsboro, Tex, 3/13/16; s. William Marvin Martin and Daisy Beavers M; m. 5/14/41 to Margaret Ann Mash; c. Sherry, Jim and Nancy. Educ: Hillsboro Jr. Col; Univ. Tex. Polit. & Govt. Pos: Mayor, Hillsboro, Tex, 46-48; Tex. State Sen, 12th Dist, 48-63; secy. of State, Tex, 63-66; Attorney Gen, Tex, 67-; del, Dem. Nat. Conv, 68. Mil. Serv: Coast Guard, 42-45. Mem: Hill Co. Bar Asn.(pres, 61-62); Mason; Lions; K. of P; Shrine; Scottish Rite; Am. Legion. Rel: Presbyterian. Legal Res: P.O. Box 257, Hillsboro, Tex. 76645. Mailing Add: 5314 Western Hills Dr, Austin, Tex. 78731.

MARTIN, DAVID O. R
Wis. State Assemblyman
b. Appleton, Wis, 3/7/31. Educ: Univ. Mich, B.S. Polit. & Govt. Pos: Wis. State Assemblyman, 60- Bus. & Prof. Pos: Traffic Analyst with paper co. Mil. Serv: Army Corps of Engrs, 54-56. Mem: Jaycees Bd. Neenah-Menasha, 59-61. Mailing Add: 521 Haylett St, Neenah, Wis. 54956. (1967)

MARTIN, DAVID THOMAS R
U.S. Rep, Nebr.
b. Kearney, Nebr, 7/9/07; m. to Margaret Taylor; c. David K, Patricia Maloney and John L. Educ: Dartmouth Col. Polit. & Govt. Pos: Nebr. State Rep. Chmn, 49-54; mem, Rep. Nat. Cmt, 52-54; U.S. Rep, 60- Bus. & Prof. Pos: Retail lumber bus. in Kearney. Mem: Elks; Shriner. Rel: Presbyterian. Legal Res: Kearney, Nebr. Mailing Add: 500 4th St. S.E, Washington, D.C. 20003.

MARTIN, EDA C. R
b. Lisbon, N.H; widow. Educ: Bus. Col. grad. Polit. & Govt. Pos: N.H. State Sen, 59-67; Constitutional Conv, 56; N.H. State Rep, 51, 53, 55, 57, 61, 63; Secy. & Treas, Grafton City Rep. Comm. Bus. & Prof. Pos: Off. mgr, 36 yrs, Parker Drug Stores, Inc. Mem: Past Matron, Mt. Eustis Chap. OES; Colonial Club; DAR; Mayflower Soc; Am. Legion Aux; N.H. Hist. Soc; Littleton C. of C; Profile Women's Rep. Club. Rel: Methodist. Mailing Add: 42 Pleasant St, Littleton, N.H. 03561. (1967)

MARTIN, EDWIN M.
b. Dayton, Ohio 5/21/08; m. to Margaret Milburn; c. Mrs. Pedro Sanjuan and Edwin M, Jr. Educ: Northwest. Univ, B.A, 29. Polit. & Govt. Pos: Economist, Cent. Statist. Bd, 35-38; with Bur. of Labor Statist, 38-40, War Prod. Bd, 40-44 and Off. of Strategic Serv, 44-45; career officer, U.S. Dept. of State For. Serv, 45-; chief, Div. of Japanese and Korean Econ. Affairs, 45-47; acting chief, Div. Occup. Areas Econ. Affairs, 47-48; dep. dir, Off. of Int. Trade Policy, 48-49; dir, Off. of European Regional Affairs, 49-52; spec. asst. to Secy. of State, 52-53; dep. chief, U.S. Mission to NATO and European Orgn, Paris, 53557; minister-counsr, London, 57-60; Asst. Secy. of State for Econ. Affairs, 60-62; Asst. Secy. of State for Inter-Am. Affairs, 62-64; U.S. Ambassador, Argentina, 64-68; chmn, Develop. Assistance Cmt, 68- Legal Res: 911 Caldwell St, Piqua, Ohio 45356. Mailing Add: 16 Villa Said, Paris 16, France.

MARTIN, ERNEST D. D
Okla. State Sen.
b. Hugo, Okla, 4/13/22; s. James E. Martin and Maude Estes M; m. 3/12/46 to Helton Ineta Hegwood; c. Larry Lynn, Anita Susan and Terry Lee. Educ: Am. Acad. of Art, Chicago, Ill, 40-42; Univ. Okla. Sch. of Pharmacy, B.S, 50; Oupha. Polit. & Govt. Pos: Okla. State Sen, 64- Bus. & Prof. Pos: Pres, 5th Dist, Okla. Pharm. Asn, 58- Mil. Serv: Entered as Pvt, 42, Air Force, released as S/Sgt, 46; Good Conduct and Am. Theater Medals. Mem: Am. Legion; Mason (32°), Scottish Rite; Rotary. Rel: Baptist. Mailing Add: Box 51, Hoxbar Route, Ardmore, Okla. 73401.

MARTIN, ERSEL R
Chmn, Knox Co. Rep. Cmt, Ky.
b. Heidrick, Ky, 2/13/17; s. Chester Martin and Rosa Patterson M; m. 8/1/37 to Claudia Blevins; c. Douglas R, Donnie L. and Diana Lynn. Educ: Boone High Sch, grad, 35. Polit. & Govt. Pos: Chmn, Knox Co. Rep. Cmt, Ky, 56-60 & 64- Bus. & Prof. Pos: Merchant, 46- Mil. Serv: Entered as Pvt, Army, 41, released as 2nd Lt, 45, after serv. in 149th Inf, 38th Div, Pac. Area; Ky. Nat. Guard, 35. Mem: Mason. Rel: Protestant. Mailing Add: Heidrick, Ky. 40949. (1967)

MARTIN, FRANK A, JR. D
R.I. State Rep.
b. Providence, R.I, 8/15/29; m. to Ann T. Educ: Providence Col, 52. Polit. & Govt. Pos: R.I. State Rep, 60-; alternate del, Dem. Nat. Conv, 68. Bus. & Prof. Pos: Real estate and ins. Mil. Serv: Navy, 2 years. Mailing Add: 25 Nathaniel Ave, Pawtucket, R.I. 02860. (1967)

MARTIN, GRAHAM A.
U.S. Ambassador to Italy
b. Mars Hill, N.C, 9/22/12; m. to Dorothy Wallace; c. Three. Educ: Wake Forest Col, B.A, 32, LL.D, 69. Polit. & Govt. Pos: Aide to dep. adminstr, Nat. Recovery Admin, 33-36; br. chief, Soc. Security Bd, 36-41, Fed. Security Agency. 41-42 & 46; War Assets Admin, 46-47; career officer, U.S. Dept. of State For. Serv, 47-; attache and coordinator, European Regional Admin. Affairs and counsr, Paris, 47-54; mem. faculty, Air War Col, 55-57; spec. asst. to Dep. Under Secy. of State, 57-59; spec. asst. to Under Secy. of State, 59-60; U.S. Rep, UN European Off. and other Int. Orgns, Geneva, 60-62; dep. U.S. coordinator, Alliance for Progress, 62-63; U.S. Ambassador to Thailand, 63-67; spec. asst. to the Secy. of State, 67-69; U.S. Ambassador to Italy, 69- Bus. & Prof. Pos: Newspaper correspondent, 32-33. Mil. Serv: Col, 42-46. Legal Res: Thomasville, N.C. Mailing Add: U.S. Dept. of State Foreign Service, Washington, D.C. 20520.

MARTIN, JAMES DOUGLAS R
b. Tarrant, Ala, 9/1/18; s. Richard Edward Martin and Mary Graham M; m. 12/27/59 to Patricia Byrd Huddleston; c. James Douglas, Jr, Annette Graham and Richard Huddleston. Polit. & Govt. Pos: Cand, U.S. Senate, 62; U.S. Rep, Seventh Dist, Ala, until 66; cand, Gov. Ala, 66; del, Rep. Nat. Conv, 68. Bus. & Prof. Pos: Pres, Assoc. Industs. of Ala. and Am. Oil Jobbers. Mil. Serv: Entered as Pvt, Army, released as Maj, after serv. as battery comdr, artil, with Gen. Patton's Third Army, Europe and intel. officer with Army of Occupation. Mem: Gadsen-Etowah C. of C.(pres); Kiwanis (pres. and lt. gov); co. chmn. and area blood chmn, Am. Red Cross. Rel: Methodist. Mailing Add: P.O. Box 407, Gadsden, Ala. 35902.

MARTIN, JAMES GRUBBS R
Mem. Bd, Mecklenburg Co. Cmnr, N.C.
b. Savannah, Ga, 12/11/35; s. Rev. Arthur M. Martin and Mary Grubbs M; m. 6/1/57 to Dorothy Ann McAulay; c. James G, Jr. and Emily W. Educ: Davidson Col, B.S, 57; Princeton Univ, M.S. and Ph.D, 60; Omicron Delta Kappa; Gamma Sigma Epsilon; Beta Theta Pi (Nat. v.pres. and mem, Bd. Trustees, currently). Polit. & Govt. Pos: Precinct chmn, Rep. Party, Davidson, N.C, 65-66; mem. bd, Mecklenburg Co. Cmnr, 66-, chmn, 67-68; del, Rep. Nat. Conv, 68. Bus. & Prof. Pos: Richardson Assoc. Prof. Chem, Davidson Col, 60- Publ: 'Stereochemistry of the Diels-Alder Reaction,' Chem. Rev, 60; plus others. Mem: Charlotte Symphony (tuba); N.C. High Sch. Football Off. Asn. Rel: Presbyterian; deacon and tenor soloist. Legal Res: Greenway St, Davidson, N.C. 28036. Mailing Add: Box 697, Davidson, N.C. 28036.

MARTIN, JIMMIE LEEWOOD D
S.C. State Rep.
b. Aynor, S.C, 8/24/34; s. Marvin P. Martin, Sr. and Eva Hucks M; m. 4/10/55 to Betty Jean Jones; c. Melony, Jimmie Leewood and Tanner Shay. Educ: Univ. of S.C, B.S, 61. Polit. & Govt. Pos: S.C. State Rep, 69- Bus. & Prof. Pos: Pres, Exchange Realty Serv, 66 and Martin & Assocs, 67. Mil. Serv: Airman, Navy, 53-55. Mem: Mason; Shrine; Cayce-West Columbia C. of C; Gr. Columbia C. of C; Jaycees; Moose; WOW; Century Club, Univ. of S.C; chmn, Lexington Co. Heart Fund. Rel: Methodist. Legal Res: 929 Indigo Ave, Cayce, S.C. 29033. Mailing Add: 1611 Augusta Rd, West Columbia, S.C. 29169.

MARTIN, JOHN ALFRED D
S.C. State Sen.
b. Shellman, Ga, 4/11/21; s. James A. Martin and Ada Bass M; m. to Mary M. Boulware; c. Linda, John, Jr, Marianne and Dubose Rivers. Educ: Univ. S.C, LL.B, 47. Polit. & Govt. Pos: S.C. State Rep, 51-52; S.C. State Sen, 53- Bus. & Prof. Pos: Lawyer. Mil. Serv: Navy, 43-46; Lt.(jg), Naval Res. Mailing Add: Box 298, Winnsboro, S.C. 29180. (1967)

MARTIN, JOHN BUTLIN R
Cmnr. on Aging, Dept. of Health, Educ. and Welfare
b. Grand Rapids, Mich, 10/3/09; s. John B. Martin and Althea Winchester M; m. 9/5/34 to Helen Hickam; c. Richard H, Judith Hartig and Gillian Sorensen. Educ: Dartmouth Col, A.B, 31; Oxford Univ, Rhodes scholar and B.Litt, 33; Univ. Mich. Law Sch, J.D, 36; Delta Kappa Epsilon; Phi Delta Phi. Polit. & Govt. Pos: Legal secy. to chmn, Securities and Exchange Cmn, 36-38; first asst, State Div. Securities, Ohio, 39-41; dep. dir, Nat. Off. Civil Defense, 42-44; Mich. State Sen, 17th Dist, 48-50; auditor gen, Mich, 50-54; chmn, Mich. Cmn. on Aging, 57-67; Rep. Nat. Coord. Cmt. Task Force on Aging; Rep. Nat. Committeeman, Mich, 57-68; del, Mich. State Constitutional Conv, 62-63; chmn, Gov. Spec. Cmn. Crime, Delinquency and Admin. of Criminal Justice, 67-68; del, Rep. Nat. Conv, 68; Cmnr. on Aging, Dept. of Health, Educ. and Welfare, 68-; Spec. Asst. to the President for the Aging, currently. Bus. & Prof. Pos; Partner, Bidwell, Schmidt & Martin, 46-51 and Harrington, Waer, Cary & Martin, 58-68. Mil. Serv: Entered as Lt.(jg), Naval Res, 44, released as Lt. Comdr, 46, after serv. in Off. Strategic Serv, ETO, 44-46. Mem: Grand Rapids, Mich. State and Am. Bar Asns; Am. Legion; VFW. Rel: Baptist. Legal Res: 6011 Grand River Dr. S.E, Ada, Mich. 49301. Mailing Add: 7607 Glendale Rd, Chevy Chase, Md. 20015.

MARTIN, JOHN E. R
b. Wallace, Idaho, 5/29/27; s. Chauncey H. Martin and Marie M; m. 3/18/60 to Reole A. Worbois; c. Craig R, Rodney E. Educ: Univ. of Idaho, B.A; Blue Key; Kappa Sigma. Polit. & Govt. Pos: Admin. Asst, Sen. Jordan, Idaho; Staff Asst, Sen. Dworshak, 60-62; Idaho GOP Cmt, dir, 57-60. Bus. & Prof. Pos: Ed, Emmett Index, 51-57; Aide, U.S Forest Serv (summers), 46-50. Mil. Serv: 1st Lt, U.S. Army, served in Pac, WW II. Legal Res: P.O. Box 2832, Boise, Idaho. Mailing Add: 744 Girard St, N.W, Washington, D.C. 20008. (1967)

MARTIN, JOHN L. D
Maine State Rep.
b. Eagle Lake, Maine, 6/5/41; s. Frank Martin, Jr. and Edwidge Raymond M; single. Educ: Fort Kent State Teachers Col, 59-61; Univ. of Maine, B.A, 63; grad. work in polit. sci, 63-64; Young Democrats; Treas, Public Management Club. Polit. & Govt. Pos: Mem. platform cmt, Maine Dem. Conv, 64-66; mem. Allagash-St. John Study Cmt, 64-68; pres, Maine Young Dem, 64-68; mem. and clerk, Intergovt. Rels. Cmn, 64-; mem, Aroostook Co. Dem. Cmt, 64-, treas, 69-; chmn, Eagle Lake Dem. Town Cmt, 64-; mgr. and campaign coordinator, Elmer H. Violette Campaign for U.S. Senate, 66; mem, Gov. Task Force Govt. Reorgn, 67-; chmn, Gov. Task Force Dickey-Lincoln, 67-; comptroller and adv, Edmund S. Muskie V.Presidential Campaign, 68; mem, Maine Cmn. Party Struct. and Del. Selection, 69- Mem: Nat. Educ. Asn; Treas, North. Maine General Hospital, Inc; Trustee, Peoples' Benevolent Hospital; Trustee, Eagle Lake Water & Sewer Dist; C. of C; Catholic Order of Foresters. Fort Kent, Maine Jaycees Outstanding Young Man of 67. Rel: Roman Catholic; Pres, St. Mary's Church Adv. Parish Bd. Legal Res: Church St, Eagle Lake, Maine 04739. Mailing Add: P.O. Box 111, Eagle Lake, Maine 04739.

MARTIN, JOSEPH F. R
m. to Claire M. Cornwell; c. one son. Educ: Lynn Pub. Schs. Polit. & Govt. Pos: Presently serving third term as coun. of E. Lynn ward; chmn. of coun. cmt. on celebrations and mem. pub. prop. and vet. cmts. Mil. Serv: Korean War vet. Mem: Chmn. of 63 Lynn Classical Cerebral Palsy Drive; March of Dimes; East. Improvement Asn; K. of C. Mailing Add: 17 Aubrey Terr, Lynn, Mass. 02148. (1967)

MARTIN, LARRY K. R
b. Urbana, Ohio, 7/3/38; s. Howard M. Martin and Wilma Brigner M; m. 9/1/62 to Sherrill Palmer. Educ: Kent State Univ, B.S, 62; Sigma Delta Chi, Blue Key; Phi Delta Theta. Polit. & Govt. Pos: Admin. Asst. to U.S. Sen. J. Caleb Boggs, Del, 69- Bus. & Prof. Pos: Reporter, United Press Int, Columbus, Ohio, 61-62; chief, Gongwer News Serv, Lansing, Mich, 62-63; Peace Corps vol, Monrovia, Liberia, 63-65; Capitol bur. chief, News-J. Papers, Wilmington, Del, 65-69. Mil. Serv: Pfc, Army, 61; Army Res, 61- Rel: Protestant. Legal Res: 236 Bayard Ave, Dover, Del. 19901. Mailing Add: 3505 T St. N.W, Washington, D.C. 20007.

MARTIN, LEONARD WATSON D
Tenn. State Rep.
b. Nashville, Tenn, 8/9/35; s. Henry Watson Martin and Winnie Dell Thompson M; m. 7/6/56 to Margaret Helen Holcomb; c. Lee Watson. Educ: Univ. Tenn, B.S. and J.D, 62; Phi Alpha Delta. Polit. & Govt. Pos: Tenn. State Rep, 69- Bus. & Prof. Pos: Dir, Farmers & Merchants Bank, White Bluff, Tenn, 66; Pres, Ventures, Inc, Dickson, 66-; Secy, West Hills Develop. Co, Inc, 68-69. Mil. Serv: Entered as Pvt, Marines, 53, released as S/Sgt. on 57; Capt, Marines Res, 57- Mem: Dickson Co. Bar Asn.(pres, 67); Tenn. and Am. Bar Asns; Am. Judicature Soc; Tenn. and Am. Trial Lawyers Asn; Rotary (secy, v.pres. and pres, Dickson Club, 66-69); chmn, Dickson Co. Heart Fund Dr, 66; pres, Dickson Chap, Univ. Tenn. Alumni Chap, 68; dir, Dickson Co. Red Cross Chap, 68-; Mason; Dickson Country Club; Peckerwood Club; Nat. Rifle Asn; Ky. Col. Rel: Protestant. Legal Res: Rock Church Road, Dickson, Tenn. 37055. Mailing Add: Henslee Bldg, Dickson, Tenn. 37055.

MARTIN, LINDEN R. D
b. Brownsville, Ore, 1/2/99; s. Barney S. Martin and Elva M. Savage M; m. 7/29/31 to Hyla L. Hurd. Educ: Univ. Ore. and Willamette Univ, Law, 21-25. Polit. & Govt. Pos: Chmn, Wasco Co. Dem. Party, 52-66; mem, Ore. Dem. State Exec. Cmt, 54-68; chmn, Second Cong. Dist. Dem. Party, 54-68. Bus. & Prof. Pos: Attorney-at-law, 26-39; elec. engr, 39-49; gen. contractor, 49-68. Mem: F&AM; RAM; K.T; Eastern Star (past Patron). Mailing Add: 809 W. 18th St, The Dalles, Ore. 97058.

MARTIN, LOUIS EMANUEL D
b. Shelbyville, Tenn, 11/18/12; s. Louis Emanuel Martin and Willa Hill M; m. 1/2/37 to Gertrude E. Scott; c. Trudy, Anita, Toni, Linda and Lisa. Educ: Univ. of Mich, A.B, 34. Polit. & Govt. Pos: Mem, Bd. Supvrs. Wayne Co, Mich, 2 terms in 40's; dep. chmn, Dem. Nat. Cmt, 60-, mem, McGovern Cmn, currently. Bus. & Prof. Pos: Ed. and publisher, Mich. Chronicle, 36-59; ed-in-chief, Chicago Daily Defender, 47-59; v.pres. and ed, Sengstacke Newspapers, 69- Mem: Nat. Urban League (v.pres, 65-); Overseas Press Club; Nat. Press Club; Fed. Club. Rel: Catholic. Mailing Add: 5052 S. Woodlawn, Chicago, Ill. 60615.

MARTIN, MARION E. R
Cmnr, Labor and Indust, Maine
b. Kingman, Maine, 1/14/00; d. William H. Martin and Florence MacLaughlin M; single. Educ: Bradford Acad, 17; Univ. Maine, B.A, 35; Wellesley Col, 2 years; Yale Law Sch, 36-37; Northwest. Univ. Law Sch, summer 37; hon. M.A, Bates Col, 38; hon. LL.D, Nasson Col, 53; Phi Beta Kappa; Sigma Mu Sigma; Alpha Omicron Pi. Polit. & Govt. Pos: Maine State Rep, 30-35; Maine State Sen, 35-39; Maine committeewoman, Rep. Nat. Cmt, 36-47, asst. chmn, 37-47; chmn, Bd. of Boiler Rules and Regulations, Maine, 47; cmnr, Labor and Indust, 47-; mem, Indust. Accident Cmn, 47-; chmn, Bd. of Elevator Rules and Regulations, 49; chmn, Construction Safety Bd, 55; govt. adv, Int. Labor Orgn, 58 & 59. Mem: Delta Kappa Gamma; hon. mem, Local 7, BMPIUA; Maine Tuberc. and Health Asn.(bd. dirs, 48-); Nat. Tuberc. and Respiratory Disease Asn.(bd. dirs, 55, secy. of bd, 68-); Nat. Safety Coun.(bd. dirs, 50-, exec. bd, 52-); Int. Asn. Govt. Labor Off.(pres, 50-51, mem. exec. cmt, 69-); Asn. of Labor Mediation Agencies (v.pres. exec. cmt, 69-). Distinguished Serv. Award, Am. Asn. Univ. Women, 50; Soroptomist Award of Achievement, New Eng. Region, 52; Deborah Morton Award, Westbrook Jr. Col, 64; Rosell W. Huddilston Award, Maine Tuberc. Asn, 66. Rel: Episcopal. Mailing Add: Westview Ave, Hallowell, Maine 04347.

MARTIN, ROBERT C. D
N.Mex. State Rep.
b. Duncan, Ariz, 1/2/12; s. Henry Martin and Anna Bunton M; m. to Ione Rose; c. Anna (Mrs. Wright) and Robert C, Jr. Polit. & Govt. Pos: N.Mex. House of Reps, 53- Bus. & Prof. Pos: Cattle rancher. Mem: Elks; Mason; N.Mex. Cattle Growers Asn; supvr, Virden Valley Soil Conserv. Dist; chmn, bd. of dirs, First Nat. Bank of Lordsburg. Rel: Protestant. Legal Res: Redrock, N.Mex. 88055. Mailing Add: P.O. Box 146, Lordsburg, N.Mex. 88045.

MARTIN, ROBERT HUGH D
Mo. State Rep.
b. Howard Co, Mo, 8/22/34; s. Thomas N. Martin and Edna O'Brien M; m. 12/22/59 to Deanna Coleman; c. Chris Robert and Coleman O'Brien. Educ: South. Ill. Univ, B.S, 56; Univ. Missouri-Kansas City Law Sch, J.D, 65; Theta XI. Polit. & Govt. Pos: Munic. judge, Lee's Summit, Mo, 65; asst. prosecuting attorney, Jackson Co, 66-67; prosecuting attorney, Lee's Summit, 68; Mo. State Rep, 19th Legis. Dist, 69- Mil. Serv: Entered as 2nd Lt, Air Force, 56, released as 1st Lt, 59, Capt, Res. Mem: Mo. Bar; Independence Bar Asn.(bd. dirs, 68-); Rotary; C. of C; Jr. C. of C. Distinguished Service Award, Lee's Summit Jaycees, 68. Rel: Episcopal. Mailing Add: 306 O'Brien, Lee's Summit, Mo. 64063.

MARTIN, ROGER EDWARD R
Ore. State Rep.
b. Portland, Ore, 3/10/35; s. Ray Lynn Martin and Georgianna Fay Benson M; m. 12/28/58 to Janet Joan; c. Christopher D, David J. and Kathleen E. Educ: Univ. Ore, B.S, 57; Phi Delta Theta. Polit. & Govt. Pos: Ore. State Rep, 67- Bus. & Prof. Pos: V.pres, Martin Electric Co, 65; v.pres, West. Utility Supply, currently. Mil. Serv: 2nd Lt, Army, 57-58; Capt, Army Res, 64. Mem: Rotary; Elks. Rel: Catholic. Mailing Add: 13750 S.W. Kraus Rd, Lake Oswego, Ore. 97034.

MARTIN, ROY R
b. Portsmouth, Ohio, 4/12/15; s. Charles L. Martin and Ida May Giles M; m. 5/24/63 to Betty Marie Hoffner; c. O. Bruce, Sim L, R. Douglas and David L. Educ: Ohio, Univ, 45-46; Portsmouth Interstate Bus. Col, 50; Ohio State Univ, 66. Polit. & Govt. Pos: Rep. precinct committeeman, Scioto Co, Ohio, 38-42 & 54-60; chief dep. co. treas, Scioto Co, 45-50; secy, Scioto Co. Men's Rep. Club, 46-47, v.pre, 47-48, pres, 48-50; exec. cmt. chmn, Scioto Co. Rep. Party, 54-59; admin. asst. div. engr, Ohio Dept. of Hwy, 57-59; supvr. of audits, State Auditor's Off, Ohio, 59-63; asst. to gov, Ohio, 63-; del, Rep. Nat. Conv, 68, mem, Electorial Col, Ohio, 68-69. Bus. & Prof. Pos: Dist. mgr, West. & South. Life Ins, 50-54 and Union Cent. Life Ins, 54-57. Mil. Serv: Entered as Pvt, Army, 41, released as Capt, 45, after serv. in 37th Div. and 23rd Corps, Asiatic Pac. Theatre and ETO, 42-45; Bronze Star and Am. Defense Medals; Asiatic Pac. Campaign Medal with Five Battle Stars; European Campaign Medal with One Battle Star; Good Conduct and Victory Medals. Mem: Mason; Scottish Rite; Ky. Col; Exec. Order of Ohio Commodore; Elks. Rel: Methodist. Legal Res: 1028 Stedman Ave, Portsmouth, Ohio 45662. Mailing Add: 4535-A Kenfield Rd, Columbus, Ohio 43229.

MARTIN, ROY BUTLER, JR. D
Mayor, Norfolk, Va.
b. Norfolk, Va, 5/13/21; s. Roy Butler Martin and Anne Holman M; m. 1948 to Louise Freeman Eggleston; c. Roy Butler, III and Anne Beverly. Educ: William and Mary Norfolk Div, 39-40; Univ. of Va, B.S. in commerce, 43. Polit. & Govt. Pos: Former chmn, Mayor's Youth Cmn, Norfolk, Va; former mem, Gov. Cmt. on Youth; mayor, Norfolk, 62-; former mem, exec. bd, Nat. League of Cities, mem. adv. bd. and chmn, Cmt. on Commun. Develop, currently; mem. adv. bd. and chmn, Cmt. on Commun. Develop, U.S. Conf. of Mayors, mem, VALC Zoning Procedures Cmt. and bd. of dirs, Norfolk Urban Coalition, currently. Bus. & Prof. Pos: Pres, Foote Bros. & Co. Mil. Serv: Entered as Ens, Navy, 43, released as Lt, 46, after serv. in Pac; Lt, Intel. Unit, Naval Res, 48-52. Mem: Former v.pres, Va. Munic. League, pres, currently; bd. of dirs, Norfolk Boys Club, Old Dominion Col. Educ. Found. and First Nat. Bank of Norfolk; nat. adv. bd, MacArthur Mem. Found; trustee, Tidewater Va. Develop. Coun; past pres, Norfolk Food Brokers Asn. and Young Dem. Club of Norfolk; Past Comdr, Am. Legion Post 330; former mem. bd. of dirs, Norfolk Forum, Norfolk Cerebral Palsy Training Center, Norfolk Food Dealers Asn, Tide-

water Sales Rep. Asn, Am. Red Cross of Norfolk, Va. Club, Univ. of Va. Alumni Asn. and Norfolk Coun. of Navy League; former mem, Armed Forces Cmt, C. of C. and Cmt. on Parking, Am. Munic. Asn; Harbor Club; Norfolk Yacht & Country Club; Princess Anne Country Club. Rel: Episcopal; Former mem, Vestry, Church of the Good Shepherd. Legal Res: 1519 Commonwealth Ave, Norfolk, Va. 23505. Mailing Add: City Hall, Norfolk, Va. 23510.

MARTIN, SAMUEL L. R
b. Watseka, Ill, 5/27/00; m. to Madean Meents M; c. Richard, three grandchildren. Educ: Lake Forest Col; U. of Ill. Polit. & Gov. Pos: Ill. State Sen; Ill. State Rep, 3 terms. Bus. & Prof. Pos: Farmer and stock raiser; Vice Pres, Guarantee Savings and Loan Asn. of Piper City; Dir, Vice Pres, First Trust and Savings Bank, Watseka; Pres, Hemb and Martin Mfg. Co, Murfreesboro, Tenn; Vice Pres; Concrete Prods. Co, Skokie. Rel: Presbyterian. Mailing Add: 324 Conv. Ave, Watseka, Ill. 60970. (1967)

MARTIN, SPENCER FERRIN, JR. R
b. Clinton, Mass, 10/13/23; s. Spencer Ferrin Martin and Marlitta Brockelman M; m. 8/14/54 to Caroline Smith Freeman; c. Timothy Dyer, Julianna Wells and Suzanne Clark. Educ: Yale Univ, B.S, 49; Tau Beta Pi; St. Elmo Soc. Polit. & Govt. Pos: Chmn, Lincoln Rep. Town Cmt, Mass, 64-68. Bus. & Prof. Pos: Asst. dist. traffic supt, Bell Tel. of Pa, 49-54; mgr, prfnl. staff, Arthur D. Little Inc, 54-59, New Eng. Off, 59-66. Mil. Serv: Entered as Pvt, Army Air Corps, 43, released as 1st Lt, 46, after serv. in 20th Air Force, Pac. Theater, 45-46. Mem: Lincoln Players; Valley Pond Asn. Rel: Unitarian. Mailing Add: Tower Rd, Lincoln Center, Mass. 01773. (1967)

MARTIN, THEODORE S. D
b. St. Louis, Mo, 2/23/26; s. Spero Martin and Xanthe Gregory M; m. 5/9/54 to Alexandra Peters; c. Deborah, Pamella and George. Educ: St. Louis Univ, B.S; Washington Univ, LL.B; Delta Theta Phi. Polit. Pos: Alderman, 27th Ward, City of St. Louis, Mo. Bus. & Prof. Pos: Attorney at Law, self-employed. Mil. Serv: Entered Air Force, 45, released as Pre-Aviation Cadet, 46. Mem: Am. Legion; Am, Mo. and St. Louis Bar Asns. Rel: Greek Orthodox. Mailing Add: 6060 N. Pointe, St. Louis, Mo. 63147. (1967)

MARTIN, WADE OMER, JR. D
Secy. of State La.
b. Arnaudville, La, 4/18/11; s. Wade O. Martin and Alice Mills M; m. 10/25/38 to Juliette Bonnette; c. Merle Mary, Marcelle, Wade O, III, David, Wallace and Gregory. Educ: Southwest. La. Inst, B.A, 32; La. State Univ, LL.B, 35; Gamma Eta Gamma; Kappa Sigma. Polit. & Govt. Pos: Asst. attorney gen, Baton Rouge, La, 35-40; Secy. of State, La, 44- Bus. & Prof. Pos: Attorney-at-law, 40-44. Mem: Am. and La. Bar Asns; Nat. Asn. of Secretaries of State; K. of C. Mailing Add: 210 L.S.U. Ave, Baton Rouge, La. 70808.

MARTIN, WANETA R
Secy, S.Cent. Dist. Rep. Party, Alaska
b. Price, Utah, 2/6/14; d. Carl W. Empey and Ruby Jessen E; m. 7/14/35 to John W. Martin, Jr; c. John Ace, Guy Empey, Jim I, Jill Annette and Carlos William. Educ: Brigham Young Univ, 32-33; studied under Dr. Florence Jepperson and Prof. Lund, Salt Lake City, Utah, 33-35. Polit. & Govt. Pos: Alternate to Alaska Rep. Conv, 66, del, 68; secy, S.Cent. Dist. Rep. Party, Alaska, 67-; alternate del, Rep. Nat. Conv, 68. Mem: Rep. Women of Alaska. Rel: Latter-day Saint. Mailing Add: 929 W. 12th Ave, Apt. 2, Anchorage, Alaska 99501.

MARTIN, WILLARD GORDON R
N.H. State Rep.
b. Boston, Mass, 12/12/37; s. Willard Gordon Martin and Helen Dey M; m. 9/12/59 to Mary Ann Burdett; c. Melissa Ann and Helen Elizabeth. Educ: Bates Col, A.B, 59; Harvard Law Sch, L.L.B, 62; Phi Beta Kappa; Delta Sigma Rho. Polit. & Govt. Pos: City Attorney, Laconia, N.H, 63-67; co. attorney, Belknap Co, 67-69; N.H. State Rep, 69- Bus. & Prof. Pos: Assoc, Nighswander, Lord & Martin Attorneys, 62-65, partner, 65- Mil. Serv: Entered as Pvt, Army, 63, released as SP-6, 69, after serv. in Hq, N.H. Nat. Guard. Mem: Belknap, N.H. and Am. Bar Asns; Kiwanis. Rel: Unitarian. Mailing Add: 72 Belknap St, Laconia, N.H. 03246.

MARTIN, WILLIAM CABINESS D
b. Roba, Ala, 6/17/11; s. William Cabiness Martin and Satira Wilson M; m. 4/22/57 to Adita Landry; c. William Cabiness, VII and Francisco Forrest. Educ: George Wash. Univ, A.B, 36; Nat. Univ. of Law and Econ, LL.B, 38, D.J.S, 39. Polit. & Govt. Pos: Admin. asst. patronage cmt, U.S. House Rep, 37-38 and appropriations cmt, 38-40; asst. corp. counsel, D.C, 40-42; dep. cmnr, Fla. Indust. Cmn, 46-48; chmn, Dade Co. Dem. Exec. Cmt, Fla, 62-66. Bus. & Prof. Pos: Secy. and mem, Spec. Investigating Cmn. for 11th Judicial Circuit Court, 58-60; mem, Bd. of Gov, Univ. Miami Law Cent, 59- Mil. Serv: Entered as Lt.(jg), Coast Guard Res, 42, released as Lt. Comdr, 46; Am. Theater and Victory Medals; Coast Guard Res. Ribbon with Cluster; Capt, Coast Guard Res, 64. Mem: Dade Co. Bar Asn.(pres, 59-60); Fed. Bar Asn.(v.pres, S.Fla. Chap, 59-60); Am. Bar Asn; Florida Bar. Rel: Congregational. Mailing Add: 1261 Coral Way, Coral Gables, Fla. 33134.

MARTIN, WILLIAM CLYDE D
Chmn, Sherman Co. Dem. Party, Tex.
b. Stratford, Tex, 9/26/25; s. William Clyde Martin and Hazel Brown M; m. 6/4/48 to Pauline P. Keener; c. Ted, Mary Pat, Kathleen and Denny. Educ: Tex. A & M Univ, 2 years. Polit. & Govt. Pos: Trustee, Stratford Independent Sch. Dist, Tex, 63-66; mem, Draft Bd, 63-67; chmn, Sherman Co. Dem. Party, 67- Bus. & Prof. Pos: Owner, Tip Top Farms, 49-; Tip Top Motor Supply, 65- Mil. Serv: Entered as Pvt, Army, 44, released as Sgt, 46. Mem: Am. Legion; Mason; Lions; Farmers Union; Nat. Farmers Orgn. Rel: Methodist. Legal Res: 919 N Maple, Stratford, Tex. 79084. Mailing Add: Box 691, Stratford, Tex. 79084.

MARTIN, WILLIAM McCHESNEY, JR.
b. St. Louis, Mo, 12/17/06; s. William McChesney Martin and Rebecca Woods M; m. 4/3/42 to Cynthia Davis; c. Cynthia, Diana and William, III. Educ: Yale, B.A, 28; Benton Col. of Law, 31; Columbia, part-time grad. student. 31-37. Hon. LL.D, Temple Univ, Amherst Col, Tulane Univ, Marietta Col, Wash. Univ, Trinity Col, Univ. Pa, Yale Univ. and Harvard Univ. Polit. & Govt. Pos: Mem. of bd, Export-Import Bank, 45, chmn. bd. of dirs, 46-48; Asst. Secy. of Treas, 49; U.S. exec. dir, Int. Bank Reconstruction and Develop, 49-52; chmn, Fed. Reserve Bd, 51-70. Bus. & Prof. Pos: Mem, N.Y. Stock Exchange, 31-38; publisher and ed, Econ. Forum, 32-34. Mil. Serv: Entered as Pvt, Army, 41, released as Col, 45. Mem: Chmn, bd. trustees, Berry Sch; trustee, Johns Hopkins Univ, Yale Corp. and For. Serv. Educ. Found; West Side Tennis Club; Yale Club; Metrop. Club; Alibi Club; Chevy Chase Club. Rel: Presbyterian. Mailing Add: 2861 Woodland Dr. N.W, Washington, D.C. 20008.

MARTIN, WILLIAM ROY D
Chmn, Fayette Co. Dem. Exec. Cmt, Ala.
b. Millerville, Ala, 5/29/03; s. John Simeon Martin (Methodist Minister) and Lelia Ophelia Strong M; m. 8/1/31 to Frankie A. Nuckols; c. John Arthur; grandchildren, Mary Frances, John A, Jr. and Teresa Ann. Educ: High Sch, Elkmont, Ala, 24; Bus. Courses, Birmingham & Montgomery, Ala. and Nashville, Tenn. Polit. & Govt. Pos: Chmn, Fayette Co. Dem. Exec. Cmt, Ala, 44- Mem: Boy Scout master; Farm Bur; 4H Counselor; Lions (held all offices); Mason (dist. lectr, 14th dist. Lodge of Ala); Charles Baskerville Lodge, Fayette (Worshipful Master, 5 times); AF&AM (Sr. Grand Steward, 67-68); Col, Gov. Staff; Boosters Club. Citation from F.D. Roosevelt for bond sales during World War II. Rel: Methodist; Steward and former trustee and supt, Sunday Sch, First Methodist Church, Fayette. Mailing Add: P.O. Box 388, 401 Winston St, Fayette, Ala. 35555.

MARTINEK, VIOLA E. D
b. Melvin, Iowa, 3/15/18; d. Frank Knapp (deceased) and Rika Roelofsen K; div; c. Shirley Rae. Educ: Melvin Consolidated Schs, 11 years. Polit. & Govt. Pos: Precinct committeewoman, Precinct 1, Dem. Cent. Cmt, Iowa, 58-; mem, Dem. Cent. Cmt, 58-; del, Dem. Nat. Conv, 64; secy, Fifth Dist. Cmt. on Polit. Educ, Iowa Fedn. Labor, AFL-CIO, 66-; mem, State Dem. Sustaining Fund, 66-; mem, Nat. Dem. Participating Fund, 66- Bus. & Prof. Pos: Leader, Brownie Scout Troop, 42-51; dir, Established Girl Scout Camp, 46 & 47; labor rep, United Fund, 65. Mem: Amalgamated Meat Cutters and Butcher Workers of N.Am; Webster Co. Fedn. of Labor (secy); Iowa Commun. Serv. Staff, Iowa Fedn. Labor, AFL-CIO; Union counsr; Rehabilitation Proj; YWCA; Am. Legion; Am. Nat. Red Cross (Red Cross Disaster Serv, adv, voc. rehabilitation chmn. state wide planning cmt. region 3); Nat. Rehabilitation Asn; Planning and Zoning Cmn. City, Ft. Dodge. Rel: Lutheran. Mailing Add: 211 Ave. E, Ft. Dodge, Iowa 50501.

MARTINES, MARY-ALICE WALLACH D
Mem. Exec. Cmt, Outagamie Co. Dem. Party, Wis.
b. Oak Park, Ill, 6/19/30; d. Andrew Sylvester Wallach and Marion Dee W; m. 8/23/58 to Hugo Martines; c. Mario Charles, Suzanne Carla, Sarah Catherine and David Stephen. Educ: Rosary Col, River Forest, Ill, B.A, 51; Northwest. Univ, M.A, 56. Polit. & Govt. Pos: Secy, McCarthy for Pres. Cmt, Outagamie Co, Wis, 68; alternate del, Dem. Nat. Conv, 68; mem. Exec. Cmt, Outagamie Co. Dem. Party, 69- Mem: V.chmn, Fox Valley Human Rights Coun; co-chmn, Fish Community Serv; Grape Boycott Cmt, Appleton & Fox Valley. Rel: Roman Catholic. Mailing Add: 129 N.Lawe St, Appleton, Wis. 54911.

MARTINEZ, ALEX G. D
N.Mex. State Sen.
b. 1926. Educ: St. Michael's Col; Col. Santa Fe. Polit. & Govt. Pos: N.Mex. State Rep, 63-66; N.Mex. State Sen, 67- Bus. & Prof. Pos: Agent for AT&SF Rwy. Mil. Serv: Army, Pac. Theater, 43-45; Purple Heart with Two Clusters. Mem: Am. Legion; VFW; Kiwanis; Order of Purple Heart; YMCA (bd. dir); bd. dir, United Fund; C. of C. Rel: Catholic. Mailing Add: 1949 Hopi Rd, Santa Fe, N.Mex. 87501.

MARTINEZ, ELVIN L. D
Fla. State Rep.
b. Tampa, Fla, 1935; married; c. Four. Educ: Univ. Tampa; Stetson Univ, B.A. and LL.B. Polit. & Govt. Pos: Fla. State Rep, 67-; del, Dem. Nat. Conv, 68. Bus. & Prof. Pos: Attorney. Mem: Pres, W. Tampa Optimist Club; Co, Fla. State and Nat. Bar Asns. Mailing Add: 1717 N. Howard Ave, Tampa, Fla. 33607. (1967)

MARTINEZ, LEVI D
b. Cerro, N.Mex, 11/10/22; s. Delfino Martinez and Dulcinea Arellano M; m. 6/11/50 to Clotilda Lobato; c. Bernadette, Yvette, Dolores, Levi, Jr, Henrietta Theresa and Emilio. Educ: Adams State Col, B.A, 48; Univ. Colo, LL.B, 51; Bd. of Editors, Rocky Mt. Law Review, 50-51; Phi Delta Phi; pres. of Student Body, Adams State Col, 48. Polit. & Govt. Pos: Co. attorney, Costilla Co, Colo, 53-55; v.pres, Young Dem. Pueblo Co, 56-58; secy, Young Dem. Colo, 57; chmn, Precinct 20, Dem. Party, Pueblo Co, 57-62; dep. dist. attorney, Tenth Judicial Dist, Pueblo, 62-64; alternate del-at-lg, Dem. Nat. Conv, 64; co-founder, Mexican Orgn. for Latin Defense; Independent Party cand. for Gov, Colo, 67. Bus. & Prof. Pos: Private practice of law, 51-; pres. and major stock holder, Nationwide Builders and Whitman Hotel, currently. Mil. Serv: Entered as Pvt, Army, 42, released as Sgt, 46, after serv. in S.Pac; New Guinea Campaign Star; S.Pac. Ribbon. Publ: 'Alien Land Laws vs. United Nations Charter' Rocky Mt. Law Review, 12/50 and National Law Digest, 51. Mem: Pueblo Co, Am. and Colo. Bar Asns; Citizens Serv. Orgn; C. of C. Letterman, Track Team, Adams State Col, 48. Rel: Catholic. Legal Res: 1740 Alexander Circle, Pueblo, Colo. 81001. Mailing Add: 213 W. First National Bank Bldg, Pueblo, Colo. 81003.

MARTINEZ COLÓN, HECTOR M. New Progressive, P.R.
Sen, P.R. Senate
b. Ponce, P.R, 3/27/29; s. Francisco Martinez and Carmen Colón Colón M; m. 4/10/55 to Percida Maldonado Figueroa; c. Mayra del Carmen, Hector Carlos, Hector Cesar, Hector Manuel and Hector Javier. Educ: Univ. P.R, B.A, 50, B.L, 53. Polit. & Govt. Pos: Sen, P.R. Senate, 69- Mem: Mason. Rel: Catholic. Legal Res: Exten. Alhambra A-55, Ponce, P.R. 00731. Mailing Add: Box 1048, Ponce, P.R. 00731.

MARTINIS, JOHN ANTHONY D
Wash. State Rep.
b. Everett, Wash, 6/4/30; s. Paul Martinis and Pearl Marincovich M; m.

9/25/50 to Virginia Olich; c. Paulett, John, Tracy, Christie, and Marty. Educ: Everett Jr. Col, 48-49. Polit. & Govt. Pos: Port Cmnr, Everett, Wash, 68-; Wash. State Rep, 38th Dist, 69- Bus. & Prof. Pos: Owner, Bob's Sporting Goods, currently. Mem: Elks; Wash. State Sportsmans Coun; Eagles; Wash. State Environmental Coun. Rel: Catholic. Mailing Add: 2304 Eighth St, Everett, Wash. 98201.

MARTON, LARRY BRUCE D
Coordinator Int. Info. Prog, U.S. Dept. Agr.
b. New York, N.Y, 6/25/24; s. Michael Marton (deceased) and Helen Weiss M; m. 6/26/42 to Fanchon Pickrell; c. Keith Ian, Kenneth Lawrence, Kathryne Jan (Mrs. John Carhart), and Kraig Jonathon. Educ: Ariz. State Univ, B.A. and M.A, 49; Kappa Delta Pi; Phi Delta Kappa; Psychology Club; Ariz. Press Club; '49 Club; ed, Helios. Polit. & Govt. Pos: Admin. asst. to Gov. Ariz, 57-58; acting personnel dir. and press liaison, Ariz. Corp. Cmn, 59-62; pres, Mesa Young Dem, 62; admin. asst. to U.S. Rep. George F. Senner, Jr, Third Dist, Ariz, 63-67; coordinator int. info. prog, U.S. Dept. Agr, 67- Bus. & Prof. Pos: Feature and ed. writer, Mesa Tribune, 51-57; publicity dir, Producer's Life Ins, Co, 56; pres, Marste Consult, Inc, 62. Mil. Serv: Entered as Pvt, Air Force, 42, released as Pfc, 45, after serv. in Inf, U.S, 45. Mem: Nat. Asn. of Secondary Principals; Burro Club, Nat. Educ. Asn; Cong. Secretaries Club; Elks; Kiwanis; Ariz. State Soc; YMCA; Fed. Ed. Asn; Orgn. Prfnl. Employees Dept. Agr; U.S.D.A. Employees Coun. Rel: Methodist. Mailing Add: 11119 Byrd Dr, Fairfax, Va. 22030.

MARTY, JAMES FLOYD 'JIM' R
b. Ardmore, Okla, 3/1/36; s. James Ray Marty and Betty Shinn M; m. 5/25/56 to La Keta Jo Bellis; c. Bruce Wayne, La Keta Le and Lisa Dawn. Educ: Univ. Okla, 3 years. Polit. & Govt. Pos: Chmn, Seminole Co. Rep. Cent. Cmt, Okla, 65-66. Bus. & Prof. Pos: Secy-treas, Okla. Water Law Coun, 65-66. Mem: Okla. and Nat. Jaycees; Seminole Jaycees (past pres. and past state dir). Rel: Church of Christ. Mailing Add: 526 N. First, Seminole, Okla. 74868.

MARTY, LAWRENCE A. R
U.S. Cmnr, Sweetwater Co, Wyo.
b. Platte Co, Nebr, 6/17/26; s. Herman L. Marty and Frances J. Harvey M; m. 8/8/65 to Nellie M. Moerke. Educ: Wayne State Teachers Col, 44-46; Creighton Sch. of Law, 46-47 and 51-52; Univ. Wyo, LL.B, 54; Delta Theta Phi. Polit. & Govt. Pos: Munic. judge, Green River, Wyo, 58-60; U.S. Cmnr, Sweetwater Co, Wyo, 58-; chmn, Sweetwater Co. Rep. Cent. Cmt, 60-64 & 68-; alternate del, Rep. Nat. Conv, 64; Rep. State Committeeman, Sweetwater Co, 64-66. Bus. & Prof. Pos: Attorney-at-law, 54- Mem: Am. and Wyo. Bar Asns; Lions (past pres. and zone chmn). Rel: Lutheran. Legal Res: 391 Hilcrest Way, Green River, Wyo. 82935. Mailing Add: P.O. Box 231, Green River, Wyo. 82935.

MARTZ, JOHN E D
b. Minersville, Pa, 7/5/03; s. Joshua Martz and Debra Evans M; m. 6/4/60 to Isabella Farrell. Polit. & Govt. Pos: Treas, Northumberland Co. Dem. Party, Pa, 51-55; del, Dem. Nat. Conv, 68. Bus. & Prof. Pos: Ins. broker, 29-69; publisher, Mt. Carmel Examiner, 53-69. Mem: F&AM; Consistory. Legal Res: 119 N. Oak St, Mt. Carmel, Pa. 17851. Mailing Add: 117-19 N. Oak St, Mt. Carmel, Pa. 17851.

MARUSKA, HARVEYDALE
b. Angus, Minn, 1921; married; c. Three daughters. Educ: N.Dak. Agr. Col. Polit. & Govt. Pos: Minn. State Rep, 58 & 60; Minn. State Sen, 62-66. Bus. & Prof. Pos: Grain farmer. Mem: Dir, Marshal Co. Agr. Asn; Toastmasters Int.(area Gov); Mason (Past Master). Rel: Presbyterian; Elder and Trustee, Presby. Church. Mailing Add: Route 1, Angus, Minn. 56712. (1967)

MARVEL, BILLY BRYAN D
Chmn, Butler Co. Dem. Cmt, Mo.
b. Bloomfield, Mo, 4/6/13; s. Lewis W. Marvel and Maude Mitchell M; m. 10/27/36 to Clarabelle Davis; c. Louise (Mrs. Essary), Emily (Mrs. Penn) and David Roosevelt. Educ: Southeast Mo. State Univ, 1 year. Polit. & Govt. Pos: Alderman, Poplar Bluff City Coun, Mo, 59-69; chmn, Butler Co. Dem. Cmt, 63-; del, Dem. Nat. Conv, 68. Bus. & Prof. Pos: Owner and operator, Marvel Music Co, Mo, 47- Mem: Mason; Scottish Rite; Shrine. Rel: Protestant. Mailing Add: 406 N. C St, Poplar Bluff, Mo. 63901.

MARVEL, RICHARD DOUGLAS R
Nebr. State Sen.
b. Hastings, Nebr, 12/8/17; s. Archie Douglas Marvel and Ruth Capps M; m. 5/17/41 to Oline Ida Lindemann; c. Douglas James and Anne Elizabeth. Educ: Univ. Leipzig, Germany; Hastings Col, B.A, 40; Univ. Nebr, M.A, 60 & Ph.D, 66. Polit. & Govt. Pos: Co. chmn, Rep. Party, Nebr, 54-58; Nebr. State Sen, 51-55 & 59-, chmn, Legis, Budget Cmt. Mil. Serv: Entered as Pvt, Army, 42, released as T/Sgt, 45, after serv. in 119th AAA Group Hq, S.Pac, 43-45. Mem: Am. Legion (dept. comdr, Nebr, 46-47); VFW; Rotary; YMCA. Rel: Presbyterian. Mailing Add: 919 N. Lincoln Ave, Hastings, Nebr. 68901.

MARVIN, GUY L. R
b. Greene, 7/31/03; m. to Lucille Botsford. Educ: Lowell Sch. of Bus, Binghamton. Polit. & Govt. Pos: N.Y. State Assemblyman, 58-66; bd. of supvr, Town of Greene, 41-58; chmn, 49-58; tax collector, Town of G eene, 15 years; Greene Village bd. of trustees, 4 years. Bus. & Prof. Pos: Owner, Cornell Pencil Co, Greene. Mem: Norwich C. of C; former pres, N.Y. State Supvrs. Asn; former p. master, E. Light Lodge 126, F&AM; Greene Chap. 106, R.A.M, Greene Rotary Club. Rel: Episcopalian. Mailing Add: Greene, N.Y. 13778. (1967)

MARWELL, EDWARD MARVIN D
b. Brookline, Mass; s. Nathan Marwell and Ethel Shapiro M; m. to Grace Glass; c. Stuart Evan, Emily, David George and Joshua Lenard. Educ: Columbia Col, A.B, 43; Columbia Univ, Sch. Eng, B.S, 44; Zeta Beta Tau. Polit. & Govt. Pos: Trustee, Mt. Kisco, N.Y, 55-59, dep. mayor, 59-, chmn, Human Rights Cmn, currently; del, Dem. Nat. Conv, 68. Bus. & Prof. Pos: Engr, Gen. Precision Lab, 47-61; pres, Curtis Instruments, Inc, Mt. Kisco, N.Y, 61- Mil. Serv: Entered as Aviation Cadet, Air Force, 43, released as 1st Lt, 46, after serv. in Hq, Fifth AFSC, Pac, 45-46. Rel: Judaism. Mailing Add: Leonard St, Mt. Kisco, N.Y, 10549.

MARX, ELANOR F. Independent
b. 4/13/16; married; c. three, two step-children. Educ: Utica Conservatory of Music and Sch. of Dramatic Art; Rollins Col. Polit. & Govt. Pos: N.H. State Rep, 63-67. Bus. & Prof. Pos: Former Editor-Publisher of weekly newspaper and political columnist. Mem: Former sch. bd. mem; Asn. of Lawyers Wives of the N.H. Bar Asn; Bd. of Dir. and Past Pres, Commun. Club; Past Pres, Parents Club; Bd. of Dir, Rockingham Hosp. Auxiliary; Pink Ladies Serv; Rockingham Hosp. 1967 Legal Res: Box 56, Alstead, N.H. No mailing address available. (1967)

MARX, EMIL FRANCIS D
b. Botkins, Ohio, Dec, 1892; s. Michael Albert Marx and Whilomena Brinniger M; m. 6/28/21 to Mary Ruth Eckert. Educ: St. Joseph Col, Rensselaer, Ind, 3 years. Polit. & Govt. Pos: Serv. dir, City of St. Marys, Ohio, 34-35; adj. gen, Ohio, 35-39; chmn, Auglaize Co. Dem. Party, 40-68; chmn, Auglaize Co. Bd. Elec, 42-69. Bus. & Prof. Pos: Mem. sect. bd. govs, Joint Twp. Mem. Hosp, 47-68. Mil. Serv: Entered as Pvt, Army and Nat. Guard, 14, released as Col, 42, after serv. in Sixth Inf, World War I, Bachret, Argonne Drive, St. Mehiel and two drives in Belgium, 17-19; Mex. Border Serv, 16-17; Res, 19-42 (Ret). Mem: Past Comdr, St. Marys Post Am. Legion 323; past comdr, VFW; Post 9289, DAV; Eagles; K. of C; C. of C. Received plaque for being Dem. Co. Chmn. for more than 25 years from Dem. Nat. Hq. Rel: Catholic. Mailing Add: 208 N. Pear St, St. Marys, Ohio 45885.

MARZANO, FRANK G. D
Wash. State Rep.
b. Tacoma, Wash, 1922; m. to Angel M; c. Four. Educ: High sch. Polit. & Govt. Pos: Wash. State Rep, currently. Bus. & Prof. Pos: Driver salesman. Mil. Serv: Army; Coast Guard. Mem: Amvets; Bellarmine Boosters; Christopher Columbus Soc. Mailing Add: 2501 S. Melrose, Tacoma, Wash. 98405. (1967)

MASCO, DOROTHY BERYL R
Secy, Archuleta Co. Rep. Cent. Cmt, Colo.
b. Adelaide, S.Australia, 3/16/18; d. Albert Edward Hersey and Ida Tisher H; m. 1/10/44 to Charles Frederick Masco. Educ: Adelaide High Sch, S.Australia, 4 years. Polit. & Govt. Pos: Secy, Archuleta Co. Rep. Cent. Cmt, Colo, 65- Bus. & Prof. Pos: Sales Counsr, Fuller Brush Co, Salt Lake City, Utah, 65. Mem: Woman's Civic Club (past pres). Rel: Methodist. Mailing Add: Box 412, Pagosa Springs, Colo. 81147.

MASCOLO, FREDERIC EDWARD D
Mem, Waterbury Dem. Town Cmt, Conn.
b. Waterbury, Conn, 7/24/29; s. Edward Mascolo and Clelia Menichino M; m. 4/23/55 to Irene J. Zoli; c. Frederic D. and Edward D. Educ: Seton Hall Univ, B.S, 51; Georgetown Univ. Law Sch, LL.B, 53; Phi Alpha Delta. Polit. & Govt. Pos: Mem, Conn. Dem. State Cmt, 62-64; city comptroller, Waterbury, 63-65; mem, Waterbury Dem. Town Cmt, 63-; alternate del, Dem. Nat. Conv, 68. Bus. & Prof. Pos: Attorney at Law, 54-; instr. bus. law, Mattatuck Commun. Col, 67- Mil. Serv: Entered as Pvt, Army, 55, released as SP-4, 57, after serv. in Tenth Inf. Div, Europe, 55-57. Mem: Conn. State and Waterbury Bar Asns; Unico; Ital. Am. Dem. Club; Incorporator, Waterbury Hosp; Conn. Heart Asn; YMCA (bd. dirs). Rel: Catholic. Mailing Add: 107 Eastfield Rd, Waterbury, Conn. 06708.

MASHBURN, TELFAIR JAMES D
b. Flomaton, Ala, 8/22/07; s. Telfair James Mashburn and Florrye Bell McWilliams M; m. to Ida Belle Turberville; c. Julia (Mrs. Laurence Stern Morgan), Deborah, Telfair James, III. Educ: Univ. of Ala, B.A, 28; LL.B, 36. Polit. & Govt. Pos: Judge, 28th Judicial Circuit Court, 49-53, 64-; pres, Ala. Asn. Circuit Judges, 53; Ala. State Rep, 63-66. Bus. & Prof. Pos: Lawyer. Mil. Serv: Entered as Lt.(jg), Naval Res, 42, released as Lt. Comdr, 45; Res, 45-63, Comdr. (Ret). Mem: Mason; WOW; VFW (state comdr, 53-54); Red Cross. Rel: Baptist. Mailing Add: Box 192, Bay Minette, Ala. 36507.

MASK, WILLIAM GLENN R
Chmn, Jack Co. Rep. Party, Tex.
b. Perrin, Tex, 2/20/21; s. Roe Dolph Mask and Pearly Byers M; m. 12/30/44 to Clara Mae Cromeans; c. Michael Glenn. Educ; Univ. Tex. Col. Pharm, 38-41, 43-44; Baylor Univ. Col. Med, M.D, 48; U.S. Navy Med. Sch, 51-52; Tulane Med. Sch. Ophthalmology, 63-64; Phi Beta Pi. Polit. & Govt. Pos: Chmn, Jack Co. Rep. Party, Tex, 62- Bus. & Prof. Pos: Physician & Surgeon, 48- Mil. Serv: Entered as A/S, Navy, 41, released as Lt. Comdr, Naval Res, 59; after serv. in Med. Corps, S.W. Pac, 42-43, Korea, 50-51; Good Conduct and Pre-Pearl Harbor Medals; Am. Theater Ribbon; Pac. Theater Ribbon with 2 Stars; China Area, Occup. Japan, Korea and UN Serv. Medals; Lt. Comdr.(Ret), Med. Corps, Naval Res, 59. Mem: Tex. and Am. Med. Asns; Tex. and Am. Acads. of Gen. Practice; VFW; Jack Co. Hist. Soc; Farm Bur; Jacksboro C. of C; W. Tex. C. of C; Lions (pres, Jacksboro Hinoon Lions Club, 68-69). Outstanding Citizen Award, Jacksboro Tex. C. of C, 66. Rel: Protestant. Mailing Add: 401 North Third, Jacksboro, Tex. 76056.

MASLOFF, SOPHIE D
Secy, Pa. Fedn. Dem. Women
b. Pittsburgh, Pa, 12/23/17; d. Louis Friedman and Jennie F; m. 2/12/39 to Jack Masloff; c. Linda. Educ: Fifth Ave. High Sch, grad, 36. Polit. & Govt. Pos: Secy, Allegheny Co. Dem. Women's Guild, Pittsburgh, Pa, 40-; Secy, Pa. Fedn. Dem. Women, 67-; alternate del, Dem. Nat. Conv, 68. Bus. & Prof. Pos: Chief Investr, Allegheny Co. Court of Common Pleas, Pittsburgh, Pa, 40- Mem: B'nai B'rith; Hadassah. Rel: Jewish. Mailing Add: 3566 Beechwood Blvd, Pittsburgh, Pa. 15217.

MASON, BRUCE BONNER D
b. Cleburne, Tex, 12/19/23; s. Joseph Lee Mason and Daisy Bonner M; m. 12/13/46 to Jacqueline Tenery; c. Douglas Lee. Educ: N.Tex. State Col, B.S, 47; Tex. Christian Univ, M.A, 49; Univ. Tex, Austin, Ph.D, 52; Pi Sigma Alpha; Men's Independent Campus Asn. Polit. & Govt. Pos: Field survey officer, Tex. State Approval Agency, 48; consult, Ill. Co. Probs. Cmt, 58-60; pres, Champaign Co. Dem. Fedn. of Ill. Chap, 59; Dem. precinct committeeman, Tempe, Ariz, 64-68; state co-chmn, Ariz. McCarthy for Pres, 68; del, Dem. Nat. Conv, 68. Bus. & Prof. Pos: Asst. prof, Northwest. State Col, La,

52-53, Memphis State Col, 53-54, and Univ. Fla, 54-58; res. asst. prof, Univ. Ill, Urbana, 58-60; prof, Ariz. State Univ, 60- Mil. Serv: Entered as Cadet, Army Air Corps, 42, released as Sgt, 45, after serv. in Fourth Air Force, Nev, 43-45. Publ: Extra-Party Organizations in Illinois Politics, Univ. Ill, 60; Arizona General Election Results, 1911-60, 61 and co-auth, Constitutional Government in Arizona, 3rd ed, 68, Ariz. State Univ. Mem: Am, South. and West. Polit. Sci. Asns; Am. Soc. for Pub. Admin, West. Govt. Research Asn; Am. Civil Liberties Union; Ariz. Dem. Coun. B.S. with highest degree. Rel: Unitarian. Mailing Add: 320 East Fairmont Dr, Tempe, Ariz. 85281.

MASON, CLARENCE EDWARD R

b. Paint Rock, Tex, 11/21/24; s. William Harry Mason and Maggie Williams M; m. 12/8/51 to Sondra Vannette Wagnon; c. Clarence Edward II, Linda Gail, and Lisa Jane. Polit. & Govt. Pos: Pres, Parmer-Bailey Co. Young Rep, Tex, 62-64; chmn, Parmer Bailey Co. Rep. Cmt, 64-66. Mil. Serv: Entered as Pvt, Army, 44, released as Pfc, 45, after serv. in ETO, 44; Good Conduct Medal; Purple Heart. Rel: Church of Christ. Mailing Add: Route 2, Box 232, Muleshoe, Tex. 79347.

MASON, DREW R

b. Boone, Iowa, 2/23/29; s. George E. Mason and Bertha Wilkin M; m. 8/12/50 to Janet Miller; c. John Jeffrey and Joel Lynn. Educ: Univ. Iowa, B.A, in Polit. Sci, 50. Polit. & Govt. Pos: Fund raising consult. and exec. secy, Okla. Rep. State Cmt; campaign coordinator, Bellmon for Gov. of Okla, 62; admin. asst. to Gov. Henry Bellmon, 62-66; exec. asst. to Gov. Dewey Bartlett, 67; nat. finance dir, Nixon for President Cmt, Wash, D.C, 67-68; campaign coordinator, Bellmon for U.S. Senate, Okla, 68, admin. asst. to U.S. Sen. Henry Bellmon, Okla, 69- Mil. Serv: Entered as Draftee, Army, 51, released as Pfc, 53, after serv. in 82nd ABN Div, 505 ABN Regt, Ft. Bragg, N.C; Parachute Badge. Rel: Protestant. Legal Res: Oklahoma City, Okla. Mailing Add: 3303 Parkside Terr, Fairfax, Va. 22030.

MASON, EDWYN E. R

N.Y. State Assemblyman

b. De Peyster, N.Y; m. 1941 to Melva Bettinger; c. Martha Anne and Richard Eric. Educ: Oswego State Teacher's Col, B.S, 38; Syracuse Univ; Tex. A&M Col; Univ. Minn; Albany Law Sch, LL.B. Polit. & Govt. Pos: Former mem, Selective Serv. Bd. and town bd. and former justice of peace, Stamford, N.Y; N.Y. State Assemblyman, 52-, chmn, Assembly Agr. Cmt. and v.chmn, Joint Legis. Cmt. on Interstate Affairs. Bus. & Prof. Pos: Instr. in shop courses; attorney, Rusmore, Mason, Marcus & Crocker, 41- Mil. Serv: Army Mil. Police. Mem: Am. Legion; Del. Co, N.Y. and Am. Bar Asns; Del. Co. Hist. Soc; Odd Fellows; Mason; Rotary; Audubon Soc; Grange; Farm Bur; Sullivan and Schoharie Co. Hist. Asns; counsel, N.Y. State Arms Collectors Asn. Award for outstanding contrib. to Am. Legion Boys State, N.Y. State Am. Legion, 68; Citation of Merit and Plaque by Rabbi Jacob Joseph School, The Mother Yeshiva of Am, 69. Rel: Presbyterian. Mailing Add: Box 236, Hobart, N.Y. 13788.

MASON, JULIEN J. D

Va. State Del.

b. Colonial Beach, Va, 9/9/16; m. to Carolyn Jule Waite. Educ: William and Mary Col, A.B, 36; Univ. Va, LL.B; Kappa Alpha. Polit. & Govt. Pos: Substitute judge, Caroline Co, Va; Va. State Del, 66- Bus. & Prof. Pos: Lawyer. Mil. Serv: Entered as 2nd Lt, Army Inf, Ft. Benning Officers Cand. Sch, World War II, released as Maj, after serv. in 24th Div, Judge Adv. Gen. Corps, Overseas; Bronze Star, Philippines. Mem: Am. and 15th Judicial Circuit Bar Asns; Va. State Bar Asn.(past pres); Am. Legion (past Comdr); Omicron Delta Kappa; Seven Soc; Commonwealth Club; Lions (past pres). Rel: Episcopal. Mailing Add: Box 525, Bowling Green, Virginia 22427. (1967)

MASON, LOUIS, JR. D

City Councilman, Pittsburgh, Pa.

b. Minneapolis, Minn, 3/9/15; s. Louis Mason and Blanche Yancey M; m. 5/26/41 to Dorothea Scott Harris. Educ: Univ. Minn, B.S, 40; Duquesne Univ, 45; Univ. Pittsburgh, M.A, 52; Omega Psi Phi; Loendi Club. Polit. & Govt. Pos: Asst. dir, Mayor's Cmn. Fair Employ. Practices, Pittsburgh, 53-55; dep. dir, Mayor's Cmn. Human Rels, 55-63, exec. dir, 63-67; city councilman, Pittsburgh, 67-; del, Dem. Nat. Conv, 68. Bus. & Prof. Pos: Asst. dir, Indust. Rels, Urban League, Pittsburgh, 45-47, dir, 47-53. Mil. Serv: Pvt, Army Inf, 43. Publ: The Extent of Membership and Participation of a Minority Group in Selected Trade Unions in Allegheny Co, 50; The Role of a Public Agency in Breaking Through Barriers to Open Occupancy, 56; Controlled Occupancy or Free Choice?, Cmn. on Human Rels, 63. Mem: Nat. Asn. Soc. Workers; Nat. Asn. Intergroup Rels. Off; Soc. Pub. Admin; Pittsburgh Personnel Asn; former mem, U.S. Steelworkers of Am; IBT; Hod Carriers Union; Dining Car Employees Union and Hotel and Restaurant Workers Union. Rel: Episcopal; mem, Brain Trust Cmt. Legal Res: 931 Clarissa St, Pittsburgh, Pa. 15219. Mailing Add: 510 City County Bldg, Pittsburgh, Pa. 15219.

MASON, MAURICE D

Chmn, Porter Co. Dem. Cent. Cmt, Ind.

b. Cannelton, Ind, 11/9/14; s. Bert E. Mason and Elsie Richey M; m. 10/12/32 to Catherine M. Brunner; c. Marcella June, Robert Dow and Cynthia Kay. Educ: High Sch. Polit. & Govt. Pos: Chmn, Porter Co. Dem. Cent. Cmt, Ind, 60- Bus. & Prof. Pos: Printer, Cannelton Newspaper, 32-40; make-up foreman, Vidette Messenger, 40-48; publisher and owner, Porter Co. Herald, 48- and Kouts Times, 51- Mem: Trustee, Porter Mem. Hosp, Valparaiso; C. of C; Mason; Shrine; Moose; Elks. Rel: Methodist. Legal Res: 111 Sigler St, Hebron, Ind. 46341. Mailing Add: Box 7, Hebron, Ind. 46341.

MASON, NORMAN CHRISTY D

Chmn, Somerset Co. Dem. Party, Md.

b. Crisfield, Md, 1/9/16; s. Leonard Fillmore Mason, Sr. and Catherine Christy M; m. 3/20/37 to Eloise Ida Redden; c. Norman C, Jr. and Catherine Jane. Educ: High sch. grad. Polit. & Govt. Pos: Mem, East. Shore State Hosp. Bd, Md, 4 years; mem, Somerset Co. Welfare Bd, 4 years; chmn, Md. Dem. State Cent. Cmt, 50-66; chmn, Md. Motion Picture Bd, 56-66 and Md. Motion Picture Censor Bd, 58-66; alternate del, Dem. Nat. Conv, 64; judge, Md. Tax Court, 67-; chmn, Somerset Co. Dem. Party, currently. Bus. & Prof. Pos: Coal and concrete bus, Crisfield, Md, 35- Mem: Rotary; Elks; Crisfield Country Club. Rel: Methodist. Mailing Add: 321 Broadway, Crisfield, Md. 21817. (1967)

MASON, WILLIE C. R

Mem. Exec. Cmt, D.C. Rep. Party

b. Washington, D.C, 6/3/18; s. Conder Mason and Mattie Robinson M; m. 8/13/61 to Clarice Walden; c. Crystal Shirlee. Educ: Am. Col. Life Underwriters, Chartered Life Underwriter, 63. Polit. & Govt. Pos: Sgt, U.S. Park Police, Dept. Interior, 54-59; mem. exec. cmt, D.C. Rep. Party, 67- Bus. & Prof. Pos: Branch mgr, J.E. Jones Ins. Agency, 59-63; ins. consultant, N.Y. Life Ins. Co, 63- Mil. Serv: SPA 2/C, Navy, 44-46. Mem: Life Underwriters Asn; Am. Col. Chartered LifeUnderwriters; F&AM; Consistory (32°); AAONMS. Rel: Methodist. Mailing Add: 1770 Verbena St. N.W, Washington, D.C. 20012.

MASSA, SALVATORE D

b. Bristol, R.I, 4/5/10; m. to Marcelle Collins. Educ: Bristol Schs. Polit. & Govt. Pos: R.I. State Rep, 64-67. Bus. & Prof. Pos: Mechanic and operator of garage and used car lot. Mem: Credit Cmn, Bristol Credit Union; Lions (past pres, Bristol Club); Eagles (past pres). Mailing Add: 337 State St, Bristol, R.I. 02809. (1967)

MASSAD, ANTHONY M. D

Okla. State Sen.

b. Shidler, Okla, 6/15/28; s. Michael J. Massad and Adelaide M; m. 6/4/50 to Mary Jean Rahhal; c. Cynthia Jean, Cathy Ann and Michael John. Educ: Okla. Mil. Acad; Okla. Univ; Okla. Univ. Law Sch; Delta Theta Phi. Polit. & Govt. Pos: Okla. State Sen, 65- Mil. Serv: Entered as 2nd Lt, Army, 50, released as Maj, Army Res, 65, after serv. in ETO. Mem: Tillman Co. Bar Asn. (pres, 61-62); Frederick C. of C. (pres, 59); Rotary; Am. and Okla. Bar Asns. Outstanding Citizen Award, 63. Rel: First Christian Church. Legal Res: 1100 Rebecca Rd, Frederick, Okla. 73542. Mailing Add: Box 606, Frederick, Okla. 73542.

MASSAD, ERNEST LOUIS D

b. Brinkman, Okla, 12/25/08; s. Namey Massad and Shafiga Kouri M; m. 1/30/39 to Mozelle Sockwell; c. Michael Louis and Elaine Mozelle. Educ: Okla. Univ, maj. in psychol, 28-35; v.pres, Student Coun. Polit. & Govt. Pos: Mem. sch. bd, Ardmore, Okla, 56-66 and pres, 60-66; mem, Okla. State Voters Cmt, 66-; Dep. Asst. Secy. of Defense, Reserve Affairs, 68-69. Bus. & Prof. Pos: Chmn. bd, United Life Ins. Co, Ardmore, Okla, 61-68 and pres, 62-68. Mil. Serv: Entered as 1st Lt, Army, 40, released as Col, 46, after serv. in First Carrier Div, 82nd Airborne and 11th Airborne Div, Pac. Theatre, 44-45; Maj. Gen.(Ret), Army Res, 68; Distinguished Serv. Medal; Silver Star; Legion of Merit; Bronze Star with Oak Leaf Cluster; Purple Heart; Okla. Distinguished Serv. Medal; Reserve Officers of U.S. Distinguished Serv. Award. Publ: 'Are the Reserve Forces Receiving A Fair Shake?,' Armed Forces Mgt. Mag, 8/69. Mem: Pres, Okla. Reserve Officers Asn; Life Underwriters Asn; Am. Legion; VFW (comdr, Ardmore Chap); Mil. Order of World Wars; Mason (32°); Lions. State Americanism Award, 57; Lebanese Man of Year, West. Fedn, 63. Rel: Methodist. Legal Res: 816 Rosewood, Ardmore, Okla. 73401. Mailing Add: 107 Hinkle St, Ardmore, Okla. 73401.

MASSARI, PHILLIP D

Colo. State Rep.

b. Segundo, Colo, 4/12/13; s. Domenic Massari (deceased) and Angelina Pecorelli M.(deceased); m. 6/6/36 to Mary Margaret Spota; c. Phyllis Jean. Educ: Trinidad State Jr. Col. Polit. & Govt. Pos: V.pres, Young Dem, Colo, 34-36; social worker, Las Animas Co. Dept. Pub. Welfare, 36-48; probation officer, Third Judicial Dist, 48-; Colo. State Rep, 52-, chmn, Fish and Park Cmt, Colo. House of Rep; del, Dem. Nat. Conv, 60 & 68. Mil. Serv: Pvt, Army, 43-44. Mem: Columbian Fedn; Izaak Walton League; Colo. Parole & Probation Asn; DAV. Received Legis. Conservationist Award by Colo. Wildlife, Nat. Wildlife Fedn. and Sears-Roebuck Found, 66. Rel: Catholic. Mailing Add: 407 Goddard Ave, Trinidad, Colo. 81082. (1967)

MASSARI, VINCENT D

Colo. State Sen.

b. Luco nei Marsi, Italy; s. Domenico Massari and Angela Pecorelli M; m. 8/3/17 to Amalia Perasso; c. Angelina (Mrs. Martella) and Rose (Mrs. Chesler). Educ: Sem, Penne, Italy. Hon. LL.D, South. Colo. State Col; hon. D.Jour, Univ. Toronto. Polit. & Govt. Pos: Colo. State Rep, 54-64; Colo. State Sen, 64-, mem, Legis. Coun, Colo. State Senate, currently. Bus. & Prof. Pos: Asst. ed, L'Unione, 17-21, ed. and publisher, 21-47; owner and asst. mgr, Massari Travel Agency, 21-; dir, First Fed. Savings and Loan Asn, Pueblo, Colo, 34- Publ: Contrib. ed, Colorado, Denver, Il Progresso Italo-Americano, N.Y. and La Parola del Popolo, Chicago. Mem: Pres, Fidelity Lodge, 32-; past pres, Protective and Beneficient Lodge; Nat. pres, Columbian Fedn, 37-; treas, United Socs. of Pueblo, 38-; Kiwanis. Received Star of Solidarity from the President of Italy for cementing good rels. between U.S and Italy; Cert. of Appreciation, Sertoma Club, Pueblo, Colo. State Am. Legion and Colo. Dent. Asn; Serv. Award, Kiwanis Club; hon. life membership, Civil Serv. Asn. of Colo. Legal Res: 216 Lincoln St, Pueblo, Colo. 81005. Mailing Add: 322 S. Victoria Ave, Pueblo, Colo. 81003.

MASSENBURG, KATHERINE BLACK R

Rep, Nat. Committeewoman, Md.

b. Baltimore, Md, 7/1/21; d. Walter Evan Black and Margaret Rice B; div; c. George Yellott, III and Walter Black. Educ: Randolph-Macon Woman's Col, A.B, 43; Johns Hopkins Univ; Phi Beta Kappa; Tau Kappa Alpha; Phi Beta Phi. Polit. & Govt. Pos: Secy, Md. Fedn. Young Rep, 51-53, co-chmn, 57-59; first v.pres, Md. Fedn. Rep. Women, 59-63, pres, 63-64; tech. dir, Decennial Census, Seventh Cong. Dist, 60; mem, State Rep. Cent. Cmt. and chmn, Third Legis. Dist, 62-66; mem, Baltimore Commun. Rels. Cmn, 63-65; Rep. Nat. Committeewoman, 64-; admin. asst. to Mayor T.R. McKeldin, Baltimore, 65-67; chmn, Md. Cmn. on Status of Women, 68- Bus. & Prof. Pos: Teacher, jr. high sch, 44-45; law clerk and librarian, Marshall, All, Carey & Doub, 45-47. Mem: Pi Beta Phi Alumnae; Randolph-Macon Woman's Col. Alumnae; United Christian Citizens; League Women Voters; Urban League; Md. Asn. for Retarded Children; Md. Ment. Health Asn; Citizens Planning and Housing Asn; Md. Women's Coun. Rel: Baptist. Mailing Add: 5608 Purlington Way, Baltimore, Md. 21212.

MASSEY, ALTON D

Miss. State Rep.

b. Lobutcha, Miss, 12/18/08; s. Ira Irving Massey and Virginia Taylor M;

single. Educ: Milsaps Col, 30-31; Holmes Jr. Col, 31-32; Univ. Miss, LL.B, 37; Alpha Tau Omega. Polit. & Govt. Pos: Miss. State Sen, 36-40; mayor, Kosciusko, Miss, 46-51; mem, State Vet. Bd, 48-54; mem, Vet. Farm and Home Bd, 56-60; Miss. State Rep, 64- Bus. & Prof. Pos: Attorney, 37-; motel and restaurant bus, cotton and tree farming. Mil. Serv: Entered as Pvt, Air Force, 42, released as Cpl, 45, after serv. in 441st Troup Carrier Squadron, Ninth Air Force, 43-45. Mem: Miss. Bar Asn; Eastern Star; Mason; Shrine; WOW; VFW; Am. Legion; DAV; Lion (dist. gov, Lions Int, gov. and secy); C. of C. Rel: Methodist. Mailing Add: P.O. Box 189, Kosciusko, Miss. 39090.

MASSEY, HORACE S. T. D
V.Pres, Calif. Dem. Coun.
b. Detroit, Tex, 9/10/10; s. Walter Dorset Massey and Ella Belle Rogers M; m. 9/20/35 to Lillian Frances Hildreth; c. Ronald Creel, Hugh Garrison, David Carl, Donald Walter and Lillian Virginia. Educ: Self educated in civil eng, through correspondence courses. Polit. & Govt. Pos: Mem, Kern Co. Dem. Cent. Cmt, Calif, 60-62 & 64-66, v.chmn, 62-64 and chmn, 69-; dist. dir, Calif. Dem. Coun, 61-63, v.pres, 63-; mem, Calif. Dem. State Cent. Cmt, 63-64 & 68-; alternate del, Dem. Nat. Conv, 64. Bus. & Prof. Pos: Job supt, Griffith Co, 48-58, estimator-supt, 58- Mil. Serv: Pfc, Okla. Nat. Guard, 28-29. Mem: Bakersfield Engrs. Club and Builders Exchange Club; Elks; NAACP; Int. Union of Operating Engrs. 12. Rel: Protestant. Mailing Add: 312 McCord Ave, Bakersfield, Calif. 93308. (1967)

MASSEY, JAMES CLEMENTS D
Chmn, Blount Co. Dem. Exec. Cmt, Ala.
b. Locust Fork, Ala, 12/11/27; s. Clements Morgan Massey and Rosseye Wilder M; m. 1947 to Betty Joyce Sargent; c. Deborah Joyce (Mrs. Gary F. Cornelius), James Michael and Rebekah Michele. Educ: High Sch. grad. Polit. & Govt. Pos: Chmn, Blount Co. Dem. Exec. Cmt, Ala, currently. Bus. & Prof. Pos: Owner, Massey Auto Parts, 11 years. Mem: Nat. Star Route Mail Carriers Asn; Dem. Nat. Cmt; Mason (past Master, Locust Fork Lodge); Shrine; Cumberland Lake Country Club. App. Hon. Lt. Col. Aide-de-Camp, Ala. State Militia, 68. Rel: Baptist. Mailing Add: P.O. Box 41, Locust Fork, Ala. 35097.

MASSEY, JOHN LEWIS D
Okla. State Sen.
b. Durant, Okla, 5/21/36; s. Emmett Massey and Jenny Bryant M; m. 5/30/59 to Marion Joyce Vanderpool; c. Mike and Gregg. Educ: Southeast. State Col, B.S, 60; Blue Key; Sigma Tau Gamma. Polit. & Govt. Pos: Okla. State Rep, 60-64; Okla. State Sen, currently. Mil. Serv: Entered as Pvt, Army, 54, released as Sgt, 57. Rel: Baptist. Mailing Add: Box 721, Durant, Okla. 74701. (1967)

MASSICOTTE, JOSEPH J. D
Mem, Conn. State Dem. Cent. Cmt.
b. Middletown, Conn, 9/5/96; s. Frank X. Massicotte and Catherine Carroll M; m. 4/15/23 to Madeline M. Callahan, wid; c. John J. Educ: N.Y. Univ. Polit. & Govt. Pos: Dep. comptroller, Bridgeport, Conn, 32-35; del, Conn. Constitutional Conv, 65; chmn, Bridgeport Dem. Town Party, currently; mem, Conn. State Dem. Cent. Cmt, currently; alternate del, Dem. Nat. Conv, 68. Bus. & Prof. Pos: Chief cost acct, Manning, Maxwell & Moore, 17-40; acct, Remington Arms Co, 40-49; secy, Dual-Lite Co, Inc, 49- Mil. Serv: Pvt, Army Med. Corps, 19. Mem: K. of C.(4°); Algonquin Club; Elks; Hibernian, John Kennedy Br. Rel: Catholic. Mailing Add: 80 Cartright St, Bridgeport, Conn. 06604. (1967)

MASTANDREA, FRANK J. R
State Committeeman, N.Y. Rep. Cmt.
b. Bronx, N.Y, 7/4/20; s. Angelo Mastandrea and Angelia Petrone M; m. 1947 to Isabela Guadagno; c. Frank, Jr, Robert and Michelle. Educ: N.Y. Indust. High Sch. Polit. & Govt. Pos: Leader, 95th Assembly Dist. Rep. Party, N.Y, 63; exec. leader, 86th Assembly Dist. Rep. Party, 65; state committeeman, N.Y. Rep. Cmt, 66-; sr. del, N.Y. State Constitutional Conv, 67; alternate del, mem. exec. br. govt. cmt, mem. cmt. on labor, civil serv. and pensions, v.chmn. subcmt. vet. affairs and author of 25 proposition, Rep. Nat. Conv, 68; commun. rels. specialist, N.Y. State Narcotic Addiction Control Cmn, 68- Bus. & Prof. Pos: Pres, SMS Parts and Serv, Inc, 49-66. Mil. Serv: Entered as Pvt, Air Force, 42, released as T/Sgt, after serv. in Ninth Air Force, ETO, 44-45; Three ETO Citations. Mem: CWV (Comdr, Post 390); VFW (dist. Comdr, N.Y. State Chap, nat. dep. chief of staff); 42nd Precinct Youth Coun. (chmn); Police Athletic League (exec. dir); Exec. N.Bronx Businessman's Asn; Job Placement Coord. Urban Leader of the Bronx. Citation of Merit, Police Athletic League, 63; Citation, Nation's Bus. Week, 65; Citation, Future Mag, 66; Outstanding Bronx Businessman, Bronx Jaycees, 67; Nat. Commun. Leader Award, 68. Rel: Catholic. Mailing Add: 11 Oak Lane, Pelham Manor, Bronx, N.Y. 10803.

MASTEN, LEAH MAE R
b. Lyndon, Vt, 4/6/14; m. to Gerald Masten; c. One son and two daughters. Educ: Lyndon Inst. Polit. & Govt. Pos: Sch. dir, Vt, currently; petit juror, Essex Co, 3 times; Vt. State Rep, 63-67. Bus. & Prof. Pos: Former tel. operator; housewife; libr. trustee. Rel: Congregational. Mailing Add: Box 267, North Concord, Vt. 05858. (1967)

MASTERMAN, HAROLD R
Chmn, Hull Rep. Town Cmt, Mass.
b. Boston, Mass, 7/26/23; s. Jacob Masterman and Anne Roffman M; m. 2/8/45 to Esther Dores; c. Wayne, Linda and Susan. Polit. & Govt. Pos: Mem, Hull Planning Bd, Mass, 58; v.chmn, Hull Housing Authority, 67; chmn, Hull Rep. Town Cmt, 68- Bus. & Prof. Pos: Salesman, Boston Edison Co, Boston, Mass, 49, mgr, 53, supvr, 55, div. head, 59, pub. rels. dist. mgr, 68- Mil. Serv: Entered as Pvt, Marine Corps, 43, released as Sgt, 45, after serv. in Third Div, S.Pac, Theatre, 43-45; Presidential Unit Citation; Asiatic-Pac. Theatre Citation. Mem: Elec. Inst. Boston; AF&AM; Consistory; Shrine; Boston chmn, United Fund Campaign, 63; hon. life mem. Gr. Boston C. of C. Rel: Jewish. Mailing Add: 90 Kingsley Rd, Hull, Mass. 02045.

MASTERS, HAROLD WILLIAM R
b. Kansas City, Mo, 10/30/17; s. Bert Hale Masters and S. Ellen Fortner M; m. to Peggy Jean Payne. Educ: Univ. Kansas City, B.A, 56. Polit. & Govt. Pos: Precinct Capt, Kansas City Rep. Party, Mo, 38-42 & 46-60; ed, A Republican Report, 58-66; rep. cand. Jackson Co. Assessor, 66; rep. cand, U.S. Rep, Fifth Dist, Mo, 68. Bus. & Prof. Pos: Merchandiser, Masters Grain Co, Kansas City, 58- Mil. Serv: Army, Ordnance Dept, serv. in Theatre Overhead, Southwest Pacific Theatre, 42-45. Mem: Kansas City Bd. of Trade; Kansas City Feed Club; Am. Legion; Mo. Hist. Soc; Jackson Co. Hist. Soc; Int. Rel. Coun; Nat. Rifle Asn. Rel: Baptist. Mailing Add: 5300 Brookside Blvd, Kansas City, Mo. 64112.

MASTERS, LEONARD E. R
b. Ranchester, Wyo, 9/25/07; m. to Margery; c. Two. Educ: Calif. Col. Polit. & Govt. Pos: Pres, Dayton Fire Dist, Wyo; former Wyo. State Rep. Bus. & Prof. Pos: Rancher. Mem: Dayton-Ranchester Rotary; C. of C; Elks; Big Horn Permittees Orgn; Farm Bur; Sheridan Co. Hereford Asn; leader, 4-H Coun, 11 years; Sheridan Co. Fair Bd. Mailing Add: OZ Ranch, Box 107, Ranchester, Wyo. 82839. (1967)

MASTERS, RICHARD STEARNS R
Chmn, Susquehanna Co. Rep. Cmt, Pa.
b. Kingsley, Pa, 6/14/14; s. Alva J. Masters and Clara Stearns M; m. 12/28/32 to Eloise Williams; c. Joyce (Mrs. Richard Berish), Marcia (Mrs. Gary Housel), Betsy, Richard W. and Jacqueline. Educ: Harford Voc. High Sch; Univ. Scranton, Evening course in pub. speaking. Polit. & Govt. Pos: Dir, Mt. View Joint Schs, Pa, 45-55; Chmn, Susquehanna Co. Rep. Cmt, 52-; del, Rep. Nat. Conv, 68. Bus. & Prof. Pos: Pres, Masters Contracting Corp, 44. Mem: F&AM; Shrine. Rel: Congregational. Mailing Add: Kingsley, Pa. 18826.

MASTERS, ROBERT J. D
Exec. Secy, Beaver Co. Dem. Cmt, Pa.
b. Midland, Pa, 11/5/30; s. Benjamin Masters and Antoinette Viotte M; m. 6/20/59 to Nancy Martino; c. Barbara Anne and Robert Martin. Educ: Grove City Col, A.B, 51; Univ. of Pittsburgh Law Sch, LL.B, 54; Phi Alpha Delta. Polit. & Govt. Pos: Past chmn, Citizens Cmt. for Kennedy-Johnson and Citizens Cmt. for Johnson-Humphrey; committeeman, Midland Dem. Party, Pa, 58-; solicitor, Midland, Pa. and Midland Sch. Dist, 58-64; Asst. Dist. Attorney, Beaver Co, 59-62; exam, Pub. Utility Cmn, 62-64; exec. secy, Beaver Co. Dem. Cmt, Pa, currently. Bus. & Prof. Pos: Partner, Suffoletta & Masters Law Firm, 57- Mil. Serv: Spec. agent, Army Counter Intel. Corps, 55-57. Mem: Beaver Co, Pa. and Am. Bar Asns; Nat. Dist. Attorney's Asn; Elks; Sons of Italy; K. of C; St. Anthony Club. Rel: Roman Catholic. Mailing Add: 1079 Virginia Ave, Midland, Pa. 15059.

MASTERSON, WILLIAM ANTHONY D
b. N.Y.C, 6/25/31; s. John Patrick Masterson and Helen O'Hara M; m. 8/25/56 to Marcia Grace Williams; c. Mark, Mary, Timothy and Barbara. Educ: Univ. Calif, Los Angeles, B.A. in Hist, 53, J.D, 58; Order of the Coif. Polit. & Govt. Pos: Del, Dem. Nat. Conv, 68. Bus. & Prof. Pos: Partner, Sheppard, Mullin, Richter & Hampton, Law Firm, 62- Mil. Serv: Entered as Pvt, Army, 53, released as Cpl, 55, after serving in Inf, Continental U.S, 53-55. Publ: Articles on tech. subj. in various legal periodicals. Mem: Am. Bar Asn; State Bar of Calif; Calif. Club; Cmt. for Calif. Rel: Roman Catholic. Mailing Add: 1342 Circle Dr, San Marino, Calif. 91108.

MASTICS, GEORGE E. R
Ohio State Rep.
b. Cleveland, Ohio, 1931; married; c. Five. Educ: West. Reserve Univ, B.A, 53, Law Sch, LL.B, 56. Polit. & Govt. Pos: Ohio State Rep, 67-; Chief Asst. State Attorney Gen. Bus. & Prof. Pos: Lawyer. Mem: Fairview Park GOP Club (past pres). Mailing Add: 4587 Concord Dr, Fairview Park, Ohio 44126.

MASTIN, PHILIP OLIN, JR. D
Dep. chmn, Oakland Co. Dem. Cmt, Mich.
b. Wayne, Mich, 5/27/30; s. Philip Olin Mastin and Gracia Ruth Hayward M; m. 1947 to Donna June Keck; c. Dawn (Mrs. Michael Massong), Cheryl and Philip, III. Educ: S. Macomb Commun. Col, 3 years. Polit. & Govt. Pos: Alternate dem. del, precinct six, Hazel Park, Mich, 62-64; city councilman, Hazel Park, 62-68 and mayor-pro-tem, 62, 66 & 68; treas, Oakland Co. Dem. Cmt, 65 and dep. chmn, 65-; co. supvr, Oakland Co, 65-; Hazel Park Bd. Supvr. Alternate Del, Southeast Mich. Coun. Govt, 66-68; alternate del, Dem. Nat. Conv, 68; Dem. supvr. caucus chmn, Oakland Co, 68- Bus. & Prof. Pos: Automotive chassis designer, Ford Motor Co, Mich, 55-57; sr. automotive chassis designer, Chevrolet Div, Gen. Motors Corp, 57-65; ed, Oakland Dem. Newsletter, 65- Mem: Soc. Automotive Engrs; Am. Soc. Tool Engrs; past pres, Hazel Park Jr. C. of C; UAW; Methodist Men's Club of Hazel Park. Outstanding Young Man of the Year, Hazel Park; Distinguished Serv. Award, Hazel Park Jaycees, 65. Rel: Methodist. Mailing Add: 526 E. Harry, Hazel Park, Mich. 48030.

MASTRANGELO, EVELINO WILLIAM D
Treas, Lake Co. Cent. and Exec. Dem. Cmts, Ohio
b. Cleveland, Ohio, 10/20/23; s. Dominic Anthony Mastrangelo and Filomena Fatica M; m. 6/16/51 to Elizabeth Benedict; c. Mark, Lisa, Susan and Ellen. Educ: Ohio State Univ, B.S. in educ, Ohio State Col. of Law, J.D; Alpha Phi Delta; Delta Theta Phi. Polit. & Govt. Pos: Spec. counsel, Off. of Attorney Gen, State of Ohio, 58-62; mem, Bd. of Elecs, 58-, chmn, currently; dir. of law, City of Wickliffe, Ohio, 62-; treas, Lake Co. Dem. Cent. and Exec. Cmts, currently, chmn, currently; del, Dem. Nat. Conv, 68. Bus. & Prof. Pos: Attorney, 53- Mil. Serv: Entered as Pvt, Army, 43, released as Sgt, 46, after serv. in 310th Ord. Bn, ETO, 44-46; Am. Theater Ribbon; Europe-Africa-Middle East Theater Ribbon with one Bronze Star; Good Conduct and World War II Victory Medals. Mem: Am. Legion; Exchange Club; Elks; Lake Co. Bar (pres); Amvets (judge adv); Nat. Inst. of Munic. Law Officers Asn; Ohio State and Am. Bar Asns; Ohio State Univ. Alumni Asn. Rel: Roman Catholic. Mailing Add: 36629 Ridge Rd, Willoughby, Ohio 44094.

MASTRANGELO, RICHARD EDWARD R
Exec. Dir, Mass. Rep. State Cmt.
b. Watertown, Mass, 5/14/38; s. Louis Mastrangelo, M.D. and Helen G. Decost M; single. Educ: Boston Univ. Col. of Gen. Educ, A.A, 57, Sch. of Pub. Rels. and Commun, B.S. in Pub. Rels, 59, Sch. of Law, J.D, 62; Tau Mu Epsilon; Scarlet Key; Chi Gamma Epsilon; Media; v.pres, Boston Univ.

Student Govt; New Eng. Sectional chmn, Alpha Phi Omega. Polit. & Govt. Pos: Chmn, Mass. Col. Rep. Caucus, 57-58; campaign staff asst. to U.S. Sen. Laverett Saltonstall, 60; town meeting mem, Watertown, Mass, 61-, clerk, adv. bd. of rev, 60-61 and clerk, personnel bd, 62-64; campaign mgr, Quinlan for State Sen. Cmt, 62; mem. credentials Cmt, Mass. State Rep. Conv, 62; chmn. Mass. del, Young Rep. Nat. Conv, 63 & 65; mem. exec. cmt, Mass. Rep. State Cmt, 63-65, exec. dir, 69-; chmn, Mass. Coun. of Young Rep. Clubs, 63-65; alternate del-at-lg, Rep. Nat. Conv, 64; asst. dir. of orgn, Richardson for Lt. Gov. Cmt, Mass, 64; pres, Mass Young Rep. Asn, 65; Young Rep. Nat. Committeeman, Mass, 65-67; spec. asst. to Lt. Gov, Mass, 65-67; asst. attorney gen, Chief Vet. Div, Mass, 67-69; chmn, Watertown Rep. Town Cmt, 68-; selectman, Watertown, 68- Bus. & Prof. Pos: Attorney-at-law, 62- Publ: The Anatomy of a State Senate Campaign, 66. Mem: Mass. and Boston Bar Asns; dir, Boston Univ. Gen. Alumni Asn, and Mass. Bay Chap, Nat. Found; Lions. Named Brother of Year, Zeta Upsilon Chap, Alpha Phi Omega, 58, Distinguished Serv. Key, 59; Named Man of Year, Boston Univ, 59. Rel: Roman Catholic. Mailing Add: 267 School St, Watertown, Mass. 02172.

MATHENY, GORDON R
N.Dak. State Rep.
b. Blackwater, N.Dak, 8/29/14; s. James Ira Matheny and Martha Spillers M; m. 6/18/50 to Wylma Wolters; c. Gary Edward, Bruce Allen, Nancy Kay and Jo Ann. Educ: Garrison High Sch, 4 years. Polit. & Govt. Pos: N.Dak. State Rep, McLean Co, 69-; dist. chmn, McLean Co. Rep. Party, currently. Mem: N.Dak. Stockmen's Asn; McLean Co. Farm Bur. Rel: Protestant. Mailing Add: Emmet, N.Dak. 58534.

MATHER, RICHARD F. R
b. 1919. Polit. & Govt. Pos: N.Mex. State Rep. until 67. Bus. & Prof. Pos: Gen. mgr, Creamland Dairies, Inc. Mil. Serv: Naval Aviator, 4½ years. Mem: Rotary; Exec. Asn. of Gr. Albuquerque. Rel: Presbyterian. Mailing Add: Parkland Circle S.E, Albuquerque, N.Mex. 87108.

MATHER, WILLIAM S. R
Mont. State Rep.
b. Lewistown, Mont, 5/19/22; s. W.S. Mather and Anne Beckman M; m. 7/22/44 to Dorothy Martin; c. William, III and Donald. Educ: Univ. Mont; Sigma Alpha Epsilon; Phi Delta Phi. Polit. & Govt. Pos: Chmn, Musselshell Co. Rep. Cmt, Mont, 50-58; city attorney, Roundup, Mont, 51-65; dep. co. attorney, 55-65; del, Rep. Nat. Conv, 60; Mont. State Rep, Musselshell Co, 65-67, Yellowstone Co, 67-, majority whip, Mont. House Rep, 67-69, majority floor leader, 69- Bus. & Prof. Pos: Partner, Mercer & Mather, Attorneys, 48-51, Mather & Ask, Attorney, 55-65 and Moulton, Bellingham, Longo & Mather, 65- Mil. Serv: Entered as Pvt, Army, 42, released as Capt, 46, after serv. in ETO; Combat Inf. Badge. Mem: Elks; VFW. Rel: Episcopal. Mailing Add: 2227 Green Terrace Dr, Billings, Mont. 59102.

MATHES, DONALD TAYLOR R
b. Detroit, Mich, 10/2/28; s. Lloyd Merrill Mathes and Vera Taylor M; m. 6/11/49 to Bernice Ann Knight; c. Denise Ann, Dawn Marie and Donna Fay. Educ: Wayne Univ, 2 years. Polit. & Govt. Pos: Co. clerk, Kalamazoo Co, Mich, 67-68; admin. asst. to U.S. Rep. Garry Brown, Third Dist, Mich, 69- Bus. & Prof. Pos: Employ. interviewer, Chrysler Corp, Dodge Div, 48-53; off. mgr. and asst. secy, Detroit Bowling Asn, 53-54; resident mgr, Watling, Lerchen & Co, 54-64; gen. mgr, Wayside Corp, 64-66, Mathes Corp, 66-67. Mil. Serv: Aviation Cadet, Air Force 47-48. Mem: Mason; Battle Creek C. of C. Rel: Protestant. Legal Res: Kalamazoo, Mich. Mailing Add: 15105 Columbine Way, Rockville, Md. 20853.

MATHESON, DONALD STUART D
b. Cheraw, S.C, 11/8/03; s. D.S. Matheson and Esten Jennings M; m. 11/4/33 to Elizabeth Drane Webb; c. Elizabeth Webb. Educ: Presby. Col. of S.C; N.C. State Univ, B.S, 25; Univ. N.C, M.A, 32. Polit. & Govt. Pos: Agr. agent, Orange Co, N.C, 35 years; N.C. State Sen, 63-68. Bus. & Prof. Pos: Real estate. Mem: Research Triangle Planning Cmt; Three Co. Libr. Bd; bd, Hillsborough Hist. Soc; Co. Indust. Develop. Bd; Lions. Distinguished Serv. Award, Nat. Co. Agr. Agents Asn, 45. Rel: Episcopal; Vestryman, St. Matthew's Episcopal Church, Hillsboro, 40-, treas, 55-64. Mailing Add: P.O. Box 634, Hillsboro, N.C. 27278. (1967)

MATHESON, GORDON CAMERON R
Mem, North Smithfield Rep. Town Cmt, R.I.
b. North Smithfield, R.I, 3/27/30; s. Col. Guy Peter MacClean Matheson and Flora MacDonald M; m. Margaret Mary Dwyer; c. Christine Lynn, Gordon Cameron, Jr. and Kimberly Ann. Educ: Univ. of R.I, 3 years; Sales Analysis Inst, 1 year; Sigma Alpha Epsilon. Polit. & Govt. Pos: Mem, Chafee for Gov. and O'Donnel for Lt. Gov. Campaign Cmt, R.I, 62; mem, North Smithfield Zoning Bd. of Rev, 63-64; mem, North Smithfield Rep. Town Cmt, 64-; campaign mgr, 66 and chmn, 68-69; adv. staff and coordinator, O'Donnel For Lt. Gov. Cmt, 64-68; coordinator, DiPrete For Cong. Cmt, North Smithfield, 67; cand, R.I. State Senate, 30th Dist, 68; mem, R.I. Real Estate Cmn, 69- Bus. & Prof. Pos: Sales rep, Sun Oil Co, Providence, R.I, 54-68 and land dept. rep, 68- Mil. Serv: Entered as Pvt, Army, 51, released as Cpl, 53, after serv. in 306th Field Hosp, Europe, 52-53. Mem: R.I. Petroleum Asn; F&AM; Cumberland Civic Center. Rel: Episcopal. Legal Res: North Smithfield, R.I. Mailing Add: 70 Bellevue Ave, Union Village, Woonsocket, R.I. 02895.

MATHESON, L. KEITH R
b. W. Stockbridge, Mass, 4/3/09; married; c. two girls, one boy. Educ: N.Y Univ; Sheldon Col. Polit. & Govt. Pos: N.H. State Rep, 57-67; town moderator; health officer; town auditor. Bus. & Prof. Pos: Real estate; operator of large serv. sta. Mem: Chocorua Lodge, No. 83; F&AM; Ellacoya No. 43; Eastern Star; Grange; PTA. Rel: Congregational; Licensed Lay Preacher. Mailing Add: Box 126, Center Harbor, N.H. 03226.

MATHEWS, CHARLES T. D
Ala. State Rep.
b. Ashland, Ala, 11/16/17; single. Educ: Jacksonville State Col, B.A, 39, LL.B, 52; Univ. Ala. Polit. & Govt. Pos: City attorney, Clay City and Ashland, Ala; Ala. State Rep, 55-59 & 67-; Ala. State Sen, 63-66. Bus. & Prof. Pos: Lawyer. Mil. Serv: Lt, Army, World War II. Mem: Shrine; Mason. Rel: Methodist. Mailing Add: Box 355, Ashland, Ala. 36251. (1967)

MATHEWS, ELBERT G.
b. Troy, N.Y, 11/24/10; married. Educ: Univ. Calif, Berkeley, B.A, 30. Polit. & Govt. Pos: Career officer, U.S. Dept. of State For. Serv, 35-; v.consul, Vancouver, 35-36 and Australia, 37-40; third secy, Managua, 40-43; second secy, Kabul, 43-46; consul, Calcutta, 46-47; asst. chief, Off. of S.Asian Affairs, 47-49, dir, 49-51; consul gen, Istanbul, 51-53; Imperial Defense Col, 53-54; Dep. Chief of Mission, Oslo, 54-55; mem, Policy Planning Staff, 55-57, Dep. Asst. Secy. for Policy Planning, 57-59; U.S. Ambassador to Liberia, 59-62; dir, Off. of Inter-African Affairs, 62-64; U.S. Ambassador to Nigeria, 64-69; coordinator sr. seminar in for. policy; Dept. of State, 69- Bus. & Prof. Pos: Statistician, Inst. of Child Welfare, Univ. Calif, 30-31 & 32-33; acct, 33-35. Legal Res: Lafayette, Calif. Mailing Add: c/o U.S. Dept. of State Foreign Service, Washington, D.C. 20521.

MATHEWS, HARLAN D
Tenn. Cmnr. of Finance and Admin.
b. Walker Co, Ala, 1/17/27; m. 1947 to Betty Cox; c. Stanley, Richard and Lester. Educ: Jacksonville State Col, B.A, 49; Vanderbilt Univ, M.A; awarded scholarship, 49-50, by Inst. of Soc. Sci. to study pub. admin. at Vanderbilt Univ. Polit. & Govt. Pos: Employee, State Planning Cmn, 50-54; mem, Budget Staff, 55-59; appointed Dep. Cmnr. Finance and Admin, 59; appointed Tenn. Cmnr. Finance and Admin, 61- Mil. Serv: Navy, 44-46. Mem: Tenn. and Nat. Munic. Finance Officers Asn; Nat. Asn. State Auditors, Comptrollers and Treas; Nat. Asn. of State Budget Officers. Rel: Baptist. Mailing Add: State Capitol, Nashville, Tenn. 37219.

MATHEWS, JOHN E, JR. D
Fla. State Sen.
b. Jacksonville, Fla, 6/20/20; m. to Gwendolyn Howard; c. Josiah Game, Kimball Irene, Barbara Alice and John Elie III. Educ: Emory Univ, AB, 42; Harvard Law Sch, LL.B, 48; Phi Beta Kappa; Pres, ODK; Chmn, Honor Coun; Pres. Student Body; designated best debator in Grand Eastern Tournament, sophomore year; Lincoln's Inn Soc. and Root Club at Harvard. Polit. & Govt. Pos: Dep. cmnr, Fla. Indust. Cmn, 50-51; Fla. State Rep, Duval Co, 56-62; Fla. State Sen, Duval Co, 62-, pres, Fla. State Sen, 69- Bus. & Prof. Pos: Lawyer. Mil. Serv: Lt. Comdr, Naval Res; U.S. Navy, World War II, Bronze Star; 8 major battles (Pacific). Mem: Jacksonville C. of C; Dir, 56 March of Dimes; Commun. Chest; Sigma Chi; AAONMS; Scottish Rite; Mason (32°); Exchange Club; Morocco Temple, pres. of Black Camel Fund. Received Balfour Award as most representative Sigma Chi in Southeast. Rel: Methodist. Mailing Add: 1530 American Heritage Building, Jacksonville, Fla. 32202.

MATHEWS, LAURENCE CARROLL D
b. Patterson, Wash, 8/23/19; s. Frank Elmer Mathews and Lois Carroll M; m. 5/5/43 to Carol Jean Bruce; c. Joan Carol and Bruce Alan. Educ: Cent. Wash. Col. of Educ, B.A, in Ed, 40; Univ. of Wash, B.S.C.E, 51. Polit. & Govt. Pos: Cmnr. of pub. works, Yakima, Wash, 56-59; del, Dem. Nat. Conv, 68. Bus. & Prof. Pos: Teacher, pub. schs, Friday Harbor, Wash, 40-41 and East Wenatchee, Wash, 46-47; asst. city engr, Walla Walla, Wash, 52; consult. engr, Gray & Osborne, Yakima, Wash, 53-56; pub. works cmnr, Yakima, Wash, 56-59; engr, Portland Cement Asn, hq, Seattle, Wash, 59-67, regional dir, Manpower Training Prog, Skokie, Ill, 67- Mil. Serv: Entered as Pvt, Air Force, 43, released as S/Sgt, 45, after serv. in 12th Material Squadron and 23rd Depot Supply Squadron, Mediterranean, 43-45. Mem: Nat. Soc. of Prfnl. Engrs; Am. Soc. of Agr. Engrs. Rel: Unitarian. Legal Res: 805 S. 17th Ave, Yakima, Wash. 98902. Mailing Add: P.O. Box 1362, Yakima, Wash. 98901.

MATHEWS, ROY PALMER R
Chmn, Baca Co. Rep. Cent. Cmt, Colo.
b. Coolidge, Kans, 12/18/98; s. Lewis Franklin Mathews and Katie Palmer M; m. 7/22/22 to Hazel Irene Lent; c. Lewis Earl and Maj. James R. Educ: High Sch. and Salt City Bus. Col, Hutchinson, Kans. Polit. & Govt. Pos: Secy, Baca Co. Rep. Cent. Cmt, Colo, 18-30, chmn, 30-41 & 48-; chmn, Local Draft Bd. during World War II; Baca Co. coordinator between Sportsmen and cattlemen for Commanche Grass Lands, currently. Bus. & Prof. Pos: Asst. cashier, First Nat. Bank, Springfield, Colo, 21-22 and Bishop, Calif, 23; secy, Springfield Abstr. Co, 26-27; pres, Baca Co. Abstr. Co, 47-69; trustee, Colo. Exp. Sta, Springfield, 53-69. Mem: Shrine, Commandery, RAM, Coun, past master, Blue Lodge 158, AF&AM. Rel: Methodist. Mailing Add: 801 Main St, Springfield, Colo. 81073.

MATHEWS, VINCENT R. D
Wis. State Assemblyman
b. Watertown, Wis, 6/8/12. Educ: Carroll Univ, B.A, 34. Polit. & Govt. Pos: Alderman, Waukesha, Wis, 47-51; Wis. State Assemblyman, 58- Bus. & Prof. Pos: Former personnel work in dept. store; ins. agent. Mem: Boy Scouts; YMCA; Commun. Chest. Mailing Add: 242 E. Park Ave, Waukesha, Wis. 53186. (1967)

MATHIAS, CHARLES McC, JR. R
U.S. Sen, Md.
b. Frederick, Md, 7/24/22; s. Charles McCurdy Mathias and Theresa McElfresh Trail M; m. 11/8/58 to Ann Hickling Bradford; c. Charles Bradford and Robert Fiske. Educ: Yale Univ, 43-44; Haverford Col, B.A, 44; Univ. Md, LL.B, 49. Polit. & Govt. Pos: Asst. attorney gen, Md, 53-54; city attorney, Frederick, 54-59; Md. State Del, 59-60; U.S. Rep, Sixth Dist, Md, 60-69, mem, House Judiciary and D.C. Cmts, U.S. House of Rep; U.S. Sen, Md, 69- Bus. & Prof. Pos: Practice of law, Frederick, Md. Mil. Serv: Entered as Seaman, Navy, 42, released as Ens, 46; Capt, Naval Res. Mem: Pres, Hist. Soc. Frederick Co; bd. assocs, Hood Col; officer, Children's Aid Soc; Frederick Co. and Md. State Jr. C. of C; trustee, Episcopal Free Sch. and Orphan House. Rel: Episcopal. Legal Res: New Design Rd, Frederick, Md. 21701. Mailing Add: U.S. Senate, Washington, D.C. 20510.

MATHIAS, ROBERT BRUCE R
U.S. Rep, Calif.
b. Tulare, Calif, 11/17/30; m. to Melba Wiser; c. Romel, Megan and Marissa.

Educ: Stanford Univ, A.B, 53. Polit. & Govt. Pos: U.S. Rep, Calif, 67- Bus. & Prof. Pos: Freelance TV, 56-62; owner, Bob Mathias Sierra Boys Camp, 62- Mil. Serv: Marine Corps, 54-56; Capt, Res. Mem: Elks; Amateur Athletic Union; U.S. Olympians. Olympic Decathlon Champion, 48 & 52; Sullivan Award; Outstanding Young Man Award, Jr. C. of C. Rel: Methodist. Legal Res: Calif. Mailing Add: Room 1008 Longworth House Office Bldg, Washington, D.C. 20515.

MATHIS, JAMES WESLEY D
b. Lena, Miss, 9/17/34; married. Educ: Sigma Nu. Polit. & Govt. Pos: Miss. State Rep, 64-68. Bus. & Prof. Pos: Gen. ins. Mem: Wow; Rotary; Jaycees; Leake Co. C. of C; pres, E. Cent. Jr. Col. Alumni Asn; Citizens Coun; Travelers Club; Cent. Miss. Archery Club. Rel: Baptist. Mailing Add: Box 26, Carthage, Miss. 39051. (1967)

MATHIS, RALPH C.
b. 1910; m; c. Five. Educ: Drake Univ, grad; Iowa State Univ. and Univ. Iowa, grad. work. Polit. & Govt. Pos: Iowa State Rep, 66; Justice of the Peace. Bus. & Prof. Pos: Farms and manages a hybrid seed bus; sch. teacher, 5 years. Mem: Treas, Iowa State Univ. Agr. Develop. Cmt. Rel: Christian; Chmn. Bd, Elkhart Christian Church. Mailing Add: Elkhart, Iowa 50073. (1967)

MATHISEN, CHRIS D
m. to Mary Calhoun; c. Chris Tyler. Polit. & Govt. Pos: Admin. Asst, Rep. Harrison, 50-63; admin. asst, U.S. Rep. Marsh, Va. currently. Bus. & Prof. Pos: Ed. Dept, Wash. Evening Star, 34-42, 46-50. Mil. Serv: Navy, serv. in Off. of Chief Cable Censor; U.S.S. John C. Butler (DE 339); Navy News Correspondent, Asiatic-Pac. Theater. Mem: Nat. Press Club; Audubon Naturalist Soc. of Cent. Atlantic States, former dir; Wash. Newspaper Guild, former v.pres; Am. Soc. Pub. Admin. Mailing Add: 4019 N. Randolph St, Arlington, Va. 22207.

MATHNA, WOODROW WILSON R
Mayor, Lorain, Ohio
b. Gibsonburg, Ohio, 3/27/13; s. Clarence Mathna and Effie Rosenberry M; m. 6/22/38 to Kathleen Dillon; c. Patrick Allen and Margaret Rose. Educ: High sch. and part time courses. Polit. & Govt. Pos: Fourth Ward Councilman, Rep. Party, Ohio, 56-61; Mayor, Lorain, Ohio, currently. Mem: Life mem. Ohio PTA; Elks; Kiwanis; K. of P. Rel: Evangelical United Brethren Church. Mailing Add: 507 W. 32nd St, Lorain, Ohio 44055.

MATLACK, DON D
b. Halstead, Kans, 6/18/29; s. Orval Matlack and Blanche Harris M; m. 6/10/51 to Ardena Williams; c. Lucinda Donn, Roxanne, Terry Clyde, Rex William and Timothy Alan. Educ: Kans. State Univ, Manhattan, B.S, 51; Washburn Univ, LL.B, 57; Delta Tau Delta. Polit. & Govt. Pos: Dep. co. attorney, Sedgwick Co, Kans, 57-59; Kans. State Sen, 65-68; del, Dem. Nat. Conv, 68; mem, Kans. Civil Serv. Bd, 69. Bus. & Prof. Pos: Partner, Blair, Matlack, Rogg & Foote Attorneys, 59- Mil. Serv: Entered as Seaman Recruit, Navy, 51, released as Lt.(jg), 54, after serv. in Korea, 52-53; Korean Serv. and UN Ribbons; Lt, Naval Res, 56. Mem: Am. Bar Asn; Am. Trial Lawyers Asn; Mason; Consistory; Shrine; Am. Legion; Lions. Rel: Methodist. Mailing Add: 615 Elaine, Clearwater, Kans. 67026.

MATO, LOUIS V. D
Wis. State Assemblyman
b. Pogradec, Albania, 7/20/03. Educ: Bus. Col, 21-22. Polit. & Govt. Pos: Mem. bd, Eau Claire Co, Wis, 52-; Wis. State Assemblyman, 62- Bus. & Prof. Pos: Former restaurant operator; salesman for chef's supplies. Mem: Civic and serv. progs, Eau Claire Co. Mailing Add: Fairchild, Wis. 54741. (1967)

MATSON, MAURICE JOHN R
Chmn, Kingsbury Co. Rep. Cent. Cmt, S.Dak.
b. Hetland, S.Dak, 8/17/21; s. Myrum Matson and Galena Mydland M; single. Educ: Augustana Col, S.Dak, B.A, 43; Gladstonian Soc. Polit. & Govt. Pos: State cent. committeeman, Kingsbury Co. Rep. Cmt, 60-65; mem, S.Dak. Bd. Mil. Affairs, 61-69; mem, S.Dak. Rep. Adv. Coun, 61-; chmn, S.Dak. Rep. Fair Bldg. Cmt, 62-65; chmn, Kingsbury Co. Rep. Cent. Cmt, 65- Mil. Serv: Entered as Midn, Navy, 43, released as Lt.(jg), 46, after serv. in LCI (L) Flotilla 1, Mediterranean Theater, 43-45; Europe-Africa-Middle East Campaign Medal with Three Battle Stars; Am. Campaign Medal; Victory Medal. Mem: Am. Legion; VFW. Rel: Lutheran. Mailing Add: Hetland, S.Dak. 57244.

MATSUNAGA, SPARK MASAYUKI D
U.S. Rep, Hawaii
b. Kauai, Hawaii, 10/8/16; s. Kingoro Matsunaga and Chiyono Fukushima M. (both deceased); m. 8/6/48 to Helene Hatsumi Tokunaga; c. Karen Chiyono, Keene Goro, Diane Yukie, Merle Masae and Matthew Masao. Educ: Univ. Hawaii, B.Ed, 41; Harvard Law Sch, LL.B, 51; Real Dean; Phi Kappa Phi; Pi Gamma Mu; Casner Law Club; King's Bench; Sigma Lambda; Univ. Theatre Guild; YMCA; Saber and Chain; Varsity Debate. Polit. & Govt. Pos: Vet. counsr, Surplus Prop. Off, Dept. of Interior, 45-47; chief priority claimants div, War Assets Admin, 47-48; mem, Terr. War Mem. Found, 47-48 and Gov. Cmt. on Housing, 47-48; mem, Hawaii Statehood del. to Cong, 50-54; chmn. rescue serv, Civil Defense Agency, 51-52; asst. pub. prosecutor, City and Co. of Honolulu, 52-54; Oahu Co. committeeman and exec. bd. mem, Dem. Party of Hawaii, 52-54; del. co. and state Dem. conv, 52-62, serv. on Resolutions, Rules and Platform Cmts; mem. relocation adv. cmt, Honolulu Redevelop. Agency, 53-54; pres, Dem. Precinct Club, First Precinct, Fourth Dist, 53-55; Hawaii Territorial Rep, 54-59, Majority Leader, 59, chmn, Judiciary Cmt. and Juvenile Ct, Recreation and Welfare Cmt, v.chmn, Tourism and Land Cmts, mem, Finance Cmt; v.chmn, Citizens for Kennedy and Johnson; Hawaii, 56-59; pres, Dem. Precinct Club, Third Precinct, 16th Dist, 59-64; mem, Pac. War Mem. Cmn, Hawaii, 60-63; U.S. Rep, Hawaii, 63-, chmn, Subcmt. on Domestic Mkt. and Consumer Rels, Cmt. on Agr, mem, Post Off. and Civil Serv. Cmt. and secy, House Dem. Steering Cmt, U.S. House of Rep; del, Dem. Nat. Conv, 68. Bus. & Prof. Pos: Stevedore and warehouseman, 31-34; bookkeeper and sales clerk, gen. merchandise store, 34-37; attorney-at-law, 54-63. Mil. Serv: Entered as 2nd Lt, Army, 41, released as Capt, 46, after serv. in 100th Inf. Bn, 442nd Inf. Regt, African-European-Asiatic Theatres, 41-45; Lt. Col, Judge Adv. Gen. Corps, Army Res, 63-; Bronze Star Medal with V; Purple Heart Medal with Oak Leaf Cluster; Army Commendation Medal; Asiatic-Pac. Campaign Ribbon; African-European Campaign Ribbons; Five Battle Stars; Am. Theater Ribbon; Combat and Expert Inf. Badges. Publ: 'An Experiment in Speech Correction,' Hawaii Educ. Rev, 51. Mem: Am. Bar Asn; Hawaii Bar Asn.(cmt. on ethics, 58-60); Cmt. on Hawaii Rules of Criminal Procedure; exec. bd, Hawaii Chap, World Brotherhood and Soc. for Crippled Children and Adults; bd. dir, Honolulu Coun. for Soc. Agencies; pres. and bd. mem, Naturalization Encouragement Asn; chmn, v.chmn, bd. mem, Kaimuki YMCA; pres, Univ. Hawaii Presch. PTA; v.pres, Aliiolani Sch. PTA; Lions; v.chmn, Friends of Rizal Soc; Harvard Club of Hawaii; Club 15; pres, Club 100; comdr. and judge advocate, DAV; chmn, United Vet. Legis. Cmt; chmn, AJA Vet. Coun; mem, MIS Vet. Club. Received YMCA Serv. to Youth Award, Boy Scouts Meritorious Serv. Award, DAV Nat. Merit Award, War Assets Admin. Meritorious Serv. Award, Japanese-Am. Citizens League Nat. Nisei of the Biennium Award. Rel: Episcopal. Legal Res: 1022 Bethel St, Honolulu, Hawaii 96813. Mailing Add: House of Representatives, Washington, D.C. 20515.

MATTAR, EDWARD PAUL, III R
b. Buffalo, N.Y, 3/15/39; s. Joseph Mattar and Anne Abraham M; single. Educ: St. Francis Col; Univ. Buffalo Sch. Law; Mt. Vernon Sch. Law, LL.B; Georgetown Univ. Polit. & Govt. Pos: D'Youville Col. Chmn, Nixon for President, 60; mem. campaign staff, N.Y. Supreme Court Justice Frederick M. Marshall, 61 & 67; asst. to West. N.Y. coordinator, Citizens for Rockefeller-Javits, 62; dir. col. and youth activities, asst. to nat. campaign coordinator and exec. dir. polit. sci. internship prog, Rockefeller Nat. Campaign Staff, 64; cand, U.S. Rep, 41st Dist, N.Y, 68. Bus. & Prof. Pos: Exec. secy, assoc. nat. dir. and publ. dir, Nat. Crusaders Youth Fedn, 57-59; elem. teacher, Diocese Buffalo, 59-60; instr. parliamentary law, pub. speaking, and contemporary Am. probs, adult educ. center, D'Youville Col, 60-62; exec. ed, Programme Book Rev. Serv, 63-66; high sch. teacher govt, Arlington Co. Pub. Schs, 64-65; dean students, admin. asst. to exec. v.pres, Peace Corps Liason and instr. bus. law, East. Col, 65-66; ed. TV/USA and exec. v.pres, U.S. Asn. TV Viewers, 65-67; pres, Century Twenty One Limited, 67-; instr. sch. law, grad div, Canisius Col, 68. Publ: Barry Goldwater: A political indictment, 64. Mem: Trustee, USA/TV; cmnr, Nat. Accrediting Cmn. for Tech. Educ; bd. dir, John Howard Soc; bd. dir, Buffalo Coun. World Affairs; pres, Niagara Frontier Chap, Aiding Leukemia Stricken Am. Children; judge, Cath. Youth Orgn. Cultural Progs; Buffalo Area C. of C; Am. Asn. Univ. Prof; Capitol Hill Club; Admin. Mgt. Soc; Independent Cath. Action Now; Allentown Asn; Ment. Health Asn. Erie Co; Buffalo World Hospitality Asn; Nat. Educ. Asn; Coalition for Action, Unity and Soc. Equality; past bd. dir, Nat. Coun. Cath. Youth; past del, Conf. Commun. Living; Erie Co. Civil Defense (past telephone commun. coordinator). Rel: Catholic. Mailing Add: 17 Court St, Buffalo, N.Y. 14202.

MATTHEEUSSEN, FLOYD J. D
b. Chicago, Ill, 3/29/30; m. to Barbara Marie Schindler; c. Karen, Joseph. Educ: Elmhurst Col, B.A. degree; West. Mich. Univ, M.A. degree; pursued post grad. work. Polit. & Govt. Pos: Mich. State Rep, 64-66; Berrien Co. chmn. to the Dem. State Cmn. on Agr. Bus. & Prof. Pos: Fruit farmer; served in pub. educ. as a teacher, prin. and supt. Mil. Serv: Army, educ. specialist, Pusan, Korea. Mem: YMCA; Am. Fedn. of Teachers; polit. action chmn, NAACP, Benton Harbor Br; chmn, Berrien Co. Citizens Cmt. for Sound Govt, pres. Berrien Co. Dem. Club; asst. scout master and adv. to the Explorers. Rel: United Church of Christ; mem, State Bd. Dirs. of Mich. Conf. Mailing Add: RFD 2, Box 193, Benton Harbor, Mich. 49022. (1967)

MATTHEWS, CAREY D
Fla. State Rep.
b. N.Y.C, 9/16/22. Educ: Amherst Col; Yale Univ; Columbia Univ; Columbia Law Sch, A.B. and LL.B. Polit. & Govt. Pos: Former Asst. Attorney Gen, Fla; Fla. State Rep, 60-66 and currently; del, Dem. Nat. Conv, 68. Bus. & Prof. Pos: Attorney; gen. counsel, Dade Co. Classroom Teacher's Asn. Mil. Serv: Marines, Korea, World War II, wounded in action three times; Marine Corps Res; awarded eight Am. and for. combat decorations and citations. Mem: Fla. Bar; First and Fifth Marine Div. Asns; Hialeah-Miami Springs DAV; Phi Gamma Delta. Mailing Add: 123 N.E. 79th St, Miami, Fla. 33138. (1967)

MATTHEWS, CHARLES DAWSON D
Chmn, Ark. State Dem. Cmt.
b. Little Rock, Ark, 2/12/39; s. John Pope Matthews and Martha Dawson M; m. 6/10/61 to Susan Ann Scully; c. Michael Dawson, James Patrick, Martha Ann and William Scully. Educ: Georgetown Univ, B.S. in Eng, 61; Univ. Ark, LL.B, 64; pres, Sr. Class, 60-61; Georgetown Univ. Varsity Swimming Team (capt); Univ. Ark. Student Bar Asn.(pres); assoc. ed, Univ. Ark. Law Rev; Blue Key. Polit. & Govt. Pos: Ark. State Rep, Pos. One, Dist. 22, 66-68; chmn, Ark. State Dem. Cmt, 68- Bus. & Prof. Pos: V.pres. and mem. bd. dirs, Matthews Co. and Crestwood Develop. Co, North Little Rock. Mem: Pulaski Co, Ark. and Am. Bar Asns; C. of C.(bd. dirs, North Little Rock Chap); YMCA (bd. dirs); Ark. Asn. for the Crippled (pres); Ark. Kidney Found. (pres). Outstanding Freshman Mem, 66th Gen. Assembly; Outstanding Cath, Bishop Fletcher Award, 64; Outstanding Young Man Award, North Little Rock Jaycees, 67. Rel: Catholic. Legal Res: 3604 North Hills Blvd, North Little Rock, Ark. 72116. Mailing Add: 1505 Lakewood House, North Little Rock, Ark. 72116.

MATTHEWS, DONALD RAY D
b. Micanopy, Fla, 10/3/07; s. D. H. Matthews and Flora A. M; m. 1941 to Sara Lewis M; c. Carolyn, Ann, Donald Ray, Jr. Educ: Univ. of Fla, B.A, M.A; Alpha Phi Epsilon; Pi Gamma Mu; Tau Kappa Alpha; Fla. Blue Key; Scabbard and Blade; Sigma Phi Epsilon. Polit. & Govt. Pos: Fla. State Rep, 35, mem, Cmt. on Appropriations; U.S. Rep, Fla, 52-67. Bus. & Prof. Pos: Sch. teacher; High Sch. prin; admin. staff, Univ. of Fla, 16 years; serv. as Dir. of Fla. Union, Student Activity center, and Dir. Alumni Aff; instr. Am. Inst, Santa Fe Jr. Col, Gainesville, Fla, 67- Mil. Serv: Inf, 4 years; discharged as Capt. Mem: Asst. State 4-H agent for Fla, 10 summers; past Dist. Gov. Lions Int; past Chmn, Fla. Coun. for the Blind; past Pres, Gainesville Kiwanis Club; past Chmn, Alachua Co. Chap. Nat. Found. for Infantile Paralysis; Am. Legion; K. of P; Gainesville C. of C; Elks; Moose; past Pres,

Nat. Asn. of Col. Unions; Phi Kappa Phi. Rel: Presbyterian; Elder, First Presbyterian Church, Gainesville. Mailing Add: 2611 S.W. Eighth Dr, Gainesville, Fla. 32601.

MATTHEWS, DORSEY RUDOLPH D
Ga. State Rep.
b. Emma, Ga, 8/26/13; s. John Bailey Matthews and Carrie Johnson M; m. 12/24/38 to Elizabeth Taylor; c. Melanie Sue, Lawton Virgil, Judith Elizabeth and Hugh Dorsey. Educ: Moultrie High Sch, 31. Polit. & Govt. Pos: Ga. State Sen, 47th Dist, 55-56; Ga. State Rep, 59- Bus. & Prof. Pos: Farmer; dir, Flue-Cured Tobacco Stabilization Coop. of U.S. Mem: Pres, Colquitt Co. Farm Bur, 50-53. Named Ga. Master Farmer, 54. Rel: Methodist. Mailing Add: Route 1, Moultrie, Ga. 31768. (1967)

MATTHEWS, JAMES MADISON, JR. D
Ark. State Rep.
b. Dumas, Ark, 9/29/44; s. James Madison Matthews and Annie Mae Lock M; div. Educ: Henderson State Col, 62-63; Ark. A&M Col, 64; Univ. of Ark, 65-66. Polit. & Govt. Pos: Ark. State Rep, Lincoln and Desha Co, 69- Bus. & Prof. Pos: Asst. mgr, Matthews, Inc, 66. Mem: Dir, Ark. LP Gas Asn; Ark. Automobile Dealers Asn; Jaycees; C. of C. Rel: Baptist. Legal Res: Hwy. 54 E, Dumas, Ark. 71639. Mailing Add: P.O. Box 127, Dumas, Ark. 71639.

MATTHEWS, RICHARD CARROLL R
Md. State Del.
b. Hampstead, Md, 7/11/26; s. Arthur Jennings Matthews and Gladys Bishop M; m. 12/29/45 to Dorothy Ann Hale. Polit. & Govt. Pos: Mem, Carroll Co. Rep. Cent. Cmt, Md, 62-66; Md. State Del, currently. Bus. & Prof. Pos: Owner, Matthews Tire Co, 46- Mem: Lions; C. of C. Rel: Methodist. Mailing Add: 111 Taylor Ave, Hampstead, Md. 21074. (1967)

MATTHEWS, RICHARD MOORE D
b. Cambridge, Md, 4/18/27; s. Robert Hutchin Matthews and Beulah Moore M; m. 12/19/56 to Doris Lee Melvin; c. Valerie Lee and Richard Moore, Jr. Educ: Univ. of Md. Law Sch, LL.B, 53; Delta Theta Phi. Polit. & Govt. Pos: Md. State Del, 59-67. Mil. Serv: Pvt. and seaman, Army and Maritime Serv, 45-47, serv. in U.S. and Mediterranean. Mem: Dorchester Co. and Md. Bar Asns; Cambridge Yacht Club; Dorchester Hist. Soc; Lions. Rel: Protestant. Legal Res: 5 West End Ave, Cambridge, Md. 21613. Mailing Add: 314 High St, Cambridge, Md. 21613.

MATTHEWS, ROBERT D
b. Shelbyville, Ky, 9/14/23; s. Robert F. Matthews, Sr. and Zerelda Baxter; m. 3/23/45 to Betty Buntin; c. Charles K. and Alan. Educ: Col. of William and Mary, B.A, 43; Univ. Va, LL.B, 48; Kappa Alpha. Polit. & Govt. Pos: Asst. attorney gen, Ky, 55-60, exec. secy. to gov, 60, cmnr. of finance, 60-63 and Attorney Gen, 64-68. Bus. & Prof. Pos: Gen. law practice, Matthews & Matthews Law Off, Shelbyville, Ky, 48-; rancher, Tex, 50-53. Mil. Serv: Entered as A/S, Navy, 43, released as Lt, 46, after serv. in N. Atlantic and S. Pac. Theaters. Mem: Am. and Ky. Bar Asns; Rotary; Mason. Rel: Presbyterian. Mailing Add: 1428 W. Main St, Shelbyville, Ky. 40065. (1967)

MATTHEWS, ROBERT CHAPPELLE D
Ga. State Rep.
b. Athens, Ga, 11/01/08; s. Vincent Matthews and Susan Dorsey M; m. 9/15/65 to Dorothy Harris. Educ: Univ. of Ga, 33; South. Law Sch, LL.B, 34; Sigma Alpha Epsilon. Polit. & Govt. Pos: Ga. State Rep, 49-, chmn, Univ. System Cmt. of the House, 50-53 & 57-; mem, South. Regional Educ. Bd, 50-, secy-treas, 58-60, mem. legis. adv. cmt; mem, Ga. Sci. and Tech. Cmt, 65; mem, Ga. Coun. to Improve Educ, 68. Bus. & Prof. Pos: Attorney-at-law; mem, bd. of gov, Ga. Bar Asn, 56-58 and chmn, legis. cmt, 69- Mil. Serv: U.S. Cavalry, retired. Mem: Ga. Nuclear Cmn, origin; Ga. and Am. Bar Asns; Am. Judiciary Soc; Elks; Athens City Club; Ga. Farm Bur. Outstanding Alumni Award, Univ. of Ga, 64. Rel: Methodist. Legal Res: 190 Rutherford Lane, Athens, Ga. 30601. Mailing Add: 306 Souther Mutual Bldg, Athens, Ga. 30601.

MATTHEWS, VIRGIL E(DISON), JR. D
Councilman-at-lg, Charleston, W.Va.
b. LaFayette, Ala, 10/5/28; s. Virgil Edison Matthews (deceased) and Izetta Ware M. (deceased); m. 1/23/60 to Shirley Elizabeth McFatridge; c. Brian Keith, Michael André and Deborah Michele. Educ: Univ. Ill, Urbana, B.S, 51; Univ. Chicago, S.M, 52, Ph.D, 55; Sigma Xi; Phi Lambda Upsilon; Cosmopolitan Club. Polit. & Govt. Pos: Councilman-at-lg, Charleston, W.Va, 67-; del, Dem. Nat. Conv, 68. Bus. & Prof. Pos: Clerk, registr. off, Univ. Chicago, 51 and teaching asst. chem, 51-52; part-time instr. and prof. chem, W.Va. State Col, 55-; res. chemist, res. and develop. dept, Union Carbide Corp, W.Va, 54-67 and proj. scientist, 67- Publ: 'Improved Synthesis of Salts and Esters of Nitroacetic Acid,' 60 and 'Synthesis of 1,1'-Bis (tri-n-dodecylsilyl) ferrocene,' 62, J. Organic Chem. Mem: Am. Chem. Soc; fel, Am. Inst. Chemists; Brit. Chem. Soc; fel, Am. Asn. Adv. Sci; Alpha Phi Alpha; Optimist Int; life mem, NAACP. Rel: Baptist. Mailing Add: 835 Carroll Rd, Charleston, W.Va. 25314.

MATTHEWS, WILLIAM JOSEPH R
Chmn, Hardeman Co. Rep. Exec. Cmt, Tenn.
b. Middleburg, Tenn, 11/15/92; s. William Morrow Matthews and Martha Ann Burrus M; m. 10/1/16 to Lillian Long; c. Mary Louise (Mrs. Pulliam); granddaughters, Diane and Debra. Educ: Cent. High Sch, Bolivar, Tenn, grad. Polit. & Govt. Pos: Asst. postmaster, Tenn, 18-30; chmn, Hardeman Co. Rep. Exec. Cmt. and mem. Elec. Cmn, 22- Bus. & Prof. Pos: Formerly operator, chain of silent movies and supermarket, ticket agent, Greyhound Bus Co. and Ill. Cent. R.R, and cotton buyer for numerous firms; night supvr, State Hosp, Bolivar, Tenn, 31-32; asst. chief patrolman, Naval Air Sta, Millington, 43-44, Chief patrolman, 45; cotton buyer and bookkeeper, Bolivar Gin Co, 45- Rel: Baptist. Mailing Add: 729 N. Jones, Bolivar, Tenn. 38008. (1967)

MATTINGLY, MACK FRANCIS R
Chmn, Eighth Dist. Rep. Party, Ga.
b. Anderson, Ind, 1/7/31; s. Joseph H. Mattingly and Beatrice Wayts M; m. 6/16/57 to Carolyn Longcamp; c. Jane L. and Anne L. Educ: Ind. Univ, B.S. in Mkt. and Econs, 57. Polit. & Govt. Pos: Chmn, Eighth Dist. Goldwater Campaign, Ga, 64; del, Rep. Nat. Conv, 64, Sgt-at-Arms, 68; v.chmn, Eighth Dist. Rep. Party, 64-66, chmn, 66-; Rep. cand. for U.S. Rep, Eighth Dist, Ga, 66; mem, Ga. State Rep. Cent. Cmt, 66-; presidential elector, Rep. Party, Ga, 68; mem, State Rep. Exec. Cmt, 68- Bus. & Prof. Pos: Prod. scheduling, Arvin Industs, 57-59; sales rep, Int. Bus. Machines Corp, 59- Mil. Serv: Entered as Pvt, Air Force, 51, released as S/Sgt, 55, after serv. in Strategic Air Command. Mem: Rotary; Glynn Co. & Waycross-Ware Co. C. of C; Glynn Co. Cmt. of 100. Rel: Methodist; trustee and chmn. off. bd, St. Simons Methodist Church. Mailing Add: 4315 Tenth St, East Beach, St. Simons Island, Ga. 31522.

MATTINGLY, REX MAX R
Chmn, Bernalillo Co. Rep. Cent. Cmt, N.Mex.
b. Lucy, N.Mex, 5/25/19; s. Eugene Aloysus Mattingly and Linnie Beard M. m. 7/9/41 to Laura Elizabeth Treat; c. Sharon Gay, Sally Ann and Lloyd Eugene. Educ: Univ. N.Mex. Polit. & Govt. Pos: Chmn, Bernalillo Co. Rep. Cent. Cmt, N.Mex, 65-; chmn, N.Mex. Rep. State Cent. Cmt, 67-68; mem, Rep. Nat. Cmt, 67-68; del, Rep. Nat. Conv, 68. Bus. & Prof. Pos: Brakeman, South. Pac. R.R, 41-42; partner, Mattingly Oil Co, 46- Mil. Serv: Entered as Aviation Cadet, Air Force, 42, released as 1st Lt, 45, after serv. in Cent. Flying Command. Mem: Mason; Scottish Rite; Shrine; Elks; N.Mex. Club. Rel: Protestant. Mailing Add: 288 Placitas Rd. N.W, Albuquerque, N.Mex. 87107.

MATTOX, ELMER GOOCH D
b. Portland, Tenn, 2/28/08; s. Charlie Mattox and Bertha Duffer M; m. 12/12/35 to Frances Louise Kelly; c. Charles Frederic. Educ: Portland High Sch. grad; Bus. Admin. and Salemanship Courses. Polit. & Govt. Pos: Alderman, Gallatin City Coun, Tenn, 53-59; Sumner Co. Campaign mgr. for Gov. Frank Clement; hon. col, staff, Gov. Frank Clement; Sumner Co. Campaign mgr. for Gov. Buford Ellington, 58 & 66; del, Dem. Nat. Conv, 60, 64 & 68. Bus. & Prof. Pos: Own and operate, Mattox Oil Co, Gallatin, Tenn. Mem: Tenn. Indust. Cmt, Gallatin; mem. of official bd, C. of C; Lions; Mason; Blue Grass Country Club; Farm Bur; Gallatin Country Club. Football, and golf, winner of several golf trophies. Rel: Methodist; Member of Official Board, First Methodist Church, Gallatin. Mailing Add: 804 Harris Dr, Gallatin, Tenn. 37066.

MATTOX, RAY D
b. Jessup, Ga, 3/10/27; m. to Dorothy Sullivan; c. Marie Ann and Susanne. Educ: Fla. South. Col, B.S; Univ. Fla, LL.B. Polit. & Govt. Pos: Fla. State Rep, 56-68; alternate del, Dem. Nat. Conv, 68. Bus. & Prof. Pos: Attorney-at-law. Mil. Serv: Lt, Army Res; War Serv, Navy. Mem: Jr. C. of C; Am. Legion; Lions. Rel: Baptist. Mailing Add: 749 Ave. M,S.E, Winter Haven, Fla. 33880. (1967)

MATTOX, VERNA D. R
Mem, Calif. Rep. State Cent. Cmt.
b. Washington, Nebr, 7/14/16; d. Fred C.H. Dalgas and Jacobina Madsen D; m. 4/19/41 to Tilden Mattox; c. Frederick and Judy Ann. Polit. & Govt. Pos: Secy, Manhattan Beach Recreation Cmn, Calif, 50-51; pres, S.Bay Club of Fed. Rep. Women, 62-63; co-chmn, S.Bay Citizens for Goldwater, 64; alternate del, Rep. Nat. Conv, 64; mem, Calif. Rep. State Cent. Cmt, 64-; current events chmn, Speaker's Bur, Los Angeles Co. Bd, Calif. Fedn. Rep. Women, 64-, chmn, Speaker's Bur, South. Div. Bd, 66-, transportation chmn, 66-; alternate, 46th Assembly Dist, Rep. Cent. Cmt, 65-; second v.pres, Los Angeles Co. Fedn. Rep. Women, 67-68, pres, 69- Bus. & Prof. Pos: Exec. secy. to v.pres, Pac. Finance Corp, 40-42; co-owner and operator, Tilden's Sport Shop, 43- Mem: Auxiliary Children's Home Soc. Rel: Presbyterian. Mailing Add: 22647 B Nadine Circle, Torrance, Calif. 90505.

MATTRAN, GERALD CHARLES R
Exec. Secy, Oak Park Rep. Orgn, Ill.
b. Chicago, Ill, 2/21/33; s. Albert Charles Mattran and Catherine O'Connor M; m. 7/2/55 to Nancy Dilzer; c. Mary Frances, Mark Gerald and Kathleen Marie. Educ: DePaul Univ; Univ. Chicago, M.A, 66, Ph.D, 70; Alpha Delta Sigma (pres, 56). Polit. & Govt. Pos: Auditor, Oak Park Twp, Ill, 66-; exec. secy, Oak Park Rep. Orgn, 67-; alternate del, Rep. Nat. Conv, 68. Bus. & Prof. Pos: Sales prom. mgr, Haywood Publ. Co, 58-62; sales mgr, Am. Dent. Asn, 62-65; asst. prof, Chicago City Col, 67-69; research assoc, Univ. Chicago, 69- Mil. Serv: Entered as Seaman Recruit, Navy, 51, released as PO 2/C, after serv. in U.S.S. Kimberly DD-521 and U.S.S. Turner DDR-834; Good Conduct Medal; Korean Serv. Medal with Two Battle Stars; UN Medal; Presidential Unit Citation; Syngman Rhee Citation; China Serv. Medal; Navy Occup. Medal; Nat. Defense Serv. Medal. Publ: 'Oak Park Community Profile,' Omnibus Mag, 65; Politics From the Inside Up, Follett, 66; plus others. Mem: Orgn. Am. Historians; Am. Hist. Asn; Oak Park Hist. Soc.(pres, 68); Oak Park Coun, K. of C. Rel: Catholic. Mailing Add: 617 S. Oak Park Ave, Oak Park, Ill. 60304.

MATTSON, JOHN B, JR. R
b. Newton, Mass, 1/28/31; s. John Benhard Mattson and Elma Helena M; m. 6/5/59 to Nancy Wilburn; c. John Edward, Thomas Michael and Robert Wilburn. Educ: Mass. Inst. of Tech, B.S. in indust. eng, 48; Univ. N.Mex, M.S. in nuclear eng, 59; Harvard Grad. Sch. of Bus. Admin, M.B.A, 61; pres. and treas, Phi Kappa Sigma. Polit. & Govt. Pos: Former chmn, Bernalillo Co. Rep. Platform Cmt; former N.Mex. State adv. for Teenage Rep; N.Mex. State Rep, 14th Dist, 65-68, former mem, Judiciary and Educ. Legis. Cmts. Bus. & Prof. Pos: Teacher econ. and bus. admin, Burdett Col, 60-61; pres. and dir, Mecca Computer Systs, Inc, 68- Mil. Serv: Entered as 2nd Lt, Army, 52, released as 1st Lt, 54. Mem: Nat. Soc. Prfnl. Engrs; pres, Harvard Club of N.Mex; Mason; Elks. Golf, bowling, fishing, photography; reading history and current affairs. Mailing Add: 1513 Cedar Ridge N.E, Albuquerque, N.Mex. 87112.

MATTSON, ROBERT W. DFL
b. Virginia, Minn, 8/25/24; m. to Shirley Kunze; c. Robert, Jr, Susan, Marsha, Polly Ann. Educ: Va. Jr. Col; Univ. Minn, B.S.L, 49, LL.B, 50. Polit. & Govt. Pos: Attorney Gen, 64-66; chief of legal sect, Los Angeles Ordinance Dist, 50-53; spec. asst. Attorney Gen, Jan, 55; asst. Attorney Gen, Mar, 55; dep. Attorney Gen. for Highways, June, 55; chief dep. Attorney Gen, 58. Bus. & Prof. Pos: Lawyer; private practice, Minneapolis, 60-64. Mil. Serv: Army, combat inf; Purple Heart. Mailing Add: 2410 Overlook Dr, Bloomington, Minn. 55404. (1967)

MATUS, MARGARET ANNA D
b. West Wyoming, Pa, 7/12/25; d. Joseph Matus and Eva Udinsky M; single. Educ: Am. Univ, B.A, 52. Polit. & Govt. Pos: Secy, Hoover Cmn. Cmt. on Orgn. of Exec. Br, 47-48 and U.S. Civil Serv. Cmn, 45-49; admin. asst. to U.S. War Claims Cmn, 49-53, U.S. Nat. Security Training Cmn, 53-54, U.S. Rep, John Lesinski, 16th Dist, Mich, 55-64, U.S. Rep. N. Neiman Craley, 19th Dist, Pa, 65-66 and U.S. Rep. Richard McCarthy, 39th Dist, N.Y, 67- Legal Res: Arlington, Va. Mailing Add: 238 House Office Bldg, Washington, D.C. 20515.

MAUBERRET, CLAUDE, JR. D
Assessor, Second Munic. Dist, New Orleans, La.
b. New Orleans, La, 2/11/22; s. Claud Mauberret, Sr. and Bessie Morrill M; m. 6/4/59 to Diane Bennett; c. Claude, Catherine and Lee. Educ: Auburn Univ, D.V.M; Kappa Alpha Order; Omega Tau Sigma. Polit. & Govt. Pos: Vet, La. State Racing Cmn, 48-59; mem, La. Dem. State Cent. Cmt, 52-; assessor, Second Munic. Dist, New Orleans, 60-; mem, La. Racing Cmn, First Cong. Dist, 64- Bus. & Prof. Pos: Vet, Self-employed, 47- Mil. Serv: Entered as Pvt, Army, 42, released as Pfc, 44. Mem: Am. Vet. Med. and La. Vet. Med. Asns; Int. Asn. Assessing Officers. Rel: Catholic. Mailing Add: 218 N. St. Patrick St, New Orleans, La. 70119. (1967)

MAUGHAN, RICHARD JOHNSON D
Chmn, Davis Co. Dem. Cent. Cmt, Utah
b. Logan, Utah, 11/13/17; s. Heber Chase Maughan and Ragna Johnson M; m. 7/12/46 to Laura Dell Torgeson; c. Margith Christine, Joyce, Eloise, Richard and Mary Frances. Educ: Utah State Univ, B.S, 48; Univ. of Utah, Salt Lake City, J.D, 51; Pi Sigma Alpha; Phi Alpha Delta. Polit. & Govt. Pos: Asst. Attorney Gen, State of Utah, 51-53; chmn, Salt Lake Co. Young Dem, 53-55; secy, Utah State Dem. Finance Cmt, 53-55; dem. cand, Utah State Legis, 66; chmn, Davis Co. Dem. Cent. Cmt, 66-; dem. cand, U.S. House Rep, First Cong. Dist, 68; mem, Utah State Bd. Higher Educ, 69; mem. exec. cmt, West. Interstate Cmn. for Higher Educ, 69; mem, Utah State Cmt. for Polit. Reform, 69. Bus. & Prof. Pos: Chmn, Continuing Legal Educ. Cmt, Utah State Bar Asn, 62-; mem. and chmn. bd. trustees, Utah State Univ, 65-69; past pres, Davis Co. Bar Asn. Mil. Serv: Entered as Pvt, Air Force, 42, released as Sgt, 45. Mem: Utah State Bar Asn.(chmn, 62-); Davis Co. Bar Asn. (past pres); Salt Lake Co. Bar Asn; admitted to practice in all State Courts, Fed. Dist. and Circuit Court of Appeals and U.S. Supreme Court; Salt Lake Exchange Club (bd. dirs, 65-67). Rel: Latter-day Saint. Legal Res: 500 East Tenth N, Bountiful, Utah 84010. Mailing Add: 615 Kearns Bldg, Salt Lake City, Utah 84101.

MAUGHMER, FRED H, JR. R
b. Savannah, Mo. 6/26/27; s. Fred H. Maughmer and Ruth Hine M; m. 1/17/59 to Laura McNair; c. Douglas and Holly. Educ: U.S. Mil. Acad, West Point, N.Y, B.S, 49; Univ. Mo, LL.B, 57; Phi Delta Phi; Beta Theta Pi. Polit. Pos: Mo. State Rep, 65-67; mem, Mo. State Sen. Redistricting Cmn, 61. Prof. Pos: Attorney-at-Law, 57- Mil. Serv: Entered as Seaman 1/C, Navy, 45, released as 1st Lt, 54, after serv as Jet Fighter Pilot, Alaskan Air Command, 52-54; Victory Medal; Korean Serv. and Air Force Long Serv. Ribbons; Maj, Mo. Air Nat. Guard, 61- Mem: Mo. Bar; Am. Bar Asn; Am. Legion; Masons, Scottish Rite, Shrine; Lions, Int. Rel: Episcopal. Mailing Add: 417 W. Main St, Savannah, Mo. 64485. (1967)

MAUGHMER, KARROL JUNE R
Mem, Calif. Rep. State Cent. Cmt.
b. Franklin Co, Ga, 4/7/32; d. Oren Bowers and Clara Cleveland B; c. Patricia Elizabeth, Phillip Robert and Susan Karrol Educ: High sch, grad. Polit. & Govt. Pos: Pres, Thousand Oaks Rep. Women, Calif, 64; assoc. mem, Calif. Rep. State Cent. Cmt, 65, mem, 65-; co-chmn, Finch for Lt. Gov, Ventura Co, Calif, 66; adv, Calif. Lutheran Col. Rep. Youth, 66-; pres, Ventura Co. Fedn. Women, Calif, 67-68; co. women's chmn, Nixon for Pres, 68. Mem: Thousand Oaks Art Asn; NAACP, Ventura Co; bd. dirs, Mary Health of the Sick Hosp. Guild. Commendation from City of Thousand Oaks for initiating Green Power Found. Day in the Valley. Mailing Add: 1875 Village Court, Thousand Oaks, Calif. 91360.

MAULE, ELROY D
Iowa State Rep.
b. Mondamin, Iowa, 5/16/13; s. Charles Riley Maule and Jennie McElroy M; m. 1/1/33 to Evangeline Mae Wickersham; c. John Robert and Mary Louisa. Educ: Univ. Iowa, B.A. in sci, 36; Univ. Colo, grad. study, 38; Univ. Chorus; wrestling team; conf. champion, small bore rifle. Polit. & Govt. Pos: Twp. trustee, Iowa, 46-50; mem, Agr. Stabilization and Conserv. Cmt, 46-48 and Farm Security Admin. Bd, 53-55; Iowa State Rep, 57-, majority leader, Iowa House of Rep, 65-66, chmn, Iowa Drainage Study Cmt, mem, Lewis and Clark Develop. Cmt, Iowa Legis. Research Cmt, mem. Gov. Tax Study Cmt, Iowa-Nebr. Boundary Cmt, chmn, ways and means cmt. and ranking mem, appropriations cmt, 61, mem, Iowa Manpower Voc. Educ. Cmt, nat. legis. research conf. and coun. State Govts; co. Dem. Chmn, 68- Bus. & Prof. Pos: Inst, Shueyville High Sch, Cedar Rapids, Iowa, 36-41, prin, 39-41; farmer, 41- Mem: Iowa State Hist. Soc; Iowa Archeol. Soc; Univ. Iowa Alumni Asn; Nat. Educ. Asn; Am. Aberdeen Angus Asn; Farmers Union; Farm Bur; C. of C; Boy Scouts; Isaac Walton League; Outdoor Club; West. Iowa Exp. Farm Asn; Methodist Men. Rel: Methodist. Mailing Add: R.R. 2, Onawa, Iowa 51040.

MAURO, GUY J. D
V.Chmn, Columbiana Co. Dem. Exec. Cmt, Ohio
b. Alliance, Ohio, 9/19/11; s. Anthony T. Mauro and Mary Ungaro M; m. 5/20/44 to Catherine E. Morrow; c. Eileen, James and Mary Kay. Educ: Ohio Northern Univ, 29-30; Ohio State Univ, B.A, 33 and LL.B, 36; Theta Kappa Phi. Polit. & Govt. Pos: Asst. prosecuting attorney, Columbiana Co, Ohio, 38-40; del, Dem. Nat. Conv, 52 & 68, alternate del, 60 & 64; chmn, Columbiana Co. Welfare Adv. Bd, 63-65; v.chmn, Columbiana Co. Dem. Exec. Cmt, currently. Mil. Serv: Entered as Pvt, Army, 42, released as 1st Lt, 46, after serv. in 13th Armored Div, ETO, 45; Bronze Medal. Mem: Ohio Bar Asn; Columbiana Co. Bar Asn.(pres, 69); Am. Legion; K. of C.(4°); past pres. and Lt. Gov, Salem Kiwanis; tres, Columbiana Co. Cath. Serv. Bur, 64-68. Rel: Catholic. Mailing Add: 544 E. State St, Salem, Ohio 44460.

MAUTZ, ROBERT THEODORE R
b. Portland, Ore, 3/11/05; s. Charles William Mautz and Alice Viola Varner M; m. 11/22/33 to Marguerite Tarbell; c. Susan (Mrs. O.R. Peterson Jr), Robert Tarbell and Carl Eugene. Educ: Univ. Ore, LL.B, 27; Kappa Sigma; Phi Delta Phi. Polit. & Govt. Pos: Mem, Bd. Bar Exams, Ore, 33-40; mem, Ore. Racing Cmn, 48-56; mem, Rep. Nat. Cmt, 56-60; mem. bd. gov, Ore. State Bar, 60- Bus. & Prof. Pos: Sr. partner, Mautz, Souther, Spaulding, Kinsey & Williamson, 50- Mem: Fel, Am. Col. Trial Lawyers; Am. Bar Found; Int. Asn. Ins. Counsel; Am. Judicature Soc; Nat. Legal Aid Asn; hon. mem, Nat. Asn. State Racing Cmnrs; Multnomah Athletic Club (past pres); Arlington Club (past secy); Waverly Country Club (past pres). Mailing Add: Standard Plaza, 1100 S.W. Sixth Ave, Portland, Ore. 97204.

MAUZY, OSCAR HOLCOMBE D
Tex. State Sen.
b. Houston, Tex, 11/9/26; s. Harry Lincoln Mauzy and Mildred Kincaid M; m. 12/22/57 to Aglaia Dixie; c. Catherine Anne, Charles Fred and James Stephen. Educ: Univ. of Tex, B.B.A, 50 and LL.B, 52; Delta Theta Phi. Polit. & Govt. Pos: Pres, Young Dem. Club Dallas Co, Tex, 53-55; nat. committeeman, Young Dem. Clubs Tex, 54-56; Dem. precinct chmn, 62-66; Tex. State Sen, 23rd Dist, 67- Mil. Serv: Entered as A/S, Navy, 44, released as Radarman 3/C, 46; Pac. Theater of Operations with 12 Stars. Mem: Am. and Dallas Bar Asns; State Bar of Tex; Dallas Asn. of Trial Attorneys; Am. and Tex. Trial Lawyers Asns; Suuth Oak Cliff Kiwanis; hon. withdrawal card, Oil Workers Int. Union. Rel: Unitarian. Legal Res: 1338 Acapulco Dr, Dallas, Tex. 75232. Mailing Add: 1601 National Bankers Life Bldg, Dallas, Tex. 75201.

MAUZY, THAMES L. R
b. Warsaw, Ind, 11/13/08; s. Charles A. Mauzy and Mae Harmon M; m. 7/30/33 to Helen K. Nelson; c. T. Lamdon and Sharon Kay. Educ: Anthony Wayne Col, Bus. Admin, 29; Alpha Gamma Upsilon. Polit. & Govt. Pos: Mem. town bd, Winona Lake, Ind, 48-56; Ind. State Rep, 67-69. Bus. & Prof. Pos: Spec. sales rep, Hibbard Spencer Bartlett, 30-35; sales and promotion, Sears Roebuck & Co, 35-39; sales mgr, Mellencamp Furniture, 39-42; personnel and labor rels, Arnolt Motors Corp, 42-45; owner-mgr, Home Furniture Mart, 46-66. Mem: Rotary; Elks; Mason; Scottish Rite; Shrine; dir, C. of C, Credit Bur. and Area Facilities Planning Cmt; Columbia Club; Nat. Soc. State Legis. Recipient ACI Award for Retail Excellence, 62; Skeet Champion, Kosko Club, 47. Rel: Presbyterian. Mailing Add: 1025 Country Club Lane, Warsaw, Ind. 46580.

MAXHAM, DONALD HOWARD R
b. Worcester, Vt, 9/22/01; m. to Marjory Hinkley; c. One son, four daughters. Educ: Montpelier Seminary, 22. Polit. & Govt. Pos: Overseer of the poor and tax collector, Vt, 53-; Vt. State Rep, 61-67. Bus. & Prof. Pos: Fur farmer. Rel: Methodist. Mailing Add: Worcester, Vt. 05682. (1967)

MAXHAM, PAUL B. R
b. Concord, N.H, 12/1/02; s. George A. Maxham and Lenora K. M; m. 9/19/68 to Anita Daleo; c. Dawn A. (Mrs. Robert W. Bennett) and Editha L. (Mrs. Robert Hall); two grandchildren. Educ: Concord Pub. Schs; Boston Sch. Anatomy and Embalming. Polit. & Govt. Pos: N.H. State Rep, 47-67; former chmn, Pub. Welfare and State Inst. Cmn. Bus. & Prof. Pos: Former mem. and chmn, N.H. State Bd. of Funeral Directing and Embalming. Mem: N.H. Funeral Dirs. and Embalmers Asn.(past pres); Nat. Funeral Dirs. Asn; Mason; Shrine. Rel: Protestant. Mailing Add: 48 West St, Concord, N.H. 03301.

MAXWELL, CHARLES BRENTLEY R
b. Wilsonburg, W.Va, 8/1/05; s. David Inman Maxwell and Bessie May Fittro M; m. 12/22/28 to Imogene Rittenhouse; c. William Edward. Educ: Salem Col, spring 23, summers 24 & 25. Polit. & Govt. Pos: With Post Off. Dept, Clarksburg, W.Va, 24-63, retired as U.S. Civil Serv. Exam. in Charge, Post Off; Clarksburg, 63; chmn, Harrison Co. Rep. Exec. Cmt, 65-69. Bus. & Prof. Pos: Bus. mgr, Mountaineer Post Off. Clerk, 63-68. Mil. Serv: Lt, W.Va. State Guard, 44-47. Mem: United Nat. Asn. of Post Off. Clerks (nat. v.pres, 50-58, pres, W.Va. State Br, 58-61); Elks; Moose; Sons of Union Vet. of the Civil War. Rel: United Methodist. Mailing Add: 225 Howard St, Clarksburg, W.Va. 26301.

MAXWELL, CLINTON WILLIAM R
b. Grand Forks, N.Dak, 2/22/27; s. P.E. Maxwell and Orpha Clinton M; m. 12/25/52 to Lillian Mattson; c. twins, Clinton W. and Sally D, Sandra L. and Jana K. Educ: Univ. of Minn, B.S. in Civil Eng, 51. Polit. & Govt. Pos: Chmn, Lake Co. Rep. Cmt, Minn, 64-68. Bus. & Prof. Pos: Civil engr, Reserve Mining Co, 51- Mil. Serv: Entered as Pvt, Army, 44, released as Sgt, 47. Mem: Mason (32°): Shrine. Rel: Episcopal. Mailing Add: 33 Evans, Silver Bay, Minn. 55614. (1967)

MAXWELL, DIAMOND AI R
b. Concord, N.H, 4/6/93; s. George Herbert Maxwell and Mary Ellen Brooks M; wid; c. Mary Ellen (Mrs. Chagnon), Jean Andrews (Mrs. Harford), Robert Austin, Janice Ruth (Mrs. Robinson) and Diamond A. Educ: Pub. schs. Polit. & Govt. Pos: N.H. State Rep, retired. Bus. & Prof. Pos: Printing and publishing. Rel: Protestant. Mailing Add: 39 Main St, Henniker, N.H. 03242.

MAXWELL, JAMES LIVINGSTON D
b. Tulsa, Okla, 5/12/26; s. William Raymond Maxwell and Mary Pauline O'Donnell M. Educ: Okla. State Univ, B.A, 50; Sigma Chi. Polit. & Govt. Pos: Mayor of Tulsa, Okla. and mem. bd. dirs, Utility bd, mem, City Cmn, Metrop. Area Planning Cmn, Park and Recreation Cmn. and bd. dirs, Airport Authority, 58-66; consult, U.S. Econ. Develop. Admin, 67-68; private consult, 68- Mailing Add: 4124 E. 46th Place, Tulsa, Okla. 74135.

MAXWELL, ROBERT HAMILTON R
Chmn, Rep. Exec. Cmt.
b. Atmore, Ala, 9/25/27; s. William Randolph Maxwell and Mary Talmadge; m. 8/18/50 to Hattie Mallory King; c. Richard King, David Hamilton. Educ: Univ. Ala, B.S, 49, LL.B, 51; Phi Eta Sigma; Sigma Chi; Phi Alpha Delta. Polit. & Govt. Pos: Secy, Escambia Co. Rep. Exec. Cmt, Ala, 62-66, chmn, 66-; mem. nominating cmt, Ala. Rep. State Conv, 66 and chmn, credentials cmt, 68;

mem, Ala. Rep. Exec. Cmt, 66- Mil. Serv: Entered as Pvt, Marine Corps, 44, released as Pfc, 46, after serv. in Cent. Pac. and N.China Theaters. Mem: Lions; Am. Legion. Rel: Baptist. Legal Res: 201 E. Oak St, Atmore, Ala. 36502. Mailing Add: P.O. Box 587, Atmore, Ala. 36502.

MAXWELL, STEPHEN LLOYD R
b. 1921. Educ: Univ. Minn, 39-40 & 46-47; Morehouse Col, B.A, 42; St. Paul Col. of Law, B.S.L, 53. Polit. & Govt. Pos: Asst, attorney, Ramsey Co, Minn, 59-64; corp. counsel, St. Paul, 64-66; Cand. for U.S. Rep, 66; Munic. Court judge, St. Paul, 67-68 and Dist. Court judge, 68- Bus. & Prof. Pos: Zone dep. collector, Bur. of Internal Revenue, 45-46, auditor, 48; acct, St. Paul & Munic. Auditorium, 48-51; spec. agent, investr, Off. Price Stabilization, 51-53; Attorney in pvt. practice, 53-59. Mil. Serv: Coast Guard, World War II; Comdr, Naval Res. Mem: Bd. of Dirs, St. Paul Chap, Am. Red Cross; YMCA; St. Paul United Fund and Coun, Inc. Mailing Add: 882 Carroll Ave, St. Paul, Minn. 55104.

MAY, ALFRED A. R
Chmn, First Cong. Dist. Rep. Party, Mich.
b. Wash, D.C, 2/24/06; s. Isadore May and Mina David M; m. 11/24/28 to Sylvia S. Scheer; c. Nancy and Alan A. Educ: Univ. Md, B.A, 24; Nat. Univ. LL.B, 29; Phi Sigma Delta. Polit. & Govt. Pos: Spec. agent, Fed. Bur. of Invest, 29-31; Asst. U.S. Attorney, 31-33; chmn, Loyalty Investigating Cmt, Detroit, Mich; chmn, First Cong. Dist, Rep. Party, 61-; Wayne Co. Pub. Adminstr, 65; del, Rep. Nat. Conv, 68. Mil. Serv: Chief Investr, Army Air Corps, 42-45, serv. in Intel. Unit, U.S, Presidential Citation. Mem: Mich. State and Fed. Bar Asns; Probus Club; pres, Detroit Round Table for Catholics, Jews and Protestants; Nat. Conf. of Christians and Jews, Inc. Award of Merit, Weizmann Inst. of Sci, Rehovoth, Israel; Night of Charity Award, Maryglade Col; Builder of Brotherhood Award, Nat. Conf. of Christians and Jews. Rel: Jewish. Mailing Add: 17610 Fairway Dr, Detroit, Mich. 48221.

MAY, BERNICE HUBBARD D
City Councilman, Berkeley, Calif.
b. Colusa Co, Calif, 9/29/97; d. William Henry Hubbard and Virginia Milton H; m. 9/12/40 to Samuel C. May, wid. Educ: Univ. of Calif, Berkeley, A.B, 19; Phi Beta Kappa; Alpha Omicron Pi; Prytanean Honor Soc. Polit. & Govt. Pos: Exec. secy. exten. div, Univ. Calif, 23-40, asst. dir, Eng. Sci. & Mgt. War Training, 41-45; cmnr, San Francisco Bay Conserv. and Develop. Cmn; trustee, Berkeley Pub. Libr; city councilman, Berkeley, Calif, 59-; mem. exec. cmt, Asn. Bay Area Govt, 68-; cmnr, Bay Area Transportation Study Cmn, 68-69. Mem: Sierra Club; Calif. Conserv. Coun; League of Women Voters Calif.(state pres, 47-49); Am. Asn. Univ. Women; NAACP; Women's Faculty Club, Univ. Calif. Legal Res: 16 Roble Rd, Berkeley, Calif. 94705. Mailing Add: City Hall, Berkeley, Calif. 94704.

MAY, CATHERINE BARNES R
U.S. Rep, Wash.
b. Yakima, Wash, 5/18/14; d. Charles H. Barnes and Pauline V. B; m. 1/18/43 to James O. May; c. James Collins and Melinda Ellen. Educ: Univ. Wash, M.Ed, 36; Alpha Chi Omega. Polit. & Govt. Pos: Wash. State Rep, 52-58; U.S. Rep, Wash, Fourth Dist, 59- Mem: Wash. Asn. for Retarded Children; Bus. & Prfnl. Women; Young Rep. Fedn; hon. mem, Zonta, Altrusa and Soroptimist Clubs. Rel: Episcopal. Legal Res: P.O. Box 1666, Yakima, Wash. 98901. Mailing Add: 2332 Rayburn House Office Bldg, Washington, D.C. 20515.

MAY, CLARENCE EDWARD D
b. Weyers Cave, Va, 4/12/03; s. William Henry May and Eliza Jane Rankin M; m. 2/2/28 to Frances Zoll; c. Clarence Edward, Jr. Educ: Bridgewater Col, B.A, 24; Univ. Va, M.A, 31; Tau Kappa Alpha; Pi Delta Epsilon; Lambda; Valedictorian of both high sch. and col. classes. Polit. & Govt. Pos: Councilman, Bridgewater Town Coun, Va, 56-58; mayor, Bridgewater, 58-68; del, Nat. and State Dem. Conv, 64; precinct chmn, Bridgewater Dem. Party and committeeman, Rockingham Co. Dem. Party. Bus. & Prof. Pos: Teacher Eng, Cristobal High Sch, 41-42; asst. commandant, Fork Union Mil. Acad, 42-44; prin, Copeland Park Sch, 44-45 and Culpeper High Sch, 45-46; prof. Eng. and dir. pub. rels, Bridgewater Col, 46-68. Mem: S.Atlantic Mod. Lang. Asn; Mason. Rel: Protestant Episcopal. Mailing Add: 421 E. College, Bridgewater, Va. 22812.

MAY, EDGAR
b. Zurich, Switz; 6/27/29, naturalized U.S. citizen, 54; s. Ferdinand May and Renee Bloch M; wid. Educ: Northwest. Univ, B.J, with highest distinction, 57; Kappa Tau Alpha. Polit. & Govt. Pos: Mem, Pres. Task Force War Against Poverty, 64; asst. dir, Off. Econ. Opportunity, 64-68; spec. adv. to U.S. Ambassador to France, 68- Bus. & Prof. Pos: Reporter, ed, Bellows Falls, Vt. Times, 51-53; reporter, Chicago Tribune, 55-57; free lance writer, Europe, 57; reporter, Buffalo Evening News, 58-61; dir, Pub. Welfare Projs, State Charities Aid Asn, 62-64. Mil. Serv: Cpl, Army, 53-55. Publ: The Wasted Americans, 64. Page One Award, Buffalo Newspaper Guild, 58; Walter O. Bingham Award, 59; Pulitzer Prize for local reporting, 61; Merit Award, Northwest. Univ. Alumni Asn, 62. Mailing Add: Muckross, Springfield, Vt. 05156.

MAY, EDWIN HYLAND, JR. R
b. Hartford, Conn, 5/28/24; s. Edwin Hyland May and Dorothy Wells Hannum M; m. 7/19/47 to Jean Blease; c. Edwin H, III, Laura Wells and Lisa Barrie. Educ: Wesleyan Univ; Olin Scholar; Mystical Seven; Chi Psi. Polit. & Govt. Pos: U.S. Rep, Conn, 57-58; chmn, Conn. State Rep. Party, 58-62; chmn, Northeast. State Rep. Chmn. Asn, 59-62; Cand. for Gov, Conn, 62; cand, U.S. Sen, Conn, 68; alternate del, Rep. Nat. Conv, 68. Bus. & Prof. Pos: Partner, R.C. Knox and Co, 48-56; pres, May, Potter and Murphy Inc, 56- Mil. Serv: Entered as Pvt, Army Air Force, 42, released as 2nd Lt, 45, after serv. in Fourth Air Force; Pilot's Wings. Mem: Past pres, Hartford and Conn. Jr. C. of C; U.S. Jaycees (v.pres, 54); Gr. Hartford C. of C.(dir); Conn. C. of C; Wethersfield Country Club; Originator of Prfnl. Golfers Asn. Ins. City Open Golf Tourney. Rel: Protestant. Legal Res: 802 Prospect St, Wethersfield, Conn. 06109. Mailing Add: 1 American Row, Hartford, Conn. 06103.

MAY, JAMES WOODROW D
b. Marysville, Calif, 1/20/19; s. Harry May and Inez Bothwell Raye M; m. 11/1/47 to Patricia Joy Criss; c. Robert Lee and Lyle Bradley. Educ: Yuba Jr. Col, $1\frac{1}{2}$ years. Polit. & Govt. Pos: Mem, Sierra Co. Dem. Cent. Cmt, Calif, 62-65 and chmn, 65-68. Mem: PTA; Little and Babe Ruth League Baseball; Boy Scouts; Cub Scouts; 4-H Club; Lumber and Sawmill Workers, AFL. Mailing Add: Box 561, Loyalton, Calif. 96118.

MAY, JOHN AMASA D
b. Graniteville, S.C, 10/30/08; s. John Amasa May, Sr. and Martha Randall M; m. 1/6/37 to Louise McCreary Ariail; c. Pamela Amasa. Educ: Wofford Col, A.B, 31; Harvard Univ. Law Sch, 31-32; Univ. S.C. Law Sch, LL.B, 34; Phi Delta Phi; Sigma Alpha Epsilon. Polit. & Govt. Pos: Judge of City Court, Aiken, S.C, 34-35; S.C. State Rep, Aiken Co, 35-66; Col. on Staff of Gov. Olin D. Johnston and Ransome J. Williams; mil. secy, Gov. S.C; chief, Div. of Outdoor Recreation, S.C, 66-; app. by President Johnson, mem, Nat. Adv. Coun. on Historic Preservation, currently. Bus. & Prof. Pos: Sr. mem, Law Firm, May, Rich and Grant, 53-60; pres, Fedelity Home, Finance Co, 53-60. Mil. Serv: Entered as 2nd Lt, Army, 41, released as Maj, 46, after serv. in Inf, ETO and War Crime Trials, 43-46; Maj, Army Res, 45; Bronze Star; Pre-Pearl Harbor, German Occupation and Good Conduct Medals. Publ: South Carolina Secedes, Univ. of S.C. Press, 60; History of St. Johns Methodist Church, Book Shop Press, 62; Tall Pines, Tidwell Press, 64. Mem: Knight of Sovereign Mil. Order, Temple of Jerusalem; hon. assoc. mem, UDC; Bd. of Dirs, South. Heritage Found; past comdr, Dept. of S.C, Am. Legion, 55-56, nat. historian, 69-; past dist. gov, Lions Clubs of S.C, 40-41; Omar Temple Shrine; Mason; VFW; past pres, Aiken C. of C, 55-60; Nat. comdr-in-chief, Sons of Confederate Vet; past comdr-in-chief, Order of Stars and Bars; chmn, S.C. Confederate War Centennial Cmn. Nat. Award of Distinction, U.S. Civil War Centennial Cmn. Rel: Methodist. Mailing Add: Mayfields, Aiken, S.C. 29801.

MAY, RONALD ALAN R
Gen. Coun, Rep. Party, Ark.
b. Waterloo, Iowa, 9/8/28; s. John W. May and Elsie Finlayson M; m. 8/18/50 to Naomi Gray; c. Sarah, Jonathan, Andrew and Rachel. Educ: Univ. Iowa, B.A, 50; Vanderbilt Univ, LL.B, 53; Phi Beta Kappa; Order of the Coif. Polit. & Govt. Pos: Gen. counsel, Rep. Party, Ark, 69- Bus. & Prof. Pos: Partner, Wright, Lindsey & Jennings, attorneys, Ark, 58- Mil. Serv: Entered as Pvt, Army, 46, released as Cpl, 47, after serving in 7th Div, Korea, 46-47. Mem: Pulaski Co, Ark, and Am. Bar Asns; Top of the Rock Club; Country Club of Little Rock. Rel: Episcopal. Legal Res: 4014 S. Lookout, Little Rock, Ark. 72205. Mailing Add: 1600 Tower Bldg, Little Rock, Ark. 72201.

MAY, STEPHANIE MIDDLETON D
Treas, Caucus of Conn. Dem.
b. New York, N.Y, 4/16/28; d. Thomas Hazelhurst Middleton and Ruth Stephens M; m. 10/21/49 to John Walter May; c. Elizabeth and Geoffrey. Educ: Stephens Col, 2 years; Columbia Univ, 1 year. Polit. & Govt. Pos: Bd. mem, Nat. Cmt. for Sane Nuclear Policy, 58-68; chmn, Conn. Dissenting Dem, 67; secy-treas, McCarthy for Pres, Conn, 67-68; del, Dem. Nat. Conv, 68; treas, Caucus of Conn. Dem, 69- Bus. & Prof. Pos: Prfnl. portrait sculptor, currently. Mem: Fel, Royal Soc. Arts; Conn. Acad. Fine Arts; Jr. League of Hartford; United World Federalists; Another Mother for Peace. Sculptor of the Eleanor Roosevelt Peace Award. Rel: Episcopal. Mailing Add: 113 Duncaster Rd, Bloomfield, Conn. 06002.

MAY, TIMOTHY JAMES D
b. Denver, Colo, 8/3/32; s. Thomas H. May (deceased) and Helen O'Conner M; m. 8/24/57 to Monica Anita Gross; c. Stephanie, Maureen, Cynthia, Timothy, Jr. and Anthony. Educ: Catholic Univ. of Am., B.A, 54; Georgetown Law Center, LL.B, 57 and LL.M, 60; Blue Key; Phi Kappa; Phi Delta Phi. Polit. & Govt. Pos: Acting chief counsel, Senate Subcmt. on Stockpiling and consult, Exec. Off. of the President, 61-63; managing dir, Fed. Maritime Cmn, 63-66; gen. counsel, Post Off. Dept, 66-69. Bus. & Prof. Pos: Law clerk, Judge Danaher, U.S. Court of Appeals, D.C, 57-58; assoc. mem, Covington & Burling, 58-61; partner, Patton, Blow, Verrill, Brand and Boggs, 69- Publ: 'The Status of Federal Maritime Commission Shipping Regulation Under Principles of International Law,' Georgetown Law Jour, 3/66. Mem: Am, Fed. and Inter-Am. Bar Asns; Jr. C. of C; Washington Bd. of Trade. Rel: Roman Catholic. Legal Res: Denver, Colo. Mailing Add: 5611 Namakagan Rd, Sumner, Md. 20016.

MAY, WALLACE G. R
Chmn, Lenawee Co. Rep. Cmt, Mich.
b. Hart, Mich, 12/23/17; s. Max G. May and Maud Weirich M; m. 9/28/41 to Eunice Weaver; c. Garry and Debra. Educ: Mich. State Univ, D.V.M, 41; Alpha Psi. Polit. & Govt. Pos: Precinct work in state elec, Mich, 62 & 64; chmn, Lenawee Co. Rep. Cmt, Mich, 65-; citizens adv. coun. mem. to Adrian Bd. Educ, 68-69. Mem: PTA (counc. chmn, 67-69). Rel: Baptist. Mailing Add: 4974 W. Toledo Rd, Adrian, Mich. 49221.

MAY, WILLIAM J. S. D
Wash. State Rep.
b. England, 1902; m. to Pearl M; c. Three. Educ: High Sch; Spec. courses in adver. and elec. Polit. & Govt. Pos: Wash. State Rep, currently; exec. secy, Spokane Labor Coun. Mem: Elks. Mailing Add: W. 711 Waverly Pl, Spokane, Wash. 99205. (1967)

MAYBANK, BURNET R. D
Chmn, Charleston Co. Dem. Party, S.C.
b. Charleston, S.C, 5/2/24; s. Burnet R. Maybank and Elizabeth Myers M; m. 1/27/48 to Marion Mitchell; c. Burnet R. and Marion M. Educ: Citadel, B.S, 47; Univ. of S.C. Law Sch, LL.B, 50; Phi Alpha Delta; Sigma Alpha Epsilon. Polit. & Govt. Pos: S.C. State Rep, 52-58; Lt. Gov, S.C, 58-62; chmn, Charleston Co. Dem. Party, S.C, currently. Bus. & Prof. Pos: Attorney-at-law. Mil. Serv: Entered as Cadet, Army, 42, released as 1st Lt, 45; after serv. in 394th Heavy Bomb Group, Eighth Air Force, ETO; Air Medal; Distinguished Flying Cross. Mem: Am. and S.C. Bar Asns; Am. Trial Lawyers Asn; VFW; Sertona. Civil Air Patrol. Rel: Episcopal. Legal Res: 2 Water St, Charleston, S.C. 29401. Mailing Add: 31 Broad St, Charleston, S.C. 29402.

MAYBERRY, CLIFTON E. R
Chmn, Lawrence Co. Rep. Cmt, Mo.
b. Highlandville, Mo, 9/9/09; s. Frank Mayberry and Betty Brown M; m. 1/1/32 to Anna Delphe Emlet; c. Lois Ann and George Franklin. Educ: High

Sch. Polit. & Govt. Pos: Judge, East. Dist, Lawrence Co, Mo, 50-54; chmn, Lawrence Co. Rep. Cmt, 58- Bus. & Prof. Pos: Owner and operator, Mayberry's Supermarket, 36-; owner and operator, Mayberry's Floral & Nursery. Mil. Serv: Pvt, Mo. Nat. Guard Medics Corps, 44-46. Mem: Rotary. Rel: Baptist. Legal Res: Route 3, Mt. Vernon, Mo. 65712. Mailing Add: Box 411, Mt. Vernon, Mo. 65712.

MAYBERRY, D. VINCENT D
Iowa State Rep.
b. Atlantic, Iowa, 1916; m. 1939 to Betty Jean Brobeil; c. Merilla and Gwen. Educ: Morningside Col; Univ. of Iowa. Polit. & Govt. Pos: Iowa State Rep, currently. Bus. & Prof. Pos: Former newspaper publisher; formerly with Fed. Dept. of Justice; poultry processor. Mem: Lions; Am. Legion; C. of C. Rel: Catholic. Mailing Add: 2802 16th Ave. N, Ft. Dodge, Iowa 50501. (1967)

MAYBORN, FRANK WILLIS D
b. Akron, Ohio, 12/7/03; s. Ward C. Mayborn and Nellie C. Welton M; m. 4/20/47 to Wythel Killen. Educ: Univ. Colo, B.A, 27. Polit. & Govt. Pos: Mem, Tex. State Dem. Exec. Cmt, 48; del, Dem. Nat. Conv, 68. Bus. & Prof. Pos: Employee, Dallas News, 26 and North Tex. Traction Co, Ft. Worth, 27-29; bus. mgr, Temple Tel, Tex, 29-45, ed, pres. and publisher, 45-; operator and pres, Radio Sta. KTEM, Temple, 36-; pres. and dir, Bell Broadcasting Co, Temple, 36-, Bell Publishing Co, Temple, 45- and Sherman Dem. Co, 45-; owner, Sherman Dem, Tex, 45-; founder and operator Radio Sta. WMAK, Nashville, 47-54; pres, part owner and operator, Killeen Herald, Tex, 52-; pres. and dir, Killeen Herald Publ. Co, Tex, 52-; pres, part owner and operator, Taylor Press, Taylor, Tex, 59-; pres. and dir, Taylor Publ. Co, Tex, 59-, Channel 6, Inc, 62-, FWM Properties, 65- and Co. Developers, Inc, 67- Mil. Serv: Entered as Pvt, Army, 42, released as Maj, 45 after serv. in ETO; Bronze Star Medal. Mem: dir, 1st Nat. Bank, Temple; dir, Temple Indust. Found.(pres, 63); mem. adv. coun, Univ. Tex. Journalism Found, 64-66; mem. adm. develop. bd, Tex. Indust. Cmn; mem. A&M Adv. Coun, Dept. of Journalism, 59; Baylor Univ. Broadcast Coun, 64-65; bd. dir, Temple Boys Choir, 69; bd. dir, Waco Symphony Asn, 68-69; adv. bd, Scott and White Hosp. Found, Temple; Tex. State Hist. Surv. Cmt, 66-69; Tex. Hist. Found, 67 & 68; Ft. Hood Civilian Adv. Cmt, 63-; Am. Soc. Newspaper Ed; Tex. Daily Press League (dir, Tex. Sunday Comic Sect); Temple C. of C.(dir. and past pres); Retail Merchants Asn. Temple; Tex. Daily Newspaper Asn.(past pres); South. Newspaper Publishers Asn.(pres, 62, chmn. bd, 63); Phi Kappa Psi; Sigma Delta Chi; Mason; Wash. Nat. Press Club; Ft. Worth Advert. Club (past pres); Dallas Athletic Club; Temple Co. Club; Headliner Club; Dallas Lancers Club; The President's Club, 66-69. Recipient Outstanding Citizens Award, Temple, Tex, 48; Tex. Award for Outstanding Serv. VFW, 55. Rel: Presbyterian, Deacon. Legal Res: 603 W. Shell Ave, Temple, Tex. 76501. Mailing Add: 17 S. Third, Temple, Tex. 76501.

MAYER, ANITA ENGELKING D
Chmn, Austin Co. Dem. Party, Tex.
b. Wallis, Tex, 11/20/14; d. William George John Engelking and Mattie Louise Sprain E; m. 12/30/35 to Bruno Martin Mayer; c. William Martin. Educ: S.W. Tex. Col, 33-35. Polit. & Govt. Pos: Dem. chmn, Precinct 15, Tex, 64-66; chmn, Austin Co. Dem. Party, 66- Bus. & Prof. Pos: Bank teller, River Oaks Bank, Houston, Tex, 52-69. Rel: Lutheran. Mailing Add: Box 236, Wallis, Tex. 77485.

MAYER, KATHARINE R
Mem, N.Mex. State Rep. Finance Cmt.
b. Santa Fe, N.Mex, 5/16/05; d. George Harvey Van Stone and Mary Robert Hurt V; m. 2/28/36 to Walter Max Mayer; c. Thomas Walter and James William. Educ: Colo. Col, grad. 28, summa cum laude; Phi Beta Kappa. Polit. & Govt. Pos: Del, Rep. Nat. Conv, 44, 48 & 66; past mem, Rep. State, Co, City Cent. Cmts, 20 years; state co-chmn, Citizens for Eisenhower, 52; mem. bd. dir, N.Mex. Pub. Welfare Dept, 52-56; mem. bd. regents, N.Mex. State Hosp, 58-60; mem. and secy. bd. of regents, Mus. of N.Mex, 8 years; v.chmn, N.Mex. Coun. on Crime and Delinquency; mem, N.Mex. State Rep. Finance Cmt, currently. Mem: Founder and mem, Maternal and Child Health Center, 32 years (four times past pres); founder and 27 years mem. bd, Santa Fe Boys Club; past pres, Santa Fe Chap, N.Mex. Heart Asn; Opera Asn. of N.Mex.(pres, 64, 65, 66 & 67, mem. bd, 8 years). Rel: Episcopal. Mailing Add: 132 E. De Vargas St, Santa Fe, N.Mex. 87501.

MAYER, WILLIAM HUGHES R
b. St. Louis, Mo, 12/4/21; s. Albert A. Mayer and Idabelle Hughes M; m. 10/23/42 to Janet Clark; c. Susan L.(Mrs. Michael Randall), Katherine H. and Margaret H. Educ: Univ. Wis, B.A, 47; Phi Eta Sigma. Polit. & Govt. Pos: Treas, Multnomah Co. Cent. Cmt, Ore, 60; admin. asst. to U.S. Sen. Robert W. Packwood, Ore, 69- Bus. & Prof. Pos: Acct, Haskins and Sells, CPA's, 47-48; off. mgr, Gabriel Boiler Co, 49-53, Soule Steel Co, Portland, Ore, 53-54; secy-treas, Donald M. Drake, Co, 54-69. Mil. Serv: Entered as Pvt, Army, 43, released as T-4, 46 after serv. in 178th U.S. General Hospital SHAEF, 44-46. Mem: Multnomah Athletic Club. Rel: Presbyterian. Mailing Add: 6800 Algonquin Ave, Bethesda, Md. 20034.

MAYER, WILLIAM SNYDER R
Conn. State Rep.
b. West Haven, Conn, 11/7/24; s. Stanley B. Mayer and Aldenia Snyder M; m. 7/21/45 to Florence Scranton; c. Wendy R, Alan S. and Robin E. Educ: St. Louis Univ, B.S, 48. Polit. & Govt. Pos: Chmn, E. Granby Planning & Zoning Cmn, 54-62; mem, E. Granby Rep. Town Cmt, 54-; E. Granby rep, Capitol Regional Planning Agency, 57-59; Conn. State Rep, currently. Mil. Serv: Entered as Pvt, Army Air Force, 43, released as 1st Lt, 45, after serv. as Pilot, Italy, 44-45; Air Medal with five Clusters. Mem: C.of C; Grange. Rel: Congregational. Mailing Add: Melody Lane, East Granby, Conn. 06026.

MAYERS, THOMAS CRAWFORD R
b. Boston, Mass, 3/21/09; s. Walter James Mayers and Alice Crawford M; m. 11/9/30 to Alice M. Henry; c. Thomas C, Jr, Mary Alice, Lawrence M, Marjorie A, Paul M, Ruth M, Eileen, Rosemary and Brenda. Educ: Boston Latin Sch; Harvard Col, B.A, 30. Polit. & Govt. Pos: Former mayor, Stamford, Conn. Bus. & Prof. Pos: Personnel mgr, Bloomingdale's, 47-48, mgr. New Rochelle Br, 48-53, Stamford Br, 54-62 and dir. br. store develop, 62-63. Mem: K. of C.(4°); dir, Stamford Family & Children's Servs; dir, Stamford Chap, Am. Red Cross; hon. mem, Rotary. Rel: Roman Catholic. Mailing Add: 64 Hope St, Stamford, Conn. 06906. (1967)

MAYFIELD, BOBBY M. D
b. 1926. Educ: N.Mex. State Univ, B.S. and M.S. Polit. & Govt. Pos: N.Mex. State Rep, 61-69. Bus. & Prof. Pos: Farmer. Mil. Serv: Pilot, Strategic Air Command, 11 years. Mem: Mason. Rel: Protestant. Mailing Add: P.O. Box 458, Mesilla Park, N.Mex. 88046. (1967)

MAYFIELD, FRANK HENDERSON, JR. R
Ohio State Rep.
b. Cincinnati, Ohio, 7/20/39; s. Frank Henderson Mayfield and Queenee Jones M; m. 1/30/58 to Judith Radnbaugh; c. Deborah Francis, David Glen, Diana Lee and Frank Henderson III. Educ: Univ. N.Carolina, Chapel Hill, A.B; Univ. Cincinnati Law Sch, 2 years; Chase Law Sch, LL.B; Phi Alpha Delta. Polit. & Govt. Pos: Mem, City Planning Cmn, Cincinnati, Ohio, 66-67; Ohio State Rep, 67th Dist, 68- Rel: Methodist. Legal Res: 1280 Hershel Ave, Cincinnati, Ohio 45208. Mailing Add: 280 Central Trust Bldg, Cincinnati, Ohio 45202.

MAYHALL, JAMES ELWIN R
Chmn, Cumberland Co. Rep. Cent. Cmt, Ill.
b. Cumberland Co, Ill, 12/25/23; s. William Mayhall and Myrtle Borror M; m. 5/17/46 to Marilyn L. Claybaugh; c. James David and Teri Lynn. Educ: Neoga Twp. High Sch, Ill. Polit. & Govt. Pos: City clerk, Neoga, Ill, 48-50; co. chmn, Citizens for Nixon, 60; chmn, Cumberland Co. Rep. Cent. Cmt, 64- Bus. & Prof. Pos: Agent, Metrop. Life Ins. Co, 53-55; asst. mgr, Frank Kern Mfg. Co, Neoga, Ill, 55- Mil. Serv: Entered as Pvt, Army, 42, released as Cpl, 46, after serv. in ETO; Am. Campaign Medal; European-African-Mid. East. Theater Ribbon with 3 Bronze Battle Stars; Good Conduct and Victory Medals. Mem: Rep. Co. Chmn. Asn. of Ill; Am. Legion; Odd Fellows. Rel: Presbyterian. Legal Res: 736 Pine Ave, Neoga, Ill. 62447. Mailing Add: 118 E. Sixth St, Neoga, Ill. 62447.

MAYHALL, ROY D
Mem, Ala. Dem. State Exec. Cmt.
b. Haleyville, Ala, 4/28/01; s. Wesley Vowell Mayhall and Mary Williams M; m. 9/3/22 to Louise Alcott Roberson; c. Doris (Mrs. Roberts), Travis Earl and Reba (Mrs. Brown). Educ: Univ. Ala, LL.B, 23. Polit. & Govt. Pos: City Attorney, Haleyville, Ala, 27-43; solicitor, Winston Co, 31-43; mem, Ala. Dem. State Exec. Cmt, 33-, chmn, 55-59 & 63-67; gov, Dist. 34, 36-37; Ala. State Rep, 38-42; chmn, Winston Co. Dem. Exec. Cmt, 39-43; circuit judge, 14th Judicial Circuit, 43-65; del, Dem. Nat. Conv, 60 & 68; supernumerary circuit judge, 65- Mem: Lions Int. Rel: Baptist. Legal Res: 818 Eighth Ave, Jasper, Ala. 35501. Mailing Add: P.O. Box 847, Jasper, Ala. 35501.

MAYHEW, ELDON JAY R
b. Trousdale, Kans, 11/1/16; s. Allen A. Mayhew and Mary Wood M; m. 8/3/38 to Helen Moore; c. John D, Robert J. and Allen E. Educ: Kans. State Col, 34-38; Colo. Sch. of Mines, Prof. Eng. Degree in Geol, 41; Phi Delta Theta; Mortar & Ball; ROTC. Polit. & Govt. Pos: Committeeman, Co. Rep. Cmt, 55-63; committeeman and del, Co. Rep. Conv, 57-63; del, State Rep. Conv, 63-67; Utah State Rep, 63-67, mem, Appropriations Cmt, Utah House of Rep; mem. adv. bd, State Geol. Survey, 63- and State Tech. Serv. Cmn, 66- Bus. & Prof. Pos: Proj. engr, Colo. Sch. Mines Research Found; opers. mgr, Great Lakes Carbon Corp, 46-50, Owner mgr, Utah Mud Co, 50-55, Mayhew Engrs, 50-, Apex Exploration Co. and Empire Surveys, 52-57 and Moab Brine Co, 60-; v.pres, Skyline Labs, Wheat Ridge, Colo, 68-; v.pres, Terrasearch, Inc, 68- Publ: 'Perlite, the New Industrial Mineral,' Int. Mining Corp, 6/51; 'Concentrated Subsurface Brines in the Moab Region, Utah,' Utah Geol. Survey, 6/65. Mem: Colo. and Utah Mining Asns; Am. Inst. Mining Engrs; Am. Asn. of Petrol Geols; Am. Geophys. Union; Am. Asn. for the Adv. of Sci; Am. Inst. Prof. Geologists; Jeggerson Co. Indust. Develop. Cmt; Elks; Moab Golf and Country Club; C. of C; bd. dir, Colo. Sch. Mines Alumni Asn; Rolling Hills Country Club. Licensed contractor and surveyor and certified prof. geologist and engr; Mo. Valley 145 Wrestling Champion, 37; Southwest. Intercollegiate Champion, 36; Rocky Mt. Intercollegiate Champion, 38. Rel: Episcopal. Mailing Add: 600 S. Youngfield Court, Denver, Colo. 80228.

MAYHEW, HARRY ENNIS D
b. Milford, Del, 4/16/06; s. James Henry Mayhew and Delila A. Deputy M; m. 7/28/28 to Frances L. Abbott; c. Harry E, Jr, William J. and Susan A. Educ: High sch. and exten. courses in transportation and pub. speaking. Polit. & Govt. Pos: Del. State Rep. and Speaker, House of Rep, 54-58; Del. State Sen, 62; acct, Joint Finance Cmt, Del. State Legis; mem, State Forestry Cmn, Del, currently. Bus. & Prof. Pos: V.pres, Victor Lynn Lines, Inc, 46; owner-operator, Milford Ice & Coal Co, Del, currently. Mem: Rotary; Mason (32°); Shrine; Consistory; Scottish Rite; Tall Cedars. Rel: Protestant. Legal Res: 602 N. Walnut St, Milford, Del. 19963. Mailing Add: P.O. Box 304, Milford, Del. 19963.

MAYNARD, OLIVIA BENEDICT 'LIBBY' D
Recording secy, Mich. State Dem. Cent. Cmt.
b. Cincinnati, Ohio, 6/24/36; d. Samuel Benedict and Elizabeth Carruthers B; div; c. Elizabeth, Benjamin and John. Educ: Sweet Briar Col, 54-57; George Wash. Univ, B.A, 58; Univ. Mich, currently; Student Govt. Exec. Bd; Bum Chums; Choir; World Affairs Club. Polit. & Govt. Pos: Recording secy, Mich. State Dem. Cent. Cmt, 67-; del, Dem. Nat. Conv, 68; mem, Mich. Polit. Reform Cmn, 69; mem, Genesee Co. Dem. Exec. Cmt. and Women's Div. Exec. Cmt, 69- Mem: Am. Civil Liberties Union; Am. for Dem. Action; Flint Urban League; Flint League Women Voters. Rel: Episcopal. Legal Res: 2026 Calumet, Flint, Mich. 48503. Mailing Add: 900 W. Michigan Ave, Lansing, Mich. 48915.

MAYNARD, PAUL JOSEPH R
Chmn, Pawtucket Rep. City Cmt, R.I.
b. Pawtucket, R.I, 7/16/41; s. John H. Maynard and Helen Laffey M; m. 11/30/63 to M. Janice Ford; c. M. Kim. Educ: Univ. R.I, 3 years; Bryant Col, 1 year. Polit. & Govt. Pos: Charter mem. and mem. nominating cmt, Pawtucket Young Rep. Club, R.I, 65, pres, 68, chmn. bd, 69; mem. and Fourth Ward secy, Pawtucket Rep. City Cmt, 67-, chmn, 68-; mem, R.I. State Rep.

Cent. Cmt, 69- Bus. & Prof. Pos: Sales rep, Hamilton Mgt. Corp, Denver, Colo, 64-65; sales rep, Hudson Pulp & Paper Corp, N.Y.C, 65-66, sr. salesman, 66-69 and asst. dist. mgr, 69- Mil. Serv: Entered as Seaman Recruit, Navy, 59, released as Hospitalman 3/C, 62, after serv. in Physical Therapy Dept, Newport Naval Hosp. Publ: 'Service to Humanity,' Rhody Jaycee, 8/65. Mem: Knights of the Grip; Pawtucket LeFoyer Club (past state chmn, past state dir, and past local dir); United Cerebral Palsy Campaign Cmt. (city chmn, 64 & 65); Meat Cutters and Food Store Workers (Past Shop Steward); St. Mary's Holy Name Soc. Spoke and Spark Plug Awards, Jaycees; Speak Up Jaycee Award, Pawtucket Jaycees; Speak Up Jaycees Award and Best Proj. of the Year Award, 66, R.I. Jaycees. Rel: Roman Catholic. Mailing Add: 128 Clifford St, Pawtucket, R.I. 02860.

MAYNARD, RICHARD EDWARDS D
Committeeman, Ill. Dem. Cent. Cmt.
b. Monmouth, Ill, 1/15/33; s. Clayton Dale Maynard and Sydnie Edwards M; m. 8/23/53 to Jennievee Ola Blackman; c. Richard Edwards, Jr, Ronald Eugene, Roger Eric, Robert Eldon and Jane Elisabeth. Educ: West. Ill. Univ, 2/3 year. Polit. & Govt. Pos: Sheriff, Mercer Co, Ill, 58-62; precinct committeeman, Mercer Precinct 2, 62-; supt. of Veterans Assistance, Mercer Co, 67-; committeeman, Ill. Dem. Cent. Cmt, 44th Dist, 68- Bus. & Prof. Pos: Ins. and real estate broker, Ford & Maynard Agency, Aledo, Ill, 63- Mil. Serv: Entered as Pfc, Army, 52, released as Cpl, 53, after serv. in 44th FA Bn, Fourth Inf. Div, Europe. Mem: AF&AM, Aledo; VFW, Mercer Co; Am. Legion; Mason (32°), Moline Valley; 40 et 8, Rock Island; Aledo Jr. C. of C. Rel: Methodist. Mailing Add: 407 S.E. Fifth Ave, Aledo, Ill. 61231.

MAYNARD, ROBERT RAYMOND D
Mem, Dem. Town Cmt, Bristol, Conn.
b. Bristol, Conn, 6/6/25; s. Montcalm F. Maynard and Emma Gosselin M; m. 8/23/52 to Margaret Mary Dwyer; c. Christopher T, Timothy J. and Lisa C. Educ: Wesleyan Univ, A.B, 52; Univ. Va. Sch. Law, LL.B, 55. Polit. & Govt. Pos: Registrar of voters, Conn, 48-52; asst. corp. counsel, Bristol, 55-59; chmn, Fifth Dist. Dem. Town Cmt, 60-64; city corp. counsel, Bristol, Conn, 63-65; chmn, Bristol Dem. Town Cmt, 64-66; legal counsel, Bristol Redevelop. Agency, 65-; mem, Dem. Town Cmt, Bristol, currently. Bus. & Prof. Pos: Attorney, Missal, Hanrahan & Grabowski, 55-59; attorney-at-law, 59- Mil. Serv: Pvt, Army, 2nd Inf. Div, 43-46; Purple Heart; Combat Inf. Badge; ETO Ribbon with Three Battle Stars. Mem: Am. Legion; DAV; Franco-Am. War Vets; Conn, Hartford Co. and Bristol Bar Asns; K. of C; United Fund; Family Serv. Rel: Roman Catholic. Legal Res: Brightwood Rd, Bristol, Conn. 06010. Mailing Add: 120 Laurel St, Bristol, Conn. 06010.

MAYNARD, ROBERT TILSON D
b. Oakland, Calif, 9/27/26; s. Percy Hardy Maynard and Jackie Schelnick M; m. 12/23/58 to C. Jean Fain; c. Stephen Patrick. Educ: San Jose State Col, grad; Santa Clara Univ. Law Sch, grad; past pres, Psi Chi. Polit. & Govt. Pos: Chmn, Parks & Recreation Cmt, Santa Clara, Calif, 63-64 and Transportation Policy Cmt, 66; mayor, Santa Clara, 66-68. Bus. & Prof. Pos: Attorney at Law, private practice, 59- Mil. Serv: Entered as A/S, Navy Seabees, 44, released as EM 3/C, 46, after serv. in 143rd Naval Construct. Bn, Pac; Am. Theater and Philippine Theater Ribbons; Good Conduct Medal. Mem: State and Co. Bar Asns; pres, Penn Div. League of Calif. Cities; Elks; Nat. Rifleman's Asn. Mailing Add: 1469 Bergin Place, Santa Clara, Calif. 95051. (1967)

MAYNARD, WILLIAM R
b. 1917. Educ: Univ. N.H; Boston Univ. and Law Sch. Polit. & Govt. Pos: Spec. Justice of Munic. Court of Plymouth, N.H, 41-55; mem, Gov. Legal Counsel, 59; U.S. Attorney for Dist. of N.H, 54-61; Attorney Gen, N.H, 61-66; chmn, N.H. Cmt. on Interstate Coop; secy, N.H. Cmt. Study Uniform State Laws; mem, N.H. Judicial Coun, N.H. Ballot Law Cmt; N.H. Bd. of Trust Co, Inc. and N.H. Bd. of Control. Bus. & Prof. Pos: Lawyer; extensive practice before state and fed. courts. Mailing Add: R.F.D. 3, Concord, N.H. 03301.

MAYNE, WILEY R
U.S. Rep, Iowa
b. Sanborn, Iowa, 1/19/17; m. 1/5/42 to Elizabeth Dodson M; c. Martha Elizabeth, Wiley Jr. and John. Educ: Harvard Col, B.S, cum Laude, 38; Harvard Law Sch, 38-39; Univ. Iowa Law Sch, J.D, 41. Polit. & Govt. Pos: Spec. agent, Fed. Bur. Invest, 41-43; Nat. Committeeman Young Rep, 48-52; nat. v.chmn, Young Rep, 49-51; Eisenhower Chmn. for Woodbury Co, Iowa, 52; cmnr, Uniform State Laws, 56-60; U.S. Rep, Iowa, 67- Bus. & Prof. Pos: Partner, law firm, Shull, Marshall, Mayne, Marks & Vizintos, 46-66; pres, Sioux City Symphony Asn, Iowa, 47-53 and Sioux City Symphony Found, 54-66; exec. committeeman, Int. Asn. Ins. Counsr, 61-64; pres, Iowa State Bar Asn, 63-64; chmn, Midwest Region Rhodes Scholar Selection Cmt, 64-66; mem, house of del, Am. Bar Asn, 66-68. Mil. Serv: Entered Navy, 43, released as Lt.(jg), 46, after serv. in Pac, Atlantic and European Theaters; Naval Res. Mem: Sioux City, Iowa State and Am. Bar Asns; Am. Col. Trial Lawyers; Scottish Rite (33°); Mason. Sioux City Bar Award of Merit, 60. Rel: Presbyterian. Legal Res: Iowa. Mailing Add: 506 Cannon House Office Bldg, Washington, D.C. 20515.

MAYO, ROBERT PORTER R
Dir, Bur. of the Budget
b. Seattle, Wash, 3/15/16; s. Carl Asa Mayo and Edna Alberta Nelson M; m. 8/28/42 to Marian Aldridge Nicholson; c. Margaret Alice, Richard Carl, Carolyn Ruth (Mrs. Gregory Brown) and Robert Nelson. Educ: Univ. Wash, A.B, magna cum laude, 37, M.B.A, 38; Phi Beta Kappa; Pilgrim Club; Concert Band. Polit. & Govt. Pos: Research dir. and tax auditor, Wash. State Tax Corp, 38-41; from econ. analyst to asst. to secy. for debt mgt, Off. of Secy. of Treas, 41-60; staff dir, Pres. Cmn. Budget Concepts, 67; dir, Bur. of the Budget, 69- Bus. & Prof. Pos: V.pres. trust investment and public affairs, Continental Ill. Bank and Trust Co. of Chicago, 60-69. Mem: Financial Analysts Soc. of Chicago; Inst. of Chartered Financial Analysts; Chicago Asn. of Commerce and Indust.(v pres, research and statistics); Am. Econ. Asn; Am. Finance Asn; Am. Statist. Asn; Asn. Bus. Econ; Cosmos Club, Wash, D.C; Carderock Springs Swimming and Tennis Club, Bethesda, Md; Trout Valley Asn, Cary, Ill. Rel: Methodist. Legal Res: 33 Little Marryat Rd, Trout Valley, Cary, Ill. 60013. Mailing Add: 6909 Granby St, Kenwood Park, Bethesda, Md. 20034.

MAYO, WILLIAM PATRICK D
Secy-Treas, Beaufort Co. Dem. Exec. Cmt, N.C.
b. Asheville, N.C, 10/9/26; s. John Augustus Mayo and Harriet Sawyer M; m. 4/25/57 to Anna Ball Arthur; c. Anna Ball and William Patrick, Jr. Educ: Univ. N.C, A.B, 49, LL.B, 53; Phi Alpha Delta; Phi Gamma Delta. Polit. & Govt. Pos: Mem, Off. Attorney Gen, N.C, 54-56 and staff, N.C. State Bar, 56; prosecuting attorney, Beaufort Co. Recorder's Court, 57-67; secy-treas, Beaufort Co. Dem. Exec. Cmt, 58-63 & 67-, chmn, 63-67; pres, Beaufort Co. Young Dem. Club, 61. Bus. & Prof. Pos: Town attorney, Belhaven, N.C, 64-65 and Aurora, 64-68; Beaufort Co. Attorney, 68- Mil. Serv: Entered as Seaman 2/C, Naval Res, 45, released as Seaman 1/C, 46, after serv. in Am. Theater; Victory Medal. Mem: N.C. and Am. Bar Asns; Kiwanis; Am. Legion. Rel: Presbyterian. Legal Res: Riverside Park, Washington, N.C. 27889. Mailing Add: P.O. Box 635, Washington, N.C. 27889.

MAYO, WILLIAM TAYLOR 'BILLY' D
Cmnr, Fla. Pub. Serv. Cmn.
b. Summerfield, Fla, 12/10/17; s. Nathan Mayo and Nora Newsom M; m. 8/6/39 to Elizabeth Blalock; c. William T, Jr, Elizabeth Jean, Nathan Michael and Joseph Bryan. Educ: Univ. Fla. Polit. & Govt. Pos: Cmnr, City Cmn, Tallahassee, Fla, 50-54 & 56-62; mayor, Tallahassee, 53-54; interstate hwy. adminstr. and bd. mem, Fla. State Rd, Dept, 61-64; cmnr, Fla. Pub. Serv. Cmn, 64- Bus. & Prof. Pos: Co-owner, Mayo-Mingledorff Motors. Mem: Exchange Club; Elks; Nat. Asn. of R.R. and Utilities Cmnrs. Rel: Methodist. Legal Res: 1548 Lee Ave, Tallahassee, Fla. 32303. Mailing Add: 700 S. Adams St, Tallahassee, Fla. 32304.

MAYOR, JAMES MILLER R
b. Newport, Ark, 11/6/32; s. E. Allan Mayor and Elizabeth Hastings M; m. 11/16/54 to Helen Elizabeth Jones; c. Melissa Ann and Michael Allan. Educ: Univ. Houston, B.S. in govt, 53; Sigma Alpha Epsilon. Polit. & Govt. Pos: Precinct chmn, Harris Co. Rep. Party, Tex, 64-65, co. chmn, 65-68; mem, Harris Co. Young Rep. Club; del, State Rep. Conv, 64 & 66; mem, Harris Co. Cmnrs. Court, Redistricting Cmt, 66- Bus. & Prof. Pos: Dist. Mgr, Int. Circulation Distributors, Hearst Magazines, 62- Mil. Serv: Entered as 2nd Lt, Army, 54, released as 1st Lt, 56, after serv. as Aide-de-Camp to III Corps Artil. Commanding Gen, Ft. Hood, Tex, 18 months. Mem: Tex. Bill of Rights Found; Houston Coun. on World Affairs; Univ. Houston Alumni Asn. Rel: Methodist. Mailing Add: 9642 Meadowcroft, Houston, Tex. 77042. (1967)

MAYS, JAMES McCOY D
Ala. State Rep.
b. Hamilton, Ala, 9/11/11; s. William Augusta Mays and Harriet M; m. 7/17/35 to Edith Cruit; c. Robert William and James Cruit. Educ: Birmingham-South. Col, A.B, 33; Auburn Univ, M.S, 39; Omicron Delta Kappa. Polit. & Govt. Pos: Ala State Rep, Dist. 39, Escambia Co, 67- Mem: Pres, Escambia Co. Teacher's Asn, 40; pres, Lions Club; Farm Bur; Escambia Co. Cattlemen's Asn. Rel: Methodist. Mailing Add: 1111 Pressly St, Atmore, Ala. 36502.

MAYS, ROBERT ALAN R
Financial V.Chmn, Adams Co. Rep. Cent. Cmt, Ill.
b. Quincy, Ill, 10/16/21; s. Howard L. Mays and Edna Best M; m. 11/2/46 to Alice Morrison, div, 7/11/68; m. 3/8/69 to Anne Markley Frank; c. Richard Howard, Alan Morrison, Jeffrey Douglas and Elise. Educ: Northwest. Univ, B.S. in Indust. Mgt, 43; Phi Gamma Delta. Polit. & Govt. Pos: Cmnr, Quincy Park Dist, Ill, 47-; precinct committeeman, 60-; Adams Co. chmn, United Rep. Fund of Ill, 60-, memb. bd. gov, 63-; financial v.chmn, Adams Co. Rep. Cent. Cmt, Ill, 62- Bus. & Prof. Pos: Sales mgr, Flava Mfg. Co, 49-; pres, Miss. Valley Canteen Serv. Co, 55- Mil. Serv: Entered as Ens, Navy, 42, released 46, after serv. in Supply Corps, re-entered as Lt. Comdr, 51-52, serv. in 4th Fleet, Korea. Mem: Kiwanis; Am. Legion; Quincy Consistory, Lambert Lodge AF&AM. Rel: Congregational. Mailing Add: 1682 Hampshire St, Quincy, Ill. 62301.

MAYS, TROY A. R
Chmn, Spalding Co. Rep. Party, Ga.
b. Atlanta, Ga, 2/25/29; s. Troy E. Mays and Mary Knight M; m. Aug. 1947 to Dorothy Ponder; c. Deborah, Sherry and Terri. Educ: Ga. Inst. Tech, B.T.E. Polit. & Govt. Pos: Treas, Sixth Dist. Rep. Party, Ga, 64-66; v.chmn, Spalding Co. Rep. Party, 66-68, chmn, 68- Rel: Baptist. Legal Res: 925 Springer Dr, Griffin, Ga. 30223. Mailing Add: P.O. Box 97, Griffin, Ga. 30223.

MAZAN, WALTER L. R
Asst. Secy. for Pub. Affairs, Dept. of Transportation
b. Center Rutland, Vt, 6/5/21; s. Lawrence W. Mazan and Henrietta Mazur M; m. 7/14/56 to Lee Duffy; c. Walter Lawrence, II, Lorilee, Michelle and Michael. Educ: Middlebury Col, 42; Univ. Vt, B.S, 49. Polit. & Govt. Pos: Acting dir, Civil Defense, Vt, 51-57; mem. staff state and local defense planning, Off. of Emergency Planning, Wash, D.C, 57-63; spec. asst. for fed-state rels, Off. of Emergency Preparedness, 63-67, dep. dir. of liaison, 67-69, acting dir. of liaison, 69; asst. secy. for pub. affairs, Dept. of Transportation, currently. Bus. & Prof. Pos: Polit. campaign consult, Montpelier, Vt, 49; ins. adjuster, Gen. Adjust. Bur, Inc, 49-51. Mil. Serv: Entered as Sgt, Army Air Corps, 42, released as Pilot, 46, after serv. in various units; various mil. awards and decorations. Publ: Numerous articles with regard to position. Mem: Charter pres, Exec. Off. Pres. Toastmasters' Club; pres, v.pres. and mem, Nat. Conf. of State Socs; Vt. State Soc. Fed. Outstanding Performance Award. Rel: Catholic. Legal Res: Vermont. Mailing Add: 4856 N. 35th Rd, Arlington, Va. 22207.

MAZEWSKI, ALOYSIUS ALEX R
b. North Chicago, Ill, 1/5/16; s. Felix Mazewski and Harriet Konieczny M; m. 6/27/48 to Florence W. Heider; c. Aloysius A, Jr. and Marilyn. Educ: DePaul Univ. Col. Law, LL.B, 40. Polit. & Govt. Pos: Former committeeman, 45th Ward Rep. Orgn, Chicago, Ill; Master in Chancery, Superior Court, Cook Co, 63-64; alternate del, Rep. Nat. Conv, 64; dir, Nationalities Div, Ill, 64-; mem, exec. cmt, Cook Co. Rep. Cent. Cmt, 64-, attorney, 65-; chmn, Nationalities Cmt, Cook Co, 65- Bus. & Prof. Pos: Practicing Attorney-at-law, 40- Mil. Serv: Entered as Pvt, Army, 42, released as Capt, 46, after serv. in Med. Admin. Corps; Maj, Officers Res. Corps; Army Commendation Medal. Mem: Fed, Am, Ill. and Chicago Bar Asns; pres, Advocates Soc, 64; Judicature Soc;

pres, Polish Nat. Alliance; Lions; Moose; Amvets; Am. Legion; Elks. Rel: Roman Catholic. Legal Res: 3813 Medford Circle, Northbrook, Ill. 60061. Mailing Add: 1520 W. Division St, Chicago, Ill. 60622.

MAZOR, LEON LOUIS D
Committeeman, Ill. Dem. Cent. Cmt.
b. Chicago, Ill, 10/8/03; s. Louis Mazor and Sarah Gordon M; m. 9/9/60 to Ida Karp; c. Joseph Allen and Frances Bennet. Educ: Crane Jr. Col, 18-20; Chicago Kent Col. of Law, J.D, 25; Alpha Signa Iota. Polit. & Govt. Pos: Attorney, Union Ridge Water Co, 58-61; pres, Norwood Park Twp. Dem. Orgn, 58-; attorney, Norwood Park Twp. Fire Protection Dist, 59- and Norwood Park Twp. Street Lighting Dist, 60-; Justice of the Peace, Norwood Park Twp, 61-64; magistrate, Circuit Court, Cook Co, 64-66; committeeman, Ill. Dem. Cent. Cmt, currently. Bus. & Prof. Pos: Dir, Gamble Coker Corp; dir. and secy-treas, Alliance Mercantile Corp; dir, O.V.B. Finance Corp; v.pres, Suburban Land Investment Asn; dir, Barrington Hills Develop. Co. Mem: Ill. and Northwest Bar Asns; Decalogue Soc. of Lawyers; Mason; Scottish Rite; Shrine; Temple Sholom; Univ. of Chicago Found. for Emotionally Disturbed Children. Rel: Jewish. Legal Res: 1909 Washington, Park Ridge, Ill. 60068. Mailing Add: 134 N. LaSalle St, Room 1300, Chicago, Ill. 60602.

MAZUR, JOHN D
Chmn, Northumberland Co. Dem. Cmt, Pa.
b. Sagon, Pa, 7/7/26; s. George Mazur and Theresa Povelchak M; m. 10/9/48 to Lorraine Ann Nebroski; c. Paula, John, Jr, Karen and Seth. Educ: Pa. Mil. Col. Polit. & Govt. Pos: Cent. v.pres, Pa. Young Dem, 58-60, dir, 60-64; city chmn, Mt. Carmel, Pa, 59-64; chmn, Northumberland Co. Dem. Cmt, Pa, currently; alternate del, Dem. Nat. Conv, 68; chmn, 17th Cong. Dem. Asn. Bus. & Prof. Pos: Dept. engr, Ford Motor Co, 52-56; chief automobile engr, Bur. of Traffic Safety, 56-61; pres, Licoma Coal Co, 62-64; mfr. rep, 64- Mil. Serv: Entered as Seaman 2/C, Naval Res, 44, released as Seaman 1/C RM, 45; Victory Medal and Atlantic Theater Ribbon. Mem: Rotary Int; VFW; Am. Legion; Moose; Elks; Am. Soc. for Qual. Control; SAM; Am. Asn. Motor Vehicles Admin. Hon. Mention, All Am. Wrestling Team, 48. Rel: Greek Catholic. Mailing Add: 338 E. Ave, Mt. Carmel, Pa. 17851.

MAZZA, JOSEPH M, JR. D
Vt. State Rep.
b. Mineville, N.Y, 5/8/05; m. to Mary T. Perrino; c. five sons. Educ: Mineville, N.Y. pub. schs. Polit. & Govt. Pos: Mem, Prudential Com. Fire Dist. Two; Justice of the Peace; town grand juror; Vt. State Rep, 61- Bus. & Prof. Pos: Owner, grocery store. Mem: Lions; Colchester Sch. Bd, 55-; Vt. Realtors. Rel: Catholic. Mailing Add: R.F.D, 3, Winooski, Vt. 05404. (1967)

MAZZIE, E. C. 'BILL' R
b. Merced, Calif, 5/4/12; m. Dec. 1950 to Lorraine Gardiner; c. Toby James. Educ: Fresno State Col, 4 years. Polit. & Govt. Pos: Chmn, Arnett for Congress, 62; Kern Co. co-chmn, Reagan for Gov, 66 and Nixon for President, 68; del, Rep. Nat. Conv, 68; mem, Calif. Rep. State Cent. Cmt, 68-69; mem, Calif. State Bd. Agr, 69- Bus. & Prof. Pos: Co-owner, Mazzie Farms, Arvin, Calif, 40-69; owner, A.F.C. Inc, Edison, 69; pres, Globe Farms, Arvin and Vacation Coordinators, Bakersfield, 69. Rel: Catholic. Mailing Add: 5263 Kent Dr, Bakersfield, Calif. 93306.

MAZZIE, LORRAINE GARDINER R
b. Bakersfield, Calif, 8/10/18; d. Anna Gardiner; m. to E.C. 'Bill' Mazzie; c. Toby James. Educ: Fresno State Col, 4 years. Polit. & Govt. Pos: Chmn, Arnett for Cong, Kern Co, Calif, 62, Reagan for Gov, 66 and Nixon for Pres, 68; mem. finance cmt, Knight for Gov; mem, Calif. State Bd. of Tourism, 67-; mem, Calif. Rep. State Cent. Cmt, 68-69. Bus. & Prof. Pos: Co-owner, Mazzie Farms, Arvin, Calif, 40-; treas, A.F.C. Inc, Edison, Calif, 55-; v.pres, Globe Farms, Arvin, Calif, 69-; dir, Butte Valley Farms, Arvin Calif. and Vacation Coordinators, Bakersfield, Calif, 69- Rel: Protestant. Mailing Add: 5263, Kent Dr, Bakersfield, Calif. 93306.

MAZZOLI, ROMANO LOUIS D
Ky. State Sen.
b. Louisville, Ky, 11/2/32; s. Romano Mazzoli and Mary Ioppolo M; m. 8/1/59 to Helen Dillon; c. Michael Romano and Andrea Marie. Educ: Univ. Notre Dame, B.Sc, 54; Univ. Louisville, LL.B, 60; Omicron Delta Kappa; Phi Kappa Phi. Polit. & Govt. Pos: Del, Dem. Nat. Conv, 68; Ky. State Sen, 68- Mil. Serv: Entered as Pvt, Army, 54, released as Cpl, 56, after serv. in Alaska, 55-56. Mem: Am, Ky. and Louisville Bar Asns. Outstanding Freshman Sen, Ky. Gen. Assembly, 68. Rel: Roman Catholic. Mailing Add: 939 Ardmore Dr, Louisville, Ky. 40217.

MAZZUCA, EUGENE F. D
Mo. State Rep.
b. St. Louis, Mo, 9/25/24; m. 2/26/49 to Mary Mae Allman; c. Gene Vito and Joseph Vito. Educ: St. Louis pub. and parochial schs. Polit. & Govt. Pos: Dep. tax auditor, earning div, Off. of Collection of Revenue, St. Louis, Mo; mem, 24th Ward Regular Dem. Orgn, 19 years; dep. constable, St. Louis, 11 years, app. constable, 62; Mo. State Rep, 64- Bus. & Prof. Pos: Mem. staff, Int. Revenue Serv, U.S. Treas. Dept, 3 years; sales mgr, local and nat. concerns. Mil. Serv: Army, 43-46. Rel: Catholic. Mailing Add: 6215 Victoria Ave, St. Louis, Mo. 63139. (1967)

MEACHAM, AL D
b. Poweshiek City, Iowa, 1921; m. 3/11/45 to Lois Clifton; c. Michael, Casey and Connie. Educ: Grinnell Col, B.A, 47. Polit. & Govt. Pos: Grinnell-Newburg Bd. of Educ, Iowa, 61-64; Poweshiek City Rep. to State Assembly of Sch. Bd, 62; Iowa State Rep, 66; secy, Iowa State Senate, 67. Bus. & Prof. Pos: Farmer; merchant; pres, Agri-Serv, Inc; chmn, Iowa Merit Employ. Cmn, 68. Mil. Serv: Navy, World War II Vet, three years. Mem: 4-H Club Leader, five years; Rotary; Eagles; Am. Legion; Toastmasters, Int. Rel: Protestant. Mailing Add: Route 1, Grinnell, Iowa. 50112.

MEACHAM, CHARLES HARDING R
Cmnr, Fish & Wildlife Serv, Dept. of the Interior
b. Newman, Calif, 9/21/25; s. Vernon A. Meacham and Sara Paulsen M; m. 6/22/46 to June Lorraine Yunker; c. Charles Paulsen and Bruce Herbert. Educ: Utah State Univ, B.S, 50; two nat. scholastic fraternities. Polit. & Govt. Pos: Biologist, Calif. Dept. of Fish and Game, Stanford Univ, 50-56 and Alaska Dept. of Fisheries, Wrangell, Alaska, 56-59; regional supvr, Regions II and III, Alaska Dept. of Fisheries, 59-68; dir, Int. Fisheries, Off. of Gov, Juneau, 68-69; cmnr, Fish & Wildlife Serv, Dept. of the Interior, 69- Mil. Serv: Entered as Pvt, Marines, 43, released as Pfc, 46, after serv. in Marine Raiders, S.Pac. Theatre, 44-46; S.Pac. Theatre Ribbon; Navy Unit and Presidential Unit Citations; Good Conduct Medal. Mem: Adv. and cmnr, Int. N. Pac. Fisheries Cmn; adv, Alaska Cmnrs. of Pac. Marine Fisheries Cmn; sr. mem, Alaska-Japan Fisheries Panel & Joint Research Venture; U.S. State Dept. Fisheries Adv. Cmt; cmnr, Great Lakes Fisheries and Int. Pac. Salmon Fisheries Cmns; Am. Legion; Elks; Am. Fisheries Soc; Wildlife Soc; Pac. Fisheries Biologist; Int. Asn. of Game, Fish and Conserv. Cmnrs. Rel: Presbyterian. Legal Res: 2612 Turnagain Pkwy, Anchorage, Alaska 99503. Mailing Add: Dept. of the Interior, Washington, D.C. 20240.

MEACHUM, ROBERT LEWIS D
Chmn, Lapeer Co. Dem. Party, Mich.
b. Saginaw, Mich, 8/14/39; s. Jake Lewis Meachum and Frieda Ann Gilmore M; m. 8/1/64 to Patsy Marlene Barner; c. Jake Lewis and John Edgar. Educ: Mich. State Univ, B.S, 63. Polit. & Govt. Pos: Chmn, Lapeer Co. Dem. Party, Mich, 67-; alternate del, Dem. Nat. Conv, 68. Mem: Nat. and Mich. Asns. Teachers Voc. Agr; Nat. and Mich. Educ. Asns; Mich. Farm Bur. State Farmer Degree, Mich. Asn. Future Farmers of Am. Rel: Lutheran-Mo. Synod; dir, Christian Educ. Mailing Add: 1650 Bowers Rd, Lapeer, Mich. 48446.

MEAD, ED V. D
b. 1923. Educ: Bus. Col. Polit. & Govt. Pos: N.Mex. State Sen, 61-67; Lt. Gov, 59-60; Bernalillo Cty. Comm, 56. Bus. & Prof. Pos: Wholesale bakery exec. Rel: Baptist. Mailing Add: Box 604, Albuquerque, N.Mex. 87103. (1967)

MEAD, JOHN J. S. R
Dep. Co. Attorney, Westchester Co, N.Y.
b. Waccabuc, N.Y. 5/10/08; s. Joseph Mead and Louise Griswold; m. 4/6/40 to Barbara Whitehill; c. George S, Betty Louise (Mrs. Tubman) and John J.S, Jr. Educ: Princeton Univ; N.Y. Law Sch. Polit. & Govt. Pos: Justice of the Peace, Lewisboro, N.Y, 32-34, supvr, 34-42 & 56-60; N.Y. State Assemblyman, 61-65; dep. co. attorney, Westchester Co, 66- Mil. Serv: Entered as 1st Lt, Marine Corps, 42, released as Maj, 46, after serv. in Pac. Theater; Am, Pac. and Good Behavior Ribbons; 1 Battle Star. Mem: Westchester Bar Asn; Am. Legion; Lions. Rel: Episcopal. Mailing Add: Waccabuc, N.Y. 10597.

MEADE, RALPH ALLISON D
Ala. State Rep.
b. Birmingham, Ala, 7/30/28; s. Cooper Cedone Meade and Ada Vastie Allison M; m. 6/20/48 to Nancy Jo Brown; c. Gregory Allison, Nancy Dianne, Vicki Gail and James Cooper. Educ: Cherokee City Pub. Schs. Polit. & Govt. Pos: Ala. State Rep, DeRalb and Cherokee Co, 58- Bus. & Prof. Pos: Mgr, WAGC radio sta, Centre, Ala. Mem: Mason; Shrine. Rel: Baptist. Mailing Add: Box Q, Centre, Ala. 35960.

MEADER, GEORGE R
b. Benton Harbor, Mich, 9/13/07; s. Robert Eugene Meader and Jennie Editha Gibson M; m. 11/19/28 to Elizabeth Barbara Faeth; c. Robert Eugene and Katherine Elizabeth (Mrs. Vandelly). Educ: Ohio Wesleyan Univ, 23-25; Univ. of Mich, A.B, 27, Law Sch, J.D, 31. Polit. & Govt. Pos: Charter bd. mem, Mich. Fedn. Young Rep, 32; pres, Washtenaw Co. Young Rep. Club, Mich, 32; prosecuting attorney, Washtenaw Co, 41-43; counsel, Truman-Mead Spec. Cmt. Invest. Defense Prog, 43-45; chief counsel, Mead Spec. Cmt. Invest. Defense Prog, U.S. Senate, 45-47; chief counsel, Fulbright Subcmt. Invest. Reconstruction Finance Corp, U.S. Senate Banking & Currency Cmt, 50; U.S. Rep, Second Dist, Mich, 51-65; assoc. counsel, Joint Cmt. on Orgn. of Cong, 65-67, chief counsel, 67-68. Bus. & Prof. Pos: Counsel, Mich. Merit Syst. Asn, 39-41. Publ: Review of book entitled Congress, Its Contemporary Role, by Ernest Griffith, Mich. Law Review, 6/56; 'Congressional Investigations: Importance of the Fact-Finding Process,' Univ. of Chicago Law Review 51; 'Limitations on Congressional Investigations,' Mich. Law Review, 4/49. Mem: Am, Mich. and Dist. of Columbia Bar Asns; Ann Arbor Kiwanis (pres, 39); Elks; Capitol Hill Club; Columbia Country Club. Admitted to practice before U.S. Supreme Court; Golf, chess, foreign languages. Rel: Methodist. Legal Res: 1060 Baldwin, Ann Arbor, Mich. 48104. Mailing Add: 3360 Tennyson St. N.W, Washington, D.C. 20015.

MEADORS, ALBERT MURRIL R
Chmn, Wash. Co. Rep. Cent. Cmt, Ind.
b. Salem, Ind, 3/1/01; s. Elbert W. Meadors and Lillie E. Colglazier M; m. 12/16/28 to Ella Mae Frances Wilt. Educ: High Sch. Polit. & Govt. Pos: Del, Rep. State Conv. for many years; co. relief chmn; co. finance chmn, Wash. Co. Rep. Cent. Cmt, Ind, 50-56, city chmn, 55-59, chmn, 58-; presidential elector, Ninth Dist. Ind, 68. Bus. & Prof. Pos: Motor Truck & Bus Business and Wholesale Bus. & Farm Produce, 21-50; farmer, 30-; milk procurement, Salem Cheese & Milk Co, Salem, Ind, 51-; auto license br. mgr. Mem: Red Men; K. of P; Salem Lions; Farm Bur; Co. Fair (secy); Lions (pres); Ind. Motor Traffic Asn. (past pres); State of Ind. Coun, Sagamore of the Wabash. Rel: Christian Church N.Am. Legal Res: 103 W. Homer St, Salem, Ind. 47167. Mailing Add: P.O. Box 167, Salem, Ind. 47167.

MEADOWCROFT, WILLIAM HOWARTH R
Mem, Wash. State Rep. Finance Cmt.
b. Seattle, Wash, 1/30/29; s. Albert Henry Meadowcroft and Lillian Howarth M; m. 3/2/57 to Elizabeth Weyerhaeuser; c. Laura Hunt, Elizabeth Mills, Anne Weyerhaeuser, Mark Howarth and David Walker. Educ: Univ. Puget Sound; Harvard Bus. Sch. Polit. & Govt. Pos: Co-finance chmn, Pierce Co. Rep. Finance Cmt, 62-64; del, Rep. Nat. Conv, 64; precinct committeeman, Pierce Co. Rep. Cent. Cmt, 64-66; mem, Wash. State Rep. Finance Cmt, currently. Bus. & Prof. Pos: Personnel asst, Weyerhaeuser Co, 49-52, mgr. mkt. planning, 54-60, new prod. div, 60-65, asst. to exec. v.pres, 65-68 and asst. to pres, 68-; dir, Puget Sound Nat. Bank, Tacoma, Wash, currently. Mil Serv: Naval Air Reserve, 47-54. Mem: Elks; Tacoma Club; trustee, Univ. Puget Sound; Wash. Athletic Club; Tacoma Golf & Country Club. Rel: Episcopal. Legal Res: 23 Forest Glen Lane S.W, Tacoma, Wash. 98498. Mailing Add: Tacoma Bldg, Tacoma, Wash. 98402.

MEADOWS, AUSTIN RUEL D
b. Alexander City, Ala, 12/24/99; s. Little Benjamin Meadows and Martha Annie Carter M; m. 3/16/36 to Eleanor Hooper. Educ: Jacksonville State Normal Sch, Ala; Univ. Ala, B.S. and M.S; Columbia Univ, Ph.D; Phi Beta Kappa. Polit. & Govt. Pos: Admin. pos, State Dept. Educ, Ala, 29-46; state supt. educ, 46-51, 55-59 & 63-67; O.P.S. dir, Birmingham, Ala, 51-52; co. supt. educ, Madison Co, Ala, 52-54, asst. state supt. educ, 59-62. Bus. & Prof. Pos: Mem, White House Conf. Educ. and Admin, 45-55; mem, exec. cmt, South. States Work Conf, South. Regional Educ. Bd, 50 and Ala. Educ. Asn; chmn, Planning Cmt. of the Study Cmn, Chief State Sch. Officers. Publ: Safety and Economy in School Bus Transportation; numerous articles on sch. bus transportation, sch. admin. and pub. releases to the press of Ala. on pub. educ. in Ala. Mem: Lions; Masons. Varsity football and basketball, Jacksonville State Normal Sch. Rel: Baptist. Legal Res: 3658 Cleveland Ave, Montgomery, Ala. 36105. Mailing Add: State Dept. of Education, Montgomery Ala. 36104.

MEADOWS, DAVID BREACY D
Committeeman, Washoe Co. Dem. Party, Nev.
b. Ennis, Tex, 1/3/12; s. Joe Meadows and Anna Thompson M; m. 10/16/42 to Ella Mae Filmore. Educ: Butler Col, Sem. training, 42-45. Polit. & Govt. Pos: Committeeman, Washoe Co. Dem. Party, Nev, 65- Bus. & Prof. Pos: Pastor, Mt. Zion Baptist Church, Reno, Nev, 47-65; mgr, Cannery Sales Mkt, 61-63 and Pennysaver Mkt, Reno, 65; night mgr, Food King Mkt, 63-65. Prfnl. Boxing, 30-33. Rel: Baptist. Mailing Add: 541 Elko Ave, Reno, Nev. 89502. (1967)

MEARES, CARL WHITTEN D
b. Fair Bluff, N.C, 9/10/07; s. Ellis Meares; Minnie Anderson M; m. 7/7/39 to Margaret Bracy; c. Carolyn, Carl, Jr, Mary Lee. Educ: Mars Hill Col, 27-29; Univ. N.C, 29-31. Polit. & Govt. Pos: N.C. State Sen, 63-66. Bus. & Prof. Pos: Gen. farm supply merchant; operator, tobacco warehouse; Ford automobile dealer; dir, First Union Nat. Bank. Mem: Rotary Club; Shrine; trustee, Mars Hill Col. Rel: Baptist. Mailing Add: Fair Bluff, N.C. 28439. (1967)

MEBUS, CHARLES FILLMORE R
Pa. State Rep.
b. Abington, Pa, 6/15/28; s. Geoge Brinker Mebus and Estelle Claxton Negus M; m. 7/26/58 to Joy Campbell Robbins; c. Lisa Jane Campbell. Educ: Pa. State Univ, B.S. in chem, 49 and B.S. in sanit. eng, 51; Scabbard and Blade; Pershing Rifles: v.pres, Sigma Alpha Epsilon, 50-51. Polit. & Govt. Pos: Mem, Montgomery Co. Rep. Cmt, Pa, 60-; Pa. State Rep, 65- Bus. & Prof. Pos: V.pres, George B. Mebus, Inc, 53- Mil. Serv: Entered as 2nd Lt, Army, 51, released as 1st Lt, 53, after serv. in 354th Eng. Construct. Bn, Germany, 52-53; German Occup. Medal; NATO Ribbon; Capt, Army, Res, 60. Mem: Am. Soc. Civil Engrs; Pa. Soc. Prfnl Engrs; Consult. Engs. Coun. Pa; Am. Soc. Testing & Materials; Am. Water Works Asn; Nat. Soc. State Legislators; Rotary; Navy League; VFW; Dist. Cmt, Boy Scouts; former mem, Jaycees. Rel: Episcopal; Layreader in Episcopal Church. Mailing Add: 214 Maple Ave, Wyncote, Pa. 19095.

MECHAM, ALLAN ELISON R
Utah State Rep.
b. Oakley, Idaho, 4/7/11; s. Elmer B. Mecham and Sarah A. Elison M; m. 6/5/36 to Marion Dixon; c. George Michael, Craig Worthington, Allan Dixon and Rosemary. Educ: George Wash. Law Sch; Univ. Utah, J.D; Hague Acad. of Int. Law, Holland; Sigma Chi. Polit. & Govt. Pos: Utah State Rep, Majority Leader, State House of Rep, 67-68; del, Rep. Nat. Conv, 68. Bus. & Prof. Pos: Attorney-at-law, Clyde, Mecham & Prat, Salt Lake City, Utah, currently. Mil. Serv: ROTC. Mem: Utah and Am. Bar Asns; Alpine Country Club. Rel: Latter-day Saint. Mailing Add: 2681 Sherwood Dr, Salt Lake City, Utah 84108.

MECHAM, LEONIDAS RALPH R
b. Murray, Utah, 4/23/28; s. Leonidas DeVon Mecham and Minnie Frame M; m. 8/10/50 to Barbara Folsom; c. Mark L, Meredith, Richard O, Stephen F. and Alison. Educ: Univ. Utah, B.S. magna cum laude, 51; George Wash. Univ, J.D, 57; Harvard Univ, M.P.A, 64, fel. pub. admin, 65-66; Phi Kappa Phi; Phi Eta Sigma. Polit. & Govt. Pos: Legis. asst. to U.S. Sen. Wallace F. Bennett, Utah, 52-58, admin. asst. and counsel, 58-65; asst. to the pres. for spec. projs, Univ. Utah, 65-67, v.pres. for econ. and commun. develop, 67-69; spec. asst. to the Secy. of Commerce for Regional Econ. Coord, 69; exec. secy, Fed. Adv. Coun. on Regional Econ. Develop, 69; fed. co-chmn, Four Corners Regional Cmn, 69- Bus. & Prof. Pos: V.pres. and gen. counsel, Olympus Research Corp, Salt Lake City, Utah, 68-69. Mem: Nat. Coun. of Univ. Research Adminstr; Am. Soc. for Pub. Admin; Am. Polit. Sci. Asn; Utah and Salt Lake Co. Bar Asns; D.C. Bar; Adult Educ. Asn; Nat. Adv. Exten. Asn. Awarded one of the first four and the highest Cong. Staff Fels. by a bipartisan House-Senate Leadership Adv. Cmt. for the Am. Polit. Sci. Asn, 63. Rel: Latter-day Saint. Legal Res: 54 N. Wolcott St, Salt Lake City, Utah 84103. Mailing Add: 11337 Willowbrook Dr, Potomac, Md. 20854.

MECHEM, EDWIN LEARD R
b. Alamorgordo, N.Mex, 7/2/12; s. Edwin Mechem and Eunice Leard M; m. 12/30/32 to Dorothy Ellen Heller; c. Martha (Mrs. M. Vigil), John, Jesse (deceased) and Walter. Educ: N.Mex. State Univ, 30, 31 & 35; Univ. Ark, LL.B, 39. Polit. & Govt. Pos: With U.S. Reclamation Bur, 32-35; agent, Fed. Bur. Invest, Tex, Ark. and Calif, 42-45; Gov. of N.Mex, 51-54, 57-58 & 61-62; U.S. Sen, N.Mex, 62-64; del, Rep. Nat. Conv, 68. Bus. & Prof. Pos: Lawyer, 39-; partner, Darden, Mechem & Sage, Las Cruces, N.Mex, 65- Mem: Am. Law Inst.(mem. cmt. on govt. security). Rel: Methodist. Legal Res: 333 Capri Arc, Mesilla Park, N.Mex. 88047. Mailing Add: Drawer 578, Las Cruces, N.Mex. 88001.

MECKEL, VIVIAN MILLER R
b. Kiowa, Kans, 7/1/16; s. Oswald Karl Meckel and Ella Miller M; m. 6/11/39 to Florence Ilo Brumitt; c. Marilyn Bernice, Marsha Kay, Mark Douglas and Maria Michele. Educ: Ft. Hays Kans. State Col, A.B. in Chem, 38; Phi Mu Alpha; Seventh Cavalry; pres, Eng. Soc. Polit. & Govt. Pos: Dist. chmn, Young Rep, Kans, 48-50; precinct committeeman, Rep. Party, 48-66; chmn, Ellis Co. Rep. Party, 52-62; chmn, Gov. Cultural Arts Adv. Coun, 65-66; Kans. State Rep, 65-66. Bus. & Prof. Pos: Pres, Hays Music Co, Inc, 39-; mem, Bd. of Dirs, Farmers State Bank, Hays, Kans, 48- Mil. Serv: Entered as Seaman 2/C, Navy, 43, released as PO 3/C, 45. Mem: Nat. Bd. Dir, Nat. Asn. of Music Merchants, 63-67; Bd. Dir, Cent. Baptist Sem, Kansas City, 62-66; Bd. of Dir. and Exec. Cmt, Hadley Med. Center, Hays, Kans, 56-; Bd. of Dir, High Plains Ment. Health Cent, 63-; Music Educators Nat. Conf; Mason; Shrine; Rotary; Am. Legion; Smoky Hill Country Club. Rel: Baptist. Mailing Add: 2000 Pershing Dr, Hays, Kans. 67601.

MEDAIRY, BERNARD JOHN, JR. D
b. Baltimore, Md, 1/11/21; s. Bernard John Medairy and Elizabeth Loretta Codd M; m. 5/25/54 to Patricia Joan Beach; c. Bernard John, III, Paul Beach and Nicholas Brice. Educ: Univ. Md, 46-48; Univ. Md. Law Sch, LL.B, 52; Delta Theta Phi; Taney Senate. Polit. & Govt. Pos: Md. State Del, 62-66; Dem. nominee, Md. State Sen, 66. Bus. & Prof. Pos: Private practice of law, Baltimore Co, Md, 52- Mil. Serv: Entered as A/S, Navy, 44, released as Photographer's mate 3/C, 46, after serv. in S.Pac, Philippines and China. Mem: Baltimore Co, Md. State and Am. Bar Asns; SAR; Soc. of the War of 1812 in Md; K. of C; Baltimore Co. and Md. Hist. Socs; Nat. Geneal. Soc; Towson Lodge 469, Elks. Won first prize with The Medairy Family of Maryland, Parker Geneal. Contest, sponsored by Md. Hist. Soc, 65. Rel: Roman Catholic. Legal Res: 229 Dunkirk Rd, Baltimore Co, Md. 21212. Mailing Add: 204 Courtland Ave, Towson, Md. 21204.

MEDDERS, MARION WARDNER R
Mem, Ala. State Rep. Exec. Cmt.
b. Marion, Ala, 2/5/25; s. Marion A. Medders and Lola A. M; m. 7/22/45 to Dorothy B; c. Martha Lois: Davis Samuel and Mary Elizabeth. Educ: Cent. Wesleyan Col, Th.B, 45; Univ. Ala; Troy State Col. Polit. & Govt. Pos: Mem, Ala. State Rep. Exec. Cmt, 66-; chmn, Autauga Co. Rep. Party, Ala, 66- Mem: Past Lt. Gov, past pres. local club and dist. chaplain, Civitan Int. Rel: Methodist. Legal Res: 893 Newton St, Prattville, Ala. 36067. Mailing Add: P.O. Box 422, Prattville, Ala. 36067.

MEDLOCK, THOMAS TRAVIS D
S.C. State Rep.
b. Joanna, S.C, 8/28/34; s. M.K. Medlock and Mayme DuBose M; single. Educ: Univ. of S.C. Law Sch, 56-59; Wofford Col, A.B, 56; Phi Beta Kappa; Blue Key. Polit. & Govt. Pos: Asst. Attorney Gen, S.C, 61-62; S.C. State Rep, currently. Bus. & Prof. Pos: Lawyer, private practice, Columbia, S.C. Mem: Pres, United Cerebral Palsy of Midlands Carolina. Rel: Wesley Mem. Church. Mailing Add: 1421 Bull St, Columbia, S.C, 29201. (1967)

MEEDS, LLOYD D
U.S. Rep, Wash.
b. Dillon, Mont, 12/11/27; c. Michael R, Marcia L and Michelle Jean. Educ: Everett Jr. Col; Gonzaga University of Law, LL.B, 58. Polit. & Govt. Pos: Elec. Snohomish Co. prosecuting attorney, Wash, 62; dep. prosecuting attorney, Spokane and Snohomish Co; U.S. Rep, Wash, 64- Bus. & Prof. Pos: Lawyer; admitted to Wash. State Bar, 58; engaged in private practice of law in Everett, Wash, 2 yrs, in asn. of Hunter, Meeds & French. Mil. Serv: Navy, 46. Mem: Kiwanis Int; Eagles; Wash. State Bar Asn; Snohomish Co. Bar Asn. (v.pres); Snohomish Co. Young Dem.(former pres); Gonzaga Law Young Dem; Phi Alpha Delta. Legal Res: Everett, Wash. 98201. Mailing Add: U.S. House of Representatives, Washington, D.C. 20515.

MEEHAN, ANDREW MARTIN R
b. Phila, Pa, 5/29/36; s. Austin A. Meehan and Dorothy McNulty M; m. 5/23/59 to Jane Ellen Smith; c. Ann Marie, Jane, Andrew and Stephen. Educ: La Salle Col, 1 year; Villanova Univ, 1 year. Polit. & Govt. Pos: Pres, Northeast Young Rep, Pa, 58-60; v.chmn, Phila. Young Rep, 60-62, chmn, 62-, bd. of adv, Pa. Young Rep, 64-66; 63rd ward leader, Phila. Rep. Cmt, 65-; mem, Phila. Rep. Policy Cmt, 66-; del, Rep. Nat. Conv, 68. Mem: Bd. dir, Men of Med. Mission; v.chmn, Fox Chase Commun. Coun. Various awards for activity in Young Rep. Rel: Roman Catholic. Mailing Add: 1004 Rhawn St, Philadelphia, Pa. 19111.

MEEHAN, LEO JOHN D
Chmn, Will Co. Dem. Cent. Cmt, Ill.
b. Clayton, Iowa, 9/14/23; s. James Jacob Meehan and Frances Eva Meder M; m. 12/27/47 to Margaret Frances Rooney; c. John James, Jane Frances and Sarah Nicollette. Educ: State Univ. Iowa, B.Sc, 50; Pi Kappa Alpha. Polit. & Govt. Pos: Chmn. and precinct committeeman, Will Co. Dem. Cent. Cmt, Ill, 56-; dir, Co. Chmns. Orgn, Ill; Ill-Mich. Canal Supt, Div. of Waterways, 61-69; alternate del, Dem. Nat. Conv, 68. Bus. & Prof. Pos: Sales rep, Gordon Pontiac, Joliet, Ill. and Travel Center, Inc, Lockport, Ill, 69-; ins. broker; real estate salesman. Mil. Serv: Entered as A/S, Coast Guard, 42, released as Seaman 1/C, 46; Good Conduct Medal. Mem: Am. Legion; Old Timers Baseball Asn; K. of C; Irish Fel. Club of Chicago; Holy Name Soc; Moose; Marycrest Homeowners Asn. Distinguished Serv. Award, Will Co. Young Dem, Ill. Rel: Roman Catholic. Mailing Add: 2209 McDonough St, Joliet, Ill. 60436.

MEEK, FRED R
Kans. State Rep.
b. Idana, Kans, 3/24/02; s. Milo Edgemont Meek and Ella Henrietta Long M; m. 10/16/31 to Nellie Florine Trechsel; c. Alice Lee (Mrs. Gayle Peterson), Frederick Trechsel and Paul Taylor. Educ: Auburn Univ, B.S, 24. Polit. & Govt. Pos: Precinct Committeeman, Rep. Party, Kans, 28-; mem, Co. Soil Conserv. Serv. Bd, 47-57, and chmn, 4 years; Rep. co. chmn, 52-60, alternate del, Rep. Nat. Conv, 56, del, 64; Kans. State Rep, 55- Bus. & Prof. Pos: Farmer, 26- Mem: Kans. Farmers Union (pres, 60); mem. bd. dirs, Coop. Mkt. Asn, Kansas City, 52-64; bd. dirs, Far-Mar-Co; Masonic Bodies; Elks; Farm Bur; Farm Coop. Rel: Presbyterian. Mailing Add: Idana, Kans. 67453.

MEEK, WALTER BUCHANAN D
Miss. State Rep.
b. Memphis, Tenn, 1/13/26; married. Educ: Univ. Miss; Pi Kappa Alpha. Polit. & Govt. Pos: Miss. State Rep, currently. Bus. & Prof. Pos: Attorney; ins; farmer. Mem: Am. Legion; Am. and Miss. Bar Asns. Rel: Methodist. Mailing Add: Route 1, Eupora, Miss. 39744.

MEEKER, ANTHONY 'TONY' R
Ore. State Rep.
b. Amity, Ore, 3/18/39; s. Phillip Edwin Meeker and Mable Iona Davis M;

m. 9/1/62 to Carolyn Morton; c. Tracy Michelle. Educ: Willamette Univ, B.A, 61; Omicron Delta Kappa; Beta Theta Pi. Polit. & Govt. Pos: Ore. State Rep, Fifth Dist, 69- Bus. & Prof. Pos: Asst. mgr, Burlingham Meeker Co, Amity, Ore, 66-69. Mil. Serv: Entered as 2nd Lt, Air Force, 61, released as 1st Lt, 65, after serv. in Strategic Air Command and Pac. Air Force, U.S. and Vietnam, 65; Two Oak Leaf Clusters; Air Force Commendation Medal. Mem: Am. Legion; Lions; C. of C; Ore. Agr. Bus. Coun. Rel: Methodist. Mailing Add: 110 Rosedale, Amity, Ore. 97101.

MEEKER, FREDERICK EDWARD D
b. Burlington, Iowa, 4/29/47; s. Harley Fred Meeker and Mathy Hirstein M; Educ: Burlington Commun. Col, 65-67; Univ. North. Iowa, 2 years; Kappa Delta Pi. Polit. & Govt. Pos: Del-at-lg, Dem. Nat. Conv, 68; student sen, Univ. North. Iowa, 68-69; pres, Iowa Young Dem, 68-69. Commencement speaker, Burlington Commun. Col, 67. Rel: Methodist. Legal Res: R.R. 1, Mediapolis, Iowa 52637. Mailing Add: 514 S. Third Ave. E, Newton, Iowa 50208.

MEEKER, GEORGE WILBER D
b. Larned, Kans, 3/5/22; s. George Lindley Meeker and Bertha Hewson M; m. 7/1/44 to Helen Margaret Sorensen; c. Larry George and Douglas Alton. Educ: Garden City Commun. Jr. Col, grad, 41; Kans. State Univ, B.S. in Bus. Admin, 43; Phi Delta Theta; Alpha Kappa Psi. Polit. & Govt. Pos: Treas, Sunrise Sch. Bd, Finney Co, Kans, 48-58; Rep. precinct committeeman, 52-58; mem. and chmn, Agr. Stabilization and Conservation Cmt, U.S. Dept. of Agr, Garden City, 60-62; Kans. State Rep, Finney Co, 63-69; Dem. cand, U.S. House of Rep, 68. Bus. & Prof. Pos: Farmer, stockman and businessman, Garden City, Kans, 47-69; mem. exec. bd, Wheat & Wheat Foods Found, Chicago, Ill, 65-69; pres, Scott City Grain Co, Inc, Kans, 66-69; treas, bd. dir, Hi-Plains Enterprises, Leoti, 66-69; chmn. bd. dir, West. Grain, Inc, Wichita, 67-69; trustee, Hertzler Research Found, Halstead, 68-69; pres, adv. bd. mem. asn, Life of Am, Wichita, 68-69; past mem, bd. dir. Great Plains Wheat, Inc, Wash, D.C. Mil. Serv: Entered as Aviation Cadet, Navy Air Corps, 43, released as Lt.(jg), 46, after serv. aboard U.S.S. Gilbert Islands, Pac. Theatre, 45-46; Philippine Liberation Ribbon; plus others. Mem: Kans. Asn. of Wheat Growers (pres, 64-67); Nat. Asn. of Wheat Growers (pres, 68); Elks; Am. Legion; C. of C; Grange. Rel: United Church of Christ. Mailing Add: 1401 E. Hackberry, Garden City, Kans. 67846.

MEEKER, JAMES GEORGE D
b. Jamestown, N.Dak, 7/15/37; s. Donald Betts Meeker and Abigail W. Klenk M; m. 8/27/60 to Jane F. Sheridan; c. Jeffrey Lynn, Julie Ann and John Donald. Educ: Jamestown Col, 55-57; Univ. N.Dak, B.A, 59; Pa. State Univ, 65-66; Blue Key; Beta Theta Pi. Polit. & Govt. Pos: Admin. asst. to Sen. Quentin N. Burdick, N.Dak, 67- Bus. & Prof. Pos: Dir. of news and info, Univ. N.Dak, 60-61; polit. reporter, Fargo Forum, 61-65. Mem: U.S. Senate Asn. of Admin. Asst. Fel. Wash. Journalism Center, 66-67. Rel: Presbyterian. Legal Res: 1442 14th St. S, Fargo, N.Dak. 58102. Mailing Add: 5920 Walton Rd, Bethesda, Md. 20034.

MEEKER, LEONARD CARPENTER
U.S. Ambassador to Romania
b. Montclair, N.J, 4/4/16; s. Irving Avard Meeker and Elizabeth Louise Carpenter M; m. 10/27/47 to Christine Rhoda Halliday; c. Richard Halliday, Charles Carpenter and Sarah Louise. Educ: Amherst Col, A.B, 37; Harvard Univ, LL.B, 40. Polit. & Govt. Pos: Off. of Gen. Counsel, Treas. Dept, 40-41; Off. of Solicitor Gen, Dept. Justice, 41-42; with Off. of Legal Adv, Dept. State, 46-51, asst. legal adv, 51-61, dep. legal adv, 61-65, legal adv, 65-; U.S. Ambassador to Romania, 69- Bus. & Prof. Pos: Attorney; admitted to D.C. Bar, 40 and Calif. Bar, 41. Mem: Bd. trustees, Potomac Sch, 59-, chmn, 60-63; Am. and Fed. Bar Asns; Am. Soc. Int. Law; St. Nicholas Soc. City of New York. Mailing Add: 3000 Chain Bridge Rd. N.W, Washington, D.C. 20016.

MEEKHOF, GEORGE R
Chmn, Missaukee Co. Rep. Party, Mich.
b. McBain, Mich, 11/28/23; s. Myne G. Meekhof and Johanna Lucas M; m. 4/26/46 to Clarice M. Fredricks; c. Judy (Mrs. Nederhoed), Joyce, Maxine, Marcia, Johanna, Carol, George, Dean and David. Educ: Midwest Motive Trade Inst, 6 months; Mich. State. Polit. & Govt. Pos: Del, Mich. State Rep. Conv, 64-68; justice of the peace, Riverside Twp, 65; finance chmn, Missaukee Co. Rep. Party, 66 & 67, treas, 67, chmn, 69-; mem. sch. bd, McBain Pub. Schs, 66- Bus. & Prof. Pos: Farmer until 58; partner, Don's Auto Clin, 58- Mil. Serv: Entered as Pvt, Army, 43, released as S/Sgt, 45, after serv. in 3803 Qm. Truck Co, ETO; Good Conduct Medal; Meritorious Serv. Award. Rel: Reformed Christian Church. Mailing Add: Route 2, McBain, Mich. 49657.

MEEKISON, DAVID D
Chmn, Henry Co. Dem. Exec. and Cent. Cmts, Ohio
b. Napoleon, Ohio, 12/12/13; s. George A. Meekison and Vadae G. Harvey M; m. to Mary Frances Shaff: c. Maureen (Mrs. Houppert), David Francis and Beth Ann. Educ: Harvard Col, 31-33; Ohio State Univ. Law Sch, LL.B, 36; Phi Delta Phi. Polit. & Govt. Pos: Chmn, Henry Co. Dem. Exec. and Cent. Cmts, Ohio, 49-; chmn. and v.chmn, Henry Co. Bd. of Elec, Ohio, 50- Bus. & Prof. Pos: Pres, Henry Co. Bar Asn, 59-63. Mil. Serv: Entered as Lt.(jg), Naval Res, 44, released as Lt.(sg), 46. Mem: Elks; Port Clinton Yacht Club; Harvard Club of Toledo. Rel: Protestant. Legal Res: 318 W. Washington St, Napoleon, Ohio 43545. Mailing Add: 609 N. Perry St, Napoleon, Ohio 43545.

MEEKS, CORDELL DAVID D
Chmn, Bd. Co. Cmnrs, Wyandotte Co, Kans.
b. Little Rock, Ark, 9/25/14; s. Charles Arthur Meeks and Mossie Green M; m. 12/22/40 to Cellastine Dora Brown; c. Marlene, Cordell D, Jr, Marcena and Marquita. Educ: Univ. of Kans, A.B, 38, Sch. of Law, LL.B, 40, J.D, 68; past pres, Upsilon Chap, Alpha Phi Alpha. Polit. & Govt. Pos: Asst. co. prosecuting attorney, Wyandotte Co, Kans, 47-51; del, Dem. Nat. Conv, 48 & 64; mem, Wyandotte Co. Bd. Cmnrs, 51-, chmn, 65-; pres, Democracy Inc, 57- and Wyandotte Co. Dem. Officeholders Asn, 64-66. Bus. & Prof. Pos: Co-founder and dir, Douglass State Bank, 47, v.pres, 64-; sr. mem, Meeks, Whyte, Wallace & Meeks, Law Firm, 58. Publ: 'The Right To Peace And Quiet,' The Kans. City Kansan, 65. Mem: Am, Kans. and Wyandotte Co. Bar Asns; Nat. Asn. of Co. Officials; AF&AM; dir, Greater Kans. City Chap, Univ. of Kans. Alumni Asn; Exec. Cmt. Kans. Coun, Boy Scouts; v.chmn, educ. cmt, Nat. Asn. Counties, 66-67, bd. dir, 69-; secy-treas, Mid-Am. Coun. of Govt, 68- Admitted to practice before U.S. Supreme Court, 66. Rel: First African Methodist Episcopal Church. Mailing Add: 600 Oakland Ave, Kansas City, Kans. 66101.

MEEKS, JOHN NEAL D
V.Chmn, Stark Co. Dem. Party, Ohio
b. Canton, Ohio, 7/20/31; s. John H. Meeks and Vergie Riel M; m. 9/27/58 to Joan D. Bullard; c. Sandra, John, David and Paul. Educ: Ohio Univ, B.S.C, 54; Blue Key; Theta Chi. Polit. & Govt. Pos: Dem. precinct committeeman, Stark Co, Ohio, 60-; controller, Stark Co. Engr. Off, 62-66; mem, Stark Co. Dem. Exec. Cmt, 62-; Fed. Aid coordinator, Stark Co, 66-; v.chmn, Stark Co. Dem. Party, 66-; founding mem, Citizens for Humphrey, 68; del-at-lg, Dem. Nat. Conv, 68. Bus. & Prof. Pos: Gen. agent, Mich. Life Ins. Co, 58-60; pres, McKinley Bus. Col, Canton, Ohio, 60-62; pres, JM & Assocs, 66- Mil. Serv: Entered as 2nd Lt, Air Force, 54, released as 1st Lt, 57, after serv. in 79th Fighter Bomber Squadron, 20th Fighter Bomber Wing, Royal Air Force Sta, Eng, Third Air Force, 55-57, Capt, Air Force Res. Mem: Elks; Sertoma; NAACP; Pro Football Hall of Fame Club; Canton Ex-Newsboys Asn; Fraternal Order Police Assocs; Stark Co. Hist. Soc; YMCA; Canton Art Inst. Awards from United Fund of Stark Co, YMCA and Salvation Army; Man of Year Award, Jefferson-Jackson Men's Club. Rel: Presbyterian. Mailing Add: 603 22nd St. N.W, Canton, Ohio 44709.

MEEKS, JULIUS PAUL, JR. D
Ala. State Rep.
b. Birmingham, Ala, 7/18/28; s. Julius Paul Meeks and Alice Mabel Jenkins M; m. to Ella Joan Marsh; c. Marsha Leigh. Educ: Univ. of Ala, B.S, 51; Birmingham Sch. of Law, LL.B, 57. Polit. & Govt. Pos: Ala. State Rep, 62- Bus. & Prof. Pos: Insurance. Mil. Serv: U.S. Army, Lt, 51-53. Mem: Eagles. Rel: Christian Church. Mailing Add: 333 Bank for Savings Bldg, Birmingham, Ala. 35203.

MEEKS, WILLIAM THOMAS, JR. D
b. Atlanta, Ga, 10/01/14; s. William Thomas Meeks and Dolly Colwell M; single. Educ: Clarkesville A & M, 30; Young Harris Jr. Col, 35. Polit. & Govt. Pos: Ga. State Rep, 63-66, 49-50, 47. Bus. & Prof. Pos: Merchant; farmer. Mil. Serv: WW II, discharged S/Sgt. 11/09/45; Am. & Asiatic-Pacific Theatre Ribbons; Good Conduct Medal. Mem: Mason; Elk; Am. Legion. Rel: Protestant. Mailing Add: Blairsville, Ga. 30512. (1967)

MEENAN, PATRICK HENRY R
Wyo. State Rep.
b. Casper, Wyo, 9/24/27; s. Hugh Martin Meenan and Margaret Kelly M; m. 12/30/50 to Shirley Louise Byron; c. Maurya Ann, Kevin Patrick, Michael James and Patricia Kelly. Educ: Univ. Notre Dame, B.S.C. cum laude, 49. Polit. & Govt. Pos: Councilman, City of Casper, Wyo, 56-65, v.mayor, 61, mayor, 62 & 65; U.S. del, Int. Union of Local Authorities, 61; Wyo. State Rep, 69- Bus. & Prof. Pos: CPA, Raab, Roush & Gaymon, 49-53, partner, 60-69; asst. treas, Williston Oil & Gas Co, 53-55; partner, Meenan & Higgins, CPA, 55-60; pres, KATI & KAWY(FM), 64- Mem: Am. Inst. CPA; Wyo. Soc. CPA; Nat. and Wyo. Asns. Broadcasters; CBS Affil. Asn; K. of C; Elks; Eagles; Lions; C. of C,(dir); Casper Country Club. Jaycee Young Man of the Year, 62; Distinguished Pub. Servant, 65; Jaycee Boss of the Year, 66. Rel: Roman Catholic. Legal Res: 3070 E. Fourth, Casper, Wyo. 82601. Mailing Add: Box 481, Casper, Wyo. 82601.

MEES, VEARLE ABBIE R
b. Alpena, S.Dak, 1/29/14; d. Roy Washington Neumeyer and Abbie Louisa Wentzel N; m. 12/13/41 to Harold Alfred Mees; c. Kay Ann and Karla Ardene. Educ: North. State Teacher's Col, Aberdeen, 1½ years; Leadership Club. Polit. & Govt. Pos: Precinct committeewoman, Jerauld Co. Rep. Club, S.Dak, 61-69, v.chmn, 65-69. Mem: V.chmn, Alpena Sch. Bd. of Educ; Progressive Study Club; Home Makers Exten. Club; WSCS; life mem, PTA. Rel: Methodist. Mailing Add: R.R. 2, Alpena, S.Dak. 57312.

MEGEATH, WILLIAM A. D
b. Rock Springs, Wyo, 10/18/13; m. to Josephine; c. Four. Educ: Univ. of Wyo, B.S. Polit. & Govt. Pos: Former Wyo. State Rep; mem, Uinta Co. Dem. Cmt. Bus. & Prof. Pos: Mgr, Freemans Bar; owner, garage and serv. sta. Mem: Lions; C. of C. Rel: Presbyterian. Mailing Add: 416 Main St, Evanston, Wyo. 82636. (1967)

MEGGS, MARGARETTE BROWN R
b. Detroit, Mich, 8/19/10; d. Edward George Brown and Mary Ellen O'Leary McGeary B; m. 8/25/32 to Charles Winfield Meggs; c. Brown, Toby Wiley, Peggy White and Victoria Meade. Educ: Marymount Col, N.Y. Polit. & Govt. Pos: Rep. nominee for Calif. State Sen. and for Presidential Elector, 64; city councilwoman, Grass Valley, Calif, 64-66; former mem, Calif. State Rep. Cent. Cmt. Bus. & Prof. Pos: Lectr, currently. Mil. Serv: Driver for Naval Aid, 11th Naval Dist, 41-44. Published short stories; prize winning art. Rel: Catholic. Mailing Add: 320 Moss, Laguna Beach, Calif. 96251. (1967)

MEHOLCHICK, STANLEY A. D
Pa. State Rep.
b. Ashley, Pa, 1/1/17; s. Albert Meholchick (deceased) and Margaret Miller M; m. to Viola F. Rowinski; c. Margaret, Paulette, Violet, Bernice, Stanley, Jr, and George. Educ: St. Leo's Parochial Sch, Ashley, Pa. Polit. & Govt. Pos: Sch. dir, Ashley Borough, Pa, 48-57 & 61-65; Dem. chmn, Second Legis. Dist, 50-54; Pa. State Rep, 54- Bus. & Prof. Pos: Breaker-repairman, Huber Colliery, Glen Alden Corp. Mem: United Mine Workers, Local 7779; Lions; Elks; United Sportsmen of Pa; Tatra Club; Holy Name Soc; Holy Rosary Post 274. Rel: Holy Family Church. Mailing Add: 3 Sively St, Ashley, Pa. 18706. (1967)

MEHURON, VARNUM R. R
b. Ira, Vt, 9/18/91; m. to Addie M. Parker. Educ: Ira Pub. Sch. Polit. & Govt. Pos: Vt. State Rep, 31, 63, 65; sch. dir, 19-22; selectman, 27-60; justice of the peace, 36- Bus. & Prof. Pos: Retired marble worker. Mem: Masons; Eastern Star. Rel: Baptist. Mailing Add: RFD 1, West Rutland, Vt. 05727. (1967)

MEIDINGER, ROLAND E. R
b. Fredonia, N.Dak, 4/15/13; s. John J. Meidinger and Amelia M; m. 4/2/62 to Shirley E. Rolfs; c. Andrea J. Educ: Univ. of the Pac, B.S, 36. Polit. & Govt. Pos: N.Dak. State Sen, 53-65, mem, Legis. Research Cmn, N.Dak. State Senate, 55-65; Rep. Nat. Committeeman, N.Dak, 63-68; mem, N.Dak. Higher Educ. Facilities Cmn, 65-67; alternate del, Rep. Nat. Conv, 68. Bus. & Prof. Pos: Pres, State Bank of Streeter, 53-68; trustee, Jamestown Col, 56-; pres, R.E. Meidinger Co. Inc, 61-; pres, Stutsman Co. State Bank, 65- Mem: Mason; Shrine; Jester; Elks; Rotary. Rel: Methodist. Mailing Add: 733 Fifth St. N.E, Jamestown, N.Dak. 58401.

MEIER, BEN R
N.Dak. Secy. of State
b. Logan City, N.Dak, 8/1/18; m. 1944 to Clara Kaczynski; c. Lynn and Bernie. Educ: Dak. Bus. Col; Sch. of Banking, Univ. Wis. Polit. & Govt. Pos: N.Dak. Secy. of State, 54-; acting gov. of N.Dak, 61; v.chmn, Nat. Conf. States Bldg. Codes and Standards, currently. Bus. & Prof. Pos: Farming, until 41; banking at Napoleon, Gackle and Hazleton, N.Dak, 8 years; real estate bus, Bismarck, 53-; pres, Mandan Security Bank, 59- Mem: Sons of Norway; N.Dak. Bankers Asn; Nat. Asn. Secretaries of State (past pres). Mailing Add: Bismarck, N.Dak. 58501.

MEIER, ERVIN A. R
Mayor, Wauwatosa, Wis.
b. Milwaukee, Wis, 9/17/97; s. William Meier and Minnie Mahnke M; m. 7/19/28 to Olga Wolf; c. Arlene M. (Mrs. Donald J. Koch) and Corene V. (Mrs. James O. Klippel). Educ: Correspondence college courses. Polit. & Govt. Pos: Mayor, Wauwatosa, 64- and alderman. Bus. & Prof. Pos: Pres, League of Wis. Munic. Mem: Milwaukee Typographical Union 23; pres, Kiwanis and Wauwatosa PTA; Mason; Shrine; K. of P. Rel: Methodist; United Brethren Church. Legal Res: 2564 North 81st St, Wauwatosa, Wis. 53213. Mailing Add: 7725 West North Ave, Wauwatosa, Wis. 53213.

MEIER, HAROLD ELLSWITH R
Wyo. State Rep.
b. Denver, Colo, 2/6/32; s. Henry A. Meier and Ruth Winsor M; m. 9/1/58 to Joan Carrol Preis; c. Scott Winsor, Celia Ann and Douglas Conrad. Educ: Univ. Wyo, B.S. in Geol, 54, J.D, 59; Omicron Delta Kappa; Chi Gamma Iota; Kappa Sigma. Polit. & Govt. Pos: Co. and Prosecuting Attorney, Fremont Co, Wyo, 66; Wyo. State Rep, 69- Mil. Serv: Army Eng. Corp, 54-56. Mem: Am. Bar Asn; Mason; Consistory; Shrine; Lions; Elks. Rel: Lutheran. Legal Res: 342 Parks St, Lander, Wyo. 82520. Mailing Add: 150 N. Third, Lander, Wyo. 82520.

MEIER, WILLIAM HENRY D
Chmn, Kearney Co. Dem. Cent. Cmt, Nebr.
b. Lincoln, Nebr, 12/23/04; s. Otto William Meier and Mary G. Bothwell M; m. 8/12/34 to Amelia Mabel Utter; c. William E, Joel F. and Sarah (Mrs. Arnold Peterson). Educ: Univ. Nebr, A.B, 26, J.D, 30; Paladian Lit. Soc; Delta Theta Phi. Polit. & Govt. Pos: Spec. agent, Fed. Bur. Invest, Denver, Colo. and Birmingham, Ala, 30-31; Nebr. State Sen, 32-34; attorney, Fed. Land Bank, Omaha, 34-36; police magistrate, Minden, 38-40; chmn, Kearney Co. Dem. Cent. Cmt, 38-40,& 65-; mem, Nebr. State Dem. Cent. Cmt, 40-42, chmn, 50-54 and mem, 54-58; govt. appeal agent, Kearney Co. Selective Serv, 40-42 & 48-49; asst. U.S. Dist. Attorney, Omaha, 42-45; mem. Minden Sch. Bd, 45-48 and pres, 46-48; mem, Kearney Co. Selective Serv. Bd, 45-47; Nebr. Dem. Pres. Elector Designate, 48; chmn, Dem. First Cong. Dist. Conv, 48-50; mem, Kearney Co. Sch. Reorgn. Cmt, 49-54; co. attorney, Kearny Co, 59-67, dep. co. attorney, 67- Bus. & Prof. Pos: Mem, Matschullat, Meier and Matschullat, Attorneys, Lincoln, 30-33; attorney, Minden, 36-67; partner, Meier & Adkins, Attorneys, 67- Mem: Am, Nebr, Tenth Judicial Dist. and Kearny Co. Bar Asns; AF&AM; Mason (32°) Shrine; Lions; past dist. gov, Lions Int, 50-51; Odd Fellows; pres, Minden C. of C, 50. Man of the Year, Minden C. of C, 50; Cong. Selective Serv. Medal. Rel: Presbyterian. Legal Res: 305 N. Tower Ave, Minden, Nebr. 68959. Mailing Add: P.O. Box 267, Minden, Nebr. 68959.

MEIKLE, KATHLEEN HURST D
State Dir, U.S. Savings Bonds Div, Dept. Treas.
b. Pawnee, Okla, 1/11/16; d. Waldo Ross Hurst and Nora Tippits H; m. 11/17/33 to John H. Meikle; c. John Roger and Mellanee (Mrs. Kirk I. Cronquist). Educ: Stevens Henager Col. Polit. & Govt. Pos: V.chmn, Cache Co. Young Dem, Utah, 54-57; mem, Cache Co. Dem. Exec. Cmt, 54-61; secy-treas, Smithfield Dist. One Dem. Party, Utah, 54-66; del, Dem. Nat. Conv, 56, 60 & 64; mem, West. States Dem. Conf, 57; co-chmn, Utah State Dem. Cent. Cmt, 57-61; field secy. to U.S. Sen. Frank E. Moss, 59-60, mem, State Adv. Cmn, U.S. Cmn. on Civil Rights, 62-; mem, Utah State Small Bus. Adv. Coun, U.S. Small Bus. Admin, 64-; state dir, U.S. Savings Bond Div, Dept. of Treas. Bus. & Prof. Pos: Retail dealer, Midwest. Homes, 62-68; mgr, broker, Mt. States Realty, 63-66; owner and broker, Meikle Real Estate, 66- Mem: State Asn. Real Estate Bd; Smithfield Civic Club; PTA; Farmers Union; One Hundred Club; Utah Dem. Women's Club; Toastmistress Club; C. of C; Fed. Exec. Asn.(Utah Chap); Am. Soc. Pub. Admin.(bd, mem, Utah Chap, 67-). Only woman panelist on Secy. of Agr. Land and People Conf. Portland, Ore, 62; Superior Serv. Award, Spec. Serv. Award and Secy. Cert, U.S. Savings Bonds Div, Dept. Treas, 68. Rel: Latter-day Saint. Mailing Add: 785 South 650 East, Bountiful, Utah 84010.

MEINECKE, ROBERT LEE R
Chmn, Lamb Co. Rep. Party, Tex.
b. Plainview, Tex, 12/31/30; s. Robert Lee Meinecke and Nannie Wilson M; m. 5/13/51 to Patricia Mae Vaughn; c. Jackye, Sheree and Mitzi. Educ: Tex. Tech. Col, B.S. in Agronomy, 53. Polit. & Govt. Pos: Chmn, Lamb Co. Rep. Party, Tex, 65- Bus. & Prof. Pos: Farmer, currently. Mem: Mason; Farm Bur: Girl Scouts. Rel: Methodist. Mailing Add: Route 1, Olton, Tex. 79064.

MEIS, MARTHA F. R
Assoc. Mem, Calif. Rep. State Cent. Cmt.
b. Oyens, Iowa, 9/12/13; d. John Meis and Susan Homan M; single. Educ: Mt. St. Mary, Cherokee, Iowa, B.A, 34; Univ. Calif, Los Angeles, postgrad. eng. courses, 44-45. Polit. & Govt. Pos: Assoc. mem, Calif. Rep. State Cent. Cmt, 50-; v.pres, Los Angeles Co. Rep. Assembly, 52-53; v.pres, Calif. Rep. Assembly, 56-57 and 62-63; mem. and secy, Los Angeles Co. Rep. Cent. Cmt, 58- and v.chmn. exec. cmt, 67-69. Bus. & Prof. Pos: Indust. engr, N.Am. Rockwell Corp, Los Angeles Div, 42- Publ: Time Study Manual, N.Am. Aviation, Inc, Los Angeles Div, 58. Mem: Soc. Applied Indust. Eng; Soc. Women Engrs; Soc. Adv. Mgt; C. of C, Women's Div. Rel: Roman Catholic. Mailing Add: 7002 Ramsgate Place, Los Angeles, Calif. 90045.

MELAS, NICHOLAS J. D
Chmn. Exec. Cmt, Fourth Ward Dem. Orgn, Chicago, Ill.
b. Chicago, Ill, 8/22/23; s. John Melas and Christina Pappas M; m. 1/29/61 to Irene Prasopoulos; c. Christina and Elizabeth. Educ: Univ. Chicago, Ph.B, 46, S.B, 48; Univ. Chicago Grad. Sch. of Bus, M.B.A, 50; Beta Gamma Sigma; Phi Gamma Delta; The Quadrangle Club. Polit. & Govt. Pos: Chmn, Cook Co, Ill. Vet. for Paul H. Douglas, 48; admin. asst. to Sheriff of Cook Co, 54-59; chmn, Young Dem. of Cook Co, 55-56; supvr. of collections, Dept. of Revenue, Ill, 61; city sealer, Chicago, 61-62; trustee, Metrop. Sanit. Dist, Greater Chicago, 62-; chmn. exec. cmt, Fourth Ward Dem. Orgn, Chicago, 62-; alternate del, Dem. Nat. Conv, 68. Bus. & Prof. Pos: Proj. dir, Indust. Rels. Center, Univ. Chicago, 50-54; owner, N.J. Melas & Co, Gen. Ins, 63- Mil. Serv: Entered as Pvt, Army, 43, released as Pfc, 45, after serv. in 411th Inf. Regt, 103rd Div, ETO, 44 and 45; Purple Heart; Bronze Star. Mem: Am. Acad. of Polit. and Soc. Sci: Indust. Rels. Res. Asn; Am. Legion; Am. Vet. Cmt; dir, Church Fedn. of Greater Chicago; Chicago Urban League; Crusade of Mercy, Hyde Park Kenwood Commun. Conf. Wrestling, 2nd place, Big Ten, 42, 1st place, Midwest A.A.U, 42. Rel: Greek Orthodox; v.pres, St. Constantine and Helen Greek Orthodox Church. Legal Res: 5000 E. End Ave, Chicago, Ill. 60615. Mailing Add: 100 E. Erie St, Chicago, Ill. 60611.

MELBOURNE, MAXINE JOYCE R
Mem, Valencia Co. Rep. Cent. Cmt, N.Mex.
b. Cortez, Colo, 2/12/37; d. John Theodore Dunning and Effie Snyder D; m. 7/20/57 to Ralph Melbourne; c. Ralph Patrick and Nancy Jeanne. Educ: Mesa Jr. Col, Colo, 54-55; Draughon's Bus. Col, Albuquerque, N.Mex, 55. Polit. & Govt. Pos: Block capt, Rep. Party, Bernalillo Co, N.Mex, 60, precinct div. chmn, 63-65, Rep. chmn, Precinct 31, 67-; del, N.Mex. Rep. State Conv, 61-68; chmn. by-laws cmt, Rep. Women Valencia Co, 66; mem, Valencia Co. Rep. Cent. Cmt, 66-; chmn, Poll Workers Sch, 66 & 68; chmn, Women of Nixon, 68; alternate del, Rep. Nat. Conv, 68. Mem: PTA; East. Valencia Co. Little League Auxiliary. Rel: Episcopal. Legal Res: El Camino de Sandia Rd, Bosque Farms, N.Mex. 87105. Mailing Add: Route 1, Box 711 XX, Albuquerque, N.Mex. 87105.

MELBOURNE, RALPH R
Mem, N.Mex. Rep. State Cent. Cmt.
b. Albuquerque, N.Mex, 2/29/32; s. Ralph Melbourne (deceased), stepfather, Carl Schlick and Ernestine Wilson Melbourne S; m. 7/20/57 to Maxine Joyce Dunning; c. Ralph Patrick and Nancy Jeanne. Educ: Univ. N.Mex, B.B.A, 55. Polit. & Govt. Pos: Block worker, Rep. Party, Bernalillo Co, N.Mex, 60; mem, Bernalillo Co. Rep. Cent. Cmt, 61-63; del, N.Mex. Rep. State Conv, 61-68; mem. rules and order of bus. cmt, 68; chmn, Bernalillo Co. Rep. Finance Cmt, 63-65; mem, Bernalillo Co. Rep. Exec. Cmt, 63-65; treas, Bernalillo Co, 65; mem, Valencia Co. Rep. Cent. Cmt, 66-; mem, Valencia Co. Rep. Exec. Cmt, 66-; mem, N.Mex. Rep. State Cent. Cmt, 66-; finance chmn, East. Valencia Co, 67-69; chmn. campaign advert, Valencia Co, 68; chmn, Nixon for Pres. Cmt, Valencia Co, 68; hon- sgt-at-arms, Rep. Nat. Conv, 68; orgn. v.chmn, Dist. One, Rep. Party, Valencia Co, 69-; cmnr, Regional Housing Authority, N.Mex, 69- Bus. & Prof. Pos: Head teller, E.Cent. Off, Albuquerque Nat. Bank, N.Mex, 52-56; v.pres. and loan officer, Standard Mortgage Co. Inc, 56-63; v.pres. and sr. loan officer, Sandia Savings & Loan Asn, 63-69; lectr. and teacher real estate finance, career series, Univ. N.Mex, 66-69. Mem: Albuquerque Mortgage Bankers Asn.(past v.pres. and pres); Albuquerque Consumer Credit Asn.(past mem. bd. dirs); Albuquerque Bd. Realtors (past mem. finance cmt); PTA (past pres, Bosque Farms); past v.pres. and coach and currently umpire, East. Valencia Co. Little League; Los Lunas Jaycees (past secy-treas); Bernalillo Co. Red Cross (past mem. bd. dirs). Rel: Episcopal. Legal Res: El Camino de Sandia Rd, Bosque Farms, N.Mex. 87105. Mailing Add: Route 1, Box 711 XX, Albuquerque, N.Mex. 87105.

MELCHER, JOHN D
U.S. Rep, Mont.
b. Sioux City, Iowa, 9/6/24; m. 12/1/45 to Ruth Klein; c. Terry, Joan, Mary, Robert and John. Educ: Univ. Minn, 1 year; Iowa State Univ, D.V.M, 50; Phi Zeta. Polit. & Govt. Pos: City alderman, Forsyth, Mont, 53-55, mayor, 55-61; Mont. State Rep, Rosebud Co, 61-62 & 69; Mont. State Sen, 63-67; former mem, Mont. Legis. Coun; Dem. Cand. for U.S. Rep, Mont, 66; U.S. Rep, Mont, 69- Bus. & Prof. Pos: Partner, Yellowstone Valley Vet. Clinic, Forsyth, Mont, currently; operator, cattle feedlot, 56- Mil. Serv: Army, 43-45, with serv. in 76th Inf. Div, Third Army, ETO; Purple Heart; Combat Infantryman's Badge. Legal Res: Forsyth, Mont. Mailing Add: Room 1504, Longworth House Office Bldg, Washington, D.C. 20515.

MELICH, MITCHELL R
b. Bingham Canyon, Utah, 2/1/12; s. Joseph Melich and Mary Kalembar M; m. 6/3/35 to Doris Snyder; c. Tanya (Mrs. Noel L. Silverman), Dr. Michael E, Nancy (Mrs. Robert A. Ossana) and Robert A. Educ: Univ. Utah, LL.B, 34; Kappa Sigma. Polit. & Govt. Pos: City attorney, Moab, Utah, 34-55; co. attorney, Grand Co, 40-42; Utah State Sen, 42-50; mem, bd. regents, Univ. Utah, 59-64; Rep. Nat. Committeeman, Utah, 61-63; Rep. cand for Gov. of Utah, 64; consult. on staff of Congressman Sherman P. Lloyd, 67-69; former mem, Utah Legis. Coun; former mem, Utah Colo. River Water Bd; alternate del, Rep. Nat. Conv, 68; solicitor, Dept. of Interior, Wash, D.C, 69- Bus. & Prof. Pos: Secy. and dir, Utex Exploration Co, Utah, 53-62; pres, Uranian Reduction Co, 54-62; consult. to pres, Atlas Minerals, 62-67; mem. bd. dirs, Ideal Nat. Ins, 62-69; mem. bd, Salt Lake City First Security Bank, 62-69. Mem: Utah and Am. Bar Asns; chmn, Salt Lake City Coun. For. Rels; Cmt. Designing Educ. for Future; Utah Ballet Soc; Hon. Col. Corps, Utah; Alta Club; Salt Lake Country Club; Mason; Shrine. Rel: Congregational. Legal Res: Salt Lake City, Utah. Mailing Add: 4100 Cathedral Ave. N.W, Washington, D.C. 20016.

MELLAND, ROBERT BRUCE R
N.Dak. State Sen.
b. Fargo, N.Dak. 8/7/29; s. Russell O. Melland and Gunvor Wichmann M;

m. 9/1/49 to Helen Elaine Burau; c. James Bruce and Deborah Jean. Educ: Jamestown Col, 47-48; Concordia Col, 48-49. Polit. & Govt. Pos: Del, N.Dak. Rep. State Conv, 51; mem. adv. cmt, Stutsman Co. Rep. Party, 51-54, co. patronage cmt, 53-54 and finance chmn, 64-66; N.Dak. State Sen, Dist. 29, 67- Mem: Elks; Mason; Shrine; Eagles; C. of C.(pres, 57); Lions (pres, 58); pres, Jamestown Indust. Develop. Corp, 58-66; v.pres, Crippled Childrens Sch, 58-; trustee, Jamestown Col, 66- Rel: Lutheran. Legal Res: 225 Third Ave. S.E, Jamestown, N.Dak. 58401. Mailing Add: Box 112, Jamestown, N.Dak. 58401.

MELLEN, MELBA J. R
Mem, Calif. Rep. State Cent. Cmt.
b. Bonham, Tex, 8/5/27; d. Graham F. Gurden and Ethel Russell G; m. 10/1/59 to Richard A. Mellen; c. Richard G, Mark S. and Fredric A. Educ: Cent. High Sch, Jackson, Miss, grad, 45; Millsaps Col, 45-47; Vikings, Millsaps Col. Polit. & Govt. Pos: Chmn, Bus. Women's Cmt, Rep. Assocs, Los Angeles, Calif, 69-; mem, Calif. Rep. State Cent. Cmt, 69- Rel: Protestant. Mailing Add: 10724 Garfield Ave, Culver City, Calif. 90230.

MELLO, DONALD RAY D
Nev. State Assemblyman
b. Owensboro, Ky, 6/22/34; s. Jack Mello (deceased) and Gladys (Peggy) Jasper M; m. 2/18/56 to Barbara Jane Woodhall; c. Donald Jack and David William. Educ: Univ. of Nev, 53-55; Lambda Chi Alpha. Polit. & Govt. Pos: Nev. State Assemblyman, 63-, mem, Legis. Cmn. Sub-Cmt. to Study State Hosp. Probs, 67-68, first Alternate, Legis. Cmn, 67-68, mem, 69-71, mem, Legis. Cmn. Sub-cmt. to Study State Uniform Consumer Credit Code—Consumer Protection, 69-71. Bus. & Prof. Pos: Brakeman, South. Pac. Co, 55-61, conductor, 61- Mil. Serv: Inactive Naval Res. Mem: Elks, Reno Lodge No. 597; F&AM, Nev. Benjamin Franklin Lodge 45; Eagles, Aerie No. 2625; Sparks Dem. Club; past mem. bd. dir, C. of C; Brotherhood of Railway Trainmen, Lodge 726; mem. bd. dir, Young Audiences of North. Nev, Inc; Sons of Italy. Capt, Sparks High Sch. Track Team, 53; Record Holder of 220 yd. dash. Rel: Emmanuel Baptist. Mailing Add: 2590 Oppio St, Sparks, Nev. 89431.

MELLO, HENRY JOHN D
Supvr, Santa Cruz Co, Calif.
b. Watsonville, Calif, 3/27/24; s. John C. Mello and Margaret S. Travers M; m. 2/26/49 to Helen A. Burns; c. John H, Stephen F, Michael B. and Timothy S. Educ: Hartnell Col. Polit. & Govt. Pos: Chmn, Santa Cruz Co. Dem. Cent. Cmt, Calif, 60-66; cmnr, Local Agency Formation Cmn, 64-66; supvr, Santa Cruz Co, 67- Mem: Elks; Native Sons of the Golden West; Boy Scouts; Refrigerating Engrs. & Technicians Asn. Rel: Catholic. Legal Res: 32 White Rd, Watsonville, Calif. 95076. Mailing Add: P.O. Box 47, Watsonville, Calif. 95076.

MELONEY, JOHN MITCHELL
b. Walton, N.Y, 1/14/23; s. Henry Mitchell Meloney and Charlotte More M; m. 5/28/49 to Virginia Shannon Malany. Educ: Cornell Univ, 42-43; Univ. Minn, 44; Univ. Stockholm, Sweden, 46. Polit. & Govt. Pos: Organizer, polit. pressure groups for World Fed. Govt, throughout U.S. and Scandinavia, 44-49; chmn, West. N.H. Eugene McCarthy Campaign, 68; del, Dem. Nat. Conv, 68. Bus. & Prof. Pos: Reporter and ed, various newspapers, N.Y, N.H. and Fla, 40-59; dist. mgr, King Meritt & Co, N.H, Vt. and Fla, 59-64; east. regional dir, Am. Youth Hostels, Inc, 64- Mil. Serv: Entered as Pvt, Army, 43, released as Sgt, 46, after serv. in OSS, ETO, 44-46; ETO Ribbon; Good Conduct Medal. Mem: Sigma Delta Chi; Nat. Recreation and Parks Asn; Mason; Rotary; Sierra Club; Appalachian Mt. Club; Alaska Conserv. Soc; state bd. dirs, N.H. Civil Liberties Union, 68. Rel: Protestant. Legal Res: 95 Winter St, Claremont, N.H. 03743. Mailing Add: Box 59, Claremont, N.H. 03743.

MELOY, FRANCES EANES D
b. Richmond, Va, 10/15/18; d. David Dance Eanes and Annie Woodward E; m. 8/2/41 to Samuel William Hubbard Meloy; c. William Stephen; Arthur David and Patricia Anne. Educ: Mary Wash. Col. Polit. & Govt. Pos: Subsupvr, Elections, Prince Georges Co, Md, 62-63; campaign mgr, Joseph D. Tydings, 64; mem, Md. Status of Women Cmn, 65-66; Md. State Del, 64-66. Mem: Past v.pres, South. Convocation, Episcopal Churchwomen, Wash, 61-65; v.pres, Am. Cancer Soc, Prince Georges Co, 62-64; treas, Forest Garden Club, 63-64; dir, Prince Georges Chap, Am. Red. Cross, 65-69; Owls. Rel: Episcopal. Mailing Add: Box 210 Billings Lea, Upper Marlboro, Md. 20870.

MELOY, FRANCIS EDWARD, JR.
U.S. Ambassador to the Dominican Repub.
b. Wash, 3/28/17; s. Francis Edward Meloy and Anne Teresa Connor M. Educ: Am. Univ, B.A, 39; Yale Univ, M.A, 42. Polit. & Govt. Pos: Mem, Diplomatic Serv, 46-; v.consul, Dhahran, Saudi Arabia, 46-49; assigned to Off. of the Secy. of State, 49-53; detailed to NATO Defense Col, Paris, France, 53; second secy. and consul, Am. Embassy, Saigon, Vietnam, 53, first secy. and consul, 54; first secy. and consul, Paris, France, 56-57; mem, U.S. Mission to NATO, Paris, 57-58; detailed to Imperial Defense Col, London, Eng, 59-60; spec. asst. to Dep. Under Secy. of State for Polit. Affairs, 60-62; dir. Off. of West. European Affairs, 62-64; minister and dep. chief of mission, Am. Embassy, Rome, Italy, 64-69; U.S. Ambassador to the Dominican Repub, 69- Mil. Serv: Lt. Comdr, Naval Res, 42-46. Mem: U.S. del, first Australia, New Zealand and U.S. Coun. Meeting, Honolulu, Hawaii, 52; tenth NATO Coun. Meeting, Paris, France, 52; Metropolitan Club; City Tavern Asn, Wash. Legal Res: 2909 P St. N.W, Washington, D.C. 20007. Mailing Add: U.S. Embassy, Santo Domingo, Dominican Republic.

MELROSE, A. RAE D
b. China, 10/2/94; s. John C. Melrose and Margaret R. M; m. to Mona Kies; c. Andrew R, Mona M.(Mrs. Altiery) and Nancy M.(Mrs. Albertson). Educ: Lenox Col, B.A, 1915; Columbia Univ, M.A, 1920. Polit. Pos: Iowa State Rep, 1966; Chmn, Draft Bd; Airport Cmn; Chmn, Planning and Zoning Cmn; City Dem. Chmn, 50-57. Bus & Prof. Pos: Ins. Agent since 1927; High Sch. Prin, 16-27. Mil. Serv: WWI Vet; Distinguished Serv. Cross; Purple Heart. Mem: C. of C; Lions Club; Am. Legion; VFW; Masons; K. of P; Trustee, Munic. Hosp. Rel: Congregationalist. Mailing Add: 609 N. Johnson, Charles City, Iowa 50616. (1967)

MELTON, EMORY L. R
Treas, Barry Co. Rep. Cent. Cmt, Mo.
b. McDowell, Mo. 6/20/23; s. C.R. Melton and Pearly Wise M; m. 6/19/49 to Jean Sanders; c. Stanley and Russell. Educ: Univ. Mo, LL.B, 45. Polit. & Govt. Pos: Prosecuting attorney, Barry Co, Mo, 47-51; treas, Barry Co. Rep. Cent. Cmt, Mo, currently. Bus. & Prof. Pos: Pres, Melton Publns, Inc, 60- Mil. Serv: Entered as Pvt, Army, 45, released as Sgt, 46, after serv. in Criminal Invest. Div, Pac. Theater, 45-46. Mem: Mason; Lions. Rel: Baptist. Mailing Add: Cassville, Mo. 65625.

MELTON, G. T. D
b. Tennille, Ga, 11/2/11; m. to Sarah Morrison; c. Mrs. Jack Argersinger, T. Morrison and Patricia. Educ: Fla. South. Col, A.B, 33. Polit. & Govt. Pos: Fla. State Sen, 58-67. Bus. & Prof. Pos: Distributor of petroleum prod. Mem: C. of C, former dir; Elks; Moose; Rotary, former dist. gov; Fla. State Golf Asn, former pres; Lake City Country Club. Rel: Methodist, former chmn. of bd. Mailing Add: P.O. Box 971, Lake City, Fla. 32055. (1967)

MELTON, JOHN CALVIN R
b. El Paso, Tex, 7/27/29; s. John Graham Melton and Elsie Ruth Briggs M; m. 10/11/52 to Midge Rinehart; c. Cathy, Frederick, Gregg and Kurt. Educ: Tex. West. Col, 46-48; Univ. Tex, Austin, 56-57; Univ. Tex, Dent. Br, D.D.S, 61; Omicron Kappa Epsilon; Sigma Alpha Epsilon; Delta Sigma Delta. Polit. & Govt. Pos: Block worker, Rep. Party, Las Cruces, N.Mex, 64-65; mem, Rep. Cent. Cmt, Las Cruces, 65-69; chmn, Co. Rep. Precinct Affairs Cmt, 65-66; chmn, Rep. Co. Cmt, 66-69; mem, State Rep. Cent. Cmt, 66-69; mem, State Rep. Exec. Cmt, 68-69. Bus. & Prof. Pos: Mem. dent. staff, Mem. Gen. Hosp. Mil. Serv: Entered as Pvt, Army, 51, released as 1st Lt, 53, after serv. in 65th Inf. Regt, 3rd Inf. Div, Fecom, Korea, 53; Combat Infantrymans Badge, Korean Serv. Medal with Two Battle Stars; Nat. Defense Serv. Medal; UN Serv. Medal. Mem: Southwest Dist, N.Mex. and Am. Dent. Asns; Dona Ana Dent. Soc.(pres, 66); pres, Co. Coun. of Dona Ana Co. PTA. Rel: Episcopal. Legal Res: 1300 Park St, Las Cruces, N.Mex. 88001.

MELTON, MITCHELL WESLEY D
Pa. State Rep.
b. Phila, Pa, 4/6/43; s. Mitchell Melton and Ethel I. Hall M; m. to Evelyn Jean Reddick; c. Tyrone Eugene and Donna Marie. Educ: Pa. Inst. Criminology, Dipl, 63. Polit. & Govt. Pos: Dem. committeeman, 32nd Ward, 18th Div, Pa, 64-; Pa. State Rep, 196th Legis. Dist, 68- Bus. & Prof. Pos: Ins. agent, N.C. Mutual Life Ins. Co, 65-67; revenue investr, Phila. Dept. Collections, Sanit. Div, 67-68. Mem: Phila. Jr. C. of C.(past chmn, Neighborhood Youth Corps cmt). Rel: African Methodist Episcopal. Mailing Add: 1843 N. Taney St, Philadelphia, Pa. 19121.

MELTON, QUIMBY, JR. D
Ga. State Rep.
b. Americus, Ga, 2/12/22; s. Quimby Melton, Sr. and Mary Davenport M; m. 6/30/43 to May Kenimer Wingfield; c. Oliver Quimby III, Mary Wingfield, Laura Barnett and Leila Davenport. Educ: Baylor Sch, 39; Univ. Ga, A.B, 42; La Salle Exten, LL.B, 57; Woodrow Wilson Col. of Law, LL.B, 61; Kappa Alpha. Polit. & Govt. Pos: Ga. State Rep, 59- Bus. & Prof. Pos: Ed, Griffin Daily News, 45-; attorney-at-law, 61- Mil. Serv: Lt, World War II; Purple Heart. Mem: Mason; Elks; Gridiron; Bd. of Regents, Univ. System of Ga, 55-60; pres, Ga. Press Asn, 55-56; State Progs. Study Cmn, 54. Man of the Year in Griffin, 58; wrote and edited, Hist. of Griffin, 59. Rel: Methodist. Mailing Add: Griffin Daily News, Griffin, Ga. 30223.

MELTON, RALPH H. R
Mo. State Rep.
b. Dadeville, Mo, 7/23/19; s. John Otis Melton and Millie Holman M; m. 4/13/56 to Betty Walsh; c. Nancy Jane, Twyla Jean. Educ: High sch. grad. Polit. & Govt. Pos: Mo. State Rep, 64- Bus. & Prof. Pos: Milk trucking line owner and operator for 13 years; presently owns and operates Hi-View Registered Jersey Farm with brother. Rel: Methodist. Mailing Add: Dadeville, Mo. 65635.

MELVIN, JARRETT GREEN 'JERRY' D
Fla. State Rep.
b. Bonifay, Fla, 7/22/29; s. Carlton Alexander Melvin and Ruby Newton M; m. 6/7/68 to Patricia Ann Shelly Emminizer; c. Shelly Ann and JayGee. Educ: Col. of Charleston, 2 years; Am. Univ; Fla. State Univ, Eglin Air Force Base Exten; Pi Kappa Phi; Athletic Coun; Student Coun. Polit. & Govt. Pos: Pres, Okaloosa Co. Young Dem, 56; nat. committeeman, Fla. Young Dem, 57; legis. asst, U.S. Rep. Bob Sikes, 56-59; Fla. State Rep, Seventh Dist, 68- Bus. & Prof. Pos: Asst. radio station mgr, WCNH, Quincy, Fla, 50-54; writer, develop. proj, Playground Daily News, Ft. Walton Beach, Fla, 61-62; exec. mgr. Okaloosa Island Authority, 62-; owner, J.G. Melvin Bus. Serv, 63-; secy-treas, Prfnl. Bldg, 66- Mil. Serv: Nat. Guard. Mem: Northwest Fla. Press Club; Fla. Pub. Rels. Coun; Kiwanis; C. of C.(exec. mgr, Ft. Walton Beach Chap, 54-56 & 59-61, mem, Destin and Niceville-Valparaiso Chap); Miracle Strip Coun; Gulf Beach Resort Asn; W.Fla. Natural Resources Coun; Adult Adv. Coun, Okaloosa-Walton Jr. Col; Game Fish Protective Asn. Most Talented High Sch. Sr, 47; Mr. Col. of Charleston, 48; Freshman C. of C. Scholarship, 55; Runner-up, Allen Morris Award, Outstanding Freshman Legis, 69. Rel: Methodist. Mailing Add: 840 Santa Rosa Court, OIB, Ft. Walton Beach, Fla. 32548.

MELVIN, KATHLEEN O'HARA R
b. Syracuse, N.Y, 11/27/30; d. Henry Russell O'Hara and Doris Bolton O; m. 8/7/54 to Crandall Melvin, Jr; c. Crandall Melvin III. Educ: Syracuse Univ, B.A, 51; Pi Gamma Mu; Kappa Kappa Gamma. Polit. & Govt. Pos: V.pres, Onondaga Co. Young Rep. Club, N.Y, 50-52; Miss Eisenhower For N.Y. State, 52; co-chmn, Youth For Eisenhower, Onondaga Co, 52; secy. Bd. of Gov, Asn. N.Y. State Young Rep. Clubs, 52-54; N.Y. State Rep. Upstate Finance Cmt, 62-64; v.chmn, Onondaga Co. Rep. Cmt, 64-68. Bus. & Prof. Pos: Tech. writer, Gen. Elec. Co, Syracuse, 51-56. Mem: Women of Rotary of Syracuse (past pres); YWCA (treas, Syracuse and Onondaga Co. Chap); Cent. N.Y. Girl Scout Coun.(first v.pres); first v.pres, Auxiliary to Commun. Gen. Hosp. of Gr. Syracuse. Rel: Unitarian-Universalist. Mailing Add: 604 Balsam St, Liverpool, N.Y. 13088.

MENAKER, EDWARD GOWARD D
Chmn, Waynesboro Dem. City Cmt, Va.
b. Newark, N.J, 4/10/19; s. George Menaker and Sara Goward M; m. 9/6/41 to Elizabeth Dresbold; c. Richard Glen and Lawrence James. Educ: Columbia Col, A.B, 38; Columbia Univ, M.A, 39; Union Col, N.Y, 46-47. Polit. & Govt. Pos: V.chmn, Waynesboro Dem. City Cmt, Va, 65-66, chmn, 69-; mem. bd. trustees, Waynesboro Pub. Libr, 66; del, Dem. Nat. Conv, 68. Bus. & Prof. Pos: Teacher, Altaraz Sch, Monterey, Mass, 40-41; engr. and various eng. mgt. pos, Gen. Elec. Co, Schenectady, N.Y. and Waynesboro, Va, 46-; value control mgr, Compagnie Bull, Gen. Elec, Paris, France, 67. Mil. Serv: Entered as Pvt, Army, 42, released as Maj, 46, after serv. in 308th Bombardment Group, 14th Air Force, China-Burma-India Theatre, 44-45, Maj.(Ret), Air Force; Bronze Star Medal; Unit Citation; Theatre Ribbons with 6 Battle Stars. Publ: 'Fundamentals of Infrared Hot Box Detection,' IEEE Transactions, 64. Mem: Nat. Soc. Prfnl. Engrs; Inst. Elec. and Electronic Engrs; Scout cmnr, Stonewall Jackson Area Coun. and del, Nat. Coun, Boy Scouts. Silver Beaver Award, Boy Scouts. Rel: Jewish. Mailing Add: 1824 Westminster Rd, Waynesboro, Va. 22980.

MENASCO, HORACE R
Dep. Asst. Secy. for Labor Standards, Dept. of Labor
Mailing Add: Dept. of Labor, 14th & Constitution Ave. N.W, Washington, D.C. 20210.

MENDALL, RALPH BERTRAND, JR. R
b. Middleboro, Mass, 2/20/21; s. Ralph B. Mendall and Marjorie Kendall M; m. 11/30/46 to Florence S. Snyder; c. Geoffrey S. and Melissa M. Educ: Univ. of Mass; Kappa Sigma. Polit. & Govt. Pos: Mem and finance chmn, Plympton Rep. Town Cmt, Mass, 58-, chmn, 60-68; mem, Plympton Finance Cmt, 62-63; mem, Silver Lake Regional High Sch. Bd, 63-64; mem, Indust. Cmn, Plympton, 69- Bus. & Prof. Pos: Claims Examiner, Liberty Mutual Ins. Co, 54-66. Mil. Serv: Entered as Pvt, Army, 42, released as T/Sgt, 51, after serv. in Signal Corps, ETO and Korea; Good Conduct Medal; ETO Medal with Two Battle Stars; Am. Theater, Victory and Japanese Occupation Medals; Presidential Citation with Two Clusters. Mem: Assoc. mem, Plymouth Co. Rep. Club; Plympton Commun. Garden Club (conserv. chmn). Rel: Protestant. Mailing Add: RFD, Grove St, Plympton, Mass. 02367.

MENDELSOHN, ROBERT H. D
Supvr, San Francisco Co. Bd. of Supvr, Calif.
b. Iowa City, Iowa, 1/11/38; s. Matthew Mendelsohn and Esther Jacobs M; m. 1/25/57 to Ingrid Levin; c. Scott. Educ: Univ. Calif, Berkeley, A.B. cum laude, 59; Coro Found, San Francisco, Cert, 61; Pi Sigma Alpha; Honor Student Soc; Interfraternity Scholastic Honor Soc. Polit. & Govt. Pos: Supvr. commun. serv, San Francisco Redevelopment Agency, Calif, 61-64; admin. asst, State Sen. J. Eugene McAteer, 64-67; San Francisco v.chmn, Kennedy for Pres. Campaign, 68; state-wide chmn, Educators for Cranston, 68; del, Dem. Nat. Conv, 68; supvr, San Francisco Co. and City Bd. of Supvr, 68- Bus. & Prof. Pos: Asst. prof. polit. sci, San Francisco State Col, 67-; lectr, Nat. Coun. Jewish Women, 68 & 69; dir. develop, Century Consultants, Inc, 68-; consult, Daniel Yankelovich, Inc, 68-; lectr. grad. sch. soc. welfare, Univ. Calif, 69- Mil. Serv: Entered as Pvt, Marine Corps Res, 56, released as Pfc, 62, after serv. in Sixth Commun. Co, Fourth Marine Div. Publ: Voice of the People (w. Florence Randall), Century Commun, 69. Mem: Calif. League for Handicapped (bd. dirs); Multi-Culture Inst.(bd. dirs); Coun. Civic Unity (bd. dirs); Proj. ABLE (bd. dirs); Health Professions Coun; Bay Area Health Facilities Planning Asn; San Francisco Ment. Health Adv. Bd; San Francisco Econ. Opportunity Coun; S.Center Libr.(adv. bd); S. Mkt. Boys (adv. bd); Jr. C. of C; League of Calif. Cities; Joint Cmt. Bay Area Regional Orgn.(citizens adv. cmt); Jewish Commun. Rels. Coun; AntiDefamation League; B'nai B'rith; Am. Fedn. Teachers; Union State Employees; Bay Area Soc. Planning Coun. One of Monthly Men Worth Watching, Gr. San Francisco C. of C. Mag, San Francisco Bus. Rel: Jewish. Legal Res: 11 Santa Monica Way, San Francisco, Calif. 94127. Mailing Add: 235 City Hall, San Francisco, Calif. 94102.

MENDENHALL, BETTY LEE D
Colo. State Dem. Cent. Committeewoman
b. York, Nebr, 12/6/20; d. John Benton Perry and Elizabeth Hart P; m. 12/23/42 to Robert N. Mendenhall; c. Susan Lee and Carol Anne. Educ: Christian Col, A.A, 39; Univ. of Nebr, B.A, 42; Phi Theta Kappa; Phi Sigma Iota; Delta Gamma. Polit. & Govt. Pos: Dem. precinct committeewoman, El Paso Co, Colo, 62-; El Paso Co. Dem. Exec. Committeewoman, 63-; Colo. State Dem. Cent. Committeewoman, 65- Mem: Colo. Springs Opera Asn; Citizens Coun. for Pub. Sch; League of Women Voters; PTA; YWCA. Am. Civil Liberties Union; Girl Scouts. Rel: Episcopal. Mailing Add: 30 Boulder Crescent, Apt. 4P, Colorado Springs, Colo. 80902.

MENDENHALL, JOHN CECIL R
Iowa State Rep.
b. Ponca, Nebr, 1/20/04; s. Ivan Mendenhall and Lena Millee M; m. 6/29/40 to Margareta Leyh; c. Phyllis (Mrs. Francis Ward) and Milo. Educ: Sioux City Col. Bus & Commercial Law, 2 years. Polit. & Govt. Pos: Town councilman, New Albin, Iowa, 32-54, mayor, 54-69; mem, Sch. Bd. Adv. Coun, New Albin, 66-; representative, Tourism Coun, northeast Iowa, 67-; town rep, Co. Civil Defense, 68-69; Iowa State Rep, Allamakee Co, 69- Bus. & Prof. Pos: Owner & operator, Mendenhall Lumber Co, 27-67, Mendenhall Concrete Prod, 34-67 and Mendenhall Construction, 34-67. Publ: 'Progress,' 1/15/67 and 'Positive Thinking,' 6/16/67, Allamakee J. Mem: Mason; Farm Bur; Hist. Soc; New Albin Commun. Club (past pres). Rel: Methodist; church treas, chmn. finance cmt, mem. official bd, trustee chmn, lay leader and cert. lay speaker. Legal Res: Box H, New Albin, Iowa 52160. Mailing Add: State Capitol, Des Moines, Iowa 50319.

MENDENHALL, SAMUEL BROOKS D
S.C. State Rep.
b. Rock Hill, S.C. 1/1/36; s. George Wallace Mendenhall and Margaret Love Good M; m. 3/10/62 to Carolyn King; c. Robert Bratton and Mary Margaret. Educ: Univ. of S.C, A.B, LL.B, 62; Phi Kappa Sigma; Omicron Delta Kappa; Kappa Sigma Kappa; Justice, Phi Alpha Delta; pres, Euphradian Lit. Soc, 58-59; Chmn, Univ. Young Dem. Club, 58. Polit. & Govt. Pos: Chmn, York City Hist. Cmt, S.C; v.chmn, Dem. Party, Ebenezer Precinct, 62. Bus. & Prof. Pos: Lawyer. Publ: Author of numerous articles on local hist. and co-auth. of book, Plaxco-Robinson. Mem: Elks; Jaycees (secy); SAR (secy), dir, S.C. Soc; York City Hist. Soc.(pres, 59-62); S.C. Hist. Soc. Rel: Presbyterian. Mailing Add: Box 342, Rock Hill, S.C. 29730.

MENDEZ, JUSTO A. New Progressive, P.R.
Sen, P.R. Senate
b. Lares, P.R, 9/8/17; s. Justo Méndez and Cristina Rodríguez M; m. 9/6/42 to Provi Oliver; c. Provinés (Mrs. Humberto Torres), Justo and Lumen. Educ: Col. Agr. and Mech. Arts, Mayaguez, P.R, B.S. in Chem. Eng, 42; Phi Sigma Alpha. Polit. & Govt. Pos: Chmn. exec. cmt, Statehood Rep. Party, P.R, 66-67; first v.pres, United Statehooders, 67-68; interim pres, New Progressive Party, 69; Sen. and Minority Floor Leader, P.R. Senate, 69- Bus. & Prof. Pos: Chief chemist, Cent. Los Caños, 42, gen. supt, 46-58; exec. v.pres, Cent. Fed. Savings and Loan Asn, 58-64; pres, San Martin Mortgage & Investment Corp, 64-67. Mil. Serv: Entered as Pvt, Army, 43, released as T/5, 46, after serv. in Malaria Control Unit, Caribbean; Am. Defense Medal; World War II Medal; Victory Medal; Good Conduct Medal. Publ: Arecibo Harbor Feasibility Study, 51; 'Preliminary Work with the Filtration of Effluences of Rotary Cane Mud Filters, annual meeting, Sugar Tech. Asn, 54; 'Co-operative Progress in Puerto Rico, 27th Session of the Am. Inst. of Cooperativism, Purdue Univ, 55. Mem: P.R. Col. Engrs, Architects and Surveyors; P.R. Chem. Soc; Inter-Am. Planning Soc; Prfnl. Engrs; Lions Int. Rel: Catholic. Legal Res: C-71 Ebano St, Golden Gate Development, Caparra, P.R. 00920. Mailing Add: G.P.O. Box 4067, San Juan, P.R. 00936.

MENDEZ, LIONEL FERNANDEZ D
P.R. State Sen.
b. Cayey, P.R, 1/24/15; s. Benigno Fernandez Garcia and Maria Luisa Mendez; m. 11/2/52 to Ana Usera; c. Ana Milagros and Lionel. Educ: Univ. P.R, B.A, 30; Georgetown Univ, LL.B, 38. Polit. & Govt. Pos: Assoc. mem, P.R. Labor Res. Bd, 45-48; P.R. State Sen. from Senatorial Dist. Guayama, 48-; chmn, Cmn. on the Judiciary (Penal), U.S. Senate, 48-56, chmn, Cmn. on the Judiciary (Civil) of the Senate, 56-, mem. Cmn. on Finance, Cmn. on Health, Cmn. on Commonwealth and Munic. Govt, Cmn. on Elecs. and Personnel, Cmn. on Interior Govt. and Cmn. on Spec. Affairs and Impeachment Proc, 56-; mem, Constitutional Conv, 51; del, Dem. Nat. Conv, 68. Mil. Serv: Entered as Pvt, Army, 42, released as Warrant Officer, after serv. in Judge Adv. Off, Antilles Command; Army Commendation Ribbon. Mem: P.R. and Am. Bar Asns; Casino De Puerto Rico. Rel: Roman Catholic. Legal Res: Cayey, P.R. Mailing Add: P.O. Box 2326, San Juan, P.R. 00903.

MENEFEE, MAYNARD TURNER R
Iowa State Rep.
b. Adair, Iowa, 10/15/07; s. Avery John Menefee and Myrtle Turner M; m. 12/28/30 to Dorothy Mabel Newell; c. Myron Newell. Educ: Adair High Sch, grad, 25. Polit. & Govt. Pos: Mem, Farmer's Home Admin. Cmt, Dallas Co, 49-50 and Fayette Co, Iowa, 57-60; dep. assessor, Fayette Co, 57-67; chmn, Fayette Co. Rep. Party, 66-68; Iowa State Rep, 69- Bus. & Prof. Pos: Pres, Dallas Co. Farm Bur, 45-47; mem, Farm Coop. Bd, Dallas Co, 46-48. Mem: Farm Bur. Fedn; Farm Coop; Golf and Country Club. Master Farmer Award, 48. Rel: United Presbyterian. Mailing Add: R.R. 2, Fayette, Iowa 52142.

MENENDEZ-MONROIG, JOSE M. New Progressive, P.R.
Sen, P.R. Senate
b. San Juan, P.R, 6/22/17; s. Albert Seaman Menéndez and Agustina Monroig M; m. 8/3/46 to Lyda M. Cortada; c. José Antonio and Michele Marie. Educ: Univ. P.R, B.A, 39, LL.B, 41; Phi Sigma Alpha; AFDA. Polit. & Govt. Pos: Assoc. attorney, Pub. Serv. Cmn, 46; adjudicator, Vet. Admin, 47; Sen, P.R. Senate, 69- Mil. Serv: Entered as 2nd Lt, Army, 41, released as Capt, 46, after serv. in 295th Inf, Caribbean Command, 41-45 and 296th Inf, Pac. Theatre, 45-46; Caribbean Theatre Medal. Mem: Am. Bar Asn; Colegio de Abogados de P.R; Lay-adv, San Antonio Abad Col. Rel: Catholic. Legal Res: 54 Krug St, Santurce, P.R. 00911. Mailing Add: Box 3183, San Juan, P.R. 00904.

MENES, PAULINE H. D
Md. State Del.
b. New York, N.Y, 7/16/24; d. Arthur Benjamin Herskowitz and Hannah H; m. 9/1/46 to Melvin Menes; c. Sandra Jill, Robin Joy and Bambi Lynn. Educ: Hunter Col, B.A, 45; Norris '45-House Plan. Polit. & Govt. Pos: Secy, Prince Georges Co. Independent Dem, Md, 62; chief clerk, Supvr. of Elecs, Md, 63; secy, Prince Georges Co. Dem. Steering Cmt, 66; Md. State Del, 67- Bus. & Prof. Pos: Economist, Qm. Corps, 45-47; geographer, Army Map Serv, 49-50; substitute teacher, Prince Georges Pub. High Schs, Md, 65-66. Rel: Jewish. Mailing Add: 3517 Marlbrough Way, College Park, Md. 20740.

MENGEL, ELDON R. R
Chmn, Fallon Co. Rep. Party, Mont.
b. Apex, Mont, 4/3/16; s. Roy Mengel and Gretchen Young M; m. 3/11/67 to Francis Kron; c. Irene, Ray and Joan. Educ: Baker High Sch, grad. Polit. & Govt. Pos: Chmn, Fallon Co. Rep. Party, Mont, 66- Bus. & Prof. Pos: Owner, T&M Electric, 47- Mil. Serv: Entered as Pvt, Army, 40, released as 1st Lt, 46, after serv. in 96 Signal Bn; China-Burma-India, 43-45. Mem: Am. Legion; Lions. Rel: Baptist. Mailing Add: 326 Kimbel, Baker, Mont. 59313.

MENNING, C. J. R
Cmnr, Douglas Co, S.Dak.
b. Douglas Co, S.Dak, 9/3/96; married; c. Six. Educ: Grade schs. Polit. & Govt. Pos: Elected to S.Dak. Legis, 28, 30, 60, 62 and 64, State Rep, until 66; cmnr, Douglas Co, 68- Bus. & Prof. Pos: Farmer and bulk oil dealer; mem, Temple Time Radio Cmt. Rel: Reformed Church in Am. Mailing Add: Corsica, S.Dak. 57328.

MENSING, A. L. R
Iowa State Rep.
b. 10/27/96; married; c. two sons. Polit. & Govt. Pos: Former Mayor of Lowden; former Postmaster; former Co. Rep. Chmn; Iowa State Rep, 51-65 & 67- Bus. & Prof. Pos: Gen. mercantile bus, 15-53; chmn. bd. and dir, Am. Trust and Savings Bank of Lowden. Mil. Serv: Navy, World War I. Rel: Protestant. Mailing Add: Lowden, Iowa 52255.

MENTELE, EDWARD MATHEW D
b. Roswell, S.Dak, 8/15/14; s. Herman Mentele and Catherine Eich M; m. 5/24/38 to Frances Haas; c. Kae (Mrs. Phelan), Jeanne (Mrs. Ed Ledbetter), Reginald, Dixie, Richard, Steven and Laurie. Polit. & Govt. Pos: Del, Dem. Nat. Conv, 68; Davidson Co. chmn, Robert Kennedy Campaign, S.Dak, 68. Mem: Mitchell Bd. of Realtors (secy-treas, 54-56 & 67-69, pres, 56-58); Independent Ins. Agents; United Commercial Travelers; Elks; Mitchell Country Club; K. of C. Rel: Roman Catholic. Legal Res: R.R. 4, Mitchell, S.Dak. 57301. Mailing Add: Box 456, Mitchell, S.Dak. 57301.

MENTON, PAUL C. D
Mass. State Rep.
b. Cambridge, Mass, 4/15/25; s. Patrick A. Menton and Lucy A. Comfort M; m. 9/9/50 to Mary T. Regan; c. Christopher, Robert, Jayne, Brian and Carol. Educ: Suffolk Univ. Law Sch, LL.B, 53. Polit. & Govt. Pos: Parole officer, Youth Serv. Bd. Cmt, Mass, 51-53; mem, sch. cmt, Watertown, 52-53; spec. agent, Fed. Bur. Invest, 53-58; mem, Fifth Dist. Mass. State Dem. Cmt. and v.chmn, 68-; Mass. State Rep, 59- Bus. & Prof. Pos: Attorney-at-Law, Watertown, Mass, 58- Mil. Serv: Entered as Recruit, Marine Corps, 43, released as Cpl, 46, after serv. in S.Pac. Theater. Publ: 'Truth in Lending.' Mem: Mass, Watertown, Waltham and Weston Bar Asns; Mass. and Fed. Bars; Mass. Trial Lawyers Asn; Elks; K. of C; Am. Legion; Marine Corps League. Rel: Catholic. Mailing Add: 100 Robbins, Watertown, Mass. 02172.

MENTOR, JOSEPH PERRINE R
Wash. State Rep.
b. Covington, La, 8/25/33; s. Joseph Peter Mentor and Seleta P. Bridges M; m. 6/25/55 to Joan Lene'a Brix; c. Joseph P, Jr, James O. and Judith E. Educ: Univ. Wash, B.A, 56; Chi Phi. Polit. & Govt. Pos: Finance chmn, Kitsap Co. Rep. Party, Wash, 67-68; Wash. State Rep, Tenth Dist, 69- Bus. & Prof. Pos: Owner, Mentor Construction, 56-; dir, Kitsap Co. Bank, 69- Mem: Nat. Asn. Home Builders (Kitsap Co. past pres, dir, Kitsap Co. Chap, Legis. cmt, Nat. Asn); Cub Scout Master; Olympic Peninsula Enterprises (past v.pres, mgt. cmt); Bremerton C. of C.(spec. action cmt. for civic affairs Forward Thrust); Gov. Task Force Cmt. on Balancing the Creation of Indust. Jobs with Protection of Environ. Rel: Lutheran. Legal Res: Route 4, Box 2350, Bremerton, Wash. 98310. Mailing Add: 830 Pacific, Bremerton, Wash. 98310.

MENTZ, W. DEWEY D
b. Gap Mills, W.Va, 9/30/08; s. William M. Mentz and Mary Young M; m. 9/21/41 to Elizabeth Harris; c. William M, II. Educ: Capitol City Commercial Col; Alderson Jr. Col. Polit. & Govt. Pos: W.Va. House of Dels, 62-66. Bus. & Prof. Pos: Sales mgr; former rep. of finance div. of Ford Motor Co. Mil. Serv: WWII, Inf. replacement. Mem: Masonic Chap; Welch Commandery 27; Beni Kedem Shrine; White Shrine; McDowell Cty. Shrine Club; Modern Woodmen; LOOM; Welch Lions Club; Am. Legion; former dep. comdr, W.Va. 40 et 8; post comdr, McDowell Cty. Post 8, 48-49, 2nd dept. v.comdr, 49-50; Vets. Coun, W.Va. Dept. of Vets. Affairs; former pres, Young Dem. Club, McDowell Cty; Ky. Col; chmn, McDowell Cty. March of Dimes Drive, 56; chmn, McDowell Cty. TB Seals for 61; chmn, Vets. for Johnson Cmt, McDowell Cty; co-chmn, McDowell Cty. Centennial 1957 Comm. Rel: Presbyterian; elder, former Sunday Sch. supt; former pres, Men's Bible Class. Mailing Add: Welch, W.Va. 24801. (1967)

MENZ, JOSEPH R
b. Dak. Territory, 7/15/83; widower. Educ: N.Dak. State Univ. of Agr. and Applied Sci. Polit. & Govt. Pos: N.Dak State Rep, elected in 57 and 61; former Register of Deeds; Cty. Judge and Clerk of Court of Sioux Cty. Mailing Add: Ft. Yates, N.Dak. 58538. (1967)

MERCORELLA, ANTHONY J. D
N.Y. State Assemblyman
b. 3/6/27; s. Sante Mercorella and Josephine Bozzuti M; m. 6/16/56 to Maria De Lucia; c. Anne, Susan, Robert and Carole. Educ: L.I. Univ, A.B, 49; N.Y. Univ, 49; Fordham Univ. Law Sch, LL.B, 52. Polit. & Govt. Pos: Law asst, Civil Court, Bronx Co, N.Y.C, 55-65; N.Y. State Assemblyman, 85th Assembly Dist, currently. Bus. & Prof. Pos: Partner, Mercorella & Kase, N.Y.C, currently. Mil. Serv: Entered in Navy, 45, released in 46, after serv. in U.S.S. Helena, Pac. and European Theatre; European and Pac. Service Awards. Mem: V.pres, Bronx Co. Bar Asn; dir, Columbian Lawyers Asn, First Dept; Columbus Esca Alliance, Inc; Local Sch. Bd. Dist. 23-24; Sons of Italy; All-Am. Coun, Nat. Dem. Cmt; Nat. Conf. of Christians and Jews; Mary, Queen of Peace Coun; K. of C; St. Claire's Post 617; Cath. War Vet; bd. adv, Asn. for Children with Retarded Mental Develop, Inc. Rel: Roman Catholic. Legal Res: 1363 Astor Ave, New York, N.Y. 10469. Mailing Add: 600 Madison Ave, New York, N.Y. 10022.

MERCURO, TOBIA GUSTAVE R
Chmn, 28th Legis. Dist. Rep. Cmt, Va.
b. East Orange, N.J, 10/30/33; s. Tobia Mercuro and Louise Pelosi M; m. 12/20/59 to Barbara Ann Beckwith; c. Thomas Tobia and Virginia Louise. Educ: Newark Col. Eng, B.S, Mech. Eng, 55; Univ. Wis, Milwaukee, 56-58; Xavier Univ, 59-60; Pi Tau Sigma. Polit. & Govt. Pos: Treas, Warren Co. Rep. Cmt, Va, 66-68 and chmn, 68-; chmn, 28th Legis. Dist. Rep. Cmt, Farquier, Rappahanock and Warren Co, 69- Bus. & Prof. Pos: Supvr, mfg. engr, Allis-Chalmers Mfg. Co, Ohio, 55-61; asst. plant mgr, Philip Carey Mfg. Co, N.J, 61-63; v.pres. and gen. mgr, Riverton Lime & Stone Co, Va, 63- Mem: Dir, Nat. Limestone Inst; Va. Aggregates Asn; Struct. Clay Prod. Inst; Cincinnati Chap, Am. Inst. Indust. Engrs.(past pres); dir, Warren Co. C. of C; Warren Co. Indust. Cmn; Rotary; Izaac Walton League; United Fund of Warren Co.(past pres). Mailing Add: 325 Amherst Dr, Front Royal, Va. 22630.

MEREDITH, HARRY R. D
b. Waynesville, Ohio, 7/29/98; s. Sam Meredith and Sallie Robinson M; m. 9/1/25 to Eugenia W. Whitaker; c. Richard Eugene. Educ: Ohio North. Univ, J.D, 25; Univ. Cincinnati. Polit. & Govt. Pos: Legal counsel to Gov. Frank J. Rausche, Ohio; precinct committeeman, Dem. Party, 20-26 & 28-36; chmn, Allen Co. Dem. Cmt, 42-50; chmn, Dem. State Platform Cmt, 3 times; del, Dem. Nat. Conv, 4 times; mem, U.S. Selective Serv. Bd. of Appeals, during World War II; chmn, Ohio State Dem. Cent. Cmt, 50-68. Bus. & Prof. Pos: Gen. counsel and mem. bd. dirs, Lima Mem. Hosp, Ohio. Mil. Serv: Midn, Navy, 18-19. Publ: Various papers on legal matters before local Bar Asns; articles on chattel mortgages and small loan financing, Finance News & Quarterly Report. Mem: Am. Bar Asn; Cmt. on Judicial Admin, Ohio State Bar Asn, 52-58; pres, Allen Co. Bar Asn, 48-50; Mason (32°); Comdr, Am. Legion, Post 96, 36-37; Elks; Kiwanis; K. of P. Ky. Col. Rel: Protestant. Mailing Add: 1211 Lakewood Ave, Lima, Ohio 45805.

MEREDITH, MANUTAFEA EDWARD R
Rep, Am. Samoa House of Rep.
b. Fagatogo, Tutuila, American Samoa, 9/20/36; s. Edward Ripley Meredith and Galoane Ioane M; m. 2/28/60 to Tina S. Faumuina; c. Edmund, Francis, Belmyra A, Elsie A, Gordon D.A. and Peter M. Educ: Samoana High Sch, Pago Pago, 3 years. Polit. & Govt. Pos: Rep, Am. Samoa House of Rep, Tenth Dist, 69- Bus. & Prof. Pos: Credit officer, Bank of Am. Samoa, Pago Pago, 58- Mem: Lions; Am. Samoa Red Cross Chap.(treas); Am. Samoa Athletic Asn. Rel: Catholic. Mailing Add: Leloaloa, Tutuila, Pago Pago, American Samoa 96920.

MERIDETH, HORACE LAVELLE, JR. D
Miss. State Rep.
b. Greenville, Miss, 12/7/30; married. Educ: Phi Alpha Delta. Polit. & Govt. Pos: Miss. State Rep, 60- Bus. & Prof. Pos: Attorney. Mem: Exchange Club; Am. Legion; VFW; Wash. City, Miss. State, and Am. Bar Asns; C. of C. Rel: Baptist. Mailing Add: Box 99, Greenville, Miss. 38701.

MERINO, S. Q. D
b. Santa Rita, N.Mex, 3/4/29; s. Jesus A. Merino and Gregoria Quinones M; m. 7/5/49 to Otilia Renteria; c. Carlos R, Lupita R, Oscar R, Mary Ellen and Samuel Ray. Educ: Compton Clartown High Sch, 2 years; Hurley High Sch, 2 years. Polit. & Govt. Pos: Del, Dem. Nat. Conv, 68; mem, N.Mex. State Parks and Recreation Cmn, N.Mex. State Safety Mine Adv. Bd. and N.Mex. Civil Rights Cmn, currently. Bus. & Prof. Pos: Hosp. bd. mem, Grant Co, N.Mex. Mil. Serv: Entered as A/S, Navy, 46, released as Seaman 1/C, 48, after serv. aboard U.S.S. President Hayes, Pac. Theater. Mem: VFW; USW (pres, Local 890, 63-69); Lulacs. Rel: Catholic. Legal Res: 313 Nevada St, Hurley, N.Mex. 88043. Mailing Add: P.O. Box 363, Bayard, N.Mex. 88023.

MERKEL, KENNETH J. R
Wis. State Assemblyman
b. Marshfield, Wis, 8/9/26. Educ: Mich. State Col; Marquette Univ, 49; Univ. of Wisconsin, Milwaukee Grad. Sch. Polit. & Govt. Pos: Mem, Elm-Brook Rep. Unit; Wis. State Assemblyman, 64- Bus. & Prof. Pos: Elec. engr. Mil. Serv: Army Air Force, World War II Vet. Mem: Registered Prfnl. Engrs; Wis. Soc. of Prfnl. Engrs; K. of C; John Birch Soc; Americans for Constitutional Action; former mem, Nat. Machine Tool Builders Elec. Standards Cmt. Mailing Add: 3405 N. Brookfield Rd, Brookfield, Wis. 53005. (1967)

MERKLE, CHRIS A. R
Pub. Utilities Cmnr, S.Dak.
b. Eureka, S.Dak, 11/26/92; married; c. Two. Educ: North. State Teachers Col, Aberdeen, grad; Univ. S.Dak. Law Sch, grad. Polit. & Govt. Pos: Supvr. of City Schs, Bowdle, S.Dak, 15-17; State's Attorney, McPherson Co, 25-29, Co. Judge, 31-39; mayor, Leola, 34-39; Pub. Utilities cmnr, S.Dak, 39, 44, 50, 56 & 62- Mil. Serv: Aviator, Army Air Force, 17-19. Mem: Mason; Shrine; Eastern Star. Rel: Methodist. Mailing Add: Pierre, S.Dak. 57501.

MERLINO, JOSEPH PIEDMONT D
N.J. State Assemblyman
b. Trenton, N.J, 7/15/22; s. Pasquale Merlino (deceased) and Margarittia Fuccello M.(deceased); m. 4/26/49 to Molly J. McGoogan; c. Claire Margaret, Mary Nell, Kate, James Richard and Joseph McGoogan. Educ: Col. South Jersey, 40-42; Seton Hall Col, B.S.S, 48; Fordham Univ. Law Sch, L.L.B and J.D, 51; Int. Rels. Soc.(pres, 46-47); Student Coun.(pres, 47-48); Pre-Legal Soc.(pres, 46-48); Glee Club (v.pres, 47-48). Polit. & Govt. Pos: Attorney, Mercer Co. Rent Control, N.J, 54-58; asst. prosecutor, Mercer Co, 59-66; city attorney and dir. Dept. of Law, Trenton, 66-; N.J. State Assemblyman, Mercer Co, Dist. 6-B, 68- Bus. & Prof. Pos: Practicing attorney, Trenton, 52- Mil. Serv: Pvt, Army, serv. in 103rd Hospital Ship Co, ETO, 43-45. Mem: Mercer Co, N.J. and Am. Bar Asns; Am. Judicature Soc; Trenton Symphony Asn.(dir); v.pres, Trenton Theater-in-the-Park; Am. Arbitration Asn; Int. Narcotic Enforcement Officers Asn; Asn. for the Arts of the N.J. State Museum; Nat. Inst. of Municipal Law Officers; Trustee, Delaware Valley United Fund; Nat. Soc. of State Legislators (secy, N.J. Chap); Fermi Federation; Elks; K. of C; Unity League. Rel: Roman Catholic. Legal Res: 25 Whittier Ave, Trenton, N.J. 08618. Mailing Add: 516 S. Clinton Ave, Trenton, N.J. 08611.

MERLO, JOHN D
Ill. State Rep.
b. Chicago, Ill, 9/12/12; m. to Meryle State; c. Three. Educ: DePaul Univ; Phi Kappa Alpha. Polit. & Govt. Pos: Former secy. to Edward J. Barrett, 44th Ward Committeeman, Ill; Ill. State Rep, currently; alternate del, Dem. Nat. Conv, 68. Bus. & Prof. Pos: Mem. staff, Chicago Park Dist, 33- Mem: C. of C.(past pres, v.pres, bd. of dirs. and mem. exec. cmt, Lincoln Park Chap); past pres, Holy Name Soc. and Lake View Men's Club; Park West Commun. Asn; Ballarmine Club; Lions. Outstanding Vol. Award, March of Dimes, 62. Rel: St. Clement's Church, Usher, 27 years. Mailing Add: 3018 Sheridan Rd, Chicago, Ill. 60657. (1967)

MEROLA, ARTHUR EUGENE D
b. Burlington, Vt, 12/6/29; s. Frank Merola and Stella Sorriento M; single. Educ: Johnson State Col, 2 years; Champlain Col, 1 year; Country Sch. of Photog. Polit. & Govt. Pos: Inspector of elec, Vt, 63-64; alderman, Ward Five, 65-67; Vt. State Rep, Dists. 1-7, 67-69. Mil. Serv: Entered as Airman, Air Force, 51, released as Airman 1/C, 55, after serv. in ETO. Mem: Burlington Downtown Athletic Club; Burlington Vets. Club. Photog, Stamps and Coins; Vt. State Softball Cmnr. Rel: Catholic. Mailing Add: 126 Maple St, Burlington, Vt. 05401. (1967)

MERRELLI, GEORGE D
b. Ramsey, Ohio, 2/19/11; s. Concetto Merrelli and Angeline Forti M; m. to Jean Marie Wojciechowski; c. Laura Ann, Leona Ann, Robert George and Richard Donald. Mem: Eagles; Holy Name Soc. Rel: Catholic. Mailing Add: 23301 Middlesex Dr, St. Clair Shores, Mich. 48080. (1967)

MERRICK, SAMUEL VAUGHAN D
b. Cynwyd, Pa, 3/24/14; s. Rodney K. Merrick and Mary Gordon M; m. 8/22/47 to Eleanor Perry; c. John Rodney, Melvin Gregory and Thaddeus. Educ: Univ. Pa, B.A, LL.B; Phi Beta Kappa. Polit. & Govt. Pos: Spec. asst. gen. counsel, Nat. Labor Rel. Bd, 50-55; staff mem, U.S. Senate Labor Cmt, 59-61; spec. asst. to the Secy. of Labor for Legis. Affairs, 61-68; spec. counsel to Mayor, Boston, Mass, 68- Rel: Catholic. Mailing Add: 401 N St. S.W, Washington, D.C. 20024.

MERRIFIELD, GEORGE R. R
N.H. State Rep.
b. Sunapee, N.H, 4/1/08; married; c. Four. Polit. & Govt. Pos: N.H. State Rep, 57- Rel: Methodist. Mailing Add: Sunapee, N.H. 03782. (1967)

MERRILL, D. BAILEY R
b. Hymera, Ind, 11/22/12; s. Harry D. Merrill and Bertrice Bailey M; m. 12/26/39 to Josephine Drehrer. Educ: Ind. State Univ, A.B, 33 and J.D, 37. Polit. & Govt. Pos: U.S. Rep, Eighth Dist, Ind, 53-54. Bus. & Prof. Pos: Lawyer, Merill, Schroeder & Johnson, 37-52 & 55-; teacher, Hymera High Sch, Ind, 33-35. Mil. Serv: Entered as Pvt, Army, 42, released as Capt, 46, after serv. in 291st Field Artil. Observation Bn, ETO, 44-46; Bronze Star; Heroic Action, Ardennes Campaign, Rhinelands Campaign and Cent. Europe Campaign Ribbons. Mem: Am, Ind. State and Evansville Bar Asns; Rotary; Am. Legion; VFW; Evansville Petrol. Club; Columbia Club, Indianapolis; Nat. Lawyers Club, Wash, D.C. Rel: Baptist. Legal Res: 20 Adams Ave, Evansville, Ind. 47713. Mailing Add: 301 Union Federal Bldg, Evansville, Ind. 47708.

MERRILL, HUGH DAVIS D
Ala. State Rep.
b. Anniston, Ala, 4/12/13; s. Hugh Davis Merrill and Martha Chitwood M; m. 12/28/51 to Martha Holcombe; c. Hugh, David, Paul and Nancy. Educ: Univ. Ala, A.B, 35, LL.B, 37; Sigma Alpha Epsilon. Polit. & Govt. Pos: Del, Dem. Nat. Conv, 44, 52, 56 & 64; mem, State Dem. Cmt, Ala, 51-58; Ala. State Rep, 55- Mil. Serv: Entered as Pvt, Army, 44, released as Lt, 46, after serv. in Judge Adv. Gen. Dept. Mem: Mason; K. of P; Kiwanis; Am. Legion. Rel: Baptist. Legal Res: 2312 Ridgeview Rd, Anniston, Ala. 36201. Mailing Add: P.O. Box 1498, Anniston, Ala. 36201.

MERRILL, PELHAM JONES D
Assoc. Justice, Supreme Court of Ala.
b. Heflin, Ala, 12/1/07; s. Walter Benjamin Merrill and Lilla Jones M; m. 8/21/36 to Gladys Morrison. Educ: Univ. of Ala, A.B, 26; Univ. of Ala, LL.B, 34. Polit. & Govt. Pos: Ala. State Rep, 36-38, & 46-51, speaker pro-tem, Ala. House Rep, 49-51; mem, State Dem. Exec. Cmt, Ala, 36-40; chmn, Cleburne Co. Dem. Exec. Cmt, 36-42; assoc. justice, Supreme Court of Ala, 53- Mil. Serv: Entered as 2nd Lt, Army Air Corps, 42, released as Maj, 46; Col. Air Force Res. Rel: Baptist. Mailing Add: 2008 Commodore St, Montgomery, Ala. 36106.

MERRILL, SHIRLEY KIMBALL R
N.H. State Rep.
b. West Peabody, Mass, 9/11/22; d. Linwood Kimball and Carrie Sawyer K; m. 11/16/46 to Charles Allison Merrill; c. John Charles and Nancy Sawyer. Educ: Univ. N.H, B.S, 44; Alpha Xi Delta. Polit. & Govt. Pos: N.H. State Rep, 67-; alternate del, Rep. Nat. Conv, 68; mem, Lebanon City Coun, 68- Mem: Lebanon Woman's Club (pres); Alice Peck Day Hosp. Auxiliary (pres). Rel: Protestant. Mailing Add: 22 Perley Ave, Lebanon, N.H. 03766.

MERRILL, WILLIAM HALE D
b. E. Milton, Mass, 5/27/23; s. William McKinley Merrill and Augusta F. MacMahon M; m. 5/1/65 to Evelyn Ryska; c. Richard H. and Ann. Educ: Dartmouth Col, B.A, 47; Yale Law Sch, LL.B, 50; Phi Kappa Psi. Polit. & Govt. Pos: Asst. U.S. Attorney, Detroit, Mich, 61-66; del, Dem. Nat. Conv, 68. Mil. Serv: Entered as Pvt, Army Air Corps, 43, released as Sgt, 46. Mailing Add: 2805 Hickory Grove, Bloomfield Hills, Mich. 48013.

MERRIMAN, RUSSELL FIELD R
Chmn, Vt. Rep. State Cmt.
b. New Bedford, Mass, 12/23/28; s. Reginald S. Merriman (deceased) and Violet Boudreau Merriman L; stepfather, Edwin E. Lindsey; m. 7/9/55 to Jean M. Morrison; c. Linda Ann, Susan Elizabeth and Robert Lindsey. Educ: Vt. Col, Montpelier, 2 years. Polit. & Govt. Pos: Chmn, Montpelier Rep. City Cmt, Vt, presently; chmn, Vt. Rep. State Cmt, 69- Bus. & Prof. Pos: Supt. agencies, Union Mutual Fire Ins. Co, 60-65, asst. to pres, 65-68, corp. secy, 68- Mil. Serv: Entered as Pvt, Army, 46, released as Sgt, 47, after serv. in 62nd Signal Bn, Pac. Eighth Army, 46-47. Mem: Vt. Ins. Fieldmen's Asn; New Eng. 1752 Club; Kiwanis; Elks; F&AM. Rel: Protestant. Mailing Add: 159 State St, Montpelier, Vt. 05602.

MERRITT, HUGH L. D
V.Chmn, Surry Co. Dem. Exec. Cmt.
b. Mount Airy, N.C, 4/8/08; s. William E. Merritt and Caroline Kochititzky M; m. 4/29/39 to Emma Rice; c. Emma Jane, Julia Frances (Mrs. Fuller), Nancy Elizabeth (Mrs. Ball) and Hugh L, Jr. Educ: Univ. N.C, B.S, 29; Alpha Kappa Phi; Pi Kappa Phi. Polit. & Govt. Pos: N.C. State Rep, 65-67; v.chmn, Surry Co. Dem. Exec. Cmt, 68- Bus. & Prof. Pos: Hosiery mfr. and mem. bd. dir, Renfro Hosiery Mills Co, 68-69; mem. bd. trustees, North. Hosp. of Surry Co, 68-69; dir, Nat. Asn. Hosiery Mfrs, 68-69. Mem: Mason; K.T; Shrine. Rel: Methodist. Mailing Add: Country Club Rd, Mount Airy, N.C. 27030.

MERRITT, JANET BURTON SCARBOROUGH D
Ga. State Rep.
b. Americus, Ga, 1/4/09; d. Robert Henry Scarborough and Janet Augusta Burton S; m. 6/6/33 to Samuel Mickleberry Merritt; c. Thomas Burton, Mary Ella and Janet. Educ: Valdosta State Col, B.A, 59. Polit. & Govt. Pos: Mem, Third Dist. Dem. Cent. Cmt-at-lg; mem, Andersonville Prison Park Develop. Cmt; Ga. State Rep, 68th Dist, 64-, mem, Appropriations Cmt, Ga. House of Rep, mem, Welfare Cmt. and chmn, Juvenile Affairs Subcmt, mem, Univ. Ga. Cmt. and secy, Long Range Prog. subcmt. Bus. & Prof. Pos: Teacher, pub. schs, Ga. Sch. Syst, 28-33; licensed real estate broker; nat. accredited flower show judge. Mem: DAR (mem. nat. bd, 60-62, adv. bd, Tamasee DAR Sch, 62-65, nat. v.pres, 63-66, nat. finance cmt, 68-71, hon. life state regent, Ga. Soc); trustee, Meadow Garden Bd, 62-68; Red Cross nurses aide and organizing chmn. Gray Ladies, Sumter Co. Chap. Am. Red Cross, 64; parliamentarian, Federated Garden Clubs Sumter Co, 64 and Am. Bus. & Prfnl. Women; town chmn, Colonial Dames Asn, 64-66; Civil Defense Cmt, Women's Cmt, Ga; Ga. Music Teachers Asns; Daylily Garden Club; Jr. Welfare League Americus; Chi Omega Mothers Club, Univ. of Ga. Rel: Episcopal. Mailing Add: 234 W. Dodson St, Americus, Ga. 31709.

MERRITT, TOM R
Ill. State Sen.
b. Rossville, Ill, 10/20/11; m. to Martha Sandusky; c. Tom, Jr. and Judy. Educ: De Pauw Univ; Purdue Univ. Polit. & Govt. Pos: City treas, Ill, 37-41; mem. bd. suprvs, 47-64, Rep. Precinct Committeeman, 50-64; chmn, Vermilion Co. Rep. Cent. Cmt, 62-64; Ill. State Sen, 44th Dist, 65- Bus. & Prof. Pos: Owner, Tom Merritt & Co, gen. ins, real estate and farm loan bus; dir. and v.chmn. bd, Wellington State Bank. Mem: Charter mem. and past pres, Hoopeston Rotary Club; Mason; Shrine; Moose; Farm Bur; Vermilion Co. and Ill. Asn. Ins. Agents; C. of C; Am. and Ill. Soc. Prfnl. Farm Mgrs. and Rural Appraisers. Del, White House Conf. on Children and Youth, 60. Rel: Methodist. Mailing Add: 858 E. Lincoln St, Hoopeston, Ill. 60942.

MERRYWEATHER, THOMAS L. D
Chmn, Dorchester Co. Dem. Party, Md.
b. Cambridge, Md, 5/23/20; married. Educ: Cambridge pub. schs. Polit. & Govt. Pos: Md. State Del, 59-67; chmn, Dorchester Co. Dem. Party, currently. Bus. & Prof. Pos: Wholesale beer distributor. Mil. Serv: Air Force, 43-45. Mem: Cambridge Vol. Fire Co; Elks; Moose; Am. Legion; Cambridge Country Club; Cambridge Yacht Club. Rel: Christ P.E. Church, Cambridge; Vestryman. Mailing Add: R.D. 3, Cambridge, Md. 21613. (1967)

MERSHON, JOHN CARL D
Ky. State Representative
b. Ludlow, Ky, 6/20/01; s. Ernest C. Mershon and Mary Ellen Jordan M; m. 9/20/24 to Dolores Wanda Blair. Educ: Ludlow, Ky. High Sch. Polit. & Govt. Pos: Police Chief, Kenton, Co, Ky, 46-62, Police Dispatcher, 62-66; Ky. State Rep, 66th Dist, 68- Bus. & Prof. Pos: Photo engraver, Process Engraving Co, Cincinnati, Ohio, 16-22 & 26-35; fireman, Southern R.R, 22-25; salesman, Heidelberg Brewing Co, Covington, Ky, 35-46 and Ky. Liquor & Wine Co, Newport, 66-69. Rel: Catholic. Mailing Add: 620 Church St, Ludlow, Ky. 41016.

MERSHON, JOHN J. D
N.Mex. State Rep.
b. 1908. Educ: Okla. Baptist Univ. Polit. & Govt. Pos: N.Mex. State Rep, 59- Bus. & Prof. Pos: Farmer. Mem: Mason. Rel: Protestant. Mailing Add: P.O. Box 268, Cloudcroft, N.Mex. 88317.

MERTZ, EDWARD F. D
Wis. State Assemblyman
b. Milwaukee, Wis, 8/15/90. Educ: Badger State Bus. Col; Reisch Aerm. Sch. of Auctioneering, Mason City, Iowa, 1960. Polit. & Govt. Pos: Secy, Dem. Co. Cmt, Wis, 4 years; chmn, Dem. Co. Finance Cmt, 10 years; mem, Wis. State Dem. Cent. Cmt, 44-48; del, Dem. Nat. Conv, 44, 48 & 52; Wis. State Assemblyman, 48-56 & 64-; mem, Milwaukee Co. Bd, 56-60. Bus. & Prof. Pos: Licensed Engr; Appraiser, Semiretired; Formerly Law Clerk, Bldg. Contractor, Operated Tavern and Restaurant. Mil. Serv: World War I Vet, Army, 17-19. Mem: Past Comdr, Am. Legion Post; Chaplain, Firing Squad, 9 years; VFW; Badger Fisherman's League; AFL-CIO Local; Northwest Old Settlers Club, Lions Int. Mailing Add: 3112 W. Silver Spring Dr, Milwaukee, Wis. 53209.

MERTZ, J. HAROLD R
Ind. State Rep.
b. Holyoke, Colo, 1896; m. to Esther Simons; c. Dr. Joanne and Mrs. Phyllis Punshon. Educ: Purdue Univ, B.S; Columbia Univ, M.Ed. Polit. & Govt. Pos: Ind. State Rep, 67- Bus. & Prof. Pos: Teacher, 23-38; purchasing agent, city schs, 38-48; prin, Logansport High Sch, 48-63; farm owner; dir, State Bank of Burnettsville; dir, Holding Corp. for Logansport High Sch. Stadium and Lincoln Jr. High Sch. Mem: Exec. bd, Three Rivers Coun. Boy Scouts; past pres, Kiwanis. Rel: Presbyterian. Mailing Add: 2521 North St, Logansport, Ind. 46947.

MESKILL, THOMAS J. R
U.S. Rep, Conn.
b. New Britain, Conn, 1/30/28; m. to Mary T. Grady; c. Maureen, John, Peter, Eileen and Thomas. Educ: Trinity Col, B.S, 50; Univ. Conn. Law Sch, 56; N.Y. Univ. Sch. of Law; ed, Law Rev, Univ. Conn. Polit. & Govt. Pos: Mayor, New Britain, Conn, 62-64; mem, Constitutional Conv, Hartford, 65; U.S. Rep, Conn, 66- Bus. & Prof. Pos: Attorney, partner Meskill, Dorsey, Sledzik, and Walsh; corp. counsel, 65- Mil. Serv: 1st Lt, Air Force, 50-53. Mem: Conn, New Britain, Hartford Co. and Fla. Bar Asns; former pres, New Britain Jaycees and New Britain Coun. of Soc. Agencies; Daly Coun; K. of C; Elks; Am. Legion. Distinguished Serv. Award, New Britain Jaycees, 64. Rel: Catholic. Legal Res: New Britain, Conn. Mailing Add: 6830 Silver Lane, Annandale, Va. 22003.

MESPELT, ROY W. D
City Councilman, El Cerrito, Calif.
b. Berkeley, Calif, 12/12/24; s. Roy L. Mespelt and Winifred G. Hills M; m. 2/14/49 to Barbara L. Kerner; c. Carol Lynne and Mark Steven. Educ: Berkeley High Sch, grad, 43. Polit. & Govt. Pos: City councilman, El Cerrito, Calif, 64-; committeeman, Calif. Dem. Party, 68. Mem: Lions; F&AM; Jr. C. of C; bd. dirs, Contra Costa Epilepsy League; life mem, Castro PTA. Silver Key Award, El Cerrito Jr. C. of C, twice. Rel: Lutheran. Mailing Add: 7320 Plank Ct, El Cerrito, Calif. 94530.

MESSER, ERNEST BRYAN D
N.C. State Rep.
b. Waynesville, N.C, 12/21/13; s. of Forrest W. Messer and Effie Furr M; m. 1/11/36 to Jincy Owen Bryan C; c. Mrs. Clyde Poovey, Jr. Educ: Carson

Newman Col, B.A, 35. Polit. & Govt. Pos: Chmn, Haywood Co. Dem. Exec. Cmt, N.C, 58-62; mem, Haywood Co. Planning Bd; rep, Gen. Assembly, 63; N.C. State Rep, currently. Bus. & Prof. Pos: Teacher and basketball coach, Haywood Co. Sch, 35-39; supvr, Wood Procurement Dept, Champion Papers, Inc. Mil. Serv: Lt, Navy, 42-45. Mem: Lions; Toastmasters; Am. Legion; VFW; bd. of dirs, Haywood Co. Ment. Health Asn; Champion YMCA; Champion Credit Union; Haywood Co. Hist. Asn. Rel: Baptist; Teacher, Adult Sunday Sch. Class. Mailing Add: 15 Forest View Circle, Canton, N.C. 28716. (1967)

MESSERLY, FRANCIS L. R
Iowa State Sen.
b. Cedar Falls, Iowa, 4/21/15; s. Edward Messerly and Essie M; m. to Mary Hamlin; c. Carol and Randy. Educ: Grad. Finchford. Polit. & Govt. Pos: Bd. Supvrs, Black Hawk Co, Iowa, 50-60, Iowa State Rep; Iowa State Sen, currently. Bus. & Prof. Pos: Bus. Bldg. Contractor; Operated Gen. Merchandise Bus, 10 years. Mem: Odd Fellows; Masons; Farm Bur; Izaak Walton League. Rel: Finchford Community Church. Mailing Add: Route 3, Cedar Falls, Iowa 50613.

MESSERLY, ROBERTA G. (MRS) D
b. Youngstown, Ohio; d. Patrick J. and Nora Barrett Cronin; m. to George D. Messerly. Polit. & Govt. Pos: Admin. Asst. to Rep. Kirwan. Mem: Bus. & Prfnl. Women's Club, Youngstown, Ohio. Legal Res: Youngstown, Ohio. Mailing Add: 4943 Eskridge Terr, N.W, Washington, D.C. 20016. (1967)

MESSMER, JACK GUSTAPHE R
b. Hamburg, Germany, 8/29/99; U.S. citizen; s. Johames Th. Messmer and Anna Lange M; m. to Lucille D. Rieck; c. George, Fern and Ricky. Educ: Univ. of Kiel, W. Germany; Univ. of Art, Munich; Technical Univ, Munich, C.E. and A.E. Polit. & Govt. Pos: Mem, Park Bd, Indianapolis, Ind, 35; city host, Indianapolis; mem, Collier Co. Port Authority, Fla; former chmn, Collier Co. Rep. Exec. Cmt. Bus. & Prof. Pos: Pres, Jack G. Messmer Construct. Co. Emerson Riley Realty Corp, Northview Develop. Corp, College Realty Corp, Messmer Realty Co, Capitol Develop. Corp. and Prima Invest. Corp, 30-62. Mil. Serv: Kaisers Army, 17, released as Lt.(jg), 19, after serv. in Russia & France; Iron Cross; Hansa Cross; Knight of Order of Serv, W. Germany. Publ: Articles on water sports for yachting mag. and several newspapers. Mem: Pres, Naples Players; commodore emeritus, three Yacht Clubs; past comdr, U.S. Coast Guard Auxiliary; hon. life mem, Optimists; Shrine; York Rite, Scottish Rite; Indust. Cmt, C. of C; Rel: Lutheran. Mailing Add: 672 16th Ave. S, Naples, Fla. 33940. (1967)

MESSNER, GEORGE DONALD R
Chmn, Brookings Co. Rep. Cmt, S.Dak.
b. Brookings, S.Dak, 9/30/13; s. Frank Lawrence Messner and Hariette Alstot M; m. 8/17/42 to Leola Joyce Storsteen; c. Frank David. Educ: S.Dak. State Univ, B.S; Blue Key; Scabbard and Blade. Polit. & Govt. Pos: Co. cmnr, Brookings Co. Cmn, S.Dak, 63-65 and chmn, 65-; chmn, Brookings Co. Rep. Cmt, 64- Bus. & Prof. Pos: Math. teacher and coach, Gregory High Sch, 35-38 and Milbank High Sch, 39-48; farm mgr, 48- Mil. Serv: Res. Officer, no active service. Rel: Presbyterian. Mailing Add: 313 20th Ave, Brookings, S.Dak. 57006. (1967)

METAYER, ELIZABETH NENER D
b. Boston, Mass, 8/21/11; d. John Willoughby Nener and Lucy Phillips N; m. 6/30/35; wid; m. 4/27/47 to Edward Achille Metayer; c. Richard Edward Metayer and Gael Metayer (Mrs. Corbin). Educ: Harvard Univ, 2 years; Hickox Secy. Sch. grad. Polit. & Govt. Pos: Mem, Braintree Town Meeting, Mass. 12 years; chmn, Braintree Tech. Adv. Cmt. Transportation, 66-69; mem, Braintree Dem. Town Cmt, 67- Publ: 'Cabbages and Kings,' weekly column, Braintree Observer Forum, currently. Mem: Pres, Braintree Point Woman's Club; pres. second dist, Past Pres. Club Mass; second v.pres, Past Chmn. Club Mass; vet. chmn, Braintree Philergians; Braintree Hist. Soc; Braintree League Women Voters (founding and past pres). Rel: Catholic. Mailing Add: 33 Arthur St, Braintree, Mass. 02184.

METCALF, GEORGE R. R
b. Auburn, N.Y, 2/5/14; m. to Elizabeth Bradley; c. Five. Educ: Princeton Univ, B.A, 36; Columbia Grad. Sch. of Journalism, M.S, 37. Polit. & Govt. Pos: Mem, Nat. Munic. League and Citizens Union of N.Y.C, 37-38; chmn, Auburn Housing Authority, 49-; N.Y. State Sen, 50-66; constructed pub. housing project for low income families in coop. with State Div. of Housing, 51; cand, U.S. House of Rep, N.Y, 68. Bus. & Prof. Pos: Publisher, Auburn Press, 38-41; columnist, Citizen Advertiser. Mil. Serv: Sixth Armored Div, World War II, ETO; Silver Star. Mailing Add: R.D. 2, Auburn, N.Y. 13021. (1967)

METCALF, JACK HOLACE R
Wash. State Sen.
b. Marysville, Wash, 11/30/27; s. John Read Metcalf and Eunice Grannis M; m. 10/3/48 to Norma Jean Grant; c. Marta Jean, Gayle Marie, Lea Lynn and Beverly Ann. Educ: Pac. Lutheran Col, B.A. & B. of Educ, 51; Univ. Wash, grad. work, 65-66. Polit. & Govt. Pos: Wash. State Rep, 60-64; pres, Wash. Fedn. Young Rep. Clubs, 64; Wash. State Sen, 21st Dist, 67-; cand, U.S. Sen, Wash, 68. Mil. Serv: Pvt, Army, 46-47. Mem: State Bd. of Dirs, Wash. Educ. Asn, 59-61 and State Legis. Cmt, 57-58; local unit pres, Everett Asn. of Classroom Teachers, 56-57; Lynnwood Kiwanis; Edmonds Rod & Gun Club; bd. of dirs, Snohomish Co. Vols. of Am. Rel: Protestant. Mailing Add: 7421 46th W, Mukilteo, Wash. 98275.

METCALF, JOHN ALBERT R
Minn. State Sen.
b. Durand, Wis, 8/10/04; s. John Sala Metcalf and Minnie Sweitzer M; m. 11/7/27 to Ina Mae DeMarce; c. Irene Thresa, Mary Ellen and Nancy Lee. Educ: St. Mary's Col, Minn, B.S, 27; Univ. Minn, Minneapolis. Polit. & Govt. Pos: Minn. State Sen, Carver, Scott and LeSueur Co, 55- Bus. & Prof. Pos: Supt. schs, Swanville, 29-36; supt. schs, Shakopee, 36-45; pres, Shakopee Commercial, 45-46 & 52-54; supt. schs, Burnsville, 55-67; mem. bd. dirs, Metrop. Hosp. Planning, 62; supt. schs, Bricelyn, 67-68. Mem: Sch. Execs. (pres, Dist. 22 Chap, 31-34); K. of C.(Grand Knight, 40-42); pres, Missota Conf, 61-63. Man of the Year, Upper Miss. Waterways Asn, 61; Bishop Heffron Award, St. Mary's Col, 62; John Metcalf Jr. High Sch, Burnsville, so named in 63; Commun. Serv. Award, Shakopee Jaycees, 66. Rel: Catholic. Mailing Add: 534 Holmes, Shakopee, Minn. 55379.

METCALF, LEE D
U.S. Sen, Mont.
b. Stevensville, Mont, 1/28/11; m. 1938 to Donna Hoover; c. Jerry (foster son). Polit. & Govt. Pos: Assoc. Justice, Mont. Supreme Court, 46; U.S. Rep, Mont, 53-54; U.S. Sen, Mont, 60- Bus. & Prof. Pos: Lawyer. Legal Res: Helena, Mont. Mailing Add: 427 Senate Office Bldg, Washington, D.C. 20510.

METCALF, NEIL D
b. Hartford, Ala, 11/10/21; s. Ramsey L. Metcalf and Jimmilee M. M; single. Educ: Univ. of Ala, B.S, 43. LL.B, 48; Univ. of Tex, 48-49, grad. study in pub. law; Pi Kappa Alpha; Phi Alpha Delta. Polit. & Govt. Pos: App. Asst. Attorney Gen. of Ala, 49; asst. securities cmnr; Ala. State Sen, 54-58 & 62-66. Bus. & Prof. Pos: Lawyer, in private practice in Geneva, 52- Mil. Serv: Army, Capt, 43-46; served 30 months overseas on staff of Gen. Douglas MacArthur as psychol. warfare officer; active duty, 50, 15 months in Korea on staffs of Gen. MacArthur and Ridgeway; currently state staff, Ala. Nat. Guard. Mem: Exec. committeeman of Jr. Bar Asn, 48; pres, Geneva Chap. Young Dem. Club, 50; WOW; Elks; Am. Legion; VFW. Rel: Baptist. Mailing Add: Geneva, Ala. 36340.

METCALFE, RALPH HAROLD D
Alderman, Chicago City Coun, Ill.
b. Atlanta, Ga, 5/29/10; s. Maj. Clarence Metcalfe and Mayme Attaway M; m. 7/20/47 to Madalynne Fay Young; c. Ralph H, Jr. Educ: Marquette Univ, Wis, Ph.B, 36; Univ. South. Calif, Westwood, M.S, 39; Alpha Psi; Alpha Sigma Nu. Polti. & Govt. Pos: Committeeman, Third Ward Dem. Cmt, Chicago, Ill, 52-; alderman, Third Ward City Coun, Chicago, 55-; alternate del, Dem. Nat. Conv, 56 & 64, elector, 60 and del, 68; chmn, Cmt. Bldgs. and Zoning, City Coun, Chicago, Ill, 65, pres-pro-tem, city coun, 69; mem, Northeast. Ill. Metrop. Area Planning Cmn, Chicago, 69. Mil. Serv: Entered as Pvt, Army, 42, released as 1st Lt, 45, after serv. in Transportation Corps; Legion of Merit. Mem: Am. Legion; Amvet; Int. Platform Asn. James A. Hoey Award; Ecumenic Int. Justice. Rel: Catholic. Legal Res: 4530 S. Michigan Ave, Chicago, Ill. 60653. Mailing Add: 45 E. 47th St, Chicago, Ill. 60653.

METTLER, JOE H. D
Chmn, Fifth Dist. Dem. Cmt, Ind.
b. Wells Co, Ind, 6/13/13; s. Frank Mettler and Blanche Fuller M; m. 4/20/35 to Theresa Osterholt; c. John and Patrick. Educ: Ind. Tech, 31. Polit. & Govt. Pos: Mem, Wells Co. Dem. Cmt, Ind, 34-36 and Dem. Precinct Committeeman, 46-48; secy, Huntington Co. Dem. Cmt, 48-54, co. chmn, 54-56; field rep. to State Rep. J. Ed Roush, 58-68, chmn, Roush for Cong. Cmt, 68; chmn, Fifth Dist. Dem. Cmt, 59-; mem, Gov. Ins. Cmn, Ind, 60-; del, Dem. Nat. Conv, 68. Publ: 'How to Sell Accident and Health to Business and Professional People,' Nat. Underwriters, 58. Mem: Pres, Huntington Co. Ins. Bd, 52-54, Ft. Wayne Accident and Health Bd, 54-56 and Huntington Co. Jaycees, 46-48; C. of C; K. of C; Moose; Elks; Kiwanis; Izaak Walton League. Rel: Roman Catholic. Legal Res: 710 Flax Mill Rd, Huntington, Ind. 46750. Mailing Add: 616 N. Jefferson, Huntington, Ind. 46750.

METTLER, ROLLIN WOODRUFF, JR. D
Conn. State Rep.
b. West Haven, Conn, 7/2/32; s. Rollin Woodruff Mettler and Helen Shaw M; m. 8/19/50 to Elizabeth Manthey Zorn; c. Linda Anne, Judith, Joan Carol and Frederick Woodruff. Educ: Choate Sch, Conn, dipl, 46; Yale Univ, B.A, 50. Polit. & Govt. Pos: Mem, Indust. Develop. Cmn, Hamden, Conn, 63-65; Conn. State Rep, 96th Assembly Dist, 67-68 & 69- Bus. & Prof. Pos: Pres, Mettler Piano Showrooms, Inc, New Haven, Conn, 50-60, Mettler & Assocs, Hamden, 60-63 and Circuit-Wise, Inc, North Haven, 64- Mem: Rotary. Rel: Lutheran. Mailing Add: 61 Carmalt Rd, Hamden, Conn. 06517.

METZ, DANIEL DODDS R
Chmn, Lincoln Co. Rep. Cent. Cmt, Kans.
b. Lincoln, Kans, 12/22/37; s. Theodore Melrose Metz and Wilma Dodds M; m. 8/6/66 to Lynne Lieurance; c. Michael Ted. Educ: Washburn Univ, A.B, 59, Law Sch, J.D, 66; Kappa Sigma; Phi Alpha Delta. Polit. & Govt. Pos: Asst. Attorney Gen. of Kans, 66-68; chmn, Lincoln Co. Rep. Cent. Cmt, Kans, 68-; Lincoln Co. attorney, Kans, 69- Bus. & Prof. Pos: Dir, Lincoln Co. Develop. Corp, 68- Mil. Serv: Entered as Ens, Naval Res, 59, released as Lt, 62, after serv. in U.S.S. St. Paul, 60-62; Res, 62-, Lt. Comdr. Mem: Am, Kans. and Northwest Kans. Bar Asns. Mailing Add: 713 N. Second, Lincoln, Kans. 67455.

METZENBAUM, HOWARD MORTON D
b. Cleveland, Ohio, 6/4/17; s. Charles I. Metzenbaum and Anna K. Klafter M; m. 8/8/46 to Shirley Louise Turoff; c. Barbara Jo, Amy Beth, Susan Lynn and Shelley Hope. Educ: Ohio State Univ, B.A, 39, LL.B, 41; Order of the Coif; Phi Eta Sigma; Tau Epsilon Rho. Polit. & Govt. Pos: Pub. Panel mem, War Labor Bd, 42-45; Ohio State Rep, 43-46; Ohio State Sen, 47-50; mem, Judicial Coun, Ohio, 49-50; former mem, Ohio Dem. State Exec. Cmt; del, Dem. Nat. Conv, 68. Bus. & Prof. Pos: Chmn. of the bd, Airport Parking Co. of Am, 58- and Int. Tel. & Tel. Consumer Serv. Corp, 66-; dir, Capital Nat. Bank of Cleveland, 62- and Norwalk Truck Lines, Inc, 66. Rel: Jewish. Mailing Add: 18500 N. Park Blvd, Shaker Heights, Ohio 44118.

METZGER, DAVID F. D
Polit. & Govt. Pos: Chief probation officer, Del. Cty. Juvenile Court; exec. bd. mem, Ind. State Probation-Parole Asn; Ind. State Rep, -66. Mil. Serv: Navy, Korean Conflict. Mem: Pres, Muncie Commun. Welfare Coun; Ind. Youth Coun; Muncie Human Rights Comm; Masonic Order; Elks; Lions. Rel: Presbyterian. Mailing Add: 2210 W. Memorial Dr, Muncie, Ind. 47302. (1967)

METZGER, EDWARD R
N.Dak. State Rep.
b. Willa, N.Dak, 4/14/27; s. William Metzger and Elizabeth Miller M; m. 9/5/53 to Alyce Mae Ellison; c. Edward J, Cynthia R, Marty Rae and Joy Marie. Educ: Hebron High Sch, grad, 45. Polit. & Govt. Pos: Co-v.chmn, N.Dak. Dem. Non-Partisan League; precinct committeeman, Dem. Party, N.Dak, 63-66; N.Dak. State Rep, 32nd Dist, 67- Mil. Serv: Entered as Pvt, Army, 45, released as Sgt, 47, after serv. in 907 Counter Intel. Corps, ETO. Mem: Elks; Am. Legion; VFW; Int. Brotherhood of Electrical Workers; Bis-

marck Mfrs. Trades and Labor Assembly; bd. mem, Salvation Army; Urban Renewal Cmt. Rel: Lutheran. Mailing Add: 410 Shady Lane, Bismarck, N.Dak. 58501.

METZNER, CARROLL E. R
Chmn, Second Cong. Dist. Rep. Party, Wis.
b. Milwaukee, Wis, 4/24/19; s. Edwin F. Metzner and Anna Mathilda Clara Henke M; m. 8/12/44 to Peggy Joan Hausse; c. Bruce Carroll Stokes and Margot Andrea. Educ: Univ. Wis. Exten, 37-39; Northwestern Univ, B.S, 41; Univ. Wis. Law Sch, LL.B, 43. Polit. & Govt. Pos: Alderman, Madison, Wis, 51-56; Wis. State Assemblyman, 54-58; secy, Citizens for Better Govt, 61-64; mem. exec. cmt, Dane Co. Rep. Party, 61-65 and chmn, 65-69; mem. ins. laws revision adv. cmn, Wis. Legis. Coun, 67-; alternate del, Rep. Nat. Conv, 68; chmn, Second Cong. Dist. Rep. Party, Wis, 69- Bus. & Prof. Pos: Attorney, Aberg, Bell, Blake & Metzner. Mem: Dane Co. Bar Asn.(chmn. legis. & judiciary cmt, 65-69 and judicial selection cmt, 66-69); Wis. State Bar Asn; Am. Bar Asn; Fedn. of Ins. Counsel; pres, Am. Bus. Club, 56-57; Lions Int; Defense Res. Inst; trustee, Methodist Hosp, 62- Rel: Congregational Christian. Legal Res: 733 Huron Hill, Madison, Wis. 53711. Mailing Add: 16 N. Carroll St, Madison, Wis. 53703.

MEUNIER, ALEX J. R
Wis. State Sen.
b. Brussels, Wis, 11/9/97. Educ: Algoma Teachers Col, 1917. Polit. & Govt. Pos: Wis. State Assemblyman, 43-49; alternate, Rep. Nat. Conv, twice; undersheriff, Wis, 12 years, sheriff, 4 years; mem, Conserv. Cong; Rep. Nat. Committeeman; Wis. State Sen, 63- Bus. & Prof. Pos: Owner and operator, orchard, 40-46; teacher, 9 years; ins. rep. Mil. Serv: Army, 1918. Mem: Dir, C. of C; Church Men's Club; former pres, Northeast Wis. Life Underwriters Asn. Mailing Add: 106 S. Ithaca Ave, Sturgeon Bay, Wis. 54235.

MEYER, ALICE C. D
Committeewoman, Second Dist. Dem. Party, N.J.
b. Niagara Falls, N.Y, 3/3/31; d. Harold Cripe and Nina Belangie C; m. 8/3/57 to Alan S. Meyer; c. Robert Alan and Julie Ellen. Educ: Albion Col, B.A, 53; N.Y. Law Sch, currently. Polit. & Govt. Pos: Committeewoman, Second Dist. Dem. Party, N.J, 65-; exec. dir, Bergen Co. Vol. for McCarthy, 68; alternate del, Dem. Nat. Conv, 68; mem, exec. bd, Bergen Co. Dem. Coalition, N.J, 68- Bus. & Prof. Pos: Clerk, N.Y. Pub. Libr, N.Y, 53-54; sr. res, Am. Petroleum Inst, 54-58. Mem: Am. Civil Liberties Union of N.J.(educ. dir, Newark, 69, exec. bd, Bergen-Passaic Chap, currently); Bergen Co. Health and Welfare Coun; Bergen Co. Women Strike for Peace; Bergen Co. Fair Housing Coun; Tenafly Fair Housing Cmt. Rel: Ethical Culture. Mailing Add: 43 Buff Rd, Tenafly, N.J. 07670.

MEYER, ANNE HEINEMAN D
Mem, Hall Co. Dem. Exec. Cmt, Fla.
b. Mainz, Germany, 5/31/25; d. Richard L. Heineman and Anna Berney H; m. 1/19/47 to Sylvan Meyer; c. Erica Heineman, David Norman, II and Jason Berney. Educ: Col. of Charleston, B.S, 45. Polit. & Govt. Pos: Active campaign worker for local, state and nat. Dem. Cands, 47-69; mem. and secy, Chestatee Libr. Bd, 6 years; del, Dem. Nat. Conv, 64; mem, Hall Co. Young Dem, Ga, 64-69; co-chmn, Oper. Support, Ninth Cong. Dist. and Hall Co. chmn, Ninth Dist. Dem. Women's Conf; mem, Hall Co. Dem. Exec. Cmt, 66-; mem, Citizens Adv. Cmt. on Urban Renewal, 66-69. Bus. & Prof. Pos: Woman's dir, prom. mgr, WCSC, Charleston, S.C, 44-47; columnist, writer, part-time woman's ed, The Daily Times, Gainesville, Ga, 47- Mem: PTA; founder and pres, Garden Club; past pres, Study Club; past mem, League of Women Voters; Educ. Cmt, Model Cities Prog, Gainesville, Ga. Became Am. Citizen, 47. Rel: Jewish. Mailing Add: 248 W. Rivo Alto, Miami, Fla. 33139.

MEYER, ARLIE H. R
Mo. State Rep.
b. St. Charles, Mo, 8/12/05; s. Edward Meyer and Sophie Grie M; m. 6/14/33 to Flora Anna Haferkamp; c. Donald Edward and Robert Allen. Educ: St. Charles Pub. Schs, 10 years. Polit. & Govt. Pos: City councilman, St. Charles, Mo. 35-39, co. assessor, St. Charles Co, 53-65; Mo. State Rep, 67- Bus. & Prof. Pos: Real estate salesman. Mem: Mo. Real Estate Asn; Elks (Exalted Ruler, Lodge 690); Moose; Am. Red Cross; pres, Mo. State Assessors Asn. Rel: United Church of Christ. Mailing Add: 234 Thomas, St. Charles, Mo. 63301.

MEYER, ARMIN HENRY
U.S. Ambassador to Japan
b. Ft. Wayne, Ind, 1/19/14; m. to Alice James; c. Kathleen Alice. Educ: Capital Univ, B.A, 35, LL.D; Ohio State Univ, M.A, 41. Polit. & Govt. Pos: News ed, chief, Bur. News, Off. War Info, 44-45; pub. affairs off, FS Auxiliary, Baghdad, 46-48; career officer, U.S. Dept. State For. Serv, 48-, second secy, Baghdad, 48, first secy. and consul, Beirut, 52-55, first secy, counsr, Kabul, 55-57, dep. dir, Off. S.Asian Affairs, 57-58; dep. dir. and dir, Off. Near E. Affairs, 58-60, dep. asst. secy. state for Near E. and S. Asian Affairs, 61; U.S. Ambassador to Lebanon, 62-65; U.S. Ambassador to Iran, 65-69; U.S. Ambassador to Japan, 69- Bus. & Prof. Pos: Pub. rels. officer, 35-39; asst. prof. and dean of men, Capital Univ, 40-42. Mil. Serv: Off. of War Info. State Dept. Meritorious Serv. Award, 58. Legal Res: Lincoln, Ill. Mailing Add: U.S. Embassy, Tokyo, Japan.

MEYER, CARL A. D
b. Cumberland, Iowa, 12/15/03; married; c. Twelve. Educ: Pub. Schs. Polit. & Govt. Pos: N.Dak. State Rep, 59-66. Bus. & Prof. Pos: Farmer; rancher. Mem: Farmers Union; Farm Bur; N.Dak. Stockmen's Asn; 4-H Leader. Mailing Add: Box 1000, Flasher, N.Dak. 58535. (1967)

MEYER, CHARLES APPLETON R
Asst. Secy, Bur. of Inter-Am. Affairs, Dept. of State
Legal Res: Pa. Mailing Add: Dept. of State, 2201 C St. N.W, Washington, D.C. 20520.

MEYER, CLARENCE ARDELL HENRY R
Nebr. State Attorney Gen.
b. Pender, Nebr, 9/1/10; s. William C. Meyer and Bertha Schultz M; m. 7/22/41 to Francis Boughn. Educ: Univ. Nebr, A.B; Univ. Nebr. Col. Law, J.D, 33; Sigma Alpha Epsilon; Phi Delta Phi. Polit. & Govt. Pos: Mem. staff, U.S. Dept. Justice, 40-42 and Nebr. Dept. Labor, 46-49; Asst. Attorney Gen, Nebr, 49-52; dep. attorney Gen, 52-60, Nebr. State Attorney Gen, 60- Bus. & Prof. Pos: Lawyer, 33-40. Mil. Serv: Entered as 2nd Lt, Air Force, 42, released as Maj, 46, after serv. in Air Transport Command, China-Burma-India, 43-46; Bronze Star; Distinguished Unit Citation; Chinese Air Force Medal. Publ: 'State Taxation in Nebraska,' 1/55 and 'Analysis of Business Lotteries,' 3/55, Nebr. Law Rev; 'Arrest, Search & Seizure,' Nebr. State Bar J, 4/67. Mem: President Nixon's Task Force Crime and Law Enforcement; Nat. Asn. Attorneys Gen.(exec. cmt. chmn, criminal law cmt); Am. Law Inst; Am. Legion; Lincoln, Nebr. and Am. Bar Asns. Lewis E. Wyman Award, 65. Rel: Lutheran. Legal Res: 3210 Van Dorn, Lincoln, Nebr. 68502. Mailing Add: Statehouse, Lincoln, Nebr. 68509.

MEYER, FRANK R
b. Portage Twp, Mich, 8/16/13; s. Albert Meyer and Cora Ebelink M; m. 6/17/42 to Bertha Ronda; c. Thomas Jay, James Edward, John Albert and Barbara Ann. Educ: West. Mich. Univ, A.B, 35; Univ. Mich, A.M, 39; Columbia Univ; Mich. State Univ. Polit. & Govt. Pos: Admin. asst. to U.S. Rep. Gerald R. Ford, 55- Bus. & Prof. Pos: Teacher, 35-53; Ford Found fellow, 53-54. Rel: Christian Reformed. Legal Res: Grand Haven, Mich. 49417. Mailing Add: 5203 Fenwood Ave, Washington, D.C. 20021.

MEYER, FRANK STRAUS Conservative, N.Y.
V.Chmn, Conservative Party, N.Y.
b. Newark, N.J, 5/9/09; s. Jack F. Meyer and Helene Straus M; m. 10/11/40 to Elsie Bown; c. John Cornford and Eugene Bown. Educ: Princeton Univ, 26-28; London Sch. of Econ, 32-34; Univ. Chicago, 34-38; Balliol Col, Oxford, B.A, 32, M.A, 54. Polit. & Govt. Pos: Chmn, Cmt. on Int. Affairs and v.chmn, Conservative Party, N.Y, currently; mem. bd. dirs, Am. Conservative Union. Bus. & Prof. Pos: Sr. ed, National Review, 57- Mil. Serv: Entered as Pvt, Army, 42, released as Cpl, 43. Publ: The Moulding of Communists, Harcourt, Brace, 61; In Defense of Freedom, Henry Regnery Co, 62; co-author, What is Conservatism?, Holt, 64; The Conservative Mainstream, Arlington-House, 69. Mem: Philadelphia Soc; Am. Polit. Sci. Asn; Princeton Club of N.Y; Nat. Press Club; Am. Legion; U.S. Chess Fedn. Mailing Add: Ohayo Mt. Rd, Woodstock, N.Y. 12498.

MEYER, FRED CHARLES D
Chmn, Howard Co. Dem. Party, Nebr.
b. Palmer, Nebr, 10/13/18; s. Ernest Henry Meyer and Adele Belefeldt M; m. 12/24/42 to Maxine Ann Matousek; c. Donita Mae, Vikkie Darlene and Lori Jo. Educ: Merrick Co. High Sch, Nebr. Polit. & Govt. Pos: Chmn, Howard Co. Dem. Party, Nebr, 64-; mem, State Sch. Bd. Unit 10. Mil. Serv: Entered as Pvt, Army, 42, released as S/Sgt, 46, after serv. in 108 Gen. Hosp, ETO; Good Conduct Medal; Oversea's Campaign Ribbon with 3 Battle Stars. Mem: Pres, Howard Co. Feeder's and Breeder's Asn, 60-64; Lions; Eagles; Am. Legion; Leiderkrantz Club; St. Paul Country Club. Selected as Distinguished Young Farmer, Howard Co. C. of C, 64. Rel: Missouri Synod Lutheran. Mailing Add: R.R. 2, St. Paul, Nebr, 68873. (1967)

MEYER, J. THEODORE R
Ill. State Rep.
b. Chicago, Ill, 4/13/36; s. Joseph Theodore Meyer and Mary E. McHugh M; m. 8/19/61 to Mary Lou Bartholomew; c. Jean Frances and J. Theodore, III. Educ: John Carroll Univ, B.S, 58; DePaul Univ. Col. of Law, LL.B, 62. Polit. & Govt. Pos: Ill. State Rep, 28th Dist, 67-68 & 69- Bus. & Prof. Pos: Self-employed attorney, 63- Mem: Am, Ill. State, Chicago and South Side Bar Asns; Mt. Greenwood Lions; Ill. State Hist. Soc; Beverly Hills Univ. Club; The Oriental Inst. Rel: Catholic. Mailing Add: 10444 S. Kedzie Ave, Chicago, Ill. 60655.

MEYER, JOHN P. R
b. Danville, Ill, 8/17/20; c. six. Educ: U. of Notre Dame, B.S.C, 42; U. of Notre Dame Law Sch, passed Ill. State Bar Exam, 46. Polit. & Gov. Pos: Elected to Ill. State Sen, 52, 56, 60; Ill. State Rep, 48, 50; Chmn, Ill. Cmt. on Narcotics; U.S. Del. to UN Cmt. on Narcotic drugs at Geneva, Switz, 60. Bus. & Prof. Pos: Lawyer. Mil. Serv: W.W. II, U. S. Army, entered as Pvt; cmn. at Fort Sill, Okla, 43, assigned to 14th Armored Div, 3 1/2 years, tow overseas; attained rank of Capt. in field artillery; awarded Bronze and Silver Stars. Mem: Am. Legion; 40 et 8; Amvets; Chmn, Vermilion Co. Young Rep. Orgn, 50-51. Mailing Add: 406 W. Clark, Champaign, Ill. (1967)

MEYER, JOHN RICHARD 'JACK' R
Chmn, Clay Co. Rep. Cent. Cmt, Ill.
b. Olney, Ill, 4/5/23; s. Ralph G. Meyer and Lena Bunnell M; m. 12/23/44 to Ruth Ann Schwager; c. Carol, Paul and Janet. Educ: Wash. Univ, LL.B, 47, J.D, 68. Polit. & Govt. Pos: Spec. asst. attorney gen, Ill, 59-61 & 69-; chmn, Clay Co. Rep. Cent. Cmt, Ill, 68- Mil. Serv: Entered as A/S, Naval Res, 43, released as Lt.(jg), 45, after serv. in LST Flotilla Staff 36, Pac. Theatre, 44-45. Mem: Ill. State Bar Asn; Ill. and Am. Trial Lawyers Asns; Kiwanis. Rel: Christian. Mailing Add: 717 N. Main St, P.O. Box 67, Flora, Ill. 62839.

MEYER, NORMAN J. D
b. Wilkes-Barre, Pa, 8/5/30; s. Nathan H. Meyer and Helen Goldstein M; m. 8/23/53 to Shirley F. Nast; c. Lee Ann, Jack R, Neal J. and Joanne. Educ: Syracuse Univ, 47-48; Pa. State Univ, B.S. in physics, 51, M.S. in physics, 53; Univ. South. Calif, 52-53; Univ. Calif, Los Angeles, Ph.D. in physics, 59; Sigma Xi; Sigma Pi Sigma. Polit. & Govt. Pos: Mem, Orange Co. Dem. Cent. Cmt, Calif, 59-, v.chmn, 60-62, chmn, 62-66; mem, Calif. State Dem. Party, 60-66; mem. exec. bd. and steering cmt, 62-66; del, Dem. Nat. Conv, 64; mem. bd. trustees, Fairview State Hosp, Costa Mesa, Calif, 64-68. Bus. & Prof. Pos: Sr. engr, HRB-Singer, State Col, Pa, 51-52; research scientist, Aeronutronic Div, Philco, Newport Beach, Calif, 59-61; staff physicist, Marshall Labs, Torrance, 61-62; asst. dir, LTV Research Center, West Div, Anaheim, 62-; v.pres, 32nd Dist. Agr. Asn, Orange Co. Fair, 66-; v.pres. and mem. bd. dir, Hearing Conserv. Serv, Inc, Commerce, currently. Publ: Several tech. articles, J. of Chem. Physics and J. of Acoustical Soc. of Am. Mem: Am. Physical Soc; Acoustical Soc. of Am; Am. Asn. for Advancement of Sci; Soc. Sigma Xi; Sigma Pi Sigma; Mason; bd dirs, Orange Co. Easter Seal Soc. and Orange Co. Jewish Commun. Coun; regional adv. bd, Anti-Defamation League,

Pac. Southwest Region; Univ. Calif, Los Angeles Alumni Asn; pres. elect, Orange Co. Jewish Commun. Coun, 66- Rel: Jewish. Mailing Add: 2988 Ceylon Dr, Costa Mesa, Calif. 92626.

MEYER, WALTER L. D
Mo. State Rep.
b. St. Louis, Mo, 2/25/23; m. 7/17/43 to Audrey Marie Merklin; c. Lawrence, Daniel and Maureen. Educ: Southwest High Sch, St. Louis. Polit. & Govt. Pos: Alderman of Bellefontaine Neighbors, 53-57, mayor, 57-63; chmn, Symington for President for Local 1102 and North Co. Area Chmn, Citizens for Kennedy, 60; Mo. State Rep, 62-, chmn. rds. and hyws. cmt, Mo. House of Rep, mem, educ. and workman's compensation cmts; Dem. Committeeman, St. Ferdinand Twp, 64; alternate del, Dem. Nat. Conv, 68. Bus. & Prof. Pos: Employed 28 years with Emerson Elec. Co. as exp. tool maker in Engr. Div, Elec. and Spaceonics Div. Mem: Bellefontaine Neighbors, Mo; past pres, Northwest Kiwanis Club; past mem. exec. bd, Christian Bros. Col. Father's Club; Hathaway-Riverview Terr. Improv. Asn; area chmn, Red Cross for N. St. Louis Co; charter mem, Surrey Lane Athletic Asn; exec. cmt, St. Louis Co. League of Munic. with sub-cmts. on zoning and legis; pres, Annapolis Fathers Club of the Naval Acad; Local 1102, IUE-AFL-CIO, having held off. of secy-treas. and steward, app. del. to St. Louis Labor Coun; exec. cmt, Gr. St. Louis IUE-AFL-CIO COPE; area chmn, Friends of Scouting and March of Dimes. Rel: Catholic. Mailing Add: 9495 Yorktown Dr, Bellefontaine Neighbors, Mo. 63137.

MEYER, WILLIAM D
b. Bluffton, Ind, 11/2/04; s. Jacob Meyer and Ida Mae Beeler M; m. 5/19/27 to Josephine DeLong; c. Wilma Jean and Marcia Jo. Polit. & Govt. Pos: Dem. precinct committeeman, Ind, 36-40; mem. adv. bd, Harrison Twp. Wells Co, Ind, 36-40; del, Ind. State Conv, 58 & 60; del, Dem. Nat. Conv, 60 & 64; chmn, Farmers Home Admin, 62-64. Mem: Mason; Eastern Star; AASR; Ind. Bur. Rel: Protestant. Mailing Add: R.R. 2, Bluffton, Ind. 46714.

MEYER, WILLIAM BENEDICT D
Mem, Calif. Dem. State Cent. Cmt.
b. Santa Ana, Calif, 3/13/23; s. J. Meyer, Jr. and Connie Chavez M; m. 7/27/69 to Barbara Wangsness; c. Judy (Mrs. Tom Leichtfuss), Susan (Mrs. David McCrory), Roger P. and Bruce M. Educ: Long Beach State Col, B.A. with honors, 52, M.A, 53; Univ. Calif, Los Angeles; Univ. South. Calif; Phi Theta Kappa. Polit. & Govt. Pos: Pres, Orange Dem. Club, 64-65 and E. Orange Co. Dem. Coun, 65-66; dir, 35th Cong. Dist. Calif. Dem. Coun, 66-67; chmn, Orange Co. Dem. Fedn, 67-69; mem, Orange Co. Dem. Cent. Cmt. and chmn. of Dem. Clubs, 68-; mem, Calif. State Dem. Cent. Cmt, 68- Bus. & Prof. Pos: Counsr, Orange Co. Juvenile Hall, 45-54; teacher, Fullerton Jr. Col, 54- Mil. Serv: Pvt, Marines, 44-45, with serv. in Fourth Bn, U.S; Good Serv. Medal. Mem: Calif. Teachers Asn; past pres, Fullerton Jr. Col. Faculty Asn; Calif. Jr. Col. Faculty Asn; Nat. Educ. Asn; Calif. Asn. of Teachers of English; Am. Asn. Univ. Prof; Mod. Lang. Asn. Rel: First Christian. Mailing Add: 701 E. Palmdale, Orange, Calif. 92667.

MEYERS, CHARLES WALTER, SR. D
Mem, Calif. Dem. State Cent. Cmt.
b. San Francisco, Calif, 8/15/21; m. 2/3/51 to Alene J. Aviani M; c. Charlene Marie, Charles Walter, Jr. Educ: City Col. of San Francisco; Univ. of San Francisco; Golden Gate Col. Polit. & Govt. Pos: Calif. State Assemblyman, 48-67; mem, Calif. Dem. State Cent. Cmt, currently. Bus. & Prof. Pos: Assoc. automobile bus. Mil. Serv: Army, 43-46; Corps of Engrs. Mem: NSGW; Soc. of Mkt. Boys; Univ. of San Francisco Alumni Asn; Hibernians; Am. Legion; DAV; Eagles; K. of C; Steuben Soc; Lions; Druids; United Nationalities of San Francisco; bd. of dir, Sacred Heart and City Col. Alumni Asn; dist. committeeman, Boy Scouts. Mailing Add: 579 Wildwood Way, San Francisco, Calif. 91342. (1967)

MEYERSON, A. FREDERICK D
N.Y. State Sen.
b. Paterson, N.J, 2/2/18; s. Max Meyerson and Rose Prince M; m. 12/21/47 to Shirley Kahan; c. Gregory and Norma. Educ: St. John's Univ, Col. Arts & Sci, B.A, 45, Law Sch, LL.B, 43. Polit. & Govt. Pos: Admin. asst. to Congressman, Eugene J. Keogh; counsel, Joint Legis. Cmt. Reapportionment; law secy, Justice Victor L. Anfuso, Supreme Court, Kings Co, 63; law asst, Supreme Court, Kings Co, 67; law secy, Justice Abraham J. Multer, Supreme Court, 68; N.Y. State Sen, 15th Sen. Dist, 69- Bus. & Prof. Pos: Mem. Law Firm, Arab & Meyerson, 47- Mem: Temple Sinai (pres); 75th Precinct Youth Coun; East N.Y. Commun. Activities (bd. dirs); 38th Assembly Dist. Regular Dem. Orgn.(v.pres); B'nai B'rith (past pres. East N.Y. Lodge); United Jewish Appeal; Fedn. Jewish Philanthropies; Arthritis and Rheumatism Found. Highland Park Commun.(past pres); Coun. Better East N.Y; N.Side Commun. Cabinet; East N.Y. Coun. Jewish Nat. Fund.(past pres); active in sale of Bonds for Israel; past co-chmn, Arlington-Bushwick Boy Scouts Drives. Guest of Honor Dinner, United Jewish Appeal; Guest of Honor Dinner, East N.Y. Brownsville Div. Fedn. Jewish Philanthropies. Rel: Hebrew. Legal Res: 14 Van Siclen Court, Brooklyn, N.Y. 11207. Mailing Add: 186 Joralemon St, Brooklyn, N.Y. 11201.

MEYNER, ROBERT BAUMLE D
b. Easton, Pa. 7/3/08; s. Gustave Herman Meyner and Mary Sophia Baumle M; m. 1/19/57 to Helen Day Stevenson. Educ: Lafayette Col; Columbia Univ. Law Sch. Polit. & Govt. Pos: N.J. State Sen, Warren Co, 48-52; del, Dem. Nat. Conv, 48-68; Gov, N.J, 54-62. Bus. & Prof. Pos: Lawyer, 36-54; partner, law firm, Meyner and Wiley, 62-; adminstr, Cigarette Advert. Code, 64- Mil. Serv: Entered as Lt.(jg), Navy, 42, released as Comdr, Naval Res, 66. Mem: Elks; Eagles; Odd Fellows; Moose; Rotary; C. of C; fel, Am. Bar Found; Am, N.J. State, Warren, Hudson and Essex Co. Bar Asns; Grange; Essex (Newark), Columbia Univ. and River (N.Y.) Clubs; Amvets; Am. Legion; VFW. Legal Res: 16 Olden Lane, Princeton, N.J. 08540. Mailing Add: 24 Commerce St, Newark, N.J. 07102.

MEZVINSKY, EDWARD M. D
Iowa State Rep.
b. Ames, Iowa, 1/17/37; m. to Myra; c. Margot, Vera, Elsa and Eve. Educ: Univ. Iowa, B.A, 60; Univ. Calif, M.A. and J.D; Omicron Delta Kappa. Polit. & Govt. Pos: Legis. asst. to Congressman Neal Smith, Iowa, 65-67; Iowa State Rep, Johnson Co, currently. Bus. & Prof. Pos: Lawyer, Iowa City, Iowa. Presidential commendation for work to protect the public in areas of traffic and highway safety and meat inspection. Legal Res: 620 River St, Iowa City, Iowa 52240. Mailing Add: House of Representatives, State House, Des Moines, Iowa 50319.

MICHAEL, JAMES HARRY, JR. D
Va. State Sen.
b. Charlottesville, Va, 10/17/18; s. James Harry Michael, Sr. and Reuben Shelton M; m. 12/18/46 to Barbara Elizabeth Puryear; c. Jarrett Elizabeth and Victoria von derAu. Educ: Univ. Va, B.S, 40; Univ. Va. Law Sch, LL.B, 42; Omicron Delta Kappa; Raven Soc. Polit. & Govt. Pos: Va. State Sen, 22nd Dist, 68- Bus. & Prof. Pos: Lectr, Univ. Va. Law Sch, 49-53; mem. bd, Charlottesville Pub. Schs, 51-62; exec. dir, Univ. Va. Inst. of Pub. Affairs, 52; mem. bd. gov, St. Anne's Sch, Charlottesville, 52-; assoc. judge, Juvenile and Domestic Rels. Court, 54-67; spec. master in patent cases, U.S. Dist. Court, West. Dist. of Va, 60- Mil. Serv: Entered as Ens, Navy, 42, released as Lt. Comdr, 46 after serv. in various commands, Southwest Pac. Theatre, 43-45; Comdr, Naval Res. Mem: Charlottesville-Albemarle, Va. and Am. Bar Asns; Nat. Consumer Finance Asn; Va. and Am. Trial Lawyers Asns; Am. Judicature Soc; Elks; Fraternal Order of Police; Farmington Country Club; Boar's Head Club; Redland Club; Charlottesville Heart Asn; Charlottesville Cmt. on For. Rels; Civil League of Charlottesville and Albemarle Co. Rel: Episcopal. Legal Res: 900 Rugby Rd, Charlottesville, Va. 22903. Mailing Add: P.O. Box 895, Charlottesville, Va. 22902.

MICHAEL, PATRICIA M. R
V.Chmn, Colo. State Rep. Cent. Cmt.
b. Steubenville, Ohio, 12/13/26; d. Frank P. May and Mabel Cunningham M; m. to Robert K. Michael; c. Terry, Randy and Pat. Educ: Univ. Ill, B.A; Soc. Illustrators; Delta Gamma. Polit. & Govt. Pos: V.chmn, Colo. State Rep. Cent. Cmt, 67- Mailing Add: 7075 Roaring Fork, Boulder, Colo. 80302.

MICHAEL, ROBERT KERN R
Chmn, Boulder Co. Rep. Cent. Cmt, Colo.
b. Centralia, Ill, 10/7/23; s. Earl Brantly Michael and Mae Kern M; m. 4/10/47 to Patricia Jean May; c. Terrence B, Wm. Randolph and John Patrick. Educ: DePauw Univ, 41; Univ. Colo, 42-45; Beta Theta Phi. Polit. & Govt. Pos: Rep. precinct committeeman, Boulder, Colo, 62-64; ed, Colo. Govt. Annual, Colo. State Rep. Hq, Denver, 64-66; chmn, Boulder Co. Rep. Cent. Cmt, Colo, 66- Bus. & Prof. Pos: Owner, Ready-to-Wear, Ore, 46-53; real estate broker, Boulder, Colo, 54-69; mgr, Automobile Agency, 59-63. Publ: 'Colorado Governmental Annual,' Colo. Rep. Cent. Cmt, 64-66. Mem: Lions Int; Jaycee Int.(Sen, local pres. and state v.pres). Rel: Episcopal. Mailing Add: 7075 Roaring Fork Trail, Boulder, Colo. 80302.

MICHAELS, ERNEST EDWIN R
b. Watertown, S.Dak, 9/30/97; s. Herman Frederick Michaels and Bertha R. Rau M; m. 6/12/26 to Elizabeth Shedd; c. Elizabeth Ann (Mrs. Edward V. Mochel) and Edwin Shedd. Educ: S.Dak. State Univ, B.S, 20, D.Eng, 59; Univ. Ill, M.S, 22; Sigma Xi. Polit. & Govt. Pos: Mem, Citizens' Supvy. Cmt, Personnel Bd, Jefferson Co, Ala, 39; mem. adv. cmt, Birmingham Br, Nat. Youth Admin, 40; chmn, Smoke Abatement Cmt, Birmingham, 40-41; mgt. mem, Labor-Mgt. Cmt, Birmingham Area, War Manpower Cmt, 43-45; indust. mem, War Labor Bd, Atlanta Region, 45; nominee for U.S. Rep, Third Dist, Ill, 62; del, Rep. Nat. Conv, 64 & 68; chmn. adv. bd, 19th Ward Chicago Rep. Party, Ill, 64-68. Bus. & Prof. Pos: Field engr, S.Dak. Hwy. Cmn, 20; research grad. asst, Eng. Experimental Sta, Univ. Ill, 20-22; engr, Chicago Bridge and Iron Co, 22-24, chief draftsman, 24-27, asst. mgr. opers, 27-30, mgr, Birmingham, Ala. Plant, 30-47, v.pres. and dir, 46-52, mgr. of opers, 47-52, exec. v.pres. and dir, 52-56, pres. and dir, 56-62. Mil. Serv: Entered as Pvt, Army, 17, released as Sgt, 19; Battle Clasps for Defensive Sector, Aisne-Marne Offensive, Aisne Offensive, St. Mihiel Offensive and Meuse-Argonne Offensive. Mem: Am. Soc. Civil Engrs; past pres, Steel Plate Fabricators' Asn; former chmn, Welding Research Coun; West. Soc. of Engrs; Newcomen Soc; Univ. Club of Chicago; Am. Legion; Econ. Club of Chicago; South Shore Country Club; Second Div. Asn; Capitol Hill Club. Rel: Bethany Union. Legal Res: 7059 S. Shore Dr, Chicago, Ill. 60649. Mailing Add: 5077 Sandy Shore Ave, Sarasota, Fla. 33581.

MICHAELS, GEORGE M. D
N.Y. State Assemblyman
m. to Helen Wetzler. Educ: Cornell Univ, 31; Brooklyn Law Sch, LL.B, 33. Polit. & Govt. Pos: Mem, Auburn City Coun, N.Y, 49; mem, Auburn Bd. of Educ, 60-; mem, N.Y. State Dem. Adv. Coun; N.Y. State Assemblyman, 60-66 & 68- Bus. & Prof. Pos: Lawyer, Sr. Mem, Michaels, Cuddy and Bertrand, Auburn, N.Y. Mil. Serv: Marine Corps, 42-45, discharged as Capt; Presidential Unit Citation and Navy Commendation Medal for Serv. in Pac. Mem: N.Y. State Adv. Coun. on Ment. Health; N.Y. State Bar Asn.(Cmt. on Fed. Constitution, 68-); past pres, Cayuga Co. Bar Asn; past pres, Auburn Vets. Coun; past Comdr, W. Mynderse Rice Post No. 97, Am. Legion; Elks; Mason; Anar Grotto; VFW; 40 et 8; Marine Corps League; B'nai B'rith; Cayuga Co. Museum; Auburn Golf and Country Club; Owasco Yacht Club. Rel: Jewish; Past Pres, Congregation B'nai Israel, Auburn, N.Y. Mailing Add: 10 Norman Ave, Auburn, N.Y. 13021.

MICHAELSON, JULIUS COOLEY D
R.I. State Sen.
b. Salem, Mass, 1/26/22; s. Carl Michaelson and Celia Cooley M; m. 11/20/50 to Rita Castowitz; c. Mark C. and Jeffrey S. Educ: Boston Univ. Law Sch, LL.B, 47; Brown Univ, A.M, 67. Polit. & Govt. Pos: Pub. counsel, Utility Rate Cases, 57-58; del, State Constitutional Conv, R.I, 57-58; R.I. State Sen, 63-, chmn, Dem. Steering Cmt, R.I. State Senate, 67-68, Dep. Majority Leader and v.chmn, Cmt. on Health, Educ. and Welfare, 69; del, Dem. Nat. Conv, 68; mem. cmt. state-urban rels, Coun. State Govts, 69; mem, R.I. Cmn. on Interstate Coop, 69. Bus. & Prof. Pos: Attorney, currently. Mil. Serv: Entered as Pvt, Army, 43, released as 1st Lt, 46. Mem: R.I. Bar Asn.(secy, 59-); Am. and Mass. State Bar Asns; Nat. Soc. State Legislators (mem. bd. dirs, 66-); Am. Arbit. Asn. Rel: Jewish. Mailing Add: 78 Lorraine Ave, Providence, R.I. 02906.

MICHALS, CHARLES R
Chmn, Marin Co. Rep. Cent. Cmt, Calif.
b. Cleveland, Ohio, 3/3/24; s. Charles Michals (deceased) and Tessie Kyros M; m. 4/28/46 to Amelia Cocallas; c. Mary Anne and Patricia Amelia. Educ: N.Y. Univ, 43-44; Univ. of Calif. Exten, cert. in indust. rels, 60. Polit. & Govt. Pos: Pres, Marin Co. Young Rep, Calif, 62; chmn, Goldwater Rally, Young Rep. Nat. Conv, San Francisco, Calif, 63; press aide, Rep. Nat. Conv, 64, alternate del, 68; pres, Marin Rep. Coun, 64; exec. dir, Marin Christopher for Gov. Primary Campaign, 66; v.chmn, Marin Reagan for Gov. Cmt, 66; chmn, Marin Co. Rep. Cent. Cmt, 67-; chmn, Bay Area Region Asn. of Rep. Co. Cent. Cmt. Chmn. of Calif, 68-; mem. exec. cmt, Calif. Rep. State Cent. Cmt, 69- Bus. & Prof. Pos: Pub. affairs specialist, govt. rels. staff, Standard Oil Co. of Calif, 49- Mil. Serv: Entered as Pvt, Army, 43, released as Sgt, 45, after serv. in 104th Inf. Div, ETO, 44-45; Bronze Star Medal; Three Battle Stars. Publ: Ed, 'Chevron Chemical News,' 63-68; contrib, The Standard Oiler, 68- Mem: Commonwealth Club. Recipient of First Rep. Man of Year Award, Marin Rep. Coun, 69. Rel: Episcopal. Mailing Add: 71 Via Cheparro, Greenbrae, Calif. 94904.

MICHALSKI, CLEMENS FRANCIS D
b. Milwaukee, Wis, 4/21/02; s. Lawrence Michalski and Juilian Ratajczyk M; m. 6/24/24 to Patricia Sequenz; c. Caroline (Mrs. Bagin), Patricia Ann (Mrs. Mueller) and Robert Lawrence. Educ: South Division High School. Polit. & Govt. Pos: Wis. State Assemblyman, 34-36; alderman, 12th Ward, Milwaukee, Wis, 36-52; U.S. Marshal, East. Dist. Wis, 52-56; sheriff, Milwaukee Co, 56-60, co. clerk, 60-69. Mem: Milwaukee Soc; South Div. Civic Asn; Metrop. Civil Defense Cmt; Nat. Asn. Co. Off; Nat. Sheriffs Asn; Polish Roman Cath. Union; St. Jude's League; St. Joseph's Home for Children Asn; K. of C; Milwaukee Pere Marquette Coun. Rel: Catholic. Mailing Add: 3300 W. Oklahoma Ave, Milwaukee, Wis. 53215.

MICHALSKI, EDWARD K. D
b. Hamtramck, 1/6/20; married; c. Carol Ann (Mrs. McCarthy), Judith E. (Mrs. Gillerman), Carl, Edward, Patrick. Polit. & Govt. Pos: Mich. State Rep, 60-66; served as v.chmn, Wayne Co. Dem. Orgn; mem, Dem. State Cent. Comm. and 1st Dist. Dem. Comm. Mil. Serv: Navy. Mem: Dad's Club; Holy Name Soc; Polish Nat. Alliance; Pulaski Dem. Club; VFW, Post 7170; Am. Legion; Polish Legion of Am. Vets; Dom Polski Asn. of N. Detroit; Croation Home Asn; Moose; K. of C, Cardinal Mercier Coun; E. Outer Dr. Home Improv. Asn; Jayne Home Owners Asn; N. Detroit Polit. Club. Rel: Catholic; St. Bartholomew Catholic Church. Mailing Add: 20161 St. Aubin, Detroit, Mich. 48234. (1967)

MICHAUD, DENIS JOSEPH D
b. Portland, Ore, 1/19/40; s. Joseph Ernest Michaud and Rosemary Bone M; m. 10/15/60 to Thora Darleen Wright; div; c. Denis Joseph, Jr. 'Skip' and Darleen Elise 'Demi'. Educ: Ventura Col, 2 years; Univ. Calif, Santa Barbara, A.B, 64, Univ. Calif, San Francisco Med. Center, Pharm.D, 68; Dean's List; Alpha Lambda Sigma; Kappa Psi (pres, 66-67); Cal Club. Polit. & Govt. Pos: V.pres, Assoc. Students, Pharm. Sch, Univ. Calif, San Francisco, 66-67, pres, med. sch, 67-68; chmn, Univ. Calif. Statewide Assoc. Student Body President's Coun, 67-68; co-chmn, Humphrey for President Cmt, Pacifica, Calif, 68; state chmn, Students for Kennedy, 68; v.chmn, Calif. Kennedy for President Cmt, 68; del, Dem. Nat. Conv, 68; alternate committeeman, San Mateo Co. Dem. Cent. Cmt, 68-69. Bus. & Prof. Pos: Drug consult, Teamsters Security Fund, San Francisco, 68-69; and Prepaid Prescriptions, Inc, Los Angeles, 69- Mil. Serv: Entered as Airman Recruit, Navy, 57, released as Airman, 60, after serv. in Counter-Measures Dept, Naval Air Missile Test Center, Calif, 58-60. Mem: Am. and Calif. Pharmaceut. Asn; Univ. Calif. Pharmaceutical Sch. Alumni Asn.(bd. gov); founder, Calif. Kennedy Action Corps (pres). Mailing Add: 5305 Rosemead Blvd, San Gabriel, Calif. 91776.

MICHEL, ROBERT HENRY R
U.S. Rep, Ill.
b. Peoria, Ill, 3/2/23; s. Charles John Michel and Anna Baer M; m. 12/26/48 to Corinne Ellen Woodruff; c. Martin Scott, Bruce Woodruff, Laurie Lee and Robin Ward. Educ: Bradley Univ, B.S. in Bus. Admin, 48; Sigma Nu; Pi Kappa Delta; pres, Jr. Class, Bradley Univ. Polit. & Govt. Pos: Admin. asst. to U.S. Rep. Harold Velde, 49-56; U.S. Rep, 18th Cong. Dist, Ill, 57-; del, Rep. Nat. Conv, 64 & 68. Mil. Serv: Entered as Pvt, Army, 42, discharged as disabled vet, 46, after serv. as Combat Infantryman, Eng, France, Belgium and Germany; Bronze Star; Purple Heart and Four Battle Stars. Publ: 'Congress Must Control REA,' Pub. Utilities Quart, 11/62; 'REA Encroachment—Is the End in Sight?,' Pub. Utility Surv, 5/65; 'Reorganization of the Committees on Government Operations and Minority Control of Investigations' in We Propose: A Modern Congress, McGraw-Hill, 66. Mem: DAV: Am. Legion; life mem, Mil. Order of Purple Heart, VFW and Amvets; Peoria Asn. of Commerce; 85th Cong. Club (pres); Ill. State Soc.(pres, 66); Peoria Ad Club; Cosmopolitan Int; Orpheus Club; Creve Coeur Coun. Boy Scouts; YMCA; Ahepa; Creve Coeur Club of Peoria; Mt. Hawley Country Club of Peoria. Distinguished Alumnus Award, Bradley Univ, 61. Rel: Apostolic Christian. Legal Res: 1029 N. Glenwood, Peoria, Ill. 61606. Mailing Add: 2112 Rayburn House Office Building, Washington, D.C. 20515.

MICHELS, JOHN RUDOLF R
N.H. State Rep.
b. White Plains, N.Y, 6/16/44; s. Rudolf Karl Michels and Ilse Gruner M; single. Educ: Holy Cross Col, Worcester, Mass, A.B, 66; Harvard Bus. Sch, Sept. 69- Polit. & Govt. Pos: Summer intern for Sen. Robert F. Kennedy, 65; N.H. State Rep, 69- Bus. & Prof. Pos: Real estate broker, Danbury, N.H, 62- Mil. Serv: Entered as Pvt, Army, 66, released as 1st Lt, 68, after serv. in 29th Civil Affairs Co, Vietnam, 68, Res, 68-; Distinguished Grad, Officers Cand. Sch. Mem: Winnipesaukee Yacht Club; Am. Legion. Rel: Roman Catholic. Mailing Add: North Rd, Danbury, N.H. 03230.

MICHELS, LLOYD JOHN D
b. Minneauwakan, N.Dak, 2/23/05; s. James Jerome Michels and Anna Christene Fugle M; m. to Winifred Mae Claypool; c. Anne Corrine, Robert James and Marcia Lynn. Polit. & Govt. Pos: Mont. State Rep, 49-59; Mont. State Sen, Sheridan Co, 59-66. Mem: Secy-treas. of bd. of dirs, Farmers Union Grain Terminal Asn, St. Paul, Minn; Elks; Farmers Union. Rel: Catholic. Mailing Add: Medicine Lake, Mont. 59247.

MICKELSON, BOB J. D
Chmn, Columbia Co. Dem. Cent. Cmt, Wash.
b. Wilson Creek, Wash, 6/16/21; s. Eos Mickelson and Barbara Moore M; m. 9/1/46 to Donna M. Cutts; c. Helen Cristine and Stephanie Ann. Educ: Kinman Bus. Univ; Idaho State Univ; Univ. N.Mex. Polit. & Govt. Pos: Chmn, Columbia Co. Dem. Cent. Cmt, Wash, 64- Bus. & Prof. Pos: Former farm employ. supvr. and agr. supvr; farm cost acct, Green Giant Co, currently. Mil. Serv: Entered as Seaman, Navy, 42, released as SK 1/C, 53, after serv. in Pac. Area; Am. Area and Asiatic-Pac. Area Campaign Ribbons; Good Conduct and World War II Victory Medals. Mem: Am. Legion; Wash. State Big Game Coun; Columbia Co. Sportsmen. Letterman in football, Univ. N.Mex, 45. Rel: Congregational. Mailing Add: 702 N. First, Dayton, Wash. 99328.

MICKELSON, FRANK LESLIE D
Mo. State Rep.
b. Freeman, Mo, 1/25/11; m. 8/17/39 to Alberta Marie Rutt. Educ: Cent. Mo. State Col; Univ. Mo, B.S. Polit. & Govt. Pos: Treas. and ex officio collector of revenue of Cass Co, Mo, 41-53; Mo. State Rep, 52-56 & 63- Bus. & Prof. Pos: Sch. teacher; farmer. Mem: Mason; Lions. Rel: Baptist. Mailing Add: R.F.D. 1, Freeman, Mo. 64746.

MICKELSON, GORDON MAX R
Wyo. State Rep.
b. Denver, Colo, 7/28/26; s. James Francis Mickelson and Mae Stewart M; m. 7/26/44 to Margaret Gilchrist; c. Corliss (Mrs. Wayne Poindexter, James Stewart, II, Gordon Max, II, Eric Lynn, Margaret Leigh, Thomas Mark and Mildred Kay. Educ: Univ. Wyo, B.S. in agr, 50; Sigma Chi. Polit. & Govt. Pos: Wyo. State Rep, 65-; del, Rep. Nat. Conv, 68. Bus. & Prof. Pos: Rancher, Circle Cattle Co, 44- Mil. Serv: Entered as Pvt, Army, 44, released as Tech. Sgt, 46, after serv. in 78th Div, 310 Inf, ETO, 44-46; ETO Ribbon; Presidential Unit Citation. Mem: Am. Legion; VFW; Wyo. Stock Growers; AF&AM; Shrine; Eastern Star; Sublette Co. Farm Bur; Hist. Soc; trustee, Congregational Commun. Church. Rel: Protestant. Mailing Add: Box 189, Big Piney, Wyo. 83113.

MICKLE, CHARLES ABRAHAM R
Field Coordinator, Fla. Rep. Party
b. Greenhill, Ind, 8/30/99; s. James Henry Mickle and Sarah Ellen Delaney M; m. 7/9/24 to Berniece Caroline Stearman; c. Joan Azubah (Mrs. John Byron Lefforge) and Richard James. Educ: Northwest. Sch. of Commerce, 25; LaSalle Exten. Univ, 27. Polit. & Govt. Pos: Sch. trustee, Citrus Co, Fla, 66-67; chmn, Citrus Co. Rep. Exec. Cmt, 67-68; organizer and pres, Rep. Club Citrus Co, Fla, 67-68; mem, Citrus Co. Port Authority, 67-68; field coordinator, Fla. Rep. Party, 68- Bus. & Prof. Pos: Warehouse supt, inventory control, Acme Steel Corp, Chicago, Ill, 22-26; foundry supt, pattern inventory, Harrison Steel Co, Attica, Inc, 33-41; works mgr, Steel Sales Corp, Chicago, Ill, 41-44; sales mgr, Albert M. Siegel Steel, 44-47; self employ. plumbing, heating and home bldg, 47-66; real estate broker, Land Develop. and Real Estate, currently. Mil. Serv: Entered as Pvt, Army, 18, released 19, after serv. in ETO; reenlisted, Pfc, 20-21. Mem: West Coast Realtors (bd. dirs); World War I Vet; AARP; Rep. Club Citrus Co; Beverly Hills Civic Asn. Rel: Methodist. Mailing Add: 12 N. Washington St, Lecanto, Fla. 32661.

MICOLEAU, CHARLES JUDD D
Legis. Research Dir, Maine Dem. Party
b. Englewood, N.J, 2/8/42; s. Henri LeBrec Micoleau and Emily Moody M; m. Dec, 67 to Judith Frary. Educ: Bowdoin Col, B.A, 63; Sch. of Advanced Int. Studies, Washington, D.C, M.A, 65; Chi Psi. Polit. & Govt. Pos: Dir. Work Training, Maine Health & Welfare Dept, 65-67; Legis. Research Dir, Maine Dem. Party, 68-; V.Chmn, Augusta Dem. City Cmt, 68-; Pres, Maine Young Dem, 68- Bus. & Prof. Pos: Exec. Secy, Casco Bay Island Develop. Asn, 67-; Dir, Job Corps Recruitment, New Eng. AFL-CIO Coun, 69. Publ: 'A Proposal to Reduce Welfare Costs' Maine Townsman, 12/66; 'The Secret War: Myths, Morals and Misconceptions,' The Central Intelligence Agency, D.C. Heath & Co, 68. Mem: Am. Fedn. of State, Co. and Munic. Employees; Maine Conf. of Soc. Welfare. Mailing Add: 31 Chapel St, Augusta, Maine 04330.

MIDDENDORF, HENRY STUMP, JR. Conservative Party, N.Y.
Chmn, N.Y. Co. Cmt, Conservative Party
b. Baltimore, Md, 2/23/23; s. Henry Stump Middendorf and Sarah Kennedy Boone M; single. Educ: Harvard Univ, A.B, 45, J.D. cum laude, 52; N.Y. Univ, LL.M, 57; ed, Harvard Law Review, 51-52; Lincoln's Inn Soc. Harvard Law Sch; treas, Harvard Lampoon; Hasty Pudding-Inst. of 1770; Owl Club. Polit. & Govt. Pos: Mem, N.Y. Co. Rep. Cmt, 55-61; counsel, Nat. Draft Goldwater Cmt. and Goldwater for Pres. Cmt, 62-64; mem, N.Y. Conservative Party State Cmt, 62-; chmn, Judicial Selection Cmt, First Judicial Dist. Conservative Party, 64-; chmn, Petitions Cmt, N.Y. Co. Conservative Party, 65- and Judicial Selection Cmt, 66-; chmn, N.Y. Co. Conservative Party Cmt, 66-; mem, N.Y. Conservative Party State Exec. Cmt, 66-; counsel, Nixon Finance Cmt, 68. Bus. & Prof. Pos: Assoc, Milbank, Tweed, Hope & Hadley, 52-56 and Gilbert & Segall, 56-59; private practice of law, 59- Mil. Serv: Entered as Pvt, Army, 44, released as 1st Lt, 46, after serv. in Japanese Army of Occupation. Publ: Ed, Law Today, 63- Mem: Am, N.Y. State and Independent Bar Asns; Asn. of the Bar of the City of New York; Am. Legion; Union Club; N.Y. Genealogical and Biographical Soc. Rel: Episcopal. Legal Res: 236 E. 36th St, New York, N.Y. 10016. Mailing Add: 36 W. 44th St, New York, N.Y. 10036.

MIDDENDORF, JOHN WILLIAM, II R
U.S. Ambassador to the Netherlands
b. Baltimore, Md, 9/22/24; s. Harry Stump Middendorf and Sara Boone M; m. 3/7/53 to Isabelle J. Paine; c. Frances Paine, Martha Stone, Amy Ward, John William, IV and Ralph Henry. Educ: Holy Cross, B.S, 45; Harvard, A.B, 47; N.Y. Univ, Grad. Sch. Bus. Admin, M.B.A, 54. Polit. & Govt. Pos: Mem. exec. cmt, Greenwich Rep. Town Cmt, 58-, Greenwich Rep. Town Meeting, 60- and Rep. Cong. Boosters Club, 64-; treas, Rep. Nat. Cmt, 64-69; del, Rep. Nat. Conv, 68; U.S. Ambassador to the Netherlands, 69- Bus. & Prof. Pos: Employee, Bank of Manhattan Co, 47-52; employee, Wood, Struthers & Co, 52-58, partner, 58-61; partner, Middendorf, Colgate & Co, 62-; chmn. of Assocs, John Carter Brown Libr. and mem. vis. cmt. fine arts, Harvard Univ, currently. Mil. Serv: Ens, Naval Res, 43-46; serv. in Pac. Theater. Publ: Invest-

ment Policies of Fire and Casualty Insurance Companies, 54. Mem: Am. Antiq. Soc; Walpole Soc; bd, Roundhill Commun. Church of Greenwich; trustee, N.Y. Hist. Soc, Greenwich Hist. Soc, Middlesex Sch, Boys Club of N.Y. and Heritage Found. of Old Deerfield; Union Club, N.Y; Anglers Club; Round Hill Club; Field Club; Capital Hill Club; Downtown Asn, N.Y. Club of Odd Vols; benefactor, Metrop. Mus. of Art. Mem, U.S. Olympic Games Cmt.(field hockey); former pres, Field Hockey Asn. of Am. Legal Res: 36 Husted Lane, Greenwich, Conn. 06830. Mailing Add: 80 Broad St, New York, N.Y. 10004.

MIDDLEMAS, JOHN ROBERT D
Fla. State Rep.
b. Panama City, Fla, 7/4/36; s. Lott Warren Middlemas and Cecelia Kuhlman M.(deceased); m. 6/29/58 to Kendall Hood; c. John Robert, Jr, Mary Cecelia and Davis Lawson. Educ: Emory Univ, B.A, 57; Alpha Epsilon Upsilon; Sigma Alpha Epsilon. Polit. & Govt. Pos: Mem, Fla. Libr. and Hist. Cmn, 65-66; Fla. State Rep, 66- Mil. Serv: Entered as Pvt, Nat. Guard, 58, released as Sgt, 64, after serving in Panama City, Fla. Mem: Kiwanis; Elks; Jaycees. Rel: Presbyterian. Legal Res: 451 S. Palo Alto Ave, Panama City, Fla. 32401. Mailing Add: P.O. Box 166, Panama City, Fla. 32401.

MIDDLESWART, JAMES IRA D
Iowa State Rep.
b. Indianola, Iowa, 4/8/12; s. David Allen Middleswart and Eva Morgan M; m. 6/10/36 to Geraldine Ann Denly; c. Phyllis Ann (Mrs. Geyer), La Verne David and Irene Marie. Educ: Simpson Col, 32. Polit. & Govt. Pos: Asst. cmnr, Soil Dist, Iowa; Iowa State Rep, currently. Mem: Pres, Warren Co. Farm Bur, 55-57; Isaac Walton League; pres, Sheriff's Posse; Iowa Flying Farmers. Sweepstakes winner, Des Moines Register and Tribune Soil Conserv. Contest, 65. Rel: Methodist. Mailing Add: R.R. 2, Indianola, Iowa 50125. (1967)

MIDDLETON, B. R. 'BEV' D
Va. State Del.
b. Norfolk Co, Va, 9/7/28; s. Erby George Middleton and Thelma Wood M; m. 4/8/50 to Ann Wayne Minor; c. John R, Wayne M. and Beverly A. Educ: Va. Polytech. Inst, B.S. in E.E, 51; Sigma Delta Psi; Scabbard and Blade; German Club. Polit. & Govt. Pos: Va. State Del, 68- Mil. Serv: Entered as 2nd Lt, Army, 51, released as 1st Lt, 53, after serv. in Signal Corps, European Theatre, 51-53. Mem: Nat. Employ. Counsr. Asn; Am. Inst. of Elec. Engrs; Elec. League of Norfolk (pres, 58); Kiwanis (pres, 62). Rel: Protestant. Mailing Add: 1612 Wakefield Dr, Virginia Beach, Va. 23455.

MIDDLETON, BLANCHE JONES D
b. Senath, Mo; d. Ivan T. Jones (deceased) and Annie E. Kimbrow J; m. 9/23/49 to Harvey Middleton; c. Jo Ann. Educ: High Sch; Draughon's Bus. Univ, Springfield, Mo. Polit. & Govt. Pos: Admin. asst. to U.S. Rep. Orville Zimmerman (deceased), 37-48 and to U.S. Rep. Paul C. Jones, 48-69. Bus. & Prof. Pos: Secy, Hardesty & Limbaugh, Attorneys, Cape Girardeau, Mo, 28-30; secy, Orville Zimmerman, Attorney, Kennett, Mo, 30-32; secy-bookkeeper, liquidation of defunct banks, First Nat. Bank, Campbell, Mo. and Rector, Ark, 32-34; secy, Bradley & McAnally, Attorneys, Kennett, Mo, 34-37. Mem: Cong. Secy. Club; Eastern Star. Rel: Methodist. Legal Res: Kennett, Mo. 63857. Mailing Add: 5841 Nebraska Ave. N.W, Washington, D.C. 20015.

MIDDLETON, CLYDE WILLIAM R
Ky. State Sen.
b. Cleveland, Ohio, 1/30/28; s. Edward George Middleton and Eleanor Mertz M; m. 8/14/54 to Mary Ann Janke; c. Ann Eleanor, David Edward, Richard Carl and John Clyde. Educ: U.S. Naval Acad, B.S, 51; Xavier Univ, Ohio, M.B.A, 62; Phi Kappa Psi. Polit. & Govt. Pos: Pres, Kenton Co. Young Rep, Ky, 60-61; chmn, Kenton Co. Rep. Party, 61; Rep. cand. for Cong, Fourth Dist, 62 & 64; chmn, Fourth Dist. Young Rep, 63; Ky. State Sen, 24th Dist, 67- Bus. & Prof. Pos: Buyer, Procter & Gamble Co, Cincinnati, Ohio, 57-64; field underwriter, N.Y. Life, Cincinnati Off, 64- Mil. Serv: Entered as Seaman Recruit, Navy, 46, released as Lt.(jg), 55, after serv. on U.S.S. Menifee (APA 202), Far East-Korean War, 51-53 and on U.S.S. Steinaker (DDR 863), East Coast-Mediterranean, 53-55, Lt. Comdr, Res, 55-69; World War II Victory, Japanese Occup, Nat. Defense, China Serv; Korean War and UN Korean Medals. Mem: Nat. Asn. Life Underwriters; VFW; pres, Covington Optimist Club. Hon. Mention Award, Ky. Pub. Health Asn. for work as chmn. of Ky. Comprehensive Health Planning Coun, 69. Rel: Lutheran. Legal Res: 30 Ft. Mitchell Ave, Covington, Ky. 41011. Mailing Add: P.O. Box 546, Covington, Ky. 41012.

MIDDLETON, EDWIN G. R
Rep. Nat. Committeeman, Ky.
b. Louisville, Ky, 6/11/20; s. Charles G. Middleton and Anita Gheens M; m. 7/11/42 to Mary Jane Lampton; c. Edwin Gheens, Anita G. and Huntley L. Educ: Univ. Va, B.A, 41; Univ. Louisville, LL.B, 48. Polit. & Govt. Pos: Finance chmn, Citizens for Eisenhower, 52; chmn, Louisville and Jefferson Co. Rep. Exec. Cmt, 58-63; del, Rep. Nat. Conv, 64; Rep. Nat. Committeeman, Ky, 65- Bus. & Prof. Pos: Partner, Middleton, Seelbach, Wolford, Willis and Cochran, 48; chmn, Louisville and Jefferson Co. Children's Home, 56-60; trustee, Louisville Collegiate Sch, 56-, Louisville Country Day Sch, 57-64 and Univ. Louisville, 64-; dir, Am. Life and Accident Ins. Co. Mil. Serv: Entered as Pvt, Marine Corps, 41, released as Major, 46, Bronze Star; Purple Heart. Mem: Am, Ky. and Louisville Bar Asns; Louisville Country Club (pres. and dir). Legal Res: 6401 Transylvania Ave, Harrods Creek, Ky. 40027. Mailing Add: 501 S. Second, Louisville, Ky. 40202.

MIDDLETON, JACK LUCAS R
Chmn, Eighth Dist. Rep. Cmt, Va.
b. The Plains, Va, 2/17/21; s. John Preston Middleton and Glenna Lucas M; m. 6/16/57 to Barbara Austin Gerow. Educ: Va. Polytech. Inst, B.S, 43; Cotillion Club. Polit. & Govt. Pos: Chmn, Fauquier Co. Rep. Cmt, Va, 52-; chmn, Eighth Dist. Rep. Cmt, 58-; finance chmn, Rep. Party of Va, 63-66; del, Rep. Nat. Conv, 68. Bus. & Prof. Pos: Owner, Jack L. Middleton Real Estate & Ins, The Plains, Va, 48- Mil. Serv: Entered as 2nd Lt, Army, released as Capt, 46, after serv. in Pac. Theatre, 45-46; Commendation Award. Mem: Nat. Asn. Real Estate Bd; charter mem, Lions; charter mem, VFW; co-founder & dir, Old Dominion Eye Bank & Res, Inc. Rel: Episcopal. Mailing Add: Drawer A, The Plains, Va. 22171.

MIDDLETON, JAMES EDWARD D
b. Centerville, Tex, 1/17/23; s. Howard J. Middleton and Ninnie Wilson M; m. 4/10/45 to Winnie Lee Nobles; c. Carolyn Joyce (Mrs. Anthony Hall, Jr), Barbara Doris (Mrs. Joseph Henderson), James Edward, Jr. and Toni LaVette. Educ: Tex. South. Univ, 42-45. Polit. & Govt. Pos: Alternate del, Dem. Nat. Conv, 68. Bus. & Prof. Pos: Secy-treas, Laborers Int. Union 18, 60-69 and South. Tex. Laborers Dist. Coun, 65-69. Mem: Victory Lodge 19; YMCA; Citizen C. of C; Houston Urban League; Harris Co. and Houston United Fund; A. Phillip Randolph Inst. Rel: Baptist. Mailing Add: 2102 Rosedale, Houston, Tex. 77004.

MIDDLETON, RICHARD HOXIE R
b. New York, N.Y, 3/17/25; m. to Martha Alice Haugh M. Educ: W.Va. Univ; Univ. of Va, B.S; Sigma Chi. Polit. & Govt. Pos: Va. State Del, 62-68. Bus. & Prof. Pos: Farmer; pres, The Tire Center, Inc. Mil. Serv: Air Force. Mem: Charlottesville Ed. Found. Sch. Bd; Va. Hereford Breeders Asn.(past pres. and past dir); Atlantic Rural Exposition, Inc.(past dir); dir, Va. Engr. Found. and Charlottesville Ed. Found; Belfield Sch,(past dir). Rel: Episcopal. 1967 Legal Res: Charlottesville, Va. No mailing address available. (1967)

MIDGETT, LORIMER WILLARD D
Chmn, 1st Dist. Dem. Conv, N.C.
b. Mann's Harbor, N.C, 2/9/11; s. Ellis Bradford Midgett and Matilda Tillett M; m. 6/3/33 to Margaret White. Educ: Univ. of N.C, A.B, 32. Polit. & Govt. Pos: Mem, Pasquotank Co. Cmn, N.C, 38-41; mem, N.C. Retirement Cmn, 41-43; N.C. State Rep, 43-44; N.C. State Sen, 47-49; chmn, First Dist. Dem. Conv, 50-; mem. bd, Dept. of Conserv. & Develop, 59-65. Bus. & Prof. Pos: V.pres, Albemarle Savings & Loan, 50-; mem. bd, C. of C. of U.S, 52-54; pres, Indust. Bank, 54- Mil. Serv: Entered as Lt.(jg), Navy, 43, released as Lt. Comdr, 46, after serv. in Naval Intel, Pac. Theater. Mem: Elks; Kiwanis; VFW; Am. Legion. Rel: Methodist. Legal Res: 1619 Rochelle Dr, Elizabeth City, N.C. 27909. Mailing Add: P.O. Box 428, Elizabeth City, N.C. 27909.

MIDGLEY, GRANT WINDER D
b. Salt Lake City, 8/2/11; s. John George Midgley and Anna Grant M; m. 12/28/42 to Marsha Ballif; c. Marsha, John Ballif and Jane. Educ: Univ. of Utah, B.S, 32; Phi Kappa Phi. Polit. & Govt. Pos: Utah State Rep, 41-44; Utah State Sen, 45-48; admin. asst. to U.S. Sen. Moss, Utah, 65- Legal Res: Salt Lake City, Utah. Mailing Add: 6212 31st St. N.W, Washington, D.C. 20015.

MIDYETT, THOMAS EARLE, SR. D
b. Jackson, Tenn, 12/8/18; s. James Ashley Midyett and Ruth Batchelor M; m. 5/30/43 to Dorothy Louise Birchett, wid; c. Thomas E, Jr. and James Henry. Educ: Union Univ, B.S, 41. Polit. & Govt. Pos: Mem, Madison Co. Sch. Bd, Tenn, 54-61; del, Dem. Nat. Conv, 56 & 64; del, Constitutional Conv, Tenn, 60; Tenn. State Rep, 61-67. Bus. & Prof. Pos: Farmer and merchant, Birchwood Farms, 30. Mil. Serv: Pvt, Army, 41, Med. Discharge. Mem: Elks; Moose; VFW; Farm Bur; Am. Legion. Rel: Baptist. Mailing Add: Old Bells Rd, Jackson, Tenn. 38303. (1967)

MIEDEMA, ERNEST JOHN R
N.Dak. State Rep.
b. Marion, N.Dak, 1/5/32; s. Andrew Miedema and Ruth Rohrbeck M; m. 5/26/51 to Elinor Darlene Sortland; c. Larry Ernest, Darryl Wayne and Gwen Lynette. Polit. & Govt. Pos: Rep. precinct committeeman, 63rd precinct, N.Dak, 64-; N.Dak. State Rep, 24th Dist, 68- Bus. & Prof. Pos: Owner, Auction City Sales Inc, N.Dak, 58- Mem: C. of C.(mem-officer, Valley City Chap, 63-); Gr. N.Dak. Asn.(dir, 66-69); Kiwanis; Valley City Planning Cmn. Rel: Free Lutheran. Legal Res: 1220 Tenth St, S.W, Valley City, N.Dak, 58072. Mailing Add: P.O. Box 830, Valley City, N.Dak. 58072.

MIERA, ERNEST D
N.Mex. State Rep.
b. 1916. Educ: Univ. of Calif, Los Angeles. Polit. & Govt. Pos: Co. cmnr, N.Mex, 4 years; N.Mex. State Rep, 55-56 & 61- Bus. & Prof. Pos: Salesman; advert. Mil. Serv: Army Air Force, 3½ years, overseas with Ninth Air Force Night Fighter Squadron, Eng, France, Germany, ETO, 44-45. Mem: Rotary; K. of C; VFW; Hoo-Hoo Lumberman's Asn; Bernalillo Betterment Asn; v.pres, Bernalillo Credit Union; adv. mem, First State Bank of Bernalillo; People to People Int. Mailing Add: P.O. Box 485, Bernalillo, N.Mex. 87004. (1967)

MIERA, RUBEN D
b. Algodones, N.Mex, 10/25/24; s. Fred Miera and Marianna Lovato M; m. 5/19/46 to Pauline Garcia; c. Rosemarie, Diana and Christopher. Educ: N. N.Mex. Normal Sch, El Rito. Polit. & Govt. Pos: Asst. Secy. of State, N.Mex, 55-59; admin. asst, N.Mex. Bur. of Revenue, 59-60; asst. state auditor, N.Mex, 61-62; dir, N.Mex. Dept. of Courtesy and Info, 63-; former chmn, Sandoval Co. Dem. Party. Mil. Serv: Entered as A/S, Navy, 43, released as Hosp. Apprentice 1/C, 46. Mem: Am. Legion. Rel: Catholic. Mailing Add: Algodones, N.Mex. 87001. (1967)

MIERS, MILEY L, II D
Fla. State Rep.
b. Montgomery, Ala, 2/6/27; s. Miley L. Miers and Luna Browder M; m. 9/7/59 to Patricia Malloy; c. Melanie Anne, Michelle Lynn, Michael Lawrence and Miley L, II. Educ: Univ. Ala, 3 years; Wash. Univ, A.B, D.D.S. Polit. & Govt. Pos: Pres, Independent Student Govt. Assoc, Univ. Ala, 46-47; Fla. State Rep, Leon, Franklin and Wakulla Co, 66- Mil. Serv: Entered as A/S, Navy, 44, released as Photo M 1/C, 46, after serv. in aerial photography, U.S. Mem: Am. Acad. Dent. Practice Admin; fel, Am. Col. of Dentists; Am. Prosthodontic Soc; Am. Equilibration Soc; pres, N.W. Dist. Dent. Soc. of Fla, 62; pres, N.Fla. Dent. Research Cmt, 66; pres. elect, Fla. State Dent. Soc, 69, former secy, 2nd v.pres. and 1st v.pres; Rotary; YMCA; Toastmaster. Rel: Methodist. Legal Res: 614 Short St, Tallahassee, Fla. 32303. Mailing Add: 1213 Miccosukee Rd, Tallahassee, Fla. 32303.

MIERS, MORGAN L. D
Chmn, Decatur Co. Dem. Cent. Cmt, Ind.
b. Greensburg, Ind, 3/22/19; s. Roy H. Miers and Ruth Lundmark M; m.

4/24/46 to Nansi L. Harries; c. Twins, David and Melodi. Educ: Purdue, B.S.A, 41; Sigma Delta Chi; Sigma Nu. Polit. & Govt. Pos: Chmn, Decatur Co. Dem. Cent. Cmt, Ind, currently; del, Dem. Nat. Conv, 64 & 68; treas, Ninth Dist. Dem. Cent. Cmt. Mil. Serv: Entered as 2nd Lt, Army Artillery, 41, released as Capt, 46, after serv. in 28th Inf. Div, 108th Field Artillery and 229th Field Artillery, ETO; Bronze Medal; Purple Heart; ETO Ribbon. Mem: Mason; Scottish Rite; Elks; Am. Legion; Farm Bur. Rel: Methodist. Mailing Add: R.R. 4, Greensburg, Ind. 47240.

MIFFLIN, EDWARD B. R
Pa. State Rep.
b. Philadelphia, Pa, 9/26/23; s. E. Lawrie Mifflin and Edna A. Parker M; m. to Joan Lynne Davis; c. Five. Educ: Swarthmore Col, B.A; mem, Soccer Team; Phi Kappa Psi; mem. staff, Student Newspaper. Polit. & Govt. Pos: Rep. jr. committeeman, Pa, 58-62; Rep. borough chmn, 58-; city tax assessor, 60-63; Pa. State Rep, 62- Bus. & Prof. Pos: Secy-treas. and dir, two textile firms. Mil. Serv: Air Force, 43-45, 15th Air Force, Navigator, 23 Combat Missions over Cent. Europe; 1st Lt, Air Force Res, 46-51. Publ: Contributing author on baseball statistics, Sporting News, St. Louis. Mem: Boy Scouts; Commun. Chest; Jr. C. of C; pres, Phi Kappa Psi Alumni Asn; Munic. Assessors Asn. Mailing Add: 419 Drew Ave, Swarthmore, Pa. 19081. (1967)

MIGLAUTSCH, THOMAS JOHN D
b. Milwaukee, Wis, 11/1/13; s. Frank L. Miglautsch and Clara Klann M; m. to Dorothy Storer; c. Karen (Mrs. Soukup) and Thomas, Jr. (deceased). Educ: Univ. Mich, Ann Arbor, 35; Univ. Wis, Milwaukee, 32-33 and 37-38; Teachers Lifetime Cert, Wis. Polit. & Govt. Pos: Chmn, Waukesha Co. Dem. Party, Wis, 54-56; chmn, Second Cong. Dist. Dem. Party, 57-60; mem, Wis. Dem. Party State Admin. Cmt, 57-62; v.chmn, Wis. Gov. Cmn. on Human Rites, 59-65; ed, chmn, Wis. Democrat, 60; del, Dem. Nat. Conv, 60, 64 & 68. Bus. & Prof. Pos: Pres, Advantage Ad, Inc, 47- Mailing Add: 1221 Jenkins Dr, Oconomowoc, Wis. 53066.

MIHLBAUGH, ROBERT HOLLERAN D
Committeeman, Ohio State Dem. Cent. Cmt.
b. Lima, Ohio, 6/17/32; s. Edward P. Mihlbaugh and Mary Holleran M; m. 10/29/60 to Barbara Synck; c. Robert E.H. and Michael Patrick. Educ: Univ. Notre Dame, B.A. with honors, 54, J.D, 57. Polit. & Govt. Pos: Mem, Ohio State Adv. Bd, Small Bus. Admin, 65-68 and Nat. Adv. Bd, 66-68; committeeman, Ohio State Dem. Cent. Cmt, 66-; del, Dem. Nat. Conv, 68. Publ: Comprehensive Marketing Manual, Marathon Oil Co, 63; 'Sale-Leaseback Financing,' Ohio Bar Asn, 3/63. Mem: Hon. lifetime mem, Ohio State Bar Asn; Am. Bar Asn; K. of C; Elks; Eagles. Rel: Catholic. Legal Res: 1471 W. Market St, Lima, Ohio 45805. Mailing Add: Mihlbaugh Bldg, Lima, Ohio 45804.

MIHO, KATSUGO R
Hawaii State Rep.
b. Kahului, Maui, Hawaii, 5/15/22; s. Katsuichi Miho and Ayano M; m. 5/12/56 to Laura Masuko Iida; c. Carolyn Mariko, Arthur Kengo, Celia Yukiko and Ann Takako. Educ: Univ. Hawaii, B.A, 49; George Wash. Univ. Law Sch, LL.B, 53. Polit. & Govt. Pos: Hawaii State Rep, 59-, Minority Attorney, Hawaii House of Rep, 59, Asst. Minority Floor Leader, 63-64 and Minority Leader, 65. Bus. & Prof. Pos: Attorney, Fong, Miho, Choy & Roginson, 54- Mil. Serv: Entered as Pvt, Army, 43, released as Pfc, 46, after serv. in 442nd Regimental Combat Team; Rome-Arno, North Appennines Rhineland, Cent. Europe, Am, Europe-Africa-Middle East and Asiatic-Pac. Serv. Medals; Good Conduct and Victory Medals; Army Res, 49-55. Mem: Am. and Hawaiian Bar Asns; Univ. of Hawaii Bd. of Athletic Control; Univ. of Hawaii Athletic Found; pres, 442nd Vets. Club of Honolulu, 67; chmn, Oahu Chap, Nat. Found. March of Dimes; Lions; Waikiki Athletic Club; sustaining mem, Univ. of Hawaii YMCA; life mem, Univ. of Hawaii Alumnae Asn; Bd. of Councillors, Kuakini Hosp. & Home; George Wash. Univ. Law Asn; (exec. cmt). Rel: Protestant. Mailing Add: 3458 Pinao St, Honolulu, Hawaii 96822.

MIKVA, ABNER J. D
U.S. Rep, Ill.
b. Milwaukee, Wis, 1/21/26; s. Henry Abraham Mikva and Ida Fishman M; m. 9/19/48 to Zorita Wise; c. Mary Lane, Laurel Ida and Rachel Shaine. Educ: Univ. Wis, 46-47; Wash. Univ, 47-48; Univ. Chicago Law Sch, J.D, 51; Order of the Coif; Phi Beta Kappa; Phi Sigma Delta. Polit. & Govt. Pos: Law clerk to Justice Sherman Minton, U.S. Supreme Court, 51-52; Ill. State Rep, 56-66; U.S. Rep, Ill, 69- Bus. & Prof. Pos: Partner, Devoe, Shadur, Mikva and Plotkin, Attorney's, 52-68. Mil. Serv: Entered as Pvt, Air Force, 44, released as 2nd Lt, 45, after serv. as navigator Air Force Training Command. Publ: 'Two Perspectives on Civil Rights,' Univ. Chicago Law Rev, 65. Mem: Bd. of Mgrs, Chicago Bar Asn, 62-64; Am. and Ill. State Bar Asns; City Club of Chicago; Am. Vets. Cmt; B'nai B'rith; Lions; Hyde Park-Kenwood Commun. Conf; bd. mem, Chicago Urban League and Inst. for Psychoanalysis; former bd. mem, Am. Civil Liberties Union and Independent Voters of Ill; former bd. mem, Jewish Family and Commun. Servs. Chosen Outstanding Freshmen Rep, Ill. Newspapermen Covering Springfield, 56; Voted, One of the Ten Outstanding Young Men of Chicago, Jr. Asn. of Commerce and Indust, 61; Winner of Page One Award, Chicago Newspaper Guild, 65; Recipient for Five Straight Terms of the Best Legis. Award, Independent Voters of Ill. Rel: Jewish. Legal Res: 5545 S. Kenwood Ave, Chicago, Ill. 60637. Mailing Add: 1532 Longworth House Office Building, Wash, D.C. 20515.

MILAM, MOBLEY MEADOWS D
b. Los Angeles, Calif, 8/11/23; s. Benjamin Milam (deceased) and Pearl Meadows M; m. 8/24/57 to Jean Lemon; c. Ben Robert, Mark Whitney and Dawn Elaine (deceased). Educ: Univ. Calif, Berkeley, A.B. & LL.B. Polit. & Govt. Pos: Dep. pub. defender, Los Angeles, Calif, 51; dep. dist. attorney, Imperial Co, 51-54; city attorney, Calexico, 54-60; Pres, Calexico Dem. Club, 59-64; dir, 45th Dist. Agr. Asn, 61-66, pres, 66; chmn, Imperial Co. Dem. Cent. Cmt, 64-68. Mil. Serv: Entered as Pvt, Army, 43, released as 1st Lt, 45, after serv. in 491st Bomb Squadron, China-Burma-India; Maj, Air Force Res; Two Battle Stars. Mem: Am. Legion; C. of C; Elks; Kiwanis; Native Sons of Golden West; Calif. State Bar; Imperial Co. Bar Asn. (secy, 53, pres, 60). Rel: Protestant. Legal Res: 18 Palm Dr, Calexico, Calif. 92231. Mailing Add: P.O. Box 628, Calexico, Calif. 92231. (1967)

MILBURN, BERYL BUCKLEY R
Pres, Tex. Fedn. Rep. Women
b. Los Angeles, Calif, 4/2/20; d. Edmund Langford Buckley and Beryl Meeks B; m. 6/3/41 to Malcolm Long Milburn; c. Beryl Langford, Malcolm Long, Jr. and Michael Noyes. Educ: Univ. of Tex, B.A, 41; Kappa Kappa Gamma. Polit. & Govt. Pos: Alternate del, Rep. Nat. Conv, 56, del, 64 & 68; committeewoman, Rep. State Exec. Cmt, Tex, 56-65, secy, 63-65; state dir, Woman Power for Tower Campaign, 66; pres, Tex. Fedn. Rep. Women, 67-; mem. state adv. cmt, Women for Nixon, 68. Mem: Jr. League of Austin; Settlement Club; Pan-Am. Round Table; Med. Referral Serv. (past chmn. of bd); past mem. of bd. of Austin Diocese, Catholic Charities; past mem. of exec. cmt, Tex. Law Enforcement & Youth Found. Rel: Roman Catholic. Mailing Add: 2606 Pecos St, Austin, Tex. 78703.

MILDER, MYRON HARRY R
b. Omaha, Nebr, 1/13/27; s. Hymie Milder and Ella Braunstein M; m. 3/2/58 to Lois Lee Rodin; c. Myron H, II and Emily I. Educ: George Wash. Univ, 46-47; Univ. Nebr, Omaha, B.S, 48; Zeta Beta Tau. Polit. & Govt. Pos: Conv. chmn, Midwest Coun. of Young Rep, 54; chmn, V.President Nixon's Visit and Meeting in Omaha, Douglas Co. Rep. Party, Nebr, 54; del, Co. and State Rep. Conv, 54-68; bd. mem, Omaha City Planning Cmn, 55-57; mem, Douglas Co. Rep. Cent. Cmt, 58; del, Rep. Nat. Conv, 68. Mil. Serv: HA 2/C, Navy, 44-46, serv. in U.S. Naval Hosp, San Diego, and Officer's Training Unit, Moscow, Idaho. Mem: Am. Legion; Mason; Shrine; YMCA; pres, Omaha Jr. C. of C, 56-57, Nebr. Jr. C. of C, 59-60 and v.pres, U.S. Jr. C. of C, 60-61. Omaha's Outstanding Young Man of 59. Rel: Jewish. Legal Res: 133 S. Elmwood Rd, Omaha, Nebr. 68132. Mailing Add: Milder Oil Co, 26th and Dorcas St, Omaha, Nebr. 68105.

MILES, DANIEL BLACK D
b. Marshall, Mo, 11/19/17; s. Frank Weir Miles and Ellen Eugenia Black M; m. 11/2/49 to Kathleen Neill White; c. Daniel Black II, Ellen Eugenia Mahlon White, Jane Kathleen, Frank Weir, III. Educ: Mo. Valley Col, Marshall, Mo, 36-39; Univ. of Mo, 39-40; Sigma Delta Chi; Sigma Nu. Polit. & Govt. Pos: Admin. asst, Sen. Edward V. Long, Mo, 60-69. Bus. & Prof. Pos: State ed, Daily Pantograph, Bloomington, Ill, 46-50; ed-publisher, Mo. Daily Dem, Clinton, Mo. Eye, Montrose-Tydings-Urich Herald and Henry Co. Kayo, presently. Mil. Serv: Army Res, Sgt, 42-46. Mem: Mo. Press Asn; chmn, Freedom of Info; v.pres, Cent. Mo. Press Asn; Kans. City Press Club; Dem. Eds. of Mo; Am. Legion; N.W. Mo. Press Asn; NEA; Clinton, Mo. C. of C. Best Ed. Awards, Mo. Press Asn; Commun. Betterment Award. Rel: Episcopal. Mailing Add: c/o Democrat Publishing Co, 210-12 S. Washington St, Clinton, Mo. 64735.

MILES, ETHEL LOLA R
V.Chmn, Gregory Co. Rep. Cent. Cmt, S.Dak.
b. Newcastle Nebr, 10/28/01; d. James Albert Curry and Elizabeth Gould C; wid; c. Audrey (Mrs. Weldon Harris), Russell John, Wilodyne (Mrs. E.E. Bruce) and Wilva (Mrs. V. Lloyd Whitley). Educ: Newcastle High Sch, Nebr, grad, 20; Wayne State Col, summer, 23. Polit. & Govt. Pos: V.chmn, Gregory Co. Rep. Cent. Cmt, S.Dak, 64- Mem: Burke Womans Club; Pleasant Hour Extension Club; Local 4-H Club Leader, 29 years; State 4-H Leaders Asn; participate, Great Plains Conservation Program. Third place winner in Co. Conservation Program, 68. Rel: Baptist. Mailing Add: R.R, Burke, S.Dak. 57523.

MILES, HUGH E. D
Polit. & Govt. Pos: Ind. State Sen, -66. Bus. & Prof. Pos: Printing salesman, Indianapolis Printing Co. Mil. Serv: Navy. Mem: Am. Legion; Masonic Lodge. Rel: Baptist. Mailing Add: 6930 Daneby Circle, Indianapolis, Ind 46220. (1967)

MILES, MARY JO D
Mem, Calif. Dem. State Cent. Cmt.
b. Lincoln, Nebr, 5/22/22; d. Robert Don Latsch and Hattie Ogden L; m. 11/16/51 to Richard Samuel Miles; c. Linda Latsch and Steven Latsch. Educ: Vassar Col, 40-41; Univ. Nebr, B.A, 44; Kappa Alpha Theta. Polit. & Govt. Pos: Mem, Santa Barbara Co. Dem. Cent. Cmt, Calif, 68-; mem, Calif. Dem. State Cent. Cmt, 68- Bus. & Prof. Pos: Inspector for U.S. Signal Corps at West. Elec, 44-45; advert. mgr. and exec. secy, Latsch Bros, 45-51; v.pres, Miles Enterprises, 63- Mem: Jr. League; League of Women Voters; Commun. Arts Music Asn; Inter-Agency Coun. on Smoking & Health; Am. Cancer Soc; Channel City Women's Forum; Int. Platform Asn; Santa Barbara Regional Med. Prog. Charles Garvin Award for Improv. in Stationery Indust; Brand Names Found. Award, 49. Rel: Presbyterian. Mailing Add: 611 Las Palmas Dr, Santa Barbara, Calif. 93105.

MILES, THOMAS JAMES R
b. Dallas, Tex, 11/6/28; s. Thomas Miles and Hattie M. Chandler M; wid; c. Donnell O, Gregory T, Florence F, Lovette P, Thomas J, III and Antoinette. Educ: Golden Gate Col, degree, 52; Univ. Calif. Grad. Sch, 1 year; Lincoln Univ, 3 years; Kappa Phi. Polit. & Govt. Pos: V.chmn, United Voters, Inc, 54; exec. secy, Rep. Group, Alameda Co, Calif, 66-69; chmn, Concerned Berkeley Citizens, 68; alternate del, Rep. Nat. Conv, 68; chmn, 17th Rep. Assembly Dist, El Club Tegano, Rep. Minority Adv. Cmt. and Calif. Rep. Assembly Urban Affairs Cmt, 69- Bus. & Prof. Pos: Pres, Thomas J. Miles Realty & Finance Co, 60-; chmn, Monterey Savings Center, 67- Publ: 'Negro Buying Power,' News Week, 64; 'Black Business,' Bay Viewer Mag, 67. Mem: Nat. Notary Asn; participating mem, U.S. C. of C; Paragon's Inc; Golden Gate Col. Alumni Asn; Kappa Phi; W. Oakland Improv. Club; W. Oakland Notary Asn. Award for outstanding coordinator of workers in the 17th Assembly Dist, Calif. Co. Cent. Cmt, 68 and for outstanding leadership in Ph. Asn, 56. Rel: Methodist. Mailing Add: 3251 Grove St, Oakland, Calif. 94609.

MILFORD, CHARLES PATRICK D
b. Carnesville, Ga, 4/19/35; s. Clarence Arlington Milford and Gladys South M; m. 12/7/68 to Rachel Olivia Turpin; c. Richard Keith Walters (stepson). Educ: Univ. Ga, A.B, 57, LL.B, 59; Phi Alpha Delta. Polit. & Govt. Pos: Co. attorney, Franklin Co, 59-; Ga. State Rep, Franklin Co, 63-64. Bus. & Prof. Pos: Mem. bd. dirs, Gillespie Bros. Co, Inc, Carnesville, Ga, currently. Mem: Ga. Bar Asn; North. Circuit Bar Asn. (secy-treas, 62-63 & 65-66); Franklin Bldg. and Loan Asn. (mem. bd. dirs. and exec. v.pres);

Savannah Valley Prod. Credit Asn.(mem. bd. dirs); Jaycees (pres, Franklin Co. Chap, 64-65); Lions (pres, Carnesville Club, 65-66); Farm Bur; secy-treas, Poplar Springs United Methodist Campground. State of Ga. Award for Govt. Affairs, 64; sponsored by Ga. Jaycees to rep. Ga. at Govt. Affairs Sem, Wash. D.C, 64. Rel: Methodist; Church Sch. Supt; Choir; Church Lay Leader; Mem, Bd. of Admin. Affairs; Del to Annual Conf. Mailing Add: P.O. Box 247, Carnesville, Ga. 30521.

MILFORD, WILLIAM DOYLE D
Ga. State Rep.
b. Toombs Co, Ga, 12/15/42; s. Arthur Doyle Milford and Elizabeth Anderson M; m. 10/21/66 to Barbara Gail Ayers. Educ: Univ. Ga, B.B.A, 66; Sigma Phi Epsilon. Polit. & Govt. Pos: Ga. State Rep, 69- Bus. & Prof. Pos: Owner, supermkt. and farmer, Hartwell, Ga, 68-69. Mil. Serv: Entered as E-1, Army, 66, released as E-4, 68, after serv. First Army Div. Mem: Jaycees; Am. Legion. Rel: Baptist. Mailing Add: Route 3, Hartwell, Ga. 30643.

MILHOLLIN HENRY ROBERTS D
b. Broxton, Ga, 2/01/23; s. J. Henry Milhollin and Laurie Roberts M; m. 8/14/48 to Venita Joan Paulk; c. Laurie Suzane, Henry Ralph, George Roberts, Kathy Louise. Educ: Gordon Mil. Col, S. Ga. Col; Univ. of Ga, B.S, 49. Polit. & Govt. Pos: Ga. State Rep, 59-66. Bus. & Prof. Pos: Farmer, fertilizer & seed dealer; Douglas Peanut Co. Mil. Serv: U.S.A.F, WW II, 42-45. Mem: Mason No. 386; Lions; Elks; Shriner, Hasson Temple. Rel: Methodist. Mailing Add: RFD 2, Douglas, Ga. 31533. (1967)

MILIAS, GEORGE WALLACE R
Calif. State Assemblyman
b. Gilroy, Calif, 9/20/26; s. George C. Milias, Jr. and Geneve Wallace M; m. 7/23/63 to Mary Ann Rodeck. Educ: San Jose State Col, B.A. in hist. and polit. sci; Stanford Univ, M.A. in hist; Phi Mu Alpha; Phi Alpha Theta; Sigma Alpha Epsilon. Polit. & Govt. Pos: Mem, Grand Jury, Santa Clara Co, Calif, 54, foreman, 56; chmn. Host Cmt, Rep. Nat. Conv, 56, mem. Rules Cmt, 60, chmn. housing cmt, 64 and del, 68; pres, Calif. Rep. Assembly, 57; mem, Rep. Nat. Cmt, 58-60; state chmn, Calif. Rep. Party, 58-60; mem, Santa Clara Co. Planning Cmn, 58-60, v.chmn, 61, chmn, 62; Calif. State Assemblyman, 22nd Dist, 62-, chmn. Cmt. on Natural Resources and Conserv, mem. Elec. and Constitutional Admendments Cmt. and Govt. Admin. Cmt, currently. Bus. & Prof. Pos: Rancher and hotel operator. Publ: Hiram Johnson, Governor of California, Stanford Univ. Press, 49. Mem: Stanford and San Jose State Alumni Asns; Santa Clara Co. Exec. Bd, Boy Scouts, 62; Sierra Club; Rotary; Native Sons of the Golden West; Commonwealth Club; Elks. Nat. Young Rep. Hall of Fame, 60. Rel: Catholic. Legal Res: R.R. 1, Box 35, Gilroy, Calif. 95020. Mailing Add: 405 Alberto Way, Los Gatos, Calif. 95030.

MILLEN, FLOYD H. R
Iowa State Rep.
b. Watertown, S.Dak, 5/17/19; s. Homer E. Millen and Pearle Wright M; m. 2/15/42 to Betty Coffin; c. James Randall, Robert Gregg and David Craig. Educ: Iowa State Univ, 37-38; Nev. Sch. of Mines, 39-41. Polit. & Govt. Pos: Iowa State Rep, Jefferson-Van Buren Co, 63-, Majority Floor Leader, Iowa House of Rep, 67-68, Speaker Pro-Tempore, 69. Bus. & Prof. Pos: Pres, Valley Limestone & Gravel, Inc, 46- Mil. Serv: Entered as Pvt, Army, 42, released as 2nd Lt, 46, after serv. in 618th Light Engr. Equip. Co, Southwest Pac, Philippines, 45; Philippines campaign. Mem: Am. Mil. Engr; Sch. Bd; C. of C; Nat. Limestone Inst; Am. Roadbuilders Asn; Iowa Limestone Producers Asn; Shrine; Consistory; Elks; Am. Legion; VFW; Isaac Walton; I Club; Dads Asn. Rel: Methodist. Mailing Add: Farmington, Iowa 52626.

MILLER, ADIN R. R
b. S.Dak, 9/22/02; married. Educ: Minot State Teachers Col, B.A; Univ. Minn, M.A. Polit. & Govt. Pos: N.Dak. State Rep, 61-66. Bus. & Prof. Pos: Ins. Mailing Add: Beach, N.Dak. 58621.

MILLER, ALBERT EDWARD R
Chmn, Hartford Rep. Town Cmt, Conn.
b. Hartford, Conn, 4/26/27; s. George Miller and Sophie Sayet M; m. 6/18/61 to Barbara Smith; c. Jeffrey W. and Kimberlee B. Educ: Syracuse Univ, B.S; N.Y. Univ. Grad. Sch, finance. Polit. & Govt. Pos: Mem, Small Bus. Adv. Cmt, Conn; pres. and pub. rels. dir, Young Rep. Party; chmn, Hartford Rep. Town Cmt, 66- Bus. & Prof. Pos: Instnl. sales mgr, Bache & Co, Hartford, Conn. Mil. Serv: Seaman, Navy Air Corps, 45-46. Mem: Mason; bd. of dirs, Hartford Jewish Fedn; Eagles; B'nai B'rith; Beth Israel Men's Clubs; H.A.R.C. Rel: Hebrew. Mailing Add: 180 Terry Rd, Hartford, Conn. 06105. (1967)

MILLER, ALBERT VIRGIL D
b. Gainesville, Miss, 8/12/26; married. Educ: Phi Delta Phi. Polit. & Govt. Pos: Miss. State Rep, 56-68. Bus. & Prof. Pos: Lawyer. Mem: Am. Legion; Farm Bur; Miss. State Bar Asn; Rotary; Mason; Delta Coun. Rel: Baptist. Mailing Add: Rolling Fork, Miss. 39159. (1967)

MILLER, ALBERTA MERYL D
b. Hutchinson, Kans, 11/27/15; d. Frank M. Spaniol and Edith Lofthouse S; m. 9/27/34 to Jay Duvall Miller; c. Gladys (Mrs. Blea) and Jay D, Jr. Educ: Hays State Teacher's Col. Polit. & Govt. Pos: Former secy, Gov. Office and Asst. State Purchasing Agent; mem, Platform Cmt, Dem. Nat. Conv, 64; hon. mem, N.Mex. Young Dem; secy, Capitol Bldg. Improv. Cmn; ex-officio mem, Pub. Employees Retirement Bd, State Canvassing Bd, Capitol Custodian Cmn. and State Cmn. Pub. Records; Secy. of State, N.Mex. until 67; state dir, Civil Defense and Mobilization, 68- Bus. & Prof. Pos: Trainmaster's clerk, Santa Fe Rwy; off. mgr, several Albuquerque firms; area rep. for N.Mex, Nat. Bus. Woman, 69- Mem: Adv. bd, N.Mex. Div, Am. Automobile Asn; legis. cmt, State YMCA Youth and Govt. Cmt; adv. bd, N.Mex. Chap, Am. Mothers Cmt; legis. chmn, State Federated Bus. & Prfnl. Women and Am. Legion Auxiliary; Duke City Bus. & Prfnl. Women; affil, Int. Zonta. Honored speaker, Purple Heart Conv, 64; Citation, Mil. Order of Purple Heart; selected 1 of 5 Outstanding Women, Duke City Bus. & Prfnl. Women, 65; off. recognition, all br. Armed Forces, Am. Asn. Retired Persons and Nat. Asn. Civil Serv. Retired Employees. Rel: Episcopal. Legal Res: 423 Pueblo Solano N.W, Albuquerque, N.Mex. Mailing Add: 340 Berger St, Santa Fe, N.Mex. 87501.

MILLER, ALEX D
Dem. Nat. Committeeman, Alaska
Mailing Add: 312 11th Ave, Fairbanks, Alaska 99701.

MILLER, ARTHUR Independent
b. N.Y.C, 10/17/15; s. Isadore Miller and Augusta Barnett M; m. to Ingeborg Morath; c. Rebecca, Robert and Jane. Educ: Univ. Mich, A.B, 38, hon. D.H.L. Polit. & Govt. Pos: Del, Dem. Nat. Conv, 68. Publ: Death of a Salesman, 49; The Crucible, 55; After the Fall, 64; plus others. Rel: Jewish. Mailing Add: Roxbury, Conn. 06783.

MILLER, B. READ R
b. Louisville, Ky, 1/12/34; s. Eugene Hunter Miller and Mary Adair Motley M; m. to Nancy Ann Norris; c. Mary Ann, Martha Adair, Ann Norris, B. Read, Jr. and John Hunter. Educ: Univ. Ky, 56-59; Univ. Ky. Law Sch. Phi Delta. Phi; Phi Sigma Kappa. Polit. & Govt. Pos: Del, Ky. Rep. State Conv, 62, Fayette Co. Rep. Conv, 62 and Ky. Young Rep. State Conv, 65; precinct chmn. and mem. finance cmt, Rep. Party, Ky, 64; former chmn, Woodford Co. Rep. Exec. Cmt. Mem: Blue Grass Claims Asn; Spindletop Hall Club; Woodford Co. Country Club; Fayette Co. Young Rep. Club; Blue Grass Lincoln Club. Rel: Episcopal; Vestry, St. John's Episcopal Church. Mailing Add: 112 Shaw Ave, Versailles, Ky. 40383. (1967)

MILLER, BETTY JANE D
b. Bluefield, W.Va, 4/22/27; d. Maurice R. Francis and Verna V. Hall F; m. 6/6/48 to John L. Miller; c. Margaret Beth and Alan Douglas. Educ: Ohio Univ, B.S, 48; Phi Beta Kappa. Polit. Pos: Colo. State Rep, 65-67. Rel: Episcopal. Mailing Add: 1265 S. Depew, Denver, Colo. 80226.

MILLER, CHARLES H. DFL
Minn. State Rep.
b. 1918; married; c. Six. Educ: Wabasha High Sch; Ins. sch, Des Moines, Iowa; Nat. Rural Elec. Coop. Asn, dipl. in mgt. and finance. Polit. & Govt. Pos: Clerk, Watopa Twp, Minn, 9 years; clerk, Rural Sch. Dist, 15 years; Minn. State Rep, 63-64 & 67- Bus. & Prof. Pos: Owner and operator, Idle Hour Game Farm Restaurant, Wabasha, Minn, formerly; owner, farm, Wabash Co, formerly. Mailing Add: Kellogg, Minn. 55945. (1967)

MILLER, CHARLES P. D
Iowa State Rep.
b. Harbor Beach, Mich, 4/29/18; s. William H. Miller and Anna V; m. 8/3/46 to Virginia Mae Ferrington; c. Five sons and one daughter. Educ: Jr. Col; Palmer Chiropractic Col. Polit. & Govt. Pos: Iowa State Rep, currently. Bus. & Prof. Pos: Chiropractic, 52- Mil. Serv: Navy, Active duty, Active res, 46-51. Mem: Past Pres, Chiropractic Soc. of Iowa; Past Pres. and Past area Gov, Toastmasters Int; Exec. Bd. Mem, S.E. Iowa Coun. of B.S, 12 years; Mem, Bd. of Control, Int. Chiropractors Asn; K. of C; Eagles; Elks; VFW; Am. Legion; Lions; United Commercial Travelers; Travelers Protective Asn. Mailing Add: 801 High St, Burlington, Iowa 52601.

MILLER, CHARLES ROBERT R
Committeeman, Ill. Rep. Cent. Cmt.
b. Carlinville, Ill, 3/9/23; s. Cuyler C. Miller and Gertrude Hunter M; m. 3/14/43 to Claribelle Otwell; c. Mary Katherine, Robin Ann (Mrs. Ron Sawyer), Gail Alden, Suzanne and Rebecca Lynn. Educ: Blackburn Univ, 41-42; Kans. Univ, E.E, 43. Polit. & Govt. Pos: Committeeman, Ill. Rep. Cent. Cmt, 54- Bus. & Prof. Pos: Farmer, chief engr, Radio WSMI, Litchfield, Ill, 54-59; electronics technician, Rogers Plumbing & Wiring, 59- Mil. Serv: Civilian, Wright Field, Ohio, War Dept. Mem: V.pres, Ill. Jaycees, nat. dir, U.S. Jaycees; Lions Int; pres, Ill. Valley Livestock Feeders Asn. SPOKE Award and Spark Plug Award, Ill. Jaycees; Key Man Award, U.S. Jaycees. Rel: Methodist. Mailing Add: R.R. 4, Carlinville, Ill. 62626.

MILLER, CLARENCE E. R
U.S. Rep, Ohio
b. Lancaster, Ohio, 11/1/17; s. Clarence E. Miller, Sr. and Delores Lloyd M; m. 12/25/36 to Helen Brown; c. Ronald and Jacqueline (Mrs. Thomas Williams). Educ: Int. Correspondence Sch, dipl, 56. Polit. & Govt. Pos: Mem. city coun, Lancaster, Ohio, 57-62 & 63, mayor, 64-65; U.S. Rep, Tenth Dist, Ohio, 67- Bus. & Prof. Pos: With Ohio Fuel Gas Co, 36; elec. engr. Mem: Elks; YMCA; exec. cmt, Lancaster Commun. Improv. Corp; U.C.T. Citation of Merit for Commun. Serv, Jr. C. of C. Rel: First Methodist. Legal Res: 1430 E. Main St, Lancaster, Ohio 43130. Mailing Add: 128 Cannon House Office Bldg, Washington, D.C. 20515.

MILLER, CLARENCE R. D
Ky. State Rep.
b. Louisville, Ky, 1909. Educ: Clark Bus. Col. Polit. & Govt. Pos: Ky. State Rep, 56- Bus. & Prof. Pos: Credit Mgr. Mem: Mason; Mose Green Dem. Club. Mailing Add: 614 E. Brandeis Ave, Louisville, Ky. 40217. (1967)

MILLER, CLAUDE J. R
b. Grant City, Mo, 6/19/22; s. Franz Edward Miller and Lucy Ewing M; m. 4/7/56 to Martha Loraine Murren; c. Kathy Ann and Linda Kay, stepdaughter, Cheryl C. Lister and step-son, Mark E. Lister. Educ: Northwest Mo. State Col, one year. Polit. & Govt. Pos: V.chmn, Worth Co. Rep. Cmt, Mo, 60-62 & 64-65, chmn, 66-68. Mil. Serv: Entered as Pvt, Army, 42, released as Sgt, 46, after serv. in Med. Corps, Seventh Command; Good Conduct Medal. Mem: Farm Bur. Rel: Christian Church; Deacon, Grant City Christian Church. Mailing Add: R.R. 3, Grant City, Mo. 64456. (1967)

MILLER, CLYDE L. D
Secy. of State, Utah
b. Salt Lake City, Utah, 1/1/10; s. Mark M. Miller and Louella McArthur McMullin M; m. 10/2/54 to Reva Lee Carlson; c. Roberta Lee, Clyde Alton, Carey Mae, Diane Marie, Linda Rae, Mark Miles and Daniel Duncan. Educ: Univ. Utah, B.S, 34. Polit. & Govt. Pos: Utah State Rep, 51-52; Utah State Sen, 59-64; Secy. of State, Utah, 65- Rel: Latter-day Saint. Legal Res: 374 E. Haven Ave, Salt Lake City, Utah 84115. Mailing Add: Room 203, State Capitol Bldg, Salt Lake City, Utah 84114.

MILLER, DARREL R. DFL
married; c. three. Polit. & Govt. Pos: Cand, Minn. State Rep, 66; Co. Bd. Mem. Bus. & Prof. Pos: Owns and operates 614 acre dairy farm. Mem: Chmn, tractor pulling contest; Rural Olmsted chmn, March of Dimes, 2 years; v.pres, New Haven Farmers Union; Olmsted Co. secy-treas. for the union; Dodge Co. Fair Bd, dir; Rural Co. chmn, Heart Fund, 66; v.chmn, New Haven Twp, A.S.C. Olmsted Co's. outstanding young farmer, 64. Rel: Methodist. Mailing Add: Pine Island, Minn. 55963. (1967)

MILLER, DEAN E. D
b. Caldwell, Idaho, 9/26/22; s. Dean W. Miller and Mary Meek M; m. 8/20/45 to Josephine Ney; c. Dean Joseph, Nicholas G, Thomas F, Mary M. and Patrick J. Educ: Univ. Idaho, LL.B, 49; Phi Alpha Delta; Beta Theta Pi. Polit. & Govt. Pos: Co. chmn, Dem. Party, Idaho, 50-54; state committeeman, 54-56, regional coordinator, 56-; chmn, Idaho McCarthy for Pres. Campaign, 68; del, Dem. Nat. Conv, 68. Mil. Serv: Entered as Pvt, Army, 42, released as 1st Lt, 45, after serv. in 531 Field Artillery Bn, Cent. and S.Pac, 43-45; Army Res.(Ret); Asiatic-Pac. Soc. Ribbon; 3 Battle Stars; Philippine Liberation Medal. Mem: Am. Bar Asn; Am. Legion; Elks(pres, Idaho State Asn); Rotary Int; K. of C; pres, Univ. Idaho Alumni Asn. Rel: Roman Catholic. Mailing Add: 2201 Washington, Caldwell, Idaho 83605.

MILLER, DOROTHY JENILEE D
Pres, Kans. Fedn. of Women's Dem. Clubs
b. Dodge City, Kans, 7/30/24; d. Cecil Ballard Middaugh and Ida Beatrice Cody M; m. 9/22/48 to Garnett Earl Miller; c. Stephen Wayne and Mark William. Educ: Newton High Sch, Kans, 38-42. Polit. & Govt. Pos: Dem. precinct committeewoman, First Precinct, Kans, 54-; pres, Harvey Co. Fedn. Dem. Club, 56-69; prog. chmn, Kans. Fedn. Women's Dem. Clubs, 58-59, v.pres, 63-66, pres, 66-; v.chmn, Harvey Co. Dem. Cent. Cmt, 60-62; Dollar for Dem. chmn, Kans. Dem. State Cmt, 60, 62 & 63, Fourth Dist. registrn. chmn, 62 & 64; del, Dem. Nat. Conv, 68. Mem: Kans. Day Women's Club, Topeka, Kans; Native Sons and Daughters, Topeka; VFW Auxiliary, Newton; Newton PTA Coun. Rel: Episcopal; past pres, Couple's Club and finance chmn, Women's Orgn, St. Matthews Episcopal Church, Newton, Knas. Mailing Add: 704 Elm St, Newton, Kans. 67114.

MILLER, DOROTHY RISLEY R
Conn. State Rep.
b. East Hartford, Conn, 4/1/20; d. John Strong Risley, Jr. and Winifred Irene Cooley R; wid; c. Diane Rdelle. Educ: Manchester High Sch, Conn, grad, 38. Polit. & Govt. Pos: Mem, Rep. Town Cmt, Bolton, Conn, 54-, secy, 56-61, chmn, 61-63; Conn. State Rep, Bolton, 59-63 and 51st Dist, 69-; mem, Nat. Order of Women Legislators, 59-; mem, Conn. Order of Women Legislators, 59-, secy, 69; committeewoman from 35th Dist, Conn. State Rep. Cent. Cmt, 60-63. Bus. & Prof. Pos: Clerk, supvr. and secy, Etna Life & Casualty, Hartford, 38-63 & 66-; secy, Henry S. Beers, retired exec, 64- Mem: Tolland Co. Rep. Assocs.(organizer and first pres, in 60, now defunct); Tolland Co. Rep. Women's Asn. (former pres, now defunct); Second Cong. Dist. Rep. Women's Asn.(presently dist. v.pres). Rel: Methodist; mem, Women's Soc. of Christian Serv, United Methodist Church, Bolton (pres, 65-67). Mailing Add: Cook Dr, Box 485, RFD 2, Bolton, Conn. 06040.

MILLER, EDWARD TYLOR R
b. Woodside, Md, 2/1/95; s. Guion Miller and Annie E. Tylor M; m. 11/14/42 to Josephine Ford; c. Theodore G. Educ: Yale, B.A, 16; Phi Beta Kappa; Omicron Delta Kappa; Psi Upsilon; Fence Club; Yale Football; Y Men's Asn. Polit. & Govt. Pos: Cand. for state's attorney, Talbot Co, Md, 23; referee in bankruptcy, U.S. Dist. Court, Md, 24-42; chmn, Md. State Rep. Cent. Cmt, 26-29; police court and juvenile justice, Talbot Co, 35-39; mem, Nat. Rep. Cong. Cmt, and chmn. auditing cmt, 47-59; U.S. Rep, First Dist, Md, 47-59; v.chmn, U.S. del, UN Conf. on Law of the Sea, Geneva, Switzerland, 60; mem, Rep. Nat. Cmt, 60-64; cand. for U.S. Senate, 62; del. and mem. platform cmt, Rep. Nat. Conv, 64; mem, Constitutional Conv. Cmn, Md, 65-; del, State Constitutional Conv, 67- Bus. & Prof. Pos: Attorney-at-law, sr. partner, Miller, Wheeler, Thompson & Thompson, Easton, Md, 20- Mil. Serv: 2nd Lt, Army, 17-19, serv. with Inf, France, 42-46, serv. with 319th and 320th Inf, 80th Div, Gen. Hq. France and N.Africa, European, Mediterranean and China-Burma-India Theaters; Collar, Chinese Order of Cloud and Banner; Medaille de St. Mihiel; numerous serv. ribbons including World War I with 4 Battle Stars and World War II with 2 Battle Stars; Col. (Ret), Army Res, 55. Mem: Am, Md. State and Talbot Co. Bar Asns; Mason (32°), Shrine; Elks; Am. Legion; VFW; Fence Club; 14 W. Hamilton St. Club; Chesapeake Bay and Miles River Yacht Clubs. Rel: Society of Friends. Mailing Add: The Pines, Easton, Md. 21601.

MILLER, EDWINA R. D
b. Adel, Ga, 5/10/24; d. James Alfred Jones and Aline Williams J; 2nd marriage, 11/20/49 to Alex Miller; c. Paul Michael Beneke, Jan Aline and Alex, III. Educ: St. Joseph's Infirmary, Atlanta, Ga; Madison Press Club. Polit. & Govt. Pos: Campaign secy, Proxmire for Gov. Clubs, Wis, 54; state secy, Kefauver for Pres. Club, Wis, 56; capitol secy, Wis. State Sen. Wm. Proxmire, 57-58; off. mgr, Second Dist, U.S. Sen. John F. Kennedy for Pres, 59 & 60; campaign secy, U.S. Rep. Robt. Kastenmeier, 60, 62 & 64; former chmn, Dane Co. Dem. Party. Rel: Lutheran. Mailing Add: 118 Bradford Lane, Madison, Wis. 53714. (1967)

MILLER, ELIZABETH RUBY R
Iowa State Rep.
b. Marshalltown, Iowa, 8/24/05; d. Stephen Shank and Lenora Burns S; m. 9/5/23 to John Bascom Miller; c. John Bascom, Jr, Edward James, Mary Lorse (Mrs. Tom Speas) and Betty Arlene (Mrs. Russell Weeden Jr). Educ: Marshalltown High Sch, grad, 23. Polit. & Govt. Pos: Co. pres, Iowa Fedn. Rep. Women, 65-66, State Campaign Chmn, 68-69; Iowa State Rep, 69- Bus. & Prof. Pos: Chmn, Home Nursing, Red Cross, 50-60; co. rural chmn, Cancer Soc, 55-56. Mem: Gen. Fedn. Women's Clubs; Farm Bur; Iowa Hist. Soc. Outstanding Civic Leader of Am, 67. Rel: United Church of Christ. Mailing Add: R.R. 3, Marshalltown, Iowa 50158.

MILLER, EMMA GUFFEY D
Dem. Nat. Committeewoman, Pa.
b. Guffey Station, Pa, 7/6/74; d. John Guffey and Barbaretta Hough G; m. 10/28/05 to Carroll Miller (deceased); c. William Gardner, twins John Guffey and Carroll, Jr. and Joseph F. Guffey. Educ: Alinda Acad, Pittsburgh; Bryn Mawr Col, A.B, 98; Pi Delta Phi; pvt. tutoring. Polit. & Govt. Pos: First Precinct Committeewoman, Seventh Ward, Pa, 20-30; del, Dem. Nat. Conv, 24-68; mem, Pittsburgh Mayor's Cmt, George Wash. Bicentennial, 32; mem, State Dem. Cmt. and Co. Dem. Cmt; Dem. Nat. Committeewoman, 32-; mem, Pa. State Coun. Educ. and Pa. State Welfare Cmt, 35-39; chmn. adv. bd, Pa. Nat. Youth Admin, 35-43; mem, Gov. Defense Cmt. for Pa, 40; Presidential elector, 40 & 44; pres, for Life Nat. Woman's Party Sponsoring the Equal Rights Amendment, currently. Bus. & Prof. Pos: Mem: bd. trustees, Slippery Rock State Col, Pa, 33-; mem. planning cmt, Japan Int. Christian Univ. Found, 58. Publ: 'Romance of the National Pike,' West. Pa. Mag; 'No Meat for a Month,' Mine Workers J; 'The Equal Rights Amendment,' New Times. Mem: Consumers League, 10-14; Parent Teachers, 15-18; League of Women Voters, 21-25; nat. adv. bd, Women's Orgn. Nat. Prohibition Reform, 29-33; chmn. women's activities, Pa. Fed. Constitution Commemoration, 37-38; Asn. Pa. Teachers Cols, 37-39; v.chmn, Pa. 300th Anniversary Cmt, 38-39; Am. Jewish Cong; pres. for life, Nat. Woman's Party. Nat. Chmn, Distinguished Daughter of Pa, 55; Women's Dem. Club of Slippery Rock renamed Emma Guffey Miller Club of Slippery Rock, Pa, 65. Rel: Episcopal. Mailing Add: Wolf Creek Farm, R.D. 2, Slippery Rock, Pa. 16057.

MILLER, ETHEL ALLEN R
V.Chmn, Genesee Co. Rep. Cmt, N.Y.
b. Rochester, N.Y, 5/3/04; d. William V. Allen and Blanche Bullock A; m. 11/7/25 to Francis James Miller, Sr; c. Francis J, Jr, Joan E. and Patricia (Mrs. Webster A. Chapman). Educ: Rochester Bus. Sch, 2 years. Polit. & Govt. Pos: Past Pres. and V.Pres, Genesee Co. Women's Rep. Club, N.Y; Past V.Pres and Pres, Eighth Judicial Dist. Women's Rep. Club; V.Chmn, Genesee Co. Rep. Cmt, 67- Mem: Eastern Star (dist. dep. and Grand Matron); life mem, Am. Heart Asn; West. N.Y. Heart Asn.(mem. bd); N.Y. State Heart Asn (mem. bd); Stafford Co. Club. Rel: Presbyterian. Mailing Add: 53 Rochester St, Bergen, N.Y. 14416.

MILLER, EVERETT HOWARD R
Vt. State Rep.
b. Hartland, Vt, 9/13/04; m. to Luella M. Merriam; c. Two. Educ: Vt. State Agr. Sch, Randolph. Polit. & Govt. Pos: Selectman, 5 years; sch. dir, 12 years; Vt. State Rep, 51 & 65- Bus. & Prof. Pos: Retired farmer; dir. and pres, Inter-State Trust Co; dir, 1st Nat. Bank, White River, Vt; Mary Hitchcock Mem. Hosp. Corp, Hanover, N.H. Rel: Protestant. Mailing Add: Hartland, Vt. 05048. (1967)

MILLER, FRANCES MIRON D
V.Chmn, Brown Co. Dem. Cmt, Ind.
b. Kankakee, Ill, 4/29/14; d. Thomas Novellette Messina and Nellie Rickard M; m. to Louie Frank Miller; c. 13; 22 grandchildren. Polit. & Govt. Pos: Precinct v.committeewoman, Brown Co. Dem. Cmt, Ind, 56-60, co. recorder, v.chmn, 60-; treas, Brown Co. Dem. Women's Club, 63-64, v.pres, 65-66; mem, Ind. Dem. Women's Club, 65-66; secy, Tri-Co. Off. Econ. Opportunity, Bartholemew, Brown and Jackson Co. Mem: Bd, Farm Bur; Ment. Health Bd; secy, Tri-Co. Off. Econ. Opportunity Commun. Action. Rel: Nazarene. Mailing Add: Nashville, Ind. 47448. (1967)

MILLER, FRANK L. D
Chmn, Beauregard Parish Dem. Exec. Cmt, La.
b. Dry Creek, La, 6/18/10; s. S. Nathan Miller and Emma Heard M; m. 12/31/31 to Versie Welborn; c. Franklin D, Rose (Mrs. Gallien), William N, John R. and Kathy. Educ: Northwest. State Col, B.A, 31, M.E, 59; Sigma Tau Gamma. Polit. & Govt. Pos: Mem, Beauregard Parish Dem. Cmt, La, 33-59; chmn, Beauregard Parish Dem. Exec. Cmt, 59- Bus. & Prof. Pos: Teacher, Beauregard Parish Sch. Bd, 31-33, prin, 33-69. Mem: Beauregard Parish Teachers Asn; La. Teachers Asn.(v.pres, 63, pres, 64); Nat. Educ. Asn; F&AM, DeRidder Lodge; DeRidder Kiwanis Club; Beauregard Parish Farm Bur. Kiwanian of the year, 67. Rel: Baptist. Legal Res: 628 Le Compte St, DeRidder, La. 70634. Mailing Add: P.O. Box 447, DeRidder, La. 70634.

MILLER, FRANKLIN D
V.Chmn, N.Y. State New Dem. Coalition
b. Brooklyn, N.Y, 2/5/22; s. Leon Miller and Sadie Berger M; m. 3/13/46 to Bernice Gerenstein; c. Sandra M.(Mrs. Seth Greenberg) and Patricia L. Educ: Col. of the City of N.Y, 38-42; Brooklyn Law Sch, LL.B, 48; N.Y. Univ, LL.M, 51; Alpha Sigma Lambda. Polit. & Govt. Pos: Dem. Cong. Cand, Sixth Dist, N.Y, 68; v.chmn, Queens Co. New Dem. Coalition, 68-69 and N.Y. State New Dem. Coalition, 69- Mil. Serv: Entered as Pvt, Army, 42, released as T/5, 46, after serv. in Signal Corps, S.Pac. Theatre and Philippines, 45-46; Area Awards with Two Battle Stars. Mem: Am. and Queens Co. Bar Asns; Am. and N.Y. Trial Lawyers Asns; Am. Juridical Soc; Flushing Lawyers Club (pres, 66); Mason; Douglaston Lodge; K. of P; pres, Little Neck-Douglaston Civic Asn; Deepdale Gardens Commun. Coun.(past pres). Rel: Jewish. Mailing Add: 60-03 Hewlett St, Little Neck, N.Y. 11362.

MILLER, FREMONT W. R
Wyo. State Sen.
b. Burris, Wyo, 12/29/18; m. to Bernice; c. Four. Educ: Colo. State Univ. Polit. & Govt. Pos: Mem, Dubois Sch. Bd, Wyo; Wyo. State Rep, 4 terms; Wyo. State Sen, 67- Bus. & Prof. Pos: Honey producer and cattle rancher; adv. bd. mem, Big Horn Nat. Life Ins. Co. Mem: Fremont Co. Cattlemen's Asn; Sioux Honey Asn; Farm Bur; Am. Legion; Sch. Bd. Asn. Rel: Lutheran. Mailing Add: Burris, Wyo. 82435. (1967)

MILLER, GEORGE A. D
Okla. State Sen.
b. Montrose, Colo, 4/3/27; s. George A. Miller and Verdie Sallee M; m. 6/17/48 to Mary Evelyn Cox; c. George Edward, Mary Ann, John David and Robert Walter. Educ: Okla. State Univ, Assoc. Degree in Eng, 50. Polit. & Govt. Pos: Okla. State Sen, Dist. 13, 64- Bus. & Prof. Pos: Chief eng, KADA Broadcasting, Inc, 50-62; news dir, East. Okla. TV, Inc, 54- Mil. Serv: Entered as Seaman 1/C, Navy, 45, released 46. Rel: Church of the Nazarene. Mailing Add: 1021 E. 6, Ada, Okla. 74820.

MILLER, GEORGE PAUL D
U.S. Rep, Calif.
b. San Francisco, Calif, 1/15/91; s. Joseph Miller and Margaret Anson M; m. 5/21/27 to Esther M. Perkins; c. Ann. Educ: St. Mary's Col, Calif, B.S, 12. Polit. & Govt. Pos: Exec. secy, Calif. Div. of Fish and Game; Calif. State Assemblyman, 52nd and 53rd sessions; adv. to U.S. Ambassador to UN on Peaceful uses of outer space; U.S. Rep, Calif, 44-, chmn, Sci. and Astronaut. Cmt, U.S. House of Rep, currently. Bus. & Prof. Pos: Civil engr. Mil. Serv: Command Lt, Army, F.A, 17; grad, 30th Class, sch. of fire, Ft. Sill, Okla, 18. Mem: Nat. Hist. Publ. Cmn; Am. Legion (past 1st v.comdr, Dept. of Calif); Lions; Eagles; Elks. Legal Res: 1424 Benton St, Alameda, Calif. 94501. Mailing Add: House Office Bldg, Washington, D.C. 20515.

MILLER, HANS R. Non-Partisan
Educ: Univ. Minn. Sch. of Agr; Henry George Sch. of Soc. Sci, N.Y. Polit. & Govt. Pos: Cand, Minn. State Rep, 66; former co. chmn, Farmer Labor Party; Agr. Dept. Adjust. Cmt. during the Depression; state supvr, Voc. Training and Re-employ. for Nat. Defense during WWII. Bus. & Prof. Pos: Retired builder and contractor; former dairy farmer; worked for Fed. Govt, 7 years, labor admin. and pub. rel. Mem: Charter mem, Minn. REA. Mailing Add: 2918 7th Ave, N, Anoka, Minn. 55303. (1967)

MILLER, HARLAN WALTER D
Chmn, Wetzel Co. Dem. Exec. Cmt, W.Va.
b. Epperly, W.Va, 9/12/20; s. Clarence Preston Miller and Elsie Mae Trout M; m. 2/12/44 to Elaine Broyles Blake; c. Joyce Elaine, Anita Roxie and Harlan Corbett. Educ: U.S. Navy Turbo Elec. Sch, Sound Motion Picture Tech. Sch. and Elec. Sch. Polit. & Govt. Pos: Pres, Wetzel Co. Young Dem, W.Va, 58-61; secy. exec. cmt, W.Va. State Young Dem, 59-61, mem, 61-64; chmn, Wetzel Co. Dem. Exec. Cmt, 64-; mem, Grant Dist, Wetzel Co. Dem. Exec. Cmt, 68- Bus. & Prof. Pos: Electrician, Union Carbide Chems. Co, 45- Mil. Serv: Entered as A/S, Navy, 40, released as CPO, 45, after serv. in S.Pac; South Pacific Theater, North Atlantic Theater and Asiatic Theater Ribbons. Mem: Mason (32°), Shrine; VFW; Am. Legion; Pine Grove Sportsman Club. Rel: Methodist. Mailing Add: Hastings, W.Va. 26365.

MILLER, HARRIET EVELYN D
b. Council, Idaho, 7/4/19; d. Colwell Miller and Vera Crome M; single. Educ: Whitman Col, B.A, 41; Univ. of Pa, M.A, 49; Univ. of Mont, grad. study; Phi Beta Kappa; Psi Chi; Phi Kappa Phi; Alpha Chi Omega. Polit. & Govt. Pos: Secy, Missoula Co. Young Rep, Mont, 52-53; nat. committeewoman, Mont. Young Rep, 54-56; supt. of pub. instr, Mont, 57-68. Bus. & Prof. Pos: Med. technician, U.S. Govt. Civil Serv, Ft. Lewis, Wash, 42-44; research chemist, Atlantic Refining Co, Phila, Pa, 44-50; student personnel adminstr, Univ. of Mont, 50-53, assoc. dean of students, 54-56; free-lance writer, 53-54. Publ: Ed, Elephant Trumpetings, Mont. Young Rep, 53-54; auth, 'Problems of Financing Quality Education in Montana,' Col. of Educ. Record, Univ. of Idaho, spring 65. Mem: Am. and Mont. Asns. of Sch. Adminstrs; Am. Libr. Asn; life mem, Mont. Cong. of Parents and Teachers; hon. life mem, Mont. Asn. and Future Homemakers of Am; Delta Kappa Gamma; Nat. and Mont. Educ. Asns; Coun. of Chief State Sch. Officers; hon. mem, Blackfoot Indian Tribe; Adv. Cmt. on New Educational Media, U.S. Off. of Educ; Soroptimist Int; Am. Asn. Univ. Women; Bus. & Prfnl. Women's Club; Lewis & Clark Humane Soc; Mont. Conserv. Coun; Educ. Adv. Cmt. for Girl Scouts of Am; bd. of trustees, Int. Jour. for the Educ. of the Blind. Selected Woman of the Year by Assoc. Press, 64. Rel: Methodist. Mailing Add: 1029 Mauldin, Helena, Mont. 59601. (1967)

MILLER, HENRY A. R
b. Centerville, Wash, 5/16/07; s. John A. Miller and Elizabeth J. Garner M; m. 6/9/33 to Florence Scott; c. John Douglas and James Henry. Educ: Univ. of Wash, B.B.A, 29; Phi Beta Kappa; Beta Gamma Sigma; Beta Alpha Psi. Polit. & Govt. Pos: Dir, Centerville Sch. Dist. 215, 41-49; chmn, Klickitat Co. Cmt. on Sch. Orgn, 50-54 and Klickitat Co. Rep. Cent. Cmt, 67-68; cmnr, Klickitat Co, 55-66 and Pub. Utility Dist. one, 68- Bus. & Prof. Pos: Chmn. bd. of dirs, Klickitat Valley Bank, Goldendale, Wash, 68-69. Mem: Centerville Grange; Wash. Cattlemen's Asn; C. of C. Rel: Protestant. Mailing Add: Centerville, Wash. 98613.

MILLER, HERBERT SIDNEY D
b. New York, N.Y, 5/4/25; s. Thomas Peter Smith and Ruth Uffner S; m. Aug. 54 to Anne Broy; c. Rachel, Jonathan, Rebecca and Ruth. Educ: Syracuse Univ, 1 year; Adelphi Col, B.A, 49; Georgetown Univ, LL.B, 58; Pi Gamma Mu. Polit. & Govt. Pos: Intel. analyst, Air Force, Wash, D.C, 51-58; dep. legis. counsel, Ore. State Legis, 58-59; exec. secy, Ore. Legis. Cmt. on Criminal Law, 59-61; trial attorney, criminal div, Dept. Justice, Wash, D.C, 61-65; adv, narcotics and drug addiction, President's Crime Cmn, 66-67; mem, Fairfax Co. Crime Cmn, Va, 66-67; del, Dem. Nat. Conv, 68; precinct chmn, Fairfax Co. Dem. Cmt, 68- Bus. & Prof. Pos: Sr. research attorney, Inst. Criminal Law and Procedure, Georgetown Univ. Law Ctr, 65-68; dep. dir, 68- Mil. Serv: Entered as Pvt, Air Force, 43, released as 2nd Lt, 46, after serving in 20th Air Force, Mariannas Islands, 45-46; Battle Stars. Publ: 'Report of Legislature Interim Committee on Criminal Law', Ore. Legis, 61; The role of Counsel in the Sentencing Process, Bender, 69; Probation (report on minimum standards for criminal justice for Am. Bar Asn) to be publ. in 69. Mem: Pres, Local Citizens Asn, 64-65; officer and mem. exec. cmt, Fairfax Co. Fedn. Citizen's Asn, 65-69; chmn, Citizens Cmt. on Crime and Delinquency, currently. Outstanding Citizen Award, Local Citizens Asn, 66. Rel: Unitarian. Mailing Add: 1654 Wainwright Dr, Reston, Va. 22070.

MILLER, HOWARD A, JR. R
m. to Patricia Winters; c. Coleen and Michael. Educ: Cornell Univ; Law Sch, Temple Univ. Polit. & Govt. Pos: Can, U.S. Rep, Mass; del, Rep. State Conv, 66 & 67; chmn, Franklin Planning Bd. Bus. & Prof. Pos: Past chmn, Franklin Indust. Develop. Cmn; chem. engr, dist. mgr, Rohm & Haas Co. Mil. Serv: Army Chem. Corps. Mem: Chmn, Worcester Co. Cancer Crusade, 69. Rel: Roman Catholic. Mailing Add: 27 Brushwood Hill, Franklin, Mass. 02038.

MILLER, HOWARD BENJAMIN D
b. Newark, N.J, 7/11/37; s. Morris Miller and Rose Weissman M; m. 9/8/57 to Shirley Joanne Shubin; c. Marc Louis, Alex Edward and Craig Andrew. Educ: Pepperdine Col, B.A, 57; Univ. Chicago Law Sch, J.D, 60; Order of the Coif. Polit. & Govt. Pos: Alternate del, Dem. Nat. Conv, 68. Bus. & Prof. Pos: Law clerk to Chief Justice Roger J. Traynor, Calif. State Supreme Court, San Francisco, 60-61; attorney, Los Angeles, 61-65, prof. law, Univ. South. Calif, Los Angeles, 65- Mem: State Bar Calif. Rel: Jewish. Mailing Add: 13555 Bayliss Rd, Los Angeles, Calif. 90049.

MILLER, JACK LEE R
b. Parkersburg, W.Va, 3/28/28; s. William Guy Miller and Rosetta Batten M; m. 12/28/54 to Roseanne Williams; c. Glenn and Gaylene. Educ: W.Va. Univ, A.B, 50; Univ. Mich, LL.B, 54; Sigma Chi. Polit. & Govt. Pos: Former Parkersburg City Prosecutor and Wood Co. Asst. Prosecuting Attorney, W.Va; W.Va. State Del, 60-62; W.Va. State Sen, 62-69; cmnr, W.Va. Dept. of Finance and Admin, 69- Bus. & Prof. Pos: Attorney-at-Law, 15 years. Mil. Serv: Navy, 46, PO 3/C; Air Force Officer, 50. Mem: Mich, Mo. and W.Va. Bar Asns; W.Va. Law Sch. Asn; Wood Co. Bar Asn; Am. Legion (Past Post Comdr; Asst. Chief Counselor, Am. Legion Mountaineer Boys' State); Moose; Elks; Farm Bur; Mason. Selected as Centennial Sports Great for Contribution to and Participation in High Sch. and Collegiate Wrestling, 63. Rel: United Methodist. Legal Res: 2905 Morningside Ave, Parkersburg, W.Va. 26101. Mailing Add: Commissioner, Department of Finance and Administration, State Capitol Building, Charleston, W.Va. 25305.

MILLER, JACK RICHARD R
U.S. Sen, Iowa
b. Chicago, Ill, 6/6/16; s. Forest W. Miller and Blanche M.(deceased); m. 8/1/42 to Isabelle Browning, 'Jerry'; c. Janice (Mrs. John Flanagan), Judy (Mrs. John McLaughlin), James and Jaynie. Educ: Creighton Univ, A.B, cum laude, 38; Cath. Univ, A.M, 39; Columbia Univ, LL.B, 46; State Univ. Iowa Col. Law, post-grad. study, 46; Alpha Sigma Nu; Alpha Chi Kappa. Hon. LL.D, Parsons Col, Fairfield, Iowa, 62, Creighton Univ, Omaha, Nebr, 66, Loras Col, Dubuque, Iowa, 66 and Wesleyan Col, Mount Pleasant. Polit. & Govt. Pos: Iowa State Rep, 55-56; Iowa State Sen, 57-60; U.S. Sen, Iowa, 61-; del, Rep. Nat. Conv, 68. Bus. & Prof. Pos: Attorney, Off. of Chief Counsel, Int. Revenue Serv, Wash, D.C, 47-48; asst. prof. law, Univ. Notre Dame Col. of Law, 48-49; tax lawyer, Sioux City, Iowa, 49-60. Mil. Serv: Entered as 1st Lt, Air Force, 42, released as Lt. Col, 46, after serv. in Air Force Hq, Wash, D.C, Faculty U.S. Army Command and Gen. Staff Sch, Ft. Leavenworth, Kans. and China-Burma-India ETO; Brig. Gen, Air Force Res, currently. Publ: Co-auth, Prentice-Hall Tax Ideas Serv; numerous articles on taxation in various tax and legal periodicals, farm jour, and trade publ. Mem: Iowa, Nebr. and Am. Bar Asns; life mem, Am. Law Inst; Res. Officers Asn; Rotary; Elks; Moose; Eagles; K. of C; Izaak Walton League; Am. Legion; VFW; Amvets. Rel: Catholic. Legal Res: 3718 Jackson St, Sioux City, Iowa 51104. Mailing Add: 4313 New Senate Office Building, Washington, D.C. 20510.

MILLER, JAMES R. D
Chmn, Ky. Dem. State Cent. Exec. Cmt.
b. Vicksburg, Miss, 3/31/16; m. to Tommie Melton. Educ: Pub. schs, Vicksburg, Miss. Polit. & Govt. Pos: Precinct worker and committeeman, Dem. Party, Ky; mem, Gov. Cmn. on Econ. Develop; mem. bd, Ky. Dept. of Agr; chmn, Daviess Co. Dem. Cmt. and Daviess Co. Dem. Exec. Cmt; mem, Ky. Dem. State Cent. Cmt; del, Dem. Nat. Conv, 68; chmn, Ky. Dem. State Cent. Exec. Cmt, currently. Bus. & Prof. Pos: Mgr, Rural Elec. Coop, 37- Mil. Serv: EM 1/C, Naval Res, 42-44. Mem: Owensboro C. of C.(pres, 57); Ky. C. of C.(bd, 59-61); Jr. C. of C.(pres, Owensboro Chap, 48); Mason (past master); Shrine; Boy Scouts (pres, Audubon Coun, 55-56, mem, Regional Exec. Cmt. and Nat. Bd. Dirs). Silver Beaver and Silver Antelope Awards, Boy Scouts; Silver Key, Gold Key and Distinguished Serv. Award, U.S. Jaycees; Honor Award, Future Farmers of Am. Rel: Methodist. Legal Res: 4418 Greenacres Dr, Owensboro, Ky. 42301. Mailing Add: P.O. Box 709, Owensboro, Ky. 42301.

MILLER, JAMES ROGERS, JR. R
b. Sandy Spring, Md, 6/15/31; s. James Rogers Miller and Mary Cecil M; m. 4/27/57 to Jo Anne Trice; c. James R, III, Andrew Cecil and Merrie Hamilton. Educ: Wesleyan Univ, A.B, 53; Georgetown Law Sch, LL.B, 55; Alpha Delta Phi. Polit. & Govt. Pos: V.pres, Montgomery Co. Young Rep. Club, Md, 59-60; treas, Marylanders for Mathias, 60; Md. State Del, 62-66, former chmn, Montgomery Co. Del, Md. State House of Del; mem, Legis. Coun. of Md, 63-66; co. chmn, Mathias Cong. Cmt, 64. Bus. & Prof. Pos: Partner and attorney, Miller, Miller & Canby, 56- Mem: Am, Med. and Montgomery Co. Bar Asns; pres, Rockville C. of C; v.pres, Montgomery Co. C. of C; Md. Jr. C. of C; Camp Echo Lake; March of Dimes; Heart Fund; Fair Representation Cmt. Rel: Baptist. Mailing Add: 4812 Great Oak Rd, Rockville, Md. 20853. (1967)

MILLER, JOHN D. D
b. 1932. Educ: Univ. of Ky, B.S. and LL.B. Polit. & Govt. Pos: Former Ky. State Rep. Bus. & Prof. Pos: Attorney-at-law. Mil. Serv: Ky. Nat. Guard. Rel: Unitarian. Mailing Add: 519 Griffith Ave, Owensboro, Ky. 42301.

MILLER, JOHN E. D
Ark. State Rep.
b. Melbourne, Ark, 3/2/29; s. Green H. Miller and Annie Gray M; m. 11/5/49 to Ruby Robertson; c. David, Martha and Naomi. Educ: Ark. State Col, B.S, 49. Polit. & Govt. Pos: Co. and circuit clerk, Melbourne, Ark, 52-56; Ark. State Rep, 59- Bus. & Prof. Pos: Owner, John E. Miller Ins. Agency, 59- Mem: Farm Bur; Farmers Unions; pres, Ark. Co. Clerk's Asn, 55-56; Lions; Eastern Star; Mason (32°); RAM; PTA. Rel: Baptist. Mailing Add: Melbourne, Ark. 72556.

MILLER, JOHN J. D
Clerk, N.J. State Gen. Assembly
b. Newark, N.J, 10/11/23; m. to Madeline; c. Patricia Anne. Educ: Fordham Univ, B.S. in Econ. Polit. & Govt. Pos: Pres, Irvington Dem. Club, N.J; former v.chmn, Irvington Housing Authority; Dem. Munic. chmn, Irvington; N.J. State Assemblyman, 62-63; clerk, N.J. State Gen. Assembly, currently. Bus. & Prof. Pos: Owner, John T. Miller Ins. Agency, Irvington. Mil. Serv: Navy, Aviator, World War II and Korean War; Comdr, Naval Res, heading Air Intel. Unit, Naval Air Sta, N.Y. Mem: Formerly v.pres, Irvington C. of

C; trustee, Welfare Fedn. of Newark; pres, Irvington Jaycees; Am. Legion; Elks; Rotary; Essex Co. Ins. Agents Asn. Mailing Add: 46 Ridgewood Ave, Irvington, N.J. 07111. (1967)

MILLER, JOHN JOSE D
Calif. State Assemblyman
b. Savannah, Ga, 7/28/32; s. Fred Miller, Sr, and Minnie Emond M; m. 1/24/62 to Joyce Kolheim McNair; c. Duncan McNair and Heather Joyce. Educ: Talladega Col, A.B, 54; Howard Univ. Sch. of Law, J.D, 57; Boalt Hall of Law, Univ. of Calif, Berkeley, LL.M. Cand; Alpha Phi Alpha; Int. House; class and student body pres. and Avery Speech Award, Talladega, Col, 54; W.H.C. Brown fel, Howard Univ, 55-57; Walter Perry Johnson grad. research fel. law, Univ. Calif, Berkeley, 58-59. Polit. & Govt. Pos: Mem, Berkeley Housing Adv. & Appeals Bd, Calif, 62-65; mem, Bd. of Libr. Trustees, Berkeley, 64-65; mem, Bd. of Educ, 64-66, pres, 65-66; Calif. State Assemblyman, 17th Dist, 66- Bus. & Prof. Pos: Partner, Miller & George, Oakland, Calif, 65- Publ: Assoc. ed, Howard Law J, 67. Mem: Calif. State Bar Asn; Am. Acad. of Polit. and Soc. Sci; Univ. of Calif. Men's Faculty Club; Oakland grad. Chap, Alpha Phi Alpha. Rel: Episcopal; mem. Bishop's Cmt, Diocese of Calif. Legal Res: 1187 Amador Ave, Berkeley, Calif. 94707. Mailing Add: State Capitol, Sacramento, Calif. 95814.

MILLER, JOHN L. R
N.J. State Sen.
b. Tarentum, Pa, 8/6/25; m. to Doris Worrell; c. John L, III, Marianne and Jennifer. Educ: Col. of S.Jersey; Rutgers Univ. Law Sch, LL.B, 52; assoc. ed, Rutgers Law Rev, 51-52. Polit. & Govt. Pos: N.J. State Sen, currently. Bus. & Prof. Pos: Sr. partner, Miller, Myers, Matteo & Davis, Attorneys. Mil. Serv: Navy, Pac. Theatre, hon. discharged 46. Mem: Camden Co. and N.J. State Bar Asns. Mailing Add: State House, Trenton, N.J. 08625.

MILLER, JOHN ROBERT R
Cmnr. of Agr, Ky.
b. Tompkinsville, Ky, 6/5/20; s. Harlan Ross Miller and Ina Chapman M; m. 6/30/42 to Naomi Bowman; c. Rhoda Beth, John Robert, II and Joseph Jesse. Educ: West. Ky. State Col, B.S. in Agr, 48; Univ. Ky, M.S. in Agr. Educ, 55. Polit. & Govt. Pos: Cmnr. of Agr, Ky, 68- Bus. & Prof. Pos: Voc. agr. teacher, Tompkinsville High Sch, 50-67. Mil. Serv: Entered as Pvt, Army Air Force, 42, released as Sgt, 46, after serv. in Air Force, U.S; Good Conduct Medal; plus others. Mem: Ky. and Nat. Educ. Asns; Farm Bur; Nat. Farmers Orgn; Livestock Improv. Asn. Rel: Protestant. Legal Res: Route 3, Tompkinsville, Ky. 42167. Mailing Add: 807 Leawood Dr, Frankfort, Ky. 40601.

MILLER, JOHN S. D
b. Murray, Iowa, 1921; s. Mr. and Mrs. Ge. Miller; m. 10/14/45 to Helen E. Roberts; c. Barbara, Stephen, Richard and Maryann. Educ: Storm Lake Pub. Schs. Polit. Pos: Iowa State Rep, 1966; served as 6th Dist. V.Chmn. on Polit. Educ. Bus. & Prof. Pos: Hy-Grade Food Prods; Iowa State Ins. license, represents Equitable Assurance Soc. Mil. Serv: U.S. Army, 40-45, awarded Bronze Star. Mem: Cub Scouts; Boy Scouts; Amvets; VFW; Elks; Meatcutters Union, Local 191. Rel: Church of Christ. 1967 Legal Res: 17 Freeseway Dr, Robins, Route 1, Marion, Iowa. No mailing address available. (1967)

MILLER, JOHN WILLIAM R
Mayor, Kokomo, Ind.
b. Kokomo, Ind, 2/19/12; s. Matthew Miller and Alpha Burns M; m. 10/24/38 to Frances Rachel Carter; c. Jane Ellen (Mrs. Webster), Burtis Ann and Elizabeth. Educ: Purdue Univ, B.S, 33, M.S, 38; Skull and Crescent; Sigma Alpha Epsilon; P Men Club. Polit. & Govt. Pos: City councilman, Kokomo, Ind, 45-48, mayor, 60- Bus. & Prof. Pos: Pres, Ind. Munic. League, 62-63. Mem: Mason; Scottish Rite; Shrine; Elks. Mem. and Letterman, Purdue Track Team. Rel: Methodist. Mailing Add: 1929 S. Main, Kokomo, Ind. 46901. (1967)

MILLER, JOSEPH ABRAHAM, JR. D
b. Fruitdale, Ala, 9/10/14; married. Polit. & Govt. Pos: Former Miss. State Rep. Bus. & Prof. Pos: Tel. co. owner and mgr. Mem: Lions; Rotary. Rel: Church of the Brethren. Mailing Add: Box 487, Leakesville, Miss. 39451. (1967)

MILLER, JOSEPH KERR R
b. Upper Sandusky, Ohio, 12/23/08; s. Harry C. Miller and Eva Smith M; single. Educ: Upper Sandusky High Sch, Ohio. Polit. & Govt. Pos: Mem, Ohio Rep. State Cent. Cmt, 40-69, secy-treas, 48-69; mem, City Coun, Upper Sandusky, 48-50, mem, Bd. Elec, currently. Bus. & Prof. Pos: Auto body worker and painter, Ford Garage, 29-69. Mem: Mason; A.A.S.R. Rel: Presbyterian. Mailing Add: 720 S. Seventh St, Upper Sandusky, Ohio 43351.

MILLER, KEITH HARVEY R
Gov. of Alaska
b. Seattle, Wash, 3/1/25; s. Hopkins Keith Miller and Margaret Harvey M; m. 12/26/53 to Diana Mary Doyle. Educ: Univ. Wash, B.A, 52. Polit. & Govt. Pos: Alaska State Rep, 62-66; del, Rep. Nat. Conv, 64; Secy. of State Alaska, 66-69; Gov. of Alaska, 69- Bus. & Prof. Pos: Pres, Olympia Holly Farm, Wash, 49-53 and United Collection Serv, Inc, Seattle, 54-57; homesteader, Talkeetna, Alaska, 59-62. Mil. Serv: Army Air Force, 43-45. Mem; Alaska Life Underwriters Asn; Am. Legion; Lions; Elks. Rel: Methodist. Mailing Add: Pouch A, Juneau, Alaska 99801.

MILLER, KENNETH WALTON R
Ill. State Rep.
b. Hillsdale, Ill, 10/18/12; s. Jesse Miller and Bertha Ellison M; m. 1/1/36 to Ruth E; c. Stanley A, Charles A. and Jean A. Educ: Univ. Iowa, B.A, 34, J.D, 36. Polit. & Govt. Pos: Ill. State Rep, 39th Dist, 63-64, 67-68, 69- Bus. & Prof. Pos: Sr. mem, Miller & Helm, Attorneys. Mil. Serv: Entered as Ens, Naval Res, 43, released as Lt.(jg), 45, after serv. in Pac. Theater. Mem: Am, Ill. and Whiteside Co. Bar Asns; past comdr, VFW; past pres, Sterling Rotary Club. Rel: Congregational. Legal Res: 1410 Ave. H, Sterling, Ill. 61081. Mailing Add: 405 Second Ave, Sterling, Ill. 61081.

MILLER, LEROY S. R
Iowa State Rep.
b. Clarinda, Iowa, 11/28/14; s. L.F. 'Fleet' Miller and Inez Stitt M; m. 2/14/35 to Beulah Otte; c. Marcia and Nancy. Educ: Iowa Farmers Degree. Polit. & Govt. Pos: Mem, Shenandoah City Coun; mem, Yorktown Sch. Bd; Iowa State Rep, currently. Bus. & Prof. Pos: Owner and operator, implement bus, Shenandoah, 22 years; farmer, 13 years. Mem: Farm Bur; former mem, 4-H and Future Farmers of Am; Mason; Elks; Izaak Walton League; past pres, Jr. C. of C. and Sr. C. of C. Rel: Presbyterian; Elder, deacon and trustee. Mailing Add: 305 W. Clarinda Ave, Shenandoah, Iowa 51601.

MILLER, LORNA MARIE D
V.Chmn, Chippewa Co. Dem. Party, Wis.
b. Valley City, N.Dak, 8/27/29; d. John E. Clancy and Frances Starke C; m. 8/23/58 to Anton J. Miller; c. Michelle, Renee and Shawn. Educ: Valley City State Teachers Col, N.Dak, 3 years. Polit. & Govt. Pos: Chmn, Barnes Co. Young Dem, N.Dak, 45; chmn. and nat. committeewoman, N.Dak. Young Dem, 51-56; secy-treas, Humphrey for Pres. Cmt, Eau Claire Co, Wis, 60; v.chmn, Eau Claire Co. Dem. Party, 60; secy-treas, Chippewa Co. Dem. Party, 65, v.chmn, 69-; secy-treas, McCarthy for Pres. Cmt, Chippewa Co, 68; del, Dem. Nat. Conv, 68. Bus. & Prof. Pos: Teacher, Hazen, Ypsilanti, West Fargo, N.Dak, 49-51; fieldworker, N.Dak. Farmers Union, 51-58; educ. dept. dir, Wis. Farmers Union, 58-; exec. dir, African-Latin Am. Farm Coop. Seminar, Nat. Farmers Union and Agency Int. Develop. Contract, Kamp Kenwood, Chippewa Falls, Wis, summers 66 & 67. Mem: Cmn. Voc. Opportunities for Rural Youth; North. Great Lakes Resource Develop. Cmt; Nat. Educ. Asn; Farmers Union; Am. Civil Liberties Union. Rel: Catholic. Mailing Add: 714 Park Circle, Sun Prairie, Wis. 53590.

MILLER, MARILYN RUTH D
b. N.Y.C, 11/7/32; d. Julius H. Robinson and Claire E. Eisenberg R; separated; c. Hilary Elizabeth. Educ: Columbia Univ, B.S. in English, 57. Polit. & Govt. Pos: Judicial Del, 84th Assembly Dist. Dem. Party, N.Y, 61-67, Leader, 66-; mem, Bronx Co. Dem. Cmt, 61-68; Del, N.Y. State Dem. Conv, 66; Alternate Del, Dem. Nat. Conv, 68; Asst. to Borough Pres, Bronx, 68- Bus. & Prof. Pos: Teacher, N.Y.C. Pub. Sch. Syst, 58-62; Asst. teacher, Marble Hill Nursery Sch, 65-68. Mem: Benjamin Franklin Reform Dem. Club; League of Women Voters; Intergroup. Volunteer Serv. Award, Leake & Watts Children's Home. Rel: Jewish. Mailing Add: 3020 Johnson Ave, Bronx, N.Y. 10467.

MILLER, MARVIN EUGENE R
Pa. State Rep.
b. Lime Rock, Pa, 5/28/27; s. Roy Kling Miller and Emma Whitmyer M; m. 7/7/45 to Arlene Louise Geibe; c. Marvin E, Jr. and Lorrie L. Polit. & Govt. Pos: Dir, Lancaster Co. Young Rep, Pa, 61-62; mem, Pa. House Campaign Cmt, 64 & 66; research aide and writer, Rep. Floor Leader Staff, Pa. House of Rep, 66; Pa. State Rep, 67- Bus. & Prof. Pos: Sports ed. and asst. city ed, Intelligencer J, 46-58; ed, Lititz Record-Express, 58-60; reporter and asst. ed, Lancaster New Era, 60-66; ed, Octorara Newspapers, 66- Mil. Serv: Pvt, Marine Corps, 45, serv. in Recruit Depot, Parris Island. Mem: Pa. Legis. Correspondents Asn; Woodridge Swim Club; Quarterback Club of Lancaster; Lancaster Sportswriters & Broadcasters Asn; Citizens for Decent Literature, Lancaster. Winner, six statewide prizes in newspaper reporting, Pa. Newspaper Publishers Asn. Rel: Moravian Church. Mailing Add: 501 Valley Rd, Lancaster, Pa. 17601.

MILLER, MARY ELLEN R
b. Tulsa, Okla; d. Howard Malcolm Sivadon and Elsie Clark S; m. 12/10/45 to Raymond Joe Miller; c. William Joe and Anne Marie. Educ: Univ. Tulsa, 41-44; Univ. Ala. Exten, 56-58. Polit. & Govt. Pos: Secy, Tulsa Co. Young Rep. Club, Okla, 42-44; secy, Eisenhower-Nixon Hq, Mobile, Ala, 56; del, Rep. Nat. Conv, 60 & 64; mgr, Nixon-Lodge Hq, Mobile, 60; charter pres, Mobile Rep. Women's Club, 60; mgr, McNally for Mayor, 61; chmn, First South. Regional Rep. Women's Conf, 61; charter pres, Ala. Fedn. of Rep. Women, 62; dir, Women's Activities, Martin for Senate, 62; del, Biennial Conv. Nat. Fedn. Rep. Women, 62 & 64; field representative, Rep. Nat. Cmt, 62-64; campaign mgr, Edwards for Cong, First Dist, Ala, 64; educ. dir, Tulsa Co. Rep. Party, Okla, 66-68; spec. asst. to chmn, Nat. Rep. Cong. Cmt, 67- Bus. & Prof. Pos: Private secy. to supt, Phillips Petroleum Co, Venezuela, S.Am, 46-54; mgr, Albert Plan, Mobile, Ala, 55-62; prin. and teacher, Perry Christian Sch, Marion, 65-66. Publ: Handbook for Alabama Republican Women, 62 & 66. Mem: Bus. and Prfnl. Women's Clubs; Am. Bus. Women; Southwest. Art Asn; VFW Auxiliary; Tulsa Philharmonic Soc, Inc. State of Miss. Award for Outstanding Serv. in Creating a Two Party Syst, 63; Annual Award to Outstanding Women's Rep. Club of Ala. Named the Mary Ellen Miller Award in 66. Rel: Protestant. Legal Res: 4562 E. 39th St, Tulsa, Okla. 74135. Mailing Add: 3000 Connecticut Ave. N.W, Apt. 216, Washington, D.C. 20008.

MILLER, MAYNE WILLIAMS D
b. Johnson City, Tenn, 10/16/23; s. Robert Rush Miller and Gertrude Williams M; m. 7/17/54 to Mariko Terasaki; c. Robert Rush, Timothy, Mayne Cole and Terence Haynes. Educ: Vanderbilt Univ, LL.B, 48. Polit. & Govt. Pos: Chmn, Natrona Co. Dem. Cent. Cmt, Wyo, 60 & 68-69; exec. secy, Wyo. Dem. State Cent. Cmt, 61, 62 & 63; del, Dem. Nat. Conv, 64, alternate del, 68. Bus. & Prof. Pos: Partner, Kefauver, Duggan & Miller, Attorneys-at-Law, Chattanooga, Tenn, 50-53; attorney-at-law, Casper, Wyo, currently; chmn. bd, West. Nat. Bank of Casper, 67-69. Mil. Serv: Entered as Pvt, Army, 42, released as 1st Lt, 56, after serv. in Judge Adv. Gen. Corps. Mem: Natrona Co, State of Wyo. and Am. Bar Asns; Am. Trial Lawyers Asn; Lawyer-Pilots Asn. Rel: Unitarian. Legal Res: 111 W. 14th, Casper, Wyo. 82601. Mailing Add: 123 S. Center, Casper, Wyo. 82601.

MILLER, MELVIN M. R
b. Cleveland, Wis, 10/24/26; s. Amos William Miller and Matilda Neuhaus M; m. 4/26/58 to Linda Jane Kik; c. Duane A, Jay M, Timothy A. and Andrea Jane. Educ: Univ. Wis, B.S, 51, Law Sch, LL.B, 53. Polit. & Govt. Pos: Counsel, House Cmt. on Small Bus, 53-54; attorney-adv, Dept. Health, Educ. & Welfare, 55-56; admin. asst. to U.S. Rep. Glenard P. Lipscomb, Calif, 57 minority clerk, House Admin. Cmt, 69- Mil. Serv: Entered as A/S, Navy, 45, released as Seaman 2/C, 46. Mem: Nat. Lawyers Club. Rel: Presbyterian. Mailing Add: 6206 Kellogg Dr, McLean, Va. 22101.

MILLER, MIDGE LEEPER D
Mem, Nat. Steering Cmt, New Dem. Coalition
b. Morgantown, W.Va, 3/8/22; d. Lorimer Victor Cavins and Neva Adams

C; m. 11/5/44 to H. Dean Leeper, wid. 9/26/55; m. 5/12/63 to Edward Ernst Miller; c. Steven Lloyd, David Dean, Linda Jean and Kenneth Chandran Leeper and Mark Finley, Sterling Davey, Jeffrey Scoon, Nancy Jean and Randall Conrad Miller. Educ: Univ. Mich, B.S, 44; Yale Divinity Sch, audit, 54-57; Univ. Wis, Madison, M.A, 62. Polit. & Govt. Pos: Corresponding secy, Dane Co. Dem. Party, Wis, 1 year, v.chmn, 66-67; dist. rep, West Madison Dem. Party, 3 years; del, Dem. Nat. Conv, 68 and mem. platform cmt; mem, Wis. State Steering Cmt, McCarthy Campaign, 68; mem, Nat. Steering Cmt, New Dem. Coalition, currently. Bus. & Prof. Pos: Prog. dir, YWCA, Conn. and Mich, 44-46; asst. dean in letters and sci, Univ. Wis, 60-66 and coordinator of univ. relig. activities, 66-68. Mem: YWCA. Rel: Methodist. Mailing Add: 1937 Arlington Place, Madison, Wis. 53705.

MILLER, MITCH D
Ga. State Rep.
b. Mentone, Ala, 10/4/30; s. Henry Thomas Miller and Ruthie Jane M; m. 2/19/50 to Minnie Lyn Martin; c. Charles Martin and Myron Baynor. Educ: Univ. Ga, 58-59; Ohio State Univ, 62. Polit. & Govt. Pos: Ga. State Rep, 67- Bus. & Prof. Pos: Logistics mgt, U.S. Air Force, 48-63; regional mkt. mgr, Emerson Elec. Co, 63-; mgt. and mkt. consult, self-employed, 63- Mem: Am. Legion; Moose; Mason; Scottish Rite; Shrine. Rel: Methodist. Mailing Add: 3859 Mathis St, Macon, Ga. 31206.

MILLER, NEIL J. D
Idaho State Rep.
b. Blackfoot, Idaho, 10/28/29; s. Earl J. Miller and Nora Marlow M; m. 6/19/49 to Mary Stott; c. Debra (Mrs. Orchard), John, Jay, Ann and Layne. Educ: Idaho State Univ, 1 year; Utah State Univ, 1 year. Polit. & Govt. Pos: Idaho State Rep, Dist. 27, 66- Bus. & Prof. Pos: Owner, Miller Honey Co. 49- and Miller Transportation Co, 64-67. Mem: Idaho Honey Producers Asn.(pres, 2 terms); Rotary; Elks. Rel: Latter-day Saint. Mailing Add: 61 N. Shilling Ave, Blackfoot, Idaho 83221.

MILLER, NORMAN LEE D
Asst. Attorney Gen, Mich.
b. Detroit, Mich, 1/31/36; s. Anthony J. Miller and Irene Orlowski M; m. 6/30/62 to Carol Andrea Rouse; c. Norman L, Jr. and Kristina Jeanne. Educ: Univ. Mich, A.B, 57, Law Sch, LL.B, 60; v.pres, Nat. Newman Apostolate; Sigma Nu; Phi Delta Phi; Gilbert & Sullivan Soc. Polit. & Govt. Pos: Mem, First Cong. Dem. Orgn, Mich, 61-64; mem. exec. bd, 14th Cong. Dem. Orgn; Asst. Attorney Gen, Mich, 63-; del, Dem. Nat. Conv, 64. Bus. & Prof. Pos: Sr. partner, Paruk & Miller, Attorneys, 62-; asst. dean, asst. prof. of law and dir. urban law prog, Univ. Detroit Sch. of Law, 65- Publ: 'Urban Law,' Univ. Calif. Law Rev, summer 66. Mem: State Bar of Mich; Detroit and Am. Bar Asns; Am. Asn. of Law Sch. Profs; The Players of Detroit. Rel: Roman Catholic. Legal Res: 1653 Newcastle Rd, Grosse Pointe Woods, Mich. 48236. Mailing Add: 1100 Washington Blvd. Bldg, Detroit, Mich. 48226.

MILLER, PETER J. R
Ill. State Rep.
b. June 16, 1909; c. five. Educ: Ill. Mil. Col, Abington; Northwest. Univ. Polit. & Govt. Pos: Former park supvr, Chicago, Ill, 11 years; former secy, Ill. State Athletic Cmn, 5 years; Ill. State Sen, 2 terms; Ill. State Rep, 56-; mem, Ill. State Rep. Cmt, currently; del, Rep. Nat. Conv, 68. Bus. & Prof. Pos: Former paymaster, Sanit. Dist, Chicago; former phys. educ. teacher, parochial grammar schs; Olympic skating coach, 40 & 48. Mem: Dir. spec. events, Cath. Youth Orgn, 17 years; past pres, Amateur Skating Unions of U.S. Legal Res: 1840 N. Rutherford Ave, Chicago, Ill. 60635. Mailing Add: 5719 W. Fullerton, Chicago, Ill. 60644. (1967)

MILLER, RALPH ROSS D
La. State Rep.
b. Norco, La, 4/27/34; s. Homer F. Miller, Sr. and Emma Cambre M; m. 7/18/59 to Anne M. Blanchard; c. Ross A, Gregory A, Maria C. and Maureen J. Educ: La. State Univ, B.S, 56, J.D. and LL.B, 58; Gamma Eta Gamma; Pi Tau Pi; Newman Club. Polit. & Govt. Pos: La. State Rep, Third Dist, St. Charles, St. John and St. James Parish, 68- Bus. & Prof. Pos: Attorney at Law, 59- Mil. Serv: Entered as Pvt, Army, 61, released as S/Sgt, 62, after serv. in 159th Evacuation Hosp, Ft. Sill, Okla; Army Commendation Medal; La. Cross. Mem: Am, La. State and Jefferson Bar Asns; 29th Judicial Dist. Bar Asn.(past pres); Lions; K. of C; Kiwanis; Jaycees. Rel: Roman Catholic. Legal Res: 626 Spruce St, Norco, La. 70079. Mailing Add: P.O. Box 190, Norco, La. 70079.

MILLER, ROBERT CHARLES R
State Field Dir, Rep. Party of Wis.
b. Keego Harbor, Mich, 12/27/27; s. Clinton B. Miller, Sr.(deceased) and Marguerite Sievers M; m. 2/12/49 to Mary Lou Horsley; c. Judith Ann, Todd Emerson and Robert C, Jr. Educ: Pontiac Sr. High, Mich, grad, 46. Polit. & Govt. Pos: Chief investr. for Prosecuting Attorney, Oakland Co, Mich, 51-56; precinct del, Mich. State Rep. Conv, 52-58; v.pres, Oakland Co. Lincoln Rep. Club, 54-56; pres, Pontiac Rep. Club, 56; Rep. nominee for Mich. State Rep, 56; acting postmaster, Pontiac, Mich, 58-60; exec. dir, Capitol Hill Asn. and Club, D.C, 62 & 63; exec. secy, Eisenhower 74th Birthday Dinner, 63; exec. dir, D.C. Rep. Cmt, 63-65; state field dir, Rep. Party of Wis, 65-; Rep. committeeman, Precinct One, Ward Three, Madison, Wis, 67- Bus. & Prof. Pos: Radio announcer, WCAR, Pontiac, Mich, 43-46, WTAC, Flint, 48-50; police officer, Pontiac Police Dept, 50-51; sales mgr, Cadillac-Oldsmobile Dealer, Pontiac, 56-62. Mil. Serv: Entered as A/S, Navy Aviation, 46, released as Seaman 1/C, AMM, 48, after serv. in Basic Training Squadron, Pensacola Air Base and Corey Field, Fla, 47-48; Am. Theatre Ribbon and Victory Medal, World War II. Mem: Elks, Pontiac, Mich; Madison Press Club, Wis; East Side Bus. Men's Asn, Madison. Rel: Methodist. Mailing Add: 5217 Queensbridge Rd, Madison, Wis. 53714.

MILLER, ROBERT EVANS D
b. Glover's Gap, W.Va, 1/18/08; s. Charles Elmer Miller and Nettie Morris Wells M; div; c. Charles Evans, George Raymond and Carolyn Jane (Mrs. Baird). Educ: Fairmont High Sch, W.Va, grad, 25; W.Va. Univ, 25-26; Registered Pharmacist, Ariz, 28; La Salle Extension, 30-33. Polit. & Govt. Pos: State drug inspector, Ariz, 46; Clerk of Superior Court, Maricopa Co, 62-66; nominee for U.S. Rep, Ariz, 68. Bus. & Prof. Pos: Apprentice in pharm, Stidger & Barry, W.Va, 21-23; owner and operator retail pharmacies, Gila Bend, Ariz, 33-37 and Phoenix, 46-62. Mil. Serv: Entered as Pvt, Army, 42, released as T/Sgt, 45, after serv. in Med. Dept. Publ: Ed, 'Arizona Sentinal,' Phoenix, 49; ed. and publisher, 'The Maverick,' Ariz. Weekly, 49-51. Mem: Secy, Ariz. Pharmacist's Guild (Phoenix Cent. Labor Coun, 41); v.comdr, Am. Legion Post 75, Phoenix; charter mem, Glendale Kiwanis. Nominated Man of Year, Phoenix, 48. Rel: University of Life Church. Mailing Add: 2202 E. Dobbins, Phoenix, Ariz. 85040.

MILLER, ROBERT GORDON R
City Councilman, San Jose, Calif.
b. Los Angeles, Calif, 9/19/37; s. Leslie Miller and Ethel Morningstar M; m. 5/31/58 to Vivian Marie Teresi; c. John Evers, Michéle Marie and Michael Scott. Educ: San Jose State Col, 58; Delta Upsilon. Polit. & Govt. Pos: City councilman, San Jose, Calif, 65-, mem, Personnel and Streets and Traffic Cmts, chmn, Cmt. on Pub. Health, Safety and Emergency Serv. and Solid Waste Disposal Cmt, coun. rep, Sanit. Dist. 4 Adv. Bd, coun. liaison to Adv. Bd. Pub. Health and San Jose City Col. Dist, coun. rep. to mem. Exec. Cmt. and chmn. Goals and Orgn. Cmt; v.pres, Bay Area Govt, 66, pres, 67; v.mayor, San Jose, 66-68. Bus. & Prof. Pos: Pres, C.D.S, Inc, contract drapery serv, San Jose, Calif, 59-; city operations mgr, Kaiser Engrs, 68- Mem: Life mem, San Jose Jr. C. of C, dir, 60-61, v.pres, 62-63, pres, 63-64; chmn, Calif. State Jr. C. of C, 61, dir, 61-62; dir, Gr. San Jose C. of C, 63-64, co-chmn, Finance Cmt, 64-65; pres, Santa Clara Co. Dent. Health Asn, 63-65; coun, San Jose YMCA, 64-65; Rotary; membership capt, Coord. Arts Coun, 65; patron mem, San Jose Light Opera Asn, 63-65 and San Jose Symphony Asn, 64-65; dir, Metro A of San Jose, 65, Speakers Bur. Chmn, 64; Better Bus. Bur; dir, San Jose Concert Series Adv. Bd, 64; Sen, Jr. Chamber Int; Holy Names Soc; Master Plan Adv. Cmt, San Jose Jr. Col. Dist. Bd, 64-65; v.chmn, Commun. Theater Bonds Drive, 64; sponsor, Boys' City Boys' Club, 65; Prfnl. Men's Sodality Santa Clara, 65; Downtown San Jose Lay Apostolate, 65. Achievements: Selected Outstanding mem, San Jose Jr. C. of C, 60-62; Outstanding State Dir, Calif. Jr. C. of C, 62; one of Outstanding Young Men of Am, 64; San Jose's Outstanding Young Man of Year, 64; Distinguished Citizen of San Jose, 65; grand juror, Santa Clara Co. Grand Jury, 65. Rel: Roman Catholic. Legal Res: 3394 Beacon Lane, San Jose, Calif. 95124. Mailing Add: 1775 South First St, San Jose, Calif. 95112.

MILLER, ROBERT JOHN R
Dep. Co. Clerk, San Diego Co, Calif.
b. High River, Alta, Can, 6/29/14; s. William Orson Miller and Nell Glenn Fletcher M; m. 12/31/37 to Mary Elizabeth Mickelson; c. Fletcher John. Educ: Interstate Bus. Col, 33-34; N.Dak. State Univ, 32; Balboa Univ. Law Sch, LL.B, 51 and pres, Student Body. Polit. & Govt. Pos: Dep. co. clerk, San Diego Co, Calif, 59-; dep. clerk, Superior Court of Calif, 59-; mem, Calif. Rep. State Cent. Cmt, 67-; cand. for bd. of supvr, First Dist, San Diego Co, 68. Bus. & Prof. Pos: CPA, Calif, 46- Mil. Serv: Entered as Pvt, Marine Corps Res, 43, released as Cpl, 46, after serv. in MAG 32, First Marine Air Wing, Philippine Islands and China, 44-46; Good Conduct Medal. Mem: Mason; life mem. and comdr, Amvets of World War II, Post 35, San Diego, Calif; Oper. Hospitality Cmt. for For. Officers; YMCA; charter mem, Ocean Beach Town Coun. Inc; PTA; pres, San Diego Co. Employees Asn. and Superior Court Clerks Asn. of the State of Calif; spec. dep. sheriff, San Diego. Rel: Lutheran; Past pres, First Lutheran Church. Mailing Add: 4612 Coronado Ave, San Diego, Calif. 92107.

MILLER, ROBERT LOUIS R
Ky. State Rep.
b. Louisville, Ky, 12/22/33; s. Louis Beeler Miller and Kathryn Mather M; m. 12/1/64 to Ellen Harvin; c. Virginia Lavern. Educ: Ky. Sch. Embalming, 62; Univ. Louisville, 62-63. Polit. & Govt. Pos: Ky. State Rep, 37th Legis. Dist, 67- Bus. & Prof. Pos: Secy-treas, Louis B. Miller & Son Funeral Home, Inc, 54- Mil. Serv: Entered as Pvt, Marines, 51, released as Pfc, 54 after serv. in H Co, Third Bn, Eighth Marines, Second Marine Div, 51-54. Mem: Cent. Dist. Funeral Dirs. Asn. (pres-secy-treas, 66-69); Funeral Dirs. Asn. of Falls Cities (dir, 68-); F&AM; RAM; Optimists. Rel: Southern Baptist. Mailing Add: 410 Christopher Place, Louisville, Ky. 40214.

MILLER, RODERICK LUKE R
Mem, La. Rep. State Cent. Cmt.
b. Reddell, La, 10/20/24; s. Cleophas Mark Miller and Isabelle Michot M; m. 6/19/47 to Clemencia Clotworthy; c. Thomas J, Kenneth G, John G, Jeanine Marie, Julie Ann, Emile F, Carmel T. and Normand C. Educ: Univ. Southwest. La, B.A, 47; Loyola Univ. of the South, LL.B. and J.D, 50; Pi Gamma Mu; Phi Lambda Beta; Sigma Alpha Sigma; Sigma Pi; LeCercle Francais; St. Thomas More Law Club; Inter-Fraternity Coun.(secy). Polit. & Govt. Pos: La. State Rep, Lafayette Parish, 66-68; mem, La. Rep. State Cent. Cmt, 19th Representative Dist, 67-; alternate del, Rep. Nat. Conv, 68. Mil. Serv: Entered as Pvt, Army Air Corps, 43, released as 2nd Lt, 46, after serv. in Am. Theater, recalled as 2nd Lt, Air Force, 51, released as 1st Lt, 52, after serv. in 358th Bombardment Squadron, Strategic Air Command, Am. Theater. Mem: Lafayette Bar Asn.(secy-treas, 50's); La. State and Am. Bar Asns; K. of C.(4°); Kiwanis; Am. Legion; Farm Bur; Boy Scouts (Evangeline Area Coun). Lafayette's Young Man of the Year, Jaycees Distinguished Serv. Award, 56; Boy Scouts Red Hat with Green Feather. Rel: Roman Catholic. Legal Res: 311 N. Sterling St, Lafayette, La. 70501. Mailing Add: P.O. Box 2069, Lafayette, La. 70501.

MILLER, ROSS MATTHEW, JR. D
City Councilman, Compton, Calif.
b. Boston, Mass, 2/19/28; s. Ross M. Miller and Beatrice Burson M; m. 8/11/62 to Iris Rodgers; c. Cheryl and Adrienne. Educ: Howard Univ, B.S, 47, M.D, 51; Alpha Phi Alpha. Polit. & Govt. Pos: Park and recreation cmnr, Compton, Calif, 62; Trustee, Compton High Sch, 65; city councilman, Compton, 67-; del, Dem. Nat. Conv, 68. Bus. & Prof. Pos: Instr. surg, Univ. Calif, Los Angeles and Harbor Hosp, 66-; chief of staff, Dominguez Valley Hosp, 66-; surg. chmn, Nat. Med. Asn, 67- Mil. Serv: Entered as Lt.(jg), U.S. Pub. Health Serv, 54, released as Lt, 56, after serv. at Nat. Cancer Inst, Bethesda, Md. Publ: 'Wound Seeding as the Cause of Failure in Surgical Treatment of Cancer', J. Nat. Cancer Inst, 56. Mem: Nat, Am, Calif. and Los Angeles Co.

Med. Asns; Charles R. Drew Med. Soc; fel. Am. Col. Surgeons; fel. Int. Col. Surgeons; dipl. Am. Bd. Surg. Man of the Year Award, Compton Negro Businessmen and Prfnl. Asn. Rel: Baptist. Mailing Add: 1319 Atlantic Dr, Compton, Calif. 90220.

MILLER, ROY A. R
Iowa State Rep.
b. 8/26/06; married; c. Three daughters. Educ: Cedar Rapids Bus. Col. Polit. & Govt. Pos: Past pres, Earlville Sch. Bd, Iowa; city councilman; Iowa State Rep, 63-65 & 67- Bus. & Prof. Pos: Former Earlville fire chief; former operator, farm implement and motor truck bus; farm owner. Mem: Past pres, Rotary. Rel: Methodist; Mem, Church Bd. Mailing Add: 713 S. Main, Monticello, Iowa 52310. (1967)

MILLER, S. LEE R
Chmn, Longmeadow Rep. Town Cmt, Mass.
b. Schenectady, N.Y, 9/18/32; s. Sidney E. Miller and Huldah C. Blossey M; m. to Joan A. Martinez; c. Julie Ann, Carolyn Jean and Tracy Joan. Educ: Yale Univ, B.A, 54; Univ. of Va. Law Sch, LL.B, 57; Sigma Nu Phi. Polit. & Govt. Pos: Chmn, Longmeadow Rep. Town Cmt, Mass, 67-; chmn, Hampden Co. Rep. Cmts, 69. Bus. & Prof. Pos: Mem. staff, trust dept, First Nat. Bank, St. Petersburg, Fla, 57-58; attorney, law dept, Aetna Life Affiliated Co, Hartford, Conn, 59-60; trust officer, trust dept, Third Nat. Bank of Hampden Co, Springfield, Mass, 60- Mem: Va. State Bar; Fla. State Bar; Conn. Bar Asn; Am. Bar Asn; dir. Springfield Chap, Am. Red Cross; asst. treas, Chestnut Knoll; treas, Hampden-Berkshire Tuberc. and Respiratory Disease Asn, 68-; pres, Estate Planning Coun. of Hampden 69; Exchange Club of Springfield; pres, Springfield Chap, Mass. Soc. for the Prev. of Cruelty to Children, 68-, v.pres, Pioneer Valley Dist, 69; endowment cmt, Metrop. Springfield Y.M.C.A, corporator, Pioneer Valley United Fund, Inc; pres, Springfield Jr. C. of C, 62; regional chmn, U.S. Jr. C. of C, 63; pres, Univ. Club of Springfield, 66-67; corporator, Wesson Maternity Hosp. Admitted to practice before the U.S. Supreme Court. Mailing Add: 33 Ellington St, Longmeadow, Mass. 01106.

MILLER, SCOTT, JR. R
Ky. State Sen.
b. 1927. Educ: Univ. of Louisville Law Sch, LL.B. Polit. & Govt. Pos: Mem, Young Rep. Club; Ky. State Sen, 58-; chmn, Rep. Caucus, 62. Bus. & Prof. Pos: Attorney-at-law. Rel: Episcopal. Mailing Add: 26 Rio Vista Dr, Louisville, Ky. 40207. (1967)

MILLER, TERRY R
Alaska State Sen.
b. San Francisco, Calif, 11/10/42; s. Conrad B. Miller and Nellie W. Wright M; m. 7/20/63 to Terry L. Niemann. Educ: Univ. Alaska, B.A, 65; Alpha Kappa Psi; Alpha Phi Omega. Polit. & Govt. Pos: North Pole City Coun, Alaska, 63-66; assemblyman, Fairbanks North Star Borough, 63-66, presiding officer of assembly, 64-66; Alaska State Rep, 66-68; Alaska State Sen, 69- Bus. & Prof. Pos: Businessman. Mailing Add: Box 118, North Pole, Alaska 99705.

MILLER, THOMAS ROWLAND D
Treas, Jefferson Co. Dem. Cmt, Ky.
b. Louisville, Ky, 5/6/06; s. Thomas Richard Miller and Maud Isaacs M; m. 7/8/35 to Barbara Simmons. Educ: Univ. Chicago, 23-25; Univ. Louisville, 65-66. Polit. & Govt. Pos: Dem. precinct capt, 60-68; Dem. ward man, 64-68; cand. for alderman, Louisville, Ky, 65; admin. asst. to cmnr. of highways, 66-67; del, Dem. Nat. Conv, 68; treas, Jefferson Co. Dem. Cmt, Ky, 68- Bus. & Prof. Pos: Restaurateur, Miller's Dairy Bar, Louisville, Ky, 39-45, Miller's Grill, 46-64 and Teeken's Bakery, 54-65; real estate salesman, McGill & McGill, 64-66; mgr, Alan Nash, Realtor, 68-69. Mil. Serv: Entered as Pvt, Army, 43, released as Cpl, 46, after serv. in 604th Ord. Ammunition, Mediterranean Theatre, 44-46; Bronze Star. Mem: Assoc. mem, Louisville Bd. of Realtors; Cath. Bus. and Prof. Men's Club; Esquire Club; NAACP; YMCA. Ky. Col. Rel: Catholic. Mailing Add: 215 N. 46th St, Louisville, Ky. 40212.

MILLER, THOMAS WOODNUTT R
b. Wilmington, Del, 6/26/86; s. Charles Robert Miller and Abigail Morgan Woodnutt M; m. 1913 to Katherin Tallman (deceased 45); c. Thomas L. and Mrs. George P. Bissell, Jr; m. 1946 to Eleanor Taylor. Educ: Sheffield Sci. Sch, Yale Univ, Ph.B, 08; Delta Phi (nat. pres, 16-17); St. Elmo Club, New Haven. Polit. & Govt. Pos: Secy. State, Del, 13-15; U.S. Rep, Del, 15-17; chmn, Del. State Coun. Defense, 17; Alien Property Custodian, 21-25; mem, Am. Battle Monuments Cmn, 23-26; founder, Nev. State Park Syst, 35, chmn, Nev. State Park Cmn, 35-37, 52-59 & 67-; supvr, U.S. Grazing Serv, Nev. and Calif, 36-42; chmn, Nev. State Coun. Defense, 42-46; staff field rep, U.S. Vet. Employ. Serv. for Fourteen West. States, 46-57; mem, Nev. Coun. Civil Defense, 51-59; chmn, Park & Hort. Cmn, Reno, 63-66, mem, Recreation and Park Cmn, 66- Bus. & Prof. Pos: Rolling mill foreman, Bethlehem Steel Co, S.Bethlehem, Pa, 08-09; ranching and mining, Nev, many years. Mil. Serv: Plattsburg Mil. Training Camp, N.Y, 15; entered as Pvt, Inf, 17, released as Lt. Col, 19, after serv. in First Del. Inf. and 114th Inf, 29th Div, Ft. McClelland, Ala, as Ord. and Machine Officer, 79th Div, A.E.F, one year, France, Meuse-Argonne Offensive, Lt. Col, Res, 19-21, serv. as Exec. Officer 315th Inf; cited in div. orders, by Commanding Gen. 79th Div, for gallantry in action under enemy fire and by Gen. Pershing for especially meritorious serv. with the 79th Div, France; Purple Heart. Publ: Contrib, various conserv. publ. Mem: Am. Legion (pres, Founders of Am. Legion, presided over caucus, Paris, 15-17 & 19, past Nat. Comdr, Dept. Comdr. of two states and Nat. Exec. Committeeman from both states, sr. mem. cmt); pres, FIDAC, 24-25; F&AM; Reno Consistory; Kerak Temple of the Shrine; Nat. Sojourners; Univ. Club Chicago; Reno Press Club; Hist. Soc. Del. and Nev; Navy League U.S; Am. Red Cross (bd. chmn, Sierra Nev. Chap, 68-69); Desert Coun. and many Mil. and Civic Orgn. Rel: Episcopal; mem, Episcopal Found. Nev, 54-58, Vestry, Jr. Warden and Sr. Warden, mem. Bishop's Exec. Coun, 63-67, Trinity Church. Mailing Add: 1419 S. Arlington Ave, Reno, Nev. 89502.

MILLER, VICTOR A. D
b. St. Nazianz, Wis, 8/26/16; s. John Miller and Francis Hornick M; m. 6/18/41 to Isabel Grimm; c. John, Mary, Jane, Meg and Mark. Educ: Valders High Sch; Marquette Univ. Polit. & Govt. Pos: Del, Dem. Nat. Conv, Roosevelt, Truman, Stevenson and Kennedy; chmn, Manitowoc Co. Dem. Party, Wis, 47-57; mem, Citizen's for Kennedy, Vol. Dem. Cmt. and Campaign Cmt, Dem. Party. Bus. & Prof. Pos: Officer, John Miller Supply Co, 40; lawyer, 40-; chmn. tax sect, Wis. Bar Asn, 65. Mem: Am. and Wis. Bar Asns; Manitowoc Co. Bar Asn.(pres, 66); Lions (dist. gov, 58); Elks; K. of C. (mem, exec. cmt, Nat. Coun. Cath. Men, 66). Oratorio Pro-Dei Award; Holy Name Nat. Serv. Award. Rel: Catholic. Mailing Add: St. Nazianz, Wis. 54232.

MILLER, WARD MacLAUGHLIN R
b. Portsmouth, Ohio, 11/29/02; s. Henry Ward Miller and Annis MacLaughlin M; m. 7/23/32 to Marian Elizabeth Dillon; c. Ward MacLaughlin, Jr, Whitney Dillon, Henry James, Marian W, Annis Bennett (Mrs. Edward C. Reinkoester, II and Rosamond (Mrs. Jerome Dean French). Educ: Ohio State Univ, A.B; Harvard Univ, A.M; Phi Gamma Delta; Sigma Delta Psi; Foreign Policy Asn, Harvard Univ. Polit. & Govt. Pos: Mem, Ohio State Bd. of Educ, 55-; U.S. Rep, 6th Dist, Ohio, 60-61. Prof. Pos: Pres, Portsmouth Real Estate Bd, Ohio, five separate terms; dir, Ohio Asn. of Real Estate Bds, five separate terms and trustee, three separate terms. Mem: Royal Inst. of Philos, London, Eng; Modern Language Asn; Am. Asn. for the Adv. of Sci; Rel: Presbyterian. Mailing Add: Beechwood Heights, Portsmouth, Ohio 45662. (1967)

MILLER, WESTON WALTERS R
Chmn, Adams Co. Rep. Cent. Cmt, Wash.
b. Ritzville, Wash, 3/17/10; s. Weston Otis Miller and Elizabeth Maude Walters M; m. 11/21/42 to Erma Lula Strate; c. Richard Walters and Brian Henry. Mem, Honor Soc, Col. of Probate Counsel. Polit. & Govt. Pos: Prosecuting attorney, Adams Co, Wash, 39-43; chmn, Adams Co. Rep. Cent. Cmt, Wash, 58- Mil. Serv: Entered as Lt.(jg), Naval Res, 42, released as Lt. Comdr, after serv. in Pac. Theater. Mem: Wash. State and Am. Bar Asns; pres, C. of C; past-post comdr, Am. Legion; Odd Fellows; F&AM. Rel: Methodist. Legal Res: 607 S. Adams, Ritzville, Wash. 99169. Mailing Add: Box 497, Ritzville, Wash. 99169.

MILLER, WILLIAM EDWARD R
b. Lockport, N.Y, 3/22/14; s. Edward J. Miller and Elizabeth Hinch M; m. 2/26/43 to Stephanie Wagner; c. Elizabeth Ann, Mary Karen, William E, Jr, and Stephanie Catherine. Educ: Notre Dame Univ, B.A, 35; Alban Law Sch, LL.B, 38. Polit. & Govt. Pos: Asst. dist. attorney, Niagara Co, N.Y, 46-49, dist. attorney, 49-51; U.S. Rep, N.Y, 51-64; former chmn, Rep. Nat. Cmt. and Cong. Campaign Cmt; cand for Vice President, U.S, 64; del, Rep. Nat. Conv, 68. Bus. & Prof. Pos: Attorney-at-law, 39- Mil. Serv: Entered as Pvt, Army, 42, released as 1st Lt, 46. Mem: VFW; Elks; Tuscarora Club of Lockport; Lockport Town and Country Club; Buffalo Country Club. Hobby: Golf. Rel: Catholic. Legal Res: 418 Willow St, Lockport, N.Y. 14094. Mailing Add: 1500 Liberty Bank Bldg, Buffalo, N.Y. 14202.

MILLER, WILLIAM ERNEST R
b. Johnson City, Tenn, 2/3/08; s. Samuel Ernest Miller and Grace Barlow M; m. 12/1/34 to Carolyn Gies; c. Mrs. Charles E. Wright, Jr. Educ: Univ. Tenn, A.B, 30, hon. J.D, 68; Yale Law Sch, LL.B, 33; Phi Beta Kappa; Order of the Coif; Scabbard and Blade; Phi Alpha Delta; Sigma Alpha Epsilon. Polit. & Govt. Pos: Del, Constitutional Conv. of Tenn, 33; presidential elector, 40; chancellor, First Chancery Div. of Tenn; chief judge, U.S. Dist. Court, Middle Dist. of Tenn, 55-; mem, Tenn. Adv. Coun. on Higher Educ. Act of 1966. Bus. & Prof. Pos: Lectr. law, Vanderbilt Law Sch; mem, Cox, Epps, Miller & Weller, Law Firm, Johnson City, Tenn, 33-55. Mil. Serv: Entered as 1st Lt, Army Air Force, 42, released as Maj, 45; Commendation award. Publ: Contrib. to law reviews. Mem: Admitted to Tenn. Bar, 33; Am, Tenn. and Nashville Bar Asns; hon. mem, Va. and Fed. Bar Asns; Am. Law Inst; Tenn. Hist. Soc; Int. Platform Asn; Nat. Lawyers Club, Wash, D.C; trustee and mem. athletics bd, Univ. Tenn; chmn, Rhodes Scholarships Selection Cmt. for Tenn; Rotary; Cumberland Club; Round Table; Belle Meade Country Club; Am. Legion. Award of Merit, Univ. of Tenn. Law Sch, 66. Rel: Methodist. Legal Res: 228 Vaughns Gap Rd, Nashville, Tenn. 37205. Mailing Add: 824 U.S. Courthouse, Nashville, Tenn. 37203.

MILLER, WILLIAM M. 'FISH BAIT' D
Doorkeeper, U.S. House of Rep.
b. Pascagoula, Miss, 7/20/09; m. to Mable Breeland; c. Sarah Patsy. Educ: Harrison-Stone-Jackson Jr. Col, Miss; George Washington Univ. Law Sch; Atlanta Law Sch, LL.D. Polit. & Govt. Pos: Doorkeeper, U.S. House of Rep, 49-53 & 55- Mem: Mason; Shrine. Legal Res: Pascagoula, Miss. Mailing Add: 3119 N. Harrison St, Arlington, Va. 22207.

MILLER, ZELL BRYAN D
b. Young Harris, Ga, 2/24/32; s. Stephen Grady Miller and Birdie Bryan M; m. 1/15/54 to Shirley Ann Carver; c. Murphy Carver, Matthew Stephen. Educ: Young Harris Jr. Col, 51; Univ. of Ga, A.B, 57, M.A, 58; one year's work toward Ph.D. Polit. & Govt. Pos: Ga. State Sen. (50th dist.), 63-66, (40th dist.), 61-62; Mayor, Young Harris, 60. Bus. & Prof. Pos: Prof. Mil. Serv: U.S.M.C, 53-56, Pvt.-Sgt; Good Conduct Medal. Mem: Master Mason. Misc: Published Master's Thesis, 'The Admin. of E.D. Rivers as Gov. of Ga,' 170pp. Rel: Methodist; Steward. Mailing Add: Young Harris, Ga. 30582. (1967)

MILLESON, RONALD KINSEY D
Chmn, Harrison Co. Dem. Cent. & Exec. Cmt, Ohio
b. Freeport, Ohio, 8/11/34; s. Arthur H. Milleson and Mary G. Kinsey M; m. 10/14/56 to Carol Ann Carson; c. Richard G, Mary Lynn, Greg Arthur and James Roland. Educ: Freeport Local High Sch, grad, 52. Polit. & Govt. Pos: Chmn, Harrison Co. Cent. & Exec. Cmt, Ohio, 62-; mayor, Freeport, 63-; v.chmn, Ohio Chmn. Orgn, 68- Bus. & Prof. Pos: Ins. agent, self-employed, 61-; v.pres, Freeport Press, Inc, 63- Rel: Protestant. Mailing Add: 111 Philadelphia St, Freeport, Ohio 43973.

MILLETT, H. SAWIN, JR. R
Maine State Rep.
b. Waterford, Maine, 10/8/37; s. Howard S. Millett and Marguerite Hulbert M; m. 8/30/57 to Barbara Shaw; c. Kenneth Jack, Kerry Don, Kathy Jo-Ann and

Karla Di-Ann. Educ: Bates Col, B.S, 59; Univ. Maine, M.Ed, 67. Polit. & Govt. Pos: Maine State Rep, currently. Mem: AF&AM. Rel: Protestant. Mailing Add: Box 27, Dixmont, Maine 04932.

MILLETT, HAROLD R
S.Dak. State Rep.
b. Sorum, S.Dak, 1/7/18; married; c. Dean and Mark. Educ: Agr. at State Col. Polit. & Govt. Pos: S.Dak. State Rep, 62- Bus. & Prof. Pos: Rancher. Mem: Mason; VFW; Am. Legion. Mailing Add: Reva, S.Dak. 57651. (1967)

MILLETTE, THEODORE JOSEPH D
Miss. State Rep.
b. Greenville, Miss, 11/11/30; married. Educ: Univ. of Miss; Phi Delta Theta; M Club. Polit. & Govt. Pos: Miss. State Rep, currently. Bus. & Prof. Pos: Real estate and ins; tug boat rentals. Mem: Elks; Moose; Am. Legion; C. of C; Quarterback Club; Rotary; Alumni Asn. Univ. of Miss. Rel: Catholic. Mailing Add: 1255 Washington Ave, Pascagoula, Miss. 39567. (1967)

MILLHOUSE, CLIFFORD JOHN R
Chmn, Genesee Co. Rep. Cmt, Mich.
b. Flint, Mich, 4/25/27; s. Clifford Millhouse and Etta J. Wolverton M; m. 9/17/49 to Helen Gene Graybill; c. Marlia, Susan and David. Educ: Gen. Motors Inst, B.B.A, 52; Sigma Alpha Epsilon. Polit. & Govt. Pos: Treas, Genesee Co. Rep. Cmt, Mich, 67-69, chmn, 69- Bus. & Prof. Pos: Partner, Millhouse & Holaly, 60-; dir, Genesee Merchants Bank & Trust Co, 67- Mil. Serv: Entered as Pvt, Air Force, 46, released as Cpl, 47, after serv. in Air Univ, Maxwell Field, Ala. Mem: Am. and Mich. Asns. CPA; dir. and treas, Flint Golf Club. Rel: Presbyterian. Legal Res: 1325 Beard, Flint, Mich. 48503. Mailing Add: 1800 Genesee Towers, Flint, Mich. 48502.

MILLICAN, MANYON MEADOWS R
b. Harriman, Tenn, 10/16/26; s. Roscoe Claude Millican and Mary E. M; m. 6/8/54 to Amelia Jean Wheeler; c. Mark Steven, Janice Carlene and Barry Scott. Educ: Univ. Chattanooga, 45-46, 48-49; South. Col. Pharm, Mercer Univ, B.S, 52; pres, Kappa Psi, 52; Pi Kappa Alpha. Polit. & Govt. Pos: Precinct chmn, Jefferson Co. Rep. Party, Ala, 60, mem. exec. cmt, 62-65; precinct capt, Jefferson Co. Young Reps, 60, v.chmn. and regional coordinator, six major precincts, 61; dir. orgn, Rep. Party of Ala, 62-64, exec. dir, 64-66. Bus. & Prof. Pos: Med. Serv. rep, CIBA Pharmaceutical Corp, 52-59 and Warner-Chilcott Labs, 59-62; co-trustee, B D & F Assoc, Polit. Mgt. Firm, 67- Mil. Serv: Entered as A/S, Navy, 46, released as Seaman 1/C, 47, after serv. in USS George K. MacKenzie, Atlantic, 46-47. Publ: 'Republicans: Let's Face Facts,' Personal Manuscript Mailed to Selected Rep, 5/64. Mem: Am. Pharmaceutical Asn. Rel: Baptist. Legal Res: 1308 Old Springville Rd, Birmingham, Ala. 35215. Mailing Add: 16 Office Park Circle, Suite 12, Birmingham, Ala. 35223.

MILLIGAN, IDA VICTORIA COLLINS R
b. N.Y.C; married. Educ: Mass. Polit. & Govt. Pos: N.H. State Rep, until 67. Bus. & Prof. Pos: Former lawyer. Rel: Christian Science. Mailing Add: 618 S.E. 29th Terr, Ocala, Fla. 32670.

MILLIKEN, JOHN GORDON D
Chmn, Arapahoe Co. Dem. Cent. Cmt, Colo.
b. Denver, Colo, 5/12/27; s. William Boyd Milliken and Margaret Marsh M; m. 6/13/53 to Marie Machell; c. Karen Marie, Douglas Gordon, David Tait and Anne Alain. Educ: Yale Univ, B.S. in Indust. Admin, 49, B.E. in Civil Eng, 50; George Wash. Univ, 51-52; Univ. Colo, M.S. in Mgt, 66, D.B.A, 69; Tau Beta Pi; Sigma Iota Epsilon; Beta Gamma Sigma. Polit. & Govt. Pos: Civil engr, U.S. Dept. Interior, Bur. of Reclamation, Denver, Colo. and Wash, D.C, 49-55; pres. and dir, S.E. Englewood Water Dist, Colo, 63-; dir, S.Englewood San. Dist, 65-; mem. adv. cmt, Arapahoe Co. Dem. Cent. Cmt, 66-68, chmn, 69-; Dem. precinct committeeman, Arapahoe Co, 68-69. Bus. & Prof. Pos: Asst. to plant mgr, Stanley Aviation Corp, Denver, Colo, 55-56; prin. mgt. engr. adv. progs. and mgr. orgn. and procedures dept, Aerospace Div, Martin Marietta Corp, 56-64; mgt. engr, Safeway Stores, Inc, 64-66; research economist and assoc. prof, Denver Research Inst, Univ. Denver, 66- Mil. Serv: Entered as Pvt, Army, 45, released as Pfc, 46, after serv. in Med. Dept, Am. Theatre, 45-46; World War II Victory Medal. Publ: The Channels of Technology Acquisition in Commercial Firms and the NASA Dissemination Program (with J. Gilmore and others), NASA, Wash, 67; Contract Research and Development Adjuncts of Federal Agencies (with J.G. Welles and others), 69 and Economic and Social Impact of Recreation at Reclamation Reservoirs: An Exploratory Study of Selected Colorado Reservoir Areas (with H.E. Mew, Jr.), 69, Univ. Denver Research Inst. Mem: Acad. of Mgt; Yale Eng. Asn. Rel: Congregational. Mailing Add: 6502 S. Ogden St, Littleton, Colo. 80120.

MILLIKEN, ROGER R
Mem, Rep. Nat. Finance Cmt.
b. N.Y.C, 10/24/15; s. Gerrish Hill Milliken and Agnes Gayley M; m. 6/5/48 to Justine Van Rensselaer Hooper; c. Justine Van Rensselaer, Nancy, Roger, Jr, David Gayley and Weston Freeman. Educ: Yale Univ, A.B, 37. Polit. & Govt. Pos: S.C. elector, Nat. Elec, 56; del, Rep. Nat. Conv, 56, 60, del-at-lg, 64 & 68 and mem, Platform Cmt, 56 & 60; state finance chmn, S.C. Rep. Party, 59-63; mem, Rep. Nat. Finance Cmt, 63- Bus. & Prof. Pos: Dir, Mercantile Stores Co, Inc, 39-, First Nat. City Bank, N.Y, 47, W.R. Grace & Co, 53 and Westinghouse Elec. Corp, 62; pres. and dir, Deering Milliken, Inc, 47- Rel: Episcopal. Legal Res: 627 Otis Blvd, Spartanburg, S.C. 29302. Mailing Add: 234 S. Fairview Ave, Spartanburg, S.C. 29302.

MILLIKEN, WILLIAM GRAWN R
Gov, Mich.
b. Traverse City, Mich, 3/26/22; s. James Thacker Milliken and Hildegarde Grawn M; m. 10/5/45 to Helen Wallbank; c. William, Jr. and Elaine. Educ: Yale Univ, B.A, 46. Hon. LL.D, Univ. Mich, East. Mich. Univ, Cent. Mich. Univ. and Detroit Inst. Tech; L.H.D, North. Mich. Univ. Polit. & Govt. Pos: Chmn, Grand Traverse Co. Rep. Cmt, 6 years; dir, Gr. Mich. Found, cmnr, Mich. Waterways Cmn, 47-55; mem, U.S. State Dept. Intercult. Exchange Prog, W.Germany, 53; Mich. State Sen, 60-64, Majority Floor Leader, Mich. State Senate, 63-64; Lt. Gov, Mich, 64-69, Gov, 69- Bus. & Prof. Pos: Pres, J.W. Milliken, Inc, currently. Mil. Serv: Entered as Pvt, Army Air Force, released as S/Sgt, after serv. in 50 Combat Missions as Waist Gunner on a B-24; Purple Heart; Air Medal with 2 Oak Leaf Clusters; ETO Ribbon with 3 Battle Stars. Mem: Past pres, Traverse City C. of C; mem. bd. trustees, Northwest. Mich. Col, 3 years; mem. bd. counsr, Smith Col; past pres, Scenic Trails Coun, Boy Scouts. Rel: Congregational. Legal Res: Traverse City, Mich. 49684. Mailing Add: Office of the Governor, Lansing, Mich. 48903.

MILLION, CLARENCE H. D
Polit. Pos: Ind. State Rep, until 66. Bus. & Prof. Pos: Seed merchant and farmer; former teacher of voc. agr. and phys. educ, 20 years. Mem: Elks; Lions; Masons; Scottish Rite, Shrine; Bi-co. C. of C; Ind. Seed Certification Comm; Ind. Crop Improv. Asn; Wabash Valley Asn. Rel: Methodist. Mailing Add: 4 E. Monroe St, Williamsport, Ind. 47993. (1967)

MILLS, BILLY GENE D
b. Waco, Tex, 11/19/29; s. Roosevelt Mills and Genevieve Donahue M; m. 6/20/53 to Rubye Maurine Jackson; c. Karol M, Karen G, John S, William K. and James E. Educ: Compton Col, A.A, 49; Univ. Calif, Los Angeles, B.A, 51; Univ. Calif, Los Angeles Law Sch, LL.B, 54; Nu Beta Epsilon; Kappa Alpha Psi. Polit. & Govt. Pos: Dep. probation officer, Los Angeles Co, 57-60; councilman, Eighth Dist, Los Angeles City Coun, Calif, 63-; chmn, Los Angeles Co. Dem. Cent. Cmt, 67-68. Bus. & Prof. Pos: Release engr, Douglas Aircraft Corp, 54-55; attorney-at-law, assoc. with Herman English, 60-63; attorney-at-law, Firm of Mink, Mills & Neiman, 68- Mil. Serv: Entered as Pvt, Army, 55, released as Specialist, 3/C, 57, after serv. in Off. of Adj. Gen, Far East Command. Mem: Am. and Calif. Bar Asns, and mem, Judicial Admin. Sect; Langston Law Club; Am. Judicature Soc; mem. of the Bar, Supreme Court of the U.S; Angel City Lodge 18 F&AM, Los Angeles Consistory 26 (33°), Egyptian Temple 5, United Supreme Council; The Urban League; YMCA; Int. Asn. of Machinist Union; Bldg. Serv. and Maintenance Employees Int. Union. Rel: Baptist; Charter mem, Laymen's League, Trinity Baptist Church. Legal Res: 3621 Third Ave, Los Angeles, Calif. 90018. Mailing Add: Room 237, City Hall, 200 N. Spring St, Los Angeles, Calif. 90012.

MILLS, CHARLES J. D
b. Greensburg, 10/20/08; s. the late George H. Mills and Nellie Hayden M; m. to Emma McChesney; c. one. Educ: Greensburg Bus. Sch; Westinghouse Tech. Sch; Univ. of Pgh. Night Sch. Polit. & Govt. Pos: Pa. State Rep, 44-67; Dem. committeeman, 6 years; Dem. City chmn, Greensburg, 2 years. Bus. & Prof. Pos: Gen. ins. bus. Mem: Elks 511; Moose 1151; Eagles 577; Youngwood Lions Club. Mailing Add: RFD 1, Box 622, Greensburg, Pa. 15601.

MILLS, DON D
Pres, Ky. Young Dem.
b. McLean Co. Ky, 5/1/36; s. Elbert R. Mills and Maurine Plain M; single. Educ: Univ. Ky, A.B.J, 58; Edinburgh Univ, 58-59; Univ. Ky. Sch. of Diplomacy, 59-60; Lamp and Cross; Sigma Delta Chi; Alpha Tau Omega. Polit. & Govt. Pos: Publicity chmn, Breathitt Gubernatorial Campaign, 62-63; press secy. to Gov. Edward T. Breathitt, 63-67; del, Dem. Nat. Conv, 68; pres, Ky. Young Dem, 69- Bus. & Prof. Pos: Ed, The Lexington Herald, 68- Mil. Serv: Entered as 2nd Lt, Army, 60, released as 1st Lt, 62, after serv. in Inf. and Civil Affairs; Army Res, 10 months. Mem: Frankfort Jaycees. Rotary Found. fel, to study in Scotland; One of Three Outstanding Young Men in Ky, Ky. Jaycees, 65. Rel: Methodist. Mailing Add: The Lexington Herald, 239 W. Short, Lexington, Ky. 40507.

MILLS, ELLSWORTH LUTHER, II R
Committeeman, Ill. Rep. Cent. Cmt.
b. Chicago, Ill, 5/12/26; s. Ellsworth L. Mills and Mary Roberts M; m. 4/23/49 to Betty Annette Masters; c. Ellsworth L, III, Karen Clark, Martha Roberts and Juliana Knight. Educ: Missouri Valley Col, 44-45; Northwest. Univ, 46-47; Sigma Nu. Polit. & Govt. Pos: Precinct committeeman, Rep. Party, Lake Co, Ill, 52-; chmn, Deerfield Twp. Rep. Party, 64-68; committeeman, Ill. Rep. Cent. Cmt, 66-; mem, Lake Co. Rep. Cent. Cmt, 68- Bus. & Prof. Pos: Progressive student, International Harvester, Memphis, 47-50; asst. sales mgr, Bastian Blessing Co, Chicago, 50-66; sales rep, Joseph Dixon Crucible Co, Chicago, 66- Mil. Serv: Entered as Aviation Cadet, Naval Air Corps, 44, released, 47, after serv. in Training Units. Mem: Am. Foundrymen's Soc; Liquified Petroleum Gas Asn; Chicago Curling Club; Am. Legion; St. Andrews Soc. of Ill; Boy Scouts (leader 61-) Rel: Episcopal. Mailing Add: 1870 Dale Ave, Highland Park, Ill. 60035.

MILLS, FRANCES JONES D
b. Gray, Ky; d. William Harrison Jones, M.D. and Bertie Steeley J; m. 7/24/49 to Gene Mills. Educ: Union Col; East. State Teachers Col; Cumberland Col. Polit. & Govt. Pos: Co. chmn, Cmt. for Gov. Bert Combs, 58; precinct chmn, Dem. Party, Ky, 60-65; Ky. State Rep, 61-62, asst. to Speaker, Ky. House of Rep, 63; mem, Nat. Cmt. on Higher Educ, 63- and Gov. Cmt. on Status of Women, 65-; del, Dem. Nat. Conv, 64 & 68; Dem. Nominee for Cong, 64; mem, Int. Dem. Platform Cmt; state chmn. for U.S. Senate Race, 68; Dem. Nominee, Ky. State House of Rep, 69. Bus. & Prof. Pos: Teacher, Gray Sch. Syst, Lynn Camp High Sch. and Ft. Mitchell High Sch, Dayton, Ohio, 8 years; med. asst. to her father, Dr. Jones, 50-60. Mem: Int. Temple Cmt, Past Grand Rep. to N.Y. and Past Worthy Matron, Eastern Star; Federated Women's Club; Whitley Co. Med. Auxiliary; Bus. & Prfnl. Women's Club; White Shrine. Won Nat. Award for Best Publ. of Booklet on Emergency Preparedness 'What Would You Do?,' Nat. Asn. of Civil Defense Dir, V.I, 67. Mailing Add: Box 15, Gray, Ky. 40734.

MILLS, FRED MOORE, JR. D
N.C. State Rep.
b. Wadesboro, N.C, 3/26/22; s. Fred Moore Mills and Zeta Fetzer M; m. 12/28/53 to Frances Lee Davis; c. Fred M, III and James Fetzer. Educ: Univ. N.C, B.S. Commerce, 50; Phi Kappa Sigma. Polit. & Govt. Pos: N.C. State Sen, 63-66; N.C. State Rep, 67- Bus. & Prof. Pos: Farmer. Mil. Serv: T/Sgt, 42-45. Mem: Moose. Rel: Presbyterian; Deacon. Mailing Add: 607 Camden Rd, Wadesboro, N.C. 28170. (1967)

MILLS, GOVAN D
Chmn, Barber Co. Dem. Cent. Cmt, Kans.
b. Lake City, Kans, 10/6/07; s. Govan Mills and Margaret Hittle M, 'Maggie'; m. 12/30/30 to Margaret McKenzie; c. Beulah Margaret (Mrs. Harbaugh), Govan Clifton and Hannah Louise (Mrs. Clarke). Educ: Kans. State Univ, B.S,

30. Polit. & Govt. Pos: Secy-treas, Barber Co. Dem. Cent. Cmt, Kans, 36-38, chmn, 62-; twp. treas, 38-44; precinct committeeman and mem, Cent. Cmt, 52-60; alternate del, Dem. Nat. Conv, 68. Bus. & Prof. Pos: Teacher, Haviland High Sch, Kans, 31-32, Lacrosse High Sch, 32-34 and Larned High Sch, 34-36; owner and operator, Mills Ranch, Lake City, 37-66; organizer and pres, S. Cent. Tel. Asn, Inc, Medicine Lodge, 52-66. Mem: Mason; Consistory; Shrine. Rel: Christian Church. Mailing Add: Lake City, Kans. 67071.

MILLS, JAMES C. R
Mem, Dona Ana Co. Rep. Cent. Cmt, N.Mex.
b. Sparks, Okla, 8/8/20; s. Cecil A. Mills and Mable C. Ward M; m. 1/13/45 to Pearl A. Muller; c. John C. and Richard A. Educ: Okla. Univ, B.S. in elec. eng, 42. Polit. & Govt. Pos: Chmn, Dona Ana Young Reps, N.Mex, 60-62 and chmn, Dona Ana Co. Rep. Cmt, 63-64; del, Rep. Nat. Conv, 64; mem, Dona Ana Co. Rep. Cent. Cmt, 66- Mil. Serv: Entered as A/S Navy, 42, released as Aviation Chief Radioman, 46, after serv. in Patrol Squadron 44, Combat, S.Pac; Air Medal; Good Conduct Medal; Mariana Campaign Ribbon; Victory Medal; Asiatic-Pac. Theater Ribbon. Publ: Dona Ana Co, Status of the Two Polit. Parties, 64. Mailing Add: 3035 Fairway Dr, Las Cruces, N.Mex. 88001.

MILLS, JAMES R. D
Calif. State Sen.
b. San Diego, Calif, 6/6/27; m. 1/9/59 to Joanna Rohrbough M. Educ: San Diego State Col, B.A, M.A; Univ. London. Polit. & Govt. Pos: Calif. State Assemblyman, 60-66; Calif. State Sen, 67-; del, Dem. Nat. Conv, 68. Bus. & Prof. Pos: Teacher and writer (an authority on the hist. of San Diego and South. Calif). Mil. Serv: Army, 50-53. Mem: Urban League; San Diego Hist. Soc; San Diego Soc. for Maritime Research; C. of C; Am. Legion; NAACP; VFW; G.I. Forum; F&AM. Mailing Add: 341 U.S. Grant Hotel, San Diego, Calif. 92101.

MILLS, KENNETH ADOLFO D
b. San Francisco, Calif, 3/20/24; s. Carley Mills and Beatrice Stahl M; m. 11/17/62 to Elizabeth Elstad; c. Polly, Penny and John. Educ: Princeton Univ, A.B, 48; Phi Beta Kappa; Dial Lodge. Polit. & Govt. Pos: V.chmn, N.Y. Cmt. Dem. Voters, 67-69; del, Dem. Nat. Conv, 68; chmn, New Dem. Coalition, Manhattan, 69; leader, 66th Dem. Assembly Dist, 69- Bus. & Prof. Pos: Dir. research and promotion, KATZ TV, N.Y.C, 48-; pres, Princeton Broadcasting Corp. Mil. Serv: Entered as A/S, Navy, 43, released as Seaman 3/C, 46; Good Conduct Medal. Mem: Broadcasters Promotion Asn.(bd. dirs); Mailing Add: 1349 Lexington Ave, New York, N.Y. 10028.

MILLS, KENNETH ARMOUR D
Maine State Rep.
b. Lynn, Mass, 9/3/99; s. Frederick Ellsworth Mills and Edith Mavis Armour M; m. to Irene Mae Hickey. Polit. & Govt. Pos: V.chmn, Eastport Dem. Cmt, Maine, 64-; committee mem, Washington Co. Dem. Party, 64-; Maine State Rep, 65-66 & 69-; mem, State Dem. Platform Cmt, 66-68; mem, Eastport City Coun, 68- Mil. Serv: Pvt, Army, World War I, with serv. in 40th Div, European Theatre. Mem: Am. Legion; Border Hist. Soc; Perry Improv. Asn. Rel: Protestant. Mailing Add: 56 High St, Eastport, Maine 04631.

MILLS, MAX MILO R
b. Marshalltown, Iowa, 8/26/20; m. 1945 to Carmel Bellini; c. Sally, Jeffrey, Carol. Educ: Univ. of Chicago; Drake Univ, Juris Dr; Washington Univ; Northwest. Univ; Iowa State Univ. Polit. & Govt. Pos: Iowa State Sen, -66; former co. attorney. Bus. & Prof. Pos: Practicing attorney with law firm Mills and Grimes; v.pres, Tallyho Transport, Inc. and McIntire Travel Agency; pres, Big Timber Cattle Co, breeders of purebred Angus cattle and operators of over 1,000 acres of farm land. Mil. Serv: Marine Corps, Feb. 42-Jan. 46, Maj, engaged as combat officer in 8 Pac. campaigns. Awarded 2 Purple Hearts and the Silver Star. Mem: Lions Club; Adult Educ. Coun; Various civic, fraternal and patriotic bodies; past pres, Marshalltown C. of C. Rel: Episcopal. Mailing Add: 146 N. 5th St, Marshalltown, Iowa 50158. (1967)

MILLS, MILES E. D
Ill. State Rep.
b. Vandalia, Ill; m. to Margaret M; c. Edward, Laurene, Pauline and Forrest. Educ: Cols. of Ill, Kans, Mont. Polit. & Govt. Pos: City supt, Altamont City Schs, 4 years; village prin; supt. schs, Effingham Co, 8 years; chief dep. sheriff, Effingham Co, 2 years; Ill. State Rep, 6 terms. Bus. & Prof. Pos: Rural teacher, 28 years; Life and Casualty Ins, 3 years. Mem: Effingham Lodge No. 149 AF&AM; Danville Valley Scottish Rite Consistory. Rel: Methodist. Mailing Add: 602 S. 2nd St, Effingham, Ill. 62401.

MILLS, MORRIS HADLEY R
Ind. State Rep.
b. West Newton, Ind, 9/25/27; s. Howard S. Mills and Bernice Hadley M; m. 8/8/54 to Mary Ann Sellars; c. Douglas, Frederic and Gordon. Educ: Earlham Col, A.B, 50; Harvard Grad. Sch. of Bus. Admin, M.B.A, 52. Polit. & Govt. Pos: Ind. State Rep, Marion Co, 69- Bus. & Prof. Pos: Secy-treas, Maplehurst Farms, Indianapolis, Ind, 52-59; pres, 59-61; partner, Mills Bros. Farms, 61- Mil. Serv: Entered as Pvt, Army, 46, released as Tech. 4/C, 47 after serv. in Engrs, Japan, 46-47. Mem: Lions; Farm Bur. Rel: Quaker. Legal Res: 7332 W. Thompson Rd, Indianapolis, Ind. 46241.

MILLS, NEWT V. D
b. Calhoun, La, 9/27/99; s. Henry E. Mills and Minervia A. Sanford M; m. 9/23/59 to Margaret Elizabeth Sunny. Educ: State Normal Col, La, 22; La. Tech, 23-25; La. State Univ, 29. Polit. & Govt. Pos: Mem, Presidential Electoral Col, 36; Col, staff of Gov. R.W. Leche, La, 36-40; U.S. Rep, Fifth Cong. Dist, La, 37-43. Bus. & Prof. Pos: Real estate, farmer, timber, cattle, gas and oil; sch. teacher and prin. for 11 yrs. Honored recognition for participation in celebration of formation of Constitution, U.S. Constitution Sesquicentennial Cmn, 37. Rel: Assembly of God. Mailing Add: 715 Loop Rd, Monroe, La. 71201.

MILLS, OKEY ANDREW D
Treas, Raleigh Co, W.Va.
b. Sweenyburg, W.Va; s. Rufus Clayton Mills and Dora Arizona Cook M; m. 4/4/51 to Letty Mae Neely. Educ: Beckley Col, W.Va; pres, Kappa Theta Phi and Phi Gamma Theta; ed, Flight of Blue Hawk; Beckley Col. Basketball. Polit. & Govt. Pos: Sheriff, Raleigh Co, W.Va, 49-52, 57-60 & 65-; Sgt-at-Arms, W.Va. House of Del, 53 & 54; chmn, Raleigh Co. Dem. Exec. Cmt, 58-; treas, Raleigh Co, 65- Bus. & Prof. Pos: Safety instr, W.Va. Dept. of Mines, 55 & 56; bus. mgr, Pinecrest Sanit, 61. Mil. Serv: Entered as Pvt, Army, 42, released as S/Sgt, after serv. in 508 Parachute Inf, 82nd Airborne, ETO; Bronze Star; Purple Heart with cluster; ETO Ribbon with 4 Stars and Bronze Invasion Arrowhead; Good Conduct, Victory and Occupation Medals; Am. Defense Ribbon; Presidential Unit Citation; Unit Citations, France, Belgium and Holland. Mem: Lions Int; Am. Legion; VFW; DAV; W.Va. Sheriff's Asn; Elks; Moose. Baseball, State Centennial Sports Great Co. of Raleigh. Rel: Baptist. Mailing Add: Box 516, Crab Orchard, W.Va. 25827. (1967)

MILLS, RICHARD COKE, JR. D
b. Waco, Tex, 5/16/38; s. Richard Coke Mills and Olivia Rucker M; m. to Margaret Schuler. Educ: South. Methodist Univ, 56-59; Baylor Univ, A.B, 60, LL.B, 65; Alpha Tau Omega; Phi Alpha Delta. Polit. & Govt. Pos: Dem. Precinct Chmn, Waco, Tex, 60; del, Tex. State Dem. Conv, 60, 64, 66 & 68; alternate del, Dem. Nat. Conv, 68; v.chmn, Melennan Co. Humphrey-Muskie Campaign Cmt, 68. Mem: Waco-McLennan Co. Jr. and Sr. Bar Asns; State Bar of Tex; Am. Judicature Soc; Waco Jr. Bar (dir, 67-68); Waco Legal Aid Found.(dir, 68 & 69); Waco Jaycees (dir); Dem. Supper Club; YMCA; Muscular Dystrophy Asn.(pres, cent. Tex. Chap, 69). Rel: Methodist. Legal Res: 116 Lake Air East, Waco, Tex. 76710. Mailing Add: 604 First National Bldg, Waco, Tex. 76701.

MILLS, ROBERT GRAY R
b. Ararat, N.C, 3/25/32; s. Ellis Washington Mills and Stella Ann Forkner M; m. 10/17/49 to Jacqueline Sams; c. Vickie Gray and Lydia Ann. Educ: Pilot Mountain High Sch, grad. Polit. & Govt. Pos: Former chmn, Surry Co. Exec. Cmt, N.C; del, Rep, Nat. Conv, 64. Bus. & Prof. Pos: Pres, Riverside Hosiery Mills Inc, 57-61; owner, Blueridge Cookie Co, 61- Mem: Mason; v.pres, Long Hill Develop. Asn; pres, Longhill Ruritan Club; Farm Bur. Rel: Quaker. Mailing Add: Ararat, N.C. 27007. (1967)

MILLS, THOMAS PERRY R
S.Dak. State Rep.
b. Tiffen, Ohio, 8/21/21; s. Clifton Newton Mills and Erma Alice Davis M; m. 8/30/47 to A. Marie La Craft; c. Ken. Educ: S.Dak. State Univ, B.S. in Pharm, 47; Blue Key; Pharm. Soc. Polit. & Govt. Pos: Mem. and past chmn, State Interprfnl. Cmt, S.Dak, 52-; mem, State Vet. Cmt, 56-58; S.Dak. State Rep, Minnehaha Co, 67- Mil. Serv: Entered as Pvt, Army, 42, released as Cpl, 45, after serv. in 175th Inf. Regt. Co. D, 29th Inf. Div, 11th Mobile Radio Unit, ETO, 44-45; ETO Ribbon with 5 Campaign Stars; Am. Theater Ribbon; Army of Occup. Medal; Good Conduct Medal; Meritorious Serv. Plaque with 1 Cluster; Combat Infantryman's Badge; Div. Citation Band. Mem: Sioux Falls Pharm. Asn.(pres, 56-58); S.Dak. and Am. Pharmaceut. Asns; Nat. Asn. of Retail Druggists; Asn. of Prfnl. Pharmacists; Nat. Asn. of Rexall Druggists; S.Dak. State Univ. Alumni Asn.(past pres); Upper Midwest Chap, Nat. Kidney Found; dir, Sioux Falls Boy's Club; Am. Legion; Elks; Shrine; Consistory; Mason; Optimist Int.(past gov); Sioux Falls Club (past pres. and lt. gov). Rel: Congregational. Mailing Add: 2601 Arcadia Rd, Sioux Falls, S. Dak. 57105.

MILLS, WILBUR D. D
U.S. Rep, Ark.
b. Kensett, Ark, 5/24/09; m. 5/27/34 to Clarine Billingsley; c. Martha Sue and Rebecca Ann. Educ: Hendrix Col; Harvard Law Sch. Polit. & Govt. Pos: Co. and probate judge of White Co, Ark, 34-38; U.S. Rep, Ark, currently. Bus. & Prof. Pos: Lawyer. Mem: Admitted to practice law before Supreme Court of Ark, 33 and Supreme Court of U.S, 39; Mason (33°). Rel: Methodist. Legal Res: Kensett, Ark. Mailing Add: 2701 Connecticut Ave, Washington, D.C. 20008.

MILLS, WILLIAM DONALD D
b. Maysville, N.C, 10/8/32; s. Leo Bell Mills and Mildred Jones M; m. 1/25/52 to Donniere Morton; c. William Donald, Jr. and Robert Duane. Educ: E. Carolina Col. Polit. & Govt. Pos: Onslow Co. Cmnr, N.C, 59-64; former N.C. State Rep. Bus. & Prof. Pos: Appliance and furniture bus. Mil. Serv: Army, 51-52, Cpl, E-4. Mem: South. Retail Furniture Asn; Sea Side Lodge No. 429, Swansboro, N.C; Consistory; Sudan Temple, New Bern, N.C; Moose; Eastern Star. Rel: Methodist; Supt, Belgrade Methodist Church, 54-60, trustee, 62-; pres, Methodist Men's Club, 59-60. Mailing Add: Route 1, Maysville, N.C. 28555. (1967)

MILLS, WILLIAM LARRY R
b. Boise, Idaho, 5/16/12; s. William John Mills and Katherine Josephine Leary M; m. 6/16/37 to Beatrice B. Milligan; c. Sharon Ann and Patrick Joseph. Educ: Carroll Col, Helena, Mont, 30-32; Univ. Idaho, B.S, 37 and M.S, 47. Polit. & Govt. Pos: Precinct committeeman, Boise Co. Rep. Party, Idaho, 38-40; Idaho State Rep, Boise Co, 40-42, Latah Co, 46-52 and Ada Co, 62-66; admin. asst. to U.S. Rep. Budge, Idaho, 51-54. Bus. & Prof. Pos: Dir. govt. affairs, Boise Cascade Corp, 54- Mil. Serv: Entered as Pvt, Army, 43, released as T/Sgt, 46; Combat Inf. Badge; Saipan, Okinawa and Asiatic-Pac. Campaign Ribbons. Mem: K. of C; Elks; Am. Legion; Arid Club; Hillcrest Country Club. College letters in baseball, basketball and football. Rel: Roman Catholic. Legal Res: 85 Horizon Dr, Boise, Idaho 83702. Mailing Add: P.O. Box 200, Boise, Idaho 83701.

MILLSAP, CLAUDE, JR. R
b. Los Angeles, Calif, 6/17/20; s. Claude Millsap and Marie B. Postal M; m. to Pamela Lynne; c. Norma Jean (Mrs. Strickland) and Linda Lou. Educ: Univ. South. Calif, B.A. in bus. admin, 53. Polit. Pos: Del. and chmn, Alternate Delegation, Rep. Nat. Conv, 64; chmn, Southeast. Alaska Senate Dist, Rep. Party and mem, Alaska State Cent. Cmt, 62-64; chmn, 4th House Legis. Dist, Rep. Party, 60-62. Govt. Pos: Chmn, Greater Juneau Borough, 63. Bus. & Prof. Pos: Pres, Juneau Credit Serv. Co, Inc. and Cal-Dustrial Engrs, Inc. Mil. Serv: Entered as A/S, Coast Guard, 41, released as Boatswain Mate 1/C, 46, after serv. in Coast Guard Cutter, Aurora W46 in N.Pac, Bering Sea and Aleutian Islands. Mem: Bd. Dirs, Salvation Army and C. of C; Am. Legion; Elks; Nat. Munic. League; Alaska Munic. League; Rotary Int; Pioneer Alaska

Lobbyists Soc; Territorial Sportsmen, Inc. Rel: Episcopal. Legal Res: Apt. 11, Cheechako Apt, Douglas, Alaska 99824. Mailing Add: Box 353, Douglas Alaska 99824. (1967)

MILMORE, THOMAS ALOYSIUS D
Chmn, Weston Dem. Town Party, Conn.
b. Brooklyn, N.Y, 3/21/24; s. Thomas Aloysius Milmore and Mary Smith M; m. 6/12/54 to Eleanor Bourne; c. Susan, Thomas, Jr, Roland and Kevin. Educ: Columbia Univ, 1 year. Polit. & Govt. Pos: Cmt. mem, Weston Dem. Town Party, Conn, 64, chmn, 65- Bus. & Prof. Pos: Asst. advert. mgr, Philco, N.Y, 51-54; creative dir, Norm Advert, 54- Mil. Serv: Entered as Pvt, Army, 42, released as Sgt, 45, after serv. in 551st Field Artil Bn, ETO, 44-45. Rel: Catholic. Mailing Add: Steephill Rd, Weston, Conn. 06880.

MILNAR, CAROL VIRGINIA R
b. St. Paul, Minn, 7/13/24; d. Elmer H. Peterson and Nannie Blomquist P; m. 1/12/66 to Walter H. Milnar; c. Janet (Mrs. Jeske), Nancy Chalupa and Allen Chalupa. Polit. & Govt. Pos: Chairwoman, S.St. Paul Rep. Cmt, Minn, 62-63 and Dakota Co. Rep. Cmt, 63; first v.chairwoman, First Cong. Dist. Rep. Cmt, 63-65; alternate del, Rep. Nat. Conv, 64; chmn, Minn. Capitol Rep. Tour Guides, 65. Mem: Pres, PTA; guardian coun, Jobs Daughters; League of Women Voters; Young Rep. League. Rel: Presbyterian. Mailing Add: 333 Ridge Rd, Palm Springs, Calif. 92262.

MILONE, SALVATORE ANTHONY R
b. Rockville Centre, N.Y, 7/19/07; s. Dominick Milone and Elisa Pacielli M; m. 6/16/35 to Margaret Annunziato, wid; c. Elissa (Mrs. Joseph G. Metz) and Richard D. Educ: St. Agnes High Sch; Brooklyn Polytech. Inst. Polit. & Govt. Pos: Pres, Rockville Centre Rep. Club, N.Y, 49-51; mem. bd. gov, Columbian Rep. League, 50-60; Rep. village leader, Rockville Centre, 54-; treas, Hempstead Rep. Town Orgn, 55-66, chmn, finance cmt, 66-; alternate del, Rep. Nat. Conv, 56, 60 & 64; chmn, Nassau Co. Rep. $100 Plate Dinner, 61-66; mem, Gov. 350th Anniversary Cmt. for N.Y, 59; mem. bd. gov, Home Rule Party, Rockville Centre; del, Judicial Dist. Conv; former Rep. State Committeeman. Bus. & Prof. Pos: Exec. v.pres, Dominick Milone, Inc, 25-; mem. bd. dirs, People's Savings and Loan Asn, 62-; mem. bd. dirs, Chemical Bank N.Y. Trust Co, 64- Mem: Bd. gov, L.I. Bldg. Cong;Kiwanis;Nassau Co. Cerebral Palsy Bd;past pres, Northwest Civic Asn. of Rockville Centre;K. of C;Holy Name Soc;Knight of Papal Order of Holy Sepulchre; affil. mem, Soc. of Mary; bd. trustees, Molloy Catholic Col. for Women, Rockville Centre, N.Y. and adv. bd. trustees, 63-66; Bishop's Cmt. of the Laity for Catholic Charities, Diocese of Rockville Centre; warden, Civil Defense; Patrolmen's Benevolent Asn; capt, Rockville Centre Fire Dept; pres, Ment. Health Bd. of Nassau Co, 64. Rel: Roman Catholic. Mailing Add: 19 Bradford Court, Rockville Centre, N.Y. 11570

MILSTEAD, GEORGE L. D
b. Ferriday, La, 12/25/22; s. George L. Milstead and Etta Mae Willis M; m. 2/14/49 to Clara Virginia Sutherland; c. Barbara Ann. Educ: Am. Univ, B.S. Polit. & Govt. Pos: Admin. asst. to Rep. Jones, Ala. Bus. & Prof. Pos: Cong. liaison rep, Civil Serv. Cmn, 56-63; supv, CIA, 51-52. Mil. Serv: Air Force, 1st Lt, 416th Night Fighter Squadron, pilot, Europe; Maj, U.S.A.F.R. Mailing Add: 4205 Linden St, Fairfax, Va. 22030. (1967)

MILTICH, PAUL ANDREW R
b. Virginia, Minn, 10/30/19; s. Andrew D. Miltich and Mary Pope M. (deceased); m. 5/17/44 to Sylvia S. Schumann; c. Andrew Paul and Marianne April. Educ: Univ. Minn, B.S, 41 and postgrad. work, 42; Delta Pi Lambda; Lambda Alpha Psi. Polit. & Govt. Pos: Dep. cmnr, Saginaw Co. Pub. Schs, Mich, 46; press secy. to House Rep. Leader, Gerald R. Ford, 66- Bus. & Prof. Pos: Teacher and drama dir, Breck Sch. for Boys, St. Paul, 41-42; teacher, Saginaw Pub. Schs, Mich, 46; reporter and asst. city ed, Booth Newspapers of Mich, 46-57, Wash. Correspondent, 57-66. Mil. Serv: Entered as Pvt, Army, 42, released as Cpl, 46, after serv. in Transportation Corps, European Theater, 44-45; Good Conduct Medal; European Campaign Ribbon. Mem: Former mem, Standing Cmt. of Correspondents, House and Senate Press Galleries. Rel: Congregational; former mem, Bd. of Benevolences and Soc. Action Bd. Mailing Add: 11104 Inwood Ave, Silver Spring, Md. 20902.

MIMS, LAMBERT CARTER
Mayor, Mobile, Ala.
b. Uriah, Ala, 4/20/30; s. Jeff Carter Mims and Carrie Lambert M; m. 8/17/46 to Reecie Phillips; c. Dale Phillips and Louis Daniel. Educ: Blackshear High Sch, Uriah, Ala, grad. Polit. & Govt. Pos: Pub. works cmnr, Mobile, Ala, 65-68, mayor, 68- Bus. & Prof. Pos: V.pres, Ala. Chap, Am. Pub. Works Asn, 68, pres, 69. Publ: For Christ and Country, Fleming H. Revell Co, 69. Rel: Baptist. Legal Res: 3366 Childers St, Mobile, Ala. 36605. Mailing Add: 111 S. Royal St. (P.O. Box 1827), Mobile, Ala. 36601.

MINARIK, FRANK STUYVESANT D
b. New York, N.Y, 1/3/98; s. Joseph Minarik and Anna Pesek M; m. 4/21/24 to Clarabel Smith, wid. 2/4/47; c. Smith, Clara Joe (Mrs. Fisher) and Mary Ann (Mrs. Lane). Educ: Univ. Tenn, B.A, 23; St. Lawrence Univ, LL.B, 29; Phi Delta Phi. Polit. & Govt. Pos: Chmn, Pima Co. Dem. Party, Ariz, 52-54 & 58-60; v.chmn, Ariz. Dem. Party, 54-56; Dem. Nat. committeeman, Ariz, 60-64; chmn. Dist. 7F, Pima Co. Dem. Party, Ariz, 66- Bus. & Prof. Pos: Trustee, Trinity Univ, Tex; dir, Beacon Found. for Retarded Children; bd. mem, Hire the Handicapped, 46-; co-founder, Square and Compass Crippled Children's Clin, Tucson, Ariz, 49, pres, 49- Mem: Nat. Conf. Christians and Jews; Mason; Shrine; Scottish Rite; K.T. Eagles Award for Commun. Serv, 51; Sportsman of the Year, K. of C, 53; Outstanding Commun. Serv. Award, Nat. Conf. Christians and Jews, 55. Rel: Presbyterian. Mailing Add: 2025 N. Wilmont, Tucson, Ariz. 85616.

MINCKS, JACOB BENJAMIN D
b. Davis Co, Iowa, 8/26/13; s. Joseph Otis Mincks and Susan Squires M; m. 8/31/35 to Mildred Mae Cottrell; c. Larry and Linda (Mrs. James Grant). Polit. & Govt. Pos: Chmn, Wapello Co. Dem. Cent. Cmt, Iowa, 53-58; mem, Labor Adv. Cmt, Dem. Nat. Conv, 56; Iowa State Sen, 58-66; mem, Iowa Civil Rights Cmt, 61-63; mem, Iowa Adv. Cmt. on Workmen's Compensation, 63-68; mem, Iowa Adv. Cmt. to Soc. Welfare, 65-67. Bus. & Prof. Pos: Exec. v.pres, Iowa Fedn. of Labor, AFL-CIO, 61-68. Publ: Questions and Answers on Iowa Workmen's Compensation, 63; Questions and Answers on Iowa Employment Security Act, 67. Mem: UAW; Eagles. Rel: Protestant. Mailing Add: 108 S. Adella, Ottumwa, Iowa 52501.

MINEAR, LEON PIERSON
b. San Antonio, Tex, 3/20/15; s. Joseph H. Minear and Monnie M. Guin M; m. 8/20/39 to Dolores F. Goetzee; c. Roger Leon. Educ: San Francisco State Col, A.B. cum laude, 38; Stanford Univ, M.A, 41, Ed.D, 47; Phi Delta Kappa; Kappa Delta Pi; Sigma Alpha Eta. Polit. & Govt. Pos: Mem, Ore. Coun. on Arts and Humanities; chmn, Gov. Policy Planning Cmn. for Human Resources; educ. consult, For. and State Govt; research consult, U.S. Off. Educ; adv. to U.S. Cmnr. Educ; secy, Gov. Adv. Coun. on Juvenile Insts, 55-61; mem, Selective Serv. State Appeals Bd, 58-65; chmn, Portland Metrop. Youth Cmn, 60-61; mem, Interagency Legis. Cmt. on Migratory Labor and Ore. Outdoor Educ. Cmt, 61-64; supt. pub. instr, Ore, 61-68; mem, President's White House Cmt. on Aging and President's Cmt. on Voc. Educ, 62; dir, U.S. Off. of Educ. Study for Nat. Syst. Regional Research Centers, 62-63; chmn, Higher Educ. Coord. Coun, 63 & 65; mem, Gov. Cabinet; mem, White House Conf. on Educ, 65; dir, div. of voc. and tech. educ, Off. of Educ, Dept. Health, Educ. and Welfare, 68- Bus. & Prof. Pos: Teacher, elem. and jr. and sr. high schs, Oakland, Calif, 38-42; demonstration teacher, Univ. Calif, summers, 40-42, v.prin, sec. demonstration, summer sch, 46; flight radio officer, Pan Am. World Airways, 42-43, sr. commun. rep, S.Pac, 44; asst. supt. training, 44, supt. training, 45-46; v.prin, Carmel High Sch, Calif, 46-47; asst. prof. educ, Univ. Denver and asst. to dean, Denver Jr. Col, 47-49; pres, Stockton Jr. Col, 49-52; prin, Benson Polytech. Sch, 52-61; mem, ed. adv. bd, Grolier Soc. Mil. Serv: Entered as Ens, Navy, released as Lt.(jg), 53, after serv. in Pac. Publ: Co-auth, educ. textbooks; articles in educ. jour. Mem: Dir, Ford Found. Study for Ore. Educ. Improv, 62-66; conductor, Monterey Regional Symphony, 46-47; Denver Commun. Symphony; Carmel Found, Inc; Monterey Symphony Asn; Denver Businessmen's Symphony Asn; pres, Portland High Sch. Prin. Asn; 56-57; Harvard-Lexington Exp. Prog; state chmn. and nat. bd. dirs, Save the Children Fedn; Ore. Mus. of Sci. and Indust; Ore. Hist. Soc; Univ. Coun. for Educ. Admin, Ohio State Univ; educ. cmt, C. of C; Coun. Chief State Sch. Officers; Nat. Center for Adv. Study of Educ. Admin; Ore. Sch. Activities Asn; Pac. Research Center; Inst. for Am. Strategy; Educ. Policies Cmn; nat. steering cmt, Educ. Cmn. of the States; dir, Carnegie Found. Study of State Sch. Admin; Am. Asn. Sch. Adminstr; Nat. and Ore. Educ. Asns. Rel: Reorganized Latter-day Saint. Legal Res: 4241 Alderbrook, Salem, Ore. 97302. Mailing Add: Office of Education, Dept. of Health, Education and Welfare, Room 5102, Seventh and D St. S.W, Washington, D.C. 20202.

MINEHART, THOMAS ZENO, II D
Chmn, Pa. State Dem. Cmt.
b. Philadelphia, Pa, 5/23/07; s. John R. Minehart, M.D. and Katherine Violet Cosgrove M; m. 10/3/36 to Janet Mulvany; c. Janet Elisabeth (Mrs. Maupay), Thomas Z, III, Marylee, Charles R. and John R. Educ: Temple Univ, A.B, 29; Temple Univ. Sch. Law, LL.B, 33; Blue Key; Theta Upsilon Omega. Polit. & Govt. Pos: Spec. attorney, Commonwealth of Pa, 35; city councilman, Phila, Pa, 36; chief area rent attorney, Off. Price Admin, 43; auditor gen, Pa, 61-65, state treas, 65-69; chmn, Pa. State Dem. Cmt, 66-; del, Dem. Nat. Conv, 68. Bus. & Prof. Pos: Attorney-at-law, admitted to practice before Courts of Phila, Pa. Supreme and Superior Courts, U.S. Dist. Court and U.S. Circuit Court of Appeals. Mem: Pa. and Phila. Bar Asns; Nat. Asn. of State Auditors; Comptrollers and Treas; Ft. Wash. Volunteer Fire Co; Gwynedd Valley Sportsmen's Club; Rainbow Fishing Club. Rel: United Church of Christ. Legal Res: 408 Bellaire Ave, Fort Washington, Pa. 19034. Mailing Add: 735 P. S.F. Bldg, 12 S. 12th St, Philadelphia, Pa. 19107.

MINER, BARBARA PAULA D
b. Wilkes-Barre, Pa, 5/17/28; d. Al Werth; m. 1/23/50 to Floyd F. Miner; c. Linda, Floyd F, Jr. and Jimmy. Educ: Emory Univ, B.S. and R.N, 48; Univ. Miami; Dade Jr. Col, Nat. Registered Parliamentarian, 66; Delta Delta Delta. Polit. & Govt. Pos: Mem, Dade Co. Dem. Exec. Cmt, Fla, 58-66, v.chmn, 62-66; secy, treas. and parliamentarian, Dem. Women's Club Fla, 61-; secy, treas, chmn. bd. and parliamentarian, Dade Co. Dem. Woman's Club, 61-; mem, Gov. Cmt. on Cold War Educ, 62; co-chmn, Dade Co. Get-Out-the Vote Dr, 62; mem, Dade Co. Young Dem, 62-66; mem, S.Dade Young Dem, 62-66; del, Dem. Nat. Conv, 68; chmn, Dade Co. Woman's Presidential, Gubernatorial, State Legis. and Local Campaigns. Bus. & Prof. Pos: Registered nurse and off. mgr, Dr. J.A. Speropoulos, Miami, 48-63; exec. dir, Dade Co. Leukemia Soc, 63-65; secy-treas, and mem. bd, Miner, Inc, 63- Publ: Columnist, 'Questions and Answers,' Dade Co. Dem. Woman's Club. Bul. Mem: Miami Gaveliers Parliamentary Law Unit; Nat. and Fla. Asns; Parliamentarians; Fla. Unit. of Registered Parliamentarians; Nat. Asn. Registered Parliamentarians; Alcoholic Rehabilitation Cmt.(citizen's adv. cmt. for Harbor Light and mem. bd. dirs, 62); Coral Gables Civic Asn.(pres, 62-66); United Fund of Dade Co.(block capt, 58-61, neighborhood chmn, 62, area chmn, 63); March of Dimes (block capt, 60, 61 & 64, sect. chmn, 62, area co-chmn, 63); Girl Scouts (Brownie Troop leader, 58-60, mother's cmt, 60-62); Oper. Educ. (chmn, Dade Co, 62); Children Home Soc; Am. Red Cross (off. vol, 61-63); Miami Woman's Club; PTA (mem. bd. St. Stephen's Chap, 58-59, mem. fund raising events, 61-66). Silver Torch Award for Commun. Serv. and Humanitarian Efforts, Dade Co, 63; runner-up, Most Outstanding Young Woman Award, Dade Co, 64. Rel: Episcopal: Sunday Sch. Teacher, 56-66; mem. fund raising projs, 60-; co-sponsor Episcopal Young Churchman, 61-63. Legal Res: 6617 Santona Ct, Coral Gables, Fla. 33134. Mailing Add: 506 Ainsley Bldg, 14 N.E. First Ave, Miami, Fla. 33132.

MINER, ROBERT GRAHAM
U.S. Ambassador to Sierra Leone
b. Scranton, Pa, 1/16/11; married. Educ: Hamilton Col, B.A, 34; Yale Univ, M.A, 42. Polit. & Govt. Pos: Analyst, Off. of Strategic Serv, 42-43; Career Officer, U.S. Dept. of State For. Serv, 46-; consul, Athens, 48-51; first secy, Imp. Defence Col, 51-52; first secy, Paris, 52-55; officer-in-charge, Dominion Affairs, 55-56; consul gen, Istanbul, 56-60; dir, Off. of Greek, Turkish and Iranian Affairs, 60-62; U.S. Ambassador to Trinidad and Tobago, 62-67 and Sierra Leone, 67- Bus. & Prof. Pos: Instr, Athens Col, 34-35, Robert Col, Istanbul, 35-37 and Hamilton Col, 37-40. Mil. Serv: Lt, Navy, 43-46. Mailing Add: U.S. Dept. of State Foreign Service, Washington, D.C. 20521. (1967)

MINER, S. NORTON R
Chmn, Salisbury Rep. Town Cmt, Conn.
b. Salisbury, Conn, 3/28/11; s. Samuel Corning Miner and Fanny Maria Peckham M; m. 6/18/37 to Isabel O. Keller; c. Linda (Mrs. Malcolm MacLaren, Jr). Educ: Mass. Inst. Tech, B.Arch, 36; Phi Kappa Sigma. Polit. & Govt. Pos: Chmn, Salisbury Rep. Town Cmt, Conn, 65- Mailing Add: Lime Rock Rd, Lakeville, Conn. 06039.

MINER, STANLEY PINGREY R
b. Brooklyn, N.Y, 11/5/99; s. George Ephraim Miner and Hattie Sawyer M; m. 10/6/28 to Catherine Gerwig Jones; c. Mary Ann, Catherine Sawyer and Constance Gerwig. Educ: Dartmouth Col, B.S, 22; Phi Delta Theta; Casque and Gauntlet Sr. Soc. Polit. & Govt. Pos: Vt. State Rep, Dist. 65, 65-68. Bus. & Prof. Pos: With Bell Tel. Co, Pa, 22 and N.Y. Tel. Co, 23-61. Mil. Serv: Pvt, Army, 18. Mem: Trustee, Vt. Hist. Soc; past pres, Dartmouth Club of Bergen Co, N.J; pres, Dartmouth Club of Hanover, N.H. Area. Rel: Congregational. Mailing Add: Gaysville, Vt. 05746. (1967)

MINETTO, JOHN A. R
Conn. State Sen.
b. Naugatuck, Conn, 1893; married. Polit. & Govt. Pos: Conn. State Rep, 45-55; Conn. State Sen, 55- Mailing Add: 191 Albert St, Torrington, Conn. 06790. (1967)

MINGE, JERRY LEE D
b. Rome, Ga, 9/23/34; s. Willie Lee Minge and Mary Moore M; m. 3/27/58 to Carol Tilman Bland; c. Mary Angela, Jennifer Bland and Anne Marguerite. Educ; Darlington Sch. for Boys, 53; Univ. of Ga, B.B.A. and LL.B; Sigma Nu; Phi Delta Phi. Polit. & Govt. Pos: Ga. State Rep, Floyd Co, Dist. 13, 65-67; judge, Floyd City Court, 67-68. Bus. & Prof. Pos: Partner, Hamilton, Anderson & Minge, Attorneys, 60- Mem: Am, Ga. and Rome Bar Asn; past pres, Rome Jaycees; Young Dem; Elks; Mason; Nine O'Clock Cotillion Club; Coosa Country Club. Rel: Baptist. Legal Res: 519 E. Eleventh St, Rome, Ga. 30161. Mailing Add: P.O. Box 746, Rome, Ga. 30161.

MINGLIN, HARRY J. R
Chmn, Sac Co. Rep. Party, Iowa
b. Lavinia, Iowa, 10/2/00; s. William E. Minglin and Dora King M; m. 2/2/24 to Muriel Ann Wheeler. Educ: Onarga, Ill. High Sch, grad, 18. Polit. & Govt. Pos: Postmaster, Ulmer, Iowa, 39-45; finance chmn, Sac Co. Rep. Party, 58-61, chmn, 61-; alternate del, Rep. Nat. Conv, 64. Bus. & Prof. Pos: Owner and ed, Auburn Enterprise & Tri-Co. Spec, 45- Mem: Lions, Auburn, Iowa; Farm Bur; Jephtha Lodge 201; Abu Bekr Temple, Sioux City; York Rite, Sac City; Scottish Rite Bodies, Sioux City Consistory; Commercial Clubs of Auburn, Lake View and Wall Lake. Rel: Methodist. Mailing Add: Auburn, Iowa 51433.

MINGO, JACK R
Mem, Calif. Rep. State Cent. Cmt.
b. Lodi, Calif, 2/28/24; s. Arthur Mingo and Rose Prinzo M; m. 11/14/45 to Helene K. Wade; c. Linda, Jack, Jr, Kathleen and Rick. Educ: Sacramento Col. Commerce, Acct. Maj, 46-49; McGeorge Col. Law, 50-51. Polit. & Govt. Pos: City clerk, Galt, Calif, 48-51; mem, Sacramento Co. Dem. Cent. Cmt, 50-54; mem, Sacramento Co. Bd. Supvr, 59-62; mem, Sacramento Co. Rep. Cent. Cmt, 66-; mem, San Joaquin Co. Rep. Cent. Cmt, 66-; mem, Calif. Rep. State Cent. Cmt, 66- Bus. & Prof. Pos: Pub. acct, Sacramento, 48-; investment broker, Jack Mingo & Co, 56-; life ins. broker, 63- Mil. Serv: Entered as Pvt, Army, serv. in SCU 1913, Camp White, Ore, 43. Publ: 'Governmental Reorganization,' Local newspapers, 60. Mem: Nat. Asn. Securities Dealers; Calif. Soc. Pub. Acct; Mason; Shrine; Scottish Rite; Kiwanis. Rel: Protestant. Mailing Add: 2766 Lacy Lane, Sacramento, Calif. 95821.

MINISH, JOSEPH GEORGE D
U.S. Rep, N.J.
b. Throop, Pa, 9/1/16; s. George Minish and Angelina M; m. to Theresa La Capra; c. George, James and Joyce. Educ: Dunmore High Sch, Pa. Polit. & Govt. Pos: Mem, Newark Cmt. on Econ. Develop, N.J; v.chmn, Essex Co. Welfare Fedn, 2 years, trustee, 6 years; U.S. Rep, N.J, 63- Bus. & Prof. Pos: Exec. secy, Essex-West Hudson Co. CIO, 7 years; secy-treas, Essex-West Hudson Labor Coun. AFL-CIO. Mil. Serv: World War II. Mem: K. of C; Elks; Ment. Health Asn. of Essex Co; exec. cmt, Green Acres Citizens Group. Legal Res: West Orange, N.J. 07052. Mailing Add: 438 Cannon House Office Bldg, Washington, D.C. 20515. (1967)

MINK, PATSY TAKEMOTO D
U.S. Rep, Hawaii
b. Maui, Hawaii, 12/6/27; d. Suematsu Takemoto and Mitama Tateyama T; m. 1/27/51 to John Francis Mink; c. Gwendolyn. Educ: Univ. Hawaii, B.A, 48; Chicago Law Sch, J.D, 51; Delta Sigma Rho. Hon. LL.D, Lindenwood Col, 65; L.H.D, Wilson Col, 65. Polit. & Govt. Pos: Charter pres, Young Dem. of Oahu, 54-56; attorney, Territorial Legis, 55 & 60; state pres, Young Dem, Hawaii, 56-58; Hawaii State Rep, 56-58; Nat. v.pres, Nat. Young Dem, 57-59; Hawaii State Sen, 58-59 & 62-64; U.S. Rep, Hawaii, 65-, mem, Educ. and Labor Cmt. and Interior and Insular Affairs Cmt, U.S. House of Rep, 65; mem, House-Senate Ad Hoc Cmt. on Poverty; secy-treas, 89th Dem. Cong. Club, 65-; mem, Cong. for Peace Thru Law, 65-; v.pres, Dem. Study Group, 67-; mem, Dem. Nat. Cmt. Cmn. on Rules Rev; mem. adv. cmt. on state-urban rels, Coun. of State Govts, 68. Bus. & Prof. Pos: Lectr, Univ. Hawaii, 52-56 & 59-62; attorney at law, 53-65. Mem: Hawaii and Am. Bar Asns; Am. Asn. for UN (former dir, Hawaii Chap); NAACP; former dir, Hawaii Asn. to Help Retarded Children; YMCA, Lanakila Crafts and Palama Settlement. Nisei of the Biennium Award, Japanese-Am. Citizens League, 66; Distinguished Am. Woman Honoree, Grand Temple Daughters and Grand Lodge of the Elks, 67; Leadership for Freedom Award, 68. Rel: Protestant. Legal Res: 94-1037 Maikai St, Waipahu, Oahu, Hawaii 96797. Mailing Add: 228 Cannon House Office Bldg, Washington, D.C. 20515.

MINN, MOMI PEARL D
Hawaii State Rep.
b. Honolulu, Hawaii, 1/28/20; d. Hoon Ting and Healani Kuawela T; m. 8/4/42 to Philip P. Minn; c. Philip Nathan, Geraldine Healani, Michael Puiki and Phyliss Momi. Educ: Univ. Hawaii. Polit. & Govt. Pos: Precinct secy, Dem. Party, Hawaii; mem, Dem. Co. Cmt; Dem. Nat. Committeewoman, Hawaii, 64-; Hawaii State Rep, 67- Mem: DAV Auxiliary; Women in Construction. Mailing Add: 86-127 Kakaiapola St, Waianae, Oahu, Hawaii 96792. (1967)

MINN, PHILIP P. D
Chmn, Hawaii Dem. State Finance Cmt.
b. Hana, Maui, Hawaii, 8/31/17; s. Eui Sik Minn and Hana Lee M; m. 8/4/42 to Momi Pearl Ting; c. Philip Nathan, Geraldine Healani, Michael Puiki and Phyliss Momi. Educ: Univ. Hawaii. Polit. & Govt. Pos: Cent. committeeman, Tenth Dist. Dem. Party, Hawaii, 50-62, chmn, 62-66; Hawaii State Rep, 54-66; chmn, Hawaii Dem. State Finance Cmt, currently; alternate del, Dem. Nat. Conv, 68. Bus. & Prof. Pos: Owner and mgr, P. Minn Plant Nursery and Landscaping Co, 45- Mil. Serv: Entered as Sgt, Army, 40, released as 1st Sgt, 44; Capt, Hawaii Nat. Guard Res, currently; Pac. Theater and Guadalcanal Campaign Ribbons. Mem: Hawaii Asn. of Nurserymen (past pres; dir, currently); Am. Asn. of Nurserymen; Am. Asn. of Landscape Contractors; Am. Legion; K. of C; Farm Bur; Civitans; life mem, DAV. Coached football, McKinley Alumni and Iolani High Schs. Rel: Roman Catholic. Mailing Add: 86-127 Kakaiapola St, Waianae, Oahu, Hawaii 96792. (1967)

MINOW, NEWTON NORMAN D
b. Milwaukee, Wis, 1/17/26; s. Jay A. Minow and Doris Stein M; m. 5/29/49 to Josephine Baskin; c. Susan Nell, Mary Rose and Martha Louise. Educ: Univ. Mich; Northwest. Univ, B.S, 49 and LL.B, 50; Order of the Coif; recipient, Wigmore Award. Hon. LL.D, Brandeis Univ, 63, Univ. Wis, 63 and Northwest. Univ, 65. Polit. & Govt. Pos: Law clerk to Chief Justice of Supreme Court Fred M. Vinson, 51-52; admin. asst. to Gov. Adlai E. Stevenson, Ill, 52-53; spec. asst. to Adlai E. Stevenson in Presidential Campaigns, 52 & 56; gen. counsel and secy, Nat. Bus. and Prfnl. Cmt. for Kennedy-Johnson, 60; chmn, Fed. Commun. Cmn, 61-63; alternate del, Dem. Nat. Conv, 68. Bus. & Prof. Pos: Assoc, Mayer, Meyer, Austrian & Platt, 53-55; partner, Stevenson, Rifkind & Wirtz, 55-61; exec. v.pres, gen. counsel and dir, Encyclopedia Britannica, Inc, 63-65; trustee, Rand Corp, 65-; sr. partner, Leibman, Williams, Bennett, Baird and Minow, 65-; dir, Barnaby's, Inc; dir, Dynascan Corp, 66-, FAS Int, Inc, 67-, Berger-Kent Spec. Fund, Inc, 68- and FCB Cablevision, Inc, 69- Mil. Serv: Entered as Pvt, Army, 44, released as Cpl, 46. Publ: Equal Time: The Private Broadcaster and the Public Interest, Atheneum Publishers, 64; contrib, As We Knew Adlai, Harper & Row, 66. Mem: Am, Ill, Chicago and Wis. Bar Asns; fel. Am. Bar Found; bd. of lay trustees, Univ. of Notre Dame; dir. and chmn, Chicago Educ. TV; dir, Nat. Educ. TV, Stevenson Inst. of Int. Affairs, Nat. Book Cmt. and Nat. Civil Serv. League; adv. bd, George Foster Peabody Radio and TV Awards, 20th Century Fund, Nat. Acad. of TV Arts and Sci, Northwest. Alumni Asn, Chicago Coun. For. Rels. and Midland Authors; Legal, Econ, Exec, Mid-Am. and Law Clubs; Standard Club, Chicago; Northmoor Country Club, Highland Park; Fed. City Club, D.C. Named One of Ten Outstanding Young Men in Chicago, Jr. C. of C. and Indust, 60 and One of Ten Outstanding Young Men in U.S, 61; George Foster Peabody Award, 61. Rel: Jewish. Legal Res: 375 Palos Rd, Glencoe, Ill. 60022. Mailing Add: Room 3200, One First National Plaza, Chicago, Ill. 60670.

MINSHALL, WILLIAM E. R
U.S. Rep, Ohio
b. E. Cleveland, Ohio, 10/24/11; m. to Frances Smith; c. William Edwin, III, Werner Ellis and Peter Charles. Educ: Univ. of Va; Cleveland Law Sch, LL.B; admitted to bar 40. Polit. & Govt. Pos: Gen. Counsel to Maritime Admin, 53-54; U.S. Rep, Ohio, 54-, mem, U.S. House of Rep, cmt. on appropriations, subcmts, defense and transportation; mem, Bd. of Visitors to U.S. Mil. Acad, 61-62, U.S. Naval Acad, 63-65 and U.S. Air Force, 66-; del, Rep. Nat. Conv, 68. Bus. & Prof. Pos: Attorney-at-law. Mil. Serv: Enlisted Dec. 40 as Pvt, Army and serv. in ETO, G-2 Sect, Hq. III Corps, released Mar. 46, Lt. Col. Legal Res: Lakewood, Ohio 44107. Mailing Add: 2243 Rayburn House Office Bldg, Washington, D.C. 20515.

MINTZ, HYMAN E. R
b. South Fallsburg, N.Y, 10/6/08; m. to Miriam Evans; c. two. Educ: Cornell Univ, A.B, 29, LL.B, 31. Polit. & Govt. Pos: N.Y. State Assemblyman, 50-66. Bus. & Prof. Pos: Lawyer, Monticello, N.Y. Mem: F&AM; Elks; B'nai B'rith; K. of P; Lions; Shrine. Rel: Jewish. Mailing Add: South Fallsburg, N.Y. 12779.

MIRABELLI, MICHAEL ANTHONY D
State Treas, Nev.
b. Union City, N.J, 6/2/22; s. Carmine Mirabelli and Filomena Silvagni M; m. 3/10/43 to Betty Ann Beezer. Educ: Univ. Nev, B.A. Polit. & Govt. Pos: Cmnr, Washoe Co, Nev, 61-62; State Treas, Nev, 63- Bus. & Prof. Pos: Teacher, Las Vegas Sch. Syst, Nev, 51-52; mgr, Stamppli's Record Room, 52-55; owner, M.I.K. Inc, 56-66. Mil. Serv: Entered as Pvt, Air Force, 42, released as Sgt, 45, after serv. in Eighth Air Force, Eng, 45. Mem: Elks; K. of C; dir, YMCA; nat. del, Am. Cancer Soc. Rel: Roman Catholic. Mailing Add: 805 Sharrow Way, Carson City, Nev. 89701. (1967)

MIRANDA JIMENEZ, MAXIMINO New Progressive, P.R.
Sen, P.R. Senate
v. Villalba, P.R, 6/15/31; s. José Miranda and Silvana Jiménez M; m. 4/11/53 to Antonia Ilia Colón Gonzalez; c. Maximino, José Alberto and Ivelisse. Educ: Cath. Univ, P.R, LL.B, 66. Polit. & Govt. Pos: Sen, Dist. of Ponce, P.R. Senate, 69- Bus. & Prof. Pos: Sec. sch. teacher, Dist. of Villalba, P.R, 60-67. Mil. Serv: Entered as Pvt, Army, 51, released as SP-2, 56, after serv. in 30th Inf. Regt, Third Div, Korea, 53-55; Good Conduct Medal. Mem: Legal adv, Am. Legion Post 27; appelate mem, local bd, Selective Serv. 75. Rel: Catholic. Legal Res: Muñoz Rivera St, Villalba, P.R. 00766. Mailing Add: Barceló 12 A, Villalba, P.R. 00766.

MIRIKITANI, PERCY KIYOSHI R
Hawaii State Sen.
b. Honolulu, Hawaii, 5/1/17; s. Hiakutaro Mirikitani and Masa Iketaka H; m. 5/10/41 to Lavina Jane Spoonamore. Educ: Univ. of Hawaii, B.Ed. and Fifth Year Cert, 41; Tulane Law Sch, J.D, 52; Phi Alpha Delta; La Societe de Civile Droite. Polit. & Govt. Pos: Dep. attorney gen. and

adminstr. of the attorney gen. off, Hawaii, 53-59; Hawaii State Rep, 59-66; Hawaii State Sen, 66- Bus. & Prof. Pos: Teacher, Washington Jr. High Sch, Honolulu, 41-42; construction supt, U.S. Army, Corps of Engrs, Honolulu, 42-45; realtor, developer and bus. consult, Hawaiian Bus. Brokerage, Honolulu, 45-49; attorney-at-law, Mirikitani, Mirikitani & Namaka, Honolulu, 59-; legal counsel, Honolulu Police Reserve. Mem: Hawaii and Am. Bar Asns; Am. Judicature Soc; Univ. of Hawaii Alumni Asn; Tulane Alumni Asn; Honolulu Bd. of Realtors; Nat. Asn. of Realty Bd; Hawaiian Govt. Employees Asn; Honolulu Police Old Timers; Hawaii State Investr. Asn; Prfnl. Photographers Asn; Hawaii State Capital Fine Arts Cmt; C. of C. (bd. of dirs, Honolulu Japanese Chap); Eye of the Pac. Guide Dogs; Honolulu Acad. of Arts; Honolulu Symphony Soc; YMCA; Boy Scouts; Bishop Museum Asn; Cystic Fibrosis Asn; Friends of Iolani Palace; Hawaii Asn. to Help Retarded Children. Named Outstanding Citizen as an Attorney, McKinley High Sch, 67. Rel: Congregational; Mem, Bd. of Trustees, Central Union Church. Legal Res: 240 Makee Rd, Parkview Apt, P.H. 'A', Honolulu, Hawaii 96815. Mailing Add: P.O. Box 8483, Honolulu, Hawaii 96815.

MISBAUER, BENEDICT 'BEN' D
Mo. State Rep.
b. St. Louis, Mo, 11/11/13; m. 1932; c. Mrs. Madeline Woolem and Mrs. Elsa Meadows. Educ: St. Louis Parochial and Pub. Schs. Polit. & Govt. Pos: Mem, Eighth Ward Dem. Orgn, Mo; Mo. State Rep, 59- Bus. & Prof. Pos: Engaged in the air conditioning maintenance bus. Mem: Elks. Rel: Catholic. Mailing Add: 3015 Hawthorne Blvd, St. Louis, Mo. 63104. (1967)

MISHLER, EVERETT MONROE D
b. New Paris, Ind, 9/29/18; s. Milton Mishler and Nina Moyer M; m. 12/6/39 to Kathryn Louise Stahly; c. Kermit, Marlene, Jerry, Grace, Howard, Rex, Carolan and Dan. Polit. & Govt. Pos: Ind. State Rep, Elkhart Co, 65-66. Mem; Farm Bur; Nat. Farmers Orgn; Elkhart Co. Farm Bur. Coop. Asn. Ind. Rep, Nat. 4-H Club Conf, 39. Rel: Church of the Brethren, mem, gen. bd, 69-70; dir, Elkhart Co. Coun. Churches, 69-71. Mailing Add: R.R. 1, New Paris, Ind. 46554.

MISHOE, W. FRANK D
b. Greeleyville, S.C, 11/27/19; s. Fred Mishoe and Margaret Rodgers M; m. 11/13/46 to Mamie Lee Boyd. Educ: Univ. of S.C, 39-40. Polit. & Govt. Pos: Mayor, Greeleyville, S.C, 51-54; S.C. State Sen, 61-66. Bus. & Prof. Pos: Farmer and merchant; owner of Santee Milling Co. Mil. Serv: Army, 41-44, served 21 months with 145th Inf, 37th Div, Pac. Theatre of Opers. Mailing Add: Greeleyville, S.C. 29056. (1967)

MISKA, WALTER JOHN R
R.I. State Sen.
b. Fall River, Mass, 10/17/21; both parents deceased; m. 2/23/46 to Bertha V. Witkowicz; c. Jeanne Marie and Walter Joseph. Educ: B.M.C. Durfee High Sch, Fall River, Mass, grad, 39. Polit. & Govt. Pos: R.I. State Sen, Dist. 46, 67- Bus. & Prof. Pos: Owner-operator, Miska Rug Outlet, 48-69; Polish prog. dir, Radio WALE, Fall River, Mass, 63-69, news dir, 68-69. Mil. Serv: Entered as Seaman, Navy, 42, released as ARM 1/C, 46, after serv. in Photog. Reconnaissance (VD-1), S.E. Pac. Theatre, 43-46; 4 Air Medals. Rel: Roman Catholic. Mailing Add: 3216 E. Main Rd, Portsmouth, R.I. 02871.

MISURACA, MALCOLM ANTHONY D
Mem, Calif. Dem. State Cent. Cmt.
b. Glendale, Calif, 5/31/37; s. Louis J. Misuraca and Gertrude Marie Schucking M; m. 9/12/62 to Karen Christine Quistgard; c. Melinda, Andrea and Jessica. Educ: Georgetown Col, B.S. in Soc. Sci, 59; Univ. Calif. Sch. of Law, Berkeley, LL.B, 62; Calif. Law Rev, 60-62, Book Rev. Ed, 61-62. Polit. & Govt. Pos: Chmn, Yuba Co. Dem. Cent. Cmt, Calif, 66-68; del, Dem. Nat. Conv, 68; mem, Calif. Dem. State Cent. Cmt, 68- Mem: Calif. Bar Asn; Am. Bar Asn.(chmn, food and drug cmt, Admin. Law Sect, 63); exec. coun, Calif. Conf. Barristers, 65-67. Mailing Add: 632 Cristmont, Yuba City, Calif. 95991. (1967)

MITCHELL, ALBERT KNELL R
b. Clayton, N.Mex, 6/25/94; s. Thomas Edward Mitchell and Linda Knell M; 2nd m. 6/27/57 to Natalie Galbraith; c. Linda (Mrs. Davis) and Albert Julian. Educ: Cornell Univ, Class of 17; Gnome Club; Owl and Key. Polit. & Govt. Pos: N.Mex. State Rep, 27-29; nominee, Gov, N.Mex, 37; U.S. Sen, 41; mem. and chmn, Rep. Nat. Conv. Cmts; committeeman, Rep. Nat. Cmt, N.Mex, 42-65; v.chmn, Rep. Nat. Cmt, 62-65; mem, Nat. Cmn. on Food Mkt, 65- Bus. & Prof. Pos: Pres, T.E. Mitchell & Son, Albert, N.Mex, 34-; dir, Albuquerque Production Credit Corp, 38-, S.E.C. Corp, El Paso, 39-, First Nat. Bank, Raton, N.Mex, 40-, Ideal Basic Industries, Inc, 45- and Colo. Interstate Corp, Colorado Springs, 55-; chmn. bd. and dir, Nat. Livestock Tax Cmn, Denver, Colo, 57- Mil. Serv: Pvt, Field Artil. Officers Training, Camp Zachary Taylor, Louisville, Ky, 18. Mem: Pres, Am. Nat. Livestock Asn, 36-37, Am. Hereford Asn, 27-28 & 56-57 and Am. Quarter Horse Asn, 46-49 & 54; dir, Int. Livestock Exposition, Chicago (past pres. and chmn. bd. and dir); 1st v.pres, Nat. West. Livestock Show, Denver, 48-; trustee, Cornell Univ, Ithaca, N.Y, 49-; regent, N.Mex. State Univ, 40-46; Chicago Club; Denver Club; Albuquerque Petrol. Club; Mason (32°); Shrine; chmn. bd, Nat. Cowboy Hall of Fame, 56-; dir. and chmn. exec. cmt, Lovelace Found. Albuquerque. Rel: Episcopal. Mailing Add: Tequesquite Ranch, Albert, N.Mex. 87733.

MITCHELL, BRUCE TYSON R
Mem, Calif. Rep. Cent. Cmt.
b. San Francisco, Calif, 11/6/28; s. John Robert Mitchell and Lorraine Tyson M; m. 10/14/51 to Adrienne Means Hiscox; c. Mark Means. Educ: Stanford Univ, B.A, 49, LL.B, 51; El Cuadro Eating Club. Polit. & Govt. Pos: Chmn, Tri-City Young Rep, Calif, 57; mem, San Mateo Co. Rep. Cent. Cmt, 60-, v.chmn, 62-64, chmn, 64-; mem, Calif. Rep. Cent. Cmt, 64-; treas, Asn. of Rep. Co. Cent. Cmt. Chmn. of Calif, 67-; alternate del, Rep. Nat. Conv, 68. Bus. & Prof. Pos: Estate adminstr, Crocker-Anglo Nat. Bank, 55-57; sr. counsel and asst. secy, Utah Construction & Mining Co, 57- Mil. Serv: Entered as Seaman, Navy, 52, released as Lt.(jg), 55, after serv. in Naval Forces Far East; Lt, Naval Res; Am. Defense Medal; Korean and UN Campaign Ribbons. Mem: San Francisco, Calif. and Am. Bar Asns; Am. Judicature Soc; Am. Soc. Corp. Secretaries; Mason; Commonwealth Club of Calif; Jaycees (Past exec. v.pres. and dir). Rel: Congregational. Mailing Add: 165 Redwood Dr, Hillsborough, Calif. 94010.

MITCHELL, BRYAN FRANKLIN R
Mem, W.Va. State Rep. Exec. Cmt.
b. Petersburg, W.Va, 8/31/27; s. Bryan Mitchell and Esther Forman M; m. 6/18/65 to Grace Holden; c. Tammy Ann and William Clifford. Educ: Washington and Jefferson Col; Pa. State Col. of Optometry; Honor Soc. Polit. & Govt. Pos: Mem, Grant Co. Young Rep. Club, W.Va, 52; chmn, State Young Rep. Club, 58; chmn, Grant Co. Rep. Cmt, 60-; mem, W.Va. State Rep. Exec. Cmt, 60- Bus. & Prof. Pos: Optometrist, 54- Mil. Serv: Entered as Seaman, Navy, 65, released as Hosp. Apprentice 1/C, 66. Mem: Am. Optom. Asn; Am. Legion; Odd Fellows; Mason. Rel: Presbyterian. Legal Res: Judy St, Petersburg, W.Va. 26747. Mailing Add: Box 38, Petersburg, W.Va. 26747.

MITCHELL, C.C. Conservative
b. Lyon Co; c. Two. Educ: Univ. Minn. Law Sch. Polit. & Govt. Pos: Minn. State Sen, 46-66; Mille Lacs Co. Attorney, 8 years. Bus. & Prof. Pos: Lawyer. Mailing Add: 106 S. 5th Ave, Princeton, Minn. 55371.

MITCHELL, CARLTON ADGER D
S.C. State Rep.
b. Anderson, S.C, 7/5/07; s. Robert Foster Mitchell and Margret Buchanan M; m. 11/11/33 to Zilla Bakter Sears; c. Fleurette Ann (Mrs. Joe B. Fendley), Donna Sue (Mrs. Howard B. Parker) and Cephus Jared. Educ: O'Neil Ross Col, Ft. Wayne, Ind, early 30's in basic sci; Standard Inst. of Therapeutics, York, Pa, N.D, 37; Cent. States Col, Eaton, Ohio, summers, 58, 59 & 61. Polit. & Govt. Pos: Sch. trustee, Reedy Fork Sch, Seneca Area, 44-49 & 50-53; S.C. State Rep, 57-, second v.chmn, Mil. Pub. and Munic. Affairs Cmt, 61- Bus. & Prof. Pos: Physician and owner, Shady Brook Sanatorium, 46- Mem: Nat. Eclectic Med. Asn. Rel: Baptist; mem. and Deacon, Reedy Fork Baptist Church, 50- Legal Res: Route 6, Seneca, S.C. 29678. Mailing Add: Shady Brook Sanatorium, Seneca, S.C. 29678.

MITCHELL, CECIL DARRELL R
Chmn, Okmulgee Co. Rep. Cmt, Okla.
b. Seminole, Okla, 7/28/30; s. Virgil Custer Mitchell and Della Sublett M; m. 5/31/49 to Minnie Ruth Boatman; c. Malcolm Victor and Martha Vonne. Educ: Pub. Schs. Polit. & Govt. Pos: Chmn, Okmulgee Co. Rep. Cmt, Okla, currently. Bus. & Prof. Pos: Driller's asst, Newsom-Mills Drilling Co, 49-52; pipe liner, Mid-Continent Pipe Line, 52-65; bldg. contractor, M & C Construction Co, 65-; independent oil operator, Mitchell Oil Co. Rel: Assembly of God. Mailing Add: 1219 E. Ninth, Okmulgee, Okla. 74447.

MITCHELL, CHARLENE Communist Party
Secy, Cmn. on Black Liberation, Communist Party, U.S.A.
b. Cincinnati, Ohio, 6/8/30; d. Charles Alexander and Naomi Taylor A; div; c. Steven. Educ: Herzl Jr. Col, A.A, 50. Polit. & Govt. Pos: Mem, Ill. State Bd, Labor Youth League, 49-55; admin. secy, South. Calif. Communist Party, 57-60, chmn. Negro cmn, 63-67; mem. nat. cmt, Communist Party, U.S.A, 57-, U.S. presidential cand, 68, secy, Cmn. on Black Liberation, 68- Bus. & Prof. Pos: Head bookkeeper, importing firm, South. Calif, 62-68. Mailing Add: 23 W. 26th St, New York, N.Y. 10010.

MITCHELL, CHARLES B. R
Miss. State Rep.
b. Carthage, Miss, 12/6/25; s. Clarence B. Mitchell and Lessie Jolly M; m. 12/24/47 to Kathleen Yates; c. Karen, Nancy and Jan. Educ: Millsaps Col, B.A, 49; Lambda Chi Alpha. Polit. & Govt. Pos: Miss. State Rep, Hinds Co, 68- Mil. Serv: Entered as Pvt, Army, 44, released as Cpl, 46, after serv. in 239th Gen. Hosp, ETO, 44-46. Mem: Jackson Asn. Life Underwriters (pres, 62-63); Miss. Chartered Life Underwriters Asn.(v.pres, 61-62); Kiwanis. Rel: Methodist; Chmn. bd. stewards, Christ Methodist Church, 64-65. Legal Res: 5627 Concord Dr, Jackson, Miss. 39211. Mailing Add: P.O. Box 12301, Jackson, Miss. 39211.

MITCHELL, CLARENCE M, III D
Md. State Sen.
b. St. Paul, Minn, 12/14/39; married. Educ: Gonzaga High Sch, Wash, D.C; Univ. of Md; Morgan State Col. Polit. & Govt. Pos: Mem, Young Dem. of Md; Md. State Del, 63-67; Md. State Sen, 67-; alternate del, Dem. Nat. Conv, 68. Bus. & Prof. Pos: Pres, Real Estate Co. Mem: YMCA; NAACP; Kappa Alpha Psi; Baltimore Jr. C. of C. Rel: Methodist; mem, off. bd, Sharp St. Methodist Church. Mailing Add: 1239 Druid Hill Ave, Baltimore, Md. 21217.

MITCHELL, COY J. D
b. Dellwood, Fla, 9/22/18; m. Jessie Roberts; c. Martha Charlotte, Coy Lynn and Dean Allison. Educ: Linely Bus. and Prfnl. Sch, Hot Springs, Ark. Polit. & Govt. Pos: Fla. State Rep, 62-66. Bus. & Prof. Pos: Dent. technician. Mil. Serv: Army, Med. Detachment, SCU 1448. Mem: Farm Bur; Am. Legion (former Comdr); chaplain, 40 et 8; Mason (treas, coun); K.T.(treas); Eastern Star; Elks (former trustee). Rel: Baptist; secy-treas, Adult II Sunday Sch, First Baptist Church, Marianna, Fla. Mailing Add: Box 26, Marianna, Fla. 32446. (1967)

MITCHELL, DON Conservative
b. Princeton, Minn; married; c. Six. Educ: Sch. of Agr, Univ. of Minn. Polit. & Govt. Pos: Minn. State Rep, 56 & 64-68; chmn, Nobles Co. Agr. Stabilization & Conserv. Cmt, 57; area census supvr, 60; postmaster, Minn. State House of Rep, 63. Bus. & Prof. Pos: Farmer. Mem: Round Lake Farmers Elevator; Adult 4-H leader; bd. mem, Nobles Co. Coop. Oil Asn. Mailing Add: Round Lake, Minn. 56167. (1967)

MITCHELL, DONALD J. D
b. Ft. Dodge, Iowa, 1914; s. Michael J. Mitchell and Mary Howard M. Educ: State Univ. of Iowa, A.B, J.D, 37. Polit. & Govt. Pos: Asst. co. attorney, Iowa, 38-41; chmn, Webster Co. Dem. Cmt, 48-53; mem, Dem. Nat. Cmt, 53-68, mem, exec. cmt, 62-68; del, Dem. Nat. Conv, 68. Bus. & Prof. Pos: Lawyer, Ft. Dodge, Iowa. Mil. Serv: Army, World War II. Mem: Am. Legion; Elks; Moose; K. of C. Rel: Catholic. Mailing Add: 610 Snell Bldg, Ft. Dodge, Iowa 50501. (1967)

MITCHELL, DONALD J. R
Majority Whip, N.Y. State Assembly
b. Ilion, N.Y, 5/8/23; m. to Greta Levee; c. Gretchen, Cynthia, Allen. Educ: Hobart Col; Columbia Univ, B.S; Columbia Univ. Teachers Col, M.A. Polit. & Govt. Pos: Mem, Herkimer Town Coun, N.Y, 54-57; mayor, Herkimer, 57-60, mem, Zoning Bd. Appeals, 63-64; N.Y. State Assemblyman, 64-, Majority Whip, N.Y. State Assembly, 69- Bus. & Prof. Pos: Optometrist, 50-; mem, N.Y. State Bd. Optometry Examiners. Mil. Serv: Navy, World War II and Korea, 5 years. Mem: Pres, Mohawk Valley Conf. Mayors, 57-63; naval rep. three man mil. adv. cmt, Optometry's Nat. Orgn; Mohawk Valley Optometric Soc; past officer or dir, Herkimer Red Cross, Cancer Soc, Libr, Washburn Mem, Boy Scouts, Cub Scouts and Kiwanis; mem, Mason; Elks; Am. Legion; VFW; Rod and Gun Club. Rel: First Methodist, mem. off. bd, Herkimer First Methodist Church. Mailing Add: Herkimer, N.Y. 13350.

MITCHELL, GEORGE JOHN D
Dem. Nat. Committeeman, Maine
b. Waterville, Maine, 8/20/33; s. George J. Mitchell and Mary Saad M; m. 8/29/59 to Sally Heath; c. Andrea. Educ: Bowdoin Col, B.A, 54; Georgetown Univ, LL.B, 60; Sigma Nu. Polit. & Govt. Pos: Trial attorney, U.S. Dept. of Justice, Wash, D.C, 60-62; exec. asst. to U.S. Sen. Edmund S. Muskie, 62-65; chmn, Maine Dem. State Cmt, 66-68; del, Dem. Nat. Conv, 68; Dem. Nat. committeeman from Maine, 68- Bus. & Prof. Pos: Attorney, Jensen & Baird, Portland, Maine, 65- Mil. Serv: Entered as 2nd Lt, Army, 54, released as 1st Lt, 56, after serv. in Army Counter Intel, Berlin, Germany, 55-56. Mem: Am. Bar Asn. Rel: Roman Catholic. Mailing Add: 107 Falmouth Rd, Falmouth, Maine 04105.

MITCHELL, GEORGE TRICE R
b. Marshall, Ill, 1/20/14; s. Roscoe Addison Mitchell and Alma Elizabeth Trice M; m. 6/21/41 to Mildred Aletha Miller; c. Linda Sue (Mrs. Keith L. Miller) and Mary Kathryn. Educ: Purdue Univ, B.S. in Mech. Eng, 35, grad. sch, 35-36; George Wash. Univ, M.D, 40; Smith-Reed-Russell Med. Soc; Acacia; Alpha Kappa Kappa. Polit. & Govt. Pos: Mem. state coun, Ill. Med. Polit. Action Cmt, 66-; alternate del, Rep. Nat. Conv, 68. Bus. & Prof. Pos: Gen. practice of med, Marshall, Ill, 46-; mem. bd. of dir, 1st Nat. Bank, 49-, v.pres, 66- Mil. Serv: Entered as 1st Lt, Army Med. Corps, 41, released as Lt. Col, 46, after serv. in Army Air Force, West. Flying Training Command and Air Force Redistribution Command, 41-46. Mem: Am. Med. Asn; Ill. State Med. Soc; Am. Acad. of Gen. Practice; Clark Co. Med. Soc; Aesculapian Soc. of the Wabash Valley; Terre Haute Acad. of Med; Mason (32°); Shrine; Am. Legion; Rotary; Ill. Agr. Asn; Capitol Hill Club; Country Club of Terre Haute. Distinguished Serv. Award, Jaycees, 66. Rel: Methodist. Mailing Add: R.R. 2, Marshall, Ill. 62441.

MITCHELL, HARLAN ERWIN D
b. Dalton, Ga, 8/17/24; s. Douglas Wright Mitchell, Sr. and Mary Erwin M; m. 9/24/43 to Helen Jones; c. Harlan Erwin, Jr, Marilyn Helen and Leslie Lee (Mrs. Taylor). Educ: The Citadel; Univ. Ga. Sch. Law, LL.B, 48; Gridiron; Sigma Alpha Epsilon; Delta Theta Phi. Polit. & Govt. Pos: Solicitor-gen, Cherokee Judicial Circuit, 53-56, judge, Superior Court, 57-58; U.S. Rep, Ga, 58-61; Ga. State Sen, 43rd Dist, 60-62. Mil. Serv: 1st Lt, Air Force, 43-46 & 51-52; Air Medal with 2 Stars; Pac. Ribbon with 2 Battle Stars. Mem: Ga, Am. and Conasauga Circuit Bar Asns; Elks; Am. Legion; VFW. Rel: Methodist. Mailing Add: 612 Miller St, Dalton, Ga. 30720.

MITCHELL, HENRY REDMAN D
Miss. State Rep.
b. Amory, Miss, 12/6/06; married. Polit. & Govt. Pos: Miss. State Rep, currently. Bus. & Prof. Pos: Farmer and dairy bar operator. Mem: Mason. Rel: Baptist; Deacon and teacher of young people. Mailing Add: Route 1, Amory, Miss. 38821. (1967)

MITCHELL, HUGH BURNTON D
b. Great Falls, Mont, 3/22/07; s. Harry Browne Mitchell and Mary Greening M; m. 9/17/38 to Kathryn Herkimer Smith; c. Bruce C. and Elizabeth S. Educ: Dartmouth Col, 25-29; Phi Kappa Psi. Polit. & Govt. Pos: U.S. Sen, Wash, 45-46; U.S. Rep, 1st Dist, Wash, 49-53. Bus. & Prof. Pos: Partner, Martin Van Lines, 53-60; chmn, Gaco Western, Inc, 56-; pres, Alaska Van & Storage Co, Inc, 56-; pres, Alaska Terminals, Inc. and Alaska HHG Movers, Inc, 61- Publ: 'The Prospect for Fiscal Responsibility,' Wash. Educ. Mag, 3/66. Mem: Chmn, Cmt. for Wash. Tax Reform; C. of C; Wash. Athletic Club; Munic. League of Seattle. Rel: Unitarian. Mailing Add: 3220 Magnolia Blvd. W, Seattle, Wash. 98199.

MITCHELL, J. HAROLD R
Utah State Rep.
b. Parowan, Utah, 9/15/95; s. William C. Mitchell and Laurette Orton M; m. 6/7/23 to Bertrude Seeley; c. Florence (Mrs. Glenn Russell), Harold Seeley, JoAnne (Mrs. Bob R. Adams) and Peggy Laurette (Mrs. Thomas Dobrusky). Educ: Uath State Univ, B.S, 23; Univ. Utah, summer 30; Univ. Ariz, M.A, 40; Phi Delta Kappa; Pi Kappa Alpha. Polit. & Govt. Pos: Utah State Rep, 57-58 & 65- Bus. & Prof. Pos: Athletic coach, Safford High Sch, Safford, Ariz, 23-24, prin, 24-40 and supt. of schs, 40-47. Mem: Pres, Iron Co. Farm Bur, 2 terms; Rotary. Rel: Latter-day Saint. Mailing Add: 27 S. 100 East, Parowan, Utah 84761.

MITCHELL, JOHN C. D
Chmn, Nebr. State Dem. Cent. Cmt.
b. Kearney, Nebr, 12/17/24; s. Charles P. Mitchell and Athena Kapotas M; m. to Mary J. Kafasis; c. John Charles, II. Educ: Nebr. State Col, Kearney, B.A, 47; Georgetown Univ. Sch. of Law, LL.B, 50. Polit. & Govt. Pos: Dollar-a-Year Man, U.S. Treas. Dept, 46; police judge, Kearney, Nebr; justice of peace, Buffalo Co, Nebr; chmn, Buffalo Co. Dem. Cmt, 58-; del, Dem. Nat. Conv, 64; chmn, Nebr. State Dem. Cent. Cmt, 64- Bus. & Prof. Pos: Nat. ~~Gen.~~ Gen. Legal Counsel and Parliamentarian, U.S. Jr. C. of C, 53-57; mem, Supreme Court Pattern Jury Instruction Cmt, 65-68. Mem: Am. and Buffalo Co. Asns; Cmt. for Practice and Procedure, Nebr. State Bar Asn; Am. Trial Lawyers Asn; former mem, Am. Judicature Soc; nat. committeeman for Nebr, Am. Asn. of Trial Attorneys; bd. dir, Nebr. Asn. of Trial Attorneys; Kearney Commun. Concert Asn; Kearney Bd. of Adjustments; Buffalo Co. Red Cross; Alpha Tau Omega Alumni Asn; Nebr. State Col. Alumni Asn. Selected Most Valuable Mem. Editorial Staff Georgetown Law J, Served as Leading Article Ed, and was on Staff for $2\frac{1}{2}$ Years, Submitting Recent Decisions and notes; Most Valuable Citizen Award, City of Kearney, Nebr, 57; Am. Dem. Rep. to Iran Polit. Cong, 67. Rel: Greek Orthodox; Bd. of Trustees, Holy Trinity Greek Orthodox Church. Legal Res: 3024 Paddock, Omaha, Nebr. 68124. Mailing Add: 1130 First National Bank, Omaha, Nebr. 68102.

MITCHELL, JOHN NEWTON R
Attorney Gen. of U.S.
b. Detroit, Mich, 9/5/13; s. Joseph Charles Mitchell (deceased) and Margaret Agnes McMahon M. (deceased); m. to Martha Beall; c. John Newton, III, Jill Elizabeth (Mrs. Edwin C. Reed) and Martha. Educ: Fordham Univ, 32-34; Fordham Univ. Law Sch, LL.B, 38; St. John's Univ. Law Sch, postgrad. study, 38-39. Polit. & Govt. Pos: Campaign mgr, Richard Nixon for Pres, 68; Attorney Gen. of U.S, 69- Bus. & Prof. Pos: Attorney-at-law, Caldwell & Raymond, N.Y.C, 38-42, Caldwell, Trimble & Mitchell, 42-66 and Nixon, Mudge, Rose, Guthrie, Alexander & Mitchell, 67-68. Mil. Serv: Comdr, Navy, 43-46, with serv. in Motor Torpedo Boats, Pac. Theatre. Mem: Sect. on local govt, Am. Bar Asn; N.Y State Bar Asn; past pres, Munic. Bond Club and Munic. Forum of N.Y; dir. and trustee, Am. Coun. to Improve Our Neighborhoods; dir, Nat. Housing Conf. Legal Res: Rye, N.Y. Mailing Add: U.S. Dept. of Justice, Washington, D.C. 20530.

MITCHELL, LELAND DEWIGHT D
Membership Coordinator, Fourth Dist. Dem. Party, Mich.
b. Charlottesville, Ind, 1/20/02; s. Charles C. Mitchell and Mollie Mae Heckleman M; wid, 58; m. 6/6/59 to Dorothy Meade Mackey; c. Roger, Clarence J. and Robert L. Mitchell, D. Daniel Mackey (stepson) and Mrs. Debora Carter (stepdaughter). Educ: Palmer Sch. of Chiropractic, Davenport, Iowa, D.C, 21; West. Mich. Univ, Kalamazoo, Pre-med, 43; Phi Delta Phi. Polit. & Govt. Pos: Cand, U.S. Cong, 62; chmn, Fourth Cong. Dist. Dem. Party, Mich, 62-64; del, Dem. Nat. Conv, 68; mem, Fourth Dist. Cent. Cmt, currently; mem, Dem. State and Nat. Asn, currently; membership coordinator, Fourth Dist. Dem. Party, Mich, 69- Bus. & Prof. Pos: Pres, Mitchell Hosp, 52-67. Mem: Life mem. resident adv. bd, Alexander Hamilton Life Ins. Co. Am; Nat. Coun. Chiropractic Roentgenologists; Mich. State Chiropractic Asn. (pres, dist. two, 46-48); Nat. Chiropractic Asn; Rotary. Citation of Honor, Alexander Hamilton Ins. Co, 68. Rel: Protestant. Legal Res: 123 N. Main St, Three Rivers, Mich. 49093. Mailing Add: P.O. Box 206, Three Rivers, Mich. 49093.

MITCHELL, LESTER ELBRIDGE, SR. R
N.H. State Rep.
b. Campton, N.H, 3/9/88; s. Samuel Mitchell and Pamelia Homans M; m. to Ethel V. Newton (deceased); c. Ruth (Mrs. Robert Loring), Lester, Jr, Lilla (Mrs. George Sjostrand), Alice (Mrs. Philip Chapman), Mildred (Mrs. Philip Therard) and Arlen (Mrs. Kenith Horton). Educ: New Hampton, 2 years. Polit. & Govt. Pos: Road agent, Campton, N.H, 19-34 and moderator, 28-69; N.H. State Rep, Campton, 33, 35 & 69-; N.H. State Sen, Dist. 3, 39, 63 & 65. Bus. & Prof. Pos: Inspector, State Liquor Cmn, 40-60. Mem: Jr. Order United Am. Mechanics; Grange. Rel: Protestant. Mailing Add: R.F.D, 1, Plymouth, N.H. 03264.

MITCHELL, LOREN H. D
b. Council Bluffs, Iowa, 9/27/42; s. Lewis Mitchell and Elouise Williamson M; single. Educ: Drake Univ, B.A, 64; Stanford Univ. Sch. Law, 64-67; Phi Beta Kappa; Omicron Delta Kappa. Polit. & Govt. Pos: Admin. asst, League of Iowa Munic, 63-65; pres, Drake Univ. Young Dem, 63-64; exec. dir, Young Dem. Clubs of Iowa, 63-64; del, Dem. Nat. Conv, 64; mem. bd. dirs, Young Dem. Clubs of Am, 64-65; former v.pres, Stanford Young Dem, Calif. Rel: Latter-day Saint. Mailing Add: 509 W. Tenth Ave. N, Estherville, Iowa 51334. (1967)

MITCHELL, MAXINE K. R
Secy, Tuscarawas Co. Rep. Exec. and Cent. Cmts, Ohio
b. New Philadelphia, Ohio, 10/4/19; d. Philip Getzman King and Etta Wilson K; m. 2/27/43 to Robert Wilson Mitchell; c. Marilyn and Louise. Educ: Beckwith Bus. Col, 1 year. Polit. & Govt. Pos: Secy, Ohio State Bur. Motor Vehicles, 39; cashier, secy. to chief auditor, div. pub. assistance, Ohio State Dept. Pub. Welfare, 43; secy, U.S. Dept. Defense Transportation Corps. of Engrs, 43; receptionist, Ohio State Hwy. Dept, 47; mem, Tuscarawas Co. Rep. Bd. Elections, 58-; secy, Tuscarawas Co. Rep. Exec. and Cent. Cmts, 56- Bus. & Prof. Pos: Secy. to bldg. engr, Kaiser Shipbuilding, Portland, Ore, 43-44; secy, Curtiss-Wright, 45. Mem: Beta Sigma Phi; Eastern Star; adv, 4-H, 10 years mem, exten. adv. cmt; vol. wives, C. of C; Union Hospital Auxiliary; Nat. and Ohio Fedn. Rep. Women; Qui Vive Lit. Club; New Phila. Chmn. Women's Div, United Commun. Fund. Rel: Methodist. Mailing Add: 719 Oak St. N.W, New Philadelphia, Ohio 44663.

MITCHELL, MINNIE ALICE R
State Treas, Wyo.
b. Crawford, Nebr, 4/15/92; d. Charles Nelson Millhollin and Lucy Parker M; m. 7/31/16 to James Roy Mitchell (deceased); c. Gordon LeRoy and twins, Bernice Fern and Beryl (Mrs. O. Calvin York). Educ: Univ. Wyo. Summer Sch. Polit. & Govt. Pos: State treas, Wyo, 52-55 & 67-, state auditor, 55-67. Mem: Pres, Nat. Asn. State Auditors, Treas, and Comptrollers, 66; Am. Legion Auxiliary; Eastern Star (grand treas, 56-66); Altrusa Club (past pres). Boss of Year, Nat. Secy. Asn, 61. Rel: Methodist. Legal Res: 2520 Deming Blvd, Cheyenne, Wyo. 82001. Mailing Add: State Treasurer's Office, Capitol Bldg, Cheyenne, Wyo. 82001.

MITCHELL, NICHOLAS WILFRED D
Mass. Gov. Councillor
b. Fall River, Mass, 1/15/13; s. John Mitchell and Malvina Lafleur M; m. 4/20/42 to Rita T. Blake; c. John B. and Barbara A. Educ: Private tutoring and schooling for Registered Pharmacist, Mass, grad, 37. Polit. & Govt. Pos: Mem. bd. dir, Pub. Welfare, Fall River, Mass, 53-56, city coun, 61-62, 63-65 & 65-67, Dem. committeeman, 65- and mayor, 68-; gov. councillor, First Dist, 64-66, 66-68 and 69-; del, Dem. Nat. Conv, 68. Bus. & Prof. Pos: Owner, Mitchell's Pharm, 47- Mil. Serv: Entered as Pvt, Army Air Force, 42, released as T/Sgt, 46, after serv. in Eighth and Ninth Air Force, ETO, 43-

46; Good Conduct Medal; ETO Ribbon; Two Bronze Stars. Mem: Life mem, Mass. Pharmacist Asn; Fall River Druggist Asn.(pres, 54-55); life mem. Southeast Mass. Druggist Asn.(pres, 60-61); Kiwanis (past pres); Ahepa; Elks; life mem. Amvets; life mem. VFW; Fran Co. Am. War Vets; Am. Legion; life mem. DAV; Moose; K. of C; Lt, Colonial Navy of Mass. Rel: Catholic. Mailing Add: 105 Garden St, Fall River, Mass. 02720.

MITCHELL, RALPH WILSON D
Ky. State Rep.
b. Greensburg, Ky, 9/30/12; s. William Wilson Mitchell and Harriet Hatcher M; m. 6/19/37 to Rena Holt Wadlington; c. Ralph Seldon and Courtney W. Educ: Centre Col, A.B, 33; Jefferson Sch. Law, LL.B, 39; Harvard Law Sch, 47; Beta Theta Pi. Polit. & Govt. Pos: Co. judge, Shelby Co, Ky, 52-64; Ky. State Rep, 58th Dist, 68- Bus. & Prof. Pos: Clerical staff, Procter & Gamble, Cincinnati and Louisville, 33-41, salesman, Tenn. and W.Va, 41-42; contract rep, Curtis-Wright, Louisville, 42-43; attorney-at-law, Shelbyville, Ky, 47- Mil. Serv: Entered as Pvt, Marines, 43, released as Sgt, 46, after serv. in 12th Air Warning Squadron. Mem: Ky. Bar Asn; Am. Trial Lawyers Asn; Am. Judicature Soc; Nat. Asn; Probate & Bank Attorneys; Rotary. Rel: Presbyterian. Mailing Add: 119 Adair, Shelbyville, Ky. 40065.

MITCHELL, RICHARD O. D
b. Omega, Ga, 1/28/18; m. Sara Sanders; c. Richard O, Jr, Kathy, Mark and Michelle. Educ: Univ. of Ga; Fla. State Univ; Univ. of Miami Law Sch, LL.B, 53. Polit. & Govt. Pos: Fla. State Rep, 56-66. Bus. & Prof. Pos: Attorney-at-law. Mil. Serv: Commanding Officer, Coast Guard Organized Res. Training Unit, Tallahassee; U.S. Coast Guard, World War II. Mem: Legal Div, Red Feather; Citizenship and Legis. Cmts, Fla. Bar Asn; Legis. Cmt, C. of C; Red Cross; Salvation Army; bd. of dirs, Easter Seal Soc; Optimist Club; Am. Legion (former comdr); VFW (former Comdr. and Judge Advocate); Mason; Shrine; Phi Alpha Delta. Rel: Baptist; Deacon. Mailing Add: P.O. Box 806, Tallahassee, Fla. 33502. (1967)

MITCHELL, ROBERT E. R
Tres, Los Angeles Co. Rep. Cent. Cmt, Calif.
s. Graham Mitchell and Helen Leonard M; m. 10/3/53 to Sarah S. Christensen; c. William, Susan, Cathleen and John. Educ: Univ. South. Calif, 48-53; Univ. South. Calif. Law Sch, 53-56; Squires; Knights; Sigma Phi Epsilon; Blue Key; Skull and Dagger; pres, Asn. Men Students. Polit. & Govt. Pos: Past chmn, 66th Assembly Dist. Rep. Cent. Cmt. and 19th Cong. Dist. Rep. Cent. Cmt, Calif; mem. exec. cmt, Calif. Rep. State Cent. Cmt; alternate del, Rep. Nat. Conv, 68; treas, chmn, Cand. Research and Develop. Cmt, mem, Budget and Expenditures Cmt. and Exec. Cmt, Los Angeles Co. Rep. Cent. Cmt, 68-; co-chmn. ad hoc cmt, Non-Partisan Citizen Cmt, 69. Bus. & Prof. Pos: Attorney, Iverson & Hogoboom, 56, Parker, Stanbury, Reese & McGee; attorney, self-employed, 63- Mil. Serv: Entered as Pvt, Army, 46, released as Cpl, 48, after serv. in 24th Inf. Div, Japanese Occup. Mem: Legion Lex, Univ. South. Calif. Law Sch. Support Group; past mem, bd. dirs, La Mirada C. of C; bd. dirs, Norwalk C. of C; Norwalk Kiwanis; Los Angeles Co. Art Museum; Los Angeles Co. Hist. Soc; Los Angeles World Affairs' Coun; chmn, State Social Welfare Bd. Rel: Protestant. Legal Res: 15622 Olive Branch Dr, La Mirada, Calif. 90638. Mailing Add: 13917 San Antonio Dr, Norwalk Calif. 90650.

MITCHELL, ROBERT S. D
Chmn, Tenth Cong. Dist. Dem. Party, Mich.
b. Edenville, Mich, 3/10/22; s. Estey William Mitchell and Mary Barron M; m. 6/11/53 to Carole Hunt. Educ: Flint Jr. Col, Assoc. in Eng, 47; Wayne State Univ, 47-48. Polit. & Govt. Pos: Chmn, Midland Co. Dem. Party, Mich, 54-59 & 63-68; chmn, Tenth Cong. Dist. Dem. Party, 69- Mil. Serv: Entered as Pvt, Air Force, 42, released as Cpl, 66, after serv. in Continental U.S.A, 42-46. Rel: Methodist. Mailing Add: 2615 St. Marys Dr, Midland, Mich. 48640.

MITCHELL, RUDOLPH D
S.C. State Rep.
b. Saluda, S.C, 9/6/26; s. Thomas S. Mitchell and Mary Sue Bledsoe M; m. 7/30/49 to Lenora Werts; c. Randy and Molly. Educ: Hollywood High Sch, 43. Polit. & Govt. Pos: Dir, Farm Bur; S.C. State Rep, 63- Bus. & Prof. Pos: Pianist with The Ivory Keys; dairy farmer. Mil. Serv: Army, 45-47, ETO. Mem: Home Mission Bd, South. Region, Advent Christian Church; Grange (Master, Higgins Grange). Young Farmer of the Year for Saluda Co, S.C, 60. Rel: Christian Church; Sunday Sch. supt, Hickory Grove Advent Christian Church. Mailing Add: Route 5, Saluda, S.C. 29138. (1967)

MITCHELL, STEPHEN A. D
b. Rock Valley, Iowa, 3/3/03; s. Stephen A. Mitchell and Dorothy Higgins M; m. 2/16/31 to Evelyn Miller; c. Dr. Stephen A, Jr, Michael W.(deceased) and John A. Educ: Creighton Univ, 24; Georgetown Univ. Law Sch, LL.B, 28; Phi Alpha Delta. Hon. LL.D, De Paul Univ, Chicago and St. Bernard's Col, Ala. Polit. & Govt. Pos: Chief, French Div. of Lend-Lease Admin, 42-44, and French Div. Wartime Econ. Affairs, U.S. Dept. of State, 44-45; co. chmn, Campaign Cmt, Adlai E. Stevenson for Gov, 48; chief counsel, Chelf Cmt. to Invest. the U.S. Dept. of Justice, 52; chmn, Dem. Nat. Cmt, 52-55, mem. cmt. on rules and conv. procedure, 69; chmn, Adv. Cmt. on Rules, Dem. Nat. Conv, 52 & 56, del, 56, 64 & 68, counsel, Rules Cmt, 60-64; chmn, Eugene McCarthy Conv. Cmt, 68; v.chmn, Humphrey for Pres. Cmt, 68. Bus. & Prof. Pos: Partner, Taylor, Miller, Busch and Boyden, 33-42; with, Gen. Motors Acceptance Corp, Wash, D.C, and N.Y.C, 24-32; partner, Mitchell and Russell, Lawyers, Chicago, Ill, Mitchell & Mitchell, Santa Fe and Taos, N.Mex. and predecessor firms, 45-; lawyer, Taos and Santa Fe, N.Mex, 61- Publ: Elms Street Politics, Oceana Press, 59; co-author, As We Knew Adlai, 66. Mem: Bd. of trustees, De Paul Univ; bd. regents, Mus. of N.Mex. Rel: Roman Catholic. Legal Res: Talpa Route, Ranchos de Taos, N.Mex. 87557. Mailing Add: P.O. Box 486, Taos, N.Mex. 87571.

MITCHELL, THOMAS R
Chmn, Clark Co. Rep. Cent. Cmt, Idaho
b. Ft. Benton, Mont, 4/27/96; s. Alexander Mitchell and Mary Ellen Coleman M; m. 9/20/19 to Bessie May Finch; c. Warren T, T.C. and Donald R. Polit. & Govt. Pos: Rep. precinct committeeman, Clark Co, Dubois, Idaho, 64-68; chmn, Clark Co. Rep. Cent. Cmt, 68- Mil. Serv: Entered as Fireman 3/C, Navy, 17, released as Engr, 2/C, 19. Mem: Lions; Am. Legion. Rel: Christian. Mailing Add: P.O. Box 173, Dubois, Idaho 83423.

MITCHELL, THOMAS MARVIN D
b. Dalton, Ga, 12/18/35; s. Paul M. Mitchell and Violet King M; single. Educ: Mid. Tenn. State Col, B.S, 58. Polit. & Govt. Pos: Ga. State Rep, 63-66. Bus. & Prof. Pos: Construction contractor. Mil. Serv: Ga. Nat. Guard, 58- Rel: Baptist. Mailing Add: 1500 Underwood St, Dalton, Ga. 30720. (1967)

MITCHELL, WENDELL WILKIE D
b. Montgomery, Ala, 9/4/40; s. Furman Gastle Mitchell and Pearl Burnum M; m. 8/23/64 to Rosalind McBride; c. Peter Maury. Educ: Auburn Univ, B.S, 62; Univ. Ala, LL.B, 65; Squires Sophomore Hon, pres, Pi Kappa Phi and Debate Team and Coun. and ed, Tiger Cub, Auburn Univ; Phi Alpha Delta. Polit. & Govt. Pos: Admin. asst. to Congressman Tom Bevill, Ala, 67-68 and to U.S. Sen. James B. Allen, 69- Bus. & Prof. Pos: Partner, Law Firm of Hawkins, Rhea & Mitchell, Gadsden, Ala, 65-66. Mem: U.S. Senate Asn. of Admin. Asst; Ala. Bar Asn; Bar of the U.S. Supreme Court; Ala. Jaycees. Outstanding Jaycee Pub. Speaker, Ala, 66. Rel: Church of Christ. Legal Res: W. Sixth St, Luverne, Ala. 36049. Mailing Add: 5925 Fifth St. N, Arlington, Va. 22203.

MITCHELL, WILLIAM HENRY D
b. Tylertown, Miss, 8/23/35; married. Polit. & Govt. Pos: Miss. State Rep, 60-68. Bus. & Prof. Pos: Farmer and cattleman. Mem: WOW; Jaycees; C. of C; Farm Bur; Cattlemen's Asn. Rel: Baptist. Mailing Add: Route 2, Tylertown, Miss. 39667. (1967)

MITCHLER, ROBERT W. R
Ill. State Sen.
b. Aurora, Ill, 6/4/20; s. John L. Mitchler and Clara Rub M; m. 6/16/50 to Helen L. Drew; c. John Drew, Kurt David and Heidi Louise. Educ: Aurora Col, Ill, B.S, 53. Polit. & Govt. Pos: Chmn, Kendall Co. Young Rep. Club, Ill; precinct committeeman, Kendall Co. Rep. Party, 63; Ill. State Sen, 65- Bus. & Prof. Pos: Sales and pub. rels, North. Ill. Gas Co, 58. Mil. Serv: Chief Yeoman, Navy, Pac. Theater, 41-46 and Japan and Korean Theaters, 50-52, mem, Mil. Armistice Negotiations at Pan Mun Jom, Korea, on Staff of Adm. C. Turner Joy; 13 medals and decorations in World War II and Korean War, including Navy Commendation Ribbon and Combat 'V' for combat serv. in Korean War. Mem: Moose; Mason; Scottish Rite; Shrine; Am. Legion; VFW; 40 et 8; Ill. Police Asn; Ill. Rep. Vet. League. Rel: Methodist. Mailing Add: Hill Spring Oaks, Route 1, Box 250, Oswego, Ill. 60543. (1967)

MITLIN, LAURANCE ROBERT D
b. Brooklyn, N.Y, 2/8/47; s. Norman Mitlin and Luceille Liston M; single. Educ: Miss. State Univ, Nat. Merit scholar, 65, B.A, 69; Pi Delta Epsilon; Omicron Delta Epsilon. Polit. & Govt. Pos: Pres, Young Dem. Club, Miss. State Univ, 67-; alternate del, Dem. Nat. Conv, 68; mem. exec. cmt, Loyalist Dem. Party, Oktibbeha Co, Miss, 68- Bus. & Prof. Pos: Assoc. ed, Reflector, Miss. State Univ, 68-69. Mem: Am. Civil Liberties Union; Miss. Collegiate Press Asn.(secy-treas, 68-69). Mailing Add: 513 Poplar Rd, Starkville, Miss. 39759.

MITTNESS, LEWIS T, JR. D
Wis. State Assemblyman
b. LaCrosse, Wis, 7/29/29. Educ: Wis. State Col, B.S, 54; Univ. Wis, M.E, 58. Polit. & Govt. Pos: Wis. State Assemblyman, 64- Bus. & Prof. Pos: Teacher; formerly, drive-in owner and mgr. Mil. Serv: Army, 51-53. Mem: Nat, State and Local Educ. Asns. Mailing Add: 730 N. Ringold St, Janesville, Wis. 53545.

MIWA, RALPH M. D
b. Honolulu, Hawaii, 1/4/25; s. Nobuichi Miwa and Fuyu Hashimoto M; m. 6/23/51 to Hilda N. Odan; c. Colin Odan, Lani-Ann and Marie M. Educ: Univ. Hawaii, B.A, 48 and M.A, 50; Johns Hopkins Univ, Ph.D, 53; Phi Beta Kappa; Univ, Ford Found, Laucheimmer and Hawaii Vet. fels; Pi Sigma Alpha. Polit. & Govt. Pos: Research analyst, Fed. Govt, 54-57; admin. asst, Sen. Inouye, Hawaii, 63-66; del, Dem. Nat. Conv, 68. Bus. & Prof. Pos: Assoc. prof. polit. sci, Univ. Mo, 57-61. Mil. Serv: S/Sgt, Intel, Army, 44-46. Mem: Am. Polit. Sci. Asn; Asian Studies Asn; UN Asn. of U.S; Am. Pub. Admin. Asn. Mailing Add: 3038 Waipuna Rise, Honolulu, Hawaii 96822.

MIX, JOHN PARSON D
Idaho State Sen.
b. Boise, Idaho, 10/15/34; s. John Parson Mix and Jean Mary Holden M; m. 6/24/56 to Shirley Rae Blick; c. Stephanie Jo, Jeffrey Paul and Tracy Jo. Educ: Univ. Idaho, B.A, 56; Phi Delta Theta. Polit. & Govt. Pos: Idaho State Sen, Fifth Dist, 68- Bus. & Prof. Pos: Mgr, KLER Radio, Orofino, Idaho, 58-59; sta. mgr, KRPL Radio, Moscow, 59-63, pres. and gen. mgr, 63- Mil. Serv: Entered as 2nd Lt, Army, 56, released as 1st Lt, 58, after serv. in 288th AFA Bn, Europe, 57-58; Capt, Res, 58- Mem: Nat. Asn. Broadcasters; Idaho State Broadcasters Asn.(pres, 69); Elks; VFW; Jaycees; Lions; C. of C; Univ. Idaho Alumni Asn. Distinguished Serv. Award, Moscow Jaycees, 66; Man of Action Award, Moscow C. of C, 67. Rel: Methodist. Mailing Add: P.O. Box 360, Moscow, Idaho 83843.

MIXON, BILLY PEARSON R
b. Augusta, Ga, 7/9/28; s. Chas. Eugene Mixon and Josephine Collins M; m. 6/14/52 to Ida Few Bigbie; c. Charles McLendon, William Pearson, Margaret Few and Jennifer Collins. Educ: Citadel, 45-47; Univ. of Ga. Law Sch, 47-49 and 53 to 54; Pi Kappa Alpha. Polit. & Govt. Pos: Chmn, Muscogee Co. Rep. Exec. Cmt, Ga, 63-66; v.chmn, Exec. Cmt, 3rd Cong. Dist. Bus. & Prof. Pos: Principal Hall-Mixon & Assocs, 59-; agent and dist. agent, Nat. Life Ins. Co. of Vt, 57-; agent, Prudential Life Ins. Co, 54-57. Mil. Serv: Entered as Pvt, Army, 49, released as 1st Lt, 53, after serv. in 2nd Inf. Div, 9th Regiment, Korea; Combat Infantry Badge; Unit Citations and Awards. Mem: President, Columbus, Ga, Estate Planning Coun, 65-66; Am. Soc. Chartered Life Underwriters; Million Dollar Round Table. Rel: Methodist. Mailing Add: Sunset Rd, Green Island Hills, Columbus, Ga. 31904. (1967)

MIXON, HARRY D
b. Ocilla, Ga, 11/11/28; s. Warren R. Mixon and Martha Van Sutton M; m. 8/26/48 to Lila Louise Lee; c. Sharon Louise and Warren Lee. Educ: S. Ga. Col, 55; Univ. of Ga. Law Sch, 59; Pi Sigma Alpha; Phi Alpha Delta. Polit. & Govt. Pos: Ga. State Rep, 61-68. Bus. & Prof. Pos: Law clerk. Mem: Shrine. Rel: Baptist. Mailing Add: First State Bank Bldg, Ocilla, Ga. 31774. (1967)

MIXSON, WILLIAM EDWARD D
b. Fairfax, 10/28/24; s. M.C. Mixson and Nonie Dowlings M; m. to Marlene Hart. Educ: Wofford Col, B.A, 49. Polit. & Govt. Pos: Past pres. Jr. C. of C; magistrate Allendale Twp, 58-62; S.C. State Rep, until 66. Bus. & Prof. Pos: Merchant, Mixson's Dept. Store; partner M & W Florist and Hampton Shoe Center. Mil. Serv: Navy, 42-46. Mailing Add: Main St, Allendale, S.C. 29810.

MIYAKE, HOWARD Y. D
Majority Leader, Hawaii House of Rep.
b. Honolulu, Hawaii, 10/16/18; s. Kan Noburu Miyake and Tei Yamamoto M; m. 5/26/48 to Juanita Devereux-Arnez. Educ: Univ. Hawaii, B.A, 40; Univ. Colo. Law Sch, LL.B, 54; Real Dean Award, 40; Rothgerber Appellate Award, 54; Phi Alpha Delta. Polit. & Govt. Pos: Mem, Hawaii Dem. Party Cent. Cmt, 58-66; Hawaii Territorial Rep, 58; Hawaii State Rep, Majority Leader and chmn, Majority Caucus and House Policy Cmt, 59-; mem. exec. cmt, Nat. Conf. of State Legis. Leaders, 59-61; mem, West. Regional Conv, Coun. of State Govt, Cmt. on Educ. and Humanities and Cmt. on Uniform Laws, West. Interstate Conf. on Higher Educ. and Nat. Conf. on Intergovt. Rels. of State Legis. Leaders; del, Hawaii Constitutional Conv, chmn, Cmt. of the Whole Article II and v.chmn, Legis. Powers and Functions, 68. Bus. & Prof. Pos: Mem, State Comprehensive Health Planning Cmt, State Ment. Health Planning and Coord. Cmt, 3 years, State Planning Cmt. on Rehabilitation and chmn, State Conf. on Archit. Barriers, 66; mem, Gov. Cmt. on Employ. of Handicapped, 8 years; trustee, Lanakila Crafts, Inc, 6 years; trustee, Honolulu Theater for Youth; past bd. mem, Honolulu Commun. Theater. Mil. Serv: Entered as Pvt, Army, 41, released as Capt, 47, after serv. in 100th Inf. Bn, Mil. Intel. Serv, 298th Inf. Regt, Hawaii, Europe and Africa; Capt.(Ret), Army Res; Silver Star; Bronze Star; Purple Heart; Combat Inf. Badge; 3 campaign ribbons. Mem: Hawaii Bar Asn; past dir, Hawaii Red Cross; dir, Hawaii Asn. to Help Retarded Children, 10 years; DAV (past Comdr, Dept. of Hawaii); Cent. YMCA (past trustee); Am. Judicature Soc; Aloha United Fund (mem, Budget Cmt); Lions Int.(Kuhio Den); Hawaii Fedn. for Blind; hon. mem, Abilities Unlimited; past pres, Club 100; Citizens Study Club of Oahu; Am. Japanese Ancestry Vet. Coun. Kokua Man's Award, Abilities Unlimited, 66. Rel: Christian. Mailing Add: 3236 Kaohinani Dr, Honolulu, Hawaii 96817.

MIYAKE, NOBORU R
b. Waimea, Kauai, Hawaii, 4/19/96; s. Katsuhei Miyake and Tama Izumi M; m. 8/30/30 to Yone Kagawa; c. Roy Takashi, Will Edward and Vee Nobuko (Mrs. Robert Yamafuki). Educ: Correspondence course in Elec. Eng. and Law. Polit. & Govt. Pos: Hawaii State Sen, 52-67; Territorial Rep, Hawaii, 48-52; supvr, Co. of Kauai, 29-31 and 33-42. Bus. & Prof. Pos: Pres. and mgr, Waimea Garage, Ltd, 21-66; pres. and mgr, Waimea Elec. Co, 21-53. Mil. Serv: Sgt, Hawaii Nat. Guard, 16-17; Supply and 1st Sgt, 2nd Hawaiian Inf, Army, 17-19; mem. price admin, Hawaii, WW II; WW I Victory Medal. Mem: Charter mem. and past pres, W. Kauai Lions Club; Kauai C. of C; past comdr, Kauai Post Am. Legion; Vets. Club; W. Kauai Merchant's Asn; Trustee, Health Facilities Coun, Hawaii; trustee, Waimea Clinic. Educational Award for Higher Educ. Rel: Christian Church. Mailing Add: P.O. Box 4, Waimea, Kauai, Hawaii 96796. (1967)

MIZE, CHESTER L. R
U.S. Rep, Kans.
b. Atchison, Kans, 12/25/17; m. to Betty Muchnic; c. David, Ann and Janet. Educ: Sch. of Bus. Admin, Univ. Kans, 35-39; Phi Delta Theta. Polit. & Govt. Pos: Past mem, Atchison Pub. Sch. Syst. Bd, Kans; mem. bd. of trustees, Mt. St. Scholastica of Atchison; mem, Univ. Kans. Athletic Bd; mem. adv. bd, Sch. of Bus. Admin, Univ. Kans; U.S. Rep, Kans, 65- Bus. & Prof. Pos: Treas, Blish, Mize & Silliman Hardware Co, 45-51; owned and operated a cattle ranch in N.Mex. and a farm in Atchison Co, Kans; v.pres, Valley Co, Inc, Gen. Investment Co, 51-64. Mil. Serv: Naval Res, 40; Navy, 41-45, S. Pac. Theater; Lt. Comdr, Naval Res. Mem: Am. Legion; VFW; Kans. Farm Bur; Elks; Kans. C. of C; past chmn, Gr. Univ. Fund, Univ. Kans; chmn, Atchison Co. Savings Bond Drives, several years. Rel: Episcopal; Vestryman, Trinity Episcopal Church. Legal Res: Atchison, Kans. 66002. Mailing Add: 114 Cannon House Office Bldg, Washington, D.C. 20515.

MIZE, DWIGHT WORKMAN D
Mem, Calif. Dem. State Cent. Cmt.
b. Tulsa, Okla, 4/22/29; s. Dwight W. Mize, Sr. and Elnora Wyrick M; m. 6/16/50 to Joanne Lindamood; c. Dwight Anthony, Michelle and Gregory Warren. Educ: St. Peters High Sch, Joplin, Mo, dipl, 48. Polit. & Govt. Pos: Mem, Calif. Dem. State Cent. Cmt, 68-; mem, Small Bus. Adv. Coun, Calif, 69- Mem: Lincoln Continental Owner Club; Aircraft Owners & Pilots Asn; Elks; Rotary. Rel: Catholic. Mailing Add: 11922 Comstock Rd, Garden Grove, Calif. 92640.

MIZELL, WILMER DAVID R
U.S. Rep, N.C.
b. Vinegar Bend, Ala, 8/13/31; s. Walter David Mizell and Addie Turner M; m. 11/16/62 to Nancy Ruth McAlpine; c. Wilmer David, Jr. and James Daniel. Educ: Leakesville High Sch, Miss. Polit. & Govt. Pos: Chmn, Davidson Co. Cmn, N.C, 66; U.S. Rep, N.C, 69- Bus. & Prof. Pos: Baseball pitcher, St. Louise Cardinals, Pittsburgh Pirates and New York Mets. Mil. Serv: Entered as Pvt, Army, 53, released 55, after serv. in Hq. Unit, Detachment 1, 3442 Area Service Unit, Ft. McPherson, Ga, 53-55. Athlete of the Year, South. Baptist Sports Asn, 51; named to the Nat. League all-Star Baseball Team, 59; Distinguished Citizen's Award, George Wash. Univ, 69. Rel: Alliance Missionary. Legal Res: Route 5, Winston-Salem, N.C. Mailing Add: 1228 Longworth House Office Building, Washington, D.C. 20515.

MOAKLEY, JOHN JOSEPH D
Mass. State Sen.
b. South Boston, Mass, 4/27/27; s. Joseph A. Moakley and Mary Rita Scappini M; married. Educ: Univ. Miami; Suffolk Law Sch. Polit. & Govt. Pos: Mass. State Rep, 53-60; Mass. State Sen, 65-; del, Dem. Nat. Conv, 68. Mil. Serv: Entered as Seaman 2/C, Navy, 43, released as Seaman 1/C, 46, after serv. in Seabees, S.Pac; Philippine Liberation Medal. Mem: Mass. and Boston Bar Asns; Mass. Trial Lawyers' Asn; Am. Legion; VFW; DAV; K. of C. Rel: Catholic. Mailing Add: 1812 Columbia Rd, South Boston, Mass. 02127.

MOAN, ALFRED R. D
b. Scituate, R.I, 11/12/16; m. to Marion E. Yeaw. Educ: West Warwick High Sch. Polit. & Govt. Pos: Mem, Welfare Cmn, R.I, 4 years; mem, Hwy. Cmn, 2 years; mem, Police Cmn, 2 years; mem, Dem. Town Cmt, 6 years; mem, Town Coun, 4 years; R.I. State Rep, 59-68. Bus. & Prof. Pos: Proprietor, Moan Brothers Express Co. Mem: K. of C; Elks; Lions; C. of C; Narragansett Gun Club; Holy Name Soc. of St. Peter and Paul's Church, Phenix. Mailing Add: Knotty Oak Rd, Coventry, R.I. 02816. (1967)

MOATE, MARVIN E. D
Ga. State Rep.
b. Sparta, Ga, 9/22/10; s. Robert H. Moate and Eula Smith M; m. 12/27/42 to Margaret Carroll; c. Marvin E, Jr. and Linda Carroll. Educ: Tenth A&M Sch, 27; Atlanta Law Sch, LL.B, 32. Polit. & Govt. Pos: Ga. State Sen, 20th Dist, 39, 45-46 & 51-52; Ga. State Rep, 41, 43-44 & 53-, Speaker, Ga. State House of Rep, 55-58. Bus. & Prof. Pos: Law practice, 32-39; lumber mfr, 39-48; cotton ginner and bonded warehouse bus; v.pres, Bank of Warner Robins; v.pres, Econ. & Gen. Loan Co. Mem: Mason; Elks; Athletic Club. Rel: Methodist. Mailing Add: 608 Rabun, Sparta, Ga. 31087. (1967)

MOBERLEY, KENNETH E. R
b. Moweaqua, Ill, 10/2/07; m. 1932 to Eugenia Hammett M; c. Sandra (Mrs. Grabow), Frederic W, Kenneth E. Jr. Educ: U. of Ill. Col. of Law, 30. Polit. & Gov. Pos: Ill. State Rep, 3 terms. Bus. & Prof. Pos: Gen. Practice of Law. Rel: Ravenswood Methodist Church, officer. Mailing Add: 5118 N. Winchester Ave, Chicago, Ill. 60640. (1967)

MOBERLY, ISABEL CAROL R
Rep. Nat. Committeewoman, Mont.
b. Alliance, Alta, Can, 9/12/09; d. Carl J. Quisberg and Elizabeth Hogan Q; m. 10/6/26 to Waldo Young Moberly. Polit. & Govt. Pos: Pres, Toole Co. Rep. Women's Club, Mont, 58-60; former v.pres, Mont. Fedn. Rep. Women; v.chmn, Rep. State Cent. Cmt, Mont, 60-64; mem. exec. cmt, Rep. Nat. Cmt, Mont, 64-68, Rep. Nat. Committeewoman, Mont, 64- Bus. & Prof. Pos: V.pres, W.Y. Moberly Inc, U.S. Customhouse Broker, Sweetgrass, Mont, 55-68. Mem: Am. Legion Auxiliary, dir. Mont. Girls State, 63-65; Daughters of Nile; Eastern Star. Rel: Methodist. Mailing Add: 485 Judy Ave, Shelby, Mont. 59474.

MOBLEY, CARLTON
Assoc. Justice, Supreme Court of Ga.
b. near Hillsboro, Ga, 12/7/06; s. Jesse Aldine Mobley and Lillie Pearl Jackson M; m. 1/6/34 to Margaret Elrod; c. Margaret Elrod. Educ: Mercer Univ, B.A, LL.B. cum laude, 28; Sigma Pi; Delta Theta Phi. Polit. & Govt. Pos: U.S. Rep, Ga, 32-34; secy, Exec. Dept, 34-37; asst. attorney gen, 41-42; assoc. justice, Supreme Court of Ga, 54- Bus. & Prof. Pos: Attorney-at-law, 37-41 & 46-54. Mil. Serv: Lt. Comdr, Naval Res, 43-46. Mem: Am, Ga. and Macon Bar Asns; Mason; Shrine; Elks; Kiwanis. Rel: Baptist. Mailing Add: Judicial Bldg, State Capitol, Atlanta, Ga. 30334.

MOBLEY, ERNEST NELSON R
Calif. State Assemblyman
b. Shadyside, Ohio, 11/1/18; s. B.G. Mobley and Ethel G. Gatten M; m. 12/14/46 to Lillian Van Zant; c. Jill. Educ: Ohio Univ, B.S, 43; Tau Kappa Epsilon. Polit. & Govt. Pos: Co. admin. officer, Fresno Co, Calif, 56-62; city mgr, Santa Monica, 62-64; Calif. State Assemblyman, 33rd Dist, 67- Mil. Serv: Entered as Pvt, Army, 43, released as Capt, 46, after serv. in Sixth Armored Div, 44th A.I.B, Europe, 44-46; Lt. Col, Army Res, 46-66; Silver Star; Bronze Star with 2 Oak Leaf Clusters; Combat Inf. Badge; 5 Battle Stars; Purple Heart. Mem: Farm Bur; Shrine; Scottish Rite; F&AM; Commun. Coun; VFW; Am. Legion. Rel: Protestant. Legal Res: 907 N. Oliver, Sanger, Calif. 93657. Mailing Add: 600 W. Shaw, Suite 210, Fresno, Calif. 93704.

MOBLEY, GARRETT JUDSON D
b. Kershaw, S.C, 10/8/12; s. Jesse H. Mobley and Florence M. Floyd M; m. 10/5/37 to Kathryn Rowell. Educ: Clemson Col, B.S, 34. Polit. & Govt. Pos: Former secy. and treas, Lancaster Co. Farm Bur, pres, 50; mem, Lancaster Co. Bd. of Educ, 51-56; state dir, S.C. Farm Bur, 52; S.C. State Rep, 63-66. Bus. & Prof. Pos: Farmer. Mil. Serv: Air Force, 42-46, 2 years for. serv. in Pac. theatre. Rel: Baptist; Sunday Sch. supt. and deacon, Kershaw First Baptist Church. Mailing Add: R.F.D. 2, Kershaw, S.C. 29064. (1967)

MOBLEY, JOHN ALLEN D
Tex. State Rep.
b. Houston, Tex, 5/29/30; s. John A. Mobley and Mary McDonald M; m. 6/5/51 to Lois Ann Parker; c. James Allen and Steven Mark. Educ: Tex. A&M Univ, B.B.A, 51. Polit. & Govt. Pos: Tex. State Rep, Dist. 15-F, Gregg and Smith Co, 65-; exec. asst. to Gov. John Connolly, Tex, 67-69. Bus. & Prof. Pos: Pres. and gen. mgr, John Mobley Co, 51-61, pres, 61-; secy, Alliance Distributors, Inc, 63-; pres, Walker Chem-Spray, Inc, 64-; pres, Southwest Disposal, Inc, 65- Mem: Am. Petrol. Inst; Am. Inst. Mining Engrs; Rotary; C. of C. Rel: Presbyterian. Legal Res: 2408 Green Hills Dr, Kilgore, Tex. 75662. Mailing Add: P.O. Box 1640, Kilgore, Tex. 75662.

MOBLEY, PLEAZ WM. R
b. 1914. Educ: Union Col, A.B; Univ. Louisville; Jefferson Sch. Law, LL.B; Sigma Delta Kappa. Polit. & Govt. Pos: R.R. cmnr, Third Dist, Ky, 52-56; Fed. Judge, 56-57; Ky. State Sen, 64-69; hearing officer, Ky. Workmen's Compensation Bd, 69- Bus. & Prof. Pos: Attorney-at-law, currently; TV and radio personality. Mil. Serv: Air Force, World War II. Mem: Am. and Ky. Bar Asns; Am. Judicature Soc; Mason; Kiwanis; Eastern Star; Am. Legion; VFW. Rel: Baptist. Mailing Add: Manchester, Ky. 40962.

MOBLEY, RALPH CAROL R
b. McAlpin, Fla, 12/24/25; s. William Summerfield Mobley and Eddie Clara Walters M; m. 1/6/51 to Katherine Marie; c. Summerfield Quinn and Cynthia Marie. Educ: Auburn Univ, 46; Univ. Ga, D.V.M, 50; Alpha Psi (first pres, Lambda Chap). Polit. & Govt. Pos: Managed first GOP hq, Madison, Tenn, 64; secy, Davidson Co. Rep. Party, 64 and co-chmn, 68; chmn, Tenth Councilmanic Dist, 68; alternate del, Rep. Nat. Conv, 68. Bus. & Prof. Pos: Secy,

Tenn. Bd. Vet. Med. Exam; past pres, Davidson Co. Acad. Vet. Med. Mil. Serv: Entered as Pvt, Marine Corps, 43, released as Pfc, 46, after serving in 1st Marine Div, S. Pac. and participant in the invasion of Okinawa. Mem: Am. Vet. Med. Asn; Tenn. Vet. Med. Asn.(chmn. ethics cmt); Fla. Vet. Med. Asn; Mason; Am. Legion; Kiwanis. Awarded Kiwanian of the year, Madison Kiwanis Club, 67. Rel: Protestant. Legal Res: 325 Meneese Lane, Madison, Tenn. 37115. Mailing Add: Mobley Veterinary Clinic, 4709 Gallatin Rd, Nashville, Tenn. 37216.

MOCKLER, FRANKLIN HENRY R
b. Lander, Wyo, 9/13/35; s. Frank Carpenter Mockler and Esther Heyne M; m. 11/13/54 to Nancy Claire Fisher; c. Frank, Jayne and Steve. Educ: Univ. Wyo, 53-55; Sigma Alpha Epsilon. Polit. & Govt. Pos: Precinct committeeman, Rep. Party, Wyo, 56-66; mem, Co. Rep. Exec. Cmt, 56-66; chmn, Co. Young Rep, 60-62; former Wyo. State Rep. Bus. & Prof. Pos: Rancher, self-employed; bd. dirs, Dubois Mercantile, Ind, 63- Mem: Shrine; Farm Bur; Wyo. Stockgrowers Asn; Wyo. Retailers Asn; Dubois C. of C. Rel: Episcopal. Mailing Add: Box 275, Dubois, Wyo. 82513. (1967)

MOCULESKI, CHESTER FRANCIS D
b. Chicago, Ill, 6/9/16; s. Alexander Moculeski and Angeline Tabak M; m. 6/18/49 to Eleanor M. Lewandowski; c. Karen. Educ: Univ. Chicago, B.S, 39. Polit. & Govt. Pos: Dem. precinct committeeman, Downers Grove Twp, Du-Page Co, Ill, 60-; del, Dem. Nat. Conv, 68. Bus. & Prof. Pos: Chemist, Deavitt Labs, Chicago, 39-41; group leader, U.S. Gypsum Research Lab, 41-43; tech. rep, Rohm & Haas Co, Phila, Pa. 43-49, Glyco Chem. Co, Chicago, 49-57; sales mgr, Wallace Erickson Co, 57-59, Clintwood Chem. Co, 59-62, v.pres, 62-68, pres, 68- Mem: Am. Chem. Soc; Soc. of Cosmetic Chemists (chmn, Midwest Chap, 68). Rel: Roman Catholic. Mailing Add: 325 W. Ninth St, Hinsdale, Ill. 60521.

MOELLER, BEVERLEY BOWEN R
Mem, Ventura Co. Rep. Cent. Cmt, Calif.
b. Long Beach, Calif, 10/12/25; d. George Walter Bowen and Agnes Coffey B; m. 12/11/55 to Roger David Moeller; c. Claire Agnes, Barbara and Thomas David. Educ: Cornell Univ. and Stanford Univ. undergrad. work; Whittier Col, B.A, 56; Univ. Calif, Los Angeles, M.A, 65, Ph.D, 68; Kappa Kappa Gamma. Polit. & Govt. Pos: Mem, Ventura Co. Rep. Cent. Cmt, Calif, 59-; mem, Calif. Rep. State Cent. Cmt, 61 & 68-69; mem, Ventura Co. Grand Jury, Calif, 65; treas, Ventura Co. Commun. Action Cmt, War on Poverty, 65-66. Bus. & Prof. Pos: Instr, Valley Col, 68- Publ: 'Colnett and Tsimshian Indians, 1787, Pac. Northwest Quart, 1/66; 'Eighteenth Century Views, Hawaiian Agriculture,' Agr. Hist, 10/67; 'Phil Swing in Washington,' Doctoral Dissertation, 8/68. Mem: Am. Hist. Asn; Orgn. Am. Historians; West. Hist. Asn. Mailing Add: 801 Laguna Dr, Simi, Calif. 93065.

MOELLER, HENRY GEORGE R
b. Omaha, Nebr, 4/2/08; s. Henry Carl Moeller and Mabel Roebling M; m. 9/5/31 to Emmy C. Jetter; c. Henry George and John Roger. Educ: U.S. Naval Acad, B.A, 31. Polit. & Govt. Pos: Cmnr, S.Dak. Indust. Develop. & Expansion Agency, 61-67; mem, Rep. Nat. Cmt, S.Dak, 63-68; mem, State Adv. Coun. on Voc-Tech. Educ, 69- Bus. & Prof. Pos: Civil and mech. engr, 31-44; pres, Sioux Alfalfa Meal Co, 44-; mem. adv. bd, Nat. Bank of S.Dak. and bd. dirs, Bethesda Home for Aged. Mem: Am. Dehydrator's Asn.(past pres). Rel: Lutheran. Legal Res: 205 N. Pine St, Vermillon, S.Dak. 57069. Mailing Add: Box 576, Vermillon, S.Dak. 57069.

MOELLER, WALTER H. D
b. Indianapolis, Ind, 3/15/10; m. to Lenora Rafferty; c. Janeen (Mrs. John Arguelles). Educ: Concordia Col. and Sem, Springfield, Ill, 35; Defiance Col, A.B; Indiana Univ, M.S; Phi Delta Kappa. Polit. & Govt. Pos: U.S. Rep, Ohio, 58, 60 & 64-66. Bus. & Prof. Pos: 22 years in the ministry of Lutheran Church, 15 of which were in Ohio; 10 years instr. in Eng. composition, German, and sociol. Giffen Jr. Col. in Van Wert; farm owner. Mem: Kiwanis Club (past pres); Inst. of Human Rels; past mem, bd. of dirs, Fairfield Co. YMCA. Rel: Lutheran. Legal Res: Lancaster, Ohio 43130. Mailing Add: 435 N. J. Ave. S.E, Washington, D.C. 20003.

MOEN, CARL DONOVAN DFL
Minn. State Rep.
b. Fergus Falls, Minn, 5/24/29; s. Carl Willard Moen and Edith Ruth Lamming M; m. 1/17/49 to Geraldine Margaret; c. Barbara Jeanne, Terri Lee and Judy. Educ: Macalester Col, 2 years. Polit. & Govt. Pos: Minn. State Rep, Dist. 57A, 69- Mil. Serv: Vet. of World War II and Korean Conflict. Rel: Lutheran. Mailing Add: 24-66½ Way, Fridley, Minn. 55432.

MOERSCHEL, W. NEAL R
Del. State Rep.
b. Baltimore, Md, 12/24/30; s. William George Moerschel and Emma Hevern M; m. 5/10/53 to Thelma Wright; c. Susan, Leslie and Grant. Educ: Towson State Col, B.S, 52; Johns Hopkins Univ, B.S, 59; Delta Sigma Pi. Polit. & Govt. Pos: Councilman, Borough of Stratford, N.J, 62-63; nat. committeeman, Del. Fedn. Young Rep, 67-68; Del. State Rep, 31st Rep. Dist, 68- Bus. & Prof. Pos: Methods programmer, B&O R.R, Baltimore, Md, 57-59; syst. analyst, Honeywell Electronic Data Processing Div, Philadelphia, Pa, 59-65; mgr, data processing, Speakman Co, Wilmington, Del, 65- Mil. Serv: Entered as Seaman, Navy, 52, released as Lt.(jg), 56, after serv. in Patrol Squadron 24, Fleet Airborne Electronic Training Unit, Atlantic Fleet and Comdr. Air Force, Atlantic Fleet. Mem: Nat. Asn. Accountants. Rel: Lutheran. Mailing Add: 584 Westwood Dr, Dover, Del. 19901.

MOFFAT, JOHN WEIR R
Chmn, Schoolcraft Co. Rep. Cmt, Mich.
b. Laurium, Mich, 9/8/16; s. William Russell Moffat and Annie Weir M; m. 7/15/40 to Mary Wieber; c. John Wieber, Alec Weir, James Ramsay, Katharine Ann, Robert Bruce, Meg and David. Educ: Mich. Tech. Univ, B.S. in Mech. Eng, 39; Harvard Bus. Sch, Harvard Univ; Tau Nu Tau; Am. Soc. Mech. Engrs. Polit. & Govt. Pos: Chmn. co. bd, Schoolcraft Co, Mich, 60-61, mem. bd. supvrs, 58-62; mayor, Manistique, Mich, 60-62, city councilman, 58-62, trustee sch. bd, 62-67; dist. finance chmn, Rep. State Cent. Cmt, 67-; chmn, Schoolcraft Co. Rep. Cmt, 69- Bus. & Prof. Pos: Engr, Inland Lime & Stone Co, Inland Steel Co, Gulliver, Mich, 39-46, chief engr, 46-50, supt, 50-57, v.pres, 57-61 and v.pres. and gen. mgr, 61- Mil. Serv: Entered as 2nd Lt, Army Air Force, 41, released as Maj, 45, after serv. in Army Air Force Training Command, U.S. Theatre. Mem: Newcomen Soc. N.Am. Bd. Control Silver Medal, Mich. Tech. Univ, 68. Rel: Protestant. Mailing Add: 235 Range St, Manistique, Mich. 49854.

MOFFATT, NORBERT BASIL D
Asst. Dep. Protocol Officer, State of Calif.
b. Owen Sound, Ont, Can, 6/19/07; s. William C. Moffatt and Ellen Mary Murphy M; m. 6/23/37 to Gertrude M. Whitestone. Polit. & Govt. Pos: Hon. chmn, Tom Carrell for Senate, Calif, planning cmnr, Los Angeles, 58-61; mem, Calif. Planning Adv. Cmt, 59-64; mem, Dist. Attorney's Adv. Coun; chmn, South. Calif. World Trade Center Authority, 65-66 and v.chmn, World Trade Authority; Cong. liaison for U.S. Rep. James C. Corman; Asst. Dep. Protocol Officer, State of Calif, currently. Bus. & Prof. Pos: Formerly controller chain of 10 stores, N.Y.C. and mgr. retailing, Detroit and Cleveland, formerly; owner, jewelery stores, Reseda, Calif, 5 years, Van Nuys, 44- and Canoga Park, 46-; v.pres and dir, Lincoln Bank, 61-66. Mem: Canoga Park C. of C; Van Nuys C. of C.(v.pres); K. of C.(area dep. and Past Grand Knight, W. Valley Chap); bd. adv, Valley Children's Park Asn. and Int. Orphans, Inc; past chmn, San Fernando Valley Commun. Chest and March of Dimes; past co-chmn, YMCA Campaign; past dir, Am. Cancer soc. and past chmn, San Fernando Valley-Antelope Valley Campaign; dir, Valley Bd, United Serv. Orgn; dir, El Caballero Country Club; charter mem, Van Nuys Elks Lodge 2028 and past pres. bldg. cmt; Moose; Eagles; Lions (past pres); World Trade Club, San Francisco; past pres, Columbus Corp. and Van Nuys Bur. Mens' Asn. Walter Mendenhall Man of the Year Award; Lions Int. Citation; Lion of the Year Award; Am. Legion Award; Knight of the Year Award; Golden Rule Citation, Pac. Coast Scandinavian Vikings; Outstanding Los Angeles Co. Chmn, Am. Cancer Soc; Resolution of Commendation, Los Angeles, City Coun; Man of the Month Award, Reseda Co. Jaycees. Rel: Roman Catholic. Legal Res: 5930 Tampa Ave, Tarzana, Calif. 91356. Mailing Add: 6378 Van Nuys Blvd, Van Nuys, Calif. 91401.

MOFFETT, GEORGE CLARENCE D
b. Chillicothe, Tex, 11/20/95; s. Frank Lee Moffett and Ina Farrington M; m. 10/4/64 to Ruth Sallee; c. Patricia Joy and Frank Lee. Educ: Tex. A&M Univ, B.S, 16. Polit. & Govt. Pos: Tex. State Rep, 31-38; Tex. State Sen, 39-64. Bus. & Prof. Pos: Pres, First Nat. Bank, Chillicothe, Tex, 65- Mil. Serv: Pvt, Air Force, 18-19. Mem: Lions (charter mem. and first pres, Chillicothe Club); AF&AM (Grand Master, Tex. Masonic Grand Lodge, 55). Rel: Methodist. Mailing Add: Box 1600, Vernon, Tex. 76384.

MOFFITT, DELMONT THEODORE R
b. Woodstock, Minn, 12/21/11; s. Forest Emil Moffitt and Bertha Hester Boyer M; m. 2/14/37 to Mary Josephine Scott; c. Nancy Jo (Mrs. Milburn), Judith Ellen (Mrs. Guinn) and Mary Sue (Mrs. Zaputil). Educ: Centerville Commun. Col, 1 year. Polit. & Govt. Pos: Iowa State Rep, 61-64 & 67-68; former chmn, Appanoose Co. Rep. Cmt. Mem: Farm Bur. Skelly Agr. Achievement Award; Goodyear Award for Outstanding Achievement in Soil Conserv. Rel: Christian. Mailing Add: Route 1, Mystic, Iowa 52574.

MOGAN, V. DEVON R
b. Wichita, Kans, 12/12/26; s. Luis A. Mogan and Vera I. McDowell M; m. 11/6/48 to Catherine F. Matthews; c. Karen A. and Susan G. Educ: Benjamin Franklin Univ, B.C.S, 54 and M.C.S, 56. Polit. & Govt. Pos: Comptroller, Rep. Nat. Cmt, 63-67. Bus. & Prof. Pos: Asst. chief acct, Julius Garfinckle & Co, Inc, 56-61; consult. and acct. systs. writing, 62-63; controller-asst. treas, Diversified Educ. and Research Corp, 67-68; consult, North. Va. CPA Firm, 68- Mil. Serv: Entered as Seaman, Navy, 43, released as Hospitalman 2/C, 49, after serv. in S.Pac; Asiatic and Am. Theater Ribbons; Philippine Theater Ribbon with One Battle Star; Two Good Conduct Medals; Presidential Unit Citation; Victory Medal. Mem: Capitol Hill Club; Mason. Rel: Episcopal. Mailing Add: 9321 Brambly Lane, Alexandria, Va. 22309.

MOGFORD, JOHN L. D
Chmn, Dimmit Co. Dem. Party, Tex.
b. Menard, Tex, 10/16/13; s. Christian Alford Mogford and Bertie May Crump M; m. 10/28/38 to Mary Eleanor Rogers; c. John L, II and Mary Lynn (Mrs. Flood). Educ: Tex. A & M Univ, B.S, 37; Univ. Calif, Berkley, Chinese Language, 43; Saddle and Sirloin Club; Battalion Staff; Social Class (Rep). Polit. & Govt. Pos: Precinct Chmn, Dem. Party, Tex, 48-54; chmn, Dimmit Co. Dem. Party, 54-; Pres, Rio Grande Elec. Coop, 58-60; City Councilman, Carrizo Springs, 64- Bus. & Prof. Pos: Pres, S.Tex. Life Ins. Agents Farm Bur. Co, 68- Mil. Serv: 2nd Lt, Army, 42-45, with serv. in China-Burma-India Theatre, 43-45; Entered as 2nd Lt, Tex. Nat. Guard, 46, released as Maj, 66; Combat Inf. Medal; Bronze Star; Two Combat Stars. Mem: Pecos Valley Livestock Asn.(pres, 38-42); United Fund (pres, Carrizo Springs Chap, 69); Lions (past pres, Carrizo Springs Club). Named Number One Life Ins. Salesman, South. Farm Bur. Life Ins. Co, Jackson, Miss, 57. Rel: Baptist; Pres. bd, First Baptist Church, 62-64, Sunday Sch. Supt, 64-69. Legal Res: 200 S. 18th St, Carrizo Springs, Tex. 78834. Mailing Add: 1905 N. First St, Carrizo Springs, Tex. 78834.

MOGGED, CHARLES GEORGE R
Iowa State Sen.
b. Altamont, S.Dak, 2/22/32; s. Otto Mogged (deceased) and Ida Fritz M; m. 4/26/52 to Vivian Boyle; c. Charles George, Jr, Gregory Dean, James Stephen, Kathleen Marie and Karen Lynn. Educ: Univ. Ill, Champaign, B.S. in Agr, 54; M.S. in Econ, 59; Sigma Zeta; Phi Sigma Epsilon. Polit. & Govt. Pos: Bd. mem, Fairfield Sch. Dist, Iowa, 64-66; Iowa State Sen, Second Dist, 69- Bus. & Prof. Pos: Dist. economist, Iowa State Univ, 58-66; owner, Mogged Real Estate, 66- Mil. Serv: Entered as Pvt. E-1, Army, 54, released as Spec. 3, 56, after serv. in 113th Counterintel. Corps Detachment, Fifth Army Hq, Chicago, Ill; Letter of commendation for work as special agent; Counterintel. Corps Medal. Mem: Southeast Iowa Bd. of Realtors; Iowa Asn. of Realtors; Nat. Asn. of Real Estate Bd; Am. Farm Mgr. and Rural Appraisers; Am. Farm Econ. Asn; Rotary; C. of C, Bethany Home Bd. mem; Am. Farm Bur. Fedn; Fairfield Country Club; Walton Club. Rel: Catholic. Mailing Add: 206 Wilson Blvd, Fairfield, Iowa 52556.

MOHAMED, OLLIE D
Miss. State Sen.
b. Shaw, Miss, 2/7/25; married. Polit. & Govt. Pos: Miss. State Sen, currently. Bus. & Prof. Pos: Merchant; farmer. Mem: Mason; Scottish and York Rites; Am. Legion; VFW; Farm Bur; Retail Merchants Asn; C. of C; Delta Cotton Coun. Rel: Baptist. Mailing Add: 105 Oak St, Belzoni, Miss. 39038. (1967)

MOHLER, ROBERT EMERSON D
b. Akron, Ohio, 8/14/12; s. Reuben A. Mohler and Pearl Carter M; m. 9/5/36 to Marian Silvester; c. Janice (Mrs. James Grove), Roger A. and Jocelyn (Mrs. James Lance). Educ: Univ. Akron, A.B; Ohio State Univ, M.A; Univ. Akron Law Sch, J.D; Phi Sigma Alpha; Grad. with Distinction, Univ. Akron. Polit. & Govt. Pos: Asst. Co. Prosecutor, Summit Co, Ohio, 50-53; mem, Ohio State Dem. Exec. Cmt, 53; mem, Akron Bd. of Educ, 55-67, pres, 61 & 67; mem, Akron Police & Fire Pension Bd, 60-63; Dem. cand. for Mayor of Akron, 67; del, Dem. Nat. Conv, 68. Bus. & Prof. Pos: High sch. teacher, Akron Pub. Schs, 36-46; head of claim dept. for Akron Dist, Ins. Co. of N.Am, 47-50; instr, Law Sch, Univ. Akron, 53-56; asst. counsel, Firestone Tire & Rubber Co, 53-69. Publ: 'Articles of the History of Akron,' Summit Co. Hist. Soc. Bul, 58-65; 'Article on Improving Juvenile Court,' Nat. Coun. on Crime and Delinquency. Mem: Akron, Ohio State and Am. Bar Asns; U.S. Trademark Asn; Summit Co. Hist. Soc.(pres); Adv. Cmt. to Summit Co. Juvenile Court (pres); Citizens Adv. Cmt. to Akron Pub. Schs; Akron Child Guidance Center Cmt. Akron Bar Asn. Award for Merit, Civic Activities; Cert. Merit, Akron United Fund. Rel: Episcopal. Mailing Add: 321 Mull Ave, Akron, Ohio 44313.

MOHLING, CARL LOUIS D
b. Waverly, Iowa, 9/2/24; s. Albert Mohling and Ida Dins M. (deceased); m. 2/14/58 to Agnes Marie Bolton; c. Steven John, Caroline Ann and Sarah Beth. Educ: Wartburg Col, 1½ years. Polit. & Govt. Pos: Dem. precinct chmn, Jefferson Twp, Iowa, 64-68; chmn, Bremer Co. Dem. Party, 66-68. Rel: Lutheran. Mailing Add: R.R. 3, Waverly, Iowa 50677.

MOHN, JAMES FRANKLIN D
N.C. State Rep.
b. Pender Co, N.C, 7/26/10; s. Frank C. Mohn and Hattie Harrelson M; m. 7/17/32 to Lyde Mae Carter; c. James F, Jr, Donald C, Robert H, Kay M. (Mrs. Gasperson), Frederick H. and David J. Educ: Duke Univ, 42. Polit. & Govt. Pos: Mayor, Richland Twp, N.C, 38-39 & 42-43, councilman, 40-41; mem, Onslow Co. Bd. Cmnr, 48-49 & 55-59, chmn, 50-51; N.C. State Rep, 67- Bus. & Prof. Pos: Pres, J.F. Mohn Mercantile Co, J.F. Mohn & Sons Tractor Co, J.F. Mohn & Sons Oil Co. and J.F. Mohn & Sons Grain Co. Mem: Pres, Lions, 38-40 & 52-53; Moose. Rel: Baptist. Mailing Add: 103 Foy St, Richlands, N.C. 28574. (1967)

MOHRFELD, FRED R
Iowa State Rep.
b. Tama, Iowa, 12/23/11; married; c. two daughters. Educ: Tama High Sch. Polit. & Govt. Pos: Mem, Tama Sch. Bd, Iowa; Iowa State Rep, 67- Bus. & Prof. Pos: Owner, serv. sta, motel and cafe, 34 years; mem, Standard Oil Adv. Coun, 2 years; businessman, real estate, currently. Mem: Toledo Commercial Club Bd; Lions (past pres); Mason (Master). Rel: Methodist. Mailing Add: 1203 S. Broadway, Toledo, Iowa 52342.

MOLINARO, GEORGE D
Wis. State Assemblyman
b. Kenosha, Wis, 10/1/02. Educ: Bus. Col. Polit. & Govt. Pos: Mem, Co. Bd, Wis, 39-47; Wis. State Assemblyman, 46- Bus. & Prof. Pos: Automobile worker; bank pres. Mem: Life mem, local co. fair asn.(former dir). Mailing Add: 424 44th St, Kenosha, Wis. 53140. (1967)

MOLL, CHARLES PHILLIP D
b. St. Louis, Mo, 8/28/33; s. Charles P. Moll, Sr. and Mildred Winterer M; m. 6/25/55 to Arlene Jasper; c. Richard Bradley, Ronald Brian and Pamela Lynn. Educ: St. Louis Univ, B.S. in Commerce, 56, LL.B, 58, J.D, 69; Phi Delta Phi. Polit. & Govt. Pos: Treas, Franklin Co. Dem. Club, Mo, 62-63; prosecuting attorney, Franklin Co, 60-64; del-at-lg, Dem. Nat. Conv, 68. Mem: Am. and Mo. Bar Asns; Am. Trial Lawyers; Am. Judicature Soc; K. of C; C. of C; Lions; Elks. Rel: Roman Catholic. Legal Res: 114 Oak, Washington, Mo. 63090. Mailing Add: Box 101, Washington, Mo. 63090.

MOLL, OTTO RUDOLPH R
Committeeman, Ill. Rep. Cent. Cmt.
b. Altamont, Ill, 6/15/99; s. Rudolph Moll and Elizabeth Yagow M; m. 6/15/29 to Rachel E. Hartmeister; c. Judith (Mrs. James Barth) and David Eugene (deceased). Educ: McKendree Col, 1 year. Polit. & Govt. Pos: City treas, Altamont, Ill, 30-67; v.chmn. and chmn, Effingham Co. Sch. Survey Cmt, 46-50; mem, Effingham Co. Bd. Sch. Trustees, 50-; committeeman, Ill. Rep. Cent. Cmt, 66- Bus. & Prof. Pos: Registered pharmacist, 23-; pharmacist and mgr, Drug Store, 14-31. Mil. Serv: Pvt, McKendree Students Army Training Corps Unit, 18. Mem: Am. Legion (serv. officer, 35 years); Lions Int.(past pres, Altamont Club, 2 terms, zone chmn, 4 terms); Int. Lutheran Laymens League; Int. Lutheran Hour (dist. rep, 10 years). Rel: Lutheran. Legal Res: 107 Edwards, Altamont, Ill. 62411. Mailing Add: Box 212, Altamont, Ill. 62411.

MOLLERE, JULES GUSTAVE D
La. State Sen.
b. New Orleans, La, 5/22/21; s. Jules G. Mollere, Sr. and Maria L. Benson M; m. 4/21/45 to Miriam Ruth Chevis; c. Jeanine(Mrs. Ludwig), Judith, Nanette and Jules G, III. Educ: Tulane Univ, B.B.A, 42, Post-grad. work in admin, 49; Loyola Univ.(La), LL.B, 49; Delta Theta Phi. Polit. & Govt. Pos: Sch. bd. mem, Jefferson Parish, La, 53-59; La. State Rep, 61-64; La. State Sen, 64- Bus. & Prof. Pos: Acct, Jules G. Mollere & Assocs, Jefferson Parish, 46-; attorney, Mollere & Barbera, 49-; dir, Metairie Savings Bank & Trust Co, 59- Mil. Serv: Entered as A/S, Navy, 42, released as Lt.(sg), after serv. in anti-submarine warfare, S.Pac, 43-46. Mem: Am, La. and Jefferson Parish Bar Asns; urban develop. bd, Brookings Inst; cmt. on rev. of judicial articles of La. Constitution, La. Law Inst; La. Cmt. on Govt. Mgt. and Efficiency; bd. dirs, Our Lady of the River Convent; Rotary (past pres, Metairie Club); Young Men's Bus. Club; VFW; plus others. Rel: Protestant. Legal Res: 300 Cedar Dr, Metairie, La. 70005. Mailing Add: 2341 Metairie Rd, Metairie, La. 70001.

MOLLOHAN, ROBERT H. D
U.S. Rep, W.Va.
b. Grantsville, W.Va, 9/18/09; s. Robert P. Mollohan and Edith Witt M; m. to Helen M. Holt; c. Robert H, Alan B. and Kathryn M.(Mrs. Moats). Educ: Glenville Col; Shepherd Col. Polit. & Govt. Pos: Former chief miscellaneous tax div. and cashier, U.S. Internal Revenue Bur, W.Va; former dist. mgr. and state personnel dir, Works Projs. Admin; state dir, 1940 Census; former supt, W.Va. Indust. Sch. for Boys; former U.S. marshal, North. Dist, W.Va; former clerk, U.S. Senate Cmt. on D.C; U.S. Rep, W.Va, 53-56 & 69- Mem: Elks; Eagles; Moose. Rel: Baptist. Legal Res: Fairmont, W.Va. Mailing Add: 314 Cannon Office Bldg, Washington, D.C. 20515.

MOLYNEAUX, SILAS ROBARRE D
b. Houghton, N.Y, 4/14/16; s. John Robert Molyneaux and Pearl Ingersoll M; m. 8/27/38 to Elenore Mae Kaltenborn; c. Joel Edward and Leslie Lenore. Educ: Houghton Col, B.A, 36; Columbia Univ, M.A, 48. Polit. & Govt. Pos: Dem. cand. for N.Y. State Sen, 65; chmn, Dem. Town Cmt, Somerset, N.Y, 65-68; del, Dem. Nat. Conv, 68. Bus. & Prof. Pos: Spec. asst. to pres, State Univ. N.Y. Col, Buffalo, 64-69. Mil. Serv: Entered as Pvt, Air Force, 42, released as Col, 64, after serv. in U.S. and Far East Areas, 43-64, Regular Officer,(Ret); Legion of Merit; Army Commendation Medal; Numerous Battle Stars and Serv. Ribbons. Mem: Phi Delta Kappa; Air Force Asn; Mason; Lions; Quiet Birdmen. Rel: Protestant. Mailing Add: 1152 Hartland Rd, Barker, N.Y. 14012.

MONACELLI, WILLIAM ANTHONY D
Chmn, Orleans Co. Dem. Cmt, N.Y.
b. Albion, N.Y, 3/14/12; s. Horace Monacelli and Hyacinth Lombard M; m. 12/18/59 to Betty Francis; c. Dona Kay (Mrs. Heywood), Don William and Jill Marie. Educ: Hamilton Col, A.B, 32; post grad. study, Univ. Rochester Union Col, on a Gen. Elec. Physics Fel. and Hamilton Col, on a Nat. Sci. Found. Math. Fel; Pi Delta Epsilon; Emerson Literary Soc. Polit. & Govt. Pos: Mayor, Village of Albion, 51-54 & 66-, trustee, 65-66; chmn, Orleans Co. Dem. Cmt, N.Y, 63-; research clerk, N.Y. State Legis. Cmt. on Conserv, 65-67 and Joint Legis. Cmt. on Indust. and Labor Conditions, 68-69; mem, Orleans Co. Bd. of Elec, 67-; mem. bd. gov, Fedn. of Italian-Am. Dem. Orgn, State of N.Y, 67- Bus. & Prof. Pos: Sci. and math. instr, Albion Cent. Sch, N.Y, 35-55 & 62-; Orleans Co. correspondent and photographer, Rochester Gannett Newspapers, 38-64; Orleans Co. correspondent for Buffalo Eve. News, 40-; sci. and math. instr, Lockport Sr. High Sch, N.Y, 56-62; Sunday columnist, Rochester Dem. and Chronicle, 60-64. Mil. Serv: Entered as Meteorol. Cadet, Army Air Corps, 42, released as 1st Lt, 46, after serv. as Weather Officer, Tech. Training Command, Chanute Field, Ill, 42-46. Publ: Orleans County Historical Political Chronology, Eddy Printing, Albion, N.Y, 65. Mem: Albion and N.Y. Teachers Asn; Nat. Educ. Asn; Northwest. Frontier Asn. Village Off.(pres, 66-67); N.Y. State Conf. Mayors; N.Y. State Asn. of Upstate Rural Co. Dem. Chmn; Rotary (past pres. and 25 year mem, Albion Club); Am. Legion (past comdr. and past Orleans Co. comdr. and hon. life mem, Sheret Post); Orleans Voiture; 40 et 8; Elks; Italian Sons and Daughters of Am; Moose; St. Mary's Athletic Club; pres, Orleans Co. Semi-Pro Baseball League, 34-52; pres, Orleans Co. Babe Ruth Baseball League, 62- Rel: Roman Catholic. Legal Res: 34 S. Clinton St, Albion, N.Y. 14411. Mailing Add: Box 29, Albion, N.Y. 14411.

MONAGAN, JOHN STEPHEN D
U.S. Rep, Conn.
b. Waterbury, Conn, 12/23/11; s. Charles A. Monagan and Margaret Mulry M; m. 5/23/49 to Rosemary Anne Brady; c. Charles A, Michael, Parthenia, Laura and Susan. Educ: Dartmouth Col, A.B, 33; Harvard Law Sch, LL.B, 37; Alpha Delta Phi; Sphinx. Polit. & Govt. Pos: Pres, Bd. Alderman, Waterbury, Conn, 40-42 and mayor, 43-48; U.S. Rep, Conn, Fifth Dist, 59-, mem, Govt. Opers. Cmt, U.S. House of Rep, 59-, mem, For. Affairs Cmt, 61- and chmn, spec. studies subcmt, 62-; Cong. del. to European Conf. NATO Parliamentarians, 60; Cong. del. to Inter-Parliamentary Union Conf, 65-69; mem. exec. cmt, Am. Group of Inter-Parliamentary Union, 66; del, Dem. Nat. Conv, 68. Bus. & Prof. Pos: Dir, Waterbury Savings Bank, 58- Mem: Waterbury and Conn. Bar Asns; Fed. Bar; U.S. Supreme Court Bar; YMCA; Elks; Eagles; Ancient Order of Hibernians; Soc. of Colonial Wars; Waterbury Club. Rel: Roman Catholic. Legal Res: 103 Buckingham St, Waterbury, Conn. 06710. Mailing Add: 2331 Rayburn House Office Building, Washington, D.C. 20515.

MONAGAN, ROBERT TIMOTHY, JR. R
Speaker, Calif. State Assembly
b. Ogden, Utah, 7/5/20; s. Robert Timothy Monagan and Ora Johnson M; m. 3/17/45 to Margaret Ione Angwin; c. Michael Richard and Marilee. Educ: Univ. of the Pac, B.A, 42; alumni secy, 46. Polit. & Govt. Pos: Admin. asst, U.S. Congress, 53-54; mayor, Tracy, Calif, 59-60; Calif. State Assemblyman, 12th Dist, 61-, Minority Leader, Calif. State Assembly, 67-69 and Speaker, 69-; del, Rep. Nat. Conv, 68. Bus. & Prof. Pos: Athletic dir, Univ. of the Pac, 47-50; partner, Monagan-Miller Ins. Co, currently. Mil. Serv: Entered as Cadet, Coast Guard, 43, released as Lt.(jg), 46, after serv. in Aleutian Islands. Mem: Am. Legion; VFW; Mason; Elks; Moose; Grange; Tracy C. of C.(mgr, 50-52). Rel: Methodist. Mailing Add: 1317 El Portal, Tracy, Calif. 95376.

MONAGHAN, JOHN BERNARD D
b. Ft. Dodge, Iowa, 12/14/34; s. Joseph D. Monaghan and Mary Bradley M; m. 8/17/57 to Ann Lyn Bixby; c. Terri Lyn and Kelli K. Educ: High Sch. and Dale Carnegie Course. Polit. & Govt. Pos: Financial Coordinator, E.B. Smith Campaign Cmt, Iowa, 66; campaign mgr, V. Mayberry for State Rep, 66 and 64; del, Dem. Nat. Conv, 64; financial chmn, Webster Co. Dem. Party, 60-64. Mil. Serv: Entered as Pvt, Army, 52, released as Sgt, 58, after serv. in 134th Div. Mem: Bd. dirs, Iowa Jaycees; Ft. Dodge Country Club; Elks. Rel: Roman Catholic. Mailing Add: 3622 Forest Rd, Davenport, Iowa 52807.

MONAGHAN, THOMAS J. D
Mayor, Lancaster, Pa.
b. Mahanoy City, Pa, 7/26/14; s. Thomas J. Monaghan and Mary Scully M; m. 4/10/44 to Sylvia Krick; c. Thomas J, Mary F. and Charles P. Polit. & Govt. Pos: Sch. dir, Mahanoy City Sch. Dist, Pa, 37-42; mem, Pa. State Dem. Exec. and Policy Cmts; Dem. precinct committeeman, Lancaster, Pa, 50-60; city chmn, Lancaster Dem. Cmt, 50-60; mayor, Lancaster, 58-62 & 66-; Secy. of

Commerce, Commonwealth of Pa, 61-63; del, Dem. Nat. Conv, 68. Mil. Serv: Entered as Seaman, Navy, 42, released as SK 1/C, 45, after serv. in Pac. Theater. Mem: Elks; VFW; CWV; Moose; Eagles; Am. Legion; K. of C. Rel: Catholic. Mailing Add: 717 Hilton Dr, Lancaster, Pa. 17603.

MONAHAN, JOHN LEO D
Secy. to Speaker John McCormack, U.S. House of Rep.
b. Newton, Mass, 3/8/33; s. Francis Joseph Monahan and Mary F. Quilty M; m. 1963 to A. Jean Franklin; c. John L, Jr. Educ: Boston Col, B.A, 59. Polit. & Govt. Pos: Secy. to Majority Leader, U.S. House of Rep, 60-62, Secy. to Speaker John McCormack, 62- Mil. Serv: Entered as Pvt, Army, 55; released as Sgt, 57. Legal Res: Newton, Mass. Mailing Add: Capitol Bldg, Room H-209, Washington, D.C. 20002.

MONAHAN, MAURICE BRICE R
Chmn, Millbury Rep. Town Cmt, Mass.
b. Montreal, Que, Can, 5/21/26; s. Maurice Brice Monahan and Muriel Ethel Taylor M; m. 8/28/48 to Dorothy Evelyn Gittus; c. Brian Edward. Educ: Sir George Williams Univ, 2 years. Polit. & Govt. Pos: Mem, Millbury Rep. Town Cmt, Mass, 63-, chmn, 66-; mem. and asst. treas, Millbury Housing Authority, 67- Bus. & Prof. Pos: Sales and advert. mgr, Hunter Douglas Ltd, Montreal, 53-; claim rep, Paul Revere Life Ins Co, Worcester, Mass, 57- Mil. Serv: Pvt, Army Air Corps, 43-45, serv. in USAAFTTC, U.S. Mem: AF&AM. Rel: Protestant. Mailing Add: 44 W. Main St, Millbury, Mass. 01527.

MONCE, RAYMOND EUGENE D
Mem, Calif. Dem. State Cent. Cmt.
b. Indianapolis, Ind, 3/8/24; s. Raymond Charles Monce and Mildred Olvey M; m. 3/5/55 to Doris Ruth Anderson; c. Mark Douglas and Melissa Rae. Educ: Butler Univ, 46-48; Ind. Univ, 48-50; Calif. West. Univ, M.S.M.S, 66. Polit. & Govt. Pos: Mem, Wrightwood Sch. Bd, Calif, 58; mem, San Diego Co. Dem. Cent. Cmt, 66-; mem, Calif. Dem. State Cent. Cmt, 68- Bus. & Prof. Pos: Aerospace eng. and mgt, 48-69. Mil. Serv: Entered as A/S, Navy, 43, released as Chief Electronic Technician, 46, after serv. in U.S.S. Earl K. Olsen, European and Asiatic-Pac. Theatres, 43-46; Area Medals; Japanese Occup. Ribbon. Mem: Nat. Mgt. Asn. Rel: Protestant. Mailing Add: 2035 Helix, Spring Valley, Calif. 92077.

MONCURE, WILLIAM IRBY D
Mayor, Blackstone, Va.
b. Nottoway Co, Va, 7/23/11; s. Irby Moncure and Mattie Williams Epes M; m. 10/26/35 to Sue Seay Bagwell; c. William Irby, Jr, Conway Bagwell and Susan Epes. Educ: Col. William & Mary, Williamsburg, Va, 3 years; Univ. Richmond, LL.B, 34; Kappa Alpha. Polit. & Govt. Pos: Secy-treas, Nottoway Co. Dem. Cmt, Va, 39-63, chmn, 63-; mayor, Blackstone, 46- Mem: Mason; K. of P; Moose. Rel: Methodist. Legal Res: 210 Brunswick Ave, Blackstone, Va. 23824. Mailing Add: 103 S. Main St, Blackstone, Va. 23824.

MONDALE, WALTER FREDERICK DFL
U.S. Sen, Minn.
b. Ceylon, Minn, 1/5/28; s. The Reverend Theodore Sigvaard Mondale and Claribel Cowan M; m. 12/27/55 to Joan Adams; c. Theodore Adams, Eleanor Jane and William Hall. Educ: Macalester Col, 46-49; Univ. Minn, B.A, 51, Law Sch, LL.B, 56. Polit. & Govt. Pos: Spec. Asst. Attorney Gen, Minn, 2 years, Attorney Gen, 60-64; mem, President's Consumer Adv. Coun, 62-64; mem. credentials cmt, Dem. Nat. Conv, 64, del, 68; U.S. Sen, Second Dist, Minn, 65-, mem, Cmt. on Labor and Pub. Welfare and chmn, Subcmt. on Migratory Labor, mem, Cmt. on Banking and Currency, Spec. Cmt. on Aging and Select Cmt. on Nutrition and Human Needs. Bus. & Prof. Pos: Attorney-at-Law, Minneapolis, Minn, 56-60. Mil. Serv: Entered as Pvt, Army, 51, released as Cpl, 53, after serv. in Korea. Publ: 'Minnesota Corrupt Practices Act,' Minn. Law Review, 55. Mem: Hennepin Co, Minn. and Am. Bar Asns; former mem, Nat. Asn. Attorneys Gen; UN Asn. of U.S; Sons of Norway; Moose; Eagles; Am. Vets. Cmt, Am. Legion; Hennepin Co. Citizens League. Averell Harriman Equal Housing Opportunity Award. Rel: Presbyterian. Mailing Add: 172 Federal Courts Bldg, Minneapolis, Minn. 55401.

MONDANI, THOMAS P. D
Conn. State Rep.
b. Deep River, Conn, 8/6/34; s. Frank Mondani and Ellen Campbell M; m. 11/19/60 to Henrietta Bloch; c. Thomas, Jr. and James. Educ: Univ. Conn, B.A, 56; Univ. Hartford, M.Ed, 62. Polit. & Govt. Pos: Mem, East Haddam Dem. Town Cmt, Conn, 64-; Conn. State Rep, 73rd Dist, 67- Bus. & Prof. Pos: Salesman, Napier Co, 58-59; teacher, Moodus Schs, 59-63; dir. of research, Conn. Educ. Asn, 63- Mil. Serv: Entered as Pvt, Army, 56, released as Specialist 4, 58. Publ: The Manual for Teacher Negotiators, Educators' Press, 66. Mem: Lions; Father Kuster, K. of C; Conn. Educ. Asn; life mem, Nat. Educ. Asn. Rel: Roman Catholic. Mailing Add: Neptune Ave, Moodus, Conn. 06469. (1967)

MONDELLO, FERDINAND J. D
N.Y. State Assemblyman
b. New York, N.Y; m. to Carolyn Loppolo; c. Pamela, Phillip. Educ: Columbia Univ; Brooklyn Law Sch. of St. Lawrence Univ. Polit. & Govt. Pos: Trustee, Chippewa Dem. Club, N.Y; State Assemblyman, 60-, co-sponsor, Metcalf-Mondello Law Alcoholism, N.Y. State Assembly, 65 and Travia-Mondello Law Narcotics Addiction Control, 66, chmn, Joint Legis. Cmt. on States' Commerce, Econ. Develop, Tourism and Motor Boats, 67. Bus. & Prof. Pos: Lawyer. Mem: Chmn. bd. of dirs, Charitable ESCA Club and Regional Aid for Interim Needs, Inc, NYC; past pres, Columbian Lawyers Asn, First Judicial Dept; Bronx v.pres, Boys Towns of Italy; Dir. Bronx Chap, Multiple Sclerosis; Bronx Chmn, Hemophilia 'Life Brigade' Drive; Counsel to, N.E. Bronx Little League, C.Y.O. Sea Cadets, Sea Battalions; Bronx Shore Commun. Asn; Trustee, Parchester Chap. for Cancer Care; Spec. Events Cmts: Heart Fund, Boy Scouts; Mem. Gifts Chmn: St. Frances De Chantal New Sch. Drive, Cardinal Spellman's Drive for Seminary and New High Schs; Pres, Fathers Club of Preston Catholic High Sch, Throggs Neck Neighborhood Cmt. for Girl Scouts; St. Raymond Coun, K. of C. Rel: Catholic. Mailing Add: 256 Calhoun Ave, Bronx, N.Y. 10465.

MONDRAGON, CHARLES STEVEN, JR. D
Chmn, Costilla Co. Dem. Cent. Cmt, Colo.
b. Alamosa, Colo, 10/3/22; s. Charles Mondragon and Rose Rodriques M; m. 8/16/48 to Katherine Nigro; c. Marie Annette, Carol Louise, Charles, III and Kathy Lynin. Educ: Adams State Col, Colo, 41-43; Colo. State Col; Univ. N.Mex, B.F.A; Phi Kappa Alpha; Delta Phi Delta. Polit. & Govt. Pos: Mem, Colo. Indust. Develop. Adv. Coun, 58-59; chmn, Costilla Co. Dem. Cent. Cmt, 64-; del, Dem. Nat. Conv, 68. Bus. & Prof. Pos: Owner, The San Luis Co, 48- Mil. Serv: Entered as Pvt, Air Force, 43, released as Capt, 45, after serv. in 15th Air Force, ETO, 44-45; Capt, Air Force Res, until 58; N.Apennines, Rhineland, Arno-Po Valley, Air Combat, Balkans, North. and South. France Campaign Ribbons; Distinguished Unit Citation; ETO-African, Middle East Serv. Medal. Mem: Bd. mem, Univ. N.Mex. Vet. Asn, 47-48; K. of C. (4°); Rotary; Am. Legion. Rel: Roman Catholic. Mailing Add: P.O. Box 357, San Luis, Colo. 81152. (1967)

MONDRAGON, ROBERT A. D
N.Mex. State Rep.
b. La Loma, N.Mex, 7/27/40; s. Severo Mondragón and Lucia Aragón M; m. 11/28/68 to Bell Urrea; c. Julian Jaramillo, Geraldine Jaramillo and Robert Anthony. Educ: Albuquerque High Sch, grad, 58. Polit. & Govt. Pos: N.Mex. State Rep, Bernalillo Co, 67- Mem: Exec. cmt, Albuquerque Goals Prog; C. of C; Lions; Am. GI Forum; Fraternal Order of Police Assocs. Rel: Catholic. Mailing Add: 610 11th St. N.W, Albuquerque, N.Mex. 87102.

MONDRES, MARVIN D. R
Cong. Liaison Officer, Dept. of Commerce
b. N.Y.C, 6/16/25; s. Joseph R. Mondres and Estelle Margolies M; m. 11/27/52 to Roberta Claire Leder; c. Eric Myles and Gina Allyson. Educ: Cornell Univ, 42-44; Tau Epsilon Phi. Polit. & Govt. Pos: Former v.pres, Gr. Miami Young Rep. Club, Fla; chmn, Fla. Young Rep. State Conv. Cmt, 52; organizer, Dade Co. Fedn. of Young Rep. Clubs, mem. bd. dirs, in charge of all publicity and pub. rels; Rep. cand, Fla. State Rep, 54; mem, Dade Co. Rep. Exec. Cmt; former pres, W. Broward Rep. Club; mem, Broward Co. Rep. Exec. Cmt, 8 years, v.chmn, 2 years; chief campaign coordinator, J. Herbert Burke Campaigns for Broward Co. Bd. of Cmnrs, 60 & 64 and U.S. Rep, 66 & 68; v.chmn, Broward Co. Zoning Bd, Fla, 60-65; chief campaign coordinator, J.W. Stevens Campaign, Broward Co. Bd. of Cmnrs, 62; mem, Broward Co. Bd. of Adjust, 66; admin. asst. to U.S. Rep. J. Herbert Burke, Fla, 67-69; cong. liaison officer, Dept. of Commerce, 69- Bus. & Prof. Pos: Mfg. rep, Miami, Fla, 46-48; life underwriter, Aetna Life Ins. Co, 49-51; pres, Lucky's Furniture, Inc, Hollywood, Ft. Lauderdale, Miami and West Palm Beach, Fla, 52-65. Mil. Serv: Entered as A/S, Navy, 44, released as Seaman 1/C, 45. Mem: Past pres, Hollywood Civitan Club; West Hollywood C. of C.(past pres, retail merchants div); Cornell Univ. Alumni Club; Cornell Alumni Cmt. on Sec. Schs; United Fund (chmn, West Broward, bd. dirs, Broward Co); bd. dirs, Fla. State Soc. in Wash; Cong. Secy. Club; Bull Elephants Club; Poets Club; Capitol Hill Club; Elks; B'nai B'rith. Rel: Jewish. Legal Res: 4211 N. Federal Hwy, Ft. Lauderdale, Fla. 33308. Mailing Add: 9300 Arabian Ave, Vienna, Va. 22180.

MONDT, LOREN EDWARD D
Chmn, Boone Co. Dem. Cent. Cmt, Iowa
b. Boone, Iowa, 5/15/10; s. Harry A. Mondt and Minnie A.K. Leininger M; m. 3/21/33 to Annabelle Baird; c. Loren E, Jr. Educ: Boone High Sch, grad, 29; Cornell Exec. Soc, 51-64. Polit. & Govt. Pos: Chmn, Boone Co. Dem. Cent. Cmt, Iowa, 64-; committeeman, Boone Third Ward, 65-69; del, Dem. Nat. Conv, 68. Bus. & Prof. Pos: Dir, Iowa Restaurant Asn, 48-69, pres, 55-56. Mil. Serv: Entered as Seaman, Navy, 44, released as 3/C Cook, 45, after serv. in Destroyer, Pac. Theatre; Am. Area Campaign Medal; Asiatic-Pac. Area Campaign Medal with Two Bronze Stars. Mem: Exalted Ruler, Elks, Boone, 44-; VFW; Am. Legion; Kiwanis (pres, 56-57). Legion of Honor, DeMolay, 32. Rel: Methodist. Mailing Add: 605 Story St, Boone, Iowa 50036.

MONKS, BRUCE L. D
b. Lansing, Mich, 11/8/23; m; c. Mary Kathleen, Kevin, Patrice, Michael. Educ: Mich. State Univ, A.B, 45; Detroit Col. of Law, J.D, 52. Polit. & Govt. Pos: Mich. State Rep, 64-66; Justice of the Peace, Clinton Twp, 56-59 and supv, 61-65. Bus. & Prof. Pos: Lawyer. Mil. Serv: Army, Philippines, 45-46. Mem: Clinton Valley Kiwanis Club; State Bar of Mich; Macomb Co. Bar Asn; K. of C; former treas, Huron Clinton Metrop. Authority. Rel: Roman Catholic. Mailing Add: 23620 Southland Ct, Mt. Clemens, Mich. 48043. (1967)

MONKS, ROBERT A. G. R
b. Boston, Mass, 12/4/33; s. G. Gardner Monks and Katherine Knowles M; m. 7/2/54 to Millicent Sprague; c. Melinda C. and Robert C.S. Educ: Harvard Col, B.A, 54; Trinity Col, Cambridge Univ, 55; Harvard Law Sch, LL.B, 58; Phi Beta Kappa. Polit. & Govt. Pos: Chmn, City of Cambridge Rep. Cmt, Mass, 66; finance chmn, Mass. State Rep. Cmt, 67-68; del, Rep. Nat. Conv, 68. Bus. & Prof. Pos: Attorney, Goodwin, Procter & Hoar, Boston, 58-65; v.pres, Coolidge Cunningham & Monks succeeded by Gardner Assocs, Inc, 66-67; pres, C.H. Sprague & Son, Co, 68-; dir, Esterline Corp, Codex Corp. and Westmoreland Coal. Mem: Cape Elizabeth Conserv. Soc; trustee, Lenox Sch; treas, Longy Sch. Music. Rel: Episcopal; Clerk, Trustees of Donations, Protestant Episcopal Church. Legal Res: Richmond House, Ram Island Farm, Cape Elizabeth, Maine 04107. Mailing Add: Room 1600, 125 High St, Boston, Mass. 02110.

MONPLAISIR, MARIA ELLEN R
b. New York, N.Y ; m. 9/28/47 to Chester Julian Monplaisir; c. Donald Chester and Jereen Maria. Polit. & Govt. Pos: V.Chmn, James T. Ryan Conservative Club, N.Y, 62-63, chmn, 63-64; v.chmn, Richmond Co. Conservative, N.Y, 64-65, chmn, 65-69; mem, State Cmt, Conservative, N.Y, 65-69, mem, State Exec. Cmt, 66-69. Mil. Serv: Entered as A/S, Waves, 43, released as Aviation Machinist Mate 2/C, 46, after serv. in Naval Air Sta. Alameda and Livermore, Calif. and Barbers Point, T.H; Good Conduct and World War II Victory Medals; Pac. Theater Ribbon. Mem: James J. Tappen Post, Am. Legion; past pres, Richmond Co. Police Post, Am. Legion Auxiliary; Richmond Co. Commun. Planning Bd. 4. Rel: Roman Catholic. Mailing Add: 404 N. Cherry Ave, Tucson, Ariz. 85719.

MONROE, LAMAR RALPH R
b. Scipio, Utah, 12/16/20; s. Ralph Moroni Monroe and Nana E. McArthur M; m. 6/5/47 to Gwen Tuttle; c. Jeanne, Lee, Lloyd, Mark and Mary. Educ: Utah State Univ, B.S; Sigma Phi Epsilon. Polit. & Govt. Pos: Precinct chmn,

Rep. Party, Utah; Utah State Rep, Millard Co, 61-67. Bus. & Prof. Pos: V.pres, Scipio Irrigation Co, 12 years. Mil. Serv: Entered as Cpl, Army, 43, released as Capt, 46, after serv. in 75th Div, ETO; ETO Ribbon with 3 Battle Stars; 1 Bronze Star; 2 Purple Hearts. Mem: Lions; Am. Legion; pres, Co. Farm Bur, 58-61; pres, local Farm Bur. Utah Cattlemans Asn; Scipio Riding Club. Rel: Latter-day Saint. Mailing Add: Scipio, Utah 84656.

MONROE, WARREN LUDWIG D
Nev. State Sen.
b. Rocklin, Calif, 4/17/06; s. George Monroe and Alice Udbye M; m. 5/10/30 to Mary Kathleen Johnstone; c. Lawrence K. and James W. Educ: Univ. Nev, A.B; Nev. Debate Soc. Polit. & Govt. Pos: Chmn, Humboldt Co. Rep. Cmt, Nev, 32; chmn, Humboldt Co. Bd. Educ, 34-37; Nev. State Rep, 41, 43 & 47; mem, Nev. Fish and Game Cmn, 47-54, chmn, 53; mem. and past chmn. and secy, Elko Co. Dem. Cent. Cmt; mem. and past chmn, Nev. Dem. Cent. Cmt; Nev. State Sen, 58-, Majority Whip Nev. State Senate 69. Mil. Serv: Entered as Pvt, Army, 43, released as Pfc, after serv. in 106th Gen. Hosp, ETO, 45. Mem: Nev. State Press Asn.(past pres); C. of C.(v.pres. and pres-elect, Elko Chap, 66-67); Rotary (past pres, Elko Club); Elks. Legal Res: 100 Oak, Elko, Nev. 89801. Mailing Add: P.O. Box 309, Elko, Nev. 89801.

MONROE, WILLIE PARKER D
Dir, Ninth Cong. Dist, N.C.
b. Lillington, N.C, 8/24/00; d. William James Parker and Eula Register P; m. 8/17/30 to Reid Stafford Monroe; c. William Reid. Educ: Lillington High Sch; Atlanta Bus. Col, Atlanta, Ga. Polit. & Govt. Pos: Trustee, N.C. Tubercular Syst, 63-67; del, Dem. Nat. Conv, 64; dir, Ninth Cong. Dist, N.C, 64- Mem: Chmn, Legis. Cmt, Salisbury Woman's Club. Rel: Methodist; Mem, Official Bd. Mailing Add: 128 Maupin Ave, Salisbury, N.C. 28144. (1967)

MONRONEY, A. S. MIKE D
b. Oklahoma City, Okla, 3/2/02; m. to Mary Ellen Mellon; c. Michael. Educ: Univ. Okla, B.A, 24; Phi Beta Kappa; Phi Gamma Delta; Sigma Delta Chi. Polit. & Govt. Pos: U.S. Rep, Okla, 38-50; U.S. Sen, Okla, 51-68; del, Dem. Nat. Conv, 68. Bus. & Prof. Pos: Reporter and polit. writer, Okla. News, 24-28; aviation and transportation consult, Wash, D.C, 69- Collier's Award for Distinguished Cong. Serv, 45; Trophy for Pub. Serv. in Aviation, 61. Rel: Episcopal. Legal Res: 2760 32nd St. N.W, Washington, D.C. 20008. Mailing Add: 300 World Center Bldg, Washington, D.C. 20006.

MONSON, ARCH, JR. R
Mem, Calif. State Rep. Cent. Cmt.
b. Thorntown, Ind, 11/10/13; s. Arch Monson and Mabel Miller M; m. 1/10/59 to June Hammersmith; c. Eminel, Arch, III, Dwight and Jay. Educ: Moral Twp. Union High Sch, London, Ind, grad, 30. Polit. & Govt. Pos: Mem, United San Francisco Rep. Finance Cmt, Calif; tech. consult. to arrangements cmt, Rep. Nat. Conv, 56, 64 & 68, del, 68; North. Calif. chmn, George Murphy for U.S. Sen, 64; statewide coordinator, Christopher for Gov. Cmt, 66; v.chmn, State Finance Cmt. Reagan for Gov, 66; asst. treas, Rep. State Cent. Cmn, 67; co-chmn, Dobbs for Mayor Cmt, San Francisco, 68; region II chmn, Nixon-Agnew Calif. Campaign Cmt, 68; presidential elector, Calif, 68; mem, Calif. Rep. State Cent. Cmt, 69- Bus. & Prof. Pos: Pres, Monson Elec. Co, Inc, 35; West Coast mgr, Autocall Co, Fed. Sign & Signal Co, 45; pres, Holzmueller Corp, 47; pres, Pac. Auxiliary Fire Alarm Co, 59; owner-operator, St. George Ranch, Geyserville, 59. Mem: San Francisco Elec. Club; Los Angeles Elec. Club; Nat. Elec. Contractors Asn; Pac. Coast Elec. Asn; nat. exec. bd, Boy Scouts; v.pres, San Francisco C. of C; bd. dirs, San Francisco Conv. & Visitors Bur; dir, San Francisco Rotary Club; trustee, Golden Gate Col; trustee, Pac. Med. Center; past pres, Bohemian Club; Scottish Rite; KCCH; Islam Temple of the Shrine. Silver Beaver and Silver Antelope, Boy Scouts. Rel: Presbyterian. Legal Res: 2825 Broadway, San Francisco, Calif. 94115. Mailing Add: 360 Sixth St, San Francisco, Calif. 94103.

MONSON, N. PAUL R
Chmn, Polk Co. Rep. Cent. Cmt, Nebr.
b. Osceola, Nebr, 3/18/15; s. Andrew M. Monson and Hannah E. Peterson M; m. 9/18/41 to Louise Thygeson; c. Louis P. and Elizabeth A. Educ: Hastings Col; Univ. Nebr, B.S. in Agr; Pi Kappa Delta; Delta Upsilon. Polit. & Govt. Pos: Chmn, Polk Co. Rep. Cent. Cmt, Nebr, 63- Mem: Farm Bur. Rel: Lutheran. Mailing Add: Osceola, Nebr. 68651.

MONTAGUE, DAVID NICHOLLS R
First V.Chmn, Rep. Party, Va.
b. New York, N.Y, 8/23/36; s. Edgar Sclater Montague and Suzanne Garrett M; m. 6/21/58 to Carolyn Stewart Day; c. Suzanne Stewart and David Nicholls, Jr. Educ: Univ. Va, B.A, 58; Univ. Va. Law Sch, LL.B, 61; Beta Theta Pi (v. pres); T.I.L.K.A. Soc; IMP Soc. Polit. & Govt. Pos: Chmn, Hampton City Rep. Cmt, Va, 68-; first v.chmn, Rep. Party of Va, 68- Bus. & Prof. Pos: Partner, Montague, Cumming & Watkins, Attorneys, 63-67, Montague & Montague, Attorneys, 67- Mil. Serv: Entered as 2nd Lt, Army, 61, released as 1st Lt, 62, after serv. in Army Med. Training Center, Brooke Army Med. Center, Ft. Sam Houston, Tex; Capt, Med. Serv. Corps, Army Res, 62-65. Mem: Hampton, Va. State and Am. Bar Asns; Va. Trial Lawyers Asn; Am. Judicature Soc; Rotary. Rel: Episcopal. Mailing Add: 29 Hampton Roads Ave, Hampton, Va. 23361.

MONTAGUE, HARRY NICHOLS D
Vt. State Rep.
b. Jericho, Vt, 12/4/04; s. Hurd F. Montague and Bertha Nichols M; m. 4/26/37 to Eleanor Wood; c. Harry R, Richard H. and Alan W. Educ: Univ. Vt, B.S, 28; M. Ed, 39; Alpha Zeta; Kappa Phi Kappa; Zeta Chi; Univ. Vt. M. Aggie Club, Pres, 27-28. Polit. & Govt. Pos: Vt. State Rep, Dist, 4-2, 69- Bus. & Prof. Pos: High sch. prin, Newport Center, Vt, 28-31; supv. prin, Cambridge, Vt, 31-35, high sch. prin, North Bennington, Vt, 35-41; supt. schs, Chester, Vt, 41-45, Bennington Southwest Dist, 45-48, Rockingham, 48-51 and Windham Southeast dist, 51-68; retired, 68. Mem: Am. Asn. Sch. Adminstrs; New Eng. Sch. Develop. Coun; Nat. and Vt. Educ. Asns; Century Club; F&AM; Rotary Int.(past pres). Rel: Congregational. Legal Res: 14 Prospect St, Brattleboro, Vt. 05031.

MONTAGUE, RUPERT JAMES R
b. Charlotte, Vt, 5/24/06; m. to Audrey R. Young; c. Four. Educ: Johnson Normal Sch. Polit. & Govt. Pos: Mem, Bakersfield Sch. Bd, Vt, sch. dir, 49-, moderator, 60-; trustee, Brigham Acad, 59-62; Vt. State Rep, 65-67. Bus. & Prof. Pos: Supvr, Dairy Herd Improv. Mem: Mountain View Grange; F&AM. Rel: Congregational; trustee, Bakersfield Congregational Church. Mailing Add: Bakersfield, Vt. 05441. (1967)

MONTALVO, RAY GARCIA D
b. Oakland, Calif, 8/8/32; s. Adolph C. Montalvo and Stella Garcia M; m. 2/28/54 to Carmela Ferri; c. Mark Thomas and Matthew Adolph. Educ: Oakland City Col, 1 year; San Jose State Col, A.B, 59. Polit. & Govt. Pos: Del, Dem. Nat. Conv, 68. Bus. & Prof. Pos: Financial coordinator and gen. agent, Voyager Life Ins. Co, 66-; v.pres. A. & R. Marmont, Inc. and v.pres. and treas, Int. Funding Corp, Calif, currently. Mil. Serv: Entered as Pvt, Army, 52, released as Cpl, 54, after serv. in Med. Corps and Spec. Serv; Soldier's Medal, Good Conduct Medal. Mem: Million Dollar Round Table; Le Clube Democrate (Pres. Club, 67); Golden "C"; Spartan Club. Rel: Catholic. Legal Res: 4424 Ewing Rd, Castro Valley, Calif. 94546. Mailing Add: Suite 300, 235 W. MacArthur Blvd, Oakland, Calif. 94611.

MONTANO, ARMANDO D
N.Y. State Assemblyman
b. San Juan, P.R, 10/10/28; s. Armando Montano, Sr. and Serafina Ramos M; m. Sept. 1959 to Norma Silva; c. Armando, Jr, Richard, Ronald and Marc. Educ: City Col. N.Y, Bernard Baruch Br, 2 years. Polit. & Govt. Pos: Housing proj. specialist, Housing and Develop. Admin, N.Y.C, 66; founder, Robert F. Kennedy Independent Dem. Club, 66; N.Y. State Assemblyman, 68- Bus. & Prof. Pos: Licensed ins. and real estate broker, Montano Realty Co, Bronx, N.Y, 59- Mem: Inst. for Puerto Rican Urban Studies, Inc; chmn, Hunts Point Area Develop. Cmt; C. of C; Gr. N.Y. Ins. Brokers Asn; Puerto Rican Forum, Inc; Urban League of Gr. N.Y; NAACP; Spanish Am. Businessmen's Asn; Puerto Rican Parade, Inc; West Side Tenants Asn; Puerto Rican Crippled Children Cmt; bd. dirs, Bronx Small Bus. Develop. Center, Inc; commun. bd, Morris High Sch; secy. M.A.M.E. Prog, City Wide Small Bus. Admin. Awarded Keys to the Cities of Lackawana, N.Y. and San Juan, P.R; John F. Kennedy Libr. for Minorities Award: Puerto Rican House Award. Rel: Catholic. Legal Res: 634 Manida St, Bronx, N.Y. 10474. Mailing Add: 511 E. 149th St, Bronx, N.Y. 10455.

MONTANO, GEORGE JOHN R
Chmn, New Haven Rep. City Party, Conn.
b. New Haven, Conn, 9/28/27; s. Charles P. Montano and Lucia Macchiaroli M; m. 5/12/52 to Eleanor M. DeCapua; c. Ellyn and twins, John Charles and Stephen Michael. Educ: Holy Cross Col, B.S. in econ, 50; Holy Cross Outing Club. Polit. & Govt. Pos: Chmn, New Haven Rep. Adv. Cmt, Conn, 64-65; chmn, New Haven Rep. City Party, 66-; del, Rep. Nat. Conv, 68. Bus. & Prof. Pos: V.pres, Maplewood Realty Corp, 50-; v.pres, Montano Construction Co, 60-; pres, Nat. Diversified Investors, 62-; v.pres, Coop. Credit Corp, 64- Mem: New Haven Retail Credit Asn; Elks; Union League; Racebrook Country Club; St. Aedan Holy Name Soc; Confraternity of Christian Doctrine; Holy Cross Club. Rel: Catholic. Mailing Add: 1169 Forest Rd, New Haven, Conn. 06515. (1967)

MONTE, RAYMOND LOUIS D
b. Trenton, Mich, 7/17/31; s. Louis Monte and Elizabeth Rose Flow M; m. 8/8/53 to Marilyn June Harlow; c. Richard Dale, Randall George and Melissa Sue. Educ: Mich. State Col, B.A, 53; Mich. State Univ, M.A, 67; Theta Alpha Phi. Polit. & Govt. Pos: Chmn, Ionia Co. Dem. Party, 64-68; supvr, Ionia Co, 69. Bus. & Prof. Pos: Dir. of speech, Ionia High Sch, 56- Mil. Serv: Entered as 2nd Lt, Army, 54, released as 1st Lt, 56, after serv. in Ninth Inf. Div, German, 55-56. Mem: Speech Asn. of Am; Am. Nat. Theatre and Acad; Am. Forensic Asn. Rel: Catholic. Mailing Add: 342 Lafayette St, Ionia, Mich. 48846.

MONTGOMERY, A. HAROLD D
b. Humble, Tex, 4/19/11; s. Allie H. Montgomery and Martha Dean M; m. 2/14/45 to Azalee Wilson; c. Hal. Educ: Univ. Ark, B.A. and M.A. Polit. & Govt. Pos: La. State Sen, 60-68. Bus. & Prof. Pos: Sch. teacher, 34-41; state supvr, Dept. Educ, 41-45; state distributor of power equip, 45-; farmer and cattleman, 54-; dir, Peoples Bank & Trust, 58- and Lincoln Bank & Trust, 62- Mem: Mason (32°); Lions; Local, State and Nat. C. of C; state chmn, Free Electors; state v.pres, Soil Conserv. Dist; state pres, La. Methodist Laymen Asn. Nat. Legislator of the Year Award. Rel: Methodist. Mailing Add: Route 1, Doyline, La. 71023.

MONTGOMERY, C. (DICK) D
b. Clarksburg, W.Va, 5/23/26; s. Carl F. Montgomery and Mildred Leonard M; m. 1946 to Betty Ryan; c. Ricki Michelle, Konnie Cheryl, Marie Denise. Educ: Salem Col; W.Va. Univ. Polit. & Govt. Pos: Former W.Va. State Sen; Pine Grove City Coun; former pres, Wetzel Co. Young Dem. Club; former mem, State Young Dem. Exec. Cmt. Bus. & Prof. Pos: Tech. asst, chem. plant. Mil. Serv: Navy, WWII. Mem: LOOM; Pine Grove Civic Club; Am. Legion, former Adjutant, post 81. Rel: Christian Church. 1967 Legal Res: Pine Grove, W.Va. No mailing address available. (1967)

MONTGOMERY, CHARLES ALBERT D
b. W. Greene, Ala, 9/25/12; s. Lawrence Hardy Montgomery and Eula Leavelle M; m. 4/21/34 to Margaret Chandler; wid; c. Janis Carol (Mrs. John M. Pool), Charles Gamewell. Educ: Univ. of Ala. Polit. & Govt. Pos: Ala. State Sen, -66. Bus. & Prof. Pos: Farming and cattle raising. Rel: Methodist. Mailing Add: Eutaw, Ala. 35462. (1967)

MONTGOMERY, F. F. R
b. Oklahoma City, Okla, June 24. Polit. & Govt. Pos: Ore. State Rep, 59-68, former Speaker of the House; del, Rep. Nat. Conv, 68. Bus. & Prof. Pos: Ins. agency. Mailing Add: Box 349, Eugene, Ore. 97401. (1967)

MONTGOMERY, GEORGE F. D
Mich. State Rep.
b. Ann Arbor, Mich, 8/21/33; s. George Montgomery; m. 8/8/56 to Elizabeth Ann LeBlanc; c. Sarah Anne and Emily Jane. Educ: Wayne State Univ, B.S, 59. Polit. & Govt. Pos: Former precinct del, Dem. Party, Mich, former mem, exec. bd; del, Dem. State Conv; Mich. State Rep, 64- Bus. & Prof. Pos: Pub. sch. teacher, 58-64. Mil. Serv: Army, 56-58. Mem: Pres, Buckingham Park Civic Asn. Mailing Add: 15792 Meyers Rd, Detroit, Mich. 48227. (1967)

MONTGOMERY, GILLESPIE V. D
U.S. Rep, Miss.
b. Meridian, Miss, 8/5/20; single. Polit. & Govt. Pos: Miss. State Sen, 57-66; U.S. Rep, Miss, 67- Bus. & Prof. Pos: Life ins. co. off. and gen. ins. agent. Mem: Mason; Moose; Scottish Rite; Shrine; Optimist Club; Am. Legion; VFW; 40 et 8; past pres, Miss. Nat. Guard Asn; past pres, Miss. State Univ. Alumni Asn; pres. elect, Miss. Heart Asn. Rel: Episcopal. Legal Res: Box 1009, Meridian, Miss. 39301. Mailing Add: House of Representatives, Washington, D.C. 20515.

MONTGOMERY, JOHN WILLARD D
La. State Sen.
b. Bastrop, La, 6/2/36; s. Earl Willard Montgomery and Bernice McLeod M; m. 9/4/59 to Carolyn Ann Tucker; c. Elizabeth Ann and John Willard, Jr. Educ: Tulane Univ, B.A, 58; La. State Univ. Law Sch, LL.B, 62; Gamma Eta Gamma. Polit. & Govt. Pos: La. State Sen, Bossier-Webster Parishes, 68-; mem, La. Cmn. on Law Enforcement and Admin. of Criminal Justice. Bus. & Prof. Pos: Attorney-at-law, Fish & Montgomery, Springhill, La, 66- Mil. Serv: Entered as 1st Lt, Air Force, 62, released as Capt, 65, after serv. in Aero-Space Med. Div, Air Force Syst. Command. Mem: La. and Am. Bar Asns; Lions; Jaycees; Am. Legion. Rel: Baptist. Mailing Add: 708 5th N.E, Springhill, La. 71075.

MONTGOMERY, WAYNE SWOPE R
Mayor, Asheville, N.C.
b. Battle Creek, Mich, 4/21/25; s. Frank S. Montgomery (mother deceased); m. to Elizabeth C. Jeschke; c. Swope, Woody, Ann, Jane and Mary. Educ: DePauw Univ; Wayne State Univ; Campbell Clin. Found, Univ. Tenn; Phi Kappa Psi; Phi Rho Sigma. Polit. & Govt. Pos: Chmn, Buncombe Co. Rep. Party, N.C, 66-69; mayor, Asheville, 69- Bus. & Prof. Pos: Med. dir, West. N.C. Cerebral Palsy Clin, 57-69; chief sect. surg, Mem. Mission Hosp, Asheville, 69; mem. bd. dirs, Asheville Biltmore Col. Found and Asheville Orthopedic Hosp, currently. Mil. Serv: Lt, Naval Res. Med. Corps. Publ: 'Splint for Fracture of the Great Toe,' Armed Forces Med. J, 53; 'Experimental and Clinical Studies in Stimulation of Bone Growth,' J. South. Med. Asn, 56; 'Anterior Tibial Syndrome,' J. N.C. State Med. Soc, 58. Mem: Am. Bd. Orthopedic Surg; Am. Acad. Orthopedic Surg; Am. Acad. Cerebral Palsy; Kiwanis (pres, Asheville Club, 67); Dads Club Lee Edwards High Sch. Rel: Presbyterian. Legal Res: 55 Sunset Pkwy, Asheville, N.C. 28801. Mailing Add: Bone & Joint Clinic, Doctors Dr, Asheville, N.C. 28801.

MONTGOMERY, WAYNE WARREN R
b. Los Angeles, Calif, 12/20/26; s. Wayne Warren Montgomery Sr. and Eleanor Delong M; m. 6/13/51 to Frieda Annelies Menge; c. Wayne Warren, III, Melville William, Mary Anne, Julie Christine and Lisa Eugenia. Educ: Univ. South. Calif, 46-48; Acacia Fraternity. Polit. & Govt. Pos: Del, Rep. Nat. Conv. and mem, Rep. Nat. Platform Cmt, 60; Rep. Cong. nominee, Mont. First Dist, 62 & 64. Bus. & Prof. Pos: Owner and operator, Lakeview Ranch and Recreation Area, Lakeview Ski Lodge and Slopes and Summit Hotel. Mil. Serv: Merchant Marine, Pac. Theater, 44-46; Marine Corps, 47-67, served in Charlie Co, Fifth Marines, Korea, 52 and as commanding officer, 36th Rifle Co, Butte Mont, 60-62; Various Korean Serv. Awards and Decorations, including the Purple Heart. Mem: DAV; Am. Legion; VFW. Rel: Protestant. Legal Res: R.F.D, Monida, Mont. 59744. Mailing Add: P.O. Box K, Lima, Mont. 59739.

MONTOYA, ALFONSO T. D
N.Mex. State Sen.
Educ: Regis Col, Denver; Univ. N.Mex, B.S; George Washington Univ, LL.B; Georgetown Law Sch. Polit. & Govt. Pos: N.Mex. State Rep, 59-60; N.Mex. State Sen, 61- Bus. & Prof. Pos: Lawyer; apple orchard bus. Mil. Serv: Navy, 2 years. Rel: Catholic. Mailing Add: Ranchos de Placitas, Placitas, N.Mex. 87043. (1967)

MONTOYA, JOSEPH M. D
U.S. Sen, N.Mex.
b. Sandoval Co, N.Mex, 9/24/15; m. to Della Romero; c. Joseph II, Patrick and Lynda. Educ: Regis Col, Denver, Colo; Georgetown Univ. Law Sch, LL.B, 38. Polit. & Govt. Pos: N.Mex. State Rep, 36-40, Majority Floor Leader, N.Mex. House of Rep, 38; N.Mex. State Sen, 40-46 & 52-54, Majority Whip, N.Mex. Senate, 40; Lt. Gov, N.Mex, 46-48 & 54-56; U.S. Rep, N.Mex, 57-64; del, Interparliamentary Conf, Warsaw, Poland, Orgn; Nat. Co-Chmn, Viva Kennedy Clubs, 60; del, Mex-U.S. Interparliamentary Conf, 61-65; U.S. Sen, N.Mex, 64-, mem, Senate Cmts. on Appropriations and Pub. Works, Select Cmt. on Small Bus. and former mem, Senate Cmts. on Agr. and Forestry and Govt. Opers; Off. U.S. Observer, Latin Am. Parliamentary Conf, Lima, Peru, 65; del, Dem. Nat. Conv, 68. Bus. & Prof. Pos: Attorney-at-law; actively engaged in various bus. enterprises. Legal Res: Santa Fe, N.Mex. 87501. Mailing Add: 5403 Surrey St, Chevy Chase, Md. 20015.

MONTPLAISIR, DAVID HENRY D
b. Fargo, N.Dak, 2/11/36; s. Henry Montplaisir and Jeanette Lerum M; m. 8/28/56 to Shirley Mary Kellen; c. David Henry, Jr, Dawn Marie and Daniel Paul. Educ: Moorhead State Col, B.S, 60, M.S.E, 67; George Wash. Univ, M.S. in Pub. Admin, 68; Alpha Phi Gamma. Polit. & Govt. Pos: Chmn, Cass Co. Dem. Non-Partisan League, 63-67; N.Dak. State Rep, 65-67; v.chmn, Citizens Adv. Cmt, 66-67. Bus. & Prof. Pos: Commercial pilot; teacher, West Fargo High Sch, N.Dak, 60- Mil. Serv: Entered as A/B, N.Dak. Air Nat. Guard, 53, released as Maj, 69, after Active Duty Flight Training, 57-58; Maj, Air Force Res, 69-, currently on extended active duty; Outstanding Grad, Radar Intercept Flight Sch, Waco, Tex, 58. Mem: Phi Delta Kappa; Elks; Am. Legion; K. of C. Rel: Catholic. Legal Res: West Fargo, N.Dak. 58078. Mailing Add: 8512 Marquette, Vienna, Va. 22180.

MONZEL, L. VINCENT R
b. Alton, Ill, 8/13/20; s. H.A. Monzel and Irene Grigsby M; m. 10/26/57 to Edith Anna Luise Adam; c. Catherine Luise. Educ: Univ. Mich, A.B. in sociology, 42; Wash. Univ. and George Wash. Univ, grad. work; Phi Sigma Kappa. Polit. & Govt. Pos: Investigator, Off. Qm. Gen, Dept. Army, 48-50; mem. staff and faculty, Indust. Col. Armed Forces, 50-52; research analyst, Select Cmt. on Small Bus, U.S. House of Rep, 52-55; admin. asst. to U.S. Rep. John E. Henderson, Ohio, 55-61, U.S. Rep, Tom V. Moorehead, Ohio, 61-63 and to U.S. Rep. James T. Broyhill, N.C, 63- Bus. & Prof. Pos: Employee and pub. rels. man, Dow Chemical Co, Freeport, Tex, 46-48. Mil. Serv: Entered as Pvt, Army, 42, released as S/Sgt, 45. Mailing Add: 4701 Willard Ave, Chevy Chase, Md. 20015.

MOODY, JACK ARTHUR D
b. Moore Co, N.C, 8/26/27; s. J. Lee Moody and Lucy Ann Baldwin M; single. Educ: Campbell Col, A.A, 47; Elon Col, B.A, 49; Univ. of Richmond Sch. of Law, LL.B, 53; Delta Theta Phi, v.pres, 52. Polit. & Govt. Pos: Chmn, Fourth Cong. Dist. Dem. Club, N.C, 59; pres, Chatham Co. Young Dem. Club, 60; mem, N.C. Prison Cmn, 61; N.C. State Rep, 63-66. Bus. & Prof. Pos: Lawyer; bd. of dirs, Sanford Savings and Loan Asn, Siler City, N.C. Mil. Serv: Navy, 45-46; 1st Lt, Marine Corps, 53-55. Mem: Chatham Co. and N.C. Bar Asns; N.C. Jr. C. of C; Am. Legion; Nat. Asn. of Claimants Counsel of Am; pres, Siler City Jr. C. of C, 60. Rel: Baptist; Teacher Young Adult Sunday Sch. Class. Mailing Add: P.O. Box 189, Siler City, N.C. 27344. (1967)

MOODY, WILLARD JAMES D
Va. State Sen.
b. Franklin, Va, 6/16/24; m. to Betty Glenn Covert. Educ: Norfolk Div. of Col. of William and Mary; Univ. of Richmond, T.C. Williams Law Sch, LL.B. Polit. & Govt. Pos: Va. State Del, 56-68; alternate del, Dem. Nat. Conv, 68; Va. State Sen, 69- Mil. Serv: World War II. Mem: Portsmouth Jr. C. of C; Portsmouth-Norfolk Co. Bar Asn.(past pres); Norfolk-Portsmouth Bar Asn; Am. Bar Asn; Va. Trial Lawyers Asn; Am. Trial Lawyers Asn; Va. State Bar Asn; Portsmouth Cosmopolitan Club; bd. of dirs, Portsmouth C. of C. Rel: Baptist. Mailing Add: 120 Riverpoint Crescent, Portsmouth, Va. 23704.

MOODY, WILMA D
Dem. Nat. Committeewoman, Nev.
Mailing Add: 171 C St, Hawthorne, Nev. 89415.

MOON, CHARLES D
Wash. State Rep.
b. Sheridan, Wyo, 1923; m. to Ellen; c. Three. Educ: Wash. State Univ, B.S, D.V.M. Polit. & Govt. Pos: Wash. State Rep, currently. Bus. & Prof. Pos: Vet. Mil. Serv: Army. Mailing Add: Route 2, Box 427-A, Snohomish, Wash. 98290. (1967)

MOON, HIRAM A. D
b. Garden Valley, Tex, 12/24/13; s. Walter B. Moon and Maggie Cagle M; m. 8/19/44 to Frances Routt; c. Hiram Douglas, Phil Murray, Don B, Kay Frances and Shirley. Polit. & Govt. Pos: Del, Dem. Nat. Conv, 60, 64 & 68. Bus. & Prof. Pos: Dir, Tex. Area, Int.Union, UAW, 46- Mem: First UAW Local Union in Tex. Accompanied former President Johnson on flight from Wash, D.C. to Tex, Jan. 20, 69. Rel: Baptist. Legal Res: 3422 Rugged Dr, Dallas, Tex. 75224. Mailing Add: 310 Oak Cliff Bank Tower, Dallas, Tex. 75208.

MOON, MARJORIE RUTH D
Treas, State of Idaho
b. Pocatello, Idaho, 6/16/26; d. Clark Blakely Moon and Ruth Gerhart M; single. Educ: Pac. Univ, Ore, 44-46; Univ. Wash, Seattle, A.B, 48; Theta Sigma Phi; Phi Lambda Omicron. Polit. & Govt. Pos: Precinct committeeman, Idaho State Dem. Cent. Cmt, 58 and ed, Idaho Democrat, 58-61; Treas, State of Idaho, 63-; v.chmn, Idaho Cmn. on the Status of Women, currently. Bus. & Prof. Pos: Reporter, Pocatello Tribune, Idaho, 44 and Caldwell News-Tribune, 48-50; bur. chief, Deseret News of Salt Lake City, Boise, 50-52; publisher, Idaho Pioneer Statewide, 52-55; publisher, owner and founder, Garden City Gazette, 54-68; partner, Mod. Press Printing Plant, Boise, 58-61 and Sawtooth Lodge Dude Ranch, Grandjean, Idaho, 58-61. Mem: Idaho Press Women; Nat. Fedn. Press Women; Idaho Press Asn; Nat. Asn. of Auditors, Comptrollers and Treas; Soroptimist (treas, Boise Club). Rel: Congregational. Legal Res: 2227 Heights Dr, Boise, Idaho 83702. Mailing Add: P.O. Box 207, Boise, Idaho 83701.

MOONEY, ARTHUR AMOS R
Vt. State Rep.
b. Newport, Vt, 2/5/99; s. Raymond James Mooney and Carrie Isobelle Magoon M; m. 6/18/43 to Lucille A. Gardner; c. Arthur Richard, Winston Charles, Robert Alan and Stephen James. Educ: Newport High Sch, Vt, 4 years. Polit. & Govt. Pos: Asst. postmaster, Newport, Vt, 57; Justice of the Peace, Newport, Vt, 64-69; chmn, Newport Rep. Town Cmt, 67-69; Vt. State Rep, Dist. 17, 69- Bus. & Prof. Pos: Trustee, Vt. Baptist State Conv; pres, Vt-N.H-Maine Postal Supvr, 59-60; v.pres, Vt. Credit Union League, 60-67. Mil. Serv: Entered First Vt. Vol. Inf, Army, 17, released as Pfc, 19, after serv. in 101 AMM. TR. 26th Div, AEF, 17-19; Re-enlisted V6, Naval Res, 43, released as SP (M), 44. Mem: AF&AM; Am. Legion; Vet. of World War I; Baptist Conv; Eastern Star; Credit Union. Recipient of Superior Achievement Award, U.S. Post Off. Dept. Rel: Baptist. Mailing Add: Bluff Rd, Newport, Vt. 05855.

MOONEY, CHARLES A. D
Mayor, Fairview Park, Ohio
b. Cleveland, Ohio, 8/21/34; s. Charles A. Mooney and Helen Byrider M; m. 11/29/58 to Laurie Ryan; c. Jacqueline Ryan, Katrina Ryan, John Ryan and Charles A, IV. Educ: John Carroll Univ, B.S.S, 57. Polit. & Govt. Pos: Ohio State Rep, 59-67; del, Dem. Nat. Conv, 68; mayor, Fairview Park, Ohio, 68- Bus. & Prof. Pos: Pres, Charles A. Mooney & Co, Inc. Ins. Agency, 61-; v.pres, Tax Sheltered Benefit Plans, Inc, 64- Mil. Serv: Entered as Pvt, Army Nat. Guard, 57, released as Pfc, 58, after serv. in Signal Corps, Ft. Meade, Md. Presidents Citation, Ohio Asn. of Ins. Agents; Gr. Cleveland High Sch. Tennis Champion, 52. Rel: Catholic. Legal Res: 3869 Savoy Dr, Fairview Park, Ohio 44126. Mailing Add: 20800 Center Ridge Rd, Rocky River, Ohio 44116.

MOONEY, MICHAEL L. D
m. to Sandra Page; c. Six. Polit. & Govt. Pos: Cand, Mass. State Rep, 66. Bus. & Prof. Pos: Sales mgr. for a prfnl. and hosp. equip. co, 10 years; asst. supt, Cent. Hosp. in Somerville; bd. of dirs, Nahant Land Co. Mil. Serv: Army, 82nd Airborne Div. Mem: K. of C; DAV; Nahant Co. Club. Mailing Add: 15 Grosvenor Park, Lynn, Mass. 01902.

MOONEY, THOMAS JOSEPH, III D
Md. State Del.
b. Baltimore, Md, 9/9/31; s. Thomas Joseph Mooney, Jr. and Margaret Gisriel M; m. 7/21/56 to Geraldine Kathleen Quinn; c. Thomas J, IV, M. Megan, Patrick J. and Timothy J. Educ: Loyola Col, B.A, 50-54; Georgetown, 54-56; East. Col, LL.B, 59-60. Polit. & Govt. Pos: Md. State Del, 3rd Dist, 63- Mil. Serv: Entered as Pvt, Army, 56, released as Sgt, 58, after serv. in ETO, 57-58; Nat. Defense Ribbon. Mem: Baltimore Bar Asn; VFW; pres, Woverly Improv. Asn. Rel: Roman Catholic. Mailing Add: 828 E. 33rd St, Baltimore, Md. 21218. (1967)

MOORE, ARCH A, JR. R
Gov, W.Va.
b. Moundsville, W.Va, 4/16/23; s. Arch A. Moore and Genevieve Jones M; m. 8/11/49 to Shelley S. Riley; c. Arch A, III, Shelley Wellons and Lucy St. Clair. Educ: Lafayette Col, 43; W.Va. Univ, A.B, 48, Col. Law, LL.B, 51; pres, Beta Theta Pi, Coun. of Fraternity Pres, Sr. Men's Hon, Men's Ranking Hon. and Law Sch. Class, 51; Phi Delta Phi. Polit. & Govt. Pos: Mem, Rep. Nat. Cmt; W.Va. State Del, 52; U.S. Rep, First Dist, W.Va, 56-68, ranking mem, House Judiciary Cmt, House Select Cmt. on Small Bus, House Subcmt. on Immigration, House Spec. Cmt. on Interstate Taxation and House Select. Cmt. to Investigate Adam Clayton Powell; mem, Joint House-Senate Cmt. on Immigration and Nationality Policy and Select Cmt. on West. Hemispheric Immigration; del, Intergovt. Cmt. on European Migration; mem, James Madison Mem. Cmt; del, Rep. Nat. Conv, 60 & 64, mem, Platform Cmt. and Platform Speaker, 64; Gov, W.Va, 69- Mil. Serv: Entered as Pvt, Army, 43, released as Sgt, 45; Purple Heart; Combat Infantrymen's Badge; European Campaign Ribbon with Three Battle Stars. Mem: Am. Bar Asn; past v.pres, W.Va. Bar Asn; pres, 85th Cong. Club; W.Va. State Bar; Am. Judicature Soc; bd. dirs, Mercantile Banking & Trust Co; Moundsville C. of C; Rotary; Am. Legion; life mem, VFW and Amvets; 40 et 8; Moose; Eagles; Elks; Nat. Trail Coun. and former chmn, Mohawk Dist, Boy Scouts; Capitol Hill Club. Silver Beaver Award, Boy Scouts; Patriotic Serv. Medal, Am. Coalition of Patriotic Socs; Comdr. and Grande Officiale, Order of the Merit, Italy. Rel: Methodist; mem. off. bd, Simpson Methodist Church, Moundsville. Mailing Add: 507 Jefferson Ave, Glen Dale, W.Va. 26038.

MOORE, ARCHIE RALPH D
Chmn, Corson Co. Dem. Party, S.Dak.
b. Athboy, S.Dak, 9/11/18; s. Ralph Archie Moore and Ida Keller M; m. 6/9/51 to Dorothea Evelyn Hutton. Educ: Dakota Wesleyan Univ, 2 years; S.Dak. Univ. Law Sch, grad; Delta Theta Phi. Polit. & Govt. Pos: State's Attorney, Corson Co, S.Dak, 43-47 & 63-; judge, Corson Co, 47-59; adv. to Gov, S.Dak, 59-60; S.Dak. State Sen, 30th Dist, 59-63; chmn, Corson Co. Dem. Party, currently. Bus. & Prof. Pos: Spec. investr, State Attorney Gen. Off, 59-60. Mem: Nat. Farmers Union; McIntosh Commercial Club; S.Dak. State Bar Asn. Rel: Presbyterian. Mailing Add: McIntosh, S.Dak. 57641. (1967)

MOORE, AUBRY LEE D
Tex. State Rep.
b. Frost, Tex, 8/4/01; s. James Madison Moore and Agnes Elizabeth Wilkinson M; m. 12/27/30 to Lucille Hooker. Educ: Tex. A&M Univ, B.S. in Eng, 23; Baylor Univ, spec. bus. courses, 56-57 and 60; South. Methodist Univ, 58; Alpha Chi. LL.D, Tex. A&M Univ, 48. Polit. & Govt. Pos: Presidential elector, Tex, 64; dir-at-lg, Tri-Co. Munic. Water Dist, Tex, 65-; Tex. State Rep, currently. Bus. & Prof. Pos: Mgr, Hillsboro C. of C, 53-57; real estate and ins. broker, self-employed, 54-; dir. int. opers, Airline, 57; consult. to indust, Aircraft Mfg, 60-64. Mil. Serv: Entered as 2nd Lt, Air Force, 27, released as Brig. Gen, 53, after serv. in various Air Force Units & Commands; Asiatic Theater Ribbon with 3 Battle Stars; Am. Defense Ribbon; Distinguished Flying Cross; Legion of Merit with 2 Oak Leaf Clusters; Bronze Star Medal; Air Medal; Am. Theater Ribbon; Chinese Spec. Collar Order of Cloud and Banner; Chinese Spec. Breast Order of Cloud and Banner; Victory Ribbon; Army of Occup. Medal; Commendation Ribbon; Korean Campaign Ribbon. Mem: Nat. and Tex. Asns. of Real Estate Bds; Air Force Asn; Air Forces Hist. Found; Daedalians; Am. Legion; Press Club of Dallas. Rel: Protestant. Mailing Add: 401 Craig St, Hillsboro, Tex, 76645.

MOORE, C. ROBERT
Dep. Asst. Secy. for African Affairs, Dept. of State
b. Galena, Ill, 8/16/15; m. Joanna Daniels Moore; c. Caroline, Cynthia and Letitia. Educ: Harvard Univ, B.A, 35; N.Y. Univ, M.A, 40; Nat. War Col, 55-56. Polit. & Govt. Pos: Mem. staff, Off. of Lend-Lease Admin, 43; with For. Econ. Admin, Ankara, 43-46; career officer, U.S. Dept. of State For. Serv, 46-; mem. staff, Am. Embassy, Ankara, 46-48, officer-in-charge of Turkish Affairs, 49-52; first secy, Paris, 52-55; counsr, Ankara, 56-59; counsr. and dep. chief of mission, Phnom Penh, 59-62 and Damascus, 62-65; U.S. Ambassador to Mali, 65-68; Dep. Asst. Secy. for African Affairs, Dept. of State, 68- Bus. & Prof. Pos: Investment reviewer, banking firm, 35-43. Legal Res: Seattle, Wash. Mailing Add: U.S. Dept. of State, Washington, D.C. 20520.

MOORE, CARL RANDOLPH D
Tenn. State Rep.
b. Appalachia, Va, 2/26/30; s. Earl B. Moore and Janet L. Randolph M.(both deceased); m. 7/12/52 to Elizabeth Ann Massengill; c. Janet Lynn, Cynthia LeNoir, Dana Elizabeth and Carl, Jr. Educ: Univ. Ala, B.S. in personnel mgt, 52; Univ. S.C. and Univ. Tenn, postgrad. courses; Delta Tau Delta. Polit. & Govt. Pos: Mem, Gov. Clement's and Gov. Ellington's staff; chmn, Planning Cmn, Bristol, Tenn, 60-65; Tenn. State Rep, First Dist, Sullivan Co, 65- Bus. & Prof. Pos: Dir, Wash. Trust and Savings Bank; organizer, dir. and v.pres, Twin City Fed. Savings and Loan Asn; pres, Lee Garden Apt. Corp; v.pres, Southside Shopping Center, Inc, Johnson City and Kingsport Holiday Inns, Bristol Int. Speedway Corp. and Subsidiary Corp. and Cartenva Enterprises, Inc; bd. dirs, C/M Worldwide Personnel Syst, Inc, N.Y; personnel dir, S.E. Massengill Co, Bristol, 54-61, dir. and v.chmn. exec. cmt, 61-; pres, Carl R. Moore Enterprises, Inc, Tenn, 61- Mil. Serv: Entered as 2nd Lt, Army, 52, released as 1st Lt, 54; Good Conduct Medal. Mem: Past pres, Bristol Personnel Club; Bristol Preaching Mission, 55-57; past pres, Bristol Lions; bd. of dirs, United Fund, 57-59, pub. rels. chmn, 56-57, Spec. Gifts Div, 58-63, Budget and Admissions Cmt, 64-66; Bristol Centennial, 56; chmn, Ocanosta Dist. Meeting, Boy Scouts, 56-57, chmn, Troup 104 Cmt, 56-58; bldg. and relig. emphasis cmts, YMCA; bd. dirs, Bristol Heart Asn. and Am. Red Cross; bd. dirs. & chmn, Fund Raising Campaign, Appalachian Heart Chap, 64; past chmn, Bristol Planning Cmn; v.chmn, Tenn. Tourist & Travel Coun; bd. dirs. and chmn, Personnel Cmt, Bristol Mem. Hosp; v.pres, C. of C; Liaison Cmt, Boy Scouts; Nat. Capitol Dem. Club; Rocky Mt. Hist. Asn; past mem. bd. dirs, Bristol Country Club; Elks; Moose; Cent. Little League; Hackler-Wood Post, Am. Legion; Univ. Ala. Alumni Asn; Eagles; Lions. Outstanding Young Man of Year Award, Jr. C. of C, 57. Rel: Episcopal. Legal Res: 920 Holston Ave, Bristol, Tenn. 37620. Mailing Add: Box 3028, Bristol, Tenn. 37620.

MOORE, CAROLYN DABBS D
Mem, Dem. Exec. Cmt, Tenn.
b. Florence, S.C, 6/11/31; d. James McBride Dabbs and Jessie Armstrong D; m. 12/30/50 to Richter Hermann Moore, Jr; c. Cassandra McBride, Diana and Susan. Educ: Coker Col, 47-49; Univ. S.C, A.B. in Hist, Sociol. and Psychol, 51; Alpha Psi Omega; Int. Rels; Sigma Tau Delta; Endlish; CYD'S. Polit. & Govt. Pos: Mem, Washington Co. Dem. Exec. Cmt, Tenn, 62-; pres, Washington Co. Dem. Women, 63-64; mem, Dem. Exec. Cmt, Tenn, 64-; alternate del, Dem. Nat. Conv, 68. Bus. & Prof. Pos: Clerk ready to wear dept, Marizon's; co-owner, mgr. and sales clerk, Acad. Hill, Jonesboro, currently Mem: Jonesboro Hist. Cmn; Earth Trees and Seeds Garden Club; Asn. for the Preservation of Tenn. Antiquities; League of Women Voters; Tenn. Fedn. of Dem. Women; Univ. S.C. Alumni Asn; Univ. S.C. Educ. Found. Rel: Presbyterian. Mailing Add: 624 Depot St, Jonesboro, Tenn. 37669.

MOORE, CHARLES CARLISLE D
b. Walnut Grove, S.C, 4/13/03; s. L.G. Moore and Mary Ellen Harrison M; m. 6/24/45 to Janie Lee O'Farrell; c. Jenifer and Karen. Educ: Wofford Col, A.B, 27; Univ. S.C. Law Sch, 33. Polit. & Govt. Pos: S.C. State Rep, 37-40; S.C. State Sen, 40, 41-42 & 49-68; del, S.C. State Dem. Conv, 48; chmn. Spartanburg Army Adv. Cmt. Bus. & Prof. Pos: Sch. teacher, 5 years; partner, Moore and Stoddard, Attorneys. Mil. Serv: Maj, Army Air Force, 42-45; Maj, Army Air Force Res. Mailing Add: Box 5178, Spartanburg, S.C. 29361.

MOORE, DANA CLIFTON, JR. D
Miss. State Rep.
b. Shaw, Miss, 8/4/31; married. Educ: Univ. of Miss, LL.B, 57; Phi Delta Theta; Phi Alpha Delta. Polit. & Govt. Pos: Miss. State Rep, currently. Bus. & Prof. Pos: Lawyer. Mem: Rotary; C. of C; Farm Bur; Am. Legion. Rel: Episcopal. Mailing Add: P.O. Box 608, Cleveland, Miss. 38732. (1967)

MOORE, DANIEL KILLIAN D
b. Asheville, N.C, 4/2/06; s. Fred Moore and Lela Enloe M; m. 5/4/33 to Jeanelle Coutler; c. Edith (Mrs. Edgar B. Hamilton, Jr.) and Dan K, Jr. Educ: Univ. N.C, B.S. in Bus. Admin, 27, Law Sch, Chapel Hill, grad, 28; Phi Beta Kappa; Pi Kappa Phi. Polit. & Govt. Pos: Former Dem. precinct chmn; mem, Co. and State Dem. Exec. Cmts; mem, Cong. Adv. Cmt; N.C. State Rep, 41; solicitor, 30th Judicial Dist, N.C, 46-48; judge, Superior Court of N.C, 48-58; Gov. of N.C, 65-69; del, Dem. Nat. Convs. Bus. & Prof. Pos: V.chmn, N.C. Bd. of Water Resources; former dir, Univ. of N.C. Alumni Asn, Radio Sta. WWIT, Univ. N.C. Law Sch. Found. and N.C. R.R; former trustee, Univ. N.C; lawyer, Joyner, Moore and Howison, Raleigh, N.C, 69- Mil. Serv: Entered as Pvt, Army, 43, released as T-5, 45, after serv. in ETO and Judge Adv. Gen. Off. Mem: Mason; Rotary; Civitan. Rel: Methodist. Legal Res: Canton, N.C. 28716. Mailing Add: Joyner, Moore and Howison, Box 109, Wachovia Bank Bldg, Raleigh, N.C. 27601.

MOORE, DON, JR. D
b. Chattanooga, Tenn, 11/27/28; s. Don M. Moore and Frances Wolfe M; m. 1/23/60 to Sarah Mosley; c. Lisa Michele and Deidre LeAyne. Educ: Univ. Chattanooga, 47-48; Emory Univ. Law Sch, 49-50; Univ. Tenn. Law Sch, LL.B; 52; Phi Alpha Delta; Sigma Chi. Polit. & Govt. Pos: Tenn. State Rep, Hamilton Co, 56-58 & 64-66; Tenn. State Sen, 66-68. Bus. & Prof. Pos: Secy, Moore Bldg. Corp, 55-; partner, Moore & Wild, Attorneys, 58-; v.pres, Cigarette Vending Co. of Chattanooga, 60-; partner, Tri-State Cigar Co, 60- and Moore & Moore Contractors, 66. Mil. Serv: Entered as Pvt, Army, 46, released as Cpl, 48, after serv. in 527th M.P. Serv. Co, ETO; re-entered as Cpl, Army, 50, released as S/Sgt, 51, after serv. in 882nd Tank Bn, U.S; World War II Victory and Army of Occup. Medals. Mem: State Bar of Ga; Chattanooga, Tenn, Ga. and Am. Bar Asns; Tenn. Trial Lawyers' Asn; Elks; Am. Legion; Brainerd Hills Country Club; Chattanooga Flyers' Club; Moccasin Flying Club; Wolftever Fishing Club. Licensed private pilot. Rel: Methodist. Legal Res: 1802 Skyline Dr, Chattanooga, Tenn. 37421. Mailing Add: Suite 405 Professional Bldg, Chattanooga, Tenn. 37402.

MOORE, DON A. R
Ill. State Rep.
b. Chicago, Ill, 1/1/28; m. to Verla; c. Albert. Educ: Morgan Park Jr. Col; John Marshall Law Sch, LL.B, 50. Polit. & Govt. Pos: Rep. committeeman, Bremen Twp, Ill, 56-; asst. states attorney, 57-59; Ill. State Rep, currently; alternate del, Rep. Nat. Conv, 68. Bus. & Prof. Pos: Practicing Attorney, 12 years. Mem: Admitted to practice Law in Ill, 50 and Supreme Court of U.S, 57; Chicago, Ill, Blue Island and S. Suburban Bar Asns; Am. Judicature Soc; Lions; Boy Scouts; Moose; Mason; Jaycees; other civic, fraternal and charitable orgn. Mailing Add: 14636 S. Long Ave, Midlothian, Ill. 60445. (1967)

MOORE, DON CAGER D
Ga. State Rep.
b. Toccoa, Ga, 6/25/25; s. William Hunter Moore and Mary Elizebeth Terrell M; m. 9/21/48 to Louise Graham; c. Michael Allen and Janet Louise. Educ: Clemson Col; Tiger Alumni. Polit. & Govt. Pos: Ga. State Rep, 12th Dist, currently. Bus. & Prof. Pos: Pres, Moore Prov. Co, 65-66. Mem: WOW; Kiwanis; Touchdown Club; Peace Officers Asn; Toastmasters; Farm Bur; Young Dem; Am. Legion; Gov. Staff. Received Scholarship in Football. Rel: Baptist; past pres, Sunday Sch. Class and mem, Choir, First Baptist Church. Mailing Add: Route 4, Toccoa, Ga. 30577. (1967)

MOORE, DONALD BRUCE R
Chmn, 28th Dist. Rep. Party, N.Dak.
b. Forbes, N.Dak, 6/5/34; s. Glenn W. Moore and Alice Peterson M; m. 5/31/64 to Gwendolin Jane Oxenrider; c. Scott Alan. Educ: N.Dak. State Univ, B.S, 56; Colo. State Univ, M.S. 59; Alpha Zeta; Farm House. Polit. & Govt. Pos: Rep. committeeman, Lorraine Precinct, Dickey Co, N.Dak, 58-67; mem,

Dickey Co. Rep. Exec. Cmt, 60-62; committeeman, N.Dak. Rep. State Cent. Cmt, 62-67; mem, Bd. of Educ, Forbes, 64-67; mem, N.Dak. Rep. State Exec. Cmt, 65-68; chmn, 28th Dist. Rep. Party, 67- Bus. & Prof. Pos: Rancher and partner, Glenn W. Moore & Sons, Forbes, N.Dak, 52- Publ: 'Factors Influencing Comparisons of Hereford Bulls for Rate of Gain' J. of Animal Sci, 5/61. Mem: Sigma Xi; N.Dak. Stockmans Asn; N.Dak. Farm Bur. Certificate of Appreciation for Outstanding Service in 64 Campaign, N.Dak. Rep. Party. Rel: Presbyterian. Mailing Add: Forbes, N.Dak. 58439.

MOORE, DOROTHA HUNTLEY R
V.Chmn, Rep. Nat. Cmt.
b. Portland, Ore, 12/29/03; d. John Clyde Huntley and Verna Lyman H; m. 5/24/25 to Collis Powell Moore; c. David Huntley. Educ: Ore. Col. Educ; Univ. Ore. Polit. & Govt. Pos: Mem. exec. cmt, Ore. State Cent. Cmt, 46-56; chmn, Sherman Co. Rep. Cmt, 52-56; Rep. nat. committeewoman, Ore, 56-; v.chmn, Rep. Nat. Cmt, 64- Mem: Int. hon. Sigma Beta Phi; Eastern Star; DAR; Metrop. Club; Rep. Women's Fedn. and Dalles Club. Rel: Presbyterian. Mailing Add: Box 225, Moro, Ore. 97039.

MOORE, DUDLEY SHIELDS R
Chmn, First Cong. Dist. Rep. Cmt, Calif.
b. Sandusky, Ohio, 5/24/20; s. Albert Henry Moore and Helen Shields M; m. 3/29/49 to Lynn Tanner; c. Barbara Ann and James Dudley. Educ: Maryville Col, A.B, 42; Ind. Univ. Sch. Dent, D.D.S, 44; Univ. Calif. and Northwest. Univ, post grad. study; Delta Sigma Delta; col. letter for swimming, 41-42. Polit. & Govt. Pos: Pres, Bd. Trustees, Santa Rosa Pub. Libr, Calif, 56-; chmn, Sonoma Co. Rep. Cent. Cmt, 62-69; v.chmn, First Cong. Dist. Rep. Cmt, 63- Bus. & Prof. Pos: Dentist, Oral Surgeon, currently. Mil. Serv: Entered as Pvt, Army, 43, released as Capt, 45, after serv. in Dent. Corps, 618th Med. Co, Sixth Army, 47; Lt. Col, Air Force Res; Good Conduct Ribbon; Am. Theater Ribbon; Victory Medal; Asiatic-Pac. Theater Ribbon; Air Force Reserve Medal; Air Force Longevity Ribbon. Publ: Prfnl. articles in J. Fla. Dent. Asn, J. South. Calif. Dent. Asn. and Sonoma Co. Med. Bul. Mem: Redwood Empire Dent. Soc.(pres, 58); Calif. Dent. Asn.(dir. and mem. exec. cmt); Am. Dent. Asn; North. Calif. and Am. Soc. Oral Surgeons; fel, Int. Asn. of Oral Surgeons; C. of C.(dir); Santa Rosa Jr. C. of C.(past pres); Calif. Jr. C. of C. (state v.pres); Jr. Chamber Int. Sen; DeMolay (chmn. adv. bd, Santa Rosa Chap); Elks; Rotary; Mason; Scottish Rite (32°); Shrine. Rel: Episcopal. Legal Res: 6255 Melita Rd, Santa Rosa, Calif. 95405. Mailing Add: 1173 Montgomery Dr, Santa Rosa, Calif. 95405.

MOORE, E. BLACKBURN D
b. Wash, D.C, 4/26/97; m. to Dorothy Parker. Educ: Davidson Col; Cornell Univ. Polit. & Govt. Pos: Va. State Del, 33-68, Speaker of the House, 50-68; chmn, State Water Control Bd. Bus. & Prof. Pos: Fruit grower, farmer and banker. Rel: Presbyterian. Mailing Add: Berryville, Va. 22611. (1967)

MOORE, EDSEL FORD D
b. Moulton, 1/24/22; s. Finten T. Moore and Dessie Newman M; m. 5/27/55 to Lucy Virginia Blackburn; c. Elizabeth Ann, James Edsel. Educ: Florence State Col; Univ. of Ala. Atlanta Div. Univ. of Ga, LL.B. and LL.M. Atlanta Law Sch. Polit. & Govt. Pos: Ala. State Rep, 63-66. Bus. & Prof. Pos: Law practice. Mem: Mason. Rel: Methodist. Mailing Add: Box 31, Moulton, Ala. 35650. (1967)

MOORE, ELLEN BRYAN D
Register, State Land Off, La.
b. Baton Rouge, La, 4/13/12; d. Alexander Dunn Bryan and Louise Rhodes B; m. 1/21/44 to Darrow Haywood Moore; c. Margaret L'Mell and Ellen Victoria. Educ: La. State Univ, Baton Rouge, B.A, 34, M.A, 50; Univ. Southwest. 1 year; Tulane Univ, 1 year; Psi Chi; Delta Zeta; Phi Lambda Phi; Alpha Delta Kappa. Polit. & Govt. Pos: Register, State Land Off, La, 52-; head, Oper. Crossroads, Stevenson Campaign, Southeast U.S; chmn, Dollars for Dem; worker, Dem. Party. Bus. & Prof. Pos: Pres. and v.pres, Personal Property Mgt. Co, 32-69; realtor, Haywood Moore, 34-42; teacher, East Baton Rouge Parish Sch. Syst, 34-42; pres, Bailey Moore Construction Corp, 56-60. Mil. Serv: Entered as Pvt, Women's Army Corps, 42, released as Capt, 46, after serv. in Adj. Gen. and Surgeon Gen. Corps, Continental U.S, 4 years, Maj, Res. Mem: Hon. mem, Girls and Boys State; Nat. Bd. Am. Right of Way Asn; Nat. Bd. Nat. Conf. on State Parks; Nat. Bd. Cmt. on Status of Women (state chmn). Award for contribution to recreation movement in Am, Nat. Recreation Asn; award for youth work, Girls and Boys State; twice nominee, Delta Zeta Woman of the Year; Outstanding Alumni Award, La. State Univ, 69. Rel: Methodist. Mailing Add: 2222 Government St, Baton Rouge, La. 70806.

MOORE, FRANK EMERSON R
Pa. State Rep.
b. Rochester Mills, Pa, 12/18/33; s. Evelett Brook Moore and Alice Mae Work M; m. 1/23/53 to Peggy Lou Marshall; c. Linda Jean, Beverly Dawn, Judy Lee, David Brook and Kenneth Lisle. Educ: Marion Center High Sch, Marion Center, Pa, grad, 51. Polit. & Govt. Pos: Justice of the peace, East Mahoning Twp, 57-62; treas, Indiana Co, Pa, 65-68; Pa. State Rep, 62nd Dist, 69- Bus. & Prof. Pos: Cashier, Atlantic & Pac. Tea Co, 51; coil shear operator, Alco Aluminum Co, 52; lineman, Bell Tel. Co, 53-; real estate salesman, Almes Realty, 65. Mem: Odd Fellows; Indiana Fire Co; Fedn. of Tel. Workers; Pa. Farmers Asn; Christian Bus. Men Cmt; Rochester Mills Rod & Gun Club; Indiana Sportsmen's Club. Rel: United Presbyterian. Mailing Add: 549 Grandview Ave, Indiana, Pa. 15701.

MOORE, FRED H. D
b. Spencer, Iowa, 5/14/20; s. Earl H. Moore and Jane Kelly M; m. 8/10/45 to Helen V. McCambridge; c. Molly, Kate and Pate. Educ: Georgetown Univ, B.C, 41; Iowa Univ. Col. Law, J.D, 43; Phi Delta Phi. Polit. & Govt. Pos: Chmn, Eighth Cong. Dist. Dem. Party, Iowa, 60 and Sixth Cong. Dist. Dem. Party, 62; mem, Iowa Dem. State Cent. Cmt, 60-63; hon. col, Gov. Mil. Staff, 62; chmn, Iowa Bd. of Parole, 63-; del, Dem. Nat. Conv, 64, alternate del, 68. Bus. & Prof. Pos: V.pres, First Finance Co, 57- Mil. Serv: Entered as Cpl, Army, released as 1st Lt, 45, after serv. in 13th Armored Div, ETO, 43-45; Purple Heart; Cent. European and Am. Theater Ribbons. Mem: Am. Legion; Elks; Moose. Rel: Catholic. Mailing Add: 1002 N. Grand, Spencer, Iowa 51301. (1967)

MOORE, FRED THURMAN D
S.C. State Rep.
b. Seneca, 6/30/21; s. Alger Earl Moore and Edith Betty Stancil M; m. to Maude Elizabeth Williams; c. Fredda, Butch and Betty Joe. Polit. & Govt. Pos: S.C. State Rep, 51-56 & 63-; chmn, Coun. State Govts, 52- Bus. & Prof. Pos: Publisher-ed, Honea Path Chronicle, 20 years and gen. auctioneer and owner, Moore Auction Co, specializing in printing machinery; mem. bd. dirs, Grammer Guitar Co, Nashville, Tenn. Mil. Serv: Enlisted, 42, Navy, released as PhM 1/C, 45 after serv. in Pac. and ETO; Purple Heart. Rel: Latter-day Saint. Mailing Add: Box 505, Honea Path, S.C. 29654.

MOORE, GARNETT ST. CLAIR D
Va. State Del.
b. Max Meadows, Wythe Co, Va, 9/9/14; m. to Virginia Kathleen Kersey. Educ: Col. William and Mary, Norfolk; Univ. Va, LL.B; Omicron Delta Kappa. Polit. & Govt. Pos: Former town attorney, Pulaski and Dublin, Va; former dir, Civil Defense; Va. State Del, 54-, chmn, Courts of Justice Cmt. and Va. Adv. Legis. Coun, Va. State House of Del. Bus. & Prof. Pos: Lawyer. Mil. Serv: Navy; serv. in Shore Patrol. Mem: Va. State and Am. Bar Asns; Kiwanis; Ruritan; Elks; C. of C; former chmn, Pulaski Co. Defense Bond Cmt. Rel: Methodist. Mailing Add: 24 Fourth St. N, Pulaski, Va. 24301.

MOORE, GEORGE MANSFIELD R
Cmnr, U.S. Tariff Cmn.
b. LaGrange, Ky, 12/9/13; s. George Mansfield Moore and Mary Elizabeth Johnston M; m. 6/28/46 to Mary Caroline McCullar; c. George McCullar, James Alfred and Robert Mansfield. Educ: George Wash. Univ, A.B, 37 and LL.B, 40; Kappa Sigma. Polit. & Govt. Pos: Chief counsel, Post Office and Civil Serv. Cmn, U.S. House of Rep, 47-52; cmnr, U.S. Civil Serv. Cmn, 53-57; exec. asst. to Postmaster Gen, Post Off. Dept, 57-59, Dep. Asst. Postmaster Gen, 61, Asst. Postmaster Gen, Bur. of Transportation, 59-61; cmnr, U.S. Tariff Cmn, 69- Bus. & Prof. Pos: Assoc, Galvin, Tracy, Goehegan, Levy and Milliken, Attorneys, Cincinnati, Ohio, 46, Fairbanks, Stafford and Fairbanks, Attorneys, D.C, 52 and Ames, Hill & Ames, Attorneys, D.C, 64-69. Mem: Am. and Ky. State Bar Asns; Interstate Commerce Cmn. Practitioners Asn; Capitol Hill and Nat. Aviation Clubs. Distinguished Serv. Award, Post Off. Dept, 60. Rel: Baptist. Legal Res: 1101 Highland Dr, Silver Spring, Md. 20910. Mailing Add: U.S. Tariff Commission, Eighth and E Sts. N.W, Washington, D.C. 20436.

MOORE, HERMAN AUBREY D
N.C. State Sen.
b. Greenwood, S.C, 11/8/29; s. Herman A. Moore (deceased) and Emmie McConnell M; m. 1950 to Bete Craig; c. Leslie, Herman, III, Craig and Eric. Educ: Univ. N.C; Charlotte Col. Polit. & Govt. Pos: Pres, Mecklenburg Co. Young Dem. Club; secy, N.C. State Dem. Exec. Cmt, 52-56; dinner chmn, Jefferson-Jackson Day Dinner, 55; N.C. State Sen, 64-, Pres. Pro Tempore, N.C. State Senate, 67-69. Bus. & Prof. Pos: Dir. and mem. exec. cmt, Am. Credit Corp; state chmn, nat. trustee and mem. exec. cmt, Ducks Unlimited, Inc. Rel: Presbyterian. Mailing Add: P.O. Box 2665, Charlotte, N.C. 28201.

MOORE, ISAAC E, JR. D
b. Colo. Springs, Colo, 3/20/24; s. Isaac E. Moore, Sr. and Katherine Cole Brown M; m. 12/24/50 to Dorothy Elizabeth Williams; c. Isaac E, III and Emily L. Educ: Univ. of Colo. Law Sch, LL.B, 49. Polit. & Govt. Pos: Colo. State Rep, 64-66 and 57-60; Dist. Capt, Dem. party, 55-61 and precinct committeeman, 51-61. Mem: Colo. and Denver Bar Asns; Colo. and Am. Trial Lawyers Asns; Life mem, NAACP. Rel: Protestant. Mailing Add: 436 26th St, Denver, Colo. 80205. (1967)

MOORE, J. MAX R
Mem, Calif. Rep. State Cent. Cmt.
b. Phila, Pa, 9/14/19; s. James Thaddeus Moore and Selma Gessler Steller M; m. 9/3/41 to Mary Cowles; c. Ciss (Mrs. Robert Harris, Jr), James Cowles and John B. Educ: Stanford Univ, A.B, 41; Delta Kappa Epsilon. Polit. & Govt. Pos: Mem. libr. cmn, City and Co. of San Francisco, Calif, 56-59; pres, Bd. of Permit Appeals, San Francisco, Calif, 59-63; acting mayor, City and Co. of San Francisco, 63; mem, San Francisco Co. Bd. of Supvr, 63-64; chmn, San Francisco Co. for Reagan, 66-69; mem, San Francisco Co. Rep. Cent. Cmt, currently; treas, Rep. Exec. Cmt, currently; mem, Calif. Rep. State Cent. Cmt, currently. Bus. & Prof. Pos: Pres, Moore Mfg, Inc, 53-69; Moore Mfg. of South. Calif, 60-69 and Moore Plastic Industs, Inc, 65-69; exec. v.pres, Moore Chem. Corp, 60-69; v.pres, Signature Transportation, Inc, 63-69. Mil. Serv: Entered as A/S, Navy, 42, released as Lt.(sg), 45, after serv. in Supply Corps and Naval Air Training Command; Victory Medal; U.S. Theatre Medal. Mem: Plastic Industs, Inc; Lowell Alumni Asn.(former pres); Bohemian Club; Press Club; Rotary; Commonwealth Club; Silverado Country Club. Young Man of the Year, San Francisco, 55. Rel: Episcopal. Legal Res: 2470 Broadway, San Francisco, Calif. 94115. Mailing Add: Industrial Way and Moore Rd, Brisbane, Calif. 94005.

MOORE, JACK MITCHELL
Mayor, Beaumont, Tex.
b. Kickapoo, Tex, 8/16/06; s. William Ernest Moore and Ella Virginia Askew M; m. 9/8/27 to Della Mae Perry; c. Ray M. and Jackye Mae (Mrs. Thomas Aiena). Educ: Lon Morris Col, 25; Univ. Tex, LL.B, 28. Polit. & Govt. Pos: V.pres, French Independent Sch. Bd, 47, pres, 47-48; city councilman, Beaumont, Tex, 60-62, mayor, 62- Bus. & Prof. Pos: Admitted to Tex. bar, 28; attorney-at-law, Beaumont, 28- Mil. Serv: Inf, Army, 44. Mem: Am, Tex. and Jefferson Co. Bar Asns; Am. Judicature Asn; dir. and past pres, Beaumont Golf Asn; Beaumont Country, Beaumont and Bus. and Prfnl. Men's Clubs. Recipient, Golden Deeds Award, Exchange Club, 65. Rel: Methodist. Legal Res: 5490 Avie Lane, Beaumont, Tex. 77708. Mailing Add: San Jacinto Bldg, Beaumont, Tex. 77701.

MOORE, JAMES EDWARD D
S.C. State Rep.
b. Laurens, S.C, 3/13/36; s. Roy Ernest Moore and Mary Elizabeth Hill M; m. 1/27/63 to Mary Alicia Deadwyler; c. Erin Alicia and Travis Warren. Educ: Duke Univ, B.A, 58; Duke Univ. Law Sch, LL.B, 61; Kappa Sigma; Phi Delta Phi. Polit. & Govt. Pos: Del, S.C. State Dem. Conv, 64, 66 & 68; v.pres, City Dem. Club, Greenwood, 65, 66; S.C. State Rep, Greenwood, Co, 69- Mil.

Serv: S/Sgt, Air Nat. Guard, 58-64. Mem: Secy, Greenwood Co. Bar Asn; S.C. and Am. Bar Asns; S.C. and Am. Trial Lawyers Asns; A&FM; Moose. Rel: Baptist. Mailing Add: 405 Clairmont Dr, Druid Hills, Greenwood, S.C. 29646.

MOORE, JAMES FRANCIS R
Chmn, Alachua Co. Rep. Exec. Cmt, Fla.
b. Paducah, Ky, 7/16/25; s. Robert Allen Moore and Robbie Tatem M; m. 6/14/56 to Sarah Ann Swords; c. Jon Craig. Educ: West. Ky. State Univ, B.S. in Acct, 46; Tulane Univ, 47; Univ. Fla, 1 year; Beta Alpha Psi and Alpha Kappa Psi. Polit. & Govt. Pos: Chmn, Alachua Co. Kirk for Gov. Cmt, Fla, 66; secy, Fla. State Bd. Acct, 67-; chmn, Alachua Co. Nixon for Pres. Cmt, 68; mem, Fla. Legis. Select Coun. Post High Sch. Educ. Cmn, 68-; chmn, Alachua Co. Rep. Exec. Cmt, 68- Bus. & Prof. Pos: Prof. acct, Univ. Fla, Gainesville, 48-62; partner, Moore, Cobb & Cloud, CPA, Gainesville, 62-; mem. consult. ed. bd, Vet. Econ. J, United Publ. Corp, Cleveland, Ohio, currently. Publ: Principals of Accounting - Elementary, Univ. Fla, 53, rev. ed, 55; ed, Fla. CPA J, Fla. Inst. CPA's, Gainesville; articles in several magazines and journals. Mem: Am. and Fla. Inst. CPA; Nat. Asn. State Bd. Accts. Fla. Inst. of Certified Pub. Acct. Distinguished Serv. Award. Rel: Baptist. Legal Res: 1418 N.W. 17th St, Gainesville, Fla. 32601. Mailing Add: P.O. Box 1616, 1300 N.W. 6th St, Gainesville, Fla. 32601.

MOORE, JAMES LOUIS D
Permanent Chmn, Kansas City Clay Co. Dem. Club, Inc, Mo.
b. St. Joseph, Mo, 9/12/21; s. Charles James Moore and Bertha Hiatt M; m. 3/16/49 to Wanda Mae Farrier; c. Katherine Diane and James Edward. Educ: St. Joseph Jr. Col, grad, 41; Army Air Force Navig. Sch. Polit. & Govt. Pos: Campaign chmn, Kansas City North, Warren E. Hearnes for Gov. Mo, 64; del, Dem. Nat. Conv, 64; chmn, Clay Co. Bd. of Elec. Cmnr, Mo, 65-66; permanent chmn, Kansas City Clay Co. Dem. Club, Mo, currently. Bus. & Prof. Pos: Load dispatcher, Trans World Airlines, Mo, 46-50, crew dispatcher, 50-56 and supvr. oper. planning 56- Mil. Serv: Entered as Pvt, Air Force, 42, released as 2nd Lt, 46. Mem: T.W.A. Mgt. Club; Northland Optimist Club; Elks. Rel: Protestant. Mailing Add: 4950 N. Gladstone, Kansas City, Mo. 64119.

MOORE, JAMES RUSSELL R
Mem, Va. State Rep. Cent. Cmt.
b. Seven Mile Ford, Va, 2/23/18; s. George Cowan Moore and Nita Rector M; m. 9/17/43 to Leona Greer; c. Anita Greer and Joseph Ward. Educ: Univ. Va, B.S, 39, LL.B, 42; Sigma Nu Phi. Polit. & Govt. Pos: Chmn, Richmond Va. Rep. Cmt, 47-53; del, Rep. Nat. Conv, 52, alternate del, 68; chief asst. to U.S. Attorney E.D, Va, 53-56; chmn, Ninth Dist. Rep. Cmt, 60-61; Va. State Del, 64-66; mem, Va. State Rep. Cent. Cmt, 66- Mem: Elks; Kiwanis; Moose; Farm Bur. Fedn. Rel: Methodist. Mailing Add: 250 Stonewall Heights, Abingdon, Va. 24210.

MOORE, JAMES W. D
Shelby Co. Cmnr, Tenn.
b. Paris, Tenn, 4/24/03; s. James W. Moore and Sally Gregson M; m. 10/30/40 to Kate Miles. Educ: Union Univ; Alpha Tau Omega. Polit. & Govt. Pos: Cmnr, Memphis, Tenn, 60-66 and Shelby Co, 66- Bus. & Prof. Pos: Prfnl. baseball, 23-36, two world series, 30 & 31; taxi transportation, 36-52 and bus transportation, 40-56; real estate, 56-60. Mem: Mason (32°); Shrine; four soc. clubs; Lions. Col. on staff of Gov. Tenn. and Gov. Ky. Rel: Presbyterian. Legal Res: 95 Hollyoke Lane, Memphis, Tenn. 38101. Mailing Add: Court House, Memphis, Tenn. 38103. (1967)

MOORE, JERRY ALEXANDER, JR. R
Councilman, D.C.
b. Minden, La, 6/12/18; s. Jerry Alexander Moore, Sr. and Mae Dee Abner M; m. 1/14/46 to Ettyce Herdon Hill; c. Jerry, III and Juran D. Educ: Morehouse Col, B.A, 40; Howard Univ, B.D, 44, M.A, 57; Phi Beta Sigma. Polit. & Govt. Pos: Mem, D.C. Rep. Exec. Cmt, 67; alternate del, Rep. Nat. Conv, 68; councilman, D.C, 69- Bus. & Prof. Pos: Asst. mgr, United Serv. Orgn, New Orleans, La, 43; boy's work secy, YMCA, 44; personnel rels. officer, Port of Embarkation, 44; asst. to Pastor, 19th St. Baptist Church, D.C, 45, pastor, 46- Publ: Look to This Day, privately publ, 49. Mem: Bd. dirs, N.W. Settlement House, Uplift House, Wash. Urban League, Stoddard Baptist Home, Opportunities Industrializations Center and Wash. Metrop. Area Transit Authority. Rel: Baptist. Mailing Add: 1612 Buchanan St. N.W, Washington, D.C. 20011.

MOORE, JOHN DENIS JOSEPH R
U.S. Ambassador to Ireland
b. N.Y.C, 11/10/10; s. John Denis Joseph Moore and Julia Frances Leader M; m. 7/28/36 to Mary Foote; c. John Denis, Margaret Foote, Anne, M.D.(Mrs. Arnold L. Lisio), Julia (Mrs. Allan Dean Converse, III), Mary Faith and Martha. Educ: Yale Univ, A.B, 32; Yale Law Sch, LL.B, 35; Alpha Delta Phi. Polit. & Govt. Pos: Asst. corp. counsel, N.Y.C, 40-43; asst. dist. attorney, N.Y Co, 43-46; U.S. Ambassador to Ireland, 69- Bus. & Prof. Pos: Lawyer, White & Case, 35-38 and Burlingame, Nourse & Pettit, 38-40; v.pres, W.R. Grace & Co, N.Y.C, 46-69; dir, Grace Line, Inc, 53-69. Mil. Serv: Pvt, N.Y. Guard, 42-46, serv. in 51st Regt. Mem: Am. Bar Asn; U.S. Inter-Am. Coun. (chmn, 60-64); Ireland-U.S. Coun. (chmn, 65-68); Coun. for Latin Am.(v.chmn, 64-69); Yale Club, N.Y; Metrop. Club, Wash, D.C; Club Nacional, Lima, Peru; 1925 F. St. Club, Wash, D.C. Order of Sun, Peru; Knight of Malta, Vatican; Order of Merit, Ecuador; Order of Leopold II, Belgium; Gold Medal, Am-Irish Hist. Soc, 66. Rel: Roman Catholic. Legal Res: 33 Brooklawn Dr, Short Hills, N.J. 07078. Mailing Add: 42 Elgin Rd, Dublin, Ireland

MOORE, JOHN HARVEY D
b. Cedartown, Ga. 10/10/31; s. W. Harvey Moore and Lillian Cooper M; m. 5/13/53 to Peggy Joyce Thornton; c. John Harvey, Jr, Donald Scott and Richard Anderson. Educ: Jacksonville State Col, B.S, 52. Polit. & Govt. Pos: Ga. State Rep, 61-68. Bus. & Prof. Pos: V.pres, United Buying Serv. of Ga. and Students Assoc, Ltd, pres, Finance Investors Corp. and P.T.M. Corp, currently. Mil. Serv: Entered as Seaman Recruit, Naval Res, 52, released as Lt.(jg), 56, after serv. in Atlantic Fleet. Mem: Ga. Tech. Alumni Asn; Royal Arch Mason; Polk Co. Farm Fedn; Nat. Exchange Club; past pres, Cedartown Exchange Club and C. of C; Am. Legion; Nat. Automobile Dealers Asn; life mem, Nat. Rifle Asn; chmn. bd. dirs, Ga. Sport Shooting Asn. Tennis Letter in Col. Rel: Baptist; Supt, Intermediate Sunday Sch. Dept. Legal Res: 503 N. Cave Spring St, Cedartown, Ga. 30125. Mailing Add: P.O. Box 845, Cedartown, Ga. 30125.

MOORE, JOHN P. D
b. N.Y.C, N.Y, 3/14/16; married. Educ: Manhattan Col, B.B.A, 37; Cath. Univ. of Am. Law Sch, LL.B, 40. Polit. & Govt. Pos: Chief counsel, U.S. Sen. Subcmt. on Privileges and Elec, 52-53 & 57-58; chmn, Montgomery Co. Bd. of Property Rev, Md, 62; Md. State Del, 63-66; judge, Circuit Court, Montgomery Co, Md, 66- Bus. & Prof. Pos: Former ed-in-chief, The Young Lawyer; lawyer, currently. Mil. Serv: Navy, 44-46. Mem: Fed, Am, Md. and Montgomery Co. Bar Asns; Elks. Mailing Add: 7 Hesketh St, Chevy Chase, Md. 20015.

MOORE, JONATHAN R
Exec. Asst. to the Under Secy. of State, Dept. of State
b. N.Y.C, 9/10/32; s. Charles Frederick Moore, Jr. and Adeline Nichols M; m. 6/15/57 to Katherine Weeks Andres; c. Joan Brooke, Jennifer, Jocelyn Andres and Charles Frederick, IV. Educ: Dartmouth Col, A.B. cum laude, 54; Harvard Grad. Sch. Pub. Admin, M.P.A, 56; Kennedy Inst. of Polit, Harvard Univ, resident fel, 66-67 & fall 68; Theta Delta Chi. Polit. & Govt. Pos: Pub. affairs asst, U.S. Info. Agency, Wash, Bombay and Monrovia, 57-59; legis. asst. to U.S. Sen. Leverett Saltonstall, Mass, 59-61; politico-mil. affairs officer, Off. of Int. Security Affairs, Dept. of Defense, 61-63, spec. asst. to Asst. Secy. of Defense, 63-64; spec. asst. to Asst. Secy. of State for Far East. Affairs, Dept. of State, 64-66, pub. affairs adv. Far E. Bur, summer 66, exec. asst. to the Under Secy. of State, 69-; for. affairs adv. to Gov. Romney, Nat. Campaign for Presidential Nomination of Gov. George Romney, 67-68 and to Gov. Rockefeller, Nat. Campaign for Presidential Nomination of Gov. Nelson A. Rockefeller, 68. Rel: Protestant. Legal Res: Tonset Rd, Orleans, Mass. 02653. Mailing Add: 2407 Nordok Place, Alexandria, Va. 22306.

MOORE, KENNETH MERRILL D
Chmn, Linn Co. Dem. Cent. Cmt, Iowa
b. Massena, Iowa, 7/22/35; s. Thad Andrew Moore and Fern Schutz Moore Shearer; single. Educ: Northwest Mo. State Col, B.S, 56; Maryville Col, M.S, 57; Kappa Delta Pi; Sigma Tau Gamma. Polit. & Govt. Pos: Dem. Precinct Committeeman, Fourth Precinct, Cedar Rapids, Iowa, 66-; chmn, Linn Co. Dem. Cent. Cmt, 67-. Bus. & Prof. Pos: Teacher, Cedar Rapids Community Schs, 57-67; soc. studies dir, Linn Co. Bd. of Educ, 67-68; soc. studies coordinator, Joint Co. Syst. of Cedar, Johnson, Linn and Washington Counties, 68- Mem: Pres, Iowa Coun. for the Soc. Studies; Nat. Coun. for the Soc. Stud; Am. Hist. Asn; Orgn. of Am. Historians; Asn. for Supv. and Curriculum Develop; Nat. and Iowa State Educ. Asns; State Hist. Soc. of Iowa; Cedar Rapids Fedn. of Teachers (past pres). Rel: Methodist. Mailing Add: 514 16th St. N.E, Cedar Rapids, Iowa 52402.

MOORE, LESTER LELAND D
b. Troy, Iowa, 5/9/26; s. Forest A. Moore and Ida M. Freeman M; m. 12/1/46 to Ruth Ellen Stremlow; c. David Lee, Jeffrey Lane, Jane Ellen and Randall Scott. Educ: Simpson Col, A.B, 49; Boston Univ, S.T.B, 52 and S.T.M, 53; Univ. Iowa, grad. study, 53-54; Pi Kappa Delta; Sigma Tau Delta; Pi Gamma Mu; Alpha Phi Omega; Kappa Chi. Polit. & Govt. Pos: Mem, Gov. Cmn. on Juvenile Probs, 58-60; mem. exec. cmt, Gov. Cmn. on Alcoholism, 58-60 & 62-64 and Gov. Human Rights Cmn, 63-65; mem, Iowa UN Cmt, 64 & 66-68; admin. asst. to U.S. Rep. John R. Hansen, 65-68. Bus. & Prof. Pos: Pastor, Warren Co. Group Ministry, 46-49, South Middleboro-South Carver, Mass, 50-53, North Methodist Parish, Muscatine, 53-57, Manning-Dedham, 57-65 and Corning, 66-; chmn, S.Iowa Conf. Bd. of Christian Soc. Concerns, 62-64; del, Gen. Conf. of Methodist Church, 60-64 & 66- Mil. Serv: Entered as Pvt, Army, 44, released as Sgt, 46, after serv. in Co. A, 314th Regt, 79th Inf. Div, ETO, 44-45; Bronze Star; Good Conduct and Victory Medals; European-African, Am. and Allied Command Theater Ribbons; Combat Infantryman's Badge; Presidential Unit Citation. Publ: 'Youth Goes to the City,' Roundtable Mag, 65; 'The Christian and Politics,' Quill Mag, 66, Concern Mag, 67, and Leader Mag, 67; 'Pow-Wow,' Together Mag, 68; 'Media,' Engage Mag, 69. Finished Second in Nat. Col. Debate Tournament, 49. Rel: Methodist. Mailing Add: 605 Grove Ave, Corning, Iowa 50841.

MOORE, MARGARET W. D
b. Scottdale, Pa; d. John A. Whitaker and Ann S. Amend W; m. 6/16/30 to Phillips D. Moore; c. Phillips Daniel Moore, Jr. Educ: Ohio State Univ; Kent State Univ. Polit. & Govt. Pos: Secy. to Rep. Van Deerlin; elected, Dem. State Cent. Committeewoman, 11th Cong. Dist, 56, 58; mem, exec. cmt, secy. treas, v.chmn, Trumbull Co, Ohio, 46-; Cent. Cmt, Trumbull Co, 40; 16 years, Trumbull Co. bd. of elections. Bus. & Prof. Pos: Taught 7 years in Warren City Schs. Mem: Theta Phi Alpha; many polit. orgns; Good Samaritan Guild; St. Joseph's Riverside Hosp; Warren City Fedn. of Women's Clubs; Trumbull Toastmistress Club; Nat. Capitol Dem. Club. Rel: Catholic. Legal Res: Farmdale, Ohio. Mailing Add: 211 Cannon House Office Bldg, Washington, D.C. 20515.

MOORE, MARTHA CHRISTINE R
Mem, Ohio State Rep. Cent. Cmt.
b. Cambridge, Ohio, 11/13/18; d. C. Ellis Moore and Nannie B. Hammond M; single. Educ: Wellesley Col, 36-37; Muskingum Col, B.A, 40; Ohio State Univ, M.A, 52; Columbia Univ, post grad. study, 59; hon. mem, Nat. Collegiate Players. Polit. & Govt. Pos: Mem, Ohio State Rep. Cent. and Exec. Cmts, 50-; mem, Guernsey Co. Bd. of Electors, 56-; alternate del-at-lg, Rep. Nat. Conv, 60 and dist. alternate del, 64; mem, Guernsey Co. Exec. Cmt, 62-; precinct committeeman, Guernsey Co. Rep. Cent. Cmt, 64- Bus. & Prof. Pos: Teacher, Painesville, Ohio, 41-42 and Cambridge, 42-45; secy, Aluminum Co. of Am, 45-47; assoc. prof. speech, Muskingum Col, 48- Mem: Speech Asn. of Am; Speech Asn. of Ohio; Am. Asn. of Univ. Women. Rel: United Presbyterian. Mailing Add: 50 W. Broad St, Suite 618, Columbus, Ohio 43215. (1967)

MOORE, PRESTON JAY D
b. Colton, Okla, 2/7/20; s. Charles Felix Moore and Leta Townsend M; m. 8/29/41 to Nella Mae Reinhardt; c. Preston J, Jr. and Brown Rivers. Educ: Okla. State Univ; Univ. Okla. Polit. & Govt. Pos: Dem. nominee for Gov. of Okla, 66. Mil. Serv: Entered as Pvt, Army, 41, released as Lt, 45, after serv. in 13th Air Force; Asiac-Pac. Campaign Medal with nine Battle Stars; Distinquished Unit Badge. Mem: Am, Okla. State, and Okla. Co. Bar Asns; Mason;

Elks; Am. Legion (nat. comdr, 59); VFW; Izaac Walton League. Rel: Methodist. Legal Res: 6306 N. Villa, Oklahoma City, Okla. 73112. Mailing Add: 4040 Lincoln, Oklahoma City, Okla. 73104.

MOORE, REUBEN SPAULDING R
b. Bradford, N.H, 8/30/94; married; c. two sons. Educ: Simonds Free High Sch. Polit. & Govt. Pos: N.H. State Rep, 41-67; Postmaster (8 yrs.); Selectman (21 yrs). Bus. & Prof. Pos: Real estate and agr. Mem: Master Sunapee Lake Grange; Sullivan City, Pomona Grange; St. Peters Lodge, F&AM; Woods Royal Arch Chap, Constitutional Conv, 56. Rel: Protestant. Mailing Add: Bradford, N.H. 03102. (1967)

MOORE, ROGER ALLAN R
Gen. Counsel, Mass. Rep. State Cmt.
b. Framingham, Mass, 8/8/31; s. Ralph Chester Moore and Mabelle Taft M; m. 7/4/55 to Barbara Lee Wildman; c. Marshall Christian, Elizabeth Lee, Taft Hayden Davis and Allan Baron. Educ: Harvard Col, A.B, 53, Harvard Law Sch, LL.B, 56. Polit. & Govt. Pos: Col. dir, Young Rep. Nat. Fedn, 51-53, v.chmn, 53-57; mem, Bd. of For. Scholarships, U.S. Dept. of State, 54-58; exec. dir, Mass. Citizens for Eisenhower, 56; gen. counsel, Mass. Rep. State Cmt, 62-; del, Rep. Nat. Conv, 64; counsel, Goldwater for Pres. Cmt, 64; parliamentarian, Mass. Rep. Conv, 64 & 66. Bus. & Prof. Pos: Legal asst. to Attorney Gen. of Mass, 53-56; attorney, Ropes & Gray, 56-66, partner, 67- Publ: Chmn. bd, Nat. Rev, Inc. Mem: Boston, Mass. and Am. Bar Asns. Rel: Episcopal. Legal Res: 26 W. Cedar St, Boston, Mass. 02108. Mailing Add: 225 Franklin St, Boston, Mass. 02110.

MOORE, ROGER R. D
S.Dak. State Rep.
b. Ree Heights, S.Dak, 8/4/22; m. to Delores Griese; c. Three boys and two girls. Educ: High sch, 2 years. Polit. & Govt. Pos: S.Dak. State Rep, 62- Bus. & Prof. Pos: Farming and ins; former partsman for farm machinery and automobiles, 12 years. Mem: Am. Legion; VFW; Odd Fellows. Rel: Methodist. Mailing Add: 205 S. Park, Gettysburg, S.Dak. 57442. (1967)

MOORE, SYDNEY ALTON R
Dist. Committeeman, Rep. Party, Tex.
b. Comanche, Tex, 5/30/06; s. John Charles Moore and Minnie May Tucker M; m. 6/30/52 to Winnie May Walker; c. Charles Patrick and Robert Sydney. Educ: Thorp Spring Christian Col, 27; John Tarleton Col, B.S, 29; Univ. Calif, Los Angeles, grad. study, 29-30. Polit. & Govt. Pos: Precinct chmn, Rep. Party, Tex, 60-61, co. chmn, 61-, dist. committeeman, 68- chmn, Citizens Traffic Cmn. and mem. Planning & Zoning Cmn, 64-66. Bus. & Prof. Pos: Interior designer, Nat. Soc. of Interior Designers, 60-66. Mem: C. of C.(chmn, Lubbock Chap); A.B.C; Lions. Rel: Protestant. Mailing Add: 6006 Ave. W, Lubbock, Tex. 79415.

MOORE, THOMAS GRIFFITH D
Tex. State Rep.
b. Wichita, Kans, 10/31/15; s. Charles James Moore and Elizabeth Wilson Griffith M; m. 4/27/68 to Josephine Worsham; c. Vardeman Griffith and Robin Wilson Moore; stepchildren: William F, Bruce Ragnet, Nancy and Christopher Randolph Burrow. Educ: South. Methodist Univ, 32-35; Phi Delta Theta; Alpha Kappa Psi; Polit. & Govt. Pos: Councilman, Highland Park, Tex, 60-64; Tex. State Rep, 67- Bus. & Prof. Pos: Dir, Dallas Transit Co, 50-58; Southwest Savings Asn, 52- Mil. Serv: Entered as Seaman, Naval Res, 42, released as Lt. 45, after serv. in Submarine Force-Armed Guard, Pac. and Atlantic, Lt. Comdr, Naval Res.(Ret). Rel: Episcopal. Mailing Add: 3838 N. Versailles, Dallas, Tex. 75209.

MOORE, THOMAS JEFFERSON R
b. Loganville, Ga, 6/2/19; s. James A. Moore and Ettie Needham M; m. 10/12/40 to Ponnie McConnell; c. Delaine, Roselyn and Thomas J, Jr. Educ: Furman Univ, B.S, 40; Emory Univ, LL.B, 49. Polit. & Govt. Pos: Chmn, Sch. Bd, Grayson, Ga, 51-59; pres, Rep. Club of Gwinnett Co, Ga, 66-69; chmn, Gwinnett Co. Rep. Party, 68-69. Mil. Serv: Entered as Ens, Naval Res, 44, released as Lt.(jg), 46. Mem: Ga. and Gwinnett Co. Bar Asns; Mason; Am. Legion. Football Letter, Furman Univ. Rel: Baptist; Chmn, Church Bd, 50-66. Legal Res: R.F.D. 1, Grayson, Ga. 30221. Mailing Add: 3336 Chartwell Rd, Birmingham, Ala. 35226.

MOORE, WALTER VERNON, JR. D
b. Oakland, Miss, 2/9/27; married. Polit. & Govt. Pos: Miss. State Sen, 60-68. Bus. & Prof. Pos: Farmer. Mem: Am. Legion; Farm Bur. Rel: Methodist. Mailing Add: Oakland, Miss. 38948. (1967)

MOORE, WARNER D
Chmn, Sedgwick Cent. Cmt, Kans.
b. Silverdale, Kans, 5/25/21; s. E.D. Moore and Grace Warren M; m. 10/13/42 to Maxine Biberstein; c. Dennis and Randall. Educ: Wichita Univ, 46-48; Washburn Sch. of Law, LL.B, 50. Secy-treas, Sedgwick Co. Young Dem, Kans, 46-48; co. attorney, Sedgwick Co, 53-58; chmn, Sedgwick Co. Dem. Cent. Cmt, 66- Bus. & Prof. Pos: Mem, bd. of Urban Renewal, Wichita, Kans, 64-68. Mil. Serv: Entered as Seaman 1/C, Coast Guard, 42, released as Sonarman 1/C, 46, after serv. in U.S.S. Mengees, European and African Theatre, 43-46. Mem: Sedgwick Co. and Kans. Bar Asns; Am. Trial Lawyers Asn; Shrine; Mason (32°). Rel: Methodist. Legal Res: 6347 Eilerts, Wichita, Kans. 67218. Mailing Add: 715 Union National Bldg, Wichita, Kans. 67202.

MOORE, WILLIAM F. R
Mo. State Rep.
b. Kansas City, Mo, 12/22/28; s. William H. Moore and Mary E. Studyvin M; m. 6/11/50 to Evelyn L. Manitz; c. Jeffrey L. and Denise A. Polit. & Govt. Pos: Pres, Jackson Co. Young Rep, 66; bd. mem, Mo. Rep. Club and Mo. Fedn. Young Rep, 66-; exec. dir. and sixth ward committeeman, Jackson Co. Rep. Cmt, 66-; Mo. State Rep, Third Dist, 67- Bus. & Prof. Pos: Real estate agent, David W. Childs, Inc, Mo, 62- Mil. Serv: Entered as Pvt, Mo. Nat. Guard, 48, released as S/Sgt, 51, after serv. in 110th Eng. Bn, 35th Div. Mem: Assoc. mem, Kansas City Real Estate Bd; Mason; De Molay (Chevalier); YMCA (lay mem, Youth & Govt. State Cmt); Heart of Am. Law Enforcement Orgn; Boy Scouts (treas, Troop 78); Jr. C. of C.(past pres); hon. bd. dirs, Rockhurst Col. Rel: Lutheran. Mailing Add: 4320 Bell, Kansas City, Mo. 64111. (1967)

MOORE, WILLIAM GRAHAM R
Conn. State Sen.
b. N.Y.C, 10/21/22; s. Eugene M. Moore and Margaret Graham M; m. 12/26/41 to Shirley Flower; c. Megan, William G, Jr, Corwin F. and Shirley. Educ: Yale Univ, B.A; Delta Kappa Epsilon. Polit. & Govt. Pos: Mem, Greenwich Representative Town Meeting, Conn, 52-61; v.chmn. and mem, Conn. Rep. Finance Cmt, 64-69; chmn, Conn. Rep. Pub. Rels. Adv. Cmt, 69; Conn. State Sen, 69- Bus. & Prof. Pos: Assoc. ed, Column Mag, 47-49; reporter, Wall Street J, 49-53; assoc. ed, Fortune Mag, Time, Inc, 53-56; consult, Inquiry Eval, Inc, Indust. Mkt. Research, 56-61, pres, 61- Mil. Serv: Entered as Pvt, Army, 42, released as T/Sgt, 45, after serv. in Mil. Intel. Serv, 18th Airborne Corps, ETO, 44-45; Five Battle Stars. Publ: Poems, 1940-60, Poetry Asn. Am, 61; many articles and poems in Atlantic Monthly, New Yorker, N.Y. Times Mag, Mag. of Wall St; plus others. Mem: Asn. Indust Advertisers; N.Y. Financial Writers Asn; C. of C. Rel: Protestant. Mailing Add: Joshuatown Rd, Lyme, Conn. 06371.

MOORE, WILLIAM TYLER D
Tex. State Sen.
b. Robertson Co, Tex, 4/9/18; s. Ernest Boyd Moore and Ruby Closs M; m. 7/26/53 to Macille; c. William Tyler, Jr. Educ: Tex. A&M Univ, B.B.S, 40; Univ. Tex, Austin, LL.B, 49. Polit. & Govt. Pos: Tex. State Rep, 47-49; Tex. State Sen, 49-, pres. pro tempore, Tex. State Senate, 57. Bus. & Prof. Pos: Attorney-at-law, 48- Mil. Serv: Entered as Pvt, Army, 43, released as S/Sgt, 46, after serv. in 11th Air Force, Asiatic-Pac. Theatre, 43-46. Mem: State Bar of Tex; VFW; Am. Legion. Rel: Baptist. Legal Res: 1204 Sul Ross, Bryan, Tex. 77840. Mailing Add: P.O. Box 3967, Bryan, Tex. 77840.

MOOREHEAD, THEOVALD ERIC D
Sen, V.I. Legis.
b. Cruz Bay, St. John, V.I, 11/1/16; s. Edward Alfred Moorehead and Eugene Theodora Keating M; m. 5/18/43 to Genevieve A. Hendricks; c. Theodora Eliza. Educ: Blackstone Col. Law, LL.B; Weaver Sch. Real Estate, dipl, Lee Inst, dipl. Polit. & Govt. Pos: Immigration inspector & customs inspector, Govt. V.I, 37-41, admin. clerk, 37-41, admin. clerk, U.S. Naval Net Depot, St. Thomas, V.I, 41-44; sen, V.I. Legis, 56- Bus. & Prof. Pos: Owner, Mooie's Bar, Cruz Bay, St. John, V.I, 56-; dep. chief, St. John Fire Vol. Unit, 56-; v.pres. and mem bd. dirs, St. John Corp, 58-67; owner, Moorehead's Real Estate, 67- Mil. Serv: Entered as Pvt, Army, 44, released as M/Sgt, 55, after serv. in Pac, Am, European and Caribbean Areas; Good Conduct Medal; Am. Theatre, European Theatre and Pac. Theatre Ribbons. Mem: Nat. Asn. of Real Estate Bd; V.I. Emergency Resource Planning Cmt.(dep. dir); Am. Legion; Nat. Travel Club; PTA; St. John Celebrations Cmt; V.I. Dist. Boy Scout Coun. Certificate of Appreciation (Boy Scouts of Am). Rel: Lutheran. Mailing Add: Cruz Bay, St. John, V.I. 00830.

MOOREHEAD, TOM V. R
b. Zanesville, Ohio, 4/12/98; s. Thomas L. Moorehead and Nellie Van Horn M; m. to Louise Anderson; c. Joan (Mrs. Johnson), Janet (Mrs. Freisinger), Tom V, Jr. and Douglas A. Educ: Ohio Wesleyan Univ; George Wash. Univ. Polit. & Govt. Pos: Councilman, Zanesville, Ohio, 34-38, mayor, 38-45; Ohio State Sen, 45-60 & 63; U.S. Rep, Ohio, 61-62. Bus. & Prof. Pos: Owner, Real Estate and Ins. Agency, 32-66. Mil. Serv: Naval Air Force, 18. Rel: Presbyterian. Legal Res: 1515 Maple Ave, Zanesville, Ohio 43701. Mailing Add: 4 Main St, Zanesville, Ohio 43701.

MOORHEAD, CARLOS J. R
Calif. State Assemblyman
b. 1922; married; c. Three. Educ: Univ. Calif, Los Angeles; Univ. South Calif, LL.B. Polit. & Govt. Pos: Mem, 43rd Dist. Rep. Coun. and Rep. State Cent. Cmt; Calif. State Assemblyman, currently. Bus. & Prof. Pos: Lawyer, 20 years. Mem: Glendale Bar Asn.(past pres). Mailing Add: 1300 Beaudry Blvd, Glendale, Calif. 91208.

MOORHEAD, MRS. J. T. 'MIKE' R
Rep. State Committeewoman, Tex.
b. Lodi, Va, 12/11/11; d. Hager Harmon Michael and Frances Ellen Wilcox M; m. 3/1/30 to James Thomas Moorhead; c. Dolores (Mrs. Jerry Dugan). Educ: Bethel Woman's Col, 27-28; Carson Newman Col, 28-30; local sororities in both colleges. Polit. & Govt. Pos: Exec. secy, El Paso Rep. Party, Tex, 59-64; dir, El Paso Co. Rep. Women's Club, 59-69; precinct chmn, Rep. Party, Tex, 59-69; Rep. State committeewoman of Tex, 64-; del, Rep. Nat. Conv, 68; mem, Tex. Rep. Coun. on Fed. Employ, 69. Mem: Yearbook chmn, El Paso Woman's Club, 67-69, dir, 68-69; mem. bd, El Paso Woman's Dept. of C. of C, 69-70. Rel: Baptist. Mailing Add: 806 McKelligon Dr, El Paso, Tex. 79902.

MOORHEAD, WILLIAM SINGER, JR. D
U.S. Rep, Pa.
b. Pittsburgh, Pa, 4/8/23; s. William S. Moorhead and Constance Barr M; m. 12/23/46 to Lucy Galpin; c. William S, III, Lucy P. Galpin, Stephen Galpin and James Barr. Educ: Yale Univ, B.A, 44; Harvard Univ. Law Sch, LL.B. cum laude, 49. Polit. & Govt. Pos: Mem, Pittsburgh Art Cmn; asst. city solicitor, Pittsburgh, Pa, 54-57; secy, Allegheny Co. Housing Authority, 56-58; U.S. Rep, 14th Cong. Dist, 59- Bus. & Prof. Pos: Partner, Moorhead & Knox, Attorneys, 49- Mil. Serv: Entered as A/S, Naval Res, 43, released as Lt.(jg), 46, after serv. in Pac. Theater; Am. Campaign Ribbon; Philippine Campaign Ribbon with 1 Battle Star; Pac. Campaign Ribbon with 5 Battle Stars. Mem: Trustee, Pittsburgh Child Guid. Center and Tuberc. League of Pittsburgh; dir, West. Pa. Conservancy; Am. Legion; Amvets; VFW. Rel: Episcopal. Legal Res: 5226 Westminster Place, Pittsburgh, Pa. 15232. Mailing Add: 2418 Rayburn House Office Bldg, Washington, D.C. 20515.

MOORMAN, RICHARD ELLIOTT D
b. Louisville, Ky, 2/7/29; s. David Clark Moorman and Laura Sparrow M; m. 11/21/56 to Jean Elizabeth Gray; c. Laura, Elizabeth, Carolyn and Richard, Jr.(deceased). Educ: Univ. Ky, 48-51; Univ. Louisville, LL.B, 58; pres, Phi Alpha Delta, 57. Polit. & Govt. Pos: City attorney, Leitchfield, Ky, 60-61; dir, Ky. Tourist & Travel Cmt, 60-64; nat. committeeman, Young Dem. Clubs of Ky, 62-64, pres, 64-66; regional dir, Young Dem. Clubs of Am, 64-65; city attorney, Hardinsburg, Ky, 68-; Dem. nominee for Commonwealth Attorney, 46th Dist, Ky, 69- Bus. & Prof. Pos: Attorney, 58-; dir. and attorney, First

Fed. Savings & Loan, Leitchfield, Ky, 61-69, pres, 69- Mil. Serv: Entered as Pvt, Marine Corps, 46, released as Cpl, 48; entered Army as 2nd Lt, 52, released as 1st Lt, 53; entered active Army Res. as 1st Lt, 54, released as Capt, 62, after serv. with 100th Div, Ft. Chaffee Ark, 61-62; Bronze Star; Army Commendation Medal; Combat Inf. Badge; Korean Presidential Unit Citation; Korean Campaign, Nat. Defense Serv. and UN Serv. Ribbons. Mem: Chmn, Rough River Area Coun, Off. Econ. Opportunity and Econ. Develop; Am. and Ky. Bar Asns; U.S. Supreme Court Bar; Am. Legion (comdr, Post 81, 63-); VFW; Lions; Mason. Mem, XX Corps, Army Res. Rifle Team Nat. Matches, Camp Perry, Ohio, 62. Rel: Methodist. Legal Res: 114 S. English St, Leitchfield, Ky. 42754. Mailing Add: Box 96, Leitchfield, Ky. 42754.

MOOS, DONALD WILLIAM R
Dir. of Agriculture, State of Wash.
b. Spokane, Wash, 3/4/23; s. William F. Moos and Clara Koch M; m. 8/12/45 to Parmalee Brouillard; c. Merry K. and William Herman. Educ: City Col. New York, 44; Wash. State Univ, B.S. cum laude, 47; Phi Kappa Phi; Alpha Zeta; Lambda Chi Alpha. Polit. & Govt. Pos: Pres, Young Rep. Fedn, Wash, 56-58; temporary chmn, Rep. State Conv, 63, del-at-lg. and permanent chmn, 65; Wash. State Rep, Eighth Dist, 58-65; Dir. of Agr, Wash, 65- Mil. Serv: Entered as Pvt, Army, 42, released as S/Sgt, 45, after serv. in 110th Inf, 28th Div, ETO; Purple Heart; 3 Battle Stars; ETO Ribbon. Mem: Wash. Asn. of Wheat Growers (pres, 56); Grange (master, Waukon Chap, 51-52); F&AM; RAM; Shrine; Lions; Rotary. Rel: Methodist. Mailing Add: 2326 Vista, Olympia, Wash. 98501.

MOOSE, MARGARET RUTH R
Mem, Calif. State Rep. Cent. Cmt.
b. Pacific Grove, Calif, 11/23/33; d. Edwin Carol Moose and Marjorie Powell M; single. Educ: Monterey Peninsula Col, 1 year; Dental Nurses Training Sch, grad. Polit. & Govt. Pos: Secy, Sunnyvale Rep. Assembly, Calif, 68, mem. bd. dirs, 68- and publicity chmn. and v.pres, 69-; secy, Santa Clara Co. Gov. Reagan Favorite Son Cmt, 68; secy, Santa Clara Primary Cmt, Rafferty for U.S. Sen, 68; secy, Bradley for State Sen, 68; dir-at-lg, Calif. Rep. Assembly, 69; mem, Calif. State Rep. Cent. Cmt, 69- Rel: Catholic. Mailing Add: 1698 Ontario Drive 10, Sunnyvale, Calif. 94087.

MOOT, ROBERT C. D
Asst. Secy. of Defense
b. Orange, N.J, 6/1/11; m. to Helen Helms; c. Karen, Robert, Jr. and Gregory. Educ: N.J. Schs. Polit. & Govt. Pos: Entered Fed. Civil Serv, 46; Comptroller, Bur. of Supplies and Acct, Dept. of the Navy, comptroller, Defense Supply Agency, Dept. of Defense, 62-65, Dep. Asst. Secy. of Defense for Logistics Serv, 65-66, Asst. Secy. of Defense, 68-; Dep. Adminstr, Small Bus. Admin, 66-67, Chief Officer, 67-68. Mil. Serv: Army, World War II, released as Chief Warrant Officer. Recipient, Distinguished Civilian Serv. Award with Bronze Palm and Meritorious Civilian Serv. Award, Dept. of Defense; Exceptional Civilian Serv. Award and Meritorious Civilian Serv. Award, Defense Supply Agency; Distinguished Civilian Serv. Award, Small Bus. Admin. Legal Res: Annandale, Va. 22003. Mailing Add: Dept. of Defense, Pentagon, Washington, D.C. 20301.

MOOTY, WILLIAM LEWIS R
b. Grundy Center, Iowa, 5/23/06; s. William A. Mooty and Mary Elizabeth Kauffman M; m. 2/10/46 to Jean Leahman; c. Marcia Ann and Helen Frances. Educ: Iowa State Univ, B.A, 28, LL.B, 30; Phi Alpha Delta. Polit. & Govt. Pos: Co. attorney, Grundy Center, Iowa, 33-37; alternate del, Rep. Nat. Conv, 40; mem. city coun, Grundy Center, 46-54; Iowa State Rep, 51-57 and speaker, House of Rep, 57; Lt. Gov, Iowa, 60-66. Bus. & Prof. Pos: Private law practice, Grundy Center, Iowa, 30-42; automobile bus, 35-64; farm implement bus, 36-65; dir, Grundy Nat. Bank; farming and cattle feeding bus, 46-; cmnr, Grundy Mem. Hosp, 51- Mil. Serv: Army Air Force, Maj, 42-46. Mem: Iowa Bar Asn; Iowa Automobile Dealers Asn; Iowa Retail Farm Equip. Asn; Am. Legion; Farm Bur; Odd Fellows; Mason; Shrine; Elks. Rel: Presbyterian; Elder. Mailing Add: 802 I Ave, Grundy Center, Iowa 50638.

MORAITES, PETER R
Speaker, N.J. Assembly
b. Asheville, N.C, 6/8/22; s. Nicholas M. Moraites and Stella Englesalis M; m. 3/16/46 to Helen O'Neil; c. Ellen, Peter, John, William and Nicholas. Educ: St. John's Univ. Law Sch, LL.B, 46; Phi Delta Phi. Polit. & Govt. Pos: N.Y. Secy, U.S. Rep. Jacob Javits, N.Y; spec. asst. attorney gen, N.Y; mem, Bergen Co. Park Cmn, N.J, 60-61; N.J. State Assemblyman, 62-, speaker, N.J. Assembly, 69-; acting gov, N.J, Jan, 20, 69. Bus. & Prof. Pos: Attorney-at-law. Mem: Am. Maritime Law Asn; Lotos Club; N.Y. Athletic Club. UNICO Citizen of the Year, Tenafly Chap. Rel: Greek Orthodox. Mailing Add: Robin Lane, Alpine, N.J. 07620.

MORAN, CYRIL J. D
b. Scranton, Pa, 7/8/10; s. Frank Moran and Margaret M; m. to Mary T. Hickey. Educ: St. Thomas' Col. Polit. & Govt. Pos: Chmn, Ninth Ward Dem. Party, Scranton, Pa; sch. dir. and former pres. sch. dist, Scranton; Pa. State Rep, 62-67. Bus. & Prof. Pos: Sales rep. for Gulf Oil Corp. Mem: Dir, AAA Motor Club of Northeast. Pa; former pres. of bd. of dir, W. Side Hosp; dir, Nat. Found. Infantile Paralysis Chap; K. of C.(4°); C. of C; assoc. bd, Marywood Col, Scranton; vol. worker, LUF, Cancer, Heart, and other civic drives. Mailing Add: 825 N. Irving Ave, Scranton, Pa. 18510.

MORAN, DANIEL JOSEPH D
Chmn, Sanborn Co. Dem. Cmt, S.Dak.
b. Woonsocket, S.Dak, 1/2/38; s. Francis Cornielius Moran and Bertha Ritter M; m. 8/26/58 to Trudy Schlicht; c. Kelly Jo, Colleen Marie and Darbie Jean. Educ: North. State Col, 58-59; Dakota Wesleyan Univ, B.A, 62; Sigma Tau Delta. Polit. & Govt. Pos: Chmn, Sanborn Co. Dem. Cmt, S.Dak, 65- Bus. & Prof. Pos: Coach, Montrose, S.Dak, 62-64; prin. and coach, Letcher, S.Dak, 64-66. Mil. Serv: Entered as Pvt, Marine Corps, 56, released as Cpl, 58, after serv. in First Marine Div; Presidents Unit Citation. Mem: S.Dak. Educ. Asn; Moose. All State Basketball; State Basketball; State Baseball Tourney; Col. Football. Rel: Catholic. Legal Res: Box 21, Woonsocket, S.Dak. 57385. Mailing Add: Box 66, Letcher, S.Dak. 57359. (1967)

MORAN, J. ANTHONY D
b. Altoona, Pa, 9/8/20; s. Joseph Moran and Josephine Cuzzolina M; m. 8/14/68 to Virginia Lee Carpenter; c. Diane Narkunas, Helene Eckart and Joseph S. Educ: St. Frances Col, Pa, 37-38; Dickinson Col, 38-40; George Wash. Univ, LL.B, 49, LL.M, 50; hon. LL.D, Alliance Col, 68. Polit. & Govt. Pos: Asst. to Dep. Admin, War Assets Admin, Wash, D.C, 46-47; legal trainee, Pub. Housing Admin, 48-49; legal consult, Off. of Price Stabilization, 51; legal consult, House Select Cmt. on Astronautics & Space Exploration, 58-59; consult. to V.President Lyndon B. Johnson, 60-63; consult. to President Lyndon B. Johnson, 63-65; adv. to V.President Hubert H. Humphrey, 66-68; del, Dem. Nat. Conv, 68. Bus. & Prof. Pos: Owner, Law offices of J. Anthony Moran, Wash, D.C, 50- Mil. Serv: Entered as Pvt, Army, 42, released as Capt, 46, after serv. in OQMG, Camp Lee, Va. and Ft. Belvoir, Va; Unit Citation; Gen. Commendation. Publ: Presidential Advancemen's Manual, 64; 'Government Contracts,' Masters Thesis, 50; 'Legislative Counsel: His Washington Role,' N.Y. Law Jr, 5/67. Mem: Delta Theta Phi; Am. and D.C. Bar Asns; Air Force Asn; bd. gov, Ital. Exec. of Am; Am. Legion; Cong. Country Club. Meritorious Pub. Serv. Award, Govt. of D.C, 66. Rel: Catholic. Legal Res: 500 Coleridge Ave, Altoona, Pa. 16602. Mailing Add: 1707 L St. N.W, Washington, D.C. 20036.

MORAN, JOHN E. D
b. Providence, R.I, 11/28/12; m. to Rita M. Educ: Manhattan Col, 36. Polit. & Gov. Pos: R.I. State Sen, 57-66; Chmn. of Study Group of Blackstone Valley area of White House Conf. on Aid to Educ; Chmn, Cumberland Bd. of Canvassers, 5 yrs. Bus. & Prof. Pos: Wholesale malt beverage distributor. Mil. Serv: Navy, Lt, 44-46; Gunnery Officer on SS Nelson B. Keen in Europe and Pac. Theatres of action. Mem: BPOE, Lodge 850, Woonsocket; K. of C; St. Thomas Coun, Valley Falls; 4th Degree K. of C, Delaney Coun; Sherman-LeClerc-Monteiro Post 86, Am. Legion; finance off. for 6 yrs; Bd. of Dir, Legion Town summer camp; Friendly Sons of St. Patrick; Holy Name Soc. of St. Joseph's Church, Ashton; Hon. mem, New Eng. and R.I. Police Chiefs' Asn; Past Pres, Sons of Irish Kings. Rel: Catholic. Mailing Add: Mendon Rd, R.F.D, Cumberland Hill, Manville, R.I. 02838. (1967)

MORAN, JOHN GEARY D
b. Great Falls, Mont, 4/3/31; s. Clement M. Moran and Viola G. Geary M; m. 3/17/55 to Delores Jean Anderson; c. Michael Matthew, Michelle Marie, Colleen Katherine, Kelly Jean and Patrick Geary. Educ: West. Mont. Col, B.S, 59; Mont. Univ, grad. work, 61; Seattle Univ, grad. work, 65. Polit. & Govt. Pos: Chmn, Wheatland Co. Dem. Cent. Cmt, Mont, until 68; past mem, Mont. Dem. State Cent. Cmt. Bus. & Prof. Pos: Chmn. Eng. Dept, Centennial High Sch, Portland, Ore, currently. Mil. Serv: Entered as Pfc, Marines, 52, released as Cpl, 54, after serv. in First Bn, Fourth Marines. Mem: VFW; Am. Legion; Nat. and Mont. Educ. Asns; Jaycees. Rel: Catholic. Mailing Add: 329 S.E. 238, Troutdale, Ore. 97060.

MORAN, ROBERT DANIEL R
Adminstr, Wage and Hour and Pub. Contracts Div, U.S. Dept. of Labor
b. Brewer, Maine, 10/25/29; s. William H. Moran (deceased) and Mary Ann Flynn M; m. 5/26/56 to Joan Ellen Leonard; c. Kevin Leonard, Brian Cunningham, Mark McGuire, Sean Michael and Kathleen Kelly. Educ: Univ. Maine, B.A, 50; Boston Univ, LL.B, 52; Georgetown Law Sch, grad study in law, 58; Am. Int. Col, grad. study in bus. admin, 63; Pi Kappa Delta, Order of Debate; Phi Delta Phi. Polit. & Govt. Pos: Legis. counsel, Off. of the Secy. of Defense, Wash, D.C, 55-56; pres, Springfield Young Rep. Club, Mass, 57-58; treas, Mass. Young Rep. Asn, 61; del, Mass. Rep. State Conv, 62, del. and mem. rules cmt, 66; pub. adminstr, Hampden Co, Mass, 62-67; mil. aide to Lt. Gov. of Mass, 65-66; mem, Cmn. to Study Financing of Polit. Campaigns, 65-66; chmn, Springfield City Rep. Cmt, Mass, 65-69; chmn, Mass. Bd. of Conciliation and Arbit. and Mass. Minimum Wage Cmn, 66-69; assoc. cmnr, Mass. Dept. of Labor & Industs, 66-69; alternate del, Rep. Nat. Conv, 68; adminstr. wage and hour and pub. contracts div, U.S. Dept. of Labor, 69- Bus. & Prof. Pos: Attorney at law, 56-; labor arbitrator, 66- Mil. Serv: Entered as Pvt, Army, 53, released as 1st Lt, 55, after serv. in Off. of Secy. of Defense, Wash, D.C, 54-55; Maj, Judge Adv. Gen. Corps, Army Res, 64. Publ: Massachusetts Municipal Collective Bargaining Manual (with others), Boston Col. Bur. of Pub. Affairs, 68; 'Collective Bargaining in the Public Service,' Mass. Law Quart, 6/67; 'State Subsidized Arbitration,' Labor Law J, 10/68. Mem: Indust. Rels. Res. Asn; Boston Bar Asn.(mem. cmt. on arbit); Mass. and Hampden Co. Bar Asns; Bar of the Supreme Court of the U.S. and the U.S. Court of Mil. Appeals; Elks. Radio Sta. WACE Citation for Commun. Serv, 62. Rel: Roman Catholic. Legal Res: 258 Washington Blvd, Springfield, Mass. 01108. Mailing Add: 2501 Q St. N.W, Washington, D.C. 20008.

MORAN, ROBERT MARTIN R
N.Mex. State Rep.
b. Tulsa, Okla, 11/18/28; s. Edgar Francis Moran and Grace Marjorie Starr M; m. 6/13/59 to Brenda Anne Coogan; c. Patricia Grace, Charles Edgar and Kathleen Ann. Educ: Univ. Notre Dame, B.S.M.E, 50. Polit. & Govt. Pos: N.Mex. State Rep, Dist. 3, Lea Co, 69- Bus. & Prof. Pos: Pres, Moran Oil Producing & Drilling Corp, 55-; Dir, First Nat. Bank, Hobbs, 69- Mem: Independent Petroleum Asn; N.Mex. Oil & Gas Asn; Am. Asn. of Oil Well Drilling Contractors; Hobbs United Fund; Rotary. Rel: Catholic. Legal Res: 1000 Walker Dr, Hobbs, N.Mex. 88240. Mailing Add: P.O. Box 1919, Hobbs, N.Mex. 88240.

MORANO, ALBERT PAUL D
b. Paterson, N.J, 1/18/08; s. Anthony Morano and Clementina Belmonte M; m. 3/6/33 to Millicent J. Greco; c. Anthony Albert and Clare Anita. Educ: Greenwich Pub. Schs. Polit. & Govt. Pos: Exec. secy. to U.S. Rep. Albert E. Austin, 39-41 and U.S. Rep. Clare Boothe Luce, 43-47; unemploy. cmnr, Fourth Cong. Cmn, 47-50; U.S. Rep, Fourth Dist, Conn, 51-59; spec. asst. to U.S. Sen. Thomas J. Dodd, 62-68. Mem: Elks; K. of C.(4°); Soc. of St. Lawrence. Rel: Roman Catholic. Mailing Add: 7 Mallard Dr, Greenwich, Conn. 06830.

MORASCO, SAMUEL A. D
b. Grafton, W.Va, 9/24/20; s. John B. Morasco and Theresa Tiano M; m. 3/25/51 to Rose Lee Jones; c. David Lee. Educ: Penn Mutual Life Ins. Sch, correspondence course; Aetna Life Ins. Surety & Casualty Co; W.Va. Univ. Polit. & Govt. Pos: W.Va. State Del, 64-68. Bus. & Prof. Pos: Realtor; Owner, Morasco's Agency, ins. and real estate; pres, Grafton Area Develop. Coun. Mil. Serv: 1st Sgt, Air Force, 42-46. Mem: Elks; Am. Legion; K. of

C; Tygart Valley Develop. Asn, Inc; Kiwanis (former pres). Outstanding Citizen Award, U.S. Jaycees, 68. Rel: Catholic. Mailing Add: 40 Main, Grafton, W.Va. 26354.

MORDECAI, FRANK SELMER R
Chmn, Lamar Co. Rep. Party, Ala.
b. Fernbank, Ala, 7/6/88; s. Marion Mordecai and Jane Atkins M; m. 12/9/06 to Arrie Ridgeway; c. Marshall, Rudolph, Charlie Marion, Myrtle (Mrs. Richards), Sarah Lee (Mrs. Blair), Dot (Mrs. May), Jo Fern (Mrs. Jordon) and Faye (Mrs. Stokes). Educ: Millport High Sch, grad, 06. Polit. & Govt. Pos: Chmn, Lamar Co. Rep. Party, Ala, 63- Mem: Odd Fellows. Rel: Baptist. Mailing Add: Route 1, Fernbank, Ala. 35558.

MORE, DAVID LEWIS R
Mem, Calif. Rep. State Cent. Cmt.
b. Santa Barbara, Calif, 5/21/14; s. Warren D. More and Lucy Harriet Taylor M; m. 2/21/47 to Eleanor Ruth McCullough; c. Victoria, Diana, Elizabeth and David. Educ: Univ. Calif, Berkeley, A.B; Univ. Calif, Los Angeles Grad. Sch. of Bus. Admin, Exec. Mgt. Summer Seminar; Phi Phi; Pi Delta Epsilon; Hammer and Coffin; Triune; Pi Kappa Alpha. Polit. & Govt. Pos: Alternate mem, Los Angeles Co. Rep. Cent. Cmt, Calif, 63-68; chmn, 59th Dist. Rep. Cand. Develop. Cmt, 63-68; chmn, 26th Cong. Dist. Rep. Cand. Selection Cmt, 64; pres, 59th Dist, Calif. Rep. Assembly, 64-65; Rep. nominee for Calif. State Assemblyman, 59th Dist, 68; chmn, 59th Dist. Rep. Coord. Coun, 69-; mem, Calif. Rep. State Cent. Cmt, 69- Bus. & Prof. Pos: Pres, Rattancraft of Calif, Los Angeles, 52- Mil. Serv: Entered as Pvt, Army, 42, released as 2nd Lt, 45, after serv. in 633rd Field Artil. Bn, European-N.African Theatre, 43-45; Awarded Battlefield Cmn; Unit Citations; Six Battle Stars. Mem: Rattan Mfrs. & Importers Asn.(past pres); Rancho Park Kiwanis (past pres); Westwood Methodist Men's Club (past pres); bd. mgrs, W. Los Angeles YMCA; bd. mem, W. Area United Way; Neighborhood Youth Asn; Int. Student Center; commun. chmn, United Crusade; mem, Los Angeles C. of C; World Affairs Coun; Foreign Trade Asn. of S. Calif; Furniture Mfrs. Asn. Rel: Methodist; Served as Trustee, Treas. and Lay Leader. Mailing Add: 12218 Lawler St, Los Angeles, Calif. 90066.

MORELAND, WILLIAM ALEXANDER D
W.Va. State Sen.
b. Morgantown, W.Va, 4/21/16; s. James R. Moreland and Ethel Finnicum M; m. 8/3/40 to Ruth Russell Roberts; c. Patricia Ann (Mrs. A. Wang). Educ: W.Va. Univ, A.B, 38, Law Sch, LL.B, 40; Kappa Alpha. Polit. & Govt. Pos: Mem, Suncrest City Coun, W.Va, 46-47 and Morgantown City Coun, 48-50; W.Va. State Del, 51-58; W.Va. State Sen, 58-, Majority Leader, W.Va. State Senate, 60-68; mem, Co. Dem. Cmt, 60- Mil. Serv: Entered as 2nd Lt, Army, 41, released as Lt. Col, 46, after serv. in Am. Inf. Div, Far East Theater, 44; Lt. Col, Army Res. Mem: Monongalia Co. Bar Asn.(pres, 66-67); Nat. Conf, of State Legis. Leaders; South Region Coun. of State Govt; Rotary; Am. Legion; VFW; Moose. Rel: Presbyterian. Legal Res: 368 Rotary St, Morgantown, W.Va. 26505. Mailing Add: 821-26 Monongahela Bldg, Morgantown, W.Va. 26505.

MORELLI, CARMEN D
Mem, Windsor Dem. Town Cmt, Conn.
b. Hartford, Conn, 10/30/22; s. Joseph Morelli and Helen Carani M; m. 6/26/43 to Irene Edna Montminy; c. Richard A, Mark D. and Carl J. Educ: Boston Univ, B.S. in Bus. Admin, 49; Boston Univ. Sch. Law, LL.B, 52. Polit. & Govt. Pos: Asst. prosecutor, Windsor, Conn, 57-58, town attorney, 61; mem, Windsor Dem. Town Cmt, 57-, treas, 60-64, chmn, 64-65; Conn. State Rep, 59-60; mem, Charter Revision Cmt, Windsor, 63-64 and cmnr, Windsor Town Plan & Zoning Cmn, 65; rep, Capitol Region Planning Agency, 65. Bus. & Prof. Pos: Attorney-at-law; arbitrator, Am. Arbit. Asn, 64. Mil. Serv: Entered as Seaman, Navy, 43, released as AMM 2/C, 45. Mem: Hartford Co, Conn. State and Am. Bar Asns; Conn. Youth and Govt. Cmt; Elks; YMCA. Rel: Catholic. Mailing Add: 41 Farmstead Lane, Windsor, Conn. 06095.

MORETTI, ROBERT 'BOB' D
Calif. State Assemblyman
b. Detroit, Mich, 6/3/36; s. Marino Claudio Moretti and Mary Bestigian M; m. 8/23/58 to Marilyn Ann Stotko; c. Michael, Marina and Leslie. Educ: Univ. Notre Dame. Polit. & Govt. Pos: State committeeman, Dem. Party, Calif, 62-64 and Co. Committeeman, 63-64; consult, Calif. Legis, 63-65; Calif. State Assemblyman, 65-; del, Dem. Nat. Conv, 68; mem, Calif. Dem. State Cent. Cmt, 68- Bus. & Prof. Pos: Plant supt, Horizon Door & Window Co, 58-61; customer serv. mgr, Don Baxter, Inc, 61-63. Mem: Elks; Moose; Optimist; C. of C; PTA; Scouts. Rel: Roman Catholic. Mailing Add: 5736 Costello St, Van Nuys, Calif. 91401. (1967)

MORGAN, CLYDE NATHANIEL R
Chmn, Taylor Co. Rep. Exec. Cmt, Tex.
b. Belton, Tex, 11/2/23; s. Xenophen William Morgan and Rhoda Ella Deck M; m. 3/3/51 to Birdie Joyce Palmer; c. Clyde Nathaniel, Jr, Reinette Jean and Nancy Elaine. Educ: Abilene Christian Col, B.S, 48; Univ. of Tex. Med. Br, M.D, 53; Alpha Chi; Phi Omega Chi; Phi Rho Sigma. Polit. & Govt. Pos: Aircraft mechanic, Civil Serv, 41-43; precinct chmn, Taylor Co. Rep. Party, Tex, 64-65; alternate del, Tex. Rep. State Conv, 64, del, 66; chmn, Taylor Co. Rep. Exec. Cmt, 65-; del, Rep. Nat. Conv, 68. Bus. & Prof. Pos: Physician and surgeon, 54-; secy. staff Hendrick Mem. Hosp, 56. Mil. Serv: Entered as Pvt, Army Air Force, 43, released as 1st Lt, 46, after serv. in African and Mid. East Theaters, 45-46 and spec. assignment as personal pilot to King Ibn Saud, Saudi Arabia, 45; Am, ETO, African and Mid. East Campaign Medals; Victory Medal. Publ: 'Patients Like My Drive-In Office, Med. Econ, 63; 'Time Savers,' Patient Care, 9/67; 'Automation,' Firm Found, 4/69. Mem: Taylor-Jones Co. Med. Soc; Tex. and Am. Med. Asns; Tex. Acad. of Gen. Practice; Am. Acad. of Gen. Practice; Abilene Acad. Gen. Practice (secy, 57); Kiwanis Int; C. of C; Aircraft Owners & Pilots Asn. Med. Econ. Award, 63. Rel: Church of Christ. Legal Res: 1718 Cedarcrest Dr, Abilene, Tex. 79601. Mailing Add: 1166 Merchant St, Abilene, Tex. 79603.

MORGAN, ELDON M. D
b. Mahaska Cty, Iowa, 7/22/90; s. Saul Morgan and Jane M; m. 5/18/18 to Zana Irene Witt. Polit. & Govt. Pos: Iowa State Rep, -66. Bus. & Prof. Pos: Rural mail carrier, 42 yrs. Mil. Serv: WWI, Battery F, 163rd Artil. Brigade, AEF. Rel: First Christian Church. Mailing Add: 805 N. A, Oskaloosa, Iowa 52577. (1967)

MORGAN, FRANCES HADDON D
b. Bremerton, Wash; d. Lulu D. Haddon (deceased); m. to Osmore Morgan; c. Two daughters. Educ: Bus. Col. Polit. & Govt. Pos: Wash. State Sen, until 68; Wash. State Rep, one term. Bus. & Prof. Pos: Owner and operator, welcoming serv. Mem: Ladies of Elks; Soroptimists; PTA; Wash. Asn. for Retarded Children. Mailing Add: 948 Lower Oyster Bay Rd, Bremerton, Wash. 98310. (1967)

MORGAN, FRED H. D
Ky. State Rep.
b. 1915. Educ: Murray State Col. Polit. & Govt. Pos: Ky. State Rep, 46-, spec. session, Ky. House of Rep, 49, Majority Leader, 56 & 68; city mgr, Paducah, 52 & 54-55. Bus. & Prof. Pos: Ins. Agent. Mem: Kiwanis; Moose. Rel: Presbyterian. Mailing Add: 2057 Broad St, Paducah, Ky. 42001.

MORGAN, GEORGE ALLEN
U.S. Ambassador to Ivory Coast
b. Murfreesboro, Tenn, 12/2/05; m. to Margaret Carter; c. Anne, Gael and John. Educ: Emory Univ, Ph.B, 25, high honors; Harvard Univ, Ph.D, 30. Polit. & Govt. Pos: For. Serv. Officer, U.S. Dept. of State, 47-, First Secy, Moscow, 48-50, dir. E. Element, Off. of U.S. High Cmnr. for Germany, Berlin, 50-51, asst. dir, then dep, finally acting dir, Psychol. Strategy Bd, 51-53, counsr, Tokyo, 54-58, mem, Policy Planning Staff, 58-59, Dep. Asst. Secy. of State for Policy Planning, 59-61, v.chmn, Policy Planning Coun, 61-62, dir, Dept. of State For. Serv. Inst, 62-65, U.S. Ambassador to Ivory Coast, 65- Bus. & Prof. Pos: Instr. and tutor, Harvard Univ, 29-33; assoc. prof. philos, Hamilton Col, 33-36, Duke Univ, 36-42. Mil. Serv: Capt, Army, 42-45; Bronze Star; Croix de Guerre. Publ: Author, What Nietzsche Means, 41; Stalin on Revolution, For. Affairs, 49. Legal Res: Washington, D.C. 20007. Mailing Add: U.S. Embassy, Abidjan, Ivory Coast.

MORGAN, HANDSEL GRADY D
b. Buford, Ga, 9/20/21; s. Henry Grady Morgan and Eva Benson M; m. 3/26/49 to Joy King; c. Handsel Grady, Jr. 'Hank', Timothy King and Ann Benson. Educ: Piedmont Col, A.B, 42; Univ. of Ga, M.A, 48; John Marshall Law Sch, LL.B, 50. Polit. & Govt. Pos: Ga. State Rep, 59-64; Judge, City Court Burford, Ga, 65- Bus. & Prof. Pos: Attorney. Mil. Serv: U.S. Army, World War II; N. Africa; ETO. Rel: Methodist. Mailing Add: Buford, Ga. 30518.

MORGAN, HERBERT DOYLE D
Co. Dem. Exec. Committeeman, S.C.
b. Six Mile, S.C, 11/28/29; s. Herbert D. Morgan Sr. and Christine Jones M; m. 10/6/56 to Kate Nimmons; c. Jean N. and Robert E. Educ: U.S. Naval Acad, 47-48; Clemson Univ, B.S, 50; Univ. S.C. Law Sch, currently; Phi Alpha Delta. Polit. & Govt. Pos: Del, S.C. Dem. Conv, 58, 62, 64, 66 & 68; alternate del, Dem. Nat. Conv, 60, del, 64; Co. Dem. exec. committeeman, S.C, 64-; S.C. State Rep, 67-68. Bus. & Prof. Pos: Salesman, Am. Cyanamid Co, Wayne, N.J, 50-65; owner, Nimmons Farm Supply Co, Seneca, S.C, 58- Mil. Serv: 1st Lt, Army Res, 50-57. Mem: AF&AM; Scottish Rite (32°); Shrine; Sertoma; Seneca Jaycees (past pres); S.C. Jaycees (past int. dir); Jr. Chamber Int. Sen. Young Man of the Year, Seneca, S.C, 60. Rel: Presbyterian. Mailing Add: Clemson Rd, Seneca, S.C. 29678.

MORGAN, JACK COCHRAN D
b. Sweetwater, Tex, 3/17/28; s. John F. Morgan and Tommie Lee Cochran M; m. 1/24/53 to Millie E. Edmunds; c. Millicent and Jack, Jr. Educ: Tex. Univ, B.A. and LL.B, 50; Sigma Chi. Polit. & Govt. Pos: Asst. Co. Attorney, Kaufman Co, Tex, 50-51; Tex. State Rep, 55; City Attorney, Kaufman, 55-; former chmn, Kaufman Co. Dem. Party. Bus. & Prof. Pos: Dir, Farmers & Merchants Nat. Bank, Kaufman, 65- Mil. Serv: 2nd Lt, Air Force Res, discharged as Capt. Mem: Am, Tex. and Kaufman Co. Bar Asns; Rotary. Rel: First Christian Church. Legal Res: 1704 S. Houston St, Kaufman, Tex. 75142. Mailing Add: 108 N. Washington, Kaufman, Tex. 75142.

MORGAN, JACK H. D
b. Newton Co, Ga, 5/02/19; s. Joe Carter Morgan and Margaret Turner M; m. 6/16/45 to Barbara M. Davis; c. Barbara, Jack, Emily, Davis, John, William, Edna Sue, Dan. Educ: Heard-Mixon High Sch, 36. Polit. & Govt. Pos: Ga. State Rep, 63-64. Bus. & Prof. Pos: Farmer; pulpwood dealer; grading contractor. Mil. Serv: USN Med. Corps, WW II. Mem: Elk; Rotary. Rel: Methodist. Mailing Add: Covington, Ga. 30209. (1967)

MORGAN, JOE LEE R
b. Mars Hill, N.C, 5/14/31; s. The Rev. Frank Woodard Morgan, Sr. and Effie McDaris M; single. Educ: Berea Col, A.B, 54; North. Ill. Univ, Educ, Spring, 55; Univ. Hawaii, Ancient Hist, Spring, 56; Univ. Colo, Polit. Sci, Summers, 57-58; Univ. N.C, Educ. & Psychol, 57-58; Duke Univ, grant for Asian Studies, 59; East Tenn. State Univ, Grad. Study & Libr. Sci, Summers, 60-63. Polit. & Govt. Pos: Mem, Mecklenburg Co. Rep. Exec. Cmt. and precinct chmn, 58-60; del, N.C. State Rep. Conv, 58 & 64, 11th Dist. Cong. Conv, N.C, 62 & 64, Ninth Dist. Cong. Conv, Ga, and Ga. State Rep. Conv, 66; first v.chmn, White Co. Rep. Party, Ga, until 67. Bus. & Prof. Pos: Teacher, Lincoln Elem. Sch, Ill, 54-55, seventh and eighth grades, Charlotte, N.C, 57-59 and seventh and eighth grades, Eng, Biology and French, Madison Co. Schs, 59-63; librn, Mars Hill High Sch, N.C, 63-65; head librn, Truett-McConnell Col, Ga, 65-; regional rep, N.C. Sch. Performing Arts, 65- Mil. Serv: Entered as Pvt, Army, 55, released as Specialist 3/C, 57, after serv. in Signal Corps, Charlotte, N.C. and Schofield Barracks, Hawaii, 55-57; Good Conduct Medal; Cert. of Achievement; Specialist E4, Army Res, 58. Publ: A Librarians's Handbook, 64 and N.C. and the Admission of Kansas as a State Under the Lecompton Constitution, 66; News-Record Press; Reflections on the Scopes Evolution Trial, Biltmore Press, 65. Mem: Buncombe Co. Young Rep. Club; Young Am. for Freedom; Bd. of Policy, Liberty Lobby; Nat. and N.C. Educ. Asns; founding mem, RCA Victor Soc. Great Music; N.C. Librarian's Asn; Korean Cultural and Freedom Found, Inc; Citizen's Cmt. for Free Cuba; mem. libr. coun, initiator and past chmn, Adult Literacy Prog. and clerk, French Broad Baptist Asn; Cmt. of 100 for Better Schs, Madison Co; Madison Co. Classroom Teachers Asn.(secy-treas, 59-65); PTA (reporter and secy-treas,

Mars Hill High Sch, 63-65), Arts and Humanities Cmn, Coun. of South. Mt, Inc; Asheville Commun. Concert Asn.(Marshall area rep, 64-66). Recipient, Founding Supporter's Cert, Radio of Free Asia. Rel: Missionary Baptist; Former supt, Sunday Sch. teacher, secy. and librn, Peek's Chapel Baptist Church, Marshall, N.C. Legal Res: Route 2, Marshall, N.C. 30501. Mailing Add: 1325 N. Enota Ave. N.W, Gainesville, Ga. 30501. (1967)

MORGAN, KEN L. R
N.Dak. State Sen.
b. Fargo, N.Dak, 1915; m. to Doris Ann Stevens. Educ: Leonard Pub. Sch. Polit. & Govt. Pos: Numerous jobs during legis. sessions, 35-; precinct committeeman, Barrie Twp. and state cent. committeeman, Richland City; mem. senate, Richland, City, 56; N.Dak. State Sen, 67- Bus. & Prof. Pos: Farming. Mailing Add: Walcott, N.Dak. 58077. (1967)

MORGAN, LEWIS V, JR. R
Ill. State Rep.
b. Wheaton, Ill, 12/17/29; m. to Marilyn F. Sherman; c. Barbara, Lewis and Diane. Educ: DePaul Univ, B.A, 51; Univ. Chicago, Law Sch, J.D, 54. Polit. & Govt. Pos: Former justice peace; chmn, Ill. Cmn. Atomic Energy; asst. state's attorney, DuPage Co, 3 years; former chmn, Milton Twp. Rep. Orgn; precinct committeeman; Ill. State Rep, currently. Bus. & Prof. Pos: Lawyer, Redmond, Morgan, Mraz & Benworth. Mil. Serv: Army Artil. Corps, 2 years, Germany, 18 months. Mem: Wheaton Jaycees (past state dir); DuPage Co. Family Serv. Asn.(dir. and past v.pres); Wheaton Commun. Asn.(dir); Lions; DuPage Co. Bar Asn. Mailing Add: 1144 N. President St, Wheaton, Ill. 60187. (1967)

MORGAN, ROBERT BURREN D
Attorney Gen, N.C.
b. Lillington, N.C, 10/5/25; s. James Harvey Morgan and Alice Butts M; m. 8/27/60 to Katie Owen; c. Margaret, Mary and foster son, Rupert. Educ: East Carolina Col, B.S, 47; Wake Forest Col, LL.B, 50; Phi Sigma Pi; Phi Alpha Delta. Polit. & Govt. Pos: Precinct worker, Dem. Party, N.C, 47-; clerk of Superior Court, Harnett Co, 50-54; N.C. State Sen, 55-57, 59-61 & 63-68, Pres. Pro Tem, N.C. State Senate, 65-68, co-chmn, N.C. Legis. Res. Cmt, 65-68; Attorney Gen. of N.C, 69- Bus. & Prof. Pos: Practicing attorney, 55-; chmn. bd. trustees, East Carolina Univ, 64-; sr. partner, Morgan, Williams & Jones, Attorneys, 66- Mil. Serv: Entered as Seaman, Navy, 44, released as Lt, 53, after serv. in Am. Theater 45-46 and Korean Theater, 52; Lt. Comdr, Naval Res, 57-; Am. Theater and World War II Ribbons; Korean War Ribbon with Battle Star; UN and Armed Force Res. Medals; Navy Unit Citation. Mem: Am. and N.C. Bar Asns; Am. Trial Lawyers Asn; Rotary; Mason; Moose; Am. Legion; VFW. Rel: Baptist. Legal Res: Morgan Dr, Lillington, N.C. 27546. Mailing Add: Dept. of Justice, P.O. Box 629, Raleigh, N.C. 27602.

MORGAN, ROBERT C. D
N.Mex. State Sen.
b. 1907. Polit. & Govt. Pos: N.Mex. State Sen, currently. Bus. & Prof. Pos: Farmer and ins. agent. Mem: WOW; Rotary; Farm Bur; C. of C; Farm Loan Asn.(bd. mem); Bd. mem, Roosevelt Co. Gen. Hosp. Rel: Baptist. Mailing Add: 223 S. Main, Portales, N.Mex. 88130. (1967)

MORGAN, RUFUS JAY R
b. Tinmouth, Vt, 5/1/04; m. to Nina B. Gilman; c. two sons, two daughters. Educ: Rutland Bus. Col. Polit. & Govt. Pos: Vt. State Rep, 65-66; town lister and auditor; selectman, currently. Bus. & Prof. Pos: Woodsman. Rel: Protestant. Mailing Add: R.D, West Rutland, Vt. 05777. (1967)

MORGAN, THOMAS ELLSWORTH D
U.S. Rep, Pa.
b. Ellsworth, Pa, 10/13/06; s. William Morgan and Mary Lawson M; m. 8/26/37 to Winifred Stait; c. Mary Ann (Mrs. Gordon Youngwood). Educ: Waynesburg Col, B.S, 30; Detroit Col. of Med. and Surg, B.M, 33; Wayne Univ. M.D, 34. Hon. LL.D, Waynesburg Col, 65. Polit. & Govt. Pos: U.S. Rep, Pa, and chmn, House For. Affairs Cmt, U.S. House of Rep, currently; del, Dem. Nat. Conv, 68. Mem: Elks; Odd Fellows. Rel: Methodist. Legal Res: Fredericktown, Pa. 15333. Mailing Add: 2183 Rayburn House Office Bldg, Washington, D.C. 20515.

MORGAN, WALTER HENRY D
Tenn. State Rep.
b. Hartsville, Tenn, 1/28/03; s. Robert Forrest Morgan and Sorena Jones M; m. 12/2/22 to Hazel Marie McElhiney; c. Elizabeth Marie (Mrs. Morris), Walter Henry, Jr, Helen Ruth (Mrs. Snell), Beulah Ann (Mrs. Shumate) and Forrest Moody. Educ: Trousdale Co. High Sch; South. Sch. of Printing. Polit. & Govt. Pos: Councilman, Nashville, Tenn, 47-63; Tenn. State Rep, 67-; alternate del, Dem. Nat. Conv, 68. Bus. & Prof. Pos: Compositor, Banner-Tennessean, 29-67, supt. in composing 37-54. Mem: Mason (32°); Shrine; Int. Typographical Union. Ky. Col; Tenn. Col. Rel: Church of Christ. Mailing Add: 1915 Holly St, Nashville, Tenn. 37206.

MORGAN, WILLIAM NELSON R
Secy. and Treas, Perry Co. Rep. Exec. Cmt, Ohio
b. New Straitsville, Ohio, 8/28/35; s. Nelson Miles Morgan and Mary Millard Donnley M; m. 4/15/61 to Virginia Lee Kopis; c. William Scott, Susan Lynn and Stacy Lee. Educ: New Straitsville High Sch, grad, 54; Police & Criminal Invest. Sch, Germany, grad, 60; Ohio Bur. of Criminal Identification Sch, grad, 63. Polit. & Govt. Pos: Mem, Perry Co. Young Rep. Club, Ohio, 55-, secy, 60 and pres, 65; dist. chmn. for John D. Herbert, State Treas, 66; state v.chmn, Ohio League of Young Rep. Clubs, 66 & 67; mayor, Shawnee, Ohio, 66 & 68; co. campaign chmn, Clarence E. Miller for U.S. Rep, Ohio, 66 & 68; dist. campaign co-chmn. for Tom. V. Moorehead, Ohio State Sen, 68; state chmn, Mil. Absentee Voting Prog, 68; secy. and treas, Perry Co. Rep. Exec. Cmt, 68- Bus. & Prof. Pos: Employee, Standard Oil of Ohio, Columbus, 54-56; criminal investr. and gen. duties, Perry Co. Sheriff's Dept, 60-67; chief probation officer, Perry Co. Juvenile Court, 67-68; asst. dir, Tax Collection Dept, State Treas. Off, 68- Mil. Serv: Army, 56-60. Mem: Pres, Perry Co. Mayor's Asn, 67; exec. bd, State Mayor's Asn, 67. Robert A. Taft Serv. Award to Most Outstanding Young Rep. in State of Ohio, 68. Mailing Add: Shawnee St, Shawnee, Ohio 43782.

MORGAN, WRIGHT J. JR. R
b. Trinidad, 1/29/21. Polit. & Gov. Pos: Asst. City Attorney; Dep. Dist. Attorney for Denver; former Asst. Attorney Gen. in Legis. Ref. Off; Asst. City atty. for Westminster; Rep. committeeman, 60-; dist Capt, 62; cand. for Justice of the Peace in Jefferson Co, 60, 62. Bus. & Prof. Pos: former sch. teacher. Mailing Add: 881 Bronco Rd, Valley Vista, Denver, Colo. 80221. (1967)

MORGANTHAU, HENRY, JR.
b. N.Y.C, 5/11/91; s. Henry Morganthau and Josephine Sykes M; m. 11/21/52 to Marcelle Puthon; c. Henry, Robert and Joan. Educ: Cornell Univ, 09-10 & 12-13. Hon. LL.D, Temple Univ, 38 and Amherst Col, 42; D.H.L, Hebrew Union Col, Cincinnati, 48. Polit. & Govt. Pos: Conserv. cmnr, N.Y; chmn, Gov. Roosevelt's Agr. Adv. Cmn; mem, Taconic State Park Cmn; Govt. Farm Credit Admin, 27-33; chmn, Fed. Farm Bd, Wash, 33; Acting and Under Secy. of Treas, 33-34, Secy. of Treas, 34-35. Bus. & Prof. Pos: Publisher, Am. Agriculturist, 22-33; gen. chmn, United Jewish Appeal, 47-50, hon. chmn, 51-53; chmn. bd. gov, Hebrew Univ, 50-51 and Am. Financial and Develop. Corp. for Israel, 51-54. Mil. Serv: Lt.(jg), Navy, World War I; Medal of Merit; Grand Officer Legion of Honor; Chinese Order of Auspicious Star; Grand Cordon. Mem: Obed and Jordan Lodges; Century Country Club; Dutchess Golf and Country Clubs; N.Y.C, Metrop. and Amrita Clubs; Nat. Press Club, Wash. Rel: Jewish. Mailing Add: Hopewell Junction, N.Y. 12533. (1967)

MORGEN, GLADYS H. D
V.Chmn, Wash. State Dem. Cmt.
b. Bismark, N.Dak, 7/13/16; d. Ragner Carlander and Mary Esther Long C; m. 11/11/35 to Clarence James Morgen; c. Dennis James, David Robert, Gerald Lloyd and Randy John. Educ: Bismarck High Sch, N.Dak, 4 years. Polit. & Govt. Pos: Dem.precinct committeeman, Spokane Co, Wash, 58-; state chmn, Dem. Nat. Campaign Conf. for Women, 65; v.chmn, Spokane Co. Dem. Cmt, 66, committeewoman, 67-; v.chmn, Wash. State Dem. Cmt, 67-; pres, Wash. State Fedn. Dem. Women's Clubs, 67-; del, Dem. Nat. Conv, 68; chmn, Women for Humphrey, 68. Mem: Charter mem, St. Charles Home and Sch. Asn; mem. adv. bd, Booth Mem. Hosp. Rel: Catholic. Mailing Add: W. 2311 Walton, Spokane, Wash. 99205.

MORIAL, ERNEST NATHAN D
La. State Rep.
b. New Orleans, La, 10/9/29; s. Walter Etienne Morial (Deceased) and Leonie Moore M; m. 2/18/55 to Sybil Gayle Haydel; c. Julie Claire, Marc Haydel, Jacques Etienne and Cheri Michele. Educ: Xavier Univ, B.S. in Bus. Admin, 51; La. State Univ, Baton Rouge, J.D, 54; Alpha Phi Alpha. Polit. & Govt. Pos: Asst. U.S. attorney, New Orleans, La, 65-67; del, Dem. Nat. Conv, 68; La. State Rep, 68- Bus. & Prof. Pos: Gen. counsel, Standard Life Ins. Co, of La, Inc, 63-; treas, Autocrat Finance Co, Inc, 64-; v.pres, Royal La. Mortgage Corp, 68- Mil. Serv: Pvt, U.S. Army Intel. Corps. Mem: Am, La. State and Nat. Bar Asns; Am. Arbit. Asn; nat. advocate, Knights of Peter Claver; gen. pres, Alpha Phi Alpha. Rel: Catholic. Legal Res: 1242 Magazine St, New Orleans, La, 70130. Mailing Add: 1821 Orleans Ave, New Orleans, La. 70116.

MORIARTY, CHARLES PATRICK, JR. R
b. Seattle, Wash, 7/15/27; s. Charles Patrick Moriarty and Thelma Thurman M; m. 5/27/64 to Marion Elizabeth Pelly; c. Mark, Marion and Mary. Educ: Univ. Wash, B.A, 49, Sch. of Law, LL.B, 51; Phi Delta Phi; Phi Delta Theta. Polit. & Govt. Pos: Wash State Rep, 57-59; mem, Wash. State Statute Law Cmt, Olympia, 57-; Wash. State Sen, 59-67. Bus. & Prof. Pos: Admin. asst, U.S. Rep. Thomas M. Pelly, 53-54; partner, Moriarty, Olson, Merrick & Brindle, Attorneys, 54- Mil. Serv: Entered Army, 52, released as 1st Lt, 53, after serv. in Off. Judge Adv. Gen, Pentagon, Wash, D.C, 52-53; Maj, Army Res, 66. Mem: Seattle, King Co, Wash. State and Am. Bar Asns; Rainier Club; Seattle Tennis Club. Rel: Roman Catholic. Legal Res: Route 6, Box 6808, Bainbridge Island, Wash. 98110. Mailing Add: 1212 Olympic National Bldg, Seattle, Wash. 98104.

MORIARTY, DANIEL PATRICK D
Mem, Indianapolis City Coun, Ind.
b. Indianapolis, Ind, 3/14/06; s. Maurice John Moriarty and Mary Barton M; m. 12/30/42 to Pauline Heidt. Educ: Arsenal Tech, Indianapolis, Ind, night classes. Polit. & Govt. Pos: Former v.pres, Indianapolis City Coun, Ind, mem, currently. Mil. Serv: Entered as Yeoman 3/C, Coast Guard, 42, released as Cl.B.Mate 2/C, 44. Mem: Am. Legion; K. of C. Mailing Add: 107 N. Denny St, Indianapolis, Ind. 46201.

MORIARTY, JEREMIAH J. R
b. Buffalo, N.Y, 7/5/14; m. to Helen Rott; c. Jeremiah J, III, Karen A, Mary Ellen, Daniel J. and Thomas J. Educ: Canisius Col, grad, 36; Univ. Buffalo Law Sch, 39. Polit. & Govt. Pos: V.pres, Bd. of Educ, Franklinville Cent. Sch, N.Y, 4 years; trustee, Franklinville, 5 years; N.Y. State Assemblyman (spec. elec), 60-62; N.Y. State Sen, 62-66. Bus. & Prof. Pos: Dir, Nat. Union Bank, Franklinville, N.Y. Mil. Serv: Entered Navy, 41, released as Lt. Comdr. 46. Mem: Cattaraugus Co. Bar Asn.(dir. and past pres); N.Y. State and Am. Bar Asns; N.Y. State Asn. of Sch. Attorneys; Ischua Creek Watershed Asn; dir, Cattaraugus Co. Tuberc. Asn; C. of C.(past pres, Franklinville Chap); Franklinville Conserv. Club; Am. Legion (Past Comdr, Post 526). Mailing Add: Franklinville, N.Y. 14737.

MORIN, THOMAS LEE R
Chmn, Grant Co. Rep. Cmt, Ind.
b. North Vernon, Ind, 9/30/29; s. Harold Leroy Morin and Agnes Gardner M; m. 10/21/50 to Emily Caroline Lewis; c. Douglas Martin and Melinda Diane. Educ: Ind. Univ, A.B, LL.D. and J.D, 56; Phi Delta Phi. Polit. & Govt. Pos: Chmn, Young Rep. Club, Grant Co, Ind, 56-58; precinct committeeman, Grant Co. Rep. Party, 58-62; chmn, Grant Co. Rep. Cmt, 65-; alterante del, Rep. Nat. Conv, 68. Mil. Serv: Entered as 2nd Lt, Army, 52, released as 1st Lt, 54, after serv. in Qm. Corps. Mem: Grant Co. Ind. Bar Asn.(pres, 67); Ind. State Bar Asn.(chmn, probate trust & real property sect, 67); Am. Bar Asn; Mason; Exchange Club; Am. Legion. Mailing Add: 908 Sydney Lane, Marion, Ind. 46952.

MORIOKA, TED T. D
Hawaii State Rep.
b. Honolulu, Hawaii, 11/18/21; s. Kamekichi Morioka and Kikuno Sasagawa M; m. 6/2/45 to Alice U; c. Daniel and Lyla. Educ: Univ. Hawaii. Polit. & Govt. Pos: Mem, Eviction Appeals Bd, Hawaii Housing Authority, 59-61; mem, Traffic Safety Cmn, City and Co. of Honolulu, 59 and civil serv. cmnr, 61-64; del, Dem. Nat. Conv, 64 & 68; Hawaii State Rep, Third Legis, 65- Bus. & Prof. Pos: Advert. salesman, Yellow Pages, Hawaiian Tel. Co, 47-53, commercial engr, 53-56, budget analyst, 57-63, asst. to exec. v.pres, 63; asst. to pres, 64- Mil. Serv: Entered as Pvt, Army, 45, released as T-4, 47, after serv. in Hawaii. Mem: Lions; Hawaii State C. of C; YMCA; Honolulu Japanese C. of C. Rel: Buddhist. Mailing Add: 2618 Gardenia St, Honolulu, Hawaii 96816.

MORLEY, WALTER H. D
b. Boston, Mass, 8/5/02; s. Walter Morley and Johanna Donovan M; wid; c. two. Educ: Boston Col. H.S. Polit. & Govt. Pos: Pa. State Rep, 60-67; former ward leader 21st Ward; chmn, 59th Ward Dem. Exec. Com. Bus. & Prof. Pos: Steamfitter. Mem: Steamfitters Local Union 420. Mailing Add: 353 W. Duval St, Philadelphia, Pa. 19144. (1967)

MORLOCK, HENRY JACOB Conservative
Minn. State Rep.
b. Jordan, Minn, 4/5/05; s. Henry T. Morlock and Johanna Fehlandt M; m. 9/1/31 to Agnes Eilers; c. Phyllis (Mrs. Del Wissink), Terry and Rod. Educ: Gustavus Adolphus Col. Polit. & Govt. Pos: Mem, Bd. of Educ, 28 years; Minn. State Rep, 62- Bus. & Prof. Pos: Mink rancher; farmer. Mem: Nat. Bd. of Fur Farmers (pres, state orgn). Awarded 50 trophies for outstanding mink ranching. Rel: Lutheran. Mailing Add: 201 Second, Jordan, Minn. 55352.

MORONG, LEROY LIBBY D
b. Lubec, Maine, 5/23/17; s. Frederick W. Morong and Maude Libby M; m. 10/18/63 to Margaret; c. Louise (Mrs. Bruce Wentworth), Frank G, Edwin W. and Joel. Educ: Rockport High Sch, 4 years. Polit. & Govt. Pos: Town chmn, Dem. Party, Camden, Maine, 60-61; chmn, Knox Co. Dem. Party, 66-69; mem, Parole Bd, Maine, 66; campaign coordinator, Gov. Curtis, Knox, Waldo and Lincoln Co, 66 and Congressman Kyros, 66-69; state chmn. testimonial dinner, Curtis For Gov, 67; field rep, Exec. Dept. Munic. Coordinators Off, 69- Bus. & Prof. Pos: Owner, jewelry store, 48-56; spec. sales agent, Provident Mutual Life Ins. Co, 55-69 and supvr, 58-60. Mem: Lions (pres. and secy, Camden Club); Mason; C. of C.(mem, merchants and indust. cmts, Camden Chap); coach and pres, Pony and Little League. Rel: Baptist. Legal Res: Molyneaux Rd, Camden, Maine. 04843. Mailing Add: Box 343, Camden, Maine 04843.

MORPHIS, RICHARD W. R
b. Spokane, Wash, 1929; m. to Violet M; c. one son. Educ: Walla Walla Col, B.A. Polit. & Gov. Pos: Wash. State Rep, until 66. Bus. & Prof. Pos: Mgr, Spokane Sanitarium. Mem: Spokane Cent. Lions; Odd Fellows; Masonic Bodies. Mailing Add: 3504 Riverview Dr, Spokane, Wash. 99205. (1967)

MORPHY, TED L. D
Co. Cmnr-At-Lg, Lexington Co, S.C.
b. Lexington, Ky, 11/3/33; s. Lewis Harris Morphy and Jewel E. Deal M; m. 1/9/58 to Barbara Ann Bowers. Educ: Grad. Columbia Bus. Col, 58. Polit. & Govt. Pos: S.C. State Rep, 65-66; co. cmnr-at-lg, Lexington Co, 67- Bus. & Prof. Pos: Pres, Ted L. Morphy Enterprises, Inc. Mil. Serv: Army, 50-54; Paratroops, 82nd Airborne Div; retired for disability. Mem: Bd. dirs, W. Columbia-Cayce C. of C. and Lexington C. of C; Cayce-W. Columbia Jaycees; Farm Bur; Civitans; 40 et 8; DAV; Am. Legion; cmnr, Boy Scouts; Nat. Rivers and Harbors Cong. Rel: Baptist. Mailing Add: Lexington, S.C. 29072.

MORRAH, P. BRADLEY, JR. D
b. Lancaster, S.C, 6/13/15; s. P. Bradley Morrah and Hessie Thomson M; m. to Edna Burgess. Educ: The Citadel, A.B, 36; Duke Univ. Law Sch, 39. Polit. & Govt. Pos: S.C. State Rep, 41 & 47-48; S.C. State Sen, 53-66. Bus. & Prof. Pos: Lawyer. Mil. Serv: Vet. Mem: Bd. of visitors, The Citadel. Mailing Add: Box 10248, Greenville, S.C. 29603.

MORREALE, JOSEPH FRANCIS R
Mem, Md. Rep. State Cent. Cmt.
b. Queens, N.Y, 12/27/13; s. Angelo Morreale and Josephine Cancemi M; m. 8/22/43 to Jennie Margaret Sinacore; c. Elena, Carol, Peter and John. Educ: City Col. N.Y, B.B.A, 51; Newman Club. Polit. & Govt. Pos: Mem, Md. Rep. State Cent. Cmt, 64-; chmn, Wicomico Co. Rep. Cent. Cmt, 64-68. Bus. & Prof. Pos: Plant mgr, Lalance & Grosjean Mfg. Co, 35-51; mgt. consult, E. Norman Kagan Co, 51-55; mgt. engr, Symington Wayne Corp, 55- Mil. Serv: Entered as Pvt, Army, 41, released as Capt, 46, after serv. in 1897 Eng. Aviation Bn, Southwest Pac, 44-46; New Guinea, Philippines and Okinawa Campaign Ribbons; Personal Commendation, Palawan Engagement; Unit Citation, Leyte Engagement. Publ: 'Planning and Control,' Am. Mfr. Asn. Mfg. Series 224, 57; 'Preventive Maintenance,' 3/59 and 'Don't Gamble With Maintenance,' 1/66, Supvry. Mgt. Mem: Am. Mgt. Asn; Soc. for Adv. of Mgt; Int. Maintenance Inst; Elks. Rel: Roman Catholic. 1967 Legal Res: Salisbury, Md. No mailing address available. (1967)

MORRELL, EMILY A. D
Chmn, Arthur Co. Dem. Party, Nebr.
b. Arthur; Nebr, 4/4/19; d. Arthur W. Lemmert and Olive Maud Shaptaw L; m. 6/6/46 to Edward Morrell; c. Eddy Allen. Polit. & Govt. Pos: Postal clerk, Arthur, Nebr, 43-67; chmn, Arthur Co. Dem. Party, currently. Rel: Protestant. Legal Res: Main St, Arthur, Nebr. 69121. Mailing Add: Box 161, Arthur, Nebr. 69121.

MORRILL, ARTHUR H. R
b. 5/27/91; married; c. four. Educ: Manchester, N.H. Polit. & Govt. Pos: N.H. State Rep, -67; Trustee Town Trust Funds; Libr, Trustee; Selectman (24 yrs.). Bus. & Prof. Pos: Textiles—salesman O.H. Metals and Agr. Mil. Serv: WW I veteran. Mem: Masonic Lodge, 32nd degree Mason; Grange. Rel: Presbyterian. Mailing Add: RFD 3, Manchester, N.H. 03103. (1967)

MORRIS, ANN BARNETT R
b. Columbia, S.C, 8/25/17; d. William Dickson Barnett and Nellie Aycock Caughman B; m. 1/25/42 to Edgar Longette Morris; c. Diane Barnett (Mrs. Thomas McCullough Boulware), Edgar Longette, Jr, William Dickson and Beronica Longette. Educ: Converse Col, B.A, 38. Polit. & Govt. Pos: Pres, Richland Co. Rep. Women's Club, S.C, 62-63; alternate del, Rep. Nat. Conv, 64, del, 68; state canvass chmn, S.C. State Rep. Party, 64; Rep. nat. committeewoman, S.C, 64-68; state campaign mgr, Supt. Educ. Campaign, 66; campaign co-chmn, U.S. Rep. Albert Watson Campaign, 68. Mem: Forest Lake Country Club; Quadrille Club. Rel: Presbyterian. Mailing Add: 813 Woodland Dr, Columbia, S.C. 29205.

MORRIS, ARLINE WINIFRED D
Mem, East Lyme Dem. Town Cmt, Conn.
b. Hartford, Conn, 8/4/23; d. Louis Zephier Richards and Winifred McHugh R; m. 6/17/46 to Edward Vincent Morris; c. Brian, Pamela and Richard. Educ: Mount St. Joseph Acad; Hartford Hosp. Sch. of Nursing. Polit. & Govt. Pos: Committeewoman, Dem. State Cent. Cmt, 62-66; chmn, 20th Sen. Dist. Asn, 63-64; secy, Conn. Young Dem. and alternate del, Dem. Nat. Conv, 64; mem, East Lyme Dem. Town Cmt, Conn. and pres, East Lyme Dem. Federated Women's Club, 64- Mem: Niantic Bay Yacht Club; East Lyme Dem. Club; St. Agnes' Guild. Rel: Roman Catholic. Mailing Add: 65 Prospect Ave, Crescent Beach, Conn. 06357. (1967)

MORRIS, BENJAMIN GORDON D
b. Quinter, Kans, 1/5/40; s. Benjamin Smith Morris and Lucille Lewis M; m. 6/21/69 to Nancy Anne Johnson. Educ: Ft. Hays Kans. State Col, 57-60; Inst. of Tech. of Monterrey, Mex, 59; Univ. Kans, A.B, 60-62; Univ. Costa Rica, Exchange Prog, 61; Instituto Interamericano de Educación Politica, Dipl, 61; Univ. Kans. Sch. Law, J.D, 66. Polit. & Govt. Pos: Kans. State Rep, 104th Dist, 65-66, caucus secy, Dem. House Mem, 65-66. Bus. & Prof. Pos: Admin. dir. and prof, Inter-Am. Inst. of Polit. Educ, 62 and spec. adv. to the Dominican Repub. Govt, Inter-Am. Center of Econ. and Soc. Studies, 63; asst. to secy-treas, Inst. of Int. Labor Research, Inc, 62-63; asst. dean, Univ. Kans. Sch. of Law, 67-69. Publ: 'The Sixth Amendment's Right of Confrontation and the Non-English Speaking Accused,' Fla. Bar J, 7/67. Mem: Am. and Kans. Bar. Asns; Mo. Bar Asn.(dir. of activities, 66-67); Am. Judicature Soc; Kans. Trial Lawyers Asn. Mem: AF&AM; Mason. Rel: Protestant. Mailing Add: 12303 N. 52nd St, Tampa, Fla. 33617.

MORRIS, BREWSTER HILLARD
Asst. Chief of Mission, Berlin, Germany
b. Bryn Mawr, Pa, 2/7/09; m. to Ellen Downes. Educ: Haverford Col, B.S, 30; Oxford Univ, B.A, 32, B.Lit, 33. Polit. & Govt. Pos: Career officer, Dept. of State For. Serv, 36-; v.consul, Montreal, 36-38, Vienna, 38, Dresden, 39, Berlin, 40-41 and Stockholm, 42-44; polit. adv. staff to U.S. Mil. Govt. in Germany, 44-48; first secy, Moscow, 48-49 and Frankfort, 49-51; mem. staff, Nat. War Col, 51-52 and Off. of German Affairs, 52-54; For. Serv. Inspector, 54-57; counsr, London, 57-60; minister-counsr, Bonn, 60-63; Ambassador to Chad, 63-67; asst. chief of mission, Berlin, currently. Bus. & Prof. Pos: Investment analyst, 34-36. Legal Res: Villanova, Pa. Mailing Add: U.S. Mission, Berlin, Germany.

MORRIS, BRUCE LEO D
Conn. State Rep.
b. New Haven, Conn, 3/28/32; s. Brass Morris and Leona Foreman M; m. 4/10/53 to Gwendolyn Davis; c. Anthony E. and Bruce V. Educ: New Haven Col, 56; Colonial Sch. Tool Design, 59; Conn. State Tech. Inst, 61; Cent. Conn. State Col, 64. Polit. & Govt. Pos: Alderman, Dem. Party, 62-; Conn. State Rep, currently. Bus. & Prof. Pos: Tool designer, M.B. Electronics, 59-65, Sargent & Co, 65-66 and self-employed mfg. engr, 66- Mil. Serv: Entered as Pvt, Army 53, released as Cpl, 55, after serv. in Mil. Police, West Point, N.Y; Nat. Defense and Good Conduct Medals. Mem: Am. Soc. Tool Mfg. Engrs; Int. Elks. Rel: Catholic. Mailing Add: 280 Division St, New Haven, Conn. 06511.

MORRIS, CHARLES EDWARD R
b. Sidney, Iowa, 12/15/93; s. John J. Morris and Julia A. Lahman M; m. 10/26/14 to Clara A. Gude; c. Olin E, Bernard N. and Ruth L. (Mrs. Ross). Polit. & Govt. Pos: Liberty Precinct Rep. chmn, 16 years; Sch. Bd. mem, 14 years; past Mayor, Union, Nebr, mem, Union Fire Dept, 40 years and chief 30 years, pres, currently; mem, Village Bd, Union, 16 years; Cass Co. chmn, Rep. Cent. Cmt, 64-66; mem, Water & Sewer Cmt, Union, 65- Bus. & Prof. Pos: Farmer, 15-20; lineman, Lincoln Tel. & Tel. Co, 21; skilled laborer, Chicago Elec, 22; agent, Standard Oil Co, Nebr. 22-37; owner and operator, Morris Grocery. Mem: Chmn, Cass Co. Nebr. Centennial; state chmn, Nebr. Am. War Dads Civil Defense, currently; Cmt. Mem. of Water Shed Proj, currently; Mason (past Master, Nehawka Lodge 246); Boy Scouts Coun. Mailing Add: P.O. Box 85, Union, Nebr. 68455.

MORRIS, CHESTER R
Chmn, Sutter Co. Rep. Cent. Cmt, Calif.
b. Chicago, Ill, 11/21/32; s. Charles L. Morris and Lucille Williams M; m. 3/13/59 to Carol Mae Clark; c. Drew and Kris. Educ: Modesto Jr. Col, A.A, 57; Hastings Col. of the Law, J.D, 61; Phi Delta Phi. Polit. & Govt. Pos: Mem, Sutter Co. Rep. Cent. Cmt, Calif, 64-; chmn, 69-; mem, Calif. State Environ. Quality Study Coun, 69; mem, Calif. State Rep. Cent. Cmt, 69- Mil. Serv: Entered as Pvt, Air Force, 51, released as Sgt, 55, after serv. in Korea, 53-54; Nat. Defense Serv. Medal; Korean Serv. Medal; UN Serv. Medal; Good Conduct Medal. Mem: Yuba-Sutter Bar Asn.(secy, 69); Am. Bar Asn. of Defense Counsel; State Bar Asn. of Calif; bd. dirs, Sutter Co-Yuba City C. of C, 69. Rel: Protestant. Legal Res: 1112 Buchanan St, Yuba City, Calif. 95991. Mailing Add: P.O. Drawer A, Marysville, Calif. 95901.

MORRIS, CHRISTIAN PURTSCHER R
Mayor, Lima, Ohio
b. Lima, Ohio, 11/3/30; s. Christian P. Morris (deceased) and Helen Stolzenbach M.(deceased); m. 9/6/52 to Lillian Y. Foehrenbach; c. Debra Ann, Christian P, Jr, Mark Edward and David Remley. Educ: DePauw Univ, 48-50; Ohio State Univ, 54; Phi Sigma Alpha; Alpha Tau Omega. Polit. & Govt. Pos: Mayor,

Lima, Ohio 65- Bus. & Prof. Pos: Owner and mgr, M&M Allsports, Inc, 54-60 and Morris Brothers Allsports, Inc, 60-65; mem. bd. dirs, North Main, Inc, until 65. Mil. Serv: Entered as Seaman 2/C, Navy, 50, released as PO 1/C, 53; Korean War Ribbon; Mediterranean Theater of Operation Ribbon; Good Conduct Medal. Mem: Nat. Sporting Goods Asn; Nat. Congress of Parents & Teachers; Ohio Mayors Asn.(pres, 68-69); hon. chief, Ohio Fire Chief's Asn; Lima Area C. of C; Elks; Evening Optimist Club; U.S. Jr. C. of C; G&H Gun Club; Lima Young Rep. Club. Rel: Presbyterian. Mailing Add: 429 S. Jameson Ave, Lima, Ohio 45805.

MORRIS, COALSON C. R
b. Floydada, Tex, 7/20/16; s. William Luther Morris and Troy Coalson M; m. 2/4/42 to Jean Crawford; c. Susan, Jeffrey and Christine. Educ: Univ. South. Calif; Trojan Knignts; Sigma Sigma; Blue Key; Skull & Daggar. Polit. & Govt. Pos: Chmn, Orange Co. Rep. Cent. Cmt, Calif, 57-60; mem. exec. cmt, Calif. State Cent. Cmt, 59-61; del, Rep. Nat. Conv, 68. Bus. & Prof. Pos: Mem. bd. dirs, Kohlen-Berger Eng. Co, 63-; chmn. bd, Tustin Savings & Loan Asn, 64-; mem. and chmn. bd. dirs, Morehouse Industs. and v.pres. and treas, Maxad, Inc, currently. Mil. Serv: Entered as Ens, Navy, 43, released as Lt, 46, after serv. with Pac. Fleet. Mem: Rotary; former pres, Orange Co. Goodwill Industs; United Fund Bd, Anaheim, Calif, 54-62. Rel: Presbyterian. Mailing Add: 708 N.West St, Anaheim, Calif. 92805.

MORRIS, EARLE E, JR. D
S.C. State Sen.
b. Pickens, S.C, 7/14/28; s. Earle E. Morris, Sr. and Bernice Carey M; m. 4/12/58 to Jane L. Boroughs; c. Lynda L, Carey M, Elizabeth M. and Earle E, III. Educ: Clemson Univ, B.S, 49; Blue Key; Phi Kappa Phi. Polit. & Govt. Pos: S.C. State Rep, 50-54; del, State and Co. Dem. Convs, 50-68; del, Dem. Nat. Conv, 52, 56 & 68; pres, Pickens Co. Dem. Party, 54, 65 & 66; S.C. State Sen, Pickens Co, 54-; mem, South. Regional Educ. Bd. Cmn. on Ment. Illness, Atlanta, Ga, 58-; mem, Gov. Adv. Group on Ment. Health Planning, 63-65; mem, Interagency Coun. on Ment. Retardation Planning, 64-; mem, Nat. Adv. Ment. Health Coun, U.S. Pub. Health Serv, 65-; secy-treas, S.C. Dem. Party, 65-66, chmn, 66-68; mem, Senate Interagency Coun. on Aging, 66. Bus. & Prof. Pos: V.pres. and secy, Morris & Co, Inc, 50-; v.pres. and dir, Bankers Trust of S.C, 56-; v.pres, Gen. Ins. Agency, 57-; secy, Carolina Investors, Inc, 63- and Duncan Motor Lines, 65-. Mil. Serv: Capt, S.C. Army Nat. Guard, 51- Mem: S.C. Ment. Health Asn; S.C. Asn. for Retarded Children; v.pres, S.C. Vocational Rehabilitation Asn; S.C. Crippled Children's Soc; Mason; Shrine; Lions; Elks; former mem, Jaycees; Pickens Country Club; Poinsett Club; SAR; v.pres, S.C. Rehabilitation Soc. Rel: Presbyterian; Elder and Clerk of the Session. Legal Res: Route 2, Pickens, S.C. 29671. Mailing Add: Box 97, Pickens, S.C. 29671.

MORRIS, EUGENE, JR. R
Chmn, Cent. Dist. Fourth Cong. Dist. Rep. Party, Va.
b. Petersburg, Va, 10/26/20; s. Eugene Branch Morris and Bertha McAllister M; m. 2/28/41 to Virginia Tucker; c. Jay Lynn. Polit. & Govt. Pos: Alternate del, Rep. Nat. Conv, 68; chmn, Cent. Dist. Fourth Cong. Dist. Rep. Party, Va, 68-; chmn, Prince George Co. Rep. Party, 69- Bus. & Prof. Pos: Secy-treas, Petersburg News Agency, Inc, Va, 53- Rel: Presbyterian. Legal Res: 605 Hoke Dr, Petersburg, Va. 23803. Mailing Add: P.O. Box 670, Petersburg, Va. 23803.

MORRIS, H. H. D
Postmaster of the U.S. Congress
b. Carrollton, Ky, s. Joseph Watkins Morris and Mary M. Gullion M; m. 11/2/35 to Lyda J. Secrest. Educ: Univ. Ky, 29-31; Nat. Law Sch, LL.B, 39; Phi Beta Gamma; Kappa Sigma. Polit. & Govt. Pos: Asst, Dem. Cloak Room, U.S. House of Rep, 32-40; secy, Rep. and Sen. Chapman, Ky, 40-49; asst. clerk, U.S. House of Rep, 49-51; asst, Sen. Underwood, 51-52; secy, Rep. Watts, 52-55; Postmaster, U.S. Congress, 56- Mem: Nat. Press Club. Rel: Baptist. Legal Res: New Castle, Ky. 40050. Mailing Add: 3318 Ordway St. N.W, Washington, D.C. 20008.

MORRIS, HELENE M. R
b. Boston, Mass; wid. Educ: Lowell State Teachers Col; Boston Univ, grad. study in bus. admin. Polit. & Govt. Pos: Rep. nat. committeewoman, Fla, until 68; State Rep. Committeewoman; state treas, Rep. State Exec. Cmt; bd. mem, Fla. Fedn. of Rep. Women; mem, Women's Nat. Rep. Club, N.Y.C; v.chmn. Fla. del, Rep. Nat. Conv, 64, alternate del. and mem. host cmt, 68. Bus. & Prof. Pos: Co-owner, M Bar M Ranch, Sarasota, Fla; v.pres, Geo. L. Mesher Steel Corp, Evansville, Ind. and New Albany, Miss. Mil. Serv: 2nd Lt. to Maj, Women's Army Corps. Mem: Women's Auxiliary Mem. Hosp; Sarasota Art Asn; Am. Legion; Sarasota Co. Bd. of Zoning Appeals; Vis. Nurse Asn.(past pres. and bd. mem); Ment. Health Asn; nat. bd, Am. Inst. Parliament (cert. parliament); Capitol Hill Club, Wash, D.C; State Cmt. Fla. Vet. Affairs; bd, Korean Cultural and Freedom Found; Fla. West Coast Symphony; Asolo Opera Guild; Sarasota Music Club (past pres. and mem. bd); Mus. Coun; Boys Club Sarasota (v.pres); bd, St. Leo Col; Nat. League Am. Pen Women. Mailing Add: Le Chateau, 37 Sunset Dr, Sarasota, Fla. 33580.

MORRIS, J. HAROLD D
b. Etowah Co, Ala, 6/5/41; s. James Archible Morris and Lula Bell McCreless M; m. 1/18/64 to Margaret Ann Gibbs. Educ: Univ. Ga, B.S.Ed, 63. Polit. & Govt. Pos: Del, Dem. Nat. Conv, 64 & 68. Bus. & Prof. Pos: Teacher and coach, Paulding Co, Ga, 64-66, Atlanta Pub. Schs, 66-69. Mem: Atlanta, Ga. and Nat. Educ. Asns. Rel: Baptist. Mailing Add: 1991 Bencal Dr. S.E. Atlanta, Ga. 30316.

MORRIS, JAMES McCULLUM D
S.C. State Sen.
b. New Zion, S.C, 4/24/28; s. Harrison McCullum Morris and Janie Marie Barker M; m. 6/13/46 to Dorothy Evelyn Coleman; c. Sandra, Evelyn, Karen and Marian. Educ: Univ. S.C, LL.B, 55; Wig and Robe; Phi Alpha Delta. Polit. & Govt. Pos: S.C. State Rep, Clarendon Co, 55-62; S.C. State Sen, Clarendon-Sumter Co, 62-66 & 68- Bus. & Prof. Pos; Lawyer and farmer, 55- Mil. Serv: Pvt, Air Force, 46; re-entered 50, released as S/Sgt, 51, after serv. in Air Training Command and Troop Carrier. Mem: S.C. State Bar Asn; Ruritan; Mason; Am. Legion; Rotary. Rel: Methodist. Mailing Add: P.O. Box 22, New Zion, S.C. 29111.

MORRIS, JAMES PAXTON R
Chmn, Bernalillo Co. Rep. Party, N.Mex.
b. Tulsa, Okla, 8/12/35; s. Carl Paxton Morris and Katherine Cross M; m. 1/27/57 to Sara Ann Carpenter; c. Janna Marie, Joseph Lee and James Paxton, Jr. Educ: Univ. N.Mex, 53-57; Sigma Alpha Epsilon. Polit. & Govt. Pos: Secy-treas, Albuquerque City Campaign, N.Mex, 66; area coordinator, Bernalillo Co. Rep. Party, 67, chmn, 67-; del, Rep. Nat. Conv, 68. Bus. & Prof. Pos: Pres, Albuquerque chap, N.Mex. Motor Carriers, 67-68, bd. dirs. and mem-at-lg, N.Mex. Motor Carriers, 68-69. Mem: Pres, Delta Nu Alpha, 56-60; Kiwanis; Mason; Shrine. Rel: Christian Science. Legal Res: 11401 Baldwin, N.E, Albuquerque, N.Mex. 87112. Mailing Add: P.O. Box 853, Albuquerque, N.Mex. 87103.

MORRIS, JOHN K. D
Chmn, State Property Tax Appeal Bd, Ill.
b. Lanark, Ill, 6/3/09; s. George R. Morris and Amy A. Kenyon; m. 4/3/37 to Ealy Grobe; c. Patricia (Mrs. Schmidt) and John F.(deceased). Educ: Univ. of Ill, Urbana, Col. of Agr, B.S, 32; Sigma Mu. Polit. & Govt. Pos: Justice of the Peace, Lanark, Ill, 36-52 and mem. sch. bd; Ill. State Rep, 47-67, v.chmn, Agr. Cmt, Ill. House of Rep, chmn, Revenue Cmt, 59, 61 & 65; chmn, State Property Tax Appeal Bd, 67- Bus. & Prof. Pos: Pres, Chicagoland Angus Asn, 58-59; raises grain and livestock, specializing in purebred Aberdeen Angus cattle; real estate broker; pub. rels. and pub. develop, Daily Gazette, Sterling, Ill, 61-67. Mem: Farm Bur; Ill. Farmer's Union; Nat. Farmer's Orgn; Ill. Livestock Feeder's Asn; Grange. Named as Outstanding Agr. Legislator in Ill. by Ill. Livestock Feeder's Asn, 63. Rel: Methodist. Mailing Add: R.R. 1, Chadwick, Ill. 61014.

MORRIS, MOUNT ETNA D
b. Dade Co, Mo, 9/1/00; s. Albert G. Morris and Veda Wilson M. (deceased); m. 12/24/22 to Helen Adamson, wid; c. Mrs. D. Fred Croce, John Albert and eight grandchildren. Educ: Southwest Mo. State Col; Univ. Mo. Polit. & Govt. Pos: Mo. State Rep, 34; app. state cmnr. finance, 45; dir, Dept. of Revenue, 46, reappointed, 53 & 61; Mo. State Treas, 48, 56 & 64-69. Bus. & Prof. Pos: Organized and operated Peoples Bank, Mill, Mo, 28-36; exec. officer, Trenton Nat. Bank until 45. Mil. Serv: World War I Vet. Mem: Mason; Scottish Rite; Shrine; Am. Legion; Elks (past exalted ruler); Boy Scouts (past dist. exec. cmnr); bd. regents, Northwest State Col, 40-46; Cmn. on Legis. of Mo. Bankers Asn.(chmn, 10 years). Rel: Presbyterian; Elder. Legal Res: 1100 W. Main, Jefferson City, Mo. 59638. Mailing Add: Jefferson Bldg, Jefferson City, Mo. 59638. (1967)

MORRIS, SAM CAMERON D
Chmn, Hoke Co. Dem. Exec. Cmt, N.C.
b. Raeford, N.C, 1/16/18; s. Bruce Morris and Beulah Cameron M; m. 3/13/43 to Mary Alice Pernell; c. Sarah Frances and John Arthur. Educ: Raeford High Sch. Polit. & Govt. Pos: Pres, Young Dem. Club, 50-54; precinct chmn, Dem. Party, N.C, 54-58; chmn, Hoke Co. Dem. Exec. Cmt, 58- Mil. Serv: Entered as Sgt, Army, 40, released as Capt, 46, after serv. in Pac. Theater. Mem: Am. Legion; Kiwanis. Rel: Presbyterian. Legal Res: 110 N. Jackson St, Raeford, N.C. 28376. Mailing Add: P.O. Box 541, Raeford, N.C. 28376.

MORRIS, THOMAS GAYLE D
b. Eastland Co, Tex, 8/20/19; s. Robert Gayle Morris and Nancy Smith M; m. 6/5/47 to Corinne Stevens; c. Thomas G, II and Elizabeth Jane. Educ: Univ. of N.Mex, B.S. in Civil Eng, 48; Sigma Chi. Polit. & Govt. Pos: Chmn, N.Mex. Interstate Streams Cmn; N.Mex. State Rep, 53-58; U.S. Rep, N.Mex, 58-68. Mil. Serv: Entered as A/S, Navy, 37, released as Seaman, 44. Mem: VFW; DAV; Am. Legion; N.Mex. Farm and Livestock Bur; Nat. Reclamation Asn; N.Mex. Cattle Growers Asn; Elks; Lions. Rel: Presbyterian. Mailing Add: 2010 S. Second, Tucumcari, N.Mex. 88401.

MORRIS, WILLIAM HARRELL, JR. R
Chmn, Madison Co. Rep. Party, Tenn.
b. Memphis, Tenn, 1/5/29; s. William Harrell Morris and Rosaland Gooch M; m. 2/20/54 to Nancy Johnson; c. George Robert and Mary Elizabeth. Educ: Univ. Tenn, 2 years; Sigma Alpha Epsilon. Polit. & Govt. Pos: Co. chmn. for Goldwater, Tenn, 64; seventh dist. chmn, Young Rep, 65 & 66; seventh dist. campaign mgr. for cong. candidate, 66; pres, Jackson-Madison Co. Young Rep. Club, 66-67; chmn, Madison Co. Election Cmn, 67 & 68; chmn, Madison Co. Rep. Party, 67-; del, Rep. Nat. Conv, 68; seventh dist. chmn, Nixon-Agnew Campaign, 68. Bus. & Prof. Pos: Secy. and Sales mgr, Gooch-Edenton Wholesale Hardware Co, Inc, 55- Mil. Serv: Entered as Seaman, Navy, 51, released as PN-3, 53, after serv. in Res. Mem: Bd. dirs. of Jackson Rotary, Jackson Golf & Country Club, Youth Town of Tenn, Madison Co. Cancer Soc, C. of C, Madison Co. Tuberc. Asn. and Boy's Club of Jackson; v.pres, W.Tenn Area Boy Scout Coun. Tenn. Young Rep. of the Year, 67; City Maker award, Jackson, Tenn, 68. Rel: Methodist. Mailing Add: 37 Carlisle Dr, Jackson, Tenn. 38301.

MORRIS, WILLIAM SHELTON D
Lt. Gov, Mo.
b. Higginsville, Mo, 11/8/19; s. Cyrus Morris and Elizabeth Jung M; m. 3/30/42 to Lucile Albers; c. Lisa Sanders. Educ: Wentworth Mil. Acad; Univ. Kansas City Sch. of Law, LL.B, 48; Phi Alpha Delta. Polit. & Govt. Pos: Pres, Lafayette Co. Young Dem, Mo, 5 years; Dem. Mem, Kansas City Elec. Bd, 59-62; chmn, Kansas City Bd. of Elec. Cmnrs, 62-64; app. Pub. Adminstr, Jackson Co, 64-66; elec. Pub. Adminstr, Jackson Co, 66-68; Lt. Gov, Mo, 68- Bus. & Prof. Pos: Clerk to Asst. Trust Officer, Trust Officer and v.pres, Union Nat. Bank, 46-58; managing dir. and v.pres, Phillips Hotel, 59-68; v.pres, Monitor Investment Co. & City Builders, Inc, 59-68; pres, Kansas City Blues Hockey Club, Inc, 67-; attorney-at-law, Home Savings Bldg, Kansas City, Mo, 69- Mil. Serv: Pvt, Army, 42, released as Maj, 46 after serv. in Sixth Inf. Div, Pac; Silver Star; Bronze Star; Air Medal. Mem: Boy Scouts; Hon. Fel. of Truman Libr, Inc; Kansas City C. of C.(former dir); Kansas City Sports Cmn; bd. trustees, Wentworth Mil. Acad; Mo. Bar Asn; Kansas City Lawyers Asn; Kansas City Bar Asn; Hon. Dir. Asn. of Rockhurst Col; life mem, VFW; Mason (32°); Ararat Shrine. Rel: Methodist. Legal Res: 1278 W. Gregory, Kansas City, Mo. 64114. Mailing Add: State Capitol Building, Jefferson City, Mo. 65101.

MORRISON, ARTHUR THOMAS R
Vt. State Rep.
b. Waterford, Vt, 12/5/02; m. to Dorothy M. Pease; c. One son and three daughters. Educ: Waterford Schs, Vt. Polit. & Govt. Pos: Town auditor, 38-47; Vt. State Rep, 59- Bus. & Prof. Pos: Retired; librn, Waterford Pub. Libr, 39-53 & 59- Rel: Congregational. Mailing Add: Lower Waterford, Vt. 05848. (1967)

MORRISON, BEATRICE BETHEL D
V.Chmn, Moffat Co. Dem. Party, Colo.
b. Ladysmith, Wis, 5/20/15; d. William A. Nolton and Stella Pearl Wallace N; m. 8/10/40 to Harvey Robert Morrison; c. Jerry Robert, John Wallace and Clifford Harvey. Educ: Johnson High Sch, St. Paul, Minn, grad, 34. Polit. & Govt. Pos: Committeewoman, Dem. Party, Craig, Colo, 58-62; v.chmn, Moffat Co. Dem. Party, 62- Bus. & Prof. Pos: Plant clerk, Mt. States Tel, Craig, Colo, 52-68, tel. operator, 68- Mem: Benevolent Patriotic Order of Does (all chairs through pres, 55-; chaplain, 126 Chap, 69); Commun. Workers of Am.(secy, 57-69); Jane Jefferson Club (v.pres, 64-66). Rel: Presbyterian. Mailing Add: P.O. Box 572, Court House, Craig, Colo. 81625.

MORRISON, BESSIE MATILDA R
N.H. State Rep.
b. N.S, Can, 6/11/00; d. John L. Ross and Ida Crabbe R; wid; c. Kenneth W. (adopted). Educ: Elem. Sch, Salem, N.H, grad. eighth grade. Polit. & Govt. Pos: Treas, Libr, Salem, N.H, 3 years, trustee, 9 years; N.H. State Rep, 63-; selectman, Salem, 69- Bus. & Prof. Pos: real estate broker and notary public. Mem: Hist. Soc; Order of Woman Legislators; Rep. Women's Club; Salem and Enterprize Grange (past master); Pomona, State and Nat. Grange; Salem Women's Club (past pres); 43 Club; Owls; Eastern Star. Rel: Protestant. Mailing Add: 27 Scotland Ave, Salem, N.H. 03079.

MORRISON, C. M. 'CHUCK' D
Wyo. State Rep.
b. Casper, Wyo; single. Educ: Casper Col; Armed Forces Sch; Sorbonne Univ, Paris. Polit. & Govt. Pos: Councilman, Casper City, Wyo, 51-53; chmn, Wyo. Winter Sports Cmn. and Gov. Recreation Cmn; Wyo. State Rep, currently. Bus. & Prof. Pos: Outdoor ed, Casper Star Tribune; photographer-photo-journalist. Mem: Izaak Walton League; Wyo. Outdoor Asn; Nat. Wildlife Fedn; Wyo. Conserv. Asn; Outdoor Writers Asn. of Am; Nat. Press Photographers Asn; Casper Troopers (photographer and press reporter). Has had photo articles in 'Life,' 'Nat. Geog' and other nat. publns; recipient of thirteen Pace Maker Awards, Wyo. Press Asn; Wyo. Press Photographer of the Year, 67 & 69. Mailing Add: 3050 E. Fourth St, Casper, Wyo. 82601.

MORRISON, CLAYTON T. R
b. 12/11/03; married; c. Audrey Norton, Dorothea Callaway, June Peffers. Educ: Mich. State Univ. Polit. & Govt. Pos: Mich. State Rep, 52-66; Local sch. bd, 24 years. Bus. & Prof. Pos: Dealer in real estate, forest prods. Mem: Lions Club; Izaac Walton League; C. of C; Gideons Int. Rel: Methodist. Mailing Add: Pickford, Mich. 49774. (1967)

MORRISON, DONALD EDGAR R
Chmn, Laramie Co. Rep. Cmt, Wyo.
b. Douglas, Wyo, 11/10/26; s. Ray E. Morrison and Bertha Walker M; m. 12/18/48 to Mary Jayne Willford. Educ: Univ. Wyo, B.S. with honors, 53, M.S, 59; Beta Gamma Sigma. Polit. & Govt. Pos: Mem, Wyo. State Bd. of Accountancy, 64-, past pres; precinct committeeman, Laramie Co. Rep. Cent. Cmt, 6 years, treas, 66-67, v.chmn, 67-68, chmn, 68- Bus. & Prof. Pos: Staffman, Raab, Roush & Gaymon, CPA, 55-60, partner, 60- Mil. Serv: Entered as Pvt, Army, 44, released as T-5, 46. Mem: Am. Inst. of CPA; Wyo. Soc. of CPA; Nat. Asn. of State Bd. of Accountancy; Mason. Rel: Methodist; mem. off. bd, First Methodist Church, Cheyenne. Mailing Add: 3208 Forest Dr, Cheyenne, Wyo. 82001.

MORRISON, DOROTHY DUNN D
b. Meredosia, Ill; d. Arthur Dunn and Minnie Ellen Williams D.(deceased); m. to Dr. Joseph Paul Eldred Morrison; c. Mary Callaway, Lilian Philips and Michael Paul Eldred. Educ: Univ. Wis; Quill and Scroll, hon. jour. Polit. & Govt. Pos: Mem. staff, U.S. Rep. Chet Holifield, Calif, 45-48 and admin. asst. until 69; former mem, House Cmt. on Govt. Oper; clerk, Exec. and Legis. Reorgn. Subcmt, 49-52. Bus. & Prof. Pos: Violinist, symphony orchestra. Mem: Cong. Secy. Club (secy, 53-69, mem. bd, 62-69); P.R-Am. Women's League. Rel: Christian Church of N.Am; mem. church choir. Mailing Add: 1330 Fourth St. S.W, Washington, D.C. 20024.

MORRISON, EDWARD ALLAN Liberal
V.Chmn, N.Y. State Liberal Party
b. Brooklyn, N.Y, 4/9/33; s. Samuel Jarvis Morrison and Sara Greenwald M; m. 9/9/56 to Elaine Madge; c. Dean E, Russell J, Andrew L. and William J. Educ: Brooklyn Col, B.A; Columbia Law Sch, LL.B. Polit. & Govt. Pos: State dir, Roosevelt for Gov. Campaign; chmn, New York Co. Liberal Party; assoc. dir. and v.chmn, N.Y. State Liberal Party, currently; chmn, State Law Cmt; coordinator, Mayor John V. Lindsay Campaign, 69. Mailing Add: 280 Ninth Ave, New York, N.Y. 10014.

MORRISON, FRANK B. D
b. Golden, Colo, 5/20/05; m. 6/28/36 to Maxine Hepp; c. Frank B, Jr, David J and Jean Marie. Educ: Kans. State Col, B.S, 1927; Univ. Nebr, LL.B, 1931; Tau Kappa Epsilon; Phi Alpha Delta; Delta Sigma Rho; Pi Kappa Delta. Polit. & Govt. Pos: Co. Attorney, Red Willow and Frontier Co; Gov. of Nebr, 60-67. Bus. & Prof. Pos: Former farmer and teacher; lawyer; counsel for Frenchman-Cambridge Irrigation Dist, McCook Pub. Power Dist. and Twin Valleys Elec. Mem. Asn. Mem: Dist. Gov, Rotary Int; pres, Norris Mem. Found; dir, McCook C. of C; trustee, Lutheran Med. Center; bd. dirs, Fed. Home Loan Bank of Topeka; Am. & Omaha Bar Asn; Omaha Rotary Club; Nat. Small Bus. Admin. Adv. Coun. Mailing Add: 1100 Farm Credit Bldg, Omaha, Nebr. 68102.

MORRISON, JAMES HOBSON D
b. Hammond, La, 12/8/08; s. Benjamin M. Morrison and Florence Hobson M; m. 2/14/40 to Marjorie Abbey; c. James H, Jr. 'Hobby' and Benjamin Abbey 'Benjy'. Educ: Tulane Univ, LL.B, 35; Delta Tau Delta; Phi Delta Phi. Polit. Pos: U.S. Rep, La. 42-67. Mem: La. State and Am. Bar Asns; Eagles; Elks; City Club of Baton Rouge. Rel: Episcopal. Legal Res: R.R. 3, Box 165 M, Hammond, La. 70401. (1967)

MORRISON, MAXINE E. D
b. Greeley, Nebr, 9/18/15; d. John Frederick Hepp and Jessie Marie Martin H; m. 6/28/36 to Frank Brenner Morrison; c. Frank B, Jr, David Jon and Jean Marie (Mrs. Ben Galloway). Educ: Nebr. Cent. Quaker Col, 33-35; McCook Jr. Col, 41; Alpha Delta Pi. Polit. & Govt. Pos: Former First Lady of Nebr; Dem. cand. for U.S. Rep, 68. Bus. & Prof. Pos: Radio and TV programmer; nat. dir, customer rels, King's Food Host U.S.A, currently. Rel: Episcopal. Mailing Add: 13006 Shirley, Omaha, Nebr. 68144.

MORRISON, RAYMOND M, SR. D
Mem, Dade Co. Dem. Exec. Cmt, Ga.
b. Trenton, Ga, 4/12/99; s. William Granville Morrison and Allie Hassell Brock M; m. 6/17/28 to Lula Olivine Tate; c. R.M. Morrison, Jr. and Kathleen Rae (Mrs. Lord). Educ: Dade Co. High Sch, Ga, grad, 16; Tech High Sch, Atlanta, Ga. Polit. & Govt. Pos: Clerk, Dade Co. Superior Court, Ga, 29-40; rural letter carrier, Dade Co, 40-46; acting postmaster, Trenton, Ga, 46-51, postmaster, Dade Co, Ga, 52-56; mem, Dade Co. Dem. Exec. Cmt, 62- Bus. & Prof. Pos: Cashier, Bank of Dade, Trenton, Ga, 57-63, v.pres, 63- Mem: Mason; Lions. Rel: Methodist. Mailing Add: P.O. Box 506, Trenton, Ga. 30752.

MORRISON, ROBERT ELLIOTT D
b. Chatsworth, Ga, 10/8/28; s. John Watson Morrison and Maud Moore M; m. 2/26/49 to Martha B. Butler; c. Pamela, Michael and Diane. Educ: N.Ga. Col, B.S; Peabody Col, M.A. and E.D.S. Polit. & Govt. Pos: Chmn, Murray Co. Dem. Cmt, Ga. Bus. & Prof. Pos: Prin, Eton Elem. Sch, Ga, 64- and teacher, 62-64; asst. plant mgr, World Carpet Mills, Dalton, Ga, 60-62; asst. credit mgr, Cabin Crafts, Inc, 55-60. Mil. Serv: Entered as Pvt, Army, 45, released as Cpl, 48, after serv. in ETO; European Occupation Ribbon. Mem: Am. Legion; Masons; Ruritan; Nat. and Ga. Educ. Asns. and Dept. Elem. Sch. Principals. Rel: Baptist. Mailing Add: Box 275, Chatsworth, Ga. 30705. (1967)

MORRISON, ROBERT LEE D
Co. chmn, Clark Co. Dem. Cent. Cmt, Nev.
b. Alpena, Mich, 2/27/24; s. Dougal Lawrence Morrison and Jennie Manning M; m. 4/19/44 to Florence Rita Squire; c. Robert Dougal, Anne Mary and Shannon Kathleen. Educ: Mich. State Univ, B.S, 48; Univ. Mich, Dr.Dent.Surg, 51; Phi Kappa Phi; Omicron Kappa Upsilon; Delta Sigma Delta. Polit. & Govt. Pos: Precinct capt, Clark Co. Dem. Party, Nev, 64-65; co. chmn, Clark Co. Dem. Cent. Cmt, 68- Mil. Serv: Entered as Air Cadet, Air Force, 42, released as 1st Lt, 45, after serv. in W.Coast Flying Training Command, Pilot. Mem: Am. Dent. Asn.(v.pres, 65-66, trustee, 67-); Elks; K. of C. Rel: Catholic. Mailing Add: 1329 S. Seventh, Las Vegas, Nev. 89104.

MORRISON, SID R
Wash. State Rep.
b. Wash, 1933; s. Charles Morrison; m. to Marcella; c. four. Educ: Yakima Valley Col; Wash. State Univ, 54. Polit. & Govt. Pos: Wash. State Rep, 67- Bus. & Prof. Pos: Orchardist and nurseryman. Mem: Boy Scout Leader; Grange; PTA; Mason; past pres, Wash. Apple Cmn. and Wash. Peach Coun. Rel: Methodist. Mailing Add: Route 1, Box 220 AA, Zillah, Wash. 98953.

MORRISON, THEODORE V, JR. D
Va. State Del.
b. Atlanta, Ga, 6/15/35; s. Theodore V. Morrison and Helen Sisson M; m. 6/13/56 to Audrey Powell; c. Thomas Purnell. Educ: Emory Univ, B.A, 57, LL.B, 59; Alpha Tau Omega; Phi Delta Phi. Polit. & Govt. Pos: Va. State Del, Newport News, 68- Bus. & Prof. Pos: Attorney-at-law, Saunders, Carlton, Morrison, Stephenson & Spratley, currently. Mil. Serv: Entered as Pvt, Army Nat. Guard, 59, released as Sgt, 65. Mem: Newport News, Va. and Am. Bar Asns; Am. and Va. Trial Lawyers Asns; Am. Judicature Soc; Rotary; Propeller Club; Moose; Elks. Distinguished Serv. Award, Hampton Roads Jaycees, 68; Outstanding Young Man of 1968 Award, Va. State Jaycees. Rel: Episcopal. Mailing Add: 109 Leslie Dr, Newport News, Va. 23606.

MORRISON, ZELMA REEVES D
b. Wenatchee, Wash; d. Frank Reeves and Belle Culp R; m. to Raymond R. Morrison; c. Frank R, Betty Belle (Mrs. R.A. Vitousek, Jr) and Raeburn Rose (Mrs. Wayne Hagen). Educ: Univ. Wash, B.A; N.Y. Univ, grad student, 49-50; Chi Omega. Polit. & Govt. Pos: Complaint adv, Spokane Co. Welfare Dept, 36-41; info. exec, Off. Price Admin, 43-46; v.chmn, Wash. State Dem. Cent. Cmt, 55-59; pres, Wash. State Fedn. Dem. Women's Clubs, 55-59; mem, Dem. Nat. Cmt. from Wash, 60-67; mem. chief staff serv, Wash. State Dept. Licenses, 60- Bus. & Prof. Pos: Mem. faculty pub. rels. staff, East Wash. Col. of Educ, 46-51 and chmn. bd. trustees, 57-61. Mem: Spokane City Pan Hellenic (pres, 57-58); secy. adv. bd, Booth Mem. Hosp; Am. Asn. Univ. Women (past chmn. higher educ, Wash. State Chap); DAR; Nat. Asn. of Parliamentarians; League of Women Voters; Rebekah Assembly; Lady Lions. Named Dem. Woman of the Year, Wash. State Fedn. of Dem. Women's Clubs, 59. Rel: Episcopal. Mailing Add: 458 W. 21st Ave, Spokane, Wash. 99201. (1967)

MORRISSEY, THOMAS LAWRENCE D
Co. Attorney, Johnson Co, Nebr.
b. Tecumseh, Nebr, 11/23/36; s. Raymond B. Morrissey and Florence Elizabeth Senneff M; m. 8/18/58 to Marie A. Neukirch; c. Timothy Paul, Elizabeth Ann and Theodore Raymond. Educ: Creighton Univ, J.D, 60; Phi Alpha Delta. Polit. & Govt. Pos: Co. attorney, Johnson Co, Nebr, 63-; co. chmn, Johnson Co, Nebr, Dem. Cent. Cmt, 68-69. Bus. & Prof. Pos: Partner, Morrissey & Morrissey, Attorneys, Tecumseh, Nebr, 60-; chief council, S.E. Nebr. Crime Study Cmn, 69. Mem: Nebr. Co. Attorneys Asn; Nat. Dist. Attorneys Asn; pres, Tecumseh Country Club; Kiwanis; C. of C. Rel: Roman Catholic. Legal Res: 962 N. Fifth, Tecumseh, Nebr. 68450. Mailing Add: Box 467, Tecumseh, Nebr. 68450.

MORRONE, VERO A.
b. Westerly, R.I, 10/21/10; m. to Helen. Educ: Westerly High Sch. Polit. & Govt. Pos: Police cmnr, 4 years; town coun, 8 years; R.I. State Rep, 64-68.

Bus. & Prof. Pos: Restaurant owner. Mil. Serv: Nat. Guard. Mem: Elks (past exalted ruler, Westerly Chap); founder, Little League in R.I; K. of C. (bd. dirs); Westerly Yacht Club; Ital-Am. Club. Mailing Add: 246 Canal St, Westerly, R.I. 02909. (1967)

MORROW, FLOYD LEE D
City Councilman, San Diego, Calif.
b. Wichita Falls, Tex, 1/20/33; s. William Frank Morrow and Lillian Shipp M; m. 6/26/54 to Marlene Petersen; c. Darlene, Shawn and Lance. Educ: Univ. Tex, B.B.A, 57, LL.B, 59; Phi Alpha Delta. Polit. & Govt. Pos: Dep. city attorney, San Diego, Calif, 63-65, city councilman, 65-; mem, San Diego Co. Dem. Cent. Cmt, 64-65. Bus. & Prof. Pos: Attorney, Ryan Aeronaut. Co, 59-63; sr. partner, Morrow and Young, 65- Mil. Serv: Entered as Pvt, Marine Corps, 51, released as Sgt, 54, after serv. in 1st Marine Div, Korea; Korean Campaign Ribbon with 3 Battle Stars; Good Conduct, Nat. Defense Serv. and UN Serv. Medals. Mem: San Diego Bar Asn; Calif. & Tex. State Bar Asns; San Diego Exchange Club; co. chmn, March of Dimes; YMCA. Rel: Lutheran. Mailing Add: 7132 Belden, San Diego, Calif. 92111.

MORROW, HUGH, III D
Ala. State Sen.
B. Birmingham, Ala, 11/28/31; s. Hugh Morrow and Dorothy Thomas M; m. 7/50/60 to Jane Kaul; c. Hugh, IV, Libby Kaul and Dorothy Anne. Educ: Univ. Ala; Univ. of the South. Polit. & Govt. Pos: Ala. State Rep, 58-66; Ala. State Sen, 67- Bus. & Prof. Pos: Investment banking bus, 51-52 & 54-; v.pres. and dir, City Nat. Bank of Birmingham, 65-67; pres, Mid-South Co, Inc, 68- Mil. Serv: Army, 52-54. Mem: Mason; Shrine. Rel: Independent Presbyterian. Legal Res: 3412 Brookwood Rd, Birmingham, Ala. 35223. Mailing Add: 607 City National Bank Building, Birmingham, Ala. 35203.

MORROW, JAMES ANTHONY 'JIM' D
Miss. State Rep.
b. Clovis, N.Mex, 9/22/23; single. Polit. & Govt. Pos: Miss. State Rep, 52- Bus. & Prof. Pos: Farmer; lawyer; automobile dealer; merchant seaman. Mem: Am. Legion; 40 et 8; Mason. Rel: Episcopal. Mailing Add: P.O. Box 73, Brandon, Miss. 39042. (1967)

MORROW, ROBERT EMERY D
b. San Louis Obispo, Calif, 9/29/94; s. Robert Powell Morrow and Janie Zerelda Elkins; m. 9/21/51 to Doris Dian Richardson; c. Robert F. Morrow and Carol Jean (Mrs. Cotten). Educ: High Sch, Selma, Calif, 10-14; Spec. Mil. Sch, Galveston, Tex, 18. Polit. & Govt. Pos: Constable, Owens-Wikeiup, Ariz, 27-28, Justice of the Peace, 28-29; Ariz. State Rep, 30-41; Ariz. State Sen, 52-66; mem, Colo. River Adv. Cmt; chmn. spec. water cmt, Mohave Co. C. of C, 67-68. Bus. & Prof. Pos: Stock rancher, 12-27; horticulturist, 14-19; real estate broker, 27- Mil. Serv: Entered Marine Corps, 17, released as Pvt, 19, after serv. in 75th Co. Sixth Marine Corps, Argonne-Champaigne, Ninth French Army Corps and Von Steuban Ribbons; Purple Heart. Publ: '100 Year History of Mohave County Law Makers', Mohave Co. Miner, 12/68. Rel: Methodist. Mailing Add: P.O. Box 870 Old Port, Kingman, Ariz. 86401.

MORSE, ELIZABETH ANN 'BETTY' D
b. Sandcreek, Mich, 8/12/09; d. Arch L. Knox and Alberta Black K; m. 6/4/27 to Frank H. Morse; c. Beverly (Mrs. Clement), Joyce (Mrs. Packard) and David. Educ: High Sch. Polit. & Govt. Pos: Mem, Co. and Dem. Women's Club; alternate del, Dem. Nat. Conv, 64; del, Mich. State Conv, many times. Bus. Pos: Real Estate Saleslady, Pifer Real Estate Co. Mem: Eastern Star 224, Fairfield; Fairfields Garden Club; mem, Bd. of Econ. Opportunity. Rel: Protestant. Mailing Add: 6603 Packard Rd, Morenci, Mich. 49256. (1967)

MORSE, FRANK BRADFORD R
U.S. Rep, Mass.
b. Lowell, Mass, 8/7/21; s. Frank Young Morse and Inez Turnbull Coffin M; m. 5/7/55 to Vera Francesca Cassilly; c. Susanna Francesca and Anthony Bradford. Educ: Boston Univ, B.S, 48, LL.B, 49; Sigma Alpha Epsilon. Hon. D.Sc, Lowell Tech. Inst. Polit. & Govt. Pos: City councilman, Lowell, Mass, 52-53; attorney, U.S. Senate Cmt. on Armed Serv, 53-54; exec. secy. and chief asst. to Sen. Leverett Saltonstall, 55-58; dep. admin, Vets. Admin, 58-60; U.S. Rep, Mass, currently. Bus. & Prof. Pos: Law clerk, Chief Justice-Supreme Judicial Court of Mass, 49; attorney-at-law, Lowell, 49-53; faculty mem, Boston Univ, 49-53. Mil. Serv: Entered as Pvt, Army, 42, released as 2nd Lt, 46. Mem: U.S-Mexican Interparliamentary Group, Int. Parliamentary Union Sponsor, the Atlantic Coun; Am. Bar Asn; Am. Legion; VFW; Elks. Legal Res: 476 Beacon St, Lowell, Mass. 01850. Mailing Add: 301 Cannon House Office Building, Washington, D.C. 20515. (see addenda)

MORSE, GEORGE C. R
Vt. State Sen.
b. Danville, Vt, 12/21/92; m. to Betty Beaton; c. Two sons. Educ: Lowell Commercial Col, grad. Polit. & Govt. Pos: Sch. dir, 20; town auditor, 20-40; justice of peace, 28-; Vt. State Rep, 45 & 47; v.chmn, Caledonia City Rep. Cmt; Vt. State Sen, 49- Bus. & Prof. Pos: Fuel dealer and farmer. Mil. Serv: Pfc, Battery B, 302 F.A, World War I. Mem: Co of C.(past pres. and treas, Danville Chap, 34-); Northeast. Develop. Asn; Am. Legion (past comdr. and adj); Danville Grange (past master); Danville Green Cemetery Asn. (trustee and pres). Rel: Congregational. Mailing Add: Danville, Vt. 05829. (1967)

MORSE, MACY ELKINS D
Secy, N.H. Dem. State Exec. Cmt.
b. Molalla, Ore, 1/25/21; d. Robert Joseph Elkins and Nina Dunton E; m. 1/3/44 to Paul Henry Morse; c. Michael, Paul, Rodney, Suzanne, Gregory, Loren, William, John, Robert, Nina, Peter, James and Matthew. Educ: Ore. State Col, 2 years; Ore. Col. of Educ, grad, 41. Polit. & Govt. Pos: Secy, Dem. Women's Club, Nashua, N.H, 65-66; dir, Commun. Action Prog, Hillsboro Co. Off. Econ. Opportunity, 66; secy, Dem. Assocs. for Thought and Action, 66-67; alternate del, Dem. Nat. Conv, 68; secy, N.H. Dem. State Exec. Cmt, 68- Bus. & Prof. Pos: Sales rep, Pac. Tel. and Tel. Co, 41-44; teacher, Nashua Pub. Schs, 65. Mailing Add: 10 Beacon St, Nashua, N.H. 03060.

MORSE, MURIEL A. D
Vt. State Rep.
b. Jay, Vt, 8/14/02; m. to Fred Morse; c. Two. Educ: Jay Schs. Polit. & Govt. Pos: Town auditor, 47- Vt. State Rep, 65- Bus. & Prof. Pos: Housewife. Rel: Methodist. Mailing Add: RFD 2, Box 82, North Troy, Vt. 05859.

MORSE, RICHARD A. R
V.Chmn, N.H. Rep. State Cmt.
b. Manchester, N.H, 10/7/29; s. E.A. Morse and Rena Philbrick M; m. 10/16/65 to Maxine L. Katz. Educ: Univ. N.H, A.B, 51; Harvard Law Sch, LL.B, 56. Polit. & Govt. Pos: Chmn, Charter Rev. Cmn, Manchester, N.H, 62-63; v.chmn, N.H. Rep. State Cmt, 65- Mil. Serv: Entered as 2nd Lt, Air Force, 51, released as 1st Lt, 53, after serv. in Far East Air Forces; Air Force Commendation Medal; Korean Serv. Medal; Air Force Res. Ribbon. Mem: Kiwanis; Am. Legion; Grange; VFW; Am. and N.H. Bar Asns. Rel: Methodist. Mailing Add: 299 N. Bay St, Manchester, N.H. 03101. (1967)

MORSE, ROBERT WARREN D
b. Boston, Mass, 5/25/21; s. Walter L. Morse and Ethel E. Prince M; m. 1/25/43 to Alice M. Cooper; c. Robert W, Jr, Pamela Dean and James Prince. Educ: Bowdoin Col, B.S, 43; Brown Univ, Sc.M, 46, Ph.D, 49; Sigma Xi. Polit. & Govt. Pos: Asst. Secy. of Navy for Research and Develop, 64-66; chmn, Interagency Cmt. on Oceanography, Fed. Coun. for Sci. and Tech, 64-66. Bus. & Prof. Pos: Asst. prof. physics, Brown Univ, 49-53, assoc. prof, 53-58, prof, 58-64, head dept, 60-62, dean of col, 62-64; chmn, Undersea Warfare Cmt, Nat. Acad. Sci, 62-64; pres, Case West. Reserve Univ, 66- Mil. Serv: Entered as Ens, Navy, 43, released as Lt, 46. Publ: Over forty scientific papers in low temperature physics and acoustics. Mem: Am. Acoustical Soc.(pres, 65-66); fel, Am. Physical Soc; fel, Am. Acad. of Arts and Sci. Mailing Add: Office of the President, Case Western Reserve University, University Circle, Cleveland, Ohio 44106.

MORSE, WALTER C. D
b. Enfield, N.H, 9/19/87; married; c. Two. Educ: Bus. Col. Polit. & Govt. Pos: N.H. State Rep, 61-68; selectman; past hwy. agent; past supvr, Checklist. Bus. & Prof. Pos: Supt, woolen mill. Rel: Protestant. Mailing Add: South St, Enfield, N.H. 03748. (1967)

MORSE, WAYNE LYMAN D
b. Madison, Wis, 10/20/00; s. Wilbur Frank Morse and Jessie White M; m. 6/18/24 to Mildred Martha Downie; c. Nancy (Mrs. Hugh Campbell), Judith (Mrs. Wade Eaton) and Amy (Mrs. John Bilich). Educ: Univ. Wis, Madison, Ph.B, 23, M.A, 24; Univ. Minn, Minneapolis, LL.B, 28; Columbia Univ, J.D, 32; Phi Kappa Phi; Scabbard and Blade; Gamma Eta Gamma; Pi Kappa Alpha. Hon. LL.D, Cornell Col, 46, Drake Univ, 47, Col. of South Jersey, 47, Centre Col. of Ky, 52, Am. Int. Col, 62 and Wilberforce Univ, 66; D.Jr.Sc, Suffolk Univ, 61; Pd.D, Salem Col, 65; D.C.L, Parsons Col, 65; D.H.L, Pac. Univ, 69. Polit. & Govt. Pos: Spec. asst. to Attorney Gen. U.S, 36-38; chmn, President's Emergency Bd, U.S. Govt, 41; pub. mem, War Labor Bd, 41-44; U.S. Sen, Ore, 45-69; U.S. Rep, UN Gen. Assembly, 60; chmn, President's Spec. Bd. on Atlantic and Gulf Maritime Indust. Dispute, 63; mem, President's Spec. Emergency Bd, East Coast Longshoremen's Dispute, 65; mem, President's Spec. Bd. of Inquiry, Steel Indust. Labor Dispute, 65; chmn, President's Emergency Bd, Airlines Dispute, 66; chmn, President's Spec. Bd, R.R. Dispute, 67; del, Dem. Nat. Conv, 68. Bus. & Prof. Pos: Instr. argumentation and debate, Univ. Wis, 23-24; instr. argumentation and debate, Univ. Minn, 24-28; asst. prof. law, Univ. Ore, 29-31, dean and prof. law, 31-44; coastwide arbitrator, West Coast Maritime Indust, 35-41. Mil. Serv: 2nd Lt, Field Artil, Army Res, 23-30. Publ: 'Survey of the Grand Jury System,' Ore. Law Rev, 31; The Administration of Criminal Justice in Ore, (with Ronald H. Beattie), Univ. Ore, 32; Attorney General's Survey of Release Procedures, Fed. Industs. Press, Ft. Leavenworth, Kans, 40. Mem: Order of the Coif; SAR; Mason; Shrine; Ore-Wash. Farmers Union; Nat. Grange; hon. nat. chmn, Lawyers Cmt. Against War in Vietnam; mem. bd. trustees, Pan Am. Develop. Found. Distinguished Serv. Award, Univ. Ore, 63. Rel: Congregational. Legal Res: 595 Crest Dr, Eugene, Ore. 97405. Mailing Add: Apt. 312-S, 2500 Virginia Ave. N.W, Washington, D.C. 20037.

MORTON, AMBROSE GAINES R
b. Knoxville, Tenn, 7/17/32; s. Benjaman Andrew Morton, Jr. and Edith Jenks Gaines M; m. 7/17/49 to Patricia Sue Sterchi; c. Jenks Whitaker, Andrew Sterchi and Benjaman Karnes. Educ: Univ. Tenn. Polit. & Govt. Pos: Tenn. State Rep, until 66. Bus. & Prof. Pos: Pres, Ft. Sanders Serv. Station, Inc, 60-; pres, Vol. Helicopters Inc, 63-; mem. bd. dirs, Tenn. State Mental Health Asn, 65- Mem: Fraternal Order of Police; Civil Air Patrol; Aircraft Owners & Pilots Asn; Knox Co. Bd. Cmnrs; Tenn. Law Enforcement Officers Asn; Knox Co. Dep; Elks; West Knox Sertoma; Cherokee Country Club; Senators Club; Nat. Soc. of State Legis; Knox Co. Rep. Club. All-State football and mem, state champion track team, Knoxville High; City swimming champion, 3 years; heavyweight champion, Golden Gloves. Rel: Episcopal. Mailing Add: 416 Cherokee Blvd, Knoxville, Tenn. 37919. (1967)

MORTON, HUGH R
b. Fall River, Mass, 9/10/06; s. James M. Morton, Jr. and Nancy J. B. Brayton M; m. 9/11/35 to Anne Marshall Boos; c. William Hugh Madison and Nancy (Mrs. Alec B. Dawson). Educ: Williams Col, B.A, 27; Trinity Col, Cambridge Univ, Eng, 28; Harvard Law Sch, LL.B, 31; Chi Psi. Polit. & Govt. Pos: Mass. State Rep, 47-48; chmn, Fall River Licensing Bd, Mass, 52; state committeeman, Mass. Rep. Party, Second Bristol Dist, 52; Asst. Attorney Gen, Mass, 52-58; del, Rep. Nat. Conv, 60, alternate del, 68; chmn. exec. cmt, Mass. Rep. State Cmt, 60-62; chmn, Mass. Civil Serv. Cmn, 62- Bus. & Prof. Pos: Lawyer, Warner, Stackpole, Bradlee & Cabot, Boston, 32-35; partner, Law Firm of Lowell & Morton, 35-42; self-employed lawyer, Fall River, 45-; pres, H & M/VAPKOOL, Ltd, Freeport, L.I, 68- Mil. Serv: Entered as Lt, Navy, 42, released as Lt. Comdr, 46. Mem: Am. and Mass. Bar Asns; Mass. Trial Lawyers Asn; AF&AM; Union Club of Boston; Quequechan Club of Fall River; Acoaxet Golf Club; Am. Legion (post comdr, John Foster Stafford Post 314); trustee, Fall River Home for Aged; dir, Fall River Hist. Soc. Rel: Congregational. Mailing Add: 59 Greenlawn St, Fall River, Mass. 02720.

MORTON, ROGERS CLARK BALLARD R
U.S. Rep, Md.
b. Louisville, Ky, 9/19/14; s. David C. Morton and Mary Ballard M; m. 5/27/39 to Anne Jones; c. David and Anne. Educ: Yale Univ, A.B, 37. Polit.

& Govt. Pos: U.S. Rep, Md, 62-; del, Rep. Nat. Conv, 68; chmn, Rep. Nat. Cmt, 69- Bus. & Prof. Pos: Former farmer and businessman; experienced in bus. mgt. and pub. rels; v.pres, Ballard and Ballard, Louisville, Ky, 46-47, pres, 47-51, v.pres, after co. merged with Pillsbury Co, 51-52, presently dir. and mem. exec. cmt; mem, Civilian Adv. Bd, Air Training Command of Air Force; dir, Atlas Chem. Industs, Inc. Mil. Serv: Entered as Pvt, Army, 41, released as Capt, 45, after serv. in Field Artil. Mem: Soc. of Cincinnati; trustee, Md. Agr. Soc. Talbot Co; bd. gov. and bd. visitors, Wash. Col, Chesterton, Md; Pendennis Club, Louisville and Minneapolis; Chesapeake Bay Yacht Club. Rel: Episcopal. Legal Res: R.D.1, Easton, Md. 21601. Mailing Add: U.S. House of Representatives, Washington, D.C. 20515.

MORTON, THRUSTON B. R
b. Louisville, Ky, 8/19/07; s. David Cummings Morton and Mary Harris Ballard; m. 4/18/31 to Belle Clay Lyons; c. Thruston B, Jr. and Clay Lyons; four grandchildren. Educ: Yale Univ, A.B, 29; Alpha Delta Phi. Polit. & Govt. Pos: U.S. Rep, Ky, 46-52 & 56-69, mem. Sen. Cmt. on D.C. and Spec. Cmt. on Aging, 67-69, chmn, Rep. Sen. Campaign Cmt, 63-69, former mem, Finance and Commerce and Rep. Policy Cmts; Asst. Secy of State, 53-56; chmn, Rep. Nat. Cmt, 59-61. Bus. & Prof. Pos: V.pres, pres. and chmn. of bd, Ballard & Ballard Co, 36-51. Mil. Serv: Entered as Lt.(jg), Navy, 41, released as Lt. Comdr, 46, after serv. in Pac. Fleet, holding three separate commands; Comdr, Naval Res, 48. Mem: Adv. Cmt, Who's Who in Am. Politics; Am. Legion; VFW. Rel: Episcopal. Mailing Add: 1416 Willow, Louisville, Ky. 40204.

MORTON, WARREN ALLEN R
Wyo. State Rep.
b. Birmingham, Ala, 3/22/24; s. Lindley C. Morton and Ruth Goddard M; m. 9/28/46 to Katharine Hancock Allen; c. Frederick Lee, Allen Salisbury, Robert Coleman and Warren Goddard. Educ: Yale Univ, chem. eng, 45; Delta Psi. Polit. & Govt. Pos: Wyo. State Rep, Natrona Co, 67- Bus. & Prof. Pos: petrol. engr, Morton and Sons, 46-52; mgr, M.K.M. Oil Co, 52-66. Mil. Serv: Entered as A/S, Naval Res, 43, released as Ens, 46. Mem: Am. Petrol. Inst; Rocky Mountain Oil and Gas Asn. Rel: Episcopal. Mailing Add: 241 E. 12th St, Casper, Wyo. 82601.

MOSBACHER, EMIL, JR. 'BUS' R
Chief of Protocol, Dept. of State
b. Mt. Vernon, N.Y. 4/1/22; s. Emil Mosbacher and Gertrude Schwartz M; m. 11/24/50 to Patricia Ryan; c. Emil III, Richard Bruce and John David. Educ: Dartmouth Col, B.A, 43; Gamma Delta Chi. Hon. M.A, Dartmouth Col, 63; LL.D, L.I. Univ, 69. Polit. & Govt. Pos: Chief of Protocol, Dept. of State 69- Bus. & Prof. Pos: Trustee, Lenox Hill Hosp, 57-, chmn. joint conf. cmt, 67-, mem. exec. cmt, 67-; dir, Lily Tulip Cup Corp, 62-68; trustee, Dollar Savings Bank, 64-69, mem. exam. cmt, 67-69; dir, Police Athletic League, 67-69, Nat. Life Ins. Co, 68-69, Abercrombie & Fitch Co, 68-69 and United Merchants & Mfg. Inc, 68-69; real estate investor and oil gas producer, N.Y, currently. Mil. Serv: Navy, 43-46, Lt, with serv. in Pac, V.I. and Wash, D.C. Mem: Choate Club N.Y.(dir, 64); Choate Assocs; Westchester Co. chmn, Choate Fund for the Future Drive, 65-66; Choate Father's Asn.(v.pres, 66, pres, 67-); trustee, Choate Sch, 68-; Dartmouth Col. Class 43 (chmn, 59-64); co-chmn, Dartmouth Col. Capital Gifts Campaign, 59-60; Dartmouth Col. Clubs N.Y. and Westchester (dir); Dartmouth Col. Nat. Alumni (chmn. third century fund, 67-); Rye Country Day Sch. Father's Asn.(pres, 64-66); Real Estate Bd. N.Y; Bronx Bd. Trade; N.Y. C. of C; Westchester Co. Asn; New Rochelle Downtown Asn; Independent Petroleum Asn. Am; N.Y. Yacht Club; Ida Lewis Yacht Club; Storm Trysail Club; Royal Corinthian Yacht Club; Royal Ocean Racing Club; Noroton Yacht Club; Westchester Country Club; Am. Yacht Club; Univ. Club; Yacht Racing Asn. L.I. Sound (past exec. cmt. mem); Jr. Yacht Racing Asn. L.I. Sound (past secy. and exec. cmt. mem); Mamaroneck Frostbite Asn.(chmn, 58-61, founders cmt); U.S. Olympic Yachting Cmt; Int. One Design Class (past cmt. mem); Sailboat Training Facility; N.Am. Yacht Racing Union Olympic Cmt; U.S. Int. Sailing Asn; Int. Star Class; Mayor's Sports Cmn; Am. Red Cross (co-chmn, N.Y.C, 62). Rel: Episcopal. Legal Res: 384 Rosedale Ave, White Plains, N.Y. 10605. Mailing Add: 2650 Virginia Ave. N.W, Washington, D.C. 20037.

MOSBERG, IRVING D
b. N.Y.C, 5/6/08; m. to Eva G; c. Harold Jay. Educ: N.Y. Univ. Sch. of Commerce; St. John's Col. Sch. of Law, 30. Polit. & Govt. Pos: Mem, Local Sch. Bd. Dist, 50-54; criminal law investr, Queens Co, N.Y, 54; past pres, South Side 12th Assembly Dist. Dem. Club, Inc; past recording secy, financial secy. and second v.pres, United Exec. Dem. Club, Inc; N.Y. State Sen, until 68; asst. dist. attorney, Queens Co, 54- Bus. & Prof. Pos: Lawyer, Forest Hills, N.Y. Mem: Queens Co. Bar Asn; Queens Lawyers' Club of the Fedn. of Jewish Charities (dir); counsel to Jewish Commun. Center of Ozone Park and Rockwood Park Jewish Commun. Center; NAACP; Laurelton Jewish Center; B'nai B'rith; K. of P; Elks. Rel: Jewish. Mailing Add: 141-05 228th St, Laurelton, N.Y. 11948. (1967)

MOSELEY, DOUGLAS DEWAYNE R
b. Bowling Green, Ky, 3/24/28; s. J Lee Moseley and Eva Moore M; m. 1954 to Betty Jean Wyant; c. J Lewis, Rebekah Ellen and Leslie Ann. Educ: West. Ky. Univ, 46-49; Ky. Wesleyan Col, A.B, 52; Emory Univ, B.D, 58. Polit. & Govt. Pos: Listed with Rep. Nat. Cmt. Speakers Bur, campaign speaker for Rep. Party; alternate del, Rep. Nat. Conv, 64; mem, Ky. State Personnel Bd, 68-69, v.chmn, 69- Bus. & Prof. Pos: Minister, Methodist Church, 46-66; asst. to pres, Lindsey Wilson Col, 64- Mem: Pres, Ky. Jr. Col. Asn, 64-65. After Dinner Speaker. Mailing Add: Lindsey Wilson College, Columbia, Ky. 42728.

MOSER, FRED J. D
b. Plum City, Wis, 5/2/98. Educ: Univ. of Wis, 27, Ph.B. Polit. & Govt. Pos: Wis. State Assemblyman, 64-66; alderman; chmn, Co. Sch. Cmn. Bus. & Prof. Pos: Retired sch. adminstr, 26 years; teacher; guid. dir. Mil. Serv: Vet. Mailing Add: Cumberland, Wis, 54829.

MOSER, JOHN RICHARD R
Chmn, Butler Co. Rep. Exec. Cmt, Ohio
b. Hamilton, Ohio, 3/5/27; s. John Jacob Moser and Magdalena Buchmann M; m. 6/28/52 to Shirley N. Keats; c. Linda Kay, Janet Lee and Donald K. Educ: Miami Univ, Ohio, B.A, 50; Univ. of Cincinnati Col. of Law, LL.B, 53; Acacia. Polit. & Govt. Pos: Asst. prosecuting attorney, Butler Co, Ohio, 56-64; pres, Young Rep. of Hamilton, 59; chmn, Butler Co. Rep. Exec. Cmt, 60-; del, Rep. Nat. Conv, 64. Mil. Serv: Entered as Pvt, Army, 45, released as Sgt, 47, after serv. in 4th Armored Cavalry, ETO. Publ: Miscellaneous law review articles while at Col. of Law, Univ. of Cincinnati. Mem: Secy, Butler Co. Bar Asn, 56; Ohio and Am. Bar Asns; Am. Trial Lawyers Asn; F&AM; Scottish Rite; Shrine; Toastmasters; Exchange Club; chmn, Crippled Childrens Soc. Financial Drive, Butler Co, 66; Am. Legion; chmn, Nat. Found. Financial Drive, Hamilton, 59 & 60; chmn, Heart Fund, Hamilton, 59-60. Rel: Presbyterian; Elder. Mailing Add: 900 Sanders Dr, Hamilton, Ohio 45013.

MOSER, RAYMOND R
Mem, Calif. Rep. State Cent. Cmt.
b. Sutton, Nebr, 1/17/31; s. Theodore Moser (deceased) and Clara Hofmann M; m. 6/25/60 to Sandra Gillis; c. Mark Raymond and Gail Adele. Educ: Stockton Col, A.A, 51; Univ. Calif, Berkeley, B.S, 53; Big 'C' Soc; Kappa Sigma. Polit. & Govt. Pos: Pres, Elmwood-Claremont Rep. Assembly, Calif, 61; v.pres, Alameda Rep. Assembly, 65; Rep. nominee for Calif. State Assembly, 14th Assembly Dist, 66, 68; mem, Calif. Rep. State Cent. Cmt, 67-; exofficio mem, Alameda Co. Rep. Cent. Cmt, 66-69; v.chmn, Eastbay Rep. Alliance, Alameda Co, Calif, 69. Bus. & Prof. Pos: Salesman, Values, Inc. Real Estate, 57-59; owner, Crest Investments, 60-67, Ray Moser & Assoc, 67-69. Mil. Serv: Entered as Officer Cand, Navy, 53, released as Lt.(jg), 56 after serv. in U.S.S. Chemuno, West. Pac. and W.Coast; Lt. Comdr, Naval Res, 62. Mem: Res. Officers Asn; Rotary; Navy League. Rel: Protestant. Mailing Add: 913 Otis Dr, Alameda, Calif. 94501.

MOSES, CARL EUGENE R
Alaska State Rep.
b. Santa Cruz, Calif, 7/16/29; s. Lewis Orion Moses and Olga Carlson M; m. 10/21/53 to Christine Ann Steffensen; c. Lewis Orion and Arline Jean. Educ: Univ. Wash, 54-57. Polit. & Govt. Pos: Alaska State Rep, 12th Dist, 65- Bus. & Prof. Pos: Owner and mgr, Carl's Commercial Co, 60- Mil. Serv: Entered as Pvt, Army, 51, released as Cpl, 53, after serv. in 867 Anti-Aircraft Artil, Alaska. Rel: Russian Orthodox. Legal Res: Unalaska, Alaska. 99685. Mailing Add: P.O. Box 2199, Juneau, Alaska 99801. (1967)

MOSES, ROBERT R
b. New Haven, Conn, 12/18/88; s. Emanuel Moses and Bella M; m. 10/3/66 to Mary A. Grady; c. Barbara (Mrs. Richard J. Olds) and Jane (Mrs. Frederic A. Collins). Educ: Yale, B.A, 09; Oxford, B.A. with honors in Jurisp, 11, M.A, 13; Columbia Univ, Ph.D. in Polit. Sci, 14. Hon. A.M, Yale, 36; LL.D, Syracuse Univ, 36, Union Col, 38, Bates Col, 45, Princeton Univ, 47, Hofstra Col, 48, Columbia Univ, 52, Yale, 52, Harvard, 53, L.I. Univ, 54, Pratt Inst, 55 and N.Y. Law Sch, 61; D.E, N.Y. Univ, 50, Univ. Mich, 53, Manhattan Col, 54, Polytech. Inst. Brooklyn, 56, St. John's Univ, 59 and Univ. Buffalo, 59; L.H.D, Colgate Univ. and Fordham Univ, 59; hon. fel, Wadham Col, 60; D.F.A, Niagara Univ, 61; D.P.A, Univ. R.I, 64. Polit. & Govt. Pos: Munic. investr, N.Y.C, 13; chief of staff, N.Y. State Reconstruction Cmn, 19-21; secy. coalition cmt, N.Y.C. Munic. Campaign, 21; secy, N.Y. State Asn, 21-26; mem, State Fine Arts Cmn, 24-27; pres, L.I. State Park Cmn. and chmn, State Coun. of Parks, 24-63; chmn. Metrop. Conf. on Parks, 26-30; Secy. of State, N.Y, 27-28; mem, State Reorgn. Cmn, 27-28; chmn, N.Y. Cmt. on Pub. Improv, 27-28; Moreland Cmnr. to investigate State Banking Dept, 29; rep. mem, L.I. Sanit. Cmn, 30; mem, N.Y. Cmn, Chicago Fair, 31; chmn, Emergency Pub. Works Cmn, 33; chmn, Jones Beach State Pkwy. Authority and Bethpage Park Authority, 33-63; Rep. cand. for Gov, N.Y, 34; mem, Triborough Bridge Authority, 34, chmn, 36; sole mem, Henry Hudson Pkwy. Authority and Marine Pkwy. Authority, 34-38; N.Y.C. Park Cmnr, 34-60; del, Rep. Nat. Conv, 36; exec. off, N.Y.C. World's Fair Cmn, 36-40; del, N.Y. State Constitutional Conv, 38; chmn, Cmt. on Hwy, Pkwy. and Grade Crossings, 38; sole mem, N.Y. City Pkwy. Authority, 38; chmn, State Cmt. on Postwar Employ, 42; mem, N.Y. State Postwar Pub. Works Cmn, 42; mem, City Planning Cmn, 42-60; chief exec. off, N.Y.C. Tunnel Authority, 45-46; chmn, Consolidated Triborough Bridge and N.Y.C. Tunnel Authority, 46-48; chmn, Mayor's Emergency Cmt. on Housing and Mayor's Cmt. for Permanent World Capitol, 46; coordinator, N.Y.C. Construction, 46-60; chmn, Mayor's Slum Clearance Cmt, 48-60; mem, N.Y.C. Traffic Cmn, 49; adv, Nassau Co. Transit Cmn, 49; mem, L.I. R.R. Cmn, 50; chmn, Power Authority of State of N.Y, 54-63; coordinator of arterial projs, N.Y, 60-66; pres, N.Y. World's Fair 1964-1965 Corp, 60-67; secy, Temporary State Cmn. on Protection and Preservation of the Atlantic Shorefront, 62; mem, Mitchel Field Adv. Cmt, 63-64; mem, N.Y.C. Transportation Coun, 66- Bus. & Prof. Pos: Consult. arterial plan, Pittsburgh Regional Planning Asn, 39; Centennial lectr, Duke Univ, 39; Godkin lectr, Harvard, 39; Stafford Little lectr, Princeton, 40; employed by State of Mich. and Huron-Clinton Metrop. Authority to rev. hwy. plans for Detroit region, 42; coordinator, Surv. of Congested War Prod. Areas for Army and Navy Munitions Bd, 43; dir, Postwar Plan for Portland, Ore, 43; dir. arterial plan, Baltimore, Md, 44; consult, Ill. Superhwy. Cmn, 44; dir. arterial plan, New Orleans, La, 46; lectr, Miami Univ, 46; consult. on reconstruction of Postwar Germany, 47; consult. on arterial syst, Caracas, Venezuela, 48; chief consult. on pub. works, Cmn. on Orgn. of the Exec. Br. of U.S. Govt, 48; consult, arterial syst, Hartford, Conn, 49; consult, Int. Basic Econ. Corp, 50; dir. of report, São Paulo, Brazil, 50; report on expressway prog, New Britain, Conn, 51; dir. of report, Canton, Ohio, 52; report on new city hall, Flint, Mich, 53; lectr, Syracuse Univ, Swarthmore, Cornell and Harvard, 54; Alice Holden lectr, Smith Col, 57; Phillips lectr, Springfield, Mass. Adult Educ. Coun, 57; lectr, Cornell, 59; Conroy fel, St. Paul's Sch, Concord, N.H, 60; Lovett lectr, Pierson Col, Yale Univ, 60; Herman G. James lectr, Ohio Univ, 61; consult. to chmn, Metrop. Transportation Authority, 68- Publ: Weekly columnist and writer for mag. and newspapers on govt, parks, pub. works, housing and recreation. Mem: Trustee, Hofstra Col, 44; exec. cmt, Manhattan Col, 56-; dir, Lincoln Center for Performing Arts, 60-; bd. trustees, People-to-People, 61; chmn, Am. Pub. Works Asn, 64; bd. trustees, Hall of Sci, N.Y.C, 64-67; Nat. Cmt. for Immigration Reform, 65; bd, Make N.Y. Beautiful, 65; Cmt. for Govt. of the People, 66; mem-at-lg, Gr. N.Y. Boy Scouts Coun, 66; life mem, N.Y. Bldg. Cong, 66; Fordham Univ. Coun, 67; Phi Beta Kappa; Players, N.Y.C, Southward Ho, Bay Shore, N.Y. and Lotos, N.Y.C. Clubs. Am. Scenic and Historic Preservation Soc. Gold Medal, Columbia Univ. Medal of Merit and St. Nicholas Soc. Medal, 37; Fairmount Park Art Asn. Medal, Garden Club of Am. Medal and Roosevelt Mem. Medal, 38; Lincoln Award, Lincoln High Sch,

Brooklyn, Mass, Hort. Soc. White Medal and Bartlett Award, 39; Nat. Inst. Arts and Letters Medal, Am. Inst. Steel Construction John Lloyd Kimbrough Medal and Moles' Annual Plaque Award, 41; Rotary Club Distinguished Serv. Award, 43; Nassau Co. Bar Asn. Medallion and Nat. Sculpture Soc. for Civic Achievements Medal, 45; Nat. Inst. Soc. Sci. Gold Medal, 46; N.Y. Acad. of Pub. Educ. Medal, 50; Soc. des Architects Diplomes Medal, William Randolph Hearst Mem. Gold Medal of Gr. N.Y. Civic Center Asn. and Col. of City of N.Y. Finley Award, 51; Order of Cruzeiro Do Sol, Brazil, Bd. of Educ, City of N.Y. and Sachs Found. for Commun. Serv. Medal and W. Side Asn. of Commerce of City of N.Y. Medal, 52; Stevens Inst. Tech. Honor Award, 53; Gr. N.Y. Coun. Boy Scouts Silver Beaver Award, Metrop. A.A.U. First Gold Medal for Serv. and Holland Soc. Distinguished Achievement Medal, 54; Lord and Taylor Award, Freedoms Found. at Valley Forge George Wash. Honor Medal and Gov. of L.I. Award, 55; Named New Yorker of the Year, N.Y. Daily News, 56; Nat. Coun. of State Garden Clubs, Inc. Gold Medal, 57; L.I. Press Distinguished Serv. Award, 58; Hort. Soc. of N.Y, Inc. Spec. Award, Munic. Art Soc. Medal of Honor and Allied Professions' Medal of A.I.A, 59; Manhattan Medal Award, 60; Brooklyn Botanic Garden Forsythia Award, Bronx Bd. of Trade Pub. Affairs Award and Sales Exec. Club of N.Y. Applause Award, 61; N.Y. Mirror Welfare Fund Humanitarian Award, 62; N.Y. State Bldg. and Construction Trades Coun. Distinguished Serv. Award, Fifth Ave. Asn. Honor Award, Am. Inst. Consult. Engrs. Award of Merit, Springfield, Ill. Citizens' Cmt. Lincoln Award and God & Country Award of Bus. & Prfnl. Men's Chap. 37, St. George Asn, 63; Nat. Sculpture Soc. Spec. Citation, Nat. Arts Club Cert. of Merit, Ave. of the Americas Asn. Outstanding Achievement Award, N.Y.C. Baseball Fedn. 1963 Award, Boy Scouts Silver Buffalo, Am. Hort. Soc. Liberty Hyde Bailey Medal, Jordanian Kawkab Decoration of the First Order, Hashemite Kingdom of Jordan and City of N.Y. Medal, 64; N.Y.C. Police Dept, St. George Asn. Golden Rule Award, Lions Club of N.Y. Outstanding Achievement Award, Kings Co. Chap. of N.Y. Soc. Prfnl. Engrs. Award for construction of the Verrazano-Narrows Bridge, Legion of Valor Testimonial, Rank of Comdr, Order of Merit of Repub. of Italy, Toastmasters Int. Golden Gavel Award, Bishop Walter P. Kellenberg Medal and Bene Maerenti Medal from Francis Cardinal Spellman, 65; Fordham Civic Asn. Golden Age Man of the Year Award and St. Peter's Col. Alumni Asn. Distinguished Citizen Award, 66; Brooklyn Heights Award, Construction Man of the Year Award, City Club of N.Y. Distinguished New Yorker Medal and Suffolk Co. Coun, Boy Scouts Distinguished Citizen Award, 67; Nassau-Suffolk Hosp. Coun. Theodore Roosevelt Award and Nassau Co. Recreation and Parks Soc. Achievement Award, 68. Hon. mem, Am. Inst. of Architects, 52, Am. Soc. of Landscape Architects, 60, Am. Pub. Works Asn, 60 and N.Y. State Co. Judges Asn, 65; hon. fel, Nat. Sculpture Soc, 60; hon. chmn, Richmondtown Restoration, 63 and Prospect Park Centennial, 66; winner, Gen. Motors Better Hwy. Award Contest, 53; hon. citizen, São Paulo, Brazil, 54. Mailing Add: 1 Gracie Terr, New York, N.Y. 10028.

MOSES, WILLIAM PRESTON R
Chmn, Contra Costa Co. Rep. Cent. Cmt, Calif.
b. San Francisco, Calif, 9/29/17; s. Preston S. Moses and Marie Calderella M; m. 5/15/44 to Margaret Walker; c. Preston. Educ: Univ. of Calif; Hastings Col. of Law; San Francisco Law Sch. Polit. & Govt. Pos: Mem, Contra Costa Co. Rep. Cent. Cmt, Calif, 52-58 & 64-66, chmn, 66-; mem. and pres, Contra Costa Co. Sch. Bd, 63-; mem. exec. cmt, Calif. State Rep. Cent. Cmt, currently; mem, Calif. State Water Cmn, 67- Bus. & Prof. Pos: Partner, Pelletreau, Gowen, Moses and Porlier, San Pablo, Calif, 60- Mil. Serv: Entered as Cadet, Air Force, 41, released as 2nd Lt, 45, after serv. in S.Pac. Mem: Pres, Contra Costa Bar Asn, 58-59; Am. and Calif. Bar Asns; past comdr, Am. Legion; Elks; Eagles; Native Sons of Calif; past pres, Kiwanis. Rel: Protestant. Mailing Add: 5691 San Pablo Dam Rd, El Sobrante, Calif. 94806.

MOSHER, CHARLES ADAMS R
U.S. Rep, Ohio
b. DeKalb City, Ill, 5/7/06; m. 1929 to Harriet Johnson; c. Frederic A, Mary Jane. Educ: Oberlin Col, A.B, cum laude, 28. Polit. & Govt. Pos: Mem, Oberlin City Coun, Ohio, 45-50; Ohio State Sen, 51-60; v.chmn, Ohio Sch. Surv. Cmn, 54-55; Ohio Legis. Serv. Cmn, 55-59; U.S. Rep, Ohio, 60-; Oberlin Col. Bd. of Trustee, 64- Bus. & Prof. Pos: Employed on daily newspapers in Ill. and Wis, 29-40; pres, Oberlin Printing Co, publisher of Oberlin News-Tribune, 40-62. Legal Res: Oberlin, Ohio. Mailing Add: 4246 Warren St, Washington, D.C. 20016.

MOSHER, SOL R
Spec. Asst. to Secy. of Commerce for Cong. Rels, U.S. Dept. of Commerce
b. Chicago, Ill. 4/14/28; s. Jacob Mosher and Blanch Becker M; m. 11/1/53 to Cora E. Walker; c. Janice May and Caryn Anne. Educ: Kansas City Jr. Col, A.B, 47; Univ. Mo, Columbia, B.Journalism, 49; Sigma Delta Chi; Sigma Alpha Mu. Polit. & Govt. Pos: Admin. asst, Congressman Durward G. Hall, Mo, 61-69; Spec. Asst. to Secy. of Commerce for Cong. Rels, U.S. Dept. of Commerce, 69- Bus. & Prof. Pos: Sports Ed, Mo. Daily News Digest, Springfield, 54; news ed, Sta. KICK, 54-56; news ed, KYTV, 56-58; civic affairs mgr, C. of C, 58-60. Mil. Serv: Entered as Pvt, Army, 50, released as 1st Lt, 53, after serv. in 45th Div, Far East Command, 51-52. Mem: Bull Elephants; Mo. Soc. of Wash. Distinguished Serv. Award, Springfield C. of C. Legal Res: 3027 W. Madison, Springfield, Mo. 65802. Mailing Add: 5010 Althea Dr, Annandale, Va. 22003.

MOSHIER, TERRY ALLEN R
Chmn, Ga. Young Rep.
b. Omaha, Nebr, 7/18/36; s. Fredrick D. Moshier and Vivian Rhodes M; m. 10/6/65 to Mary Helen Riddle; c. Terry Allen, Jr. Educ: Carleton Col, B.A, 58; Univ. Nebr, M.S, 61; Sigma Xi. Polit. & Govt. Pos: Dir, Ga. Young Rep, 63-67, nat. committeeman, 67-68 and chmn, 68-; subcmt. chmn, Fulton Co. Rep. Exec. Cmt, 64-65; mem. awards cmt, Nat. Fedn. Young Rep, 67-69; elector, Ga. Rep. Party, 68; alternate del, Rep. Nat. Conv, 68; mem, Fifth Dist. Rep. Exec. Cmt, 68- Bus. & Prof. Pos: Tech. rep, Union Carbide Corp, 60-64; pres, Moshier Shoe Co, 64-67; regional sales rep, PPG Indust, 67- Mem: Soc. Paint Tech; Am. Chem. Soc; Nat. Paint Varnish & Lacquer Asn. Rel: United Presbyterian. Mailing Add: 653 Starlite Dr, Atlanta, Ga. 30305.

MOSHOFSKY, WILLIAM JAMES R
b. Beaverton, Ore, 3/30/23; s. Edward George Moshofsky and Sophia Lehman M; 1st m. to Cleda Nell Carpenter (deceased); 2nd m. 8/3/57 to Margaret Jean Utz; c. Mary Laneta, Brett William, Sally Ann and Michael James. Educ: Univ. Ore, B.S. and J.D; Alpha Tau Omega; Phi Kappa; Order of the Coif. Polit. & Govt. Pos: Mem, Legis. Counsel Staff, Ore. Legis, 55; metrop. chmn, Rockefeller for President and state co-chmn, Scranton for President, Ore. Primary, 64; alternate del, Rep. Nat. Conv, 68. Bus. & Prof. Pos: Mem. bd. of exam, Ore. State Bar, 57-60; asst. to Pres, Ga-Pac. Corp, 63-; mem. exec. cmt, Assoc. Ore. Industs, 64- Mil. Serv: Entered as Pvt, Army, 43, released as 1st Lt, 46, after serv. in 1st Inf. Div, ETO; recalled to active duty, Korean War, Army, 17 months; Bronze Star; ETO Ribbon and Victory Medal. Mem: Bd. of dirs, Portland C. of C, 64- and chmn, Legis. Coun, 63-65; chmn, Ore. Coun. on Crime & Delinquency; Kiwanis; Commun. Coun; City Club. Rel: Congregational. Mailing Add: 7680 S.W. Memory Lane, Portland, Ore, 97225. (1967)

MOSIER, LEO DeWITT DFL
Minn. State Sen.
b. Rogers, Nebr, 8/25/91; s. Franklin Stewart Mosier and Lulu Paden M; m. 12/22/16 to Caroline Marie Tschudy; c. Leo D, Jr. and Kathryn Eilene (Mrs. Hill). Educ: Northwest. Col. of Law, LL.B, 15. Polit. & Govt. Pos: Minn. State Rep, 48-62, chmn, Appropriations Cmt, Minn. State House of Rep, 57-60, Judiciary Cmt, 61-62 and Cities Cmt, 63-64; Minn. State Sen, 39th Dist, 62- Bus. & Prof. Pos: Pres, Constitution Protection Cmt, 63-66. Mil. Serv: Pvt, Minn. Nat. Guard, 6 years. Publ: Columnist, 'Dome Dairy,' Minneapolis Labor Review, 49-58; 'Legislative Look,' N. Minneapolis Post, 54-58; 'My Corner,' N. Minneapolis Post, 65-66. Mem: Minneapolis Typographical Union. Rel: Presbyterian. Mailing Add: 4340 Washburn Ave. N, Minneapolis, Minn. 55412.

MOSK, EDNA MITCHELL D
b. Winnipeg, Man, Can, 9/16/15; d. M.K. Mitchell and Katharine Blond M; m. 9/27/36 to Justice Stanley Mosk; c. Richard Mitchell. Educ: Univ. Calif, Los Angeles, 3 years; Phi Sigma Sigma. Polit. & Govt. Pos: Mem, Calif. Dem. State Cent. Cmt, 60-62; mem. exec. cmt, Econ. Opportunity Coun, San Francisco, 67-69; del, Dem. Nat. Conv, 68. Bus. & Prof. Pos: Real estate broker, 48-58. Mailing Add: 1200 California St, San Francisco, Calif. 94109.

MOSK, RICHARD MITCHELL D
b. Los Angeles, Calif, 5/18/39; s. Justice Stanley Mosk and Edna Mitchell; M; m. 3/21/64 to Sandra Lee Budnitz; c. Julie. Educ: Stanford Univ, A.B. with great distinction, 60; Harvard Law Sch, LL.B. cum laude, 63; Phi Beta Kappa; Pi Sigma Alpha; Theta Delta Chi. Polit. & Govt. Pos: Mem. staff, President's Cmn. on the Assassination of President Kennedy, 64; clerk, Calif. Supreme Court Justice Mathew Tobriner, 64-65; del, Dem. Nat. Conv, 68. Bus. & Prof. Pos: Attorney, Law Firm of Mitchell, Silberberg & Knupp, Los Angeles, Calif, 65- Mil. Serv: Entered as Airman, Air Force, 63, released as Airman 2/C, 64, after serv. in Calif. Air Nat. Guard; Lt, Naval Res, 65- Publ: 'The Use of Personal Names as Unfair Competition,' Los Angeles Bar Bul, 4/66; 'The Warren Commission and the Legal Process,' Los Angeles Bar Bul, reprinted case and comment, 2/67; book rev, Univ. Calif, Los Angeles, Law Rev, 11/68. Mem: Am, Calif, Fed, Los Angeles and Beverly Hills Bar Asns; Am. Judicature Soc; B'nai B'rith Cmt. for Calif. Woodrow Wilson Fel. Rel: Jewish. Mailing Add: 1531 San Ysidro Dr, Beverly Hills, Calif. 90210.

MOSK, STANLEY D
Justice, Calif. Supreme Court
b. San Antonio, Tex, 9/4/12; s. Paul Mosk and Minna Perl M; m. 9/27/36 to Edna Mitchell; c. Richard Mitchell. Educ: Univ. Tex, 30; Univ. Chicago, Ph.B, 33; Phi Sigma Delta. Polit. & Govt. Pos: Exec. secy. to Gov. of Calif, 39-42; judge, Superior Court, 43-59; attorney gen, 59-64; justice, Calif. Supreme Court, 64- Bus. & Prof. Pos: Pres, West. Asn. of Attorneys Gen, 63. Mil. Serv: Pvt, World War II, serv. in Coast Guard Temporary Res. Publ: Numerous articles in Am. Bar Jour, UCLA, Stanford and Calif. Law Rev. and other legal periodicals. Mem: Am. Legion; Coast Guard League; Elks; Eagles; B'nai B'rith; Vista Del Mar Child-Care Serv; Commonwealth Club of San Francisco; Town Hall of Los Angeles; Town Club of Santa Monica; all nat, state and local bar asns. Legal Res: 1200 California St, San Francisco, Calif. 94109. Mailing Add: State Building, San Francisco, Calif. 94102.

MOSS, CHARLES HOLMES D
Chmn. Llano Co. Dem. Party, Tex.
b. Temple, Tex, 12/11/15; s. Holmes Moss and Mae Ratliff M; m. 10/19/52 to Ruth Milliger; c. Marla and Sally. Educ: Univ. Tex, 2 years. Polit. & Govt. Pos: Chmn, Llano Co. Dem. Party, Tex, 64- Bus. & Prof. Pos: Rancher. Mil. Serv: Entered as Pvt, Army, 41, released as M/Sgt, 45, after serv. in Signal Corps in United States. Mem: Dir, Mohair Prom. Coun; past pres, Llano Lions Club. Rel: Methodist; mem. church bd. Mailing Add: Llano, Tex. 78643.

MOSS, FRANK EDWARD D
U.S. Sen, Utah
b. Salt Lake City, Utah, 9/23/11; s. James Edward Moss and Maud Nixon M; m. 6/20/34 to Phyllis Hart; c. Marilyn (Mrs. Armstrong), Frank Edward, Jr, Brian Hart and Gordon James. Educ: Univ. Utah, B.A, 33; George Wash. Univ, J.D, 37; Order of Coif; Phi Delta Phi; Pi Kappa Alpha. Polit. & Govt. Pos: City judge, Salt Lake City, Utah, 41-50; co.attorney, Salt Lake Co, 51-58; U.S. Sen, Utah, currently; del, Dem. Nat. Conv, 68. Mil. Serv: Entered as 2nd Lt, Army Qm. Corps, 42, released as Maj, 46, after serv. in 8th Air Force, ETO; Col, Air Force Res. Mem: VFW; Am. Legion; ROA. Rel: Latter-day Saint. Legal Res: 1848 Wasath Dr, Salt Lake City, Utah 84108. Mailing Add: Senate Office Bldg, Washington, D.C. 20510.

MOSS, JOHN EMERSON D
U.S. Rep, Calif.
b. Carbon Co, Utah; m. 9/15/35 to Jean Kueny; c. Jennifer and Allison. Educ: Sacramento Col. Polit. & Govt. Pos: Calif. State Assemblyman, Ninth Dist, 48-52, asst. Dem. Floor Leader, Calif. State Assembly, 49-52; U.S. Rep, Calif, 52-, Dep, Majority Whip, U.S. House of Rep, 62-, chmn, Subcmt. on For. Opers. and Govt. Info. and Subcmt. on Commerce and Finance. Mil. Serv: Navy, World War II. Legal Res: Sacramento, Calif. Mailing Add: Room 2185, Rayburn House Office Bldg, Washington, D.C. 20515.

MOSS, JOSEPH GIBSON D
Miss. State Rep.
b. Jackson, Miss, 4/26/22; married. Educ: Sigma Delta Kappa. Polit. & Govt. Pos: Miss. State Rep, 56- Bus. & Prof. Pos: Lawyer; farmer. Mem: Lions; Farm Bur; VFW. Rel: Methodist. Mailing Add: P.O. Box 144, Raymond, Miss. 39154. (1967)

MOSS, PAUL SIMEON, JR. D
b. Lincoln, Nebr, 1/29/35; s. Paul Simeon Moss and Roberta Cole M; m. 8/5/61 to Dixie D. Foley; c. Teresa Ann, Helen Simeone and Paul Simeon, III. Educ: Univ. of the South, 52-53; Univ. Wichita, 57-59; Nebr. State Col, B.A, 61; Pi Kappa Alpha; Psi Omega. Polit. & Govt. Pos: Speech writer, Colwell for Cong, Third Dist, 64; mem, Gov. Staff, Lincoln, Nebr, 65-67; advance man for Hubert H. Humphry, 67-68; campaign coordinator, Callan for Cong, First Dist, 68; alternate del, Dem. Nat. Conv, 68. Bus. & Prof. Pos: Teacher, Lorenzo Pub. Schs, 61-63, Sidney Pub. Schs, 63-64 and Northeastern Jr. Col, 64-65; opers. mgr, Allied Industs, Inc, 69- Mil. Serv: Pvt, Army, 54-56, serv. in 69th Antiaircraft Bn, Eng. Mem: Nat. Teachers Asn. Rel: Episcopal. Mailing Add: 4028 Dunn Ave, Lincoln, Nebr. 68502.

MOSS, THOMAS WARREN, JR. D
Va. State Del.
b. Norfolk, Va, 10/3/28; s. Thomas Warren Moss and Laura Burckard M; m. to Jane Patricia Miller; c. Elizabeth Ann, Susan Bruce and Thomas Warren, III. Educ: Va. Polytech. Inst, B.S; Univ. of Richmond, LL.B. Polit. & Govt. Pos: Former Exec. v.pres, Young Dem. Club of Va; former pres, Young Dem. Club of Norfolk; mem, Steering Cmt, Dem. Party of Norfolk Yacht and Del, 66- Bus. & Prof. Pos: Attorney-at-law. Mil. Serv: Korean War. Mem: Norfolk-Portsmouth Bar Asn; Va. State Bar Asn; Am. Bar Asn; Va. Trial Lawyers Asn; Norfolk Yacht and Country Club; Mason; Scottish Rite; Shrine; pres, Tidewater chap, Va. Polytech. Inst. Alumni Asn; Midtown Kiwanis Club. Rel: Lutheran. Mailing Add: Suite 830, Maritime Tower, Norfolk, Va. 23510.

MOSS, TRUETT W. R
Chmn, Gordon Co. Rep. Party, Ga.
b. Ranger, Ga, 3/19/30; s. Grover Downey Moss and Clara Knight M; m. 6/9/57 to Yvonne Welch; c. Kimberly, Jan and Amber. Educ: Red Bud High Sch, Calhoun, Ga, grad, 49. Polit. & Govt. Pos: Chmn, Gordon Co. Rep. Party, Ga, 66- Bus. & Prof. Pos: Mgr, Cotton Producers Asn, 53-61; agent, Prudential Ins. Co, 61- Mil. Serv: Entered as Pvt, Army, 51, released as Cpl, 53, after serv. in Mil. Police, ETO. Mem: Gordon Co. and Ga. Life Underwriters Asns; Ga. Farm Bur; Red Bud Commun. Club; Am. Legion; Mason; Kiwanis, Calhoun. Rel: South. Baptist. Legal Res: R.F.D. 1, Ranger, Ga. 30734. Mailing Add: P.O. Box 211, Calhoun, Ga. 30701.

MOSS, W. F. D
Tenn. Cmnr. of Agr.
b. Tenn, 1909; m. to Golda Siler M; c. Patsy Anne (Mrs. Paul W. Walker). Educ: Univ. Chattanooga; Univ. Tenn, B.S; N.C. State Univ, M.A. Polit. & Govt. Pos: Co. agent, Rhea and Marshall Co, Tenn, 35; dist. dairy specialist, Chattanooga area, 47; Asst. Cmnr. of Agr, Tenn, 53-, Cmnr. of Agr, currently. Bus. & Prof. Pos: Former teacher, voc. agr, Elkton and Jellico High Schs. Mailing Add: Ellington Agricultural Center, Nashville, Tenn. 37219.

MOSSNER, EUGENE DONALD D
Chmn, Saginaw Co. Dem. Cmt, Mich.
b. Saginaw, Mich, 5/27/30; s. Clarence William Mossner and Irma Schallhorn M; m. 1/7/57 to Yoko Ito; c. Christine Elaine, David Yukio and Peter John. Educ: Bay City Jr. Col, A.A, 50; Univ. Mich, A.B, 52; Wayne State Univ. Sch. Law, J.D, 55; Omicron Delta Kappa; pres, Asn. of Independent Men, 52. Polit. & Govt. Pos: Pres, Univ. Mich. Young Dem, 51-52; Wayne State Univ. Young Dem, 54-55; mem, Saginaw Co. Dem. Cmt, Mich, 52-, chmn, 69-; del, Dem. Nat. Conv, 68. Bus. & Prof. Pos: Attorney-at-Law. Mil. Serv: Entered as Pvt, Army, 55, released as Sp/c, 57, after serv. in Japan Qm. Petrol. Depot, Far East, 56-57; Good Conduct Medal; Outstanding Serv. Citation, Japan Qm. Petrol. Depot. Mem: Saginaw Co. Bar Asn.(mem. various cmts, 57-); State Bar Mich.(mem. various cmts, 57-, v.chmn, negligence law sect, 68-69, chmn, 69-); Mich. Trial Lawyers Asn.(first v.pres, 68-69, pres, 69-); Am. Trial Lawyers Asn; Am. Bar Asn; Germania of Saginaw; Mayor's Cmt. of Concern; Lutheran Sunday Sch. Teachers Asn. of Saginaw Valley. Am. Bar Asn. Most Outstanding Law Day U.S.A. Prog. Award as Chmn. of Saginaw Co. Bar Asn. Law Day U.S.A. Rel: Lutheran-Mo. Synod. Mailing Add: 3208 Midland Rd, Saginaw, Mich. 48603.

MOTLEY, CONSTANCE BAKER D
b. New Haven, Conn, 9/14/21; d. Willoughby Alva Baker and Rachel Huggins B; m. 8/18/46 to Joel Wilson Motley; c. Joel Wilson. Educ: N.Y. Univ, A.B, 43; Columbia Univ, LL.B, 46. Polit. & Govt. Pos: Mem, N.Y. State Adv. Coun. Employ. and Unemploy. Ins, 58-64; N.Y. State Sen, 64-65; pres, Manhattan Borough, 65-66; U.S. dist. judge, South. Dist. of N.Y, 66- Bus. & Prof. Pos: mem, Legal Defense and Educ. Fund, NAACP, 45-65; admitted to N.Y. Bar, 48. Mem: Asn. Bar City of N.Y. Mailing Add: 875 West End Ave, New York, N.Y. 10025.

MOTLEY, RAYMOND CHARLES D
b. Corsicana, Tex, 11/27/12; s. George Wiley Motley and Leona Deakle M; m. 7/17/43 to Doroty Goad, wid; c. Jan, Judy, Gwen and Biff. Educ: Cameron Jr. Col, 30-31; La. State Univ, 32; Trinity Univ. Tex, 36-39; Theta Kappa Nu. Polit. & Govt. Pos: Ohio State Rep, 56-60; mem, Butler Co. Dem. Club, Ohio. Bus. & Prof. Pos: Gen. Mgr, Ft. Hamilton Broadcasting Co, 61-66. Mil. Serv. Entered as Pvt, Army, 40, released as 1st Lt, 45. Mem: Sports Broadcasters Asn. of Am; Elks; Am. Legion; Ky. Col. Rel: Protestant. Mailing Add: 165 Glencross Ave, Hamilton, Ohio 45103.

MOTLOW, REAGOR D
Tenn. State Sen.
b. Lynchburg, Tenn, 2/15/98; s. Lem Motlow and Clara Reagor M; m. 1/1/28 to Jeanie Garth. Educ: Vanderbilt Univ, B.A, 19; Alpha Tau Omega; Owl; Commodore. Polit. & Govt. Pos: Tenn. State Rep, 41-62; Tenn. State Sen, 16th Sen. dist, 65- Bus. & Prof. Pos: Farmer; v.pres, Jack Daniel Distillery, Lynchburg, Tenn, 38-47, pres, 47-63, mem. bd, 63-68; mem. bd, Brown-Forman Distillers Corp, 63-68; dir. and v.pres, Farmers Bank, currently; mem, bd. trust, Vanderbilt Univ, currently. Mil. Serv: 2nd Lt, Army, 18, serv. in Inf, U.S. Mem: Am. Soc. of Engrs; Elks; Rotary; Shrine; Pendennis Club, Louisville, Ky; Am. Legion; Cumberland Club, Nashville, Tenn. Rel: Protestant. Legal Res: Treelawn, Lynchburg, Tenn. 37352. Mailing Add: P.O. Box 202, Lynchburg, Tenn. 37352.

MOTT, SAMUEL D. D
Chmn, New Shoreham Dem. Town Cmt, R.I.
b. Block Island, R.I, 12/7/09; s. Alton H. Mott and Clossie A. Ball M; m. 5/20/55; c. Susan Ellen, John R, James W, George D, Peter J, Alton H. and S. Douglas. Educ: Brown Univ, Ph.B, 32; Kappa Sigma. Polit. & Govt. Pos: Mem, Town Coun, Block Island, R.I, 49-53, pres, 67 & 68, mem. and chmn, Sch. Cmt, 49-53; R.I. State Rep, 61-62; chmn, New Shoreham Dem. Town Cmt, R.I, 61- Bus. & Prof. Pos: Asst. mgr, wine steward and room clerk, Various Knott Hotels, N.Y.C, 33-43; asst. mgr, Hotel Taft, 42-43, mgr, Hotel Blackstone and Hotel Albert, 43-46; asst. mgr, Hotel Dixie, 45-46; owner and mgr, Narragawsett Inn, Block Island, R.I, 46-; pres. and mgr, Spring House Hotel, 52-; owner and mgr, The Oar Cafe and Lounge, 67- Mem: Mason (32°); Block Island Vol. Fire Dept; Residents Asn; Eastern Star; Block Island C. of C.(pres). Rel: Protestant. Mailing Add: Block Island, R.I. 02807.

MOTTL, RONALD M. D
Ohio State Sen.
b. Cleveland, Ohio, 2/6/34; s. Milton Mottl and Anna Huml M; div; c. Ron, Jr. and Ronda. Educ: Univ. of Notre Dame, B.S, 56, LL.B, 57. Polit. & Govt. Pos: Asst. dir. of law, Cleveland, Ohio, 58-60; councilman, Second Ward, Parma City Coun, 60-61, pres, 61-66; Ohio State Rep, Dist. 51, 66-68; Ohio State Sen, Dist. 24, 68- Mil. Serv: Pvt, Army, 57; $5\frac{1}{2}$ years in Res. Rel: Roman Catholic. Mailing Add: 6407 Virginia Ave, Parma, Ohio 44129.

MOULDS, ELIZABETH FRY D
Mem, Calif. Dem. State Cent. Cmt.
b. San Pedro, Calif, 11/9/41; d. Donald Hume Fry, Jr. and Pauline Fraser F; m. 8/29/64 to John Fryer Moulds III; c. Donald Bancroft and Gerald Bennett. Educ: Sacramento State Col, B.A, 63; Univ. Calif, Berkeley, M.A, 64; Woodrow Wilson fel; Phi Kappa Phi; Young Dem. Polit. & Govt. Pos: Mem, Calif. Dem. State Cent. Cmt, 68- Bus. & Prof. Pos: Instr. Political Science, Col. of San Mateo, 64-66; Instr. Political Science, Sacramento State Col, 66- Rel: Protestant. Mailing Add: 1995 Garden Hwy, Sacramento, Calif. 95833.

MOULTON, IDANELLE T. R
b. St. Paul, Minn, 7/30/93; wid. Educ: Schs. in St. Paul, Minn, Spokane, Wash. and Stoneham, Mass. Polit. & Govt. Pos: N.H. State Rep, 57-68; town clerk, New Durham, 8 years. Bus. & Prof. Pos: Housewife. Mem: Eastern Star; Evergreen Rebekah Lodge; New Durham Worth While Club. Rel: Baptist. Mailing Add: Route 1, P.O. Box 104, New Durham, N.H. 03855. (1967)

MOULTON, WILLIAM S. D
b. Wessington Springs, S.Dak; m. 7/14/34; c. Two. Educ: Pub. Schs. and exten. courses. Polit. & Govt. Pos: Nebr. State Sen, 51-68. Bus. & Prof. Pos: Assoc. with Roberts Dairy since 34, presently in pub. rels. dept. Mem: YMCA; Red Cross; Commun. Chest; PTA; mem. at large, Boy Scout Covered Wagon Coun, 58-59; state chmn, Hi-Y youth and govt. prog, 58-62; Elks; Mason. Rel: Methodist. Mailing Add: 3340 N. 57th St, Omaha, Nebr. 68104.

MOUNGER, WILLIAM DONALD R
State Finance Chmn, Miss. Rep. Party
b. Jackson, Miss, 3/31/26; s. William Malcolm Mounger and Veronica Robertson M; m. 1/26/56 to Jan Gore; c. William Malcolm, II and Robert Gore. Educ: U.S. Mil. Acad, B.S, 48; Univ. Okla, B.S. in Petrol. Eng, 56, M.S. in Petrol. Eng, 56; Sigma Gamma Epsilon; Pi Epsilon Tau. Polit. & Govt. Pos: Finance chmn, Rep. Party, Hinds, Miss, 64-66; state finance chmn, Miss. Rep. Party, 66-; del, Rep. Nat. Conv. and v.chmn. Miss. del, 68; mem, Rep. Exec. Cmt, Miss, 68-; finance chmn. for various campaigns for U.S. Rep. and Gubernatorial Campaigns. Bus. & Prof. Pos: Independent oil operator, Miss, 53-54; petroleum engr, Humble Oil & Refining Co, La, 57-58; petroleum engr, Deposit Guaranty Nat. Bank, Jackson, Miss, 58-60, v.pres, 60- and mem. bd. dirs, 62. Mil. Serv: Entered as 2nd Lt, Air Force, 48, released as 1st Lt, 53, after serv. in 92nd Bomb Wing, El Paso, Tex, 49-53. Mem: V.pres, Independent Petroleum Asn. Am; pres. Miss-Ala. Div, Mid-Continent Oil and Gas Asn; Miss. Geol. Soc; Miss. Landmens Asn; past pres, Petroleum Club of Jackson; Country Club of Jackson; River Hills Tennis Club; Patio Club. Rel: Presbyterian. Legal Res: 1402 Robert Dr, Jackson, Miss. 39211. Mailing Add: P.O. Box 1200, Jackson, Miss. 39505.

MOUNTS, SWANSON H. D
b. Stafford, W.Va, 2/20/09; s. Andrew Jackson Mounts and Virgie Ferrell M; m. 12/31/55 to Snowie B. Pratt; c. Mary Lou (Mrs. Hale) and Swanson H, Jr. Educ: Phelps Acad, 2 years; Waverly High Sch, 2 years. Polit. & Govt. Pos: Mgr, Nat. Reemploy. Serv, 37; court bailiff, Common Pleas Court, 60-63; clerk of courts, Pike Co, Ohio, 63-69; chief probation officer, Juvenile Court, 69- Mem: Mason (32°); York Rite; Shrine. Rel: Protestant. Mailing Add: 423 Seventh St, Waverly, Ohio 45690.

MOURSUND, ALBERT WADEL, III D
b. Johnson City, Tex, 5/23/19; s. Albert Wadel Moursund, Jr. and Mary Frances Stribling M; m. 5/8/41 to Mary Allen Moore; c. Will Stribling and Mary Moore. Educ: Univ. Tex, LL.B, 41. Polit. & Govt. Pos: Tex. State Rep, 48-52; judge, Blanco Co, 53-59; mem, Tex. Parks and Wildlife Cmn, 63-67. Bus. & Prof. Pos: Attorney-at-Law, 46-; pres, Arrowhead Co, 58; mem. firm, Moursund & Ferguson, 63-; chmn. bd. and dir, Moore State Bank, Llano, Tex, 63-; dir, Johnson City Bank, Tex, Am. Nat. Bank, Austin, Tex. Broadcasting Corp, Austin and KWTX, Waco and Texoma, Ardmore, Okla. Mil. Serv: Army Air Force, 42-46. Mem: Tex. and Am. Bar Asns; Hill Co. Bar Asn.(past pres). Rel: Baptist. Mailing Add: P.O. Box 125, Johnson City, Tex. 78636.

MOUSER, COTYS MILNER D
b. Antrim, La, 10/3/06; s. Enoch Melvin Mouser and Hattie Jackson M; m. 6/17/33 to Vestal McKenzie Mathis; c. Elizabeth (Mrs. Frank C. Fellows, Jr) and John Melvin. Educ: Univ, Tex, Austin B.B.A, 28; La. State Univ, M.A, 37; Univ. Tex, Univ. Denver and Ind. Univ, Bloomington, summers 38-39 &

50; 'B' Hall Asn. Polit. & Govt. Pos: Chief clerk, U.S. Senate Cmt. Agr. & Forestry, 51-53 & 54-, asst. chief clerk, 53-54. Bus. & Prof. Pos: Auditor and head bus. dept, Martin High Sch, Laredo, Tex, 29-40; instr. bus. admin, Sam Houston State Col, Huntsville, 40; auditor-bus. mgr, assoc. prof. bus, Northwest. State Col, 40-51; teacher personal finance and bus. math, part time, Grad. Sch. U.S. Dept. Agr, Wash, D.C, 53- Publ: Syllabi for $\frac{1}{2}$ unit Courses in Retail Selling and Consumership, Tex. State Bd. Educ; compiler annual budgets, Northwest. State Col, 43-49 and Job Study Non Academic Personnel of State Colleges, La. State Bd. Educ, 50. Mem: Gulf Coast Sch. Exec. Asn.(v.pres); La. State Teachers Asn. Bus. Educ. Sect; La. Col. Conf. Bus. Adminstr. Sec.(v.pres); AF&AM; La. Forestry Asn; Lions, Laredo; Rotary, Natchitoches. Rel: Presbyterian; former chmn. bd. deacons, Natchitoches. Legal Res: Broadway and Main St, Grayson, La. 71435. Mailing Add: 7057 Western Ave. N.W, Washington, D.C. 20015.

MOWBRAY, JOHN CODE D
Justice, Nev. Supreme Court
b. Bradford, Ill, 9/20/18; s. Thomas John Mowbray and Ellen Code M; m. 10/15/49 to Kathlyn Ann Hammes; c. John Hammes, Romy Hammes, Jerry Hammes and Terry Hammes. Educ: West. Ill. Univ, B.A, 40; Notre Dame Law Sch, J.D, 49. Polit. & Govt. Pos: Dep. dist. attorney, Clark Co, Nev, 49-53; U.S. referee, State of Nev, 55-59; state dist. judge, 59-67; justice, Nev. Supreme Court, 67- Mil. Serv: Entered as Aviation Cadet, Army, 42, released as Maj, 46. Rel: Catholic. Legal Res: 1815 S. 15th, Las Vegas, Nev. 89105. Mailing Add: Supreme Court, Carson City, Nev. 89701.

MOWRY, JOHN L. R
Iowa State Sen.
b. Baxter, Iowa, 12/15/05; s. William Mowry and Grace Lindsay Conn M; m. June, 1941 to Irene Eudora Lounsberry; c. Madelyn (Mrs. Irvine). Educ: Ohio State Univ, 27-28; Univ. Iowa, B.A, 28, J.D, 30; Sigma Chi; Phi Delta Phi; Iowa Law Rev. Polit. & Govt. Pos: Spec. agent, Fed. Bur. Invest, 30-34; spec. investr, Off. of Thomas E. Dewey, spec. prosecutor, New York Co, N.Y, 34-36; Marshall Co. attorney, Iowa, 38-41; dep. cmnr, N.Y. State Liquor Authority, 45-47; Mayor, Marshalltown, Iowa, 50-55; Iowa State Rep, 57-65 & 67-69; Iowa State Sen, 69- Bus. & Prof. Pos: Pres, Evans Abstract Co. and GMK, Inc. Mil. Serv: Intel. Div, Air Force, 41-45. Mem: Marshall Co. Bar Asn.(pres, 52); v.pres, Cmt. Uniform Commercial Code, 67; Iowa State Bar Asn; Former Agents of Fed. Bur. Invest.(past nat. pres); Marshall Co. Hist. Soc.(trustee); Lions; Shrine; Consistory. Rel: Presbyterian. Legal Res: 503 W. Main St, Marshalltown, Iowa 50158. Mailing Add: 25 N. Center St, Marshalltown, Iowa 50158.

MOYE, CHARLES A, JR. R
b. Atlanta, Ga, 7/13/18; s. Charles Allen Moye and Annie Luther Williamson M; m. 3/9/45 to Sarah Ellen Johnston; c. Henry Allen and Lucy Ellen. Educ: Emory Univ, A.B, 39, J.D, 43. Polit. & Govt. Pos: Chmn, De Kalb Co. Rep. Exec. Cmt, Ga, 52-56, Fifth Dist, 56-64 and Fourth Dist, 64-65; v.chmn, Rep. State Cent. Cmt. of Ga, 56-65; Rep. presidential elector, Ga, 64. Bus. & Prof. Pos: Partner, Gambrell, Russell, Moye & Killorin, Atlanta, Ga, 55- Mem: Am, Ga, Atlanta and Fed. Bar Asns; Asn. of Bar, City of N.Y; Am. Judicature Soc; Lawyers Club of Atlanta; Int. Asn. Ins. Counsel; Newcomen. Rel: Baptist. Mailing Add: 1317 Council Bluff Dr, Atlanta, Ga. 30329.

MOYE, JAMES M. R
Rep. Nat. Committeeman, Miss.
b. Laurel, Miss, 2/9/21; m. 2/5/44 to Mae Eleanor; c. Marilyn and Jamie. Educ: Jones Co. Jr. Col; South. Col. of Optom, Memphis, Tenn. Polit. & Govt. Pos: Mem, Laurel Sch. Bd, Miss, 61-66; chmn, Co. Campaign for Gov, 63; mem, Miss. Rep. State Exec. Cmt, 64; alternate del, Rep. Nat. Conv, 64, del, 68; v.chmn, Miss. State Rep. Party and chmn, Fifth Dist. Rep. Party, 66; chmn, Fifth Cong. Dist. Rep. Party, 66-67; Rep. Nat. Committeeman, 68- Bus. & Prof. Pos: Optometrist; pres, Miss. Optom. Asn, 54-55; mem, State Bd. of Exam. in Optom, 56-61; mem, Am. Optom. Asn, 59-, chmn, Practice Mgt. Cmt, 63-65. Mem: Past mem. bd. dirs, Laurel C. of C; Cmt. of 100, currently; bd. dirs, local Red Cross; former mem, Southeast. Area Adv. Coun. Received Distinguished Serv. Award, Laurel Jaycees, 52. Rel: Presbyterian; Elder, Trinity Presby. Church. Legal Res: 17 Glenwood Dr, Laurel, Miss. 39440. Mailing Add: 515 Fifth Ave, Laurel, Miss. 39440.

MOYED, RALPH S. R
Dir. Pub. Rels, Del. Rep. State Cmt.
b. Philadelphia, Pa, 8/26/30; s. Edward M. Moyed and Elizabeth Hartz M; m. 2/13/57 to Myra Snyder; c. Mark Goldberg (stepson), Nancy and Jonathan. Educ: Temple Univ, 49-50; New York Univ, 51-52. Polit. & Govt. Pos: Dir. pub. rels, Del. Rep. State Cmt, 69- Bus. & Prof. Pos: Reporter, Intelligencer-Lancaster, Pa, 56-61; reporter and political writer, News-Journal, Wilmington, Del, 61-69. Mil. Serv: Entered as Seaman, Navy, 50, released as PO 3/C on 54, after serv. in public relations, N.Y.C, 51-54. Rel: Jewish. Legal Res: 837 Marvel Ave, Northridge, Claymont, Del. 19703. Mailing Add: 407 Delaware Ave, Wilmington, Del. 19801.

MOYER, DON F. D
b. Zanesville, Ohio, 7/30/30; s. Meryle K. Moyer and Louanna Durant M; m. 6/16/51 to Virginia A. Durant; c. Deborah K, Tim J, Donald D, Jill Ann and Jennifer. Educ: St. Nicholas High Sch, Zanesville, Ohio, grad. Polit. & Govt. Pos: Trustee, Muskingum Co. Young Dem, Ohio, 63, pres, 66-67, mem, currently; mem, Twp. Cmt, Muskingum Co, 64 & 66; mem, Muskingum Co. Dem. Exec. Cmt, 64-69; nat. committeeman, Ohio Young Dem, 66-; alternate del, Dem. Nat. Conv, 68; mem, Ohio Dem. Exec. Cmt, 69. Bus. & Prof. Pos: Owner, grocery store, 53, Don's Laundromats, 56-, Phi-Dune Better TV, 68- and Cable-TV, 69- Mil. Serv: Naval Res, 48-55. Mem: Elks; Eagles. Rel: Catholic. Mailing Add: 264 North St, Duncan Falls, Ohio 43734.

MOYER, GLENN ROYDON D
Chmn, Lehigh Co. Dem. Cmt, Pa.
b. Allentown, Pa, 8/21/29; s. Carl E. Moyer and Irene Sechrist M; m. to Suzanne Clare Eckert; c. four. Educ: Allentown High Sch. Polit. & Govt. Pos: Chmn, Lehigh Co. Dem. Cmt, 66-; alternate del, Dem. Nat. Conv, 68. Bus. & Prof. Pos: Pres, Cutshall Agency, Inc, 61- Mil. Serv: Entered as Pvt, Army, 47, released as S/Sgt, 50. Rel: Unitarian. 1967 Legal Res: Emmaus, Pa. No mailing address available. (1967)

MOYER, RUTH ELOISE D
Secy, Iowa State Dem. Cent. Cmt.
b. Ottumwa, Iowa, 2/23/17; d. Andrew Julius Wind and Ada Mae Ward W; m. 4/20/47 to Donald Henry Moyer; c. Linda Lou (Mrs. Richard L. Cox). Educ: Stephens Col, Assoc. in Music. Polit. & Govt. Pos: Dep. recorder, Wapello Co, Iowa, 53-; Dem. precinct committeewoman, 56-; pres, Wapello Co. Dem. Women's Club, 60-62 and 64; mem, Gov. Legis. Cmt, 64-; committeewoman, Fourth Cong. Dist, Iowa, 64-; secy, Iowa State Dem. Cent. Cmt, 64-; mem, cmt. for urban renewal, Mayor's Adv. Coun, Ottumwa, 67-; pres, Dem. Women's Club, Wapello Co, 68- Mem: Past. pres, Am. Home Finding Auxiliary; Ottumwa Civic Music Asn.(treas, 58-); West End Boosters Club; Wapello Co. Asn. for Retarded Children; New Frontier Club of Iowa. Rel: Presbyterian. Mailing Add: 308 E. Elmdale Blvd, Ottumwa, Iowa 52501.

MOYERS, BILL D. D
b. Hugo, Okla. 6/5/34; s. John Henry Moyers and Ruby Johnson M; m. 12/18/54 to Judith Suzanne Davidson; c. William Cope, Alice Suzanne and John Davidson. Educ: Univ. Tex, B.J, 56; Univ. Edinburgh, 56-57; Southwest. Theol. Sem, B.D, 59; Sigma Delta Chi. Polit. & Govt. Pos: Asst. to Senate Majority Leader, U.S. Senate, 60; assoc. dir, Peace Corps, 61-63, Dep. Dir, 63; Spec. Asst. to the President, 63-67. Bus. & Prof. Pos: Publisher, Newsday, 67- Publ: 'One Thing We Learned,' For Affairs, 7/68; 'Mass Media and the Age of Dissent,' New Leader, 12/68; 'Reveille for Democrats,' Atlantic Monthly, 3/69. Mem: Trustee, Rockefeller Found; bd. of visitors, J.F.K. Sch. of Govt, Harvard Univ; bd. of dirs, Coun. on For. Rels. Rel: Protestant. Mailing Add: 76 Fourth St, Garden City, N.Y. 11530.

MOYERS, PAUL SHAY D
b. Cutlips, W.Va, 4/25/10; s. W.B. Moyers (deceased) and Carrie Bull M; m. 2/16/51 to Mabel Crisman, wid; c. Paul Bradford. Educ: Glenville State Col; W.Va. Univ, Col. of Agr; Mountain State Bus. Col; Pi Kappa Phi. Polit. & Govt. Pos: Mem. town coun, Burnsville, W.Va, 43-60; W.Va. State Del, 60-68. Bus. & Prof. Pos: Merchant. Mil. Serv: ROTC, W.Va. Univ, two years. Mem: Mason; Braxton Co. Farm Bur; W.Va. Lions Sight Conserv Found; Braxton Co. Redevelop. Asn; secy. and former pres, Burnsville Lions Club; former zone chmn. and dep. dist. gov, Lions Int; former pres, Braxton Co. Indust. Develop. Asn; pres, Braxton Co. Merchants Asn. and Farming for Better Living Coun. Rel: Baptist. Legal Res: Main Street, Burnsville, W.Va. 26335. Mailing Add: P.O. Box 8, Burnsville, W.Va. 26335.

MOYLAN, HAROLD THOMAS D
Nebr. State Sen.
b. Bayard, Iowa, 3/5/03; s. John Moylan and Margaret Ellen Ferris M; m. 2/4/29 to Margaret Ellen Emery; c. James H, Joseph W, Mary Jean, Patrick F. and Ann Marie. Educ: Creighton Univ, B.A, 28. Polit. & Govt. Pos: Nebr. State Sen, 65- Bus. & Prof. Pos: Real Estate Broker. Mem: Farm Bur; K. of C; Eagles. Rel: Roman Catholic. Mailing Add: 3862 California St, Omaha, Nebr. 68131.

MOYLAN, JAMES HAROLD D
b. Omaha, Nebr, 10/17/30; s. Harold Thomas Moylan and Margaret Ellen Emery; m. 7/9/60 to LiLa Marie Fitzgerald; c. James Patrick, Michael Thomas and Patrick William. Educ: Creighton Univ, B.S, 52, LL.B, 57; Phi Alpha Delta. Polit. & Govt. Pos: Pres, Douglas Co. Young Dem, Nebr, 59-61; dep. attorney, Douglas Co, 60-69; v.chmn, Douglas Co. Dem. Cent. Cmt, 62-66, chmn, 66-68; alternate del, Dem. Nat. Conv, 68. Bus. & Prof. Pos: Assoc. regent, St. Marys Col, Omaha, 65-; attorney-at-law. Mil. Serv: Entered as Pvt. E-1, Army, 52, released as Cpl, 54, after serv. in Hq. Co. Southwest Command, Japan, U.S. Armed Forces, Far East, 53-54; Good Conduct Medal. Mem: Iowa, Nebr. and Omaha Bar Asns; v.pres, Omaha Barristers Club, 62; mem, Creighton Univ. Alumni Coun, 63-65; Am. Legion. Rel: Roman Catholic. Legal Res: 2144 S. 84th St, Omaha, Nebr. 68124. Mailing Add: 1640 Woodmen Tower Bldg, Omaha, Nebr. 68102.

MOYNAHAN, THOMAS ALVIN D
b. Indianapolis, Ind, 11/16/38; s. Robert B. Moynahan and Mary Louise Shiel Moynahan Frey; m. 10/24/64 to Jane Ellis Drury; c. Kara Browning. Educ: Univ. Notre Dame, B.S, 60. Polit. & Govt. Pos: Del, Dem. Nat. Conv, 68. Bus. & Prof. Pos: Pres, T.A. Moynahan Properties, Inc, 64- Mil. Serv: Entered as Ens, Naval Res, 60, released as Lt, 64, after serv. in U.S.S. San Pablo and U.S.S. Alcor. Mem: Nat. Asn. Real Estate Bd; Young Pres. Orgn; C. of C; Indianapolis Athletic Club. Rel: Catholic. Legal Res: 4502 N. Delaware St, Indianapolis, Ind. 46220. Mailing Add: 850 N. Pennsylvania St, Indianapolis, Ind. 46204.

MOYNIHAN, DANIEL PATRICK D
Asst. to the President for Urban Affairs
b. Tulsa, Okla, 3/16/27; s. John Henry Moynihan and Margaret A. Phipps M; m. 5/29/55 to Elizabeth Therese Brennan; c. Timothy Patrick, Maura Russell and John McCloskey. Educ: City Col. New York, 43; Tufts Univ, B.A. cum laude, 48; Fletcher Sch. Law and Diplomacy, M.A, 49, Ph.D, 61; hon. LL.D. Polit. & Govt. Pos: Dir, P.R. Int. Rescue Cmt, 54; asst. to secy, asst. secy. and acting secy. to Gov. of N.Y, 55-58; secy. of pub. affairs cmt, N.Y. State Dem. Cmt, 58-60; mem, N.Y. State Tenure Cmt, 59-60; dir, N.Y. State Govt. Research Proj, Syracuse Univ, 59-61; del, Dem. Nat. Conv, 60; spec. asst. to Secy. of Labor, 61-62, exec. asst, 62-63, Asst. Secy. of Labor, 63-65; Asst. for Urban Affairs to the President and Exec. Secy. to the Coun. for Urban Affairs, 69- Bus. & Prof. Pos: Dir, Mass. Inst. of Tech-Harvard Univ. Joint Center for Urban Studies, 66-69; prof. educ. and urban polit, Harvard Univ. Grad. Sch. of Educ, 66- Mil. Serv: Naval Res, 44-47. Publ: Co-auth, Beyond the Melting Pot (Anisfield Award, 63), 63; Maximum Feasible Misunderstanding, Free Press, 69; author of many articles. Mem: Am. Acad. Arts and Sci; Am. Philos. Soc; Cath. Asn. Int. Peace. Recipient, Fulbright Fel, London Sch. Econ. and Polit. Sci, 50; Arthur S. Fleming Award, 56; Meritorious Serv. Award, Dept. of Labor, 64. Rel: Catholic. Legal Res: 57 Francis Ave, Cambridge, Mass. 02138. Mailing Add: The White House, 1600 Pennsylvania Ave. N.W, Washington, D.C. 20500.

MOZINGO, JAMES PIERCE, III D
S.C. State Sen.
b. Darlington, S.C, 8/24/13; s. James Pierce Mozingo, Jr. and Janie Rawls M; 2nd m. 1958 to Margaret J. Arrants; c. James Pierce, IV, Frank Lever, Wil-

liam Butler, Thomas Aladdin and Brock Arrants. Educ: Clemson Col, 31-32; Univ. S.C, LL.B, 36; Blue Key; pres, Kappa Sigma Kappa; winner, Gonzales & Keitt Oratorical Medals. Hon. LL.D, Clements Col, 68. Polit. & Govt. Pos: S.C. State Rep, 35-38; S.C. State Sen, Darlington Co, 38-; del, Dem. Nat. Conv, 40, 44, 60, 64 & 68; chmn, Darlington Co. Dem. Party, 64 & 68. Bus. & Prof. Pos: Attorney-at-law; dir, Int. Acad. of Trial Lawyers; dir. and treas, Darlington Int. Raceways, Inc; dir, Carolina Bank & Trust Co, Darlington, S.C. Mem: Am. and Int. Bar Asns; pres, Nat. Asn. of Claimants Compensation Attorneys, 52-53; Nat. pres, Am. Trial Lawyers Asn; organizer and charter mem, World Peace Through Law Conf; Nat. Motor Vehicle Safety Adv. Coun; trustee, Winthrop Col, Clemson Col. and Univ. S.C; K. of P; Mason; Shrine; Elks. Rel: Presbyterian: mem. finance cmt, Presby. Church of Darlington. Legal Res: 126 Oak St, Darlington, S.C. 29532. Mailing Add: P.O. Box 257, Darlington, S.C. 29532.

MROZINSKI, BENJAMIN ALEXANDER D
b. Baltimore, Md, 4/18/05; s. Casimir Paul Mrozinski and Pauline Gromacki M; m. 8/16/25 to Rose Mary Szocik; c. Helen Agnes. Educ: Holy Rosary Parochial Sch. Polit. & Govt. Pos: Md. State Del, 47-66; chief cmt. clerk, Baltimore City Coun, 49-55. Bus. & Prof. Pos: Conductor, Pa. R.R, 22-67. Mem: Holy Name Union; K. of C; Brotherhood of R.R. Trainmen; Polish Roman Catholic Union; Polish Am. Dem. Club. Rel: Roman Catholic. Mailing Add: 627 S. Kenwood Ave, Baltimore, Md. 21224.

MUDGE, DICK H, JR. D
b. Edwardsville, Ill, 6/9/19; s. Dick H. Mudge and Louise Gregory M; m. 7/20/46 to Jeanne Godfrey; c. Carolyn (Mrs. Morrison), Suzanne, Dick H, III and Thomas G. Educ: Harvard Univ, A.B, 40; Northwest. Univ. Law Sch, J.D, 47. Polit. & Govt. Pos: States attorney, Madison Co, Ill, 56-64; del, Dem. Nat. Conv, 68. Bus. & Prof. Pos: Lawyer, 47- Mil. Serv: Entered as Pvt, Army, 41, released as Maj, 46, after serv. in Army Air Corps as single engine fighter pilot, Europe, 43-45; Distinguished Flying Cross with 2 clusters; Air Medal with 3 clusters. Mem: Am. and Ill. Bar Asns; Wilderness Soc. Legal Res: 736 Randle St, Edwardsville, Ill. 62025. Mailing Add: 224 St. Louis St, Edwardsville, Ill. 62025.

MUDGETT, GALEN EARL, SR. R
b. Randolph, Vt, 10/24/22; m. to Hazel C. Bicknell; c. one son and four daughters. Educ: Vt. State Sch. of Agr. Polit. & Govt. Pos: Sch. dir, 9 years; Vt. State Rep, 65-66; dist. councilman, Agway, Inc; clerk, bd. selectmen. Bus. & Prof. Pos: Dairy farming. Mem: Farm Bur; Agway, Inc. Rel: Congregational. Mailing Add: South Royalton, Vt. 05068. (1967)

MUELLER, AUGUST B. Conservative
Minn. State Rep.
b. Arlington Twp, Minn. Educ: St. Olaf Col. Polit. & Govt. Pos: Minn. State Rep, 41- Bus. & Prof. Pos: Partner, farming. Mailing Add: Arlington, Minn. 55307. (1967)

MUELLER, FREDERICK HENRY R
b. Grand Rapids, Mich, 11/22/93; s. John Frederick Mueller and Emma Matilda Oesterle M; m. 5/22/61 to Pauline Crane Kessler; c. Frederick Eugene and Marcia Joan. Educ: Mich. State Univ, B.S, 14, LL.D, 59; Tau Beta Pi. Polit. & Govt. Pos: Asst. Secy. of Commerce, 55-58, Undersecy. of Commerce, 58-59, Secy. of Commerce, 59-61. Bus. & Prof. Pos: Gen. partner, Mueller Furniture Co, 14-55; pres. and gen. mgr, Grand Rapids Industs, Inc, 41-46; pres, Furniture Mutual Ins. Co, 41-55; pres, Butterworth Hosp, 45-55; mem. gov. bd, Mich. State Univ, 45-57; pres, United Hosp. Fund, Inc, 48-55; mem. bd. dirs, Detroit Edison Co. and Fruehauf Corp. Mem: Nat. Asn. Furniture Mfrs.(pres, 34-35); C. of C.(pres, Grand Rapids Chap, 40-41); Mason (33°); Shrine; Rotary (past dist. gov); Capitol Hill, Metrop. and Bird Key Yacht Clubs; Univ. Club. of Sarasota. Mailing Add: Box 3436, Sarasota, Fla. 33578.

MUELLER, HAROLD F. D
b. Manly, Iowa, 7/6/06; s. Gottlieb J. Mueller and Bertha Stoecker M; m. 1/2/31 to Marcella Bergland; c. Don, Eugene, Ray, Mary (Mrs. Griffith) and Paul. Educ: Iowa State Univ, B.S, 29; Theta Chi. Polit. & Govt. Pos: Iowa State Rep, 59-66, chmn, Agr. Cmt, Iowa House of Rep, 65. Bus. & Prof. Pos: Dir. and chmn. bd, Manly State Bank and dir. and v.pres, Worth Co. Coop. Oil Co, currently. Mem: Elks. Rel: United Methodist. Mailing Add: Manly, Iowa 50456.

MUELLER, INEZ LEE D
Mem, Galveston Co. Dem. Exec. Cmt, Tex.
b. Live Oak Co, Tex, 11/15/16; d. John Dobie and Alice Inez Coffman D; m. to Hugo Albert Mueller; c. Mitzi Inez and Tanya (Mrs. A.H. Jaridly). Polit. & Govt. Pos: Mem. steering cmt, Galveston Co. Dem. Club, Tex, 60-66; presiding judge for co. and state elec, 60-69; Galveston Co. Dem. chmn, Precinct 47, 60-; mem, Galveston Co. Dem. Exec. Cmt, 60-; mem, State Dem. Exec. Cmt, Tex, 62-66; committeewoman, 17th Sen. Dist. Dem. Exec. Cmt, 62-66; alternate del, Dem. Nat. Conv, 68. Mem: OCAWIU (past pres. auxiliary and mem. Sr. Mem. Club); Mainland Cent. Labor Union (past dir. Women's Activities Dept); Galveston Co. Civic Music Asn; Order of Sons of Hermann; Mainland Sr. Citizens Coun; Golden Age Club; Women's Soc. of Christian Serv; Philathea Class; Girl Scout leader for 12 years. Rel: Methodist; primary Sunday sch. supt, First Methodist Church of Texas City. Mailing Add: 816 13th Ave. N, Texas City, Tex. 77590.

MUELLER, JACK FREDERICK R
b. Cheyenne, Wyo, 11/10/41; s. Frederick John Mueller and Ellen Crago M; single. Educ: Univ. Wyo, B.A, 63; Kappa Delta Pi, Omicron Delta Kappa, Iron Skull, Phi Epsilon Phi, Sigma Chi. Polit. & Govt. Pos: Chmn, Univ. Young Rep, 60-63; educ. sen, Student Body Senate, Univ. Wyo, 61-62, pres. pro tempore, 62-63; del, Young Rep. Nat. Conv, 61, 63, 65, 67 & 69; del, Wyo. Rep. Conv, 62, 66 & 68; region dir, Young Rep. Nat. Fedn, 63-65, nat. v.chmn, 65-67, regional co-dir, 69; chmn, Laramie Co. Young Rep, 65-; precinct committeeman, Rep. Party, Laramie Co, 66-68; del, Rep. Nat. Conv, 68; Young Rep. State Chmn, 69. Bus. & Prof. Pos: Teacher, high sch, Tex, 63-64, Wyo, 64-65; dir. civil defense educ, Wyo. Dept. Educ, 65-, consult. driver educ, 67- Mem: Am. Driver and Traffic Safety Educ. Asn; Farm Bur; Wyo. Hist. Soc; Laramie Co. Hist. Soc; Univ. Wyo. Alumni Asn; Asn. State Dirs. Safety and Driver Educ. Sigma Chi best Pledge, 59-60, outstanding senior, 63. Rel: Lutheran Missouri Synod. Mailing Add: 3822 Capitol, Cheyenne, Wyo, 82001.

MUELLER, L.C. R
N.Dak. State Rep.
b. Madison, S.Dak, 4/6/94; married; c. Four. Educ: Pub. schs. Polit. & Govt. Pos: N.Dak. State Rep, 55-66 & currently; mayor, Oakes, N.Dak; chmn, Dickey Co. Rep. Party, 68. Bus. & Prof. Pos: Auto dealer; farmer. Mem: Mason; Am. Legion; Lions; N.Dak. Water Users Asn.(first pres). Mailing Add: Oakes, N.Dak. 58474. (1967)

MUENSTER, THEODORE R. D
b. Beatrice, Nebr, 10/15/40; s. Theodore R. Muenster, Sr. and Marcelene Goble M; m. 3/5/65 to Karen Nelsen; c. Theodore R, III. Educ: Univ. Nebr, B.A. in hist. and polit. sci, 62, grad. work in polit. sci, 63-64; Pi Sigma Alpha. Polit. & Govt. Pos: Pres, Univ. Nebr. Young Dem, 61-62; regional dir, Young Dem. Clubs of Am, 61-63; nat. committeeman, Young Dem. Clubs of Nebr, 62-64; spec. asst. to Gov. of Minn, 63-64; alternate del, Dem. Nat. Conv, 64; spec. asst. to U.S. Rep. Clair A. Callan, 65-68. Bus. & Prof. Pos: Grad. teaching asst, Univ. Nebr, 63-64; adminstr, Univ. S.Dak, currently. Mem: Jr. C. of C; Nebr. Food for Peace Cmt; Nebr. Fair Campaign Practices Cmt. Rel: Unitarian. Mailing Add: 604 Kennedy St, Vermillion, S.Dak. 57069.

MUFTIC, FELICIA BOILLOT D
Mem, Colo. State Dem. Cent. Cmt.
b. Muskogee, Okla, 2/27/38; d. Lowell Francois Boillot and Geneva Halstead B; m. 9/6/61 to Michael Muftic, M.D; c. Tanya, Teddy and Mariana. Educ: Free Univ. Berlin, 58-59; Northwest. Univ, B.A. in Polit. Sci, 60; Alpha Lambda Delta; Kappa Kappa Gamma. Polit. & Govt. Pos: Co-capt, dist. 14B, Denver, Colo, 67-; mem, Colo. State Dem. Cent. Cmt, 69- Rel: Protestant. Mailing Add: 2683 S. Niagara, Denver, Colo. 80222.

MUHLESTEIN, GEORGE R
Chmn, Wasatch Co. Cent. Cmt, Utah
b. Provo, Utah, 3/15/05; s. John N. Muhlestein and Martha Liechty M; m. 4/28/26 to Ella A. Clark; c. Harold G, John Clark, Ralph Kent, Marna (Mrs. Grant Patch), LaRae (Mrs. Gene Whiting) and Kathryn (Mrs. Phil Wright). Educ: Lincoln High Sch, Orem, Utah, 4 years. Polit. & Govt. Pos: Chmn, Wasatch Co. Rep. Cent. Cmt, Utah, 67- Mem: Pres, Provo, Utah Retail Grocers Asn, 55-57; Am. Dairy Asn; C. of C; Am. Farm Bur. Fedn; Rotary; AFL. Rel: Latter-day Saint. Mailing Add: R.F.D, Heber City, Utah 84032.

MUHM, JAMES R. R
Capt. Legis. Dist. 13 Rep. Party, Colo.
b. Torrington, Wyo, 8/20/25; married. Educ: Univ. Wyo, B.S, 50. Polit. & Govt. Pos: Capt, Legis. Dist. 13 Rep. Party, Colo, 68- Bus. & Prof. Pos: Research scientist, Martin Marietta Corp, Denver, Colo, 67- Mil. Serv: Entered Navy, 43, released as Lt. Comdr, 54, after serv. in Pac. and Alaska Theatre. Mailing Add: 1747 S. Locust St, Denver, Colo. 80222.

MUI, THOMAS LAWRENCE D
b. Honolulu, Hawaii, 4/29/33; s. King-Chau Mui and Fung-Ching Ng M; m. 4/15/61 to Lois Thom; c. Elisa, Eric. Educ: Univ. of Hawaii, B.A, 54; Fordham Univ, LL.B, 59; N.Y. Univ, 59-60; Newman Club. Polit. & Govt. Pos: Exec. Asst, U.S. Rep. S.M. Matsunaga, D-Hawaii; Claim Examiner, Dept. Health, Educ. & Welfare, N.Y.C, 59-60; Dep. Prosecuting Attorney, Honolulu, 60-62. Bus. & Prof. Pos: Attorney, Matsunaga, Mui, & Gedan, Honolulu, 62-; Secy, Spec. Counsel, Amalgamated Leather Cos. of Del; V.pres, Heritage Investment Co; V.pres, Counsel Caatex Corp. of Honolulu. Mil. Serv: U.S. Army, 54-56, Pfc. Mem: Dir, Chinese Civic Asn; Chinese C. of C; Am. Rose Soc. Rel: Catholic. Mailing Add: 339 Puamamane St, Honolulu, Hawaii 96821. (1967)

MULARZ, RUTH LOUISE D
V.Chmn, Pitkin Co. Dem. Party, Colo.
b. Chicago, Ill, 2/1/29; d. Ernest W. Larson and Sophia Markgraff L; m. 11/9/63 to Theodore L. Mularz; c. Anne Catherine and Mark Andrew. Educ: Carleton Col, B.A. in Econ. Polit. & Govt. Pos: V.Chmn, Pitkin Co. Dem. Party, Colo, 69- Bus. & Prof. Pos: Admin. asst, Int. Minerals & Chem. Corp, Skokie, Ill, 53-59; exec. secy. for Herbert Bayer, Aspen, Colo, 59-63. Rel: Lutheran. Legal Res: White Horse Springs, Aspen, Colo. 81611. Mailing Add: P.O. Box 166, Aspen, Colo. 81611.

MULFORD, DAVID DONALD R
Calif. State Assemblyman
b. Oakland, Calif, 8/27/15; s. David Roscoe Mulford and Mabelle Bush M; m. 6/7/42 to Virginia Adams; c. David Adams, Donna Adams (Mrs. James Randall Moren), Patricia Ann and Donald Adams. Educ: Univ. Calif, A.B, 39; Theta Delta Chi; Kappa Alpha Theta. Polit. & Govt. Pos: Calif. State Assemblyman, 57-, majority caucus chmn, Calif. State Assembly, mem, Constitutional Rev. Cmn. and Ways and Means, Intergovt. Rels. and Urban Affairs and Housing Cmts, ex-officio mem, Assembly Rules Cmt, chmn, Subcmt. on Fire Prev. and Residential Safety and Ways and Means Subcmt. on Capital Outlay, 69-70 Budget; del, Rep. Nat. Conv, 60, 64 & 68. Bus. & Prof. Pos: West Coast mgr, Music Corp. of Am, San Francisco and Beverly Hills, 46-49; pres, Mulford Co, 49-64; partner, Mulford, Poulton and Orr Ins. Brokers, 65- Mil. Serv: Entered as 2nd Lt, Army, 40, released as Lt. Col, 46, after serv. in Am. Theater, 4th Army, 30th Inf. Regt, 3rd Div. and Asiatic Pac. Theater, 9th Amphibious Task Force and ETO, Allied Force Hq; Lt. Col, Army Res; Army Commendation Medal; Order of Crown, Italy; ETO, Asiatic-Pac. and Am. Theater Ribbons. Mem: The Family; Native Sons of the Golden West; Univ. Calif. Alumni Asn; Hastings Col. of Law Alumni Asn; Calif. Hist. Soc; Oakland Mus. Asn; E. Clampus Vitus; Jesters; Am. Legion; Guardsmen; Mason; K.T, KCCH, Shriner; Internation Supreme Coun, DeMolay; Elks; Piedmont Coun, Boy Scouts; Children's Hosp. Med. Center; Bay Counties Peace Officers Asn; Musicians Union Local 6; Reserve Officers Asn; Irish-Israeli Soc. of San Francisco; life mem, Calif. Cong. of Parents and Teachers; YMCA; Commonwealth Club; San Francisco Press Club; High Twelve and Breakfast Club, Berkeley; Lake Merritt Breakfast Club, Oakland; Men's Club of Piedmont; Jr. League. Man of the Year Award, Hastings Col. Law. Rel: Protestant. Mailing Add: 145 Hillside Ave, Piedmont, Calif. 94611.

MULGREW, THOMAS JAMES D
Chmn, Dubuque Co. Dem. Cmt, Iowa
b. Dubuque, Iowa, 11/20/20; s. Russell J. Mulgrew and Genevieve Meysembourg M; m. 5/16/53 to Joan Virginia Kiernan; c. Tom, Kate, Joe, Laura, Tess, Sam and Jennie. Educ: Loras Col, A.B, 39-43. Polit. & Govt. Pos: Chmn, Dubuque Co. Dem. Cmt, Iowa, 62-; del, Dem. Nat. Conv, 64, alternate del, 68. Bus. & Prof. Pos: V.pres, Mulgrew Blacktop, Inc, 53-; pres, Center Grove Land Co, 61-, 4-M Corp, 64- and Asphalt Paving Asn. of Iowa, 65- Mil. Serv: Entered as Pvt, Air Force 43, released as 2nd Lt, 45, after serv. in Cent. Flying Training Command, 44-45. Mem: Elks; Am. Legion; Dubuque Golf and Country Club; v.pres, Loras Alumni Asn. Derby Grange Slalom Champion, 64-65. Rel: Roman Catholic. Mailing Add: R.R. 1, Dubuque, Iowa 52001.

MULHALL, ALLA NELSON D
b. Salina, Utah, d. Arthur Nelson and Anna Ludvigson N; m. 9/2/33 to Thomas Edward Mulhall. Educ: Univ. Utah, B.A. Polit. & Govt. Pos: V.chmn, Voting Dist. and Sen. Dist. Dem. Party, at present; Utah State Rep, Dist. 14, Salt Lake Co. until 67; party worker for more than 25 yrs. Bus. & Prof. Pos: Teacher and librarian, Salt Lake City Schs, Utah for 27 yrs. Mem: Order of Women Legis; Utah Educ. Asn. Rel: Unitarian. Mailing Add: 1475 Murphy's Lane, Salt Lake City, Utah 84106. (1967)

MULHERN, JOHN FRANCIS D
b. New York, N.Y, 1/19/38; s. John Joseph Mulhern and Bridget Gilhouly M; single. Educ: Cathedral Col, B.A, 60; Cath. Univ, S.T.B, 64; Intercultural Inst, P.R, 64. Polit. & Govt. Pos: Del, Dem. Nat. Conv, 68; mem, King's Co. Dem. Coalition, N.Y, 68. Bus. & Prof. Pos: Dir, Independence Commun. Center and Wallabout Commun. Center, 66-, dir, Brooklyn Navy Yard Develop. and Brooklyn Legal Serv. Corp. A, 67- Publ: 'Urban Housing Problems,' Tablet, 65. Rel: Catholic. Mailing Add: 263 Marcy Ave, Brooklyn, N.Y. 11211.

MULHOLLAND, JOE HENRY D
b. Phila, Miss, 8/26/34; single. Polit. & Govt. Pos: Miss. State Sen, until 68. Bus. & Prof. Pos: Farmer and sch. teacher. Mem: Rotary; Farm Bur; C. of C. Rel: Church of God. Mailing Add: Route 3, Collinsville, Miss. 39325. (1967)

MULLEN, JAMES G. D
Educ: Suffolk Univ; U.S. Naval Air Acad, Pensacola. Polit. & Govt. Pos: Town meeting mem; del. to state convs, 54-64; one of two incumbent reps. from dist; serves in House as clerk of cmt. on aeronaut. Bus. & Prof. Pos: Affiliated with Mullen Construction. Mil. Serv: Maj, Marine Corps. Mem: Several vets. and fraternal orgns. Mailing Add: 1355 Canton Ave, Milton, Mass. 02186. (1967)

MULLEN, JOHN H. R
Committeeman, Conn. Rep. State Cent. Cmt.
b. Stafford Springs, Conn, 2/15/09; s. Joseph E. Mullen and Anna Mellon M; m. 4/19/41 to Eleanor Niemiec. Educ: Stafford High Sch, Stafford Springs, Conn. Polit. & Govt. Pos: Conn. State Rep, 45-49; mem, Conn. Rep. State Finance Cmt, 49; Conn. State Sen, 35th Dist, 51; committeeman, Conn. Rep. State Cent. Cmt, 52-; alternate del, Rep. Nat. Conv, 56, 60 & 64, del, 68. Bus. & Prof. Pos: Owner, Mullen Ins. Agency, 38; dir, Stafford Savings Bank and Stafford Savings & Loan Assoc; adv. mem, Conn. Bank & Trust Co, Stafford Springs, Conn. Mem: Rotary (past secy, Stafford Club); K. of C.(4°). Rel: Catholic. Legal Res: 10 W. Main St, Stafford Springs, Conn. 06076. Mailing Add: P.O. Box 85, Stafford Springs, Conn. 06076.

MULLEN, MARTIN P. D
Pa. State Rep.
b. Phila, Pa, 7/29/21; s. John Mullen and Nellie McDermott M. Educ: Wharton Evening Sch. of Univ. of Pa, cert. of proficiency in bus. admin; Brooklyn Law Sch. and Temple Univ. Sch. of Law, LL.B. Polit. & Govt. Pos: Pa. State Rep, 54- Bus. & Prof. Pos: Attorney; admitted to practice before the Phila. Superior and Supreme Courts of Pa, the U.S. Dist. Court, 3rd Circuit Court of Appeals of the East. Dist. of Pa. Mil. Serv: Air Force, Sgt, 42-46; New Caledonia, Australia, Solomons, New Guinea, Philippines. Mem: Am. Legion. Mailing Add: 5332 Glenmore Ave, Philadelphia, Pa. 19143.

MULLENDORE, HERBERT JACK R
Ind. State Rep.
Polit. & Govt. Pos: Ind. State Rep, currently. Bus. & Prof. Pos: Commercial pilot; airport owner and operator; farmer. Mil. Serv: Navy pilot. Mem: Pres, Johnson Co. Red Cross; Mason; Aviation Trades Asn; Farm Bur; Franklin C. of C. Rel: Christian Church. Mailing Add: R.R. 3, Franklin, Ind. 46131.

MULLER, ELLA ELIZABETH R
Mem, Calif. Rep. State Cent. Cmt.
b. Nashville, Ill, 2/12/94; d. Samuel A. Muller and Caroline Koenemann M; single. Educ: South. Ill. Univ, 1 year; Univ. Calif, Los Angeles and Univ. South. Calif, summer semesters. Polit. & Govt. Pos: Precinct worker in city, co, state and nat. campaigns; chmn, Campaign Hq, 54-; mem, Calif. Rep. State Cent. Cmt, 64-; mem, Los Angeles Co. Rep. Cent. Cmt, 48th Assembly Dist, 67-68. Bus. & Prof. Pos: Formerly teacher, Ill; mem. staff, Criminal Div, Los Angeles Co. Clerk's Off, 13 years. Mem: Eastern Star; Royal Neighbors of Am; Highland Park Rep. Women, Federated. Rel: Presbyterian. Mailing Add: 153 Roselawn Place, Los Angeles, Calif. 90042.

MULLER, MARILYN JOAN DFL
b. Minneapolis, Minn, 8/30/32; d. Edgar W. Ozmon and Martha Scheer O; m. to Paul A. Muller; c. Laurits and Elise. Educ: Univ. Minn, B.A, 68; Univ. Interam, Saltillo, Mex, 68; Woodrow Wilson fel. designate. Polit. & Govt. Pos: Chairwoman, Hennepin Co. Dem-Farmer-Labor Party, 63-65; mem, Minn. State Dem. Cent. and Exec. Cmts, 63-65; del, Dem. Nat. Conv, 64. Mailing Add: 4504 Drew Ave. S, Minneapolis, Minn. 55410.

MULLIN, WILLIAM EDWARD, JR. DFL
b. Minneapolis, Minn, 4/15/34; s. W. Edward Mullin and Mary Hester M; singled. Educ: Georgetown Univ, 52-54; Univ. Minn. Law Sch, B.S.L, 56, LL.B, 58. Polit. & Govt. Pos: Attorney, U.S. Dept. of Justice, Wash. D.C, 58-60; spec. asst. attorney gen, Minn, 60-63; chmn, Dem-Farmer-Labor Ward Club, Edina-Hopkins, 63; mem, Nat. Adv. Coun, Small Bus. Admin, 66-67; chmn, Hennepin Co. Dem-Farmer-Labor Party, Minn, 67-68. Bus. & Prof. Pos: Attorney, Law Firm of Erickson, Popham, Haik & Schnobrich, 63-64; attorney and partner, Mullin, Galinson, Swirnoff & Weinberg, 64- Mem: Hennepin Co. and Fed. Bar Asns; Minn. State Bar Asn.(mem, Admin. Law and Antitrust Cmts.); Am. Bar Asn.(mem, Antitrust Sect); Minn. Hist. Soc; Minn. Civil Liberties Union; Citizens' League. Rel: Catholic. Legal Res: 17 S. First St, Minneapolis, Minn. 55401. Mailing Add: 2200 Dain Tower, Minneapolis, Minn. 55402.

MULLINS, DAVID WALKER D
Chmn, Logan Co. Dem. Party, W.Va.
b. Stollings, W.Va, 12/29/23; s. Roy Mullins and Freda Walker M; m. 3/20/45 to Jacqueline Wampler Friel; c. James Walker, Vernon Nathaniel, Ruth Ellen and Linda Fay. Educ: W.Va. Univ, A.B. and B.S; Med. Col. of Va, M.D; Delta Tau Delta; Phi Beta Pi. Polit. & Govt. Pos: W.Va. State Sen, 64-68; mem, Logan City Dem. Exec. Cmt; chmn, Logan Co. Dem. Party, W.Va, 69- Bus. & Prof. Pos: Physician and surgeon. Mil. Serv: World War II, ERC, AUS, former med. officer, Naval Res. Mem: Am. Med. Asn; W.Va. Acad. Ophthalmology and Otolaryngology. Rel: Protestant. Mailing Add: Logan, W.Va. 25601. (1967)

MULREED, JAMES NELSON D
b. Stamford, Conn, 9/7/97; s. William Patrick Mulreed and Harriet Fisk M; m. 6/12/24 to Frances T. Murphy; c. Mary E. (Mrs. French), Francis W, James E. and Agnes B. (Mrs. Toth). Educ: Marrietta Col; Alpha Di Gamma. Polit. & Govt. Pos: Fourth dist. rep, Stamford Bd. of Rep, 49-55; mem, Conn. Hoover Cmn, 59-63; Conn. State Rep, 59-66. Bus. & Prof. Pos: Photographer, McClelland & Pratt, 15-17; employ. mgr. and staff mem. cost dept, Elec. Specialty Co, 22-29; owner, Stamford Ignition & Battery Serv, 29-37; machinist, Petroleum Heat & Power Corp, 38-40 and Norma Hoffman Bearings Corp, 40-65. Mil. Serv: Entered as Pvt, Army, 17, released as Pfc, 19, after serv. in Ambulance Serv; Croix de Guerre with Star, France. Mem: K. of C; Hibernians; Stamford Good Govt. Asn; Am. Legion; Lodge 1666 Int. Asn. of Machinists. Rel: Roman Catholic. Mailing Add: 53 Crane Rd, Stamford, Conn. 06902. (1967)

MULROONEY, FRANK LEO D
Chmn, Vilas Co. Dem. Party, Wis.
b. Mt. Hope, Wis, 1/27/98; s. Edward Mulrooney and Agnes Cull M; m. 10/11/29 to Catherine Ellen Morrison; c. Patrick Edward, Michael James and Timothy Francis. Educ: Marquette Univ, Ph.G, 18; Wis. Real Estate Sch. & Univ. Exten, passed examining bd. exam, 68. Polit. & Govt. Pos: Chmn, Vilas Co. Dem. Party, Wis, 59-62 & 67-, v.chmn, 64-67; mem, Gov. Cmt, Employment of Handicapped, 61-68; mem, President's Cmt, Employment of Handicapped, 61-; alderman, City Coun, Eagle River, Wis, 61-; supvr, Co. Bd, Vilas Co, 65-; mem, Adv. Coun. Small Bus. Admin, Minn. and Wis. Dist, 68- Bus. & Prof. Pos: Pharmacist and pres, Mulrooney Drug Co, Inc, Eagle River, Wis, 24-69; dir, loan dept, First Nat. Bank, 51-; owner and operator, Mulrooney Realty, 68- Mem: C. of C; Conservation Clubs; K. of C; Rotary. Rel: Roman Catholic. Legal Res: 303 Third St, Eagle River, Wis. 54521. Mailing Add: Mulrooney Drug Co, Inc, 107 E. Wall St, Eagle River, Wis. 54521.

MULTER, ABRAHAM J. D
Justice, Supreme Court of N.Y.
b. Manhattan, N.Y, 12/24/00; s. Max Multer (deceased) and Emma Rock M. (deceased); m. to Bertha L; c. Robert K. and Howard C. Educ: City Col, N.Y, eve. classes; Brooklyn Law Sch, LL.B. and LL.M; Yeshiva Univ, LL.D; pres, Marshall Soc; nat. practor, Iota Theta. Polit. & Govt. Pos: Counsel to Dem. leader, N.Y. State Assembly and to many city, state and fed. legis. cmts; spec. counsel to Mayor, N.Y.C; spec. asst. Attorney Gen. in elec. matters, 10 years; former v.chmn, Kings Co. and N.Y. State Dem. Law Cmts; former exec. mem, pres, secy, chmn, Civil Serv. Cmt. and organizer Civil Serv. Sch, Kings Hwy. Dem. Club; former mem, N.Y. State Dem. Cmt. and Kings Co. Exec. Cmt; U.S. Rep, N.Y, 47-67, mem, Banking and Currency, Small Bus, D.C. and Joint Defense Prod. Cmts, U.S. House of Rep, Zone Two Dem. Whip; Justice, Supreme Court of N.Y, 67- Bus. & Prof. Pos: Former mem, Rayfiel and Multer and Multer, Nova and Seymour. Mil. Serv: Coast Guard Res, World War II. Mem: Brooklyn, N.Y. State and Inter-Am. Bar Asns; Fed. Bar Asn. D.C, N.Y, N.J. and Conn; N.Y. Law Inst; Am. Judicature Soc; Am. Soc. Int. Law; Brooklyn-Manhattan Trial Lawyers Asn; Am. Polit. Sci. Asn; lay bd, Coney Island Hosp; adv. bd, East Midwood Jewish Center; pres. coun, Yeshiva Univ; former chmn. lawyers cmt, Jewish Nat. Fund; v.chmn, Albert Einstein Med. Col. Cmt; former pres, Men's Club, Temple Beth Emeth and Coney Island YMHA; United Hebrew Immigrant Aid Soc; exec. cmt, Fedn. Jewish Philanthropies; life mem, Hebrew Inst. L.I; trustee, Union Am. Hebrew Congregations; Jewish Theol. Sem; Synagogue Coun. Am; Zionist Orgn. Am; Am. Friends Hebrew Univ; B'nai B'rith; B'nai Zion; Jewish Chatauqua Soc; former del, Nat. Fedn. and Metrop. Conf. Temple Brotherhoods; bd. dir, Ocean Front and Shorefront YMHA and YWHA Brooklyn; Coast Guard Auxiliary; Coast Guard League; dir, Nottingham Civic Asn; past pres, P.S. 193 PTA; Mason; Elks; K. of P; Boy Scouts; Flatbush Boys Club; Police Athletic League; Men's League, Brooklyn Jewish Commun. Coun; hon. fel, Archaeol. Inst. Am; hon. trustee, Boys' High Sch. Alumni Asn. Admitted to practice law before U.S. Supreme Court, U.S. Court Mil. Appeals and many fed. dept. Rel: Jewish; V.pres, Temple Beth Emeth. Mailing Add: Supreme Court, Civic Center, Brooklyn, N.Y. 11201.

MULVEY, HAROLD M. D
b. New Haven, Conn, 12/5/14; s. Michael Mulvey and Bessie M; m. 11/21/53 to Genevieve Carroll; c. Ann. Educ: Fordham Univ, B.S, 38; Law Sch, LL.B, 41. Polit. & Govt. Pos: Attorney Gen. of Conn, until 67; app. asst. Corp. Counsel New Haven, 54; Corp. Counsel, New Haven, 61-63. Bus. & Prof. Pos: Lawyer, admitted to N.Y. Bar, 42, Conn. Bar, 49; admitted to practice in U.S. Dist. Court for South. Dist. of N.Y, U.S. Dist. Court for Conn. Firm, Mulvey, Falsey and Shay. Mil. Serv: Coast Guard, Lt, with serv. on sub chaser, Atlantic, Comdr, LST, Iwo Jima, Okinawa and Japan. Mem: Knights of St. Patrick, New Haven; Grads. Club of New Haven; New Haven City Bar Asn; Conn. State and Am. Bar Asns. Mailing Add: 244 McKinley Ave, New Haven, Conn. 06515. (1967)

MUNDT, KARL EARL R
U.S. Sen, S.Dak.
b. Humboldt, S.Dak, 6/3/00; s. F. J. Mundt and Rose E. Schneider M; m. 6/24/24 to Mary E. Moses. Educ: Carleton Col, A.B, 23; Columbia Univ, A.M, 27; Delta Sigma Rho; Pi Kappa Delta. Hon. degrees, Riders Col, N.J, St. John's Univ, N.Y, Huron Col, Dakota Wesleyan Univ. and S.Dak. Sch. of Mines and Tech, S.Dak. Polit. & Govt. Pos: Co-chmn, Nat. Rep. Cmt. Speakers Bur, First Eisenhower-Nixon Campaign; mem, S.Dak. Game and Fish Cmn, 30-36; U.S. Rep, S.Dak, 39-49; U.S. Sen, S.Dak, 49-, mem, for. rels, appropriations and govt. opers cmts. Bus. & Prof. Pos: Chmn. speech dept, Gen. Beadle State Col, 27-36; secy-treas, Mundt Loan and Investment Co, Madison, S.Dak, 27-38. Publ: Articles in Reader's Digest, Cosmopolitan, Liberty Magazine, This Week and many others. Mem: Mason, Shrine; Odd Fellows; Elks; Isaak Walton League. Rel: Methodist. Mailing Add: Madison, S.Dak. 57042.

MUNFORD, DILLARD R
First V.Chmn, Ga. Rep. Orgn.
b. Cartersville, Ga, 5/13/18; s. Robert Sims Munford and Katherine Aubrey M; m. 9/6/41 to Lillie Shepherd Davis; c. Dillard, Jr, Page S, Mary Aubrey, Robert D. and Henry A. Educ: Ga. Inst. Tech, B.S. in Mech. Eng. Polit. & Govt. Pos: Past pres, Young Pres. Orgn, Ga, 63; finance chmn, Howard Callaway for Gov, 64; mem, Ga. State Rep. Exec. Cmt. and asst. chmn, Exec. Cmt, 64-; first v.chmn, Ga. Rep. Orgn, currently; alternate del, Rep. Nat. Conv, 68. Bus. & Prof. Pos: Pres, Munford Co, 46-62; chmn. bd, Atlantic Co, 62-; past div. v.pres, Nat. Asn. Mfgrs; pres. and chief exec. officer, Jackson-Atlantic, Inc, 68- Mil. Serv: Entered as 2nd Lt, Army, 42, released as Capt, 45, after serv. in Aleutian Islands; Pac. Campaign Ribbon. Rel: Methodist. Legal Res: 1065 W. Paces Ferry Rd, Atlanta, Ga. 30327. Mailing Add: P.O. Box 7701 Sta. C, Atlanta, Ga. 30309.

MUNGER, HARRY LEONARD D
Mem, Minn. DFL State Cent. Cmt.
b. Fergus Falls, Minn, 10/29/27; s. Harry Lyman Munger and Elsie Zuelsdorph M; m. 6/23/51 to Barbara Jean Kobe; c. Mark, David and Anne. Educ: Univ. of Minn, B.S, 52; St. Paul Col. of Law, LL.B, 56; Delta Theta Phi. Polit. & Govt. Pos: Chmn, St. Louis Co. DFL Party, Minn, 58-60; state del, Minn. DFL Conv, 58-; mem, Minn. DFL State Cent. Cmt, 58-; Eighth Dist. DFL Party, 64-67; special munic. judge, Duluth 64-; del, Dem. Nat. Conv, 68. Bus. & Prof. Pos: Lawyer, McDonald & Munger, Duluth, Minn, 56- Mil. Serv: Entered as Pvt, Air Force, 45, released as Pfc, 47, after serv. in U.S; Good Conduct Medal. Mem: Minn. Bar Asn; Trial Lawyers of Am; Moose; Issac Walton; Clean Air. Col. Court of Honor, St. Paul Col. of Law. Rel: Episcopal. Mailing Add: 2402 Chambersburg, Duluth, Minn. 55811.

MUNGER, WILLARD M. DFL
Minn. State Rep.
b. 1911. Educ: Univ. of Minn. Polit. & Govt. Pos: Minn. State Rep, 55-65 & 67-; mem, Water Pollution Control Adv. Cmn; mem, Zoological Bd. and Zoological Adv. Cmn; food sect. chief, Off. Price Stabilization; mem. mkt. inspection serv, dairy and food div, State Dept. of Agr, and state grain inspection serv, Minn. Bus. & Prof. Pos: Pres, Willard Enterprises, Inc; former grocer. Mailing Add: 7408 Grand Ave, Duluth, Minn. 55807. (1967)

MUNIZ, RAUL D
Tex. State Rep.
b. Floresville, Tex, 6/4/32; s. Raul R. Muniz and Beatrice Trevino M; m. 2/28/54 to Esther Patino; c. Frank Rey, Ruth and Raul, III. Educ: Tex. West, B.A. and M.Ed; Phi Alpha Theta. Polit. & Govt. Pos: Tex. State Rep, 64- Mil. Serv: Entered as Pvt, Army, 54, released as Cpl, 56, after serv. in 97th Engrs. Mem: TSTA; Nat. Educ. Asn. Rel: Methodist. Mailing Add: 9923 Fenway Dr, El Paso, Tex. 79925. (1967)

MUNLEY, MARION L. D
b. Buffalo, N.Y; d. Martin J. Langan (deceased) and Julia Walsh L; m. to Robert W. Munley; wid; c. two sons. Educ: Marywood Col; Powell Sch. of Bus. Polit. & Govt. Pos: Pa. State Rep, 47-67; elected Secy. of the House, 65; Young Dems. of Lackawanna Cty; Blakely Dem. Club; Jermyn Dem. Club; Women's Dem. Club of Mayfield. Mem: Organizer and pres. of 20th Ward Dem. Women's Club; Am. Legion Auxiliary; Archbald Civic Asn. Mailing Add: 175 Spruce St, Archbald, Pa. 18403. (1967)

MUNLEY, ROBERT WILLIAM D
b. Archbald, Pa, 11/22/30; s. Robert W. Munley and Marion Langan M; m. 7/30/60 to Bernadine Munley; c. Marion, Bernadine, Robert W, III, Daniel and Christopher. Educ: Univ. of Scranton, B.S, 52; Temple Univ. Sch. of Law, LL.B, 58. Polit. & Govt. Pos: Asst. dist. attorney, Lackawanna Co, Pa, 60-; chmn, Dem. Cmt, Archbald, Pa, 63-66; del, Dem. Nat. Conv, 68; Dem. nominee, dist. attorney, Lackawanna Co, 69. Bus. & Prof. Pos: Partner, Fallk and Munley, 59-65, Munley and Munley, 65-68 and Munley and Pieski, 68- Mil. Serv: Entered as Pvt, Army, 53, released as Cpl, 55, after serv. in 841st Eng-Aviation Bn, Korea. Mem: Phi Delta Phi; Pa. Bar Asn; Boy Scouts (mem. exec. bd, Forest Lake Coun); Am. Red Cross (mem. bd. of dirs, Scranton Chap). Rel: Roman Catholic. Mailing Add: 352 Main St, Archbald, Pa, 18503.

MUNNELL, WILLIAM ARTHUR D
b. Marshalltown, Iowa, 10/9/20; m. 4/6/40 to Charlotte Hayduk; c. William John, Mary Louise, Betty Jean and David Brian. Educ: Univ. of South. Calif, A.B. and LL.B. Polit. & Govt. Pos: Calif. State Assemblyman, 50-61; judge, Superior Court, Calif, 61- Mil. Serv: Vet. World War II. Mailing Add: 226 Peacock Lane, Montebello, Calif. 90640.

MUÑOZ, PADIN RENE Popular Dem, P.R.
Pres, Fifth Dist. Popular Dem. Party, P.R.
b. Las Marías, P.R, 1/2/25; s. Manuel Muñoz Torrellas and Teresa Padín Mártir T; m. 4/22/44 to Gloria Maria del Castillo Aponte; c. Carmen Gloria, Ileana Margarita, Betsy and René José. Educ: Univ. P.R, B.A, 46, Col. Law, LL.B, 49. Polit. & Govt. Pos: P.R. Rep, 52-60; munic. assemblyman, San Juan City, 62-64; P.R. Sen, First Dist, San Juan City, 64-68; pres, Fifth Dist. Popular Dem. Party, currently. Mem: Exchange Club; Colegio de Abogados de P.R. Rel: Catholic. Legal Res: Tulipán 171, Urbanización San Francisco, Río Piedras, P.R. 00920. Mailing Add: Calle Alesia 1000, Puerto Nuevo, P.R. 00920.

MUNOZ-MARIN, LUIS Popular D
P.R. Sen-at-lg.
b. San Juan, P.R, 2/18/98; s. Luis Munoz-Rivera and Amalia Marin; m. to Ines Maria Mendoza; c. Munita, Luis II, Vivian and Victoria. Educ: Georgetown Univ, 12-16. Polit. & Govt. Pos: Secy, Resident Cmnr. P.R. in Wash, D.C, 16-18; P.R. Sen-at-lg, 32 & 65-; founder and pres, Popular Dem. Party, 38; pres, P.R. Sen, 41-48; gov, Territory of P.R, 48-52, Commonwealth of P.R, 52-65; mem, Constitutional Assembly P.R, 51; formerly econ. cmnr. for P.R. in U.S; mem. gen. secretariat, Pan-Am. Conf, Havana. Bus. & Prof. Pos: Founder and ed, El Batey; ed. and publisher, La Democracia; ed, La Revista de Indies, 18-19. Publ: Borrones, 17; Madra Haraposa (in collab), 17; contrib, Am. Mercury, Nation, New Repub. and For. Affairs. Rel: Catholic. Mailing Add: Capitol, San Juan, P.R. 00903. (1967)

MUNOZ-RIVERA, LUIS D
V.Pres, Dem. Party of P.R.
b. Cayey, P.R, 4/10/16; s. Jose Munoz and Clemencia Rivera M; m. 12/17/64 to Dulce Fernandez; c. Luis and Marya. Educ: Univ. of P.R, B.B.A, 51 and LL.B, 60; Syracuse Univ, M.P.A, 54. Polit. & Govt. Pos: Auditor, San Juan, P.R, 47-54, dir. of the budget, 54-59; mem. cent. bd, San Juan Popular Dem. Cmt, 50-; del, P.R. Constitutional Conv, 51-52; P.R. State Sen, 61-68; treas, P.R. Dem. State Cmt, 62-; 1st v.pres, San Juan Popular Dem. Party, 65-69; del, Dem. Nat. Conv, 68; v.pres, Dem. Party of P.R, 68- Mem: Am. Bar Asn; bd. of dirs, Bar Asn. of P.R, 62-63; v.pres, P.R. Soc. Pub. Admin, 66- Rel: Catholic. Legal Res: Apt. 9W, 61 King's Court, San Juan, P.R. 00911. Mailing Add: Box 1892, Hato Rey, P.R. 00919.

MUNROE, KENNETH GEORGE D
Chmn, Del Norte Co. Dem. Cent. Cmt, Calif.
b. Crary, N.Dak, 5/20/23; s. John Barkley Munroe and Bertha Powell M; m. 7/9/49 to Erma Juanita Kostic; c. Dalie (Mrs. Jack Morgan), Victoria, Rex, John and Anthony. Educ: Tillamook High Sch, 4 years. Polit. & Govt. Pos: Chmn, Del Norte Co. Dem. Cent. Cmt, 65- Bus. & Prof. Pos: Log scaler, Tillamook Log Scaling & Grading, 49-56; log scaler, N.Calif. Log Scaling Bur, 56-58; timber mgr, McNamara & Peepe, 58- Mil. Serv: Entered as Pvt, Army, 39, released as Sgt, 45, after serv. in Inf, Pac. Theatre, 42-44; Combat Infantryman's Badge; Victory Medal; Am. Defense Serv. Medal; Am. Theatre Serv. Medal. Mem: Forest Forum; Log Scaling Asn. North. Calif; C. of C; Elks; Am. Legion; VFW; Boy Scouts. All-State Post Comdr. of VFW, 65-67. Rel: Protestant. Mailing Add: 917 Hamilton Ave, Crescent City, Calif. 95531.

MUNSEY, EVERARD D
Chmn, Arlington Co. Dem. Cmt, Va.
b. Washington, D.C, 9/25/33; s. Virdell E. Munsey and Mildred Wood M; m. 9/20/56 to Bernice Wilson; c. Wanda Louise, Allan Coll, Andrew Everard and Carolyn Jane. Educ: Yale Univ, B.A. magna cum laude, 55; Harvard Univ, M.P.A, 67; Pi Sigma Alpha. Polit. & Govt. Pos: Legis. asst. to U.S. Rep. Henry Reuss, 63-68; v.chmn, Arlington Co. Dem. Cmt, Va, 65-66, chmn, 67-; info. coordinator, United Dem. for Humphrey, 68; del, Dem. Nat. Conv, 68; asst. dir. pub. affairs for news and dir. research, Dem. Nat. Cmt, 68. Bus. & Prof. Pos: Reporter, Wash. Post, 57-63; asst. exec. secy, Nat. Planning Asn, 69- Mil. Serv: Entered as Pvt, Army, 55, released as Pfc, 57, after serv. in 6966th Spec. Detached Unit, 56-57. Mem: Am. Polit. Sci. Asn; Am. Acad. Polit. and Soc. Sci. Am. Polit. Sci. Asn. distinguished pub. affairs reporting award, 62 and cong. staff fel, 66-67. Rel: Congregational. Mailing Add: 2389 N. Kenmore St, Arlington, Va. 22207.

MURAKOWSKI, ARTHUR R. D
Ind. State Rep.
b. East Chicago, Ind, 3/15/25; s. Ben Murakowski and Clara Krolikowski M; m. 10/23/54 to Lucille Pawlus; c. Arthur J, Janis, Judith, Mark, Karen and Thomas. Educ: Northwest. Univ, Evanston, B.S, 50; Beta Theta Pi. Polit. & Govt. Pos: Clerk, Co. Assessors Off, Ind, 54-68, supvr, N.Twp. Assessors Off, 68; Ind. State Rep, 65- Mil. Serv: Entered as Seaman 3/C, Navy, 43, released as Fireman 1/C, 46, after serv. aboard Destroyer-Minelayer, Pac. Mem: Am. Legion. Most Valuable Football Player to Team, Northwest. Univ, 47-48, All Am. Honors, 48. Rel: Catholic. Mailing Add: 256 Dyer Blvd, Hammond, Ind. 46320

MURCH, BERTRAND LOUD D
b. Minneapolis, Minn, 9/25/96; s. George L. Murch and Christine Grund M; m. 4/30/17 to Hazel C. Winkley; c. Lucille C.(Mrs. Jonjak), Roberta L.(Mrs. Wright), Carol C.(Mrs. Schroeder) and James W. Educ: W. and Cent. High Sch, 4 years. Polit. & Govt. Pos: Chmn, Rusk Co. Progressive Party, Wis, 36, Chippewa Co. Dem. Party, 58 and Barron Co. Dem. Party, 68; pres, Wis. Farmers for Humphrey, 60; del, Dem. Nat. Conv, 68. Bus. & Prof. Pos: Dairy farmer, Rusk Co, Wis, 18-46; turkey producer, Chippewa Co, 46-60; semi-retired turkey laborer, 61- Rel: Methodist. Mailing Add: Route 1, Barron, Wis. 54812.

MURFIN, WILLIAM FLOYD R
Assoc. Adminstr, Small Bus. Admin.
b. Anderson, Ind, 8/28/25; s. Floyd Frank Murfin and Della Fowler M; 2nd m. 3/4/62 to Jean Wilson; c. Carole, Robyn, James, Charles and Harold. Educ: Ferris State Col, Big Rapids, Mich, B.S, 50. Polit. & Govt. Pos: Chmn, Rep. Activities Cmt, Fla, 64-65; pres, Martin Co. Young Rep. Club, 65-66; chmn, Rep. State Exec. Cmt, Fla, 66-69; mem, Rep. Nat. Cmt, 66-69; del, secy. of host cmt. and chmn, Fla. Del, Rep. Nat. Conv, 68; assoc. adminstr, Small Bus. Admin, Wash, D.C, 69- Bus. & Prof. Pos: Mem, Fla. Bd. of Pharmacy. Mil. Serv: Seaman, Navy, European Theatre, 43-46. Mem: Elks. Rel: Protestant. Legal Res: P.O. Box 723, Hobe Sound, Fla. 33455. Mailing Add: 1441 L St. N.W, Washington, D.C. 20005.

MURNINGHAN, MAX ERNEST R
b. St. Johns, Mich, 8/18/24; s. Ernest R. Murninghan and Gladys Smith M; m. 4/19/47 to Patricia Anne Planck; c. Marsha Marie, Mark Windsor, Laurie Danaher and Patrick Hartman. Educ: Purdue Univ, 46; Mich. State Univ, 47. Polit. & Govt. Pos: Mem, city coun, Lansing, Mich, 54-61, pres, 60-61,

mayor, 65-69; mem, Ingham Co. Bd. Supvrs, 55-61; pres, Conf. of Mayors, 67- Bus. & Prof. Pos: Owner, Murninghan Printing Co, Lansing, 50-54; realtor, Lansing, 61-65; chmn. employer-employee rels. cmt. and trustee, Mich. Munic. League, 67- Mil. Serv: Marine Corps Res, World War II; Purple Heart. Mem: Bd. dirs, United Commun. Chest; Lansing Safety Coun; Ingham Co. Chap, Red Cross; Nat. Found. Ment. Health Cmt; pres. bd. dirs, Lansing Conv. Bur; Gr. Lansing C. of C; Am. Legion; VFW; Marine Corps League; First Marine Div. Asn. Rel: Methodist. Legal Res: 115 S. Jenison St, Lansing, Mich. 48915. Mailing Add: City Hall, Lansing, Mich. 48933.

MURPHY, ARTHUR POWELL D
Idaho State Sen.
b. Sandpoint, Idaho, 5/18/98; s. Thomas Edward Murphy and Mary Elizabeth Purdy M; m. 4/5/28 to Anietta Inola Rolfs; c. Michael Arthur, Colleen Joyce (Mrs. Cornell) and Terrance William. Educ: High sch, Sandpoint, Idaho 2 years. Polit. & Govt. Pos: Idaho State Rep, Shoshone Co, 39-43 & 51, Asst. Majority Leader, 41, Asst. Minority Leader, 43 and Minority Leader, 51, Idaho State House of Rep; Idaho State Sen, 57-, Majority Leader, 59, Minority Leader, 67 and Caucus Chmn, 69, Idaho State Senate; del, Dem. Nat. Conv, 68. Mem: Mullan Coun; pres, C. of C; first civil defense dir, Shoshone Co; dir, United Crusade; Cataldo Mission; Wallace Mus; Elks; Eagles. Batting Awards and Diamond Lapel Button, Oakland Championship Coast League, 27. Rel: Presbyterian. Mailing Add: 127 Mill. St, Mullan, Idaho 83846.

MURPHY, ASHLEY MONROE D
b. Atkinson, N.C, 8/14/09; s. John Alexander Murphy, Sr. and Mary Campbell M; m. 1/18/47 to Alice Hill Reeves; c. Priscilla Katherine. Educ: N.C. State Col; Univ. N.C; Emory Univ, A.B, LL.B, 34; Alpha Lambda Tau. Polit. & Govt. Pos: Mem, State Dem. Exec. Cmt, 53-62; N.C. State Rep, 53-66; del, Dem. Nat. Conv, 56 & 60. Bus. & Prof. Pos: Trustee, Univ. N.C, Greensboro and Pembroke State Col; farmer; ins. dealer. Mil. Serv: Army, Sgt, 42-45, with serv. in Africa and Italy, First Armored Div, 27th FA. Mem: Elks; Atkinson Ruritan Club (secy, 50-52); Am. Legion; VFW; dir. and v.pres, N.C. Agr. Found, 58-59; Boy Scouts (educ. adv). Rel: Presbyterian. Mailing Add: Atkinson, N.C. 28421. (1967)

MURPHY, AUSTIN J. D
Pa. State Rep.
b. North Charleroi, Pa, 6/17/27; s. Austin J. Murphy and Evelyn Spence M; m. to Eileen Romona McNamara; c. Colleen, Erin, Brian, Maureen, Sheila and Holly. Educ: Duquesne Univ, A.B, 48; Univ. of Pittsburgh, LL.B, 52. Polit. & Govt. Pos: Boro auditor, Speers, Pa, 49-51, Boro Councilman, 51-55; mem, Dem. Cmt, 53-55; asst. dist. attorney, Wash. Co, 56-57; Pa. State Rep, 59- Mil. Serv: Entered as Pvt, Marines, 44, released 46; Marine Corps. Res, 48-50. Mem: Pa. and Am. Bar Asns; Am. Trial Lawyers Asn; Am. Legion. Rel: Catholic. Legal Res: 699 Maple Dr, Monongahela, Pa. 15063. Mailing Add: 308 Fallowfield Ave, Charleroi, Pa. 15022.

MURPHY, CHARLES SPRINGS D
b. Wallace, N.C, 8/20/09; s. William Murphy and Kate Westbrook M; m. 12/24/31 to Kate Chestney Graham M; c. Courtenay, Westbrook and Elizabeth. Educ: Duke Univ, A.B, 31; LL.B, 34; Order of the Coif; Delta Sigma Phi; Pi Gamma Mu; Omicron Delta Kappa. Polit. & Govt. Pos: Past pres, Nat. Capitol Dem. Club; mem, Off. of Legis. Counsel, U.S. Senate, 34-47; admin. asst. to President, U.S, 47-50; spec. counsel to President, U.S, 50-53; counsel to Dem. Nat. Adv. Coun, 57-60; Under Secy. of Agr, 61-65; chmn, Civil Aeronaut. Bd, 65-68; counselor to President, U.S, 68-69. Bus. & Prof. Pos: Lawyer, mem. firm Morison, Murphy, Clapp & Abrams, 53-61 and Morison, Murphy, Abrams & Haddock, 69- Mem: Mem, bd. of visitors, Duke Sch. of Law; Brookings Adv. Cmt. on Pres. Transition, 60; Am, D.C, N.C, and Fed. Bar Asns. Rel: Methodist. Mailing Add: Greenbriar Lane, Annapolis, Md. 21401.

MURPHY, DENNIS EDWARD, JR. D
b. Concord, N.H, 9/9/42; s. D. Edward Murphy and Viola Hall M; m. 10/8/66 to Janice Helene Janovic. Educ: Univ. N.H, B.A. in govt; Pi Gamma Mu; Pi Sigma Alpha. Polit. & Govt. Pos: Mem, N.H. State Dem. Cmt, 64-66; N.H. State Rep, 65-66; spec. asst. to Gov. John W. King, N.H, 66-69. Bus. & Prof. Pos: Consult, Resources Develop. Center, Univ. N.H, 69- Rel: Roman Catholic. Legal Res: Center Hill Rd, Epsom, N.H. 03234. Mailing Add: R.D, Gossville, N.H. 03239.

MURPHY, EWELL EDWARD, SR. D
Chmn, Tom Green Co. Dem. Cmt, Tex.
b. Weatherford, Tex, 5/12/95; s. Robert W. Murphy and Maude Baker M; m. 6/15/23 to Lou Phillips; c. E.E. Murphy, Jr. and Mary Lou (Mrs. Williams). Educ: Cumberland Univ, LL.B; Nat. Univ, LL.B; Georgetown Univ, B.F.S. Polit. & Govt. Pos: Chmn, Tom Green Co. Dem. Cmt, Tex, 35-; chmn. selective serv. appeal bd, North Judicial Dist, Tex, 40-; presidential elector, 62. Bus. & Prof. Pos: Practicing attorney, San Angelo, Tex, 17-; co. attorney, 19-20; mem, D.C. Bar, 21-30. Mil. Serv: Entered as Pvt, 17, released as 2nd Lt, 19, after serv. in 133rd Machine Gun Bn, 36th Div, AEF, France. Mem: VFW; DAV; Am. Legion; Mason (32°); Shrine. Rel: Baptist. Mailing Add: 615 Central, San Angelo, Tex. 76901. (1967)

MURPHY, FRANK, JR. R
Calif. State Assemblyman
b. Santa Cruz, Calif, 1/19/34; s. John Francis Murphy and Marjorie Liebbrandt M; m. 7/7/62 to Christine A. Allegrini; c. Michel Louise and Katherine Anne. Educ: Univ. of Santa Clara, A.B, 55 and LL.B, 57. Polit. & Govt. Pos: Consult, Joint Interim Cmt. on Equalization and Assessment Practices, Calif. Legis, 57; Calif. State Assemblyman, 31st Dist, 67-, chmn, Criminal Procedure Cmt, Calif. State Assembly, 69- Bus. & Prof. Pos: Assoc, Murphy & Adams, 57-58 & 61-66; partner, Murphy & Murphy, 66-68 and Murphy, Murphy & Black, 68- Mil. Serv: Entered as Lt.(jg), Navy, 58, released as Lt, 61, after serv. as Legal Officer, Beeville, Tex, 58-59 and Long Beach, Calif. 59-61. Mem: Calif. and Santa Cruz Co. Bar Asns; Am. Cancer Soc; Leukemia Soc, Inc; Lions; Elks; K. of C; Navy League; Miss Calif. Pageant Bd. of Dirs. Rel: Catholic. Legal Res: 33 Eastridge Dr, Santa Cruz, Calif. 95060. Mailing Add: P.O. Box 634, Santa Cruz, Calif. 95060.

MURPHY, GEORGE LLOYD R
U.S. Sen, Calif.
b. New Haven, Conn, 7/4/02; s. Mike Murphy; m. 1926 to Julie Johnson M; c. Dennis and Melissa (Mrs. Robert W. Ellis III). Educ: Yale Univ. Polit. & Govt. Pos: Del. to four Rep. Nat. Conv, in charge of progs, 56 & 60; chmn, Calif. Rep. State Cent. Cmt, 53-54; U.S. Sen, Calif, 64-, mem, Senate Armed Serv. and Labor and Pub. Welfare Cmts; chmn, Nat. Rep. Sen. Cmt, 67-69. Mem: Past pres, AFL-CIO affil. Screen Actors Guild, bd. dirs, 15 years. Appeared in four Broadway Shows and 45 Motion Pictures; recognized by Army, Navy, Marine Corps, Air Force and Coast Guard for activities in entertainment during World War II; received awards and honors from U.S. Dept. of State, Am. Red Cross, Friendly Sons of St. Patrick, USO, Boy Scouts, Cancer Prev. Soc. and Univ. South. Calif; received first Nat. Award given by Nat. Conf. of Christians and Jews. Legal Res: Beverly Hills, Calif. Mailing Add: 452 Senate Office Bldg, Washington, D.C. 20510.

MURPHY, IRA H. D
Tenn. State Rep.
b. Memphis, Tenn, 9/8/28; s. George Murphy and Margaret Ross M; m. to Rubye Bland. Educ: Tenn. State Univ, B.S, 50; N.Y. Univ, LL.B, 55, LL.M, 57; Kappa Delta Pi; Alpha Phi Alpha. Polit. & Govt. Pos: Tenn. State Rep, Dist. Six, 68- Bus. & Prof. Pos: Attorney at law, Memphis, Tenn. Mil. Serv: Army. Mem: Mason; Shrine; Elks. Rel: Seventh Day Adventist. Legal Res: 411 S. Orleans, Memphis, Tenn. 38126. Mailing Add: 626 Vance Ave, Memphis, Tenn. 38126.

MURPHY, JACK M. R
Lt. Gov, Idaho
b. Shoshone, Idaho, 1925. Educ: Idaho State Univ; Univ. Utah, B.S. in Econ. and Acct. and LL.B, 51. Polit. & Govt. Pos: Idaho State Sen, 12 years, Minority Leader, Idaho State Senate, 59, Majority Leader, 61, pres. pro tem, 63, 65 and spec. session 66; Lt. Gov, Idaho, 67- Bus. & Prof. Pos: Attorney; cattle rancher. Mailing Add: P.O. Box 506, Shoshone, Idaho 83352. (1967)

MURPHY, JAMES E. R
Mont. State Rep.
b. Laredo, Mo, 11/6/10; s. John F. Murphy and Ida Warren M; m. to Sylvia J. Brassett; c. Mary Patricia. Educ: William Jewell Col, A.B, 35; George Washington Univ, LL.B, 39; Sigma Nu. Polit. & Govt. Pos: Mont. mem, Columbia Interstate Compact Cmn, 54-; mem, Pac. Northwest River Basons Cmn; mem, Rep. Nat. Cmt, Mont, 60-; Mont. State Rep. and chmn, Judiciary Cmt, Mont. State House of Rep, 67- Mil. Serv: Entered as Pvt, Army, 42, released as 1st Lt, 46. Mem: Mont. and Am. Bar Asns; Mason; Shrine; Elks. Rel: Lutheran. Mailing Add: 604 Woodland, Kalispell, Mont. 59901.

MURPHY, JAMES E. D
Ky. State Rep.
b. 1929. Educ: Xavier Univ. Polit. & Govt. Pos: Ky. State Rep, 60-; former city cmnr, Newport; del, Dem. Nat. Conv, 64 & 68. Bus. & Prof. Pos: Real estate broker and ins. broker. Mem: Elks; K. of C; Fraternal Order of Police. Rel: Catholic. Legal Res: 2246 New Linden Rd, Newport, Ky. 41071. Mailing Add: 335 York St, Newport, Ky. 41071.

MURPHY, JOHN FRANCIS D
Vt. State Rep.
b. Ludlow, Vt, 2/22/23; s. Thomas James Murphy and Fern Agnes Batch M; m. 4/19/52 to Floribel Ann La Pine; c. John Francis, Jr. Educ: High sch. Polit. & Govt. Pos: Chmn, Rep. Town Cmt, Ludlow, Vt, 62-64, dist. chmn, 64-66, co. chmn, 64-68; Vt. State Rep, 68- Rel: Catholic. Legal Res: Pleasant St, Ludlow, Vt. 05149. Mailing Add: P.O. 125, Ludlow, Vt. 05149.

MURPHY, JOHN FRANCIS D
S.Dak. State Rep.
b. 7/19/30; married; c. Timothy Patrick and Catherine Ann. Educ: St. John's Univ, B.A; Univ. Minn, LL.B. Polit. & Govt. Pos: S.Dak. State Sen, 65-66; S.Dak. State Rep, 69- Bus. & Prof. Pos: Attorney. Mil. Serv: Army, 52-54. Mem: Elks; Am. Legion; VFW; K. of C. Rel: Catholic. Mailing Add: Elk Point, S.Dak. 87025.

MURPHY, JOHN FRANCIS D
State Committeeman, Mass. Dem. Party
b. Brockton, Mass, 10/28/38; s. Ambrose Francis Murphy and Rose Ethel Welch M; m. 10/11/59 to Caroline Elizabeth Corcoran; c. John Francis, Jr, Julie Grace, James Ambrose and Jeanne Rose. Educ: Col. of the Holy Cross, B.S, 60; Boston Univ. Law Sch, 2 year; founder, Holy Cross Young Dem. Polit. & Govt. Pos: Mem, Planning Bd, Brockton, Mass, 63, mem, Dem. Ward Cmt, 64 and mem, Bd. of Zoning Appeals, 67; state committeeman, Mass. Dem. Party, 64-; v.chmn. rules cmt, Dem. State Conv, 66; pres, Mass. Electoral Col, 68. Bus. & Prof. Pos: Research asst. to Secy. of State Kevin H. White, Mass, 61 and admin. asst, 64; admin. asst. to Mayor Kevin H. White, Boston, Mass, 68. Mem: K. of C; Young Dem; Citizens Adv. Cmt. for City of Brockton, Mass; mem. bd. of dirs, Wimbeldon Beach Asn. Rel: Catholic. Mailing Add: 34 James St, Brockton, Mass. 02402.

MURPHY, JOHN MICHAEL D
U.S. Rep, N.Y.
b. Staten Island, 8/3/26; s. Frank Murphy; Florence M; m. to Patricia Hart; c. Deirdre, John and Eve. Educ: Amherst Col; U.S. Mil. Acad, B.S. Polit. & Govt. Pos: U.S. Rep, N.Y, 62-, mem, Cmts. on Interstate and For. Commerce and Merchant Marine and Fisheries U.S. House of Rep; del, N.Y. State Constitutional Conv, 67; mem, Franklin Delano Roosevelt Mem. Cmn; del, Dem. Nat. Conv, 68. Bus. & Prof. Pos: Gen. mgr. for Frank Murphy, contract carrier of Staten Island, 56-62; Pres, Cleveland Gen. Transport Co, Inc, 57; mem. bd. dirs, Empire State Hwy. Transportation Asn, 60. Mil. Serv: Enlisted in Army, 44, Pvt, promoted to Cpl. and commissioned 2nd Lt, 45, app. to W. Point, 46, Korean vet, served as platoon leader, co. comdr. and intel. officer in ninth Inf. Regt; promoted to 1st Lt, 50 and Capt, 53-56; awarded Distinguished Serv. Cross; Bronze Star with Oak Leaf Cluster; Commendation Ribbon with Oak Leaf Cluster; Combat Inf. Badge; Parachute Badge; Korean Serv. Medal with 6 Battle Stars; Chungmu Distinguished Serv. Medal. Mem: Am. Legion; VFW; K. of C. Rel: Catholic. Legal Res: Staten Island, N.Y. Mailing Add: 1134 Longworth House Office Bldg, Washington, D.C. 20515.

MURPHY, JOSEPH RICHARD R
Del. State Rep.
b. 1934. Educ: Univ. Scranton, Pa. Polit. & Govt. Pos: Del. State Rep, 67- Bus. & Prof. Pos: Teacher, Wilmington High Sch; assembly line supvr, Avon Prods, Inc, Newark. Mil. Serv: Korean Conflict. Mem: Boy Scouts (health and safety chmn, Capitol Trail Dist); K. of C; bd. dirs, Scythian Mutual Fund. Rel: Catholic. Mailing Add: 171 Brookside Blvd, Brookside Park, Del. 19711. (1967)

MURPHY, LAWRENCE P. D
N.Y. State Assemblyman
b. N.Y.C; s. Daniel F. Murphy and Mary M; m. to Theresa Byrne; c. Phillip Francis, Lawrence P. Jr, Brian Paul and Dennis Byrne. Educ: St. Patrick's Cathedral Grammar Sch, page to late Patrick Cardinal Hayes; St. Francis Xavier High Sch; Fordham Col; Fordham Law Sch. Polit. & Govt. Pos: N.Y. State Assemblyman, 45-; mem. bd. dirs, 42nd Assembly Dist. Dem. Club. Bus. & Prof. Pos: Attorney, Brooklyn, N.Y. Rel: Catholic. Mailing Add: 4408 Flatlands Ave, Brooklyn, N.Y. 11234.

MURPHY, MARGARET ANNA D
Md. State Del.
b. Baltimore, Md, 6/24/08; d. Edward Fuhr and Ada Hodges F; m. 8/14/53 to John Oliver Murphy; c. William W. Wilbourn; four grandchildren. Educ: St. Joseph's Monastery, 8 years. Polit. & Govt. Pos: Del, Dem. State Conv, 60; Md. State Del, 60-, chmn, Legis. Cmt. Bus. & Prof. Pos: Owner, Confectionery Store, Baltimore, 54- Mem: Women's Asn. of Allied Beverage Industs, Inc; Poplar Ridge Improv. Asn. of Anne Arundel Co; Maccabees Fraternal Soc. (past pres); Md. & D.C. Fraternal Cong.(past pres); House of Dem; 3-4-5 Dem. Club (past pres, Ladies Auxiliary, 65-67 & 68-69); Morrell Park & Vicinity Commun. Asn, Inc; VFW Auxiliary; Am. Legion Auxiliary. Rel: Catholic. Mailing Add: 1927 Griffiss Ave, Baltimore, Md. 21230.

MURPHY, MARGARET ANSBORO D
b. Albany, Vt, 12/26/83; m. to Eugene Stephen Murphy, wid; c. Four sons. Educ: Craftsbury Acad, grad; several summer sessions at U.V.M. Polit. & Govt. Pos: Vt. State Rep, 57-66; town auditor, 58- Bus. & Prof. Pos: Retired teacher; libr. trustee. Mem: PTA; Northeast. Vt. Dev. Asn; St. Anne's Soc; Vt. Retired Teachers. Rel: Catholic. Mailing Add: Lowell, Vt. 05847. (1967)

MURPHY, MARY CATHERINE DFL
Mem, Dem-Farmer-Labor State Exec. Cmt, Minn.
b. Duluth, Minn, 10/25/39; d. James Lloyd Murphy (deceased) and Gertrude Yost M.(deceased); single. Educ: Col. of St. Scholastica, B.A. in Hist, 61; Univ. Minn, summers, 64, 68 & 69; Student Coun; pres, Day Student's Orgn; pres, Class of 1961. Polit. & Govt. Pos: Alternate del, Dem. Nat. Conv, 64, del, 68; alternate del, Eighth Dist. and State Dem. Conv, 64, 65 and del, 68; 59th Dist. Sustaining Fund chmn, Minn. Dem-Farmer-Labor Cent. Cmt, 65-66; v.pres, Duluth Dem-Farmer-Labor Women, 65-67; secy, Duluth Dem-Farmer Women, 65-67; v.chairwoman, 59th Legis. Dist, Dem-Farmer-Labor Party, Minn, 66-68; del, St. Louis Co. Dem. Conv, 66-68; del, Dem-Farmer-Labor State Cent. Cmt, 68-; mem, Dem-Farmer-Labor State Exec. Cmt, 69-; chairwoman, Eighth Cong. Dist, Dem-Farmer-Labor Party, 69- Bus. & Prof. Pos: Teacher, Clover Valley High Sch, 61-64 and Duluth Cent. High Sch, 64- Mem: Alpha Delta Kappa; Duluth Teachers Asn.(v.pres, 68-70); Nat. Conf. of Parents and Teachers; Am. Fedn. of Teachers; Am. Asn. for the UN; Am. Asn. of Univ. Women; Col. of St. Scholastica Alumni Asn; Duluth Dem-Farmer-Labor Women (pres, 66); Minn. Dem-Farmer-Labor Women's Fedn; Friends of the Duluth Pub. Libr; Daughters of Isabella. Community Leader of Am. Award, 68. Rel: Roman Catholic. Mailing Add: 6794 Arrowhead Rd, Duluth, Minn. 55811.

MURPHY, NORBERT CLINTON D
Chmn, Delta Co. Dem. Cmt, Mich.
b. Escanaba, Mich, 9/24/31; s. John Kevill Murphy and Merceda Middlebrook M; single. Educ: St. Norbert Col, 49-50; North. Mich. Univ, B.A, 58; Alpha Phi Omega. Polit. & Govt. Pos: Precinct del, Delta Co. Dem. Party, Mich, 64-68; mem, Delta Co. Dem. Exec. Cmt, 66-68; chmn, Delta Co. Dem. Cmt, 68- Bus. & Prof. Pos: Pres, West Br. Educ. Asn, Mich, 60-61; del, Mich. Dept. of Classroom Teachers, 69- Mil. Serv: Entered as Pvt, Air Force, 51, released as Airman 1/C, 54, after serv. in Air Training Command, 51-54; Good Conduct and Nat. Defense Serv. Medals. Mem: Escanaba, Mich. and Nat. Educ. Asns; Elks; Delta Co. Alumni Club and Golden Wildcat Club of North. Mich. Univ. Campus Citizenship Award. Rel: Catholic. Mailing Add: 505 S. 13th St, Escanaba, Mich. 49829.

MURPHY, PETER C, JR. R
Finance Chmn, Ore. Rep. State Cent. Cmt.
b. Portland, Ore, 9/17/36; s. Peter C. Murphy, Sr. and Dorothy Zingleman M; m. 7/23/60 to Marcella Jubitz; c. Peter C. III, Mark, Amanda, Anna and Marcella. Educ: Univ. Notre Dame, B.A, 58. Polit. & Govt. Pos: Del, Rep. Nat. Conv, 68; finance chmn, Ore. Rep. State Cent. Cmt, 68- Bus. & Prof. Pos: Gen. Mgr, The Murphy Co, Portland, Ore, 61-; dir, Pac. Logging Cong, 64-67 & 68-71; pres, Eugene Bombers Football Club, 65-68; pres, Continental Football League-West. Div, 66-67; dir, Condominiums Northwest, Salem, 69-72. Mil. Serv: Airman 2nd Class, Air Nat. Guard of Ore, discharged, 64. Mem: Rotary; C. of C; Eugene Country Club. Perfect Attendance Award throughout four years of high sch. Rel: Roman Catholic. Mailing Add: 2410 W. 22nd, Eugene, Ore. 97405.

MURPHY, PETER JOHN D
N.H. State Rep.
b. Dover, N.H, 8/8/45; s. John R. Murphy and Thega Winslow M; single. Educ: Univ. N.H. Polit. & Govt. Pos: N.H. State Rep, 67-; mem, Gov. Task Force on Juvenile Delinquency, 68- Named Outstanding Youth of New Eng, 67; Named Commun. Leader of Am, 67- Rel: Roman Catholic. Legal Res: 15 Richardson Dr, Dover, N.H. 03820. Mailing Add: State House, Room 200, Concord, N.H. 03301.

MURPHY, RICHARD JAMES D
b. Baltimore, Md, 10/15/29; s. James Fitzgerald Murphy and Thais Victoria Brady M; single. Educ: Univ. N.C, A.B. in Econ, 51, grad. study, 52; Phi Beta Kappa; Phi Eta Sigma; nat. pres, U.S. Nat. Student Asn, 52-53; Order of the Golden Fleece; Order of the Old Well; pres, N.C. State Student Legis. Polit. & Govt. Pos: Mem, Nat. Capital Dem. Club; mem, U.S. Nat. Cmn. on UNESCO, 51-53; exec. dir, Young Dem. Div, Dem. Nat. Cmt, 56-61, mem, Cmt. on Polit. Orgn. 58-60; exec. secy, Young Dem. Clubs of Am, 56-61; dir. arrangements, Dem. Platform Cmt, and assoc. dir, Advance Platform Hearings, Dem. Nat. Conv, 60; nat. coordinator, Young Voters for Kennedy-Johnson, 60; alternate mem, President's Cmt. on Employee Mgt. Coop, 61; mem, Subcabinet Group on Civil Rights, 61-63; mem, Inaugural Cmts, 61 & 65; asst. postmaster gen, 61-69; nat. chmn, Young Dem. Nat. Conv, 64 & 65; alternate mem, Cabinet Cmt, Staff Retirement Systs, 65. Mil. Serv: Entered as Pvt, Army, 53, released as Pfc, 55, after serv. in Army Ord. Corps, Aberdeen Proving Grounds; Good Conduct and Nat. Defense Medals. Publ: Assoc. ed, Democratic Digest, 57-60. Mem: Am. del, Int. Student Conf, Copenhagen, 53, Atlantic Conf, Polit. Youth Leaders, Paris, 58 and Universal Postal Union Centennial, Paris, 63; bd. mem, United Givers Fund, Wash, D.C, 66-; chmn, Orgn. Cmt, United Givers Fund, Govt. Unit, 63, 64 & 65, Kennedy Libr. Drive, 64 and Savings Bond Drive, 66. Former permanent panelist, Col. News Conf, ABC Network; William A. Jump Found. Award for Meritorious Achievement in Pub. Admin, 62. Rel: Unitarian. Mailing Add: 9912 Harrogate Rd, Bethesda, Md. 20034. (1967)

MURPHY, ROBERT EDWARD D
b. Frederic, Wis, 9/19/31; s. Edward L. Murphy and Irene Rogers M; m. 6/7/58 to Judy Beddor; c. Patrick, Kathleen, Marjorie, Monica and Bridget. Polit. & Govt. Pos: Secy-treas, Polk Co. Dem. Party, Wis, 54-58, chmn, 59-65, mem. exec. cmt, 65-66; supvr, Town of Georgetown, 59-66. Bus. & Prof. Pos: Secy, Japs-Olson Printing Co, Minneapolis, Minn, currently. Rel: Catholic. Mailing Add: 1470 W. 35th St, Minneapolis, Minn. 55408.

MURPHY, ROBERT J. D
b. Casper, Wyo, 6/29/21; m. to Sally; c. nine. Educ: Univ. of Wyo. and Law Sch, Univ. of Wyo. Polit. & Govt. Pos: Wyo. State Sen; served two terms -67. Bus. & Prof. Pos: Lawyer. Mem: K. of C; Elks; Am. Legion; C. of C. Rel: Catholic. Mailing Add: 1025 S. Center, Casper, Wyo. 82601. (1967)

MURPHY, ROBERT JOSEPH, III R
Mem, Calif. Rep. State Cent. Cmt.
b. Summit, N.J, 6/3/36; s. Robert Joseph Murphy, Jr. and Catherine Ames M; m. 8/3/62 to Judith Ann Miller; c. Catherine Elizabeth. Educ: Brown Univ, A.B, 58; Stanford Law Sch, LL.B, 66; Sigma Chi. Polit. & Govt. Pos: Law clerk, U.S. Senate Interior Cmt, 65; legis. intern, Calif. State Assembly, 66-67, asst. counsel, Assembly Judiciary Cmt, 67-68, legis. asst. to Assemblyman William T. Bagley, 68-; mem, Calif. Rep. State Cent. Cmt, 69- Bus. & Prof. Pos: Attorney-at-Law, Bagley, Bianchi & Sheeks, private law firm, San Rafael, Calif, 68- Mil. Serv: Entered as Ens, Navy, 58, released as Lt, 63, after serv. in Fighter Squadron 92, Naval Air Force, Pac. Fleet, 60-61, Lt. Comdr, Res, 66-; Designated a Naval Aviator, 59. Mem: Calif. and Marin Co. Bar Asns; Commonwealth Club; Marin Rep. Coun; Naval Reserve Asn. Mailing Add: 65 Oak Knoll Dr, San Anselmo, Calif. 94960.

MURPHY, ROBERT T, SR. D
V.Chmn, Civil Aeronaut. Bd.
b. Providence, R.I, 3/5/15; s. John C. Murphy and Margaret Hourahan M; m. 9/30/40 to Anna Meenagh; c. Robert T, Jr, Brian P. and Richard J. Educ: Providence Col, A.B, 36; Georgetown Univ. Law Sch, LL.B, 40. Polit. & Govt. Pos: Chief counsel, U.S. Senate Campaign Expenditures Cmt, 44-45; counsel, Aviation Subcmt, U.S. Senate Commerce Cmt, 56-61; mem, Civil Aeronaut. Bd, 61, v.chmn, 61- Bus. & Prof. Pos: Private practice of law, Wash, D.C. and R.I, 39-61. Mem: Bar of Dist. of Columbia and R.I; Am. and Fed. Bar Asns; Am. Judicature Soc; Counselors. Admitted to practice before Supreme Court of U.S, 46. Rel: Catholic. Legal Res: 2 Bayberry Rd, Narragansett, R.I. 02882. Mailing Add: 7315 Lynnhurst St, Chevy Chase, Md. 20015.

MURPHY, RUPERT LEO
Cmnr, Interstate Commerce Cmn.
b. Bromville, Ga, 7/27/09; s. Luther H. Murphy and Ardelia Woodruff M; m. 4/18/31 to Marion Kerlin; c. Rupert L. Educ: Atlanta Law Sch, LL.B, 38, LL.M, 39; Delta Theta Phi; Delta Nu Alpha. Polit. & Govt. Pos: Past pres. and chmn, Gov. S. Traffic League; cmnr, Interstate Commerce Cmn, 55- Bus. & Prof. Pos: Correspondent and rate clerk, Atlanta Freight Tariff Bur, Ga, 25-29; asst. traffic mgr, Fulton Bag and Cotton Mills, Atlanta, 29-42; traffic mgr. and attorney, Ga-Ala. Textile Traffic Asn, Atlanta, 42-55. Mem: Am. and Ga. Bar Asns; Asn. Interstate Commerce Cmn. Practitioners; Am. Soc. Traffic and Transportation; past v.pres, Nat. Indust. Traffic League; past gen. chmn, S.E. Shippers Adv. Bd; Mason; Shrine; Transportation Club, Atlanta. Rel: Presbyterian. Legal Res: Apt. B-114, 1400 S. Joyce St, Arlington, Va. 22202. Mailing Add: Interstate Commerce Commission, 12th St. and Constitution Ave, Washington, D.C. 20423.

MURPHY, THOMAS BAILEY D
Admin. Floor Leader, Ga. House of Rep.
b. Bremen, Ga, 3/10/24; s. William Harvey Murphy and Leita Jones M; m. 7/22/46 to Agnes Bennett; c. Michael L, Martha L, Marjorie Lynn and Mary June. Educ: N.Ga. Col, 43; Univ. Ga. Law Sch, 49. Polit. & Govt. Pos: Chmn, Bremen Bd. of Educ, Ga; Ga. State Rep, 61-, Admin. Floor Leader, Ga. House of Rep, 67- Bus. & Prof. Pos: Attorney. Mil. Serv: Navy, 43-46. Rel: Baptist. Mailing Add: Route 2, Bremen, Ga. 30110.

MURPHY, THOMAS J. D
Ind. State Rep, -66. Bus. & Prof. Pos: Attorney; faculty mem, Marian Col. Mil. Serv: Army, 54-56. Mem: Notre Dame and Ind. Univ. Alumni Asns; Ind. and Indianapolis Bar Asns. Rel: Catholic. Mailing Add: 21 N. Hawthorne Lane, Indianapolis, Ind. 46219. (1967)

MURPHY, THOMAS JOHN DFL
b. St. Paul, Minn, 12/9/37; s. Edward Charles Murphy and Appolonia L. Wise M; m. 8/24/57 to Mary Alice Hughes; c. Jerome Joseph, Mary Bridgit, Shannon Marie, Alice Anne, Collene Jane and Patricia Rose. Educ: Col. St. Thomas, B.A, 68. Polit. & Govt. Pos: Dem-Farmer-Labor caucus chmn, 32nd Precinct, Minn, 64, 66 & 68; del, Ramsey Co. Dem-Farmer-Labor Conv, 64, 66 & 68, Fourth Dist. Dem-Farmer-Labor Conv, 66 & 68, State

Dem-Farmer-Labor Conv, 68 and Dem. Nat. Conv, 68; Dem-Farmer-Labor cand, Minn. State Rep, 68; del, Minn. Dem-Farmer-Labor Cent. Cmt, 68-69; mem, Ramsey Co. Dem-Farmer-Labor Exec. Cmt, 68-69; chmn, Dist. 48B, Minn. Dem-Farmer-Labor Party, 68-69. Bus. & Prof. Pos: Prod. control supvr, Univac Div. of Sperry Rand, Roseville, Minn, 60-66, pre-prod. engr, 64-66, prod. supvr, 66-69 and pricing engr, Blue Bell, Pa, 69- Mil. Serv: Entered as Pvt, Army, 57, released as Cpl, 59, after serv. in 8th Army Headquarters, Seoul, Korea, 57-58. Rel: Catholic. Legal Res: 1672 Lincoln Ave, St. Paul, Minn. 55105. Mailing Add: 35 E. Seventh St, Lansdale, Pa. 19446.

MURPHY, WILLIAM J. R
Ill. State Rep.
b. Sioux City, Iowa, 10/12/15; m. to Virginia Floren M; c. Three sons. Educ: John Marshall Law Sch, Chicago, 2½ years. Polit. & Govt. Pos: Former pres, bd. of educ; Ill. State Sen, currently, majority leader, 73rd Gen. Assembly, Ill. State Senate. Bus. & Prof. Pos: Presently operates a Real Estate Bus. and Ins. Bus. Mem: Co. Bd. of Realtors; Lions; Sportsmen Asn; Alumnae Soc; Moose; Elks; Lions; Eagles; Am. Legion. Mailing Add: R.R. 1, Box 607, Antioch, Ill. 60002. (1967)

MURPHY, WILLIAM MALCOLM, JR. D
Mem, Kent Co. Dem. Cmt, Del.
b. Americus, Ga, 12/18/27; s. William Malcolm Murphy and Gussie Dell Harbuck M; single. Educ: George Washington Univ: Corcoran Sch. of Fine Arts; Ford Mkt. Inst, N.Y.C, 62-68; Wesley Col, 68. Polit. & Govt. Pos: V.pres, Kent Co. Young Dem, Del, 60-61, pres, 65-66, treas, 66-67; mem, Kent.Co. Dem. Cmt, 62-; alternate nat. committeeman, Young Dem. Am, 63-65, nat. committeeman, 65-68; alternate del, Dem. Nat. Conv, 64 & 68; mem, Dem. State Cmt, 66-; pres. and founder, 31st Dist. Dem. Club, 68-69, bd. dir, 69; dir, Kent Co. Civil Defense, 69- Bus. & Prof. Pos: V.pres. and asst. mgr, Murphy's Hardware, 64-; pres, Kennersley Marina and Yacht Club, 65-68. Mil. Serv: Entered as Pvt, Army, 46, released as T/Sgt, 48, after serv. in Am. Theater. Mem: Prfnl. Sales Mgrs; Kent Island Yacht Club; Kennersley Yacht Club; Elks; co-founder, treas. and mem. bd. dirs, Del. Arts Soc, Inc. Painting; Yachting. Rel: Presbyterian. Mailing Add: 1437 Nathaniel Mitchell Rd, Dover, Del. 19901.

MURPHY, WILLIAM T. D
U.S. Rep, Ill.
b. Chicago, Ill, 8/7/99; m. to Rose McInerney; c. William T, Jr, John P. and Rosemary. Educ: Loyola Univ. Law Sch, LL.B, 26; Delta Theta Phi. Polit. & Govt. Pos: Alderman, Chicago City Coun, Ill, 35-39, mem. cmt. on finance, 38-59 and cmt. on rules exec. cmt, 41-59, chmn. cmt. on labor mgt, 40-47 and cmt. on planning, 47-59, mem, Chicago Plan Cmn, 47-59; Dem. ward committeeman, 17th Ward, Chicago, 40-53; del, Dem. Nat. Conv, 44, 48, 52 & 56; U.S. Rep, Ill, 59-, mem. cmt. on for. affairs and subcmt. on Africa, 59-69, mem. subcmt. on Asian and Pac. affairs, 65-68 and chmn, 69-, mem. subcmt. on Near East, 65-69, mem. spec. study mission to Africa, 60, Southeast Asia, 63, Communist countries, 64 and Asia, 65; mem, Can-U.S. Interparliamentary Group, 60-68. Bus. & Prof. Pos: Licensed prfnl. engr. and registered land surveyor; Lawyer, admitted to Ill. State Bar, 27 and U.S. Supreme Court, 44. Mil. Serv: Vet. of World War II. Mem: Fed. Bar Asn; Lambda Alpha Int; chmn, St. Bernard's Hosp. Bldg. and Charity Cmt, 35-49; Lions; Moose; Ahepa; K. of C; Am. Legion; Amvets. Commemorative Medal, Nat. Assembly of S.Vietnam, 63; Tenth Commemorative Medal, Assembly of Captive Nations, 63; Commemorative Medal of the Knesset, Jerusalem, Israel, 66; rep. of the Speaker of U.S. House of Rep. at dedication of new parliament bldg, Jerusalem, Israel, 66. Legal Res: Chicago, Ill. Mailing Add: 1628 House Office Bldg, Washington, D.C. 20515.

MURRAH, WILLIAM NOLAN, JR. R
First V.Chmn, Third Cong. Dist. Rep. Party, Ga.
b. Columbus, Ga, 10/27/34; s. William Nolan Murrah and Mary Huguley M; m. 9/9/55 to Barbara Ann Greene; c. William Nolan and Lee Allan. Educ: Univ. Ga, 3 years; Emory Univ. Law Sch, A.B. & LL.B; Harvard Law Sch, 1 year; SAE; Phi Delta Phi. Polit. & Govt. Pos: Chmn, Young Rep. Club, Muscogee Co, Ga, 64-66; chmn, Muscogee Co. Rep. Cmt, 66-68; chmn, Nixon-Agnew Cmt, 68; del, Rep. Nat. Conv, 68; first v.chmn, Third Cong. Dist. Rep. Party, 68- Bus. & Prof. Pos: Law asst, Supreme Court of Ga, 61; v.pres, secy. and gen. counsel, Royal Crown Cola Co, 61- Mil. Serv: Entered as 2nd Lt, Air Force, 58, released as Capt, 61, after serv. in 3800 ABW, Maxwell AFB, Ala, 58-61. Mem: Am. and Ga. Bar Asns; Am. Judicature Soc. Rel: Baptist. Mailing Add: 1829 Park Dr, Columbus, Ga. 31906.

MURRAY, DONALD WILLIAM D
b. Bancroft, Iowa, 6/1/23; s. William A. Murray and Elizabeth M. McDonald; m. 2/20/50 to Ardelle B. Fischer; c. Michael C, Bryan K, Stephen W, Michele A. and Diana L. Educ: St. Thomas Col, 41-42; Iowa State Univ, 42-43; Pa. Mil. Col, 44. Polit. & Govt. Pos: Mem, City Coun, Bancroft, Iowa, 45-59, Mayor, 59-61; Greenwood Twp. Dem. chmn, 48-58; Kossuth Co. Dem. chmn, 58-62; Dem. State Cent. committeeman, 63-68; chmn, Sixth Dist. Dem. Party, 63-68; del, Dem. Nat. Conv, 64 & 68; Iowa State Sen, 64-68. Bus. & Prof. Pos: Mgr. and owner, Murray Elevator, Inc, Bancroft, Iowa, 45-68; farm mgr. and owner, Murray Farms Co, 45-69; securities, real estate broker and ins. salesman, 68-69. Mil. Serv: Entered as Pvt, Army, 43, released as Pfc, 46. Mem: Nat. Asn. of Real Estate Bds; Nat. Asn. Life Underwriters; Nat. Asn. State Legislators; K. of C; Am. Legion; Cath. Order of Foresters. Rel: Roman Catholic. Mailing Add: 502 E. Seventh St, Ankeny, Iowa 50021.

MURRAY, EDWARD THOMAS D
Chmn, Martin Co. Dem. Exec. Cmt, Fla.
b. New York, N.Y, 12/25/98; s. Thomas Murray and Eve Stubberfield M; m. 9/21/21 to Arminda Long Case; c. Dorothy (Mrs. Ralph Wheelock) and William J. Educ: Norris High Sch, N.Y, grad, 14. Polit. & Govt. Pos: Dem. chmn. and leader, Eighth Ward, Essex Co, N.J, 33-55; chmn, Martin Co. Dem. Exec. Cmt, Fla, 60- Bus. & Prof. Pos: Inspector, License Div, Dept. Pub. Safety, Newark, N.J, 34-55. Mil. Serv: Entered as Pvt, Army, 15-19, serv. in Fifth and Seventh Cavalry, 28th Inf, First Div, 17-18. Mem: VFW Post 4194; Vet. World War I, Barracks 851. Rel: Catholic. Mailing Add: 667 Cleveland Ave, Stuart, Fla. 33494.

MURRAY, ERWIN L. D
b. Emporium, Pa, 7/15/20; s. Riley A. Murray and Francis Schwab M; m. 1/1/46 to Leah K. Zerbe; c. Erwin, Jr. and June Elizabeth. Educ: Emporium High Sch, grad; Curtis Wright Tech. Polit. & Govt. Pos: Chmn, Cameron Co. Dem. Party, Pa, 58-62; Pa. State Rep, 63-66; cmnr, Cameron Co, 68- Bus. & Prof. Pos: Mechanic and owner of garage; co-owner, Murray Aircraft Repair. Mil. Serv: Entered as Pvt, Air Force, 42, released as S/Sgt, 44, after serv. in 4th Airdrome, 5th Air Force, S. Pac. Mem: Dir, Emporium Civil Defense; VFW; Emporium Vol. Fire Dep, Fire Dept. Rescue Squadron and Ambulance Squadron; pilot, Civil Air Patrol, 705th Squadron. Rel: Protestant. Mailing Add: 201 Hemlock St, Emporium, Pa. 15834.

MURRAY, FRANK D
Secy. of State, Mont.
b. Butte, Mont, 2/28/07; s. Bernard Murray (deceased) and Harriet Tracey M. (deceased); m. 6/27/35 to Geraldine Alice Jones. Educ: High Sch. and various home-study courses. Polit. & Govt. Pos: Mem, Exec. Cmt, Mont. State Dem. Cent. Cmt, 30-, secy, 44-56; dep. clerk and recorder, Silver Bow Co, Butte, Mont, 33-37; trustee, Sch. Dist. 1, Butte, Mont, 37-38; state store mgr, Mont. Liquor Control Bd, 37-39; clerk of Mont. Supreme Court, 42-57; del, Dem. Nat. Conv, 52, 64 & 68; Secy. of State, Mont, 57- Mem: Nat. Asn. of Secretaries of State (v.pres, pres, 69-); United Commercial Travelers of Am; Elks; Eagles; AF&AM; Shrine. Has devoted much time to civic and fraternal affairs, including safe-driving and fund raising campaigns for res. in polio, cancer, tuberc, arthritis and rheumatism. Legal Res: 825 Hauser Blvd, Helena, Mont, 59601. Mailing Add: Secretary of State, State Capitol, Helena, Mont. 59601.

MURRAY, FRANK A, JR. D
Precinct Chmn, Dem. Party, N.Mex.
s. Frank A. Murray and Effie Mae Robinson M; m. 6/22/43 to Velma Rierson; c. Frank, III and George. Educ: East. N.Mex. Univ, 40-41. Polit. & Govt. Pos: Alternate del, Dem. Nat. Conv, 60, del, 64; precinct chmn, Dem. Party, N.Mex, 61- Bus. & Prof. Pos: Mgr, Cortez Hotel, N.Mex. 48-51, De Soto Hotel, 51-53; owner, Clovis Cab and Rent a Car, 53-60 and Aztec Lounge, 61-; pres, Aztec Bowling Corp, 63- Mil. Serv: Entered as Pvt, Army Air Force, 42, released as Cpl, 46, after serv. in Aircraft Radio Lab, Wright Field, Research and Develop. Command. Mem: Elks; Am. Legion; K. of C; Rotary Int. Rel: Catholic. Legal Res: 1425 Reid Clovis, N.Mex. 88101. Mailing Add: Box 549, Clovis, N.Mex. 88101. (1967)

MURRAY, GEORGE E. R
Mo. State Rep.
b. St. Louis, Mo, 8/9/23; s. George E. Murray and Marie C. Straub M; m. 11/20/48 to Elizabeth Russell Cooper; c. Elizabeth, George, III, Peggy and Mary Kathleen. Educ: Wash. Univ, LL.B. & B.S in B.A, 48; Delta Theta Phi; Beta Theta Pi. Polit. & Govt. Pos: City Attorney, Fenton, Mo, 57-66; mem, Gov. Cmn. Dent. Care of Handicapped Children, 62-; Mo. State Rep, 38th Dist, 67- Bus. & Prof. Pos: Partner, Bialson, Murray & Ebert, Attorneys, currently. Mil. Serv: Pvt, Army, 42-44. Mem: Elks; Am. Legion. Rel: Catholic. Mailing Add: 3 Williamsburg Rd, Creve Coeur, Mo. 63141.

MURRAY, HARVEY P, JR. R
Pa. State Rep.
b. Sunbury, Pa, 6/28/34; s. Harvey P. Murray and Anna M. Wray M; m. to Nancy Lou Kunkel. Educ: Wharton Sch. Finance and Commerce, Univ. Pa, B.S; Univ. Pa, LL.B; Rotary Int. Fel, Trinity Col. Law Sch, Univ. Dublin, 58-59; Am. Univ. grad. work; past pres, Theta Xi. Polit. & Govt. Pos: Former publicity dir, Snyder Co. Rep. Cmt, Pa; former chmn, Snyder Co. Young Rep; former mem, Selinsgrove Broough Coun; Pa. State Rep, 63- Bus. & Prof. Pos: former service with Central Intel. Agency, U.S; mem. ed. staff, Sunbury Daily Item (part-time), 52- Mil. Serv: Army, 59; Res, currently. Mem: Snyder Co. and Pa. Bar Asns; C. of C; Am. Legion Home Asn; Moose; Rotary Int. Rel: Lutheran. Mailing Add: 106 W. Pine St, Selinsgrove, Pa. 17870.

MURRAY, JAMES JOSEPH, III D
b. Boston, Mass, 12/31/33; s. James J. Murray and Anne L. Gurvin M; m. 5/7/54 to Alma Marie Tefrault; c. James, Paul, Laura and Douglas. Educ: Harvard Univ, A.B, 55; Pi Eta; Harvard Varsity Club. Polit. & Govt. Pos: Munic. chmn, Regular Dem. Orgn, River Vale, N.J, 63-68; councilman, Twp. River Vale, 64 & 65-68 and police cmnr, 65-66; mem. polit. adv. staff, Sen. Harrison Williams, 64-65; policy staff mem, Lord Cmt, Gov. Richard J. Hughes, 65-67; campaign cmt. mem, Cong. Henry Helstoski, 68; mem. steering and coord. cmt, N.J. Vol. for McCarthy, 68; co. chmn, Dem. Co. Cmt. for McCarthy, 68; del, Dem. Nat. Conv, 68. Bus. & Prof. Pos: Col. rep, Prentice-Hall Inc, 57-59, field ed, 59-60, polit. sci. ed, 60-69 and ed-in-chief of soc. sci, 66-69; pres, Winthrop Publishers Inc. & mem. bd. of dirs, 69- Mil. Serv: Entered as 2nd Lt, Marine Corps, 55, released as 1st Lt, 57, after serving in 2nd Marine Div, Camp Lejeune, N.C, 55-57. Mem: Am. Polit. Sci. Asn; Am. Acad. Polit. & Soc. Sci; N.J. State Dem. Cmt. Rel: Catholic. Mailing Add: 25 Highland Circle, Wayland, Mass. 01778.

MURRAY, JOHN HIRAM R
Chmn, Leavenworth Co. Rep. Party, Kans.
b. Leavenworth, Kans, 1/28/14; s. Roy Murray and Floy Burt M; m. 10/1/39 to Dorothy Lord; c. Richard Lord and John Hiram, Jr. Educ: Univ. Kans, LL.B, 38, J.D, 68; Delta Chi; Phi Alpha Delta. Polit. & Govt. Pos: Police judge, Leavenworth, Kans, 39-41, co. attorney, 43-49; city attorney, Easton, 49; Kans. State Rep, 49-57; del, Rep. Nat. Conv, 52; city attorney, Lansing, Kans, 57; Kans. State Sen, 57-65; Cmnr, Perry Dam, 64; city attorney, Basehor, Kans, 65; chmn, Leavenworth Co. Rep. Party, 66- Bus. & Prof. Pos: Gen. practice of law, 38-; attorney, Citizens' Mutual Bldg. & Loan Asn, 49- Mil. Serv: Entered as Ens, Navy, 44, released as Lt.(jg), 46, after serv. in Amphibious Forces, Pac. Theater. Mem: Leavenworth Co, Kans. and Am. Bar Asns; Am. Judicature Soc; Lions (past pres); Eagles; Elks; Am. Legion; VFW; Mason (Past Grand Master, Kans, 61 and mem, Kans. Masonic Home Bd); York Rite; Scottish Rite; KCCH (32°); Shrine; Hi-12 (past state pres); Cushing Mem. Hosp. Bd; Salvation Army Adv. Bd; DeMolay; Legion of Honor; Jesters; Sojourners. Rel: Presbyterian; Elder. Mailing Add: 1020 S. Fourth St, Leavenworth, Kans. 66048.

MURRAY, JOHN J. D
b. Fort Dodge, Iowa, 9/15/26; s. Walter E. Murray and Ursula Ennis M; m. 9/8/51 to Joan D. Schwab; c. Shelia, Stephen and Michael. Educ: Univ. Iowa Col. of Law, grad, 52. Polit. & Govt. Pos: Chmn, Webster Co. Dem. Cmt, Iowa, 64-66 and 53-56; chmn, Iowa Develop. Cmn, 65-66 and mem. and v.chmn, 63, 64-65; Iowa State Rep, 62-64; co. attorney, 59-60; del, Dem. Nat. Conv, 60. Bus. & Prof. Pos: Chmn. Bd, Iowa Surety Co, 65-; officer & dir, Hawkeye Nat. Life Ins. Co, 65-, Beaver Creek Distillery, 65- and Farm Investors, Inc, 64-; dir, First Nat. Bank, Fort Dodge, 64- Mil. Serv: Sgt, Army, 45. Mem: Dir, Fort Dodge C. of C; 65; Iowa and Am. Bar Asns; Iowa Acad. of Trial Lawyers; Iowa Defense Inst. Rel: Catholic. Mailing Add: 704 Crest Ave, Fort Dodge, Iowa 50501. (1967)

MURRAY, JOHN JOSEPH, JR. R
V.Mayor, San Mateo, Calif.
b. San Francisco, Calif, 7/18/14; s. John Joseph Murray, Sr. and Margaret Rose Flaherty M; m. 9/14/40 to Hallie M. Butler; c. John Joseph, III, Jeanne, Maureen and William. Educ: St. Joseph's Col, Mountain View, Calif, A.A. magna cum laude, 34; Univ. San Francisco, A.B, 37; Univ. Calif. and Golden Gate Col, postgrad. courses. Polit. & Govt. Pos: Mem. staff, Dept. of Soc. Welfare, Calif, 38-39 and San Francisco Pub. Welfare Dept, 39-41; city councilman, San Mateo, 65, v.mayor, 66-67 & 69-, mayor, 67-68, mem, San Mateo Coun. of Mayors; exec. cmt, Regional Planning Cmt, Bay Front ad hoc subcmt. and del, Asn. Bay Area Govt, 68; mem, San Mateo Co. Rep. Finance Cmt, 69; mem, Calif. Rep. State Cent. Cmt, 69. Bus. & Prof. Pos: Columnist, San Francisco Cath. Monitor and The Leader, 39-46; coordinator, Bethlehem Steel Corp, San Francisco, 41-45; v.pres, John J. Murray Co, Inc, 46-54, pres, 54; v.pres. and exec. dir, Peninsula Mfrs. Asn, San Mateo, Calif, 68. Publ: Contrib, San Mateo Times, 61-, Burlingame Advance Star, 61-, Serra Int. Mag, 61- and West. Cities Rev, 61- Mem: Painting and Decorating Contractors Asn; Univ. San Francisco Alumni Asn; St. Joseph's Col. Alumni Asn; S.San Mateo Home Owner's Asn.(bd. dir, 62-65); San Mateo Toyonaka Sister City Asn, 63; Elks; pres, Peninsula Symphony Asn; St. Gregory's Men's Club; St. Mary's Col. Assocs.(bd. dir, 61, pres, 63-66); K. of C; Hibernians; United Irish Socs; Serra Int.(pres, San Mateo Club, gov. dist. three, v.pres. and bd. dir); Commonwealth Club of Calif; chmn, San Mateo Bus. Leadership Coun; bd. dir, San Mateo Commun. Action Coun; bd. dir, North. Calif. Indust. Educ. Coun; bd. dir, Bay Area Soc. Planning Coun; San Mateo Co. Hist. Soc; Coyote Point Yacht Club; NAACP. Dist. Gov. Plaque and Int. Officer's Plaque, Serra Int; President's Award, St. Mary's Col, Moraga, Calif; K. of C. Citizenship Plaque; St. James A.M.E. Zion Church Appreciation Award; Church of Latter-day Saints Brotherhood Award. Rel: Catholic. Mailing Add: 257 Del Mar Way, San Mateo, Calif. 94403.

MURRAY, KENNETH JOHN D
b. New York, N.Y, 2/7/25; s. Peter Murray and Winifred McGaw M; m. to Majbritt Victoria Gustavsson; c. Peter and Robin. Educ: Univ. Chicago, B.A; Loyola Univ. Law Sch, J.D. Polit. & Govt. Pos: Chmn, Wauwatosa Dem. Party, Wis, 60; exec. dir, Milwaukee Co. Dem. Party, 62; v.chmn, Fourth Cong. Dist. Dem. Party, 62-64; del, Dem. Nat. Conv, 64; chmn, Milwaukee Co. Dem. Statutory Cmt, Wis, 66-69. Bus. & Prof. Pos: Contract adminstr, Ford Motor Co, 55-57; purchasing agent, Blackhawk Mfg. Co, 57-60; mgr. purchasing and personnel, Applied Power Int, 60-65 and mgr. supply and admin, 65- Mil. Serv: Entered as Pvt, Army, 43, released as Cpl, 46, after serv. in ETO. Mem: Wis. Bar Asn. Mailing Add: 617 N. 67th St, Wauwatosa, Wis. 53213. (1967)

MURRAY, LOUIS A. D
Minn. State Rep.
b. East Grand Forks, Minn, 9/16/13; s. William S. Murray and Mary E. M; m. to Jean Laretta Mankie; c. Michael William,Daniel Louis, Patricia Jean, Timothy Brian, Kathleen Ann and Mary Theresa. Educ: Northern State Teachers Col, 37-39; Univ. N.Dak, 45-46. Polit. & Govt. Pos: Munic. judge, East Grand Forks, Minn, 45-49, alderman, 49-51, mayor, 64-67; Minn. State Sen, 51-63; Minn. State Rep, 67- Mil. Serv: Entered as Pvt, Army, 40, released as Technician 4/C, 45, after serv. in Corps Engrs, Southwest Pac. Mem: Elks; Eagles; Am. Legion; K. of C.(4°). Rel: Roman Catholic. Mailing Add: 828 River Dr, East Grand Forks, Minn. 56721. (1967)

MURRAY, MENTON JOSEPH D
Tex. State Rep.
b. Dayton, Ohio, 10/25/07; s. James Joseph Murray and Katherine Menton M; m. 12/27/38 to Betty Nosler; c. Betty Marie and Menton, Jr. Educ: Rice Univ, 25-28; Univ. Tex, Austin, LL.B, 31; Tejas Club, McLaurin Law Soc. Polit. & Govt. Pos: Judge Corp. Court and Justice of the Peace, Harlingen, Tex, 38-42; dist. dir. and attorney, Off. Price Admin, Harlingen, 42-44; chmn, Cameron Co. Dem. Exec. Cmt, 46-48; Tex. State Rep, 48- Bus. & Prof. Pos: Partner, McCullough, Murray & McCullough, Harlingen, 57- Mil. Serv: Entered as Lt.(jg), Navy, 44, released as Lt, 46, after serv. in Communications, Phillipines, 45-46. Mem: Cameron Co. Bar Asn. (past pres); Tex. State Bar Asn; K. of C; Lions Int; Am. Legion. Dean, House of Rep, Tex, 63. Rel: Catholic. Legal Res: 1022 E. Pierce, Harlingen, Tex. 78550. Mailing Add: Box 2244, Harlingen, Tex. 78550.

MURRAY, MICHAEL WEBSTER D
Mem. Exec. Cmt, Ariz. Dem. Party
b. Sioux Rapids, Iowa, 7/9/35; s. Frank Murray and Myrna Webster M; single. Educ: St. John's Univ, Collegeville, Minn, B.S, 57; Univ. Ariz, J.D, 64; Phi Delta Phi. Polit. & Govt. Pos: Dem. precinct committeeman, 14th precinct, Pima Co, Ariz, 64-; mem. exec. cmt, Pima Co. Dem. Cmt, 66-; pres, Young Dem. of Gr. Tucson, 68; magistrate, City of Tucson, 68; del, Dem. Nat. Conv, 68; referee juvenile court, Pima Co. Superior Court, 68-; mem. Exec. cmt, Ariz. Dem. Party, 68-; mem, Ariz. Cmn. Party Structure and Del. Selection, 69. Bus. & Prof. Pos: Attorney-at-law, Tucson, 64-; pres, Southwest. Fiduciaries, Inc, Tucson, 69- Mil. Serv: Entered as Pvt, Marines, 56, released as 1st Lt, 60, after serv. in First and Third Marine Div, 57-60; Res, 66-, Maj; Am. Defense Ribbon. Mem: V.pres, Tucson Chap; Am. Trial Lawyers Asn; Pima Co. and Ariz. Bar Asns; v.pres, Marine Corps Reserve Officers Asn; Young Dem. of Ariz; Nucleus Club; Tucson Press Club; Am. Legion. Admitted to practice before Supreme Court of Ariz. and Fed. Dist. Court for Ariz. Rel: Catholic. Mailing Add: 3943 E. Broadway, Tucson, Ariz. 85711.

MURRAY, RICHARD DAVID R
b. Hiles, Wis, 6/10/38; s. Walter Andrew Murray and Jeanette Ann Bell M; m. 6/4/60 to Martha Linn Hanson; c. Richard David, David Oscar and Thomas Padraic. Educ: Univ. Wis, Madison, B.S, 61. Polit. & Govt. Pos: Rep. cand, U.S. Rep, Second Dist, Wis, 68; spec. asst, legis, Dept. Health, Educ. and Welfare, 68- Bus. & Prof. Pos: Sales trainee, Standard Oil, Milwaukee, Wis, 61, sales rep, Madison, 61-62, sales analyst, 62-64, merchandiser, Chicago, Ill, 64-65, sales mgr, 65-66; v.pres, Nasco Industs, Inc, 66-69. Mem: Nat. W Club; C. of C; Univ. Wis. Alumni Asn; Ft. Atkinson Beautification & Improv. Coun; United Fund; Rotary; Ft. Atkinson Sports Coun; Voc. & Tech. Serv. Adv. Cmt. Winner of Three Letters in Basketball, Univ. Wis. Rel: Lutheran. Legal Res: 325 Hillcrest Dr, Ft. Atkinson, Wis. 53538. Mailing Add: 1705 Old Stage Rd, Alexandria, Va. 22308.

MURRAY, ROBERT S. R
N.Mex. State Rep.
b. Washington, D.C, 11/23/37; s. Robert S. Murray, Sr. and Elizabeth Swartz M; m. 8/3/57 to Laurel Wilch; c. Robert M, Richard K. and Jennifer Lynne. Educ: Colo. Agr. & Mech. Col, 56; Univ. N.Mex, 57; Pi Kappa Alpha. Polit. & Govt. Pos: N.Mex. State Rep, 69- Mil. Serv: Nat. Guard. Rel: Presbyterian. Mailing Add: S.V. Star Route, Alameda, N.Mex. 87114.

MURRAY, ROGER STEPHEN D
Chmn, Missoula Co. Dem. Cent. Cmt, Mont.
b. Butte, Mont, 2/25/31; s. Roger Stephen Murray, Sr. and Opal Elizabeth Saxton M; m. 7/14/56 to Helen Elizabeth Hartman; c. Elizabeth Ann, Rose Marie and Joseph Frederick. Educ: Carroll Col, 2 years; Univ. Mont, B.A, 58. Polit. & Govt. Pos: Dem. precinct committeeman, Helena, Mont, 54-56 and Missoula, 58-60; city alderman, Missoula, 62-64; mem, Missoula Co. Bd. of Health, 62-64; chmn, Missoula Co. Dem. Cent. Cmt, 65-; mem. exec. cmt, Mont. State Dem. Cent. Cmt, 66-68. Bus. & Prof. Pos: Chief crew clerk, North. Pac. Railway, 48- Mil. Serv: Entered as Seaman Recruit, Coast Guard, 50, released as Yeoman 2/C, 53, after serv. in Combat Readiness Group, Korea, 51-53; Am. Defense Medal; Korean Defense Medal; Purple Heart; Good Conduct Medal. Mem: Elks; Moose; Eagles; Brotherhood of Railway Clerks. Rel: Catholic. Mailing Add: 1904 River Rd, Missoula, Mont. 59801.

MURRAY, RONALD J. D
Chmn, Campbell Co. Dem. Party, Tenn.
b. Harlan, Ky, 4/10/30; s. Don M. Murray and Emma Wilburn M; m. 8/27/57 to Billie Jean Hatmaker. Educ: Univ. Tenn, 3 years; Univ. Ky, 1 year; Stetson Univ, 1/4 year. Polit. & Govt. Pos: Justice of the Peace, La Follette, Tenn, 60-66, state probation officer, 69-; chmn, Campbell Co. Dem. Party, 64-66 & 69- Bus. & Prof. Pos: Basketball coach, La Follette Schools, 57-67. Mil. Serv: Entered as Pvt, Army, 51, released as Cpl, 54, after serv. in 82nd Airborne Div; Good Conduct Medal. Mem: VFW; Am. Legion; Eagles; Senator's Club; Jaycees. Rel: Baptist. Mailing Add: 400½ South Ave, La Follette, Tenn. 37766.

MURRAY, THAD S. D
b. Norfolk, Va, 10/17/19; s. Charles B. Murray and Blanche Thomas Spiers M; m. 12/18/49 to Nan Astin M; c. Thad Neil and Stephen Kent. Educ: Randolph-Macon Col. Polit. & Govt. Pos: Admin. asst, U.S. Rep. Porter Hardy, Jr, Va, 47-69; exec. asst. to U.S. Sen. Spong, Va, currently. Bus. & Prof. Pos: Off. mgr, Norfolk Br, Giffels & Valet, Architects and Engrs, 42-44; dist. mgr, Mass. Mutual Life Ins. Co, Norfolk, 44-45; publicity dir, Am. Red Cross, Norfolk, 45-46; v.pres, James & Murray, Inc, Real Estate and Ins, 45-47. Mem: Jaycees (state secy, 44-45 past pres, Norfolk Chap, 46-47); bd. dirs, Norfolk YMCA, 45-46; dir, Cong. Employees Fed. Credit Union. Rel: Methodist. Legal Res: Norfolk, Va. Mailing Add: 10513 Cedar Ave, Fairfax, Va. 22030.

MURRAY, THOMAS F. D
b. Silesia, Mont, 7/29/16; s. John Murray and Rose Baker M; m. 1/24/42 to Helen Hargreaves; c. Terry, Betty, John and Patricia. Educ: Univ. Mont, LL.B, 45-50. Polit. & Govt. Pos: City attorney, Superior, Mont, 53-56; dep. attorney, Missoula Co, 56-57; city councilman, Missoula, 59-63; chmn, Missoula Co. Dem. Cent. Cmt, 60-65, mem, 65-69; del, Dem. Nat. Conv, 68. Bus. & Prof. Pos: Partner, Law Firm of Garnaas, Murray & Hall, 59- Mil. Serv: Entered as Pvt, Army, 41, released as 1st Lt, 45, after serv. in 35th Inf. Div, ETO, 44-45; Purple Heart; Bronze Star; Normandy Campaign, Central Europe Campaign, Battle of Ardennes and Germany Campaign Ribbons. Mem: Mont. State and West. Mont. Bar Asns; Elks; Moose; K. of C. Rel: Catholic. Mailing Add: 728 S. Third St. W, Missoula, Mont. 59801. (1967)

MURRAY, TOM D
b. Jackson, Tenn, 8/1/94; single. Educ: Union U, B.A; Cumberland U, LL.B; Sigma Alpha Epsilon. Polit. & Gov. Pos: U.S. Rep, Tenn, 42-66; Elec. Dist. Attorney Gen, 12th Judicial Circuit of Tenn, 22; Resigned, 33, to become assoc. with Off. of Solicitor of Post Off. Dept. in Wash, until 42; former mem, State Dem. Exec. Cmt. of Tenn; Del. to Dem. Nat. Conv, 28, 32, 36; Chmn, Dem. Exec. Comm. of Madison Co, 24-33. Bus. & Prof. Pos: Practiced Law in Jackson; taught sch, 2 yrs. Mil. Serv: Army; mem, Am. Expeditionary Forces in France; discharged 1919. Mem: Cmdr, John A. Deaver Post of Am. Legion, Jackson; Vice Cmdr, Legion for the State of Tenn; VFW. Legal Res: Jackson, Tenn. Mailing Add: The Congressional, Washington, D.C. 20013. (1967)

MURRAY, WILLIAM McGARRY R
Wyo. State Rep.
b. Cheyenne, Wyo, 1/14/24; s. Edward F. Murray and Mary McGarry M; m. 10/21/43 to Therese Popp; c. Dianne (Mrs. Bruce Twine), Katheryne, Mary, and William. Educ: N.Mex. Mil. Inst, 2 years; Colo. Col, 1 year; Univ. Wyo, B.A. Polit. & Govt. Pos: Wyo. State Rep, Laramie Co, 69- Bus. & Prof. Pos: Salesman, Murray Ins. Agency, 47, partner, 55 and sr. partner, 62. Mil. Serv: Entered as Pvt, Marine Corps, 43, released as Cpl, 46, after serv. in Sixth Marine Div, 15th Regt, Pac. and Orient; Presidential Unit Citation. Mem: Nat. Asn. of Surety Bond Producers; Elks; VFW; Am. Legion; Rotary; Turtles; C. of C; K. of C. Boss of Year, Nat. Secy. Asn, 66. Rel: Catholic. Mailing Add: 2843 Olive Dr, Cheyenne, Wyo. 82001.

MURRELL, CECIL BOYD R
Mem, Calif. Rep. State Cent. Cmt.
b. Lebanon, Ky, 9/11/09; s. Richard Murrell and Mary Carter M; m. 4/15/46

to Ursula Elizabeth Pruitt; c. Mary Virginia (Mrs. Williams). Educ: Univ. Calif, Los Angeles, A.B, 33; Hastings Col. Law, 34-37. Polit. & Govt. Pos: Hearing exam, Los Angeles Police Dept, Calif, 57-; pres, Coun. of Orgn. Against Vice, Los Angeles, 60-; Rep. nominee for Calif. State Sen, 29th Sen. Dist; mem. adv. cmt, Dist. Attorney of Los Angeles Co, Calif, 64-; mem, Rep. Assocs, 65-68; mem. exec. cmt, Los Angeles Co. Rep. Cent. Cmt, 66-68; mem, Calif. Rep. State Cent. Cmt, 66-; pres, Cosmopolitan Rep. Voters Club, Inc, 68- Bus. & Prof. Pos: Sr. partner, Murrell & Embry Real Estate Co, 46-; gen. agent, Golden State Mutual Ins. Co, Los Angeles, 57-60; publisher, Los Angeles Sun, 61-62. Mil. Serv: Entered as Steward, Merchant Marine, 41, released as Lt.(jg), 46, after serv. in Far East Area. Publ: Series of articles in Los Angeles Times, Los Angeles Herald-Examiner, neighborhood newspapers and some Negro publ, 60- Mem: Alumni Asn. Univ. Calif, Los Angeles; bd. dirs, United Serv. Orgn; life mem, NAACP. Cert. of Appreciation, Boys' Clubs of Am, 66; Plaque of Appreciation for sponsoring Olympic Qualifying Trip of Los Angeles Group; other plaques for outstanding commun. serv. Rel: Presbyterian. Mailing Add: 2905½ S. Western Ave, Los Angeles, Calif. 90018.

MURROW, CALVIN COOLIDGE R
N.C. State Sen.
b. Aberdeen, N.C, 7/6/24; s. John L. Murrow, Sr. and Maggie Leonard M; m. 1/4/46 to Mildred Jones; c. Jeznne (Mrs. Edwards) and Michael C. Educ: High Point Col. Polit. & Govt. Pos: N.C. State Sen, 68- Bus. & Prof. Pos: Co-owner and secy-treas, Country Furniture Co, CLC Rentals and Murrow's Transfer, High Point, N.C, currently. Mil. Serv: Entered as Pfc, Third Marines Div, 42, released as Cpl, 46, after serv. in Pac. Mem: Exchange Club; C. of C. Rel: Quaker. Mailing Add: 506 Overbrook Dr, High Point, N.C, 27262.

MURTHA, JOHN PATRICK D
Pa. State Rep.
b. New Martinsville, W.Va, 6/17/32; s. John Patrick Murtha and Mary Edna Ray M; m. 6/10/55 to Joyce Bell; c. Donna Sue, John Mark and Patrick Clark. Educ: Wash. & Jefferson Col; Univ. Pittsburgh; Ind. Univ. of Pa, B.A, 61; student coun. Polit. & Govt. Pos: Dem. nominee for U.S. Rep, 68; Pa. State Rep, 72nd Legis. Dist, 69- Bus. & Prof. Pos: Pres, Johnstown Minute Car Wash, 57-; mem, bd. dir, Commun. Nursing Serv, currently. Mil. Serv: Pvt, Marines; Lt. Col, Marine Corps Res; Bronze Star Medal; Vietnamese Cross of Gallantry; Two Purple Hearts. Publ: Ser. of six articles, 'Jungle Warfare,' Res. Marine, 61; 'Intelligence in Vietnam,' Marine Corps Gazette, 1/68. Mem: Pres, Conemaugh Valley ROA; dist. cmnr, W.Dist, Boy Scouts. Legal Res: 109 Colgate Ave, Johnstown, Pa. 15906. Mailing Add: 711 Somerset St, Johnstown, Pa. 15906.

MUSCH, WARREN ROY R
Secy, Cass Co. Rep. Cent. Cmt, Ill.
b. Virginia, Ill, 10/25/21; s. Roy John Musch and Gertrude Anderson M; m. 6/23/44 to Haroldine Ruth Husted; c. Randal Lee and Cordel Roy. Educ: Ill. Col, A.B, 43; Phi Alpha Literary Soc. Polit. & Govt. Pos: Secy, Cass Co. Rep. Cent. Cmt, Ill, 66-; Rep. committeeman, precinct 14, Cass Co, currently. Bus. & Prof. Pos: Farmer, Virginia, Ill, 46- Mil. Serv: Entered as Pvt, Marines, 43, released as 1st Lt, 46, after serv. in Hq. Co, Third Bn, 28th Marines, Fifth Marine Div. and Hq, Sixth Marines, Second Marine Div, Pac. Theatre, 44-46. Mem: Sangamon Valley Farm Bus. Farm Mgt. Asn; AF&AM; Consistory; Shrine; Am. Legion; Kiwanis; Elks; Farm Bureau. Rel: Presbyterian. Mailing Add: Route 2, Box 62, Virginia, Ill. 62691.

MUSE, RAYMOND O'NEAL D
Chmn, Swain Co. Dem. Exec. Cmt, N.C.
b. Bryson City, N.C, 5/28/28; s. Harley Raymond Muse and Ida Chambers M; m. 12/15/46 to Doris Glenda Tallent; c. Glenda Neil, Daniel, Rita Kim, Margaret Ann and Jeffery Scott. Educ: Swain Co. Schs, 12 years; Swain Co. High Sch, Postgrad, Bookkeeping & Typing, 1 year. Polit. & Govt. Pos: Chmn, Swain Co. Dem. Exec. Cmt, N.C, 65- Bus. & Prof. Pos: Mgr, Bennett's Drug Store, Bryson City, N.C, 58- Mil. Serv: Seaman 2-V6, Navy, 46. Mem: Jaycees; Maroon & White Club; dir, C. of C. Rel: Baptist. Mailing Add: Box 42, Bryson City, N.C. 28713.

MUSGRAVE, HAROLD MILLER R
b. East St. Louis, Ill, 2/22/11; s. John Curtis Musgrave and Maude Miller M; m. 2/27/36 to Margaret Eleanor Copple; c. Sondra Sue (Mrs. Charles H. Salem) and Pamela (Mrs. David G. Taggart). Educ: East St. Louis High Sch, grad, 28. Polit. & Govt. Pos: Chmn, Dist. 8-J Maricopa Co. Rep. Cmt, Ariz, 66-; Alternate Del, Rep. Nat. Conv, 68. Bus. & Prof. Pos: Real Estate Broker, 61- Mem: Gothic Lodge, AF&AM; Consistory; Shrine; Elks. Rel: Protestant. Mailing Add: 5810 N. 12th Ave, Phoenix, Ariz. 85013.

MUSGRAVE, JOE EDWARD R
Okla. State Rep.
b. Pawhuska, Okla, 8/13/94; s. John Wesley Musgrave and Margaret Frances Steer M; m. 6/12/13 to Madge C. Howard; c. Lyle J, Ken H. and Joe E, Jr. Polit. & Govt. Pos: Okla. State Rep, 43-47, 51-53, 55-57 & 62- Bus. & Prof. Pos: Pres, Stainless Steel Mfg. Co, Kans. City, Mo, 39-41; independent ins. underwriter, Bankers Life Co, Okla, 41- Mem: C. of C; KCCH (32°), Mason; Shrine. Rel: Baptist. Legal Res: 4911 S. Madison, Tulsa, Okla. 74105. Mailing Add: Suite 404, 1307 S. Boulder, Tulsa, Okla. 74119. (1967)

MUSGROVE, GLENN BURKE D
Tex. State Rep.
b. Vernon, Tex. 3/31/41; s. Lowell Glenn Musgrove and Dale Dora Burke M; single. Educ: Univ. of Tex, Austin, eng. and bus. courses, 59-66; South Methodist Univ, 66; nat. presidential rep, Alpha Phi Omega; Tejas. Polit. & Govt. Pos: Tex. State Rep, Dist. 53, 67-, sponsor of Tex. Dangerous Drug Laws, 67 and 69 Acts. Bus. & Prof. Pos: Admin. Asst. to Gordon McLendon, Dallas, 66; exec. asst. to H.L. Hunt, 66-67; pres, Breckenridge Oil Well Servicing and Salvage, 69- Mem: Am. Soc. of Chem. Engrs; Lions (hon. mem, Breckenridge Chap); Jaycees; Elks; Breckenridge Country Club; Am. Legion (coordinator, Tex. Chap. Boys State Prog, 65-). SAR Medal of Honor; Chicago Tribune Award; Selected Outstanding Student, Univ. of Tex, 63; Univ. of Tex. Barry Whitaker Leadership Award; Named Hon. Citizen of 20 Tex. Cities; Recipient of Local and State Americanism Awards. Rel: Methodist. Legal Res: South Oakwood, Breckenridge, Tex. 76024. Mailing Add: Miller Bldg, Breckenridge, Tex. 76024.

MUSGROVE, WILLIAM L. D
Chmn, San Joaquin Co. Dem. Cent. Cmt, Calif.
b. Lodi, Calif, 3/24/43; s. James Cleo Musgrove and Oressa Huckins M; m. Alberta Fegan; c. John William and guardian for: Michele, Dorri and James Musgrove. Educ: Stockton Col, A.A, 63; Sacramento State Col, B.A, 67; San Francisco State Col; San Diego State Col; San Joaquin Delta Col; pres, Stockton Col. Student Asn; Econ. Club; Rho Eta Sigma; Circle K. Polit. & Govt. Pos: Pres, Lodi Dem. Club, Calif, 66-68; Dist. 15 dir, Calif. Dem. Coun, 67; mem. exec. cmt, 15th Dist. Coun. of Dem. Clubs, 67-; v.pres, Dem. of Cent. Calif, 67- and first v.pres, 69-; mem. and mem. exec. cmt, Calif. Dem. State Cent. Cmt, 68-; chmn, San Joaquin Co. Dem. Cent. Cmt, 68- Mem: Am. Fedn. of Grain Millers. Rel: Protestant. Mailing Add: 8458 San Pablo Way, Stockton, Calif. 95207.

MUSHNICK, SAMUEL WINIKER R
b. Milford, Mass, 3/2/31; s. Morris Charles Mushnick and Judith Winiker M; m. to Janice Rosen; c. Cindy Beth. Educ: Burdett Col; Bentley Col. Polit. & Govt. Pos: Chmn, Medway Town Rep. Cmt, Mass, 64-68. Mil. Serv: Entered as Seaman, Navy, 62, released as DK 2. Mem: Mason; Am. Legion; VFW; Mass. Dep. Sheriff Asn. Rel: Hebrew. Mailing Add: 14 High St, Medway, Mass. 02053. (1967)

MUSICK, VIRGIL LEE D
b. Taylor Co, Tex, 12/11/06; s. Julian Edgar Musick and Martha Lee M; m. 8/5/28 to Bertha Briggs; c. Linda Kay and Anita. Educ: Tex. Tech. Col. Polit. & Govt. Pos: Mem, Tex. Aeronaut. Cmn, 47-53; chmn, Taylor Co. Dem. for Lyndon B. Johnson, Tex, 54-64; mem, Taylor Co. Campaign Cmt. for Gov. John Connelly; del, Dem. Nat. Conv, 60 & 64; adv, Small Bus. Admin, Tex, 64- Bus. & Prof. Pos: Owner, Seven-Up Bottling Co. of Abilene and San Angelo, Tex, 47- Mil. Serv: Civilian Flight Instr, 42-45. Mem: Past master, Abilene Lodge 559 AF&AM; past potentate, Suez Shrine Temple, San Angelo, Tex; past pres, Tex. Bottlers Asn. Rel: Baptist. Legal Res: 1933 River Oaks Rd, Abilene, Tex. 79605. Mailing Add: P.O. Box 2318, Abilene, Tex. 79604. (1967)

MUSKEY, NICHOLAS CHRIS R
Mem, Calif. Rep. State Cent. Cmt.
b. St. Paul, Minnesota, 4/21/10; s. Chris John Moschogianis and Kalliopi Yiannakoulis M; m. 1/27/41 to Claramay Franing. Educ: Univ. Minn, 1 year; Univ. Calif, Los Angeles, Exten. Div, 1 year; City Col. of Los Angeles, Exten. Div, 1 year; Univ. South. Calif, Exten. Div, 1 year. Polit. & Govt. Pos: Rep. precinct chmn, 42nd Assembly Dist, Calif, 52, registrn. chmn, 63-64; dir. 21st Dist, Calif. Rep. Assembly, 60, dir. 27th Dist, 61, pres. 42nd Assembly Dist, 61-62, dir-at-lg, 66, v.pres, 67, dir. 28th Dist, 69; mem, Calif. Rep. State Cent. Cmt, 63-, mem. rules cmt, 66-69; pres, Burbank Rep. Assembly, 65; pres, All Rep. Assembly, 66; v.pres, Los Angeles Co. Rep. Assembly, 66-67. Bus. & Prof. Pos: Co-owner and mgr, Off. Photos, Inc, Hollywood, Calif, 46-47; traffic mgr, Teleways Radio Prod, 48; asst. mgr, Acousti-Glas, Inc, Burbank, 49-50; owner and operator, Magnolia Grill, N.Hollywood, 50-51; asst. mgr, Radio Sta. KBLA, Burbank, 52-53; plant mgr, Rol-Fol Table Co, Inc, Van Nuys, 53-55; personnel dir, Hycor Div, Int. Resistance Corp, Sylmar, 55-56; production mgr, Wizard Mfg. Co, N. Hollywood, 56; owner and operator, Blackwater Mining Co, Death Valley, 56-58; mgr, Bekins Film Center, Hollywood, 58-66; mgr, Producers Film Center, 66- Mil. Serv: Entered as Pvt, Marine Corps, 40, retired as CWO-4, 66, after serv. in Second Marine Div, S.Pac. Theater, 40-46, Res, 46-66; Two Presidential Citations; Res. Medal; Pac. Theater Medal; Am. Theatre Ribbon. Mem: Soc. of Motion Picture and TV Engrs; TV Film Asn.(secy-treas); South. Calif. Motion Picture Coun.(adv. bd); life mem, Second Marine Div. Asn.(currently mem, Calif. Chap); life mem, Marine Corps Reserve Officers Asn. Rel: Greek Orthodox. Mailing Add: 15751 Morrison St, Encino, Calif. 91316.

MUSKIE, EDMUND SIXTUS D
U.S. Sen, Maine
b. Rumford, Maine, 3/28/14; s. Stephen Muskie and Josephine Czarnecki M; m. 5/29/48 to Jane F. Gray; c. Stephen Oliver, Ellen, Melinda, Martha and Edmund S, Jr. Educ: Bates Col, B.A, 36; Cornell Univ. Law Sch, LL.B, 39; Phi Beta Kappa; Delta Sigma Rho; Phi Alpha Theta. Hon. LL.D, Bates Col, Univ. Maine, Portland Univ, Bowdoin Col, Colby Col, Lafayette Col, Univ. Buffalo and Nassan Col; D.P.A, Suffolk Univ. Polit. & Govt. Pos: Maine State Rep, 46-51, Minority Leader, Maine House of Rep, 48-51 and chmn, Subcmt. on Air and Water Pollution of Pub. Works; Maine dist. dir, Price Stabilization, 51-52; Dem. Nat. Committeeman, 52-54; Gov, Maine, 55-59; U.S. Sen, Maine, 59-; del, Dem. Nat. Conv, 68; Dem. Vice Presidential Cand, 68. Bus. & Prof. Pos: Law practice, Waterville, Maine, 40-55. Mil. Serv: Entered as Ens, Navy, 42, released as Lt.(jg), 45, after serv. as Eng. Officer, European and Pac. Theaters; 3 Battle Stars. Mem: Waterville, Kennebec Co, Maine and Mass. Bar Asns; Commercial Law League; Lions; Elks; Amvets. First Popularly Elected Dem. Sen. from Maine. Rel: Roman Catholic. Legal Res: Waterville, Maine 04901. Mailing Add: 5409 Albia Rd. N.W, Washington, D.C. 20016.

MUSSER, VIRGIL LEE D
Pres, Young Dem. Clubs. of Am.
b. Marshallville, Ohio, 8/3/34; s. Leland V. Musser and Delpha Garman M; m. 6/18/55 to Dorothy Ann Hook; c. Scott Alan and Julie Ann. Educ: Col. of Wooster, B.A, 56; West. Reserve Univ. Sch. of Law, LL.B, 59; Phi Alpha Delta; Pi Sigma Alpha. Polit. & Govt. Pos: Pres, Col. Wooster Young Dem, 54-55; State coordinator, Ohio Col. Young Dem, 55; pres, Wayne Co. Young Dem, 55, Young Dem. of Cuyahoga Co, 56-57, Stark Co. Young Dem, 64 and Ohio League of Young Dem. Clubs, 64-66; pres, Young Dem. Clubs of Am, 65-; city solicitor, Massillon, Ohio, 66-; cand, U.S. House of Rep, 16th Dist, Ohio and del, Dem. Nat. Conv, 68. Mil. Serv: Entered as Pvt, Army Res, 59, released as Spec. 4, 65. Mem: Jr. Bar Cmt, Ohio State Bar Asn, 64; Cleveland, Stark Co. and Massillon Bar Asns; nat. pres, Col. of Wooster Alumni Asn, 69-; past pres, Varsity Letterman's Asn, Col. of Wooster; pres, Am. Asn. of Young Polit. Leaders; one of founders and bd. dirs, Yes-Actt; United Fund Bd, West. Stark Co; pres, Stark Co. War on Poverty Cmt; Jaycees; Ur-

ban League; Boy's Club; pres, Social Planning Coun. West. Stark Co; exec. cmt, Atlantic Alliance of Young Polit. Leaders and U.S. Youth Coun. First alternate del, World Assembly of Youth Cong, Toyko, 66. Rel: Methodist. Legal Res: 301 Sheri Dr. N.E, Massillon, Ohio 44646. Mailing Add: Massillon Bldg, Massillon, Ohio 44646.

MUSSEY, WILLIAM HOWARD R
Ohio State Rep.
b. Chicago, Ill, 8/24/13; s. Charles F. Mussey and Mabel Hill M; m. 1/21/39 to Elizabeth Ann Dowdney; c. Elizabeth Jean and Ann Louise. Educ: Ohio State Univ, 31-35. Polit. & Govt. Pos: Ohio State Rep, 12th Dist, 67- Bus. & Prof. Pos: Gen, mgr, Clermont Sun Publishing Co, Inc, 53-66. Mil. Serv: Ohio Nat. Guard, 29-40; also entered as Pvt, Army, 42, released as Major, 53, after serv. in 37th and 33rd Inf. Div, Korean Mil. Advisor Group, S.Pac. and Japan; President Commendation Medal, 2 awards; Philippine Campaign, Japan Occupation, Am. Theater and Korean Ribbons. Mem: Nat. and Ohio Newspaper Asns; Cincinnati Advertisers Club; Am. Legion, Batavia Post 237; Batavia Businessmens Asn; Little Miami River Develop. Asn; past pres, Batavia Rotary Club. Rel: Presbyterian; Chmn, Bd. Trustees, Batavia Presbyterian Church. Mailing Add: 150 Riverside, Batavia, Ohio 45103.

MUSSLEWHITE, CHARLES BENTON D
b. Lufkin, Tex, 9/21/31; s. Robert Chilton Musslewhite and Mildred Guinn M.(deceased); m. 6/13/53 to Rosanne Dickson; c. Charles Benton, Jr, Guinn and David Dickson. Educ: South. Methodist Univ, B.B.A, 53, LL.B, 54; Georgetown Univ, LL.M, 57; Order of Woolsack; Cycen Fjodr; Blue Key; South. Methodist Law J; Barristers; Phi Delta; Phi Alpha Delta. Polit. & Govt. Pos: Del, State Dem. Conv, 60-68, mem, Permanent Resolutions Cmt, 60; adv, Nat. Coun. on Phys. Fitness, 61-64; field rep, Nat. Dem. Cmt, 62; mem, Nat. Adv. Cmt. on Area Redevelop, 62-63; cong. cand, Seventh Cong. Dist, Tex, 62 & 64; v.pres, Dem. Club, Angelina Co, 68; del, Dem. Nat. Conv, 68; legis. asst. to Sen. Ralph Yarborough, Tex, 69- Bus. & Prof. Pos: Partner, Burford, Ryburn & Ford, Attorneys, Dallas, Tex, 58-59; Musslewhite & Musslewhite, Lufkin, Tex, 59-68 and Musslewhite, Maroney & Cely, 68- Mil. Serv: Entered as 1st Lt, Army, 55, released as Capt, 57, after serv. at Judge Adv. Gen. Corps Hq, Dept. of the Army, Pentagon, 55-57; Army Res; Commendation Ribbon with Medal Pendant. Publ: Articles on the Democratic National Convention, Angelina Co. Free Press, 68. Mem: Bd. dir, Tex. Trial Lawyers Asn; Tex. Bar Asn; Am. Trial Lawyers Asn; Lufkin Lions Club. Rel: Methodist. Legal Res: 1511 Reen St, Lufkin, Tex. 75901. Mailing Add: c/o Sen. Ralph Yarborough, Senate Office Bldg, Washington, D.C. 20510.

MUSTO, JAMES A. D
Pa. State Rep.
b. Pittston Twp, Pa, 10/12/99; s. Ralph Musto (deceased) and Louise M; m. to Rose M. Frushon; c. Six sons and two daughters. Educ: Pittston Twp. Pub. Schs. Polit. & Govt. Pos: Former pres, Pittston Twp. Sch. Bd, Pa; Pa. State Rep, 48- Bus. & Prof. Pos: Formerly worked in the breaker and mines; barber and merchant. Mailing Add: 61 Bryden St, Pittston Twp, Pa. 18640. (1967)

MUSTO, WILLIAM V. D
N.J. State Sen.
b. Union City, N.J, 3/27/17; m. 1/3/46 to Rhyta Palmerini; c. Patrick and Patricia. Polit. & Govt. Pos: N.J. State Assemblyman, 46-65, Minority Leader, N.J. State Assembly, 53; mem, bd. of cmnr, Union City, N.J, 54-, mayor, 62; N.J. State Sen, 65- Bus. & Prof. Pos: Attorney-at-law. Mil. Serv: Army, 4½ years. Mem: Chmn. of many charity drives and affil. with many civic, fraternal and church orgn. Rel: Catholic. Mailing Add: 321 23rd St, Union City, N.J. 07087.

MUTCH, DUANE R
N.Dak. State Sen.
b. Grand Forks, N.Dak, 5/13/25; married; c. Three. Educ: Pub. Schs. Polit. & Govt. Pos: N.Dak. State Sen, 59-61 and currently. Bus. & Prof. Pos: Bulk Oil Distributor. Mil. Serv: World War II. Mem: Am. Legion; DAV. Mailing Add: Larrimore, N.Dak. 58251. (1967)

MUTHS, SHERMAN LEWIS, JR. D
Miss. State Rep.
b. Gulfport, Miss, 11/22/32; s. Sherman L. Muths and Margaret Tomlinson M.(deceased); m. 8/15/59 to Celia Carter; c. Sherman L, III. Educ: Univ. Miss, B.B.A, 54 and LL.B, 60; Phi Alpha Delta; Sigma Nu. Polit. & Govt. Pos: Miss. State Rep, currently. Mil. Serv: Entered as 2nd Lt, Air Force, 54, released as 1st Lt, 57, after serv. as Navigator, Military Air Transport Serv, 55-57; Capt, Office of Staff Judge Advocate, Air Force Res, 60- Mem: Pres, Miss. Jr. Bar, 64-65; 2nd v.pres, Miss. State Bar, 65-66. Rel: Methodist. Legal Res: 4105 Washington Ave, Gulfport, Miss. 39501. Mailing Add: 2300 14th St, Gulfport, Miss. 39501. (1967)

MUTSCHER, GUS FRANKLIN D
Speaker, Tex. House of Rep.
b. William Penn Community, Tex, 11/19/32; s. Gus Mutscher and Gertie Goeke M; m. 6/7/69 to Donna Axum; c. Miss Lisa Buckley. Educ: Blinn Jr. Col, grad, 52; Univ. of Tex, Austin, B.B.A, 56; Gamma Delta; int. pres, Collegiate Lutheran Orgn; Blinn Baseball Letterman; Blinn Debate Team state champion; class pres. Polit. & Govt. Pos: Del, Dem. State Conv, Washington Co, 58-68; Tex. State Rep, 29th Dist, 60-, speaker, Tex. House of Rep, 69-; del, Dem. Nat. Conv, 68. Bus. & Prof. Pos: Field rep. for Borden Co, Houston, 59. Mil. Serv: Entered as 2nd Lt, Army, 56, released as 1st Lt, 59, after serv. in Mil. Police. Named Outstanding Young Businessman of Harris Co, 59; Jr. C. of C. Outstanding Young Texan Award, 67; Distinguished Alumnus Award, Col. of Bus. Admin, Univ. of Tex, 69; Elected to the South. Conf. Adv. Cmt. of the Coun. of State Govt, 69. Rel: Lutheran. Legal Res: 307 N. Ross, Brenham, Tex. 77833. Mailing Add: Speaker's Apt, State Capitol, Austin, Tex. 78711.

MUTZ, JOHN M. R
Ind. State Rep.
s. John L. Mutz and Helen Massie M; m. 6/21/58 to Carolyn Jane Hawthorne; c. John Mark and Diana Caryl. Educ: Northwest. Univ, B.S, 57 and M.S, 58; Pi Alpha Mu; Beta Theta Pi. Polit. & Govt. Pos: Chmn, Allegheny Co. Young Rep, Pa, 59-60; chmn, Lawrence Twp. Young Rep, 64-65; Lawrence Twp. chmn, Marion Co. Rep. Party, 66-67; Ind. State Rep, 67- Bus. & Prof. Pos: V.pres, Circle Leasing Corp, 62-; secy-treas, Burger Chef of Louisville Inc, 64- Publ: Equipment Leasing for Financial Institutions, Mid-Continent Bank, 65. Mem: Jr. C. of C. Mailing Add: 5940 E. 79th St, Indianapolis, Ind. 46250.

MYDLAND, GORDON J. R
Attorney Gen, S.Dak.
b. Lake Preston, S.Dak, 5/12/22; m. to Lorraine Grange; c. John. Educ: S.Dak. State Col, B.S, 47; Univ. S.Dak, LL.B, 56. Polit. & Govt. Pos: Brookings Co. States Attorney, S.Dak, 59-62; S.Dak. State Sen, 63-68; S.Dak. Code Compilation Cmnr, 63-69; Attorney Gen, S.Dak, 69- Bus. & Prof. Pos: Lawyer, Cheever & Mydland until 69. Mil. Serv: Navy, 43-46. Mem: S.Dak. Bar Asn; Rotary; Am. Legion; VFW. Rel: Lutheran. Mailing Add: State Capitol, Pierre, S.Dak. 57501.

MYER, CALVIN HARLEY D
Treas, C.Z. Regional Dem. Party
b. Mansfield, Ohio, 7/6/32; s. Calvin Charles Myer and Inez Louise Wright M; div. Educ: Ashland High Sch, Ohio, dipl, 49; U.S. Air Force Inst. and on base col. exten. courses in Electronics. Polit. & Govt. Pos: Treas, C.Z. Regional Dem. Party, 68- Bus. & Prof. Pos: Engr-in-charge, Caribbean Area UNIVAC, Fed. Syst. Div, Sperry Rand Corp, 66- Mil. Serv: Entered as Pvt, Air Force, 51, released as S/Sgt, 60, after serv. in First Pilot Bomber Squadron, Fla, Caribbean, Germany and gen. West. European Area, 52-57; German Occup. Medal; Good Conduct Medal with Cluster; Nat. Defense Medal; UN Medal; Sharpshooter. Mem: Soc. of Philatelic Am; Am. Philatelic Soc; Am. Soc. of the Repub. of Panama; VFW; Albrook/Howard Officers Club. Rel: Protestant. Legal Res: P.O. Box 934, Albrook, C.Z. Mailing Add: P.O. Box 934, APO, New York, N.Y. 09825.

MYERS, BOB J. D
Mem, Calif. Dem. State Cent. Cmt.
b. Brawley, Calif, 1/27/40; s. Billy E. Myers and Lavada Oliver M; div; c. Kari Lynne, Robert Michael, Danielle Marie and William Randolph. Educ: San Diego State Col, B.A, 63; Sacramento State Col, M.A, 69. Polit. & Govt. Pos: Dem. nominee, Calif. State Assembly, 66; mem, Calif. Dem. State Cent. Cmt, 66-; pres, Bus. & Prfnl. Dem. of Imperial Co, Calif, 68. Mem: Calif. Teachers Asn. Mem, Experienced Teachers Fel. Prog. in Mexican Am. Educ, Sacramento State Col, 68-69. Rel: Episcopal. Mailing Add: 7707 College Town Dr. 12, Sacramento, Calif. 95826.

MYERS, CLAY R
Secy. of State, Ore.
b. Portland, Ore, 5/27/27; s. Henry Clay Myers and Helen Mackey M; m. 10/1/55 to Elizabeth Lex Arndt; c. Richard Clay, Carolyn Elizabeth and David Hobson. Educ: Univ. Ore, B.S, 49; Northwest. Col. of Law, 50-52; Lambda Chi Alpha, Sigma Nu Phi. Polit. & Govt. Pos: Asst. Secy, State, Ore, 65-66, Secy State, 68-; del, Rep. Nat. Conv, 68. Bus. & Prof. Pos: Property mgr, Trust Dept, First Nat. Bank, 49-53; with Conn. Gen. Life, Ore, 53-59, state mgr, 60-62; v.pres, Ins. Co. of Ore, 62-65. Mil. Serv: Navy, U.S. Coast Guard Acad. Mem: Ore. Estate Planning Coun; Nat. Asn. Life Underwriters; Ore. Asn. Health Underwriters; Ore. Life Mgr. Asn; Willamette Tuberc. and Health Asn; bd, Willamette Chap. Red Cross; bd, Soc. Work Careers; Portland City Club; Portland C. of C; Elks; v.pres. and chmn, endowment fund, Portland Jr. Symphony; Am. Legion. DeMolay Legion of Honor. Rel: Episcopal. Legal Res: 1610 Fir St. S, Salem, Ore. 97302. Mailing Add: 121 State Capitol, Salem, Ore. 97310.

MYERS, DAISY LOVELAND R
b. Woodford, Vt, 6/17/05; wid. Educ: Bennington High Sch. Polit. & Govt. Pos: Chmn, Rep. Town Cmt; mem, Bennington Co. Rep. Cmt; Town Auditor, Bennington, Vt, 58-; Vt. State Rep, 59-66. Bus. & Prof. Pos: Retired. Mem: Treas, Woodford Cemetery Cmt; dir, Regional Hwy. Coun. Rel: Episcopal. Mailing Add: Box 275, Bennington, Vt. 05201. (1967)

MYERS, FERN HOLT D
Chmn, Stone Co. Dem. Cent. Cmt, Mo.
b. Reeds Spring, Mo, 2/29/12; d. James Newton Holt and Winnie Stewart H; m. to William Rush Myers, wid. Educ: Southwest Mo. State Col, 2 years. Polit. & Govt. Pos: Chmn, Stone Co. Dem. Cent. Cmt, Mo, 66- Mailing Add: Crane, Mo. 65633.

MYERS, J. HOWARD D
Clerk, W.Va. State Senate
b. Berkeley Co, W.Va, 10/24/01; s. James C. Myers and Lillie E. M; m. 2/6/37 to Elizabeth M. Trump. Educ: Shepherd Col; W.Va. Univ; Kappa Sigma. Polit. & Govt. Pos: Sheriff, Berkeley Co, W.Va, 38-45; state exec. dir, Off. Civil Defense, 45; clerk, W.Va. State Senate, 45-; campaign chmn, Kilgore Campaign, 46; chmn, W.Va. State Dem. Exec. Cmt, 48 & 53-56; gen. campaign chmn, Dem. Party, 52. Mem: Mason (32°); Shrine; Elks. Mailing Add: Clerk of the State Senate, State Capitol Bldg, Charleston, W.Va. 25305.

MYERS, J. W. D
Wyo. State Sen.
b. Evanston, Wyo, 6/5/07; m. to Fern; c. four. Educ: Univ. of Wyo, B.S. Polit. & Govt. Pos: Wyo. State Rep, 4 years; Wyo. State Sen, 57- Bus. & Prof. Pos: Livestock; rancher. Mem: Mason; Wyo. Farm Bur; Wyo. Stockgrowers; Wyo. Taxpayers; Wyo. Develop. Asn. Mailing Add: R.D. 1, Evanston, Wyo. 82930. (1967)

MYERS, JACK FREDONDO R
b. Roosevelt, Okla, 1/17/32; s. Fred M. Myers and Minnie N. Anderson M; m. 9/21/52 to Margie A. Fitzgerald; c. Teresa Kay, Kirby Gene and Jack, Jr. Educ: Okla. State Univ, 49-50; Pershing Rifles. Polit. & Govt. Pos: Precinct secy, Dem. Party, Okla, 54-56; chmn, Kiowa Co. Rep. Party, 63-69; cand. for Okla. State Rep, 64; chmn, State Agr. Stabilization & Conserv. Serv. Cmt, U.S. Dept. Agr, 69- Bus. & Prof. Pos: Bd. mem, Kiowa Co. Farm Bur, 54-62, secy, 57-58. Mil. Serv: Entered as Pvt, Army, 50, released as Cpl, 52, after serv. in 45th Inf. Div, Japan and Korea, 51-52; Combat Infantryman Badge; Good Conduct Ribbon; UN Serv. Medal; Japan Occup. Medal; Korean War Medal with three Battle Stars. Mem: Farm Bur; Am. Legion; VFW. Rel: First Baptist. Mailing Add: Rt. 1, Snyder, Okla. 73566.

MYERS, JAMES FRANK D
b. Plains, Ga, 6/21/20; s. James Frank Myers and Mary Givan M; m. 5/31/53 to Marion Joyce Nelson; c. Mary Joyce, Barbara Jean and James Frank, III. Educ: Univ. Ga, B.S. in Commerce, 41, LL.B, 48; Phi Delta Phi; Sigma Alpha Epsilon; Gridiron Club. Polit. & Govt. Pos: Ga. State Rep, 49-50; mayor, Americus, Ga, 61-62; alternate del, Dem. Nat. Conv, 64; secy, Ga. State Bd. of Health, 64-65; solicitor gen, Southwest. Judicial Circuit, Ga, 65-68. Bus. & Prof. Pos: Lawyer, 47-; pres, Builtwell Homes, Inc, 62-64. Mil. Serv: Entered as Aviation Cadet, Navy Air Corps, 42, released as Lt, 45, after serv. in Patrol Bombing Squadron 53, S.Am, S.Pac. and Japan; Air Medal with two Oak Leaf Clusters. Mem: Elks; Am. Legion; VFW. Rel: Baptist. Legal Res: 506 Pine View Dr, Americus, Ga. 31709. Mailing Add: P.O. Box 507, Americus, Ga. 31709.

MYERS, JAN D
Auditor, Kans. Fedn. Women's Dem. Clubs
b. Coffeyville, Kans, 11/14/27; d. Ernest E. Royer and Frances Hodge R; m. 11/19/48 to Jack Allen Myers; c. Marsha Jan, Monica Jane, Melisa Jo, Jack Allen, Jr. and Frederick Wm. Educ: Cent. Mo. State Col, 47-48. Polit. & Govt. Pos: Co. and dist. officer, Johnson Co. Young Dem, Kans, 54-62 & 63-66; precinct committeewoman, Johnson Co. Dem. Party, 56-62 & 65-70; secy, Johnson Co. Dem. Women's Club, 57-59, v.pres, 63-69, first v.pres, 69-70; secy, Co. Dem. Cmt, Midland, Mich, 62; v.pres, Kans. Fedn. Women's Dem. Clubs, 63-69, auditor, 69-; v.chmn, Third Cong. Dist. Dem. Party, Kans, 64-66; alternate del, Dem. Nat. Conv, 64 & 68; Third Dist, Women Doer of 66; state chmn, Kans. Women for Humphrey-Muskie, 68, Johnson Co. chmn, 68. Mem: Kans. Parent and Teachers Orgn; secy-treas, Salvation Army, Merriam, Kans, 58-62; secy, Merriam Civic Improv. Cmt, 58-62; Boy Scouts; Camp Fire Girls; Girl Scouts. Painting, arts and crafts. Rel: Presbyterian. Mailing Add: 3911 W. 68th Terr, Prairie Village, Kans. 66208.

MYERS, JOHN T. R
U.S. Rep, Ind.
b. Covington, Ind, 2/8/27; s. Warren E. Myers and Myra Wisher M; m. 5/30/53 to Carol Carruthers; c. Carol Ann and Lori Jan. Educ: Ind. State Univ, B.S, 51; Sigma Pi. Polit. & Govt. Pos: U.S. Rep, Ind, 67- Mil. Serv: Entered as Pvt, Army, 45, released as S/Sgt, 46, after serv. in ETO; Maj, Army Res. Mem: Reserve Officers Asn; VFW; Am. Legion; Mason; Shrine; Elks; Lions; Wabash Valley Asn. Rel: Episcopal. Legal Res: 921 Second St, Covington, Ind. 47932. Mailing Add: U.S. House Office Building, Washington, D.C. 20515.

MYERS, KENNETH MORTON D
Fla. State Sen.
b. Miami, Fla, 3/11/33; s. Stanley C. Myers and Martha Scheinberg M; m. 1969 to Ursula. Educ: Univ. N.C, A.B, 54; Univ. Fla. Law Sch, LL.B, 57; Phi Beta Kappa; pres, Phi Alpha Delta; Pi Sigma Alpha; Tau Epsilon Phi; Freshman swimming team; track and fencing teams; pres, Debate Coun. and mem, Debate Team; Student Coun; Student Hon. Court; Order of Golden Fleece; exec. ed, Univ. Fla. Law Review; state champion, Law Sch. Moot Court Competition. Polit. & Govt. Pos: Fla. State Rep, 64-68; mem, City of Miami Pension Bd; trustee, City of Miami Pension Syst; mem, Agency Oper. Cmt. and Agency Oper. Steering and Appeals Cmt, United Fund; Fla. State Sen, 69- Allen Morris Award, Most Valuable Second Term Mem. in House of Rep, 67; St. Petersburg Times Capitol press poll, One of Ten Most Valuable Members of the House of Rep, 67; Miami Jr. C. of C. Award, Outstanding Young Man of Miami, 67; Fla. Jr. C. of C. Award, One of Five Outstanding Young Men of Fla, 67; Allen Morris Award, Outstanding First Termer in Fla. State Senate, 69. Rel: Jewish. Legal Res: 2451 Brickell Ave, Miami, Fla. 33129. Mailing Add: 1150 S.W. First St, Miami, Fla. 33130.

MYERS, PAUL J. R
Mayor, Ft. Myers, Fla.
b. Springfield, Ohio, 3/10/30; s. Marcus M. Myers and Jennie Bradshaw M; m. 3/25/50 to Arlene Marie Teach; c. Jay Paul, Curtis Lee, Matthew Mark and Laura Lynn. Educ: Cedarville Col, Cedarville, Ohio. Polit. & Govt. Pos: Bd. mem, Lee Co. Bd. of Pub. Instr, 61-65; mayor, Ft. Myers, Fla, 62- Mem: Kiwanis; Elks; Moose; Ft. Myers Symphony; Am. Cancer Soc; Lee Co. Rep. Club. Rel: Presbyterian; Elder, First Presby. Church. Legal Res: 1221 Canterbury Dr, Ft. Myers, Fla. 33901. Mailing Add: P.O. Box 2217, Ft. Myers, Fla. 33901. (1967)

MYERS, ROBERT LEE, III D
b. Camp Hill, Pa, 5/15/28; s. Robert Lee Myers, Jr. and Evelyn Mary Mentzer M; m. 6/21/58 to Helen Johnson; c. Robert Lee, IV, Katharine Manley and William Frederick. Educ: Col. William & Mary, A.B, 51; Dickinson Sch. Law, LL.B, 53; Theta Delta Chi; Corpus Juris Soc, Dickinson Sch. Law. Polit. & Govt. Pos: Cand, Dist. Attorney, Cumberland Co, Pa, 59; cong. cand, 19th Cong. Dist, Pa, 68. Bus. & Prof. Pos: Secy. & dir, Mt. Allen Corp, Lemoyne, Pa. Mil. Serv: Entered as Pvt, Army, 46, released as T-5, 47, after serv. in Third Armored Cavalry, U.S, 46-47. Publ: 'Decedent's Estates—Conclusiveness of Probate,' Dickinson Law Rev, 52-53. Mem: Cumberland Co. Bar Asn. (exec. cmt, 69); Pa. Bar Asn. (standing cmt. on econ. of law practice, 69); Am. Bar Asn; Am. Trial Lawyers Asn; Pa. Trial Lawyers Asn; F&AM; trustee, Harrisburg Symphony Asn; Lions (charter mem, Lower Allen Twp. Club); Eagles; bd. dir, Hemlock Girl Scout Coun; v.pres. & trustee, W. Shore Pub. Libr. Asn; chmn, Camp Hill Civil Serv. Cmn; W. Shore C. of C; chmn, legis. action cmt, W. Shore Country Club; mem. bd. mgt. and v.pres, Harris Ferry Chap, SAR; Gen. Alumni Asn, Dickinson Sch. Law. Rel: Presbyterian; Deacon and secy, bd. trustees, Camp Hill Presby. Church. Mailing Add: 2300 Market St, Camp Hill, Pa. 17011.

MYERS, RODERICK DOUGLAS R
Chmn, Pueblo Co. Rep. Cent. Cmt, Colo.
b. West Grove, Iowa, 10/16/32; s. Raymond Carl Myers and LaVelle Lamb M; single; foster son, Charles T. Conway. Educ: Colo. State Col, A.B. and teaching cert, 54, Colo. State Bd. Voc. Educ, Adult Educ. Cert, 56; Colo. State Univ. and Adams State Col, adv. study; Blue Key; Colvin Bus. Soc; Distributive Educ. Clubs of Am; Int. Rels. Club; Pi Omega Pi; Sigma Phi Epsilon; Lambda Gamma Kappa; DeMolay Club; Canterbury Club. Polit. & Govt. Pos: Chmn, Colo. Springs High Sch. Rep. Club, 48-50; chmn, Colo. State Col. Young Rep. League, 52-54; chmn, Pueblo Co. Young Rep. League, Colo, 58-62; cand. for Colo. State Rep, Pueblo Co, 58 & 60; committeeman and mem. exec. cmt, Pueblo Co. Rep. Cent. Cmt, Colo, 58-65, chmn, 65-; chmn, Third Cong. Dist. Young Rep. League, 60-62; bonus mem, Colo. State Rep. Cent. Cmt, 60-62; campaign mgr, State Supreme Court Justice, 62; pub. rels. dir, Third Dist. Goldwater Campaign, 64. Bus. & Prof. Pos: Coordinator, Distributive Educ, Pueblo Pub. Schs, 54-; pres, Myers Enterprises, 57-62; owner, Myers Land and Cattle Co, 60-64; pres, Roderick Douglas Myers Found, 60-; v.pres, King Bus. Col. Inc. and Pueblo Employ. Serv, 60-; owner, Trading Post Co, 62- Mil. Serv: Entered as Pvt, Army, 55, released as 2nd Lt, 57, after serv. in 554th and 89th Div, Antiaircraft; 1st Lt, Qm. Corps, Army Res, 57-64. Mem: Pueblo, Colo. and Nat. Educ. Asns; Nat. Sales Exec. Asn; Asn. of Sales Ralley Speakers; Pueblo C. of C; Beulah Valley C. of C; dir, Pueblo Chap, Am. Red Cross, Pueblo YMCA, Pueblo Co. Nat. Found. and Camp Crocket Boys Ranch; Elks; past pres, Pueblo Civitan; past Lt. Gov, Colo. Civitan; Pueblo D.E. Alumni Asn. Animal and bird trainer. Rel: Episcopal. Legal Res: The Mikado, P.O. Box 158, Beulah, Colo. 81023. Mailing Add: 1440 E. River St, Pueblo, Colo. 81001.

MYERS, RUFUS H, JR. D
b. Indianapolis, Ind, 8/11/42; s. Rufus H. Myers, Sr. and Susie B. Price M; m. 4/8/62 to Brenda L. Ewell; c. Michael Raymond and Mia Reneé. Educ: Ind. Univ; Howard Univ. Polit. & Govt. Pos: 11th dist. chmn, Ind. State Young Dem. and mem. human rights cmt, 64-66; chief dep, Marion Co. Voters Registrn, 64-65; Marion Co. Probate Court, 65-66; legis. asst. to U.S. Rep. Andrew Jacobs, Jr, 66-68, admin. asst, 68- Rel: Presbyterian. Mailing Add: 1120 W. 37th St, Indianapolis, Ind. 46208.

MYERS, WADE ALEXANDER D
b. Emporia, Kans, 5/29/29; s. Wade E. Myers and Lucille Metz M; m. 7/9/52 to Donna Rae Bess; c. Wade Douglas and Kym-Eric. Educ: Washburn Univ, B.A, 51, LL.B, 56; Delta Theta Phi; Phi Delta Theta. Polit. & Govt. Pos: Judge, Lyon Co, Kans, 57-61; Kans. State Sen, 61-65; del, Dem. Nat. Conv, 64. Bus. & Prof. Pos: Attorney, 56-67. Mil. Serv: Entered as 2nd Lt, Air Force, 53, released as 1st Lt, 55, after serv. in 15th Air Force Hq. Intel. Mem: Am. Legion; Lions; C. of C. Rel: Catholic. Mailing Add: 1242 Luther, Emporia, Kans. 66801.

MYERS, WALTER, JR. D
b. Indianapolis, Ind, 6/9/14; s. Walter Myers and Katharine Lyons M; div; m. 11/26/52 to Jane Weldon; c. Dennis. Educ: Yale Col; Yale Law Sch; Tau Kappa Epsilon; Phi Alpha Delta. Polit. & Govt. Pos: Dep. prosecutor, Marion Co, Ind, 39-40; attorney, Indianapolis Sanit. Bd, 48-51; ward chmn, Dem. Co. Cmt, 48-54; judge, Appellate Court of Ind, 59-62, Supreme Court of Ind, 63-68. Bus. & Prof. Pos: Mem, Law Firm of Myers, Northam & Myers, 39-59; lectr. bus. law, Butler Univ, 42-66. Mem: Am, Ind. State and Indianapolis Bar Asns; Lawyers Asn. of Indianapolis; Lawyers Club; F&AM; Scottish Rite; Shrine; Indianapolis C. of C; bd. dirs, Marion Co. Tuberc. Asn, Ment. Health Asn. and YMCA; Indianapolis Athletic Club; Woodstock Country Club; Hon. Order of Ky. Col; Sagamore of the Wabash; mem. and past pres, Ind. Dem. Club. Rel: Presbyterian; Mem, Bd. of Deacons. Mailing Add: 1136 West 56th St, Indianapolis, Ind. 46208. (1967)

MYERS, WARD G. R
Wyo. State Rep.
b. Perry, Iowa, 9/17/02; m. to Glenna L; c. two. Educ: Mil. Acad. Trade Sch. Polit. & Govt. Pos: Wyo. State Rep, currently, Speaker Pro-Tem, Wyo. State House of Rep, 69- Bus. & Prof. Pos: Garage owner. Mem: C. of C. (dir); Wyo. Automobile Dealers Asn. (past dir, v.pres, 68-); Farm Bur; Mason (Past Master, 48-); Shrine; Eastern Star (Past Worthy Patron, 48-); Elks. Wyo. Dealer of the Year Award, 66. Rel: Episcopal. Mailing Add: Lovell, Wyo. 82431.

MYERS, WILLIAM BLACKWELL D
Mem, Calif. Dem. State Cent. Cmt.
b. Powell, Miss, 12/28/04; s. William Blackwell Myers and Alice Spencer M; m. 8/23/64 to Margaret May Maddux; c. Alice Lynne and Nancy Jeane. Educ: Univ. Ark, 24-26; Ark. Law Sch, LL.D, 29. Polit. & Govt. Pos: 18th Cong. Dist. co-chmn, Calif. Dem. State Cent. Cmt, 66-68, mem, 66-; mem, Kern Co. Dem. Cent. Cmt, 66-, chmn, 68- Bus. & Prof. Pos: Farm owner, 49- Mil. Serv: Entered as 2nd Lt, Air Force, 26, released as Lt. Col. (Ret), 65, after serv. in Civilian Conserv, Intel. and Civil Affairs, 34-48. Mem: Elks; Mason; Am. Legion; DAV; Retired Officers Asn; Bakersfield Dem. Club. Rel: Methodist. Mailing Add: 1 Montrose St, Bakersfield, Calif. 93305.

MYERS, WILLIAM GEORGE R
Chmn, Martin Co. Rep. Exec. Cmt, Fla.
b. Kittanning, Pa, 9/28/30; s. William George Myers and Emma A. Webb M; m. 6/19/52 to Carol Anne Edgar; c. Jacqueline Jolane, William George, Bradley Stephen, Brian Jeffry, Barry Douglas and Jennifer Sue. Educ: Univ. Pittsburgh, B.S, 52, Sch. Med, M.D, 56; South Side Hosp, Pittsburgh, Pa, internship, 56-57, med. residency, 57-58; Nu Sigma Sigma; Alpha Omega Alpha; Tau Kappa Alpha; Nu Sigma Nu. Polit. & Govt. Pos: Precinct committeeman, exec. cmt. and cand, co. cmnr, 64; charter pres, Young Rep. Martin Co. Fla, 64-66; del. Young Rep. Nat. Conv, 65; chmn, Cand. Selection Cmt, 65-66; chmn, Martin Co. Rep. Exec. Cmt, 65-; co-chmn, Martin Co. Kirk for Gov, 66. Bus. & Prof. Pos: Secy, Martin Memorial Hosp. Med. Staff, 65. Mem: Tri-County Med. Soc; Fla. Med. Soc; Am. Med. Asn; Fla. Med. Polit. Action Cmt; Am. Acad. Gen. Practice; Am. Geriatric Soc; C. of C. (bd. dirs, Hobe Sound, 63-66, pres, 62-64); bd. dirs, Heart Asn. of Palm Beach, 63-66; pres, Martin Co. YMCA, 66; Hobe Sound Civic Asn; Co. Conserv. Cmt; Martin Co. Hist. Soc; DeMolay; K. of P. Rel: Lutheran. Legal Res: 9 East Coconut Way, Hobe Sound, Fla. 33455. Mailing Add: P.O. Box 625, Hobe Sound, Fla. 33455. (1967)

MYHRA, NORMAN L. D
b. Amherst, Wis, 2/17/25. Educ: Milwaukee Voc. Sch. Polit. & Govt. Pos: Wis. State Assemblyman, 60-67. Bus. & Prof. Pos: Former life ins. agent. Mil. Serv: Army, Inf, 43-45; Mil. Order of Purple Heart; Army and Navy Union. Mem: VFW; past post comdr, Am. Legion; adj. and past comdr. local chap, now dep. judge advocate, DAV. Mailing Add: 2317 Welsby Ave, Stevens Point, Wis. 54481.

MYLES, THOMAS EBERLY D
W.Va. State Del.
b. Fayetteville, W.Va, 10/24/22; s. T.A. Myles and Rovena Eberly M; m. 5/23/43 to Virginia Lee Marshall; c. Steven and Philip. Educ: W.Va. Inst. Tech, A.B, 46, Col. Law, LL.B, 49. Polit. & Govt. Pos: W.Va. State Del, 55-, Majority Leader, W.Va. State House of Del, 57-60 & 67-68. Bus. & Prof. Pos: Attorney-at-law, 49- Mil. Serv: Entered as Pvt, Air Force, 42, released as S/Sgt, 45; Purple Heart; Air Medal with 4 Oak Leaf Clusters; 5 Campaign Ribbons. Mem: Mason; Shrine; Elks; Am. Legion. Rel: Presbyterian. Mailing Add: 123 Goddard Ave, Fayetteville, W.Va. 25840.

N

NABERS, (JOSEPH) LYNN D
Tex. State Rep.
b. Brownwood, Tex, 3/31/40; s. Joseph Dudley Nabers and Ima Lou Littlefield N; m. 10/3/59 to Mary Scott; c. Joseph Scott and Timothy Lynn. Educ: N.Tex. Univ, 58-59; Howard Payne Col, B.S, 62; Baylor Univ, J.D, 68; Phi Delta Phi; Lambda Chi. Polit. & Govt. Pos: Tex. State Rep, 64th Legis. Dist, 68- Bus. & Prof. Pos: Attorney-at-law, 68. Mem: Am. Tex. and Brown Co. Bar Asns; Brownwood C. of C; Farm Bur; Sportsmans Club; Brownwood Jaycees; Knife and Fork Club; Brownwood Country Club; Rotary; Brown Co. Youth Fair Asn. Rel: Baptist. Mailing Add: 3506 Durham, Brownwood, Tex. 76801.

NABORS, CHARLES JAMES, JR. D
b. Cleveland, Ohio, 1/11/34; s. Charles James Nabors and Melissa Denola Collum N; m. 6/25/61 to Joan Frances Washington; c. Brian Charles and Claire Kelley. Educ: Wabash Col, A.B, 55; Univ. Utah, Ph.D, 65; Markle scholar in Acad. Med, 69. Polit. & Govt. Pos: Del. and mem. credentials cmt, Dem. Nat. Conv, 68; Dem. rep to Utah Elec. Law Cmt, 68- Bus. & Prof. Pos: Instr, Univ. Utah, 65, asst. prof, 67- Mil. Serv: Airman, Air Force, Air Force Res, 65. Publ: Abstr, articles and chap. in 32 sci. publ. Mem: Am. Asn. Adv. Sci; N.Y. Acad. Sci; Endocrine Soc; Radiation Research Soc; Reticuloendothelial Soc; Sigma Xi. Rel: Episcopal. Mailing Add: 1638 Lakewood Dr, Salt Lake City, Utah 84117.

NABORS, OLLIE WILSON D
Ala. State Sen.
b. Gadsden, 7/1/26; s. Wallace Scott Nabors and Lola Atkins N; m. 12/18/49 to Leatha Jeanette Thornton; c. Peggy Jeanette. Educ: Univ. Ala, LL.B, 50; Farrar Order of Jurisprudence; Omicron Delta Kappa; Quadrangle. Polit. & Govt. Pos: U.S. Cmnr, 58-62; Ala. State Rep, 62-66; Ala. State Sen, 67- Bus. & Prof. Pos: Law. Mil. Serv: Navy, 3 years. Rel: Baptist. Mailing Add: First City National Bank Bldg, Suite 202, Gadsden, Ala. 35901.

NADDY, DONALD WILLIAM D
Co. Cmnr. of Marshall Co, S.Dak.
b. Kidder, S.Dak, 1/12/17; s. William Edward Naddy and Anna Impecoven N; single. Educ: North. State Col, 1st Grade Teachers Cert, 36. Polit. & Govt. Pos: Twp. clerk, Marshall Co, S.Dak, 41-, co. cmnr, currently; S.Dak. State Rep. and Asst. Minority Leader, 58-66. Bus. & Prof. Pos: Dir, Co. Crop Improv. Asn, currently, Marshall Co. Coop. Asn, 54-, N.East Research Farm, 58- and Adv. Cmt, Agr. Div, S.Dak. State Univ, 60- Mem: Odd Fellows; Farmers Union. Mailing Add: Britton, S.Dak. 57430.

NADEN, ROBERT WILLIAM R
Chmn, Hamilton Co. Rep. Cent. Cmt, Iowa
b. Osage, Iowa, 5/6/21; s. William I. Naden and Ruth Gardner N; m. 11/8/42 to Dorothy Marie Russell; c. Russell Thomas, Janet Marie, Candace Carol and Leah Margaret. Educ: Webster City Jr. Col, 2 years; Iowa State Univ, 2 years. Polit. & Govt. Pos: Iowa State Rep, 55-64, Majority Floor Leader, Iowa House of Rep, 61 & 62, Speaker, 63 & 64; chmn, Hamilton Co. Rep. Cent. Cmt, 67- Mil. Serv: Entered as Seaman 1/C, Navy, 42, released as Lt.(jg), 46, after serv. as Eng. Officer, Landing Ship, Tank 920, Pac. Theatre, 45-46. Mem: Mason; High Twelve; Kiwanis; Am. Legion. Rel: Methodist. Legal Res: 600 Parkway Dr, Webster City, Iowa 50595. Mailing Add: P.O. Box 237, Webster City, Iowa 50595.

NAFTALIN, ARTHUR D
b. Fargo, N.Dak, 6/28/17; s. Sandel Naftalin and Tillie Bresky N; m. 7/3/41 to Frances Marie Healy; c. Mark, David and Gail. Educ: N.Dak. Agr. Col, 34-36; Univ. Minn, B.A, 39, M.S, 42, Ph.D, 48; Hon. LL.D, Univ. N.Dak, 69. Polit. & Govt. Pos: Trustee, Nat. Center Educ. in Polit. and Nat. Inst. Pub. Affairs; secy. to Hubert H. Humphrey, Mayor of Minneapolis, Minn, 45-47; mem, Adv. Cmn. Intergovt. Rels; Cmn. of Admin, Minneapolis, 54-60; bd. dir, Citizens League of Gr. Minneapolis, 54-; consult. ICA, Mich. State Univ. Proj, Saigon, Vietnam, 57; Surgeon Gen. Adv. Cmt, Urban Health Affairs, 62-; mayor, Minneapolis, 61-69. Bus. & Prof. Pos: Ed. staff, Fargo Forum, 34-36; managing ed, Minn. Daily, Univ. Minn, 36-39, staff, 38-39; ed. staff, Minneapolis, Tribune, 39-41; instr, A.S.T.P. and teaching asst. polit. sci, 41-45; syndicated newspaper columnist, Minn. Polit. Roundup, Minn. Newspapers, 45-54; assoc. prof, Univ. Minn, 47-54; consult, Pub. Affairs Div, Ford Found, 60; prof, sch. pub. affairs, Univ. Minn, Minneapolis, 69- Publ: 'Personality, Work, Community: An Introduction to Social Science' (with others), 53. Mem: Nat. Munic. League; U.S. Conf. Mayors (hon. pres, 69); Am. Munic. Asn.(past exec. cmt); Am. Soc. Pub. Admin; Nat. League of Cities; League Minn. Munic; Urban Coalition (nat. steering cmt); Nat. Acad. Pub. Admin; Harvard Univ. Prog. Tech. & Soc; New Towns 69. C.C. Ludwig Award for Outstanding Munic. Serv, 69. Mailing Add: 66 Seymour Ave. S.E, Minneapolis, Minn. 55414.

NAGEL, GLADYS S. R
V.Chmn, Lapeer Co. Rep. Exec. Cmt, Mich.
b. Detroit, Mich, 9/4/12; m. 5/10/39 to John Q. Nagel; c. David B, Edna N. (Mrs. McComb) and Mary C. Educ: Wayne State Univ. Polit. & Govt. Pos: V.chmn, Lapeer Co. Rep. Exec. Cmt, Mich. and v.chmn, Seventh Cong. Dist. Rep. Party, currently. Bus. & Prof. Pos: Housewife; Aberdeen-Angus breeder; 4-H Club leader; recording secy, mem. nat. coun. and ed. of Newsletter, Mich. Div, Woman's Nat. Farm and Garden Asn; v.pres, Essex Brass Corp. Mem: Pres, Mich. Angus Auxiliary; del. and former mem, Bd. of Soc. Serv, Suncrest. Recipient of 4-H Meritorious Serv. Award. Rel: Church of Christ Scientist. Mailing Add: 2669 Sutton Rd, Metamora, Mich. 48455.

NAGEL, HAROLD DERRER R
b. Stockton, Ill, 4/2/20; s. Otto Nagel and Ella Derrer N; m. 5/31/47 to Patricia Nichols; c. Thomas, Ann and Susan. Educ: Univ. Dubuque; Northwest. Univ. Sch. Law. Polit. & Govt. Pos: Precinct committeeman, Jo Daviess Co, Ill, state's attorney, 48-64. Mil. Serv: Entered as Pvt, Army, 43, released as S/Sgt, 45, after serv. in Mediterranean Theater. Mem: Ill. and Am. Bar Asns; Lions; Mason. Rel: Evangelical United Bretheren. Mailing Add: 421 E. Benton, Stockton, Ill. 61085. (1967)

NAGELVOORT, BERNARD CHARLES R
b. Detroit, Mich, 8/7/30; s. Bernard August Nagelvoort and Caroline Lamport N; m. 2/2/57 to Mary Lucie Holmes; c. Bernard Peter, Jonathan Holmes, Adam Winston and Charles Wendell. Educ: Mich. State Univ, B.S, 53; Univ. Mich, B.B.A, 57; Alpha Zeta; Sigma Phi Epsilon. Polit. & Govt. Pos: Chmn, Newaygo Co. Rep. Cmt, Mich, 60-62, secy, 63-64; admin. asst. to Congressman Vander Jagt, 66- Bus. & Prof. Pos: Mgt. trainee, Gerber Prod. Co, Fremont, Mich, 57-58, statist. analyst, mkt. research, 59-63, sr. analyst, 63-66. Mil. Serv: Entered as Pvt. E-1, Army, 53, released as Cpl, 55 after serv. in Finance Corps, Germany; Good Conduct Medal. Mem: Am. Mkt. Asn. Young Man of the Year Award, 62 and Outstanding Proj. Chmn. Award, 64, Jaycees. Rel: Congregational; Deacon, Fremont, Mich. Congregational Church, 66. Legal Res: 5613 S. Green St, Fremont, Mich. 49412. Mailing Add: 9112 Quintana Dr, Bethesda, Md. 20034.

NAGER, EDWARD D
Wis. State Assemblyman
b. N.Y, N.Y, 7/22/27. Educ: City Col. of N.Y, B.S, 50; Univ. Wis. Law Sch, LL.B, 55. Polit. & Govt. Pos: Mem, Madison City Planning Cmt, 65; asst. dist. attorney, Dane Co, 60-62; Wis. State Assemblyman, 62-; alternate del, Dem. Nat. Conv, 68. Bus. & Prof. Pos: Attorney. Mil. Serv: Army Air Force, 45-47. Mailing Add: 840 Spaight St, Madison, Wis. 53703.

NAGLE, DANIEL LEE D
b. Davenport, Iowa, 2/9/37; s. James Ray Nagle and Roma E. Meien N; single. Educ: St. Ambrose Col, B.A, 62. Polit. & Govt. Pos: Justice of peace, Winfield Twp, Iowa, 60, councilman, Long Grove, 61; Iowa State Rep, 65-66; asst. fire chief, Long Grove Vol. Fire Dept. and mem, North Scott Citizen's Cmt, currently. Mil. Serv: Entered as Pvt, Army Nat. Guard, 60, released as SP-4, 63; SP-4, Army Res, currently. Mem: Scott Co. Justice of the Peace Asn; Nat. Soc. of Legislation; Izaak Walton League; pres, Long Grove Civic League, currently; K. of C. Rel: Catholic. Mailing Add: Box 75, Long Grove, Iowa 52756. (1967)

NAHIL, SAM J. R
N.H. State Rep.
b. Lawrence, Mass, 10/3/05; married; c. one. Educ: Lawrence High Sch. Polit. & Govt. Pos: N.H. State Rep, 51- Bus. & Prof. Pos: Barber shop and real estate. Mem: Elks; C. of C. Rel: Catholic. Mailing Add: 62 South St, Claremont, N.H. 03743.

NAKAMURA, YOSHIRO D
b. Ninole, Hawaii, 6/9/26; s. Toyomatsu Nakamura and Tora Tanaka N; m. 12/20/53 to Jane Sachiko Kitagawa; c. John K. Educ: Univ. Hawaii, B.A, 50; Univ. Minn. Law Sch, LL.B, 56. Polit. & Govt. Pos: City Councilman, City and Co. of Honolulu, 61-; del, Dem. State Conv, 66. Bus. & Prof. Pos: Pres, Polynesian Hotels, Inc, 65-; attorney at law, 59- Mil. Serv: Pvt, Army, 45-47; reentered serv. as 2nd Lt, Army, 50, released as 1st Lt, 53, after serv. in Hawaiian Training Center. Mem: Lions. Rel: Non-denominational. Legal Res: 1728 Eames St, Wahiawa, Hawaii 96786. Mailing Add: 702-A California Ave, Wahiawa, Hawaii 96786. (1967)

NAKASHIMA, S. STEPHEN R
b. Fresno, Calif, 1/29/22; s. Hiroshi Nakashima and Hiteyo Koga N; m. 4/20/47 to Sally Sato; c. Dale H, Jann Marie, Lex Lyle and Mona Jane. Educ: Univ. Calif, Berkeley, B.S, 48; Univ. Calif, Law Sch, J.D, 51; Beta Alpha Psi. Polit. & Govt. Pos: Del, Rep. Nat. Conv, 68; mem, State Bd. Med Exam, 69- Bus. & Prof. Pos: Attorney, 55- Mil. Serv: Entered as Pvt, Army, 45, released as S/Sgt, 46. Mem: Calif. Soc. of CPA; Asn. of Attorney, CPA; Calif. State Bar Asn; Am. Judicature Soc; Rotary. Rel: Methodist. Legal Res: 1565 Cherry Glen Way, San Jose, Calif. 95125. Mailing Add: 760 N. First St, San Jose, Calif. 95112.

NAKASIAN, SAMUEL R
b. Turkey, 12/5/15; s. Barabed Nakasian and Perouz N; m. 9/5/51 to Patricia Stirling Prochnik; c. Patricia Stephanie, Samuel Stirling, Suzanne Price and Stacey Price. Educ: N.Y. Univ, A.B, 40; Grad. Faculties, Columbia Univ, M.A, 41; Georgetown Univ. Law Sch, LL.B, 46. Polit. & Govt. Pos: Economist, U.S. Off. Price Admin, Wash. D,C, 42-43; sr. economist, War Foods Admin, 43; prin. economist, U.S. Bur. of the Budget, 44-47; chief price br, Econ. Coop. Admin, 48-51; spec. counsel, U.S. Dept. Justice, 51-52; Rep. cand. for U.S. Rep, N.Y. 25th Cong. Dist, 68. Bus. & Prof. Pos: Practicing attorney, own firm, Wash, D.C, 51-57 and N.Y.C, 57-68; mem. coun, State Univ. N.Y. Binghamton, 67-; sr. partner, Manning, Nakasian & Carey, N.Y.C, currently. Publ: 'Manufacturers' Problems Under Price Control,' Harvard Bus. Rev, 52; 'Security of Foreign Petroleum Resources,' Polit. Sci. Quart, 53; 'International Judicial Process,' Georgetown Law J, 53. Mem: Asn. of the Bar of the City of N.Y; Siwanoy Country Club. Rel: Protestant. Mailing Add: 22 Sunny Brae, Bronxville, N.Y. 10708.

NALETTE, JOSEPH C. D
N.H. State Rep.
b. Canada; married; c. Seven. Polit. & Govt. Pos: N.H. State Rep, 57- Bus. & Prof. Pos: Retired. Mem: A.C.A; pres, St. Vincent de Paul Soc. of St. Marie's Parish; Third Order St. Francis; Holy Name Soc. Rel: Catholic. Mailing Add: 259 Notre Dame Ave, Manchester, N.H. 03102. (1967)

NALLY, JOHN JOSEPH R
Mem, Colo. State Rep. Cent. Cmt.
b. Kansas City, Kans, 1/23/31; s. John F. Nally and Julia Mae Spillane N; m. 6/6/59 to Mary Elizabeth Callahan 'Beth'; c. Liza Renee, Scott John and Christina Diane. Educ: Donnelly Jr. Col, Kansas City, Kans, 50-51; Univ. Colo, B.S. in Acct, 59. Polit. & Govt. Pos: Campaign mgr. for U.S. Rep. Don-

ald G. Brotzman, Colo, 66 & 68, Colo. field rep, 67-; treas, Jefferson Co. Young Rep, 66-67; alternate, Nat. Young Rep, 67; del, Colo. State Rep. Conv, 68; mem, Colo. State Rep. Cent. Cmt, 69- Bus. & Prof. Pos: CPA, Peat, Marwick, Mitchell & Co, Denver, Colo, 59-62; internal auditor, Colo. Fuel & Iron Corp, 62-64; controller, West. States Leasing Co, 64-65, Unidyne Industs, Inc, 65-66; CPA, John J. Nally & Assocs, 66- Mil. Serv: Entered as Airman Air Force, 52, released as Airman 1/C, 55, after serv. in 374th Troop Carrier Group, Far East Air Force, 54-55; Nat. Defense Serv. Medal; Korean Serv. Medal; UN Serv. Medal; Good Conduct Medal. Mem: Am. Inst. Cert. Pub. Acct; Colo. Soc. Cert. Pub. Acct; Nat. Asn. Acct; Alameda W. Kiwanis; Univ. Colo. Alumni Asn; Columbine Hills Civic Asn; Industs. for Jefferson Co. Rel: Catholic. Mailing Add: 5675 W. Chestnut Ave, Littleton, Colo. 80120.

NANCE, KENNETH ROBERT D
Okla. State Rep.
b. Mt. Carmel, Ill, 10/1/41; s. M.J. Nance and Leona Lee Pike N; m. 8/31/63 to Barbara Sue Hennessey; c. Barry Wayne. Educ: Oklahoma City Univ, B.A, 63, Sch. Law, J.D, 68; Univ. Okla, 63-64; Kappa Alpha Order. Polit. & Govt. Pos: Research assoc, Okla. Legis. Coun, 64-67; dir, Okla. Cmn. Fiscal Struct, 67; Asst. Attorney Gen, Okla, 68; Okla. State Rep, 68- Bus. & Prof. Pos: Attorney at law, 68- Mem: Okla. and Am. Bar Asns; Pi Sigma Alpha; Phi Delta Phi; Jaycees; C. of C. Outstanding Young Man of Capitol Hill, 68. Rel: Methodist. Mailing Add: 1141 S.W. 54th, Oklahoma City, Okla. 73109.

NANGLE, JOHN FRANCIS R
Mem, Rep. State Cmt, Mo.
b. St. Louis, Mo, 6/8/22; s. Sylvester A. Nangle and Thelma B. N; m. 4/22/50 to Andrea Urseth; c. John F, Jr. Educ: Univ. Mo, B.S. in Pub. Admin, 43; Wash. Univ, J.D. & LL.B, 48; Phi Delta Phi. Polit. & Govt. Pos: City attorney, Brentwood, Mo, 53-62; committeeman, Jefferson Twp. Rep. Party, 58-; mem, Rep. State Cmt, 58-; mem, St. Louis Co. Rep. Cent. Cmt, 58-, chmn, 60-61; pres, Mo. Rep. Vet. League, 59-60; pres, Mo. Asn. of Rep, 60-61; spec. asst. counsr, St. Louis Co, 62-; del, Rep. Nat. Conv, 68. Bus. & Prof. Pos: Lawyer, Clayton, Mo, 48- Mil. Serv: Entered as Pvt, Army, 43, released as 1st Sgt, 46 after serving in 655th Engr. Bn, ETO; Res, 46-63, Capt. Mem: St. Louis Co, Mo. and Am. Bar Asns; Mason; John Marshal Rep. Club; mem. bd, Edgewood Children's Home; Rotary. Rel: Protestant. Mailing Add: 9 Southcote Rd, Brentwood, Mo. 63144.

NANKEY, RALPH WALLACE Conservative, N.Y.
Chmn, Oneida Co. Conservative Party, N.Y.
b. Lockport, N.Y, 5/2/27; s. Nelson L. Nankey and Jennlyn M. Kiska N; m. 10/21/50 to Charlene A. Hall; c. Georgia A, Pamela M. and Kurt M. Educ: Univ. Buffalo, B.S, 50 and M.S, 54. Polit. & Govt. Pos: Chmn, Oneida Co. Conservative Party, N.Y, 64- Bus. & Prof. Pos: Sr. dynamicist, Bell Aircraft Corp, 50-54; consult. engr, Glenn L. Martin Co, 54-55; consult. engr, Gen. Elec. Co, 55- Mil. Serv: Entered as A/S Naval Res, 45, released as Seaman 2/C, 46. Mem: Am. Soc. Mech. Engrs; Am. Inst. Aeronautics & Astronautics; Soc. of Sigma Xi; F&AM; Aircraft Owners & Pilots Asn; Utica Conservative Party Club; Oneida Co. Patriotic Soc; Bd. of Policy, Liberty Lobby; Air Force Asn. Rel: Lutheran. Mailing Add: 32 Devereux Lane, Whitesboro, N.Y. 13492.

NAPIER, DONALD DUDLEY, JR. R
Dep. State Finance Chmn, Tex. Rep. Party
b. St. Paul, Minn, 1/6/21; s. Donald Dudley Napier and Florence Holm N; m. 4/15/46 to Mary Ann Prowell; c. Mary Pryor, Donald Dudley, III and Margaret Prowell. Educ: Univ. Minn, 41; Univ. Houston, B.S, 49; Chi Psi. Polit. & Govt. Pos: Finance chmn, Ft. Bend Co. Rep. Party, Tex, 50-; mem, Tex. Rep. Party, 60-, v.chmn. finance cmt, 64-66, dep. state finance chmn, currently; v.chmn, Friends of John Tower, 65; finance co-chmn, Sen. John Tower Campaign Cmt, 65-66; alternate del, Rep. Nat. Conv, 68. Bus. & Prof. Pos: Secy-treas, McCormick Steel Co, 50-62; v.pres, Metals and Tubes, Inc, 63-65; v.pres, South-West Abrasive Co, 66. Mil. Serv: Entered as Pvt, Army, 42, released as T/Sgt, 46, after serv. in 15th Inf, Third Div, ETO; Good Conduct Medal; nominee, Bronze Star. Mem: Bd. mem, Alumni Asn. Univ. of Houston and Tex. Inst. of Child Psychiatry; VFW; Am. Legion; Houston Country Club; Ft. Bend Country Club. Ranking jr. tennis player; capt, Univ. Houston team. Rel: Episcopal. Mailing Add: 315 Hillcrest Dr, Richmond, Tex. 77469. (1967)

NAPOLITANO, RICHARD A. D
b. Chicago, Ill, 9/7/16; c. Marie Antoinette, Kristine, Kathryn, Charles. Educ: Marquette Inst; DePaul Univ. Col. of Law; Delta Theta Phi. Polit. & Govt. Pos: Ill. State Rep, 5 terms; Asst. State's Attorney, 47-53. Mem: 31st Reg. Dem. Orgn; Alamo Post; Am. Legion; Justinian Soc. of Lawyers; Admitted Ill. Bar, 47. 1967 Legal Res: Chicago, Ill. No mailing address available. (1967)

NARUSIS, BERNARD V. R
Spec. Asst. Attorney Gen, Ill.
b. West Frankfort, Ill, 6/12/29; s. John Norusis and Constance Wiltrakis N; m. 6/19/59 to Regina Gyte Firant; c. Victor John and Ellen Marie. Educ: South. Ill. Univ, B.A, 52; Northwest. Univ. Grad. Commerce Div, M.B.A, 54; Univ. of Ill. Law Sch, J.D, 58; Int. Rels. Club; Phi Alpha Delta. Polit. & Govt. Pos: 22nd Cong. Dist. Bd. Gov, Ill. Young Rep. Orgn, 58-59; village attorney, Oakwood Hills, Ill, 59-; Rep. precinct committeeman, McHenry Co. Rep. Cent. Cmt, 62-, chmn. adv. cmt, 64-66; del, Judicial Conv, Appellate Court of Ill, Second Dist, McHenry Co, 64 and Ill. State Rep. Conv, 64 & 68; del, Rep. Nat. Conv, 68; spec. asst. attorney gen, Ill, 69- Bus. & Prof. Pos: Law assoc, Joseph P. Smith, Mattoon, Ill, 58-59 and Steinbrecher & Narusis, Crystal Lake, 59-68; partner, Narusis & Narusis, Cary, 69- Mil. Serv: Entered as Pvt, Army, 47, released as Sgt, 49, after serv. in 123rd Signal Photo Det, Korea 48-49; re-entered as Pvt, Army, 54, released as Pfc, 55, after serv. in 356th Rwy. Transportation Bn, Korea; 2nd Lt, Army Res; Occup. Medal; World War II Medal; Korean Liberation Medal; Nat. Defense Medal. Mem: Bd. of dirs, Cary-Grove Commun. Hosp. Asn, Inc. Rel: Catholic. Mailing Add: 213 W. Lakeshore Dr, Cary, Ill. 60013.

NARVID, ETHEL GALLAY D
b. N.Y.C, Dec. 25; d. James Gallay and Manya Helfant G; div; c. Natalie and Michael. Polit. & Govt. Pos: Field secy. to city councilman, Los Angeles, Calif, 56-60; mem. exec. cmt, Calif. Dem. State Cent. Cmt, 60-64; field representative to U.S. Rep, 60-68. Bus. & Prof. Pos: Asst. to Pres, Coro Found, Los Angeles, Calif, currently. Rel: Jewish. Mailing Add: 8741 Shoreham Dr, Los Angeles, Calif. 90069.

NASH, NORRIS JEWELL D
Ga. State Rep.
b. Lilburn, Ga, 6/17/26; s. William Henry Nash and Berta Guthrie N; m. to Elizabeth K; c. Norman J, Terry, Melvin Maurice, Velva Alyce and Anita Jewell. Educ: Lilburn High Sch, grad. Polit. & Govt. Pos: Ga. State Rep, 67- Bus. & Prof. Pos: Chmn. bd. and pres, Mortgage Acceptance Corp, Metrop. Land Develop. & Invest. Corp, Nash & Sturdivant Grading Contractors, Inc, Gwinnett-DeKalb Realty, Inc. and N & N Builder's, Inc. Mem: Mason. Rel: Baptist. Legal Res: 1471 Jennifer Lane, Lilburn, Ga. 30247. Mailing Add: P.O. Box 6, Lilburn, Ga. 30247.

NASH, PHILLEO D
b. Wisconsin Rapids, Wis, 10/25/09; s. Guy Nash and Florence Philleo N; m. 11/2/35 to Edith Rosenfels; c. Margaret Helen and Sally. Educ: Wisconsin, A.B, 32; Chicago, Ph.D, 37; Sr. Honors, Wis; Sigma Xi; fel, Am. Anthrop. Asn. Polit. & Govt. Pos: Cmnr, Bur. of Indian Affairs, 61-66; asst. to Asst. Secy. of Interior, 61; Lt. Gov. of Wisconsin, 59-61; chmn, Dem. Party of Wis, 55-57; admin. asst. to the President of United States, 52-53. Bus. & Prof. Pos: Consult. anthropologist, 66-; pres, Biron Cranberry Co, 46-; spec. asst, The White House Office, 46-52; spec. asst. to Dir, Off. of War Info, 42-46; lectr, Univ. Toronto, 37-41. Publn: Religious Revivalism on Klamath Reservation. Mem: Theta Delta Chi; Soc. for Appl. Anthrop; Wis. Cranberry Growers Asn. Rel: Congregational. Legal Res: 810 Third St, Wisconsin Rapids, Wis. 54494. Mailing Add: 540 N St. S.W, Washington, D.C. 20024. (1967)

NASH, VICTORIA C. 'VICKI' D
Activities Coordinator, Nev. State Dem. Cent. Cmt.
b. Buffalo, Kans, 4/18/15; d. Garnet E. Carpenter and Gladys Rozell Anderson C; m. 10/26/47 to William Michael Nash, Jr; c. Wm. M, III, David J, Mary Jo, Thomas L, Anoinette Michele, Dorothy Reneé and Paul Joseph and 9 grandchildren. Educ: Univ. Toledo; Southwest. Univ; Hastings Col. of Law. Polit. & Govt. Pos: Hq. mgr. for Grant Sawyer for Gov, 58, precinct orgn, 62; precinct orgn. chmn, Washoe Co, 58-60; publicity dir, Nev. State Dem. Cent. Cmt, 60-, secy, 64-66, activities coordinator, currently; del, West. Dist. Nev. Women's Dem. Clubs. Bus. & Prof. Pos: Church secy, Ohio, 32-39; law librn, Calif, 43-47; legis. reporter and free lance polit. columnist, 59-; owner and mgr, Vicki Nash Assocs, Inc, Advert. Agency, 59-; legis. reporter, Reno Newspapers, Inc. and polit. analyst, Reno Eve. Gazette, currently. Mil. Serv: Entered as Y 3/C, Coast Guard Res, 44, released as Y 2/C, 45. Mem: Soroptimists; Reno Press Club; Advert. Club; St. Mary's Hosp. Guild; PTA; Nat. Bus. & Prfnl. Women; Dem. Woman's Club. Rel: Catholic. Legal Res: 3250 Everett Dr, Reno, Nev. 89503. Mailing Add: P.O. Box 5477, Reno, Nev. 89503.

NATCHER, WILLIAM H. D
U.S. Rep, Ky.
b. Bowling Green, Ky; m. 6/17/37 to Virginia Reardon; c. Celeste (Mrs. White) and Louise (Mrs. Lewter). Educ: West. Ky. State Col, A.B; Ohio State Univ, LL.B. Polit. & Govt. Pos: Fed. conciliation cmnr, West. Dist. Ky, 36-37; co. attorney, Warren Co, Ky, 37, served three 4 year terms; past pres, Young Dem. Clubs Ky, 41-46; past pres, Bowling Green Bar Asn; commonwealth attorney, Eighth Judicial Dist, 51-53; U.S. Rep, Ky, 53-, mem. cmt. appropriations, U.S. House Rep. Bus. & Prof. Pos: Practicing attorney, Bowling Green, Ky, since Mar. 18, 34. Mil. Serv: Navy, 42-45. Mem: Kiwanis Club; Odd Fellows; Am. Legion Post 23; 40 et 8 Mammoth Cave Voiture 1146. Rel: Baptist. Legal Res: Bowling Green, Warren Co, Ky. Mailing Add: 4201 Massachussetts Ave, Washington, D.C. 20016.

NATHAN, RICHARD PERLE R
Asst. Dir, U.S. Bur. of the Budget
b. Schenectady, N.Y, 11/24/35; s. Sidney Robert Nathan and Betty Green N; m. 6/5/57 to Mary McNamara; c. Robert Joseph and Carol Hewit. Educ: Brown Univ, B.A. magna cum laude, 57; Harvard Univ, M.P.A, 59, Ph.D, 66; Phi Beta Kappa; Theta Delta Chi. Polit. & Govt. Pos: Legis. asst. to Sen. Keating, N.Y, 59-62; dir, domestic policy research, Gov. Rockefeller, 63-64; assoc. dir, Nat. Adv. Cmt. on Civil Disorders, Wash, D.C, 67-68; President Nixon's Transition Task Forces on Pub. Welfare and Intergovernmental Fiscal Rels, 68; asst. dir, U.S. Bur. of the Budget, 69- Bus. & Prof. Pos: Research assoc, Brookings Inst, Wash, D.C, 66-69; prof. lectr, Am. Univ, 66-68. Publ: 'The Policy Setting: Analysis of Major Post-Vietnam Federal Aid Policy Alternatives' and 'The Case for Tax Sharing—a Political View,' In: Revenue Sharing and Its Alternatives, Vol. II, Joint Econ. Cmt, U.S. Cong, 67; 'The Potential Impact of General Aid for Four Selected States,' In: Fiscal Issues in the Future of Federalism, Cmt. Econ. Develop, 68; 'Jobs and Civil Rights, the Role of the Federal Government in Promoting Equal Opportunity in Employment and Training,' U.S. Cmn. of Civil Rights, 69. Rel: Reform Jewish. Mailing Add: 7503 Cayuga Ave, Bethesda, Md. 20034.

NATHANSON, CHARLES R
Dep. Minority Leader, R.I. State Senate
b. Providence, R.I, 11/24/22; s. Joseph George Nathanson and Jeannette Rosefield N; m. 6/24/50 to Adelaide M. Richmond; c. J. George, Caroline and Mindelle. Educ: Brown Univ, A.B, 44. Polit. & Govt. Pos: Chmn. bd. canvassers, Warwick, R.I, 58-63; mem, Ninth Ward Rep. Cmt. and Warwick Rep. City Cmt, 62-; del, R.I. Constitutional Conv, 64-68; R.I. State Sen, 19th Dist, 67-, Dep. Minority Leader, R.I. State Senate, 69- Bus. & Prof. Pos: Gen. mgr, Solvol Chem. Co, Inc, 50-63, pres. and treas, 63- Mil. Serv: Entered as Pvt, Army, 44, released as Sgt, 46, after serv. in 294th Field Artil. Observation Bn, ETO, 45. Mem: Am. Chem. Soc; Am. Asn. Textile Chemists & Colorists; Am. Asn. Textile Technologists; F&AM; E. Greenwich Yacht Club; Quidnessett Country Club. Rel: Episcopal. Mailing Add: 1 Joyce Glen, Warwick, R.I. 02886.

NATION, BILL D
b. Lingle, Wyo, 5/28/25; s. Wade Oliver Nation and Marie Voss N; m. 12/11/46 to Joanne Ida Petersen; c. Michael William, Martin Charles, Nancy Jo and Molly Marie. Educ: Cheyenne High Sch, Grad. Polit. Pos: Wyo. State Rep, 65-67; mayor, Cheyenne, 62-66. Bus. & Prof. Pos: Real Estate

salesman, Searle-McCue Realty, 66-; photographer, Nation Studio, 48-62 and Frontier Studio, 46-48. Mil. Serv: Entered as Seaman, Navy, 43, released as Gunner's Mate 3/C, 46, after serv. in Pac. Theater. Mem: V.pres, Wyo. Asn. Munic; U.S. Conf. of Mayors; Nat. League of Cities; Int. Platform Asn; Adv. Coun. on Naval Affairs; VFW; Am. Legion; Elks; Eagles; Exchange Club; C. of C; Wyo. Soc. for Crippled Children; Toastmasters Club 798; Past pres, PTA; chmn, Scout-O-Rama; membership chmn, YMCA; Cancer Soc; Southeast Ment. Health Asn. Jaycee Distinguished Serv. Award, 59. Rel: Congregational. Mailing Add: 123 W. 27th St, Cheyenne, Wyo. 82001. (1967)

NAUJOCK, EVELYN KATSIS R
Mem, Calif. Rep. State Cent. Cmt.
b. Chicago, Ill, 12/21/20; d. Sotirios Katsis and Panayiota Karageorge K; m. 12/12/42 to Claude Otto Naujock; c. Frederick August and Claude Arthur. Educ: Austin High Sch, Chicago, Ill, grad, 39. Polit. & Govt. Pos: Mem, Calif. Rep. State Cent. Cmt, 67- Bus. & Prof. Pos: Secy-Treas, Toolmasters, Inc, San Gabriel, Calif, 53. Mem: Bd. dir, Samaritan Home for Children, Inc, Valinda, Calif; Eastern Star; East San Gabriel Valley Rep. Women's Club; White Shrine of Jerusalem; charter pres, South Hills High Sch. P.T.A, West Covina, Calif. Rel: Protestant. Mailing Add: 2832 E. Lark Hill Dr, West Covina, Calif. 91790.

NAURISON, MORTON STANLEY R
Mem, Rep. Nat. Cmt.
b. Springfield, Mass, 7/2/10; s. James Z. Naurison and Helen Ruth Granstein N; m. 11/30/39 to Florence Lillian Johnson; c. Edward. Educ: Boston Univ, B.S, 32; Phi Alpha. Polit. & Govt. Pos: Chmn, By-law Cmt, Wales, Mass, 67; mem, Rep. Nat. Cmt, currently. Bus. & Prof. Pos: Treas, Naurison Jewelry Co, Inc, Palmer, Mass, 39- Mem: Retail Jewelers Asn; AF&AM; RAM; RSM. Rel: Hebrew. Mailing Add: Lake Shore Dr, Wales, Mass. 01081.

NAVE, MARSHALL TONEY R
b. Elizabethon, Tenn, 7/14/28; s. John L. Nave and Gladys Arnold N; m. 9/19/62 to Nettie Lee Slemp; c. Terri Sue. Educ: Steed Col. Tech. Polit. & Govt. Pos: V.chmn, Carter Co. Court, Tenn, 60-66; magistrate, Elizabethton, 60-66, Tenn. State Sen, until 68. Bus. & Prof. Pos: Dir, Carter Co. Memorial Hosp, chmn, East Tenn. Hosp. Asn, trustee, Carter Co. Rescue Squadron and acct, Tenn. Eastman Co, currently. Mil. Serv: Entered as Seaman, Navy, 43, released as PO 1/C, 45, after serv. in S.Pac; Asiatic-Pac-European Theater Ribbons; Occupation Medal; Am. Campaign Ribbon; Presidential Citation. Mem: VFW (past state comdr); Tenn. and Nat. Legis. Cmt. Rel: Methodist. Mailing Add: Edgewood Ave, Elizabethton, Tenn. 37643. (1967)

NEADERHISER, JACK I. D
Polit. & Govt. Pos: Ind. State Rep, 61-68; former officer, Int. Brotherhood of Elec. Workers. Bus. & Prof. Pos: Commun. Indust. Mil. Serv: Army. Mem: Am. Legion; VFW; Eagles. Rel: Methodist. Mailing Add: 2217 Fourth Ave, Terre Haute, Ind. 47804. (1967)

NEAL, CASWELL FINCHER D
Educ: N.Mex. Mil. Inst; Univ. Okla; Univ. Tex, LL.B, grad work; Sigma Nu; Delta Theta Phi. Polit. & Govt. Pos: N.Mex. State Sen, 61-68; past Nat. Dir, N.Mex. Jaycees. Bus. & Prof. Pos: Lawyer. Mil. Serv: Air Force, 1st Lt, B-24 pilot. Mem: Jaycees (past pres, Carlsbad Chap); Mason. Rel: Methodist. Mailing Add: P.O. Drawer N, Carlsbad, N.Mex. 88220. (1967)

NEAL, FRED WARNER D
Mem, Calif. State Dem. Cent. Cmt.
b. Northville, Mich, 8/5/15; s. Frank Stephenson Neal and Bertha Fendt N; m. 1/2/52 to Marian Katherine Prindle; c. Susan (Mrs. Buckingham), Frank S, II, John Walker and Bruce Walker. Educ: Univ. Mich, B.A. and M.A, 37, Ph.D, 55; Harvard Univ, 42-43; Karlova Univ, Prague, 49; Univ. Paris, 50; Nieman fel, 42; Alpha Beta Phi; Sphinx; Michigamua. Polit. & Govt. Pos: Consult. on Russian affairs, U.S. State Dept, 46-49; chmn. for. policy cmt, Calif. Dem. Coun, 64-69; nominee, U.S. Rep, 24th Dist, Calif, 68; chmn, McCarthy for President Campaign, 24th Dist, 68; alternate del, Dem. Nat. Conv, 68; mem, Calif. State Dem. Adv. Cmt, 68; mem, Calif. State Dem. Cent. Cmt, 69- Bus. & Prof. Pos: Asst. to pres, State Univ. N.Y, 49; Fulbright professorship, France, 50 & 61; asst. prof. polit. sci, Univ. Colo, 51-56; assoc, Am. Univs. Field Staff, 54-55; assoc. prof, Univ. Calif, Los Angeles, 56-57; prof. and chmn. faculty in int. rels, Claremont Grad. Sch, 57-; Rockefeller Found. grants, 61 & 65; consult, Center for Study of Dem. Insts, 64- Mil. Serv: Entered as Ens, Naval Air Force, 43, released as Lt, 46, after serv. in Russia and Siberia, 43-46; Navy Expeditionary Medal. Publ: U.S. Foreign Policy and the Soviet Union, Center for Study of Dem. Insts, 61; War and Peace and Germany, W.W. Norton, 62; Yugoslavia and the New Communism, 20th Century Fund, 62. Mem: Am. and West. Polit. Sci. Asns; Int. Studies Asn; Asn. Adv. Slavic Studies; Am. Asn. Univ. Prof; Nat. Cmt. for Sane Nuclear Policy. Fel, San Diego State Col. Inst. World Affairs; Hon. Commandant, March Air Force Base. Rel: Methodist. Mailing Add: 210 E. Foothill, Claremont, Calif. 91711.

NEAL, HARVEY IVAN R
Chmn, Keya Paha Co. Rep. Party, Nebr.
b. North Platte, Nebr, 10/3/40; s. John Ivan Neal and Onetta Harvey N; m. 4/18/63 to Janet Gray; c. Jeffery Dean and Jacqueline Ann. Educ: Miltonvale Wesleyan Col, A.A, 59; Univ. Nebr, B.S. and J.D; Phi Alpha Delta. Polit. & Govt. Pos: Chmn, Keya Paha Co. Rep. Party, Nebr, 66-; co. attorney, Keya Paha Co, 67- Bus. & Prof. Pos: Partner, Weddel & Neal Attorneys, Springview, Nebr, 64-; dir, First Nat. Bank of Springview, 67- Mem: Am, Nebr. State and Fifteenth Judicial Dist. Bar Asns; Springview Serv. Club. Rel: Methodist. Mailing Add: Box 248, Springview, Nebr. 68778.

NEAL, HENRY G. D
b. Fortson, Ga, 11/24/24; s. Charles Minchen Neal and Frances Morgan N; single. Educ: Univ. Ga, B.B.A, 43; Lumpkin Law Sch, LL.B, 48; Kappa Sigma; pres, Interfraternity Coun. and Student Vet. Orgn; Omicron Delta Kappa; Blue Key. Polit. & Govt. Pos: City attorney, Thomson, Ga, 52-54; co. attorney, McDuffie Co, 52-56; asst. attorney gen, Ga, 59-66; exec. secy, bd. regents, Univ. Syst. of Ga, 66- Bus. & Prof. Pos: Assoc, Knox & Neal, Attorneys, 48-59; chmn, Drafting Subcmt, Criminal Law Study Cmt, 62- Mil. Serv: World War II; grad. OCS; Combat Inf. Badge; Purple Heart with Oak Leaf Cluster. Mem: Past pres, Rotary, Toombs Circuit Bar Asn. and Kilpatrick Associational Brotherhood; Am. Legion; VFW; speakers bur, State C. of C; past scoutmaster, Boy Scouts, finance chmn, 55 and exec. bd, Ga-Carolina Coun; Scabbard & Blade; Phi Delta Phi. Rel: Baptist; Lay speaker; past pres, Brotherhood and past supt, Sch. Adult Dept. Mailing Add: P.O. Box 46, Thomson, Ga. 39824.

NEAL, JAMES HUSTON D
b. 11/11/22; married. Educ: Sigma Delta Kappa. Polit. & Govt. Pos: Miss. State Rep, 60-68. Bus. & Prof. Pos: Radio and TV broadcasting; attorney. Mem: Sons of Confederate Vets; Jackson Touchdown Club. Rel: Presbyterian. Mailing Add: Camellia Lane, Jackson, Miss. 39204. (1967)

NEAL, THOMAS V. D
Colo. State Rep.
b. El Paso, Tex, 1/10/22; s. Dr. T. V. Neal and Nora Green N. (deceased); m. 7/7/44 to Beverly Jo Fitzsimmons; c. Tina, Maureen and Fitz. Educ: Baylor Univ, B.A, 48; Northwest. Univ, M.A, 53. Polit. & Govt. Pos: Staff aide, Cong. Wayne N. Aspinall, Fourth Dist, Colo, 56-61; chmn, Fourth Cong. Dist. Dem. Cent. Cmt, 63-65; Colo. State Rep, 20th Dist, 66- Bus. & Prof. Pos: Teacher, Durango Pub. Sch. Syst, Colo, 48-56 & 61-69; publisher, Silverton Standard, Colo, 63-65. Mil. Serv: Entered as Pvt, Army Air Force, 43, released as T/Sgt, 45, after serv. in Eighth Air Force, ETO, 44-45. Rel: Episcopal. Mailing Add: 2055 W. Second Ave, Durango, Colo. 81301.

NEAL, VERNON D
Tenn. State Sen.
b. Byrdstown, Tenn, 10/10/31; s. Levi Piercen Neal and Mary Della Cope N; m. 2/16/58 to Mona Joyce Mahan; c. Belinda Sue, Jeffrey Dale and Melissa Gail. Educ: Tenn. Tech. Univ, B.S, 52; Univ. Tenn, LL.B. and J.D, 56; Phi Delta Phi. Polit. & Govt. Pos: City attorney, Algood, Tenn, 60-68; Tenn. State Rep, Putnam Co, 62-66; Tenn. State Sen, 13th Sen. Dist, 66-; mem, Gov. Task Force for Vocational Rehabilitation, 68. Bus. & Prof. Pos: Attorney-at-law, Cookeville, Tenn, 57- Mem: Putnam Co, Tenn. and Am. Bar Asns; Mason; Optimist; Farm Bur. Rel: Baptist. Mailing Add: 1008 Oaklawn Dr, Cookeville, Tenn. 38501.

NEAL, WILLIAM HENRY, JR. R
Tenn. State Rep.
b. Bristol, Tenn, 2/23/15; s. William Henry Neal and Ella Hughes N; m. 4/25/42 to Edith Poole; c. George Henry. Educ: Bristol, Tenn. High Sch, grad, 35. Polit. & Govt. Pos: Tenn. State Rep, 68- Bus. & Prof. Pos: Sales mgr, Charles J. Lowery Agency, 55-57, Affiliated Realtors, 57-68 and Brown Agency, 68-69. Mem: Pres, Real Estate Bd. of Bristol; C. of C; past exalted ruler, Bristol Elks Lodge 232; past gov, Bristol Moose Lodge 633; past state pres, Travelers Protective Asn; v.pres, United Fund; pres, Boys Club. of Bristol; v.pres, Little League; past grand patron, Eastern Star. Twenty five Year Vet. Award and Silver Beaver Award, Boy Scouts; Medallion and Man and Boy Award, Boys Club; 25 Club Award; Gov. Merit Award; Moose Award. Rel: Methodist. Mailing Add: 1141 Indian Hill Dr, Bristol, Tenn. 37620.

NEALE, GENEVIEVE SHACKELFORD D
b. Bates City, Mo, 12/10/15; d. Walter William Shackelford and Lavenia Rannabargar S; m. 6/27/37 to John Vance Neale; c. John Vance, Jr, James Courtney and Robert Carter. Educ: Cent. Mo. State Col, 33-36; Cornell Univ, 37; Kappa Delta Pi: Beta Alpha; Alpha Phi Delta. Polit. & Govt. Pos: N.H. State Rep, 58-62; mem, Hanover Dem. Cmt, 58-, women's chmn, 59-64; treas, N.H. Order of Women Legis, 59-62, first v.pres, 63-65; secy, N.H. State Dem. Cmt, 60-68; mem, Gov. Cmt. Children and Youth, 61-65; mem, N.H. Econ. Growth Surv. Cmt, 61-65, and Hanover Finance Cmt, 62-63; v.chmn, Grafton Co. Dem. Cmt, 62-66; trustee, Robert Frost Mem. Home, 65-69; mem, N.H. State Bd. Educ, 66- Bus. & Prof. Pos: Teacher, Concordia Schs, Mo, 34-36 and Oak Grove Schs, 36-37; asst. in research, Dartmouth Eye Inst, 37-40; v.chmn, Hanover Coun. Commun. Serv, N.H, 60-62; trustee, Spaulding Youth Center, 60-66, mem. exec. bd, 63-66; dir, N.H. Coun. Better Schs, 62-69, mem. exec. bd, 64-69; pres, N.H. Soc. Welfare Coun, 65-66. Mem: Nat. Cmt. Support Pub. Schs; League of Women Voters (exec. bd, 55-58); N.H. Ment. Health Asn.(dir, 60-61); trustee, Upper Valley Coun. Ment. Retarded; Hanover Conserv. Coun. Rel: Congregational. Mailing Add: 55 Lyme Rd, Hanover, N.H. 03755.

NEBLETT, WILLIAM EDWIN D
Chmn, Lunenburg Co. Dem. Cmt, Va.
b. Lunenburg Co, Va, 6/1/96; s. William Edwin Neblett and Rosa Hite N; m. 7/12/30 to Virginia Louise Akers; c. Virginia Akers. Educ: William and Mary Col, 15-17; Wash. and Lee Univ, LL.B, 22; Kappa Sigma. Polit. & Govt. Pos: Commonwealth attorney, Va, 24-48; mem, Lunenburg Co. Dem. Cmt, Va, 35-, chmn, 61-; cmnr. accounts, Lunenburg Co, 60. Mil. Serv: Entered as Pvt, Army, 17, released as Cpl, 19, after serv. in 318th Inf, 80th Div, Artois Sect, St. Mihiel Meuse Argonne Forest, 18-19. Mem: Va. State Bar; Va. and Am. Bar Asns; Va. Trial Lawyers Asn; AF&AM; RAM; Am. Legion; Kiwanis. Rel: Episcopal. Mailing Add: Lunenburg, Va. 23952.

NEDZI, LUCIEN NORBERT D
U.S. Rep, Mich.
b. 5/28/25; m. to Margaret Garvey; c. Lucien A, Bridget K, Brendan T. and Gretchen T. Educ: Univ. of Mich, A.B. in Econ, 48; Univ. of Detroit Law Sch, 49; Univ. of Mich. Law Sch, LL.B, 51. Polit. & Govt. Pos: Wayne Co. Pub. Adminstr, Mich, 55; del, Dem. Nat. Conv, 60 & 68; U.S. Rep, Mich, 62-; U.S. del, Interparliamentary Union. Bus. & Prof. Pos: Attorney-at-law. Mil. Serv: World War II, 20 months overseas duty, Philippines and Japan; Korean War. Mem: Admitted Mich. Bar, Jan. 52; numerous commun, fraternal, and legal orgn. Rel: Catholic. Legal Res: Detroit, Mich. Mailing Add: 1125 Longworth House Office Bldg, Washington, D.C. 20515. (1967)

NEE, KAY EVANGELINE (Radio-TV name: Kay Bonner) DFL
Mem. Exec. Cmt, Woman's Suburban Dem. Club, Minn.
b. Plummer, Minn; d. David Thomas Boner and Helena Franken B; m. 4/19/47 to William Joseph Nee; c. Christopher, Nicole, Lisa and Rachel. Educ: Col. St. Catherine, B.A, 41; Univ. Minn, grad. work in Eng. and theater, 47; Delta

Phi Lambdi; pres, Eng. Club; Collegiate Players. Polit. & Govt. Pos: Chairwoman, Anoka Co. Dem-Farmer-Labor Party, mem, State Cent. Cmt. and Third Dist. Exec. Cmt, 62-65; mem-at-lg, Minn. State Exec. Cmt, 63-65; del, Dem. Nat. Conv, 64; mem. exec. cmt, Woman's Suburban Dem. Club, Minn, 65-; mem, Gov. Cmn. on Status of Women, currently. Bus. & Prof. Pos: Dir, Woman's Prog, Kate, 41-43; free lance actress, 43-45; radio actress, WTCN, 45-50; free lance Radio-TV actress-writer, 50-52; Radio-TV writer-producer, Manson-Gold-Miller, 52-54; TV dir, WCCO-TV, 54-56; Radio-TV writer-producer, White-Herzog-Nee, Inc, 56-; TV Dir. for McCarthy for President Campaign, 68. Publ: Eugene J. McCarthy, United States Senator (w. William J. Nee), Gilbert Press, 64. Mem: Past bd. mem, Minneapolis Mayor's Cmn. on Human Rels; Woman's Advert. Club. of Minneapolis; past exec. bd. mem, past rep. to Cent. Labor Union and past del. to Nat. Conv, Am. Fedn. of TV and Radio Artists; League of Women Voters; Anoka Co. Polit. Action League; Commun. Theatre. Rel: Catholic. Mailing Add: 219 Logan Park Way, N.E, Fridley, Minn. 55432.

NEE, PATRICK WILLIAM D
b. Boston, Mass, 11/22/38; s. Coleman Nee and Mary Cooke N; m. 8/28/65 to Mary Margaret Schuh. Educ: Harvard Sch. of Bus. Admin; Boston Col. Law Sch; Univ. Notre Dame. Polit. & Govt. Pos: Mass. State Rep, 62-66. Bus. & Prof. Pos: Pres, Boston Spectator, Inc. Rel: Catholic. Mailing Add: 758 E. Fifth, South Boston, Mass. 02127. (1967)

NEEDHAM, DAISY EUDORA R
Mem, La. State Rep. Cent. Cmt.
b. St. Helena Parish, La, 12/26/99; d. Archie Carter Lambert and Sally Epperson L; m. 12/29/21 to Patrick Michael Needham; c. Gerald. Educ: High Sch. Polit. & Govt. Pos: Mem, La. State Rep. Cent. Cmt, St. Helena Parish. Rel: Protestant. Legal Res: St. Helena Parish, Greensburg, La. 70441. Mailing Add: R.F.D 1, Box 59, Kentwood, La. 70444.

NEEDHAM, JAMES JOSEPH R
Cmnr, Securities and Exchange Cmn.
b. Woodhaven, N.Y, 8/18/26; s. James Joseph Needham and Amelia Pasta N; m. 7/1/50 to Dolores Anne Habick; c. James Joseph, Robert John, Dolores Anne, Michael and Catherine. Educ: St. John's Univ, B.B.A, 51; Cornell Univ, Naval V-5 Prog, 44-46. Polit. & Govt. Pos: Cmnr, Securities and Exchange Cmn, 69- Bus. & Prof. Pos: Acct, Price Waterhouse & Co, N.Y.C, 47-54; partner, R.T. Hyer & Co, Port Washington, N.Y, 54-57 and A.M. Pullen & Co, N.Y.C, 57-69. Mil. Serv: Entered as A/S, Naval Res, 44, released as Seaman 2/C, 46. Mem: Am. Inst. and N.Y. State Soc. of CPA; N.Y. C. of C; L.I. Asn; Acct. Club. of Am, Inc; N.Y. Credit and Financial Mgt. Asn; Cath. Acct. Guild of the Diocese of Rockville Centre; Wheatley Hills Golf Club, East Williston (former treas. and dir); City Mid-Day Club; Serra Club of Nassau (past pres); Cornell Club of Nassau Co. Rel: Catholic. Legal Res: Bethesda, Md. Mailing Add: Room 800, 500 N. Capitol St, Washington, D.C. 20549.

NEEDHAM, MICHAEL J. D
Pa. State Rep.
b. Scranton, Pa, 10/8/10; s. Daniel E. Needham and Catherine McLoughlin N. Educ: St. Patricks High Sch. Polit. & Govt. Pos: Pa. State Rep, 46-54; 58-; mem, Young Dem. of Lackawanna Co. Mil. Serv: Ninth Armored Div, 19th Tank Bn; lost both legs in Battle of the Bulge. Mem: Gun & Rod Club of W. Scranton; Am. Legion; Bone Hill Athletic Asn; Luzerne Boosters Sportsmen Club; W. Scranton High Sch. Booster Club; VFW; DAV; Irish-Am. Club; St. Patrick's Booster Club (past pres); St. Patricks Holy Name Soc; K. of C; Cath. War Vets.(past comdr, St. Patrick's Chap). Rel: Catholic. Mailing Add: 324 S. Hyde Park Ave, Scranton, Pa. 18504. (1967)

NEEDHAM, THOMAS H. R
R.I. State Sen.
b. Providence, R.I, 6/30/22; s. Marcus J. Needham (deceased) and Margaret A. Brennan N. (deceased); m. 9/10/47 to Ursula F. McHale; c. Clair Ann, Thomas W, Jane F. and Mark W. Educ: Providence Col, Ph.B. cum laude, 46; Boston Univ, LL.B, 48, LL.M, 51; Theta Chap, Delta Epsilon Sigma; lit. ed, 46 Yearbook, Providence Col; mem, Student Coun. and sr. class pres, Boston Univ. Polit. & Govt. Pos: Del, two constitutional conv, 50's; v.pres, Warwick Young Rep, R.I, 54; asst. city solicitor, Warwick, 54; mem, trial coun, Dept. of Pub. Works, 65-67; R.I. State Sen, Dist. 13, 67- Mil. Serv: Entered as Pvt, Army, 42, released as Sgt, 46, after serv. in 1282nd Combat Engrs, European and Pac. Theatres, 43-46; Army Res, 50-, Lt. Col, 68- Publ: 'Changes in Article XV of the U.S. Code of Military Justice,' R.I. Bar J. Mem: Bd. dir, Legal Aid Soc, 60-; R.I. cmnr, Cmnr. for Uniform State Laws, 63-; R.I. and Am. Bar Asns; Am. Arbit. Asn; Fed. Bar for R.I; U.S. Court of Mil. Appeals; Nat. Found. March of Dimes and Big Sisters of R.I; K. of C. (4°); Aquila Club; Cranston Mens Rep. Club; Providence Col. and Boston Univ. Alumni Asns; Mal Brown Club of Providence Col. Rel: Roman Catholic. Legal Res: 19 Berwick Lane, Cranston, R.I. 02905. Mailing Add: 403 S. Main St, Providence, R.I. 02903.

NEELY, MARION ROBERT R
Chmn, Johnson Co. Rep. Cent. Cmt, Iowa
b. Billings, Mont, 12/7/23; s. Ralph Bilyeau Neely and Frances McCrary N; m. 7/13/52 to Marilyn Joan Long; c. Robert H. and Susan K. Educ: Univ. Iowa, B.S.C, and J.D; Phi Delta Phi. Polit. & Govt. Pos: Asst. attorney gen, Iowa Dept. of Justice, 59-61; asst. bar exam, Iowa State Bar Exam, 61-64; chmn, Johnson Co. Rep. Cent. Cmt, Iowa, 64-; police judge, Iowa City Police Court, 66- Bus. & Prof. Pos: Territory mgr, John Deere Plow Co, Moline, 51-56. Mil. Serv: Entered as Pvt, Army, 43, released, 46, after serv. in 94th Div, ETO. Mem: Iowa State and Am. Bar Asns; Am. Legion; Kiwanis; Mason; Shrine; C. of C. Rel: Methodist. Legal Res: 1127 Wylde Green Rd, Iowa City, Iowa 52240. Mailing Add: 608 Iowa State Bank Bldg, Iowa City, Iowa 52240. (1967)

NEEPER, ALICE E. D
b. Woodville, Ohio, 6/4/12; d. Val Arnold and Anna Herkel A; m. 11/26/39 to Guy E. Neeper; c. Ralph and Nancy. Educ: Hiram Col; Sigma Mu Sigma; Hiram Col. Glee Club Soloist; col. paper reporter. Polit. & Govt. Pos: Mem, S. Toledo Women's Dem. Club; Ohio State Rep, Nov-Dec, 54; Lucas Co. Charter Cmn, 58-; Dem. cand, Ohio State Sen, Dist. One, 66. Bus. & Prof. Pos: Former Cost-Acct, Du Pont de Nemours & Co. Mem: Past pres, Auxiliary of Engr. Soc. of Toledo; Ohio State Univ. Mothers Club; pres, Samagama, 69-; Toledo Mus. of Art; trustee, Maumee Valley Hist. Soc, 67- Life mem, Lutheran Women of Am, recognition of serv. by Augsburg Lutheran Church Women, 55, Toledo. Rel: Lutheran. Mailing Add: 4115 Green Glen Rd, Toledo, Ohio 43614.

NEFF, CLARENCE EVERETT R
Ill. State Rep.
b. New Berlin, Ill, 8/3/09; s. Jesse James Neff and Elizabeth Ferira N; m. 9/27/47 to Elaine Droste; c. Janice Elaine and Charles Edward. Educ: Tristate Col, elec. eng, 32, civil eng, 33; Phi Sigma. Polit. & Govt. Pos: Finance chmn, Henderson Co. Rep. Cent. Cmt, Ill, 50-56, chmn, 56-; mayor, Stronghurst, Ill, 50-63; Ill. State Rep, 63- Bus. & Prof. Pos: V.pres, Monco Fertilizer Co, 59-64, pres, C.E.Neff Co, 41-, Bank of Stronghurst, 46-, Midstates Liquid Fertilizer Co, 59-64 and Gladstone Grain Co, 60- Mem: Elks; Masons, Shriners; v.pres, Ill. Implement Dealers Asn; Ill. Automobile Asn; Ill. Agr. Asn. Rel: Lutheran. Mailing Add: Stronghurst, Ill. 61480.

NEFF, EDWIN DeFREES R
Asst. Pub. Rels. Dir, Rep. Cong. Cmt.
b. Ft. Collins, Colo, 1/24/12; s. Charles Melvin Neff and Louis DeFrees N; m. 7/2/42 to Alice Fitzhugh; c. Alice Louise and Carola Grayson. Educ: Dartmouth Col, A.B, 35; Columbia Univ, M.S, 36; Kappa Kappa Kappa. Polit. & Govt. Pos: Mem. staff, Rep. Cong. Cmt, 59-69, asst. pub. rels. dir, 69- Bus. & Prof. Pos: Med. and sci. reporter, Wash. Times-Herald, 37-41 & 45-52, chief ed. writer, 52; press dir, U.S. C. of C, 52-59. Mil. Serv: Entered as Ens, Naval Res, 42, released as Lt.(sg), 45, after serv. in Com. 14, Commun, Pac. Theatre, 43-45; Pac. Theatre Ribbon. Mem: Nat. Press Club of Wash, D.C. Rel: Protestant. Legal Res: Md. Mailing Add: 5804 Ridgefield Rd, Washington, D.C. 20016.

NEFF, FRANCINE IRVING R
b. Albuquerque, N.Mex, 12/6/25; d. Edward Hackett Irving and Georga Henderson I; m. 6/7/48 to Edward John Neff; c. Sindle and Edward Vann. Educ: Cottey Jr. Col. for Women, 46; Univ. N.Mex, B.A, 48; Phi Theta Kappa; Mortar Bd; Phi Kappa Phi; Pi Lambda Theta; Sigma Alpha Iota; Alpha Delta Pi. Polit. & Govt. Pos: Rep. div. chmn, 52nd Dist, Bernalillo Co, N.Mex, 66-68; N.Mex. State Adv, TAR, 66-68; mem, N.Mex. State Young Rep. Exec. Bd, 66-68; N.Mex. State chmn, Women for Nixon-Agnew, 68; del. and mem. permanent orgn, Rep. Nat. Conv, 68; mem, Rep. State Cent. Cmt, 68 & 69; mem, Zia Fedn. Rep. Women, 68-69; mem, Bernalillo Co. Exec. Bd, 69. Mem: PEO; PTA; Auxiliary, N.Mex. Soc. CPA; Albuquerque City Panhellenic; Albuquerque Mortar Bd. Alumnae Asn; Alpha Delta Pi Alumnae; leader, Camp Fire Girls, 7 years; past den mother, Cub Scouts. Rel: Episcopal. Mailing Add: 1509 Sagebrush Trail, S.E, Albuquerque, N.Mex. 87112.

NEFF, JOHN F. D
b. Indianapolis, Ind, 1/30/37; s. Henry R. Neff and Gertrude D. N; m. 7/2/60 to Lynn Mary Clippinger; c. Andrew C. and Jill Lynn. Educ: De Pauw Univ, Greencastle, Ind, A.B, 59; Ind. Univ. Law Sch, Indianapolis, LL.B, 62; Sigma Alpha Epsilon; Phi Delta Phi. Polit. & Govt. Pos: Ind. State Rep, 64; asst. city attorney, Indianapolis, 67; Marion Co. Attorney, 68; mem, Metropolitan Planning Cmn, 69; mem, Metropolitan Bd. of Zoning Appeals, 69. Mem: Indianapolis and Ind. State Bar Asns. Rel: Methodist. Mailing Add: 322 Circle Tower, 5 E. Market, Indianapolis, Ind. 46204.

NEFUSSY, ELI MAURICE R
b. New Bedford, Mass, 5/6/35; s. Maurice Eli Nefussy and Marcia Horenstein N; m. 3/13/64 to Lois Ann Horvitz; c. David Harvey and Lisa Harriet. Educ: Suffolk Univ. Sch. Law; Boston Univ. Polit. & Govt. Pos: Chmn, New Bedford City Rep. Cmt, Mass, 63-66; pres, Exchange Club of New Bedford, 69- Mil. Serv: Entered as Airman Basic, Air Force, 59, released as Airman 2/C, 60. Mem: Mem. Bd. Dirs, Volunteers of Am; Exchange Club; Jewish Commun. Center; High Sch. Alumni Asn. Rel: Jewish. Legal Res: 19 Whiteweed Dr, North Dartmouth, Mass. 02747. Mailing Add: 460 County St, New Bedford, Mass. 02744.

NEFZGER, DONALD DEANE D
b. Vida, Mont, 11/5/21; s. Charles Henry Nefzger and Katie Kathern McFarlane N; m. 9/1/50 to Anna Marie Schlenker; c. Daniel Charles, Deanna Rae and Darrel Allan. Educ: High sch, Wolf Point, Mont. Polit. & Govt. Pos: Mont. State Rep, 64-67; co. chmn, McCone Co. Dem. Cent. Cmt, 68-69; adv. mem. to co. cmnr, McCone Co, 68- Bus. & Prof. Pos: Dir, Agr. Soil Conserv. and sch. bd; mem. staff, Dept. Judge Advocate State Mont. VFW, currently. Mil. Serv: Entered as Pvt, 42, released as Cpl, 45, after serv. in 12th Bomb Group, Asiatic-European Theater; Presidential Citation; Asiatic Campaign and ETO Campaign Ribbons; Good Conduct; Nine Battle Stars. Mem: Past Post Comdr, VFW, Past Dist. Comdr and Dept. Surgeon, at present; charter mem, Elks. Rel: Congregational. Mailing Add: Vida, Mont. 59274.

NEGLEY, HARRY HULL, JR. R
Coroner, Huntingdon Co, Pa.
b. Crafton, Pa, 2/18/09; s. Harry Hull Negley and Anne St. C. Williamson N; m. 2/11/30 to Helen Louise McIlroy; c. Harry H, III. Educ: Univ. Pittsburgh, B.S, 34; Univ. Pittsburgh Med. Sch, M.D, 34. Polit. & Govt. Pos: Coroner, Huntingdon Co, Pa, 64-; Del, Rep. Nat. Conv, 68. Bus. & Prof. Pos: Gen. Surgeon, J.D. Blair Mem. Hospital, Huntingdon, 47-, pres. of staff, 65-67 and chief of staff, 68- Mem: Mason; Shrine. Rel: Presbyterian. Legal Res: Oneida Heights, Huntingdon, Pa. 16652. Mailing Add: 808 Washington St, Huntingdon, Pa. 16652.

NEGLEY, NANCY BROWN D
b. Houston, Tex, 10/31/27; d. George Rufus Brown and Alice Pratt B; m. 4/16/49 to Alfred Walter Negley; c. Leslie Nelson (Mrs. Reagin McAllister), Alice Pratt and W. Walter. Educ: Pine Manor Jr. Col, grad, 48. Polit. & Govt. Pos: V.chmn, Tex. State Dem. Exec. Cmt, 62-65; mem, San Antonio Fine Arts Cmn, 66- Mem: Exec. cmt. Int. Expos, Hemis Fair, 68; San Antonio Fine Arts Coun; trustee, Witte Mus; bd. San Antonio Arts League; treas, San Antonio Art Inst; chmn, Southwest Craft Center; bd, San Antonio Conserv. Soc; Tex. Coun. for Higher Educ; bd, Tex. Hist. Theatre Found; v.chmn, San Jose

Mission; bd. and dir, Southwest Found. Research and Educ; Fiesta San Antonio Cmn. Rel: Episcopal. Mailing Add: 155 Bushnell Ave, San Antonio, Tex. 78212.

NEGRI, DAVID D
Mem, Calif. Dem. State Cent. Cmt.
b. Burbank, Calif, 1/29/27; s. Morris Negri and Sarah Massoth N; m. 11/19/65 to Sharon Alleta; c. Donald Howard, Debra Susan, Sharon Anne, Kari Alleta and Renea Sari. Educ: Univ. Calif, Los Angeles, A.A, 51; Stanford Univ, B.A, 52, LL.B, 54; Phi Eta Sigma; Beta Gamma Sigma; mem, Moot Court Bd; co-chmn, Marion Rice Kirkwood Moot Court Competition. Polit. & Govt. Pos: Treas, San Fernando Valley Dem. Club, 50; mem, Fernando Dem. Club, 58; mem. lawyer's cmt, Rudd Brown for Cong, 58; 41st assembly dist. co-ordinator, Glenn Anderson for Lt. Gov, 58; del, 21st Cong. Coun, 58-60; del, 41st Assembly Dist. Coun, 58-66; pres, San Fernando Dem. Club, 59; chmn, Tom Carrell Testimonial Dinner, 59; discussion leader, Calif. Dem. Issues Conf, 59; chmn. exec. cmt, Elect. of Tom Carrell, 59-60; del, Dem. Issues Conf. and Endorsing Conv, 59-66; mem, Calif. Dem. State Cent. Cmt, 60, 62 and currently; mem, Los Angeles Co. Dem. Cent. Cmt, 60, 62, 64 and currently, secy, 60-62, chmn. of delegation, 62-66; trustee, 41st Assembly Dist. Coun, 60-61; del, 22nd Cong. Dist. Coun, 60-66; mem, Adv. Cmt. for Tom Carrell, 62 & 64; co-ordinator, Gov. Campaign for Northeast San Fernando Valley, 62; registrn. chmn, N.E. Valley Area, Los Angeles Co. Cmt, 63-64; v.chmn, 22nd Cong. Dem. Coun, 64-65; del, Gov. Conf. on Youth, 66; mem, Mexican-Am. Polit. Asn; charter mem, Gov. Club San Fernando Valley, 66; Calif. State Assemblyman, 41st dist, 66-68, mem, Cmn. of the Californias, Assembly Transportation and Commerce Cmt. and Assembly Munic. and Co. Govt. Cmt, Calif. State Assembly, 66-68; Calif. State Rep. at Detroit Smog Hearings and Inspecting Rapid Transit Systems in Montreal and Toronto, Can, 68. Mil. Serv: Entered as A/S, Maritime Serv, 44, released as Ens, 47, after serv. as chief radio operator in High-Octane Tankers, S.Pac. Mem: San Fernando C. of C; City Cmt. for New Fire And Police Sta, San Fernando, 56; chmn, Commerce and Industry Commun. Chest Campaign, 57; trustee, San Fernando Valley Bar Asn, 57 & 60; pres, San Fernando-Sylmar Co-ordination Coun, 57-58; Mil. Manpower Cmn, 57-59; Cmt. for Bldg. New Holy Cross Hospital, 58; chmn, N. Cent. Area Apr. Cancer Crusade, 59; chmn, N. Valley March of Dimes, 59; Elks; Am. Bar Asn; Am. Judicature Soc; appt. by City of San Fernando Planning Cmt. of Los Angeles to implement Gov. Prog. on Juvenile Delinquency, 59-60; Sylmar Civic Asn, 59-60; White House Conf. on Prevention of Delinquency for San Fernando Co-ordination Coun, San Fernando, 59; del, Urban Renewal Cmt, San Fernando Valley, Welfare Planning Coun, 61; pres, San Fernando Lions, 61-62, tail twister, 55, treas, 56, co-chmn, Fiesta Queen Contest, 56, chmn, 57, bd. dirs, 58-59, third v.pres, 59, first v.pres, 59-60, zone chmn, 62-63; Commun. Rels. Cmt, 62-68; pres, Knollwood Property Owners Asn, 62-63; Legal Aid and Lawyers Reference Asn. San Fernando Valley Bar, 62; bd. dirs, San Fernando Valley Legal Serv, Inc, 65-66; Latin Am. Civic Asn; Mexican-Am. C. of C, 66; N. Valley Jewish Commun. Center; judge, YMCA Students in Govt. Contest. Rel: Jewish. Legal Res: 16834 Blackhawk St, Granada Hills, Calif. 91344. Mailing Add: 563 S. Brand Blvd, San Fernando, Calif. 91340.

NEIBEL, CLEMETT LEE R
b. Pomona, Calif, 11/25/05; s. Ira Lee Neibel and Blanche Day N; m. 11/18/33 to Dorothy Leezer. Educ: Pomona Col, B.A, 27. Polit. & Govt. Pos: Chmn, Rep. Assocs, Pomona Sect, Calif, 62-63; mem, Calif. Rep. State Cent. Cmt, 63-69; chmn, Cmt. to Re-elect Congressman Glenard P. Lipscomb, 24th Dist, 64 & 69; mem, Dist. Attorney's Adv. Coun, 65-69; co-chmn, Cmt. to Elect Evelle Younger, Dist. Attorney, Los Angeles Co, 67; chmn, Pomona Mall Cmn, 68- Bus. & Prof. Pos: Dist rep, South. Calif. Edison Co, 37-; v.pres, Civic Center Corp, Pomona, 66- Mem: Pac. Coast Elec. Asn; Town Hall; Univ. Club Claremont; Hist. Soc. Pomona Valley; Pomona Cent. Bus. Dist; Kiwanis; San Dimas Serv. Club; affil. mem, Pomona Valley Bd. Realtors. Rel: Congregational; Moderator. Mailing Add: 1914 Yorba Dr, Pomona, Calif. 91767.

NEIKIRCHER, JOHN R
b. Cleveland, N.Dak, 9/3/22; married; c. Three. Educ: Bus. Col. Polit. & Govt. Pos: N.Dak. State Rep, 53-66; chmn, Co. Red Cross. Bus. & Prof. Pos: Ins. Mem: Mason; Elks; Nat. Asn. of Life Underwriters (pres). Mailing Add: Jamestown, N.Dak. 58401. (1967)

NEILL, MARSHALL A(LLEN)
Assoc. Justice, Wash. State Supreme Court
b. Pullman, Wash, 8/23/14; s, Roy A. Neill and Maude Cameron N; m. 8/15/38 to Marion Hackedorn; c. Marjorie Mitchell, Martha Vance and Howard M. Educ: Wash. State Univ, Pullman, Wash, B.A, 36; Univ. Idaho, Moscow, LL.B, 38; Phi Alpha Delta; Sigma Alpha Epsilon. Polit. & Govt. Pos: City attorney, Pullman, Wash, 38-52; Wash. State Rep, 49-56; Wash. State Sen, 57-67; assoc. justice, Wash. State Supreme Court, 67- Bus. & Prof. Pos: Dir, First Nat. Bank of Pullman, Wash, 47-63; dir, Old Nat. Bank of Wash, Spokane, 63-67. Mil. Serv: Ensign, Navy, 44, released as Lt.(jg), 46, after serv. in Amphibious Forces, Pac, 45-46. Mem: Am. Bar Asn; Am. Judicature Soc; Am. Col of Probate Counsel; Nat. Asn. of Univ. and Col. Attorneys; Elks; Mason; Am. Legion; VFW; Mil. Orders of World Wars; Kiwanis; Farm Bur. Rel: Episcopal. Mailing Add: Route 6, Box 395, Olympia, Wash, 98501.

NEISLER, ROBERT PRESTON R
Chmn, Fifth Cong. Dist. Rep. Party, S.C.
b. Kings Mountain, N.C, 8/11/36; s. Joseph Andrew Neisler and Annie Lee Miller N; m. 5/30/59 to Nora Jane Deese; c. Robert Preston, Jr, Matthew Ramseur and Christopher Edgar. Educ: Lenior Rhyne Col, B.S, 60; Sigma Phi Epsilon. Polit. & Govt. Pos: Del, S.C. State Rep. Conv, 62; pres, Rep. Party, Pageland Precinct, S.C, 62-64; finance chmn, Chesterfield Co, Rep. Party, 64-66; state exec. committeeman, S.C. Rep. Party, 66-68; adv, S.C. TAR, 66; mem, Dirkson Dinner Cmt, 67; del, Rep. Nat. Conv. and S.C. rep. to permanent orgn. cmt, 68; chmn, Fifth Cong. Dist. Rep. Party, 68-; mem, S.C. State Steering Cmt, 69- Bus. & Prof. Pos: Pres, Chesterfield Yarn Mills, Pageland, S.C, 59-; v.pres, Lucky Strike Yarn Mills, Shelby, N.C, 63- Mem: Jaycees (pres, Pageland Chap. 61); chmn, Chesterfield Co. Soc. Crippled Children and Adults, 63; finance chmn, Chesterfield Co. Asn. Retarded Children, 68- Rel: Associate Reformed Presbyterian. Legal Res: Route 1, Pageland, S.C. 29728. Mailing Add: Chesterfield Yarn Mills, Pageland, S.C. 29728.

NEISTEIN, BERNARD S. D
Ill. State Sen.
b. Chicago, Ill; m. to Alice N; c. Donald, Evaly Mary. Educ: Crane Col; DePaul Comm. Sch; DePaul Univ. Polit. & Govt. Pos: Master in Chancery, Circuit Court of Cook Co; bailiff, Munic. Court of Chicago; Ill. State Rep, 57-59; Ill. State Sen, 59-; del, Dem. Nat. Conv, 68. Mil. Serv: Entered as Pvt, Army, released as Lt. after receiving a direct overseas cmn. from Gen. Spaatz. Mem: Vice Pres, Hebrew Center; Am. Legion; Jewish War Vets; Moose; Chicago Bar Asn.(cmt. on membership, 4 years); Ill. and Am. Bar Asns; Ill. and Am. Asns. Defense Lawyers. Mailing Add: 4123 W. Harrison St, Chicago, Ill. 60624. (1967)

NELSEN, ANCHER R
U.S. Rep, Minn.
b. Renville Co, Minn, 10/11/04; s. Nels Peter Nelsen and Elisabeth Anderson N; m. 1929 to Ilo Irene Zimmerman; c. Richard, Bruce and Miriam (Mrs. Sommerness). Educ: Brownton High Sch. Polit. & Govt. Pos: Minn. State Sen, McLeod Co, 36-48; Lt. Gov, Minn, 53; administr, Rural Electrification Admin, 53-56; U.S. Rep, Minn, Second Cong. Dist, 59- Mem: AF&AM; Minn. Farm Bur. Rel: Lutheran. Legal Res: Route 4, Hutchinson, Minn. 55350. Mailing Add: 2329 Rayburn House Office Bldg, Washington, D.C. 20515.

NELSON, ALAN DALE R
Mem: Minn. Rep. Cent. Cmt.
b. Morgan, Minn, 5/31/31; s. Reynold W. Nelson and Rachel L. Zellmar N; m. 6/19/54 to Beatrice Marie Teal; c. Debra Marie, Sandra Dale, Barbara Ann and Steven Alan. Educ: Madison High Sch, Minn, grad, 49. Polit. & Govt. Pos: Cmnr, Stevens Co, Minn, 62-65; chmn, Stevens Co. Welfare Bd, 65; chmn, Stevens Co. Rep. Party, 67-; mem, Minn. Rep. Cent. Cmt, 67- Bus. & Prof. Pos: Agent, State Farm Ins. Co, 54- Mil. Serv: Entered as E-1, Army, 49, released as E-4, 52, after serv. in B. Battery, 175th F.A. Bn, 47th Div, 49-52. Mem: Instr, Red Cross; Minn. Rescue and First Aid Asn; Kiwanis (past pres); Mason; Morris C. of C; W.Cent. Life Underwriters Asn; Nat. Asn. Life Underwriters. Rel: Protestant. Mailing Add: 507 W. Sixth St, Morris, Minn. 56267.

NELSON, ALBERT L. D
b. Dover, N.H, 10/14/95; married; c. two. Educ: Dover Schs. Polit. & Govt. Pos: Trustee, Wentworth-Douglas Hosp; selectman, Ward I, Dover, N.H, former mem, city council; mem, Sch. Bd, 2 terms; N.H. State Rep, until 68. Bus. & Prof. Pos: Foreman, North East Tel & Tel. Co. 42 years, 6 months, retired. Mem: Mason; Dover Gridiron Club (co-founder). Rel: Episcopal. Mailing Add: 642 Central Ave, Dover, N.H. 03820. (1967)

NELSON, ALICE MARY R
Secy, Idaho Rep. State Cent. Cmt.
b. Kootenai, Idaho, 1/13/29; d. John Orr and Grace Hibbard O; m. 9/12/48 to James Wesley Nelson; c. Mark Stephen, Leslie Ann and Jon Wesley. Educ: Sandpoint High Sch, grad. Polit. & Govt. Pos: State Committeewoman, Bonner Co, Idaho, 56-66; secy, Idaho Rep. State Cent. Cmt, 64- Rel: Lutheran. Mailing Add: 509 S. Boyer Ave, Sandpoint, Idaho 83864.

NELSON, DAVID ALDRICH R
Gen. Counsel, Post Off. Dept.
b. Watertown, N.Y, 8/14/32; s. Carlton Low Nelson and Irene Aldrich N; m. 8/25/56 to Mary Ellen Dickson; c. Federick D, Claudia B. and Caleb E. Educ: Hamilton Col, A.B, 54; Cambridge Univ, 54-55; Harvard Law Sch, LL.B, 58; Phi Beta Kappa; Emerson Lit. Soc. Polit. & Govt. Pos: Gen. Counsel, Post Off. Dept, 69- Bus. & Prof. Pos: Assoc, Squire, Sanders & Dempsey, Cleveland, Ohio, 58-67, partner, 67-69. Mil. Serv: Off. of the Gen. Counsel, Dept. Air Force, Wash, D.C, 59-62. Mem: Cleveland, Am. and Ohio State Bar Asns; admitted to practice before the Supreme Court of Ohio, The U.S. Dist. Court for the North. Dist. of Ohio, the U.S. Court of Appeals for the Sixth Circuit and the U.S. Supreme Court. Rel: Congregational. Legal Res: Montgomery Co, Md. 20854. Mailing Add: Post Office Dept, Washington, D.C. 20260.

NELSON, DIXIE LEE R
Chmn, Benton Co. Rep. Cent. Cmt, Ore.
b. San Francisco, Calif, 3/31/31; d. Irvin Heber Anderson and Dixie Doolittle A; m. 10/4/58 to Thomas Edward Nelson; c. Eric Marshall, Katherine Lee, Elizabeth Ann and Patricia Marie. Educ: Univ. Utah, B.A, 60; Air Force ROTC Sponsor Corps. Polit. & Govt. Pos: Chmn, Benton Co. Rep. Affairs Coun, 65-66; v.chmn, Wilson for State Rep. Cmt, 66; v.chmn, Area Four, Benton Co. Rep. Party, 66-67, chmn, 67-68; chmn, Benton Co. Rep. Precinct Orgn, 67-68; v.chmn, Montgomery for Secy. of State Cmt, 68; chmn, Benton Co. Rep. Cent. Cmt, 68- Bus. & Prof. Pos: French teacher, Corvallis High Sch, Ore, 62-63; secy, Whitney Ball Ins, 64-65; Coop. Mgrs. Asn, 65-69. Rel: Episcopal. Mailing Add: 7015 N.W. Mountain View Dr, Corvallis, Ore. 97330.

NELSON, FRANK R
b. Omaha, Nebr, 11/15/83; s. Paul Nelson and Margretha Ulrickson N; m. 12/5/12 to Sarah E. Hull (deceased); m. 6/6/46 to Lena A. Mortensen; c. Paul and Margretha Ellen (Mrs. Kayor). Polit. & Govt. Pos: Nebr. State Sen, 49-67; treas, Scott Twp; twp. clerk, treas, Justice of Peace and assessor, Paddock Twp; dir. of Sch. Bd, Dist. 170, Holt Co, Nebr. Bus. & Prof. Pos: Treas, Paddock Union Cemetery Asn, 35- and Farmers Union Coop. Oil, Gas and Produce, 38-35. Rel: Lutheran. Mailing Add: Anncar Route, O'Neill, Nebr. 68763. (1967)

NELSON, FRANK V. R
Utah State Rep.
b. Salt Lake City, Utah, 10/22/19; s. N. Fred Nelson and Florence Littlewood N; m. 9/5/47 to Jean Anderson; c. Eric V, Jeff V, Kent A. and Ron A. Educ: Univ. of Utah, B.S, J.D, 49. Polit. & Govt. Pos: Utah State Rep, 65- Mil. Serv: Entered as Aviation Cadet, Navy, 42, released as Lt, 46, after serv. in Navy Air Corps, Pac. Mem: Utah State Bar and Salt Lake Co. Bar; Counsel, Utah Mfrs. Asn. Rel: Latter-day Saint. Mailing Add: 1866 Wasatch Dr, Salt Lake City, Utah 84108.

NELSON, GARY KENT R
Attorney Gen, Ariz.
b. LaCrosse, Wis 7/12/35; s. Angus Nelson and Nora Nederloe N; m.

6/20/59 to Juanita Gay Moen; c. Bradley, Byron and Douglas. Educ: Ariz. State Univ, B.S, 57; Univ. Ariz, LL.B, 62; Phi Eta Sigma; Phi Kappa Phi; Delta Sigma Phi; Phi Delta Phi. Polit. & Govt. Pos: Law Clerk to Justice Fred C. Struckmeyer, Jr, Ariz. Supreme Court, 62-63; Asst. Attorney Gen, Off. Attorney Gen, Ariz, 64-68, Attorney Gen, 68- Bus. & Prof. Pos: Assoc, Kramer Roche, Burch & Streich law firm, Phoenix, 63-64. Mil. Serv: Entered as 2nd Lt, Army, 57, released as 1st Lt, 59, after serv. in Mil. Intel, Unit, Fifth Army, 58-59; Capt, Res, 59-64. Mem: Ariz, Maricopa Co. and Am. Bar Asns; Nat. Asn. of Attorneys Gen; S. Mt. Lions; adv. bd. of Theodore Roosevelt Coun, Boy Scouts; chmn, Ariz. State Justice Planning Agency. Rel: Lutheran. Legal Res: 131 W. Gary Way, Phoenix, Ariz. 85041. Mailing Add: Room 159, Capitol Bldg, Phoenix, Ariz. 85007.

NELSON, GAYLORD ANTON D
U.S. Sen, Wis.
b. Clear Lake, Wis, 6/4/16; s. Dr. Anton Nelson; m. 1947 to Carrie Lee Dotson. Educ: San Jose State Col, 39; Law degree Univ. Wis, 42. Polit. & Govt. Pos: Wis. Legis, 48; gov, Wis, 58-62; U.S. Sen, Wis, 62-, chmn, U.S. Senate Subcmt. on employment, manpower and poverty which handles Off. Econ. Opportunity Legis. Mil. Serv: Army, 46 months, serv. in Okinawa Campaign. Legal Res: Madison, Wis. Mailing Add: 3812 Kenilworth Dr, Chevy Chase, Md. 20015.

NELSON, GEORGE NEIL D
b. Buford, Ark, 3/13/14; s. George Newton Nelson and Nannie Jane Davis N; m. 12/31/40 to Euna Mae Langston; c. Robert Neil, Larry Gene and Thomas Lee. Educ: Fort Logan Clerical Sch, Army; Hocott Bus. Col, Mountain Home, Ark. Polit. & Govt. Pos: Alderman, City of Mountain Home, Ark, 36-42; pres, bd. educ, Mountain Home Sch. Dist, 52-; chmn, Baxter Co. Dem. Cent. Cmt, 56-; chmn, Baxter Co. Elec. Cmn, 56-; secy, Baxter-Marion Co. Indust. Develop. Cmn, 62- Bus. & Prof. Pos: Cashier and dir, Peoples Bank, Ark, 48-; dir, First State Bldg. & Loan Asn, 61-; dir. and pres, Ozark Bus. Corp, 62- Mil. Serv: Entered as Pvt, Air Force, 43, released as Sgt, 46, after serv. in U.S. Mem: Am. Legion; Rotary Club (past pres, Mountain Home Chap). Rel: Baptist; Deacon and teacher men's Bible class. Mailing Add: 920 S. Baker St, Mountain Home, Ark. 72653. (1967)

NELSON, H. IVAN R
b. 7/16/06; m. 1927; c. 6. Educ: Commercial Col; Dakota Wesleyan. Polit. & Govt. Pos: S.Dak. State Sen, 64-66; Draft Bd; Sch. Bd; Indian Cmn. Bus. & Prof. Pos: Rancher; real estate; ins. agent. Mem: Am. Legion. Rel: Methodist. Mailing Add: 556 W. Ninth St, Winner, S.Dak. 57580.

NELSON, HAROLD ROBERT R
b. Rosalie, Nebr, 11/19/24; s. Karl John Nelson and Esther Johnson N; m. 8/18/47 to Betty Lou McFarlin; c. Larry Lee, Gale Duane, Judy Jo, Cindy Sue, Penny Lynn, Lori Faye and Peggy Ann. Educ: NPFS, St. Mary's Col, Calif; NFTS Cornell Col, Iowa and Univ. Okla; WTS, Glendale Col, Ariz; NATTC, Jacksonville, Fla. Polit. & Govt. Pos: County chmn, Rep. Party, 64-66 and precinct chmn, 58-64. Bus. & Prof. Pos: Chmn, Thurston Co. Farm Bur, 59-65. Mil. Serv: Entered as Aviation Cadet, Naval Air Force, 43, released as AEM 3/C, 46, Dutch Harbor, Alaska. Mem: Am. Farm Bur; Am. Legion. Honorable mention State Football tackle, Regimental Wrestling champion, St. Mary's Pre-Flight Sch. Rel: Protestant. Mailing Add: Rosalie, Nebr. 68055. (1967)

NELSON, HAROLD S.
b. Owatonna, 1890; married; c. 2. Educ: Univ. of Minn; Kings Col, Univ. of London, Eng. LL.B. Polit. & Govt. Pos: Steele Co. Attorney, Minn, 21-34; Minn. State Sen, 54-66. Bus. & Prof. Pos: Lawyer in firm of Nelson. Mil. Serv: Mexican Border Serv: World War I and World War II. Mailing Add: 363 E. Broadway, Owantonna, Minn. 55060.

NELSON, HELEN M. R
b. Hoquiam, Wash; m. 5/7/33 to Lanpher Wyman Nelson. Educ: In-Serv. Mgt. and Leadership Training Courses; Dale Carnegie Course, grad; Mid. Mgt. Training, Univ. South. Calif, 64. Polit. & Govt. Pos: Attended Fed. Civil Defense Conf. Wash, D.C, 51; former mem, Mayor's Cmt. for New Libr, Aberdeen, Wash; former civil defense secy, Grays Harbor Co. Bd; former mem, State Coun. on Aging Cmt; spearheaded reorganization, Grays Harbor Women's Rep. Club, 57-58; precinct worker, State GROW Prog, 57-; committeewoman, Wash. Rep. State Cmt, 60-64; hostess and observer, Rep. Nat. Cmt. Meeting, Seattle, Wash, 62; mem, Wash. Rep. State Cent. and Exec. Cmts, 63-64; mem. pub. rels. cmt, Co. Cent. Cmt. and Women's Club; mem, Gov. Cmn. Status of Women, 63-; alternate del, Rep. Nat. Conv, 64, observer and Nixon vol, 68; State Conf. Chmn, Wash, D.C, 65; pres, Rep. Women's Club, 65-66; Rep. area co-chmn, Dist. Two, Grays Harbor Co, 65-67; dist. two co. cmnr, currently; Rep. precinct committeewoman, Aberdeen, 66-; del. or alternate del, all state Rep. conv; attended all Rep. Women's Fedn. State Conv, Conf. and Dist. and Workshop Meetings in Off. Capacity; del, Rep. Nat. Cmt. Women's Conf, Wash, D.C, 69. Bus. & Prof. Pos: Formerly v.pres, Dean & Nelson Home Construction Co; dept. head, Pac. Northwest Bell, 42-62; co-owner and mgr, Nelde Manor Apt, Aberdeen, 60- Mem: Del, Nat. Fedn. Women's Clubs, Wash, D.C, 65; former mem, Salvation Army Bd. and Polio Bd; treas, Commun. Center, 61-; past pres, Grays Harbor Soroptimist Club; past state pres, Wash. Fedn. of Bus. and Prfnl. Women's Clubs, 63-64; past pres, Grays Harbor Coun. of Tel. Pioneers; past v.pres, Commun. Concerts Asn; past v.pres, Dale Carnegie Club; Tel. Pioneers of Am; VFW Auxiliary; Lady Elk; Friends of the Libr; Knife and Fork; Grays Harbor Country Club; Ocean Shores Country Club; exec. cmt, United Good Neighbors; ment. health bd, Alcoholism Coun. Bd; Grays Harbor C. of C.(conducting action course in practical polit); regional chmn, Status of Women subcmt. under pub. affairs, Soroptimist Fedn. of Americas and Northwest. Region. Named State Woman of Achievement for Commun. Serv, Wash. State Fedn. of Bus. and Prfnl. Women's Clubs, 61; Merit Cert, Am. Red Cross and Nat. Found. Infantile Paralysis. Rel: United Presbyterian; Past pres, Womens Asn, United Presby. Church, Aberdeen. Mailing Add: 600 N. Eye St, Aberdeen, Wash. 98520.

NELSON, HERMAN G. R
Committeeman, Ill. Rep. Cent. Cmt.
b. Rock, Mich, 3/8/02; s. Edward Nelson and Esther Nilsson N; m. 5/14/60 to Margaret Diana Hagan King; c. Ruth Mae, Margaret (Mrs. Albert E. Myers), Clyde King and Lisa (Mrs. Larsen). Educ: Augustana Col, A.B, 26; studied in univs. in Sweden, 29-30; Rho Nu Delta. Polit. & Govt. Pos: Mem, Winnebago Co. Bd. of Supvr, Ill, 35-49, chmn, 45-46; mem. and v.chmn, New Sweden Tercentenary Cmn. of Ill, 38; mem. and v.chmn. Ill. Swedish Pioneer Centennial Cmn, 48; committeeman, Ill. Rep. Cent. Cmt, 50- Bus. & Prof. Pos: Ed. staff writer, Rockford Morning Star, Rockford, Ill, 26- Publ: Numerous articles for Am. Swedish Monthly, Lutheran Companion and other mag. Mem: Swedish Hist. Soc. of Rockford (former pres, secy, currently); Swedish Pioneer Hist. Soc.(first v.pres); John Ericsson Rep. Club of Winnebago Co; Ill. League. Decoration of Knight of Swedish Order, Royal Order of Vasa; New Sweden and Swedish Pioneer Decorations; KFUM Decoration; U.S. Treasury Silver Award for Sale of Bonds; Ind. Order of Viking Plaque. Rel: Lutheran. Legal Res: 215 Calvin Park Blvd, Rockford, Ill. 61107. Mailing Add: News Tower, Rockford, Ill. 61101.

NELSON, HOWARD I. Conservative
Minn. State Sen.
b. Milltown, Wis, 11/25/12; m. to Dorothy M. Palmquist; c. Five. Educ: Milltown Union Free High Sch. Polit. & Govt. Pos: Past pres, Lindstrom Center City Sch, PTA; pres, Chicago Chain of Lakes Asn; Minn. State Rep, 59-61; Minn. State Sen, 62- Bus. & Prof. Pos: Owner and operator of meat mkt. and frozen food locker bus; former firechief of Lindstrom Vol. Fire Dept. Mem: Minn. Frozen Food Locker Asn.(past pres); Chicago Lakes Sportsmen's Club (past pres); Nat. Inst. of Locker and Freezer Provisioners (dir, 68, 2nd v.pres, 69); AF&AM (past master); Eastern Star (past patron). Rel: Lutheran; Past Councilman, Trinity Lutheran Church. Mailing Add: Lindstrom, Minn. 55045.

NELSON, JACK W. R
Mem, Okla. State Rep. Exec. Cmt.
b. Sherman, Tex, 12/20/18; s. Robert Cliett Nelson and Effie Mae O'Hara N; m. 1/9/49 to Bobby Pennington; c. Christopher Anne and Kimberly Elizabeth. Educ: Univ. Tex; Austin Col, B.A, 43; U.S. Naval Res. Midshipman Sch, Notre Dame Univ; Honor Soc, Phi Sigma Alpha; capt, Varsity Football. Polit. & Govt. Pos: Precinct chmn, Tulsa, Okla, 60-62; mem, Tulsa Co. Rep. Cent. Cmt, 60-65; mem, Okla. State Rep. Cmt, 61-65; mem, Tulsa Co. Rep. Exec. Cmt, 61-; dist. dir, Tulsa Co. Rep. Party, 63, chmn, 63-66; mem, Okla. State Rep. Exec. Cmt, 63-; del, Rep. Nat. Conv, 64. Bus. & Prof. Pos: V.pres, City Transit Systs, Inc, 46-50; admin. asst. to pres, Austin Col, 50-51; spec. rep, Prudential Ins. Co. Am, 51-56; asst. v.pres, Alexander & Alexander, Inc, 59- Mil. Serv: Entered as Seaman Recruit, Navy, 42, released as Lt, 46, after serv. as Capt. Motor Torpedo Boat, Squadron, 31, Pac. Area; Navy Commendation; Navy Medal; Am. Theater and Pac. Theater Ribbons; Philippine Liberation Medal; Commanding Officer, Naval Res. Surface Div, 58-62; comdr, Naval Res, currently. Mem: Tulsa Exchange Club, Elks; Men's Forum; Life Underwriters Asn; C. of C; Navy League; ROA. Rel: Christian Church; Elder, Harvard Ave. Christian Church. 1967 Legal Res: Tulsa, Okla. No mailing address available. (1967)

NELSON, JOHN CLIFFORD R
Chmn, Rio Grande Co. Rep. Cent. Cmt, Colo.
b. Walters, Okla, 12/11/21; s. Edward Nelson (deceased) and Goldie Wills N; m. 5/20/44 to Eva Frances Schutte; c. Jo Ann and Michael Jon. Educ: Cameron Jr. Col, ½ year. Polit. & Govt. Pos: Rep. committeeman, Precinct 14, Rio Grande Co, Colo, 64-66; del, Rep. State Conv, 65; chmn, Rio Grande Co. Rep. Cent. Cmt, 68- Bus. & Prof. Pos: Mgr-meat-cutter, Wholesale-Retail Meat Plant, 38-58; customer serv. rep, Public Service Co. Colo, 58- Mil. Serv: Entered as Pvt, National Guard, 39, released as Cpl, 40, after serv. in Signal Sect-Battery D, 168th Field Artil. Mem: Elks; Monte Vista Lions Club (past pres, mem. bd); Monte Vista Old Timers Boys Baseball Asn.(bd. mem, treas); Monte Vista Country Club (past bd. mem); San Luis Valley Chap, Nat. Found.(mem. bd). Rel: Catholic. Mailing Add: Rt. 2, East of Homelake, Monte Vista, Colo. 81144.

NELSON, LeROY JAMES D
Chmn, Menominee Co. Dem. Party, Mich.
b. Spalding, Mich, 7/28/22; s. Hans Peter Nelson and Florence Mae Vincent N; m. 6/15/42 to Theadora Mae Fillion; c. LeRoy William, Michael James, Sharman Ann, John Robert and Georgeanne Marie. Educ: Bay de Noc Commun. Col, credits; Mich. Tech. Univ, 1 year. Polit. & Govt. Pos: Treas, Powers Spalding Sch. Bd, Mich, 49-53; br. mgr, Secy. of State, 56-66; Dem. cand. for Mich. State Sen, 62 & 64; dep. dir. equalization dept, Menominee Co, Mich, 66-; del, Dem. Nat. Conv, 68; chmn, Menominee Co. Dem. Party, Mich, 68-; mem. exec. cmt, 11th Cong. Dist. Dem. Party, 68-69, chmn. commun. and educ, 69- Mil. Serv: Entered as Seaman 1/C, Navy, 42, released as SM 2/C, 45, after serv. in 3rd and 5th Fleets, Asiatic-Pac. Theatre and Philippine Liberation, 43-45. Mem: Int. Asn. Assessing Officers; Am. Legion; K. of C. Rel: Catholic. Mailing Add: Box 5, Powers, Mich. 49874.

NELSON, LESLIE H. Non-Partisan
b. Hadley, Minn, 1909; married; c. 2. Educ: Slayton Pub. Schs; Minn. Mortuary Sci. Licensee. Polit. & Govt. Pos: Minn. State Rep, 64-66. Bus. & Prof. Pos: Owner-operator Nelson Funeral Home and Nelson Furniture Store, Slayton; bd. mem. Slayton Fed. Savings & Loan Asn; pres, Minn. Investment Co. Rel: Lutheran; Bd. Mem, Sunday Sch. Supt, Christ Lutheran Church. 1967 Legal Res: Slayton, Minn. No mailing address available. (1967)

NELSON, MARTIN A. R
Assoc. Justice, Minn. Supreme Court
b. Hesper, Iowa, 2/21/89; m. 1920 to Merle Henifin; c. Arthur M. and Enid M. (Mrs. Jesmer). Educ: Pharmaceutical course, registered pharmacist, 12; St. Paul Col. of Law, LL.B, 16. Polit. & Govt. Pos: Del, Rep. Nat. Conv, 28, del-at-lg, 32; chmn, Mower Co. Rep. Party, Minn; v.chmn, Minn. State Rep. Cmt; Rep. nominee for gov, Minn, 34 & 36; judge, Dist. Court, Austin, Minn, 44-65; mem, Dist. Court Bench, 44-; assoc. justice, Minn. Supreme Court, 53- Bus. & Prof. Pos: Asst. to the attorney and trust officer, Capitol Trust Co, St. Paul, Minn, 16-17; partner, law off, Gen. Arthur W. Wright, Austin, Minn, 19-27 and law firm of Nelson & Plunkett, 27-44; trustee, St. Olaf Hosp, Austin, 22 years, pres. bd, 10 years. Mil. Serv: Entered as Enlisted, Army, 17, released as 2nd Lt, 19, after serv. as Cadet, Aviator in training at four different airfields and instr. in aerial gunnery flying at field where last stationed,

World War I. Mem: Am, Minn. and Ramsey Co. Bar Asns; Kiwanis (pres, Austin Chap, 24); Elks (life mem, Austin Lodge and dist. dep. to the Grand Exalted Ruler, South Minn, 25); Mason (32°, Master, Austin Lodge, 29 and Grand Orator, Minn. Grand Lodge, 42); Am. Legion; 40 et 8; OX5 Club; Shrine (life mem, Osman Temple); Torske Klubben, Minneapolis and Six O'Clock Club, Minneapolis (past pres). Lutheran; Former Deacon and Bd. Mem, St. Olaf Lutheran Church, 29 years. Mailing Add: 515 S. Cleveland Ave. St. Paul, Minn. 55116.

NELSON, MAYNARD DALE R
b. Lake Crystal, Minn, 8/29/22; s. Wilbur Roy Nelson and Bernice Warren N; m. 2/12/48 to Franque Mattoon; c. Dianne, Cynthia, Sandra, Martha, Andrea and Maynard Stuart. Educ: Univ. Calif, 45-48; Phi Delta Theta. Polit. & Govt. Pos: Chmn, Sacramento Co. Young Rep, Calif, 59; pres, Rep. Assocs, Sacramento, 63; mem. exec. cmt, Calif. Rep. State Cent. Cmt, 64-69; chmn, Sacramento Co. Rep. Cent. Cmt, 65-68; cand, Calif. State Assembly, Third Assembly Dist, Sacramento Co, 68; pres, Calif. Asn. of Rep. Cent. Cmt. Chmn, 68. Mil. Serv: Entered Air Force, 43, released as Capt, 45, after serv. in 15th Air Force, Italy; ETO Ribbons with 8 Battle Stars; Air Medal with 4 Oak Leaf Clusters; Distinguished Flying Cross. Mem: Bd. of dirs, Sacramento Metrop, YMCA, 64-, Goodwill Industs. and Sacramento Coun. of Churches, 64-65, Commun. Welfare Coun, 59-65 and Family Serv. Agency, 58-65. Rel: Baptist. Mailing Add: 5300 Fair Oaks Blvd, Carmichael, Calif. 95608.

NELSON, NORMAN BERNARD D
b. Great Falls, Mont, 8/24/17; s. Nikolai Nelson and Jessie Hansen N; m. 10/15/55 to Neoma Virgie Phillips; c. Rocco Curttiss, Suzzanne Carol, Montgomery Bernard, Brent Phillips and Travis Nikolai. Educ: High Sch, Veblen, S.Dak, 1 year. Polit. & Govt. Pos: Dem. precinct committeeman, Anchorage, Alaska, 52-62; precinct committeeman, King Co, Wash, 63-; pres, North End Dem. Club, King Co, 64-66; del, King Co. Dem. Cent. Cmt, 64-69; del, Wash. State Dem. Conv, 64, 66 & 68; del, Dem. Nat. Conv, 68. Bus. & Prof. Pos: Pres, Alaska Creamery Prod, Inc, Anchorage, 58-62; secy-treas, Investment Contractors, Inc. and pres, Trend Investment, Inc, Seattle, Wash, 64- Mil. Serv: Entered as Pvt, Army Air Force, 43, released as Cpl, 46, after serv. in 389th Air Serv. Group, Asiatic Pac. Theatre, 45-46; Good Conduct, Victory, Am. and Asiatic Pac. Theatre Medals. Mem: Am. Civil Liberties Union; NAACP; United Brotherhood of Carpenters and Joiners of Am. Rel: Unitarian Mailing Add: 19311 45th N.E, Seattle, Wash. 98155.

NELSON, RAY O. R
Chmn, Grant Co. Rep. Party, S.Dak.
b. Pierre, S.Dak, 11/20/11; s. Archie J. Nelson and Mary Etta Craddock N; m. 5/3/41 to Elizabeth Marie Clarke; c. John K, David G. and Julie A. Educ: Pierre High Sch, grad, 30. Polit. & Govt. Pos: Chmn, Grant Co. Rep. Party, S.Dak, 68- Bus. & Prof. Pos: Mem, Small Bus. Admin. Adv. Council, 68- Mil. Serv: Entered as Pvt, Army, 42, released as Chief Warrant Off, 54 after serv. in 196th Inf. Bn, African European Theatre, Alaska. Mem: Am. Legion; VFW; Mason. Mailing Add: Big Stone City, S.Dak. 57216.

NELSON, RAYMOND D
Mem, Dem. State Cmt, R.I.
b. Providence, R.I, 9/2/21; s. Nels H. Nelson and Lillie Swanson N; m. 7/3/43 to Shirley Alice Crane; c. David C, Rebecca R. and Marc A. Polit. & Govt. Pos: Admin. asst. to U.S. Sen. Claiborne Pell and mem, Dem. State Cmt, R.I, currently. Bus. & Prof. Pos: Reporter, Providence J, 46-60, bur. chief, 50-60. Mil. Serv: Entered as A/S, Navy, 42, released as PO 3/C, 45, after serv. in ETO; Good Conduct Medal. Mem: Nat. Press Club; U.S. Sen. Admin. Assts. and Personal Secy; U.S. Sen. Press Secy. Club; Sen. Staff Club; Cong. Secy. Club; The Burro Club. Rel: Lutheran. Legal Res: 43 Hillard Ave, Warwick, R.I. 02886. Mailing Add: 6118 Wilson Lane, Bethesda, Md. 20034.

NELSON, RICHARD CURTIS R
b. Billings, Mont, 1/14/28; s. Cedric Henry Nelson and Maude Magill N; m. 12/21/51 to Patricia Beckler; c. Richard C, Jr, Thomas Alan, Christopher Henry and Jonathan Edward. Educ: Ore. State Col, Corvallis, 45-46; Univ. Nebr, Lincoln, 48-49; Univ. Nebr. Col. Med, Omaha, M.D, 53; Phi Rho Sigma. Polit. & Govt. Pos: Treas, Yellowstone Co. Rep. Cent. Cmt, Mont, 60-69; del, Rep. Nat. Conv, 68. Bus. & Prof. Pos: Physician. Mil. Serv: Entered as Pvt, Army, 45, released as Sgt, 47, after serv. in Army Ground Forces Bd. Four, U.S, 46-47. Mem: Am. Col. Physicians; Am. Soc. Internal Med; Am. Med. Asn; Rotary. Rel: Methodist. Mailing Add: 3108 Arvin Rd, Billings, Mont. 59102.

NELSON, ROBERT R. D
W.Va. State Del.
b. Boone Co, W.Va, 10/9/35; s. Joda Fulton Nelson and Opal W. Hunter N; m. Apr. 60 to Mary Lucinda Abruzzino; c. Phillip and Christine. Educ: Marshall Univ, A.B. in Polit. Sci, 60, M.A, 69; George Wash. Univ. Polit. & Govt. Pos: W.Va. State Del, 64-; admin. asst. to U.S. Rep. Ken Hechler, Fourth Dist, W.Va, currently. Mil. Serv: Marine Corps, 53-57. Rel: Protestant. Legal Res: 1416 Washington Blvd, Huntington, W.Va. 25701. Mailing Add: P.O. Box 1965, Huntington, W.Va. 25712.

NELSON, ROLF TIMOTHY R
Minn. State Rep.
b. St. Paul, Minn, 11/23/40; s. Rev. Dr. Clifford Ansgar Nelson and E. Bernice N; single. Educ: Gustavus Adolphus Col, 59-60; Univ. of Singapore, Malaya, 60; Univ. of Minn, B.A, 62 and LL.B, 65. Polit. & Govt. Pos: Precinct chmn, Robbinsdale Rep. Party, Minn, 66; Minn. State Rep, Dist. 31-B, currently. Bus. & Prof. Pos: Attorney-at-Law. Mil. Serv: Entered as Pvt, Army, 57, released as Sgt. Maj, 66; Sgt. Maj, Army Res. Mem: Hennepin Co. and Minn. State Bar Asns; North Hennepin Kiwanis; Minn. State Sheriff's Asn; Friend of North Hennepin Jr. Col. Rel: Lutheran. Mailing Add: 3615 Beard Ave N, Robbinsdale, Minn. 55422.

NELSON, T. BARDEN R
b. West Pawlet, Vt, 9/12/99; m. to Hazel Williams; c. Three. Educ: Albany Bus. Col. Polit. & Govt. Pos: Mem, Rutland Co. Tax Appeal Bd Vt, 6 years; former overseer of poor; Vt. State Rep, 51-55 & 65-66; selectman, West Pawlet, Vt, currently. Bus. & Prof. Pos: Farmer. Mem: F&AM (past Master); AAONMS. Rel: Protestant. Mailing Add: West Pawlet, Vt. 05761. (1967)

NELSON, TALMAGE L. D
Chmn, Lauderdale Co. Dem. Exec. Cmt, Tenn.
b. Ripley, Tenn, 11/6/89; m. 12/17/17 to Vicy Black, Sally Shoffner, 58, Girlean Clifft, since 64; c. Mrs. Willie Lee Allen. Educ: Grade sch, tenth grade. Polit. & Govt. Pos: Chmn, Lauderdale Co. Dem. Exec. Cmt, Tenn, 66- Bus. & Prof. Pos: Sch. teacher, Home Co, Tenn, 13-16; owner and operator, 4 Dept. Stores, 20-63, retired. Mil. Serv: Cpl, Army, AEF, 18. Mem: Col, Gov. Staff, Tenn; Mason; Eastern Star; Am. Legion; Am. Farm Bur. Rel: Methodist. Mailing Add: 160 Lake Dr, Ripley, Tenn. 38063.

NELSON, THOMAS FOWLER R
b. New York, N.Y, 7/12/30; s. Clarence E. Nelson and Janet Fowler N; m. 2/14/59 to JoAnna Uihlein; c. Clare, Jennifer and Sally. Educ: Amherst Col, B.A, 52; Yale Law Sch, LL.B, 55; Phi Beta Kappa; Order of the Coif. Polit. & Govt. Pos: Alternate del, Rep. Nat. Convs, 60 & 64; chmn, Milwaukee Co. Young Rep, Wis, 60-62; v.chmn, Wis. Fedn. of Young Rep, 61-63; cand. for Cong, Fifth Dist, 62; chmn, East Side Rep. Club, Milwaukee, 64-66; coordinator, Milwaukee Co. Rep. Party, Wis, 66-67; state cmnr. of securities, Wis, 67- Bus. & Prof. Pos: Attorney and advisor, Off. of Secy. of Air Force, 55-58; attorney, Whyte, Hirschboeck, Minahan, Harding & Harland, Milwaukee, Wis, 58-64; asst. v.pres, Loewi and Co, Inc, invest. bankers, Milwaukee, Wis, 64-67. Mil. Serv: Entered as 2nd Lt, Air Force, 55, released as 1st Lt, 58. Rel: Presbyterian. Mailing Add: 3403 Circle Close, Madison, Wis. 53705.

NELSON, W. C. 'BERT' DFL
b. White Bear Lake, Minn, 8/29/10; s. Charles G. Nelson and Josephine Kjellberg N; m. to Alice E; c. Marjorie A.(Mrs. Lammers) and Charles G. Educ: St. Paul Col. Law; Delta Theta Phi. Polit. & Govt. Pos: Treas, Renville Co. Dem-Farmer-Labor Cmt, Minn, 54-56, secy, 56-62, chmn, 64-68. Rel: Lutheran. Mailing Add: Spicer, Minn. 56288.

NELSTEAD, KEITH TORVAL R
Mem. Exec. Cmt, Yellowstone Co. Rep. Cent. Cmt, Mont.
b. Ekalaka, Mont, 10/2/26; s. Torval E. Nelstead and Ella Kjelshus N; m. 11/26/55 to Verene Will; c. Randall, Sheri and Kevin. Educ: Univ. Mont, B.A, 50; Phi Delta Theta; Lutheran Students Asn; Young Rep. Polit. & Govt. Pos: Ward leader, Yellowstone Co. Rep. Cent. Cmt, Mont, 62-64, precinct committeeman, 62-66; alternate del, Mont. Rep. Conv, 64, precinct coordinator, 64-68, del, 68 and statist. chmn, 68-69; del, Rep. Nat. Conv, 68; mem. exec. cmt, Yellowstone Co. Rep. Cent. Cmt, 68- Bus. & Prof. Pos: Mem. acct. dept, Mont. Power Co, 51. Mil. Serv: Entered as A/S, Navy, 44, released as Seaman 1/C, 46 after serving in Pac, 45-46. Mem: Mason; Elks; Optimists; Am. Legion; Rep. Club Yellowstone Co.(charter mem. and dir, 66-68). Rel: Lutheran. Mailing Add: 2941 Miles Ave, Billings, Mont. 59102.

NERO, PAT D
R.I. State Sen.
b. Providence, R.I, 9/16/19; m. to Lee Geremia. Educ: Boston Univ, B.M, 42, LL.B, 44. Polit. & Govt. Pos: R.I. State Sen, 61-, mem, Senate Dem. Steering Cmt. and chmn, Cmn. to Study Minimun Standards in Music and Arts; del, Constitutional Conv, 58. Bus. & Prof. Pos: Prfnl. violinist and conductor, mem, Providence Sch. Dept. and Recreation Dept, conductor, U.F. McCall Orchestra and Nickerson House Little Symphony, formerly; attorney-at-law. Mil. Serv: Capt, Marine Corps, 3 years; R.I. Marine Corp Res, formerly. Mem: R.I, Am. and Fed. Bar Asns; Justinian Soc; Boston Univ. Alumni Asn; Cranston Lions Club; West Warwick Elks; K. of C; Fraternal Order of Police; Matacomet Country Club; Am. Legion; Ital-Am. War Vets; Providence Police Asn; Knightsville Libr. Asn; Teachers and Musicians Unions. Mailing Add: 681 Park Ave, Cranston, R.I. 02910.

NESBITT, CHARLES R. D
Chmn, Okla. Corp. Cmn.
b. Miami, Okla, 8/30/21; s. Charles R. Nesbitt and Irma L. Wilhelmi N; m. 6/6/48 to Margot Dorothy Lord; c. Nancy Margot, Douglas Charles and Carolyn Jane. Educ: Univ. of Okla, B.A, 42; Yale Univ. Law Sch, LL.B, 47; Phi Beta Kappa; Phi Delta Phi; Pe-Et. Polit. & Govt. Pos: Mem, legal cmt, Interstate Oil Compact Cmn, 57-59; spec. counsel to Gov. and Corp. Cmn. of Okla, 57-60; Attorney Gen, Okla, 63-67; mem, Corp. Cmn. of Okla, 68-; chmn, 69- Bus. & Prof. Pos: Private practice of law, 49-62 & 67- Mil. Serv: Entered as 2nd Lt, Army, 42, released as Maj, 46, after serv. in ETO; ETO and Cent. European Campaign Ribbons. Mem: Lions; Okla. Sci. and Art Found; Okla. Art Center; Okla. Symphony Soc; VFW; Am. Legion; Nat. Asn. of Rate Cmnrs; Okla. and Am. Bar Asns. Rel: Episcopal. Mailing Add: 401 N.W. 16th, Oklahoma City, Okla. 73103.

NESMITH, CARL DALTON D
b. Brooksville, Marshall Co, Ala, 2/24/23; s. Elliott Freeman and Ella Pearl Berry N; m. 6/12/48 to Vivian Vashti Brittain; c. Pamela Susan, Carl Dalton, Jr, Sallie Marie. Educ: Univ. of Ala, Bus. Admin, LL.B, 50. Polit. & Govt. Pos: Ala. State Rep, 63-66; Co. Solicitor, 53-59; judge of Intermediate Court of Blount Co, 51-53. Mil. Serv: Navy, 43-46; Army, 48-53, attaining rank of Lt. Mem: Mason. Rel: Baptist. Mailing Add: Box 561, Oneonta, Ala. 35121. (1967)

NESSMITH, PAUL E, SR. D
Ga. State Rep.
b. Statesboro, Ga, 11/24/08; s. Benjamin David Nessmith and Sarah Moseley N; m. 8/30/36 to Eloise Smith; c. Paul Edward Jr, William Benjamin. Educ: Cave Springs Consolidated High Sch, 27. Polit. & Govt. Pos: Ga. State Rep, 63- Bus. & Prof. Pos: Past pres, Commun. Farm Bur; Ga. Agr. Commodities Authority; Ga. Agr. Commodity Cmt. for Peanuts; Chmn, Southeast. Peanut Adv. Cmt, 61-. Mem: C. of C; K. of P; Ga. Ton Per Acre Peanut Club; Ga. Bale and Half Cotton Club; 100 Bushel Corn Club; 1000 Bushel Corn Club. Ga. Master Farmer, 61. Rel: Baptist. Mailing Add: RFD 4, Statesboro, Ga. 30458. (1967)

NESVIG, JEROME D
b. Buxton, N.Dak, 1911; married; c. Ten. Polit. & Govt. Pos: N.Dak State Sen, 59-66; chmn, Prod. Mkt. Asn, Traill Co, 6 years. Bus. & Prof. Pos:

Farmer. Mem: Farmers Union; Farm Bur; Masonic Lodge; Shrine. Mailing Add: Buxton, N.Dak. 58218. (1967)

NETTELS, GEORGE E, JR. R
b. Pittsburg, Kans, 10/20/27; m. 7/19/53 to Mary Joanne; c. Christopher Bryan, Margaret Anne, Katherine Anne and Rebecca Jane. Educ: Univ. Kans, B.S. in Civil Eng, 50; Tau Beta Pi; Omicron Delta Kappa. Polit. & Govt. Pos: Precinct committeeman, Kans. Rep. Party, 60-; mem, City Zoning Cmt, 63-65; mem, Kans. Cmt. Civil Rights, 65-; mem, Pittsburgh Sch. Bd, 65-; chmn, Kans. State Rep. Party, 66-68; del, Rep. Nat. Conv, 68. Bus. & Prof. Pos: Rock Quarrying, John J. Stark Contractors; pres, Midwest Minerals, Inc, 68- Mem: Chmn. of bd, Nat. Limestone Inst, Washington, D.C; Kans. Limestone Asn; past mem, Univ. Kans. Alumni Bd; Kans. State C. of C.(v.pres). Rel: Presbyterian. Mailing Add: 509 W. Quincy Pittsburg, Kans. 66762.

NETZLEY, ROBERT E. R
Ohio State Rep.
b. Laura, Ohio, 12/7/22; s. Elmer Netzley and Mary Ingle N; m. 7/28/44 to Marjorie Lyons; c. Kathleen, Carol Anne and Robert. Educ: Miami Univ, B.S. in bus, 47; Phi Kappa Tau. Polit. & Govt. Pos: Pres, Miami Co. Young Rep. Club, Ohio, 52-54; chmn, Miami Co. Rep. Cent. and Exec. Cmts, 58-; Ohio State Rep, Seventh Dist, 61- Bus. & Prof. Pos: Secy-treas. and part owner, Netzley Oil Co, 47-; v.pres, Romale Inc, 61- Mil. Serv: Entered as A/S, Navy, 42, released as Ens, 46, after serv. in Okinawa and Pac, 45; Purple Heart; Am. & Pac. Theaters. Mem: Am. Legion; VFW; Miami Co. Heart Coun; Grange; Laura Lions; West Milton C. of C; Bradford C. of C; Farm Bur; Tuberc. & Health Asn. of Miami Co. Rel: United Church of Christ Mailing Add: 2750 Pemberton Rd, Laura, Ohio 45337.

NEU, ARTHUR ALAN R
Iowa State Sen.
b. Carroll, Iowa, 2/9/33; s. Arthur Nicholas Neu and Martha Margaret Frandsen N; m. 4/4/64 to Mary Naomi Bedwell; c. Arthur Eric and Mary Martha. Educ: Wentworth Mil. Acad, 50-52; Northwest. Univ, B.S. in Bus. Admin, 55; Northwest. Univ. Sch. Law, J.D, 58; Georgetown Univ. Sch. Law, LL.M. in Taxation, 60; Acacia. Polit. & Govt. Pos: Iowa State Sen, 67- Mil. Serv: Entered as 1st Lt, Army, 58, released as Capt, 62, after serv. in Judge Adv. Gen. Corps, Mil. Dist, Wash. Mem: Various cmts, Iowa Bar Asn; Am. Bar Asn; Rotary; Am. Field Serv. Selected to attend Eagleton Inst. of Polit, Miami, Fla, 68. Rel: Presbyterian. Legal Res: 801 N. Adams St, Carroll, Iowa 51401. Mailing Add: 721 N. Main St, Carroll, Iowa 51401.

NEUBERGER, KATHERINE R
Mem. Exec. Cmt, N.J. Rep. Nat. Cmt.
b. New York, N.Y, 4/30/07; d. Samuel Kridel and Elsie Wallach K; m. 3/7/29 to Harry H. Neuberger; c. Susan (Mrs. Donald M. Wilson), Joan (Mrs. Henry M. Woodhouse). Educ: Barnard Col, B.A, 27; postgrad, Columbia, 32-33. Polit. & Govt. Pos: Mem. bd, Monmouth Co. Orgn. Soc. Serv, 37-59; mem, Rep. Nat. Cmt. for N.J; mem. v.pres. and bd. mgrs, N.J. Reformatory for Women, 40-57; mem, N.J. Law Enforcement Coun, 52-57, chmn, 54-57; del-at-lg, Rep. Nat. Conv, 60 & 64, alternate del-at-lg, 68; mem, N.J. Rep. Nat. Cmt, 61-, mem. exec. cmt, 69- Mem: Am. Asn. Univ. Women; Cosmopolitan Club (N.Y.C); mem. bd, Family Serv. Soc, Monmouth Co, 59-; Nat. Fedn. Rep. Women (mem. exec. bd, 59-61); N.J. Fedn. Rep. Women (pres, 57-61); chmn, Home Serv. Corps, Monmouth Co. Chap. A.R.C, 40-46; trustee, Montclair State Col, 67- Rel: Episcopal. Mailing Add: 628 Middletown Lincroft Rd, Lincroft, N.J. 07738.

NEUBERGER, MAURINE BROWN D
b. Cloverdale, Tillamook Co, Ore; m. 7/11/64 to Dr. Philip Solomon. Educ: Ore. Col. of Educ, Monmouth; Univ. of Ore; Univ. of Calif, Los Angeles. Polit. & Govt. Pos: Ore. State Rep, 51-55; mem. bd. dirs, Am. Asn. for UN; mem, President's Cmn. on Status of Women; U.S. Sen, Ore, 60-66. Bus. & Prof. Pos: Teacher in pub. schs. of Milton-Freewater, Newberg and Portland, Ore; writer and photographer. Rel: Unitarian. Legal Res: 1910 S.W. Clifton St, Portland, Ore. 92702. Mailing Add: 2475 Virginia Ave, Washington, D.C. 20037. (1967)

NEUHAUS, RICHARD JOHN D
Mem. Admin. Cmt, N.Y. State New Dem. Coalition
b. Pembroke, Ont, Can, 5/14/36; s. Clemens Henry Neuhaus and Ella Prange N; single. Educ: Concordia Col, B.A, 55; Concordia Theol. Sem, B.D, 60; Wash. Univ, 57-60; Wayne State Univ, summer, 58. Polit. & Govt. Pos: Chmn, Commun. Dist. Planning Bd, Brooklyn, N.Y, 64-66, Williamsburg Commun. Progress Center, 65-66 and Brooklyn Dem. Renewal, 67-68; del, Dem. Nat. Conv, 68; mem. steering cmt, Kings Co. Dem. Renewal, N.Y, 68-; mem. admin. cmt, N.Y. State New Dem. Coalition, 68- Bus. & Prof. Pos: Pastor, St. Paul's Lutheran Church, Massena, N.Y, 60-61 and Church of St. John Evangelist, Brooklyn, 61-; ed, Una Sancta, N.Y.C, 64-; assoc. ed, Worship Mag, Collegeville, Minn, 67- Publ: The Politics of the Future, Macmillan, fall 69; Theology and the Kingdom of God, Westminster, 69; 'Super-General Hershey,' Commonweal, 1/68; plus others. Mem: Nat. Cmt. for Sane Nuclear Policy (mem. exec. cmt, N.Y. Orgn, 67-); chmn, Lutheran Human Rels. Asn, 62-65; chmn, Clergy and Laymen Concerned about Vietnam, 64-; Dept. of Int. Affairs; Nat. Coun. of Churches; Nat. Liturgical Conf. Cath. Press Award, 68. Rel: Lutheran. Mailing Add: 195 Maujer St, Brooklyn, N.Y. 11206.

NEUMAN, JEROLD JOE R
Chmn, Trinity Co. Rep. Cent. Cmt, Calif.
b. Oelwein, Iowa, 3/11/31; s. Emil William Neuman and Nancy Dudley N; m. 4/12/52 to Barbara Anne Huddleson; c. Jerold Joe, Jr, Michael Aaron, Rachelle Anne, Renee Aline and Kenneth Eugene. Educ: West. Baptist Bible Col, B.A, 57; Calif. State Col, 59-60; San Jose State Col, 64; Univ. Calif, Berkeley, 65; Chico State Col, 65, 66 & 69; Humboldt State Col, 66-67. Polit. & Govt. Pos: Mem, Trinity Co. Rep. Cent. Cmt, Calif, 66- and chmn, 69-; mem, Calif. Rep. State Cent. Cmt, 69- Bus. & Prof. Pos: Pastor, Commun. Church, Friant, Calif, 57-59; mgr. of paint stores, San Francisco, Oakland, San Jose and Hayward, Calif, 59-63; teacher, Ruth Sch, Ruth, Calif, 63-64; teacher-prin, Hoaglin-Zenia Sch, Zenia, Calif, 64-67 and Coffee Creek Sch, Trinity Center, Calif, 67- Mil. Serv: Entered as SR, Navy, 58, released as CS 3, 52, after serv. in China and Korean War. Mem: Calif. and Trinity Co. Teacher's Asns; Nat. Educ. Asn. Rel: Baptist. Legal Res: Minnehaha Creek, Trinity Center, Calif. 96091. Mailing Add: Coffee Creek School, Trinity Center, Calif. 96091.

NEUMANN, FREDERICK SLOAN R
b. Dallas, Tex, 3/7/13; s. Ernest Neumann and Mary Sloan N; m. 12/27/37 to Gertrude Shoemaker; c. Madelyn (Mrs. J.L. Harden) and Frederick Sloan, Jr. Educ: Lamar Jr. Col, 33-35. Polit. & Govt. Pos: Chmn, Jefferson Co. Rep. Exec. Cmt, Tex, 56-60; del, Rep. Nat. Conv, 60 & 64; committeeman, Second Dist, Tex. State Rep. Exec. Cmt, 60-62; mem, Tex. State Hq. Rep. Cmt, 62-68; dir, Lubbock Regional Off. of the Small Bus. Admin, 69- Bus. & Prof. Pos: Gen. mgr, Barge Transport Corp, 38-42; v.pres. and gen. mgr, Harms Marine Serv, Inc, 46-50; gen. mgr. and pres, Neu-Way Rug Cleaners, Inc, 50-69. Mil. Serv: Entered as Seaman, Maritime Serv, 42, released as Lt, 45; Atlantic and Pac. Theater Ribbons. Mem: Rotary; U.S. C. of C; Beaumont Club; Young Men's Bus. League. Rel: Episcopal. Legal Res: 6711B Hartford, Lubbock, Tex. 79413. Mailing Add: P.O. Box 10107, Lubbock, Tex. 79408.

NEUMANN, ROBERT G. R
U.S. Ambassador to Afghanistan
b. Vienna, Austria, 1/2/16; m. to Marlen Eldredge; c. Ronald E. and Gregory W. Educ: Univ. of Rennes, Diplome Superieur, 36; Geneva Sch. Int. Studies, 37; Univ. Vienna, 38; Amherst Col, M.A, 40; Univ. Minn, Shevlin Fel, 39-40, Ph.D, 46; Haynes Found. Fel, 50-51; Soc. Studies Research Coun. Fel, 50-51; Fulbright Fel, France, 54-55. Polit. & Govt. Pos: Adv, Secy. to Defense, Int. Security Affairs, Am. Del, NATO Ministerial Conf, Paris, 62; U.S. Ambassador to Afghanistan, 66- Bus. & Prof. Pos: Instr, State Teachers Col, Oshkosh, Wis, 41-43; lectr, Univ. Wis, 46-47; prof, Univ. Calif, Los Angeles, 57-69, dir, Inst. Int. and For. Studies, 59-66; ed. writer, Los Angeles Times, 52-59; chmn, Int. Rels. Sect, Town Hall, 56-62; dir, Am. Seminar in Polit. Econ. and Soc. Sci, Nice, France, 57. Mil. Serv: Army, 42-46. Publ: European and Comparative Government, 68, 4th ed; plus articles. Hon. medal, Univ. Brussels, 55; Legion of Honor, France, 57; Officers Cross, Order of Merit, Fed. Repub. of Germany, 63. Legal Res: 611 Moreno Ave, Los Angeles, Calif. Mailing Add: U.S. Embassy, Kabul, Afghanistan.

NEUNHERZ, LISE JUNGSHOVED R
Rep. State Committeewoman, Mass.
b. Copenhagen, Denmark, 4/29/37; d. Kaj Einar Jungshoved and Gerda Nielsine Schmidt J; div; c. Monika. Educ: Walnut Hills Sch, Cincinnati, Ohio, 53-56; Newton-Wellesley Hosp. Sch. of Nursing, Mass, R.N, 59. Polit. & Govt. Pos: Secy, Third Worcester Sen. Rep. Orgn, Mass, 62-66 and v.chmn, 66-; v.chmn, Westminster Rep. Town Cmt, 62-68; del, Rep. State Conv, 64, 66 & 68; chmn. legis. activities cmt, Fitchburgh Women's Rep. Club, 66-68; Rep. State Committeewoman, 66-; del. and secy. Mass. del, Rep. Nat. Conv, 68. Mem: Newton-Wellesley Hosp. Sch. of Nursing Alumni Asn. Rel: Protestant. Legal Res: 26 Nichols St, Westminster, Mass. 01473. Mailing Add: Box 294, Westminster, Mass. 01473.

NEVILLE, WILLIAM VINKLEY, JR. D
Ala. State Rep.
b. Montgomery, Ala, 7/23/34; s. William Vinkley Neville and Mildred Greene N; m. 4/8/61 to Anna Gisladottir; c. William Vinkley, III and Margaret Gudrun. Educ: Auburn Univ, B.S, 56; Univ. Va, LL.B, 59; Phi Kappa Phi; Omicron Delta Kappa; Scabbard and Blade; Arnold Air Soc; Delta Sigma Pi; Phi Eta Sigma; Pi Kappa Alpha. Polit. & Govt. Pos: Mem. and secy, Eufaula City Dem. Exec. Cmt, Ala, 64-; Ala. State Rep, 67- Bus. & Prof. Pos: Attorney-at-Law, 62- Mil. Serv: Entered as 2nd Lt, Air Force, 59, released as 1st Lt, 61, after serv. in Off. of Staff Judge Adv, 4238th Combat Support Group, Barksdale Air Force Base, La; Capt, Air Force Res; Air Defense Command Commendation Cert. Mem: Am, Ala. and Barbour Co. Bar Asns; Am. Trial Lawyers Asn; Rotary; Eufaula Heritage Asn; Eufaula Art Asn. Rel: Methodist. Legal Res: W. Broad St, Eufaula, Ala. 36027. Mailing Add: P.O. Box 239, Eufaula, Ala. 36027.

NEVILLS, WILLIE L. R
Mem, Bd. of Supvr, St. Clair Co, Ill.
b. Scooba, Miss, 5/28/14; s. Henry Nevills and Callie Nave N; div; c. Dellar (Mrs. Robert L. Murphy) and Antoinette (Mrs. James Davis). Polit. & Govt. Pos: Chmn, East St. Louis Rep. Party, Ill, currently; mem, bd. of Supvr, St. Clair Co, currently. Mil. Serv: T/5, Army, 41-45, with serv. in 184 Qm, S.Pac. Theatre; Five Serv. Medals. Rel: Protestant. Mailing Add: 1432 Market Ave, East St. Louis, Ill. 62201.

NEVINS, RICHARD D
Mem, Calif. State Bd. of Equalization
b. Los Angeles, Calif, 4/21/21; s. Richard Nevins and Katharine Tilt N; m. 5/16/46 to Mary Lois Minton; c. Richard, Jr, William McCay and Henry Minton. Educ: Yale Univ, A.B, 42. Polit. & Govt. Pos: Southern chmn, Calif. Fedn. Young Dem, 54-56, pres, 56-58; mem, Los Angeles Co. Dem. Cent. Cmt, 54-58; mem, Calif. State Dem. Cent. Cmt, 54-; del, Dem. Nat. Conv, 56, 60 & 64; mem, Calif. State Bd. Equalization, Fourth Dist, 59- Bus. & Prof. Pos: Ins. Solicitor, Marsh & McLennan, 46-58. Mil. Serv: Entered as Pvt, Army, 43, released as Cpl, 46, after serv. in Weather Serv, Air Force, U.S. Mem: Los Angeles, Metrop. Chap. Am. Soc. for Pub. Admin, Los Angeles Urban League; Pasadena Chapter NAACP. Rel: Episcopal. Mailing Add: 561 Bradford St, Pasadena, Calif. 91105.

NEW, HARRY E. R
b. Greenville, S.C, 10/8/13; s. Adolph G. New and Maude Ellen Worley N; m. 1/12/41 to Geraldine Hall; c. Mary Elizabeth (Mrs. Gill), Harry E, Jr. and William G. Educ: Clemson Univ, B.S, 35. Polit. & Govt. Pos: Rep. precinct chmn, Hidenwood, Va, 64-68; chmn, Newport News Rep. Party, 68-69; precinct chmn, City Rep. Cmt, 69- Bus. & Prof. Pos: Mgr, tech. sales serv, Chemstrand Corp, 53-56; supvr, Dow Badische Co, Williamsburg, Va, 57- Mil. Serv: Entered as 1st Lt, Army, 42, released as Maj, 46, after serv. in Shaef, European Theatre, 45-46; Army Res. Mem: Phi Psi; Textile Quality Asn; A&FM; Gideon Int; Int. Order of St. Luke. Rel: Methodist. Mailing Add: 118 Crittenden Lane, Newport News, Va. 23606.

NEW, JACK L. D
m. to Corrinne; c. Four. Educ: Ind. Univ, 48. Polit. & Govt. Pos: Research dir, Ind. Dem. State Cent. Cmt, 48-51; dep. dir. and acting dir, Ind. Off. of Price Stabilization, 51-53; mem, Hancock Co. Coun, 59-60; exec. secy. to Gov. Matthew E. Welsh throughout Mr. Welsh's term; treas, State of Ind, 65-66. Bus. & Prof. Pos: Operator, off. furniture bus, 53- Rel: Methodist. Mailing Add: P.O. Box 73, Greenfield, Ind. 46140.

NEW, JAMES GRANT R
b. Thomaston, Ga, 6/9/37; s. William LaFayette New and Minnie Lee Grant N; single. Educ: Ga. Inst. Tech, 56-58; Middle Ga. Col, 58-60; Univ. Ga, 60. Polit. & Govt. Pos: Ninth Dist. chmn, Goldwater Campaign, Ga, 64; chmn, Jackson Co. Rep. Party, 64-68; treas, Ninth Dist. Rep. Party, 64- Bus. & Prof. Pos: V.pres. and gen. mgr, Commerce Tel. Co, Inc, 60- Mil. Serv: Entered as Airman, Air Nat. Guard, 60, released as Airman 1/C, 66, after serv. in 116th Mil. Air Transport Serv, Ga. Mem: Ga. Tel. Asn; U.S. Independent Tel. Asn; Jr. C. of C; Am. Legion; Commerce and Ga. C. of C. Rel: Episcopal. Mailing Add: 208 S. Elm St, Commerce, Ga. 30529. (1967)

NEW, WILLIAM MADISON R
b. Washington, Ga, 3/9/26; s. Arlie Mobley New, Sr. and Caroline Ellington N; m. 8/12/46 to Anne Gilmore; c. Dianne, Caroline, Patricia, Nedra, Mary Jo and Virginia Lee. Educ: West Georgia Col; North Carolina State and Univ. of Göttengen. Polit. & Govt. Pos: Secy, Dist. Rep. Party, Ga, 64; alternate del, Rep. Nat. Conv, 64; mem, Ga. State Rep. Cent. Cmt, 64-66; chmn, Bd. Educ, 65-66. Bus. & Prof. Pos: Pres. and gen. mgr, Thomaston Tel. Co, 63-; dir, Bank of Upson, 65-; pres, Ga. Tel. Asn, 66-67. Mil. Serv: Entered as Pvt, Army, 44, released as Sgt, 46, after serv. in 309 Inf, ETO; Combat Inf. Badge; various campaign ribbons. Mem: VFW; Elks; Moose; Scottish Rite Mason; York Rite Mason; Shrine; Kiwanis; past master, Blue Lodge. Rel: Presbyterian. Legal Res: 108 Dianne Dr, Thomaston, Ga. 30286. Mailing Add: Box 845, Thomaston, Ga. 30286.

NEWBERGER, SHEL D
b. Chicago, Ill, 11/30/25; s. Oscar Newberger and Fannie Grodsky N; m. 10/22/46 to Natalie Bernard; c. Steven Oscar, Richard Bernard, David Eli and Jill Helen. Educ: Univ. Chicago, B.A, 44. Polit. & Govt. Pos: Exec. dir, Bowles for Pres. Cmt, 60; v.pres, Evanston Regular Dem. Orgn, 60-61; Evanston Twp. Dem. Committeeman, Ill, 61-66; alderman, Ninth Ward, Evanston, 67- Bus. & Prof. Pos: Pres, Apollo Containers Inc, 64- Rel: Jewish. Mailing Add: 1800 Cleveland St, Evanston, Ill. 60202.

NEWBERRY, JAMES H. D
b. 1918. Educ: West. Ky. Univ, B.S. Polit. & Govt. Pos: Ky. State Rep, 58-60; Ky. State Sen, 64-66; chmn, Educ. Cmt, 66. Bus. & Prof. Pos: Rep, Dairy Equip Co; dairy farmer. Mem: Ky. Farm Bur; C. of C; Hiseville Baptist Church Brotherhood (pres); charter mem, Hiseville Lions Club (past dir. and v.pres); Dist. Lions Club (former zone chmn. and dep. gov). Rel: Baptist. Mailing Add: Hiseville, Ky. 42152. (1967)

NEWBURY, GEORGE A. D
R.I. State Rep.
b. Newport, R.I, 7/6/39; s. George Edward Newbury and Helen Shea N; m. 5/15/65 to Janet Kerrigan; c. Christopher and Jennifer. Educ: Univ. San Francisco, A.B, 61 and M.A, 63. Polit. & Govt. Pos: R.I. State Rep, 66-, chmn, spec. legis. cmn. studying state scholarship prog, R.I. House Rep, currently. Bus. & Prof. Pos: Stock Broker, G.H. Walker & Co, 67- Mem: Irish-Am. Athletic Asn; Hibernians; K. of C. Rel: Roman Catholic. Mailing Add: 9 Hammond St, Newport, R.I. 02840.

NEWCOME, THOMAS W. Non-Partisan
Minn. State Rep.
b. St. Paul, Minn, 1923; married; c. Six. Educ: Univ. Minn, B.S.L; St. Paul Col. of Law, LL.B. Polit. & Govt. Pos: Former mem, Sch. Bd. Dist. 832, Mahtomedi, Minn; former Ramsey Co. Pub. Defender, 57-59; spec. munic. judge, White Bear Lake, 59-61, mayor, 61-63; Minn. State Rep, 64- Bus. & Prof. Pos: Lawyer. Mil. Serv: Army, Inf, 42-46 & 50-52. Mem: Minn. and Ramsey Co. Bar Asns; Am. Legion; VFW; Lions. Mailing Add: 2374 Joy Ave, White Bear Lake, Minn. 55110.

NEWELL, GRAHAM STILES R
Vt. State Rep.
b. St. Johnsbury, Vt, 11/27/15; s. George Graham Newell and Maud Berry N; single. Educ: Univ. Chicago, A.B, 38, A.M, 49. Polit. & Govt. Pos: Mem, Vt. Cmn. on Interstate Coop, 53-; Vt. State Sen, 55-65; mem. bd. of mgrs, Coun. State Govts, 57-65; mem, Adv. Cmn. on Intergovt. Rels, 62-64; mem, New Eng. Bd. of Higher Educ, 58-64; Vt. State Rep, 53-55 & 67- Bus. & Prof. Pos: Latin Instr, St. Johnsbury Acad, Vt, 38-47; assoc. prof, Lyndon State Col, 59-64, chmn. dept. Soc. Sci, 59-, prof, 64- Publ: Ed, 1966 Vermont Almanac and Government Guide, Vt. Rep. State Cmt. Mem: Pres, Vt. Hist. Soc, 65-; Classical Asn. of New Eng; Am. Hist. Asn; Am. Asn. Univ. Profs; dir. Vt. chap, Am. Civil Liberties Union; dir, Vt. Coun. on World Affairs. Alumni Citation for Pub. Serv, Univ. Chicago, 61. Rel: Congregational. Mailing Add: 8 Park St, St. Johnsbury, Vt. 05819.

NEWELL, HENRY CHASE R
N.H. State Rep.
b. Derry, N.H, 6/30/08; s. Charles Edward Newell and Harriett Chase N; m. 2/12/36 to Catherine Parmenter; c. David P. and Jean N. (Mrs. Hunneyman). Educ: Dartmouth Col, A.B, 30. Polit. & Govt. Pos: Draftsman and designer, N.H. Hwy Dept, 35-37 & 38-39; archit. designer, N.H. Tramway Cmn, 37-38; N.H. State Rep, 59-63 & 67- Bus. & Prof. Pos: Struct. designer, Stone & Webster Eng. Corp, 40-41; architect and engr, N.H, 45-; ed, N.H. Engineering, 52-54. Mem: Am. Soc. Civil Engrs; N.H. and Nat. Soc. Prfnl. Engrs; Mason. Rel: Congregational. Mailing Add: 166 School, Concord, N.H. 03301.

NEWHALL, DAVID, III R
b. Philadelphia, Pa, 12/6/37; s. David Newhall, Jr. and Jane Martyn Dunn N; single. Educ: Princeton Univ, A.B, 61; treas, Princeton Tower Club. Polit. & Govt. Pos: Admin. asst. to Richard S. Schweiker, U.S. Rep, Pa, 63-69, now U.S. Sen, 69-; campaign asst. to Gov. William W. Scranton, Rep. Presidential Campaign, 64. Bus. & Prof. Pos: Reporter, Phila. Eve. Bul, summers 55-57 & 60, full time, 58-59; mgr, Bell Tel. Co, Pa, 61-63. Mem: Princeton Club of Wash, D.C; bd. gov, Princeton Tower Club. Rel: Protestant. Legal Res: 411 Washington Lane, Ft. Washington, Pa. 15301. Mailing Add: 521 Seventh St. S.E. Washinton, D.C. 20003.

NEWHOUSE, GERALD FRANCIS R
Chmn, Alpena Co. Rep. Party, Mich.
b. Alpena, Mich, 11/27/40; s. Clarence John Newhouse and Frances Ranis-zewski N; m. 8/10/68 to Kathryn Mae Beemer. Educ: Alpena Commun. Col, Assoc. Polit. Sci. Polit. & Govt. Pos: Supvr, Alpena Co, Mich, 68-; chmn, Alpena Co. Rep. Party, 69- Mem: Nat. Barbers Asn; Mich. Asn. of Supvr; K. of C.(3rd° and 4th°, pres, Credit Union, 68-70); Local 237 AFL-CIO; Alpena Jaycees (past state v.pres. Mich, 66-68); A-Club; C. of C. Rel: Roman Catholic. Legal Res: 1203 S. Fourth St, Alpena, Mich. 49707. Mailing Add: Route 3, Alpena, Mich. 49707.

NEWHOUSE, IRVING R
Wash. State Rep.
b. Mabton, Wash, 10/16/20; s. John Newhouse and Tina Bos N; m. 7/14/45 to Ruth Gardner; c. Joyce (Mrs. Darrel Downing), James, Linda, Laura, Daniel and Dorothy. Educ: Wash. State Univ, B.S, 43; Alpha Zeta; Mu Beta Beta; Alpha Gamma Rho. Polit. & Govt. Pos: Wash. State Rep, Dist. 8A, 65- Bus. & Prof. Pos: Pres, Yakima Co. Cattlemen, 55-57; pres, Wash. Beef Coun, 58-59; pres, Yakima Co. Farm Bur, 60-63; dir, Sunnyside Valley Irrigation Dist, 62-; dir, Sunnyside C. of C, 66-; dir, Valley Mem. Hosp, 67- Mil. Serv: Entered as A/S, Naval ROTC, 43, released as Lt.(jg), 46, after serv. in Landing Ship, Tanks, Pac, 43-45. Mem: Elks; Farm Bur; Wash. Cattlemans Asn; Hop Growers of Am. Rel: Christian Reformed. Mailing Add: Route 1, Box 130, Mabton, Wash. 98935.

NEWKIRK, ROSA H. D
b. Richmond, Va, 12/1/28; d. Charles Taylor Henderson and Emma Overton H; m. 3/19/48 to Kermit Liston Newkirk, Sr; c. Kermit Liston, Jr, Charles Henderson and Bruce Howard. Educ: Commun. Col. Philadelphia, 67. Polit. & Govt. Pos: Committeewoman, Dem. Party, Pa, 60-; acct. clerk, Orphan's Div. Common Plea Court, 61-; mem. bd. gov, Dem. Women's Club, 62-68; alternate del, Dem. Nat. Conv, 68; treas, Concerned Women for Humphrey, 68; financial secy, Dem. Women's Forum, 69. Bus. & Prof. Pos: Pres, Home and Sch. Asn. Kearny Sch, 62-64 and North. Liberty Fed. Credit Union, 66- Mem: Friend Neighborhood Guild (asst. secy. bd); St. Paul Baptist Human Relation Cmt.(chmn. housing); Penn Town Homes Improv. Cmt. (pres); Philadelphia Cmt. to Aid Biafra Children (co-chmn); educ. chmn, Hub 1, Model City Program. Citation from Human Relation Cmn. and Home and Sch. Asn. Rel: Baptist. Mailing Add: 674 Franklin Place, Apt. E, Philadelphia, Pa. 19123.

NEWLIN, WILBUR E. R
b. Mooresville, Ind, 2/19/15; s. Elgar A. Newlin and Martha Ann Welborn N; m. 5/5/40 to Kathryn Harris; c. Teresa Elizabeth (Mrs. Sherow) and Harris E. Educ: Earlham Col, 35-36. Polit. & Govt. Pos: Cmnr, Hendricks Co, Ind, 56-64; Ind. State Sen, 65-68. Mem: Mason. Rel: Friends. Mailing Add: R.R. 2, Box 35, Mooresville, Ind. 46158. (1967)

NEWMAN, BOBBY GENE D
Ark. State Rep.
b. El Dorado, Ark, 10/1/26; s. Benton Albert Newman and Mary Roan N; m. 11/23/51 to Mary Elizabeth Raper; c. Brad Kevin and Elizabeth Lacye. Educ: Ouachita Baptist Univ, B.A, 50; Univ. Tex, Austin, 50-51; Univ. Ark, Fayetteville, M.S, 51. Polit. & Govt. Pos: Justice of Peace, Smackover, Ark, 65-68; Ark. State Rep, 69- Bus. & Prof. Pos: Mgr. and v.pres, Smackover Ins. Agency, 60-; mem. exec. cmt, Ark. Asn. Ins. Agents, 66-67. Mil. Serv: A/S, Navy, 44 released as F 1/C, 46, after serv. South Pacific, 45-46. Mem: Lions; Am. Legion. Rel: Baptist. Legal Res: 606 E. 12th, Smackover, Ark. 71762. Mailing Add: Box 52, Smackover, Ark. 71762.

NEWMAN, CLARENCE BENTON 'BUDDIE' D
Miss. State Rep.
b. Valley Park, Miss, 5/8/21; married. Polit. & Govt. Pos: Miss. State Sen, 48-52; Miss. State Rep, 52-, mem. and chmn, House Ways and Means Cmt, mem, Legis. Recess Study Cmt. and House Rules Cmt, Miss. House of Rep; mem, State Agr. and Industrial Bd, State Cmn. of Budget and Accounting, and past chmn, South. Coun. State Govt. Bus. & Prof. Pos: Farmer. Mem: Am. Legion; 40 et 8; VFW; Delta Coun; Miss. Mfg. Asn; Miss. Cattlemen's Asn; Assoc, C. of C. Exec; Pub. Rels. Assoc. of Miss; bd. dirs, Rivers and Harbors Asn. of Miss, Miss-Ala. Div. of Mid-Continent Oil & Gas Asn, and Issaquena Co. Farm Bur; past dir, Miss. Econ. Coun, State Farm Bur, State C. of C. and Miss. Div, Am. Cancer Soc. Rel: Baptist; Mem. Bd. of Deacons, Valley Park Baptist Church. Mailing Add: Box 200, Valley Park, Miss. 39177.

NEWMAN, CYNTHIA STAIR R
Rep. Nat. Committeewoman, Va.
b. Minneapolis, Minn, 3/24/22; d. John Stewart Dalrymple and Bernice Barber D; m. 5/16/58 to Carson Boru Newman, wid; c. Robert Hamill, Nancy Stair and Pamela Barber Zimmerman and Tracy Stewart and Christopher Carson Newman. Educ: Smith Col, 39-42; Univ. Va. Law Sch, LL.B, 44. Polit. & Govt. Pos: V.chmn, Va. State Rep. Party, 52-56 & 62-68, finance chmn 59-62; Rep. Nat. Committeewoman, 56-58 & 68-; del, Rep. Nat. Conv, 68. Bus. & Prof. Pos: Attorney, UNRRA, 44-45; nat. dir, Rep. Open Forums, 46-48; asst. to chmn, Rep. Sen. Cmt, 48-50; pres, Waters Travel Serv, 63-66. Mem: Am. and Va. Bar Asns; Am. Soc. Travel Agents; Soroptimists; bd. dirs, Metrop. Wash. YWCA. Rel: Unitarian. Mailing Add: 3535 Half Moon Circle, Falls Church, Va. 22044.

NEWMAN, DAN L. D
Secy, Mont. State Dem. Party
b. Butte, Mont, 5/16/37; s. Dave Newman and Elve A. Lundgren N; m. 8/17/57 to Dianna Mack; c. Bradley, Lance and Dava Jean. Educ: West. Mont. Col, B.S; Humbolt State Col; Carroll Col. Polit. & Govt. Pos: Finance chmn, Mont. State Dem. Cent. Cmt, 64-; chmn, Lewis & Clark Co. Dem. Cent. Cmt, 66-; mem. exec. bd, Mont. State Dem. Party, 67-, secy, Mont. State Dem. Party, 69-; asst, U.S. Rep. Arnold Olson, 68- Bus. & Prof. Pos: Teacher, 57-60; owner, Newman and Assocs, 60-68. Mem: Mont. and Int. Pilots Asns. Rel: Catholic. Legal Res: 1423 Stuart St, Helena, Mont. 59601. Mailing Add: 347 N. Last Chance Gulch, Helena, Mont. 59601.

NEWMAN, HAGGARD WRIGHT D
b. Hendersonville, Tenn, 9/6/14; s. John Franklin Newman and Mary F. Carter N; m. 7/23/37 to Gradie Leigh Hollaman. Educ: Gallatin High Sch, 2 years; Falls Bus. Col, Nashville, 1 year. Polit. & Govt. Pos: Del, Dem. Nat. Conv, 68. Bus. & Prof. Pos: Bookkeeper, Old Hickory Coal & Ice Co, 35-39; mgr, Jackson Ice & Coal Co, Tenn, 39-43 & 46-47; asst. mgr, Indust. Ice Co, Mobile, Ala, 47-49; pres, J.F. Newman & Son Inc, Hendersonville, Tenn, 49-, Newman Trucking Co, currently; v.pres, Newman & Freels Garden Center, currently; secy-treas, Newman & Hayes Ins. Co, 63- Mil. Serv: Entered as Pvt, Army, 43, released as S/Sgt, 46, after serv. in 44th Armed Inf-Sixth Armored Div, European Theatre, 44-46; Bronze Star; Purple Heart with 2 clusters; Good Conduct Medal; Presidential Citation; Combat Inf. Badge; French Citation. Mem: Grad. feeder adv, Ralston-Purina Co, St. Louis, Mo; VFW Post 9851; Am. Legion Post 105; DAV; Mason; Hendersonville Civic Club. Hon. Col, Gov. Staff, State of Tenn. Rel: Methodist. Legal Res: 1110 Saunders Ave, Madison, Tenn. 37115. Mailing Add: P.O. Box 6, Hendersonville, Tenn. 37075.

NEWMAN, JEFFREY PAUL D
b. Los Angeles, Calif, 9/21/42; s. Robert Ross Newman and Rose Stein N; m. 1/31/64 to Ellen Gottlieb; c. Lisa Michele and Matthew Aaron. Educ: Stanford Univ, A.B, 63; Univ. Calif, Berkeley, LL.B, 66; George Wash. Univ, 66-68; Phi Beta Kappa; Theta Delta Chi. Polit. & Govt. Pos: Attorney, U.S. Off. Econ. Opportunity, Wash, D.C, 66-67; admin. asst. to U.S. Rep. Jeffery Cohelan, 67- Bus. & Prof. Pos: Financial analyst, Trans World Airlines, N.Y.C, 63 and Munsingwear Inc, Minneapolis, Minn, 65. Mem: Am. Bar Asn; Order of the Coif. Rel: Jewish. Legal Res: 10558 Camarillo St, North Hollywood, Calif. 91602. Mailing Add: 123 Seventh St. S.E, Washington, D.C. 20003.

NEWMAN, MARY B. R
Mass. State Rep.
b. Philadelphia, Pa, 2/15/09; d. Worrall E. S. Temple and Florence May T; m. 3/30/38 to Edwin B. Newman. Educ: Swarthmore Col, Pa; Phi Beta Kappa; Am. Asn. Univ. Women. Polit. & Govt. Pos: V.pres, Mass. Fedn. Women's Rep. Orgn; Mass. State Rep, 53-54 & 57-; mem. pub. welfare adv. cmt, Mass. Dept. Pub. Welfare, 55-56; mem, Mass. Parole Bd, 55-57; co-chmn, Rep. State Platform Cmt, 66; del, Dem. Nat. Conv, 68. Bus. & Prof. Pos: Secy. and asst. to the Comptroller, Swarthmore Col, 31-41; mem. exec. staff, Am. Friends Serv. Cmt, 41-46. Mem: League of Women Voters; YWCA; Cambridge Civic Asn; NAACP; Urban League; Mass. Coun. of Churches Bd; Alliance of Cambridge Settlements Bd; Cambridge Commun. Center Bd; Cambridge Boat Club; Porsche Club of Am; Bus. & Prfnl. Women's Club; U.C.S. Budget Cmts; Bd. Mgrs, Swarthmore Col. Contributor, Tufts Assembly on Mass. Legis; 1st ed, League of Women Voters, 'Mass. State Government-A Citizen's Handbook,' Harvard Press, 53. Rel: Society of Friends. Mailing Add: 5 Willard St, Cambridge, Mass. 02138. (1967)

NEWMAN, THEODORE ROOSEVELT, JR. R
Mem, D.C. Rep. Cmt.
b. Birmingham, Ala, 7/5/34; s. Theodore R. Newman and Ruth Oliver N; m. 7/25/59 to Constance Berry. Educ: Brown Univ, A.B, 55; Harvard Law Sch, LL.B, 58; Kappa Alpha Psi. Polit. & Govt. Pos: Attorney, U.S. Dept. Justice, Wash, D.C, 61-62; mem, D.C. Rep. Cmt, 68- Mil. Serv: Entered as 1st Lt, Air Force, 58, released as 1st Lt, 61, after serv. in 66th Tactical Reconnaissance Wing, Europe, 58-61. Mem: Am. and D.C. Bar Asns; Asn. Trial Attorneys; Am. Judicature Soc. Rel: Unitarian. Mailing Add: 7924 16th St. N.W, Washington, D.C. 20012.

NEWSCHWANDER, CHARLES E. R
Wash. State Sen.
b. Tacoma, Wash, 1920; m. to Emma N; c. four. Educ: Univ. Puget Sound; Univ. Ore. Dent. Sch. Polit. & Govt. Pos: Former Wash. State Rep; Wash. State Sen, currently. Bus. & Prof. Pos: Dentist. Mil. Serv: Navy, Korean Conflict. Mem: Lions; Mason. Mailing Add: 2140 Bridgeport Way, Tacoma, Wash. 98466. (1967)

NEWSOM, DAVID D.
Asst. Secy. of State for African Affairs
b. Richmond, Calif, 1/6/18; m. to Jean Craig N; c. John, Daniel, Nancy, Catherine and David. Educ: Univ. of Calif, Berkeley, B.A, 38; Columbia Univ, M.S, 40; Pulitzer traveling scholar, 40-41. Polit. & Govt. Pos: Third secy, Karachi, 47-50; career officer, U.S. Dept. of State For. Serv, 47-; second secy, Oslo, 50-51; second secy, Baghdad, 51-53; pub. affairs officer, U.S. Info. Agency and consul, Baghdad, 53-55; off. in charge, Arabian Peninsula Affairs, 55-58; Nat. War Col, 59-69; first secy, London, 60-62; dir, Off. of N.Africa Affairs, 63-65; U.S. Ambassador to Libya, 65-69; Asst. Secy. of State for African Affairs, 69- Bus. & Prof. Pos: Newspaper reporter, 38-41; newspaper publisher, 46-47. Mil. Serv: Navy, Lt, 42-46. Commendable Serv. Award, U.S. Info. Agency for Serv. in Iraq, 55; Meritorious Serv. Award, State Dept, 58. Legal Res: Berkeley, Calif. Mailing Add: Dept. of State, Washington, D.C. 20520.

NEWSOM, GEORGE EDWARD R
Mem, Polk Co. Rep. Exec. Cmt, Iowa
b. Berwick, Iowa, 8/31/19; s. John B. Newsom (deceased) and Alease S. Hankie N; m. 9/5/37 to Mercedes M. Zink. Educ: Des Moines Pub. Schs, 24-36. Polit. & Govt. Pos: Precinct committeeman, Polk Co. Rep. Party, Iowa, 66 & 69; mem, Polk Co. Rep. Cent. Cmt, 66 & 69; campaign mgr, William H. Huff for Iowa House Rep, 68; alternate del, Rep. Nat. Conv, 68; zone leader, 21 precincts, Polk Co, 68 & 69; mem, Polk Co. Rep. Exec.Cmt, 69- Bus. & Prof. Pos: Gen. contractor, 25 years. Mil. Serv: Entered as Pvt, Army, 43, released as Sgt, 46, after serv. in 690th Engr. Base Equip. Co, Pac. Theatre, 44-46; Am. Pac. Theatre Ribbon; Victory Ribbon; Good Conduct Medal; Presidential Unit Citation. Mem: AF&AM; Mason (32°); Shrine; Elks; U.S. Power Squadrons. Rep. Precinct Committeeman's Award, Polk Co. Iowa, 66. Rel: Presbyterian. Mailing Add: 7202 Oak Brook Dr, Urbandale, Iowa 50322.

NEWTH, THOMAS M. R
b. Methuen, Mass, 3/15/11; s. Asa T. Newth and Helen M. Burnham N; m. 6/22/35 to Constance M. Nicholas; c. Marilyn Louise (Mrs. Hale) and Ellen Marie. Educ: Okla. City Univ, 32; Suffolk Law Sch, Boston, LL.B, 36. Polit. & Govt. Pos: Mem, Rep. Town Cmt, Swampscott, Mass, 48-, town meeting mem, 48-64 and secy, Town Finance Cmt, 48-52; Mass. State Rep, Eighth Essex Dist, 53-68, minority whip, 65-68; clerk, Dist. Court of South Essex, 68; spec. justice, Dist. Court South Essex, 69- Bus. & Prof. Pos: Pres, Essex Co. Legis. Asn, 57-58, treas, 60-61. Mem: Am, Essex Co, Mass. and Lynn Bar Asns; Bench and Bar Golfing Soc; Mass. Rep. Club; Mass. Legis. Asn; Ionic Club of Swampscott (past treas); Swampscott Club; Mason; Upper Swampscott Improv. Asn.(past pres). Rel: Congregational. Legal Res: 4 Parsons Dr, Swampscott, Mass. 01907. Mailing Add: 31 Exchange St, Lynn, Mass. 01901.

NEWTON, BETTY MAE R
Chmn, Harper Co. Rep. Party, Kans.
b. Hays, Kans, 7/31/29; d. Patrick Coady and Sylvia Fink C; m. 6/5/50 to Bob H. Newton; c. Bob Bradley, David Scott and Lauri Ann. Educ: Kans. State Univ, 3 years; Kappa Delta. Polit. & Govt. Pos: Rep. precinct committeewoman, Harper Co, Kans, 66-; chmn, Harper Co. Rep. Party, 68- Rel: Episcopal. Mailing Add: 115 E. Spring, Anthony, Kans. 67003.

NEWTON, BLAKE TYLER D
Mem, Va. State Dem. Cent. Cmt.
b. Hague, Va, 10/21/89; s. Edward Calston Newton and Lucy Tyler N; m. 7/29/13 to Bertha Lawrence; c. Edward Calston, Blake Tyler, Jr. and Bertha Lawrence (Mrs. Davison). Educ: Col. of William and Mary, B.A, 10 and M.A, 41; Phi Beta Kappa; Pi Kappa Alpha. Polit. & Govt. Pos: Supt. schs, Westmoreland and Richmond Co, 13-54; mem, Va. State Bd. of Educ, 37-57, pres, 46-57; Va. State Sen, 56-66; mem, Westmoreland Co. Dem. Cmt. and Va. State Dem. Cmt, currently. Bus. & Prof. Pos: Counsel and dir, Farmers Bank of Hague, 20-66. Mem: Past Master, Masonic Lodge 212, Westmoreland: William & Mary Col. Alumni Soc; Va. State Bar; Va. State Bar Asn; Northern Neck of Va. Bar Asn; Va. and Nat. Educ. Asns; Northern Neck of Va. Hist. Soc. Rel: Episcopal; Vestryman, Cople Parish Episcopal Church, 13-66. Mailing Add: Hague, Va. 22469.

NEWTON, DAVID LANIER D
b. Norman Park, Ga, 4/07/14; s. G.W. Newton and Elizabeth Barber N; m. 9/15/34 to Opal Mae Benton; c. David G, Gerald Wayne, Franklin Lanier, Tapley Fennon, Alice Susan, Cathryn Rebecca, John Steven, William Allen. Educ: Abraham Baldwin Agr. Col, 34-35. Polit. & Govt. Pos: Ga. State Rep, 57-66; Colquitt Co. Bd. of Educ, 53-, Chmn, 60- Bus. & Prof. Pos: Farmer; Dir, Quitman-Adel Nat. Farm Loan Asn, 52-; Dir, Cotton Producers Asn, Moultrie Store, 52- Mem: Mason. Rel: Missionary Baptist. Mailing Add: RFD 2, Norman Park, Ga. 31771. (1967)

NEWTON, DAVID TIMOTHY R
Chmn, Cumberland Co. Rep. Party, N.C.
b. Central, S.C, 5/15/26; s. Doc Miles Newton and Alma Nalley N; m. 6/5/48 to Lila Meriam Kendrick; c. Robert Kendrick and Neil Gregory. Educ: Clemson Col, B.S, 50; Iota Lambda Sigma. Polit. & Govt. Pos: Mem, exec. cmt, Cumberland Co. Rep. Party, N.C, 62-, treas, 64-66, chmn, 66-; mem, exec. cmt, N.C. State Rep. Party, 68- Bus. & Prof. Pos: Sch. teacher, Fayetteville City Sch, N.C, 50-55; real estate and bus. broker, 55- Mil. Serv: Entered as Seaman, Navy, 44, released as AMM 3/C, 46, after serv. in Vero Beach Naval Air Sta, Fla, 44-46. Mem: Jaycees; Toastmaster; YMCA. Rel: Nazarene. Legal Res: 2513 S. Edgewater Dr, Fayetteville, N.C. 28303. Mailing Add: P.O. Box 3365, Fayetteville, N.C. 28305.

NEWTON, ROBERT EDWARD D
Iowa State Rep.
b. Muscatine, Iowa, 7/11/31; s. Walter C. Newton and Emma Marie McSwiggen N; single. Educ: State Univ. Iowa, B.A, 56; Cath. Univ. Am, M.A, 59, Ph.D, 65; Phi Beta Kappa; Nat. Newman Hon. Soc; Distinguished mil. grad. Polit. & Govt. Pos: Admin. aide to Gov. Loveless, Iowa, 57; mem. civilian staff, Comptroller of Army, 58 and Army Chief of Transportation, 59; Iowa State Rep, Scott Co, 69- Bus. & Prof. Pos: Instr. soc. sci, Norwich Univ, 62-65; asst. prof. polit. sci, Va. Polytech. Inst, 66-67; assoc. prof. polit. sci, St. Ambrose Col, 67- Mil. Serv: Entered as Pvt, Army, 51, released as 1st Lt, 54 after serv. in European Command, 52-54; German Occup. and Korean Conflict Medals. Publ: 'Edward S. Corwin and American Constitutional Law, J. Pub. Law, winter 65. Mem: Am, Midwest and Int. Polit. Sci. Asns; Am. Soc. Polit. and Legal Philos; Am. Judicature Soc; State Hist. Soc. Iowa; Am. Asn. Univ. Prof; K. of C. Rel: Roman Catholic. Legal Res: 1325 W. Eighth St, Davenport, Iowa 52802. Mailing Add: State Capitol, Des Moines, Iowa 50319.

NEZEZON, MARIE ANN D
V.Chmn, Niagara Co. Dem. Cmt, N.Y.
b. Buffalo, N.Y, 1/6/22; d. John J. Sauers and Mary Baumgartner S; m. 5/11/46 to Stephen J. Nezezon; c. Mary (Mrs. Robert Saxon), Janet A, Ann-Marie and Pamela J. Educ: Girls voc. high sch, 3 years; leadership course, sponsored by Julia Berlove. Polit. & Govt. Pos: Fourth Ward Committeeman, Niagara Co. Dem. Cmt, N.Y, 58-69, v.chmn, 64-; pres, Women's Club, N. Tonawanda, 62-64; chmn, women's div, Niagara Co. Dem. Party, 62-69; clerk and secy, Bd. of Elec, 67-69. Bus. & Prof. Pos: Cashier, Gen. Motors, formerly; mem. staff, Curtis-Wright Plant, formerly; Electric City Box Co, formerly; head cashier, Bell's I.G.A, currently. Mem: Retail Merchants Union; Unknown Club, Waitress Union; N. Tonawanda and Buffalo Bowling Leagues. Head Cashier of the Year; Pres. Bowling Trophy; 500 Bowling Award; High Three Game Award. Rel: Catholic. Mailing Add: 607 Witmer Rd, N. Tonawana, N.Y. 14120.

NICE, HARRY WHINNA, III R
Md. State Del.
b. Baltimore, Md, 12/9/35; s. Deeley K. Nice and Ann Barnes N; m. 8/26/61 to Mary Anne Lohmeyr; c. Christa Graham. Educ: Johns Hopkins Univ; Univ. Baltimore Sch. of Law, LL.B; Phi Gamma Delta. Polit. & Govt. Pos: Secy, Third Dist, Rep. Club, Md, 66; Md. State Del, Third Dist, currently. Bus. & Prof. Pos: Asst. treas, Union Trust Co, Md, 53-64; invest. banker, Midderdorf, Colgate & Co, 64- Mil. Serv: Army Res, 53-61. Mem: Bond Club of Baltimore, Md; Merchants Club; Maryland Club. Rel: Episcopal. Mailing Add: Stevenson, Md. 21153.

NICELY, WILLIAM PERRY AMOS R
W.Va. State Del.
b. Parkersburg, W.Va, 10/23/22; s. Perry Nicely and Anna Elizabeth Posey N; m. 7/12/47 to Marjorie Faith Meadows; c. Cynthia Annette, Gregory Warren and William P.A, Jr. Educ: Marietta Col, spec. courses. Polit. & Govt. Pos: Mem. bd. trustees, W.Va. Univ; mem, Coun. Econ. Educ; bd. dir, Union Mission; W.Va. State Del, 54-58 & 64-; dir, Wood Co. Civil Defense, 59-65; dist. supvr, Fourth Cong. Dist. Census, 60; del, Rep. Nat. Conv, 68. Bus. & Prof. Pos: V.pres. and dir, Mt. State Bank; co-owner, Nicely Realty, Inc, 46-48; real estate developer, William P.A. Nicely, 48- Mil. Serv: Entered as Pvt, Air Force, 43, released as Sgt, 45, after serv. in 475 Bomber Squadron B-29's, Pac, Guam, Saipan and Iowa Jima, 44-45; Good Conduct Medal; Theater Ribbons and Three Stars. Mem: Mason (32°, Knight Templer); Lions Int.(dist. gov, 51-52); Am. Legion; Wood Co. Farm Bur; campaign chmn, Mid-Ohio Valley United Fund, 66; South Parkersburg Improv. Asn; Interstate Coop; Scottish Rite; United Commercial Travelers. 100% Dist. Gov. Award, 52; Outstanding Lions Serv. Award Commun. Serv, 54, 56 & 60; United Fund Award, 66. Rel: Methodist. Mailing Add: 400 Camden Ave, Parkersburg, W.Va. 26101.

NICHOLAS, HARRY K. R
b. Dover, N.J, 5/27/23; m. to Adelaide Amundsen; c. Three. Educ: Muhlenberg Col, B.S, 44; Columbia Univ, M.S, 51; Omicron Delta Kappa; Lambda Chi Alpha. Polit. & Govt. Pos: Apprentice training supvr, N.J. Dept. of Educ, 46-50; info. asst. and Am. House Dir, U.S. Info. Agency, Germany, 54-57; and info. asst, U.S. Rep. Harold C. Ostertag, N.Y, 57-64; admin. asst, U.S. Rep. Barber B. Conable, Jr, N.Y, 65- Bus. & Prof. Pos: Reporter, Newark News, N.J, 51-54. Mil. Serv: Aviation Cadet, Navy, 44-45. Rel: Methodist. Mailing Add: 4505 Starr Jordan Dr, Burke, Va. 22015.

NICHOLAS, W. J. 'JACK' R
Wyo. State Rep.
b. Gillette, Wyo, 1/8/27; s. Tom Nicholas and Mary M. McKean N; m. 12/26/49 to Alice Howison; c. Patricia, John Philip, Robert and Lillian. Educ: Casper Jr. Col; Univ. Colo; Univ. Kans; Univ. N.Mex; Kans. State Col, Univ. Wyo, J.D. Polit. & Govt. Pos: Dep. co. and prosecuting attorney, Fremont Co, Wyo, 53-56; city attorney, Shoshoni, 58- and Lander, 62-; committeeman, Precinct Five, Lander, Wyo. and state committeeman, Fremont Co; treas, Wyo. State Rep. Cmt; presidential elector for Wyo, 68; Wyo. State Rep, currently. Mil. Serv: Entered as Pvt, Army, 44, released as Pfc, 46, after serv. in 11th Inf. Regt, 5th Inf. Div. Mem: Am. and Wyo. State Bar Asns; Wyo. Peace Officers Asn; Wyo. Stockgrowers Asn; Am. Legion; Judge Advocate, Wyo. State Am. Legion Auxilliary; Nat. Ski Patrol Syst. and legal adv, North. Rocky Mt. Div; Elks; Rotary Int; past pres, Lander Rotary Club and Fremont Co. Bar Asn; Aircraft Owners and Pilots Asn; former mem, AFL Hodcarriers Local, Casper jurisdiction; dir, Sinks Canyon Ski Club; former dir, Lander C. of C. and Lander Golf Club; legal officer, Lander Selective Serv. Syst; dir, Nat. Outdoor Leadership Sch; cmnr. and v.chmn, Wind River Housing Authority, U.S. Housing and Urban Develop. complement of Wind River Indian Reservation; trustee and treas, Old South Pass Hist. Preserve. Rel: Catholic. Legal Res: 417 S. Third St, Lander, Wyo. 82520. Mailing Add: Nicholas Bldg, Lander, Wyo. 82520.

NICHOLS, BENJAMIN D
Exec. Bd. Mem, N.Y. State New Dem. Coalition
b. Staten Island, N.Y, 9/20/20; s. Nathan Nichols and Minnie Minkin N; m. 9/10/42 to Ethel Gertrude Baron; c. Mary Dolores and Jeffery Norman. Educ: Cornell Univ, B.E.E, 46 and M.E.E, 49; Univ. Alaska, Ph.D, 58; Eta Kappa Nu. Polit. & Govt. Pos: Committeeman, Tompkins Co. Dem. Party, N.Y, 64-; exec. bd. mem, N.Y. State New Dem. Coalition, 69- Bus. & Prof. Pos: Prof. elec. eng, Cornell Univ, 58- and head, Off. Teacher Prep, 68-; dir, Elem. Sci. Educ. Serv, Inc, Watertown, Mass, 64-65. Mil. Serv: Entered as Pvt, Army, 43, released as T/4, 45, after serv. in Anti-Aircraft Ord. Maintenance, ETO, 44-45; Good Conduct Medal. Publ: 'Geomagnetic Disturbances in the Upper Atmosphere.' J. Proc. of Inst. Radio Engrs, 58; 'Teaching Science Can Be Fun,' Instructor, 66; 'Elementary Science Study—Two Years Later,' In: Readings in Science Education for the Elementary School, MacMillan, 67. Mem: Sigma Xi; Am. Geophys. Union; sr. mem, Inst. Elec. and Electronics Engrs; Am. Soc. Eng. Educ; Cornell Soc. Engrs; Am. Asn. Univ. Prof.(former chmn, Cornell Chap). Cover picture and article, Cornell Engr, 5/66. Mailing Add: 109 Llenroc Court, Ithaca, N.Y. 14850.

NICHOLS, CHARLES E.
Mayor, Belleville, Ill.
b. Lebanon, Ill, 4/19/08; s. Stephen Edmund Nichols and Bess Jones N; m. 1/19/40 to Rosalie Sanders; c. June and Charles E, Jr. Educ: McKendree Col, A.B, 29; Pi Kappa Delta; Alpha Mu Omega. Polit. & Govt. Pos: Justice of the Peace, Lebanon, Ill, 32-39; alderman, Belleville, 46-61, Mayor, 61- Bus. & Prof. Pos: Sch. prin, Belleville Pub. Sch, 29-57. Publ: Income Tax Problems of Teachers, Thesis, 48. Mem: Rotary Club; Optimists. Rel: Methodist. Mailing Add: 300 S. Jackson, Belleville, Ill. 62220.

NICHOLS, DAVID A. R
b. Lincolnville, Maine, 8/6/17; s. George E. Nichols and Flora E. Pillsbury N; single. Educ: Bates Col, A.B. magna cum laude, 42; Univ. Mich, J.D, 49; Delta Sigma Rho; Phi Beta Kappa. Polit. & Govt. Pos: Chmn, Maine Coun. Young Rep, 50-54; pres, New Eng. Coun. Young Rep, 52-54; mem, Maine Exec. Coun, 55-57; chmn, Maine State Rep. Cmt, 60-64; former Rep. Nat. Committeeman, Maine. Bus. & Prof. Pos: Gen. practice of law, Camden, Maine, 49- Mil. Serv: Army Air Force, 42-45. Mem: Fel. Am. Bar Found; Am, Maine State and Mass. Bar Asns; Maine Trial Lawyers Asn. (past pres); pres, Camden Educ. Found. and Camden Develop. Corp; Bates Col. Alumni Asn.(past pres); Rotary (past pres); Odd Fellows; VFW. Mailing Add: Box 76, Lincolnville, Maine 04849.

NICHOLS, DAVID ALLEN D
Chmn, Pub. Rels. Cmt, S.Dak. Dem. Coalition
b. Lyons, Kans, 2/4/39; s. Arthur Alvin Nichols and Merle Allen N; m. 5/30/60 to Esther Frances Wells; c. Preston David, John Kennedy and Yolanda Joy. Educ: Southwest Col, B.M, 60; Northwest. Univ, M.M, 64; Roosevelt Univ, M.A, Hist, 69; Ind. Univ. grad. study, 61; Alpha Mu. Polit. & Govt. Pos: Precinct capt, Cook Co. Dem. Party, Ill, 64; co-chmn, Beadle Co. for Robert F. Kennedy, S.Dak, 68; del, State Dem. Conv, S.Dak, 68; alternate del, Dem. Nat. Conv, 68; subcmt. chmn, S.Dak. Dem. Party Reform Cmn, 69-; chmn, pub. rels. cmt, S.Dak. Dem. Coalition, 69- Bus. & Prof. Pos: Dir. orchestras, Huron Independent Sch. Dist, S.Dak, 60-63 and Northfield Sch. Dist. 225, Ill, 64-67; asst. prof. humanities and hist, Huron Col, S.Dak, 67-69. Mem: Nat. and S.Dak. Educ. Asns; UN Asn. Rel: Presbyterian. Mailing Add: 706 Illinois S.W, Huron, S.Dak. 57350.

NICHOLS, FRED HAROLD R
b. Vinland, Kans, 6/26/00; s. Burton E. Nichols and Kate Peppard N; m. 6/26/21 to Alice M. Bryson; c. Frank L, Richard L, Vern L, Mason L. and Joyce L. (Mrs. James T. Maxwell). Educ: High Sch. and Night Sch, Struct. Eng. Polit. & Govt. Pos: Chmn, Barton Co. Rep. Cent. Cmt, Mo, 66-68. Bus. & Prof. Pos: Farmer, 21-24; carpenter, 24-35; self-employed, 35-37; carpenter and construction supt, 37-47; construction supt, Seth E, Geim & Assocs, 48-49, Fretto Construction Co, 56-57, Williamson & Loebsack, Engr-Architects, 58-64 and Van Doren-Hazard-Stallings-Schnacke, 65- Mem: Rotary; Odd Fellows. Rel: Christian Church. Mailing Add: 1503 Gulf, Lamar, Mo. 64759. (1967)

NICHOLS, HASKELL L. R
b. Homer, Mich, 7/28/96; m. 1922 to Mary Townsend; c. Dr. John Nichols, Dr. Mary E. (Mrs. Bentley), Dr. Ann (Mrs. Clark), Dr. Don Nichols. Educ: Graduated from Aerial Gunnery Sch, Selfridge Field, Mt. Clemens, 18; Hillsdale Col; Valparaiso Univ; Univ. of Ill; Univ. of Mich. Polit. & Govt. Pos: Mich. State Sen, 42-66; Mich. House of Reps, 38-42; 32-36. Bus. & Prof. Pos: Attorney. Mil. Serv: WWI. Mem: Eagles; Moose; Masons; Elks; Kiwanis Club; Jackson Country Club; Moslem Shrine Club. Rel: Presbyterian. Mailing Add: 703 S. Webster, Jackson, Mich. 49203. (1967)

NICHOLS, HENRY LYONS R
b. Danville, Ky, 8/4/91; s. John M. Nichols and Boone Bush N; m. to Floss Taylor, wid; c. Mrs. Ebb G. Bell and Mrs. John Elmer Sims. Educ: Centre Col, 07-08. Polit. & Govt. Pos: City councilman, Danville, Ky, 18-22 & 35-37, mayor, 38-53; chmn, Boyle Co. Rep. Cmt, until 68. Bus. & Prof. Pos: Pres. and treas, Danville Laundry and Dry Cleaning Co, Inc, 42- Mem: F&AM (past master, Franklin Lodge, 28, past high priest, Danville Chap. 4, past TIM, Danville Coun. 3, past comdr, Ryan Commandery 17, past grand comdr, Grand Commandery of Ky). Rel: Methodist; Chmn. on Finance. Mailing Add: 337 W. Broadway, Danville, Ky. 40422. (1967)

NICHOLS, HUGH LLEWELLYN, II D
b. Cincinnati, Ohio, 3/7/25; s. Harold Davis Nichols and Martha Taylor N; m. 12/21/46 to Doreen Sherman; c. Nancy (Mrs. Wood), Betsy S, Judy L. and Amy G. Educ: Miami Univ, B.A, 47; Univ. Cincinnati, LL.B, 49; Phi Kappa Tau. Polit. & Govt. Pos: Dep. dir, Clermont Co. Bd. Elec, Ohio, 55-64; jury cmnr, Fed. Dist. Court, South. Dist, Ohio, 67-; del, Dem. Nat. Conv, 68. Mil. Serv: Entered as A/S, Navy, 43, released as Ensign, 46, after serv. in USS PC 1209, Atlantic. Mem: Clermont Co, State and Am. Bar Asns; Rotary; F&AM; Scottish Rite; Shrine; Am. Legion. Rel: Presbyterian. Mailing Add: 145 Wood St, Batavia, Ohio 45103.

NICHOLS, JOHN WILLIAM R
Chmn, Elbert Co. Rep. Cent. Cmt, Colo.
b. Denver, Colo, 8/27/31; s. William R. Nichols and Rozellah Wilson N; m. 8/25/56 to Nancy Lou Wilfert; c. Diane Kay, Roger William and Robert John. Educ: Univ. Colo. Polit. & Govt. Pos: Mem. bd. trustees, Simla, Colo, 57-60; Colo. State Rep, 61-65; chmn, Elbert Co. Rep. Cent. Cmt, 65-; mayor, Simla, Colo, 66-; treas, Colo. Rep. Co. Chmn. Asn, 66- Bus. & Prof. Pos: V.pres, Nichols Tillage Tools Inc, 57- Mil. Serv: Entered as Seaman Recruit, Navy, 51, released as Hospital Corpsman 2/C, 55, after serv. in Am. and Pac. Theaters, 54-55. Mem: AF&AM; Simla Vol. Fire Dept; Consistory, Colo. Co. Officials and Employees Retirement Asn. (bd. dirs, 68-). Mailing Add: P.O. Box 275, Simla, Colo. 80835.

NICHOLS, ROBERT CECIL D
Tex. State Rep.
b. Norphlet, Ark, 7/15/28; s. John Henry Nichols and Nancy Phelps N; m. 4/24/48 to Lynda Hazel Slocum; c. Joanne (Mrs. Strickland) and Wayne. Educ: Kokomo High Sch, Miss. Polit. & Govt. Pos: Committeeman, Tex. State Dem. Exec. Cmt, 59-67; Tex. State Rep, 67-; alternate del, Dem. Nat. Conv, 68. Bus. & Prof. Pos: Welder, Rheem Mfg, 48- Mem: USW, Local 2883. Rel: Baptist. Mailing Add: 7517 Crofton, Houston, Tex. 77028.

NICHOLS, WILLIAM FLYNT D
U.S. Rep, Ala.
b. Amory, Miss, 10/18/18; s. William Francis Nichols and Daisy Williams N; m. 1/30/43 to Carolyn Funderburk; c. Memorie, Margaret Lynn and William Flynt. Educ: Auburn Univ, B.S, 39, M.S, 41; A Club; Blue Key; Scabbard & Blade; Gamma Sigma Delta; O.D.K. Polit. & Govt. Pos: Ala. State Rep, 59-63; Ala. State Sen, 63-66; U.S. Rep, Ala, 67- Bus. & Prof. Pos: Agronomist and v.pres, Sylacauga Fertilizer Co, 47-67. Mil. Serv: Entered as 2nd Lt, Army, 42, released as Capt, 47, after serv. in 45th Field Artil. Bn, Eighth Inf, Atlantic Theater, 42-47; Purple Heart; Bronze Star, Three Major Battle Stars and other awards. Mem: Mason; Shrine; Zamora Temple; Sylacauga Bd. Educ: Am. Legion; DAV. Progressive Farmer Man of the Year Award; Most Outstanding Mem. Ala. Senate, Capitol Press Corps, 65. Rel: Methodist; Past Chmn. Bd, First Methodist Church. Legal Res: Capital Dr, Sylacauga, Ala. 35150. Mailing Add: 1037 Longworth House Office Bldg, Washington, D.C. 20515.

NICHOLS, WILLIAM PRESTON R
Electronic Data Processing Chmn, Monroe Co. Rep. Cmt, Mich.
b. Kevil, Ky, 6/17/31; s. Felix R. Nichols and Verna Wray N; m. 6/25/55 to Joanne L. Kinzel; c. William Paul and Robert David. Educ: Detroit Col. of Law, 59-64; Wayne State Univ, B.S. in Educ, 68. Polit. & Govt. Pos: Chmn, Monroe Co. Dem. Party, 59-61 and 67-68, secy, 61-63; Justice of Peace, Monroe, Mich, 59-63; Dem. nominee for State Sen, 60; mem, Monroe Co. Rep. Cmt, 68 and electronic data processing chmn, 69-; del, Rep. State Conv, 68; prog. coordinator, Off. of Econ. Opportunity, 69- Bus. & Prof. Pos: Welfare supvr, Detroit Welfare Dept, Mich, 55-59; justice court clerk, Frenchtown

Twp. Justice Court, 64-69; sch. teacher, Monroe and Jefferson Sch. Syst, 68-69. Mil. Serv: Navy, 50-51, with serv. in U.S.S. ODAX, Submarine Div. Mem: VFW. Mailing Add: 2789 N. Monroe St, Monroe, Mich. 48161.

NICHOLSON, CARL JOSEPH R
Chmn, Hancock Co. Rep. Party, Ind.
b. Greenfield, Ind, 1/16/16; s. Orval Leroy Nicholson and Effie Gilland N; m. 5/2/35 to Julian Elizabeth Dismore; c. David, Joseph and Robert. Educ: Greenfield High Sch, 30-34. Polit. & Govt. Pos: Precinct committeeman, Hancock Co. Rep. Party, Ind, 37-66; trustee, Brandywine Twp, 54-58; inspector new rd. construction, Ind. State Hwy. Dept, 54-58; dir, Ind. Sch. Lunch Div, Ind. Dept. Pub. Instr, 67-69; mem. exec. cmt, Ind. Rep. State Cent. Cmt, 68; educ. consult, Ind. State Supt. Pub. Instr, 69-; chmn, Hancock Co. Rep. Party, currently. Bus. & Prof. Pos: Owner and operator, farm, Greenfield, Ind, 36-60; ins. agent, All Am. Life and Casualty Co, Park Ridge, Ill, 58-66; mem. bd, Ind. Sch. Food Serv. Asn, 67- Mem: Mason; Moose; Hancock Co. Farm Bur; Ind. state v.chmn, Future Farmers Am. Hoosier Farmer Award, 34; Twenty-five mem. Pin Award, Masonic Lodge, 68. Rel: Methodist. Mailing Add: R.R. 4, Greenfield, Ind. 46140.

NICHOLSON, CHARLES GLANZ R
Pa. State Rep.
b. Philadelphia, Pa, 10/31/19; s. George Nicholaus Nicholson and Nellie Glanz N; m. 48 to Jean B. Billman; c. Craig Glanz and Bruce Allen. Educ: Univ. Pa, certif. in bus. admin, 48; Night Watch Honor Soc; Phi Sigma Kappa. Polit. & Govt. Pos: Cmnr, Upper Moreland Twp, Pa, 64-65; Pa. State Rep, 65- Bus. & Prof. Pos: Pres, Glanz, Behm & Herring Inc, 55- Mem: Past pres, Philadelphia Carpet & Upholstery Club. Rel: Presbyterian. Mailing Add: 2325 Pioneer Rd, Hatboro, Pa. 19040.

NICHOLSON, EDWARD EATON R
Iowa State Sen.
b. Elkhart, Ill, 1/15/04; s. John Edward Nicholson and Laura Montgomery N; m. 2/14/31 to Helen Elizabeth Kay; c. James Edward and Susan Kay (Mrs. Buchheit). Educ: Millikin Univ, 25-29; Delta Sigma Phi. Polit. & Govt. Pos: Iowa State Sen, Scott Co, 68- Bus. & Prof. Pos: Prin, Consolidated Grade Sch, Hartsburg, Ill, 24-25, Beason, 25-26; prod. engr, Purity Bakeries of Ill, 29-31; owner, bakery, Lawrenceburg, Ind, 31-37; v.pres. and sales mgr, Warren-Nicholson Co, Davenport, Iowa, 37-68. Mem: Dir, Nat. Sales Exec, 48-50; Mason; Commandery; Templar; Shrine; Iowa and Ill. Farm Bur; Davenport C. of C.(pres, 47); Navy League of U.S; Outing Club; Rock Island Arsenal Club; Univ. Iowa Club; Quarterback Club; pres, Quad City Navy League Coun, 69. Rel: Episcopal. Mailing Add: 49 Kenwood Ave, Davenport, Iowa 52803.

NICHOLSON, JOE DAVID D
b. Pomeroy, Wash, 6/20/14; s. Ora David Nicholson and Eva Huckshorn N; m. 3/16/51 to Phyllis Ellen Blakemore. Polit. & Govt. Pos: Precinct committeeman, Nez Perce Co. Dem. Cent. Cmt, Idaho, 52-, chmn, 54-69; alternate del, Dem. Nat. Conv, 60; dep. sheriff, Nez Perce Co, 61; officer, Nez Perce Co. Vets. Serv, 63-; Unit Lt, Am. Legion Auxiliary State Police, Idaho, 65- Mil. Serv: Entered as Pvt, Army Air Force, 42, released as Sgt, 45, after serv. in Eighth and Ninth Air Force, Fifth Air Disarmament Group, ETO, 43-45; Rhineland, Central Europe, Air Offensive Europe and Ardennes Forest Campaign Ribbons. Mem: Am. Legion (comdr, Lewis-Clark Post 13, 65-66); Am. Red Cross (bd. dirs, Lewis-Clark Chap, 65-); 40 et 8; VFW; Elks; Nat. Sheriffs' Asn. Rel: Episcopal. Legal Res: 423 18th St, Lewiston, Idaho 83501. Mailing Add: P.O. Box 501, Lewiston, Idaho 83501. (1967)

NICHOLSON, RALPH WILLIAM D
b. Chicago, Ill, 1/30/16; s. Wheelock Steele Nicholson and Violet Israel N; m. 7/4/42 to Rosemary Elizabeth Kleutgen. Educ: Univ. Chicago, A.B, 36; Phi Kappa Psi. Polit. & Govt. Pos: Asst. postmaster gen, Post Off. Dept, 61-69; v.pres. finance and treas, Corp. Pub. Broadcasting, 69- Bus. & Prof. Pos: Ed, Gen. Electric Co, 36-39; asst. off. of the pres, Univ. Chicago, 39-41; various positions ending as mgr, New York off. and dir, Fuller & Smith & Ross, 46-61. Mil. Serv: Entered as Pvt, Marine Corps, 41, released as Capt, 46, after serv. in Pac, 43-45; Letter of Commendation with Ribbon for Serv. in Okinawa; Maj, Marine Corps Res, 46-57. Mailing Add: 15 Fourth St. S.E, Washington, D.C. 20003.

NICKEL, DIETER H. R
Chmn, Rep. Orgn. Lincoln Co, Wis.
b. Minneapolis, Minn, 7/27/36; s. Theodore Hoelty-Nickel and Irma Von-Hafen N; m. 8/19/61 to Pamela Wiedenheft; c. Theodore Karl and Kathy Lyn. Educ: Valparaiso Univ, BA, 58, LL.B, 60; Pi Kappa Alpha; Phi Alpha Delta. Polit. & Govt. Pos: Dist. attorney, Lincoln Co, Wis, 62-66; chmn, Rep. Orgn. Lincoln Co, 65-; v.pres, Merrill Area Schs. Bd. Educ, 67- Bus. & Prof. Pos: Secy, Lincoln Co. Bar Asn, 63, v.pres, 64, pres, 65. Mil. Serv: Entered as Pvt, Marine Corps Res, 60, released as Cpl, 66, after serv. in 95th Rifle Co, 61-66. Mem: Am. Bar Asn; State Bar of Wis; Lions (pres, Merrill Chap); Jaycees. Rel: Lutheran. Mailing Add: 315 Center Ave, Merrill, Wis. 54452.

NICKELL, JAMES D. R
b. Huntington, W.Va, 9/30/24; s. Dennie T. Nickell and Nettie Hollon N; m. 12/28/46 to Mary Hagan Caywood; c. Anne Jeanell, Robert Hagan, Phillip Hollon, James Dennis, Mary Patricia, Mark O, Edward Caywood and Margaret Taft. Educ: Pa. State Col, Air Corps Cadet Training, 43-44; Univ. Ky, B.S, 48; Alpha Tau Omega. Polit. & Govt. Pos: Nat. committeeman, Young Rep. Clubs Ky, 51-53, pres, 53-54; field mgr, Border & South. Young Rep. Nat. Fedn, 52; v.pres, Young Rep. Nat. Fedn, 55-57; del, Rep. Nat. Conv, 60; chmn, Boyd Co. Rep. Exec. Cmt, 60-66; cand. U.S. House Rep, 68. Mil. Serv: Entered as Pvt, Army, 43, released as S/Sgt, 45, after serv. in Co. L, 311th Inf. Regt, 78th Div, ETO; Soldiers Medal; Bronze Star with Cluster; Purple Heart with Cluster; Combat Infantryman's Badge; ETO Ribbon with 3 Stars. Mem: Pres, Ashland Bd. of Realtors, 55-56; dir, Ky. State Real Estate Asn, 55-56; Nat. Asn. of Real Estate Bds; past pres, Ashland Alumni Asn, Univ. Ky; Elks Lodge 350; Am. Legion. Rel: Episcopal. Mailing Add: 1022 Bath Ave, Ashland, Ky. 41101.

NICKERSON, EUGENE HOFFMAN D
Co. Exec, Nassau Co. Govt, N.Y.
b. Orange, N.J, 8/2/18; s. Hoffman Nickerson and Ruth Constance Comstock N; m. 9/19/43 to Marie-Louise Steiner; c. Marie-Louise, Lawrie H, Stephanie W. and Susan A. Educ: Harvard Univ, B.A, 41; Columbia Univ. Law Sch, LL.B, 43; Bd. of Visitors, Columbia Law Sch. Polit. & Govt. Pos: Law secy. to Judge Augustus N. Hand, U.S. Circuit Court of Appeals, 43-44; law secy. to Chief Justice Harlan F. Stone, U.S. Supreme Court, 44-46; zone chmn, Roslyn Harbor, N.H, 53-55; v.chmn, Nassau Co. Dem. Cmt, N.Y, 55-61; counsel, Gov. Cmt. Pub. Employee Security, 56-58; mem, Law Rev. Cmn, N.Y, 58-59; chmn, transportation cmt, Regional Coun, 62; officer, Roslyn Dem. Club; co. exec, Nassau Co. Govt, 61, 64 & 67-; chmn, Mitchel Field Planning Cmt, 63; mem, adv. coun. pub. welfare, U.S. Dept. Health Educ. and Welfare, 64; mem, Pub. Off. Adv. Coun. to Off. Econ. Opportunity, 66; del, Dem. Nat. Conv, 68. Bus. & Prof. Pos: Assoc, Law Firm, Milbank, Tweed, Hope & Hadley, 46-51; mem. law firm, Hale, Stimson, Russell & Nickerson, 52-61. Publ: Ethics in Government, New York, 64; Mobilize for Democracy, 66; articles for law rev, legal and prfnl. mag. Mem: Am. and Nassau Co. Bar Asns; Asn. Bar of City of N.Y; Am. Law Inst; Am. Judicature Soc. Rel: Episcopal. Mailing Add: 495 Bryant Ave, Roslyn Harbor, N.Y. 11576.

NICKERSON, GRANT NORWOOD R
Chmn, Woodbridge Rep. Town Cmt, Conn.
b. Boston, Mass, 8/14/12; s. Ambrose Norwood Nickerson and Maud P. Grant N; m. 9/11/37 to Audrey Lee Bishop; c. Jeffrey R. and Stewart D. Educ: Amherst Col, B.A, 33; Yale Law Sch, LL.B, 36; Phi Kappa Psi. Polit. & Govt. Pos: Chmn, Woodbridge Rep. Town Cmt, Conn, 63; selectman, Woodbridge, Conn, 64- Bus. & Prof. Pos: Partner, Wiggin & Dana, New Haven, Conn, 36- Mem: New Haven Co, Conn. and Am. Bar Asns; Quinnipiac Club. Rel: Congregational. Legal Res: Deer Run Rd, Woodbridge, Conn. 06525. Mailing Add: P.O. Box 1832, New Haven, Conn. 06508.

NICKERSON, REGINALD LEE R
Chmn, Raynham Rep. Town Cmt, Mass.
b. Chatham, Mass, 5/3/26; s. George William Nickerson and Norma O'Brien N; m. 1/19/52 to Harriette Brabrook; c. Ronnie Lee, William Leonard, Brian Mason, Robert Eric and Barry Lincoln. Educ: Univ. Mass, B.B.A, 51; Q.T.V; Adelphia. Polit. & Govt. Pos: Mem, Cemetery Cmt, Raynham, Mass, 60-68; chmn, Raynham Rep. Town Cmt, 66-; mem. sch. cmt, Bridgewater-Raynham Regional Sch, 68- Bus. & Prof. Pos: Registered Rep, Chas. A. Day & Co, Inc, 65- Mil. Serv: Entered as Aviation Cadet, Army Air Force, 44, released as Sgt, 46; Res, 46-, Maj; Am. Theatre Medal; Good Conduct Medal; World War II Victory Medal; Air Force Reserve Medal. Mem: Am. Legion; Air Force Asn; Raynham Lions Club (past pres); pres, Raynham Pub. Libr, 67-69. Rel: Episcopal. Mailing Add: 255 Leonard St, Raynham, Mass. 02767.

NICKOLOFF, ROBERT STOKELY DFL
b. Hibbing, Minn, 4/10/29; s. Constantine Anton Nickoloff and Miriam Stokely N; m. 2/11/56 to Anne H. Nickerson; c. Sara K. and Charles A. Educ: Wesleyan Univ, B.A, 51; Univ. Mich. Law Sch, LL.B, 55; Phi Delta Phi; Beta Theta Pi. Polit. & Govt. Pos: First v.chmn, Eighth Cong. Dist. Dem-Farmer-Labor, Minn, 62-66, chmn, 66-68; mem, Nat. Pub. Adv. Cmt. for Area Redevelop, 62-65; mem, Dem-Farmer-Labor State Cent. Cmt, 62-; spec. asst. attorney gen. for econ. develop, Minn, 62-; mem, Nat. Pub. Adv. Cmt. Regional Econ. Develop, 62-; del, Dem. Nat. Conv, 64; mem, Minn. Dem-Farmer-Labor Exec. Cmt, 66- and Gov. Bus. Adv. Cmn, 66- Bus. & Prof. Pos: Partner law firm, Nickoloff and Bischoff, Hibbing, Minn, 56-; pres. and counsel, First Fed. Savings & Loan Asn. Hibbing, 64-; mem. bd. dirs, Fed. Home Loan Bank, Des Moines and Channel 10, Inc, 64-; secy-treas, Range TV Cable Co, Inc, 65-; first v.pres, Savings and Loan League of Minn, 66. Mil. Serv: Entered as Pvt, Marine Corps Res, 48, released as Capt, 52, after serv. in Korea; all Citations for 1st Marine Div, 51-52 and Three Battle Stars. Mem: Am. and Minn. Bar Asns; Rotary; Mason; Shrine; Elks; Moose; Am. Legion; VFW; Hibbing C. of C; Algonquin Club; Mesaba Country Club. Rich Prize for Outstanding Sr. Thesis, Wesleyan Univ, 51. Rel: Episcopal. Mailing Add: 3802 First Ave, Hibbing, Minn. 55746. (1967)

NICKS, ROY SULLIVAN D
b. Chapel Hill, Tenn, 6/30/33; s. Richard D. Nicks and Cora Sullivan N; m. Jan. 60 to Barbara Jean Love; c. Beverly Jean and Richard Matthew. Educ: Mid. Tenn. State Univ, B.S, 55; South. Regional Training Prog. sponsored by Univs. Ala, Ky. and Tenn, Cert, 56; Univ. Tenn, Knoxville, M.A, 57; Memphis State Univ, Memphis, Ed.D, 69. Polit. & Govt. Pos: Instr. and Training Officer, Univ. Tenn, 56-57; Sr. Budget Analyst, Tenn. State, 60-61, Dep. Cmn. of Finance, 61-63, Cmn. Pub. Welfare, 63-65; statewide coordinator of U.S. Senate Campaign for Frank Clement, May to Nov. 66; asst. to gov, Tenn, 65-67; asst. to pres, Memphis State Univ, 67-69, v.pres. admin, 69- Bus. & Prof. Pos: Pres, Tenn. Conf. Soc. Welfare, 65-66; pres, Am. Pub. Welfare Asn, 69- Mil. Serv: Entered as Pvt, Army, 57, released as Spec. 3/C, 59, after serv. in Seventh Army Support Command. Publ: 'Welfare in the Seventies,' Tenn. Pub. Welfare Record, June 69; 'Comprehensive Community College,' Educ. Quart, Spring 69. Rel: Methodist. Mailing Add: 3854 Central Ave, Memphis, Tenn. 38111.

NICOLAS, TOUFIC D
Chmn, Nueces Co. Dem. Party, Tex.
b. Tampico, Mex, 9/28/26; s. Adib Nicolas and Badeeha Nosser N; m. 7/30/53 to Anna Cuccia; c. Sally Ann and Sandra Rose. Educ: Univ. Tex, Austin, B.A, 49, LL.B, 50. Polit. & Govt. Pos: Exec. dir, Legal Aid Soc, Corpus Christi, Tex, 56-59; chmn, Nueces Co. Dem. Party, 63-64 & 66- Bus. & Prof. Pos: Partner, Horkin, Nicolas & Morris, Attorneys, Tex, 63- Mil. Serv: Entered as Pvt, Army, 46, released as Pfc, 47, after serving in 35th Inf. Div, Far East, 46-47, recalled as Pvt, 52, released as 1st Lt, 54, after serv. in Ft. Lewis, Wash, 52-54. Mem: Nueces Co. Bar Asn.(dir, 65-67); State Bar, Tex. Rel: Greek Orthodox. Legal Res: 4633 Monette, Corpus Christi, Tex. 78412. Mailing Add: P.O. Box 28, Corpus Christi, Tex. 78403.

NICOLL, DONALD EUGENE D
b. Boston, Mass, 8/4/27; s. George Densham Nicoll and Mary Strang N; m. 6/18/49 to Hilda Katherine Farnum; c. Hugh Marlin, Jonathan Seth, Melissa and Jessica. Educ: Colby Col, A.B, 49; Pa. State Univ, M.A, 52. Polit. &

Govt. Pos: Exec. secy, Maine Dem. Party, 54-56; mem. adv. cmt. polit. orgn, Dem. Nat. Cmt, 57-60; admin. asst. to U.S. Rep. Frank M. Coffin, Maine, 57-61; legis. asst. and news secy, U.S. Sen. Edmund S. Muskie, Maine, 61-62, admin. asst, 62-, mgr, Sen Muskie's V.Presidential Campaign, 68. Bus. & Prof. Pos: Radio and TV news ed, WLAM and WLAM-TV, Lewiston, Maine, 51-54. Mem: Exec. cmt, D.C. Citizens for Better Pub. Educ. Rel: Unitarian. Legal Res: High St, Buckfield, Maine 04220. Mailing Add: 3914 Livingston St. N.W, Washington, D.C. 20015.

NICOLSON, DON D
b. Cooperstown, N.Dak, 2/23/92; married; c. Three. Educ: N.Dak. State Univ. of Agr. and Applied Sci. Polit. & Govt. Pos: N.Dak. State Rep, 57-66; twp. supv. Bus. & Prof. Pos: Farmer, grain buyer, implement dealer. Mem: Mason; Shrine. Mailing Add: Carrington, N.Dak. 58421. (1967)

NIEHOFF, H. RICHARD PETERSEN R
Chmn, Ohio Rep. Finance Cmt.
b. Cincinnati, Ohio, 6/8/18; s. Harry P. Niehoff and Norma Petersen N; m. 9/6/47 to Betty M. LeVeque; c. Peter, Christopher, Patricia and Elsa. Educ: Princeton Univ, A.B, 38; Harvard Law Sch, LL.B, 41; Univ. Glasgow, 45. Polit. & Govt. Pos: Asst. attorney gen, Ohio, 41-47; del, Rep. Nat. Conv, 60, 64 & 68; chmn, Ohio Rep. Finance Cmt, currently. Bus. & Prof. Pos: Attorney-at-law; v.pres, Fifty W. Broad, Inc. and the LL. Leveque Co, Inc, 47-; dir, Ohio Nat. Bank, 66- Mil. Serv: Entered as 2nd Lt, Army, 41, released as Maj, 46, after serv. in 80th Inf. Div, ETO. Mem: Am. and Ohio Bar Asns. Master of Fox Hounds, Rocky Fork Headley Hunt. Rel: Presbyterian. Legal Res: Havens Corners Rd, Gahanna, Ohio 43020. Mailing Add: 50 W. Broad St, Columbus, Ohio 43215.

NIELSEN, ALFRED R
Iowa State Rep.
b. Defiance, Iowa, 12/9/01; s. Jesse Nielsen and Bertha N; m. 2/3/29 to Leta Arlene Morrison; c. Ruthann (Mrs. Milton Barry), Marlin, Marie (Mrs. Lee McLaughlin). Educ: Shelby Co. Schs. Polit. & Govt. Pos: Helped orgn. and was pres, Shelby Co. Good Rds. Asn; voting del, Farm Bur, 5 years; pres, Irwin Commun. Sch. Bd, 5 years; Iowa State Rep, currently. Bus. & Prof. Pos: Owns and operates 520 acres in Shelby and Crawford Counties. Mem: Trustee, Evangel. United Brethren Church; Masonic Lodge; Shrine; Eastern Star. Rel: Evangelical United Brethren. Mailing Add: Defiance, Iowa 51527.

NIELSEN, HELGA RAGNHILD SORENSEN DFL
Chmn, Second Dist. Dem-Farmer-Labor Party, Minn.
b. Hutchinson, Minn, 2/25/07; d. Alfred Sorensen and Sine Sorensen S; m. 2/15/29 to Niels Kusk Nielsen; c. Else (Mrs. Paul Anderson) and Sine (Mrs. Lief Duus). Educ: Minn. Bus. Col, grad. Polit. & Govt. Pos: Secy, McLeod Co. Dem-Farmer-Labor Party, Minn, 46; second v.chairwoman, Dem-Farmer-Labor Party, Minn, 51-58, chairwoman, Second. Dist. Dem-Farmer-Labor Party, 58-; dep. registrar, Motor Vehicle Div, Minn, 55-; del, Dem. Nat. Conv, 68. Bus. & Prof. Pos: Sales and inventory, Sederstrom Variety, Hutchinson, 38; clerical reconciliation statist, Kraft Foods Co, Hutchinson, 42-51; secy, Melvin J. Peterson, Attorney-at-Law, 52-55; secy, John Keefe, Attorney-at-law, 55-58. Mem: Eastern Star; Rebekah Lodge; Auxiliary, Charles McLaughlin Post 906; Hutchinson Bus. & Prfnl. Women; C. of C; Burns Manor Hutchinson Munic. Nursing Home (bd. dirs); Mem. Home Coun; Hutchinson Voc. Sch.(adv. bd). Bus. Woman of the Year, Hutchinson Bus. & Prfnl. Womens Club, 67. Rel: Lutheran. Mailing Add: 635 Harmony Lane, Hutchinson, Minn. 55350.

NIELSEN, NIELS J. D
b. Clinton, Iowa, 7/29/96; m. 1923 to Edna Aagard; c. three. Educ: Clinton and Emmet Co. Schs. Polit. & Govt. Pos: Iowa State Rep, -66; Sch. Bd. Bus. & Prof. Pos: Retired from farming and owns 160 acre farm; V.Pres, Ringsted Tel. Co. Mil. Serv: WWI. Mem: past comdr. and chaplain, Am. Legion; Izaak Walton League; Kiwanis; Iowa Lutheran Welfare Coun. Farm Bur. Rel: Lutheran. 1967 Legal Res: Clinton, Iowa. No mailing address available. (1967)

NIELSEN, VIGO GILBERT, JR. R
b. Boston, Mass, 7/26/42; s. Vigo G. Nielsen and Margaret Young N; single. Educ: Yale Univ, B.A, 64; Coro Found. Pub. Affairs Internship, Los Angeles, Calif, 65; Sr. Soc; soc. serv. orgns. Polit. & Govt. Pos: Admin. asst. to Calif. State Assemblyman Houston I. Flournoy, 66; assoc. mem, Calif. Rep. State Cent. Cmt, 66-67, mem, 68-69; asst. dep. state controller, 67-68; chief admin. officer, Calif. State Assembly, 69; exec. asst. to Lt. Gov. of Calif, 69- Bus. & Prof. Pos: Mem, bd. dir, small Calif. corp, 68- Mil. Serv: Entered as Pvt, Army, 65, released as Pfc, 66, after serv. in 418th Mil. Intel. Detachment; Airman, Calif. Air Nat. Guard Res, 69-; Letter of Commendation, Ft. Ord, Calif, Cert. of Achievement, Army Intel. Sch, Ft. Holabird, Md. Mem: Calif. Rep. League; Ripon Soc. Rel: Episcopal. Legal Res: 16 Saddleback Rd, Rolling Hills, Calif. 90274. Mailing Add: 6399 S. Land Park Dr, Sacramento, Calif. 95831.

NIELSON, ELDON DENZEL R
b. Hunter, Utah, 12/4/20; s. Hiram David Nielson and Augusta Ek N; m. 12/13/42 to Geraldine Rasmussen; c. Dennis Lon, Karen Gae and Karla Sue. Educ: Univ. Utah, A.B, 46; Univ. Ill, Ph.D, 48; Phi Eta Sigma; Alpha Chi Sigma. Polit. & Govt. Pos: Mem. exec. cmt, Citizens United Reform Effort, Albany, N.Y, 61-62; chmn, Forsyth Co. Rep. Party, 63-66; alternate del-at-lg, Rep. Nat. Conv, 64; mem. exec. cmt, N.C. Rep. Party, 64-69; Rep. cand. for Cong, Fifth Dist, N.C, 68; Forsyth Co. chmn, Scientists and Engr. for Nixon, 68. Bus. & Prof. Pos: Instr. biochem. and nutrition, Univ. South. Calif, 49-50; head biochem. research sect, Upjohn Co, 50-57, Armour Pharmaceutical Co, 57-59 and Sterling-Winthrop Research Inst, 59-62; mgr. biol. research, R.J. Reynolds Tobacco Co, 62- Mem: Am. Chem. Soc; Endocrine Soc; Soc. for Indust. Microbiol; Animal Care Panel; Am. Inst. of Biol. Sci; Am. Asn. for Adv. of Sci; Am. Mgt. Asn; Elks; C. of C. Rel: Unitarian. Mailing Add: 3521 Kirklees Rd, Winston-Salem, N.C. 27104.

NIELSON, GERALDINE R. R
N.C. State Sen.
b. Hunter, Utah; d. Lon Rasmussen and Susan Lewis R; m. to Dr. Eldon D. Nielson; c. Dennis Lon, Karen Gae and Karla Sue. Educ: State Univ. N.Y. at Albany, 60-62; Univ. N.C, B.S, 64 and M.Ed, 65; Sigma Alpha; Delta Pi Epsilon. Polit. & Govt. Pos: N.C. State Sen, 22nd Dist, 66-; del-at-lg, Rep. Nat. Conv, 68, mem. platform cmt, 68. Bus. & Prof. Pos: Off. mgr, Freshmans Wholesale & Mfg. Jewelry, Salt Lake City, Utah, 43-46; secy. to the architect, Univ. Ill, 47. Mem: League of Women Voters; Bus. & Prfnl. Women's Club (first v.pres, 69-); Forsyth Co. Fedn. of Rep. Women; Nat. Educ. Asn; Nat. Bus. Educ. Asn; Orgn. Women Legislators. Hon. Ky. Colonel, Gov. Louise B. Nunn, 68. Rel: Unitarian. Mailing Add: 3521 Kirklees Rd, Winston-Salem, N.C. 27104.

NIELSON, HOWARD CURTIS R
Utah State Rep.
b. Richfield, Utah, 9/12/24; s. Herman Taylor Nielson and Zula May Curtis N; m. 6/18/48 to Julia Adams; c. Noreen, Elaine, John, Mary Lee, James, Jean and Curtis. Educ: Univ. Utah, B.S. in math, 47; Univ. Ore, M.S. in math, 49; Stanford Univ, M.B.A. in bus. admin, 56 and Ph.D. in bus. admin. and statistics, 58; Phi Beta Kappa; Phi Kappa Phi; Sigma Xi; Pi Mu Epsilon; Sigma Pi Sigma; Order of Artus. Polit. & Govt. Pos: Del, Rep. Co. Conv, 60-69; dist. chmn, Rep. Party, Utah, 62, Provo precinct chmn, 67-69; del, Rep. State Conv, 62-69; res. dir, State Rep. Party, 67-69; Utah State Rep, 67-, mem, Joint Legis. Budget-Audit Cmt, 67-, Majority Leader, Utah House of Rep, 69- Bus. & Prof. Pos: Asst. instr, Univ. Utah, 46-47; grad. asst, Univ. Ore, 47-49; sr. statistician, Calif. & Hawaiian Sugar Ref. Corp, 49-51; research statistician and economist, Stanford Research Inst, 51-57; prof. statist, Brigham Young Univ, 57-; mgr. and sr. statistician, C-E-I-R, Inc, 63-65, consult, currently; consult, Riches Research Corp, Bur. Internal Revenue, Hill Air Force Base, Univ. Wyo. Bur. of Bus. Research, Hercules, Inc, GCA Corp, Fairchild Semiconductor, EG&G and Univ. Utah, currently. Mil. Serv: Entered as Pvt, Army, 43, released as Sgt, 46, after serv. in 13th Signal Air Warning Bn, Am. and Philippines, 44-46; Good Conduct Medal; Am. and Pac. Theater Ribbons. Publ: America's Demand for Wood, Weyerhauser Timber Co, 54; Population Trends in United States Through 1975, Stanford Research Inst, 55-57; Experimental Designs Used in Industry, Brigham Young Univ, 65. Mem: Scientific Research Soc; Inst. Math. Statist; Am. Soc. for Qual. Control; Am. Statist. Asn.(mem, nat. coun. and pres, Utah Chap); West. Econ. Asn; Viking Social Unit, Brigham Young Univ; Kiwanis. Rel: Latter-day Saint. Mailing Add: 580 Sagewood Ave, Provo, Utah 84601.

NIERENGARTEN, ROGER JOSEPH DFL
b. St. Cloud, Minn, 11/19/25; s. Henry C. Nierengarten and Rose Wimmer N; m. 10/4/54 to Dolores Rosalind Lehman; c. Therese Ann, Catherine Mary and Mary Elizabeth. Educ: St. John's Univ, Minn, B.A, 48; Marquette Univ, J.D, 51; Delta Theta Phi. Polit. & Govt. Pos: Admin. asst. to Mayor, St. Cloud, Minn, 54-56; Torrens exam, Stearns Co, 55-; co. attorney, Stearns Co, 63- Mil. Serv: Army Paratroops, World War II; Legal Dept, Army Engrs, 51. Mem: St. Cloud Exchange Club; VFW; Am. Legion; Elks; K. of C; Stearns Benton, Seventh Judicial Dist, State and Am. Bar Asns; Minn. Co. Attorneys Asn; Nat. and Dist. Attorneys Asns; Minn. and Am. Trial Lawyers Asns. Mailing Add: Route 2, St. Cloud, Minn. 56301.

NIEWOEHNER, CARL H. D
b. Kirkwood, Mo, 10/9/25; m. 3/24/51 to Gloria E. Mercer; c. Eric. Educ: Mo. Valley Col, Marshall, Mo; Cent. Col, Fayette, Mo; Columbia Univ, N.Y.C; Univ. Mo, Columbia, B.S, Civil Eng, 49. Polit. & Govt. Pos: Bd. dirs, Boone Co. Cerebral Palsy Asn; Mo. State Rep, 64-66. Bus. & Prof. Pos: Registered prfnl. engr; Chief engr, Laclede Steel Co, New Orleans, La; chief engr, Plasteck, Inc, Poteau, Okla; gen. mgr, Riback Industs, Columbia, Mo; self employed consult. engr, specializing in struct. design and construction supv, 58- Mil. Serv: Naval Res, 38 months, radar and sonar specialist and served as commanding officer of a subchaser. Mem: Mo. Soc. Prfnl. Engrs.(legis. cmt); RAM; K.T; Consistory (32°); Scottish Rite; Shrine; Alleppo Grotto (past monarch); Little Dixie Kiwanis Club (past pres. and secy); C. of C; Am. Legion; Am. Soc. Civil Engrs; Construction Specifications Inst; Nat. Soc. Prfnl. Engrs; Mo. Acad. Sci; Boone Co. Young Dem; Centralia 500 Dem. Club. Rel: Christian Church. Mailing Add: R.F.D. 5, Columbia, Mo. 65201. (1967)

NIGH, GEORGE PATTERSON D
Lt. Gov. of Okla.
b. MacAlester, Okla, 6/9/27; s. Wilber R. Nigh and Irene Crockett N; m. 10/19/63 to Donna Skinner Mashburn; c. Mike Mashburn and Georgeann. Educ: East. Okla. A&M, 46-48; East Cent. State Col, B.A, 50. Polit. & Govt. Pos: Okla, State Rep, 51-59; Lt. Gov. of Okla, 59-63 & 67-; Gov. Okla, 63. Bus. & Prof. Pos: Teacher, McAlester, Okla. High Sch, 51-58; grocery store, 54-62; pub. rels, 63-66. Mil. Serv: Entered as A/S, Navy, 46, released as Aviation Boatswain Mate 3/C, 47. Mem: Mason (32°); Shriner; Lions; Am. Legion. Rel: Baptist. Legal Res: 8321 Picnic Lane, Oklahoma City, Okla. 73127. Mailing Add: State Capitol Bldg, Oklahoma City, Okla. 73105.

NIKITAS, CHRISTUS M. D
b. Fitchburg, Mass, 7/3/23; married; c. four. Educ: Fitchburg State Col, B.S. in Educ. Polit. & Govt. Pos: N.H. State Rep, until 67; chmn, N.H. Jr. Col. Cmn. Bus. & Prof. Pos: Field underwriter for Mass. Mutual Life Ins. Co. Mil. Serv: U.S.A.F, S/Sgt. Mem: Aurora Lodge AF&AM; pres, Northwest Homeowners' Asn. Rel: Greek Orthodox. Mailing Add: 39 Marie Ave, Nashua, N.H. 03060. (1967)

NIKOLAY, FRANK LAWRENCE D
Wis. State Assemblyman
b. Day, Wis, 9/1/22; s. Jacob Nikolay and Anna Illig N; m. 8/3/57 to Mary Elizabeth Gisvold. Educ: Univ. Wis, LL.B, 48. Polit. & Govt. Pos: City attorney, Abbotsford, Wis, 48-; supvr, Clark Co, 49-51; dist. counsel, Off. of Price Stabilization, Green Bay, 51; asst. U.S. Attorney, 52, U.S. Attorney, West. Dist. Wis, 52-54; Wis. State Assemblyman, Clark Co, 59-66 & 68-, Majority Floor leader, Wis. State Assembly, 65-66, asst. Dem. Floor Leader, 69-; v.chmn, Dem. Party, Wis, 63- Mil. Serv: Entered as Pvt, Wis. Nat. Guard, 40, released as 2/C PO, 46, after serv. in 32nd Inf. Div, Army, Navy Air Corps and Navy, S.Pac, 45-46; Judge Adv, Wis. Army Nat. Guard, 46-; Asiatic Pac. Theater Ribbon; Philippine Liberation, Japanese Occup. and Pre-Pearl Harbor Medals. Mem: Am, Wis. and Clark Co. Bar Asns; Am. Legion; VFW; K. of C. Rel: Catholic. Legal Res: Abbotsford, Wis. 54405. Mailing Add: Box 455, Colby, Wis. 54421.

NILES, DALWIN J. R
N.Y. State Sen.
b. Schenectady, N.Y, 9/5/14; s. John J. Niles and Carrie M. Anderson N; m. 11/4/50 to Mary C. Heagle; c. David A. and Jeffrey A. Educ: Union Col, 32-34; Albany Law Sch, LL.B, 37. Polit. & Govt. Pos: Counsel, N.Y. State Senators, 47-52; judge, Fulton Co. Family Court, 53-65; N.Y. State Sen, 65- Bus. & Prof. Pos: Attorney, Murphy & Niles, 39- Mil. Serv: Entered as Pvt, Army, 41, released as Maj, 46, after serv. in Third Army Judge Adv. Corps, ETO, 45-46; Commendation Ribbon; Maj, Inactive Res. Mem: Fulton Co, N.Y. State and Am. Bar Asns; Mason; Am. Legion; Moose; VFW; Eagles; Lions. Rel: Presbyterian. Mailing Add: 502 S. William St, Johnstown, N.Y. 12095.

NILES, IRVING RUSSELL D
Kans. State Rep.
b. Olivet, Kans, 12/12/14; s. Frank B. Niles and Pearl Goodman N; m. 11/5/50 to Carrol Dean Ramsey; c. Frank B, Nancy K. and Norma D. Educ: Univ. Kans, 32-34; Kans. State Univ, B.S. in Agr, 37. Polit. & Govt. Pos: Supvr, Osage Co. Soil Conserv. Dist, Kans, 53-; Kans. State Rep, 55-57, 59-61 & 67-; mem, Osage Co. Farm Home Admin. Cmt, 63-66. Bus. & Prof. Pos: Farmer; co-owner, Plodium Bowling Alley, currently. Mil. Serv: Entered as A/S, Naval Res, 42, released as Lt, 46, after serv. in Amphibious Div, S.Pac. and Pac. Theatres, 42-45; Pac. Theatre Ribbon with Four Battle Stars. Publ: Columnist, 'Sounding Board,' Nat. Observer. Mem: Farm Bur; Grange; Am. Legion. Rel: Methodist. Mailing Add: R.R. 1, Lyndon, Kans. 66451.

NILSON, HERBERT TOMLIN R
Chmn, Carlisle Town Rep. Cmt, Mass.
b. Cambridge, Mass, 11/27/24; s. Nils William Nilson and Blanche Tomlin N; m. 10/12/55 to Elizabeth R. Lewis. Educ: Bryant & Stratton Bus. Col, Assoc, 48. Polit. & Govt. Pos: Mem, Lexington Rep. Town Cmt, Mass, 52-56; mem, Bedford Rep. Town Cmt, 58-63, mem. exec. cmt, 60-62; mem, Bedford Bd. Health, 59-63, chmn, 61-63, health agent, 64-69; mem. and chmn, Carlisle Rep. Town Cmt, 68- Bus. & Prof. Pos: Salesman, Sonotone, Boston, Mass, 48-49; salesman and dist. mgr, Libby MacNeilt and Libby, Boston, 49-57; sales mgr, Sands Taylor and Wood, Cambridge, 57-59 and C.E. Merry Co, Newton, 59-62. Mil. Serv: Entered as Pvt, Army, 43, released as T/Sgt, 46, after serv. in Med. Corp, ETO, 44-46; European Theatre Ribbon with Five Battle Stars; Good Conduct Medal. Mem: Grocery Mfg. New Eng; Northeast. Mass. Asns. Bd. Health; Nat. Asn. Watch and Clock Collectors. Rel: Episcopal. Mailing Add: Bedford Rd, Carlisle, Mass. 01741.

NIMMERRICHTER, LORETTA R
Md. State Del.
b. Wash. D.C, 6/2/31; d. Edward Joseph Moran and Maude Johnson M; m. 10/13/50 to Francis Joseph Nimmerrichter; c. Lawrence and Susan. Educ: Greenbrier Col, 2 years. Polit. & Govt. Pos: Judge, Orphan's Court, Charles Co, Md, 62-66; Md. State Del, 66-; pres, Charles Co. Rep. Women, 67-69. Bus. & Prof. Pos: Secy, Providence Hosp, Wash, D.C, 49-50 and Navy Yard, 50-51. Mem: S. Md. Fedn. of Women; women's br, Izaak Walton League; Aircraft Owners Pilots Asn; chmn, Co. Hist. Soc; Soc. for Restoration of Port Tobacco. Rel: Baptist. Legal Res: Route 1, Box 126, Waldorf, Md. 20601. Mailing Add: State House, Annapolis, Md. 21401.

NIMROD, JOHN JOSEPH R
Mem, Cook Co. Rep. Cent. Cmt, Ill.
b. Chicago, Ill, 5/1/22; m. to Dorothy Ingeborg Paul; c. Lisbeth, Noelle and twins John and Joseph. Educ: Univ. Ill, 40-41; Ill. Inst. Tech, 41-42; Northwest. Univ, B.S, Indust. and Mech. Eng, 50. Polit. & Govt. Pos: Auditor, Niles Twp, Ill, 61-65, supvr, 65-; civil defense dir, Skokie, 61-65; cand. for trustee, Chicago Metrop. Sanit. Dist, 62; admin. asst. to pres, Cook Co. Bd. Cmnrs, 63-; custodian, Cook Co. Properties, Cook Co. Sheriffs Off, 63-; campaign coordinator for William J. Scott, Cook Co, 64; committeeman, Niles Twp. Rep. Cmt, 66-; mem, Cook Co. Rep. Cent. Cmt, 66-; asst. state campaign dir. for Gov. Richard B. Ogilvie, 68; alternate del, Rep. Nat. Conv, 68; asst. dir, Dept. Revenue, Ill, 68-; cand. for U.S. Rep, 13th Dist, Ill, 69. Bus. & Prof. Pos: Consult. engr, Adams Steele Co, Chicago, Ill, 53-56; pres, Temrock Inc, Barrington, 56-63; faculty asst, Bd. Pre-Sch. Educ, Skokie. Mil. Serv: Entered Army, 43, released as 1st Lt, 46, after serv. in ETO; recalled as Capt, 50-52, serv. as combat adv. to Army of South Korea; Bronze Star; Combat Inf. Badge; UN Medal; Four Battle Stars; Presidential Citation; Wohrung (Korean) Medal. Publ: Ed, Korean-American Dictionary; co-auth, Township Government Today, 68. Mem: Regional dir, Heart Fund, 53; Leaning Tower YMCA (gov. mem); Twp. Off. Ill. Asn.(dir. and v.pres, former pres. state auditors div, guest lectr); Twp. Off. of Cook Co.(pres, dir. and founder); Amvets (past comdr); Am. Mgt. Asn; Ill. Soc. Plastic Engrs; Northwest Univ. Alumni Asn; Mason; Shrine. Humanitarian Award, Welfare Coun, 68. Rel: Presbyterian; Elder, Former Trustee and Sunday Sch. Supt. Mailing Add: 9216 Kildare Ave, Skokie, Ill. 60076.

NIMS, DARYL HALLETT D
b. Des Moines, Iowa, 1923; s. Harold H. Nims and Aline N; m. 12/28/45 to Margaret Rasmussen; c. Nyle, Nancy, Nadine, Norine, Normagene and Nichelle. Educ: Drake Univ, B.S. in mkt, 47; Sigma Alpha Epsilon. Polit. & Govt. Pos: Mem, Story Co. Develop. Cmt, Iowa, formerly; Iowa State Sen. until 66. Bus. & Prof. Pos: Pres. and gen. mgr, Nims Sportsman's of Ames. Mil. Serv: Air Force, 2nd Lt, pilot, B-25. Mem: Elks; Am. Legion; Izaak Walton League; Nat. Sporting Goods Asn; Ames C. of C. Mailing Add: 815 Murray Dr, Ames, Iowa 50010.

NINBURG, DANIEL HARVEY D
Mem, Calif. Dem. State Cent. Cmt.
b. Newark, N.J, 4/30/28; s. Samuel Hillel Ninburg and Beatrice Love Mecklin N; m. 8/15/66 to Margaret Mary Malley; c. Michael Hillel and twins, Eliot Patrick and Rebecca Anne. Educ: Cornell Univ, A.B, 49; Univ. Zurich Sch. Med, 54-55; Univ. Buffalo Sch. Med, M.D, 59; Alpha Epsilon Delta; Alpha Omega Alpha; Sigma Alpha Mu; Nu Sigma Nu. Polit. & Govt. Pos: Mem, Campaign Cabinet, Richard T. Hanna for Cong, 34th Dist, Calif, 64, 66 & 68; mem, Calif. Dem. State Cent. Cmt, 66-; co-chmn. Humphrey-Muskie Campaign, Orange Co, Calif, 68; cand. for Calif. Del. to Dem. Nat. Conv, 68. Bus. & Prof. Pos: Chmn. bd, Southland Ambulance Serv, Inc, Buena Park, Calif, 62-; chief of staff, Anaheim Gen. Hosp, 65-67; chmn. bd, Studio Soest, Inc, Van Nuys, 66- Mem: Am, Calif, Orange Co. and Aerospace Med. Asns; Am. Acad. Gen. Practice (pres, Orange Co. chap, 68); Anaheim C. of C.(dir, 64-65); Am. Jewish Cmt.(chmn, Orange Co. Chap, 66-). Rel: Hebrew. Legal Res: 1208 Rowan St, Anaheim, Calif. 92801. Mailing Add: 1781 W. Romneya Dr, Anaheim, Calif. 92801.

NINOS, ANTHONY D
Chmn, Brevard Co. Dem. Exec. Cmt, Fla.
b. Lockport, N.Y, 2/7/19; s. Nickolas Ninos and Bessie Calafates N; m. 6/20/54 to Georgia G. Georgas. Educ: Alfred Univ. Exten, Lockport, 37-38; Alfred Univ, 38-41; Ceramic Eng. Soc; Delta Sigma Phi. Polit. & Govt. Pos: Councilman, Cocoa, Fla, 59-63, mayor, 61-63; population cmnr, Ninth Judicial Circuit, 64; cmnr, Fla. Dept. of Vet. Affairs, 64-67; Fla. State Rep, 66-67; chmn Brevard Co. Dem. Exec. Cmt, 69- Bus. & Prof. Pos: Former pres. and dir, Teletronics, Inc, Cocoa, Fla; former pres. and dir, Boca Raton Enterprises; pres. and dir, Laycock Brevard Co, Cocoa and Cocoa Enterprises, Inc, currently. Mil. Serv: Entered as Pvt, Army, 42, released as Pfc, 45, after serv. in Third Armored Div, ETO, 43-45; Four Bronze Battle Stars; Distinguished Unit Badge; Two Campaign Medals; Letter of Commendation. Mem: Dir, Fla. Hotel and Motel Asn; dir, Cape Kennedy Restaurant Asn; Elks; VFW; comdr, Am. Legion; pres, Kiwanis; Civilian-Mil. Coun; adv. bd, Salvation Army; pres, Cocoa Jr. C. of C. Legal Res: 112 Riverside Dr, Cocoa, Fla. 32922. Mailing Add: P.O. Box 1060, Cocoa, Fla. 32922.

NISBET, EUGENE G. D
Mem, Calif. Dem. State Cent. Cmt.
b. Virginia, Ill, 1896; single. Educ: Univ. of South. Calif; Stanford Univ. Polit. & Govt. Pos: Mayor, Upland, Calif, 12 years, mem. city coun, 16 years; Calif. State Sen, 54-66; mem, Calif. Dem. State Cent. Cmt, currently. Bus. & Prof. Pos: Citrus grower. Mil. Serv: Army, overseas. Mem: Past Comdr, Post 73, Am. Legion. Mailing Add: 200 E. 13th St, Upland Calif. 91786. (1967)

NISSEN, RALPH ALBERT R
Mem, Calif. Rep. State Cent. Cmt.
b. Livermore, Calif, 7/2/11; s. Louis John Nissen and Florence Watkins N; m. 4/9/39 to Eleanor Marie Schneider; c. Florence Jeanne (Mrs. Peter Passof), Paula Louise (Mrs. Harold Miller, Jr) and Louis John, III. Educ: Univ. Calif, Davis, 35-36; Sacramento State Col, 61; Phi Alpha Iota. Polit. & Govt. Pos: Chmn, Williams Unified Sch. Bd, Calif, 40-64; chmn, Colusa Co. Rep. Cent. Cmt, 56-60; mem, Calif. Rep. State Cent. Cmt, 56-; Rep. nominee, Fourth Dist, Calif. State Sen, 63; mem, Gov. Cmn. For. Trade, 66-; chmn, Calif. Expos. and Fair Exec. Cmt, 68- Bus. & Prof. Pos: Owner and mgr, Nissen Enterprises, farming, 37-69; dir, Bank of Agr, 67- Publ: Numerous articles on rice, Am. Farm Bur. Mem: Rice Growers Asn. Calif.(dir, 43-); Calif. State Sec. Agr. Adv. Bd; Irrigation Dist. Asn.(pres, 69-); Calif. Farm Bur. Fedn.(v.pres, 55-59); Univ. Calif, Davis Alumni Asn.(dir, 68-); Odd Fellows; Arbockle Golf Club; Farm Bur; Commonwealth Club, San Francisco; Comstock Club, Sacramento. Calif. 4-H Alumni Award, 59, Nat. Finalist. Rel: Presbyterian. Legal Res: Husted Rd, Williams, Calif. 95987. Mailing Add: P.O. Box 216, Williams, Calif. 95987.

NISSLEY, ELEANORE STEFFENS R
Committeewoman, N.J. Rep. State Cmt.
b. New York, N.Y; d. Emil William Steffens and Gertrude Urchs S; m. 6/28/49 to Warren Walmer Nissley, Jr; c. James Edward, Virginia Gale, Peter Bradford and Debra Lou. Educ: Skidmore Col; New York Univ, B.S, 49. Polit. & Govt. Pos: Committeewoman, Bergen Co. Rep. Cmt, N.J, 53-; munic. chmn, Ridgewood, N.J, 60-61; pres, Bergen Co. Rep. Women's Club, 62-68; officer, Bergen Co. Rep. Orgn, 62-; committeewoman, N.J. Rep. State Cmt, 64-; officer, N.J. Fedn. Rep. Women, 65-67 & 68-; del, Rep. Nat. Conv, 68; campaign mgr, Bergen Co, 68. Bus. & Prof. Pos: Sch. teacher, Tucson, Ariz, 49. Mem: Women's Club Ridgewood; Col. Club Ridgewood; Valley Hosp. Auxiliary; Bergen Co. Women's Rep. Club; League of Women Voters; Urban League; N.W. Bergen Ment. Health Asn. Over the Top Award, Commun. Chest, 67. Rel: Presbyterian. Mailing Add: 145 Phelps Rd, Ridgewood, N.J. 07450.

NISWANDER, CALVIN ELROY R
Chmn, Lewis Co. Rep. Party, Idaho
b. Winchester, Idaho, 4/26/25; s. Virgil Elroy Niswander and Esther Lehman N; m. 12/21/47 to Kathleen Mae Smith; c. Linda Louise, Carol Ann and Cheryl Marie. Educ: Univ. Idaho, 2 years. Polit. & Govt. Pos: City councilman, Craigmont, Idaho, 68-; pres, Clearwater Econ. Develop. Asn, 68-; chmn, Lewis Co. Rep. Party, 68- Mil. Serv: Entered as A/S, Navy, 44, released as AETM 1/C, 46, after serv. on U.S.S. Ala, 45-46. Mem: Am. Legion; Mason. Mailing Add: Craigmont, Idaho 83523.

NITSCH, JOHN CHRISTIAN R
b. Oberlin, Kans, 4/4/95; s. Paul Nitsch and Thresia Nitschinger N; m. 12/6/16 to Martha M. Lueke; c. Milton A. Educ: Grand Island Bus. Col. Polit. & Govt. Pos: Del, Rep. Nat. Conv, 64. Bus. & Prof. Pos: Pres, West. Retail Implement & Hardware Asn, Kansas City, Mo, 49-50; pres, Nat. Hwy. U.S. 83 Asn, 50-52. Mem: Capital Hill Club, Wash, D.C; Rotary Club. Rel: Lutheran. Mailing Add: 202 E. Oak St, Oberlin, Kans. 67749.

NITSCHKE, ELMER CLARENCE R
Wis. State Assemblyman
b. Burnett, Wis, 5/20/11; s. Edward Charles Nitschke and Ida Strauss N; m. Oct, 1934 to Marjorie Ruth Sutton; c. Marlene (Mrs. Robert Linde), Judith (Mrs. Lynn Cundy) and Gene. Polit. & Govt. Pos: Wis. State Assemblyman, Dodge Co, 49- and Dep. Sheriff; Sch. Bd. Mem. Bus. & Prof. Pos: Secy. and treas, Burnett & Beaver Dam Mutual Ins. Co, 54-66; dir, Hustisford Farmers Mutual Ins. Co, 56-; secy, Oak Grove Farmers Mutual Ins. Co, 61- Mem: Elks; Eagles; Odd Fellows; Mason. Rel: Protestant. Mailing Add: 208 Hamilton St, Beaver Dam, Wis. 53916.

NITZE, PAUL HENRY D
b. Amherst, Mass, 1/16/07; s. William A. Nitze and Anina Hilken N; m. 12/2/32 to Phyllis Pratt; c. Heidi, Peter, William, II and Phyllis. Educ: Harvard Univ, A.B, 28; New Sch. Soc. Res; Pratt Inst, Johns Hopkins Univ, LL.D. Polit. & Govt. Pos: Finance dir, Off. Coordinator, Inter-Am. Affairs, 41-42; chief metals and minerals br, Bd. Econ. Warfare, 42-48; dir. for procure-

ment and develop. br, For. Econ. Admin, 43-44; spec. consult, War Dept; dir. and then v.chmn, U.S. Strategic Bombing Surv, 44-46; dep. dir, Off. Int. Trade Policy, 46; dep. to asst. secy. for econ. affairs, Dept. State, 48-49, dir. policy planning staff, 50-53; asst. secy. for int. security affairs, Dept. Defense, 61-63; Secy. of Navy, 63-67; Dep. Secy. Defense, 67-69. Bus. & Prof. Pos: Chmn. bd. dirs, Aspen Skiing Corp, 46-; pres, For. Serv. Educ. Found, Wash, D.C, 53-61; Dillon Read & Co, invest. bankers, N.Y.C, 29-38, v.pres, 39-41; pres, P.H. Nitze & Co, Inc, 38-39; bd. overseers, Harvard Univ, 67-; dir, Am. Security & Trust Co, Wash, D.C, 69-, Schroder's Ltd, London, Eng, 69- and Shroder's Inc, N.Y.C, 69-; trustee, Johns Hopkins Univ, 69- Publ: U.S. Foreign Policy, 45-55. Recipient, Medal for Merit. Legal Res: La Plata, Md. Mailing Add: 3120 Woodley Rd. N.W, Washington, D.C. 20350.

NIX, JAMES ELMER R
b. Ellisville, Miss, 10/24/31; s. Robert L. Nix and Gladys Strahan N; m. 11/16/56 to Rosemary Cochrane; c. Georgia Lee, Susan Paulette, James Elmer, Jr. and Robert Leroy, II. Educ: Univ. Miss, 3 years; Jefferson Med. Col, Phila, M.D, 56; Kappa Sigma; Phi Chi. Polit. & Govt. Pos: Hinds Co. del, Miss. State Rep. Conv, 68; alternate del-at-lg, Rep. Nat. Conv, 68; chmn, Precinct 51, Hinds Co, Miss, 68; mem, Hinds Co. Rep. Exec. Cmt, 68; mem, Hinds Co. Rep. Cent. Cmt, 68. Mil. Serv: Capt, Air Force, 57-59; 2789 Air Force Hosp. Mem: Miss. State, Am. and South. Med. Asns; Am. Acad. Orthopaedic Surgeons; Miss. Orthopaedic Soc; Jackson Club. Rel: Presbyterian. Legal Res: 2332 Twin Lakes Circle, Jackson, Miss. 39211. Mailing Add: 1151 N. State St, Jackson, Miss. 39201.

NIX, ROBERT N. C. D
U.S. Rep, Pa.
b. Orangeburg, S.C, 9/9/05; s. Nelson Cornelius Nix and Sylvia Benjamin N; m. to Ethel Lanier; c. Robert N.C. Educ: Lincoln Univ, A.B, 21; Univ. of Pa, LL.B, 24; Omega Psi Phi. Polit. & Govt. Pos: Spec. dep. attorney gen, escheats div, Pa. Dept. of Revenue and spec. asst. dep. attorney gen, Pa, 34-38; mem, Policy Cmt, Dem. Campaign Cmt, Phila, 53-, co-chmn, Inter-Rels. Cmt, 53-; del, Dem. Nat. Conv, 56, 60, 64 & 68; treas, Dem. Co. Cmt, 58; U.S. Rep, Pa, 58- Bus. & Prof. Pos: Lawyer, 25- Mem: Phila. Citizens Cmt. Against Juvenile Delinquency; Phila. Bar Asn; NAACP; YMCA; Am. Woodmen; Elks; Pyramid Club of Phila. Rel: Baptist. Legal Res: 2139 N. 22nd St, Philadelphia, Pa. 19121. Mailing Add: 2201 Rayburn House Office Bldg, Washington, D.C. 20515. (1967)

NIX, WILLIAM DALE, JR. 'BILL' R
Chmn, Hemphill Co. Rep. Party, Tex.
b. Amarillo, Tex, 6/9/41; s. William Dale Nix and Mary Alice Quattlebaum N; m. 8/3/63 to Nelwyn 'Puddin' Hermann; c. William Dale Todd. Educ: Tex. A&M Univ, B.A, 63, grad. work, 66; Church Divinity Sch. of the Pac, 63; Sigma Tau Delta; corps comdr, Tex. A&M Cadet Corps; Ross Volunteer Honor Guard. Polit. & Govt. Pos: Chmn, Hemphill Co. Rep. Party, Tex, 66-; key Rep, 68-; 18th Cong. Dist. chmn, Ralph Yarborough Retirement Fund Dr, 69- Bus. & Prof. Pos: V.pres. and ranch mgr, Nix Cattle Co, Inc, 66-; secy, Beef Cattle Co. Inc, 68- Mil. Serv: Entered as 2nd Lt, Army, 64, released as 1st Lt, 66, after serv. in Adv. Group to the La. Nat. Guard; Capt, Army, Res, 68-69. Mem: Tex. and Southwest. Cattle Raisers Asn; Am. Nat. Cattlemen's Asn; chmn, Co. Beef Cattle Improv. Cmt; chmn, Co. Sch. Bd; Tex. Cattle Feeders Asn; Am-Int. Charolais Asn. Outstanding Young Rancher, 67-68; Freedom's Found. Award, 66. Rel: Episcopal; Clerk of the Vestry, St. Matthew's Episcopal Church, Pampa, Tex. Mailing Add: 611 Cedar, Canadian, Tex. 79014.

NIXON, DAVID LEE R
N.H. State Rep.
b. Concord, Mass, 3/19/32; s. Louis Gerard Nixon and Alice Patricia Williams N; m. 7/10/54 to Janet Emily Rich; c. Leslie Carr, Melanie Dru, Wendy Whyte, Amy Williams, David Lee, Jr. and Louis Gerard II. Educ: Wesleyan Univ, A.B, 53; Univ. Mich. Law Sch, LL.B, 58; sr. class pres, Wesleyan Univ. and Univ. Mich. Law Sch; Olin scholarship and White fel, Wesleyan Univ; Theta Nu Epsilon; Mystical Seven Honor Soc; Cannon Honor Soc; pres, Chi Psi; Barristers Honor Soc. Polit. & Govt. Pos: Supvr. of checklist, New Boston, N.H, 61-63; trustee of trust funds, 62-64; legal counsel, New Boston, N.H. and New Boston Sch. Dist, 64-, moderator, 66-; rep. to Gen. Court, New Boston and Francestown, N.H, 69-; N.H. State Rep, Hillsboro Dist. Five, 69-, v.chmn, Cmt. on Ways and Means, N.H. House of Rep, 69- Mil. Serv: Enterec as Pvt, Army Signal Corps, 53, released as Pfc, 55, after serv. in AAA-Nike Command, Second Army, Ft. Mead, Md, 54-55; Good Conduct Medal; Korean Serv. Medal. Publ: Brief in Support of Unification of New Hampshire Bar Association, N.H. Bar J, fall 68. Mem: N.H. Bar Asn.(secy-treas, 65-69, chmn. cmt. on legis, 69-); Am. Bar Asn.(N.H. State Chmn, cmt. on enforcement on disciplinary standards); Manchester, and Int. Bar Asns; Am. Trial Lawyers Asn; Am. Arbit. Asn; N.H. Estate Planning Coun; N.H. Moderators Asn; Nat. Asn. Bar Execs; Phi Delta Phi; AF&AM (Master, Pac. Lodge 45); dir, Manchester Family Serv. Soc, 59-61; v.pres. and dir, N.H. Soc. Welfare Coun, 60-63; pres, Tri-Mountain Baseball League, 62-64; corporator, Manchester Savings Bank, N.H, 67-69; trustee, Robert Frost Homestead Found, 67-; pres, Duston's Golf Course, 68- Co-capt, high sch. and col. football teams; honor grad, U.S. Army Southeast. Signal Corps, Cryptography Sch; Meritorious Serv. Cert, N.H. Bar Asn; one of two N.H. legis. selected for participation in Eagleton Inst-Rutgers Univ. Legis. Seminar, summer 69. Rel: Protestant; Elder, New Boston Commun. Church, 65-69. Mailing Add: Old Coach Rd, New Boston, N.H. 03070.

NIXON, RICHARD M(ILHOUS) R
President, United States
b. Yorba Linda, Calif, 1/9/13; s. Francis A. Nixon and Hannah Milhous N; m. 6/21/40 to Patricia Ryan; c. Patricia and Julie (Mrs. Dwight David Eisenhower II). Educ: Whittier Col, A.B, 34; Duke Univ. Law Sch, LL.B, 37; Order of Coif. Polit. & Govt. Pos: Attorney, Off. of Price Admin, Wash, D.C, 42; U.S. Rep, Calif, 47-51; U.S. Sen, Calif, 51-52; Vice President, United States, 52-60; Rep. cand. for President, United States, 60; Rep. nominee for Gov, Calif, 62; President, United States, 69- Bus. & Prof. Pos: Lawyer, Whittier, Calif, 37-42; dir, Investors; dir, Harsco Corp; counsel, Adams, Duque & Hazeltine, 61-63; partner, Nixon, Mudge, Rose, Guthrie, Alexander & Mitchell, N.Y, 64-68. Mil. Serv: Lt. Comdr, Navy, 42-46. Publ: Six Crises, 62. Mem: Trustee, Whittier Col, 39-68; chmn. bd, Boys' Clubs of Am, 64-68. Rel: Society of Friends. Legal Res: San Clemente, Calif. Mailing Add: The White House, 1600 Pennsylvania Ave, Washington, D.C. 20500.

NIXON, THOMAS GLENN 'TOMMY' D
b. Moselle, Miss, 6/9/25; married. Polit. & Govt. Pos: Former Miss. State Rep. Bus. & Prof. Pos: Mortician. Mem: Am. Legion; VFW. Rel: Methodist. Mailing Add: 12 Lindsey Dr, Laurel, Miss. 39440. (1967)

NOAH, DONALD WITHERELL R
Chmn, Mitchell Co. Rep. Cent. Cmt, Kans.
b. Beloit, Kans, 10/3/28; s. Ralph Henry Noah and Grace Elizabeth Summers N; m. 4/19/53 to Maxine Noreen James; c. Mark James and Michael Don. Educ: Univ. Kans, A.B, 50, LL.B, 52; Phi Alpha Delta. Polit. & Govt. Pos: Secy-treas, Mitchell Co. Rep. Cent. Cmt, Kans, 58-64, chmn, 64-; city attorney, Beloit, Kans, 60-65. Mil. Serv: Capt, Kans. Nat. Guard, 48-66. Mem: Am. and Kans. Bar Asns; Elks; Rotary. Rel: Methodist. Legal Res: 502 W. Main, Beloit, Kans. 67420. Mailing Add: Box 298, Beloit, Kans. 67420.

NOAH, KEITH S. R
Chmn, Floyd Co. Rep. Cent. Cmt, Iowa
b. Charles City, Iowa, 7/18/20; s. Stanley A. Noah and Nora Tucker N; m. 9/22/43 to Helen J. Zastrow; c. Ronald K, Steven C, Eric D. and Nancy H. Educ: Univ. Iowa, B.A, 42, J.D, 48; Phi Delta Theta. Polit. & Govt. Pos: Chmn, Third Dist. Young Rep, Iowa, 50; chmn, Floyd Co. Rep. Cent. Cmt, 52; city attorney, Charles City, 54-58; chmn, Floyd Co. Rep. Cent. Cmt, 65-; mem, Iowa State Higher Educ. Facilities Cmn, 69- Mil. Serv: Entered as Pvt, Air Force, 42, released as 1st Lt, 46, after serv. in Air Corps, Pac. Theatre, 44-46. Mem: Am. and Iowa State Bar Asns; Am. Trial Lawyers Asn; Charles City C. of C.(pres, 51); Charles City Lions Club (pres and dep. dist. gov); v.pres, Winnebago Coun. Boy Scouts; Elks; Am. Legion; Mason. Rel: Methodist. Legal Res: 4 Glen Oak Circle, Charles City, Iowa 50616. Mailing Add: 200 N. Johnson St, Charles City, Iowa 50616.

NOBLE, FREDA GOLDEN D
V.Chmn, Third Cong. Dist. Dem. Cmt, Ind.
b. Brook, Ind, 12/27/06; d. Charles Lee Spitler and Lula Whiting S; m. 2/24/25 to John Edward Noble; c. Richard Lee (deceased), Patricia (Mrs. DeClercq), Norma (Mrs. Kovach) and Kenneth George. Educ: Ind. Univ. Exten. Polit. & Govt. Pos: Clerk, Bd. Pub. Works and Safety, South Bend, Ind, 41-51; secy, Third Cong. Dist. Dem. Cmt, 53-66, v.chmn, 66-; v.chmn, St. Joseph Co. Dem. Party, 53-; city clerk, South Bend, 55-63; assoc. dir. dept. tourism, State of Ind, 64-67; mem. bd. registrn, South Bend, 67- Mem: Bus. & Prfnl. Women's Club (past local pres, state officer); South Bend Altrusa Club (past treas); Am. Legion Auxiliary (past pres); 40 et 8; Gold Star Mothers; Women of the Moose; chmn. bd, North. Ind. Children's Hosp; State Ment. Health Asn. (adv. coun). Dem. of the Year, Young Dem, 61; Woman of the Year, Bus. & Prfnl. Women, 64. Rel: Roman Catholic. Mailing Add: 1114 Harvey St, South Bend, Ind. 46616.

NOBLE, JOE CLARK R
b. St. Joseph, Mo, 11/23/31; s. Norval J. Noble and Eva Hickman N; m. 12/18/52 to Darlene Podlesak; c. Carol Jo. Educ: Univ. Va, Judge Adv. Gen. Course, U.S. Army; Univ. Nebr. Col. Bus. Admin, B.S, Univ. Nebr. Col. Law, J.D, 58; Phi Delta Phi. Polit. & Govt. Pos: Info. chmn, M-O-R-E chmn, Phelps Co. Rep. Party, Nebr, 64-66. Bus. & Prof. Pos: City Attorney, Holdrege, Nebr, 65-66; co. attorney, Phelps Co, 67- Mil. Serv: 2nd Lt, Finance Corps, Army, 53-55, 1st Lt, Judge Adv. Gen. Corps, 58-59, Capt, 1st Inf. Div, Fifth Army Res, 59- Mem: Phelps Co. Bar Asn.(past pres); Am. Trial Attorneys Asn; Nebr. State Bar; Am. Bar Asn; Elks; Jaycees (past bd. dirs); Mason. Rel: Presbyterian; Bd. of Trustees. Legal Res: 1422 Garfield Dr, Holdrege, Nebr. 68949. Mailing Add: 417 West Ave, Holdrege, Nebr. 68949.

NOBLE, MERRILL E. D
b. Savoy, Ill, 12/5/96; s. James Houston Noble and Harriett Baird N; m. 6/19/20 to Martha Van Petten; c. James Van Petten, Merrill Emmett and Margaret (Mrs. R.D. Bentley). Educ: Univ. Ill, LL.B, 20; N.Mex. Highlands Univ, LL.D; Theta Delta Chi; Phi Delta Phi. Polit. & Govt. Pos: City attorney, Las Vegas, N.Mex, 24-25 & 49-53; dist. attorney, Fourth Judicial Dist, N.Mex, 37-45; mem, N.Mex. State Dem. Cent. Cmt, 42-43; mem, N.Mex. State Dem. Exec. Cmt, 46-50; justice, N.Mex. Supreme Court, 60-69. Bus. & Prof. Pos: Pres. bd. regents, N.Mex. Highlands Univ, 37-43; trustee, Southwest. Legal Center, 55-56. Mem: Pres, N.Mex. State Bar, 55-56; N.Mex. State Bar Cmn, 50-57; chmn, N.Mex. Bar Asn. Cmt. on Ethics, Grievances and Discipline, 52-55; pres, San Miguel Co. Bar Asn, 39-42. Award as Alumnus of the Month, Univ. Ill, Apr. 67; Award, Nat. Coun. of Crime and Delinquency. Legal Res: 716 Zia Rd, Santa Fe, N.Mex. 87501. Mailing Add: P.O. Box 848, Santa Fe, N.Mex. 87501.

NOBLE, ROY V. D
Ga. State Sen.
b. Crisp Co, Ga, 5/27/09; s. A.J. Noble and Minnie Spradlin N; m. 3/29/34 to Nine Myrtle Bush; c. Roy V. Jr, Myrtle Angela, John Lee, Rose Elaine. Educ: Cordile High Sch, 27. Polit. & Govt. Pos: Ga. State Sen, 19th Dist, 63-; mem, Dooly Co. Bd. Educ. and Dooly Co. Hosp. Bd. currently. Bus. & Prof. Pos: Farmer, ginner, warehouseman; Pres, Dooly Co. Farm Bur, 59-62; mem, State Farm Bur. Bd, 61-62. Mem: Mason; Shrine. Rel: Baptist; Deacon. Mailing Add: RFD 3, Vienna, Ga. 31092. (1967)

NOBLITT, HARDING COOLIDGE D
Mem, Clay Co. Dem. Cent. Cmt, Minn.
b. Marion, N.C, 10/31/20; s. Walter Tate Noblitt and Nellie Mae Horton N; m 7/3/43 to Louise Hope Lester; c. Walter Thomas. Educ: Berea Col, B.A, 42; Univ. Chicago, A.M, 47, Ph.D, 55; Phi Kappa Phi; Pi Gamma Mu; Tau Kappa Alpha; Pi Kappa Delta. Polit. & Govt. Pos: Del, Dem-Farmer-Labor State Conv, Minn, 58, 60, 62, 64 & 68; alternate del, 66, chmn. platform cmt, 68; Youth Coordinator, 61-62; nominee for cong, Seventh Dist, Dem-Farmer-Labor Party, 62; mem, Gov. Citizens Coun. on Aging, 63-66; co-chmn, Profs. for Johnson-Humphrey, Minn, 64; del, Dem. Nat. Conv, 64; mem, Clay Co. Dem. Cent. Cmt, 66- Bus. & Prof. Pos: Asst. prof, Concordia Col, Moorhead, Minn, 50-53, assoc. prof, 53-56, prof, 56- and chmn. dept. polit. sci, 64-; act-

ing ed, Discourse: A Review of the Liberal Arts, 59-60, mem. ed. bd, currently. Mil. Serv: Entered as Pvt, Army, 43, released as T/Sgt, 46, after serv. in 16th Armored Div, 79th Inf. Div, 1st U.S. Inf. Div, ETO, 45-46; European-African-Mid. East. Campaign Medal with Two Bronze Stars; Meritorious Serv. Citation. Publ: 'Intentions of Founding Fathers in Separating Church and State,' Discourse, Jan, 58; 'A Case Study in Practical Politics,' Proc. of the Minn. Acad. of Sci, Vol. 31, No. 1, 1963. Mem: Am. Polit. Sci. Asn; Acad. of Polit. Sci; Am. Acad. of Polit. and Soc. Sci; Am. Legion; VFW. Rel: Presbyterian. Mailing Add: 2014 S. 4th St, Moorhead, Minn. 56560.

NOCE, ROBERT NICHOLAS R
b. Bridgeport, Conn, 7/9/21; s. Nicholas Americus Noce and Anna Clark N; m. 12/24/42 to Marion Evelyn Spielman; c. Roberta and Christina. Educ: Fordham Univ, B.S. Polit. & Govt. Pos: Justice of the peace, Danbury, Conn, 64-; mem, Bd. of Tax Rev, 65-; former chmn, Danbury Rep. Town Cmt. Bus. & Prof. Pos: Pres, Gr. Danbury Bd. of Realtors, Inc, 64. Mil. Serv: Entered as Pvt, Army, 42, released as T/Sgt, 46, after serv. in Fourth S.C, Am. Theater; Am. Theater Serv. Ribbon; Good Conduct and Victory Medals; Army Commendation Award. Mem: Order Sons of Italy in Am; Exchange Club of Danbury; Rep. Men's Club; Union Lodge 40; AF&AM; Soc. of Real Estate Appraisers; Am. Right of Way Asn; Danbury Club; Nat, State and Local Real Estate Bds; Ridgewood Country Club. Named Danbury Realtor of the year, 64. Rel: Protestant. Legal Res: 13 Virginia Ave, Danbury, Conn. 06810. Mailing Add: P.O. Box 189, Danbury, Conn. 06810.

NOCK, JOHN DIX, JR. R
b. Baltimore, Md, 8/18/22; s. John Dix Nock and Carolyn Osmond N; m. 4/2/48 to Mary Edith Justice; c. John Dix, III, William Justice, Edith Duvall, Henry Page and Thomas Osmond. Educ: The Citadel, A.B. in Eng, 43; N.C. State Col, Raleigh, M.S. in Eng, 53. Polit. & Govt. Pos: Rep. precinct chmn, Cheraw, S.C, 62; campaign chmn, Chesterfield Co. for Strom Thurmond, 64; chmn, Chesterfield Co. Rep. Party, 64-68; mem, Selective Serv. Bd, 13, Chesterfield Co, 10 years. Bus. & Prof. Pos: Shrimping indust, Charleston, S.C, 48-50; engr, Becker Sand & Gravel, Cheraw, 53-68; pres, Family Camping Corp, Seamont, Inc, Cheraw, S.C, 68- Mil. Serv: Entered as Lt, Army, 43, released as Capt, 46, after serv. as parachutist, 11th Airborne Div, Pac. Theater. Mem: Nat. Quartz Producers Coun; Mason; Am. Legion; Boy Scout Coun. Silver Beaver, Boy Scouts. Rel: Episcopal. Legal Res: Seamont Family Campground, Route 1, Box 18P, St. Augustine, Fla. 32084. Mailing Add: P.O. Drawer 329, St. Augustine, Fla. 32084.

NOCK, MARY L. D
Md. State Sen.
b. Green Hill, Md; d. William Thomas Layfield and Lula Taylor L; m. 4/11/25 to Garland Nock. Educ: Beacom Bus. Col, Wilmington, Del; Delta Gamma Kappa. Polit. & Govt. Pos: Md. State Del, 47-55; mem, Md. State Legis. Coun, 53-54 & 59-; Md. State Sen, 55-, pres-pro-tem, Md. State Senate, 59-, chmn. educ. cmt, 59-66. Bus. & Prof. Pos: Mem. Bd. and Exec. Cmt, Educ. Cmn. of the States; mem, South. Regional Educ. Bd, 59- Mem: Past pres, Jr. Bd. Peninsula Gen. Hosp; Green Hill Yacht and Country Club; Eastern Star; John B. Parsons Auxiliary; hon. mem, Soroptimists Int; hon. life mem, Md. Cong. of Parents and Teachers. Eleanor Roosevelt Achievement Award for Outstanding Achievements in Pub. Affairs; Recipient of Citation for Christian Citizenship, Nat. Coun. of Churches. Rel: Methodist. Legal Res: 914 Camden Ave, Salisbury, Md. 21801. Mailing Add: P.O. Box 488, Salisbury, Md. 21801.

NOE, JAMES ALBERT D
b. West Point, Ky, 12/21/93; s. John M. Noe and Belle McRae N; m. 5/7/22 to Anna Gray Sweeney; c. Gay, James Albert and Linda McRae. Educ: Country schs. Polit. & Govt. Pos: Former mem, Dem. Nat. Cmt, La; La. State Sen, 32-34 & 36-40; Lt. Gov, La, 34-36, Gov, 36; del, Dem. Nat. Conv, 68. Bus. & Prof. Pos: Owner-operator, plantations in Ouachita and Tensas Parishes; owner-operator, radio stas. KNOE, KNOE FM and KNOE TV, Monroe, La. and radio sta. WNOE and WNOE FM, New Orleans, La; engaged in oil and natural gas bus. in Ark, La. and Tex. Mil. Serv: Entered as Pvt, Army, released as Lt, after serv. in 369th Inf, World War I. Rel: Presbyterian. Mailing Add: Knoe Rd, Monroe, La. 71201.

NOECKER, MARY LOU D
Secy, Piatt Co. Dem. Cent. Cmt, Ill.
b. Monticello, Ill, 3/2/28; d. Chester D. Hayes and Hazel Hosler H; m. 3/20/47 to Donald N. Noecker; c. A. Scott, Joseph K, Cindy D. and Kelly Lou. Educ: Mansfield Commun. High Sch, 4 years. Polit. & Govt. Pos: Dem. Precinct Committeeman, Monticello, Third Dist, Ill, 60-68; Secy, Piatt Co. Dem. Cent. Cmt, 60- Mem: Piatt Co. Heart Asn.(Monticello chmn, 64-68); Red Cross Bloodmobile Prog.(Monticello chmn, 66-69); Farm Bur. Rel: Methodist. Legal Res: 800 W. William, Monticello, Ill. 61856. Mailing Add: 1 Westfair, Jacksonville, Ill. 62650.

NOEL, JAMES ELLSWORTH R
Chmn, Gove Co. Rep. Cent. Cmt, Kans.
b. Quinter, Kans, 8/19/28; s. Floyd K. Noel and Phyllis N. Sharp N; m. 11/21/59 to Beverly Kay Shook; c. Anna Thea, Floyd Garnett, Megan Michele and Nels Patric. Educ: Ft. Hays Kans. State Col, 46-47; Univ. Kans, A.B, 59, LL.B, 60. Polit. & Govt. Pos: Co. treas, Gove Co, Kans, 51-55, 62-65, co. attorney, 65-67; Mayor, City of Grainfield, 61-62; precinct committeeman, Grainfield Twp, 66-68; chmn, Gove Co. Rep. Cent. Cmt, 68- Bus. & Prof. Pos: Gandy dancer, Union Pac. R.R, Grainfield, Kans, 47-51; bookkeeper and billing clerk, Grainfield Tel. Co, Inc, 51, secy-treas, 60-; ins. adjuster, Universal Adjust. & Inspection Co, Colby, 60-69. Mem: N.W. Kans. Bar Asn; Kans. Bar Asn; Mason; Lions; Theodore Gary chap, Independent Tel. Pioneer Asn. Rel: Methodist. Mailing Add: Grainfield, Kans. 67737.

NOEL, JOSEPH WALTER R
Mem, Calif. State Rep. Cent. Cmt.
b. Pittsburgh, Pa, 6/1/29; s. Harry C. Noel (deceased) and Mary Irwin N; m. 5/29/68 to Roberta Hunt; c. Parker. Educ: Santa Monica City Col, A.A, 52; Univ. South. Calif, B.S, 54. Polit. & Govt. Pos: Mem, Calif. State Rep. Cent. Cmt, 68- Bus. & Prof. Pos: Assoc, Albritton Co, Los Angeles, 57-63; owner, J.W. Noel & Co, 63-68; v.pres, Newport Oil & Gas, Inc, 68- Mil. Serv: Entered as Pvt, Army, 54, released as Sp-4, 56, after serv. in 32nd Brigade, Europe, 55-56. Mem: Nat. Asn. Life Underwriters; Calif. Asn. Life Underwriters (v.pres); West Los Angeles Life Underwriters Asn.(pres); Westside Estate Planning Coun; Westwood Jr. C. of C.(pres); Commun. Chest (bd. of dirs); Riveria Tennis Club Town Hall Los Angeles; Los Angeles World Affairs Coun. Jaycee of the Year, Jr. C. of C; Outstanding State Dir. Leadership Award, Commun. Chest. Rel: Presbyterian. Legal Res: 16554 Sunset Blvd, Pacific Palisades, Calif. 90272. Mailing Add: 606 N. Larchmont 203, Los Angeles, Calif. 90004.

NOEL, PHILIP WILLIAM D
Mayor, Warwick, R.I.
b. Providence, R.I, 6/6/31; s. Seraphin Joseph Noel and Emma B. Crudeli N; m. 10/20/56 to Joyce Anne Sandberg; c. Linda Joyce, Joseph Walter, Lori Anne and Thomas Philip. Educ: Brown Univ, A.B. in Econ, 54; Georgetown Univ, LL.B, 57; Delta Tau Delta. Polit. & Govt. Pos: City Councilman, Warwick, R.I, 60-66 and mayor, 67-; del, Dem. Nat. Conv, 68. Bus. & Prof. Pos: Attorney-at-law, 58-67. Mil. Serv: Entered as Seaman, Naval Res, 53. Mem: Am, R.I. and Kent Co. Bar Asns; K. of C; Elks; Friendly Sons of St. Patrick; Brown Football Asn; Kiwanis. Distinguished Serv. Award, R.I. and Warwick Jaycees. Rel: Roman Catholic. Mailing Add: 14 Leroy Ave, Warwick, R.I. 02889.

NOGAY, WALTER WILLIAM D
Chmn, Hancock Co. Dem. Exec. Cmt, W.Va.
b. Pittsburgh, Pa, 10/30/21; s. Anthony W. Nogay and Veronica Jamrozik N; m. 9/3/49 to Julia Valeriana Guz; c. Thomas Anthony, Valerie Maryanna, Ellen Jaye and Arlie Raymond. Educ: Weir High Sch, Weirton, W.Va. Polit. & Govt. Pos: Exec. committeeman, Hancock Co. Dem. Exec. Cmt, W.Va, chmn, currently. Bus. & Prof. Pos: Owner, Nogay and Sons Movers. Mil. Serv: Entered as Pvt, Army, 42, released as Cpl, 46, after serv. in Gq. Btry. 414th Armored FA Bn, ETO, 45; Good Conduct Medal; Am. Theatre Ribbon; European-African-Mid. East. Theatre Ribbon; World War II Victory Ribbon. Mem: Life mem. VFW; Am. Legion; charter mem. Brooke-Hancock Ment. Health Asn; Gr. Weirton Serv. Coun; Fraternal Order of Police Assocs.(past pres, Weirton Chap); World War II Last Man's Club (past commandant, Weirton Chap); Movers and Warehouseman's Asn. Rel: Roman Catholic. Mailing Add: 3225 West St, Weirton, W.Va. 26062.

NOGUCHI, GEORGE KOJI D
b. Honolulu, Hawaii, 2/29/36; s. Yozo Noguchi and Masae Yoshida N; single. Educ: Univ. Hawaii, B.A, 61; George Wash. Univ. Law Sch, LL.B, 66; Omicron Delta Kappa. Polit. & Govt. Pos: Chmn, Students for Kennedy Cmt, 60; dir, Young Dem. Oahu Co, 61-62, pres, 62-63; mem, Dem. State Campaign Cmt, 62; chmn. educ. cmt, Legis. Affairs Cmt, Young Dem. Clubs Am, 66-; Hawaii State Rep, 66-68. Bus. & Prof. Pos: Dir, Honolulu Stadium Ltd, Hawaii, 60-61. Mil. Serv: Entered as Pvt, Army, 54, released as SP-3, 57. Mem: Univ. Hawaii Alumni Asn; St. Louis Alumni Asn. Mailing Add: 2718-E Waiaka Rd, Honolulu, Hawaii 96814. (1967)

NOLAN, GEORGE EDWARD D
b. St. Albans Bay, 3/23/00; m. to Florence Loyer; c. Three. Educ: Pub. and parochial schs, St. Albans. Polit. & Govt. Pos: Vt. State Rep, 59-65; treas, Caledonia Co. Dem. Cmt; Town and Co. Dem. Cmt; selectman, 51-54; committeeman for Caledonia Co. A.C.P, 47-54. Bus. & Prof. Pos: Retired mgr. Cloverdale and First Nat. stores, 16 years; operated a dairy farm, 17. Mil. Serv: Vt. Nat. Guard, 22-26. Mem: Modern Woodmen of Am; Brownson Coun; K. of C. Rel: Catholic. Mailing Add: RFD 1, Hardwick, Vt. 05843. (1967)

NOLAN, JOHN STEPHAN R
Dep. Asst. Secy. for Tax Policy, Treas. Dept.
b. Cincinnati, Ohio, 1/12/26; s. Edward L. Nolan and Florence Wetterer N; m. 9/5/49 to Adeline Jean Mosher; c. Michael C, Joyce P, Matthew M, John G. and Elizabeth A. Educ: Univ. N.C, Chapel Hill, B.S, 47; Harvard Law Sch, LL.B. magna cum laude, 51; Phi Beta Kappa; Beta Gamma Sigma; Delta Sigma Pi; Scholarship Key. Polit. & Govt. Pos: Mem, Adv. Group to Cmnr. of Internal Revenue, Internal Revenue Serv, 67-68; Dep. Asst. Secy. for Tax Policy, Treas. Dept, 69- Bus. & Prof. Pos: Acct, Pentland, Purvis, Keller & Co, Miami, Fla, 47-48; partner, Miller & Chevalier, Wash, D.C, 51-69; adj. prof. law, Georgetown Law Sch, 56-59. Mil. Serv: Entered as A/S, Naval Res, 44, released as Ens, 46; re-entered as Lt.(jg), 52-54; Lt.(Ret), Naval Res, 67. Publ: 'Uncertain Tax Treatment of Stock Redemptions,' Harvard Law Rev, 52; 'Deferred Compensation Planning—Special Situations,' N.Y. Univ. Fed. Tax Inst, 65; Personal Holding Companies Under the 1964 Act,' Tulane Tax Inst, 65. Mem: Am. Bar Asn.(v.chmn, sect. of taxation, 66-69); Bar Asn. of D.C; Fed. Bar Asn; Barristers; Metrop. Club; bd. visitors, South. Methodist Univ, currently. Rel: Catholic. Legal Res: 10904 Stanmore Dr, Potomac, Md. 20854. Mailing Add: Treasury Dept, 15th and Pennsylvania Ave. N.W, Washington, D.C. 20220.

NOLAN, MAE ELLA R
b. San Francisco, Calif, 9/20/86; d. William Henry Hunt and Annie Irene McHugh H; m. 3/23/13 to John Ignatius Nolan, wid; c. Corliss Theresa (Mrs. Frank E. Guenther). Educ: St. Vincent's Convent of San Francisco; Bus. Col, San Francisco. Polit. & Govt. Pos: U.S. Rep, 5th Cong. Dist, Calif, 23-25. Mem: Olympic Club. Rel: Catholic. Mailing Add: 400 Hyde St, San Francisco, Calif. 94109.

NOLAN, MONICA D
Dem. State Cent. Committeewoman, Ohio
b. Covington, Ky, 12/28/14; d. James Lawrence Nolan and Mary Murphy N; single. Educ: Univ. Cincinnati, A.B, 35. Polit. & Govt. Pos: Adv. Cmt, Cincinnati Pub. Recreation Cmn, Ohio; mem. bd. dirs, Cincinnati Citizens Sch. Cmt; mem. adv. bd, Hamilton Co. Welfare Dept; mem, Mayor's Cmt. on Youth, Cincinnati; mem. steering cmt, Hamilton Co. Dem. Party; del. and mem. rules cmt, Dem. Nat. Conv, 56, del-at-lg, 64 & 68; Dem. Cand. for U.S. Rep, First Dist, Ohio, 62; Dem. State Cent. Committeewoman, Ohio, currently. Bus. & Prof. Pos: Registered rep. of N.Y. Stock Exchange, Hayden Stone, Inc, Cincinnati, Ohio. Mil. Serv: Served with Am. Red Cross in Greenland, India and Germany, World War II. Mem: Women's Nat. Dem. Club; Speakers Bur, N.Y. Stock Exchange; Asn. Alumnae of Sacred Heart; Women's Adv. Cmt, U.S. Lawn Tennis Asn. Former Ohio State Tennis

Champion; Mademoiselle Magazine Award for Outstanding War Work, 43. Rel: Roman Catholic. Mailing Add: 3547 St. Charles Place, Cincinnati, Ohio 45208.

NOLAND, JAMES ALFRED, JR. R
Mo. State Sen.
b. Macks Creek, Mo, 2/2/27; s. James Alfred Noland, Sr. and Martha Allen N; m. 3/27/58 to Janice Mae Pueser; c. Claire Ellen, Cynthia Janice and Cecilia Diane. Educ: Southwest Mo. State, B.S. in educ, 63; Mo. Univ, M.A. in educ, 64. Polit. & Govt. Pos: Mo. State Rep, 56-68; co. tax collector, 58; Mo. State Sen, 68- Bus. & Prof. Pos: Prin, Pub. Sch, 48-56; prof. psychol, Cent. Methodist Col, 65-66. Mil. Serv: Entered as Pvt, Army, 45, released as Cpl, 47, after serv. in 13th Air Force, Philippine Islands, 46-47. Mem: AF&AM (Past Master); Linn Creek Odd Fellows (Past Noble Grand and Dist. Dep. Grand Master); Lake of the Ozarks Am. Legion (Past Commander); Eastern Star. Rel: Baptist. Mailing Add: Osage Beach, Mo. 65065.

NOLEN, JAMES RICHARD D
Mass. State Rep.
b. Holyoke, Mass, 4/17/33; s. James Robert Nolen and Katherine Dillon N; single. Educ: Harvard Col, A.B; Columbia Univ, M.S; Portia Law Sch, LL.B. Valedictorian of Law Sch. class. Polit. & Govt. Pos: Mass. State Rep, 59-; alternate del, Dem. Nat. Conv, 68. Bus. & Prof. Pos: Attorney at Law, 65- Mil. Serv: Pvt, Army. Rel: Roman Catholic. Mailing Add: 25 Homecrest Ave, Ware, Mass. 01082. (1967)

NOLTING, FRED WAYNE D
Iowa State Rep.
b. Frederika, Iowa, 8/21/32; s. Fred W. Nolting and Ida Sauerbrei N; m. 12/7/51 to Wilma A. Cordray; c. Fred W, Jr. and Melody Ann. Educ: East Waterloo High Sch, Iowa, grad, 49; Nat. Camera Repair Sch, Denver, Colo, grad, 58. Polit. & Govt. Pos: Dem. precinct committeeman, Precinct 6, Ward II, Waterloo, Iowa, 62-; del, Dem. Nat. Conv, 68; secy-treas, Third Cong. Dist. Cmt. on Polit. Educ, 68-; Iowa State Rep, Black Hawk Co, 69- Mem: Midwest Labor Press Asn.(Iowa v.pres, 68-); Soc. of Photo Technologists; UPFAW (recording secy, Local 46, 58-61, pres, 61-69, v.pres, Dist. Coun. 3, 68-); AMCBW. Rel: American Lutheran. Legal Res: 1716 Patton Ave, Waterloo, Iowa 50702. Mailing Add: State House, Des Moines, Iowa 50319.

NONNENMACHER, NICHOLAS THADDEUS R
b. Oyster Bay, N.Y, 1/24/21; s. Nicholas Adam Nonnenmacher and Jennie Spellman N; m. 2/9/46 to Kathleen Virginia Bubb; c. Jeanne Marie, Mary Louise, Matthew Joseph, Mark, Therese Marie, Christine Marya, Elizabeth Ann, Regina Kathleen and Michele Yvonne. Educ: N.Y. Univ, B.Aero.E. Polit. & Govt. Pos: Research Specialist on Subversive Activities, Am. Legion Nat. Hq, Wash, 49-53; admin. asst. to U.S. Rep. Donald C. Bruce, Ind, 61-64, U.S. Rep. Glenn Andrews, Ala, 65-66 and U.S. Rep. Henry C. Schadeberg, Wis 67-; Rep. cand, U.S. Cong, Eighth Dist, 66. Bus. & Prof. Pos: Pres, The Christianform, 49-69, pub. affairs consult, 67-69. Mil. Serv: Aviation Cadet, AAC, 41; retired as Maj, Air Force, 49; Mil. Air Mission to Brazil; Hq. U.S. Armed Forces S.Atlantic; 510th Fighter Squadron, 405th Fighter Group, France, World War II; Purple Heart; Air Medal with Clusters; Am. and ETO Ribbons; Wings of Brazilian A.F, U.S. Commendation Ribbon. Mem: K. of C. Mailing Add: 5408 Wehawken Rd, Bethesda, Md. 20016.

NORD, LARRY RICHARD R
Ohio State Rep.
b. Petersburg, Ohio, 5/22/37; s. Richard Norman Nord and Thelma Baun N; m. 6/16/61 to Patricia Lee Baun; c. Christopher Baun and Brian Andrew Baun. Educ: Youngstown State Univ, B.S. in Educ; Westminster Col, M.S. in Admin; grad. study, Kent State Univ. and Akron Univ; Theta Chi. Polit. & Govt. Pos: Trustee, Champion Twp, Ohio, 66-68; Ohio State Rep, 98th Dist, 69- Bus. & Prof. Pos: Instr, Youngstown State Univ, 64-; high sch. prin, Southington Local Schs, 65-66, supt, 67-68. Mem: Ohio, Nat. and Trumbull Educ. Asns; Northeast. Ohio Teacher Asn; Lions; Optimists; Jr. C. of C; F&AM; Odd Fellows; K. of P; Aut Mori Grotto; Giddings. Rel: Lutheran. Mailing Add: 288 Durst Dr. N.W, Warren, Ohio 44483.

NORD, OSCAR R
b. Churchs Ferry, N.Dak, 11/23/21; s. Arvid Nord and Agnes Sulland N; m. 2/14/42 to Dorothy Helen Weiss; c. Gary Duane, Mark Curtis, Patricia Kay, Nancy Rae and Allan Oscar. Educ: Churches Ferry, High Sch, N.Dak, grad, 39. Polit. & Govt. Pos: Mem, legis. lobby, Farm Bur, N.Dak, 64-65, 66-67 and 68-69; chmn, Dist. 15 Rep. Party, N.Dak, 67-68; mem; N.Dak. Rep. State Cent. Cmt, 67-68; mem, State Farmers For Nixon, 68; mem, State Personal Property Tax Cmn, 68-69. Mil. Serv: Entered as Pvt, Army, Ord. Corps, 42, released as 1st Sgt, 45, after serv. in 148 Tire Repair Co, ETO, 43-45. Mem: Farm Bur.(chmn, Ramsey Co. Bur, 63-64, dir. dist. four, N.Dak. Bur, 65-, v.chmn, 66-67); Elks; 40 et 8; Churchs Ferry Rural Fire Dept; VFW; Churchs Ferry Men's Club; Am. Legion; U.S. Durum Growers; N.Dak. Stockman. Rel: Lutheran. Mailing Add: Churchs Ferry, N.Dak. 58325.

NORDBERG, NILS LOVERING R
Mass. State Rep.
b. Woburn, Mass, 11/6/34; s. Nils Lambert Nordberg and Eleanor Lovering N; m. 9/17/60 to Linda Chesley; c. Ellen Lovering and Susan Currier. Educ: Cornell Univ, B.S, 56; Alpha Tau Omega. Polit. & Govt. Pos: Rep. precinct rep, Town Meeting, Reading, Mass, 63-69, mem, Rep. Town Cmt, 66-; Mass. State Rep, 69- Mil. Serv: Entered as 2nd Lt, Army, 56, Maj, Res, Army Qm. Corps, 56- Mem, Cornell Soc. Hotelmen; Mass. Restaurant Asn.(chmn. legis. cmt. & v.pres, 66-69); Nat. Restaurant Asn; AF&AM, Reading Royal Arch Chap, Medford Coun. RSM; K.T; Shrine; Reading Jaycees (pres, 62-63); Reading Taxpayers Asn; Mass. Taxpayers Found; Nat. Fedn. Independent Bus; East. Middlesex Ment. Health Asn; pres, Stoneham C. of C. 63-64. Rel: Protestant. Mailing Add: 32 Pennsylvania Ave, Reading, Mass. 01867.

NORDIN, JOHN HERMAN DFL
b. Sweden, 6/19/92; s. Jonas Nordin and Kristina Person N; m. 11/30/14 to Julia O. Martinson (deceased); 6/25/48 to Eva V. Susa; c. Inga, Rudolph, Alma, Ruth, Esther, Hazel and John, Jr. Polit. & Govt. Pos: Minn. State Rep, 33-38, 47-55 & 57-66; mayor, Columbia Heights, 45-46. Bus. & Prof. Pos: Secy, C. of C, Columbia Heights, 47-49; pres, E. Bethel Fed. Credit Union, 65-66. Mem: Highway 65 Asn.(pres, 5 years); Highway 56 Asn.(secy, 10 years); E. Bethel Booster Club (pres, 9 years). Rel: Lutheran. Legal Res: Lakeview Point, E. Bethel Village, Minn. 55005. Mailing Add: Soderville, Minn. 55304. (1967)

NORE, HERBERT E. R
Nebr. State Sen.
b. Albion, Nebr, 6/16/11; s. Elias Nore and Signie Hovland N; m. 10/31/40 to Catherine Garber; c. Ellen (Mrs. Nordhauser), Betsy and Anne. Educ: Univ. Nebr, B.S; Alpha Zeta; Farm House. Polit. & Govt. Pos: Mem, City Park Bd, Genoa, Nebr, 55-, Commun. Hosp. Bd, 60- and Commun. Develop Corp. Bd, 67-; pres, Nance Co. Econ. Develop. Cmt, 65-; Nebr. State Sen, 65- Mem: Rotary; Elks; Lions; C. of C.(pres, Genoa Chap, 64); first v.pres, Loup Basin Asn, 67- Honors Convocation, Univ. Nebr. Rel: Lutheran. Mailing Add: Genoa, Nebr. 68640.

NOREIKA, LOUISE A. D
b. Burkburnett, Tex, 7/10/23; d. Robert Edward Lee McMillian and Annie Cavin M; m. 7/14/44 to James G. Noreika. Educ: Okla. Univ, 38-39; Okla. City Univ, 41; Beverley Bus. Col, Chicago, Ill, 46-47. Polit. & Govt. Pos: Precinct chmn, past 17 years and ward coordinator for Village, Okla, currently; women's coordinator, State Civil Defense Prog, 50-52; pub. rels. dir, Okla. Semi-Centennial Cmn, 56-58; secy, Okla. State Legis, past 10 sessions; second v.pres, State Fedn. of Dem. Women, 67-69; dep. exam, State Exam. and Inspector's Off, State Capitol, 67-; alternate del, Dem. Nat. Conv, 68; pres, Fifth Dist. Fed. Dem. Women's Clubs, Okla, 69- Bus. & Prof. Pos: Employed in radio and TV field on several occasions; free-lance pub. rels. and publicity for various organizations. Mil. Serv: Entered as Pvt, Women's Army Corps, 42, released as Capt, 45, after serv. in Third Air Force and Ninth Air Force, ETO, 43-45; Five battle stars. Mem: Okla. Pub. Rels. Asn; Northside Dem. Women's Club (past pres); State Jefferson Bryan Club (Fifth Dist. v.pres, 68-); Preceptor, Alpha Chap, Beta Sigma Phi; Galatea Chap, Am. Bus. Women's Asn. Okla. Woman of the Year, 1957; Woman of the Year, Galatea Chap, Am. Bus. Women's Asn, 69. Rel: Catholic. Mailing Add: 2624 Abbey Rd, Oklahoma City, Okla. 73120.

NORGREN, LEIGH HYATT R
b. Denver, Colo, 6/15/27; s. Carl A. Norgren and Juliet E. Lien N; m. 3/29/52 to Loretta Marie Boothe; c. Karen Marie, Virginia Phay; Kimberly Gene and Carl Boothe. Educ: Univ. Colo, 46-48; Purdue Univ, mech. eng, 48-50; Beta Theta Pi; Pi Tau Sigma. Polit. & Govt. Pos: Precinct committeeman; chmn, Arapahoe Co. Rep. Finance Cmt; bd. mem, Colo. United Rep. Fund; state chmn, Legis. Training Cmt; Colo. State Rep, Arapahoe Co, 67-68. Bus. & Prof. Pos: Pres, Phys. & Surg. Supply, 60-66; pres, Leigh H. Norgren & Co, v.pres. and dir, Carl A. Norgren Co. and dir, Security Nat. Bank and Colo. Fed. Savings & Loan Asn, currently. Mil. Serv: Navy, 45-46. Mem: Arapahoe Co. Budget Adv. Cmt. Mailing Add: 3106 Cherryridge Rd, Englewood, Colo. 80110. (1967)

NORHEIM, GORDON L. DFL
Polit. & Govt. Pos: (Cand.) Minn. State Rep; fire capt, Minneapolis; employed fire dept. 14 yrs; Int. Asn. of Fire Fighters, Local 82, secy. and bus. agent, 61-63; Minneapolis Cent. Labor Union Coun, trustee, 61-63; recording secy, 63-66; Minn. Fedn. of Labor AFL-CIO, v.pres, 64-; 2nd Ward DFL Club Exec. Bd, 64- Mem: United Labor Cmt; AFL-CIO Cope. Mailing Add: 2933 40th Ave, S, Minneapolis, Minn. 55406. (1967)

NORMAN, DOVIE S. R
V.Chmm, Simpson Co. Rep. Party, Miss.
b. Pinola, Miss, 1/30/15; d. Robert Ernest Spencer and Ida Finch S; m. 12/8/36 to Thomas D. Norman. Educ: High Sch. Polit. & Govt. Pos: V.chmn, Simpson Co. Rep. Party, Miss, 64- Bus. & Prof. Pos: Merchant, 44. Rel: Baptist. Mailing Add: R.R. 2, Mendenhall, Miss. 39114.

NORMAN, JACK D
b. Nashville, Tenn, 7/20/04; s. Chas. H. Norman and Bertha Chambers N; m. 7/28/26 to Carrie Sneed; c. Jack, Jr, Dr. Robert, Seth W, Carolyn (Mrs. Tune) and Julian. Educ: Vanderbilt Univ, LL.B, 26. Polit. & Govt. Pos: Mem, Tenn. State Dem. Exec. Cmt, 36-66, secy, 36-44 and chmn, 48-52; del. to all Dem. Convs. from 36-66, twice del. v.chmn; chmn, Tenn. State Dem. Convs, 66, 64, 60, 56 and 52; mem, Nat. Dem. Exec. Cmt, 48-52; mem, Electoral Col, 33. Prcf. Pos: Special Counsel for Tenn. in Prosecution Gas Frauds and Prosecution Impeachment of Judge Shoofield; dist. attorney gen. pro-tem to prosecute Reece Frauds; spec. counsel in Ins. Rate Investigations, City of Nashville. Mem: Past pres, Nashville Bar Asn; Tenn. and Am. Bar Asns; Am. Col. of Trial Lawyers; Am. Judicature Soc; Trial Lawyers Asn; past comdr, Nashville Commandery, York Rite, knight comdr, Scottish Rite, Mason; past potentate, Al Mench Temple Shrine; past sovereign, Red Cross of Constantine; past dir, Order of Jesters. Mailing Add: 213 Third Ave, North Nashville, Tenn. 37201. (1967)

NORMAN, ROBERT CLAUDE D
b. Washington, Ga, 6/28/19; s. Robert Claude Norman and Louise Johnson N; m. to Mary Coward; c. Claudia Diane, Mary Louise, Robert Claude, Jr. and Laura Anne. Educ: Univ. Ga, A.B, 40, LL.B, 42; Sigma Chi; Phi Beta Kappa; Omicron Delta Kappa; Blue Key; Phi Delta Phi; Spinx. Polit. & Govt. Pos: Chmn, Ga. Ports Authority, 59-66, gen. counsel, 63-66. Bus. & Prof. Pos: Assoc, Hull, Willingham & Towill, 45; partner, Hull, Towill & Norman, 46- Mil. Serv: Entered as Ens, Navy, 41, released as Lt. Comdr, 45. Publ: Legal articles pub. in Ga. Bar Journal. Mem: Augusta, Ga. and Am. Bar Asns; Am. Col. of Probate Counsel; Am. Col. Trial Lawyers; Kiwanis; Cmt. of 100; C. of C; Pinnacle Club of Augusta. Rel: First Baptist. Legal Res: 3111 W. Lake Forest Dr, Augusta, Ga. 30904. Mailing Add: 10th Floor, Southern Finance Bldg, Augusta, Ga. 30902.

NORMAN, SETH WALKER D
Secy, Tenn. State Dem. Exec. Cmt.
b. Nashville, Tenn, 4/6/34; s. Jack Norman and Carrie Sneed N; m. 10/10/58 to Mary Gennette Sain; c. Thomas Jay, Frances Gennette and Jack. Educ: Vanderbilt Univ, 2 years; Nashville YMCA Night Law Sch, LL.B; Sigma Chi. Polit. & Govt. Pos: Tenn. State Rep, 83rd Gen. Assembly, 62-64; pres, Davidson Co. Young Dem, Tenn, 64-65; secy, Davidson Co. Dem. Primary Bd,

66-67; secy, Tenn. State Dem. Exec. Cmt, 67-; del, Dem. Nat. Conv. and mem. platform cmt, 68. Mil. Serv: Entered as Airman Basic, Air Force, 53, released as 1st Lt, 57, after serv. in 581st Air Resupply Squadron, Far East Air Force and 3rd Air Transport Squadron, Mil. Air Transport Serv, Capt, Res, 57-61; Nat. Defense Serv. Medal; Korean Conflict Medal; UN Medal. Mem: Tenn. and Nashville Bar Asns; Davidson Co. Trial Lawyers Asn; AAONMS; Royal Order of Jesters; Am. Legion; VFW; C. of C. Rel: Presbyterian. Legal Res: 4005 Newman Place, Nashville, Tenn. 37204. Mailing Add: 213 Third Ave. N, Nashville, Tenn. 37201.

NORMANDIN, MARGARET EULALIE D
N.H. State Rep.
b. Laconia, N.H, 7/8/24; d. Fortunat Ernest Normandin and Susie Jane Seymour N; single. Educ: Montreal Univ, Can, 42-43; Univ. N.H, Durham, B.A, 46; Portia Law Sch, Boston, Mass, LL.B, 49; mem. Kappa Beta Pi Int. Legal Sorority. Polit. & Govt. Pos: Chmn, Gov. cmn. status women, 63; N.H. State Rep, 63-; mem, Judiciary Cmt, N.H. House of Rep, 63-68; alternate del, Dem. Nat. Conv, 68. Bus. & Prof. Pos: Instr, Gunstock Jr. Col, 65. Mem: N.H. Order of Women Legislators (pres, 63); Bus. & Prfnl. Women's Club (pres, 63-64); trustee, Gunstock Jr. Col; N.H. Voc. Inst.(bd. exam); Adv; Coun, 4-H; incorporator, Lakes Region Gen. Hosp; exec. bd, Lakes Region Family Serv; Laconia C. of C; Altrusa Club; State Bd. of Child & Family Serv; dir, N.H. Cath. Charities. Rel: Roman Catholic. Legal Res: 189 Union Ave, Laconia, N.H. 03246. Mailing Add: 135 Church St, Laconia, N.H. 03246.

NORMILE, PAUL RAYMOND D
b. Cleveland, Ohio, 6/20/08; s. John J. Normile and Mary Morgan N; m. 6/2/30 to Catherine Mary Hetzer; c. Paul R, Jr, Timothy J, John J. and Kay Frances. Educ: Pittsburgh Musical Inst, 28-29. Polit. & Govt. Pos: Mem, Aliquippa Borough Coun, Pa, 38, pres, 40; del, Dem. Nat. Conv, 64. Mem: Dir. Dist. 16, USW. Rel: Roman Catholic. Mailing Add: 864 Lovingston Dr, Pittsburgh, Pa. 15216.

NORRELL, CATHERINE DORRIS D
b. Camden, Ark; d. William Frank Dorris and Lucinda Rose Whitehead D; m. 10/26/22 to W. F. Norrell, wid. Feb, 1961; c. Julia J. Educ: Ouachita Baptist Col, Ark, 19-20; Univ. of Ark, 28. Polit. & Gov. Pos: U.S. Rep, Ark, 61-63; Dir, Dept. State Reception Center, Honolulu; Dep. Asst. Secy. State for Educ. and Cultural Affairs; Women's Nat. Dem. Club; Dem. Wives Forum. Bus. & Prof. Pos: Dir, music dept, Ark. A. and M. Col, 32-38; teacher, pub. schs, 20-24. Mem: Am. Legion Auxiliary; For. Serv. Asn; Nat. Order Women Legis; Nat. Coun. Women U.S; Am. Newspaper Women's Club; Bus. and Prfnl. Women's Clubs; past Worthy Grand Matron Ark, Order of Eastern Star; past pres, Cong. Club; Int. Club; English-Speaking Union; Waikiki Soroptimist Club; Woman's Auxiliary of Salvation Army. Mailing Add: 2456 A Sonoma St, Honolulu, Hawaii 96822.

NORRIS, ALAN E. R
Ohio State Rep.
b. Westerville, Ohio, 8/15/35; s. James Russell Norris and Dorothy A. Schrader N; m. 4/15/62 to Nancy Jeanne Myers; c. Tom Edward Jackson and Tracy Elaine. Educ: Univ. of Paris, La Sorbonne, Cert, 56; Otterbein Col, B.A, 57; N.Y. Univ. Sch. of Law, LL.B, 60; Phi Alpha Theta; Theta Alpha Phi; Phi Sigma Iota; Phi Delta Phi; Pi Kappa Phi; Pi Kappa Delta; ed, Col. Newspaper; 4 varsity letters, track. Polit. & Govt. Pos: Law clerk for Ohio Chief Justice Kingsley A. Taft, 60-61; asst. law dir, Westerville, Ohio, 62-67, chmn. zoning bd, 62-67; committeeman, Franklin Co. Rep. Cent. Cmt, 62-; Ohio State Rep, 59th Dist, 67- Bus. & Prof. Pos: Partner, Metz, Bailey & Norris, 62- Publ: 'Delay in the Court,' 4/60 and 'The Law's Delay in Ohio,' 7/60, Ohio Bar. Mem: Am, Ohio State and Columbus Bar Asns; SAR; Blendon Lodge 339 F&AM; Horeb Chap, 3, RAM; Zabud Coun 99, RSM; Mizpah Chap. 38, Eastern Star; Kiwanis Int. Jaycee Distinguished Serv. Award, 67. Rel: United Methodist. Mailing Add: 58 W. College Ave, Westerville, Ohio 43081.

NORRIS, PALMER WHITTEN 'PETE' R
Mem, Jefferson Co. Rep. Exec. Cmt, Ala.
b. Birmingham, Ala, 11/29/32; s. Defour Witzar Norris and Callie Dee Shaw N; m. 12/9/62 to Ann Elizabeth Deaver; c. Palmer Whitten, Jr. and Melissa Ann. Educ: Univ. Ala, B.S, 57; Birmingham Sch. Law, LL.B, 62, J.D, 68. Polit. & Govt. Pos: Rep. precinct chmn, Jefferson Co. Precinct 17, Ala, 63-; mem, Jefferson Co. Rep. Cmt, 64-; Rep. party poll watcher, 64 & 68; cand, Ala. House Rep, Place 14, 14th Dist, 66; coordinator, Perry Hooper Campaign for U.S. Sen, 68; del. and permanent chmn, Jefferson Co. Rep. Conv, 68; recruitment chmn, Jefferson Co. Rep. Party, 68; del, Ala. Rep. Conv. and mem. resolutions cmt, 68; alternate del, Rep. Nat. Conv, 68; legal counsel, Jefferson Co. Rep. Cmt, 68-; mem, Jefferson Co. Rep. Exec. Cmt, 68- Bus. & Prof. Pos: With Hayes Int. Corp, 58; from clerk to asst. auditor, First Nat. Bank of Birmingham, 59-63; attorney-at-law, 63- Mil. Serv: Entered as A/S, Navy, 51, released as YNT 3, 53, after serving in Transport Sq. 24, Fleet Aircraft Serv. Sq. 76, Pt. Lyauty, French Morroco and London, Eng. Mem: Birmingham and Ala. Bar Asns; past pres. and founder, Gardendale Libr. & Accreditation Fund. Rel: Conservative Baptist; mem. bd. deacons, First Conservative Baptist Church, training union dir, moderator bus. meetings and substitute Sunday sch. teacher. Legal Res: 1904 Norris Circle, Fultondale, Ala. 35068. Mailing Add: 2501 B N. 30th Ave, Birmingham, Ala. 35207.

NORRIS, PAUL GIFFORD, JR. R
b. Grinnell, Iowa, 12/3/04; s. Paul Gifford Norris and Edna Hand N; m. 2/6/29 to Garnet Ulmer (deceased) and 4/7/53 to Amy Talmadge; c. David Ulmer, Paul G, III, Donald Nixon (deceased) and Richard P. Talmadge (stepson). Educ: Grinnell Col, B.A; Sigma Delta Chi. Polit. & Govt. Pos: Del, Rep. Nat. Conv, 56 & 68; Rep. precinct committeeman, Marshall Co, Iowa, 60-64; mem, state platform cmt, 66; del, several co. and state Rep. conv. Bus. & Prof. Pos: Reporter and re-write man, City News Bur, Chicago, Ill, 25; reporter and sports ed, Times-Rep, Marshalltown, Iowa, 27-29, state ed, 29-33, asst. city ed, 33-36, city ed, 36-46, gen. mgr, 48-49, ed. and publisher, 49-; news dir, Radio Sta. KFJB, 46-48, gen. mgr, 49- Mil. Serv: Entered as Pvt, Iowa State Guard, 42, released as Maj, 47, after serv. in Co. H, 2nd Regt. Publ: Newspaper articles and ed. Mem: Am. Soc. of Newspaper Ed; Am. Newspaper Publishers Asn; Elks; Rotary (past pres, Marshalltown Club); Legion of Guardsmen (past nat. comdr); chmn, bd. dir, Des Moines Blue Cross Plan; mem, bd. dir, Iowa Blue Shield; past v.pres, Iowa Asn, Amateur Athletic Union. George Washington Medal for Ed. Writing, Freedom Found. at Valley Forge, 54; Iowa Master Ed-Publisher, 56; Master Columnist, Iowa Press Asn; Distinguished Alumnus Award, Grinnell Col, 57. Rel: United Methodist. Legal Res: 301 N. Ninth St, Marshalltown, Iowa 50158. Mailing Add: Times-Republican, Marshalltown, Iowa 50158.

NORRIS, RAYMOND R
Chmn, Jackson Co. Rep. Cmt, Ky.
b. Waneta, Ky, 10/28/11; s. Ben Norris and Maggie Lunsford N; m. 2/27/36 to Bessie Barnett; c. Lewis Ray and Kenneth Leon. Educ: McKee High Sch, Ky, two years. Polit. & Govt. Pos: Mem. sch. bd, McKee, Ky, 42-; chmn, Jackson Co. Rep. Cmt, 68- Bus. & Prof. Pos: Bus driver, 30; salesman, 30-36; merchant, McKee, Ky, 37-69; real estate salesman. Mem: Mason. Twenty year pen, Ky. Sch. Bd. Asn. Rel: Baptist. Mailing Add: Water St, McKee, Ky. 40447.

NORRIS, RUSSELL EARL, JR. Conservative, N.Y.
V.Chmn, Southern Tier Region, Conservative Party, N.Y.
b. Johnson City, N.Y, 11/23/29; s. Russell Earl Norris and Nora Bailey N; m. 8/9/52 to Winona Lillie Seislove; c. Scott Royce, Anita Kay, Mark Andrew, John Russell and Lori Anne. Educ: Rochester Inst. Tech, A.Appl. Sci, 50; Bucknell Univ, B.S, 53. Polit. & Govt. Pos: Chmn, Conservative Party Club of Broome Co, N.Y, 62-64; v.chmn, Southern Tier Region, Conservative Party, N.Y, 63-; mem, Conservative Party State Exec. Cmt, 64- Bus. & Prof. Pos: Assoc. tech. writer, Int. Bus. Machines Corp, 67- Mil. Serv: Entered as Pvt, Army, 53, released as Pfc, 55; after serv. in Develop. & Proof Servs. Ord. Corps, Aberdeen Proving Grounds; Good Conduct Medal. Mem: Am. Ord. Asn; Soc. Tech. Writers and Publishers; Endicott Optimists' Club; Am. Legion; Young Am. for Freedom. Rel: Presbyterian. Mailing Add: 212 N. Willis Ave, Endwell, N.Y. 13760.

NORRIS, WILLIAM A, JR. D
Wyo. State Sen.
b. Cheyenne, Wyo, 7/29/25; s. William A. Norris and Ethel Warlaumont N; m. 6/28/51 to Jeanette Clarke; c. W.A, III. Educ: Ga. Sch. Tech, 3 years; Univ. Wyo, B.S. in Eng. Polit. & Govt. Pos: Wyo. State Rep, 51-52 & 55-56; Wyo. State Sen, 57-; Dem. Nat. Committeeman, Wyo, 61-; del, Dem. Nat. Conv, 68. Bus. & Prof. Pos: Pres, Wortham Mach. Co, 51- Mil. Serv: Entered as Pvt, Army, 43, released as Lt, 45, after serv. in Army Engrs. Mem: Am. Legion; Rotary. Rel: Catholic. Mailing Add: 320 W. Seventh Ave, Cheyenne, Wyo. 82001.

NORRIS, WILLIAM ALBERT D
b. Turtle Creek, Pa, 8/30/27; s. George Norris and Florence Clive N; m. 6/4/50 to Catherine Horn; c. Barbara, Donald, Kim and Alison. Educ: Princeton Univ, A.B, 51; Stanford Univ, LL.B, 54; Phi Beta Kappa; exec. ed, Stanford Law Rev; Order of the Coif. Polit. & Govt. Pos: Mem, Calif. State Dem. Cent. Cmt, 59-66; campaign mgr, Rudd Brown Cong. Campaign, 60; mem, Calif. State Bd. Educ, 61-67, v.pres, 66-67; co-chmn. South. Calif. Campaign to Reelect Gov. Brown, 62; del, Dem. Nat. Conv, 64 & 68, mem. rules cmt, 68; chmn, South. Calif. Steering Cmt, Campaign Against Proposition 14, 64; mem, Coord. Coun. Higher Educ, 64-66; treas, Thomas Braden for Lt. Gov. Campaign, 66; trustee, Calif. State Cols, 67-; v.chmn, Kennedy Pres. Campaign, Calif, 68; mem. exec. cmt, Tom Bradley for Mayor Campaign, 69. Bus. & Prof. Pos: Spec. asst. attorney gen. of Calif. for Colo. River Litigation; assoc, Northcutt Ely, Wash, D.C, 54-55; law clerk to Justice William O. Douglas, U.S. Supreme Court, 55-56; assoc, Tuttle & Taylor, 56-60, partner, 60-; spec. counsel, President Kennedy's Cmn. Airlines Controversy, 61. Mil. Serv: Navy, 45-47. Mem: Am, Calif. State and Los Angeles Co. Bar Asns; Town Hall, Los Angeles; Alumni Bd. of Visitors, Stanford Law Sch, 58-64; dir, Constitutional Rights Found, 67- Legal Res: 1540 San Pasqual, Pasadena, Calif. 91106. Mailing Add: 609 S. Grand Ave, Los Angeles, Calif. 90017.

NORRIS, WILLIAM E. R
Chmn, Riverside Co. Rep. Cent. Cmt, Calif.
b. Phila, Pa, 9/29/37; s. T.E. Norris and Kathryn B. McMahan N; m. 6/20/58 to Nancy Sheryl Johnson; c. William Tyler, Julie Anna and Trevor Edwin. Educ: Stanford Univ, B.A; Kappa Alpha. Polit. & Govt. Pos: Chmn, Personnel Cmn, City of Riverside, Calif, 64-69; del, Rep. Nat. Conv, 68; chmn, Riverside Co. Rep. Cent. Cmt, Calif, 68- Bus. & Prof. Pos: Pres, McMahan's, Norris Div, 60-69; dir, Jr. Achievement. Mil. Serv: Entered as Ens, Navy, 58, released as Lt.(jg), 60, after serv. in U.S.S. Yorktown CVS-10. Mem: Exchange Club. Rel: Protestant. Legal Res: 4542 Beacon Way, Riverside, Calif. 92501. Mailing Add: 6807 Airport Dr, Riverside, Calif. 92504.

NORSWORTHY, ISIAH D
b. Kirbyville, Tex, 5/31/25; s. Willie Newton Norsworthy and Amis Allen N; m. 10/2/42 to Ruth Marie Bean; c. John Douglas, Beverly Ruth, Ethel Vernell, Marilyn Elaine, Rodney Isiah and Bryan Donovan. Educ: Bishop Col, Marshall, Tex, 1 year; Inter-Baptist Theol, Houston, B.Th, D.D, 69; Commun. Club; PTA. Polit. & Govt. Pos: Former pres, Votes League; v.pres, Seventh Cong. Votes League, Lufkin, Tex, 66; alternate del, Dem. Nat. Conv, 68. Bus. & Prof. Pos: Pastor, Dixie Baptist Church, 64- Mil. Serv: Entered as Pvt, Air Force, 43, released as 1st Sgt, 48, after serv. in 1008 Qm; Good Conduct Medal; Rifle Expert Badge. Mem: Most Worshipful Prince Hall Grand Lodge of Tex. and jurisdictions. Rel: Baptist. Mailing Add: Route 1, Box 44-A, Kirbyville, Tex. 75956.

NORTH, JOHN-CLARENCE D
Md. State Sen.
b. Tilghman, Md, 8/25/22; s. Robert Risdon North, Jr. and Effie E. Tarr N; m. 4/25/53 to Vivian Marina Butt; c. John-Clarence, Jr, Steven Matthew and Amy Elizabeth Effie. Educ: Univ. of Baltimore, LL.B, 47; Phi Beta Gamma. Polit. & Govt. Pos: Md. State Del, 51-55; Md. State Sen, 55- Bus. & Prof. Pos: Attorney at Law, 47- Mil. Serv: Entered as Yeoman 3/C, Navy, 42, released as Chief Specialist, 46; South Pac. Theater Ribbon, plus others. Mem: Am, Md. and Talbot Co. Bar Asns; Am. Judicature Soc; Am. Ord. Asn; Odd Fellows; Elks; K. of P; Am. Legion; VFW; Mason (32°); Shrine; Isaac Walton League. Rel: Methodist. Mailing Add: 220 S. Harrison St, Easton, Md. 21601.

NORTH, RAYMOND D. D
b. Douglas, Okla, 9/7/32; s. John Jacob North and Ruby Jewel Cooper N; single. Educ: Okla. A&M Col, A.B, 57; Okla. Univ, LL.B, 60; Xi Mu; Phi Eta Sigma; Phi Alpha Theta; Omicron Delta Kappa; Phi Kappa Phi; Vets. Club, Young Dems; Pi Gamma Mu; Arts & Sci. Hon. Soc. Polit. & Govt. Pos: Asst. co. attorney, Garfield Co, Okla, 60-63; del, Dem. Nat. Conv, 64. Mil. Serv: Entered as Recruit, Army, 50, released as Sgt, 53, after serv. in Eighth Army, Korea. Mem: Okla. and Am. Bar Asns; C. of C; Odd Fellows. Rel: Christian Union. Mailing Add: 1714 E. Cedar, Enid, Okla. 73701.

NORTH, SALLY ANNE R
Chmn, Mackinac Co. Rep. Cmt, Mich.
b. Battle Creek, Mich, 5/30/34; d. Sidney M. Greensmith and Mildred E. Brooks G; m. 4/25/53 to Walter H. North; c. Thomas Brian, David Allen and James Ryan. Educ: Battle Creek Cent. High Sch, 4 years. Polit. & Govt. Pos: Mem, Calhoun Co. Young Rep, Mich, 64; bd. mem, Battle Creek Rep. Women's Club, 64-; del, Rep. State Conv, 68-69; trustee, Moran Twp. Bd. Educ, 68-; chmn, Mackinac Co. Rep. Cmt, 69-; secy, 11th Dist. Rep. Cmt, 69- Mem: Mackinac Straits Hosp. Auxiliary. Rel: Protestant. Mailing Add: Boulevard Dr, St. Ignace, Mich. 49781.

NORTHEY, HARRY THOMAS R
Mont. State Sen.
b. Silver Bow, Mont, 5/5/11; s. William John Northey and Bessie Rickard N; m. 8/30/36 to Dorcas Keach; c. John William, Elizabeth (Mrs. Peter Odegard), Thomas Keach, Richard Merrill and Harry Leonard. Educ: Missoula Co. High Sch, dipl, 31. Polit. & Govt. Pos: Missoula Sch. Bd. trustee, Sch. Dist. 1, Mont, 50-62; mem, Missoula Park Bd, 52-53 and Missoula Police Cmn, 56-57; Mont. State Rep, Missoula Co, 63-65 & 67-69; Mont. State Sen, Dist. 26, 69- Bus. & Prof. Pos: Dir, Missoula First Fed. Savings & Loan, Mont, 68- Mem: Pres, Mont. Transfer and Warehousemen's Asn, 42; dir, Mont. Motor Transport Asn, 68-; past pres, West. Mont. Fish and Game Asn; past pres, Missoula Active Club; West. Mont. Coun. on Alcoholism and Drugs; Lions; Elks; Am. Movers Conf; C. of C; United Commercial Travelers; Mont. Wildlife Fedn; Missoula Bus. Builders. Rel: Presbyterian. Mailing Add: 514 Daly Ave, Missoula, Mont. 59801.

NORTHINGTON, ARCH EWING D
b. Clarksville, Tenn, 10/18/09; s. Sterling Neblett Northington and Eugenia Rollow N; wid. Educ: Vanderbilt Univ; Del Sq. Psi; Delta Tau Delta. Polit. & Govt. Pos: Cmnr. of Ins. and Banking, Tenn, 53-59; chmn, Gov. Cmt. on Employ the Physically Handicapped, 61-62; mem, President's Cmt. on Employ the Physically Handicapped, 61-63; alternate del, Dem. Nat. Conv. 68. Bus. & Prof. Pos: Entered ins. bus, Nashville, Tenn, 28 later moving to Clarksville, formed King and Northington Agency, 33, assoc, King, Northington & Frost, Inc, currently; v.pres, World Serv. Life Ins. Co, Ft. Worth, Tex, currently. Mil. Serv: Entered as Pvt, Army, 42, released as 1st Lt, 45, after serv. in 235 Ord. Base Group, ETO. Mem: Mason (32°); Shriner; past chmn, Montgomery Co. Red Cross; Am. Legion (past Comdr. Post 7, past Dist. Comdr, Tenn. and chmn, Vet. Employ. Div); pres, Clarksville C. of C, 64-65; pres, Tenn. Tourist Develop. Asn; bd. mem, State of Tenn. Retirement Syst. for Co. Paid Judges; state nat. dir. for Insurors of Tenn. to Nat. Asn. of Ins. Agents; v.pres, Insurors of Tenn, 59-60, pres, 60-61; past chmn. exec. cmt, Nat. Asn. of Ins. Cmnr, served on several cmts, v.pres, 57 and pres, 58; bd. dirs, United Serv. Orgn, North. Bank of Tenn, Servico Inc, Memphis, Am. Food Mach. Corp. and Montgomery Co. Ice Co, Clarksville. Tenn. Jaycee Award for Good Govt, 54; Pres. Award, Nat. Asn. of Ins. Agents, 63. Rel: Presbyterian; Chmn, Bd. of Deacons, First Presby. Church, Clarksville, Tenn. Legal Res: 220 Porters Bluff Rd, Clarksville, Tenn. 37040. Mailing Add: P.O. Box 888, Clarksville, Tenn. 37040.

NORTHRUP, ARTHUR HARRY R
Ind. State Rep.
b. Indianapolis, Ind, 6/3/20; s. Leonard E. Northrup and Margaret Couden N; m. to Deborah Lee Norris; c. Arthur H, Jr. and Nancy. Educ: Harvard Col, A.B. with Honors, 42; Grad. Sch. Bus. Admin, Harvard Univ, M.B.A, 46; Univ. Mich. Law Sch, J.D, 49; Coolidge Prize, Harvard Debating Club; Harvard Glee Club. Polit. & Govt. Pos: Elec. inspector or judge, Indianapolis, Ind, 50-64; asst. city attorney, Indianapolis, 51-54 & 68-; pres, Wash. Twp. Rep. Club, 65-67; dep. elec. cmnr, Indianapolis, 67; Ind. State Rep, 69- Bus. & Prof. Pos: Mem. law firm, Gregg, Fillion, Hughes & Northrup, 50-; secy, Ind. Corp. Survey Cmn, 57-; mem, Ind. Trust Code Study Cmn, 69. Mil. Serv: Entered as A/S, Navy, 44, released as Spec. Q 2/C, 46, after serv. in Naval Commun, U.S; Navy Unit Commendation Medal. Publ: 'Sales Taxes, Exclusions and Extensions,' Vanderbilt Law Rev, 58; 'Marital Deduction: The Street Case,' Notre Dame Lawyer, 60; 'Trust Administration in Indiana,' Ind. State Bar Asn, 65. Mem: Ind. State Bar Asn.(chmn, Probate, Trust and Real Property Sect, 68-); Am. Bar Asn.(mem, Probate, Trust & Real Property Sect, 69-); Indianapolis Bar Asn; Bar Asn. Seventh Fed. Circuit; Am. Judicature Soc; past comdr, John H. Holliday Post Am. Legion; past judge advocate, 11th Dist. Ind. Am. Legion; past pres, Ind. Harvard Club; past pres, Harvard Bus. Sch. Club Indianapolis; Mason; Scottish Rite; Murat Shrine; secy, Summer Mission Sick Children. Rel: Christian Scientist. Legal Res: 4050 N. Adams Court, Indianapolis, Ind. 46204. Mailing Add: 1212 Merchants Bank Bldg, Indianapolis, Ind. 46204.

NORTHRUP, L. DONALD R
Wyo. State Sen.
b. Braymer, Mo, 6/8/06; m. 12/22/66 to Jane D. Clark; c. two. Educ: Univ. of Iowa. Polit. & Govt. Pos: Mem. adv. coun, Big Horn Nat. Forest; mem. adv. bd, Powell Research Sta.(past pres); dir, Wyo. Sch. Trustees Asn; past pres, Big Horn Basin Sch. Trustees Asn; mem, Powell Sch. Bd, 15 years, clerk, 5 years; chmn, Educ. Cmt; mem, Wyo. Youth Coun; Wyo. State Rep, until 66; Wyo. State Sen, 67- Bus. & Prof. Pos: Farmer and feeder. Mem: Rotary Int; Masonic Lodge; Odd Fellows Lodge; Elks; Farm Bur; C. of C; Wyo. Stock Growers Asn. Rel: Methodist. Mailing Add: Star Route, Box 56, Powell, Wyo. 82435.

NORTON, CLYDE MONROE D
N.C. State Sen.
b. Marion, N.C, 3/7/16; s. Jasper Monroe Norton and Sarah Hensley N; m. 5/13/44 to Janet Nodine Norton; c. Kenneth, Tommy, Sarah. Polit. & Govt. Pos: Alderman, Old Fort, N.C, 52-54; mem, Bd. Co. Cmnrs, McDowell Co, 56-65, v.chmn, 60-; N.C. State Sen, 63- Bus. & Prof. Pos: Owner and mgr, retail furniture store, 45-; partner and pres, Norton-Ramsey Motor Lines, furniture carrier, Southwest. States, 67- Mem: Mason (Master, Joppa Lodge 401); C. of C; N.C. Hist. Asn. Rel: Baptist; Deacon, First Baptist Church, Old Fort, N.C, 46- Mailing Add: P.O. Box 477, Old Fort, N.C. 28762.

NORTON, FRANCIS CARLETON R
Chmn, Barnstable Rep. Town Cmt, Mass.
b. Hyde Park, Mass, 4/5/18; s. John Francis Norton and Margaret Victoria Morris N; wid. Educ: Hobart Col, 1 year. Polit. & Govt. Pos: Chmn, Barnstable Rep. Town Cmt, Mass, 66-; mem, Rep. Nat. Cmt, currently. Bus. & Prof. Pos: Career life underwriter, New Eng. Mutual Life Ins, 40-42; licensed Mass. Real Estate Broker, currently. Mem: Hobart Col. Club Boston; Century Club Hobart Col; Independent Mutual Agents of New Eng; Nat. Asn. Mutual Ins. Agents; Barnstable Civic Asn; Rep. Club Mass; Middlesex Club. Rel: Episcopal; License Lay-Reader. Mailing Add: Route 6-A, P.O. Box 66, Cummaquid, Mass. 02637.

NORTON, FRED CARL DFL
Minn. State Rep.
b. Minneapolis, Minn, 8/19/28; s. Henry Wachs Norton and Lois Nash N; m. 3/22/52 to Martha C. Holman; c. Cynthia, Jeffrey Pierce and Katharine. Educ: Wesleyan Univ, B.A, 50; Univ. Minn, LL.B, 55; Psi Upsilon. Polit. & Govt. Pos: Attorney, Dept. Taxation, Minn, 55-56; spec. asst. attorney gen, 56-63, asst. attorney gen, Minn, 63-66; mem, Minn State Dem-Farmer-Labor Cent. Cmt; Minn. State Rep, Dist. 46A, 67- Mem: Minn. and Ramsey Co. Bar Asns; Bd. of Dir, Capitol Commun. Services and Dale Selby Action Coun; v.pres, Northwest. Lawn Tennis Asn. Rel: Unitarian. Mailing Add: 701 Fairmount Ave, St. Paul, Minn. 55105.

NORTON, PHILIP JEFFREY R
b. Edgartown, Mass, 8/30/92; s. Clement Norton and Minnie L. Blodget N; m. 11/8/33 to Louise M. Wood; c. Philip Jeffrey, Jr. and Clement Scott. Educ: Edgartown High Sch. Polit. & Govt. Pos: Register of Deeds, Dukes Co, Mass, 18-, Clerk of Dist. Court, 27-62; Town Clerk, Edgartown, 19-55. Mem: Martha's Vineyard Lodge AF&AM. Rel: Methodist. Mailing Add: W. Tisbury Rd, Edgartown, Mass. 02539.

NORTON, WILLIAM HAYDEN D
b. Pierce, Nebr, 3/29/26; s. William Wendell Norton and Catherine Hayden N; m. 4/6/50 to Nancy Rogers Sayre; c. William Hayden, Jr. and Lisa Dale. Educ: Univ. Nebr, LL.B, 51; Phi Delta Phi; Sigma Alpha Epsilon. Polit. & Govt. Pos: Chmn, Nebr. Power Review Bd, 64-69; attorney, Polk Co, Nebr, 55-67; chmn, Gov. Cmt. on Educ, 66; mem, Nebr. Resources Cmt. Mil. Serv: Cadet, Air Force, 44-46. Mem: Am, Nebr, Local and Dist. Bar Asns; Nebr. Co. Attorneys Asn; Nat. Dist. Attorneys Asn; Mason, Scottish Rite, Shrine; Am. Legion; 40 et 8; plus others. Rel: Methodist. Mailing Add: Osceola, Nebr. 68651.

NORTON, WILLIAM J. D
b. Anderson, Ind. 3/10/28; s. Byron E. Norton and Denise S. Lannoy N; m. 11/28/68 to Nancy Lee Forbes. Educ: Univ. Notre Dame, B.S; Georgetown Univ, LL.B, 51, J.D, 54, LL.M, 55. Polit. & Govt. Pos: Asst. prosecutor, Madison Co, Ind, 55-57; chmn, Madison Co. Dem. Cent. Cmt, 58-64; Dem. nominee, U.S. Rep, Ind, 68. Bus. & Prof. Pos: Asst. counsel, Navy Dept, 54-55; attorney, 55- Mil. Serv: Entered as Pvt, Army, 1½ years, released as Sgt, 47, after serv. in Mil. Gov. Germany, ETO. Mem: Elks; Am. Legion; K. of C. Rel: Catholic. Mailing Add: 715 Anderson Bank Bldg, Anderson, Ind. 46017.

NORVELL, DAVID L. D
N.Mex. State Rep.
b. Kansas City, Mo, 1/31/35; s. Kenneth J. Norvell and Mildred Lagers N; m. 8/9/57 to Marivee Trentman; c. Teresa Jean, Connie, David, Jr. and Felicia. Educ: Northeast. State Col, B.S. in Hist, 55; Okla. Univ, LL.B, 58; Delta Theta Phi; Phi Sigma Epsilon. Polit. & Govt. Pos: N.Mex. State Rep, 63-, speaker, N.Mex. House Rep, 69- Bus. & Prof. Pos: Partner, Blythe & Norvell Law Off, 59- Mem: Am. Bus. Club. Rel: Catholic. Legal Res: 1105 Fairway Terrace, Clovis, N.Mex. 88101. Mailing Add: P.O. Drawer E, Clovis, N.Mex. 88101.

NORVELL, JAMES RANKIN D
b. Hayden, Colo, 9/24/02; s. Robert Elias Norvell and Jean Curry Ralston N; m. 4/21/27 to Mabel Elizabeth Keeley. Educ: Univ. Colo, A.B, 23, J.D, 26; Phi Delta Phi; Delta Sigma Rho; Alpha Sigma Phi. Polit. & Govt. Pos: Justice, Court of Civil Appeals, San Antonio, Tex, 40-56; justice, Supreme Court Tex, 57-68. Bus. & Prof. Pos: Trustee, Law Sch, St. Mary's Univ, 46-, prof. law, 69-; chmn. judicial sect, Tex. State Bar Found, 55, fel, 60. Publ: 'Oran M. Roberts and the Semicolon Court,' Tex. Law Rev, 59; 'The Ames Case Revisited,' S.W. Hist. Quart, 62; 'The Supreme Court of Texas,' 1961-1965, Houston Law Rev, 64. Mem: Am. Judicature Soc; Am. Bar Asn; State Bar Tex; Am. Soc. Legal Hist; Tex. State Hist. Soc; Philos. Soc. Tex; Mason (33°); Scottish Rite Mason. Rel: Episcopal. Legal Res: 7707 Broadway, San Antonio, Tex. 78209. Mailing Add: 2700 Cincinnati Ave, San Antonio, Tex. 78228.

NORVELL, JOHN HUGH R
Chmn, Wexford Co. Rep. Party, Mich.
b. Tuscola, Ill, 10/9/16; s. William Thomas Norvell and Minnie Mabis N; m. 8/16/51 to Betty Louise Hill; c. Stephanie Lynn, Robert Curtis, John Hugh, Jr. and Darryl Zane. Educ: Tuscola Commun. High Sch. Polit. & Govt. Pos: Chmn, Wexford Co. Rep. Party, Mich, 64- Bus. & Prof. Pos: Dist. supvr, Texaco Inc, 53- Mil. Serv: Entered as Pvt, Army, 42, released as 1st Lt, 45, re-entered as Capt, 51; Lt. Col, Army Res, presently. Mem: Mason. Rel: Baptist. Mailing Add: 1005 Sunset Lane, Cadillac, Mich. 49601.

NORVELL, RICHARD D
b. Nashville, Tenn, 6/6/21; s. Richard Owen Norvell and Margaret Parker N; m. 6/8/43 to Mary Elizabeth Manning; c. Margaret Parker, Richard Manning and Owen Maury. Educ: Vanderbilt Univ, 2 years; Sigma Alpha Epsilon. Polit. & Govt. Pos: City cmnr, Forest Hills, 61-64; Tenn. State Rep, 65-68. Mil. Serv: Entered as Aviation Cadet, Army Air Force, 42, released as Capt, 45, in Tactical Air Command, 51-52; Am. Theater, European-African Theater

and Asiatic Theater Ribbons. Mem: V.pres, Tenn. Bldg. Materials Asn, 66-67; SAR; Lions. Rel: Episcopal. Legal Res: 5325 Stanford Dr. N, Nashville, Tenn. 37215. Mailing Add: P.O. Box 178, Nashville, Tenn. 37202.

NOTERMAN, JOSEPH PAUL D
b. Covington, Ky, 9/18/07; s. Ollie G. Noterman (deceased) and Katherine Schuessler N.(deceased); m. 7/1/35 to Mildred Nancy Tomlinson; c. Peter Allen, Esq. and Nancy Lucille. Polit. & Govt. Pos: Del, Dem. Nat. Conv, 68. Bus. & Prof. Pos: Salesman, Remington Rand Inc, 36-46; dist. sales mgr, Nationwide Ins. Co, 46-51, Ins. agent, 51- Mem: Greater Wilkes-Barre Dem. Club; Nat. Cmt. for Sane Nuclear Policy; Am. Civil Liberties Union; New Dem. Coalition. Mailing Add: 200 Horton St, Wilkes-Barre, Pa. 18702.

NOTHERN, AUSTIN R
Kans. State Rep.
b. Salina, Kans, 10/8/38; s. Glen A. Nothern and Gay Austin N; m. 6/6/63 to Marianna Bantleon Hoover; c. Brent A. and Mary Elizabeth. Educ: Univ. Colo, B.A, 60; Washburn Univ. Sch. Law, LL.B, 64; N.Y. Univ, LL.M, 67; Sigma Alpha Epsilon; Phi Alpha Delta. Polit. & Govt. Pos: Kans. State Rep, 44th Dist, 69- Bus. & Prof. Pos: Attorney-at-law, Topeka, Kans, 64-; lectr. taxation, Washburn Law Sch, 64- Mem: Kans. Bar Asn; Topeka Active 20-30 Club. Rel: Episcopal. Mailing Add: 200 Woodlawn, Topeka, Kans. 66606.

NOTTE, JOHN ANTHONY, JR. D
b. Providence, R.I, 5/3/09; s. John Anthony Notte and Eva Rondina N; m. Sept, 1934 to Marie Joan Huerth; c. John A, III and Joyce Ann. Educ: Providence Col, A.B, 31; Boston Univ. Sch. Law, LL.B, 35; Alpha Phi Delta. Hon. LL.D, Univ. R.I. Polit. & Govt. Pos: Gov, R.I, 61-62, lt. gov, 59-60 and secy. of state, 57-58; secy. to U.S. Sen. Theodore Francis Green, R.I, 48-56; pres, Young Dem. of R.I, 49-50. Prof. Pos: Attorney and sr. partner, Notte & Notte, 63- Mil. Serv: Entered as Lt.(jg), Navy, 43, released as Lt.(sg), 46, after serv. in African and Mediterranean Theaters, 43-45; ETO Ribbon with 2 Bronze Stars; Mediterranean and Am. Theater Ribbons. Mem: Am. and R.I. Bar Asns; Elks; VFW; Am. Legion; DAV; K. of C; Metacomet Golf Club; Pleasant Valley Country Club; Aurora Civic Asn. Hobbies: Golf; Oil Painting. Rel: Roman Catholic. Mailing Add: 716 Fruit Hill Ave, North Providence, R.I. 02908. (1967)

NOVAK, ANTHONY F. D
Ohio State Sen.
b. Cleveland, Ohio, 1924; married. Educ: Fenn Col. Polit. & Govt. Pos: V.chmn, Ohio Tax Study Cmn; Ohio State Rep, 55-65, Ohio State Sen, 65-; del, Dem. Nat. Conv, 68. Bus. & Prof. Pos: Pub. acct. Mil. Serv: Army, World War II. Mem: Pub. Accts. Soc.(former pres, Cleveland Chap). Mailing Add: 6218 St. Clair Ave, Cleveland, Ohio 44103. Mailing Add: State Capitol Bldg, Columbus, Ohio 43215. (1967)

NOVAK, EDWARD G. DFL
Minn. State Sen.
b. 4/16/17; married; c. Three. Educ: Col. of St. Thomas; Univ. Minn. St. Paul Col. of Law, B.S.L and LL.B. Polit. & Govt. Pos: Minn. State Sen, 58- Bus. & Prof. Pos: Attorney; agent, Fed. Bur. Invest, Tex, Ill. and N.Y; served as enforcement officer and attorney in several govt. agencies. Mailing Add: 1424 Arundel St, St. Paul, Minn. 55117. (1967)

NOVAK, ETHEL V. R
b. Honor, Mich, 1/2/04; d. Isaac Jerome Mead and Ada A. St. Clair M; m. 5/26/61 to Richard George Novak; c. Marguerite (Mrs. Menerey), Gerald E. Quintel and Marie L. (Mrs. Clark). Educ: Bible Holiness Seminary, Owosso, Mich. Polit. & Govt. Pos: Chmn, Benzie Co. Rep. Cmt, 63-65; worked on Agr. Survey, 52-53; precinct worker; mem, Election Bd. and Draft Bd. Bus. Pos: With Floor Covering Store, 45-54; secy. and buyer, Furniture Store, 38-46; F.C.C. operator, part time. Rel: Missouri Synod Lutheran. Mailing Add: 8703 Deadstream Rd, Honor, Mich. 49640. (1967)

NOVAK, JAMES B. Conservative, N.Y.
Chmn, Schoharie Co. Conservative Party, N.Y.
b. Biste, Hungary, 9/13/13; s. James B. Novak and Mary Bidlen N; m. 8/17/35 to Catherine S. Reese; c. Catherine, James, Warren and Bruce. Polit. & Govt. Pos: Chmn, Schoharie Co. Conservative Party, N.Y, 63- Mem: IUE (past mem. exec. bd). Rel: Roman Catholic. Mailing Add: Schoharie, N.Y. 12157. (1967)

NOVAK, LARRY F. D
b. Valatie, N.Y, 7/16/22; s. Martin M. Novak and Mary Newrocky N; single. Educ: High Sch. grad. Polit. & Govt. Pos: Town chmn, Kinderhook, N.Y, 49-66; chmn, Columbia Co. Dem. Party, 63-66. Bus. & Prof. Pos: Owner, Novak Bowling Supplies, 50-66; v.pres, Valatie Savings & Loan, pres, 67- Mil. Serv: Entered as A/S, Navy, 42, released as B/M 1/C, 46; 12 Ribbons. Mem: VFW; Am. Legion; past pres, St. Clause Club; mem, 12 Columbia Co. Dem. Clubs; Polish Commun. Club; Elks. Rel: Catholic. Mailing Add: Valatie, N.Y. 12184.

NOVAK, STANLEY D
Mich. State Sen.
b. Salemsville, Pa, 3/9/11; married; c. Stanley Jay and Terry Lee. Educ: Pub. schs. in Pa. Polit. & Govt. Pos: Mich. State Sen, 54- Bus. & Prof. Pos: Former UAW-CIO int. rep; former bus. agent of the boilermakers union. Mil. Serv: Navy, S. Pac. and Asiatic Theatres. Mem: Elks; VFW; Amvets; NAACP; Polish Nat. Alliance. Rel: Catholic. Mailing Add: 5901 Elmer, Detroit, Mich. 48210.

NOVOTNY, FRANK D
S.Dak. State Sen.
b. 9/20/03; m. 10/12/36 to Helen Haki; c. Marylyn, Thomas. Educ: Elem. Sch, 8 years. Polit. & Govt. Pos: Twp. clerk; S.Dak. State Sen, 64- Bus. & Prof. Pos: Farmer; dir, Charles Mix Elec. Asn; E. River Elec. Power Coop. Dir. Rel: Catholic. Mailing Add: Lake Andes, S.Dak. 57356.

NOWACK, DONALD ROBERT D
Ohio State Rep.
b. Cleveland, Ohio, 2/23/24; s. Andrew Nowack and Harriet Michalke N; m. 6/2/45 to Audrey M. Polak; c. Kenneth Brian, Cheryl Lynne, Keith Bradley and Mark Brandon. Educ: Cleveland Col; Fenn Col. Polit. & Govt. Pos: Mem: Garfield Heights Dem. Orgn, Cuyahoga Co. Dem. Exec. Cmt, Safety Coun. of Garfield Heights and Fire and Police Pension Bds; councilman, Ward Four, Garfield Heights, Ohio, 60-65, pres. coun, 65-66; Ohio State Rep, Dist. 45, 67- Bus. & Prof. Pos: Supvr, Sunnyvale Farms, 46-66; spec. agent, John Hancock Mutual Ins. Co, 66- Mem: PTA (chmn, juvenile protection and safety, Garfield Heights Jr. High Sch, chmn, legis. Garfield Park Elem. Sch); Alliance of Poles; Friends of Retarded Children; Friends of Libr; Little Theatre Group; F&AM; Tax Policy Action Cmt, Citizens League; Little League; Cub Scouts; past mem, Teamsters. Rel: Protestant; Deacon, Garfield Trinity Church, 63- Legal Res: 10212 Russell Ave, Garfield Heights, Ohio 44125. Mailing Add: State Capitol Bldg, Columbus, Ohio 43215. (1967)

NOWELL, JOHN C, JR. D
b. Trenton, Tenn, 12/28/20; s. John C. Nowell, Sr. and Ida Johnson N; m. 3/10/55 to Charlotte Somervill Dickinson; c. John Dickinson and Thomas Somervill. Educ: Univ. Mo, Columbia, A.B. & B.S; Rutgers Univ. Sch. Law, 50-51; Vanderbilt Univ, J.D, 53; Beta Sigma Pi; Phi Gamma Delta. Polit. & Govt. Pos: Chmn, Gibson Co. Libr. Bd, 54-60 and 66-69; Tenn. State Rep, 62-66; del, Dem. Nat. Conv, 68. Mil. Serv: Entered as 2nd Lt, Army, 43, released as Capt, 46, after serv. in 84th Inf. Div, ETO, 44-45; Bronze Star; ETO Ribbon with 3 Battle Stars. Publ: 'Advertising and the Buyers Remedies, Vanderbilt Law Rev,' 53. Mem: Am. and Tenn. Bar Asns; Gibson Co. Bar. Asn.(pres, 64-66); Am. Legion (dist. comdr, 59-60, post comdr, 61-62); VFW; Elks; Rotary (pres, Trenton Club, 63-64). Rel: Protestant. Legal Res: Old Jackson Rd, Trenton, Tenn. 38382. Mailing Add: Courtsquare, Trenton, Tenn. 38382.

NOWICKI, JOSEPH F. X. R
b. Yonkers, N.Y, 10/18/22; s. Joseph A. Nowicki and Sophye T. Wojciechowski N; m. 7/1/50 to Catherine McLoughlin; c. Joseph, Paul, Peter, Michael, Catherine, Patrick and Ann. Educ: Fordham Col, B.S; Fordham Law Sch, LL.B. Polit. & Govt. Pos: Del, N.Y. State Rep. Conv, 58, 62 & 66; asst. attorney, Rockland Co, 58-59; pres, N.Y. State Asn. of Young Rep. Clubs, 59-60; counsel to Lt. Gov. of N.Y. State, 60-61; N.Y. State Assemblyman, 61-64. Bus. & Prof. Pos: Certified trial counsel by Judge Advocate Gen, Navy, 51; partner, Granik, Garson, Silverman & Nowicki, Esquires, 60-; Rockland Co. Counsel, Eastchester Savings Bank, 60-; pres, Orange & Rockland Indust. Develop. Corp, 65- Mil. Serv: Entered as Pvt, Marine Corps, 42, released as 2nd Lt, 46, after serv. in 2nd Marine Div, Pac. Theater; recalled to active duty, 50, released as Capt; Pac. Campaign Ribbon with 1 Battle Star; Am. Defense Ribbon; Presidential Unit Citation. Mem: K. of C.(4°); dir, Nanuet Rotary Club; Elks; Am. Legion; VFW; hon. mem, Ancient Order of Hibernians; Rockland Co. Campaign dir, March of Dimes, 57-59; pres, Rockland Co. Coun. Boy Scouts, 68- 880 yd. Champion, IC4A and NCAA, All-Am. Track Team, 43. Rel: Roman Catholic. Mailing Add: 149 N. Middletown Rd, Nanuet, N.Y. 10954.

NOWLAN, JAMES DUNLAP R
Ill. State Rep.
b. Kewanee, Ill, 9/8/41; s. Robert J. Nowlan and Barbara Dunlap N; single. Educ: Univ. Ill, Urbana, B.A. with high honors in polit. sci, 63, M.A, 65; Skull & Crescent Soc; Sigma Nu. Polit. & Govt. Pos: Mem. staff, Ill. State Cent. Cmt, 63-64; Ill. State rep, 69- Bus. & Prof. Pos: Ed, Stark Co. News, 62-63; army instr, Black Hawk E. Col, Kewanee, Ill, 69- Mil. Serv: Entered as 1st Lt, Army, 66, released as Capt, 68, after serv. in Ft. Gordon, Ga. and Fifth Army Hq, Ft. Sheridan, Ill; Capt, Army Res, 68-; Army Commendation Medal. Mem: Sigma Delta Chi; Mason; Am. Legion. Rel: Congregational. Mailing Add: 209 S. Miller, Toulon, Ill. 61483.

NOWLIN, JAMES ROBERTSON D
Tex. State Rep.
b. San Antonio, Tex, 11/21/37; s. William Forney Nowlin and Jeannette Robertson N; single. Educ: Trinity Unit, B.A. and M.A; Univ. Tex. Sch. Law, LL.B. Polit. & Govt. Pos: Legal counsel, labor and pub. welfare cmt, U.S. Senate, 65-66; Tex. State Rep, 67- Bus. & Prof. Pos: Attorney, Kelso, Locke & King, San Antonio, 63- Mil. Serv: Entered as 2nd Lt, Army, 59, released as Capt, 12/68, after serv. in Res, Ft. Lee, Va, 59-60. Mem: State Bar of Tex; Am, San Antonio and San Antonio Jr. Bar Asns; Am. Judicature Soc; C. of C; Jr. C. of C; Mex. C. of C; LULAC (mem. coun. 16); Research and Planning Coun. Outstanding Young Man of the Year, Trinity Univ. & San Antonio Jr. C. of C, 67. Rel: Presbyterian. Legal Res: 3223 Howard St, San Antonio, Tex. 78212. Mailing Add: 635 Milam Bldg, San Antonio, Tex. 78205.

NOWOTNY, GEORGE EDWARD, JR. R
Ark. State Rep.
b. New Braunfels, Tex, 10/18/32; s. George Edward Nowotny and Margaret Voight N; m. 8/14/54 to Lura Duff Elliston; c. Edward Duff, George Edward, III and Addison Dance. Educ: Univ. Tex, B.S, 55; Phi Eta Sigma; Sigma Gamma Epsilon; Phi Beta Kappa; Delta Tau Delta. Polit. & Govt. Pos: Ark. State Rep, 67-, Minority Leader, Ark. House of Rep, 67-; committeeman, Nat. Resources, Interstate Oil Compact Cmn, 67-; alternate del, Rep. Nat. Conv, 68; mem. bd. dir, South. Regional Bd, Nat. Conf. of Rep. Legislators, 69- Bus. & Prof. Pos: Geophysicist, affiliate of Standard Oil Co, Caracas, Venezuela, Havana, Cuba, Buenos Aires, Argentina, Okla, Utah and Mich, 56-61; consult, geologist, Barton & Nowotny, Ft. Smith, Ark, 61-63; owner, Nowotny & Co, real estate and personal investments, 63-69. Mem: Am. Asn. Petroleum Geologists; Soc. Explor. Geophysicists; Asn. Petroleum Landmen; Nat. Exchange Club; Int. Platform Asn; United Commercial Travelers of Am; bd. dir, Am. Red Cross, past pres, Sebastian Co. Chap; Ark. Asn. for Crippled, Inc; C. of C; sustaining mem, Westark Coun, Boy Scouts; past chmn, Commercial Div, United Fund Campaign. Rel: Episcopal. Legal Res: 18 Berry Hill, Ft. Smith, Ark. 72901. Mailing Add: 301 First Federal Bldg, Ft. Smith, Ark. 72901.

NOYES, CHESTER DREW R
N.H. State Rep.
b. Stewartstown, N.H, 5/24/00; s. Fred Hutchins Noyes and Carrie Drew N; m. 2/2/36 to Dorothea Smith; c. Clement Drew, Robert M, James D, John S, Jane (Mrs. Holbrook) and William C. Educ: Colebrook Acad, dipl. Polit. & Govt. Pos: Supvr. of check list, Stewartstown, N.H, 23-29, selectman, 29-36, rd. agent, 36-38, auditor, 36-44, town and sch. moderator, 40-69 and chmn. munic. budget cmt, 69; chmn, Stewartstown Rep. Town Cmt, 46-69;

del, Rep. Constitutional Conv, N.H, 48 & 64; N.H. State Rep, 65-; clerk, Coos Co. Rep. Del. and mem. finance cmt, 69. Bus. & Prof. Pos: Dir, Coop. Exten, Coos Co, N.H, 48-62; v.pres, Coos Co. Farm Bur, 52-54; dir, United Farmers of New Eng, 55-62 and Farm and Home Admin, 58-61; coun, White Mt. Region, 58-69; dir, Merrimack Farmers Exchange Inc, 62-69. Mil. Serv: Pvt, Students Army Training Corps, 18, with serv. in Col. Unit. Mem: Am. Legion; Mason; Eastern Star; exec. cmt, Vershire Shop and Schs; trustee, Northeast Kingdom Ment. Health Serv. Inc. Recipient of Serv. Award, Univ. of N.H, for Outstanding Contrib. to Exten. Prog; First Prize for N.H. in New Eng. Green Pastures Contest, 49 & 52; Cert. of Merit for Outstanding Layman; Named Hon. Mem, Future Farmers of Am. Rel: Methodist; Chmn. Admin. Bd, local church; lay leader, North. Dist. N.H. Conf. Legal Res: R.F.D. 2, Stewartstown, N.H. 03576. Mailing Add: R.F.D. 2, Colebrook, N.H. 03576.

NOYES, RICHARD CUNNINGHAM R

b. New Haven, Conn, 12/5/21; s. Edward Simpson Noyes and Phyllis Cunningham N; m. 12/21/42 to Harriet Elizabeth Sayre; c. Mary B, Carolyn S. and Phyllis C. Educ: Yale, B.A, 42; Berzelius; Beta Theta Pi. Polit. & Govt. Pos: Conn. State Rep, Farmington, 57-67; mem, Rep. Platform Research Cmt, 62 & 66; mem, Cmn. on Intergovt. Coop, 63-66. Mil. Serv: Entered as Ens, Naval Res, 42, released as Lt, 46, after serv. in Pac. Theater for 44 months, reentered as Lt, 52, released as Lt. Comdr, 53, after Officer Cand. Sch; Navy Combat Commendation Ribbon; Asiatic-Pac. Theater Medal with Eight Battle Stars; Am. Area Ribbons; Defense, Victory and Philippine Liberation Medals. Mem: Am. Mgt. Asn; Mfrs. Asn. Hartford Co. (exec. v.pres. and secy, 64). Rel: Protestant. Mailing Add: Prattling Pond Rd, Farmington, Conn. 06032.

NUCIFORO, ANDREA FRANCESCO D

Mass. State Sen.

b. Pittsfield, Mass, 7/14/27; s. Francesco Nuciforo and Mary Alberti N; m. 11/18/61 to Irene G; c. Sara Jane, Andrea F, Jr, John F. and Mark Robert. Educ: Rutgers Univ, Class of 52; Boston Univ. Sch. Law, LL.B, 55. Polit. & Govt. Pos: Mass. State Sen, currently. Bus. & Prof. Pos: Attorney at law, 55- Mil. Serv: Entered as Pvt, Air Force, 45-46. Mem: Itam Lodge, 2147, Pittsfield, Mass; Ital. Am. Club; Polish Commun. Club; Mass. Legislators Asn. Rel: Catholic. Legal Res: 222 Velma Ave, Pittsfield, Mass. 01201. Mailing Add: 27 Willis St, Pittsfield, Mass. 01202.

NUCKOLLS, KENNETH RUSSELL R

Chmn, Whatcom Co. Rep. Party, Wash.

b. Westboro, Mo, 12/12/21; s. Russell Kohler Nuckolls and Vesta Andrews N; m. 12/8/45 to Dorothy Ilene Kerr; c. Ellen (Mrs. Alan Rickis), Russell Kenneth and Sara Jo. Educ: Mont. State Univ, 4 years; Alpha Gamma Rho. Polit. & Govt. Pos: Del, Wash. State Rep. Conv, 54-; Rep. precinct committeeman, Bellingham, Wash, 57-, ward capt, 59-64; asst. finance chmn, Whatcom Co. Rep. Party, 63-66, state committeeman, 65-66; pres, Wash. Second Dist. Rep. Club, 64-66; mem, Gov. Adv. Cmn, Wash, 64-; chmn, Whatcom Co. Rep. Party, 66- Bus. & Prof. Pos: Mem. bd. dirs, Mt. Baker Recreation Co, 64-, pres, 67- Mil. Serv: Entered as Cpl, Inf, 43, released as 1st Lt, 46, after serv. in 35th Inf. Div, ETO, 44-45. Mem: Kiwanis (v.pres, 57-58, pres, 59); United Good Neighbors (mem. bd. dirs, 59-65, pres, 63); C. of C. (bd. dirs, 59-65); Elks; Bellingham Golf & Country Club; Bellingham Yacht Club. Outstanding Citizen Award, 67. Rel: Congregational. Mailing Add: 2811 Lynn, Bellingham, Wash. 98225.

NUGENT, JAMES PATRICK D

Mont. State Rep.

b. Butte, Mont, 10/21/22; s. Patrick William Nugent and Gertrude White N; m. 6/3/47 to Theresa Marie Willems; c. James Patrick, Jr, John William, Teri Ann, Joseph Micheal and Tina Marie. Educ: 5 Year Plumbing Apprenticeship; Int. Corr. Sch, Plumbing & Steam Fitting, Dipl, 48 and Refrig. & Air Conditioning, Dipl, 49. Polit. & Govt. Pos: Chmn, Missoula City Park Bd, Mont, 62-; alderman, Missoula, 63-; Mont. State Rep, 67- Bus. & Prof. Pos: Mem. exec. bd, Plumbers Union 459, 55-58 and chmn. finance cmt, 59-62. Mil. Serv: Entered as Pvt, Air Force, 42, released as Sgt, 45, after serv. in Europe-Africa-Mid. East Theater, 43-45; East. African Mid. East. Theater Ribbon; Good Conduct Medal. Mem: Eagles; K. of C; VFW; VFW Cootie's; Missoula Plumbers Union; St. Francis Home and Sch; St. Francis Xavier Holy Name Soc; Cath. High Sch. Found; West. Mont. Fish and Game Asn. Mont. All State Guard, 40-41, Butte High Sch. Rel: Roman Catholic. Mailing Add: 637 Alder St, Missoula, Mont. 59801.

NUGENT, JOHN JOSEPH D

b. North Kingstown, 10/25/12; m. to Rose H. Educ: Providence Col, 33; Boston Col. Law Sch, LL.B, 40. Polit. & Govt. Pos: Roving clerk, R.I. House of Rep, 41-42, clerk of house finance cmt, 46-48; R.I. State Rep, 49-58; mem, Judicial Coun, 50-64; attorney gen, R.I, 58-66; mem, Bar Asn. Adv. Cmt. on Amendments to the Law, exec. cmt, R.I. Dem. State Cmt, Fed. Dist. Court, U.S. Supreme Court, U.S. Court of Mil. Appeals and U.S. Court of Appeals; chmn, Criminal Law Cmt, Nat. Asn. of Attorneys Gen, 61-65, chmn, East. States Regional Conf. Cmt, 62-63 and mem. exec. cmt, 63-64; del, Dem. Nat. Conv, 68. Bus. & Prof. Pos: Attorney-at-law. Mil. Serv: Navy gunnery officer in European and Pac. areas with rank of Lt, 3½ years. Mem: Sons of St. Patrick of Capitol Hill; Soc. of Friendly Sons of St. Patrick: R.I. and Am. Bar Asns; Am. Legion, Roger Williams Post; VFW, Water-Langston Post. Voted winner of Wyman Award by all the attorneys gen. of U.S, 64. Mailing Add: 11 Observatory Ave, North Providence, R.I. 02911. (1967)

NUNALLY, BRIG. GEN. VAN D, JR.

b. Baxter, Putnam Co, Tenn, 3/9/17; m. to Frances Ditty N; c. Linda, Ann. Educ: Alumnus of Baxter Sem, University of Chattanooga; Various Army serv. schs. Polit. & Govt. Pos: Mem, State Adj. Gen. Staff, 51; Asst. Adj. Gen, 55; Tenn. Adj. Gen, 61-67. Mil. Serv: Enlisted, Army, 41; commissioned, 42; Co. Cmdr. in tank destroyer bn, served in France, Germany, Czechoslovakia; served at Army field forces hq. at Ft. Monroe, Va; Staff and Faculty, Armory Sch, Ft. Knox, Ky. Mem: Am. Legion Post 5; Mason; Shriner. Rel: Methodist. Mailing Add: Sidco Dr, Nashville, Tenn. 37204.

NUNN, LOUIE B. R

Gov, Ky.

b. 3/8/24; m. to Buela Cornelius Aspley; c. Five. Educ: Bowling Green Bus. Univ; Univ. Cincinnati; Univ. Louisville, law degree. Polit. & Govt. Pos: Elected judge of Barren Co, Ky, 53; mgr, Eisenhower-Cooper-Morton Campaign, 56 and Cooper and Morton Campaigns, 60 & 62; del, Rep. Nat. Conv, 68; Gov, Ky, currently. Mil. Serv: Army, World War II, 3 years. Mem: Mason; Past Comdr, Barren Co. Post, Am. Legion; past pres, Glasgow PTA; past v.pres, Rotary and C. of C; past dist. pres, Ky. Welfare Asn. Named One of the Three Outstanding Young Men of Ky. in 1956. Rel: Christian Church; Chmn, Bd. of Elders, First Christian Church of Glasgow. Mailing Add: State Capitol, Frankfort, Ky. 40601.

NUNN, MYRTA MAE D

V.Chmn, Lincoln Co. Dem. Cent. Cmt, Kans.

b. Bunker Hill, Kans, 2/17/28; d. William Leslie Boyd and Winifred Groves B; m. 3/9/52 to Grant Elwood Nunn, Jr; c. Kevin Boyd, Kent Grant and Kraig Jon. Educ: Hope Rural High Sch, Kans, 4 years. Polit. & Govt. Pos: V.chmn, Lincoln Co. Dem. Cent. Cmt, Kans, 66- Mem: Epsilon Sigma Alpha; Am. Legion Auxiliary; treas, Lincoln Carnegie Libr. Bd. Rel: Methodist. Mailing Add: 413 E. Court St, Lincoln, Kans. 67455.

NUNNERY, JIMMIE ERNEST D

S.C. State Rep.

b. Ft. Lawn, 10/21/30; s. M.A. Nunnery and Iva Marie Jordan N; m. 4/11/67 to Marie Little; c. William Stanley and Melvin Ernest. Educ: Palmetto Mil. Acad, 54; Univ. S.C. Polit. & Govt. Pos: Rural chmn, Co. United Fund, S.C; pres, Co. Farm Bur, 6 years; mem, Serv. and Exchange Cmn; Co. Bd. of Dirs, 47-62; v.pres, S.C. Farm Bur. Fedn, 62-64; dir, Chester Co. Tuberc. Asn, 62-64; co. magistrate, Dist. Three, 63-64; mem. Area Redevelopment Cmn; dir, Chester Co. Bd. of Commerce and Develop; del, Dem. Nat. Conv, 68; S.C. State Rep, currently. Bus. & Prof. Pos: Farmer, real estate and investments. Mil. Serv: S.C. Nat. Guard, Capt. Mem: Mason; Past Master, Richburg Masonic Lodge 89 AF&AM; Hejaz Shrine Temple; Elks. Rel: Baptist. Mailing Add: Route 1, Ft. Lawn, S.C. 29714.

NURMINEN, BIRGER DFL

Minn. State Rep.

b. Cloquet, 1904; m. to Bertha Hagen; c. Ardith (Mrs. Kane) and Harold. Polit. & Govt. Pos: Mem, adv. cmt, U.S. Dept. of Agr, 61; Minn. State Rep, 64- Bus. & Prof. Pos: Farmer and turkey grower. Mailing Add: Route 1, Aitkin, Minn. 56431.

NURSE, H. KENNETH D

b. Dunlap, Iowa, 12/13/18; s. Mr. and Mrs. Howard W. Nurse; m. 2nd time to Elaine Blake; c. Linda and Dennis. Educ: Iowa State Univ, 47, degree, voc. educ. Polit. & Govt. Pos: Iowa State Sen, until 66. Bus. & Prof. Pos: Real estate bus; Regional supvr, Gen. Life of Iowa Ins. Co. in a six co. area; Taught voc. agr. at Hartley High Sch; Taught vets-on-farm training in O'Brien Co; Farm mgt. work. Mem: Masonic Lodge, Kiwanis Club. Rel: Methodist. Mailing Add: 550 W. Maple, Hartley, Iowa 51346. (1967)

NUTTELMAN, NORBERT R

Wis. State Assemblyman

b. LaCrosse Co, Wis, 3/8/11. Educ: W. Salem High Sch. Polit. & Govt. Pos: Mem. local br, Fed. Farm Home Admin, 56-60; Wis. State Assemblyman, 60-, chmn, Agr. Cmt, Wis. State Assembly, 67- Bus. & Prof. Pos: Farmer, 26- Mem: 4-H (committeeman); Wis-Am. Dairy Asn; Breeders Coops (officer); Interstate Fair Asn; Kiwanis; C. of C; West Salem PTA (past pres); LaCrosse Milk Prod. Asn. (officer); Nat. Award. Superior Achievement in Agr. and Commun. Serv, Fed. Farm Home Admin, 52. Mailing Add: Route 1, West Salem, Wis. 54669.

NUTTER, G. WARREN R

Asst. Secy. of Defense for Int. Security Affairs

b. Topeka, Kans, 3/10/23; m. 1946 to Jane Calvert Couch; c. Coleman, Terry, Anne and William. Educ: Univ. Chicago, A.B, 44, A.M, 48 and Ph.D, 49; Phi Beta Kappa. Polit. & Govt. Pos: Asst. Secy. of Defense for Int. Security Affairs, 69- Bus. & Prof. Pos: With Cent. Intel. Agency, 51-53; former faculty mem, Lawrence Col. and Yale; mem. research staff and dir, Study of Soviet Econ. Growth, Nat. Bur. of Econ. Research, 54-67; Paul Goodloe McIntire prof. econ, chmn. of the dept. and dir. Thomas Jefferson Center, Univ. Va, 57-69. Mil. Serv: World War II, ETO; 1st Lt, Army Res; Bronze Star; Combat Infantryman's Badge; Three Battle Stars. Publ: Some Observations on Soviet Industrial Growth, Columbia, 57; Growth of Industrial Production in the Soviet Union, Princeton, 62; The Strange World of Ivan Ivanov; plus others. Recipient, Gavel Award, Am. Bar Asn, 68. Legal Res: Charlottesville, Va. 22902. Mailing Add: Dept. of Defense, Pentagon, Washington, D.C. 20301.

NYBERG, HARRY E. R

N.H. State Rep.

b. 12/31/92; married; c. One. Educ: Heeser Bus. Col. Polit. & Govt. Pos: Former ward clerk and alderman; N.H. State Rep, 23- Bus. & Prof. Pos: Former employee, N.E. Tel. & Tel. Co; retired. Mem: Tel. Pioneers of Am. Rel: Lutheran. Mailing Add: 121 Wellington Rd, Manchester, N.H. 03104. (1967)

NYE, GERALD PRENTICE R

b. Hortonville, Wis, 12/19/92; s. Irwin Raymond Nye and Phoebe Ella Prentice N; m. to Ann J. Munch; c. Marjorie E, Robert G. and James P; m. 12/14/40 to Marguerite Johnson; c. Gerald P, Jr, Richard J. and Deborah M. Educ: High sch, Wittenberg, Wis, grad, 11. Polit. & Govt. Pos: U.S. Cmnr, Fryburg, N.Dak, 16-18; mem, Sch. Bd, Cooperstown, N.Dak, 24-25; U.S. Sen, N.Dak, 25-45; asst. cmnr, Fed. Housing Admin, 60-63; mem. prfnl. staff, U.S. Senate Cmt. on Aging, 63-66. Bus. & Prof. Pos: Ed, Hortonville Rev, 11-14; ed, Creston Iowa Daily Plain Dealer, 14-15; ed, Fryburg, N.Dak. Pioneer, 16-20; ed, Cooperstown, N.Dak. Sentinel-Courier, 21-25; pres, Records Eng, Inc, Washington, D.C, 45-60; consult, 66. Publ: Reports by U.S. Senate Cmts, including, Teapot Dome Investigation and reports resulting from 2 year Select Cmt. Study of Munitions Industry and Causes of War, 25-45. Mem: Masons; Shrine; K. of P; Burning Tree Country Club; Columbia Country Club. Rel: Lutheran. Legal Res: 3213 Farmington Dr, Chevy Chase, Md. 20015. Mailing Add: 1108 16th St. N.W, Washington, D.C. 20036.

NYE, WILLIAM B. D
Ohio State Sen.
b. Akron, Ohio, 9/1/33; s. Richard A. Nye and Ruth Fairheart N; m. 8/31/57 to Linda Broughton; c. Kimberly Lynn, Erik William and Kevin Richard. Educ: Univ. Akron, B.A, 57; Univ. Mich. Law Sch, J.D, 60; Phi Sigma Alpha; Theta Chi. Polit. & Govt. Pos: Asst. law dir, Akron, Ohio, 61-62; attorney-exam, Ohio Bur. of Workmen's Compensation, 62-64; del-at-lg, Ohio League of Young Dem; former Ohio State Rep; del, Dem. State Conv, mem. platform cmt. and chmn. credentials cmt, 68; Ohio State Sen, currently. Bus. & Prof. Pos: Contract Analyst, Gen. Dynamics Corp, 61. Mil. Serv: Entered as Airman, Air Force, 54, released as Airman 2/C, 55; Korean Serv. Medal. Mem: Akron and Ohio Bar Asns; Citizens for Land and Water Use. Rel: Protestant. Mailing Add: 2367 E. Market St, Akron, Ohio 44312.

NYGAARD, K.O. D
b. DeLamere, N.Dak, 6/16/06; married; c. Two. Educ: N.Dak. State Univ. of Agr. and Applied Sci. Polit. & Govt. Pos: N.Dak. State Rep, 61-66; dir, N.S.R. Electric Coop. Bus. & Prof. Pos: Farmer. Mem: Farmers Union. Mailing Add: DeLamere, N.Dak. 58022. (1967)

NYQUIST, DEAN ALLEN R
Minn. State Sen.
b. Brule, Wis, 1/24/35; s. William Theodore Nyquist and Lilly Lindberg N; m. 9/9/61 to Marie Evangeline Nelson; c. Leland Everette, Jeanette Marie and Frederick Stuart. Educ: N.Dak. State Univ, B.S.E.E, 56; William Mitchell Col. Law, LL.B, 61; Tau Beta Pi; Phi Kappa Phi; Sigma Phi Delta; Phi Beta Gamma. Polit. & Govt. Pos: Del, Minn. Rep. State Conv, 66 & 68; mem. resolutions cmt, Hennepin Co. Conv, 66, parliamentarian, 68-69; Minn. State Sen, 67-, caucus chmn, Minn. State Senate, 66, chmn. corrections subcmt, 67-68. Mem: Minn. State and Hennepin Co. Bar Asns; Toastmaster's Club (pres, 66); Honneywell Engrs. Club (prog. chmn, 64-65); Northport Citizen's Asn.(bd. dirs); C. of C; Fly-Well Flying Club. Brooklyn Center's Outstanding Young Man, 68; One of Minn. Ten Outstanding Young Men. Rel: Covenant; Chmn, Brookdale Covenant Church. Mailing Add: 3707 53rd Place N, Minneapolis, Minn. 55429.

O

OAKES, JAMES LOWELL R
b. Springfield, Ill, 2/21/24; s. James Lowell Oakes; m. to Rosalyn M. Landon; c. Cynthia, Elizabeth and James, Jr. Educ: Harvard, A.B, 45, Law Sch, LL.B, 47. Polit. & Govt. Pos: Vt. State Sen, Windham Co, 61-64; Attorney Gen, Vt, until 69. Mem: Vt. Bar Asn.(first v.pres, 69); Bd. Bar Exam. Rel: Universalist-Unitarian. Legal Res: Guilford Vt. Mailing Add: 225 Main St, Brattleboro, Vt. 05301.

OAKES, ROY SIDNEY R
V.Chmn, Hamblen Co. Rep. Party, Tenn.
b. Gresham, Ore, 9/22/28; s. Henry Sidney Oakes and Gertrude Witt O; m. 9/22/52 to Elise Frazier; c. Karen Jane and Timothy Frazier. Educ: Knoxville High Sch, 4 years. Polit. & Govt. Pos: V.chmn, Hamblen Co. Rep. Party, Tenn, 59-; mem, Morristown Sch. Bd, 62-; magistrate, Hamblen Co. Quarterly Court, 66-; alternate del, Rep. Nat. Conv, 68. Bus. & Prof. Pos: V.pres-secy, Oakes Motor Co. Inc, 50- Mil. Serv: Entered as Pvt, Army, 47, released as T/Sgt, 51, after serv. in Seventh Div, Pac. Theatre, 47-49. Mem: F&AM; Kerbela Temple; Elks; Moose; Morristown Country Club; C. of C. Rel: Presbyterian. Legal Res: 2007 Magnolia Ave, Morristown, Tenn. 37814. Mailing Add: P.O. Box 8, Morristown, Tenn. 37814.

O'BANNON, ROBERT P. D
Ind. State Sen.
Polit. & Govt. Pos: Past pres, Corydon C. of C. pres, Dem. Ed. Asn, 46-47; pres, Hoosier State Press Asn, 51-52; Ind. State Sen, 51-; chmn, State Budget Cmt. Bus. & Prof. Pos: Ed. and publisher, Corydon Dem; mgr, O'Bannon Publishing Co. Mil. Serv: World War I. Mem: Harrison Co. Farm Bur; Harrison Grange; Am. Legion; Mason; Scottish Rite; K. of P; Rotary. Rel: Methodist. Mailing Add: 118 Elliott Ave, Corydon, Ind. 47112. (1967)

OBENSHAIN, RICHARD DUDLEY R
V.Chmn, Third Dist. Rep. Cmt, Va.
b. Abingdon, Va, 10/31/35; s. Samuel Shockley Obenshain and Josephine Mathews Dudley O; m. 7/15/61 to Helen Nottingham Wilkins; c. Mark Dudley, Anne Scott and Kate Boyce. Educ: Bridgewater Col, B.A, 56; N.Y. Univ. Sch. Law, LL.B, 59; Phi Delta Phi. Polit. & Govt. Pos: Chmn, Young Rep. Fedn. Va, 61-64; del, Rep. Nat. Conv, 64; Rep. cand. for Cong, Third Dist, Va, 64; v.chmn, Third Dist. Rep. Cmt, Va, 64-; Rep. Cand. for Attorney Gen, Va, 69. Bus. & Prof. Pos: Partner, McGuire, Woods & Battle, 66-69; dir, Blue Cross Va, 68-69. Mil. Serv: Marine Corps Res. Mem: Am. and Va. State Bar Asns; Am. Judicature Soc. Rel: Presbyterian. Mailing Add: 5505 Toddsbury Rd, Richmond, Va. 23226.

OBERDORFER, LOUIS F. D
b. Birmingham, Ala, 2/21/19; s. A. Leo Oberdorfer and Stella Maud Falk O; m. 7/31/41 to Elizabeth Weil; c. John Louis, Kathyrn Lee, Thomas Lee and William L. Educ: Dartmouth Col, A.B, 39; Yale Univ, LL.B, 46. Polit. & Govt. Pos: Law clerk to Justice Hugo H. Black, 46-47; asst. attorney gen, tax div, Dept. of Justice, 61-65. Bus. & Prof. Pos: With Paul, Weiss, Wharton and Garrison, 47-51, Cox, Langford, Stoddard and Cutler, 51-61 and Wilmer, Cutler & Pickering, D.C; co-chmn, Lawyers Cmt. for Civil Rights Under Law, 67-69. Mil. Serv: Capt, Army, 41-46. Mem: Am, Fed, D.C. and Ala. Bar Asns; Metrop. Club. Mailing Add: 1423 Kirby Rd, McLean, Va. 22101.

OBERHANSLEY, MILLY D
Utah State Rep.
b. Brewster Nebr, 5/28/20; d. Robert E. Cox and Eleanor Jarvis C; m. 3/17/48 to Rex E. Oberhansley; c. Judy (Mrs. Roldo Bliss) and Carole. Educ: Broken Bow, Nebr. Sch. Syst, grad, 38; Success Bus. Col, Denver Colo, 39-40. Polit. & Govt. Pos: Charter mem, Kearns Town Coun, Utah, 52-57 & 58-64; mem. bd. dirs, Kearns Improv. Dist, 58-69; mem, Planning and Zoning Cmn, Salt Lake Co. Govt, 58-; State Coun. of Defense, 65-67; Utah State Rep, 67-68 & 69-, mem, Legis. Coun, Utah House of Rep, 67-68, Higher Educ. Cmt. and Manpower Planning Coun, 69-; v.chmn. bd. dirs, Salt Lake Co. Commun. Action Prog, 68- Bus. & Prof. Pos: Personnel Specialist, Eimco Corp, 57-; chmn, Salt Lake Businessmen's Exec. Coun, Crime and Prev. Unit, Salt Lake City Police Dept, 68-69. Mem: Charter mem. and past pres, Kearns Ladies Civic Club. Commun. Serv. Award, Kearns C. of C, 66; Outstanding Citizen Award, Kearns, 69. Mailing Add: 5186 South 4620 West, Kearns, Utah 84118.

OBERMILLER, EDWARD D
Treas, Clinton Co. Dem. Cent. Cmt, Iowa
b. Clinton, Iowa, 3/6/24; s. Henry Obermiller and Alma Gladhill O; m. 4/27/45 to Claire Cramm; c. John W. and Susan. Educ: Clinton High Sch. Polit. & Govt. Pos: Treas, Clinton Co. Dem. Cent. Cmt, Iowa, 58-; del, Dem. Nat. Conv, 68; co. coordinator, John C. Culver Campaign, 69. Bus. & Prof. Pos: Millwright, Clinton Corn Processing Co, 48-65, safety coordinator, 68-; bus. rep, Local 6, Am. Fedn. Grain, 65-68. Mil. Serv: Entered as A/S, Navy Air Force, 42, released as AMM 2/C, 45. Mem: Clinton Engr. Club; Clinton Toastmaster Club 1319; mem. bd. dirs, United Fund of Clinton, Salvation Army and Respiratory and Tuberc. Bd; Moose; Amvets; VFW. Rel: Lutheran. Legal Res: 860 S. Bluff Blvd, Clinton, Iowa 52732. Mailing Add: P.O. Box 227, Clinton, Iowa 52732.

OBERWAGER, FRANCES ROBERTSON R
V.Chmn, Columbia Co. Rep. Cmt, N.Y.
b. Salem, N.Y, 2/22/23; d. James Wood Robertson and Julia Roche R; m. to Edwin R. Oberwager. Educ: Wash. Acad, Salem, N.Y, grad; Albany Training Sch. for Nurses, grad. Polit. & Govt. Pos: V.chmn, Columbia Co. Rep. Cmt, N.Y, currently; ex-officio mem, Rep. Clubs Columbia Co; pres, Women's Rep. Club, Columbia Co; chmn, Rep. Party Activities for Annual Columbia Co. Fair; del, Annual Conv, Nat. Fedn. Women's Rep. Clubs, Wash, D.C; mem, Third Judicial Dist. Rep. Exec. Cmt; exec. rep, Rep. Women 28th Cong. Dist. Rep. Women; former alternate del, N.Y. State Rep. Cmt. State-Wide Gubernatorial Nominating Conv. Bus. & Prof. Pos: Mem. staff and asst. to supt, Child's Hosp, Albany, N.Y, 46-59, acting supt, 59-61. Mem: Eastern Star; Women's Club of Chatham; Kinderhook Garden Club, Inc; Columbia Golf and Country Club; Columbia Mem. Hosp. Auxiliary; Ghent Vol. Firemen's Auxiliary. Rel: Lutheran; communicant, Christ Evangelical Lutheran Church. Mailing Add: Church St, Ghent, N.Y. 12075.

OBEY, DAVID R. D
U.S. Rep, Wis.
b. Okmulgee, Okla, 10/3/38; m. 1962 to Joan Lepinski; c. Craig David. Educ: Univ. of Wis, M.A. in Polit. Sci, 60. Polit. & Govt. Pos: Mem, Admin. Cmt. Wis. Dem. Party; Wis. State Assemblyman, 60-69; U.S. Rep, Wis, 69-, mem, House Cmt. on Pub. Works, subcmts. on Rivers and Harbors, Flood Control, Pub. Bldgs. and Grounds and Ad Hoc Subcmt. on Appalachia. Bus. & Prof. Pos: Real estate broker. Mem: Optimists; K. of C; dir, Friends of the Menominees. Legal Res: 515 N. Ninth Ave, Wausau, Wis. 54401. Mailing Add: 1417 Longworth Bldg, Washington, D.C. 20515.

O'BLOCK, PATRICK MICHAEL D
b. Chicago, Ill, 9/1/19; s. Mathew O'Block and Ellen Mullaney O; m. 6/21/41 to Helen P. Burns; c. Kenneth, Dennis, Patricia, Peggy, Kathy, Mickey and Nancy. Educ: Am. Tech. Soc. Sch. of Commerce. Polit. & Govt. Pos: Trustee, Hazel Crest, Ill, 60-62, mayor, 62-65; dir. civil defense, Cook Co. Ill, 63-67 & 69-; committeeman, Thornton Twp. Dem. Party, 64-; secy, Ill. Racing Bd, 67-69; del, Dem. Nat. Conv, 68; dir, John F. Kennedy Campaign for Thornton Twp, Ill. Bus. & Prof. Pos: Mgr, Superior Match Co, Chicago, 49-53; sales territory mgr, Diamond Nat. Corp, 53-63; spec. events dir, Maywood Park Race Track, currently. Publ: 'Lite up and Live,' Prog, Hwy. Safety, Ill. Mem: Moose; Kiwanis; K. of C. Recipient of Boy Scout Award, 64; Humanitarian South Suburban Mayors Award of Dedication; Gov. of Ill. Safety Award. Rel: Catholic. Mailing Add: 15126 Drexel Ave, South Holland, Ill. 60473.

O'BRIEN, BERNARD F. D
Pa. State Rep.
b. Miners Mills, Pa, 3/5/14; s. Michael J. O'Brien and Ellen Rogan O; m. to Agnes McDonnell; wid; c. ten. Educ: Coughlin High Sch, Wilkes-Barre, Pa. Polit. & Govt. Pos: Pa. State Rep, 62- Bus. & Prof. Pos: Stereotyper. Mem: Active in United Fund, Mercy Hosp. Bldg. Fund, and W-B Indust. Fund Orgns; I.S. & E.U, AFL-CIO, Cent. Labor Union; Allied Trades Coun; K. of C; Eagles; Stereotyper's Union, (pres, 12 years). Mailing Add: 28 Hillard St, Wilkes-Barre, Pa. 18702. (1967)

O'BRIEN, BERNARD F, JR. D
b. 11/11/34; s. Former Rep. Bernard F. O'Brien; married; c. Laura Ann, Kathleen Marie. Educ: Univ. of Detroit; Mich. State Univ. Polit. & Govt. Pos: Mich. State Sen, 64-66; served as a page for several years under his father. Bus. & Prof. Pos: Self employed in the real estate and ins. bus. Mem: K. of C, 3°; pres, Vernor Junction Bus. Men's Asn. Rel: Catholic. Mailing Add: 1581 Calvary St, Detroit, Mich. 48233. (1967)

O'BRIEN, CARL W. D
b. Pontiac, Mich, 4/1/30; married; c. Shaun, Tracy, Darcy, Brett, Rory, Keely, Daniel. Educ: Wayne State Univ. Polit. & Govt. Pos: Mich. State Sen, 64-66; past pres. Oakland Co. Young Dems; chmn. 19th Cong. Dist. Young Dems, at present a mem; original mem. exec. coun, Dem. Polit. Action Cmt. Bus. & Prof. Pos: Inspector, Qual. Standards Dept, Gen. Motors Corp; staff writer for Radio Sta. WORS-FM. Mil. Serv: Army, Korean Conflict. Mem: Guardian of the crippled children of the Easter Seal Soc; hon. mem, Pontiac Creative Arts Asn, mem. of UAW, Local 596; Oakland Co. Dem. Cmt. Mailing Add: 513 Moore St, Pontiac, Mich. 48057. (1967)

O'BRIEN, CHARLES A. D
Chief Dep. Attorney Gen, Calif.
b. Lawrence, Mass, 9/1/25; s. E.W. O'Brien and Genevieve Scanlon O; m. 9/17/54 to Marie Fox; c. Devin, Brennan and Erin. Educ: Harvard Univ, A.B, 50; Harvard Law Sch, LL.B, 53. Polit. & Govt. Pos: Asst. attorney gen, Calif, 59-60, chief asst. attorney gen, 60-61, exec. secy. to gov, 61-62, chief dep. attorney gen, 62- Mil. Serv: Combat Inf, ETO, 43-45. Publ: Articles in

various law reviews and general circulation mag. Mem: San Francisco, Los Angeles and Calif. Bar Asns. Rel: Catholic. Mailing Add: 6000 State Bldg, San Francisco, Calif. 94102.

O'BRIEN, CHESTER J. R
Educ: Northeast. Univ; Lincoln Inst. Polit. & Govt. Pos: Mem, rep. town cmt; v. pres, Arlington Young Reps. Club; del. to Mass. Young Rep. Asn. Bus. & Prof. Pos: Sen. engr, local elec. firm. Mailing Add: 101 Thorndike St, Arlington, Mass. 02174. (1967)

O'BRIEN, DANIEL JOHN D
Dem. Nat. Committeeman, Vt.
b. Burlington, Vt, 12/15/33; s. Leo O'Brien, Sr. and Mary Mabel Hayes O; m. to Sandra Corey; c. Stephanie and Molly. Educ: Cathedral High Sch, Burlington, Vt. Polit. & Govt. Pos: Chmn, South Burlington Dem. Town Cmt, Vt, 57-62; mem, Cmt. on Town Govt, 58-69; Justice of the Peace, 60-; mem, Bd. of Civil Authority, 60-; chmn, Chittenden Co. Dem. Cmt, 62-64; chmn, Vt. State Dem. Cmt, 64-68, chmn. exec. cmt, 68-; mem, Vt. State Bd. of Health, 65-; Dem. Nat. Committeeman, Vt, 68-; mem. bd. of gov, Med. Center Hosp. of Vt, 68-; mem, Small Bus. Admin. Adv. Coun, Vt, 68- Bus. & Prof. Pos: Partner, O'Brien Bros. Cattle Dealers, South Burlington, Vt, 57-; pres, Forest Park Realty Corp, 68-; v.pres, Realty Sales Inc, 69- Mem: Vt. Cattlemen's Asn; Farm Bur; North Farms; K. of C; Eagles; Ethan Allen Club; Burlington Country Club. Rel: Roman Catholic. Legal Res: 113 Patchen Rd, South Burlington, Vt. 05401. Mailing Add: P.O. Box 2184, South Burlington, Vt. 05401.

O'BRIEN, DONALD EUGENE D
b. Marcus, Iowa, 9/30/23; s. Michael John O'Brien and Myrtle Toomey O; m. 4/15/50 to Ruth Virginia Mahon; c. Teresa, Brien, John and Schiuvaun. Educ: Creighton Univ, LL.B, 48; Gamma Eta Gamma. Polit. & Govt. Pos: Co. attorney, Sioux City, Iowa, 55-58, munic. judge, 59-60; U.S. attorney, North. Dist, Iowa, 61-67; campaign aide to Robert Kennedy, Iowa, Nebr, S.Dak, 68; conv. coordinator for Senator McGovern, 68, del, Dem. Nat. Conv, 68; South. Calif. coordinator for H. Humphrey, 68. Mil. Serv: Entered as Pvt, Army Air Force, 42, released as 1st Lt, 45, after serv. in 390th Bomb Group, ETO, 44-45; Distinguished Flying Cross; Five Air Medals; Presidential Citation. Mem: Iowa Bar Asn; K. of C; Amvets; Am. Legion. Rel: Catholic. Legal Res: 3126 Jones St, Sioux City, Iowa 51104. Mailing Add: 916 Grandview Blvd, Sioux City, Iowa 51101.

O'BRIEN, DONALD J. D
b. Chicago, Ill; m. to Helen McGinnis; c. Five. Educ: DePaul Univ. Col. Commun, Col. Law, LL.B, 36; admitted to bar, 36; Phi Alpha Delta; Phi Beta Epsilon. Polit. & Govt. Pos: Committeeman, 14th Ward, Regular Dem. Orgn, Ill; Ill. State Sen, 67th-73rd Gen. Assemblies. Bus. & Prof. Pos: Law practice; trial lawyer. Mem: K. of C.(4°); Chicago, Ill. State and Am. Bar Asns; Trial Lawyers; fel. Int. Acad. Trial Lawyers. Mailing Add: 1102 W. Garfield Blvd, Chicago, Ill. 60621. (1967)

O'BRIEN, DOROTHY GERTRUDE D
Dem. Nat. Committeewoman, Ill.
b. DeKalb, Ill, 2/8/19; d. James S. O'Brien and Mary Carton O; single. Educ: St. Joseph Hosp. Sch. Nursing, nursing diploma, 40; DePaul Univ, B.S, 44, Law Sch, 54-56; Kappa Beta Pi. Polit. & Govt. Pos: Chairwoman, DeKalb Co. Dem. Cent. Cmt, Ill, 56-60; mem. adv. cmt, Dem. Nat. Cmt, 58-60; state chairwoman, Ill. State Dem. Cent. Cmt, 58-64; del. and mem. Platform Cmt, Dem. Nat. Conv, 60, 64 & 68; precinct committeewoman, Afton Twp. Dem. Party, 62-; Dem. Nat. Committeewoman, Ill, 64-; mem. defense adv. cmt. on women in the serv, Defense Dept, 64-66; v.chmn, Dem. Midwest Conv, 65-67. Mil. Serv: Entered as Asst. Nurse Officer, U.S. Pub. Health Serv, 45, released as Sr. Asst. Nurse Officer, 52, after serv. in Nutrition Div, 1 year and Venereal Disease Control Div, 6 years. Mem: St. Joseph Hosp. Alumnae Asn, Chicago; Women's Bd, St. Joseph Hosp, Chicago; Nat. League for Nursing; Am. Legion Post 66; NAACP; Nat. Farmers Union; DeKalb Co. Farmers Union (secy, 56-58); mem, Atlantic Coun. for NATO and del. to Atlantic Cong, London, Eng, 59. Rel: Roman Catholic. Mailing Add: R.R. 2, DeKalb, Ill. 60115.

O'BRIEN, E. D. D
Mich. State Rep.
b. Detroit, Mich, 6/4/20; m. 1941 to Margaret M. Johnson; c. Dayle R. Educ: Evening classes, Wayne State Univ, two years. Polit. & Govt. Pos: Mich. State Rep, 56- Mil. Serv: S/Sgt, Army, 44-46 with combat in Italy. Mem: Am. Legion, D.S.R. Post; VFW, Ft. Gratiot Post; Amvets, Post 57; Native Born Detroiter's Club; Gratiot Ave. Improv. Asn; Park-Dr. Ravendale Improv. Asn; Friendly Sons of St. Patrick; Fedn. of Filipinos of Mich.(hon. mem.). Mailing Add: 13392 Promenade Ave, Detroit, Mich, 48213.

O'BRIEN, JADINE R. D
b. Whitman, Mass, 8/27/31; d. John F. Raynes and Eunice Nesmith R; m. 11/2/52 to John B. O'Brien; c. Joy J. and Jill J. Educ: Westbrook Jr. Col, 51; Univ. Maine, B.S, 66. Polit. & Govt. Pos: V.Chmn, Portland City Dem. Cmt, Maine, 62-63; secy, Cumberland Co. Dem. Cmt, 63-64; mem, Maine State Dem. Cmt, two terms, 64-68; del, Maine Asn. of Dem. Women, 64-; field coordinator, Congressman Peter N. Kyros, 67-; del, Dem. Nat. Conv, 68. Bus. & Prof. Pos: Chmn, subcmt, Maine Coun. Fed. Agencies, 69- Mem: Altrusa Club of Portland; League of Women Voters; Model Cities - Health Task Force. Rel: Episcopal. Mailing Add: 194 Pleasant Ave, Portland, Maine 04103.

O'BRIEN, JOHN F. X. D
Md. State Del.
b. Baltimore, Md, 1/26/36; s. John Mitchell O'Brien and Anne Zerhusen O; m. 9/24/66 to Mary Ellen Foppiano; c. Kelly. Educ: Univ. Baltimore, LL.B, 64. Polit. & Govt. Pos: Md. State Del, 67- Mil. Serv: Entered as Pvt, Army, 56, released as Pfc, 58, after serv. in 11th Armored Cavalry, Germany, 57-58. Rel: Roman Catholic. Mailing Add: 6405 Alta Ave, Baltimore, Md. 21206.

O'BRIEN, JOHN FITZGERALD D
Committeeman, Ill. Dem. Representative Cmt.
b. Springfield, Ill, 5/6/28; s. Edward L. O'Brien and Mary Murphy O; m. 5/6/61 to Sharon L. Fassero; c. Marjorie ann and Polly Ann. Educ: Local sch. Polit. & Govt. Pos: Pres, Young Dem. of Sangamon Co, 60-62; committeeman, Ill. Dem. Representative Cmt, 62-; asst. clerk, Ill. House of Rep, 69- Bus. & Prof. Pos: Owner, O'Brien Ins. Agency, Springfield, Ill, 54- Mil. Serv: Entered as Pvt, Army, 46, released as S/Sgt, 51, after serv. in Second Inf. Div, Korea, 50-51; Sgt. Maj, Army Res, currently; Combat Inf. Badge. Mem: K. of C; Elks; Secy. and treas, Sons of Erin. Rel: Roman Catholic. Legal Res: 2427 Sussex Rd, Springfield, Ill. 62703. Mailing Add: P.O. Box 2346, Springfield, Ill. 62705.

O'BRIEN, JOHN JOSEPH D
Vt. State Sen.
b. New Bedford, Mass, 4/29/97; widower; c. Two. Educ: New Bedford Schs. Polit. & Govt. Pos: Vt. State Sen, 59-; mem, Lake Champlain Waterway Cmn. Bus. & Prof. Pos: Retired, formerly sports promoter. Mem: Elks (past exalted ruler). Rel: Catholic. Mailing Add: 33 Hayden Pkwy, S. Burlington, Vt. 05401. (1967)

O'BRIEN, JOHN L. D
Wash. State Rep.
b. Seattle, Wash, 1911; m. to Mary; c. six. Educ: Bus. Col; West. Inst. of Prfnl. Acct. Polit. & Govt. Pos: Wash. State Rep, 41-, Majority Leader, Wash. House of Rep, 51 & 65, Minority Leader, 53, 63, 67 & 69, Speaker of the House, 55-61. Bus. & Prof. Pos: CPA. Mil. Serv: Coast Guard; Temp. Res. Mem: Eagles; K. of C; Wash. Athletic Club; Rainier Bus. Men's Club; Wash. Soc. of CPA; Am. Inst. CPA (past mem. of bd); mem. exec. cmt. and past pres, Nat. Conf. of State Legis. Leaders. Mailing Add: 5041 Lake Washington Blvd. S, Seattle, Wash. 98118.

O'BRIEN, JOSEPH K. D
b. Kingston, Pa, 3/29/40. Educ: Providence Col, B.A; U. of R.I. Polit. & Gov. Pos: R.I. State Rep, 64-66; Exec. Secy. Rhode Islanders for Newport-Jamestown Bay Bridge; Pres, Young Citizens for Urban Renewal. Bus. & Prof. Pos: Stock Broker. Mem: Young Dem; Ancient Order of Hibernians; K. of C; Newport Co. C. of C. 1967 Legal Res: 14 Catherine St, Newport, R.I. No mailing address available. (1967)

O'BRIEN, LAWRENCE FRANCIS D
b. Springfield, Mass, 7/7/17; s. Lawrence O'Brien, Sr. and Myra Sweeney O; m. 5/30/44 to Elva Lena Brassard; c. Lawrence Francis, III. Educ: Northeast. Univ, LL.B, 42. Hon. Ph.D, in law, West. New Eng. Col, 62; hon. Ph.D. in pub. admin, Northeast. Univ, 65; hon. Ph.D. in law, Villanova Univ. and hon. Ph.D. in Humanities, St. Anselm's Col, 66. Polit. & Govt. Pos: Dir. orgn, Second Cong. Dist. Dem. Campaigns, Mass, 46, 48 & 50; admin. asst. to U.S. Rep. Foster Furcolo, Mass, 48-50; dir. orgn, J. F. Kennedy Senate Campaigns, Mass, 52 & 58 and Kennedy-Johnson Campaign, 60; spec. asst. to President for Cong. Rels, 61-65; dir. orgn. Johnson-Humphrey Campaign, 64; Postmaster Gen, U.S. Post Off. Dept, 65-68; former Dem. Nat. Chmn. Bus. & Prof. Pos: Former mgr, family bus. enterprises; bd. pres. and bus. mgr, West. Mass. Hotel Fund, 52-58; in pub. rels, 58-60. Mil. Serv: Army, 43-45. Publ: The O'Brien Manual, Dem. Nat. Cmt, 60, revised 62 & 64. Mem: Elks; Am. Legion. Mailing Add: Upper Beverly Hills Rd, West Springfield, Mass. 01089. (1967)

O'BRIEN, LEO, JR. D
Vt. State Sen.
b. Burlington, Vt, 2/5/31; s. Leo O'Brien, Sr. and Mary Mabel Hayes O; m. 4/12/58 to Stella T. Cotrupi; c. Maureen, Leo, III, Kathleen, Bridget, Joanne and Patrick. Educ: St. Michael's Col, 49-50; Univ. Vt, B.A. in polit. sci, 54-57; Ethan Allen Club. Polit. & Govt. Pos: Mem, S. Burlington Dem. Cmn, Vt, 54-; Chittenden Co. Dem. Cmn, 56-; S. Burlington Planning Cmn, 60-68; Cmn. Admin. Coord, 63-64; Vt. State Rep, 63-69, Minority Leader, Vt. House of Rep, 66-68, mem, Joint Fiscal Cmt, 68; trustee, Univ. of Vt. & State Agr. Sch, 65-; assoc. trustee, St. Michael's Col, 67-; del, Dem. Nat. Conv, 68; mem, Interstate Coop. Cmn, 69-; Vt. State Sen, Chittenden-Grand Isle Dist, 69- Bus. & Prof. Pos: Partner, O'Brien Brothers Cattle Sales, S. Burlington, Vt, 57-; v.pres, Forest Park Realty Corp, 68-; pres, Realty Sales, Inc, 69- Mil. Serv: Entered as Seaman Recruit, Navy, 50, released as PO 2/C, 54, after serv. in Atlantic Fleet, 51-54; Nat. Defense Serv. Medal. Mem: Vt. and N.Y. Cattle Dealers Asns; Burlington Veterans Club; Elks; Farm Bureau; Grange; Am. Legion. Distinguished Serv. Award, Jr. C. of C, 64. Rel: Catholic. Mailing Add: 200 Old Farm Rd, South Burlington, Vt. 05401.

O'BRIEN, LEO WILLIAM D
b. Buffalo, N.Y, 9/21/00; m. 1925 to Mabel Jean. Educ: Niagara Univ, 22; hon. degrees from Univ. of Alaska, Univ. of Niagara and Sienna Col. Polit. & Govt. Pos: U.S. Rep, N.Y, 52-67; mem. of Alaska Int. Rail and Hwy. Cmn; floor mgr. for Alaska and Hawaii Statehood Bills. Bus. & Prof. Pos: Newspaperman, 22-52; as radio and TV commentator won Nat. Awards, 50-51. Mailing Add: 160 S. Manning Blvd, Albany, N.Y. 12208. (1967)

O'BRIEN, MILES S. D
b. Oelwein, Iowa, 10/8/17; s. Edward R. O'Brien and Mary E. Hagan O; m. 7/1/47 to Cora A. Osheim; c. Ruth A, Kathleen A, Mary H, Edward R, James R, William M, Michael T. and Michelle M. Educ: Univ. Iowa, Law, 35-42; Beta Theta Pi; Phi Delta Phi. Polit. & Govt. Pos: Del, Dem. State Conv, 42- and Dem. Nat. Conv, 68; finance chmn, Fayette Co. Dem. Party, 46-50. Bus. & Prof. Pos: Attorney-at-law, Oelwein, Iowa, 42- Mil. Serv: Entered as Aviation Cadet, Air Force, 43, released as Pfc, 45, after serv. in Cent. Flying Training Command. Mem: Fayette Co. and Iowa State Bar Asns; Am. Trial Lawyers Asn; Elks; Am. Legion. Rel: Catholic. Legal Res: 11 First Ave, N. E, Oelwein, Iowa 50662. Mailing Add: 409 Sixth Ave, S.E, Oelwein, Iowa 50662.

O'BRIEN, MYRTLE A. D
b. Parnell, Iowa, 7/22/98; d. John Cosgrove Toomey and Honorah Hanson T; m. 6/21/21 to Michael John O'Brien; wid; c. Patricia (Mrs. Aiken), Donald E, Michael T, John T, Robert J, Philip H, Thomas H. and Shiuvaun (Mrs. Nasypany). Educ: Iowa State Teachers Col, 17. Polit. Pos: Precinct committeewoman, Dem. Party and del. Co. Convs, 46-; del, Dem. Nat. Conv, 64, State Convs, 38-42. Mem: Catholic Women's League; Am. Legion Auxiliary;

Dem. Woman's Club; St. Margaret Circle; Blessed Sacrament Confraternity; Trinity Mothers Club. Rel: Catholic. Mailing Add: 2509 Jones, Sioux City, Iowa 51102. (1967)

O'BRIEN, WILLIAM J. R
State Auditor, Minn.
b. Jacksonville, Fla, 2/19/30; m. to Eleanor Kennedy; c. Katherine, Alice, Julia and Deborah. Educ: Cornell Univ, 47-49; Univ. of Minn, Minneapolis, B.B.A, 52; Univ. of Chicago. Polit. & Govt. Pos: Minn. State Rep, 63-67; cmnr, Minn. Dept. of Econ. Develop, 67; State Auditor of Minn, 69- Bus. & Prof. Pos: St. Paul account exec. for Chicago based investment counseling firm, presently. Mem: St. Paul Children's Hosp.(mem, bd. of trustees and finance cmt, former mem, exec. cmt, former corporate secy); Minn. Hist. Soc.(former dir. and mem. of exec. cmt, mem, finance cmt, chmn, Ft. Snelling restoration cmt). Rel: Catholic. Legal Res: 734 Woodbridge Dr, St. Paul, Minn. 55118. Mailing Add: Office of the State Auditor, 309 Administration Bldg, St. Paul, Minn. 55101.

O'BRIEN, WILLIAM W. D
R.I. State Rep.
b. Augusta, Maine, 5/28/17; m. to Margaret. Educ: Cranston High Sch. Polit. & Govt. Pos: Pres, Cranston Nat. Div. of Little League, R.I; mem. city coun, Cranston, 61-62 and chmn, Recreation Cmt; R.I. State Rep, 64- Bus. & Prof. Pos: Materials collector. Mailing Add: 217 Aqueduct Rd, Cranston, R.I. 02910. (1967)

OCASEK, OLIVER ROBERT D
Ohio State Sen.
b. Bedford, Ohio, 11/2/25; s. Jack Barney Ocasek and Olive Drabek O; m. 6/18/55 to Virginia Mae Hejduk. Educ: Kent State Univ, B.Sc, 46, M.A, 51; West. Reserve Univ, 51-56; Phi Delta Kappa; Asn. for Higher Educ; Nat. Educ. Asn; Sigma Nu. Polit. & Govt. Pos: Twp. trustee, Sagamore Hills, Ohio, 49-60, precinct committeeman, 52-; Ohio State Sen, 58-; pres, Young Dem. of Ohio, 62-64; v.pres, Young. Dem. of Am, 63-65. Bus. & Prof. Pos: Teacher, Richfield High Sch, Ohio, 46-50 and Stow High Sch, 50-51; prin, Tallmadge High Sch, 51-60; instr, Kent State Univ, 60; assoc. prof. of educ, Akron Univ, 61- Publ: School Finance, Ohio's Schs, 65. Distinguished legislator award from several orgns. Rel: Presbyterian. Mailing Add: 7665 Gannett Rd, Northfield, Ohio 44067.

OCHS, TILLMAN PAUL R
Kans. State Rep.
b. Boyd, Kans, 6/3/10; s. Peter L. Ochs and Lydia Resner O; m. 7/20/43 to Edlyn L. Fehr; c. Gary Alan and Stephen Douglas (deceased). Educ: Lakeland Col, 1 year. Polit. & Govt. Pos: Kans. State Rep, 109th Dist, 66- Bus. & Prof. Pos: Grain elevator operator, Peter L. Ochs, 29-39; pres, Peter L. Ochs Elevators, Inc, 62- Mil. Serv: Entered as Pvt, Air Force, 41, released as 1st Sgt, 45, after serv. in Third Staff Squadron, Sherman Field, Ft. Leavenworth, Kans. Mem: Kans. Independent Oil & Gas Asn; Kiwanis; Am. Legion. Rel: Protestant. Mailing Add: 271 W. 8th St, Hoisington, Kans. 67544.

OCKERMAN, FOSTER D
b. Nelson Co, Ky, 9/17/20; s. R. F. Ockerman and Anna Clara Sweazy O; m. 8/25/50 to Joyce Ann Harris; c. Foster, Jr, Jefferson and Ann Ward. Educ: Univ. of Ky, B.A. and LL.B. Polit. & Govt. Pos: City attorney, Lexington, Ky, 50-54; Ky. State Rep, 54-59; cmnr, Dept. Motor Transportation, Commonwealth of Ky, 59-62; mgr, Successful Primary and Gen. Elec. Dem. Gubernatorial Campaign, 63; chmn, State Dem. Cent. Exec. Cmt, Ky, 64-66. Prof. Pos: Attorney at Law, 46- Mil. Serv: Entered as Seaman, Navy, 42, released as Lt, 46, after serv. Pac. Theater. Mem: Am, Ky. and Fayette Co. Bar Asns; Am. Legion; Elks; Mason. Rel: Methodist. Legal Res: 211 S. Hanover Ave, Lexington, Ky. 40502. Mailing Add: 259 W. Short St, Lexington, Ky. 40507.

O'CONNELL, JOHN JAMES D
b. Tacoma, Wash, 4/30/19; s. Michael O'Connell and Margaret Caulfield O; m. to Margaret Hatchell; c. Michael, Mary Margaret, Kathleen, Maureen, Patricia and Rosemary. Educ: Gonzaga Univ. Sch. of Law, LL.B, 42. Polit. & Govt. Pos: Former precinct committeeman, Wash. Dem. Party; pres, Wash. Young Dem, 48; asst. city attorney, Tacoma, 48-50; prosecuting attorney, Pierce Co, 50-56; attorney gen, State of Wash, 56-68; Dem. Nominee for Gov, State Wash, 68. Bus. & Prof. Pos: Attorney-at-Law, Tacoma, Wash, 46-48 and currently. Mil. Serv: Entered as Pvt, Army, 42, released as 1st Lt, 46, after serv. in S.Pac. Mem: Pres, Nat. Asn. Attorneys General, 63; past pres, Western Asn. Attorneys General; former mem, exec. bd, Mt. Rainier Boy Scout Coun; chmn, State Employee's Retirement Bd; chmn, Spec. Cmt. on Interstate Taxation, Coun. State Govts; Kiwanis; Elks; Eagles; VFW; Am. Legion; Serra Club; K. of C. Elected Outstanding Attorney General in Nation by Nat. Asn. of Attorneys General and presented Wyman Award, 61. Rel: Catholic. Legal Res: 614 N. J St, Tacoma, Wash. 98403. Mailing Add: 14th Floor, Puget Sound Bank Building, Tacoma, Wash. 98402.

O'CONNELL, JOHN W. D
b. Kalispell, Mont, 11/14/09; s. William H. O'Connell and Margaret O'Connor O; m. 6/12/36 to Claudia Lewis; c. Jerry Anne and Charles Lewis. Educ: Northwest. Bus. Col, Spokane, Wash. Polit. & Govt. Pos: Mem, Rivers & Harbor Cmt, Mont, 46-48; mayor, Columbia Falls, Mont, 46-49; chmn, Sitka Dem. Precinct Cmt, Alaska, 60-63; mem, State Econ. Develop. Cmt, 63-64; mayor, Sitka, Alaska, 63-67; former Alaska State Rep; v.pres, Alaska Munic. League, 65-66, pres, 66-67; mem, Gr. Sitka Borough Assembly, 65-67. Bus. & Prof. Pos: Pres, Southeast. Plumbing Contractors, 60-61. Mil. Serv: Entered as Seaman 3/C, Navy, 44, released as Machinist's Mate 3/C, 46, after serv. in 86th N.C.B, Pac; Pac. Theater and Okinawa Ribbons. Mem: Elks; Moose; Am. Legion; VFW. Rel: Catholic. Mailing Add: 233 Lincoln, Box 242, Sitka, Alaska 99835.

O'CONNELL, KENNETH JOHN D
Assoc. Justice, Ore. Supreme Court
b. Bayfield, Wis, 12/8/09; s. Daniel W. O'Connell and Kathryn B. Smith O; m. 7/3/64 to Esther Foster; c. Daniel and Thomas. Educ: Univ. of Wis, Madison, LL.B, 33, S.J.D, 34; Order of the Coif; Omicron Delta Tau. Polit. & Govt. Pos: Mem, Wis. Tax Cmn, 34; chmn, Statute Rev. Coun, Ore, 50-54; Assoc. Justice, Ore. Supreme Court, 58-; v.chmn, Ore. Constitutional Rev. Cmn, 61-63. Bus. & Prof. Pos: Assisted in prep. of restatement of Law of Property for Am. Law Inst, 33-34; asst. prof. of law, Univ. of Ore. Law Sch, 35-40, assoc. prof, 40-44 and prof, 47-58; practice of law, Darling and Vonderheit, Eugene, Ore, 44-47. Publ: Personal Property Outlines (5), privately published, 57; Oregon Laws on Surveying, State Agency; articles for Ore. Law Rev, 36-67. Am. and Ore. State Bar Asns; Am. Judicature Soc; Law and Soc. Award of Merit, Ore. State Bar, 53; Distinguished Serv. Award, Univ. of Ore, 67; Appointment to Order of Coif Triennial Awards Cmt. Legal Res: Route 3, Box 681-8, Salem, Ore. 97302. Mailing Add: Supreme Court Bldg, Salem, Ore. 97310.

O'CONNELL, MAURICE J. D
b. Baltimore, Md, 12/22/26; m. Educ: Loyola Col, B.S. Polit. & Govt. Pos: Md. State Del, 63-67. Mil. Serv: Navy and Md. State Guard. Mailing Add: 5520 Bucknell Rd, Baltimore, Md. 21206. (1967)

O'CONNELL, RICHARD T. R
b. Newark, N.J, 2/15/28; s. Daniel T. O'Connell and Margaret DeLeeuw O; m. 9/10/65 to Mary Geraldine Norris. Educ: Univ. Vt, B.A; Univ. Miami, LL.B; Tau Kappa Alpha. Polit. & Govt. Pos: Mem, Old Saybrook Bd. Educ, Conn, 60-66; mem, Old Saybrook Charter Cmn, 63-65; chmn, Old Saybrook Rep. Party, until 68. Bus. & Prof. Pos: Attorney, 55- Mil. Serv: Entered as A/S, Navy, 45, released as Seaman 1/C, 46. Nat. Col. Debating Champion, 50. Legal Res: Anchorage Lane, Old Saybrook, Conn. 06475. Mailing Add: 709 Boston Post Rd, Old Saybrook, Conn. 06475. (1967)

O'CONNELL, WILLOUGHBY L. D
Postmaster, Nevada, Mo.
b. Nevada, Mo, 4/20/26; s. Emmett L. O'Connell and Helen Columbia O; m. 8/9/52 to Mary Jane Morgan; c. Timothy Patrick. Educ: Univ. Mo, B.S. in bus, 50. Polit. & Govt. Pos: Chmn, Midwestern Conf, Young Dem. Clubs of Am, 59-61; state pres, Young Dem. Clubs, Mo, 59 & 60, nat. committeeman, 62-63; chmn, Vernon Co. Dem. Cmt, Mo, 63-66; chmn, Fourth Cong. Dist. Dem. Party, 63-66; postmaster, Nevada, 69- Bus. & Prof. Pos: Mgr, Nev. Auto Parts, 50- Mil. Serv: Entered as Seaman 2/C, Navy, 44, released as Seaman 1/C, 46; Asiatic, European and Am. Theater Ribbons. Mem: Elks; Am. Legion; Athletic Alumni Coun, Univ. Mo. Rel: Catholic. Mailing Add: 611 South Adams, Nevada, Mo. 64772.

O'CONNOR, CAROLYN OLD D
b. Sheffield, Ala, 11/17/42; d. George Joseph Armstrong and Ruby Old A; m. 9/3/66 to James David O'Connor. Educ: Univ. Ala, B.S, 65; Mortar Bd; Pi Mu Epsilon; Alpha Lambda Delta; Phi Beta Kappa; Zeta Tau Alpha. Polit. & Govt. Pos: Alternate del, Dem. Nat. Conv, 68; publicity chmn, Madison Co. Dem. Club, Ala, 68- Bus. & Prof. Pos: Comput. programmer, Boeing Co, Huntsville, Ala, 65-67, technical lead comput. appln, 67- Mem: Seattle Prfnl. Eng. Employees Asn. Rel: Baptist. Mailing Add: 3724 Oakdale Court N.W, Huntsville, Ala. 35810.

O'CONNOR, EARL E. R
Justice, Supreme Court of Kans.
b. Paola, Kans, 10/6/22; s. Nelson O'Connor and Mayme Scheetz O; m. 5/24/62 to Jean Ann Timmons; c. Nelson L, Clayton E. and Gayle A. Educ: Univ. Kans, B.S, 47, LL.B, 50; Beta Gamma Sigma; Phi Alpha Delta. Polit. & Govt. Pos: Asst. co. attorney, Johnson Co, Kans, 52-53, probate and juvenile judge, 53-55; judge, Tenth Judicial Dist, Kans, 55-65; Justice, Supreme Court, Kans, 65- Mil. Serv: Entered as Pvt, Army, 42, released as 1st Lt, 46, after serv. in Transportation Corps, ETO; Col, Army Res, 46- Mem: Am. and Kans. Bar Asns; Inst. Judicial Admin; Mason; Rotary. Rel: Methodist. Mailing Add: 2120 W. 32nd, Topeka, Kans. 66611.

O'CONNOR, EUGENE PAUL D
b. Buffalo, N.Y, 7/18/34; s. Eugene Francis O'Connor, mother deceased; m. 12/29/62 to Gretchen Miller; c. Eugene Paul, Jr, Peter M, Moira and Michael P. Educ: Univ. Notre Dame, B.S. in Commerce, 56; Univ. Buffalo, LL.B, 59. Polit. & Govt. Pos: Asst. U.S. attorney, U.S. Justice Dept. West. Dist. N.Y, 61-64; attorney, Union Free Sch. Dist. Nine, Sloan, N.Y, 65-68; Dem. cand, U.S. House Rep, 40th Dist, N.Y, 68. Bus. & Prof. Pos: Attorney-at-law, Cosgrove & O'Connor, 66- Mem: Am. and Erie Co. Bar Asns; Am. Football Coaches Asn; YMCA; Notre Dame Alumni Club, Buffalo; West. N.Y. High Sch. Football Coaches Asn. Rel: Roman Catholic. Mailing Add: 68 Fairbanks Ave, Buffalo, N.Y. 14223.

O'CONNOR, FRANK DANIEL D
Justice, N.Y. Supreme Court
b. N.Y.C, 12/20/09; s. James O'Connor and Margaret Collins O; m. 7/25/41 to Mary Kearney; c. M. Kevin, Thomas S. and Terrence C. Educ: Niagara Univ, B.A, 32; Brooklyn Law Sch, LL.B, 34. Hon. LL.D, Niagara Univ, 64. Polit. & Govt. Pos: N.Y. State Sen, 49-52 & 55; dist. attorney, Queens Co, 56-65; pres, N.Y.C. Coun, 66-68; del, Dem. Nat. Conv, 68; justice, N.Y. Supreme Court, 69- Mil. Serv: Entered as Seaman, Coast Guard, 42, released as Ens, 45, after serv. in N.Pac. Mem: N.Y. State and Queens Co. Bar Asns; Asn. of the Bar, N.Y.C; N.Y. State Dist. Attorneys Asn; Niagara Univ. Alumni Asn; VFW; Am. Legion; K. of C, Champlain Coun; Elks; Am-Irish Hist. Soc; Nat. Conf. of Christians and Jews; Big Brothers. Rel: Roman Catholic. Mailing Add: 8426 Charlecote Ridge, Jamaica Estates, N.Y. 11432.

O'CONNOR, GENE ANTHONY D
Chaffee Co. Cmnr, Colo.
b. Salida, Colo, 9/20/28; s. Eugene Timothy O'Connor and Antoinette Eussen O; m. 4/19/54 to Diane Estella Gregg; c. Kevin Eugene, Kelly Patrick, Kerry Brian, Kasey Sean, Kirby Gregg and Karen Aileen. Educ: High Sch, Salida, Colo. and Holy Cross Abbey, Canon City. Polit. & Govt. Pos: Chaffee Co. Cmnr, Colo, 57- Bus. & Prof. Pos: Rancher; agent, Standard Oil Co, 54- Mil. Serv: Inactive Naval Res, 47-55. Mem: K. of C; Past Exalted Ruler, Elks. Rel: Catholic. Legal Res: 801 Poncha Blvd, Salida, Colo. 81201. Mailing Add: Box 329, Salida, Colo. 81201. (1967)

O'CONNOR, J. RAYMOND R
Chmn, Winchester Rep. Town Cmt, Conn.
b. Winsted, Conn, 2/18/02; s. John F. O'Connor and Mary A. Wheeler O; m.

8/22/32 to Jeannette Soucy; c. John F. and Robert E. Educ: Gilbert High Sch, 4 years. Polit. & Govt. Pos: Mem, Winsted Vol. Fire Dept, 25-; mem. bd. finance, Winchester, Conn, 41-53; Conn. State Rep, 51-53 & 55-57; chmn, Winchester Rep. Town Cmt, 66- Bus. & Prof. Pos: Asst. engr, Conn. Light & Power Co, 23-67, retired, 67. Mem: Elks; Union Engine Co. One, Winsted Vol. Fire Dept.(treas); Old Newgate Coon Club (secy). Rel: Roman Catholic. Mailing Add: 11 Cottage St, Winsted, Conn. 06098.

O'CONNOR, JAMES DAVID D
b. Detroit, Mich, 7/25/40; s. Edward Daniel O'Connor and Genevieve Kathleen Trinkwell O; m. 9/3/66 to Carolyn Old Armstrong. Educ: Univ. South. Miss, B.S. in Math. with honors, 62; Auburn Univ. Grad. Sch, 62 & 64-65; Nat. Defense Educ. Act Fel; Kappa Mu Epsilon; Pi Mu Epsilon; Auburn Dem. Club. Polit. & Govt. Pos: Del, Dem. Nat. Conv, 68; prog. chmn, Madison Co. Dem. Club, Ala, 68- Bus. & Prof. Pos: Comput. programmer, Boeing Co, Seattle, Wash, 63-64, technical lead, Huntsville, Ala, 65-67, supvr. space flight simulations, 67-68, 2nd level supvr. flight simulations, 69- Mil. Serv: Entered as E-1, Marine Corps Res, 61, released as E-2, 67. Mem: Seattle Prfnl. Eng. Employees Asn; Boeing Mgt. Asn; Am. Astronaut. Soc. Mailing Add: 3724 Oakdale Court N.W, Huntsville, Ala. 35810.

O'CONNOR, JEREMIAH F. D
b. N.Y, 5/18/33; m; c. Four. Educ: Rice High Sch; Iona Col, New Rochelle, N.Y. Polit. & Govt. Pos: Former N.J. State Sen; twp. cmt, libr. bd; bd. of adjust. planning bd, 63-64; mayor, Saddle Brook, 65; Dem. Mayors Orgn. Bus. & Prof. Pos: Sales mgr, Bell & Howell Co, Phillipsburg Div. Mem: Bergen Co. Hist. Asn; Jaycees; K. of C, St. Ann's Coun; Bergen Irish Asn. Rel: Catholic. 1967 Legal Res: Trenton, N.J. No mailing address available. (1967)

O'CONNOR, LAWRENCE JOSEPH, JR. D
Cmnr, Fed. Power Cmn.
b. Tulsa, Okla, 12/29/14; s. Laurence Joseph O'Connor and Bess Yarbrough O; single. Educ: Rice Univ, A.B, 36; Harvard Univ, M.B.A, 38; Beta Alpha Psi. Polit. & Govt. Pos: Asst. dir, Off. of Oil and Gas, U.S. Dept. of Interior, 59- and adminstr, Oil Import Admin, 60-; cmnr, Fed. Power Cmn, 61- Bus. & Prof. Pos: Acct, Haskins & Sells, 38-45; v.pres. & treas, Goldston Oil Corp, 45-58; dir. & v.pres, Houston Dist, Independent Petroleum Asn. of Am, 54-58, chmn, Tax Study Cmt. and mem. cmts. dealing with oil and gas supply and demand, natural gas, oil and gas productive capacity, etc; consult, 58-59. Publ: 'Regulation and Accounting,' The Fed. Acct, fall, 64; 'Regulatory Commission Authority Over Published Financial Statements of Utilities,' Jour. of Accountancy, 5/65; 'The Positive Side of FPC Accounting Regulations from the Investor's Standpoint,' Investment Dealers Digest, 10/65. Mem: Harvard Bus. Sch. Club of Wash, D.C; Rice Univ. Club of Wash; Houston Country Club, Tex; Cong. Country Club, Wash, D.C. Rel: Roman Catholic. Legal Res: 2828 Bammel Lane, Houston, Tex. 77006. Mailing Add: Room 4110, General Accounting Office Bldg, 441 G St. N.W, Washington, D.C. 20426.

O'CONNOR, PATRICK J. D
Mo. State Rep.
b. St. Louis, Mo, 9/7/31; m. 9/12/59 to Judith Slawson; c. Patrick James, Jr. Educ: Wellston High Sch. Polit. & Govt. Pos: Mem, Citizens for John F. Kennedy for President Cmt; del, Mo. State Dem. Conv, 60; Mo. State Rep, 62-; acting treas, Dem. Nat. Cmt, currently. Bus. & Prof. Pos: Thomas J. Sheehan Heating Co. Mil. Serv: Army. Mem: Pipefitters Local 562; Airport Twp. Dem. Club. Rel: Catholic. Mailing Add: 12618 Weskan Lane, Bridgeton, Mo. 63042. (1967)

O'CONNOR, WILLIAM THOMAS DFL
Chmn, Brown Co. Dem-Farmer-Labor Party, Minn.
b. Belle Plaine, Minn, 10/2/34; s. William Francis O'Connor and Grace Dwyer O; m. 2/16/64 to Mary Kay Manley; c. Timothy, Catherine and Daniel. Educ: Col. St. Thomas, B.A, 59; William Mitchell Col. of Law, LL.B, 64; Inns of Court; Educ. Club. Polit. & Govt. Pos: Chmn, Brown Co. Dem-Farmer-Labor Party, Minn, 64-; asst. co. attorney, Brown Co, Minn. 64- Mem: Minn. and Am. Bar Asns; Am. Trial Lawyers Asn; Am. Judicature Soc; K. of C; Serra Club of New Ulm; K. of C.(state advocate). Rel: Catholic. Mailing Add: 805 S. Broadway, New Ulm, Minn. 56073.

O'CONOR, ROBERT, JR. R
Chmn, Webb Co. Rep. Party, Tex.
b. Los Angeles, Calif, 6/22/34; s. Robert O'Conor and Frances Robinson O; m. 11/21/61 to Ana Lourdes Navarrete; c. Anne Frances and Robert Daniel. Educ: Univ. Tex, Austin, B.A, 56 and LL.B, 57. Polit. & Govt. Pos: Chmn, Jack Cox for Gov. Cmt, Webb Co, Tex, 62; chmn, Webb Co. Rep. Party, 68- Mil. Serv: Res, Capt, U.S. Army, 62. Mem: Am. and Tex. Bar Asns; Laredo Bar Asn.(pres, 69); Tex. Trial Lawyers Asn; Am. Judicature Soc; Kiwanis (secy, 68-69); Elks; C. of C. Rel: Catholic. Legal Res: 2202 Ash St, Laredo, Tex. 78040. Mailing Add: P.O. Box 298, Laredo, Tex. 78040.

ODA, HOWARD KAZUMI R
Hawaii State Rep.
b. Wahiawa, Oahu, Hawaii, 7/3/31; s. Joseph Tatsumi Oda and Hatsumi Ishi O; m. 7/4/54 to June Shizuko Eto; c. Terri Jo and Robert Joe. Educ: Ohio State Univ, 54; La Crosse State Univ, B.S, 58; Univ. Hawaii, Prfnl. Cert; Phi Kappa Epsilon; L Club. Polit. & Govt. Pos: Dist. chmn, Wahiawa, Oahu, Hawaii Rep. Party, 65; Hawaii. State Rep, 66-; del, State Constitution Conv, 68. Bus. & Prof. Pos: Teacher, Dept. of Educ, Hawaii, 58-66; supvr, tax. annuity, Grand Pac, Honolulu, 68. Mil. Serv: Sgt, Army, 51-54, served in 343 Gen. Hosp, Far East; UN Korean Unit Citation; Nat. Defense Serv. Medal. Legal Res: 1912 Leimoni Pl, Wahiawa, Oahu, Hawaii 96786. Mailing Add: Iolani Palace, Honolulu, Hawaii 96813.

O'DEA, RICHARD W. 'DICK' DFL
Minn. State Rep.
b. St. Paul, Minn, 7/17/16; married; c. Four. Educ: Univ. Minn. Polit. & Govt. Pos: Former mayor, Willernie, Minn; Minn. State Rep, 53- Bus. & Prof. Pos: Quality control anal, Whirlpool Corp. Mailing Add: 92 Wildwood Beach Rd, Mahtomedi, Minn. 55115. (1967)

ODEGAARD, GARY MARTIN D
Wash. State Sen.
b. Bellingham, Wash, 2/28/40 to Harold Kristian Odegaard and Laurel Clark O; m. 6/8/63 to Kathleen Marit Fifield; c. Gregory Martin and Jeffrey Arthur. Educ: West. Wash. State Col, B.A. in Educ, 62; Univ. Wash, summers, 63-67. Polit. & Govt. Pos: Wash. State Sen, 20th Dist, 69-, chmn, Senate Pub. Insts. Cmt, Wash. State Senate, 69; mem, Joint Interim Cmt. Educ; chmn, Subcmt. Occup. and Voc, Instnl. and Adult Educ. Cmt. Mem: Int. Reading Asn; Nat, Wash. and Centralia Col. Educ. Asns; pres, Black River Educ. Asn, 63-64 and Onalaska Educ. Asn, 66-68; Lewis Co. Pomona Grange and Alpha Grange 154 (officer); Elks, Chehalis, Wash. 500 Hour Award, Wash. Educ. Asn. Rel: Presbyterian. Mailing Add: Star Route 1, Box 1 A, Onalaska, Wash. 98570.

ODELL, CHARLES R
b. Salem, Mass, 1/6/28; s. Harry Albert Odell and Edna Faulkner O; m. 11/21/56 to Dale Rolene Kelly Nichols; c. David Lyle, Charles Dwight and Kelly Nichole. Educ: Western Wash. State Col, B.A, 52; chmn, Evergreen Student Conf, 51. Polit. & Govt. Pos: Treas, Wash. State Young Rep, 57; pres, Kitsap Co. Young Rep, 57; chmn, Kitsap Co. Rep. Cent. Cmt, 59-61 & 63-64; del, Rep. Nat. Conv, 64; admin. asst. to U.S. Rep. Thomas M. Pelly, 65- Bus. & Prof. Pos: Teacher, South Kitsap Schs, 52 & 55-65. Mil. Serv: Entered as A/S, Navy, 45, released as C.S. 3/C, 48. Mem: Am. Fedn. of Teachers; Elks; Am. Legion; Bull Elephant Club; past pres, South Kitsap Active Club and South Kitsap Little League. South Kitsap Teacher of The Year, 63-64. Rel: Baptist. Legal Res: Kitsap County, Wash. Mailing Add: 1112 Spotswood Dr, Silver Spring, Md. 20904.

O'DELL, FORD E. R
b. Norwalk, Ohio, 10/24/00. Educ: Ohio Pub. Schs. Polit. & Govt. Pos: Pa. State Rep, 56-67; 2 terms pres. of the Pa. Retail Jewelers' Asn; 11 years secy, Erie Infantile Paralysis Asn; bd. of dirs, Drs'. Osteopathic Hosp. of Erie. Bus. & Prof. Pos: Owns jewelry bus. Mem: Perry Lodge 392 F&AM; Consistory Commandery; Shrine and all of the affil. bodies; Moose; past exalted ruler of Elks 67; Erie Add Club; Erie Kennel Club; Erie Better Bus. Bur; Erie Kiwanis Club. Rel: Presbyterian. Mailing Add: 7898 E. Lake Rd, Erie, Pa. 16511. (1967)

O'DELL, ROBERT W. R
Wash. State Rep.
b. Camas, Wash, 1924; m. to Jeanne; c. Three. Educ: Whitman Col, B.A; Willamette Col. of Law; Phi Delta Theta. Polit. & Govt. Pos: Wash. State Rep, currently. Bus. & Prof. Pos: Attorney-at-law. Mem: Lions. Mailing Add: 2022 N.W. Benton, Camas, Wash. 98607.

ODEM, SUE EDNA R
b. St. Joseph, Tenn, 7/3/16; d. William Luther Tidwell and Elizabeth Richardson T; m. 7/11/36 to Grady V. Odem; c. Kay (Mrs. Rippy, Jr) and Susan (Mrs. Falls). Educ: Florence Bus. Col, Ala. Polit. & Govt. Pos: Publicity Chmn, Hardin Co. Fedn. Rep. Women's Club, at present; registrar, Hardin Co. Elec. Cmn, 65-66; co-chmn, Hardin Co. Rep. Cmt, Tenn, 58-66; alternate del, Rep. Nat. Conv, 64; co-chmn, Pres. Elec. Campaign, 60. Bus. & Prof. Pos: News Correspondent, Jackson Sun, 60- and Nashville Banner, 53-; assoc. ed, Savannah Courier Newspaper, 61-62. Publn: Several feature stories in various newspapers. Mem: Garden Club; TVA Women's Club; Savannah Country Club. Hobbies: Flower arranging and stage directing. Rel: Methodist. Mailing Add: 2410 Park St, Savannah, Tenn. 38372. (1967)

ODEN, WILLIAM EMMETT D
Ala. State Sen.
b. Franklin Co, Ala, 11/2/09; s. George Walter Oden and Rebecca Gibson O; m. 12/27/35 to Charlene Cunningham. Educ: Howard Col, A.B, 40. Polit. & Govt. Pos: Ala. State Rep, 51-63; Ala. State Sen, 63- Bus. & Prof. Pos: Banker and cattle farmer. Mem: Mason. Rel: Baptist. Mailing Add: 402 High St. N.W, Russellville, Ala. 35653.

ODGAARD, JOHN EDMUND 'JACK' R
b. Omaha, Nebr, 12/4/41; s. Medrick C. Odgaard and Hildegarde P. Theewen O; m. 12/28/66 to Sandra Jean Johannes; c. Eric Christopher and Jacqueline Terese. Educ: Wayne State Col, 60-61; Univ. Md, Heidelberg W. Germany, 62-63; Univ. Nebr, 65-66. Polit. & Govt. Pos: Admin. asst. to U.S. Rep. Dave Martin, Nebr, 69- Bus. & Prof. Pos: Surveyor, Adv. Commun. Engr, Strategic Air Command, Nebr, 60; lineman, Union Pac. R.R, Nebr, Colo. and Wyo, 65; reporter, Lincoln Eve. J, Nebr, 65-66; polit. features ed, Columbus Daily Tel, 66-69. Mil. Serv: Entered as Pvt. E-1, Army, 61, released as E-4, 64, after serv. in 509th Airborne Inf, Eighth Inf. Div, Europe, 62-64; Army Commendation Medal; Good Conduct Medal; Eighth Inf. Div. Noncommissioned Officer Acad. Distinguished Grad; Trooper of Month Award; Seventh Army Lang. Sch. Cert; Parachutist Wings. Mem: Sigma Delta Chi, Nat. and Nebr; Nat. and Nebr. Press Photographers Asn; Columbus Press Club; Am. Legion; VFW; K. of C; Columbus Commun. Action Team; Platte Col. Citizens Adv. Coun; Izaak Walton League; Nat. Rifle Asn; C. of C; Nebr. Soc. of Wash, D.C. Freedoms Found. George Wash. Honor Medals, 62 & 64; Platte Col. Founder's Plaque; Columbus C. of C. Distinguished Cmt. Chmn; Inland Daily Newspaper Asn. First Place Photo Series; Nebr. Press Photographers Awards. Rel: Roman Catholic. Legal Res: 1671 23rd Ave, Columbus, Nebr. 68601. Mailing Add: 2435 Drexel St, Vienna, Va. 22180.

O'DOHERTY, KIERAN Conservative, N.Y.
State V.Chmn, Conservative Party, N.Y.
b. New York, N.Y, 8/8/26; s. Edward O'Doherty and Mary Kirk O; married. Educ: City Col. of N.Y, A.B, 50; Columbia Law Sch, LL.B, 53; Phi Beta Kappa; Phi Alpha Delta. Polit. & Govt. Pos: Pres, City Col. Young Rep. Asn, N.Y, 49-50; exec. mem, Queens Co. Cmt. for Taft, 52; pres, Queens Co. Young Rep. Asn, 53-55; mem, Queens Co. Rep. Cmt, 53-56; Conservative Party Cand. for U.S. Sen, 62 for U.S. Rep, 17th Cong. Dist, 64; co-founder and first state chmn, Conservative Party, N.Y, 62, chmn, Nat. Affairs Cmt. and mem, State Exec. Cmt, state v.chmn, currently; mem, Adv. Assembly, Am. Conservative Union, 65-; Conservative Party Campaign Chmn, Wm. F. Buckley, Jr. for Mayor, N.Y.C, 65; cand. for Lt. Gov, N.Y, 66. Bus. & Prof. Pos: Mgr, Stagshead Restaurant, Inc, 53-55; assoc, William G. Mulligan, Esq, 55-57 and Royall, Koegel & Rogers, 57-65; attorney-at-law, N.Y.C. and L.I,

65-68; gen. counsel, Status Mkt. Corp, 68- Mil. Serv: Entered as Pvt, Army, 44, released as Technician 5th Grade, 46, after serv. in 4th Armored Div, ETO, 45-46. Publ: 'The Buckley Campaign,' Nat. Rev. Mag, 10/65. Mem: N.Y. State Bar Asn; Cath. War Vets; Cmt. for Monroe Doctrine; Cmt. of One Million Against Admission of Communist China to UN; Nat. Adv. Bd, Young Am. for Freedom; bd. gov. and trustee, Daytop Village, Narcotics Center, 68- Frequent panelist and debater, including many TV and radio appearances in N.Y.C. Rel: Roman Catholic. Mailing Add: 360 First Ave, New York, N.Y. 10010.

ODOM, COLQUITT HURST D
Ga. State Rep.
b. Waynesboro, Ga, 3/19/23; s. Horace Houston Odom and Emma Parnell O; m. 12/20/47 to Frances Ashley Dunbar; c. Colquitt H, Jr. and Carol Lee. Educ: Univ. of Ga, LL.B, 50; Demosthenian Lit. Soc; Delta Theta Phi; X Club; Gridiron. Polit. & Govt. Pos: Ga. State Rep, 59-; solicitor, City Court of Albany, 63-64. Bus. & Prof. Pos: Attorney-at-law. Mil. Serv: U.S. Coast Guard, World War II, 42-46. Mem: VFW; Am. Legion; Moose; Albany Bar Asn; Elks. Dir. of Happy House, Inc. and Boys and Girls Club of Albany. Rel: Presbyterian. Mailing Add: 1218 Third Ave, Albany, Ga. 31705.

O'DONNELL, ALFRED PETER JOSEPH, JR. R
b. Elyria, Ohio, 7/20/16; s. Alfred Peter Joseph O'Donnell and Bernice Mary Schnitzler O; m. 11/29/47 to Mary Jo Keyes; c. Kathy Joyce, Alfred, III, Dianna Marie, Richard M, Leslie Hope, Jayce Estell, Gale Ann and Jeffrey Edward. Polit. & Govt. Pos: City councilman-at-lg, Elyria, Ohio, 56-58; mem, Lorain Co. Bd. Elec, 62-66; chmn, Lorain Co. Rep. Cent. Cmt, 64-68. Bus. & Prof. Pos: Pres, O'Donnell Paint & Wallpaper Co. Inc, 50-66. Mil. Serv: Entered as Pvt, Army, 41, released as 1st Lt, 45, after serv. in S.Pac, 44-45. Mem: K. of C. Rel: Roman Catholic. Mailing Add: 402 Middle Ave, Elyria, Ohio 44035. (1967)

O'DONNELL, GLADYS R
Pres, Nat. Fedn. Rep. Women
b. Whittier, Calif; d. George Osmer Berry and Esther Livingston B; wid; c. Lorraine M.(Mrs. Doyle) and James Lloyd, Jr; Five Grandchildren. Educ: Long Beach City Col, 46-47; Long Beach State Col, 48; Univ. South. Calif, 49. Polit. & Govt. Pos: Mem, Rep. State Cent. Cmt, Calif, 52-, v.chmn, 56-60 and secy, 60-62; pres, Long Beach Coun. Rep. Women, 52-54; pres, Calif. Fedn. Rep. Women, 56-57; pres, Nat. Fedn. Rep. Women, 68- Bus. & Prof. Pos: Partner, Hydro-Test Tubing Serv, 52-; Owner-Operator, O'Donnell Oil Co, 60- Mem: PEO; Nat. Aeronaut. Asn; Aviation Breakfast Club; 99 Club; Long Beach C. of C; Independent Petroleum Producers Asn; Soroptimist Aerial Trophy; Amelia Earhart Trophy; Diamond Jubilee Celebrity Award, Long Beach, Calif. Rel: Methodist. Legal Res: 5610 Las Lomas Ave, Long Beach, Calif. 90815. Mailing Add: 1026 16th St. N.W, Wash, D.C. 20036.

O'DONNELL, JAMES A. D
b. Bethlehem, 6/3/03; s. John J. O'Donnell and Susan Purcell O; m. to Mary F. Wagner; c. one. Educ: Penn. State Exten. Sch. Polit. & Govt. Pos: Pa. State Rep, 58-67; del. to Dem. Nat. Conv, 56; court tipstaff, Northampton Co. Bus. & Prof. Pos: Plumbing and heating contractor. Mem: Former mem. of Plumbers and Steamfitters Local 670 in Allentown. Mailing Add: 30 W. Fourth St, Bethlehem, Pa. 18015. (1967)

O'DONNELL, JAMES P. D
Pa. State Rep.
b. Phila, Pa, 12/20/20; s. James P. O'Donnell and Anna Hope O; m. to Laura; c. Two. Educ: Drexel Inst; St. Joseph's Col; Univ. Pa. Polit. & Govt. Pos: Dem. chmn, Ward Campaign Cmt, Pa; Dem. mem, Ward Exec. Cmt; Pa. State Rep, 58- Bus. & Prof. Pos: Former regional dir, Bur. Inspection, Dept. Labor and Indust; plumber. Mil. Serv: Navy, Machinist Mate 1st Class, 4 years; served on submarines, on 8 patrol runs in China, Japan, Philippines, Guam, Panama and W.Indies. Mem: Plumbers Union 690; Am. Legion; VFW; comdr, Sub. Vet. World War II. Mailing Add: 2636 S. 66th St, Philadelphia, Pa. 19142. (1967)

O'DONNELL, JAMES T. D
b. Denver, Colo, 6/14/98; married; c. Three; 14 grandchildren. Polit. & Govt. Pos: Colo. State Rep, 57-63 & 67-69. Bus. & Prof. Pos: Retired Denver police detective. Mil. Serv: Vet, World War I and World War II. Mem: DAV; Am. Legion; former v.pres, Police Pension Asn; bd. of dirs, Vet. Affairs; Boilermakers; Helpers Union; Brotherhood of Locomotive Firemen and Enginemen. Mailing Add: 2100 Magnolia St, Denver, Colo. 80207. (1967)

O'DONNELL, JOHN JOSEPH D
b. Philadelphia, Pa, 1/30/09; s. John Joseph O'Donnell and Sarah Shankland O; single. Educ: Girard Col, grad, 26. Polit. & Govt. Pos: Mem, ward cmt, 40th Ward Dem. Cmt, Pa, currently; asst. dir, Co. Audits, 61-; alternate del, Dem. Nat. Conv, 68. Mil. Serv: Entered as Pvt, Army, 42, released as M/Sgt, 45, after serv. in Ground Forces, 4278th Qm. Depot Co, Cent. Pac. Base Command. Rel: Roman Catholic. Mailing Add: 8410 Brewster Ave, Philadelphia, Pa. 19153.

O'DONNELL, JOSEPH H, JR. R
Mem. Exec. Cmt, R.I. Rep. State Cent. Cmt.
b. North Smithfield, R.I, 5/22/25; s. Joseph H. O'Donnell, Sr. and Anna McCarthy O'D; m. to Yolande Cavedon; c. Sharon, Diane, Jennifer, Ellen, Christopher and John. Educ: Providence Col; Maine Maritime Acad, grad. Polit. & Govt. Pos: Mem, N. Smithfield Sch. Cmt, R.I, 56-62; State Dir. of Admin, 63-66; Lt. Gov. of R.I, 67-69; mem. exec. cmt, R.I. Rep. State Cent. Cmt, 69-; chmn, N. Smithfield Rep. Town Cmt, presently. Bus. & Prof. Pos: Keough-Kirby Assocs, Inc; asst. treas, Woonsocket Color & Chem. Co; mem. of corp, Hickory Color & Chem. Co. Mil. Serv: Merchant Marines. Mem: Chmn, Providence Chap, Nat. Found. Infantile Paralysis; corp. mem, Woonsocket Hosp. and Mercy Hosp. Rel: Catholic. Mailing Add: 11 Getchell St, North Smithfield, R.I. 02908.

O'DONNELL, KENNETH P. D
b. Worcester, Mass; s. Cleo O'Donnell, Sr; m. to Helen Sullivan; c. Ken, Jr, Kevin, Kathy, Mark and Helen. Educ: Harvard. Polit. & Govt. Pos: Associated with the early sen. campaigns of John F. Kennedy; asst. counsel to Senate Rackets Cmt; former asst. to President Kennedy and President Johnson; directed White House staff under President Kennedy; cand, Gov. of Mass, 66; worked for Robert F. Kennedy in campaign for pres, 68; mem. of exec. cmt. and leader of fight for Vietnam Peace Plank, Dem. Nat. Platform Cmt, 68; serv. as co-chmn. with Terry Sanford and Arthur Goldberg, Humphrey-Muskie Citizens Cmt, 68. Mil. Serv: Air Force, lead bombardier, B-29 Squadron stationed in Eng; distinguished Flying Cross; was shot down and escaped. Capt, Harvard Football Team. Mailing Add: 56 Lochstead Ave, Jamaica Plain, Mass. 02130.

O'DONNELL, PETER, JR. R
State Chmn, Tex. Rep. Party
b. Dallas, Tex, 4/21/24; s. Peter O'Donnell and Annette Campbell O; m. 11/22/52 to Edith Jones; c. Ann, Carol and Ruth. Educ: Univ. of the South, B.S, 47; Wharton Grad. Div, Univ. Pa, M.B.A; Phi Beta Kappa; Phi Delta Theta. Polit. & Govt. Pos: Mem, RNC Task Force on Fed. Fiscal & Monetary Policy, Tex; Rep. chmn, Precinct 143, Dallas, 56-69; chmn, Dallas Co. Rep. Party, 59-; state chmn, Tex. Rep. Party, 62-; mem. exec. cmt, Rep. Nat. Finance Cmt, 64-; chmn, South. Asn. Rep. State Chairmen, 65-; del, Rep. Nat. Conv, 68. Mil. Serv: Entered as Seaman, Naval Res, 43, released as Lt.(jg), 46. Mem: Dallas Asn. of Investment Analysts; trustee, Univ. of the South; adv. trustee, Univ. Dallas and Grad. Research Center; trustee, South. Methodist. Univ. Found. for Bus. and Econ. Rel: Episcopal. Legal Res: 4300 St. John's Dr, Dallas, Tex. 75205. Mailing Add: 4275 First National Bank Bldg, Dallas, Tex. 75202. (1967)

O'DONNELL, PHILIP CONROY D
Mass. State Rep.
b. Peabody, Mass, 7/29/15; s. Patrick F. O'Donnell and Julia Conroy O; div; c. Jacqueline and Charles. Educ: Peabody High Sch, 5 years. Polit. & Govt. Pos: Coun, Peabody City Coun, Mass, 46-51; mayor, Peabody, 52-61; cmnr, Mass. Alcoholic Beverages Control Cmn, 60-61; Mass. State Rep, 67- Mil. Serv: Entered as Pvt, Army Air Force, 42, released as T/Sgt, 45, after serv. in 22nd Photo Reconnaissance Squadron, ETO, 42-45; Bronze Star. Rel: Roman Catholic. Mailing Add: 27 Harris St, Peabody, Mass. 01960.

ODORISIO, ROCCO A. R
b. Wayne, Pa, 10/12/00; s. Camillo Odorisio and Raffaela D'Aloise O; m. to Helen Ritter. Educ: Radnor Twp. Schs. Polit. & Govt. Pos: Sch. dir, Radnor Twp, Pa, 35-50; mem, Del. Co. Housing Authority, 57-; Pa. State Rep, 58-68; cmnr, Sixth Ward Radnor Twp, 60- Mil. Serv: Army, with Machine Gun Co, 11th Inf, 28th Div, Mil. Police Hq, Div. of Criminal Invest, 2nd Army Hq, Base Sect. 9, Am. Forces in Germany. Mem: Treas, Mem. Libr. of Radnor Twp; pres, Radnor Fire Co; Am. Legion; 40 et 8; Mason. Mailing Add: 402 W. Wayne Ave, Wayne, Pa. 19807. (1967)

O'DOWD, GEORGE EDWARD D
b. Brunswick, Vt; m. to Mary Johnson; c. Two. Educ: Brunswick Schs. Polit. & Govt. Pos: Mem, Sch. Bd, Vt; selectman; Vt. State Rep, 65-67. Bus. & Prof. Pos: Farmer; retired. Mem: Farm Bur. Rel: Catholic. Mailing Add: North Stratford, N.H. 03884. (1967)

OEHLSEN, ROBERT W. D
b. State Center, Iowa, 5/25/21; s. Walter Oehlsen and Clara O; m. 1/11/41 to Esther Knutson. Educ: State Col, Iowa, Cedar Falls, 1 year. Polit. & Govt. Pos: Iowa State Rep, -66; former mayor of Radcliffe. Bus. & Prof. Pos: Owned and operated a variety store at Radcliffe 15 years; now engaged in farming. Mil. Serv: Army, 4 1/2 years, 34th Inf. Div; took part in African and Ital. campaigns; hon. discharged 45; presently serving in Iowa Nat. Guard; Capt. Mem: Post comdr. Am. Legion 4 terms; continuous membership in Post 315, Am. Legion at Radcliffe. Rel: Lutheran. Mailing Add: Radcliffe, Iowa 50230. (1967)

OESTERLING, DONALD OSWALD D
Pa. State Sen.
b. Butler, Pa, 6/2/27; s. Victor K. Oesterling, Sr. and Marjorie Oswald; m. 12/22/47 to Ann McDowell; c. Michael James, Dawn, Peter J. and Matthew John. Educ: Capital Univ, B.S. in bus. admin, 50. Polit. & Govt. Pos: Investigator, Pa. Dept. of Revenue, 61-63; Pa. State Sen, 21st Dist, 64-; mem, Butler Co. Dem. Exec. Cmt; precinct committeeman, Dem. Party; mem. adv. coun, Pa. Crime Cmn, presently; mem, State Coun. of Civil Defense, presently. Bus. & Prof. Pos: Former radio farm dir, Radio Sta. WISR, Butler, Pa; v.pres. and chmn. of bd, Regal Prod. for Indust, Inc, presently; pres, Dows Ins. Agency, presently; mem. bd. of regents and exec. cmt, Capital Univ, Columbus, Ohio, presently. Mil. Serv: Seaman, Navy, 45-46, serv. in Atlantic Theater; Good Conduct and Am. Theater Ribbons. Mem: Unionville Grange 1971 and Pomona Grange; United Commercial Travelers Coun. 465; Butler Little Theater; Mercer Rd. Vol. Fire Co; VFW Post 249; Am. Legion Post 778; Center Twp. Athletic Asn; assoc. dir, Butler Co. Soil Conserv. Dist; Butler Co. Child Welfare Adv. Cmt; past pres, Center Twp. PTA and Butler Jr. C. of C; June Dairy Month Cmt. chmn, Agr. Cmt, Butler Area C. of C, 59; co-chmn, Commun. Chest Drive; publicity cmt, Nat. Plowing Contest and Conserv. Expos, 58; Past Exalted Ruler and hon. life mem, Elks Lodge 170; pres, West. Dist, Pa. State Elks Asn; bd. mem, Butler Co. Ment. Health Asn; past pres, Butler Co. Safety Coun; Pa. Rural Safety Coun; past secy-treas, Butler Co. Fair and Agr. Asn; former space mgr, Butler Farm Show. Received Pa. Future Farmers Am. Citation for WISR for excellence in agr. programming, 59; Hon. Keystone Farmer Degree, Pa. Future Farmers Am, 61 and Hon. Chap. Farmer Degree, Evans City Chap; Gov. Safety Award, 63; Cert. Achievement, Agr. Stabilization and Conserv. Serv, U.S. Dept. Agr, 64. Rel: Lutheran. Mailing Add: 307 Sunset Dr, Butler, Pa. 16001.

OESTMANN, ARTHUR FRED D
Chmn, Nemaha Co. Dem. Party, Nebr.
b. Auburn, Nebr, 8/15/04; s. Ernest Oestmann and Mina Heidzig O; m. 8/18/29 to Theresa Rogge; c. Juanalee (Mrs. Richard Alden) and Rita (Mrs. Robert Seiler). Educ: Rohrs, Dist. 80 Rural Sch, 6 years. Polit. & Govt. Pos: Chmn, Nemaha Co. Dem. Party, Nebr, 61-; del, Dem. Nat. Conv, 64. Bus. & Prof. Pos: Owner and operator, farm, Auburn, Nebr, 28-69. Mem: Men of the Church. Rel: Lutheran; Supvr, construction of church, 60. Mailing Add: 1405 H St, Auburn, Nebr. 68305.

O'FARRELL, THOMAS RICHARD D
Md. State Sen.
b. Westminster, Md, 6/17/15; s. Joseph Lawrence O'Farrell and Alberta A. McCaffrey O; m. 9/18/38 to Gertrude O'Mara; c. Rosalie Ann (Mrs. Breeding), Mary Patricia (Mrs. Friese), Sharon Kathleen (Mrs. Jones), Alberta Agnes, Thomas Richard, Jr. and Mary Katherine. Polit. & Govt. Pos: Past pres, Caroll Co. Dem. Club, Md; Md. State Del, 59-65, mem. House Ways and Means Cmt, Educ. Cmt, Vet. and Civil Defense Cmts; Spec. Cmt. Taxation and Fiscal Matters, Chesapeake Bay and Tributaries Cmt. and Judicial Proceedings Cmt, Md. House Del; Md. State Sen, Carroll Co, 65- Bus. & Prof. Pos: Ins. broker, The Travelers Indemnity Co; real estate broker; horse-breeder, Windy Hills Farm; auctioneer, Nat. Horse Sales, Inc. Mem: Md. State Fair Bd; K. of C; New Mkt. Hounds; Md. Horsebreeders Asn. Rel: Catholic. Legal Res: Route 3, Sullivan Rd, Westminster, Md. 21157. Mailing Add: 15 Court St, Westminster, Md. 21157.

OFFICER, ALBERT FITZPATRICK, JR. 'PAT' D
Chmn, Overton Co. Dem. Party, Tenn.
b. Livingston, Tenn, 3/12/34; s. Albert Fitzpatrick Officer and Leliabel Dale O; m. 12/3/56 to Curtis Marie Dodson; c. Albert Fitzpatrick, III, David Curtis, Michael Dale and Jane Ann. Educ: Tenn. Tech. Univ, B.S, 56; Vanderbilt Univ, LL.B, 61; Delta Theta Phi. Polit. & Govt. Pos: Asst. dist. attorney gen, Fifth Judicial Circuit, Tenn, 62-; Overton Co. chmn, for Lyndon B. Johnson for Pres, 64; chmn, Overton Co. Dem. Party, 66-; chmn, Hubert H. Humphrey for Pres. Cmt, Livingston, 68. Mil. Serv: Entered as Pfc, Army, 56, released as Specialist 4, 58 after serving in Hq. Detachment Med. Training Center, Ft. Sam Houston, Tex, 56-58. Mem: Am. and Tenn. Trial Lawyers Asns; Tenn. Bar Asn; Nat. Dist. Attorney Asn; Am. Judicature Soc; Jr. C. of C.(pres, Livingston Chap, 64). Rel: Disciples of Christ. Legal Res: Greenfield Dr, Livingston, Tenn. 38570. Mailing Add: Officer Bldg, S.E. Corner Public Square, Livingston, Tenn. 38570.

OFFUTT, DAVID ALLEN R
Chmn, Yuba Co. Rep. Cent. Cmt, Calif.
b. Independence, Mo, 1/29/40; s. R.S.S. Offutt and Iris Wood O; m. 7/6/63 to Laetitia A. Warren; c. Michael David. Educ: Univ. Notre Dame, B.A, 61; Boalt Hall Law Sch, Univ. Calif, J.D, 64. Polit. & Govt. Pos: Yuba Co. chmn, Reagan for Gov, Calif, 66; chmn, Yuba Co. Rep. Cent. Cmt, 67-; gen. chmn, Shumway for Cong, 68. Bus. & Prof. Pos: Chmn, Orgn. and Exten. Cmt, Boy Scouts-Butte Area Coun, 67; assoc. ed, Calif. Trial Lawyers, 68-69. Mem: Calif. Trial Lawyers Asn; Am. Trial Lawyers Asn; Yuba-Sutter Bar Asn. (chmn, 66); Am. Bar Asn; Yuba-Sutter Tuberc. Soc.(bd. dirs, 66-69); bd. dirs, Lions, 67; bd. dirs, C. of C, 69; Boy Scouts Am; K. of C. Rel: Catholic. Mailing Add: 1163 Rideout Way, Marysville, Calif. 95901.

O'GARA, FRANK L. D
Mo. State Rep.
b. Kansas City, Mo. 4/10/22; s. John J. O'Gara and Josephine W. Wall O; m. 10/26/59 to Patricia A. Kramer; c. John J, Mary Joe, Frank L, Jr. and Patricia Anne. Rockhurst Col, 1 year; St. Benedict's Col. Polit. & Govt. Pos: Constable, Fourth Magistrate Dist, Jackson Co, Mo, 58-; Mo. State Rep, Second Dist, Jackson Co, 69- Mil. Serv: Entered as A/S, Coast Guard, 42, released as Seaman 1/C, 46, after serv. in South Pacific, 42-45. Rel: Catholic. Mailing Add: 808 W. 33rd, Kansas City, Mo. 64111.

OGDAHL, HARMON T. Conservative
Minn. State Sen.
b. Minneapolis, Minn, 1917; married; c. Five. Educ: Univ. Minn; Hamline Univ. Polit. & Govt. Pos: Alderman, Minneapolis, Minn, 13th Ward, 59-62; Minn. State Sen, 62- Bus. & Prof. Pos: Pres, Peoples Fed. Savings & Loan. Mil. Serv: Army, 42-46, Pac. Theatre. Mailing Add: 5026 Morgan Ave. S, Minneapolis, Minn. 55419.

OGDEN, CARL D
Fla. State Rep.
b. Jacksonville, Fla, 8/27/29; s. Garrett Franklin Ogden and Catherine Cante O; m. 6/29/57 to Dorothy Christine Shook; c. Bradley John and Gregory Carl. Educ: Jacksonville Univ, 2 years. Govt. & Polit. Pos: Fla. State Rep, 68- Bus. & Prof. Pos: Pres, CarlOgden,Agency Inc, Jacksonville, Fla, 62- Mil. Serv: Entered as Pvt, Air Force, 47, released as S/Sgt, 51, after serv. in Alaskan Air Command, Korean Conflict. Mem: Mason; Optomist Int; Southville Businessmen's Club; Cmt. of 100; C. of C. Rel: Presbyterian. Legal Res: 539 Mandalay Rd, Jacksonville, Fla. 32216. Mailing Add: 6565 Beach Blvd, Jacksonville, Fla. 32216.

OGDEN, EDWIN BENNETT, JR. R
Chmn, Adams Co. Rep. Party, Miss.
b. Chattanooga, Tenn, 8/26/04; s. Edwin Bennett Ogden and Mary Curlett Broderick O; m. 12/2/36 to Nancy Hamilton Allen; c. Nancy (Mrs. Paul Rogers), Mary (Mrs. Martin Ratcliffe), Anne Louisa Wilkinson and Ellen Allen. Educ: Cathedral High Sch, Natchez, Miss, 3 years. Polit. & Govt. Pos: Del, Rep. Nat. Conv, 68; mem, Adams Co. Rep. Elec. Cmn, Miss, 69-; chmn, Adams Co. Rep. Party, Miss, 69- Bus. & Prof. Pos: Civilian forage master, U.S. Army Remount Depot, Camp Lee, Va, 19-20; partner, Ogden & Co, Havana, Cuba, 22-60 and Natchez, Miss, 60- Mil. Serv: 2nd Lt, Army Res, 31-36. Mem: Am. Club; Biltmore Forest Country Club; Boston Club; Adams Co. Farm Bur; Miss. Econ. Coun; Miss. Feed and Grain Asn; Miss. Valley Asn; Miss. Wholesale Grocers' Asn; Natchez-Adams Co. C. of C; Nat. Feed Mfrs. Asn; Nat. Food Brokers Asn; Rotarians of Cuba in Exile; Rotary. Rel: Catholic. Legal Res: 309 S. Commerce St, Natchez, Miss. 39120. Mailing Add: P.O. Box 1106, Natchez, Miss. 39120.

OGG, JACK CLYDE D
Tex. State Rep.
b. Kansas City, Mo, 9/7/33; s. William J. Ogg and Mildred Owens O; m. 1/1/59 to Constance Sue Harner, 'Connie'; c. Kimbra Kathryn. Educ: Univ. Houston, B.S, 57; S.Tex. Col. of Law, LL.B, 62; Phi Theta Kappa; Pi Kappa Alpha; Phi Alpha Delta; Inter-Fraternity Coun. Polit. & Govt. Pos: Tex. State Rep, 66- Bus. & Prof. Pos: Attorney-at-law, 62- Mem: Phi Alpha Delta Legal Fraternity Alumni Asn; Houston and Tex. Bar Asns; Jr. C. of C; Westbury Civic Club; Univ. Houston and S.Tex. Col. of Law Alumni Asns; Pi Kappa Alpha Alumni Asn; Univ. Houston Cougar Club and Cager Club Boosters; Univ. Houston Ex-Lettermen's Alumni Asn; Houston Touchdown Club. Outstanding Alumnus of Phi Alpha Delta Legal Fraternity, 68; Outstanding Alumnus of S.Tex. Col. of Law, 68; Outstanding Young Houstonian, 68. Rel: Episcopal. Legal Res: 761 Kuhlman, Houston, Tex. 77024. Mailing Add: 711 Main Bldg, Suite 1010, Houston, Tex. 77002.

OGILVIE, OSCAR PHILLIPS D
Chmn, Red River Parish Dem. Exec. Cmt, La.
b. Shreveport, La, 11/5/98; s. Oscar Phillips Ogilvie and Anna Harper O; m. 8/10/22 to Sarah Elizabeth Brown; c. Betty Jean (Mrs. Fear, Jr). Polit. & Govt. Pos: Mem, Coushatta Town Coun, La, 28-32; mem, Red River Parish Dem. Exec. Cmt, 32-, chmn, 36-; mayor, Coushatta, 40-46. Mem: Mason; Lions; Farm Bur. Rel: Methodist. Legal Res: Springville Ave, Coushatta, La. 71019. Mailing Add: Box 383, Coushatta, La. 71019. (1967)

OGILVIE, RICHARD BUELL R
Gov. of Ill.
b. Kansas City, Mo, 2/22/23; s. Kenneth S. Ogilvie and Edna Mae Buell O; m. 2/11/50 to Dorothy Louise Shriver; c. Elizabeth. Educ: Yale Univ, B.A, 47; Chicago Kent Col. Law, LL.B, 49; Beta Theta Pi; Phi Alpha Delta. Polit. & Govt. Pos: Chmn, Young Rep. Orgn, Cook Co, Ill, 54; asst. U.S. Attorney, Chicago, 54-55; spec. asst. to U.S. Attorney Gen, 58-60; sheriff, Cook Co, Ill, 62-68; pres, Bd. Cmnrs, Cook Co, 66-69; del, Rep. Nat. Conv, 68; Gov. Ill, 69- Bus. & Prof. Pos: Partner law firm, Lord, Bissell & Brook, 55-58; Stevenson, Conaghan, Hackbert, Rooks & Pitts, 60-62. Mil. Serv: Entered as Pvt, Army, 42, released as Sgt, 45, after serv. in 781st Tank Bn, ETO, 44-45; Purple Heart; ETO Ribbons. Mem: Am, Fed, Ill. State and Chicago Bar Asns; Soc. Trial Lawyers; Legal Club; Mason; Shrine; Union League Club; Sangamo Club; City Club; Am. Legion; Moose; Law Club; Chicago Club; Mid Am. Club; Illini Country Club; Amvets. Rel: Presbyterian. Mailing Add: Executive Mansion, Springfield, Ill. 62701.

OGILVIE, ROBERT S. R
b. Pittsburgh, Pa; married. Educ: Univ. of Pittsburgh. Polit. & Govt. Pos: Pa. State Rep, 52-67; adv. bd. of Harrisburg Hosp; mem, Nat. Security Cmt. Bus. & Prof. Pos: Retired dist. sales mgr, Tex. Co, 58; taught math. and sci. Mil. Serv: WWI, 2 years, enlisted to Lt. Mem: Masonic bodies; comdr, Post 27 Am. Legion, 47-48; 40 et 8, Mil. Order of World Wars; Nat. Sojourners; York Camp Heroes of 76; Judge Advocate of Mil. Order of World Wars; Am. Legion Dept. chmn. of Scotland Sch. for Vets. Children, 12 years; Am. Legion; mem. and past pres. of Harrisburg Lions Club, Harrisburg Pitt Club, and Colonial County Club; Lehigh Valley Club, Allentown; Pa. Soc, Green T-Square Club; Quarter Century Club of N.Y.C; Harrisburg Rep. Club; Old Timers Athletic Club; Joint Vets. Coun. of Gr. Harrisburg; Harrisburg C. of C. Mailing Add: 2619 N. Second St, Harrisburg, Pa. 16511. (1967)

OGLE, ALICE NICHOLS R
Mem, Calif. Rep. State Cent. Cmt.
b. Azusa, Calif, 8/6/25; d. Charles Leslie Nichols and Mary Murphy N; m. 3/20/48 to Robert Eugene Ogle; c. Mary, Janet, John, Nancy, Vernon and Bobby. Educ: Occidental Col, B.A, 48; Zeta Tau Zeta. Polit. & Govt. Pos: Chmn, 43rd Assembly Dist. Rep. Precinct Orgn, Calif, 66; v.chmn, Los Angeles Co. United Rep. Precinct Orgn. Steering Cmt, 67-68 & 69-; mem, Calif. Rep. State Cent. Cmt, 67-; alternate mem, Los Angeles Co. Rep. Cent. Cmt, 67-, mem. data processing cmt, 68- Bus. & Prof. Pos: Teacher, Glendale Unified Sch. Dist, 48. Mem: Am. Asn. Univ. Women; Nat. Charity League; La Providencia Guild of Children's Hosp. Calif. Rep. State Cent. Cmt. Precinct Leadership Award, 68. Rel: Methodist. Mailing Add: 720 S. Bel Aire Dr, Burbank, Calif. 91501.

OGLE, ELLEN KNIGHT R
Mem, Fla. Art Cmn.
b. Chicago, Ill, 5/27/03; d. James Seaton Knight and Alma Matilda Fredricka Peterson K; m. 12/30/30 to Arthur Hook Ogle; c. Jamie (Mrs. Allen Osborne Shafer) and Carolyn (Mrs. Norman Bluhm). Educ: Univ. Wis, B.A, 24; Art Inst. Chicago, 25-27; Cleveland Art Inst, 44 & 45; Alpha Phi. Polit. & Govt. Pos: Rep. precinct committeewoman, Broward Co, Fla, 63-; finance chmn, Broward Co. Rep. Party, 65; mem, Fla. Art Cmn, 67-; alternate del, Rep. Nat. Conv, 68. Rel: Congregational. Mailing Add: 510 Lido Dr, Ft. Lauderdale, Fla. 33301.

OGLESBY, GLADYS MARTIN D
Ark. State Rep.
b. Stamps, Ark, 3/11/03; d. Francis Leon Ward and Minnie Nelson W; m. to William Harry Martin, 10/6/23, Lowman H. Oglesby, 10/8/65; c. William H. Martin, Jr. Educ: Stamps High Sch, Ark, grad, 20; Bush Conservatory of Music, Chicago, Ill, summer 21. Polit. & Govt. Pos: Justice of the Peace, Lafayette Co, Ark, 63; Ark. State Rep, 63-, sponsor, Ark. Legis. Act 224, 67. Bus. & Prof. Pos: Bookkeeper and teller, Bodcaw Bank, Stamps, Ark, 41-52; payroll clerk and bookkeeper, R.H. Davis Rd. Contractor, 52-61; part-time radio and script writing and radio commentator, KVMA Radio Sta, Magnolia, 53-; free lance writing, 53-; mgr, Stamps C. of C. Off, 61-66. Publ: Articles for several newspaper Sunday mag. sect. Mem: Nat. Asn. of State Legislators; Bus. & Prfnl. Women's Club; Stamps Home Improv. Club; C. of C. One of two Outstanding Women in Commun, Bus. & Prfnl. Women's Club, 66. Rel: Baptist; leader of Training Union Group and asst. teacher of Adult Women's Sunday Sch. Class, First Baptist Church, Stamps. Legal Res: Oak Grove Rd, Stamps, Ark. 71860. Mailing Add: P.O. Box 275, Stamps, Ark. 71860.

OGLESBY, JAMIE WHITE R
b. Elberton, Ga, 1/2/29; s. Hoke Cecil Oglesby and Mattie Fortson O; m. 10/31/51 to Delpha Elizabeth Folmer; c. Cathy Elizabeth and Jamie White, Jr. Educ: North Ga. Col. Polit. & Govt. Pos: Chmn, Second Dist. Rep. Party, Ga; Ga. State Rep, Thomas Co, 64-68, former Minority Leader, Ga. House of Rep. Bus. & Prof. Pos: Pres, Oglesby-Nunnally Corp, 54-66. Mil. Serv: Entered as Recruit, Army, 51, released as 2nd Lt, 53, after serv. in 76th A.W. Bn, Korea; Good Conduct Medal; Distinguished Serv. Award; plus others. Mem: Elks; Moose; YMCA; Rotary; Am. Legion; VFW; Glen Orven Country Club; Am. Monument Asn; Monument Builders of Am; exec. bd, PTA. Rel: Presbyterian; Elder. Mailing Add: 119 Parkway Dr, Thomasville, Ga. 31792. (1967)

O'GORMAN, FRANCIS EDMUND R
b. N.Y.C, 7/18/19; s. John J. O'Gorman and Elizabeth Sheehan O; m. 12/29/49 to Elizabeth McClelland; c. Jean Mary, Kathleen, Christine, Francis E, Jr, Barbara Ann, Susan and Anne Elizabeth. Educ: Cath. Univ. of Am, B.A, 39; Fordham Univ. Grad. Sch. English. Polit. & Govt. Pos: U.S. Probation Officer, mid. dist, Pa, 57-62; admin. asst, U.S. Rep. Joseph McDade, Pa, 63- Bus. & Prof. Pos: Grammar Sch. teacher, St. Bernard's Sch, N.Y.C, 39-40, high sch. teacher, 40-41, Barnard Sch. for Boys, 46-49; instr. in Eng, Marywood Col, 49-57 and Univ. Scranton, 52-57. Mil. Serv: Entered as Pvt, Army Air Force, 41, released as Capt, 46, after serv. in Eighth Air Force, Eng, First Air Div, ETO, 42-45; Lt. Col, Air Force Res, inactive; Unit Citation; ETO Ribbon with Six Battle Stars; Am. Theatre Ribbon; Victory Medal Publ: Moon of the Devil (short story), 47; The Day of the Bomb, Sign Mag, 48; The Wheat (second place award, nat. short story contest), 53. Mem: Cath. War Vet; Rotary; hon. mem, Lions Club, Carbondale, Pa; hon. life mem, TAR, Pa. Rel: Roman Catholic. Legal Res: 929 Grandview St, Scranton, Pa. 18509. Mailing Add: 101 N. Carolina Ave, S.E, Washington, D.C. 20003.

O'GRADY, EUGENE P. D
Chmn, Ohio Dem. Party
b. Cleveland, Ohio, 7/18/20; s. Michael J. O'Grady and Anne Sweeney O; m. 11/20/48 to Patricia Feller; c. Michael P, Thomas J, Francis P, Mary Elizabeth, Mary Jude, Mary Anne, Richard K, Mary Catherine, Mary Rita, Mary Therese, Mary Christine and John E. Educ: John Carroll Univ, A.B, 49; Cleveland Marshall Law Sch, 48-52. Polit. & Govt. Pos: Court bailiff and secy, Judge Donald F. Lybarger, Common Pleas Bench and united appeal campaign mgr, Common Pleas Court, Cuyahoga Co, Ohio, 50-62; mem, Cuyahoga Co. Dem. Exec. Cmt, 17 years; chmn, Paul F. Ward for Attorney Gen, 54; chmn, Suburban Elec. Cmt, 55; hq. mgr, Bartunek for Mayor Campaign, 55; chmn, Young Dem. for DiSalle for Gov, 58; past pres, Cuyahoga Co. Young Dem; co-chmn, Young Dem. for Kennedy; former state dir, U.S. Savings Bonds Div. and U.S. Treas. Dept; asst. dir, Ohio State Dept. Commerce, 62, dir, 62-63; v.chmn, State Water Pollution Bd; gov. rep, Interstate Oil Compact Cmn. and mem. exec. cmt; mem, Ohio State Civil War Centennial Cmn, 62-63; pub. rels. staff mem, Burr Commun. Agency, Toledo-Cleveland, 63-; field dir, Elec. of Int. Pres. of USW, I.W. Abel, 64-65; field dir, reelec. campaigns of U.S. Sen. Stephen M. Young, Ohio, primary and gen. elec, 64; field dir, defeat of Issue No. 3, "the 1964 lame duck session" apportionment plan adopted by the Rhodes admin. as part of his Four Issues Prog, 65; chmn, Ohio Dem. Party, 68-; exec. dir, Ohio Dem. State Exec. Cmt, currently. Bus. & Polit. Pos: Ins. claims adjustor, Aetna Casualty & Surety Co, Ohio, 48-50. Mil. Serv: Army Air Corps, 42-45, S/Sgt, with serv. as Crew Chief, Athletic Dir, Tech. Writer and Instr. Mem: John Carroll Alumni Asn; Hibernians (past state historian and past pres, div. 5); Holy Name Soc.(past pres). Rel: Roman Catholic. Mailing Add: 1294 Bronwyn Ave, Columbus, Ohio 43204.

O'HAIR, ALLYN W. D
b. Dickinson, N.Dak, 11/18/10; s. James W. O'Hair and Adeline Weigum O; m. 3/5/36 to Agnes E. Armstrong; c. Jerry Paul, Andy Thomas, Bonnie Alice and Mary Agnes. Polit. & Govt. Pos: Mont. State Rep, Park Co, 63-67. Mem: Pres, Park Co. 4-H Coun; Hon. mem, Kiwanis; Citizens Conf. Cmt. Mailing Add: Box 955, Livingston, Mont. 59047. (1967)

OHANIAN, CHARLES D
Mass. State Rep.
b. Watertown, Mass; s. Cyrus Ohanian. Educ: Univ. Conn. Polit. & Govt. Pos: Mass. State Rep, 64-; alternate del, Dem. Nat. Conv, 68. Bus. & Prof. Pos: Dir. phys. educ, Mass. Div. of Youth Serv; pres, Charles Laminating Co. Mil. Serv: Army, Commun. Office of the Chief of Staff, Pentagon, Wash, D.C. Mailing Add: 16 Whites Ave, Watertown, Mass. 02172.(1967)

O'HANLON, ISAAC HAWLEY D
N.C. State Rep.
b. Fayetteville, N.C, 9/5/11; s. George A. O'Hanlon (deceased) and Dora Hawley O. (deceased); m. 9/1/35 to Emma Merle Sikes; c. William Hawley and Edward Wilkings. Educ: Wake Forest Col, 30-35. Polit. & Govt. Pos: Mem. bd. trustees, E. Carolina Univ, 53-59; N.C. State Rep, 53-55, 63- Bus. & Prof. Pos: Owner and mgr, Antex Exterminating Co, Inc; mem. bd. trustees, Vardell Hall, Red Springs, N.C; mem. Methodist Col. Found. Mem: Fayetteville C. of C; N.C. Pest Control Asn; Fayetteville Camelia Club; Fayetteville Rose Club; K. of P; Kiwanis Club (pres, 59, Lt. Gov). Rel: Episcopal; Mem, Vestry. Legal Res: 3605 Morganton Rd, Fayetteville, N.C. 28304. Mailing Add: P.O. Box 475, Fayetteville, N.C. 28302.

O'HARA, DONALD J.
b. Niagara Falls, N.Y, 12/8/28; s. James A. O'Hara and Pearl Paltrovitch O; m. to Helen Crowell; c. Mary Margaret, Maureen, Katherine, Julianne, Jane, Christine and Constance. Educ: Purdue Univ, Army Specialized Training Prog; Niagara Univ, B.B.A, 50. Polit. & Govt. Pos: Councilman, Niagara Falls, N.Y, 63-64; N.Y. State Assemblyman, 65; city mgr, Niagara Falls, 67- Bus. & Prof. Pos: Owner-operator, ins. brokerage firm, Niagara Falls, N.Y, 56-60; partner, retail liquor store, 56-66; instr. and attendance teacher, Niagara Falls Bd. of Educ, 60-64; lectr, Niagara Univ, 62-63. Mil. Serv: Entered as Pvt, Army, 43, released as T/Sgt, 46, after serv. in ETO; Bronze Star; Combat Inf. Badge. Mem: Int. City Mgr. Asn; N.Y. State City Mgr. Asn; bd. of dirs, Niagara Coalition; K. of C; Am. Legion; Amvets; Moose; First Friday Club; Holy Name Soc; Lions; bd. of dirs, Niagara Falls Philharmonic Orchestra; bd. of dirs, Cath. Youth Orgn, Diocese of Buffalo; hon. chmn, Cystic Fibrosis, 63-64; parish chmn, Cath. Charities, 68-69. Rel: Catholic. Mailing Add: 741 Park Place, Niagara Falls, N.Y. 14301.

O'HARA, JAMES GRANT D
U.S. Rep, Mich.
b. Washington, D.C, 11/8/25; s. Raphael McNulty O'Hara and Neta Lloyd Hemphill O; m. 2/14/53 to Susan Puskas; c. Ray, Thomas, Patrick, Brendan, Mary Kathryn, Brigid and Neal. Educ: Univ. of Mich, A.B, 54 and LL.B, 55. Polit. & Govt. Pos: U.S. Rep, Mich, 59-; del, Dem. Nat. Conv, 68. Mil. Serv: Army, 43, released as Sgt, 46, after serv. in 11th Airborne Div, Pac. Theater, 44-45. Mem: K. of C; DAV; Am. Legion; VFW. Rel: Roman Catholic. Legal Res: 45306 Cass Ave, Utica, Mich. 48087. Mailing Add: House of Representatives, Washington, D.C. 20515.

O'HARA, MARY EVELYNE R
b. Stantonsburg, N.C, 11/28/14; d. Peter Redmon Flora and Sara Evelyne Summerlin F; m. 2/14/41 to Leonard Thomas O'Hara; c. Elaine Michele (Mrs. George Walker Pettit, Jr) and Thomas Michael. Educ: Flowers Bus. Sch, 2 years. Polit. & Govt. Pos: V.pres, Rep. Club, Hatboro, Pa, 46 & 47, pres, New Paltz, N.Y, 55-57; del, N.Y. State Dem. Conv, 54 and Rep. Nat. Conv, 68; committeewoman, Ulster Co. Dem. Cmt, N.Y, 56; dir. pub. rels, Ky. Federated Women's Club, 59-60 and Ky. Off. Pub. Info, 68-69; state and co. committeewoman, Ky, 67-69; precinct capt. and elec. worker, pub. rels. and publicity, several elec; coordinator pub. affairs, Gov. Louie B. Nunn, Ky, 68- Bus. & Prof. Pos: Secy, cashier, pub. rels. officer, receptionist, newspaper writer, personnel interviewer and real estate broker. Rel: Protestant. Mailing Add: 540 Albany Rd, Lexington, Ky. 40502.

O'HARA, RICHARD E. D
N.H. State Rep.
b. Gorham, N.H, 9/12/21; married; c. Three. Educ: Gorham State Col. Polit. & Govt. Pos: N.H. State Rep, currently. Mil. Serv: 42-46. Mem: VFW. Rel: Protestant. Mailing Add: 25 Promenade, Gorham, N.H. 03581. (1967)

O'HEARN, TAYLOR WALTERS R
b. Shreveport, La, 7/7/07; s. Ernest Paul O'Hearn and Mattie Walters O; m. 2/22/46 to Gladys Bookout; c. Patrick, Jerry (Mrs. Meier) and Paul Kennon, stepson. Educ: Baylor Univ; Centenary Col. Polit. & Govt. Pos: Former La. State Rep; mem. bd, La. Polit. Action Coun, 65- Bus. & Prof. Pos: Mem. exec. bd, State CPA Asn, 54-55; Comdr, Lowe-McFarlane Am. Legion, 61; mem, Law Firm of O'Hearn & Gerhardt, currently. Mil. Serv: Entered as Ordinary Seaman, Navy, 44, released as PO 2/C, 45, after serv. in Fleet Air Wing 14. Mem: La. CPA Soc; CPA Inst. of Am; Shreveport, La. and Am. Bar Asns; Am. Trial Lawyers Asn; Mason; Shrine; Am. Legion; 40 et 8; C. of C. Past chmn, Brotherhood Cmn, Southern Baptist Conv. Rel: Baptist. Legal Res: 2509 Grand View, Richardson, Tex. 75080. Mailing Add: O'Hearn & Gerhardt, 1012 Slattery Bldg, Shreveport, La. 71101.

O'HEARN, TRAVE E. R
Iowa State Rep.
b. Davenport, Iowa, 7/13/39; s. Trave V. O'Hearn and Helene Shanley O; single. Polit. & Govt. Pos: Mem. bd, Young Am. for Freedom; mem, Am. Conservative Union; Iowa State Rep, Scott Co. Subdist. Three, 69- Mil. Serv: Pfc, Marines. Mem: Conveyors' Equip. Mgf. Asn.(mem. bd); Davenport C. of C.(mem. adv. coun); Elks. Rel: Roman Catholic. Mailing Add: P.O. Box 1145, Davenport, Iowa 52801.

OHLSEN, FERDINAND ALBERT R
Chmn, Morton Co. Rep. Party, N.Dak.
b. Jackson Co, Mo, 5/15/17; s. Gunnar S. Ohlsen and Ruth O; m. 10/28/39 to Dorotha Maye Gautier; c. John Ferdinand, Richard Albert and Janice Kay. Polit. & Govt. Pos: Pres. sch. bd, Pitcher Sch. Dist, Jackson Co, Mo, 46-54; pres, Mandan Bd. Cmnrs, N.Dak, 56-60; precinct committeeman, Morton Co. Rep. Party, N.Dak, 58-62, mem. exec. bd, 62-64, chmn, 64-; del, Rep. State Conv, 60 & 62. Bus. & Prof. Pos: Employee, Am. Oil Co. Mandan, N.Dak, 36-, shift foreman, 54-, pres, Employees Credit Union, 56-60; owner, Pitcher Sch. Bus. Serv, Mo, 50-54. Mem: AF&AM; Elks; Lions; indust. cmn, Mandan C. of C, 57. Rel: Presbyterian; trustee and elder. Mailing Add: 704 Third Ave. N.W, Mandan, N.Dak. 58554.

OHRENSTEIN, MANFRED D
N.Y. State Sen.
b. Mannheim, Germany, 8/5/25; s. Markus Ohrenstein and Fannie Hollander O; m. 9/1/57 to Marilyn Bacher; c. Nancy Ellen and David Jonathan. Educ: Brooklyn Col, cum laude, 48; Harlan Fiske Stone scholar, Columbia Univ. Law Sch, 51; Brooklyn Col. Hon. Soc. Polit. & Govt. Pos: Asst. dist. attorney, N.Y. Co, N.Y, 54-58; N.Y. State Sen, 61- Bus. & Prof. Pos: Private law practice, 58-61; partner, Karpatkin, Ohrenstein & Karpatkin, 61- Mil. Serv: 1st Lt, Judge Adv. Gen. Corps, Army, 52-54; Capt, Army Res, currently. Mem: N.Y. Co. Lawyers Asn; Nat. Gov. Coun, Am. Jewish Cong; N.Y. State Bd. of Am. for Dem. Action; mem. bd, N.Y. Shakespeare Festival. Rel: Jewish. Mailing Add: 215 W. 90th St, New York, N.Y. 11024. (1967)

OKA, KENNETH D
b. N.Y.C, 7/31/16; s. Samuel Oka and Bessie Weiner O; m. 6/6/41 to Gertrude Heller; c. Barbara, Michele Lee (Mrs. Doner), Stephanie and Jonathan Kenneth. Educ: City Col. New York, B.S.S, 37; Harvard Univ, LL.B, 40. Polit. & Govt. Pos: Justice of the peace and judge, small claims court, Miami, Fla, 45-57; mayor, Miami Beach, 57-59 & 61-63, councilman, 59-61 & 63-65; dir-in-chief, Sister City Prog, People to People, 65-66; del, Dem. Nat. Conv, 68. Mem: Past pres, Miami Beach Jr. C. of C; past exalted ruler, Miami Beach Elks Club. Outstanding Civic Leader of the Year, Miami Beach, Fla, 59. Rel: Jewish. Legal Res: 2801 Fairgreen Dr, Miami Beach, Fla. 33140. Mailing Add: 407 Lincoln Rd, Miami Beach, Fla. 33139.

OKADA, HIDEO D
Committeeman, Hawaii State Dem. Cent. Cmt.
b. Waipahu, Hawaii, 6/15/10; s. Denjiro Okada and Matsu Imai O; m. 11/23/35 to Matsuko Hashinmoto; c. Marlene Kikuko (Mrs. Hirata), Glenn Kenji and Richard Masahiro. Educ: Mid-Pac. Inst. High Sch, Honolulu, Hawaii, grad, 32. Polit. & Govt. Pos: Del, Hawaii State Dem. Conv, 48-68; v.chmn, Oahu Co. Dem. Party, Hawaii, 64-66; chmn, Waipahu Dem. Precinct Club, 66; committeeman, Hawaii State Dem. Cent. Cmt, 69- Bus. & Prof. Pos: Bus. agent, ILWU, 50; Mem. adv. coun, Leeward Oahu Commun. Col, 69. Mem: Waipahu Businessmen's Asn.(dir, 68); Waipahu Young Farmers (pres, 64); Waipahu Orchid Soc.(pres, 67); Waipahu Baseball Club(pres, 68); Waipahu Commun. Asn.(pres, 66-68); Wailani Neighborhood Asn; Leeward YMCA; Int. Longshoremen's Union (secy, 46-). Rel: Buddhist. Mailing Add: 94-111 Farrington Highway, Waipahu, Hawaii 96797.

OKANE, BERNARD PATRICK D
b. Jefferson Co, Colo, 11/30/20; s. Barney Okane and Elizabeth McCallon O; m. 10/25/58 to Mary Joanne Little; c. Patrick, Sean, Kevin and Kelly. Educ: Univ. Denver and Law Sch. Polit. & Govt. Pos: Committeeman capt, Dem. Party, Colo; dist. attorney, 1st Judicial Dist, 56-60; Colo. State Rep,

54-56. Bus. & Prof. Pos: Attorney, 51- Mil. Serv: Entered as Pvt, Army Air Force, released as 1st Sgt, 46. Mem: Colo. and 1st Judicial Dist. Bar Asns; Am. Legion; DAV; VFW. Rel: Catholic. Mailing Add: 13100 West 72nd Ave, Arvada, Colo. 80002. (1967)

O'KEEFE, ARTHUR B, JR. D
Mem, Madison Town Dem. Cmt, Conn.
b. Orange, Conn, 6/6/12; s. Arthur B. O'Keefe and Marie Kerrigan O; m. to Jane Gamble; c. Jane Kerrigan and Arthur B, III. Educ: Yale Univ; George Wash. Univ, A.B, 33; Georgetown Univ, LL.B, 35; Kappa Beta Phi. Polit. & Govt. Pos: Mem, West Haven Town Dem. Cmt, 36-40; prosecuting attorney, Munic. Court West Haven, 49-51; chmn, Madison Town Dem. Cmt, 52-66, mem, 66-; dep. attorney gen, Conn, 59-67. Bus. & Prof. Pos: Mem, O'Keefe, Gillooly & Votto, until 64; owner, Law Firm, O'Keefe & O'Keefe, 64- Mil. Serv: Entered as Pvt, Brit. Army, 41, released as Capt, 45, after serv. in 51st Highland Div, Black Watch, Royal Highland Regt; Brit. Campaign Ribbons for serv. in N.W. European and other European Campaigns; Overseas Medals; Victory Medal; Col, Conn. State Guard, 59-65. Mem: New Haven Co, Conn. and Am. Bar Asns; Am. Judicature Soc; Am. Trial Lawyers Asn; Century Club; Am. Criminal Lawyers Asn; Ins. Co. Bar; Am. Legion; K. of C. (4°); Knights of St. Patricks; Elks. Rel: Roman Catholic. Legal Res: Neptune Ave, Madison, Conn. 06443. Mailing Add: 152 Temple St, New Haven, Conn. 06510.

O'KEEFE, JAMES L. D
Pub. Adminstr, Cook Co, Ill.
b. Chicago, Ill, 1/8/10; s. Raymond T. O'Keefe and S. Monahan O; m. 6/19/34 to Josephine Killian; c. James L, Jr, William J. and Dennis M. Educ: Northwestern Univ, B.A, 31; Chicago-Kent Col. of Law, J.D, 36; Phi Delta Phi; Law Club; Phi Kappa Sigma. Polit. & Govt. Pos: Master in Chancery, Circuit Court, Ill, 45-65; del, Del. Nat. Conv, 48, 52, 56, 60, 64 & 68, chmn. host cmt, 52 & 56; pub. adminstr, Cook Co, Ill, 61- Bus. & Prof. Pos: Sr. partner, O'Keefe, O'Brien, Hanson & Ashenden, 37-; dir, Great Lakes Supply Corp. and Nat. Blvd. Bank of Chicago, at present. Mem: Chicago, Ill. and Am. Bar Asns; Chicago Club; Mid-Day Club; Evanston Golf Club; Country Club of Fla; Ocean Club; past pres, Northwest. Univ. Club, Chicago and West. Golf Asn; Chicago Dist. Golf Asn.(pres); U.S. Golf Asn.(exec. cmt); Rel: Roman Catholic. Legal Res: 1420 N. Sheridan Rd, Wilmette, Ill. 60091. Mailing Add: 5100 First National Plaza, Chicago, Ill. 60670.

O'KEEFE, JOHN CORNELIUS D
b. Chicago, Ill, 8/29/27; s. John Edward O'Keefe and Anna McCollum O; m. 10/17/64 to Marilyn Joy Laurin Campbell; c. John Cornelius, Jr, Timothy Terence and Daniel Laurin; stepchildren: Robert Bruce Campbell and Laurie Lanay Campbell. Educ: Rollins Col; Claremont Men's Col, B.A, 52; Kappa Alpha. Polit. & Govt. Pos: State Inheritance tax appraiser, Los Angeles Co, Calif, 59-62; exec.dir, Calif. Dem. State and Nat. Cmts, 63-64; mem, Los Angeles Co. Dem. Cmt, 66; mem, Calif. Dem. State Cmt, 66 and 69; active in Gov. Brown's, Mayor Yorty's and various congressmen's, state sen. and assemblymen's campaigns. Bus. & Prof. Pos: Owner and pres, O'Keefe Co, Investment Bankers, 52-; field secy, Coun. of Profit Sharing Industs, 53-54; asst. to pres, Ampex Corp, 54-58; bank organizer, Bakersfield Nat. Bank and Alhambra Nat. Bank, 65-68; chmn. of the bd, Dirs. Life Ins. Co, 66-69. Mil. Serv: Entered as Seaman, Navy, 44, released as Seaman 1/C, 45 after serv. in Nat. Res, Pac. Theatre. Rel: Unitarian. Mailing Add: 917 Mt. Washington Dr, Los Angeles, Calif. 90065.

O'KEEFE, MICHAEL HANLEY D
La. State Sen.
b. New Orleans, La, 12/1/31; s. Judge Arthur J. O'Keefe, Jr. and Eleanora Gordon O; m. to Jean Ann Van Geffen; c. Michael Hanley, Jr. and Erin Elizabeth. Educ: Loyola Univ, B.A, Sch. Law, LL.B; Blue Key. Polit. & Govt. Pos: Chmn, La. Cmn. Interstate Coop; La. State Sen, Third Dist, 57-, Senate Floor Leader, La. State Sen, 64- chmn, Coun. Govt. Reorgn. & Goals for La. Cmt, La. State Senate; del, Dem. Nat. Conv, 68. Bus. & Prof. Pos: Attorney and partner, O'Keefe and O'Keefe, New Orleans, La; former mem. faculty, Loyola Univ. Eve. Div. Mil. Serv: Army, 2 years, serv. as Asst. Provost Marshal, Ft. Hood. Mem: Am, La. and New Orleans Bar Asns; Cub Scout Master, Boy Scouts; exec. cmt, Total Commun. Action, Inc; La. mem. bd. mgr, Coun. State Govt; bd. dirs, Citizens for Adv. Pub. Educ. and Greater New Orleans Tourist and Conv. Cmn; Res. Officers Asn; Pub. Affairs Research Coun; Bur. Govt. Research; Jr. C. of C; K. of C; Holy Name Soc; Young Men's Bus. Club; Friends of Cabildo; Crescent City Concert Asn. (exec. cmt); La. Civil Serv. League; Loyola Univ. Speaker's Bur; Kiwanis; Am. Automobile Asn.(adv. bd, La. Div); Lake Vista Property Owners Asn. (past pres); Holiday Club (past pres); La. Coun. Music and Performing Arts (v.pres); chmn. bd, Repertory Theatre, New Orleans. Outstanding Young Man of Year Award, Jr. C. of C, 64. Rel: Roman Catholic. Legal Res: 4 Gull St, New Orleans, La. 70124. Mailing Add: 813 American Bank Bldg, New Orleans, La. 70130.

O'KEEFFE, WHITNEY CARTER R
Mem, Ga. Rep. State Cmt.
b. Brooklyn, N.Y, 1/6/35; s. Edwin Hope O'Keeffe and Reba Carter O; m. 12/29/61 to Marion Eliza Gaines; c. Whitney Carter, Jr and William Davis. Educ: Ga. Inst. Tech, B.I.E, 61; Wharton Grad. Div, Univ. Pa, M.B.A, 65; Chi Phi. Polit. & Govt. Pos: First v.chmn, Fifth Dist. Rep. Party, Ga, 64-66; first v.chmn, Ga. Rep. Party, 65-66; mem, Ga. Rep. State Cmt, 64-; mem, Fulton Co. Rep. Cmt, 64- Bus. & Prof. Pos: Asst. treas, Trust Co. of Ga, 62-69, v.pres, 69- Mil. Serv: Entered as Pvt, Army, 57, released as Specialist 3/C, 58. Mem: Am. Inst. of Indust. Engrs; Am. Inst. of Banking; U.S. Jaycees, dir, Atlanta Humane Soc. Rel: Baptist. Mailing Add: 997 Wadsworth Dr. N.W, Atlanta, Ga. 30318.

O'KELLEY, WILLIAM CLARK R
Gen. Counsel, Ga. Rep. Party
b. Atlanta, Ga, 1/2/30; s. Ezra Clark O'Kelley and Theo D. Johnson O; m. 3/28/53 to Ernestine Allen; c. Virginia Leigh and William C, Jr. Educ: Emory Univ, A.B, 51, LL.B, 53; Sigma Chi, Omicron Delta Kappa; Phi Delta Phi. Polit. & Govt. Pos: Asst. U.S. Attorney, North. Dist. Ga, 59-61; v.chmn, Ninth Cong. Dist. Rep. Party, 66-68; city attorney, Norcross, 67-; alternate del, Rep. Nat. Conv, 68; gen. counsel, Ga. Rep. Party, 68- Bus. & Prof. Pos: Partner, O'Kelley, Hopkins & Van Gerpen, Atlanta, 61-; dir. and corp. secy, Gwinnett Bank & Trust Co, 67- Mil. Serv: Entered as 1st Lt, Air Force, 53, released as 1st Lt, 58, after serving in Strategic Air Command, U.S, 53-55, Japan, 54, Morocco, 55-57; Capt, Air Force Res, resigned. Mem: Am, Ga. State, Atlanta and Gwinnett Bar Asns; Lawyers Club of Atlanta; Kiwanis (past pres, Peachtree-Atlanta Club); Gwinnett C. of C. (past v.pres). Rel: Baptist. Legal Res: 550 Ridgecrest Dr, Norcross, Ga. 30071. Mailing Add: 2250 National Bank of Georgia Bldg, Atlanta, Ga. 30303.

OKEY, EUGENE P. D
Dem. Campaign Chmn, Stark Co, Ohio
Married; c. Four. Educ: Kent State Univ; William McKinley Law Sch. Polit. & Govt. Pos: Pres, Canton Chap, Nat. Sojourners, Ohio; pres, Jefferson-Jackson Dem. Club; Dem. campaign chmn, Stark Co, 66- Bus. & Prof. Pos: Law firm of Bernabel, Okey and Korey. Mil. Serv: Intel. Officer, ETO and Pac. Theater, World War II; Provost Marshall, Va. Mil. Dist, Korean War. Mailing Add: 1525 49th St. N.W, Canton, Ohio 44709. (1967)

OKIYAMA, JESUS CARBULLIDO D
Sen, Guam Legis.
b. Agat, Guam, 8/2/13; s. Francisco K. Okiyama and Ana C. Carbullido O; m. 6/27/42 to Josefina M. Leon Guerrero; c. John Anthony and Frank Vincent. Educ: Guam High Sch. Polit. & Govt. Pos: Chmn, Commerce and Trade Cmn, Guam Cong, 46-50, chmn, Cmt. on Housing and Transportation, 50-52; chmn, Cmt. on Govt. Opers, Guam Legis, 52-64, chmn, Far E. Trade Mission, 56; Guam rep, S.Pac. Econ. Conf, 62; del, Hawaii Statehood Celebration; del, Dem. Nat. Conv, 64 & 68; Dem. Nat. Committeeman, 64-; Sen, Guam Legis, 66-, spec. asst. to Minority Mem, 66; chmn, for. trade cmt, West. State Conf. Bus. & Prof. Pos: Mgr, Wholesale Div, Guam Commercial Corp, 46-52; pres. and owner, Okie & Young Co, 56-62. Mem: Young Men League of Guam; Guam Eagle; Triple A Club of Yona. Rel: Roman Catholic. Legal Res: Yona, Guam 96910. Mailing Add: P.O. Box 373, Agana, Guam 96910.

O'KONSKI, ALVIN E. R
U.S. Rep, Wis.
b. Kewaunee, Wis; m. to Veronica Hemming. Educ: Wis. State Col, bachelor of educ. degree; Univ. of Wis; Univ. of Iowa. Polit. & Govt. Pos: U.S. Rep, Wis, 42-, dean of Wis. del; mem, Armed Serv. Cmt. and D. C. Cmt; pres, World Bill of Rights Asn, 45; former dir, Free World Forum and World League to Stop Communism; mem, Katyn Massacre Cmt, 52. Bus. & Prof. Pos: Pres, WAEO-TV Inc, Rhinelander, Wis; former owner of WOSA and WLIN, radio stas. at Wasau and Merrill, Wis; former publisher of newspaper, Hurley, Wis; taught at Itasca Jr. Col. in Minn, Ore. State Col. in Ore, and Univ. of Detroit, Mich. Voted Most Distinguished Am. for 45 by For. Lang. Press for his work against communism; Awarded Polonia Restitutia, Highest Medal of Free Poland; ranked first among all Congressmen in Am. Hist. test conducted by United Press; capt. of debating team 3 years and pres. of student body 2 years, Wis. State Col; capt, Univ. of Wis. Big Ten Championship Debating Team. Legal Res: Rhinelander, Wis. Mailing Add: 507 D St. S.E, Washington, D.C. 20003.

OLANDER, GENE M. R
Co. Attorney, Shawnee Co, Kans.
b. Bartlesville, Okla, 10/31/32; s. Eugene Olander and Mary Lucile Tucker O; m. 6/29/63 to Charlotte Maye Barnett; c. Pamella Jean, Cynthia Anne and Mary Lucile. Educ: Kans. State Univ, B.S, 60; Washburn Univ. Sch. of Law, LL.B, 63; Blue Key; Phi Delta Theta; Phi Alpha Delta. Polit. & Govt. Pos: Precinct Committeeman, Shawnee Co. Rep. Cmt, Kans, 62-, chmn, 66-68; State Chmn, Kans Collegiate Rep, 63-64; Chmn, Shawnee Co. Young Rep, 64-66; alternate del, Rep. Nat. Conv, 68; co. attorney, Shawnee Co, Kans, 69- Mil. Serv: Entered as E-1, Navy, 51, released as E-5, 55, after serv. in U.S.S. Rasher SSR 269, Pac. Theatre, 53-55. Mem: Topeka and Kans. Bar Asns; Nat. Dist and Kans. Co. Attorneys Asns; Kans. Peace Officers; Elks; Kiwanis; Eagles; Am. Legion. Rel: Protestant. Mailing Add: 2200 Fairlawn Rd, Topeka, Kans. 66614.

OLDHAM, CHAUNCEY MARLING R
Secy, Guernsey Co. Rep. Exec. Cmt, Ohio
b. Cambridge, Ohio, 8/15/88; s. Isaac J. Oldham and Margaret Ford; wid; c. Alice Esther (Mrs. Walker K. Wilson), Morris M, Robert Grant, Walter Jay (deceased). Educ: Col. of Wooster, summers 07, 08, 10 & 11. Polit. & Govt. Pos: Bailiff, Cambridge Munic. Court, Ohio, 52-66; mem, Guernsey Co. Rep. Exec. Cmt, Ohio, 16-, secy, 68- Bus. & Prof. Pos: Teacher, grade sch, Ohio, 07-09 and Mecca Twp, Cortland, 11-12; teacher and prin, Barton, Ohio, 09-11; investr, Bd. of Real Estate Exam, Columbus, 30-31. Mem: Grange; Valley Grange; Guernsey Co. Pomona Grange; Ohio State Grange; Nat. Grange. Rel: United Presbyterian. Mailing Add: 419 N. Seventh St, Cambridge, Ohio 43725.

OLDHAM, EDWIN L. D
Chmn, Polk Co. Dem. Exec. Cmt, Tenn.
b. Alamo, Tenn, 6/16/13; s. Virgil S. Oldham and Lurline Lewis O; m. 8/3/35 to Flora Pate; c. Loel E. and Larry V. Educ: High Sch. Polit. & Govt. Pos: Former v.chmn, precinct chmn. and committeeman, Polk Co. Dem. Exec. Cmt, Tenn, chmn, presently. Bus. & Prof. Pos: Supvr, Tenn. Copper Co, 48- Mem: Past master, Master Masons, past high priest, RAM; past pres, Ruritans, Rotary and PTA. Rel: Baptist. Mailing Add: Ducktown, Tenn. 37326.

OLDHAM, SARAH SMITH D
b. Lafayette, Tenn, 1/6/36; d. Wesley Clay Smith and Lillie Jones S; m. 6/12/56 to Paul Dean Oldham; c. Bruce Nelson; Educ: Macon Co. High Sch, Lafayette, Tenn, dipl, 54. Polit. & Govt. Pos: Mem, Cmt. for Re-elec. of Anderson for Cong, 66 & 68; del, Tenn. State Dem. Conv, 68; alternate del, Dem. Nat. Conv, 68. Bus. & Prof. Pos: State correspondent, Nashville Banner, 67- Mem: Dem. Women's Club; PTA. Rel: Baptist. Legal Res: 208 Main St, Lafayette, Tenn. 37083. Mailing Add: P.O. Box 223, Lafayette, Tenn. 37083.

OLDS, GLENN A.
U.S. Ambassador-Rep, UN Econ. and Soc. Coun.
b. Sherwood, Ore, 2/28/21; s. Glenn Alvero Olds and Hazel Ross O; m.

6/20/44 to Eva B. Spelts; c. Linda (Mrs. Robert Haynes) and Richard. Educ: Willamette Univ, A.B. magna cum laude, 42; Garrett Theol. Sem, B.D. with highest distinction, 45; Northwest. Univ, Swift travelling fel, 44-45, M.A. with honors, 45; Yale Univ, Robinson fel, 45-46, Ph.D, 48; Omicron Delta Kappa; Tau Kappa Alpha; Blue Key; Omicron Delta Sigma. Hon. D.D, Willamette Univ, 55; D.H, Springfield Col, 65; Academico Honoris Causa, Mexican Acad. Int. Law, 67; hon. academician, China Acad, Taiwan, 67; L.H.D, Inter-Am. Univ, P.R, 68. Polit. & Govt. Pos: Mem, Am. Seminar to Europe, 50; leader, Am. Seminar to the Union of Soviet Socialist Repub, 57; consult. to President Eisenhower, Stockholm Conf. on Educ, 60; consult, Peace Corps, 61; consult, President's Coun. on Juvenile Delinquency, 61-62; consult, President's Coun. on Youth and Phys. Fitness, 61-63; former consult, Disarmament and Arms Control Cmn; consult, Govt. of Liberia, 62; consult, Ministry of Educ, Nigeria, 62; spec. asst. to Sargent Shriver, War on Poverty, 64; mem, exec. cmt, Alliance for Progress, Mass-Colombia, 64-65; chmn, seminar, educ. and cult. exchange, White House Conf. on Int. Educ, 65; convenor and host, N.Am. Conf. on Univs. Role in the Quest for Peace, Int. Center, L.I, 67, U.S. rep, convening cmt, Univs. Role in the Quest for Peace, Rome, Italy, 67; U.S. rep, Conf. on Latin Am. in the Last Quarter of the Twentieth Century, Mexico City, Mex, 68; U.S. rep, Conf. on the Future of the UN, Dubrovnik, Yugoslavia, 68; spec. asst. for policy and manpower develop. to President Richard M. Nixon, 68-69; U.S. rep, Kyoto Conf. on U.S-Japan Rels, 69; U.S. Ambassador-Rep, UN Econ. and Soc. Coun, 69- Bus. & Prof. Pos: Student pastor, Methodist Churches, Harrisburg and Brooks, Ore, 39-40; dir. youth, First Methodist Church, Salem, Ore, 40-42 and Oak Park, Ill, 43-45; dir, Wesley Found, Yale Univ, 45-47, asst. in instr, univ, 47-; assoc. prof. philos. and ethics, Garrett Theol. Sem. and vis. prof. philos, Northwest. Univ, 48-51; asst. prof. philos, DePauw Univ, 48-; chaplain and prof, Univ. Denver, 51-54; dir, Cornell Univ. United Relig. Work, 54-58; pres, Springfield Col, 58-65; dean int. studies and world affairs, State Univ. N.Y. Syst, 65-68; adv, Nat. Asn. of Int. Rels. Clubs, 67-68; consult, Universidád de O'riente, Venezuela, 68. Mem: Pres, Alpha Psi Zeta Found, 54; cmn. on student personnel, Am. Coun. on Educ, 56-58; prog. cmt, Nat. Coun, YMCA, 59-65; adv. coun, Nat. Coun, Boy Scouts, 60; cmn. on the arts, Am. Asn. of Cols, 60-62; trustee, World Literacy Found, 60-62; Nat. Citizen's Adv. Cmt. on Commun. Campaigns and Welfare, 62; trustee, Albert Schweitzer Found, 62-65; exec. cmt, Nat. Surv. of Commun. Health Serv, 64-65; adv. bd, U.S-France Inst. of Am. Studies, Paris, 66-68; exec. cmt, int. educ, Nat. Asn. of State Univ. and Land Grant Cols, 66-68; adv. bd, int. training, Am. Soc. of Pub. Admin, 67-68; trustee, Dag Hammarskjold Col, 68; v.pres, Metrop. Area Coun. for Int. Recreation, Cult, and Lifelong Educ, N.Y.C, 68; v.chmn, educ. and world affairs, Coun. on Univ. Int. Progs, 68. Nat. fel, Nat. Coun. on Relig. in Higher Educ, 46; Outstanding Teacher Award, Univ. Denver, 53; Outstanding Citizen Award, City of Springfield, Mass, 65. Legal Res: Apt. C, 400 E. 56th St, New York, N.Y. 10022. Mailing Add: 799 United Nations Plaza, New York, N.Y. 10017.

OLENICK, STEPHEN R. D
Auditor, Mahoning Co, Ohio
b. Youngstown, Ohio, 10/18/10; s. Joseph Stephen Olenick and Veronica Yasechko O; m. 6/17/39 to Ann Slifka; c. Bernice (Mrs. Krispinsky), Carole (Mrs. Morris) and Robert. Educ: South High Sch, Youngstown, Ohio, grad, 29. Polit. & Govt. Pos: City councilman, Youngstown, Ohio, 46-54; Ohio State Sen, 55-62; auditor, Mahoning Co, 62-; alternate del, Dem. Nat. Conv, 64, del, 68. Bus. & Prof. Pos: Supreme auditor, Slovak Cath. Sokol, Passaic, N.J, 55-62, supreme treas, 62- Mem: Chmn, local govt. div, United Appeal; dir, Red Cross; C. of C; v.pres, Baseball Town USA Oldtimers; pitcher, Nat. Amateur Baseball Fedn. Champions; v.pres, Co. Off. Asn. Ohio; co-chmn. legis. cmt, Auditors Orgn, Ohio; First Cath. Slovak Union; Greek Cath. Union; Polish Nat. Alliance; Arco Vet. Club; K. of C. Citation, Buckeye Sheriffs Asn; Citation, from Ohio Attorney Gen; C. of C. Award. Rel: Roman Catholic; Councilman, St. Matthias Church, 13 years. Mailing Add: 3022 Rush Blvd, Youngstown, Ohio 44502.

OLESON, OTTO H. D
N.H. State Rep.
b. Jefferson, N.H, 6/2/15; s. Otto W. Oleson and Goldine Stellings O; m. 11/30/40 to Eilleen Garland; c. Otto G, Eric J. and Faith (Mrs. Belanger). Educ: Berlin High Sch, N.H, 4 years. Polit. & Govt. Pos: N.H. State Rep, 65-; del, Dem. Nat. Conv, 68. Mil. Serv: Entered as C.M. 3/C, Navy, 43, released as C.M. 1/C, 45, after serv. in Naval Construction Bn, Pac. Theatre. Mem: Grange; Am. Legion; F&AM. Rel: Protestant. Mailing Add: 10 Hamlin Ave, Gorham, N.H. 03581.

OLIPHANT, S. PARKER R
Mem, D.C. Rep. State Cmt.
b. Washington, D.C, 10/26/27; s. A. Chambers Oliphant and Ruth Larner O; m. 6/2/62 to Martha Carmichael; c. Leonard Carmichael and Samuel Duncan. Educ: Princeton Univ, B.S, 49; Dial Lodge. Polit. & Govt. Pos: Rep. precinct worker, Wash, D.C, 49-52 and precinct chmn, 54-68; mem, D.C. Rep. State Cmt, 60- Bus. & Prof. Pos: Treas, William P. Lipscomb Co, 49- Mem: Wash. Bldg. Cong; Rotary; Chevy Chase Club; Metrop. Club. Rel: Presbyterian. Mailing Add: 4977 Glenbrook Rd. N.W, Washington, D.C. 20016.

OLIVER, CHARLES PRESTON D
Chmn, McMinn Co. Dem. Exec. Cmt, Tenn.
b. Sutherland, Ashe Co, N.C, 4/27/11; s. Roy Oliver and Lucy Cornett O; m. 4/25/40 to Grace Matthews. Polit. & Govt. Pos: Chmn, McMinn Co. Dem. Exec. Cmt, Tenn, presently. Bus. & Prof. Pos: Owner and operator, Oliver's Trading Post, 47-; secy. and treas, Skateland, Inc, 58- Rel: Baptist. Mailing Add: Route 1, Niota, Tenn. 37826.

OLIVER, CLINTON D
b. Glennville, Ga, 10/18/22; s. Alfred Green Oliver and Ruth Sikes O; m. 12/21/52 to Mary Frances Smith; c. Clinton Paul, Jr, Francine, Bert Smith, David Green, Julie Ann, John Hampton and Mary Ruth. Educ: Glennville High Sch, 39; Ga. Teachers Col, 2 years. Polit. & Govt. Pos: Ga. State Sen, 63-64. Bus. & Prof. Pos: Gulf Oil Distributor. Mil. Serv: Army, World War II, 43-46, M/Sgt, commissioned 2nd Lt, Inf, 45, Maj, Corps of Engrs, U.S. Army Res.(Ret); Three Bronze Serv. Stars for Battle Participation in Campaigns of North. France, Ardennes and Rhineland. Mem: Phila. Lodge 73, F&AM, Glennville; Alee Temple; AAOS, Savannah. Rel: Baptist. Legal Res: R.F.D. 4, Glennville, Ga. 30427. Mailing Add: P.O. Box 237, Glennville, Ga. 30427.

OLIVER, COVEY THOMAS D
U.S. Exec. Dir, Int. Bank for Reconstruction and Develop.
b. Laredo, Tex, 4/21/13; s. Pheneas Roan Oliver and Jane Covey Thomas O; m. 12/28/46 to Barbara Hauer; c. Jane Covey, Lucy Boulware, Woodlief Hauer, Scotti Longan and Jefferson Thomas. Educ: Univ. Tex, B.A. summa cum laude, 33 and LL.B. summa cum laude, 36; Columbia Univ, LL.M, 53 and Jur. Sci. Dr, 54; Phi Beta Kappa; Phi Delta Phi. Polit. & Govt. Pos: Sr. attorney, Bd. of Econ. Warfare, 42; chief econ. controls sect, Am. Embassy, Madrid, 42-44; head various divs, Dept. State, 44-49; mem. U.S. del, Paris Peace Conf. and other delegations, 46-49; Am. mem, Inter-Am. Juridical Cmt, Orgn. Am. States, 63-; Ambassador Extraordinary and Minister Plenipotentiary to Colombia, 64-66; Asst. Secy. of State for Inter-Am. Affairs, 67-69; U.S. coordinator, Alliance for Progress, 67-69; U.S. exec. dir, Int. Bank for Reconstruction and Develop, Int. Finance Corp, Int. Develop. Asn, 68-; spec. asst. to Secy. of Treas, 69- Bus. & Prof. Pos: Admitted to Tex. Bar, 36; mem. law faculty, Univ. Tex, 36-41; prof. law, Univ. Calif, Berkeley, 49-56, Univ. Pa, 56-69, Hubbell Prof. Law, 69-; Fulbright scholar and lectr, Univ. São Paulo, 63; mem. bd. of ed, Am. J. of Int. Law, 69- Publ: Assoc. reporter, Restatement of the Foreign Relations Law of the U.S, 63; The Inter-American Security System and the Cuban Crisis, 64; 'Foreign and Human Relations with Latin America,' For. Affairs, 4/69; plus others. Am. Soc. of Int. Law (v.pres, mem. exec. coun, 68-); Am. Bar Asn; Int. Law Asn; For. Serv. Asn; Order of the Coif; Chancellors. Grand Cross, Order of Boyaca, Repub. of Colombia, 66. Legal Res: 4210 Spruce St, Philadelphia, Pa. 19104. Mailing Add: 161 Law Bldg, University of Pennsylvania, Philadelphia, Pa. 19104.

OLIVER, FLOYD D
Colo. State Sen.
b. Kersey, Colo, 2/15/11; s. Ross Oliver and Mary Jackson O; m. 9/22/29 to Lillie May Kennedy; c. Floyd, Jr, William James and Mary Patricia. Polit. & Govt. Pos: Precinct committeeman, Colo, 40-; Colo. State Sen, 57-; mem, Civil Serv. Cmn, 69- Bus. & Prof. Pos: Pres, Colo. Water Well Asn, 34, Oliver Well Works, Inc, 35- and Nat. Water Well Asn, 59; mem, Colo. State Hwy. Adv. Bd, 48-52 and Conv. Cmt. on Fed-State Rels, 66-67. Mem: Rotary; Elks; C. of C. Rel: Congregational. Mailing Add: 800 19th St, Greeley, Colo. 80631.

OLIVER, JACK LARONSO D
b. Birmingham, Ala, 3/14/18; s. Sidney Oliver and Mary Lee Foster O; m. 7/1/42 to Jean Bickley; c. George E. and Virginia P. Educ: Cleveland Col, 1 year. Polit. & Govt. Pos: Bailiff Municipal Court, Cleveland, Ohio, 63-66; Secy. to Serv. Dir, Cleveland, 66-67; alternate del, Dem. Nat. Conv, 68; info. chief, Cleveland City Coun, Ohio, 68- Bus. & Prof. Pos: Self-employed in Pub. Relations, 52-63. Mem: Am. Fedn. of State, Co. and Municipal Employees. Rel: Protestant. Mailing Add: 643 E. 117th St, Cleveland, Ohio 44108.

OLIVER, JACK PHILLIP R
Ohio State Rep.
b. Rochester, Ind, 10/16/31; s. Mark Oliver and Lorene Drudge O; m. 7/30/55 to Martha Lee Krieder; c. Steven Matthew and Amy Lou. Educ: Ball State Univ, B.S. Ed, 54; Sigma Tau Gamma. Polit. & Govt. Pos: Ohio State Rep, Third Dist, 69- Bus. & Prof. Pos: Sec. teacher, Brown Co. Sch. Dist, Ind, 54-56 and Franklin Monroe Sch. Dist, Darke Co, Ohio, 56-57. Mem: Ohio Educ. Asn; Ohio and Darke Co. Coaches Asns; Southwest Ohio and Darke Co. Teachers Asns. Rel: United Methodist. Mailing Add: 503 W. First, Arcanum, Ohio 45304.

OLIVER, RAY D
Chmn, Montgomery Co. Dem. Party, Mo.
b. Montgomery City, Mo, 7/26/06; s. E.S. Oliver and Sallie J. Bosley O; m. 6/14/41 to Vera Virginia Tate; c. Barbara Jen (Mrs. March) and Thomas Ray. Educ: High sch. Polit. & Govt. Pos: Chmn, Montgomery Co. Dem. Party, Mo, 64- Bus. & Prof. Pos: Self-employed. Mil. Serv: Army, 41. Mem: Kiwanis. Rel: Baptist. Mailing Add: 615 N. State, Montgomery City, Mo. 63361. (1967)

OLIVER, ROBERT G. D
Conn. State Rep.
b. San Diego, Calif, 6/5/40; s. Robert John Oliver and Esmeralda Godfrey O; m. 1/27/68 to Barbara A. Cooney. Educ: Yale Univ, B.A. magna cum laude, 62, Yale Law Sch, LL.B, 65. Polit. & Govt. Pos: Mem, First Ward Dem. Cmt, Conn, 61-69; alderman, First Ward New Haven, 65-67; Conn. State Rep, 104th Dist, 66- Bus. & Prof. Pos: Attorney at law, Daggett, Colby & Hooker, Conn, currently. Mil. Serv: Coast Guard Res, 65-67; Naval Res, 67-, Lt. Mem: New Haven Co. Bar Asn; Knights St. Patrick; Off. Urban Affairs; Archdiocese Hartford (pres. bd. dirs); Dwight Area Asn; Hill Inter-Agency Coun. Rel: Roman Catholic. Legal Res: 55 Parmelee Ave, New Haven, Conn. 06510. Mailing Add: P.O. Box 603, New Haven, Conn. 06503.

OLIVER, STELLA GRACE R
V.Chmn, Phillips Co. Rep. Party, Colo.
b. Inland, Nebr, 10/17/93; d. Charles Eugene Ingalsbe and Mary Ardell Lee I; wid; c. Lois Stella (Mrs. Biddle) and Shirley Jeanne (Mrs. Peterson). Educ: Grammer Sch, West Inland, Nebr, 8 years; High Sch, Kennesaw, 1 semester. Polit. & Govt. Pos: Rep. Committeewoman, Seventh Precinct, Colo, 47, 49, 51, 53, 55, 57, 59, 61, & 63, and Precinct one, 65; v.chmn, Phillips Co. Rep. Party, Colo, 67- Mem: Eastern Star; Bus. and Prfnl. Women's Club; Phillips Co. Rep. Women's Club (pres); chmn, East Phillips Co. Cancer Crusade; organizer Phillips Co. Hist. Soc. & Mus; DAR. Rel: Methodist. Mailing Add: 440 S. Phelan Ave, Holyoke, Colo. 80734.

OLIVIER, CHARLES J. R
V.Chmn, Rockingham Co. Rep. Cmt, N.H.
b. N.Y.C, 9/27/14; s. Charles C. Olivier and Margaret Müller O; m. 10/1/38 to Helen Senko; c. Denise, Richard A. and Laurence C. Educ: Seamen's Inst. Navigation Sch. Polit. & Govt. Pos: Selectman, Chester, N.H, 56-65, mem. sch. bd, 65-68; chmn, Rockingham Co. Rep. Cmt, 67-68, v.chmn, 69- Bus. & Prof. Pos: Sales mgr, N.E. area, Wire Rope Mfg, 42- Mil. Serv: Entered as Pvt, Army, 33, released as Pfc, 36, after serv. in 27th and 18th Inf. Div. Mem: Lions; N.H. and Maine Good Roads Asns; New Eng. R.R. Club. Rel: Protestant. Mailing Add: Chester, N.H. 03036.

OLMERT, JOSEPH PHILLIP R
Chmn, Lee Co. Rep. Party, S.C.
b. Washington, D.C, 6/14/16; s. Joseph Peter Olmert and Catherine Gannon O; m. 7/15/44 to Jacqueline F. McCutchen; c. Joseph Phillip, Jr, Sarah Darrington, Henley McCutchen and Bryan Jenkins. Polit. & Govt. Pos: Chmn, Lee Co. Rep. Party, S.C, 63- Bus. & Prof. Pos: Mgr. feed opers, Bishopville Milling Co, 52-66. Mil. Serv: Entered as Pvt, Marine Corps, 45, released as Pvt. 1/C, 46. Mem: Past pres. and mem. bd. dirs, Bishopville Rotary. Silver Beaver Award, Boy Scouts. Rel: Presbyterian; Elder. Mailing Add: 222 S. Heyward, Bishopville, S.C. 29010. (1967)

OLRICH, FRANK EDWIN D
b. Oakland, Calif, 10/20/43; s. Dr. Frank Moore Olrich and Helen Zielasko O; m. 3/15/69 to Mary Michael Sommers; c. Jeanne Diane, Kelley Michelle and Anna Kathleen. Educ: Stanford Univ, A.B, 65 and M.A, 66; Phi Delta Kappa; Sigma Chi. Polit. & Govt. Pos: Campaign asst, Mark Sullivan for Cong, 66; legis. asst, Calif. State Legis, 67-; campaign asst, John Vasconcellos for Assembly, 68; alternate del, Dem. Nat. Conv, 68. Bus. & Prof. Pos: Asst. dean of fraternities, Stanford Univ, summer 66; intern in pub. affairs, Coro Found, 66-67. Mem: San Jose Jaycees; Stanford Alumni Asn. Rel: Protestant. Legal Res: 3230 Loma Verde Dr, San Jose, Calif. 95117. Mailing Add: 5949 Lake Crest Way, No. 8, Sacramento, Calif. 95822.

OLSEN, ARNOLD D
U.S. Rep, Mont.
b. Butte, Mont, 12/17/16; s. Albert Olsen (deceased) and Anna O; m. to Margaret Williams; c. Margaret Rae (Mrs. David Childs), Anna Kristine and Karen Synneve. Educ: Montana Sch. of Mines; Montana State Univ. Law Sch, LL.B; Phi Delta Phi. Polit. & Govt. Pos: Attorney Gen, Mont; U.S. Rep, Mont, 60-, mem, Pub. Works Cmt, Post Off. and Civil Serv. Cmt, and chmn, Postal Rates Cmt, U.S. House Rep. Bus. & Prof. Pos: Lawyer. Mil. Serv: Navy, World War II, 4 years overseas duty. Mem: Am. Legion; VFW; Am. Vet. of World War II; Silver Bow Lodge 48 AF&AM; Scottish Rite; Bagdad Temple of the Shrine; Scandinavian Fraternity of Am; Elks; Eagles. Legal Res: Helena, Mont. Mailing Add: 4244 50th St, Washington, D.C. 20016.

OLSEN, NEVA ARGALA R
V.Chmn, Ziebach Co. Rep. Party, S.Dak.
b. Opal, S.Dak, 11/30/25; d. Eldafanso Beltran Forrester and Mary Sophia Daugherty F; m. 7/23/47 to Edgar Alton Olsen; c. Erling Alton, Erdean Anson and Eulene Rae. Educ: Faith High Sch, grad. Polit. & Govt. Pos: Del, Rep. Nat. Conv, 64; mem. elec. bd, Redelm Precinct, S.Dak, 66 & 68; v.chmn, Ziebach Co. Rep. Party, 66- Bus. & Prof. Pos: Clerk, Kelly's Super Valu, 44-47. Mem: Farm Bur; Ziebach Co. Rep. Party; Ziebach Co. 4-H Leader's Asn; Bethel Ladies Aid. Rel: Lutheran. Mailing Add: Box 5C, Dupree, S.Dak. 57623.

OLSEN, RAY D
b. Baker, Ore, 1904; m. to Ellen O. Educ: Bus. Col. Polit. & Govt. Pos: Wash. State Rep, until 66; mem, Seattle Civic Center Cmn, presently; legis. aide to King Co. Coun, presently. Mem: Elks; Eagles; Wash. Athletic Club; Swedish Club. Mailing Add: 1400 Hubbell Pl, Apt. 710, Seattle, Wash. 98101.

OLSEN, VAN ROGER R
b. Sanish, N.Dak, 5/25/33; s. Oswald J. Olsen and Nettie E. Vanderhauf O; m. 9/20/58 to Myrna Louise Farroh; c. Matthew G. and Jennifer M. Educ: Univ. of Mont, B.A, 58; Phi Sigma Kappa. Polit. & Govt. Pos: Chmn, Cass Co. Young Rep, N.Dak, 62-63; info. dir, N.Dak. Rep. Party, 65; admin. asst. to U.S. Rep. Mark Andrews, N.Dak, 65- Bus. & Prof. Pos: Salesman, yellow pages, Northwest. Bell Tel. Co, Minneapolis, Minn, 58-59; sales prom. mgr, Farmhand Co, 59-60; acct. exec, Flint Advert. Agency, Fargo, N.Dak, 60-65. Mil. Serv: Entered as E-1, Army, 54, released as E-4, 55, after serv. in Vet. Serv. Corps, Hawaii, 14 months. Rel: Episcopal. Mailing Add: 622 Crocus Dr, Rockville, Md. 20850.

OLSON, ALEC GEHARD D
Minn. State Sen.
b. Mamre Twp, Kandiyohi Co, Minn, 9/11/30; s. Axel Gehard Olson and Florence R. Hoglund; m. 7/3/57 to Janice Ruth Albecht; c. Alan G, Dennis A, Deron Jon and Eric W. Educ: High Sch, grad, 48; U.S. Dept. Agr. Grad. Sch, course in econ, 67. Polit. & Govt. Pos: Co. Dem-Farmer-Labor Chmn, Kandiyohi Co, Minn, 54-57; Dem-Farmer-Labor Chmn, Seventh Cong. Dist, 58-62; U.S. Rep, Minn, 62-66; asst. to secy. agr, U.S. Dept. Agr, 67; del, Dem. Nat. Conv, 68; Minn. State Sen, 69- Bus. & Prof. Pos: Ins. rep, Nat. Farmers Union Serv. Corp, 54-62; account exec. with investment firm, Kelly & Morey, 69- Mem: Nat. Asn. of Security Dealers; Elks. Rel: Lutheran. Mailing Add: 1905 S.W. 5th St, Willmar, Minn. 56201.

OLSON, ALEX R
b. Sweden, 2/26/96; married; c. 4. Educ: High sch. Polit. & Govt. Pos: S.Dak. State Rep, 44-46, 62-66; S.Dak. State Sen, 48-52; former sch. bd. mem. and co. cmnr. Bus. & Prof. Pos: Retired farmer-stockman. Mem: Masonic Lodge; Oriental Consistory; El Riad Shrine. Rel: Presbyterian. Mailing Add: Martin, S.Dak. 57551. (1967)

OLSON, CURTIS R
N.Dak. State Auditor
b. Barnes Co, N.Dak, 3/26/09; m. to Violet Rassmuson; c. Two. Educ: Minneapolis Sch. of Bus. Polit. & Govt. Pos: Mem, State Water Conserv. Cmn, N.Dak, 10 years; mayor, Valley City, 8 years, past mem, Valley City Coun; N.Dak. State Rep, 40-44; N.Dak. State Auditor, 56- Bus. & Prof. Pos: Automobile and gasoline dealer in Valley City, 28-56. Mem: Mason; Elks. Rel: Congregational. Mailing Add: C/o State Capitol, Bismark, N.Dak. 58501.

OLSON, DAGNY V. R
Pres, N.Dak. Fedn. of Rep. Women
b. Maddock, N.Dak, 8/15/14; d. Bertheus Olson and Carolina Engen O; single. Educ: Minnewaukan High Sch, grad. Polit. & Govt. Pos: Reporter for N.Dak. Senate, ten sessions and 1 spec. session; chmn. fund raising events, Ramsey Co. Rep. Party, six years; pres, N.Dak. Fedn. of Rep. Women, 67-; del, Rep. Nat. Conv, 68. Bus. & Prof. Pos: Office Court Reporter, Second Judicial Dist. N.Dak, 49- Mem: Bus. and Prfnl. Women's Clubs of N.Dak; Nat. and N.Dak. Shorthand Reporters Asns. Elected N.Dak. Rep. Woman of the Year, 69. Rel: Lutheran. Mailing Add: Box 618, Devils Lake, N.Dak. 58301.

OLSON, DONALD WAYNE R
b. Eau Claire, Wis, 8/19/23; s. Melvin Oscar Olson and Agnes Fossum O; m. 11/29/59 to Theresa M. Gauthier. Educ: St. Olaf Col, B.A, 47; Univ. of Minn, M.A, 50; St. Paul Col. of Law, B.S.L, 56; Blue Key. Polit. & Govt. Pos: Motor transport inspector, Minn. R.R. & Warehouse Cmn, 50-53; res. asst, Minn. Legis. Res. Cmt, 53-56; legis. asst. to U.S. Sen. Edward J. Thye, 56-58; cong. liaison, U.S. Small Bus. Admin, 59-60; admin. asst. to U.S. Rep. Ancher Nelsen, Minn, 61- Mil. Serv: Entered as Pvt, Army Air Corps, 42, released as Flight Officer, 45, after serv. in Continental U.S. Mem: Past pres, Ravenwood Park Citizens Asn. and Minn. State Soc; St. Olaf Col. Alumni Club of Wash, D.C; Capitol Hill Club. Rel: Lutheran. Mailing Add: 6204 Colmac Dr, Falls Church, Va. 22044.

OLSON, FLORENCE MAY D
V.Chmn, N.Dak. Dem. Non-Partisan League
b. Enderlin, N.Dak, 5/28/20; d. Oswald Hjalmer Sveum and Clara Olson S; m. 9/24/39 to Dale Conroy Olson; c. Terry Dale and Kurt David. Educ: Enderlin Pub. Sch, 12 years. Polit. & Govt. Pos: Dem. precinct committeeman, Moore Twp, N.Dak, 58-; secy, Ransom Co. Women's Dem. Non-Partisan League, 60-62 and pres, 62-64; dist. dir, Dem. Non-Partisan League Women's Activities, 62-65; adv. and organizer, Ransom Co. Young Dem, 62-66; chmn, Ransom Co. Dem. Non-Partisan League Orgn, 62-68; chmn. in charge of tent mgt. and selling of novelties, Dem. Non-Partisan League, Plowville, N.Dak, 64; v.pres, N.Dak. Women's Dem. Non-Partisan League, 65-67; state chmn, Nat. Campaign Conf. Wash, D.C, and '4 for 66' Vol. Prog, 66; campaign rep, state cand. for labor, Earl Anderson, 66 and state cand. for secy. of state, Clara Wheelihan, 68; mem, state campaign cmt, 66 & 68; chmn. dist, 27 and regional dir, Dem. Non-Partisan League, 66-68; v.chmn, N.Dak. Dem. Non-Partisan League, 66-; del, Dem. Nat. Conv, 68; served on, Rural Vol. for Humphrey, 68. Mem: Royal Neighbors of Am; Moore Hustler Homemakers; Am. Legion Auxiliary; VFW Auxiliary. Rel: Lutheran. Mailing Add: Enderlin, N.Dak. 58027.

OLSON, GARY MILES R
Chmn, Skamania Co. Rep. Cent. Cmt, Wash.
b. Portland, Ore, 7/18/31; s. Reubin Alexander Olson and Greta Ehert O; single. Educ: Pac. Univ, 55-59, treas, Assoc. Students, 3 years; Intercollegiate Knights; Blue Key; Pi Delta Epsilon. Polit. & Govt. Pos: Committeeman, Cascade Precinct, Skamania Co, Wash, 65-; chmn, Skamania Co. Rep. Party, 66-; chmn, Skamania Co. Civil Serv. Cmn, 66-; chmn, Skamania Co. Rep. Cent. Cmt, 66- Bus. & Prof. Pos: Salesman, N.Y. Merchandise Co, Portland, Ore, 59- Mil. Serv: Entered as Seaman Recruit, Navy, 50, released as YN 3, 54, after serv. in Amphibious Force, USS LSM 161, Korean Conflict, 52-53; Good Conduct Medal; Nat. Defense Serv. Medal; UN Korean Serv, 2 stars; Korean Presidential Unit Citation. Rel: Protestant; Treas, North Bonneville Commun. Church, 10 years. Mailing Add: Box 97 R, North Bonneville, Wash. 98639.

OLSON, GILLMAN C. D
b. Cooperstown, N.Dak, 12/28/05; married; c. Four. Educ: Pub. Schs. Polit. & Govt. Pos: N.Dak. State Rep, 55-66. Bus. & Prof. Pos: Farmer and livestock trucker. Mem: Griggs Co. Livestock Asn; Farmers Union Livestock Truckers Asn. Mailing Add: Route 1, Cooperstown, N.Dak. 58425. (1967)

OLSON, JACK R. R
Lt. Gov, Wis.
b. Kilbourn, Wis, 8/29/20; s. Grover Olson and Jane Zimmerman O; m. to Eleanor Lang; c. Jill and Sally. Educ: Univ. of Wis, 38-39; West. Mich. Univ, B.S, 42. Polit. & Govt. Pos: Chmn, Columbia Co. Rep. Party, Wis, 57-60; Wis. State chmn, Vol. for Nixon, 63-64; Lt. Gov, Wis, 63-64 & 67- Bus. & Prof. Pos: Pres, Wis. Vacationland Coun, 52-57; dir, Bur. of Bus. Reserach, Univ. Hawaii, 61; dir, Wis. Trade Mission to Europe, 64; exec. chmn, Wis. World's Fair Participation Corp, 64-65; official rep, Wis. European Trade Mission, 65; mgr, Olson Boat Co, Wisconsin Dells. Mil. Serv: Entered as Enlisted man, Navy, 42, released as Lt.(jg), 46, after serv. in N. Atlantic. Mem: Pres, North. Great Lakes Area Coun, 58; dir, Wis. Good Roads. Asn. and West. Mich. Univ. Alumni Asn; Wis. State chmn, March of Dimes, 65-66; Am. Legion; dir, Wisconsin Dells C. of C. Mem, West. Mich. Univ. undefeated and united football team, 41; Distinguished Alumnus Award, West. Mich. Univ, 64. Rel: Presbyterian. Legal Res: 834 Meadow Lane, Wisconsin Dells, Wis. 53965. Mailing Add: State Capitol, Madison, Wis. 53702. (1967)

OLSON, JEROME ARNOLD R
Chmn, Lake of the Woods Co. Rep. Cmt, Minn.
b. Dunn Co, N.Dak, 6/13/14; s. Carl Peter Olson and Emma Wisted O; m. 5/29/42 to Barbara Ella Watson; c. Carl, Stuart and Clare. Educ: High Sch. Polit. & Govt. Pos: Chmn, Lake of the Woods Co. Rep. Cmt, Minn, 58- Mil. Serv: Entered as A/S, Navy, 42, released as A.E.M. 1/C, 45, after serv. in ETO; Good Conduct Medal; ETO Ribbon. Mem: Am. Legion; Farm Bureau. Rel: Lutheran. Mailing Add: North Route, Williams, Minn. 56686.

OLSON, JOHN L.
Minn. State Sen.
b. Worthington, Minn, 1906; married; c. Four. Educ: Nobles Co. Pub. Schs. Polit. & Govt. Pos: Minn. State Sen, 58- Bus. & Prof. Pos: Livestock farmer; 2 terms, Adv. Coun, Inst. of Agr, Univ. Minn. Mem: Past pres, Minn. Swine Producers Asn; exec. cmt. and past pres, Minn. Livestock Breeders Asn; 29 years, supt, Sunday Sch, First Lutheran Church of Worthington; secy. of churchmen, Lutheran Church of Am. Portrait in Minn. Livestock Hall of Fame. Rel: Lutheran. Mailing Add: Route 2, Box 13, Worthington, Minn. 56187.

OLSON, KATHLEEN W. 'KAY' R
V.Chmn, Mellette Co. Rep. Party, S.Dak.
b. Wood, S.Dak, 2/22/27; d. James Harlan Danker and Theresa Cordes D; m. 7/18/51 to Eugene R. Olson; c. Warren E, Dale W. and Barbara K. Educ:

Univ. of S.Dak, B.S, 50; Alpha Xi Delta. Polit. & Govt. Pos: Secy, Mellette Co. Rep. Party, S.Dak, 53-60 and v.chmn, 60-; del, Rep. State Conv, 66. Mem: Eastern Star; Am. Legion Auxiliary; Gen. Fedn. of Women's Clubs. Rel: Methodist. Mailing Add: White River, S.Dak. 57579.

OLSON, KENNETH C. D
b. Rock Springs, Wyo, 12/12/37; s. Clarence E. Olson and Bessie Day O; m. 12/21/60 to Linda A. Massey; c. Kristal F, Eric K. and Mark K. Educ: Univ. Utah, 5 yrs. Polit. Pos: Utah State Rep, 65-67; del, Voting Dist, 65. Bus. & Prof. Pos: Dir, Special Serv, Bd. Educ, Salt Lake City, presently. Exchange student to Germany; Am. Field Serv. Prog. Rel: Church of Jesus Christ of Latter Day Saint. Mailing Add: 3856 Lee Maur St, Salt Lake City, Utah 84119. (1967)

OLSON, LESLIE O. R
b. Bethune, Col, 8/13/28; s. Oscar A. Olson and Iva May Rowbotham O; m. 6/15/58 to Anne Marie Granieri; c. Leslie Anne, Michael Douglas and Lynda Marie. Educ: Univ. of Nebr, 53-54; Univ. of Colo, 55; West. State Col. of Colo, B.A, 57; Lambda Delta Lambda; Kappa Delta Mu; West State Col. Vet. Asn. Polit. & Govt. Pos: Cand, U.S. Rep, Dist. Four, Mo, 68. Bus. & Prof. Pos: Field engr, defense projs. div, West. Elec. Co, Concord Mass, Grand Forks, N.Dak. and Montgomery, Ala, 57-61, planning engr, mfg. div, Lee's Summit, Mo, 61-69. Mil. Serv: Entered as Pvt, Marine Corps, 48, released as S/Sgt, 52, after serv. in First Marine Air Wing, Korean Theatre, 50-51; Good Conduct Medal; Presidential Unit, Army Unit and Korean Presidential Unit Citations; Korean Serv. and UN Serv. Medals. Mem: Inst. of Elec. and Electronic Engrs; registered prfnl. engr, Mo; Kiwanis Int; Lee's Summit Club; VFW; Lee's Summit Rep. Club; bd. of dirs, Lee's Summit Hosp. Asn; bd. of dirs, Heart of Am. United Fund; exec. Cmt, Jackson Co. United Fund; Jackson Co. Hist. Soc. Rel: Protestant. Mailing Add: 820 Pleasant Dr, Lee's Summit, Mo. 64063.

OLSON, MAURICE ALAN D
Chmn, Day Co. Dem. Party, S.Dak.
b. Pierpont, S.Dak, 4/8/26; s. Olen Enger Olson and Alice Moe O; m. 6/30/50 to Mildred Aileen Erickson; c. Debra Ann, Cynthia Ruth, Barbara Louise, Jerald Keith and Ronald Mark. Educ: Pierpont & Langford High Sch, grad; Augustana Col, S.Dak, 48-49; Kappa Theta Phi. Polit. & Govt. Pos: Precinct committeeman, Egeland Precinct, S.Dak, 60-64; chmn, Day Co. Dem. Party, 66- Mil. Serv: Entered as Pfc, Army, 50, released as Sgt, 52, after serv. in 196 Regimental Combat Team, Alaska, 51-52; Good Conduct Medal. Mem: Nat. Farmers Union; Nat. Farmers Orgn; Am. Legion. Rel: Lutheran. Legal Res: R.R. 2, Waubay, S.Dak. 57273.

OLSON, RICHARD CARL D
b. St. Paul, Minn, 9/13/22; s. Eric Lawrence Olson and Thelma Lydia Augustine O; m. 11/1/47 to Patricia L. Pushor; c. Paul (deceased), Mark, Thomas, Melissa and Jeffrey. Educ: Univ. Ariz, B.A. Polit. & Govt. Pos: Dist. secy, U.S. Rep. Stewart L. Udall, Ariz, 55-60; legis. asst, U.S. Rep. Morris K. Udall, Ariz, 61-68, exec. asst, 69- Bus. & Prof. Pos: Reporter, city ed, Tucson Daily Citizen, 50-55; pub. rels. consult, Richard Olson & Assoc, 55-61. Mil. Serv: Navy, Pac. Theater. Mem: Sigma Chi; chmn, Tucson Cmn. on Human Rels. Legal Res: Tucson, Ariz. Mailing Add: 1807 Mt. Pleasant Dr, McLean, Va. 22101.

OLSON, ROBERT CHARLES R
b. Minneapolis, Minn, 7/3/34; s. Charles Joseph Olson, Jr. and Margaret Nelson O; m. 7/31/53 to Marjorie Marie Heutmaker; c. Wendy Anne, Thomas Robert, Paul Joseph and Anne Marie. Educ: Univ. Minn, Exten. Div, 56-62. Polit. & Govt. Pos: Mem, Winona Co. Rep. Cmt, Minn, 63-, chmn, 65-67. Bus. & Prof. Pos: Mgr, N.W. Bell Tel. Co, 62-67; instr, Am. Inst. Banking, 64-; gen. mgr, Technigraph Corp, currently. Mil. Serv: Entered as Recruit, Naval Air Res, 52, released as PO 3/C, 60, after serv. in Air Support Squadron SF 612. Mem: Dir, Winona Rotary, 65-; chmn, gov. affairs cmt, Winona C. of C, 64-66; pres, bd. dirs, Winona Jr. Achievement, 63-65; pres. and bd. of dirs, Winona Commun. Chest. Rel: Catholic. Mailing Add: 479 Olmstead, Winona, Minn. 55987.

OLSON, VERN FRANK R
Chmn, Chippewa Co. Rep. Cmt, Minn.
b. Buffalo, Minn, 7/23/24; s. Frank Olson and Elvera Nelson O; m. 7/26/46 to Shirley Trovatten; c. Kristine, Kirk and Lee. Educ: Purdue Univ, 43-44; Cornell Univ, 44; Univ. Minn, B.S, 49, D.V.M, 51; A.G.R. Polit. & Govt. Pos: Chmn, Chippewa Co. Rep. Cmt, Minn, 68- Mailing Add: Box 280, Clara City, Minn. 56222.

OLSON, WAYNE H. DFL
b. Swanville. Educ: Macalester Col; Univ. of Minn. Law Sch. Polit. & Govt. Pos: Dep. attorney gen. under Miles Lord; chief dep. under Walter F. Mondale, conserv. cmnr, 60-63; state chmn, Young Dem-Farmer-Labor, 65. Bus. & Prof. Pos: Lawyer. Mil. Serv: 5th Air Force, Navigator, Pac. Theater. Mailing Add: 2043 Bayard Ave, St. Paul, Minn. 55116. (1967)

OLSON, WESLIE W. R
b. Isanti, Minn, 2/23/03; s. Olof L. Olson and Amanda Soderstrom O. (both deceased); m. 11/2/40 to Loraine Helen Branson; c. Ronald Wesley and Eugene Randall. Educ: Univ. of Chicago; Univ. of Minn, B.B.A, 32; Pershing Rifles; bus. mgr. and publisher, Soc. Dir. and Who's Who in the Twin Cities, 33. Polit. & Govt. Pos: Mayor, Quincy, Ill, 61-69; chmn, Cent. Ill. Expressway Cmt, 63-; mem, Civil Defense Adv. Bd, Ill, 64- Bus. & Prof. Pos: Gen. credit mgr, Gardner-Denver Co, Quincy, Ill, 39-42; asst. dir. acct, Am. Red. Cross, S. Pac, 42-46; dist. mgr, Equitable Life Assurance Soc, Quincy, Ill, 46-50; Pontiac dealer, Louisiana, Mo, 50-57; mgr, Home Builders Dept, Gem City Elec. Co, Quincy, Ill, 58-61. Mil. Serv: Nat. Guard; Medal of Freedom from Gen. MacArthur for work in New Guinea and Philippines for Am. Red Cross. Mem: Hon. mem, High Twelve and Toastmasters; bd. dirs, Toastmaster Int, 48; life mem, Univ. Minn. Alumni Asn. and Optimists Int; Elks; Moose; Mason; Blue Lodge, Shriners, Jesters; Ill. Police Asn; Ill. Sheriff's Asn; Navy League; Capitol Hill Club; past pres, Ill. Munic. League and Tri-State Mayors Asn. Hon. Mayor, Mooseheart; Ky. Col; Adm, Nebr. Navy. Rel: Congregational. Mailing Add: 3210 Crestview Dr, Quincy, Ill. 62301.

OLSSON, ELEANOR R
V.Chmn, Allegan Co. Rep. Exec. Cmt, Mich.
b. Elberta, Ala, 5/19/31; m. 9/8/56 to James Olsson; c. Carol and James. Polit. & Govt. Pos: Precinct del. and chmn; v.chmn, Allegan Co. Exec. Cmt, Mich, currently; v.pres, Women's Rep. Club. Bus. & Prof. Pos: Statist—gathering info. and figures for scheduling, planning and projecting. Mem: Secy, PTA, 2 years and coun, 3 years; treas, W.Mich. PTA Conf, 2 years; bd. mem, DeGraaf Nature Center; vol, Head Start Day Care Center; Sch. Room Mother. Rel: Congregational; Choir mem, 18 years, chmn, Church Circle, 2 years. Mailing Add: 89 E. 37th St, Holland, Mich. 49423.

OLVER, JOHN WALTER D
Mass. State Rep.
b. Honesdale, Pa, 9/3/36; s. T. Horace Olver and Helen Fulleborn O; m. 9/12/59 to Rose Alice Richardson. Educ: Rensselaer Polytech. Inst, B.S, 55; Mass. Inst. Tech, Ph.D, 61; Sigma Xi; Phi Lambda Upsilon. Polit. & Govt. Pos: Mass. State Rep, Second Hampshire Dist, 69- Bus. & Prof. Pos: Instr, Mass. Inst. Tech, 61-62; asst. prof, Univ. Mass, Amherst, 62-69. Publ: 14 articles in chem, anal. research jour. Mem: Am. Chem. Soc; Electrochem. Soc. Legal Res: 1333 West St, Amherst, Mass. 01002. Mailing Add: Box 699 Amherst, Mass. 01002.

O'MALLEY, BERNARD JOHN D
b. Des Moines, Iowa, 9/20/37; s. George Edward O'Malley and Grace Johnson O; m. 5/2/64 to Loni J. Jonins;c. Christine, Linda and Diane. Educ: Creighton Univ, A.B, 59, J.D, 61; Delta Theta Phi. Polit. & Govt. Pos: Iowa State Rep, Polk Co, 65-68, asst. minority floor leader, 67-68. Bus. & Prof. Pos: Assoc. Law Firm, Connolly, O'Malley and Conley, 61- Mem: Am, Iowa and Polk Co. Bar Asn; K. of C. Rel: Catholic. Mailing Add: 4101 39th St. Place, Des Moines, Iowa 50310.

O'MALLEY, DAVID DONALD D
Wis. State Assemblyman
b. Waunakee, Wis, 11/12/12; s. Thomas P. O'Malley and Martha Monks O; wid; c. Thomas Patrick, Maureen and David, Jr. Educ: Univ. Wis, 36-38. Polit. & Govt. Pos: Wis. State Assemblyman, 59-; treas, Dave Co. Dem. Statutory Cmt, currently. Rel: Catholic. Mailing Add: 315 W. Main, Waunakee, Wis. 53597. (1967)

O'MALLEY, GEORGE E. D
Iowa State Sen.
b. Bouton, Iowa, 9/18/05; m. 1933 to Grace Johnson; c. George, Jr, Bernard, Jean, John, Dennis, Richard, Brian, Kathleen, Michael and Joseph. Educ: Creighton Univ, A.B. and LL.B, 30. Polit. & Govt. Pos: Chief enforcement attorney, Iowa Price Admin, World War II; Iowa State Sen, 49-, Minority Leader, Iowa State Senate, 55th-58th Gen. Assemblies, former Pres. Pro Tem; del, Dem. Nat. Conv, 68. Bus. & Prof. Pos: Farmer, Dallas Co; attorney. Mem: Former State Dep, K. of C. of Iowa; Boy Scouts; C. of C; Kiwanis; state co-chmn, Nat. Conf. of Christians and Jews. Mailing Add: 420 Royal Union Bldg, Des Moines, Iowa 50309. (1967)

O'MEARA, GEORGE F, JR. D
State Committeeman, Mass. Dem. Party
b. Lowell, Mass, 6/29/21; s. George F. O'Meara and Clara T. Mahoney O; m. 1/26/56 to Estelle R. Paguette; c. George F, III, Mary K. Peskouitz and Mark S. Educ: Lowell High Sch, 39. Polit. & Govt. Pos: State committeeman, Mass. Dem. Party, 64-; city coun, Lowell, Mass, 65-68; alternate del, Dem. Nat. Conv, 68; fed-state liaison officer, Gr. Lowell Area Planning Cmn, currently. Rel: Roman Catholic. Mailing Add: 521 Rogers St, Lowell, Mass. 01852.

OMHOLT, ELMER V. R
State Auditor, Mont.
b. Great Falls, Mont, 3/29/20; s. Kristian Omholt and Ellen W. Johnson O; m. 12/22/46 to Audrey Mae Haralson; c. Kris Henry and Myrna Ellen. Educ: North. Mont. Col, 38-40. Polit. & Govt. Pos: Justice of peace, Teton Co, Mont, 50; Mont. State Rep, Teton Co, 51-55, chmn, Workmen's Compensation and Engrossing Cmts, Mont. House of Rep, v.chmn, Mil. Affairs Cmt, mem, Fish and Game Cmt. and Banking and Ins. Cmt; mayor, Dutton, Mont, 58; past mem, Teton Co. Juvenile Court Bd; state ins. cmnr, investment cmnr. and fire marshal, 62-; State Auditor, Mont, 62- Bus. & Prof. Pos: In auto implement bus, 45-50; with gen. ins. agency, 50-62. Mil. Serv: Entered as Pvt, Army, 40, released as 1st Lt, 45, after serv. in 34th Inf. Div, European-African Theater; Purple Heart. Mem: Fedn. of Ins. Coun; pres, Dutton Chap, Am. Red Cross; dist. comdr, Am. Legion, 48; DAV; Retired Officers Asn. Rel: Lutheran. Mailing Add: 915 12th Ave, Helena, Mont. 98601.

OMOHUNDRO, BAXTER HARRISON R
Dir. of Pub. Info, Dept. of Health, Educ. and Welfare
b. Denver, Colo, 12/27/25; s. Baxter Allen Omohundro and Mary Ferree O; m. 12/30/44 to Shirley Arlese Spruill; c. Sue Carol (Mrs. Ronald Goble), Baxter Allen, Patricia (Mrs. Thomas Williams) and Janet Lee. Educ: El Camino Col. Polit. & Govt. Pos: Dir. of Pub. Info, Dept. of Health, Educ. and Welfare, 69- Bus. & Prof. Pos: Reporter-photographer, Long Beach Independent Press-Tel, 48-57, regional bur. chief, 57-61, city ed, 61-64; Wash. correspondent, Ridder Newspapers, 64-69. Mil. Serv: Entered as A/S, Navy, 43, released as Yeoman 2/C, 46, after serv. in Landing Ship, Tank Flotilla 36 Staff, Asiatic-Pac. Theatre, 45. Mem: Nat. Press and Capitol Hill Clubs. Rel: Protestant. Mailing Add: 3134 W. Ox Rd, Herndon, Va. 22070.

O'NEAL, DUDLEY LEE, JR. D
b. Andalusia, Ala, 1/13/24; s. Dudley L. O'Neal (deceased) and Mary Louise Perrenot O; m. 9/15/51 to Mildred E. Johns; c. Dudley L, III, Lizabeth P. and Francis W. J. Educ: The Citadel, 41-43; Univ. Ala, A.B, 47, Univ. of Ala. Law Sch, LL.B, 50; Kappa Sigma; Phi Delta Phi. Polit. & Govt. Pos: Attorney, Dept. Justice, 51; criminal investr, Fed. Housing Admin, 53-54; trial attorney, Civil Serv. Cmn, 54-55; asst. counsel. subcmt. housing, U.S. Sen, 55-61, co-staff dir. and chief counsel, 61-69, and staff dir. and gen. counsel, banking and currency cmt, 69- Bus. & Prof. Pos: Lawyer, Andalusia, Ala, 50-51. Mil. Serv: Entered as Pvt, Army Corps Engrs, 43, released as Capt, 46, after serv. in Sixth Army Hq, Southwest Pac. Theatre, 44-46; recalled as Capt, 51-52, served in 866 Engr. ANV Bn; Bronze Star with Oak Leaf Cluster; Legion

of Merit; Army Commendation Medal with Two Oak Leaf Clusters. Mem: VFW; WOW. Rel: Episcopal; Trustee, St. Thomas Episcopal Church. Legal Res: Andalusia, Ala. 36240. Mailing Add: 8611 Dixie Place, McLean, Va. 22101.

O'NEAL, JOHN BARNWELL D
Mem, Ga. State Dem. Exec. Cmt.
b. Blackshear, Ga, 10/22/20; s. John B. O'Neal, Jr. and Carol Anita Nelson O; m. 2/25/45 to Phyllis Johnson; c. Patricia, Pamela, John, IV and Peggy. Educ: Univ. Ga, B.S; Med. Col. Ga, M.D. Polit. & Govt. Pos: Mayor, Elberton, Ga, 54-56; mem, Gov. Cmn. Efficiency and Econ. in Govt, 62-66; del, Dem. Nat. Conv, 64; mem, Ga. State Dem. Exec. Cmt, currently. Bus. & Prof. Pos: Dir, First Nat. Bank, Elberton, Ga; pres, Elberton Civic Center, 67- Mil. Serv: Entered as 1st Lt, Army, 45, released as Capt, 48, after serv. in Med. Corps. Mem: Med. Asn. of Ga; Am. Med. Asn; Am. Soc. Abdominal Surgeons; pres, Elberton C. of C, 63-65; Rotary Club Elberton (pres, 69-70); dir, Citizens Cmt. Reorgn. State Legis, 68-69. Rel: Methodist. Mailing Add: 33 Chestnut St, Elberton, Ga. 30635.

O'NEAL, MASTON EMMETT, JR. D
U.S. Rep, Ga.
b. Bainbridge, Ga, 7/19/07; s. Maston Emmett O'Neal and Bessie Birch Matthews O; m. 6/4/34 to Mary Charlotte Tyson; c. Susan Charlotte (Mrs. Jerry M. Bowden) and Maston Emmett, III. Educ: Marion Mil. Inst, A.A, 25; Davidson Col, A.B, 27; Emory Univ. Law Sch; Pi Kappa Alpha. Polit. & Govt. Pos: Solicitor gen, Albany Judicial Circuit, Ga, 40-64; U.S. Rep, Second Dist, Ga, 64- Mil. Serv: Entered as Seaman, Navy, 44, released as Lt, 46, after serv. in Pac; Asiatic-Pac. Campaign Medal with Battle Star; Navy Occupation Serv. Medal with ASA Clasp; Am. Campaign Medal; Victory Medal. Mem: Am. and Ga. Bar Asns; pres, Solicitors Gen. Asn. of Ga; dir, Nat. Asn. of Co. & Prosecuting Attorneys; Scottish Rite; Mason; Am. Legion; VFW; Am. Farm Bur. Fedn; Ga. and Fla. Hist. Socs; Bainbridge Country Club. Rel: Presbyterian; Moderator, Presbytery of Southwest Ga. Legal Res: 805 Alice St, Bainbridge, Ga. 31717. Mailing Add: 453 Cannon House Office Bldg, Washington, D.C. 20515. (1967)

O'NEIL, C. MICHAEL D
b. Keene, N.H, 9/12/40; married; c. one. Educ: Northwest. Univ; Keene State Col; presently attending Keene State Col. majoring in Govt. and Econ. Polit. & Govt. Pos: N.H. State Rep, -67; Selectman, Ward I. Rel: Catholic. Mailing Add: 17 Gardner St, Keene, N.H. 03431. (1967)

O'NEIL, FRANK M. D
b. New York, 10/2/06; s. Patrick Henry O'Neil and Ailean Steward O; m. to Lois Decker. Educ: Hamilton Col, B.A. Polit. & Govt. Pos: Pa. State Rep, 54, 58, 64-67; mem. bd. of dirs. of Red Cross; pres, Du Bois Area Develop. Coun; chmn, Non-Partisan Get Out-and-Vote Campaign; dir, civil defense; pres, Young Dems; rep. Auditor Gen's. Dept; mem. Pa. Bur. Traffic Safety representing the Gov's. Traffic Safety Coun. Mil. Serv: Air Force, overseas. Mem: Chmn, fund drs; treas, Du Bois Blood Bank; pres, Du Bois Lions Club; mem. of other fraternal and soc. orgns; past comdr, Am. Legion; cmt. mem. Nat. Am. Legion; mem. and legis. officer, VFW. Rel: Methodist. Mailing Add: 421 Garfield Ave, Du Bois, Pa. 15801. (1967)

O'NEIL, JAMES E. R
N.H. State Rep.
b. N.Y.C, 1/22/21; married; c. Four. Educ: Univ. N.H. Polit. & Govt. Pos: Moderator, Sch. Bd, N.H; N.H. State Rep, 59-; mem, N.H. Rep. State Cent. Cmt, 68- Bus. & Prof. Pos: Sch. consult. Mil. Serv: Aviation Topographic Engrs, Pac. Rel: Protestant. Mailing Add: Box 151, Chesterfield, N.H. 03443. (1967)

O'NEILL, ALYSE STERN R
State Committeewoman, Fla. Rep. Party
b. Phila, Pa, 9/8/24; d. Arthur Hartman Stern and Frances Fox S; m. 3/7/58 to Paul Joseph O'Neill; c. Pamela J, Barton J, Paul J, Jr. and Paige J. Educ: Phila. Bus. Sch, grad, 43; Univ. Pa, 43. Polit. & Govt. Pos: Pres, Biscayne Women's Rep. Club, Fla, 64-66; campaign activities chmn, Fla. Fedn. Rep. Women, 64-66, finance chmn, 66-67; state committeewoman, Fla. Rep. Party, Dade Co, 66-; Rep. cand, Fla. State Rep, 67; del, Rep. Nat. Conv, 68; finance chmn, Riviera Women's Rep. Club, Miami, currently; v.chmn, Dist. 11, Rep. Exec. State Cmt. of Fla, currently; chmn, Rep. Women's Action Coun, 69- Bus. & Prof. Pos: Pvt. secy. to attorney, Maximillian J. Klinger, 43; registr. at sch, Pa. Inst, 49-50. Mem: PTA; Retarded Children; Children's Serv. Bur; charter mem, Am. for Constitutional Actions. Rel: Jewish. Mailing Add: 1260 N.E. 97th St, Miami Shores, Fla. 33138.

O'NEILL, C. WILLIAM R
Justice, Ohio Supreme Court
b. Marietta, Ohio, 2/14/16; s. Charles Thompson O'Neill and Jessie Arnold O; m. 7/29/45 to Betty Estelle Hewson; c. Charles William and Peggy. Educ: Marietta Col, A.B, 38; Ohio State Univ. Col. Law, LL.B, 42; Phi Beta Kappa; Pi Kappa Delta; Delta Upsilon. Hon. L.H.D, Marietta Col, 53; hon. LL.D, Defiance Col, 53, Ohio Univ, W.Va. Univ, Steubenville Col. and Miami Univ, 57, Wilberforce Univ. and Heidelberg Col, 58. Polit. & Govt. Pos: Pres, Wash. Co. Young Rep. Club, Ohio, 38; Ohio State Rep, 39-50, speaker, Ohio House of Rep, 47-48 and minority leader, 49-50; chmn, Ohio State Rep. Conv, 48; attorney gen, Ohio, 51-56, Gov, 57-58; del, Rep. Nat. Conv, 52 & 56, v.chmn. Ohio del, 56; justice, Ohio Supreme Court, 60- Mil. Serv: Entered as Pvt, Army, 43, released as S/Sgt, 46, after serv. in 976th Engrs, ETO, 44-45; Normandy Campaign and Battle of the Bulge Ribbons. Mem: Am, Ohio State, Columbus and Wash. Co. Bar Asns; pres, Marietta Col. Alumni Asn, 47-48; pres, Ohio State Univ. Col. of Law Asn; bd. trustees, Delta Upsilon Educ. Found; Am. Legion; VFW; Amvets; Grange; Elks; bd. dirs, Univ. Club; Mason; Shrine; Scottish Rite; York Rite; K. of P; Odd Fellows; Rebekahs; YMCA (v.pres. nat. coun); bd. trustees, Riverside Hosp. One of Ten Outstanding Young Men in the U.S, 51. Rel: First Community Church; Mem. bd. of gov. Mailing Add: 1560 London Dr, Columbus, Ohio 43221.

O'NEILL, HENRY MARTIN, JR. R
Treas, Ohio Rep. Finance Cmt.
b. Columbus, Ohio, 3/6/35; s. Henry Martin O'Neill, Sr. and Jane Downey O; m. 11/28/64 to Patricia Griffin Kelley; c. Kelley Patricia and Shane Downey. Educ: Ohio State Univ, B.S, 57; Beta Theta Pi. Polit. & Govt. Pos: Chmn. Franklin Co. Div, Ohio Rep. Finance Cmt, 65-, treas, 68-; del, Rep. Nat. Conv, 68. Mil. Serv: Entered as 2nd Lt, Army, 57, released as 1st Lt, 60, after serv. in First Cavalry Div, Far East, Korea, 57-60; Ohio Nat. Guard, Capt, 60- Named One of the Ten Most Outstanding Young Men of the Year, Jr. C. of C, 63 & 67, Recipient of SPOKE Award for Outstanding First Year Jaycee. Rel: Roman Catholic. Mailing Add: 138 S. Parkview Ave, Columbus, Ohio 43209.

O'NEILL, JAMES JOSEPH D
State Committeeman, Mass. Dem. Party
b. Lawrence, Mass, 3/20/27; s. William A. O'Neill and Mary E. Creeley O; m. 6/3/50 to Mary H. Coupe; c. William A, James J, Jr. and Joseph L. Educ: Merrimack Col, N.Andover, Mass, 47-51. Polit. & Govt. Pos: Alderman and dir. pub. property and parks, Lawrence, Mass, 64-; state committeeman, Fifth Essex, Mass. Dem. Party, 69- Mil. Serv: Entered as A/S, Navy, 44, released as Seaman 1/C, 46. Mem: Pres, Little League Boosters and S.Lawrence Little League; Lawrence British Club; Fifth Essex Social and Dem. Lodge; LaSalle Club; Elks; K. of C; Am. Legion. Rel: Catholic. Legal Res: 558 S. Union St, Lawrence, Mass. 01841. Mailing Add: Room 201, City Hall, 200 Common St, Lawrence, Mass. 01840.

O'NEILL, JOSEPH THOMAS R
Minn. State Rep.
b. St. Paul, Minn, 11/13/31; s. Joseph Thomas O'Neill and Marie Agnes O'Connell O; m. 9/11/54 to Marianne Kenefick; c. Kathleen, Joseph, Maureen, Thomas, John, Michael and Kevin. Educ: Univ. Notre Dame, B.A, 53; Univ. Minn. Col. of Law, LL.B, 56. Polit. & Govt. Pos: Minn. State Rep, 67- Bus. & Prof. Pos: Partner, O'Neill, Burke & O'Neill, presently. Mil. Serv: Entered as Lt, Air Force, 56, released as 1st Lt, 59, after serv. in Judge Adv. Br, Mil. Air Transport Serv; Capt, Air Force Res. Mem: Fed, Am, Minn. State and Ramsey Co. Bar Asns; Am. Judicature Soc; Jr. Chamber Int. Sen; pres, St. Paul Jr. C. of C, 64-65. Rel: Roman Catholic. Mailing Add: 1381 Summit Ave, St. Paul, Minn. 55105.

O'NEILL, NORRIS LAWRENCE D
Conn. State Rep.
b. Newark, N.J, 5/26/26; s. Phillip A. O'Neill and Ellen Leary O; m. 8/5/50 to Shelagh Heffernan; c. Megan and Gunning. Educ: Brown Univ, 46-48; Rutgers Law Sch, LL.B, 51. Polit. & Govt. Pos: Conn. State Rep, 67- Bus. & Prof. Pos: Partner, O'Neill, Steinberg and Lapuk, Attorneys, Hartford and secy, Motorlease Corp, Farmington, currently. Mil. Serv: Entered as Pvt, Army, 44, released as Pfc, 46. Mem: Hartford Co, Conn. and Am. Bar Asns; dir, Community Renewal Team, 63-67; pres, Greater Hartford Urban League, 63-67; dir, Neighborhood Legal Serv, 66-; dir, Greater Hartford Community Coun, 66- Rel: Roman Catholic. Legal Res: 202 Terry Rd, Hartford, Conn. 06105. Mailing Add: 50 State St, Hartford, Conn. 06105.

O'NEILL, OREN GEORGE D
b. Rapid City, S.Dak, 4/18/29; s. George F. O'Neill and Lucille Lewis O; m. to Vinita Jean Mayberry; c. Jo Ann (Mrs. Fletcher), Stanley, Shawn and Oren David. Educ: Long Beach City Col, A.A, 48; Univ. Calif, Los Angeles, B.A, 50, M.A, 52 and J.D, 55. Polit. & Govt. Pos: Mem, Calif. Dem. State Cent. Cmt, until 69. Bus. & Prof. Pos: Private law practice, Gardena and Porterville, Calif, 56-; dep. dist. attorney, Tulare Co, Calif, 59-61 and dep. pub. defender, 63-69. Mem: West. Econ. Asn; Nat. Legal Aid and Pub. Defenders Asn; Am. and Calif. Trial Lawyers Asns; Calif. Pub. Defenders Asn. Admitted to practice before the U.S. Supreme Court. Rel: Catholic. Legal Res: 345 North E St, Porterville, Calif. 93257. Mailing Add: 16 W. Oak Ave, Porterville, Calif. 93257.

O'NEILL, PAUL JOSEPH R
b. Pleasantville, N.J, 2/16/13; s. Paul J. O'Neill, Sr. and Kathryn Veronica Henderson O; m. 3/7/58 to Alyse Stern; c. Paul, Jr. and Paige; stepchildren, Pamela and Barton. Educ: Rider Col, B.B.A, 34; Naval War Col. Staff Sch, 45; Skull and Sabres; first pres, Beta Zi Chap, Delta Sigma Pi; pres, Interfraternity Coun. Polit. & Govt. Pos: Pres, Action thru Educ. Club, 63-65; chmn, Dade Co. Right to Vote Cmt, Fla, 64; Rep. nominee for U.S. Cong, Third Dist, Fla, 64; pres, Miami Shores Men's Rep. Club, 64-65; Rep. nominee, Fla. State Legis, 65 & 66; chmn, Dade Co. Rep. Exec. Cmt, 66-69; app, Subversive Activities Control Bd, Wash, D.C, 69- Bus. & Prof. Pos: Mgr. New Eng. Br, Dorland Advert. Agency, 38-41; secy-treas, Atlantic City Newspapers, N.J, 46-51; with Newberger & Co, 51-55 and A.C. Allen & Co, 56-57; assoc. mgr, Hayden Stone, 60-66, mgr. Miami Br, 67-69. Mil. Serv: Entered as Lt.(jg), Navy, 42, released as Lt. Comdr, 46, after serv. in Naval Units, FAW 10, VP 11 and 101, S.W. Pac. Theater and Philippines, 42-45; Comdr, Ready Res; mil. ribbons and two battle stars. Mem: Dir, Miss Am. Beauty Pageant, Atlantic City, N.J, 47-55; treas. and mem. bd. gov, Atlantic City Hosp, 48-55; Fla. State Comprehensive Health and Planning Cmn; Am. Legion; Acacia; Mason; Elks; Rep. Clubs; Miami Tiger Bay Polit. Club. Letters in varsity track, football and swimming, Rider Col; Fla. Outstanding Rep. Co. Chmn, 67. Rel: Presbyterian. Mailing Add: 1260 N.E. 97th St, Miami, Fla. 33138.

O'NEILL, THOMAS P, JR D
U.S. Rep, Mass.
b. 12/9/12; s. Thomas P. O'Neill and Rose Anne Tolan O; m. 6/17/41 to Mildred Anne Miller; c. Rosemary, Thomas III, Susan, Christopher and Michael. Educ: Boston Col, A.B, 36. Polit. & Govt. Pos: Mass. State Rep, 36-52, minority leader, Mass. State House of Rep, 47-48, speaker of the house, 47-52; mem, Cambridge Sch. Cmt, 46-47; U.S. Rep, Mass, 52-; del, Dem. Nat. Conv, 68. Bus. & Prof. Pos: Ins. Legal Res: Cambridge, Mass. Mailing Add: 2601 Woodley Pl, Washington, D.C, 20008.

O'NEILL, WILLIAM G. D
b. Arcadia, Fla, 2/14/21; m. to Betty Arnold; c. Margaret Jean and Deborah. Educ: Univ. Fla, LL.B, 49; Univ. Fla, Hall of Fame, 47; Fla. Blue Key; Student Exec. Coun; assoc. ed, F Book. Polit. & Govt. Pos: Prosecuting attorney, Marion Co, Fla, 54-55; Fla. State Rep, 56-66. Bus. & Prof. Pos: Attorney. Mil. Serv: Army Air Force and Army Ground Forces, Signal Corps, Pac. Theater, World War II. Mem: Former chmn, Ocala Pub. Safety Cmn; bd. dirs, Am. Red Cross; former chmn, Nat. Found. for Infantile Paralysis;

C. of C; financial dr. chmn, Boy Scouts; former pres, Marion Co. Bar Asn; Fla. Bar; Am. Bar Asn; Sigma Phi Epsilon; Am. Legion; 40 et 8; WOW; Odd Fellows. Rel: Presbyterian. Mailing Add: P.O. Box 253, Ocala, Fla. 32670. (1967)

ONION, CECIL R. D

b. Corydon, Ind, 11/13/08; s. Edgar T. Onion and Myrtle M. Pearson O; m. 1/29/29 to Thelma L. Duley; c. Bobby T, Patsy (Mrs. Neil Hoeppner), Billy R, Harold, Stephen and Donna. Educ: Ind. State Univ, 2 years; Spencerian Bus. Col, grad. Polit. & Govt. Pos: Postmaster, Civil Serv, 29-33; trustee, Redevelop. Cmn, Ft. Wayne, Ind, 64-; del, Dem. Nat. Conv, 68. Bus. & Prof. Pos: Dispatcher, Gen. Elec. Co, Ft. Wayne, Ind, 40-63; pres, Cent. Labor Coun, AFL-CIO, Ft. Wayne, 52-56; pres, Local 901, IUE, AFL-CIO, Ft. Wayne, 56-63, secy-treas, Dist. Coun. Eight, Indianapolis, 63- Rel: Protestant. Legal Res: 1928 Steup Ave, Ft. Wayne, Ind. 46808. Mailing Add: 2138 E. 52nd St, Indianapolis, Ind. 46205.

O'PAKE, MICHAEL ALLEN D

Pa. State Rep.

b. Reading, Pa, 2/2/40; s. Michael Edward O'Pake and Anna Masler O; single. Educ: St. Joseph's Col, Pa, A.B, 61; Univ. Pa. Law Sch, LL.B, 64; Alpha Sigma Nu. Polit. & Govt. Pos: Aid and Clerk, Pa. Superior Court, 65-66; Pa. State Rep, 69- Bus. & Prof. Pos: Attorney-at-law, Marx, Ruth, Binder & Stallone, Reading, Pa, 66- Mem: Am. and Pa. Bar Asns; Optimist (pres, Reading, Pa. Club, 68); Elks; Firemen's Asns. Named Distinguished Young Man of Berks Co. by Reading Jaycees, 68. Rel: Roman Catholic. Mailing Add: 1525 Schuylkill Ave, Reading, Pa. 19601.

OPP, NORMAN D

Chmn, Hughes Co. Dem. Party, S.Dak.

b. Eureka, S.Dak, 3/11/32; s. Christ G. Opp and Marie Hieb O; m. 9/17/55 to Lauretta Naasz; c. Harvey H, Curtis D, June M. and Carol J. Educ: High Sch, Eureka, S.Dak, 4 years. Polit. & Govt. Pos: Dep. sheriff, Hughes Co, S.Dak, 57-60, dep. co. treas, 58-60, co. treas, 61-63; chmn, Hughes Co. Dem. Party, 66- Bus. & Prof. Pos: Restaurant owner, 63-65; ins. salesman, Norman Opp Ins. Agency, 65- Mil. Serv: Entered as Pvt, Marines, 52, released as Sgt, 56, after serv, in 3rd Marine Div, Japan & Korea, 54-55; several Medals. Mem: Odd Fellows; Am. Legion; Pierre Encampment 46; VFW; S.Dak. Health Underwriters; S.Dak. Life Underwriters. Awards in law enforcement work; Cert. Health Underwriter Award; Builders Club Mem. Award, 66, 67 & 68. Rel: Protestant. Mailing Add: 202 N. Tyler Ave, Pierre, S.Dak. 57501.

OPPERMAN, LEONARD D

Ind. State Sen.

b. South Bend, Ind, 2/7/28; s. Leo Opperman and Antoinette Glicksman O; m. to Barbara Alpern; c. Richard, Jerrold, David, Kim and Laura. Educ: Ind. Univ, A.B, 50; Univ. Chicago, M.A, 58. Polit. & Govt. Pos: Ind. State Rep, 62-63; Ind. State Sen, 64- Bus. & Prof. Pos: Mgr, Sunshine Cleaners, Inc, 50-; lectr, Ind. Univ, 60- Mil. Serv: Entered as Pvt, Army, 46, released as Sgt, 47, after serv. in Kirtland Field, N.Mex. Mem: Am. Polit. Sci. Asn. Rel: Jewish. Mailing Add: 1429 E. Colfax, South Bend, Ind. 46617.

ORBECK, EDMUND N. D

Alaska State Rep.

b. West Union, Minn, 9/16/15; s. Joseph S. Orbeck and Mary E. Gans O; m. 1941 to Sherry C. Hanson; c. John E. and Sharon L. Educ: Winona Teachers Col; Columbia Col. Polit. & Govt. Pos: City councilman, Fairbanks, Alaska, 57-59; Alaska State Sen, 60-64; Alaska State Rep, Dist. 16, 64- Bus. & Prof. Pos: Bus. mgr, Laborers Union, Fairbanks, Alaska, 50- Mem: Past pres, Toastmasters, Fairbanks Club; Kiwanis; NAACP; Grange; Elks; Moose; Eagles. Played prfnl. football, LA Bulldogs and Hollywood Rangers, during war years. Mailing Add: 1033 Lathrop St, Fairbanks, Alaska 99701.

ORDMAN, ARNOLD D

Gen. Counsel, Nat. Labor Rels. Bd.

b. Somersworth, N.H, 2/16/12; s. Maurice J. Ordman and Anna Pierce O; m. to Evelyn Ruth Sisson; c. Edward Thorne and Alfred Bram. Educ: Boston Univ, A.B, 33; Harvard Law Sch, LL.B, 36; Phi Beta Kappa. Polit. & Govt. Pos: Mem, Nat. Labor Rels. Bd, 46-, chief counsel to chmn, 61-63, gen. counsel, 63- Bus. & Prof. Pos: Pvt. practice of law, Salem, Mass, 37-42. Mil. Serv: Entered as Ens, Naval Res, 42, released as Lt.(sg), 45, after serv. in Pac; Certificate of Commendation; Atlantic, ETO, Pac, Iwo Jima and Okinawa Campaign Ribbons. Mem: Int. Soc. for Labor Law and Soc. Action; Am. Asn. for Adv. Sci. Rel: Jewish. Mailing Add: 4701 Willard Ave, Chevy Chase, Md. 20015.

O'REILLY, JOHN P. D

Mo. State Rep.

Educ: Christian Bros. Col, A.B; St. Louis Univ, LL.B. Polit. & Govt. Pos: Mo. State Rep, 33-34 & 48- Mil. Serv: Army, Sgt, 18-19, Judge Adv. Gen. Dept, 10th Div. Rel: Catholic. Mailing Add: 2124 A Adelaide, St. Louis, Mo. 63107. (1967)

ORLEBEKE, CHARLES J. R

Exec. Asst. to Secy, Dept. of Housing and Urban Develop.

b. Grand Rapids, Mich, 10/27/34; s. Joe Orlebeke and Wilhelmina Plekker O; m. 2/27/61 to Faith Holtrop; c. Evagren, Alison and Britany. Educ: Calvin Col, B.A, 57; grad. study fel, Mich. State Univ, 57-60, M.A, 60, Ph.D, 65; Fulbright scholarship, Univ. Sydney, 60-61. Polit. & Govt. Pos: Res. asst, Romney for Gov. Cmt, Mich, 62; admin. asst. to Gov. Romney, 63-66 and exec. asst, 67-69; exec. asst. to Secy, Dept. of Housing and Urban Develop, Wash, D.C, 69- Publ: 'The Calare By-Election,' Australian Polit. Studies Asn. News, 2/61; 'Ambition & Organization: The Liberal Party (N.S.W.),' Australian Polit, Cheshire, 66; 'Executive Branch Has New Look,' Mich. Challenge, 2/67. Mem: Am. Polit. Sci. Asn; assoc. mem, Am. Soc. Pub. Admin. Rel: Protestant. Mailing Add: 5215 Roosevelt St, Bethesda, Md. 20014.

ORLINSKY, WALTER SIDNEY D

Md. State Del.

b. Baltimore, Md, 5/19/38; s. Harry Myer Orlinsky and Donya Fein O; m. 6/19/61 to Jo-Ann Mayer; c. Eric Gustav. Educ: Johns Hopkins Univ, A.B, 60; Univ. Md. Law Sch, LL.B, 64; Pi Delta Epsilon; Phi Alpha Delta; Alpha Epsilon Pi. Polit. & Govt. Pos: Coordinator, Kennedy Registrn. Drive, Kennedy for Pres, 60; clerk, Baltimore City Coun, Md, 63-64; Johnson-Humphrey Registrn. Chmn, Baltimore City Dem. Nat. Cmt, 64; nat. committeeman, Young Dem. Md, 64-66; Gen. counsel's off, Post Off. Dept, 65; v.pres, Mt. Royal Dem. Club, currently; Md. State Del, 67-, mem. econ. matters cmt. and joint cmt. orgn. and procedure, Md. House Del, chmn. metrop. affairs cmt. Bus. & Prof. Pos: Bd. mem, Colonial Savings & Loan Asn, 64-65. Publ: 'Baltimore Needs a Mass Transit System', Baltimore Illustrated Press, 7/64. Mem: Jr. Bar Asn. of Baltimore; Am. Bar Asn; Acad. of Polit. Sci; Johns Hopkins Club; B'nai B'rith; Wilderness Soc; New Era Dem. Club; Nat. Trust for Historic Preservation; Am. Civil Liberties Union; Am. Jewish Cong; chmn. bd. of dirs, Baltimore Tutorial Project, Inc; Histadrut (nat. bd. mem); Habonim Alumni (nat. bd. mem). Rel: Jewish. Legal Res: 1530 Bolton St, Baltimore, Md. 21217. Mailing Add: 341 St. Paul Place, Baltimore, Md. 21202.

ORME, FERN HUBBARD R

Nebr. State Sen.

b. Opportunity, Nebr, 4/17/03; m. 6/28/47 to E.W. Orme (deceased). Educ: Univ. Nebr, A.B, 24, B.F.A, 28, M.A, 30; Colo. A&M, 31-47; Univ. of Wash, correspondence course, 42; Delta Kappa Gamma. Polit. & Govt. Pos: Mem, Lincoln Post War Planning Cmt, 45-57, White House Conf. on Children and Youth, 50-54, Nebr. Civil Defense Adv. Bd, 51-55, Lincoln Traffic Cmn, 52-56; secy, Lincoln Bd. of Health; 46-47; mem, Lincoln City Coun, 46-56 and v.pres, 51-55; Rep. cand, Nebr. State Sen, 56; Nebr. State Sen, 59-66 & 68-; alternate del, Rep. Nat. Conv, 60; v.pres, Rep. Women's Club, 62; Rep. cand, Lt. Gov, Nebr, 66. Bus. & Prof. Pos: Teacher, dramatics, Univ. of Nebr, 24-26, Eng. and dramatics, Nebr. Sch. of Agr, 26-27 and Irving Jr. High Sch, 28-43; supvr. sec. distributive educ, Lincoln Pub. Schs, 42-47; classes in human rels. and selling tech, two stores, Lincoln, Nebr, 45-46 and class in personality develop. and pub. contacts, Credit Women of Lincoln, 47. Mem: Bd, Delta Kappa Gamma, 48-49 & 52-53; Lancaster Co. Centennial Cmt; Lincoln-Lancaster Safety Coun; Lincoln Univ. Club; Lincoln Country Club; Inter-Com Club; Malone Commun. Center; Child Guid. Center, Inc; Commun. Adv. Health Coun; Madonna Home Lay Adv. Bd; Lancaster Co. Coun. for Ment. Health; Lincoln Alumni Club, Univ. of Nebr; Gov. Cmt. on the Status of Women; Nebr. Welfare Asn; Nebr. Art Asn; Nebr. Pub. Health Asn; Nebr. State Hist. Soc; Coun. for Nebr. Cultural Resources; State and Nat. Asns. of Parliamentarians; Gov. Cmt. on Ment. Retardation; Ak-Sar-Ben; Nebr. Coun. of Better Educ; Nebr. Alumni Asn; Gov. Citizens Study Cmt. on Ment. Retardation; State Adv. Cmt. for Visually Handicapped; Nebr. Retired Teachers Asn; League of Women Voters; Altrusa; Daughters of the Nile; Am. Legion Auxiliary; Nat. Cmt. for Support of the Pub. Schs; Nat. Order of Women Legislators; Am. Interprfnl. Inst; Nat. Asn. of Retired Teachers; Nat. Asn. of Rehabilitation; Legis. Ladies League; Unicameral Club; Women's Div, Lincoln C. of C.(bd. of dirs, 42-44 & 58-60); pres, Lincoln Teachers Asn, 43-45, trustee, 46-47; chmn, Pub. Rels. and Legis. Cmt, Dist. 1, Nebr. State Educ. Asn, 44-45; Am. Asn. of Univ. Women (pres, Lincoln Br, 43-46, Nebr. pres, 48-52, mem. Nebr. adv. bd, 52-54, Nebr. legis. chmn, 54-55, mem, nat. status of women cmt, 54-58 and co-chmn, Nebr. status of women cmt, 55-56); speaker, Lancaster Co. Red Cross Dr, 47; co-chmn, Lincoln March of Dimes Dr, 47-48; mem. of bd, Lincoln-Lancaster Child Guid. Center, 48-50, Lincoln-Lancaster Co. Ment. Health Asn, 56-65, Govt. Research Inst, 59, Lincoln-Lancaster Commun. Emergency Shop, 59-63, Lincoln-Lancaster Co. Heart Coun, 61-65, Lincoln Hosp. Coun, Lincoln Pre-Sch. for the Visually Handicapped, Inc, 65- and Blood Bank, 69-; Coun. of Women's State Orgns.(secy-treas, 49-50, pres, 50-52); life mem, Lincoln Women's Club, 49-; chmn, State Cmt. on Mid-Century White House Conf. on Children and Youth, 50-54; secy, Nebr. Civil Defense Adv. Cmt. for Women's Affairs, 53-55; chmn. adv. bd, Lancaster Asn. for Retarded Children, Inc, 56-58; secy, Gateway Manor, Inc, 59-; YWCA (v.pres. and mem. of bd, 61-64, mem. Lin-Co-Y cmt. of mgt, 65-); Coun. of State Govt.(mem. steering cmt. for Midwest. regional conf, 62-65, alternate del, 62, chmn. Nebr. del, 63, chmn. Nat. conv, 64); bd. of trustees, Nebr. Heart Asn, 62-64; mem. adv. bd, Christian Record Benevolent Asn, 63-; incorporator and mem. bd. of dirs, Coun. on Alcoholism, 63-; Vol. Bur.(mem. of bd, 65-66, sustaining mem, 67-); mem-at-lg, Lincoln Found, 68- Headliner Award, Lambda Chap, Theta Sigma Phi, Univ. of Nebr, 52; Citation for Christian Citizenship, United Church Women, 55; Honored at Pub. Affairs Luncheon, Women's Div. of Lincoln C. of C, 59; Awarded Distinguished Citizen in Women's Activities Honors, Lincoln, 59; One of Five Women Honored by Lincoln Bus. and Prfnl. Club, 61; Citation for Contribution to pub. Educ, Lincoln Educ. Asn, 64; Cited for Role in Bldg. State Support for Construction of Women's Phys. Educ. Bldg, Univ. of Nebr, 68; Woman of Achievement Award, Nebr. Fedn. of Bus. and Prfnl. Clubs, 69. Rel: Presbyterian. Mailing Add: 3025 Sheridan Blvd, Lincoln, Nebr. 68502.

ORME, LILA MORTON D

Mem, Calif. Dem. State Cent. Cmt.

b. Chicago, Ill; d. Evan John Morton and Delilah Munro M; div; c. Lila Jeanne (Mrs. Whitlow), Maynard E. and Evan M. Educ: Univ. Calif, Berkeley, B.S. and M.S, 29; Beta Gamma Sigma; Gamma Epsilon Pi. Polit. & Govt. Pos: Mem, Calif. Dem. State Cent. Cmt, 44-; mem, Fresno Co. Dem. Cent. Cmt, 44-50 and exec. secy, 48-50 and 58-60; mem. campaign cmts, Roosevelt-Truman and Downey, 44, Phillips, 46, Truman, 48, Sisk, 54 & 58 and Humphrey, 68; v.chmn, Cong. Dist. Dem. Cent. Cmt, 46-48; pres, Fresno Co. Dem. Women, 46-47, 67-69 and voter registrn. chmn, 58-; alternate del, Dem. Nat. Conv, 48; Fresno Co. v.chmn, Stevenson-Sparkman, 52; asst. conv. mgr, Calif. Dem. Coun, 58, 59 and 60; coordinator, registrn. drives, 58, 60 & 62; campaign coordinator, Fresno Co. Brown Campaign, 62 and Salinger, 64; managed hq, Trombetta, 67 and United Dem, 68; co. women's chmn, Cranston Campaign, 68; co-chmn. and mgr. hq, Hardy for City Coun, 69; secy, Dem. of Cent. Calif, 69- Bus. & Prof. Pos: Copy writer, Honig-Cooper Advert, Seattle, Wash, 29-30 and J. Walter Thompson, San Francisco, Calif, 32-35; asst. to advert. mgr, United Prune Growers, 30-32; instr. in Eng, Fresno State Col, Calif, 55-56 and 60-61. Mem: Fresno Women's Civic Coun.(pres, 54-55); Am. Asn. Univ. Women; bd. dirs, San Joaquin Valley Town Hall; PTA. Mailing Add: 1035 E. Michigan Ave, Fresno, Calif. 93704.

O'ROURKE, JAMES F. X. R

Mayor, Yonkers, N.Y.

b. N.Y.C, 3/11/20; s. John Patrick O'Rourke and Beatrice McAvoy O; m.

8/21/41 to Evelyn Cooke; c. James, Colleen, Brian, Kathleen, Kevin, Eileen, Mary, Sean, Ann, Michael, Tara, Keri and Brenden. Educ: Manhattan Col, B.S, 39; Georgetown Univ, M.D, 43. Polit. & Govt. Pos: Councilman, Third Ward, Yonkers, N.Y. 63-67, Majority Leader, 65-67; chmn, Coun. Cmt. on Transit and Commun, Coun. Cmt. Educ, Libraries and Mus, Cmt. on Narcotics and Drug Abuse and Cmt. on Natural Disaster; v.chmn, Urban Renewal Agency; mem, Cmt. on Capital Budget and Cmt. Zoning and Recreation, trustee, Uniformed Serv. Pension Fund, currently; v.mayor, Yonkers, N.Y, 66-67 and mayor, 67- Bus. & Prof. Pos: Mem. of staff, Columbia Presby. Med. Center, Yonkers Gen. Hosp. and St. John's Riverside Hosp, currently. Mil. Serv: Entered as 1st Lt, Army, released as Maj, after serv. in Bn. Aide Surgeon, 100th Inf. Div, ETO; Purple Heart; Bronze Star. Publ: Yonkers Advisory Committee on Narcotics and Drug Abuse Report, 1/65. Mem: Dipl, Am. Bd. Ophthalmology; fel, Am. Col. Surgeons; Yonkers Acad. Med; Yonkers Hist. Soc; YMCA; Amackassin Club; Am. Legion; bd. dirs, Colts Boy's Club (past pres); K. of M.(affil. of the Bros. of the Christian Sch, Yonkers). Rel: Catholic. Mailing Add: 4 Delavan Terr, Yonkers, N.Y. 10703.

O'ROURKE, PETER EDWARD R
b. Detroit, Mich, 11/14/33; s. Randall Michael O'Rourke and Alice White O; m. 9/30/67 to Susan Ellen Gehrke; c. Kathleen Ann. Educ: Wayne State Univ, B.A, 55; Detroit Col. of Law, J.D, 58; Delta Theta Phi. Polit. & Govt. Pos: Rep. nominee for U.S. Rep, 68; mem, Mich. Employment Security Appeal Bd, 69- Bus. & Prof. Pos: Partner, Porritt, Hegarty & O'Rourke, 63-67 and Elsman, Young & O'Rourke, 67-69. Mil. Serv: Entered as Ens, Coast Guard, 58, released as Lt.(jg), 62, after serv. aboard U.S. Coast Guard Cutter Basswood, Chief Law Enforcement, Ninth Coast Guard Dist, 58-62; Lt. Comdr, Coast Guard Res, 69. Mem: Dir, Mackinac Island Yacht Club. Rel: Catholic. Mailing Add: 1652 Hawthorne, Grosse Pointe, Mich. 48236.

O'ROURKE, ROBERT EMMETT R
Umatilla Co. Port Cmnr, Ore.
b. Pendleton, Ore, 9/29/37; s. William Edward O'Rourke and Ida Walters O; m. 7/24/65 to Mary Lou Lazinka; c. Shawn Robert. Educ: Univ. Portland, 55-58; Northwest. Col. Law, Lewis & Clark Col, LL.B, 61. Polit. & Govt. Pos: Mem, Port of Umatilla, info. officer, Umatilla Co. Develop. Cmn. and Water and Resources Develop. Cmt; chmn, Umatilla Co. Rep. Cent. Cmt, 64-66; Umatilla Co. Port Cmnr, Ore, 66-; mem. exec. cmt, Adv. Cmt. to Ore. Legis, 67-68. Bus. & Prof. Pos: Partner, Kottkamp & O'Rourke, Attorneys, 65-; dir, Ore. Reclamation Cong, 68-; dir, Inland Empire Waterways Asn, 69- Mil. Serv: Pvt, Army Nat. Guard, 61-63, serv. in Co. B, 2nd Bn, 186th Inf. Mem: Am. and Ore. Bar Asns; Am. Trial Lawyers Asn; Elks; Rotary; Nat. Reclamation Asn. Rel: Roman Catholic. Legal Res: 2429 S.W. Olson, Pendleton, Ore. 97801. Mailing Add: Box 1023, Pendleton, Ore. 97801.

O'ROURKE, THOMAS F. D
b. Manchester, N.H, 11/14/33; married; c. two. Educ: St. Anselm's Col. Polit. & Govt. Pos: N.H. State Rep, -67; Hillsborough Co. Dem. Cmt. Bus. & Prof. Pos: Supvr. Mil. Serv: USN, 4 yrs, Good Conduct Medal. Mem: Indust. Mgt. Club; Am. Legion. Mailing Add: 91 Harrison St, Manchester, N.H. 03104. (1967)

OROZCO, JOSEPH WILLIAM R
Mem, Calif. Rep. State Cent. Cmt.
b. Guadalajara, Jalisco, Mex, 5/5/21; s. Jose David Orozco and Carmen Alcayde O; m. 12/22/68 to Olga Hortencia Corrales; c. Cynthia Margaret, David William and James Francis. Educ: Univ. Puebla, Mex, Degree in Econ, 52. Polit. & Govt. Pos: Mem, Mayor's Citizens Adv. Cmt, Los Angeles, Calif, 61-; mem, Calif. Rep. State Cent. Cmt, 64-; mem, Dist. Attorney's Adv. Coun, Los Angeles, 65-; mem, Los Angeles Co. Rep. Cent. Cmt, 66-; mem, 48th Assembly Dist. Rep. Cent. Cmt, 66-; South. Calif. rep. to Gov, Calif, 67-68; Republican nominee, U.S. Rep, Calif, 68; mem. exec. cmt, Los Angeles Co. Rep. Cent. Cmt, 68; mem. and pres. bd. trustees, Los Angeles City Jr. Col. Dist. One, 69- Bus. & Prof. Pos: Trustee, Queen of Angeles Clinic and Research Found, Los Angeles, Calif, 67-; mem. bd. dirs, Health & Respiratory Disease Asn, Los Angeles Co, 68- Mil. Serv: Entered as Pvt, Army, 42, released as M/Sgt, 45, after serv. in Mil. Intel. Serv, Second Inf. Div, ETO, 43-45; Chief Warrent Officer, Army Res, currently. Mem: Am. Legion; ROA; Elks; K. of C; Inter-Am. Club Los Angeles. Man of the Year Award, Inter-Am. Club, 67; Citations from Am. Cancer Soc, Health & Respiratory Disease Asn. Los Angeles Co; Papal Blessing, 62. Rel: Catholic. Legal Res: 748 Silver Lake Blvd, Los Angeles, Calif. 90026. Mailing Add: 202 S. Broadway, Los Angeles, Calif. 90012.

ORR, FREDDIE RAY D
Tex. State Rep.
b. Dallas, Tex, 2/9/38; s. Willis Orr and Audra Hill O; m. 9/4/59 to Lottie Jacquline King; c. Anglea Lee and Greg. Educ: N.Tex. State Univ, B.S, 60; Pi Kappa Alpha. Polit. & Govt. Pos: Mem, DeSoto City Coun, Tex, 64; Tex. State Rep, Dallas Co, 66- Bus. & Prof. Pos: Pres, Gr. Dallas South Inc; mem. bd. of dirs, DeSoto Indust. Found. Mem: Lions (officer, DeSoto Chap); Jaycees (officer, DeSoto Chap). Named Outstanding Citizen of DeSoto Under 35. Rel: Church of Christ. Legal Res, 309 Woodhaven, DeSoto, Tex. 75115. Mailing Add: P.O. Box 10, DeSoto, Tex. 75115.

ORR, JAMES WEAVER R
Chmn, Wharton Co. Rep. Party, Tex.
b. Emporia, Kans, 3/23/37; s. William Howard Orr and Naomi Matilda Williams O; m. to Rebecca Ann Moore; c. James Steven. Educ: Sam Houston State Col, B.S, 64; Univ. Tex. Dent. Sch, D.D.S, 68; Xi Psi Phi. Polit. & Govt. Pos: Chmn, Wharton Co. Rep. Party, Tex, currently. Bus. & Prof. Pos: Private practice of gen. dent, currently. Mil. Serv: Entered as Pvt. E-1, Army, 55; Grad, Army Artil. and Missile Officer Cand. Sch, Ft. Sill, Okla, 59. Mem: Guadalupe Valley Dist. Dent. Soc; Tex. and Am. Dent. Asns; Nat. Soc. Preventive Dent; Nat. Rehabilitation Asn; Rotary. Rel: Protestant. Mailing Add: Hwy. 71 N, El Campo, Tex. 77437.

ORR, JOHNNY LYNCH D
b. Florence, Ala, 4/20/37; s. Frank Howard Orr Jr. and Lola Lynch O; m. 6/16/57 to Mary Wellden; c. Johnny Lynch, Jr. Educ: Union Univ, Tenn, B.A; Alpha Tau Omega. Polit. & Govt. Pos: Primary and gen. Elec. campaign mgr. for Buford Ellington, Rutherford Co, Tenn, 66; del, Dem. Nat. Conv, 68. Bus. & Prof. Pos: Teacher and coach, Athens Jr. High Sch, Ala, 59-60; agent, Mutual Savings Life Ins. Co, 60-63, agency mgr, 63-68, regional mgr, 68- Mem: Nat. Asn. Life Underwriters; Stones River Country Club; Rotary; Jaycees. Rel: Baptist. Legal Res: 141 Cherry Lane, Murfreesboro, Tenn. 37130. Mailing Add: P.O. Box 1296, Murfreesboro, Tenn. 37130.

ORR, JUANITA ELOIS D
Mem, Calif. Dem. State Cent. Cmt.
b. West Palm Beach, Fla, 4/18/33; d. Joseph Alexander Orr and Eula Terry O; single. Educ: Fla. A&M Univ, B.S, 54; N Y. Univ, M.A, 58; Alpha Kappa Alpha. Polit. & Govt. Pos: Chmn, Get-Out-Vote Cmt, Johnson Campaign, 64 and Get-Out-Vote Cmt, Contra Costa Co. Brown for Gov. Campaign, 66; treas, Key Dem. Women, 66 and pres, 69-; co-chmn, Voter Registrn. Cmt, 66-68; mem, Contra Costa Co. Finance Cmt. and Co. Campaign Adv. Cmt, gen. campaign, 68; minority co-chmn, Humphrey Campaign, 68; dist. coordinator, Miller for State Sen, 68; mem, Calif. Dem. State Cent. Cmt, 68- Bus. & Prof. Pos: Teacher, Palm Beach Co. Schs, Fla, 54-57, N.Y.C. Pub. Schs, 58-59 and Mt. Diablo United Sch. Dist, Concord, Calif, 63-69; reading specialist, U.S. Army Dependent Schs, France and Germany, 59-63. Mem: Nat. and Mt. Diablo Unified Dist. Educ. Asns; Calif. Teachers Asn; NAACP; Am. Asn. of Univ. Women. Rel: Baptist. Mailing Add: 4462 Clayton Rd, Concord, Calif. 94521.

ORR, LON GREER D
b. Dixon, Mo, 4/3/34; s. Clay Henry Orr and Thelma Stahl O; m. 9/1/56 to Marilyn Walters; c. Julie Claire, Lon Greer, II, Christopher John Tillman and Amy Joan. Educ: Univ. Mo-Columbia, 52-56; N.Y. Inst. Finance, 64; Beta Theta Pi; Baseball Letterman; Univ. Mo. Student Govt. Asn. Polit. & Govt. Pos: Del, Mo. Young Dem. Conv, 57, 58 & 59; pres, Jasper Co. Young Dem, 57-59; mem. exec. cmt, Mo. Young Dem, 58 & 59, seventh dist. chmn, 58-59; admin. asst. to Congressman Charles H. Brown, Seventh Dist, 59-60; Lawrence Co. del, Mo. State Dem. Conv, 64; southwest Mo. coordinator, True Davis for U.S. Sen. Campaign, 68; chmn. Lawrence Co. del, Mo. State Dem. Conv, 68; mem, Businessman for Humphrey Cmt, 68; del, Dem. Nat. Conv, 68. Bus. & Prof. Pos: Salesman, Life Ins, Joplin, 56-59; Angus cattle breeder, Eaglecrest Farm, Sarcoxie, 60; stockbroker, Christopher & Co, Joplin, 64- Mem: Licensed Security Broker in Mo, Okla, and Kans; life member of Mo. Hist. Soc; Miller Bd. Educ.(v.pres, 65-68); F&AM; Scottish Rite (Knight Comdr, Court of Honor, 64); Shrine; Eastern Star; York Rite; Rotary; Univ. Mo. Alumni Asn; Elks; Twin Hills Country Club; Nat. Farmers Orgn. Rel: Episcopal; Licensed Lay Reader of W.Mo. Episcopal Diocese, 63- Legal Res: Eaglecrest Farm, Sarcoxie, Mo. 64862. Mailing Add: 211 West 4th, Joplin, Mo. 64801.

ORR, LORRAINE R
Chmn, Nebr. State Rep. Cent. Cmt.
b. Nebr, 1921; m. 7/20/40 to James W. Orr; c. Jeffrey Lee. Educ: Bus. Col, San Francisco, 2 years. Polit. & Govt. Pos: Pres, Lincoln Co. Rep. Women's Orgn, Nebr, 4 years; mem, Nebr. State Rep. Cent. Cmt, v.chmn, 64-67, chmn, 67- Bus. & Prof. Pos: Bookkeeper, 42-58. Mem: Ak-sar-ben; Nebr. Bowling Asn; Lincoln Co. Red Cross (drive secy, 4 years). Rel: Presbyterian. Mailing Add: 402 S. Jefferson, North Platte, Nebr. 69101.

ORR, RICHARD ARTHUR R
Mem, Monroe Town Coun, Conn.
b. Mansfield, Ohio, 11/23/28; s. Samuel Henderson Orr and Lena A. Dulfer O; m. 4/18/48 to Dorothy Louise Hunt; c. Nancy Louise, Susan Jean and Douglas James. Educ: Mass. Inst. of Tech, 46-48; Univ. Bridgeport. Polit. & Govt. Pos: Mem, Monroe Rep. Town Cmt, Conn, 61-, chmn, 62-68; mem, exec. cmt, Fairfield Co. Rep. Cmt, 62-68; Justice of the Peace, 62-; del. and mem. campaign orgn. cmt, Conn. Rep. Coun, 63; del, Conn. State Rep. Conv, 64 & 66 and Spec. Conv, 65; mem, Fifth Cong. Dist. Rep. Cmt, 64-, chmn, 66-68; secy, Mid. Sch. Bldg. Cmt, 65- and High Sch. Bldg. Cmt, 67-; spec. dep. sheriff, 66-; mem, Gr. Bridgeport Regional Planning Agency, 68-; pres, Whitney Commun. Center, 69; mem, Monroe Town Coun, 69- Bus. & Prof. Pos: Machine designer, Wheeling Steel Corp, W.Va, 49-52; designer, Sikorsky Aircraft, 52-61, sr. dynamics engr, 61-64, sr. design engr, 64-66 and proj. engr, 66-; mem. faculty, Bridgeport Eng. Inst. Mem: Am. Helicopter Soc; Bridgeport Engrs. Club; chmn, St. Peter's Nursery Sch, 61-65; treas, Monroe Lions, 62-64, dir, 64- and pres, 69-; Monroe Rep. Club; Monroe Hist. Soc; Mass. Inst. Tech. Alumni Asn. Recipient of 22 Awards for Photographic Work; Holder of Patent 3, 176, 939, Assigned to United Aircraft Corp. Rel: Episcopal; Keyman, St. Peter's Episcopal Church, 63-68, former Vestryman and Del. to Diocesan Conv. Mailing Add: 40 Woodlawn Rd, Monroe, Conn. 06468.

ORR, ROBERT DEWEY D
b. Clinton, Okla, 4/13/21; s. Robert Dewey Orr and Lillie O; m. 9/15/47 to Caroline Engelhart; c. Robert W, Kathleen Ann, Carol Lynn, Renee Marie and Cynthia Barbara. Educ: Northern State Col, B.S, 53; Univ. of S.Dak, M.A. in Hist. and Govt, 56. Polit. & Govt. Pos: Del, State Dem. Conv, 58; mem, platform cmt, S.Dak. Dem. Party, 58; finance chmn, Co. Dem. Party, 58-62; S.Dak. State Rep, 62-66. Bus. & Prof. Pos: Teacher polit. sci. and econ, 54-60; owner & mgr, Robert D. Orr Real Estate and Ins. Co, 58-66, O & R Investment Co, 64-66 and ROR Enterprises, Inc, 65-66; owner, Indust. and Commercial Consults, 68-; prof, Presentation Col, Aberdeen, S.Dak, 68- Mil. Serv: Army, 39-45, serv. in Combat Engrs, Signal Corps and Qm. Corps, 45th Div, Algeria, French Morrocco, Tunisia, Rome-Arno, North Apennine and Po Valley, 42-45; Bronze Serv. Award with 5 Overseas Serv. Bars; European-African-Middle Eastern Theater Serv. Medal with Lapel Button; Am. Defense Serv. Medal with 4 Discharge Emblems. Publ: History of Aviation in South Dakota, State Univ. of S.Dak. Press, 66; 'The Nation Wept' in John Fitzgerald Kennedy, U.S. Govt. Printing Off, 64. Mem: Am. Legion; Rotary. Rel: Methodist. Legal Res: 416 Sixth Ave. S.E, Aberdeen, S.Dak. 57401. Mailing Add: 609 Citizens Bldg, Aberdeen, S.Dak. 57401.

ORR, ROBERT DUNKERSON R
Ind. State Sen.
b. Ann Arbor, Mich, 11/17/17; s. Samuel Lowry Orr and Louise Dunkerson O; m. 12/16/44 to Joanne Wallace; c. Robert D, Jr, Marjorie R. and Susan S. Educ: Yale Univ, B.A, 40; Harvard Bus. Sch, 42; Delta Kappa Epsilon; Scroll and Key. Polit. & Govt. Pos: Chmn, Center Twp. Adv. Bd, Ind, 50-54;

treas, Vanderburgh Co. Eisenhower Cmt, 52; leader, Eval. Team to Vietnam for For. Opers. Div, 54; precinct committeeman, Rep. Party, Ind, 54-62; alternate del, Rep. Nat. Conv, 56; chmn, Ind. Scranton Cmt, 64; treas, Eighth Dist. Rep. Cmt, 56-68; chmn, Vanderburgh Co. Rep. Cent. Cmt, 65-; Ind. State Sen, 69- Bus. & Prof. Pos: Exec. v.pres, Orr Iron Co, 46-60; v.pres-dir, Hahn, Inc, 57-69; dir, Sign Crafters Inc, Evansville, 57-, PAR Indust, 60-, Dixson, Inc, Grand Junction, Colo, 62-, Erie Invest, Evansville, 65- and Indian Industs, 67-; pres. & dir, Indian Archery Corp, 62-65. Mil. Serv: Entered as Pvt, Army, 42, released as Maj, 46, after serv. in Qm. Corps, Alaska, S.W. Pac, Philippines, Okinawa, Japan; Legion of Merit. Mem: Rotary; Evansville Country Club; Evansville Petroleum Club; former mem, Jaycees; Columbia Club; trustee, Hanover Col. Distinguished Serv. Award, Jaycees, 53. Rel: Presbyterian. Legal Res: R.R. 8, Box 97, Evansville, Ind. 47711. Mailing Add: P.O. Box 3397, Evansville, Ind. 47701.

ORR, ROY LEE D
Committeeman, Tex. State Dem. Party
b. Dallas, Tex, 10/2/32; s. Willis Walker Orr and Audra Hill O; m. 7/3/52 to Jessie Janice Gallagher; c. Valorie Sue, Roxie Karen, Lei Ann and John Timothy. Polit. & Govt. Pos: Pres, De Soto Independent Sch. Dist, Tex, 61-67; chmn, charter cmn, City of De Soto, 68-69; committeeman, Tex. State Dem. Party, 23rd Senatorial Dist, 68- Mil. Serv: Entered as Pvt, Air Force, 50, released as Sgt, 52, after serv. in 443rd Troop Carrier Wing. Mem: Tex. and Am. Bankers Asns; Tex. and Dallas Agents Asns; De Soto C. of C.(pres, 62-63, 68-69); Oak Cliff C. of C; Gr. Dallas South Inc; Dem. Cmt. Responsible Govt; Lions Int.(pres, De Soto Club, 53-55, 63-64, dep. dist. gov, 56-57); Order of the Blue Goose. Outstanding Citizen Under Age 35, 63. Rel: Church of Christ. Legal Res: 320 Woodhaven Dr, De Soto, Tex. 75115. Mailing Add: Box 10, De Soto, Tex. 75115.

ORRICK, WILLIAM HORSLEY, JR. D
b. San Francisco, Calif, 10/10/15; s. William Horsley Orrick and Mary Downey O; m. 12/5/47 to Marion Naffziger; c. Mary Louise, Marion and William H, III. Educ: Yale Univ, B.A, 37; Univ. Calif, LL.B, 41. Polit. & Govt. Pos: Del, Dem. Nat. Conv, 56, 60, 64 & 68; asst. attorney gen, Civil Div, U.S. Dept. Justice, 61-62, Antitrust Div, 63-65; dep. undersecy. state, Calif, 62-63. Bus. & Prof. Pos: Assoc, Orrick, Herrington, Rowley & Sutcliffe, 41-50, partner, 50-51 & 65- Mil. Serv: Entered Army, 42, released as Capt, 46, after serv. in Mil. Intelliegence. Rel: Episcopal. Legal Res: 6 Presidio Terrace, San Francisco, Calif. 94118. Mailing Add: 405 Montgomery St, San Francisco, Calif. 94104.

ORTIZ, RUDY A. D
Chmn, Bernalillo Co. Dem. Party, N.Mex.
b. Santa Fe, N.Mex, 11/16/32; s. Tony J. Ortiz and Luisita Perea O; m. 2/23/57 to Angeline Oyaca; c. Marc R, Martin R, Marquita R. and Marlisa R. Educ: Col. Santa Fe, B.A, 55; Univ. N.Mex, grad. study, 67- Polit. & Govt. Pos: Treas, Bernalillo Co. Dem. Party, N.Mex, 67-68, chmn, 69-; N.Mex. state chmn, McCarthy for Pres. Campaign, 68; del, Dem. Nat. Conv, 68; bd. mem, New Dem. Coalition, Nat. Dem. Party, 68- Bus. & Prof. Pos: Ins. exam, State of N.Mex, 55-67; exec. v.pres. & dir, West. Am. Life Ins. Co, 67- Mil. Serv: Entered Navy, 55, released as DK-3, 57 after serv. on U.S.S. Nerus As-17. Mem: Nat. Asn. Life Co. Rel: Catholic. Legal Res: 1727 Truman, N.E, Albuquerque, N.Mex. 87110. Mailing Add: P.O. Box 409, Albuquerque, N.Mex. 87103.

ORTIZ STELLA, CRUZ Popular Dem, P.R.
P.R. State Sen.
b. Maunabo, P.R, 1900; s. Juan Cruz Ortiz Pagán and Julia Stella Lebrón; m. 10/24/24 to Carolina Gordils Benet; c. Norma, Edgardo, Osvaldo, Humberto and Diana. Educ: Univ. P.R, LL.B. Polit. & Govt. Pos: Munic. Judge and Registr. of Property, P.R; P.R. State Rep, 41-44; P.R. State Sen, 45- Publ: Los Oros se Vislumbran; La Caravana Oscura; Misa del Alba; plus others. Rel: Catholic. Legal Res: Atanasio Cuadra St, Humacao, P.R. 00661. Mailing Add: Noya & Hernández, P.R. 00661.

ORTIZ, WILLIE V. R
b. Chimayo, N.Mex, 10/2/21; s. Ursulo Ortiz and Anita Velarde O; m. 7/3/47 to Edith June Ellis; c. Joy Ann. Educ: St. Michael's Col, N.Mex, B.S, 58. Polit. & Govt. Pos: Chmn, Santa Fe Co. Rep. Cmt, N.Mex, 59-64; v.chmn. and mem, Exec. Cmt, N.Mex. State Rep. Cent. Cmt, formerly; mem, Gov. Reorganization of State Govt, 67-; mem, State Personnel Bd, 69- Bus. & Prof. Pos: Mem. bd. of dirs, Loretto Acad, Santa Fe, N.Mex, 58-63; mem. adv. cmt, Southwest. Coop. Educ. Lab, 66- Mil. Serv: Entered as Pvt, Army, 42, released as Cpl, 45, after serv. in Intel. Dept, S.Am. and S.Pac. Mem: V.pres, Scholarship Cmt, St. Michael's Col; secy, St. Michael's Col. Alumni Asn. Rel: Catholic. Mailing Add: 119 W. Lupita Rd, Santa Fe, N.Mex. 87501.

ORTIZ-TORO, ARTURO R
Chmn, P.R. Rep. Party
b. Ponce, P.R, 11/18/96; s. Carlos Ortiz de Landázuri y Rodas and Elisa del Toro Labarthe O; m. 2/24/18 to Zoraida Córdova Mattei; c. Earline (Mrs. Rogers), Lisette (Mrs. Veve) and Arturo A. Educ: Univ. Pa. Law Sch, LL.B; pres, Phi Chi Delta. Polit. & Govt. Pos: Mem, Superior Bd. of Health, P.R, 26-40; First Asst. Attorney Gen. and Acting Attorney Gen, P.R, 28-33; mem, San Juan Selective Serv. Bd; Rep. Statehood Party of P.R; cand, Resident Cmnr. of P.R; del, Rep. Nat. Conv, 52, 56, 60, 64 & 68; P.R. State Sen, 60-68; chmn, P.R. Rep. Party, currently. Bus. & Prof. Pos: Pres, Furniture Finance Corp, 40; dir, El Faro Develop. Corp; treas, Copa Construction Corp, currently. Mem: Pres, San Juan Chap, Am. Legion, 31; pres, San Juan Chap, Univ. Pa. Club, 32; pres, Cornell-Pa. Club, 33; pres, San Juan Chap, Civil Legion; Fed, Inter-Am. and Am. Bar Asns; v.pres, P.R. Bar Asn, 37; Coast Guard League; Gen. Alumni Soc. of Univ. Pa; Ateneo Puertorriqueño; C. of C; El Morro Officers Club; Order of Ky. Col; Nat. Soc. State Legislators. Rel: Catholic. Legal Res: Marbella St. 58, Condado, Santurce, P.R. 00907. Mailing Add: P.O. Box 4646, San Juan, P.R. 00905.

OSBORN, CLAYTON E. R
N.H. State Rep.
b. 11/28/95; married; c. Five. Educ: Churchville and Oakfield, N.Y. Polit. & Govt. Pos: Former dep. sheriff, N.Y. State; mem, city coun, N.H, 9 years; supt, Portsmouth Pub. Works, 7 years; several ward off, Portsmouth; N.H. State Rep, 61- Bus. & Prof. Pos: Over 40 years experience in construction and mgt; retired engr. Mil. Serv: World War I. Mem: Past Exalted Ruler, Elks; Past Comdr, Post and Co. Am. Legion; F&AM; Vet. World War I; past pres, Sherburn Civic Asn; past pres, PTA. Rel: Protestant. Mailing Add: 42 Harvard St, Portsmouth, N.H. 03801. (1967)

OSBORN, GEORGE W. R
V.Chmn, Greene Co. Rep. Cmt, N.Y.
b. Windham, N.Y, 7/24/98; s. George W. Osborn and Clara Goslee O; m. 10/6/23 to Florence Dodge. Educ: Albany Bus. Col. Polit. & Govt. Pos: Mem, Bd. of Educ, Windham High Sch, N.Y, sch. dir. and town supvr, 16 years; v.chmn, Greene Co. Rep. Cmt, N.Y, 58- Bus. & Prof. Pos: Owner, summer resort, Osborn House, Windham, N.Y, 15-46. Mem: Mason (Past Master, High Priest, Past Dist. Deputy). Rel: Protestant. Mailing Add: Windham, N.Y. 12496.

OSBORN, MICHAEL KINDIG D
Mem, Colo. State Dem. Cent. Cmt.
b. Columbia, S.C, 11/3/40; s. Donald Olin Osborn and Ora Clark O; m. 4/18/62 to Nancy Ellen Engquist; c. Jennifer Kennedy and Thomas Rodd. Educ: Univ. Colo, 58-59; Mankato State Col, B.A, 63; Alpha Tau Omega. Polit. & Govt. Pos: Dist. coordinator, Citizens for Kennedy, 68; alternate del, Dem. Nat. Conv, 68; corresponding secy, Colo. Young Dem, 68-; precinct committeeman, Jefferson Co. Dem. Cent. Cmt, Colo, 68-, dist. v.capt, 68-69, dist. capt, 69-; mem, Colo. State Dem. Cent. Cmt, 69- Bus. & Prof. Pos: Dept. supvr, Rocky Mountain Bank Note Co, Denver, Colo, 63-; ed, Mountain Free Press, 67-68, Jefferson Papers, 69- Mil. Serv: Entered as Pvt.E-1, Marine Corps Res, 61, released as Cpl. E-4, 67, after serv. in Marine Air Control Squadron 23, Fourth Marine Air Wing, 63-67. Publ: Columns, articles and editorials, Mountain Free Press and Jefferson Papers. Mem: Counselor, Jefferson Co. Vol. Probation Prog; Am. for Dem. Action. Rel: Unitarian. Mailing Add: 4661 Estes St, Arvada, Colo. 80002.

OSBORNE, EARL THOMAS D
Judge, Ky. Court of Appeals
b. Ballard Co, Ky, 7/10/20; s. Willie Claude Osborne and Dovie Bradford O; m. Nov. 1943 to Helen Cooper; c. William P, Thomas Lee, Phyllis Jo and Debora Jane. Educ: Univ. Ky, LL.B, 50; Phi Alpha Delta. Polit. & Govt. Pos: Circuit Judge, 42nd Judicial Dist, Ky, 57-67; Judge, Ky. Court Appeals, 67- Mil. Serv: Entered as Pvt, Air Force, 40, released as 1st Lt, 45, after serv. in 438 Troop Carrier Group, 90th T. C. Sq, ETO, 43-45; Air Medal with Two Oak Leaf Clusters. Mem: Ky. State and Am. Bar Asns; Am. Legion; VFW. Rel: Methodist. Mailing Add: Route 5, Benton, Ky. 42025.

OSBORNE, EDWARD BERYL D
Chmn, Clermont Co. Dem. Cent. and Exec. Cmts, Ohio
b. Indian Hill, Ohio, 7/30/19; s. Jesse Price Osborne and Jessie Jordan O; m. 2/25/41 to Rosemary White; c. Karen. Educ: Wilmington Col, B.S. in educ, 42; Univ. Cincinnati Col. of Law, LL.B, 48. Polit. & Govt. Pos: Secy, Clermont Co. Dem. Cent. and Exec. Cmts, Ohio, 56-64, chmn, 64-; precinct committeeman, Dem. Cent. Cmt, 56-; mem, Clermont Co. Bd. of Elecs, 57-60, chmn, 60- Mil. Serv: Entered as Pvt, Army, 42, recalled, 51, released as 1st Lt, 52, after serv. in 95th Div, 70th Div, 81st Div. & 1st Cavalry, S. Pac. & Korea, Japan, 42-46, 51-52; Bronze Star; Second Award Combat Infantryman's Badge; Bronze Arrowhead; Pac. Theater Ribbons with four Battle Stars; Japanese Army of Occup. Medal; Korean Campaign Ribbon; Philippine Campaign Ribbon. Mem: Clermont Co. and Ohio Bar Asns. Rel: Methodist. Mailing Add: 2262 Cedarville Rd, Goshen, Ohio 45122.

OSBORNE, JULIAN HANMER D
Chmn, Richmond Dem. City Cmt, Va.
b. Keysville, Va, 8/9/13; s. Patrick Henry Osborne and Georgie Hanmer O; m. 11/17/41 to Annabelle Howe; c. Jane (Mrs. Nelson Johnson). Educ: Randolph Macon Col, 31-32; Hampden Sydney Col, 32-33; Univ. Richmond Eve. Sch. Bus, 46-48; Kappa Alpha; Alpha Tau Chap. Polit. & Govt. Pos: Del, Va. Dem. State Conv, 52, 56, 60, 64 & 68; pres, Young Dem. Club Richmond, 59-60; mem, Richmond Dem. City Cmt, 59, first v.chmn, 62-65, chmn, 65-; chmn, Richmond Hemrico Campaign for House Del, 67; chmn, 36th Dem. Legis. Dist, 67, secy, 69-; del, Dem. Nat. Conv, 68; mem, Third Cong. Dist. Dem. Cmt, 68-; Dem. nominee, Cmnr. of Revenue, 69. Bus. & Prof. Pos: Employee, Commonwealth of Va, 41-66; exec. dir, Lumber Mfg. Asn. Va, 66-67; lobbyist, Gen. Assembly of Va, 68-69. Mem: Mason; Scottish Rite (32°); Shrine; Jamestown Soc. Rel: Presbyterian. Mailing Add: 2010 Monument Ave, Richmond, Va. 23220.

OSBORNE, RAY C. R
Lt. Gov, Fla.
b. Winston Salem, N.C, 9/7/33; s. Rufus Charles Osborne and Maggie Prevette O; m. 10/21/61 to Mary Thom White; c. Molly Payne. Educ: N.C. State Col, B.S, 55; Univ. of N.C, LL.B, 61; Kappa Sigma; Phi Psi; Delta Theta Phi. Polit. & Govt. Pos: Fla. State Rep, 64-68; alternate del, Rep. Nat. Conv, 68; Lt. Gov, Fla, 69-; mem. Exec. Cmt, Nat. Conf. Lt. Gov, 69- Mil. Serv: Entered as 2nd Lt, Army, 55, released as 1st Lt, Third Armored Div, 57. Mem: Am. Bar Asn; Am. Judicature Soc; St. Petersburg Yacht Club; Univ. Club; Dragon Club. Rel: Episcopal. Legal Res: 115 18th Ave. N, St. Petersburg, Fla. 33704. Mailing Add: P.O. Box 1562, Tallahassee, Fla. 32302.

OSBOURN, D. R. 'OZZIE' D
Mo. State Rep.
b. Upton, Mo, 12/14/23; s. Moses Henry Osbourn and Opal L. Stottlemyre O; m. 8/28/50 to Lois M. Meeker; c. Doran M. and Lori Lynn. Educ: Southwest Mo. State Col, B.S, 46; Univ. Mo, Columbia, M.E, 48; Phi Delta Kappa. Polit. & Govt. Pos: Mo. State Rep, Dist. 99, 67- Bus. & Prof. Pos: Athletic dir. and basketball coach, Hannibal-LaGrange Col, 48-50 and Holy Rosary High Sch, 56-58. Mil. Serv: Entered as Pvt, Army Air Force, 43, released as AC 44, after serv. in 326CTD, East. Command, 43-44; Good Conduct Medal. Mem: Mo. Jr. Col. Athletic Asn.(v.pres); Moose; Elks; Lions; Grange; VFW; Farm Bur. Rel: Christian Church of N.Am. Mailing Add: Route 2, Palmyra, Mo. 63461.

OSGOOD, H. DAVISON, JR. R
Chmn, First Dist. Rep. Cong. Cmt, Maine
b. Haverhill, Mass, 4/2/32; s. Harold D. Osgood and Ruth H; Frecker O; m.

12/28/57 to Judith F. Piper; c. Sarah F. and Margaret J. Educ: Bowdoin Col, A.B, 53, James Bowdoin Scholar and Rhodes Scholar nominee; Univ. Mich. Law Sch, LL.B, 56; Stonier Grad. Sch. of Banking, Rutgers, 64; pres, Theta Delta Chi; pres, Lawyers Club, Mich; Delta Theta Phi. Polit. & Govt. Pos: Former committeeman, Cumberland Co, Maine Rep. State Cmt; mem. and past chmn, Scarborough Rep. Town Cmt; town moderator, Scarborough, 63-67; alternate del, Rep. Nat. Conv, 64; chmn, First Dist. Rep. Cong. Cmt, Maine; selectman, Scarborough. Bus. & Prof. Pos: Mem. faculty, Colby Col. Estate Planning and Tax Inst, 64, 66 & 67; pres, Corporate Fiduciaries Asn. of Maine, 65-67; v.pres. and sr. trust officer, Canal Nat. Bank, Portland, Maine. Publ: Thesis 'The Law of Pourovers and the Uniform Testamentary Additions to Trusts Act,' 64. Mem: Maine and Cumberland Bar Asns; State of Maine Estate Planning Coun; Cumberland Club; past chmn. and pres, Portland Club; Portland Cmt. on For. Rels; past pres, Bowdoin Club of Portland and Portland Players. Mem. 1949 Macmillan Arctic Expedition; 1953 Bowdoin Meddiebempster European United Serv. Orgn. Tour. Rel: Episcopal. Mailing Add: Thunder Rock Farm, Scarborough, Maine 04074.

OSGOOD, THOMAS ANDREW D
Mem, Humboldt Co. Dem. Cent. Cmt, Calif.
b. Los Angeles, Calif, 7/13/46; s. Lloyd W. Osgood, Jr. and Jo Veta Powell O; single. Educ: Los Angeles Pierce Col, 64-65; Humboldt State Col, B.A, 69; Green and Gold Key; Sigma Pi. Polit. & Govt. Pos: Pres, Assoc. Student Body, Humboldt State Col, 67-68; alternate del, Dem. Nat. Conv, 68; mem, Humboldt Co. Dem. Cent. Cmt, Calif, 69- Bus. & Prof. Pos: Div. Pres, Los Angeles Christian Endeavor, 64-65; col. prog. dir, Humboldt State Col, 68-69. Rel: Protestant. Legal Res: 7056 Lindley Ave, Reseda, Calif. 91335. Mailing Add: 550 24th St, Arcata, Calif. 95521.

O'SHAN, DAVID R
b. 8/6/95; married; c. three. Educ: N.Y. and Mass. Agr. Col. Polit. & Govt. Pos: N.H. State Rep, -67. Bus. & Prof. Pos: Retired. Mil. Serv: WWI, Co. I, 103 Inf, 26th Div, wounded and gassed. Mem: Am. Legion; VFW, N.H. Vet. Asn; Chmn, State Vet. Council, 103rd Inf Vet. Asn; Vet. of WWI of the USA Inc. Rel: Protestant. Mailing Add: 25 Pine St, Laconia, N.H. 03246. (1967)

OSHEIM, DONALD R
S.Dak. State Rep.
b. Rosholt, S.Dak, 8/20/19; s. Lawrence C. Osheim and Anna Erdahl O; m. 11/17/42 to Reva Terry; c. Elizabeth, David and Robert. Educ: Univ. S.Dak, LL.B, 48; Kappa Sigma; Delta Theta Phi. Polit. & Govt. Pos: City attorney, Watertown, S.Dak, 59-62; S.Dak. State Rep, currently, speaker pro tem, S.Dak. House Rep, 69-; mem. bd. regents, Augustana Col, 68- Bus. & Prof. Pos: Practicing attorney, Stover, Beardsley & Osheim, 52-56 and Beardsley, Osheim & Wagner, 65. Mil. Serv: Pilot, Navy Air Corps, 41, released as Lt.(sg), 45; Air Medal; Pac. Theater Ribbon. Mem: Am. and S.Dak. Bar Asns; Past Exalted Ruler, Elks; Lions. Rel: Lutheran. Mailing Add: 1381 Crestview Dr, Watertown, S.Dak. 57201.

OSHEL, VAL R
b. Harrisburg, Ill, 3/5/26; s. James Clyde Oshel and Della McKinney O; m. 5/16/49 to Shirley Louise Walker; c. Michael Val. Educ: Univ. Ill, 47-48; South. Ill. Univ, 55-58. Polit. & Govt. Pos: City Cmnr, Harrisburg, Ill, 63-67; Mayor, Harrisburg, 67-69; Rep. cand, U.S. Rep, Ill, 68; asst. dir, Ill. Dept. of Pub. Works, 69- Mil. Serv: Entered as A/S, Navy, 44, released as Signalman 3/C. 46, after serv. in S. Pac. Theatre, 45-46. Mem: Mason; Elks. Rel: Baptist. Legal Res: 103 N. Granger, Harrisburg, Ill. 62946. Mailing Add: 525 W. Cook, Springfield, Ill. 62701.

O'SHIELDS, JAMES EARL D
b. Joanna, 9/22/19; s. James Monroe and Eunice Elizabeth Wood O; m. 6/30/46 to Dorothy Ragsdale O. Educ: Univ. of S.C. Law Sch, LL.B, 50. Polit. & Govt. Pos: S.C. State Rep, 63-66. Bus. & Prof. Pos: Lawyer. Mil. Serv: Army, 41-45; Co. C, 107th Antiaircraft Artil. Mem: Deacon, First Baptist Church of Hemingway; adjutant Hemingway Post 84, Am. Legion, 56; 40 et 8. Mailing Add: Box 397, Hemingway, S.C. 29554.

OSHIKI, KAZ D
b. Hawthorne, Calif, 10/25/24. Educ: Drake Univ, B.S; Univ. of Wis, M.S. Polit. & Govt. Pos: Admin. asst. Rep. Kastenmeier, Wis. Mil. Serv: S/Sgt, U.S. Army, WWII, with serv. in S. and W. Pac. Mailing Add: 5600 Broad Branch Rd, Washington, D.C. 20015.

OSHIRO, ROBERT CHOSEI D
Hawaii State Rep.
b. Wahiawa, Hawaii, 11/19/24; s. Chozun Oshiro (deceased) and Matsuru Tanaka O; m. 2/8/51 to Ruth Taeko; c. Roberta Mary, Marcus Robert and Susan Ruth. Educ: Univ. Hawaii, B.A, 49; Duke Univ, LL.B, 52, LL.M, 53; Phi Delta Phi; Newcomen Soc. Polit. & Govt. Pos: Dist. chmn, Ninth Dist. Dem. Party, Hawaii, 56, councilman, Third Precinct, Ninth Dist, Dem. Party, 57; v.chmn, Fifth Sen. Dist. Territorial Dem. Cent. Cmt, 58-60; Hawaii State Rep, 59-; chmn, Dem. Fact Finding Cmt. and For. Trade Cmt, West. State Dem. Conf, 61-62; chmn, Hawaii State Dem. Cent. Cmt, 62-68. Bus. & Prof. Pos: Attorney, 54-; lectr. bus. law, Univ. Hawaii, 55-57. Mil. Serv: Entered as Pvt, Army, 44, released as Pfc, 46. Mem: Am. and Hawaii Bar Asns; Wahiawa Lions (pres, 62-63); v.pres, Wahiawa Gen. Hosp. Asn; Leilehua Alumni Asn.(past pres); Wahiawa Jr. C. of C.(past dir); Wahiawa C. of C; Honolulu Symphony Soc.(v.pres). Dean Award for Undergrad. Research, University Hawaii, 59. Rel: Protestant. Legal Res: 55 Kalie St, Wahiawa, Hawaii 96786. Mailing Add: P.O. Box 1149, Wahiawa, Hawaii 96786.

OSHRIN, ALBERT SIDNEY D
b. N.Y.C, 11/25/14; s. Harry H. Oshrin and Emma Goodman O; m. 9/14/62 to Dorothy Hauser; c. Terrie Ann, Laurie Alison, Diette, Patrice Margo and Eric. Educ: Univ. Ariz, 32; N.Y. Univ, 33. Polit. & Govt. Pos: Del, Dem. Nat. Conv, 68. Bus. & Prof. Pos: Pres, Oshrin Hosp, 47-; owner, Cortaro Cotton & Cattle Co, 50-68, Quien Sabe Ranch, 61-68. Mil. Serv: Entered as Pvt, Army, 41, released as Capt, 46, after serv. in 853rd Engr. Aviation Bn, China-Burma-India, 42-46. Mem: Old Pueblo Club; Su Pima Asn; Ariz. Cotton Grower Asn; Sahuro Rotary; Ariz. Crop Improv. Asn. Rel: Hebrew. Legal Res: 500 W. Orange Grove Rd, Tucson, Ariz. 85704. Mailing Add: P.O. Box 3943, Tucson, Ariz. 85717.

OSMERS, FRANK C, JR. R
b. Leonia, N.J, 12/30/07; m. 11/7/42 to Marguerite Marsh Udall; c. Two. Educ: Williams Col. Hon. LL.D, Fairleigh Dickinson Univ, 61. Polit. & Govt. Pos: Secy, Bergen Co. Rapid Transit Asn; City councilman, Haworth, N.J, 30-34 and mayor, 35-36; N.J. State Assemblyman, 36-38, chmn, Cmt. on Taxation and Investigating Cmt. on Gubernatorial Campaign Vote Frauds, N.J. State Assembly, 37; mem, Nat. Rep. Club; U.S. Rep, N.J, 39-42 & 51-64, mem, Spec. Cmt. on Nat. Defense Migration, U.S. House of Rep, 39-42, wrote first Cong. bill to provide scholarships in sci. and math for needy col. students, 51-64, mem, Armed Serv. Cmt. and Armed Serv. Spec. Cmt. on Cent. Intel. Agency; pres, Bergen Co. Safety Coun. and foreman, Bergen Co. Grand Jury, 47; chmn, Bergen Co. Rep. Cmt, N.J, 48-52; exec. adminstr, Bergen Co, 68- Bus. & Prof. Pos: Mfg. jeweler, gem expert, appraiser and v.pres, Frank C. Osmers Co, Inc, 25-39; former dir, North. Valley Savings and Loan Asn; licensed real estate broker, N.J; publisher and commercial printer, 46- Mil. Serv: Entered as Pvt, Army, 42, released as Maj, 46, after serv. in Inf, Philippine and Okinawan Campaigns, Korean Occup; Bronze Star; Maj, Army Res. Mem: Nat. Press Club; Brotherhood of Traveling Jewelers; ROA; Am. Legion; VFW; Elks; Mason; 77th Div. Asn, 306th Inf. Asn; Haworth Men's Club; Rotary; former mem, bd. gov, Englewood Hosp; Mayors' Asn. of Bergen Co. Rel: Congregational. Mailing Add: Tenafly, N.J. 07670.

OSORIO, ELROY THOMAS LEIALOHA R
Rep. Nat. Committeeman, Hawaii
b. Hilo, Hawaii, 9/6/24; s. Emil M. Osorio and Eliza Kamakawiwoole O; m. 11/18/44 to Clara Kuulei Kay; c. Leoannalissa N, Elroy T.L, Jr, Jonathan K, David K, Mathew J. and Emil C.K. Educ: St. Louis High Sch, Honolulu, grad, 42. Polit. & Govt. Pos: Supvr, Hawaii Co, Hawaii, 61-64; chmn, Hawaii Co. Rep. Party, 63-64; Rep. Nat. Committeeman, Hawaii, 65-; del, Rep. Nat. Conv, 68. Bus. & Prof. Pos: Pres, Big Island Realty Inc, 63-; pres, Nalei Hotel, 65- Mil. Serv: Merchant Marine, 43-46; Capt, Army Res, currently. Mem: Elks; Lions Int; Hawaiian Civic Club; first dir. from the State of Hawaii to the Nat. Asn. of Co. Officials, 62-64. Rel: Congregational. Legal Res: 1303 Kalanianaole Ave, Hilo, Hawaii 96720. Mailing Add: 175 Banyan Dr, Hilo, Hawaii 96720. (1967)

OSOS, TOBY D
b. Michigan City, Ind, 6/11/21; d. Joseph P. Osos and Ann Kerkla O; single. Educ: Univ. Minn; Calif. State Univ. at Los Angeles. Polit. & Govt. Pos: Pres, Calif. Fedn. Young Dem, 52-54; secy, Young Dem. Clubs of Am, 53-55; dir, Calif. Dem. Coun, 54-60, v.pres, 61-65; del, Dem. Nat. Conv, 60 & 64; co-chmn, Calif. State Dem. Cent. Cmt, 60-66. Bus. & Prof. Pos: Psychometrist aid, Univ. Chicago, 44-46; psychometrist, Pasadena City Schs, 47-52; sr. mgt. consult, Griffenhagen-Kroeger Inc, 53- Mem: Dir, Pasadena YWCA, 49-54 & 65-; v.pres, Nat. Employed Women's Coun, 51-54; Am. Civil Liberties Union; League of Women Voters; NAACP; Altrusa; Pub. Personnel Asn; Am. Soc. for Pub. Admin; West. Govt. Res. Asn; Women's City Club. Legal Res: 475 S. Oakland Ave, Pasadena, Calif. 91106. Mailing Add: P.O. Box 164, Pasadena, Calif. 91102.

OSSIAN, CONRAD R
Iowa State Rep.
b. Stanton, Iowa, 1900; m. 11/15/22 to Mabel Swanson; c. Donald and Crystal. Educ: Luther Col, Wahoo, Nebr. Polit. & Govt. Pos: Mem, Stanton Sch. Bd, Iowa 14 years; Montgomery Co. Bd. Supvrs; Iowa State Rep, currently. Bus. & Prof. Pos: Owned and operated, Stanton Grocery and Prod. Firm, 19 years; farm owner. Mem: Rotary; Mason; Izaak Walton League; Farm Bur. Rel: Lutheran. Legal Res: Stanton, Iowa 51573. Mailing Add: State Capitol, Tenth and Grand Ave, Des Moines, Iowa 50319. (1967)

OSTENDORF, ALVIN FRED R
Chmn, Washington Co. Rep. Party, Ill.
b. Nashville, Ill, 12/4/25; s. John Fred Ostendorf and Alvina Blumhorst O; m. 6/5/54 to Doris Laura Kersten; c. Mary, John, Marsha and Marlene. Educ: LaSalle Exten. Univ, LL.B, 69. Polit. & Govt. Pos: Mem, Grade Sch. Bd, Addieville, Ill, 57-66; precinct committeeman, Plum Hill Twp, 64-; chmn, Washington Co. Rep. Party, 68- Bus. & Prof. Pos: Farmer and trucker, 54- Mil. Serv: Entered as Pvt, Nat. Guard and Air Force, 48, released as Sgt, 57, after serv. in 44th Div. and 3310 T.T. Wing; Serv. Ribbon. Mem: Gov. Adv. Coun; Farm Bur; Churchmen's Fel. Rel: United Church of Christ. Mailing Add: R.R. 2, Nashville, Ill. 62263.

OSTER, HENRY J. D
Chmn, Davison Co. Dem. Cmt, S.Dak.
b. Ind, 5/4/94; s. Anton Oster and Maria Leven O; m. 6/12/17 to Margaret K. Kimber, wid; c. Francis B, Margaret M, Mary K. (Mrs. Barnes), Anthony W, Matilda (Mrs. Fritza), June D. (Mrs. Hoag), Phyllis T. (Mrs. Lambert), Ruth Ann (Mrs. Cone) and John H. Polit. & Govt. Pos: Justice of the peace and twp. clerk for several years; S.Dak. State Rep, 27-28; S.Dak. State Sen, 40-42, 48-50 & 54-65; mayor, Ethan, S.Dak, 61-64; chmn, Davison Co. Dem. Cmt, S.Dak, 64- Bus. & Prof. Pos: Committeeman, Triple A and chmn, Pub. Schs for several years; dir, Prod. Credit, 31-33; pres, Davison Co. Coop. Tel. Co, 20 years; pres, Ethan Coop. Lumber Asn, 41- Mem: Chief ranger, Cath. Foresters; Local and Co. Farmers Union (pres); Nat. Farmers Orgn. Rel: Catholic. Mailing Add: Ethan, S.Dak. 57334.

OSTER, JOHN EDWARD R
b. Holgate, Ohio, 3/15/83; s. William Oster and Elizabeth Fox O. Educ: Ohio North. Univ, B.S, 07, Litt.B, 08, B.Pd. and LL.B, 09; Ohio State, Columbia and Harvard Univs; Lincoln Mem. Univ, L.H.D, 17. Polit. & Govt. Pos: Speaker, Rep. Nat. Cmt, 10-; spec. speaker, LaGuardia Campaign for Mayor N.Y.C, 33; specialist in debates at cols. for Hoover Pres. Campaign, 28; N.Y. Co. Rep. Cmt, 16-21; mem, Legal Adv. Bd. 166, World War I. Bus. & Prof. Pos: Pres, Real Estate Corp, 63-; lectr. govt, polit, sociol. & econ, City Col. N.Y, 16-63; supvr, N.Y. Adult Educ. Prog, 36-37; courses in sociol, bus. and real estate law over Munic. Broadcasting Sta. Air Col. for N.Y. Bd. of Educ, 35; ed, World Court Mag, 15-16; pres, Pub. Serv. Holding Corp. Publns:

Polit. and Econ. Doctrines of Chief Justice Marshall, 15; ed, The Orgn. Repub. and Metropolis Mag. Mem: Am. Sociol. Soc; fel, Am. Geog. Soc; Am. Inst. Criminal Law and Criminol; AAAS; Am. Folklore Soc; Am. Econ. Asn; Stable Money Asn; Foreign Policy Asn; Am. Acad. Polit. & Soc. Sci; Am. Soc. Int. Law; Harlem Bd. Commerce; dir, Dante League Am; Ohio Soc; Am. Asn. UN; NEA; Adult Educ. Asn; Progressive Educ. Asn; Clubs: Nat. Travel, N.Y. Econ, Hamilton Rep, 13th Assembly Dist. Rep, Harvard, Athene, Verdi and Story-Tellers. Medal for patriotic serv, Treas. Dept, 19; Four Minute Man; Victory minute speaker; orator at Grant's Tomb on 30th anniversary of his burial. Mailing Add: 362 Riverside Dr, New York, N.Y. 10025. (1967)

OSTER, TONY W. D
b. Ethan, S.Dak, 3/11/25; s. Henry J. Oster and Devonia L. Puetz; m. 1/23/49; c. Charles, James, Francis, Steven, Geralyn and Michele. Educ: High sch. Polit. & Govt. Pos: S.Dak. State Rep, Davison Co, 64-66. Bus. & Prof. Pos: Financial secy, Cath. Order Foresters, 25 years; treas, Local Sch. Bd, 58-; supvr, Soil Conserv. Dist, 5 years; chmn, Davison Co. Nat. Farmers Orgn, 68-69; farmer. Mem: Nat. Farmers Orgn; Farmers Union. Rel: Catholic. Mailing Add: Ethan, S.Dak. 57334.

OSTERTAG, HAROLD CHARLES R
b. Attica, N.Y, 6/22/96; s. Otto John Ostertag and Frances Julia Briem O; m. 6/25/19 to Grace Jean Bryson. Educ: Chamberlain Mil. Inst. Polit. & Govt. Pos: N.Y. State Assemblyman, 32-50; U.S. Rep, 39th and 37th Cong. Dist, N.Y, 50-64. Bus. & Prof. Pos: Asst. v.pres, Traffic Dept, New York Cent. Syst. Mil. Serv: Entered as Musician, Army, 17, released as Sgt, after serv. in 55th Pioneer Inf, AEF. Mem: Elks; Am. Legion; VFW; World War I Veterans; Farm Bur; Silverlake, N.Y.C. of C; Tamarac, Fla. C. of C; Tamarac Yacht Club. Rel: Presbyterian. Legal Res: Westside, Silver Lake, Perry, N.Y. 14530. Mailing Add: 73 Palm Club, Pompano Beach, Fla. 33062.

O'SULLIVAN, PATRICK BRETT D
Chief Justice, Conn. Supreme Court
b. Derby, Conn, 8/11/87; s. Thomas Jefferson O'Sullivan and Margaret Brett O; m. 6/19/13 to Marguerite Lawton; c. Thomas, James, Robert and Patricia. Educ: Yale Col, B.A, 08; Georgetown Col, 09; Yale Law Sch, LL.B, 13; Phi Delta Phi; Corbey Court. Polit. & Govt. Pos: Secy-treas, Conn. State Dem. Cmt, 14-16, chmn, 30-31; Conn. State Sen, 16-17; U.S. Rep, Conn, 23-25; judge superior court, 31-50; assoc. justice, Conn. Supreme Court, 50-57, chief justice, 57-; chmn, State Parole Syst, 57-59; co-chmn, Conn. State Constitutional Conv, 65. Bus. & Prof. Pos: Assoc. prof, Yale Law Sch, 47- Mil. Serv: Entered as Ens, Navy, 17, released as Lt. Comdr, Naval Res, 35. Mem: Conn. and New Haven Co. Bar Asns; Am. Legion; VFW. Rel: Roman Catholic. Legal Res: 823 Walnut Hill Rd, Orange, Conn. 06477. Mailing Add: County Court House, New Haven, Conn. 06510.

O'SULLIVAN, VIRGIL D
b. Colusa Co, Calif; m. to June; c. Kathleen, Deborah, Kevin, Drusilla, Gregory and Pollyanna. Educ: Univ. of Calif, 39; Boalt Hall Sch. of Law, LL.B, 47. Polit. & Govt. Pos: Former chmn, Colusa Co. Vets. Cmt, Calif; former dep. dist. attorney, Colusa Co; Calif. State Sen, 58-66. Bus. & Prof. Pos: Law practice since 48; engaged in farming and livestock raising. Mem: Pres, Colusa Co. Bar Asn; Commonwealth Club; Elks; K. of C; Grange; Farm Bur; Calif. Wool Growers Asn; Cattlemen's Asn; Rice Growers Coop; Prune and Apricot Asn; Bean Growers Asn; past comdr. of Am. Legion, Williams Post 214; dir, Colusa Co. Hist. Soc. Mailing Add: Box 427, Williams, Calif. 95987.

OSWALD, ROBERT HOLMES D
b. Birmingham, Ala. 1/26/28; s. Charles Alfred Oswald, Jr. and Jeannette Bibby O; m. 7/23/66 to Betty Jean Robinson; c. Robert, Jr, Robyn and Rebecca. Educ: Millsaps Col, 46-47; Tulane Univ, 47-49; Jackson Law Sch, LL.B, 51; Sigma Delta Kappa. Polit. & Govt. Pos: City prosecutor, Pascagoula, Miss, 53-56, city attorney, 56-60; chmn, Jackson Co. Dem. Exec. Cmt, 56-68; secy, Young Dem. of Miss, 57-59, pres, 61-63; chmn, Miss. Dem. Conf, 66. Bus. & Prof. Pos: Attorney-at-law, 52. Mil. Serv: Entered as A/S, Navy, 45, released as Seaman 1/C, 46, after serv. in U.S.S. Sargent Bay and U.S.S. Tripoli, Pac. Theatre; Victory Medal; Asiatic-Pac. Theatre Medal. Mem: Am, Miss. and Jackson Co. Bar Asns; Am. Legion; pres, Optimist Club, Pascagoula, Miss, 69. Rel: Baptist. Legal Res: Bayou Oaks, Gautier, Miss. 39553. Mailing Add: P.O. Box 189, Pascagoula, Miss. 39567.

OSWALD, ROBERT LEON R
Cong. Liaison Officer, Interstate Commerce Cmn.
b. Glendale, Los Angeles, Calif, 10/31/35; s. Theodore Lewis Oswald and Cora Ruth Youngberg O; m. 6/5/67 to Frances Dianne Biegelmeier; c. Robert Scott. Educ: Univ. Md, B.A, 60; George Wash. Univ. Sch. Law, J.D, 64; First Honor Convocation; Delta Theta Phi. Polit. & Govt. Pos: Admin. asst. to Chief Hearing Examiner, Interstate Commerce Cmn, Wash, D.C, 61-64, legal asst. to Dir. Bur. Enforcement, 64-65, cong. liaison officer, Interstate Commerce Cmn, 69-; spec. asst. for research & develop. contracts to Dir, Nat. Career Inst, Nat. Inst. Health, 65-66; admin. asst. to U.S. Rep. William S. Mailliard, Calif, 67-69; field rep, Ohio United Citizens for Nixon-Agnew, 68; staff asst, Rockefeller Cong. Steering Cmt, 68; assoc. mem, Calif. Rep. State Cent. Cmt, 69- Mil. Serv: Entered as Pvt, Air Force, 53, released as Sgt, 57 after serv. in 1254th Air Transport Group, Wash; Group Conduct Medal; Nat. Defense Medal. Mem: DAV. Outstanding Law Student Award, George Wash. Univ. Law Sch, 64; Outstanding Brother Award Region Four, Delta Theta Phi; Outstanding Serv. Award, Student Bar Asn, George Wash. Univ. Sch. Law; Achievement Cert, D.C. Bar Asn; Distinguished Scholarship Cert, Univ. Md. Rel: Protestant. Legal Res: 4734 H La Villa Marina, Marina Del Rey, Calif. 90291. Mailing Add: 101 E St. S.E, Washington, D.C. 20003.

OTENASEK, MILDRED D
Dem. Nat. Committeewoman, Md.
b. Baltimore, Md, 2/6/14; d. Frank Busick and Josephine Cook B; m. 6/9/37 to Dr. Frank J. Otenasek. Educ: Col. of Notre Dame, Md, A.B, 36; Johns Hopkins Univ, Ph.D, 39. Polit. & Govt. Pos: V.chmn, State Dem. Cent. Cmt, Md, 48-56; pres, United Dem. Women's Clubs of Md, 55-57; Dem. Nat. Committeewoman, Md, 56-; del, Dem. Nat. Conv, 68. Bus. & Prof. Pos: Assoc. prof. econ, Trinity Col, 40-54; assoc. prof. econ. & polit. sci, Notre Dame Col, 56- Mem: Catholic Cmn. on Intellectual and Cultural Affairs. Rel: Roman Catholic. Mailing Add: 219 Northway, Baltimore, Md. 21218.

OTIS, JAMES CORNISH, JR.
Assoc. Justice, Minn. Supreme Court
b. St. Paul, Minn, 3/23/12; s. James Cornish Otis and Winifred Brill O; c. Emily R. (Mrs. Thach), James D. and Todd H. Educ: Yale Univ, B.A, 34; Univ. Minn, LL.B, 37; Phi Delta Phi; Zeta Psi. Polit. & Govt. Pos: Judge, Munic. Court, St. Paul, Minn, 48-54; Second Dist. Court, 54-61; assoc. justice, Minn. Supreme Court, 61- Prof. Pos: Partner, Law Firm, Otis, Faricy & Burger, 37-48. Mem: Minn. State and Am. Bar Asns; v.pres, Minn. State Bar Found; Am. Judicature Soc; Nat. Coun. Crime & Delinquency (Coun. of Judges); Inst. of Judicial Admin; trustee, Children's Hosp, Wilder Found, St. Paul Acad. and Hamline Univ; Am. Law Inst. Rel: Unitarian. Legal Res: 475 Grand Ave, St. Paul, Minn. 55102. Mailing Add: 230 State Capitol, St. Paul, Minn. 55101.

O'TOOLE, THOMAS J. D
Chmn, Muskegon Co. Dem. Cmt, Mich.
b. Muskegon, Mich, 7/20/26; m. to Patricia A; c. Thomas J, Kathleen, Mary Louise, Daniel, John, Margaret and Sarah. Educ: Marquette Univ; Univ. Mich. Law Sch. Polit. & Govt. Pos: Spec. asst. attorney gen, Mich, 61-; mem, zoning appeals bd, Muskegon, 68; chmn, Muskegon Co. Dem. Cmt, 69- Bus. & Prof. Pos: Attorney-at-law. Mem: Muskegon Br, NAACP; Muskegon Co. Bar Asn; Nelson Improv. Cmt. Mailing Add: 1329 Fourth St, Muskegon, Mich. 49440.

OTSTOTT, JESSE LEE D
Chmn, Greeley Co. Dem. Cent. Cmt, Kans.
b. Athens, Ill, 1/23/11; s. Jesse Hughie Otstott and Lola Mae Long O; m. 4/24/60 to Eva Marie Groff Warne; c. Sammie Mauk, John, Robert, Delaine, Clark and Maynard Warne and Richard Eugene Otstott. Educ: Preston High Sch, Kans, 27-31. Polit. & Govt. Pos: Chmn, Greeley Co. Dem. Cent. Cmt, Kans, 50-; Greeley Co. centennial chmn. Bus. & Prof. Pos: Sta. agent, Mo. Pac. R.R. Co, 42- Mem: Transportation Commun. Employees Union. 25 year Pin, Mo. Pac. R.R. Co, 67. Rel: Catholic. Mailing Add: Box 248, Tribune, Kans. 67879.

OTT, ALEXANDER REGINALD D
Mem, Dem. State Cent. Cmt, Mich.
b. Picayune, Miss, 6/9/31; s. Fred Ott and Violette Armstrong O; m. 6/7/52 to Izolla Gaddies; c. Alexander R, II, La Sharna M, Wendell W. and Veronical Y. Educ: Alcorn Agr. & Mech. Col, Miss, 51-52; Dillard Univ, La, 54-55; Flint Col, Mich, 56-57. Polit. & Govt. Pos: Chmn, Genesee Co. Dem. Publicity Cmt, Mich, 66-67; mem, Genesee Co. Dem. Exec. Cmt, 66-68; mem, Genesee Co. Bldg. Authority, Flint, 67-; mem, Dem. State Cent. Cmt, Seventh Dist, 67-; del, Dem. Nat. Conv, 68. Bus. & Prof. Pos: Owner, Restaurant, Flint, Mich, 57-59; v.pres. Local 659, UAW, Mich, 65-68; int. rep, UAW, Flint, 68- Mil. Serv: Entered as Basic Airman, Air Force, 52, released as Airman 1/C, 54, after serv. in Mil. Transportation, Far East. Air Command, 53; Good Conduct Medal. Mem: UAW; Genesee Co. Bldg. Authority Cmt; Flint Urban League; NAACP; Flint Commun. Civic League; Elks; Am. Legion; Cent. Budget Cmt, Red Feather Orgn; mem. adv. bd. Genesee Co. Skill Center, Flint Col. Labor Studies and League of Women Voters; mem. bd. dirs, Oak Knoll Park; dir, Big Brother of Flint, Inc, Genesee Co. Ment. Health, Mich. State Asn. Ment. Health, and Red Feather Bd; pres, Jefferson Sch. PTA; Rel: Protestant. Mailing Add: 753 Lyndon Ave, Flint, Mich. 48505.

OTT, T. TRUETT D
Fla. State Sen.
b. Osyka, Miss, 10/25/10; s. W.J. Ott and Margaret Alexandria O; m. 1/21/42 to Anita Williams; c. Sandra Ellen, Thomas William, Gary Truett and Hugh Justin. Educ: Hinds Jr. Col, Miss, 37-39; Univ. Fla, LL.B, 48; Phi Alpha Delta; Phi Delta Theta. Polit. & Govt. Pos: Fla. State Sen, 25th Dist, 66- Bus. & Prof. Pos: Mem, Bd. of Dirs, Peoples Bank of Tampa, 66. Mil. Serv: Entered as Aviation Cadet, Army Air Corps Flying Sch, 41, released as Maj, 46, after serv. as Asst. Dir. Opers. and Training, Caribbean Defense Command, Cent. and S.Am; recalled, 50 and released as Lt. Col, after 17 months, Korean Conflict. Publ: Florida Civil Trial Practice, Fla. Bar Manual, 63. Mem: Bd. of Dirs, Tampa-Hillsborough Co. Bar Asn, 64-66; Bd. of Dirs, Tampa YMCA, 60-66 and pres, 66; Fla. Bar Asn; Am. Trial Lawyers Asn; Acad. of Fla. Trial Attorneys; Ye Mystic Krewe of Gasparilla; Mason; Univ. of Southern Fla. Found; Tampa Art Inst. Outstanding Serv. Award by United Fund. Rel: Baptist. Legal Res: 614 S. Oregon, Tampa, Fla. 33606. Mailing Add: 101 E. Kennedy Blvd, Tampa, Fla. 33602.

OTTE, CARL D
Wis. State Assemblyman
b. Sheboygan, Wis, 6/24/23; s. John Otte and Magdalena Verconteren O; m. 11/1/48 to Ethel Dorothy Braatz; c. Allen Carl, Jane Karen, Julie Beth and Lynn Carol. Educ: Central High Sch, Sheboygan, grad. Polit. & Govt. Pos: Mem, Co. Bd, Sheboygan, Wis, 62-68, Parking Cmn, 65-68, Advisory Cmt. Commun. Develop, 68 and Police and Fire Cmn, 68-; Wis. State Assemblyman, currently. Mil. Serv: Entered as Pvt, Army, 43, released as Pfc, 45, after serv. in 478th Ord. Evacuation Co, ETO, 44-45. Mem: Local 325 Amalgamated Meat Cutter and Butcher Workmen of North Am; Local 95 Am. Fedn. of Musicians. Rel: Lutheran. Legal Res: 1440 S. 22nd St, Sheboygan, Wis. 53081. Mailing Add: 10 West, State Capitol, Madison, Wis. 53702.

OTTERMAN, ROBERT JAMES D
Mem. Exec. Bd, Dem. Cent. Cmt. Summit Co, Ohio
b. Akron, Ohio, 7/29/32; s. John L. Otterman and Marguerite Rauch O; m. 8/4/51 to Caroly Marie Anzaldi; c. John Robert and Robyn Marie. Educ: Akron Univ, B.A, Soc. Studies, 58 and M.A, Admin, 64; Lambda Chi Alpha. Polit. & Govt. Pos: Mem. exec. bd, Summit Co. Young Dem, Ohio, 63-65 & 68-, second v.pres, 65-66, 1st v.pres, 66-67, pres, 67-68; precinct committeeman, Summit Co. Dem. Party, 65-, youth coordinator, 67-, teen Dem. adv, 68-; col. adv, Akron Univ. Dem. Party, 67-; mem. exec. bd, Dem. Cent. Cmt. Summit Co, 67-; alternate del, Dem. Nat. Conv, 68. Bus. & Prof. Pos: Rep, Akron Educ. Asn, 64-65, legis. chmn. and mem. bd. dirs, 65-67; mem. legis. cmt, Ohio Educ. Asn, 65-66. Mil. Serv: Entered as Pvt, Marines, 50, re-

leased as Sgt, 54, after serv. in Seventh Marines, Korea, 52-53. Mem: Kent. Area Pupil Personnel Coun; Hilltop Guid. Coun; Akron Counselor's Asn; Ellet Citizens Asn; Summit Co. Ment. Health Asn. S.P.O.K.E. Award, Akron Jaycees, 65. Rel: Catholic; Pres, Cath. Relig. Prog, St. Matthew Church. Mailing Add: 738 Plainfield Rd, Akron, Ohio 44312.

OTTERSON, LAURA GUNDERSON R
Mem, Minn. State Rep. Cent. and Exec. Cmts.
b. Aneta, N.Dak, 8/17/07; d. John George Gunderson and Bertha Magoris G; m. 1/19/29 to Everett H. Otterson; c. Richard D. and David L. Educ: Mt. Ida Sch. for Girls, Newton, Mass. Polit. & Govt. Pos: Active in N.Dak. Rep. Party, 28-35; active in S.Dak. Rep. Party, 35-41; coordinator, Dr. Walter Judd's Campaign Cmt, Minn, 42-62; precinct chairwoman, 11th Ward Rep. Party, Minneapolis, chairwoman, 54-56; v.chairwoman, Fifth Cong. Dist. Rep. Party, 57-61, chairwoman, 61-65; del, Rep. Nat. Conv, 64; mem, Minn. State Rep. Cent. and Exec. Cmts, presently. Rel: Episcopal. Mailing Add: 716 E. 44th St, Minneapolis, Minn. 55407.

OTTERSON, MARGARET LaVERNE R
Mem, Calif. Rep. State Cent. Cmt.
b. Newcastle, Calif, 4/7/28; d. Virgil Vaugh Gilman and Nara Ann O'Donoghue G; m. 12/7/47 to Roy Wallace Otterson; c. Val Stanford, Donna Irene, Gail LaVerne and Hap Leonard. Educ: Notre Dame High Sch, Marysville, Calif, dipl, 46. Polit. & Govt. Pos: Mem, Glenn Co. Rep. Cent. Cmt, Calif, 64-, precinct chmn, 69-; mem, Calif. Rep. State Cent. Cmt, 64- Mem: Willows Monday Afternoon Club; Glenn Rep. Women's Fedn. Rel: Protestant. Mailing Add: Route 1, Box 307-A, Willows, Calif. 95988.

OTTERSTEIN, ADOLPH WILLIAM D
b. Denver, Colo, 12/9/06; s. Adolph William Otterstein and Eva Manhardt O; m. 8/14/29 to Margaret Louise Henderson; c. Adolph W, III and Evanne. Educ: Columbia Univ, B.S, 30; Stanford Univ, M.A, 33; Phi Mu Alpha; Phi Delta Kappa; Delta Chi. Polit. & Govt. Pos: Mem, Pueblo City Coun, Colo, 50-52; del, Dem. Nat. Conv, 68. Bus. & Prof. Pos: Head music dept, San Jose State Col, 30-42; pres, Otterstein & Co, Pueblo, Colo, 45- Mil. Serv: Entered as Pvt, Army Air Corps, 42, released as T/Sgt, 45, after serv. in 52nd Army Air Corp Band, U.S. Publ: Baton In Motion, Carl Fischer, Inc, 37. Mem: Life mem. Musicians Union; Am. Legion (past comdr, Post 2); Elks; Sertoma Club; C. of C; Pueblo Country Club. Rel: Episcopal. Mailing Add: 2001 Greenwood St, Pueblo, Colo. 81003.

OTTINGER, EDWARD E. R
Mo. State Rep.
b. St. Louis, Mo, 7/16/34; s. Alva Ottinger and Vera Hilbert O; single. Educ: Mo. Univ, B.S, 57. Polit. & Govt. Pos: Mo. State Rep, 60th Dist, currently. Mil. Serv: Entered as Seaman, Naval Air Res, 53, released as PO 3/C, 61. Mem: Real Estate Bd. of Metrop. St. Louis; dir, Associated Ins. Agents. & Brokers, 66; Nat. Asn. of Independent Fee Appraisers; Real Estate Salesmen Asn. of South St. Louis (pres, 64); Toastmasters. Rel: Presbyterian. Mailing Add: 5912 Loughborough, St. Louis, Mo. 63109.

OTTINGER, RICHARD LAWRENCE D
U.S. Rep, N.Y.
b. N.Y.C, 1/27/29; s. Lawrence Ottinger and Louise O; m. to Betty Ann Schneider; c. Ronald, Randall, Lawrence and Jenny Louise. Educ: Cornell Univ, B.A, 50; Harvard Law Sch, LL.B, 53; Georgetown Univ, grad study in int. law, 60-61. Polit. & Govt. Pos: Contract mgr, Int. Coop. Admin, 60-61; second staff mem. and dir. progs. Latin Am, West. Coast, Peace Corps, 61-64; U.S. Rep, N.Y, 25th Dist, 65-; del, Dem. Nat. Conv, 68. Bus. & Prof. Pos: Assoc, Wall Street Firm of Cleary Gottlieb, corp. and int. law practice, 55-56; partner, law firm, Kridel and Ottinger, N.Y.C, 56-60. Mil. Serv: Entered Air Force, 53, released as Capt, 55. Mem: Am, Inter-Am, Int, N.Y.C, Westchester Co. and Yonkers, N.Y. Bar Asns; nab. bd. dirs, UN Asn. of U.S; Westchester Co. Asn; bd. dirs, Westchester Childrens Asn; Cornell Univ. Coun; Tuskegee Inst, Nat. Adv. Coun; bd. dirs, Scarborough, Halsted Schs. Admitted to practice before U.S. Court of Appeals Second Circuit and U.S. Supreme Court, 60. Rel: Jewish. Legal Res: 235 Bear Ridge Rd, Pleasantville, N.Y. 10570. Mailing Add: 129 Cannon House Office Bldg, Washington, D.C. 20515.

OTTO, ARNOLD EUGENE D
b. Aurora, Nebr, 7/4/33; s. W. Gordon Otto and Wilma M. Arnold O; m. 8/21/67 to Phyllis June Rohay. Educ: Northwest Schs, Portland, Ore, dipl, 55; Univ. of Nebr, B.S, 69. Polit. & Govt. Pos: Del, Dem. Nat. Conv, 60 & 64; treas, Hamilton Co. Dem. Cent. Cmt, 60-64, chmn, 64-66; justice of the peace, Monroe-Phillips Precinct, 65-69. Bus. & Prof. Pos: Bookkeeper, Otto's Serv, Phillips, Nebr, 53-67; notary pub, Nebr. Sept. of State, Lincoln, 59-69; clerk, U.S. Post Off. Dept, Phillips, 61-67; asst. dir, Nebr. Civil Defense, 64-69; Health Prog. Rep. I, Off. of Migrant Health, Gering, 69- Mem: Speech Asn. of Am; Nebr. Speech Asn; Nat. Conf. of Christians and Jesw; U.S. Cmt. for the UN; Nebr. Sheriffs' and Peace Officers Asn; Nev. Wildlife Fedn, Inc; Boy Scouts; Am. Red Cross. Rel: Seventh Day Adventist. Mailing Add: Phillips, Nebr. 68865.

OTTO, CARL J. D
b. Mitchell, Nebr, 3/26/16; m. to Ruth; c. 2. Educ: Univ. of Wyo, B.S. Polit. & Govt. Pos: Wyo. State Rep, first term, -67. Bus. & Prof. Pos: Farmer and rancher; spec. agent Farmers Union Ins; former elem. and high sch. teacher. Mil. Serv: WWII, Combat. Mem: Lutheran Laymen's League; PTA; Farmers Union; Wheat Growers Asn, Goshen Co. Wheat Growers Asn, pres; Goshen Co. Stock Growers Asn; Am. Legion; VFW. Rel: Lutheran. Mailing Add: Route 1, Yoder, Wyo. 82244. (1967)

OTTO, HENRY P. R
b. Pittsburgh, 1/19/12; s. William Otto and Henrietta Rall; m. to June Turba; c. one. Educ: Pittsburgh Pub. Schs. Polit. & Govt. Pos: Pa. State Rep, 62-67; former mem, 44th Dist. Rep. State Cmt; former v.chmn, Penn Hills Rep. Cmt; Allegheny Co. Rep. Cmt. Bus. & Prof. Pos: Advert. exec; v.pres. Advert. Distributors of Am, Pgh; formerly held various admin. poss. with the H.J. Heinz Co. Mem: Former officer, Penn Hills Lions Club; Elks; Moose; Masonic bodies. Mailing Add: 361 Long Rd, Penn Hills, Pittsburgh, Pa. 15235. (1967)

OUBRE, GEORGE THURMAN D
La. State Sen.
b. Norco, La, 4/27/30; s. Lezin C. Oubre and Marguerite Bradley O; m. 6/30/51 to Barbara Williams; c. Joanne K, George T, Jr, Katherine L, John D. and Barbara L. Educ: Southeast. La. Col; La. State Univ, B.A, 52; Tulane Univ, LL.B, 57; Alpha Omega. Polit. & Govt. Pos: Asst. Dist. Attorney, 29th Judicial Court, La, 60-68; La. State Sen, 17th Dist, 68- Bus. & Prof. Pos: Attorney-at-law, Norco, La, 57-; pres, Credit Bur. of St. Charles Parish. Mil. Serv: Entered as Pvt, Army, 52, released as S/Sgt, 54, after serv. in Adjutant Gen. Corps, U.S. Mem: La. State, Am. and 29th Judicial Dist. Bar Asns; Lions; Riverlands Golf & Country Club; Kiwanis; East St. Charles Civic Coun; C. of C; Sun Villa. Rel: Roman Catholic. Legal Res: 777 Good Hope St, Norco, La. 70079. Mailing Add: #9 Apple St, Norco, La. 70079.

OURS, LARKIN B. R
W.Va. State Del.
b. Dorcas, W.Va, 4/4/17; s. George E. Ours and Sallie Bond O; m. 4/4/37 to Helen V. Keller; c. Sally Ann (Mrs. Ralph Dunkie). Educ: Pub. Schs. of Grant Co. Polit. & Govt. Pos: W.Va. State Del, 54- Bus. & Prof. Pos: Farming and livestock. Mem: Mason; former pres, Grant Co. Coop. Farm Serv; former pres, Grant Co. Farm Bur; dir, Am. Hereford Breeders Asn; W.Va. and Grant Co. Hereford Breeders Asns; W.Va. Poultry Asn; Grant Co. Rod and Gun Club; Petersburg Indust. Develop. Corp. Rel: Baptist. Legal Res: Dorcas, W.Va. 26835. Mailing Add: State Capitol, Charleston, W.Va. 25305. (1967)

OURS, RALPH WARDEN R
b. Portland, Ohio, 6/5/09; s. Charles Gilbert Ours and Harriet Frances Jones O; m. 10/3/36 to Murl Irene Trussell; c. Paul and Betty (Mrs. Gaul). Polit. & Govt. Pos: Twp. trustee, Ohio, 50-65; chmn, Ohio Rep. State Cent. Cmt, 58-68. Mem: Mason; Grange. Rel: Protestant. Mailing Add: Long Bottom, Ohio 45743. (1967)

OUSLEY, ROY GLENN D
Chmn, Union Co. Dem. Party, Tenn.
b. Loyston, Tenn, 4/12/11; s. Jacob Milus Ousley and Myrtle Longmire O; m. 3/29/36 to Dottie D. Davis; c. Betty C, Rosemary, Glenda Sue and Wanda Inez. Educ: Univ. Tenn. Polit. & Govt. Pos: Former chmn, Tenn. Dem. Exec. Cmt; chmn, Union Co. Dem. Party, 69- Bus. & Prof. Pos: Cashier, Union Co. Bank, 50- Mem: F&AM. Rel: Methodist. Mailing Add: Maynardville, Tenn. 37807. (1967)

OUTLAND, GEORGE E. D
b. Santa Paula, Calif, 10/8/06; s. Elmer Garfield Outland and Stella Martha Faulkner O; m. 12/2/38 to Ruth Merry; c. George Faulkner and John Warner. Educ: Whittier Col, A.B, 28; Harvard Univ, A.M, 29; Yale Univ, Ph.D, 37. Polit. & Govt. Pos: Mem, Calif. State Dem. Cent. Cmt, 42-52; U.S. Rep, Calif, 43-46; del, Dem. Nat. Conv, 44 & 48; chmn, Calif. State Dem. Policy Cmt, 46-48; mgr, Roosevelt for Gov. Campaign, Primary Elec, 49-50. Bus. & Prof. Pos: Asst. dir, Boys' Work, Hale House, Boston, 28-30; dir, Denison House, Boston, 29-33; dir, Boys' Work, Los Angeles Neighborhood House, 33-35; dir, South. Calif. Fed. Transient Serv, 34-35; dir, New Haven Commun. Col, 35-36; instr, Yale Univ, 35-37; asst. prof, Santa Barbara State Col, 37-43; prof, San Francisco State Col, 47- Publ: Boy Transiency in America, Santa Barbara State Col. Press, 39; Sociological Foundations of Education, with J. Roucek, Crowell, 40; numerous articles in scholarly jours. and 2 in Readers' Digest. Mem: Nat. Cmt. for an Effective Cong; Bd. of Dirs, Consumers Union, 7 years and Pub. Affairs Inst, 46-64. Achievements: More than 20 appearances on nat. broadcasts, including Town Meeting of the Air, Wake-up America and American Forum of the Air. Rel: Methodist Episcopal. Legal Res: 528 Font Blvd, San Francisco, Calif. 94132. Mailing Add: 1600 Holloway, San Francisco, Calif. 94132.

OUTLAW, NIGLE C. D
Chmn, Garza Co. Dem. Exec. Cmt, Tex.
b. San Gabriel, Tex, 5/9/97; s. Elmer Alpheus Outlaw and Zora Barclay O; m. 2/17/26 to Mildred Lorena Pate; c. Zora Anne (Mrs. Evans) and Alma Louise (Mrs. Boone). Educ: Baylor Univ, LL.B, 25; Senate and Barrister's Temple. Polit. & Govt. Pos: Spec. co. and dist. judge on various occasions; co. attorney, Crosby Co, Tex, 29-30; presidential elector, Tex. Dem. Party, 32 & 56; conciliation cmnr, Fed. Govt, 33-35; co. surveyor, 39-40; co. attorney, Garza Co, Tex, 41-42; appeal agent, Selective Serv, 42-62; chmn, Garza Co. Dem. Exec. Cmt, 57-; v.chmn, Dem. State Conv, 60. Mil. Serv: Entered as Pvt, Army, 17, released as Sgt, 19, after serv. in 3rd U.S. Cavalry, France, 17-19; Victory Medal; French Campaign Ribbon. Mem: Past pres, Garza Co. Bar Asn; past pres, South Plains Bar Asn; Tex. State Bar Asn; Am. Legion; VFW. Rel: Methodist. Legal Res: Lubbock Rd, Post, Tex. 79356. Mailing Add: Box 206, Post, Tex. 79356.

OVERBY, HOWARD THOMAS D
b. Buford, Ga, 6/14/15; s. James Floyd Overby and Sallie Thomas O; m. 8/8/47 to Lalla Green Nimocks; c. Currie Nimocks, Sally, Howard Thomas, Jr. Educ: Mercer Univ; Univ. of Ga, LL.B, 37; S.A.E. Fraternity; Phi Alpha Delta. Polit. & Govt. Pos: Ga. State Rep, 63-66, 57-58, 51-52, 47-48; Ga. State Sen, 61-62, 55-56, 49-50; Attorney, Hall Co, 57-58; Asst. Solicitor Gen, Northeast. Circuit, 49-50. Bus. & Prof. Pos: Attorney; admitted to Gainesville, Ga. Bar, 38. Mil. Serv: U.S. Army, WW II, 1st Lt. Mem: Mason; Shriner; Elk; Odd Fellows; Red Men; Lions; Moose; Am. Legion. Rel: Baptist. Mailing Add: 1173 Riverside Dr, Gainesville, Ga. 30501. (1967)

OVERMAN, HENRY 'BUD' D
b. 1927. Educ: Villa Madonna Col, B.A. Polit. & Govt. Pos: Former Ky. State Rep; alternate del, Dem. Nat. Conv, 68. Bus. & Prof. Pos: Sales rep, Boehmer Paint Co. Mil. Serv: Army. Mem: Assoc. mem, Jaycees. Rel: Catholic. Mailing Add: 29 Bivouac Place, Ft. Thomas, Ky. 41075. (1967)

OVERPECK, LEM FRANKLIN R
b. Belle Fourche, S.Dak, 9/18/11; s. Tyler S. Overpeck and Lulu Temple O; m. 8/21/39 to Helen E. Brewer; c. Gretchen (Mrs. Haahr), Janifer (Mrs. Farquhar), Lizabeth (Mrs. Manning), and Marylu. Educ: Univ. S.Dak, LL.B, 36; Phi Delta Phi; Phi Delta Theta. Polit. & Govt. Pos: States attorney, Butte

Co, S.Dak, 39-41 & 46-50; del, Rep. Nat. Conv, 48; pres, Bd. Regents, 54-60; S.Dak. State Sen, 63-64; lt. gov, 64-68. Mil. Serv: Entered as Lt.(jg), Naval Res, released as Lt, 46. Mem: S.Dak. and Am. Bar Asns; Am. Judicature Soc; Int. Soc. of Barristers; Am. Legion; Elks; Mason; Shrine. Rel: Episcopal. Mailing Add: 1208 Eighth Ave, Belle Fourche, S.Dak. 57717.

OVERSTREET, FREDERICK HEISKELL R
Chmn, 19th Representative Dist. Rep. Party, Hawaii
b. Ft. Pierce, Fla, 9/17/20; s. Seaborn Franklin Overstreet and Elizabeth Heiskell O; m. 3/18/60 to Dorothy Jean Barnett; c. Mary Ann Elizabeth and Catherine Ann. Educ: Mercer Univ, B.A; Alpha Tau Omega. Polit. & Govt. Pos: Rep. precinct chmn, 13th Precinct, Tenth Dist, Hawaii, 67-68; chmn, Citizens for Reagan, 68; alternate del, Rep. Nat. Conv, 68; chmn, 19th Rep. Dist. Rep. Party, Hawaii, 69- Bus. & Prof. Pos: Field rep, Gen. Motors Acceptance Corp, Wash, D.C, 55-58; loan rep, First Hawaiian Bank, Honolulu, 58-62; pres. and gen. mgr, Pac. Investment Inc, Honolulu, 62- Mil. Serv: Entered as Pvt, Army, 51, released as Sgt. 1/C, 55, after serv. in 8057 Army Unit, Korea, 51-55; Nat. Defense Unit Citation (4); UN Ribbon; Korean Campaign Medal with 4 Stars. Mem: Lodge Les Progres de L'Oceanie; F&AM; York Rite; Elks; Rotary. Rel: Episcopal. Mailing Add: 4211 Halupa St, Honolulu, Hawaii 96818.

OWEN, BEN D
Miss. State Rep.
b. Columbus, Miss, 7/12/21; s. Frank Owen and Mary Askew O; m. 6/12/49 to Mary Jane Collins; c. Lydia Watson, Frank Caleb, Marsha Ethridge, David Collins, Mary Jane and Judith Sharp. Educ: Univ. Miss, B.S, 42, LL.B, 47; Phi Delta Theta. Polit. & Govt. Pos: Miss. State Rep, 64- Mil. Serv: Entered as Lt, Army, 42, released as Capt, 46, after serv. in Pac. Theater, 42-45. Mem: Lowndes Co, Miss. and Am. Bar Asns; Lowndes Co. Farm Bur; Am. Legion; VFW; Elks; Moose; Kiwanis Int; Ole Miss. Alumni Asn; Ole Miss. M Club. Rel: Baptist. Legal Res: Route 3, Box 136 Columbus, Miss. 39701. Mailing Add: P.O. Box 1001, Columbus, Miss. 39701.

OWEN, CLYDE CRADDOCK 'JACK' D
Cmnr, Ala. Pub. Serv. Cmn.
b. West Blocton, Ala, 10/1/15; s. Clyde Craddock Owen and Pat O; m. 10/15/43 to Mary Frances Landers; c. Jane Larraine (Mrs. Morris, Jr.), Mary Katherine (Mrs. Davis, Jr) and Clyde Craddock, Jr. Educ: Auburn Univ, B.S, 39; Blue Key; Alpha Gamma Rho. Polit. & Govt. Pos: Cmnr, Ala. Pub. Serv. Cmn, 47-51 & 67-, pres, 51-65. Bus. & Prof. Pos: Asst. co. agent, Ala. Exten. Serv, 39-42; owner, Owen Lumber Co, Tuscaloosa, 45-47; bus. consultant, Montgomery, 65-66. Mil. Serv: Entered as Cadet, Marines, 42, released as Lt, 45, after serv. in Southwest Pac. Theatre, Luzon and Mindinao; Distinguished Flying Cross; the Air Medal. Mem: Mason; Shrine. Rel: Episcopal. Legal Res: 1864 S. Hull St, Montgomery, Ala. 36104. Mailing Add: P.O. Box 991, Montgomery, Ala. 36102.

OWEN, DAVID CARROLL R
Kans. State Sen.
b. Hermitage, Ark, 8/10/38; s. Robert Carroll Owen and Lois M. Clanton O; m. 7/5/58 to Beverly Ann Lewis; c. Debbie, Beth and Melissa. Educ: Ohawa Univ, B.A, 60. Polit. & Govt. Pos: Kans. State Sen, 69- Bus. & Prof. Pos: V.pres, Overland Park State Bank, Kans, currently. Mil. Serv: Army Res, 7 years. Mem: Cosmopolitan; C. of C. Rel: Protestant. Mailing Add: 7701 W. 100th, Overland Park, Kans. 66212.

OWEN, G. STAFFORD D
b. Maysville, Mo, 8/6/99; m. 3/1/24 to Esta Dice. Educ: Drake Univ, Des Moines, Iowa; Northwest Mo. State Col, Maryville; Mo. Wesleyan Col. Polit. & Govt. Pos: Mo. State Rep, 54-66. Bus. & Prof. Pos: Kans. City Life Ins. Co, 47-; engaged in retail clothing bus, 25 years; taught and was prin. in the Mo. pub. schs, 6 years. Mem: Masons; Moila Shrine; charter mem. Maysville Rotary Club. Rel: Christian Church. Mailing Add: Sheridan St, Maysville, Mo. 64469. (1967)

OWEN, HENRY D.
b. N.Y, N.Y, 8/26/20; m. 3/56 to Hertha Stockreiter; c. Two. Educ: Harvard Univ. A.B, 41. Polit. & Govt. Pos: Economist, Off. of Price Admin, 41-42; econ, Intel. Research, 46-55; U.S. State Dept. of State, 46-69, mem, Policy Planning Staff, 55-62, dep. counselor and v.chmn, Policy Planning Coun, 62-66, chmn, 66-69; dir, For. Policy Studies Prog, The Brookings Inst, 69- Mil. Serv: Lt, U.S. Navy, 42-46. Meritorious Serv. Award, State Dept, 62. Mailing Add: 2946 University Terr, Washington, D.C. 20016.

OWEN, KENNETH E. D
b. Jerome, Iowa, 9/1/18; m. 1937 to Frances Hamm; c. Keith, Diana. Educ: Centerville Jr. Col. Polit. & Govt. Pos: Iowa State Secy. of Agr, 64-66; Iowa State Sen, 56th - 58th Gen. Assemblies. Bus. & Prof. Pos: actively engaged in farming since 1936. Mem: 4-H mem. and long-time leader; various agr. organs. Received the Iowa Master Swine Producers award in 1953. Mailing Add: Plano, Iowa 52581. (1967)

OWEN, L. DICK, JR. D
Ala. State Rep.
b. Bay Minette, Ala, 4/10/19; s. L. D. Owen and Kate Lee O; m. 9/15/49 to Annie Ruth Heidelberg; c. L. D, III. Educ: Univ. Ala, B.S, 41; Pi Kappa Phi. Polit. & Govt. Pos: City councilman, Bay Minette, Ala, 60-63; judge of probate, Baldwin Co, 63-64; Ala. State Rep, presently. Mil. Serv: Entered as 2nd Lt, Army, 41, released as Capt, 46, after serv. in 82nd A/B Div, ETO, 43-45; 2 Bronze Stars; Combat Inf. Badge; ETO Theater Ribbon with 6 Campaign Stars; Lt. Col.(Ret), Army Res, 62. Mem: Ala. State Comdr, VFW, 50; Am. Legion. Rel: Baptist. Legal Res: 211 11th St, Bay Minette, Ala. 36507. Mailing Add: Box 45, Bay Minette, Ala. 36507.

OWEN, SANK EDWARD R
Chmn, Monroe Co. Rep. Party, Miss.
b. Aberdeen, Miss, 2/12/27; s. Sank Owen and Louise Howell O; single. Educ: Miss. State Univ, B.S, 47; George Peabody Col. Teachers, M.A, 55; v.pres, YMCA, Miss. State Univ; pres, Miss. Club, George Peabody Col. for Teachers. Polit. & Govt. Pos: Committeeman, Monroe Co. Rep. Party, Dist. 2, Miss, 64-68; campaign mgr. for Rubel Phillips, cand. for Gov. of Miss, Monroe Co, 67; chmn, Monroe Co. Rep. Party, Miss, 68- Mil. Serv: Entered as Recruit, Army, 50, released as S/Sgt, 52, after serv. in 45th Inf. Div, Korean Conflict, 51-52; Good Conduct Medal and Ribbons. Publ: 'Articles to Holly Springs,' South Reporter, 1951-55; 'Why I Chose Peabody,' Peabody Reflector, 56. Mem: Nat, Miss. and Amory Educ. Asns; Miss. Folklore Soc; secy, Marshall Co. Educ. Asn, 53-54; secy, Monroe Co. Educ. Asn, 58-59; pres, Aberdeen Educ. Asn, 62-63; Amory Lions (dep. gov, Lions Int. 30-A, 65-66); Am. Legion. Teacher of the Year Award for Aberdeen, 60; Runner-Up for Miss. Teacher of the Year, 60. Rel: Methodist. Legal Res: Route 2, Box 18, Aberdeen, Miss. 39730. Mailing Add: P.O. Box 182, Amory, Miss. 38821.

OWENBY, WILLIAM EMILY R
Chmn, Union Co. Rep. Party, S.C.
b. Mooresville, N.Carolina, 12/10/28; s. James F. Owenby and Inez Toney O; m. 12/17/49 to Raymoth Jane Wood; c. William Barry, James Christopher and John Preston. Educ: Wofford Col, 3 years. Polit. & Govt. Pos: State Exec. Committeeman, Union Co. Rep. Party, S.C, 64-68, chmn, 68- Bus. & Prof. Pos: Qual. control supvr, Excelsior Woolen Mill, Union, S.C, 58-69, color develop. mgr, 69- Mil. Serv: Entered as A/S, Navy, 46, released as Qm. 2/c, 49 after serv. in U.S.S. Little Rock cruiser and U.S.S. Hamilton minesweeper, ETO, 46-49; European Theatre, Occupation, African Asiatic Theater and Good Conduct Medals; World War II Victory Medal. Mem: Am. Soc. for Qual. Control; C. of C; AF&AM; Am. Legion; Hejas Temple AAONMS. Rel: Baptist. Mailing Add: 312 Catawba St, Union, S.C. 29379.

OWENS, BILLY E. D
b. Bardwell, Ky, 9/8/24; s. Ike Owens and Inez Dodson O; m. 12/21/46 to Naomi Johnson; c. Ricky Ray and Randol Edward. Educ: Arlington High Sch. Polit. & Govt. Pos: Mem, Henry Co. Court, Tenn, 65-; del. and co-chmn, Pub. Info. Cmt, Tenn. Constitutional Conv, 65-66; del, Dem. Nat. Conv, 64; pub. chmn, Henry Co. Dem. Cmt, 64; state exec. committeeman, Young Dem. Club, Ky, 57-58; chmn, draft bd, Carlisle Co, Ky, 55. Bus. & Prof. Pos: Owner, Owens Adjustment Serv, 60-; pres, Southall Adjustment Serv, 57-60; staff adjuster, Serv. Ins. Co, N.Y, 51. Mil. Serv: Entered as Pvt, Army, 43, released as Cpl, after serv. in Vet. Corps, China-Burma-India, reentered serv. 50, released, 51. Mem: Elks; Am. Legion; VFW; C. of C; Optimist; Paris Country Club. Rel: Missionary Baptist. Legal Res: 601 S. Dunlap, Paris, Tenn. 38242. Mailing Add: P.O. Box 606, Paris, Tenn. 38242.

OWENS, DON R
Mo. State Sen.
b. Beaufort, Mo, 8/7/05; s. Dr. I. M. Owens and Mollie Richardson O; m. 9/21/33 to Caroline Raaf; c. Robert and William D. Educ: Jennings High Sch, Mo, grad, 23. Polit. & Govt. Pos: Past city treas. of Gerald, Mo; past pres, Gerald Sch. Bd; mem, Franklin Co. Rep. Cent. Cmt, 22 years; Mo. State Sen, 62- Mem: AF&AM; Scottish Rite; Shrine; Eastern Star; Lions. Rel: Evangelical Reformed; former pres, St. Pauls Evangelical Reformed Church of Gerald. Mailing Add: 374 S. Bernhardt Ave, Gerald, Mo. 63037.

OWENS, DOUGLAS WAYNE D
b. Panguitch, Utah, 5/2/37; s. Joseph Owens and Ruth Dodds O; m. 8/18/61 to Marlene Wessel; c. Elizabeth, Henry Douglas, Sarah Ruth and Stephen W. Educ: Univ. Utah Col. Law, J.D, 64; Phi Delta Phi. Polit. & Govt. Pos: Rocky Mt. Coordinator, Kennedy for Pres. Cmt, 68; asst. to Sen. Frank E. Moss, Utah, 63-69; del, Dem. Nat. Conv, 68 and mem. Platform Cmt; asst. to U.S. Sen. and Senate Majority Whip Edward M. Kennedy, 69- Bus. & Prof. Pos: Attorney-at-law, Salt Lake City, Utah, 65-68. Mem: Utah, Salt Lake Co. and Am. Bar Asns. Rel: Latter-day Saint. Legal Res: Salt Lake City, Utah. Mailing Add: 3243 Highland Lane, Fairfax, Va. 22030.

OWENS, ERWIN D
b. Canon, Ga, 2/9/20; s. William Gladstone Owens and Eddythe Baker O; m. 5/3/52 to Margaret Alice Richards; c. Richard Erwin, Dudley Kenneth. Educ: Univ. of Ga, 41. Polit. & Govt. Pos: Ga. State Sen, 61-66. Bus. & Prof. Pos: Hatchery owner. Mil. Serv: U.S.A.F, WW II, 41-45. Rel: Methodist. Mailing Add: Dahlonega, Ga. 30533. (1967)

OWENS, FRANK CAPERS D
S.C. State Sen.
b. Columbia, S.C, 12/17/98; s. Lawrence B. Owens, M.D. and Clara Capers O; m. 11/8/23 to Ida Hand; c. Frances Rebecca, Vivian Capers and Louise Beacham. Educ: Univ. S.C, B.S, 19; S.C. Med. Col, M.D, 23; Kappa Alpha; Blue Key. Polit. & Govt. Pos: Mayor, Columbia, S.C, 46-50; S.C. Chmn, Med. Adv. Cmt. to Selective Serv, 52-67; v.chmn. exec. cmt, S.C. Bd. of Health and mem. exec. cmt, S.C. Pollution Control Authority, 55-67; S.C. State Sen, Richland Co, 66- Mil. Serv: Entered as Capt, Air Force, 42, released as Lt. Col, 45, after serv. in Air Serv. Command and Med. Corps. Mem: Am, Southern, S.C. and Columbia Med. Asns; Am. Legion; 40 et 8; Mason, Shrine; Lions; Elks; Forest Lake Country Club; Palmetto Club. Rel: Episcopal. Legal Res: 431 Edisto Ave, Columbia, S.C. 29205. Mailing Add: 1319 Laurel St, Columbia, S.C. 29201.

OWENS, HOLLIS M, JR. D
Chmn, Rutherford Co. Dem. Exec. Cmt, N.C.
b. Avondale, N.C, 4/3/23; s. Hollis Monroe, Sr. and Jessie Jenkins O; m. 9/1/48 to Frances Smith; c. Mary Frances, Hollis Monroe, III. Educ: Wofford Col, A.B, 43; Duke Univ. Law Sch, LL.B, 49; Lambda Chi Alpha (pres, 43); Phi Alpha Delta. Polit. & Govt. Pos: Solicitor, Rutherford Co. Recorder's Court, N.C, 52-58; pres, Rutherford Co. Young Dem. Club, 53; mem, Cmn. of Reorgn. of State Govt, 61-63; N.C. State Rep, 61-66; mem, Legis. Coun, 63-65; chmn, Rutherford Co. Dem. Exec. Cmt, 68- Bus. & Prof. Pos: Lawyer. Mil. Serv: Army, Sgt, 43-45, Inf. Div; Purple Heart; Bronze Star, 3 Battle Stars. Mem: N.C. State Bar; N.C. Bar Asn; Rutherford Co. Bar Asn. (pres, 53); pres, Methodist Men's Club, 55; v.chmn, bd. of stewards, 56; supt, Adult Dept, 58-61; pres, Rutherford Co. Club, 66; pres, Rutherford Co. Red Cross Drive, 53; pres, Rutherfordton Jr. C. of C, 59; trustee, Isothermal Commun. Col, 64- Rel: Methodist. Mailing Add: 204 Fernwood Dr, Rutherfordton, N.C. 28139.

OWENS, HUGH FRANKLIN D
Cmnr, U.S. Securities and Exchange Cmn.
b. Muskogee, Okla, 10/15/09; s. James Francis Owens and Elizabeth Turner

O; m. 12/27/34 to Louise Simon; c. Julie (Mrs. William Charles Pickens). Educ: Univ. Ill, A.B, 31; Univ. Okla, LL.B, 34; Phi Delta Phi; Sigma Chi, Significant Sig Award. Polit. & Govt. Pos: Adminstr, Okla. Securities Cmn, 59-64; cmnr, Securities and Exchange Cmn, Wash, 64- Bus. & Prof. Pos: Assoc, Cummins, Hagenah & Flynn, Chicago, Ill, 34-36; assoc, Rainey, Flynn, Green & Anderson, Oklahoma City, Okla, 36-48; mem. bd. dirs, Salvation Army, Oklahoma City Commun. Fund, 38-41; partner, Hervey, May & Owens, Oklahoma City, 48-51; div. attorney, Superior Oil Co, Midland, Tex, 51-53; gen. counsel, Nat. Assoc. Petrol. Co, Tulsa, 53; attorney-at-law, Oklahoma City, 53-59; mem. part time faculty, Okla. City Univ. Law Sch, 57-64. Mil. Serv: Naval Res, World War II. Mem: Bar, U.S. Supreme Court; exec. cmt, Nat. Asn. R.R. and Utility Cmnr; hon. life mem, Kans. Bar Asn; Okla. Bar Asn; Retired Officers Asn; U.S. Jr. C. of C, v.pres, 40-41; Oklahoma City C. of C; bd. dirs, K. of C; Clubs, Metrop. and Chevy Chase. Mailing Add: Securities and Exchange Commission, 500 N. Capitol, Washington D.C. 20549.

OWENS, JAMES KING, JR. R
Chmn, Pickens Co. Rep. Exec. Cmt, Ala.
b. Birmingham, Ala, 10/18/30; s. James King Owens and Beatrice Geer O; m. 10/30/53 to Vivian Thompson; c. James, III and Yolande V. Educ: Univ. of Ala, B.S, 53; Beta Gamma Sigma; chap. pres, Alpha Kappa Psi. Polit. & Govt. Pos: Mem, Pickens Co. Rep. Exec. Cmt, Ala, 62-64, secy-treas, 64-65 and chmn, 65-; trustee, Pickens Co. Hosp. Bd, 66- and Hale Mem. Tuberc. Hosp, 68-; councilman, Gordo Town Coun, 68- Bus. & Prof. Pos: Cashier, Bank of Gordo, Ala, 57- and v.pres, 66-; agency mgr, Owens Ins. Agency, Inc, 67- Mil. Serv: Entered as A/S, Navy, 54, released as Lt.(jg), 57, after serv. in Naval Air Sta, Pensacola, Fla; Lt. Comdr, Naval Res, 63-; Nat. Defense Serv. Medal; Naval Reserve Medal. Mem: Past chmn, Region IV, Ala. Bankers Asn; past pres, Gordo Rotary; Naval Reserve Asn; Reserve Officers Asn; secy, Knolls Country Club; Indian Hills Country Club. Rel: United Methodist. Legal Res: Sullivan Addition, Gordo, Ala. 35466. Mailing Add: P.O. Box 27, Gordo, Ala. 35466.

OWENS, RONALD D
N.J. State Assemblyman
b. Newark, N.J, 2/4/30; s. Leroy and Eleanor O; m. to Louise Redding; c. Randall Scott, Pamela Tracy. Educ: Rutgers Univ, B.A, 53; Seton Hall Law Sch, 59. Polit. & Govt. Pos: Mem, Newark Bd. of Educ, N.J, 63-66; asst. corp. counsel, Newark, 66-69; N.J. State Assemblyman, presently. Bus. & Prof. Pos: Teacher, Newark Pub. Sch. Syst, N.J, 55-; law clerkship under Ferdinando J. Biunno, Esq, Off. of the U.S. Rep. Peter W. Rodino, Jr, 59-; lawyer, Newark, presently. Mil. Serv: Signal Corps, 53-55. Mem: Essex Co, N.J. and Am. Bar Asns; exec. bd, Newark Br. NAACP. Mailing Add: 84 Barclay St, Newark, N.J. 07102.

OWENS, RUTH JOHNSON D
Dem. Nat. Committeewoman, Ala.
m. to Wyatt Owens; c. Two. Polit. & Govt. Pos: Formerly active with Young Dem; personal secy, Gov. Folsom, Ala, 55-58; Dem. Nat. Committeewoman, Ala, 60-; del, Dem. Nat. Conv, 68. Mailing Add: 1208 Vista Lane, Birmingham, Ala. 35203.

OWENS, STANLEY ALBERT D
Va. State Del.
b. Canon, Ga, 2/10/07; m. to Janet Rebecca Trusler. Educ: Emory University Law Sch, Atlanta; University of Ga. Law Sch, Athens, LL.B, 31; Pi Kappa Alpha; Phi Alpha Delta. Polit. & Govt. Pos: Past dir, Va. State C. of C; v.pres, Commonwealth's Attorneys' Asn, 59; Commonwealth attorney, Prince William Co, 44-60; Va. State Del, 60- Bus. & Prof. Pos: Lawyer; pres, Piedmont Tel. Co, Manassas; pres. & gen. counsel, Piedmont Fed. Savings and Loan Asn, Manassas; dir. & v.chmn. of Bd, The Nat. Bank of Manassas. Mem: Kiwanis (past pres); Ruritan (past pres. and past Lt. Gov); Gr. Manassas C. of C. Rel: Baptist. Mailing Add: Box 109, Manassas, Va. 22110.

OWENS, THOMAS JEROME D
Chmn, Sangamon Co. Dem. Cmt, Ill.
b. Springfield, Ill, 10/24/20; s. Harry Grant Owens and Nonie Bowe O; m. 4/10/48 to Lela Williams; c. Terrance and Virginia L. Polit. & Govt. Pos: Chmn, Sangamon Co. Dem. Cmt, Ill, 60-; supt. Buildings & Grounds, State of Ill, 64- Mil. Serv: Entered as Pvt, Army, 42, released as M/Sgt, 46, after serving in 96th Inf. Div, South Pacific. Mem: Ill. Landscape Contractors Asn; Licensed Tree Expert; Cent. Ill. Nurseryman's Asn; Am. Legion; VFW, 96th Inf. Div. Asn; K. of C. Rel: Catholic. Mailing Add: R.R. 2, Pleasant Plains, Ill. 62677.

OWENS, WILLIAM E. D
Mem. Bd. Co. Cmn, Martin Co, Fla.
b. Palm Beach, Fla, 10/7/25; m. to Ronda Stephens; c. Jaima, William E. Jr, and Heather. Educ: Univ. of Fla, BS, BA, 1950. Polit. & Govt. Pos: Planning and Adv. Bd. of City of Stuart, charter mem. and two years as first chmn; three terms, including chairmanship, supvr, Martin Co. Soil Conserv. Dist. Bd. of Supvrs; Fla. State Rep, 62-66; mem, Bd. of Co. Cmn, Martin Co, 68- Bus. & Prof. Pos: Citrus Fruit Grower; Charter Mem, Bd. of Dirs, First Fed. Savings and Loan Asn. of Martin Co. Mil. Serv: 2 years Army Air Force. Mem: Bd. of dirs, Martin Co. Chap, Am. Red Cross, former chmn; bd. of dirs, Martin Co. Fair Asn; former pres, Martin Co. Farm Bus; Phi Delta Theta; Mason; former pres, Kiwanis Club of Indiantown; former lt. gov, Div. 13, Fla. Dist, Kiwanis Int. Grandfather, State Legislator and Palm Beach Co. Tax Assessor; Father, Palm Beach Co. Tax Assessor; Fishing; Golf. Rel: Presbyterian, Elder and Supt. of Sunday Sch. Mailing Add: Route 1, Box 194, Stuart, Fla. 33494.

OWENS, WILLIAM EDWARD, JR. 'BILL' D
Ala. State Rep.
b. Gadsden, Ala, 5/31/28; s. William Edward Owens, Sr. and Ophelia Tolbert O; m. 11/22/49 to Julia Crosby; c. William E, III and Lila Ann. Educ: Univ. of Ala, Gadsden Center, 53-56. Polit. & Govt. Pos: Ala. State Rep, 63- Bus. & Prof. Pos: Secy-treas, W.E. Owens Lumber Co, Inc, Ala, presently. Mem: Gadsden Exchange Club (pres, 59); Etowah Co. Home Builders Asn; mem, State Bldg. Cmn, 63-67. Rel: Baptist. Mailing Add: 1243 Sangster Rd, Gadsden, Ala. 35901.

OWLES, FAE BIDGOOD D
Pres, Dem. Women's Club, Fla.
b. Dublin, Ga, 11/23/32; d. Grover Cleveland Bidgood and Henrietta Turner B; m. 6/12/54 to Frederick George Owles, Jr; c. Margaret Alyson and Frederick George, III. Educ: Shorter Col, 50-52; Polymnian Social Soc; Shorter Soc. Coun. Polit. & Govt. Pos: Mem. bd. of dirs. and precinct committeewoman, Orange Co. Dem. Exec. Cmt, 56-66, area co-ordinator, 60-66; pres, Winter Park Dem. Women's Club, 61-62; v.pres, Fla. Dem. Women's Club, 62-64, secy, 64-66, pres, 66-; del-at-lg, Dem. Nat. Conv, 64, del, 68. Mem: League of Women Voters; bd. of dirs, Winter Park Youth Center; past pres, Auxiliary, Am. Inst. of Architects; former, Jr. Serv. League of Winter Park. Selected Woman of the Week, Orlando Daily Newspapers, Inc. Rel: Roman Catholic. Mailing Add: 531 Worthington Dr, Winter Park, Fla. 32789.

OXLEY, MYRON B. D
b. Marion, Iowa, 9/14/22; s. Ralph Oxley and Mary O; m. 2/16/56 to Jean Liabo; c. three. Educ: Marion High Sch. Polit. & Govt. Pos: Iowa State Rep, -66; Dem. Committeeman, Marion Twp. 10 years. Bus. & Prof. Pos: Livestock and Grain Farmer. Mem: Hawkeye Angus Asn; four Coops; Masonic Lodge, A.F. & A.M. No. 6, Marion, Iowa. Rel: Methodist. Mailing Add: Route 2, Marion, Iowa 52302. (1967)

OZINGA, FRANK M. R
Ill. State Sen.
b. Chicago, Ill, 8/30/14; s. Martin Ozinga and Wilma Hoving O; m. 1/5/38 to Grace Stob; c. Wilma, Martin, Ronald, Janice and Marcia. Educ: Cent. YMCA Col, A.A, 34; Chicago Kent Col. of Law, LL.B, 38. Polit. & Govt. Pos: Asst. attorney gen, Ill, 49-; asst. probate judge, Cook Co, 48-56; Ill. State Sen, 56- Bus. & Prof. Pos: Chmn. of the Bd, 1st Nat. Bank of Evergreen Park, Ill, 49- Mil. Serv: Entered as Ens, Navy, 44, released as Lt.(jg), 46. Mem: Chicago, Am. and Ill. Bar Asns; Lions. Rel: Christian Reformed Church. Legal Res: 9626 S. Homan Ave, Evergreen Park, Ill. 60642. Mailing Add: 3101 W. 95 St, Evergreen Park, Ill. 60642.

OZZARD, WILLIAM E. R
Mem, N.J. Rep. State Cmt.
b. Weehawken, N.J, 6/15/15; s. James H. Ozzard and Josephine Bergman O; div; c. Suzanne Lee (Mrs. Cruver) and Kathryn E. Educ: Rutgers Univ. and Ind. Univ, pre-law, 3 years; N.Y. Univ. Sch. of Law, LL.B; N.Y. Univ. Law Rev. Asn. Polit. & Govt. Pos: Acting gov, N.J. 63; former N.J. State Sen, Somerset-Hunterdon Co, pres, N.J. State Senate, 63, former Minority Leader; mem, N.J. Rep. State Cmt, 69- Bus. & Prof. Pos: Law partner, Beekman, Ozzard & Mauro, currently. Mil. Serv: Entered as Pvt, Army, 44, released as 1st Lt, 46, after serv. as Asst. Adj. Gen, 3rd Army Hq, ETO; ETO Campaign Ribbon with Three Battle Stars. Mem: Am, N.J. and Somerset Co. Bar Asns; Rotary Int. Rel: Presbyterian. Legal Res: 1908 Mountain Top Rd, Somerville, N.J. 08876. Mailing Add: 27 N. Bridge St, Somerville, N.J. 08876. (1967)

P

PAARLBERG, DON R
Dir. of Agr. Econ, U.S. Dept. of Agr.
b. Oak Glen, Ill, 6/20/11; s. Henry P. Paarlberg and Grace Int-Hout P; m. 6/23/40 to Eva Louisa Robertson; c. Don, Jr. and Robert Lynn. Educ: Purdue Univ, B.S, 40; Cornell Univ, M.S, 43, Ph.D, 46; Sigma Xi; Alpha Gamma Rho. Polit. & Govt. Pos: Asst. to the Secy, U.S. Dept. of Agr, 53-57, asst. secy, 57-58, dir. of agr. econ, 69-; spec. asst. to the President, 58-61, food for peace coordinator, 60-61. Bus. & Prof. Pos: Prof, Purdue Univ, 46-53, Hillenbrand prof. agr. econ, 61-69. Publ: Food (with F.A. Pearson), Knopf, 44; American Farm Policy, Wiley, 64; Great Myths of Economics, New Am. Libr, 68. Mem: Am. Econ. Asn; Am. Agr. Econ. Asn; Am. Farm Bur. Fedn. Best Teacher Award, Purdue Univ, 61 & 68; Award for Distinguished Serv. to Am. Agr, Am. Soc. of Farm Mgrs, 66. Rel: Methodist. Legal Res: 1214 Hayes, West Lafayette, Ind. 47906. Mailing Add: D705, 2440 Virginia Ave. N.W, Washington, D.C. 20037.

PACARRO, RUDOLPH D
Hawaii State Rep.
b. Watertown, Honolulu, Hawaii, 10/6/27; s. Frank Suan Pacarro and Juliana Adorna P; m. 6/10/50 to Mabel Jean Cortezan; c. Rudolph, William, Catalino, Clarence Alexander and Randolph Scott. Educ: St. Louis Col, Honolulu; Colo. State Col. Educ; Univ. Hawaii. Polit. & Govt. Pos: Hawaii State Rep, 12th Dist, 63- Bus. & Prof. Pos: Asst. mgr, Sky Room Restaurant, Int. Airport, 59-61; realtor-salesman, Manoa Realty Co, 61-; pres, First Filipino Finance Corp, 63- Mem: Dist. cmnr, Boy Scouts, Kam Dist; dir, Police Activities, Puunmi and Lanakila; Kamehameha Lions; pres, Maemae Sch. PTA; Filipino C. of C. Rel: Congregational. Mailing Add: 1747 Skyline Dr, Honolulu, Hawaii 96817. (1967)

PACE, FRED V. D
b. Gravois Mills, Mo, 4/6/19; m. 6/5/43 to Agnes Friedly; c. Mary Kay, Jean Ann, Bill and John. Educ: Cent. Mo. State Col, Warrensburg; Univ. of Mo, Columbia; B.S, Agr. Polit. & Govt. Pos: Mo. State Rep, 64-66. Bus. & Prof. Pos: Farmer and in real estate; teacher Morgan Co. Rural Schs, supvr. for vets. on Farm Training Prog. and Univ. of Mo. Exten. Serv. Mil. Serv: Army, Pac. Theater. Mem: Am. Legion, Post 104; Kiwanis Club; Lodge 320; AF&AM. Rel: Baptist. Mailing Add: RFD 2, Barnett, Mo. 65011. (1967)

PACE, GEORGE H. D
b. Crystal Lake, Ill, 11/21/16; m. 4/16/44 to Dazzie V. Rosser. Educ: Univ of Ill, Urbana, A.B. Polit. & Govt. Pos: Mo. State Rep, 60-66. Bus. & Prof. Pos: Owns and operates a motel. Mil. Serv: Army, 41-45. Mem: Trustee, Methodist Church; AF&AM; Scottish Rite and Shrine; Kiwanis; Am. Legion; Marion Co. Young Dems. Rel: Methodist. Mailing Add: 415 Hafner, Hannibal, Mo. 63401. (1967)

PACE, JOSEPH L. D
b. San Francisco, Calif, 5/4/17; s. Garland Pace and Luella Udall P; m. 3/24/42 to Pauline Clyde; c. Nathan, Craig, Maurio, Malcolm, Shana, Tia and

Nichole. Educ: Brigham Young Univ, A.B, 38; Univ. Chicago, M.D, 42. Polit. & Govt. Pos: V.mayor, San Jose, Calif, 62-64, mayor, 64-66 and mem. city coun, 66-67. Bus. & Prof. Pos: Gen. med. practice, San Jose, Calif, 46- Mil. Serv: Lt, Navy Med. Corps, 42-46, with serv. as Flight Surgeon. Mem: Am. Med. Asn; Acad. of Gen. Practice. Rel: Latter-day Saint. Mailing Add: 1871 The Alameda, San Jose, Calif. 95126.

PACE, LORIN NELSON R
Speaker, Utah House of Rep.
b. Miami, Ariz, 8/15/25; s. Levi Wilson Pace and Sentella Nelson P; m. 7/26/50 to Marilynn Haymore; c. Grant Franklin, Lee Wendell, Stanley Lorin, Mark Leonard, Lorraine, Maurine, Lynn Haymore, Deanna and Bradley Wilson. Educ: Brigham Young Univ, B.A, 51; Univ. Utah Col. Law, LL.B, 53, J.D, 67. Polit. & Govt. Pos: For. serv. officer, U.S. Dept. State, 55 & 56; Utah State Rep, Dist, 17, 65-, Speaker, Utah House of Rep, 69- Bus. & Prof. Pos: Attorney-at-law, Richfield, Utah, 54 & 55, Salt Lake City, 60-; mission pres, Latter-day Saint Church, Argentina and Chile, 56-60. Mil. Serv: Cadet, Air Force, World War II. Mem: Utah Bar Asn. Rel: Latter-day Saints. Mailing Add: 2386 Olympus Dr, Salt Lake City, Utah 84117.

PACHECO, FERMIN D
b. Chacon, N.Mex, 4/27/16; s. Juan A. Pacheco and Corina Maestas P; m. 12/5/34 to Mary Amelia Martinez; c. Fermin, Jr, Jacob E. and Paul John. Educ: Highlands Univ. Polit. & Govt. Pos: Chmn, Mora Co. Dem. Cent. Cmt, N.Mex, 62-68. Bus. & Prof. Pos: Owner, wholesale petrol. bus, 46- Mem: Charter mem, Mora Lions. Rel: Presbyterian. Legal Res: 100 Main St, Mora, N.Mex. 87732. Mailing Add: P.O. Box 337, Mora, N.Mex. 87732. (1967)

PACHECO, HENRY W. D
R.I. State Rep.
m. to Charlotte Sousa; c. two. Educ: Bristol Schs. Polit. & Govt. Pos: Mem, Bristol Sewer Cmn, R.I, 54-61, chmn, 2 years; mem, Bristol Town Cmt, 20 years; past treas, Bristol Fourth of July Cmt; dep. sheriff, Bristol Co, 61-63; R.I. State Rep, 66-, mem, Joint Cmt. of Highway Safety and Cmt. on Labor, R.I. House of Rep; chmn, Cmn. to Study Automobile Inspection Stations, 66- Bus. & Prof. Pos: Asst. sales mgr, Asselin Chevrolet, Warren, R.I. Mil. Serv: Navy, World War II. Mem: Portuguese-Am. Dem. Club of R.I. Mailing Add: 69 Fox Hill Ave, Bristol, R.I. 02809.

PACK, DAVID M. D
Attorney Gen. and Reporter, Tenn.
b. Sevierville, Tenn, 11/4/21; m. to Ruth Dixon; c. Pamela Dixon and David, Jr. Educ: Univ. of Tenn, A.B. and J.D, 48. Polit. & Govt. Pos: Chancellor, 13th Chancery Div, 54-57; Asst. Attorney Gen, Tenn, 57-63; Tenn. State Cmnr. of Highways, 63-67; Tenn. State Cmnr. of Ins. and Banking, 67-69; Attorney Gen. and Reporter, Tenn, 69- Bus. & Prof. Pos: Practiced law in Sevierville, Tenn. until 54. Mil. Serv: Army, $3\frac{1}{2}$ years, 42-46. Rel: Baptist. Mailing Add: Supreme Court Bldg, Nashville, Tenn. 37219.

PACKARD, DAVID R
Dep. Secy. of Defense
b. Pueblo, Colo, 9/7/12; s. Sperry Sidney Packard and Ella Lorna Graber P; m. 4/8/38 to Lucile Salter; c. David Woodley, Nancy Anne (Mrs. Robin Burnett), Susan and Julie Elizabeth. Educ: Stanford Univ, B.A, 34, E.E, 39; Univ. of Colo, 34; Alpha Delta Phi; Tau Beta Pi; Sigma Xi. Hon. Sc.D, Colo. Col, 64; LL.D, Univ. of Calif, 66. Polit. & Govt. Pos: Dep. Secy of Defense, 69- Bus. & Prof. Pos: Dir, Am. Mgt. Asn, 56-59, v.pres-at-lg, 59-69; dir. and mem. exec. cmt, Stanford Research Inst, 58-69; mem, adv. bd, Hoover Inst. on War, Peace and Revolution, 58-69; dir, Pac. Gas & Elec. Co, 59-69; dir, Calif. State C. of C, 62-69; dir, Crocker-Citizens Nat. Bank, 63-69; dir, Nat. Merit Scholarship Corp, 63-69; dir, Gen. Dynamics Corp, 64-69; dir, U.S. Steel Corp, 64-69; chmn. of bd. and chief exec. officer, Hewlett-Packard Co, 64-69; dir, U.S. Churchill Found, 65-69. Mem: Palo Alto Bd. of Educ, 48-56; trustee, Stanford Univ, 54-69, pres. of bd, 58-60 and 1st v.pres, 60-67; trustee, Colo. Col, 66-69; Univ. Research Assoc, 65-69; hon. life mem, Instrument Soc. of Am; Inst. of Elec. and Electronics Eng; Phi Beta Kappa; Links Club, N.Y.C; Pac. Union and Bohemian Club, San Francisco; Calif. Club, Los Angeles. Legal Res: 26580 Taaffe Ave, Los Altos Hills, Calif. 94022. Mailing Add: Dept. of Defense, The Pentagon, Washington, D.C. 20301.

PACKRONI, TELIO D
b. Mt. Sterling, 12/18/15; s. Benjamin Packroni and Florence Pierangelini P; m. to Jeannette M. Townsend; c. four. Educ: Masontown High Sch. Polit. & Govt. Pos: Pa. State Rep, 64-67; Tax Collector, 46-53, 58-65; Tax Assessor, 44-45; dir, Fayette Co. Blind Asn. Bus. & Prof. Pos: Co-owner Masontown Printing Co. Mailing Add: Box 788, N. Water St, Masontown, Pa. or 212 S. Main St, Masontown, Pa. 15461. (1967)

PACKWOOD, ROBERT WILLIAM R
U.S. Sen, Ore.
b. Portland, Ore, 9/11/32; s. Frederick William Packwood and Gladys Taft P; m. 11/25/64 to Georgie Ann Oberteuffer; c. William Henderson. Educ: Willamette Univ, A.B, 54; N.Y. Univ. Sch. Law, LL.B, 57; Beta Theta Pi. Polit. & Govt. Pos: Chmn, Multnomah Co. Rep. Cent. Cmt, Ore, 60-62; Ore. State Rep, 63-69; U.S. Sen, Ore, 69- Publ: Campaign Techniques, a book on the techniques of successful campaigning in Ore, 63, 65 & 67. Mem: Am, Ore. and Multnomah Co. Bar Asns; World Affairs Coun. of Ore; Civil Theater; Jr. C. of C. Named One of Three Outstanding Young Men, Ore, 66; Portland's Jr. First Citizen, 67; Ore. Speaker of the Year, 68. Rel: Unitarian. Legal Res: 1050 S.W. Englewood Dr, Lake Oswego, Ore. 97034. Mailing Add: 7030 Longwood Dr, Bethesda, Md. 20014.

PADDOCK, DARVEN LEVERE R
Mem, Calif. Rep. State Cent. Cmt.
b. Minneapolis, Minn, 2/7/08; s. Hattel Barthalemew Paddock and Minnie Vona Harrison Moore P; m. 8/11/46 to Arlette Hope Martin; c. Beverly Elizabeth (Mrs. Thomas J. Carney). Educ: Aero Industs. Tech. Inst, 1 year; Southwest. Law, 1 year; Calif. Inst. of Tech, 1 year. Polit. & Govt. Pos: Secy, North. San Bernadino Co. Hoover Campaign, Calif, 32; pres, 43rd Dist. Rep. Assembly, Calif, 57; regional dir. and chmn, various cmts, Calif. Rep. Assembly, 58-65 and v.pres, 61 and 64; cand, State Treas, 62; v.pres, Los Angeles Co. Rep. Assembly, 62-63; former assoc. mem, Calif. Rep. State Cent. Cmt, mem, 67-; mgr. of many polit. campaigns over the years in South. Calif. and also pub. rels. work for various cand. Bus. & Prof. Pos: Clerical and secretarial work, South. Pac. Co, Los Angeles and Indio, Calif, 25-29; supvr. of Off. Serv, Am. Potash & Chem, Trona, Calif, 30-35; asst. to pres, West. Fruit Growers, Los Angeles, Calif, 35-39; staff work, Lockheed Aircraft, Burbank, Calif, 39-44; owner and mgr, Paddock's Stationery, Glendale, Calif, 44-; independent studies for mgt. on syst, methods and orgn. Publ: Ed, The Hour and High Twelvian; various articles in Al Malaekahn and News Press. Mem: Int. Platform Asn; v.pres, South. Calif. Booksellers Asn, 52-53; Nat. Fedn. Independent Bus; v.pres, Calif. Asn. of High Twelve Clubs; AF&AM; K.T; RSM; Royal Arch; Shrine (past chmn, San Fernando Valley Clubs); moose; Club San Moritz; Town Club; C. of C; Lions; past pres, Toastmasters; former v.pres, Glendale Merchants Asn; former adv, Glendale Youth Coun; pub. rels. work for various drives, progs. and orgn. Rel: Lutheran; Former pres, Cathedral Choir and former secy, Soc. Ministry, First Lutheran Church, Glendale, Calif. Mailing Add: 3640 Emanuel Dr, Glendale, Calif. 91208.

PADGETT, C. WARD D
Chief Mine Inspector, Okla.
b. Puxico, Mo, 12/8/10; s. Charles Ward Padgett and Nell Smith P; m. 10/12/40 to Dorothy Nell Tate; c. Vanetta Sue (Mrs. James Welsh) and Charles Ward. Educ: Mining eng. courses, Ind. State Univ, Univ. Ill. and U.S. Bur. Mines exten. classes; study of long wall mining, Eng. Polit. & Govt. Pos: Chief mine inspector, Okla, 63-; mem, Appeal Bd. for Selective Serv, 4 years; chmn, Gov. Coun. Develop. of Coal Indust. in Okla; mem, Adv. Cmt. Reclamation; mem. coal and coke div, Southwest Shipper's Adv. Bd; mem. solid fuels div, Off. Emergency Planning. Bus. & Prof. Pos: Mine Foreman, Little Betty Mining Corp, 35-38; mine foreman, Crescent Coal Co, 38-40, mine supt, 40-48; gen. supt. Ky. operations, Bell & Zoller Coal Co, 48-53, gen. supt. all operations, 53-60; asst. div. supt. of mining, Lone Star Steel Co, 60-63. Publ: Author of numerous papers on safety, production, long wall mining and other mining systems, publ. in organizational proceedings. Mem: Mine Inspectors' Inst. of Am.(bd. dirs); Am. Inst. of Mining; Metallurgical & Petroleum Engrs; West. Ky. Mining Inst; Nat. Mine Rescue Asn; Nat. Asn. State Mine Inspection Agencies (v.chmn); Rotary; Shrine; Boy Scout Coun; Salvation Army (adv. bd). Rel: Baptist. Legal Res: 528 E. Seneca, McAlester, Okla. 74501. Mailing Add: 251 Capitol Bldg, Oklahoma City, Okla. 73105.

PADGETT, WILLIAM DAVID D
Treas, State Dem. Exec. Cmt, Ga.
b. Forest City, N.C, 3/22/27; s. L.B. Padgett and Louise Blanchard P; m. 48 to Dorothy R. Bennett; c. Gail Blanchard, Ted Ross, Nancy Ann and Cameron Mitchell. Polit. & Govt. Pos: Treas, State Dem. Exec. Cmt, Ga, 61- Bus. & Prof. Pos: Asst. secy, Trust Co. of Ga, 56-58, asst. v.pres, 58-60, v.pres, 60-; dir, Ga. Ment. Health Asn, 60; treas, Ga. Bankers Asn, 63-64; trustee, Ga. Sch. Banking, 64-65; dir. and v.chmn, Builtwell Homes, Inc. Mil. Serv: Staff Officer, U.S. Maritime Cmn, 44-47. Mem. F&AM; Atlanta Athletic Club; West Pines Golf Club. Rel: Methodist. Legal Res: 308 Price Ave, Douglasville, Ga. 30134. Mailing Add: P.O. Drawer 4418, Atlanta, Ga. 30302.

PADILLA, HERNAN New Progressive, P.R.
Majority Floor Leader, P.R. House of Rep.
b. Mayaguez, P.R, 5/5/38; s. Hernan Padilla and Luisa Ramirez P; m. 7/22/61 to Laura Cestero; c. Herman F. and Ingrid Y. Educ: Univ. P.R, B.S, 59; Univ. Md, M.D, 63; Univ. Hosp, Rio Piedras, P.R. Internal Med. Specialty, 64-67; Rush Club, Univ. Md. Sch. Med; Phi Sigma Alpha. Polit. & Govt. Pos: Mem, Young Rep, 64; del, Rep. Nat. Conv, 65; v.pres, Polit. Action Cmt, P.R. Rep. Party, 65; co-organizer, United Statehooders Asn, 67; v.pres-at-lg, New Progressive Party, P.R, 68, rep-at-lg, 68-; Majority Floor Leader, P.R. House of Rep, 69- Bus. & Prof. Pos: Instr. phys. sci, Univ. P.R, 59, med, 67-69, asst. attending in med, 69- Mil. Serv: Entered Army Nat. Guard, 54, currently serv. as Capt, Med. Corps, Hq. Detachment, P.R. Nat. Guard. Publ: One Year Experience with Closed Kidney Biopsies. Rel: Catholic. Mailing Add: D-42 Junquera, Villa Andalucía, Rio Piedras, P.R. 00926.

PADULA, LOUIS J. R
b. Ielsi, Italy, 4/30/05; m. to Elda Tremalio; c. Michelle, Robert. Educ: Miami Univ. (Ohio); Ohio State Law Sch. Polit. & Govt. Pos: Majority leader Conn. House of Reps, 63-67; Legis. Coun, 57-65; mem. Conn. Constitutional Conv, 65; asst. majority leader of House, 61; asst. minority leader of House, 59; Conn. State Rep, 46, 55-67. Mil. Serv: Army, 42, served overseas in a spec. detachment of Mil. Intel; awarded Bronze Star for heroism during the Salerno D-Day landing in Italy. Mailing Add: 31 Buckingham Place, Norwalk, Conn. 06851.

PAFFORD, ROBERT C. 'BOBBY' D
Ga. State Rep.
b. Lanier Co, Ga, 6/7/30; s. Leo E. Pafford and Georgie Lee P; single. Educ: S. Ga. Col, 47-49; Ga. South. Col, B.S, 49-51. Polit. & Govt. Pos: Ga. State Rep, Lanier Co, 61-64, 97th Dist, 65- Mil. Serv: Entered as Pvt, Army, 51, released as T/Sgt, 54, after serv. in Security Agency. Mem: Ga. Farm Bur; VFW; Kiwanis Int. Rel: Methodist. Mailing Add: Box 415, Lakeland, Ga. 31635. (1967)

PAGANO, MARIO A. R
Del. State Rep.
b. 1912. Educ: Univ. of Ala; N.Y. Univ. Polit. & Govt. Pos: Del. State Rep, 67-; alternate del, Rep. Nat. Conv, 68. Bus. & Prof. Pos: Mech. drawing teacher and develop. engr, DuPont Co; owner, Anchor Eng. Co. and Pec Kay Tool Co. Mem: Past pres, Delpark Civic Asn; past pres, Millcreek Men's Rep. Club; Kiwanis. Mailing Add: 5 Duff Circle, Delpark Manor, Wilmington, Del. 19808. (1967)

PAGE, DONALD KENNETH D
b. Cleveland, Ohio, 3/24/28; s. Kenneth Elmer Page and Barbara Schuneman P; m. 8/13/52 to Gretchen Ann Grothe; c. Michael William. Educ: Woodrow Wilson High Sch, Los Angeles, Calif, grad. Polit. & Govt. Pos: Dem. nominee, Calif. State Assemblyman, 54th Dist, 68; mem, Mayor's Adv. Coun,

Councilman Adv. Coun, Northeast Planning Adv. Cmn. and Glassell Park Improv. Asn. Bus. & Prof. Pos: Owner, Page TV, Los Angeles, Calif, 53- Mil. Serv: Entered as A/S, Merchant Marines, 45, released as Lt.(sg), 50. Mem: C. of C.(coord. coun); K. of C; Boy Scouts; YMCA; life mem. PTA; Highland Park Rescue Serv; T-Timers Inc; Little Flower Assocs; Campfire Girls; Optimist (life mem, past pres, Breakfast Optimist Club, Highland Park and past pres, Optimist Club El Sereno); plus others. Rel: Catholic. Mailing Add: 2749 Lompoc St, Los Angeles, Calif. 90065.

PAGE, FUGATE FOSTER R
b. Uniontown, Ohio, 11/9/09; s. Hugh Fugate Page and Emma French P; m. 5/7/54 to Lois Plummer. Educ: Uniontown High Sch, grad, 28. Polit. & Govt. Pos: Dep. co. auditor, Franklin Co, Columbus, Ohio 50-63; asst. cashier, State Treas. Off, Columbus, 63-65; admin. asst. to Treas, Ohio, 65-; mem, Franklin Co. Rep. Exec. Cmt; alternate del, Rep. Nat. Conv, 68. Bus. & Prof. Pos: Asst. gen. foreman, Columbus Div, Curtis Wright Aviation, 42-46; field rep, Franklin Brewery, Columbus, 46-50; owner-mgr, Aimes Employ. Serv, 50-52; real estate sales mgr, part-time, Mallory Realtor. Mem: Columbus Leadership Conf; Nat. Bus. League, United Negro Col. Fund; Mayors Adv. Bd, Columbus Urban League; Mason; Elks; first v.pres, Ohio State Asn. Rel: Methodist. Mailing Add: 1837 Franklin Ave, Columbus, Ohio 43205.

PAGE, LEONARD A, JR. R
State Committeeman, Wyo. Rep. Party
b. New York, N.Y, 3/10/28; s. Leonard A. Page and Mary McDonough P; m. 6/30/56 to Joan Mahoney; c. Leonard III, Francis M, Anne Marie and Helen. Educ: Iona Col, B.B.A, 49. Polit. & Govt. Pos: V.chmn, Carbon Co. Rep. Cent. Cmt, Wyo, 61-65, chmn, 63-68; councilman, Rawlins, 62-65, mem. pub. utilities bd, 65-67; mem, Wyo. State Printing Coun, 68-69; State Committeeman, Wyo. Rep. Party, 68- Bus. & Prof. Pos: Acct, Joseph Froggatt & Co, 49-51; acct, budget dept, New York, 51-52; asst. controller, Am. Broadcasting Co, San Francisco, Calif, 52-57; chief acct, West. Nuclear Inc, 57-60; partner, Hawkins & Page CPA's, 60- Mil. Serv: Entered as Pvt, Air Force Res, 48, released as Capt, 59. Mem: Wyo. Soc. CPA's; Am. Inst. CPA's; Lions; Elks. Rel: Catholic. Legal Res: Happy Hollow, Rawlins, Wyo. 82301. Mailing Add: Box 459, Rawlins, Wyo. 82301.

PAGE, MATTHEW JOHN D
V.Chmn, Wash. Co. Dem. Orgn, Miss.
b. Greenville, Miss, 11/16/29; s. Johnny Page and Mollie Turnbull P; m. 7/6/60 to Vivian Miller Patton; c. Letha Ann. Educ: Tougaloo Col, B.S, 52; Meharry Med. Col, M.D, 56; Omega Psi Phi. Polit. & Govt. Pos: Mem. Miss. Adv. Cmt, U.S. Civil Rights Cmn, 67-; del, Dem. Nat. Conv, 68; v.chmn, Wash. Co. Dem. Orgn, Miss, 68- Mil. Serv: Entered as 1st Lt, Air Force, 57, released as Capt, 59, after serv. in 40:81st Hosp. Unit, Northeast Air Command, 57-59; Capt, Air Force Res, 59-; Air Force Commendation Medal. Mem: Nat. and Am. Med. Asns; C. of C; Herbert Lee Commun. Center; Miss. Coun. Human Rels. Rural Serv. Award, Off. Econ. Opportunity, 68. Rel: Protestant. Mailing Add: 239 N. Florida St, Greenville, Miss. 38701.

PAGE, RAY R
Supt. of Pub. Instr, Ill.
b. New Berlin, Ill, 12/8/21; s. Warren Page and Pearl Taylor P; m. 6/6/43 to Kathryn Kincaid; c. Kenneth Ray and Marcia Kay. Educ: Western Ill. Univ, B.Ed, 43; Univ. Ill, M.S, 51; State Life Gen. Supvy. Cert, Off. of Pub. Instr, State of Ill, 52; Phi Delta Kappa. Hon. Ed.D, Merrimack Col, Mass, 66; hon. LL.D, Eureka and McKendree Cols, Ill, 68. Polit. & Govt. Pos: Supt. of Pub. Instr, Ill, 63-; mem, United Rep. Fund of Ill. and Sangamon Co. Young Rep. Club; del. and secy. Ill. del, Rep. Nat. Conv, 64, del, 68. Bus. & Prof. Pos: Teacher and coach, Auburn High Sch, Ill, 45-46, Chebanse High Sch, 46-49 and Springfield High Sch, 54-62; dist. supt, prin. and teacher, Williamsville Sch. Dist, 49-54. Mil. Serv: Entered as Air Cadet, Army Air Force, 43, released as Flight Officer, 45; Received Wings as Flight Officer, 45; World War II Victory Medal. Publ: Many publications released by virtue of my position. Mem: Coun. of Chief State Sch. Officers; Nat. and Ill. Educ. Asns; Am. and Ill. Asns. of Sch. Adminstrs; Am. Fedn. of Teachers; Nat. and Ill. Asns. of Sec. Sch. Prin; Ill. High Sch. Asn; Mason; Shrine; Elks; Am. Bus. Club; Am. Legion; YMCA. Rel: Christian Church. Legal Res: 101 Pinehurst Dr, Springfield, Ill. 62704. Mailing Add: Room 302, State Office Bldg, Springfield, Ill. 62706.

PAGE, S. RONDALL 'RONNIE' R
b. Mt. Vernon, Ill, 4/10/37; s. Sebern H. Page and Opal Slayden P; m. 12/28/58 to Carolyn Ruth Kelley; c. Kellye Denise and Shannon Colleen. Educ: Mt. Vernon High Sch, grad, 55. Polit. & Govt. Pos: Cand. U.S. House Rep, Sixth Cong. Dist, Tenn, 68. Bus. & Prof. Pos: Talent host, WLAC-TV, Nashville, Tenn, 59-65; bus. mgr, Chuck Wagon Gang, 65-68; pres, Ronnie Page Org, 68- Publ: I Pledge Allegiance, Page Publ, 68. Mem: Gospel Music Asn. (bd. dirs). Performances, United Serv. Orgn, Europe, Korea, N.Africa, Spain, Vietnam. Rel: Southern Baptist. Mailing Add: Box 450, Hendersonville, Tenn. 37075.

PAGE, SEWELL A. D
b. Ryegate, Vt, 12/30/25; m. to Adell Bailey; c. Three. Educ: Groton High Sch. Polit. & Govt. Pos: Commun. committeeman, Agr. Stabilization & Conserv. Serv, Vt; town lister, 60; Vt. State Rep, 65-67. Bus. & Prof. Pos: Farmer. Mem: Farm Bur; N.E.M.P.A; bd. dirs, Corinth D.H.I.A. Rel: Congregational. Mailing Add: South Newbury, Vt. 05051. (1967)

PAGE, STANLEY HAYNES R
Chmn, Guilford Rep. Town Cmt, Conn.
b. New Haven, Conn, 5/5/42; s. Harry Logan Page, Jr. and Hazel Langdon P; m. 10/10/64 to Laura Dudley; c. Claudia Haynes and Katharine Wilcox. Educ: Mitchell Col, A.S, 62; New Haven Col, 62-63. Polit. & Govt. Pos: Treas, Guilford Rep. Town Cmt, Conn, 67-69, chmn, 69-; justice of the peace, Guilford, 69- Bus. & Prof. Pos: V.pres, Page Hardware & Appliance Co, Guilford, 63- Mem: Guilford Jaycees (past pres, v.pres. and dir); Guilford Vol. Fire Dept. (past pres, Eagle Hose Co. 2). Rel: Protestant. Mailing Add: Murray Lane, Guilford, Conn. 06437.

PAGE, WAYNE HAROLD R
Chmn, Hyde Park Rep. Town Cmt, Vt.
b. Hyde Park, Vt, 9/25/22; s. Ernest C. Page and Leila Whittemore P; m. 9/1/42 to Sylvia Ward; c. Nancy and Karen. Educ: Univ. of Vt, B.S. in elec. eng, 43. Polit. & Govt. Pos: Chmn, Hyde Park Rep. Town Cmt, Vt, 56-; former chmn, Lamoille Co. Rep. Cmt; mem, Vt. Rep. State Cmt. Bus. & Prof. Pos: Prfnl. engr, Vt. Mil. Serv: Entered as Pvt, Army, 43, released as Capt, 46, after serv. in 100th Inf. Div, ETO; re-entered for serv. with 43rd Inf. Div, 50-51; Bronze Star with Cluster; Presidential Unit Citation with Cluster; Combat Infantryman's Badge; Europe-Africa-Mid. East Campaign Ribbon with 3 Battle Stars; Brig. Gen, 86th Armored Brigade, Vt. Nat. Guard. Mem: Canadian Inst. of Mining & Metall; Vt. Soc. of Eng; VFW; Am. Legion; Vt. Horse Shows Asn; Nat. Guard Asn. of U.S; Asn. United States Army. Rel: Protestant. Mailing Add: The Elms, Hyde Park, Vt. 05655.

PAGEL, GARY JAMES DFL
Mem, Minn. State Dem-Farmer-Labor Cent. Cmt.
b. St. Paul, Minn, 4/17/40; s. R. Emil Pagel and Lucille Finson P; single. Educ: Univ. Minn, A.A, 61; St. Cloud Col, B.A, 63; Tau Kappa Epsilon. Polit. & Govt. Pos: Founder, Young Dem-Farmer-Labor Clubs, 61; chmn, West St. Paul Dem-Farmer-Labor Party; mem, Dakota Co. Cent. Cmt, 61-; alternate del, Dem. Nat. Conv, 64; mem, Minn. State Dem-Farmer-Labor Cent. Cmt, 66- Mil. Serv: Airman, Air Force Res, 65. Mem: C. of C; BRCA. Rel: Lutheran. Mailing Add: 398 Rehnberg Place, West St. Paul, Minn. 55118. (1967)

PAGEL, JOHN THEODORE R
Chmn, Crawford Co. Rep. Cmt, Ga.
b. Wilkes Barre, Pa, 1/13/22; s. John Theodore Pagel, Sr. and Jessie Coons P; m. 10/21/45 to Mary Bradley Douglas; c. John Theodore, Mary Lucile, Jessica Lynn and Jennifer Joyce. Polit. & Govt. Pos: 1st v.chmn, Crawford Co. Rep. Cmt, Ga, 60-64, chmn, 64- Bus. & Prof. Pos: V.pres, W.F. Bradley Lumber Co, 48-55; pres, Roberta Sand & Gravel Co, 60- Mil. Serv: Entered as A/S, Navy, 41, released as Aviation Electrician 1/C, 46; Victory Medal; South Pac. Theater Ribbon; Marshall Islands Ribbon with Battle Star. Mem: Mason; Am. Legion; Kiwanis Inst. Rel: Methodist. Mailing Add: Box 307, Roberta, Ga. 31078.

PAIEWONSKY, RALPH D
b. St. Thomas, V.I, 11/9/07; s. Isaac Paiewonsky and Rebecca P; married; c. Two. Educ: N.Y. Univ, B.S. in Chem, 30. Polit. & Govt. Pos: Mem, People's Party, V.I, 36; organizer, Dem. Club for participation in nat. polit, 36; mem. and chmn, Munic. Cmt, 36-46; chmn, Legis. Assembly, V.I, 36-46; chmn, St. Thomas and St. John Munic. Coun, 36-46; mem. of del. to present needs of V.I. to Cong, 39; del, Dem. Nat. Conv, 40 & 44; Dem. Nat. Committeeman, V.I, 40-60; mem, V.I. Senate Organic Act Adv. Cmt. and Citizens' Adv. Cmt. for Home Rule, 52-60; adv. to Legis. to Caribbean Cmn, 58-60; chmn, Jackson-Jefferson Day Dinner, 58 & 60; mem, Spec. Tax Cmt. for C. of C. and V.I. Legis. to present V.I. tax legis. case before Cong, 59-60; gen. chmn, Gov. Adv. Cmt. on Tourism and Trade, 60; pres, V.I. Bd. Trade, 60; hon. mem, Inaugural Rule Cmt, 60; Gov, V.I, 61-69. Bus. & Prof. Pos: Mgr, St. Thomas Apothecary Hall, 30; extensive research with sea water fermentation from which rum distillation process developed, 32; mgr, A.H. Riise Distilling Co, 33-49, pres, 49-; pres, Apollo Theater, Inc. and Center Theater, Inc, 48-; pres, A.H. Riise, Inc, 49; mem. bd. dirs. and pres, W.I. Ins. Co, 54-58; organizer, W.I. Bank and Trust Co, 54, mem. bd. dirs, chmn. exec. cmt. and v.pres, 54-59; pres, W.I. Investment Corp, 54-58, mem. bd. dirs, 54-60. Mem: St. Thomas Dem. Club; charter mem, Dem. Capital Club; F&AM (32°); Shrine; 750 Club. Rel: Hebrew. Mailing Add: Charlotte Amalie, St. Thomas, V.I. 00801. (1967)

PAINE, HARRY ALLEN D
b. Bement, Ill, 9/25/11; s. Harry Allen Paine and Ida Sowers P; m. 5/15/37 to Virginia Fayen. Educ: Univ. Cincinnati, M.E; Pi Tau Sigma; Omicron Delta Kappa; Iota Chi Epsilon. Polit. & Govt. Pos: Alternate del, Dem. Nat. Conv, 68. Bus. & Prof. Pos: Asst. to v.pres, Geometric Tool Co, New Haven, Conn, 40-48; v.pres, Fed. Bryant Machinery Co, Chicago, 48- Mem: Am. Soc. Tool and Mfg. Engrs. Rel: Unitarian. Mailing Add: 3226 University Ave, Highland Park, Ill. 60035.

PAINE, THOMAS OTTEN D
Adminstr, NASA
b. Berkeley, Calif, 11/9/21; s. George Thomas Paine and Ada Louise Otten P; m. 10/1/46 to Barbara Helen Taunton Pearse; c. Marguerite Ada, George Thomas, Judith Janet and Frank Taunton. Educ: Brown Univ, A.B, 42; Stanford Univ, M.S, 47, Ph.D, 49; Sigma Xi; Delta Kappa Epsilon. Hon. D.S.C, Brown Univ, 69. Polit. & Govt. Pos: Chmn, Santa Barbara Scientists and Engrs. for Johnson and Humphrey, 64; chmn. spec. task force, Dept. of Housing and Urban Develop, 67; dep. adminstr, NASA, 68, acting adminstr, 68-69, adminstr, 69- Bus. & Prof. Pos: Research assoc, Stanford Univ, 47-49; research assoc, Gen. Elec. Research Lab, Schenectady, N.Y, 49-50, mgr, Gen. Elec. Meter & Instruments Lab, Lynn, Mass, 51-58, mgr, eng. applications, Gen. Elec. Research & Develop. Center, Schenectady, N.Y, 58-63, mgr, Tempo, Gen. Elec. Center for Adv. Studies, Santa Barbara, Calif, 63-68. Mil. Serv: Entered as Midn, Naval Res, 42, released as Lt, 46, after serv. in Submarine Serv, Pac. and Southwest Pac. Areas, 42-46; Commendation Ribbon; Submarine Combat Award with Two Stars. Publ: 'Magnetic Properties of Fine Particles,' chap. in Magnetic Properties of Metals and Alloys, Am. Soc. for Metals, 59; 'The City as an Information Network,' presented at the Inst. of Elec. and Electronic Engrs. Int. Conv, G.E. Tempo, 3/22/66; 'Space and National Security in the Modern World,' Air Force and Space Digest, 5/69. Mem: N.Y. Acad. of Sci; Am. Phys. Soc; Inst. Elec. and Electronic Engrs; Am. Inst. Mining, Metallurgical and Petroleum Engrs; Am. Soc. for Metals; Inst. of Metals, London; Soc. for the Hist. of Tech; Newcomen Soc, London; Naval Hist. Found; U.S. Naval Inst; Am. Inst. Aeronaut. and Astronaut; fel, Am. Astronaut. Soc; Cosmos Club; Army and Navy Club; Nat. Space Club; Nat. Aviation Club; Submarine Vet. of World War II; NAACP; Am. Asn. Adv. Sci. Rel: Unitarian. Legal Res: Berkeley, Calif. Mailing Add: National Aeronautics and Space Administration, 400 Maryland Ave. S.W, Washington, D.C. 20546.

PAINI, ARTHUR WILLIAM D
Chmn, Warren Co. Dem. Party, N.J.
b. Phillipsburg, N.J, 3/2/19; s. Secondo Paini and Anna Belardinelli P; m. 5/3/41 to Catherine A. Gallagher; c. Richard A. and Lynn A. Educ: Mich.

State Col, 62. Polit. & Govt. Pos: Cmnr, Phillipsburg, N.J, 50-59, mayor, 58-62, cmnr. st. and pub. improv, 64-; freeholder, Warren Co, 59; alternate del, Dem. Nat. Conv, 60, dist. del, 64 & 68; chmn, Warren Co. Dem. Party, 63-; sergeant-at-arms Warren Co. Dist. Court. Bus. & Prof. Pos: Contractor and builder, Phillipsburg, 45-65; gen. supt, Delaware River Joint Toll Bridge Cmn, 64- Mil. Serv: Entered as Cadet, Army Air Force, 43, released as 2nd Lt, 45. Mem: Dir, Joseph H. Firth Youth Center; Elks (trustee); Warren Chem. Fire Co; Unico; Am. Legion; K. of C; C. of C.(exec. secy, Phillipsburg Chap, 59-62). Civic Citation, Lafayette Col, 60; Outstanding Citizens Award, Unico. Rel: Catholic. Mailing Add: 708 Wilbur Ave, Phillipsburg, N.J. 08865.

PAINTER, JAMES MEDFORD R
Chmn, Page Co. Rep. Cmt, Va.
b. Stanley, Va, 11/2/24; s. Harvey Mahlon Painter and Della Petefish P; m. 12/25/44 to Mildred Elizabeth Bradley; c. James L, Theresa S, Larry A, Timothy R, Craig L. and Phillip M. Educ: Stanley High Sch, grad, 43; AAF Clerical Sch, Denver, Colo, 1 year. Polit. & Govt. Pos: Justice of the Peace, Page Co, Va, 56-63; councilman, Stanley, Va, 57-63 and 69-; mem. bd. of supvr, Page Co, 64-67; chmn, Page Co. Rep. Cmt, 67- Mil. Serv: Entered as Pvt, Air Force, 43, transferred to Army, released as S/Sgt, 46, after serv. in Co. C, 116th Inf. Regt, ETO, 1 year; ETO, Am. Theatre, Occup. and Good Conduct Ribbons. Mem: VFW; Ruritan Club; Boy Scout Cmt; Fire Dept. Rel: Baptist. Mailing Add: P.O. Box, 165, Stanley, Va. 22851.

PALAZZI, JOHN R
State Chmn, Rep. Nat. Cmt, N.H.
b. West Boylston, Mass, 5/27/18; m. 1944 to Phebe Lamphere; c. Suzanne and Frank. Educ: High Sch, grad, 36. Polit. & Govt. Pos: Former chmn, N.H. Rep. State Cmt; state chmn, Rep. Nat. Cmt, N.H, currently. Bus. & Prof. Pos: Pres, Palazzi Corp. and Frank Palazzi & Sons, Inc. Mil. Serv: Air Force. Mem: New Eng. and N.H. Water Pollution Cmts. Mailing Add: 134 N. Main St, Concord, N.H. 03301. (1967)

PALERMO, CONSTANCE JOAN R
V.Chmn, Lake Co. Rep. Cent. Cmt, Colo.
b. Denver, Colo, 4/3/36; d. George Arthur Durbin and Vera Marjory Newman D; m. 10/22/64 to Robert Lee Palermo; c. Gloria, Chris, Ray, Lydia and Barbara. Educ: North High Sch, Denver, ½ year; Weldona High Sch, 3 years; Emily Griffith Opportunity Sch, Denver, License in Cosmetology. Polit. & Govt. Pos: V.pres, Lake Co. Rep. Women, 69-; v.chmn, Lake Co. Rep. Cent. Cmt, 69- Bus. & Prof. Pos: Hairdresser, 56-64. Mem: Colo. Fedn. of Rep. Women; Mt. Massive Golf Club. Rel: Catholic. Mailing Add: 617 W. Sixth St, Leadville, Colo. 80461.

PALEVSKY, MAX D
b. Chicago, Ill, 7/24/24; s. Isadore Palevsky and Sarah P.(deceased); div; c. Madeleine and Nicholas. Educ: Univ. Chicago, Ph.B. and B.S, 48. Polit. & Govt. Pos: Del, Dem. Nat. Conv, 68; mem, Dem. Adv. Cmt, Los Angeles, Calif, 68- Bus. & Prof. Pos: Research analyst and mathematician, Bendix Aviation Corp, Los Angeles, Calif, 52-56; gen. mgr, v.pres. and dir, Packard Bell Computer Corp, 57-61; pres. and dir, Scientific Data Systs, Inc, El Segundo, 61-, chmn. bd, Sci. Data Syst. Israel, Ltd, Haifa, 68- Mil. Serv: Entered as Pvt, Army Air Force, 42, released as Capt, 46, after serv. in Air Corps, S.Pac. Publ: Section in Computer Handbook, 'The Digital Differential Analyzer,' McGraw-Hill, 62. Mem: Inst. Elec. and Electronics Engrs; Beverly Hills Tennis Club, Calif. Mailing Add: 755 Stradella Rd, Los Angeles, Calif. 90024.

PALLADINO, VINCENT OLIVER R
b. Waterbury, Conn, 4/23/29; s. Vincent Aurelio Palladino and Aurora Oliver P; m. 11/15/52 to Marie Margaret Baumgartner; c. Mark Oliver, Kim Marie, Eric Joseph and Kirk Vincent. Educ: Wash. & Jefferson Col, B.A, 51; Univ. Conn, M.A, 59; Lambda Chi Alpha. Polit. & Govt. Pos: Chmn, Watertown Rep. Town Cmt, Conn, 64-66; charter mem, Young Rep. Club of Watertown, 64-; chmn, Watertown Bd. of Tax Rev, 68- Bus. & Prof. Pos: Advert. mgr, Town Times Newspaper, 61-62; ed. and publisher, Conn. Jaycee J, 61-62; pres, Paldon Truck Serv, Inc, 61-; real estate broker, self-employed, 65-; ed. and publisher, monthly newsletter, Rep. Register, 64-66; teacher of Eng, Crosby High Sch, Waterbury, Conn, 66-; ed, Watertown Annual Town Report, 68 & 69. Mil. Serv: Entered as Pvt, Army, 51, released as Cpl, 53, after serv. in 71st Antiaircraft Artil. Gun Bn, Ft. Belvoir, Va. Publ: 'Town Government Change,' Action, U.S. Jr. C. of C, 62. Mem: Jr. Chamber Int. Senate; publicity dir, Watertown C. of C, 63-64; Litchfield Co. Sheriff's Asn; dir, Watertown Chap, Am. Red Cross, chmn, 64-65; Conn. state chmn, Wash. & Jefferson Col. Capital Fund Dr; chmn. exec. cmt, Miss Watertown Pageant Asn, Inc, 68- Govt. Affairs Award, Conn. Jaycees, 62, Conn. State Spark Plug Award, 63, Outstanding Old Timer Award, 65; Jr. Chamber Int. Senate 3543, 63; Distinguished Serv. Award, Watertown Jaycees, 64. Rel: Roman Catholic. Mailing Add: 433 Woodbury Rd, Watertown, Conn. 06795.

PALM, NANCY DALE R
Chmn, Harris Co. Rep. Party, Tex.
b. Nashville, Tenn, 4/14/21; d. Dillard Young Dale and Mary Bishop D; m. 7/4/42 to William Morrison Palm, M.D. Educ: Vanderbilt Univ, B.A, 42; secy. and charter mem, Vanderbilt chap. Mortar Board; Gamma Phi Beta; Athenians; Lotus Eaters; Int. Rels. Club. Polit. & Govt. Pos: Rep. Precinct chmn, Dist. 274, Harris Co, Tex, 64-68; v.chmn, Harris Co. Rep. Party, 68, chmn, 68- Bus. & Prof. Pos: Pub. rels. secy, Harris Co. Med. Soc, 51-57. Twenty-five years of med, civic, polit. and soc. serv. work and extensive church work. Rel: Presbyterian. Mailing Add: 612 E. Friar Tuck Lane, Houston, Tex. 77024.

PALMBERG, MAURICE EDWIN R
Chmn, Hamilton Co. Rep. Cent. Cmt, Nebr.
b. Aurora, Nebr, 2/2/32; s. Edwin J. Palmberg and Esther Swanson P; m. 10/23/54 to Barbara Ann Axelson; c. Kurt Jeffrey and Karen Ann. Educ: N. Park Col, A.A, 52. Polit. & Govt. Pos: Chmn, Hamilton Co. Rep. Cent. Cmt, Nebr, 64- Bus. & Prof. Pos: Partner, Palmberg Auto Supply, Inc, 62. Mil. Serv: Entered as Pvt, Army, 52, released as Cpl, 54, after serv. in 5th Armored Div. Mem: Lions. Rel: Evangelical Covenant Church. Mailing Add: 920 16th, Aurora, Nebr. 68818.

PALMBY, CLARENCE DONALD R
Asst. Secy. of Agr. for Int. Affairs and Commodity Prog, Dept. of Agr.
b. Eagle Bend, Minn, 2/22/16; s. Ernest F. Palmby and Addie Hartbeck P; m. 9/21/40 to Mildred Janet Davis; c. Gail Alice (Mrs. John Geidl), Philip David and Thomas Orin. Educ: Univ. Minn, B.S, 40. Polit. & Govt. Pos: Chmn, Garden City Rep. Party, Minn, 53-55; chmn, Commodity Stabilization Serv. State Cmt, Dept. of Agr, St. Paul, 55-56; assoc. dir, Grain Div, Commodity Stabilization Serv, Wash, D.C, 56-57, dir, 57, dep. adminstr, serv, 57-58, assoc. adminstr, 58-61, pres, Commodity Credit Corp. and Asst. Secy. of Agr. for Int. Affairs and Commodity Prog, 69-; exec. v.pres, Feed Grains Coun, 61-69. Bus. & Prof. Pos: Farmer, 40-53. Mem: Alpha Zeta; RAM; Farm Bur. 4-H Club Alumni Award, 54; Skelly Award for Superior Achievement in Agr, 55; Superior Serv. Award, Dept. of Agr, 60; Leader of Commerce Award, Ital. Govt, 68. Rel: Methodist. Mailing Add: 4506 32nd Rd. N, Arlington, Va. 22207.

PALMER, DWIGHT WENDELL R
Chmn, Telfair Co. Rep. Party, Ga.
b. Glenwood, Ga, 10/17/39; s. James Aubrey Palmer and Juanita Windham P; m. 4/20/69 to Mary Vivion Young. Educ: S.Ga. Col, 57-59; Ga. South. Col, 59-60. Polit. & Govt. Pos: Chmn, Telfair Co. Rep. Party, Ga, 68- Bus. & Prof. Pos: Owner, Palmer Furniture Co, McRae, 64- Mil. Serv: Entered as Pvt, Army, 61, released as SP-4, 64, after serv. in 32nd Mil. Police Detachment, Counter Intel, Europe, 61-64. Mem: Jaycees (Rebel Corps); C. of C; Lyons; Elks. Rel: Baptist. Mailing Add: P.O. Box 4, McRae, Ga. 31055.

PALMER, GEORGE ARNOLD D
b. Swampscott, Mass, 4/23/13; s. George W. Palmer and Sarah E. Fitch P; m. 9/10/35 to E. Maxine Sweetser. Polit. & Govt. Pos: Maine State Rep, 65-67. Bus. & Prof. Pos: Founder and mgr, George A. Palmer Ins. Agency, 58- Mem: RAM; Odd Fellows; Lions; Grange. Mailing Add: Phillips, Maine 04966. (1967)

PALMER, GEORGE VINCENT D
Chmn, Schenectady Co. Dem. Cmt, N.Y.
b. Schenectady, N.Y, 12/5/20; s. Nicholas L. Palmer and Evelyn Cruise; single. Educ: Hobart Col, B.A, 42; Cornell Univ, Army Specialized Training Prog, 43; Albany Law Sch, LL.B, 49; Phi Beta Kappa; Justinian Soc; Law Rev. Bd; ed, Hobart Col. Student Newspaper. Polit. & Govt. Pos: Asst. city attorney, Schenectady, N.Y, 50-51; town attorney, Rotterdam, 58-59 & 64-69; chmn, Schenectady Co. Dem. Cmt, 61-; mgr, Conv. Campaigns for Rep. Samuel S. Stratton for Gov. and U.S. Senate nominations, 62 & 64; mem, N.Y. State Dem. Exec. Cmt, 63- Mil. Serv: Entered as Pvt, Air Force, 42, released as Sgt, 46, after serv. in West. Flying Training Command. Mem: Schenectady Co. Bar Asn. Rel: Catholic. Legal Res: 1037 Roberta Rd, Schenectady, N.Y. 12303. Mailing Add: 650 Franklin St, Schenectady, N.Y. 12305.

PALMER, GLEN DANIEL R
Chmn, Kendall Co. Rep. Party, Ill.
b. Yorkville, Ill, 3/4/93; s. Daniel F. Palmer and Harriett A. Healy P; m. 4/15/36 to Grace Irene Lagerquist; c. William A, Patricia (Mrs. Kowal), Priscilla R. and Glenda (Mrs. Richter). Educ: Univ. of Wis. Polit. & Govt. Pos: Supt, State Game Farm, Ill, 25-29; chmn, Kendall Co. Rep. Party, 46-; dep. state treas, Ill, 51-53, dir. of conserv, 53-61; asst. to U.S. Rep. Charlotte T. Reid, Ill, and in charge, 15th Dist. Off, 63- Bus. & Prof. Pos: Dist. and spec. agent, Northwestern Mutual Life Ins. of Milwaukee, Wis, 27- Mem: Lions; Izaak Walton League; Yorkville Businessmen's Asn; Mason, Shrine and Consistory. Rel: Methodist. Mailing Add: Game Farm Rd, Yorkville, Ill. 60560.

PALMER, HAZEL R
b. Climax Springs, Mo, 8/11/03; d. John William Palmer and Nancy Jane Hutton P; single. Educ: Nat. Univ. Law Sch, J.D, 32; past dean, Omicron Chap, Kappa Beta Pi; past pres, Cy Pres Club. Polit. & Govt. Pos: Asst. prosecuting attorney, Pettis Co, Mo, 37-39, collector of revenue, 42-55; chmn, Pettis Co. Rep. Party, 42 & 64-67; chmn, Bus. and Prfnl. Women's Cmt, Nat. Fedn. Rep. Women's Clubs; mem. bd, Mo. Fedn. Rep. Women's Clubs; past pres, Pettis Co. Rep. Women's Clubs; mem, Nat. Security and Peace Subcmt, Rep. Cmt. on Prog. and Progress; cand. for U.S. Sen, Mo, 58; del. and mem. platform cmt, Rep. Nat. Conv, 60, del-at-lg. and mem. credentials cmt, 64; mem, State Rep. Cmt, 62-68; City and Co. Rep. Committeewoman; mem, Nat. Adv. Cmt, Women for Nixon-Agnew, 68; mem, Citizens' Adv. Coun. on Status of Women, app. by President Nixon, 69- Bus. & Prof. Pos: Attorney-at-law, 32-; partner, Palmer and Palmer, until 58. Mem: Am. and Mo. Bar Asns; past pres, Pettis Co. Bar Asn. and Women's Bar Asn. Mo; Nat. Asn. Women Lawyers; Nat. Bd, Women's Med. Col. Pa; past pres, Nat. Fedn. Bus. & Prfnl. Women's Clubs, 56-58, Mo. Fedn. and Sedalia Bus. & Prfnl. Women's Clubs; Past Worthy Matron, Eastern Star; Knife and Fork Club; C. of C; Int. Hon. Mem, Beta Sigma Phi; past pres, Commun. Chest and United Fund. Hon. Ky. Col; Adm, Great Navy of Nebr, 58. Rel: Baptist; bd. trustees, First Baptist Church of Sedalia. Legal Res: 901 S. Vermont, Sedalia, Mo. 65301. Mailing Add: 323-325 Commerce Bldg, Sedalia, Mo. 65301.

PALMER, JOSEPH, II
U.S. Ambassador to Libya
b. Detroit, Mich, 6/16/14; s. Robert Woodbury Palmer and Helen Marie Bush P; m. 5/10/41 to Margaret McCamy Jones; c. Joseph Woodbury, Heather Gordon and Thomas Jones. Educ: Harvard, S.B, 37; Georgetown Sch. of For. Serv, 37-38; For. Serv. Sch, Dept. of State, 41. Polit. & Govt. Pos: For. serv. officer, Dept. of State, 39; v.consul, Mexico City, 40-41 and Nairobi, Kenya, 41-45; asst. chief, Div. African Affairs, Dept. of State, 45-49 and acting chief, 48; second secy. and consul, London, 49-50 and first secy. and consul, 50-53; dep. dir, Off. European Regional Affairs, Dept. of State, 53-56 and acting dir, 55; Dep. Asst. Secy. of State for African Affairs, 56-58; Am. Consul Gen, Rhodesia and Nyasaland, 58-60; U.S. Ambassador to Nigeria, 60-64; Dir. Gen. For. Serv, 64-66; Asst. Secy. of State for African Affairs, 66-69; U.S. Ambassador to Libya, 69- Mem: Am. For. Serv. Asn. Rel: Episcopal. Legal Res: 5414 Kirkwood Dr, Washington, D.C. 20016. Mailing Add: U.S. Embassy, Tripoli, Libya.

PALMER, KENNETH A. D
b. Long Beach, Calif, 3/29/28; s. Albert V. Palmer and Betty Beals P; m. 2/12/50 to Diana Edward; c. Linda K, Kenneth H, William C. and Eric M. Educ: Palos Verdes Col, Rolling Hills, Calif, A.A, 51; Univ. Calif, Santa Barbara, 1 year; North. Ill. Univ, 1 year. Polit. & Govt. Pos: Mgr, several cand. and ballot campaigns, South. Calif; chief consult, Majority Caucus, Calif. State Legis, 66; dir, 19th Dist. Agr. Asn, Calif, 66-; consult, Calif. Arts Cmn, 67; del, Dem. Nat. Conv, 68. Bus. & Prof. Pos: Reporter, Santa Barbara News-Press, 51-56, San Francisco Call Bul, United Press, 56; swing wire ed. and asst. city ed, San Jose Mercury, 56-60; dir. pub. rels, Rockford Col, Ill, 60-64; dir. pub. rels. and advert, Santa Barbara Savings & Loan, 64-65; partner, Palmer-Larson-Bateman, Inc, Santa Barbara, 65- Mil. Serv: Entered as Seaman, Navy, 45, released as Journalist 2/C, 49, after serv. in Submarine Force, Pac. Fleet, First Task Fleet, Pac. Theater; Good Conduct Medal; Pac. Theater Medal; World War II Victory Medal; Am. Theater Medal. Publ: 'Politicial-Governmental Public Relations in a Democracy,' (chap), In: Professional Public Relations, Univ. Calif. Press, 68. Mem: Accredited, Pub. Rels. Soc. Am; Am. Col. Pub. Rels. Asn; Internal Coun. Indust. Ed; West. States Asn. Advert. Agencies; dir, Direct Relief Found; dir, Santa Barbara Symphony; dir, Chance, Inc; Montecito Country Club; foreman pro tem, Santa Barbara Co. Grand Jury, 66 & 68. Rel: Protestant. Legal Res: 1135 High Rd, Santa Barbara, Calif. 93103. Mailing Add: 120 E. Dela Guerra St, Santa Barbara, Calif. 93101.

PALMER, MERLE FRANKLIN D
Pres. Pro Tempore, Miss. State Senate.
b. Pontotoc Co, Miss, 3/11/19; s. William Judson Palmer and Hesperia Faulkner P; c. William J, II. Educ: Univ. of Md. Polit. & Govt. Pos: Former munic. judge, Miss; city attorney, Pascagoula; prosecuting attorney, Jackson Co, Miss, 48-52; Miss. State Rep, 60-64; Miss. State Sen, 64-, Pres. Pro Tempore, Miss. State Senate, 68- Bus. & Prof. Pos: Lawyer. Mem: Past exalted ruler, Elks; World Travelers Asn; Ole Miss. Alumni Asn; Farm Bur; C. of C; Jackson Co, Miss. and Am. Bar Asns. Rel: Baptist. Legal Res: 1016 Cherubusco St, Pascagoula, Miss. 39567. Mailing Add: Box 59, Pascagoula, Miss. 39567.

PALMER, MILDRED L. R
N.H. State Rep.
Married. Educ: Boston Secretarial Sch. Polit. & Govt. Pos: Mem, Rockingham Co. Rural Area Develop. Cmn, N.H; former co-chmn, Rockingham Co. Women's Rep. Club; mem, finance cmt, Rockingham Co. Exten. Serv. Coun; N.H. State Rep, 55-; mem, Bd. of Invest, 56-60; mem, Constitutional Conv, 56-63; clerk, Rockingham Co. Del, 57-61; mem, Legis. Coun; chmn, Fiscal Cmn, 63, mem, Judiciary Cmt, Cmt. on Interstate Coop; mem, exec. cmt, Rockingham Co. Rep. Party, 61-69. Mem: Eastern Star (Past Matron; secy, 3 years); Pythian Sisters Grange. Mailing Add: N. Main St, Plaistow, N.H. 03865.

PALMER, THOMAS GERALD, JR. D
Mem, Calif. Dem. State Cent. Cmt.
b. San Francisco, Calif, 1/10/31; s. Thomas Gerald Palmer and La Homa Clark P; m. 4/10/60 to Susan Ann Benedict; c. Sally Ann, Peter Jon, Linda Ann and Thomas III. Educ: Col. San Mateo, 2 years. Polit. & Govt. Pos: Mem, Calif. Dem. State Cent. Cmt, currently. Mil. Serv: Entered as A/S, Navy, 52, released as YN/3, 53, after serv. in U.S.S. Telfair APA210, Japan and Korea, 52-53; four Serv. Ribbons. Mem: Calif. Dry Cleaners Asn; Peninsula Dry Cleaners Asn.(pres, 67); Int. Laundry-Dry cleaners Asn; C. of C. (mem. bd. dirs, San Bruno C. of C, 60-64); Elks. Rel: Methodist. Mailing Add: 2990 Arguello Dr, Burlingame, Calif. 94010.

PALMER, TOM CARROLL, JR. D
b. Greenville, S.C, 6/30/25; s. Tom Carroll Palmer and Frances Cleveland P; m. 7/6/47 to Margaret Adele Rigby; c. Steven Rigby and Susan Victoria. Educ: N.Ga. Col, 42-43; Mercer Univ, 43; Univ. Pittsburgh, 44; Univ. Ga, 45-46; Lambda Chi Alpha. Polit. & Govt. Pos: Ga. State Rep, 55-60 & 66-68; councilman, Pelham, 57-58; nat. committeeman, Ga. Young Dem, 57-58; mem, DeKalb Co. Ment. Health Adv. Cmt. Bus. & Prof. Pos: Owner, Retail Seafood & Poultry Mkt, 45-57; exec. secy, Ga. Asn. Finance & Loan Co, 58-60; exec. secy, Ga. Independent Auto Dealers, 61; asn. mgr, Asn. Mech. Contractors of Atlanta, Inc, 62-; exec. dir, Piping Promotion Trust, 64-69. Mil. Serv: Aviation Cadet, Army Air Corps, 43-45; Good Conduct Medal; Am. Theatre Ribbon. Mem: Am. Soc. of Sanit. Engrs; Ga. and Am. Socs. of Asn. Execs; Am. Legion; Rotary; Exchange Club; Mason; RAM; bd. of trustees, Doctor's Hosp, Tucker, Ga. Rel: Baptist; Deacon. Legal Res: 3800 Montford Dr, Chamblee, Ga. 30005. Mailing Add: 742 Ponce de Leon Place N.E, Atlanta, Ga. 30306.

PALMER, VINCENT A, JR. R
Chmn, Wayne Co. Rep. Cmt, N.Y.
b. Rochester, N.Y, 10/6/25; s. Vincent A. Palmer and Francis Ashley P; m. 11/24/62 to Eleanor C. Filmer; c. Scott Ashley and Craig Fillmore. Educ: Univ. Rochester, 46-47; Rochester Inst. of Tech, 46-47. Polit. & Govt. Pos: Chmn, Williamson Rep. Cmt, N.Y, 64-69; alternate del, Rep. Nat. Conv, 68; chmn, Wayne Co. Rep. Cmt, 68- Bus. & Prof. Pos: Secy, Cheetham and Ascherman, Inc, Williamson, N.Y, 63-; mem, exec. cmt, Myers Commun. Hosp, Sodus, 65-; asst. v.pres, Egbert F. Ashley Co, Rochester, 67-; v.pres, Realtage Corp. of Am, 69- Mil. Serv: Entered as Pvt, Army Air Force, 43, released as S/Sgt, 45, after serv. in 466th Bomb Group, Eighth Air Force, ETO, 45; Air Medal, Four Oak Leaf Clusters. Mem: Pres, Upstate Chmn. Asn: Am. Legion; Rochester Yacht Club; Pultneyville Civic Asn; Mason. Rel: Episcopal. Mailing Add: 215 E. Lake Rd, Pultneyville, N.Y. 14538.

PALMER, WALTER HENDERSON R
Chmn, Weston Rep. City Cmt, Mass.
b. Wayland, Mass, 3/15/29; s. Sanford Denison Palmer and Helma Henderson P; m. 3/21/53 to Caroline Cannon Watt; c. Rebecca Wells, Walter Stevenson, Susan Breed and Amy Lord. Educ: Harvard Col. Polit. & Govt. Pos: Asst. to campaign mgr, Lodge for Sen. Cmt, 62; exec. secy, Mass. State Rep. Cmt, 63-65; chmn, Weston Rep. City Cmt, 64-; cand. for Mass. Exec. Coun, Second Dist, 66; polit. consult, Campaign Consult, Inc, 66- Bus. & Prof. Pos: Investment broker, A. C. Allyn & Co, 57-62; dir. of human rels, Assoc. Industs. of Mass, 65-; pres, Boston Urban Coalition, Inc. 68- Mil. Serv: Entered as Pvt, Nat. Guard, 48, released as Sgt. 1/C, 55. Publ: 'The disoriented,' Forum Mag, May-June, 66. Mem: Pres, Greater Boston Jr. C. of C, 62. Rel: Unitarian. Mailing Add: 222 Boston Post Rd, Weston, Mass. 02193.

PALMER, WILLARD VINCENT D
b. Macy, Ind, 9/24/13; s. Frank M. Palmer and Edna Hatch P; m. 9/10/33 to Mary Elizabeth Harris; c. James V. and Ann Palmer. Educ: Ind. Univ, 32-33; Delta Chi. Polit. & Govt. Pos: Dem. precinct committeeman, Peru, Ind, 52-62; del, Dem. State Conv, 60 & 64; del, Dem. Nat. Conv, 64 & 68. Bus. & Prof. Pos: Partner, Bitzler Locker Co, Peru, Ind, 46-50; owner, Palmer Cattle Co. and Palmer Farms, 50-66; owner, El River Feedlot and Argos Feedlot and co-owner, Peru Motor Lodge, currently. Mem: Nat. Farmers Orgn; Elks; Mason; Scottish Rite; Shrine; Missinewa Country Club. Rel: Christian Church. Legal Res: 53 N. Fremont, Peru, Ind. 46970. Mailing Add: Box 92, Peru, Ind. 46970.

PALMER, WILLIAM DARRELL D
Iowa State Sen.
b. Iowa City, Iowa, 1/13/35; s. George D. Palmer and Florence I. Middour P; m. 6/27/53 to Evelyn L. Johnson; c. William Nick, Tony Robert and Amanda Kaye. Educ: Life Underwriters Training Course, grad, 59; Col. of Life Underwriters, at present. Polit. & Govt. Pos: Former Iowa State Rep, Polk Co; Iowa State Sen, Polk Co, 68- Bus. & Prof. Pos: Asst. dist. mgr, John Hancock Mutual Life Ins. Co, 58; pres, Palmer and Assocs, Inc, Gen. Ins. Agency, presently. Mem: East Gate Masonic Lodge; Jr. C. of C; Life Underwriters Asn; hon. mem, Local 164, United Rubber Workers, AFL-CIO, hon. mem, Local 82, Ins. Workers of Am. Rel: Methodist. Mailing Add: 2948 Easton Blvd, Des Moines, Iowa 50317.

PALMER, WILSON D
Ky. State Sen.
b. 1917. Educ: Univ. of Ky. Polit. & Govt. Pos: Mem, Bd, Regents, East State Col, Ky; mem, Rural Elec. Bd; mem, Hosp. Bd; Ky. State Sen, 62-; alternate del, Dem. Nat. Conv, 68; chmn, Harrison Co. Dem. Party, 69- Bus. & Prof. Pos: Farmer. Mem: Farm Bur. Rel: Christian Church N.Am. Mailing Add: Route 3, Cynthiana, Ky. 41031. (1967)

PALMIERI, JAMES JOHN D
Conn. State Rep.
b. Waterbury, Conn, 11/30/13; s. Alphonse Palmieri and Marie Rosa Nervo P; m. 9/16/39 to Pauline Krowchenko; c. Paula Marie, James, Jr. and John. Educ: High Sch. Polit. & Govt. Pos: Conn. State Rep, 62- Bus. & Prof. Pos: Sales rep, Metrop. Life Ins, 41; proprietor, Palmieri Ins. Agency, 55. Mil. Serv: Entered as Pvt, Army, 42, released as S/Sgt, 45, after serv. in 8th Inf, ETO; Bronze Star; Purple Heart; Presidential Citation; Combat Inf. Badge. Mem: Elks; VFW; Italian Am. Dem. Club; K. of C. Rel: Catholic. Legal Res: 65 Meriline Ave, Waterbury, Conn. 06702. Mailing Add: 51 W. Maine St, Waterbury, Conn. 06702.

PALMISANO, ANGELO FRANK D
b. Baltimore, Md, 3/7/16; s. John Palmisano and Agata Ragonese P; m. 11/11/36 to Adelaide R. Giardina; c. Agatha M. L. and Angela M. Educ: Baltimore Jr. Col; Sigma Alpha Epsilon. Polit. & Govt. Pos: Md. State Del, 63-68. Bus. & Prof. Pos: Serv. supt, Walter H. Hick, Inc, 47-59; pres. and mgr, Hick's Auto Serv, Inc, 59- Mem: K. of C. Rel: Catholic. Mailing Add: 4049 The Alameda, Baltimore, Md. 21218.

PALMORE, JOHN STANLEY, JR. D
b. Ancon, Canal Zone, Panama, 8/6/17; s. John Stanley Palmore and Antoinette Gonzalez P; m. 7/31/38 to Eleanor Gertrude Anderson; c. John W. Educ: West. Ky. State Col, 34-36; Univ. Louisville, LL.B, 39; Phi Alpha Delta. Polit. & Govt. Pos: Chief of legal br, Jeffersonville Qm. Depot, Ind, 46-47; city prosecuting attorney, Henderson, Ky, 49-53, city attorney, 53-55; commonwealth's attorney, Fifth Judicial Dist, Ky, 55-59; judge, Court of Appeals of Ky, 59- Bus. & Prof. Pos: Attorney-at-law, Henderson, Ky, 39-59. Mil. Serv: Entered as A/S, Navy, 42, released as Lt, 46, after serv. in Supply Corps, Pac. Area, 45; recalled as Lt, Navy, 51, released 52, after serv. in Bur. Supplies and Accts, D.C; Pac. Theater Ribbon with One Star, Okinawa; Atlantic Theater and Victory Ribbons. Publ: 'After the Verdict,' Ky. State Bar J, 1/62; 'Sentencing and Correction—Black Sheep of the Criminal Law,' Fed. Probation, 12/62. Mem: Ky. State and Am. Bar Asns; Am. Judicature Soc; Henderson Co. Farm Bur; Am. Legion; VFW; Moose; Elks; F&AM; Scottish Rite; AAONMS. Rel: Episcopal. Legal Res: Henderson, Ky. 42420. Mailing Add: Room 201, State Capitol, Frankfort, Ky. 40601.

PALUCH, LEO LEON D
Mayor, Allen Park, Mich.
b. Detroit, Mich, 1/15/17; s. August Paluch and Katherine Czynar P; m. to Angeline Skupien; c. Leo W. and Angela. Educ: Mich. Tech. Inst, 49. Polit. & Govt. Pos: Charter cmnr, Allen Park, Mich, 56, councilman, 57-63, mayor, 63- Bus. & Prof. Pos: Elec. contractor, 49- Mil. Serv: Entered as Pvt, Army, released as Sgt; Pac. Combat Ribbons; Good Conduct Medal. Mem: Joint Coun. of Elec. Contractors, Detroit; Am. Legion; VFW; Polish Legion of Am. Vet; K. of C. Rel: Catholic. Mailing Add: 15623 McLain, Allen Park, Mich. 48101. (1967)

PALUMBO, MARIO JOSEPH D
W.Va, State Sen.
b. N.Y.C, 4/13/33; s. Jack Palumbo and Nancy Alfonso P; m. 5/10/69 to Louise Corey. Educ: Morris Harvey Col, B.S, 54; Col. Law, W.Va. Univ, LL.B, 57; Order of the Coif; mem, Law Rev. Polit. & Govt. Pos: W.Va. State Sen, Eighth Dist, 69- Bus. & Prof. Pos: Partner, Law Firm of Woodroe, Kizer & Steed, Charleston, W.Va, 58-69 and Campbell, Love, Woodroe & Kizer, 69- Mil. Serv: Maj. and Legal Officer, 130th Spec. Opers. Group, W.Va. Air Nat. Guard Res. Mem: Am, W.Va. and Kanawha Co. Bar Asns; W.Va. State Bar; Elks; Army and Navy Club; Tennis Club; Exchange Club. Litton Award, Nat. Asn. of Intercollegiate Athletics Basketball Tournament, 53. Rel: Catholic. Mailing Add: 19 Bradford St, Charleston, W.Va. 25301.

PANCOAST, G. SIEBER R
Pa. State Rep.
b. Audubon, N.J, 6/16/14; s. Garfield Pancoast and Frances M. Rood; m. to

Muriel E. Brandt; c. two. Educ: Ursinus Col, B.S; Univ. of Pa, A.M. and Ph.D. Polit. & Govt. Pos: 2nd v.pres, Montgomery Co. Boroughs Asn, Pa; mem, Nixon Vol, 60; mayor, Borough of Collegeville, 61-65; co-chmn, Montgomery Co. Rep. Campaign Cmt. in primary elec, 62; Montgomery Co. adminstr, ACTION, 62; chmn. winter registrn. period, Registrn. Dr. for Montgomery Co. Rep. Cmt, 63-64. Bus. & Prof. Pos: Prof. Mil. Serv: Naval Res, Ens. and Lt. (j.g.), 44-46. Mem: Several prof. socs; former Consistory; Lions Clubs. Rel: United Church of Christ. Mailing Add: 122 W. 7th Ave, Collegeville, Pa. 19426.

PANDICK, MARGARET L. D
V.chmn, Delaware Co. Dem. Cmt, N.Y.
b. Delhi, N.Y; d. Ernest A. Leal and Margaret Simon L; m. 5/30/36 to Andrew Lawrence Pandick, wid. 3/20/63; c. Linda A. (Mrs. Victor A. Franzese) and Thomas O'Donnell. Educ: Binghamton Beauty Sch, Binghamton, N.Y, 34. Polit. & Govt. Pos: Dep. cmnr, Delaware Co. Bd. of Elec, N.Y, 58-; secy. & treas, Elec. Cmnr. Asn, N.Y, 68-; v.chmn, Delaware Co. Dem. Cmt, 67- Bus. & Prof. Pos: Hair stylist, Jean King Studio, Bay Shore, L.I, 35-36 and McLean's Dept. Store, Binghamton, N.Y, 36-42. Mem: Bus. & Prfnl. Women; Village Improvement Soc, Delhi, N.Y. Rel: Presbyterian. Mailing Add: 15 Clinton St, Delhi, N.Y. 13753.

PAPANDREA, EDWARD JAMES D
b. Meriden, Conn, 6/13/26; s. James N. Papandrea; single. Educ: Univ. Hartford, Bus. Admin, 60; N.Y. Univ, Cert. Retailing, 62. Polit. & Govt. Pos: Mem, Dem. Town Cmt, Meriden, Conn, 57-59, chmn, 59-65; dir. personnel, Meriden, 65- Bus. & Prof. Pos: Mgr, Papandrea Jewelers, 47-65. Mil. Serv: Entered as A/S, Navy, 44, released as Fireman 1/C, 46; Am, European and Pac. Theater Ribbons. Mem: Elks; K. of C; VFW; Lions. Rel: Catholic. Legal Res: 32 Lincoln Terr, Meriden, Conn. 06450. Mailing Add: 61 W. Main St, Meriden, Conn. 06450.

PAPANDREA, JOHN FRANCIS D
Asst. Majority Leader, Conn. House of Rep.
b. San Giovanni Calabria, Italy, 8/3/34; s. Joseph G. Papandrea (deceased) and Rose M. Mule P; m. 6/4/60 to Marianne Petrus; c. Anne Marie. Educ: Fairfield Univ, B.S, 56; Univ. Conn. Sch. Law, LL.B, 59; Acquinas Acad. Polit. & Govt. Pos: Mem. Charter Rev. Cmn, Meriden, Conn, 59-61; mem, Meriden City Coun, 62-66, City Coun. Minority Leader, 62-64, Majority Leader, 64-66, chmn, By-Laws Cmt, 62-66 and chmn, Zoning Rev. Cmt, 64-66; Conn. State Rep, 78th Dist, 67-, Asst. Majority Leader, Conn. House of Rep, 69-; mem, Gov. Cmns. on Probate Rev. and Youthful Wards of the State; mem, Legis. Coun. Cmt. for Rev. of Legis. Rules; mem, Gov. Revenue Task Force, 69. Mil. Serv: Pvt, Conn. Nat. Guard, 59-62. Mem: Conn. Bar Asn. (mem, Cmn. of Rev. of Family Law); counsel, Meriden Parents Without Partners, Meriden Latin Am. Soc. and Conn. Hairdressers and Cosmetologists; Unison Club; Mt. Carmel Holy Name Soc; Meriden Latin Am. Scholarship Cmt. Rel: Roman Catholic. Legal Res: 66 Orchard Hill Rd, Meriden, Conn. 06450. Mailing Add: 31 Pratt St, Meriden, Conn. 06450.

PAPE, CARL E. R
Chmn, Boone Co. Rep. Party, Ill.
b. Clinton, Iowa, 3/12/10; s. August C. Pape and Anna D. Jensen P; m. 8/6/32 to Helen A. Nowak; c. Robert C. Educ: Belvidere High Sch. Polit. & Govt. Pos: Hwy. cmnr, Belvidere Twp, Ill, 47-; dir, Twp. Officials of Ill, 54-64 & 66-, first v.pres, 64-65; precinct committeeman, Rep. Party, 9 years; chmn, Boone Co. Rep. Party, currently; del, Rep. Nat. Conv, 68. Mem: Int. counsr, Lions Int. and dist. gov, 60-61. Rel: Protestant. Mailing Add: 1624 S. State St, Belvidere, Ill. 61008.

PAPEN, FRANK O'BRIEN D
N.Mex. State Sen.
b. Las Vegas, N.Mex, 12/2/09; s. John A. Papen and Helen O'Brien P; m. 1942 to Julia S. Stevenson; c. Michele. Educ: De LaSalle Inst, Chicago, Ill. Polit. & Govt. Pos: N.Mex. State Rep, 57-58; del, N.Mex. Constitutional Conv, 69; N.Mex. State Sen, 69- Bus. & Prof. Pos: Chmn. Bd, Chaparral Broadcasting Co; pres, Loretto Develop. Co, Shopping Center; pres, Frank O. Papen & Co, Ins, 50-; dir, First Nat. Bank Dona Ana Co, 54-, exec. v.pres, 57-60, pres, 60-; mem, N.Mex. State Invest. Coun, 63-67; mem, N.Mex. Dept. Develop. Adv. Coun, 67-68. Mil. Serv: Fourth Army liaison Officer, ROTC Dona Ana Co, 68. Mem: Kiwanis Club; past dir, Am. Red Cross; Commun. Concert Asn.(past pres); Knight Comdr, Holy Sepulchure; K. of C.(4°); Alpha Kappa Lambda (bd. adv); Las Cruces Country Club; Lancers Club; Am. Bankers Asn.(savings bond chmn. N.Mex, 64-66, v.chmn, 12th regional adv. cmt. banking practices and policies, 65-66, adv. cmt. fed. legis, 65-); N.Mex. Bankers Asn.(exec. cmt, 65-66); S. New Mex. Chap. AUSA (pres, 68-69); Citizen of the Year Award, N.Mex. Asn. Realtors, 68. Rel: Catholic. Legal Res: 2250 E. Missouri, Apt. 3A, La Cruces, N.Mex. 88001. Mailing Add: First National Bank of Dona Ana County, 500 S. Main St, Las Cruces, N.Mex. 88001.

PAPPAGIANIS, GEORGE S. D
Attorney Gen, N.H.
b. Nashua, N.H, 4/23/24; s. Spiros George Pappagianis and Spiridula Geoldasis P. Educ: Harvard Univ, B.A, 46; Boston Univ, LL.B, 49. Polit. & Govt. Pos: N.H. State Rep, 53-57 & 59-64, N.H. Legis. Coun, 55-56 & 59-60; dep. attorney gen, N.H, 64-66, attorney gen, 66- Mem: Am, N.H. and Nashua Bar Asns. Mailing Add: 29 Charlotte Ave, Nashua, N.H. 03060.

PAPPAS, LEAH AGLAIA D
b. Ogden, Utah, 3/23/36; d. George Thomas Pappas and Maria Harames P; single. Educ: Univ. Utah, 54-57 & 62-63; Col. of St. Mary of the Wasatch, B.A, 59. Polit. & Govt. Pos: Mem, Las Vegas Dem. Cent. Cmt, Nev, 67-69; mem, Las Vegas Young Dem, 67-69; alternate del, Dem. Nat. Conv, 68. Bus. & Prof. Pos: Teacher, Bishop Gorman High Sch, Clark Co. Sch. Dist, 59-69. Mem: Nat. Educ. Asn; N.Y. State and Nev. State Teachers Asns. Rel: Greek Orthodox. Mailing Add: 1729 Oakey Blvd, Las Vegas, Nev. 89105.

PAPPAS, PETE R
Ill. State Rep.
b. Silvis, Ill, 10/14/27; s. Thomas John Pappas and Despina Lemonides P; m. 5/17/54 to Patricia Karras: c. Thomas John, George Christopher and Matthew Peter. Educ: St. Ambrose Col, 45 & 48; Idaho State Col, 49. Polit. & Govt. Pos: Supvr, 19th Cong. Dist. Census, Ill, 60; asst. supvr, Rock Island Co. Bd. Supvr, 60-66; Ill. State Rep, 44th Dist, currently. Bus. & Prof. Pos: Partner, Dio Realty Co. and River Realty Co; pres, Mid-Continent Terminal & Storage, Inc. and Port of Rock Island. Mil. Serv: Entered as A/S, Navy, 45, released as Printer 3/C, 48, after serv. in Submarine Force, Pac. Theater. Mem: Mason; Shrine; Elks; Rotary; C. of C. Rel: Creek Orthodox. Mailing Add: 2920 32nd St. Court, Rock Island, Ill. 61201. (1967)

PAPY, BERNIE, JR. D
b. Key West, Fla, 2/14/30; m. to Marilyn Malpass; c. Karen Lynne, Lisa Anne and Bernie C, III. Educ: Univ. of Fla, B.S. and B.A, 54; Phi Delta Theta. Polit. & Govt. Pos: Fla. State Rep, 64-68. Bus. & Prof. Pos: Gasoline distributor; ins. agent. Mil. Serv: Coast Guard, 3 years. Mem: Jaycees. Rel: Presbyterian. Mailing Add: 905 Von Phister St, Key West, Fla. 33040.

PAQUIN, HENRY L. D
b. Pawtucket, R.I, 8/15/18; m. to Doris Masse. Educ: Tolman High Sch, 36. Polit. & Govt. Pos: R.I. State Rep, 61-66; secy, Dem. Party, Pawtucket, R.I; city clerk, Pawtucket, 66- Bus. & Prof. Pos: Financial planner, real estate broker. Mil. Serv: 1st Lt, 41-45, ETO. Mailing Add: 228 Bucklin St, Pawtucket, R.I. 02861.

PARADISE, ELSIE M. R
V.Chmn, Niagara Co. Rep. Cmt, N.Y.
b. Niagara Falls, N.Y, 4/13/30; d. Michael Paul Luch and Anna Furcak L; m. 11/6/48 to A. John Paradise; c. Evelyn J, Lorraine, John, Joan, Joel and Ann. Educ: St. Cyril's Acad, Danville, Pa, 4 years. Polit. & Govt. Pos: Rep. Committeeman, Niagara Co, N.Y, 62-; v.chmn, Niagara Co. Rep. Cmt, 64-; research asst, N.Y. State Senate, 66-69. Named outstanding young Rep. woman, 63 and outstanding Rep. woman, 64. Rel: Catholic. Mailing Add: 2433 Linwood Ave, Niagara Falls, N.Y. 14305.

PARCELL, LEW W. D
Chmn, San Juan Co. Dem. Cent. Cmt, Colo.
b. Beverly, Ohio, 9/17/88; s. William Parcell and Nellie Jane Deal P; m. 11/19/14 to Elva Jane Glanville; c. Wallace G. Educ: Ohio Northern Univ. Polit. & Govt. Pos: Chmn, San Juan Co. Dem. Cent. Cmt, Colo, currently; mem, Colo. Dem. State Exec. Cmt, 69- Bus. & Prof. Pos: Owner, Silverton Elec. Lighting Co, 16-66; owner, Circle Route Garage, 20-56. Mem: Elks; Rotary. Mailing Add: P.O. Box 67, Silverton, Colo. 81433. (1967)

PARDRIDGE, MARILYN JONES R
Publicity Dir, Pima Co. Rep. Cent. Cmt, Ariz.
b. Chicago, Ill, 10/28/24; d. Marvin Willman Jones and Mae Hatcher J; m. to Clinton Edward Pardridge (deceased); c. Candace (Mrs. Ronald Langlas), Julie (Mrs. Ben Allgood), Katherine and Margaret. Educ: Monmouth Col, 42-43. Polit. & Govt. Pos: Asst. mgr, Gubernatorial Campaign, Ariz, 60; precinct committeewoman, Pima Co. Rep. Cent. Cmt, 60-, publicity dir, 66-; nat. committeewoman, Young Rep. League, 61; asst. mgr, Senate Campaign, Ariz, 62; mem. bds, Pima Co. and Pantano Rep. Women, 62-66; second v.chmn, Ariz. State Rep. Cent. Cmt, 63-65; state orgn. chmn, Pres. Campaign, 64; hon. Asst. Sgt. at Arms, Rep. Nat. Conv, 64; publicity chmn, Trunk N Tusk Club, 67-69; chmn, Ariz. Women for Nixon, 68; co-chmn, Ariz. Nixon for Pres. Cmt, 68; chmn, Pima Co. Slate Cmt, 68; del, Rep. Nat. Conv, 68. Publ: Co-ed, Wingtips; Pima County Republican Manual, 63; auth, Training Course for Precinct Committeeman and Party Workers, 65. Mil. Serv: Lt. Col, Ariz. Wing Civil Air Patrol, 55-59. Mem: Tucson Press Club; chmn, Assoc. Officers Wives Club, 56-66. Nat. Award, Civil Air Patrol, 57-58. Rel: Protestant. Mailing Add: 6342 E. Malvern, Tucson, Ariz. 85710.

PARDUE, ERWIN R
Mem, Calif. Rep. State Cent. Cmt.
b. Erwin, Tenn, 7/22/39; s. Salomon Bradia Pardue and Berlyn Shell P; single. Educ: YMCA Jr. Col, 2 years. Polit. & Govt. Pos: Mem, Calif. Rep. State Cent. Cmt, and 20th Assembly Dist. Rep. Coun, 69-; mem, Calif. Rep. Assembly and Calif. Rep. League, 69- Bus. & Prof. Pos: Pres, Blue Ridge Shipping & Trading Inc, 69. Mil. Serv: Seaman Recruit, Navy, 58; E-5, Navy Res, with serv. in U.S. Seventh Fleet, 62. Mem: Marine Exchange; Jr. C. of C; Optimist (v.pres, El Camino Chap); Club Sailors Union Pac. Rel: Baptist. Mailing Add: 510 Bush, San Francisco, Calif. 94108.

PARDUN, PATRICIA JANE R
V.Chmn, Iowa Rep. State Cent. Cmt.
b. Independence, Iowa, 10/23/24; d. Allen Smith and Myra Mattice S; m. 11/13/43 to W. Glen Pardun; c. Paulette (Mrs. Brossman), Anthony Allen and Pamela (Mrs. Dunlap). Educ: Univ. Dubuque, 1 year; Univ. Iowa, 2 years. Polit. & Govt. Pos: Rep. precinct committeewoman, Harrison Twp, Benton Co, Iowa, 53-68; v.chmn, Benton Co. Cent. Cmt, 54-58; pres, Rep. Women's Club, 62-64; state prog. chmn, Iowa Coun. of Rep. Women, 62-64; second dist, v.chmn, Iowa Rep. State Cent. Cmt, 58-62, fourth dist. v.chmn, 64-68, state v.chmn, 66-; del, Rep. Nat. Conv, 68; Bus. & Prof. Pos: Secy, Buchanan Co. Title & Loan, 41-43, Allen Smith, Attorney-at-Law, 43-56 and Brandon Consolidated Sch, 56-58. Mem: Red Cross; Iowa Farm Bur; Navy Mothers; Am. Legion Auxiliary; PTA; Federated Women's Club; Wapsipinicon Golf Club. Rel: Methodist. Mailing Add: R.F.D. 1, Brandon, Iowa 52210.

PARENTEAU, CAROLYN BLANCHE R
Chmn, Northfield Rep. Town Cmt, Mass.
b. Gill, Mass, 1/25/21; d. Frank A. Zak and Mary Niedbala Z; m. 5/11/46 to Raymond J. Parenteau. Educ: Nazareth Col, 40; Katherine Gibbs Secretarial Sch, 42. Polit. & Govt. Pos: Secy, Northfield Rep. Town Cmt, Mass, 53-65, v.chmn, 66 and chmn, 66-; mem-at-lg, Franklin Co. Rep. Club, 62-69; Northfield Rep. coordinator, Edward W. Brooke for Attorney Gen. Campaign Cmt, 64 and for U.S. Sen, 66; campaigner, Gov. John A. Volpe, 64 & 66, Lt. Gov. Elliot L. Richardson, 64, Attorney Gen. Elliot L. Richardson, 66 and Lt. Gov. Francis Sargent, 66; campaigner, Mass. State Rep. Silvio O. Conte, First Dist, 64 & 66, Mass. State Sen. Charles A. Bisbee, Jr, Franklin-Hampshire Dist, 64, Mass. State Sen. John D. Barrus, Franklin-Hampshire Dist, 66 and Mass. State Rep. Winston Healy, First Franklin Dist, 64 & 66; pres, Franklin Co. Rep. Women's Club, 65-67; campaign mgr, Attorney Raymond J. Fontana for Gov. Coun, Eighth Dist, 66-68; aide, Rep. State Committeewoman, Franklin

Co. Dist, 68; chmn, Franklin Co. Registrn. Voter Dr, 68; mem. nominating cmt, Mass. Fedn. Rep. Women, 69. Bus. & Prof. Pos: Owner and operator, Fairview Gardens Greenhouses, 51-69; secy-v.chmn, Pioneer Valley Regional Sch. Dist. Cmt, 61-69; mem, Rep. Club of Mass, 67-69; secy. and mem. adv. bd, Greenfield Commun. Col, 67-; mem, Greenfield Commun. Col. Found, Inc, 69. Mem: Mass. Flower Growers Asn; Mass. Sch. Cmt. Asn; chmn. and treas, Northfield Girl Scouts Little House; Northfield Garden Club (past pres); secy, Northfield Village Improv. Soc; Northfield Civic Coun. Appreciation Badge, Girl Scouts. Rel: Catholic. Mailing Add: 8 Main St, Northfield, Mass. 01360.

PARENTEAU, MARC DUANE R
Chmn, Red Lake Co. Rep. Cmt, Minn.
b. Crookston, Minn, 11/20/36; s. Aurelius J. Parenteau and Della V. Perusse P; m. 8/23/58 to Constance Lynn Kiewel; c. Marc E, Greg J, Jill M, Pamela L. and Gary R. Educ: Marquette Univ, 4 years; Delta Sigma Pi. Polit. & Govt. Pos: Village clerk and treas, Brooks, Minn, 62-; chmn, Red Lake Co. Rep. Cmt, currently. Bus. & Prof. Pos: Secy-treas, Brooks Cheese Factory, 61- Mem: Elks; Minakwa Country Club. Football Capt, Cathedral High, 53. Rel: Catholic. Mailing Add: Brooks, Minn. 56715.

PARILLO, JOSEPH, JR. R
b. New Haven, Conn, 9/16/22; s. Joseph Parillo, Sr. and Rose Cutarelli P; m. 1/4/48 to Christine Marie DeMidio; c. Rosemary, Jack and Joseph, III. Educ: Bryant Col, B.S. in Bus. Educ, 52; Alpha Theta Chi. Polit. & Govt. Pos: Rep. committeeman, 13th Ward, Third Dist, Schenectady, N.Y, 54-69; pres, 13th Ward Rep. Club, 55-59; Rep. ward chmn, 13th Ward, 59-69; secy, Schenectady Co. Men's Rep. Club, 61-67; v.chmn, Schenectady Co. Rep. Cmt, 66-69; staff asst. to Congressman Daniel E. Button, 29th Cong. Dist, 67-69. Bus. & Prof. Pos: Acct, Gen. Elec, Schenectady, N.Y, 46-69. Mil. Serv: Entered as Pvt, Army, 43, released as Pfc, 45, after serv. in 731st Field Artil. Bn, ETO, 44-45; Am. Serv. Medal; Good Conduct Medal; Expert Rifleman Medal; European-African-Mid. East. Serv. Medal. Mem: Cost Acct. Asn; Am. Legion; Ital-Am. Vet; VFW; Sons of Italy; Holy Name Soc; League of the Holy Family. Lady of Mt. Carmel Holy Name Merit Award for Man of the Year for Commun. and Church Involvement. Rel: Catholic. Mailing Add: 466 Hulett St, Schenectady, N.Y. 12307.

PARIS, JAMES W. D
Ga. State Rep.
b. Dallas, Ga, 3/25/21; s. Elijah F. Paris and Mary Tyler P; m. 5/7/44 to Grace L. Harbin; c. Patsy Latrell. Educ: Univ. of Ga, B.B.A, 49, LL.B, 52. Polit. & Govt. Pos: Mem, Barrow Co. Dem. Exec. Cmt, Ga; co. attorney; Ga. State Sen, 57-58; Ga. State Rep, 59- Bus. & Prof. Pos: Attorney. Mil. Serv: Air Force, Sgt, World War II, ETO; Silver Star. Mem: Mason; Elks; VFW; Am. Legion; Lions. Rel: Baptist. Mailing Add: 306 W. Wright St, Winder, Ga. 30680. (1967)

PARISH, DAVID ANDREW D
Mayor, Madisonville, Ky.
b. Madisonville, Ky, 11/28/99; s. Rufus Lee Parish and Martha James P; single. Educ: U.S. Naval Acad; Sch. of Pharmacy. Polit. & Govt. Pos: Mayor, Madisonville, Ky, 46-; chmn, Hopkins Co. Dem. Party, 60- Bus. & Prof. Pos: Registered pharmacist, 22- Mem: Elks; Mason (32°), trustee, Rizpoh Shrine and past pres, chmn, Hopkins Co. Develop. Corp, Youth Found. and Madisonville Hosp. Bd; Madisonville Country Club. Rel: Methodist. Mailing Add: 54 Woddill Ave, Madisonville, Ky. 42431. (1967)

PARISH, JERRY EDWARD R
Chmn, Claiborne Co. Rep. Party, Miss.
b. Wichita Falls, Tex, 2/14/18; s. Ruben Parish and Leah Eskridge P; m. 6/27/44 to Carol L. Schwartz; c. Paul M, Richard J. and David C. Educ: Draughons Bus. Col, 38; Tex. A&M, 38-42; Hardin Col, 46-51. Polit. & Govt. Pos: Chmn, Claiborne Co. Rep. Party, Miss, 68- Bus. & Prof. Pos: Partner-mgr, ranching-farming-dairy bus, 46-51; livestock specialist, Basic Formula Labs, Inc, 51-54; quality control specialist, Westinghouse Elec. Corp, 54-63; indust. rels, Allied Chem. Corp, 63-68; engr, Westinghouse Elec. Corp, 68- Mil. Serv: Entered as Aviation Cadet, Air Force, 42, released as 1st Lt, 45, after serv. in Sixth Air Force, Panama Canal, 42-45; Air Medal with Oak Leaf Cluster. Mem: Am. Soc. Tool and Mfg. Engrs; Kiwanis; Am. Legion. Rel: Catholic. Mailing Add: Box 174, Port Gibson, Miss. 39150.

PARISH, RICHARD JUSTUS DFL
b. Little Swan, Minn, 1/4/14; s. John L. Parish and Mary Ruth Sundburg P; m. 6/24/39 to Audrey Louise Hanson; c. Carol (Mrs Compton), Mary (Mrs. Gibson), Jane and Richard. Educ: Olivia High Sch, Minn; Hamline Univ, St. Paul, B.A; Minneapolis Col. of Law, LL.B; Kappa Phi Kappa. Polit. & Govt. Pos: Minn. State Sen, 62-67, Minn. State Rep, 59-62; mem, Metrop. Planning Cmn, 57-58; mem, secy-treas. & pres, Sch. Bd, Dist. 281, Robbinsdale, 49-58. Bus. & Prof. Pos: Attorney-at-Law, Parish & Parish, 46- Mil. Serv: Entered as Ens, Navy, 44, released as Lt.(jg), 46, after serv. in Armed Guard, Asiatic Pac; Am, Philippine and Asiatic Pac. Campaign Ribbons. Mem: Minn. State and Hennepin Co. Bar Asns; VFW; Am. Legion; Robbinsdale C. of C; Minn. Hist. Soc; Shrine. Rel: Methodist. Mailing Add: 2565 Vale Crest Rd, Golden Valley, Minn. 55422. (1967)

PARISH, TAT D
Chmn, Berrien Co. Dem. Cmt, Mich.
b. Waupaca, Wis, 7/23/40; m. to Margaret; c. Amy and Tat David. Educ: Hamline Univ; Harvard Law Sch. Polit. & Govt. Pos: Asst. city attorney, St. Joseph, Mich, 67-69; asst. prosecutor, Berrien Co, 68-; cand. for prosecutor, 68; village attorney, Stevensville, 69-; chmn, Berrien Co. Dem. Cmt, 69- Bus. & Prof. Pos: Attorney-at-law. Mailing Add: 600 Main St, St. Joseph, Mich. 49085.

PARK, COREY Y.S. D
b. Honolulu, Hawaii, 10/9/46; s. Francis H.Y. Park and Kyoko Hirai P; single. Educ: Univ. Hawaii, B.A, 68; Univ. Mich. Law Sch, currently; Omicron Delta Kappa. Polit. & Govt. Pos: Del, Dem. Nat. Conv, 68; precinct pres, Dem. Party, Hawaii, currently. Publ: Article in Student Travel in America, 68. Mailing Add: 46-036 Kumoo Place, Honolulu, Hawaii 96744.

PARK, DOUGLAS CAMPBELL R
Chmn, Wellfleet Rep. Town Cmt, Mass.
b. Boston, Mass, 9/29/17; s. Thaddeus Carlton Park and Priscilla Campbell P; m. 8/22/42 to Nona Gleason. Educ: Jamaica Plain High Sch. Polit. & Govt. Pos: Dep. Sheriff, Barnstable Co, Mass, 62-; mem, Bd. Appeals, Wellfleet, Mass, 64-66 & 67-, selectman, 66-67; chmn, Lower Cape Rep. Coun, 65, secy, 66-; chmn, Wellfleet Rep. Town Cmt, 66- Mil. Serv: Entered as Apprentice, Navy, 34, released as CMM, 54, after serv. in various Atlantic and Pac. actions, 41-45. Mem: AF&AM; Wellfleet Assocs; Wellfleet Assocs. Taxpayers Group. Rel: Protestant. Legal Res: 14 E. Commercial St, Wellfleet, Mass. 02667. Mailing Add: Box 46, Wellfleet, Mass. 02667.

PARK, HAZEL I. R
N.H. State Rep.
b. Hackensack, N.J, 1/6/92; widow; c. two. Educ: Packard Sch, N.Y.C. Polit. & Govt. Pos: Former postmaster, Lyme, N.H; former chmn, Lyme Recreational Coun; N.H. State Rep, 63- Mem: Utility Club of Lyme. Rel: Protestant. Mailing Add: Box 144, Lyme, N.H. 03768.

PARK, WILLIAM ANTHONY D
Chmn, 18th Dist. Dem. Orgn, Idaho
b. Blackfoot, Idaho, 6/4/34; s. William Clair Park and Thelma Shear P; m. 6/26/61 to Elizabeth Jane Taylor; c. Susan Elizabeth, William Adam and Patricia Anne. Educ: Boise Jr. Col, Idaho, A.A, 54; Univ. Idaho, B.A, 58, L.L.B, 63; Phi Alpha Delta; Kappa Sigma. Polit. & Govt. Pos: Pres, Ada Co. Young Dem, Idaho, 65-66; chmn, 18th Dist. Dem. Orgn, 67-; del, Dem. Nat. Conv, 68. Bus. & Prof. Pos: Self-employed attorney, 63- Mil. Serv: Entered as Pvt, Army, 56, released as Pfc, 57, after serv. in Qm. Corps, Phila. Qm. Depot. Mem: Idaho State and Boise Bar Asns; City Club of Boise; Crane Creek Country Club. Rel: Episcopal. Mailing Add: 315 Schmeizer Lane, Boise, Idaho 83706.

PARK, WILLIAM HENRY R
b. Bradley, Okla, 8/31/26; s. Leonard Napolean Park and Ona Goodrich P; m. 12/18/48 to Myrtle Jean Spurlock; c. Karen Marie and Mary Lou. Educ: Fresno State Col, A.B. in geol, 53; Univ. of Southern Calif, post grad. work. Polit. & Govt. Pos: Assoc. oil and gas engr, Calif. State Div. Oil & Gas, 53; 28th Assembly Dist. Precinct Chmn, Rep. Cent. Cmt, 62-65; mem, Calif. State Rep. Cent. Cmt, 64-66; city councilman, Bakersfield, Calif; admin. asst. Rep. Bob Mathias, 18th Dist, Calif, currently. Bus. & Prof. Pos: Farmer, 46-56; owner of serv. sta, 49-51. Mil. Serv: Entered as A/S, Navy, 44, released as Electricians Mate 3/C, 46; Pac. Theater Ribbon. Publ: 7 technical reports on Subsurface Geology, Calif. State Div. Oil & Gas Summary of Operations, 54- Mem: Am. Asn. of Petrol. Geologists; Am. Inst. of Prfnl. Geologists; Am. Petrol. Inst; Taft Masons, Bakersfield Scottish Rite; Eastern Star; Nat. Riflemans Asn; Am. Legion. Rel: Baptist. Legal Res: Bakersfield, Calif. Mailing Add: 9717 Commonwealth, Fairfax, Va. 22030.

PARKER, ALVA J. D
Polit. & Govt. Pos: N.Mex. State Rep, 59-69; mem, Legis. Coun, 61-; Roosevelt Co. cmnr, 4 years. Bus. & Prof. Pos: Rancher. Mil. Serv: Army, 3 years, 33 months overseas. Mem: Am. Legion; VFW. Rel: Baptist. Mailing Add: N. Star Route, Elida, N.Mex. 88116. (1967)

PARKER, ANN L. R
Mem, Calif. Rep. State Cent. Cmt.
b. Sacramento, Calif, 5/2/26; d. Harold Byron La Forge and Marjory Slade L; m. 7/30/50 to Wendell R. Parker; c. Donald, David and Lisa. Educ: Univ. of Calif, A.B. and Teacher's Cert; Prytanean. Polit. & Govt. Pos: Rep. precinct chmn, Contra Costa Co, Calif, 61-64; mem, Contra Costa Co. Rep. Cent. Cmt, alternate mem, 64-; mem, Calif. Rep. State Cent. Cmt, 62-. Bus. & Prof. Pos: Teacher, 49-50. Mem: Am. Asn. of Univ. Women; life mem. PTA. Rel: Presbyterian. Mailing Add: 134 Danefield Place, Moraga, Calif, 94556.

PARKER, BARRY T. R
N.J. State Assemblyman
b. Mt. Holly, N.J, 12/12/32. Educ: Bordentown Mil. Inst, 50; Bucknell Univ, A.B, 54; Rutgers Univ, LL.B, 60. Polit. & Govt. Pos: N.J. State Assemblyman, currently. Bus. & Prof. Pos: Attorney and mem. Law Firm, Parker, McCay and Crisuolo, Mount Holly. Mem: Secy-treas, Burlington Co. Bar Asn; rules cmt, N.J. State Bar Asn; N.J. Compensation Asn; trustee, Good Intent Fire Co; dir, C. of C; Rotary; Elks; F&AM; Tall Cedars of Lebanon; Ducks Unltd, Beach Haven Marlin and Tuna Club; Nat. Wildlife Fedn. Mailing Add: 115 High St, Mt. Holly, N.J. 08060. (1967)

PARKER, BEN P. D
b. Tenaha, Tex, 7/14/23; s. H.C. Parker and Nora Smith P; m. 5/18/65 to Dorothy Burwick; c. Judy Lee (Mrs. John Latham) and Alice Jan. Educ: Univ. Tex, Austin, 40-43. Polit. & Govt. Pos: Mem. city coun, Center, Tex, 45-49; chmn, Shelby Co. Dem. Party, 46-56; alternate del, Dem. Nat. Conv, 68. Bus. & Prof. Pos: Pres, Pep Motor Co, Center, Tex, 46-56; v.pres, First Nat. Bank, 60-65; pres, Mem. Hosp, 65-69. Mil. Serv: Entered as Cadet, Air Force, 43, released as Sgt, 46, after serv. in Fifth Air Force, S.W. Pac. Theatre; Philippine Liberation, Luzon, West. Pac, Am. Theatre Campaign and Asiatic Pac. Campaign Medals. Mem: Mason (32°); York Rite; K.T; Shrine. Rel: Methodist. Mailing Add: P.O. Box 32, Center, Tex. 75935.

PARKER, CARL ALLEN D
Tex. State Rep.
b. Port Arthur, Tex, 8/6/34; s. H. A. Parker and Juanita Christian P; m. 1/30/60 to Beverly Stiegler; c. Valerie Lynn, Christian Ann and Carl Allen, Jr. Educ: Univ. Tex; Phi Dalta Phi. Polit. & Govt. Pos: Tex. State Rep, 62- Bus. & Prof. Pos: Partner, Long & Parker. Mil. Serv: Entered as Lt.(jg), Naval Res, 58, Lt. Comdr, currently. Mem: Tex. Bar Asn; Tex. Trial Lawyers Asn; Lions; Jaycees; Mental Health Asn. Rel: Baptist. Mailing Add: 3549 Sixth St, Port Arthur, Tex. 77640.

PARKER, DONALD CONANT R
Mem, Ala. Rep. Exec. Cmt.
b. Union Springs, Ala, 7/27/26; s. Donald Wright Parker and Mabel Moore P; m. 12/28/47 to Alla Maye Springer; c. Donald M, David C. and Roger C. Educ: Auburn Univ, B.S, 50; Phi Kappa Phi; Alpha Zeta; Xi Sigma Pi. Polit.

& Govt. Pos: Secy, Bullock Co. Rep. Exec. Cmt, Ala, 62-64, chmn, 64-; v.chmn, Bullock Co. Bd. of Educ, 62-68, chmn, 68-; mem, Ala. Rep. Exec. Cmt, currently. Bus. & Prof. Pos: Partner, Springer Lumber Co, 51-, Builders Supply Co, 56- and Parker Bros, Union Springs, Ala, 63- Mil. Serv: Entered as A/S, Navy, 44, released as RM 3/C, 46, after serv. in West. Pac. Mem: Lions; Am. Legion; chmn, Bullock Co. Chap, Am. Red Cross. Rel: Presbyterian. Mailing Add: 209 W. Hardaway, Union Springs, Ala. 36089.

PARKER, EARL, SR.
Educ: Chillicothe Bus. Col, Mo. Polit. & Govt. Pos: N.Mex. State Sen, -67; 10 years Mayor of Estancia; 2 years Torrance Co. Cmnr. Bus. & Prof. Pos: Farm machinery dealer; spec. rep, First Nat. Bank of Belen. Mem: Rotary, A.F. & A.M. Rel: Methodist. Mailing Add: P.O. Box 497, Estancia, N.Mex. 87016. (1967)

PARKER, GEORGE WARREN R
b. Joplin, Mo. 5/16/23; s. William McKinley Parker and Eva Payne P; m. 11/14/42 to Lois Elizabeth Oberpriller; c. Peggy (Mrs. William L. Wheeler, Jr), Suzanne (Mrs. Palmer Nichols, Jr), George W, Jr. and Della Jo. Educ: Univ. Md, B.S, 53; Univ. Mo, grad. study; hon. mem, Theta Xi. Polit. & Govt. Pos: Civil defense dir, Columbia, Mo, 62; cand. for Mo. State Rep, Boone Co, 62; state v.pres, Mo. Asn. of Rep, 62; exec. dir, Mo. Rep. State Cmt, 63-66; Mo. State Rep, 120th Dist, 67-69 and secy, Rep. Caucus. Bus. & Prof. Pos: Assoc. prof. air sci, Univ. Mo, 58-61; ins. rep, Accacia Mutual Life Ins. Co, 61-62; real estate salesman, Boone Realty Co, Mo, 62-63; asst. ed, monthly newspaper, Mo. Rep, 64-66, ed, 66. Mil. Serv: Entered as Pvt, Army Air Corps, 40, released as Maj, 61, after serv. in 397th Bomb Group, ETO, 44-45, China, 46-49 and Alaska, 55-58. Distinguished Flying Cross; Air Medal with Two Silver Oak Leaf Clusters; Purple Heart with Oak Leaf Cluster. Mem: Masonic Bodies; Am. Legion; Kiwanis; past pres, PTA, Arlington; secy-treas, Big Bros, Inc; state secy, Alaska Jaycees, 57; Fairbanks United Fund Bd; chmn, Ladd Air Force Base Commun. Fund Drive. Outstanding Young Man of Fairbanks, 57; Distinguished Serv. Award, U.S. Jr. C. of C. Rel: Unitarian. Mailing Add: 819 Crestland, Columbia, Mo. 65201.

PARKER, H. SHELDON, JR. R
Pa. State Rep.
b. Pittsburgh, Pa, 4/14/38; s. H. Sheldon Parker and Elizabeth Matthews P; m. 3/26/69 to Sara Ann Lawler. Educ: Williams Col, B.A, 61; Univ. Pittsburgh, M.A, 65; Pi Sigma Alpha. Polit. & Govt. Pos: Committeeman, 45th Sen. Dist. Rep. Party, Pa, 65-66; chmn, Mt. Lebanon Twp. Rep. Party, 66; Pa. State Rep, 67-; alternate del, Rep. Nat. Conv, 68. Bus. & Prof. Pos: Dir. pub. rels, and investment broker, Kay, Richards & Co, Pittsburgh, currently. Mil. Serv: Pvt, Nat. Guard Res, 62-66. Publ: The State of Allegheny, 65. Mem: Pittsburgh Econ. Club; hon. mem. Dormont-Mt. Lebanon Sportmen's Club. Rel: Presbyterian. Legal Res: 195 Mt. Lebanon Blvd, Apt. 214, Pittsburgh, Pa. 15228. Mailing Add: 155 Union Trust Bldg, Pittsburgh, Pa. 15219.

PARKER, HARVIE ALLEN D
b. Desoto Parish, La, 5/19/10; s. J.C. Parker and Chloe Moseley P; m. 8/5/33 to Juanita Elois Christian; c. Carl Allen, Karen Joy and Harvie Bruce. Educ: Oak Grove High Sch, Logansport, La. Polit. & Govt. Pos: Mayor, Port Arthur, Tex, 61-63; precinct chmn, Jefferson Co. Dem; COPE Del, OCAWIU Local 4-23; del. Nat. Dem. Conv, 64. Bus. & Prof. Pos: Gen. agent, Ky. Cent. Life Ins, 55-; part-owner, Crown House Restaurant, 66; Oil pumper, Gulf Oil Corp, 31-; financial secy-treas, OCAWIU Local 4-23, 52-55; pres, 55-, int. rep, 55-56 and 57. Mem: Evening Lions Club; Eagles Lodge; OCAWIU Local 4-23. Rel: Church of Christ. Mailing Add: 4101 Dryden Rd, Port Arthur, Tex. 77640. (1967)

PARKER, HENRY WALSTEIN D
Ga. State Rep.
b. Woodcliff, Ga, 10/24/10; s. Henry Hollis Parker and Annie Bargeron P; m. 12/30/29 to Mary Walton Pierce; c. Ronald Phillip, Pamela Anita. Educ: Emory at Oxford, 26-27; grad. Ga. Normal Sch, 28. Polit. & Govt. Pos: Ex-Officio Justice of Peace, 80th Militia Dist, Screven Co, Ga; mem, Bd. of Educ, 38-58; Ga. State Rep, 59-, served on Sch. Cmn. created by 1960 Gen. Assembly, v.chmn, House Educ. Cmt, 62- and mem, Appropriations Cmt, Ga. House of Rep, currently; mem, Gov. Cmn. on Educ, 63. Bus. & Prof. Pos: Farmer; sawmill operator. Mil. Serv: ROTC at Emory. Mem: Worshipful Master, Bay Branch Lodge No. 575, F&AM; Scottish Rite; Mason; Shrine; pres. local chap, Farm Bur, 42-52. Hon. Ed.D. conferred by Ga. House of Rep, 67. Rel: Missionary Baptist. Mailing Add: Sylvania, Ga. 30467.

PARKER, JOHN RAINEY, JR. R
Chmn, Sampson Co. Rep. Exec. Cmt, N.C.
b. Little Rock, Ark, 11/12/31; s. John Rainey Parker and Ollie Leigh Marlette P; m. 6/10/60 to Jean Elizabeth Gale; c. John Rainey, III and Sarah Elizabeth. Educ: Univ. N.C, A.B. in chem, 57, Law Sch; Pi Alpha Delta. Polit. & Govt. Pos: Cand, N.C. State Sen, 64; pres, Sampson Co. Young Rep. Club, 65-66; chmn, Sampson Co. Rep. Exec. Cmt, 66-; co. attorney, Sampson Co, currently. Bus. & Prof. Pos: Assoc, Butler & Butler, 57-63; attorney-at-law, 63- Mil. Serv: Entered as Pvt, Army, 53, released as Sgt, 56, after serv. in Korean Commun. Zone; Good Conduct Ribbon. Mem: Am, N.C. and Sampson Co. Bar Asns; N.C. State Bar; past pres, Clinton Jr. C. of C. Rel: Presbyterian. Legal Res: Faison Hwy, Clinton, N.C. 28328. Mailing Add: P.O. Box 27, Clinton, N.C. 28328.

PARKER, L. L. FOX, JR. D
Chmn, Presidio Co. Dem. Party, Tex.
b. Tahoka, Tex, 12/22/17; s. Lilbrun Louis Fox Parker and Beatrice Thomas P; m. 9/20/58 to Maxine Tietschert Newton; c. Elizabeth and step children, Royce V, Tim M, David Ray, Elizabeth L. and Larue E. Educ: Tex. Col. Arts and Indust; Sul Ross State Col. Polit. & Govt. Pos: Rep. precinct chmn, Tex, 61-63; chmn, Presidio Co. Dem. Party, 63-; co-chmn, Cong. Liaison Cmt, 64-65; chmn. liaison cmt, 16th Dist, Dem. Party, 65- Mem: Rotary; C. of C.(pres, Marfa Branch, 61-64). Rel: Baptist. Legal Res: 106 S. Yale, Marfa, Tex. 79843. Mailing Add: P.O. Box 946, Marfa, Tex. 79843. (1967)

PARKER, LEON DOUGLAS R
Chmn, Stanly Co. Rep. Exec. Cmt, N.C.
b. Albemarle, N.C, 10/4/20; s. Raymond Swink Parker and Bessie Mae Arey P; m. 10/17/42 to Sue Louise Trott; c. Sue Trott (Mrs. McIntyre) and Ruty Arey. Educ: Wake Forest Col, 37-38. Polit. & Govt. Pos: Justice of the Peace, Stanly Co, N.C, 62-68; v.chmn, Stanly Co. Rep. Exec. Cmt, 64-68, chmn, 68-; magistrate, N.C. Dist. Court, 68- Bus. & Prof. Pos: Newspaper prod, Stanly News and Press, Albemarle, N.C, 17 years; owner-operator, Carolina Printing Co, 3 years. Mil. Serv: Entered as Pvt, Army, 42, released as Cpt, 45, after serv. in Mil. Police, ETO, 43-45. Mem: Lions; DAV; VFW; Stanly Co. Law Enforcement Officers Asn. Rel: Methodist. Legal Res: South Main St, New London, N.C. 28127. Mailing Add: Drawer 308, New London, N.C. 28127.

PARKER, LETHA MARY R
Secy. Exec. Cmt, Sedgwick Co. Rep. Cent. Cmt, Kans.
b. Clearwater, Kans, 12/30/05; d. Joseph Harvey Kirk and Flora A. Cummins K; m. 7/22/28 to Moses C. Parker; c. Dr. Robert N, D.V.M, Dr. Harold L, M.D. and Dorothy Anne (Mrs. Ronald T. McDonald). Educ: Emporia State Teachers Col. and Friends Univ. Polit. & Govt. Pos: Rep. committeewoman, Ninnescah Twp, Kans, 60; secy. exec. cmt, Sedgwick Co. Rep. Cent. Cmt, 64-; alternate del, Rep. Nat. Conv, 68; dir, Lincoln Rep. Club, 5th Dist; past pres, local Rep. club; Rep. ward chmn, Ninnescah Twp. Bus. & Prof. Pos: Teacher, grade sch, 24-28 & 29-30; prin, Enterprise Sch, Wichita, Kans, 29-30; housewife, 41- Publ: Co-ed, Clearwater Hist. Book, 61. Mem: Eastern Star (Worthy Matron, Ninnescah Chap. and off. in Clearwater Chap, 63-). Mother of the Year, local chap, Bus. & Prfnl. Women's Club. Rel: Baptist. Mailing Add: R.R. Clearwater. Kans. 67026.

PARKER, MARSHALL JOYNER D
b. Seaboard, N.C, 4/25/22; s. Dr. Carl P. Parker and Bertha Joyner P; m. 12/8/43 to Martha Nimmons; c. Anna, Susan and Alice. Educ: Univ. of N.C, B.S, 44; Sigma Nu. Polit. & Govt. Pos: City councilman, Seneca, S.C, 52-54; trustee, Oconee Co. Bd. Sch. Trustees, 53-56; S.C. State Sen, 57-67; mem, S.C. Tax Study Cmt, 59-64; Dem. nominee, U.S. Sen, S.C, 68; del, Dem. Nat Conv, 68. Bus. & Prof. Pos: Businessman and owner, Oconee Dairies. Mil. Serv: Marine Corps, 43-46. Mem: Lions; Am. Legion; VFW. Rel: Methodist; Mem. Bd. Stewards and Trustee, St. Mark Methodist Church, Seneca, 47-56. Mailing Add: Box 945 Seneca, S.C. 29678. (1967)

PARKER, MARY EVELYN D
State Treas, La.
b. Fullerton, La, 11/8/20; d. Racia E. Dickerson and Addie Graham D; m. to W. Bryant Parker (deceased); c. Mary Bryant and Ann Graham. Educ: Northwest. State Col, B.A, 41; La. State Univ, Dipl. Soc. Welfare, 43. Polit. & Govt. Pos: Personnel adminstr, War Dept, 43-47; exec. dir, La. Dept. Commerce and Indust, 48-52; Nat. Dem. Committeewoman, 48-52; chmn, La. Bd. Pub. Welfare, 50-51; cmnr. pub. welfare, La. State Dept. Pub. Welfare, 56-63; cmnr, Div. Admin, La, 64-67; state treas, La, 68-; chmn, State Bond Cmn, 68- Bus. & Prof. Pos: Social worker, La, 41-42; ed. weekly newspaper, Oakdale, La, 47-48; life insurance salesman, Baton Rouge, La, 52-56. Mem: Pres, La. Conf. Social Welfare, 59-61; chmn, White House Conf. on Children and Youth, La. Group, 60; chmn, Women's Div, United Givers Fund Dr, 52; mem. bd. dirs, Woman's Hosp, Baton Rouge, La. Rel: Baptist. Mailing Add: 2768 McCarroll Dr, Baton Rouge, La. 70809.

PARKER, MAURICE R. D
b. Ft. Morgan, Colo, 6/30/17; s.J. Charles Parker, Sr. and Eunice Mengel P; m. 9/17/45 to Florence Lee Barnes; c. Sharon Kay (Mrs. Stewart A. Leach), Rhonda Lou, Sue Lorayne, Kip Alan and Kitti Jean. Educ: Ft. Morgan High Sch, Colo, 32-36. Polit. & Govt. Pos: Dem. chmn, Precinct 25, Colo, 52-69; chmn, Morgan Co. Farmers for Kennedy, 60; chmn, Morgan Co. Farmers, Knous for U.S. Sen, 60; del, Fourth Cong. Dist. Dem. Party, Colo, 60, 62 & 68; del, Dem. State Conv, 60, 62, 66 & 68; mem, Morgan Co. Cmt, Romer for U.S. Sen, 66; mem, Rural Citizens for Hubert H. Humphrey Campaign, 68; campaign field worker, Colo. Fourth Cong. Dist. for Humphrey Campaign, 68; alternate del, Dem. Nat. Conv, 68. Bus. & Prof. Pos: Co. committeeman, Farm Home Admin, 50-52; pres, Morgan Co. Farmers Union, 57-63; dir, Brush Farmland Coop, Inc, 62-64; dir, Colo. Rural Rehab. Corp, 62-; v.pres, Rocky Mt. Farmers Union, 63-; dir, Ft. Morgan Rural Fire Bd, 64-; bd. mem. Morgan Co. Planning Cmn, 68- Mil. Serv: Entered as Pvt, Air Force, 41, released as Cpl, 45, after serv. in 12th Bomb Group, ETO and Middle East. Theatres and China-Burma-India Theatre; Good Conduct Medal; Unit Citation Award in ETO; European and Middle East Campaign Ribbon with 5 Battle Stars; Asiatic and China-Burma-India Campaign Ribbon with 2 Battle Stars. Mem: Farmers Union (pres. Ft. Morgan Local 274, 55-56); Elks; VFW; Am. Legion; Dem. Century Club; Ft. Morgan Toastmasters; past pres, Methodist Men; bd. mem, United Methodist Church, 56-64; Farmers Union Serv. Asn.(dir. and v.pres). Rel: Methodist. Mailing Add: R.R. 1, Ft. Morgan, Colo. 80701.

PARKER, NANCY BAUHAN R
V.Chmn, First Dist. Rep. Party, Wis.
b. Orange, N.J, 11/30/29; d. Alexander Bauhan and Margaret Weedon B; m. 8/11/51 to George Safford Parker, II; c. George Safford, III, Elizabeth Weedon, Martha Eleanor and Patricia Jeffris. Educ: Pembroke Col, Brown Univ, A.B, 51; Univ. Mich, 51-52. Polit. & Govt. Pos: Precinct survey worker, Janesville Rep. Party, Wis, 60, voter registrn. chmn, 62, campaign activities chmn, 64 and v.chmn, 65-67; chmn, Mobilization of Rep. Enterprise, Rock Co. Rep. Party, Wis, 66-69 and co-chmn, Mobilization of Rep. Enterprise, First Cong. Dist. Rep. Party, 67-69; co-chmn, First Cong. Dist. Nixon for Pres. Cmt, 68; mem, Wis. Develop. Authority, 69-; v.chmn, First Cong. Dist. Rep. Party, 69-; mem. exec. cmt, Rep. Party, Wis, 69-; mem, Rock Co. Rep. Party; sustaining mem, Nat. Cmt. Rep. Party; mem, Janesville Fedn. Rep. Women. Mem: Janesville Woman's Club; YWCA; Rock Co. Hist. Soc; Early Janesville Restoration Soc; Mercy Hosp. Auxiliary; Lake Forest Acad. Ill. Mothers Asn; Trinity Episcopal Churchwomen. Rel: Episcopal. Mailing Add: 700 St. Lawrence Ave, Janesville, Wis. 53545.

PARKER, O. ROY D
b. Wayside, W.Va, 3/15/02; s. of L.B. Parker and Martha Nelson P; m. 6/4/32 to Margaret Julia Oxley; c. Delma Jean, Mary Ella, Frederick Lee, Gatha Marie and Teresa Kay. Educ: Concord Col, B.A, 31; Duke Univ; W.Va. Univ, A.M, 40. Polit. & Govt. Pos: W.Va. State Sen, 54-66. Bus. & Prof. Pos: High sch. prin. and farmer. Mem: Mason; Odd Fellows; WVEA; secy, Greenville Ruritan Club; former pres, Union Rotary Club. Rel: Methodist. Mailing Add: Union, W.Va. 24938. (1967)

PARKER, PETER R
b. Baltimore, Md, 3/31/31; s. Walter Giles Parker and Marion Matthews P; m. 5/29/54 to Gail Munson; c. Beth Harrison, Peter, Jr, Todd Matthews and George Everett, III. Educ: Friends Sch, Baltimore, Md, 37-49; Yale Univ, B.A, 53; Harvard Law Sch, LL.B, 59; Zeta Psi; Lincoln's Inn; Holmes Club. Polit. & Govt. Pos: Mem, Rep. State Cent. Cmt, Md, 62-68, chmn, Third and First Legis. Districts and mem. Exec. Cmt, 66-68; mem, Mayor's Cmt. on Housing Law Enforcement, 63-69; pres, Bd. of Supervisors of Elec, Baltimore, 67-69; del, Rep. Nat. Conv, 68; peoples counsel, State of Md, 68- Bus. & Prof. Pos: dir, Algonquin Corp, Glazed Products, Inc, Regent Bldg. Co, Financial Acceptance Corp. and Lydian Corp; assoc, Semmes, Bowen & Semmes, Baltimore, 60-66; partner, White Page & Lentz, 67- Mil. Serv: Entered as Ens, Navy, 53, released as Lt.(sg), 57, after serv. in Korean War, 53-56, Lt. Cmdr, Res; Letter of Commendation. Mem: Maritime Law Asn; Am, Md. State and Baltimore City Bar Asns; Md. Club; Merchants Club; L'hirondelle Club. Rel: Presbyterian. Mailing Add: Three Chancery Sq, Baltimore, Md. 21218.

PARKER, ROBERT ELLIOTT, JR. D
Chmn, Nansemond Co. Dem. Exec. Cmt, Va.
b. Suffolk, Va, 12/8/27; s. Robert Elliott Parker, Sr. and Jamie Duke P; m. 12/29/51 to Jessie Penny Wilkins; c. Penny Lee and Patricia Lynn. Educ: Col. of William and Mary, A.B. in Bus Admin, 51. Polit. & Govt. Pos: Chmn, Nansemond Co. Dem. Exec. Cmt, Va, 63- Bus. & Prof. Pos: Owner, Parker & Co, Suffolk, Va, 56-, pres, 66; mem. bd. dirs, Williamsburg Life Ins. Co, Baltimore, Md, 64-, regional v.pres, 66. Mil. Serv: Entered as Pvt, Army, 46, released as Sgt, 47; re-entered as 2nd Lt, released as 1st Lt, 53, after serv. in Korea; Air Medal with 2 Oak Leaf Clusters; Commendation Medal. Mem: Suffolk Asn. of Ins. Agents; Lions; Liberty Spring Ruritan Club. Rel: Christian Church. Mailing Add: 120 Benton Rd, Suffolk, Va. 23434.

PARKER, ROBERT L. R
Committeeman, Tex. Rep. State Exec. Cmt.
b. Roby, Tex, 12/12/23; s. Tom H. Parker and Thelma McCombs; m. 10/31/43 to Dorothy G. Stevenson; c. Lynnda Diane, Robert Evans and Julie Anne. Educ: Tex. A&M Univ, Agr, 40-46. Polit. & Govt. Pos: Finance chmn, Lamar Co. Rep. Party, 66-69; alternate del, Rep. Nat. Conv, 68; del, Rep. State Conv, 68; committeeman, Tex. Rep. State Exec. Cmt, 69- Bus. & Prof. Pos: Instr. agr, Rotan and Seymour Vocational Sch, Tex, 47-50; terracing contractor, 47-50; rancher and farmer, Paris, 50-54; exec. v.pres, Tex. Sesame Growers, Inc, 54-66; pres, Paris Milling Co, 66- Mil. Serv: Entered as Pvt, Army, 43, released as 1st Lt, 46, after serv. in 380th Field Artil. Bn, 102nd Inf. Div, ETO, 44-45; Army Res; Bronze Star Medal; Europe-Africa-Middle East Campaign Medal with two Bronze Stars; Am. Theatre Campaign Medal; World War II Victory Medal. Mem: Tex. Seedsman Asn. (bd. dir); South. Seedsman Asn; Tex. Grain and Feed Asn; Nat. Grain and Feed Dealers; Am. Feed and Am. Seed Trade Asns; Rotary; VFW; Am. Legion; Farm Bur; Farmers Union; pres, Lamar Co. C. of C. Rel: Methodist. Mailing Add: 3640 Clarksville St, Paris, Tex. 75460.

PARKER, WALT E. D
Tex. State Rep.
b. Ft. Worth, Tex, 7/23/17; s. Lemuel Hicks Parker and Ethel Nancy Bradley P; m. 1/20/41 to Mildred Brock; c. Walter E, Jr. Educ: N.Tex. State Univ, B.S, 40; Tex. Christian Univ, M.A, 47; Lambda Chi Alpha. Polit. & Govt. Pos: Chmn, Denton Park Bd, Tex, 58-63; mem, Denton Sch. Bd, 67-68; Tex. State Rep, 69- Bus. & Prof. Pos: Off, Am. Football League, currently. Mil. Serv: Entered as Pvt, Air Force, 42, released as Capt, 46, after serv. in 505th Heavy Bomb Group, S.Pac. Theatre, 43-46; Capt, Air Force Res, Korea, 51-53. Mem: Southwest Football Off. Asn; Mason; Shrine; Scottish Rite; Rotary. Rel: Methodist. Legal Res: Woodland Hills Dr, Route 2, Denton, Tex. 76201. Mailing Add: Box 1279, Denton, Tex. 76201.

PARKERSON, WILLIAM FRANCIS, JR. D
Va. State Sen.
b. Rocky Mt, N.C, 6/16/20; m. to Nancy Ellen Davis. Educ: Univ. of Richmond, B.A, 41; Wash. and Lee Univ, LL.B, 47; Kappa Alpha; Phi Alpha Delta. Polit. & Govt. Pos: Commonwealth attorney, Henrico Co, Va, 57-61; Va. State Del, 62-63; Va. State Sen, 64- Bus. & Prof. Pos: Lawyer. Mil. Serv: Lt. Col, Judge Adv. Gen. Corps, Army Res. Mem: Sons of the Revolution in the State of Va; Am. Legion. Rel: Episcopal. Mailing Add: 508 W. Dr. Circle, Richmond, Va. 23229. (1967)

PARKHURST, JOHN C. R
b. Springfield, Ill, 7/14/20; s. Laird C. Parkhurst and Pauline Wlley P; m. 1/5/46 to Harriet Vance; c. Vance C, Christina L, Peter L, John W, Nancy A. and Robert C. Educ: Wabash Col, B.A, 42; Univ. Mich. Law Sch, LL.B, 48; Pi Kappa Alpha; Phi Gamma Delta. Polit. & Govt. Pos: Mem, Peoria Co. Bd. Supvr, Ill, 49-58, chmn, 57-58; Ill. State Rep, 59-69, former Minority Whip, Ill. House of Rep. Mil. Serv: Entered as Pvt, Air Force, 42, released as Sgt, 45, after serv. in 40th Mobile Commun. Squadron, ETO; Bronze Star; ETO Campaign Ribbons. Mem: Peoria Co. and Ill. State Bar Asns. Rel: Presbyterian. Mailing Add: 1607 W. Margaret St, Peoria, Ill. 61604. (1967)

PARKIN, JOHN WILBUR R
Wis. State Assemblyman
b. Rochester, Minn, 4/10/18; s. Wilbur L. Parkin and Verta Cowles P; m. 9/21/38 to Clyle Mundahl; c. Susan (Mrs. B.K. Te Strake) and Todd. Educ: Univ. Minn, 2 years; Phi Kappa Sigma. Polit. & Govt. Pos: Mem, Wood Co. Bd. Supvr, Wis, 62-, chmn, 68-; Wis. State Assemblyman, 69- Bus. & Prof. Pos: Pres, Parkin Dairy, Marshfield, Wis, 42; P.I.C. Co, Inc, 49; Wis. Independent Dairys, Madison, 58. Mem: V.pres, Nat. Independent Dairies Asn, 56; pres, Marshfield Rotary and C. of C; Elks; Boy Scouts; United Fund. Silver Beaver; Hon. Future Farmer; Hon. Girl Scout. Rel: Presbyterian. Mailing Add: 907 S. Oak Ave, Marshfield, Wis. 54449.

PARKINSON, DR. GAYLORD BENTON, JR. R
Chmn, Nat. Rep. State Chmn. Adv. Cmt.
b. Chicago, Ill, 11/18/18; s. Gaylord Benton Parkinson and Helen Simpson P; m. 6/27/42 to Harriet Weber; c. Peter Riley, Christopher Jon and Gaylord B, III. Educ: San Diego State Col, 36-40; Temple Med. Sch, 40-43; Sigma Chi. Polit. & Govt. Pos: Chmn. exec. cmt, Rep. Assocs, San Diego, Calif, 61-63, mem. bd. of trustees, 63-66; v.chmn, Calif. Rep. State Cent. Cmt, 62-64, chmn, 64-67; chmn, West Conf. Rep. State Chmn, 65-67 and Nat. Rep. State Chmn, Adv. Cmt, 65- Bus. & Prof. Pos: Physician and surgeon, Obstetrics and Gynecology, 46- Mil. Serv: Entered as Lt.(jg), Navy, 43, released as Lt, 46, after serv. as Asst. Surgeon, Med. Corps, Pac. Area, 45-46. Mem: San Diego Med. Soc; San Diego Obstetrics & Gynecology Soc; Calif. Med. Asn; Am. Med. Asn; Rotary, C. of C; Childrens Home Soc; Commun. Chest. Rel: Presbyterian. Legal Res: 10260 Fuerte Dr, La Mesa, Calif. 92041. Mailing Add: 350 S. Magnolia, El Cajon, Calif. 92020.

PARKINSON, HARVEY VINCENT R
Mem, Calif. Rep. State Cent. Cmt.
b. Long Beach, Calif, 2/24/25; s. William N. Parkinson and Ruth R. P; m. 3/17/50 to Alice Fraser; c. Garrett F, Bradford F. and Tracy F. Educ: Univ. Calif, Los Angeles, B.A, 50; Delta Sigma Phi. Polit. & Govt. Pos: Mem, Calif. Rep. State Cent. Cmt, currently; alternate mem, 64th Assembly Dist. Rep. Cent. Cmt, currently. Bus. & Prof. Pos: Pres, House-Parkinson Ins. Inc, Canoga Park, Calif, 56-69; v.pres, Johnson, Parkinson & Dodge, Inc, Woodland Hills, 69- Mil. Serv: Entered as Pvt, Army, 43, released as S/Sgt, 46, after serv. in West. Pac. Base Command, 44-46; Asiatic Pac. Campaign, Am. Campaign, Good Conduct and World War II Victory Medals; Meritorious Unit Award. Mem: Independent Ins. Agents Asn. of San Fernando Valley (past pres); Calif. and Nat. Asns. Ins. Agents; Canoga Park C. of C.(past pres); past pres, Assoc. C. of C. of San Fernando Valley; life mem, Canoga Park Jaycees (past pres); Canoga Park Kiwanis (past pres); past chmn, West Valley Rep. Boosters Club; Am. Legion; VFW; Elks. Received resolutions from Calif. State Assembly, Los Angeles City Coun, Los Angeles Co. Bd. Supvr, Mayor City of Los Angeles and Calif. State Senate; Commun. Serv. Awards, Canoga Park C. of C. Rel: Christian Science. Legal Res: 5821 Rolling Rd, Woodland Hills, Calif. 91364. Mailing Add: P.O. Box 813, Woodland Hills, Calif. 91364.

PARKS, CLIFTON Conservative
Minn. State Sen.
Married. Polit. & Govt. Pos: Minn. State Rep, 52-60; Minn. State Sen, 62- Bus. & Prof. Pos: Attorney. Mailing Add: 805 Degree of Honor Bldg, St. Paul, Minn. 55101. (1967)

PARLANTE, ALFONSO D
b. Italy, 9/22/97; s. Lazzaro Parlante and Anna Nigro P; married; c. 2; 3 grandchildren. Educ: Night Sch, W.Va. Polit. & Govt. Pos: Pa. State Rep, 52, 58-67; former state inheritance tax appraiser; pres. First Ward Civic Asn; Dem. ward leader since 52; John B. Stetson Co, 47-53; Die setter U.S. Mint, 43-47; Gen. foreman U.S. Fed. Housing Cmn. until 43; coal miner. Mem: AFL CIO. Mailing Add: 1506 E. Moyamensing Ave, Philadelphia, Pa. 19147. (1967)

PARMELEE, ALICE EMMONS R
V.Chmn, East Hartland Rep. Town Cmt, Conn.
b. East Hartland, Conn, 8/12/03; d. Edward Ellsworth Emmons and Marie Miller E; m. 12/27/24 to Gladwin E. Parmelee; c. Elliot L. and Hubert E. Educ: High Sch, Simsbury, Conn. Polit. & Govt. Pos: Conn. State Rep, 43-45 & 53-55; chmn, East Hartland Rep. Town Cmt, 55-68, v.chmn, 68-; Town tax collector, 56- Rel: Congregational. Mailing Add: Hartland Rd, East Hartland, Conn. 06027.

PARNAGIAN, ARAM R
N.H. State Rep.
b. Lawrence, Mass, 4/18/05; s. Ardash Parnagian and Mariam Ementian P; m. 4/19/34 to Siran Siranoosh Sarkisian; c. Evlyn Miriam (Mrs. Mamigonian) and Elaine Margaret (Mrs. Hashem). Educ: Mass. Radio Inst, 2 years; Lowell Inst, 2 years; Franklin Inst, 2 years. Polit. & Govt. Pos: Rep. chmn, Ward Four, Dover, N.H, 66-67; N.H. State Rep, Dist. 19, 67- Bus. & Prof. Pos: Real estate broker, N.H; asst. to mgr, Chelsea Radio, Chelsea, Mass, 24-28; mgr. radio dept, Morgan Furniture, Boston, 28-30; pres, Am. Radio Corp, N.H, 34-65. Mem: U.S. Power Squadrons (squadron comdr, dist. legis. officer); Mason; Scottish Rite; Shrine; Eastern Star; N.H. State Rep. Party. Rel: Episcopal. Mailing Add: 6 Renaud Ave, Dover, N.H. 03820.

PARNELL, DALE PAUL R
Supt. Pub. Instr, Ore.
b. Monmouth, Ore, 7/16/28; s. Archie S. Parnell; mother deceased; m. 5/24/47 to Beverly Lush; c. Sue, Paul, Teresa, Steve and Tim. Educ: Willamette Univ, B.A, 51; Univ. Ore, M.A, 56, D.Ed, 64; Phi Delta Kappa. Polit. & Govt. Pos: Precinct committeeman, Lane Co, Rep. Party, Ore, 60-64; supt. pub. instr, Ore, 68- Bus. & Prof. Pos: Teacher, Salem and Springfield, Ore, 50-54; v.pres. and prin, Springfield Sr. High Sch, 54-60; supt, Lane Co. Schs, Eugene, 60-65; pres, Lane Commun. Col, Eugene, 65-68; vis. prof, Univ. Ore, Eugene and Ore. State Univ, Corvallis, summer 64-68; consult, Am. Jr. Col. Asn. on Develop. Commun. Cols. Mem: Ore. Commun. Col. Asn; Ore. Commun. Col. Pres. Coun; Am. and Ore. Asn. Sch. Adminstrs; State Educ. Coord. Coun; State Manpower Adv. Cmt; State and Co. PTA Orgn; Cmnr. Educ. Cmn. of the States; State Manpower Coord. Cmt; Lions; Co. Youth Study Bd, YMCA; res. bd, Eugene-Springfield Metrop. Civic Club; C. of C. Indust. Cmt; past co. dir, United Appeal; Bd. mem, Lane Co. Ment. Health Asn; chmn, Young Life Cmt. Springfield Man of the Year Award, 66; State Golden Torch Award, Bus. & Prfnl. Women; Man of the Year Award, Ore. Admin. Mgt. Soc, 66. Rel: Nazarene. Legal Res: 2115 Jewel N.W, Salem, Ore. 97304. Mailing Add: Oregon Board of Education, 318 Public Service Bldg, Salem, Ore. 97310.

PARRAN, JOHN THOMAS, JR. D
b. Baltimore, Md, 2/5/26; s. John Thomas Parran and Sarah Virginia Elliott P; m. to Christel H. Educ: Charlotte Hall Acad; The Citadel; Univ. of Md, B.A, 50. Polit. & Govt. Pos: Former pres, Young Dem. of Charles Co, Md; Md. State Del, 55-59; Md. State Sen, 59-67; chmn, Tri Co. Coun. for South. Md, currently. Bus. & Prof. Pos: Real estate and ins. broker, The Parran Agency, Indian Head, Md, currently. Mil. Serv: Army, 44-46. Mem: Former dir, Charles Co. C. of C; former v.pres, Charles Co. Jr. C. of C; regional dir, Boy Scouts; Indian Head Bus. Asn; Lions; Moose; Am. Legion. Rel: Episcopal. Mailing Add: Parran Lane, Indian Head, Md. 20640.

PARRIS, GEORGE NICK D
Mem. Exec. Bd, Macomb Co. Dem. Cmt, Mich.
b. Norfolk, Va, 5/14/21; s. Nick George Parris and Katherine Cummings P; m. 2/7/48 to Phyllis Jane Bunker; c. Kathi, Nikki, Lorri, Sherri, Janni, Nickolas and George N, II. Educ: Pontiac Bus. Inst, 40-42; Univ. Mich, A.B. in Econ, 48; Wayne State Univ, LL.B. cum laude, 51; Gold Key; Sigma Nu Phi; Delta Epsilon Pi. Polit. & Govt. Pos: Asst. prosecuting attorney, Macomb Co, Mich, 52, prosecuting attorney, 61-; v.chmn, Macomb Co. Dem. Cmt, 54-56, mem. exec. bd, 60-; del, Co. and State Dem. Conv, 54-; pub. adminstr, Macomb Co, 55-57; pres, United Dem. of Warren, 55-59; del, Dem. Nat. Conv, 64. Bus. & Prof. Pos: Instr, Wayne State Univ. Law Sch, 50-51; dir. priorities, ceiling prices and CMP, Udylite Corp, 51; mem. bd. dirs, Warren Bank, 56-60 & 66-67; mem. bd. dirs, Abbey Mem. Hosp, 66. Mil. Serv: Entered as Aviation Cadet, Army Air Force, 42, released as 1st Lt, 45, after serv. in 446th Bomb Group, 707th Squadron, ETO, 44; Distinguished Flying Cross; ETO Ribbon with Four Battle Stars; Air Medal with Three Clusters. Publ: 'The Incorporation of a City,' Macomb Dem, 9/56; 'The Prosecuting Attorney,' Farm and Home News, 1/63; 'Reapportionment of County Boards of Supervisors,' Mich. Courthouse Rev, 10/65. Mem: Bd. dirs, Mich. Prosecuting Attorneys Asn, 61-67, v.pres, 65-66 and pres, 66-67; v.pres, Mich. United Co. Officers Asn, 64-67; Am, Mich. and Macomb Bar Asns; Nat. Dist. Attorneys Asn; Cmt. to Revise the Criminal Code; Criminal Jurisp. Cmt; Crime Prev. Center Cmt; F&AM; Shrine; Odd Fellows; Eagles; VFW; Amvets; Am. Legion; Goodfellows; South. Mich. Asn. of Chiefs of Police; United Dem. of Warren; Macomb Co. Big Brothers; Lions. Outstanding Young Man of Year, Warren Jaycees, 53-54; Father of Year, Macomb Co, 56. Rel: Greek Orthodox. Legal Res: 27520 Santa Ana, Warren, Mich. 48093. Mailing Add: Prosecuting Attorney, Macomb County Bldg, Mount Clemens, Mich. 48043. (1967)

PARRISH, EVERETT L. D
Exec. Dir, W.Va. State Aeronaut. Cmn.
b. 11/9/20; s. Edward Parrish and Mildred P; m. to Ella Mae Fugate; c. Patricia, Wallace and Helen. Educ: Air Mech. Tech. Sch, Chanute Field, Ill; Cadet Col. Training Detachment, Univ. Tenn; Lodwick Aviation Mil. Acad, Avon Park, Fla; Grad. Fighter Pilot, Class 44-K, Adv. Flying Sch, Napier Field, Cothan, Ala; MATS Aircraft Comdr. Sch, Palm Beach, Fla; South. Airways Helicopter Sch, Mineral Wells, Tex; Aircraft Crash Investr. Sch, Phoenix, Ariz. Polit. & Govt. Pos: State Probation and Parole Officer, 48-51 & 52-53; admin. asst, Air Nat. Guard, Kanawha Airport, Charleston, W.Va, 54-58; Army Aviation Supvr, Wood Co. Airport, Parkersburg, W.Va, 58-62; exec. dir, W.Va. State Aeronaut. Cmn, 62- Mil. Serv: Entered Mil. Serv. Dec. 40; World War II, five years, overseas, 42-43; Korea, 51-52; Eight years active serv, U.S. Army and USAF; Rated Sr. Pilot in U.S. Army and USAF; Attained rank of Maj, 61; Completed 25 years mil. serv. Dec. 1965; Assigned Aviation Staff Officer, U.S. Army Nat. Guard, State Hd. and Hd. Detachment. Mailing Add: State Capitol, Charleston, W.Va. 25305. (1967)

PARRISH, ROBERT AMBROSE R
Chmn, Barton Co. Rep. Party, Kans.
b. Oklahoma City, Okla, 3/3/27; s. George E. Parrish and Leta Faye Dodson P; m. 9/1/49 to Mary Belle Pollock; c. Cheryl C, Cynthia D. and Robert A, Jr. Educ: Univ. Kansas, Lawrence, B.S, 50; Scabbard & Blade; Pershing Rifles; Sigma Nu; Alpha Kappa Psi. Polit. & Govt. Pos: Committeeman, Rep. City Cmt, Great Bend, 61; pres, Great Bend City Coun, 63; committeeman, Barton Co. Rep. Cent. Cmt, 66, chmn, 68; chmn, Barton Co. Rep. Party, 68-; mayor, Great Bend, 69- Bus. & Prof. Pos: Automobile dealer, Parrish Motor Co, Great Bend, Kans, 50- Mil. Serv: Entered as Pvt, Army Air Force, 45, released as Cpl, 46, after serv. in Air Training Command, U.S, Capt, Res, 46-54. Mem: American Legion, Mason; Elks; Rotary. Rel: Protestant. Mailing Add: 1911 McKinney Dr, Great Bend, Kans. 67530.

PARRISH, W. F, JR. R
Committeeman, Okla. Rep. Party
b. Ada, Okla, 9/8/39; s. William Fletcher Parrish and Helen Emeline Dawson P; m. 8/12/61 to Elizabeth Ann Tennis; c. Laurie Ann and Cynthia Lynn. Educ: Univ. Okla, 57-58; E.Cent. State Col, B.A, 61; Univ. Okla. Col. of Law, LL.B, 63; Phi Delta Phi. Polit. & Govt. Pos: Del, Rep. Nat. Conv, 68; committeeman, Okla. Rep. Party, 69- Bus. & Prof. Pos: Partner, Nicklas, Parrish & Saenz, Attorneys, 63- Publ: Numerous articles, Okla. Law Rev, 61-64. Mem: Comanche Co. and Okla. Bar Asns; Am. Judicature Soc. Commended by joint resolution of Okla. Legis. and by Okla. Bar Asn. for serv. to Judiciary Cmt. in preparing and implementing statutes for judicial reform, 68. Rel: Presbyterian; Elder, Presby. Church, Lawton, Okla. Legal Res: 1329 Cherry, Lawton, Okla. 73501. Mailing Add: 516 D Ave, Lawton, Okla. 73501.

PARRY, DAVID THOMAS D
b. Seattle, Wash, 4/22/33; m. 6/25/60 to Susan Kathryn Meyers. Educ: Pac. Univ, B.A, 55; Am. Univ, M.A, 61. Polit. & Govt. Pos: Research asst. to U.S. Sen. Hartke, Ind, 62; admin. asst. to U.S. Rep. Long, Md, 65-68. Bus. & Prof. Pos: Asst. prof. polit. sci, Pac. Univ, 62-64. Mil. Serv: Cpl, Army, 56-57. Mem: Am. Polit. Sci. Asn; West. Polit. Sci. Asn; Cong. Secy. Club; Burro Club; Wm. A. Wheeler Asn. for Politically Obscure. Mailing Add: 3210 17th N.W, Washington, D.C. 20010. (1967)

PARRY, JOHN WALDO D
b. Vernal, Utah, 4/7/96; s. John M. Parry and Emma Lenore Jacob P; m. 8/8/65 to Annie Marie Noble Bishop. Educ: Utah State Univ, 16-20; Sorbonne Univ, Paris, 19; Debating Soc. Polit. & Govt. Pos: Chief clerk, Utah State House of Rep, 37, 41-47 & 59; state personnel dir, Utah, 41-48; Utah State Rep, 65-67. Bus. & Prof. Pos: Asst. mgr, Elsinore Flour Mills, 20-25; licensed securities dealer, Utah and Nat. Asn. Securities Dealers. Mil. Serv: Entered as Pvt, Army, 17, released as Cpl, 19, after serv. in 91st Div, Inf, Meuse-Argonne, St. Miheil and Defensive Sector Medals. Mem: World War I Vets, Barracks 1479; Sons of Utah Pioneers. Basketball and Tennis Teams. Rel: Latter-day Saint. Mailing Add: 178 N. Main, Salt Lake City, Utah 84103.

PARSEKIAN, NED J. D
Pres, Ridgewood Dem. Club
b. Springfield, Mass, 8/29/21; s. Martin Parsekian and Lucy Solakian P; m. 12/23/50 to Corinne Anton; c. Donna Lynn, Nancy, Sandra and Thomas. Educ: N.Y. Univ, 41-42; Columbia Univ. Sch. of Gen. Studies, 46-47; Columbia Univ. Sch. of Law, LL.B, 50. Polit. & Govt. Pos: Dept. attorney gen, N.J, 55; dir, Div. of Workmen's Compensation, 55-59 and Div. of Motor Vehicles, 59-64; N.J. State Sen, Bergen Co, 65-67; del, Dem. Nat. Conv, 68; Dem. Cand. for Gov, 69; pres, Ridgewood Dem. Club, 69- Bus. & Prof. Pos: Attorney and Counsel-at-Law. Mil. Serv: Entered as Aviation Cadet, Army Air Force, 43, released as 1st Lt, 46, after serv. in 319th Bomb Group, Pac. Theatre, 45-46. Mem: Fed. Bar Asn, N.Y; Int. Asn. of Indust. Accident Bds. and Cmns; Am. Asn. of Motor Vehicle Adminstrs; Bergen Co. and N.J. State Bar Asns; mem. of the Bar of N.J, N.Y. and Wash, D.C; Columbia Law Sch. Alumni Asn; Am. Judicature Soc. Named as Legislator of the Year, Freeholders Asn. of N.J, 66; Carl Holderman Award, Americans for Dem. Action, 66. Rel: Protestant. Mailing Add: 276 Orchard Place, Ridgewood, N.J. 07450.

PARSHALLE, EVE R
Press Chmn, Fedn. Rep. Women, Calif.
b. N.Y.C, Dec. 24; wid; c. Jere. Educ: Privately educated in N.Y, Eng. maj. Polit. & Govt. Pos: Pres, Wilshire Rep. Women's Club, Federated, Calif, 4 terms; exec. secy, Hollywood Rep. Cmt, 4 years; press chmn, Calif. Fedn. Rep. Women, 67- Bus. & Prof. Pos: Owner and publisher, Rep. Women's Newspaper; owner and publisher, Dog Mag. Publ: Dogs of the World, 35; Our Lord's Miracles, selected and prepared in Braille; Kashmir Bridge Women; Women In Politics; plus others. Mem: Gr. Los Angeles Press Club; Nat. Fedn. Rep. Women; Am. Soc. Composers, Authors and Publishers. Author of four books selected and prepared in Braille by the Libr. Cong. Rel: Christian Science. Mailing Add: 5930 Franklin Ave, Hollywood, Calif. 90028.

PARSLEY, FRANCES ELAINE R
V.Chmn, Ky. Rep. State Cent. Cmt.
b. Brownsville, Ky, 2/28/24; d. Frederick Hilery Vincent and Mattie Meredilh V; m. 5/27/43 to Andrew Gus Parsley, Sr; c. Nancy Sue and Andrew Gus, Jr. Educ: West. Ky. Univ, 2 years. Polit. & Govt. Pos: Crew leader, Ky. State Dept. Commerce, 42-46; Rep. precinct leader, Edmonson Co, 42-69; chmn, Edmonson Co. Rep. Party, 46-68; chmn, Second Dist. Rep. Party, 46-69; state chmn, Pyramaiding for 62, 62; co.chmn, Friend for Morton, 62; state chmn, Wunn for Gov, 63; state chmn, Goldwater for Pres, 64; mem. state bd. Ky. Rep. Clubs, 68; v.chmn, Ky. Rep. State Cent. Cmt, 68- Bus. & Prof. Pos: Elem. Teacher, Edmonson Co, 42-46. Mem: Eastern Star; Brownsville Home maker Club; Warren Co. Rep. Club; Univ. High PTA. Church Attendance Awards; Citation for Record Attendance of Ky. Rep. State Cent. Cmt. Rel: Baptist. Legal Res: Brownsville, Ky. 42210. Mailing Add: Box 304, Brownsville, Ky. 42210.

PARSLEY, MERLE DAVID D
b. Ambrose, N.Dak, 4/8/36; s. Glen Thomas Parsley (deceased) and Margaret Stepp P; m. 6/3/61 to Judith Katherine Kelly; c. Glenn Peter, Kelly Marie and Michael Timothy. Educ: Minot State Teachers Col, B.S, 61; Phi Sigma Pi; Col. Toastmasters. Polit. Pos: Idaho State Rep, Bonner Co, 65-67; nat. committeeman, Young Dem. Clubs of N.Dak, 61, pres, 60 and v.pres, 59. Prof. Pos: Teacher, Sandpoint, Idaho, 61-66. Mil. Serv: Entered as Airman Basic, Air Force, 53, released as Airman 1/C, 57, after serv. in Air Task Force 12, Formosa and Far East; Good Conduct Medal; Nat. Defense Ribbon; Airman Wings, radio operator. Rel: Roman Catholic. Mailing Add: Cocolalla, Idaho 83813. (1967)

PARSON, ELMER S, JR. R
Secy, Wyo. Rep. State Cmt.
b. Denver, Colo, 12/26/29; s. Elmer S. Parson and Ruth I Buchanan P; m. 12/27/53 to Mary Jean Reimer; c. Dean R. and Anne I. Educ: Univ. of Colo, B.A, 57. Polit. & Govt. Pos: Treas, Natrona Co. Young Rep, Wyo, 61-62; ward capt, Natrona Co. Rep. Cent. Cmt, 62-67 and chmn, 67-; state committeeman, Wyo. Rep. Party, 66-67; secy, Wyo. Rep. State Cmt, 68- Bus. & Prof. Pos: Explor. geologist, Continental Oil Co, Casper, Wyo, 57-69 and True Oil Co, 69. Mil. Serv: 2nd Lt, Army, 52-53, with serv. in 459 Egn. Bn, Korea. Mem: Am. Asn. Petroleum Geologists; Wyo. Geol. Asn; Rocky Mt. Oil & Gas Asn; C. of C; Wyo. Oil Industs. Cmt. Rel: Methodist. Mailing Add: 3120 E. Fifth, Casper, Wyo. 82601.

PARSONS, ALBERT ROY R
Secy, Piatt Co. Rep. Cmt, Ill.
b. Forrest, Ill, 11/18/00; s. Albert Parsons and Flora Christoff P; m. 3/21/23 to Mabel Esther Mott; c. Mary Carolyn (Mrs. Chapman). Educ: LaSalle Extension Univ, 2 year course salesmanship & Bus. Mgt. Polit. & Govt. Pos: Mem. sch. bd, Monticello, Ill, 36-40; city clerk, Monticello, 37-69; Rep. precinct committeeman, Piatt Co, 50-; secy, Piatt Co. Rep. Cmt, 50-; twp. supvr, Piatt Co. Bd. of Supvr, 67- Bus. & Prof. Pos: Steam locomotive fireman, Chicago Div, Wabash R.R, 20-23; ticket agent and cashier, Union Station, Chicago, Ill, 23-29; agent, Railway Express, Forrest and Monticello, 30-52; cashier, First State Bank, 53-67. Mem: AF&AM; Consistory; Mason; Farm Bur; Rotary. Rel: Methodist. Mailing Add: 504 E. Lafayette St, Monticello, Ill. 61856.

PARSONS, HAROLD PAUL D
Chmn, Harlan Co. Dem. Cmt, Ky.
b. Barbourville, Ky, 10/22/37; s. Curtis Sam Parsons and Estle Grant P; m. 6/13/56 to Barbara Ann Ballard; c. Gregory and Bridgette. Educ: Union Col, A.B, 58; Univ. Ky, Lexington, 61-65. Polit. & Govt. Pos: Councilman, Evarts, Ky, 62-65; adv. mgr, Harlan Co. Referendum, 64-; alternate del, Dem. Nat. Conv, 68; co-chmn, Harlan Co. Dem. Fund Raising Cmt, 69; chmn, Harlan Co. Dem. Cmt, 69- Bus. & Prof. Pos: Teacher, Harlan Co. Bd. of Educ, 58-; v.pres, Mack's Super Mkts. Inc, 63-; pres, East. Broadcasting, 66- Mem: Harlan Co. C. of C; F&AM; Evarts Lions Club (pres); Evarts Fish and Game Club. Rel: United Church of Christ. Mailing Add: Box 181 A, Evarts, Ky. 40828.

PARSONS, J. GRAHAM
b. N.Y.C, 10/28/07; m. to Margaret Boulton; c. two daughters. Educ: Yale Univ, B.A, 29; N.Y. Univ. Grad. Sch. Bus. Admin; Phi Beta Kappa. Polit. & Govt. Pos: Career officer, U.S. Dept. of State For. Serv, 36-; vice counsul, Havana, Cuba, 36-38 and Mukden, 38-40; third secy, Ottawa, 40-42; asst.

chief, Div. of Brit. Commonwealth Affairs, 45; secy, U.S. Sect, Permanent Joint Bd. on Defense of Can. and the U.S, 46-47; second secy, Rome, 47-48; first secy, New Delhi, 48-50; mem. staff, Nat. War Col, 50-51; dep. dir. and acting dir, Off. of European Regional Affairs, 51-53; counsel, Tokyo, 53-56; U.S. Ambassador, Laos, 56-58; Dep. Asst. Secy. of State for Far East. Affairs, 58-59; Asst. Secy. of State for Far East. Affairs, 59-61; U.S. Ambassador, Sweden, 61-67; sr. for serv. inspector, 67-69; State Dept. Adv, Indust. Col. of the Armed Forces, 69- Bus. & Prof. Pos: Security analyst, 31-32; private secy, U.S. Ambassador, Japan, 32-36. Legal Res: New York, N.Y. Mailing Add: c/o U.S. Dept. of State, Washington, D.C. 20521.

PARSONS, JAMES CECIL R
b. Brooklyn, N.Y, 6/17/25; s. George Parsons and Edith Yates P; single. Educ: Pac. Union Col, B.A, 48; Columbia Univ. Teachers Col, M.A, 49, prfnl. diploma, 57; Phi Delta Kappa; Kappa Delta Pi. Polit. Pos: Precinct committeeman, Dist. Rep. Orgn, 60-66; chmn, Health Welfare and Educ. Cmt, 63-64; Alaska State Rep, 60-64; del, Nat. Rep. Conv, 64, Alaska State Rep. Conv, 62-64 and Dist. Rep. Conv, 60, 62 and 64. Govt. Pos: Chmn, Anchorage City Park and Recreation Bd, 64-, mem, 59-; mem. and clerk, Anchorage Independent Sch. Dist. Bd. of Educ, 54-56. Prof. Pos: Prof, Psychol, Alaska Methodist Univ, 60-; private practice, Psychol, 59-; clinical psychologist, Alaska Div. of Ment. Health, 53-60 and Harding Hosp, Worthington, Ohio, 51-53; res. counselor, Univ. Minn, 50; counselor, teacher, Ozark Acad, Gentry, Ark, 49-50. Mil. Serv: Entered as Pvt, Army Med. Corps, 44, released as S/Sgt, 46, after serv. in Southwest. Pac, 45-46; Good Conduct Medal; Philippine Military Merit Award, Govt. of Philippines. Mem: Am. Psychological Asn; Am. Personnel and Guidance Asn; Nat. Educ. Asn; Coun. on Exception Children; Acad. of Religion & Ment. Health; Kiwanis. Rel: Seventh-day Adventist. Mailing Add: Alaska Methodist Univ, Anchorage, Alaska 99504. (1967)

PARSONS, JEWEL ETTA D
Co. Cmnr, Nye Co, Nev.
b. Joplin, Mo, 4/21/07; d. William George Conner and Estella V. Hoover C; m. 4/3/54 to Elton Parsons; c. Yvonne Alice (Mrs. Lawton) and Carl Vernon Haas, Jr. Polit. & Govt. Pos: Mem. exec. bd, Nev. Fish & Game Cmn, 52-60; chmn, Esmeralda Co. Cmn, 60-63; Nev. State Assemblyman, 65-66; co. cmnr, Nye Co, 69- Bus. & Prof. Pos: Pres, Coaldale Inn, Inc, 59-; v.pres, Parsons Construction Co, 65- Mem: Tonopah-Goldfield Dove Elks Does; Eastern Star. Rel: Baptist. Mailing Add: Coaldale Via Tonopah, Nev. 89049.

PARSONS, JOANNA GABLE D
V.Chmn, Tenth Cong. Dist. Dem. Cmt, Ga.
b. Canon, Ga, 10 /8/24; d. Benjamin Claude Gable and Martha Rucker G; m. 8/17/41 to Henry Hodgson Parsons; c. Betsy Gayle (Mrs. Eugene P. Carswell), Henry Randolph, Della Meridee and Joseph Rucker. Educ: Porter Col, grad, 52. Polit. & Govt. Pos: Probation officer, Clarke Co. Juvenile Court, Ga, 56-60; mem, Ga. State Bd. for Children and Youth, 63-67; mem. campaign cmt, Clarke Co. Dem. Party, 64; hon. secy. to Ga. Del, Dem. Nat. Conv, 64; campaign mgr. for Sam Caldwell for Cmnr. of Labor, 66; campaign mgr. for Jimmy Carter for Gov, 66; mem. bd. trustees, Tallulah Falls Sch, 66-; mem, Clarke Co. Dem. Exec. Cmt, 66-; v.chmn, Tenth Cong. Dist. Dem. Cmt, currently. Bus. & Prof. Pos: Off. mgr. and secy, First Christian Church, 52-56; owner, Jo's Secretarial Serv, 59-; admin. asst, Soc. Sci. Res. Inst, 60- Mem: Altrusa; Ga. Probation Asn; Girl Scouts; Athens-Clarke Co. Ment. Health Asn; Athens Trojan Club; Ga. Cong. of Parents and Teachers; Dem. Party of Ga; Ga. Fedn. of Women's Clubs; Farm Bur; v.pres, President's Coun. of Athens. Presented medal by Gov. Carl E. Sanders; named Woman of Year in Volunteer Pub. Serv, Athens, 64. Rel: First Christian. Legal Res: 1744 S. Milledge Ave, Athens, Ga. 30601. Mailing Add: P.O. Box 5073, Athens, Ga. 30604. (1967)

PARSONS, JOHN WELSEY R
Chmn, Warren Co. Rep. Party, Iowa
b. Hartford, Iowa, 6/27/08; s. Preston M. Parsons and Frena M. Laverty P; m. 8/29/42 to Ruth A. Greenwalt; c. Max, David and Pamela. Educ: Iowa State Univ, $2\frac{1}{2}$ years; Lambda Chi Alpha. Polit. & Govt. Pos: Finance chmn, Warren Co. Rep. Party, Iowa, 52-63, co. chmn, 63-; alternate del, Rep. Nat. Conv, 64. Mem: Mason; Rotary. Simpson Col. Distinguished Serv. Award, 60. Rel: Methodist. Legal Res: 104 W. Euclid, Indianola, Iowa 50125. Mailing Add: Box 292, Indianola, Iowa 50125.

PARSONS, ROGER ALAN R
Chmn, Watonwan Co. Rep. Party, Minn.
b. Fargo, N.Dak, 4/15/27; s. James L. Parsons and Edith Burmeister P; m. 8/5/50 to Louise Josephine Montressor; c. Patricia, Margaret, Susan, Robert, Kathryn and Janice. Educ: Univ. Minn, B.S. and M.D. Polit. & Govt. Pos: Chmn, Watonwan Co. Rep. Party, Minn, 62- Bus. & Prof. Pos: Pvt. practice of med, St. James, Minn, 54- Mil. Serv: Entered as Pvt, Army, 45, released as T-3, 46, after serv. in Finance Dept, Ft. Jackson, S.C. Mem: Blue Earth Valley Med. Soc.(pres, 65); Minn. State Med. Soc; Am. Med. Asn; Am. Acad. of Gen. Practice; K. of C. Rel: Roman Catholic. Mailing Add: 417 Second Ave. S, St. James, Minn. 56081.

PARSONS, SAMUEL A. R
b. Peru, N.Y, 4/9/99; married. Educ: Holyoke, Mass. Trades Sch. Polit. & Govt. Pos: Town clerk and treas, Vt; Vt. State Rep, 39-41 & 47-67. Bus. & Prof. Pos: Formerly assoc. with the machine tool indust. Rel: Protestant. Mailing Add: Bomoseen, Vt. 05732. (1967)

PARSONS, WILLARD ERNEST R
b. Jacksonville, Fla, 6/21/36; s. Willard E. Parsons and Eva Crosby P; m. 8/20/60 to Sally Galloway; c. Leslie and Lauren. Educ: Univ. Fla, B.S, 58, LL.B, 62; Delta Theta Phi; Sigma Alpha Epsilon. Polit. & Govt. Pos: Republican nominee, U.S. Rep, Fla, 68. Bus. & Prof. Pos: Attorney-at-law, 62- Mil. Serv: 1st Lt, Air Force Res. Mem: Jacksonville Bar Asn.(exec. cmt, 67); Fla. and Am. Bar Asns; Commercial Law League Am; Shrine; Master Mason; Scottish Rite; Jacksonville Jr. C. of C. Rel: Presbyterian. Legal Res: 1612 Kingswood Rd, Jacksonville, Fla. 32207. Mailing Add: 762 Florida National Bank Bldg, Jacksonville, Fla. 32202.

PARTAIN, DAVID OWEN D
Ark. State Sen.
b. Ozark, Ark, 8/10/19; s. David Sidney Partain and Beulah Owen P; m. 12/11/54 to Norma Mathews; c. Paige. Educ: Univ. Ark, LL.B, 42; Delta Theta Phi; Sigma Phi Epsilon. Polit. & Govt. Pos: Prosecuting attorney, 15th Judicial Dist, Ark, 47-50; city attorney, Van Buren, 57-58; Ark. State Sen, Third Sen. Dist, 67- Bus. & Prof. Pos: Attorney-at-law, 45- Mil. Serv: Entered as Pvt, Air Force, 42, released as 1st Lt, 45, after serv. in 12th Air Force, 414th Squadron, N.Africa and Italy, 43-44; Air Medal with Cluster; Theatre Ribbons. Mem: Local and Ark. Bar Asns; Rotary; VFW; Am. Legion; Mason. Rel: Presbyterian. Legal Res: 7 Mabel Nell Rd, Van Buren, Ark. 72956. Mailing Add: P.O. Box 442, Van Buren, Ark. 72956.

PARTCH, ROBERT FREDERICK R
b. New Haven, Vt, 5/12/99; s. Frederic M. Partch and Sarah Field P; m. 10/4/24 to Edna May Sweetser; c. Nancy (Mrs. O'Bryan) and Martha (Mrs. Whitney). Educ: Boston Univ, B.B.A, 22; Delta Sigma Pi. Polit. & Govt. Pos: Alderman, 45-46, 60-61; Vt. State Rep, 63-68. Bus. & Prof. Pos: Former agent for Metrop. Life Ins. Co, 30 years; retired. Mil. Serv: Students Army Training Corps, Boston Univ, 3 months; World War I. Mem: Am. Legion; pres, Vergennes Rotary Club, 51-52. Rel: Congregational. Mailing Add: 8 N. Maple St, Vergennes, Vt. 05491.

PARTEE, CECIL A. D
Ill. State Sen.
b. Blytheville, Ark; m. to Paris A. P; c. Paris I. and Cecile A. Educ: Tenn. State Univ, B.S. cum laude bus. admin; Northwest. Univ. Law Sch, J.D. Polit. & Govt. Pos: Pres, 20th Ward Reg. Dem. Orgn; asst. state's attorney, Cook Co, Ill, 8 years; Ill. State Sen, 66- Mem: Cook Co, Chicago, Ill. State and Am. Nat. Bar Asns; NAACP; Urban League. Rel: Congregational. Mailing Add: 5836 S. Michigan Ave, Chicago, Ill. 60637. (1967)

PARTELLO, CHARLES HAMILTON D
b. Des Moines, Iowa, 10/23/25; s. Alfred Leland Partello and Edith H. Nelson P; m. 11/26/60 to Gloria Joyce Heinecke; c. James M, Wayne K, Glen L, Linda M. and Cheryl C. Educ: Loyola Col, 2 years. Polit. & Govt. Pos: Sylmar Dem. Club del, Calif. Dem. Coun, 64-67; pres, Sylmar Dem. Club, 65-69; v.pres, 41st Assembly Dist. Dem. Party, 66; v.pres, 22nd Cong. Dist. Dem. Party, 67; club del, South. Calif. Dem. Party, 68-69, dir, 41st Assembly Dist. and mem, bd. gov, 69; mem, Calif. Dem. State Cent. Cmt, 68-69. Bus. & Prof. Pos: Dir. pub. rels, Commun. Workers of Am, 64-68; mem, exec. bd, Coun. on Polit. Educ, Los Angeles Co. Fedn. of Labor, 66-68. Mil. Serv: Entered as Seaman, Navy, 44, released as PO 2/C, 46, after serv. in Aviation Photo Squadron, Asiatic Pac. Theatre; M/Sgt, Air Nat. Guard, Air Force Res, 50-69; Navy Unit Commendation; Good Conduct Medal; Am. Campaign Medal; Asiatic Pac. Medal; World War II Victory Medal; Nat. Defense Medal; Armed Forces Reservist Medal; Small Arms Expert Medal; UN Medal; Calif. Fed. Serv. Medal; Watts Serv. Medal. Mem: Tel. Pioneers of Am; Am. Legion; C. of C. Rel: Methodist. Mailing Add: 12955 Tarquin St, Sylmar, Calif. 91342.

PARTRIDGE, HENRY F. D
b. Lincolnton, Ga, 2/15/02; s. William Preston Partridge and Mary Reynolds P; m. 2/15/27 to Frances Leo Morrison, wid; c. Henry Will, Anne Jeanette, Thomas Allen, Laura Lee, Franklin Preston. Educ: Agnes Pub. Sch. Polit. & Govt. Pos: Ga. State Rep, 63-64. Bus. & Prof. Pos: Farmer; lumberman; ginner; merchant. Rel: Baptist. Mailing Add: Lincolnton, Ga. 30817. (1967)

PARTRIDGE, SANBORN R
Vt. State Rep.
b. Proctor, Vt, 4/30/15; single. Educ: Amherst Col, B.A, 36; Harvard Bus. Sch, 38; Yale Law Sch, LL.B, 39; Yale Grad. Schs, M.S. in Geol, 47; Sigma Xi, Phi Beta Kappa. Polit. & Govt. Pos: Town grand juror, 40-41; town agent, 42; mem, Rutland Roadway and Reapportionment Study Cmt; Vt. State Rep, 61-; alternate del, Rep. Nat. Conv, 68. Bus. & Prof. Pos: Geologist; educator; trustee, U.V.M; pres. trustees, Proctor Free Libr. Mil. Serv: Air Force, Pvt. to 1st Lt, 42-46. Mem: Geological Soc. of Am; Societe Geologique de France; Boy Scouts (pres, Green Mt. Coun); Am. and Rutland Co. Bar Asns; Green Mt. Club; Vt. Hist. Soc; Appalachian Mt. Club; Sierra Club. Rel: United Church of Christ; trustee, Union Church. Mailing Add: 62 Ormsbee Ave, Proctor, Vt. 05765. (1967)

PARYS, RONALD G. D
b. Milwaukee, Wis, 10/7/38; s. Casimir George Parys and Gladys Bernice Olson P; m. 4/9/60 to Margarete Kauth; c. Brian George, Cheryl Ann, Lynn Marie and Dawn Marie. Polit. & Govt. Pos: V.chmn, 13th Ward Dem. Party, Wis; Wis. State Assemblyman, 13th Dist, Milwaukee Co, 65-67. Bus. & Prof. Pos: Material control, Cornell Paper Prod, 56-57; buyer, Northwest. Food Prod. Co, 57-59; foreman and purchasing supvr, Ben-Hur Mfg, 59-62; indust. appraiser, Fidelity Appraisal Co, 62-65 and Am. Appraisal Co, 65- Mil. Serv: S/Sgt, E-6, Army Res, 55-66. Mem: Polish Nat. Alliance; 13th Ward Commun. Coun; Twin Arch Sportsman Club; St. Casimir Civic & Athletic Club; St. Mary Athletic Club. Rel: Roman Catholic. Mailing Add: 1221 E. Clarke St, Milwaukee, Wis. 53212.

PASBACH, EARL FRANCIS D
R.I. State Rep.
b. Chicago, Ill, 11/28/29; s. Earl F. Pasbach and Mary White P; single. Educ: La Salle Acad, Providence, R.I, 3 years; Providence Col, B.S; Boston Col. Law Sch, LL.B; Albertus Magnus Club. Polit. & Govt. Pos: Legal asst, Off. of Solicitor, U.S. Dept. Labor, 59-60; law clerk, Assoc. Justice Thomas H. Roberts, Supreme Court, R.I, 61-62; attorney, Off. Appeals, Nat. Labor Rels. Bd, Wash, D.C, 62; R.I. State Rep, 87th Dist, 69- Mil. Serv: Entered as Pvt, Army, 54, released as Cpl, 56, after serv. in 3440th ASU, Ft. Benning, Ga. Mem: Pawtucket Bar Asn; Lions. Rel: Roman Catholic. Mailing Add: 591 Willett Ave, East Providence, R.I. 02915.

PASCAVIS, GLENN J. D
b. Rudolph, Wis, 2/20/29; s. Leonard Frank Pascavis and Elizabeth Mary Schmick P. Educ: Wausau Bus. Col, acct, 51. Polit. & Govt. Pos: Clerk

Gen, Wis. Rapids, Wis, 53; v.chmn, Wood Co. Dem. Party, 62-64, chmn, 64-66; v.chmn, Wis. Seventh Dist. Dem. Party, 65-69; Dem. cand. for Wis. State Assemblyman, 66 & 68. Mem: Childrens Serv. Soc; Wis. Seventh Dist. Cmt. on Polit. Educ; Cent. Labor Coun; Ushers Club; Holy Name Soc; 1075 City Union. Rel: Catholic. Mailing Add: 530 18th Ave. S, Wisconsin Rapids, Wis. 54494.

PASCHALL, JOSHUA ERNEST D
N.C. State Rep.
b. Wilson Co, N.C, 8/9/96; s. Joshua Walter Paschall and Sally Poole P; m. 12/18/19 to Claire Hodges; c. Julia (Mrs. Charles W. Mauze) and Col. James E. Educ: Univ. N.C, Chapel Hill, 17; Atlantic Christian Col, N.C, A.B, 18, hon. LL.D, 61; Am. Exten. Univ, Calif, LL.B, 26. Polit. & Govt. Pos: Mem, N.C. Banking Cmn, 61-65; mem, Wilson Planning & Zoning Cmn, N.C, 63-65; N.C. State Rep, 64-, chmn, Hwy. Safety Cmt, N.C. State House of Rep; pres, Coastal Plain Planning & Develop. Cmn, 65-66. Bus. & Prof. Pos: Dir, Wilson Savings & Loan Asn, N.C, 31-, pres, 44-; dir, Branch Banking & Trust Co, 42-, pres, 52-64. Mil. Serv: Entered as HA 3/C, Naval Res. Forces, 18, released as Phm 3/C, 19; Liberty Medal. Mem: Am, N.C. and Wilson Co. Bar Asns; mem. and v.chmn. bd. of trustees, Atlantic Christian Col, Wilson, N.C; pres, N.C. Bankers Asn, 60-61; Wilson C. of C; Elks; Moose; Am. Legion; Newcomen Soc. of N.Am. Rel: Christian Church; Trustee, First Christian Church, Wilson, N.C. Legal Res: 1718 Wilshire Blvd, Wilson, N.C. 17893. Mailing Add: First Union National Bank Bldg, Wilson, N.C. 17893.

PASCOE, D. MONTE D
b. Des Moines, Iowa, 1/4/35; s. Donald Leslie Pascoe and Marjorie Powers P; m. 8/3/57 to Patricia Hill; c. Sarah Lynn, Edward Llewellyn and William Arthur. Educ: Dartmouth Col, A.B, 57; Stanford Law Sch, LL.B, 60; Psi Upsilon; Casque and Gauntlet. Polit. & Govt. Pos: State co-ordinator, Humphrey for Pres, Colo, 68; Dem. dist. capt, Denver, Colo, 67-69. Bus. & Prof. Pos: Partner, Ireland, Stapleton, Pryor & Holmes, 60- Mem: Denver, Calif. and Am. Bar Asns; Colo. Bar Asn.(chmn, water law sect, 66-67); Law Club of Denver; Phi Delta Phi; Denver Club; Cactus Club; Colo. Dartmouth and Stanford Asns; secy and dir, Denver Area Jr. Achievement. Rel: Presbyterian; Elder, Montview Blvd. Presbyterian Church. Mailing Add: 744 Lafayette St, Denver, Colo, 80218.

PASHBY, FAWN D
b. 4/23/03; m. 1/12/27; c. 4. Educ: Elem. Sch; Correspondence Dale Carnegie Course. Polit. & Govt. Pos: S.Dak. State Sen, 64-66; S.Dak. State Rep, 59-61; Police and Fire Cmnr. of Pierre; Co. chmn. of Red Cross and Co. chmn. for Ment. Health Dr. Bus. & Prof. Pos: Operating a trailer court and 2 apt. houses; formerly farmed until 37, oil dealer, car dealer, motel operator. Mem: Pierre Fire Dept; 4° Knight; Elks; Eagle Lodge; Isaac Walton League; Pierre Sports, Inc. Rel: Catholic. Mailing Add: 120 W. Pleasant Dr, Pierre, S.Dak. 57501. (1967)

PASHLEY, KATHRYN GRAHAM D
b. Phila; d. Francis P. Graham (deceased) and Irene Minford G; m. to Wilfred Pashley; wid; c. Wilfred J. Educ: Cath. High Schs. of Phila. Polit. & Govt. Pos: Pa. State Rep, 54-67; chmn, 56th Ward Dem. Exec. Cmt; past pres, 35th Ward Dem. Women's Auxiliary; first v.pres. Women's Dem. Club of Phila; alternate del. 56, 60 Dem. Nat. Convs. from Fifth Cong. Dist. Mem: Capt. Infantile Paralysis Campaign. Recipient Distinguished Serv. Cert. of Am. Legion, 60. Mailing Add: 8123 Henning St, Philadelphia, Pa. 19111. (1967)

PASMA, JAMES JAY D
Chmn, Hill Co. Dem. Cent. Cmt, Mont.
b. Helena, Mont, 1/16/33; s. James M. Starr and Evelyn Anderson S; adopted by Jay P. and Elsie F. Pasma; m. 8/20/55 to Virginia Mae Shaffer; c. Zarren James, Victoria Star, Farol Marie and Zane Jay. Educ: GED, 53. Polit. & Govt. Pos: Chmn, Hill Co. Dem. Cent. Cmt, Mont, 65-; secy, Mont. State Senate, 67; finance chmn, Mont. Dem. State Cent. Cmt, 67-68; del, Dem. Nat. Conv, 68; Dem. cand. for state treas, 68; co. chmn. and committeeman-at-lg, Mont. Dem. State Exec. Cmt, 68- Bus. & Prof. Pos: Owner, Pasma Pet Shop, Havre, Mont, 67-; technician, North. Mont. Col. Mil. Serv: Entered as Pvt. E-1, Marines, 52, released as Sgt, 55, after serv. in Fleet Marine Force, Pac. Force, Hawaii, Calif. and Idaho, 53-55; 1st. Sgt. E-8, Army Nat. Guard Res, Troup E, 163rd Armored Cavalry, Havre, Mont, 55-67; Nat. Defense Ribbon; 10 Year Armed Forces Reserve Medal; numerous state nat. guard medals. Mem: Eagles; unit pres, coun. pres. and state citizenship chmn, Mont. PTA; scoutmaster, Boy Scouts, 56-66. Rel: Episcopal. Legal Res: 1055 Boulevard Ave, Havre, Mont. 59501. Mailing Add: P.O. Box 94, Havre, Mont. 59501.

PASSANNANTE, WILLIAM F. D
N.Y. State Assemblyman
b. New York, N.Y, 2/10/20. Educ: N.Y. Univ, grad, 40; Harvard Law Sch, grad, 48. Polit. & Govt. Pos: Asst. U.S. Attorney for South. Dist. of N.Y, 48-53; Legis. Counsel to pres, N.Y.C. Coun, 54; N.Y. State Assemblyman, 55- Bus. & Prof. Pos: Lawyer; pres, Cosmopolitan Trucking Corp; dir, Charles Passannante Sons, Inc. Mil. Serv: Army, 41-45. Mem: Fed. Bar Asn; N.Y. State Dist. Attorneys Asn; Greenwich Village Asn; local planning bd, Grand St. Boys Asn; Am. Legion; N.Y. Cmt, Albert Einstein Col. of Med; Columbian Soc; K. of C; Lions. Rel: Catholic. Mailing Add: 72 Barrow St, New York, N.Y. 10014.

PASSMAN, OTTO ERNEST D
U.S. Rep, La.
b. Washington Parish, near Franklinton, La, 6/27/00; married. Polit. & Govt. Pos: U.S. Rep, La, 46- Bus. & Prof. Pos: Owner, Passman Investment Co, Monroe, La, currently. Mil. Serv: Officer, U.S. Navy, World War II. Mem: Past State Comdr, Am. Vet. of World War II, Inc; Am. Legion; Scottish Rite Mason (33°); Red Cross of Constantine of York Rite of Freemasonry; Past Grand Master, Grand Lodge of the State of La, F&AM; Grand Cross Court of Honour, Scottish Rite Mason. Rel: Baptist. Legal Res: Monroe, La. 71201. Mailing Add: The Congressional, Washington, D.C. 20003.

PASTORE, JOHN O. D
U.S. Sen, R.I.
b. Providence, R.I, 3/17/07; s. Michelle Pastore and Erminia Asprinio P; m. 7/12/41 to Elena Elizabeth Calto; c. Dr. John O, Jr, Frances (Mrs. Albert Scheuer) and Louise Marie. Educ: Northeast. Univ, LL.B, 31. Hon. LL.D, Providence Col, R.I. State Col. and Brown Univ; Ed.D, R.I. Col. of Educ; Sc.D, R.I. Col. of Pharm. and Bryant Col; hon. degrees, Univ. R.I, Northeast. Univ, Salve Regina Col, New Bedford Inst. Tech, Phila. Col. of Textiles and Sci, Suffolk Univ, and Villanova Univ. Polit. & Govt. Pos: R.I. State Rep, 35-37; asst. attorney gen, R.I, 37-38 & 40-49; lt. gov, R.I, 44-45 and gov, 45-50; U.S. Sen, R.I, 50-, mem, Senate Appropriations Cmt, Senate Commerce Cmt. and Senate Dem. Policy Cmt, v.chmn. and past chmn, Joint Cmt. on Atomic Energy; mem, U.S. del, Gen. Assembly of UN, 55, cong. adv. to U.S. del, with reference to establishing a new Int. Atomic Energy Agency, 56; senate-designee, Geneva Conf. on the Peaceful Uses of Atomic Energy, 55, 58 & 61 and Initial Conf. on the Int. Agency in Vienna, 57; keynote speaker, Dem. Nat. Conv, 64, del, 68. Legal Res: Cranston, R.I. Mailing Add: Room 3215, New Senate Office Bldg, Washington, D.C. 20510.

PATE, OSCAR PERRY D
Chmn, Sabine Co. Dem. Exec. Cmt, Tex.
b. Etoile, Tex, 12/5/95; s. Wilber Franks Pate and Evaline Reynolds P; m. 8/5/20 to Vera J. Bennett; c. Mattie Pauline (Mrs. N.A. Podhaiski), Oscar Glenn, Harold Valjean and Jane (Mrs. Francis Rawson). Polit. & Govt. Pos: Supt. of pub. instr, Sabine Co, Tex, 19-23; chmn, Sabine Co. Dem. Exec. Cmt, 26-28 and currently; vet. serv. officer, Sabine Co, 58-66. Bus. & Prof. Pos: Independent contractor, 35-61. Mil. Serv: Entered as Pvt, Army, 17, released as 1st Sgt, 19, after serv. in Co. A, 360th Inf, 90th Div, Marne-St. Mehiel-Muse-Argonne Offensive, 18; Purple Heart; Capt, Tex. State Guard, 40-45. Mem: Tex. Forestry Asn; Boy Scouts; Bronson Lodge 893 AF&AM; 2nd Dist. Comdr, Dept. of Tex. Am. Legion, 64-66. Silver Beaver Award, Boy Scouts. Rel: Methodist. Mailing Add: P.O. Box 427, Hemphill, Tex. 75948. (1967)

PATERNOSTER, FRANCIS RICHARD D
b. Downsville, N.Y, 7/19/12; s. George Paternoster and Angie Miller P; m. 1/8/44 to Rebecca Retz; c. John Miller, Mark Bouck and Andrea Retz. Educ: Cornell Univ, A.B, 34, Cornell Law Sch, LL.B, 36. Polit. & Govt. Pos: Del. Co. Estate Tax Attorney, N.Y. State Dept. of Taxation and Finance, 54-58; Dist. Attorney, Del. Co, N.Y, 58; chmn, Del. Co. Dem. Party, 59-64; del, Dem. Nat. Conv, 60. Bus. & Prof. Pos: Asst. ed, Am. Law Reports, 36; attorney-at-law, 37- Mil. Serv: Entered as Pvt, Army, 41, released as Capt, 46, after serv. in 36th Div, ETO. Mem: Pres, Del. Co. Bar Asn, 52-54; Am. and N.Y. State Bar Asns; Am. and N.Y. State Trial Lawyers Asns; Am. Judicature Soc; N.Y. State Dist. Attorneys Asn; Am. Legion; VFW. Rel: Protestant. Legal Res: 39 Gardiner Place, Walton, N.Y. 13856. Mailing Add: 144 Delaware St, Walton, N.Y. 13856.

PATERSON, BASIL A. D
N.Y. State Sen.
b. N.Y.C, 4/27/26; s. Leonard J. Paterson and Evangeline Rondon P; m. 5/24/53 to Portia Hairston; c. David and Daniel. Educ: St. John's Col, B.S, 48; St. John's Univ. Sch. of Law, LL.B, 51; Kappa Alpha Psi. Polit. & Govt. Pos: N.Y. State Sen, 27th Dist, 65- Bus. & Prof. Pos: Attorney-at-law, Paterson & Michael, 57-67 and Paterson, Michael & Murray, 68- Mil. Serv: Pvt, Army, 43. Eagleton Inst. of Polit. Award, 67; Distinguished Serv. Award, Guardians Asn. N.Y. Police Dept, 68. Rel: Catholic. Legal Res: 400 Manhattan Ave, New York, N.Y. 10026. Mailing Add: 315 W. 125th St, New York, N.Y. 10027.

PATMAN, WRIGHT D
U.S. Rep, Tex.
b. Patman's Switch, Cass Co, Tex, 8/6/93; m. 2/14/19 to Merle Connor (deceased); m. 10/9/68 to Pauline Tucker; c. Three. Educ: Cumberland Univ, LL.B, 16. Polit. & Govt. Pos: Dist. attorney, Fifth Judicial Dist, Tex, 5 years; Tex. State Rep, 4 years; U.S. Rep, Tex, 28-, chmn, Banking and Currency Cmt, U.S. House of Rep, currently, v.chmn, Joint House and Sen. Defense Prod. Cmt, chmn, House and Sen. Joint Econ. Cmt, and mem. House Select Cmt. on Small Bus, currently; del, Dem. Nat. Conv, 68. Mil. Serv: Army, 1st Lt, 17-19, machine gun officer. Mem: Elks; Mason; Eagles; Shrine; Am. Legion; DAV; assoc. mem, Nat. Press Club; State Bar Asn. Admitted to practice before Supreme Court of the U.S. Rel: Baptist. Legal Res: Texarkana, Tex. Mailing Add: 2328 Rayburn House Office Bldg, Washington, D.C. 20515.

PATRICELLI, ROBERT E. R
Dep. Asst. Secy. of Planning and Eval. for Interdept. Affairs, Dept. of Health, Educ. and Welfare
b. Hartford, Conn, 1939; m. to Susan Schaffer; c. Two. Educ: Wesleyan Univ, grad, 61; Fulbright Scholar, Univ. of Paris, 62; Harvard Law Sch, LL.B, 65; Phi Beta Kappa; mem. bd. ed, Law Rev. Polit. & Govt. Pos: Worked with Rep. John V. Lindsay on Voting Rights Act of 1965; app. White House Fel, 65; mem. staff, spec. projs. on Vietnam, Cong. presentations and departmental admin, Off. of Secy. of State Dean Rusk, 65-66; minority counsel for Senate Subcmt. on Employ, Manpower and Poverty and chief legis. and policy aide on urban affairs to Sen. Jacob Javits, N.Y, 66-69; consult, Nat. Adv. Cmn. on Civil Disorders; Dep. Asst. Secy. of Planning and Eval. for Interdept. Affairs and spec. asst. to the Secy. for Urban Affairs Coun, Dept. of Health, Educ. and Welfare, 69- Legal Res: Woodacres, Md. 20016. Mailing Add: Department of Health, Education and Welfare, 330 Independence Ave. S.W, Washington, D.C. 20201.

PATRICK, DANNY L. R
Ark. State Rep.
b. Delaney, Ark, 7/8/41; s. Dan E. Patrick and Audie M. Van Brunt P; m. 8/20/65 to Kathryn L. O'Neal; c. Jerry Lee and Tonya Lucille. Educ: Univ. Ark, B.S.E, 65. Polit. & Govt. Pos: Ark. State Rep, 67- Bus. & Prof. Pos: Teacher and coach, Huntsville High Sch, Ark, 64- Mem: Ark. Educ. Asn; Ark. Coaches Asn; Ark. Cmn. Crime and Law Enforcement; Ark. Coun. Pub, Elem. and Sec. Educ. Mailing Add: General Delivery, Delaney, Ark. 72723.

PATRICK, FRED LAFOREST D
b. Adele, Ky, 4/6/89; s. Benjamin Franklin Patrick and Mary Elizabeth Taulbee P; m. 5/5/08 to Anna Wetherington; c. Earl Franklin, Volita Elvira and Clyde Truman. Polit. & Govt. Pos: Co. supt. of schs, Creek Co, Wolfe

and Depew, Okla, 13; mayor, Depew, 15-16; co. assessor, Creek Co, 21-33; mayor, Sapulpa, 56-58; chmn, Creek Co. Dem. Party, 64-67. Mem: Pres, Creek Co. Farmers Union; organizer, First PTA in Okla. and Indian Territory Cowboy and Pioneer Asn, 06; pres, First Teachers Union in Okla; pres, Rural Teachers Asn. in Okla, 14; past pres, Lions, Sapulpa; pres, State Assessors Asn. and Creek Co. Bar Asn; pres, Crippled Children's Progress; Past Exalted Ruler of Odd Fellows; 50 year mem. of Elks; Masonic Bodies; Past Patron, Eastern Star, six times. Won several state championships in track and field events; outran Jim Thorpe, 19; won U.S. Saddle Bronc Riding Championship under the tutorage of Will Rogers; Hon. Ky. Col. Rel: Christian Church; Elder, First Christian Church in Sapulpa. Legal Res: 1302 University St, Sapulpa, Okla. 74066. Mailing Add: Box 428, Sapulpa, Okla. 74066.

PATRICK, JAMES FAIRCHILD R
Chmn, Wayne Co. Rep. Party, Ky.
b. Louisville, Ky, 2/21/09; s. Samuel J. Patrick and Virginia Fairchild P; m. 3/25/60 to Ruth Marie Hucaby. Educ: Lexington Sr. High Sch, Grad, 27; Univ. Ky, 28; Pi Kappa Alpha. Polit. & Govt. Pos: Chmn, Wayne Co. Rep. Party, Ky, 62-64 and 68-; admin. asst. to Hwy. Cmnr, 68- Bus. & Prof. Pos: Oil and gas operator, Ky, 39- Mem: Ky. Oil and Gas Asn; Independent Petroleum Asn. of Am; Mason; Shrine; Kiwanis; Wayne Co. Sportsman Club; Monticello - Wayne Co. C. of C; Hon. Order of Ky. Colonels. Rel: Baptist. Legal Res: 117 Michigan Ave, Monticello, Ky. 42633. Mailing Add: Box 381, Monticello, Ky. 42633.

PATRICK, MARY LOUISE R
Secy, Okla. Rep. State Cmt.
b. St. Paul, Minn, 2/3/29; d. John H. Stoffels and Anne M. Conlin S; m. 4/6/53 to Richard A. Patrick; c. Mark S, Gregg A. and Timothy K. Educ: Mech. Arts High Sch, 4 years. Polit. & Govt. Pos: Ed, Okla. Rep. News, 66-; secy, Okla. Rep. State Cmt, 67- Rel: Methodist. Legal Res: 11213 Dover Court, Yukon, Okla. 73099. Mailing Add: 103 N.W. 23rd St, Oklahoma City, Okla. 73103.

PATRICK, MARY VERONICA D
b. Seattle, Wash, 3/29/10; d. John Michael Pappas and Helen Anagnostu P; m. 5/20/37 to William Bryan Patrick; c. John Bryan. Educ: Munson's Secy. Col, grad, 31. Polit. & Govt. Pos: Chmn, Goshen Co. Dem. Cent. Cmt, 56-58; state committeewoman, Wyo. State Dem. Cent. Cmt, 60-64, former vice chairwoman. Bus. & Prof. Pos: Secy-treas. and dir, Patrick Brothers, Inc, 63-; secy-treas, Laramie River Water Users, Inc, 64- Mem: Am. Nat. Cow-Belles, pres, Wyo. State Cow-Belles, 50-51; Jay Em Women's Club. Rel: Episcopal. Mailing Add: c/o Patrick Ranch, Torrington, Wyo. 82240.

PATRIDGE, CORBET LEE D
Miss. State Sen.
b. Ruleville, Miss, 9/20/23; married. Polit. & Govt. Pos: Field agent, Govt. Bur; Miss. State Rep, 56-60; Miss. State Sen, currently. Bus. & Prof. Pos: Agriculturalist; former teacher of Voc. Agr; pub. rels. rep, Nat. Cotton Coun. Rel: Baptist. Mailing Add: P.O. Box 347, Schlater, Miss. 38952. (1967)

PATTEN, DAVID IVY D
La. State Rep.
b. Wisner, La, 12/11/23; s. Ivy Edward Patten and Mattie Amelia Harrell P; m. 6/11/41 to Ethel Inez Ewing; c. David Mancil, Carolyn Diane (Mrs. Wallace Morace), Ronald Wayne and Sandra Jeanette. Educ: CCC Sch, Frinklington, La, 41. Polit. & Govt. Pos: La. State Rep, 63-, mem, Contingency Expenses Cmt, 63, Judiciary Cmt, 63, Health, Welfare and Charitable Insts. Cmt, 63 and Appropriations Cmt, 66, chmn, Pub. Works and Insts. Cmt; head, Indust. Develop. Prog, 64-69. Bus. & Prof. Pos: Pres, Patten's Welding Co, Inc, 52; designer of Patten Steel Bldg, 52; inventor, Suspension Cable Bldg, patented shelter structure, 62. Mil. Serv: Entered as Pvt, Air Force, 43, released as Cpl, 46, after serv. in First Ord, 509th Composite Group, 'first atomic bomb group,' Am. and Asiatic-Pac. Theaters, 43-46; Two Battle Stars; Good Conduct Medal; Victory Medal, World War II. Mem: Mason (32°); Am. Legion; C. of C.(pres, Catahoula Parish Chap, 64). Named Outstanding Personality of the South. Invited to Presidential Prayer Breakfast and attended twice. Rel: Pentecostal. Mailing Add: 1102 First St, Jonesville, La. 71343.

PATTEN, EDWARD JAMES D
U.S. Rep, N.J.
b. Perth Amboy, N.J, 8/22/05; m. to Anna Quigg, 2/22/36; c. Catharine M. Educ: Newark State Col; Rutgers Law Sch, LL.B; Rutgers Univ, B.S, Educ. Polit. & Govt. Pos: Pres. bd, Salvation Army; mem, N.J. Dem. State Cmt; chmn, Middlesex Co. Dem. Cmt, 34-36; Mayor, Perth Amboy, 34-40; Co. Clerk, Middlesex Co, 40-54; campaign mgr, Robert B. Meyner, 53-57; Secy. of State, N.J, 54-62; U.S. Rep, N.J, 62-, mem, Appropriations Cmt. Bus. & Prof. Pos: Lawyer, 27; teacher pub. schs, 27-34. Mem: Eagles; Moose; Elks; Kiwanis; K. of C; Nat. Conf. of Christians and Jews; C. of C; NAACP; past pres, Middlesex Bar Asn; Am. Judicature Soc. Recipient of Outstanding Citizenship Award from Am. Heritage Found. and B'nai B'riths Brotherhood Award. Legal Res: Perth Amboy, N.J. 08861. Mailing Add: U.S. House of Representatives, Washington, D.C. 20515.

PATTEN, ZEBOIM CARTTER D
Councilman, Hamilton Co. Dem. Cmt, Tenn.
b. Chattanooga, Tenn, 2/2/03; s. Zeboim Cartter Patten and Sarah Avery Key P; m. 8/19/31 to Elizabeth Nelson Bryan; c. Sarah Key (Mrs. P.H. Gwynn), Emma Berry (Mrs. B.A. Casey, Jr), Worcester Allen Bryan and Zeboim Cartter, III. Educ: Cornell Univ; Chi Phi. Hon. D.C.L, Univ. of the South. Polit. & Govt. Pos: Tenn. State Rep, 59-61; del, Constitutional Conv, 65-66; councilman, Hamilton Co. Dem. Cmt, 66- Bus. & Prof. Pos: Dir, Vol. State Life Ins. Co, 30- and Hamilton Nat. Bank, 60-; chmn. bd. of trustees, Bonny Oaks Sch, 50-; chmn. bd, First Fed. Savings & Loan Asn, 55-; trustee, Univ. Chattanooga, 56- Publ: A Tennessee Chronicle, 53; Signal Mountain and Walden's Ridge, 62. Mem: Mountain City Club; Elks; Am. Legion; C. of C; Tenn. Hist. Cmn; Chatanoogans, Inc; Tenn. Conserv. League; Keep Tenn. Green Asn. Rel: Episcopal. Legal Res: 406 N. Palisades Dr, Signal Mountain, Tenn. 37377. Mailing Add: 831 Georgia Ave, Chattanooga, Tenn. 37401.

PATTERSON, BENJAMIN (BEN)
b. Hibbing, Minn, 1910; married; c. Two. Educ: Univ. N.Dak, B.S, Commerce. Polit. & Govt. Pos: Dir, Minn. Resort Asn; Minn. State Sen, 62-67; mem, North. Great Lakes Resource Develop. Cmt. Bus. & Prof. Pos: Resort owner. Mem: V.pres, Minn. Arrowhead Asn. Mailing Add: Pines Resort, Deer River, Minn. 56636.

PATTERSON, BOB LEE R
Chmn, Newton Co. Rep. Party, Mo.
b. Boulder City, Mo, 9/25/24; s. Guy Patterson and Mary Ruth Green P; m. 7/25/46 to Betty Jean Sappington; c. Alan Lee, Jacky Dale and Jenna Lyn. Educ: Stella High Sch, 4 years. Polit. & Govt. Pos: Chmn, Newton Co. Rep. Party, Mo, 68- Bus. & Prof. Pos: Partner, Jeffers-Patterson Motor Co, 59- Mil. Serv: Entered as Seaman, Navy, 44, released as Seaman 3/C, 66, after serv. in S.Pac. Theatre, 44-46; Three Battle Stars. Mem: Pres, Crowder Col. Found, 2 years; Lions; AF&AM (past Master, Stella Lodge 538); Eastern Star (past Worthy Patron, Stella Lodge 438). Rel: Church of Christ. Mailing Add: 215 E. McKinney, Neosho, Mo. 64850.

PATTERSON, CHARLES VAUGHAN D
Tex. State Rep.
b. Taylor, Tex, 1/18/44; s. Claude Warren Patterson and Lois Stiles P; m. 7/6/68 to Elise Thayer. Educ: Univ. Tex, Austin, B.A, 67; St. Mary's Univ, San Antonio, 65-66; Beta Theta Pi. Polit. & Govt. Pos: Col. intern, Rep. Nat. Cmt, 63; clerk to U.S. Rep. Homer Thornberry, 63-64 and to State Sen. Charles F. Herring, 65; Tex. State Rep, 69- Bus. & Prof. Pos: Assoc, Patterson Bros. Ins, 68- Mil. Serv: 2nd Lt, Tex. Nat. Guard, Army Res, 67-; Am. Spirit of Honor Medal for display of outstanding leadership best expressing the Am. Spirit: honor, initiative, loyalty and high example to comrades in arms, awarded by the Citizens Cmt. for the Army, Navy and Air Force, Inc, Ft. Polk, La, 67. Mem: Jr. C. of C. Rel: Methodist. Mailing Add: Box 1159, Taylor, Tex. 76574.

PATTERSON, EARL EDGAR R
Chmn, Precinct Orgn, Third Cong. Dist. Rep. Party, Va.
b. Oklahoma City, Okla, 4/14/23; s. Earl Patterson and Bessie Elmira Threadkill P; m. 11/17/56 to Alice Jean May; c. Patricia Ann and Robert Earl. Educ: Univ. Okla, B.S.Ch.E, 44, M.Ch.E, 47; Mass. Inst. Tech, Sc.D. in Chem. Eng, 50; Tau Beta Pi; Sigma Tau; Sigma Xi; Alpha Chi Sigma; Delta Chi. Polit. & Govt. Pos: Chmn, Chesterfield Co. Rep. Cmt, Va, 61-66; chmn, precinct orgn, Third Cong. Dist. Rep. Party, 62- Mil. Serv: Entered as A/S, Naval Res, 44, released as Ens, 46, after serv. in Pac, 45-46; Lt. Comdr, Navy Res, 46-65. Mem: Am. Inst. Chem. Engrs; Am. Chem. Soc; Am. Soc. Metals; Indust. Research Inst. Rel: Disciples of Christ. Mailing Add: 8318 Whitewood Rd, Richmond, Va. 23235.

PATTERSON, FRANK GROVER D
Okla. State Rep.
b. Chillicothe, Mo, 5/31/89; s. Jack Patterson and Laura Belle Henderson P; m. 8/1/08 to Elizabeth C. Pike; c. Lois (Mrs. Hughes), Louise (Mrs. Kennedy) and Bennie Pike (Mrs. Smetana). Polit. & Govt. Pos: Cmnr, Co. Govt, 32-42; Okla. State Rep, 59- Bus. & Prof. Pos: Ed. and publisher, Grandfield Enterprise, 17-55. Rel: Baptist. Mailing Add: 601 Second St, Grandfield, Okla. 73546.

PATTERSON, GRADY LESLIE, JR. D
State Treas, S.C.
b. Abbeville Co, S.C, 1/13/24; s. Grady Leslie Patterson, Sr. and Claudia McClain P; m. 12/22/51 to Marjorie Harrison Faucett; c. Grady Leslie, III, Steven G, Marjorie Lynne, Laura Anne, Amy Susan and Mary Beth. Educ: Clemson Univ, 42-43; Univ. Ala, 43; Univ. S.C, LL.B, 50; Kappa Sigma. Polit. & Govt. Pos: Co. serv. officer, Abbeville Co, S.C, 50; asst. attorney gen, S.C, 59-66, state treas, 67- Mil. Serv: Entered as Pvt, Army Air Corps, 43, entered Res, as Lt, 46, after serv. in 45th Fighter Squadron, Pac-Iwo Jima, 45; Air Force Res, serv. during Korean War, 50-52, Berlin Call Up, 61-62; Col, S.C. Air Nat. Guard, 47-, Opers. Officer, 52-58; Air Medal with 2 Oak Leaf Clusters; Presidential Unit Citation; Distinguished Unit Citation; Army of Occup. Medal; World War II Victory Medal; Am. Campaign Medal; Nat. Defense Serv. Medal; Armed Forces Res. Medal; Air Force Longevity Serv. Award with Oak Leaf Cluster; Combat Readiness Medal; Small Arms Expert Marksmanship Ribbon; 20 year Res. Medal; 20 year Active State Serv. Medal; Berlin Crisis Medal. Mem: S.C. Bar Asn; Nat. Asn. of State Auditors, Comptrollers and Treas; Munic. Finance Officers Asn; Am. Legion; Mil. Order of World Wars; Air Force Asn; Nat. Guard Asns. of S.C. and U.S; Shrine. Rel: Presbyterian. Legal Res: Tugaloo Ave, Calhoun Falls, S.C. 29628. Mailing Add: 3016 Petigru St, Columbia, S.C. 29204.

PATTERSON, HUGH MORRIS D
b. Monticello, Ark, 12/16/09; s. Samuel Jasper Patterson and Lily Davis P; m. 1/19/41 to Mildred McDavid. Educ: Ark. Col, B.A, 31; Univ. Tex, Austin, J.D, 37; Delta Theta Phi. Polit. & Govt. Pos: Chmn, Connally Steering Cmt, Houston, Tex, 63-69; mem, Tex. Civil Judicial Coun, Austin, 63-69; del, Dem. State Conv, 64 & 68; mem, Pres. Club, 64-68; mem, City Charter Cmt, Houston, 65-67; del, Dem. Nat. Conv, 68. Bus. & Prof. Pos: Athletic coach, Searcy High Sch, Ark, 31-35; sr. partner, Baker, Botts, Shepherd & Coats, Houston, Tex, 38- Mil. Serv: Entered as Lt.(jg), Naval Res, 42, released as Lt. Comdr 46, after serv. in Amphibious Forces, U.S. Atlantic-Mediterranean and Pac. Theatres; Lt. Comdr.(Ret), Naval Res; Serv. Medals for Am, European and Pac. Areas; two Battle Stars; Philippine and Japan Occup. Medals. Mem: Houston, Tex. and Am. Bar Asns; Am. Judicature Soc; Tex. Law Rev. Asn; Houston C. of C.(dir); Houston Club (dir); Austin Club; Lakeside Country Club (pres, 59-61). Student Ed, Tex. Law Rev. Rel: Presbyterian. Legal Res: 510 Westminster, Houston, Tex. 77024. Mailing Add: 1600 Esperson Bldg, Houston, Tex. 77002.

PATTERSON, J. F. D
Mo. State Sen.
b. Portageville, Mo, 9/7/07; m. 3/31/29 to Mary Belle Gaddy; c. J.R, Betty Jo (Mrs. B.L. Thompson) and five grandchildren. Educ: Southeast Mo. State Col. Polit. & Govt. Pos: Mo. State Sen, 51-; exec. mgr, Caruthersville C. of C, 8 years; chmn, Bootheel Dem. Club, Southeast Mo. Bus. & Prof. Pos: Asst. organizer, v.pres. and dir. pub. rels, Mark Twain Life Ins. Co, home off, Jefferson City, Mo; exec. mgr, Bank of Hayti, Hayti, Mo, over five years; mech. and elec. eng, currently. Selected the Second-Most Valuable Mem. of Gen. Assembly and Presented Awards by St. Louis Globe-Dem, 61 & 63. Mailing Add: 112 W. 18th St, Caruthersville, Mo. 63830. (1967)

PATTERSON, J.O, JR. D
Tenn. State Sen.
b. Memphis, Tenn, 5/28/35; s. Bishop J.O. Patterson, Sr. and Deborah Mason P; div; c. James O, III and Aaron L. Educ: Fisk Univ, A.B, 58; De Paul Univ. Law Sch, J.D, 63; Blue Key; Alpha Phi Alpha; Phi Alpha Delta. Polit. & Govt. Pos: City councilman, Memphis, Tenn, 68-; Tenn. State Sen, 69- Mem: Memphis & Shelby Co. Bar Asn; NAACP. Rel: Church of God in Christ. Mailing Add: 224 S. Danny Thomas Blvd, Memphis, Tenn. 38126.

PATTERSON, J. TYLER, JR. R
b. Milford, Conn, 4/28/08; m. 1933 to Sarah Sands; c. James, David and Marjorie (Mrs. Maxim). Educ: Yale Col, B.A, 30; Yale Law Sch, LL.B, 33. Polit. & Govt. Pos: Dep. judge, Town Court of Milford, Conn, 38-42; mem. and chmn, Old Lyme Bd. of Educ, 47-53; Conn. State Rep, 50-67, Majority Leader, Conn. State House of Rep, 61, Speaker of the House, 63-67; mem, Conn. Cmn. on Intergovt. Coop, 55-59; mem, Legis. Coun, 59-67; mem, Conn. Constitutional Conv, 65. Mailing Add: Neck Rd, Old Lyme, Conn. 06371.

PATTERSON, JAMES F. R
Chmn, Geauga Co. Rep. Cent. Cmt, Ohio
b. Cleveland, Ohio, 2/16/42; s. Samuel A. Patterson and Iona Lauser P; m. 7/27/63 to Nancy Wilson; c. Susan Leigh and David Wilson. Educ: Ohio State Univ, B.S, 64; Alpha Gamma Rho. Polit. & Govt. Pos: Mem, Geauga Co. Libr. Bd, Ohio, 67-68 and Geauga Co. Bd. Educ, 68; chmn, Geauga Co. Rep. Cent. Cmt, 68-; co. comnr, Geauga Co, 69- Bus. & Prof. Pos: Farmer, Patterson Fruit Farm, 64- Mem: Ohio State Hort. Soc; West Geauga Jr. C. of C; Ohio State Univ. Alumni Asn; Ohio Farm Bur. Fedn. Rel: Methodist. Mailing Add: 7282 Mulberry Rd, Chesterland, Ohio 44026.

PATTERSON, JOHN FRANCIS D
Chmn, Grant Co. Dem. Party, Wis.
b. Leadmine, Wis, 2/3/30; s. Bernard John Patterson and Zita Mary McKenna P; m. 6/1/53 to Charlotte Marie Osterhaus; c. Earl John, Gregory Arthur, David Bernard, Margaret Mary, John Thomas and Paul Raymond. Educ: Platteville State Univ, 48-49; Marquette Univ, B.S. Journalism, 49-52; Sigma Delta Chi. Polit. & Govt. Pos: Mem. sch. bd, Bloomington, Wis, 59-64; mem. state adv. bd, Farmers Home Admin, 61-64; chmn, Grant Co. Dem. Party, 65- Mailing Add: R.F.D, Bloomington, Wis. 53804.

PATTERSON, JOHN MALCOLM D
b. Goldville, Ala, 9/27/21; s. Albert Love Patterson and Agnes Louise Benson P; m. 10/19/47 to Mary Jo McGowin; c. Albert L, III and Barbara Louise. Educ: Univ. Ala, LL.B, 49; Phi Eta Sigma; Alpha Tau Omega; Phi Alpha Delta; Omicron Delta Kappa. Polit. & Govt. Pos: Attorney Gen, Ala, 55-59, Gov, 59-63. Mil. Serv: Entered as Pvt, Artil, 40, released as Maj, 46; reentered serv. as Maj, Artil, 51, released as Maj, 53, after serv. in Africa, Italy and ETO; African, Italian, French and German Campaign Ribbons; Bronze Star Medal; Lt. Col, Artil. Res. Mem: Ala, and Am. Bar Asns; Am. Legion; VFW; WOW; Elks; Eagles; Lions and Cattleman Asn. of Ala. Rel: Methodist. Legal Res: 210 Felder Ave, Montgomery, Ala. 36104. Mailing Add: 33 S. Perry St, Montgomery, Ala. 36104.

PATTERSON, LaFAYETTE D
b. Clay Co, Ala, 8/23/88; s. Delona Patterson and Mary Sorrell P; m. 12/24/42 to Lucille Loflin; c. Geraldine, LaFayette, Jr, Arline, Delona (deceased) and Miriam. Educ: Jacksonville State Col, Ala; Birmingham-Southern Col, A.B. and Hon. LL.D; Leland-Stanford Univ, Calif, M.A. Polit. & Govt. Pos: Dem. cand. for presidential elector, Ala, 68; asst. to Secy. of Agr. and asst. to War Food Adminstr, Dept. of Agr, Washington, D.C; Agr. Adjustment Admin, Washington, D.C; U.S. Rep, Ala, 26-32; del-at-lg, Dem. Nat. Conv. Bus. & Prof. Pos: Prof, Hist. and Polit. Sci, Athens Col, Ala, 65-; pres, Patterson Travel Serv, Inc, Raleigh, N.C, 52-65; prof, Hist. and Polit. Sci, Southern Union Col, Ala, 48-51 and Jacksonville State Col; supt. of educ, Tallapoosa Co, Ala; farmer. Mem: Former mem, Rotary Club and number of other civic clubs; Nat. Educ. Asn; Am. Asn. of Col. Profs. Rel: Presbyterian. Mailing Add: 602 Wesley Dr, Montgomery, Ala. 36111.

PATTERSON, MAC V. R
b. Worth Co, Ga, 9/17/29; s. Robert Andy Patterson and Lillie Scott P; m. 4/4/53 to Doris Cothran; c. Gary Preston, Michael Berry and Farrell Kirk. Educ: Furman Univ, 55-56. Polit. & Govt. Pos: Former S.C. State Rep. Bus. & Prof. Pos: Gen. contractor, Mac V. Patterson, Inc, 63-; assoc, Trammell & Fayssoux Real Estate, 67- Mil. Serv: Entered as Pvt, Army, 51, released as Pfc, 53, after serv. in 923rd Ambulance Duty, Korea. Mem: Christian Businessmen's Fel. Rel: Baptist; charter mem, asst. treas, brotherhood pres, mem. budget and bldg. cmts. and church coun, Edwards Rd. Baptist Church. Legal Res: 6 Wimborne Lane, Greenville, S.C. 29607. Mailing Add: 600 E. North St, Greenville, S.C. 29601.

PATTERSON, MARGOT TRUMAN D
m. to H.F. (Pat) Patterson; wid; c. Chris Truman and David Francis. Educ: Univ. of S.Dak; Vermillion Univ. of Mich, Ann Arbor; Univ. of Mo, Columbia. Polit. & Govt. Pos: Mo. State Rep, 65-66. Bus. & Prof. Pos: Instr. in TV, radio and speech, Stephens Col, 46-53; asst. prof, continuing educ, Univ. of Mo, Columbia, 67- Mem: Women's Dem. Club of Columbia; Boone Co. Federated Women's Dem. Club; Young Dem. Clubs of Mo, Inc; Boone Co. Young Dem. Rel: First Christian. Mailing Add: 109 W. Burnam, Columbia, Mo. 65201.

PATTERSON, PAT J. R
Mem, Oklahoma Co. Rep. Exec. Cmt, Okla.
b. Oklahoma City, Okla, 3/16/20; s. D. Clarence Patterson and Alice Wattenbarger P; m. 10/20/43 to Ann Beard; c. Nancy and James W. Educ: Univ. Okla, 39-40; Oklahoma City Univ, LL.B, 50; Sigma Alpha Epsilon. Polit. & Govt. Pos: Nominee, U.S. Sen, Okla, 66; mem, Oklahoma Co. Rep. Exec. Cmt, 66-; del, Rep. Nat. Conv, 68; del. to several state conv. Bus. & Prof. Pos: Acct-partner, Patterson Audit Co, Oklahoma City, 47-50; attorney-at-law, 50- Mil. Serv: Flying Cadet, Army Air Force, 41, released as Lt. Col, after serv. in 5th Bomb Group, 13th Air Force, Southwest Pac. Theatre, 44-45; Distinguished Flying Cross; Air Medal with 7 Clusters; Philippine Liberation Medal with 3 Stars; Pac. Theatre Medal with 9 Stars; Am. Theater, Am. Defense and World War II Victory Medals. Publ: Church School by Mail (3 vols), Episcopal Diocese of Okla, 60. Mem: Am. Judicature Soc; various Bar Asns; Kiwanis; Am. Legion. Rel: Episcopal. Legal Res: 1115 Huntington, Oklahoma City, Okla. 73116. Mailing Add: 6403 N.W. Grand Blvd, Oklahoma City, Okla. 73116.

PATTERSON, RUTH M. R
b. Guthrie, Okla; single. Polit. & Govt. Pos: Former positions with city, co. and state govt, 26 years; Okla. State Rep, 65-69. Bus. & Prof. Pos: Businesswoman, 15 years; operating farm properties, 10 years. Mailing Add: 215 N. Elm St, Guthrie, Okla. 73044.

PATTERSON, WILMA RANDOLPH D
Chmn, Dist. 13 Dem. Party, Idaho
b. Hartville, Mo, 5/7/09; d. Arthur C. Randolph and Elizabeth Jordan R; m. 5/29/30 to Ray Patterson, wid; c. Carolyn Rae (Mrs. Stone). Educ: Nampa High Sch, grad, 26. Polit. & Govt. Pos: Chmn, Canyon Co. Dem. Cent. Cmt, Idaho, 58-66; chmn, Dollars for Dem, 66-67; chmn, Dist. 13 Dem. Party, 68- Bus. & Prof. Pos: Dir, Southwest Idaho Develop. Asn, 67-69. Publ: Humorous articles, Idaho Daily Statesman, 69. Mem: Nampa, Idaho and Nat. Bds. of Realtors. Selected as Realtor of the Year, 68. Rel: Christian Church. Legal Res: R.R. 3, Nampa, Idaho 83651. Mailing Add: 1512 First St. S, Nampa, Idaho 83651.

PATTISALL, RICHARD CHAPMAN D
Chmn, Roanoke Co. Dem. Cmt, Va.
b. Norton, Va, 1/29/38; s. Richard O'Dell Pattisall and Mary Coxe; m. 7/1/61 to Mary Jane Howard; c. Richard Chapman Jr. and Jennifer Howard. Educ: Univ. N.C, Chapel Hill, A.B, 60, LL.B, 62; Phi Gamma Delta. Polit. & Govt. Pos: V.pres, Halifax Co. Young Dem. Club, N.C, 65; asst. commonwealth attorney, Roanoke Co. Va, 68; pres, Roanoke Co. Young Dem. Club, 68; substitute munic. judge, Roanoke, 68; del, Dem. Nat. Conv, 68; v.pres, Va. Young Dem. Club, 69; chmn, Roanoke Co. Dem. Cmt, 69- Bus. & Prof. Pos: Attorney, Crew and House, Roanoke Rapids, 62-65; attorney and v.pres, Roanoke Am. Corp, Roanoke, 66-68; attorney, private practice, 69- Mil. Serv: Platoon Leaders Class Prog, Marine Corps, 59-60. Mem: Va. and N.C. State Bar; Va. State and Roanoke Bar Asns; Am. Judicature Soc; Delta Theta Phi; Jaycees. Outstanding Leader, N.C. Dem. Party, 65; named One of Outstanding Young Men of Am. 69. Rel: Presbyterian. Mailing Add: 4827 Glenbrook Dr. S.W, Roanoke, Va. 24018.

PATTISON, ORVILLE HOYT R
N.Mex. State Rep.
Educ: N.Mex. State Univ, B.S, Agr. Eng. with Honors; Univ. of Dayton, 12 hours; Alpha Zeta; Sigma Tau; Tau Kappa Epsilon. Polit. & Govt. Pos: N.Mex. State Rep, 63-, Minority Whip, N.Mex. State House of Rep, 65-66, v.chmn, House Agr. Cmt, 69- Bus. & Prof. Pos: Agr. engr. and farmer. Mil. Serv: 1st Lt, Air Force, 52-54, served in Engr. Air Research and Develop. Command, Wright-Patterson Air Force Base, Ohio. Mem: Farm Bur; Clovis Stockyards Asn; N.Mex. Wool Growers Asn. Rel: Presbyterian. Mailing Add: Star Route, Box 58, Clovis, N.Mex. 88101.

PATTON, CLAUDE HERBERT R
City Councilman, Lexington, Va.
b. Abingdon, Va, 11/9/28; s. James Godfrey Patton and Katherine Jones P; m. 6/21/50 to Eleanor Jane Taylor; c. Claude H, Jr, Olivia Lynn, John Fewell and Karen Taylor. Educ: Va. Mil. Inst, B.S. in Civil Eng, 50. Polit. & Govt. Pos: Chmn, Rockbridge Co. Rep. Party, Va, 66; city councilman, Lexington, 69- Bus. & Prof. Pos: Sales engr, Tri-State Equipment Co, Memphis, Tenn, 50-51; engr, E.I. Dupont Co, H-Bomb Project, Aiken, S.C, 51-53; sales engr, Carter Machinery Co, Roanoke, 53-55 & 57-61; exec-secy, Va. Mil. Inst. Alumni Educ. Fund, Lexington, 61-66; mgr, John Norman's Col. Town Shop, 66- Mil. Serv: Entered as 2nd Lt, Air Force, 55, released 1st Lt, 57, after serv. in NEAC Air Installations, Resolution Island, 55-56 and Craig Air Force Base, Selma, Ala, 56-57. Mem: Lexington Merchants Asn.(dir); Tri Brook Country Club (past v.pres); Lexington Golf Club (dir); dir, Rockbridge-Lexington Bd. of Ment. Health; C. of C.(dir, Lexington Chap). Rel: Presbyterian; Deacon. Mailing Add: 3 Courtland Center, Lexington, Va. 24450.

PATTON, ELBERT EARL, JR. R
Ga. State Sen.
b. Atlanta, Ga, 6/27/27; s. Elbert Earl Patton and Ella Britt Hall P; m. 3/19/49 to Mary Louise Morris; c. Thomas Earl, Richard Morris and Dorothy Louise. Educ: Ga. Inst. of Tech, B.S, 49; Sigma Chi. Polit. & Govt. Pos: State campaign chmn, Young Rep. Fedn. and del, Young Rep. Conv, 54-55; cand. for Atlanta Aldermanic Bd, 65; mem, Atlanta, Fulton Co. Local Govt. Study Cmn, 66; mem, Ga. State Rep. Cmt. and Ga. Fifth Cong. Dist. Cmt, 65; chmn, Fulton Co. Rep. Party, 66-68; Rep. cand, U.S. Sen, Ga, 68; mem, Rep. Ga. State Cent. Cmt, 68-; Ga. State Sen, 69- Bus. & Prof. Pos: with Proctor and Gamble, 49-51 and Hungerford and Assocs, 54-57; dir. of sales, Opelika Welding Machinery, Inc, 57-64; owner, Patton Assoc, 64- Mil. Serv: Navy, 44-46; reentered serv. as 2nd Lt, Air Force, 51, released as 1st Lt, 53, after serv. in 62nd Troop Carrier Squdron, Japan-Korea Theater, 52-53; Air Medal with Three Battle Stars; Presidential Unit Citation with Two Oak Leaves; Korean Campaign and Southeast Asia Ribbons. Mem: V.chmn, Bd. of Mgt, YMCA; Atlanta Quarterback Club; Capitol Hill Club; Cherokee Town and Country Club. Rel: Presbyterian. Legal Res: 669 Starlight Dr. N.E, Atlanta, Ga. 30305. Mailing Add: 38 Old Ivy Rd. N.E, Atlanta, Ga. 30305.

PATTON, JAMES E. R
b. Ford Co, Ill, 7/16/95; m. 6/14/26 to Gladys Utley; c. James A, William U. and Roger D. Educ: State Col, Cedar Falls, Iowa. Polit. & Govt. Pos: Iowa State Rep, until 68; served in all elective off. of Del. Co. Farm Bur. Bus. & Prof. Pos: Owns 350 acre farm near Manchester, where he was engaged in turkey prod, dairying and beef cattle; retired, 59. Mem: Mason; Shrine; Eastern Star; El Kahir Temple; Am. Legion. Rel: Presbyterian. Mailing Add: 144 W. Howard, Manchester, Iowa 52057. (1967)

PATTON, JAMES R. D
Educ: N.M.M.I, B.S, N.M. State Univ, 6 hours grad. work. Polit. & Govt. Pos: N.Mex. State Sen, 60-66; N.Mex. State House of Reps, 57-59. Bus. & Prof. Pos: Merchant. Mil. Serv: WWII, Korean War. Mailing Add: Drawer P, Las Cruces, N.Mex. 88001. (1967)

PATTON, JAMES WILLIAM R
Kans. State Rep.
b. Hiawatha, Kans, 5/10/16; s. David Wright Patton and Lois Jane Babcock P; m. 3/26/43 to Lyla Alice Peterson; c. Nora Jane (Mrs. Stanfill), Michael David and James A. Educ: Highland Jr. Col, 33-34; Kans. State Univ, B.S, 37; Univ. Wis. Grad. Sch. Banking, grad, 64; Northwest. Univ. Nat. Trust Sch, grad, 66; Gamma Sigma Delta; Farm House. Polit. & Govt. Pos: Chmn, Soil Conserv. Dist, Brown Co, Kans, 58-66; Kans. State Rep, 53rd Dist, 66- Bus. & Prof. Pos: Farmer, Hiawatha, Kans, 37-40 & 46-61; dir, Farm Bur. Mutual Ins. Co, Kans. Farm Life Ins. and Kans. Farm Bur. Ins. Co, 61-66; v.pres, trust officer and dir, Citizens State Bank & Trust, Hiawatha, 61- Mil. Serv: Entered as Pvt, Army Air Force, 40, released as Maj, 46, after serv. in 463rd H Bomb Group, 15th Air Force, ETO, 43-44; Silver Star Medal; Distinguished Flying Cross with Cluster; Air Medal with Clusters; Presidential Unit Citation; French Croix De Guerre with Palm; European and Am. Theatre Ribbons. Mem: Kans. Bankers Asn; Kans. Soc. Farm Mgr. & Appraisers; Kans. Farm Bur.(dir, 61-66); Brown Co. Farm Bur; Brown Co. Ment. Health Asn; Kans. State Univ. Alumni Asn.(past mem. bd. dirs). Leader of the Year Award, Kans. Farm Bur; Balance Farming Award, N.E. Kans. Rel: Methodist; church trustee. Legal Res: R.R. 2, Hiawatha, Kans. 66434. Mailing Add: Box 360, Hiawatha, Kans. 66434.

PATTON, JOHN W. D
Iowa State Sen.
b. Ford Co, Ill, 4/27/05; m. 1/30/32 to Alma Becker; c. Lois Jean and Douglas John. Educ: Pub. Sch. Polit. & Govt. Pos: Iowa State Sen, 65- Bus. & Prof. Pos: Dir, Rural Elec. Co; farmer. Mem: Mason. Rel: Methodist. Mailing Add: Aurora, Iowa 50607.

PATTON, JOHN W. R
Wyo. State Sen.
b. Glendive, Mont, 10/16/30; m. to Virginia; c. Five. Educ: Mont. State Col, 1 year; West. Mont. Col. of Educ, 1 year. Polit. & Govt. Pos: Mem, Sheridan City Coun, Wyo, 59-60; Wyo. State Rep, 61-66; Wyo. State Sen, 66-, mem, Cmt. on Interstate Compact on Educ. and Legis. Interim Cmn, Wyo. State Sen, chmn, Health, Educ. and Welfare Cmt, 69-; chmn, Title III ESEA Adv. Coun, 68-; chmn, Motor Pool Coun, 69-; mem, Wyo. Educ. Coun, 69- Bus. & Prof. Pos: Real estate and ins. Mem: Elks; Eagles; Jr. C. of C; Rotary; Boy Scouts; pres, Cent. Wyo. Coun; Aircraft Owners & Pilots Asn; AF&AM; past pres, C. of C. Received award as Wyo. Outstanding Young Man of the Year, 59. Rel: Episcopal. Mailing Add: 343 Loucks St, Sheridan, Wyo. 82801.

PATTON, WILLIAM B. R
Chmn, Waseca Co. Rep. Cmt, Minn.
b. Mitchell, S.Dak, 2/19/22; s. Blake F. Patton and Myrle J.B. Bratsberg P; m. 12/8/46 to Marvyl Beck; c. Paul B, Daniel S, Patti L. and Robert B. Educ: Mason City Jr. Col, A.A, 41; Univ. Minn. Law Sch, B.S.L. and J.D, 43, Bus. Sch, M.A, 48; Sigma Alpha Epsilon. Polit. & Govt. Pos: Chmn, Waseca Co. Rep. Cmt, Minn, 59-; city attorney, Waseca, 60-66; co. attorney, Waseca Co, 67- Bus. & Prof. Pos: Teaching asst, Univ. Minn. Bus. Sch, Minneapolis, 47-48; attorney, Stone, Iversen & Patton, Waseca, 48-50; partnership in garage, Patton Chevrolet Co, 50-57; attorney, Iversen & Patton, 57- Mil. Serv: Entered as Seaman, Naval Res, 41, released as Lt.(sg), 46, after serv. in Pac. and Asian Command, 43-46; Philippine Combat Ribbon with Battle Star; Bronze Star; Navy and Marine Corps Medal. Mem: Am. and Minn. Bar Asns; Am. and Minn. Trial Lawyers Asns; Nat. Dist. Attorneys Asn; Am. Legion; VFW; Rotary; C. of C; Waseca Lakeside Club. Rel: Congregational. Legal Res: 819 Fifth Ave. S.E, Waseca, Minn. 56093. Mailing Add: 213 N. State St, Waseca, Minn. 56093.

PAUKEN, THOMAS WEIR R
b. Victoria, Tex, 1/11/44; s. Thomas Nicholas Pauken and Patricia Weir P; single. Educ: Georgetown Univ, A.B. in Govt, 64, M.A. in Govt, 66. Polit. & Govt. Pos: Staff asst. to Sen. John Tower, 61-62; staff asst. to Rep. Bill Stinson, 62-64; mem. res. div, Rep. Nat. Cmt, 64; nat. chmn, Col. Rep. Nat. Cmt, 65-67. Publ: 'The New Campus Left,' Am. Security Coun, 10/65. Mem: Founder and chmn, Nat. Student Cmt. for Defense of Vietnam. Rel: Catholic. Legal Res: 5838 Meaders Lane, Dallas, Tex. 75230. Mailing Add: 1625 Eye St. N.W, Washington, D.C. 20006. (1967)

PAUL, EDMUND LAURENCE D
b. Rutland, Vt, 4/11/03; div; c. Two. Educ: Rutland, Vt. and Lawrence, Mass. schs. Polit. & Govt. Pos: Vt. State Rep, 63-66; justice of peace; assoc. of Mary Fletcher Hosp. Bus. & Prof. Pos: R.R. sta. agent. Mem: Order of R.R. Telegraphers; St. Edmund's Asn. Rel: Catholic. Mailing Add: Alburg, Vt. 05440. (1967)

PAUL, FREDA NOBLE D
b. Ansted, Fayette, W.Va, 11/26/15; d. Clifton Edward Noble and Mamie Neal N; m. 12/31/38 to Bosher Hubert P; c. Wanda Lou (Mrs. Charles Cummings). Educ: Marshall Univ, B.A. and M.A; Alpha Sigma Alpha. Polit. & Govt. Pos: W.Va. State Del, 64-68. Bus. & Prof. Pos: Educator. Mem: Eastern Star; Am. Asn. of Univ. Women; Woman's Club of Beverly Hills; Huntington Bird Club; Chesapeake and Ohio Hosp. Auxiliary; Dem. Woman's Club of Huntington. Rel: Baptist. Mailing Add: 2814 Washington Blvd, Huntington, W.Va. 25705.

PAUL, HERBERT O. D
b. Wharton Co, Tex, 4/24/02; s. A.C. Paul and Nellie Obenhaus P; m. 1/6/34 to Ruth Boothe; c. Julie (Mrs. Charlie Joyce). Polit. & Govt. Pos: Del, Precinct, Co. and State Dem. Conv, Tex, many times; del, Dem. Nat. Conv, 68; mem, Tex. Emergency Resources Planning Cmn, currently; mem. adv. bd, Statewide Planning for Voc. Rehabilitation Serv, Tex, currently. Bus. & Prof. Pos: Businessman, farmer and rancher, currently. Mem: Mason; Lions; C. of C; Brotherhood of Locomotive Engrs.(chmn. and legis. rep, Tex. State Legis. Bd, 54-). Rel: Baptist. Legal Res: 1707 W. 31st, Austin, Tex. 78703. Mailing Add: 1010 Lavaca St, Room 312, Austin, Tex. 78701.

PAUL, JOHN ABBOTT R
Chmn, Harrisonburg Rep. Town Cmt, Va.
b. Panama, C.Z, 3/22/38; s. Seymour Paul and Ruth Jane Abbott P; m. 6/7/63 to Bonnie Dold Lineweaver; c. Penelope Jane and John Abraham. Educ: Washington & Lee Univ, Va, B.A, magna cum laude, 59, Law Sch, LL.B, magna cum laude, 62; Univ. Va, Charlottesville, 59-60; Order of the Coif; Omicron Delta Kappa. Polit. & Govt. Pos: Chmn, Harrisonburg Rep. Town Cmt, Va, 65-; secy, Bi-Racial Cmn, Harrisonburg, 66-68; alternate del, Rep. Nat. Conv, 68; city attorney, Harrisonburg, 68- Bus. & Prof. Pos: Attorney, U.S. Atomic Energy Cmn, Germantown, Md, 62; attorney at law, Harrisonburg, 65-; asst. prof. govt, Madison Col, 66- Mil. Serv: Entered as Lt, Army, 62, released as Capt, 65, after serv. in Judge Adv. Gen. Corp. Mem: Am, Va. and Rockingham Bar Asns; Elks; VFW; Am. Legion; Harrisonburg Jaycees (dir); Rockingham Chap. Va. Mus. Fine Arts (past pres); Rockingham Hist. Soc. Rel: Episcopal; Vestryman and Sunday Sch. Teacher, Emmanuel Episcopal Church. Mailing Add: 504 S. Mason St, Harrisonburg, Va. 22801.

PAUL, MADELINE RULE R
b. Vershire, Orange, Vt, 8/6/92; wid. Educ: Thetford Acad, 10. Polit. & Govt. Pos: Vt. State Rep, 59-61 & 65-66; secy, Rep. Town Cmt; secy. and treas, Orange Co. Rep. Cmt; Libr. trustee. Bus. & Prof. Pos: Retired; former teacher, merchant and ins. agent. Mem: Eastern Star (charter mem, past matron, and present secy, Lake Fairlee Chap. 98); U.I. Club (secy). Rel: Congregational; Secy, W. Fairlee Congregational Church. Mailing Add: West Fairlee, Vt. 05045. (1967)

PAULEY, EDWIN WENDELL D
Mem, Calif. Dem. State Cent. Cmt.
b. Indianapolis, Ind, 1/7/03; s. Elbert L. Pauley and Ellen Van Petten P; m. 10/23/37 to Barbara Jean McHenry; c. Edwin W, Jr, Stephen McHenry, Susan (Mrs. Hillyer) and Robert Van Petten. Educ: Univ. Calif, B.S, 22 and M.S, 23, hon. LL.D, 56. Polit. & Govt. Pos: Regent, Univ. Calif, 39-, chmn. bd. regents, 56-58 & 60-62; petroleum coordinator for European War on Petroleum Lend-Lease Supplies for Russia and the United Kingdom, 41; treas. and secy, Dem. Nat. Cmt, 41-43; indust. and commercial adv, Tri-Part Potsdam Conf, 45; U.S. Ambassador, Allied Cmn. on Reparations, 45-46; Spec. Asst. Secy. of Army, 47; spec. adv. on reparations to Secy. of State, 47-48; mem, Calif. Dem. State Cent. Cmt, currently. Bus. & Prof. Pos: Founder and chmn. bd, Pauley Petroleum Inc, Los Angeles, Calif; mem, bd. trustees, Occidental Col; mem. governing bd, Ga. Mil. Acad; dir, West. Airlines and Eversharp, Inc. Mem: Pres, Los Angeles World Affairs Coun. Rel: Protestant. Legal Res: 9521 Sunset Blvd, Beverly Hills, Calif. 90210. Mailing Add: 10000 Santa Monica Blvd, Los Angeles, Calif. 90067.

PAULEY, HARRY R. D
W.Va. State Del, Speaker of House
b. Keystone, McDowell, W.Va, 2/19/07; s. Emory Preston and Etta Redmond P; m. 8/3/27 to Jessie M. Lambert; c. Harriet E.(Mrs. George N. Peraldo). Educ: Bus. training courses. Polit. & Govt. Pos: W.Va. State Del. and Speaker, W.Va. House of Del, currently; chmn, McDowell Co. Dem. Party, currently. Bus. & Prof. Pos: Contracting, real estate and coal bus, currently v.pres, Bank of Iaeger. Mem: Mason; Odd Fellows; Rotary. Rel: Methodist. Mailing Add: Iaeger, W.Va. 24844. (1967)

PAULEY, JACK L. D
b. Drybranch, Kanawha, W.Va, 11/30/38; s. Jess W. Pauley and Belva Slack P; single. Educ: Morris Harvey Col, B.A; Marshall Univ; Psi Sigma Psi; Tau Kappa Epsilon Int; Tau Kappa Epsilon. Polit. & Govt. Pos: Mem. adv. bd, 62-63; chmn, Membership Dr. for Young Dem. Club; pres, Morris Harvey Young Dem. Club; W.Va. State Del, 64-66. Bus. & Prof. Pos: Jr. high sch. teacher. Mem: Elks; Young Dem. Club; Nat. Educ. Asn; WVEA; Am. Fedn. of Teachers; Alumni Asn; Upper Kanawha Valley Coon Hunters Club, Inc. Rel: Baptist. Mailing Add: Surface St, East Bank, W.Va. 25067. (1967)

PAULIN, CAMILLE A. R
Chmn, Montague Rep. Town Cmt, Mass.
b. Wotton, Que, Can, 2/2/07; s. Achille T. Paulin and Eugenie Leroux P; m. 8/14/33 to Anita C. Roy; c. Jeannette T.(Mrs. Gerald T. Smart), L. Roy, Philip E, Francis E, Rita G.(Mrs. John A. Sak), George A, Adele M. and Camilla A.(Mrs. Douglas F. Pratt). Educ: Master Barbers of Am, Art and Sci. of Barbering, grad. Polit. & Govt. Pos: Cmnr,.Bd. Registrn. of Barbers, Mass, 54-57 & 66-; chmn, Montague Rep. Town Cmt, 57-59 & 64-; treas, Franklin Co. Rep. Club, 61-; mem, Rep. Club, Mass, 61-66; mem, Montague Bd. of Health, 67-, secy, 68- Bus. & Prof. Pos: Registered Barber, 33-; registered instr, Art and Sci. of Barbering. Mem: Rotary; Turners Falls C, K. of C; Int. Union Am, Journeymen Barbers; assoc, Master Barbers of Am; Hampshire-Franklin Coun. Boy Scouts, 47-57; pres, St. Anne's Guild. Rel: Roman Catholic. Mailing Add: 23 Fifth St, Turners Falls, Mass. 01376.

PAULINO, LEONARDO SAN NICOLAS D
Sen, Guam Legis.
b. Inarajan, Guam, 9/20/25; s. Vicente Torres Paulino and Ana Camacho San Nicolas P; m. 6/26/47 to Cleotilde Cruz Camacho; c. Crescencia P.(Mrs. Rudy L.G. Baza), Alvina C, Margaret Mary, Mildred Ann, Elaine Sylvia, Andrew C, Leonard, James, Vincent, Gerard and Eugene. Educ: George Wash. High Sch, Guam, 45-47. Polit. & Govt. Pos: Finance chmn, Dem. Party, Guam, 67-68; Sen, Guam Legis, 67- Bus. & Prof. Pos: School teacher, Dept. of Educ, Govt, Guam, 47-49; bus. mgr, Pac. Meat & Produce Corp, 49-54; gen. mgr and proprietor, Meat Market, 54- Rel: Roman Catholic. Legal Res: Route 4, Sinajana, Guam 96910. Mailing Add: P.O. Box 951, Agana, Guam 96910.

PAULL, RICHARD CARY R
Chmn, Westport Point Rep. Town Cmt, Mass.
b. Framingham, Mass, 12/26/41; s. Richard Paull and Lucia Beecher Kerr P; m. 6/15/63 to Martha Caroline Holman; c. Richard Cranston. Educ: Harvard Col, B.A, 63; Boston Univ. Sch. of Law, LL.B, 66; Hasty Pudding. Polit. & Govt. Pos: Mem, Westport Point Rep. Town Cmt, Mass, 67-, finance chmn, 68, chmn, 68- Bus. & Prof. Pos: Lawyer, Paull & Paull, New Bedford, Mass, 66- Mem: Mass. and New Bedford Bar Asns; Wamsutta Club. Mailing Add: 15 Cape Bial Lane, Westport Point, Mass. 02791.

PAULO, WALTER H. R
Ohio State Rep.
b. Mansfield, Ohio; m. to Dorothy Catlin; c. Mrs. Gloria Jean Meerman.

Polit. & Govt. Pos: Ohio State Rep, 67-; alternate del, Rep. Nat. Conv, 68. Bus. & Prof. Pos: Mem. staff, Pan Atlas Travel Serv; chmn. bd. Isaly Dairy Co, 24-65. Mem: Kiwanis; Int. Inst; YMCA; C. of C; South Side Bus. and Civic Club; St. Albans Lodge; Farm Bur; past pres, Youngstown Fresh Air Camp, Mahoning Saddle and Bridle Asn; Youngstown Dairy Coun; past chmn, Am. Red Cross, Youngstown Charity Horse Show, United Appeal; dir, Jr. Achievement, Mahoning Nat. Bank; exec. cmt, Youngstown Area Develop. Found; chmn, Mahoning Co. U.S. Savings Bond Sales. Rel: Christian. Mailing Add: State Capitol Bldg, Columbus, Ohio 43215. (1967)

PAULSON, CLAYTON CLARENCE D
b. Ogden, Iowa, 6/9/01; s. Herman Paulson and Katherine Kruse P; m. 5/3/21 to Albey Louise Arduser; c. Conrad. Educ: Pub. schs, N.Dak. Polit. & Govt. Pos: Twp. assessor, Marion, N.Dak, 12 years; N.Dak. State Sen, 56-66; mem, Agr. Stabilization Conserv. Serv, 63- Bus. & Prof. Pos: Farmer; dir. and secy, Marion Equity Elevator, 15 years. Mem: Farmers Union; pres, N.Dak. Dairy Show, one year, dir, 12 years. Judge of cattle, Brandon and Winnipeg Can. Shows; received ribbons and awards for championship purebred cattle shown at N.Dak. and Can. Fairs. Mailing Add: Marion, N.Dak. 58466.

PAULSON, HERMAN R
S.Dak. State Rep.
b. Hudson, S.Dak, 1/2/16; m. to Edna Peterson; c. Helen, Louise, Donna, Paul, Donald and Harlan. Educ: Augustana Acad, Canton, S.Dak. Polit. & Govt. Pos: Mem. bd, Canton Inwood Hosp; mem. twp. bd, 15 years; mem. sch. bd, 9 years; S.Dak. State Rep, 60- Bus. & Prof. Pos: Farming and livestock feeder. Rel: Lutheran. Mailing Add: Hudson, S.Dak. 57034. (1967)

PAULSON, WILLIAM LEE
Assoc. Justice, N.Dak. Supreme Court
b. Valley City, N.Dak, 9/3/13; s. Alfred Parker Paulson and Inga Wold P; m. 9/8/38 to Jane Elizabeth Graves; c. John Thomas and Mary Elizabeth. Educ: Valley City State Col, B.A, 35; Law Sch, Univ. of N.Dak, LL.B, 37; Beta Theta Pi; Phi Delta Phi. Polit. & Govt. Pos: States Attorney, Barnes Co, N.Dak, 41-50, Valley City, 59-66; Assoc. Justice, N.Dak. Supreme Court, 67- Bus. & Prof. Pos: Mem. bd. of dirs, Am. Nat. Bank of Valley City, N.Dak, 38- and Valley City Civic and Commerce Bank, 54-60. Mem: Jaycees (pres, Valley City Chap, 44, regional v-pres, N.Dak. Chap, 45); pres, Barnes Co. Bar Asn, 55; N.Dak. State and Am. Bar Asns; Am. Judicature Soc; pres, N.Dak. States Attorneys Asn, 64; state dir, Nat. Dist. Attorneys Asn, 64-65; Elks; K. of P; AF&AM; Shrine; Farm Bur; N.Dak. Farmers Union; N.Dak. Peace Officers Asn. Rel: Episcopal; Chancellor of the Episcopal Church of N.Dak. Legal Res: 361 College St. S.W, Valley City, N.Dak. 58072. Mailing Add: 1009 E. Highland Acres Rd, Bismarck, N.Dak. 58501.

PAULY, GREGORY EMIL R
Chmn, Calumet Co. Rep. Party, Wis.
b. Manitowoc, Wis, 2/23/26; s. Emil Joseph Pauly and Eulalia Becker P; m. 8/7/48 to Dolores Langenfeld; c. Jeffrey Emil, Susan Louise, Michael Adolph and Robert Gregory. Educ: Marquette Univ, B.S, 51. Polit. & Govt. Pos: Chmn, Calumet Co. Rep. Party, Wis, 66- Bus. & Prof. Pos: Dir, Nat. Asn. of Direct Selling Companies, 54. Mil. Serv: Seaman, Navy, 44-46, released after serv. in Armed Guard, ETO. Rel: Roman Catholic. Mailing Add: 1712 Circle Dr, New Holstein, Wis. 53061.

PAULY, HELEN
b. Galena, Mo, 3/7/05; d. Jackson Grant Short and Permelia Long S; m. 9/5/22 to Fred W. Pauly; wid; c. Mary P. and John Frederick. Educ: Ozark Wesleyan Acad; Wichita Bus. Col. Polit. & Govt. Pos: Secy. to U.S. Rep. O. Clark Fisher, currently. Mem: Past matron and past dist. dep. grandmatron, Eastern Star; Church of Epiphany. Rel: Episcopal. Legal Res: San Angelo, Tex. Mailing Add: 439 New Jersey Ave. S.E, Washington, D.C, 20003.

PAVETTI, FRANCIS JAMES D
Committeeman, Conn. Dem. State Cent. Cmt.
b. New Haven, Conn, 12/14/31; s. Frank J. Pavetti and Ellen Dawson P; m. 7/5/58 to Sally Thomas; c. Leah. Educ: Univ. Conn, B.S, 53; Boston Col. Law Sch, LL.B, 59; Sigma Chi. Polit. & Govt. Pos: Law clerk for Judge J. Joseph Smith, U.S. Dist. Court, 59-60; chmn, Waterford Dem. Town Cmt, Conn; mem, Waterford Develop. and Indust. Cmn, 62-66; committeeman, Conn. Dem. State Cent. Cmt, currently; mem, Rules Cmt, Conn. Dem. Party, 64. Bus. & Prof. Pos: Attorney, Dupont, Pavetti & Dupont, 66- Mil. Serv: Entered as 2nd Lt, Air Force, 53, released as 1st Lt, 55; 1st Lt, Air Force Res. Mem: Cmt. on Judicial Admin, Am. Bar Asn; Cmt. on Uniform Laws and Fed. Bench Bar Cmt, Conn. Bar Asn; New London Co. Bar Asn; Advocate, K. of C; Elks; secy. and trustee, Eugene O'Neil Mem. Theater Found. Rel: Roman Catholic. Mailing Add: 8 Woodbine St, Waterford, Conn. 06385.

PAVICH, EMIL SAM D
Chmn, Pottawattamie Dem. Cent. Cmt, Iowa
b. Council Bluffs, Iowa, 7/30/31; s. Guy Pavich and Josephine Pavelich P; single. Polit. & Govt. Pos: Pres, Pottawattamie Co. Young Dem, 56; precinct committeeman, Pottawattamie Dem. Cmt, 58-; seventh dist. committeeman, Iowa Young Dem, 59-60 and v.pres, 60-62; treas, Pottawattamie Dem. Cent. Cmt, Iowa, 64-66 and chmn, 66-; mem, Govt. Cmt. on Employ. of the Physically Handicapped, 66-68. Mil. Serv: Entered as Pvt, Army, 52, released as Pfc, 54. Mem: Local 50, Grain Millers Union; Pottawattamie Co. Historical Soc; trustee, Council Bluffs Cmt. on Polit. Educ, 58-60. Rel: Catholic. Mailing Add: 1706 15th Ave, Council Bluffs, Iowa 51501.

PAVLAK, RAYMOND DFL
Minn. State Rep.
b. 1926; married; c. Four. Educ: St. Thomas Col; St. Paul Col. of Law. Polit. & Govt. Pos: Minn. State Rep, 64- Bus. & Prof. Pos: Lawyer with Beaudoin and Pavlak; formerly assoc. with Cert. Pub. Acct. firm. Mil. Serv: Navy. Mem: Bar asns; various civic and fraternal orgns. Mailing Add: 817 Park Lane, South St. Paul, Minn. 55075. (1967)

PAVLAK, ROBERT LEO Independent
Minn. State Rep.
b. St. Paul, Minn, 7/18/24; s. Leo R. Pavlak (deceased) and Pauline Wolanski P. (deceased); m. 4/7/51 to Edel Ruth L. Monrad; c. Catherine, Mary, Susan, Christine, Robert, Jr. and David; guardian for Steven and Douglas Monrad. Polit. & Govt. Pos: Minn. State Rep, Dist. 43A, 67- Bus. & Prof. Pos: Sgt, Police Dept, St. Paul, Minn; coordinator, St. Paul Civil Defense Police. Mil. Serv: Entered as Pvt, Marine Corps Res, 42, released as Cpl, 45, after serv. in Pac; Pac. Theater Ribbons; Sgt, Army Res, 50. Mem: Little League (Riverview dir); Winter Carnival Jr. Royalty (chmn, S.Wind Cmt); past pres, Baker Playground Asn, St. Matthews Men's Club and St. Matthews Home and Sch; Humboldt High Sch. and Douglas-Bryant PTA; past v.pres, Police Local 985. Rel: Catholic. Mailing Add: 116 W. Belvidere, St. Paul, Minn. 55107. (1967)

PAWLEY, WILLIAM DOUGLAS
b. Florence, S.C, 9/7/96; s. Edward Porcher Pawley and Irene Wallace P; m. 7/25/19 to Annie Hahr Dobbs; div; m. 6/30/43 to Edna Earle Cadenhead; c. William Douglas, Annie Hahr (Mrs. Hobert Boomer McKay) and Irene Wallace (Mrs. Kenneth H. Hearn). Polit, & Govt. Pos: U.S. Ambassador to Peru, 45-46, Brazil, 46-48; del, Inter-Am. Conf. for Continental Peace and Security, Brazil, 47; spec. asst. to Secy. of State, UN Gen. Assembly, 48, del, Ninth Int. Conf. of Am. States, Bogotá, Columbia, 48; spec. asst. to Secy of Defense, Paris, and to Secy. State, D.C, 51; del, NATO Conf, Lisbon, 52; spec. assignment, Dept. of State, 54. Bus. & Prof. Pos: Pres, Co. Nacional Cubana de Aviacion Curtiss, Havana, 28-32; pres, Intercontinent Corp, N.Y. and China Nat. Aviation Corp, Shanghai, 33, Hindustan Aircraft Co, Bangalore, India, 40; pres. and owner, Miami Transit Co. and Miami Beach Rwy. Co, 54-62; dir, Fla. Nat. Bank. of Miami; pres, Talisman Sugar Corp, Fla, 64. Mem: Sponsor's cmt, Liberation of Cuban POW; cmt. of 21, Indust. Develop. Coun, Miami; chmn, bd. gov, Gr. Miami Philharmonic Soc; trustee, Miami-Dade Jr. Col. and United Fund; Miami-Dade Co. C. of C; nat. bd, Boys' Clubs Am. Organized Flying Tigers, Am. Vol. Group, World War II, 40; Man of Year award, Alianza Interamericana, 59. U.S. Medal for Merit; Air Medal, Peru; Grand Cross, Brazil; Grand Cross, Cuba; Order of the Brilliant Star, Rep. of China. Legal Res: 2555 Lake Ave, Sunset Island 2, Miami Beach, Fla. Mailing Add: Suite 711, 100 Biscayne Tower, 100 Biscayne Blvd, Miami, Fla. 33132.

PAXSON, C. ARMONDE D
Va. State Del.
b. Waterford, Va, 10/30/05; m. to Helen Post P. Educ: Mercersburg Acad; Univ. Va; Phi Alpha Delta; Phi Sigma Kappa. Polit. & Govt. Pos: Va. State Del, 62-; alternate del, Dem. Nat. Conv, 68. Bus. & Prof. Pos: Dir, Citizens Bank and Trust Co, Tandem Corp, Davis Motors, Murphy Ins. and Travel Inc. Mem: Mem. cmt. on unauthorized practice of law, Coun. of Va. State Bar; past chmn, Va. Conf. of Bar Pres; past pres, Charlottesville-Albermarle Bar Asn; bd, Charlottesville-Albermarle Ment. Health Asn; Charlottesville-Albermarle C. of C; Va. and Am. Bar Asn; Am. Judicature Soc; Am. Col. Trial Lawyers; Va. Trial Lawyers Asn; Belgian Nautical Research Asn; Am. Acad. of Polit. and Soc. Sci; Nautical Research Guild; Farmington Club; Redland Club, pres, 63-64; past pres, Kiwanis; past exalted ruler, Elks; Student Aid Found; Va. Yacht Club; Fedn. of Ins. Counsel; Navy League. Rel: Baptist. Mailing Add: 435 Park St, Charlottesville, Va. 22901.

PAXTON, RALPH EUGENE R
Mem, La. State Rep. Cent. Cmt.
b. Boone, Iowa, 12/11/01; s. Charles Cook Paxton and Mary Catharine Teagarden P; m. 12/19/25 to Cleve Squires Welsh; c. Ward Robert (deceased). Educ: Iowa State Univ, B.S. in Elec. Eng, 24, E.E, 29; Eta Kappa Nu; Kappa Sigma. Polit. & Govt. Pos: Mem, La. State Rep. Cent. Cmt, currently; chmn, Washington Parish Rep. Party. Mil. Serv: Entered as Lt, Naval Res, 42, released as Lt. Comdr, 45, after serv. in Naval Mine Sweeping Trial Bd; Am. Theater Ribbon; Chief of Naval Operations Letter of Commendation. Mem: Soc. Am. Military Engrs; Inst. Elec. and Electronics Engrs; Am. Legion; Rotary; C. of C. Iowa State and Nat. Honors in basketball. Rel: Protestant. Mailing Add: 1628 Piney Branch Rd, Bogalusa, La. 70427.

PAYNE, DALE L. R
b. Smith Co, Kans, 11/27/17; m. Nov. 1948 to Eleanor Petrasek. Educ: Glendale Jr. Col, Glendale, Calif; Walla Walla Col, Wash. Polit. & Govt. Pos: Nebr. State Sen, until 68. Bus. & Prof. Pos: Real estate broker and bldg. contractor; former mgr, Nebr. New Car Dealers Asn. and Omaha Zone Chevrolet Dealers Asn. Mem: Am. Legion. Mailing Add: 3309 Madison, Bellevue, Nebr. 68005. (1967)

PAYNE, EDWARD M, III D
b. White Sulphur Springs, 3/9/36; s. E.M. Payne, Jr. and Genevieve Wyatt P. (deceased); single. Educ: Davidson Col, B.A, 58; Univ. Va, LL.B, 62. Polit. & Govt. Pos: Secy. and mem. bd. dirs, Beckley-Raleigh Co. YMCA; mem, Planning and Zoning Cmn. of Beckley; chmn, Beckley Dem. Exec. Cmt, 63; City Attorney for Beckley, 63; W.Va. State Del, 64-68; Bus. & Prof. Pos: Secy. and mem. bd. dirs, Beckley Bus. Develop. Corp; mem. bd. dirs, Bank of Raleigh and McCreery Coal Land Co; exec. v.pres. and mem. bd. dirs, Piney Coking Coal Land Co; pres, E.M. Payne Co; lawyer. Mil. Serv: Commissioned 2nd Lt, Army, 58; now serving as 1st Lt, Army Res. Mem: Moose; Elks; Rotary; Jr. C. of C; Black Knight Country Club; Beckley-Raleigh Co. C. of C; W.Va. State Bar; Am, W.Va, and Raleigh Co. Bar Asns; Rel: Episcopal. Legal Res: 1014 Johnstown Rd, Beckley, W.Va. 25801. Mailing Add: Law Bldg, Beckley, W.Va. 25801. (1967)

PAYNE, FREDERICK GEORGE R
b. Lewiston, Maine, 7/24/04; s. Frederick George Payne and Nellie Grant Smart P; m. to Ella Hodgdon; c. E. Thomas and Putnam. Educ: Bentley Col. of Acct. and Finance, Boston, Mass; Kappa Pi Alpha. Polit. & Govt. Pos: Mayor, Augusta, Maine, 35-41; Cmnr. of Finance and Budget Dir, Maine, 40-42; Gov, 49-53; U.S. Sen, Maine, 53-59. Bus. & Prof. Pos: Chief disbursement auditor, N.E. Div, Publix Theaters Corp, 25-29; gen. mgr. of theaters, Maine and N.H. Theater Co, 29-35; indust. develop. consult, Cent.

Maine Power Co, 37-40; bus. and indust. consult, self employed, 59- Mil. Serv: Entered as Capt, Air Force, 42, released as Lt. Col, 44; Air Force Commendation Medal. Publ: Author of legislation including Housing for Aged, Study of Effects of Atomic Fallout and Aid to Distressed Areas. Mem: Am. Legion; Lions; numerous charitable orgns. Rel: Protestant. Mailing Add: Main St, Waldoboro, Maine 04572.

PAYNE, GARY EDISON D
Okla. State Rep.
b. Denison, Tex, 10/31/44; s. Thomas Edison Payne and Jeanne Landram P; m. 3/27/66 to Suzanne Major Farris. Educ: Okla. State Univ, B.S; Univ. Okla. Sch. Law, LL.B; Sigma Nu; Phi Alpha Delta; Young Dem; Student Union Activities Bd; Interfraternity Coun. Polit. & Govt. Pos: Committeeman, Okla. State Univ. Young Dem, 62-63; Okla. State Rep, 69- Bus. & Prof. Pos: Legis. intern, Okla. Legis. Coun, 66-67; asst. to legal officer, State Dept. Pub. Safety, 68; attorney-at-law, Atoka, Okla, 69- Mil. Serv: 2nd Lt, Okla. Nat. Guard, 69- Mem: Am, Okla, Atoka Co. and Marshall Co. Bar Asns; Marshall Co. Jr. C. of C; Atoka Co. C. of C; Okla. State Univ. Alumni Asn; Order of the Red Red Rose. Lew Wentz Scholarship; Ford Found. Legis. Intern Grant. Rel: Baptist. Legal Res: Box 427, Madill, Okla. 73446. Mailing Add: Box 250, Atoka, Okla. 74525.

PAYNE, HOWARD E. R
Chmn, Exec. Cmt, Mich. Rep. State Cent. Cmt.
b. Conneaut, Ohio, 4/3/34; s. Berton E. Payne and Phyllis Hughes P. Educ: Cleveland Inst. of Art, BFA, 56. Polit. & Govt. Pos: Mem. bd. dirs, Dearborn Heights Rep. Club, Inc, 60-; precinct del, 15th Cong. Dist. Rep. Party, Dearborn Heights, 64-, chmn. precinct develop, 64-, second v.chmn, 68-; del, Rep. State Conv, 64-; mem. exec. cmt, Mich. Rep. State Cent. Cmt, 65-, chmn. exec. cmt, 67-; mem. exec. cmt, Mich. Rep. State Finance Cmt, 67-; del, Rep. Nat. Conv, 68. Bus. & Prof. Pos: Indust. Designer and Design Consultant, Ford Motor Co, Dearborn, 56- Mem: Elks; Dearborn Inter-Faith Action Council. Mailing Add: 6101 Burger Ave, Dearborn Heights, Mich. 48127.

PAYNE, JOHN HOWARD R
b. Hartford City, Ind, 8/21/06; s. William E. Payne and Katharine Curry P; m. 8/18/32 to Eelene Roberts; c. Katharine, Elizabeth and John. Educ: Butler Univ, B.S, 27; Univ. Cincinnati, M.A, 28 and Ph.D, 30; Univ. of Munich, 31; Sigma Xi; Alpha Chi Sigma. Polit. & Govt. Pos: V.chmn, Hawaii State Bd. Educ, 61-63; mem, State Rep. Cent. Cmt; chmn, Honolulu Co. Rep. Party, Hawaii, 65-67. Bus. & Prof. Pos: Res. chemist, E.I. du Pont de Nemours, 30-32; prof, Univ. Hawaii, 32-40; dir. of research, Pac. Chem. & Fertilizer Co, 40-47; head dept. sugar tech, Hawaiian Sugar Planters Asn, 48-67; v.pres, Am. Factors Assocs, Honolulu, 67- Publ: Principles of Sugar Technology, Elesevier, 55-57; tech. papers in publ. of Am. Chem. Soc, Int. Soc. of Sugar Cane Technologists, Hawaiian Sugar Technologists and diversified sugar jour. Mem: Am. Chem. Soc; fel, Am. Inst. of Chemists; Int. Soc. of Sugar Cane Technologists; Am. Asn. for Adv. of Sci; Int. Cmn. for Uniform Methods of Sugar Analyses. Rel: Protestant. Mailing Add: 2260 Cooper Rd, Honolulu, Hawaii 96822.

PAYNE, JOSEPH BEVLEY R
b. Leesburg, Va, 12/15/94; s. Appleton C. Payne and Emma N. Kirby P; m. 11/20/19 to Mary Ellen Roby. Polit. & Govt. Pos: Md. State Del, 35-66. Mil. Serv: Pvt, Army, 17-24; Purple Heart. Mem: Am. Legion; Lions; Mason (32°); Ali Ghan Shrine; Eagles; Moose; K. of P. Rel: Baptist. Mailing Add: 409 E. Potomac, Brunswick, Md. 21716. (1967)

PAYNE, NANCY KENT R
b. Lynchburg, Va, 12/6/35; d. Cloyd Martin and Nancy Mann Johnson Martin Wright; m. 2/2/60 to John Miller Payne; c. Nancy Garland and Mary Margaret. Educ: Phillips' Bus. Col, Lynchburg, Va, 1 year; Randolph-Macon Woman's Col, spec. courses, currently. Polit. & Govt. Pos: Secy, Lynchburg Rep. City Cmt, Va, 52-53, mem, 54-55 & 60-65, v.chmn, 60-62; sixth dist. rep, Young Rep. Exec. Cmt, 54-55; v.chmn, Young Rep. Fedn. of Va, 55-57, secy, 58-60; sixth dist. rep, Va. Rep. Adv. Legis. Cmt. Sub-cmt. on Voting Laws, 63-; Rep. mem, Lynchburg Electorial Bd, 65-; v.chairwoman, sixth dist. Va. Rep. Exec. Cmt, 67-69; alternate del, Rep. Nat. Conv, 68. Bus. & Prof. Pos: Advert. Dir, Baldwin's Dept. Store, Lynchburg, 52-54; mem. make-up, The Daily Progress Newspaper, Chville, 54-55; asst. soc. ed, The Lynchburg News, Lynchburg, 56-57; adv. copywriter, Heironimus of Roanoke, 57-58; advert. dir, Rucker-Rosenstock Dept. Store, Petersburg, 58-60. Mem: The Jr. League of Lynchburg; DAR (mem. bd, Lynchburg Chap). The Lynchburg Jr. Woman's Club; Boonsboro Country Club; The Capitol Hill Club, Washington, D.C. Recognized as the world's youngest store advert. mgr. at age 17. Rel: Presbyterian; Choir, First Presbyterian Church. Mailing Add: 106 Linden Ave, Lynchburg, Va. 24503.

PAYNE, ROBERT FORREST, JR. R
Mont. State Rep.
b. Bozeman, Mont, 7/21/28; s. Robert F. Payne, Sr. and Edith Proffitt P; m. 2/14/47 to Irene A. Swandal; c. Larry R, James H. and Janice E. Educ: Wilsall High Sch, Mont, dipl, 46. Polit. & Govt. Pos: Mont. State Rep, Missoula Co, 69- Bus. & Prof. Pos: Mgr. retail yards, Anaconda Bldg. Materials Co, 5 years. Mil. Serv: Entered as Pvt, Marines, 45, released as Pfc, 46. Mem: Elks; Mason. Rel: American Lutheran. Mailing Add: 3109 Park St, Missoula, Mont. 59801.

PAYNE, S. TILFORD, JR. R
Chmn, Louisville and Jefferson Co. Rep. Exec. Cmt, Ky.
b. Louisville, Ky, 9/6/14; s. S. Tilford Payne and Ethel Longest P; m. 4/26/47 to Anne M. Brown; c. Anne Tilford and Edith Brown. Educ: Washington and Lee Univ, LL.B, 37; Phi Delta Phi; Pi Kappa Alpha. Polit. & Govt. Pos: Chmn, Rep. Policy Cmt, 58-61; chmn, Louisville and Jefferson Co. Rep. Exec. Cmt, Ky, 63-; alternate del, Rep. Nat. Conv, 68. Bus. & Prof. Pos: Treas, Louisville Bar Asn, 59, secy, 60. Mil. Serv: Entered as Pvt, Marine Corps, 42, released as Cmnr. Warrant Officer, 46, after serv. in 3rd Marine Air Wing, S.Pac; Pac. Theater Ribbon. Mem: Am. and Ky. Bar Asns; Rotary. Rel: Presbyterian. Mailing Add: 405 Mayfair Lane, Louisville, Ky. 40207.

PAYTON, HENRY N. D
b. Coweta Co, Ga; s. Eugene Payton and Ida Dyer P; m. 9/21/46 to Rosemary Bates; c. Gail and Suzanne. Educ: Woodrow Wilson Col. of Law, 40. Polit. & Govt. Pos: Mem. staff, State of Ga. Dept. of Law, 46; asst. attorney gen, Ga, 47-48; Ga. State Rep, 57-64. Bus. & Prof. Pos: Attorney-at-law. Mil. Serv: Capt, Army, 42-46. Rel: Methodist. Mailing Add: Newnan, Ga. 30263.

PAYTON, WILLIS OSBORNE D
Chmn, Valley Co. Dem. Party, Idaho
b. Preston, Idaho, 12/11/11; s. Chester Hall Payton and Louise Jacobson P; m. 10/23/33 to Opal Nevada Beard. Educ: West Jordan High Sch, grad. Polit. & Govt. Pos: Idaho State Rep, 51-53; Idaho State Committeeman, Valley Co, 51-55; del, Dem. Nat. Conv, 60, 64 & 68, chmn. Idaho Del, 68; chmn, Valley Co. Dem. Party, Idaho, and mem, Idaho Dem. State Exec. Cmt, 66-; Idaho chmn, Humphrey-Muskie Campaign Cmt, 68; del, Dem. Nat. Conv, 68. Bus. & Prof. Pos: Pres, Payton Construction Co. Inc, 57-66, chmn. bd. dirs, 66-; pres. bd. dirs, Centennial Corp. Inc, 64- Mem: Idaho Lodge 1, AF&AM, Boise Consistory (32°), El Korah Temple, Shrine Club; Elks Lodge 310. Rel: Congregational. Mailing Add: W. Lakeshore Dr, McCall, Idaho 83638.

PCIONEK, PAULINE ANNA D
Committeewoman, Genesee Co. Dem. Party, N.Y.
b. Elba, N.Y, 5/26/28; d. Paul Starowicz and Anna Stanek S; m. 7/29/50 to Richard Thomas Pcionek; c. Richard Thomas, Jr. and twins, James Gregory and Joanne Georgine. Educ: Elba Cent. Sch, Regents Dipl, 46. Polit. & Govt. Pos: Dem. cand. for Tax Collector, Batavia, N.Y, 63; secy, Genesee Co. Dem. Women's Club, 64-69, treas, 69-; secy-treas, Batavia Dem. Cmt, 64-; v.chmn, Genesee Co. Dem. Party, 65-67 & 69-, committeewoman, 65-; Dem. elec inspector, Batavia, 66- Bus. & Prof. Pos: Pvt. secy. to Prin. H. W. Vanderhoof, Elba Cent. Sch, N.Y, 46-55. Mem: Polish Falconettes; Batavia Firemen's Auxiliary. Citizenship Award, Elba Cent. Sch. Faculty, 46; Dansforth Award, Elba Cent. Sch. Classmates, 46. Rel: Roman Catholic. Mailing Add: 7902 Bank St. Rd, Batavia, N.Y. 14020.

PEABODY, ARTHUR H. D
N.H. State Rep.
b. Pelham, N.H, 12/23/90; wid; c. two. Educ: Pelham schs. Polit. & Govt. Pos: N.H. State Rep, 29-; former selectman and moderator. Bus. & Prof. Pos: Retired Chief of Police. Mem: Past master, Pelham Grange and Hillsborough Co. Pomona Grange; Past Dep, N.H. State Grange; Police Relief Asn; Hillsborough Co. Law Enforcement Asn. Rel: Protestant. Mailing Add: Box 144, Peabody Rd, Pelham, N.H. 03076. (1967)

PEABODY, ENDICOTT D
b. Lawrence, Mass, 2/15/20; s. The Rt. Rev. Malcolm E. Peabody and Mary Parkman P; m. 6/24/44 to Barbara Welch Gibbons; c. Barbara, Endicott, Jr. and Robert Lee. Educ: Harvard Col, A.B, 42; Harvard Law Sch, LL.B, 48. Polit. & Govt. Pos: Gov. Coun, Third Coun. Dist, Mass, 55-56; cand. for Attorney Gen, 56 & 58; cand. for Gov, Mass, 60, 62 & 64, Gov, Mass. 63-64; del, Dem. Nat. Conv, 60, 64 & 68; asst. regional counsel, Off. Price Stabilization; regional counsel and asst. to dir, Small Defense Plants Admin, Boston, Mass; cand, U.S. Sen, Mass, 66; asst. dir, Off. of Emergency Preparedness, Exec. Off. of the President, 67-68; chmn. sports cmt, President's Cmn. on U.S-Mex. Border Develop. and Friendship, 67-69. Bus. & Prof. Pos: Founder and partner, Peabody, Koufman & Brewer, 52-62; counsel, Roche & Leen, Boston, Mass, 65-66; founder and partner, Peabody, Rivlin, Kelly, Cladouhos & Lambert, Wash, D.C, 69- Mil. Serv: Entered as Ens, Navy, 42, released as Lt, 45, after serv. in Submarine Serv, two war patrols in the Far East; Presidential Unit Citation; Silver Star; Commendation Ribbon. Mem: Global Strategy Conf, Naval War Col, 65; mem. bd. dirs, World Affairs Coun; first marshal, Harvard Law Sch, 58; state chmn, Heart Fund, 60 and Mass. Ment. Health Campaign, 57; Harvard Law Sch. Asn; Am. Vet. Cmt; Harvard Varsity Club; Cambridge Tennis Club; Cambridge Skating Club; Union Boat Club; Mass, Boston, Cambridge, Fed. and Am. Bar Asns; bd. adv, Wash. Cent. YMCA; Harvard Club of Wash; Harvard Law Sch. Asn. of D.C; Wash. Athletic Club; Touchdown Club of Wash; Fairfax Hunt; Middletown Valley Hunt; Nat. Steeplechase and Hunt Asn, L.I. Named Outstanding Lineman of 41; Knute Rockne Mem. Trophy; Named Outstanding Football Player in New Eng, 41; Bulger-Lowe Trophy; Named One of the Seven Outstanding Young Men of Boston, 54. Rel: Episcopal. Legal Res: Cambridge, Mass. Mailing Add: 1730 M St. N.W, Washington, D.C. 20036.

PEABODY, MALCOLM E, JR. R
Dep. Asst. Secy. for Equal Opportunity, Dept. of Housing and Urban Develop.
b. 1928; married; c. Two. Educ: Harvard Col. and Harvard Grad. Sch. of Bus. Admin, grad. Polit. & Govt. Pos: Former exec. secy, N.Y. State Cmn. for Human Rights; chmn, Gov. Adv. Cmt. on Civil Rights, Mass, 63-64; chmn, Spec. Legis. Cmn. on Low Income Housing, Boston, 64-65; staff adv. and mem. Mayor's Cmt. on Minority Housing, Boston Redevelop. Authority, 65-66; cand, U.S. House of Rep, Third Mass. Dist, 68; Dep. Asst. Secy. for Equal Opportunity, Dept. of Housing and Urban Develop, 69- Bus. & Prof. Pos: Merchandise mgr. and controller, Butcher Polish Co, Malden, Mass; exec. dir, Interfaith Housing Corp, Boston, 66-68. Mil. Serv: Officer, Air Force, 52-53. Legal Res: Mass. Mailing Add: Dept. of Housing and Urban Development, 451 Seventh St. S.W, Washington, D.C. 20410.

PEACE, WILL K. R
Ky. State Rep.
b. 1905. Educ: Berea Col. Normal Sch; Union Col, B.S. Polit. & Govt. Pos: Ky. State Rep, 56 & 62- Bus. & Prof. Pos: Sch. prin. Mem: Mason. Rel: Baptist. Mailing Add: Williamsburg, Ky. 40769. (1967)

PEAK, AUDREY R. R
b. Green Co, Ill, 10/20/10; d. Howard S. Reavis and Effie Irene Cochran R; m. 8/25/27 to J. Ralph Peak; c. George R, Sam A. and Norah Irene. Educ: Ill. Col, grad. Polit. & Govt. Pos: Chmn, Ill. Rep. Cent. Cmt, 42-68 and chmn, Women's Div, 54-68; dir-at-lg, Cook Co. Rep. Cent. Cmt, 54-68; former mem, Rep. Nat. Cmt; del, Rep. Nat. Conv, 68. Mem: Treas, Scott Co. Chap, Salva-

tion Army, 55-68; State Women's Adv, Nat. Polio Found, 57-68; chmn, Scott Co. Tuberc. Asn. and Health Improv. Asn, 56-58; dist. chmn, Scott Co. Welfare Asn, 46-48, secy, 46; woman's dir, State Life of Ill; chmn. various fund dr, Girl Scouts; secy, Winchester Swimming Pool Asn; treas, Scott Co. Polio Found, 36- Mem: Winchester Women's Club (pres, 44-46); Eastern Star (past Worthy Matron). Rel: Baptist; past pres, Baptist Ladies Aid and past chmn, Baptist Aid Circle. Mailing Add: Fernwood Farm, Barrington, Ill. 60016. (1967)

PEARCE, PAUL LANGSTON R
Chmn, Wilbarger Co. Rep. Party, Tex.
b. Tyler, Tex, 6/23/30; s. Paul L. Pearce, Sr. and Bernardine Brookshire P; m. 4/9/55 to Mandy Hoover; c. Paul Davis, Patrick L. and Pamela. Educ: E.Tex. State Univ, B.S, 52; Baylor Univ. Col. Dent, D.D.S, 62; Psi Omega; Kappa Sigma. Polit. & Govt. Pos: Chmn, Wilbarger Co. Rep. Party, Tex, currently. Mil. Serv: Entered as 2nd Lt, Air Force, 52, released as 1st Lt, 56; Pilots Wings; Capt, Air Force Res, presently. Mem: Lions. Rel: Baptist. Legal Res: 3225 Bismarck St, Vernon, Tex. 76384. Mailing Add: P.O. Drawer 1700, Vernon, Tex. 76384.

PEARL, DOROTHY WAITE R
Chmn, Antrim Co. Rep. Party, Mich.
b. Kalamazoo, Mich, 2/20/96; d. Benjamin Asa Waite and Nellie Fisher W; m. 12/19/19 to Norton Harris Pearl (deceased); c. Ann (Mrs. Bretz), Betty (Mrs. Beeby), Jane (Mrs. Martin) and Dorothy (Mrs. Malasky). Educ: West. Mich. Univ, 4 years; Wayne State Univ, grad. work. Polit. & Govt. Pos: Dir. women's prog, Mich. State Civil Defense, 50-51; asst. dir. women's prog, Off. Civil Defense, Wash, D.C, 51-58; nat. dir. women's prog, Off. Civil and Defense Mobilization, 58-64; chmn, Antrim Co. Rep. Party, Mich, 64- Bus. & Prof. Pos: Teacher, Detroit Pub. Schs, 18-40. Publ: 'Parliamentary Points,' 50. Mem: Nat. Rep. Cmt; Am. Legion Auxiliary; Gen. Fedn. Womens Clubs; DAR; Nat. Asn. Parliamentarians; Eastern Star; Legion of Honor (Chevalier). Rel: Episcopal. Mailing Add: P.O. Box 33, Eastport, Mich. 49627.

PEARRE, JEROME R
Republican Representative Committeeman, 40th Ill. Dist.
b. Pontiac, Ill, 5/25/08; s. Louis Victor Pearre and Mary Louise Kent P; m. 9/3/37 to Erma Williams; c. James Alden and Victoria Louise (Mrs. Bond). Educ: Dartmouth Col, A.B, 30; Ill. State Univ, B.E, 31; Phi Beta Kappa; Phi Kappa Psi; Delta Omicron Gamma; Green Key. Polit. & Govt. Pos: Republican representative committeeman, 40th Ill. Dist, 60- Bus. & Prof. Pos: Securities salesman, Morgan-Guaranty Bank, 30; hist. instr, Pontiac High Sch, Ill, 32; city ed, Pontiac Daily Leader, 33-45, publisher, 45-69; secy-treas, Pontiac Leader Publ. Co, 45-69. Mem: Ill. and Inland Daily Press Asns; Am. Newspaper Publishers Asn; Pontiac Pub. Libr. Bd. Trustees; Rotary; Elks; Rel: Protestant Episcopal. Mailing Add: 206 N. Court St, Pontiac, Ill. 61764.

PEARS, DON R. R
Mich. State Rep.
b. Buchanan, Mich, 9/18/99; married; c. Donna Pickering and Charlene Simpson. Educ: Univ. Mich; Univ. Notre Dame; West. Mich. Univ, grad. Polit. & Govt. Pos: Mich. State Rep, 56-62 & 64-; former register of deeds and co. clerk of Berrien Co. Bus. & Prof. Pos: Real estate broker. Mil. Serv: World War I and II. Mem: Am. Legion; VFW (past comdr); Amvets; World War I Vets; Odd Fellows; Elks. Rel: Protestant. Mailing Add: 104 Lake St, Buchanan, Mich. 49107. (1967)

PEARSALL, C. BRUCE R
Mem, Nassau Co. Rep. Cmt, N.Y.
b. Amityville, N.Y, 8/27/20; s. Augustus A. Pearsall and Ella Edna Wade P; m. 6/17/49 to Virginia Lee Savoye; c. C. Bruce, Diana and Jeffrey Paull. Educ: Univ. Pa, B.S. in Econ, 42; St. Johns Univ. Sch. Law, LL.B, 48; Phi Delta Phi; Sigma Chi. Polit. & Govt. Pos: Asst. dist. attorney, Nassau Co, N.Y, 53-56; del, Rep. Nat. Conv, 60 & 64; mem, N.Y. State Rep, Cmt, 62-63; chmn, Oyster Bay Rep. Cmt, 62-65; dir, Nassau Co. Rep. Campaign, 64; mem, Nassau Co. Rep. Cmt, N.Y, currently. Mil. Serv: 1st Lt, Marine Corps, 42-46 & 51-52; Mariannas Campaign Ribbon; Cent. Pac. Theatre Ribbon; Letter of Commendation. Rel: Protestant. Mailing Add: 53 Bay Dr, Massapequa, N.Y. 11758. (1967)

PEARSON, ENID IRENE R
City Councilman, Palo Alto, Calif.
b. Venice, Calif, 8/21/24; d. Arthur Williams and Gertrude Emelia Ortquist W; m. 8/4/51 to Paul Alfred Pearson; c. Paul Arthur, Merit Lee, Barbara Emelia and Cecilia Irene. Educ: Mont. State Univ, B.A. in chem, 47; Am. Chem. Soc. Polit. & Govt. Pos: Mem, Nat. Redwood Scenic Rd. and Trail Cmt, 65-67; city councilman, Palo Alto, Calif, 65- Bus. & Prof. Pos: Chemist, Gen. Elec. Atomic Energy Plant, Hanford, Wash, 47-51 and Stanford Res. Inst, Calif, 51-52; secy-treas, Pearson Electronics, Inc, 58- Mem: Legis. chmn, parliamentarian and treas, Addison PTA, 57-65, coun. rep. and recording secy, 63; traffic chmn. and co-founder, Palo Alto Residents' Asn, 59-61; exec. bd, Citizens for Regional Planning, 61 and Citizens for Regional Trafficways, 62; Tax Override Citizens Adv. Cmt. on Pub. Info. for Palo Alto Sch. Dist, 63; chmn, Palo Altans for Recreation and Conserv. Open Sites, 63-65; co-founder, Richland, Wash. Bd, Am. Asn. Univ. Women and mem, Palo Alto Br. Co-sponsor, Palo Alto Planning Ordinance, 60-62 and Reduction of Council Term from Six to Four Years; sponsor, Palo Alto Park Dedication Charter Amendment. Rel: Protestant. Mailing Add: 1200 Bryant St, Palo Alto, Calif. 94301.

PEARSON, ERIC GUSTAV R
Chmn, Cohasset Rep. Town Cmt, Mass.
b. Waltham, Mass, 10/26/28; s. Carl Gustav Pearson and Margit Grening P; m. to Evelyn Lois Forest; c. Margit Linnea, Eric Gustav, Jr. and Carla Grace. Educ: Boston Univ, 47-48. Polit. & Govt. Pos: Mem, Personnel and Classification Cmt, Cohasset, Mass, 56-61; chmn, Cohasset Rep. Town Cmt, 67-; del, Rep. Platform Conv, 67-68; chmn, Nixon Reception, Cohasset, 68; mem, Selective Serv. Bd. 126, Weymouth, 68- Publ: 'Medicaid Revision Plan,' Mass. Rep. Party Platform, 67; 'Medicaid Proclamation,' Cohasset Town Meeting, 67. Mem: Nat. and Mass. Auto Dealers Asns; Crysler-Plymouth Dealer Coun.(dist. chmn, 67-); Mason; Am. Field Serv.(pres, Cohasset Chap, 59); Royal Arch; Rotary (pres, Cohasset Club, 56); Knights Templar; Jaycees; Cohasset Commun. Center; Boy Scouts (instnl. rep, mem. Old Colony Coun). Rel: Congregational; Building chmn, Beechwood Congregational Church. Mailing Add: 72 Church St, Cohasset, Mass. 02025.

PEARSON, HENRY CLYDE R
Va. State Sen.
b. Ocoonita, Va, 3/12/25; s. Henry James Pearson and Nancy Elizabeth Seals P; m. 7/26/56 to Norma Jean Calton; c. Elizabeth Frances and Timothy Clyde. Educ: Union Col, 46-49; Univ. Richmond Law Sch, LL.B, 52; Delta Theta Phi. Polit. & Govt. Pos: Va. State Del, 53-56; Asst. U.S. Dist. Attorney, West. Dist, Va, 56-61; Rep. nominee for Gov, 61; Va. State Sen, 68- Bus. & Prof. Pos: Attorney-at-law, Jonesville, Va, 52-56 and Roanoke, 61- Mil. Serv: Entered as Seaman, Navy, 43, released as PO, 46, after serv. in Atlantic and Pac. Theatres; European and Asiatic Commendations. Mem: Roanoke, Va. and Am. Bar Asns; Va. and Am. Trial Lawyers Asns; Am. Judicature Soc; past pres. and present bd. mem, Roanoke Valley United Cerebral Palsy; v.pres, State United Cerebral Palsy; adv. cmt, cent. coun, Roanoke PTA and pres, Oak Grove Elem. Sch. PTA, 68-69; past comdr, Post 33, Am. Legion; 40 et 8; Shrine; Mason (32°). Rel: Methodist. Legal Res: 4545 Laurelwood Dr. S.W, Roanoke, Va. 24018. Mailing Add: 131 W. Kirk Ave, Roanoke, Va. 24011.

PEARSON, JAMES BLACKWOOD R
U.S. Sen, Kans.
b. Nashville, Tenn, 5/7/20; m. 1946 to Martha Mitchell; c. Jimmy, Tommy, Billy and Laura Alice. Educ: Duke Univ, 40-42; Univ. Va. Law Sch, grad, 50; admitted to the Bar, 50. Polit. & Govt. Pos: City attorney, Westwood, Fairway and Lenexa, Kans, 52-61; asst. co. attorney, 52-54; probate judge, Johnson Co, 54-56; Kans. State Sen, 56-60; chmn, Kans. State Rep. Party for a short time; U.S. Sen, Kans, 62- Bus. & Prof. Pos: Attorney-at-law. Mil. Serv: Pilot, Navy, 43-46, based at Naval Air Sta, Olathe, Kans. Legal Res: Prairie Village, Kans. 66108. Mailing Add: New Senate Office Building, Washington, D.C. 20510.

PEARSON, JIMMY RAY D
Ind. State Rep.
b. Gallatin, Tenn, 7/21/35; s. Paul Anderson Pearson and Evelyn Braswell P; m. 1/9/60 to Patricia Kay McCartin; c. Kimberly Louise and Mark Alan. Educ: Morehead State Univ, 54-55; Univ. Hawaii, 57; Ind. Univ, 60-61, 65-67. Polit. & Govt. Pos: Regional dir, Ind. Dept. Commerce, 65-66; Ind. State Rep, 33rd Dist, 67- Bus. & Prof. Pos: Dir, New Hope Sch. for Retarded Children, Ind, 66- Mil. Serv: Entered as Pvt, Army, 55, released as Specialist, 58, after serv. in Pac; Expert Rifleman Badge; Good Conduct Medal. Mem: Elks; Redmen; Fraternal Order of Police. Rel: Catholic. Mailing Add: 31 Rosewood Dr, Jeffersonville, Ind. 47130.

PEARSON, LEON P. D
Ala. State Rep.
b. Elmore Co; m. to Eunice Conner; c. one and one granddaughter. Educ: Elmore Co. Sch. Polit. & Govt. Pos: Ala. State Rep, 67- Bus. & Prof. Pos: Construction and material bus; formerly restaurant motel and automobile supply bus. Mem: Master Mason; WOW; Farm Bur; Cattlemen's Asn. Rel: Presbyterian. Mailing Add: 1248 S. Main St, Prattville, Ala. 36067. (1967)

PEARSON, LLOYD EDWARD R
Mem, Bureau Co. Rep. Cent. Cmt, Ill.
b. Putnam Co, Ill, 2/15/10; s. Edward William Pearson and Hannah Swanson P; m. 8/19/35 to Gwendolyn Marjorie Williams; c. Judith Pearson (Mrs. Andersen), and Jerome Lloyd; grandchildren, Lynn Andersen. Educ: High Sch, grad, 27. Polit. & Govt. Pos: Rep. precinct committeeman, Arispie Twp, Ill, 33-; mem, Bureau Co. Rep. Cent. Cmt, Ill, 33-; supvr, Arispie Twp, 57-; civil defense dir, Bureau Co, 62-64; mem, Bureau Co. Exten. Serv, 64-68, chmn, 3 years. Bus. & Prof. Pos: Farmer, 65- Mem: Adv. bd, Perry Mem. Hosp, 40-; Tiskilwa Blue Lodge; Elks; Shrine; Consistory. Rel: Lutheran. Mailing Add: R.F.D. I, Tiskilwa, Ill. 61368.

PEARSON, RAY D
Secy, Tex. State Dem. Exec. Cmt.
b. Buda, Tex, 10/27/25; s. Jesse L. Pearson and Ophelia Wolff P; m. 7/24/55 to Shirley Joyce Turner; c. Brent Evan and Robert Turner. Educ: Sam Houston State Teachers Col, B.B.A, 49; Univ. Tex, LL.B, 55. Polit. & Govt. Pos: 29th Sen. Dist. committeeman, State Dem. Exec. Cmt, 60-61 & 62-63; secy, Tex. State Dem. Exec. Cmt, currently; del, Dem. Nat. Conv, 64 & 68. Bus. & Prof. Pos: Partner, Pearson and Speer, 55- Mil. Serv: Entered as Seaman, Navy, 43, released as Motor Machinist, 3/C, 46. Mem: Tex. and El Paso Co. Bar Asns; Sheriff's Posse, El Paso; Kiwanis. Rel: Methodist. Legal Res: 2506 N. Stanton St, El Paso, Tex. 79902. Mailing Add: 702 El Paso Nat. Bank Bldg, El Paso, Tex. 79901. (1967)

PEASE, DONALD JAMES D
Ohio State Rep.
b. Toledo, Ohio, 9/26/31; Russell E. Pease and Helen Mary Mullin P; m. 8/29/53 to Jeanne Camille Wendt; c. Jennifer. Educ: Ohio Univ, B.S.J. and M.A, 54; Univ. Durham, Eng, 54-55; Phi Eta Sigma; Omicron Delta Kappa; Delta Tau Delta. Polit. & Govt. Pos: Chmn. pub. utilities cmt, Oberlin, Ohio, 60-61; mem. city coun, Oberlin, 62-64; Ohio State Sen, 65-66; Ohio State Rep, 68- Bus. & Prof. Pos: Co-ed, Oberlin News-Tribune, Ohio, 57-66. Mil. Serv: Entered as 2nd Lt, Army, 55, released as 1st Lt, 57, after serv. in Qm. Corps. Publ: 'Recruiting for Weekly Journalism,' 63 and 'The Editor in Politics,' 10/65, Grassroots Ed; 'Teachers Perform,' Rockefeller Found. Quart, 12/68. Rel: Protestant. Mailing Add: 143 E. College St, Oberlin, Ohio 44074.

PEASE, FLOYD H. R
Wyo. State Rep.
b. Arnold, Nebr, 6/27/98; s. Jonathan Pease and Mary Morgan P; wid; c. Floyd Tim and Glen Eugene. Educ: Nebr. State Teachers Col, 1 year. Polit. & Govt. Pos: Treas, Goshen Co, Wyo, 43-67; Wyo. State Rep, 67- Mil. Serv: Pvt, Army, 18. Mem: Odd Fellows; Am. Legion; Lions; Farm Bur. Rel: Presbyterian. Mailing Add: 519 W. 15th Ave, Torrington, Wyo. 82240.

PEASE, LUCILLE CURRIE R
Chmn, Ashfield Rep. Town Cmt, Mass.
b. Cornish, Maine, 3/11/25; d. Eugene Kelvie Currie and Nora Pugsley C; m. 12/24/47 to Ralph Sanford Pease; c. Norene. Educ: Fitchburg State Col, B.S.Ed. Polit. & Govt. Pos: Chmn, Ashfield Rep. Town Cmt, Mass, 65- Bus. & Prof. Pos: Teacher, Shrewsbury, Mass, 46, Newton, 46-48, Ashfield, 48-52 and Conway, 62- Mem: Union, Mass. and Franklin Co. Teacher's Asn; Am. Legion Auxiliary (dept. pres, 65-66, nat. exec. committeewoman, 66-67, area A child welfare chmn, 66-67, area A educ. and scholarship chmn, 68-69); 8 et 40 (dept. chapeau, 67-68, area A child welfare chmn, 68-69); Eastern Star; Women's Club. Rel: Protestant. Mailing Add: Main St, Ashfield, Mass. 01330.

PEASE, ROGER DE VERE R
Chmn, Black Hawk Co. Rep. Party, Iowa
b. Littleton, Iowa, 7/1/30; s. Lawrence A. Pease and Grace Hayward P; m. 7/21/51 to Mary Ann Beatrice Herberg; c. Lynell, Randy, Kevin and Lynor. Educ: High Sch, 4 years. Polit. & Govt. Pos: Chmn, Black Hawk Co. Rep. Party, Iowa, 68- Bus. & Prof. Pos: Cost anal. clerk, John Deere Tractor Works, Waterloo, Iowa, 54- Mil. Serv: Seaman Storekeeper, Naval Res, 52-53, with serv. in U.S.S. Hickox, Korea. Mem: Mason (32°); AF&AM; Shrine; AAONMS; Eastern Star; El Kahir Oriental Band; Am. Legion; John Deere Supvr. Club; Nat. Campers and Hikers Asn. Rel: Presbyterian. Mailing Add: 1299 St. Andrews Ave, Waterloo, Iowa 50701.

PEAVEY, JOHN THOMAS R
Idaho State Sen.
b. Twin Falls, Idaho, 9/1/33; s. Arthur Jacob Peavey and Mary Thomas P; m. 6/19/57 to Luelle Lundgren; c. David, Karen and Tom. Educ: Northwest. Univ, B.S. in Civil Eng; Phi Delta Theta. Polit. & Govt. Pos: Committeeman, Idaho Rep. Party, 62-68; alternate del, Rep. Nat. Conv, 68; chmn, Legis. Dist. 21 Rep. Party, 68-69; Idaho State Sen, Dist. 21, 69- Mil. Serv: Entered as 2nd Lt, Marines, 57, released as 1st Lt, 60, after serv. U.S. Naval Mission to Haiti, 59-60. Mem: Idaho Cattleman's Asn.(dir, 65-68); dir, Am. Sheep Producers Coun, 68-; Idaho Woolgrowers Asn; Elks. Rel: Methodist. Mailing Add: 904 Tenth St, Rupert, Idaho 83350.

PEAVY, JAMES EDWIN R
Parliamentarian, Ga. Rep. Party
b. Cuthbert, Ga, 3/22/20; s. John McKenzie Peavy and Addie Belle Peak P; m. 7/8/51 to Audrey Carolyn Beasley; c. James E, Jr, and Julie Ann. Educ: Univ. Ga, B.B.A, 47; Mercer Univ, A.B. cum laude, 48, Walter F. George Sch. Law, LL.B. cum laude, 49; Phi Alpha Delta; Kappa Sigma. Polit. & Govt. Pos: Asst. secy, Rep. Exec. Cmt, Ga, 64-66, mem, 64-68; chmn, Ware Co. Rep. Cmt, 64-; asst. treas, Ga. Rep. Party, 66-68, parliamentarian, 68-; v.chmn, Eighth Dist. Rep. Cmt, 68- Mil. Serv: Entered as Pvt, Air Force, 42, released as S/Sgt, 45, after serv. in Hq. USAFISPA and Hq. SoPacBaCom, Asiatic Pac, 43-45; Asiatic-Pac. Serv. Medal with Bronze Star; Am. Serv. Medal; Victory Medal; Philippine Liberation Medal; Good Conduct Medal. Publ: Insurance Section in Mercer Law Review, 56. Mem: Am. Judicature Soc; Am. Bar Asn; bd. of gov, Ga. Bar Asn, 62-64; past pres, Waycross Bar Asn; pres, Waycross Circuit Bar Asn; Ga. Exchange Clubs. Rel: Baptist. Mailing Add: 1504 Satilla Blvd, Waycross, Ga. 31501.

PEAY, JOHN H. D
b. Clarksville, Tenn, 4/22/35; s. Austin Peay and Martha Orgain P; m. 6/3/58 to Gail Sigmon; c. John H, Jr, Frank Austin and Ross Evans. Educ: Univ. Tenn, B.S, 57 and J.D, 60; Phi Delta Phi; Order of the Coif. Polit. & Govt. Pos: Tenn. State Rep, 63-68; legis. coun. mem, 68- Bus. & Prof. Pos: Dir. operating coun, United Serv. Orgn, 65-68. Publ: 'Punitive Damages,' Tenn. Law Rev, 60. Mem: Am. and Tenn. Bar Asns; past pres, Montgomery Co. Bar Asn. and Kiwanis; Moose. Rel: Methodist. Legal Res: Waverly Rd, Clarksville, Tenn. 37040. Mailing Add: P.O. Box 606, Clarksville, Tenn. 37040.

PECHAN, ALBERT RAYMOND R
Majority Whip, Pa. State Senate
b. Ford City, Pa, 5/13/02; s. Ludwig Pechan and Theresa Greenmandel P; m. 11/4/65 to Elizabeth Tenerowicz. Educ: Univ. Pittsburgh, D.D.S, 28; Psi Omega; Omicron Delta Kappa; Omicron Kappa Upsilon. Polit. & Govt. Pos: Mem. bd. educ, Ford City, Pa, 29-59; Rep. State Committeeman, 41st Dist, Pa, 34-52; alternate del, Rep. Nat. Conv, 40, Sgt. at Arms, 52, 56 & 60; trustee, Ind. Univ. of Pa, 47- and Univ. Pittsburgh, 63-; Pa. State Sen, 41st Dist, 48-, majority whip, Pa. State Senate, 55-, v.chmn, Cmt. on Pub. Health and Welfare and mem, Rules Cmt; chmn, Armstrong Co. Rep. Party, 58-64. Bus. & Prof. Pos: Dentist, 28-65. Mil. Serv: Entered as Pvt, Army, 42, released as Maj, 46, after serv. in 114th Gen. Hosp. as Chief of Prosthetics, U.S. and European Theaters; Lt. Col, Army Res; ETO and Am. Theater Ribbons. Publ: 'Admission Standards of Pennsylvania Medical Schools,' Pa. Med. Asn. Jour, 8,9 & 10/67. Mem: Pres, Pa. Acad. Gen. Dent, 67; fel, Am. Col. of Dent, Int. Col. of Dent. and Am. Acad. of Gen. Dent; Am. Asn. for the Adv. of Sci; Elks; Eagles; K. of P; Odd Fellows; Mason; adv. bd, Salvation Army; dir, West. Pa. Cerebral Palsy Asn; 40 et 8; Boy Scouts; Crippled Children Cerebral Palsy; former chmn, Easter Seal Campaign; v.chmn, Cancer Crusade, Pa, 67, chmn, 68; Shrine; dept. chmn, Am. Legion Legis. Cmt; VFW Legis. Cmt. Pa. Dentist of the year, 57; Pitt Letterman of Distinction; Pa. Young Rep. Hall of Fame; Humanitarian Award; Benjamin Rush Award; Distinguished Serv. Awards, Pa. Am. Legion and VFW. Rel: Episcopal; former trustee, Pittsburgh Diocese of Episcopal Church; former Judge Ecclesiastical Court of Pittsburgh Diocese. Legal Res: 903 Fifth Ave, Ford City, Pa. 16226. Mailing Add: P.O. Box 272, Ford City, Pa. 16226.

PECK, BARBARA MAY R
Chmn, Pinal Co. Rep. Cmt, Ariz.
b. Jackson, Mich, 5/11/26; d. Robert Frederick Rockwell and Mae Boger R; m. 3/8/52 to Vinton Meade Peck; c. Ronald Craig, Pamela Mae and Patricia Meade. Educ: Jackson Bus. Univ, 1 year. Polit. & Govt. Pos: Committeeman, Pinal Co. Rep. Cmt, 62-, v.chairwoman, 64-68, chmn, 68-; v.pres, Apache Junction Rep. Women, 63, pres, 64, treas, 65, 68; dep. registrar, Pinal Co. Recorder, 66, 68 & 69; alternate del, Rep. Nat. Conv, 68; chmn. of nominations, Ariz. State Rep. Women, 68, membership chmn, 69. Bus. & Prof. Pos: Bookkeeper, Kennedy Hardware, Anchorage, Alaska, 51, 52; off. mgr, Peck & Peck Construction, 59, 69. Mem: C. of C; Youth Boosters; Beta Sigma Phi; PTA. Named Woman of the Year by Beta Sigma Phi. Rel: Methodist. Legal Res: 1574 Boila St, Apache Junction, Ariz. 85220. Mailing Add: Route 1, Box 1574, Apache Junction, Ariz. 85220.

PECK, GEORGE W. D
Polit. & Govt. Pos: Ariz. State Rep, 61-62; Ariz. State Sen, 62-67. Bus. & Prof. Pos: Gen. mgr, Cashion Gin Co. Mailing Add: 6813 N. 37th Dr, Phoenix, Ariz. 85019.

PECK, RAYMOND STUART D
Mass. State Rep.
b. New Bedford, Mass, 12/10/22; s. Walter Peck and Gertrude E. Costa P; m. 8/23/43 to Eleanor Louise Bouchie; c. Robert Earl and Brenda Joyce. Educ: Dartmouth High Sch; Providence Bus. & Trade; Kingston Trade. Polit. & Govt. Pos: Mem. town meeting, Dartmouth, Mass, 51-66, mem, Recreation Cmn, 59-62 and mem, Bd. of Pub. Welfare and selectman, 62-64; vet. agent, 62-63; Mass. State Rep, 64-; alternate del, Dem. Nat. Conv, 68. Bus. & Prof. Pos: Owner, Smith Mills Sport Supply, 62- and Dartmouth Golf Driving Range, past 17 years. Mem: K. of C, St. Isidore; Farmer Coun; Rotary. Rel: Roman Catholic. Mailing Add: 25 Summit Ave, N. Dartmouth, Mass. 02747. (1967)

PECKHAM, RUFUS W, JR. R
Secy, D.C. Rep. Cmt.
b. New York, N.Y, 1/25/28; s. Rufus W. Peckham and Virginia Selden P; single. Educ: Am. Univ. B.S, 53; Wash. Col. of Law, LL.B, 57; Alpha Tau Omega; Delta Theta Phi. Polit. & Govt. Pos: Dep. clerk, D.C. Court of Gen. Sessions, 56-59; nat. v.chmn, Young Rep. Nat. Fedn, 59-61; mem, D.C. Rep. Cmt, 60-, secy, 68-; gen. counsel, D.C. Young Rep. Club, 63-64; field coordinator, Rep. Nat. Cmt, 64. Bus. & Prof. Pos: Underwriter, Aetna Casualty & Surety Co, 53-56; regional dir. of state rels, Wine Inst, 59-63; attorney, Shipley, Akerman & Pickett, 65- Mil. Serv: Entered as Pvt, Marine Corps, 46, released as Sgt, 48, after serv. in 2nd Marine Div, U.S. and Caribbean Area from 46-48; 2nd Lt, Marine Corps Res, 52; Marine Corps Res. Medal; Am. Campaign and World War II Victory Medals; Occupation Serv. and Nat. Defense Medals. Mem: Am. and D.C. Bar Asns; Int. Asn. of Chiefs of Police; Lt, Metrop. Police Reserve Corps, D.C; Am. Legion; SAR; Georgetown Citizens Asn; life mem, Nat. Rifle Asn; Metrop. and Capitol Hill Clubs, D.C. Outstanding Serv. Award, Metrop. Police Dept, D.C, 69. Rel: Episcopal. Legal Res: 2501 Que St. N.W, Washington, D.C. 20007. Mailing Add: 1108 National Press Bldg, Washington, D.C. 20004.

PECSI, ANDREW D
b. Hungary, 11/25/01; s. Ferdinand Pecsi (deceased) and Julia Gutwein P. (deceased); m. 11/10/27 to Helen Hanisko; c. Andrew L, Charles F, Louis E, James A, Nancy (Mrs. Munshower) and Elaine (Mrs. Scully). Educ: Col, $1\frac{1}{2}$ years. Polit. & Govt. Pos: Asst. to chief of property mgt, Vet. Admin, $6\frac{1}{2}$ years; asst. chief rent inspector and head of comparable rent adjust, Off. of Price Admin, 5 years; alternate del, Dem. Nat. Conv, 68; mem. and asst. treas, 59th Ward Dem. Exec. Cmt, Phila, Pa, currently. Bus. & Prof. Pos: Clerk for correspondent, For. Banking and Travel Serv, 15-20; secy and gen. mgr. and head of liquidating trustees, bldg. and loan asn, 22-40; owner and operator, real estate and travel serv, 22-42; pres, Cedar Ridge Park Realty Corp. Publ: German Hungarian Business Advertising Book. Mem: German Hungarian Businessmen's Asn.(orgn. secy). Rel: Roman Catholic. Mailing Add: 127 W. Harvey St, Philadelphia, Pa. 19144.

PEDEN, KATHERINE GRAHAM D
b. Hopkinsville, Ky, 1/2/26; d. William Edward Peden and Mary Gorin P; single. Educ: Hopkinsville High Sch, grad, 44. Polit. & Govt. Pos: Co-chmn, Breathitt for Gov. Primary, Ky, 62-63 and Dem. Party, 63; Cmnr. of Commerce, Ky, 63-67; mem, Nat. Adv. Cmn. on Civil Disorders, 67-68; Dem. cand, U.S. Sen, Ky, 68; mem, Nat. Dem. Party Cmn. on Del. Selection and Party Structure, 69; bd. of dirs, Dem. Woman's Clubs of Ky, 69. Bus. & Prof. Pos: Mgr. and other positions, Radio Sta. WHOP, Hopkinsville, Ky, 44-58, v.pres, 58-; pres, Radio Sta, WNVL, Nicholasville, 65-; indust. consult, currently. Mem: Pres, U.S. Fedn. Bus. & Prfnl. Women's Clubs, 61-63. Rel: Christian Church. Legal Res: 2118 S. Virginia, Hopkinsville, Ky. 42240. Mailing Add: 981 S. Third St, Louisville, Ky. 40203.

PEDEN, PRESTON E. D
b. Duke, Okla, 6/28/14; married; c. Four. Educ: Univ. Okla, A.B, 36 and LL.B, 39. Polit. & Govt. Pos: Attorney for State Ins. Fund, Okla, 39-42; U.S. Rep, Okla, 46-47; counsel for Cmt. on Interior and Insular Affairs, U.S. House of Rep, 49-53; regional counsel for Bur. of Land Mgt, Dept. of Interior, Alaska, 50; dir, Govt. Affairs Div, Chicago Asn. Commerce and Indust, 54- Bus. & Prof. Pos: Lawyer, 46- Mil. Serv: Entered as Pvt, Army, 42, released as Capt, 46, after serv. as Forward Observer, 87th Inf. Div. and Prosecutor and Judge in Mil. Govt. Courts of Upper Bavaria; Bronze Star. Mem: Okla. State Bar. Mailing Add: 30 W. Monroe, Chicago, Ill. 60603.

PEDERSEN, ESTHER IRENE R
Mem, Calif. Rep. State Cent. Cmt.
b. Elizabeth, N.J, 7/22/00; d. Wilson John Kline and Cora Behler K; m. 6/15/25 to Clarence Edwin Pedersen; c. Shirley (Mrs. Charles O. Parent) and Don Edwin. Educ: San Juan Union High Sch, grad. Polit. & Govt. Pos: Secy, Oakland Health Dept, Calif, 20-25; pres, Berkeley Rep. Bus. and Prfnl. Women, 57 & 69-; chmn, United Rep. Calif, Thousand Oaks Unit 200, 64-; mem, Calif. Rep. State Cent. Cmt, 69- Bus. & Prof. Pos: Secy, Union Oil Co. of Calif, 25-28; secy, Oakland Defense Coun, 42-44. Mem: Eastern Star (Past Matron, Grand Rep. of Mass. in Calif, 68-); Daughters of Nile; Royal Neighbors of N.Am; East Bay Past Matrons Asn.(pres, 55); Independent Order of Foresters; Sons of Norway; Ladies Oriental Shrine; band dir, Mo-Li-La Court, 53). Rel: Christian Scientist. Mailing Add: 790 Vincente Ave, Berkeley, Calif. 94707.

PEDERSEN, HENRY FREDERICK, JR. R
Nebr. State Sen.
b. Omaha, Nebr, 12/16/29; s. Henry Frederick Pedersen, Sr. and Jessica Gough P; m. 4/16/55 to Sara Ann Campbell; c. Scott Campbell and Lisa Jane. Educ: Univ. Omaha, 47-48; Univ. Nebr, B.S.L, 51; Creighton Col. of Law,

LL.B, 53; Phi Delta Phi; Delta Tau Delta; Scabbard and Blade. Polit. & Govt. Pos: Asst. city prosecutor, Omaha, Nebr, 56-58; ward chmn, Douglas Co. Rep. Party, 60-62, co. chmn, 62-64; Nebr. State Sen, 64- Bus. & Prof. Pos: Attorney-at-law in private practice, 55-58 & 63-; attorney with legal dept. of an ins. co, 58-63. Mil. Serv: Entered as 2nd Lt, Army, 53, released as 1st Lt, 55, after serv. in Mil. Police and Judge Adv. Gen. Corps, Am. Theater; Maj, Army Res, Judge Adv, at present. Mem: Am. Trial Attorneys; Nebr. Bar Asn; Mason; Am. Legion; Danish Brotherhood; Optimists. Rel: Presbyterian. Mailing Add: 1114 S. 79th St, Omaha, Nebr. 68124.

PEDERSEN, RICHARD F.
Counsr, Dept. of State
b. Ariz, 2/21/25; married; c. Three. Educ: Univ. Pac, B.A, 46; Stanford Univ, M.A, 47; Harvard Univ, Ph.D, 50. Polit. & Govt. Pos: With Dept. of State, 50-, U.S. Mission to UN, 53-69, adv. on Econ. and Soc. Affairs, 53-56, adv. on Polit. and Security Affairs, 56-59, chief of Polit. Sect, 59-64, counsr, U.S. Mission, 64-66, sr. adv. to U.S. Rep. to UN, 66-67, dep. U.S. Rep. in UN Security Coun, 67-69, counsr, Dept. of State, 69- Bus. & Prof. Pos: Col. instr. in int. rels, law and govt, 49-50. Mil. Serv: Army, 43-45. Legal Res: 5011 Rockmere Court, Sumner, Md. 20016. Mailing Add: Department of State, 22nd and C St, Washington, D.C. 20520.

PEDERZANI, PAUL P, JR. D
Mem, Dem. State Cent. Cmt, R.I.
b. Plymouth, Mass, 6/29/25; s. Paul P. Pederzani and Ida Balboni P; m. 6/7/47 to Marjoria Louise Rodgers; c. Paul P, III and Keith J. Educ: Providence Col, A.B; Boston Col, J.D. Polit. & Govt. Pos: Mem, North Kingstown Dem. Town Cmt, R.I, 59-69, v.chmn. and chmn, 65-69; town solicitor, Exeter, 63-64; mem, Dem. State Cent. Cmt, 65-; clerk and assoc. Judge, Second Dist. Court, R.I, 69- Mil. Serv: Entered as Pvt, Army, 43, released as Pfc, 45, after serv. in 42nd Inf. Div, ETO, 44-45; Maj, Army Res, 49-; Bronze Star; Purple Heart; Combat Inf. Badge. Mem: Wash. Co. Bar Asn. (pres, 66-67); R.I. Bar Asn.(chmn, cmt. continuing legal educ, 66-); ROA; Judge Adv. Gen. Asns; North Kingstown C. of C; S.Co. Rod and Gun Club; S.Co. Elks. Rel: Catholic. Mailing Add: 98 Glenwood Dr, North Kingstown, R.I. 02852.

PEDIGO, KENNETH RAY D
Ind. State Sen.
b. Indianapolis, Ind, 5/22/28; s. Lawrence Gaylon Pedigo and Avalee Kemp P; m. 1/22/48 to Ruby Pollyann McGuffey; c. Michael K. and David L. Educ: Cent. Col. Ind, 61-65. Polit. & Govt. Pos: Ind. State Sen, Marion & Johnson Counties, 64-, chmn, Interstate Coop. Cmt, Ind. State Senate, 64-68, Ind. Transportation Study Cmt, 67-68 and Admin. Bldg. Coun, 67-68, ranking mem, Pub. Polity Cmt, 64-68 and Cities and Towns Cmt, 67-68, mem, Judiciary Cmt, 64-68, Affairs of Marion Co. Cmt, 64-68, Tax Study Cmt, 67-68, Finance Cmt, 67-68 and Appointments of Claims Cmt, 67-68; local chmn, Marion Co. Bldg. Cmt. Appeals Bd, 66-; bd. mem, Nat. Cmt. on Coun. of State Govts. and Midwest Regional Cmt. on Hwys. Transportation & Safety; mem, State Study Cmt. on Hwy. Needs & Financing of Rds. & Sts. and State Cmt. on Independent Living for Aged Citizens; mem, Nat. Cmt. on Interstate Coop. Coun. of State Govts. Bus. & Prof. Pos: Secy-treas, Pedigo Jewelers, Inc, 46-; v.pres, Pedigo Wholesale Imports Inc, 60- Mil. Serv: Entered as Seaman 3/C, Navy,44, released as Coxswain, 46, after serv. in S.Pac. Area. Mem: Dir, Nat. Jewellers Guild, 57-58; Sertoma; Southport Masonic Lodge; Fountain Square Businessman's Asn; chmn, Subcmt. on Mass Rapid Transportation, Nat. Coun. of State Govts; midwest. states' rep, Nat. Hwy. and Safety Cmt. Rel: Presbyterian. Mailing Add: 6010 S. East St, Indianapolis, Ind. 46227.

PEEBLES, ROBERT R
Secy, Scioto Co. Rep. Exec. Cmt, Ohio
b. Portsmouth, Ohio, 2/26/08; s. Samuel Coles Peebles and Helena Salmon P; div; c. Pamela Lee. Educ: Ohio State Univ, B.S, 31; Alpha Tau Omega. Polit. & Govt. Pos: Rep. Precinct Committeeman, Scioto Co, Ohio, 46-; Sixth Dist. Committeeman, Rep. State Cent. Cmt, 50-54; area rep, programmed all housing for Atomic Installation in Portsmouth Area, Dept. of Housing and Urban Develop, 52-54; secy, Scioto Co. Rep. Exec. Cmt, 69- Mil. Serv: Entered as Lt, Army, 40, released as Maj, 46, after serv. in 37th Div. Field Artil, S.E. Pac, 42-45. Mem: Mason; Elks; Am. Legion; VFW. Rel: Presbyterian. Legal Res: 26 Streich Apt, Portsmouth, Ohio 45662. Mailing Add: Box 720, Portsmouth, Ohio 45662.

PEEBLES, ROBERT CARLEY D
Chmn, Neshoba Co. Dem. Exec. Cmt, Miss.
b. Philadelphia, Miss, 8/27/92; s. Robert Harrison Peebles (deceased) and Martha Jayroe P. (deceased); m. 9/13/17 to Sara Tay Rouse; c. Martha Tay (Mrs. Conn), Robert Marvin, Sara Frances (Mrs. Howell) and Charlene (Mrs. Webb). Educ: Miss. Col. Polit. & Govt. Pos: Co. supt. of educ, Neshoba Co, 19-24; chmn, Neshoba Co. Dem. Exec. Cmt, Miss, 64- Bus. & Prof. Pos: Dist. mgr, Mutual Life Ins. Co, N.Y, 24-42; ed. and publisher, Neshoba Democrat, 26-28; pres. and mgr, Peebles Ins. Agency, Inc, 54- Mil. Serv: Entered as Pvt, Army, 17, released as 2nd Lt, 18, after serv. in 162 Depot Brigade; re-entered as 1st Lt, 42, released as Maj, 46, after serv. in Inf, Mil. Police; hon. Ret. Res. Mem: Mason; Rotary; C. of C.(former pres, Philadelphia, Neshoba Co, Miss. Chap); Am. Legion (former comdr). Rel: Methodist. Legal Res: 537 Jefferson, Philadelphia, Miss. 39350. Mailing Add: Box 271, Philadelphia, Miss. 39350. (1967)

PEEKE, HARMAN V.S. D
Mem, Calif. Dem. State Cent. Cmt.
b. San Francisco, Calif, 12/19/37; s. Edwin S. Peeke, M.D. and Helen Turner P; m. 11/30/63 to Shirley Donelan. Educ: San Francisco State Col, B.A. & M.A; Univ. of South. Calif, Ph.D, 66. Polit. & Govt. Pos: Canvassing coordinator, McCarthy for Pres. Campaign, San Francisco, 68; dist. off. mgr, Newsom for State Sen. Campaign, 68; pres, Vol. for New Polit, 68-69; mem, Calif. Dem. State Cent. Cmt, 69- Bus. & Prof. Pos: Post-doctoral research fel, Univ. of Calif. Med. Center, San Francisco, 66-68, asst. prof. of med. psychol, 68- Mem: Sigma Xi. Rel: Unitarian. Mailing Add: 154 Clifford Terr, San Francisco, Calif. 94117.

PEEL, DAVID WALKER D
b. Bentonville, Ark, 1/4/91; s. David Walker Peel and Frances Arrington P; m. 1/16/21 to Mary Courtney Briscoe; c. Mary Briscoe, John Terry, David Walker, III and Barbara Courtney. Educ: Univ. Ark. Polit. & Govt. Pos: Mayor, Bentonville, Ark, 34-40; chmn, Ark. Workmen's Compensation Cmn, 40-54; chmn, Benton Co. Dem. Cent. Cmt, 54-68. Bus. & Prof. Pos: Attorney-at-law, 12-20; cashier, First Nat. Bank, Bentonville, 20-30. Mil. Serv: Entered as Pvt, Army, 17, released as 1st Lt, 19, after serv. in 34th Inf, France; Purple Heart. Mem: Rotary; Am. Legion. Rel: Presbyterian. Legal Res: Bentonville, Ark. 72712. Mailing Add: 503 W. Central, Bentonville, Ark. 72712.

PEELER, JAMES ALFRED, JR. D
Chmn, Tenn. Dem. Exec. Cmt.
b. Covington, Tenn, 11/8/13; s. James Alfred Peeler and Jennie Huffman P; m. 10/12/62 to Mildred Brown; c. Meredith and James Alfred, III. Educ: Byars Hall High Sch, grad, 32. Polit. & Govt. Pos: Mem, Tenn. Dem. Exec. Cmt, 57-59, chmn, 59-; del, Dem. Nat. Conv, 68. Bus. & Prof. Pos: Farmer and owner of cotton gin, Covington, Tenn, 32- Mil. Serv: Entered as Pvt, Army, 42, released as 1st Lt, 46, after serv. as Finance Officer, Far E. Air Force, 43-46; Good Conduct Medal; Am. Theatre Ribbon; Asiatic Pac. Theatre Ribbon with two Bronze Serv. Stars; World War II Victory Medal. Mem: Am. Legion; VFW. Rel: Methodist. Mailing Add: 803 W. Liberty Ave, Covington, Tenn. 38019.

PEEPLES, JOE H. D
b. Zolfo Springs, Fla, 1/22/14; m. to Emma Bethea; c. Joann, Joe H. and John. Educ: Pub. Schs. Polit. & Govt. Pos: Fla. State Rep, 42-66. Bus. & Prof. Pos: Cattleman; recreation, hunting. Rel: Baptist. Mailing Add: Venus, Fla. 33960. (1967)

PEERY, WALTER H. R
State Treas, Kans.
b. Huron; m. 1927 to Florence Popejoy. Educ: Atchison High Sch. Polit. & Govt. Pos: State Treas, Kans, 60- Bus. & Prof. Pos: Working in father's merchandise store; in acct. dept, wholesale grocery firm; asst. cashier in bank; mgr. of corp. Mem: Elks; Am. Legion. Rel: Presbyterian. Mailing Add: 90 State Capitol, Topeka, Kans. 66612.

PEET, ANSON WALTER R
b. Shelburne, Vt, 3/21/05; m. to Dorothy Ayer; c. three. Educ: Burlington Bus. Col. Polit. & Govt. Pos: Vt. State Rep, 35, 59 & 63-66; selectman; lister; sch. dir; overseer of poor; town moderator. Bus. & Prof. Pos: Retired farmer. Mil. Serv: Vt. Nat. Guard, 24. Rel: Protestant. Mailing Add: RFD, Shelburne, Vt. 05482. (1967)

PEEVER, LEONARD B. R
b. Southport, Eng, 2/17/97; married; c. one. Educ: Methuen and Boston, Mass. Polit. & Govt. Pos: N.H. State Rep, until 68; chmn. bd. trustees and parole bd, N.H. State Prison; selectman; mem, Bd. of Trade; dir, Granite State Elec. Power Co; dir, Salem Trust Co; dir, Salem Coop Bank; druggist. Mil. Serv: A.E.F. Europe. Mem: Mason; Shrine; Am. Legion; VFW; Eastern Star; Kiwanis. Mailing Add: 12 Granite Ave, Salem, N.H. 03079. (1967)

PEIRCE, EUGENE WILLARD, JR. R
N.Mex. State Rep.
b. Oak Park, Ill, 3/20/31; s. Eugene W. Peirce and Elisabeth Leonard P; m. 8/8/53 to Letitia Creveling; c. Robert E, Mary E, Margaret E. and Anne Letitia. Educ: Univ. of N.Mex, B.B.A, 53; Delta Sigma Pi; Pi Sigma Alpha; Phi Delta Theta. Polit. & Govt. Pos: Precinct chmn, Rep. Party, N.Mex, 64; mem, Co. Exec. Cmt, 65-; N.Mex. State Rep, 65-, Minority Whip, N.Mex. House of Rep, 66-68. Bus. & Prof. Pos: Agent, Southwest. Life, 58- Mil. Serv: Entered as 2nd Lt, Air Force, 53, released as Capt, 57, after serv. as Pilot; Capt, Air Force Res. Mem: Million Dollar Round Table; Chartered Life Underwriter; lt. gov, Div. II, Southwest Dist. Kiwanis. Selected as Outstanding Young Man of Year, Jaycees, 67. Rel: Episcopal. Mailing Add: 2708 Tennessee N.E, Albuquerque, N.Mex. 87110.

PEIRCE, WALTER H. R
b. Rapid City, S.Dak. Polit. & Govt. Pos: Bd. of Dirs, G.V.E.A, 63-69. Bus. & Prof. Pos: Civil engr. Mem: Am. Soc. of Civil Engrs; Lions. Rel: Presbyterian. Mailing Add: P.O. Box 5091, College, Alaska 99701.

PEIRSON, MARY WOOD R
Asst. Secy, Del. Rep. State Cmt.
b. Phila, Pa, 4/8/22; d. Edgar N. Wood and Mary Hedderman W; m. 4/8/43 to David D. Peirson; c. Mary (Mrs. Harris), Barbara(Mrs. Mathers), David R, Kathleen, Patti Lynn and Donald James. Educ: Univ. of Chattanooga, B.S. Chem, 42; Gamma Sigma Epsilon; Beta Beta Beta. Polit. & Govt. Pos: Alternate committeewoman, St. Georges Hundred, 58-69; asst. secy, Del. Rep. State Cmt, 62- Bus. & Prof. Pos: Chemist, Hercules Powder Co, Wilmington, Del, 42 and Tenn. Valley Authority, Chattanooga, Tenn, 43; teacher, St. Paul's, Delaware City, Del, 66-69. Mem: Am. Asn. of Univ. Women; Bus. and Prfnl. Women; Farm Bur. Rel: Catholic. Mailing Add: R.D. 2, Box 43, Middletown, Del. 19709.

PEISCH, FRANCIS ROBERT R
Vt. State Rep.
b. Minneapolis, Minn, 2/9/18; s. Archibald M. Peisch and Josephine P; m. 10/26/46 to Mary Virginia Hogan; c. Thomas E, Stephen A, Elizabeth H, Richard F, Christopher L, Andrew P, Robert D. and Ann D. Educ: Dartmouth Col; Univ. Wis, A.B, 39; Harvard Law Sch, LL.B, 42; Delta Kappa Epsilon. Polit. & Govt. Pos: Mem, State Bd. of Health, Vt, 55-67; clerk, Fourth Ward, 63-65; Vt. State Rep, 67- Mil. Serv: Entered as Cadet, Army Air Corps, 42, released as 1st Lt, 46, after serv. in 54th Troop Carrier Wing, S.W. Pac. Area; Five Campaign Stars. Mem: Gov, Ethan Allen Club, 62-64. Rel: Catholic. Legal Res: Appletree Point, Burlington, Vt. 05401. Mailing Add: P.O. Box 954, Burlington, Vt. 05401.

PÉLADEAU, MARIUS B.
b. Boston, Mass, 1/27/35; s. Marius Péladeau, M.D. and Lucienne Beaudoin P; single. Educ: St. Michael's Col. Winooski Park, Vt, B.A; Boston Univ,

M.S. in journalism; Georgetown Univ, M.A. in literature; Sigma Delta Chi. Polit. & Govt. Pos: Admin. asst. and press secy. to U.S. Rep. Joseph P. Vigorito, Pa, currently. Publ: The Verse of Royall Tyler, Univ. Press of Va, 68; The Prose of Royall Tyler, Vt. Hist. Soc. and Charles E. Tuttle Co, Inc, 69. Mem: Colonial Soc. of Mass; Vt. Hist. Soc; Co. of Mil. Historians; White House Correspondents Asn. Mailing Add: 613 A St. N.E, Washington, D.C. 20002.

PELHAM, GLENN D
b. Cairo, Ga, 6/16/28; s. Paul David Pelham and Eula Glenn P; single. Educ: Mercer Univ, A.B, 51; John Marshall, LL.B, J.D, 62; Blue Key; Omicron Delta Kappa; Delta Sigma Pho; Tau Kappa Alpha; Alpha Tau Omega. Polit. & Govt. Pos: Ga. State Sen. (10th dist.), 63-66, (7th dist.), 57-58. Bus. & Prof. Pos: Sch. teacher; Dir. of Forensics, 61-, Emory Univ. Misc: 'Who's Who In Am. in the South & S.W,' Outstanding Young Men in Am, 64; Leading Men in the U.S, 65. Rel: Methodist. 1967 Legal Res: Cairo, Ga. No mailing address available. (1967)

PELKEY, FRANCES BAILEY D
b. Montgomery Center, 2/21/16; m. to Herman A. Pelkey; c. four. Educ: Richford High Sch; Burlington High Sch. Polit. & Govt. Pos: Vt. State Rep, 63-67; postmaster, 40-60; secy, Dem. Town Cmt. and chmn, Dist. Dem. Cmt; town clerk. Bus. & Prof. Pos: Storekeeper and mother. Mem: Pres, Ladies of St. Ann; secy. to State OWL's; town chmn, March of Dimes, 5 years; chmn, Town Humane Soc; former mem, Grange, secy. 2 years; pianist. Rel: Catholic. Mailing Add: Box 67, Highgate Center, Vt. 05459. (1967)

PELL, CLAIBORNE D
U.S. Sen, R. I.
b. N.Y.C, 11/22/18; s. Herbert Claiborne Pell and Matilda Bigelow P; m. Dec. 1944 to Nuala O'Donnell; c. Herbert III, Christopher, Dallas and Julia. Educ: Princeton Univ, A.B. cum laude, 40; Columbia Univ, A.M. Polit. & Govt. Pos: Spec. asst. at San Francisco UN Conf; exec. asst. to R.I. Dem. State Chmn, 52 & 54; consult, Dem. Nat. Cmt, 53-60; Dem. Nat. Registrn. Chmn, 56; chief del. tally clerk, Dem. Nat. Conv, 56, 60, 64 & 68; with U.S. For. Serv. and State Dept, 7 years; U.S. del. to Intergovt. Maritime Consultative Orgn. in London, 59; v.pres, Int. Rescue Cmt, until 60; mem, Nat. Coun. of Refugees; treas, Am. Immigration Conf; U.S. Sen, R.I, 60-; del, Dem. Nat. Conv, 68. Bus. & Prof. Pos: Bus. exec; investments. Mil. Serv: Entered Coast Guard prior to World War II, released as Lt; Capt, Coast Guard Res, currently. Decorated by France, Italy, Portugal and Knights of Malta. Legal Res: Newport, R.I. Mailing Add: 325 Old Senate Office Bldg, Washington, D.C. 20510. (1967)

PELL, KATHERINE D. 'KAY' D
b. Lafayette, Ind, 4/15/14; d. Benjamin F. Dunwoody and Della Siefers D; m. 9/5/40 to Kalman Louis Pell; c. Larry and John. Educ: Purdue Univ, B.S, with distinction, 36; Wellesley Col, M.S, 38; Univ. Idaho, post-grad. work in law and polit. sci; Alpha Lambda Delta; Kappa Delta Pi; Sigma Xi; Mortar Board. Polit. & Govt. Pos: Committeewoman, Modoc Point Precinct, Klamath Co, Idaho, 47-49; committeewoman, Idaho State Dem. Cmt. from Latah Co. Cent. Cmt, 53-57 and 61-66; co. assessor, Latah Co, 57-61; mem. policy cmt, State Dem. Cent. Cmt, 61-66; chmn, State Oper. Support, 61-66; del, Dem. Nat. Conv, 64; mem, Citizens Adv. Cmt, Lewiston, Idaho, 68-69. Bus. & Prof. Pos: Dir, Girl Scouts, Brookline, Mass, 37-38; commun. recreation dir, Moorestown, N.J, 38-40 and Reading, Pa, 40-42; United Serv. Orgn. dir, YWCA, Wash, D.C, during World War II; registered investment rep, Investment Income Serv, Inc, 61-66; research asst, Bur. of Pub. Affairs Research, Univ. Idaho, 61-66; exec. dir, Community Action Agency, Inc, Lewiston, Idaho, 66-; pres, Idaho State Community Action Prog. Dirs. Asn, 68-69. Publ: Handbook for Elected Municipal Officials in Idaho, 63, Salaries and Fringe Benefits in Idaho Municipalities, 64 (both w. William O. Lewis) and A Handbook for County Officials in Idaho, (w. H. Sydney Duncombe), 66; Bur. of Pub. Affairs Research, Univ. Idaho. Mem: League of Women Voters; Am. Asn. Univ. Women; Genesee Civic Asn; PTA; Bus. and Prfnl. Women's Clubs, C. C. of C. Rel: Methodist. Mailing Add: 2516 Sunset Dr, Lewiston, Idaho 83501.

PELLEGRINI, PHILIBERT L. D
Mass. State Sen.
m. Nancy Quinzani. Polit. & Govt. Pos: Mass. State Sen, 62 and currently; chmn, Bd. of Selectmen, last year of term; chmn, Town Zoning Bd. of Appeals. Bus. & Prof. Pos: Practicing attorney. Mailing Add: 17 Cheswick Rd, Arlington, Mass. 02174. (1967)

PELLY, THOMAS MINOR R
U.S. Rep, Wash.
b. Seattle, Wash, 8/22/02; s. Bernard Pelly and Elizabeth Minor P; m. 5/24/27 to Mary Taylor; c. Thomas M, Jr. and Mrs. Chas. P. Moriarty, Jr. Polit. & Govt. Pos: U.S. Rep, Wash, 53- Mem: Alpha Kappa Psi; pres, Seattle C. of C, 49-51; Rainier, Seattle Yacht, Wash. Athletic and Capitol Hill Clubs; Cong. Golf & Country Club. Rel: Episcopal. Legal Res: Route 6, Box 6808, Bainbridge Island, Wash. 98110. Mailing Add: 2211 Rayburn House Office Building, Washington, D.C. 20515.

PELOQUIN, BRUCE SIMON D
Wis. State Assemblyman
b. Chippewa Falls, Wis, 11/3/36; s. Frank Simon Peloquin and Anna Marie Normand P; m. 9/16/66 to Stephanie Baker; c. Tracy Claire. Educ: Wis. State Univ, B.A. in bus. and psychol, 66; Beta Upsilon Sigma. Polit. & Govt. Pos: Co. bd. supvr, Chippewa Co, Wis, 64-66; Wis. State Assemblyman, Chippewa Co, 65-; mem, exec. cmt, Chippewa Co. Dem. Party, 66. Bus. & Prof. Pos: Supvr, U.S. Rubber Co, Eau Claire, Wis, 58; Clerical worker, Minn. Mining & Mfg. Co, 61. Mem: K. of C. Various Journalism Awards, Col. and High Sch. Publ. Rel: Catholic. Mailing Add: R.R. 5, Box 357, Chippewa Falls, Wis. 54729.

PELOQUIN, J. CAMILLE, SR. D
R.I. State Rep.
b. Manville, R.I, 1/24/28; s. Theodore Peloquin (deceased) and Alma Dupuis P; m. 2/5/49 to Phyllis Cook; c. J. Camille, Jr, Linda Louise, Ronald N. and Theodore A. Educ: R.I. Col. Polit. & Govt. Pos: Mem, Lincoln Dem. Town Cmt. and Manville Dem. Dist. Cmt, R.I, 57; R.I. State Rep, 64- Bus. & Prof. Pos: Inspection and gage control; foreman, Anti-Submarine Warfare Div, Raytheon Co, 60- Mil. Serv: Entered Army, 45, released as Sgt, 47, after serv. in Inf. as cook, Pac-Manila Theater. Mem: Manville Fireman's Asn. and Fire Dept; Montcalm and Roosevelt Clubs; Lincoln C. of C. Rel: Catholic. Mailing Add: 1412 Old River Rd, Manville, R.I. 02838.

PELOSI, RONALD D
Supvr, San Francisco Bd. of Supvr, Calif.
b. San Francisco, Calif, 11/2/34; s. John Pelosi and Corinne Bianchi P; m. 8/10/56 to Barbara Newsom; c. Cynthia Sharon, Brennan John, Matthew Francis and Caroline Ann. Educ: Stanford Univ, A.B, 56; Georgetown Univ. Grad. Sch, 56-57. Polit. & Govt. Pos: Mem, San Francisco Co. Dem. Cent. Cmt, Calif, 60-64; mem, Calif. State Dem. Cent. Cmt, 62-64; mem, San Francisco Planning Cmn, 64-67, pres, 66; del, Dem. Nat. Conv, 68; supvr, San Francisco Bd. of Supvr, Calif, 68- Bus. & Prof. Pos: Stock broker, Brush Slocumb & Co, San Francisco, mem. firm, N.Y. Stock Exchange, 57-61, J. Barth & Co, 61- Rel: Roman Catholic. Mailing Add: 18 Sixth Ave, San Francisco, Calif. 94118.

PELTIER, HARVEY A, JR. D
La. State Sen.
b. Thibodaux, La, 1/18/23; s. Harvey A. Peltier and May Ayo P; m. 6/30/45 to Irma Geheeb; c. Patricia E, Harvey A, III and Mary Ellen. Educ: Spring Hill Col, B.S, 44. Polit. & Govt. Pos: La. State Sen, 15th Sen. Dist, 64- Mil. Serv: A/S, Navy, 43. Mem: Life mem, Am. Legion; Amvets; DAV; Nicholls Century Club; Nicholls Col. Club; Thibodaux Cardinal Club; Thibodaux Tiger Club; La. State Univ. and Spring Hill Col. Alumni Asns; 40 et 8; Lafourche Ins. Exchange; Am. Quarter Horse Asn; Palomino Horse Breeders of Am, Inc. Named Outstanding Citizen by VFW; Grand Marshall, Thibodaux Fire Dept. Rel: Roman Catholic. Legal Res: 102 Cherokee St, Thibodaux, La. 70301. Mailing Add: P.O. Box 779, Thibodaux, La. 70301.

PELTON, CHARLES HOWARD R
Iowa State Rep.
b. Clinton, Iowa, 8/15/40; s. Charles H. Pelton and Rosanna Howard P; single. Educ: Univ. Iowa, B.A, 62 and LL.B, 66; Phi Delta Phi; Alpha Tau Omega. Polit. & Govt. Pos: Iowa State Rep, 67- Bus. & Prof. Pos: Attorney-at-Law, Clinton, Iowa, 66- Mem: Clinton Co, Iowa State and Am. Bar Asns; Iowa Alumni Asn. Rel: Presbyterian. Mailing Add: 601 Wilson Bldg, Clinton, Iowa 52732.

PELZER, MAX O. R
Chmn, Emmet Co. Rep. Party, Iowa
b. Griswold, Iowa, 11/23/31; s. Irvin Pelzer and Dollie Sothman P; m. 7/10/55 to Bonnie Krueger; c. Mark, Sheryl, Scott and Todd. Educ: Iowa State Univ. Polit. & Govt. Pos: Chmn, Emmet Co. Rep. Party, Iowa, currently. Mil. Serv: Entered as Seaman, Navy, 51, released as At-2, 55, after serv. in Morocco. Mem: Kiwanis; VFW; Isaak Walton League; Farm Bur; Am. and Iowa Bar Asns. Rel: Methodist. Mailing Add: 113 N. Sixth St, Estherville, Iowa 51334.

PEMBER, ROBERT WAYNE D
b. Knox, Ind, 7/23/11; s. Ira Mansfield Pember and Eura Mae Fout P; m. 8/14/41 to Marie Delcena Bissonnette; c. Marimae (Mrs. Wayne Harrington), Bobbette Marie, Carol Ann and Janice Joy. Educ: St. Paul High Sch, Ind, grad, 30; Naval Supply Sch. and Naval Justice Sch, grad. Polit. & Govt. Pos: Chmn, Iosco Co. Dem. Party, Mich, 65-67; acting postmaster, Hale, 67- Mil. Serv: Entered as A/S, Navy, 35, released as Lt, Signal Corps, 57, after serv. in U.S.S. Lexington, CV-2, C.A.S.U.4, C.A.S.U.31, U.S.S. Caloosahatchee AO-98, U.S.S. Elokomin AO-55 and U.S.S. Orion AS-18, Lt.(Ret), 58; Am. Defense Medal; Asiatic-Pac. Medal; ETO Medal. Mem: Mason; Am. Legion; VFW. Rel: Christian. Mailing Add: R.R. 1, Box 80, Hale, Mich. 48739.

PEMBERTON, CLARENCE LILLY D
Chmn, Caswell Co. Dem. Exec. Cmt, N.C.
b. Fayetteville, N.C, 7/23/08; s. Clarence Lilly Pemberton, Sr. and Mary Norcott P; m. 3/16/40 to Anne Elizabeth Watkins; c. Mary Norcott, Elizabeth Nelson and Emalv de Jarnette. Educ: Carleton College, B.A; Minn. College of Law, LL.B; Kappa Sigma; Adelphic Soc. Polit. & Govt. Pos: Judge, Caswell Co, N.C, 38-50, attorney, 50-66; chmn, Caswell Co. Dem. Exec. Cmt, N.C, 50- Bus. & Prof. Pos: Pres, 17th Judicial Dist. Bar, 53 & 58. Mil. Serv: Entered as Seaman 2/C, Navy, 43, released as Qm 3/C, 46, after serv. in S.Pac. Mem: Rotary; Am. Legion; VFW; Farm Bur. Rel: Episcopal. Legal Res: 200 Fifth St, Yanceyville, N.C. 27379. Mailing Add: Box 7, Yanceyville, N.C. 27379.

PEMBERTON, JOHN DE J, JR. R
b. Rochester, Minn, 1919; div; c. Four daughters and one son. Educ: Swarthmore Col, B.A, 40; Harvard Law Sch, 47. Polit. & Govt. Pos: Chmn. of Minn. Br, Am. Civil Liberties Union, 55-58, mem. exec. bd. of Minn, 58-62, exec. dir, 62- Bus. & Prof. Pos: Assoc. prof, law, Duke Univ, 47-50; lawyer, 50- Mil. Serv: Am. Field Serv. ambulance units, 41-45. Publ: Assoc. ed, Law and Contemporary Probelms, J. Legal Educ, 49-50. Mem: Former mem, Rochester City Charter Cmn; C. of C; Minn. Fair Employ. Practices Cmn; Minn. Adv. Cmt. to U.S. Civil Rights Cmn. Rel: Quaker. Mailing Add: American Civil Liberties Union, 156 Fifth Ave, New York, N.Y. 10010.

PEMBLE, CARL AUGUST D
Secy, St. Croix Co. Dem. Party, Wis.
b. Clarendon, Ark, 11/9/03; s. Harold Edward Pemble and Emma Sophia Ostermann P; m. 1/1/26 to Alice Sturm; c. Rose Marjorie (Mrs. Gene Wilson) and Audrey Alta (Mrs. DeLone Halverson). Educ: Univ. Minn, B.S, 31; Univ. Wis, River Falls, 54-56; Alpha Chi Sigma. Polit. & Govt. Pos: Del, Wis. State Dem. Conv, several years; chmn, St. Croix-Pierce McCarthy for Pres. River Falls, 68; Tenth Dist. Dem. Cand. for Wis. State Sen, 68; del, Dem. Nat. Conv, 68; secy. St. Croix Co. Dem. Party, currently. Bus. & Prof. Pos: Chief chemist, West. Crucible Steel Co, Minneapolis, Minn, 23-27; instr. chem, physics and math, N.Dak. State Sch. Sci, 27-29; chief chemist, Waldorf Paper Prod. Co, St. Paul, Minn, 29-32, develop. engr, 33; research engr,

Adam Hoche, St. Paul, 32; develop. engr, personal work, 32-33 laundry truck driver and organizer, Laundry Workers Union, AFL, 33-40; teacher chem, Augsburg Col, 39; mgr, Pemble Labs, St. Paul and River Falls, 39- Mem: Am. Chem. Soc; Fedn. Am. Scientists; Wis. Acad. Arts & Sci; Laundry Workers Union; Save the St. Croix, Inc; New Dem. Coalition. Rel: Unitarian-Universalist. Mailing Add: R.R.3, River Falls, Wis. 54022.

PEÑA, MANUEL, JR. D
Ariz. State Rep.
b. Cashion, Ariz, 11/17/24; s. Manuel Peña and Elvira Gomez P; m. 6/13/45 to Aurora Cruz; c. Yolanda, Mary Ann, Henry, Estevan, Patricia, Geraldine and Manuel, III. Polit. & Govt. Pos: Cmt. mem, Ariz. State Dem. Party, 62-66, asst. dir. voter registrn, 64; exec. secy, State Athletic Cmn, asst. co. chmn, Maricopa Co. Dem. Party and legis. area chmn, Eighth Dist. Dem. Party, 64-66; Ariz. State Rep, 67- Bus. & Prof. Pos: Pres, Peña Realty & Trust Co. and owner, Peña Ins. Agency, 51-; stockholder, Home Security Finance Co, 64- and v.pres, 64-65. Mil. Serv: Entered as Pvt, Army, 45, released as Pfc, 46, after serv. in 31st Inf. Regt, S.Pac. Theatre. Mem: Am. Legion; VFW. Rel: Catholic. Legal Res: 3728 W. Willetta, Phoenix, Ariz. 85009. Mailing Add: 823 W. Adams, Phoenix, Ariz. 85007.

PENDERGAST, M. ABBOTT R
b. Reading, Pa, 2/20/20; s. Ralph E. Pendergast and Ann Boone P; m. 7/1/50 to Margueritte Craig; c. Margueritte Elizabeth, Craig Abbott and Margaret Anne. Educ: Valley Forge Mil. Acad, Wayne, Pa; Univ. Pa, Wharton Sch. Exten. Polit. & Govt. Pos: Chmn, Rep. Town Cmt, 52-56 and co. committeeman, 56-60; selectman, Kennebunk Port, Maine, 57-63 and chmn. bd, 3 years; Maine State Rep, until 68; secy, Cmt. on Pub. Utilities. Bus. & Prof. Pos: Registered rep, Hayden Stone & Co, 60-62 and Bache & Co, 62- Mil. Serv: Entered as Pvt, Army, 43, released as Pfc, 46, after serv. in 11th Inf. Bn, First Armored Div, Italy and 85th Mountain Inf. Regt, 10th Div, ETO; ETO Ribbon with Four Battle Stars; Distinguished Unit Citation, Co. B, 11th Inf, Plazzo, Italy; Good Conduct Ribbon; plus others. Mem: Newcomen Soc. in N.Am; Mason; Shrine; Am. Legion; div. v.capt, U.S. Coast Guard Auxiliary. Rel: Congregational. Mailing Add: 100 North St, Kennebunk Port, Maine 04046. (1967)

PENDERGRAFT, PHYLLIS M. R
V.Chairwoman, Seventh Dist. Rep. Party, Va.
b. Henrico Co, Va, 6/17/34; m. 9/30/61 to Gradon O'Kelly Pendergraft, Jr; c. Jimese Lynne. Educ: Clifton Forge High Sch, Va, 4 years; Dunsmore Bus. Col, Va, 52-53. Polit. & Govt. Pos: Pres, Waynesboro Rep. Women, Va, 64-66; v.chairwoman, Seventh Dist. Rep. Party, 66-; temporary chmn, 19th Sen. Conv, 67; del, State Rep. Conv, 67,68, 69 and Nat. Rep. Conv, 68 served on platform cmt, Rep. 68. Bus. & Prof. Pos: Secy, Gen. Elec. Co, Waynesboro, Va, 59-67, receptionist, 67- Mem: Waynesboro Beautification Cmt; Rep. Women's Club; Waynesboro Friends of Libr. Rel: presbyterian. Legal Res: 1308 Crofton Ave, Waynesboro, Va. 22908. Mailing Add: Box 26, Waynesboro, Va. 22980.

PENDERGRASS, ORVILLE DEXTER R
b. Near Bakersfield, Mo, 12/26/10; s. Alford Horton Pendergrass and Fannie Morris P; m. 7/4/39 to Dorthy Huse; c. Max, Jane, Louise and Leon. Educ: Southwest Mo. Col, 38-41; LaSalle Exten. Univ, 31-34. Polit. & Govt. Pos: Dep. prosecuting attorney, Baxter Co, Ark, 55-65; Ark. State Rep, 65-67. Mem: Ark. State Bar Asn; pres, Baxter-Marion Bar Asn, 55-58; Mason, Royal Arch Chap; Farm Bur; Lions; past pres, Baxter Co. Fair Asn. Rel: Methodist; past chmn. of bd; chmn, Cmn. on Christian Social Concerns, at present. Mailing Add: 511 Main St, Mountain Home, Ark. 72653.

PENDLETON, DON MILTON R
Chmn, Lincoln Co. Rep. Party, N.C.
b. Lincoln Co, N.C, 2/12/35; s. Kermit Pendleton and Eula Beam P; m. 6/7/59 to Lessy Sain; c. Don Milton, Jr. and Kermit Clay. Educ: Wake Forest Law Sch, LL.B, 58. Polit. & Govt. Pos: Chmn, Lincoln Co. Rep. Party, 65- Mem: Lincoln Co. C. of C.(pres, 65). Rel: Baptist. Legal Res: 119½ E. Main St, Lincolnton, N.C. 28092. Mailing Add: P.O. Box 159, Lincolnton, N.C. 28092.

PENDLETON, DONALD GREY D
Va. State Del.
b. Lynchburg, Va, 1/11/32; m. to Shirley Elizabeth Ewers. Educ: Phillips Bus. Col; Lynchburg Col, B.A, Polit. Sci; Univ. Va, LL.B. Polit. & Govt. Pos: Asst. Trial Judge of Amherst Co; former pres, Y.D.C; chmn, Dem. Exec. Cmt; Va. State Del, 66- Bus. & Prof. Pos: Attorney. Mil. Serv: Korean War, 49-53. Mem: Va. State Bar, Va. Trial Lawyers Asn; Am. Trial Lawyers Asn; Ruritan; WOW; Mason; Odd Fellows; Am. Legion; Jr. C. of C; Va. Nat. Guard Asn. Legal Res: Vista Dr, Amherst, Va. 24521. Mailing Add: P.O. Box 493, Amherst, Va. 24521. (1967)

PENDLETON, EDMUND E, JR. R
Chmn, D.C. Rep. State Cmt.
b. St. Louis, Mo, 6/8/22; s. Edmund E. Pendleton and Katharine Burum P; m. to Josephine C. Culbertson; c. 5 daughters. Educ: Wharton Sch. Finance and Commerce, Univ. Pa, B.S. in econ, 42; Georgetown Univ. Law Sch, J.D, 48; George Wash. Univ. Sch. of Law, LL.M, 50. Polit. & Govt. Pos: Pres, Young Rep. Club of D.C, 48-49 and 53-54; confidential asst. to Asst. Secy. of Agr, U.S. Dept. of Agr, 55-57; counsel for minority, Senate Subcmt. on Nat. Policy Machinery, 60; mem, D.C. Rep. State Cmt, and chmn, 69- Bus. & Prof. Pos: Partner, Culbertson, Pendleton and Pendleton, 48- Mil. Serv: Army, 42-46. Mailing Add: Suite 312, 1155 15th St. N.W, Washington, D.C. 20005.

PENDLETON, EUGENE BARBOUR, JR. D
Va. State Del.
b. Louisa Co, Va, 4/2/13; s. Eugene Barbour Pendleton, M.D. and Virginia Goodman P; m. 6/18/38 to Mildred McLean; c. Jane P.(Mrs. Wootton), M.D, Sally Anne (Mrs. Campbell), Nancy P. (Mrs. Wheeler), Susan P.(Mrs. Riley) and Martha C. Educ: Va. Mil. Inst, 1 year; Hampden-Sydney Col, 3 years; Sigma Chi. Polit. & Govt. Pos: Mem, bd. of supvrs, Louisa Co, Va, 39-42; co. treas, Louisa Co, 46-56; state tax consult, 56-58; state treas, Va, 58-62; Va. State Del, 66- Bus. & Prof. Pos: Mgr, ins. agency, Louisa Co, Va, 38-42; bd. of dirs, South. Bank and Trust Co; treas, South. States Coop, 61-; bd. of trustees, Richmond House for Boys. Mil. Serv: Entered as Ens, Naval Res, 42, released as Lt. (sg), 45, after serv. in Armed Guard, ETO, 43-45; Bronze Star and Citation. Mem: Kiwanis; Co. Club of Va; Downtown Club; Nat. Asn. Comptrollers and Treas; Bond Club of Va; Treas. Asn. of Va; Mason; Scottish Rite; Shrine; Am. Legion; Mil. Order of World Wars; Navy League; VFW; Farm Bur; Century Club of Va. Commonwealth Club. Rel: Christian Church; Bd. of Elders, Seventh St. Christian Church. Mailing Add: 4708 Rolfe Rd, Richmond, Va. 23226.

PENDLETON, RAYMOND A. R
N.Mex. State Sen.
Polit. & Govt. Pos: N.Mex. State Sen, currently; mem, city coun; mem, sch. bd. Bus. & Prof. Pos: Businessman and engr. Mem: Lions; C. of C. Mailing Add: Box 8, Roy, N.Mex. 87743.

PENETAR, DANIEL LAWRENCE D
b. Dunmore, Pa, 8/3/16; s. Lawrence Penetar and Frances Morano P; m. 11/15/52 to Anne Notarianni; c. Daniel, Jr, Lawrence and Martin. Educ: Wharton Sch. Bus, Univ. Pa, 35; Univ. Scranton, B.A, 40; Fordham Univ. Law Sch, LL.B, 47. Polit. & Govt. Pos: Solicitor, Borough of Dunmore, Pa, 60-; chmn, Lackawanna Co. Dem. Party Annual Dinner, 62; pres, Lackawanna Co. Ital-Am. Dem. League, 66; solicitor, Lackawanna Co. Bd. of Assessors, 67; alternate del-at-lg, Dem. Nat. Conv, 68. Bus. & Prof. Pos: Pres, Carp Realty Co. Inc, Scranton, Pa, currently, Holiday Finance Corp, Dunmore, currently; v.pres, J.N. Realty Co. Inc, Scranton, currently; assoc. and partner, Miller & Penetar, Law Firm, currently. Mil. Serv: Pvt, Army, 44, serv. in Armored Div. Mem: Lackawanna Co, Pa. and Am. Bar Asns; Am. Legion; Elks; Lions. Rel: Roman Catholic. Legal Res: 2216 Jefferson Ave, Dunmore, Pa. 18512.

PENFIELD, JAMES KEDZIE
b. N.Y.C, 4/9/08; m. to Anne Boardman; c. Kedzie Anne. Educ: Stanford Univ, A.B, 29. Polit. & Govt. Pos: Career officer, U.S. Dept. of State For. Serv, 30-; v.consul, Mexico, 30-31 and Canton, 31-33; lang. officer, Mukden, 33-34 and Peiping, 34-36; consul, Yannanfu, 36-38, Godthaab, Greenland, 40-42 and Chungking, 42-44; dep. dir, Off. of Far East. Affairs, 45-48; counsr, Prague, 48-50 and London, 50-54; dep. chief of mission, Vienna, 54-56; counsr, Athens, 56-58; Dep. Asst. Secy. of State for African Affairs, 58-61; U.S. Ambassador to Iceland, 61-67; sr. for. serv. inspector, 67- Legal Res: Longbranch, Wash. 98351. Mailing Add: c/o U.S. Dept. of State, Washington, D.C. 20520.

PENISTON, LOUIS T. D
b. 1919. Educ: Georgetown Col; Univ. of Louisville, LL.B. Polit. & Govt. Pos: Ky. State Rep, 46, 52-54 & 60-68. Bus. & Prof. Pos: Attorney. Mil. Serv: Air Force. Mem: Mason; Elks; Am. Legion. Rel: Baptist. Mailing Add: New Castle, Ky. 40050. (1967)

PENIX, BILL D
Secy, Craighead Co. Dem. Cent. Cmt, Ark.
b. Jonesboro, Ark, 10/10/22; s. Roy Penix and Billie Broadway P; m. 1/21/45 to Marian Fox; c. Susan Ellen, Bill Jr, Charley and Jane Lee. Educ: Univ. Ark, B.A, 43, LL.B, 49; Blue Key; Phi Alpha Delta; Sigma Chi. Polit. & Govt. Pos: Dep. prosecuting attorney, Craighead Co, Ark, 49-55; secy, Craighead Co. Dem. Cent. Cmt, 58-; mem, Jonesboro Sch. Bd, 67-; del, Dem. Nat. Conv, 68; state campaign mgr, Fulbright for Senate, 69; mem, State Dem. Cent. Cmt, 69. Bus. & Prof. Pos: Lawyer, Penix & Penix, Jonesboro, Ark, 49- Mil. Serv: Entered as Pvt, Army, 42, released as 1st Lt, 46, after serv. in C.H.Q. Signal Opers, Southwest-Pac, 44-46; Army Res, Maj.(Ret); Asiatic-Pac. Campaign Medal with three stars; Philippine Liberation Medal with two stars. Mem: Craighead Co, Ark. and Am. Bar Asns; Am. Legion; Lions. Rel: Methodist. Legal Res: 1011 Neville Ave, Jonesboro, Ark. 72401. Mailing Add: P.O. Box 1306, Jonesboro, Ark. 72401.

PENIX, CHAUNCEY EDWARD D
Chmn, Young Co. Dem. Exec. Cmt, Tex.
b. Big Spring, Tex, 7/23/03; s. Stephen Austin Penix and Forra Argie Lindsey P; m. 12/28/25 to Mildred Tidwell. Educ: Univ. Tex. Polit. & Govt. Pos: Co. attorney, 27-30; asst. dist. attorney, Tex, 32-34; chmn, Young Co. Dem. Exec. Cmt, 41- Bus. & Prof. Pos: Pres, Graham Fed. Savings & Loan Asn, 52-66. Mil. Serv: Entered as 2nd Lt, Army Air Force, 42, released as Lt. Col, 45, after serv. in ETO, 42-45; Bronze Star; French Croix De Guerre with Silver Star; Victory and Serv. Medals. Mem: Pres, Young Co. Bar Asn, 53; Tex. Bar Asn; Am. Legion; Mason; Eastern Star; County Club; Lions. Rel: Baptist. Mailing Add: Box 666, Graham, Tex. 76046.

PENN, FRANK REID D
N.C. State Sen.
b. Reidsville, N.C, 9/2/17; s. Charles Ashby Penn and Stella Edrington P; m. 12/19/43 to Roberta Winton; c. Roberta, Frank R, IV, Anne Spencer, Charles Ashby and Edrington J. Educ: Univ. N.C, 4 years; Beta Theta Pi. Polit. & Govt. Pos: Cmnr, Rockingham Co, N.C, 64-66; N.C. State Sen, 66- Bus. & Prof. Pos: Secy-treas, Penn, Inc, Reidsville, N.C, currently. Mil. Serv: Entered as Pvt, Army, 41, released as 1st Lt, 46, after serv. as Co. Comdr, 818th Tank Destroyer Bn, ETO, 45-46; ETO Medal; Five Oak Leaves; Bronze Star; Purple Heart. Mem: Elks; Mason (32°); Rotary; Am. Legion; VFW. Rel: Presbyterian. Legal Res: 1202 Crescent Dr, Reidsville, N.C. 27320. Mailing Add: P.O. Box 720, Reidsville, N.C. 27320.

PENN, MARIE MOORE D
Mem, Madison Co. Dem. Exec. Cmt, Tenn.
b. La Grange, Ga, 2/17/04; d. John Wesley Moore (deceased) and Mary Ann Edmondson (deceased); m. to Rev. I. Garland Penn, Jr, wid; c. Kathryn P. (Mrs. Carr). Educ: Lane Col, B.A, 53; Univ. Calif, Los Angeles, M.A, 62; Nat. Educ. Asn; Sigma Gamma Pi; pres, City Federated Clubs. Polit. & Govt. Pos: Mem, Tenn. State Dem. Adv. Cmt; mem, Madison Co. Dem. Exec. Cmt, currently; v.chmn, Mayor's Citizens Adv. Cmt, Jackson, currently; mem, Dem. Woman's Adv. Cmt. for Hubert H. Humphrey; alternate del, Dem. Nat. Conv, 68; treas, Jackson Dem. Club, Tenn, 68-; mem, State Bd. of Dirs. for Ment. Health; secy, West. State Ment. Inst. Vol. Serv. Publ: Three Decades of Christian Service, Christian Methodist Episcopal Church. Mem: Nat. Asn. of

Women Deans and Counsel; Personnel Workers Asn; Pres, Jackson Fedn. of Colored Women's Club; Civic Pride Club; Int. Platform; life mem, NAACP; adv. mem, Marquis Biographies Libr. Soc. Serv. Award, Nat. Found. March of Dimes; Commun. Leader of Am. Plaque, 69; Named Woman of the Year and Recipient of Achievement Award, Omega Psi Phi Fraternity; Plaque from Missionary Inst. of Christian Methodist Episcopal Church; Serv. Award, Lane Col. Rel: Methodist. Mailing Add: 816 N.Hays Ave, Jackson, Tenn. 38301.

PENN, THOMAS AZOR D
Ark. State Sen.
b. Lynn, Ark, 4/1/23; s. Joseph Richard Penn and Pearl Osburn P; m. 6/7/47 to Mary Trice Dalton; c. Richard Lewis and Thomas Jackson. Educ: Ark. State Col, B.A, 47; George Peabody Col, M.A, 57. Polit. & Govt. Pos: Ark. State Sen, 59- Bus. & Prof. Pos: Teacher, Cave City, Ark, 47-50; prin, Dalton, 50-55; supt. of schs, Black Rock, 55-66 and Cave City, 66- Mil. Serv: Entered as Pvt, Army, 43, grad. Air Force Cadets, Luke Field, Phoenix, Ariz, 44, released as 2nd Lt, 2nd Flying Training Command, 45. Mem: Mason; Shrine (32°); Farm Bur; Lions; Ark. Sch. Adminstrs. Asn; Ark. Educ. Asn; Nat. Educ. Asn. Rel: Church of Christ. Mailing Add: Cave City, Ark. 72521.

PENN, WILLIAM FRANK R
Mem, State Rep. Cent. Cmt, Calif.
b. Cordell, Okla, 10/17/29; s. Liebert Penn and Dorothy Courtney P; m. 4/17/62 to Barbara Dean White; c. Michelle and Cheryl. Polit. & Govt. Pos: E.Kern rep. for Reinecke, Calif, 68-69; E.Kern rep. for Goldwater, 68; alternate, Kern Co. Rep. Cent. Cmt, Bakersfield, 68-; mem, State Rep. Cent. Cmt, 69- Bus. & Prof. Pos: Editor-Mgr, La Feria News, La Feria, Tex, 50-61; dir, photo and advert, A.V. Press, Palmdale, Lancaster, Calif, 61-67; Publisher, The Enterprise, Boron, Calif, 67-69. Mem: Professional Photographers of Am; Rotary Int. (past pres); Y's Mens Club (past pres). State Award for Weekly Newspapers, Tex, 61, 'Outstanding Soil Conservation Issue.' Rel: Baptist. Legal Res: 27464 Hiway 58, Boron, Calif. 93516. Mailing Add: P.O. Box 747, Boron, Calif. 93516.

PENNELL, RUSSELL ADAMS D
Chmn, Sagadahoc Co. Dem. Cmt, Maine
b. Topsham, Maine, 5/30/22; s. Charles Sewall Pennell and Bertha Marion French P; m. 11/15/40 to June Theresa Simpson; c. Nancy Lee (Mrs. Clifford Card), Sharon Anne (Mrs. Charles Meserve, Jr), Ramona June (Mrs. Foster B. Meserve, Sr) and William Russell. Educ: Greeley Inst, agr, 1 year; Bath Iron Works Shipfitter Sch, 1 year; Navy Great Lakes Serv. Sch, shipfitter. Polit. & Govt. Pos: Town treas. and tax collector, Bowdoin, Maine, 64-; dep. sheriff, Sagadahoc Co, 64-; town chmn, Bowdoin Dem. Party; chmn, Sagadahoc Co. Dem. Cmt, 66-; chmn. of original Muskie for 72 Club, 69- Bus. & Prof. Pos: Tree surgeon; welder; burner; commercial farmer and commercial fisherman; shipfitter, Bath Iron Works, 4 years; heavy equip. operator, Union Local No. 4, 9 years; off. mgr. and claims adjuster, Barrows Transfer & Storage Co, 10 years; foreman, Maine Cent. R.R, currently. Mil. Serv: Entered as A/S, Navy, 43, released as Shipfitter 2/C, 46, after serv. in M.T.B. (PT. Boats); Squadron No. 32, S.Pac. Theatre, 44-46; Bronze Star for Guadalcanal; Bronze Star for Russell Islands. Mem: Elks. Rel: Baptist. Legal Res: Meadow Rd, Bowdoinham, Maine 04008. Mailing Add: R.F.D. 2, Bowdoinham, Maine 04008.

PENNINGTON, BROOKS MADDOX, JR. D
Ga. State Sen.
b. Madison, Ga, 10/21/27; s. Brooks Maddox Pennington, Sr. and Lucille Braswell P; m. 8/14/53 to Jacquelyn Christian; c. Brooks Maddox III, Penny Almand, Robert Braswell, William Dan. Educ: N.Ga. Col; Univ. of Ga. Polit. & Govt. Pos: Chmn, Morgan Co. Cmnrs, Ga, 60-; Ga. State Rep, 62; Ga. State Sen, 45th Dist, 63- Bus. & Prof. Pos: Seedsman, offices & plants in Madison, Vidalia, Moultrie, Atlanta & Winder, Ga, & Columbia, S.C; Secy, Morgan Co. Indus. Bd, 58-. Mil. Serv: World War II, 43-46; Korean War, 51-52. Mem: Elks; comdr, VFW Post 2557, 53-56; pres, Ga. Seedsman Asn, 60-61; chmn, Morgan Co. Hosp. Authority, 59-61; Legis. Cmt. of the Am. Seed Trade Asn; v.pres, Morgan Co. C. of C, 59; past v.pres, Morgan Co. Band Booster Club; Stone Mt. Mem. Cmt, 59-62; dir, Madison Kiwanis Club, 62-; past pres, Morgan Co. Touchdown Club. Rel: Methodist; Officer of Bd, Pennington Methodist Church. Mailing Add: Crawford St, Madison, Ga. 30650.

PENNINGTON, HARRY LUCAS D
Ala. State Rep.
b. Wetumpka, Ala, 9/3/19; s. William Matthew Pennington and Bernadine Williams P; m. 5/30/64 to Mary Evelyn Higgins; c. Harry Lucas, Jr. and Mary Melanie. Educ: Univ. Ala, A.B, 41, LL.B, 50; Sigma Chi. Polit. & Govt. Pos: Circuit solicitor, Madison Co, Ala, 51-52; circuit judge, 23rd Judicial Circuit, 55-61; Ala. State Rep, 63-, mem. and Second V.Chmn, Ala. Space Sci. Cmn, 65-; pres-pro-tem, Florence State Univ, 68- Bus. & Prof. Pos: Pres, Huntsville Lumber Co, Inc, 59-; chmn. bd. dir, The Bank of Huntsville, 68- Mil. Serv: Entered as 2nd Lt, Army, 41, released as Maj, 46, after serv. in Coast Artil. Corps, ETO, 45-46. Mem: Huntsville Lions; Am. Legion; VFW. Recipient of the Bonnie D. Hand Award as the Outstanding Mem. of the 1967 Regular Sessions House of Rep, State of Ala. as Selected by the Vote of the Members of the 1967 Capital Press Corps. Rel: Trinity Methodist. Legal Res: 5720 Criner Rd, Huntsville, Ala. 35801. Mailing Add: 809 Shoney Dr. S.W, Huntsville, Ala. 35801.

PENNINGTON, LUTHER B, JR. R
b. Plattsburg, N.Y, 12/16/21; married; c. two. Educ: Houghton Col, B.A, 59; Boston Univ. Sch. of Theology, S.T.B, 63. Polit. & Govt. Pos: N.H. State Rep, -67. Bus. & Prof. Pos: Clergyman. Rel: Protestant. 1967 Legal Res: Epping, N.H. No mailing address available. (1967)

PENNINGTON, WILLIAM ALTON D
Chmn, Va. Independent Party
b. Newport News, Va, 1/13/11; m. to Margaret Allen Alton. Educ: Col. William and Mary, pre-med; Med. Col. of Va, M.D, 37. Polit. & Govt. Pos: Dir. and first pres, Va. Wildlife Fedn; Va. State Del, 60; chmn, George Wallace Campaign, Va, 68; chmn, Va. Independent Party, 69- Bus. & Prof. Pos: Physician. Mil. Serv: Entered Army, 42, released as Capt, Med. Corps, 45; Bronze Star. Rel: Baptist. Mailing Add: Buckingham, Va. 23721.

PENNY, JAMES F, JR. D
N.C. State Rep.
b. Harnett Co, N.C, 10/23/37; s. James F. Penny, Sr. and Marie Abernathy P; m. May, 67 to Judith Hardee; c. Anne Marie and James F, III. Educ: Campbell Col, A.A, 58; Univ. N.C, Chapel Hill, B.S. in Bus. Admin, 60; Wake Forest Univ. Sch. Law, LL.B, 64; Phi Delta Phi. Polit. & Govt. Pos: Treas, Harnett Co. Dem. Exec. Cmt, N.C, 65-67; N.C. State Rep, 69- Mem: Harnett Co. Bar Asn.(v.pres, 69-); N.C. State Bar Asn; Am. Bar Asn.(mem. gen. practice cmt, 69-70); Baptist Grove Ruritan Club. Rel: Baptist. Mailing Add: P.O. Box 937, Lillington, N.C. 27546.

PENTECOST, CAYCE LaFON D
Cmnr, Tenn. Pub. Serv. Cmn.
b. Tenn, 6/1/18; s. Thomas Cayce Pentecost and Carrie LaFon P; single. Educ: Univ. of Tenn, B.S, 40 and LL.B, 47; Omicron Delta Kappa; Phi Delta Phi; Sigma Phi Epsilon. Polit. & Govt. Pos: Tenn. State Rep, 47; Asst. U.S. Attorney, 47-48; exec. counsel to Gov. of Tenn, 53; cmnr, Tenn. Pub. Serv. Cmn, 53- Mil. Serv: Entered Navy, 42, released as Lt, 46, after serv. in Air Corps, S. Atlantic and Southwest Pac; Lt. Col, Tenn. Nat. Guard. Mem: Dir. exec. cmt, Tenn. Heart Asn; Am. Legion; VFW; Mason; Shrine; Elks; Tenn. Bar Asn. Rel: Baptist. Legal Res: Dresden, Tenn. 38225. Mailing Add: State Capitol, Nashville, Tenn. 37219.

PENTLAND, ROBERT D
Mo. State Sen.
b. Bowhill, Scotland, 2/7/08; m. 4/25/35 to Irma Seaman; c. Judith Alleyn (Mrs. Schreyer), Shelia Marion (Mrs. Pudlowski), William Robert and four grandchildren. Educ: Pub. schs. of Benld, Ill. Polit. & Govt. Pos: Mo. State Sen, 48- Bus. & Prof. Pos: Bus. rep, Teamsters Union, Local 688; coal miner; grocery clerk; warehouseman. Mil. Serv: Fifth Marine Div, 2 years. Mem: 12 Ward Dem. Orgn; Cleveland High Sch. Dad's Club. Mailing Add: 6429 Gravois, St. Louis, Mo. 63116. (1967)

PENTON, MARBY ROBERT D
Miss. State Rep.
b. Gautier, Miss, 8/23/22; married. Polit. & Govt. Pos: Miss. State Rep, currently. Bus. & Prof. Pos: Attorney-at-law; attorney, Ocean Springs Munic. Separate Sch. Dist. Mem: Miss. State and Jackson Co. Bar Asns; Commercial Law League; adv, Jackson Co. Legal Secy. Asn; Lions (exec. cmt, Ocean Springs Club); Cub Scouts; PTA; Am. Legion; VFW. Rel: Protestant. Mailing Add: 206 Washington Ave, Ocean Springs, Miss. 39564.

PEOPLES, CHARLES FREDERICK R
Chmn, Stoneham Rep. Town Cmt, Mass.
b. Somerville, Mass, 10/11/11; s. George Peoples and D.A. McIntyre P; m. 1/29/39 to Helen Bryce Brown; c. Bonnie Bryce (Mrs. Michaud) and Jane Anne. Educ: Northeast. Univ, B.S.Ch.E, 35; LL.B, 45; Sigma Delta. Polit. & Govt. Pos: Mem, Planning Bd, Stoneham, Mass, 51-54; mem, Stoneham Rep. Town Cmt, 57-; chmn, 67-; asst. attorney gen, Commonwealth of Mass, 66-67, mem, Div. Commun. Affairs, currently. Bus. & Prof. Pos: Civil engr, 35-; attorney at law, 51- Mil. Serv: Entered as Pvt, Army, 40, released as Maj. C.E, 46, after serv. in ETO and Pac. Theatres; Res, 46-, Lt.Col. Mem: Boston Soc. Civil Eng; Am. Soc. Mil. Eng; Infantry Asn; Mass. Bar Asn; Am. Trial Lawyers Asn; Mason; VFW; Am. Legion. Rel: Protestant. Mailing Add: 455 Main St, Stoneham, Mass. 02180.

PEPPER, CLAUDE D
U.S. Rep, Fla.
b. Dudleyville, Ala, 9/8/00; s. J.W. Pepper and Lena C. Talbot P; m. 12/29/36 to Mildred Irene Webster. Educ: Univ. Ala, A.B, 21; Harvard Law Sch, LL.B, 24; Phi Beta Kappa; Kappa Alpha; Omicron Delta Kappa; Sigma Upsilon; Phi Alpha Delta; Blue Key. Hon. LL.D, McMaster Univ, 41, Univ. Toronto, 42, Univ. Ala, 42 and Rollins Col, 44. Polit. & Govt. Pos: Mem, Fla. State Dem. Exec. Cmt, 28-29; Fla. State Rep, Taylor Co, 29-30; mem, Fla. State Bd. Pub. Welfare, 31-32 and Bd. Law Exam, 33-34; U.S. Sen, Fla, 36-51, chmn, Senate Cmt. on Inter-Oceanic Canal, U.S. Senate, mem, Select Cmt. on Small Bus, mem, Senate For. Rels. Cmt, 37-47 & 49-50, mem, Senate Cmts. on Mil. Affairs, Patents, Commerce and Labor and Pub. Welfare, Senate Subcmt. on Wartime Health and Educ, 43-46, chmn, Subcmt. on Mid. East and mem, Subcmt. on Latin Am; U.S. Senate del, Interparliamentary Union, The Hague, 38 and Dublin, 50; del. and chmn. Fla. del, Dem. Nat. Conv, 40 & 44, alternate del, 48, 52, 56, 60, 64 & 68; U.S. Rep, Third Cong. Dist, Fla, 62-67, 11th Cong. Dist, 67-, mem, House Rules Cmt, U.S. House of Rep, chmn, House Select Cmt. to Investigate Crime, 69-, mem, House Cmt. on Internal Security, 69- Bus. & Prof. Pos: Teacher, pub. schs, Dothan, Ala, 17-18; instr. law, Univ. Ark, 24-25; attorney-at-law, Perry, Fla, 25-30 and Miami Beach, 30-36; Marfleet lectr, Univ. Toronto, 42; officer and dir, Wash. Fed. Savings and Loan Asn, Miami Beach. Mil. Serv: Pvt, Students Army Training Corps, Co. A, Univ. Ala, 18. Publ: Articles in law rev, mag. and newspapers. Mem: Int, Inter-Am, Am, Dade Co, Tallahassee, Miami Beach and Coral Gables Bar Asns; exec. coun, Fla. State Bar Asn, 34; Asn. of Bar of City of N.Y; lt. gov, West. Div, Fla. Kiwanis Int; former mem. bd. dirs, C. of C. of Americas; Am. Legion; 40 et 8; Mason; Shrine; Elks; Moose; Jefferson Island Club; Harvard Club Wash. and Miami; Army Navy Club; Coral Gables, Miami Shores, Army Navy and La Gorce Country Clubs. Albert Lasker Pub. Serv. Award, 67; Eleanor Roosevelt-Israel Humanities Award, 68. Rel: Baptist. Legal Res: 2121 N. Bayshore Dr, Miami, Fla. 33137. Mailing Add: Room 432, Cannon House Office Bldg, Washington, D.C. 20005.

PERALA, REINO A. D
b. Maple, Wis, 8/28/15. Educ: Univ. of Wis. Law Sch, LL.B, 43. Polit. & Govt. Pos: Wis. State Assemblyman, 52-68; justice of the peace; served on Interstate Ports Cmn. Bus. & Prof. Pos: Attorney; operates Hotel in Superior. Mailing Add: 824 N. 22nd St, Superior, Wis. 54301. (1967)

PERCIVAL, ELIZABETH THOMPSON R
b. Sundance, Wyo, 7/21/19; d. Nathaniel Hugh Thompson and Edith Gould T; m. 9/15/38 to Paul Phillip Percival; c. Dorothy Rae (Mrs. Whiteaker) and William Paul. Educ: Blackhills Teachers Col, 3 years. Polit. & Govt. Pos: Del, Wyo. Rep. Conv, 54-, serv. on Credentials, Platform and Nomination Cmts. at various times; cmt. work at precinct, col and state level; Rep. precinct committeewoman, Niobrara Co, 56-69; pres, Niobrara Co. Rep. Womans Club, 64-67. Mem: Easter Star; Wyo. Cow Belles; Federated Rep. Womans Club. Rel: Episcopal. Mailing Add: Box 1238, Lusk, Wyo. 82225.

PERCY, CHARLES HARTING R
U.S. Sen, Ill.
b. Pensacola, Fla, 9/27/19; s. Edward H. Percy and Elizabeth Harting P; m. 8/27/50 to Loraine Diane Guyer; c. Sharon Lee, Roger, Gail and Mark. Educ: Univ. Chicago, A.B, 41; Phi Delta Phi; Alpha Delta Phi. Hon. LL.D, Ill. Col, 61, Roosevelt Univ, 61 and Lake Forest Col, 62; H.H.D, Willamette Univ, 62. Polit. & Govt. Pos: Spec. ambassador and personal rep. of the President to presidential inauguration ceremonies in Peru and Bolivia, 56; chmn, Rep. Nat. Finance Cmt, 57-59; U.S. Sen, Ill, 67-; del, Rep. Nat. Conv, 68. Bus. & Prof. Pos: Sales trainee and apprentice, Bell and Howell, 38, mgr, war coord. dept, 41-43, asst. secy, 43-46, corp. secy, 46-49, pres, 49-61, chief exec. officer, 61-63, chmn. bd. dirs, 61-66; sales prom, Crowell-Collier Pub. Co, 39; dir, Harris Trust and Savings Bank. Mil. Serv: Navy, Lt, 43-45. Mem: Trustee, Calif. Inst. Tech; trustee, Ill. Inst. Tech, 50-54; trustee, citizens bd. and dir, alumni found, Univ. Chicago; co-chmn, Nat. Conf. Christians and Jews, Chicago, 54; Chicago Asn. Commerce; dir, Am. Mgt. Asn; Nat. Photog. Mfrs. Asn; Am. Ord. Asn; Photog. Soc. of Am; Chicago Club; dir, Econ. Club; dir, Execs. Club; Commercial Commonwealth Club. One of Ten Outstanding Young Men, U.S. Jr. C. of C, 49; World Trade Award, 55; Nat. Sales Exec. Mgt. Award, 56; officer, French Legion of Honor, 61. Legal Res: Wilmette, Ill. Mailing Add: 1200 New Senate Office Bldg, Washington, D.C. 20510. (1967)

PEREIRA, STEPHEN EDWARD D
Mem, Calif. Dem. State Cent. Cmt.
b. Oakland, Calif, 1/7/40; s. John J. Pereira and Katherin Silva P; m. 7/4/65 to Barbara Lou; c. Annely and Thomas Allen. Educ: Stockton Col, A.A, 61; San Francisco State Col, B.A, 63. Polit. & Govt. Pos: Mem, Calif. Dem. State Cent. Cmt, 65- Bus. & Prof. Pos: Soc. worker, San Joaquin Co. Welfare Dept, 64-65; teacher, St. Marys of the Assumption Sch, 65-66; teacher, Stockton Unified Sch. Dist, 66- Mem: Am. Fedn. Teachers. Rel: Roman Catholic. Mailing Add: 2255 Crafton Way, Stockton, Calif. 95204.

PERENICK, CHARLES HENRY R
Chmn, Pittsfield Rep. City Cmt, Mass.
b. North Adams, Mass, 9/30/33; s. Salvatore Perenick and Rosalie Mancuso P; m. 6/20/59 to Margaret Ann McLaughlin; c. Kimberley Ann, Charles H, Jr. and Daniel Anthony. Educ: Norwich Univ, B.A, 56; Portia Law Sch, Boston, Mass, 1 year; Pres, Alpha Chap, Theta Chi; Freshmen Class Pres. Polit. & Govt. Pos: Treas, Ward Four, Pittsfield Rep. City Cmt, 63-67, chmn, 67-; mil. aide to Gov. Volpe, Berkshire Co, 64-68; secy. to Gov. Volpe, State House Boston, 66-67; admin. asst, Mass. Rep. State Cmt, 67-68; secy. for appointments for state serv, Gov. Sargent, State House, 69- Bus. & Prof. Pos: Police officer, State of Mass, 57-62; teacher, Pittsfield High Sch, 62-65. Mil. Serv: Entered as Pvt, Nat. Guard, 50, presently, Capt, serv. in Adjutant Gen. Staff. Mem: Venerable Mass. Sons of Italy; K. of C; United Commercial Travelers; Nat. Guard Officers Asn; Mass. Nat. Guard Asn; Teachers Fedn. Rel: Catholic. Mailing Add: 38 Emerson Ave, Pittsfield, Mass. 01201.

PEREZ, JOAQUIN ARRIOLA D
Sen, Guam Legis.
b. Agana, Guam, 3/14/16; s. Pedro Leon Guerrero Perez (deceased) and Ana Alvarez P.(deceased); m. 4/15/39 to Macrena Aquiningoc; c. Patricia (Mrs. J.P. Castro), David Jose, Frank Anthony and Anne Julia. Educ: George Wash. Univ. spec. prog. Pub. Admin, 64-65. Polit. & Govt. Pos: Acct. clerk, Govt. Guam, 35-46; chmn, ways and means cmt, Guam Legis, 48-50; Sen, Guam Legis, 50-61 & 68-, v.chmn, rules cmt, 50-56, chmn, 56-61, chmn. trade and tourism cmt, 68-; asst. dir, Govt. of Guam Pub. Works, 61-67. Bus. & Prof. Pos: Asst. gen. mgr, Guam Commercial Corp. Inc, 46-49; pres. and gen. mgr, Island Serv. Co. Inc, 49-53; pres. and mgr, Perez Enterprise, Inc, 56- Mem: Young Men's League of Guam; Lions; PTA; charter mem. Legis. Leaders Conf. Am. Rel: Roman Catholic. Legal Res: Ipao-Tamuning, Guam 96910. Mailing Add: P.O. Box 456, Agana, Guam 96910.

PERICONI, JOSEPH F. R
b. 1911. Polit. & Govt. Pos: Pres, Borough of Bronx 61-66; formerly N.Y. State Sen, Bronx Dist; former mem, N.Y.C. Transit Authority; mem, N.Y. State Liquor Authority. Prof. Pos: Attorney; dir, Washington Heights Fed. Savings and Loan Asn, 65- Mailing Add: c/o Washington Heights Fed. Savings and Loan Association, 1390 St. Nicholas Ave, New York, N.Y. 10032. (1967)

PERKINS, CARL D. D
U.S. Rep, Ky.
b. Hindman, Ky, 10/15/12; s. J.E. Perkins and Dora Calhoun P; m. to Verna Johnson; c. Carl Christopher. Educ: Caney Jr. Col; Jefferson Sch. of Law. Polit. & Govt. Pos: Commonwealth attorney from 31st Judicial Dist, Ky, 39; mem, Ky. Gen. Assembly, 40; Knott Co. Attorney, 41-48; counsel, State Dept. of Hwy, 48; U.S. Rep, Ky, 48-, chmn, House Educ. and Labor Cmt, U.S. House of Rep, currently. Bus. & Prof. Pos: Attorney-at-Law. Mil. Serv: World War II, ETO, participated in battle of N. France, the Ardennes, The Rhineland and Cent. Europe. Mem: Am. Legion; Mason. Rel: Baptist. Legal Res: Knott Co, Ky. Mailing Add: 2252 Rayburn House Office Bldg, Washington, D.C. 20515.

PERKINS, CECIL RAY D
Chmn, Jessamine Co. Dem. Party, Ky.
b. Nicholasville, Ky, 2/11/24; s. Homer Perkins and Martha Peel P; m. 3/25/43 to Louise Underwood; c. Glen, Jennings, Cecil Ray, Jr, and Marty. Educ: Nicholasville High Sch. Polit. & Govt. Pos: Tax cmnr, Jessamine Co, 56-61; chmn, Jessamine Co. Dem. Party, Ky, 64- Rel: Christian. Legal Res: 316 E. Oak St, Nicholasville, Ky. 40356. Mailing Add: P.O. Box 31, Nicholasville, Ky. 40356. (1967)

PERKINS, JOHN BURTON D
Miss. State Rep.
b. Jackson, Miss, 1/8/39; s. Claude Lee Perkins (deceased) and Louise Sweat P; m. to Lyda Carol Brand; c. Ike, Christy, Thomas and John West. Educ: Millsaps Col, B.A. in Hist, 61; Univ. Miss, work on Masters, 62-63; Int. Rels. Club; Alpha Tau Omega. Polit. & Govt. Pos: Docket and reading clerk, Miss. State Senate, 62; Miss. State Rep, Lauderdale Co, 68- Bus. & Prof. Pos: Pub. rels. staff, Charles Sullivan Gubernatorial Campaign, 63; reporter, Jackson Daily News, 63-65; city hall reporter, The Meridian Star, 64-65 and managing ed, 66- Mil. Serv: Entered as Pvt, Army Res, 61, released as E-4, 67. Mem: Miss. and La. Assoc. Press Asn; Big Eight Writers Asn; N.Meridian Optimist Club; Farm Bur; Fraternal Order of Police; State Cmn. of Law Enforcement Assistance. Rel: Methodist. Mailing Add: 2407 Poplar Springs Dr, Meridian, Miss. 39301.

PERKINS, LARRY LEE R
Iowa State Rep.
b. Des Moines, Ia, 1/8/37; s. Lowell V. Perkins and Helen Francis Yates P; m. 6/15/63 to Nelda Jean Hesseltine; c. Teresa Gaye, Laura Jean, Anita Francis and Larry Virtus. Educ: Roosevelt High Sch, Des Moines, grad, 54. Polit. & Govt. Pos: Iowa State Rep, Pottawattamie Co, 69- Bus. & Prof. Pos: Lumber salesman, 61-68; commercial decorator, 68-; bar and night club owner, 68- Mil. Serv: Air Force. Mem: Elks. Rel: Methodist. Legal Res: 2544 Ave. M, Council Bluffs, Iowa 51501. Mailing Add: 2825 Center, Des Moines, Iowa 50312.

PERKINS, MILDRED KELLEY R
Mem, Rep. Nat. Cmt.
b. Littleton, N.H, 7/6/08; d. Fred Kelley and Carlotta Kimball K; m. 4/19/33 to Francis Eaton Perkins; c. Harold Wilder and Francis Eaton, Jr. Educ: Plymouth State Col, B.E, 30; Forensic Club; Pan Athenian. Polit. & Govt. Pos: Pres, Concord Women's Rep. Club, N.H, 51-52; asst. treas, N.H. State Rep. Cmt, 52, asst. chmn, 57 & 65-68; pres, N.H. Federated Rep. Women's Clubs, 56-57; mem. rev. cmt, Nat. Fedn. Rep. Women, 57, v.chmn. finance cmt, 58-59, prog. chmn, 60, membership chmn, 61-64 and fourth v.pres, 65-67; mem, Rep. Nat. Cmt, currently; Rep.Nat. Committeewoman, N.H, 68- Bus. & Prof. Pos: Instr. soc. sci, N.H. and N.J. Pub. Schs. Mem: Concord Bd. Educ, N.H; trustee, N.H. Univ. Complex, Univ. N.H, Plymouth State Col. and Keene State Col; mem. N.H. YMCA Youth and Govt. Cmt, 65-69; Eastern Star; past pres, West Concord Garden Club; Concord Women's Col. Club; co-rounder and dir, N.H. Lawyers' Wives Orgn; charter mem. and past pres, N.H. Hosp. Auxiliary; Civil War Centennial Cmn; secy, Concord Bicentennial Corp. Rel: Episcopal. Mailing Add: 5 Glendale Rd, Concord, N.H. 03301.

PERKINS, TALFORD O. R
b. Bentonville, Ark, 11/8/25; s. Thomas William Perkins and Ora E. Crissy P; m. 5/15/48 to Lovie O'Neil Davis; c. Linda Ann, Talford, Jr, Sandra Louise and William Edward. Educ: Trade sch, grad. in electronics. Polit. & Govt. Pos: Chmn, McDonald Co. Rep. Cent. Cmt, Mo, 64-67. Bus. & Prof. Pos: Fire chief, Southwest City Fire Dept, presently. Mil. Serv: Entered as Pvt, Army Air Force, 44, released as Sgt. Mem: Mason; Am. Legion; Indust. Develop. Commercial Club; Tesa. Rel: Methodist. Mailing Add: Southwest City, Mo. 64863.

PERKINS, WILLIAM H, JR. D
b. Rushville, Ill, 8/4/21; s. William Hiler Perkins, Sr. and Sarah Elizabeth Logsdon P; m. 1/14/49 to Eileen Margaret Nelson; c. Gary Douglas. Educ: Ill. Col, 39-40. Polit. & Govt. Pos: Asst. Sgt. at Arms, Dem. Nat. Conv, 52 & 56, del-at-lg, 64 & 68; spec. asst. to chmn, Dem. Nat. Cmt, President John F. Kennedy Campaign, 60; asst. chmn. and treas, Sen. Stuart Symington for Pres. Cmt, 60; mem. Presidential Inaugural Cmt, 61, 65 & 69; mem, Nat. Armed Forces Mus. Adv. Bd, Smithsonian Inst; mem, Ill. Atomic Energy Cmn, currently; Exec. Cmt, Nat. Conf. of State Legis. Leaders; Ill. Gov. Youth Traffic Safety Cmn. and Gov. Adv. Coun, Div. of Health Planning and Resource Develop. Bus. & Prof. Pos: Legis. rep, CNA Financial Corp; pres. and dir, Ins. Fedn. of Ill, Inc; bd. mem, Exec. Cmt, Ins. Econ. Soc. of Am; mem. bd. trustees, John F. Kennedy Col, Nebr. Mil. Serv: Entered as Pvt, Army, 44, released as Technician 5/C, 46; UN Citation for Serv. as Mil. Aide to former Prime Minister Anthony Eden and Brit. Ambassador the Earl of Halifax at the founding of the UN in 45; Good Conduct Medal. Mem: Int. Platform Asn; Mason; Consistory; Shrine; Nat. Capital Dem. Club; Legis. Cmt, Ill. State C. of C. Rel: Methodist. Legal Res: 52 N. Cowley Rd, Riverside, Ill. 60546. Mailing Add: 310 S. Michigan Ave, Chicago, Ill. 60604.

PERLIN, MORTON J. D
Treas, Fla. Conf. on Concerned Dem.
b. Chicago, Ill, 12/14/34; s. Sam Perlin and Jean Feinboldt P; m. 8/26/59 to Charlotte Weiss; c. Jesse and Asher. Educ: Univ. Fla, A.B, 55 and LL.B, 62; Phi Alpha Delta; Zeta Beta Tau. Polit. & Govt. Pos: Pres, South Broward Young Dem, Hollywood, Fla, 63-65; exec. v.pres, Young Dem. Clubs of Fla, 66 and secy, 67; treas, Fla. Conf. of Concerned Dem, 67-; state campaign coordinator, Sen. Eugene J. McCarthy, 68; del, Dem. Nat. Conv, 68. Mil. Serv: Entered as Pvt, Army, 55, released as E-4, 57, after serv. in Japan, 56-57; Good Conduct Medal. Publ: 'The Agency Shop,' Fla. Law Rev, 62. Mem: Fla. and Broward Co. Bars; Am. Trial Lawyers Asn; Fla. Acad. of Trial Lawyers; South Broward Bar Asn.(treas, 65); Am. for Dem. Action; Nat. Cmt. for Sane Nuclear Policy; Am. Civil Liberties Union; Gr. Miami Urban League; Am. Jewish Cmt. Selected as a Citizenship Clearing House Cong. Intern, 60; selected as an Outstanding Young Man of Am, Jaycees, 66; selected as the Outstanding Young Dem. of Fla, 67. Rel: Jewish. Mailing Add: 700 N. Park Rd, Hollywood, Fla. 33021.

PERLOFF, MAYER WILLIAM D
Ala. State Rep.
b. New Orleans, La, 9/2/26; s. Samuel Perloff and Rebecca Mitchell P; m. 10/16/60 to Lottie Jordan; c. Samuel Richard and Robert Jeffery. Educ: Univ. Ala, B.S, 49, LL.B, 57; Univ. Md, LL.B, 53. Polit. & Govt. Pos: Ala. State Rep, 67- Mil. Serv: Pvt, Army, 43, released as Capt, 46, after serv. in Inf, Europe, 44-46. Mem: Mobile and Ala. Bar Asns; Mason; C. of C; VFW; Mobile Co. Wildlife Asn; Elks; Shrine. Rel: Jewish. Legal Res: 3909 Radnor, Mobile, Ala. 36608. Mailing Add: 205 Van Antwerp Bldg, Mobile, Ala. 36602.

PERLOS, ALEXANDER CHARLES D
b. Bitolj, Yugoslavia, 7/15/30; s. Charles Perlos and Anastasia Prchevich P; m. 9/11/55 to Ruth P. Apkarian; c. Charles A, Mark N, Pamela A. and Alexander C. Educ: Mich. State Univ, B.A, 53; Univ. Wis, LL.B, 57; Phi Delta Phi. Polit. & Govt. Pos: Pres, Young Dem, Mich. State Univ, 50; del, Dem. State Conv, 57-64; circuit court cmnr, 59; pub. adminstr, Jackson Co, Mich, 62-; chmn, Jackson Co. Dem. Cmt, Mich, 63-68. Bus. & Prof. Pos: Partner Rappleye & Perlos, Law Off, 61-; pres, Jackson Realty Corp, 62- Mem: Cmt. on Defense of Indigents; Am. Bar Asn; Mich. and Wis. Bar Asns; Am. Trial Lawyers Asn. Rel: Eastern Orthodox. Legal Res: 5040 Brookside Dr, Jackson, Mich. 49203. Mailing Add: 302 Reynolds Bldg, Jackson, Mich. 49201. (1967)

PERPICH, A. J. DFL
Minn. State Sen.
b. 1932. Educ: Hibbing Jr. Col; Marquette Univ, Grad. Polit. & Govt. Pos: Minn. State Sen, 67- Bus. & Prof. Pos: Dentist. Mem: Duluth Dist. Dental Soc; Einar Lauley Toastmasters Club. Mailing Add: 108 Third Ave. N, Virginia, Minn. 55792. (1967)

PERPICH, DR. RUDOLPH G. DFL
Minn. State Sen.
b. Carson Lake, Minn, 1928; married; c. two. Educ: Hibbing Jr. Col; Marquette Univ, D.D.S. Polit. & Govt. Pos: Mem, Hibbing Sch. Bd, 56-62; Minn. State Sen, 62- Bus. & Prof. Pos: Dentist. Mil. Serv: Army, 46-47. Mailing Add: Woolworth Bldg, Hibbing, Minn. 55746. (1967)

PERRIN, CARL ELLIS D
Committeeman, Conn. State Dem. Cent. Cmt.
b. Ripton, Vt, 5/24/31; s. Floyd E. Perrin and Alice M. Hayes P; m. 2/10/51 to Dorothy Winifred Kerr; c. Susan J, Scott K, Carla E. and Mark J. Educ: Hartford Pub. High Sch; Dale Carnegie Courses. Polit. & Govt. Pos: Pres, Young Dem. Club, Cheshire, Conn, 58-60; del, Conn. Dem. State Conv, 60, 62, 64 & 68; chmn, Cheshire Dem. Town Cmt, 60-67; committeeman, Conn. Dem. State Cent. Cmt, 66-; selectman, Cheshire, 68- Bus. & Prof. Pos: Sales mgr, Frank P. Keefe & Co, 58-61, br. mgr, 61-66. Mil. Serv: Entered as Pvt, Air Force, 50, released as S/Sgt, 52, after serv. in 103rd Fighter Group. Rel: Protestant. Mailing Add: 227 Taylor Ave, Cheshire, Conn. 06410.

PERRIN, FRANK G. R
b. Osceola, Ark, 12/13/27; married. Educ: Riverside Mil. Acad, Gainesville, Ga; U.S. Naval Acad, B.S, 51; Georgetown Univ. Sch. of Law, LL.B, 59. Polit. & Gov. Pos: Md. State Del, 63-67. Mil. Serv: Navy, 45-47; Marines, 51-57. Mem: Md. Bar. Mailing Add: Box 8, Waldorf, Md. 20601. (1967)

PERRY, BOBBY GERALD (B.G.) D
Miss. State Sen.
b. Memphis, Tenn, 9/25/31; single. Educ: Phi Alpha Delta; Phi Delta Epsilon; Phi Delta Kappa. Polit. & Govt. Pos: Miss. State Sen, currently; mem, DeSoto Bd. of Realtors. Bus. & Prof. Pos: Real estate broker; attorney. Mem: Miss. Farm Bur; N. DeSoto Civic Club; DeSoto Co. Bar Asn; Miss. and Am. Bar Asns. Rel: Lutheran. Mailing Add: Corner Horn Lake and Church Rd, P.O. Box 121, Horn Lake, Miss. 38637. (1967)

PERRY, CHARLES A, JR. R
b. Providence, R.I, 8/27/19; m. to Rita. Educ: Bryant Col; Brown Univ; Univ. of Mich; Syracuse Univ. Polit. & Govt. Pos: Mem, N. Kingstown Town Coun, 50-56; mem, N.Kingstown Sr. High Sch. Bldg. Cmt; R.I. State Sen, 63-68 Bus. & Prof. Pos: Asst. dir, Blue Cross and Physician's Serv. Mem: Boy Scouts; Lions. Mailing Add: 43 W. Washington St, Wickford, R.I. (1967)

PERRY, CHRISTOPHER LAWRENCE R
b. Bay Shore, N.Y, 9/28/38; s. Glen. C.H. Perry and Sylvia Wallau P; m. 3/25/60 to Barbara Ward; c. Jeffrey Lawrence and Kimberly Paige. Educ: Princeton Univ, A.B. cum laude in polit, 57; Columbia Univ. Grad. Sch. of Journalism, M.S, 62; Colonial Club. Polit. & Govt. Pos: Dir. pub. rels, Del. Rep. State Cmt, 66-69; exec. asst. to Gov. Russell W. Peterson, 69- Bus. & Prof. Pos: Reporter, News-J. Papers, Wilmington, Del, 62-65, bur. chief and polit. columnist, Dover; writer, press rels, Bethlehem Steel Corp, 65-66. Mem: Del. News Club. Rel: Episcopal. Mailing Add: 69 Oakcrest Dr, Dover, Del. 19901.

PERRY, CLARENCE WINDFIELD R
Vt. State Rep.
b. Chittenden, Vt, 12/8/80; m. to Flora L. Durkee; c. Five. Educ: Chittenden Elem. Schs. Polit. & Govt. Pos: Lister, Chittenden, Vt, 07-14, 50-61, town clerk and treas, 10-35, selectman, 41-44; Vt. State Rep, 12, 27, 49 & 57- Bus. & Prof. Pos: Former grocery clerk; retired. Mem: Mason. Mailing Add: Chittenden, Vt. 05737.

PERRY, DOYLE D
b. Choctaw Co, Miss, 6/28/06; married. Polit. & Govt. Pos: Miss. State Sen, until 68. Bus. & Prof. Pos: Sch. adminstr. Rel: Baptist. Mailing Add: Route 1, Box 149, Louisville, Miss. 39339. (1967)

PERRY, ELDRIDGE WELLS D
b. Buena Vista, Ga, 8/31/22; s. Clarence Eldridge Perry and Mary Wells P; m. 6/06/43 to Doris Lillian Lane; c. Mary Pauline. Educ: Abraham Baldwin Agr. Col; Univ. Ga. Polit. & Govt. Pos: Justice of the peace, 807th G.M. Dist, Ga, 52-; Ga. State Rep, 57-58 & 63-66; Ga. State Sen, 24th Dist, 59-60. Bus. & Prof. Pos: Ins; grocery bus. Mem: Mason. Rel: Methodist. Mailing Add: Buena Vista, Ga. 31803.

PERRY, JESSE LAURENCE, JR. R
V.Chmn, Tenn. State Rep. Exec. Cmt.
b. Nashville, Tenn, 10/15/19; s. Jesse Laurence Perry and Mamie White P; m. 11/5/49 to Susan Taylor White; c. Robert Laurence and Judith Foulds. Educ: Univ. of the South, 35-37; Vanderbilt Univ, B.A. magna cum laude, 41; Harvard Univ, M.B.A, 43; Phi Beta Kappa; Omicron Delta Gamma; Pi Kappa Alpha. Polit. & Govt. Pos: Pres, Davidson Co. Young Rep, Tenn, 41-48; nominee, Tenn. State Rep, Sixth Dist, 48; chmn, Fifth Dist. Rep. Exec. Cmt, 50-54; campaign mgr, Mid. Tenn, 56-66; v.chmn, Tenn. Rep. State Exec. Cmt, 56-; del, Rep. Nat. Conv, 60 & 68 and v.chmn, Tenn. Del, 60; mem, Spec. Cmt. Urban Develop, Rep. Nat. Exec. Cmt, 62. Bus. & Prof. Pos: Treas, J.L. Perry Co, Nashville, Tenn, 47-48, v.pres, 49-54 and pres, 54- Mil. Serv: Entered as Pvt, Army, 43, released as Capt, 46, after serv. as Fiscal Dir, Finance Dept, Seventh Serv. Command, 44-46. Mem: Am. Acad. Polit. Sci; Nat. Advert. Fedn; Nat. Sales Exec. Coun; past pres, Nat. Off. Mgt. Asn; Tenn. Ment. Retardation Adv. Coun, 66-; dir. and first v.pres, Tenn. Asn. Retarded Children, 54-62; bd. dirs, Davidson Co. Coun. Retarded Children, 54-62; mem. bd, Jr. Achievement, 55-68; mem. bd. trust, Edgehill Sch; bd. adv, Salvation Army, 58-; secy. and mem. bd, Botanical Tenn. Garden & Fine Arts Center; hon. col, Staff Gov. Tenn; Nat. Soc. SAR; Tenn. Horsemen's Asn; Vol. State Horsemen's Asn; United Hunts Racing Club; Mid. Tenn. Pony Club (treas, 62-68); U.S. Pony Club; Nat. Young Pres. Orgn; U.S. C. of C; Nashville C. of C; Nashville Exchange Club (former officer and mem. bd); Nashville Sewanee Club; Harvard Club of Nashville; Nashville City Club; Hillwood Country Club, Nashville; Richland Country Club, Nashville; Capital Hill Club, Wash, D.C; Am. Legion; ROA; Elks. Rel: Episcopal. Mailing Add: 4434 E. Brookfield Dr, Nashville, Tenn. 37205.

PERRY, JOSEPH, JR. D
b. E. Providence, R.I, 6/17/11; m. to Mary. Educ: E. Providence High Sch. Polit. & Govt. Pos: R.I. State Rep, 57-66; former mem, E. Providence Recreation Bd; E. Providence Citizen Econ. Bd. Bus. & Prof. Pos: Funeral dir. Mem: Past pres, Holy Ghost Brotherhood of Charity; Warren Ave. Bus. Asn; Holy Ghost Beneficial Brotherhood of R.I; Portuguese-Am. Athletic Club; Golfer Athletic Club; Holy Name Soc. of St. Francis Xavier Church; assoc. mem, Fraternal Order of Police, E. Providence. Mailing Add: 254 Warren Ave, East Providence, R.I. 02914.

PERRY, LEON WHELESS R
Chmn, Vance Co. Rep. Party, N.C.
b. Franklin Co, N.C, 4/21/16; s. Richard Redding Perry and Alma Wheless P; m. 8/17/45 to Lucille Elizabeth Floyd; c. Frances Ann, Margaret Floyd (Mrs. Finch), Barbara Lynne, Mary Elinor, Julia Elizabeth and Leon Wheless, III. Educ: Edward Best High Sch, dipl, 34. Polit. & Govt. Pos: Chmn, Vance Co. Rep. Party, 68- Bus. & Prof. Pos: Owner, Perry Lumber Co, Henderson N.C, 39-; partnership, Suburban Mgt. Co, Norfolk, Va, 55-; pres, Cross Roads Enterprises, Norfolk, 55-; pres, Henderson Properties, Inc, Baton Rouge, La, 55- and Cape Canaveral, Fla, 68-; owner, various farming operations, 59-; partner, Atlantic Garden Apt, Cape Canaveral, 68- Rel: Batpist. Mailing Add: 2027 Oxford Rd, Henderson, N.C. 27536.

PERRY, MILDRED MARY D
V.Chmn, Fourth Cong. Dist. Dem. Party, Wis.
b. Milwaukee, Wis, 9/27/20; d. Frank Joseph Lamboy and Marie Kruzela L; m. 11/10/41 to Roger Frank Perry; c. Kandis Denis (Mrs. Birmingham), Margo Christine, Patricia Jean, Douglas Kent and Scott Richard. Educ: N.Div. High Sch, 4 years; Voc. Sch, 1 semester. Polit. & Govt. Pos: Chmn, Seventh Sen. Dist. Dem. Party, Wis, 60-62; Dem. committeeman, Second Ward, Franklin, 60-62 & 64-; secy, Dem. Womens Cmt, 61-64 & 67; mem, Gov. Cmn. Status of Women, 64-; secy, Fourth Cong. Dist. Dem. Party, 65-67, treas, 67-, v.chmn, 69-; v.chmn, Greenfield, Greendale, Hales Corners, and Franklin Dem. Unit, 67-; del, Dem. Nat. Conv, 68; mem, sch. bd, Sch. Dist. Five, Franklin, 68- Bus. & Prof. Pos: Secy, City of Franklin Bd. of Health, 64-; secy, Milwaukee Local 9, Off. & Prfnl. Employees Int. Union, 65- Mem: Off. & Prfnl. Employees Int. Union Local 9; Czechoslovak Soc. Am; 4-H Club; City of Franklin Cmt. on Polit. Educ. Pin and wristwatch for vol. work for Franklin Cmt. on Polit. Educ. endorsed cand. Mailing Add: 7744 S. N. Cape Rd, Franklin, Wis. 53132.

PERRY, PETER E. D
Pa. State Rep.
b. Phila, Pa, 6/22/01; m. 4/15/26 to Rephaela Procopio; c. Bernice G. (Mrs. Harry J. Doyle), Richard P. and Peter E, Jr. Polit. & Govt. Pos: Pa. State Rep, currently. Bus. & Prof. Pos: Pres, Chas. H. Howell & Co, Inc; dir, E. Germantown Bldg. & Loan Asn. Mem: Nat. Paint Salesmen's Club; W.Oak Lane Lions; W.Oak Lane Commun. Asn. Rel: Roman Catholic. Mailing Add: 1020 Lakeside Ave, Philadelphia, Pa. 19126.

PERRY, RALPH KENNETH R
b. Westminster, Md, 1/11/28; s. Charles Kenneth Perry and Dorothy Reifsneider P; m. 8/10/57 to Margaret Anne Beale; c. Douglas Keith and Diane Beth. Educ: Princeton Univ, B.S.E, 50; Phi Beta Kappa; Princeton Campus Club. Polit. & Govt. Pos: Chmn, East Longmeadow Rep. Town Cmt, Mass, 63-68; chmn, Hampden Co. Rep. Campaign Cmt, 64-68; alternate del, Rep. Nat. Conv, 68. Bus. & Prof. Pos: Supvry. and tech. pos, Monsanto Co, Springfield, Mass, 53-62, tech. supvr, 62-64, resident supt, 64-68 and prod. adminstr, St. Louis, Mo. 68- Mil. Serv: Entered as Pvt, Army, 51, released as Cpl, 53, after serv. in Chem. Corps, 51-53. Mem: Am. Inst. Chem. Engrs; Princeton Alumni Asn, West. Mass. Rel: Congregational. Mailing Add: 52 Berry Road Park, St. Louis, Mo. 63122.

PERRY, RANDOLPH HOPE D
b. Charlottesville, Va, 9/14/90; s. Eugene Augustus Perry and Martha Jefferson Terrell P; wid. Educ: Pub. sch, Charlottesville, Va. Polit. & Govt. Pos: Sgt, Charlottesville, Va, 23-56, postmaster, 42-48; admin. asst. to Gov. Va, legis. sessions, 50-52; del, Dem. Nat. Conv, 68. Bus. & Prof. Pos: Salesman, James E. Jarman, 08-14; Montague Furniture Co, 14-18. Mil. Serv: Entered as Pfc, Army, 18, released as Sgt. 1/C, 19, after serv. in Base Hosp. 41, France; French Medal of Honor. Mem: Mason; Elks; Am. Legion; VFW. Rel: Episcopal. Mailing Add: 12 Altamont Apts, Charlottesville, Va. 22901.

PERRY, ROBERT A. D
Wash. State Rep.
b. New York, 1921; m. to Nancy P; c. four. Educ: USMS Sch. of Eng. Polit. & Govt. Pos: Wash. State Rep, fourth term, currently. Mil. Serv: Officer, Merchant Marines. Mailing Add: 1154 N. 92nd, Seattle, Wash. 98103. (1967)

PERRY, ROGER J. D
W.Va. State Del.
b. Baltimore, Md, 5/4/30; s. William P.C. Perry and Mary Shutt P; m. 1/20/55 to Wanda Paxson; c. Julia D. Educ: Washington & Lee Univ, B.A. and LL.B; Lambda Chi Alpha. Polit. & Govt. Pos: City attorney, Ranson, W.Va, 59-63; mem. bd. of health, Jefferson Co, 60-; W.Va. State Del, 68- Bus. & Prof. Pos: Practising attorney, Avey & Steptoe, Charlestown. Mil. Serv: Entered as 1st Lt, Judge Adv. Gen. Corps, Army, 55, released 57, after serv. in Hq. Seventh Army, U.S. Mem: W.Va. State Bar; Jefferson Co. Bar Asn.(pres); C. of C.(dir); Jaycees (v.pres); bd. of mgrs, Charlestown Gen. Hosp. Rel: Episcopal. Legal Res: The Hill, Charles Town, W.Va. 25414. Mailing Add: P.O. Box 93, Charles Town, W.Va. 25414.

PERRY, WALTER EMMETT, JR. D
b. Birmingham, Ala, 1/19/27; s. Walter Emmett Perry and Helen Powell P; m. 11/19/46 to Elizabeth Dorgan; c. Walter Emmett, III, Augustus Proal Dorgan, Elizabeth Powell, Sophia Louise Jovillian. Educ: Univ. of Ala, B.A, 47 and LL.B, 50. Polit. & Govt. Pos: Ala. State Rep, 55-66. Bus. & Prof. Pos: Attorney-at-law, Birmingham, Ala, 50- Mil. Serv: Navy, 44-46, 52-54. Rel: Episcopal. Mailing Add: 429 Frank Nelson Bldg, Birmingham, Ala. 35203.

PERS, JOHN F. D
b. Hammond, Ind, 5/28/11; s. George W. Pers and Lena P; wid; c. Mary J, Janet C, Ruth A, John F, Jr, Rosemary and Nora. Polit. & Govt. Pos: Assessor of N. Twp, Lake Co, Ind, 53-; chmn, First Cong. Dist. Dem. Party, 62-68; mem, Gov. Ins. Adv. Bd, 64-68; mem, Lake Co. Tax Adjustment Bd. Bus. & Prof. Pos: Pres, Pers Agency, Inc, 34-; pres. and v.pres, Ind. Twp. Assessors Asn. Mem: Int. Asn. of Assessing Officers; C. of C; K. of C; Elks; Moose; Lions; Eagles; Notre Dame Club; various polit. clubs. Am. Legion Merit Awards. Rel: Roman Catholic. Mailing Add: 550 141st St, Hammond, Ind. 46327.

PERSKIE, MARVIN D. D
b. Atlantic City, N.J, 7/29/20. Educ: Lafayette Col, A.B; Univ. Pa. Law Sch, LL.B; Phi Beta Kappa. Polit. & Govt. Pos: Former N.J. State Assemblyman. Bus. & Prof. Pos: Attorney at law, Wildwood, N.J; solicitor, Avalon and West Wildwood, N.J; Avalon Sewerage Authority. Mil. Serv: World War II and Korean Conflict; adv. to Israeli Armed Forces, 49; Marine Corps Res, Lt. Col.(Ret); Silver Star; Navy Commendation Medal; Purple Heart. Mem: Am, N.J. and Cape May Co. Bar Asns; Am. Trial Lawyers Asn; U.S. Mil. Court of Appeals; Crescent Temple; Variety Club; Nat. Rifle Asn; First Marine Corps Div. Asn; Am. Legion; VFW; DAV; Epilepsy Found; Elks; Lions. Legal Res: 6800 Atlantic Ave, Wildwood Crest, N.J. 08260. Mailing Add: 3311 New Jersey Ave, Wildwood, N.J. 08260. (1967)

PERSON, CURTIS STANDIFER, JR. D
Tenn. State Sen.
b. Memphis, Tenn, 11/27/34; s. Curtis S. Person, Sr. and Helen Hamilton P; m. 7/7/57 to Peggy Joyce Moore; c. Kathleen, Curtis, III and Patrick. Educ: Memphis State Univ, B.S, 56; Univ. Miss, LL.B, 59; Phi Alpha Theta; Phi Alpha Delta; Kappa Sigma; Memphis State Golf Team. Polit. & Govt. Pos: Spec. dep. sheriff, Shelby Co, Tenn, 60-; Tenn. State Rep, 14th Dist, 66-68; Tenn. State Sen, 31st Sen. Dist, 68-, mem, Educ, Judiciary and Gen. Welfare Cmts, Tenn. State Senate, secy, 22 Mem. Shelby Co. Legis. Del. and Senate Rep. Caucus, 69-; appointed by city coun. to Memphis Censor Rev. Bd, 69- Bus. & Prof. Pos: Partner, Curtis Person Chevrolet Co, 53- Mem: Shrine, Al Chymia Temple, Scottish Rite, Mason (32°); dir, Boys' Club of Memphis, Girls' Club of Memphis, Memphis Navy League and Southern Golf Asn; charter pres, Memphis State Rebounders; exec. dir, Memphis Open Golf Tournament; pres-elect, Memphis State Univ. Nat. Alumni Asn; pres, Memphis-Shelby Co. Ment. Health Asn; v.pres, Liberty Bowl Festival Asn; dir, Boy Scouts, Recreation Serv. for the Handicapped, Inc. and Memphis Sesquicentennial, Inc; Jr. C. of C; Highland Hundred, Inc; committeeman, Colt Firearms Nat. Commemorative Cmt; past trustee, Memphis State Found; vol. worker, Shelby United Neighbors. Winner, several golf tournaments. Rel: Presbyterian; Jr. Deacon & Sunday Sch. Teacher, Second Presbyterian Church. Mailing Add: 445 Colonial Rd, Memphis, Tenn. 38117.

PERT, EDWIN HARRY D
b. Bath, Maine, 5/27/33; s. Perleston Lincoln Pert, Sr. and Katherine M. White P; single. Educ: Univ. Maine, B.A. in govt, 54; Sigma Phi Epsilon. Polit. & Govt. Pos: Publicity dir, Sagadahoc Co. Dem. Cmt, 50, chmn, 54; publicity dir, Maine Dem. State Cmt, 51; pres, Young Dem. Clubs of Maine, 52-53; exec. secy, Maine Dem. Party, 57-60; Maine State Rep, 99th Legis. and mem, Maine Civil War Centennial Cmn, 59-60; secy, Maine State Senate, 65-68. Bus. & Prof. Pos: News dir, Radio Sta. WJTO, 61; state rep, Nat. Found. March of Dimes, 61-65. Mil. Serv: Entered as 2nd Lt, Army, 55, released as 1st Lt, 57, after serv. in 32nd Inf. Regt, 7th Inf. Div, Korea. Mem: Sagadahoc Pomona Grange. Rel: Congregational. Legal Res: Seguinland Rd, Five Islands, Maine 04546. Mailing Add: P.O. Box 36, Five Islands, Maine 04546.

PESEK, ROBERT JOSEPH D
Chmn, Lavaca Co. Dem. Party, Tex.
b. Sweet Home, Tex, 10/14/22; s. Thomas James Pesek and Rosie Janak P; m. 9/12/50 to Amelia Strauss; c. Thomas Lee, Marianne, Judy Rose, Connie Sue and Joyce Marie. Educ: Tex. Univ, B.B.A, 47; Harvard Univ; Tex. Christian Univ; Delta Sigma Pi. Polit. & Govt. Pos: Pres, Lavaca Co. Flood Bd, Tex, 64-66; chmn, Lavaca Co. Dem. Party, currently. Bus. & Prof. Pos: Dir, Monument Builders of Southwest, 65-66, pres, 69- Mil. Serv: Entered as Seaman, Naval Res, 42, released as Lt.(jg), 46, after serv. in Amphibious Forces; Philippines and Okinawa Invasion Medals. Mem: K. of C; Lions (pres, 69-); Vol. Fire Dept. of Hallettsville; C. of C.(pres); Farm Bur. Rel: Catholic. Legal Res: 417 S. Main St, Hallettsville, Tex. 77964. Mailing Add: P.O. Box 292, Hallettsville, Tex. 77964.

PESKIN, BERNARD M. D
Mem, Cook Co. Dem. Cent. Cmt, Ill.
b. Chicago, Ill, 9/22/22; m. to Arlene P; c. Barbara and Robert. Educ: Wilson Jr. Col; Ill. Inst. of Tecn; John Marshall Law Sch; admitted to the Bar, 50; Tau Epsilon Phi. Polit. & Govt. Pos: Ill. State Rep, 4 terms, chmn, House Cmt. Banks and Savings and Loans, 74th Gen. Assembly; Dem. committeeman, Northfield Twp, 68-; mem, Cook Co. Dem. Cent. Cmt, 68- Bus. & Prof. Pos: Partner, Deutsch and Peskin. Mil. Serv: Army Signal Corps in China Theatre of Operations; Mem: Am, Chicago and Ill. State Bar Asns; Decalogue Soc. of Lawyers; life mem, Art Inst; trustee, Northbrook Lodge B'nai B'rith; dir, Twin Orchard C. of C; City Club and Covenant Club of Chicago; past secy, Ill. Cmn. on Children; chmn, Metrozone Adv. Coun. on Retardation; past dir, Little City, Inc. and Evanston Hillel Found. Best Legislator Award, Independent Voters of Ill, 72nd, 73rd and 74th Gen. Assemblies; Distinguished Serv. Award, Ill. Welfare Coun, 65. Rel: North Shore Congregation Israel. Mailing Add: 7 Timber Lane, Northbrook, Ill. 60062.

PETEET, PORTER WEAVER R
b. Greenwood, Miss, 11/24/10; s. Arch Peteet and Mollie Bunch P; m. 5/18/40 to Millard Ruth Whittington; c. Margaret Lynne, Portia Anne (Mrs. Lary) and Rebecca Whittington. Educ: Univ. Miss, B.A, 31; Duke Univ. Sch. of Law, LL.B, 35; Pi Gamma Mu; Order of the Coif; Sigma Alpha Epsilon; Phi Delta Phi. Polit. & Govt. Pos: Attorney, Off. Price Admin, Atlanta, Ga. and Memphis, Tenn, 42-43; dist. dir, Bur. Census, Greenwood, Miss, 50; mem, Dem. Munic. Exec. Cmt, 61-63; mem, Rep. Munic. Exec. Cmt, 65-; mem, Munic. Exec. Cmt. Rep. Party, Greenwood, 66-; alternate del, Rep. Nat. Conv, 68. Bus. & Prof. Pos: Attorney-at-law, 35-41 & 45- Mil. Serv: Entered as Lt.(jg), Naval Res, 43, released as Lt, 45, after serv. in Fleet Radio Unit, Pac, 43-45, Res, Comdr.(Ret); Am. Defense, Pac. Theatre, Victory and Naval Res. Medals. Mem: Miss. State Bar; Leflore Co. Bar Asn.(pres); Am. Legion; VFW; Greenwood Rotary Club (pres). Rel: United Methodist. Legal Res: 308 E. Adams St, Greenwood, Miss. 38930. Mailing Add: P.O. Box 263, Greenwood, Miss. 38930.

PETERS, ALICE BOYE R
Secy, Fresno Co. Rep. Cent. Cmt, Calif.
b. Sanger, Calif, 9/11/13; d. Erik Albert Boye and Henrika Hansen; m. 11/3/33 to Arnold Davis Peters; c. Robert D. and Valerie (Mrs. White). Educ: Univ. Calif, Berkeley, 30-31. Polit. & Govt. Pos: Mem, Calif. Rep. State Cent. Cmt, 58; secy, Alameda Co. Rep. Cent. Cmt, 62; secy, Fresno Co. Rep. Cent. Cmt, 69- Mem: Beta Sigma Phi. Rel: Episcopal. Mailing Add: 1425 N. Farris, Fresno, Calif. 93728.

PETERS, EDWARD EMIL, JR. R
Mem, Allegheny Co. Rep. Cmt, Pa.
b. Pittsburgh, Pa, 2/9/95; s. Edward E. Peters and Florence Creps P; m. 4/17/24 to Gladys M. Sullivan; c. Edward E, III and Mary Christine (Mrs. Albert J. Ossman, Jr). Polit. & Govt. Pos: Mem, Allegheny Co. Rep. Cmt, Pa. and chmn, White Oak Rep. Cmt, 57-; del, Rep. Nat. Conv, 64. Bus. & Prof. Pos: Pres, Peters Packing Co, 51-56 and Terra Alta Stockyard, Inc, 53- Mil. Serv: Entered as Pvt, Air Force, 18, released as Sgt. 1/C, 19. Mem: Mason; City Farmers of Allegheny Co; Elks; Boys Club of White Oak; Youghiogheny Country Club; Pittsburgh Athletic Asn; pres, Livestock Mkt. Asn; Vets. of World War I. Rel: Lutheran. Mailing Add: 1668 Lincoln Way, White Oak Boro, McKeesport, Pa. 15131. (1967)

PETERS, EVERETT R. R
Ill. State Sen.
b. Champaign Co, Ill; m. 1920 to Evelyn Messinger P; c. five. Educ: Univ. Ill. Polit. & Govt. Pos: Ill. State Sen, sixth term, currently; Ill. State Rep, three terms. Bus. & Prof. Pos: Ins. Mil. Serv: World War I Vet. Mem: Am. Legion. Mailing Add: 501 S. Fifth St, St. Joseph, Ill. 61873. (1967)

PETERS, FORNIA DUNGAN R
Tenn. State Rep.
b. Elizabethton, Tenn, 4/3/29; s. William Michael Peters and Rosa Colbaugh P; m. 4/3/48 to Peggy Ann Elliott; c. Rebecca Lane and Lisa Anne. Educ: E.Tenn. State Univ, 2 years; Univ. Va, grad. Polit. & Govt. Pos: Tenn. State Rep, Carter Co, 68- Bus. & Prof. Pos: Banker, 47-; v.pres, Carter Co. Bank, 65- Mem: Regional pres. and treas, Am. Inst. of Banking; all banking groups; Mason; Mod. Woodman; Nat. Rifleman; officer, Kiwanis, C. of C, Easter Seal Soc, United Fund, Hist. Soc, Hunting and Fishing Club and PTA. Rel: Baptist. Mailing Add: 1115 Broad St, Elizabethton, Tenn. 37643.

PETERS, JACOB JOHN D
Chmn, Greene Co. Dem. Party, Iowa
b. Wellsburg, Iowa, 1/28/09; s. John Peters and Rena Voss P; m. 4/20/35 to Wilmuth Jane Luther; c. Danial J. and foster children Lloyd G. DeMoss and Sheila Ann DeMoss (Mrs. Johnston). Educ: Iowa State Univ, B.S, 32; Delta Tau Delta. Polit. & Govt. Pos: Chmn, Washington Twp. Dem. Party, Iowa, early sixties; chmn, Greene Co. Dem. Party, 68- Bus. & Prof. Pos: Teacher and coach, Albion, Iowa High Sch, 32-34; prin. and teacher voc. agr, Rippey High Sch, 34-59, teacher math, sci. and shop, 59- Mem: Iowa State and Nat. Educ. Asns; Iowa Voc. Agr. Asn; Mason; Eastern Star; Farm Bur; Lions; dir, Off. Econ. Opportunity; scoutmaster, Boy Scouts, 20 years. 25 year Agr. Award, Sears Roebuck; 25 years perfect attendance in Lions. Rel: Methodist; Sunday Sch. Teacher, 20 years. Mailing Add: Rippey, Iowa 50235.

PETERS, JAMES ELBERT R
b. Samson, Ala, 3/2/33; s. Matthew M. Peters and Willie Snow Hagan P; m. 5/31/56 to Melba Raines; c. James Elbert, Jr. and Carol Anita. Educ: Auburn Univ, BSEE, 58; Univ. Ala, 62-64; Eta Kappa Nu; Tau Beta Pi; Lambda Chi Alpha. Polit. & Govt. Pos: Del, Ala. Rep. State Conv, 64 & 68; Rep. Nominee for Tax Collector, Madison Co, Ala, 66; ward chmn, Rep. Party, Huntsville, Ala, 66-68; mem, Madison Co. Rep. Exec. Cmt, 66-; alternate del, Rep. Nat. Conv, 68; chmn, Huntsville Rep. City Cmt, 68- Bus. & Prof. Pos: Instrumentation engr, Vitro Corp. Am, 59-61; engr, Brown Eng. Co, 61-65; engr, Boeing Co, 65-68, supvr, 68- Mil. Serv: Entered as Pvt, Air Force, 50, released as S/Sgt, 54, after serv. in Air Security Serv, 51-54. Mem: Inst. Elec. and Electronics Eng; Am. Ord. Asn; Boeing Mgt. Asn; Civitan Club; Am. Legion. Rel: Church of Christ. Mailing Add: 1701 Jeannette Circle, N.W, Huntsville, Ala. 35805.

PETERS, MAXWELL R
Mem, Ala. Rep. Exec. Cmt.
b. Montgomery, Ala, 8/14/25; s. William Marcus Peters, M.D. and Pearl Maxwell P; m. 4/22/49 to Glorious Glaze; c. William Marcus and Maxwell Lee. Educ: St. John's Univ, Minn, 43-44; Univ. Ala, B.A, 49, LL.B, 51. Polit. & Govt. Pos: Judge, Recorder's Court, Northport, Ala, 57-; exec. dir, Northport Housing Authority, 60-62; v.chmn, Tuscaloosa Co. Rep. Cmt, 65-; mem. nominating cmt, Rep. State Conv, 66 & 68; mem, Ala. Rep. Exec. Cmt, 67-; mem, State Rep. Finance and Budget Cmt, 67-; del, Rep. Nat. Conv, 68. Mil. Serv: Entered as Pvt, Air Force, 43, released as S/Sgt, 46 after serving in Eighth Air Force, ETO, 45; Air Medal. Mem: Tuscaloosa Co, Ala. and Am. Bar Asns; Am. Legion. Rel: Methodist. Legal Res: 302 Main Ave, Northport, Ala. 35476. Mailing Add: 312 First National Bank Bldg, Tuscaloosa, Ala. 35401.

PETERS, RALPH R. R
b. Unionville, Pa, 2/2/01; s. John Orvis Peters and Laura Mae Sholl P; m. 6/15/29 to Kathryne Ellen Davis; c. Stella Ellen, Ralph R. Jr. Educ: Pa. State Univ, B.S, 28; mem, Dairy Judging Team; Dairy Sci. Club; exec. secy, Del. State Soc, Delta Theta Sigma. Polit. & Govt. Pos: State dir, Farmers Home Admin, Baltimore, Md, 55-58; legis. asst. to Sen. Williams, 57-58; admin. asst. to U.S. Sen. Williams, Del, 59- Mem: Agr. Exten. Serv; Farm Bur.(exec. secy-treas, Del. Farm Bur, 55-57). Mailing Add: 304 South St, Smyrna, Del. 19977.

PETERS, RAYMOND ELMER D
Assoc. Justice, Calif. Supreme Court
b. Oakland, Calif, 4/17/03; s. Frank Joseph Peters and Mabel Whitaker P; m. 7/23/28 to Marion Estabrook; c. Janet (Mrs. Garrison) and Douglas Kirk (deceased). Educ: Univ. Calif, A.B, 25; J.D, 27; Delta Theta Phi. Polit. & Govt. Pos: Chief law secy, Calif. Supreme Court, 29-39; presiding justice, Dist. Court Appeal, 39-59; assoc. justice, Calif. Supreme Court, 59- Mem: Conf. Calif. Judges (former pres); Boalt Hall Alumni Asn.(former pres); Commonwealth Club; Sutter Club. Legal Res: 1576 Hawthorne Terr, Berkeley, Calif. 94708. Mailing Add: State Bldg, San Francisco, Calif. 94102.

PETERS, ROBERT Conservative, N.Y.
b. Cobalt, Conn, 1/2/41; s. Albert G. Peters and Camille E. Rada P; single. Educ: Am. Theatre Wing, N.Y, grad, 61. Polit. & Govt. Pos: Former chmn, Exec. Cmt, N.Y. Co. Cmt, Conservative Party, N.Y. Bus. & Prof. Pos: Prfnl. actor, 60- Mem: Am. Fedn. TV and Radio Artists. Dir, Antionette Perry Awards, 62-63. Rel: Episcopal. Mailing Add: 300 E. 71st St, New York, N.Y. 10021. (1967)

PETERS, WILLIAM COOPER D
Chmn, Colquitt Co. Dem. Exec. Cmt, Ga.
b. Moultrie, Ga, 5/7/22; s. William Cleveland Peters and Elizabeth Cooper P; m. 12/31/50 to Ellen Brown; c. John Clifton, Luellen, Floyd and Louise. Educ: Univ. Ga, A.B, 49, LL.B, 50; Kappa Sigma. Polit. & Govt. Pos: Justice of Peace, Ga, 53-; mem, Colquitt Co. Dem. Exec. Cmt, 60-, chmn, 64-; co. attorney, Colquitt Co, 68-69; recorder, City of Moultrie, 69- Bus. & Prof. Pos: Lawyer, 51- Mil. Serv: Entered as Pvt, Army, 42, released as 1st Lt, 46, after serv. in Air Transport Command, China-Burma-India, 44-46; Capt, Air Force Res; Air Medal with One Cluster. Mem: Ga. and Am. Bar Asns; State Bar of Ga; South. Circuit Bar (v.chmn, 69); Kiwanis; Mason; Am. Legion; Elk; VFW. Rel: Presbyterian. Legal Res: 25 Pine Valley, Moultrie, Ga. 31768. Mailing Add: P.O. Box 2, Moultrie, Ga. 31768.

PETERS, WILLIAM H, JR. D
b. Baltimore Co, Md, 1/26/14; married. Educ: Baltimore Co. Pub. Schs. Polit. & Govt. Pos: Md. State Del, 63-67; Chase-Bengies Dem. Club; 15th Dist. Dem. Club; Free State Dem. Club; 28th Precinct Dem. Club; del, Constitutional Conv, Md, 67-68; chief judge, Tax Appeal Court, Baltimore Co, 67- Bus. & Prof. Pos: Restaurateur; secy, bd. of dir, Back and Middle River Bldg. & Loan Asn. Mem: Bd. of dir, Essex-Middle River C. of C; membership cmt, Md. Savings-Share Ins. Corp; former pres, Baltimore Co. Licensed Beverage Asn; Md. Restaurant Asn; Md. State Licensed Beverage Asn; former pres, East. Blvd. Lions Club; Masons; Shrine; Baltimore Yacht Club. Mailing Add: 1528 Eastern Ave, Essex, Md. 21221.

PETERSEN, ARNOLD Socialist Labor Party
b. Odense, Denmark, 4/16/85. Polit. & Govt. Pos: Nat. secy, Socialist Labor Pary, 14-69. Publ: 'Constitution of the United States,' N.Y. Labor News, Fifth Printing, 63, 'Theocracy or Democracy,' 44 and 'Daniel De Leon, Social Architect,' Vol. I, 41, Vol. II, 53. Legal Res: Teaneck, N.J. Mailing Add: P.O. Box 200, Brooklyn, N.Y. 11202.

PETERSEN, DONALD HARRY R
Mem, Fresno Co. Rep. Cent. Cmt, Calif.
b. Oakland, Calif, 11/18/26; s. Harry E. Petersen and Emma Fridell P; m. 5/31/58 to Carol Hall; c. Erika and Ronald Hall. Educ: Univ. Redlands, B.A, 50. Polit. & Govt. Pos: Co. chmn, 33rd Assembly Campaign, Selma, Calif, 66; founding pres, Selma Chap, Calif. Rep. Assembly, 66; organizing chmn, Fresno Co. Coord. Rep. Assembly, 67; v.pres, Selma Rep. Assembly, 67-; dir, Calif. Rep. Assembly, 68; mem, Fresno Co. Rep. Cent. Cmt, 69-; mem, Calif. Rep. State Cent. Cmt, currently; mem, Selma Planning Cmn, currently. Bus. & Prof. Pos: Field rep, Aetna Life & Casualty, Los Angeles, Calif, 50-55, agency supt, Portland, Ore, 56-60, agency mgr, Seattle, Wash, 61-66; owner, Selma Ins. Agency, Calif, 66- Mil. Serv: Entered as A/S, Naval Res, 44, released as PO 3/C, 46, after serv. in Destroyer 592, Pac. Theater, 45-46. Mem: Independent Ins. Agents Asns. of Fresno Co. and Calif; Nat. Asn. Ins. Agents; Elks; Rotary (pres, Selma Club); dir, Selma Dist. C. of C; Selma Commun. Club (past pres). Rel: United Presbyterian; Elder, St. Andrew Church; chmn, Agr. and Labor Study Cmn, Synod of the Sierra. Mailing Add: 2477 Country Club Lane, Selma, Calif. 93662.

PETERSEN, LORRAINE FRANCES R
Chmn, Washburn Co. Rep. Party, Wis.
b. Spooner, Wis, 7/2/23; d. Raymond Clifford Barager and Pearl Hawkins B; m. 11/13/44 to Marshall Martin Petersen; c. Judith Carol. Educ: Spooner High Sch, grad, 41. Polit. & Govt. Pos: V.chmn, Washburn Co. Rep. Party, Wis, 63-66, chmn, 66-; secy, Tenth Cong. Dist. Rep. Party, 65- Bus. & Prof. Pos: Real Estate Broker, Petersen Realty, Inc, 65- Mem: Wis. Realtors Asn; Nat. Asn. Real Estate Bd; chmn, Young Am. Medal Awards Cmt, 68-69; Gov. Cmt. on Children and Youth, 66-69; Am. Legion Auxiliary; Spooner Hosp. Auxiliary. Rel: Catholic. Mailing Add: 401 Bashaw, Spooner, Wis. 54801.

PETERSEN, MARCI D
Secy, Young Dem. Clubs of Am.
b. Consumers, Utah; d. (father deceased) Lucy Mikkelsen; div; c. Kevin, Susan and Mark. Educ: Ogden Bus. Col, Utah, 1 year. Polit. & Govt. Pos: Nat. committeewoman, Young Dem. of Nev, 63-67, exec. secy, 67-; secy, Young Dem. Clubs of Am, 67-; alternate del, Dem. Nat. Conv, 68. Bus. & Prof. Pos: Legal secy, Las Vegas; slot arcade mgr, 67 & 68. Rel: Catholic. Legal Res: Las Vegas, Nev.

PETERSMEYER, VALLEA CORNELIA R
Chmn, Warren Co. Rep. Cmt, Mo.
b. Hank Point, Mo, 2/15/11; d. Allie Lee Monroe and Vina Iuka Trail M; m. 6/7/36 to Fredrick Detrich Petersmeyer; c. Merlyn Fredrick. Educ: Cent. Wesleyan Col, summers, 29-38; Northeast State Col, summer, 39. Polit. & Govt. Pos: Mem, Warren Co. Rep. Party, 60-, committeewoman, Elkhorn Twp, Ward 2, 60-; v.pres, Warren Co. Rep. Cmt, 62-66, chmn, 66- Mem: Mo. State, Nat. and Warren Co. Teachers Asns; Rebekah; Band Booster's Club; Warrenton Study Club; Dorcas Soc; Parent-Teacher Orgn.(pres, Warrenton Chap, 50-56 and Warren Co. Chap, 52-54). Rel: Protestant. Mailing Add: 405 N. 47th, Warrenton, Mo. 63383.

PETERSON, ANDRIENNE TOSSO D
Treas-secy, Lake Co. Dem. Party, Colo.
b. Leadville, Colo, 10/28/24; d. Andrew Tosso and Florence Maffei T; m. to Leo V. Peterson, wid; c. Leandrea. Educ: Leadville High Sch, Colo, grad, 41. Polit. & Govt. Pos: Recording secy, Lake Co. Jane Jefferson Club, Colo, 58-60, v.pres, 60-61 and pres, 61-66; treas-secy, Lake Co. Dem. Party, 68- Bus. & Prof. Pos: Deputy clerk, Lake Co. Court, Leadville, 58-64; commodity clerk, Lake Co. Welfare Dept, 62-65; eng. secy, Bechtel Engrs, 65-67, med. secy, Leadville Med. Center, 67- Mem: Annunciation Church Rosary and Altar Soc. Rel: Catholic. Legal Res: 135 E. Third St, Leadville, Colo. 80461. Mailing Add: Box 558, Leadville, Colo. 80461.

PETERSON, ARTHUR LA VERNE R
b. Glyndon, Minn, 6/27/26; s. John Martin Peterson and Hilda Moline P; m. 6/14/52 to Connie L. Harr; c. J. Martin, II, Rebecca Ruth, Donna Harr and Ingrid Bliss. Educ: Yale Univ, A.B, 47; Univ. South Calif, M.S. in pub. admin, 49; Univ. Minn, Ph.D, 62; Pi Sigma Alpha; Phi Mu Alpha; Sigma Phi Epsilon. Polit. & Govt. Pos: Wis. State Assemblyman, 51-55; staff dir, Scholars for Nixon-Lodge, 60; mem, Delaware, Ohio Civil Serv. Cmn, 61-62; chmn, Ohio Civil Rights Cmn, 62-65; spec. consult. to chmn, Rep. Nat. Cmt, 60-61, admin. asst. to chmn, 65-66, staff dir. platform cmt, 68-; staff dir, Rep. Coord. Cmt, 65-66. Bus. & Prof. Pos: Prof. polit, Wis. State Univ, Eau Claire, 54-59; dir, Inst. of Practical Polit, Ohio Wesleyan Univ, 61-65; pres, Thunderbird Grad. Sch. Int. Mgt, Phoenix, Ariz, 66- Mil. Serv: A/S, Navy, 44-46; Capt, Marine Corps, 51-52, serv. in Easy Co, 2nd Bn, 7th Regt, 1st Marine Div, Korea; Presidential Unit Citation; Victory Medal; Korean Conflict Ribbon. Publ: Electing the President, with Dan Ogden, Chandler Press, San Francisco, 64, revised ed, 68. Mem: VFW; Marine Corps League; Mason. Rel: Congregational; Lay Minister. Mailing Add: Thunderbird Graduate School of International Management, P.O. Box 191, Phoenix, Ariz. 85001.

PETERSON, BARBARA PRESTON R
b. Kenmare, N.Dak, 7/19/28; d. Harry Earl Preston and Althea Hard P; m. to Kermit Svein Peterson (deceased); c. Stefan Kermit, Sarajane Althea, Seth Preston and Sabin Svein. Educ: Univ. N.Dak, 3 years; Kappa Alpha Theta. Polit. & Govt. Pos: Pres, Minot Rep. Women's Club, N.Dak, 66-68; del, Rep. Nat. Conv, 68; secy. and v.chairwoman, Fifth Dist. Rep. Party, 68; mem, Congressman Tom Kleppe Spec. Cmt, 68-69. Rel: Presbyterian. Mailing Add: 1508 Seventh Ave. N.W, Minot, N.Dak. 58701.

PETERSON, BERNICE LETITIA R
b. McClellandtown, Pa, 7/13/25; d. Samuel W. Shuss and Zola Felten S; m. 8/24/46 to Robert A. Peterson, Sr; c. Robert A, Jr, Taylor E, and Ginger G. Educ: Slippery Rock Col, B.S, 46; Hon. Sci. Soc. Polit. & Govt. Pos: Former chmn, Nansemond Co. Rep. Party, Va. Bus. & Prof. Pos: Teacher, Nebr. Sch. for the Visually Handicapped, 68-69. Mem: PTA; Nat. Educ. Asn; Nebr. City Educ. Asn; Nebr. State Educ. Asn; Asn. for Educ. of the Visually Handicapped. Rel: Christian Church. Mailing Add: 909 12th Ave, Nebraska City, Nebr. 68410.

PETERSON, BETTY ANN D
Mem, Colo. Dem. State Exec. Cmt.
b. Waco, Tex, 7/12/29; d. James Herbert Guthrie and Verna Elsie Jones G; m. 11/27/52 to Wallace Bennett Peterson; c. Wallace Bennett, Jr, Kenneth James, David Wayne, Kathryn Verna, Ronald Lee and Nancy Ann. Educ: Univ. Tex, 48-49; Rosenberg Col, St. Gallen, Switz, 49; European Command Finance Center, Friedborg, Germany, cert, 50. Polit. & Govt. Pos: Dist. capt. and committeewoman, Arapahoe Co. Dem. Party, Colo, 62-69, oper. support chmn, 67-68; Arapahoe Co. chmn, 35th Jefferson-Jackson Dinner, 67; mem, Colo. State Credentials Cmt, 68; Arapahoe Co. Chmn, Ladies for Humphrey-Muskie, 68; chmn, Arapahoe Co. Sen. Dist. 22, 68-; Arapahoe Co. Campaign Chmn. to re-elect President Johnson, 68; mem. Colo. Dem. State Cent. Cmt, 68-69 and State Exec. Bd, 69; chmn, Jefferson-Jackson 'Who Me' Luncheon, 69; mem, Colo. Dem. State Exec. Cmt, 69- Bus. & Prof. Pos: Secy, War Crimes Trial, Dachau, Germany, 47; reservations clerk, Braniff Air Lines, Love Field, Dallas, Tex, 51; receptionist for Dr. Cecil I. Stell, Dallas, 52; model, The Parisian, Wichita Falls, 53. Publ: Feature editor, Petticoat Press, Sheppard Air Force Base, Tex, 53-54. Mem: Easter Seal Soc; Red Cross Volunteer, Eastridge Sch; Englewood Jane Jefferson Club (officer); Lowry Retired Officer's Wives Club; PTA (budget study for Cherry Creek High Sch); East Arapahoe Coun. Human Rels; Lowry Armed Forces Judo Asn.(officer); score keeper, Little League. Centennial Dist. Den Mother's Training Award, 65; cert. of appreciation, Channel 6 Coun. Educ. TV, 68; Dem. 'In 68' award. Rel: Lutheran; Sunday Sch. dir, First Evangel. Lutheran Church, Shreveport, La; Sunday Sch. Teacher, Lutheran Church, Bossier City, La. and Denver, Colo. Mailing Add: 2420 S. Lima, Denver, Colo. 80232.

PETERSON, BEVERLY JANE R
Mem, Calif. Rep. State Cent. Cmt.
b. Burlington, Wis, 11/16/26; d. Edmund Herbert Peterson and Clara Lucht P; single. Educ: Stout Inst, Menomonee, Wis, 45; Univ. South. Calif, Los Angeles, Cert, Modular Mgt. for Exec. Woman Conf, 63. Polit. & Govt. Pos: Staff asst, Los Angeles Co. Cent. Cmt, Calif, 60; TAR chmn, Los Angeles Co. Young Rep, 61; chmn, tel. cmt. East. div, Nixon for Gov, 62; assoc. mem, Calif. Rep. State Cent. Cmt, 64-66; mem, 69-; chmn, Women's Bus. Cmt, Rep. Assocs, 66; treas, Playa Del Rey Rep. Women's Fedn. Club, 66-68; asst. in Gov. off, Sacramento, 66-67; dir, Lincoln Rep. Club, 68; alternate mem, Los Angeles Co. Cent. Cmt, 68- Bus. & Prof. Pos: Long distance operator, supvr, force clerk, serv. rep, Wis. Tel. Co, 47-55; serv. rep, South. Bell Tel. Co, 55-56; supvr. bus. off, Wis. Tel. Co, 56-60; serv. rep. and hostess, Disneyland exhibit, Pac. Tel. Co, 60-62, tel. sales supvr, 62-64, employ. interviewer, 64-68 and asst. traffic operating mgr, 68- Rel: Lutheran. Mailing Add: 8354 Manitoba St, Apt. 5, Playa Del Rey, Calif. 90291.

PETERSON, CHARLES THOMAS R
Chmn, Blue Earth Co. Rep. Party, Minn.
b. Elmore, Minn, 9/22/16; s. Carl David Peterson and Queen Emerson P; m. 9/9/46 to Marguerite Mary Sexton; c. Mary Pat (Mrs. Fasnacht), John Charles, Margaret Joan, Kathleen Jane and Ann Marie. Educ: Univ. Minn, B.S. in Law and J.D, 38; Delta Theta Phi. Polit. & Govt. Pos: Chmn, Blue Earth Co. Rep. Party, Minn, 67-; mem, Minn. Rep. State Cent. Cmt, 67- Bus. & Prof. Pos: Secy, Mankato Police Civil Serv. Cmn, Minn, 62-; secy-treas, Minn. Valley Ment. Health Center, 66-; spec. munic. judge, Mankato, 68- Mil. Serv: Entered as Pvt, Army, 41, released as Pfc, 44, after serv. in 202nd Coast Artil. Bn, Asiatic-Pac. Area, 42-44; Bronze Star; Good Conduct Medal; Asiatic-Pac. Medal. Mem: Am, Minn. and Blue Earth Co. Bar Asns; Sixth Judicial Bar Asn.(pres, 67-68); Lions; pres, Mankato Jr. C. of C, 51-52; bd. trustees, Mankato YMCA; Am. Legion. Rel: Catholic. Mailing Add: 108 Dell-Oak Knoll, Mankato, Minn. 56001.

PETERSON, DAVID C. D
Ga. State Rep.
b. Walker Co, Ga, 2/20/01; s. Warren David Peterson and Mary Smith P; m. 8/25/29 to Julia Howard; c. David Stanley and Robert Dwight. Educ: Young Harris Jr. Col, 24; Univ. Ga, 30. Polit. & Govt. Pos: Ga. State Rep, 63- Bus. & Prof. Pos: Teacher and prin, 22- Mem: Civitan; first pres, Austell Civitan, 30. Rel: Methodist. Mailing Add: RFD, Kathleen, Ga. 31047. (1967)

PETERSON, DONALD OLIVER D
Co-Chmn, New Dem. Coalition
b. Renville, Minn, 3/9/25; s. Edgar Clarence Peterson and Jessie Henderson P; m. 1/12/46 to Roberta 'Bobbie' Anne Taylor; c. Gregory Alan, Terri Lynn, Stephanie Jo and Kirk Dale. Educ: Butler Univ, 43; Univ. Minn, 46-47; Macalester Col, 48. Polit. & Govt. Pos: Various precinct and co. Dem. Party Off. in Minn, S.Dak. and Wis, 50-; chmn, Tenth Dist. Dem. Party, Wis, 67-; del, Dem. Nat. Conv, 68; mem, Wis. Dem. State Cent. Cmt, currently; co-chmn, New Dem. Coalition, currently. Bus. & Prof. Pos: V.pres. and sales mgr, Black River Dairy Prod, Eau Claire, Wis, 66- Mil. Serv: Entered as Pvt, Air Corps, 43, released as 1st Lt, 46, after serv. in Fifth Air Force, S.Pac. Theatre, 45-46; Air Medals. Rel: Unitarian. Mailing Add: 1406 State St, Eau Claire, Wis. 54701.

PETERSON, ELLY M. R
Asst. Chmn, Rep. Nat. Cmt.
b. New Berlin, Ill; m. to Col. William Peterson. Educ: William Woods Col; Northwest. Univ; Suburban Bus. Col. Polit. & Govt. Pos: Aide to state chmn. Lawrence Lindemer, Mich, 58-61; State Field Serv. Mgr, 61; mem. and former officer, Eaton Co. and Charlotte Rep. Cmts; v.chmn, Rep. State Cent. Cmt, Mich, 61-65, chmn, 65-69; exec. dir, women's div, Rep. Nat. Cmt, 63, asst. chmn, Rep. Nat. Cmt, 64- and Nat. committeewoman, Mich, 68-; Rep. cand, U.S. Sen, 64; addressed Rep. Nat. Conv, 64; del-at-lg, Rep. Nat. Conv, 68. Bus. & Prof. Pos: Hosp. secy, Am. Red Cross, 2 years overseas, former co. pres. and former dir, regional blood prog. Mem: Am. Legion Auxiliary; Lansing Bus. and Prfnl. Women's Club; Urban League; Ingham Co. Rep. Bus. Women's Club; charter mem, Eaton Co. Rep. Women's Club; NAACP; former officer, Am. Cancer Co. Cmt. Rel: Congregational. Legal Res: Tirrill Rd, Route 2, Charlotte, Mich. 48813. Mailing Add: c/o Republican National Committee, 1625 Eye St. N.W, Washington, D.C. 20005.

PETERSON, ESTHER EGGERTSEN D
b. Provo, Utah, 12/9/06; d. Lars E. Eggertsen and Annie Nielsen E; m. 5/28/32 to Oliver A. Peterson; c. Karen Kristine, Eric Niels, Iver Echart and Lars Erling. Educ: Brigham Young Univ, A.B, 27; Columbia Univ, M.A, 30. Hon. degrees, Smith, Bryant, Montclair, Simmons and Hood Cols, Carnegie Inst. Tech, Northeast. Univ, Univ. of South. Utah and West. Col. for Women. Polit. & Govt. Pos: Campaign worker, Dem. Party, 42-46 & 58-64; adv. to U.S. Del, Int. Labor Orgn. Conf, Geneva, Switz, 61 & 64; exec. v.chmn, President's Cmt. on Status of Women, 61-63; Asst. Secy. of Labor, U.S. Dept. of Labor, 61-68, dir, Women's Bur, 61-64; spec. asst. to the President for consumer affairs and chmn, President's Cmn. on Consumer Interests, 64-68. Bus. & Prof. Pos: Teacher, indust. dept, Boston YWCA; Winsor Sch. and Br. Agr. Col, Cedar City, Utah, 27; asst. dir. educ, Amalgamated Clothing Workers of Am, 39-44, Wash. legis. rep, 45-48, legis. rep, Indust. Union Dept, AFL-CIO, 57-61. Mem: Hon. mem, Am. Home Econ. Asn. and Phi Chi Theta Club; assoc. mem, Am. Newspaper Women's Club; Nat. Dem. Club; League of Women Voters; Am. Asn. Univ. Women; Nat. Consumers League; YWCA; Bus. & Prfnl. Women. Mailing Add: 7714 13th St, N.W, Washington, D.C. 20012.

PETERSON, FRANCIS L. R
b. Colfax, Wis, 1/23/04. Educ: Boyceville High Sch. Polit. & Govt. Pos: Wis. State Assemblyman, 64-66; Mem, Village Bd, 34-36, Co. Bd, 36-39. Bus. & Prof. Pos: Merchant since 28; formerly, store clerk. Mem: Past Pres, Church Coun; Past Pres, Y.G.O.P; Treas, Sch. Bd, 32-52; Dunn Co. Park Bd; Hosp. Bd. Mailing Add: Boyceville, Wis. 54725. (1967)

PETERSON, GILMAN F. D
b. New Eng, N.Dak, 4/14/13; married; c. Five. Educ: Pub. Schs. Polit. & Govt. Pos: N.Dak. State Rep, 61-66; Sch. and Twp Bds; supv, Soil Conserv. Dist. Bus. & Prof. Pos: Farmer. Mem: Stockmen's Asn. Rel: Lutheran. Mailing Add: New Eng, N.Dak. 58647. (1967)

PETERSON, GUNNAR ARON JULIUS R
Chmn, Avon Rep. Town Cmt, Mass.
b. Svedala, Sweden, 6/17/00; s. Hjalmar Sigfrid Peterson and Matilda Svenson P; m. 12/23/23 to Betty Carlson; c. Earl Edmund and Elaine Marguerite (Mrs. Sawler). Educ: High sch, Sweden, 15. Polit. & Govt. Pos: Chmn, Avon Bd. Health, Mass, 44-65; chmn, Avon Rep. Town Cmt, 68- Bus. & Prof. Pos: Shipper, E.C. Hall Co, 24-62; foreman, Alfred G. Peterson & Sons, Inc, 62- Mem: Scandinavian Fraternity of Am.(former supreme officer); Vasa Order of Am; Southeast. Asn. of Bd of Health (founder, first pres. and hon. exec. bd. mem, emer); YMCA; Mass. Rep. Cmt. Rel: Lutheran. Mailing Add: 544 W. Main St, Avon, Mass. 02322.

PETERSON, HARRIETT MONROE R
Mem. Exec. Cmt, Calif. State Rep. Cent. Cmt.
b. Hood River, Ore, 5/14/21; d. George Henry Monroe and Carrie Candee M; m. 6/28/53 to Clarence W. Peterson. Educ: Willamette Univ, B.A, 43; Syracuse Univ, M.A, 45. Polit. & Govt. Pos: Chaplain, Calif. Fedn. Rep. Women, 55-60, recording secy, 61-63, pres. cent. div, 64-67 and v.pres. from cent. div, 68-69; Rep. precinct worker, 12 years; mem, Calif. State Rep. Cent. Cmt, 58-, mem. exec. cmt, 67-; pres, Tracy Rep. Women, 62-63; alternate del, Rep. Nat. Conv, 68. Bus. & Prof. Pos: Head resident of freshman dormitory, Univ. of Redlands, 45-48; dean of women, Stockton Col, 48-51 and Col. of the Pac, 48-53. Mem: Nat. and Calif. Asns. of Deans of Women; Delta Kappa Gamma; Pi Lambda Theta; Alpha Kappa Delta; Quota Club; Am. Asn. Univ. Women; PEO; Am. Field Serv. Cmt; Tracy Women's Club; Hosp. Auxiliary; assoc. mem, Children's Home Soc. Jr. Women's Club Citizen of the Year Award, Tracy, 61. Rel: Presbyterian. Mailing Add: 1457 Holly Dr, Tracy, Calif. 95376.

PETERSON, HARRY WILLIAM DFL
Minn. State Rep.
b. Canby, Minn, 1/16/06; s. Frank J. Peterson and Helga M. Johnson P; m. 5/30/41 to Leona Marie Bromert; c. Carole Ann, Donna M, Stuart J. and Douglas P. Educ: Yellow Medicine Co. Pub. Schs. Polit. & Govt. Pos: Sch. official, Rural Dist, 48-58; twp. officer, 50-60; Minn. State Rep, 65- Bus. & Prof. Pos: Life-time farmer, La qui Parle Co, Minn. Mem: Former state officer, Minn. Farmers Union; mem. and officer of various farm coop, dir. of two. Rel: Lutheran. Mailing Add: Route 2, Madison, Minn. 56256. (1967)

PETERSON, HJALMAR REGINALD R
b. Boston, Mass, 9/26/07; s. Alfred G. Peterson and Clara W. Ostrom P; m. to Ellen J. Olson; c. Joan (Mrs. Allan MacEachern) and Janet (Mrs. Paul Weatherbee). Educ: Bentley Col, grad; Boston Univ. and Northeast. Univ, advanced courses; past pres, Northeast Univ. Small Bus. Mgt. Assocs. Polit. & Govt. Pos: Past mem, Bd. of Gov, Commercial Club of Brockton; past chmn, Cardinal Cushing Gen. Hosp; Hosp. Fund Dr; Brockton City Rep. Chmn, Mass, 45-49; mem, city coun, Brockton, 50-54, mayor, 56-57; del, Rep. State Conv, 50-62; del, Rep. Nat. Conv, 56, 60, 64 & 68. Bus. & Prof. Pos: Pres, Alfred G. Peterson & Sons, Inc. and Mackedon Mfg. Co, Inc; dir, Canvas Products Asn. Int. and Mass. Bank and Trust; past. pres, New Eng. Awning & Canvas Products Asn. Mem: Dir, Thorney Lea Golf Club; past pres, Old Colony Advert. Club; past chmn, Greater Brockton United Fund Campaign and Red Cross Campaign; past. dir, Brockton C. of C; Mason (32°); Paul Revere Lodge, Aleppo Temple Shrine; Elks; Vega Club; past pres, Brockton Kiwanis. Rel: Baptist. Legal Res: 103 Braemoor Rd, Brockton, Mass. Mailing Add: 491 W. Main St, Avon, Mass. 02322.

PETERSON, IRENE M. D
b. Enid, Okla; d. Frank Nathan Ludlum and Lillian Underkoffler L; div. Educ: Study of law, 27-35; Univ. Mo, 42-44. Polit. & Govt. Pos: V.pres, Young Dem. of Ill, 36-38; admin. asst. to. U.S. Rep. Leonor K. Sullivan, Mo, 67- Bus. & Prof. Pos: Secy. and jr. partner, Sturtz & Ewan, Kewanee, Ill, 27-38; asst. to trust officer, Security Trust Co, St. Louis, Mo, 38-39; asst. to chief counsel, pres. and chmn. bd, Mo. Pac. R.R. Co, 40-66; asst. to publisher, St. Louis Globe-Dem, 66. Mem: Am. Coun. of R.R. Women; Bus. & Prfnl. Women's Club St. Louis (past pres); Altrusa Club St. Louis (past v.pres); Group Action Coun. Gr. St. Louis (past chmn); Group Action Coun. Women's Club (pres); plus others. Outstanding Working Woman Award, Downtown St. Louis, Inc. Rel: Catholic. Legal Res: 4615 Lindell Blvd, St. Louis, Mo. 63108. Mailing Add: 1400 S. Joyce St, Apt. A-1009, Arlington, Va. 22202.

PETERSON, JAMES E. R
Ill. State Rep.
b. Chicago Heights, Ill, 6/8/31; s. Emil. J. Peterson and Danola Conley P; m. 12/26/53 to Dorothy Warner; c. James, Jodie, Robert, Christian and Carolyn. Educ: Chicago Teacher's Col, B.E, 61, grad. work; Loyola Univ, grad. work. Polit. & Govt. Pos: Soc. studies supvr, Off. of Supt. Pub. Inst, Ill, 65-66; committeeman, 19th Ward Rep. Orgn, Chicago, 66-; mem. exec. cmt, Cook Co. Rep. Cent. Cmt, 66-, v.chmn. exec. cmt, 69-; dep. co. treas, Cook Co, 66-; trustee, Cook Co. Employees' Annuity and Benefit Fund, 67-; mem. adv. cmt, Ill. State Off. Pub. Instr, 67-; Ill. State Rep, 28th Dist, 69- Bus. & Prof. Pos: Sch. teacher, Bd. Educ, Chicago, Ill, 61-65. Mil. Serv: Entered as Pvt, Air Force, 49, released as Pfc, 50, after serv. in Air Training Command. Publ: A Manual for History Teachers, edited for Off. of Supt. Pub. Instr, 66. Mem: Ill. Co. Treas. Asn; Munic. Finance Off. Asn; Am. Mgt. Asn; Beverly Hills Univ. Club; Ill. Athletic Club; Swedish Club of Chicago; Elks; Morgan Park Improv. Asn. Rel: Catholic. Legal Res: 11002 S. Hoyne Ave, Chicago, Ill. 60643. Mailing Add: 118 N. Clark St, Chicago, Ill. 60602.

PETERSON, JAMES HARDIN D
b. Batesburg, S.C, 2/11/94. Educ: Univ. of Fla, LL.B, 14; Phi Alpha Delta; Fla. South. Col, Dr. of Humanities, 47. Polit. & Govt. Pos: Spec. Counsel, W. Coast Inland Navigation Dist, 51-; Spec. Counsel, Territory of Guam, 51-52; Chmn, Cmn. of Application of Fed. Laws to Guam, 51; U.S. Rep, Fla, 33-51; Chmn, Dem. Steering Cmt, 33-51; Polk Co. Solicitor, Fla, 23-31; Polk Co. Prosecuting Attorney, 22-23; City Attorney, Lakeland, Fla, 16 1/2 yrs. Bus. & Prof. Pos: Attorney. Mem: Am, Fla, Lakeland Bar Asns; Am. Judicature

Soc; Kiwanis; A.L; Mason; former mem, Bd. of Trustees, Nat. Trust for Hist. Preservation; Pres, Ridge Coun. Boy Scouts, 51-52; Chmn. of Bd, Fla. Heart. Asn, 50-53. Misc: Recipient of Awards: Nat. Audubon Soc, 54; Fla. Wildlife Conservation Award, 55; Certificate of Appreciation, Nat. Conf. of State Parks; Achievement Medal, Univ. of Tampa; Distinguished Alumnus Award, Univ. of Fla, 63. Rel: Methodist. Mailing Add: 217 E. Lime St, Lakeland, Fla. 33801.

PETERSON, JERRY BURNS R
Okla. State Rep.
b. Oak Park, Ill, 8/18/28; s. Frank Lindell Peterson and Dorothy Cassingham P; m. 3/11/51 to Audrey Jean Dickens; c. David A. and Lorraine A. Educ: Purdue Univ, B.S. in chem. eng, 50; Univ. Ill, LL.B, 56; Nat. Honor Soc; Sigma Chi. Polit. & Govt. Pos: Chmn, Kay Co. Young Rep, Okla, 60-61; chmn, Kay Co. Rep. Party, 61-63; del, Rep. Nat. Conv, 64; Okla. State Rep, 66- Bus. & Prof. Pos: Patent lawyer, Continental Oil Co, 57-59, supvr. of Trademarks and Licenses, 59-66, supvr. of Patent Prosecution, 66-69, supvr. of Patents and Trademarks, 69- Mil. Serv: Entered Army, 50, released 52, after serv. in 9771 Tech. Serv. Unit, Dugway Proving Ground, Utah. Mem: Kay Co, Ill, Okla. and Am. Bar Asns; Am. Patent Law Asn; U.S. Supreme Court Bar; C. of C. Rel: Lutheran. Mailing Add: 141 Whitworth, Ponca City, Okla. 74601.

PETERSON, JOHN H. Conservative
b. Norway, 1901; married; c. Five. Educ: Rock Co. Pub. Schs. Polit. & Govt. Pos: Minn. State Rep, 62-66; dir, Pope Co. Fed. Land Bank Asn; former twp. assessor and sch. bd. mem. Bus. & Prof. Pos: Farmer and auctioneer. Mem: Chmn, Pope Co. Hist. Soc; Sunday Sch. Supt, 20 years. Mailing Add: Route 2, Glenwood, Minn. 56334. (1967)

PETERSON, JOHN K. L. R
b. Plainfield, N.J, 4/2/20; s. Edwin C. Peterson and Margaret P; m. 3/13/48 to Anne Elizabeth Robinson. Educ: Pa. State Univ, B.S, 40. Polit. & Govt. Pos: Exec. v.pres, Capitol Hill Assocs, D.C, 63-68, pres, 68- Bus. & Prof. Pos: Owner and mgr, Radio Sta. WTHE, S.C, 55-63. Mil. Serv: Entered as Pvt, Air Force, 42, released as Tech Sgt, 45, after serv. in 706th Sq. 446th Bomb Group, Second Div; Eighth Air Force, ETO; Good Conduct Medal; Air Medal with Six Oak Leaf Clusters; Distinguished Flying Cross with Oak Leaf Cluster. Mem: Wings Club; Peidmont Club; Nat. Press Club; Capitol Hill Club; Founder, and pres, Poets Club, Wash, D.C; dir. pub. rels, HERO Cmt. Rel: Presbyterian. Legal Res: 334 Constitution Ave. N.E, Washington, D.C. 20002. Mailing Add: Drawer 1919, Washington, D.C. 20013.

PETERSON, JUNE ROZELLE D
Chairwoman, Union Co. Dem. Party, S.Dak.
b. Akron, Iowa, 6/22/20; d. Ivan Arthur Finzen, Sr. and Rozelle Lewison F; m 6/22/44 to Lewis Paul Peterson; c. Paulene (Mrs. Terry Harkness). Educ: Westmar Col, 38. Polit. & Govt. Pos: Secy-treas, Union Co. Dem. Party, S.Dak, 62-64, v.chairwoman, 64-66 and chairwoman, 66-; crew leader, Farm Census, Union and Clay Co, 64 and Civil Defense Census, 67. Mem: Farmers Union (educ. and youth dir, past 16 years). Educ. Dir. 15 year Award, Farmers Union. Rel: Lutheran. Mailing Add: Route 2, Box 32, Alcester, S.Dak. 57001.

PETERSON, KAY G. D
b. Argyle, Minn, 1/5/09; d. Archibald W. Headrick and Grace M. Nutt H; m. 4/9/52 to Henry G. Peterson; c. Henry, Jr. Educ: Univ. N.Dak; Valley City State Col, grad. Polit. & Govt. Pos: Chairwoman, Kittson Co. Dem. Party, Minn, 52-68; chairwoman, Seventh Cong. Dist. Dem. Party, 52-; chairwoman, dist. Kennedy and Johnson Campaigns; del, Dem. Nat. Conv, 60, 64 & 68; Mem: Co. Educ. Asn; Nat. Music Soc; Eastern Star; Minn. Educ. Asn; Nat. Educ. Asn; Legion Auxiliary Hosp Guild. Rel: Presbyterian. Mailing Add: Karlstad, Minn, 56732. (1967)

PETERSON, LOWELL D
Wash. State Sen.
b. Pateros, Wash, 1921; m. to Ruth; c. three. Polit. & Govt. Pos: Wash. State Sen, currently. Bus. & Prof. Pos: Oil distributor. Mil. Serv: Navy. Mem: Am. Legion; Eagles; Elks. Mailing Add: Box 188, Concrete, Wash. 98237.

PETERSON, M. BLAINE D
b. Ogden, Utah, 3/26/06; s. Peter Peterson and Rachel Thomas; m. 5/18/31 to Lucile Parry; c. Richard B, Julia Raye, Thomas P. and Mary Lu. Educ: Weber Col, A.B.A; Univ. Utah, B.A, 31; Georgetown Law Sch, LL.B. 38. Polit. & Govt. Pos: Mem, Exec. Offs. Food for Peace Staff Orgn, 63; U.S. Rep, Utah, 61-62; Utah State Rep, 55-56; attorney, Weber Co, Utah, 42-50. Prof. Pos: Lawyer, 41- Mem: Am, D.C. and Utah Bar Asns; pres, Monticello C. of C, 56; v.pres, Lions Club, Monticello, 56. Rel: Latter-day Saint. Mailing Add: 512 Eccles Bldg, Ogden, Utah 84401. (1967)

PETERSON, M.F.
Supt. of Pub. Instr, N.Dak.
b. Bowman Co, N. Dak; m. 1938 to Gladys Swenson; c. Gail, Carole and Pauline. Educ: Concordia Col, B.A; Master of Sci. Educ, Univ. of N. Dak. Polit. & Govt. Pos: Past pres, Cent. States Conf; mem. exec. cmt, Midwest Work Conf. on Rural Educ; dep. supt. of pub. instr, N.Dak, 47, supt. of pub. instr, 51-; former mem. bd. dirs, Coun. of Chief State Sch. Officers, pres, 67-68; exec. dir. and secy, State Bd. of Pub. Sch. Educ. Bus. & Prof. Pos: High sch. teacher, coach and supt, various schs, N.Dak. Publ: Ed, County Superintendents Handbook, 48 & 59, Compilation of School Laws of North Dakota, 57 and School Boards Manual, 66; plus one other. Mem: Gr. North Dakota Asn; Mason; Kiwanis; N.Dak. Educ. Asn; N.Dak. Asn. of Sch. Adminstr. Rel: Lutheran. Mailing Add: State Capitol, Bismarck, N.Dak. 58501.

PETERSON, MERLE FRANCIS D
b. Mt. Carmel, Ill, 3/6/16; s. Claude Roscoe Peterson and Edith Dixon P; m. 11/19/39 to Deloris Ellegood. Educ: Ark. State Univ, Jonesboro, B.S, 38. Polit. & Govt. Pos: Committeeman, Dem. Party, Ark, 48-60; Ark. State Sen, 61-66; del, Ark. Constitutional Conv, 69- Bus. & Prof. Pos: Owner and mgr, Dumas Motor Co, 39- Mil. Serv: Entered as Pvt, Air Force, 42, released as Capt, 45, after serv. in 489th Squadron, 340th Bomb Group, Mediterranean, 43-45; N.African, Southern Italy, Sicily and Corsica Campaign Ribbons. Mem: Nat. and Ark. State Auto Dealers Asns; U.S, Ark. and Dumas C. of C; Lions; Am. Legion; Farm Bur. Benjamin Franklin Quality Dealer Award, 69. Rel: Methodist. Legal Res: 117 Brasfield, Dumas, Ark. 71639. Mailing Add: P.O. Box 66, Dumas, Ark. 71639.

PETERSON, PAUL AMES D
b. Los Angeles, Calif, 2/17/28; s. Thaddeus Ames Peterson and Norma Brown P; m. 6/27/53 to Cynthia Atchley; c. Daniel C, Andrew G, Matthew A. and James F. Educ: Univ. of Calif, Berkeley, B.A. in Econ, 53 and LL.B, 56; Phi Beta Kappa; Order of the Coif. Polit. & Govt. Pos: Pres, San Diego Co. Dem. Prfnl. Club, 62; state inheritance tax appraiser, 63-66; chmn, San Diego Co. Cmt. to Elect Lyndon B. Johnson as U.S. President, 64; chmn, San Diego Co. Dem. Cent. Cmt, Calif, 64-66; chmn, San Diego Co. Cmt. to Re-Elect Gov. Edmund G. Brown, 66; co-chmn, San Diego Co. Cmt. to Elect Alan Cranston as U.S. Sen, 68; treas, San Diego Co. Cmt. to Elect Humphrey President, 68. Bus. & Prof. Pos: Instr. law, Calif. West. Law Sch, Univ. San Diego Law Sch. and Univ. Calif. Exten, 6 years. Mil. Serv: Entered as Pvt, Army, 46, released as T/Sgt, 48, after serv. in Hq, 24th Corps, Korea; Good Conduct Medal; Korean Theatre Ribbon. Publ: Numerous articles in Calif. Law Rev, Calif. State Bar J. and Dicta. Mem: San Diego Co. Bar Asn.(v.pres, 64); C. of C.(v.chmn, Govt. Affairs Cmt, San Diego Chap, 65); Calif. State Bar Asn.(chmn, Cmt. on Continuing Educ, 66-67); Fed. and Am. Bar Asns; secy, Citizens Interracial Cmt; Rotary; DAV (former mem). Rel: Presbyterian. Mailing Add: 911 Skylark Dr, La Jolla, Calif. 92037.

PETERSON, PAUL KENNETH R
Pub. Serv. Cmnr, Minn.
b. Minn, 4/13/15; s. Rev. Karl E. Peterson and Emma M. Sellin P; m. to Jean A. Erickson; c. Jane Ann, Paula K. and Carol Jean. Educ: North Park Col, Ill, A.A, 34; Univ. Minn, B.A, 36; Minn. Col. Law, LL.B, 51; William Mitchell Sch. of Law, J.D, 69; Delta Sigma Rho; Delta Theta Phi. Polit. & Govt. Pos: Minn. State Rep, 46-54; mem, Bd. Park Cmnrs, 55; mayor, Minneapolis, 57-61; mem, Nat. Bd. U.S. Conf. Mayors, 58 & 59; Pub. Serv. Cmnr, Minn, 66- Bus. & Prof. Pos: Mem. faculty, Minn. Sch. Bus, 46-48; instr, Adult Pub. Speaking & Human Rels, 46-61; admitted to practice, all courts in Minn. and all Fed. Courts including U.S. Supreme Court, 54. Mil. Serv: Entered as Seaman, 2/C, Navy, 42, released as Lt.(sg), 46, after serv. in Composite Squadron, Fighter Squadron, Pac. Theatre, 43-45; Naval Res, 45-63, Lt. Comdr.(Ret); U.S. Defense, European Theatre and Pac. Theatre Medals. Mem: Am. Legion; VFW; Minn. Citizens League. Outstanding Young Man of Minn, 49; Time Mag, 100 Newsmakers of Tomorrow, 54. Rel: Presbyterian. Legal Res: 3332 Edmund Blvd, Minneapolis, Minn. 55406. Mailing Add: 400 State Office Bldg, St. Paul, Minn. 55101.

PETERSON, ROBERT E. D
b. Rochester, Ind, 3/8/30; s. Clarence Cleveland Peterson and Beulah Marie Russell P; m. 9/12/65 to Martha Ann Coplen. Educ: Purdue Univ, B.S. in Agr, 52; Ind. Univ, J.D, 64; Phi Delta Phi; Alpha Zeta; Alpha Gamma Rho; Acacia; Scabbard and Blade; Purdue Order of Mil. Merit. Polit. & Govt. Pos: Auditor, Fulton Co, Ind, 57-61; Ind. State Sen, 61-68. Mil. Serv: Entered as 2nd Lt, Army, 52, released as 1st Lt, 54, after serv. in 52nd Field Artil. Bn, 24th Inf. Div, Korea; Bronze Star. Mem: Fulton Co. and Ind. State Bar Asns; Kiwanis; Am. Legion. Rel: Baptist. Legal Res: 302 West 11th St, Rochester, Ind. 46975. Mailing Add: 110 B East Eighth St, Rochester, Ind. 46975. (1967)

PETERSON, ROBERT EARL R
Del, Minn. Rep. State Exec. Cmt.
b. Glen, Minn, 2/10/27; s. Brynolf C. Peterson and Edith Barhite P; m. 6/27/53 to Doraine Lois Anderson ; c. Janet Lee, Robert Earl, Jr. and Lisa Ann. Educ: Bethel Col, 47-49; Univ. Minn, Minneapolis, B.A, Econ, 51. Polit. & Govt. Pos: Campaign mgr, Anoka Co. Rep. Party, Minn, 62; third v.chmn, Anoka Co. Rep. Cmt, 63, chmn, 64-65, third dist. chmn, 65-69; del, Rep. Nat. Conv, 68; del, Minn. Rep. State Exec. Cmt, 69- Bus. & Prof. Pos: Salesman, General Mills, 51-53; salesman, Standard Engineering, 53-54; supvr, Montgomery Ward, 55-56; materials mgr, Union Brass, 56-65; salesman-owner, Peterson Enterprises, 65- Mil. Serv: Entered as Seaman 2/C, Navy, 45, released as Seaman 1/C, 46, after serv. in Casu 33, Far East. Mem: Minn. Soc. for Indust. Engrs; Twin City Purchasing Agents Asn; Nat. Purchasing Agents Asn, Carpenter's Union. Rel: Baptist. Mailing Add: 4645 Fifth St. N.E, Minneapolis, Minn. 55421.

PETERSON, ROBERT L. D
b. Bisbee, N.Dak, 6/24/91; s. C.P. Peterson and Hedda Anderson P; m. 7/9/30 to Dorothy S. Steiger. Educ: N.Dak. State Univ, 3 years; pres, Agr. Club. Polit. & Govt. Pos: Postmaster, 34-60; mem, Towner Co. Draft Bd, N.Dak, World War II; del, Dem. Nat. Conv, 68. Mil. Serv: Entered as Enlisted Co. Cook, 309th Field Signal Bn, 17, released as Cook, 19, after serv. in France and Germany. Mem: Assoc, N.Dak. Chap, Nat. Asn. Postmasters; U.S. Civil Serv. Cmn; Am. Legion; Mason; Farmers Union; N.Dak. Wild Life Asn; plus others. Awards for serv. on the Draft Bd. throughout World War II. Rel: Presbyterian; Treas, local church. Mailing Add: Box 244, Bisbee, N.Dak. 58317.

PETERSON, RUSSELL WILBUR R
Gov, Del.
b. Portage, Wis, 10/3/16; s. John Anton Peterson and Emma Marie Anthony P; m. 6/30/37 to Eva Lillian Turner; c. Russell Glen, Peter Jon, Kristin Havill and Elin. Educ: Univ. Wis, B.S, 38, Ph.D, 42; Phi Beta Kappa; Sigma Xi; Phi Eta Sigma; Phi Lambda Upsilon. Polit. & Govt. Pos: Chmn, Finance Cmt, Del. State Rep. Party, 65-68; gov, Del, 69- Bus. & Prof. Pos: Research mgr. and supvr. textile fibers dept, E.I. du Pont de Nemours & Co, Wilmington, Del, 46-51, tech. supt, Seaford, Del. and Kinston, N.C, 51-52, asst. plant mgr, Kinston, N.C, 53-54, research dir, Wilmington, Del, 54, merchandising mgr, 54-55, research dir, 55-59, tech. dir. new prod, 59-62, dir. research and develop. div, develop. dept, 63-69. Publ: 'Engineering of Fabrics from Blends with Synthetic Fibers,' Textile Inst. J. Processing, 58; 'The Impact of New Product Development on Agribusiness,' Found. for Am. Agr, 66; 'New Venture Management in a Large Company,' Harvard Bus. Rev, 5-6/67. Mem: Am. Chem. Soc; Am. Asn. Advan. Sci; Textile Inst; Soc. Chem. Indust; Pris-

oners Aid Soc; Commun. Serv. Coun; Gr. Wilmington Develop. Coun; Three-S-Citizens' Campaign; Del. Citizens Crime Cmn; Kiwanis; Nat. Conf. Christians & Jews; Mason; Grange. William A. Vrooman Award, 64; Nat. Conf. Christians & Jews Award, 66; Del. Alpha Phi Alpha Fraternity Award, 66; Josiah Marvel Cup Award, 66; Nat. Munic. League Citizenship Award, 67; hon. fel, Textile Research Inst, 69. Rel: Unitarian. Legal Res: Governor's House, Dover, Del. 19901. Mailing Add: Legislative Hall, Dover, Del. 19901.

PETERSON, TED G. R
Wash. State Sen.
b. Seattle, Wash, 1/4/04; s. Olaf G. Peterson and Hulda Anderson P; m. 9/17/31 to Ruth E. Frank; c. Karen (Mrs. William McKinley) and Ted G, Jr. Educ: Univ. of Wash. Polit. & Govt. Pos: Wash. State Sen, currently. Bus. & Prof. Pos: Pres, wholesale equip. and supply co, currently. Mil. Serv: Wash. Nat. Guard, 4 years. Mem: Mason; Shrine; past int. dir, Lions Int; Elks. Rel: Baptist. Mailing Add: 2345 N.W. Blue Ridge Dr, Seattle, Wash. 98177.

PETERSON, VAL R
U.S. Ambassador, Finland
b. Oakland, Nebr, 7/18/03; s. Henry C. Peterson and Hermanda Swanberg P; m. 6/6/29 to Elizabeth Howells Pleak. Educ: Wayne State Col, A.B, 27; Univ. Nebr, A.M, 31 and additional grad. study, 31-33. Hon. LL.D, Midland Col, Muhlenberg Col, Tex. Lutheran Col, Fairleigh-Dickinson Univ. and Stetson Univ. Polit. & Govt. Pos: Secy. to Gov. Dwight Griswold, Nebr, 41-42; mem, Mo. Basin Inter-Agency Cmt, 47-52; Gov, Nebr, 47-53; chmn, Mo. River State Cmt, 48-52 and Nat. Gov. Conf, 52; admin. asst. to President Eisenhower, 53; sat in cabinet by presidential invitation, participated in Nat. Security Coun. meetings and presided over several White House Gov. and Mayor's Conf, Eisenhower Admin; U.S. rep, various NATO meetings; mem, Cmn. on Inter-Govt. Rels, 53-55; Fed. Civil Defense Adminstr, 53-57; U.S. Ambassador, Denmark, 57-61; del, Rep. Nat. Conv, 60, 64 & 68; chmn, Nebr. State Centennial Cmn, 61-62; regent, bd. regents, Univ. Nebr, 63-66, pres, 65; U.S. Ambassador, Finland, 69- Bus. & Prof. Pos: Instr, Nebr. Pub. Schs, 25-30 and Univ. Nebr, 30-33; supt, Elgin Schs, 33-39; publisher, Elgin Rev, 36-46; dir, J.M. McDonald Co, Hastings, Nebr, 56-66; v.pres. and adminstr, J.M. McDonald Found, Inc, 61-65, v.chmn. bd, 61-66; dir, Investors Life Ins. Co, Nebr, 61-69; chmn. bd. dirs, Life Investors Nebr, Omaha, 62-69; dir, First Nat. Bank, Hastings, 63-; pres, Wayne State Found, Wayne, 63-; chmn. bd, Investors Growth Indust, Inc, Omaha, 69- Mil. Serv: Entered as Capt, Army Air Corps, 42, released as Lt. Col, 46, after serv. in Hq, China-Burma-India Theatre; Air Force Res, 46-63; Bronze Star Medal; Asiatic-Pac. Theatre Serv. Medal. Mem: Pres, Coun. State Govt, 52; chmn, Nebr. Heart Asn. Fund Dr, 62 and Nebr. Div, Am. Cancer Soc, 64; exec. coun, Nebr. Asn. for 4-H Develop, 64-67; Int. Club; Nat. Press Club; Omaha Club; Lochland Country Club; York Rite; Scottish Rite; Shrine; KCCH; Am. Legion; VFW; Air Force Asn; Rotary; mem-at-lg, Nat. Coun. Boy Scouts. Pilots Single Engine Fixed-Wing Aircraft and Helicopters; Dept. Air Force Exceptional Serv. Award; Am. Red Cross Citation for Work in Disaster Relief; Decorated with Grand Cross of Dannebrog by King Frederick IX of Denmark. Rel: Lutheran. Legal Res: Hastings, Nebr. Mailing Add: American Embassy, Helsinki, Finland.

PETERSON, WALTER RUTHERFORD R
Gov, N.H.
b. Nashua, N.H, 9/19/22; s. Walter Rutherford Peterson and Helen Reed P; m. 11/24/49 to Dorothy Donovan; c. Margaret and Andrew. Educ: Col. William & Mary; Univ. N.H; Dartmouth Col, B.A, 47; Beta Theta Pi. Polit. & Govt. Pos: Chmn, Hillsborough Co. Rep. Cmt, N.H, 52-64; mem, Budget Cmt, Peterborough, 55-61; N.H. State Rep, 61-68, majority leader, N.H. House of Rep, 61-68 and speaker, 65-68; Gov, N.H, 69- Bus. & Prof. Pos: Realtor, The Petersons, Peterborough, 49-68; dir, Nat. Asn. Real Estate Bds, 58-62; pres, N.H. Realtors Asn, 60-61. Mil. Serv: Naval overseas officer, 42-46. Mem: Dir, Peterborough Indust. Develop. Corp; trustee, Monadnock Savings Bank, Jaffrey, New Hampton Sch, Univ. N.H. and Dartmouth Col; Lions; VFW; Am. Legion; Elks; Grange. Rel: Episcopal. Legal Res: E. Mountain Rd, Peterborough, N.H. 03458. Mailing Add: State House, Concord, N.H. 03301.

PETIT, LAURIER TELESPHORE R
b. Acton Vale, Canada, 5/8/02; m. to Alice Passini; c. two. Educ: Feller Inst, Grande Ligne, Canada. Polit. & Govt. Pos: Auditor, 35-; justice of peace; chmn, Rep. Town Cmt; past chmn, Orleans Co. Rep. Party; dir, NEMPA; treas, Orleans Co. Farm Bur; Vt. State Rep, 49-51 & 63-66. Bus. & Prof. Pos: Farming. Mem: Past master, Memphremagog Grange 424, Newport; past master, Memphremagog Lodge 75, F&AM; Eastern Star; Mason (32°). Rel: Baptist. Mailing Add: RFD 2, Newport, Vt. 05855. (1967)

PETITO, MICHAEL N. D
Supvr, Oyster Bay, N.Y.
b. Brooklyn, N.Y, 7/1/26; s. Michael A. Petito and Rose Margaret Rotunno P; m. 1/14/56 to Adeline Ballatore; c. Margaret Rose, Barbara Ann, Caroline and Catherine. Educ: St. Francis Col, N.Y. Fordham Law Sch; Debating Teams; pres, Student Coun; Polit. Sci. & Civics Clubs; voted Man Most Likely to Succeed by graduating class. Polit. & Govt. Pos: Dep. cmnr. pub. welfare, Nassau Co, N.Y, 61-63; chmn, Nassau Co. Del, State Dem. Conv, chmn, Task Force on Narcotics, Nassau Co; chmn, standing cmt. of pub. safety, Nassau Co. Bd. of Supvrs; Nassau Co. Rep. on Conserv, Fish and Wildlife Mgt. Bd; supvr, Oyster Bay, N.Y, 64-; nominee, Judge of the Family Court, 69. Bus. & Prof. Pos: Attorney-at-law; organized and established Topic House, first treatment center for addicts in Nassau Co. Mil. Serv: Entered Army, 43, released as Pfc, after serv. in ETO; Good Conduct and Victory Medals. Mem: Official, Nassau Co. Chap, Nat. Conf. Christians and Jews; adv. bd, Cath. Interracial Conf; Elks; Lions; Am. Legion; VFW; K. of C; Sons of Italy. Admitted to Practice before U.S. Supreme Court. Rel: Roman Catholic. Mailing Add: Knollwood Rd, Syosset, N.Y. 11791.

PETITPREN, VINCENT J. D
Mich. State Rep.
b. Mt. Clemens, Mich, 9/24/27; m. to Joan Phillips; c. Vincent, Victoria, Peter, Patricia and Paula. Educ: Univ. Ill; East. Mich. Univ; Wayne State Univ, B.S, M.A, grad. work, currently; Pi Kappa Delta. Polit. & Govt. Pos: Mem, Westland Twp. Planning Cmn, Mich, 61-63; Mich. Educ. Legis Cmt, 63; Westland Twp. Recreational Coun, 63-65; Mich. State Rep, 64-66 & 68- Bus. & Prof. Pos: Former prof, East. Mich. Univ; worked in Peace Corps prog. training young people to teach in Somolia, Africa; publisher and ed, The Mich. Teacher. Mil. Serv: Navy, Korean Conflict. Publ: Auth, Community College Act, 66. Mem: Pres, Wayne Fedn. Teachers, 58-60; v.pres, Mich. Fedn. Teachers, 62-64; Am. Asn. Univ. Prof; Am. Asn. Jr. Col; Mich. Higher Educ. Asn; Asn. Student Teachers; Crisis Club; Wayne-Westland Human Rels. Asn; Am. Red Cross Disaster Cmt; Kiwanis; VFW; C. of C. Mich. State Scholarship, 50-51; Nat. Sci. Found. scholarship, 61; U.S. Navy Honorman; Outstanding Teacher Award, 61. Rel: Roman Catholic. Mailing Add: 30810 Palmer Rd, Westland, Mich. 48185.

PETRICH, JOHN A. D
b. Tacoma, Wash, 1919; m. to Margaret P; c. six. Educ: U. of Wash; Santa Clara U; Georgetown U. Law Sch. Polit. & Gov. Pos: Wash. State Sen, until 66 Wash. State Rep, one term. Bus. & Prof. Pos: Attorney. Mem: Elks. Mailing Add: 706 Wash. Bldg, Tacoma, Wash. 98402. (1967)

PETRIE, DONALD A. D
b. Charleston, W.Va, 4/27/21; s. James MacFarlin Petrie and Emma O. Leunig P; m. 6/27/42 to Ruth Hauser; c. Ann Elizabeth and James MacFarlin. Educ: Hofstra Col, 1 year; Univ. of Chicago, B.A; Univ. of Chicago Law Sch, J.D. Polit. & Govt. Pos: Dir, Am. Found. for Continuing Educ, 61-64; mem, Nat. Adv. Coun. of the U.S. Travel Serv, 62-63; dir, Int. Schs. Serv, 62-64; chmn, Nassau Co. Coun. for Water Resources, 63-65; mem, Hosp. Rev. Bd, Nassau Co, 63; mem, Peace Corps Nat. Adv. Coun, 64-69; del, Nat. Dem. Conv, 64 and 68; pres, Peace Corps Vol. Fund, 65-; trustee, Hofstra Univ, 68- Bus. & Prof. Pos: Attorney-at-law, D'Ancona, Pflaum, Wyatt & Riskind, Chicago, Ill, 47-55; v.pres. and exec. v.pres, The Hertz Corp, Chicago, Ill. and N.Y.C, 55-60; pres, Hertz Am. Express Int, N.Y.C, 60-61; attorney-at-law, 61-62; chmn. of exec. cmt, Avis, Inc, Garden City, N.Y, 62-66; partner, Lazard Freres & Co, N.Y.C, 66- Mil. Serv: Entered as Pvt, Army, 43, released as S/Sgt, 46, after serv. in 315th Air Serv. Group, CBI. Mem: Am, Nassau Co, Ill. and Chicago Bar Asns; Asn. of the Bar of the City of New York; New York Stock Exchange; Union League of Chicago; Nat. Lawyers Club. Rel: Unitarian. Legal Res, 83 Chelsea Rd, Garden City, N.Y. 11530. Mailing Add: 44 Wall Street, 14th Floor, New York, N.Y. 10005.

PETRIS, NICHOLAS C. D
Calif. State Sen.
b. Oakland, Calif, 2/23/23; m. 9/16/51 to Anna Vlahos. Educ: Univ. Calif, A.B; Stanford Law Sch, LL.B. Polit. & Govt. Pos: V.pres, Calif. Dem. Coun, San Francisco Bay Area, 56-58; Soc. Serv. Bur; Bd. Mgrs; mem, Redevelop. Agency of Oakland, 57-58; Calif. State Assemblyman, 58-66; Calif. State Sen, 67- Bus. & Prof. Pos: Attorney-at-law. Mil. Serv: Army, Anti-aircraft Artil. Mem: Turtles; Eagles; Plymouth Lodge; Mason; UPEC; Alameda Bar Asn; NSGW; Elks; past pres, Greek Orthodox Church, Oakland; Coun. of Churches; Friends of Oakland Pub. Libr; trustee, Anatolia Col, Salonica, Greece and Patten Bible Col, Oakland, Calif; dir, Multi-Culture Inst, San Francisco, Bay Area Coun. on Soc. Planning and North. Calif. Kidney Found; Save San Francisco Bay Asn; Greek Am. Progressive Asn; Am. Hellenic Educ. Progressive Asn; Mexican Am. Polit. Asn; NAACP. Selected as Man of the Year, Calif. Kidney Found, 68. Rel: Greek Orthodox. Legal Res: 15 Crestmont Dr, Oakland, Calif. 94619. Mailing Add: State Capitol, Sacramento, Calif. 95814.

PETRO, JOHN WILLIAM R
Asst. Attorney Gen, Ohio
b. Cleveland, Ohio, 3/12/40; s. William John Petro and Lila Janca P; single. Educ: Univ. Md, 58-59; John Carroll Univ, B.S. in Soc. Sci, 63; West. Reserve Univ, J.D, 65; Phi Delta Phi. Polit. & Govt. Pos: Counsel, Ohio Crime Cmn; pres. and v.pres, Brooklyn Bd. Educ, Ohio, 65; asst. attorney Gen, 67-; cand, 20th dist, U.S. House Rep, 68; mem, 20th dist, Ohio Rep. State Cent. Cmt; mem, Cuyahoga Co. Rep. Exec. Cmt. Bus. & Prof. Pos: Gen. mgr, Murphy Parking Co; v.pres, Center-Lube Corp, currently; attorney, currently. Mem: Various bar Asns; Bd. Governors, West. Reserve Univ. Law Sch; Brooklyn Rep. Club (pres, 66-68); Brooklyn Safety Coun; Exec. Cmt. Southwest Cultural Arts, Inc. Legal Res: 8606 Outlook Dr, Brooklyn, Ohio 44144. Mailing Add: Terminal Tower, Cleveland, Ohio 44113.

PETRONI, ROMEO GENO R
b. Ridgefield, Conn, 1/17/29; s. Geno Petroni and Madalina Frattini P; m. 5/22/54 to Catherine L. Carroll; c. Carla, Elise and Marisa. Educ: Syracuse Univ, Edward L. Ballard Mem. Scholarship and B.A, 50; Fordham Univ. Sch. Law, LL.B, 53. Polit. & Govt. Pos: Town attorney, Ridgefield, 58-63; Conn. State Rep, 61-66, mem, Cities and Boroughs, Elec, Corp. and Judiciary and Govt. Functions Cmts, Conn. House of Rep; mem, Interim Legis. Cmt. to Create Judicial Dist. for Conn, 64; cand. for U.S. Rep, Conn, 66; mem, Rep. State Cent. Adv. Cmt. on Labor, currently; legal counsel to Rep. minority leader, Conn. Gen. Assembly, 67-; chmn, Fifth Cong. Dist. Orgn. GOP-5, 69- Bus. & Prof. Pos: Mem. adv. bd. dirs, Ridgefield Branch, Conn. Nat. Bank; with claims dept, Allstate Ins. Co, 55-58; attorney-at-law, Ridgefield, 58- Mil. Serv: Entered as Pvt, Army, 53, released a Pfc, 55. Mem: Conn. and Danbury Bar Asns; bd. dirs, Conn. Legal Aid Soc; legal adv, Italian-Am. Mutual Aid Soc, K. of C, Ridgefield Fire Dept, Keeler Tavern Preservation Soc. and AFL-CIO Local 316; 1st pres, Rep. Men's Club, Ridgefield and Ridgefield Human Rights Asn; officer, Ridgefield Lions; incorporator, Ridgefield Commun. Center and Ridgefield Br, Boys Club Am. Award, Conn. Rep. Labor League, 65. Rel: Catholic. Mailing Add: Shadow Lane, Ridgefield, Conn. 06877.

PETROVIC, ALEX M. D
b. Kans. City, Mo, 9/23/22; m. 7/29/44 to Frances M. Diesko; c. Frances Anne, Alex Michael, Teresa Marie, Christopher John, Mark Stefano, Anastasia Lia. Educ: Rockhurst Col, Kans. City, Mo. Polit. & Govt. Pos: Mo. State Rep, 62-66; city treas. of Sugar Creek, 5 1/2 years; Sugar Creek Sch. Bd; past pres. Sugar Creek Bus. & Prof. Club. Bus. & Prof. Pos: Br. mgr. of Independence Office of Waddell & Reed, Inc; Prin. Underwriters of United Funds, Inc, Kans. City, Mo. Mil. Serv: Marine Corps, T/Sgt, enlisted 42, served in S. Pac. with First and Second Marine Airwing Intel. Sect; Received personal

commendation from Adm. Marc Mitscher. Mem: Past pres. St. Mary's High Sch. Parents Club; former grand knight of K. of C; Jackson Co. Coun. 343 and mem. 4°; past pres. of Independence Sertoma Club; Instnl. rep. of Troop 268, Wagon Wheel Dist Boy Scouts; Tribe of Mic-o-say; Family Agencies Budget Cmt. of the Commun. Chest; Independence C. of C; VFW, Post 3976, Sugar Creek; Am. Legion Post 21, Independence. Rel: Catholic. Mailing Add: 11606 Burton, Sugar Creek, Mo. 64054. (1967)

PETTIBON, GEORGE T. R
Chmn, Beaver Co. Rep. Exec. Cmt, Pa.
b. Rochester, Pa, 12/13/22; s. Arthur W. Pettibon and Hazel Sutherland P; m. 10/4/44 to Josephine P. Phillips; c. George T, II, Dean A, Lynn Dee and Timothy E. Educ: Washington & Jefferson Col, B.S, 44; Beta Theta Pi. Polit. & Govt. Pos: Co. Cmnr, Beaver Co, Pa, 68-; committeeman, Center Twp. Rep, 68-; chmn, Beaver Co. Rep. Exec. Cmt, 68- Mailing Add: 107-108 Beaver Trust Bldg, Beaver, Pa. 15009.

PETTIGREW, RICHARD ALLEN D
Fla. State Rep.
b. Charleston, W.Va, 6/10/30; s. Grady L. Pettigrew and Otella Lee Overton P; m. 3/8/54 to Ann Moorhead; c. Jill Elizabeth and Grady L, II. Educ: Univ. Fla, B.A, 53 and LL.B, 57; Tau Kappa Alpha; Phi Eta Sigma; Phi Alpha Delta; Fla. Blue Key; Phi Delta Theta. Polit. & Govt. Pos: Pres, Dade Co. Young Dem, Fla, 60-61; nat. committeeman, Young Dem. Clubs of Fla, 61-62, pres, 63-64; Fla. State Rep, 63-, chmn, Govt. Orgn. and Efficiency Cmt. and speaker-designate for 71-72 session, Fla. House of Rep; state chmn, Young Citizens for Johnson, 64. Bus. & Prof. Pos: Attorney, Walton, Lantaff, Schroeder, Carson & Wahl, 57- Mil. Serv: Entered as 2nd Lt, Air Force, 53, released as 1st Lt, 55, after serv. in 67th Reconnaissance Tech. Wing, Korea and Japan, 54-55; Korean Campaign Ribbons; Capt, Air Force Res. Publ: 'Another Look at that Forbidden Word Insurance,' Vol. X, Univ. Fla. Law Rev, 58; 'Constitutional Reform-Forging the Effective Governing Framework,' Fla. Planning and Develop, 66. Mem: Am, Fla. and Dade Co. Bar Asns; Phi Alpha Delta Alumni Asn. Allen Morris Awards, Second-Session Mem. Showing Greatest Develop, 65 session, first runner-up, Most Effective in Cmt, 67 session and Most Valuable Mem. of the House, 69 session; St. Petersburg Times Poll Award, One of Ten Most Valuable Mem. of House of Rep, 65 & 67 sessions. Rel: Protestant. Mailing Add: 740 Ingraham Bldg, Miami, Fla. 33131.

PETTIS, JERRY LYLE R
U.S. Rep, Calif.
b. Phoenix, Ariz, 7/18/16; m. to Shirley McCumber; c. Yvonne, Peter and Deborah. Educ: Pac. Union Col, B.A, 38. Polit. & Govt. Pos: U.S. Rep, Calif, 66-, mem, Cmt. Sci. and Astronaut, Subcmt, Space Sci. and Applns. and Sci. Research and Develop, Cmt. House Adminis. and Subcmt. Printing, U.S. House of Rep. Bus. & Prof. Pos: Businessman and rancher; v.pres, Loma Linda Univ. Mil. Serv: Flight instr. search and rescue pilot, Civil Air Patrol, Air Transport Command Pilot in Pac. Theatre. Rel: Seventh-day Adventist. Mailing Add: 24934 Tulip Ave, Loma Linda, Calif. 92354.

PETTIT, H. FOSTER D
Ky. State Rep.
b. 1930. Educ: Univ. of Va, B.A, LL.B; U.S. Army Lang. Sch. Polit. & Govt. Pos: Ky. State Rep, 64- Bus. & Prof. Pos: Attorney, Mil. Serv: Air Force. Mem: Fayette Co, Ky. and Am. Bar Asns; Kiwanis. Rel: Presbyterian. Mailing Add: 605 Russell Ave, Lexington, Ky. 40508. (1967)

PETTIT, HOWARD GORDON, JR. R
Chmn, Oconee Co. Rep. Party, S.C.
b. Spartanburg, S.C, 11/4/22; s. Howard Gordon Pettit and Elsie Dye P; m. 7/7/51 to Eleanor Fay Gilreath; c. Susan Lynn, Nancy G, Catherine Ann and Howard Gordon, III. Educ: Univ. S.C, B.S, 49, Law Sch, 52; Phi Delta Phi; Kappa Sigma Kappa; Pi Kappa Phi. Polit. & Govt. Pos: Chmn, Oconee Co. Rep. Party, S.C, 62-64 & 66-; state exec. committeeman, 64-66. Mil. Serv: Entered as Pvt, Army, 42, released as 1st Lt, 46, after serv. in 65th Div, American Div, 77th Div. & 11th Airborne Div, Pacific; Asiatic Pac. Campaign Medal with Bronze Star; Japanese Occup. Medal; Am. Theater Campaign Medal; Philippine Liberation Medal; Victory Medal; Capt, Army Res, 46-64. Mem: Am, S.C. and Oconee Co. Bar Asns; Elks. Legal Res: N. Catherine St, Walhalla, S.C. 29691. Mailing Add: P.O. Box 99, Walhalla, S.C. 29691.

PETTITT, JAMES VANONI R
Mem, Calif. Rep. State Cent. Cmt.
b. Soledad, Calif, 6/16/04; s. Thomas B. Pettitt and Edith L. Vanoni P; m. 10/3/29 to Helen Hamilton; c. Nancy (Mrs. Robert J. Stedelin) and Tom H. Educ: Healds Bus. Col, 2 years. Polit. & Govt. Pos: Dep. assessor, Monterey Co, Calif, 46-62; mem, Congressman Burt L. Talcott Cong. Cmt, 66-69; mem, Calif. Rep. State Cent. Cmt, 68- Bus. & Prof. Pos: V.pres, Pettitt Lands Inc, 39-69; secy, Pettitt & Lavernelto, Real Estate and Ins, 58-69; dir, Mee Mem. Hosp, 62 & 69. Mil. Serv: Pvt, Field Artil, Army Res, 21-27. Mem: Nat. Inst. of Farm & Land Brokers; Monterey Co. Cattlemen's Asn.(secy, 46-56); C. of C.(pres, 56); pres, King City Stampede, 58-64; pres, Salinas Valley Fair, Kings City, 68 & 69; Shrine; Mason (Trustee, King City Lodge, 50-69); Odd Fellows; Scottish Rite; Eastern Star. Rel: Episcopal; Past Sr. Warden. Legal Res: 316 N. Mildred St, King City, Calif. 93930. Mailing Add: P.O. Box 965, King City, Calif. 93930.

PETTY, GEORGE BEVERLY, JR. D
S.C. State Rep.
b. Bowling Green, S.C, 9/8/11; s. George Beverly Petty and Daisy Adams P; m. 1943 to Hattie Lee Faires. Educ: Gastonia High Sch, Gastonia, N.C, 29. Polit. & Govt. Pos: S.C. State Rep, 63- Bus. & Prof. Pos: Navy, retired; farmer. Mil. Serv: Navy, 40-60, (retiring as Chief PO); served aboard U.S.S. Lexington (CV2); U.S.S. Hornet (CV8); U.S.S. Lexington (CV16); U.S.S. Harry E. Hubbard (DD 748); received Presidential Unit Citation. Mem: Mason; Elks. Rel: Presbyterian; Elder, Bethesda Presbyterian Church. Mailing Add: Box 105, RFD 1, Rock Hill, S.C. 29730. (1967)

PETTY, JOHN R.
Asst. Secy. for Int. Affairs, Treas. Dept.
b. Chicago, Ill, 4/16/30; m. 5/11/57 to H. Lee Mills; c. Lawrence T, Robert D, George M. and Victoria L. Educ: Brown Univ, 47-51. Polit. & Govt. Pos: Rapporteur, Coun. on For. Rels, 53-61; former mem, Export Subcmt, Defense Indust. Adv. Coun. and Export Action Cmt, Nat. Export Expansion Coun; Dep. Asst. Secy. for Int. Affairs, Treas. Dept, 66-68, Acting Asst. Secy. for Int. Affairs, 68, Asst. Secy. for Int. Affairs, 68- Bus. & Prof. Pos: Mem. training prog, Chase Manhattan Bank, New York, 53-55, mem, Int. Dept, Africa, West. European and Mid. East Area, 55-61, asst. treas, West. European Area, 58-61, asst. v.pres, Paris Br, 61-63, v.pres. and div. exec. Worldwide Projs. Div, New York, 63-66. Mil. Serv: Lt.(jg), Destroyers, Pac. Fleet, 51-53. Exceptional Serv. Award, Treas. Dept, 68; Received Arthur S. Flemming Award as One of the Ten Outstanding Young Men in the Fed. Serv. in 68 & 69. Legal Res: West Lake Stable Rd, Tuxedo Park, N.Y. 10987. Mailing Add: Treasury Dept, 15th and Pennsylvania Ave, Washington, D.C. 20220.

PEYTON, ANGUS E. D
Cmnr, Dept. of Commerce, W.Va.
b. Kanawha Co, W.Va, 2/22/27; m. to Ruth Raftery; c. Ruth Morgan, Mary Lisa and Angus MacDonald. Educ: Princeton Univ, B.A. in Econ, 49; Univ. Va, LL.B, 52. Polit. & Govt. Pos: Former asst. prosecuting attorney, Kanawha Co; former asst. attorney gen; cmnr, Dept. of Commerce, W.Va, 65- Bus. & Prof. Pos: Lawyer; dir, Kanawha Valley Bank, Slab Fork Coal Co. and W.Va. Bldg. and Loan Asn; former assoc. with Firm of Payne, Minor, Ray Loeb & Prince. Mem: W.Va. State and Kanawha Co. Bar Asns. Legal Res: Charleston, Kanawha Co, W.Va. Mailing Add: Fourth Floor, E. Wing, Capitol, Charleston, W.Va. 25305. (1967)

PEZAK, JOHN D
Pa. State Rep.
b. Mayfield, Pa, 10/25/13; s. Harry Pezak and Rose Katchmar P; m. to Mary Kasiewski; c. two. Educ: Jessup High Sch. Polit. & Govt. Pos: Mem, 23rd Ward Dem. Cmt; committeeman, 24 years; Pa. State Rep, 64- Bus. & Prof. Pos: Supvr; dir, Bridesburg Fed. Credit Union. Mem: AFL-CIO; St. Jude Soc; Progressive Am. Ukranian Club; Am. Ukranian Citizens League; Harmonia Club; C.W.V. Post 471; St. Nicholas Club. Mailing Add: 2332 Margaret St, Philadelphia, Pa. 19137. (1967)

PEZMAN, ALFRED LEONARD D
b. Qunicy, Ill, 1/23/18; s. Sol Pezman and Sarah Josephson P; m. 2/25/48 to Cleora Ludwig; c. Sheryl E. and Barbara Kay. Educ: Univ. Ill, A.B, 42, J.D, 45. Polit. & Govt. Pos: Pres, Univ. Ill. Young Dem, 41-42; chief enforcement attorney, Off. Price Stabilization, 51-52; state's attorney, Brown Co, Ill, 52-56; chmn, Brown Co. Dem. Cent. Cmt, 52-56 and Adams Co. Dem. Cent. Cmt, 62-65; tech. adv, Ill. Youth Cmn, 61-63; precinct committeeman, Second Dist, Melrose 62-; judge, Ill. Court of Claims, 63-69. Bus. & Prof. Pos: Gen. counsel, Trio Mfg. Co, 57-60; secy, Condee, Inc; pres, Adams Co. Abstract & Title Co. and Nova Prod, Inc. Mem: Ill. State, Adams Co. and Brown Co. Bar Asns; Optimists; Elks; Hardin Lodge 44 AF&AM, Quincy Consistory, Ansar Shrine; exec. bd, Saukee Area Coun, Boy Scouts; past pres, United Fund Adams Co; life mem, Univ. Ill. Alumni Asn. Silver Beaver Award, Saukee Area Coun, Boy Scouts. Rel: Jewish. Legal Res: R.R. 4, Quincy, Ill. 62301. Mailing Add: Illinois Bank Bldg, Quincy, Ill. 62301.

PFAENDER, THOMAS PAINE R
Chmn, Brown Co. Rep. Cmt, Minn.
b. New Ulm, Minn, 1/30/98; s. William Pfaender, Jr. and Sophia Berndt P; single. Educ: Normal Col, Am. Gymnastic Union, 25; Univ. Minn, grad. study; Phi Epsilon Kappa. Polit. & Govt. Pos: Exec. secy, Brown Co. Rep. Hq, Minn, 64; chmn, Brown Co. Rep. Cmt, 65-; Presidential Elector, 68. Bus. & Prof. Pos: Dir, dept. of health and phys. educ, New Ulm Pub. Schs, Minn, 31-63; camp dir, St. Louis Co. 4-H Club Camp, 37-64. Mil. Serv: Entered as Pvt, Inf, 16, released as Sgt, 17; Mex. Border Serv. and World War I Serv. Ribbons. Mem: Chmn. first aid cmt, Brown-West Nicollet Co. Red Cross, 46-; pres, Jr. Pioneer Asn, 64-; Am. Legion; Mason; Fel of the Am. Asn. for Health, Phys. Educ. and Recreation; life mem, Minn. for Health, Phys. Educ. and Recreation; hon. life mem, St. Louis Co. 4-H Clubs. Decorated by Mexican Govt. for fostering int. cultural rels, 68. Rel: Unitarian. Mailing Add: 900 S. Broadway, New Ulm, Minn. 56073.

PFALTZ, HUGO MENZEL, JR. R
N.J. State Assemblyman
b. Newark, N.J, 9/23/31; s. Hugo M. Pfaltz and Mary E. Horr P; m. 9/29/56 to Marilyn Muir; c. Elizabeth W, William M. and Robert L. Educ: Hamilton Col, B.A, 53; Harvard Law Sch, L.L.B, 60; N.Y. Univ. Sch. Law, L.L.M, 64; Phi Beta Kappa; Lambda Chi Alpha. Polit. & Govt. Pos: Committeeman, Rep. Party, Summit, N.J, 62-68; del, N.J. Constitutional Conv, 66; chmn, Rep. City Cmt, Summit, 67; N.J. State Assemblyman, Dist. 9C, 68- Bus. & Prof. Pos: Documents clerk, UN, 53; attorney, McCarter & English, Esquires, Newark, N.J, 60-62; attorney, Bourne and Noll, Esquires, Summit, N.J, 62- Mil. Serv: Entered as A/S, Navy, 53, released as Lt.(jg), 57, after serving in Patrol Squadron 24, Mediterranean, 54-56; Res, 57-63, Lt. Publ: ' "In Terrorem" ne Terreamus', Ky. Law J, 64. Mem: Am, N.J, Essex Co, Union Co. and Summit Bar Asns; Am. Judicature Soc; Beacon Hill Club. Rel: Unitarian. Legal Res: 118 Prospect Street, Summit, N.J. 07901. Mailing Add: 382 Springfield Ave, Summit, N.J. 07901.

PFALZGRAF, HAROLD ARCHER R
Co. Attorney, Sumner Co, Kans.
b. McPherson, Kans, 5/4/33; s. Charles Archer Pfalzgraf and Esther Brooks P; m. 10/9/53 to Carol Louise Ginavan; c. Linda and Douglas. Educ: McPherson Col, B.A, 59; Washburn Univ. Sch. Law, LL.B, 62; Delta Theta Phi. Polit. & Govt. Pos: Asst. Attorney Gen, Kans, 62-63; Probate and Juvenile Judge, Sumner Co, 63-66, Co. Attorney, 67-; Rep. Precinct Committeeman, 64-65; chmn, Sumner Co. Rep. Cmt, 68-69; pres, Fifth Cong. Dist. Lincoln Day Club, 69. Mil. Serv: Entered as Pvt, Army, 53, released as Cpl, 55, after serv. in 82nd Airborne-Paratroopers. Mem: Sumner Co, Am. and Kans. Bar Asns; Elks; Am. Legion; C. of C; Rotary. Rel: Methodist. Legal Res: 1115 N. Jefferson, Wellington, Kans. 67152. Mailing Add: Court House, Wellington, Kans. 67152.

PFEFFER, LEO D
Chmn, Champaign Co. Dem. Party
b. Seymour, Ill, 11/26/08. Educ: Univ. Ill. Polit. & Govt. Pos: Supt, Inst.

Farms, Ill; chmn, 22nd Cong. Dist. Dem. Party; precinct committeeman, 20 years; Ill. State Rep, 6 terms; chmn, Champaign Co. Dem. Party, currently. Bus. & Prof. Pos: Operator of grain and livestock farm; state hwy. policeman. Mem: Farm Bur; Elks; Moose. Mailing Add: Seymour, Ill. 61875. (1967)

PFEIFFER, LOLITA DAWSON D
b. Lynn, Mass, 5/13/45; d. Eugene Ellsworth Dawson and Arlene W. Clark D; m. 6/22/68 to Raymond Smith Pfeiffer. Educ: Chatham Col, B.A, 67; pres, Chatham Col. Soc. Bd, 66; soc. coordinator, Chatham Col, 67. Polit. & Govt. Pos: Alternate del, Dem. Nat. Conv, 68. Bus. & Prof. Pos: Develop. officer, Keuka Col, Keuka Park, N.Y, 67-69; dir. of alumnae rels, Helen Bush Sch, Seattle, Wash, 69- Mem: Am. Alumni Coun. Rel: Congregational. Legal Res: 109 E. Lake Rd, Pen Yan, N.Y. 14527. Mailing Add: 2839 Perkins Lane W, Seattle, Wash. 98199.

PFEIFFER, WILLIAM LOUIS R
b. Buffalo, N.Y, 5/29/07; s. John A. Pfeiffer and Louise J. Lechleiter P; m. 5/3/24 to Olive Edna Williams P; c. Jacqueline Clair (Mrs. William Paul Lueth), Betty Lou (Mrs. Frank Coburn, Jr). Educ: Tech. high Sch. Polit. & Govt. Pos: U.S. Rep, N.Y, 49-51; Chmn, N.Y. Rep. State Cmt, 49-53; del, Rep. Nat. Conv, 52; Dep. Comptroller, N.Y. State, 46-48; Exec. Asst, N.Y. State Comptroller, 43-46; Co. personnel officer, Erie Co. Bd. Supvrs, 42-43; Secy, Erie Co, N.Y. Rep. Cmt, 41-42; Mem, N.Y. State Jour. Clerks Staff, 39-40; Chief Aide to N.Y. State Rep. Cong. Cmt, 38; Bd. Trustees, Albany Savings Bank. Bus. & Prof. Pos: Pres, William L. Pfeiffer Co, Inc, Syria Corp. and Lake George Lochlea, Inc; Chmn, U.S. Hoffman Machinery Corp, 53-55; V.Pres, Radmetals, Inc; Dir, Hydraulic Press Mfg. Co, United Whelan Corp. and Commercial State Bank & Trust Co. Mem: Odd Fellows; Albany Country Club; Capital Hill Clubs (Buffalo and Wash.); Lotos Club, NYC. Cited by U.S. Treas. Dept. for outstanding serv. in sale of war bonds. Rel: Presbyterian. 1967 Legal Res: Old Westbury, N.Y. No mailing address available. (1967)

PFEILSTICKER, MARION AUGUST DFL
b. Reads Landing, Minn, 1/3/19; s. August Pfeilsticker and Blanche Davison P; m. 6/2/41 to Mary Ann Kreye; c. James, David, Thomas, Gerald, Stephen, Mary Lucy, Peter, Charles and Donald. Educ: Rochester State Jr. Col. Polit. & Govt. Pos: Chmn, Wabasha Co. Dem-Farmer-Labor Party, Minn, 64-67; mem, Minn. State Dem-Farmer-Labor Cent. Cmt, 64-67; co. del, Minn. State Conv, 64 & 66; acting postmaster, Wabasha, Minn, 67- Bus. & Prof. Pos: Self employed in agr, 30 years. Rel: Roman Catholic. Mailing Add: R.R, Wabasha, Minn. 55981.

PFROMMER, CHRISTOPHER F, III D
b. Newcastle, Del, 3/2/35; s. Christopher F. Pfrommer and Ethel Brown Stengle P; m. 2/24/62 to Linda Lee Winklepleck; c. Melinda Catherine and Susan Lee. Educ: Northwest. Univ, B.A, 57; Delta Kappa Epsilon. Polit. & Govt. Pos: Aide to U.S. Rep. Clarence D. Long, Md, 63-; pres, Young Dem, Baltimore, Md, 65 and 66. Bus. & Prof. Pos: Reporter, Baltimore Sun Papers, 59-62; stringer assignments, Newsweek, N.Y. Post and N.Y. Daily News. Mil. Serv: Pvt, Army, 57-59 with serv. as Ed, Pentagram News, Mil. Dist. of Wash, D.C. Publ: Article on missile base Sentry Dogs, Grit Mag, 64; 'Who Bothers to Vote for Them?' Baltimore Mag, 9/66. Mem: Jr. C. of C; Univ. Club of Baltimore; Award from Md-Del. Press for Feature Writing, 66. Rel: Episcopal. Mailing Add: 4416 Norwood Rd, Baltimore, Md. 21218.

PHEIFFER, WILLIAM TOWNSEND R
b. Purcell, Okla, 7/15/98; s. William Pheiffer and Susan Harrison P; m. 3/20/54 to Frances Uihlein. Educ: Univ. South. Calif; Univ. of Okla; Chi Phi; Phi Alpha Delta; Delta Sigma Rho. Polit. & Govt. Pos: U.S. Rep, 16th Dist, N.Y, 40-43; exec. asst. to chmn, Rep. Nat. Cmt, 44-46; U.S. Ambassador to the Dominican Republic, 53-57; alternate del, Rep. Nat. Conv, 68. Bus. & Prof. Pos: Mem, Bd. of Dirs. of various bus. corp. Mil. Serv: Capt, Army, 43-44, serv. in Cavalry; Award of Merit. Mem: Pres, Amarillo Bar Asn, Tex, 36-37; Mason; past post comdr, Am. Legion; Metrop. Club, N.Y.C; Lake Placid Club, Lake Placid, N.Y; Everglades Club, Palm Beach, Fla. Rel: Unitarian. Mailing Add: 480 Park Ave, New York, N.Y. 10022.

PHELAN, ELLEN SKAE R
Mem, Mich. Higher Educ. Cmn.
b. Detroit, Mich, 6/10/05; d. Edward Askin Skae and Florence Hammond S; m. 1/9/32 to James J. Phelan, Jr; c. Mary Meade (Mrs. Theodore H. Fuger, Jr), Florence Hammond (Mrs. Peter J. Connolly), Ellen Skae (Mrs. David M. Hamilton) and Anne Barry. Polit. & Govt. Pos: Alternate del, Rep. Nat. Conv, 60, del, 64; past v.chmn, Seventh Cong. Dist. Exec. Cmt, Mich. State Rep. Cent. Cmt; past chmn, Exec. Cmt, Lapeer Co. Rep; past secy, Dryden Bd. Educ; mem, Mich. Higher Educ. Cmn, presently. Bus. & Prof. Pos: Pres, Detroit Recreation Co; v.pres, Hammond Bldg. Co; pres, Superior Land Co, 54- Mem: Mich. Farm Bur; Jr. League of Detroit; Nat. Rep. Club, N.Y.C; Country Club of Detroit and Lapeer Co. Country Club. Rel: Roman Catholic. Mailing Add: Skaphe Hill Farms, 5860 Barber Rd, Metamora, Mich. 48455.

PHELPS, EDNA MAE D
Pres, Okla. Fedn. Dem. Women's Clubs.
b. Tulsa, Okla, 6/12/20; d. William Harold Hough and Nedda Pearl Jerome H; m. 9/10/42 to Joe Elton Phelps; c. Ronald Jerome and Joelton Mark. Educ: Okla. State Univ, B.A, 42; Okla. Col. Lib. Arts, 60; Okla. Univ. 65; Theta Sigma Phi; Kappa Delta Pi; Fourth Estate. Polit. & Govt. Pos: Publicity chmn, Seminole Co. Dem, 63-65; pres, Seminole Co. Dem. Women's Club, 65-67; chmn. of club presidents cmt, Okla. Fedn. Dem. Women's Clubs, 65-67, pres, 67-; chmn, Precinct 1, Ward 4, Seminole Co, 65-69; del. and Okla. rep. on credentials cmt, Dem. Nat. Conv, 68. Bus. & Prof. Pos: Ed, Okla. Live Stock News; pub. rels. asst, Tulsa C. of C. Mem: Bd. of trustees, Seminole Pub. Libr; Investment Club in Seminole Co. (past pres); Seminole PTA (past pres); Mod. Lit. Club (past pres); active in Cub Scout and Boy Scout work, Heart Fund and Cancer Drives. Rel: Presbyterian; church women's auxiliary (past pres). Mailing Add: 916 Lee Ave, Seminole, Okla. 74868.

PHELPS, JO MINOR R
Secy, Ga. Rep. Party
b. N.Y.C, 11/4/34; d. Henry Daniels Minor and Elizabeth Creecy Clark M; m. 7/2/69 to Arthur Crane Phelps; c. Sharon Roberts, Melody Roberts and Lenor Roberts. Educ: A.L. Miller Sr. High Sch, Macon, Ga. Polit. & Govt. Pos: Goldwater Volunteer, Houston Co, Ga, 64; first pres, Rep. Woman's Club, 65; Rep. precinct v.chmn, Houston Co, 66; v.chairwoman, Houston Co. Rep. Party, 68; secy, Ga. Rep. Party, 68- Bus. & Prof. Pos: Real Estate salesman, KEG Realty Co, Warner Robins, Ga, 68- Mem: Cert. dir, Am. Contract Bridge League. Rel: Presbyterian. Legal Res: 105 Maid Marion Court, Warner Robins, Ga. 31093. Mailing Add: 1654 Watson Blvd, Warner Robins, Ga. 31093.

PHELPS, PHELPS D
b. Bonn, Germany, 5/4/97; s. Franz von Rottenburg and Marion Phelps R; single. Educ: Williams Col, A.B, 22; Fordham Law Sch, LL.B, 27; Psi Upsilon; Delta Theta Phi. Hon. LL.D, Univ. Santo Domingo, 53. Polit. & Govt. Pos: Dep. cmnr, N.Y. Vets. Relief Cmn, 22-33; N.Y. State Assemblyman, 24-28 & 37-38; del, Dem. Nat. Conv, 36, 56 & 60; N.Y. State Sen, 39-42; gov, Am. Samoa, 51-52; U.S. Ambassador to Dominican Repub, 52-53; mem, Palisades Interstate Park Cmn, 56-; del, N.J. State Constitutional Conv, 66. Bus. & Prof. Pos: Exec. ed, Chelsea Clinton News; investment counsel. Mil. Serv: Entered as Cadet Pfc, Royal Flying Corps, 17, released, 19, reentered as 1st Lt, Army, 42, released as Capt, 46, after serv. in legal sect, GHQ-SCAB; ETO and N.African, Asiatic and Am. Theater Campaign Ribbons; 2 Victory Medals. Publ: 'Our Defences Within and Without,' 32; America on Trial, 33. Mem: Bd. trustees, Ment. Health Asn, Greenville Hosp, Jersey City and Urban League, Essex Co; bd. mem, Hudson Co. Tuberc. and Health Asn; bd. dirs, N.J. Br, Am. Asn. for UN and Int. Inst. of Jersey City; Past Exalted Ruler, N.Y. Lodge 1, Elks; Grand St. Boys Asn; Am. Legion; VFW; Army Navy Club; Univ. Club; Sons of Revolution; Soc. Colonial Wars; Union League Club; Nat. Capital Dem. Club; chmn, adv. bd, Salvation Army, Jersey City; March of Dimes Campaign Chmn, Jersey City, 60-62 and Hudson Co, 62-65; chmn, UN Day, Jersey City, 63-65. George Washington Carver Award, 62; Knight Comdr, King George I, Greece; Annual Award, Urban League of Essex, Co, 66. Rel: Episcopal. Mailing Add: Fairmount Hotel, 2595 Kennedy Blvd, Jersey City, N.J. 07306.

PHELPS, VICTOR E. D
b. Hill, N.H, 4/16/93; married; c. 3. Educ: Proctor Acad. Polit. & Govt. Pos: N.H. State Rep, 41,45,49, 55-67; Town and Sch. treas; fire warden; fire chief; water cmnr; plumber and electrician. Mem: Grange; Mason; Eastern Star; Fish and Game Club; Merrimack Co. Fire Wardens Asn. Rel: Unitarian. Mailing Add: Andover, N.H. 03216. (1967)

PHELPS, WILLIAM C. R
Mo. State Rep.
b. Nevada, Mo, 5/5/34; m. 9/5/64 to Betsy Breidenthal. Educ: Univ. of Mo, Columbia, A.B, Econ. and Bus, 56, LL.B, 59; Omicron Delta Kappa; Mystical Seven; Beta Theta Pi. Polit. & Govt. Pos: Pres, Univ. Student Union Bd, 56; Mo. State Rep, 60-; state-wide campaign mgr. for U.S. Sen. nominee Crosby Kemper, 62; minority whip 73rd Assembly; pres, Mo. Asn. of Rep, 63. Bus. & Prof. Pos: Assoc. with law firm of Morrison, Hecker, Cozad and Morrison of Kans. City, Mo; former part-time teacher of gen. econ. Mil. Serv: Army, active duty; Army Res, Capt. Mem: Am. Bar Asn; Mo. Bar; Lawyers Asn. of Kans. City; Kans. City Bar Asn. Rel: Episcopal. Mailing Add: 843 W. 56th St, Kansas City, Mo. 64113. (1967)

PHILBIN, PHILIP JOSEPH D
U.S. Rep, Mass.
b. Clinton, Mass, 5/29/98; m. to Lillan Sunberg, wid; c. Mary Ellen Bamby (Mrs. Scansaroli) and Ann Blenda. Educ: Harvard Col, A.B. 20; Columbia Univ. Law Sch, 24, LL.B. Polit. & Govt. Pos: Former spec. counsel, U.S. Senate Cmt. on Educ. and Labor; former referee, Dept. of Labor; former mem. adv. bd, Mass. Unemploy. Compensation Cmn; U.S. Rep, Mass, 43-; chmn, Clinton Town Finance Cmt, currently; del, Dem. Nat. Conv, 68. Bus. & Prof. Pos: Attorney, businessman and farmer. Mil. Serv: World War I. Legal Res: Clinton, Mass. Mailing Add: 2372 Rayburn House Office Bldg, Washington, D.C. 20515. (1967)

PHILBRICK, ROBERT D. D
N.H. State Racing Cmnr.
b. New York, N.Y, 11/19/28; s. John Philbrick and Anna Brooks P; m. 7/13/57 to Vesta Ann Peters; c. Celeste, Patrick, Brendan, Robert, Jr. and Sarah. Educ: Fordham Univ, 51. Polit. & Govt. Pos: Pres, Fordham Univ. Dem. Club, 47-51; chmn. col. div, N.Y. Dem. State Cmt, 50-51; state committeeman, N.H. Dem. Party, 58-; chmn, Hillsborough Co. and Milford Town Dem. Parties, N.H; N.H. State Racing Cmnr, currently; alternate del, Dem. Nat. Conv, 68. Bus. & Prof. Pos: New Eng. Rep, Rollins Co, New York, 56- Mil. Serv: Entered as 2nd Lt, Army, 51, released as 1st Lt, 53, after serv. in Korea; Far East Campaign Ribbon; Korean Campaign Ribbon with five Battle Stars. Mem: Nat. Asn. State Racing Cmnrs; K. of C; VFW; Am. Legion; Elks. Rel: Roman Catholic. Mailing Add: 50 Elm St, Milford, N.H. 03055.

PHILIP, JAMES PEYTON, JR. R
Ill. State Rep.
b. Elmhurst, Ill, 5/26/30; s. James Peyton Philip, Sr. and Elsa Gerhardt P; m. 12/12/64 to Judith Ann Haines; c. Cynthia Kay. Educ: Kans. City Jr. Col, 49-50; Kans. State Col, 52-53. Polit. & Govt. Pos: Treas, Elmhurst Young Rep. Club, Ill, 60; chmn, DuPage Co. Young Rep. Orgn, 61-63; admin. asst. to 14th Cong. Dep. Gov, Ill. Young Rep. Orgn, 61-63; admin. asst. to Chmn. Bd, 63, Jr. Nat. Committeeman, 63-65, pres, 65-; auditor, York Twp, 65-; Ill. State Rep, 37th Dist, 66- Bus. & Prof. Pos: Asst. mgr, Edison Bros. Stores, Inc, 49-53; sales rep, Pepperidge Farm, Inc, 53-54, sales promotion supvr, 54-60, sales promotion mgr, 60-62, dist. sales mgr, 62- Mil. Serv: Entered as Pvt, Marine Corps, 50, released as Cpl, 52. Mem: Suburban Bus. Mgt. Coun; Grocery Mgt. and Sales Exec. Club. of Chicago; Merchandising and Exec. Club. of Chicago; Ill Twp. Officials Asn; Am. Legion; Elks; Medinah Temple, DuPage Shrine Club. Hunting and fishing. Rel: Episcopal. Mailing Add: 488 E. Crescent, Elmhurst, Ill. 60126.

PHILIPPI, CRAIG M. D
Chmn, Cumberland Co. Dem. Party, Ill.
b. Greenup, Ill, 3/14/06; s. James Philippi and Delia Mattoon P; m. 6/28/24 to Ethel Maye Mitchell; c. Robert and Margaret (Mrs. Mayer). Educ:

Greenup High Sch, Ill. Polit. & Govt. Pos: Chmn, Cumberland Co. Dem. Party, Ill, 54- Rel: Protestant. Mailing Add: 208 E. Pleasant St, Greenup, Ill. 62428.

PHILLIPS, ALICE SNIDER D
b. Shuqualak, Miss, 10/29/20; m. to John Alton Phillips, wid. Polit. & Govt. Pos: Miss. State Rep, until 66; former Dem. nat. committeewoman; mem. adv. cmt. of Nat. Found. and Salk Inst. Bldg. Fund. Bus. & Prof. Pos: Artist; designer; tree farmer. Mem: Past gov, Pilot Club Int; Farm Bur; Fashion Group, Inc; Miss. Art Asn; DAR. Rel: Baptist. Mailing Add: Macon, Noxubee Co, Miss. 39341. (1967)

PHILLIPS, ANDREW CRAIG D
Supt. of Pub. Instr, N.C.
b. Greensboro, N.C, 11/1/22; s. Guy B. Phillips; m. 1943 to Mary Martha Cobb; c. Martha Gatlin, Andrew Craig, Jr, Elizabeth Cobb and Eva Craig. Educ: Univ. N.C, Chapel Hill, M.A, 46, Ed.D, 56. Polit. & Govt. Pos: Supt, Winston-Salem Schs, N.C, 57-62 and Charlotte-Mecklenburg Schs, 62-67; state supt. Pub. Instr, 69-; mem, Gov. Cmn. to Study the N.C. Pub. Sch. Syst, currently, mem, Steering Cmt, currently; mem, Nat. Citizens Cmt. on Pub. TV, currently; mem, President's Cmn. on Ment. Health for Children, currently. Bus. & Prof. Pos: Admin. v.pres, Richardson Found, Greensboro, N.C, 67-68. Mil. Serv: Entered as Ens, Naval Res, released as Lt, 46, after serv. in European and Pac. Theatres, 43-46. Mem: Am. Asn. of Sch. Adminstr, bd. dir, Nat. Acad. for Sch. Execs; South. Asn. of Cols. and Schs; Nat. and N.C. Educ. Asns; bd. visitors, Divinity Sch, Duke Univ. Winston-Salem Young Man of the Year, 57. Rel: Methodist. Legal Res: 717-C, Hawes Court, Raleigh, N.C. 27608. Mailing Add: Education Bldg, Raleigh, N.C. 27602.

PHILLIPS, CHANNING EMERY D
Dem. Nat. Committeeman, D.C.
b. Brooklyn, N.Y, 3/23/28; s. Porter W. Phillips, Sr. and Dorothy A. Fletcher P; m. 12/22/56 to Jane Nabors; c. Channing Durward, Sheilah Nahketeh, Tracy Jane, Jill Celeste and John Emery. Educ: Va. Union Univ, B.A, 50; Colgate Rochester Divinity Sch, B.D, 53; Drew Univ. Grad. Sch, 53-56; Alpha Kappa Mu; Alpha Phi Alpha. Hon. D. D, Pac. Sch. Relig. and Mary Holmes Col. Polit. & Govt. Pos: Mem, D.C. Cmnr. Coun. on Human Rels, 65-; chmn. D.C. del. and mem. platform cmt, Dem. Nat. Conv, 68, mem. rules reform cmt, 69; Dem. Nat. Committeeman, D.C, 68- Bus. & Prof. Pos: Sr. minister, Lincoln Temple, United Church of Christ, D.C, 61-; exec. pres, Housing Develop. Corp, 67- Mil. Serv: Entered as Pvt, Air Force, 46, released as Sgt, 47 after serv. in U.S, 46-47. Publ: 'The University and Revolution' in The University and Revolution, Am. Univ, (in press). Mem: Nat. Asn. Housing and Redevelop. Officials; Nat. Coun. Black Churchmen. Pittsburgh Courier Top-Hat Award, 68. Rel: United Church of Christ. Mailing Add: 1373 Locust Rd. N.W, Washington, D.C. 20012.

PHILLIPS, CHARLES EUGENE R
Secy, Knox Co. Rep. Cent. Cmt, Ohio
b. Mount Vernon, Ohio, 11/25/33; s. Charles Cliffton Phillips and Anna Geneva Kirkpatrick P; m. 9/24/60 to Diana M. James; c. Douglas Michael, Charles Robert, Heidi Sue and James Eugene. Educ: Cornell Univ, B.S. in Agr, 56; Alpha Gamma Rho. Polit. & Govt. Pos: Secy, Knox Co. Rep. Cent. Cmt, Ohio, 61-; chmn, Knox Co. Cmnr, 62-; secy, Knox Co. Young Rep. Club, 63; secy, Knox Co. Rep. Exec. Cmt, 65- Mem: Second v.pres. and trustee, Mt. Vernon Jaycees, 57; v.pres. and trustee, Knox Co. Farm Bur, 57-; chmn, Knox Co. Civil Defense, 64-68; pres, Knox Co. Commun. Action Cmt, 65-67; trustee, Knox Co. Mental Health Clinic, 65-; adv, Knox Co. 4-H Guernsey Calf Club, 68-; C. of C. Cert. of Merit, Mt. Vernon Jaycees, 61-62; Outstanding Young Farmer, 65. Rel: Methodist; Bd. Mem, Gay St. Methodist Church, 60-65. Mailing Add: Route 2, Mills Lane, Mt. Vernon, Ohio 43050.

PHILLIPS, CHARLES FRANKLIN, JR. R
V.chmn, Lexington Rep. Cmt, Va.
b. Geneva, N.Y, 11/5/34; s. Charles F. Phillips and Evelyn C. Minard P; m. 6/22/57 to Marjorie Hancock; c. Charles F, III and Susan H. Educ: Univ. of N.H, A.B, 56; Harvard Univ, Ph.D. in Econ, 60; Phi Beta Kappa; Pi Gamma Mu; Pi Sigma Alpha; Beta Gamma Sigma; Omicron Delta Epsilon; Beta Theta Pi; Sr. Men's Honor Soc. Polit. & Govt. Pos: Mem, Buena Vista-Lexington-Rockbridge Rep. Cmt, Va, 59-64, chmn, 64-67; v.chmn, Lexington Rep. Cmt, 67- Bus. & Prof. Pos: Prof. of Econ, Wash. and Lee Univ, 59- Publ: Competition in the Synthetic Rubber Industry, Univ. of N.C. Press, 63; The Economics of Regulation, Richard D. Irwin, Inc, 65, revised ed, 69; Registered Bank Holding Companies, Bd. of Gov, Fed. Reserve System, 67. Mem: Am. and South. Econ. Asns; Am. Mkt. Asn; pres, Lexington Kiwanis, 66. Rel: Presbyterian. Mailing Add: 414 Morningside Dr, Lexington, Va. 24450.

PHILLIPS, CHARLES WILEY D
N.C. State Rep.
b. Randolph Co, N.C, 6/25/97; s. Jesse Lee Phillips and Fannie Waddell P; m. 1924 to Lela Wade Phillips; c. Wade, Carolyn, Charles, Jr, Barbara Ann. Educ: Univ. N.C, Chapel Hill, A.B, 21; Columbia Univ, M.A, 27. Hon. LL.D, Univ. N.C, Greensboro, 67. Polit. & Govt. Pos: Pres, State Cong. of PTA, N.C, 43-45 and State Educ. Asn, 45-46; N.C. State Rep, 63- Bus. & Prof. Pos: Prin, Greensboro Pub. Schs, 12 years; dir. pub. rels, Woman's Col, Univ. N.C, 27 years; dir. of exp. in TV teaching in N.C, 57-61; acting dir, Greensboro Div, Guilford Col, 65-66; retired. Mil. Serv: Army, Cpl. Mem: N.C. Educ. Asn; Rotary Int, dist. gov, 32-33, 63-64; Rotary Club of Greensboro, pres, 29-30, secy, 41-66. Rel: Methodist; Church Sch. teacher; former dist. lay leader. Mailing Add: 210 S. Tremont Dr, Greensboro, N.C. 27403.

PHILLIPS, DAVID JULIUS D
Secy, McLean Co. Dem. Cent. Cmt, Ill.
b. Lebanon, Pa, 10/24/24; s. Lloyd W. Phillips and Henrietta Hairhouse P; m. 2/18/50 to Lorraine F. Burzynski; c. Mary Margaret and John David. Educ: Woodrow Wilson High Sch, Long Beach, Calif, grad. Polit. & Govt. Pos: Staff aide, House Appropriations Cmt, U.S. House of Rep, 80th Cong; speech writer, Dem. cand. for U.S. Rep, U.S. Sen. and Pres; founding mem, All-Ill. Cmt. for Humphrey-Muskie. Bus. & Prof. Pos: Staff reporter, Omaha World-Herald, Nebr, 48; ed. and publisher, Wash. Co. Review Herald, 49-52; mem. pub. rels. hq. staff, Union Pac. R.R, 52-56; mem. staff, State Farm Ins. Co, 56-, asst. v.pres, currently. Mil. Serv: Entered as Pvt, Army Paratroops, 42, released as Sgt, 45, after serv. in 101st Airborne Div, ETO, 44-45; Bronze Star; Army Commendation Medal; French Croix de Guerre; Belgian Croix de Guerre; Orange Lanyard, Holland; Presidential Unit Citations with Cluster; Combat Inf. Badge; Parachutist's Badge. Mem: Pub. Rel. Soc. of Am; Chicago Press Club; Bloomington Country Club. Two Silver Anvil Trophies, Pub. Rels. Soc. of Am; Pub. Rels. Award, Fedn. for Railway Progress; Best Campaign Award, Chicago Publicity Club. Rel: Roman Catholic. Mailing Add: 104 S. Ruth Rd, Bloomington, Ill. 61701.

PHILLIPS, DAYTON EDWARD R
Chancellor, First Judicial Div, Tenn.
b. Shell Creek, Tenn, 3/29/10; s. Avery Phillips and Bertha Shell P; m. 5/11/60 to Jessie Lynnwood Hill; stepsons, Jeter E. Wardrep, III and James C. Wardrep; grandchild, Brian Wardrep. Educ: Milligan Col, Tenn; Univ. Tenn. Law Sch; Nat. Univ. Law Sch, J.D. Polit. & Govt. Pos: Del, Rep. Nat. Conv, 3 times; co. attorney, Carter Co, Tenn, 36-40; states attorney gen, Tenn, 40-46; U.S. Rep, First Cong. Dist, Tenn, 46-50; chancellor, First Judicial Div, Tenn, 52- Bus. & Prof. Pos: Pub. sch. teacher, 30-31; attorney-at-law, 34- Mil. Serv: Enlisted Army, 42, released, 45, after serv. in Counter Intel. Corps, ETO; Five Battle Stars; ETO Ribbon; Good Conduct and Sharp Shooter Medals. Mem: Tenn. Bar Asn; Shrine; Mason; Elks; VFW; Am. Legion; State Pres, Young Rep. Club, Tenn. Named Outstanding Hon. Citizen of Year of Carter Co, 66. Rel: Baptist. Mailing Add: 1410 Burgie St, Elizabethton, Tenn. 37643.

PHILLIPS, E. BRADFORD R
Pres, Alaska State Senate
b. Lansing, Mich, 10/20/25; s. Wendell W. Phillips and Nathalie E. Dean P; m. June, 1949 to Patricia Dawn Shanly, wid; c. Shiela Toi. Educ: Univ. of Alaska; Mich. State Univ; Univ. of Tenn; Univ. of Miami, Fla; B.B.A, 50; Cornell Univ, M.I.L.R, 52; Pi Kappa Phi. Polit. & Govt. Pos: Chmn, Alaska Civil Rights Adv. Cmt, 58-60; councilman and mayor pro tem, Anchorage City Coun, 56-61; Alaska State Sen, 61-, Majority Leader, Alaska State Senate, 61-69, Senate Pres, 69- Bus. & Prof. Pos: Asst. prof, Alaska Methodist Univ, Anchorage, 59-60. Mil. Serv: Entered as Aviation Cadet, Army Air Corps, 43, released as Pfc, 46. Mem: Lions Int; Rotary Int; Am. Legion; Carpenters Union; Elks; Alaska Native Brotherhood; dir, Anchorage C. of C, Alaska, 60-61 and Anchorage Jr. C. of C, 54-55. Outstanding Young Man of the Year Award, Jr. C. of C, 58. Rel: Protestant. Legal Res: 303 W. 16th Ave, Anchorage, Alaska 99501. Mailing Add: Box 34, Anchorage, Alaska 99501.

PHILLIPS, GIFFORD D
b. Washington, D.C, 6/30/18; s. James Laughlin Phillips and Alice Conyngham Gifford P; m. 1953 to Joann Grace Kocher; c. James Laughlin, Alice Katherine and Marjorie G. Educ: Stanford, 36-38; Yale Univ, grad, 42. Polit. & Govt. Pos: Co-chmn, Commun. Groups for Stevenson, 52; del, Dem. Nat. Conv, 52-64; South. Calif. finance chmn, State Dem. Cent. Cmt, 55-56, co-chmn. finance cmt, 58-62; treas, Vol. for Stevenson, 56; co-chmn, Commun. Groups for Pat Brown, 58; mem, Calif. Housing Cmn, 59-62; mem, Attorney Gen. Adv. Cmt. on Constitutional Rights, Calif, 62; South. Calif. finance chmn, McCarthy for President Campaign, 68. Bus. & Prof. Pos: Publisher, Frontier Mag, 50-, until merger with The Nation, 67, assoc. publisher, The Nation, 67-; pres, United Properties of Am, 10 years. Mil. Serv: Pvt, Army, 42-43. Publ: Editorials, Frontier Mag, 50-; contributions to various art publ. Mem: Trustee, Phillips Collection, D.C. and Pasadena Art Mus; bd. of dirs, Univ. of Calif. at Los Angeles Arts Coun; bd. dirs, Int. Coun. and trustee, Mus. of Modern Art, N.Y.C; adv. coun, Gallery of Modern Art, D.C. Mailing Add: Suite 302, 825 S. Barrington Ave, Los Angeles, Calif. 90049.

PHILLIPS, GLENN STEPHENS D
Ga. State Rep.
b. Harlem, Ga, 10/07/01; s. Forrest H. Phillips and Luna Legwen P; m. 8/06/24 to Willie Pate Hudson; c. Glenn S. Jr. (deceased). Educ: Richmond Acad; Univ. of Ga. Polit. & Govt. Pos: Mayor, Harlem, 25-27 & 52-53; ordinary, Columbia Co, 28-37; chmn. bd. trustees, Harlem Sch. Dist, 36-43; Ga. State Sen, 37-38; Ga. State Rep. 41-47 & 53-; revenue cmnr, 47-48. Bus. & Prof. Pos: Ice and cold storage plant. Mem: Mason; Elk. Rel: Baptist. Mailing Add: Box 26, Harlem, Ga. 30814. (1967)

PHILLIPS, J. TAYLOR D
b. Greenville, S.C, 8/20/21; s. Walter Dixon Phillips and Martha Taylor P; m. 12/18/54 to Mary Elizabeth Parrish; c. John Allen, Mary Susan, Linda Lea and Julia Taylor. Educ: Glenville State Col, 49-51; Mercer Univ, LL.B, 55. Polit. & Govt. Pos: Ga. State Rep, 59-62; Ga. State Sen, 27th Dist, 63-64, resigned; judge, City Court, Macon, 64-66; judge, State Court, Bibb Co, 66- Bus. & Prof. Pos: Attorney-at-law, 54-; dir. of trial practice, Mercer Univ. Law Sch, 68- Mil. Serv: Marine Corps, World War II, 42-46; Korean Conflict, 50-51, Sgt; Presidential Unit Citation, Purple Heart, 3 Battle Stars, Good Conduct Medal. Mem: Mason; Scottish Rite; Shrine. Rel: Methodist. Mailing Add: Macon, Ga. 31201.

PHILLIPS, JIMMY D
b. Angleton, Tex, 5/17/13; s. Frank Phillips and Cora Cannan P; m. 8/30/38 to Esther Heyne; c. Jimmy, Jr. and Mike. Educ: Univ. Tex, Law, 7 years. Polit. & Govt. Pos: Tex. State Rep, 41-44; Tex. State Sen, 47-61; del, Dem. Nat. Conv, 48-60, 64 & 68; mem, Tex. Dem. State Cmt, currently. Bus. & Prof. Pos: Lawyer, State of Tex. Bar Asn, 41- Mil. Serv: Entered as Pvt, Army, 43, released as Sgt, 45, after serv. in Mil. Intel. Mem: State Bar of Tex; Brazoria Co. Bar Asn; Tex. Ex-Students Asn; Brazoria Co. Dem. Club; Pres. Club; Brazoria Co. Fair Asn; Houston Club; Petroleum Club; Int. Club; C. of C; Odd Fellows; Austin Headliners Club; Austin Citadel Club. Rel: Episcopal. Legal Res: Baileys Prairie, Angleton, Tex. 77515. Mailing Add: Drawer JJ, Angleton, Tex. 77515.

PHILLIPS, JOEL PATRICK, JR. R
b. Orange Co, Fla, 8/23/21; s. Joel Patrick Phillips and Grace Harrop P; m. to Elizabeth Bryant; c. Robert Patrick, John Harrop and Barbara Grace. Educ: Maryville Col; Rollins Col. Polit. & Govt. Pos: Rep. State Committeeman, Fla, 56-60; del, Rep. Nat. Conv, 60 & 64; zoning cmnr, Orange Co;

fed. jury cmnr, Mid. Court Dist, Fla. Bus. & Prof. Pos: Exec. v.pres. and gen. mgr, Plymouth Citrus Growers Asn. Mil. Serv: Entered as Pfc, Army Air Corps, 43, released as Capt, Air Force Res, after serv. in China-Burma-India Theater; Liberation of China Medal and one battle star. Mem: Mason; pres, Boy Scout Coun. Rel: Baptist. Legal Res: 2233 Howard Dr, Winter Park, Fla. 32789. Mailing Add: Box 1063, Winter Park, Fla. 32789.

PHILLIPS, KEVIN PRICE R
Spec. Asst. to the Attorney Gen. of the U.S.
b. N.Y.C, 11/30/40; s. William Edward Phillips and Dorothy Price P; m. 9/21/68 to Martha Eleanor Henderson. Educ: Colgate Univ, A.B, 61; Univ. Edinburgh, 59-60; Harvard Law Sch, LL.B, 64; Phi Beta Kappa. Polit. & Govt. Pos: Admin. asst. to U.S. Rep. Paul Fino, 64-68; spec. asst. to campaign mgr, Nixon for Pres. Cmt, Nat. Rep. Presidential Campaign, 68; Spec. Asst. to the Attorney Gen. of the U.S, 69- Publ: The Emerging Republican Majority, Arlington House, 69. Mem: N.Y. State and D.C. Bars. Rel: Protestant. Mailing Add: 3261 Arcadia Place N.W, Washington, D.C. 20015.

PHILLIPS, LEWIS MILTON D
Chmn, Schley Co. Dem. Exec. Cmt, Ga.
b. Macon Co, Ga, 4/21/21; s. William Henry Phillips and Sue Oliver P; m. 9/17/44 to Constance Ann Fox; c. Diane (Mrs. Avret) and Patricia (Mrs. Berry). Educ: Numerous mil. schs; pre-flight col. training; Univ. Nebr, grad. command pilot, 18 months. Polit. & Govt. Pos: Chmn, Scheley Co. Dem. Exec. Cmt, Ga, 58- Bus. & Prof. Pos: Mgr, Ga. Consol. Construction Co, 50-52; owner and mgr, Phillips Lumber Co, 52-60. Mil. Serv: Entered as Pvt, Air Force, 41, released as Capt, 45, after serv. in Eighth Air Force, 385th Bomb Group, ETO, 44-45; Air Medal. Mem: Mason; Elks; Am. Legion; Lions; Shrine. Rel: Baptist. Mailing Add: Box 321, Ellaville, Ga. 31806.

PHILLIPS, LUCAS D. D
Va. State Del.
b. Indian Valley, Floyd Co, Va, 12/07/03; m. to Elizabeth Littlejohn. Educ: George Wash. Univ. Polit. & Govt. Pos: Va. State Del, 54-; former mayor, Leesburg and trial justice for Loudoun Co. Mil. Serv: World War II. Mem: Mason; Lions; Moose; Am. Legion; Va. Bar Asn. Rel: Presbyterian. Mailing Add: Box 409, Leesburg, Va. 22075. (1967)

PHILLIPS, MARGARET LOUISE R
b. Huron, S.Dak, 5/14/05; d. Lars A. Melum and Anna Louisa Gunderson M; m. 8/25/40 to Bert Phillips; c. Richard Melum. Educ: Huron Col, 24-25. Polit. & Govt. Pos: Vice chairwoman, Beadle Co. Rep. Party, S.Dak, 50-56, precinct committeewoman, 54; mem, S.Dak. Rep. State Cent. Cmt, 56-66; del. and mem. panel 3, Platform Cmt, Rep. Nat. Conv, 64. Bus. & Prof. Pos: Owner, rental, real estate and bldg. bus, 40-; owner, builders supply and plumbing bus, 48-69; owner and operator, farm, 66- Mem: Pres, Home Bd. Trustees, Grand Chap, S.Dak. Eastern Star, 65; Bus. & Prfnl. Women's Club; Rep. Federated Women's Club; State Farm Bur; Past Matrons and Patron Asn; Study Club, Jr. C. of C. Rel: Lutheran. Mailing Add: 806 Kansas Ave. S.E, Huron, S.Dak. 57350.

PHILLIPS, NANCY LEE D
b. Wewoka, Okla, 8/4/37; d. Emory Lee Chaney and Hazel Williams C; m. 6/13/58 to Ted Morton Phillips; c. Ted Steven and Stuart Chaney. Educ: Lindenwood Col, 1 year; Univ. Okla, 2 years; Young Democrats. Polit. & Govt. Pos: Pres, Seminole Co. Dem. Women's Club, Okla, 64-65; pres, Fourth Dist, Okla. Fedn. of Dem. Women's Clubs, 65-67, pres, Third Dist, 67-, State chmn. Campaign 68 Cmt, 68; Dist. chmn, Operation Support Workshop, 67; State co-chmn. nominating cmt, Okla. Dem. Conv, 68; alternate del, Dem. Nat. Conv, 68; chmn, Resolutions Cmt, Okla. Fedn. Dem. Women's Clubs State Conv, 68, chmn, Rules Cmt, 69. Mem: C. of C; Mod. Lit. Club; Univ. Okla. Alumni Asn; Okla. Press Asn. Rel: Presbyterian. Mailing Add: 1011 Hwy. Nine West, Seminole, Okla. 74868.

PHILLIPS, ORVILLE D
Polit. & Govt. Pos: Ind. State Rep, 63-66. Bus. & Prof. Pos: Ohio Co. farmer; bank dir; dir, Ohio Valley Bldg. and Loan Co; pres, Aberbeen-Pate Water Co. Mem: Farm Bur; Farmers Union; N.F.O; former mem, AFL union. Rel: Protestant. Mailing Add: Route 1, Rising Sun, Ind. 47046. (1967)

PHILLIPS, PAUL S. R
b. Rushville, Ill, 4/13/12; s. Ralph E. Phillips and Frances Speed P; m. 11/4/39 to Mary Ellen Bohborst; c. Nancy E, Robert E. and Patricia Sue Educ: Univ. Ill, 3 years; Beta Kappa. Polit. & Govt. Pos: Precinct committeeman, DeWitt Co. Rep. Cmt, Ill, 62- Bus. & Prof. Pos: V.pres, Independent Farm Agents Ill, 68- Mil. Serv: Entered as 1st Lt, Army, 42, released as Maj. 47, after serv. in 613th Ord. Bn; ETO. Mem: Chartered Property and Casualty Underwriter (cent. Ill. Chap); Am. Legion; VFW; Elks; Rotary. Rel: Protestant. Legal Res: R.R. 2, Clinton, Ill. 61727. Mailing Add: 118 E. Main St, Clinton, Ill. 61727.

PHILLIPS, RALPH BOYD D
Chmn, Baker Co. Dem. Cmt, Ga.
b. Damascus, Ga, 7/15/03; s. Benjamin Faulton Phillips and Rhodie Catherin Poole P; m. 7/31/32 to Verna Taylor; c. Ralph Boyd, Jr. Polit. & Govt. Pos: Committeeman, Baker Co. Dem. Cmt, Ga, 34-, secy-treas, 34-62, chmn, 62-; justice of the peace, Ga, 36-69; mem, Gen. Lewis B. Hershey's Adv. Bd, 27 years; candidate for state rep. twice, for state sen. once, and for co. comnr. in 68. Bus. & Prof. Pos: Gen. merchant, milling, farming and live stock raising since 18. Mem: Farm Bur. Rel: Church of God. Mailing Add: Route 1, Damascus, Ga. 31741.

PHILLIPS, RALPH WILLARD D
Chmn, Highland Co. Dem. Exec. Cmt, Ohio
b. Cleveland, Ohio, 10/19/31; s. Frank J. Phillips and Gertrude Myers P; m. 12/14/56 to Charlotte Ann Gossett; c. Michael Lee, Todd Franklin and John Robert. Educ: Findlay Col, 49-51; Ohio North. Univ, B.A, with honors, 57, J.D, with honors, 58; Georgetown Univ, 59-60; Theta Alpha Phi, Alethean; Sigma Delta Kappa, Young Dem, Mummers, Jr. Bar Asn. Polit. & Govt. Pos: Pres, Ohio North. Univ. Young Dem, 56-57; mem, State Young Dem. Exec. Cmt, 56-57; solicitor, Village Greenfield, Ohio, 60-61; mem, Ohio League of Young Dem. Exec. Cmt, 64-68; trustee, Tri-Co. Commun. Col, 65-69; chmn, Highland Co. Dem. Exec. Cmt, 67-; mem, Greenfield Exempted Village Sch. Dist. Bd. Educ, 68-69; secy, Sixth Dist. Dem. Conf, 68- Bus. & Prof. Pos: Partner, Duncan and Phillips, Attorneys, 60-69; secy, Greenfield Indust. Develop. Fund, Inc, 62-69; secy. and dir, Dupar, Inc, 65-69; secy. and trustee, Commun. Improv. Corp. of Greenfield, 65-69; mem, Ohio Bar Legal Ethics Cmn, 68-69. Mil. Serv: Entered as Pvt, Army, 52, released as Sgt, 55, after serv. in Seventh Division, Korea, 53-54; Korean Service Medal, Good Conduct Medal, Presidential Unit Citation. Mem: Am. and Ohio Bar Asns; Highland Co. Bar Asn. (pres, 65-66); Am. Acad. Polit. and Soc. Sci, Am. Judicature Soc, Ohio and Am. Trial Lawyers Asn; Mason, Royal Arch, Elks, Rotary, Dad's Club, Jr. C. of C. Numerous law school prizes. Rel: Methodist. Mailing Add: Rt. 1, Greenfield, Ohio 45123.

PHILLIPS, REECE W. R
Chmn, St. Francis Co. Rep. Party, Ark.
b. Malvern, Ark, 11/7/21; s. Samuel Bruce Phillips and Rozilla Bailey P; m. 9/16/47 to Bettye Francis Martin; c. Linda Lou and James Allen. Educ: Univ. Ark, B.S.A, 47; Iowa State Univ, D.V.M, 52; Alpha Zeta; Alpha Gamma Rho. Polit. & Govt. Pos: Chmn, St. Francis Co. Rep. Party, 64- Mil. Serv: Entered as A/S, Naval Res, 43, released as Lt.(jg), 46, after serv. in Asiatic-Pac. Theater, 44-46; Campaign ribbons. Mem: Ark. Practitioners Asn.(pres, 60); Am, Ark. and Memphis and Shelby Co. Vet. Med. Asns; Am. Legion; C. of C; Lions; Mason; Shrine; Forrest City Country Club; Farm Bur. Rel: Methodist. Legal Res: 230 Virginia Circle, Forrest City, Ark. 72335. Mailing Add: 2400 E. Broadway, Forrest City, Ark. 72335.

PHILLIPS, RICHARD I.
Acting Asst. Secy. for Pub. Affairs, Dept. of State
b. Artesia, N.Mex, 4/2/11; s. Edward Frazier Phillips and Florence Idler P; m. 4/23/65 to Katherine Mayberry. Educ: Univ. Nebr, 28-29; Univ. South. Calif, A.B, 32, J.D, 34; Phi Beta Kappa. Polit. & Govt. Pos: Second secy, Am. Embassy, Montevideo, Uruguay, 46-48, Caracas, Venezuela, 48-51; polit. adv. to U.S. Del. to UN, Paris, France, 51-52; consul, Am. Consulate, Nairobi, Kenya, 52-54, Guadalajara, Mex, 57-58; regional planning officer, Dept. of State, 54-57, pub. affairs adv, Bur. of Inter-Am. Affairs, 58-61, spec. asst, Bur. of Pub. Affairs, 61-63, dir, off. of news, 63-64, dep. asst. secy, 64-69, acting asst. secy, 69- Bus. & Prof. Pos: Attorney, Los Angeles, Calif, 34-35; auditor, Singer Sewing Machine Co, Argentina, 35-36; partner, Law firm of Marval, Rodriguez, Lareta and O'Farrell, Buenos Aires, 36-41; exec. secy, Coord. Cmt. for Uruguay, Montevideo, 41-45. Publ: Income Tax Laws of Argentina, Marval, Rodriguez, Lareta & O'Farrell, 39. Mem: State Bar of Calif; Am. Club, Buenos Aires, Argentina; Rotary Club; Am. Asn, Montevideo, Uruguay; Int. Club, Wash, D.C; Ecuator Club, Nairobi, Kenya. Commendable Serv. Award, Dept. of State, 59. Rel: Protestant. Mailing Add: 3901 45th St. N.W, Washington, D.C. 20016.

PHILLIPS, RUBEL LEX R
b. Alcorn Co, Miss, 3/29/25; s. William Thomas Phillips and Ollie Fare P; m. to Margaret James; c. Rubel Lex, Jr. and William James. Educ: Milsaps Col, B.A, 48; Univ. Miss, LL.B, 51; Phi Alpha Delta; Omicron Delta Kappa; Lambda Chi Alpha. Polit. & Govt. Pos: Circuit court clerk, Alcorn Co, Miss, 52-56; pub. serv. cmnr, North. Dist, Miss, 56-58; Rep. nominee for Gov, 63 & 67; del, Rep. Nat. Conv, 68. Mil. Serv: Entered as Seaman, Navy, 43, released as Ens, 47, after serving in Destroyers - S. Pac, 46-47; Comdr, Naval Res, Retired. Mem: Am. and Miss. Bar Asns; Am. Legion; VFW. Alumnus of the Year, Millsaps Col, 56; Outstanding Young Man, Jackson, 59; Outstanding Young Man, Miss, 59. Rel: Baptist. Mailing Add: 3960 Eastline Dr, Jackson, Miss. 39211.

PHILLIPS, W. FRED D
Okla. State Sen.
b. Picher, Okla, 12/29/24; s. Oscar Lee Phillips and Elizabeth Sanders P; m. 10/25/46 to Alice Lorene Fite; c. W. Fred, Jr, Richard Lee, Judy Lynn and David Michael. Educ: Northeast. A&M Col, Petroleum Eng, 2 years; Univ. Okla, 2 years; Tulsa Univ. Sch. Law, LL.B, 60; Phi Beta Gamma. Polit. & Govt. Pos: Asst. co. attorney, Miami, Okla, 65-66; Judge, Ottawa Co, 67-68; Okla. State Sen, Dist. One, 69- Bus. & Prof. Pos: Engr, Byron Jackson Co, Los Angeles, Calif, 49-52; engr, Pac. Pumps Inc, Los Angeles and Tulsa, 52-65; Attorney-at-Law, Miami, Okla, 65- Mil. Serv: Entered as Seaman, Navy Air Force, 43, released as ORDN 1/C, 45, after serv. in Squadron 116, Pac. Theatre, 44-45; Three Air Medals; Presidential Unit Citation. Mem: Mason (32°); Shrine; Am. Legion; VFW; Kiwanis; Lions Int. Rel: Protestant. Legal Res: 221 I N.E, Miami, Okla. 74354. Mailing Add: Box 848, Miami, Okla. 74354.

PHILLIPS, WALTER E. D
Chmn, Oktibbeha Co. Dem. Exec. Cmt, Miss.
b. Starkville, Miss, 10/2/20; s. William Porter Phillips and Ada Hollingsworth P; m. 2/3/40 to Gloria S. Shook; c. Walter Ellis, Jr. and Bryan Thomas. Educ: Miss. State Univ, B.S; Univ. Miss. Law Sch. Polit. & Govt. Pos: City clerk, Starkville, Miss, 48-50; chmn, Oktibbeha Co. Dem. Exec. Cmt, 64-; north. dist. rep, Miss. Real Estate Cmn, 65-69, chmn, 69- Bus. & Prof. Pos: Partner, Mutual Ins. Agency, 50- Mil. Serv: Entered as Pvt, Army, released as Cpl, 46, after serv. in Armored Field Artil, Asiatic Pac. Mem: Mason; Jr. C. of C; Am. Legion; 40 et 8; Kiwanis. Rel: Methodist. Legal Res: 200 S. Washington St, Starkville, Miss. 39759. Mailing Add: P.O. Box 8, Starkville, Miss. 39759.

PHILLIPS, WATSON RANDOLPH D
Ga. State Rep.
b. Shiloh, Ga, 3/29/40; s. Thomas Watson Phillips and Ruth Chapman P; single. Educ: W.Ga. Col, A.B. in Eng, 66. Polit. & Govt. Pos: City councilman, Shiloh, Ga, 64-66; Ga. State Rep, Dist. 38, 69- Mem: C. of C. Rel: Baptist. Mailing Add: Route 1, Shiloh, Ga. 31826.

PHILLIPS, WILLARD L, JR. 'BILL' R
b. Elkins, W.Va, 4/26/41; s. Willard Lewis Phillips and Norma Wiseman P; m. 11/26/65 to Marion Elaine Fusia. Educ: Potomac State Col, A.A, 61; W.Va. Wesleyan Col, B.S, 64; pres, Phi Kappa Omega and Pan-Hellenic Coun;

v.pres, Circle K Club; Potomac State Col. Student Coun; staff, col. newspaper; Potomac State Singers; W.Va. Wesleyan Col. Young Rep. Club. Polit. & Govt. Pos: Dir, W.Va. Col. Young Rep. Clubs, 61-63; mem, exec. bd, Region III Col. Young Rep, 61-63; mem. col. serv. cmt, Region III Young Rep. Nat. Fedn, 61-63 and mem. exec. bd, 63-66; mem. state exec. cmt, Young Rep. W.Va, 61-63 and pres, 63-67; dir. of orgn, Benedict for Cong. Campaign, 62 and Benedict for U.S. Senate, 64; dir. of orgn, Randolph Co. Rep. Exec. Cmt, 62 and secy-treas, 66; pres, Young Rep. Club Randolph Co, 63; staff mem, State Rep. Exec. Cmt, 64; city councilman, Elkins, W.Va. 65. Mem: Am. Pharmaceut. Asn; exec. secy, W.Va. State Pharmaceut. Asn, 66; Nat. Asn. of Retail Druggists; Nat. Coun. of State Pharmaceut. Execs; Elks; Randolph Co. Soc. for Crippled Children and Adults; Randolph Co. Heart Unit; Del, NATO Conf. of Young Polit. Leaders, Oxford, Eng, 65. Rel: Evangelical United Brethren. 1967 Legal Res: Elkins, W.Va. No mailing address available. (1967)

PHILLIPS, WILLIAM HARRISON D
Del. State Rep.
b. 1897. Educ: Bethel Pub. Sch. Polit. & Govt. Pos: Del. State Rep, 61- Bus. & Prof. Pos: Farmer; pres, Laurel Flour & Feed Mills, Inc. Mem: Hope Lodge; Mason (past grand master); NUR Temple (past potentate); C. of C.(former pres); Rotary (former pres). Rel: Methodist. Mailing Add: Laurel, Del. 19956. (1967)

PHILLIPS, ZENO JOSEPH D
b. West Columbia, Tex, 1/31/04; s. Zeno J. Phillips and Mary Narbon P; single. Educ: Sam Houston State Col, 21-24. Polit. & Govt. Pos: Admin. asst. to U.S. Rep. Omar Burleson, Tex, 41- Mil. Serv: Entered as PO 1/C, Navy, 41, released as Chief PO, 45, after serv. in 95th Naval Construction Bn, Pac. Theatre. Mem: VFW; Am. Legion; Cong. Secy. Club; Sons of the Repub. of Tex. Rel: Presbyterian. Legal Res: Abilene, Tex. Mailing Add: 2369 Rayburn Off. Bldg, Washington, D.C. 20515.

PHILPOTT, ALBERT LEE D
Va. State Del.
b. Philpott, Henry Co, Va, 7/29/19; s. John Elkania Philpott and Mary Gertrude Prillaman P; m. 1941 to Katherine Apperson Spencer; c. Judy (Mrs. Marstiller) and Albert Lee, Jr. Educ: Richmond Col. of Univ. of Richmond, B.A, 41; Univ. of Richmond Law Sch, LL.B, 47; Lambda Chi Alpha. Polit. & Govt. Pos: Commonwealth's Attorney, Henry Co, Va, 52-58; Va. State Del, 58- Bus. & Prof. Pos: Attorney-at-law, 47- Mil. Serv: Entered as Pvt, Army Air Force, 41, released as 1st Lt, 45, after serv. in 2nd Air Force. Mem: Lions; Va. State Bar; Am, Va. State and Martinsville-Henry Co. Bar Asns; Elks; Moose; K. of P; past comdr, Bassett Am. Legion Post No. 11. Rel: Methodist. Mailing Add: Bassett, Va. 24055.

PHINNEY, CARL L. D
b. Marble Falls, Tex, 10/22/04; s. C.D. Phinney and Lillie Shugart P; m. 8/17/28 to Louise Snow; c. Louise Snow (Mrs. Josef Caldwell) and Carl Lawrence, Jr. Educ: Univ. Tex. Law Sch, 21-27. Hon. LL.D, Howard Payne Col, 64. Polit. & Govt. Pos: Chief clerk, Tex. House of Rep, 21-27; secy. to Gov. Dan Moody, Tex, 27; Commanding Gen, 36th Inf. Div, Tex. Nat. Guard, 53-61, former mem, Gen. Staff Cmt. on Nat. Guard and Reserve Policy, Chief of Staff, Army; mem, Reserve Forces Policy Bd, Dept. of Defense, 57-60; chmn, Securities Bd. and former mem, Bd. of Control, Tex; former chmn, Precinct 131, Dallas Co; campaign mgr, Lyndon B. Johnson for U.S. Sen, N.E. Tex, 48; chmn, Kennedy-Johnson Campaign, Dallas Cong. Dist, 60; supvr, President's Club, Northeast Co, Tex, 63-68; vol. campaign worker, Nat. Dem. Cmt, 64; coordinator, Dallas Dist. Nat. Dem. Ticket, 64. Bus. & Prof. Pos: Sr. partner, Phinney, Hallman, Pulley and Livingstone, Dallas, Tex. Mil. Serv: Entered as Pvt, Tex. Nat. Guard, 25, retired as Lt. Gen, 61, after serv. in 36th Inf. Div, 27-61, ETO, 43-44; ETO Ribbon with 3 Bronze Battle Stars and Bronze Arrowhead; Am. Theater, Am. Defense and Commendation Ribbons; Silver Star; Legion of Merit; Italian Cross of Officer Cavalier, Order of Saints Maurizio and Lazarra; Distinguished Serv. Medal, Heritage Found, Tex, 58. Mem: Am, Tex. and Dallas Bar Asns; life mem. and former v.pres, Nat. Guard Asn, U.S; Mil. Order World Wars; Mason; Scottish Rite; KCCH (32°), Shrine; City Club; Dallas Country Club; Army and Navy Club; Preston Trails Golf Club; Soc. Mayflower Descendents; Am. Legion. Rel: Methodist. Legal Res: 4204 Shenandoah, Dallas, Tex. 75205. Mailing Add: 4555 First National Bank Bldg, Dallas, Tex. 75202.

PHINNEY, GEORGE LEON D
V.Pres, Laurens Dem. City Cmt, S.C.
b. West Union, S.C, 5/21/21; s. James Marvin Phinney and Eleanor Keys P; m. 11/22/41 to Rae Rhoden; c. Larry, Margaret and Allison. Educ: High Sch; Sch. Commerce, Atlanta, Ga. Polit. & Govt. Pos: Chmn, Laurens Co. Planing and Develop. Bd, S.C, 56-; nat. dir, Nat. Export Coun, 64-65; nat. dir, Small Bus. Admin, 64-; v.pres, Laurens Dem. City Cmt, currently; del, Dem. Nat. Conv, 68. Bus. & Prof. Pos: Pres, Laurens Oil Co, 48- and First Nat. Bank, 62- Mil. Serv: Entered as Pvt, Air Force, 43, released as Flight Officer, 45. Mem: Am. Legion; Past Potentate, Hejaz Temple, Palmetto Lodge 19. Rel: Presbyterian. Mailing Add: 161 Moreland Ave, Laurens, S.C. 29360.

PHINNY, GEORGE KEIL R
Chmn, Brazoria Co. Rep. Party, Tex.
b. Oil City, Pa, 12/27/13; s. Thomas Frank Phinny and Karen Keil P; m. 10/7/44 to Nann Campbell; c. Nancy Keil. Polit. & Govt. Pos: Chmn, Precinct 17, Rep. Party, Tex, 60-64; chmn, Brazoria Co. Rep. Party, 62- Bus. & Prof. Pos: Control operator, Butadiene Plant, Dow Chem. Co, 52- Mil. Serv: Entered as Pvt, Army, 39, released as Capt, 45, after serv. in Field Artil, S.W. Pac. Mem: Local 564, Int. Union Operating Engrs; bd. dirs, Bay Area Heart Asn; chmn, Brazoria Co; Brazosport Sr. High Sch. PTA. Rel: Protestant. Mailing Add: 923 W. 8th St, Freeport, Tex. 77541.

PHIPPS, ALGER MILLER R
b. Clintwood, Va, 1/27/97; s. Columbus Phipps and Margaret Skeen P; m. 1/15/49 to Mary Thelma Lloyd. Educ: Emory and Henry Col, B.A, 20; Univ. Richmond; Sigma Nu Phi. Polit. & Govt. Pos: Rep. Co. chmn, Va, until 67. Mem: Mason (3°). Rel: Baptist. Mailing Add: Clintwood, Va. 24228. (1967)

PHIPPS, LUTHER JAMES D
b. Orange Co, N.C, 3/20/98; s. Charles Reid Phipps and Connie (Kate) Weaver P; m. 6/23/24 to Vivian Jane Lassiter; c. Vivian Lassiter (Mrs. Edward G. Bond) and Jamesina Dana (Mrs. William G. Gordon). Educ: Univ. N.C, B.S. in Civil Eng, 22, Univ. of N.C. Law Sch, 22-24; Phi Alpha Delta; Phi Gamma Delta. Polit. & Govt. Pos: Judge, Chapel Hill Recorder Court, N.C, 33-39 & 64-68; judge, Orange Co. Recorders Court, 47-63; chmn, Orange Co. Dem. Exec. Cmt, 59-68; N.C. State Rep, 63; mem, Historic Hillsborough Cmn, 63-, chmn, 67-; dist. judge, 15th Dist, N.C, 68- Mil. Serv: Pvt, Army, 18. Mem: N.C. Bar Asn; past pres, Chapel Hill Rotary; dept. comdr, Am. Legion, 63-64. Rel: Baptist. Legal Res: 315 Pittsboro St, Chapel Hill, N.C. 27514. Mailing Add: Box 838, Chapel Hill, N.C. 27514.

PHOEBUS, HARRY T. JR. R
b. Somerset Co, Md, 11/27/28; married. Educ: Charlotte Hall Mil. Acad; Univ. of Md, B.A, 48, LL.B, 51. Polit. & Gov. Pos: Md. State Sen, 64-67. Bus. & Prof. Pos: Attorney to Somersel Co. Bd. of Ed, Welfare Bd, Bd. of Co. Cmnrs. Mil. Serv: Army, 52-54. Mem: C. of C; Fire Dept; Farm Bur; Elks; Lions; Rotary Club; Am. Legion. Mailing Add: Crisfield, Md. 21817. (1967)

PICKARD, A. MAC D
b. Buena Vista, Ga, 6/01/10; s. A.K. Pickard and Edith McCrary P; m. 9/11/32 to Martha Nell Gloer; c. William McCrary, Joseph Aldine and Martha Kay. Educ: Columbus High Sch, 28. Polit. & Govt. Pos: Mem, City Dem. Cmt, 45-58; Ga. State Rep, 49-68; mem, Gov. Staff, 55-58. Bus. & Prof. Pos: V.pres. pub. rels, Gas Light Co. of Columbus. Mem: Rotary; C. of C; Jr. C. of C.(dir, 36-41); Merchants Asn; Mason; Elks (exalted ruler, No. 1639, 46-47, trustee, Columbus Chap, 47-49 and state v.pres, Ga. Asn, 48). Rel: Baptist. Mailing Add: 1701 Crest Dr, Columbus, Ga. 31906. (1967)

PICKARD, ALBERT MARSHALL R
Chmn, Willacy Co. Rep. Party, Tex.
b. Pecan Gap, Tex, 8/22/22; s. Lawrence E. Pickard and Laura Ross P; m. 7/31/46 to Billie Conley; c. Marsha Ann and Robert Marshall. Educ: Texas A&M Univ, D.V.M, 43. Polit. & Govt. Pos: Chmn, Willacy Co. Rep. Party, Tex, 63- Bus. & Prof. Pos: Mem, Livestock cmt, Rio Grande Valley Agr. Adv. Cmt, 67-69. Mil. Serv: Entered as Lt, Army, 43, released as Capt, 46, after serv. in 124th Cavalry, China-Burma-India, 44-45. Publ: 'Brucellosis; Eradication vs. Control,' The Cattleman, 1/66. Mem: Rio Grande Valley Vet. Med. Asn.(pres, 67-68); Tex. Vet. Med. Asn; Farm Bur.(v.pres, Willacy Co. Chap, 67-68, pres, Raymondville Chap, 68-69); Tex. and Southwest. Cattle Raisers Asn; Rio Grande Valley Santa Gertrudis Breeders. Rel: Methodist. Legal Res: Two miles N. Highway 77, Raymondville, Tex. 78580. Mailing Add: P.O. Box 657, Raymondville, Tex. 78580.

PICKARD, DWIGHT A. D
b. N.Ware, N.H, 9/9/91; m. to Beatrice J. Fairbanks; c. two. Educ: Black River Acad, 13. Polit. & Govt. Pos: Chmn, Dem. Town Cmt, 14 years; selectman, 7 years; Vt. State Rep, 61-68; financial secy, T.W.U.A, 2 years. Bus. & Prof. Pos: Tree farmer and orchardist; retired, 30 years in textile indust. Mil. Serv: Cpl, Hq. Co, 302 Field Artil, 17-19; Nat. Guard, 20-23. Rel: Catholic. Mailing Add: RFD 1, Cavendish, Vt. 05142. (1967)

PICKARD, MORRIS GLENN D
b. Burlington, N.C, 6/17/19; s. Alfred Leroy Pickard and Ola Snipes P; m. 1/9/45 to Mary Ellen Hayes; c. Morris Glenn, Jr, Thomas Alfred and Frederick Walker. Educ: Campbell Jr. Col, 39-41; Presbyterian. Jr. Col, 41-42; Elon Col; Univ. N.C. Law Sch, LL.B, 48. Polit. & Govt. Pos: Past pres. and life mem, Burlington Jr. C. of C; mem, Burlington Planning and Zoning Cmn, 48-56; mem, Alamance Co. Bd. of Electors, 52-60; pres, Alamance Co. Young Dems Club, 53; N.C. State Rep, 61-68. Bus. & Prof. Pos: Pres, Bareco, Inc; secy, Abner Sales, Inc. and Hunter TV, Inc; dir, Super Mart, Inc; mem, N.C. Coun. on Ment. Retardation. Mil. Serv: Naval Res. as Lt. Comdr, 42-45. Mem: Alamance Co. Bar Asn; N.C. State Bar Asn; 15th Judicial Dist. Bar; N.C. Bar Asn; Elks; Moose; Am. Legion; Mason; RAM; K.T; Oasis Temple; Shrine. Rel: Methodist. Mailing Add: 119 Sherwood Dr, Burlington, N.C. 27215. (1967)

PICKENS, FRANKLIN ACE D
Tex. State Rep.
b. Borger, Tex, 8/19/36; s. A.O. Pickens and Rhoda Shaw P; m. 12/17/66 to Dianna Barnard. Educ: Univ. Tex, B.B.A, 58, J.D, 62; Univ. of Tex. Cowboys; Delta Kappa Epsilon; Phi Alpha Delta. Polit. & Govt. Pos: Tex. State Rep, Dist. 68, Odessa, 64- Bus. & Prof. Pos: Attorney-at-law, McDonald & Pickens, Odessa, 63-68 and Shafer, Gilliland, Davis, Burton & McCollum, 68- Mil. Serv: Entered as Seaman, Navy, 55, released as Lt.(jg), 60, after serv. in East Coast and Mediterranean Theaters, 58-60; Lt. Comdr, Naval Res; Armed Forces Expeditionary Medal. Mem: Tex. and Ector Co. Bar Asns; Tex. Jr. and Ector Co. Jr. Bar Asns; Odessa C. of C; Odessa Jr. C. of C; Lay citizens Award for Outstanding Serv. to Educ, Phi Alpha Kappa, 65-66. Rel: Episcopal. Legal Res: 2751 Fair Palms, Odessa, Tex. 79760. Mailing Add: P.O. Box 1552, Odessa, Tex. 79760.

PICKENS, JOHN KENNETH D
b. Groton, N.Y, 2/26/18; s. John Kenneth Pickens and Helen Caswell P; div; c. John K, III, Polly Ann and Patricia (Mrs. Lawrence Swanson). Educ: George Washington Univ, A.B, 39 and LL.M, 49; Harvard Law Sch, LL.B, 42. Polit. & Govt. Pos: Trial attorney, Nat. Labor Rels. Bd, 48-50; mem, Alexandria City Coun, 61-64 & 68-; mem. and gen. counsel, North. Va. Regional Planning and Econ. Develop. Cmn, 61-66; chmn, Nat. Capitol Regional Planning Coun, 63-65; mem, Potomac River Basin Adv. Cmn, 68-; mem, Environ. Health Policy Cmt, Metrop. Wash. Coun. of Govts, 68- Bus. & Prof. Pos: Partner, Dawson, Guffin, Pickens & Riddell, Wash, D.C, 50- and Pickens and Stevens, Alexandria, Va, 62-; gen. coun. Am. Nursing Home Asn, 60- and Nat. Asn. of Practical Nurses Educ. and Serv, 65- Mil. Serv: Entered as Ens, Navy, 44, released as Lt, 47, after serv. in ETO; N.Am. and ETO Campaign Ribbons and 2 Stars. Mem: Am, Fed, Inter-Am. and Va. Bar Asns; Int. Platform Asn; Am. Inst. of Parliamentarians; Nat. Trust for Preservation; Am. Legion; VFW; Army-Navy Club; mem. of Bar of U.S. Supreme Court, N.Y, Va, D.C. and U.S. Courts of Appeal for Second, Fourth, Fifth, Sixth,

Seventh and Tenth Circuits; Asn. for Preservation of Va. Antiq. Rel: Protestant. Legal Res: 800 S. Washington St, Alexandria, Va. 22314. Mailing Add: Box 93, Alexandria, Va. 22313.

PICKERING, CHARLES WILLIS R
b. Hebron, Miss, 5/29/37; s. Robert W. Pickering and Lucille Anderson P; m. 6/19/59 to Margaret Ann Thomas; c. Paige Elizabeth, Charles Willis 'Chip,' Allison Ann and Mary Christi. Educ: Jones Co. Jr. Col, 55-57; Univ. Miss, B.A. with distinction, 59, LL.B. with distinction, 61; Phi Delta Phi; Omicron Delta Kappa (pres, 60-61); Tau Kappa Alpha (pres); Ole Miss Debate Club (pres, 58-59); Phi Kappa Phi; Pi Sigma Alpha; Claiborne Soc; Sigma Chi. Polit. & Govt. Pos: City prosecuting attorney, Laurel, Miss, 62; prosecuting attorney, Jones Co, 64-68; candidate for state legis, 67; del, Rep. Nat. Conv, 68; chmn, Fifth Cong. Dist. Campaign for Nixon, 68. Bus; & Prof. Pos: Attorney-at-law, 61; assoc. partner, Gartin and Hester, 61-62; partner, Gartin, Hester & Pickering, 62- Mem: Jones Co. Bar Asn.(past secy-treas); Miss. and Am. Bar Asns; Kiwanis; Jaycees (former v.pres); past pres. and v.pres, Jones Co. 4-H Adv. Coun; dir, Jones Co. March of Dimes Campaign, 62; past chmn, Jones Co. Chap. of Nat. Found; co-chmn. of prful. div, United Givers Fund Campaign in Laurel, 63; mem. bd. dirs, Jones Co. Chap. of Am. Red Cross; campaign dir, Jones Co. Heart Fund Drive, 67; pres, Jones Co. Heart Fund, 68; mem. bd. dirs, Laurel C. of C; Miss. Farm Bur; Laurel Booster Club; Univ. Miss. Alumni Asn. Selected by Laurel Jaycees as Outstanding Young Man of the Year, 63 and Outstanding Civic Leaders of Am, 67; selected by Miss. Jaycees as one of three Outstanding Young Men of the Year, 63. Rel: Baptist; deacon, First Baptist Church, Laurel, teacher of adult Sunday Sch. class and past Sunday Sch. Supt. Mailing Add: P.O. Box 713, Laurel, Miss. 39440.

PICKERING, GEORGE ROSCOE, JR. D
Tenn. State Rep.
b. Clarksville, Tenn, 8/12/12; s. George Roscoe Pickering and Annie Geneva Nichols P; m. 12/30/34 to Dorothy Heflin; c. Bobby Dean, William Howard and Linda Gail. Educ: Austin Peay State Univ, B.S. in Elem. Educ, 33. Polit. & Govt. Pos: Tenn. State Rep, 68- Bus. & Prof. Pos: Livestock specialist, Tenn. Farm Corp, Clarksville, 40; Farmer and livestock breeder, Pickering Farms, 60- Mem: Farm Bur; Tenn. Livestock Asn. Rel: Church of Christ; Deacon. Mailing Add: Route 1, Adams, Tenn. 37010.

PICKERING, GRACE LIPPINCOTT R
b. Marlton, N.J, 7/12/13; d. Henry Samuel Lippincott and Mabel Sara Ballinger L; m. 10/20/34 to Edward Pickering, III; c. William Doughten, George L. and Susan Elizabeth. Educ: Phila. Bus. Col, grad, 31. Polit. & Govt. Pos: Secy, Middletown Twp, Planning Cmn, Pa, 54-58; committeewoman, Bucks Co. Rep. Cmt, 56-66; v.pres, Middletown Twp. Rep. Club, 58; pres, Bucks Co. Coun. Rep. Women, 61-65; alternate del, Rep. Nat. Conv, 64. Mem: Past pres, Neshaminy Elem. and High Sch, PTA and Langhorne Sorosis; chmn, Langhorne Hist. Cmt; Rep. Women of Pa; past pres, Four Lanes End Garden Club. Rel: Society of Friends. Mailing Add: 803 Libby Lane, Langhorne, Pa. 19047.

PICKERING, ROBERT S. R
Pres, Defiance Co. Bd. of Cmnrs, Ohio
b. Defiance, Ohio, 1914; s. Art J. Pickering and Vera Seyboldt P; m. 1/1/38 to Naomi Meyer; c. Duane and Diane. Educ: Defiance Pub. Schs, Ohio. Polit. & Govt. Pos: Pres, Defiance Co. Bd. of Cmnrs, Ohio, 63-; cent. committeeman of Tiffin. Bus. & Prof. Pos: Mgr. fars; organizer, bus. orgn. Yoke Fellow House; retired tool, die maker, Aero Prod. Div, Gen. Motors, 17 years; Am. Steel Package Co.(All-Star Prod); Swift & Co. Rel: Evangelical United Brethren. Mailing Add: Route 2, Defiance, Ohio 43512. (1967)

PICKETT, JOHN F. D
Conn. State Sen.
b. Middletown, Conn, 1930; married. Polit. & Govt. Pos: Conn. State Sen, 59- Bus. & Prof. Pos: Attorney. Mailing Add: 164 Court St, Middletown, Conn. 06457. (1967)

PICKETT, LAWRENCE EDWIN R
Chmn, Green Co. Rep. Party, Ky.
b. Greensburg, Ky, 11/12/17; s. Henry Clayton Pickett and Bessie Rogers P; m. 4/30/39 to Ruby Christine Nienn; c. Connie M.(Mrs. Driggers) and Lawrence E, Jr. Polit. & Govt. Pos: Jailer, Greensburg, Ky, 50-54, sheriff, 55; chmn, Green Co. Rep. Party, Ky, 58- Mem: C. of C; Ky. Fox Hunters Asn. Rel: Methodist. Mailing Add: 108 Riverview St, Greensburg, Ky. 42743.

PICKETT, ROBERT McQUILLIOUS R
Chmn, Daviess Co. Rep. Party, Ind.
b. Daviess Co, Ind, 9/25/23; s. Thomas Laiken Pickett and Belva Alyce White P; div; c. Pricilla Jeanne. Educ: Washington High Sch, Ind, grad. Polit. & Govt. Pos: Rep. precinct committeeman Daviess Co, Ind, 52-58; secy-treas, City Rep. Cmt, Washington, 53; chmn, Daviess Co. Young Rep, 53-58; mem, Daviess Co. Rep. Finance Cmt, 54-; mgr, License Br, Bur. Motor Vehicles, 57-61; mem, Seventh Dist. Rep. Cmt, 57-66, treas, 64-66; chmn, Daviess Co. Rep. Party, 57-; mem, Eighth Dist. Rep. Cmt, 66-; treas, Win With Whitcomb Cmt, 68; presidential elector, 68; mem. exec. cmt, Rep. State Cmt, 68-; dir. R.R, Dept. Pub. Serv. Cmn, Ind, 69- Mem: Mason; Scottish Rite; Shrine; Elks; Moose; Odd Fellows; United Transportation Union. Rel: Protestant. Mailing Add: 12 Harned Ave, Washington, Ind. 47501.

PICKETT, THOMAS AUGUSTUS D
b. Travis, Tex, 8/14/06; s. James D'Aubigne Pickett and Helen Augusta Mackey P; m. 8/30/38 to Alice Louise Watson; c. Helen Louise, Alice Melinda. Educ: Palestine Bus. Col; Univ. of Tex. Polit. & Govt. Pos: U.S. Rep, Tex, 45-51; Dist. Attorney, 3rd Jud. Dist. of Tex, 35-44; Co. Attorney, Anderson Co, Tex, 31-34. Bus. & Prof. Pos: V.Pres, Asn. Am. R.R, 61-; V.Pres, Nat. Coal Asn, 52-61; law practice in Palestine, Tex. Mailing Add: Association of American Railroads, Transportation Bldg, 815 17th St. N.W, Washington, D.C. 20006.

PICKLE, J. J. 'JAKE' D
U.S. Rep, Tex.
b. Roscoe, Tex, 10/11/13; s. J.B. Pickle and Mary P; married; c. Peggy, Dick McCarroll and Graham McCarroll. Educ: Univ. Tex, B.A. Polit. & Govt. Pos: Area dir, Nat. Youth Admin, 38-41; dir, Tex. Dem. State Exec. Cmt, 57-60; mem, Tex. Employ. Cmn, 61-63; U.S. Rep, Tex, 63- Bus. & Prof. Pos: Entered radio bus. as one of the co-organizers of Radio Sta. KVET, Austin, Tex; pub. rels. and advert. bus. Mil. Serv: Navy, 3½ years in Pac. Theatre. Legal Res: Austin, Tex. Mailing Add: 3900 Watson Place, Washington, D.C. 20016.

PICKLE, LOUISE ELIZABETH D
Mem, Fla. State Dem. Exec. Cmt.
b. Blakely, Ga, 3/26/07; d. Lewis Harrison Pickle (deceased) and Ida Elizabeth Hoover P.(deceased); single. Educ: Univ. Fla, B.A, 40; Fla. State Univ, M.A, 48; Duke Univ; Univ. Pa, Wills Eye Inst, Phila. and Univ. Pa. Hosp, grad. work; Kappa Delta Pi. Polit. & Govt. Pos: Asst. enrolling clerk, Fla. House of Rep, 38-40; secy, various cmts. in Fla. Legis; ed. daily proceedings Fla. Legis, Bostwick Legis. Bur, Jacksonville; del. from Third Dist. Fla, Dem. Nat. Conv, 40 & 48, del-at-lg, 64; v.chmn, Wash. Co. Dem. Exec. Cmt, 48, mem, currently; presidential elector, 52; mem, Fla. State Dem. Exec. Cmt, 61- and mem, Adv, Legis, Audition and Credentials Cmts. Bus. & Prof. Pos: Teacher and educator of youth and adults with varying exceptionalities, spec. work with the gifted and partially seeing. Mem: Nat. and Fla. Educ. Asns; Int. Coun. for Exceptional Children; Am. Childhood Educ. Asn; Cong. of Parents and Teachers; hon. mem, Fla. Sheriff's Bur; League of Women Voters; Women's Club; Garden Club. Rel: Methodist. Mailing Add: 105 W. Church St, Chipley, Fla. 32428.

PICKRELL, ROBERT W. R
b. Prescott, Ariz, 11/25/22; s. Charles U. Pickrell and Anne H. Wallace P; m. 10/10/47 to Nancy Emerson. Educ: Univ. Ariz, A.B, 47; LL.B, 49; Phi Gamma Delta; Phi Delta Phi. Polit. & Govt. Pos: Attorney, Ariz. Indust. Cmn, 51-53; asst. attorney gen, Ariz, 53-55; attorney, Avondale, 56-58; attorney gen, Ariz, 60-67. Bus. & Prof. Pos: Admitted to Ariz. Bar, 49; assoc, Gentry & Gentry, Wilcox, Ariz, 49-51; mem, Pickrell, Hunter, Bartlett & Penn, Phoenix, 55-60. Mem: Bd. dirs, Phoenix United Fund; Family Serv. of Phoenix; Family Debt. Counselors, Phoenix; Maricopa Co. Legal Aid Soc.(1st v.pres; exec. dir, 56-57); Am. Bar Asn; Maricopa Co. Bar Asn.(v.pres, 60); State Bar Ariz.(v.chmn, Cmt. Legal Aid). Rel: Episcopal; Mem, Vestry. Mailing Add: 33 W. State St, Phoenix, Ariz. 85007. (1967)

PICÓ, RAFAEL D
b. Coamo, P.R, 12/29/12; s. Arturo Picó and María Teresa Santiago P; m. 2/12/38 to María Teresa Vidal; c. María Teresa and Isabel Victoria. Educ: Univ. of P.R, A.B, with high honors in econ. and hist, 32; Clark Univ, M.A. in geog, 34, Ph.D. in geog, 38. Hon. LL.D, Clark Univ. and East. Mich. Univ, 62; hon. Lit.D, Catholic Univ. of P.R, 66. Polit. & Govt. Pos: Chmn, P.R. Planning Bd, 42-55; Secy. of Treas, P.R. Dept. of Treas, 55-57; pres, Govt. Develop. Bank for P.R, 58-64; spec. econ. rep. to President Kennedy in the Dominican Repub, 62; P.R. State Sen, 64-68. Bus. & Prof. Pos: Instr. geog, 34-38, assoc. prof, 40-42 and prof, 43; instr. geog, Cath. Univ. Am, 38-40; lectr. on geog. of P.R, Univ. P.R, 46-48; chmn. finance cmt, Banco Popular de P.R, 65-68, dir, 65- and v.chmn. of the bd, 68- Publ: La Nueva Geografía de Puerto Rico, Parte I, Geografía Física and Parte II, Geografía Económica; Puerto Rico, Planificación y Acción; Geographic Regions of Puerto Rico; ed, Special School Map of Puerto Rico, Rand McNally and Co. Mem: Pres, P.R. Soc. Financial Analysts; Soc. for Int. Develop; Munic. Finance Officers Asn; Am. Soc. for Pub. Admin; hon. mem, Am. Geog. Soc; life mem, Alumni Asn, East. Mich. Univ; trustee, Catholic Univ. of P.R; visiting cmt, Dept. of City and Regional Planning, Mass. Inst. Tech, 65-68; hon. life mem, Asn. of Am. Geogrs; Inter-Am. Planning Soc. Rel: Roman Catholic. Legal Res: 564 Independencia St, Reparto Baldrich, Hato Rey, P.R. 00919. Mailing Add: Box 1502, Hato Rey, P.R. 00918.

PIENTA, LILLIAN LOUISE D
Mem. Exec. Bd, Calif. Dem. State Cent. Cmt.
b. Little Rock, Ark, 7/4/27; d. Dan Hackney and Sue E. Jackson H; m. 11/10/51 to Leonard Edward Pienta; c. Wayne Howard, William Howard and Stephen Edward. Educ: San Diego High Sch, Calif, grad. Polit. & Govt. Pos: Campaign coordinator, 77th Assembly Dist, Calif, 64-65; precinct chmn, 77th Assembly Dist. Dem. Cent. Cmt, 65; hq. secy, San Diego Co. Dem. Cent. Cmt, 66; admin. asst. to U.S. Sen. Aaron W. Quick, 40th Sen. Dist, Calif, 66; legis. secy. to U.S. Assemblyman F. James Bear, 79th Dist, Calif, 67-68; off. mgr. 37th Cong. dist. campaign, U.S. Rep. Lionel Van Deerlin, Calif, 68; del, 37th Dist. Dem. Co. Coun. and Calif. Dem. Coun, currently; mem. exec. bd, Calif. Dem. State Cent. Cmt, 68-; secy, U.S. Rep. Lionel Van Deerlin, 60- Bus. & Prof. Pos: Clerk, Fed. Civil Serv, NAS North Island-San Diego, 44-45 and S.Pac. R.R, San Francisco, 47-48; secy, NAS North Island-San Diego, 51-54; secy. personnel dept, Rohr Corp, Chula Vista, Calif, 59-61. Mem: Nat. City Dem. Club (exec. bd, secy. and prog. chmn); Chula Vista Dem. Club; United Commun. Dem. Club; Calif. Dem. State Cent. Cmt.(women's div). Mailing Add: 3116 Bonita Mesa Rd, Bonita, Calif. 92002.

PIEPLOW, E.C. R
S.Dak. State Sen.
b. 11/9/17; m. 8/5/39; c. Mike. Educ: Kans. State Univ, B.S. Polit. & Govt. Pos: Past mem, Bd. Educ. and Park Bd, Aberdeen, S.Dak; S.Dak. State Sen, 67- Bus. & Prof. Pos: Formerly with Radio Stas. KABR and KSDN; v.pres, First Nat. Bank of Aberdeen, currently. Mil. Serv: Lt. Comdr, Navy, World War II. Mem: Shrine; Elks; Am. Legion; Lions; past pres, Aberdeen Jaycees and C. of C; mem. bd. dirs, S.Dak. Crippled Children; pres. adv. bd, Presentation Col; past pres. bd, Brown Co. Tuberc. and Health Asn. Rel: Presbyterian. Mailing Add: 1415 N. Third, Aberdeen, S.Dak. 57401.

PIERAS, JAIME, JR. R
Rep. Nat. Committeeman, P.R.
b. San Juan, P.R, 5/19/24; s. Jaime Pieras and Inés López-Cepero P; m. 6/6/53 to Elsie Castañer; c. Awilda Inés and Jaime Roberto. Educ: Catholic Univ. Am, B.A, 45; Georgetown Univ, LL.B, 48; Phi Kappa; Nu Sigma Beta; Phi Delta Phi. Polit. & Govt. Pos: Gen. counsel, Tourism Bur, P.R, 53; mem, Finance Cmt, San Juan Electoral Campaign, 60, chmn, 64; alternate del, Rep. Nat. Conv, 64, del, 68; chmn, Finance Cmt, Statehood Rep. Party, P.R.

and mem, Polit. Action Cmt; Rep. Nat. Committeeman for P.R, 68- Bus. & Prof. Pos: Assoc, Luis E. Dubón Law Off, 49-52 and Hartzell, Fernández & Novas Law Off, 53-59; partner, Pieras & Torryella Law Off, 59- Mil. Serv: Pvt, Army, 46-47; Victory Medal; Mediterranean Theater of Operations Ribbon; 2nd Lt, Army Res, 49-51. Mem: Am. and P.R. Bar Asns; Fed. Bar Asn. of P.R; C. of C; K. of C; Catholic Univ. Am. Alumni Asn; Georgetown Univ. Alumni Asn; Rotary; San Juan Country Club. Rel: Roman Catholic. Legal Res: 1 Washington Ave, Condado, San Juan, P.R. 00907. Mailing Add: P.O. Box 507, Hato Rey, P.R. 00919.

PIERCE, A. ROBERT, JR. R
Mo. State Rep.
b. Cape Girardeau, Mo, 1/7/39; s. Alois Robert Pierce, Sr. and Mary Elizabeth Parker P; m. 8/5/61 to Sharon Ann Boone; c. Robert Parker, Elizabeth Ann and David Stuart. Educ: Southeast Mo. State Col, 57; Wash. Univ, A.B, 61, Law Sch, LL.B, 63; Omicron Delta Kappa; Tau Kappa Epsilon. Polit. & Govt. Pos: Pres, Cape Girardeau Young Rep. Club, Mo, 65; city councilman, Cape Girardeau, 65-68; mayor, 68; Mo. State Rep, 69- Bus. & Prof. Pos: Attorney-at-law, Oliver, Oliver & Jones, Cape Girardeau, Mo, 63-68; attorney-at-law, Cape Girardeau, 68- Mem: Cape Girardeau Co. and Am. Bar Asns; State of Mo. Bar Asn; Rotary; Jaycees. Outstanding Young Man in State of Mo, Jaycees, 66. Rel: Methodist. Mailing Add: 2544 Ranchito, Cape Girardeau, Mo. 63701.

PIERCE, ALFRED R. D
Mayor, Camden, N.J.
b. Camden, N.J, 10/21/20; s. Russell M. Pierce; m. to Barbara Adell Markert; c. Barbara Jane, Debra Star and Alfred R, Jr. Educ: Rutgers Col; Dickinson Sch. of Law. Polit. & Govt. Pos: Solicitor and mem. bd. educ, Camden, N.J, 50-59; cmnr, Camden, 59-61, mayor, 59-; cmnr, Delaware River Port Authority, 62-69, chmn, 69- Mil. Serv: Entered as Cadet, Air Force, 41, released as Capt, 45, after serv. in ETO; Air Medal with 3 Clusters; Serv. Ribbons. Rel: Protestant. Mailing Add: 420 Hillside Ave, Camden, N.J. 08105.

PIERCE, CHARLTON LOUIAN D
Committeeman, Fla. State Dem. Party
b. Milledgeville, Ga, 6/2/05; s. Frank Gardner Pierce and Ida Combes P; m. 6/18/31 to Ina Geraldine Hill; c. Charlina Brown. Educ: Ga. Mil. Col, Milledgeville, Ga, 20-24; Mercer Univ, 24-28; Univ. Cincinnati, summers, 32-34; Ohio North. Univ, J.D, 39; Blue Key; Sigma Nu; Sigma Delta Kappa. Polit. & Govt. Pos: Committeeman, Leon Co. Dem. Party, Fla, 47-; chmn, Leon Co. Dem. Exec. Cmt, 59-; field counsel, Fed. Nat. Mortgage Asn, 60-; former campaign mgr, Adlai Stevenson, John F. Kennedy and Hubert Humphrey Cmts; committeeman, Fla. State Dem. Party, 66- Bus. & Prof. Pos: Supv. prin, Ohio high sch, Coal Grove, 34-38; teacher, Leon High Sch, Tallahassee, Fla, 45-46, asst. supt, 46-48; attorney-at-law, Tallahassee, 48- Mil. Serv: Flight Instr. Instrument Flying, Air Force, 43-45; serv. in Air Transport Command, Blackstone, Va. Mem: Tallahassee Bar Asn; Mason (32°); Elks (past Exalted Ruler Lodge 177); Am. Legion. Rel: Protestant. Legal Res: 102 W. Jefferson St, Tallahassee, Fla. 32301. Mailing Add: 117 Broward St, Tallahassee, Fla. 32301.

PIERCE, CLARENCE ALBERT, JR. D
Miss. State Rep.
b. Thornton, Miss, 10/1/28; single. Educ: Beta Theta Pi. Polit. & Govt. Pos: Miss. State Rep, 52-; staff asst, U.S. Sen. Eastland, Miss, currently. Mem: Omicron Delta Kappa; SAR; Mason. Rel: Episcopal. Mailing Add: Box 277, Vaiden, Miss. 39176.

PIERCE, DANIEL MARSHALL D
Ill. State Rep.
b. Chicago, Ill, 3/31/28; s. Hyman A. Pierce and Thelma Udwin P; m. 6/27/53 to Ellen M. Field; c. Andrew F, Anthony D. and Theodore M. Educ: Harvard Col, A.B, 49, Harvard Law Sch, LL.B, 52; Lincoln's Inn Soc. Polit. & Govt. Pos: V.chmn, Lake Co. Dem. Cent. Cmt, Ill, 59-62; hearing officer, Ill. Commerce Cmn. and Interstate Commerce Cmn, 61-64; committeeman, Ill. State Dem. Cent. Cmt, 62-66; mem, Ill. Reapportionment Cmn, 63; alternate del, Dem. Nat. Conv, 64; Ill. State Rep, 65- Bus. & Prof. Pos: Partner, Law firm of Altheimer, Gray, Naiburg, Strasburger & Lawton, 66- Mil. Serv: Entered as Pvt, Army, 52, released as Capt, Air Force, 54, after serv. in Judge Adv. Gen. Dept, Flying Training Air Force. Mem: Am, Ill. State and Chicago Bar Asns; Am. Legion. Rel: Jewish. Mailing Add: 1923 Lake Ave, Highland Park, Ill. 60035.

PIERCE, GEORGE ADAMS D
b. Carlsbad, N.M, 5/21/43; s. Jack Cowell Pierce and Shirley Adams P; m. 6/20/64 to Paula Kay Hasslocher. Educ: Fairleigh Dickinson Univ, B.A, 69; New Sch. for Soc. Res, 69- Polit. & Govt. Pos: Committeeman, Morris Co. Dem. Party, N.J, 68; del, Dem. Nat. Conv, 68; asst. campaign mgr, Fifth Cong. Dist. Dem. Party, N.J, 68-69; pres. and charter mem, Boerum Hill Independent Dem, Brooklyn, N.Y, 69- Bus. & Prof. Pos: Asst. prod. mgr, Huntley & Crane, New Brunswick, N.J, 65-67; asst. prom. dir, Afco, N.Y.C, 68-69. Mil. Serv: Entered as Airman Basic, Air Force, 63, released as Airman 1/C, 65, after serv. in Air Force Security Serv, NATO. Mem: Am. Civil Liberties Union; Scientists Inst. for Pub. Info; Center for Study of Dem. Insts; Boerum Hill Asn. Mailing Add: 208 Dean St, Brooklyn, N.Y. 11217.

PIERCE, GRACE WAGNER R
V.Chmn, Kent Co. Rep. Cmt, Del.
b. Coatesville, Pa, 5/9/26; d. Jacob Heinly Wagner and Grace Quaintance Wallace W; married to Willard Lemar Pierce; c. Linda Lee, Barry Wallace Clark and Susan Butler. Educ: Goldey Col, 1 year; Wesley Jr. Col, 1 year. Polit. & Govt. Pos: Rep. committeewoman, 29th Dist, Kent Co, Del, 66-69; chmn. of vol, Kent Co. Rep. Campaign, 68; del, Rep. Nat. Conv, 68; prog. chmn, Del. Fedn. Rep. Women, 68 & 69; v.chmn, Kent Co. Rep. Cmt, 69- Bus. & Prof. Pos: Secy-treas, Pierce's Pharmacies Inc, Dover, Del, 58- Mem: Jr. bd, Kent Gen. Hosp; Palmer Home; Rehoboth Art League; Maple Dale Country Club; Capitol Green Commun. Center; Wilmington Soc. Fine Arts. Ribbons and awards for watercolors entered in art shows. Rel: Presbyterian. Mailing Add: 535 American Ave, Dover, Del. 19901.

PIERCE, JOHN H. R
Mont. State Rep.
b. Billings, Mont, 7/30/17; s. George R. Pierce and Margret L. Morrison P; m. 2/10/48 to Lucille M. Klipstein; c. Jon C. Educ: Univ. Mont, B.S, 40; Tau Kappa Alpha; Phi Delta Theta. Polit. & Govt. Pos: Mont. State Rep, Dist. Nine, 53- Bus. & Prof. Pos: Secy, George R. Pierce, Inc, 55-; pres, Pierce Flooring Inc, Mont, 67- Mil. Serv: Entered as Pvt, Army, 42, released as 1st Lt, 57, after serv. in San Francisco Ordnance Dist. Mem: Am. Legion; Mason; Scottish Rite; Shrine; Kiwanis. Rel: Methodist. Mailing Add: 1312 Parkhill Dr, Billings, Mont. 59102.

PIERCE, JUNIUS JULIUS D
Ala. State Sen.
b. Montgomery, 7/11/05; s. Junius Julius Pierce and Carrie Pinkston Jones P; m. 9/26/34 to Mildred Anna Patterson; c. Mildred Ann (Mrs. Bobby J. Russell), Junius Julius III. Educ: Ala. Polytech. Inst, 24-26; Emory Univ, 26-27; Univ. of Ala, 27-28. Polit. & Govt. Pos: V.chmn, Montgomery Park and Recreation Bd, Ala, 49-56; Ala. State Rep, 59-66; Ala. State Sen, 67- Bus. & Prof. Pos: Real estate and ins. bus, 28- Rel: Presbyterian. Mailing Add: 2448 Carter Hill Rd, Montgomery, Ala. 36106.

PIERCE, NATHANIEL PETER D
Mem, Calif. Dem. State Cent. Cmt.
b. Berry, Tex, 9/18/28; s. Nathaniel Pierce and Idelma Brook P; m. to Marjorie Joan Steward; c. Anothy, David, Robert, Steven, Kenyon and Natlie. Educ: Holy Cross Sch, 9 years. Polit. & Govt. Pos: Mem, San Joaquin Co. Dem. Cent. Cmt, Calif, 65-69; mem, Housing Bd. Appeals, 66-69; mem, San Joaquin Co. Grand Jury, 69-; mem, Calif. Dem. State Cent. Cmt, 69- Mem: Pres, Proj. Identity; pres, Boggs Tract Neighborhood; Nat. Alliance Businessmen (mem. bd). Four Awards. Rel: Catholic. Mailing Add: 409 S. Los Angeles Ave, Stockton, Calif. 95203.

PIERCE, WILLIAM D
b. Chicago, Ill, 1/28/98; c. three; six grandchildren. Educ: Valparaiso Col, 16-17. Polit. & Gov. Pos: Ill. State Rep, 7 terms; Labor-Mgt. Cmt, 41; Pres, his local union. Bus. & Prof. Pos: Machinist in a Rockford factory, 39- Mil. Serv: Army. Mem: Post 342, VFW. Rel: Lutheran. Mailing Add: 305 Hunter Ave, Rockford, Ill. 61108. (1967)

PIERRE, GEORGE D
b. Chesaw, Wash, 1926; single. Educ: Chaffey Col; Loyola Univ; Univ. of S. Calif; Univ. of Wash. Polit. & Govt. Pos: Wash. State Rep, until 66. Bus. & Prof. Pos: Prfnl. writer since 50. Publ: Autumn's Bounty, 59 and Indian Country, 64, Amerindic Lore Press. Mem: DAV; VFW; Marine Corps League; Am. Legion; K. of C; Scout Leader, 63, installed as Chief of Colville Confederated Tribes; Writer's Guild of Am; Los Angeles Adventurers Club. Mailing Add: 13002 Via Del Sol, Whittier, Calif. 90601.

PIERSON, ILETA FAYE D
V.Chmn, Third Cong. Dist. Dem. Cmt, Colo.
b. Lamar, Colo, 10/12/30; d. Selby Norman Sterrett and Olive Carver S; m. 3/20/49 to Paul Eugene Pierson; c. Kay (Mrs. Weimer), Carol, Douglas, Randal, Gary and Victor. Educ: Lamar High Sch, grad, 48. Polit. & Govt. Pos: Precinct committeewoman, Prowers Co. Dem. Cmt, Colo, 66-69; co-chmn, Prowers Co. Cmt. for Rep. Frank E. Evans for Cong, 68; treas, Prowers Co. Jane Jefferson Club, 68-69; v.chmn, Third Cong. Dist. Dem. Cmt, 69- Bus. & Prof. Pos: Secy, Lamar Jr. High Sch, 64- Rel: Methodist. Mailing Add: R.R. 2, Lamar, Colo. 81052.

PIKE, CHARLES ADAMS R
b. Lisbon, Ohio, 4/3/15; s. Charles Chester Pike and Etta Adams P; m. 8/2/46 to Gretchen Adelaide Parker; c. Charles Ashley and Robert Parker. Educ: Ohio State Univ, B.S. in bus. admin, 42; Ohio State Univ. Col. of Law, LL.B, 48. Polit. & Govt. Pos: Village solicitor, Lisbon, Ohio, 52-58; treas, Columbiana Co. Rep. Cent. and Exec. Cmts, Ohio, 57-60, v.chmn, 60-62, chmn, 62-68; spec. asst. prosecutor, Columbiana Co, 58-60; mem, Columbiana Co. Bd. Elec, 60-; del, Rep. Nat. Conv, 68. Bus. & Prof. Pos: Attorney-at-Law, 48- Mil. Serv: Entered as Pvt, Army, 42, released as Capt, 45, after serv. in 345th Inf. Regt, 87th Inf. Div, ETO, 44-45; Combat Infantryman's Badge; Purple Heart; Bronze Star; Silver Star. Mem: Columbiana Co, Ohio State and Am. Bar Asns; Rotary; F&AM; Am. Legion. Rel: Methodist. Legal Res: 12 Prospect St, Lisbon, Ohio 44432. Mailing Add: P.O. Box 205, Lisbon, Ohio 44432. (1967)

PIKE, EMILY GOODLOE R
Chmn, San Francisco Co. Rep. Cent. Cmt, Calif.
b. Boston, Mass, 12/29/21; d. Frederick Albert Pike and Emily Duncan Simmons P; single. Educ: Mt. Holyoke Col, A.B, 43. Polit. & Govt. Pos: Nat. committeewoman, Calif. Young Rep, 52; secy, Young Rep. Nat. Fedn, 53-55; women's v.chmn, San Francisco Co. Rep. Cent. Cmt, 56-60, secy, 60-62, commun. coordinator, 64-66, treas, 67-69, chmn, 69-; alternate del, Rep. Nat. Conv, 60 & 68; secy, Calif. Rep. State Cent. Cmt, 61 & 62, mem. exec. cmt, 66-68; pres, Golden Gate Rep. Women's Club, Federated, 64-66; secy, Calif. Rep. League, 65 & 66; North. Calif. v.chmn, Reagan for Gov, 66; v.chmn, Calif. Women's Adv. Cmt. for Nixon, 68. Bus. & Prof. Pos: Secy, Off. of Strategic Serv, Wash, D.C, 44-47, Doubleday & Co, New York and San Francisco, 47-49, San Francisco Chronicle, San Francisco, 50-55 and Bechtel Corp, 55- Mem: Calif. Heritage Coun; San Francisco Symphony Asn; San Francisco Chap, UN Asn; San Francisco Chap, Am. Red Cross. Rel: Presbyterian. Mailing Add: 1800 Broadway, San Francisco, Calif. 94109.

PIKE, OTIS GREY D
U.S. Rep, N.Y.
b. Riverhead, N.Y, 8/31/21; s. Otis G. Pike and Belle Lupton P; m. 1/6/46 to Doris A. Orth; c. Lois, Douglas and Robert. Educ: Princeton Univ, A.B. magna cum laude in govt. & polit, 46; Columbia Univ. Sch. of Law, LL.B, 48. Hon. LL.D, Adelphi Univ, 64, L.I. Univ, 67. Polit. & Govt. Pos: Del, Dem. Nat. Conv, 52, 54 & 68; Justice of Peace, Riverhead, N.Y, 53-60, cand, 49; U.S. Rep, N.Y, 61-, mem, House Armed Serv. Cmt, 61-, U.S. House of Rep. Bus. & Prof. Pos: with Griffing & Smith, 49-53; private practice, 53-63; partner, law firm of Pike, Behringer & Hurley, Riverhead, L.I, N.Y, 63- Mil.

Serv: Entered Navy Air Corps, 42, released as Capt, 46, after serv. as Marine Corps Pilot, 14 months as dive bomber pilot in Solomon Island campaign and 8½ months as night fighter pilot at Peleliu, Okinawa and Peking; 5 air medals. Mem: Past dir, Riverhead Free Libr. and Cent. Suffolk Hosp; Rotary; VFW; Am. Legion; Suffolk Co. Bar Asn; Riverhead Lodge F&AM; v.pres. and dir, Long Island Home, Ltd; sponsor, Nat. Jewish Hosp, Denver, Colo; coun-mem-at-lg, Suffolk Co. Coun, Boy Scouts; sponsor, Montauk Youth, Inc. Annual Brotherhood Award, Odd Fellows Welfare Guild, 65; Medal of Merit, Jewish War Veterans, Nassau-Suffolk Dist. Coun, 65. Rel: Congregational; Past trustee, First Congregational Church of Riverhead. Legal Res: 132 Ostrander Ave, Riverhead, N.Y. 11901. Mailing Add: 339 Cannon House Office Bldg, Washington, D.C. 20515.

PIKE, SUMNER TUCKER R
b. Lubec, Maine, 8/30/91; s. Jacob Clark Pike and Mary Tucker P; single. Educ: Bowdoin Col, A.B, 13. Polit. & Govt. Pos: Mem, U.S. M.E.C, 39-41; mem, Securities Exchange Cmn, 40-46; dir, Off. Price Admin, 42-46; mem, U.S. Atomic Energy Cmn, 46-51; chmn, Maine Pub. Utility Cmn, 53-56; Maine State Rep, 59-68. Bus. & Prof. Pos: Secy, Continential Ins. Co, 25-28; v.pres. and dir, Case Pomery & Co, 28-39. Mil. Serv: Entered as Civilian Cand, Army, 17, released as Capt, 19, after serv. in Coast Artil. Mem: Mason; Metrop. Club; Univ. Club; Lambs Club; India House; Downtown Athletic Club; N.Y.C. Club. Mailing Add: 2 Church St, Lubec, Maine 04652. (1967)

PIKE, THOMAS POTTER R
b. Los Angeles, Calif, 8/12/09; s. Percy Mortimer Pike and Elizabeth Potter P; m. 6/15/31 to Katherine Keho; c. John Keho, Josephine (Mrs. Barnes) and Mary Katherine (Mrs. Coquillard). Educ: Stanford Univ, A.B. in Econ, 31; Alpha Delta Phi. Polit. & Govt. Pos: Chmn, Los Angeles Co. Rep. Finance Cmt, Calif, 49-52 and Calif. Rep. State Finance Cmt, 52-53; dep. asst. secy, Defense, Supply and Logistics, Wash, D.C, 53-54, asst. secy, 54-56; spec. asst. to President Eisenhower, 56 & 58; spec. asst. to Secy. of Defense in charge of Mil. Assistance Prog, 56-57; chmn, Calif. Nixon for Pres, 60; v.chmn, Los Angeles Co. Nixon Finance Cmt, 68; del, Rep. Nat. Conv, 68. Bus. & Prof. Pos: Mem. staff, Republic Supply Co, Los Angeles, Calif, 31-38; pres. and founder, Thomas P. Pike Drilling Co, 38-53; chmn. bd. and chief exec. officer, Pike Corp. of Am, 58-65; v.chmn. bd, Fluor Corp, Ltd, currently. Mem: Calif. Club; Bohemian Club; Univ. Club; Valley Hunt Club. Rel: Roman Catholic. Mailing Add: 1475 Circle Dr, San Marino, Calif. 91108.

PILCH, ALEX D
Mich. State Rep.
b. Aurora, Ill, 3/18/13; s. Albert Pilch and Sofia Ulm P; m. 7/3/41 to Loretta M. St. Jacques; c. Laural A. and Francis A. Educ: Wayne State Univ; Univ. Mich. Rackham Br, Detroit. Polit. & Govt. Pos: Dir, Dept. Research & Info, Dearborn, Mich, 50-66; Dem. precinct del, 16th Cong. Dist, 54-67; mem, Draft Bd. 202, Dearborn, 62-66; Mich. State Rep, 67- Bus. & Prof. Pos: News ed, Dearborn Press, Mich, 40-48; Dearborn Guide, 49-50; correspondent, Wash. News Serv, D.C, 39-40. Mil. Serv: Entered as Pvt, Army, 43, released as T/5, 46, after serv. in Field Artil. and Coast Artil, U.S. and European Theater, 45-46; European Theater Battle Star. Publ: Numerous trade mag. articles on munic. govt. Mem: K. of C; Kiwanis; Elks; VFW; Goodfellows. Award for Best Munic. Pub. Rels. Prog, Govt. Pub. Rels. Asn, 58 and Nat. League of Cities, 60. Rel: Catholic. Mailing Add: 1793 Venice, Dearborn, Mich. 48124.

PILCHARD, MARK O. D
b. Pocomoke City, Md, 3/20/24; married. Educ: Stockton Pub. Schs. Polit. & Govt. Pos: Md. State Del, 59-67. Bus. & Prof. Pos: Farmer and Hybrid Seed Corn agent. Mem: Former v.pres, Md. Jr. C. of C; former pres, Pocomoke Jr. C. of C; Farm Bur; bd. dir, Worcester Co. Ment. Health Asn; Md. Swine Producers Asn; Mason; Shrine. Received citation as Outstanding Young Man, 58, presented by Pocomoke Jr. C. of C. Mailing Add: R.D. 3, Pocomoke, Md. 21851.

PILCHER, JAMES BROWNIE D
Chmn, Fulton Co. Dem. Party, Ga.
b. Shreveport, La, 5/19/29; s. James Reese Pilcher and Mattie Brown P; m. 1/21/51 to Frances Maxine Pettit; c. Lydia Dean, Martha Claire and Jay Bradley. Educ: La. State Univ, B.S, 52; John Marshall Univ, LL.B, 55; Emory Univ, 58; Kappa Phi Kappa; Nu Beta Epsilon. Polit. & Govt. Pos: Pres, Fulton Co. Young Dem. Club, Ga, 62-63; committeeman, Ga. Dem. State Exec. Cmt, 62-66; legal counsel to speaker of Ga. House of Rep, 62-; pres, Young Dem. Clubs. of Ga, 63-64; assoc. city attorney, Atlanta, 65-; chmn, Fulton Co. Dem. Party, 69- Bus. & Prof. Pos: Pres, Atlanta Health Coun, 66-; pres, Active Voters, 67-69. Mem: Mason (32°); pres, Atlanta Jaycees, 61-62. Rel: Baptist. Legal Res: 434 Brentwood Dr. N.E, Atlanta, Ga. 30305. Mailing Add: 2614 First National Bank Bldg, Atlanta, Ga. 30303.

PILE, C. H. D
b. 1899. Polit. & Govt. Pos: State rural hwy. foreman, Ky, 37-42; magistrate, 53-63; Ky. State Rep, 64-68. Bus. & Prof. Pos: Farmer. Rel: Baptist. Mailing Add: Guston, Ky. 40142. (1967)

PILLERS, GEORGE WYLIE, JR. R
Chmn, Clinton Co. Rep. Cent. Cmt, Iowa
b. Lincoln, Nebr, 8/17/14; s. George Wylie Pillers and Caroline Gilster P; m. 10/20/40 to Esther Luella Brandt; c. George Wylie, III and James Leigh. Educ: Col. of Bus. Admin, B.S, 35; Univ. Nebr. Col. of Law, LL.B, 37; Law Fraternity; Phalanx. Polit. & Govt. Pos: Purchasing and contracting officer, Ft. Wayne Ord. Depot, Mich, 41-43, fiscal officer, 43-44, chief stock control officer, 44-45; renegotiation attorney, legal div, Off. Cheif Ord, Detroit, 45; chmn, Clinton Co. Rep. Cent. Cmt, Iowa, 62- Bus. & Prof. Pos: Sr. partner, Pillers & Pillers. Mil. Serv: Entered as 2nd Lt, Army, 40, released as Lt. Col, 46, after serv. in Qm. Corps, Off. Chief of Ord, Detroit, Mich; Certificate of Commendation, Ord. Dept; Army Inactive Res, 46-54. Mem: Nebr. State, Iowa State and Am. Bar Asns; Aircraft Owners & Pilots Asn; Nat. Defense Transportation Asn; Am. Legion; Univ. Nebr. Alumni Asn; Sustaining mem, Rep. Action Fund; Farm Bur; pres, Clinton Co. Bar Asn, 68-69; Lutheran Lawyers Asn; Asn. ICC Practioners; C. of C.(v.pres, Clinton Chap, 63-66); Clinton Baseball Club, 59-66 (secy); Clinton Rotary (pres, 58). Rel: Lutheran; Chmn. Bd. of Dirs, Mo. Synod, Iowa Dist. East. Legal Res: 1036 Fifth Ave. N, Clinton, Iowa 52732. Mailing Add: 200 Joyce Bldg, Clinton, Iowa 52732.

PILLION, JOHN R. R
b. Conneaut, Ohio, 8/10/04; m. 1927 to Charlotte Reese; c. One daughter. Educ: Cornell Univ, LL.B, 27. Polit. & Govt. Pos: Former city court judge and corp. counsel, Lackawanna, N.Y; N.Y. legislator, 41-50; U.S. Rep, N.Y, 53-65. Bus. & Prof. Pos: Law practice, N.Y, 28-52; pres, Bison Storage & Warehouse Corp, presently. Rel: Presbyterian. Mailing Add: 7551 Lake Rd, Lake View, N.Y. 14085.

PILLSBURY, SALLY WHITNEY R
b. Minneapolis, Minn, 10/17/24; d. Wheelock Whitney and Katharine Kimball W; m. 1/4/47 to George Sturgis Pillsbury; c. Charles A, George S, Jr, Sarah Kimball and Katharine Whitney. Educ: Smith Col, B.A, 46. Polit. & Govt. Pos: Chairwoman, Eighth Ward Rep. Party, Minneapolis, Minn, 52-54; finance chairwoman, vol. cmt. for Rep. Clark MacGregor, 60, 62, 64 & 66; chairwoman, 31st Legis. Dist. Rep. Party, 62-63; state chairwoman, Walter Judd for Pres, 63-64; v.chairwoman, Hennepin Co. Rep. Cmt, 63-65; dep. chmn, Minn. Rep. Finance Cmt, 65-67. Mem: Young Rep. League; Rep. Workshop: Grow Cmt; Citizen's League Minneapolis; Madeira Sch. Corp, Washington D.C; Woodhill Country Club, Wayzata; Seminole Club, Palm Beach, Fla; trustee, Concord Acad, Concord, Mass. Rel: Presbyterian. Mailing Add: 1320 Bracketts Point Rd, Wayzata, Minn. 55391.

PILOT, LARRY R.
b. 4/22/40; m. to Lynne Joyce. Educ: Wayne State Univ, B.Sc. in Pharm, 62, grad. sch, Bus. and Pharm. Admin, 62-63; Univ. Detroit Law Sch, 63-64; Cath. Univ. of Am. Law Sch, J.D, 67; Omicron Delta Kappa (Sophomore Citation); Mackenzie Hon. Soc; Phi Delta Chi (Scholarship Award); Am. Pharmaceutical Asn. Serv. Award; Johnson and Johnson Award; Rexall Mortar and Pestle Award. Polit. & Govt. Pos: Spec. asst. to Asst. Secy. Health and Sci. Affairs, Dept. of Health, Educ. and Welfare, 69- Bus. & Prof. Pos: Detroit Area Field Interviewer, med. mkt. research, Mich, 62-64; instr. mgt. and mkt, Wayne State Univ, 62-63; pharmacist, Oakwood Hosp, Dearborn, 62-63; field rep, Mich. State Pharmaceutical Asn, 62 & 63; pharmacist, Hennessy's Prescription Pharmacy, East Detroit, 63-64; asst. dir, div. of commun, Am. Pharmaceutical Asn, 64-68; pub. rels. mgr, Spec. Projects, Pharmaceutical Mfrs. Asn, 66-67, secy, Narcotics Cmt. and attorney, 68-69. Mem: Va. and D.C. Bars; registered pharmacist, Mich. and D.C; exec. dir, pharmacists, United Citizens for Nixon-Agnew; gen. counsel, D.C. Jaycees, 68-69; bd. dirs, D.C. Downtown Jaycees; Am. Bar Asn; Am. Pharmaceutical Asn; Am. Soc. Hosp. Pharmacists; Delta Theta Phi. Legal Res: 5805 University, Detroit, Mich. 48224. Mailing Add: 1815 N. Hartford St, Arlington, Va. 22201.

PILOT, LYNNE JOYCE R
b. Cleveland, Ohio, 5/10/40; d. Kenneth George Widlitz and Irene Darden W; m. 4/6/68 to Larry Robert Pilot. Educ: John Carroll Univ, summer 57; Miami Univ, B.S. in Eng. and Hist-Govt, 62, Educ. Cert, Eng. and Soc. Studies; George Wash. Univ, Grad. Studies in Polit. Sci, 64; Nat. Law Center, George Wash. Univ, J.D. with honors, 69; Dean's List, high honors, 3 years, soc. chmn, Zeta Tau Alpha, 2 years, exec. secy. and mem, exec. coun, mem, House Coun, Assoc. Women Students, Asn. for Childhood Educ, Inter-Residence Coun. and Sr. Class Exec. Bd, chmn, Sr. Week Cmt, queen, Newman Club, attendant, Rose of Delta Sigma Pi and attendant Sesquicentennial Queen, Miami Univ. Polit. & Govt. Pos: Admin. and legis. asst. to U.S. Rep. Donald D. Clancy, Ohio, 69- Mem: Va. State and D.C. Bar Asns; Miami Univ. Alumni Asn.(v.pres, 2 years); Am. Law Students Asn; Student Bar Asn.(exec. bd, elected officer and night sch. rep); bd. gov. and student-faculty curriculum cmt, George Wash. Univ; Quart. correspondent, Kappa Beta Pi. Legal Res: South Euclid, Ohio. Mailing Add: 1815 N. Hartford St, Arlington, Va. 22201.

PINANSKI, VIOLA R. R
b. Boston, Mass, 6/24/98; d. Julius Rottenberg and Fannie Berg R; m. 8/10/20 to Abraham E. Pinanski, wid; c. Jean (Mrs. Dietz), Joan (Mrs. Morse), Jane and June (Mrs. Schiff). Educ: Wellesley, B.A. and fel; Harvard Sch. of Educ; Shakespeare Soc; Wellesley Club; hon. L.H.D, Suffolk Univ. Polit. & Govt. Pos: Mem. adv. cmt, Brookline, Mass, 34-36, mem. sch. cmt, 36-; del, Rep. Nat. Cmt, 51, 55 & 59; U.S. Del, WHO, 57; del, Rep. Nat. Conv, 60; mem, Mass. Civil Defense Cmt. and Harrington Willis Educ. Cmt. Bus. & Prof. Pos: Trustee, Peter Bent Brigham Hosp, New Eng. Med. Center and Beth Israel Hosp. Mem: Adv. Cmt, Nat. Inst. Neurol. Diseases; hon. life mem. Am. Hosp. Asn; hon. fel. Am. Col. Hosp. Adminstrs; dir, Nat. Citizens Cmt, WHO; Int. Fedn. Hosp; Royal Soc. Health; Friends of Switzerland. Leadership Award, Nat. Soc. Christians and Jews. Rel: Jewish. Mailing Add: 283 Buckminster Rd, Brookline, Mass. 02146.

PINCKNEY, FRANCIS DOUGLAS D
Adj. Gen, S.C.
b. Mt. Pleasant, S.C, 3/11/00; s. Francis Douglas Pinckney and Mary Lee Adams P; m. 11/14/23 to Mary Davie Bull; c. Mary (Mrs. Allan W. Wendt) and Alice (Mrs. John W. Evans). Educ: Col. of Charleston, 18-20; Command and Gen. Staff Col, 42. Polit. & Govt. Pos: Adj. Gen, S.C, 59- Bus. & Prof. Pos: Owner and mgr, auto accessory bus, 20-40. Mil. Serv: Entered as Maj, Army, 40, released as Col, 46, after serv. in 30th Inf. Div. and Ord. Corps, ETO, 44-46; Maintenance Officer, S.C. Nat. Guard, 47-59; Maj. Gen, Army Res, 59; Commendation Medal. Mem: Am. Legion; VFW; Mil. Order of World Wars; Asn. of U.S. Army; Rotary. Silver Beaver, Boy Scouts. Rel: Episcopal. Mailing Add: 1726 Maplewood Dr, Columbia, S.C. 29205.

PINE, CHARLES WARREN D
Mem. Exec. Cmt, Maricopa Co. Dem. Finance Cmt, Ariz.
b. Providence, R.I, 2/9/15; s. Charles Joseph Pine and Edna Kempf P; div; c. Charles Arthur and Elinor P.(Mrs. Iglinski). Educ: Providence Evening Col, 34-37; Brown Univ, exten. courses, 49-51. Polit. & Govt. Pos: Secy. eighth ward cmt, Providence Cem. Cmt, R.I, 36-38, chmn. speakers bur, 38; secy, Young Men's Dem. League of R.I, 38-41; del, Dem. Nat. Conv, 68; publ. rels. dir, Ariz. Humphrey-Muskie Cmt, 68; Dem. precinct capt, Maricopa Co, 68-; mem. exec. cmt, Maricopa Co. Dem. Finance Cmt, 69-; mem, Ariz. Dem.

Leadership Conf, 69- Bus. & Prof. Pos: Newspaperman and free lance writer, New Eng. newspapers, 34-42; managing ed, R.I. Herald News, 46; pres, Charles W. Pine & Assoc, Providence, R.I, 47-52; teacher, Providence YMCA Jr. Col, 49-50; teacher, Johnson and Wales Bus. Sch, 49-51; publicity dir, Valley Nat. Bank of Ariz, 53-63; pres. and owner, Charles W. Pine & Assoc, Publ. Rels. & Advert, 63- Mil. Serv: Entered as Pvt, Army Air Corps, 43, released 44, after serv. in Troop Carrier Command, 43-44. Publ: 'What Should You Expect of a Public Relations Man?'; 'Dispelling Some Myths About Public Relations'; 'Moderation in Politics,' plus more than 40 others. Mem: Accredited mem, Pub. Rels. Soc. Am.(dir, 60-64, mem. assembly delegates, 66-67); Phoenix Press Club; Phoenix Advert. Club; Phoenix Execs. Club (pres, 63-64); pres, Maricopa Jr. Col. Found, 68; Kiva Club; Ariz. Artists Guild; Comprehensive Health Planning Coun; Communitywide Orgn. for Drug Abuse Control; Bus. Adv. Cmt, Phoenix Gen. Hosp; C. of C; Phoenix Art Mus; Am. Legion; Nucleus Club of Maricopa Co. Cert. Achievement, Indust. Col. of the Armed Forces, 58; City Father Award, Phoenix City Coun, 60; Percy Award, Phoenix Pub. Rels. Soc; 61; Maricopa Med. Soc. Award for Extraordinary Commun. Serv, 62; Advert. Man of the Year Award, Phoenix Advert. Club, 66. Rel: Congregational; Moderator, Ariz. Congregationalist Conf, 56-57; dir, Congregational Conf. of South. Calif. & Southwest, 57-60. Legal Res: 1400 E. Thomas Rd, Apt. 110, Phoenix, Ariz. 85014. Mailing Add: 1112 TowneHouse, 100 W. Clarendon, Phoenix, Ariz. 85013.

PINE, DAVID ANDREW D
b. Washington, D.C, 9/22/91; s. David Emory Pine and Charlotte McCormick P; m. 7/8/59 to Elenore E. Townsend; c. (1st marriage) Elizabeth Pine Dayton. Educ: Georgetown Univ, LL.B, 13, hon. LL.D, 54; Georgetown Univ, grad. work, 13-14. Polit. & Govt. Pos: Confidential clerk to U.S. Attorney Gen, 14-16; law clerk, 16-17; asst. attorney, Dept. of Justice, 19; spec. asst. to U.S. Attorney Gen. in West. States, 19-21; Chief Asst. U.S. Attorney, D.C, 34-37; U.S. Attorney for D.C, 38-40; judge, U.S. Dist. Court for D.C, 40-, chief judge, 59-61, sr. judge, 65- Bus. & Prof. Pos: Attorney-at-law, D.C, 21-34; mem, Easby-Smith, Pine & Hill, Attorneys, 25-29. Mil. Serv: Capt, Inf, assigned to Provost Gen, World War I. Mem: Am. and D.C. Bar. Asn; past pres, Lawyers and Barristers Clubs; Metrop. and Chevy Chase Clubs. Rel: Episcopal. Mailing Add: U.S. Courthouse, Washington, D.C. 20001.

PINE, JAMES ALEXANDER D
Md. State Sen.
b. Princeton, W.Va, 8/12/12; s. Lewis Alexander Pine and Mary Bridges P; m. 3/4/44 to Charlotte Elissa Weikinger; c. James Alexander, Frank Carlton, Mary Frederick and Nancy Lee. Educ: Univ. W.Va, B.S, 38; Univ. Md. Law Sch, LL.B, 44. Polit. & Govt. Pos: Counsel, Baltimore Co. Bd. of Co. Cmnrs, Md, 50-51; first co. solicitor for Baltimore Co, 51-53; Md. State Sen, 58-, chmn, Exec. Nominations Cmt, Md. State Senate, 61, majority leader and chmn, Finance Cmt, 62, chmn, Intergovt. Coop, 63-64, Exec. Nominations Cmt, 65 and Econ. Affairs Cmt, 67, 68 & 69; mem, Legis. Coun, 58-; del, Dem. Nat. Conv, 68. Mem: Baltimore Co. and Md. State Bar Asns; Lions; Moose; Elks; Mason; Shrine; Baltimore Yacht Club; Boumi Temple; Farm Bur; numerous Dem. Clubs. Legislator of the Year Award, Metrop. newspapers in Baltimore area, 61. Rel: Baptist; former trustee, Calvary Baptist Church, Towson. Mailing Add: Thornhill, Baldwin, Md. 21013.

PINEGAR, RICHARD LEE D
b. Des Moines, Iowa, 1/19/26; s. Alfred R. Pinegar and Myrtle T. Pearce P; m. 2/14/51 to Mary Leona Kooyman; c. Richard L, Jr, Ted Thomas and Mary Lee. Educ: Drake Univ, B.C.S. and J.D. Polit. & Govt. Pos: Pres, Young Dem, Iowa, 54-56; state finance chmn, Harold E. Hughes for Gov. Campaign, 62; del, Dem. Nat. Conv, 64 & 68; finance chmn, Fifth Cong. Dist. Dem. Party, Iowa, 66-69. Bus. & Prof. Pos: Attorney-at-law, 50- Mil. Serv: Entered as Pvt, Army, 44, released as Pfc, 45, after serv. in 78th Inf. Div, ETO, 44-45; Combat Infantryman's Badge; Purple Heart. Mem: Am. Trial Lawyers Asn; dir, Iowa Acad. Trial Lawyers. Rel: Protestant. Legal Res: 2900 S.W. 23rd St, Des Moines, Iowa 50321. Mailing Add: 310 Key Bldg, Des Moines, Iowa 50309.

PINEO, FRED BENJAMIN, JR. D
State Committeeman, Maine Dem. Party
b. Columbia Falls, Maine, 7/19/09; s. Fred Benjamin Pineo and Lucy Higgins P; m. 6/27/31 to Shirley Grant; c. Lucille (Mrs. Charles Pittman), Bernice (Mrs. Robert Gardner), Ellis L, Dale G. and Loyce (Mrs. Paul Worcester). Educ: Columbia Falls High Sch, Maine, 4 years. Polit. & Govt. Pos: Town chmn, Columbia Falls, Maine, 8 years and 68-; chmn, Washington Co. Dem. Party, 62-66, treas, 66-; state committeeman, Maine Dem. Party, 66-; del, Dem. Nat. Conv, 68. Mem: Subordinate, Pomona, State and Nat. Granges; dep. master, Maine State Grange. Rel: Methodist. Mailing Add: Columbia Falls, Maine 04623.

PINERO, EMILIO R. D
Exec. V.Chmn, Dem. Cent. Cmt, P.R.
b. San Juan, P.R, s. Emilio Jimenez Pinero and Celia Umpierre; div; c. Emilio F, Roberto R. and Lilliane J. Educ: Georgetown Univ, 41-43; Univ. P.R, B.S, 46; Univ. Va, B.C.E, 52; Mass. Inst. Tech, 54; Phi Sigma Alpha; pres, Athletic Cmn; Student Coun; Honor Roll. Polit. & Govt. Pos: Sgt-of-arms, Dem. Cent. Cmt, P.R, 59-63, exec. v.chmn, 63-; mem, Adv. Coun. to Mayor of San Juan, 65-66; del, Dem. Nat. Conv, 68. Bus. & Prof. Pos: Mem, Nat. Adv. Coun. of Small Bus. Admin, 63- Mil. Serv: Army. Mem: Am. Soc. Civil Engrs; P.R. Soc. Civil Engrs. Rel: Catholic. Mailing Add: Box 10788, Capaira Heights Sta, P.R. 00922. (1967)

PINKETT, FLAXIE MADISON D
Dem. Nat. Committeewoman, D.C.
b. St. Louis, Mo, 11/30/17; d. John Randolph Pinkett and Flaxie Holcombe P; div. Educ: Howard Univ, B.A, 36; Delta Sigma Theta. Polit. & Govt. Pos: Del, Dem. Nat. Conv, 68; mem, Mayor's Cmt. on Employ. of Handicapped, 68; trustee, Bd. of Higher Educ, D.C, 68; mem, Dem. Cent. Cmt, D.C, 68-; Dem. nat. committeewoman, D.C, 68-; mem, Criminal Justice Coord. Bd, 69; mem, Mayor's Cmt. on Crime and Delinquency, 69. Bus. & Prof. Pos: Mem, Pub. Welfare Adv. Coun, D.C. Dept. Pub. Welfare, 60-66; mem. and chmn, Supt. Adv. Coun. D.C. Schs, 65-67; mem, adv. coun, Dept. Voc. Educ, D.C, 67-68. Publ: Many Shades of Black, William Morrow & Co, 69; 'How to Succeed in Business by Really Trying.' Mem: D.C. Health & Welfare Coun. Howard Univ. Alumni award, 64; Bus. Woman of the Year award, State Fedn. Bus. & Prof. Women's Clubs, 68; Citizens Merit award for pub. serv, D.C. Bd. Cmnr; 9 awards for outstanding achievements in bus. & commun. endeavors given by local bus. and commun. orgn, 58-69. Rel: Episcopal. Legal Res: 4210 Argyle Terr. N.W, Washington, D.C. 20011. Mailing Add: 1507 Ninth St. N.W, Washington, D.C. 20001.

PINKHAM, ERNEST L. R
b. Concord, N.H, 10/28/09; married. Educ: Coe-Brown Acad, Northwood, N.H. Polit. & Govt. Pos: Trustee of trust funds and former selectman; N.H. State Rep, 51-67. Bus. & Prof. Pos: Funeral dir. Mem: N.H. Funeral Dirs. Asn; Nat. Funeral Dirs. Asn; Grange; Mason; Eastern Star. Rel: Protestant. Mailing Add: Northwood, N.H. 03261.

PINKSTON, FRANK CHAPMAN D
Ga. State Rep.
b. Ludowici, Ga, 2/9/23; s. Alexander Gordon Pinkson, Sr. and Kathleen Chapman P; m. 3/14/48 to Lucille Park Finney; c. Frank Chapman, Jr. and Calder Finney. Educ: Walter F. George Sch. Law, Mercer Univ, LL.B, 47; Sigma Nu. Polit. & Govt. Pos: Ga. State Rep, 81st Dist, 69- Mil. Serv: Entered as Pvt, Army, 43, released as Cpl, 46, after serv. in Finance Corps. and Ordnance Corps, Eng, France, Belgium, Germany; Lt. Col, Judge Adv. Gen. Corps, currently. Mem: Pres, Trust Div, Ga. Bankers Asn, 64-; State Bar, Ga; Macon Bar Asn; Elks; Civitan Club; Nat. Found; Boy Scouts. Rel: Baptist. Mailing Add: 3077 Stuart Dr, Macon, Ga. 31204.

PINNEY, A. SEARLE R
b. New Milford, Conn, 9/14/20; s. J. Searle Pinney and Elsie Martha Lightfoot P; m. 1/10/53 to Evelyn Roberts. Educ: Tufts Univ, B.A, 42; Harvard Univ. Law Sch, LL.B, 48. Polit. & Govt. Pos: Conn. State Rep, 54-60; minority leader, Conn. House of Rep, 59; chmn, Conn. Rep. State Cent. Cmt, 61-67; alternate del, Rep. Nat. Conv, 68. Bus. & Prof. Pos: Attorney; town counsel, Brookfield, Conn; assoc, bd. of dirs, Fairfield Co. Trust Co; corporator, Savings Bank of Danbury; trustee and treas, Wooster Sch. Mil. Serv: Entered as Pvt, Air Force, 42, released as 2nd Lt, 45, after serv. in ETO. Mem: Hon. mem, Sheriff's Asn; Am, Conn. and Danbury Bar Asns; Tufts Alumni Asn; Ridgewood Country, Hartford and Danbury Clubs. Rel: Congregational. Legal Res: Brookfield, Conn. 06804. Mailing Add: c/o Pinney, Hull, Payne and Van Lenten, 26 West St, Danbury, Conn. 06810.

PINNEY, HARRY WARD D
b. Bloomfield, Conn, 9/19/07; s. Harry B. Pinney and Mary Ward P; m. 9/29/34 to Marguerite Scheele; c. John Scheele and Jean (Mrs. Dimitrios K. Tartsinis). Polit. & Govt. Pos: Mem, Town Dem. Cmt, 28-; judge, Town Court, Bloomfield, Conn, 39-40; cmnr, Metrop. Dist. Cmn, 40-52; cmnr, Town Planning & Zoning Cmn, 43-57; chmn, Sch. Bldg. Cmt, 51-; secy, Gr. Hartford Flood Cmn, 55-; Conn. State Rep, Bloomfield, 59-67; chmn, Charter Revision Cmn, 63-65; v.chmn, Bloomfield Indust. Cmn, 66-; mem, Bloomfield Town Coun, 67- Bus. & Prof. Pos: Owner, H.Ward Pinney Agency, 64-; assoc. bd. mem, Conn. Bank & Trust Co. Mem: City Club of Hartford; K. of C; Lions; Hopemeadow Country Club; C. of C. Citizenship Award, Bloomfield Lions; 59; Award for Dedicated Serv. to the Town of Bloomfield and the State of Conn, 67. Rel: Roman Catholic. Mailing Add: 150 Mountain Ave, Bloomfield, Conn. 06002.

PINNICK, SIRIA F. R
V.Chmn, Newaygo Co. Rep. Party, Mich.
b. San Francisco, Calif, 5/13/26; d. Joseph Pieri and Rita P; m. 2/15/47 to Joseph Francis Pinnick; c. Cristine, Patricia, Kathleen and Thomas. Educ: Commerce High Sch, grad, 43. Polit. & Govt. Pos: Del, Mich. Rep. State Cent. Cmt, 62-; v.chmn, Newaygo Co. Rep. Party, Mich, 64- Bus. & Prof. Pos: Reporter, Fremont Times Indicator-Weekly. Mem: Ramshorn Country Club (dir. and secy); Gerber Hosp. Auxiliary. Rel: All Saints Church. Mailing Add: 121 N. Merchant, Fremont, Mich. 49412.

PINO, JOHN HARDY D
Idaho State Rep.
b. El Paso, Tex, 7/17/27; s. John Lynn Pino and Madaline Francis P; m. 1/17/50 to Delta Ila Bennett; c. Lynda Dee, Cynthia Ann, Michelle and Paul Kevin. Educ: Idaho State Univ, 1 year. Polit. & Govt. Pos: Idaho State Rep, 66- Mil. Serv: Entered as A/S, Navy, 45, released as F 1/C, 46, after serv. in U.S.S. Bottineau, Pac. Theatre. Mem: VFW; Elks. Mailing Add: 3629 Hawthorne Rd, Pocatello, Idaho 83201.

PINO, JOSE ORTIZ, III D
N.Mex. State Sen.
b. Santa Fe, N.Mex, 5/2/32; s. Frank Ortiz y Davis and Maria Garcia D; m. 1/19/52 to Yolanda Cardenas; c. Jose, IV and Maria. Educ: N.Mex. State Univ, B.A, 54. Polit. & Govt. Pos: Co. cmnr, Santa Fe Co, N.Mex, 58-62; N.Mex. State Sen, Santa Fe Co, 64-; chmn, State Parks Cmn, 66-68; spec. asst, Gov. David F. Cargo, 68- Bus. & Prof. Pos: Restaurant owner, La Mancha Original Native Foods. Mil. Serv: Entered as 2nd Lt, Army, 54, released as 1st Lt, 56, after serv. in 370th A.I.B, Munich, Germany; ETO, 55. Mem: Santa Fe C. of C. Introduced and had passed First Anti-Billboard Law in U.S. Rel: Catholic. Mailing Add: Galisteo, Via Lamy, N.Mex. 87540.

PINSKY, ESTHER F. D
Committeewoman, State Dem. Cent. Cmt.
b. Bellaire, Ohio, 2/14/00; d. Harry Pinsky and Rina Lubitz P; single. Educ: Ohio State Univ, LL.B, 28; Kappa Beta Pi. Polit. & Govt. Pos: Chairwoman, Belmont Co. Dem. Party, Ohio, 32-36; city solicitor and police prosecutor, Bellaire, 32-36 & 46-48; 18th Dist. committeewoman, State Dem. Cent. Cmt, 36-; asst. attorney gen, Ohio, 37-39; chmn, Belmont Co. Elec. Bd, 50-54; v.chmn, Ohio State Dem. Exec. Cmt, 50-56 & 64-68; trustee and 2nd v.pres, Pub. Elec. Officials of Ohio, 53-54; mem, Nat. Dem. Platform Conv, 56; v.chmn, Southeast Dist. Fed. Dem. Women of Ohio, 56-58; mem, Ohio State Dem. Platform Conv, 58 60, 62, 64 & 66; del. and mem. rules cmt, Dem. Nat. Conv, 68. Bus. & Prof. Pos: Dir, Weir-Cove Dairy Co, Weirton, Ohio, 36-; dir, Cloverdale Dairy Co, Wheeling, W.Va, 36-, asst. treas, 54-; mem. adv. cmt. for adult educ, Ohio Univ, presently. Mil. Serv: Pvt, W.A.A.C, 43.

Mem: Am. Judicature Soc; Ohio State and Belmont Co. Bar Asns; Am. Trial Lawyers Asn; Ohio Attorney General's Asn; Int. Pilot Club of Bellaire; dir, Belmont Co. Chap, Am. Red Cross, 44-48 and 54-, chmn, 60-62, chmn. fund campaign, 44-54; Bd. Health, Bellaire; mem. family law cmt, Am. Bar Asn. Rel: Jewish. Mailing Add: 4135 Harrison St, Bellaire, Ohio 43906.

PINTAR, ANTON JAMES D
Chmn, Houghton Co. Dem. Cmt, Mich.
b. Painesdale, Mich, 6/17/40; s. Anton Joseph Pintar and Evelyn Allen P; m. 9/1/62 to Barbara Jane Kangas P; c. Anton John, Daniel James, Thomas Joseph, Sarah Jane and Edward Jonas. Educ: Mich. Tech. Univ, B.S, 62; Ill. Inst. Tech, Ph.D, 68; Phi Kappa Phi; Phi Lambda Upsilon; Phi Eta Sigma; Sigma Rho. Polit. & Govt. Pos: Chmn, Houghton Co. Dem. Cmt, Mich, 69- Bus. & Prof. Pos: Tech. asst, IIT Research Inst, 62-66; asst. prof, Mich. Tech. Univ, 66- Publ: Measurement of Surface Viscosity, Ill. Inst. Tech, 68. Mem: Am. Inst. Chem. Engrs; Am. Chem. Soc. Rel: Roman Catholic. Mailing Add: 641 Second St, Ripley, Hancock, Mich. 49930.

PINTAR, MICHAEL ANTHONY DFL
Field Rep, Minn. Dem-Farmer-Labor Party
b. Keewatin, Minn, 5/13/35; s. Michael John Pintar and Ann Frances Podomanick P; m. 9/7/57 to Joelle Rae Gallant; c. Charles Joseph, Michele Patrice and Michael Clement. Educ: Hibbing Jr. Col, pre-law, 56; Bemidji State Col, B.A. in educ. and hist, 58; Georgetown Univ, grad. study; Tau Beta Gamma. Polit. & Govt. Pos: Mem, Minn. Young Dem-Farmer-Labor Cmt, 56-60; mem, Second Dist. Exec. Cmt. and State Cent. Cmt, Dem-Farmer-Labor Party and chmn, Sibley Co. Dem-Farmer-Labor Party, 60-65; del, Dem. Nat. Conv, 64, alternate del, 68; field rep, Minn. Dem-Farmer-Labor Party, 65-; mem, Humphrey-Muskie Cmt, 68. Bus. & Prof. Pos: Instr, Am. hist. and speech, Henderson Sch. Syst, Minn, 60-64; educator soc. probs, Rush City High Sch, 64-65. Mil. Serv: Entered as E-1, Army EGR, Recon, 58, released as E-4, 60. Mem: Minn. Valley Improv. Asn; Minn. Educ. Asn; K. of C; Elks. Rel: Catholic. Mailing Add: 110 Donovan Dr, Grand Rapids, Minn. 55744.

PIOTROWSKI, LILLIAN D
b. Chicago, Ill. Educ: Chicago Teachers' Col; Loyola Univ, Ph.B; Pi Gamma Mu. Polit. & Govt. Pos: Ill. State Rep, 7 terms; pres, Ladies' Dem. Club of 22nd Ward; Div. of Sch. Attendance, Bd. of Educ; Juvenile and Adult Probation Officer; Dep. Sheriff in Criminal and Juvenile Courts of Chicago; alternate del, Dem. Nat. Conv, 68. Mem: Polish Alma Mater; St. John's Lodge; Isadore's Soc; Moose; Order of Women's Legis; Am. Polish Women's Civic Club. Mailing Add: 2819 W. 38th Place, Chicago, Ill. 60632. (1967)

PIPER, ROBERT LEWIS D
b. Hartford, Conn, 11/11/32; s. Lewis A. Piper and Anna Zink P; m. 8/23/58 to Lenore S. Levin; c. Lisa Rebecca and Marc Lewis. Educ: Transylvania Col, A.B, 54; Syracuse Univ, M.A, 59, Ph.D, 65; Acad. of Int. Law. Polit. & Govt. Pos: Chmn, Albion Dem. Cmt, Mich, 63-67; del, Dem. Nat. Conv, 64; mem, resolutions cmt, Mich. Dem. State Conv, 64 & 67; mem. and chmn, Calhoun Co. Bd. of Canvassers, 64-66. Bus. & Prof. Pos: Asst. prof. polit. sci, Albion Col, 62-67; assoc. prof. polit. sci, Antioch Col, Yellow Springs, Ohio, 67-; dir, Phila. Center, Antioch-Putney Grad. Sch, 67- Mil. Serv: Entered as Pvt, Army, 55, released as Pfc, 57, after serv. in Ninth Inf. Regt, Yukon Command. Publ: Ed, American Political Parties: Vehicle for Decision Making?; political science articles. Mem: Am. Polit. Sci. Asn; Am. Asn. Univ. Prof; Midwest Conf. Polit. Scientists; State Bd, Am. Civil Liberties Union of Mich, 63-67; Youth and Govt. Cmt, Mich. YMCA, 66-67. Rel: Protestant. Mailing Add: 546 W. Ellet, Philadelphia, Pa. 19119.

PIPER, RODNEY E. D
Polit. & Govt. Pos: Ind. State Sen, until 68. Bus. & Prof. Pos: Owner, Assoc. Advert. and Specialty Co. Mil. Serv: Marine Corps, participated in first invasions on Guadalcanal. Mem: Kiwanis Club; Moose; Amvets. Mailing Add: 3207 W. Jackson Blvd, Muncie, Ind. 47304. (1967)

PIPER, WILLIAM G. R
Pa. State Rep.
b. Phila, 2/16/06; s. Hugh B. Piper and Rosina Goodman P; m. to Ida C. Greenawalt; c. Susan C. Educ: Pub. Schs. of Phila. Polit. & Govt. Pos: Investr, Pa. Liquor Control Bd, 34-43; mem, Spring Twp. Sch. Bd, 47; justice of the peace, 53-; pres, Pa. State Claimmen's Asn, 54-55; Pa. State Rep, 56, 60-; pres, Lincoln Park Civic League, 60; pres, Berks Co. Magistrates Asn, 61; pres, Pa. Magistrates Asn, 62; mem, Berks Co. Rep. Exec. Cmt, Berks Co. Rep. Cmt. and Berks Co. Adv. Coun, presently. Bus. & Prof. Pos: Mem, Pa. State Hwy. Patrol, 25-31; gen. ins, 43- Mem: Pres. Berks Co. Lodge 71 Fraternal Order of Police, 37-38; C. of C; Kiwanis Club of Reading; Masonic bodies; local fire cos. Rel: Community Church. Mailing Add: 202 Harvard Blvd, Lincoln Park, Reading, Pa. 19609.

PIRNIE, ALEXANDER R
U.S. Rep, N.Y.
b. Pulaski, N.Y, 4/16/03; m. to Mildred S; c. Bruce R. and Douglas J. Educ: Cornell Univ, A.B; Cornell Law Sch, LL.B, admitted to the bar, 26; mem, Cornell Law Sch. Coun; past pres, Judge Advocates Asn. Polit. & Govt. Pos: U.S. Rep, N.Y, 58-, mem, Armed Serv. Cmt, U.S. House of Rep. Bus. & Prof. Pos: Began practice of law with Miller, Hubbell & Evans, Utica, now designated Evans, Pirnie & Burdick. Mil. Serv: Commissioned 2nd Lt, 24; vol. for active duty, 42; released as Col. after serv. on staff assignments, ETO; Bronze Star and Legion of Merit. Mem: Liberty Lodge 959, FAAM; Yahnundasis Scottish Rite Bodies; past potentate, Ziyara Temple AAOMS; Am. and N.Y. State Bar Asns; past pres, Oneida Co. Bar Asn. and Cornell Law Asn. Legal Res: 12 Slaytonbush Lane, Utica, N.Y. 13501. Mailing Add: 200 C St. S.E, Washington, D.C. 20003.

PIRO, VINCENT JOSEPH D
Mass. State Rep.
b. Somerville, Mass, 5/15/41; s. Guy T. Piro and Anna Lonardo P; m. 6/15/63 to Karen Lee Kelley; c. Lisa Noelle and Vincent, Jr. Educ: Salem State Col, B.S.Ed, 64, M.Ed, 66; Beta Chi. Polit. & Govt. Pos: Mem, Dem. Ward and City Cmt, Mass, 63; local alderman, 65-, v.pres, Bd. Aldermen, 65, pres, 66; ex-officio mem, Sch. Cmt, 66; v.chmn, Somerville Dem. Cmt, 68; Mass. State Rep, 68- Bus. & Prof. Pos: Elem. sch. teacher, Wakefield Syst, Mass, 64-69, asst. princ, 66-69. Mem: Mass. Cities and Towns; Mass. Teachers Asn; Mass. Legislators Asn; Elks; Moose; Dante Club; Ward 2 and Somerville Civic Asns. Rel: Catholic. Mailing Add: 482 Medford St, Somerville, Mass. 02145.

PISANI, JOSEPH R. R
N.Y. State Assemblyman
b. New Rochelle, N.Y, 8/31/29; s. Louis M. Pisani and Kathryn C. Ferrara P; m. 12/27/53 to Joan L. Marchiano; c. Frank, Louis, Kathryn and Theresa. Educ: Iona Col, A.B, 50; Fordham Univ. Law Sch, J.D, 53; N.Y. Univ. Law Sch, 56; Fordham Law Rev. Asn; Delta Theta Phi. Polit. & Govt. Pos: City prosecutor, New Rochelle, N.Y, 62-64, city councilman, 64-66; N.Y. State Assemblyman, 66- Bus. & Prof. Pos: Partner, Gaynor, Freeman, Glick & Pisani, 58- Mil. Serv: Entered as Seaman, Navy Res, 53, released as Lt.(jg), 66, after serv. in U.S, 53-56. Mem: New Rochelle Bar Asn; Westchester Bar Asn.(mem. city court cmt); N.Y. State Bar Asn; Criminal Courts Bar Asn. Westchester Co; dir, Commun. Chest, former mem. Agency Rels. and Budget Cmt; Jr. C. of C.(past state v.pres, local pres. and youth chmn); Iona Col. Alumni Asn.(past pres, v.pres); former dir, Ment. Health Asn; past dir, C. of C; adv, Downtown Asn; adv. and charter mem, Westchester Cmt. for Educ; Young Men's Rep. Club (past pres. and mem. exec. bd, youth tackle league and mem. bd. dirs); dir, Rep. League; past Commanding Officer, Sea Cadets, Elks, K. of C, Am. Legion and Aviglianese Soc, del. and nat. trustee; ROA and YMCA Youth Cmt; past chmn, Orgn. Fund Drive, Am. Red Cross; charter mem. and treas, Westchester Rowing Asn; 1965 chmn, Noodle Golf Tournament, Fund Raising Campaign for Boys Town of Italy, 66-68 and Westchester Dir. and New Rochelle Chmn; N.Y. State Pilots' Asn; Police Pilots' Asn. Rel: Roman Catholic. Legal Res: 18 Fairview Place, New Rochelle, N.Y. 10805. Mailing Add: 271 North Ave, New Rochelle, N.Y. 10801.

PISANO, PAUL J. D
Pres, Cranston City Coun, R.I.
b. Providence, R.I, 7/11/39; s. Alessio P. Pisano and Josephine Caito P; m. 6/9/62 to Carol Santoro; c. Holly Ann and Alison Mary. Educ: Providence Col, A.B, 61; Georgetown Univ. Law Sch, J.D, 64; Friar's Club; Delta Theta Phi. Polit. & Govt. Pos: Clerk, U.S. Sen, 62-64; campaign mgr, R.I. State Rep. Edward L. Maggiacomo, 66; chmn, Cranston Dem. City Cmt, R.I, 66 & 68; alternate del, Dem. Nat. Conv, 68; mem, R.I. Supreme Court Investigating Cmt, 68-; pres, Cranston City Coun, R.I, 69- Bus. & Prof. Pos: Partner, Law Firm, Almonte, Lisa & Pisano at present; Law Prof, Roger Williams Col, 67-68. Publ: author numerous articles, R.I. Bar J, 66- Mem: Am. Bar Asn; Am. Trial Lawyers Asn; Am. Judicature Soc; R.I. Bar Asn.(ed. bd, jour, 66-, v.chmn, young lawyers sect, 67); K. of C; C. of C; Cmnr, Boy Scouts. Eagle of the Cross Award; Named Outstanding Catholic Youth of Am. Rel: Roman Catholic. Mailing Add: 57 Birchwood Dr, Cranston, R.I. 02920.

PISCOPO, PATSY J. R
b. Waterbury, Conn, 7/14/27; s. John Piscopo and Filomena Minucci P; m. 2/19/55 to Frances B. Laffey; c. John E, Joyce R, Robert T, Nancy J. and Linda P. Educ: Am. Int. Col, B.A; Alpha Sigma Delta; Varsity Club. Polit. & Govt. Pos: Dir, Libr. Bd, Thomaston, Conn, 58-60; chmn, Rep. Town Cmt, 60-66; 1st selectman, Thomaston, 65- Bus. & Prof. Pos: Teacher, Swift Jr. High, 52-65. Mil. Serv: Entered as A/S, Navy, 45, released as Seaman, 1/C, 46. Mem: Pres, Watertown Teacher's Asn, 60-64; chmn, Prog. Cmt, PTA, 64; Rod & Gun Club; Am. Legion; VFW; Leiderkrantz Singing Soc; Am. Int. Col. Alumni; Young Rep; Litchfield Co. Police Asn; Street & Hwy. Off. Asn. Sportsmanship award, 51; earned numerals in freshman year and letter in football, jr. and sr. years; capt. rowing team, sr. year, earned letter, 3 years; popularity award, King of Winter Carnival, 50. Rel: Catholic. Legal Res: 38 Laurel Dr, Thomaston, Conn. 06787. Mailing Add: 158 Main St, Thomaston, Conn. 06787.

PITCHESS, PETER J. R
b. Salt Lake City, Utah, 2/26/12; s. John P. Pitchess and Rena Demos P; m. 2/27/38 to Athena Takis; c. John P. and Andrew T. Educ: Univ. Utah, B.S. and LL.B; Justice of Phi Alpha Delta; pres, Barristers Club, Univ. Utah Law Sch. Hon. LL.D, Los Angeles Pac. Col. Polit. & Govt. Pos: Sheriff, Co. of Los Angeles, 58- and undersheriff, 53-58; spec. agent, Fed. Bur. Invest, 40-52. Mem: Pres, Calif. State Peace Officers' Asn, 65-66 and 64-65; Int. Asn. of Chiefs of Police; Calif. State Sheriff's Asn; mem-at-lg, Los Angeles Area Coun, Boy Scouts; Disaster Law Enforcement Coordinator, Region 1, State of Calif; San Marino Lodge and affiliated Masonic fraternities. Rel: Greek Orthodox. Mailing Add: 1110 Paloma Dr, Arcadia, Calif. 91006. (1967)

PITHOUD, NAIDA R
Chmn, Clark Co. Rep. Cent. Cmt, Wash.
b. Woodward, Iowa, 6/14/10; d. Leon Edwin Mouser and Theda Belle Rhoads M; m. 3/26/38 to Myron Almon Pithoud; c. Laurel Jean (Mrs. Elden) and Ralph William McGinn. Educ: Jackson High Sch, Council Bluffs, Iowa, 4 years. Polit. & Govt. Pos: Precinct committeeman, Clark Co. Rep. Cent. Cmt, Wash, 43-, secy, 54-56, v.chmn, 58-62, chmn, 62- Bus. & Prof. Pos: Partner, M.A. 'Pete' Pithoud-Elec. Contractor, 46-53. Mem: Eastern Star; Shrine; Daughters of the Nile; Vancouver Civic Club; Rep. Women's Club of Clark Co. Rel: Methodist. Mailing Add: 2311 N.E. 119th St, Vancouver, Wash. 98665.

PITT, RICHARD LEWIS D
b. Moscow, Idaho, 5/28/27; s. Perry Emerson Pitt and Alice Wiley P; m. 6/5/49 to Grace Velma Farnsworth; c. Richard Scott and Craig Perry. Educ: Gonzaga Univ, LL.B, 53. Polit. Pos: Precinct committeeman, Dem. Party, 60-62. Govt. Pos: Prosecuting attorney, Island Co, Wash, 62- Bus. & Prof. Pos: Head attorney, Legal Div, Regional Off, Allstate Ins. Co, Seattle, Wash, 54-62; attorney, private practice, 53-54. Mil. Serv: Entered as Pvt, Army, 45, released as Pfc, 46, after serv. in Mil. Police, ETO. Mem: Am. and Wash. Bar Asns; Nat. Dist. Attorneys Asn; Lions; C. of C. Rel: Methodist. Mailing Add: Route 2, Box 667, Oak Harbor, Wash. 98277. (1967)

PITTENGER, JOHN CHAPMAN D
Pa. State Rep.
b. Phila, Pa, 5/23/30; s. Nicholas Otto Pittenger and Cornelia Chapman P;

single. Educ: Harvard Col, B.A, 51; Harvard Law Sch, LL.B, 58. Polit. & Govt. Pos: Mem, Lancaster Co. Dem. Exec. Cmt, 60-; dist. leader, Ninth Ward, Lancaster, 60-; Pa. State Rep, 65-67 & 69-; dir. of research, Minority Caucus, Pa. State House of Rep, 67-69. Bus. & Prof. Pos: Attorney-at-law, 58-65; adj. instr, govt, Franklin and Marshall Col, 60 & 63- Mil. Serv: Entered as Pvt. E-1, Army, 52, released as 1st Lt, 55, after serv. in Inf, Transportation Corps. Mem: Lancaster Co, Pa. and Am. Bar Asns. Rel: Society of Friends. Mailing Add: 307 N. West End Ave, Lancaster, Pa. 17603.

PITTENGER, PHILIP OSBORN R
Mich. State Rep.
b. Worthington, Minn, 8/9/29; s. Glenn H. Pittenger, Sr. and Mildred Derbyshire P; m. 6/11/55 to Patricia E. Howell; c. Pamela M. and Penni N. Polit. & Govt. Pos: V.pres, Ingham Co. Young Rep, Mich, 55; exec. asst. Bagwell for Gov. Cmt, 58 & 60; exec. asst. Romney for Gov. Cmt, 62 & 64; exec. asst. Gov. George Romney, 63-65; dep. cmnr, Mich. Corp. & Securities Cmt, 65; chief dep. dir, Mich. Dept. Licensing & Regulation, 66; Mich. State Rep, 58th Legis. Dist, 67- Bus. & Prof. Pos: Conv. bur. mgr, Lansing C. of C, 53-56; mgr, Howell C. of C, 57. Mem: Bd. dir, Proj. HOPE; North PTA (pres); Old Newsboys Asn; Cath. Mens Club; Commun. Chest; K. of C. Rel: Catholic. Mailing Add: 6218 Norburn Way, Lansing, Mich. 48910. (1967)

PITTLE, RONALD DAVID D
b. Washington, D.C, 10/7/38; s. Phillip Burnette Pittle and Frances Hannah Connelly P; m. 8/10/61 to Allyne Marie Hayden; c. Karin Stacy and Kristin Elise. Educ: Univ. Md, B.S.E.E, 63; Univ. Wis, M.S.E.E, 65, Ph.D, 69; Tau Beta Pi; Eta Kappa Nu; Pi Mu Epsilon; Phi Theta Kappa. Polit. & Govt. Pos: Alternate del, Dem. Nat. Conv, 68; del, Wis. State Dem. Conv, 69. Bus. & Prof. Pos: Electrical engr, Goodard Space Flight Center, Greenbelt, Md, 63; instr, electrical eng, Univ. Wis, Madison, 63-69; electrical engr, U.S. Army, Fort Meade, Md, 66. Mil. Serv: Entered as E-1, Navy, 56, released as E-5, 59, after serv. in U.S.S. Samuel B. Roberts, Destroyer Force-Atlantic Fleet, 57-59; Good Conduct Medal. Publ: 'Competitive Interaction Studies,' Journal of The Franklin Institute, 11/66. Mem: Dem. Party of Wis. Rel: Unitarian. Mailing Add: 15 Sherman Terr, Madison, Wis. 53704.

PITTMAN, EDWIN LLOYD D
Miss. State Sen.
b. Hattiesburg, Miss, 1/2/35; m. to Barbara Peel. Educ: Hattiesburg High Sch, grad. Polit. & Govt. Pos: Miss. State Sen, presently. Bus. & Prof. Pos: Attorney-at-law. Mem: Jr. C. of C; Hub Dist. of Boy Scouts. Rel: Baptist. Mailing Add: 2101 Arcadia St, P.O. Box 1445, Hattiesburg, Miss. 39401.

PITTMAN, FRANK SHIELDS, JR. D
b. Rocky Mount, N.C, 5/9/46; s. Frank Shields Pittman and Virginia Blackwell P; single. Educ: N.C. State Univ, Assoc. Agr; Kappa Alpha Order. Polit. & Govt. Pos: Student campaign mgr, Mel Broughton for Gov, Raleigh, N.C, 68; alternate del, Dem. Nat. Conv, 68. Bus. & Prof. Pos: V.pres, Farmers Supply Co, Enfield, N.C, 69- Mem: N.C. Young Dem. Club. Rel: Baptist. Mailing Add: 813 Church St, Scotland Neck, N.C. 27874.

PITTMAN, KENNETH ALEXANDRIA D
Chmn, Exec. Cmt, Dem. Party, N.C.
b. Louisburg, N.C, 11/22/92; s. John W. Pittman and Pattie Selema Horton P; m. to Maude Baynor; c. Maude Baynor Foy (Mrs. Cutts) and grandchildren Kenneth Lee and Laura Ellen. Educ: Wake Forest Col, LL.B, 16; The Dozen Club. Polit. & Govt. Pos: Mayor, Ayden, N.C, 17, Pitt Co, N.C, 25; N.C. State Rep, Pitt Co, 25; mem, N.C. Cmn. Study Cancer Control; N.C. State Sen, Seventh Dist, 41-43; govt. appeal agent and chmn, Civilian Defense for Greene Co, World War II; judge, Superior Court; chmn. precinct cmt, Dem. Party, N.C, chmn. exec. cmt, currently. Bus. & Prof. Pos: Practice of law; former sch. teacher and prin. Mil. Serv: Entered as Pvt, Army, World War II, released as M/Sgt; Mil. Cross. Mem: Eighth Judicial Dist. Bar Asn.(pres); Exec. Club; AF&AM; Ayden Rotary (former pres); Snow Hill Rotary (former pres). Presented a bronze plaque inscribed Gentleman, Judge and Lawyer, by people of N.C; named Mr. Dem. and Pres. Emeritus, Dem. Exec. Cmt. Rel: Methodist. Legal Res: 102 N. Greene St, Snow Hill, N.C. 28580. Mailing Add: P.O. Box 155, Snow Hill, N.C. 28580. (1967)

PITTMAN, RICHARD EDWARD R
V.Chmn, First Dist. Rep. Party, Ga.
b. Lyons, Ga, 8/19/36; s. John Walker Pittman and Carrie Bell Burns P; m. 5/2/61 to Alice Faye Hunter; c. Angela and Jennifer. Educ: Toombs Cent. High Sch, grad, 55. Polit. & Govt. Pos: Co. chmn, Toombs Co. Rep. Party, Ga, 66-68; v.chmn, First Dist. Rep. Party, 68- Mil. Serv: Capt. Army Nat. Guard, 54-69. Mem: Moose; Farm Bur; Nat. Guard Asn. of U.S. Rel: Baptist. Mailing Add: Route 1, Glenwood, Ga. 30428.

PITTMAN, WALTER JAMES, JR. D
b. Bailey, N.C, 10/7/11; s. Walter James Pittman and Leelah Shelton P; m. 4/26/51 to Mary Lucile Thomas; c. Mary Lou and Walter James, III. Educ: Wake Forest Col, LL.B, 34; Chi Tau; Gamma Eta Gamma. Polit. & Govt. Pos: Chmn, Wilson Co. Bd. of Elec, N.C, 38-42; admin. asst. to U.S. Rep. L.H. Fountain, second dist, N.C, 53- Rel: Methodist. Legal Res: 1614 W. Nash St, Wilson, N.C. 27893. Mailing Add: 2400 Rayburn House Office Bldg, Washington, D.C. 20515.

PITTS, HUDIE D
b. Wayne Co, Miss, 2/12/05; married. Polit. & Govt. Pos: Miss. State Sen, 60-68. Bus. & Prof. Pos: Farmer; livestock raiser; operator George Co. stockyard. Mem: Mason; Lions Club; Farm Bur. Rel: Baptist. Mailing Add: Route 2, Lucedale, Miss. 39452. (1967)

PITTS, JON WILL R
Mem, Ala. Rep. State Exec. Cmt.
b. Clanton, Ala, 6/25/32; s. Percy McGraw Pitts, Sr. and Mytle L. Reynolds P; single. Educ: Univ. Ala, Tuscaloosa, A.B, 54, LL.B, 56; Fla. State Univ, Urban and Regional Planning, 69-; Sigma Alpha Epsilon. Polit. & Govt. Pos: Page, Rep. Nat. Conv, 52; organizer and pres, Students for Eisenhower-Nixon, Univ. Ala, Tuscaloosa, 52; Chilton Co. campaign mgr, Nixon for Pres. Cmt, 60; mem, Ala. Young Rep. State Exec. Cmt, 60-62; organizer and first pres, Chilton Co. Young Rep. Club, 62; Rep. nominee for Co. Solicitor, Chilton Co, 62, co. attorney, 64-68; mem, Ala. Rep. State Exec. Cmt, 62-; chmn, Chilton Co. Rep. Party, 66-68. Bus. & Prof. Pos: Attorney-at-law, Pitts and Lathan, Clanton, Ala, currently. Mem: Mason; exec. secy, Chilton Co. C. of C, 58-64; pres, Chilton Co. Bar Asn, 68- Rel: Methodist. Legal Res: 102 Second St. St, Clanton, Ala. 35045. Mailing Add: Pitts and Lathan, Attorneys-at-Law, 409 Log Dam Rd, Clanton, Ala. 35045.

PITTS, KNOX D
Chmn, Bedford Co. Dem. Exec. Cmt, Tenn.
b. Elkton, Tenn, 4/28/16; s. Rufus Knox Pitts and Inez Puckette P; m. 7/21/38 to Mildred Steele; c. Knox, III and John Steele. Educ: Oglethorpe Univ, A.B, 35. Polit. & Govt. Pos: Admin. asst. to U.S. Rep. Joe L. Evins, Tenn, 47; del, Dem. Nat. Conv, 56, 60, 64 & 68; chmn, Bedford Co. Dem. Exec. Cmt, Tenn, 55-; dep. state campaign mgr. for Lyndon Johnson, 64. Bus. & Prof. Pos: Owner, Knox Pitts Plumbing & Elec. Supply Co, Shelbyville, Tenn, 47- Mil. Serv: Entered as Pvt, Army, 42, released as 1st Lt, 45, after serv. in 147th Qm. Depot Co, ETO, 43-45. Mem: Lions; Am. Legion; VFW; DAV; Nat. Farm Orgn; Farm Bur. Mailing Add: 613 Kingree Rd, Shelbyville, Tenn. 37160.

PITTS, NOAH ODAS, JR. R
Mem, N.C. State Rep. Exec. Cmt.
b. Glen Alpine, N.C, 4/11/21; s. Noah Odas Pitts and Maude Simpson P; m. 1/23/45 to Lillian Riggan; c. Elizabeth Hill, Barbara Gene, Noah Odas, III and Grady Riggan. Educ: Duke Univ, 41-43; Kappa Alpha. Polit. & Govt. Pos: Chmn, Precinct Four, Burke Co, N.Y, 54-60; pres, Burke Co. Young Rep, 58-59; co. chmn, Rep. Party, Burke Co, 60-; mem, N.C. State Rep. Exec. Cmt, 60- Bus. & Prof. Pos: V.pres, Morganton Savings & Loan, 61-; v.pres, Pitts Lumber, Inc, 61-; secy. and treas, Burke Lumber, Inc, 61-; mem. bd. of trustees, Grace Hosp, 64-; pres, Burke Construction Co, Inc, currently. Mil. Serv: Entered as Ens, Navy, 43, released as Lt.(jg), 45, after serv. in Pac. Theatre; ETO and Pac. Theatre Ribbons. Mem: Carolina Builder's Asn; Morganton C. of C.(dir, 61-65, pres, 68); Morganton Merchants Asn; Mimosa Hills Golf Club; Lenoir Country Club. Rel: Methodist. Legal Res: 510 Riverside Dr, Morganton, N.C. 28655. Mailing Add: P.O. Box 338, Morganton, N.C. 28655.

PIVONKA, CHARLES AUGUST D
V.Chmn, Rush Co. Dem. Party, Kans.
b. Timken, Kans, 8/2/04; s. Frank Pivonka and Mary Bizek P; m. 10/8/29 to Ludmila Pechanec; c. Maurice Charles and Barbara Jane (Mrs. Robert Upson). Educ: Rush Co. Sch. Dist. 19, 9 years. Polit. & Govt. Pos: V.chmn, Rush Co. Dem. Party, Kans, 69- Bus. & Prof. Pos: Farmer and ins. salesman; pres, Co. Farmers Union. Mem: Lions; Farmers Union; Nat. Farmers Orgn. Rel: Catholic. Mailing Add: Timken, Kans. 67582.

PIXLEY, THEODORE R, SR. D
Chmn, Calhoun Co. Dem. Party, Mich.
b. 7/15/24; m. to Hilda M; c. Theodore R, Jr, Timothy John and Stephen David. Educ: Univ. Detroit, B.S; Univ. Detroit Law Sch. Polit. & Govt. Pos: Former city attorney, Clare, Mich; chmn, Calhoun Co. Dem. Party, 69- Bus. & Prof. Pos: Attorney-at-law. Mem: K. of C; former dir. and treas, Legal Aid Soc, Calhoun Co; VFW; Delta Theta Phi; Blue Key. Admitted to practice law in Mich, 52, U.S. Court of Appeals and U.S. Supreme Court. Legal Res: Route 6, Box 630, 20544 Bedford Rd, Battle Creek, Mich. 49017. Mailing Add: 265 Capitol N.E, Battle Creek, Mich. 49014.

PIZARRO, FEDERICO Popular Dem, P.R.
b. Rio Grande, P.R, 7/24/34; s. Federico Pizarro Gonzalez and Carmen Santiago G; single. Educ: Univ. P.R, B.S, 49, B.A, 59, LL.B, 63. Polit. & Govt. Pos: Active in polit. activities of the Popular Dem. Party, P.R, currently; mem, Dem. Party Cmt. of P.R, currently; del, Dem. Nat. Conv, 68. Bus. & Prof. Pos: Pres, Eastern Finance Corp, 66. Mil. Serv: Entered as 2nd Lt, Army, 51, released as Capt, 56, after serv. in 11th Airborne Div; Capt, Army Res; Sr. Parachutist Badge; Nat. Defense Serv. Medal. Mem: Pres, Asn. of P.R. Small Loan Co. and Rio Grande Jr. C. of C, 68. Rel: Catholic. Legal Res: 153 San Juan St, Rio Grande, P.R. 00745. Mailing Add: Box 468, Rio Grande, P.R. 00745.

PLAISANCE, VERNON RAYMOND R
Minn. State Rep.
b. Elk River, Minn, 2/29/32; s. Daniel Plaisance and Anna Collette P; m. 7/5/55 to Joan Johnsen; c. Stephen, Deborah, Diane, Linda, James, John, Thomas, David and Donald. Educ: St. Thomas Col, St. Paul, Minn, B.A, 55. Polit. & Govt. Pos: Minn. State Rep, 69- Bus. & Prof. Pos: Adminstr, Maple Manor Nursing Home, currently. Mem: Minn. Nursing Asn; K. of C. Rel: Catholic. Mailing Add: 9741 Foley Blvd, Coon Rapids, Minn. 55433.

PLANER, RICHARD ANDREW D
Chmn, Onondaga Co. Dem. Cmt, N.Y.
b. Syracuse, N.Y, 12/1/31; s. Charles P. Planer (deceased) and Jessica Kirby P.(deceased); single. Educ: Univ. St. Michael's Col, Univ. Toronto, 51-53; Army Lang. Sch, Monterey, Calif, honors grad. in Russian, 55; Syracuse Univ, A.B, 59, doctoral cand, currently. Polit. & Govt. Pos: Exec. secy, Onondaga Co. Dem. Cmt, N.Y, 66-67, chmn, 68-; research dir, N.Y. State Joint Legis. Cmt. on Migrant Labor, 68. Bus. & Prof. Pos: Teacher and chmn, soc. studies, Marcellus High Sch, 59-64; personnel asst, off. dean of men, Syracuse Univ, Syracuse, 65-66; dir, pub. rels. and develop, Maria Regina Col, 67- Mil. Serv: Entered as Pvt, Army Security Agency, 54, released as Specialist 5/C, 56, after serv. in Far East, Japan, 55-56; Good Conduct and Nat. Defense Serv. Medals. Mem: Am. Asn. Jr. Cols; Cent. N.Y. Col. Pub. Rels. Asn; Am. Legion; Optimist Club (bd. dirs, Syracuse Chap); Syracuse Liederkranz Club; Tipp-Off Found.(bd. dirs); Syracuse Press Club. Rel: Roman Catholic. Legal Res: 13 Centennial Dr, Syracuse, N.Y. 13207. Mailing Add: 105 W. Seneca Turnpike, Syracuse, N.Y. 13205.

PLANT, MARY ANN D
b. Centerburg, Ohio, 12/22/96; d. Frank W. Cotton and Lavina Keller Helt C; m. 3/21/22 to William D. Plant, Sr; c. William D, Jr. and James Phillip. Educ: Otterbein Univ, 14; Kent State Univ, teachers degree, 15. Polit. & Govt.

Pos: Supvr. and off. mgr, Summit Co. Treas. Off, Ohio, 33-53, chief dep. and off. mgr, 53-; precinct committeewoman, Dem. Cent. Cmt, 34-66; charter mem. and pres, Dem. Pub. Affairs Study Club, 39-42; rep, Dem. Exec. Cmt, State Dem. Conv, 48-66; organizer and hon. life mem, Akron Women's Dem. Club, 60-66; chairwoman, Akron City Dem. Cmt, 60-66; former dir. women's activities, Summit Co. Dem. Exec. Cmt. Bus. & Prof. Pos: Comptometer operator, Firestone Tire & Rubber, 18-20; off. mgr, Ralph Barr Printing Co, 24-25; acct. and systs. installer, Akron Typographical Asn, 25-26; off. mgr, Cahill Provision Co, 28-31; stenographic supvr, B.F. Goodrich Co, 31-33. Publ: Weekly columnist, Summit Co. Democrat, 45-59; various articles on politics, State & Party Publ. Mem: Nat. Newspaper Women's Asn; Nat. Data Processing Asn; Ohio Treasurer's Asn; Bus. & Prfnl. Women's Clubs of Ohio; Altrusa Club; Akron for Citizen's for Progress; Daughter's of Am; bd. mem, Girl Scouts; pres, Akron YWCA; Kent State Alumni Asn; Sr. Citizen's of Summit Co; City and County Safety Bldg. Cmt; Family & Children's Serv. Soc. Akron Woman of Year for Civic Group Participation, 57. Rel: United Church of Christ. Mailing Add: 644 Hillsdale Ave, Akron, Ohio 44303. (1967)

PLANTE, CHARLES LARRY D
b. Minot, N.Dak, 8/8/31; s. Charles Joseph Plante and Alda Charlebois P; m. 6/16/56 to Mary Ann Vandegrift; c. Patricia, Charles, Peter, Kathleen and Jonathan Jacob. Educ: St. John's Univ, Minn, B.A, 53; Univ. Mont, M.A, 54; Georgetown Univ, completed class work for Ph.D, 56-58; Phi Alpha Theta. Polit. & Govt. Pos: Mem. staff, Sen. W. Lawyen, N.Dak, 56-59; legis. admin. asst. to Sen. T. Dodd, 60-61; asst. to dir, Bur. of Land Mgt, U.S. Dept. of Interior, 61; admin. asst. to Sen. Q. Burdick, N.Dak, 62-68; assoc. dir, U.S. Peace Corps, 67-68. Bus. & Prof. Pos: Self-employed consult, Nat. Kidney Found. and George Wash. Found, 68- Mil. Serv: Entered as Pvt, 54, released as Cpl, 56. Publ: Collaborator, Volume on Pub. Lands, Dept. of Interior, article in First Homesteader and pamphlets, Dept. of Interior, 61. Rel: Catholic. Mailing Add: 1088 Manning St, Great Falls, Va. 22066.

PLANTE, PETER PAUL D
b. Gracefield, Que, Can; 8/3/20; s. Edgar M. Plante and Georgianna Monahan P; m. 9/4/48 to Rita M. Donahue; c. Therese, Maura, Stephen, Anthony, Kathleen, Maryanna, Margaret, Jeanne, Thaddeus J, Christina and Robert. Educ: Univ. Western Ontario, B.A, 43; Univ. Detroit, J.D, 49; assoc. ed, Univ. of Detroit Law Review, 49. Polit. & Govt. Pos: Town agent, Norwich, Vt, 56-63, justice of peace, 56-58; bd. mem, Norwich Town Sch. Dist, 58-62; v.chmn, Dresden Sch. Dist, 62; judge, Hartford Munic. Court, 63-67; consult. on inter-state schs, Vt. State Bd. of Educ, 66- Bus. & Prof. Pos: Dir, Gateway Motors, Inc, 56-; incorporator, Dartmouth Savings Bank and dir. and incorporator, Mary Hitchcock Mem. Hosp, 59- Mil. Serv: Entered as Pvt, Army, 43, released as Sgt, 46, after serv. with Mil. Police. Mem: Past pres, Windsor Co. Bar Asn; Am. Bar Asn; Third v.pres, Vt. Bar Asn, 69-; Am. & Vt. Trial Lawyers Asns; K. of C; past pres, White River Junction Rotary Club. Rel: Roman Catholic. Legal Res: 12 Church St, Norwich, Vt. 05055. Mailing Add: Municipal Bldg, White River Junction, Vt. 05001.

PLANTZ, DONALD JAMES R
Dir, Pub. Rels. and Info. for V.I.
b. Watertown, N.Y, 2/5/24; s. Charles Henry Plantz and Margaret Smith P. (deceased); m. 7/24/53 to Emily Bulman. Educ: Cornell Univ, B.A, 48; Stanford Univ, 48-49; Book and Bowl Club. Polit. & Govt. Pos: Pub. rels. dir, Rep. Party of the V.I, 67-69 and campaign chmn, 68; dir, Pub. Rels. and Info. for V.I, 69- Bus. & Prof. Pos: Owner, Donald J. Plantz Advert. and Pub. Rels, St. Thomas, V.I, 59-, Plantz Chem, 63- and V.I. Cards. Mil. Serv: Entered as Pvt, Air Force, 42, released as Capt, 46, after serv. in Third Air Commando Group, Pac. Theatre, 44-46; Capt, Air Force Res; Three Air Medals; Pac. Theatre Ribbon; China-Burma-India Theatre Ribbon; New Guinea Campaign, Philippine Campaign and Japanese Occup. Forces Medals. Publ: Sweeney Squadron, Doubleday & Dell, 61-62; Marked for Death, Monarch, 64. Mem: Overseas Press Club of Am; Nat. Swimming Pool Inst; U.S. Diplomatic Courier Asn. Legal Res: Botany Bay, St. Thomas, V.I. 00801. Mailing Add: P.O. Box 1476, St. Thomas, V.I. 00801.

PLASKETT, JAMES M. D
Ind. State Sen.
Educ: Hanover Col, 30; Beta Theta Pi. Polit. & Govt. Pos: Sheriff, Clark Co, Ind, 30, surveyor, 41-44; Ind. State Sen, 63- Bus. & Prof. Pos: Sch. prin. and farmer. Mil. Serv: Army engr. Mem: Mason; VFW; Am. Legion; PTA; ISTA. Rel: Methodist. Mailing Add: New Washington, Ind. 47162. (1967)

PLATT, FAUN R
Chmn, Lenawee Co. Rep. Party, Mich.
b. Thawville, Ill, 1/12/02; m. 8/19/25; c. Dr. Thomas E. and Richard. Educ: Ill. Normal; Seina Heights Col; Mich. State Univ. Polit. & Govt. Pos: V.chmn, Dist. Rep. Party, 2 years and reelected 2 years; v.chmn, Lenawee Co. Rep. Party, Mich, 5 years, chmn, 2 years; former mem, Mich. Rep. State Cent. Cmt; alternate del, Rep. Nat. Conv, 60; del, Women's Fedn. in Wash, 67. Bus. & Prof. Pos: Sch. teacher, 15 years; juvenile co. agent; probation officer for probate court. Mem: Grange; Eastern Star. Awarded Silver Plaque for Outstanding Work for the Rep. Party, 68. Mailing Add: 7616 Tipton Hwy, Tipton, Mich. 49287.

PLATT, HARVEY J. R
b. St. Johns, Ariz, 9/12/06; s. Henry John Platt and Masylvia Peterson P; m. 3/9/50 to Merle Ballantyne; c. Jo Ann (Mrs. Hovious), Jay, Valerie, Richard and Marcor. Educ: Brigham Young Univ, 25-26; Univ. Ariz, B.A; Delta Chi. Polit. & Govt. Pos: Chmn, Apache Co. Rep. Cmt, Ariz, 56-61 & 68-69; alternate del, Rep. Nat. Conv, 60 & 64; dir, Ariz. Dept. of Econ. Planning and Develop, 64-69 and v.chmn, 68-69. Bus. & Prof. Pos: Dir, Ariz. Frozen Foods Corp, 48- Mem: Ariz. Cattle Growers Asn; Ariz. Farm Bur; Am. Nat. Cattlemens Asn; Ariz. Cattle Feeders Asn.(chmn, 44-45); pres, Apache Co. Farm Bur, 68-69. Rel: Latter-day Saint. Legal Res: 195 E. Cleveland, St. Johns, Ariz. 85936. Mailing Add: Box 426, St. Johns, Ariz. 85936.

PLATT, JAMES WILLIAM D
Utah State Rep.
b. Salt Lake City, Utah, 8/24/32; s. Charles Edward Platt and Nina Parry P; m. 7/27/51 to Darlene Catherine Alder; c. Eda Debra (Mrs. James D. Fife, Jr), Jae Tamira and Lorine Devon. Educ: West High Sch, Salt Lake City, Utah, 4 years. Polit. & Govt. Pos: Treas. and pub. rels. officer, Sen. Dist. Dem. Party, Utah, 65; chmn, Legis. Dist. Dem. Party, Salt Lake City, 68; mem, Dem. Cent. Cmt, 69; Utah State Rep, 69- Bus. & Prof. Pos: Criminal investr, Salt Lake City Police Dept, Utah, 56; self employed in pub. rels. and advert, 62; plant supvr, PPP Inc, Salt Lake City, 64; announcer and prod, KMOR Radio, 66; pub. rels. dir, Utah Peace Officers Asn, 69- Mem: Int. Footprinters Asn; Utah Peace Officers Asn; Elks. Mailing Add: P.O. Box 892, Salt Lake City, Utah 84110.

PLATT, JOE-ANN ELIZABETH R
Nat. Secy, Young Rep. Nat. Fedn.
b. Moline, Ill, 9/27/33; d. Joe W. Sowder and Elizabeth G. Fulton S; m. 6/15/52 to John B. Platt, Jr; c. Judith B, Jeb B, Jo-Ellyn E. and Joe B. Educ: Awarded 4 year scholarship, Pa. Col. for Women, 51; Univ. Md. Polit. & Govt. Pos: V.chmn, Scott Co. Young Rep, Iowa, 60; campaign coordinator, J. Kenneth Stringer Campaign for U.S. Senate, 60; precinct committeewoman, Scott Co. Rep. Party, 60-; mem. staff, Rep. Nat. Conv, 64; nat. committeewoman, Young Rep. of Iowa, 65-; state chmn, Young Iowans for Miller, U.S. Sen. Jack Miller Campaign, 66; coordinator, Scott Co. Rep. Campaign, 66-69; del-at-lg, Rep. Nat. Conv, 68; mem. state adv. cmt, Richard Nixon for President, 68; state campaign coordinator, successful campaign of Lt. Gov. Roger W. Jepsen, 68; chmn, Iowa State Finance Cmt, Young Rep. Nat. Fedn, 69-, nat. secy, 69- Bus. & Prof. Pos: Secy-treas, J.P.D. Company, Inc, The Home Place; secy, Platt & Assocs, Inc; prfnl. syst. installationist, Diebold, Inc, through Platt & Assocs, currently. Mem: C. of C.(Womens Bur, Davenport Br); Davenport Human Rels. Cmn.(secy); Miss. Valley Press Club (mem. bd); Davenport Chap, Federated Women's Club of Iowa; trustee, Ava M. Preacher Mem. Trust; Am. Cancer Soc.(chmn. bus. and indust. cmt, Scott Co. Chap). Rel: Episcopal. Mailing Add: 1122 W. 51st St, Davenport, Iowa 52806.

PLATT, THOMAS C. R
Committeeman, Suffolk Co. Rep. Cmt, N.Y.
b. New York City, N.Y, 5/29/25; s. Collier Platt and Louise Lusk P; m. 6/25/48 to Ann Byrd Symington; c. Ann Byrd, Charles Collier, Thomas C, III and Elizabeth Louise. Educ: Yale Col, B.A, 47, Law School, L.B, 50; Phi Delta Phi; Fence Club. Polit. & Govt. Pos: Asst. U.S. Attorney, East Dist, N.Y, 53-56; committeeman, Suffolk Co. Rep. Cmt, N.Y, 57-; village attorney, Laurel Hollow, 57-; alternate del, Rep. Nat. Conv, 64 & 68; del, Rep. State Conv, N.Y, 66. Bus. & Prof. Pos: Mem. law firm, Bleakley, Platt, Schmidt, Hart & Fritz, presently. Mil. Serv: Entered as A/S, Navy, 43, released as Ens, 46, after serv. in Atlantic. Mem: N.Y. State, Nassau Co. and N.Y.C. Bar Asns; dir, Huntington C. of C, 66-69. Rel: Episcopal. Legal Res: 448 West Neck Rd, Lloyd Harbor, N.Y. 11743. Mailing Add: 120 Broadway, New York, N.Y. 10005.

PLAXICO, ROBERT LAWRENCE D
S.C. State Exec. Committeeman, Laurens Co.
b. Cherokee Co, S.C, 12/26/98; s. John Emmett Plaxico and Zulia Borders P; m. 10/1/26 to Frances Elizabeth Tribble; c. Robert L, Jr. Educ: Erskine Col, 2 years. Polit. & Govt. Pos: Chmn, Laurens Co. Dem. Party, S.C, 54-64; alternate del, Dem. Nat. Conv, 56, del, 64; S.C. State Exec. Committeeman, Laurens Co, S.C, 64-; mem, Bd. Cmnrs. for the Mentally Retarded for S.C, 68-, presently v.chmn. Bus. & Prof. Pos: Secy-treas, D.E. Tribble Co, 28-; chmn, Bd. Trustees, Whixtten Village, 57- Mem: Past Master, Campbell Lodge F&AM; past pres, Clinton Kiwanis; past pres, Clinton C. of C. Rel: Assoc. Reformed Presbyterian. Legal Res: 205 N. Woodrow St, Clinton, S.C. 29325. Mailing Add: Box 356, Clinton, S.C. 29325.

PLECHNER, RICHARD FREDERICK R
N.J. State Del.
b. New York, N.Y, 11/25/32; s. Walter W. Plechner and Sophie Coppersmith P; m. 9/4/54 to Eleanor A. Schenck; c. Ann Louise, Walter George, Ellen Marie, Paul Frederick and Barbara Sue. Educ: Rutgers Univ, B.A, 54, LL.B, 59; Phi Delta Phi. Polit. & Govt. Pos: Chmn, Middlesex Co. Young Rep, 63-64; del, Rep. Nat. Conv, 64; chmn, Young Rep. of N.J, 64-65; Planning Bd. Attorney, Madison Twp, N.J, 64-65, Zoning Bd. Attorney, 64-67 and Munic. Attorney, 65; Zoning Bd. Attorney, Borough of Carteret, 65; v.chmn, Young Rep. Nat. Fedn, 65-66; nat. dir, Young Americans for Fedn, 65-67; N.J. State Del, 68- Bus. & Prof. Pos: Attorney-at-law, Metuchen, N.J, 60- Mil. Serv: Entered as 2nd Lt, Army, 55, released as 1st Lt, 57, after serv. in 29th Inf. Regt. Combat Team, Ft. Benning, Ga; Capt, Army Res. Mem: Am. Bar Asn. Rel: Dutch Reformed. Mailing Add: 62 Oak Ave, Metuchen, N.J. 08840.

PLEWA, CASMERE JOSEPH R
b. Hamtramck, Mich, 7/26/26; s. George Plewa and Mary Mazur P; m. 9/1/56 to Veronica Lucy Zwolak; c. Robert, Michael and David. Educ: Univ. Detroit, B.M.E, 51; Tau Beta Pi; Pi Tau Sigma; Sigma Alpha Epsilon. Polit. & Govt. Pos: Mem, Warren Recreation Cmn, Mich, 62-64; mem, Warren Libr. Cmn, 62-, chmn, 67-; precinct del, Rep. Party, 62-; treas, Macomb Co. Rep. Campaign Cmt, 66; dist. chmn, 12th Dist. Rep. Party, 67-; del, Rep. Nat. Conv, 68. Bus. & Prof. Pos: Sr. mfg. process engr, Fisher Body, GMC, 51-64; sr. mfg. process engr. and cost analyst, Ford Motor Co, 64- Mil. Serv: Entered as Pvt, Army, 44, released as T-5, 46, after serv. in Gen. Hq, Pac. Theatre, 46; Presidential Citation; Overseas Serv. Ribbons; Good Conduct Medal. Mem: Eng. Soc. Detroit; Bernadine Homeowners Asn.(past chmn. and treas). Bausch & Lomb Sci. Award; Am. Legion Sch. Award. Rel: Roman Catholic. Mailing Add: 27761 Lorraine, Warren, Mich. 48093.

PLIMPTON, THEODORE FERRY R
b. Sturbridge, Mass, 7/25/01; s. George Lincoln Plimpton and Etta Ione Ferry P; m. 7/24/29 to Dorothy Janet Bugbee; c. James David and Thomas Lincoln. Educ: Wesleyan Univ, A.B, 21; Mass. Inst. Tech, 23-24; Harvard Bus. Sch, 50; Delta Kappa Epsilon. Polit. & Govt. Pos: Rep. Precinct committeeman, 60-68; del, Ind. State Conv, 62, 64 & 68; treas, St. John Twp. Rep. Orgn, 62-; police cmnr, Schererville, Ind, 64-68; Rep. ward chmn, Schererville, 66-; del, Rep. Nat. Conv, 68; pres, N.W. Ind. Crime Cmn, 69- Bus. & Prof. Pos: Instr. physics, Phillips Acad, Andover, Mass, 21-23; mem. staff, Inland Steel Co, East Chicago, Ind, 24-29, asst. supt. blast furnaces, 30-40, supt, 41-50, asst. gen. mgr, 51-56, asst. to v.pres, mfg. and research, 57-65.

Mem: Am. Iron and Steel Inst; Am. Inst. of Mining, Metallurgical and Petroleum Engrs; Asn. of Iron and Steel Engrs; Blast Furnace and Coke Asn; West. Soc. of Engrs; Soc. for the Adv. of Mgt; Kiwanis; Elks; pres, East Chicago, Ind. C. of C; trustee, Tilton Sch, N.H; pres, East Chicago Boy Scout Coun. Silver Beaver, Boy Scouts. Rel: Methodist. Mailing Add: 7 Hawthorn Place, Schererville, Ind. 46375.

PLOESER, WALTER CHRISTIAN R
b. 1/7/07; s. Christian D. Ploeser and Maude E. Parr P; m. 8/17/28 to Dorothy Annette Mohrig; c. Ann (Mrs. George E. Berg) and Sally (Mrs. William Chapel, III). Educ: City Col. of Law and Finance, St. Louis, Mo. Hon. LL.D, Norwich Univ, 48; Hon. Dr, Nat. Univ. of Asuncion, Paraguay. Polit. & Govt. Pos: Mo. State Rep, 31-32; founder and pres, Young Rep. Fedn. of Mo. 34-35; subcmt. chmn, Rep. Nat. Prog. Cmt, 37-39; U.S. Rep, Mo, 41-49; chmn, St. Louis Co. Rep. Finance Cmt, 52-56; U.S. Ambassador to Paraguay, 57-59; Rep. Nat. Committeeman, Mo, 64-66. Bus. & Prof. Pos: Chmn. bd, Ploeser, Watts & Co, Ins, 33-; dir, Wesbter Groves Trust Co. and Wehrenberg Theatres. Mem: Mason (33°); Scottish Rite; York Rite; Sovereign Grand Inspector Gen, Scottish Rite in Mo; Past Grand Master, Int. DeMolay; former chmn. nat. affairs, Metrop. St. Louis C. of C; Mo. Athletic and Noonday Clubs; Ins. Bd. of St. Louis, Mo; Gilead Hunting and Fishing Club. Cert. of Merit, U.S. Navy; Freedom Found. Award, 49; Grand Cross of Repub. of Paraguay, 59. Rel: Christian Scientist. Mailing Add: Hawthorne, Box 251, R.R. 1, Manchester, Mo. 63011.

PLOTNICK, MAURICE DANIEL D
b. Richmond, Va, 3/1/21; s. David Joseph Plotnick (deceased) and Ann Levi P; m. to Sandra Jean Romick; c. Rochelle, David, Sara Lynn, Barbara, Michael, Ann Lee and Alan Towb. Educ: Univ. Richmond, Va, 40-41; Univ. Calif, Los Angeles, 45-48; Scabbard and Blade; Arnold Air Soc; Omicron Delta Kappa. Polit. & Govt. Pos: Chmn, Anchorage Precinct 24, Alaska, 48-66; del, Dem. State Conv, 60, 62, 64 & 66; pres, Anchorage Dem. Club and chmn, Alaska UN Day, 64; Alaska State Rep, 64-66. Bus. & Prof. Pos: Dir, O.T. Land Develop. Corp, v.pres, Romick-Alaska Land Develop. and pres, Fed. Disbributing Co. Inc, 66. Mil. Serv: Entered as Pvt, Army Air Corps, 41, released as Capt, 58, after serv. in Alaskan Air Command; Soldier's, Victory, Navy Life Saving, Good Conduct, Berlin Airlift and Korean Medals; Am. and Caribbean Theater Ribbons; World War II Ribbon; Air Forces Res, Retired. Publ: Publisher, Alaskan Air Command Air Intelligence Rev, 49-52. Mem: C. of C.(bd. dirs, Anchorage Chap, 57); Lions Int.(past pres); Bd. of YMCA; Am. Red Cross; Nat. Conf. of Christians and Jews; Am. Legion; VFW; Alaskan Methodist Univ. Participant in floating Ice Island in Arctic; first JATO assists in Taku Glacier take off in 1950. Rel: Jewish. Legal Res: 1511 Second Ave, Douglas, Alaska 99824. Mailing Add: Box 429, Douglas, Alaska 99824. (1967)

PLOWMAN, FRANCIS WILDS R
b. Dover, Del, 10/2/02; s. Garrett Hyuson Plowman and Beulah Wilds P; m. 4/6/40 to Elizabeth Crozer Buckhead; c. Suzanne (Mrs. Auteis), Joan (Mrs. Partridge) and Francis W, Jr. Educ: Wash. and Lee Univ, B.S, 24; Omicron Delta Kappa; Beta Gamma Sigma; Phi Epsilon Pi. Polit. & Govt. Pos: Finance chmn, Rep. Party, Pa, 66-67; alternate del, Rep. Nat. Conv, 68. Bus. & Prof. Pos: V.pres, Scott Paper Co, Phila. Mem: Union League. Rel: Episcopal. Mailing Add: 425 Swarthmore Ave, Swarthmore, Pa. 19081.

PLUMADORE, HAYWARD HENRY R
Chmn, Franklin Co. Rep. Cmt, N.Y.
b. Lyon Mt, N.Y, 7/13/13; s. Herbert Plumadore and Ceceila Minney; m. 9/10/40 to May Furnia; c. Jan H, Karen (Mrs. Jurascheck) and Brett. Educ: St. Lawrence Univ, B.S, 40; Albany Law Sch, LL.B, 43 and J.D, 68; Xi Chap, Phi Sigma Kappa. Polit. & Govt. Pos: Supvr, Town of Harrietstown, N.Y, 50-55 & 58-61; chmn, Franklin Co. Rep. Cmt, 52-62 & 67-; N.Y. State Assemblyman, Franklin Co, 60-65; mem, N.Y. Rep. State Cmt, 67- Bus. & Prof. Pos: Attorney-at-law, 43- Mil. Serv: Pvt, N.Y. Nat. Guard, 35-38; entered as Ens, Navy, 43, released as Lt. Comdr, 47, after serv. in Amphibious Forces, European, N.African and Am. Theatres; Lt. Comdr, Inactive Naval Res, currently; Purple Heart; Am. and N.African Theatre Ribbons; European Theatre Ribbon with Two Stars. Mem: Am. Legion; VFW; Amvets; Elks; Moose (4°); K. of C.(4°). Judge Advocate, Fourth Dist. N.Y. Am. Legion; Judge Advocate, St. Lawrence Valley Coun, VFW. Rel: Catholic. Legal Res: Lower Saranac Lake, Saranac Lake, N.Y. 12983. Mailing Add: 52 Broadway, Saranac Lake, N.Y. 12983.

PLUNKETT, LAMAR R. D
Ga. State Sen.
b. Jesup, Ga, 3/23/11; s. James Edgar Plunkett and Cora Estelle Hemphill P; m. 10/9/40 to Ava Frances Sewell; c. Lamar R, Jr, Thomas S. and Elizabeth Ann. Educ: Mercer Univ, Macon, Ga, B.S.C, 31; U.S. Mil. Acad, 31-32; Blue Key; Sigma Nu. Polit. & Govt. Pos: Ga. State Sen, 30th Dist, 63-, chmn, Appropriations Cmt, Ga. State Senate, 67- Bus. & Prof. Pos: V.pres, Warren Sewell Clothing Co, 45-; pres, LaMar Mfg. Co. 54-; pres, Bowdon Mfg. Co, 59- Mil. Serv: Entered as 2nd Lt, Air Corps, 42, released as Lt. Col, 45, after serv. in U.S. Mil. Acad, Stewart Field, N.Y; Lt. Col. Air Force Res, 45- Mem: Bd. control, South. Regional Educ. Bd; Shrine; Mason; Lions; Am. Legion. Rel: Baptist. Mailing Add: 50 Morris St, Bowdon, Ga. 30108.

POAGE, WILLIAM ROBERT 'BOB' D
U.S. Rep, Tex.
b. Waco, Tex, 12/28/99; s. William A. Poage and Helen Conger P; m. 2/14/38 to Frances Cotton. Educ: Univ. Colo; Univ. Tex; Baylor Univ, A.B. and LL.B, hon. LL.D, 67. Polit. & Govt. Pos: Tex. State Rep, 25-29; Tex. State Sen, 31-37; U.S. Rep, Tex, 36-, chmn, Cmt. on Agr, U.S. House of Rep, currently; Am. del. to the Interparliamentary Union, 47- Bus. & Prof. Pos: Attorney-at-law, Waco, 24-36. Mem: Am. Legion. Legal Res: Waco, Tex. Mailing Add: 228 Second St. S.E, Washington, D.C. 20003.

POBUDA, ROBERT E. R
V.Chmn, Macomb Co. Rep. Party, Mich.
b. Chicago, Ill, 11/27/28; m. 8/8/53 to Betty Ann Getman; c. Daniel, Michael, Carol and Jonathan. Educ: B.A, M.A. and Ed.S. Polit. & Govt. Pos: V.chmn, Macomb Co. Rep. Party, Mich, currently. Bus. & Prof. Pos: Dir. of extended serv, Warren Consolidated Schs, Mich. Mem: Lions. Legal Res: 31812 Sankuer Dr, Warren Mich. 48093. Mailing Add: Warren Consolidated Schools, 29900 Lorraine, Warren, Mich. 48093.

POCHÉ, MARC B. D
Exec. Asst, Ninth Cong. Dist. Dem. Party, Calif.
b. New Orleans, La, 5/1/34; s. Marcel A. Poché and Marie Belmar P; m. 6/30/56 to Therese Kremer; c. Matthew, Anne and Michelle. Educ: Univ. of Santa Clara, B.A. summa cum laude, 56; Univ. of Calif, Berkeley, J.D, 61; bd. of ed, Calif. Law Rev; Alpha Sigma Nu. Polit. & Govt. Pos: Spec. hearing officer, U.S. Dept. of Justice, 67-68; Dem. nominee, Calif. State Assembly, 25th Dist, 68; mem, Santa Clara Co. Dem. Cent. Cmt, 68-; exec. asst, Ninth Cong. Dist. Dem. Party, 69- Bus. & Prof. Pos: Attorney-at-law, San Jose, Calif, 62-69; assoc. prof. of law, Univ. of Santa Clara, 65-67, prof. of law, 69- Mil. Serv: Entered as 2nd Lt, Marines, 56, released as 1st Lt, 58, after serv. in Second Marine Air Wing, 56-58. Publ: 'Federal Abstention Doctrine,' Calif. Law Rev, 61; 'Uninsured Motorist Legislation in California,' Hastings Law Rev, 62. Mem: Am, Calif. and Santa Clara Co. Bar Asns; Am. Asn. of Univ. Counsel; Marine Corps Officers Asn; Sierra Club; Serra Club. Ryland Debate Prize. Rel: Catholic. Legal Res: 1650 University Ave, San Jose, Calif. 95126. Mailing Add: 999 W. Taylor, San Jose, Calif. 95126.

PODCASY, BERNARD JOHN D
Prothonotary, Luzerne Co, Pa.
b. Ashley, Pa, 8/12/20; s. Joseph J. Podcasy and Catherine Pierozak P; m. 6/29/46 to Jane Mercedes Ladner; c. Bernard A, Susan and Melissa. Educ: Univ. Toronto, B.A, 42; Georgetown Univ. Sch. of Law, LL.B, 48. Polit. & Govt. Pos: Solicitor, Ashley Borough Coun, 51-60; asst. dist. attorney, Pa, 60-61, asst. dep. attorney gen, 60-62; Prothonotary, Luzerne Co, 62- Mil. Serv: Entered as Pvt, Army, 42, released as Capt, 47, after serv. in 179th Inf, 45th Div, ETO; ETO Ribbon with 3 Stars; Combat Infantryman Badge; Purple Heart with 2 Clusters. Mem: Wilkes-Barre Law & Libr. Asn; K. of C; Order of Alhambra; VFW; Am. Legion; Amvets; DAV. Rel: Roman Catholic. Mailing Add: 36 St. Mary's Rd, Wilkes-Barre, Pa. 18702.

PODELL, BERTRAM L. D
U.S. Rep, N.Y.
b. Brooklyn, N.Y, 12/27/25; s. Hyman Podell and Henrietta Menaker P; m. 2/15/53 to Bernice Posen; c. Stephen, Ellen and Gary. Educ: St. John's Univ, B.A; Brooklyn Law Sch, LL.B. Polit. & Govt. Pos: N.Y. State Assemblyman, 54-68; U.S. Rep, N.Y, 68- Bus. & Prof. Pos: Attorney, Podell & Podell, Esquires, New York, currently. Mil. Serv: Entered as Seaman, Navy, 44, released as HA 1/C, 46. Publ: 'Condemnation Proceedings: Protest of Assessments,' N.Y. Law J, 12/67; 'Consolidation of Local Government as a Greater Means to Economy and Efficiency in New York State,' 67; 'Joint Legislative Committee on Penal Institutions Report,' N.Y. State Assembly, 68. Mem: Many civic and philanthropic orgn. Rel: Jewish. Legal Res: 153 Rugby Rd, Brooklyn, N.Y. 11226. Mailing Add: 1712 Longworth House Office Bldg, Washington, D.C. 20515.

PODESTA, ROBERT A. R
Asst. Secy. of Commerce for Econ. Develop.
b. Chicago, Ill, 10/7/12; s. Andrew D. Podesta and Agnes Frazer P; m. 12/26/36 to Corrine Agnes Murnighan; c. Carol Ann (Mrs. Foley), Mary Ellen (Mrs. Burke), Kathleen (Mrs. Mehigan) and Robert A. Educ: Northwestern Univ, B.S.B.A, 44. Polit. & Govt. Pos: Rep. Cand, U.S. House Rep, third dist, Ill, 68; Asst. Secy. of Commerce for Econ. Develop, 69- Bus. & Prof. Pos: V.pres, treas. and dir, Julien Collins & Co, 45-49; Managing Partner, Cruttenden, Podesta & Miller, 49-63; sr. v.pres, mem. exec. cmt. and dir, Walston & Co. Inc, 63-64; sr. v.pres, treas. and dir, The Chicago Corp, 65-69. Mem: Gov, Investment Bankers Asn. Am, Am. Stock Exchange and Midwest Stock Exchange; mem, Chicago Bd. Trade; trustee, DePaul Univ, St. Mary's Col, Ind. and Mundelein Col. Rel: Catholic. Legal Res: 9319 S. Hamilton, Chicago, Ill. 60604. Mailing Add: Apt. 801, Watergate West, 2700 Virginia Ave. N.W, Washington, D.C. 20037.

PODGORSKI, ANTHONY (AL) DFL
b. St. Paul, Minn, 1903; married; c. Two. Educ: St. Paul Schs. Polit. & Govt. Pos: Minn. State Rep, 45-66. Bus. & Prof. Pos: Owner and operator of gasoline filling sta. Mem: Active in civic, commun, and church work. Mailing Add: 642 Van Buren Ave, St. Paul, Minn. 55104. (1967)

POE, McDONALD, SR. D
b. Hon, Scott Co, Ark, 12/26/00; s. Alfred Caleb Poe and Ethel Park P; m. 6/3/29 to Florence Hawk; c. McDonald, Jr, M.D, Frances (Mrs. Fulton) and Charles Alfred, Ph.D. Educ: Univ. Ark. Col. Arts and Sci, B.A. with honors, 23; Univ. Ark. Law Sch, LL.B. with honors, 27; Phi Alpha Delta; Skull and Torch, Univ. Ark. Col. Arts and Sci; Pi Kappa Alpha. Polit. & Govt. Pos: Sch. dir, Waldron High Sch, Ark, 35-60; city attorney, Waldron, 35-68; Ark. State Rep, Scott Co, 47-49; Ark. State Sen, Fifth Sen. Dist, 49-53; del, Dem. Nat. Conv, 68. Bus. & Prof. Pos: Practicing attorney, 27-; dairyman, farmer and owner several bus. bldg, currently. Mil. Serv: Army ROTC, 18-20, Sgt. Publ: Prepared Ark. Ed. to Wickersham Crime Report, 28-29; Mem. Legis. Cmt. that prepared report on higher educ, 51-53. Mem: Ark. Bar Asn; Mason. Rel: Methodist. Mailing Add: P.O. Box 40, Waldron, Ark. 72958.

POEPOE, ANDREW KELIIKUNIAUPUNI R
Asst. Minority Floor Leader, Hawaii House of Rep.
b. Honolulu, Hawaii, 5/2/35; s. Abraham Poaiki Poepoe and Dorothy Espinda P; m. 9/20/58 to Jaya L. Ramulu; c. Stephen and Alan. Educ: Yale Univ, B.S, 57. Polit. & Govt. Pos: V.chmn, Eighth Dist. Rep. Party, Hawaii, 64-; Hawaii State Rep, 67-, asst. minority floor leader and minority whip. Bus. & Prof. Pos: Indust. engr, Castle & Cooke Terminals, 57-62 and Dole Co, 62- Mem: Soc. for Adv. of Mgt; Effective Citizens Orgn; Friends of the East-West Center; Kaneohe Yacht Club; Koolaupoko Hawaiian Civic Club; Jaycees; Commun. Coun. Coach, Iolani High Sch. Rowing Team. Rel: Congregational. Mailing Add: 456 Wanaao Rd, Kailua, Hawaii 96734.

POFF, RICHARD H. R
U.S. Rep, Va.
b. Radford, Va, 10/19/23; m. 6/24/45 to Jo Ann Topper; c. Rebecca Topper,

Thomas Randolph and Richard H. Educ: Roanoke Col; Univ. Va. Law Sch, LL.B; Sigma Nu Phi. Hon. LL.D, Roanoke Col, 69. Polit. & Govt. Pos: U.S. Rep, Va, 53- Bus. & Prof. Pos: Partner, Dalton, Poff & Turk, attorneys, Radford, Va. Mil. Serv: B-24 bomber pilot; awarded Distinguished Flying Cross. Mem: Jr. C. of C; Lions; Mason (32°); Moose; Am. Legion; VFW. Rel: Presbyterian. Legal Res: Radford, Va. 24141. Mailing Add: 2228 Rayburn House Office Bldg, Washington, D.C. 20515.

POFFENBARGER, JOHN TALLMAN R
W.Va. State Sen.
b. Charleston, W.Va, 10/15/35; s. L.F. Poffenbarger and Virginia E. Jarrette P; m. 4/7/62 to Susan Gidley; c. Matthew Tallman and Kathryn E. Educ: Va. Mil. Inst, Lexington, Va, B.A, 58; W.Va. Univ, LL.B, 61. Polit. & Govt. Pos: City attorney, Dunbar, W.Va, 64-; W.Va. State Sen, 67-; chmn, W.Va. Clean Elec. Cmt, Rep. Party, 67-; attorney, Urban Renewal, Dunbar Urban Authority, 69- Mil. Serv: Entered as 2nd Lt, Army, released as Capt, 69, after serv. in Judge Adv. Gen. Corps. Publ: Defenses of the Poor in Criminal Cases, 65. Mem: Kanawha Co. Bar Asn.(mem. exec. cmt, 67-69); Am. Bar Asn.(reporter, W.Va. Indigent Rep. Study, 65); Kanawha Legal Aid Soc.(mem. exec. cmt, 67-); Am. Judicature Soc. Mailing Add: 1516 Kanawha Ave, Dunbar, W.Va. 25064.

POHLENZ, DEAN R
b. Blue Hill, Nebr, 7/14/20; s. Chris P. Pohlenz and Nettie Smith P; m. 5/22/42 to Mary Margaret Schmidt; c. Paul Dean, Peggy J. Educ: Univ. Nebr, 40; Indust. Col. of Armed Forces, 56-57; Sigma Delta Chi; Sigma Phi Epsilon. Polit. & Govt. Pos: Admin. asst. to U.S. Sen. Hruska, Nebr, currently; dep. asst. dir, Off. of Emergency Planning, Wash, 53-61. Bus. & Prof. Pos: Lectr. Naval War Col; Indust. Col. of Armed Forces; reporter, Nebr. State Jour, Lincoln, 37-53. Mil. Serv: Army, Pvt, 42-46; served as correspondent with Stars and Stripes, ETO; Distinguished Serv. Award; OCOM. Mem: Bd. gov. Nebr. State Soc. Rel: Methodist. Legal Res: Lincoln, Nebr. Mailing Add: 5303 Marlyn Dr, Bethesda, Md. 20027. (1967)

POINDEXTER, GORDON WALLACE, JR. R
Chmn, Waynesboro Rep. Town Cmt, Va.
b. Richmond, Va, 9/14/26; s. Gordon Wallace Poindexter, Sr. and Mary Boyd P; m. 10/18/52 to Lucy Seaman; c. Gordon Wallace, III. Educ: E.Carolina Col, B.S, 51; Univ. Richmond, LL.B, 59; Omicron Delta Kappa. Polit. & Govt. Pos: Chmn, Waynesboro Rep. Town Cmt, Va, 68- Mil. Serv: Entered as Pvt, Marines, 43, released as Maj, 66, after serv. in Pac. and Korea; Res, Maj. (Ret); Purple Heart. Rel: Episcopal. Mailing Add: Box 1140, Waynesboro, Va. 32920.

POINDEXTER, JAMES BERNARD D
b. Guyandotte, W.Va, 1/26/02; s. James Chalmers Poindexter and Maria Henrietta Tauber P; m. 8/7/26 to Thelma Lavenia Johnson; c. Thelma Bernice and Dr. James Bernard, Jr. Educ: Marshall Univ; Ohio Col. of Dent. Surgery; Univ. Louisville, D.D.S, 27; Psi Omega; Omicron Kappa Upsilon. Polit. & Govt. Pos: Mem, Huntington Bd. Park Cmnrs, 18 years; W.Va. State Del, 54-58 & 60-66. Bus. & Prof. Pos: Dentist and oral surgeon; staff mem, Huntington Hosps. Mem: Dipl. Am. Bd. Oral Surg; Am. Dent. Asn; Mid-Atlantic Soc. of Oral Surgeons; Am. Soc. of Oral Surgeons; Am. Col. of Dentists; Am. Dent. Soc. of Anesthesiology; former pres, W.Va. and Huntington Dent. Socs; Mason; Shrine; Elks; Rotary; Huntington C. of C; Ky. Col. Rel: Episcopal. Mailing Add: 1139 Fourth Ave, Huntington, W.Va. 25701. (1967)

POINTER, JAMES EDGAR, JR. D
Secy-Treas, Gloucester Co. Dem. Cmt, Va.
b. Gloucester Co, Va, 9/22/22; s. James Edgar Pointer and Lucy Lillie Minor P; m. 1/24/47 to Catherine Haseltine Jones; c. James Edgar, III and Steven David. Educ: Col. of William & Mary, B.S, 43 and B.C.L, 47; Sigma Pi. Polit. & Govt. Pos: Acting commonwealth's attorney, Gloucester Co, Va, 53-54, commonwealth's attorney, 54-63; attorney, co. sch. bd, 54-; secy-treas, Gloucester Co. Dem. Cmt, 54-; aide-de-camp to Gov. of Va, 58-; cmnr. of accts, Gloucester, 62-; campaign mgr. and area coordinator, Lyndon B. Johnson Presidential Campaign, Va, 64; First Cong. Dist. del, Dem. Nat. Conv, 64; Gloucester Co. campaign mgr, William B. Spong, Jr. for U.S. Senate, 66 and William C. Battle for Gov. of Va, 69. Bus. & Prof. Pos: Partner, Du Val & Pointer, 51-54; dir. and asst. secy, Bank of Gloucester, Va, 54-; dir, Francis N. Sanders Nursing Home, Inc, 59-; partner, Pointer & Feild, Attorneys at Law, Gloucester, 59- Mil. Serv: Entered as Midn, Naval Res, 43, released as Lt.(jg), 46, after serv. in Pac. Theatre, 44-45. Mem: Am. Legion; pres, C. of C. of Gloucester Co. Rel: Episcopal. Mailing Add: Gloucester, Va. 23061.

POINTER, SAM CLYDE, JR. R
V.Chmn, Ala. State Rep. Exec. Cmt.
b. Birmingham, Ala, 11/15/34; s. Sam Clyde Pointer and Elizabeth I. Brown P; m. 10/18/58 to Paula Purse; c. Minge C. and Sam C. Educ: Vanderbilt Univ, A.B, 55; Univ. Ala. Law Sch, LL.B, 57; N.Y. Univ. Grad. Sch. Law, LL.M. in Taxation, 58; Founder's scholarship; Kenneson fel; Phi Beta Kappa; Phi Eta Sigma; Farrah Order of Jurisp; bd. ed, Ala. Law Rev; Sigma Chi; Phi Delta Phi. Polit. & Govt. Pos: Del, State and Co. Rep. Conv, Ala, 62, 64, 66 & 68; ballot security officer, Rep. Party of Ala, 63-67, legal counsel, 65-; mem, Ala. Rep. State Exec. Cmt, 64-, v.chmn, 65-; mem, Jefferson Co. Rep. Exec. Cmt, 65; city attorney, Mountain Brook, 65-; alternate del, Rep. Nat. Conv, 68. Bus. & Prof. Pos; Assoc, Brown & Pointer, Attorneys, Birmingham, 57-60; partner, Brown, Pointer & Pointer, 60- Mil. Serv: Pvt, Army, 57, Maj, Res, currently. Publ: Miscellaneous articles, Ala. Law Rev, 56-57; General Election Manual for Poll Officials, 3 ed, 64, 66 & 68. Mem: Am, Ala. and Birmingham Bar Asns; Am. Judicature Soc; Nat. Inst. Munic. Law Officers; Panel of Arbitrators, Fed. Mediation and Conciliation Serv; ROA; Rotary; C. of C; dir, Ala. Found. Speech and Hearing. Outstanding Grad. of Inn, Phi Delta Phi. Rel: Episcopal. Legal Res: 4027 Winston Way, Birmingham, Ala. 35213. Mailing Add: 807 Massey Bldg, Birmingham, Ala. 35203.

POIZNER, JOSEPH JACOB D
Chmn, Third Cong. Dist. Dem. Party, Kans.
b. Russia, 6/10/05; s. Jacob Poizner and Sarah Campbell P; m. 11/29/31 to Bess Mnookin, wid. 11/29/61; c. Sherman and Michael; m. 4/30/65 to Dorothy Supica Owens. Educ: Kans. City Sch. Law, LL.B, 29. Polit. & Govt. Pos: Dep. adminstr. war bonds, U.S. Treas. Dept, 42-43; dep. attorney, Wyandotte Co, Kans, 43-45; mem, Kans. State Hwy. Cmn, 58-62; chmn, Wyandotte Co. Dem. Cent. Cmt, 64-66; dep. city attorney, Kansas City, 65-66; chmn, Third Cong. Dist. Dem. Party, 68-; mem, Kans. Water Resources Bd, 68- Bus. & Prof. Pos: Controller and v.pres, Helzberg's Diamond Shop, 44-49. Mil. Serv: Entered as Pvt, Kans. State Guard, released as 1st Lt, 46, after serv. as Adj, Third Bn. Mem: Wyandotte Co, Kans, Mo. and Am. Bar Asns, Interstate Cmn. Practitioner; Nat. Soc. Pub. Accts; B'nai B'rith; Army Asn. U.S; Kansas City Area C. of C.(pres, 69-); Kans. State C. of C. Rel: Jewish. Legal Res: 117 Lombardy Dr, Kansas City, Kans. 66102. Mailing Add: 645 Ann Avenue Bldg, Kansas City, Kans. 66101.

POKORNY, FRANK R. D
b. Cleveland, Ohio, 1924; married; c. Three. Educ: John Carroll Univ; Clevland-Marshall Law Sch, LL.B, 55. Polit. & Govt. Pos: Ohio State Rep, 59-68; del, Dem. Nat. Conv, 68. Bus. & Prof. Pos: Actuary, Workmen's Compensation Serv. Co. Mil. Serv: Army. Mailing Add: 7039 Brecksville Rd, Independence, Ohio 44131. (1967)

POLACK, ROBERT R
Chmn, La. Young Rep. Fedn.
b. Waltham, Mass, 3/31/45; s. Joseph Albert Polack and Ann Godchaux P; single. Educ: Princeton Univ, A.B, 67; La. State Univ. Law Sch, 67-69; Phi Alpha Delta; Cloister Inn of Princeton Univ. Polit. & Govt. Pos: Pres, Princeton Conservative Club, 64-65; exec. secy, La. Young Rep. Fedn, 64, 67-68, chmn, 68-; exec. dir, Sixth Dist. Rep. Party, La, 65; del, Young Rep. Nat. Conv, 65, 67 & 69; pres, Baton Rouge Young Rep, La, 67; mem, East Baton Rouge Parish Rep. Exec. Cmt, 67-; treas, Col. Rep. Nat. Cmt, 67-69; alternate del, Rep. Nat. Conv, 68; dir, La. Rep. Polit. Action Bd, 68- Outstanding La. Young Rep, 67. Rel: Jewish. Mailing Add: 4332 Claycut Rd, Baton Rouge, La. 70806.

POLANCO-ABREU, SANTIAGO D
b. Bayamón, P.R, 10/30/20; s. Santiago Polanco and Ana Abreu de P; m. 1944 to Viola Orsini. Educ: Univ. P.R, B.A, 41, LL.B, 43. Polit. & Govt. Pos: Legal adv, Tax Court, P.R, 43; P.R. State Rep, 48-64, chmn. cmt. finance, P.R. House Rep, v.chmn. cmt. interior govt. appointments and impeachment proc, mem. cmt. rules and calendar, chmn, judiciary cmt, 52-56, speaker, 63; mem, P.R. Constitutional Conv, 51-52; resident cmnr. of P.R. in Wash, D.C, 65-68. Bus. & Prof. Pos: Practice of law, Isabela and San Juan, P.R, 44-62. Publ: Political Status of Puerto Rico, Brookings Inst, 65; 'Economic Development of Puerto Rico,' Vital Speeches, 9/65. Mem: Fed, Am. and P.R. Bar Asns; P.R. Atheneum; Asn. of Am. Writers; Am. Soc. of Writers; hon. mem, P.R. Bar Asn. in New York; Asn. for Liberty and Democracy; Rotary; Lions; PanAm. Gun Club. Target Shooting Award; Citizen of the Year Award, Inst. of P.R, N.Y, 64. Rel: Catholic. Mailing Add: Corchado St, Isabela, P.R. 00662. (1967)

POLAND, BILL MERLE D
Alaska State Sen.
b. Artesia, N.Mex, 7/7/12; s. William Poland and Mary Clark P; m. 1/1/49 to Kathryn Eleanor Kennedy; c. Bradley Melvin, Patrick Kennedy, Kathleen (Mrs. Theodore R. Carlsen) and Shannon Elizabeth. Educ: Univ. Kans, 31-33. Polit. & Govt. Pos: City mgr, Kodiak, Alaska, 57-64; chmn, adv. bd, Alaska Dept. Fish & Game, 58-62, mem, 62-; Alaska State Rep, 65-66, chmn, Local Govt. Cmt. and mem, Resources Cmt, Alaska State House of Rep, 65-66; Alaska State Sen, 67-, mem, Local Govt. Cmt. and State Affairs Cmt, Alaska State Senate, 67-68 and Commerce Cmt. and Resources Cmt, 69- Bus. & Prof. Pos: Self-employed serv. sta, Kans, 34-40; paymaster, Seims-Drake, Kodiak, Alaska, 40-41; supt. fuel depot, Kodiak Naval Sta, 41-47; self-employed, big game guiding and outfitting, 47-57 & 64-; bus. mgr, Barr & Assocs. Consult. Engrs, 65. Mem: Elks; C. of C; Kodiak Island Guides Asn; League of Alaska Cities. Legal Res: 135 Rezanoff Dr, Kodiak, Alaska 99615. Mailing Add: Box 45, Kodiak, Alaska 99615.

POLANSKY, DANIEL J. R
Treas, Kings. Co. Rep. Cmt, N.Y.
b. Brooklyn, N.Y, 5/4/06; s. Harry Polansky and Minnie Cantor P; m. 6/28/31 to Eva Bresler; c. Edwin Herbert and Sanford. Educ: St. Lawrence Univ, LL.B, 27; Kappa Phi Sigma. Polit. & Govt. Pos: Asst. attorney gen, N.Y. State Dept. Law, 44-63, asst. attorney gen. in charge of labor bur, 63-; chmn. bd. dirs, 13th Assembly Dist. Rep. Club, 51-64, 42nd Assembly Dist. Rep. Club, 64-; alternate del, Rep. Nat. Conv, 56 & 64; Presidential Elector, Rep. Party, N.Y, 68; treas, 42nd Dist. Kings Co. Rep. Cmt, currently. Mem: Cmt. Labor and Indust. Rels, Brooklyn Bar Asn; C. of C; Canarsie Lodge, B'nai B'rith; Vanderveer Gardens Civic Asn. Cong. Selective Serv. Medal, 46; Vanderveer Gardens Civic Asn. Citation, 60; B'nai B'rith Citation, 63. Rel: Jewish. Mailing Add: 966 E. 104th St, Brooklyn, N.Y. 11236.

POLASKI, FRANK D
Pa. State Rep.
b. Erie, Pa, 12/19/04; s. Michael Polaski and Mary Orlemanski P; m. to Rose Tomczak; c. Four. Educ: Univ. Mich, A.B; Northwest. Univ. Law Sch, J.D; Gannon Col. Sch. of Bus. Admin. Polit. & Govt. Pos: Mem, War Refugee Relief Cmt, 39-42; Pa. State Rep, 64-. Bus. & Prof. Pos: Off. mgr. Mil. Serv: Air Force, 42-45. Mem: Ill. Bar; Eastside Fedn; Am. Legion. Mailing Add: 1051 E. 24th St, Erie, Pa. 16503.

POLEN, J. DEAN D
b. New Alexandria, Ohio, 8/13/00; s. John W. Polen and Eva B. Criswell P; m. to Thelma M. Wood; c. Dean W. and Robert C. Polit. & Govt. Pos: Cmnr, Pa. Hist. and Mus. Cmn, 59-, mem, Pa. State Bd. Pub. Welfare, 59-, Pa. Indust. Develop. Authority, 56- and Pa. Cmn. on Interstate Coop; chmn, West. Wash. Co. Sch. Authority; Pa. State Rep, 59-66, 49-56, 45-46 and 41-42; mem, Wash. Co. Dem. Exec. Cmt, 36-66, chmn, Wash. Co. Dem. Cmt, 62-63; mem, Wash. Co. Bd. Sch. Dirs, 37-52 and Independence Twp. Sch. Bd, 33-51. Bus. Pos: Dir, Cong. Life Ins. Co. Phila; independent coal, oil and gas operator, 46-66; employee, Pittsburgh and W.Va. Rwy, 16-46. Mem: Traffic and Transportation Asn. Pittsburgh; Odd Fellows; Moose; Order of R.R. Telegraphers; Pa. Hist. Asn; bd. dirs, Bradford House Hist. Asn. and Wash. Co.

Tuberc. and Health Asn; Pa. Citizens Coun; West. Pa. Conservancy; Avella C. of C; YMCA. Rel: Presbyterian. Mailing Add: Morningside Dr, Avella, Pa. 15312. (1967)

POLEN, ROBERT CAYLOR R
W.Va. State Del.
b. Moundsville, W.Va, 7/15/35; s. Lloyd Polen and Iva Caylor P; m. 4/11/57 to Kathern Rose Kramer; c. Mark Allen, John Robert and Cynthia June. Educ: W.Va. Univ, 53-56. Polit. & Govt. Pos: W.Va. State Del, Marshall Co, 66- Bus. & Prof. Pos: Research chemist, PPG Industs, Natrium, W.Va, 56-67 and qual. control supvr, 67- Mem: 4-H Leader, Moundsville Beavers Club; Sanford Grade Sch. PTA; Marshall Co. Pin Wearers Asn; pres, Marshall Co. 4-H Leaders Asn. Rel: Baptist. Mailing Add: 1701 Third St, Moundsville, W.Va. 26041.

POLHILL, MAXINE LAUGHLIN R
V.Chmn. in Charge Women's Div, Ill. Rep. State Cent. Cmt.
b. Industry, Ill, 8/8/08; d. Edward Theodore Laughlin and Jessie Aline Holmes L; m. 6/25/31 to Ray Burdett Polhill; c. Allen R, Ray L. and Lee N. Educ: West. Ill. State Teachers Col, B.Ed, 29; Home Econ. Club; Diana Klub; Delta Kappa Gamma; G.A.A. Polit. & Govt. Pos: Chmn, Carroll Co. Rep. Party, 44-63; pres, Fedn. Rep. Womens Club's of Carroll Co, 45-47; committeewoman, 16th Cong. Dist, 61-; v.chmn. in charge Women's Div, Ill. Rep. State Cent. Cmt, 67- Bus. & Prof. Pos: Teacher home econ, High Sch, Stockton, Ill, 29-31. Mem: Am. Asn. Univ. Women; Eastern Star; PTA; Fedn. Women's Clubs; Fedn. Rep. Women's Clubs; Civic Music Asn; Carroll Co. Welfare Cmt, Wysox Twp. Libr. Bd. Rel: Methodist. Mailing Add: 214 W. Fifth, Milledgeville, Ill. 61051.

POLI, NANCY CAROL D
b. Almo, Idaho, 4/30/30; d. Dante Ricci and Izaette Edwards R; m. 11/7/48 to Felice John Poli, Jr; c. Stephen John (deceased), Carol Izaette and Catherine Lorraine. Educ: Yerington High Sch, Nev, grad, 48. Polit. & Govt. Pos: Del, Dem. Nat. Conv, 68. Publ: Column in Nev. Farm Bur. Agr. and Livestock J. Mem: State womens chmn, Nev. Farm Bur. Fedn; pres, Lyon Co. Cancer Soc. Rel: Latter-day Saint. Mailing Add: Box 1012, Yerington, Nev. 89447.

POLICASTRO, PAUL D
N.J. State Assemblyman
b. Newark, N.J, 8/29/00; s. Antonio Policastro and Rosa Ammiano P; m. 7/1/49 to Sarah Martin. Educ: Rutgers Univ, LL.B, 24. Polit. & Govt. Pos: Mem, bd. of adjustment and zoning bd, Newark, N.J, 53-54; trustee, Essex Co. Youth House, 60-62; N.J. State Assemblyman, 62-, asst. majority leader, 66, majority leader, 67. Bus. & Prof. Pos: Lawyer, 24- Mil. Serv: Pvt, Air Force, 42-43. Mem: Essex Co. Bar Asn; Elks Lodge 21. Rel: Catholic. Mailing Add: 7 Crescent Court, Newark, N.J. 07106.

POLING, B. NOEL R
b. Kenna, 12/17/27; s. James B. Poling and Ada Ernestine Skeen P; m. 11/4/50 to Evelyn M. Harpold; c. Michael Noel, Jenni Le, Stephen B. and Randy. Educ: Chicago Sch. of Engr. Polit. & Govt. Pos: Former mem, Jackson Co. Rep. Cmt, W.Va; former pres, Young Rep. Club Jackson Co; Asst. State Fire Marshal, 57-59; W.Va. State Del, 60-68; alternate del, Rep. Nat. Conv, 68. Bus. & Prof. Pos: Elec. engr. and appliance dealer. Mil. Serv: Army, 2 years. Mem: AF&AM; Rotary; Odd Fellows; Jaycees; IBEW. Rel: Baptist. Mailing Add: Main St, Ripley, W.Va. 25271. (1967)

POLING, CLARENCE C. D
b. Needmore, Ind, 7/29/99; married; c. Two. Educ: Pub. Schs. Polit. & Govt. Pos: N.Dak. State Rep, 51-66; Co. Cmnr, presently. Bus. & Prof. Pos: Farmer. Mailing Add: Williston, N.Dak. 58801.

POLIQUIN, ARTHUR D
N.H. State Rep.
b. Nashua, N.H, 11/27/10; married; c. One. Educ: Detroit Col. Polit. & Govt. Pos: Alderman-at-large, N.H, two years; alderman, 12 years; former clerk and moderator; N.H. State Rep, presently. Mem: Steward at Club Soc; pres. Club Soc, 25 years; former pres. Garde Rochambeau; dir. St. Jean Club; dir. St. Jean Soc; former pres. Soc. Assocs, Inc. Rel: Catholic. Mailing Add: 6 Ninth St, Nashua, N.H. 03060.

POLITANO, FRANK JAMES D
Chmn, Somerset Co. Dem. Party, N.J.
b. N.Y.C. 10/26/18; s. Frank Politano and Nellie Suriano P; m. 10/24/37 to Antoinette Burolla; c. Carol Ann (Mrs. Cicerelle), Linda (Mrs. Lunger), Jaime, Robert and Diane. Educ: Fordham Univ, 36-37. Polit. & Govt. Pos: Mem, City Planning Bd, Manville, N.J, 50-53; secy, Zoning Bd. Adjust, Manville, 51-54; pres, Bd. Health, Manville, 51-54; mem. adv. bd, N.J. Planning Cmn, 54-55; munic. chmn, Manville Dem. Party, 52-54; mem, Somerset Co. Planning Bd, 65-67; chmn, Somerset Co. Dem. party, 66- Bus. & Prof. Pos: Indust. Eng. Div, Johns-Manville Corp, Manville, N.J, 41-55; pres-broker, Garden State Realty Co, Somerville, 55-; confidential aide to Cmnr. of Labor and Indust, Trenton, 67-; exec. dir, N.J. Alliance of Businessmen, New Brunswick, 68- Mil. Serv: Entered as Seaman 2nd Class, Navy, 43, released as Specialist 1st Class, after serv. in Pac. Theatre, 43-45; Am. Theatre Medal; Pac. Theatre Medal. Mem: Somerset Co. Bd. Realtors (past pres); Am. Legion; VFW. Rel: Roman Catholic. Legal Res: 770 Old Farm Rd, Somerville, N.J. 08876. Mailing Add: 208 E. Main St, Somerville, N.J. 08876.

POLITZER, S. ROBERT D
Chmn, Marin Co. Dem. Cent. Cmt, Calif.
b. N.Y.C, 9/16/29; s. Sigmund Politzer and Emma Linzer P; m. 12/6/57 to Olive Webb; c. Cassandra Deborah, Nicholas Charles (deceased) and Adam Webb. Educ: Cooper Union Art Sch, N.Y.C, Archit, 52; Columbia Univ. Sch. of Archit, 52-54. Polit. & Govt. Pos: Pres, Sausalito Dem. Club, Calif, 63-64; chmn, Marin Co. Coun. of Dem. Clubs, 64-65; first cong. dist. dir, Calif. Dem. Coun, 65-67; v.chmn, Marin Co. Dem. Cent. Cmt, 67-68, chmn, 68-; co-chmn, Sixth Cong. Dist. Dem. Caucus, 68-; mem. exec. cmt, Calif. Dem. State Cent. Cmt, 68- Bus. & Prof. Pos: Designer and job capt, John Carl Warnecks & Assocs, 61-63; project architect, Anshen & Allen, Architects, 63-68; prin, archit. practice, 68- Mem: Trustee, Sausalito Found. Rel: Jewish. Mailing Add: 29 Glen Dr, Sausalito, Calif. 91965.

POLK, NORMAN E. D
b. Somerset Co, Md, 8/12/02; married. Educ: Worcester Co. Pub. Schs. Polit. & Gov. Pos: Md. State Del, 58-67; Md. State Cmn. on the Aging; Navy Civilian Adv. Coun. Bus. & Prof. Pos: Lumberman and Farmer. Mem: Pocomoke C. of C; Bd. of Dir, McCready Mem. Hosp; former Pres, Delmarva Lumbermen's Asn; Farm Bur; former Pres, Pocomoke Rotary Club; Elks; Terrapin Club. Rel: Trustee, Pitts Creek Presbyterian Church. Mailing Add: Pocomoke, Md. 21851. (1967)

POLLACK, WILLIAM E. R
b. Chicago, Ill, 12/2/08; c. Three. Educ: Northwest. Univ, B.S, Polit. Sci, 30; Law Sch, J.D, 33. Polit. & Govt. Pos: Ill. State Rep, 50-68, Rep. Whip, Ill. House Rep, 69th, 70th and 71st Gen. Assemblies, minority leader, 72nd and 73rd Gen. Assemblies; dir, 33rd Ward Regular Rep. Club, Inc. Bus. & Prof. Pos: Gen. practice of law. Mem: Am, Ill. and Chicago Bar Asns; Mason; Shrine. Selected by the Legis. Correspondents Asn, as outstanding legis. in 71st Gen. Assembly. Mailing Add: 3829 N. Seeley Ave, Chicago, Ill. 60618. (1967)

POLLARD, FRED G. D
Lt. Gov, Va.
b. Richmond, Va, 5/7/18; s. Robert Nelson Pollard and Mary Faulkner Butler P; m. 12/1/62 to Jane Elliott De Jarnette; c. Lewis Butler, Nelson Carter, Emily Rosamond and Elizabeth Dozier Lee. Educ: Univ. Va, B.A, 40, LL.B, 42. Polit. & Govt. Pos: Va. State Del, 50-65; Lt. Gov, Va, 66-; del, Dem. Nat. Conv, 68. Bus. & Prof. Pos: Attorney, partner, Williams, Mullen & Christan, 46- Mil. Serv: Lt, Navy, 42-46. Rel: Presbyterian. Mailing Add: 510 State Planters Bank Bldg, Richmond, Va. 23219.

POLLARD, ODELL R
State Chmn, Rep. Nat. Cmt, Ark.
b. Union Hill, Ark, 4/29/27; s. Joseph F. Pollard and Beulah Scantlin P; m. 2/8/53 to Sammy Lane Lewis; c. Laura Lane, Paula Lynn and Mark. Educ: Miss. Col; Tulane Univ; Univ. Ark, LL.B. Polit. & Govt. Pos: Former mem. gen. counsel, White Co. Rep. Cmt, Ark, $2\frac{1}{2}$ years, mem, 58-; mem, Rep. Exec. Cmt, Ark, 60-; state chmn, Rep. Nat. Cmt, currently; del, Rep. Nat. Conv, 68. Bus. & Prof. Pos: Attorney. Mem: Am, Ark. and White Co. Bar Asns. Rel: Methodist. Legal Res: 407 W. Race Ave, Searcy, Ark. 72143. Mailing Add: P.O. Box 36, Searcy, Ark. 72143.

POLLARD, VIOLET McDOUGALL D
b. Glengarry Co, Ont, Can, 7/17/89; d. Peter P. McDougall and Ellen Robertson M; m. 7/31/33 to John Garland Pollard; wid. Educ: Regina Col, Sask. and George Wash. Univ. Law Sch; Kappa Beta Pi. Polit. & Govt. Pos: Exec. secy. to four successive gov, Va, 19-33; alternate del. or del, Dem. Nat. Conv, 36-, mem. Platform Cmt; Dem. nat. committeewoman, Va, 40-68; chmn, Inter-Agency Cmt. on Recreation, 53-56. Bus. & Prof. Pos: Assoc. dir, Va. Mus. Fine Arts, 40-56. Mem: Pres, Richmond Woman's Club, 61-63; v.pres, Historic Richmond Found, 60-61; life mem. Asn. for Preservation of Va. Antiquities; King and Queen Hist. Soc. and Va. Mus. of Fine Arts; bd. mem, Richmond Symphony Orchestra; Country Club of Va; 2300 Club; Colony Club. Rel: Presbyterian. Mailing Add: 1015 W. Franklin St, Richmond, Va. 23220.

POLLARD, WILLIAM DONALD 'BILL' D
Treas, Benton Co. Dem. Cent. Cmt, Wash.
b. Baker, Ore, 12/17/37; s. William Henry Pollard and Claudia I. Wallace P; m. 1/14/61 to Hope Esperanza Maria Cayetana Gonzales; c. William Donald, Jr. and Richard Martin. Educ: Univ. Wash, 56-59; Univ. Ore. Postgrad. Exten, Portland, 63; Mgt. Center. of Cambridge, Burlington, Mass, 69. Polit. & Govt. Pos: Dem. committeeman, Precinct 51, Benton Co, Wash, 66-; treas, Benton Co. Cent. Cmt, 66-; Richland chmn, Kennedy for Pres. Cmt, 68; del, Benton Co. Dem. Conv, 68; del, Fourth Dist. Dem. Conv, 68; del, Wash. State Dem. Conv, 68; alternate del, Dem. Nat. Conv, 68. Bus. & Prof. Pos: Clerk-typist, Burns and Roe, Inc, Richland, Wash, 61-62, design draftsman, 62-64; sr. elec. designer, Vitro Corp. Am, Richland and N.Y, 64-68; eng. designer, Atlantic Richfield Hanford Co, Richland, 68- Mem: Richland Commun. Coun. (chmn, 68); Tri-City Latin Am. Asn; bd. dirs, Gr. Rural Opportunities in Wash, Inc; Dem. Seeking a Newer World; Wash. Citizens for Migrant Affairs; Toastmasters Int; Benton Co. Dem. Club; Jaycees. Rel: Unitarian. Mailing Add: 519 Cascade, Richland, Wash. 99352.

POLLEY, IRA
Supt. of Pub. Instr, Mich.
b. Haines, Alaska, 6/18/17; m. 8/22/53 to Margaret Mary Foley; c. Vincent Ira and John William. Educ: Ind. Univ, B.A, 38; Soc. Sci. Research Coun. fels, 41-42 & 47; spec. student, London Sch. of Econ, 53-54; Univ. Minn, Ph.D, 54; Phi Beta Kappa; Pi Sigma Alpha. Polit. & Govt. Pos: Admin. asst, Off. of Civilian Defense, 42; from asst. to assoc. procedural analyst, War Prod. Bd, 42; field exam. and indust. rels. analyst, Nat. Labor Rels. Bd, Minneapolis, Minn. and Wash, D.C, 42-47 & 48-51; regional dir. and regional chmn, U.S. Wage Stabilization Bd, Region Eight, Minneapolis, 51-53; budget exam. for educ, Dept. of Admin, Mich, 56-59, exec. asst. to state controller and budget exam. for higher educ, 59-60, Acting State Controller, 60, State Controller and secy. to state admin. bd, 60-62; exec. secy, Constitutional Reform Study Cmn, 60; dir. of research and staff, Gov. Adv. Cmt. on Reorgn. of State Govt, 60-61; exec. secy, Constitutional Conv. Planning Cmn, chmn, Mich. Cmn. on Interstate Coop, mem, State Bldg. Cmn, chmn, Gov. Coord. Cmt. on Area Redevelop. Admin. and mem, Steering Cmt. Constitutional Conv. Coop. Cmt, Lansing, 61; exec. dir, Mich. Coun. of State Col. Pres. and secy, Mich. Coord. Coun. for Pub. Higher Educ, 62-; Supt. of Pub. Instr, Mich, 66- Bus. & Prof. Pos: Teaching Asst, Univ. Minn, 38-41; asst. prof, Mich. State Univ, 47-48; research assoc, dept. of pub. admin, Wayne State Univ, 54-55; vis. assoc. prof, dept. of polit. sci. and acting assoc. dir, Pub. Admin. Center, Univ. Minn, 55-56; lectr, dept. of polit. sci, Mich. State Univ, winter 64. Publ: Wage Stabilization in Region 8; co-auth, Constitutional Revision; 'Program Development and Control,' In: Changing Perspectives in Public Administra-

tion. Mem: Am. Polit. Sci. Asn; Am. Soc. Pub. Admin; panel mem, Am. Arbit. Asn; Mayor Bowerman's Cmt. on Efficiency in City Govt; bd. of gov, Gr. Mich. Found. Legal Res: 935 Audubon Rd, East Lansing, Mich. 48823. Mailing Add: Dept. of Education, Lansing, Mich. 48903.

POLLOCK, HOWARD W. R
U.S. Rep, Alaska
b. Chicago, Ill, 4/11/20; m. to Maryanne Passmore; c. Ron, Pam Randy, Patty and Ricky. Educ: Univ. Houston Sch. of Law, LL.B, 55; Mass. Inst. Tech, Sloan Fel, 59-60, M.S. in indust. mgt, 60; nat. pres, Phi Theta Kappa, 40; nat. v.pres, Am. Law Student Asn, 54, nat. pres, 54-55; chmn. bd. gov, 55. Polit. & Govt. Pos: Territorial Rep, Alaska Territorial Legis, 53-55; dir, Oper. Statehood, Alaska and Oper. Statehood, Hawaii, 58-59; dir, Alaska World Affairs Coun, 60-65; former cand. for Rep. nomination for Gov, Alaska; Alaska State Sen, 60-62 & 64-66, Minorty Whip, Alaska State Senate, 64-65; mem, Alaska State Rep. Cent. Cmt. and committeeman, Rep. South-cent. Dist; U.S. Rep, Alaska, 67-; del, Rep. Nat. Conv, 68. Bus. & Prof. Pos: Personnel mgr, Mare Island Cafeteria Syst, Vallejo, Calif, 44-45; sales mgr, Zippet Venetian Mfg. Corp, 46-47; salary and wage analyst, Civilian Personnel Off, Ft. Richardson, 48-49; civilian personnel officer, Ft. Richardson and Hq, U.S. Army, Alaska, 49-51; chief contract and claims dept, Morrison-Knudsen Co, White Alice Commun. Syst, 55-56; pres, Falcon Alaska Oil Co, corp. secy. and legal counsel, North. Serv, Inc, subsidiary Fed. Elec. Corp, maintenance and oper, White Alice Commun. Syst, 57-59; pres, Rural-Tel; practicing attorney and sr. mem, Pollock and Assocs, 60-65; dir, Alaskan Seafoods, Inc. and pres, Alaska Gold and Other Prod, Inc, 60-65. Mil. Serv: Engr-Apprentice, Ordinary Seaman, Maritime Serv, 36-37, Seaman, Navy, 41, released as Lt. Comdr, 46, after serv. overseas. Mem: Alaska, Anchorage, Tex. and Am. Bar Asns; 1st pres, Anchorage UN Asn, 56; pres, Alaskan Prospectors Soc, 50; life mem, U.S. Jaycees; Anchorage C. of C; K. of C; Elks; Kiwanis Int; Am. Legion; VFW; Alaska Native Brotherhood. Outstanding student, Univ. Houston, 55; grad. of year, Phi Delta Phi, 55; selected 1 of 10 Outstanding Young Men in U.S, U.S. Jr. C. of C, 55; admitted to practice law before U.S. Supreme Court, 60; George Washington Honor Medal, Am. Freedom Found, 66; 4 big game trophies honored in Records of N.Am. Big Game, polar bear, grizzly bear, mountain sheep and caribou. Rel: Catholic. Legal Res: Anchorage, Alaska. Mailing Add: 1507 Longworth House Office Bldg, Washington, D.C. 20515.

POLLOCK, STEPHEN W, SR. R
N.H. State Rep.
b. Locse, Hungary, 10/9/93; married; c. Two; Two grandchildren. Educ: Bus. Sch. Polit. & Govt. Pos: Retired dep. chief, Keene Fire Dept, N.H; mem. city coun, Keene, N.H, 24-25 & 54-55; N.H. State Rep, 63- Mil. Serv: Mexican Border Serv, Bn. Sgt. Maj, 16; World War I, serv in France, 17-19, released as 2nd Lt. Mem: Life mem, Am. Legion (past comdr); life mem. Elks (past exalted ruler). Mailing Add: 34 Douglas St, Keene, N.H. 03431. (1967)

POMEROY, BENJAMIN SHERWOOD R
Mem, Minn. Rep. State Cent. Cmt.
b. St. Paul, Minn, 4/24/11; s. Benjamin A. Pomeroy and Florence Anne Sherwood P; m. 6/25/38 to Margaret L. Lyon; c. Benjamin A, Sherwood R, Catherine Ann and Margaret Dawn. Educ: Iowa State Univ, D.V.M, 33; Cornell Univ, M.S, 34; Univ. Minn, Ph.D, 44; Phi Kappa Phi; Cardinal Key; Gamma Sigma Delta; Phi Zeta; Alpha Gamma Rho. Polit. & Govt. Pos: Chmn, Spec. Cmts. to Nat. Poultry Improv. Plans, U.S. Dept. of Agr, 48, mem, Adv. Cmt. to Poultry Inspection, Consumer & Mkt. Serv, 63; blockworker, 12th precinct, 10th Ward, Minn, 56-59, precinct officer, 59-60; chmn, 43rd South. Legis. Dist. Rep. Party, 60-61; chmn, Fourth Dist. Rep. Cmt, 61-63 & 67-69; mem, Minn. Rep. State Exec. Cmt, 61-65 & 67-69; chmn, Ramsey Co. Rep. Cmt, 61-65, mem, 65-; del, Rep. Nat. Conv, 64; mem, Adv. Cmt. on Vet. Med, Food and Drug Admin, 65; mem, Minn. Rep. State Cent. Cmt, 65- Bus. & Prof. Pos: Instr, asst. prof. and assoc. prof, Col. of Vet. Med, Univ. Minn, St, Paul, 34-48, prof, 48- and head dept. vet. bact. and pub. health, 53- Publ: Diseases and Parasites of Poultry, (w. Barger and Card), 58; contributing auth, Diseases of Poultry, Biester and Schwarte, Iowa State Col. Press, 65. Mem: Sigma Xi; Am, Minn. and Twin City Vet. Med. Asns; Soc. Exp. Biol. & Med; Am. Acad. of Microbiol; Am. Col. of Vet. Bact; Poultry Sci. Asn; St. Anthony Park Asn. Rel: Presbyterian. Mailing Add: 1443 Raymond Ave, St. Paul, Minn. 55108.

POMEROY, ELWAINE FRANKLIN R
Kans. State Sen.
b. Topeka, Kans, 6/4/33; s. Charles Franklin Pomeroy and Ada Frances Owen P; m. 9/30/50 to Joanne Carolyn Bunge; c. Janella Ruth, Duane Franklin and Carl Fredrick. Educ: Washburn Univ. of Topeka, A.B, 55; Washburn Univ. Sch. Law, LL.B, 57, J.D, 69; Pi Gamma Mu; Pi Kappa Delta; Tau Delta Pi; Delta Theta Phi. Polit. & Govt. Pos: Rep. precinct committeeman, Eighth Precinct, Eighth Ward, Kans, 61-; city attorney, Silver Lake, 64-; Kans. State Sen, 69- Bus. & Prof. Pos: Attorney-at-law, Topeka, Kans, 57-; dir. and counsel, Topeka Teachers Credit Union, 57-; pres, Topeka Escrow Serv, Inc, 60-; sr. partner, Pomeroy and Pomeroy, 64-; legal counsel, Kans. Hwy. Credit Union, 64- Publ: Contrib, Principles of Accounting, Pittman Publ. Co, 57. Mem: Topeka, Kans. and Am. Bar Asns; Am. Judicature Soc; Delta Theta Phi; Mason; Moose; Eagles; Breakfast Optimist Club. Rel: Lutheran. Legal Res: 1619 Jewell, Topeka, Kans. 66604. Mailing Add: 1415 Topeka Ave, Topeka, Kans. 66612.

POMEROY, ROBERT WATSON R
b. Buffalo, N.Y, 6/21/02; s. Robert W. Pomeroy and Lucy Bemis P; m. 9/4/30 to Estelle Bassett; c. Margaret (Mrs. Haldane) and Robert W, III. Educ: Yale Univ, Ph.B, 24. Polit. & Govt. Pos: Dir. civilian defense, Dutchess Co, N.Y, 41-42; state vet. counselor, N.Y, 46-47; N.Y. State Assemblyman, Dutchess Co, 48-64; N.Y. State Sen, 65-66; del, N.Y. State Constitutional Conv, 67. Mil. Serv: Entered as Pvt, Army, 42, released as Capt, 45, after serv. in Field Artil, ETO; ETO Ribbon. Mem: Am. Legion; hon. life mem, Am. Cancer Soc, N.Y. State Div; bd. dirs, Nat. Audubon Soc. Mailing Add: Wassaic, N.Y. 12592.

POMMER, MERLE CLAUSEN R
S.Dak. State Rep.
b. Castlewood, S.Dak, 12/19/10; s. Ollie Jay Pommer and Dora N. Clausen P; m. 6/15/40 to Mary E. Hoschied; c. Lana M. and James Brooks. Educ: High Sch, Castlewood, S.Dak, 25-29. Polit. & Govt. Pos: Pres, Hamlin Co. Young Rep, S.Dak, 31-40; S.Dak. State Rep, Dist. 36, 54-, chmn, Legis. Agr. Cmt, 58-; pres, Watertown Fed. Land Bank Asn, 56-59. Bus. & Prof. Pos: Farmer and cattle feeder. Mem: Chmn, Hamlin Co. Livestock Asn; mem. and past master, Sioux Valley Masonic Lodge 125. Rel: Presbyterian. Mailing Add: Castlewood, S.Dak. 57223.

POMMERENING, GLEN E. R
b. Milwaukee, Wis, 9/27/27. Educ: Univ. Wis, B.S, 50, LL.B, 53. Polit. & Govt. Pos: Wis. State Assemblyman, 54-66. Bus. & Prof. Pos: Attorney. 1967 Legal Res: Wauwatosa, Wis. No mailing address available. (1967)

PONEC, GERALD ROBERT D
V.chmn, Cudahy Sr. Dem. Unit, Wis.
b. Cudahy, Wis, 5/4/39; s. Jerry A. Ponec and Marie Trzecinski P; single. Educ: Spencerian Bus. Col, 57-58; Marquette Univ, night sch, 64. Polit. & Govt. Pos: Treas, Milwaukee Co. Young Dem. Clubs, Wis, 61-62; state campaign coordinator and exec. v.chmn, Young Dem. Clubs of Wis, 62-63, nat. committeeman, 63-66; chmn, Seventh Sen. Dist. Young Dem. Club, 62-64; alternate del, Dem. Nat. Conv, 64; chmn, Cudahy Sr. Dem. Unit, Wis, 64-69, v.chmn, 69-; alderman, Cudahy, 66- Bus. & Prof. Pos: Asst. mgr, Cudahy Schiff's, 60-62; asst. mgr, Computer Payroll Dept, Louis Allis Co, Milwaukee, 66. Mem: K. of C; Eagles; Wis. Sr. Citizens; Holy Name Soc. & Choir; Jaycees. Rel: Roman Catholic. Mailing Add: 5301 S. Lake Dr, Cudahy, Wis. 53110.

PONS, VICTOR MANUEL, JR. Popular Dem, P.R.
b. Rio Piedras, P.R, 4/5/35; s. Victor M. Pons and Carolina Núñez P; m. 2/26/60 to Carmen Luisa Rexach; c. Carolina Sofia, Carmen Luisa, Victor Manuel and Juan Antonio. Educ: Swarthmore Col, 2 years; Univ. P.R, B.A. magna cum laude, 56, LL.B. magna cum laude, 59. Polit. & Govt. Pos: Mem, Coun. on Higher Educ, P.R. 66-; chmn, Kennedy for Pres. Cmt, P.R, 68; del, Dem. Nat. Conv, 68; mem. cent. coun, Popular Dem. Party, P.R, 68-69. Bus. & Prof. Pos: Assoc. attorney, Fiddler, Gonzalez & Rodriguez, 59-62, partner, 63- Publ: 'Not Guilty by Reason of Insanity (A Commentary on Article 293 of the Code of Criminal Procedure)', Revista Juridica, Univ. P.R, Vol. XXVII; 'Apportionment of Damages Under the Comparative Negligence Doctrine', Revista del Colegio de Abogados de P.R, Vol. XIX. Mem: P.R, Am. and Inter-Am. Bar Asns. Rel: Roman Catholic. Legal Res: H-26 Villa Caparra, Guaynabo, P.R. 00619. Mailing Add: G.P.O. Box P, San Juan, P.R. 00936.

PONSELL, WILLIAM KING D
b. Coffee Co, Ga, 3/5/94; s. Thomas Moses Ponsell and Julia Spivy P; m. 10/03/15 to Nora Ivy Chapman; c. J. T, Melba Rose Lott, Chester Chapman, King Franklin, Marie Annette. Educ: Jamestown Sch. Polit. & Govt. Pos: Ga. State Sen. (5th dist.), 61-66; 55-56. Bus. & Prof. Pos: Farmer. Rel: Baptist. Mailing Add: Waycross, Ga. 31501. (1967)

PONZIO, ARTHUR W. D
Chmn, Atlantic Co. Dem. Cmt, N.J.
b. Glassboro, N.J; s. Vincent Ponzio and Virginia Renna P; m. 9/20/47 to Mary Kondratow; c. Virginia, Arthur, Robert and Daniel. Educ: Atlantic City High Sch, N.J; U.S. Marine Corps, Spec. Training in Eng; Int. Correspondence Sch, eng. Polit. & Govt. Pos: Mem, Young Dem. of N.J; pres, First Ward Dem. Club; Freeholder, N.J; chmn, Atlantic City Munic. Cmt; chmn, Atlantic Co. Dem. Cmt, 66-; alternate del, Dem. Nat. Conv, 68. Bus. & Prof. Pos: Asst. city engr, Atlantic City, 20 years. Mil. Serv: Entered as Pvt, Marine Corps, released as Sgt. Mem: Marine Corps League; K. of C; Alki Club; Inlet Social & Athletic Club; Allied Dem. Club; CWV. Rel: Roman Catholic. Mailing Add: 216 S. New Hampshire Ave, Atlantic City, N.J. 08401. (1967)

POOL, PENTA PRICE R
V.Chairwoman, Eddy Co. Rep. Party, N.Mex.
b. Harlengen, Tex, 2/13/28; d. H. Frank Price and Penta Simmans Price Stallard; m. 12/17/49 to Fred Franklin Pool, Jr; c. Pamela Jane (Mrs. Meadors), Penny Lynn, Patti Ann and Fred F, III. Educ: Tex. Wesleyan Col, B.S, 49; Abilene Christian Col, 49-50. Polit. & Govt. Pos: V.chairwoman, Eddy Co. Rep. Party, N.Mex, 66-; alternate del, Rep. Nat. Conv, 68. Bus. & Prof. Pos: Sci. teacher, Carlsbad Schs, 69- Mem: Am. Asn. Univ. Women; Assistance League of Carlsbad. Rel: Church of Christ. Mailing Add: 1212 W. Riverside, Carlsbad, N.Mex. 88220.

POOLE, JAMES FORD D
b. Laurens, S.C, 4/12/36; s. Oliver R. Poole and Sara Miller P; m. 10/19/61 to Martha Ray Spann; c. Stephanie Diane and Heather Jane. Educ: Benedict Col, B.S, 59; Univ. Pa, grad, 63; Alpha Phi Alpha. Polit. & Govt. Pos: V.chmn, City Planning and Zoning Cmn, Pueblo, Colo, 64- Bus. & Prof. Pos: Pres, Allied Builders Corp, Colorado Springs, Colo. and Toro Y. Leon, Inc, Pueblo, currently; educ, financial and indust. consult, Pueblo, Colo, currently. Mil. Serv: Entered as E-1, Army, 59, released as E-5, 62, after serv. in ARADCOM Choral Group, 60-62; Good Conduct Medal. Mem: Nat. Asn. of Securities Dealers; Kiwanis; Commun. Welfare Coun. Rel: Unitarian. Mailing Add: 90 Fordham Circle, Pueblo, Colo. 81005.

POOLE, JERRY WALLACE R
Dep. Asst. Secy. for Cong. Liaison, Dept. of Health, Educ. & Welfare.
b. Muskogee, Okla. 2/12/24; s. Wallace Marion Poole and Rebecca Joyce Ryan P; m. 6/12/48 to Mary Jean Bornhofen; c. Lee Ryan, Lynn Ann and Gary Wallace. Educ: Okla. State Univ, 40-43; Northwest. Univ, B.S. and M.S; Phi Eta Sigma; Sigma Delta Chi; Scabbard & Blade; Kappa Sigma. Polit. & Govt. Pos: Rep. precinct committeeman, Maricopa Co, Ariz, 58-62; mem. exec. cmt, Ariz. Rep. State Cmt, 60-62; campaign mgr. for U.S. Rep. John J. Rhodes, Ariz, 58, 60 & 62; press secy. to U.S. Sen. Paul Fannin, Ariz, 64-67; dep. asst. secy. for cong. liaison, Dept. of Health, Educ. & Welfare, 69- Bus. & Prof. Pos: Reporter, Chicago Sun-Times, 48-50; pub. rels. asst, Northwest. Univ, 50-51; reporter, polit. ed. & Wash, D.C. correspondent, Phoenix Newspapers, 51-57; partner, Poole, Hervey Assocs, Phoenix, 57-59; pub. rels. dir, Ariz. Bank, 59-63; news bur. dir, San Diego Gas & Elec. Co, 63-65; asst. to pres, Am. Petroleum Inst, 67-69. Mil. Serv: Entered as Pvt, Army, 42, released as 1st Lt, 46, after serv. in 410th Inf. 103rd Div, 7th Army, European

Theater; Purple Heart; Bronze Star Medal; Combat Infantryman Ribbon; 3 Campaign Stars. Publ: Regular news and polit. commentary columnist, Ariz. Republic, 51-57. Mem: Wash. Prfnl. Chap, Sigma Delta Chi; Nat. Press Club; Capitol Hill Club; U.S. Senate Staff Club; Crofton, Md. Golf and Country Club; Sigma Delta Chi Outstanding Grad. Award, Northwest. Univ, 48. Rel: Episcopal. Mailing Add: 6320 67th Court, Riverdale, Md. 20840.

POOLE, WILL D
Ga. State Rep.
b. Pickens Co, Ga, 4/27/01; s. D. Patterson Poole and Arminda Fowler P; m. 6/11/24 to Myrtle Henson; c. Arminda Jane (Mrs. Robert Gilbert). Educ: Jones Sch. Polit. & Govt. Pos: Councilman, Jasper, Ga, 40-48; Ga. State Rep, 61- Bus. & Prof. Pos: Retail merchant. Mem: Mason; Lions. Rel: Baptist. Mailing Add: 787 Church St, Jasper, Ga. 30143. (1967)

POOR, ROBERT LAWRENCE R
Chmn, Putnam Co. Rep. Cmt, Ind.
b. Greencastle, Ind, 12/5/33; s. John Lawrence Poor and Edna Hillis P; m. 6/19/55 to Barbara Ann Fuson; c. Cynthia Lee and Lisa Ann. Educ: DePauw Univ, A.B, 55; Lambda Chi Alpha. Polit. & Govt. Pos: Mem. city coun, Greencastle, Ind, 63; chmn, Putnam Co. Rep. Cmt, Ind, 65- Bus. & Prof. Pos: V.pres, Poor & Sons Inc, 58. Mil. Serv: Entered as 2nd Lt, Air Force, 55, released as 1st Lt, 58, after serv. in Continental Air Command, Bakalar AFB, 60; Capt, Air Force Res, 58-66. Mem: Elks; Kiwanis; Greencastle C. of C; Ind. Grain Dealers Asn; Ind. C. of C; Am. Legion. Rel: Methodist. Mailing Add: 108 Northwood Blvd, Greencastle, Ind. 46135. (1967)

POORBAUGH, JACK MORGAN R
Fla. State Rep.
b. Cleveland, Ohio, 11/3/19; s. John Milton Poorbaugh and Mianda Stewart P; m. to Patty Sue; c. John, Carl, Gregory, Paul, Cathy and Jayne. Educ: Wash. Univ, B.S. in archit, 43. Polit. & Govt. Pos: Investr, U.S. Sen, 47-53; pres, Boynton Beach-Ocean Ridge Rep. Club, Fla, 66; Fla. State Rep, currently. Bus. & Prof. Pos: Engr, Gill Construction Co, 53-55; owner, Archit. Specialties, 55-60; gen. sales mgr, Engineered Prod, 60-66. Mil. Serv: Entered as Pvt, Marine Corps, 42, released as Sgt, 46. Mem: Mason. Rel: Protestant. Mailing Add: 706 S.W. 27th Ave, Boynton Beach, Fla. 33435. (1967)

POOVEY, JULIUS REID R
N.C. State Sen.
b. Hickory, N.C, 9/24/02; s. Lloyd Willard Poovey and Nancy Thomas Reid P; m. 4/7/28 to Kathryn Violet Icard; c. J. Reid, Jr, James N, D.D.S, Maj. William B. and Nancy J. (Mrs. Walter N. Yount). Educ: Weaver Col; Lenoir Rhyne Col, 19-22. Polit. & Govt. Pos: Magistrate, Hickory, N.C, 50-62; former co. secy, precinct chmn. and precinct secy, Catawba Co. Rep. Cmt, presently exec. committeeman; N.C. State Rep, 66-68; N.C. State Sen, 68- Mil. Serv: Entered as Seaman 2/C, Coast Guard Res, 44, released as Seaman 1/C, 45, after serv. in Chesapeake Bay, Md. Mem: Am. Legion. Rel: Episcopal. Mailing Add: 61 20th Ave. N.W, Hickory, N.C. 28601.

POPE, ALEXANDER H. D
b. New York, N.Y, 6/4/29; s. Clifford H. Pope and Sarah H. Davis P; m. 9/23/50 to Harriet E. Martin; c. Stephen C, Terri M, Angela L, Virginia L. and Daniel M. Educ: Univ. Chicago, B.A, 48, Law Sch, J.D, 52; Phi Beta Kappa; Order of the Coif; pres, Univ. Chicago Student Govt, 48-49; managing ed, Univ. Chicago Law Rev, 51-52. Polit. & Govt. Pos: Mem. nat. bd, Vol. for Stevenson, 52; v.chmn, Los Angeles Co. Dem. Cent. Cmt, Calif, 58-59; legis. secy, Calif. Gov. Off, 59-61; co-chmn, Los Angeles, Brown for Gov. Cmt, 62; Los Angeles finance chmn, Californians Against Proposition 14, 64; Los Angeles chmn, Calif. Dem. Coord. Cmt, 65; consult. on S. Los Angeles Riots, Calif. Gov. Off, 65-66; mem, Calif. Hwy. Cmn, 66- Bus. & Prof. Pos: Partner, Fine & Pope, 57- Mil. Serv: Entered as Pvt, Army, 52, released as Sgt, 54, after serv. in 8th Army Hq, Korea, 53-54. Publ: 'Retroactivity of Recognition of New Foreign Governments,' 51 and 'Vertical Forestalling Under the Anti-Trust Laws,' Univ. Chicago Law Rev, 52. Mem: Pres, Inglewood Dist. Bar Asn, 67; v.pres, Westchester Coord. Coun, 59; pres, Westchester Ment. Health Clinic, 63. Rel: Unitarian. Legal Res: 7706 Boeing Ave, Los Angeles, Calif. 90045. Mailing Add: Suite 700, 9800 S. Sepulveda Blvd, Los Angeles, Calif. 90045.

POPE, CHARLES GERALD D
b. Eldorado, Mo, 12/1/27; s. Lewis B. Pope and Virginia Whited P; married; c. Georgia, Janette and Delisa Dee. Educ: Univ. of Tulsa, LL.D, 58; Sigma Nu; Delta Theta Phi. Polit. & Govt. Pos: Okla. State Sen, 65-66. Bus. & Prof. Pos: Practicing attorney. Mil. Serv: Entered as Pvt, Army, 52, released as Cpl, 54, after serv. in Korea, 53-54. Rel: Unitarian. Legal Res: 4321 S. Birmingham, Tulsa, Okla. 74105. Mailing Add: 500 W. Seventh, Tulsa, Okla. 74119. (1967)

POPE, GEORGIA HELEN R
Mem, N.Mex. State Rep. Cent. Cmt.
b. Watonga, Okla, 1/13/32; d. Arnold Julius Prickett and Fern Neal P; m. 6/1/52 to Leland Dean Pope; c. Christy Lee and Julie Beth. Educ: Okla. State Univ, 50-52. Polit. & Govt. Pos: Mem, N.Mex. State Rep. Cent. Cmt, 66-; co. chairwoman, Rep. Party of McKinley Co, 66-68, co. chmn, 68. Bus. & Prof. Pos: Substitute teacher, Gallup-McKinley Co. Schs, 57-61; ins. agent, Nat. Old Line Ins. Co, 61-64, dist. gen. agent, 64- Mem: Soroptimist (past pres); Alpha Pi-Epsilon Sigma Alpha (past pres); Eastern Star (past matron); secy, Shylock Investment Club; mother adv. and mem. adv. bd, Order of the Rainbow for Girls; Past Matron's Club (past pres); Ruth Circle of Methodist Church. Mem. of the Wall of Fame of Nat. Old Line Ins. Co. Rel: Methodist; past pres. of primary dept, past secy of the Sunday sch. and teacher, Ninth grade Sunday sch. class, First United Methodist Church of Gallup. Mailing Add: 510 Julie Dr, Gallup, N.Mex. 87301.

POPE, GREGORY J. D
N.Y. State Assemblyman
b. Medina, N.Y, 11/27/26; m. to Josephine Juliana; c. Gregory, Cynthia, Paula and Richard. Educ: Grad. Coyne Elec. Sch. & Am. Elec. Engr's Sch, Chicago, Ill; attended schs. in labor mgt. at Fredonia State Teachers Col. & Alfred Univ. Polit. & Govt. Pos: N.Y. State Assemblyman, 64- Bus. & Prof. Pos: Employed, Bell-Aero Syst. Co, Niagara Falls. Mem: UAW-CIO (pres, Local 516, del, Skilled Trades in Niagara Co. and Niagara Co. Coun, UAW-CIO-AFL); co-chmn, Bell Humanity Fund; mgr. and coach, Little League Baseball; councilor, Young Dem. Teens Orgn; Boy Scouts Programs; K. of C; Am. Legion; Eagles; VFW; Navy Marine Club; Lockport and Pomona Grange. Rel: Catholic. Mailing Add: 619 East Ave, Lockport, N.Y. 14094. (1967)

POPE, JACK D
Assoc. Justice, Supreme Court of Tex.
b. Abilene, Tex, 4/18/13; s. Dr. Andrew J. Pope and Ruth Taylor P; m. 6/11/38 to Allene Nichols; c. Jackson and Allen. Educ: Abilene Christian Col, B.A, 34; Univ. Tex, LL.B, 37. Polit. & Govt. Pos: Dist. judge, 94th Dist. Court, Tex, 46-50; assoc. justice, Fourth Court of Civil Appeals, 50-65 and Supreme Court of Tex, 65- Bus. & Prof. Pos: Attorney-at-law, Corpus Christi, Tex, 37-46. Mil. Serv: Seaman, Navy, 2 years. Publ: 'Public Impressions of the Courtroom Scene,' 2/59 and 'Broad and Narrow Issues,' 11/63, Tex. Bar J; 'The Judge and Jury,' Southwest. Legal J, 3/64. Mem: Am, San Antonio, Travis Co. and Hill Country Bar Asns; pres, Nueces Co. Bar Asn, 46; Insts. Cmt, State Bar of Tex. and Cmt. on Admin. of Justice, 58-64, chmn, Citizenship Cmt, 52-53 and Cmt. on Rules and Statutes, 59-60, pres, Judicial Sect, 61-62, Cmt. on Family Law, 52-55 and Legis. Cmt, 59; Am. Judicature Soc; Law-Sci. Inst; Am. Soc. for Legal Hist; adv. bd, Southwest. Law J; pres, Metrop. YMCA, San Antonio, 57-58, bd. dirs, 54-57, Corpus Christi YMCA, 48-50; exec. bd, Alamo Coun, Boy Scouts, 56-65. Silver Beaver Award, Boy Scouts; Rosewood Gavel Award, St. Mary's Sch. Law, 62. Rel: Church of Christ. Mailing Add: Supreme Court Bldg, Capitol Station, Austin, Tex. 78711.

POPE, JAMES WILLIAM, JR. 'BILL' D
Mayor, Pikeville, Tenn.
b. Nashville, Tenn, 2/2/38; s. James William Pope, Sr. and Givin P; m. May, 59 to Joan Smith; c. Karen Elaine, Elizabeth Ann and James William, III. Univ. Tenn; Cumberland Law Sch, LL.B; Alpha Tau Omega; Delta Theta Phi; Student Bar Asn.(pres). Polit. & Govt. Pos: Title attorney, Tenn. Valley Authority, 62-64; mayor, Pikeville, Tenn, 66-; Tenn. State Rep, Four-Co. Dist, 67-68; Dem. nominee, U.S. Rep, Tenn, 68. Bus. & Prof. Pos: Attorney, private practice, 64- Mem: Tenn. Bar Asn; dir, First Nat. Bank of Pikeville; Tenn. Munic. League; Chmn, Southeast Tenn. Develop. Dist; dir, Bledsoe Co. Gen. Hosp; Sequatchie Valley Planning & Develop. Asn.(v.chmn); charter mem, Bledsoe Co. Jaycees; charter mem, Bledsoe Young Dem. Legis. Conserv. Award, by Tenn. Conserv. League, 67; Holiday Award for a Beautiful Am, 69. Rel: Methodist. Mailing Add: P.O. Box 210, Pikeville, Tenn. 37367.

POPE, MARION THOMAS, JR. D
b. Thomaston, Ga, 9/28/27; s. Marion Thomas Pope, Sr. and Hulette Clark P; m. 7/9/66 to Judith Anita Few; c. Marion Thomas Pope, III. Educ: S. Ga. Col, B.B.A; Univ. of Ga, LL.B, 53; Sigma Nu; Delta Theta Phi. Polit. & Govt. Pos: Ga. State Rep, 63-66; Judge, Superior Courts, Blue Ridge Judicial Circuit, 67- Bus. & Prof. Pos: Attorney-at-law, Canton, Ga, 53-; gen. counsel, Ga. Jr. C. of C, 60. Mil. Serv: Navy, 45-47. Mem: Gridiron Soc; v.pres, Ga. Jr. C. of C, 56-57; pres, Canton Jr. C. of C, 58; pres, Canton Kiwanis, 59. Rel: Baptist. Legal Res: City Route 3, Canton, Ga. 30114. Mailing Add: P.O. Box 352, Canton, Ga. 30114.

POPE, SAMUEL ELIBA D
Va. State Del.
b. Southhampton Co, Va, 5/18/05; m. to Sara Holt White. Educ: Randolph-Macon Col, A.B; Va. Polytech. Inst; Kappa Alpha. Polit. & Govt. Pos: Va. State Del, 46-; del, Dem. Nat. Conv, 52; chmn. South. conf, Coun. State Govt, 69- Bus. & Prof. Pos: Farmer; pres, Southhampton Co. Bank. Mem: Mason; Ruritans; Jamestown Found. Distinguished Alumnus Award, Randolph-Macon Col, 63; Jefferson Cup Award, Asn. Va. Counties, 66. Rel: Methodist. Mailing Add: Drewryville, Va. 23844.

POPE, VERLE A. D
Fla. State Sen.
b. Jacksonville, Fla, 12/12/03; m. to Edith Taylor, wid; c. (Mrs. Richard O. Watson). Educ: Univ. Fla. Polit. & Govt. Pos: Former chmn, Bd. Co. Cmnrs, St. John's Co, Fla; former mem, Dist. Welfare Bd; Fla. State Sen, 48-, past pres, Fla. State Senate. Bus. & Prof. Pos: Real estate broker; dir, Hastings Exchange Bank. Mil. Serv: U.S. Army Air Force, World War II; European Air Medal, Eight Clusters; Pres. Citation; Croix De Guerre for St. Lo Mission. Mem: Former dir, C. of C; Hist. Soc; Res. Officers Club; Am. Legion; VFW; Mason; Kiwanis; Elks, Former Exalted Ruler; Arts Club. Golf, Fishing and Hunting. Rel: Episcopal. Mailing Add: P.O. Box 519, St. Augustine, Fla. 32084.

POPHAM, WAYNE GORDON R
Minn. State Sen.
b. Florence, S.Dak, 10/23/29; s. Samuel Russell Popham and Vera Monahan P; m. 12/10/55 to Joan Marion Nelson; c. Todd, Stephanie, Kathryn, John and Geoffrey. Educ: Univ. Minn, B.S.L, 51, LL.B, 53. Polit. & Govt. Pos: V.chmn, Hennepin Co. Rep. Cmt, Minn; chmn, Fifth Cong. Dist. Rep. Party, 61-63; Minn. State Sen, 35th Dist, 62- Bus. & Prof. Pos: Law partner, Popham, Haik, Schnobrich, Kaufman & Doty, 55- Mil. Serv: Entered as E-1, Army, 53, released as S-4, 55. Mem: Hennepin Co. and Am. Bar Asns; chmn, 64 inst, Minn. Bar Asn; Am. Judicature Soc; Minneapolis Club. Rel: Methodist. Mailing Add: 1550 Minnehaha Pkwy, Minneapolis, Minn. 55417.

POPKIN, SAMUEL LEWIS D
b. Superior, Wis, 6/9/42; s. Arnold J. Popkin and Anne R. Cohen P; single. Educ: Mass. Inst. Tech, B.S. in polit. sci. and math, 63, Woodrow Wilson fel, 64-65, Ph.D. in polit. sci, 68. Polit. & Govt. Pos: Alternate del-at-lg, Dem. Nat. Conv, 64. Bus. & Prof. Pos: Election coordinator computer anal, WBF-TV, 64; mem, Tech. Cmt, Nat. Coun. Soc. Sci. Archives, 64-66; proj. dir, Simulmatics Corp, 65-67; lectr. polit. sci, Yale, 67-68; consult, Rand Corp. and Simulmatics Corp, 68-; asst. prof. govt, Harvard, 68- Publ: Candidates, Issues and Strategies: A Computer Simulation of 1960 Presidential Election (w. I. Pool and R. Abelson), Mass. Inst. Tech, 64; plus others. Mem: Am.

Polit. Sci. Asn. Rel: Jewish. Legal Res: 1405 N. 23rd, Superior, Wis. 54880. Mailing Add: Dept. of Government, Harvard University, Cambridge, Mass. 02138. (1967)

POPPEN, HENRY ALVIN R
S.Dak. State Sen.
b. De Smet, S.Dak, 2/12/22; s. Otto H. Poppen and Sena Fransen P; m. 10/26/52 to Lorna Mildred Meyer; c. Elizabeth Ann and Nanette Mildred. Educ: Huron Col, B.A, 49. Polit. & Govt. Pos: Crew leader, 1959 Agr. Census, Kingsbury-Miner Co, S.Dak, 59, 1960 Census, Kingsbury-Beadle Co, 60; chmn, Kingsbury Co. Rep. Party, 60-65; chmn, Spirit Lake Twp. Bd, 64-; S.Dak. State Sen, Dist. 7, 67- Bus. & Prof. Pos: Partner, Poppen Brox, De Smet, S.Dak, 54-69. Mem: Kingsbury Co. Farm Bur.(v.pres, 66); Mason. Rel: Presbyterian. Mailing Add: R.R. 1, De Smet, S.Dak. 57231.

POPPER, DAVID HENRY
U.S. Ambassador to Cyprus
b. N.Y.C, 10/3/12; s. Morris Popper and Lilian Greenbaum P; m. 3/8/36 to Florence C. Maisel; c. Carol, Lewis, Katherine and Virginia. Educ: Harvard Univ, A.B, 32 and A.M, 34. Polit. & Govt. Pos: Specialist in int. orgn. affairs, Dept. of State, 45, adv, U.S. Del. to UN Gen. Assembly, 46-53 and prin. exec. officer, 49-50; asst. chief div. int. orgn. affairs, Dept. of State, 48-49 and officer in charge, UN Gen. Assembly Affairs, 49-51; dep. dir, Off. UN Polit. and Security Affairs, 51-54 and dir, 54-55; dep. U.S. Rep. for Int. Orgn, Geneva, 56-59; dep. U.S. Rep, Conf. on Discontinuance Nuclear Weapons Tests, Geneva, 59-61; sr. adv. disarmament affairs, U.S. Mission to UN, 61-62; mem, U.S. Del, NATO Ministerial Meetings, 62; dir. Off. of Atlantic Polit. and Mil. Affairs, Dept. State, 62-65; Dep. asst. Secy. State for Int. Orgn. Affairs, 65-69; U.S. Ambassador to Cyprus, 69- Bus. & Prof. Pos: Research assoc, For. Policy Asn, Inc, N.Y.C, 34-40 and assoc. ed. publ, 41-42. Mil. Serv: Capt, CWC, Mil. Intel Serv, AUS, 42-45. Publ: The Puzzle of Palestine, 38; plus various articles in prfnl. publs. Mem: Am. Polit. Sci. Asn; Am. Soc. Int. Law; Am. Acad. Polit. and Soc. Sci. Legal Res: 6116 33rd N.W, Washington, D.C. 20015. Mailing Add: U.S. Embassy, Nicosia, Cyprus.

PORTELA, THOMAS JOSEPH D
b. New York, N.Y, 9/17/23; s. Faust F. Portela and Margaret Curtin P; m. 8/14/48 to Marie Raab; c. Thomas Gregory, Jane Ellen and Patricia Anne. Educ: Manhattan Col, B.A; Fordham Univ, LL.B; St. Thomas More Law Soc; Beta Sigma. Polit. & Govt. Pos: Mem, Nassau Co. Policy Cmt, N.Y, 62-, dep. exec, 62-65, treas, 66-68, mem, Bd. Health, 69- Bus. & Prof. Pos: Attorney-at-law, 51-60; partner, Murphy & Portela, Esquires, 60-62; govt. banking officer, First Nat. City Bank, N.Y, 68- Mil. Serv: Entered as Pvt, Army Air Force, 42, released as Flight Officer, 45, after serv. in 5th Air Force, Asiatic Pac; Air Medal with Clusters; Philippine Liberation Medal; Asiatic Pac. Medal with 9 Battle Stars; Air Offense Japan Medal. Mem: Nassau Co. Bar Asn; Nassau Co. Lawyers Orgn; Elks; Am. Legion; VFW; K. of C; Boy Scouts. Rel: Roman Catholic. Mailing Add: 2732 Colonial Ave, Merrick, N.Y. 11566.

PORTELL, CLYDE F. D
b. Bonne Terre, Mo, 10/10/12; m. 2/3/50 to Ruth E. Herter; c. David, Barbara, Vicky Jane, Janet Virginia. Educ: Bonne Terre High Sch. Polit. & Govt. Pos: Mo. State Rep, 60-66; St. Francois Co. Dem. Cmt, 2 years. Bus. & Prof. Pos: Owner of an advert. bus; Pgh. Plate glassworker, 10 years; linotype operator on a Dem. newspaper, 13 years. Mil. Serv: Navy, 4 years. Mem: VFW Post 2210; Am. Legion, Post 150. Rel: Catholic. Mailing Add: 276 St. Gerard St, Ste. Genevieve, Mo. 63670. (1967)

PORTEOUS, LOUIS ROBERT, JR. R
Exec. Councillor, Maine.
b. Norwich, Conn, 3/21/23; s. Louis Robert Porteous and Florence Ann Cushman P; m. 5/14/66 to Elizabeth Lyman Decker; c. L. Robert, III, Stuart E, David C, Elizabeth and Martha. Educ: Bowdoin Col, B.A, 48; Delta Kappa Epsilon. Polit. & Govt. Pos: State chmn, Maine Rep. Finance Cmt, 58-; Maine State Sen, 61-64; exec. coun, Maine, 67- and chmn, 68; del, Rep. Nat. Conv, 68. Bus. & Prof. Pos: V.pres. and treas, Porteous, Mitchell & Braun Co, 59- Mil. Serv: Entered as A/S, Navy, 42, released as Qm. 3/C, 46, after serv. in Amphibious Div, Pac, 65-66. Mem: Dir, C. of C; dir, Area Bldg. Fund Inc; pres. and mem. bd, Portland YMCA, 53-55; pres. and bd. chmn, Maine Publicity Bur, 60-64. Young Man of Year, Portland Jaycees, 55. Rel: United Church of Christ. Mailing Add: Foreside Rd, Cumberland Foreside, Maine 04110.

PORTER, ALBERT D
Chmn, Hood Co. Dem. Party, Tex.
b. Granbury, Tex, 10/25/94; s. Luther Preston Porter and Amanda Massey P; m. 8/10/18 to Eula William (deceased); c. William Norris, Doris Jean (Mrs. Sweeney) and Garth Albert. Educ: Granbury High Sch, grad, 17. Polit. & Govt. Pos: Co. clerk, Hood Co, Tex, 36-49 & 58-; chmn, Hood Co. Dem. Party, 58- Bus. & Prof. Pos: Owner, Grocery Store, Granbury, Tex, 23-34; supt, First Methodist Sunday Sch, 28-68; pres, Tri-Co. Elec. Coop, 42-; supvr, Hood-Parker, Soil Conserv. Dist, 51- Mem: WOW. Cert. of Merit, Tex. Bank and Trust Co, Dallas, Tex. Rel: Methodist. Mailing Add: 108 S. Houston, Granbury, Tex. 76048.

PORTER, ALBERT S. D
Dem. Nat. Committeeman, Ohio
b. 11/29/04; s. Albert S. Porter Sr. and Lena May P; m. to Genevieve S; c. Lee A, Alan C. and Carol S. Educ: Ohio State Univ, B.C.E, 28; Tau Beta Pi; Sigma Xi; Pi Mu Epsilon; Texnikoi; Sigma Phi Epsilom Polit. & Govt. Pos: Del, Dem. Nat. Conv, 52, 64 & 68; cand. for mayor, Cleveland, Ohio, 53; chmn, Dem. State Conv, 58 & 66; chmn, Cuyahoga Co. Charter Cmn, 59; Ohio Favorite Son Cand. for President, 60 & 64; chmn, Dem. Exec. Cmt, 63-; Dem. Nat. Committeeman, Ohio, 64-; chmn, Cuyahoga Co. Dem. Cent. Cmt, 64- Bus. & Prof.Pos : Draftsman and asst. engr, City Plan Cmn. and City Engrs. Off, Columbus, Ohio, 25-29; engr. and consult, Cleveland Hwy. Research Bur, 29-32; asst. to div. engr, Div. 12, State Hwy. Dept, Cleveland, 32-33; chief dep. co. engr, Cuyahoga Co, 33-41 & 46-47; Cuyahoga Co. Engr, 47- Mil. Serv: Civil Engr. Corps, Navy, 41-46; Comdr, Naval Res. Mem: Cleveland, Ohio and Nat. Soc. Prfnl. Engrs; Co. Engrs. Asn. of Ohio; Am. Soc. Civil Engrs; F&AM; Al Sirat Grotto; Lake Erie Consistory (32°); Al Koran Shrine; Nat. Sojourners; Heroes of '76; SAR; Reserve Officers Asn; Reserve Officers of the Naval Serv; Am. Legion; VFW; Mil. Order of World Wars; Koran Club; Shrine Luncheon Club; dir, Acacia Country Club, 63-64; Eagles; West. Reserve Hist. Soc; Phillis Wheatley Asn; State and City Beach Erosion Bd, 47-48; Freeway Exec. Cmt, 46-51, Freeway Bd, 51-; dir. of supply, Civil Defense, 51; Hwy. Study Cmt, 49-51; Hwy. Invest. Cmt, 52, steering cmt. and chmn. prog. subcmt; Transportation Panel, Cleveland Auto Club; dir, Regional Geodetic Surv; exec. cmt, Regional Planning Cmn; City Club of Cleveland; dir, Fairview Park Savings and Loan Asn, 51-55 and Park View Fed. Savings and Loan, 65-; President's Hwy. Safety Conf, 49 & 51; Am. Roadbuilders Asn; dir, Co. Wide Traffic Surv, 52-55; bd. control, Cleveland Safety Coun; Smaller Bus. Asn; Ment. Health Cmn; exec. cmt, Metro; Cleveland Safety Coun, traffic adv. cmt, 59 and v.pres, pub. employees, 60; Nat. Asn. Co. Off, hwy. cmt, 60; Nat. Asn. C. Engrs; chmn, Co. Airport Bldg. Cmn, 58; exec. bd, Cleveland Open Golf Tournament, 64- Engr. of the Year, Cleveland Soc. Prfnl. Engrs. and Cleveland Eng. Soc, 64; K. of C. Civic Award for Commun. Serv, 64. Rel: Episcopal. Legal Res: 31179 S. Woodland Rd, Cleveland, Ohio 44115. Mailing Add: 1926 Standard Bldg, Cleveland, Ohio 44113.

PORTER, ANNABELLE CUNNINGHAM R
Chmn, Falls Church Rep. City Cmt, Va.
b. Fairfield, Ill, 11/1/06; d. Benjamin Franklin Cunningham and Lula King C; wid; c. Carter E. Educ: Arcadia Col, 18-23. Polit. & Govt. Pos: V.chmn. and voting mem, Tenth Dist. Rep. Cmt, Va, 4 years; secy, and corresponding secy, Gr. Falls Church Rep. Club, 6 years; mem. of cmts. for U.S. Rep. Joel T. Broyhill, 54-; v.chmn, Virginians for Nixon, 60; mem, Charter Rev. Cmt, Falls Church, Va, 60-61, mem, Bd. Zoning Appeals and Planning Cmn, 61-66; mem. bd. dirs, Cerebral Palsy Center, 64, conducted fund drive; chmn, Heart Fund Dr, 66; chmn, Falls Church City Rep. Cmt, 67- Bus. & Prof. Pos: Secy. to pres, Signode Corp, Ill, 27-37. Mem: League of Women Voters; Citizens for A Better City; Gr. Falls Church Rep. Women's Club; Village Preserv. Soc. Falls Church. Rel: Baptist. Mailing Add: 1015 Birch St, Falls Church, Va. 22046.

PORTER, CARLEY V. D
Calif. State Assemblyman
b. Chicago, Ill, 2/19/06; m. 10/20/34 to Marie Walton P; c. Carl William. Educ: Compton Jr. Col, Univ. South. Calif, 36; Phi Delta Kappa; Phi Kappa Tau. Polit. & Govt. Pos: Calif. State Assemblyman, 49-, chmn, Water Cmt, Calif. State Assembly, 59-; former mem, 38th Assembly Dist. Dem. Co. Cmt. Bus. & Prof. Pos: Businessman; former teacher hist. and speech, Excelsior High Sch. and Long Beach City Col. Mil. Serv: Instr, Santa Ana Army Air Base, 42-46. Mem: Vet. Serv. Center Bd, Red Cross; past pres, Compton Jr. Col. Bd. Trustees; Coord. Coun, Willowbrook; bd. trustees, Norwalk State Hosp; Rotary; Boy Scouts; Elks. Mailing Add: 1717 N. Long Beach Blvd, Compton, Calif. 90221.

PORTER, CHARLES O. D
b. Klamath Falls, Ore, 4/4/19; s. Frank Jason Porter and Ruth Peterson P; m. 3/1/43 to Priscilla Dean Galassi; c. Donald Jason, Christopher Dean, Samuel Curry and Anne Julie. Educ: Harvard Col, B.S, 44; Harvard Law Sch, LL.B, 47. Polit. & Govt. Pos: Alternate del-at-lg, Dem. Nat. Conv, 56; U.S. Rep, Ore, 56-60; del-at-lg, Dem. Nat. Conv, 60, 64 & 68; White House Consult, Food for Peace Prog, 61. Mil. Serv: Entered as Pvt, Army, 41, released as 1st Lt, after serv. in Hq, 9th Air Force; Maj, Air Force Res.(Ret) 67; Four Battle Stars; Distinguished Unit Medal. Publ: Co-auth, The American Lawyer, Univ. Chicago, 54; The Struggle for Democracy in Latin America, Macmillan, 61. Rel: United Church of Christ. Legal Res: 2680 Baker St, Eugene, Ore. 97403. Mailing Add: 200 Legal Center, 858 Pearl St, Eugene, Ore. 97401.

PORTER, DWIGHT J.
U.S. Ambassador to Lebanon
b. Shawnee, Okla, 4/12/16; m. to Adele Ritchie; c. Dwight A, James, Ellen, Barbara, Joan and Ritchie. Educ: Grinnell Col, B.A, 38. Polit. & Govt. Pos: Intern, Nat. Inst. of Pub. Affairs, 38-39; with U.S. Housing Authority, 39-41 and Dept. of Agr, 41-42 & 45-48; asst. personnel officer, Bd. of Econ. Warfare, 42; career officer, U.S. Dept. of State For. Serv, 48-; dep. dir, Displaced Persons Cmn, 48-49; chief mgt. and budget div, U.S. High Cmnr. for Germany, Frankfort, 49-52, dep. exec. dir, Bonn, 52-54; first secy, London, 54-56; coord, Hungarian Refugee Policies and Activities, 56-57; exec. dir, Bur. of Econ. Affairs, 56-57; mem. staff, Nat. War Col, 57-58; spec. asst. to Under Secy. for Polit. Affairs, 58-59; counsel. and dep. chief of mission, Vienna, 59-63; Asst. Secy. for Admin, 63-65; U.S. Ambassador to Lebanon, 65- Mil. Serv: Capt, Marine Corps, 42-45. Mailing Add: Beirut, Dept. of State, Washington, D.C. 20521.

PORTER, E. MELVIN D
Okla. State Sen.
b. Okmulgee, Okla, 5/22/30; s. Victor E. Porter and Mary Cole P; m. 12/15/55 to Jewel Ewing; c. E. Melvin, II and Joel Anthony. Educ: Tenn. State Univ, B.S, 56; Vanderbilt Univ, LL.B, 59; Sigma Rho Sigma; Kappa Alpha Psi. Polit. & Govt. Pos: Okla. State Sen, 65- Mil. Serv: Entered as Pvt, Army, 48, released as Cpl, 52 after serving in 93rd Engrs, Guam, 49-51. Mem: Am, Okla. and Okla. Co. Bar Asns; Am. Judicature Soc; NAACP; YMCA; C. of C. Kappa of the Month. Rel: Baptist. Mailing Add: 2116 N.E. 23rd St, Oklahoma City, Okla. 73111.

PORTER, LOUISE M. R
Kans. State Sen.
b. Lindsborg, Kans, 9/19/20; d. Fred E. Anderson and Agnes Elvin A; m. 9/9/45 to Walter H. Porter; c. Jane Marie and Richard Walter. Educ: Fort Hays Kans. State Col; Emporia State Teacher's Col; Colo. Univ; Delta Kappa Gamma. Polit. & Govt. Pos: Mem, Nat. and State Rep. Women's Clubs; Kans. State Sen, 64- Bus. & Prof. Pos: Teacher, 40-45; Nurse's aid in World War II, 43. Mem: Local, State, Nat. Teacher's Asns; Int. Platform Asn; Woman's Kans. Day Club; State and Nat. Woman's Fed. Clubs; former pres, Bus. & Prfnl. Women's Club; State and Nat. Livestock Asns; State Hist. Soc; Co. Exten. Bd; State and Nat. Farm Bur; C. of C; Emporia Country Club; Cancer

Surv. Asn. Worker with youth; Scouts, 4-H Leader, Church Youth and Int. Farm Youth Exchange Prog; Bd. mem, High Sch. Rel: Methodist. Legal Res: Miller Ranch, Reading, Kans. 66868. Mailing Add: State Capitol Bldg, Topeka, Kans. 66612.

PORTER, RALPH E. R
Colo. State Rep.
b. Crawford, Colo, 7/6/02; s. Everett H. Porter and Cora J. Flannary P; m. 8/30/25 to Marjorie O. Peck; c. Robert, Jack S. and Polly (Mrs. Spann). Educ: West. State Col, A.B, 27, A.M, 55; Kappa Delta Mu; W Club. Polit. & Govt. Pos: Local councilman, 28; Colo. State Rep, Dist. 58, 63- Bus. & Prof. Pos: Bus. mgr, West. State Col, 27-60; owner lumber co, 41-51; ranch and cattle owner and operator, 41-52. Mem: C. of C.(pres, Gunnison Chap, 33); Rotary (pres, Gunnison Club, 34); AF&AM(master, Gunnison Lodge, 34); Elks. Rel: Protestant. Mailing Add: Crested Butte, Gunnison, Colo. 81224.

PORTER, ROBERT LAWRENCE D
Chmn, 20th Dist. Dem. Party, N.Dak.
b. Grandin, N.Dak, 4/11/26; s. James F. Porter and Lelah M. Coleman P; m. 6/26/46 to Dolores M. Tetzlaff; c. Bonnie L. and David R. Educ: Wahpeton Sci, 1 year. Polit. & Govt. Pos: Precinct committeeman, 20th Dist. Dem. Party, N.Dak, 54-, chmn, 65- Mil. Serv: Entered as A/S, Navy, 44, released as WT 2/C, 46, after serving on U.S.S. Bootes Ak-99, Asiatic-Pac. Theatre, 44-46. Mem: Farmers Union; RR Valley Sugarbeet Growers Asn; Am. Legion; VFW. Rel: Lutheran. Mailing Add: Grandin, N.Dak. 58038.

POSESS, STANLEY D
b. N.Y.C, 11/30/25; s. Louis Posess and Bessie Levine P; m. 3/30/58 to Rose Stern; c. Nina and David. Educ: Fordham Sch. of Adult Educ, N.Y.C, 45-47; Fordham Univ. Law Sch, LL.B, 50. Polit. & Govt. Pos: Dep. Traffic Cmnr, N.Y.C, 62-66; Dem. State Committeeman, 23rd Assembly Dist, Queens, N.Y, 64-; secy. to U.S. Rep. James H. Scheuer, Bronx, N.Y.C, 66-67; del, Dem. Nat. Conv, 68; counsel, Codification Cmt. N.Y.C. Coun, 68- Bus. & Prof. Pos: Lawyer, 50- Mil. Serv: Entered as Pvt, Army, 43, released as Pfc, 45, after serv. in 100th Inf. Div, ETO, 44-45; Purple Heart. Mem: Queens Co. Bar Asn; N.Y. Co. Lawyers Asn; Queens Div, Am. Jewish Cong; NAACP; Queens PTA; North Shore Dem. Asn. Rel: Jewish. Mailing Add: 14-29 160th St, Beechhurst, N.Y. 11357.

POSEY, GROVER HAROLD D
b. Columbus, Ga, 2/9/38; s. James Herbert Posey and Marie Hollomon P; m. 7/1/61 to Merne Hines; c. Kevin Harold. Educ: Univ. Ga, A.B, 60 and LL.B, hon. grad, 62; Univ. Mich, LL.M, 63; Phi Beta Kappa; Phi Kappa Phi; Phi Alpha Delta; scholarship for Grad. Study, Univ. Mich. Polit. & Govt. Pos: Attorney, Fed. Aviation Agency, 63-66 and Nat. Aeronaut. & Space Admin, 66-67; admin. asst, U.S. Rep. Jack Brinkley, Ga, 67- Mem: Ga. State Bar. Rel: Baptist. Legal Res: Upatoi, Ga. 31829. Mailing Add: 6811 Bellamy Ave, Springfield, Va. 22512.

POSEY, JOHN A, JR. R
b. Montgomery Co, 8/5/23; m. to Ann Barton; c. 3. Educ: Howard Col; Univ. of Ala. Law Sch. Polit. & Govt. Pos: Judge of Winston Co. Court; Ala. State Rep, -66. Bus. & Prof. Pos: Practices law. Mil. Serv: Army Air Corps. Mem: Masons; Civitans; Lions; VFW; Am. Legion; C. of C. Rel: Baptist. Mailing Add: Haleyville, Ala. 35565. (1967)

POSEY, JOHN PHILLIP D
b. Dothan, Ala, 12/4/35; s. James Herbert Posey and Marie Holloman P; m. 9/18/60 to Pauline Stewart; c. Heather Patrice and Laurel Marie. Educ: Univ. Ga, B.S, 58, M.A, 59, Ph.D, 62; Phi Alpha Theta; Pi Sigma Alpha; Theta Chi. Polit. & Govt. Pos: Del, Loyal Dem. of Miss. Conv, 68; del, Dem. Nat. Conv, 68; mem, exec. cmt, Humphrey-Muskie Campaign, Forrest Co, Miss, 68; chmn, Cmt. on New Ideas and Progs, Miss. Dem. Party, 68-69; mem, New Dem. Coalition Ind, 69-; faculty moderator, Young Dem. Club St. Joseph's Col, 69- Bus. & Prof. Pos: Grad. asst. hist, Univ. Ga, 58-61, student instr, 61-62; Nat. Defense Educ. Act instr, summer 66 & 67; asst. prof, Va. Polytech. Inst, 62-66; Appalachian Univ, summer 63; assoc. prof, Univ. South. Miss, 66-69; St. Joseph's Col, Ind, 69- Publ: 'David Hunter Miller as an Informal Diplomat: The Fiume Question at the Paris Peace Conference,' 4/67, 'Soviet Propaganda, Europe, and the Russo-Polish War, 1920,' 1/68 and 'From the Diary of A.A. Polovtsov: Leadership in the Russo-Turkish War,' 4/69, South. Quart. Mem: Am. Hist. Asn; Am. Asn. for the Adv. of Slavic Studies; South. Conf. on Slavic Studies; Asn. Asian Studies. Ford Found. Fel, Inst. on Far East. Hist. and Civilization, Fla. State Univ, 65. Rel: Methodist. Legal Res: 142 W. Vine St, Rensselaer, Ind. 47978. Mailing Add: Dept. of History, St. Joseph's College, Rensselaer, Ind. 47978.

POSILLIPO, ANTHONY JOSEPH D
Supvr, Rye, N.Y.
b. Port Chester, N.Y, 12/16/07; s. Thomas Posillipo and AnnRose Grimaldi P; m. 2/8/32 to Rose Rescigno; c. AnnRose (Mrs. Rubino) and Thomas. Polit. & Govt. Pos: Trustee, Port Chester, N.Y, 41-48, mayor, 52-54; supvr, Rye, 54-; dir, Rye-Port Chester Civil Defense; cmnr, Rye Town Police Dept; chmn, Rye Town Park Cmn; minority leader, Westchester Co. Bd. of Supvr, mem, Budget, Charter, Airport, Playland, Med. Center and Legis. Cmts; del, Dem. Nat. Conv, 68. Bus. & Prof. Pos: Bus. agent, Bricklayers, Plasterers & Masons, Local 48, financial secy, 30 years; v.pres. and secy-treas, Westchester Co. Bldg. Trades Coun; dir, Port Chester-Rye Savings Bank. Mem: Dir, Port Chester Carver Center; trustee, Port Chester Pub. Libr. and United Hosp; pres. and organizer, Port Chester Little League; Am. Cmt. on Italian Migration; Ment. Health Adv. Cmt; Citizen Cmt. on Urban Renewal; Am. Red Cross Spec. Gifts Cmt; Knights of Manresa; exec. coun, Iona Col; dir, United Cerebral Palsy of Westchester; hon. chmn, Boys Town of Naples; finance cmt, Commun. Chest; N.Y. State Adv. Cmn. Indust. Bldg; pres. of bd, Middle Income Housing; pres, Port Chester Rotary Club; chmn, Port Chester Emergency Food Cmt; chmn, Carver Center Bldg. Cmt; adv. mem, Girl Scouts of Am; chmn, Columbus Day Cmt; chmn, Corpus Christi Church Bldg. Fund Drive, Corpus Christi Church Cath. Charities, Cath. Charities Guid. Clin. and Cardinal Spellman's Servicemens Club; pres, Corpus Christi Holy Name Soc; supvr, Construction of Corpus Christi Center-Convent; hon. chmn, Boys Town of Italy Fund Drive; chmn, Westchester Co. Retarded Children Fund; dir, Westchester Co. United Fund; chmn, March of Dimes Fund Drive; committeeman, Girl Scout Bldg; YMCA; Eagles; K. of C. (4°); 40/40 Club; Siwanoy Dads Asn; Elks; Foresters of Am; Italian-Am. Protection Asn; dir, Salvation Army; K. of M. B'nai B'rith Outstanding Citizen Award, 56; Key Citizen Award, Key Club of Port Chester, 59; Boys Town of Naples Achievement Award, 61; Anthony Tocci Labor and Achievement Award, 61; Don Bosco Youth Assistance Citizen Award, 63; Carver Center Key Award, 66; Man of the Year, Westchester Co. Postal Employees, 68. Rel: Roman Catholic; Trustee, Corpus Christi Church. Mailing Add: 321 Olivia St, Port Chester, N.Y. 10573.

POSNER, PAUL M. D
Chmn, Los Angeles Co. Dem. Cent. Cmt, Calif.
b. Milwaukee, Wis, 11/6/29; s. Jerome Posner and Bella Appel P; m. 12/29/64 to Germaine Jeanne Mason. Educ: Univ. Calif, Los Angeles, B.A, 52 and LL.B, 55; Pi Sigma Alpha; Alpha Phi Omega; Nu Beta Epsilon. Polit. & Govt. Pos: Mem, Los Angeles Co. Dem. Cent. Cmt, Calif, 52-, v.chmn, 62-64, chmn, 64-66 & 68-; mem. exec. bd. and steering cmt, Calif. State Dem. Cent. Cmt; chmn, Los Angeles Co. Johnson-Humphrey Campaign, 64 and Humphrey-Muskie Campaign, 68; alternate del, Dem. Nat. Conv, 64. Bus. & Prof. Pos: Attorney-at-law, Wirin, Rissman, Okrand and Posner, Los Angeles, Calif, 56; mem. panel of arbitrators, Am. Arbitration Asn, 65- Publ: 'Decade of Appeals,' (Chessman Case), Univ. Calif. Los Angeles Law Rev, 7/61. Mem: Calif. State Bar Asn; Los Angeles Co. Bar Asn; U.S. Supreme Court Bar; Nat. Asn. Defense Counsel in Criminal Cases; Lawyers Club Los Angeles; Legal Cmt, Am. Civil Liberties Union; Dem. Assocs; City of Hope; Urban League; Mayors Commun. Adv. Cmt. Rel: Jewish. Legal Res: 2722 Club Dr, Los Angeles, Calif. 90064. Mailing Add: 257 S. Spring St, Los Angeles, Calif. 90012.

POSNER, SEYMOUR D
N.Y. State Assemblyman
b. Bronx, N.Y, 5/21/25; s. Nathan Posner and Fannie Gittleman P; m. 5/31/53 to Marilyn Deutsch; c. Naomi Gila. Educ: City Col. of N.Y, B.S. in Soc. Sci, 48; N.Y. Univ, M.A. in Pub. Admin; New Sch; Univ. Paris. Polit. & Govt. Pos: Gen. cmt, N.Y. Cmt. for Dem. Voters; co-chmn, Vols. for Stevenson in the Bronx, 52; Concourse-Jefferson Independent Dem; N.Y.C. Dept. of Welfare; N.Y.C. Housing Authority, State Rent Cmn, formerly; N.Y. State Assemblyman, 65- Bus. & Prof. Pos: Past dir, Bronx Div, Am. Jewish Cong. (on leave at time of his elec); moderator, Weekly Radio Discussion Series on Commun. Probs; formerly, Urban League of Gr. N.Y, United Housing Found; pub. rels. dir, March on Wash, 63; conducts weekly pub. serv. prog, Ombudsman, Radio Sta. WEVO, currently. Mil. Serv: Inf. World War II. Publ: Author of series of articles on housing probs, El Diaro De Nueva York. Mem: Former N.Y. State housing chmn, DAV; Maccabean Post, Jewish War Vets; Borough Pres. Planning Bd; Citizen's Union; NAACP; Local 1707, Commun. and Soc. Agency Employees, AFL-CIO, formerly, Commun. Servs. Cmt, N.Y.C. Cent. Labor Coun; Asn. of Bronx Commun. Orgns; Nat. Asn. of Intergroup Rels. Offs; past chmn, Bronx Cmt. to Save Rent Controls; N.Y. State Bd. of Am. for Dem. Action, past polit. action chmn, Local 371; AFSCME; past nat. gov. coun, Am. Jewish Cong; past chmn, Neighborhood Housing and Rent Clinic. Rel: Jewish; Congregation, Adath Jeshurun, Zionist Orgn. of Am. Mailing Add: 1100 Grand Concourse, Bronx, N.Y. 10456.

POSS, EDWIN CARROLL D
b. Athens, Ga, 9/01/27; s. Summie Jewel Poss and Ruby Parker P; m. 3/20/46 to Mary George Barber; c. Jamie Carroll, John Greg (deceased) and Jeffrey Scott. Educ: Auburn Univ, 45-46; awarded Am. Legion Medal in high sch, outstanding leadership. Polit. & Govt. Pos: Ga. State Rep, 63-68. Bus. & Prof. Pos: Ins; pres. & owner, Barber & Poss Inc. Ins. Agency, Athens, 54- Mil. Serv: Navy, 46-47. Mem: Elks; Moose; Madison Co. Civic Club (dir, 60-61); Lions (zone chmn, 61-62). Rel: Methodist. Mailing Add: R.F.D. 1, Hull, Ga. 30646. (1967)

POST, MANNING J. D
b. Chicago, Ill, 1/3/18; s. Joseph Post and Esther Kaplan P; m. 6/6/43 to Florence Conrad; c. Karen Linda. Educ: Univ. Ill, 36-40. Polit. & Govt. Pos: V.chmn, Calif. Cmn. on State Govt. Orgn. and Econ, 61-69; treas, Unruh Campaign Cmt, 62-69; treas, Johnson-Humphrey Campaign Cmt, Calif, 64; finance co-chmn, Attorney Gen. Lynch Cmt, 66; chmn, Dem. Assocs. Bd. Trustees, 66-; chmn, Los Angeles Co. Real Estate Cmn, 67-; treas, Kennedy Calif. Del, 68; treas, Beverly Hills Mayor Fredric Leopold Campaign Cmt, 68; mem, Beverly Hills Parking and Traffic Cmn, 68-; del, Dem. Nat. Conv, 68. Bus. & Prof. Pos: Pres, Europa Motor Car Co, 54-; pres, Automotive Distributors Inc, 56-62; v.pres, Leshef Corp. Properties, 62-; partner, Chandler-Systs/Post Properties, 62-; partner, Von Neumann-Post Properties, 67- Mem: Brandeis Univ. Pres. Coun; Los Angeles Irish-Israeli Soc; Los Angeles Co. Mus. Art; Mus. Modern Art, N.Y; Mayors Commun. Adv. Cmt, Los Angeles. Mailing Add: 450 Trousdale Place, Beverly Hills, Calif. 90210.

POSTON, HOWARD HENRY, JR. R
Chmn, Williamsburg Co. Rep. Party, S.C.
b. Kingstree, S.C, 10/19/29; s. Howard H. Poston, Sr. and Henri Louise Johnson P; m. 7/21/51 to Mary Jo Stroud; c. John Howard, Rebecca Louise, Mary Lella, Patricia Page. Educ: Duke Univ, A.B, 51; Med. Col. of S.C, M.D, 55; Sigma Chi. Polit. & Govt. Pos: Med. dir, Williamsburg Co. Civil Defense, 60; chmn, Independent Voters of Williamsburg Co, 61-65; v.chmn, Workman for Senate Cmt, 62; chmn, Cand. Evaluation Cmt, Sixth Cong. Dist, 62-65; mem, State Bd. of Dirs, State Br, Am. Polit. Action Cmt, 62-65; mem, State Bd. of Dirs, State Br, Am. Polit. Action Cmt, 62-65; chmn, Williamsburg Co. Goldwater for Pres. Cmt, 64; med. adv, Local Selective Serv. Bd, S.C, 65; chmn, Williamsburg Co. Rep. Party, 65-; del, Rep. Nat. Conv, 68. Bus. & Prof. Pos: V.pres, Seventh Med. Dist, 59-60; alternate del, S.C. Med. Asn, 60-67, del, 68-69. Mil. Serv: Entered as 1st Lt, Air Force, 56, released as Capt, 58, after serv. in Med.C, 6606th Air Force Hosp, Goose Air Force Base, Labrador, 56-58. Mem: S.C. Acad. of Gen. Practice; v.pres, Williamsburg Co. Med. Soc, 61, pres, 62; Am. Med. Asn; Am. Acad. of Gen. Practice; Moose. Rel: Methodist. Legal Res: 1505 Fulton Ave, Kingstree, S.C. 29556. Mailing Add: 1248 Longstreet, Kingstree, S.C. 29556.

POSTON, JAMES RICHARD D
Chmn, Campbell Co. Dem. Exec. Cmt, Ky.
b. Covington, Ky, 2/4/25; s. Cecil F. Poston and Agnes Duvelius P; m. 1/31/53 to Shirley Frost; c. Susan M, James R, Melinda M, Cindy M, Jay R, Diane M, Jennifer M, Jon R. and Amy M. Educ: Denver Univ, A.B, 47; Salmon P. Chase Col. of Law, LL.B, 51; Omicron Delta Kappa; Sigma Alpha Epsilon. Polit. & Govt. Pos: Alternate del, Dem. Nat. Conv, 64; del, Ky. Constitutional Rev. Assembly, 64-67; chmn, Dem. Co. Campaign, 65-68; chmn, Campbell Co. Dem. Exec. Cmt, 69- Bus. & Prof. Pos: Counsel, Cinti Gas & Elec. Co, 58- Mem: Am, Ky. and Campbell Co. Bar Asns; bd. dirs, North. Ky. C. of C; Dan Beard Coun; bd. dirs, Boy Scouts. Named Outstanding Young Man, Campbell Co, Ky, 61; Gov. Award, Ky, 66. Rel: Catholic. Mailing Add: 131 Capri Dr, Ft. Thomas, Ky. 41075.

POSTON, RALPH R. D
Fla. State Sen.
b. Miami, Fla, 1/2/23; m. to Carolyn Davis; c. Ralph R, Jr, Dorothy Susan (Mrs. Barrier) and Sheryl Lynne. Educ: Univ. of Miami; Univ. of Houston. Polit. & Govt. Pos: Fla. State Rep, 64-66; Fla. State Sen, 67-; mem, Metro-Dade Co. Examining Bd. Bus. & Prof. Pos: Pres. of steel erection firm, Poston Bridge and Iron, Inc, founded firm, 50, started incentive mgr, 61; Dale Carnegie Instr, 56; dir, Riverside Bank Miami. Mil. Serv: Navy, World War II. Mem: Past pres, Steel and Ornamental Erectors Asn. of S. Fla, Inc; adv, Univ. of Miami Citizens Bd; bd. of dirs, Goodwill Industs; former dir, Eng. Contractors Asn; Baptist Hosp. Adv. Bd; Mason; Mahi Shrine; Scottish Rite; Kiwanis; Moose; Tiger Bay Club; DAV; past pres, Allapattah Lions; indust. develop. cmt, Fla. C. of C; Fla. Rd. Builders; dir, S. Dade Coun; indust. develop. coun, Miami-Dade C. of C; trustee, Southeast. Ironworkers Health and Welfare Cmt; President's Nat. Hwy. Safety Adv. Cmt; SAR. Rel: Methodist. Legal Res: 6282 S.W. 133rd St, Miami, Fla. 33156. Mailing Add: 3103 N.W. 20th St, Miami, Fla. 33127.

POTGETER, JAMES ALVIN R
Iowa State Sen.
b. Steamboat Rock, Iowa, 10/19/30; s. George Potgeter and Lydia Kruse P; m. 12/26/58 to Joyce Hippen. Educ: Reed Col, 48-50; Univ. Iowa, B.A, 56; London Sch. of Econ. and Polit. Sci, 56-57. Polit. & Govt. Pos: Chmn, Rep. Co. Cent. Cmt, Iowa, 63-66; Iowa State Sen, 66-, Asst. Majority Leader and chmn, Iowa Develop. Cmt, Iowa State Senate, 69-; legis. mem, Interstate Coop. Cmn, 69- Bus. & Prof. Pos: Managing partner, Geo. Potgeter Co, 59-69. Mil. Serv: Entered as Pvt, Air Force, 50, released as S/Sgt, 54, after serv. in 20th Weather Squadron, Japan, 52-54; UN and Korean Theater of Opers. Medals; Syngman Rhee Presidential Unit Citation. Mem: Rotary; Am. Legion; Farm Bur. Rel: Protestant. Mailing Add: 10 Market St, Steamboat Rock, Iowa 50672.

POTOCHNIK, STANLEY D
Chmn, Sheboygan Co. Dem. Party, Wis.
b. Sheboygan, Wis, 11/15/17; s. John Potochnik and Mary Stajduhar P; m. 7/26/47 to Evelyn Gertrude Jacobs; c. Kristi Ann and Timothy Mark. Educ: Univ. Wis, B.S. in Mech. Eng, 48; Ill. Inst. Tech, 50; Foreign Students Club. Polit. & Govt. Pos: Tech. rep. in radio, Off. Strategic Serv, India and China, 44-45; v.chmn, Sheboygan Co. Dem. Party, Wis, 60-62, treas, 63-64, chmn, 65-; exec. bd. mem, Sixth Cong. Dist. Dem. Party, 65-66. Mem: Air Pollution Control Asn; Nat. Rifle Asn; China-Burma-India Vet. Asn; Boy Scouts. Rel: Methodist. Mailing Add: 2621 N. Ninth St, Sheboygan, Wis. 53081.

POTT, GEORGE FREDERICK R
b. Pittsburgh, Pa, 6/9/14; s. George Pott and Mary McNamara P; m. 4/10/40 to Vera McKinney; c. George F, Jr. and Richard W. Educ: Univ. Pittsburgh, B.A. in bus. admin, 37; Delta Tau Delta; Yankanuck Club, Sans Souci, Ont. Polit. & Govt. Pos: Chmn, Allegheny Co. Draft Eisenhower Cmt, Pa, 48; pres, 17th Legis. Dist. Rep. Cmt, 2 terms; asst. chmn, Rep. Finance Cmt, 50; chmn, Ind. Twp. Rep. Cmt, 50-; chmn, Ind. Twp. Authority, Pa, 57-68; chmn, Businessmen's Cmn. for Scott-McGonigle, 58 and for VanZandt-Scranton, 62; mem, Platform Subcmt. on Indust. Develop. and Unemploy, 62; treas, Scranton for Pres. Cmt, 64; chmn, Allegheny Co. Rep. Exec. Cmt, Pa, 64-67; mem, Pa. Joint State Govt. Cmn. Cmt. on Taxation; del. and co-chmn. taxation cmt, Pa. Constitutional Conv, 67-68; co-chmn, West. Pa. Nixon for President Cmt, 68. Bus. & Prof. Pos: Acct, Pa. Dept. of Pub. Assistance, 37-39; indust. engr, Blawnox Steel Co, 39-46; v.pres, Int. Water Corp, Pittsburgh, Pa, 46- Mil. Serv: Entered as 2nd Lt, Army, 41, released as Maj, 45, after serv. in 437th Antiaircraft Bn, African, Tunisian and Italian Campaigns; Atlantic Theater Ribbon; ETO Ribbon with 3 Stars; Maj, Army Inactive Res. Mem: Past dir, E. Liberty C. of C; Pittsburgh C. of C; World Trade Coun; World Affairs Coun; past pres, E. Liberty Rotary; 1st pres. and organizer, Dorseyville Volunteer Fire Co; past pres, Amen Corner; Ambassador's Club; Pa. Soc; Press Club; Friends of Scouting; Mason; Dist. 730 gov, Rotary Int, 69- Rel: Protestant Episcopal. Mailing Add: 518 Saxonburg Blvd, Pittsburgh, Pa. 15238.

POTT, GEORGE P. R
Dep. Asst. Secy. for Water Quality & Research, Dept. of the Interior
Mailing Add: Dept. of the Interior, C St. between 18th & 19th St. N.W, Washington, D.C. 20240.

POTTAGE, THOMAS MICHAEL R
Legis. Asst. to U.S. Rep. H. Allen Smith, Calif.
b. Glendale, Calif, 6/23/41; s. Thomas Edward Pottage and H. Louise Mosher P; div; c. Thomas William and Edward Dean. Educ: Glendale Col, 59-61. Polit. & Govt. Pos: Past v.pres, Glendale Young Rep, Calif; past v.pres. and past pres, Glendale Unit 1, United Rep. of Calif; legis. asst. to U.S. Rep. H. Allen Smith, Calif, 68- Bus. & Prof. Pos: Reporter, San Fernando Valley Sun, Calif, 60-62; city ed, Duartean, 62-63; ed. page ed, Ledger-Independents, 63-68. Mem: Bd. dir, Flintridge Prep. Sch. Alumni Asn, 67-68. Legal Res: 2233 Florencita Dr, Montrose, Calif. 91020. Mailing Add: 7708 Arlen St, Annandale, Va. 22003.

POTTENGER, THOMAS ALEXANDER R
Ohio State Rep.
b. Harrison, Ohio, 6/9/20; s. Meade Campbell Pottenger and Gussie Marie Ingersoll P; m. 11/7/45 to Mildred Vaye Roberson; c. Tom, Jr, Barbara Marie and Laura Marie. Educ: Ohio State Univ, B.Sc. Agr. Eng, 42; Chase Law Col, Cincinnati, J.D, 62. Polit. & Govt. Pos: Ohio State Rep, 61-66; co. judge, Hamilton Co, 66-67; asst. attorney gen, 68; Ohio State Rep, 73rd Dist, 69- Bus. & Prof. Pos: Farm mgr, Century Farms, Harrison, Ohio, 46-66; attorney-at-law, 62- Mil. Serv: Pfc, Marines, 43, released as 1st Lt, 46, after serv. in Third Marine Div, Pac. Theatre, 43-45; Lt, Navy Res, 17 years; Purple Heart; Guam Campaign Ribbon; Letter of Commendation for Bravery in Action; Iwo Jima Campaign Ribbon. Mem: Cincinnati and Ohio State Bar Asns; Am. Legion; Springdale Kiwanis; Cincinnati Br, Inst. World Affairs; Hamilton Co. Rep. Club. Rel: Protestant. Mailing Add: 750 Cedarhill Dr, Cincinnati, Ohio 45240.

POTTER, CHARLES EDWARD R
b. Lapeer, Mich, 10/30/16; s. Fred Potter and Sarah Elizabeth Converse P; m. to Mary Elizabeth Bryant Wismer; c. Henry Richards Wismer, Wendy Wisner. Educ: East. Mich. Univ, A.B, 38; LL.D, 54; LL.D, Hillside Col, Mich, 55. Polit. & Govt. Pos: Adminstr, Bur. Soc. Aid, Cheboygan Co, Mich, 38-42; voc. rehabilitation adv, Retraining and Reemployment Admin, Wash, D.C, 46-47; U.S. Rep, Mich, 47-52; U.S. Sen, Mich, 52-59. Bus. & Prof. Pos: Real estate broker, securities broker and bus. consult; v.pres, Int. Develop. & Eng. Corp; dir, Nat. Capitol Life Ins. Co; pres, Charles & Potter Co, 65-; sr. partner, Potter and Kornmeier Int, currently. Mil. Serv: Army, Maj, discharged 46; 28th Inf. Div, wounded at Colmar, France, 45; decorated Silver Star; French Croix de Guerre with Silver Star; Purple Heart with 2 clusters. Publ: 'Days of Shame,' 65. Mem: Am. Battle Monuments Comt; Wash. Real Estate Bd; Nat. Asn. Securities Dealers; Nat. Rehab. Asn.(dir.); Am. Legion; DAV; VFW; Amvets; Eagles; Elk; Kiwanis. Goodwill Award, 57; Nat. Rehabilitation Asn. Pres. Award, 54; VFW Award, 51; Hero of Month, DAV, 51; Named by U.S. Jr. C. of C. One of Ten Outstanding Young Men in Am, 51. Rel: Methòdist. Legal Res: 5221 Kenewood Ave, Chevy Chase, Md. 20015. Mailing Add: 1140 Connecticut Ave. N.W, Washington, D.C. 20036.

POTTER, IRWIN LEE R
Rep. Nat. Committeeman, Va.
b. Tower City, Pa, 10/5/09; s. Harry Stewart Potter and Emma Wagner P; m. 5/28/28 to Dulcie H. Horner; c. Alan Lee. Educ: Southeast. Univ. Polit. & Govt. Pos: Chmn, Arlington Co. Rep. Cmt, Va, 48-50 and Va. Tenth Cong. Rep. Dist, 50-52; Rep. cand, Va. State Legis, 49; spec. asst. to Secy. of Labor James P. Mitchell, 54-55; asst. to chmn, Rep. Nat. Cmt, 55-66; chmn, Va. Rep. State Cmt, 56-62; Rep. Nat. Committeeman, Va, 64-; exec. dir, Rep. Cong. Campaign Cmt; del, Rep. Nat. Cmt, 68. Bus. & Prof. Pos: Partner, Potter & Wilt, 56-, Lee-Hi Indust. Park, 63- and Maplewood Assocs; dir, Arlington Trust Co, Inc, 58- and Am. Realty Trust, 66-; gen. partner, Crystal Plaza Assocs, 66-; chmn. bd, Frank R. Jelleff, Inc, currently; pres, I. Lee Potter Assocs, Inc, currently. Mem: Wash. Golf.and Country Club; Capitol Hill Club; AFL-CIO, Local 161, AF of M; Gr. Wash. Cent. Labor Coun, AFL-CIO; former pres, Arlington Symphony Asn; former dir, Home Builders Asn. of Metrop. Wash. Rel: Baptist. Legal Res: 3120 N. Wakefield St, Arlington, Va. 22207. Mailing Add: Congressional Hotel, Washington, D.C. 20003.

POTTER, JAMES B, JR. R
Los Angeles City Councilman, Calif.
b. Humansville, Mo, 10/21/31; s. James Burnie Potter and Ruth McCall P; m. 3/29/52 to Norma McKevett Teague; c. Alan M, Susan L. and James B. Educ: Univ. Mo, B.S. in indust. and personnel mgt, 58; pres. of sr. class and student body. Polit. & Govt. Pos: Los Angeles City Councilman, 2nd Dist, Calif, 63-; v.pres, Bd. of Data Admin, Los Angeles; chmn, Water and Power Cmt; v.chmn Govt. Efficiency Cmn; mem, Bldg. and Safety Cmt. and Feather River Proj. Asn. Bus. & Prof. Pos: With Behr-Manning, 58-60; with Lockheed, 60-61; Electronics Sales, 62-63. Mil. Serv: Entered as Pvt, Air Force, 52, released as S/Sgt, 56, after serv. in AACS, Korea. Rel: Protestant. Legal Res: 12205 Viewcrest Dr, Studio City, Calif. 91604. Mailing Add: 200 N. Spring St, Room 236, City Hall, Los Angeles, Calif. 90012.

POTTER, JOHN MELVIN R
b. Wisconsin Rapids, Wis, 8/16/24; s. Roy M. Potter and Ruth C. Crowns P; m. 5/5/51 to Kathleen Reeths; c. Kevin, John and Greg. Educ: Univ. of Wis, LL.B, 48; Phi Alpha Delta; Beta Theta Pi. Polit. & Govt. Pos: Del, Rep. State Conv, Wis, 47-50 & 52-65; dist. chmn, Young Rep, 48-50; dist. attorney, Wood Co, 50-57; mem, Gov. Cmt. on Cranberry Probs, Wis, 59; Wis. State Sen, 61-65; chmn, Senate Rep. Caucus, 63-64; del, Rep. Nat. Conv, 64; chmn, Gov. Conf. on Water Probs, Wis, 65-66; chmn, State Bd. Natural Resources, currently. Bus. & Prof. Pos: Partner, Graves, Casey & Potter, 48-52; private law practice, 52-61; partner, Brazeau, Brazeau, Potter & Cole, 61-66; partner, Potter, Wefel & Nettesheim, 67- Mil. Serv: Entered as Pvt, Marine Corps, 43, released as 2nd Lt, 45, re-entered 51, released as 1st Lt, 52. Mem: Pres, Wis. Caranberry Growers, 59-60; Elks; Kiwanis; Am. Legion. Rel: Catholic. Mailing Add: 950 First Ave. S, Wisconsin Rapids, Wis. 54494.

POTTER, NORMA TEAGUE R
Mem, Calif. Rep. State Cent. Cmt.
b. Oxnard, Calif, 7/11/31; d. Charles McKevett Teague and Marjorie Cowden T; m. 3/29/52 to James Burnie Potter, Jr; c. Alam McCall, Susan Lindsey and James Bruce. Educ: Stanford Univ, 49; Univ. of Calif, 50-51; Pi Beta Phi. Polit. & Govt. Pos: Assoc. mem, Calif. Rep. State Cent. Cmt, 62-66, mem, 67-; second v.pres, San Fernando Valley Rep. Womens Club, 66, pres, 67-68. Mem: Bd. of dirs, Women's Div, South. Calif. Arthritis Found. Mailing Add: 12205 Viewcrest Rd, Studio City, Calif. 91604.

POTTER, ORLANDO B. D
b. Ossining, N.Y, 1/11/28; s. Frederick A. Potter and Irene McWilliams P; m. 8/20/56 to Rose Ann Early; c. Ann Brandreth and Matthew Early. Educ: Hamilton Col, B.A, 50; Yale Univ, M.A, 55; Am. Univ, Wash, D.C, 69; Pi Delta Epsilon; Delta Upsilon. Polit. & Govt. Pos: Legis. asst. to Sen. Claiborne Pell, R.I, 62-68; Dem-Lib. cand. for U.S. Rep, 68. Bus. & Prof. Pos: Reporter, Watertown Times, N.Y, 50; copy ed, Nippon Times, Tokyo, 52; ed. writer and Wash. correspondent, Providence J-Bul, R.I, 55-62. Mil. Serv: Army, 50-52, serv. as Combat correspondent, Pac. Stars and Stripes, Korea. Mem: Nat. Press Club. Cong. Staff Fel, Am. Polit. Sci. Asn, 69. Rel: Protestant. Legal Res: Brandreth, Long Lake, N.Y. 12847. Mailing Add: 4519 Klingle St. N.W, Washington, D.C. 20016.

POTTER, RALPH WILSON R
Iowa State Sen.
b. Cedar Rapids, Iowa, 7/29/20; s. Walter D. Potter and Helen M. Pinckney P; m. 5/2/45 to Helen E. Drake; c. Robert W. and Boyd D. Educ: Franklin High Sch, grad, 38. Polit. & Govt. Pos: Mayor, Marion, Iowa, 63-68; Iowa State Sen, Sub-dist. 1, Linn Co, 69- Bus. & Prof. Pos: Assoc, Linn Co. Produce Co, Marion, 38-55; real estate broker, 55- Mil. Serv: Entered as Pvt, Marine Corps, 42, released as S/Sgt, 45, after serv. in various Marine Air Units. Mem: Am. Legion; Kiwanis; Mason; Shrine; C. of C; Farm Bur. Rel: Methodist. Mailing Add: 1950 E. Post Rd, Marion, Iowa 52302.

POTTER, S. DON R
b. Detroit, Mich, 12/15/28; married; c. Patricia, Thomas. Educ: Grad, Mich. State Univ, B.A. and M.A; Univ. of Minn, LL.B. Polit. & Govt. Pos: Mich. State Sen, 64-66; former mem, Lansing City Coun, Ingham Co. Bd. of Supvrs. Bus. & Prof. Pos: Journalist; former radio and TV news dir. Rel: Presbyterian. 1967 Legal Res: Lansing, Mich. No mailing address available. (1967)

POTTER, THOMAS EUGENE R
W.Va. State Del.
b. Pittsburgh, Pa, 6/20/33; s. Eugene William Potter (deceased) and Dorothy Studebaker P; m. 8/25/56 to Nancy Elizabeth Rapp; c. Sharon Lynn, Barton Carl and Matthew Eugene. Educ: W.Va. Univ, A.B, 55 and LL.B, 57; Phi Alpha Delta; Sigma Phi Epsilon; Mountain; Sphinx; Fi Batar Cappar. Polit. & Govt. Pos: Pres, Young Rep. Club, Kanawha Co, W.Va, 63; chmn, Bd. of Zoning Appeals, Charleston, 65-66; v.chmn, Rep. Revival in W.Va, 65-66; city solicitor, Charleston, 67-68; mem, Munic. Planning Cmn, 67-68; W.Va. State Del, 67-; chmn, W.Va. Rep. State Exec. Cmt, 68-; mem, Rep. Nat. Cmt, 68- Bus. & Prof. Pos: Lawyer and partner, Woodroe, Kizer, and Steed, 60-68; Jackson, Kelly, Holt and O'Farrell, 69- Mil. Serv: Entered as 2nd Lt, Air Force, 57, released as 1st Lt, 60, after serv. in Judge Adv. Gen. Off; Capt, Air Force Res, 68. Mem: Am, W.Va. and Kanawha Co. Bar Asns; W.Va. State Bar (past chmn, Young Lawyers Sect); past pres, Kanawha Co. Legal Aid Soc; Rotary; Cosmos; past pres, Army and Navy Club of Charleston; past pres, Charleston Tennis Club. Named Young Man of the Year by Charleston Jr. C. of C. Rel: Presbyterian. Legal Res: 637 Gordon Dr, Charleston, W.Va. 25314. Mailing Add: 1601 Kanawha Valley Bank Bldg, Charleston, W.Va. 25301.

POTTER, WILLIAM SAMUEL D
Dem. Nat. Committeeman, Del.
b. Clarksburg, W.Va, 1/10/05; s. Dorsey Read Potter and May Wheat P; m. 6/28/30 to Alice H. Harvey; c. Mary (Mrs. Kitchel), Florence (Mrs. Robb) and Renee (Mrs. Sieglaff). Educ: Univ. Va, LL.B, 27; Phi Delta Phi; Order of Coif; Phi Beta Kappa; Chi Phi. Polit. & Govt. Pos: Chmn, Seventh Ward, Wilmington, Del, 29; mem, Del. Racing Cmn, 39-45; Dem. state chmn, Del, 42-45; Dem. Nat. Committeeman, Del 55-; mem. bd. of visitors, Univ. of Va, currently; del, Dem. Nat. Conv, 68. Bus. & Prof. Pos: Gen. practice of law, Wilmington, Del, 27-; dir, Wilmington Trust Co. and Thornton Fire Brick Co; Del. Wild Lands, Inc; Del. Park, Inc; Wilmington Med. Center; Episcopal Church Sch. Found, 48-; Del. Hosp, 50-; trustee, Winterthur Mus, 52- Publ: Co-author, Delaware Corporation Annotated, 36. Mem: Am. and N.Y.C. Bar Asns; pres, Del. Bar Asn, 42-44; Soc. of Colonial Wars; dir, Del. Racing Asn; Wilmington Club; Wilmington Country Club; Farmington Country Club; Biderman Golf Club. Rel: Episcopal; Chancellor, Episcopal Diocese of Del. Mailing Add: 5826 Kennett Pike, Wilmington, Del. 19801.

POULIN, GASTON GERARD D
Committeeman, Skowhegan Town Dem. Cmt, Maine
b. St. Joseph, Que, 1/28/22; s. Joseph W. Poulin and Alida Lessard P; m. 5/29/48 to Theresa Mary Provencher; c. David and Diane. Educ: High Sch. Polit. & Govt. Pos: Selectman, Skowhegan, Maine, 55-56, mem. planning bd, 56-60; Maine State Rep, 65-66; committeeman, Skowhegan Town Dem. Cmt, currently. Bus. & Prof. Pos: Poulin's Upholstery, 46- Mil. Serv: Entered as Pvt, Army Air Force, 41, released as T/Sgt, 45, after serv. in 323rd Bomb Group, ETO; Distinguished Flying Cross; Purple Heart; Air Medal with twelve clusters; ETO Medal with four stars; Am. Theater and Pre-Pearl Harbor Ribbons; Good Conduct and Victory Medals. Mem: VFW; Am. Legion; K. of C; Eagles; Lions; C. of C; Sports Booster Club; committeeman, Boy Scouts. Rel: Catholic. Mailing Add: 24 Marie St, Winslow, Maine 04976.

POULOS, WILLIAM FREDERIC D
Okla. State Rep.
b. 1920. Educ: Univ. Tex. Polit. & Govt. Pos: Okla. State Rep, 65- Bus. & Prof. Pos: Securities dealer. Mem: Chmn. of bd, Operation Rescue; Mason. Mailing Add: 505 N. 70th East Ave, Tulsa, Okla. 74115. (1967)

POUST, CLARA ESTHER R
b. Alberta, Can, 3/24/19; d. Delbert Henry Cook and Ruby Newman C; m. 2/14/46 to Raymond J. Poust; c. Raymond, Barry, John and Tom. Educ: Bus. Col, San Francisco. Polit. & Govt. Pos: Mem, Calif. Rep. State Cent. Cmt, until 69. Mem: Past pres, Lafayette PTA; hon. life mem, Calif. PTA. Rel: Lutheran. Mailing Add: 3414 McEllen Court, Lafayette, Calif. 94549.

POUZAR, THOMAS FRANK D
Chmn, Grand Traverse Co. Dem. Party, Mich.
b. Hamtramck, Mich, 10/16/26; s. Frank Pouzar and Rose Zezulka P; m. 7/19/52 to Amanda Louise Rosenburg; c. Thomas Frank, Jr, James Edward and Linda Marie. Educ: Buckley High Sch, Mich. Polit. & Govt. Pos: Secy, Grand Traverse Co. Dem. Party, Mich, 66 & 67, chmn, 67-; mem, Ninth Dist. Exec. Bd, Mich. Dem. Party, 66-; co-chmn, 69; mem, Mich. Anti-Ballistics Missile Cmt, 69; mem, Grand Traverse Co. Jury Bd, 69- Mem: Eagles; commun. action prog. chmn. and bd. trustee, Local 945, UAW. Award on the Adv. Effective Speaking and Parliamentary Procedure Class and an Award on Collective Bargaining Technicalities, Mich. State Univ; Award on a course in Workman Compensation and Unemployment Ins; Citation by the Am. Legion Baseball Cmn. Rel: Protestant. Mailing Add: 437 Fair St, Traverse City, Mich. 49684.

POWE, WILLIAM ALISON R
Chmn, Forrest Co. Rep. Exec. Cmt, Miss.
b. Hattiesburg, Miss, 12/19/98; s. William Alexander Powe and Pauline Lee P; m. 4/12/35 to Margaret Thomas; c. Ellen Thomas and William A, Jr. Educ: Miss. State Univ, B.Sci, 20; La. State Univ, 21; Universidad Cent, Madrid, Spain, 26; Kappa Alpha; Lee Guard. Polit. & Govt. Pos: Elec. cmnr, Forrest Co, Miss, currently; chmn, Forrest Co. Rep. Exec. Cmt, 68- Bus. & Prof. Pos: Chemist, Guantanamo Sugar Co, Cuba, 21-24; supt. of fabrication, Punta Alegre Sugar Co, 25-26; salesman, Oliver Continuous Filter Co, San Francisco, Calif, 26-34; owner, Powe Machinery Co, Havana, Cuba, 34-60; ed, Sugar J, 64-68. Mil. Serv: Entered as Student, ROTC, 16, released 2nd Lt, 21, after serv. in Inf. Mem: Int. and Am. Soc. of Sugar Cane Technologists; Miss. Asn. of Soil and Water Conserv. Dist. Cmnr; Mason; Scottish Rite; Rotary; Nat. Coun, Boy Scouts. Silver Beaver Award, Boy Scouts. Rel: Episcopal. Mailing Add: 300 Sixth Ave, Hattiesburg, Miss. 39401.

POWELL, ADAM CLAYTON, JR. D
U.S. Rep, N.Y.
b. New Haven, Conn, 11/29/08; s. Adam Clayton Powell and Mattie Fletcher Schaefer P; m. Dec, 1944 to Hazel Scott; c. Adam Clayton Powell, III; m. Dec, 1960 to Yvette Marjorie Flores Diago; c. Adam Clayton Powell-Diago. Educ: Colgate Univ, B.A, 30; Columbia Univ, M.A, 32; Va. Union Univ, LL.D, 48; Shaw Univ, D.D, 49; Phi Delta Kappa; Alpha Phi Alpha. Polit. & Govt. Pos: Mem, N.Y.C. Coun, 41-43; U.S. Rep, 18th Dist, N.Y, 44-, chmn, Educ. and Labor Cmt, U.S. House of Rep, until 67. Bus. & Prof. Pos: Minister, Abyssinian Baptist Church, N.Y.C, 30-; v.pres, World Asn. of Parliamentarians. Publ: Marching Blacks, Dial Press, 44; Keep the Faith, Simon and Schuster, 68; 'Duties and Responsibilities of a Congressman,' Esquire Mag, 9/63. Mem: Mason; Shrine; Elks; Bimini Big Game Fishing Club. Rel: Baptist. Legal Res: 175 W. 137th St, New York, N.Y. 10030. Mailing Add: 2244 Rayburn House Office Bldg, Washington, D.C. 20515.

POWELL, AUSTIN CLIFFORD D
Chmn, Frederick Co. Dem. Party, Md.
b. Frederick, Md, 8/11/13; s. James Kennedy Powell and Sadie Frances Meister P; m. 11/25/31 to Annabell Lee; c. Edna Irene. Polit. & Govt. Pos: V.chmn, Md. State Dem. Cent. Cmt, 58-62, chmn, 62-66; chmn, Frederick Co. Dem. Party, 68- Mem: Eagles; Moose; Jr. Fire Co; Jeffersonian Dem. Club. Rel: Episcopal. Mailing Add: 20 E. Ninth St, Frederick, Md. 21701.

POWELL, CHARLES CARUTH D
Chmn, Coryell Co. Dem. Party, Tex.
b. Gatesville, Tex, 9/22/12; s. William Lytle Powell, Sr. and Eula Caruth P; m. 11/30/33 to Nancy Lou Routh; c. Charles Caruth and William Elmo. Educ: John Tarleton State Col, 2 years. Polit. & Govt. Pos: Mayor, Gatesville, Tex, 56-59; chmn, Coryell Co. Dem. Party, 67- Bus. & Prof. Pos: Cotton ginner, Gatesville Gin Co, Tex, 33-69. Mem: Mason. Mailing Add: 1211 E. Bridge St, Gatesville, Tex. 76528.

POWELL, CHARLES LEWIS D
S.C. State Rep.
b. Ware Shoals, S.C, 6/18/33; s. Richard Powell and Cora Ferguson P; single. Educ: Lander Col, 55. Polit. & Govt. Pos: S.C. State Rep, currently. Bus. & Prof. Pos: Trainman, Seaboard Airline R.R; farmer. Mil. Serv: Army Res, 8 years. Mailing Add: R.F.D. 4, Abbeville, S.C. 29620. (1967)

POWELL, DONALD DELOSS D
b. Madison Co, Mont, 6/17/12; s. Jonathon White Powell and Nettie Waite P; m. 12/23/33 to Alice Osborn Hay; c. Coral (Mrs. Lowry), Richard 'Dick', Robert 'Bob' and William 'Bill'. Educ: Cardwell High Sch, 27-31. Polit. & Govt. Pos: Committeeman, precinct 15, Madison Co. Dem. Party, Mont, 56- and co. chmn, 66-68. Mem: Mason (Master, Riverside Lodge 111, Jefferson Island, Mont); leader, Mt. Hollowtop 4-H Club; Eastern Star (Worthy Patron, Randall Chap. 97); Mont. Farmer's Union; Mont. Stock Growers; Mont. Wool Growers; Agr. Stabilization and Conserv. Serv. Cmt. Named Mont. Father of the Year, 53; 20 Year 4-H Leader Award; Grand Cross of Colors, Rainbow. Rel: Methodist. Mailing Add: Cardwell, Mont. 59721.

POWELL, EDWARD BAKER R
Chmn, Coryell Co. Rep. Party, Tex.
b. Gatesville, Tex, 6/17/04; s. Sam Jones Powell and Martha Hampton P; m. 11/3/21 to Louise Galloway; c. Anne Louise (Mrs. Lawrence J. Black). Educ: St. Edwards Col, 2 years. Polit. & Govt. Pos: Chmn, Coryell Co. Rep. Party, Tex, 62- Bus. & Prof. Pos: Salesman, Johnson & Johnson, Ky, 30-40, divisional sales mgr, Calif, 40-61; partner, Powell Real Estate, Gatesville, Tex, 62-69. Mem: Elks; Gatesville Country Club; dir, Red Cross, Coryell Co. Rel: Presbyterian. Legal Res: 106 N. 30th St, Gatesville, Tex. 76528. Mailing Add: Box 145, Gatesville, Tex. 76528.

POWELL, FREDDIE DELANO D
b. Kent, Ala, 5/7/32; s. Millard Lee Powell and Naomi Ruth Yates P; m. 9/21/57 to Katie Mulder. Educ: Schs. of Elmore Co. and studied acct. Polit. & Govt. Pos: Ala. State Rep, 62-66. Bus. & Prof. Pos: Acct. profession. Mem: Mason; Civitan. Rel: Congregational Christian; Deacon, Congregational Christian Church. Mailing Add: Route 1, Tallassee, Ala. 36078.

POWELL, HERBERT B. Independent
b. Monmouth, Ore, 7/13/03; s. Ira Clinton Powell and Lena Guenavier Butler P; m. 4/7/28 to Beryl King. Educ: Univ. Ore, B.S, 26; Command Gen. Staff Sch, grad, 41; Nat. War Col, 48-49; Phi Kappa Psi. Polit. & Govt. Pos: U.S. Ambassador to New Zealand, 63-68. Mil. Serv: Entered as Pvt, Ore. Nat. Guard, 19, released as Sgt, 26; entered as 2nd Lt, Army, 26, released as Gen, 61, after serv. in Hawaii, 26-41, War Dept. Gen. Staff, 42, chief of staff, 75th Inf. Div, European campaigns including Battle of the Bulge, 43-45, U.S. Army Hq, Europe, 45-47, comdr, 17th Inf. Regt. advance on Yalu River, Korea, 50, dep. G-1 manpower control and Army Gen. Staff, 51-54; comdr, 25th Inf. Div, 54-56, comdr. U.S. Army, Pac, 56; commandant, Army Inf. Sch, Ft. Benning and U.S. Army Inf. Center, 56-58; Dep. Commanding Gen, Res. Forces, Continental Army Command, 58-60; Commanding Gen, Third Army, 60; Commanding Gen, Continental Army Command, 60-63; Comdr-in-Chief, Army Atlantic, Cuban Crisis, 60-63; Distinguished Serv. Cross; Distinguished Serv. Medal; Legion of Merit with Oak Leaf Cluster; Bronze Star with Two Oak Leaf Clusters; Air Medal; Commendation Medal; Purple Heart; Combat Inf. Badge; Wings of Army Aviator; Czech. War Cross; Ulch Distinguished Serv. Medal; Presidential Citation, Repub. Korea. Mem: Army and Navy Club. Mailing Add: P.O. Box 98, Jekyll Island, Ga. 31520.

POWELL, JOHN DUANE R
Committeeman, Mo. State Rep. Party
b. Rolla, Mo, 12/9/25; s. Frank Bowman Powell and Gertrude Carpenter P; m. 4/23/49 to Ruth Hawkins; c. Jane, Anne and Frank Bowman. Educ: Univ. Mo, Rolla, 43; Triangle. Polit. & Govt. Pos: Committeeman, Mo. State Rep. Party, 62-; treas, Phelps Co. Rep. Cmt, 62-64 & 68-; del, Rep. Nat. Conv, 64. Bus. & Prof. Pos: Secy-treas, Frank B. Powell Lumber Co, currently; chmn, Adv. Coun, Forestry Dept, Univ. Mo, 64; chmn, Forestry Cmt, Mo. Conserv. Fedn, 65- Mil. Serv: Midshipman, Merchant Marine, 44-45; Pac. Theater Ribbon. Mem: Pres, Rolla Lions, 61; v.pres, Rolla C. of C, 54. Forest Conserv. of the Year Award, Conserv. Fedn. Mo, Sears Found. and Nat. Wildlife Fedn, 68; Cert. of Merit in Forestry, Univ. Mo, 68. Rel: Episcopal. Legal Res: 605 W. 11th St, Rolla, Mo. 65401. Mailing Add: P.O. Box 576, Rolla, Mo. 65401.

POWELL, JOHN WILLIAM D
Miss. State Sen.
b. Liberty, Miss, 3/4/28; s. John Wesley Powell and Nan Bond P; m. 4/25/65 to Martha Ann Burris; c. John Wesley. Educ: Southwest Miss. Jr. Col, Summit. Polit. & Govt. Pos: Miss. State Sen, 60-; mem, Citizens Coun, presently. Bus. & Prof. Pos: Self-employed, cattle and timber. Mem: Mason; Shrine; Eastern Star; Miss. Cattleman Asn; Farm Bur; Tree Farmers. Rel: Baptist. Mailing Add: Route 2, Liberty, Miss. 39645.

POWELL, KATHRYN 'KATE' R
b. Calhoun, Mo, 9/29/07; d. James Palistine Doss and Agnes Mae Mason D; m. 12/26/45 to Weston Powell, wid. 1/24/63. Polit. & Govt. Pos: Secy. and membership chmn, Lafayette Co. Federated Women's Rep. Club, Mo, 60-62; secy, Fourth Dist. Women's Federated Rep. Club, 60-64; v.chmn, Lafayette Co. Rep. Cent. Cmt, 62-66; Mo. Out State chmn, Wash. Conf, 63; v.chmn, Mo. State Rep. Party, 64-69. Mem: Past Noble Grand, Rebekah Lodge 678; Farm Bur; Mo. Farm Orgn; charter mem, Lafayette Co. Hist. Soc; Mo. State Saddle Club; Lexington Saddle Club. Show horses, matched pair, received High Hon. in 5 states. Rel: Christian Church. Mailing Add: 500 W. 32nd St, Higginsville, Mo. 64037. (1967)

POWELL, MARION LEE R
Utah State Rep.
b. Ogden, Utah, 7/14/05; s. Thomas Ezra Powell and Jane Ritchie P; m. 6/27/27 to Mildred LaVon Reeder; c. Darlene, Marcia Jane and Sally. Polit. & Govt. Pos: Utah State Rep, Seventh Dist, Weber Co, 67- Bus. & Prof. Pos: Sales clerk, Safeway Stores, 27-29, mgr. and owner, 29-46. Rel: Latter-day Saint. Mailing Add: 1161 W. 12th St, Ogden, Utah 84404. (1967)

POWELL, MARTHA BROWN R
East. V.Chmn, Va. Rep. Party
b. Battery Park, Va, 9/5/26; d. Robert Elmer Brown and Josie Lee Whitley B; m. 6/5/45 to James Melvin Powell, Sr; c. Jacqueline Faye, James Melvin, Jr. and Pactricia Luellen. Educ: Smithfield High Sch, Va, grad, 44. Polit. & Govt Pos: Pres, Isle of Wight Co. Rep. Womans Club, 61-; alternate del, Rep. Nat. Conv, 64, del. and credentials chmn, 68; chmn, Isle of Wight Co. Rep. Party, 64-68, secy, 68-; Fourth Dist. Rep.Va. Fedn. of Rep. Women, 64-; East. v.chairwoman, Va. Rep. Party, 68- Bus. & Prof. Pos: Secy, R.E. Brown & Sons, 59-; off. helper, Little's Supermkt, Smithfield, Va, 69- Mem: Smithfield Recreation Asn; UDC. Rel: Baptist. Mailing Add: Route 1, Box 75 A, Carrollton, Va. 23314.

POWELL, PAUL D
Secy. of State, Ill.
b. Vienna, Ill, 1/21/02; married. Educ: Vienna Pub. High Sch, Ill. Polit. & Govt. Pos: Former mem, State Personnel Admin. Cmn, Cmn. to Study State Govt, Legis. Coun, Intergovt. Coop. Cmn, State Revenue Laws Cmn. and Munic. Revenue Cmn, Ill; former mayor and mem. high sch. bd, Vienna, Ill; mem, Johnson Co. Dem. Cent. Cmt, 28-, chmn, currently; Ill. State Rep, 34-64, Dem. minority whip, Ill. House Rep, 45, Dem. minority leader, 47, 51, 53 & 63, speaker, 49, 59 & 61; downstate dir, Ill. State Dem. Cent. Cmt, 45-54, mem, currently; mem, Ill. Budgetary Cmn, 45-64; mem, Legis. Audit Cmn, 57-64; Secy. of State, Ill, 64-; del, Dem. Nat. Conv, 68. Bus. & Prof. Pos: Former operator, private retail and serv. estab. Mem: Dir, Ill. Asn. Co. Fairs; secy, Massac Co. Fair; AF&AM; Elks; Eagles; Moose; Shrine. Selected Outstanding Legislator of Ill, Ill. Legis. Correspondents Asn, 51-55. Legal Res: Vienna, Ill. 62995. Mailing Add: 208, State Capitol, Springfield, Ill. 62706.

POWELL, SAMUEL CLARENCE R
b. Cheyenne, Wyo, 9/26/92; s. Samuel J. Powell and Mary Delahunty P; m. 11/8/23 to Myra Grout. Educ: Notre Dame Univ, 11-12; Univ. Pa, 12-14; Georgetown Univ, J.D, 15. Polit. & Govt. Pos: Co. attorney, Weber Co, Utah, 24-26; govt. appeal agent, Selective Serv, 45-69; mem, State Bd. of Corrections, 52-59; del, Rep. Nat. Conv, 56 & 64; trustee, Weber State Col, 61-65. Bus. & Prof. Pos: Cmnr, Utah State Bar, 31-34, pres, 34; v.pres, Bank of Utah, 51-57. Mil. Serv: Entered as Seaman 2/C, Navy, 17, released as Chief Storekeeper, 18, after serv. in Supply Corp. Mem: Pres, Ogden C. of C, 40; Am. Bar Asn; Utah State Bar; Am. Law Inst; Am. Legion; Rotary. Rel: Catholic. Legal Res: 1620-29th St, Ogden, Utah 84403. Mailing Add: 621 Eccles Bldg, Ogden, Utah 84401.

POWELL, STANLEY M. R
Mich. State Rep.
b. Ionia, Mich, 7/7/98; married; c. Patricia Ann, Ronald Herbert, Larry Burton, Rex Lynn. Educ: Grad, Mich. State Univ, B.S, 20; Pi Kappa Delta; Delta Sigma Rho (hon. pub. speaking and debating fraternities). Polit. & Govt. Pos: Mich. State Rep, 30-32 & 64-; mem, Mich. State Fair Authority, 44-64; del, Constitutional Conv, 61-62. Bus. & Prof. Pos: Farmer; served as legis. counsel and dir. of pub. affairs, Mich. Farm Bur, 21-27 & 38-64; contrib. ed, Mich. Farmer Mag, 27-65. Mil. Serv: World War I. Mem: Overseer, Mich. State Grange, 28-32; mem. exec. cmt, Mich. State Grange, 32-66; former dir. and past pres, Am. Milking Shorthorn Soc; currently secy-treas, Mich. Milking Shorthorn Asn; Farm Bur; Grange; Am. Legion; Vets. of World War I of the U.S.A. Awarded citations and plaques by Mich. State Univ, Mich. Farm Bur, Mich. State Grange, Mich. Future Farmers of Am. and Mich. Asn. of Teachers of Voc. Agr. Rel: Baptist. Mailing Add: R.F.D. 1, Ionia, Mich. 48846.

POWELL, WESLEY R
b. Portsmouth, N.H, 10/13/15; s. Samuel Wesley Powell and Mary Gosse P; m. 1942 to Beverly Swain; c. Samuel, Peter and Nancy. Educ: Univ. N.H; South. Methodist Univ. Col. Law. Polit. & Govt. Pos: Asst. to U.S. Sen. Styles Bridges; staff dir, U.S. Sen, Cmt. on Appropriation and other cmts, 40-43 & 46-49; Gov, N.H, 59-63; chmn, U.S. Gov. Conf, 60-63; chmn, New Eng. Gov. Conf, 61-62. Bus. & Prof. Pos: Lawyer, publisher and businessman, 63- Mil. Serv: Army Air Corps, Bomber command, ETO. Mailing Add: Hampton Falls, N.H. 03844.

POWER, PHILIP HARWICK D
b. Ann Arbor, Mich, 6/3/38; s. Eugene Barnum Power and Sadye Harwick P; single. Educ: Univ. Mich, B.A, 60; Univ. Col, Oxford Univ, Marshall Scholar and B.A, 64; Phi Beta Kappa. Polit. & Govt. Pos: Press writer, Staebler for U.S. Rep, 62 and Staebler for Gov, 64; admin. asst. to U.S. Rep. Paul H. Todd, Jr, Third Dist, Mich, 65-66. Bus. & Prof. Pos: City ed, Fairbanks Daily News-Miner, Alaska, 61-62; staff mem, Chicago Daily News, For. News Serv, 62-64; publisher, Observer Newspaper Inc, Livonia, Mich, 66- Legal Res: 16535 Middle Belt Rd, Livonia, Mich. 48154. Mailing Add: 33050 Five Mile Rd, Livonia, Mich. 48154.

POWERS, ANNA BERTHA JOSEPHINE D
Committeeman, N.Dak. State Dem. Cent. Cmt.
b. Leonard, N.Dak, 7/10/12; d. Julius Anderson and Inga Verding A; m. 6/18/30 to Edward Lancing Powers. Educ: Leonard High Sch, grad, 30; Leonard Adult Classes, 60. Polit. & Govt. Pos: Precinct committeeman, Dem. Party, N.Dak, 50-; pres, N.Dak. Dem. Non-Partisan League Woman's Club, 60-; N.Dak. State Rep, 61-66, v.chmn, soc. welfare cmt, N.Dak. House of Rep, 65; committeeman, N.Dak. State Dem. Cent. Cmt, 61-; mem, N.Dak. Gov. Cmn. on Status of Women, 63; del, Dem. Nat. Conv, 64. Mem: Pres, Leonard Cemetery Asn; Maple River Homemaker's Club; N.Dak. Coun. of Churches, Dept. of Legis; N.Dak. Diamond Jubilee Cmt, 64. Rel: Moravian; elected to Provincial Women's Bd, North. Prov, 66-, v.pres, 69-; Elder, local Moravian Church. Mailing Add: Leonard, N.Dak. 58052.

POWERS, ARTHUR B. D
b. N.Y.C, 6/28/28; s. Arthur Prosser Powers and Helen Boyd P; div; c. Arthur B, Jr, Juliann and Martha Grace. Educ: Tufts Col; Tower Cross; Polit. & Govt. Pos: Chmn, Berlin Town Dem. Party, Conn, 55-61; Conn. State Rep, 59-61; First selectman, Berlin, Conn, 59-; spec. asst. to U.S. Sen. Thomas J. Dodd, Conn, 61-68; state chmn, Elec. of Dem. Legislators, 62; cmnr, State Water Resources Cmn, 63-; campaign mgr. for Rep. Bernard Grabowski, 64; alternate del, Dem. Nat. Conv, 64, del, 68; mem, Conn. State Dem. Cent. Cmt, 66-68. Bus. & Prof. Pos: Pres, Francis Maloney Ins. Agency, Inc, 56. Mem: New Britain YMCA; corporator, New Britain Gen. Hosp. Rel: Protestant. Mailing Add: 857 Worthington Ridge, Berlin, Conn. 06037.

POWERS, FRANK JAMES D
b. Jerseyville, Ill, 2/18/96; s. James J. Powers and Margaret O'Malley P; m. 8/19/31 to Nellie Hunt Sunderland. Educ: Central School. Polit. & Govt. Pos: Alternate del, Nat. Dem. Conv, 52-64; chmn, Jersey Co. Dem. Cmt, Ill, 8 years, hon. chmn, until 68. Bus. & Prof. Pos: Auto dealer, Sunderland Motor Co, 19-57. Mil. Serv: Entered as Pvt, Army and released as Cpl, 18. Mem: K. of C; Elks; Am. Legion; 40 et 8; Jersey Co. Farm Bur; Westlake Country Club. Rel: Catholic. Mailing Add: 708 N. State St, Jerseyville, Ill. 62052. (1967)

POWERS, GORDON F. R
Mem, Orange Co. Rep. Cent. Cmt, Calif.
b. La Grande, Ore, 4/18/16; s. George Gordon Powers and Catherine Hilma Johnson P; m. 12/11/43 to Martha Jenkins; c. Patricia B, G. Bruce and Bennett F. Educ: Univ. Wash, 34-40; Varsity Boat Club; Oval Club. Polit. & Govt. Pos: Mem, Orange Co. Rep. Cent. Cmt, Calif, 64-; mem, Calif. Rep. State Cent. Cmt, 66-; cmnr, Calif. State Bldg. Standards Cmn, 67-; v.pres, Calif. Rep. Assembly, 68- Bus. & Prof. Pos: Architect, Am. Inst. Architects, 52- Mil. Serv: Entered as Flying Cadet, Army Air Corps, 41, released as Cadet; Pvt, Army, 44-46. Mem: Am. Inst. Architects; Lions; Seal Beach and Long Beach Kids Basebal Asns; Long Beach Comets; Girls Track Club. Rel: Protestant. Mailing Add: 1545 Crestview, Seal Beach, Calif. 90740.

POWERS, JAMES EDWARD D
N.Y. State Sen.
b. Chicago, Ill, 5/30/31; s. Vincent Henry Powers and Mary La Fleur P; m. 10/12/52 to Lucille Ann De Frank; c. Scott Vincent and Valorie Ann. Educ: North. Ill. Univ, B.S, 57; Univ. Ill, M.A. in labor and indust. rels, 58. Polit. & Govt. Pos: Councilman, Chili, N.Y, 61-65; N.Y. State Assemblyman, Third Dist, 65 and 133rd Dist, 66; N.Y. State Sen, 51st Dist, 67- Bus. & Prof. Pos: Teacher, East High, Rochester, N.Y, 58-65; bank officer, Lincoln Rochester Trust of Rochester. Mil. Serv: Entered as Pvt, Air Force, 51, released as Sgt, 55. Mem: Elks; Lions; Am. Legion. Rel: Episcopal. Mailing Add: 17 Evergreen Dr, Rochester, N.Y. 14624.

POWERS, JOHN E. D
Dem. Nat. Committeeman, Mass.
b. South Boston, Mass, 11/1/10; m. to Dorothy M. Hutton; c. John E, Jr. and Dorothy (Mrs. Richard Kelly); grandchildren, John E, III, Susan Marie, Richard Jr. and Don. Polit. & Govt. Pos: Mass. State Rep, 39-46; Mass. State Sen, 46-64; clerk, Mass. Supreme Judicial Court, Suffolk Co, 64-; del, Dem. Nat. Conv, 68; Dem. Nat. Committeeman, Mass, 68- Rel: Catholic. Mailing Add: 158 M St, South Boston, Mass. 02127. (1967)

POWERS, KIERAN FRANCIS R
Chmn, Juneau Co. Rep. Orgn, Wis.
b. Mauston, Wis, 12/7/32; s. James Michael Powers and Emma Feldbruegge P; m. 8/8/59 to Dolores Rose Gilles; c. David, Donna, Sharon, Mary Louise

and Patricia. Educ: Univ. Wis, Col. of Agr, 51. Polit. & Govt. Pos: Secy, Juneau Co. Rep. Orgn, Wis, 60-66, chmn, 66-; chmn, Town Bd, Seven Mile Creek, 65-69; mem, State Bd. of Agr, 69- Mil. Serv: Pvt, Army, 57-58. Mem: Kiwanis; K. of C; Juneau Co. Agr. Soc. Rel: Catholic. Mailing Add: Lyndon Station, Wis. 53944.

POWERS, LAWTON RAYMOND R
Mem, Calif. Rep. State Cent. Cmt.
b. Bakersfield, Calif, 9/3/40; s. Stanley Norvan Powers and Virginia Dougherty P; m. 6/21/59 to Aloma Faye Bonny; c. Lawton Darren and Warren Todd. Educ: Bakersfield High Sch, Calif, grad, 58. Polit. & Govt. Pos: Mem, United Rep. of Calif, 67-69; mem, Calif. Rep. State Cent. Cmt, 67- Bus. & Prof. Pos: V.pres, and partner, Warde D. Watson Realty, Bakersfield, Calif, 64-69, pres. and partner, 69-; v.pres, Kern Commercial Properties, 67. Mem: Bakersfield Bd. Realtors; Indust. and Commercial Div, Calif. Real Estate Asn; Nat. Inst. Real Estate Brokers; Elks; Rotary. Named Certified Commercial Investment Mem. by Bd. Gov, Nat. Inst. Real Estate Brokers. Rel: Protestant. Mailing Add: 2412 Elm St, Bakersfield, Calif. 93301.

POWERS, LEONARD H. D
b. Rockwell City, Iowa, 1/4/10; s. William H. Powers and Bessie Baxter P; m. 8/12/35 to Madeline Kenney; c. James, Robert and Carol (Mrs. Barrett). Educ: Creighton Univ, Pharm. Grad, 32; Alpha Sigma Nu; Phi Delta Chi. Polit. & Govt. Pos: Chmn, Sanit. Cmn, Omaha, Nebr, 52-56; del, Dem. Nat. Conv, 68. Bus. & Prof. Pos: Pharmacist, Powers Pharm, 37-69; pres, Powers Investment Co, 46-69. Mem: K. of C. Rel: Catholic. Mailing Add: 8607 Douglas St, Omaha, Nebr. 68114.

POWERS, THOMPSON D
b. New Orleans, La, 4/29/29; s. Marion Thompson Powers and Eloise Noyes P; m. 12/18/54 to Mary Lamb; c. David, William and Thomas. Educ: Duke Univ, A.B, 51; Harvard Law Sch, LL.B, 54; Phi Beta Kappa. Polit. & Govt. Pos: Spec. asst. to Under Secy. of Labor, 61-62; dep. solicitor of Labor, 62-63; exec. asst. to the Secy. of Labor, 64-65; exec. dir, Equal Employment Opportunity Cmn, 65; registrn. chmn, Dem. State Cent. Cmt, Montgomery Co, Md, 66; mem. staff, Platform Cmt, Dem. Nat. Conv, 68. Bus. & Prof. Pos: Assoc, Steptoe & Johnson, Washington, D.C, 57-61, partner, 66- Mil. Serv: Entered as Off. Cand, Navy, 54, released as Lt.(jg), 57, after serv. in Atlantic Res. Fleet. Mem: Am. and Dist. of Columbia Bar Asns. Rel: Episcopal. Mailing Add: 5204 Keokuk St, Chevy Chase, Md. 20016.

POWERS, WILLIAM SHOTWELL R
Rep. Nat. Committeeman, Colo.
b. Elizabeth, N.J, 6/7/10; s. James P. Powers and May Statts P; m. 10/4/40 to Arlene Morrison Crane; c. Jean P. and Patricia C. Educ: Rutgers Univ, B.S. in Bus, 33, LL.B, 36; Delta Upsilon. Polit. & Govt. Pos: Rep. Nat. committeeman, Colo, currently; Colo. State Sen, 55-56; various positions, Rep. Party, 33- Bus. & Prof. Pos: Attorney and partner, Rothgerber Appel & Powers, 46- Mil. Serv: Entered as Lt, Army, 40; released as Col, 46, after serv. in West. Pac. Area; Legion of Merit; Bronze Star; Pac. Theater Ribbon; Col, Army Res. Mem: Am. and Denver Colo. Bar Asns; Am. Legion; VFW. Rel: Presbyterian. Mailing Add: 745 S. Steel St, Denver, Colo. 80209.

POYNTER, BILL CHARLES R
b. Hillman, Ark, 9/27/35; s. Sidney H. Poynter and Nina Holman P; m. 8/24/56 to Martha Carolyn Scoggins; c. Cynthia Ann, Janice Carolyn and Karen Elizabeth. Educ: Ark. Polytech. Col, B.S. in Sci. & Math, 57; Nat. Mil. Honor Soc; Sci. and Math. Club. Polit. & Govt. Pos: Pres, Texarkana Young Rep, Ark, 62-63; del, Rep. Nat. Conv. and Ark. State Rep. Conv, 64; chmn, Miller Co. Rep. Cmt, Ark, 64-66; mem, Ark. Rep. State Cent. Cmt, 64-66; chmn, Miller Co. Elec. Cmn, Ark, currently. Bus. & Prof. Pos: Geologist, Scoggins Independent Oil, 58-62; independent oil operator, 62-; trustee, South. State Col, presently; mem, Interstate Oil Compact Cmn, presently. Mil. Serv: 2nd Lt, Army, 57-58; 1st Lt, 19th Corps, Army Res, 58-65. Mem: Shreveport Geological Soc; mem, Texarkana bd. of dirs, Kiwanis Int. Rel: Baptist. Mailing Add: 11 Regency, Texarkana, Ark. 75501.

POZEN, WALTER D
b. East Orange, N.J, 10/17/33; s. Irving Joseph Pozen and Bert Protter P; m. 6/19/55 to Elizabeth Klupt; c. Agatha Elizabeth, Jonathan Walter and Thorn Lord. Educ: Univ. of Chicago Col, B.A, 52; Univ. of Chicago Law Sch, J.D, 56; Iron Mask; Owl & Serpent. Polit. & Govt. Pos: Mem, campaign staff, U.S. Sen. Harrison Williams, N.J, 58; asst. to U.S. Secy. of Interior, 61-67; del, Dem. Nat. Conv, 64, counsel, Credentials Cmt, 68. Bus. & Prof. Pos: Assoc, law firm of Strasser, Spiegelberg, Fried & Frank, Wash, D.C, 56-58; legis. counsel, Wash. Home Rule Cmt, 58; assoc. dir. and counsel, For. Policy Clearing House, 59; resident partner, Wash. off. of N.Y. law firm of Stroock, Stroock & Lavan, 67- Publ: Book reviews, Wash. Post, 60-64; Strategy for the Sixties, Prager, N.Y, 60. Rel: Jewish. Legal Res: 19 Warren Rd, Maplewood, N.J. 07040. Mailing Add: 3415 Raymond St, Chevy Chase, Md. 20015.

PRACHT, JOHN CHRISTOPHER, JR. D
b. 8/9/25; s. John C. Pracht and Catherine P; m. to Sara Eunice Sullivan; c. Chris. Educ: Vanderbilt Univ, B.A. and LL.B, 51, LL.M, Taxation, 52. Polit. & Govt. Pos: S.C. State Rep, 57-68. Bus. & Prof. Pos: Lawyer. Mil. Serv: Army, Parachute Inf, 43-46. Mailing Add: Box 136, Anderson, S.C. 29621. (1967)

PRANGE, ROBERT LOUIS R
Mo. State Sen.
b. St. Louis, Mo, 12/3/15; s. Louis Herman Prange and Adelia W. Redemeyer P: m. 7/2/40 to Mildred G. Brown; c. Barbara Ann, Marilyn Sue, Elise Marie, Louis Gordon, Robert Lee and Frederick William. Educ: Univ. Mo, Rolla, B.S.C.E, 36; City Col. Law & Finance, LL.B, 40; Alexander Hamilton Inst, 50; Tau Beta Pi; Letterman, basketball team, 34-36. Polit. & Govt. Pos: Dir, Hazelwood Sch. Bd, Mo, 63-; Mo. State Sen, 67- Bus. & Prof. Pos: Asst. div. engr, Wabash R.R, 41-44, trainmaster, 44-46; staff asst. personnel, Norfolk & West. R.R, 46- Mem: Mo. Bar Asn; dir, Spanish Lake Imp. Asn. Rel: Lutheran. Mailing Add: 12714 Bellefontaine Rd, St. Louis, Mo. 63138.

PRANGER, ROBERT JOHN Independent
Dep. Asst. Secy. of Defense for Int. Security Affairs
b. Waukesha, Wis, 11/6/31; s. John William Pranger and Alpha Rasmussen P; m. 1/30/60 to Charlotte Gifford Evans; c. Benjamin Charles and Melissa Claire. Educ: San Diego State Col, 49-52; Univ. Calif, Berkeley, B.A, 53, M.A, 57, Ph.D, 61; Phi Beta Kappa. Polit. & Govt. Pos: Dept Asst. Secy. of Defense for Int. Security Affairs, Dept. of Defense, 69- Bus. & Prof. Pos: Instr. polit. sci, Univ. Ill, Urbana, 60-61, asst. prof, 61-65; asst. prof, Univ. Ky, 65-66, assoc. prof, 66-68; lectr, Univ. Calif, Berkeley, 66; assoc. prof, Univ. Wash, 68- Mil. Serv: Entered as Pvt, Army, 54, released as Sp-3, 55, after serv. in G-2, Caribbean, 54-55. Publ: The Eclipse of Citizenship, Holt, Rinehart and Winston, 68; Action, Symbolism, and Order, Vanderbilt Univ. Press, 68; plus others. Mem: Am. Polit. Sci. Asn. Woodrow Wilson Fel, 59-60; Soc. Sci. Research Coun. Fel, 62-63. Rel: Protestant. Legal Res: 3877 45th Ave. N.E, Seattle, Wash. 98105. Mailing Add: 4512 33rd St. N, Arlington, Va. 22207.

PRATT, FREDERICK D
b. Woburn, Mass, 8/6/28; married; c. three. Educ: Bentley Col. of Acct. and Finance, Boston, Mass. Polit. & Govt. Pos: N.H. State Rep, 63-67. Bus. & Prof. Pos: Prin, Mutual Credit Corp, Keene. Mil. Serv: Navy. Mem: K. of C; Keene Lodge of Elks. Rel: Catholic. 1967 Legal Res: 42 Congress St, Keene, N.H. No mailing address available. (1967)

PRATT, JEROME D
Fla. State Rep.
b. Orlando, Fla, married; c. Five. Educ: Stetson Univ, B.A, LL.B. Polit. & Govt. Pos: City judge, Palmetto, Fla; chmn. legis. cmn, Mantee Co. Safety Cmn, currently; Fla. State Rep, 67- Bus. & Prof. Pos: Attorney. Mil. Serv: Cpl, Army, World War II. Mem: Conquistadors; C. of C; PTA (past pres, Palmetto Elem. Sch); dir, Heart Fund; Palmetto Jaycees (v.pres). Rel: Methodist. Legal Res: 2214 Seventh St, Palmetto, Fla. 33561. Mailing Add: P.O. Box 67, Palmetto, Fla. 33561.

PRATT, JOHN ALDEN R
b. Woburn, Mass, 5/22/08; s. Frank Leroy Pratt and Lena Harrington P. both deceased; m. 8/23/30 to Doris Madeline Wardwell; c. John Wardwell. Educ: Colby Acad, New London, N.H, grad, 26; Mass. Inst. Tech, 26-28; Sigma Chi. Polit. Pos: Chmn, Hancock Co. Rep. Cmt, Maine, 62-66 and finance chmn, 60-66; chmn, Castine Town Rep. Cmt, 60-66 and v.chmn, 58-60. Bus. & Prof. Pos: Dist. sales mgr, Timken Silent Automatic Div, 49-57 and York-Shipley Mfg. Co, York, Pa, 46-49. Mil. Serv: Warrant Officer, Naval Res, 43-46, serv. in S.Pac. and Atlantic Theaters; Campaign Ribbons; Inactive Res, 46-51. Mem: Hancock Lodge 4 AF&AM, Commandery, Shrine. Rel: Congregational. Mailing Add: Box 266, Green St, Castine, Maine 04421. (1967)

PRATT, JOHN McKEE D
Mem, Dem. State Cent. Cmt, Calif.
b. Syracuse, N.Y, 5/14/33; s. John Wesley Pratt and Harriett Davis P; single. Educ: Williams Col, B.A, 55; Union Theol. Sem, N.Y, B.D, 59; Columbia Univ. Law Sch, LL.B, 63; Phi Beta Kappa; Beta Theta Pi. Polit. & Govt. Pos: Dist. leader, N.Y.C. Dem. Party, 62-63; Dem. cand, U.S. Rep, 28th Dist, Calif, 68; mem, Dem. State Cent. Cmt, 69- Bus. & Prof. Pos: Legal counsel, Cmn. Relig. and Race, Nat. Coun. Churches, N.Y.C, 63-66; exec. dir, Cmn. Church and Race, S.Calif. Coun. Churches, Los Angeles, Calif, 66-68. Mem: Founder & v.pres, Lawyers' Constitutional Defense Cmt, Inc. Rel: Episcopal. Mailing Add: 17352 Sunset Blvd, Los Angeles, Calif. 90272.

PRATT, LEVI B. R
b. Wells, Vt, 1/22/09; m. to Elizabeth Shamper; c. Eight. Educ: Granville, N.Y. High Sch. Polit. & Govt. Pos: Mem, Rep. Town Cmt; chmn. bd. trustees, Wills Cemetery Improvement Asn; sch. dir; lister; moderator; Vt. State Rep, 55-61 & 65-66. Bus. & Prof. Pos: Bldg. contractor. Mem: MWA (secy, 54-). Rel: Episcopal. Mailing Add: South St, Wells, Vt. 05774. (1967)

PRATT, OSCAR C. D
b. Hopkinton, R.I, 6/21/91. Educ: Hope Valley High Sch. Polit. & Gov. Pos: R.I. State Sen, 63-66; R.I. State Rep, 59-63. Bus. & Prof. Pos: Retired. Mailing Add: RFD, Hope Valley, R.I. 02832. (1967)

PREECE, CECIL H. R
b. Ira, Va, 6/15/19; s. Joseph L. Preece and Lena Dotson P; m. 2/21/42 to Lula Crockett; c. Virginia Ann. Educ: East. Ky. State Univ. Polit. & Govt. Pos: Chmn, Buchanan Co. Rep. Cmt, Va, 66-67. Mil. Serv: Entered as A/S, Navy, 43, released as SK 2/C 105 CB, 45, after serv. in S.Pac; Am-Asiatic-Pac. Ribbon with 1 Star; Philippine Liberation Ribbon with 1 Star; Victory Medal. Mem: C. of C; Kiwanis; Shrine; Sandy Valley Lodge 17; Odd Fellows 17; El Hessa Temple; Childs Gentry VFW Post. Rel: Presbyterian. Legal Res: R.R. 1, Grundy, Va. 24614. Mailing Add: P.O. Box 807, Grundy, Va. 24614. (1967)

PREECE, RALPH ALMA R
Utah State Sen.
b. Vernal, Utah, 5/25/24; s. Alma Preece and Mary Murray P; m. 6/11/42 to Carma Ross; c. Brent R, Gerry (Mrs. Anthony Wright), Janet, Lorri and Daryl Ross. Educ: Uintah Co. Schs, 12 years. Polit. & Govt. Pos: Chmn, Uintah Co. Rep. Party, Utah, 56; city councilman, Vernal, 64-68; Utah State Rep, 67-68; Utah State Sen, 69- Bus. & Prof. Pos: Pres, Utah State Motel Asn, 64, Dinosaurland Advert. Inc, Vernal, Utah, 65; dir, Bank of Vernal, 69; pres, Serv. Ins. Agency Inc, currently. Mil. Serv: Entered as Seaman, Navy, 43, released as Gunners Mate 1/C, 46, after serv. in LCSL, Pac. Theatre, 44-46; Commendation Ribbon, Okinawa. Mem: Pres, Vernal Jr. C. of C, 55; Rotary; Elks; Farm Bur. Utah Agent of the Year, 68. Rel: Latter-day Saint. Legal Res: 195 N. Sixth West, Vernal, Utah 84078. Mailing Add: P.O. Box 728, Vernal, Utah 84078.

PRENDERGAST, JAMES FRANCIS D
Majority Whip, Pa. State House of Rep.
b. Easton, Pa, 2/5/17; s. John L. Prendergast and Elizabeth Hegarty P; m. to

Ann Naab; c. Therese, Mary, Kathleen, John, Virginia and Timothy. Educ: Lafayette Col, B.A; George Wash. Univ. Law Sch, LL.B; Sigma Nu. Polit. & Govt. Pos: Pa. State Rep, 136th Legis. Dist, 59-, Majority Caucus Secy, Pa. State House of Rep, 65-66, Minority Caucus Chmn, 67-68, Majority Whip, 69- Mil. Serv: 1st Lt.(Ret), Marine Corps Res; Purple Heart; Navy Cross in Pac. Mem: Am. Legion; K. of C; CWC; VFW; Pa. Bar Asn; Admitted to practice before Supreme Courts of Pa, Fed. Courts, D.C. Bar. Legal Res: 340 Paxinosa Ave, Easton, Pa. 18042. Mailing Add: 318 Spring Garden St, Easton, Pa. 18042.

PRENDERGAST, WILLIAM BRODERICK R
b. Bridgeport, Conn, 9/6/14; s. William B. Prendergast (deceased) and Mabel Halsey P; m. 10/12/42 to Mary Elizabeth Comeford; c. William B, Jr, Richard H, Michael J. and Martha Ann. Educ: Univ. Notre Dame, A.B, 37 and A.M, 38; Univ. of Louvain Belgium; Univ. of Chicago, Ph.D, 48. Polit. & Govt. Pos: Asst. research dir, Presidential Cmn. on Intergovt. Rels, 54-55; research dir, Rep. Nat. Cmt, 57-64; former research dir, Rep. Conf, U.S. House of Rep. Bus. & Prof. Pos: Prof. polit. sci, U.S. Naval Acad, 46-56; prof, Johns Hopkins Univ, 48-52; dir. of polit. research, Am. Broadcasting Co, 64. Mil. Serv: Entered as Pvt, Army, 42, released as Capt, 46. Rel: Roman Catholic. 1967 Legal Res: Annapolis, Md. No mailing address available. (1967)

PRESCOTT, ROBERT W. D
b. Ft. Worth, Tex, 5/5/13; s. George Washington Prescott and Una Victoria Stewart P; m. 7/16/62 to Anne-Marie Bennstrom; c. French Steele and Kirsten. Educ: Compton Jr. Col, A.A, 36; Loyola Univ, law student, 37-39. Bus. & Prof. Pos: Goodyear Tire and Rubber Co, 34-36; Challenge Cream and Butler Co, 37-39; pilot, Transcontinental and West. Airlines, 42-43; capt, China Nat. Aviation Corp, 43-44; purchaser of planes and supplies for a Mexican airline, 44-45; founder, pres, and dir, Flying Tiger Line, Inc.(formerly Nat. Skyway Freight Corp), 45- Mil. Serv: Navy, Ens, 39-42; instr, U.S. Naval Flying Sch, Pensacola, Fla, 39-41; mem, Am. Vol. Group (Flying Tigers), 41-42; flight leader, 42. Mem: Flying Tigers; A.V.G; C. of C. in Los Angeles, Oakland, Burbank, San Fransicso and Portland; dir, Air Transport Asn. Mailing Add: 7401 World Way West, Los Angeles International Airport, Los Angeles, Calif. 90009.

PRESNAL, BILLY CHARLES D
Tex. State Rep.
b. Bryan, Tex, 4/26/32; s. Will Presnal and Margie Marquart P; m. 6/6/54 to Cecille D'Aun McCoy; c. James Scott, Stephen Earl and DeAnna Kay. Educ: Tex. A&M Univ, B.S, 53, M.S, 60. Polit. & Govt. Pos: Tex. State Rep, 18th Dist, 69- Bus. & Prof. Pos: Instr, W.Tex. State Univ, 53-54; civilian counsr, Tex. A&M Univ, 62-68. Mil. Serv: Entered as 2nd Lt, Air Force, 54, released as 1st Lt, 56, after serv. in Crew Training, Air Training Command. Mem: Farm Bur. First Runner-up, Outstanding Young Farmer of Tex, 66. Rel: Methodist. Mailing Add: Route 1, Box 74, Bryan, Tex. 77801.

PRESTAGE, ETHEL MARIAN R
Mem, Calif. Rep. State Cent. Cmt.
b. Porterville, Calif, 11/15/99; d. Clinton Ellsworth Martin and Nellie Alice Hall M; m. 4/30/20 to Edgar Lewis Prestage; c. Lewis Ellsworth, Marcia Jeanette (Mrs. Allen), Margaret Ellen (Mrs. Winton) and Douglas Warren (deceased). Educ: Univ. of Calif. Polit. & Govt. Pos: Pres, Porterville Area Rep. Women, Calif, 54-64, membership chmn, 65-; mailing chmn, Tulare Co. Rep. Party; mem, Calif. Rep. State Cent. Cmt, 54- Bus. & Prof. Pos: Bookkeeper, 17-20. Mem: Adv. bd, Porterville State Hosp; Porterville Women's Club (past pres); Porterville Garden Club (past treas); Coun. of Vol.(ward brightening chmn, Porterville State Hosp); bd. mem, Tulare Co. Crippled Children's Soc. Named Porterville's woman of the year, 66. Rel: Methodist. Mailing Add: 219 S. Westwood, Porterville, Calif. 93257,

PRESTON, RUSSELL EDWARD D
b. Lowell, Mass, 9/1/30; s. Richard F. Preston (deceased) and Margaret Burke P; single. Educ: St. Anselm's Col, N.H, B.A. Polit. & Govt. Pos: Del, Dem. State Conv, 52-; mil. aide-de-camp to Gov, N.H, 63-69; alternate del, Dem. Nat. Conv, 64 & 68; cmnr, Traffic Safety Cmn, N.H, 65- Bus. & Prof. Pos: Pres. and treas, Anchorage Corp, 56-59; safety engr, Royal-Globe Ins, 59-66, supvr, 66-; corp. safety engr, Sanders Assoc. Inc, 67- Mil. Serv: Entered as Seaman, Navy, 53, released as Lt(jg), 56, after serv. in Korea; UN, Nat. Defense, Korean Theater and European Occupation Ribbons; Lt, Naval Res, at present. Mem: Soc. of Safety Engrs; Nat. Safety Coun. (exec. cmt, EEE Sect); Mass. Safety Coun; N.H. Accident Prev. Asn; Naval Res. Asn; Battleship Asn; Elks; Am. Legion. Rel: Roman Catholic. Mailing Add: 401 Central St, Manchester, N.H. 03103.

PRESTWOOD, COLON EDWARD D
Chmn, Caldwell Co. Dem. Exec. Cmt, N.C.
b. Lenoir, N.C, 4/23/13; s. James Sidney Prestwood and Cordelia Bush P; m. 1/6/34 to Nellie Pauline Ernest; c. Billie Sue and William John Taylor, Jr. Educ: Oak Hill High Sch, 9 years. Polit. & Govt. Pos: Chmn, Caldwell Co. Dem. Exec. Cmt, N.C, 66-; mem, Indust. Safety Adv. Bd, State of N.C. Dept. Labor, 69- Bus. & Prof. Pos: Foreman, Hibriten Furniture, 38-40; machine room foreman, Bernhardt Furniture, 40-46, supt, 46-43, prod. mgr, 63- Mem: Mason; York Rite; Shrine; Lions; Country Club. Rel: Methodist. Mailing Add: 520 Mountain View, Lenoir, N.C. 28645.

PRETE, JOHN DONALD D
Conn. State Rep.
b. New Haven, Conn, 9/24/34; s. John Prete and Anntoinette Siclari P; m. 10/10/59 to Marie Carmel Caruso; c. Leslie and John. Educ: Univ. Conn, B.S, 59; pres, Sigma Chi. Polit. & Govt. Pos: V.pres, West Haven Young Dem, 8 years; mem, West Haven Dem. Town Cmt, 9 years; Conn. State Rep, 63-, chmn, House Cmt. on Airports and Aircraft, Conn. House of Rep, 63-65, chmn, House Corrections Cmt, mem, Welfare Cmt. and interim exec. mem, Banking and Health Cmts, currently. Bus. & Prof. Pos: Former sales promotion asst, United Illuminating, urban develop. specialist, at present. Mil. Serv: Entered as E-4, Army, 54, released as Pfc, 56, after serv. in Army Security Agency. Mem: Fairfield Co. Advert. Asn; Conn. Chiefs of Police Asn; K. of C; Elks; Jaycees. Rel: Catholic. Mailing Add: 18 Wildwood Terr, West Haven, Conn. 06516.

PREWITT, TAYLOR ARCHIE D
Chmn, Drew Co. Dem. Cent. Cmt, Ark.
b. Selma, Ark, 10/13/86; s. Zachary Taylor Prewitt and Cora Bell Lobbin P; m. 11/27/07 to Hughetta Duncan; c. Cathryn (Mrs. McDaniel), Taylor Archie Jr. and Claudious Rowan. Educ: Hendrix Col. Polit. & Govt. Pos: Mem. Adv. Cmt, Dept. Health, Educ. and Welfare, 62-66; chmn, Drew Co. Dem. Cent. Cmt, Ark. and chmn. Elec. Cmt, currently. Bus. & Prof. Pos: Gen. merchant; retired. Mem: Bd, State Schs. for Deaf and Blind for 24 years; Farm Bur; Local Mens Clubs. Rel: Methodist; mem, Church Gen. Jurisdictional Bd. Mailing Add: Tillar, Ark. 71670.

PREYER, LUNSFORD RICHARDSON D
U.S. Rep, N.C.
b. Greensboro, N.C, 1/11/19; s. William Yost Preyer and Mary Norris Richardson P; m. 5/11/46 to Emily Irving Harris; c. L. Richardson, Jr, Mary Norris, Britt Armfield, Jane Bethel and Emily Harris, II. Educ: Princeton Univ, A.B, 41; Harvard Law Sch, LL.B, 49. Polit. & Govt. Pos: City Judge, Greensboro, N.C, 53-54; State Superior Court Judge, N.C, 61-63; U.S. Dist. Judge, N.C, 63-64; U.S. Rep. Sixth Dist, N.C, 69- Bus. & Prof. Pos: Attorney, Preyer & Bynum, Greensboro, N.C, 50-56; sr. v.pres. and trust officer, N.C. Nat. Bank, 64-; mem. bd. dirs, Re-Ins. Corp, N.Y. and dir, Richardson Corp, Greensboro, currently. Mil. Serv: Entered as Lt.(jg), Naval Res, 42, released as Lt, 46, after serv. on destroyers, Atlantic and Pac. Fleets, 42-46; Bronze Star. Mem: Am. and N.C. Bar Asns; Newcomen Soc; Kiwanis; hon. mem, Nat. Boy Scout Coun; N.C. Grange. Greensboro Young Man of the Year Award, U.S. Jr. C. of C, 54; Outstanding Civic Leader of the Year Award, Greensboro Inter-Club Coun, 68. Rel: Presbyterian; Elder and Teacher Men's Bible Class, First Presbyterian Church. Legal Res: 605 Sunset Dr, Greensboro, N.C. 27408. Mailing Add: Room 1232, Longworth Bldg, Washington, D.C. 20515.

PRICE, ED H. JR. D
b. Jacksonville, Fla, 1/1/18; m. to Elise Ingram; c. Jerald Steven. Educ: Univ. of Fla. Polit. & Govt. Pos: Former chmn, Bd. of Sch. Trustees, City Govt. Revision Cmt. and State Freeze Damage Surv. Team; former cmnr. of census, 12th Judicial Dist, Fla; formerly, mem, Mantee Co. Indust. Cmn, State Bd. of Control and State Plant Bd; Fla. State Sen, 58-66; chmn, Bradenton Housing Authority and mem, Sarasota-Bradenton Airport Zoning Adjust. Bd, currently. Bus. & Prof. Pos: Exec. v.pres, Tropicana Prods, Inc, currently. Mil. Serv: U.S. Army Med. Corps and Air Corps, World War II; Air Medal, 4 Clusters. Mem: Dir, Fla. State C. of C; trustee, Univ. of S.Fla. Found; dir, Fla. Citrus Expos; mem. adv. cmt, Fla. Citrus Mutual; former dir, Farm Bur. and Jr. C. of C; Am. Red Cross, former chmn; former v.chmn, Commun. Chest, Cmt. of 100; C. of C, former v.pres; Crusade for Freedom, former regional chmn; Fla. Agr. Coun, former secy-treas; Salvation Army; Boys Club; Crippled Children's Soc; trustee, Stetson Univ; Blood Bank; Sigma Alpha Epsilon; Kiwanis Club, former pres. Tennis, Flying. Rel: Baptist. Mailing Add: P.O. Box 338, Bradenton, Fla. 33505.

PRICE, ETHEL A. R
b. Wilkes-Barre, Pa, 12/5/09; d. Harry Aerenson (deceased) and Anna Bogart A.(deceased); m. 11/22/37 to Oliver Jones Price, wid. Educ: Coughlin High Sch, Wilkes-Barre, Pa, grad, 27. Polit. & Govt. Pos: Secy, Wilkes-Barre City Coun, 32-37; appointed city councilman, Wilkes-Barre, 56, elected city councilman, 57-67; co. cmnr, Luzerne Co, 68- Publ: Articles in Munic. J, London, Eng, Pub. Cleansing & Salvage, Edinburgh, Scotland, and Am. City, N.Y.C. Mem: Bus. & Prfnl. Women; Soroptimist Asn; bd. mem, Wyo. Valley Tuberc. Soc, Nat. Found. March of Dimes, Jewish Home, Scranton, Pa. and Luzerne Co. Retarded Children's Asn; past matron, Eastner Star; Girl Scouts; United Fund; Serve Your City Club; Hadassah, Coun. of Jewish Women; Heart Asn; Vol. at Vets. Hosp. Rel: Jewish. Mailing Add: 27 W. Hollenback Ave, Wilkes-Barre, Pa. 18702.

PRICE, GARNET ELLEN R
V.Chmn, Brule Co. Rep. Cent. Cmt, S.Dak.
b. Wessington, S.Dak, 10/15/18; d. Martin Diekhoff and Elsie Maude Franklin D; m. 1/21/44 to John Wilbur Price; c. JoEllen (Mrs. Donald Roxworthy), Cathy, Susan and John M. Educ: Huron Col, teacher cert, 38; Greeley Teacher's Col, summer sch, 41; Eulalean Literary Soc. Polit. & Govt. Pos: Rep. Precinct committeewoman, Brule Co, S.Dak, 62-66; State Cent. Committeewoman, Brule Co. Rep. Party, 64-66; v.chmn, Brule Co, Rep. Cent. Cmt, 66-; auditor clerk, Brule Co, 69- Bus. & Prof. Pos: Teacher, Canning, S.Dak, 38-41, Willow Lake, 41-42 and Timber Lake, 42-44; driver license clerk, S.Dak. State Hwy. Dept, Chamberlain, 67-69. Mem: Eastern Star (past Matron); VFW Auxilary; Am. Contract Bridge League. Rel: Congregational. Legal Res: 200 S. River St, Chamberlain, S.Dak. 57325. Mailing Add: Box 284, Chamberlain, S.Dak. 57325.

PRICE, GEORGE A. R
Md. State Del.
b. Phoenix, Md, 5/22/26; married. Educ: Mercersburg Acad, Mercersburg, Pa; Univ. of Md. Polit. & Govt. Pos: Md. State Del, 63-; dir, Baltimore Co. Conserv. Dist, Baltimore Co. Forestry Bd. and Tenth Dist. Rep. Club. Bus. & Prof. Pos: Farmer; Chmn. of the Bd, Baltimore Co. Petroleum Corp. Mem: Former Pres, Baltimore Co. Farm Bur, Md. Angus Asn; Dir, East. Nat. Livestock Showing; Baltimore Co. Hist. Soc; Hereford PTA Exec. Cmt; Chmn, Boy Scout Troop Cmt, Troop 485; Phi Kappa Sigma. Mailing Add: Stockton Farm, Phoenix, Md. 21131.

PRICE, HENRY JOHN R
b. Brooklyn, N.Y, 9/8/31; s. Henry John Price, Sr. and Helen Galvin P; m. 9/14/57 to Dianne Dula; c. Mary Anne, Lee Anne and Henry John, III. Educ: Brooklyn Col, A.B, 52; N.Y. Univ, 54; Omega Delta Phi. Polit. & Govt. Pos: Polit. ed. and columnist, Conn. Sunday Herald, 55-68; press secy, U.S. Rep. Lowell P. Weicker, Jr, Conn, 69- Bus. & Prof. Pos: Polit. reporter, Conn. Sunday Herald, Fairfield, 55-66, managing ed, 67-68. Mil. Serv: Entered as Pvt, Army, 52, released as Pfc, 54, after serv. in Stars and Stripes, Europe; Army of Occupation and Nat. Defense Medals. Publ: 'Gambling in Massachusetts,' 61, 'Alcoholism,' 62 and 'Federal and State Highway Program, Massachusetts,' 63, Havril J. Mem: VFW; Am. Newspaper Guild. News Writing Award, United Press Int, 61. Rel: Roman Catholic. Legal Res: 104 Wentworth St, Bridgeport, Conn. 06606. Mailing Add: 5724 Bradley Blvd, Bethesda, Md. 20014.

PRICE, JOHN RICHARD R
Dep. State Treas, Ind.
b. Indianapolis, Ind, 2/2/41; s. Cecil Ralph Price and Dorothy Elizabeth Emmler (deceased); m. 6/8/61 to Suzanne Cathy Lammert; c. Andrea Jean and John Richard, II. Educ: Wabash Col, B.A, 63; Ind. Univ. Sch. of Law, J.D, 68; Phi Delta Epsilon; Beta Theta Pi. Polit. & Govt. Pos: Asst. campaign mgr, Ristine for Gov. Cmt, 64; dir, Speaker's Bur, Ind. Rep. State Cent. Cmt, 64, campaign coordinator, 66, secy, 68-; dep. state treas, Ind, 67- Bus. & Prof. Pos: Attorney-at-law, Indianapolis. Mem: Am. and Ind. State Bar Asns; Columbia Club, Indianapolis. Rel: Presbyterian. Mailing Add: 11313 Lakeshore Dr, Carmel, Ind. 46032.

PRICE, LENNA WROBLINSKEE R
V.Chmn, Providence Rep. City Cmt, R.I.
b. New Bedford, Mass, 1/21/16; d. Alfred Wroblinskee and Frances E. Kot W. (both deceased); m. 2/14/42 to Maj. Albert Raymond Price, Wid; c. Terrance Martin and Frances (Mrs. Dwyer). Educ: Manhattan State Hosp, grad, 39; N.Y. Univ, 40; Walker Sch. of Radio & Drama, grad, 50; Univ. R.I, exten. sch. courses, 60-62. Polit. & Govt. Pos: Mem, 12th Ward Rep. Cmt, R.T, 45- and v.chmn; chmn, Shut-in Ballots, R.I, 64; mem, R.I. Rep. State Cent. Cmt; pres, Providence Coun. Rep. Women; v.chmn, Providence Rep. City Cmt, currently. Bus. & Prof. Pos: Private duty nurse, N.Y.C, 39-41; floor nurse, Kapiolani Maternity Hosp, Hawaii, 41; private duty nurse, Ore. and R.I; adminstr, Price Nursing Home, Inc, 46-66. Mem: R.I. Sanitarians; past pres, R.I. Nursing Homes Asn. and Smith Hill Bus. Men's Asn. Health commentator, Lady with the Lamp radio prog, 50-52. Rel: Catholic. Mailing Add: 15 Cherry St, Providence, R.I. 02908.

PRICE, MELVIN D
U.S. Rep, Ill.
b. East St. Louis, Ill, 1/1/05; s. Lawrence Wood Price and Margaret Elizabeth Connolly P; m. 7/7/52 to Garaldine Freelin; c. William. Polit. & Govt. Pos: Secy. to U.S. Rep. Edwin Schaefer, 33-43; U.S. Rep, Ill, 45- Bus. & Prof. Pos: Sports writer, East St. Louis News-Rev, 25-27; correspondent, East St. Louis, 27-33; correspondent, St. Louis Globe Dem, 33. Mil. Serv: Army, 43-44. Mem: Am. Legion; Am. Vet; K. of C; Moose; Eagles; Elks; Ancient Order of Hibernians; Nat. Press Club. Rel: Catholic. Legal Res: 426 N. Eighth St, East St. Louis, Ill. 62201. Mailing Add: 2468 Rayburn House Office Bldg, Washington, D.C. 20515. (1967)

PRICE, NEIL LAWSON R
Kans. State Rep.
b. Reading, Kans, 11/21/11; s. Tom Jones Price and Ethel A. Traylor P; m. 12/24/42 to Helen A. Droll; c. Amelia Ann (Mrs. Eicholtz), Warren Martin and Helen Jacqueline. Educ: Kemper Mil. Sch, 1 year; Kans. State Teachers Col, 2 years; Tau Kappa Epsilon. Polit. & Govt. Pos: Dir, sch. bd, 33-47; Kans. State Rep, 67-; Bus. & Prof. Pos: Pres, Lyon Co. Fair, 60-65. Mem: Farm Bur; Kans. Quarterhorse Asn; Kans. Angus Asn; Kans. and Lyon Co. Livestock Asn; 4-H Leader for 10 years. Received Nat. 4-H Alumni Recognition, Co. Honors. Rel: Methodist. Mailing Add: Route 1, Reading, Kans. 66868. (1967)

PRICE, (WILLIAM) RAYFORD D
Tex. State Rep.
b. Jacksonville, Tex, 2/9/37; s. Quanah Price and Vaye Baker P; m. 6/3/61 to Barbara Jean Ashley; c. Brett. Educ: Lon Morris Jr. Col, 2 years; Univ. Tex, LL.B, 67; Phi Delta Phi. Polit. & Govt. Pos: Tex. State Rep, Anderson and Cherokee Counties, 61- Bus. & Prof. Pos: Attorney-at-law. Mil. Serv: Entered as Pvt, Tex. Nat. Guard, 55, released as Sgt. 1/C, after serv. in 36th Div. Mem: Tex. Bar Asn; dir, E.Tex. Bar Asn, 64-; Kiwanis; Jr. C. of C; Anderson Co. C. of C; Int. Typographical Union. Rel: Methodist. Legal Res: 321 Thomas Rd, Palestine, Tex. 75801. Mailing Add: Box 00, Palestine, Tex. 75801.

PRICE, REGINALD STAUNTON D
b. Chicago, Ill, 2/21/25; s. Reginald Price and Charlotte P; m. 4/25/53 to Carla Hemphill; c. Robin Lynn and Leslie Ann. Educ: Knox Col, 46-49; Sigma Nu. Polit. & Govt. Pos: Del, Dem. Nat. Conv, 68. Bus. & Prof. Pos: Agent, Kerr Steamship Corp, New Orleans, La, 49-53; salesman, Home Lockers, Baytown, Tex, 53-54; salesman, Allstate Ins. Co, 54-58; mem. traffic opers. staff, Dalton Steamship Corp, Houston, 59, mgr, Galveston, Tex. and Mobile, Ala, 59- Mil. Serv: Entered as Seaman, Navy, 43, released as Radar Man 2/C, 46, after serv. in U.S.S. Denver, Asiatic-Pac. Theater, 44-46; Victory Medal; Asiatic-Pac. Campaign Medal with Six Stars; Philippine Liberation Ribbon; Letter of Commendation. Mem: Mobile Steamship Asn.(v.pres, 67, pres, 67-68); Mobile Port Traffic Bur.(v.pres, 4 years); MSSA-ILA PWV (trustee, 66-); C. of C.(firm rep, Mobile Area Chap). Rel: Presbyterian; Deacon, Spring Hill Presby. Church, 66-68. Mailing Add: 5509 Richmond Rd, Mobile, Ala. 36608.

PRICE, ROBERT DALE R
U.S. Rep, Tex.
b. Reading, Kans, 9/7/27; s. Ben F. Price, Sr. and Gladys A. Watson P; m. 12/29/51 to Martha Ann White; c. Robert Grant, Benjamin Carl and Janice Ann. Educ: Okla State Univ, B.S. in Agr, 51; Sigma Alpha Epsilon. Polit. & Govt. Pos: U.S. Rep, Tex, 66-, mem, Cmt. on Agr. Subcmts. on Cotton, Livestock and Grains, Sci. and Astronaut. Cmt. and Subcmts. on NASA Oversight, Manned Space Flight, U.S. House of Rep, currently; del, Rep. Nat. Conv, 68. Bus. & Prof. Pos: Rancher. Mil. Serv: Entered as Airman, Air Force, 51, released as 1st Lt, 55, after serv. in 51st Fighter Intercepters, Korea, 16th Squadron Jet Fighters, 53-54; 27 Combat Missions; Air Medal. Mem: Sigma Alpha Epsilon Alumni Asn; hon. dir, Top O Tex. Rodeo Asn; VFW; Am. Legion; Kiwanis (pres, 63); orgn. and exten. chmn, Boy Scouts; Pampa C. of C. Rel: Baptist. Legal Res: 2135 Charles, Pampa, Tex. 79065. Mailing Add: 8802 Fircrest Place, Alexandria, Va. 22308.

PRICE, ROBERT ROSS D
Chmn, Jefferson Co. Dem. Exec. Cmt, Ohio
b. Carrollton, Ohio, 11/24/26; s. Robert Henry Price and Martha Jane Dunlap P; m. 8/5/67 to Judith Renee Kerr; c. Karen Lee, Robert Kenneth, Linda Sue, Bruce Allan and Julia Adrianne. Educ: Col. of Steubenville, B.S; Univ. Pittsburgh, D.D.S; Psi Omega. Polit. & Govt. Pos: Precinct cmt. mem, Jefferson Co. Dem. Party, Ohio, 59-69; v.chmn, Jefferson Co. Dem. Party, 67-68, chmn, exec. cmt, 68-; mem, Ohio State Co. Chmn. Asn, 68-; alternate del, Dem. Nat. Conv, 68; mem, Jefferson Co. Bd. Elec, 68-; mem. exec. cmt, Ohio State Dem. Party, 69- Mil. Serv: Entered as Pfc, Army, 44, released as T-5, 46. Mem: Am. and Ohio State Dent. Asns; Ft. Steuben Dent. Soc.(pres, 65-67); Eagles; Elks; Mason; Moose; Shrine. Rel: Protestant. Mailing Add: R.D. 3, Wintersville, Ohio 43952.

PRICHARD, JAMES McMURTRY R
Chmn, Buena Vista Co. Rep. Party, Iowa
b. St. Paul, Minn, 2/7/26; s. James Skewis Prichard and Fern McMurtry P; m. 8/23/53 to Eloise Yon; c. James Yon, Thomas Warren and Jane Eloise. Educ: St. Ambrose Col, 1 year; Univ. N.Mex, 2 years; State Univ. Iowa, B.A, 47, J.D, 50. Polit. & Govt. Pos: Chmn, Buena Vista Co. Rep. Party, Iowa, 66- Bus. & Prof. Pos: Attorney-at-law, 50- Mil. Serv: Entered as Seaman, Navy, 43, released as Lt.(jg), 46, after serv. in Weather Ship, Pac. Ocean, 45-46. Mem: Buena Vista and Iowa State Bar Asns; Iowa Defense Counsel Asn; Kiwanis; Am. Legion; Mason; C. of C. Rel: Methodist. Mailing Add: 1301 W. Sixth, Storm Lake, Iowa 50588.

PRICHARD, ROBERT DANIEL R
Chmn, Monona Co. Rep. Cent. Cmt, Iowa
b. Onawa, Iowa, 1/3/28; s. Elbert Morris Prichard and Louise Bowe P; m. 7/6/52 to Elaine Ellis; c. David Ellis, John Jacob and Thomas Robert. Educ: Univ. Iowa, B.A, 50, J.D, 52; Phi Alpha Delta. Polit. & Govt. Pos: Attorney, Monona Co, Iowa, 55-62; chmn, Monona Co. Rep. Cent. Cmt, Iowa, 62- Mil. Serv: Entered as A/S, Navy, 45, released as Aviation Cadet, 46. Mem: Monona Co. Bar Asn.(pres, 58, secy, 59-63); Iowa Bar Asn.(co. membership chmn, 58-); Kiwanis (lt. gov); Mason; Scottish Rite; Shrine; Am. Legion; cubmaster, Boy Scouts. Rel: Congregational. Legal Res: 1603 Sunset Dr, Onawa, Iowa 51040. Mailing Add: Box 5, Onawa, Iowa 51040.

PRICHARD, W. M. R
Chmn, Jefferson Co. Rep. Party, Ga.
b. Dyersburg, Tenn, 6/28/13; s. Jefferson R. Prichard and Martha H. White P; m. 4/29/39 to Mabel C. Rambeau; c. Philip M. and Pamela N. Educ: Univ. Tenn, grad, 35; Sigma Phi Epsilon; Biologia Society. Polit. & Govt. Pos: City councilman, Louisville, Ga, 53-57; chmn, Jefferson Co. Rep. Party, 64- Bus. & Prof. Pos: Played prfnl. baseball, 35-37; proj. mgr, Calloway Farms, Hamilton, Ga, 37-41; co. agr. agent, Ext. Serv, 41-45; mgr. and partner, Louisville Bonded Warehouse and Abbot and Prichard, 45-59; owner and operator, Prichard Seed Farms, 59-; v.pres. and dir, Found. Seeds, Inc, Athens, Ga; dir, First Nat. Bank, Louisville Ga, currently. Mem: Farm Bur; dir, Ga. Crop Improv. Asn; dir, Sandersville Prod. Credit Asn; pres. and dir, Ga. Soybean Asn; Ga. Seed Develop. Cmn; dir, Am. Soybean Asn; Kiwanis; C. of C; chmn, Jefferson Co. Libr. Bd. Rel: Presbyterian. Legal Res: Avera Rd, Louisville, Ga. 30434. Mailing Add: P.O. Box 228, Louisville, Ga. 30434.

PRICKETT, RICHARD C. R
b. Gas City, Ind, 4/16/08; s. Lora A. Prickett and Anna Sheron P.(both deceased) m. 7/7/36 to Susan Tukey; c. Nancy A.(Mrs. Heche) and Penelope A.(Mrs. Smith). Educ: Univ. Mich, grad, 32; Kappa Tau Alpha. Polit. & Govt. Pos: Secy, U.S. Rep. George W. Gillie, 45-48; ed, Nat. Young Rep, 47-48; admin. asst. to U.S. Rep. E. Ross Adair, Fourth Dist, Ind. and U.S. Rep. William S. Hill, 49-50. Bus. & Prof. Pos: Owner and ed, Albion New Era, Ind, 40- Mem: Mason; Scottish Rite. Rel: Methodist. Mailing Add: 215 N.Orange, Albion, Ind. 46701.

PRIDGEON, DEAN M. R
Chmn, Branch Co. Rep. Party, Mich.
b. Montgomery, Mich, 6/22/21; s. Glen Dean Pridgeon and Lorene Mitchell P; m. 11/24/39 to Mary McConeghy; c. Michael, William, Barbara and Rebecca. Polit. & Govt. Pos: Twp. supvr, Montgomery, Mich, 53-65; mem, Bd. of Control Voc. Educ, 54-65; chmn, Branch Co. Zoning Cmt, 64-; mem, Mich. Rep. Agr. Coun, 65-; chmn, Branch Co. Rep. Party, currently. Mem: Mich. Farm Bur. (v.pres, 64-); Mason. Rel: Presbyterian. Mailing Add: R.F.D. 1, Montgomery, Mich. 49255. (1967)

PRIEBE, MILTON W. R
Chmn, Kingfisher Co. Rep. Party, Okla.
b. Quincy, Ill, 12/19/07; s. Friederich W. Priebe and Julia Ida Bensing P; m. 1/23/34 to Irene Faye VanWagoner. Educ: Phillips Univ, 25-28; Univ. Okla, LL.B, 33. Polit. & Govt. Pos: Co. attorney, Kingfisher Co, Okla, 38, co. judge, 42-49; Okla. State Rep, Kingfisher Co, 56-63; Rep. committeeman, Kingfisher Co, 63-68; chmn, Kingfisher Co. Rep. Party, 68- Mem: Okla. Bar Asn; Lions; Mason; Shrine; Odd Fellows. Rel: Baptist. Legal Res: 716 S. Seventh St, Kingfisher, Okla. 73750. Mailing Add: Suite 22, Pappe Bldg, Kingfisher, Okla. 73750.

PRIEST, IVY BAKER R
State Treas, Calif.
b. Kimberly, Utah; d. Orange Decatur Baker and Clara Fernley B; m. Roy Priest (deceased 59); m. 6/20/61 to Sidney W. Stevens; c. Roy Baker Priest, Mrs. J.A. Valenzuela and Mrs. Pierce Jensen, Jr. Educ: Hon. L.H.D, Elmira Col; Hon. D.Sc. in Bus. Admin, Bryant Col; Hon. LL.D, Rider Col. Polit. & Govt. Pos: Rep. Nat. Committeewoman, Utah, 44-53; v.pres, Rep. Orgn. of 11 West. States, 46-53; asst. nat. chmn, Rep. Nat. Cmt, 52-53; U.S. treas, 53-61; former dir, Gr. Los Angeles Safety Coun; state treas, Calif, 67- Publ: Green Grows Ivy. Mem: Int. Soroptimist Club; trustee, Nat. Soc. for Crippled Children and Adults; dir, Calif. Easter Seal Soc; Bus. & Prfnl. Women's Club; Women's Advert. Club of Wash. D.C; Beta Sigma Phi; Delta Zeta. Nominated one of twenty Most Outstanding Women in This Century, Women's Newspaper Ed. and Publishers Asn. Rel: Latter-day Saints. Legal Res: Suite Six, 10700 Santa Monica Blvd, Los Angeles, Calif. 90025. Mailing Add: Room 128, State Capitol, Sacramento, Calif. 95809.

PRIESTLEY, WALLACE SCHUYLER 'WALLY' D
Ore. State Rep.
b. Portland, Ore, 7/17/31; s. Wallace Soren Priestley and Florence Anne Winslow P; single. Educ: Univ. Ore; Ore. State Univ; Portland State Col;

Sigma Chi. Polit. & Govt. Pos: Ore. State Rep, currently. Mil. Serv: Entered as E-1, Navy, 51, released as E-6, 54; Good Conduct Medal. Mailing Add: 2207 N.E. Ainsworth, Portland, Ore. 97211. (1967)

PRIFREL, JOSEPH D
Minn. State Rep.
b. Moson, Hungary, 12/1/05; s. Joseph Prifrel and Helena Knobel P; m. 7/13/46 to Evelyn Heitmiller; c. Thomas, Josette, James, Robert and Kathlynn. Educ: Univ. night sch, 29-38. Polit. & Govt. Pos: Minn. State Rep, 39- Bus. & Prof. Pos: B.M. Furriers Union, Locals 52 and 57, 40; organizer, Hotel Employees Union 556, 50; bus. agent, Bldg. Employees Local 64, AFL-CIO, 51; pres, draftsmen, physicists, scientists and engrs, Honnewell, 53; secy-treas. and bus. agent, Local 149, IBT, 54. Rel: Catholic. Mailing Add: 1031 Woodbridge St, St. Paul, Minn. 55117.

PRINCE, BRADFORD H. R
N.Mex. State Rep.
Educ: N.Mex. Mil. Inst; Univ. Colo, B.A. in Journalism. Polit. & Govt. Pos: N.Mex. State Rep, 65- Bus. & Prof. Pos: Advert. and pub. rels. Mil. Serv: World War II, Korea; Capt, N.Mex. Nat. Guard. Mem: C. of C; Exec. Asn. of Albuquerque; Elks. Mailing Add: 3505 Haines Ave. N.E, Albuquerque, N.Mex. 87106. (1967)

PRINCE, EUGENE AUGUSTUS R
Sgt-at-Arms, Wash. House of Rep.
b. Thornton, Wash, 7/31/30; s. Burdett H. Prince and Lula Henning P; m. 2/28/60 to Sherri Knittle; c. Stephan Randal and Suzanne M. Educ: Wash. State Univ, B.S, 52; Alpha Zeta; Alpha Gamma Rho. Polit. & Govt. Pos: Rep. precinct committeeman, Whitman Co, Wash, 52-; bill clerk, Wash. House of Rep, 59, asst. chief clerk, 63-64, cmt. clerk, 65, sgt-at-arms, 67-; committeeman, Wash. Rep. Party, 62-64; chmn, Whitman Co. Rep. Party, 66-68; co-chmn, platform cmt, Rep. State Conv, 68. Bus. & Prof. Pos: Farmer, 52- Mil. Serv: Entered as 2nd Lt, Air Force, 54, released as 1st Lt, 56, after serv. in Transportation, Air Research and Develop. Command. Mem: Wash. Asn. of Wheat Growers (pres, 65-66); Mason; Grange; Farm Bur. Int. Farm Youth Exchange Trip to Turkey Serv. as Goodwill Ambassador, 52. Rel: Presbyterian. Mailing Add: Thornton, Wash. 99176.

PRINCE, JACK ALEXANDER R
Mem, Hall Co. Rep. Cmt, Ga.
b. Spartanburg, S.C, 9/30/28; s. Alfred Bobo Prince and Mary Dunn P; m. 6/30/51 to Patricia Ann Jewell; c. Deborah, Jesse and Rebecka. Educ: Brevard Jr. Col; Univ. N.C, A.B; Arnold Air Soc; Order of the Old Well; Student Assembly; Philantropic Literary Soc; Pi Kappa Phi. Polit. & Govt. Pos: Pres, Hall Co. Young Rep. Club, Ga, 60-64; chmn, Ninth Dist. Goldwater for Pres. Cmt, 63-64; former mem, Ga. State Rep. Cmt; alternate del, Rep. Nat. Conv, 64; Rep. cand, U.S. Rep, Ninth Dist, Ga, 64; v.chmn, Ninth Cong. Dist. Rep. Cmt, 64-66; mem, Hall Co. Rep. Cmt, Ga, 64-, v.chmn, 64-66. Bus. & Prof. Pos: Sales promotion mgr, J.D. Jewell, Inc, 54-57, gen. sales mgr, 57-59 and v.pres, 59-64; pres, Jack Prince, Inc, 65-; chmn. bd, Precast Marble, Inc, Gainesville, Ga, 66- Mil. Serv: Entered as Pvt, Army, 46, released as Capt, Air Force Res, 64, after serv. in 188th Parachute Inf, 11th Airborne Div, Japanese Occup; Victory and Japanese Occup. Medals; Parachutist Badge. Mem: Past v.pres, Ga. Poultry Fedn; research cmt, Nat. Broiler Coun; research coun, Inst. of Am. Poultry Indust; dir, South. Frozen Foods Asn; past local pres, state v.pres. and nat. dir, U.S. Jaycees; Jaycee Int. Senate; Elks; Kiwanis; VFW. Rel: Episcopal; former sr. warden and licensed lay reader. Mailing Add: 155 Piedmont Ave. N.W, Gainesville, Ga. 30501.

PRINCE, JERRY RICHARD R
Chmn, Chattooga Co. Rep. Party, Ga.
b. Summerville, Ga, 10/29/43; s. Frank N. Prince and Juanita Keith P; m. 9/15/60 to Elaine Rollins; c. Ricky and Martha. Educ: N. Ga. Col, Dahlonega, 2 years. Polit. & Govt. Pos: V.chmn, Chattooga Co. Rep. Party, Ga, 64, chmn, 64- Bus. & Prof. Pos: Mgr. Western Auto Assoc. Store, Summerville, 63- Mem: Jr. C. of C; mem. bd. dirs, Chattooga Co. Commun. Action Coun. Rel: Methodist. Mailing Add: 302 N. Hill St, Summerville, Ga. 30747.

PRINCE, SANFORD JACK, JR. R
m. to Lillian Jones; c. Lowell Bradford. Educ: Hebron Acad; Shaws Bus. Col; N.Y. Sch. Finance. Polit. & Govt. Pos: Former Maine State Rep. Bus. & Prof. Pos: Maine Publicity Bur. Mailing Add: Orr's Island, Maine. 04066. (1967)

PRINDIVILLE, JOHN D. D
b. Rutland, N.Dak, 1/3/96; s. John Patrick Prindiville and Karen Lyngved P; m. 1/28/18 to Naomi N. Barnhard; c. Dennis V, Roger J, Gerald D, John H, Gwendolyn R.(Mrs. Young) and Alan M. Polit. & Govt. Pos: Former mem, Dem. Exec. Cmt; postmaster, Rutland, N.Dak, 33-60. Bus. & Prof. Pos: Farmer, 22- Mem: K. of C. Rel: Catholic. Mailing Add: Rutland, N.Dak. 58067.

PRINGLE, CHARLES KISTNER D
b. Avon Park, Fla, 5/13/31; married. Polit. & Govt. Pos: Former Miss. State Rep; mem, State Bd. of the Am. Cancer Soc. Bus. & Prof. Pos: Attorney. Mem: Miss. and Harrison Co. Bar Asns; Biloxi Jr. C. of C. Rel: Presbyterian. Mailing Add: P.O. Box 292, Biloxi, Miss. 39533. (1967)

PRIOLEAU, DIANE THYS R
Mem, Calif. Rep. State Cent. Cmt.
b. San Francisco, Calif, 4/25/34; d. Edouard Thys and Beatrice Horst T; m. 1/5/57 to H. Frost Prioleau; c. Paul, Marc, Rene and Michelle. Educ: Wellesley Col, B.A, 55; Phi Sigma. Polit. & Govt. Pos: Sector chmn, Sacramento Co. Rep. Precinct Orgn, Calif, 64; precinct chmn, Sacramento Co. Citizens for Goldwater-Miller, 64; mem, Calif. Rep. State Cent. Cmt, 65-67, assoc. mem, 67-69, mem, 69-; sector chmn, Alameda Co. Rep. Cent. Cmt, 68; precinct chmn. and schedule coordinator, North. Calif. Rafferty for U.S. Senate, 68. Mem: Rep. Assembly; Am. Cancer Soc; Oakland Mus. Asn; Calif. Fed. Rep. Women. Rel: Episcopal. Mailing Add: 111 Woodland Way, Piedmont, Calif. 94611.

PRIOLO, PAUL V. R
Calif. State Assemblyman
b. San Francisco, Calif, 7/14/27; s. Joseph Priolo and Pauline Pizzo P; m. 11/11/51 to Anna Lee Kutz; c. Jeffrey Paul and Jan Christine. Educ: Univ. Calif, Berkeley, B.A, 51; Phi Kappa Tau. Polit. & Govt. Pos: Calif. State Assemblyman, 60th Dist, 67-, chmn, Assembly Cmt. on Elecs. and Constitutional Amendments, Calif. State Legis, 69-; mem, Assembly Cmt. on Finance and Ins, Assembly Cmt. on Housing and Urban Affairs and Joint Cmt. on Atomic Develop. and Space, currently. Bus. & Prof. Pos: Merchandise trainee, The Emporium, San Francisco, Calif, 51-52; salesman, Gen. Elec. Co, 52; factory rep, Reynolds Metals Co, 52-55; partner, Stewart Photo & Sound Co, 55-67. Mil. Serv: Entered as A/S, Naval Res, 45, released as Seaman 1/C, 46, after serv. in Pac. Theater; Pac. Theater Ribbon; Victory Medal. Mem: Master Photo Dealers and Finishers Asn; Rotary; Calif. Alumni Asn; Navy League of U.S; life mem, C. of C. and Jr. C. of C; mem. exec. bd, Crescent Bay Coun, Boy Scouts. Selected as Outstanding Young Man, Santa Monica, Calif, Jr. C. of C, 62. Rel: Roman Catholic. Legal Res: 14966 La Cumbre Dr, Pacific Palisades, Calif. 90272. Mailing Add: 12121 Wilshire Blvd, Los Angeles, Calif. 90025.

PRITCHARD, HOWARD PORTER R
Tenn. State Rep.
b. Memphis, Tenn, 1/18/34; s. Howard Wilson Pritchard and Mary Elise Porter P; m. 6/30/62 to Margaret Elizabeth Guinn; c. Howard P, Jr, and Wilson C. Educ: Univ. of the South, B.A, 56; Vanderbilt Univ. Col. of Law, LL.B, 61; Phi Delta Theta. Polit. & Govt. Pos: Tenn. State Rep, 69- Bus. & Prof. Pos: Attorney, 61- Mem: Am, Tenn, Memphis and Shelby Co. Bar Asns. Rel: Presbyterian. Legal Res: 3129 Cowden Ave, Memphis, Tenn. 38111. Mailing Add: 1101 Memphis Bank Bldg, 44 N. Second St, Memphis, Tenn. 38103.

PRITCHARD, JOEL M. R
Wash. State Sen.
b. Seattle, Wash, 1925; m. to Joan P; c. Four. Educ: Marietta Col, Ohio. Polit. & Govt. Pos: Wash. State Rep, until 66; Wash. State Sen, 66- Bus. & Prof. Pos: Mgr, Griffin Envelope Co. Mil. Serv: Infantry. Mailing Add: 1401 Broadway, Seattle, Wash. 98122.

PRITZLAFF, JOHN CHARLES JR. R
U.S. Ambassador to Malta
b. Milwaukee, Wis, 5/10/25; s. John Charles Pritzlaff and Elinor Gallun P; m. 2/10/51 to Mary Dell Olin; c. Ann Olin, John C, Barbara Whitney and Richard Gallun. Educ: Princeton Univ. Polit. & Govt. Pos: Precinct committeeman and finance chmn, Rep. Party, Milwaukee, Wis, 50-58; v.chmn, Milwaukee Co. Rep. Exec. Cmt, 57-58; chmn, Maricopa Co. Rep. Finance Cmt, Ariz, 60-63; Rep. precinct committeeman, Phoenix, 60-; Ariz. State Rep, 63-69, Rep. Whip, 65 & 66, chmn, Appropriations Cmt, v.chmn, Ways & Means Cmt, mem, Rules and State Govt. Cmts, Ariz. House of Rep, 66-69; field dir, West. region, Rep. Nat. Cmt, 64; mem, Rep. Nat. Finance Cmt, 68 & 69; U.S. Ambassador to Malta, 69- Bus. & Prof. Pos: Pres, Pritzlaff Hardware Co, Milwaukee, Wis, 56-58; v.pres, Arrow Valve Co, Phoenix, Ariz, 59-60; exec. v.pres, Oxford Life Ins. Co, Scottsdale, 60-62; chmn. bd. and treas, Repub. Property, Inc, 60-69; dir, Phoenix Capital Corp, 62-; mem. bd, Nashotah Episcopal Sem, Wis. and Thunderbird Grad. Sch. Mgt, Phoenix, 68- Mil. Serv: Entered as Pvt, Army, 43, released as T/Sgt, 45, after serv. in PI Team, ETO; Good Conduct Medal; Presidential Citation; ETO Theatre Ribbon. Mem: Nat. Soc. State Legis; Phoenix Symphony Asn; Heard Mus; San Pablo Home for Youth; St. Luke's Hosp; Scottsdale Rotary; Scottsdale C. of C; Phoenix Press Club; Wash. Capitol Hill Club; Phoenix Univ. Club; Ariz. Zool. Soc.(mem. bd); Phoenix Jr. Achievement, Inc.(mem.bd, 68). Rel: Episcopal. Legal Res: 4954 E. Rockridge Rd, Phoenix, Ariz. 85018. Mailing Add: U.S. Embassy, Valletta, Malta.

PRIVETT, ARNOLD REX D
Speaker, Okla. House Rep.
b. Maramec, Okla, 5/28/24; s. Arnold Privett and Muriel P; m. to Patricia Nichols; c. Deborah Ann, Rex Nichols and Patricia Michelle. Educ: Okla. State Univ, B.A; Kappa Sigma. Polit. & Govt. Pos: Okla. State Rep, Dist, 35, 57-, speaker, Okla. House Rep, 67-; del, Dem. Nat. Conv, 68; mem. exec. cmt, Nat. Conf. State Legis. Leaders, 69; mem, Okla. Ambassadors Corps, 69; mem. gov. bd, Coun. State Govt, 69. Mil. Serv: Entered Army 43, released, 46, after serving in Eng. Corps, S.Pac, Okinawa and Saipan. Mem: Past pres, Pawnee Co. Cattlemen's Asn; Pawnee Co. C. of C; Am. Legion; Boy Scout Committeeman; coun. mem, Will Rogers Coun; bd. dirs, Bi-State Ment. Health Found. Hon. mem. Pawnee Indian Tribe, given a headdress and name 'Bucks-Pa-Hut Pawnee-Nasharo' meaning 'Red Headed Pawnee Chief,' 67. Rel: Methodist. Legal Res: Route One, Maramec, Okla. 74045. Mailing Add: Speaker's Office, 401 State Capitol, Oklahoma City, Okla. 73105.

PROCHAZKA, JOE W. D
Chmn, Rawlins Co. Dem. Cent. Cmt, Kans.
b. Atwood, Kans, 3/20/22; s. Joseph Prochazka and Frances Dozbaba P; m. 10/12/50 to Lowana M. Stephen; c. Kathleen Ann, Joseph William, III, Lawrence J. and Mary Jo. Educ: Atwood Commun. High Sch, 39; Fairfax Aviation Sch. Polit. & Govt. Pos: Secy, Rawlins Co. Dem. Cent. Cmt, Kans, 52, chmn, 64- Bus. & Prof. Pos: Dir, Farmers Nat. Bank, 48- Mem: K. of C.(4°); Rotary. Rel: Catholic. Mailing Add: Atwood, Kans. 67730.

PROCTOR, ERNEST EARL R
Chmn, Coweta Co. Rep. Party, Ga.
b. Millen, Ga, 11/29/27; s. Ernest Earl Proctor, Sr. (deceased) and Lila Lee P; m. 6/18/54 to Barbara Watkins; c. Robert Jesse, Richard Earl and Evelyn. Educ: Emory Univ, A.B, 50, M.D, 54; Phi Beta Kappa; Alpha Omega Alpha; Kappa Alpha Order. Polit. & Govt. Pos: Mem. campaign adv. cmt, Coweta Co. Rep. Party, Ga, 64, chmn, Coweta Co. Rep. Party, 65-; mem. exec. cmt, Sixth Dist. Rep. Party, 65. Bus. & Prof. Pos: Pres, Fourth Dist. Med. Soc, 64-65; chief of staff, Coweta Gen. Hosp, 64-66; secy-treas, Med. Staff, Newman Hosp, 65-66. Mil. Serv: Entered as Pvt, Army, 45, released as 1st Lt, 48, after serv. in Army Security Agency, Pac. Hq, 46-48. Mem: Soc. Nuclear Med; Am. Med. Asn; assoc, Am. Col. Physicians; Am. Heart Asn. Rel: Baptist. Mailing Add: 209 Jackson St, Newman, Ga. 30263.

PROCTOR, HELEN JUNE R
Chmn, Leicester Rep. Town Cmt, Mass.
b. Worcester, Mass, 10/14/17; d. Ralph E. Monigle (deceased) and Estelle Lind Monigle Boyd; m. 6/5/37 to Wesley Archer Proctor; c. Cynthia (Mrs. Edward C. Kehoe, Jr), Louise (Mrs. Richard L. McKeon) and Wayne Archer. Educ: Commerce High Sch. Polit. & Govt. Pos: Hq. secy, Leicester Rep. Town Cmt, Mass, 61 & 64, finance chmn, 64-68, soc. chmn, 64-68, chmn, 68-; hq. secy, John S. Konrad for Mass. State Rep, 62; town coordinator, Stanley R. Johnson and John C. Miller for Mass. State Rep, 64; town chmn, Edward W. Brooke for U.S. Sen, 66; Leicester campaign tel. chmn, Richard M. Nixon for Pres, 68. Bus. & Prof. Pos: Bookkeeper, Independent Grocery Store, Worcester, Mass, 35-36. Publ: Month articles for Mass. State Fedn. Women's Clubs as chmn. commun. serv. for Topics Mag, 65-67 and report of New Eng. Conf, 68. Mem: Eastern Star (Past Matron); Rebekah (Past Noble Grand Idun Rebekah Lodge); life mem. Leicester Woman's Club (organizer, past pres); Women's Rep. Club Worcester Co; Worcester Commun. Concert Asn; Mother's Club, DeMolay; Flotilla 1-1004 U.S. Coast Guard Auxiliary; Mass. State Fedn. Women's Clubs (Past Clerk). Award of Merit, Mass. Rep. State Cmt, 66. Rel: Protestant. Mailing Add: 13 Breezy Green Rd, Leicester, Mass. 01524.

PROFFER, MARVIN E. D
Mo. State Rep.
b. Cape Girardeau, Mo, 2/3/31; m. 10/30/54 to Marilyn Wilson; c. Robert Kirk, Marian Louise, James Kent. Educ: Southeast Mo. State Col, Cape Girardeau; Univ. Mo, Columbia, B.S. in Educ. and M.Ed. Polit. & Govt. Pos: Alderman, city coun, Jackson, Mo; bd. dirs, Cape Girardeau Co. Dem. Cmt; hon. col, Staff of the Late Gov. James T. Blair, Jr. and Gov. John M. Dalton; Mo. State Rep, Dist. 156, 62-, formerly, chmn. Cmt. on Accts, v.chmn, Cmt. on Appropriations and mem, Roads and Hwys. Cmt, Mo. House of Rep. Bus. & Prof. Pos: Newspaper published and ed, ins. agent and owner and operator of a printing and off. supply bus, currently; theater mgr, formerly. Mil. Serv: Army, 54-55. Mem: Rotary; Jr. C. of C.(past pres); bd. dirs, Jackson C. of C; Elks; Mason; AF&AM; Lions. Selected as Outstanding Young Man of Mo, 60; Nominee for One of Ten Outstanding Young Men of Am, 64. Rel: Presbyterian; Elder, First Presby. Church, Jackson Mo, having served as Deacon, Treas, Pres. Men's Coun. and Sunday Sch. Teacher. Mailing Add: Highway 72 W, Jackson, Mo. 63755.

PROLLER, NATHAN R
b. Gloversville, N.Y, 8/20/01; m. to Mildred Fones. Educ: Corinth High Sch; Wharton Sch. of Finance and Commerce, Univ. of Pa. Polit. & Govt. Pos: N.Y. State Sen, 64-66; Past Supvr, Town of Luzerne, Warren Co; Chmn. Bd. of Supvrs, 3 yrs; Exec. Cmt, Asn. of Towns, 7 yrs; Prepared script and conducted model town bd. meetings for annual Asn. of Towns meetings, 5 yrs; dir. and exec. cmt, Adirondack Park Asn; Co-Chmn, Adirondack Northway; N.Y. State Lottery Cmnr, currently. Bus. & Prof. Pos: Pres, Proller Agency, Inc. and Nathan Proller Assocs, Inc, corps. engaged principally in ins. and real estate bus. Mil. Serv: Vet, World War II. Mem: Am. Legion; Kiwanis; Temple Beth-El, Glens Falls; Jewish War Vets; Sen. Lodge 456; F&AM; Oriental Temple, Troy; Shrine; Elks; dir, Glens Falls C. of C; dir, Sunnyview Hosp. and Rehabilitation Center. Rel: Jewish. Mailing Add: 16 Ft. Amherst Rd, Glens Falls, N.Y. 12801.

PROMINSKI, HENRY JOHN R
Fla. State Rep.
b. New Brunswick, N.J, 9/4/29; s. John Henry Prominski and Stephanie Daszewski P; single. Educ: Univ. Pa, B.A, 50; Univ. Miami, LL.B, 59; McGill Univ, LL.M, 61; Alpha Chi Rho; Delta Theta Phi; Univ. Miami Law Rev; Wig and Robe. Polit. & Govt. Pos: Fla. State Rep, Dist. 86, 66- Bus. & Prof. Pos: Village attorney, Lazy Lake and asst. to the Attorney, City of Wilton Manors, currently. Mil. Serv: Entered as Aviation Cadet, Navy, 52, released as Lt.(jg), 56, after serv. in Mediterranean; recalled to active duty, 61-62, Cuban Mobilization; Lt. Comdr, Naval Res, currently. Publ: 'Contempt of Court,' Newspaper Photographers, Miami Law Rev, 2/58; 'State, Federal and Warsaw Racial Discrimination in Union Membership,' Vol. 13, Miami Law Rev; 'Wrongful Death in Aviation,' Miami Law Rev, Fall 60. Mem: Broward, Fla. and Am. Bar Asns. Rel: Roman Catholic. Mailing Add: 2750 N.E. 29th St, Lighthouse Point, Fla. 33064.

PROPST, HOWARD B. R
Chmn, Rep. State Cent. Cmt, Colo.
b. Merino, Colo, 1924; m. to Roberta Lascelles; c. Heather, Lorre and Rebecca. Educ: Univ. Denver, B.A. Polit. & Govt. Pos: Mem, Sch. Bd. and Colo. Child Welfare Div, Colo. Dept. Welfare; secy, Logan Co. Rep. Cent. Cmt; former exec. asst. to Gov. John Love; precinct committeeman, 48-56; Colo. State Rep, 56-62; Rep. Cand, U.S. House Rep, 62; alternate del, Rep. Nat. Conv, 68; chmn, Rep. State Cent. Cmt, currently. Bus. & Prof. Pos: Rancher. Mem: State Bd. Asn; Lions; Northeast. Colo. Cattlemen's Asn. (past pres); Colo. Boy Scout Adv. Bd; leader 4-H. Legal Res: 2475 Wadsworth Blvd, Denver, Colo. 80215. Mailing Add: 2175 Dover, Denver, Colo. 80215. (1967)

PROSSER, RUFUS K. R
R.I. State Sen.
b. Manchester, N.H, 8/15/04; m. to Freda B. Educ: Grand Cent. Archit. Sch, N.Y.C. Polit. & Govt. Pos: Chmn, Charlestown Sch. Cmt, 10 years; mem, Regional Sch. Dist. Planning Bd, Charlestown, Richmond Hopkinton, 56-57; R.I. First Regional Sch. Dist; chmn, Chariho Regional High Sch. Dist, 58-60; R.I. State Rep, 61-63; R.I. State Sen, 63-67 & 69- Bus. & Prof. Pos: Officer, bldg. material concern, N.Y.C, 15 years; owner and operator, Garage and Automotive Parts Store. Mem: Elks. Mailing Add: Post Rd, Charlestown, R.I. 02808.

PROSSER, WILLIAM HAYDN R
Mayor, Altoona, Pa.
b. Altoona, Pa, 11/30/20; s. Ivor H. Prosser and Hazel C. Lightner P; m. 6/17/50 to Marian Elizabeth Croyle; c. Stephen H. and Mark W. Educ: Pa. State Univ, B.A. in Psychol, 49; Skull and Bones; pres, Asn. Independent Men; Bar Bell Club; All Col. Recreation Cmt; mem, All Col. Cabinet. Polit. & Govt. Pos: Mayor, Altoona, Pa, currently. Bus. & Prof. Pos: Social serv. worker, Dept. Pub. Assistance, 49-50; personnel dir, Puritan Sportswear Corp, 50-51; personnel mgr, SKF Industs, Inc, 51-62; consult. indust. rels, self-employed, 62- Mil. Serv: Entered as Pvt, Army, 42, released as T/5, 45, after serv. in Fifth Combat Engrs, Spec. Brigade, ETO, 43-44; ETO Ribbon with Battle Star and Arrowhead. Mem: Am. Soc. Personnel Admin; past pres, Blair Co. Indust. Rels. Asn; Pa. State Psychol. Club; VFW; Am. Legion; C. of C; Am. Bus. Club; RAM; K.T; F&AM. Rel: Methodist. Mailing Add: 505 Coleridge Ave, Altoona, Pa. 16602.

PROTAN, JOHN D
Chmn, Boone Co. Dem. Party, W.Va.
b. Holden, W.Va, 12/12/21; s. Mike Protan and Rose Telasky P; m. to Doris Chingle; c. Doris Mae, Connie Kay and John Michael. Polit. & Govt. Pos: Constable, Sylvester, W.Va, 50-60, beer cmnr, 60-64, sheriff, 64-; chmn, Boone Co. Dem. Party, W.Va, 64- Mil. Serv: Entered as A/S, Navy, released as PO 2/C, after serv. in S.Pac. Mem: Elks; Moose; Am. Legion; Mason. Mailing Add: Sylvester, W.Va. 25193. (1967)

PROUD, RICHARD FRENCH R
Nebr. State Sen.
b. Des Moines, Iowa, 1/19/22; s. George C. Proud and Florence French P; m. 7/16/50 to Jean Hancock; c. George, John and Carol. Educ: Univ. Nebr, A.B, 47; Univ. Colo, LL.B, 49. Polit. & Govt. Pos: Mem, Sch. Bd, Furnas Co, Nebr, 52-55; serv. officer, Furnas Co, 60; city attorney, Arapahoe, 60; Nebr. State Sen, presently. Mil. Serv: Entered as A/S, Navy, 43, released as Lt.(jg), 46, after serv. as Commanding Officer, LCT Group, Pac. Theater, 45. Mem: Nebr. State Bar Asn; Mason, Monument Lodge; Am. Legion. Rel: Episcopal. Mailing Add: 2224 S. 110th St, Omaha, Nebr. 68144.

PROUDFIT, JOHN GRAHAM R
Asst. Attorney Gen, N.Y.
b. Edinburgh, Scotland, 7/13/32; s. Isabel Boyd P; single. Educ: Cornell Univ, B.A, 54, Wharton Grad. Sch, Univ. Pa, M.B.A, 59; N.Y. Univ. Law Sch, LL.B, 62. Polit. & Govt. Pos: Pres, Manhattan West Rep. Club, N.Y, 67-; Asst. Attorney Gen, N.Y, 67-; alternate del, Rep. Nat. Conv, 68; Rep. cand, U.S. Rep, N.Y, 68. Mil. Serv: Entered as 2nd Lt, Air Force, 54, released as 1st Lt, 57, after serv. in Korea and Air Defense Command; Res, Capt. Mem: Asn. of the Bar of City of N.Y; Fed. Bar Asn; Citizens Union; Borough Pres. Coun. of Adv; Sierra Club. Mailing Add: 215 W. 90th St, New York, N.Y. 10024.

PROUTY, WINSTON L. R
U.S. Sen, Vt.
b. Newport, Va; m. 7/3/62 to Jeannette Herbert Hall. Polit. & Govt. Pos: Mayor, Newport, Vt, 38-41; Vt. State Rep, 41 & 45-47, Speaker, Vt. State House of Rep, 47; chmn, Vt. State Water Conserv. Bd, 48-50; U.S. Rep, Vt, 50-58; U.S. Sen, Vt, 58- Bus. & Prof. Pos: Businessman. Legal Res: Newport, Vt. 05855. Mailing Add: 5615 Ogden Rd, Washington, D.C. 20016.

PROVO, JACK MARLOWE R
b. Minneapolis, Minn, 3/11/37; s. Clarence Provo (deceased) and Alice Iverson Provo Courteau; m. 9/6/58 to Joyce Diane Olson; c. Jay and Jeffrey. Educ: Univ. Minn, B.S, 59. Polit. & Govt. Pos: Chmn, Richfield Young Rep. League Club, Minn, 62 & 63; precinct chmn, Richfield Rep. Party, 63; acting chmn, Hennepin Co. Bd. Cmnrs, 65; del, Ward, Dist. and State Convs, 5 years; del, Rep. Nat. Conv, 68. Bus. & Prof. Pos: Chmn, Hennepin Co. Welfare Bd, 65-; chmn, Ways & Means Cmt, 67-; v.pres., Minn. Welfare Asn, currently. Mem: Nat. Asn. Co. (welfare cmt); Am. Soc. Pub. Admin; Minn. Attorney Gen. Adv. Coun. Law Enforcement; YMCA (Indian guide leader); Richfield Hist. Soc; PTA (Portland Sch. legis. chmn); Kiwanis; Citizens League; Minn. Heart Asn. (Hennepin Co. Bd. dirs, state bd. dirs, state chmn). Rel: Lutheran; Chmn. Church Coun, Holy Trinity Lutheran Church. Mailing Add: 7033 Second Ave. S, Richfield, Minn. 55423.

PROVOST, PERLEY HERBERT, JR. R
b. Winooski, Vt, 6/9/25; s. Perley Herbert Provost and Evelyn Blanchette P; m. 5/19/47 to Eleanor Dorey; c. Kenneth Allen, Janice Pamela and Perley H, III. Educ: St. Michael's Col, B.A, 49; Univ. Notre Dame, M.A, 51. Polit. & Govt. Pos: Personnel dir. and admin. asst. to mayor, South Bend, Ind, 54-56; precinct committeeman, Rep. Party, South Bend, 54-60; asst. to Lt. Gov. of Ind, 61-64; chmn, St. Joseph Co. Rep. Cmt, 61-66; mem, Ind. State Rep. Cent. Cmt, 66-; former chmn, Third Cong. Dist. Rep. Party; dir, Natural Resources, Ind, currently. Bus. & Prof. Pos: Instr, St. Michael's Col, 51-52; city probation officer, South Bend, Ind, 52-54; gen. foreman, U.S. Rubber, 56-58; chief juvenile probation officer, St. Joseph Co, Ind, 58-61; pres, Allied Agency, Inc, 62-; assoc. faculty mem, Ind. Univ, South Bend, currently. Mil. Serv: Entered as Pvt, Marine Corps, 43, released as Cpl, 45, after serv. in Third Marine Air Wing and Detached Duty, Third Amphibian Corps, Pac. Theater, 43-45; Pac. Theater Ribbon with One Battle Star, Guam. Mem: Moose and Many Rep. Clubs. Winner of Letters, Hockey and Baseball. Rel: Catholic. Mailing Add: 53330 N. Ironwood Rd, South Bend, Ind. 46635.

PROXMIRE, WILLIAM D
U.S. Sen, Wis.
b. Lake Forest, Ill, 11/11/15; s. Dr. Theodore Stanley Proxmire and Adele Flanigan P; m. 12/1/56 to Ellen Hodges; c. Elsie Stillman, Theodore Stanley and Douglas Clark. Educ: Yale, B.A, 38; Harvard Bus. Sch, M.B.A. cum laude, 40, Sch. Pub. Admin, M.P.A, 48. Polit. & Govt. Pos: Wis. State Assemblyman, 51-52; U.S. Sen, Wis, 57-, chmn, Great Lakes Conf, v.chmn, Cong. Joint Econ. Cmt, mem, Banking and Currency Cmt, Senate Appropriations Cmt, Dem. Steering Cmt. and chmn, Appropriations D.C. Subcmts, U.S. Senate. Bus. & Prof. Pos: Polit. and labor reporter, Capital Times, Madison, Wis, 49; reporter, Madison Union Labor News, Wis, 50; pres, Artcraft Press, Waterloo, Wis, 53-57. Mil. Serv: Entered as Pvt, Army, 41, released as 1st Lt, 46, after serv. in Counterintel Corps. Publ: Can Small Business Survive?, Henry Regnery Co, 64. Letter in football at Yale; Yale boxing champion in 149-159 lb. weight class. Rel: Episcopal. Legal Res: 4613 East Buckeye Rd, Madison, Wis. 53716. Mailing Add: Senate Office Bldg, Washington, D.C. 20510.

PRUIT, RALPH EUGENE R
N.Mex. State Rep.
b. Blackwell, Tex, 7/31/35; s. Thurman D. Pruit and Mamie L. Choate P; m.

8/28/59 to Mary Lee Trimble; c. John D. and Larry N. Educ: Univ. of N.Mex; Carlsbad Br, N.Mex. State Univ. Polit. & Govt. Pos: N.Mex. State Rep, Curry Co, 69- Mem: Gateway Asn. of Life Underwriters; N.Mex. Farm and Livestock Bur; charter mem, West. Farm Bur. Life Century Club. Nat. Quality Award; Top Life Ins. Agent for Farm Bureau, 67 & 68. Rel: Protestant. Legal Res: 101 Commerce Way, Clovis, N.Mex. 88101. Mailing Add: 108 W. Plains, Clovis, N.Mex. 88101.

PRUITT, BOBBY MAURICE D
b. Union, 4/29/32; s. Ray C. Pruitt and Kathleen Lamb P; m. 12/31/60 to Joyce Deuser. Educ: Univ. of S.C, B.S, 54; LL.B, 60. Polit. & Govt. Pos: S.C. State Rep, 63-66; asst. Munic. Recorder of Spartanburg; mem. bd. of dir. for the visiting Nurses Asn. Bus. & Prof. Pos: Lawyer, firm of Whiteside & Pruitt. Mil. Serv: Air Force, pilot, 54-57. Mem: Secy-treas, Spartanburg Co. Bar Asn. Mailing Add: Box 1144, Spartanburg, S.C. 29301. (1967)

PRUITT, DAVID CARL, III R
b. Birmingham, Ala, 10/15/33; s. David Carl Pruitt, Jr. and Leo Reese P; single. Educ: Univ. Ala, B.S. in Commerce, 55; Alpha Kappa Psi; Pi Kappa Alpha. Polit. & Govt. Pos: Admin asst. to U.S. Rep. George Huddleston, Ala, 64-65 and to U.S. Rep. Jack Edwards, First Dist, Ala, 65- Bus. & Prof. Pos: Nat. dir, Am. Jr. Miss Pageant, 60-64. Mil. Serv: Entered as 2nd Lt, Army, 55, released as 1st Lt, 57, after serv. in Qm. Corps, Seventh Army, ETO; Outstanding Serv. Cert. Mem: Mobile Jr. C. of C; Ala. State Soc. of Wash, D.C; Univ. Ala. Alumni Asn. Rel: Methodist. Legal Res: 1250 Belle Chene, Mobile, Ala. 36609. Mailing Add: 137 House Office Bldg, Washington, D.C. 20515.

PRUITT, IRA DRAYTON D
Ala. State Rep.
b. Pine Hill, Ala, 3/4/04; s. Ira Drayton Pruitt and Mary Elizabeth Miller P; m. 11/27/35 to Elise Knox Cobb; c. Ira Drayton, Jr. Educ: Univ. Ala, LL.B, 34; Phi Alpha Delta. Polit. & Govt. Pos: Mem. town coun, Livingston, Ala, 36-51; circuit solicitor, 17th Judicial Circuit, 40-44; Ala. State Rep, 44- Bus. & Prof. Pos: Attorney-at-law, 34- Mem: Mason. Mailing Add: Livingston, Ala. 35470.

PRUITT, JAMES H. D
Fla. State Rep.
b. Cartersville, Ga, 12/16/18; m. to Mary Law; c. Lonnie, Tanya and Mike. Educ: Cartersville High. Polit. & Govt. Pos: Former mem, Juvenile Court Merit Bd. of Brevard Co, Fla; former city coun. and mayor, Eau Gallie; Fla. State Rep, 58- Bus. & Prof. Pos: Ins. and Real Estate; bd. of dirs, First Nat. Bank of Eau Gallie; pres, S. Brevard Bd. of Realtors; chmn. bd, Indialantic Beach Bank. Mil. Serv: First Cavalry Div, Heavy Artil, S.Pac; Two Battle Stars. Mem: Bd. of dirs, Orange Bowl Cmt; Am. Legion; charter mem. and former pres, Melbourne Lions and Eau Gallie Lions. Rel: Baptist. Mailing Add: P.O. Box 875, Eau Gallie, Fla. 32935.

PRUITT, LESLIE O. D
Treas, Lake Co, Ind.
b. Gary, Ind, 9/7/21; s. Leslie C. Pruitt and Katherine Untermajer P; m. 11/3/45 to Martha Mamula; c. Leslie Douglas and Kay Doreen. Educ: Univ. of Wyo. Polit. & Govt. Pos: Chief dep. treas, Lake Co, Ind, 51-62, treas, 62-; treas, Lake Co. Dem. Cent. Cmt, 62-; First Dist. chmn, State Dem. Cent. Cmt, presently. Mil. Serv: Pvt, Army, 42-45, serv. in 5th Inf. Div, ETO; Good Conduct Medal; Purple Heart; Am. Theater Ribbon; ETO Ribbon with Battle Stars. Mem: Am. Legion; VFW; DAV; Moose; Eagles; Optimists; Young Dems; K. of C. Rel: Roman Catholic. Mailing Add: 4187 Jefferson, Gary, Ind. 46408.

PRUITT, PRENTICE D
b. Bilbertown, Ala, 7/7/16; m. to Jane Vickers; c. Lettie Jane (Mrs. Tompkins) and Nancy Elizabeth. Educ: Univ. of Fla, LL.B, 1950, Jr. Class Pres. Polit. & Govt. Pos: Fla. State Rep, 53, 55 & 64-66. Bus. & Prof. Pos: Attorney. Mil. Serv: Marines, World War II. Mem: C. of C; Hist. Soc; Mason; Shriner; Kiwanis; Quarterback Club. Recreation: Fishing, Hunting, All Sports. Rel: Methodist. Legal Res: 555 E. Washington, Monticello, Fla. 32344. Mailing Add: S. Cherry St, Monticello, Fla. 32344. (1967)

PRUNTY, ROGER D. D
Dist. Capt, S.Dak. Dem. Party
b. Forestburg, S.Dak, 1/14/29; s. Glenn G. Prunty and Anna Anderson P; m. 11/1/53 to Betty Ann Johnson; c. Steven, Stephanie, Robin, Jacqueline and Susan. Educ: S.Dak. State Univ, B.S. in Econ. Polit. & Govt. Pos: Chmn, Brookings Co. Dem. Cmt, S.Dak, 59-62; chmn, Brookings Co. Dem. for Kennedy, 68; del. and mem, credentials cmt, Dem. Nat. Conv, 68; dist. capt, S.Dak. Dem. Party, 68- Mil. Serv: Entered as Pvt, Army, 51, released as Cpl, 53, after serv. in 8048th Army Unit, Far East Command. Mem: Am. Legion; C. of C. Rel: Protestant. Legal Res: 106 Jefferson Ave, Brookings, S.Dak, 57006. Mailing Add: Box 342, Brookings, S.Dak. 57006.

PRYOR, DAVID HAMPTON D
U.S. Rep, Ark.
b. Camden, Ark, 8/29/34; s. William Edgar Pryor and Susan Newton P; m. 11/28/57 to Barbara Jean Lunsford; c. David, Jr, Mark and Scott. Educ: Henderson State, Ark, 52-53; Ark. Univ, B.A, 57 and Law Sch, LL.B, 64; Blue Key; Sigma Alpha Epsilon; Phi Alpha Delta. Polit. & Govt. Pos: Ark. State Rep, 61-66; U.S. Rep, Ark, 67-, mem, House Appropriations Cmt, U.S. House of Rep, currently; del, Dem. Nat. Conv, 68. Bus. & Prof. Pos: Publisher, weekly newspaper, Ouachita Citizen, 57-60; law partner, Pryor & Barnes, 64-66. Mem: Jr. C. of C; C. of C. Selected One of Five Outstanding Young Men in Ark, Ark. Jaycees, 67. Rel: Presbvterian. Mailing Add: 3321 N. Ohio, Arlington, Va. 22207.

PRYOR, W. IRVIN R
b. Greene Co, Ind, 6/18/95; s. Levi C. Pryor and Laura Hancock P; m. to Ona Griffith; c. Ruth (Mrs. Vandeventer), Robert and William. Educ: Special training course in printing and journalism. Polit. & Govt. Pos: Co. Chmn, Rep. Party, Ind, 56-66 and 40-48; del, Rep. State Convs, 36-; del, Rep. Nat. Conv, 64, alternate del, 52. Bus. & Prof. Pos: Mem. and dir, Ind. Rep. Ed. Asn. Mem: K. of P; Red Men; past officer, Ind. Red Men Lodges; MWA· pres, C. of C, 6 yrs. and Lions, 2 terms. Rel: Christian Church; Teacher, Men's Bible Class. Legal Res: 105 East St, Worthington, Ind. 47471. Mailing Add: 114 E. Main St, Worthington, Ind. 47471. (1967)

PSATY, MARTIN MELVILLE D
b. Brooklyn, N.Y, 12/3/17; s. Charles I. Psaty and Leah Seham P; m. 10/25/42 to Claire Ringelheim; c. Beverly Rae (Mrs. Pomerantz), Alan Irwin and Madelyn Susan. Educ: Univ. Calif, Berkeley, A.B. with hons. in econs, 39; N.Y. Univ. and Columbia Univ, grad. work, 46-51; N.Y. Law Sch, LL.B, 60; Law Review; Phi Delta Phi; Hon. Econs. Fraternity; Senate Debating Soc, Univ. of Calif. Polit. & Govt. Pos: Jr. economist, Bur.of Labor Statistics, Wash, D.C, 41; chief price analyst, U.S. Army Ord. Dist, Birmingham, Ala, 43-45 and N.Y.C, 51-52, consult, Dept. of Army, N.Y.C, 52-57; N.Y. State Assemblyman, 63-65. Bus. & Prof. Pos: Secy-treas, Gr. New York Waterproofing Co, 46-; pres, Horn Waterproofing Corp, N.Y.C, 60-; pres, Psaty Horn Corp, 67- Mil. Serv: Entered as Pvt, Army, 41, released as 1st Lt, 46, after serv. in Birmingham Ord. Dist. Mem: Executives Asn. of Gr. N.Y; bd. mem, N.Y. Post, Am. Ord. Asn; Cardoza Lodge 1150 F&AM, Mason (32°), Valley of N.Y, Shrine, Mecca Temple; Gratitude Lodge, K. of P; Kew Forest Post, Jewish War Vets; Jackson Heights Post, Am. Legion; Am. Jewish Cong; Nat. Admin. Cmn. Presidents Award, Union of Nat. Orthodox Congregations of Am; Silver Shofar award, Young Israel of Am; Honored by United Jewish Appeal and Bonds for Israel. Rel: Jewish. Legal Res: 64-29 110th St, Forest Hills, N.Y. 11375. Mailhg Add: 500 Fifth Ave, New York, N.Y. 10036.

PUCHALLA, ANDREW FRANCIS D
Chmn, Huntingdon Co. Dem. Cmt, Pa.
b. Mt. Union, Pa, 11/15/11; s. Lawrence J. Puchalla and Eva Suchanec P; m. 4/20/39 to Mary Jane Mickley; c. Patricia Eva and Victoria Jane. Educ: High Sch. grad. Polit. & Govt. Pos: Chmn, Clark-Dillworth Campaign Cmt, Pa, 62; chmn, Huntingdon Co. Dem. Cmt, 64-; asst. dir, Bur. Liquor Audits, Auditor-Gen. Dept, Pa, 67- Bus. & Prof. Pos: Pres, Huntingdon Co. Indust. Develop. Coun, Inc, Pa, 55-; mem. bd, Mt. Union Area Develop. Corp, 58-, pres, 65- Publ: 'Industrial Development in Huntingdon Co,' Banker's Weekly, 5/28/58; co-author, article on indust. develop, Indust. Mkt. Magazine, 58; assisted in numerous develop. articles, Tyrone Daily Herald, 60. Mem: Lions; K. of C; exec. bd, Huntingdon Co. Cancer Soc; pres, Mt. Union C. of C; co-ordinator, Nat. Safety Coun. Defensive Driving Course, through Auditor Gen. of Pa; chmn, Capitol Hill Health Fund Dr, 69, Auditor Gen. Dept. and U.S. Savings Bond Statewide Dr, 69. Achievements: Assisted in formulating overall econ. develop. prog. for Mifflin and Huntingdon Co, 62; took major part in fund raising for econ. develop. Huntingdon Co. and Mt. Union; represented Huntingdon Co. at Indust. Develop. Show, N.Y. Coliseum. Rel: Roman Catholic. Mailing Add: 125 S. Division St, Mt. Union, Pa. 17066.

PUCINSKI, ROMAN C. D
U.S. Rep, Ill.
b. 5/13/19; m. to Aurelia Bordin; c. Two. Educ: Northwest. Univ; John Marshall Law Sch, Chicago. Polit. & Govt. Pos: Chief investr, Select Cmt. of Cong. investigating mass murder by Communists of 15,000 Polish Army Officers in World War II; U.S. Rep, 11th Cong. Dist, Ill, 58-, chmn, Spec. Task Force to Study Labor Dispute Involving Nuclear Ship Savannah, U.S. House of Rep, mem, House Cmt. on Educ. and Labor and House Cmt. on Vet. Affairs, chmn, Subcmt. on Nat. Labor Rels. Bd, 87th Cong, chmn, Ad Hoc Subcmt. on Nat. Research Data Processing and Info. Retrieval Center, 88th and 89th Cong, chmn, Standing Cmt. on Select Educ, 89th Cong, chmn, Standing Cmt. on Gen. Educ, 90th and 91st Cong; alternate del, Dem. Nat. Conv, 68. Bus. & Prof. Pos: Staff reporter and writer for Chicago Sun-Times, 38-58. Mil. Serv: Entered World War II as Pvt. in 106th Cavalry, discharged as Capt; served with 20th Global (Superfort) Air Force; led his bomber group on first B-29 bombing raid over Tokyo, 44; subsequently flew 48 missions over Japan; awarded the Distinguished Flying Cross and Air Medal with Cluster. Rel: Roman Catholic. Legal Res: Chicago, Ill. Mailing Add: 2104 Rayburn House Office Bldg, Washington, D.C. 20515.

PUCKETT, THOMAS W. D
b. Porterville, Miss, 8/23/92; wid. Polit. & Govt. Pos: Former Miss. State Rep; former mem. Game and Fish Cmn. Bus. & Prof. Pos: Farmer; merchant. Mem: Scottish Rite (32°); Shrine; Am. Legion (post comdr, twice, former dist. 5 comdr, former supv). Rel: Baptist. Mailing Add: Route 2, DeKalb, Miss. 39328. (1967)

PUFFER, ERMA E. R
Vt. State Rep.
b. Acworth, N.H, 5/13/21; m. to Raymond Puffer; c. Barbara E. (Mrs. Bradford Bliss), Gary Douglas and Raymond Henry, Jr. Educ: Leland and Gray Sem, Townshend, Vt. Polit. & Govt. Pos: Vt. State Rep, 59-; justice of the peace; moderator, Town of Vernon; v.chmn, Vernon Recreation Bd, currently; mem, Vernon Planning Cmn, currently. Bus. & Prof. Pos: V.pres. and treas, hwy. transportation and truck sales and serv. co; trustee, Family and Child Guid. Serv. and Vernon Historians, Inc, currently. Mem: Grange; Eastern Star; Farm Bur; Quota Club, Brattleboro; Vt. and Nat. Order of Women Legislators. Rel: Congregational. Mailing Add: Box 62, Vernon, Vt. 05354.

PUFFER, K(ENNETH) HART R
b. South Boardman, Mich, 4/14/10; s. George Wesley Puffer and Roma Thomas P; m. 12/24/35 to Lela Minear Baughman; c. Phyllis A, Joan L. (Mrs. Kotcher) and Karen J. Educ: West. Mich. Univ, B.S, 35; Mich. State Univ, M.A, 49; Univ. of Mich, Ph.D, 59. Polit. & Govt. Pos: Chmn, Kalkaska Co. Rep. Party, Mich, 66-68. Bus. & Prof. Pos: Supt. of schs, Flint Hoover, 53-56 and Stambaugh, 62-64; teacher, Flint, 57-62 and 64- Publ: How Good Schools Are Run, Bond Wheelwright, 62; plus others. Mem: Nat, Flint and Mich. State Educ. Asns; Mason; Justin Morgan Horse Asn; Genesee Co. Amateur Radio Club; Mich. Hist. Soc; Mich. Archeol. Soc; Int. Platform Asn. Citation for assisting Upper Peninsula Creative Writers' Asn. Rel: Methodist. Legal Res: Route 1, South Boardman, Mich. 49680. Mailing Add: Pine Hills Farm, South Boardman, Mich. 49680.

PUFFER, THOMAS RAY R
Treas, San Diego Co. Rep. Cent. Cmt, Calif.
b. Buffalo, N.Y, 3/13/31; s. Ray H. Puffer and Mildred I. Pease P; m. 8/17/68

to Patricia Lamb; c. Richard Scott and Lisa Karen. Educ: Hamilton Col, B.A, 54; Univ. Calif, San Diego, Cert. of Indust. Rels, 59; Theta Delta Chi. Polit. & Govt. Pos: Mem, San Diego Co. Rep. Cent. Cmt, Calif, 62-, treas, 69-; mem, Calif. Rep. Cent. Cmt, 66- Bus. & Prof. Pos: Corp. secy, San Diego Employers Asn, Calif, 57- Mil. Serv: Entered as 2nd Lt, Marine Corps, 54, released as Capt, 57, after serv. in First Marine Div, Camp Pendleton, Calif, 54-57. Mem: San Diego Chap, Indust. Research Asn; past pres, San Diego Active 20-30 Club; San Diego Co. Welfare Bd; Kona Kai Club. Rel: Presbyterian. Mailing Add: 7363 Florey St, San Diego, Calif. 92122.

PUGLIESE, JOSEPH MICHAEL R
Conn. State Rep.
b. Plainville, Conn, 10/16/24; s. Joseph Nunzio Pugliese and Mary Pinto P; m. 2/1/47 to Lorraine Willey; c. Joseph M, Jr, Thomas Anthony and Allan Francis. Educ: Army Commun. Sch, Tex, Cert, 43; Marc Porter Sch. of Tool & Mach. Design, Conn, Dipl, 49. Polit. & Govt. Pos: Mem, Bd. of Health, Conn, 59-61; town councilman, Plainville, 61-67 and chmn, town coun, Plainville, Conn, 67-68; Conn. State Rep, Dist. 33, 68- Bus. & Prof. Pos: Eng. Designer, New Britain Machine Co, Conn, 49-51; group leader, Production Services Corp, 51-58; tool designer, United Aircraft Corp, 58-60; dept. supvr, Atlantic Machine Co, 60- Mil. Serv: Entered as Pvt, Army, 43, released as Cpl, 46, after serving in 720 Amphibian Tractor Bn, Pac. Theatre, 44-46; Am. Theatre Ribbon, Good Conduct Medal, Pac-Asiatic Ribbon, Victory Medal. Mem: Am. Soc. of Tool and Mfg. Engrs; Farmington River Watershed Asn; Am. Legion. Rel: Roman Catholic. Mailing Add: 101 Pinnacle Rd, Plainville, Conn. 06062.

PUHAN, ALFRED
U.S. Ambassador to Hungary
b. Marienburg, Germany, 3/7/13; s. Otto Albert Puhan and Anna Machlewitz P; m. 11/5/38 to Fairfax Judd; c. Ursula, Fairfax and Frederic J. Educ: Oberlin Col, A.B, 35; Univ. Cincinnati, A.M, 37; Columbia Univ, 37-39. Polit. & Govt. Pos: Quadripartite dir, Am. Embassy, Vienna, Austria, 53-55 and dir. polit. sect, 55-57; dep. dir, Off. of Int. Affairs, Dept. State, 57-59 and dir, 59-60; exec. dir, Bur. European Affairs, Dept. of State, 60-63; dep. chief of mission, minister-counsr, Am. Embassy, Bangkok, Thailand, 62; dir. German affairs, Dept. of State, 64-68; Acting Dep. Asst. Secy. of State for Europe, 68-69; U.S. Ambassador to Hungary, 69- Bus. & Prof. Pos: Teacher, Columbia and Rutgers Univs, 37-41; dir, German Lang. broadcasts from London, 44, broadcasts from Radio Luxembourg for SHAEF, 45, various Voices of Am. Broadcasts, 46-50 and all Voices of Am. Programming, 50-53. Participated in McCloy mission to study takeover by Dept. of State of info. activities in Germany from Dept. Defense, 49. Legal Res: 1046 Clover Dr, McLean, Va. 22101. Mailing Add: Dept. of State, Budapest, Washington, D.C. 20521.

PULAKOS, GEORGE STEVE D
Chmn, Erie Co. Dem. Cmt, Pa.
b. Erie, Pa, 4/22/22; s. Steve George Pulakos and Geraldine Bolger P; m. 5/1/43 to Margaret Pauline Weindorf; c. Kathleen Ann (Mrs. Barbour) and Lynne Mary. Educ: Univ. Pittsburg Inst. of Local Govt; Gannon Col. Inst. for Commun. Develop. Polit. & Govt. Pos: Fireman, West Lake Fire Dept, Pa, 38-, hon. past chief and asst. chief, 11 years; supvr, Millcreek Twp, 62; chmn, Erie Co. Dem. Cmt, 66- Bus. & Prof. Pos: Owner-mgr, Pulakos-on-the-Lake and Sportsmen's Athletic Club, 46-61; ins. and real estate, 60-62; instr, Pa. Dept. Pub. Instr. Mil. Serv: Entered as 2nd Cook, Merchant Marine, 43, released as Chief Steward, 45, after serv. in Pac; Atlantic and Pac. Theatre Campaign Ribbons. Publ: Article on snow removal, Pa. Twp. News, 9/66. Mem: Pres, Erie Co. Asn. Twp. Off; membership cmt. and del. to House of Del, Am. Pub. Works Asn; chmn, Erie Co. Redevelop. Authority; Int. City Mgr. Asn; chmn, Resolutions Cmt, Pa. State Asn. Twp. Supvr. All-Co. Football Team, Erie Co. Rel: Roman Catholic. Legal Res: 1024 Grace St, Erie, Pa. 16505. Mailing Add: 3608 W. 26th St, Erie, Pa. 16506.

PULIDO, ALBERTO D
Dir. Nationalities Div, Mich. Dem. State Cent. Cmt.
b. Laredo, Tex, 6/7/22; s. Tomas Pulido and Ramona Zapata P; m. 6/21/52 to Domitila Serrato; c. Teresa. Educ: Detroit Col. Law, 49-50; Detroit Inst. Tech, B.A, 50; Univ. Mich. Exten. Serv, 52, 59, 64 & 65; Wayne State Univ. Law Sch, 56-57; Am. Inst. Banking; Gabriel Richard Inst, 66. Polit. & Govt. Pos: Pres, Latin Am. Cmt. on Polit. Action, Detroit, Mich, 58-59; right of way title analyst, Wayne Co. Rd. Cmn, 58-63, appraisal reviewer, 63-67, negotiator, 67-; chmn, Latin Am. affairs, nationalities div, Mich. Dem. State Cent. Cmt, 64-, asst. dir, nationalities div, 64-69, mem, policy adv. cmt, 65-66, mem, exec. bd, 16th Cong. Dist, 66-, mem, justice and equality cmt, 68-, dir, nationalities div, 69-; chmn. and founder, Latin Am. Dem. Club of Mich, 64-; mem, cmt. on apprenticeship info. center, Mich. Employment Security Cmn, 64-; precinct del, Dem. Co. and State Conv, 64-; first v.chmn, citizens area adv. cmt, Total Action Against Poverty Area 2, West. Commun. Center, 65-66; mem, mayor's policy adv. cmt, Total Action Against Poverty, 65-66; chmn, property sect, citizens adv. cmt, West. High Sch, Detroit Bd. of Educ, 66-67; mem, Mayor's Cmt. on Neighborhood Conserv. and Housing, 66-68; chmn. and founder, Mich. Huelga Cmt, 66-; mem, adv. coun, Small Bus. Admin, Mich, 67-68; alternate del-at-lg, Dem. Nat. Conv, 68; state chmn. and founder, Viva Humphrey Club, 68-; co-chmn, Jefferson-Jackson Dinner Ticket Cmt, 16th Cong. Dist, 69- Bus. & Prof. Pos: Shoe shine boy, Laredo, Tex, 32-33; dishwasher, Depot Cafe, 33-34, bartender and mgr, 34-35; cotton picker, Corpus Christi, summers 36-40; migrant laborer, sugar beet fields, Mich. and Ohio, 40-41; painter and rough carpenter, Laredo, Tex, 41-43; gas welder, Briggs Mfg. Co, Mack Plant, Detroit, Mich, 46-49; secy. and law clerk to Charles C. Benjamin, 46-49; abstractor and title exam, Burton Abstract and Title Co, 49-52; admin. asst. and chief mortgage closer, Indust. Nat. Bank of Detroit and later the Mfrs. Nat. Bank of Detroit, 52-56; real estate broker and ins. agent, 57-58; gen. mgr, Alamo Ins. Agency, 58-; gen. agent, Seguros Tepeyac, S.A, 59-68; dir, Corktown Credit Union, 60-63, pres, 64-67. Mil. Serv: Tank Comdr, Army, 43-46, with serv. in Co. C, 766th Tank Bn, Southwest Pac. Theatre of Opers; Asiatic Pac. Campaign Medal with One Bronze Star; Good Conduct Medal; Victory Ribbon with Four Overseas Serv. Bars. Mem: Finance officer, Mexican Am. Post 505, Am. Legion, 47-48, judge adv. and child welfare chmn, 48-68, serv. officer, 48-; comdr, 50-51, chmn, exec. cmt, 51-60; exec. v.pres, Mex. Am. Post 505, Mem. Home Asn, 58-59, pres, 60-68; sub-cmt. on commun. rels, Archbishop's Cmt. on Commun. Rels, 60-62; co-chmn, int. rels. cmt, Archdiocesan Coun. of Cath. Men, 61-62, chmn, 64-67; treas, Hubbard-Richard Commun. Coun, 65-66; chmn, Finance and property cmt, bd. mgt, West. Br, YMCA, 65-; dir, Delray Improv. Asn, 66-67; bd. dir, Fortier O'Grady Post 9039, VFW, Mem. Home Asn, 66-68; pres, Mexican Patriotic Cmt. of Mich, 66-68; parliamentarian, Bagley Ave. Businessmen's Asn, 66-; Vernor-Junction Businessmen's Asn; pres, U.S. Hunt Club, 67-; Am. Fedn. of State, Co. and Munic. Employees, AFL-CIO; Am. Right-of-Way Asn; Int. Platform Asn. Thirteen Cert. of Merit for the Most Outstanding Serv. Officer, 15th Dist, Detroit Dist. Asn, Am. Legion; Two Departmental Meritorious Awards, Dept. of Mich, Life Mem. Award, Mexican Am. Post 505; Three Silver Medals and Cert. for being selected as Runner-Up for Mich. Vet. of the Year for 1963, 1965 & 1967; Cert. Award in recognition of the outstanding meritorious serv. in the field of constitution and by-law writing ability, Vernor-Junction Businessmen's Asn; Cert. of Merit in recognition of commun. serv. rendered, Dictionary of Int. Biographies; Chamizal Medalion received from President Lyndon B. Johnson in commemoration of the Chamizal Agreement between the U.S. and the Repub. of Mex. Rel: Catholic. Mailing Add: 3542 28th St, Detroit, Mich. 48210.

PULLEY, WILLIAM W. R
Chmn, Butler Co. Rep. Cent. Cmt, Ohio
b. Oxford, Ohio, 3/7/29; s. Verlin L. Pulley and Corola Wood P; m. 8/22/51 to Martha Lee Lesher; c. William Lesher, Mary Lynn and Jeffrey Verlin. Educ: Dartmouth Col, A.B, 50; Miami Univ, M.B.A, 56; Phi Beta Kappa; Beta Gamma Sigma; Phi Delta Theta. Polit. & Govt. Pos: Rep. precinct committeeman, Ohio, 58; mem. exec. cmt. and area capt, Butler Co. Rep. Cent. Cmt, 60, chmn, currently; del, Rep. Nat. Conv, 68. Bus. & Prof. Pos: Sales mgr, Capitol Varsity Co, 53, gen. mgr, 66. Mil. Serv: Res, Mil. Intel, 51-57. Mem: Rotary. Rel: Methodist. Mailing Add: 150 Shadowy Hills Dr, Oxford, Ohio 45056.

PULLIAM, DONALD WOODROW D
Chmn, Boone Co. Dem. Cent. Cmt, Ill.
b. Maroa, Ill, 1/18/17; s. Joseph Cleveland Pulliam and Luvincy Seibert P; m. 3/19/41 to Ruth Elizabeth Grey; c. Sharon Ruth, Steven Donald, Michael Grey and Susan Elizabeth. Educ: Rock Valley Col, 1½ years; Univ. Ill, 4 years. Polit. & Govt. Pos: Pres, Bd. Educ, Sch. Dist. 33, Poplar Grove, Ill, 50-51; precinct committeeman, Poplar Grove Twp. Dem. Party, 58-; v.chmn, Boone Co. Dem. Cent. Cmt, 60-68, chmn, 68- Mil. Serv: Entered as Motor Machinist Mate 3/C, Navy, 44, released as Motor Machinist Mate 1/C, 45, after serv. in Pacific Theatre, 45; Philippine Liberation Medal. Mem: Am. Legion; United Auto Workers; VFW; Odd Fellows; IBT. Mailing Add: 204 West Park St, Poplar Grove, Ill. 61065.

PULLIN, ROLAND BUCKNER R
Chmn, Golden Valley Co. Rep. Party, N.Dak.
b. Refugio, Tex, 1/6/30; s. James Buckner Pullin and Edna O'Neil P; m. 6/26/55 to Norma Meredith Martin; c. Mark and Leslie. Educ: Univ. South. Calif, B.S. in Pub. Admin; Pi Sigma Alpha. Polit. & Govt. Pos: Chmn, Golden Valley Co. Rep. Party, N.Dak, currently. Bus. & Prof. Pos: Farm & ranch mgr, Martin & Martin, 66- Mil. Serv: Entered as Pvt, Marine Corps, 48, released as Sgt, 52, after serv. in Pac; Korean War Medal. Mem: Elks; Mason; Am. Legion. Rel: Congregational. Mailing Add: Sentinel Butte, N.Dak. 58654. (1967)

PURCELL, FRANCIS T. R
b. Brooklyn, N.Y, 8/11/18; m. to Barbara Kern; c. Three. Educ: Malverne High Sch. Polit. & Govt. Pos: Mem. bd. gov, Malverne Rep. Club, N.Y; trustee, Malverne, 47-54, mayor, 55-63; N.Y. State Assemblyman, 64-66; alternate del, Rep. Nat. Conv, 68. Bus. & Prof. Pos: Pres, Westwood Paper and Hardware Co, NYC; dir, Dollar Fed. Savings and Loan Asn. Mil. Serv: Army, 41-45, discharged as Capt. Mem: Past pres, Nassau Co. Village Off. Asn; Malverne Police Benevolent Asn; hon. mem, Malverne Fire Dept; Malverne Post 44, Am. Legion. Mailing Add: 25 Croyden St, Malverne, N.Y. 11565. (1967)

PURCELL, GRAHAM D
U.S. Rep, Tex.
b. Archer City, Tex, 5/5/19; s. Graham B. Purcell and Della Key P; m. 1943 to Betty Smith; c. Blaine, Kirk, Blake and Jannie. Educ: Tex. A&M Col, B.S. Agr, 46; LL.B, Baylor Univ. Law Sch, 49. Polit. & Govt. Pos: Former Juvenile Court Judge of Wichita Co, Tex; former Judge, 89th Judicial Dist; U.S. Rep, Tex, 62-; mem, Nat. Cmn. on Food Mkt, 64. Bus. & Prof. Pos: Practicing attorney, Big Spring, Tex. and Wichita Falls, Tex, 49-55. Mil. Serv: Army, 41, serv. in Africa and Italy; Lt. Col, Army Res, Armor, currently. Mem: Very active in work with juveniles, both as judge and civic worker; dist. chmn, Boy Scouts of Am. Honored twice as Outstanding Citizen of Wichita Falls. Rel: Presbyterian; Deacon, Fain Memorial Presbyterian Church of Wichita Falls. Legal Res: Wichita Falls, Tex. Mailing Add: 120 Cannon House Office Bldg, Washington, D.C. 20515. (1967)

PURCELL, HAROLD HIDMORE D
b. Louisa, Va, 2/7/20; s. John Samuel Purcell; m. to Virginia Omohundro; c. Harold Walton and Charles Flint. Educ: Univ. Va. Law Sch, LL.B; Sigma Phi Epsilon. Polit. & Govt. Pos: Va. State Del, 47-59; Va. State Sen, 59-65, mem, Steering Cmt. and Courts of Justice Cmt, Va. State Senate; Judge, Ninth Judicial Circuit, 66- Bus. & Prof. Pos: Lawyer, 46-66. Mil. Serv: Entered as Pvt, Army, 42, released as Capt, 46, after serv. in Panama Canal Zone. Mem: Lions; Am. Legion; VFW; Mason; Scottish Rite, Shrine; K. of P. Rel: Christian Church; Elder, Louisa Christian Church. Mailing Add: Louisa, Va. 23093.

PURCELL, JOE D
Attorney Gen, Ark.
Mailing Add: State Capitol, Little Rock, Ark. 72201.

PURDHOMME, LEROY H. D
b. Claremont, 6/15/97; married; c. Two. Educ: Claremont. Polit. & Govt. Pos: N.H. State Rep, 61-68. Bus. & Prof. Pos: Tool and die maker. Mem: Dad's Club; Am. Legion. Rel: Catholic. Mailing Add: 67 Central St, Claremont, N.H. 03743. (1967)

PURDY, ELLERY REDFIELD R
Vt. State Sen.
b. Geneva, N.Y. 1/6/96; m. to Katharine Aldrich; c. Two. Educ: Wharton Sch, Univ. Pa, B.S. Econ, 20; Univ. Vt, M.Ed, 41; Phi Kappa Psi. Polit. & Govt. Pos: Mem, Rutland Pension Bd, Rutland Libr. Bd, Barstow Mem. Mendon Sch. Bd; trustee, U.V.M; mem, Civil Defense Planning Cmn, 57-58; Vt. State Rep, 59-65; Vt. State Sen, 65- Bus. & Prof. Pos: Dir, Vt. Auto Asn; former teacher of hist, athletic coach and asst. prin, Rutland High Sch; instr. in summer sessions, U.V.M, Norwich and Am. Banking Inst; retired. Mil. Serv: Army, France, 17-19, Pvt. Mem: Mason; Vt. Hist. Soc; Nat. Geog. Soc; Am. Acad. of Polit. and Soc. Sci. Mailing Add: Town Line Rd, Rutland, R.F.D, Mendon, Vt. 05701. (1967)

PURDY, MARK F. D
Dem. Nat. Committeeman, N.Dak.
Mailing Add: Box 1000, Minot, N.Dak. 58701.

PURITZ, ALFRED DAVID D
V.I. Territorial Sen.
b. St. Thomas, V.I, 2/4/35; s. Alfred Sparky Puritz and Paulina Paiewonsky P; m. 5/21/53 to Phyllis Hyman; c. Shelly Linda, Jeffrey Sparky, David M. and Gregory Allan. Educ: Univ. Miami; N.Y. Univ, B.S, 55; Alpha Epsilon Pi. Polit. & Govt. Pos: Treas, Unity Party, V.I, 56-60, mem. exec. bd, 56-62; mem, Pub. Utilities Cmn, 61-63; V.I. Sen. and secy, V.I. Legis, 62-, treas, territorial cmt, 63-66. Bus. & Prof. Pos: Pres, Sparky's & Affiliates, 63-66. Mem: Dir, Nat. and Local Jaycees, 60-63; mem, C. of C, 63-66; Mem, Lq. Dealers Asn. of V.I, 60-66; Navy League; Allied mem, ASTA; Mason (32°); Scottish Rites; B'nai B'rith; President's Club; Dem. Clubs of Wash, D.C; Int. Platform Asn; Shrine Club. Rel: Jewish. Mailing Add: Charlotte Amalie, V.I. 00801. (1967)

PURNELL, KARL H. R
b. Lewisburg, 1/31/34; s. Dr. John S. Purnell and Marie Sexton P; m. to Betty Jane Bernreuter. Educ: Harvard Univ, B.A; Univ. of Pa, M.A; Delphic Club. Polit. & Govt. Pos: Pa. State Rep, 62-67; dist. dir, treas, Young Reps. of Pa, 60-62; chmn, Union Co. Cancer Crusade, 62-63. Bus. & Prof. Pos: Publisher, Union Co. J. Mailing Add: 24 S. Water St, Mifflinburg, Pa. 17844. (1967)

PURSELL, LUCILLE R
Chmn, Washington Co. Rep. Cent. Cmt, Ore.
b. Chicago, Ill, 5/29/04; d. Fred D. Hawkins and Cecelia Collins H; m. 6/17/28 to Leonard D. Pursell; c. Lucille (Mrs. David L. Weinecke) and Jacqueline (Mrs. Dan Widney). Educ: Univ. Ill, 3 years. Polit. & Govt. Pos: Precinct committeewoman, Washington Co. Rep. Cmt, 62; v.chmn, Washington Co. Rep. Cent. Cmt, 66-67 and chmn, 67- Rel: Episcopal. Mailing Add: Route 1, Box 430, Beaverton, Ore. 97005.

PURTELL, WILLIAM ARTHUR R
b. Hartford, Conn, 5/6/97; s. Thomas M. Purtell and Nora O'Connor P; m. 12/30/19 to Katherine E. Cassidy; c. William Arthur, Margaret Mary. Educ: Pub. schs, Hartford; LL.D, Trinity Col, Hillyer Col. Polit. & Govt. Pos: U.S. Sen, Conn, 52, 53-58. Bus. & Prof. Pos: Pres, treas, gen. mgr, Elec. Soldering Iron Co, Deep River, Conn; v.pres, treas, gen. mgr, Sparmak Eng. Corp, 38-52; pres, treas, gen. mgr, dir, Holo-Krome Screw Corp, Hartford, 29-52; pres, treas, gen mgr, Billings & Spencer Co, Hartford, 37-44; dir, chmn. exec. comm, 44-47; also formerly dir, Colts Mfg. Co, Hartford (Conn.) Trust Co, Veeder-Root, Inc; also various pos. other mfg. concerns. Mil. Serv: AEF, radio sect, Signal Corps, 18-19. Mem: Am. Soc. Metals; dir, Am. Supply and Machinery Mfrs. Asn; Am. Legion. Recipient Citation Nat. Conf. Christians and Jews; Merit Award, Hardware Merchants and Mfrs. Asn, 58. Rel: Roman Catholic. Legal Res: 514 Maple Ave, Old Saybrook, Conn. 06475. Mailing Add: P.O. Box 247, Deep River, Conn. 06417. (1967)

PURTLE, JOHN INGRAM D
Ark. State Rep.
b. Enola, Ark, 9/7/23, s. John Wesley Purtle and Edna Ingram P; m. 12/31/51 to Marian Ruth White; c. Jeffrey and Lisa Karen. Educ: Ark. State Col, prelaw, 46-47; Univ. Ark, J.D, 50; Phi Alpha Zeta. Polit. & Govt. Pos: Ark. State Rep, Faulkner Co, 51-53 and Pulaski Co, 69-; mem, Pulaski Co. Dem. Cent. Cmt, Ark, 67-68. Mil. Serv: Entered as Pvt, Army, 40, released as Lt, 45, after serv. in 153rd Inf, Asiatic-Pac. Theatre, 42-45, Lt. Col, Res; Am. Defense Medal; Good Conduct Medal; Am. Theater Ribbon; Asiatic-Pac. Ribbon; Aleutian Island Campaign Ribbon with Two Bronze Stars. Mem: Am. and Ark. Bar Asns; Am. Judicature Soc; Am. and Ark. Trial Lawyers Asns; Pulaski Co. Bar; Am. Legion; VFW; Kiwanis; PTA; Ment. Health Asn; Ark. Arts Center. Rel: Baptist; Deacon, Trustee. Mailing Add: 4416 West Dr, Little Rock, Ark. 72209.

PURVIS, MARY O. CARNLEY D
b. Elba, Ala, 5/23/06; d. Jefferson Albert Carnley and Mary Olive Ray C; div; c. Mary Jo (Mrs. Charlie V. Martin) and Edward E, III. Educ: Judson Col, 23-25; Samford Univ, A.B, 26; Am. Col. Chartered Life Underwriters, C.L.U, 61; Jones Law Sch, LL.B, 65. Polit. & Govt. Pos: Alternate del, Dem. Nat. Conv, 60, del, 68. Bus. & Prof. Pos: Co. home demonstration agent, Elmore Co, Ala, 29-33; spec. agent, Prudential Ins. Co, 52- Mem: Altrusa Int; Women Leaders Round Table; Nat. Asn. Life Underwriters; Am. Soc. of Chartered Life Underwriters; Montgomery Estate Planning Coun; UDC; DAR. Rel: Baptist. Legal Res: 105 Daleville Ave, Enterprise, Ala. 36330. Mailing Add: 3554 Le Bron Rd, Montgomery, Ala. 36111.

PURVIS, PERRIN HAYS D
Miss. State Sen.
b. Blue Springs, Miss, 2/24/18; married. Polit. & Govt. Pos: Miss. State Sen, currently. Mem, Miss. State Sovereignty Cmn; pres, Tupelo Bd. of Educ; Tupelo Planning and Zoning Bd; Commun. Develop. Found. Bus. & Prof. Pos: Gen. ins. agent; bd. dir, First Citizens Nat. Bank; v.pres, WTWV Channel 9 TV; v.pres, North Miss. Realty Co. Mil. Serv: World War II. Mem: Mason (32°); Shrine; WOW; Am. Legion; 40 et 8; past pres, Tupelo Kiwanis Club; Tupelo Country Club; past pres, Univ. of South. Miss. Alumni Asn. Rel: Methodist. Mailing Add: Box 791, Tupelo, Miss. 38801.

PURYEAR, BYRON NELSON D
Mem, Hampton Dem. Exec. Cmt, Va.
b. Winston-Salem, N.C, 9/22/13; s. Royal Wendell Puryear and Beatrice Sharp P; m. 3/25/34 to Gladys Thornton Bizzell; c. Alvin Nelson. Educ: Hampton Inst, trade dipl, 33. Polit. & Govt. Pos: Mem. subcmt, Va. Adv. Legis. Cmt, Richmond, 67; mem, Hampton Dem. Exec. Cmt, 67-68 & 69-; del, Va. Dem. State Conv, 68; alternate del, Nat. Dem. Conv, 68; mem, Elec. Laws Study Cmn, 68-69; mem. state cmt, Howell for Gov, 69. Publ: Booklet on Democratic Candidates, Wilson and Andrews, 63; Hampton Institute, A Pictorial Review of its First Century, 1868-1968, Privately Publ, 67; 'Know Thy Neighbor.' Mem: Life mem. NAACP (exec. bd. mem); Am. Civil Liberties Union; Citizens Orgn; Penninsula C. of C.(dir, 68); Nat. Negro Bus. League; del. U.S. C. of C; Va. Soc. Prev. Blindness (bd. mem, 68-69); Penninsula Br. Soc. Prev. Blindness (v.chmn, 68-69). Nathan W. Collier Meritorious Serv. Award, Fla. Mem. Col, 65. Rel: Baptist. Mailing Add: 2705 Shell Rd, Hampton, Va. 23361.

PUSATERI, LAWRENCE XAVIER R
Chmn, Ill. Parole and Pardon Bd.
b. Oak Park, Ill, 5/25/31; s. Lawrence Pusateri and Josephine Romano P; m. 7/9/56 to Eve M. Graf; c. Joanne, Lawrence F, Paul Leo, Maryanne and Eva. Educ: DePaul Univ. Col. Law, LL.B, summa cum laude, 53; Pi Gamma Mu Nat; Delta Theta Phi; Jr. Bar Asn. Polit. & Govt. Pos: Asst. state attorney, Cook Co, Ill, 57-59; spec. asst. to Off. of Attorney Gen, Ill, 59-60; chmn, Cook Co. Young Rep, 59-60; nat. committeeman, Ill. Young Rep, Inc, 59-61; mem, Nat. Young Rep. Fedn. Exec. Bd, 61-62; mem. and chmn, Ill. Crime Investigating Cmn, 64-68; Ill. State Rep, 64-69; chmn, Ill. Parole and Pardon Bd, 69-; mem. adv. cmt, Gov. Law Enforcement Planning Coun, Ill, currently. Bus. & Prof. Pos: Partner, Law Firm of Newton, Wilhelm, Capt, 57, after serv. as Asst. Staff Judge Advocate, Inf. Div, Continental U.S. and Europe, 53-56; 3 Letters of Commendation; Ill. Nat. Guard, 85th Inf. Div. Res, Ill. Publ: 'Search and Seizure—Illinois Exclusionary Rule,' DePaul Univ. Law Review, 59; 'Risk of Loss After Contract to Sell Real Property . . . , Ill. Bar J, 64; 'Proposed Uniform Consumer Credit Code,' Personal Financial Law Quarterly Report, 64. Mem: Am, Ill. State and W. Suburban Bar Asns; past pres, Justinian Soc. Lawyers; Chicago Bar Asn.(past mem, Bd. of Mgr, chmn, Law Day Cmt, currently); Kiwanis; Ill. State C. of C; Chicago Asn. of Commerce and Industry. Selected as One of the Ten Outstanding Young Men in Chicago, 59 & 65. Rel: Catholic. Legal Res: 905 Winston Dr, Melrose Park, Ill. 60160. Mailing Add: 105 W. Madison St, Suite 1700, Chicago, Ill. 60602.

PUTMAN, KATHLEEN MAVOURNEEN R
Mem, Ala. Rep. State Exec. Cmt.
b. Chicago, Ill, 8/31/13; d. Frank William Harvey, Jr. and Helen McJunkin H; m. 10/2/37 to Albert Michael Putman; c. Rev. Michael Dennis, Leigh Reding (Mrs. Plagens), David Jeremy, Jonathan Christopher, Timothy Harvey and Mary Kathleen. Educ: St. Mary's of Notre Dame; pres, Freshman Class. Polit. & Govt. Pos: Jefferson Co. co-chmn, Citizens for Eisenhower, Ala, 52; mem, Jefferson Co. Rep. Exec. Cmt, 52-; Ala. co-chmn, Citizens for Eisenhower, 56 and Vol. for Nixon, 60; campaign coordinator, Ala, Rep. Cong. Race, 60 and Jim Martin for Gov. Race, 66; mem, Ala. Rep. State Exec. Cmt, 62-; Justice of Peace, precinct 25, Jefferson Co, 64-68; spec. asst. to regional dir, Nixon Presidential Campaign, 68; Ala. v.chmn, Nixon Inaugural Ball, 69. Mem: Bd. mem, Vol. Cmt. of Jefferson Co. and Children's Aid Soc; Cauldron Literary Club; sustaining mem, Jr. League of Birmingham; Highland Sewing Circle; Camellia Garden Club. Rel: Catholic. Mailing Add: 1200 Saulter Rd, Birmingham, Ala. 35209.

PUTNAM, HOLLIS JAMES R
Vt. State Rep.
b. Springfield, Vt, 7/12/06; s. Solon James Putnam and Stella K. Rice P; m. 6/22/40 to Margaret Griffith; c. Hugh S. Educ: Rutland Bus. Col, Vt, grad, 26. Polit. & Govt. Pos: Vt. State Rep, 66-, chmn, Commerce Cmt, Vt. House of Rep, currently. Bus. & Prof. Pos: Cost dept. supvr, Fellows Gear Shaper Co, Springfield, Vt, 45-62, accts. payable supvr, 63-69. Mem: Nat. Asn. Accts; Nat. Soc. State Legislators; Vt. Conf. Soc. Concerns; Nat. Wildlife Fedn; Odd Fellows; C. of C; Springfield Sportsmen Asn. Rel: Congregational. Mailing Add: 115 South St, Springfield, Vt. 05156.

PUTNAM, L. D. D
Treas, Holt Co. Dem. Cmt, Nebr.
b. Wagner, S.Dak, 3/28/08; s. Dennis Putnam and Mary Cahalan P; m. 6/28/37 to Wilma Nelson; c. Daniel D. and William L; grandchildren, Shannon, Sean, Tara Marie, Mari and Anne. Educ: High Sch, Gregory, S.Dak, grad, 28. Polit. & Govt. Pos: Campaign worker, Dem. Presidential Campaigns, Al Smith, 28, Franklin D. Roosevelt, 32, 36, 40 & 44, Harry Truman, 48, Adlai Stevenson, 52, A. Harriman, 56, John F. Kennedy, 60, Lyndon Johnson, 64 and H. Humphrey, 68; del, Nebr. State Conv, 30 years; treas, Holt Co. Dem. Cmt, Nebr, 50-; alternate del, Dem. Nat. Conv, 56, del, 68. Bus. & Prof. Pos: Owner and operator, cattle ranch, S.Dak, 25-35 and Holt Co, Nebr, 35- Mem: S.Dak. and Nebr. Stock Growers Asns; Nat. Livestock Asn; Nebr. Sandhill Cattle Feeders Asn; K. of C.(4°); C. of C; O'Neill Rodeo Asn; St. Anthony Hosp. Adv. Bd.(pres, 52-67, v.pres, 67-); former pres, O'Neill Lions Club. Rel: Catholic. Mailing Add: R.R. 1, P.O. Box 191, O'Neill, Nebr. 68763.

PUTNAM, PAUL McQUEEN R
Chmn, Wharton Co. Rep. Party, Tex.
b. Houston, Tex, 10/9/20; s. Paul Thrower Putnam and Francis McQueen P; m. 6/25/48 to Anne Kathryn Porter; c. Guy McQueen and Anne Marion. Educ: Univ. Houston, 42-43. Polit. & Govt. Pos: Chmn, Wharton Co. Rep. Party, Tex, currently. Bus. & Prof. Pos: Pres, Ranch Radio, Inc. Mil. Serv: Entered as A/C Army Air Force, 42, released as Capt, 53, after serv. in 391st Bomb Group, Ninth Air Force ETO; Air Medal with Seven Clusters; ETO Ribbon with Four Battle Stars; Presidential Unit Citation. Mem: Rotary; Am. Legion. Amateur Radio- Call letters K5TSM. Rel: Presbyterian. Mailing Add: P.O. Box 767, El Campo, Tex. 77437. (1967)

PUTNAM, PEGGY JOAN R
Mem, Eighth Dist. Rep. Cent. Cmt, Mich.
b. Tuscumbia, Mo, 11/9/32; d. Norman Grant Brown Sr. and Oma Roberts B;

m. to Raymond K. Putnam (deceased); c. Michael Ray and Cindy Fay. Educ: Lexington Pub. Schs, Mich, 5 years; Caro Commun. Sch, 8 years. Polit. & Govt. Pos: Del, Almer Twp, Mich, 56-; dep. treas, 58-67; del, Mich. State Rep. Conv, 68 & 69; v.chmn, Tuscola Co. Rep. Party, 68; mem, Eighth Dist. Rep. Cent. Cmt, 69- Bus. & Prof. Pos: Legal secy, White & Williams Attorneys, 52-55; composition dept, Tuscola Co. Advertiser, 68- Mem: VFW Auxiliary; Tuscola Co. Rep. Womens Club. Rel: Methodist. Mailing Add: 3247 French Rd, Caro, Mich. 48723.

PUTNAM, RICHARD JOHNSON D
Abbeville, La, 9/27/13; s. Robert E. Putnam and Mary Mathilde Young P; m. 1/27/40 to Dorethea Gooch; c. Richard J, Jr, Claude Robert, Mary Stacy and Cynthia Ann. Educ: Spring Hill Col, Ala, B.S, 34; Loyola Univ. of the South, LL.B, 37; Delta Theta Phi. Polit. & Govt. Pos: Dist. attorney, 15th Judicial Dist, La, 48-54 and Dist. Judge, 54-61; U.S. Dist. Judge, West. Dist. of La, 61- Mil. Serv: Entered as civilian agent for training, Off. of Naval Intel, Eighth Naval Dist, released as Lt, 45, after serv. in anti submarine warfare, Atlantic and Pac. Theatres. Mem: Am, La, Fifteenth Judicial Dist. and Vermilion Parish Bar Asns; La. Dist. Judges Asn; charter mem, Abbeville C. of C; former bd. mem, Abbeville Golf & Country Club; exec. bd. mem, Evangeline Area Coun. Boy Scouts; past pres, Vermilion Dist. Boy Scouts; Am. Legion; VFW; K. of C.(4°). Rel: Catholic. Legal Res: Lafitte Rd, Abbevile, La. 70510. Mailing Add: 515 Lafitte Rd, Abbeville, La. 70510

PUTNAM, ROSE S. D
b. Burlington, Vt, 9/24/00; wid; c. Four. Educ: Hartford High Sch. Polit. & Govt. Pos: Former N.H. State Rep; former supvr. of check lists; organizer and past pres, W. Lebanon PTA; past town chmn, Lebanon Dem. Club. Bus. & Prof. Pos: Clerk-typist, stenographer and secy. Mem: Past grand regent, C.D.A, 3 years; VFW Auxiliary (past pres, Wood-Guarino Chap, 9552, past dept. secy, N.H, past musician and currently asst. musician). Rel: Catholic. Mailing Add: 25 Dana St, West Lebanon, N.H. 03766. (1967)

PUTNEY, LACEY EDWARD D
Va. State Del.
b. Big Island, Va, 6/27/28; m. to Elizabeth Harlow P. Educ: Wash. and Lee Univ, B.A, LL.B. Polit. & Govt. Pos: Va. State Del, 62-; mem, Va. Income Tax Study Cmn, 66-68; bd. trustees, Va. Baptist Hosp, Lynchburg. Bus. & Prof. Pos: Lawyer. Mil. Serv: Air Force, 50-54. Mem: Va. and Am. Trial Lawyers Asn; Am. Legion; Bedford Rotary Club; Masons; Scottish Rite; Moose. Rel: Baptist. Mailing Add: Glenn Mary, Goode, Va. 24556. (1967)

PYATT, WADE HENRY R
b. Marion, N.C, 1/12/19; s. Henry Wade Pyatt and Nola Moore P; m. 7/26/48 to Elsie Zerfass. Educ: Pittsburgh Inst. of Tech, grad. in heating & air conditioning eng, 51. Polit. & Govt. Pos: Rep. precinct chmn, McDowell Co, N.C, 58-60; v.pres, McDowell Co. Rep. Club, 62-63; chmn, McDowell Co. Rep. Party, 63-67. Bus. & Prof. Pos: Sales mgr, Miracle Maid Cookware, 52-53; serv. mgr, Hanover Iron Works, 53-56; pres, Pyatt Heating & Air Conditioning Co, 56-; pres, Pyco-Press Commercial Printers, 65- Mil. Serv: Entered as Pvt, Army, 40, released as S/Sgt, 48, after serv. in 332nd Eng, ETO; Philippine Liberation Ribbon with 1 Bronze Star; Meritorious Unit Award; Asiatic Pac. Campaign Medal with 2 Bronze Serv. Stars; Am. Defense, Am. Campaign, Good Conduct, World War II Victory and Army of Occup. Medals. Mem: N.C. Heating Asn; Nat. Heating Asn; Printing Industs. of Am; Printing Industs. of the Carolinas; Chapel Hill Commun. Develop. Club; Civitan Club; C. of C. Rel: Baptist. Mailing Add: 300 Glenwood Ave, Marion, N.C. 28752.

PYLE, CHARLES VICTOR, JR. D
S.C. State Rep.
b. Greenville, S.C, 12/24/34; s. Charles Victor Pyle and Eugenia Smith P; m. 6/8/57 to Johanna Douglas Wright; c. Louisa Douglas, Sarah Bryson and Charles Victor, III. Educ: Univ. S.C, LL.B, 59; Kappa Alpha Order; pres, Calhoun Inn, Phi Delta Phi, 59. Polit. & Govt. Pos: Asst. city attorney, Greenville, S.C, 63-65, judge, Munic. Court, 65-68; S.C. State Rep, 68- Bus. & Prof. Pos: Chmn, S.C. Traffic Court Conf, 66-67. Mem: Greenville Co. Bar Asn; S.C. Bar Asn.(chmn. young lawyers conf, 63-64, mem. exec. cmt, 65-67, circuit v.pres, 66-67); Am. Bar Asn.(mem. assoc. and adv. cmt. to standing cmt, traffic court prog, 66-); Am. Judicature Soc.(dir, 66-); Rotary; Elks. Cert. of Performance, Jr. Bar Conf, Am. Bar Asn, 64 and Traffic Court Prog. Award, 68; Dist. Serv. Award, City of Greenville, 68. Rel: Methodist; chmn. assoc. bd. of stewards, Buncombe St. Methodist Church, 61-62. Legal Res: 309 Pimlico Rd, Greenville, S.C. 29607. Mailing Add: 300 E. Coffee St, Greenville, S.C. 29601.

PYLE, GLADYS R
b. Huron, S.Dak, 10/4/90; d. John Levis Pyle and Mamie I. Shields P; single. Educ: Huron Col, A.B, 11; Chicago Univ. and Am. Conservatory of Music, 11-12. Hon. LL.D, Huron Col, 58. Polit. & Govt. Pos: S.Dak. State Rep, 23-27; Secy. of State, S.Dak, 27-31; secy, State Securities Cmn, 31-33; alternate del, Rep. Nat. Conv, 36, del, 40; U.S. Sen, S.Dak, 38-39; mem. and secy, S.Dak. Bd. of Charities and Corrections, 40-53. Bus. & Prof. Pos: Teacher, S.Dak. high schs, 12-20; life ins. agent, Northwest. Mutual Life Ins. Co, 49- Mem: Nat. Asn. Retired Teachers; Federated Bus. and Prfnl. Women; Am. Asn. of Univ. Women; Life Underwriters Asn; Am. Legion Auxiliary; Twentieth Century Club; bd. of dirs, Red Cross and Salvation Army; trustee, YWCA; Literary Coterie; PEO. Selected Lady of the Year, Beta Sigma Phi, 52, Named Int. Hon. Mem, 55; Distinguished Serv. Award, Alumni Asn, Huron Col, 56; Named Hon. Mem, Delta Kappa Gamma, 65; Selected Huron's Citizen of the Year, C. of C, 65; Christian Citizenship Award, YWCA, 65. Rel: Presbyterian. Mailing Add: 376 Idaho S.E, Huron, S.Dak, 47350.

PYLES, JOHN W. D
Assessor, Monongalia Co, W.Va.
b. Flemington, 1/28/33; s. Melford J. Pyles and Lucy L. Scarcella P; single. Educ: W.Va. Univ, B.M. and M.A; Kappa Kappa Psi. Polit. & Govt. Pos: W.Va. State Del, 63-66; chmn. legis. cmt, Monongalia Co. Classroom Teachers Asn, 62-66; del. to Nat.Educ.Asn. Nat. Conv, 62-66; mem. state legis. cmt, W.Va. Classroom Teachers Asn; pres, Monongalia Co. Young Dem. Club; dem. cand, Morgantown City Coun, 60; assessor, Monongalia Co, currently. Bus. & Prof. Pos: Pub. Sch. Teacher. Mem: Monongalia Co. Dem. Men's Club; Monongalia Co. Ment. Health Asn; Nat. Educ. Asn; W.Va. Educ. Asn; secy-treas, W.Va. Region IX Bandmasters Asn, 57. Who's Who in the East and Outstanding Young Men of Am. Rel: Baptist. Mailing Add: 121 Lorentz Ave, Morgantown, W.Va. 26505.

PYNE, LEE EDWARD R
b. Lynn, Mass, 10/30/08; s. Okes Lee Pyne and Nellie Bishop P; m. 7/14/45 to Doris Laviolette Kearns. Educ: Boston Univ, B.A. and M.A; Purdue Univ, prfnl. cert; Phi Delta Kappa. Polit. & Govt. Pos: Justice of the Peace, Ashford, Conn, 58-62, mem, Bd. Tax Rev, 60-69, chmn, currently; chmn, Ashford Town Rep. Party, 60-68. Mil. Serv: Entered as Pvt, Army, 42, released as Sgt, 45, after serv. in Med. Corps, Am. Theater. Mem: Am. and Conn. Personnel & Guid. Asns; Nat. and Windhan Educ. Asns; Conn. Educ. Asn; Nat. Voc. Guid. Asn; Am. Asn. of Sch. Adminstrs; AF&AM; Am. Legion. Rel: Baptist. Mailing Add: R.F.D. 1, Mansfield Center, Conn. 06250.

PYRROS, JAMES G. D
b. Detroit, Mich, 3/10/28; m. 9/26/65 to Betty Blougouras. Educ: Wayne State Univ, B.A, LL.B. Polit. & Govt. Pos: Admin. Asst, Rep. Nedzi, Mich; Asst. Attorney Gen. of Mich, 55-61; Aide, Slum Clearance Dir, Detroit, 50-53. Mil. Serv: U.S. Army, 53-55; Korean Serv. and UN Serv. Medals. Mailing Add: 490 M St. S.W, Washington, D.C. 20024. (1967)

PYTKO, WALTER STANLEY D
City Councilman at Large, Phila, Pa.
b. Phila, Pa, 1/19/01; s. Francis M. Pytko and Anna Boruta P; m. to Helen Stachowiak, wid; c. Helen D.(Mrs. Larios). Educ: Temple Sch. of Law, 22-26. Polit. & Govt. Pos: Mem, Phila. Co. Dem. Exec. Cmt, Pa, 32-49, secy, 39-49; Pa. State Sen, 35-39; mem, Bd. of Mercantile Appraisers, 41-43; asst. state treas, Pa, 45-49; registrn. cmnr, Dept. Licenses and Inspections, Phila, 49-52, cmnr, 52-57; managing dir, Phila. Parking Authority, 57-62; city councilman at large, Phila, Pa, 62- Bus. & Prof. Pos: Pres, Polish Beneficial Asn. and Life Ins. Co, 42- Mem: Frankford and Bridesburg Bus. Men's Asn.(pres, 24-28); Polish Am. Citizens League Pa.(pres, 25-49); Polish Am. Cong.(nat. dir, 44-58). Rel: Roman Catholic. Mailing Add: 4476 E. Thompson St, Philadelphia, Pa. 19137. (1967)

Q

QUACKENBUSH, MARGARET THOMPSON R
b. Rochester, N.Y, 12/18/06; d. Lewis W. Thompson and Jane Lee T; m. 9/19/29 to Bronson A. Quackenbush; c. Mrs. Peter A. Hager, Mrs. Charles J. Umberger and Paul H, II. Educ: Vassar Col, A.B, 29. Polit. & Govt. Pos: Alternate del, Rep. Nat. Conv, 42, del, 64; del, N.Y. State Gubernatorial Conv, 44-64; committeewoman, N.Y. State Rep. Exec. Cmt, 43-69. Bus. & Prof. Pos: Trustee, State Univ. New York, 64- Mem: Am. Asn. Univ. Women (mem. legis. cmt, 63). Rel: Protestant. Mailing Add: 1 Park Place, Herkimer, N.Y. 13350.

QUADARA, DOMINICK ROCKO D
b. Guttenburg, N.J, 6/3/27; s. Jack Quadara and Ann Q; m. 10/16/46 to Barbara Scymczak; c. Denise and Daniel. Educ: Mem. High Sch, West New York, N.J. Polit. & Govt. Pos: Mem, twp. cmt, Brick Twp, N.J, 65, councilman-at-lg, 67 and pres, Town Coun, 68-; mem, Nat. River & Harbor Cmn, U.S. Cong; del, Dem. Nat. Conv, 68. Bus. & Prof. Pos: Pres, Quadara Enterprises, Builders and Developers, currently; bd. dirs, Pineland State Bank, currently. Mil. Serv: Entered as Pvt, Army, 42, released as T-5, 46, after serv. in Army Intel, ETO. Mem: N.J. Shore Builders Asn; Nat. Asn. Home Builders; K. of C; Navy League. Rel: Catholic. Mailing Add: 625 N. Lake Shore Dr, Brick Town, N.J. 08723.

QUALLS, JAMES FRANKLIN R
b. Harriman, Tenn, 11/13/22; s. Lee Andrew Qualls and Ruby Wright Q; m. 2/22/47 to Peggy Jeanne Ball; c. James Franklin, Jr, Ruby Jeanne (Mrs. Sidney T. Stanley), Virginia Karen and Robert Lee. Educ: Univ. Tenn, Knoxville, J.D, 48; Lambda Chi Alpha; Phi Delta Phi; Omicron Delta Kappa; Scabbard and Blade. Polit. & Govt. Pos: City judge, Harriman, Tenn, 48; co. attorney, Roane Co, 54-64, co. judge, 67-; del, Rep. Nat. Conv, 68. Mil. Serv: Entered as Pvt, Army, 43, released as Capt, 46, after serv. in 222nd Inf, 42nd Div, ETO; Combat Infantryman's Badge; Purple Heart; Bronze Star with One Oak Leaf Cluster. Mem: Am. and Tenn. Bar Asns; Scottish Rite; Consistory; Shrine; F&AM; Elks; VFW; Am. Legion; 40 et 8; Jr. Order, United Am. Mechanics. Rel: Methodist. Legal Res: Webster Pike, Harriman, Tenn. 37748. Mailing Add: P.O. Drawer 509, Harriman, Tenn. 37748.

QUAM, LESLIE JAMES R
b. Toronto, S.Dak, 8/23/28; s. Herman Quam and Jennie Haynes Q; m. 9/25/55 to Lois Maye Ramynke; c. Lauren James. Educ: Toronto High Sch, 4 years. Polit. & Govt. Pos: Chmn, Deuel Co. Young Rep. S.Dak, 61-62; chmn, Deuel Co. Rep. Party, 62-67. Bus. & Prof. Pos: Farmer, Deuel Co, S.Dak, 47- Mil. Serv: Entered as Pvt, Army, 52, released as Cpl, 53, after serv. in First Div, Europe. Mem: Am. Legion; Toronto Commun. Club. Rel: Lutheran. Mailing Add: Toronto, S.Dak. 57268.

QUARKER, DOROTHY ELAINE D
b. Detroit, Mich, 2/21/22; d. Anthony Henry Quarker, Sr.(deceased) and Hortense Virginia Mann Q; single. Educ: Univ. Detroit, B.B.A; Detroit Col. Law and Wash. Col. Law, 56-59; Phi Gamma Nu. Polit. & Govt. Pos: Admin. asst. to U.S. Rep. Charles C. Diggs, Jr, Mich, 55-; mem, exec. bd, 13th Cong. Dist. Dem. Orgn, 68-; downtown forum co-chmn, Wayne Co. Dem. Cmt, currently. Bus. & Prof. Pos: From secy. to secy. gen. mgr. to asst. to off. mgr, Great Lakes Mutual Life Ins. Co, Detroit, Mich, 42-55, asst. to the pres, 55. Mem: Bd. dir. and secy, Detroit Asn. of Commerce; bd. dir. and asst. secy, Inner City Bus. Improvement Forum, Inc; educ. cmt, NAACP, Detroit Br. Rel: Protestant. Legal Res: 1705 Lafayette Towers W, Detroit, Mich. 48209. Mailing Add: 1201 E. Grand Blvd, Detroit, Mich. 48211.

QUARLES, W. GRUNDY D
Tenn. State Cmnr. of Standards and Purchase
b. Gainesboro, Tenn, 8/25/12; m. to Margaret Haile Q; c. Dr. W.G, Jr, Ben-

ton H, James Thadeus and Mary Margaret. Educ: Pub. Sch, Jackson Co. Polit. & Govt. Pos: Mayor, Gainesboro, Tenn, 3 terms; chmn, Jackson Co. U.S. Savings Bond Div; mem, State Property Admin; Tenn. State Cmnr. of Standards and Purchase, currently. Bus. & Prof. Pos: Retail Druggist, 30 years; past pres, Jackson Co. Indust. Corp. Mil. Serv: Navy, overseas, 2 years. Mem: Tenn. Pharm. Asn; Rotary (past pres); Am. Legion; VFW; Mason; Shrine; mem. bd. dirs, Goodwill Indust. of Nashville, Inc. Rel: Methodist. Mailing Add: 210 Central Services Bldg, Nashville, Tenn. 37219.

QUAST, WERNER CARL R
Mem. Exec. Cmt, Rep. State Cent. Cmt, Wash.
b. Bremen, Germany, 9/8/31; nat. U.S. citizen, 63; s. Carl Emil Quast and Anna Caroline Volkmer Q; m. 6/30/62 to Merrie C. Collins; c. David Carl. Educ: Univ. Freiburg Law Sch, 53-54; Whitman Col, B.A, 55; teaching fels, Univ. Wash, 56-58, M.A, 58, Ph.D, 66; Pi Sigma Alpha. Polit. & Govt. Pos: Chmn, Clallam Co. Rep. Cent. Cmt, Wash, 66-68, state committeeman, 68-; precinct committeeman, 68-; mem. exec. cmt, Rep. State Cent. Cmt, 69- Bus. & Prof. Pos: Exec. dir, Found. for Int. Understanding through Students, Seattle, Wash, 59-61; asst. prof. polit. sci. & philos, Peninsula Col, 62-, chmn. commun. serv. cmt, 63-, chmn. div. soc. sci, 64-66 & 68-69. Mem: West. and Pac. Northwest Polit. Sci. Asns; Asn. Higher Educ; C. of C; Port Angeles Yacht Club; trustee, Olympic Peninsula Kidney Found. Award of Fulbright travel grant, 52. Rel: Protestant. Mailing Add: 308 E. Tenth, Port Angeles, Wash. 98362.

QUATTROCCHI, ROCCO ANTHONY D
R.I. State Rep.
b. Providence, R.I, 1/13/27; s. John Quattrocchi and Virenza Di Gennaro Q; m. 1/1/51 to Dolores R. De Rosa; c. John Joseph, Cynthia Ann and Joseph Anthony. Educ: Univ. R.I, B.S, 51; Phi Kappa Theta. Polit. & Govt. Pos: R.I. State Rep, Seventh Dist, 69- Mil. Serv: Entered as Pvt, Army, 45, released as Sgt, 46, after serv. in Signal Corps, Iceland, 45-46. Rel: Catholic. Mailing Add: 15 Messina St, Providence, R.I. 02908.

QUEEN, KENNETH E. R
b. Pecksrun, 8/1/06; s. Oda Alvin Queen and Grace Wilma Crislip Q; m. 5/14/25 to Elsie White; c. Mrs. D.J. Stone, Jr, Mrs. Robert Dean, Mrs. Gene Sutton. Educ: Pub. Schs, Upshur Co; concrete engr, Int. Correspondence Sch. Polit. & Govt. Pos: W.Va. State Del, 64-68. Bus. & Prof. Pos: Gen. contractor. Mem: Moose; Elks; Blue Mason; Scottish Rite; Shrine. Rel: Protestant. Mailing Add: Buckhannon, W.Va. 26201. (1967)

QUELCH, LESLIE H. D
b. Leicester, Vt, 7/22/37; m. to Elita Goodspeed; c. Two daughters. Educ: Leicester Sch. Polit. & Govt. Pos: Vt. State Rep, 65-66. Bus. & Prof. Pos: Truck driver. Rel: Episcopal. Mailing Add: Box 196, Brandon, Vt. 05733. (1967)

QUEVEDO, HENRY ANTHONY R
Mem, Calif. Rep. State Cent. Cmt.
b. Los Angeles, Calif, 7/15/35; s. Eduardo L. Quevedo and Ida M. Thompson Q; m. 6/23/56 to Alice Montano; c. Edward, Henry, Steve, Susan and Teresa. Educ: Loyola Univ, Los Angeles, B.A. in Philos, 56; Southwest. Univ, J.D, 62; Aristonians. Polit. & Govt. Pos: Mem, Calif. Rep. State Cent. Cmt, Los Angeles Co. Cent. Cmt, 29th Cong. Rep. Cent. Cmt, 48th Assembly Rep. Cent. Cmt, Mex-Am. Polit. Asn, Coun. Latin Am. Rep. Orgns. and Pueblos of Los Angeles Rep. Asn, currently; dist. attorney, Los Angeles, 66-69; exec. dir, Inter-Agency Cmt. on Mex-Am. Affairs, 69-; spec. adv. and consult, Dept. Health, Educ. and Welfare, currently. Publ: Articles in law enforcement and Mexican-Am. probs. Mem: Coun, Angeles Girl Scout Coun; Los Angeles PTA; YMCA; East Los Angeles Jr. C. of C; Beverly Hills Optimist Club and San Fernando Gr. Valley Jr. C. of C. Rel: Catholic. Legal Res: 2766 Chadwick Circle, Los Angeles, Calif. 90032. Mailing Add: 1800 G St. N.W, Washington, D.C. 20506.

QUICK, AARON W. D
b. Kans; m. to Linda; c. 4. Educ: Pub. Sch. Imperial Co. Polit. Pos: Calif. State Sen, 1966; Calif. State Assemblyman; Agent-in-Charge, Bur. of Customs, U.S. Treas. Dept, 1960. Mem: El Centro Optimist Club; Navy League; Imperial Valley Pioneers; Life Member, Imperial-Yuma Co. Peace Officers Assoc; Past Pres, The Imperial Valley Shrine Club. 1967 Legal Res: 713 State St, El Centro, Calif. 92243. No mailing address available. (1967)

QUIE, ALBERT HAROLD R
U.S. Rep, Minn.
b. Dennison, Minn, 9/18/23; m. 6/6/48 to Gretchen Hansen; c. Fredric, Jennifer, Daniel, Joel and Benjamin. Educ: St. Olaf Col, Northfield, Minn, B.A. in Polit. Sci, 50. Polit. & Govt. Pos: Former dir, Soil Conserv. Dist, Md; former mem, Sch. Bd; Minn. State Sen, 54-58; U.S. Rep, Minn, 58-; del, Rep. Nat. Conv, 68. Bus. & Prof. Pos: Farmer. Mil. Serv: Pilot, Navy, World War II. Distinguished Serv. Award, Northfield Jr. C. of C; Young Man of the Year Award, Minn. Jr. C. of C; Distinguished Alumnus Award, St. Olaf Col. Legal Res: Dennison, Minn. 55018. Mailing Add: 710 Burnt Mills Ave, Silver Spring, Md. 20901.

QUIGLEY, JAMES MICHAEL D
b. Mt. Carmel, Pa, 3/30/18; s. James Quigley and Helen C. Laughlin Q; m. 9/8/41 to Genevieve C. Morgan; c. Ann, Joan, Claire, James, Jr, Mary and Elizabeth. Educ: Villanova Univ, A.B, 39; Dickinson Law Sch, LL.B, 42. Polit. & Govt. Pos: U.S. Rep, Pa, 54-56 & 58-60; asst. secy, U.S. Dept. Health, Educ. and Welfare, 61-65; chmn, Fed. Water Pollution Control Admin, 65-68. Bus. & Prof. Pos: V.pres, U.S. Plywood Champion Papers Inc, 68- Mil. Serv: Lt, Naval Res, 43-46. Mem: Pa. and Dauphine Bar Asns. Mailing Add: 9710 Carriage Rd, Kensington, Md. 20795.

QUIGLEY, ROBERT JOSEPH D
Chmn, Monroe Co. Dem. Cmt, N.Y.
b. Salamanca, N.Y, 3/26/24; s. Andrew M. Quigley and Pauline Elsen Q; m. 5/21/47 to Patricia Boardman; c. Sean, Timothy and Molly. Educ: Salamanca High Sch, N.Y, 4 years. Polit. & Govt. Pos: Supvr, Wheatland, N.Y, 55-66; minority leader, Monroe Co, N.Y, 63-67 and co. legislator, Second Dist, 67; del, Dem. Nat. Conv, 68; exec. secy, Monroe Co. Dem. Cmt, 68-69, chmn, 69- Mil. Serv: Entered as Pvt, Air Force, 43, released as S/Sgt, 45 after serv. in Air Drome Squadron, S.Pac, 43-45. Mem: Nat. Asn. of Co; Co. Officer's Asn; Town Supvr. Asn. of N.Y. State; N.Y. State and Rochester Real Estate Bd; Order of R.R. Telegraphers; Lions; Am. Legion; VFW; Monroe Co. Vol. Fireman's Asn; C. of C; Ancient Order of Hibernian's Club. Rel: Roman Catholic. Legal Res: 74 Main St, Scottsville, N.Y. 14546. Mailing Add: 600 Powers Bldg, Rochester, N.Y. 14614.

QUILLEN, GEORGE ROBERT R
Del. State Rep.
b. Ocean View, Del, 10/28/28; s. Robert Henry Quillen and Cora Derrickson Q; single. Educ: Beacom Bus. Col, cert, 50. Polit. & Govt. Pos: Del. State Rep, 29th Dist, 67-69, 33rd Dist, 69- Mil. Serv: Sgt, Army, 50-52, serv. in First Med. Bn, First Inf. Div, Germany, 51-52. Mem: Am. Legion; Kent Co. Archaeol. Soc; pres, Harrington Planning & Zoning Cmn, 65 & 66; C. of C. Rel: Episcopal; jr. warden, St. Stephen's Episcopal Church. Legal Res: 40 Commerce St, Harrington, Del. 19952. Mailing Add: P.O. Box 247, Harrington, Del. 19952.

QUILLEN, JAMES HENRY R
U.S. Rep, Tenn.
b. Wayland, Va, 1/11/16; s. John A. Quillen (deceased) and Hannah Chapman Q; m. 8/9/52 to Cecile Cox. Hon. LL.D, Steed Col, 63. Polit. & Govt. Pos: Tenn. State Rep, 55-63, Rep. Floor Leader, Tenn. House of Rep, 59; del-at-lg, Rep. Nat. Conv, 56, del, 64 & 68; U.S. Rep, First Dist, Tenn, 63- Bus. & Prof. Pos: Pres, Kingsport Develop. Co, Inc, Gen. Contractors, Inc, Ins. Inc, Model City Investment Corp. and Real Estate-Loans, Inc, 52-63; dir, Kingsport Nat. Bank, 59-; pres, Wofford Brothers, Johnson City, Tenn, 62-63. Mil. Serv: Entered as Ens, Navy, 43, released as Lt, 46, after serv. in Pac, 45-46; Atlantic and Pac. Theater Ribbons. Mem: Past pres, Lions, Kingsport; C. of C; Am. Legion; VFW; Elks; Eagles; Moose. Rel: Methodist. Legal Res: 1601 Fairidge Place, Kingsport, Tenn. 37660. Mailing Add: 102 Cannon House Office Bldg, Washington, D.C. 20515.

QUILLIAM, WILLIAM REED, JR. D
b. Beaumont, Tex, 1/21/29; s. William Reed Quilliam and Gladys Harned Q; m. 6/6/53 to Myrna Corinne Simmons; c. Mary Corinne, Kathryn Harned and William Reed, III. Educ: Lamar Jr. Col, 45-46; Univ. Tex, B.A. in govt, 49, B.B.A, 51 and J.D, 53; LL.M, Harvard, 69; Phi Alpha Delta; Theta Xi. Polit. & Govt. Pos: Tex. State Rep, 61-69. Bus. & Prof. Pos: Asst. prof. finance, Tex. Tech. Col, 55-56, prof. of law, 69-; practicing attorney, Lubbock, Tex, 56-58 & 60-67; trust officer, Am. State Bank, Lubbock, 59. Mil. Serv: Entered as Ens, Navy, 53, released as Lt.(jg), 55, after serv. in Seventh Fleet, Pac. Area, 53-55; Korean, UN and Nat. Defense Ribbons; Lt. Comdr, Naval Res, 60- Mem: State Bar of Tex; Lubbock Co. Bar Asn. Named Outstanding Freshman Mem, Tex. House of Rep, 61; selected as one of 36 legislators in nation to participate inf First Eagleton Inst. of Polit, State Govt. Seminar, Rutgers Univ, 66. Rel: Presbyterian. Mailing Add: 5703 Geneva, Lubbock, Tex. 79413.

QUINLAN, JOHN M. R
Mass. State Sen.
b. Natick, Mass, 7/11/35; s. Arthur William Quinlan and Margaret Everett Q; single. Educ: Harvard Col, A.B, 57. Polit. & Govt. Pos: Mem, Dover Rep. Town Cmt, 56-69; spec. asst, U.S. Sen. Leverett Saltonstall, Mass, 60-62; mem, Nat. Asn. of State Legislators, 65-, Mass. Legislators Asn, 65-, and Norwood Rep. Town Cmt, 69; exec. dir, Mass. Coun. for Constitutional Reform, 63-64; Mass. State Sen, Second Dist, Norfolk, 65-, mem, spec. cmn. to re-dist. the Mass. Gen. Court and on pub. aid to non-pub. schs, Mass. State Senate, 67-68; pres, Norfolk Co. Rep. Club, 66-; chmn, Cmt. for a Constitutional Conv, 67-; Mass. chmn, United Citizens for Nixon-Agnew, 68. Bus. & Prof. Pos: Govt. and hist. teacher, Franklin Pub. Schs, Mass, 57-60. Mil. Serv: A/2C, Air Force Res, 57-63. Mem: Mass. Adv. Coun. on Educ; Nat. Cmt. for Pub. Schs; Sacred Heart Coun, K. of C; Mass. Audubon Soc; trustee, Robert S. Hale Reservation and Boston Ballet Co; spec. gifts chmn, Nat. Found. March of Dimes, Mass. Bay Chap; dir, Old Colony Coun, Boy Scouts of Am; Jr. C. of C; Am. Fedn. of Musicians; Harvard Club of Boston. One of Mass. Ten Outstanding Young Men, Gr. Boston Jr. C. of C, 66; One of 36 Outstanding Legislators, Eagleton Inst. of Polit; Seminar on Improv. of State Legis. Rel: Roman Catholic. Legal Res: 401 Engamore Lane, Norwood, Mass. 02062. Mailing Add: 510 Washington St, Norwood, Mass. 02062.

QUINN, AUGUSTINE STATHAM R
Chmn, Tenth Dist. Rep. Party, Ga.
b. Washington, Ga, 3/3/21; s. Augustine Statham Quinn, Sr. and Nona Lewis Hill Q; m. 2/15/44 to Lois Debus; c. A.S, III, Lorenz E, William D. and Henry L. Educ: Presby. Col, 4 years; Blue Key. Polit. & Govt. Pos: V.chmn, Tenth Dist. Rep. Party, Ga, 63-64 and chmn, currently. Bus. & Prof. Pos: Salesman, Roy Morgan Agency, Mutual of Omaha, Atlanta, Ga, 44 and Ga. sales mgr, 48-55; sales dir. south. states, Home Off, Mutual of Omaha, Omaha, Nebr, 55-57; gen. agent, Mutual of Omaha, Topeka, Kans, 57-59, St. Louis, Mo, 59-63 and Augusta, Ga, 63- Mil. Serv: Entered as 2nd Lt, U.S. Inf, 42, released as 1st Lt, 43. Mem: Life Underwriters Asn; Health and Accident Asn; Boy Scouts (adv, Evans Troop); Lions; Kiwanis; United Fund; DAV; Retired Officers Asn. Past Pres. Award, Boy Scouts, Health and Accident Asn. and Life Underwriters Asn. Rel: Presbyterian. Mailing Add: 8127 Sir Galahad Dr, Evans, Ga. 30809.

QUINN, DONALD LEE R
b. Scottville, Mich, 10/26/14; s. John Ernest Quinn and Bessie Saxton Q; m. 9/26/36 to R.L. Edythe Lindgren; c. Patricia Doreen and Donald George. Educ: East. Mich. Univ. Polit. & Govt. Pos: City cmnr, Ludington, Mich, 50-51; chmn, Mason Co. Rep. Cmt, Mich, 64-68. Bus. & Prof. Pos: Dir. recreation, Ludington, 45-48. Mem: United Mine Workers, Local 12773; Dist. Cmt, Boy Scouts. Rel: Protestant. Mailing Add: R.R. 2, U.S. 10 & 31, Ludington, Mich. 49431. (1967)

QUINN, DWIGHT WILSON D
N.C. State Rep.
b. York, S.C, 9/12/17; s. William Lytle Quinn and Lucy Wilson Q; m. 2/23/36

to Marion Elizabeth Isenhour; c. Mrs. Lester U. Dodge. Educ: Night and correspondence schs. Polit. & Govt. Pos: Pres, Cabarrus Co. Young Dem. Club, N.C, 48, served on various state cmts; precinct registr, 48-50; N.C. Med. Care Cmn; N.C. State Rep, 51-; mem, Gov. Cmn. Reorgn. State Govt, 59-60, chmn, 61-62; mem, Gov. Cmt. Juvenile Delinquency, Los Angeles, Calif, 60; del, Dem. Nat. Conv, 60 & 68; mem. exec. cmt, N.C. Citizens Cmt. Better Schs, Inc. Bus. & Prof. Pos: Supvry. capacity, Cannon Mills Co. Mil. Serv: Army, 44-45. Mem: YMCA (bd. dirs. Cannon Mem. Chap); mem. Nat. YMCA Young Men's Coun; Inter-Club Coun.(past pres); adv, Hi-Y; Dist. Boy Scout Cmt; bd, Nat. Cerebral Palsy Asn; N.C. Heart Asn.(bd. dirs. and past pres, Cabarrus Co. Chap); Am. Legion (v.comdr); 40 et 8; Rotary; AF&AM; Scottish Rite; Shrine; Oasis Temple. Kannapolis Man of the Year, Jaycees, 48; Amvets Nat. Distinguished Serv. Award for Outstanding Commun. Serv, 53. Rel: Lutheran; Mem. church coun, secy. congregation, gen. supt, Sunday Sch; pres, Brotherhood, Sunday Sch. Teacher and mem. archit. and planning cmt, Kimball Mem. Lutheran Church. Legal Res: 213 S. Main St, Kannapolis, N.C. 28081. Mailing Add: P.O. Box 314, Kannapolis, N.C. 28081. (1967)

QUINN, EGBERT LYLE D
b. Pocomoke City, Worcester Co, Md, 1/8/85. Educ: Crisfield Pub. Schs. Polit. & Govt. Pos: Md. State Del, 57-67; Mayor of Crisfield, 48-54; Crisfield City Coun, 40-48. Bus. & Prof. Pos: Newspaper Ed. & Publisher. Mem: Bd. of Dir, McCready Mem. Hosp, Crisfield; Order of the Eastern Star; Masons; Elks; Crisfield Country Club; Gov. Club. Mailing Add: N. 3rd St, Crisfield, Md. 21817. (1967)

QUINN, J. HERBERT D
b. Concord, N.H, 10/12/30; s. Blanche A. Johnson (father deceased); m. 10/12/50 to Carolyn French; c. John Michael, Cynthia Ann and Timothy Patrick. Educ: St. John High Sch. Polit. & Govt. Pos: N.H. State Rep, 61-62; N.H. Gen. Court, 61-62; exec. dir, Concord Housing Authority, 61-66; mayor, Concord, N.H, 66-68. Bus. & Prof. Pos: Owner, Quinn Motor Transportation, 57-58. Mil. Serv: Entered as Recruit, Navy, 49, released as PO 3/C, 52, after serv. in Surface Anti Develop. Detachment, N. Atlantic. Mem: Nat. Housing and Redevelop. Officials; founder-dir, Concord Housing Authority; hon. Sr. Citizen Concord Sunset Club, 64, Am. Legion; VFW; Moose; Elks; Concord Vis. Nurse Asn.(dir, 62-66). Outstanding Man of the Year Award, N.H. Jr. C. of C, 63. Rel: Catholic. Mailing Add: 13 Grove St, Concord, N.H. 03301. (1967)

QUINN, JAMES L. D
b. Louisa Co, Iowa, 5/26/13; s. Robert L. Quinn and May S. Q; m. 1934 to Gretchen Helse; c. Judith, James, Robert, John, Sarah, Joseph, Michael and Matthew. Educ: Univ. Iowa, B.S. in Bus. Admin, 37. Polit. & Govt. Pos: Mem, Sch. Bd, Washington, Iowa, 40-48, former mem, Wash. Co. Draft Bd; twp. assessor, 40-50; Iowa State Rep, until 66. Bus. & Prof. Pos: Ins. agent, 37-40; farmer; with Ainsworth State Bank, 52- Mem: Mason; Shrine; Farm Bur; YMCA; State Hist. Soc. Rel: Methodist. Mailing Add: Route 2, Washington, Iowa 52353.

QUINN, JEROME F. R
Wis. State Assemblyman
b. Green Bay, Wis. Educ: Univ. Wis. Polit. & Govt. Pos: Alderman, Wis, 16 years; Brown Co. Bd, 6 years; Wis. State Assemblyman, 54- Bus. & Prof. Pos: Merchant, 30 years; real estate investment bus. Mem: Green Bay Asn. of C; W. Side Businessmen's Asn; Elks; past chmn. finance cmt, Green Bay Bd. of Educ. Mailing Add: 137 N. Oakland Ave, Green Bay, Wis. 54303. (1967)

QUINN, JOHN E. D
b. Plattsburgh, N.Y, 8/16/28; m. to Mildred Williams. Educ: Mt. Assumption Inst, Plattsburgh, Grad; Syracuse Univ; St. Lawrence Univ. Polit. & Govt. Pos: N.Y. State Sen, 64-66; Former Alderman, 3rd Ward, Plattsburgh; Finance Cmt, Plattsburgh. Bus. & Prof. Pos: Employee, N.Y. State Dept. of Correction at Dannemora. Mil. Serv: Vet, USN, serv. in China and Korean Conflict; Presidential Unit Citation. Mem: Esteemed Leading Knight, Plattsburgh Lodge of Elks; Am. Legion; VFW; Coun. 2166, K. of C. Rel: St. John's Catholic Church. Mailing Add: 36 Olivetti Pl, Plattsburgh, N.Y. 12901. (1967)

QUINN, PHILIP ANDREW D
Mass. State Sen.
b. Worcester, Mass, 2/21/10; s. James Henry Quinn and Dorothy Mulrone Q; single. Polit. & Govt. Pos: Mass. State Rep, 49-65; Mass. State Sen, 65-; alternate del, Dem. Nat. Conv, 68. Bus. & Prof. Pos: Proprietor, Hotel Massasoit, Spencer, Mass, 35-; owner, John J. Brown Ins. Agency, 58- Mil. Serv: Entered as Pvt, Air Force, 42, released as S/Sgt, 45, after serv. in 302nd Air Serv. Group, India and Burma, 45; India-Burma Ribbon with 3 Battle Stars. Mem: K. of C; Am. Legion; VFW. Rel: Roman Catholic. Mailing Add: 101 Main, Spencer, Mass. 01562.

QUINN, ROBERT H. D
Attorney Gen, Mass.
b. Boston, Mass, 1/30/28. Educ: Boston Col, A.B, 52; Harvard Law Sch, LL.B, 55. Polit. & Govt. Pos: Mass. State Rep, 57-69, speaker, Mass. House of Rep, 67-69; Attorney Gen, Mass, 69- Bus. & Prof. Pos: Attorney-at-law. Mem: Am, Mass. and Boston Bar Asns; Mass. Legislators Asn; K. of C; Boston Col. Alumni Asn; Boston Col. Varsity Club; Harvard Law Sch. Asn. of Mass. Legal Res: 32 Auckland St, Boston, Mass. 02125. Mailing Add: State House, Boston, Mass. 02133.

QUINN, THOMAS RODNEY D
b. Plattsburgh, N.Y, 11/28/33; s. Stephen T. Quinn and Rita Rooney Q; m. 8/20/55 to Sandra Davies; c. Susan Mary, Julie Ann, Thomas R, Jr, Stephen Davies, Keri Margaret and Kevin Michael. Educ: St. Michael's Col, Vt, 3 years; Albany Law Sch, grad, 58. Polit. & Govt. Pos: City tax attorney, Plattsburgh, N.Y, 63-65, city judge, 65- and acting corp. counsel, 69-; alternate del, Dem. Nat. Conv, 68. Bus. & Prof. Pos: Law clerk, 58-59; adjuster, Allstate Ins. Co, Whitesboro, N.Y, 59-60. Mem: New York State and Clinton Co. Bar Asn; Plattsburgh Elks; Dannemora Lions. Rel: Roman Catholic. Legal Res: 123 Oak St, Plattsburgh, N.Y. 12901. Mailing Add: c/o Quinn, Keable & Wylie, 68 Court St, Plattsburgh, N.Y. 12901.

QUINN, TIMOTHY ALLAN D
Chmn, Mansfield Dem. Town Cmt, Conn.
b. Methuen, Mass, 6/28/25; s. Thade A. Quinn and Marjorie Ellershaw Q; m. 11/23/52 to Julia Lynch; c. Sheila Anne. Educ: Ithaca Col, Ithaca, N.Y, B.S, 50; Univ. Conn, M.A, 52, CAGSE, 60; Kappa Gamma Psi. Polit. & Govt. Pos: Mem, Mansfield Dem. Town Cmt, Conn, 52-57 & 58-; secy, Town Govt. Study Cmt, 57, chmn, 67-; mem, Charter Cmn, Mansfield, 69- Bus. & Prof. Pos: Dir. music, Windham Pub. Schs, Conn, 57- Mil. Serv: Army Air Force, 43; Air Force Res, currently, Maj, serv. as admissions counsr, U.S. Air Force Acad. Mem: Windham Educ. Asn; Nat. Cmt. Educators Human Rights; Conn. Educ. Asn.(v.pres, pres, 69-); Nat. Educ. Asn.(resolutions cmt, 69-). Mailing Add: P.O. Box 91, Mansfield Center, Conn. 06250.

QUINN, VICTOR H. R
Chmn, Maury Co. Rep. Exec. Cmt, Tenn.
b. Lula, Ga, 10/29/25; s. Herbert Quinn and Minnie Q; m. 3/13/48 to Jean Westmoreland; c. Victor H, Jr, Suzanne and Michael. Polit. & Govt. Pos: Mem, Maury Co. Rep. Exec. Cmt, Tenn, 48-, secy, 48-60, chmn, 64-; mgr, Maury Co. Nixon Campaign, 60; magistrate, Maury Co. Court, 60-66; finance chmn, Sixth Cong. Dist. Rep. Party; jury cmnr, Middle Tenn. Dist. Fed. Court, 64-66. Bus. & Prof. Pos: Employee, Commerce Union Bank, 54-64, asst. cashier, 64-65; asst. v.pres, 65-66. Mil. Serv: Entered as A/S, Navy, 43, released as Aviation Radioman 2/C, 47, after serv. in Patrol Bomber Squadron 108, Pac, 44-47. Mem: Columbia Jaycees (pres, 60); Am. Legion; Rotary; bd. mem, Middle Tenn. Heart Asn; Maury Co. Ment. Health Asn.(pres, 66); Maury Co. Cancer Soc.(treas). Selected Maury Co. Outstanding Young Man of Year, 61. Rel: Church of Christ. Mailing Add: R.R. 6, Columbia, Tenn. 38401. (1967)

QUINN, WESLEY MARION R
b. Sumner Co, Kans, 2/21/07; s. Thaddeus Quinn and Rebecca Alice Bledsoe Q; m. 11/26/36 to Jeanne Electa Knowles; c. Stephen Knowles. Educ: Univ. N.Mex; Pi Kappa Alpha. Polit. & Govt. Pos: Mem, N.Mex. Rep. State Exec. Cmt, 48-49; mem, bd. regents, Univ. N.Mex, 50-59; former city attorney, Clovis; former chmn, Curry Co. Rep. Party; alternate del, Rep. Nat. Conv, 68. Bus. & Prof. Pos: Bar cmnr, Ninth Judicial Dist, N.Mex, currently. Mil. Serv: Entered as A/S, Navy, 42, released as Lt.(jg), 45, after serv. in Amphibious Forces, Pac. Theatre. Mem: Curry Co. and N.Mex. State Bar Asns; pres, State Bar of N.Mex, 65-66; v.chmn, Gen. Practice Sect, Am. Bar Asn, 69; Shrine; N.Mex. Club; Cmt. of Fifty. Rel: Presbyterian. Legal Res: Star Route, Clovis, N.Mex. 88101. Mailing Add: P.O. Box 490, Clovis, N.Mex. 88101.

QUIÑONES, SAMUEL R. D
b. San Juan, P.R, 8/9/04; s. Francisco Quiñones and Dolores Q; m. 12/31/39 to Clara Luz Vizcarrondo; c. Samuel René and Francisco Arturo. Educ: Univ. P.R, LL.B; pres, Asn. of Univ. Students, Univ. P.R; ed. Univ. Annual, 26; pres, Literary Soc. Univ. P.R; Phi Eta Mu. Polit. & Govt. Pos: Mem, Bd. Elec, P.R, 38-; speaker, P.R. House of Rep, 41-43; v.pres, P.R. Senate, 44-48, pres, 49-69; pres, Finance Cmt, P.R. Seante, 44; mem, Constitutional Conv. and pres, Cmn. of Exec, 50; mem, Conf. State Legis. Leaders and Nat. Legis. Leaders Conf, 56-; mem, Presidential panel, Popular Dem. Party, 60-, presidential del, 3 terms; mem, Constitutional Redistricting Bd. P.R, 64; observer, Latin Am. Parliament, 65. Bus. & Prof. Pos: Ed, La Democracia, 38-39; founder and dir. magazines, including Patria, Indice, Revista del Ateneo Puertorriqueño, Gaceta Forense and Anuario de la Universidad de P.R; pres, Cmt. on Youth Delinquency; participant at conf, Madrid's Atheneum, Spain, Center of P.R. Students in Salamanca, Brown Univ, Moral Rearmament in Mich. and Jr. Delinquency in Wash; dir. ed. cmt, Anthology of P.R. Authors. Mil. Serv: Lt. Col. and Judge Adv, State Guard P.R, 42. Publ: Temas y Letras, 3 ed; Constitucion y Convenio para Puerto Rico; Nemesio R. Canales - El Humorista de Puerto Rico. Mem: Pres, Bar Asn. P.R, 43-44; pres, P.R. Acad. Spanish Language; correspondent mem, Royal Acad. Spanish Language; bd. trustees, Univ. P.R. and Inter-Am. Univ; Soc. Journalists and Authors; Casino de P.R; pres, P.R. Atheneum, 34-36; hon. mem, bd. dirs, YMCA, 57-59; int. hon. mem, Lions, 65. Citizen of Year, P.R. Inst. N.Y, 65; awards, P.R. Inst. Literature, City of Miami, Retailers of P.R, Royal Acad. Spanish Language, Eduador's Penal Cong. and Senate of France. Rel: Presbyterian. Legal Res: Road 2, Km. 8.5 Bayamón, P.R. 00619. Mailing Add: Box 3946, San Juan, P.R. 00904.

QUIRIN, E. WILLIAN 'BILL' DFL
b. Osseola Co, Iowa, 1927; married; c. Nine (one deceased). Educ: Rochester Jr. Col. Polit. & Govt. Pos: Minn. State Rep, 64-68; del, Dem. Nat. Conv, 68. Bus. & Prof. Pos: Ins. agent, 13 years; farmer, Rochester Dairy; Home Gas Co. Mil. Serv: Navy, Pac. Theatre. Mem: Olmsted Co. DFL; Rochester Life Underwriters Asn; Minn. Heart Asn.(regional chmn, bd. of dir); K. of C; St. Johns Men's Club; St. John's Home Sch. Asn; Golden Hill PTA; VFW. Rel: St. John's Church. Mailing Add: 1804 Third Ave, S.W. Rochester, Minn. 55901. (1967)

QUIRK, CHARLES EVANS D
Chmn, Black Hawk Co. Dem. Cent. Cmt, Iowa
b. Milwaukee, Wis, 12/13/33; s. Ralph Evans Quirk and Irma Janke Q; m. 8/19/55 to Gale Marie Senty; c. Wayne, Brian and Robert. Educ: Carroll Col, B.A, 55; Harvard Divinity Sch, 55-56; McCormick Theol. Sem, B.D, 58; Univ. Iowa, 59-61 and Ph.D, 67; Tau Kappa Epsilon. Polit. & Govt. Pos: Orgn. chmn, Black Hawk Co. Dem. Cent. Cmt, Iowa, 65-67, ward leader, 64 and chmn, 67-; chmn, Iowa Legis. Subdistricting Cmn, 67; del, Dem. Nat. Conv, 68. Bus. & Prof. Pos: Pastor, First Presby. Church, Hamburg, Iowa, 61-63; asst. prof. hist, Univ. North. Iowa, 63-69, assoc. prof, 69- Publ: 'A Statistical Analysis of the Signers of the Auburn Affirmation,' J. Presby. Hist, 9-65. Mem: Presby. Hist. Soc; Am. Acad. Relig; Am. Fedn. Teachers. Rel: Presbyterian. Mailing Add: 245 Alta Vista, Waterloo, Iowa 50703.

QUIRK, JEREMIAH R
N.H. State Rep.
b. Portsmouth, N.H, 4/17/94; single. Educ: Portsmouth High Sch. Polit. & Govt. Pos: N.H. State Rep, 55-; chmn. bd. of registrs, 59-62. Bus. & Prof. Pos: Retired machinist. Mem: P.R.A. Club. Mailing Add: 140 Lincoln Ave, Portsmouth, N.H. 03801. (1967)

QUIST, KENNETH EUGENE D
b. Hinsdale, N.H, 12/26/15; s. Axel L. Quist and Esther M. Swenson Q; m. 8/26/39 to Lucille Norma Nelson; c. Lowell, Wallace, Kenneth and Jay. Educ: Cannon Falls High Sch, 34; Future Farmers of Am. Polit. & Govt. Pos: Chmn, Pierce Co. Dem. Party, Wis, 63-68; mem, State Admin. Cmt, Wis, 66- Mem: Farmers Union; Packinghouse Workers Local 167, CIO. Rel: Swedish Covenant. Mailing Add: Maiden Rock, Wis. 54750. (1967)

R

RAAP, F. CHARLES D
b. Ottawa Co, 11/4/20; married; c. Charles, Russell, Joan. Educ: Ravenna sch. syst. Polit. & Govt. Pos: Mich. State Rep, 64-66; 54-60. Bus. & Prof. Pos: Machinist at Continental Motors Corp. Mil. Serv: Navy Air Corps Vet. Mem: Bd. of dels. in charge of the West. Mich. News; Local 113, Cmt. on Polit. Educ; Eagles; Moose; Egelston Dem. Club. Mailing Add: 5853 Apple Ave, Muskegon, Mich. 49442. (1967)

RAASCH, MARY ELIZABETH R
V.Chmn, Hamlin Co. Rep. Party, S.Dak.
b. Aroya, Colo, 2/7/09; d. William Henry Rowe Ching and Annie Jardin C; m. 6/25/31 to Earl Raasch; c. Robert W, Marjorie M. (Mrs. Poppen) and Richard E. Educ: S.Dak. State Univ, 1 year; Watertown Bus. Univ, 6 months. Polit. & Govt. Pos: V.chmn, Hamlin Co. Rep. Party, S.Dak, 61- Bus. & Prof. Pos: Bookkeeper, auto co, Watertown, S.Dak, 29-31. Mem: Eastern Star; Fidelus Study Club; Rep. Federated Club. Rel: Presbyterian. Mailing Add: Rural Route, Castlewood, S.Dak. 57223.

RABBITT, RICHARD J. D
Mo. State Rep.
b. St. Louis, Mo, 10/30/35; m. 11/24/62 to Teresa Marie Molloy; c. Michael Patrick and Richard J, Jr. Educ: St. Louis Univ; St. Louis Univ. Grad. Sch, B.S, in polit. sci. and LL.B. Polit. & Govt. Pos: Mo. State Rep, 60- Bus. & Prof. Pos: Attorney-at-law. Mem: K. of C.(first grand knight, past grand knight and trustee, Coun. 5181). Rel: Catholic. Mailing Add: 4340 Forest Park, St. Louis, Mo. 63108. (1967)

RABINOWITZ, JAY ANDREW D
Assoc. Justice, Supreme Court of Alaska
b. Phila, Pa, 2/27/27; s. Milton Rabinowitz and Rose R; m. 6/14/57 to Ann Marie Nesbit; c. Judith and Mara. Educ: Syracuse Univ, B.A, 49; Harvard Law Sch, LL.B, 52. Polit. & Govt. Pos: Asst. U.S. attorney, Territory of Alaska, 58-59; dep. attorney gen, Alaska, 59-60, superior court judge, 60-65; assoc. justice, Supreme Court of Alaska, 65- Mil. Serv: Entered as Pvt, Army Air Corps, 45, released as Pfc, 46, after serv. in U.S. Rel: Jewish. Legal Res: Yankovitch Rd, Fairbanks, Alaska. 99701. Mailing Add: Box 109, Fairbanks, Alaska 99701.

RACE, HOWARD EVERETT R
Mem, Milwaukee Co. Rep. Coun, Wis.
b. Rome, N.Y, 5/9/18; s. Homer D. Race and Estelle Maude Herman R; m. 8/14/44 to Mary Theresa Thiery. Educ: Milwaukee Sch. Eng, B.S. and E.E.P; Sigma Pi Rho. Polit. & Govt. Pos: Chmn, 15th Ward Rep. Party, Milwaukee, Wis, and committeeman, 15th Dist, 61-62; mem, State Cent. Cmt, 62; alternate del, Rep. Nat. Conv, 64; Gov. campaign coordinator, Fourth Cong. Dist, 64; del. and membership chmn, Milwaukee Co. Rep. Coun, 64, mem, 66-; del. and mem. exec. cmt, Ninth Dist. Rep. Party and chmn, 18th Ward, 66- Bus. & Prof. Pos: Sr. Prfnl. Engr, Allen Bradley, 52- Mil. Serv: Entered as A/S, Navy, 42, released as AMM 2/C, 45. Mem: Plastics Engrs. Soc; Inst. Elec. and Electronics Engrs; Am. Legion. Mailing Add: 8605 W. Glendale Ave, Milwaukee, Wis. 53225.

RACE, JOHN ABNER D
b. Fond du Lac, Wis, 5/12/14; s. Lewis Frank Race and Elsie I. Sonnenburg R; m. 5/29/37 to Dorothea Schroeder; c. Marilyn (Mrs. Ronald Repp), Susan (Mrs. Robert Tadman) and Kathi. Polit. & Govt. Pos: Mem: Fond du Lac Co. Bd. of Supvr, Wis, 58-64; mem, Wis. State Bd. of Voc. and Adult Educ, 59-65; v.chmn, Sixth Dist. Dem. Party, 61-65; chmn, Fond du Lac Co. Dem. Party, 61-65; mem, Wis. Coord. Cmt. for Higher Educ, 63-64; mem, Fond du Lac Dist. Comprehensive Ment. Health Planning Cmt, 64; U.S. Rep, Sixth Dist, Wis, 65-66; Dem. Cand for U.S. Rep, Wis, 66 & 68. Bus. & Prof. Pos: Dir, Sheltered Workshop, Inc, Fond du Lac, 63-65. Mem: IAMAW; Optimists. Rel: Lutheran. Mailing Add: 402 S. Hickory St, Fond du Lac, Wis. 54939. (1967)

RACEWICZ, WILLIAM JOHN D
b. Providence, R.I, 10/31/99. Educ: Providence Tech. High Sch. Polit. & Govt. Pos: R.I. State Rep, 64-66. Bus. & Prof. Pos: Former Collector and salesman; retired. Mem: Pres, Sons of Poland Soc; v.pres, Polish Home, Providence; bd. mem, Nickerson House; Barbershoppers Singing Group. Former amateur ball player, Providence. Mailing Add: 44 Bowdoin St, Providence, R.I. 02909. (1967)

RADANT, KENNETH RAYMOND R
Chmn, Rep. Party Barry Co, Mich.
b. Owosso, Mich, 1/1/36; s. Raymond Radant and Josephine Kovacic R; m. 6/15/57 to Marjorie Ellen White; c. Karen, Steven and Joellyn. Educ: Alma Col, 3 years; Mich. State Univ, B.A, 58; Tau Kappa Epsilon. Polit. & Govt. Pos: Chmn, Rep. Party of Barry Co, Mich, 65-; alternate del, Rep. Nat. Conv, 68; supvr, Barry Co. Bd. Supvr, 68- Bus. & Prof. Pos: Pres. & gen. mgr, WBCH AM-FM, Hastings, Mich, 62- Mem: Rotary; Elks. Outstanding Serv. Award, Jr. C. of C. Rel: Episcopal. Mailing Add: 646 W. Walnut St, Hastings, Mich. 49058.

RADCLIFFE, JOHN D
Wis. State Assemblyman
b. Little Falls, Wis, 5/19/20. Educ: Tony High Sch. Polit. & Govt. Pos: Chmn, Trempealeau Co. Dem. Party, Wis; Wis. State Assemblyman, 64- Bus. & Prof. Pos: Surveyor, formerly; employee, Rubber Co, 20 years. Mil. Serv: Navy, World War II. Mem: VFW; Strum Commercial Club; Rod and Gun Club; State Horticulture Soc; past pres, Strum PTA; dist. dir, Boy Scouts; chief steward, CIO Rubber Workers, Eau Claire; past mem, Strum-Eleva Cent. High Sch. Bd; past chmn, Strum-Skyline Park Bd. Mailing Add: Box 55, Strum, Wis. 54770. (1967)

RADCLIFFE, W. O. E. 'BILL' D
b. Goldendale, Wash, 1902; m. to Francelia R; c. Two. Educ: Western Wash. State Col, B.A; U. of Wash, M.A; Phi Delta Kappa. Polit. & Govt. Pos: Wash. State Rep, until 66. Bus. & Prof. Pos: Former prin, Shuksan Jr. High Sch. Mem: Masons; Eastern Star; Grange. Mailing Add: 437 21st St, Bellingham, Wash. 98225.

RADEMAKER, JANICE MAY D
b. Lewiston, Maine, 12/14/42; d. Dr. John Adrian Rademaker and Mrs. Elizabeth Spencer R; single. Educ: Willamette Univ, B.A, 63; Martin Luther King, Jr. Inst. Social Change, Chester, Pa, Cert, 66; Univ. Ore, M.A, 67; Nat. Defense Educ. Act fel; Univ. Ore. Teaching and Research Assistantships in Sociol. and Polit. Sci; hiking clubs; col. newspaper staff. Polit. & Govt. Pos: Pres, Univ. Ore. Young Dems, 64-65; alternate del, Dem. Nat. Conv, 68. Publ: 'The Buddhist Movement in South Vietnam,' WIN magazine, May, 1968. Mem: Grad. Students in Polit. Sci. Union; Dem. Party; Civil Rights Orgn; Friends of South. Christian Leadership Conf. Rel: Quaker. Legal Res: 960 Shipping St. N.E, Salem, Ore. 97303. Mailing Add: 2551 Columbia, Apt. 1, Eugene, Ore. 97403.

RADER, BOBBY JEWETT R
Mem, Calif. Rep. State Cent. Cmt.
b. Tecumseh, Okla, 2/23/26; s. M.C. Rader and Alice Harbor R; m. 8/16/45 to Clarice Jean Brundege; c. Robin Jean and Susan Myrl. Educ: Okla. Univ, 1 year. Polit. & Govt. Pos: Mem, Calif. Rep. State Cent. Cmt, 65- Bus. & Prof. Pos: Mgr. Visalia yard, United Lumber Yards, Calif, 50-60; owner, Mother Lode Lumber Co, Mariposa, currently. Mil. Serv: Merchant Marine. Mem: Elks; F&AM; Lions. Rel: Church of Christ. Mailing Add: P.O. Box 96, Hwy. 140, Mariposa, Calif. 95338.

RADER, JOHN L. D
Alaska State Sen.
b. Howard, Kans, 2/11/27; s. Mr. and Mrs. Ralph R. Rader; m. 1951 to Carolyn Weigand; c. Tim, Matthew and Janet. Educ: Univ. Ore; Stanford Univ; Univ. Kans, B.S. in Bus. Admin, 48 and LL.B, 51. Polit. & Govt. Pos: City attorney, Anchorage, Alaska, 54-55; state attorney gen, Alaska, 59-60; Alaska State Rep, 61-68; floor leader, Alaska House of Rep, 63-64; mem. bd, Gr. Anchorage Health Dist; Alaska State Sen, 68- Bus. & Prof. Pos: Mem, Indust. Rels. Dept, Lago Oil & Transport, Netherlands, W.I, 48; employee, FE Co, 49; partner, McCutcheon, Nesbett & Rader, 51-54 and Hartlieb, Groh & Rader, 55-58 & 61-62; part-time instr. real estate law, Anchorage Commun. Col, 57; attorney-at-law. Mil. Serv: Naval Res, 45-46. Mem: Alaska Bar. Received Young Man of Year Award, Anchorage Jr. C. of C, 60. Mailing Add: Box 2068, Anchorage, Alaska 99501.

RADL, RICHARD MARTIN D
Iowa State Rep.
b. Chicago, Ill, 8/27/11; m. to Helen Bartlett; c. Richard, Peter, David, William and Mary. Polit. & Govt. Pos: Iowa State Rep, currently. Bus. & Prof. Pos: Mech. engr; owner, Illini Molded Plastics, Lisbon, Iowa. Mailing Add: Lisbon, Iowa 52253. (1967)

RADNEY, TOM D
Ala. State Sen.
b. Wadley, Ala, 6/18/32; s. James Monroe Radney and Beatrice Simpson R; m. 9/8/62 to Madolyn Boyd Anderson; c. Margaret Ellen, Sara Frances and Hollis Lee. Educ: Auburn Univ, B.S. and M.S, 52; Univ. Ala, LL.B, 55; Phi Kappa Tau; Phi Alpha Delta. Polit. & Govt. Pos: Del, Dem. Nat. Conv, 60 & 68; city judge, Alexander City, Ala, 62-; Ala. State Sen, 66- Mil. Serv: Entered as Pvt, Army, 55, released as Capt, 59, after serv. in Judge Adv. Gen. Corps. Mem: Am. Bar Asn; secy, Ala. Young Lawyers, 65; Am. Legion; Kiwanis; Elks; Mason; Shrine; Eastern Star. Rel: Methodist. Mailing Add: 234 Ridgeway Dr, Alexander City, Ala. 35010.

RADWAY, LAURENCE INGRAM D
N.H. State Rep.
b. Staten Island, N.Y, 2/2/19; s. Frederick and Dorothy R; m. 8/20/49 to Patricia Ann Headland; c. Robert Russell, Carol Sinclair, Michael Porter and Deborah Brooke. Educ: Harvard, B.S, 40, Ph.D, 50; Phi Beta Kappa. Polit. & Govt. Pos: Civilian aide to Secy. of Army; chmn, Platform Cmt, N.H. Dem. Party, 58-60; chmn, Grafton Co. Dem. Cmt, 58-62; mem, N.H. Dem. State Cmt, 58-62; prof, Nat. Security Affairs, U.S. Nat. War Col, 62-63; mem, N.H. Del, Dem. Nat. Conv, 64; N.H. State Rep, 68- Mil. Serv: Entered as Cpl, Army, 43, released as Capt, 46, after serv. in Transportation Corps, ETO and U.S, 43-46. Publ: Soldiers and Scholars, Princeton Univ. Press, 57; Mil. Behavior in Int. Orgn, Free Press of Glencoe, 62; Foreign Policy and National Defense, Scott, Foresnan & Co, 69. Mem: Am. Polit. Sci. Asn; Coun. on Foreign Rels. Rel: Protestant. Mailing Add: 22 Occom Ridge, Hanover, N.H. 03755.

RAE, MATTHEW SANDERSON, JR. R
Mem, Calif. State Rep. Cent. Cmt.
b. Pittsburgh, Pa, 9/12/22; s. Matthew Sanderson Rae and Olive Waite R; m. 5/2/53 to Janet Hettman; c. Mary-Anna S, Margaret S. and Janet S. Educ: Duke Univ, A.B, 46, LL.B, 47; Stanford Univ, 51; Phi Beta Kappa; Omicron Delta Kappa; Phi Eta Sigma; Tau Psi Omega; Sigma Nu; Phi Alpha Delta. Polit. & Govt. Pos: Pres, South Bay Young Rep, 56; parliamentarian, Los Angeles Co. Young Rep, Calif, 56; pres, 46th Assembly Dist. Rep. Assembly, 57; asst. treas, Calif. Rep. Assembly, 57-58; v.pres, Los Angeles Co. Rep. Assembly, 59-64; v.chmn, 17th Cong. Dist. Rep. Party, 60-62; mem, Los Angeles Co. Rep. Cent. Cmt, 60-64; v.chmn, 28th Cong. Dist. Rep. Party, 62-64; chmn, 46th Assembly Dist. Rep. Party, 62-64; pres, Calif. Rep. League, 66-67; mem, Calif. State Rep. Cent. Cmt, 66-, mem. exec. cmt, 66-67. Bus. & Prof. Pos: Asst. to dean, Duke Univ. Sch. of Law, 47-48; assoc, Off. of Karl F. Steinmann, Baltimore, Md, 48-49; nat. field rep, Phi Alpha Delta Law Fraternity, 49-51; research attorney, Calif. Supreme Court, 51-52; assoc,

Darling, Mack, Hall & Call, 53-55, partner, 55- Mil. Serv: Entered as Aviation Cadet, Army Air Corps, 43, released as 2nd Lt, 45, after serv. in Training Command, U.S, 43-45. Mem: Am. and South Bay Bar Asns; Am. Judicature Soc; fel. Am. Col. of Probate Counsel; Nat. Legal Aid and Defender Asn; Los Angeles Co. Bar Asn.(chmn. probate and trust law cmt, 64-66); State Bar of Calif; Lawyers Club of Los Angeles; Phi Alpha Delta (supreme advocate, 68-); Legion Lex (v.pres, 68-); Am. Legion (comdr, Allied Post, 69-); Air Force Asn; Aircraft Owners & Pilots Asn; Town Hall; Commonwealth Club; World Affairs Coun; Int. Platform Asn; Rel: United Presbyterian. Legal Res: 600 John St, Manhattan Beach, Calif. 90266. Mailing Add: 523 W. Sixth St, Room 737, Los Angeles, Calif. 90014.

RAFFERTY, MAX R
State Supt. of Pub. Instr, Calif.
b. New Orleans, La, 5/7/17; s. Maxwell L. Rafferty and De Etta Cox R; m. 6/4/44 to Frances L. Longman; c. Kathleen, Dennis and Eileen. Educ: Univ. Calif. at Los Angeles, B.A. and M.A; Univ. South. Calif, Ed.D; Phi Delta Kappa. Polit. & Govt. Pos: State supt. of pub. instr, Calif, 63- Bus. & Prof. Pos: Teacher, Trona Sch. Dist, Calif, 40-48; prin, Big Bear High Sch, Calif, 48-51; supt, Saticoy Sch. Dist, 51-55, Needles Sch. Dist, 55-61 and La Canada Sch. Dist, 61-62. Publ: Suffer, Little Children, 62. Mem: Nat. Educ. Admin; Am. Asn. Sch. Admin; Lions Int; Rotary Int. Rel: Episcopal. Mailing Add: 721 Capitol Mall, Sacramento, Calif. 95814.

RAFFL, KENNETH ALBERT R
Chmn, Randolph Co. Rep. Party, Ill.
b. Redbud, Ill, 11/17/13; s. Oswald Raffl and Adeline Bromleve R; m. 8/19/38 to Luella Schuette; c. John David. Polit. & Govt. Pos: Rep. precinct committeeman, Ill, 60; chmn, Randolph Co. Rep. Party, 64-; mem, Ill. Rep. State Cent. Cmt, currently. Bus. & Prof. Pos: Salesman, Liggett-Meyers, 35-38 and Weeke Wholesale Co, 39- Mem: Instnl. rep, Boy Scouts. Rel: Catholic. Mailing Add: 269 Summit, Redbud, Ill. 62278. (1967)

RAGAN, MARTIN D
b. Pa, 11/11/99; s. Andrew Ragan and Suzanne Ragan R; m. 2/5/24 to Suzanne Ubrin; c. Martin A.(killed in action, 44, S.Pac, USMC), George W, Donald E, Lavone (Mrs. Michael P. Balint), Suzanne (Mrs. Arthur Carrasco) and Anna Mae (Mrs. William Saunders). Educ: Pub. Schs. Brooke Co; two years night sch. in mining. Polit. & Govt. Pos: W.Va. State Del, 64-68. Mil. Serv: World War I. Mem: Secy, Non-Partisan League of United Mine Workers, Brooke Co. Rel: Presbyterian. Mailing Add: R.F.D. 1, Wellsburg, W.Va. 26070. (1967)

RAGLAND, JOE F. D
b. Newnan, Ga, 4/7/36; s. Jack H. Ragland and Elna Loftin R; m. 10/1/60 to Nancy Jayne Edwards; c. Jodie, Joe Frank and David Edward. Educ: Univ. Ga, B.B.A, 58; Sigma Nu; Alpha Phi Omega. Polit. & Govt. Pos: Ga. State Rep, Dist. 109, 67-69. Bus. & Prof. Pos: Spec. agent, Ins. Co. of N.Am, 58-60; salesman, Fickling & Walker, Inc, 60-65; owner, Ragland Realty Co, 65- Mil. Serv: Naval Res, 53-61. Mem: Elks; Exchange Club; Jaycees; C. of C. Rel: Methodist. Mailing Add: 724 Forest Lake Dr, Macon, Ga. 31204. (1967)

RAGLAND, KENNETH NEIL D
b. Beaver Dam, Ky, 4/14/30; s. Thurman Lee Ragland and Mabel Porter R; m. 8/19/61 to Jennie Lee James. Educ: Univ. Ky, A.B, 58, LL.B, 60; Phi Alpha Theta; Phi Delta Phi. Polit. & Govt. Pos: City attorney, Livermore, Ky, 62-; chmn, McLean Co. Dem. Exec. Cmt, 64-69; city attorney, Island, Ky, 65- Bus. & Prof. Pos: V.pres. and dir, First Security Bank, Island, Ky, 63-; pres. and dir, Green Valley Farm Supply Inc, Island, Ky, 63- Mem: Jaycee; Lions Club. Mailing Add: Calhoun, McLean Co, Ky. 42327.

RAGSDALE, ALBERT GEORGE D
Chmn, Phillips Co. Dem. Cent. Cmt, Ark.
b. West Helena, Ark, 5/23/13; s. George William Ragsdale and Agnes Snyder R; m. 6/6/31 to Gladys Jane Kendal; c. Norma Sue (Mrs. Surman). Educ: Woodruff High Sch, West Helena, Ark, 10 years. Polit. & Govt. Pos: Chmn, Phillips Co. Dem. Cent. Cmt, Ark, 65-; secy, Phillips Co. Election Cmnr, 65- Bus. & Prof. Pos: Owner, Albert Ragsdale Serv. Sta, 40-; consignee, Cities Serv. Oil Co, 40- Mem: Shrine. Rel: Methodist. Mailing Add: 134 Stonebrook Rd, Helena, Ark. 72342.

RAGSDALE, HOWARD ARTHUR D
b. Halfway, Mo, 7/27/12; s. William Hershel Ragsdale and Erlinda B. Jones R; m. 12/21/41 to Mary Jane Fulbright; c. William Howard, Robert Mark, Jane Carolyn, John Arthur, Judy Leora, David Herschel and Jeanne Marilyn. Educ: Goodson High Sch. Polit. & Govt. Pos: Mem, Colo. State Wheat Adv. Cmt, 60-61 and Colo. State Cmt, Agr. Stabilization and Conserv. Serv, 61; chmn, Prowers Co. Dem. Cmt, 64-67. Bus. & Prof. Pos: Farmer and rancher, wheat & cattle; mgr, Ins. Bus, Farmers Union, 57- Mil. Serv: Entered as Pvt, Army, 42, released as Pfc, 45, after serv. in 96th Inf. Div, Pac. Theater. Mem: Masonic Lodge 72, Granada, Consistory, Pueblo; York Rite; Lamar Colo; Al Kaly Shrine, Pueblo; Am. Legion; Kiwanis; Farmers Union. Rel: Baptist. Legal Res: 44 Mayhew Dr, Lamar, Colo. 81052. Mailing Add: P.O. Box 509, Lamar, Colo. 81052.

RAGSDALE, HUGH APPLETON D
N.C. State Rep.
b. Smithfield, N.C, 1/18/09; s. Thomas Smith and Ann Eliza Robinson R; m. 11/23/31 to Annie Koonce Sutton; c. Hugh Appleton, Jr, Carl Sutton and Michael Robinson. Educ: Univ. of N.C. Polit. & Govt. Pos: Rep, Gen. Assembly, N.C, 63; mem, City Coun. and Co. Bd. of Educ; N.C. State Rep, 63- Bus. & Prof. Pos: Automobile dealer; farmer. Rel: Methodist; Mem, Bd. of Stewards; Asst. Dist. Lay Leader. Mailing Add: Richlands, N.C. 28574. (1967)

RAHE, ARME NA D
V.Chmn, Del. Co. Dem. Orgn, Ind.
b. Brazil, Ind, 10/2/13; d. Thomas R. Hutson and Frances Butterman H; m. 6/15/33 to William J. Rahe Jr; c. Thomas R, Judith C. (Mrs. Morrow) and R. Kay (Mrs. Nute). Educ: Acad. Immaculate Conception; St. Francis Hosp, Nursing. Polit. & Govt. Pos: Precinct, v.chmn, Dem. Orgn, Ind, 56-58; bd. mem, Voters Registrn. Off, 57-60; v.chmn, Del. Co. Dem. Orgn, Ind, 59-; asst. mgr, Muncie Auto License Br, 60- Bus. & Prof. Pos: Self-employed, Wm. J. Rahe & Sons Inc, 48-57. Mem: Daughters of Isabella; Alter Rosary Soc; bd. dirs, Acad. Immaculate Conception Alumnae; Del. Co. Dem. Woman's Orgn; State Fedn. of Dem. Women. Rel: Catholic. Mailing Add: R.R. 2, Box 438, Muncie, Ind. 47302. (1967)

RAICHE, ROBERT EDWARD D
Minority Leader, N.H. House of Rep.
b. Manchester, N.H, 2/18/37; s. Edward Raiche and Lucienne Harris R; m. 10/4/58 to Mary Elizabeth Duval; c. Robert Edward, Jr, Denise Anne, Maureen Elizabeth, Donna Marie and Kathleen Joyce. Educ: Nathaniel Hawthorne Col, B.A, 67. Polit. & Govt. Pos: Mem, N.H. Dem. State Cmt, 65-; N.H. State Rep, 65, minority leader, 69-; alternate del, Dem. Nat. Conv, 68; chmn, Hillsborough Co. Dem. Party, 69- Bus. & Prof. Pos: Newspaper agency employee, formerly; instr, Nathaniel Hawthorne Col, 68- Mil. Serv: Entered Marine Corps, 55, released as Sgt, 61. Mem: K. of C. Rel: Roman Catholic. Mailing Add: 957 Sommerville St, Manchester, N.H. 03103.

RAIFFIE, HARRY C. D
b. St. Louis, Mo, 4/12/08; m. 3/13/38 to Sue Grunberg; c. Herbert, Leonard and Marilyn. Educ: High Sch, St. Louis. Polit. & Govt. Pos: Mo. State Rep, 52-68, Caucus Chmn, Mo. Gen. Assembly, 65. Bus. & Prof. Pos: Vending machine bus. Mem: Mason. Rel: Temple Shaare Emeth. Mailing Add: 5870a Delmar Blvd, St. Louis, Mo. 63112. (1967)

RAILSBACK, THOMAS F. R
U.S. Rep, Ill.
b. Moline, Ill, 1/22/32; m. to Patricia Sloan; c. Kathryn, Julia, Margaret Ann and Lisa. Educ: Moline Commun. Col, 1 semester; Grinnell Col, B.A. in eng, 54; Northwest. Univ. Law Sch, J.D, 57; sr. class pres, Grinnell Col; pres, Phi Delta Phi, Northwest. Univ; Phi Gamma Delta. Polit. & Govt. Pos: Ill. State Rep, 63-66; U.S. Rep, 19th Dist, Ill, 66- Bus. & Prof. Pos: Attorney, assoc. with father, Fred H. Railsback, Ill, 57-63; assoc, Graham, Califf, Harper, Benson & Railsback, Attorneys, 63-69. Mil. Serv: Army, 57-59, serv. in Legal Assistance Off, Ft. Riley, Kans. Mem: Chmn, Younger Mem. Conf, Ill. State Bar Asn; Jr. C. of C; Elks; bd. dirs, Blackhawk Chap, Am. Red Cross; pres, Grinnell Col. Alumni Bd. Dirs. Distinguished Serv. Award, Jaycees, 64; Moline's Outstanding Young Man of Year, 64. Rel: Congregational; Sunday Sch. teacher and supt, Jr. High Dept. Mailing Add: 1313 Ninth St, Moline, Ill. 61265.

RAINBOLT, AUDIE W. D
Ind. State Rep.
Polit. & Govt. Pos: Ind. State Rep, currently. Bus. & Prof. Pos: Real estate and ins. agent. Mil. Serv: Navy. Mem: New Albany Bd. of Realtors; Mason; Am. Legion; C. of C; DAV; Elks; Improved Order of Red Men; past state comdr, VFW; past pres, Independent Ins. Agents of New Albany, Inc. Rel: Methodist. Mailing Add: 4003 Green Valley Rd, New Albany, Ind. 47150.

RAINBOLT, JOHN VERNON 'MIKE' D
Chmn, Fourth Dist. Okla. Dem. Cent. Cmt.
b. Abbott, Tex, 6/23/14; s. John Bellfield Rainbolt and Venda Gray R; m. 6/16/38 to Mary Alice Power; c. John V, II, Elizabeth (Mrs. Marshall) and Charles. Educ: Univ. of Okla. Polit. & Govt. Pos: Chmn, Washita Co. Dem. Party, Okla, 39, 43, 52 & 56; del, Dem. Nat. Conv, 64 & 68; chmn, Fourth Dist. Okla. Dem. Cent. Cmt, 66- Mil. Serv: Merchant Seaman, Navy, 43-45. Mem: Am. Asn. Petroleum Landmen; Okla. City Landmen's Asn; C. of C; Okla. Good Roads Asn; Okla. and Am. Title Asns. Rel: Presbyterian. Mailing Add: 620 N. College St, Cordell, Okla. 73632.

RAINES, THOMAS LYLE R
b. Dell Rapids, S.Dak, 2/12/38; s. Homer Thomas Raines and Margret Grau R; m. 6/28/64 to Karen Joan Wilson; c. Richard Thomas. Educ: S.Dak. State Univ, B.S. in Econ, 60. Polit. & Govt. Pos: Chmn, Brule Co. Rep. Cent. Cmt, S.Dak, 66-68. Bus. & Prof. Pos: Dist. sales rep, Am. Oil Co, 61. Mil. Serv: Entered as Airman, Air Force, 60, released as S/Sgt, 66 after serv. in S.Dak. Air Nat. Guard; Airman of the year Award, 64; Expert Carbine Marksmanship Medal; Meritorious Serv. Ribbon. Mem: Nat. Rifle Asn; Nat. Guard Enlisted Men's Asn. Rel: Methodist. 1967 Legal Res: Chamberlain, S.Dak. No mailing address available. (1967)

RAINES, WILLIE E. 'JACK' D
Mem, Tazewell Co. Dem. Cmt, Va.
b. Cedar Bluff, Va, 5/29/22; s. Thomas Samuel Raines and Jennie Rasnake R; m. 7/7/46 to Otey Anderson. Polit. & Govt. Pos: Mem, Tazewell Co. Dem. Cmt, Va. 66- Bus. & Prof. Pos: Owner, Cattle farm, 45- and W.E. Raines Supply Co, 47- Mem: K.T; Mason; RAM. Rel: Presbyterian. Mailing Add: P.O. Box 747, Richlands, Va. 24641. (1967)

RAINEY, CHARLES E. 'CHUCK' R
b. Cleveland, Ohio, 8/10/32; m. to Geraldine Squier R; c. Charles E, III and Elizabeth Marie. Educ: Emory Univ; Univ. of Fla; Sigma Alpha Epsilon. Polit. & Govt. Pos: Mem, Pinellas Co. Merit Bd, Fla; Fla. State Rep, 64-68. Bus. & Prof. Pos: With Fla. Statist. Serv, Inc. Mil. Serv: Army. Mem: Pres, Clearwater Lions Club; Am. Legion; Elks; Coun. of Mens Serv. Clubs. Rel: Catholic. Mailing Add: P.O. Box 785, Clearwater, Fla. 33517. (1967)

RAINEY, DONALD GLENN D
b. Mayfield, Ky, 8/14/31; s. Frank Paul Rainey and Maudie R; m. 6/7/53 to Geraldine Edwards; c. Denis Glenn, Julie Lynn and Jill Marie. Educ: Union Univ, B.A, 53; Ga. Inst. Tech, M.S, 54; Univ. Pittsburgh, 54-55; Sigma Alpha Epsilon. Polit. & Govt. Pos: Chmn, Gov. Campaign, Tenn, 67, Gov. field rep. and mem, Gov. Staff, 68-; del, Tenn. State Dem. Conv, 68; del, Dem. Nat. Conv, 68; mem, Tenn. Conserv. Cmn, 68- Bus. & Prof. Pos: Engr, Westinghouse Elec. Corp, 57-60; instr, Union Univ, 60-62; pres, Rainey Furniture Co, Inc, 62- Mil. Serv: Entered as Pvt, Army, 55, released as Specialist, 57, after serv. in 3rd Inf, Ft. Benning, Ga. Publ: 'Purchasing News,' 59. Mem: Purchasing Agents Asn; Retail Merchants Coun.(chmn); Retail Furniture Dealers Asn. of Tenn; v.pres, Jackson C. of C; pres, United

Fund; pres, Jackson Retail Furniture Dealers Asn; pres, W.Tenn. Lect. Club; chmn, Salute to Higher Educ. Day; chmn, Civic Center Coun; secy. exec. cmt, Brotherhood Cmn. of South. Baptist Conv. Commun. Award, Jackson State Commun. Col, 62; Cited by Jackson C. of C, 62-65; Spec. Citation, Union Univ, 63; Jackson's Young Man of Year, 65; Human Rels. Award, Lane Col, 68; Spec. Award, United Fund; Col, Gov. Staff, Tenn, 68. Rel: Baptist; Lay Preacher, Deacon and Supt, W.Jackson Baptist Church. Mailing Add: 841 Skyline Dr. Jackson. Tenn. 38301.

RAINEY, HOWARD D
b. Crisp Co, Ga, 8/21/27; s. Dallas Rainey and Essie Lewis R; m. 11/13/49 to Mildred Edge; c. Marsha Lynn and Howard Mark. Educ: Ga. Southwest. Col, 47. Polit. & Govt. Pos: Ga. State Rep, 61-69. Bus. & Prof. Pos: Income tax acct; real estate agent; retail furniture operator. Mil. Serv: Ga. Nat. Guard. Mem: Farm Bur; WOW; Lions; Jr. C. of C. Rel: Baptist. Mailing Add: 201 Eighth St. S, Cordele, Ga. 31015.

RAINS, ALBERT M. D
Nat. Dem. Committeeman, Ala.
b. DeKalb Co, Ala, 3/11/02; s. Elbert Rains and Louella Campbell R; m. 12/29/39 to Allison Blair. Educ: Jacksonville State Col; Univ. Ala. Polit. & Govt. Pos: Dist. attorney, Etowah Co, Ala, 32-36; Ala. State Rep, 42-44; U.S. Rep, Ala, 45-65; Nat. Dem. Committeeman, Ala, currently. Bus. & Prof. Pos: Attorney, Rains and Rains; chmn. of Bd, First City Nat. Bank. Publ: With Heritage So Rich, Random House, 66. Mem: Am. and Ala. Bar Asns; Lions; Mason; Newcomen Soc. Rel: Baptist. Legal Res: 221 Alpine View, Gadsden, Ala. 35901. Mailing Add: Suite 204, First City National Bank Building, Gadsden, Ala. 35901.

RAINS, HOBDY G. D
Secy, Ala. Dem. State Exec. Cmt.
b. DeKalb Co, Ala, 3/29/12; s. Will G. Rains and Ola Hamrick R; m. 9/8/45 to Constance N. Goldman. Educ: Howard Col; Univ. Ala, A.B. and LL.B. Polit. & Govt. Pos: Prison supt, Ala, 39-42 and parole officer, 42-44; secy, Ala. Dem. State Exec. Cmt, currently. Bus. & Prof. Pos: Lawyer, 45- Mil. Serv: Nat. Guard, 3 years, served in Qm. Band. Mem: Field counsel, Fed. Nat. Mortgage Asn, 50-; Judicature Soc; past pres, Etowah Co. Bar Asn; Odd Fellows; Mason; Shrine. Rel: Baptist. Mailing Add: 112 Gwindale Rd, Gadsden, Ala. 35902.

RAINS, JOE F. D
Mo. State Rep.
b. Clinton, Mo, 1/24/14; m. 2/7/46 to Yvonne W. Crouch; c. Charles Allen, Joe Bill and Jerry Wayne. Educ: Cent. Mo. State Col, pub. speaking; correspondence course in bus. Polit. & Govt. Pos: Mo. State Rep, 64- Bus. & Prof. Pos: Oil and used car bus, formerly; grocery bus, 19 years. Mil. Serv: Army, 43-46, ETO, Four Bronze Stars. Mem: VFW; Am. Legion; bd. mem, Boys Club of Am; C. of C. Sedalia Grocers Asn.(pres, two terms, state pres, one term, chmn. of bd). Rel: Baptist. Mailing Add: 700 E. Tenth St, Sedalia, Mo. 65301. (1967)

RAINVILLE, HAROLD E. R
b. Chicago, Ill, 1/30/07; s. William Van Buren Rainville and Agnes Marie Ward R; m. 8/6/32 to Mariann Rita Pack; c. Nancy (Mrs. McKiernan) and Roger Harold. Educ: Northwestern Univ, B.S. in journalism, 29; Sigma Delta Chi; Pi Kappa Alpha; Mu Alpha; Hammer & Coffin. Polit. & Govt. Pos: Publicity dir, Richard J. Lyons for Sen, 37-38, State Rep. Cent. Cmt, 38 and Dwight H. Green successful campaign for Gov, 40; campaign mgr, June Smith for Ill. Supreme Court, 41-42; asst. to Len Hall, Speakers Bur, Dewey for Pres. Campaign, 44; mgr, Everett M. Dirksen for Pres. Cmt, 44; mgr, Everett McKinley Dirksen Sen. Campaigns, 50, 56, 62 & 68; alternate del-at-lg, Rep. Nat. Conv, 52 & 64; asst. to chmn, Rep. Sen. Campaign Cmt, 52-54; admin. asst. to U.S. Sen. Everett McKinley Dirksen, 53, spec. asst, 54-69. Mem: Chicago Press Club; Boswell Club; Chicago Press Vet; Ill. Press Asn; Headline Club; Pub. Rels. Soc. Am. Amvet Nat. Award, 57; Robert A. Taft Award, Midwest Col. Young Rep, 63; Cmt. of 100 Good Am. Award, 65; Ky. Colonel; Ariz. Colonel; Nebr. Adm; Am. Airlines Adm. Rel: Congregational. Legal Res: 222 Pearson E, Chicago, Ill. 60611. Mailing Add: 8 S. Michigan Ave, Chicago, Ill. 60603.

RAINWATER, WALLACE EUGENE 'GENE' D
Ark. State Rep.
b. Fort Smith, Ark, 11/4/24; s. Wallace B. Rainwater and Nona B. Plunkett R; single. Educ: Col. of The Ozarks, 42-43; Ark. A&M Col, 43-44; Northwest. Univ, 44. Polit. & Govt. Pos: Ark. State Rep, 12th Dist, 67- Bus. & Prof. Pos: Pres, Rainwater Trucking Co. Inc, Fort Smith, Ark, currently. Mil. Serv: Entered as A/S, Navy, 42, released as Ens, 46, after serv. in Standard Landing Craft Unit 62, recalled to active duty, 50, released as Lt, 52, duty in Korea and Japan; Comdr, Naval Res. Mem: Nat. Soc. of State Legis; ROA; Exchange Club; Am. Legion; Mason; U.S. Naval Inst; Farm Bureau. Rel: Methodist. Legal Res: Route 3, Box 1924, Fort Smith, Ark. 72901. Mailing Add: 1123 S. Sixth St, Fort Smith, Ark. 72901.

RAIT, GEORGE D
N.Dak. State Sen.
b. Noonan, N.Dak, 12/5/07; s. Robert Rait and Williamina Morrison R; m. 6/19/47 to Olga Hanson. Educ: Long Creek Sch, 8 years. Polit. & Govt. Pos: Commun. committeeman, Agr. Adjustment Agency, N.Dak, 37-44; bd. mem, Farmer Home Admin, 42-46; first chmn, Soil Conserv. Dist, 46-50; N.Dak. State Sen, 65-, mem, Legis. Coun, 67-, mem, Finance and Tax Cmn, 67-, mem, Coun. of State Govt. on Social Welfare, 69- Bus. & Prof. Pos: Mem, Divide Co. Fair Asn, 47-57; pres, Burke Divide Elec. Coop, 64-69; v.pres, Upper Mo. Elec. Gen. and Trans. Coop, 64-69; mem, Midwest Elec. Consumers Asn, 64-69. Mem: Farmers Union. Soil Conservation Awards. Rel: Protestant. Mailing Add: Noonan, N.Dak. 58765.

RALEY, J. FRANK, JR. D
b. Park Hall, Md, 9/13/26; s. John F. Raley and Ruth R; m. 3/5/66 to Barbara Cook; c. Kathy and John. Educ: Georgetown Univ. Polit. & Govt. Pos: Md. State Del, 55-58; cmnr, Md. Dept. of Econ. Develop, 59-62; Md. State Sen, 63-66. Bus. & Prof. Pos: Mem. bd. trustees, St. Mary's Col. and bd. dirs, Citizens Nat. Bank, currently. Mil. Serv: Entered as Pvt, Army, 45, released as Cpl, 46, after serv. in Pac. Theater, 45; Pac. Ribbon. Mem: Pres, Lexington Park C. of C, 59; Lions; VFW; Elks; Farm Bur. Mailing Add: 9 Shangri La Dr, Lexington Park, Md. 20653.

RALEY, ROBERT A. D
S.C. State Rep.
b. Jefferson, S.C, 8/17/28; s. Mack A. Raley and Ethel Reeves R; m. 10/21/51 to Pauline Rowell; c. Paulette. Educ: Presby. Jr. Col, 45-46; Newberry Col, 49-50. Polit. & Govt. Pos: Cmnr, Chesterfield Co, S.C, 58-68; S.C. State Rep, 69- Bus. & Prof. Pos: Owner, Raley Hardware Co, 55- Mil. Serv: Entered as Seaman, Navy, 46, released as FP-3, 49, after serv. in Mine Forces; Good Conduct Medal. Mem: Mason; Farm Bur. Rel: Methodist. Mailing Add: Box 158, Jefferson, S.C. 29718.

RALPH, LEON DOUGLAS D
Calif. State Assemblyman
b. Richmond, Va, 8/20/32; s. Arthur Ralph and Leanna Woodard R; m. 9/27/51 to Martha Anna Morgan; c. Martha B, Ruth L. and Leon A. Educ: Univ. Colo; Valley Col, A.A, 61. Polit. & Govt. Pos: Chmn, Los Angeles Co. Youth for Kennedy Orgn, Calif, 60; chmn, 62nd Assembly Dist, Los Angeles Co. Dem. Cmt, 62-66; dir. field orgn, Dem. Party, Calif, 63-64; coordinator for President Johnson's Campaign, 64; admin. asst. to Speaker, Calif. House of Rep, 64-66 and consult. to Speaker; Calif. State Assemblyman, 66-, chmn, Assembly Subcmt. on Urban Probs, 68-; Cent. Los Angeles campaign mgr. for U.S. Sen. Robert F. Kennedy, 68; del, Dem. Nat. Conv, 68. Bus. & Prof. Pos: Logistics analysts, N.Am. Aviation, 59-62. Mil. Serv: Entered as Pvt, Air Force, 50, released as S/Sgt, 54, after serv. in Provost Marshalls Off, Air Defense Command Hq; Good Conduct and Nat. Defense Medals. Publ: Author, California Freeway-Housing Law for Poor People, 68. Mem: Mason; Boy Scouts; life mem, NAACP. Rel: Methodist; trustee, Grant A.M.E. Church. Mailing Add: 14013 Eadall Ave, Los Angeles, Calif. 90061.

RAMBO, AGNES McKINNELL WILSON R
Secy, Eighth Dist. Rep. Party, Mich.
b. Clydebank, Scotland, 4/27/09; d. Peter Wilson (deceased) and Margaret Richmond W.(deceased); m. 9/2/26 to Melvin Peter Rambo; c. Ellen (Mrs. Haigh), Peter C, Robert and Charles A. Educ: Exten. courses, Saginaw High Sch. and Univ. Mich. Polit. & Govt. Pos: Co. and state del. Rep. Party, Mich, 56-68; precinct dir, Saginaw Co. Rep, 58-62; chmn, Nixon Campaign, 60, coordinator, 68; Saginaw Co. Bd. Supvrs, 64-68; chmn, Saginaw Co. Campaign, Robert Griffin for Sen, 68; in charge, Romney Girls, Griffin Girls and Nixon Girls, 68. Bus. & Prof. Pos: Highland Dance Teacher, 23-68. Mem: Supt, Arts and Hobbies, Saginaw Fair, 55-69; coordinator, March of Dimes, 60-65; woman's coun. rep. to city coun, Commun. Action Exec. Bd. Mem, 61-69; bd. mem, Vis. Nurse Asn, 64-69; coordinator, Muscular Dystrophy, 66-67; personnel cmt, YWCA, 67-69; Eastern Star (Past Matron, past State Committeewoman and past pres, Woman's Coun); PTA (past pres, Wash. Chap, past officer, City Coun); Girl Scouts; Coun. of the Elderly. Mailing Add: 1911 Lincoln St, Saginaw, Mich. 48601.

RAMBO, G. DAN D
Chmn, Cleveland Co. Dem. Party, Okla.
b. Marietta, Okla, 4/23/28; s. Joseph Daniel Rambo and Mae Belle Raum R; m. 2/25/69 to Carroll Ann Imle. Educ: Univ. Okla, B.B.A. in Bus, 51, M.S. in Geol, 55 and J.D, 65; Phi Eta Sigma; Delta Sigma Pi; Sigma Gamma Epsilon; Sigma Xi; Sigma Alpha Epsilon; Delta Theta Phi; Scabbard and Blade. Polit. & Govt. Pos: Chmn, Cleveland Co. Dem. Party, Okla, 65-; co. chmn, Fred Harris Campaign Orgn; state coordinator in states of Wash. and Ore. and asst. coordinator for South. Calif, del. search oper. and campaign orgn, Humphrey-Muskie Campaign; Dem. Nat. Cmt, 68; del, Dem. Nat. Conv, 68. Mil. Serv: Entered as Pvt, Marine Corps, 46, released as Pfc, 47, after serv. in Signal Bn, First Marine Div; Army Res, 49-53, 2nd Lt. Mem: Am. Asn. Petroleum Geologists; Cleveland Co, Okla. and Am. Bar Asns; Lions; C. of C; chmn, Cleveland Co. Commun. Action Found, Inc. Rel: Presbyterian. Legal Res: 511 Chautauqua Ave, Norman, Okla. 73069. Mailing Add: 118 N. Peters, Norman, Okla. 73069.

RAMIREZ, E. ALICE D
Mem, Calif. Dem. State Cent. Cmt.
b. Los Angeles, Calif, 4/29/28; d. Vicente M. Contreras and MaRefugio Vasquez C; m. 11/25/53 to Concepcion Ramirez; c. Steven, Marie Concepcion, Alice, Anthony and Sylvia. Educ: Instituto Técnico Industrial de Agua Caliente, Mexico, 4 years; Metropolitan Bus. Col, Los Angeles, Calif, 49. Polit. & Govt. Pos: Treas, Echo Park Dem. Club, Calif, 64, pres. 65-67 & 69; mem, Calif. Dem. State Cent. Cmt, 66-; chmn, 29th Cong. Dist. Coun, 68; field rep. to Assemblyman David A. Roberti, 68-; asst. secy, Los Angeles Co. Dem. Cmt, 69. Mem: Dem. Women's Forum; Latin Alliance Club; life mem, PTA; Mexican-Am. Polit. Asn; Polit. Action League of Mexican Am. Rel: Catholic. Mailing Add: 1540½ Ewing St, Los Angeles, Calif. 90026.

RAMIREZ, FLORENCIO TORRES D
Sen, Guam Legis.
b. Agana, Guam, 11/1/15; s. Jesus Borja Ramirez and Maria Palomo Torres R; m. 4/3/37 to Josefina Sablan Leon Guerrero; c. Virginia R.(Mrs. Hughes), John Paul, Florencio T, Jr, Naomi (Mrs. Debevoise), Jesus L.G, Barbara J, Elizabeth L.G, Anthony J. and Jessica L. Educ: Guam Evening High Sch, 31-34. Polit. & Govt. Pos: Clerk, Gov-Commandant's Off, U.S. Naval Sta, Guam, 31-41; supvr. clerk, Civilian Personnel Off, Off. Commanding Gen, Marianas-Bonins Command, 45-49; Councilman, Guam Congress, Dist. of Yigo, 49-50; Sen, Guam Legis, 51-; v.chmn, Dem. Party Guam, 67- Bus. & Prof. Pos: Co-owner and mgr, Guam Style Center, Dept. Store, 47-58. Mem: Young Men's League of Guam. Rel: Roman Catholic. Legal Res: Chalan-Pago Ordot, Guam 96910. Mailing Add: P.O. Box 1498, Agana, Guam 96910.

RAMMELL, ARTHUR LEON 'ART' D
Chmn, Teton Co. Dem. Party, Idaho
b. Tetonia, Idaho, 6/17/01; s. George Fredrick Rammell and Josephene Nielsen R; m. 9/8/25 to Pearl Daniels; c. Glenda (Mrs. Robert Green) and George Daniels. Polit. & Govt. Pos: Chmn, Teton Co. Dem. Party, Idaho, currently. Bus. & Prof. Pos: Life time farmer and rancher. Rel: Latter-day Saint. Mailing Add: 402 N. Main, Tetonia, Idaho 83452.

RAMOS-LOPEZ, JOSE D
b. Bayamon, P.R, 12/2/15; m. to Aida Cartagena. Educ: Univ. of P.R; St. Johns Univ. Law Sch, LL.B, 39. Polit. & Govt. Pos: Dep. cmnr, N.Y.C. Dept. of Correction, N.Y, 53-54; referee, Workmens Compensation Bd, 55-58; N.Y. State Assemblyman, 58-67; city court judge, N.Y.C, 67- Bus. & Prof. Pos: Attorney-at-law. Mem: Bronx Co, P.R. and Pan Am. Bar Asns; Melrose House; P.R. Inst; Businessmen and Profs. Cmt. for Develop. of P.R's; Spanish Cath. Action. Mailing Add: 9722 57th Ave, Rego Park, Queens, Flushing, N.Y. 11374.

RAMOS YORDAN, LUIS ERNESTO Popular Dem, P.R.
Popular Dem. Party Floor Leader, P.R. House of Rep.
b. Ponce, P.R, 2/2/15; s. Federico Ramos Antonini and Felícita Yordán R; m. 3/13/43 to Lenabelle Smith; c. Harry Luis and Lysa Lee. Educ: Lincoln Univ, B.S, 41; Faculty of Med, Nat. Univ. Mex, M.D, 47; Grad. Sch. Pub. Health, Columbia Univ, M.P.H, 54. Polit. & Govt. Pos: Consult. indust. med. and occup. health, Dept. of Labor, P.R, 55-56 and Dept. of Health, 58-59; consult. indust. med. and safety, P.R. House of Rep, 67-68; Rep. and Popular Dem. Party Floor Leader, P.R. House of Rep, 69- Bus. & Prof. Pos: Prof. pub. health, Col. Pharm, Univ. P.R, 48-50; med. dir, Arroyo City Hosp, P.R, 49-51 and Arecibo Dist. Hosp, 51-53; pres. hosp. dr, Ramos-Yordan, Inc, 57-; pres, Lenabelle & Burhans Lab, Inc, 57- and Ramos Smith Realty, Inc, 64- Mil. Serv: Entered as Capt, Army, 56, released as Maj, 58, after serv. in Med. Corps, Chief Prev. Med, Far East Command. Publ: Pathogenesis of Sprue, Mex, 47; 'Industrial Hygiene and Occupational Disease in Puerto Rico,' Indust. Med. and Surv, 2/58; 'Health to Labor Leaders for Latin American Countries,' paper presented in the Inter-Am. Cong, Vienna, Austria, 66. Mem: V.pres, Int. Cong. of Indust. Accidents, Brussels, Belgium, 58; mem. bd. dirs, Int. Cong. for the Study of Better Living and Working Conditions, Cannes, France, 56; mem, Permanent Cmn. of Occup. Med, Int. Cong. Occup. Med. Asn, 68; Med. Asn. of P.R; Am. Indust. Med. Asn. Sport Hall of Fame, P.R. Rel: Catholic. Legal Res: 40 SO and De Diego Ave, La Riviera, P.R. 00921. Mailing Add: P.O. Box 10847, Caparra Height Station, P.R. 00922.

RAMPTON, CALVIN LEWELLYN D
Gov, Utah.
b. Bountiful, Utah, 11/6/13; s. Lewellyn S. Rampton and Janet Campbell R; m. 3/10/41 to Lucybeth Cardon; c. Margaret, Janet, Anthony and Vincent. Educ: Univ. of Utah, LL.B, 40; George Washington Univ. Polit. & Govt. Pos: Admin. asst. to U.S. Rep. J.W. Robinson, 36-38; co. attorney, Davis Co, Utah, 39-41; Gov, Utah, 65-; del, Dem. Nat. Conv, 68. Bus. & Prof. Pos: Attorney-at-law, 40. Mil. Serv: Nat. Guard, 32-37; entered as 2nd Lt, Army, 37, released as Maj, 45, after serv. in ETO and U.S. Army Claims Cmn; Res. Col, Army Field Judiciary Serv; Bronze Star; Army Commendation Ribbon with Rhineland and W.Germany Battle Stars. Mem: Int. Acad. of Trial Lawyers. Rel: Latter-day Saint. Legal Res: 1270 Fairfax Rd, Salt Lake City, Utah 84103. Mailing Add: Governor's Office, State Capitol, Salt Lake City, Utah 84111.

RAMSER, HAROLD CHARLES R
b. Ashton, S.Dak; s. Frank Ramser and Fredreika Skibbe R; m. 2/3/28 to Elizabeth Eves; c. Harold C, Jr. and Philip S. Educ: Univ. South. Calif, B.A, 30; Sigma Chi. Polit. & Govt. Pos: Pres, Los Angeles Co. Rep. Assembly, Calif, 53-54; pres, Calif. Rep. Assembly, 54-55; finance chmn, Calif. Rep. State Cent. Cmt, 58-60; mem, Nat. Rep. Finance Cmt, 58-60; mem, United Rep. Finance Cmt, Los Angeles Co, 52-, chmn, 61, 62 & 63, chmn, Budget and Expenditures Cmt, 64. Bus. & Prof. Pos: Owner and pres, Upholstery Supply Co, 33-; pres, Ramser Oil Co, 53-, Enterprise Capital Corp, 66- and Rameo Industs, 58-; v.pres, Rancho Cortamadera Corp, 68- Mem: Calif. Thoroughbred Breeders Asn.(secy. and mem. bd. dirs). Rel: Episcopal. Legal Res: 870 Stone Canyon Rd, Los Angeles, Calif. 90024. Mailing Add: 1530 E. 16th St, Los Angeles, Calif. 90021.

RAMSEY, FRANCES CRAFTON R
b. Henderson, Ky, 12/25/00; d. Clarence Cooksey Crafton and Mary Ellen Robertson C; m. to Robert R. Ramsey (deceased). Educ: George Peabody Col, B.S, 22. Polit. & Govt. Pos: Former v.pres, Madison Co. Good Govt. League, N.C; former, N.C. State Rep. Bus. & Prof. Pos: Teacher home econ. and sci, State High Sch, Shop Springs, Tenn, Henderson Co. High Sch, Henderson, Ky, 26, Anderson Col, S.C, 26-28; home demonstration agent, Madison Co. Agr. Exten. Serv, 6 years; clerk, Asheville Livestock Yard, Ashville, N.C. and Newport Livestock Yard, Newport, Tenn, 37-40; bookkeeper and mgr, Asheville Livestock Yard, 40-44; owned and operated, Gen. Merchandising Store, Walnut, N.C, 49-58; owned and operated, Dairy and Tobacco farm 57-62; retired. Mem: Madison Co. Farm Bur; Marshall Book Club; Madison Co. Home Demonstration Club; chmn, Madison Easter Seal Soc, 5 years; leader, Walnut Girl Scout Troop, 106; pres, Woman's Soc. Christian Serv, teacher study courses, treas, 6 years; past secy, Madison Co. Dairy Asn; Walnut Rep. Club; Madison Civic Improvement Prog. Rel: Methodist; Steward; Sunday Sch. Class Teacher, 30 years. Mailing Add: Walnut, N.C. 27052.

RAMSEY, HARVEY KENNETH R
Chmn, Knox Co. Rep. Cent. Cmt, Ind.
b. Vincennes, Ind, 1/21/18; s. John A. Ramsey and Nora Mayall R; m. 10/11/40 to Alma B. Newton; c. Paula A, Patrick H. and Christopher A. Educ: Ind. Univ; Phi Alpha Delta. Polit. & Govt. Pos: Prosecuting attorney, Knox Co, Ind, 51-59; town attorney, Bruceville, 56-66; city attorney, Vincennes, 64-66; chmn, Knox Co. Rep. Cent. Cmt, 64- Mil. Serv: Entered as Pvt, Air Force, 41, released as Sgt, 45; Air Medal; Asiatic-Pac. Theater and Am. Theater Ribbons. Mem: Knox Co. and Ind. Bar Asns; K. of C.(3° and 4°); Am. Legion; VFW; 40 et 8; Elks; Eagles; Harmony Soc; Farm Bur. Rel: Catholic. Legal Res: 1203 Busseron, Vincennes, Ind. 47591. Mailing Add: 118 N. Seventh, Vincennes, Ind, 47591.

RAMSEY, JAMES EDWARD D
N.C. State Rep.
b. Woodsdale, N.C, 10/19/31; s. John Talmadge Ramsey and Otey Wilkins R; m. 2/27/53 to Eunice Saunders; c. Frank Talmadge, Linda Hart, David Clark and Carl Wilkins. Educ: Univ. of N.C, Chapel Hill, A.B, 53, LL.B, 58; Univ. of Hawaii, 54; pres, Chi-Psi, 52-53. Polit. & Govt. Pos: Judge, Person Co. Recorder's Court, N.C, 58-62; N.C. State Rep, 62- Bus. & Prof. Pos: Attorney-at-law, Ramsey, Long & Jackson, 58-69. Mil. Serv: Entered as Pvt, Marine Corps Res, 50, released as Capt, 55, after serv. in Hq. Squadron, Kaneohe Bay, Hawaii, 54-55. Mem: N.C. State and Am. Bar Asns; State Bar Asn; Lions (pres, 62, zone chmn, 63, dep. dist. gov, 31G, 64); Olive Hill Ruritan Club (pres, 62); Person Co. Wildlife Club; Jr. Order of Am. Mechanics (secy, 59); Marine Corps Air Sta. Toastmasters Club, 55. Outstanding Young Man of Person Co, 62. Rel: Methodist. Legal Res: White Oak Dr, Roxboro, N.C. 27573. Mailing Add: P.O. Box 601, Roxboro, N.C. 27573.

RAMSPECK, ROBERT D
b. Decatur, Ga, 9/5/90; s. Theodore R. Ramspeck and Ida Word R; m. 10/18/16 to Nobie Clay; c. Dorothy R. (Mrs. Dunson) and Betty R. (Mrs. T.D. Webb, Jr.). Educ: Atlanta Law Sch; Delta Theta Phi. Hon. LL.D, Ohio Wesleyan Univ. Polit. & Govt. Pos: Chmn, U.S. Civil Serv. Cmn; mem, Cmn. on Polit. Activity of Govt. Personnel; Financial Adv. Cmt, Montgomery Co, Md; U.S. Rep, Ga; Ga. State Rep; prosecuting attorney, City Court of Decatur; city attorney, Decatur; chief dep. U.S. marshal; dep. clerk, DeKalb Co. Superior Court. Bus. & Prof. Pos: Secy-treas, Jones, Ramspeck & Co, 19-20; attorney-at-law, 20-29; exec. v.pres, Air Transport Asn, 46-51; v.pres, East. Air Lines, Inc, 53-62; pvt. consult, Fed. Affairs, currently. Mem: Am. Bar Asn; Pub. Rel. Soc. of Am; Mason; Shrine; Elks, Nat. Dem. Club; Aero Club of Wash; Columbia Country Club; Ft. Barrington Club. Rel: Presbyterian. Legal Res: Kensington, Md. Mailing Add: 9516 W. Stanhope Rd, Kensington, Md. 20795.

RAND, JOHN WILLIAM D
Chmn, Trimble Co. Dem. Exec. Cmt, Ky.
b. Bedford, Ky, 3/7/09; s. Dr. Biddy Orange Rand and Josie Miles R; wid; c. Dr. Bernard Owen, Carolyn and Reginald W; m. 11/28/68 to Mae Shepherd Johnson. Educ: Univ. Ky. Polit. & Govt. Pos: Chmn, Trimble Co. Dem. Exec. Cmt, Ky, 36-; Dem. presidential elector, 61 & 65; del, Dem. Nat. Conv, 68. Bus. & Prof. Pos: Founder and dir, Western Pioneer of Am, Inc, and Western Pioneer Life Ins. Co, 65- Mem: Nat. Farmers Orgn; F&AM (past Master Bedford Lodge 158); Bedford Rotary Clubs (past pres). Rel: Christian Church. Mailing Add: Rand Insurance Agency, Bedford, Ky. 40006.

RAND, WILLIAM R
Leader, 66th Assembly Dist. Rep. Party, N.Y.
b. New York, N.Y, 10/11/26; s. William Rand and Barbara Burr R; m. 8/31/57 to Paula Coudert; c. Alicia, Carley Coudert and William Coudert. Educ: Yale Col, 44-45; Harvard Col, A.B, 48; Columbia Sch. Law, LL.B, 51; Delphic Soc; Kent Moot Court. Polit. & Govt. Pos: Asst. dist. attorney, N.Y. Co, N.Y, 54-59; asst. counsel to Gov, N.Y, 59-60; justice, N.Y. Supreme Court, 62; del, Rep. Nat. Conv, 64; pres, Metrop. Rep. Club, 67-69; leader, 66th Assembly Dist. Rep. Party, 69- Bus. & Prof. Pos: Partner, Coudert Brothers, 63- Mil. Serv: Entered as A/S, Navy, 44, released as Radarman 3/C, 46, after serv. in Pac. and Japanese Theatres, 45-46; Ens, Naval Res, 50-56; Pac. Theater Ribbon with Star; Japanese Occupation Medal; Am. Theater Ribbon. Mem: N.Y.C, N.Y. State and Am. Bar Asns; Racquet and Tennis Club. Rel: Protestant. Legal Res: 1150 Fifth Ave, New York, N.Y. 10028. Mailing Add: 200 Park Ave, New York, N.Y. 10017.

RANDALL, DONALD H. R
b. Brockton; m. to Isabel A. Philbrook R, 1939; c. six. Educ: Bowdoin Col, 1930 A. B. Degree; M. A, Boston Univ, 1937; MIT. Polit. & Govt. Pos: Chmn. Halifax Rep. Town Cmt; Bd. of Assessors; Pres. Marshfield Scituak Teachers Asn; Halifax Planning Bd. Syrs; Dir. Plymouth Co. Teachers Asn. Bus. & Prof. Pos: Teacher; Mgr, Auto Exchange, 1948-55; Marshfield High Sch. Teacher-Coach, 1931, Asst. Prin, 1934-42; Teacher, Stratford, Conn. and Concord; Randolph High Sch, 1944-46, Asst. Prin, Quincy Jr. High Sch. Mem: Founder S. Shore Antique Auto Club, 1951; Pres, Silver Lake Unitarian Fellowship; Parish Cmt; Pres. Randolph Church, 1935; Pres. Standing Cmt. Brockton Church 1937-50; Halifax Farmers Club, Jones River Village Club of Kingston; Dir. Steam Auto. Club of Am. Misc: Finalist Gilmore prize speaking contest; winner 1926 Lawrence Acad. of the Pillsbury prize speaking contest; Winner Bowdoin of the DeAlva Alexander speaking contest; Fairbanks Lockwood Debating Prize; Pub. a Treatise on the Culture and Microprojection of Some Free Living Protozoa. Rel: Unitarian. Mailing Add: River St, Halifax, Mass. 02338. (1967)

RANDALL, DONALD MILLARD D
Chmn, Buchanan Co. Dem. Cmt, Mo.
b. St. Joseph, Mo, 12/1/26; s. Don C. Randall and Thelma Lester R; m. 8/10/45 to Evelyn Norris; c. Donald O, Thomas and Eddie. Educ: High sch. Polit. & Govt. Pos: Committeeman, Buchanan Co. Dem. Cmt, Mo, 62-64, chmn, 64- Bus. & Prof. Pos: Serviceman, Light & Power Co, 52- Mil. Serv: Entered as Pvt, Army, 42, released as Pfc, 45, after serv. in Mil. Police, ETO and Atlantic-Pac. Theatre, 45-46; M/Sgt, Air Force Res, 49-; several medals. Mem: Mason; VFW; Am. Legion; Eagles; IBEW. Rel: Protestant. Mailing Add: 4011 Pickett Rd, St. Joseph, Mo. 64503.

RANDALL, EARLE F. R
N.H. State Rep.
b. Tilton, N.H, 3/17/96; married. Educ: Tilton Schs. Polit. & Govt. Pos: N.H. State Rep, currently. Mem: Mason; Eastern Star. Rel: Protestant. Mailing Add: Box 185, Tilton, N.H. 03276. (1967)

RANDALL, HARRY, JR. R
N.J. State Assemblyman
b. Oradell, N.J, 1/30/27; s. Harry Randall and Regina Flanagan R; m. 6/14/52 to Katharine Mary Potter; c. Elizabeth, Victoria, Thomas and Mary-Ruth. Educ: Dartmouth Col, B.A, 49; Rutgers Univ. Law Sch, LL.B, 52; Delta Tau Delta. Polit. & Govt. Pos: Mem. coun, Westwood, N.J, 58-61, pres, 60-61; city attorney, Montvale, 61- and Westwood, 63-; sch. bd. attorney, Hillsdale and Harrington Park; N.J. State Assemblyman, 62- Bus. & Prof. Pos: Partner, Randall & Randall, Attorneys, Westwood, N.J. Mil. Serv: Entered as Pvt, Army, 44, released as Sgt, 46, after serv. in Army of Occup, Japan, 45-46. Mem: Bd. dirs, Pascack Valley Bank and Trust Co; Gr. Pascack Valley C. of C.(former pres); Bergen Co. Bar Asn.(trustee, 61-69); N.J. State Bar Asn; Am. Judicature Soc; N.J. Inst. of Munic. Attorneys; N.J. Sch. Attorneys;

Boy Scouts; North Bergen Co. Coun; finance chmn, Pascack Valley Campaign, 60-61; Westwood and Pascack Valley C. of C.(past pres); Rotary (past mem. bd. dirs, Westwood Club); VFW (past Comdr, Ralph W. Lester Post 130); Westwood Craftsmen's Club (past pres); treas, Int. Commessation Asn.(treas); Dartmouth Alumni Club of Bergen Co; Elks; Westwood Rep. Club; Bergen Co. Men's Rep. Club; United Rep. Orgn. Rel: Episcopal. Mailing Add: 67 Dean St, Westwood, N.J. 07675.

RANDALL, KENNETH ALFRED R

b. Ogden, Utah, 6/22/27; s. J. William Randall and Beatrice Pingree R; m. 8/20/52 to Jeraldine Daynes Smith; c. Nancy Kay, Shelly Marie and Tami Lee. Educ: Brigham Young Univ, B.S. in finance and banking, 49 and M.S. in econs, 58; Grad. Sch. of Banking, Rutgers, The State Univ, 60. Polit. & Govt. Pos: Mem. bd. dirs, Fed.Deposit Ins. Corp, 64-65, chmn, 65- Bus. & Prof. Pos: Employee, State Bank of Provo, Utah, 47-49, asst. cashier, 49-52, cashier, 53-54, dir, 54-59, v.pres. and cashier, 59-63 and pres, 63-64. Publ: Many articles in banking publs, including Banking Mag, The Banker, Am. Banker and Mid-Continent Banker. Mem: Past mem, Nat. Bd. of Field Advisers, Small Bus. Admin; past mem. and officer, Utah Bankers Asn; Utah Chap, Bank Admin. Inst; Mountain States Chap, Robert Morris Assoc; Am. Bankers Asn; West. Independent Bankers Asn; chmn, President's Coord. Cmt. on Financial Inst; adv. coun, Assemblies for Bank Dirs. sponsored by Found. Southwest. Methodist Univ, Dallas, Tex. Rel: Latter-day Saint. Legal Res: 1027 Fir Ave, Provo, Utah 84601. Mailing Add: 12001 Old Bridge Rd, Rockville, Md. 20852.

RANDALL, M. T. 'TED' D

Fla. State Rep.

b. Ft. Myers, Fla, 11/15/24; m. to Mary Elizabeth Bunnell; c. Elizabeth, Wallace Frank and Laura Fair. Educ: Univ. Fla, B.S.F, 50; Phi Delta Theta; F Club; lettered in track. Polit. & Govt. Pos: Past chmn, Planning Cmn, Ft. Myers, Fla; past chmn, Lee Co. Citizens Tax Coun; Fla. State Rep, 64-, v.chmn, cmt. salt water conserv. and game and fresh water fish cmt, Fla. House of Rep, 67-68. Bus. & Prof. Pos: Real estate investor. Mil. Serv: Air Corps, World War II. Mem: Past pres. and dir, Lee Co. Cattlemen's Asn, Agr. and Stabilization Cmt. and United Fund of Lee Co; past dir, Edison Pageant of Light; Ft. Myers Rod and Gun Club; Ft. Myers Gun Club; Everglades Sportsman and Conservation Club; Tallahassee Rifle and Pistol Club; Am. Ord. Soc; life mem. Nat. Rifle Asn.(cert. firearms safety instr); committeeman and counsr, Boy Scouts (past chmn. bd. of rev); Mason; Shrine; Kiwanis; Royal Palm Yacht Club; PTA; C. of C; Civil Defense; Farm Bur; Soc. Am. Foresters; v.chmn, Pro-Teens Parent-Youth Coun; dir, Lee Co. Asn. for Retarded Children. Recipient of State Audubon Soc. Award for Conservationist of the Year; Received Gene Ranker Mem. Award as State's Outstanding Conservationist; Recognized for Conservation Work by Lee Co. C. of C. and Southwest Fla. Conserv. Clearing House. Rel: Episcopal; Vestryman and past jr. warden. Legal Res: 1453 Lynwood Ave, Ft. Myers, Fla. 33901. Mailing Add: P.O. Box 1668, Ft. Myers, Fla. 33902.

RANDALL, WILLIAM I. R

Mass. State Sen.

b. Framingham, Mass, 9/13/15; s. Howard B. Randall and Helen Rice R; m. 8/31/40 to Harriet Griswold; c. William G, Jonathan C. and Eleanor R. Educ: Yale Univ, B.A, 38; Harvard Law Sch, LL.B, 41. Polit. & Govt. Pos: Selectman, Framingham, Mass, 47-50; Mass. State Sen, currently; alternate del, Rep. Nat. Conv, 68. Bus. & Prof. Pos: Partner, Sheridan & Randall, attorneys, 46- Mil. Serv: Entered as Ens, Navy, 42, released as Lt, 45, after serv. in S.Atlantic. Rel: Congregational. Mailing Add: 122 Edgell Rd, Framingham, Mass. 01701.

RANDALL, WM. J. D

U.S. Rep, Mo.

b. Independence, Mo, 7/16/09; m. to Margaret L; c. Mary (Mrs. Garland Wilson, III). Educ: Jr. Col, Kansas City, Mo; Univ. of Mo; Kansas City Sch. of Law; Univ. of Kansas City. Polit. & Govt. Pos: Judge, Jackson Co. Court, Mo, 46-59; U.S. Rep, Mo, 59- Mil. Serv: World War II, serv. in Amphibious Unit, S.W. Pac. and Philippines. Legal Res: Independence, Mo. Mailing Add: 220 C. St. S.E, Washington, D.C. 20003.

RANDOLPH, CLARENCE MARVIN, JR. D

Tenn. State Rep.

b. Nashville, Tenn, 12/6/27; s. Clarence Marvin Randolph Sr. and Hattie Baugus R; m. 11/24/57 to Carolyn Sue Marshall; c. Clarence Marvin III and Charles Marshall. Educ: Union Univ, B.S, 49; Sigma Alpha Epsilon. Polit. & Govt. Pos: Tenn. State Rep, 69- Bus. & Prof. Pos: Randolph Hardware Co, Milan, Tenn, 54- Mil. Serv: Entered as Pfc, Air Force, 50, released as S/Sgt, 52, after serv. in 516th Troop Carrier Wing. Mem: Mason; v.pres, Tenn. Retail Hardware Asn; Am. Legion; dir, Milan C. of C; Elks. Rel: Methodist. Legal Res: Jackson Hwy, Milan, Tenn. 38358. Mailing Add: P.O. Box 86, Milan, Tenn. 38358.

RANDOLPH, JENNINGS D

U.S. Sen, W.Va.

b. Salem, W.Va, 3/8/02; s. Ernest Randolph and Idell Bingman R; m. Feb, 1933 to Mary Katherine Babb; c. Jennings, Jr. and Frank Babb. Educ: Salem Col, grad, 24; Tau Kappa Alpha. Hon. LL.D, Davis and Elkins Col, 39, Univ. Pittsburgh, 65, Alderson Broaddus Col, 66, W.Va. Univ, Milton Col, Waynesburg Col. and W.Va. Wesleyan Col, 67; hon. Litt.D, Southeast. Univ, 40; hon. HH.D, W.Va. State Col, 64; hon. Dr. Aeronaut. Sci, Salem Col, 43; hon. L.H.D, Maryville Col, 66. Polit. & Govt. Pos: Mem, Labor Dept. Anniversary Cmt; mem, President's and W.Va. Gov. Cmts. on Employ. of the Handicapped; U.S. Sen, W.Va, 58-; del, Dem. Nat. Conv, 68. Bus. & Prof. Pos: Ed, Green and White and The Message, Salem, W.Va, 22-23; mem. ed. staff, Clarksburg Daily Telegram, 24-25; assoc. ed, W.Va. Rev, 25-26; hon. trustee, Davis and Elkins Col. and prof. of pub. speaking and journalism, 26-32; trustee, Salem Col; asst. to pres. and dir. pub. rels, Capital Airlines, 47-58; former co-owner and assoc. ed, Randolph Enterprise-Rev, Elins; mem. adv. coun, Careers Abroad Prog; former faculty mem, Leadership Training Inst; former instr. effective speaking, Southeast. Univ. and dean, Col. Bus. and Financial Admin. Publ: 'Going to Make A Speech?' Capital Airlines, 48; co-author, Mr. Chairman, Ladies and Gentlemen, Judd and Detweiler, Inc, 39; contributor, nat. magazines. Mem: Pres, W.Va. Intercollegiate Press Asn, 22-23; bd. gov, Nat. United Serv. Orgn, 58-59; dir, Police Boys' Club, Big Bros, Cent. Br. YMCA, Elkins and W.Va. C. of C. and Claude Worthington Benedum Found; hon. mem, Kiwanis; Rotary United Sportsmen Am; Lamplighters; Transportation Asn. Am. Bd. Dirs. Alumni and Am. Asn. Airport Exec; Elkins YMCA and nat. sponsoring cmt, Youth Gov. Conf, 62-63; Moose; int. counsr. and former gov. W.Va. Clubs, Lions; Citizens Crime Cmn. Metrop. Wash; adv. bd, Nat. Coun. for Adv. Small Cols; Nat. adv. cmt, United Bus. Sch. Asn; former v.pres. and dir, Nat. Aeronaut. Asn; Nat. Adv. Coun, Embry-Riddle Aeronaut. Inst; Univ. Aviation Asn; Elkins Pilot's Club; pres, Cong. Flying Club, 44-45; former treas. and pres. airport div, Am. Road Builders Asn; Elkins Indust. Develop. Corp; Mt. State Visitors Bur; Upper Monongahela Valley Asn; W.Va. Sportsmen Unlimited; W.Va. Press Asn; Nat. Press Club; 3½ Club; Univ. Club; Salem Col. Alumni; Varsity Club; People to People; Int. Platform Asn; W.Va. Acad. Sci; W.Va. Soc. of D.C; U.S. Capitol Hist. Soc; W.Va. and Randolph Co. Hist. Socs; adv. cmt, Nat. Blinded Vet. Asn; Nat. Asn. Physically Handicapped. W.Va. Son of Year Award, W.Va. Soc. of D.C, 60; Civic Merit Award, Randolph Co. Hist. Soc, 48; Distinguished Serv. Awards, Nat. Fedn. Blind and Blinded Vet. Asn, 56 and 61 and Pres. Cmt. on Employ. Handicapped, 56 and 61; Man of Year Award, Air Line Traffic Asn, 53; awards, All Am. Aviation, 39, Wash. Bd. Trade, 45, Advert. Club, 50, Capital Airlines, 52, Wash. Reciprocity Club, 55, Wash. Host Lions Club, 56, Nat. Coun. YMCA, 58, B'nai B'rith, 61, VFW, 62, N.Y. State Cmn. for Blind, 63, D.C. Trucking Asn. and State of Israel Bonds, 65, Am. Humanics Found and W.Va. Credit Union League, 66; Youth Appreciation Award, Bowling Proprietors Asn. Am, 63; W.Virginian of the Year Award, Gazette-Mail, 64; Am. Road Builders Asn. Award for Exceptional Serv. to the Hwy. Prog, 65; Nat. Aviation Club Award for Achievement, 66; W.Va. Wesleyan Col. Founders Award, 66; Distinguished Serv. Award for Dedicated Leadership and Serv. to Develop. and Progress of Nation's Hwys, Nat. Limestone Inst, 67; Eng. News-Record Award, 68; W.Va. Speaker-of-the-Year Award, W.Va. Univ. Chap, Delta Sigma Rho-Tau Kappa Alpha, 68; Distinguished Serv. Award for Contribution to Am. Educ, Legis. Cmn. of Nat. Educ. Asn, 68; Gold Medal of Merit, VFW of U.S, 69. Rel: Seventh Day Baptist. Legal Res: Elkins, W.Va. 26241. Mailing Add: 4608 Reservoir Rd. N.W, Washington, D.C. 20007.

RANDOLPH, LEONARD WRAY D

b. Leon, Iowa, 8/1/26; s. Everett Lawrence Randolph and Ferne Pace R; m. 10/17/53 to Gloria Janice Shafer; c. Jan Theodora and Ann Elizabeth. Educ: Drake Univ, 47-50. Polit. & Govt. Pos: Spec. asst, Gov. Lawrence, Pa, 59-63; admin. asst, Rep. Rooney, Pa, 63-68; asst. dir, Nat. Found on the Arts and Humanities, currently. Bus. & Prof. Pos: Announcer, KCBC and KWDM, Des Moines, 46-52; feature writer and educ. ed, Pocono Record, Stroudsburg, Pa, 51-58; exec. dir, The Shapp Found, 63. Mil. Serv: Entered as Pvt, Army, 44, released as T-5, 46, after serv. in 184th Inf, 7th Div; Mil. Occupation of Korea and Combat Inf. Badge. Publ: Survey of Educ. Opportunities in Monroe Co, Pennsylvania; 'War on Poverty in Pennsylvania' a 60 minute film produced by the Shapp Found. Mem: Broadcasting Soc; Burro Club; Educ. Writers of Am. Legal Res: Stroudsburg, Pa. 18360. Mailing Add: 1800 G. St. N.W, Washington, D.C. 20506. (1967)

RANDOLPH, PAUL J. R

Ill. State Rep.

b. Logan Co, Ill, 9/5/05. Educ: Millikin Univ; Univ. Ill. Polit. & Govt. Pos: Ill. State Rep, 54- Bus. & Prof. Pos: Oil. Mem: Mason; Scottish Rite; Shrine; Lawson YMCA Bd; Moose; Kiwanis; Lake Shore Club; Chicago Farmers; Exec. Club. Rel: Presbyterian. Mailing Add: 850 N. DeWitt Pl, Chicago, Ill. 60611.

RANER, GUY HAVARD, JR. D

Mem, Calif. Dem. State Cent. Cmt.

b. Vicksburg, Miss, 11/7/19; s. Guy Havard Raner, Sr. and Caroline Lorraine Campbell R; m. 12/13/41 to Jane Anne Law; c. James G. Daniel L. and Janice A. Educ: Univ. of Miss, 37-40; Univ. of Mo, Columbia, B.J, 42; Univ. of Calif, Los Angeles, Sec. Teaching Credentials, 46; Univ. of South. Calif, M.A. in Polit. Sci, 56; San Fernando Valley State Col, Sec. Admin. Credentials, 65; Tau Kappa Alpha. Polit. & Govt. Pos: Cand, Calif. State Assembly, 64th Dist, 68; mem, Calif. Dem. State Cent. Cmt, 68-; mem, Los Angeles Co. Dem. Cent. Cmt, currently. Bus. & Prof. Pos: Govt. and hist. teacher and chmn. soc. studies dept, Canoga Park High Sch, Los Angeles City Unified Sch. Dist, 46- Mil. Serv: Entered as Yeoman 3/C, Naval Res, 42, released as Lt, 55, after serv. in Patrol Squadron 94, Fleet Air Wing 16, Harvard Commun. Sch, U.S.S. Bougainville, U.S.S. Shangri-La and Sch. of Naval Justice, Newport, R.I, World War II, 42-45, Brazil, Pac; Korean War, 51-52; Atlantic and Pac. Area Ribbons; Reserve Medal. Publ: Co-ed, Land Of The Free And Its Critics, Calif. Teachers Asn, 67; 'Polling the Teachers,' Calif. Soc. Sci. Rev, 10/64; 'How "Free" is the Free Secondary School?,' Jour. of Sec. Educ, 3/65. Mem: Nat. Coun. and Calif. Coun. for the Soc. Studies; South. Calif. Soc. Sci. Asn (pres); Calif. Teachers Asn; Coun. on Consumer Info; Nat. Educ. Asn; UN Asn; NAACP; Am. Fedn. of Teachers, AFL-CIO; Am. For Dem. Action; Calif. Dem. Coun. Recipient of JFK Award for Meritorius Serv. in the Field of Human Rels. Mailing Add: 22331 Devonshire St, Chatsworth, Calif. 91311.

RANEY, JAMES W. 'JIM' R

b. Fordyce, Ark, 5/8/34; s. James T. Raney and Helen Von Malcom R; m. 12/21/52 to Norma Jean Williams; c. Marla Lise, James Scott, Norman Todd and John David. Educ: Ark. A&M Col, B.S.E, 61. Polit. & Govt. Pos: Ark. State Sen, 63-66. Mil. Serv: Entered as Airman, Air Force, 52, released as Airman 1/C, 56, after serv. in 1273 AACS, France; Good Conduct and Nat. Defense Serv. Medals. Mem: Mason; Am. Legion; U.S. C. of C; Warren C. of C. All-dist. 4A football. Rel: Missionary Baptist. 1967 Legal Res: Warren, Ark. No mailing address available. (1967)

RANGEL, CHARLES B. D

N.Y. State Assemblyman

b. N.Y.C, 6/11/30; s. Ralph Rangel and Blanche Wharton R; m. 7/26/62 to Alma Carter; c. Steven. Educ: N.Y. Univ, B.S, 57; St. John's Law Sch, LL.B, 60 and J.D, 68; Phi Alpha Delta; Alpha Phi Alpha. Polit. & Govt. Pos: Asst. U.S. Attorney, N.Y. Dept. Justice, 61; counsel to Assembly Speaker, N.Y. Assembly; counsel, N.Y.C. Housing Authority and President Johnson's Draft Revision Cmt; N.Y. State Assemblyman, 72nd Assembly Dist, Harlem, 67- Mil. Serv: Entered as Recruit, Army, 48, released as Sgt, 52, after serv. in Second Inf. Div, Korea, 50-51; Purple Heart; Bronze Star; 4 Battle Stars; Presidential Citations. Mem: N.Y. State Bar Asn; 369th Vet. Asn; Elks; NAACP; CORE; Nat. Asn. State Legislators; Commun. Planning Bd.(borough pres, adv. cmt). Commun. Awards, Best Legislator, Father of the Year. Rel: Catholic. Legal Res: 74 W. 132nd St, New York, N.Y. 10037. Mailing Add: 30 Vesey St, New York, N.Y. 10007.

RANKIN, HARRY LONGINO, JR. R
Chmn, Marion Co. Rep. Exec. Cmt, Miss.
b. Columbia, Miss, 11/4/26; s. Harry Longino Rankin and Tommye Bridewell R; m. 7/17/50 to Olive Elizabeth Clower; c. Marianne, Thomas Stephen Clower, Elizabeth Carolyn and Christopher Harry Lee. Educ: Univ. Ala, Tuscaloosa, B.S. in Banking, 48; La. State Univ. Sch. of Banking of the South, 59; Harvard Univ. Sch. of Bus, sr. bank officers seminar, 60; Army Finance Sch, 50; Air Command and Staff Sch, Maxwell Air Force Base, Ala, Squadron Officers course, 51; Officers Training Sch, Shepard Air Force Base, Tex, 64; Nat. War Col, Wash, D.C, defense strategy seminar, 65; Pi Tau Chi; Sigma Chi; Alpha Chi Omega. Polit. & Govt. Pos: Col, Miss. Militia, 48; mem, Nat. States Rights Party, 48-49; chmn, Marion Co. Rep. Exec. Cmt, 59- Bus. & Prof. Pos: Teller, Citizens Bank, Columbia, Miss, 48-50, cashier, 56-57, v.pres, 52-62 & 69-; exec. v.pres, 62-69; pres, The Rankin Co, 69- Mil. Serv: Cadet Pvt, U.S.C.C, U.S.M.A, 45; re-entered as 2nd Lt, Air Force, 50, released as Capt, 55, after serv. in Japan; Maj, Miss. Air Nat. Guard, 63-; World War II Victory, Nat. Defense Serv, Korean Serv, Air Force Longevity, Air Force Res, and UN Serv. Medals. Mem: Pres, Miss. Chartered Savings and Loan Asn, 61-62; Sigma Delta Pi; v.pres, Miss. Div, Am. Automobile Asn, 59-; state exec. cmt, Asn. of Citizens Coun, 58-; Am. Legion; VFW; Air Force Asn; Nat. Guard Asns. of the U.S. and Miss; Shrine; Scottish Rite; K.T; Mason; Miss. Farm Bur; Sons of Confederate Vet; Order of the Stars and Bars; C. of C; Rotary. UDC Award; Cross of Mil. Serv, World War II and Korea. Rel: Episcopal. Legal Res: 1927 Orchard Dr, Columbia, Miss. 39429. Mailing Add: P.O. Box 391, Columbia, Miss. 39429.

RANKIN, JEANNETTE R
b. Mont, 6/11/80; d. John Rankin and Olive Pickering R; single. Educ: Univ. Mont, B.S, 02. Polit. & Govt. Pos: U.S. Rep, Mont, 17-19 & 41-43. Mem: Inst. of Social Logic. First woman ever elected to U.S. House of Rep. Legal Res: Missoula, Mont. 59801. Mailing Add: Watkensville, Ga. 30677. (1967)

RANKIN, MARTHA KELLY R
Finance Chmn, Greene Co. Rep. Party, Ohio
b. Springfield, Ohio, 10/19/96; d. Edwin Stewart Kelly and Martha Linn K; m. 5/5/42 to Stacy Barcroft Rankin; c. Fleury Velie (Mrs. Don Mackie) and Damaris Velie (Mrs. Thomas Story Jenks). Educ: Finch Sch, N.Y, grad, 16. Polit. & Govt. Pos: Chairwoman, Greene Co. Rep. Party, Ohio, 50-62 and finance chmn, 62-; del, Rep. Nat. Conv, 68. Bus. & Prof. Pos: Farmer, currently. Mil. Serv: Army Nurse, Wright-Patterson Air Force Base, 17, Ann Morgan Unit in France, 18-19; Walter Reed Hosp, Wash, D.C; Medaille de Reconnaissance, French Govt, 19. Mem: League of Women Voters; Farm Bur; Garden Club of Am. Red Cross Serv. Award. Rel: Episcopal. Mailing Add: Whitehall Farm, Yellow Springs, Ohio 45387.

RANKIN, OTWELL C. D
Chmn, Kenton Co. Dem. Exec. Cmt, Ky.
b. Harrison Co, Ky, 6/23/16; s. Grover C. Rankin and Alice Mae Townsend R; m. 12/20/40 to Katherine Prather; c. Richard, Thomas and Harry. Educ: East. State Col, Ky, B.S, 38; Xavier Univ, Ohio; Univ. Cincinnati; Phi Kappa Tau. Polit. & Govt. Pos: Chmn, Kenton Co. Dem. Exec. Cmt, Ky, 59-; mem. bd. of dirs, Fed. Home Loan Bank,Cincinnati, 63-; alternate del, Dem. Nat. Conv, 68. Bus. & Prof. Pos: V.chmn. bd. of dirs, YMCA, 64- Mem: C. of C. Rel: Methodist. Mailing Add: 114 Graves Ave, Erlanger, Ky. 41018.

RANKIN, RICHARD J. R
Chmn, Madison Co. Rep. Cent. Cmt, Mont.
b. Mingo, Iowa, 9/27/32; s. Daniel Thomas Rankin and Flossie May Hole R; m. 11/10/62 to Donna Ray Balkovetz; c. Peri Gae, Shelly Rose and Rita Jean. Educ: Billings Bus. Col, 56-58; charter pres, Circle K Club, Billings Bus. Col, 57. Polit. & Govt. Pos: Finance chmn, Madison Co. Rep. Cent. Cmt, Mont, 64-66, chmn, 66-; precinct committeeman, Madison Co. Rep. Party, 66- Bus. & Prof. Pos: Staff acct, Peat Marwick Mitchell & Co, Billings, Mont, 59-61; owner and mgr, Rankin Realty & Ins, Ennis, 62- Mil. Serv: Entered as Seaman Recruit, Navy, 52, released as RMSN, 53, after serv. in NATO Command, South. Europe. Mem: Mont. and Nat. Asns. of Real Estate Bd; state dir, Mont. Asn. of Realtors, 67-69; VFW; AF&AM; Elks. Rel: Presbyterian. Mailing Add: Box 686, Ennis, Mont. 59729.

RANNEY, THOMAS POLLOCK R
S.Dak. State Rep.
b. Aberdeen, S.Dak, 5/3/37; s. Paul T. Ranney and Elizabeth J. Antelman R; m. 4/25/65 to Rosemary Hafner; c. Bruce Daniel. Educ: Univ. S.Dak, B.A, 59 and LL.D, 63; Univ. Wyo, 61; Delta Theta Phi; Sigma Alpha Epsilon. Polit. & Govt. Pos: Dep. states attorney, Pennington Co, S.Dak, 63-64; racing judge, S.Dak. Racing Cmn, 63-66; city attorney, Rapid City, 65-; S.Dak. State Rep, 67- Mil. Serv: Entered as 2nd Lt, Army Res, 60, 1st Lt, Inf, at present. Publ: 'Search and Seizure, Return and Execution of Warrants,' S.Dak. Law Rev, Spring, 1963. S.Dak. and Pennington Co. Bar Asns; Am. Judicature Soc; Sect. on Local Govt, Am. Bar Asn; Elks; Mason; Shrine; Consistory; Jaycees. Rel: Protestant. Legal Res: 3016 Meadowbrook Dr, Rapid City, S.Dak. 57701. Mailing Add: P.O. Box 2031, Rapid City, S.Dak. 57701.

RANNEY, ZILPAH FAY R
b. Pittsfield, Vt, 5/1/90. Educ: Univ. Vt, B.A, 16; Boston Univ. Col. Lib. Arts, M.A, 38; Delta Delta Delta. Polit. & Govt. Pos: Mem, Women's Rep. Club, Vt, currently; chmn, Women's Rep. Club, Pittsfield, currently; past state secy, Order Women Legislators; trustee, Pub. Moneys, currently; former secy. and treas, Rep. Town Cmt, chmn, currently; Vt. State Rep, 61-65. Bus. & Prof. Pos: Former secy-treas, Mt. Wilcox Water Asn, Inc; retired high sch. teacher; trustee, Pub. Libr, Pittsfield, Vt, currently. Mem: Nat. and Mass. Retired Teachers Asn; Am. Asn. Univ. Women; Nat. Soc. New Eng. Women; Ladies Union; DAR; Nat. Fedn. Rep. Women; Nat. Order Women Legislators; Int. Platform Asn; Cascadnas Garden Club; 251 Club of Vt. Rel: Methodist. Mailing Add: Park Circle Dr. Pittsfield. Vt. 05762.

RANSOHOFF, BABETTE STRAUSS R
b. New York, N.Y, 3/25/04; d. Martin Strauss and Annie Jackson S; m. 2/10/26 to Arthur Lee Ransohoff; c. Martin, Jackson and Barbara (Mrs. Howard Burnett). Educ: Vassar Col, B.A, 25. Polit. & Govt. Pos: Mem, Charter Rev. Cmn, Stamford, Conn, 44-48, mem, Stamford Housing Authority, 44-50, clerk and mem. bd. representatives, 49-54 and trustee, Ferguson Libr, 65-; mem, State Rep. Platform Cmt, 50; chmn, Fairfield Co. Eisenhower-Nixon Campaign, 56; v.chmn. and mem. exec. cmt, Rep. Nat. Cmt, 59-65 and mem. Platform Cmt, 60; campaign chmn, Lowell P. Weicker, Jr. for U.S. Rep, Conn, 68. Publ: What's The U.S. to You? A Quiz, League of Women Voters of U.S, 48; 'Is Politics Your Job?,' The Methodist Woman, 50; Where Does Christian Citzenship Start?, Methodist Church, 50. Mem: Nat. Soc. for Prevention of Blindness; trustee, Stamford Mus; former bd. mem, YWCA, Family & Children's Servs. and various Rep. orgns. New Orleans Golf Champion, 30. Mailing Add: Wyndover Lane N, Stamford, Conn. 06902.

RANSOM, EDWARD DUANE R
b. Minot, N.Dak, 1/3/14; s. Edward M. Ransom and Gladys Root R; m. 10/6/40 to Margaret E. Phelps; c. Edward P, Susan M, Richard M. and Mary A. Educ: Minot State Teachers Col, 32-34; Univ. Mich, A.B, 36 and J.D, 38. Polit. & Govt. Pos: U.S. Del, Int. Maritime Law Conf, 59; gen. counsel, Fed. Maritime Bd. & Maritime Admin, 55-57. Prof. Pos: Lawyer, Lillick, Geart, Wheat, Adams & Charles, San Francisco, 38-41, 45-; partner, 50-55, 57- Mil. Serv: Lt. Comdr, Navy, 41-45. Mem: Am. Bar Asn, v.chmn, cmt. on Maritime transportation, 63, chmn, 64; Calif, Fed. and San Francisco Bar Asns; Maritime Law Asn, exec. cmt, 57-60, cmt. on Limitation Liability, cmt. on Comite-Maritime Int; Univ. Mich. Alumni Asn, dir, San Francisco Bay Area. Admitted to Calif. Bar, 39; also U.S. Supreme Court, Circuit Court Appeals for D.C. and 9th Circuit, ICC. Legal Res: 646 Haddon Rd, Oakland, Calif. Mailing Add: 311 California St, San Francisco, Calif. 94104. (1967)

RANSON, SAMUEL LEE R
Chmn, Buckingham Co. Rep. Party, Va.
b. Dillwyn, Va, 2/21/23; s. Radford Bennett Ranson, Sr. and Norah Estelle Fitzgerald R; single. Educ: Dillwyn High Sch, Va, grad, 40. Polit. & Govt. Pos: Chmn, Buckingham Co. Rep. Party, Va, 64- Bus. & Prof. Pos: Merchant, Ranson Bros, Dillwyn, Va, 46- Mil. Serv: Entered as Pvt, Army, 42, released as Cpl, 46, after serv. in Signal Corps, U.S, 42-46; Sharp Shooter, Good Conduct and Am. Victory Medals. Mem: State and Regional Defense Airlift Plan Fleet Pilot; Lions; Am. Legion; RAM (past High Priest); K.T; Shrine; Va. Farm Bur; Civil Air Patrol (squadron comdr, 54-68, major); Mason (past Master, Illustrious Master and Annointed High Priest, 3 times). Rel: Baptist. Legal Res: Dillwyn, Va. 23936. Mailing Add: P.O. Box 72, Dillwyn, Va. 23936.

RAPER, JOHN FREDERICK, JR. Non-Partisan
b. Mapleton, Iowa, 6/13/13; s. John Frederick Raper and Anna Selma Peterson R; m. 8/4/39 to Nell Marie Chesler; c. Thomas J, Larry H, Robert B. and Charles R. Educ: Drake Univ, 34-35; Univ. Wyo, LL.B, 36; Sigma Nu. Polit. & Govt. Pos: City attorney, Sheridan, Wyo, 49-53; U.S. Attorney, Dist. of Wyo, 53-61; Attorney Gen, Wyo, 63-66; Dist. Judge, Wyo, 66- Bus. & Prof. Pos: Private practice of law, 36-40, 45-50, 51-53 and 61-63. Mil. Serv: Entered as 1st Lt, Army, 40, released as Lt. Col, 45, Pac; also serv. in Korea, 50-51 as Commanding Officer, 300th FA Bn; Presidential Unit Citation; Silver Star; Commendation Medal; Am, Pac. and Korean Theater Ribbons. Mem: Am. Legion; VFW; Rotary; AF&AM; Consistory; Shrine; Eastern Star. Rel: Presbyterian. Mailing Add: 3733 Dover Rd, Cheyenne, Wyo. 82001.

RAPPANA, DUANE Conservative
Minn. State Rep.
b. Minneapolis, Minn, 1/21/24; s. Archie W. Rappana and Hilda Mattila R; m. 7/2/48 to Jean Lorain Modahl; c. Diane Jean and Richard Duane. Educ: Univ. Minn, B.A, 48. Polit. & Govt. Pos: City councilman, Third Dist, Duluth, Minn, 59-64; Minn. State Rep, 60th Dist, 64- Mil. Serv: Navy, 42-46, pilot; jet fighter pilot, Korea, 2 years; Comdr, Naval Res. Mem: Kiwanis; C. of C; W. End Bus. and Civic Club. Rel: Protestant. Mailing Add: 62 Pike Lake, Duluth, Minn. 55811.

RAPPAPORT, SAMUEL D
b. Philadelphia, Pa, 8/25/32; s. Joseph Rappaport and Goldie Evans R; div. Educ: Temple Univ, A.B, 54; Columbia Univ, LL.B, 57; Univ. Pa. Grad. Sch, 60-61. Polit. & Govt. Pos: Del. & co-chmn, Cmt. on Home Rule of Local Govt, Pa. Constitutional Conv, 67-68; spec. adv, Pa. Local Govt, Cmn, 68-; alternate del, Dem. Nat. Conv, 68. Bus. & Prof. Pos: Lawyer, Rappaport & Furman, Esqs, 60-; assoc. consult, Div. Housing and Community Renewal, State of N.Y, 63-64. Mil. Serv: Entered as recruit Army, 57, released as Sp-4, 59, after serv. in Third Med. Bn, ETO, 58-59. Mem: Pa, Phila. and Am. Bar Asns; Am. Acad. Polit. & Soc. Sci; B'nai B'rith. Admitted to practice, N.Y, 57 and Pa, 60. Rel: Jewish. Mailing Add: 812 Pine St, Philadelphia, Pa. 19107.

RAPPELET, ALBERT OTTO, 'A. O.' D
La. State Rep.
b. New Orleans, La, 9/18/10; s. Rene St. Aubin Rappelet and Evelina Terrebonne R; m. 6/10/50 to Velvina Vegas; c. Charles Gerald. Geraldine (Mrs. Bourgeois), Sharon Anne and René A.O. Educ: Warren Easton Boys High Sch, 3 years. Polit. & Govt. Pos: Field supvr, La. State Dept. Wildlife & Fisheries, 40-42; La. State Sen, 12th Sen. Dist, 48-52, 56-64; chmn. bd, Gr. Lafourche Port Cmn, 60-; La. State Rep, Eighth Rep. Dist, 68- Bus. & Prof. Pos: Self-employed retail dealer, 30-40; rice plantation owner, 42-45; gen. contractor, 45-; bldg. material dealer, 47- Mem: Int. Found. Exceptional Children (chmn. bd, 60-63); YMBC. Rel: Methodist. Mailing Add: P.O. Box 217, Galliano, La. 70354.

RARICK, JOHN RICHARD D
U.S. Rep, La.
b. Goshen, Ind,1/29/24; m. to Marguerite Gertrude Pierce; c. John Richard,

Jr, Carolyn Cherie and Laurie Lee. Educ: Ball State Teachers Col; La. State Univ; Tulane Univ, LL.B. Polit. & Govt. Pos: Dist. judge, La, 61-66; U.S. Rep, La, 67- Bus. & Prof. Pos: Attorney. Mil. Serv: Army; 2 Bronze Stars; Purple Heart; Fleur de Guerre, Belgium. Mem: Past Pres, Toastmasters; dir, Audubon Coun; Am. Legion; DAV; VFW; Civitans; Mason; Farm Bur. Rel: Protestant. Legal Res: Baton Rouge, La. Mailing Add: 1525 Longworth House Office Bldg, Washington, D.C. 20515.

RASKOSKY, EDWARD J. D
Polit. & Govt. Pos: Ind. State Rep, -66; Lake Co. dep. prosecuting attorney. Bus. & Prof. Pos: Lawyer. Mil. Serv: Navy. Mem: Eagles; Elks; Am. Legion; VFW. Rel: Catholic. 1967 Legal Res: 1042 Eaton St, Hammond, Ind. No mailing address available. (1967)

RASMUSEN, HOLGER B. R
Wis. State Sen.
b. Superior, Wis, 4/26/94. Educ: Drake Univ, Ph.G, 16. Polit. & Govt. Pos: Mayor, Spooner, Wis, 42-48; co. chmn, Civilian Defense; mem, Co. Sch. Cmt, 48-52; Wis. State Assemblyman, 49-55; Wis. State Sen, 56-58 & 62- Bus. & Prof. Pos: Pharmacist; in drugstore bus, 54 years; owner and operator, drugstore, 47 years. Mil. Serv: Navy, World War I. Mem: Sch. Bd, 24-32; active in fraternal and civic orgns. Mailing Add: 722 Franklin Ave, Spooner, Wis. 54801. (1967)

RASMUSON, ELMER EDWIN R
b. Yakutat, Alaska, 2/15/09; s. Edward Anton Rasmuson and Jenny Olson R; m. 11/4/61 to Col. Mary Louise Milligan; c. Edward, Lile (Mrs. Gibbons) and Judy. Educ: Harvard Univ, B.S, 30, A.M, 34; Phi Beta Kappa. Polit. & Govt. Pos: Officer, N.Y. Young Rep. Club, 35-39; pres, Anchorage Rep. Club, Alaska, 45-46; councilman, Anchorage, 45, chmn, City Planning Cmn, 46-49 and mayor, 64-67; mem. bd. regents, Univ. Alaska, 50-69; hon. Swedish consul, Alaska, 50-; Rep. cand. for U.S. Senate, Alaska, 68. Bus. & Prof. Pos: Chief Acct, Nat. Investors Corp, N.Y.C, 33-35; prin, Arthur Andersen & Co, 35-43; pres, Nat. Bank of Alaska, Anchorage, 43-65, chmn. bd, 65- Mem: State Soc. CPA, N.Y. and Alaska; Arctic Inst. N.Am; Elks; Mason; Pioneers of Alaska; Rotary; Explorers, Harvard. Outstanding Civilian Serv. Award from Secy. of Army; Order of Vasa, King of Sweden. Rel: Presbyterian. Legal Res: 824 W. 25th, Anchorage, Alaska 99503. Mailing Add: Box 600, Anchorage, Alaska 99501.

RASMUSSEN, A.L. 'SLIM' D
Mayor, Tacoma, Wash.
b. Everett, Wash, 1909; m. to Eleanor; c. four. Educ: Tacoma Pub. Schs. Polit. & Govt. Pos: Wash. State Rep, eight terms; former Wash. State Sen; Mayor, Tacoma, currently. Bus. & Prof. Pos: R.R. machinist, North. Pac. R.R. Mailing Add: 4031 Pacific Ave, Tacoma, Wash. 98408. (1967)

RASMUSSEN, CLARK R. D
Chmn, Iowa Dem. State Cent. Cmt.
b. Kimballton, Iowa, 7/11/34; s. H. Henning Rasmussen and Martha Jenson R; m. 9/3/56 to Joanne L. Disterhoft; c. Gregory D, Daniel H, John L. and Matthew K. Educ: Drake Univ, B.S, 57; Delta Sigma Pi. Polit. & Govt. Pos: Mem, Judicial Nominating Cmn, Second Judicial Dist; nat. committeeman, Young Dem. Clubs of Iowa, 60-62; former Iowa State Rep; exec. secy, Iowa Dem. State Cent. Cmt, formerly and chmn, currently; del, Dem. Nat. Conv, 68. Mil. Serv: Entered as Pvt, Army, 54, released as Pfc, 56. Rel: Lutheran. Mailing Add: 524 32nd, W. Des Moines, Iowa 50317. (1967)

RASMUSSEN, DONALD WOODROW D
b. Beresford, S.Dak, 4/25/19; s. A. Edward Rasmussen and Christine Anderson R; m. 1/25/44 to Mary Ellen Burns; c. Patricia and Dean. Educ: Yankton Col, B.A, 41; Univ. S.Dak, M.A, 49. Polit. & Govt. Pos: Clay Co. chmn, McGovern for Senate Cmt, S.Dak, 58; state chmn. for Kennedy-Johnson, 60; chmn, Gov. Cmt. for Children and Youth; chmn, Clay Co. Dem. Party. Bus. & Prof. Pos: Dir. of speech and drama, Huron Col, S.Dak, 46-50; teacher, Vermillion High Sch, 51-62, dir. of guid, 61-66; dir. of counseling serv, Yankton Col. Mil. Serv: Entered as Pvt, Army Air Corps, 43, released as 2nd Lt, 46. Mem: Nat. Educ. Asn; Mason; Oriental Consistory; Elks. Rel: Congregational. Mailing Add: 602 Burgess Rd, Yankton, S.Dak. 57078.

RASMUSSEN, ERIC C. R
Nebr. State Sen.
b. York Co, Nebr, 2/9/26; m. 4/20/52 to Marie Elizabeth Larsen; c. Luann Marie and Clark. Educ: Cordova High Sch. Polit. & Govt. Pos: Nebr. State Sen, 62-64 & 66-; chmn, Cmt. on Cmts, 66; mem, Nebr. State R.R. Cmts, 69- Bus. & Prof. Pos: Farmer; dir, Farmers Export Co. and FAR-MAR Co, Inc. Mil. Serv: S/Sgt, Army, 44-46, served in Artil, Pac. Mem: Past Comdr, Am. Legion Post 359; Danish Brotherhood. Rel: Lutheran. Mailing Add: RFD 2, Fairmont, Nebr. 68354.

RASMUSSEN, KURT DUEVANG D
b. Haarlev, Denmark, 1/30/39; s. Svend Rasmussen and Ruth Anna R; m. 5/27/61 to Karen Louise Hort; c. Rolf John, Karl Skjold and Rita Kay. Educ: Noncommissioned Officer Sch, Danish Army, 1 year; Omaha Univ, 1 year. Polit. & Govt. Pos: Del, Dem. Nat. Conv, 68. Mem: Pres, Danish Brotherhood Lodge No. 1; chmn. entertainment and bd. mem, Vennelyst Park; Young Dem. Rel: Lutheran. Mailing Add: 4503 S. 12th St, Omaha, Nebr. 68107.

RASMUSSEN, PAUL A. DFL
Cmnr, Minn. Pub. Serv. Cmn.
b. Lanesboro, Minn, 12/4/95; s. Henry Edward Rasmussen and Lucy Ann Gray R; m. 10/18/23 to Pearl Kathryn Amundson; c. Phyllis (Mrs. Robert Verchota), Audre (Mrs. Peter Lommen), Lucy (Mrs. Richard Randgaard) and Paul H. Educ: St. Olaf Col, B.A, 18; Pi Kappa Delta. Polit. & Govt. Pos: Cmnr, Minn. Budget Cmn, 34-38; cmnr, Minn. Pub. Serv. Cmn, 52- Bus. & Prof. Pos: Dean, Concordia Col, Moorhead, Minn, 23-34; farmer, 23- Mil. Serv: Entered as Pvt, Army, 17, released as 2nd Lt, 18, after serv. in 24th Machine Gun Co, Eighth Div, Heavy Field Artil, 17-18. Publ: Many articles and technical papers printed in magazines and books. Mem: Am. Legion; Mason; Farmers Union; Farm Bur. Rel: Lutheran. Legal Res: Marine-on-St. Croix, Minn. 55047. Mailing Add: 400 State Office Bldg, St. Paul, Minn. 55101.

RASMUSSEN, ROSS HANS D
b. Lincoln, Nebr, 1/24/17; s. Louis J. Rasmussen and Grace Kennedy R; m. 10/16/43 to Alice W. Hoegemeyer; c. Ruth Ann (Mrs. David McMaster); Janice and Nina. Educ: Univ. Nebr, B.S. in Agr, 42; Gamma Sigma Delta. Polit. & Govt. Pos: Former secy, Dodge Co. Dem, Nebr; co. supvr, Dodge Co. Bd. Supvrs, 58-60; chmn, Dodge Co. Kennedy for Pres. Campaign, 60; Nebr. State Sen, 60-68. Bus. & Prof. Pos: Owner-operator, Nu-Dwarf Turf Farm, currently; exec. secy, Nebr. State Sch. Bds. Asn, 68- Mil. Serv: Entered as 2nd Lt, Army, 43, released as 1st Lt, 45, after serv. in 87th Inf. Div, Third Army, ETO, 44-45; Bronze Star with Valor; Cent. France, Rhineland and Germany Ribbons. Mem: Pres, Nebr. Inventors Asn, 65-66; Dodge Co. Centennial Tree and Native Grass Cmt; Gov. Inter-Agency Cmt. on Ment. Retardation; Nebr. Cmt. for Children and Youth; Univ. Nebr. Alumni Asn; Am. Legion; VFW; DAV; Farmers Union; Eagles; Izaak Walton League; Elks; hon. mem. Mu Epsilon Nu. Distinguished Serv. Award, Nebr. Sch. Masters, 64 and Dept. of Rural Educ, Nat. Educ. Asn, 65. Rel: Lutheran; past deacon and treas. Mailing Add: R.R. 2, Hooper, Nebr. 68031.

RAST, HOLT D
b. Portsmouth, Norfolk Co, Va, 10/29/17; s. Lucien Holt Rast and Sarah Armanda Blake R; m. 4/11/42 to Anne Laura; c. Holt III, Bobby John, Michael James, Sue Ellen, Mary Virginia, Marian Regena, Daniel Blake, Sally Anne. Educ: Univ. of Ala, B.S, Civil Eng, 42; mem. O.D.K; pres. of 'A' Club. Polit. & Govt. Pos: Ala. State Rep, 59-66. Bus. & Prof. Pos: Co-owner of Donahoo-Rast Contracting Co. of Birmingham. Mil. Serv: Army, Corps of Engrs, maj, ETO, 42-45. Mem: Former O.D.K; pres. 'A' Club. All Am. Football. Rel: Presbyterian. Mailing Add: Box 1491, Birmingham, Ala. 35201. (1967)

RATCLIFF, FRANCES JEAN R
b. Wash, 11/12/23; d. Zeno Olen Ratcliff and Mary Elizabeth Spruill R; single. Educ: Flora MacDonald Col, 39; E. Carolina Col, B.S, 46; Literary Soc; YWCA Cabinet; Methodist Club; Home Econ. Club. Polit. & Govt. Pos: Crew leader, Bur of Census, 54; secy, First Cong. Dist. Rep. Exec. Cmt, N.C, 56-61; v.chmn, Young Rep. Exec. Cmt, 57-58, nat. committeewoman, 59-60; alternate del, Rep. Nat. Conv, 60 & 64; treas, N.C. Rep. Exec. Cmt, 62-66; v.chmn, First Cong. Dist, 64-68. Bus. & Prof. Pos: Teacher, Bethlehem Day Nursery, 46-49; partner, Zeno O. Ratcliff Farms, 50-61; secy-treas, Zeno O. Ratcliff Inc, 62-69. Mem: Matcha Pungo Garden Club; East. Rep. Club; Farm Bur; E. Carolina Col. Alumni Asn. Rel: Methodist. Mailing Add: Route 1, Pantego, N.C. 27860.

RATCLIFFE, C. R. 'BUTCH' D
b. Beardstown, Ill; m. to Margaret Stucke R; c. Kenneth. Educ: U. of Ill. Polit. & Gov. Pos: Ill. State Rep; Sheriff, Cass Co, 43-46; Del. to Dem. Nat. Conv. from 20th Cong. Dist, 44. Bus. & Prof. Pos: Automobile dealer. Mem: Am. Legion, Post 605; Cass Co. Farm Bur; Elks; Masons; Shrine; Jesters. Mailing Add: Beardstown, Ill. 62618. (1967)

RATH, ROBERT KARL D
b. Mansfield, Ohio, 1/20/22; s. Franz Rath (deceased) and Anna Werner R; (deceased); m. 4/9/43 to Ethel Bailey; c. David and Carol. Educ: Miami Univ, B.A, 48; George Washington Univ, LL.B, 50, LL.M, 51; Delta Upsilon; Phi Delta Phi. Polit. & Govt. Pos: City Solicitor, Mansfield, Ohio, 61-; del, Dem. Nat. Conv, 68. Bus. & Prof. Pos: Attorney-at-law, Mansfield, Ohio, 51- Mil. Serv: Entered as 2nd Lt, Army, 42, released as Maj, 47, after serv. in Mediterranean Theatre, European Theatre and Korea, 43-47; Col, Army Res, currently. Publ: Mansfield Code of Ordinances, Anderson Co, Cincinnati, Ohio, 54. Mem: Richland Co. and Federal Bar Asns; Reserve Officers Assoc; Mil. Govt. Asn; dir, Richland Co, Red Cross; Exchange Club; Amvets; Sons of Herman. Rel: Protestant. Legal Res: 87 Elmridge Rd, Mansfield, Ohio 44907. Mailing Add: 3 N. Main St, Mansfield, Ohio 44902.

RATHBUN, FRANK HUGO D
b. Philadelphia, Pa, 10/3/24; s. Frank Hugo Rathbun and Florence McLean R; m. 9/11/48 to Claire Eileen Sinsabaugh; c. Charity Theresa, Frank Hugo, III, Rebecca Rae and Charles Frederick. Educ: Wayne State Univ, B.A, 51. Polit. & Govt. Pos: Admin. asst. to U.S. Rep. William D. Ford, 15th Dist, Mich, 65- Bus. & Prof. Pos: Newspaper reporter, Mellus Newspapers, Lincoln Park, Mich, 51-64. Mil. Serv: Entered as Pvt, Marine Corps, 42, released as S/Sgt, 46, after serv. in Second Marine Div, S.Pac, 42-44; Guadalcanal, Tarawa, Saipan and Tinian Campaign Ribbons; Presidential Unit Citation. Mem: Mason; Shrine; Eagles; past pres, Lincoln Park Jaycees and Lincoln Park Hist. Soc. Legal Res: Allen Park, Mich. 48101. Mailing Add: 125 House Office Bldg, Washington, D.C. 20515.

RATHE, BARBARA A. D
b. New Orleans, La, 9/24/24; d. Gustave Henry Rathe and Euxenia Baccich R; single. Educ: Sacred Heart Convent, Loyola Univ. of the South, New Orleans, La. Polit. Pos: Exec. secy. to U.S. Rep. Hale Boggs, La, 49- Rel: Roman Catholic. Legal Res: 3101 Napoleon Ave, New Orleans, La. 70115. Mailing Add: 1656 32nd St. N.W, Washington, D.C. 20007.

RATHER, MARY ALICE D
b. Huntsville, Tex, 4/3/12; d. Edward Seay Rather and Mary Alice Branch R; single; adopted nephew and nieces, Edward Branch, Nancy Bond and Bethenia Morrow Rather. Educ: Univ. Tex, 2 years. Polit. & Govt. Pos: Secy. to Under Secy. of Interior, 40-41; secy. to Lyndon B. Johnson, House Rep, 41-44, U.S. Senate and House Rep, 45-53 and U.S. Sen, 55-58, admin. asst, Off. Lyndon B. Johnson, 68-; del, mem. credentials cmt. and chmn. of housing for Tex. del, Dem. Nat. Conv, 64. Bus. & Prof. Pos: Trustee and mgr, Morrow Trusts, 58- Rel: Episcopal. Mailing Add: 1900 Exposition Blvd, Austin, Tex. 78703.

RATHJE, VICTOR DEAN R
Chmn, Buchanan Co. Rep. Cent. Cmt, Iowa
b. Clinton, Iowa, 6/22/34; s. Lewis H. Rathje and Dorothy Stuedemann R; m. 11/30/56 to Rae Jean Henzen; c. Brent, Rhonda and Kendall. Educ: Iowa State Univ, B.S. in Agronomy. Polit. & Govt. Pos: Chmn, Buchanan Co. Rep. Cent. Cmt, Iowa, 64- Mil. Serv: Entered as Pvt, Army, 56, released as Sp-3, 58. Mem: Pres, Independence Jaycees; bd. of dirs, Buchanan United Fund; C. of C. Rel: Lutheran. Legal Res: 713 Ninth Ave. N.W, Independence, Iowa 50644. Mailing Add: Box 258, Independence, Iowa 50644. (1967)

RATLIFF, DAVID WADE D
Tex. State Sen.
b. Decatur, Tex, 4/20/12; s. Lemuel David Ratliff and Myra Texas Pace R; m. 7/17/31 to Priscilla Gladish; c. David Lemuel, Lynnora Ann, Mary Jane and John A. Educ: Austin Col; N.Tex. State Univ; Draughon's Bus. Col. Polit. & Govt. Pos: Tex. State Rep, 50-54; Tex. State Sen, 24th Dist, 55-; Pres. Pro tempere, Tex. Senate, 61. Mem: Pres, Exchange Club, Stamford, Tex, 47; Hon. Rotarian, Stamford, Tex; Farm Bur. Acting Gov. of Tex, 61. Rel: Christian Church. Legal Res: 1005 Wells St, Stamford, Tex. 79553. Mailing Add: P.O. Box 1123, Stamford, Tex. 79553.

RATNER, PAYNE H, JR. R
Kans. State Rep.
b. Parsons, Kans, 8/31/24; s. Payne Harry Ratner and Cliffe Dodd R; m. 6/30/50 to Adelaide Bryant Schutz; c. Payne H, III, Charlotte Bryant and Carl Tinsley. Educ: Univ. of Kans, B.S. in bus. admin, 47, LL.B, 50 and J.D, 68; Phi Delta Phi; Beta Theta Pi. Polit. & Govt. Pos: Kans. State Rep, 67- Mil. Serv: Entered as A/S, Navy, 42, released as Lt.(jg), 46, after serv. in Atlantic & Pac. Theaters. Publ: Various legal articles in Practical Lawyer and other legal publs. Mem: Mason; Elks; VFW. Rel: Episcopal. Legal Res: 227 N. Crestway, Wichita, Kans, 67208. Mailing Add: Box 306, Wichita, Kans. 67201.

RATTE, GEORGE JOSEPH R
Mem. Exec. Cmt, Worcester Rep. City Cmt, Mass.
b. Worcester, Mass, 1/8/34; s. Joseph G. Ratte; m; c. 4. Educ: Middlebury Col, B.A, 56; Sigma Phi Epsilon. Polit. & Govt. Pos: Rep. chmn, Ward Nine, Worcester, Mass, 63-; mem. exec. cmt, Worcester Rep. City Cmt, 63-; mem. exec. cmt, Worcester Co. Rep. Club, 69-; v.chmn. bd. trustees, Worcester State Hosp, currently. Bus. & Prof. Pos: Claim exam, State Mutual Am, 58- Mil. Serv: Entered as 2nd Lt, Marines, 56, released as 1st Lt, 68, after serv. in Third Marine Div. Mem: New Eng. Claim Asn; Worcester Unit, Am. Cancer Soc; Boy Scouts (chmn. orgn. and exten. Quinsigamond Dist, Mohegan Coun). One of Ten Outstanding Young Men Worcester, Jr. C. of C, 69. Rel: Catholic; Parish Coun, Christ the King Parish Worcester. Mailing Add: 47 Moore Ave, Worcester, Mass. 01602.

RATTLIFF, HERMAN W. R
Ky. State Rep.
b. Summersville, Ky, 4/2/26; s. James William Rattliff and Estill Dobson R; m. 3/18/51 to Jewell Merritt; c. David Brian and Kristi Lynn. Educ: Campbellsville Col, 2 years; Woodward Sch. Photog, 1 year. Polit. & Govt. Pos: Pres, Taylor Co. Young Rep, Ky, 53-54; v.pres, Ky. Young Rep, 54, dist. chmn, 55-56, nat. committeeman, 64-65; precinct chmn, Taylor Co. Rep. Party, 57-69; Ky. State Rep, 29th Dist, 68- Bus. & Prof. Pos: Partner, photog. studio, Campbellsville, 49- Mil. Serv: Entered as Pvt, Army, 45, released as S/Sgt, 47, after serv. in 557th Signal Bn, S.Pac. Theater, 45-46; Good Conduct Medal; S.Pac. Theater Ribbon. Mem: Ky. Prfnl. Photographers Asn; Prfnl. Photographers Asn. Am; Am. Legion; C. of C; Ky. Hist. Soc; Farm Bur; Jaycees. Outstanding Serv. Awards, Taylor Co. Jaycees, 65, 67 & 68; Outstanding Young Rep. Ky, 66. Rel: Methodist. Mailing Add: 602 Meader St, Campbellsville, Ky. 42718.

RAUCH, JOSEPH RALPH D
Chmn, Sac Co. Dem. Party, Iowa
b. Auburn, Iowa, 6/30/07; s. Charles Patrick Rauch and Anna Smith R; m. 6/30/34 to Mary Margaret Maun; c. Maxine (Mrs. Richard Bauer), Marlene (Mrs. Lester Schulte), Darlene (Mrs. Dennis Wiederin) and Kirk L. Educ: Auburn High Sch, grad, 24. Polit. & Govt. Pos: Precinct Committeeman, Sac Co. township, Iowa, 51-61; chmn, Sac Co. Dem. Party, 61- Bus. & Prof. Pos: U.S. Rubber Plant Production employee, Baldwin Rubber, Pontiac, Mich, 32-43; Gas station owner and operator, 36-38; Farmer, Auburn, Iowa, 44-50; Grocery store and locker operator, 50- Mem: Lions; K. of C; Finance Cmt, St. Mary's; Holy Name Soc; Pin Splitters Bowling League. 12 year Certificate for operating in Clover Farm Store; Trophy for 2nd best Ham in National Ham Show, Des Moines, 3rd in National contest, Omaha. Rel: Catholic. Mailing Add: Box 56, Auburn, Iowa 51433.

RAUCH, MARSHALL ARTHUR D
N.C. State Sen.
b. N.Y.C, 2/2/23; s. Nathan A. Rauch and Tillie Wohl R; m. 5/18/46 to Jeanne Girard; c. Ingrid, Marc, Peter, Stephanie and John. Educ: Duke Univ, 44; Zeta Beta Tau. Polit. & Govt. Pos: Mayor pro tem, Gastonia, N.C, 52-54 & 61-63, city councilman, 63-65; N.C. State Sen, 29th Dist, 67- Bus. & Prof. Pos: Purchasing agent, Algoden Mfg. Co. Inc, 49-53; pres. and chmn. of bd, Pyramid Mills Co, Inc, 53-, Pyramid Dye Corp, 59-, Homeside Yarns, Inc. and Nile Star Inc, 60- Mil. Serv: Entered as Pvt, Army, 43, released as Pfc, 45; Combat Infantry Medal; European Theater and Occupation Ribbons. Mem: Dir, YMCA, Salvation Army, United Fund, C. of C, Gaston Boys Club and Gaston Commun. Action; chmn, Gaston Human Rels. Cmt, 64-; pres, Assoc. Industs, 65; 1st v.pres, N.C. Asn. of Jewish Men, 66; Mason; Shrine; VFW; Am. Legion; Elks; Moose. Named Man of the Year, Jr. C. of C, 57 and Jr. Womans Club, 64; Citizen of the Year, Omega Psi Phi, 66; Received Nat. Recreation Citation, 65. Rel: Jewish. Mailing Add: 1121 Scotch Dr, Gastonia, N.C. 28052.

RAUGUST, WILLIAM C. R
Rep. Precinct Committeeman, Wash.
b. Odessa Bessarabia, Russia, 3/13/95; s. Christian Raugust and Louisa Janke R; m. 4/20/19 to Reca Heitzelman; c. Trudy, Betty, Wilma, Margaret and William. Educ: Bus. Col; correspondence courses. Polit. & Govt. Pos: Former mayor and councilman, Odessa, Wash; v.chmn, Lincoln Co. Rep. Party, 4 years, chmn, 4 years; committeeman, Wash. State Rep. Cmt, 6 years; Rep. Precinct Committeeman, 21-; Wash. State Rep, 43-49; former pres. and dir, Odessa Schs; mem, West. Policy Cmn. on Hwy, Cmt. on Hwy. Exten. and Cmt. on Water Resources, 15 West. Policy Cmn. on Hwy, Cmt. on Hwy. Exten. and Cmt. on Water Resources, 15 West. States, Coun. State Govt, also mem, Cmt. on Game Fish; mem, Joint Fact Finding Cmn. on Hwy, 47-67; Wash. State Sen, 49-67, mem, Agr. and Horticulture, Commerce, Mfr. and Licenses, Constitution, Elec. and Legis. Processes, Hwy, Liquor Control and Rules and Joint Rules Cmts, Wash. State Senate; chmn, Joint Fact Finding Cmn. on Roads and Bridges, 53-55; del, Rep. Nat. Conv, 56- Bus. & Prof. Pos: Past pres, Yankton Theol. Sem, S.Dak; past pres. and dir, Pac. N.W. Hardware and Implement Asn; mgr, Farmers Grain and Lumber Co, 16-27; mgr, Odessa Trading Co, 27-65, pres, 55-66; pres, Farmers Supply Co, Ritzville, 44-63 and Columbia Pac. Life Ins. Co, 50-63; dir, United Theol. Sem, Twin Cities, Minn. Mil. Serv: Navy, 18-19, serv. in radio commun, Univ. Wash. and Harvard Univ. Mem: Chmn, Nat. War Fund, United Serv. Orgn; Past Comdr, Am. Legion; Lions; Nat. and State Farm Bur; past pres, Odessa C. of C; past pres, Gen. Conf. of Congregational Churches. Rel: United Church of Christ; Dir, Wash. Idaho Conf; chmn. bd. deacons, United Church of Christ, Odessa. Mailing Add: Odessa, Wash. 99159.

RAUH, JOSEPH L, JR. D
b. Cincinnati, Ohio, 1/3/11; s. Joseph L. Rauh and Sara Weiler R; m. 9/1/35 to Olie Westheimer; c. B. Michael and Carl S; grandchildren, B. Michael, Jr, Suzanne and Joseph L, III. Educ: Harvard Col, B.S, 32, Law Sch, LL.B, 35; Phi Beta Kappa. Polit. & Govt. Pos: Counsel to various govt. agencies, 35-36 & 39-42; law secy. to Supreme Court Justices Cardozo and Frankfurter, 36-39; gen. dep. housing expediter, Vet. Emergency Housing Prog, 46-47; v.chmn, Dem. Cent. Cmt, Wash. D.C, 52-64, chmn, 64-67; nat. chmn, Am. for Dem. Action, 55-57 and v.chmn, currently. Mil. Serv: Entered as 1st Lt, Army, 42, released as Lt. Col, 45, after serv. as Exec. Officer, G-5, Hq, Southwest Pac. Area; Legion of Merit; Philippine Distinguished Serv. Star. Publ: Various articles on civil rights and civil liberties. Mem: Wash. counsel, UAW and Gen. Coun. Leadership Conf. on Civil Rights. Rel: Jewish. Legal Res: 3625 Appleton St. N.W, Washington, D.C. 20008. Mailing Add: 1001 Connecticut Ave. N.W, Washington, D.C. 20036.

RAULERSON, LOUIS THOMAS D
b. Haylow, Ga, 5/11/14; s. John H. Raulerson and Della Eddy R; m. 8/02/40 to Gladys P. Parrish; c. Robert Kelly, Leonard Thomas, Anita Gayle. Educ: High sch. in Clinch Co. under GI Bill. Polit. & Govt. Pos: Ga. State Rep, 55-66; Echols Co. Constable, 48-54. Bus. & Prof. Pos: Forestry; bee indust. Mil. Serv: Army. Mem: Mason. Rel: Baptist. Mailing Add: Haylow, Stockton, Ga. 31642. (1967)

RAUSCH, EUGENE E. D
Mem, Ohio Dem. Exec. Cmt.
b. Marysville, Ohio, 8/25/10; s. John M. Rausch and Caroline Rausch R; m. 8/30/35 to Mary Jo Main; c. Lynn (Mrs. Beasley). Educ: Marysville High Sch, Ohio, 4 years. Polit. & Govt. Pos: Secy. and chmn, Union Co. Dem. Exec. Cmt, Ohio, 30-; mem, Young Dem. State Exec. Cmt, 32-36; chmn, Union Co. Bd. of Elec, 36-; mem, Ohio Dem. Exec. Cmt, 69- Bus. & Prof. Pos: Asst. mgr. and mgr, City Loan Co, Marysville, Ohio, 35-61; pres, Fuller Monument Works Inc, 60- Mil. Serv: Entered as Pvt, Army, 43, released as Sgt, 46, after serv. in M.I.S, ETO, 44-46. Mem: Elks; Moose; Rotary; Am. Legion; VFW; C. of C; 40 et 8. Rel: Lutheran. Mailing Add: 230 Grand Ave, Marysville, Ohio 43040.

RAUSCHENBERGER, JOHN KENNETH R
Chmn, Kane Co. Rep. Cent. Cmt, Ill.
b. Elgin, Ill, 6/30/22; s. Carl L. Rauschenberger and Laura Eaton R; m. 3/1/47 to Shirley Mae Westerbeck; c. Laurel Ann, John K, Jr, Thomas E, Carol Jean, Steven J. and Keith W. Educ: Ellis Bus. Col, 42. Polit. & Govt. Pos: Precinct committeeman, Rep. Party, Ill, 62-; mem, Kane Co. Bd. of Supvrs, 63-; chmn, Kane Co. Rep. Cent. Cmt, 66- Bus. & Prof. Pos: Pres, Rauschenberger Furniture Co. Mil. Serv: Entered as Pvt, Army, 43, released as Sgt, 45, after serv. in 92nd Chem. Mortar Bn, ETO; ETO Ribbon with 5 Battle Stars. Mem: Pres, Kiwanis Club of Elgin, 59; pres, Fox River Valley Coun. Boy Scouts, 62-63; Elks. Rel: Episcopal. Mailing Add: 637 Prospect St, Elgin, Ill. 60120.

RAVEN, JUANITA G. R
Mem, Calif. Rep. State Cent. Cmt.
b. Vacaville, Calif, 2/21/26; d. Miguel Garcia (deceased) and Mary Caparros G; wid. Educ: San Francisco State Col, B.A, 48, M.A. in Sec. Admin, 55; San Francisco Col. for Women, M.A. in Spanish Lit, 65; Univ. Hawaii, French Lang. Cert, 58; Univ. Valencia, 60; For. Lang. Honor Soc; pres, Int. Club; Nat. Defense Educ. Act French Lang. grant, Univ. Hawaii. Polit. & Govt. Pos: Assoc. mem, Calif. Rep. State Cent. Cmt, 66-68, mem, 68-; secy, Calif. Rep. League, 68, second v.pres, 69; Twin Peaks Area chmn. for Rep. Supvr. James Mailliard, 68; assoc. mem, San Francisco Co. Rep. Cent. Cmt, 68-69. Bus. & Prof. Pos: Teacher, George Wash. High Sch, San Francisco, 50; teacher, Am. Dependent Sch, Japan, 51-54; instr, Troop Info. and Educ, Japan, 52-54; admin. asst, For. Broadcasting Info. Serv, 55; teacher, Portola Jr. High Sch, San Francisco, 57; teacher, Oakland and Skyline High Sch, 57- Mem: For. Lang. Asn. North. Calif; Calif. and Oakland Teachers Asns; social mem, Olympic Club; San Francisco Women's Tennis Club. Rel: Catholic. Mailing Add: 22 Twin Peaks Blvd, San Francisco, Calif. 94114.

RAVENSCROFT, VERNON FRANK D
Idaho State Rep.
b. Buhl, Idaho, 1/26/20; s. W. F. Ravenscroft and Fern Gould R; m. 12/28/40 to Harriett E. Burkhard; c. Marilyn Lee, Carolyn Kay, Lynell Louise (deceased), Allan Bruce, Gordon John and Bryan Dale. Educ: Univ. Idaho, B.S. in forestry, 43; Xi Sigma Pi; Alpha Phi Omega. Polit. & Govt. Pos: Grazing adminstr, Clearwater Timber Protective Asn, Orofino, Idaho, 42; exten. forester, Univ. Idaho, 42-51; trustee, sch. bd, Hagerman Consol. Schs; Idaho State Rep, Gooding Co, 63- Bus. & Prof. Pos: Part-owner and gen. mgr, Penta Post and Treating Co, Tuttle, Idaho, 51- Publ: Various bulletins and articles on forestry, Univ. of Idaho, Moscow, Idaho. Mem: Soc. of Am. Foresters; state chmn, Idaho Landholder-Sportsman Coun; Grange; Farm Bur. Rel: Methodist. Mailing Add: Box 5, Tuttle, Idaho 83354.

RAVIZZA, EUGENE ALBERT R
b. San Jose, Calif, 7/21/28; s. Albert Joseph Ravizza and Georgia Bardason R; m. 11/19/55 to Mary Dianne Schott; c. Claranne, Mark and Gregory. Educ: Univ. Santa Clara, B.E.E, 50. Polit. & Govt. Pos: Del, Rep. Nat. Conv, 64; mem, Calif. Rep. State Cent. Cmt, 64-69. Bus. & Prof. Pos: Design engr, Porter-Urgart-Skidmore-Owing-Merrill, 51-53; pres,

Cupertino Elec. Inc, 54- Mil. Serv: 1st Lt, Army, Corps. of Eng, 62. Mem: Am. Inst. Elec. Engrs; Lions; Commonwealth Club of Calif. Rel: Catholic. Mailing Add: 21343 Sarahills Dr, Saratoga, Calif. 95070. (1967)

RAVNHOLT, EILER CHRISTIAN D
b. Milltown, Wis, 2/21/23; s. Ansgar B. Ravnholt and Kristine Petersen R; m. 3/23/47 to Edna Joyce Collis; c. Eliszabeth, Ann, Margarete, Jane and Christopher. Educ: Niagara Univ, 43-44; Univ. of Minn, B.S, 48; Univ. of Southampton, Eng, 49-50. Polit. & Govt. Pos: Chmn, Blue Earth Co. Dem-Farmer-Labor Party, Minn. and first v.chmn, Second Cong. Dist. Dem-Farmer-Labor Party, 60-62; del, Dem. Nat. Conv, 60, alternate del, 64; asst. librn, U.S. Senate, 62-65; asst. to the Vice President, 65-69; admin. asst, U.S. Sen. Daniel K. Inouye, Hawaii, 69- Bus. & Prof. Pos: Teacher, Mankato Pub. Schs, Minn, 52-62. Mil. Serv: 104th Inf. Div, ETO, 44-46. Publ: 'Teachers In Politics,' Minn. Educ. Jour, 3/59; Nomination and Election of the President and Vice President of the United States, GPO, 64. Mem: Nat. and Minn. Educ. Asn. Rel: Unitarian. Mailing Add: 3566 Raymoor Rd, Kensington, Md. 20795.

RAWLINGS, CALVIN WILLIAM D
Dem. Nat. Committeeman
b. Provo, Utah, 1895; s. William S. Rawlings and Margaret Ann R; m. to Ruth Candland; c. Elaine and Joyce. Polit. & Govt. Pos: Chmn, State Dem. Party, Utah, 32-36; mem, Dem. Nat. Cmt, 48-; del, Dem. Nat. Conv, 68. Bus. & Prof. Pos: Lawyer, mem. firm Rawlings, Wallace, Robert & Black, 19- Mil. Serv: 1st Lt, Army, F.A, 17-18. Mem: Exec. cmt, Boy Scouts; life mem, Nat. Conf. Cmnrs. Uniform State Laws; Am, Utah State and Salt Lake City Bar Asns; Utah Symphony (v.pres); bd. regents, Univ. Utah. Rel: Latter-day Saint. Mailing Add: 530 Judge Bldg, Salt Lake City, Utah 84111.

RAWLINGS, GEORGE CHANCELLOR, JR. D
Va. State Del.
b. Fredericksburg, Va, 11/7/21; m. to Rosalie Dabney Saunders R. Educ: Randolph-Macon Col, B.A; Univ. Va, LL.B; Kappa Alpha Order. Polit. & Govt. Pos: Va. State Del, 64- Bus. & Prof. Pos: Lawyer. Mem: Va. and Am. Bar Asns; 39th Judicial Circuit; v.pres, Fredericksburg Agr. Fair, Inc; bd. dirs, Hist. Fredericksburg, Inc; Elks; Moose; K. of P. Rel: Baptist. Mailing Add: 321 William St, Fredericksburg, Va. 22401.

RAWLINGS, MAURICE EDWARD D
Justice, Iowa Supreme Court
b. Onawa, Iowa, 8/17/06; s. Ed Eugene Rawlings and Effie Miller R; m. Feb. 1928 to Helen C. Fowler; c. Richard Ray (deceased), Maurice F, William J, Janet (Mrs. Pulscher), Mary (Mrs. Gaukel) and Robert C. Educ: Univ. Iowa, 25-27; S.Dak. Univ. Col. Law, LL.B, 30; Phi Gamma Delta. Polit. & Govt. Pos: Co. attorney, Woodbury Co, Iowa, 35-43; Off. Price Admin. dir, Iowa-S.Dak-Nebr, 43-47; corp. counsel, Sioux City, Iowa, 48-51; mem, Sioux City Sch. Bd, 55-58; judge, Fourth Judicial Dist, 58-65; justice, Iowa Supreme Court, 65- Bus. & Prof. Pos: Adv. coun, Sgt. Floyd Area Boy Scouts, 60-; adv. bd, Boys and Girls Home, 62-68; bd. dirs, Goodwill Industs, Sioux City, Iowa, 64- Mil. Serv: Army Res, 37-42, Capt, serv. in Judge Adv. Gen. Dept, Seventh Serv. Command. Publ: 'Constitutional Balance Between Fair Trials and Free Press,' Drake Law Rev, 12/67. Mem: Am. and Woodbury Co. Bar Asns; Iowa Bar Asn.(uniform jury instr. cmt, 63-68); Am. Legion (Comdr, 49-50). Distinguished Serv. Award, Woodbury Co. Bar Asn, 68. Rel: Episcopal. Legal Res: 3433 Court St, Sioux City, Iowa 51104. Mailing Add: 608 Court House, Sioux City, Iowa 51101.

RAWLINGS, ROB ROY D
b. Westerly, 2/20/20; m. to Barbara T. Educ: Univ. of R.I; Duke Univ. Polit. Pos: R.I. State Sen, 64-66; Richmond Tax Study Comt, 62-63; Dem. State Cmt, 1962. Bus. & Prof. Pos: Self-employed, Meadow Brook Golf Course. Mem: Past Master, Hope Valley Grange; Former Pres, C. of C; Former Secy, Hope Valley Vol. Fire Asn, Inc; V.Pres, Richmond PTA; Mem, Bd. of Dir. and V.Pres, Chariho-Exeter Credit Union. Mailing Add: Wyoming, R.I. 02898. (1967)

RAWLINGS, WILLIAM VINCENT D
Va. State Sen.
b. Capron, Va, 8/17/13; s. Edgar Eley Rawlings and Irma Vincent R; m. 6/20/42 to Novella Howard Pope; c. Elizabeth C, Arthur P. and Novella Vincent. Educ: Va. Mil. Inst, B.S, 35; Univ. Va, LL.B, 38; Phi Alpha Delta; Phi Kappa Sigma. Polit. & Govt. Pos: Mayor, Capron, Va, 48-50; mem, Southampton Co. Sch. Bd, 50-56, chmn, 56-62; mem, Southampton Co. Dem. Cmt, 52-; mem. exec. cmt, Farmers for Kennedy-Johnson, 60; mem, Pres. Nat. Agr. Adv. Cmt, 61-65; chmn, Gov. Opportunities in Agr. Study; Va. State Sen, 62-; chmn, Rural Virginians for Johnson-Humphrey, 64; state campaign chmn, William C. Battle, cand. for Gov, Va. Bus. & Prof. Pos: Attorney-at-law, 38-41; exec. secy. and gen. counsel, Asn. Va. Peanut & Hog Growers, 48-69. Mil. Serv: Entered as 1st Lt, Army, 41, released as Lt. Col, 46, after serv. in ETO, 44-46; Col, Army Res, 47; Legion of Merit; Bronze Star; Croix de Guerre; Three Campaign Stars. Mem: Farm Bur; Ruritan; Grange; Am. Legion; Farmers Union; Commonwealth Club of Va. Rel: Methodist. Mailing Add: P.O. Box 126, Capron, Va. 23829.

RAWLS, JOHN LEWIS, JR. D
Va. State Del.
b. Suffolk, Va, 12/7/23; m. to Mary Helen Macklin. Educ: Va. Mil. Inst; Duke Univ; Univ. Va, LL.B. Polit. & Govt. Pos: Va. State Del, 62- Bus. & Prof. Pos: Attorney-at-Law; pres, Suffolk Oil Mill, Inc. Mil. Serv: Commissioned officer, Naval Res; Pacific Theatre, P.T. Boats, Air-Sea Rescue. Mem: Va. Club of Norfolk; Princess Anne Co. Club; Commonwealth Club; Rotary; Cedar Point Club. Rel: Congregational. Mailing Add: P.O. Box 1458, Suffolk, Va. 23434.

RAY, BILL D
Alaska State Rep.
b. Anaconda, Mont, 4/6/22; s. Eli Ray and Marchette Victoria Isabella Sabella R.(deceased); m. 4/18/46 to Jeanette Pauline Haas; c. Terry Haas and Bill Carter. Educ: Wallace High Sch, Idaho, 38. Polit. & Govt. Pos: Mem, Fish and Game Adv. Bd, Alaska, 55-59: chmn, Alcoholic Beverage Control Bd, 59-64, dir, 63-64; Alaska State Rep, Fourth Dist, 65-, v.chmn, Finance Cmt, Alaska State House of Rep, 65-66, mem, 67-68 and chmn, 69- and mem, Legis. Coun, 65-66, Legis. Audit, 67-68 and v.chmn, Legis. Audit, 69-, Alaska State House of Rep. Bus. & Prof. Pos: Owner, Bill Ray's Liquor Stores (3), 48-66. Mil. Serv: Entered as A/S, Navy, 42, released as Chief Radioman, 46, after serv. in N.Pac. and S.Pac. Command Admin; Am. Theater, Asiatic-Pac. and Good Conduct Ribbons; Victory Medal. Mem: VFW; Am. Legion; Elks; Rotary; Alaska Pioneers. Nat. Edgar Award, 63; recognized sport fishing expert (Salmon). Rel: Episcopal. Mailing Add: 108 Sixth St, Juneau, Alaska 99801.

RAY, CHESTER J. D
b. Baltimore, Md, 9/11/15; married. Educ: Baltimore pub. schs. Polit. & Gov. Pos: Md. State Del, 55; 63-67; Baltimore City Coun, 55-59; Dem. State Cent. Cmt, 51-55; V.Pres, 7th Ward Dem. Asn; 6th, 10th and 11th Wards, Dem. Clubs. Bus. & Prof. Pos: Auditor. Mil. Serv: Army. Mem: Md. Pleasure Club; YMCA. Mailing Add: 823 N. Patterson Park Ave, Baltimore, Md. 21231. (1967)

RAY, CREAD L, JR. D
Tex. State Rep.
b. Waskom, Tex, 3/10/31; s. Cread L. Ray, Sr. and Antonia Hardesty R; m. 12/25/52 to Betty Sue Atkinson; c. Sue Ann, Robert Edwin and Glenn Lawrence. Educ: Tex. A&M Univ, B.B.A, 52; Univ. Tex. Sch. Law, LL.B, 57; YMCA; A&M Hometown Club; Pre-Law Club. Polit. & Govt. Pos: Co. judge, Harrison Co, Tex, 60-62; del, Tex. State Dem. Conv, 60-68; Tex. State Rep, Dist. Three, Harrison and Panola Co, 67- Mil. Serv: Entered as 2nd Lt, Air Force, 52, released as 1st Lt, 54, after serv. in 315th Air Div, Far East, 53-54; Maj, Res, 54-65; Am. Defense, UN, Korean Defense and Ten Year Res. Serv. Medals. Mem: Harrison Co. Bar Asn.(pres, 65); State Jr. Bar of Tex. (bd. dirs, 65-67); Northeast Tex. Bar Asn.(pres, 67-68); State Bar of Tex. (v.chmn. gen. practice sect, 66); Am. Bar Asn; Am. Judicature Soc; Law Sci. Acad. Am; Int. Acad. Law and Sci; Delta Theta Phi; Am. and Tex. Trial Lawyers Asns; Am. Legion; VFW; Kiwanis; Elks; C. of C; Boy Scouts; Marshall Jaycees (pres, 59); Tex. Jaycees (v.pres, 61). Outstanding Marshall Jaycee, 60; Boss of the Year, 67. Rel: Methodist. Legal Res: 701 Slone Dr, Marshall, Tex. 75670. Mailing Add: P.O. Box 299, Marshall, Tex. 75670.

RAY, JACK BOWDOIN D
State Treas, Ga.
b. Adairsville, Ga, 10/01/13; m. 7/06/40 to Jane Moore Hamilton; c. Neal Hamilton. Educ: Univ. Ga, LL.B; Kappa Alpha; Phi Delta Phi; Gridiron Club, Sphinx and Blue Key, Univ. Ga. Polit. & Govt. Pos: Ga. State Rep, 43-61; State Treas, Ga, Nov, 61 to fill unexpired term, elected, 62- Bus. & Prof. Pos: Attorney; farmer. Mem: Mason. Rel: Methodist. Legal Res: Norwood, Ga. 30821. Mailing Add: State Capitol, Room 245, Atlanta, Ga. 30334.

RAY, JAMES R. D
Chmn, Hale Co. Dem. Party, Tex.
b. Weslaco, Tex, 3/18/35; s. Wade H. Ray and Bessie Emery R; m. 4/18/63 to Susan W. Murfee; c. Joseph Kent, James Lynn and Stephen Eugene. Educ: Tex. Tech. Col, B.A, 58; Georgetown Univ. Law Sch, 58-60. Polit. & Govt. Pos: Admin. asst. to U.S. Rep. George Mahon, 58-65; del, Dem. Nat. Conv, 68; chmn, Hale Co. Dem. Party, Tex, 68- Bus. & Prof. Pos: Cattle farming, W.Tex, 65-; instr. govt, Tex. Tech. Col, 65-; real extate and loan broker, Plainview, 68- Mil. Serv: Entered as Pvt, Tex. Nat. Guard, 54, released as 1st Lt, 68, after serving in Army Res. Rel: Baptist. Mailing Add: 1410 Canyon, Plainview, Tex. 79072.

RAY, JOHN HENRY R
b. Mankato, Minn, 9/27/86; s. John Henry Ray and Genevieve Eldredge R; m. 10/9/12 to Hama Olive Thompson; c. Virginia Thompson (Mrs. James E. Potts), John Henry III. and Gordon Ray. Educ: Univ. Minn, A.B, 08; Harvard, LL.B, 11. Polit. & Govt. Pos: Asst. to spec. rep. of Secy. of War in adjust. of War Dept. claims against Allied Govt, 19; U.S. Rep, N.Y, 53-62. Bus. & Prof. Pos: Entered law off. of Koon, Whelan and Hempstead, Minneapolis, Minn, 11; asst. secy. and asst. trust officer, Wells-Dickey Trust Co, 18; gen. attorney, Am. Tel. & Tel. Co, 24-28; gen. solicitor, 28-30, counsel, 36-42, v.pres. and gen. counsel, 42-51; v.pres, dir. and gen. counsel, West. Elec. Co, 30-36; assoc. Skadden, Arps, Slate & Timbers, Attorneys, 51- Mil. Serv: Army, 1st Lt, Judge Adv. Gen. Dept, Wash, 18-19. Mem: Am. Fed, Commun. and N.Y. State Bar Asns; Asn. of the Bar, NYC; N.Y. Co. Lawyers Asn; Beta Theta Pi; Univ. Club; Richmond Co. Country Club, N.Y. Mailing Add: 57 St. James Place, Staten Island, N.Y. 10304.

RAY, ROBERT D. R
Gov, Iowa
b. Des Moines, Iowa, 9/26/28; s. Clark A. Ray and Mildred Dolph R; m. 12/21/51 to Billie Lee Hornberger; c. Randi Sue, Lu Ann and Vicki Jo. Educ: Drake Univ, B.A. in Bus. Admin, 52, J.D, 54. Polit. & Govt. Pos: Chmn, Iowa Rep. Party, 63-; chmn, Midwest Asn. Rep. State Chmn, 65-; chmn, Nat. Rep. State Chmn. Asn, 67-; Gov, Iowa, currently. Bus. & Prof. Pos: Attorney-at-law, Ray and Crouch, Des Moines, Iowa, 54- Mil. Serv: Army, 46-48. Mem: Iowa Acad. Trial Lawyers; Am. Trial Lawyers Asn; Iowa State, Polk Co. and Am. Bar Asns; Delta Theta Phi; Alpha Kappa Psi; Omicron Delta Kappa; Sigma Alpha Epsilon; state chmn, March of Dimes, 60-62; bd. dirs, Family Serv. Rel: Disciples of Christ. Legal Res: 917 California Dr, Des Moines, Iowa 50312. Mailing Add: State Capitol, Des Moines, Iowa 50319.

RAYBALL, JOSEPH CHARLES D
b. Lowell, Mass, 6/28/32; s. Joseph Bernard Rayball and Honora Collins R; m. 9/4/55 to Rita Patricia Carnevale; c. Joseph, Mary Louise, Lisa Ann, Sharon Marie and Catherine Larkin. Educ: Leland-Powers Sch, Boston, 2 years. Polit. & Govt. Pos: Supvr. of Checklist, Salem, N.H, 65-67; del, N.H. Dem. State Conv, 66 & 68; v.pres, Salem Dem. Town Cmt, N.H, 67, pres, 68; chmn, Salem Recreation Cmn, 68; press secy. to U.S. Rep. Margaret Heckler, Mass, 68-69, admin. asst, 69- Bus. & Prof. Pos: Staff reporter, WHAV-Radio, Haverhill, Mass, 56-58; news dir, WLLH-Radio, Lowell, 58-61, news and sports dir, 64-66; pub. affairs and sports dir, WCAP-Radio, 61-64; city hall and polit. reporter, Lowell Sun Newspapers, 66-68; Boston Traveler correspondent, 66-68; news and sports dir, WCCM-Radio, Lawrence, 68-69;

Boston Globe correspondent, 68-69. Mil. Serv: Entered as Seaman Recruit, Navy, 50, released as Radarman 3/C, 54, after serv. in N.Atlantic and Mediterranean Fleets. Mem: Am. Fedn. of TV and Radio Announcers; Pub. rels. consult, Gr. Lowell Area Planning Agency, Lowell; K. of C, Andover. United Press Int. Tom Phillips Awards for Best News Story Coverage in Mass, 60, for Best Radio Ed, 64 and for Best Elec. Coverage, 68. Rel: Roman Catholic. Legal Res: 219 Main St, Salem, N.H. 03079. Mailing Add: 1602 N. Danville St, Arlington, Va. 22201.

RAYMOND, JOSEPH ROBERT D
Asst. Attorney Gen, Md.
b. Brooklyn, N.Y, 10/12/39; s. Joseph Raymond and Frances Ciauri R; m. 8/25/67 to Elizabeth Levering Royer. Educ: Georgetown Univ, A.B, 61; Georgetown Univ. Law Center, LL.B, 64; Young Dem; Mask and Bauble Dramatic Soc. Polit. & Govt. Pos: Research asst. to U.S. Sen. Daniel B. Brewster, Md, 61-64; asst. states attorney, Baltimore, 66-68; pres, Young Dem. Clubs of Md, 67-68; del, Dem. Nat. Conv, 68; asst. attorney gen, Md, 68- Mil. Serv: Entered as 2nd Lt, Army, 64, released as Capt, 66, after serv. in Defense Contract Admin. Serv. Region, Army Base, Boston, 64-66; Capt, Army Res, 69. Mem: Am, Md. State, Baltimore City and Jr. Bar Asns; Nat. Dist. Attorneys' Asn; Md. State's Attorneys' Asn; Am. Coun. of Young Polit. Leaders (bd. mem); Citizens' Cmn. on Md. Govt. (bd. mem); Md. Asn. of Mental Health (bd. mem); Citizens' Planning and Housing Asn; Mayor's Task Force on Civil Rights. Rel: Catholic. Mailing Add: 12 W. Mount Vernon Place, Baltimore, Md. 21201.

RAYMOND, RAPHAEL ROYAL R
Ore. State Sen.
b. Pendelton, Ore, 10/16/06; s. Raphael Raymond and Adeline Sutherland R; m. 7/29/26 to Gladys Adele Snyder; c. Raphael Royal, Jr. and Barbara-Lee (Mrs. Allan Pinkerton). Educ: Univ. Ore; Kappa Sigma. Polit. & Govt. Pos: Chmn, Umatilla Co. Agr. Planning Coun, 48-53; mem, Umatilla Co. Develop. Cmn, 50- and Ore. Wheat Cmn, 63-64; mem. and chmn, Umatilla Co. Budget Cmt, 51-54; Ore. State Rep, 59-62; Ore. State Sen, 65- Bus. & Prof. Pos: Dir, Pendleton Fed. Land Bank, 51-57 and Ore. Nat. Life Ins, 65- Mem: Pres, Umatilla Co. Cattle Asn, 47-48 and Ore. Wheat Growers League, 57; hon. state farmer, Ore. State Future Farmers of Am; Rotary; Mason; Shrine; K. of P; Elks; Ore. Wheat League; Farm Bur; Grange; Ore. Cattle Asn; C. of C. Rel: Presbyterian. Mailing Add: Vansycle Canyon Rd, Helix, Ore. 97835. (1967)

RAYNES, BURT FRANKLIN R
b. Clinton, Ind, 4/8/13; s. Burt Franklin Raynes (deceased) and Alfreda Johnson R.(deceased); m. 10/12/43 to Lois Schaff; c. Mark Schaff and Melissa Ann. Educ: Rose Polytech. Col, 33-35; Sigma Nu. Hon.D.Eng, Rose Polytech. Col, 68. Polit. & Govt. Pos: Mem. bd. trustees, Rep. Assocs. of San Diego Co, Calif, 63-64; mem. exec. finance cmt, Rep. Cent. Cmt, formerly; del, Rep. Nat. Conv, 68. Bus. & Prof. Pos: Asst. chief inspector, Ryan Aeronaut. Co, San Diego, Calif, 38-40; chief inspector, Rohr Corp, 40-45, works mgr, Universal Cooler Div, Marion, Ohio, 45-49; mgr. elec. furnace and rolling mill div, Newport Steel Corp, Ky, 49-53; v.pres. mfg, Rohr Corp, 53-59, sr. v.pres, 59-62, exec. v.pres, 62-63, pres. and gen. mgr, 63-65, chmn. bd, pres. and chief exec. officer, 65-; dir, Sundstrand Corp, Rockford, Ill, Bourns, Inc, Riverside, Calif. and San Diego Gas and Elec. Co, currently. Mil. Serv: Navy. Mem: Wright Bros. mem. award cmt, Soc. of Automotive Engrs. 3 years. chmn, 63; Nat. Aeronaut. Asn; bd. gov. and exec. cmt, Aerospace Industs. Asn, 67-68; v.pres. and bd. dir, Aircraft Builders Counsel; Calif. rep. bd. dir, Nat. Asn. of Mfrs; Navy League of U.S; nat. emergency cmt, Nat. Coun. on Crime and Delinquency; coun. for marine sci, Univ. South. Calif; organizer, San Diego Develop. Corp; former dir. and v.pres, Gr. San Diego Econ. Develop. Corp; former gen. chmn, fund drive, Southwest. Col; chmn, Citizens Cmt. for Educ, Sweetwater Union High Sch. Dist, currently; bd. trustees, Christian Col. and U.S. Int. Univ, currently; bd. dir, San Diego Natural Hist. Soc; San Diego C. of C.(bd. dir, Ambassadors); Riverside C. of C; bd. gov, Gr. San Diego Sci. Fair; San Diego Country Club; San Diego Yacht Club. Rel: Protestant. Mailing Add: 299 Hilltop Dr, Chula Vista, Calif. 92010.

RAYNOLDS, HAROLD, JR. D
b. Chicago, Ill, 2/7/25; m. to Ann Richards Ellis; c. two sons, two daughters. Educ: Cornell Univ, B.S. I & LR, 48; M.A, 52. Polit. & Govt. Pos: Vt. State Sen, 65-66; State Bd. of Educ, Chmn; Chmn, Forest Festival Cmt. Bus. & Prof. Pos: Journalist, teacher. Mil. Serv: U.S. Army Inf, S/Sgt, 43-45, European Theater of Opers, Purple Heart. Mem: Rotary Club; Rotary Club, Bellows Falls; Elks Club; Springfield; Elks, Lodge No. 1560. Rel: Unitarian-Universalist. Mailing Add: R.D. 2, Box 141, Springfield, Vt. 05156. (1967)

RAYNOR, JOSEPH BRYANT, JR. D
N.C. State Rep.
b. Cumberland Co, N.C, 1/26/23; s. Joseph Bryant Raynor, Sr. and Beatrice Owen R; m. 1/15/44 to Mildred Horne. Educ: Engr. and Refrigeration Sch, 44. Polit. & Govt. Pos: Mem, Bd. Selective Serv, 23 & 63; mem. exec. cmt, Cumberland Co. Young Dem. Club, N.C, 59 & 63; N.C. State Rep, 63- Bus. & Prof. Pos: Owner, Raynor Supply Co. dealer of automotive wholesale supplies; bd. of dirs, Cumberland Co. Guidance Center. Mem: Fayetteville Exchange Club; Seventy-first Ruritan Club; pres, Cumberland Co. Chap, N.C. Soc. for Crippled Children and Adults, 60; Cumberland Co. Ment. Health Asn; Cystic Fibrosis Soc; K. of P; Moose; United Commercial Travelers of Am. (past sr. counselor, 50, grand sentinel, 61, grand page, 62, grand conductor, 63, grand jr. counselor, 64); Ancient Mystic Order of Bagmen of Bagdad. Exchangite of Year, 59; Cert. of Recognition for serv. to the Nation and Selective Serv. Syst. in the admin. of the Universal Mil. Training and Serv. Act by President Lyndon B. Johnson, 64. Rel: Methodist; Camp Ground Methodist Church, bd. of stewards, 54. Mailing Add: 5234 Raeford Rd, Fayetteville, N.C. 28304.

RAYSON, LELAND HOMER D
Ill. State Rep.
b. Oak Park, Ill, 8/23/21; s. Ennes Charles Rayson and Beatrice Margaret Rowland R; m. 5/30/44 to Barbara Ellen Chandler; c. Ann Louise, John, William, Anthony, Leland, James and Thomas. Educ: Coe Col, 40-41; Univ. Rochester, A.B, 46; Northwest. Law Sch, J.D, 49; Dean's List Scholarship; Alpha Delta Phi; Phi Alpha Delta. Polit. & Govt. Pos: Sch. bd. mem, Tinley Park, Ill, 50-54, police magistrate, 51-53, police cmnr, 54-55; twp. assessor, Bremen Twp, 53-61; pres, Bremen Twp. Regular Dem. Orgn, 54-; alternate del, Dem. Nat. Conv, 60; Justice of the Peace, Bremen Twp, 61-65; cmnr, Ill. Cmn. on Low Income Housing, 65-67; Ill. State Rep, 65-; cmnr, Ill. Family Law Study Cmn, 67-; dir, Am. for Dem. Action, 68- Bus. & Prof. Pos: Attorney, Rayson and Hutchison, Tinley Park, Ill, 49-; dir, Palos-Worth Reporter, Worth, 60-; dir, Interstate Bank of Oak Forest, 68- Mil. Serv: Entered as Seaman, Navy, 43, released as Lt.(jg), 46, after serv. in Pac. Theatre, 44-45; Lt. Comdr, Naval Res, 68; Battle Star Ribbons for Pac. Theatre, Leyte Invasion and Lingayen Gulf Invasion; Am, Pac. and Philippines Theatre Ribbons. Publ: 'Face the Facts as They Are,' IVI Bellringer, 5/65; 'Abortion Law Reform in Illinois,' Student Law J, 12/68; 'Rights and Liabilities of Family Members,' Ill. Inst. for Continuing Legal Educ, Ill. State Bar Asn, 3/69. Mem: Nat. Soc. State Legis; Chicago City Club; Chicago Coun. on For. Rels; admitted Ill. Bar, 49, U.S. Dist. Courts, U.S. Court of Appeals, Fifth Circuit, U.S. Supreme Court, U.S. Tax Court and U.S. Court of Mil. Appeals; Chicago Bar Asn; Lions; C. of C; World Serv. and Finance Cmn. of the United Methodist Church. Best Freshman Citation, 66 and Best Legislator Awards, 66 & 68, Independent Voters of Ill. Rel: Protestant. Legal Res: 6500 W. 166th St, Tinley Park, Ill. 60477. Mailing Add: 16740 S. Oak Park Ave, Tinley Park, Ill. 60477.

RAZNIKOV, RICHARD ALAN D
b. Newark, N.J, 6/20/46; s. I.R. Raznikov and Phyllis Sweet R; m. 8/27/67 to Laurie Ann Cooper; c. Jessica. Educ: Univ. Calif, Berkeley, A.B, 68, Boalt Hall Sch Law, student, 68-; Pi Kappa Delta. Polit. & Govt. Pos: Pres, Marin Co. Young Dem, Calif, 62-63; mem. Nat. Exec. Cmt, Citizens for Kennedy 1968, 67-68; del, Dem. Nat. Conv, 68. Rel: Universal Life. Mailing Add: 372 Nob Hill Dr, Walnut Creek, Calif. 94598.

REA, JAMES MAGRUDER D
Mem, Md. Dem. Cmt.
b. Washington, D.C, 3/11/24; s. James Lewis Light Rea and Parthia Moulton R; m. 9/17/55 to Ora Evelyn West; c. James Magruder, Jr, Evelyn Suzanne, Mary Alice and Amy West. Educ: Univ. Md, B.A, 43, LL.B, 50. Polit. & Govt. Pos: Del, Dem. State Conv, 54 & 58; asst. co. attorney, Prince Georges Co, Md, 59; chmn, Bd. Property Rev, Prince Georges Co, 62-66; mem, Md. Dem. Cmt, 66- Bus. & Prof. Pos: Farmer, 44-50; attorney-at-law, 50- Mil. Serv: 2nd Lt, Med. Corps, 43. Mem: Md. State Bar Asn; Prince Georges Co. Bar Asn.(past pres); South. Md. Soc; Am. Legion; Marlborough Hunt Club. Rel: Episcopal. Mailing Add: Box 2155, Upper Marlboro, Md. 20870.

REA, SAMUEL A. R
Ind. State Rep.
Polit. & Govt. Pos: Ind. State Rep, 63- Bus. & Prof. Pos: Bus. broker. Mil. Serv: Navy air vet. Rel: Presbyterian. Mailing Add: 927 S. Harrison St, Ft. Wayne, Ind. 46802. (1967)

READ, BENJAMIN H. D
b. Phila, Pa, 9/14/25; s. William Bond Read and Rachel Biddle Wood R; m. 8/12/50 to Anne Lowell Keezer; c. Benjamin Huger, Dexter K, Anne L. and Mary B. Educ: Williams Col, B.A, 49; Univ. Pa, LL.B, 52; Phi Beta Kappa. Polit. & Govt. Pos: Pub. defender, Phila, Pa, 55-56; attorney adv, Legal Adv. Off, Dept. of State, 57-58; legis. asst. to U.S. Sen, Joseph Clark, Pa, 58-63; dep. exec. secy, Dept. of State, 63, exec. secy. of the Dept. and spec. asst. to Secy. of State, 63-69; acting dir, Woodrow Wilson Int. Center for Scholars, Smithsonian Inst, D.C, 69, dir, 69- Bus. & Prof. Pos: Assoc, Duane, Morris & Heckscher, Attorneys, 52-55. Mil. Serv: Marine Corps, 43-46, Pac. and China Theatre. Mem: Am, Pa. and Phila. Bar Asns; Federal City Club. Rel: Episcopal. Legal Res: 1739 Crestwood Dr. N.W, Washington, D.C. 20011. Mailing Add: Woodrow Wilson International Center for Scholars, Smithsonian Institution, Washington, D.C. 20560.

READ, HARRY AUGUSTUS SHERMAN R
Mass. State Rep.
b. Brighton, N.Y, 11/18/36; s. Harry Augustus Sherman Read and Helen White R; m. 8/6/60 to Carolyn Fish Hummel; c. Elizabeth Baylog and Bridget Wilson. Educ: Stetson Univ, B.A, 62; all-state soccer team. Polit. & Govt. Pos: Del, Rep. Pre-Primary Conv, 64 & 66; v.chmn, Sandwich Rep. Town Cmt, 64-; Barnstable Co. finance coordinator, Mass. Rep. State Cmt, 65; chmn, Sandwich Rep. Finance Cmt, 66; mem, Rep. Nat. Workshops, 66; Mass. State Rep, 67- Bus. & Prof. Pos: Teacher, hist. and govt, Bourne High Sch, 63-66. Mil. Serv: Entered as Airman 3rd, Nat. Guard, 59, released as 2nd Lt, Army, 62. Mem: Treas, Rotary; Grange. Legal Res: Grove St, Sandwich, Mass. 02563. Mailing Add: State House, Boston, Mass. 02133.

READ, MAURICE W. R
N.H. State Rep.
b. Derry, N.H, 12/26/03; s. John Louis Read and Edith Willey R; m. 7/15/26 to Dorothy Holbrook; c. Charles L. and Priscilla (Mrs. Perry). Educ: Columbia Univ, 3 years; Cent. Col. of Commerce, 1 year. Polit. & Govt. Pos: N.H. State Rep, 69- Bus. & Prof. Pos: Self employed. Mem: Mason; Kiwanis. Rel: Protestant. Mailing Add: 16 Chester Rd, Derry, N.H. 03038.

READ, WILLIAM BROOKS D
Mem, Dem. State Cent. Cmt, La.
b. Baton Rouge, La, 8/4/26; s. Frank Clifford Read, Sr. and Margaret Huck R; m. 7/30/49 to Maureen Hushar; c. Jennifer, Heather and Wendy. Educ: La. State Univ, 41-42 & 48-49; Northwest. Univ, 42-43. Polit. & Govt. Pos: Mem, Gov. Adv. Cmt. on State Penitentiary, 64; mem, Dem. State Cent. Cmt, La, 67-; del, Dem. Nat. Conv, 68; mem, Family Court Adv. Cmt, East Baton Rouge Parish, 69- Bus. & Prof. Pos: Gen. mgr, WNAT Radio, Natchez, Miss, 51; prod. mgr, Liberty Broadcasting Syst, Dallas, Tex, 51-52; owner-mgr. and free-lance writer, VoiServ, Dallas, Tex. and Baton Rouge, La, 53-54; news dir, WBRZ-TV, Baton Rouge, La, 55-64; pres, Brooks Read & Assocs, Inc, 64- Mil. Serv: Entered as Pvt, La. Nat. Guard, 48, released as 1st Lt, 55, after serv. in Mil. Intel, Army Res. Mem: Sigma Delta Chi; Press Club of Baton Rouge; Capitol Correspondents Asn. of La; adv. bd, Vol. of Am; bd. dirs, Gr. Baton Rouge Safety Coun, Oper. Upgrade and Capitol City Dem. Asn; govt. affairs cmt, Baton Rouge C. of C; Pub. Affairs Res. Coun. Rel: Episcopal. Legal Res: 1525 Cloverdale Ave, Baton Rouge, La. 70808. Mailing Add: P.O. Box 2345, Baton Rouge, La. 70821.

READER, BARBARA JEAN R
V.Chmn, Oakland Co. Rep. Exec. Cmt, Mich.
b. Howell, Mich, 10/18/18; m. 9/6/46 to Zar Anthony Reader, D.D.S; c. Zar Anthony, III, William McDowell and Susan Elizabeth. Polit. & Govt. Pos: V.chmn, Oakland Co. Rep. Exec. Cmt, Mich, currently; first v.pres, Oakland Co. Coun, Rep. Women's Clubs; precinct del, Third Precinct, Farmington Twp, Oakland Co. Rep. Party. Mem: Hon. adv, Farmington Commun. Center, Inc; Women's Soc. of Christian Serv; Detroit Dist. Dent. Auxiliary; past bd. mem, Farmington Friends of Libr; initiator and first pres, Citizens for Farmington Students, Inc; past pres. and coun. chmn, PTA. Honored by Farmington Area PTA Coun. for Outstanding Contribution to PTA. Rel: Methodist; past bd. mem, Franklin Commun. Church. Mailing Add: 28984 Wellington Rd, Farmington, Mich. 48024.

READING, JOHN HARDEN R
Mayor, Oakland, Calif.
b. Glendale, Ariz, 11/26/17; s. Cecil Virgil Reading and Lillian May Ingram R; m. 3/21/41 to Hazel Mary Swortfiguer; c. Joanna Lee (Mrs. Negley) and Ronald James. Educ: Univ. Calif, B.S, 40. Polit. & Govt. Pos: Mayor, Oakland, Calif, 66- Mil. Serv: Entered as Flying Cadet, Air Force, 40, released as Col, 46, after serv. in Second Air Command. Rel: Protestant. Mailing Add: 4735 Sequoyah Rd, Oakland, Calif. 94605.

REAGAN, BRUCE VINCENT R
b. Winnebago, Minn, 7/5/02; s. John Albert Reagan and Lena MacLaughlin R; m. 7/23/22 to Muriel Dolores Benton; c. Bruce Vincent, Jr. Educ: Yale Univ, 20-22. Polit. Pos: State chmn. emeritus, United Rep. of Calif, 65-, State chmn, 63-65; mem, State Rep. Cent. Cmt, 58-67; chmn, Region 1, Reagan for Gov, 66; del. and presidential elector, Rep. Nat. Conv, 64; pres, Pasadena Rep. Club, 54; past officer, State and Los Angeles Co. Cent. Cmts. Govt. Pos: Rep. Nominee for State Controller, Calif, 62; Calif. State Assemblyman, 47th Dist, 59-62 and 48th Dist, 49-50. Bus. & Prof. Pos: Pres, Glendale Fed. Savings and Loan; mgr, Merrill Lynch, Pasadena Off, 31-57. Mil. Serv: Entered as Capt, Army, 43, released as Maj, 46, after serv. in SHAEF and U.S. Group Control Coun, Berlin, ETO, 44-46; Army Res. until 66. Mem: Past Comdr. and life mem, Pasadena Post, MOWW; past pres, Pasadena Chap, Nat. Sojourners; pres, Los Angeles Mil. Govt. Asn; Los Angeles Econ. Round Table. Rel: Protestant. Mailing Add: 955 A South Orange Grove Blvd, Pasadena, Calif. 91105.

REAGAN, MAUREEN ELIZABETH R
Mem, Calif. Rep. State Cent. Cmt.
b. Los Angeles, Calif, 1/4/41; d. Ronald Reagan and Jane Wyman; div. Educ: Marymount Col, 1 year. Polit. & Govt. Pos: Pres, Walter Knott Rep. Women's Club, Anaheim, Calif, 66; Youth educ. chmn, Calif. Fedn. Rep. Women, South. Div, 66-67, youth activities dir, 68-69; mem, Calif. Rep. State Cent. Cmt, 67- Rel: Episcopal. Legal Res: Burbank, Calif.

REAGAN, RONALD WILSON R
Gov, Calif.
b. Tampico, Ill, 2/6/11; s. John Edward Reagan and Nelle Wilson R; m. 3/4/52 to Nancy Davis; c. Maureen Elizabeth, Michael Edward, Patricia Ann and Ronald Prescott. Educ: Eureka Col, B.A, 32, hon. M.A, 57; Tau Kappa Epsilon. Polit. & Govt. Pos: Mem, Calif. Rep. State Cent. Cmt, 64-66; Gov, Calif, 66-; del, Rep. Nat. Conv, 68; chmn, Rep. Gov. Asn, 68- Mil. Serv: Entered as 2nd Lt, Air Force, 42, released as Capt, 45. Publ: Where's the Rest of Me, Duell-Sloane & Pierce, 65. Mem: Bd. dirs, Motion Picture Indust. Coun, 49-60, pres, 55, 57; bd. dirs, Screen Actors Guild, 41-60, pres, 47-52, 59; adv. cmt, Who's Who in Am. Polit, 69; Lions; Friars. Varsity football and swimming team. Rel: Christian Church. Mailing Add: Executive Residence, Sacramento, Calif. 95814.

REAGAN, WILLIAM ANGUS D
b. Coeur d'Alene, Idaho, 12/7/26; s. William John Reagan and Mary Elizabeth Madden R; m. 12/28/53 to Claudia Jean Bales; c. Kathy Ann, Nancy Jean, Polly Lynn, Michael Emery, William Tipton, Patrick John, Mary Beth and Amy Louise. Educ: Univ. Idaho, 45-49; Gonzaga Univ, LL.B, 57; Tau Kappa Epsilon. Polit. Pos: Del, State Dem. Conv, 64; alternate del, Nat. Dem. Conv, 64. Govt. Pos: Prosecuting attorney, Kootenai Co, Idaho, 60-65. Bus. & Prof. Pos: Dir, secy. and treas, Western Frontiers, Inc, 60-; dir, Kootenai Co. Area Redevelopment Asn, 63-64. Mil. Serv: Entered as Pvt, Army, 51, released as Cpl, 62. Mem: 8th Judicial Dist. Bar Asn, State of Idaho; Am. and State Bar Asns; Am. Judicature Soc; Elks; Gyro; K. of C. Rel: Catholic. Mailing Add: 801 Indiana Ave, Coeur d'Alene, Idaho. 83814. (1967)

REAMS, FRAZIER, JR. D
b. 1929. Educ: Wash. & Lee Univ, B.A; Univ. Mich. Law Sch, LL.B. Polit. & Govt. Pos: Ohio State Sen, 2 terms; cand. for Gov, Ohio, 66; del, Dem. Nat. Conv, 68. Bus. & Prof. Pos: Attorney; broadcasting exec. Mailing Add: 3516 Ridgewood Rd, Ottawa Hills, Ohio 43606. (1967)

REARDON, HAROLD E. R
Finance Chmn, Humboldt Co. Rep. Party, Calif.
b. Cresco, Iowa, 10/20/08; s. Charles John Reardon and Mary Hogan R; m. 1937 to Ethel Rait; c. Robert Charles and Harold E, Jr. Educ: N.Dak. State Univ, B.S, 34. Polit. & Govt. Pos: Finance chmn, Humboldt Co. Rep. Party, Calif, 55- Bus. & Prof. Pos: Secy. and treas, Bridgeville Lbr. Co, 50-; owner, H.E. Reardon Realtor Co, 49- Mil. Serv: Entered as Lt.(jg), Navy, 41, released as Lt. Comdr, 45, after serv. in Pac. Theater, 42-44; Capt, Res, 44-58; Commendation from Secy. of Navy. Mem: Am. Soc. Mil. Engrs; Nat. Asn. Real Estate Brokers; Licensed Civil Engr; Mason (32°); Shrine; Nat. Farm Bur; Lions. Rel: Protestant. Mailing Add: 5169 Leonard Dr, Eureka, Calif. 95501.

REARDON, TIMOTHY JAMES, JR. D
b. Somerville, Mass, 5/18/15; s. Timothy James Reardon and Mary Ellen Keefe R; m. 12/2/43 to Betty Jane Paden; c. Timothy James III. Educ: Harvard, A.B, 38. Polit. & Govt. Pos: Mem, Kennedy Campaign Staff, 46; admin. asst. to U.S. Rep. John F. Kennedy, Mass, 47-52, spec. asst. to U.S. Sen. John F. Kennedy, 53-60 and to President John F. Kennedy, 61-63, spec. asst. for cabinet affairs. 61-64: asst. to chmn. Fed. Deposit Ins. Corp, 64-65, exec. asst. to bd. dirs, 65- Bus. & Prof. Pos: Advert. bus, Boston, 38-42. Mil. Serv: Army Air Force, Capt, 42-46. Mailing Add: 3134 Dumbarton Ave. N.W, Washington, D.C. 20007.

REAVES, HENRY L. D
Ga. State Rep.
b. Kissimmee, Fla, 8/07/19; s. Coy Reaves and Blanche Nance R; m. 2/27/48 to Frances Barker; c. Henry L. Jr. and Joan A. Educ: Osceola High Sch, 37. Polit. & Govt. Pos: Ga. State Rep, 63- Bus. & Prof. Pos: Farmer; cattleman; asst. mgr, Agr. Bus. Servs, South. Railway. Mil. Serv: 1st Lt, Army Air Force, World War II, ETO. Mem: Elks; Quitman Rotary Club (pres, 49-50, secy-treas, 1 year); pres, Brooks Co. Livestock Asn, 6 years; secy-treas, Brooks Co. Farm Bur. Rel: Baptist. Mailing Add: R.F.D. 2, Quitman, Ga. 31643.

REAVIS, CHARLES G. R
b. Yadkin Co, N.C, 5/31/92; s. George W. Reavis and Lydia Vanhoy R; m. 1/20/20 to Hattie B. Key; c. Thad, Mrs. Charles Dellinger, Clyde C, Gray, Mrs. Richard Taylor and Charles G, Jr. Educ: Yadkin Co. Pub. Schs, 99-10. Polit. & Govt. Pos: Sheriff, Yadkin Co, N.C, 31-34; N.C. State Sen, 53 & 59; N.C. State Rep, 63-66. Bus. & Prof. Pos: Co-owner and pres, Pioneer Chevrolet Co, Inc, Yadkinville, N.C. Mem: Jr. Order United Am. Mech. Rel: Methodist; Steward, 20-44, Supt. Sunday Sch, 26-30 & 44-52, Trustee, 47-52. Mailing Add: Route 3, Yadkinville, N.C. 27055. (1967)

REAVLEY, THOMAS MORROW D
Assoc. Justice, Supreme Court, Tex.
b. Quitman, Tex, 6/21/21; s. Thomas Mark Reavley and Matty Morrow R; m. 7/24/43 to Florence Montgomery Wilson; c. Thomas Wilson, Marian, Paul Stuart and Margaret. Educ: Stephen F. Austin Col, 37-39; Univ. Tex. Law Sch, B.A, 42; Harvard Law Sch, LL.B, 48. Polit. & Govt. Pos: Co. attorney, Nacogdoches Co, Tex, 51; secy. of state, Tex, 55-57; dist. judge, 167th Judicial Dist, Tex, 64-68; assoc. justice, Supreme Court, Tex, 68- Mil. Serv: Entered as Ens, Navy, 43, released as Lt, 45, after serv. in U.S.S. Cogswell and U.S.S. Ticonderoga. Rel: Methodist. Legal Res: 1312 Meriden Lane, Austin, Tex. 78703. Mailing Add: Supreme Court of Texas, Austin, Tex. 78711.

REBER, JOSEPH BRYANT, SR. D
Mont. State Sen.
b. Butte, Mont, 2/17/19; s. Edward A. Reber and Mary I. Rooney R; m. 3/23/38 to Marie E. Tauriainen; c. Joseph E, Roberta Marie (Mrs. Corette), Dianna Jean (Mrs. Riley), C. Bryant and Susan Doleros. Educ: Hon. LL.D, Carroll Col, Mont. Polit. & Govt. Pos: Finance dir, State Dem. Cent. Cmt, Mont, 54-64; del, Dem. Nat. Conv, 56, 60, 64 & 68; chmn, Kennedy for Pres, Mont, 60; mem. finance cmt, Dem. Nat. Cmt, 60-64; chmn, Businessman for Humphrey, Mont, 68; Mont. State Sen, Dist. 21, 69- Bus. & Prof. Pos: Mem. bd. adv, sch. bus. admin, Univ. Mont, 64-68; mem, Upper Midwest Research and Develop. Coun, 65-; wing comdr. with rank of Col, Mont. Civil Air Patrol, 65-66; mem. bd. regents, Carroll Col, 68- Mil. Serv: Entered as Purser, Merchant Marine, 43, released, 45, after serv. in Pac. Theatre. Mem: Elks; Eagles; K. of C; Mont. Club (pres, 66-67); Jr. C. of C.(pres, 50-52). Cert. of Merit, President's Missile Site Labor Cmn; Cert. of Merit, Univ. Mont. Sch. Bus. Admin. Rel: Catholic. Mailing Add: 801 Floweree, Helena, Mont. 59601.

RECHTIN, EBERHARDT R
Dir, Adv. Research Projs. Agency, Dept. of Defense
b. Orange, N.J, 1/16/26; s. Eberhardt Carl Rechtin and Ida Pfarrer R; m. 6/10/51 to Dorothy Diane Denebrink; c. Andrea Compton, Nina, Julie Anne, Erica and Mark Eberhardt. Educ: Calif. Inst. Tech, B.S. in Eng, 46, Ph.D, 50; Tau Beta Pi. Polit. & Govt. Pos: Dir, Adv. Research Projs. Agency, Dept. of Defense, 67- Bus. & Prof. Pos: From research engr. to asst. dir. for tracking and data acquisition, Jet Propulsion Lab, Calif. Inst. of Tech, 49-67. Mil. Serv: Entered as A/S, Naval Res, 43, released as Lt, 58, after serv. in Continental U.S, 43-46; Theater Ribbon. Publ: Articles on space commun, Astronaut, 62-67. Mem: Fel, Am. Inst. Aeronaut. and Astronaut; fel, Inst. Elec. and Electronics Engrs; Nat. Acad. of Eng. Academician, Int. Astronaut. Fedn; NASA Medal for Exceptional Sci. Achievement. Rel: Protestant. Mailing Add: 6904 Old Gate Lane, Rockville, Md. 20852.

RECKMAN, ROBERT FREDERICK R
b. Cincinnati, Ohio, 4/7/22; s. William A. Reckman and Florence Apel R; m. 12/1/45 to Mary Carleen Stone; c. Robert C, Richard F. and Mark S. Educ: DePauw Univ, A.B, 43; Univ. Cincinnati, LL.B, 48; Phi Beta Kappa; Phi Eta Sigma; Sigma Delta Chi; Blue Key; Beta Theta Pi. Polit. & Govt. Pos: Ohio State Rep, 52-68, acting speaker, Ohio House of Rep, formerly. Bus. & Prof. Pos: Dir, Corryville Bldg. & Saving Co, 47-, pres, 68-; partner, Nichols, Wood, Marx & Ginter, 61-; dir, Globe Off. Equip. Co, 64-; pres. and dir, Monarch Bldg. & Loan Asn. Co, 68- Mil. Serv: Entered as Pfc, Marine Corps, 43, released as Lt.(jg), Naval Air Corps, 46. Mem: Cincinnati Club; Cincinnatus Asn. Rel: Presbyterian. Legal Res: 330 Warren Ave, Cincinnati, Ohio 45220. Mailing Add: 900 Tri-State Bldg, Cincinnati, Ohio 45202.

RECTOR, WILLIAM GORDON 'BILL' D
Wyo. State Sen.
b. Des Moines, Iowa, 7/22/22; s. Jesse Rector and Viola O'Conner R; m. 4/20/50 to Norma Louise Watkins; c. William Gordon, Jr. and Christine Louise. Educ: Kearney State Col, B.S, 43. Polit. & Govt. Pos: Wyo. State Rep, 59-65; Wyo. State Sen, 67- Bus. & Prof. Pos: Owner, restaurant and drive inn. Mil. Serv: Marine Corps, 6 years. Mem: Jr. C. of C.(pres, 53); Quarterback Club (pres, 66-67); Elks; Am. Legion; VFW; Exec. Club; Optimists Club; Cheyenne Restaurant Asn.(pres, 57-69). Rel: Catholic. Mailing Add: 301 W. Fifth Ave, Cheyenne, Wyo. 82001.

RECTOR, WILLIAM LEE R
Committeeman, Tex. State Rep. Exec. Cmt.
b. Shawnee, Okla, 11/30/19; s. William Lee Rector and Mary Elizabeth Reese R; m. 5/3/43 to N. Jane Fielder; c. Nancy Jane and Lee Anne. Educ: Okla. State Univ, B.S, 40; Okla. Univ, M.D, 43; Blue Key; Phi Beta Pi. Polit. & Govt. Pos: Committeeman, Tex. State Rep. Exec. Cmt, 64-; chmn, Task Force

on Human Rights and Responsibilities, Rep. Party, Tex, 66-; del, Rep. Nat. Conv, 68. Bus. & Prof. Pos: Practicing physician, Med. and Surg. Clin, Wichita Falls, Tex, 50- Mil. Serv: Entered as 1st Lt, Army, 43, released as Capt, 45. Mem: Dipl, Am. Bd. Internal Med; Am. Col. Physicians. Altrusa Distinguished Civic Serv. Award, 63. Rel: Protestant. Legal Res: 2605 Amherst, Wichita Falls, Tex. 76308. Mailing Add: 1518 Tenth St, Wichita Falls, Tex. 76301.

REDD, JOHN PACKARD R
Utah State Rep.
b. Mt. Pleasant, Utah, 12/25/30; s. Leland W. Redd and Alice Vera Hunter R; m. 7/16/49 to Erma Helquist; c. Michael, David, Linda, Lowry, Audry and Kristin. Educ: Univ. Utah, B.S. in Ch.E, 59. Polit. & Govt. Pos: Precinct chmn, Rep. Party, Utah, 63-65, legis. dist. chmn, 65-67; Utah State Rep, 67-, mem. revenue and taxation, indust. develop. and appropriations cmts, Utah House of Rep, 69-, chmn. house educ. cmt, 69-; Utah cmnr, Educ. Cmn. to the States, 69- Bus. & Prof. Pos: Chem. engr, Standard Oil of Calif, 58-60; chief engr, Beeline Refining Co, 60-62; partner, Redd and Redd, Consult. Engrs, 62- Publ: 'Radiant Heating,' Heating, Piping, and Airconditioning Magazine, July, 1966. Mem: Am. Soc. Heating, Refrigerating and Air Conditioning Engrs.(pres); Am. Inst. Chem. Engrs; Utah Soc. Prfnl. Engrs. (pres. elect); Nat. Soc. of Prfnl. Engrs; C. of C; Rotary; Davis Co. Ment. Health Adv. Bd; Boy Scouts (asst. dist. cmnr, Lake Shore Dist). Utah's Engineer of the Year, 1968. Rel: Latter-day Saint. Mailing Add: 3263 South 350 West, Bountiful, Utah 84010.

REDD, LUCY D
Dem. Nat. Committeewoman, Utah
b. Blanding, Utah, 7/20/26; d. L. Frank Redd and Nettie Rebecca Rose R; single. Educ: Univ. Utah, LL.B; Phi Delta Delta. Polit. & Govt. Pos: Reference attorney, Utah State Legis, 49; dep. co. attorney, Salt Lake Co, 49; Dem. Nat. committeewoman, Utah, 60-; v.chmn, West. States Dem. Conf, 63-66, chmn, 66-; mem, Site Cmt. and Platform Cmt, Dem. Nat. Conv, 64, alternate del, 68. Mem: Am. and Utah Bar Asns; Salt Lake Co. Bar Exec. Cmt; Motor Carrier Lawyers Asn; Nat. Asn. of Co. and Prosecuting Attorneys. Rel: Latter-day Saint. Legal Res: 1235 E. Second South, Salt Lake City, Utah 84111. Mailing Add: 345 S. State St, Salt Lake City, Utah 84111.

REDDEN, JAMES ANTHONY D
b. Springfield, Mass, 3/13/29; s. James Anthony Redden and Alma Cheek R; m. 7/13/50 to Joan Ida Johnson; c. James Anthony, Jr. and William Francis. Educ: Boston Univ, 49-51; Boston Col. Law Sch, LL.B, 54. Polit. & Govt. Pos: Chmn, Jackson Co. Dem. Cmt, Ore, 57-59; Ore. State Rep, 19th Dist, 63-69, Minority Leader, Ore. House of Rep, 67; del, Dem. Nat. Conv, 68; mem, State of Ore. Pub. Employee Rels. Bd, currently. Mil. Serv: Entered as Pvt, Army, 46, released as Pfc, 48, after serv. in 118th Sta. Hosp, Japan; Japan Occup. Medal. Mem: Ore. Bar; Mass. and Jackson Co. Bar Asns; Am. Judicature Soc. Rel: Catholic. Legal Res: 518 Barnes Ave, Medford, Ore. Mailing Add: 107 E. Main, Medford, Ore. 97501.

REDDICK, RICHARD DALY R
Mem, Calif. Rep. State Cent. Cmt.
b. Huntington Park, Calif, 5/14/37; s. Benjamin Otis Reddick and Dorothy Daly R; m. 4/5/68 to Donna Lynn Palmer. Educ: Orange Coast Col, A.A. in Bus, 58; Univ. South. Calif, B.S. in Bus. Admin, 60; Tau Kappa Epsilon, Univ. South. Calif; Circle K, Orange Coast Col. Polit. & Govt. Pos: Ed, Orange Co. Rep. Challenge, Calif, 62-64; chmn, Orange Co. Young Rep, 63-64; mem, Orange Col Cmt, Murphy for U.S. Senate, 64; regional v.pres, Calif. Young Rep, 65; mem, Calif. Rep. State Cent. Cmt, 65-; chmn, Coombs for State Senate Campaign Cmt, 66; mem, San Bernardino Co. Rep. Cent. Cmt, 69-; admin. asst. Calif. State Sen. William E. Coombs, 69- Bus. & Prof. Pos: Gen. mgr, Garden Grove Free Press, Calif, 57-59; asst. publisher, Newport Harbor News-Press, Newport Beach, 59-62; owner, R.D. Reddick & Assoc, 62-65; publisher, Rialto Record Newspapers, 65-68. Publ: 'Hilltop Highlights,' Highlander & J. Newspapers, 66-68; 'Ye Ed,' column in Rialto Record Newspapers, 67-68; 'Capitol Caucus,' column in Rep. GO-Paper Mag, 69. Mem: Calif. Newspaper Publishers Asn; Alpha Delta Sigma; Twin Co. and Orange Co. Press Clubs; Nat. Press Photographers Asn; Calif. Newspaper Advert. Exec. Asn; state dir, Calif. Jaycees; Elks; Kiwanis; dist. coun, Boy Scouts; Univ. South. Calif. Alumni Club; United Fund; C. of C; Heart Fund Drive; Merchants Asn. Rel: Protestant. Legal Res: 654 S. Cactus Ave, Rialto, Calif. 92376. Mailing Add: Room 5053, State Capitol Bldg, Sacramento, Calif. 95814.

REDDY, SAMUEL, JR. R
N.H. State Rep.
b. Concord, N.H, 12/9/29; married. Educ: Hampton Acad. Polit. & Govt. Pos: Former Rep. precinct cmnr, Contoocook, N.H; auditor; N.H. State Rep, 63- Bus. & Prof. Pos: Loan officer, Mechanicks Nat. Bank, Concord, N.H. Mil. Serv: Navy, 51-55. Mem: Harris Lodge 91; F&AM, Warner, Acacia Chap. Rose Croix; Aeriel Coun. Princes of Jerusalem; Alpha Lodge of Perfection; N.H. Consistory S.P.R.S.(32°); dir. and treas. of Contoocook Valley Fair Asn. Rel: Methodist. Mailing Add: Box 146, Maple St, Contoocook, N.H. 03229. (1967)

REDEKER, STANLEY FREDERICK R
b. Lincoln, Nebr, 8/4/26; s. Frederick Julius Redeker and Fern Grant R; m. 4/15/53 to Maxine Erickson; c. Ellen Jane and Joel Stanley. Educ: Univ. Notre Dame, 2 years; Boone Jr. Col, 1 year; Stanford Univ, B.S. in Econ, 49; Zeta Psi. Polit. & Govt. Pos: mem, Iowa State Bd. of Regents, 61-64, pres, 64-; del, Rep. Nat. Conv, 68. Bus. & Prof. Pos: Owner, Redeker Furniture Co, Boone, Iowa, currently. Mil. Serv: Entered as A/S, Navy, 44, released as Seaman 2/C, 46; entered as Pvt, Army, 50, released as Cpl, 52. Mem: Lions; C. of C. Local Civic Leadership Awards. Rel: Methodist. Mailing Add: 1509 Kate Shelley Dr, Boone, Iowa 50036.

REDFEARN, B. WILSON R
Chmn, Del. Fedn. of Young Rep.
b. Chicago, Ill, 7/8/36; s. Berry Wilson Redfearn and A. Halm R; m. 4/15/61 to Patricia McIntyre; c. Braeden, Michelle, Brett and Maureen. Educ: Loyola Univ, 56; Miami Univ, B.A, 58; Northwest. Univ. Sch. Law, J.D, 61; Dean's List; Delta Tau Delta; PHID. Polit. & Govt. Pos: Dep. attorney gen, Del, 62-64; former pres, Westgate Farms Civic Asn; dep. chmn, New Castle Co. Rep. Party, currently; chmn, Del. Fedn. of Young Rep, currently; pres, New Castle Co. Young Rep; lawyer, New Castle Co. Govt, currently; officer, Polit. Region, currently; co. officer, currently; mem, Co. Rep. Exec. Cmt, currently. Bus. & Prof. Pos: Partner, Tybout & Redfearn, currently. Mem: Am. and Del. Bar Asns; YMCA; Quadril; Big Bros. Rel: Catholic. Legal Res: 131 Oldbury Dr, Wilmington, Del. 19808. Mailing Add: 920 King St, Wilmington, Del. 19801.

REDFEARN, LAURIN ROBERT D
b. Wadesboro, N.C; s. W.M. Redfearn and Cora B. Timmons R; m. 11/4/27 to Catherine Arant; c. L.R, Jr. Educ: Davidson Col, 21-22. Polit. & Govt. Pos: S.C. State Rep, 63-66; coroner of Chesterfield Co, 20 years. Bus. & Prof. Pos: Funeral Dir; pres, Redfearn Funeral Home, Inc. Mem: Worshipful master Cheraw Masonic Lodge, 39-41; pres, Lions Club; pres, Cheraw Camellia Club, 55; pres, S.C. Funeral Dirs. Asn, 57. Mailing Add: Box 343, Cheraw, S.C, 29520. (1967)

REDFERN, CARROLL IRWIN D
b. New London, Iowa, 3/25/05; s. Ray Redfern and Hannah Broeker; m. 7/3/28 to Evea Fern Wasson; c. Nancy Carol (Mrs. Thuma) and Merlin Lee. Educ: Iowa State Univ, B.S, 29; Gamma Sigma Delta. Polit. & Govt. Pos: Mem, Lee Co. Bd. of Rev, Iowa, 48-; Iowa State Rep, 64-68. Bus. & Prof. Pos: Farm mgr, Penick & Ford, Ltd, Inc, 28-29; co. agr. agent, Lee and Madison Co, Iowa, 30-40; mem. bd, Lee Co. Fair, 44-; v.pres. and pres, Iowa Fair Mgrs. Asn. Mem: Accts. Asn. of Iowa; Lions; Farm Bur. Rel: Methodist. Legal Res: 421 University St, Donnellson, Iowa 52625. Mailing Add: P.O. Box 176, Donnellson, Iowa 52625.

REDFIELD, REUBEN ROBERT D
b. N.Y.C, 12/7/19; s. Harry Redfield and Rebecca Schiffrin R; div; c. Diane and Ronald R. Educ: N.Y. Univ, B.S, 47; Sigma Tau Epsilon. Polit. & Govt. Pos: Union Co. campaign mgr, U.S. Rep. Jack B. Dunn, N.J, 60 & 62, N.J. State Assembly Dem. Cands, 62 & 64 and N.J. Sen, James McGowan, 64; alternate del, Dem. Nat. Conv, 64 & 68. Bus. & Prof. Pos: CPA, Redfield, Blonsky & Co, Elizabeth, N.J, 50-69; bd. dirs, Ment. Health Asn, Union Co, 65-69. Mil. Serv: Entered as Pvt, Air Force, 42, released as Capt, 46, after serv. in First and Second Air Force, Continental U.S. Mem: N.J. Soc. of CPA (legis. cmt, 65-68, internal revenue cmt, 69); Am. Inst. of CPA; Aircraft Owners and Pilots Asn; pres, Elizabeth Boys Club, 68-69; East. Union Co. YMCA (bd. of dirs, 68-69, treas, 69). Winner of Nat. Aeronautic Air Races, Worcester, Mass, 53 & 54. Rel: Jewish. Mailing Add: 330 W. Jersey St, Elizabeth, N.J. 07202.

REDING, LEO JOHN DFL
b. Austin, Minn, 6/6/24; s. John W. Reding and Mathilda Uschold R; m. 10/29/49 to Marian A. Thommes; c. Colleen, Maureen, Terrence, Laurie and Thomas. Educ: Col. St. Thomas, B.S. in phys. ed, 48; Tiger Club. Polit. & Govt. Pos: Chmn, Mower Co. Democrat-Farmer-Labor Party, Minn, 65-68; Alderman, Austin City Coun, 68- Mem: K. of C; UPWA. Rel: Catholic. Mailing Add: 709 12th Ave. N.W, Austin, Minn. 55912.

REDLIN, ROLLAND D
b. Lambert, Mont, 2/29/20; m. to Christine Nesje; c. Ilene, Jeannette, Lisa, Daniel and Steven. Educ: Univ. Wash; N.Dak. State Col, Minot, exten. courses. Polit. & Govt. Pos: Nominee, N.Dak. State Rep, 52; N.Dak. State Sen, 58-64; U.S. Rep, N.Dak, 64-66; Dem. cand. for U.S. Rep, N.Dak, 66 & 68. Bus. & Prof. Pos: Farming. 1967 Legal Res: Crosby, N.Dak. No mailing address available. (1967)

REDMAN, JAMES L. D
Fla. State Rep.
b. Plant City, Fla, 1/19/32; s. J.W. Redman and Madaline Miller R; m. 8/9/57 to Ruby Jean Barker; c. Susan, Pam and Jeanne. Educ: Univ. Fla, B.S.B.A, 53, LL.B, 58; Phi Kappa Phi; Kappa Alpha. Polit. & Govt. Pos: Assoc. City Judge, Plant City, Fla, 60-65; Dem. precinct committeeman, 62-66; Fla. State Rep, 66- Mil. Serv: Entered as 2nd Lt, Air Force, 54, released as 1st Lt, 56, after serv. with Auditor Gen, Tactical Air Command, European Theater. Mem: Fla. and Hillsborough Co. Bar Asns; Am. Judicature Soc; Lions; Fla. Cattlemen's Asn; Fla. Citrus Mutual. Rel: Baptist. Legal Res: 605 N. Johnson St, Plant City, Fla. 33566. Mailing Add: P.O. Drawer TT, Plant City, Fla, 33566.

REDMAN, RICHARD ELSON R
b. Elko, Nev, 9/5/38; s. Corwin Elson Redman and Mary Polich R; m. 3/21/69 to Jeanette McKellar Remsburg; c. Jacklyn Lou and Stephanie Anne. Educ: State Univ. Iowa, B.A, 60. Polit. & Govt. Pos: Exec. secy, Young Rep. Iowa, 60-63; orgn. dir, Rep. State Cent. Cmt, Iowa, 63-65, finance secy, 65-66, exec. secy, 66-69; dir, Redmond Resources, Rep. Fund Raisers, 69- Mem: Des Moines Club. Rel: Presbyterian. Mailing Add: 2307 Woodland, West Des Moines, Iowa 50265.

REDMON, FRED G. R
b. Craig, Mo, 1897; m. to Sadie; c. three. Educ: Yakima High Sch. Polit. & Govt. Pos: Official, Alcan Hwy, 42; cmnr, Yakima Co, Wash, 44-51; chmn, Wash. State Hwy. Cmn, 51-54; treas, Yakima Co, 56-63; Wash. State Sen, 64-68. Bus. & Prof. Pos: Road construction. Mil. Serv: World War I. Mem: Mason; Elks; Eagles; Am. Legion. Mailing Add: P.O Box 182, Yakima, Wash. 98901. (1967)

REDMON, HELEN CARVER D
b. Marysville, Ind, 10/16/18; d. John H. Carver and Gertrude Hanger C; m. 3/10/40 to Joseph C. Redmon; c. Rebecca (Mrs. Will F. Cheesman) and Roberta (Mrs. C. Eugene Speaker). Polit. & Govt. Pos: Pres, Dem. Ladies League, Ind, 58-62; v.chmn, Bartholomew Dem. Cent. Cmt, 58-66; mgr, Bur. of Motor Vehicles, 60-64. Bus. & Prof. Pos: Asst. treas, Hamilton Emp. Fed. Credit Union, 65- Mem: Am. Bus. Women's Asn. Mailing Add: R.R. 2, Hope, Ind. 47246.

REDMOND, THOMAS JOSEPH D
Chmn, Williamson Co. Fedn. of Dem. Leagues, Tenn.
b. Franklin, Tenn, 10/28/07; s. William Benjemin Redmond and Albinda

William R. Educ: Walden Univ; Biggins Commercial Col. Polit. & Govt. Pos: Chmn, Williamson Co. Fedn. of Dem. Leagues, Tenn. Mem: Int. Elks, (World Past Exalted Master, Mid. Tenn. Dist); J.H. Hale Coun. 91. Rel: Gay-Lea Christian Church. Mailing Add: 2818 W. Kirkwood Ave, Nashville, Tenn. 37204. (1967)

REDMOND, WILLIAM A. D
Ill. State Rep.
b. Chicago, Ill, 11/25/08; m. to Rita Riordan; c. Mary, William Patrick and Colleen. Educ: Marquette Univ; Northwest. Univ, J.D. Polit. & Govt. Pos: Village attorney, Bensenville, Ill; sch. bd. attorney; Ill. State Rep, currently. Bus. & Prof. Pos: Private law practice, Chicago, 34-42. Mil. Serv: Naval Res, released, 46, as Lt. Comdr. Mem: Am. Legion; Lions; K. of C. Mailing Add: 250 Tioga Ave, Bensenville, Ill. 60106. (1967)

REECE, LOUISE GOFF R
b. Milwaukee, Wis, 11/6/98; d. Guy Despard Goff and Louise Van Nortwick G; m. 10/30/23 to B. Carroll Reece; c. Mrs. George W. Marthens, II. Educ: Milwaukee Downer Sem, 16; Miss Spences Sch, N.Y.C, 18. Polit. & Govt. Pos: Del, Rep. Nat. Conv, 56 & 68, del-at-lg, 64; U.S. Rep, Tenn, 61-63; former Rep. Nat. Committeewoman, Tenn. Bus. & Prof. Pos: Dir. Carter Co. Bank, Elizabethton, Tenn, 40-65, v.chmn, 63-65; dir, First Nat. Bank, Jonesboro, 43-56; proprietor and mgr, Goff Properties, Clarksburg, W.Va, 54-; dir, First Peoples Bank, Johnson City, 56-, v.chmn, 63-64, chmn, 64- Mem: Bus. & Prfnl. Women's Club; Women Bankers; Colonial Dames; DAR; Daughters of 1812; Eastern Star; Chevy Chase, Sulgrave and Capitol Hills Clubs; Johnson City Country Club. Rel: Episcopal. Mailing Add: 1201 Woodland Ave, Johnson City, Tenn. 37601.

REECE, THOMAS HENRY D
b. Payson, Utah, 12/22/15; s. Thomas Edward Reece and Irene Tanner R; m. 12/15/44 to Shanna Hatch; c. Thomas Dee, Gregory Lewis, Chana Rebecca, Nancy Gay and twins, Janna and Jillayne. Educ: Brigham Young Univ, B.S, 41. Polit. & Govt. Pos: Chmn, Payson City Young Dem. Orgn, Utah, 36-40; chmn, First Dem. Dist, Payson, 48-56; chmn, Payson City Dem. Precinct, 56-62; mem, Payson City Planning Cmn, 58-66; del, Dem. Nat. Conv, 60 & 64; mem. bd. dirs, Utah Valley Day Care and Training Center, Small Bus. Cmt, West. States Dem. Conf. and chmn, Utah Co. Dem. Party, 62-66; exec. secy, Utah State Dem. Cmt, 63-66; mem, Utah State Contractors Bd, 65-66; projects coordinator, Utah State Bldg. Bd, 67- Bus. & Prof. Pos: Secy, off. mgr. and mem. bd. dirs, Davis Construct. Co, 57-62 and Great Basin Construct, Inc, 63-66; off. mgr, Leftwich Construct. Co, 63-66; sales rep. for Utah, Eastside Winery, Lodi, Calif, 65-66. Mil. Serv: Entered as Pvt, Army, 41, released as T/Sgt, 45, after serv. in 18th Engr. Regt, Corps of Engrs, Alaskan Command, 42-44. Mem: Past v.pres, Utah State Jr. C. of C; pres, Payson Jr. C. of C; secy, Provo Exchange Club; Elks; Silks & Saddle Club; Provo Ski Club. Rel: Latter-day Saint. Mailing Add: 1623 Lone Peak Dr, Salt Lake City, Utah 84117.

REED, BUFORD LESLIE D
b. Dickson, Tenn, 2/5/11; s. Masha Lloyd Reed and Martha Elizabet Stevens R; m. 6/10/44, wid; c. Buford L, Jr, Matilda Sue and James Stevens. Polit. & Govt. Pos: City alderman, Dickson, Tenn, 53-, mem. of six cmts. and chmn. of one; v.mayor, Dickson, 4 years; Tenn. State Rep, 58-68. Mil. Serv: Entered as Pvt, Army, released as 2nd Lt, 40, recalled to Nat. Guard, 40, released as Capt, 30th Inf. Div, ETO, 42; Am. Defense and ETO Ribbons. Mem: Dir, C. of C, 64-65; Am. Legion; VFW; Mason (32°); York Mason, Shriner; secy, Dickson Rod and Gun Club. Rel: Methodist. Mailing Add: 106 Lone Oak Dr, Dickson, Tenn. 37055. (1967)

REED, CARLTON DAY, JR. D
Maine State Sen.
Educ: Colby Col, B.A, 53. Polit. & Govt. Pos: Maine State Sen, currently; del, Dem. Nat. Conv, 68. Bus. & Prof. Pos: Partner, bridge bldg. bus. in Woolwich. Mem: Assoc. Gen. Contractors of Maine. Mailing Add: Woolwich, Maine 04579. (1967)

REED, CECIL ARVELL R
b. Collinsville, Ill, 10/23/13; s. William Garrett Reed and Julia Jones R; m. 1/5/36 to Evelyn Ruth Collins; c. Carole Janette, Richard Wesley, Michael James and David Cecil. Educ: High Sch. grad, 32. Polit. & Govt. Pos: Mem, City Cmn. on Human Rights, Iowa; Iowa State Rep, 67-69. Bus. & Prof. Pos: Owner, Reed Floor Co, Iowa, 43- Mem: Bd. dirs, Cedar Rapids C. of C; bd. mem, NAACP and Westside Civic Club; U.G.N. Rev. Cmt; Mason; Shrine; Elks; Kiwanis; Carpenters Local 308. Rel: Methodist. Legal Res: 1608 Mt. Vernon Ave. S.E, Cedar Rapids, Iowa 52403. Mailing Add: P.O. Box 1307, Cedar Rapids, Iowa 52406. (1967)

REED, CLARKE THOMAS R
Chmn, Miss. State Rep. Party
b. 8/4/28; s. Lyman Harlan Reed and Kathryn Reynolds R; m. 10/8/57 to Julia Brooks; c. Julia Evans, Clark T, Jr. and Reynolds Crews. Educ: Univ. Mo, B.S. in Econ, 50; Phi Gamma Delta. Polit. & Govt. Pos: Chmn, Washington Co. Rep. Party, Miss, 62-65; finance chmn, Miss. State Rep. Party, 65, chmn, 66-; del, Rep. Nat. Conv, 68; chmn, South. Asn. Rep. State Chmn, 69- Bus. & Prof. Pos: Pres, Reed-Joseph Co, 52- Mil. Serv: Entered as 2nd Lt, Air Force, 53, released as 1st Lt, 55; Commendation Ribbon. Mem: Young Presidents Orgn. Rel: Presbyterian. Legal Res: Bayou Rd, Greenville, Miss. 38701. Mailing Add: Box 479, Greenville, Miss. 38701.

REED, DANA WHITMAN R
Asst. Dep. Controller, Calif.
b. Englewood, N.J, 1/17/44; s. Alden Gratien Reed and Mildred Hansen R; m. 8/23/69 to Daralyn Ellis; c. Kelly Sue. Educ: Foothill Col, 61-63. Polit. & Govt. Pos: Asst. to U.S. Rep. Don. H. Clausen, Calif, 65-66; field rep, Reagan for Gov. Cmt, San Francisco, 66; asst. secy. of bus. and transportation, Calif, 67-68; transportation coordinator Calif. Del, Rep. Nat. Conv, 68; speakers bur. coordinator, Calif. Nixon-Agnew Cmt, 68; mem, Calif. Rep. State Cent. Cmt, 69-; asst. dep. controller, Calif, 69- Rel: Protestant. Legal Res: 762 De Soto Dr, Palo Alto, Calif. 94303. Mailing Add: 1916 Argail Way, Sacramento, Calif. 95822.

REED, DONALD H, JR. R
Fla. State Rep.
b. East Liverpool, Ohio, 2/28/33; s. Donald H. Reed and Elfreda Burbick R; m. 8/24/57 to Carole Virginia Cole; c. Pamela Cole, Donald Paul, David Andrew and Douglas Kirk. Educ: Ohio State Univ, B.A, 57; Univ. of Fla, LL.B, 60; Lambda Chi Alpha; Phi Delta Phi. Polit. & Govt. Pos: Fla. State Rep, Palm Beach Co, 63-, minority leader, Fla. House of Rep, 64-69; mem, Fla. Constitutional Rev. Cmn, 65-68 and Fla. Tax Reform Cmn, 67-69; del, Rep. Nat. Conv. and Presidential Elector, Fla, 68. Bus. & Prof. Pos: Assoc. munic. judge, Deerfield Beach, Fla. and attorney, Palm Beach Co. Sheriff's Off, 62-65; town prosecutor, Hillsboro Beach, 64-; town attorney, Highland Beach, 65-; partner, Deschler, Reed, Mowry & Poulton, currently. Mil. Serv: Entered as 2nd Lt, Army, 54, released as 1st Lt, 56, after serv. in 2nd Armored Div, ETO. Mem: Kiwanis; Mason; Jaycees; Am. Fla. and South Palm Beach Co. Bar Asns; Shrine; VFW. Nominated Outstanding Young Men of Am, Nat. Jr. C. of C, 65 and Outstanding Mem. Fla. House of Rep, 67. Rel: Presbyterian. Mailing Add: 555 S. Federal Hwy, Boca Raton, Fla. 33432.

REED, EUGENE THOMPSON, SR. D
b. Church Hill, Md, 11/1/28; s. Thomas Edward Reed, Sr. and Hallie M. Thompson R; m. 9/3/49 to Barbara Jane Thompson; c. Cheryl Lynn, Donna Jean, Thomas Merland, Cathy Ann and Eugene Thompson, Jr. Educ: H.F. Brown Voc. High Sch, dipl; Navy Printing Sch, Wash, D.C, dipl. Polit. & Govt. Pos: Committeeman, Fifth Elec. Dist, 60-68; mem, first reapportionment cmt, Del, 63; constable, Del, 63-64; chmn, Tenth Dist. Dem. Cmt, Del, 64-67, chmn, Eighth Dist. Dem. Cmt, 67-68; mem, Del. State Dem. Cmt, 64-68, Co. Dem. Exec. Cmt, 66-68; justice of the peace, 65-66 & 68-; chief state safety inspector, 67-68; alternate del, Dem. Nat. Conv, 68. Mil. Serv: Entered as Seaman 3/C, Navy, 49, released as Seaman 2/C, 50, after serv. as a Printer. Mem: AF&AM; Touchdown Club; Dem. Club (past pres); Claymont Heights Civic Asn.(past pres); mgr, Little League; Maple Lane PTA (past v.pres); Oil, Chem. and Atomic Workers Union (past chmn, Workman's Cmt); Iron Worker's Union. Rel: Methodist. Mailing Add: 2505 Lincoln Ave, Claymont, Del. 19703.

REED, EWELL RICHARD D
Tex. State Rep.
b. Plano, Tex, 2/25/34; s. Joseph Oscar Reed and Buelah Ellen Robinson R; m. 5/30/54 to Helen Colene Vest; c. Richard Dale, Malcolm Ray, Cynthia Jean and Dianna Lynn. Educ: Decatur Baptist Col, $1\frac{1}{2}$ years. Polit. & Govt. Pos: Precinct chmn, Dem. Party, Tex, 64-68; Tex. State Rep, Dist. 33, 69- Rel: Baptist. Mailing Add: 4034 Shelley Blvd, Dallas, Tex. 75211.

REED, GEORGE JOSEPH R
Chmn, U.S. Bd. of Parole
b. Haigler, Nebr, 5/31/14; s. Edwin W. Reed and Cleo Randall R; m. 10/10/38 to Lois Goetze; c. George Calvert. Educ: Pasadena Col, A.B, 38, LL.D, 53; Univ. South. Calif, grad. work, 48. East. Nazarene Col, hon. LL.D, 57. Polit. & Govt. Pos: Dep. probation officer, Los Angeles Co, Calif, 38-46; field dir, Calif. Youth Authority, 46-49; dep. dir, Minn. Youth Conserv. Cmn, 49-53; chmn, Youth Correction Div, U.S. Bd. of Parole, 53-57, chmn. and mem, U.S. Bd. of Parole, 57-64, chmn, 69-; dir, Nev. Dept. of Parole and Probation, 65-67, Lane Co. Juvenile Dept, Eugene, Ore, 68-69. Bus. & Prof. Pos: Prof. of criminology, Col. of the Sequoias, 67-68. Mil. Serv: Navy, 41-44. Publ: Crime Prevention and Community Organization, State of Minn, 50; 'Parole Better Protects Society,' Vital Speeches of the Day, 11/58; 'Treating the Youthful Offender,' Southwest Legal Found, 59. Mem: Fel. Am. Acad. of Criminology; Am. Correctional Asn; Nat. Parole Coun; Prfnl. Coun. Nat. Coun. on Crime and Delinquency. Award, Outstanding Pres. Alumni Asn, Pasadena Col; Spec. Award of Recognition, Am. Legion; Membership in Spec. Awards for Serv. to Humanities by Nat. Exchange Clubs of Am. Rel: Protestant. Legal Res: 1925 Coventry Way, Eugene, Ore. 97405. Mailing Add: 101 Indiana Ave, N.W, Washington, D.C. 20537.

REED, GLENN T. D
Chmn, Iowa Co. Dem. Cmt, Iowa
b. North English, Iowa, 1/11/20; s. Robert Reed and Gertrude Calef R; m. 10/14/39 to Pauline E. Jordan; c. Phyllis Ann, Linda Lee, John Harry and Kay Louise. Educ: North English High Sch, grad, 37. Polit. & Govt. Pos: Chmn, Iowa Co. Dem. Cmt, Iowa, 59- Bus. & Prof. Pos: Farmer, Iowa Co, Iowa, 37-51; jobber, Phillips 66 Petroleum Prods, 51- Mem: Rotary; Mason; mem, local sch. bd, 7 yrs. and co. sch. bd, 6 yrs. Hons. in High Sch, State Athletic Events. Rel: Christian Church. Mailing Add: North English, Iowa 52316.

REED, GORDON WIES R
Mem, Nat. Rep. Finance Cmt.
b. Chicago, Ill, 11/20/99; s. Frank Reed and Mary Wies R; m. 10/7/67 to Genevieve Funston; c. Tom and step daughter Susan Logan. Educ: Univ. Ill, Urbana, B.S, 22. Polit. & Govt. Pos: Chmn, Rep. Citizens Cmt, Conn, 62-65 and Rep. Finance Cmt, 64-65; del, Rep. Nat. Conv, 68; mem, Nat. Rep. Finance Cmt, 69- Bus. & Prof. Pos: Chmn, Tex. Gulf Prod. Co, 41-64; chmn. finance cmt, Am. Metal Climax, 64- Mil. Serv: Pvt, Army, 18; asst. dir. aluminum and magnesium div, War Prod. Bd, 41-44; Civilian Air Medal, 55. Publ: Reed Report on Military Air Transport Service, U.S. Air Force, 58. Rel: Methodist. Mailing Add: 100 Clapboard Ridge Rd, Greenwich, Conn. 06830.

REED, J. DUFF, III R
b. Pittsburgh, Pa, 9/28/29; s. J. Duff Reed and Alice Williams R; m. 12/1/62 to Georgine Szalay. Educ: Univ. Va, B.A; Univ. Edinburgh, grad. cert. Polit. & Govt. Pos: Press secy. to U.S. Sen. Keating, N.Y, 63-64; consult, Rep. Cmts, 65-66; press secy. to U.S. Rep. R.C.B. Morton, Md, 65-66; and Nat. Rep. Senate Cmt, 66-67; spec. asst. to U.S. Sen. Thruston B. Morton, Ky; dir. govt-indust. rels, Radio Corp. Am, currently. Bus. & Prof. Pos: Reporter, United Press Int, 54-55; acct. exec, Erwin, Wasey, Ruthrauf & Ryan, 56-57 and Doremus & Co, New York, 58-60; pres, Sorin-Hall, Inc, Wash, 61-63. Rel: Episcopal. Mailing Add: 4241 Garfield St. N.W, Washington, D.C. 20007.

REED, JOHN HATHAWAY R
b. Ft. Fairfield, Maine, 1/5/21; s. Walter Manley Reed, Sr. and Eva Seeley R; m. 3/24/44 to Cora Davison; c. Cheryl Diane and Ruth Ann. Educ: Univ.

Maine, B.S, 42; Phi Eta Kappa. LL.D, Ricker Col. and Univ. Maine. Polit. & Govt. Pos: Maine State Rep, 55-57; Maine State Sen, 57-59, Pres, Maine State Senate, 59; Gov, Maine, 60-67; mem, Nat. Transportation Safety Bd, Wash, D.C, 67- Bus. & Prof. Pos: Dir, Reed Farms, Inc, Ft. Fairfield, Maine, 42- Mil. Serv: Entered as Storekeeper 3/C, Naval Res, 42, released as Lt.(jg), 45, after serv. in Cub 17, Okinawa, Pac, 45. Mem: Rotary; Capital Hill Club; Nat. Aviation Club; U.S. Trotting Asn; Elks; K. of P; Farm Bur; Grange; AMVETS; VFW; Am. Legion; Shrine; Mason. Rel: Congregational. Legal Res: Ft. Fairfield, Maine 04742. Mailing Add: 410 O St. S.W, Washington, D.C. 20024.

REED, LESTER B. R
Md. State Del.
b. Mt. Savage, Md, 8/10/08; married. Educ: Catherman's Bus. Col, Cumberland; Int. Correspondence Schs. Polit. & Govt. Pos: Md. State Del, 39-, Minority Leader, Md. State House of Del, 59-62. Bus. & Prof. Pos: Bus. counsr, Vending Stand Dept, Md. Workshop for the Blind. Rel: Episcopal; Communicant, St. George's Episcopal Church. Mailing Add: Valley View, Mt. Savage, Md. 21545.

REED, LOIS SWALLOW R
Pres, Iowa Fedn. Rep. Women
b. Waukee, Iowa, 10/4/04; d. Alden Swallow and Cassie Graham S; m. 7/2/39 to Herbert Milton Reed. Educ: Univ. North. Iowa, A.B, 28; Theta Gamma Nu; Zeta Lit. Soc. Polit. & Govt. Pos: Precinct committeewoman, Guthrie Co, Iowa, 42-54; v.chmn, Guthrie Co. Rep. Cent. Cmt, 54-68; pres, Guthrie Co. Rep. Women, 54; chmn. legis, Seventh Dist. Rep. Women, 59-60; first v.pres, Seventh Dist. Fedn. Rep. Women, 60, pres, 61-62; recording secy, Iowa Fedn. Rep. Women, 63-64, third v.pres, 65-66, first v.pres, 67, pres, 68-; del-at-lg, Rep. Nat. Conv, 68; mem. bd. dir, Nat. Fedn. Rep. Women, 68-69. Bus. & Prof. Pos: Teacher, Guttenbery Pub. Schs, Iowa, 24-26; teacher, Waterloo Pub. Schs, 28-29; instr. educ, Oshkosh Univ, Oshkosh, Wis, 29-38; teacher, Kenilworth, Ill, 38-40; co-owner, Reed Ins. Agency, Panora, Iowa, 40- Mem: Nat, Wis, Iowa and Ill. Educ. Asns; Am. Asn. Univ. Women; Eastern Star; Daughters of Nile; Federated Women's Club; Am. Legion Auxiliary; Federated Garden Club; Iowa Libr. Asn; Za-Ga-Zig Ladies Hosp. Unit; Iowa Independent Ins. Agents; Farm Bur; Iowa Heart Asn; Iowa Poetry Day Asn. Rel: Methodist. Mailing Add: Panora, Iowa 50216.

REED, MICHAEL LEE D
b. Durant, Okla, 9/9/37; s. I.N. Reed and Daisy L. Derrick R; m. 11/9/68 to Stephanie Williams. Educ: Wash. Univ, A.B, 61; Univ. Okla, LL.B, 62; Phi Delta Phi; Sigma Nu. Polit. & Govt. Pos: Mem. staff, Gov. Okla, 60-62, counsel to Gov, 62; asst. to U.S. Sen. J. Howard Edmondson, Okla, 63-64; legis. asst. to U.S. Rep. Carl Albert, Okla, 64- Mem: Fed. and Okla. Bar Asns. Rel: Methodist. Legal Res: Durant, Okla. 74701. Mailing Add: 1600 S. Joyce, Apt. B 1404, Arlington, Va. 22202.

REED, NATHANIEL PRYOR R
b. New York, N.Y, 7/22/33; s. Joseph Verner Reed and Permelia Pryor R; m. 1/9/66 to Alita Davis Weaver; c. Nathaniel Pryor, Jr, Alita Weaver and Adrian William Weaver. Educ: Trinity Col, Conn, B.A, 55; St. Anthony Hall. Polit. & Govt. Pos: City cmnr, Jupiter Island, Fla, 65-; spec. asst. to Gov. of Fla, 67-; alternate del, Rep. Nat. Conv, 68. Bus. & Prof. Pos: V.pres, Hobe Sound Co, Fla, 59- Mil. Serv: Entered as 2nd Lt, Air Force, 55, released as Capt, 59, after serving in Intel, ETO, N.Africa and Mid.E, 55-59. Mem: Martin Mem. Hosp. Bd. Dirs; Audubon Soc: Issac Walton League. Outstanding conservationist, Fla. Wildlife Fedn. Rel: Episcopal. Mailing Add: Jupiter Island, Hobe Sound, Fla. 33455.

REED, NELL QUINLAN R
b. Parsons, Kans, 3/6/89; d. John Quinlan and Catherine Fitzgibbons Q; m. to Sen. James A. Reed, wid; c. David Quinlan. Educ: Lindenwood Col; Hon. L.H.D, Coe Col; hon. LL.D, Lindenwood Col. Polit. & Govt. Pos: Mem, Kans. City Sch. Bd, Mo, 58-; del. and mem, Platform Cmt, Rep. Nat. Conv, 64; former mem, Mo. State Cmt. Bus. & Prof. Pos: Founder & former pres, Nelly Don, Inc, 16-55; chmn. bd, Fairview Farms, Inc, Mo, 30- Mem: Bd. trustees, Midwest Res. Inst, Lindenwood Col, Kans. City Philharmonic Asn, Conservatory of Music and Performing Arts Found. Mailing Add: 5049 Wornall Rd, Kansas City, Mo. 64112.

REED, NORRIS CUMMINS, JR. D
N.C. State Sen.
b. Washington, D.C, 8/27/10; s. Norris C. Reed, Sr. and Coronilla Seibert R; m. 8/15/36 to Gertrude Murrill; c. Norris C, III. Educ: Columbus Univ, LL.B, 37. Polit. & Govt. Pos: Judge Craven Co, Recorders Court, N.C, 62-66; N.C. State Sen, 69- Mil. Serv: Entered as Pvt, Army, 43, released as Sgt, 44, after serv. in Special Training Unit. Mem: Mason; Scottish Rite; Shrine; Jesters; Am. Legion; 40 et 8. Rel: Christian. Legal Res: Country Club Rd, New Bern, N.C. 28560. Mailing Add: P.O. Box 89, New Bern, N.C. 28560.

REED, OTTWA LUTHER D
V.Chmn, Wyandott Co. Dem. Cent. Cmt, Kans.
b. Vian, Okla, 9/3/06; s. David A. Reed and Anna Luther R; m. 5/18/41 to Mary Lee Turner; c. Arvita, Ottwa Luther, Jr, Karyen Manette and Kathy Malia. Educ: Lincoln High Sch, 4 years. Polit. & Govt. Pos: Dem. committeeman, Wyandotte, Co, Kans, 50-; v.chmn, Wyandotte Co. Dem. Cent. Cmt, 54-; del, Dem. Nat. Conv, 68. Bus. & Prof. Pos: Wyandotte Co. Supt. of Roads and Bridges, Kans, 53- Mem: Master, Mason; Blue Lodge; Orient Consistory (32°); Shrine; Daughters of Isis (past adv); Kans. City NAACP (past pres); dep. chief engr, Order of Cyrenes; treas, Trouver's Club. Rel: Baptist. Mailing Add: 1500 Cleveland Ave, Kansas City, Kans. 66104.

REED, ROBERT GORDON, JR. R
Chmn, Hardin Co. Rep. Cent. Cmt, Ohio
b. Kenton, Ohio, 9/21/36; s. Robert Gordon Reed and Eva Mae Campbell R; single. Educ: Ohio State Univ, B.A, 58, LL.B, 60; Phi Delta Phi. Polit. & Govt. Pos: Chmn, Hardin Co. Rep. Cent. Cmt, Ohio, 68- Bus. & Prof. Pos: Partner, Hanna & Reed, Kenton, Ohio, 64- Mil. Serv: Entered as 1st Lt, Army, 61, released as Capt, 64, after serv. at Judge Adv. Gen. Sch, Charlottesville, Va, 61-64; Army Commendation Medal. Mem: Am, Ohio State, Hardin Co. and Logan Co. Bar Asns; Grange; Elks; Kiwanis. Rel: United Presbyterian. Mailing Add: R.R. 1, Belle Center, Ohio 43310.

REED, RONALD SWAIN, JR. D
Mo. State Rep.
b. St. Joseph, Mo, 9/11/32; s. Ronald Swain Reed and Sally Juden R; m. 12/7/63 to Nancy Jane Jones. Educ: Univ. of Mo, A.B, 54 and LL.B, 58; Phi Delta Phi; Omicron Delta Kappa; Phi Gamma Delta. Polit. & Govt. Pos: Chief asst. prosecuting attorney, Buchanan Co, Mo, 58-60; del-at-lg, Dem. Nat. Conv, 60; Mo. State Rep, 65- Bus. & Prof. Pos: Attorney-at-law, Reed & Reed, 60- Mil. Serv: Entered as 2nd Lt, Army, 54, released as 1st Lt, 56, after serv. in 7th Inf. Div, Korea. Mem: Mo. and Am. Bar Asns; Elks; Eagles; treas, St. Joseph Bar Asn; bd. of dirs, Mo. Ment. Health Asn. Outstanding Good Govt. Award, St. Joseph C. of C, 65. Rel: Methodist. Mailing Add: 2602 Francis, St. Joseph, Mo. 64501.

REED, THOMAS CARE R
Rep. Nat. Committeeman, Calif.
b. N.Y.C, N.Y, 3/1/34; s. Gordon Weis Reed and Naomi Bradley R; m. 6/15/56 to Leslie Jean Papenfus; c. Carolyn, Gordon and Andrew. Educ: Cornell Univ, B.S. in Mech. Eng, 56; Univ. South. Calif, M.S. in Elec. Eng, 59; Tau Beta Pi. Polit. & Govt. Pos: Adv-prep, pres. and v.pres. cand, Rep. Nat. Cmt, 64; North. Calif. chmn, Reagan for Gov. Cmt, 66; mem, Calif. Rep. State Cent. Cmt, 66-; appointments secy, Gov. Off, Calif, 67; del, Rep. Nat. Conv, 68; Rep. Nat. Committeeman, Calif, 68- Bus. & Prof. Pos: Weapons physicist, Lawrence Radiation Lab, Univ. Calif, 59-62, consult, 62-66; managing partner, Supercon, Ltd, 62-65; pres, Quaker Hill Develop. Corp, 65-; dir, Bradley Producing Corp, 65- Mil. Serv: Entered as 2nd Lt, Air Force, 56, released as 1st Lt, 61, after serv. in Ballistic Missile Div, 56-59. Mem: Univ. Club, San Francisco; St. Francis Yacht Club; Ramada Club, Houston. Rel: Protestant. Legal Res: P.O. Box 694, Ross, Calif. 94957. Mailing Add: 503 D St, San Rafael, Calif. 94901.

REEDE, WILLIAM SAINT ELMO D
Committeeman, Richmond Dem. City Cmt, Va.
b. Manchester, Va, 9/16/99; s. Lewis Reede and Maggie Estelle Pryor R; single. Educ: Wayland Acad, grad; Va. Union Univ. Polit. & Govt. Pos: Past pres, and past chmn. bd. dirs, People's Polit. and Civic League, Inc. and chmn. Civic Improv. Cmt, currently; mem, Richmond Welfare Bd. and Richmond Human Rels. Cmn; committeeman, Richmond Dem. City Cmt, Va, 65-; alternate del, Dem. Nat. Conv, 68. Bus. & Prof. Pos: Partner, Tippy and Georges Tonsorial, 30-; mem. exec. cmt, Va. State Fedn. Labor, 6 years. Mem: YMCA (bd. dirs, Leigh St, 20 years, Prog. membership chmn, 16 years); F&AM. Afro Newspaper Award, 45. Rel: Baptist. Mailing Add: 2406 Fluvanna St, Richmond, Va. 23224.

REEDY, GEORGE EDWARD, JR. D
b. East Chicago, Ind, 8/5/17; s. George Edward Reedy and Mary Mulvaney R; m. 3/22/48 to Lillian Greenwald; c. Michael Andrew and William James. Educ: Univ. Chicago, B.A. in Sociol, 38. Polit. & Govt. Pos: Staff consult, Armed Serv. Preparedness Subcmt, U.S. Senate, 51-52; staff dir, Minority Policy, 53-54 and Majority Policy Cmt, 55-60; spec. asst. to Vice President Johnson, 61-66; press secy, President Johnson, 64-65; mem. adv. cmn, Selective Serv, 66-67 and President's Oceanog. Cmn, 67-68; spec. consult. to the President, 68-69. Bus. & Prof. Pos: Reporter, Phila. Inquirer, summer, 37; cong. correspondent, United Press Int, 38-41 & 46-51; v.pres. and dir, Struthers Wells Corp, 66-; lectr. and writer, 69- Mil. Serv: Army Air Force, 42-45. Publ: 'Speaking for the President,' In: The Voice of Govt, Wiley, 68; Who Will Do Our Fighting For Us?, World, 69. Mailing Add: 1701 Pennsylvania Ave. N.W, Suite 407, Washington, D.C. 20006.

REEDY, W. H. D
Fla. State Rep.
b. Lothair, Ky, 8/2/16; m. to Eloise Bashor; c. Mrs. James Madison Stewart, Jr. Educ: Pub. schs, Umatilla, Fla. Polit. & Govt. Pos: Fla. State Rep, 58-62, 64- Bus. & Prof. Pos: Dir, pub. rels, Fla. Tel. Corp. Mil. Serv: Army. Mem: Past pres, Kiwanis; Jaycees; Am. Legion; Farm Bur; Mason; Elks; chmn, Lake Co. Safety Coun; dir, Lake Co. Retarded Child Asn; trustee, Montverde Acad; assoc. trustee, Howey Acad; dir, Orange Blossom Chap, FPRA; fund drive chmn, Am. Red Cross, 61, 64; chmn, S.Lake Co. Bus. Asn; Fla. Pub. Rels. Asn; past pres. and secy-treas, Lake Co. Boys Ranch Found, Inc; Coun. of State Govt. Nat. Cmt. on Code and Ordinances; Nat. Coun, Hwy. and Beautification Cmt. Gov. Citation for Outstanding Contributions to State; Bd. of Regents' Citation for Leadership in Educ. Rel: Methodist. Mailing Add: P.O. Box 48, Leesburg, Fla. 32748.

REEL, WILLIAM ALBERT, JR. D
b. Edgefield, 9/24/20; s. William Albert Reel, Sr. and Carrie Moultrie R; single. Educ: Edgefield High Sch, 38. Polit. & Govt. Pos: Mayor, Edgefield, S.C, 46-48; S.C. State Rep, 51-58; S.C. State Sen, 65-66. Bus. & Prof. Pos: Ins. and acct. Mil. Serv: S.C. Nat. Guard, Lt. Comdr, AG, EOH 51; 42-45 served with Air Force, Eighth Air Force in 306th Bomb. Gp, 30 months overseas. Mem: Mason; Lions; Am. Legion; 40 et 8. Rel: Baptist. Mailing Add: Box 210, Edgefield, S.C. 29824.

REES, THOMAS L. D
Chmn, Mitchell Co. Dem. Party, Tex.
b. San Angelo, Tex, 12/14/39; s. Horace B. Rees and Margaret Holland R; m. 8/4/62 to Margaret Diane; c. Thomas L, Jr. and Melanie Diane. Educ: Rice Univ, B.S. and B.A, 62; Baylor Univ, LL.B, 65; Phi Delta Phi. Polit. & Govt. Pos: Chmn, Mitchell Co. Dem. Party, Tex, 67-; del. to Rules and Regulation 24th Cong. Dist, 68-; v.pres, Colo. Independent Sch. Dist, Colorado City, Tex, 68-69, pres, 69- Bus. & Prof. Pos: Partner, Thompson & Rees, 65-69. Mem: State Bar of Tex; Scottish Rite. Rel: Methodist. Legal Res: 1430 Oak, Colorado City, Tex. 79512. Mailing Add: Box 1007, Colorado City, Tex. 79512.

REES, THOMAS M. D
U.S. Rep, Calif.
b. Los Angeles, Calif, 3/26/25; s. Caradoc Rees and Mildred Melgaard R; m. 4/16/60 to Leanne G. Boccardo; c. Evan B. and James C. Educ: Occidental Col, B.A, 50; Univ. Calif, Los Angeles, grad. work, 50-51. Polit. & Govt. Pos: Mem, State Dem. Cent. Cmt, Calif, 54-56; Calif. State Assemblyman, 55-62; del, Dem. Nat. Conv, 56, 60, 64 & 68; Calif. State Sen, 26th Dist, 62-65; mem, Calif. Cmn. of the Californias, 63-66 and Calif. Arts Cmn, 63-66; U.S. Rep, 26th Cong. Dist, Calif, 65-, mem, Banking and Currency Cmt, subcmts,

Domestic Finance, Int. Trade and Int. Finance, U.S. House of Rep. Bus. & Prof. Pos: Pres, Compania Del Pacifico, 52-; mem. bd, Connoisseur Wine Imports, Inc, 65-68. Mil. Serv: Entered as Pvt, Army, 43; released as Pfc, 46, after serv. in 89th Inf. Div, Third Army, ETO; Combat Inf. Badge; ETO Medal with 2 Battle Stars; Am. Theater Ribbon. Mem: Los Angeles Mus. of Art Assoc; Los Angeles World Affairs Coun; Los Angeles Opera Asn; Am. Legion. Rel: Episcopal. Legal Res: 1673 Waynecrest Dr, Beverly Hills, Calif. 90210. Mailing Add: House Office Bldg, Washington, D.C. 20515.

REES, WILLARD ANDREW 'BILLY' R
Chmn, Webster Co. Rep. Party, Ga.
b. Preston, Ga, 1/11/28; s. Willard Rees and Jessie Dell Walker R; m. 6/1/47 to Helen Melton; c. Sandra (Mrs. Wills), Peggy Sue and Kathy Ann. Educ: Webster Co. High Sch, Preston, Ga. Polit. & Govt. Pos: City Councilman, Preston, Ga, 64-; chmn, Webster Co. Rep. Party, 65- Bus. & Prof. Pos: Self-employed, farming and timber interests, 46-64; Area Mgr, Ga. Timberlands, Inc. 64- Mem: Ga. Farm Bur; Ga. Forestry Asn; Stewart-Webster Cattlemen's Asn. Rel: Baptist. Legal Res: Preston, Ga. 31824. Mailing Add: P.O. Box 63, Preston, Ga. 31824.

REES, WILLIAM H. H. D
b. Meriden, Conn, 4/30/34; s. Dr. Howard H. Rees (deceased) and Margaret Connors R; m. 9/21/63 to Joanne P. Tenedine; c. Joseph T. Educ: Yale Col, B.A, 56; Am. Col. Life Underwriters, C.L.U. Polit. & Govt. Pos: Alderman, 21st Ward, 66-67 and 1st Ward, 63-65; ward chmn, Dem. Town Cmt, 60-65; pres, New Haven Young Dem, 62; v.pres, Conn. Young Dem, 61. Bus. & Prof. Pos: Salesman, Estate and Bus. Analysis, Conn. Gen. Life Ins. Co, 56- Mil. Serv: Entered as Pvt, Nat. Guard, 59, released as Spec. 4, 65. Mem: Knights of St. Patrick; exec. cmt, Family Serv; v.chmn, Region of New Haven, Yale Alumni Fund. Rel: Roman Catholic. Legal Res: 271 Dwight St, New Haven, Conn. 06511. Mailing Add: Chapel Square, New Haven, Conn. 06510. (1967)

REESE, DANIEL GUNDER R
Secy, Christian Co. Rep. Cent. Cmt, Ill.
b. Taylorville, Ill, 12/14/27; s. Leal Wiley Reese and Helen Gunder R; m. 11/22/56 to Patricia Ann Everhart; c. Lindsey, Erin and Jill. Educ: Univ. Ill, B.S, 51; Univ. Chicago Law Sch, J.D, 54; Phi Kappa Psi. Polit. & Govt. Pos: Committeeman, 52nd Dist. Rep. Party, Ill, 62-64; treas, Christian Co. Rep. Cent. Cmt, 62-64, secy, 64-; precinct committeeman, Taylorville Twp. Rep. Party, Christian Co, 64-, chmn, 65-; alderman, Taylorville, 66-69, mayor, 69- Bus. & Prof. Pos: Dir, Christian Co. Agr. Fair Asn, 56-, secy, 57-62; attorney-at-law, Taylorville, 56-; secy. and dir, Breeze Printing Co, 64- and Taylorville Indust. Corp, currently. Mil. Serv: Entered as Pvt, Army, 54, released as Cpl, 56, after serv. in Germany. Mem: Ill. State and Christian Co. Bar Asns; Mason (32°), Shrine; Optimist; Taylorville Country Club. Rel: Presbyterian. Legal Res: 513 West Main, Taylorville, Ill. 62568. Mailing Add: 205 South Washington, Taylorville, Ill. 62568.

REESE, JAMES EDWIN R
b. Lincoln Co. Ga, 7/21/31; s. James Tankersley Reese and Georgia Emma Ginn R; m. 4/6/57 to Jeanette Ansley; c. Robert Bryan. Educ: Palmer Bus. Col. Polit. & Govt. Pos: Chmn, Columbia Co. Rep. Exec. Cmt, Ga, 64-68. Bus. & Prof. Pos: Gen. supt, Castleberry's Food Co. Mil. Serv: Entered as A/S, Navy, 49, released as AM-3, 53, after serv. in Naval Air Transportation Corps; Good Conduct Medal; Unit Citation. Mem: Mason; Civitan. Rel: Methodist. Legal Res: 4026 Brockwood St, Martinez, Ga. 30907. Mailing Add: R.R. 5, Box 564, Martinez, Ga. 30907. (1967)

REESE, NORMAN RANDOLPH D
Chmn, Lea Co. Dem. Party, N.Mex.
b. Portales, N.Mex, 1/14/18; s. George Lee Reese, Sr. and Jim Porter Jackson R; m. 9/1/40 to Shirley Beacham; c. Randolph Lee, Rebecca Lynn and Laurie Juanita. Educ: N.Mex. Mil. Inst, 35-37; Univ. Colo, LL.B, 40; Phi Delta Phi; Pi Kappa Alpha. Polit. & Govt. Pos: Dist. attorney, Lea, Eddy and Chaves Co, N.Mex, 49-52; chmn, Lea Co. Dem. Party, 68- Mil. Serv: Entered as Pvt, Air Force, 42, released as Sgt, 45, after serv. in 15th WEA Squadron, Pac. Theatre, 42-45; Air Medal; Purple Heart; Good Conduct Medal. Mem: Lea Co, N.Mex. and Am. Bar Asns; DAV; Am. Legion; VFW. Citation, DAV. Rel: Episcopal. Legal Res: 1330 Cimarron, Hobbs, N.Mex. 88240. Mailing Add: Box 1619, Hobbs, N.Mex. 88240.

REEVES, ALBERT L, JR. R
b. Steelville, Mo, 5/31/06; s. Albert L. Reeves and Martha Ferguson R; m. 10/3/35 to Eleanor Louise Glasner; c. Elaine Louise (Mrs. Padovani), Martha Emilie and Nancy Lee. Educ: William Jewell Col, A.B, 27; Univ. of Mo, LL.B, 31; Kappa Sigma; Phi Delta Phi; Pi Kappa Delta; Delta Sigma Rho. Polit. & Govt. Pos: Treas, Jackson Co. Rep. Cmt, Mo, 34-36; U.S. Rep, Mo, 47-48. Bus. & Prof. Pos: Partner, Michaels, Blackmar, Newkirk, Eager & Swanson, Kansas City, Mo, 31-50; partner, Cummings, Sellers, Reeves & Connor and predecessor firms, Wash, D.C, 49-60; sr. v.pres, dir. and secy, Utah Construction & Mining Co, Calif, 58-; dir. and secy, Marcona Corp, Cia San Juan, 61- Mil. Serv: Entered as Capt, Army, 42, released as Lt. Col, 46, after serv. in Mo. River Div, Corps. of Engrs; China-Burma-India Theater of Opers; Motor Transport Command, 468th Qm. Group and 1905th Aviation Bn; China-Burma-India and Z I Ribbons. Mem: Am. and Fed. Bar Asns; Am. Soc. of Int. Law; Acad. of Polit. Sci; DeMolay (Legion of Honor); adv. bd, CORO Found; pres. and trustee, World Affairs Coun. of North. Calif; dir, World Trade Club of San Francisco; bd. dirs, Golden Gate Chap, Am. Red Cross. Rel: Episcopal. Legal Res: 2225 Forest View Ave, Hillsborough, Calif. 94010. Mailing Add: Utah Construction & Mining Co, 550 California St, San Francisco, Calif. 94104.

REEVES, EDWARD IRVIN R
V.Chmn, 13th Dist. Rep. Party
b. Warwick, N.Dak, 4/18/15; s. Clyde Leroy Reeves and Eva Long R; m. 12/20/36 to Beatrice Ann Maurer; c. Clifford, Vicki Bea and Lori Ann. Educ: Warwick High Sch, 2 years. Polit. & Govt. Pos: V.chmn, Benson Co. Rep. Party, 50-54, chmn, 54-66; v.chmn, 13th Dist. Rep. Party, 66- Bus. & Prof. Pos: Owner, Warwick Oil Co, 56-; owner and operator, farm, currently. Mem: Elks; Farm Bur; Sheyenne Valley Rod and Gun Club. Rel: Lutheran. Mailing Add: Warwick, N.Dak. 58381.

REEVES, HELEN GRAYSON R
d. Thomas Samuel Grayson and Mary Elizabeth Hayes G; m. 4/20/27 to Thomas Hal Reeves, Wid; c. Katheryn (Mrs. J. L. Jean) and Ann (Mrs. Eddy); grandchildren; Hal and Lane Jean and Anthony Eddy. Educ: Henderson State Col, B.A, 25. Polit. & Govt. Pos: Chmn. fund raising, Eisenhower Campaign, Columbia Co, Ark, 52; pres, Columbia Co. Rep. Women, 67-68, chmn, 68-; chmn. fund raising, Nixon Campaign Columbia Co, 68; alternate del, Rep. Nat. Conv, 68. Bus. & Prof. Pos: V.pres, Farmers Bank and Trust Co. Magnolia, Ark; pres, Reeves Land and Timber Develop; chmn, City Planning Cmn, 62-66; owner, Red Bird Lumber Co. Mem: PTA (pres, 36-38); Band Parents, (pres, 45); Quota Club (pres, 50-51, lt. gov, 54); Sarusis Club (pres, 35-36). Rel: Church of Christ. Mailing Add: 1105 Lawton Circle, Magnolia, Ark. 71753.

REEVES, JAMES JERAULD D
Fla. State Rep.
b. Troy, Ala, 10/11/38; s. David Chester Reeves and Goldie Elaine Jerauld R; m. 4/10/63 to Lelia Frances Weaver; c. Cari Michelle and James Jerauld, Jr. Educ: Pensacola Jr. Col; Fla. State Univ; Stetson Univ. Col. Law, LL.B, 62; Alpha Tau Omega; Delta Theta Phi. Polit. & Govt. Pos: Fla. State Rep, Dist, 4, 66-, v.chmn, State Govt. Orgn. and Efficiency Cmt, Fla. House of Rep, currently, mem, Finance and Taxation Cmt. and Rules and Calendar Cmt, currently. Mil. Serv: Entered Marines, 56, released as Lance Cpl, 64, after serv. in Marine Corps Res. Mem: Fla. and Am. Bar Asns; Soc. of the Bar of the First Judicial Circuit; Am. Arbit. Asn; Am. Trial Lawyers Asn; pres, Fla. Jr. Miss Scholarship Found, currently; Pensacola Sports Asn; Navy League; Pensacola Jaycees (bd. dir, 63-66, first v.pres, 64-65, pres, 65-66); bd. gov, Fiesta of Five Flags, 65, 66 & 67; bd. dir, Pensacola Zool. Soc, 65-67; dist. v.pres, Fla. Jaycees, 66-67. Received the Am. Jurisp. Award for legal thesis on urban renewal at graduation; Named Jaycee of the Year by Pensacola Jaycees, 64, Selected as Outstanding Young Man of Escambia Co. and Received Distinguished Serv. Award, 66-67. Rel: Presbyterian. Legal Res: 2300 Osceola Blvd, Pensacola, Fla. 32503. Mailing Add: 98 E. Garden St, Pensacola, Fla. 32501.

REEVES, JOHN ESTILL D
b. Owenton, Ky, 11/5/02; s. Lorenzo Herman Reeves and Ada Roberts R; wid; c. Caroline (Mrs. Marvin Lampert), Robert Estill and David Roe. Educ: Univ. Ky, A.B, 26, M.A, 38; Columbia Univ, 39-40; Pi Sigma Alpha; Phi Alpha Delta. Polit. & Govt. Pos: Research assoc, Ky. Legis. Coun, 37-38; asst. state local finance officer, Ky, 38-39; admin. analyst, U.S. Dept. War, 43-44; exec. asst, Ky. Dept. Revenue, 44-45; precinct committeeman, Fayette Co. Dem. Party, 48-56 & 60-68, legis. dist. chmn, 62-68; mem, State Cmn. Legis. Reapportionment, 62-63; del, Ky. Constitution Rev. Assembly, 64-66; del-at-lg, Dem. Nat. Conv, 68; cand. for City Cmnr, Lexington, Ky, 69. Bus. & Prof. Pos: Soc. sci. teacher, Monumit Sch, Pawling, N.Y, 34-36; grad. asst, dept. polit. sci, Univ, Ky, 36-37, instr, 40-41, asst. prof, 41-60, assoc. prof, 60-68; retired. Publ: Co-auth, Fundamental of Citizenship: Kentucky Civics, Laidlaw Bros, 55; auth, Kentucky Government, Bur. Govt. Research, Univ. Ky, 60; 'The Constitution Making Process,' Ky. Law J, 11/47. Mem: Am. Polit. Sci. Asn; Nat. Munic. League; Am. Soc. Pub. Admin; Am. Asn. Univ. Prof; Omicron Delta Kappa; Optimists. Gov. award of merit for work on Constitution Rev. Assembly, 66. Rel: Unitarian. Mailing Add: 217 Woodspoint Rd, Lexington, Ky. 40502.

REEVES, R. B. 'BREEZY' D
Miss. State Sen.
b. Pike Co, Miss, 8/1/28; married. Polit. & Govt. Pos: Miss. State Sen, currently. Bus. & Prof. Pos: Lawyer. Mem: Sigma Nu; Phi Alpha Delta; C. of C; K. of P; Lions; Am. Legion. Rel: Baptist. Mailing Add: 820 Northwest St, McComb, Miss. 39648. (1967)

REEVES, THEODORE C. 'TED' R
b. Central City, Nebr, 3/17/05; m. 12/24/29 to Portia Marsh; c. Don T, Ladd M, Virginia (Mrs. Fraser) and Kathleen (Mrs. Owens). Educ: Chapman High Sch. Polit. & Govt. Pos: Mem, Nebr. Water Pollution Control Coun, currently; former mem, local sch. bd, nine years; Nebr. State Sen, 62-69. Bus. & Prof. Pos: Farmer and cattle rancher. Mem: Farm Bur.(past mem. bd. dirs. and midstate bd); past mem, Merrick Co. Extension Bd; past chmn, 4-H Bldg. Cmt. Outstanding Farmer Award, Central City C. of C, 61. Rel: Baptist. Mailing Add: R.R. 1, Central City, Nebr. 68826.

REGALIA, GWENDOLYN WHITEFORD D
Mem, Calif. Dem. State Cent. Cmt.
b. Ross, Calif, 8/7/33; d. Allan Whiteford, Jr. and Eunice Jenkins W; m. 7/1/56 to Edmund Louis Regalia; c. Douglas Whiteford, Kenneth Edmund, Phillip Allan and Constance Eunice. Educ: Santa Rosa Jr. Col, A.A, 52; Univ. Calif, Berkeley, A.B, 55 and Elem. Educ. Teaching Credential, 56. Polit. & Govt. Pos: Secy. and v.pres, Walnut Creek Dem. Club, Calif, 63-67; women's chmn. for Gov. Edmund Brown, Walnut Creek, 66; co-chmn, women's div, Contra Costa Co. Dem. Party, 66-; co. coordinator, Cranston for Senate, 68; mem, Calif. Dem. State Cent. Cmt, 68-; women's chmn, Miller for State Senate, Walnut Creek, 69. Bus. & Prof. Pos: Teacher, Oakland Pub. Schs, Calif, 56 and Berkeley Pub. Schs, 56-59; substitute teacher, Mt. Diablo Pub. Schs, Concord, 60-61. Mem: Am. Asn. Univ. Women; Walnut Creek Dem. Club; Citizens United. Rel: Unitarian. Mailing Add: 230 El Divisadero Ave, Walnut Creek, Calif. 94598.

REGAN, EDWIN J. D
b. San Francisco, 1906; m. to Julia Frances Beauman; c. Michael, Craig, Kathleen. Educ; St. Mary's Col; Univ. of Calif; Hastings Col. of Law. Polit. & Govt. Pos: Assoc. Justice, Court of Appeals, 3rd Dist, 65-; Calif. State Sen. 49-65; Dist. Attorney, Trinity Co. 34-48; First Sen. Rep. on Judicial Coun. Bus. & Prof. Pos: Practicing attorney, Weaverville. Mem: Native Sons; Elks; Commonwealth Club; Grange; Press Union League; Sacramento-San Joaquin Wine and Food Soc; Riverview Country Club, Redding. Mailing Add: Box 176, Weaverville, Calif. 96093. (1967)

REGAN, KATHRYN DELIMA R
b. South Bend, Wash, 8/14/25; d. Gordon John King and Delima Victoria Charron K; m. 8/10/45 to Joseph Earl Regan; c. Rebecca Suzanne (Mrs.

James R. Tyrrell); Kevin Paul, Michael Patrick, Philip Sean and Brian Joseph. Educ: State Col. of Wash, Bus. Course, 43-45. Polit. & Govt. Pos: Block capt, Citizens for Nixon Cmt, Wash, 60 & 68; legis. dist. chmn, Christensen for Sen. Cmt, 61-62; precinct anal. chmn, area 8, 46th Legis. Dist. Rep. Party, 62-63; del, King Co. & Wash. State Rep. Conv, 62 & 68, alternate del, 64; asst. precinct committeeman, King Co. Rep. Cent. Cmt, 62-66, task force top award winner, 62-64; mem, Rep. Speakers' Bur, Wash, 62-67; pres, Pro-Am, 63; ed, monthly publ, Y.R. Wire and mem. bd. dirs, N. King Co. Young Rep. Club, 63-64; v.chmn, Goldwater for President Cmt, 63-64; chmn, 5-20 Club, 63-64 and Evans for Gov. Banquet, 64; v.chmn, King Co. Citizens for Goldwater, 64; del. Rep. Nat. Conv, 64. Mem: Publicity chmn. and past pres, Ryther Child Center Guild, 62-66; alumnus, seminar, Found. for Econ. Educ; asst. dir, Pub. Affairs Prog. and v.chmn, Town Hall West; del, Archdiocesian Coun. of Cath. Women Conv, 59; Seattle Girl Scout Coun, 7 years; Cath. Children's Serv. Rel: Catholic. Mailing Add: 3542 N.E. 94th St, Seattle, Wash. 98115.

REGAN, OUIDA BAGGETT D

b. Pensacola, Fla, 9/6/27; d. Thomas Lloyd Baggett and Lois Byrd B; div; c. Daniel Thomas and Marcia Lynn. Educ: Huntingdon Col. Polit. & Govt. Pos: Chmn, Santa Rosa Island Authority, 55-63 and Coun. of Econ. Develop, 61-63; mem, Fla. Adv. Coun, Small Bus. Admin, 63-, Adv. Coun, Indust. Cmn. and Fiesta of Five Flags Cmn, 65- Bus. & Prof. Pos: Pres, Baggett Construct. Co, 50- Mem: Dir, Nat. Asn. of Homebuilders; dir, W. Fla. Homebuilders Asn, pres, 65; secy-treas, Fla. Homebuilders Asn, 57; dir, Gr. Pensacola C. of C, 66, v.pres, 68; trustee, Pensacola Art Asn; pres, Pensacola Chap, Zonta Int, 54; dir, Fiesta of Five Flags and pres, 64; sch. bd, Christ Episcopal Day Sch, 68-; bd, Pensacola Oratorio Soc, 69. Jr. C. of C. Good Govt. Award, 64; Fla. Indust. Fact Book dedicated to her in recognition of serv. to Fla. Rel: Episcopal. Mailing Add: The Bayshore, 825 Bayshore Dr, Pensacola, Fla. 32507.

REGAN, WALTER EDWARD R

Mem, Stanislaus Co. Rep. Cent. Cmt, Calif.
b. Butte, Mont, 10/1/26; s. Walter E. Regan (deceased) and Monida Gransberry R; m. 4/3/47 to Gloria Gene Craig; c. Deborah, Michael and Timothy. Educ: Woodbury Col. Polit. & Govt. Pos: Mem, Stanislaus Co. Rep. Cent. Cmt, Calif, 62-, chmn, 62-67; former treas, Rep. Co. Chmn. Asn. Calif; Rep. cand. for Calif. State Sen, Third Sen. Dist, 68. Mil. Serv: Entered as Pvt, Marine Corps, 43, released as Pfc, 45, after serv. in 2nd Marine Div, Pac. Mem: Am. Inst. of CPA; Calif. Soc. of CPA, dir, Greater Modesto C. of C, 63-65; dir, Stanislaus Co. Taxpayers Asn, 65-; Elks; K. of C; Serra Club; Am. Legion; past pres, Kiwanis. Rel: Catholic. Legal Res: 416 Greenwich Lane, Modesto, Calif. 95350. Mailing Add: 1016 McHenry Ave, Modesto, Calif. 95350.

REGGIE, EDMUND M. D

b. Crowley, La, 7/19/26; s. Fred Reggie and Victoria Andraous R; m. 6/17/51 to Doris Anne Boustany; c. Edmund Michael, Vicki Anne, Denis, Gregory, Mariam Alicia and Raymond. Educ: Univ. of Southwest. La, B.A, 46; Tulane Univ, LL.B, 49; Pi Kappa Delta; Blue Key; Phi Kappa Theta; La Societe du Droit Civile; Alpha Omega. Polit. & Govt. Pos: Judge, Crowley City Court, La, 50-; mem, Seventh Cong. Dist. of La, Stevenson-Kefauver Campaign, 56; mem, La. State Dem. Cent. Cmt, 56-64; chmn, Seventh Cong. Dist. and 15th Judicial Dist. Dem. Exec. Cmts, 56-63; co-chmn, La, Kennedy-Johnson Campaign, 60; presidential elector, La, 60; Am. specialist, State Dept, 61; chmn, La. Gubernatorial Inaugural Ceremonies, 64 & 68; mem, La. Mineral Bd, 64-; cmnr, La. Dept. of Pub. Welfare, 64-65; exec. dir, La. Cmn. on Exten. and Continuing Educ, currently; chmn, Kennedy Presidential Campaign in La, 68; del, Dem. Nat. Conv, 68. Bus. & Prof. Pos: Chmn. bd. dirs, Acadia Savings & Loan Asn, 57-; v.chmn. bd. dirs, La. Bank & Trust Co, 60- Publ: Obscenity and The Law, 66. Mem: Pres, Acadia Parish Bar Asn, 59; chmn, Cardinal Newman Found, 62-65; K. of C.(4°); Kiwanis; Town Club; Bayou Bend Country Club; Fed. City Club; Nat. Capital Dem. Club; Camelot Club, Baton Rouge; Lamplighter Club, New Orleans. Named Outstanding Dem. of La, La. Young Dem, 63. Rel: Catholic. Legal Res: 400 North Ave, Crowley, La. 70526. Mailing Add: P.O. Box D, Crowley, La. 70526.

REGIS, LARRY, JR. D

Utah State Rep.
b. Kenilworth, Utah, 12/33/35; s. Larry Regis and Vera Callor R; m. 6/4/59 to Virginia Lee; c. Jana, Darin and Lance. Educ: Carbon Col, A.S, 56; Brigham Young Univ, B.S; Assoc. Men Student Coun; Tau Sigma. Polit. & Govt. Pos: Pres, Young Dem, 60-62; chmn, Carbon-Emery Medicare Coun, Utah, 66; state del, co. del. and committeeman, Dem. Party, Utah, 66-68; Utah State Rep, 67-, Minority Floor Leader, Utah State House of Rep, v.chmn, Budget Audit Cmt; mem, Utah Safety Coun; mem. S. East. Utah Develop. Cmt. Bus. & Prof. Pos: Asst. dist. mgr, Hamilton Funds, 64; regional dir, Brigham Young Univ. Alumni Fund, 66. Mil. Serv: Army Res. Mem: Utah Educ Asn; UMW Local 5861, 55-56; Commun. Theater; Jr. C. of C; Four letterman and all state baseball team, high sch; football team, Brigham Young Univ; Distinguished Serv. Award, 62. Rel: Latter-day Saint. Mailing Add: R.R. 1, Helper, Utah 84526.

REGISTER, WILLIAM MORELL, JR. D

Fla. State Rep.
b. Nashville, Ga, 5/4/30; s. William Morell Register, Sr. and Georgia Mary Amanda McKinnon R; m. 12/27/57 to Roelofje Florence de Jonge; c. John Michael, Amanda, Lillian and Sabrina. Educ: Emory University, 46-48; Tufts University, A.B, 51; Stanford Law Sch, 51-53; Univ. London, 55-56; Cornell Univ, LL.B, 60; Alpha Epsilon Upsilon; Eta Sigma Psi; Delta Theta Phi; Theta Delta Chi. Polit. & Govt. Pos: Attorney, Hillsborough Co. Legis. Del; Fla, 62-63; mem, Hosp. Lay Adv. Bd, Fla, 64-; mem, Hillsborough Co. Charter Cmn, 65-66; Fla. State Rep, 66- Mil. Serv: Entered as Ens, Navy, 53, released as Lt, 59, after serv. in Embassy, London, Naval ROTC, Cornell Univ. and Korean Theater, 53-54; Comdr, Naval Res, 67; Am. Defense, UN Korean Serv. and U.S. Korean Campaign Medals; Korean Presidential Unit Citation. Mem: Am, Fla. and Tampa Bar Asns; Propeller Club; U.S. Naval Res. Asn; Mason; Am. Legion; VFW; YMCA. Rel: Episcopal. Legal Res: 3623 Beach Dr, Tampa, Fla. 33609. Mailing Add: P.O. Box 3239, Tampa, Fla. 33601.

REGNER, DAVID JOSEPH R

Ill. State Rep.
b. Chicago, Ill, 3/9/31; s. Joseph H. Regner and Catherine Schram R; m. 8/10/57 to Joan Catherine Scanlan; c. David Michael. Educ: DePaul Univ. Eve. Sch, B.S, 59. Polit. & Govt. Pos: Rep. block capt, 38th Ward, Chicago, Ill, 55-56; campaign chmn, Elk Grove Twp. Percy for Gov. Campaign, 63; pres, Young Rep, Elk Grove Twp, 64; v.pres, Elk Grove Twp. Rep. Orgn, 64, dep. committeeman, 65; auditor, Elk Grove Twp, 65; secy, Platform Cmt, Ill. State Rep. Conv, 66; Ill. State Rep, Third Dist, 67-, secy, Rep. Caucus, Ill. State House of Rep. Bus. & Prof. Pos: Self-employed ins. sales and chmn. bd, Great Lakes Franchise Syst, currently. Mem: Chicago Asn. of Life Underwriters; nominating cmt. and v.pres, Cook Co. Auditors Asn; pres, Independent Group, Chicago Jaycees, 60-61; pres, Mt. Prospect Jaycees, 62-63; v.pres, Ill. Jaycees, 63-64 and int. dir, 64-65; state chmn, Elec. Reporting, 64-65; Sch. Dist. 57 Caucus, 62-64; financial cmt, Mt. Prospect Park Dist, 62-64; gen. chmn, Mt. Prospect March of Dimes, 63. Outstanding Local Pres. and Active Jaycee, Ill. Jaycees, 63; Outstanding State V.Pres, Ill. Jaycees, 64; Spark Plug Awards, Mt. Prospect Jaycees, 64 and Chicago Jaycees, 65; Cert. of Merit, Ill. Jaycees, 65. Rel: Roman Catholic. Mailing Add: 910 S. See Gwun Ave, Mt. Prospect, Ill. 60056.

REGNIER, RICHARD OLIN R

Chmn, Tipton Co. Rep. Party, Ind.
b. Huntington, Ind, 9/3/29; s. Coleman Franklin Regnier and Ruth Plumley R; m. 6/19/54 to Margaret Ann Peters; c. Risa Ann, Mark Randall and David Brian. Educ: Wabash Col, A.B, 51; Ind. Univ, LL.B, 54; Phi Kappa Psi. Polit. & Govt. Pos: Co. Attorney, Tipton Co, Ind, 57-61, prosecuting attorney, 62-66; finance chmn, cent. cmt, Tipton Co. Rep. Party, 60-64; chmn, Tipton Co. Rep. Party, 66- Mil. Serv: Entered as Pvt, Army, 54, released as Spec. 3/C, 56. Mem: Tipton Co. and Ind. State Bar Asns; Rotary (pres, Tipton Club, 59-60); F&AM; C. of C.(pres, 60-61, dir, 61, 62, 65 & 66). Rel: Methodist. Mailing Add: 322 Columbia Ave, Tipton, Ind. 46072.

REGULA, RALPH S. R

Ohio State Sen.
b. 1925. Educ: Mt. Union Col, B.A; William McKinley Sch. of Law, LL.B. Polit. & Govt. Pos: Chmn, Stark Co. Tech. Inst. Study Cmn, Ohio; mem, Stark Co. Regional Planning Cmn, 10 years; mem, State Bd. Educ, 60-64; Ohio State Rep, 65-66; Ohio State Sen, 67- Bus. & Prof. Pos: Attorney-at-law; teacher and prin, 7 years. Mailing Add: 15 N. Main St, Navarre, Ohio 44662. (1967)

REHDER, MERLYN ALBERT R

Chmn, Sioux Co. Rep. Cent. Cmt, Iowa
b. Hawarden, Iowa, 8/22/31; s. Albert Marcus Rehder and Frieda Lange R; m. 7/12/69 to Phyllis Joan Dean. Educ: S.Dak. State Univ, B.S, with honor, 60, grad. sch, 60-63; Blue Key; Alpha Zeta. Polit. & Govt. Pos: Representative div. agr, bd. control, S.Dak. State Univ, and finance chmn, 59-60; prog. chmn, S.Dak. State Univ. Young Rep, 61-63; del, Nat. Leadership Training Sch. Young Rep, Wash, D.C, 62 & 64; del, Nat. Young Rep. Conv, 63 & 67; asst. chmn, S.Dak. Fedn. Young Rep, 63; counsr, Nat. TAR Camp, Lake Herman, S.Dak, 63 & 64; prog. chmn, Sioux Co. Young Rep, 64-67; counsr, Iowa TAR Camp, Boone, 66; chmn, Sioux Co. Rep. Cent. Cmt, 68- Bus. & Prof. Pos: Investment coun, Life Investors Inc, Cedar Rapids, Iowa, 65-; bus. mgr. and treas, Sioux Empire Col, Hawarden, 66- Mil. Serv: Entered as Pvt, Army, 53, released as Cpl, 55, after serv. in Co. "C" 47th Eng. Camouflage Bn, Fort Riley, Kans, and 5th Army, Chicago, Ill, 53-55; Good Conduct Medal. Mem: Nat. Asn. Life Underwriters; Kiwanis; Sioux Co. Farm Bur; Hawarden C. of C. Rel: Lutheran. Mailing Add: Hawarden, Iowa 51023.

REHM, IRMA SPURGEON R

V.Chmn, Kiowa Co. Rep. Cent. Cmt, Colo.
b. Chivington, Colo, 4/18/93; d. James Jefferson Spurgeon and Samantha Boley S; div; c. Robert Edward (deceased), Ruth (Mrs. Benell) and Harold Carl. Educ: Colo. State Univ, 3 years. Polit. & Govt. Pos: V.chmn, Kiowa Co. Rep. Cent. Cmt, Colo, 20-56 & 59-; secy, 26th Representative Dist. Rep. Party, 67-69; secy, 14th Sen. Dist, Rep. Party, 69- Bus. & Prof. Pos: Teacher, Chivington Pub. Sch, 12-15, 16-19 & 43-44, Eads Pub. Sch, 15-16 and Brandon Pub. Sch, 42-43; secy, Kiowa Co. Farm Bur, 67- Mem: Eastern Star; Grange; Farm Bur; secy, Women's Soc. Christian Serv. Hon. life mem, Colo. State Exten. Homemakers. Rel: United Methodist. Legal Res: 310 West 12th St, Eads, Colo. 81036. Mailing Add: P.O. Box 6431, Eads, Colo. 81036.

REHNBERG, REX DELBERT D

b. Bertrand, Nebr, 2/1/20; s. Gustaf Walter Rehnberg and Christina Fox R; m. 6/1/46 to Charlotte Taylor; c. Peter, Michael, Timothy and Nicholas. Educ: Univ. Nebr, B.S, 43; Cornell Univ, M.S, 47; Purdue Univ, Ph.D, 49; Alpha Zeta; Sigma Xi; Omicron Delta Epsilon; Alpha Gamma Rho. Polit. & Govt. Pos: Registrn. chmn, Larimer Co, Colo, 65-68; del, Larimer Co. and Colo. State Dem. Conv, 66 & 68; del, Dem. Nat. Conv, 68. Bus. & Prof. Pos: Asst. prof. econ, Univ. Ariz, 49-52; prof. econ, Colo. State Univ, 52- Mil. Serv: Entered as A/S, Navy, 43, released as Lt.(jg), 46, after serv. in Submarine Serv, Pac. Theater, 45-46. Publ: Economic and Social Structure of Costilla County, Colorado, Colo. Exp. Sta, 68; six articles, J. of Agr. Econ. Mem: Am. and West. Agr. Econ. Asns; Rocky Mt. Soc. Sci. Asn. Rel: Unitarian. Mailing Add: 1185 Westward Dr, Ft. Collins, Colo. 80521.

REHNQUIST, WILLIAM HUBBS R

Asst. Attorney Gen, Off. of Legal Counsel, U.S. Dept. of Justice
b. Milwaukee, Wis, 10/1/24; s. William Benjamin Rehnquist and Margery Peck R; m. 8/29/53 to Natalie Cornell; c. James, Janet and Nancy. Educ: Kenyon Col, 43; Stanford Univ, B.A. & M.A, 48, LL.B, 52; Harvard Univ, M.A, 49; Phi Beta Kappa; Order of the Coif; Phi Delta Phi. Polit. & Govt. Pos: Mem, Nat. Conf. Cmnrs. on Uniform State Laws, Ariz, 63-69; asst. attorney Gen, Off. of Legal Counsel, U.S. Dept. of Justice, 69- Bus. & Prof. Pos: Law clerk, Robert H. Jackson, U.S. Supreme Court, Wash, D.C, 52-53; attorney, Evans, Kitchel & Jenckes, Phoenix, Ariz, 53-55; partner, Ragan & Rehnquist, 56-57, Cunningham, Carson & Messenger, 57-60 and Powers and Rehnquist, 60-69. Mil. Serv: Entered as Pvt, Army Air Corps, 43, released as Sgt, 46, after serv. in Weather Serv, Africa-Middle East Theater. Publ: 'Supreme

Court Law Clerks,' U.S. News and World Report, 12/57; 'The Bar Admission Cases,' J. Am. Bar Asn, 3/58; 'Subdivision Trusts and the Bankruptcy Act,' Ariz. Law Rev, winter 61. Mem: Maricopa Co, Am. and Fed. Bar Asns; State Bar of Ariz; Nat. Conf. Lawyers and Realtors. Rel: Lutheran. Legal Res: Phoenix, Ariz. Mailing Add: Office of Legal Counsel, Dept. of Justice, Washington, D.C. 20530.

REIBER, PAUL D

b. Hastings, Nebr, 6/18/13; m. to Doris Marie Nelson. Educ: Nebr. Wesleyan Univ, B.A; Harvard Law Sch, LL.B. Polit. & Govt. Pos: Va. State Del, 66-67; chmn, Fairfax Co. Bd. of Equalization, currently. Bus. & Prof. Pos: Attorney-at-law. Mem: Nat. Lawyers Club; Nat. Aeronaut. Asn; Int. Aviation Club. Fairfax Educ. Asn. Award, 64. Rel: Unitarian. Mailing Add: 1158 Swinks Mill Rd, McLean, Va. 22101.

REIBMAN, JEANETTE F. D

Pa. State Sen.

b. Ft. Wayne, Ind, 8/18/16; d. Meir Fichman and Pearl Schwartz F; m. 6/20/43 to Nathan Lewis Reibman; c. Joseph, Edward and James. Educ: Hunter Col, A.B, 37; Ind. Univ. Law Sch, LL.B, 40; Sigma Delta Tau. Hon. LL.D, Lafayette Col, 69. Polit. & Govt. Pos: Attorney, Tax Amortization Br, War Dept, 40-42 and War Prod. Bd, 42-44; Pa. State Rep, 59-66, chmn, Cmt. on Educ, 59-62 and Cmt. on Twp, 65-66; Pa. State Sen, 18th Sen. Dist, 66-, mem, Educ. Corp, Judiciary, Labor and Indust, Local Govt. and Mines and Mineral Industs. Cmts, Pa. State Senate; Local Govt. Cmn; mem. adv. cmt. on teacher educ, State Coun. of Educ. and adv. cmt. on working conditions for women and children, State Dept. Labor and Indust; del, White House Conf. on Probs. of the Aging. Mem: Admitted to practice before Supreme Court of U.S, U.S. Tax Court and U.S. Dist. Court. East. Dist. of Pa; hon. mem, Delta Kappa Gama; Northampton Co. chmn, Cancer Crusade Campaign, 62; Easton chmn, Heart Dr, 68; Pa. Coun. of the Arts; bd. dirs, Forks of Del. United Fund; Northampton Co. Family Counseling Serv. Citation for Serv. from Under-Secy. of War, Robert Patterson, 44; Citation for Outstanding Serv, Pa. Dept. Pub. Instr, Am. Legion and Jr. Historians of Pa; Distinguished Daughter of Pa, 69. Rel: Jewish. Legal Res: 514 McCartney St, Easton, Pa. 18042. Mailing Add: 711 Lehigh St, Easton, Pa. 18042.

REICHARDT, WILLIAM J. D

Iowa State Sen.

b. Iowa City, Iowa, 6/24/30; s. Herb Reichardt; m. 1952 to Sue Manbeck; c. 3. Educ: State Univ. Iowa, B.A, 52; Phi Kappa Psi. Polit. & Govt. Pos: Iowa State Sen, currently. Bus. & Prof. Pos: Prfnl. football player, Green Bay Packers; pres, Reichardt's Inc, retail clothing store. Mil. Serv: 1st Lt, Air Force, 53-55. Mem: V.pres, I Club; youth activities; crusade chmn, Cancer Soc; Wakonda Country Club; Des Moines Club; YMCA; C. of C; Jr. C. of C. Founder, Little All Am. Football League. Rel: St. Augustine Church. Mailing Add: 38 Foster Dr, Des Moines, Iowa 50312. (1967)

REICHEL, RICHARD GENE R

Ohio State Rep.

b. Massillon, Ohio, 4/21/30; s. Herman Joseph Reichel and Grace Elizabeth Horst R; m. 9/13/52 to Shirley Jane Kelley; c. Timothy, Lindsay and Alan. Educ: Ohio State Univ, B.S, 52, J.D, 54; U.S. Air Force Legal Officer's Sch, grad, 54; Alpha Tau Omega; Phi Delta Phi. Polit. & Govt. Pos: Spec. asst. attorney gen, Ohio, 57; police prosecutor, Massillon, Ohio, 57-63; cmnr. registered lands, Stark Co, 59-; pres, Massillon Young Rep. Club, 60; city solicitor, Massillon, 64-65; Ohio State Rep, 92nd Dist, 67- Bus. & Prof. Pos: Dir. and gen. counsel, Massillon Cable TV, Inc, Power Cleaning and Maintenance Corp. and Massillon Measurements, Inc, currently. Mil. Serv: Entered as 2nd Lt, Air Force, 54, released as 1st Lt, 56, after serv. in Strategic Air Command. Mem: Stark Co, Ohio and Am. Bar Asns; Ohio Acad. of Trial Lawyers; Am. Trial Lawyers Asn; pres, Massillon Lawyers' Club, 63; treas, Massillon C. of C, 63-66; Stark Co. Tuberc. & Health Asn; Lions; Elks; YMCA; Boys Club. Rel: Methodist. Mailing Add: 1133 Stratford N.E, Massillon, Ohio 44646.

REICHERT, THOMAS GEORGE R

Chmn, Stearns Co. Rep. Party, Minn.

b. St. Cloud, Minn, 5/4/29; s. Edward Martain Reichert and Marion Chown R; m. 6/7/52 to Virginia Eileen Delaria; c. Thomas Patrick, Mark Edward, Paul Joseph and David John. Educ: St. Johns Univ, B.A; Univ. Minn. Col. Dent, D.D.S. Polit. & Govt. Pos: Block worker, St. Cloud Rep. Party, Minn, 62; chmn, Young Rep. League and Cong. Vol. Orgn, 64; chmn, Stearns Co. Rep. Party, 65- Mil. Serv: Entered as Basic Airman, Air Force, 52, released as Airman 1/C. Mem: Pres, St. Cloud Dent. Soc, 61; pres, St. Cloud Kiwanis; bd. of dirs, Civic Music, 62-65; bd. of dirs, C. of C, 63-; pres, St. Cloud Serra Club, 66; pub. policy cmt, Minn. State Dent. Asn, 66-; W.Cent. Dist. Dent. Soc; pres, St. Cloud Kiwanis. Lettered in Football, St. Johns Univ, 51. Rel: Roman Catholic. Mailing Add: 1229 13th Ave. N, St. Cloud, Minn. 56301.

REICHERT, WALTER STEWART R

Ky. State Sen.

b. Louisville, Ky, 8/8/29; s. Sauter Frank Reichert, Sr. and Alice Buschmann R; m. 2/9/52 to Ella Carolyn Ross; c. Walter S, Jr, Carolyn Jean, Paul Frank and David Lawrence. Educ: Univ. Louisville. Polit. & Govt. Pos: Ky. State Rep, 46th Dist, 64-66; mem, Louisville-Jefferson Co. Rep. Exec. Cmt, 65-; Ky. State Sen, 34th Dist, 66-; chmn, Ky. Del, Ohio Interstate Park Cmn, 68-; v.chmn, Tenn-Tombigbee Waterway Develop. Authority, 69- Bus. & Prof. Pos: Lab. technician, E.I. Dupont Co, 50- Mil. Serv: Entered as Airman Basic, Air Force, 50, released as Airman 1/C, 54, after serv. in 14th Air Force, Conac; Korean Victory; Good Conduct, Army Commendation and Korean Serv. Medals. Mem: Engrs. & Architects Soc; charter mem, Okolona Jaycees; Lincoln Club of Ky. Rel: United Church of Christ. Mailing Add: 4909 E. Manslick Rd, Louisville, Ky. 40219.

REID, AARON Q. D

Chmn, Hebron Dem. Town Cmt, Conn.

b. New York, N.Y, 5/8/31; s. John Reid and Gertrude Boshnick R; m. 11/15/50 to Marie Bennington; c. Linda, Sandra and Michael. Educ: Windham High Sch. Polit. & Govt. Pos: Justice of Peace, Hebron Conn; Dem. Registr. of Voters; chmn, Hebron Dem. Town Cmt, currently. Mem: Treas, Hebron Sportsman Club. Rel: Hebrew. Legal Res: Hebron, Conn. 06248. Mailing Add: R.F.D. 1, Route 85, Amston, Conn. 06231. (1967)

REID, CHARLOTTE T. R

U.S. Rep, Ill.

b. Kankakee, Ill, wid; c. Frank R. III; Edward Thompson; Patricia (Mrs. Lindner) and Susan. Educ: Ill. Col, Jacksonville, Ill. Polit. & Govt. Pos: U.S. Rep, 15th Dist, Ill, 63-, mem, Cmt. Interior & Insular Affairs, 63-67, Cmt. on Pub. Works, 65-67, Cmt. on Appropriations, 68- and subcmts, Labor, Health, Educ. and Welfare Appropriations and For. Operations, U.S. House of Rep. Bus. & Prof. Pos: Under the name of Annette King, served as N.B.C. Staff Vocalist; Vocalist for 3 years, Don McNeill's Radio Prog. Legal Res: 183 S. Fourth St, Aurora, Ill. 60505. Mailing Add: House of Representatives, Washington, D.C. 20515.

REID, DAVID EDWARD, JR. D

N.C. State Rep.

b. Asheville, N.C, 7/30/32; s. David Edward Reid and Susan Elias R; m. 9/13/58 to Beverley Jacqueline Rippard; c. Rebekah Beverley and Jacqueline Susan. Educ: Univ. N.C, A.B, 56, Law Sch, LL.B, 59; Phi Alpha Delta. Polit. & Govt. Pos: Research asst. to Chief Justice, N.C. Supreme Court, 59-60; state pres, N.C. Young Dem. Clubs, 62; chmn, State Dem. Jefferson-Jackson Day Dinner, 63; city attorney, Greenville, N.C, 65-; N.C. State Rep, 68- Mem: Pitt Co, N.C. and Am. Bar Asns; AF&AM; Moose; Kiwanis; Greenville Golf and Country Club; C. of C; Merchants Asn. Rel: Episcopal. Legal Res: 1600 E. Fifth St, Greenville, N.C. 27834. Mailing Add: P.O. Box 375, Greenville, N.C. 27834.

REID, HARRY M. D

Nev. State Assemblyman

b. Searchlight, Nev, 12/2/39; s. Harry Reid and Inez Jaynes R; m. 9/19/59 to Landra Gould; c. Lana, Rory and Leif. Educ: Col. South Utah, A.S, 59; Utah State Univ, B.S, 61; George Wash. Univ. LL.B. and J.D; Phi Kappa Phi, Pi Sigma Alpha, Phi Alpha Theta. Polit. & Govt. Pos: City attorney, Henderson, Nev, 63-65; Nev. State Assemblyman, Dist. Four, 69-, mem. judiciary and elec. cmts, Nev. State Assembly, 69- Mem: Clark Co. Bar Asn.(treas, 68); Am. Bar Asn; Nat. Inst. Munic. Law Officers; trustee, South. Nev. Mem. Hosp, Las Vegas, 65-68; Legal Aid Soc. (mem. bd. dirs, 66-67); Am. Cancer Soc,(mem. bd. dirs, 68-69)); judge, Nev. State Athletic Cmn, 65-; mem. adv. bd, Upward Bound, 68-69. Rel: Latter-day Saint. Mailing Add: 4601 Gretel Circle, Las Vegas, Nev. 89102.

REID, JAMES E. D

Chmn, Jackson Co. Dem. Cmt, Ala.

b. Grays Chapel, Ala, 10/12/96; s. John H. Reid and Carrie Lanham R; m. 8/17/21 to Beulah Prince. Educ: Draughns Bus. Col, 6 months. Polit. & Govt. Pos: Chmn, Co. Bd. of Registors, 29-35; circuit court clerk, Jackson Co, Ala, 35-40; postmaster, Scottsboro, Ala, 40-54; clerk, State Hwy. Dept, 56-62; chmn, Jackson Co. Dem. Cmt, 62- Mil. Serv: Entered as Recruit, Army, 18, released as Sup. Sgt, 18, after serv. in Second Co, Coast Artil. Corps, Pensacola, Fla. Mem: Mason; Am. Legion. Rel: Episcopal. Legal Res: 413 Jordan Lane, Scottsboro, Ala. 35768. Mailing Add: P.O. Box 456, Scottsboro, Ala. 35768.

REID, JOSEPH BRACKETT D

Mem, Newport News Dem. Exec. Cmt, Va.

b. Augusta, Ga, 3/6/07; s. Anderson Wilson Reid and Henrietta Greene R; m. 6/5/32 to Mary Frances Daniels; c. Frances (Mrs. Rayford Harris). Educ: Paine Col, 26; Morehouse Col, 27; Boston Univ; Duke Univ; Va. Union Univ; Hampton Inst. Hon. D.D, Va. Baptist Sem. and Col, 48. Polit. & Govt. Pos: Mem. bd. gov, Va. State Sch, Hampton, Va, 66-, and secy, 68; del, Va. State Dem. Conv. and Dem. Nat. Conv, 68; mem, Newport News Dem. Exec. Cmt, 68- Mem: Trustee, Va. Baptist Sem. and Col; mem. exec. bd, Friendship House; mem. exec. bd, State Baptist Conv. of Va; mem. exec. bd, Annual Hampton's Ministers Conf; F&AM; Elks (mem. Empire Coun, Elks Number 9). Offered the Invocation before the Va. Assembly and U.S. Cong; Citation from U.S. House of Rep. Rel: Baptist. Legal Res: 2105 Garner Terr, Newport News, Va. 23607. Mailing Add: Shalom Baptist Church, 1111 24th St, Newport News, Va. 23607.

REID, OGDEN ROGERS R

U.S. Rep, N.Y.

b. New York, N.Y, 6/24/25; s. Ogden Mills Reid and Helen Rogers R; m. 7/9/49 to Mary Louise Stewart; c. Stewart, Elisabeth, Michael, Ogden, William and David W. Educ: Yale Univ, A.B, 49; LL.D, Adelphi Col, 60, Jewish Theol. Sem, 61; hon. Dr. Hebrew Letters, Dropsie Col, 61; fel, Brandeis Univ. and Bar-Ilan Univ, Israel; Phi Gamma Delta; Sigma Delta Chi. Polit. & Govt. Pos: U.S. Ambassador, Israel, 59-61; chmn, N.Y. Cmn. for Human Rights, 61-62; chmn, N.Y. Int. Off. Visitors Off, 62; U.S. Rep, 26th Dist, N.Y, 62- Bus. & Prof. Pos: Pres, N.Y. Herald Tribune Societe Anonyme, 53-58; pres. and ed, N.Y. Herald Tribune, Inc, 55-59; dir, Panama Canal Co, 56-59; trustee, Hampton Inst. and L.I. Univ; mem. cmt. grad. sch, Yale Univ. Coun, 68- Mil. Serv: Entered as Pvt, Army, 43, released as 1st Lt, 46, after serv. in 11th Airborne Div; Capt, Army Res; Chevalier of the Legion of Honor. Mem: 369th Vets. Asn; dir, Atlantic Coun. of U.S; adv. coun, Sch. Int. Affairs, Columbia Univ; Coun. For. Rels; v.pres, Nat. Inst. Soc. Sci, Westchester Dist; first pres, 11th Airborne Div. Asn. South. Cross of Brazil, 56. Rel: Presbyterian. Legal Res: Ophir Hill, Purchase, N.Y. 10577. Mailing Add: 2901 Garfield Terr. N.W, Washington, D.C. 20008.

REID, PATRICIA ANN D

b. Hagerstown, Md, 8/4/32; d. Lawrence Grim Reid and Rebekah Grove Reid Wagner; single. Educ: Columbia Bus. Col, 51; Beta Sigma Phi. Polit. & Govt. Pos: Nat. committeewoman, Young Dem. Clubs of Md, 61-63, regional dir, Sixth Dist, 65-66; recording secy, Young Dem. Club of Wash. Co, 62-63, v.pres, 64-65, pres, 65-66, mem. bd. dirs, 66-67; co-dir, Wash. Co. Campaign, Presidential Elec, 64; alternate del, Dem. Nat. Conv, 64. Bus. & Prof. Pos: Order issuing clerk, Fairchild Hiller Corp, Md, 52-58, clerk-typist, 67-; secy, Bd. Co. Cmnrs, Wash. Co, 59-63; secy. to Trial Magistrate for Wash. Co, 63-67. Rel: Protestant. Mailing Add: 1217 Ravenwood Heights, Hagerstown, Md. 21740.

REID, THEODORE EDWIN D
Chmn, Transylvania Co. Dem. Party, N.C.
b. Sapphire, N.C, 4/18/89; s. Thomas Bryson Reid and Matilda Aiken R; wid; c. Flora (Mrs. Brown) and Bess (Mrs. Biggers). Educ: Brevard Inst, 07 & 08. Polit. & Govt. Pos: Co. rd. supvr, 20-24; chmn, co. bd. educ, 36-40; co. tax collector, 40-42; chmn, Transylvania Co. Dem. Party, N.C, 66- Bus. & Prof. Pos: Furniture salesman, 27-42; pres, Reid Furniture Co, 45-68. Mem: WOW; Kiwanis; Mason (past Master, Dunn's Rock Lodge 267 and Dist. Dep. Grand Master); Shrine. Rel: Baptist. Legal Res: 315 Probart St, Brevard, N.C. 28712. Mailing Add: P.O. Box 112, Brevard, N.C. 28712.

REID, THOMAS BEAUREGARD, JR. R
V.Pres, Young Rep. 3rd Cong. Dist, N.C.
b. Great Falls, S.C, 11/16/31; s. Thomas Beauregard Reid and Mary Fowler R; m. 3/21/66 to Katherine Louise Furr; c. Thomas B, III, Pamela Ann and James Walter. Educ: Erskine Col, S.C; Univ. N.C, A.B, 52, D.D.S, 56; Xi Psi Phi. Polit. & Govt. Pos: Finance chmn, Onslow Co. Rep. Party, N.C, 62-66; alternate del, Rep. Nat. Conv, 64; v.pres, Young Rep. Third Cong. Dist, N.C, 64- Mil. Serv: Entered as Seaman Recruit, Navy, 48, released as Lt, 59, after serv. in 4th Dental Corps. Mem: Secy, Onslow Co. Dental Soc, 62-64, v.pres, 65-66 and pres, 66-67; chmn. cmt. on sch. health, N.C. Dental Soc, 63-65 and del, house of del, 66-67; Am. Dent. Asn; Jacksonville Rotary Club; 1st v.pres, N.C. Easter Seal Soc; cmnr, E. Carolina Coun, Boy Scouts; Jacksonville Country Club. Rel: Methodist. Mailing Add: 4 Grove Court, Jacksonville, N.C. 28540. (1967)

REID, WILL CARR D
Mem, Exec. Cmt, Macon Co. Dem. Party, Tenn.
b. Hartsville, Tenn, 10/13/18; s. Carlton Reid and Gaither Whitney R; m. 5/9/42 to Anna Fay Cothron; c. Billie Jane, Ronald Dooley and Sam David. Educ: Trousdale Co. High Sch, dipl, 38. Polit. & Govt. Pos: Co. chmn, Johnson for Pres. Campaign, Macon Co, Tenn, 64 and Humphrey for Pres. Campaign, 68; chmn, Macon Co. Dem. Party, 62-66, mem, exec. cmt, 66- Bus. & Prof. Pos: Mgr, LaFayette Auto Parts, Tenn, 58-62; stock control, Imperial Reading, 62- Mil. Serv: Entered as Pvt, Marines, 38, released as M/Sgt, 58, after serv. in First Marine Div, Second Marine Air Wing, Pac; Purple Heart; Presidential Unit Citation; Korean Serv, UN, Asiatic Am. Theatre, Good Conduct and Pearl Harbor Medals. Mem: Am. Legion; VFW; Mason (32°); Shrine. Rel: Methodist. Mailing Add: 1002 Ellington Dr, LaFayette, Tenn. 37083.

REID, WILLIAM A. R
Chmn, Glocester Co. Rep. Party, R.I.
b. Douglas, Mass, 6/27/14. Educ: Univ. R.I, 1936; Tufts Med. Sch, M.D, 1940; Internship, R.I. Hosp, 40-42; Resident, Providence Lying-In Hosp, 42-44; Dept. of Gynecology, R.I. Hosp, 46-48. Polit. & Govt. Pos: Rep. from East Providence, R.I, 53-55; mem. town cmt, Glocester, 63-65; R.I. State Rep, 64-66; chmn, Glocester Co. Rep. Party, currently. Bus. & Prof. Pos: Physician. Mil. Serv: Capt, Med. Corps, Army, 44-46. Mem: Secy, Providence Med. Asn, 60-65; pres, R.I. Med. Soc, 65-66; Am. Med. Asn. Mailing Add: Evans Rd, Harmony, R.I. 02829. (1967)

REIDER, ROBERT W. D
Chmn, Ohio State Dem. Cent. Cmt.
b. Oak Harbor, Ohio, 5/5/16; s. Otto E. Reider and Laura Williamsen R; m. 12/27/45 to Annette Wendt; c. Robert W, Jr. Educ: Ohio Univ, B.S. in journalism, 39; Omicron Delta Kappa; Blue Key; J-Club; Sigma Delta Chi; Sigma Pi. Polit. & Govt. Pos: Ohio State Rep, 48-54; nominee for Secy. of State, Ohio, 54; mem, Ohio State Dem. Cent. Cmt, 58-, chmn, 68-; mem, Ohio State Dem. Exec. Cmt, 58-; mem, Pub. Utilities Cmn, 59-60; del, Dem. Nat. Conv, 60 & 68, del-at-lg. and mem, Credentials Cmt, 64. Bus. & Prof. Pos: Publisher and treas, Exponent Pub. Co, 45-50; pres. and founder, Ohio Radio, Inc, 61- Mil. Serv: Entered as Pvt, Army, 42, released as T/Sgt, 45, after serv. as Spec. Agent, Counter Intel. Corps, 970th Detachment, ETO; 1st Lt, Inactive Army Res; French Croix de Guerre with Silver Star, 44; Am. Campaign Serv. Medal; Europe-Africa-Middle East. Campaign Medal with 3 Bronze Stars. Mem: Past pres, Northwest. Ohio Chap, Sigma Delta Chi; nat. bd. of dirs, Ohio Univ. Alumni Asn, 69-; Elks; Eagles; Moose; Catawba Beach Club; Port Clinton Yacht Club; C. of C; Ohio Soc. of N.Y; Columbus Athletic Club. Rel: Lutheran. Legal Res: 504 E. Perry St, Port Clinton, Ohio 43452. Mailing Add: P.O. Drawer A, Port Clinton, Ohio 43452.

REIDY, JAMES BASIL, JR. D
City Councilman, Santa Monica, Calif.
b. Tucson, Ariz, 8/26/28; s. James B. Reidy and Catherine Chapman R; m. 7/20/51 to Virginia L. Nagel. Educ: Univ. Ariz, B.S. in bus. admin, 54, M.B.A, 55; Alpha Kappa Psi; Alpha Phi Omega. Polit. & Govt. Pos: City councilman, Santa Monica, Calif, currently. Bus. & Prof. Pos: Data processing rep, Int. Bus. Mach. Corp, 55- Mil. Serv: Entered as Pvt, Marine Corps Res, 48, released as T/Sgt, 61, with active duty Korean War, 51-53; Marine Corps Res. Ribbon. Mem: Vet. Serv. League; Amvets; Navy League; Marine Corps League; Jaycee Int. Selected One of California's Five Outstanding Young Men, 61. Rel: Roman Catholic. Mailing Add: 360 22nd St, Santa Monica, Calif. 90402.

REIFEL, BENJAMIN R
U.S. Rep, S.Dak.
b. Parmelee, S.Dak, 9/19/06; m. 12/26/33 to Alice Johnson Reifel; c. Loycé (Mrs. Emery G. Anderson). Educ: S.Dak. State Univ, B.S, 32; Harvard Univ, MPA, 50; DPA, 52. Polit. & Govt. Pos: U.S. Rep, S.Dak, 60-; adminstr, Bur. of Indian Affairs, U.S. Dept. Interior. Mil. Serv: Army Officer, 42-45. Named Outstanding Am. Indian, 56; Indian Coun. Fire Award, 60; Silver Antelope Award for Leadership, Boy Scouts, 60. Rel: Episcopal. Legal Res: Aberdeen, S.Dak. Mailing Add: 800 Fourth St. S.W, Apt. S-703, Washington, D.C. 20024.

REIFF, LEE HERBERT D
b. Newton, Kans, 7/6/29; s. Tillman Erb Reiff and Ione Austin R; m. 8/22/50 to Geraldine Long; c. Joseph Tillman and James Nathan. Educ: Univ. of Kans, 47-48; South. Methodist Univ, B.A, 51 and B.D, 54; Yale Univ, M.A, 57 and Ph.D, 63; Phi Beta Kappa; Blue Key; Tau Kappa Alpha; Sigma Chi. Polit. & Govt. Pos: Del. Dem. Nat. Conv, 68. Bus. & Prof. Pos: Minister, Bakerville Methodist Church, New Hartford, Conn, 54-57; asst. in instr, Yale Univ. Divinity Sch, New Haven, 58-60; asst. prof. of relig, Millsaps Col, Jackson, Miss, 60-64, assoc. prof, 65-69, prof, 69- and chmn, dept. of relig, 65-; asst. prof. of relig, McMurry Col, Abilene, Tex, 64-65. Mem: Am. Acad. Religion; Soc. of Biblical Lit; Am. Asn. of Univ. Professors; Miss. Council on Human Relations (State Bd. of Dirs, 68-); Am. Civil Liberties Union (Bd. of Dirs, Miss. affiliate, 69-); Child Develop. Group of Mississippi (Head Start Bd. of Dirs, 67-); Omicron Delta Kappa; Pi Kappa Alpha. Rel: Methodist; Ordained minister, mem. of Mississippi Conf, United Methodist Church. Legal Res: 4351 Forest Park Dr, Jackson, Miss. 39211. Mailing Add: Millsaps College, Box 15460, Jackson, Miss. 39210.

REILLY, CARL NELSON R
Committeeman, Fla. State Rep. Party
b. Cairo, Ill, 9/10/21; s. Carl Reilly and Anna Porter R; m. 9/15/45 to Virginia Claire McCoy; c. Carol Lee, Linda, Stephen, Margaret, Martha and Catherine. Educ: Univ. of Ill, B.S. in med, 42 and M.D, 45; Phi Beta Pi. Polit. & Govt. Pos: Alternate del, Rep. Nat. Conv, 64; committeeman, Fla. State Rep. Party, 66- Bus. & Prof. Pos: Intern, Cook Co. Hosp, Ill, 45-46; med. practice, Marion, Ill, 48-50; resident in med, Charity Hosp, New Orleans, La, 50-53; med. practice, Ill. and Fla, 53- Mil. Serv: Entered as Asst. Surgeon, Pub. Health Serv, 46, released as Sr. Asst. Surgeon, 48, after serv. in Hosp. Div, U.S.A. Publ: A Plan in the Tradition of American Free Enterprise to Meet the Unpredictable Costs of Major Illness, 64. Mem: Am, Fla. and South. Med. Asns; Radiological Soc. of N.Am; Am. Legion; Elks; Kiwanis. Rel: Methodist. Legal Res: Route 2, Box 947B, Punta Gorda, Fla. 33950. Mailing Add: 304 Nesbit St, Punta Gorda, Fla. 33950.

REILLY, EDWARD FRANCIS, JR. R
Kans. State Sen.
b. Leavenworth, Kans, 3/24/37; s. Edward Francis Reilly and Marian Sullivan R; single. Educ: Univ. Kans, B.A, 61; Sigma Alpha Epsilon. Polit. & Govt. Pos: Kans. State Rep, 63-64; Kans. State Sen, 64-; del, Rep. Nat. Conv, 68. Bus. & Prof. Pos: V.pres, Ed Reilly & Sons, Insurers-Realtors, 61-; v.pres, First State Bank of Lansing, 66-68; pres, Continental Developers, 66- Mil. Serv: Res. Officers Training Corps, 54-61. Mem: Elks (Exalted Ruler); Eagles; K. of C; Kiwanis; People to People; Jaycees. Henry Leavenworth award, Asn. U.S. Army, 60; Outstanding Young Man of Am, U.S. Jaycee Publ, 65; Distinguished Serv. award, Jaycees, 69. Rel: Catholic. Mailing Add: 430 Delaware, Leavenworth, Kans. 66048.

REILLY, JANE BERNADETTE R
Mem, Calif. Rep. State Cent. Cmt.
b. San Francisco, Calif, 6/26/29; d. Bernard Reilly and Jane Walsh Reilly; single. Univ. San Francisco, theology, 63; Golden Gate Col, acct, 65. Polit. & Govt. Pos: Assoc. mem, Calif. Rep. State Cent. Cmt, 67-68, mem, 69-; mem, Cmt. to Elect Calif. State Assemblymen, 69- Bus. & Prof. Pos: IBM Keypunch operator, Pac. Fruit Express, 52-55, tab operator, 55-64, revising clerk, 64-66, gen. cler, 66-69, computer programmer, 69. Mem: Bd. dirs, Calif. Pac. Club; Railway Clerk Union. Rel: Catholic. Mailing Add: 4550 California St, Apt. 2, San Francisco, Calif. 94118.

REILLY, JOHN RICHARD D
b. Dubuque, Iowa, 6/4/28; s. William Raphael Reilly and Stella Vogenthaler R; m. 1/17/53 to Susan Loosbrock; c. John R, Thomas M, Paul A, Patrick W, Marie E. and Susan K. Educ: Loras Col; State Univ. of Iowa Law Col, J.D, 55. Polit. Pos: Admin. asst. to Lawrence F. O'Brien, Dir. of Orgn, Kennedy for President, 60. Govt. Pos: Cmnr, Fed. Trade Cmn, Wash, D.C, 64-; head exec. off. for U.S. Attorneys and asst. to Dep. Attorney Gen, 61-64; trial attorney, Anti-trust Div, Justice Dept, Chicago, Ill, 55-58. Bus. & Prof. Pos: Mid-Western rep, Coun. of State Govts, Chicago, Ill, 58-60. Mil. Serv: Entered as Pvt, Air Force, 50, released as Airman 1/C, 53. Publn: Mem, Bd. of Editors, Iowa Law Review. Mem: Cong. Country Club. Rel: Catholic. Mailing Add: 6721 Newbold Dr, Bethesda, Md. 20034. (1967)

REILLY, JOSEPH MATTHEW R
N.Y. State Assemblyman
b. Glen Cove, N.Y, 7/21/27; s. T. Joseph Reilly and Catherine McCormach R; m. 4/18/59 to Margaret Mary Power; c. Joseph M, Jr, John P, Margaret C. and Paul C. Educ: Rider Col, B.S.Ed, 52; Hofstra Univ, M.S.Ed, 53. Polit. & Govt. Pos: Cmnr. acct, Glen Cove, N.Y, 56-61 and mayor-supvr, 62-65; N.Y. State Assemblyman, 66- Bus. & Prof. Pos: Teacher, North Shore Sch. Dist, 53-61; stock broker, Paine, Webber, Jackson & Curtis, 66- Mil. Serv: Entered as A/S, Navy, 45, released as Seaman 1/C, 46. Mem: Nat. Asn. of Security Dealers; Am. Legion; K. of C; Ancient Order of Hibernians; Glen Cove Rep. Club. Hon. Order of Gen. Pulaski. Rel: Roman Catholic. Mailing Add: 36 Chestnut St, Glen Cove, N.Y. 11542.

REIMCHE, RUBEN R. R
b. Harvey, N.Dak, 1910. Polit. & Govt. Pos: Mem. city coun, Antioch, Calif, 8 years; mayor, Antioch, Calif, 54-59; chmn, Contra Costa Co. Mayors Conv, 56; mem. grand jury, Contra Costa Co, 58; cand, State Sen, 68. Bus. & Prof. Pos: Mgr, Purity Supermarket, Lodi, Calif, 34, store mgr, Antioch, 37; established Mt. View Food Center, 46 and food center in Brentwood, 60. Mem: Retail Clerks Union Alameda and Contra Costa Co; North. Delicatessen Coun.(bd. dirs); Calif. Grocers Asn.(cmt. revenue and taxation); United Grocers Ltd.(bd. dirs); Bay Area Food Dealers Asn.(v.pres); Antioch Area C. of C.(dir); Antioch Kiwanis (officer and mem. bd. dirs); chmn, East Contra Costa Co. United Crusade. Rel: Methodist; Trustee, Bd. Dirs. Legal Res: 614 A Route 2, Almond Dr, Brentwood, Calif. 94513. Mailing Add: P.O. Box 428, Antioch, Calif. 94509.

REIMERS, ROBERT F. R
N.Dak. State Rep.
b. Carrington, N.Dak, 6/15/23; married; c. Two. Educ: N.Dak. State Univ. of Agr. and Applied Sci. Polit. & Govt. Pos: N.Dak. State Rep, 61- Bus. & Prof. Pos: Farmer. Mem: Elks; Mason; Shrine. Rel: Congregational. Mailing Add: R.R. 3, Carrington, N.Dak. 58421.

REINECKE, ED R
Lt. Gov, Calif.
b. Medford, Ore, 1/7/24; s. Frederick Reinecke and Helen Purucker R; m. 12/9/66 to Jean Raybeck; c. Mark, Madeline and Thomas. Educ: Calif. Inst. Tech, B.S. in Mech. Eng, 50. Polit. & Govt. Pos: Mem, Calif. Rep. State Cent. Cmt; former asst. cong. dist. precinct chmn, 27th Dist, Calif; Whip, Calif. Rep. Del, 65; del, Rep. Nat. Conv, 68; U.S. Rep, Calif, 65-69; Lt. Gov, Calif, 69- Bus. & Prof. Pos: Inventor and prfnl. mech. engr, Calif; pres, Febco, Inc, Sun Valley, Calif, 54-64. Mil. Serv: Entered Navy, 42, released as RT 2/C, 46, after serv. on Destroyer DD632, ETO and Atlantic, 44-45; Theater Ribbons. Publ: Numerous articles for trade publ. Mem: Am. Soc. Sanit. Engrs.(mem. nat. bd. dirs); West. Plumbing Off. Asn; Rep. Assocs; Am. Legion; VFW; Sun Valley C. of C.(mem. bd. dirs); Calif. State C. of C; Kiwanis (chmn, Div. 2 Cmt, Pub. and Bus. Affairs, 64); Elks. Rel: Lutheran. Mailing Add: 492 Crocker Rd, Sacramento, Calif. 95825.

REINHARD, JAMES RICHARD D
b. Pollock, Mo, 7/7/29; s. Virgil Reinhard and Meltha Anspach R; m. 12/30/58 to Shari L. Horton; c. James Kevin. Educ: Northeast Mo. State Col, 47-50; Univ. Mo-Columbia, A.B, 51, J.D, 53; Phi Sigma Epsilon; Phi Alpha Delta. Polit. & Govt. Pos: Prosecuting attorney, Sullivan Co, Mo, 55-57; alternate del, Dem. Nat. Conv, 56, asst. sgt-at-arms, 60, del, 68; prosecuting attorney, Monroe Co, 58-64; Asst. Attorney Gen, Mo, 67-68; pres. bd. regents, Northeast Mo. State Col, currently. Bus. & Prof. Pos: Partner, Law Off, Reinhard & Lawson, Paris, Mo. Mil. Serv: Entered as Pvt, Army, 53, released as Sgt, 55. Mem: Mo. Bar (bd. gov, 65-); Mason; Rotary. Rel: Presbyterian. Mailing Add: Paris, Mo. 65275.

REINHARDT, GEORGE FREDERICK
b. Berkeley, Calif, 10/21/11; m. 9/10/49 to Lillian Larke Tootle; c. George Frederick, III, Anna Aurelia, Charles Henry and Catherine Jane. Educ: Univ. Calif, A.B, 33; Cornell Univ, A.M, 35; Cesare Alfieri Inst, Florence, Italy, dipl, 37; Zeta Psi. Hon. LL.D, Mills Col, 62, Univ. Calif, 63 and Gonzaga Univ, 64. Polit. & Govt. Pos: Mem, Int. Boundary Cmt, U.S. and Mex, 35-36; career officer, U.S. Dept. State For. Serv, 37-68, v.consul, Vienna, 37-38; third secy, Tallinn, 39-40, Moscow, 40-42; Dept. of State, 42-43; asst. to USPOLAD Supreme Allied Comdr, Mediterranean Theater, 43-44 and European Theater, 45-46; second secy, Moscow, 45-46, first secy, 46-48; chief, Off. of E. European Affairs, 48, acting dir, 49, dir, 50-51; counselor, Paris, 51-55; U.S. Ambassador to Vietnam, 55-57; counselor, Dept. of State, 57-60; U.S. Ambassador to United Arab Repub. and U.S. Minister to Yemen, 60-61; U.S. Ambassador to Italy, 61-68. Bus. & Prof. Pos: Sr. dir, Europe, Stanford Res. Inst, Menlo Park, Calif, 68- Medal of Freedom, War Dept, 46. Rel: Unitarian. Mailing Add: Stanford Research Institute, Pelikanstrasse 37, 8001 Zürich, Switz.

REINHARDT, STEPHEN D
Dem. Nat. Committeeman, Calif.
b. N.Y.C, N.Y, 3/27/31; m. to Mary Treman; c. Mark and Justin. Educ: Pomona Col, B.A. cum laude, 51; Yale Law Sch, LL.B, 54; Order of the Coif. Polit. & Govt. Pos: Chmn. resolutions cmt, Calif. Dem. Coun, 61, chmn. elec. reform cmt, 62-63; mem, Calif. Adv. Cmn. Civil Rights, 63-, v.chmn, 65-; exec. cmt. mem, Dem. State Cent. Cmt, 64-66, legal counsel, 66-68; del, Dem. Nat. Conv, 68; Dem. Nat. Committeeman, Calif, 68- Bus. & Prof. Pos: Assoc, O'Melveny & Myers, Los Angeles, 57-59; assoc, Bodle & Fogel, 59-66; partner, Bodle, Fogel, Julber and Reinhardt, 66- Mil. Serv: Entered as 2nd Lt, Air Force, released as 1st Lt, after serv. in Gen. Counsel Off. Mem: Am. Bar Asn.(co-chmn, cmt. labor arbit. and law of collective bargaining agreements and cmt. on the ninth circuit, labor rels. sect, 66-); Calif. State Bar; U.S. Supreme Court; Bar of D.C. Legal Res: 127 S. Glenroy Ave, Los Angeles, Calif. 90064. Mailing Add: 3540 Wilshire Blvd, Los Angeles, Calif. 90005.

REINSTEIN, WILLIAM GEORGE D
Mass. State Rep.
b. Revere, Mass, 3/26/39; s. William F. Reinstein (deceased) and Madiline Carney R; single. Educ: Bentley's, Boston, 59-60; Boston Univ, 60-61; Harvard Exten. Courses, 62. Polit. & Govt. Pos: Mem, Revere Sch. Cmt, Mass, 64-68; mem, Northeast Regional Voc. Sch. Cmt, 66-; mem, Revere City Coun, 68-; Mass. State Rep, 69- Mil. Serv: Pvt, Army Res; Grad. Army Admin. Sch. Mem: K. of C; Elks; League for Retarded Children; past chmn, Revere Cancer and Heart Drives; chmn, Revere United Fund. Pres, Mass. Freshman Legis, 69-70. Rel: Catholic. Mailing Add: 24 Dana St, Revere, Mass. 02151.

REIS, JOHN C, JR. R
Educ: Durfee Tech (SMTI); Herricks Bus. Inst; New Eng. Tech. of Providence; GOP Polit. Sch. of Sci. Polit. & Govt. Pos: Orgn. staff mem. in the late Mass. Attorney Gen. George Fingold's bid for Gov; State conv. del; first dir, Orgn. of the Young Rep. Club, Gr. Fall River; exec. bd. mem; negotiating and contract cmt. mem; grievance bd. off. Bus. & Prof. Pos; Shortline Bus Co. Mem: K. of C, Coun. 86; Amvets; former Red Cross vol; Boys Club Alumni. Mailing Add: 55 Hemlock St, Somerset, Mass. 02720. (1967)

REISCH, HAROLD FRANKLIN R
Mo. State Rep.
b. Springfield, Ill, 8/5/20; s. Elmer J. Reisch and Belle Hergett R; m. 2/18/44 to Bessie Louise Thatcher; c. Sally Louise (Mrs. Ralph Warmack) and Susan Kay (Mrs. Richard Berkley). Educ: Ill. Wesleyan Univ, B.S, 42; United Theol. Sem, B.D, 48. Polit. & Govt. Pos: Mo. State Rep, 119th Dist, 69- Bus. & Prof. Pos: Managing ed, Country Christian Mag, 49-50; exec. bd, Mo. Coun. of Churches, 60-63; pres, Happy House, Inc, 64-; pastor, Church of Distinction; pres, Downtown Merchants Inc, 67-68. Mil. Serv: Entered as Chaplain, Army, 44, released as Capt, 46, after serv. in 1149th Combat Engr. Co, ETO, 44-46; Cert. Meritorious Serv. Mem: C. of C.(pres, 62-63); Farm Bur. Rel: Christian. Mailing Add: 1013 Falcon Dr, Columbia, Mo. 65201.

REISSING, THEODORE CHARLES, SR. R
b. Hopkins, Mich, 11/5/03; s. Charles George Reissing and Mary Ellinger R; m. 9/10/33 to Helen Martha Lauffer; c. Theodore Charles, Jr, Sue Ann (Mrs. William Mohney) and Michael George. Educ: Univ. Mich, B.A. in sci, 24. Polit. & Govt. Pos: Secy, Wayne Co. Draft Bd. 179, Mich, 56-; mem, 17th Cong. Dist. Rep. Exec. Cmt, 59-; del. and mem. rules cmt, Rep. Nat. Conv, 64; chmn, Mich. Rep. State Cent. Exec. Cmt, 65-68. Bus. & Prof. Pos: Eng. Supvr, Mich. Bell Telephone Co, 27- Mem: Assoc. mem, Inst. of Elec. and Electronics Engrs; v.pres, Nat. Bd. Govs, Univ. Mich. Alumni; Wayne Co. Human Rels Cmt; Mason; Washtenaw Country Club. Rel: Presbyterian. Mailing Add: 17225 Patton, Detroit, Mich. 48219. (1967)

REKEWEG, WILMER D R
Chmn, Paulding Co. Rep. Exec. and Cent. Cmts, Ohio
b. Woodburn, Ind, 5/9/12; s. Carl W. Rekeweg and Adele Hauke R; m. 6/29/41 to Ruth E. Morisy; c. Barbara Ann (Mrs. Joseph Thomas). Educ: Ind. Univ. Exten, Ft. Wayne, 30-31; DePauw Univ, 31; Valparaiso Univ, LL.B, 35; Sigma Delta Kappa; Debating & Oratory Soc, Valparaiso Univ. Polit. & Govt. Pos: Prosecuting attorney, Paulding Co, Ohio, 39-41; village solicitor, Oakwood and Grover Hill various times; chmn, Paulding Co. Rep. Party, 60-64; chmn, Paulding Co. Rep. Exec. and Cent. Cmts, 68- Bus. & Prof. Pos: Div. comdr, Am. Legion, Paulding-Defiance Co, mem. Buckeye Boys State Comn, 15 years, post comdr, Cottrell Boylan Post 253, Antwerp, 49 & 50, v.comdr, 66-67, finance officer, 67-69, comdr, Paulding Co, 68- Mil. Serv: Entered as Pvt, Army, 42, released as Sgt, 46 after serving in Mil. Intel. German Lang, Camp Ritchie, Md. and interviewer reception centers, Ft. Harrison and Camp Atterbury, Ind; cert. grad, German Mil. Intel. Sch, Camp Ritchie, Md. Mem: Am. Bar Asn; Am. Judicature Soc; Am. Legion; 40 et 8; assoc. mem. VFW. Rel: Lutheran-Mo. Synod. Legal Res: 317 S. William St, Paulding, Ohio 45879. Mailing Add: P.O. Box 6, Paulding, Ohio 45879.

REMSBERG, E. EARL R
Md. State Del.
b. Buckeystown, Md, 1/7/99; married. Educ: Frederick Co. pub. schs. Polit. & Govt. Pos: Md. State Del, 63-; chmn, Frederick Co. Soil Conserv. Dist. Bus. & Prof. Pos: Dairy farmer. Mil. Serv: Students Army Training Corps, 17. Mem: Farm Bur; Grange; Md. and Va. Milk Producers Asn; Dir, Frederick Co. Fed. Land Bank Asn; Lions; Mason. Mailing Add: 5 Fairview Ave, Frederick, Md. 21701. (1967)

RENAHAN, THOMAS MICHAEL, JR. R
Chmn, Mattapoisett Rep. Town Cmt, Mass.
b. New Bedford, Mass, 4/7/41; s. Thomas M. Renahan and Pauline Perry R; single. Educ: Johns Hopkins Univ, B.A, 63; Univ. Minn, Minneapolis, Nat. Defense Educ. Act fel, 63-66, M.A, 66; Georgetown Univ, Ph.D. cand, 66- Polit. & Govt. Pos: Chmn, Mattapoisett Rep. Town Cmt, Mass, 68- Bus. & Prof. Pos: Asst. prof. polit. sci, West. Ill. Univ, 68- Mem: Am. Polit. Sci. Asn. Rel: Catholic. Mailing Add: 28 Main St, Mattapoisett, Mass. 02739.

RENDA, THOMAS ANTHONY D
Iowa State Rep.
b. Des Moines, Iowa, 9/19/37; s. Anthony T. Renda and Helen Louise Reid R; m. 6/13/59 to Shirley Ann Murphy; c. Tamara Ann, Anthony T, II and John Andrew; Educ: Loras Col, B.A, 59; Drake Univ. Law Sch, B.L, 62; Cum-laude; Phi Alpha Delta. Polit. & Govt. Pos: Iowa State Rep, 64- Bus. & Prof. Pos: Attorney-at-Law, 63; pres, United Sports Inc, Des Moines, Iowa, 68-69. Mem: Am, Iowa State and Polk Co. Bar Asns. Football player for the Des Moines Vikings, 65 & 68-69. Rel: Catholic. Legal Res: 5004 S.W. 16th Place, Des Moines, Iowa 50321. Mailing Add: 312 Hubbell Bldg, Des Moines, Iowa 50309.

RENDON, RALPH ALBERT R
Mem, Calif. Rep. State Cent. Cmt.
b. Los Angeles, Calif, 3/15/37; s. Ralph Alex Rendon and Concha Duarte R; m. 12/2/67 to Patricia Ann Richardson. Educ: Univ. South. Calif, B.A, 59; Delta Sigma Phi; Trojan Knights; Trojan Squires. Polit. & Govt. Pos: Bd. dirs, Coun. Latin Am. Rep. Orgns, 67-; mem, Los Angeles Dist. Attorney's Advisory Coun, Calif, 67-; mem, Calif. Rep. State Cent. Cmt, 67- Bus. & Prof. Pos: Pub. Rels. Counselor, Self-employed, Beverly Hills, Calif, until 62; acct. exec, Bates Assocs, Whittier, 62-64; asst. pub. rels. dir, McFadden, Strauss, Eddy & Irwin, Palm Springs, 64; acct. exec, John R. MacFaden, Los Angeles, 64- Mil. Serv: Entered as Airman Basic, Calif. Air Nat. Guard, 60, released as Sgt, 66. Mem: Bd. of dirs, United Community Efforts, Inc, 67-69; Trojan Club; Town Hall of Calif; El Pueblo de Los Angeles, Inc; Santa Marta Hospital & Clinic Bldg. Fund (Bd. of dirs); Jr. C. of C; Governor's Advisory Coun. Recipient of Calif. State Assembly and Los Angeles City Coun. Resolutions, 68. Rel: Catholic. Legal Res: 284 S. Hill View Ave, Los Angeles, Calif. 90022. Mailing Add: 444 W. Duarte Rd. Arcadia. Calif. 91006.

RENFROW, HARRY G. R
b. Iowa, 3/4/90; married; c. Six. Educ: Dak. Bus. Col. Polit. & Govt. Pos: N.Dak. State Rep, 55-61. Bus. & Prof. Pos: Auctioneer and ins. agent. Mem: Mason. Rel: Presbyterian; Elder. Mailing Add: Calvin, N.Dak. 58323. (1967)

RENICK, RICHARD RANDOLPH D
Fla. State Rep.
b. Bronx, N.Y, 10/14/30; s. Ralph Apperson Renick and Rosalie Marie Dwyer R; m. 10/12/68 to Valerie E. Phillips; c. Deborah Kathleen and Karen Valerie. Educ: Univ. Miami, 2 years. Polit. & Govt. Pos: Fla. State Rep, 66- Bus. & Prof. Pos: TV film dir, WTVJ, Miami, Fla, 50-59; with Renick Prod, 60-69. Mil. Serv: Entered as 2/C Seaman, Navy, 47, released as Radio Seaman, 50, after serv. in U.S.S. Conserver, Pac. Mem: Miami State Employees Local 545, 64-; Int. Photographers Local 666, 65-; Am. Legion; Kiwanis; Elks; Jaycees; K. of C; Moose. Rel: Catholic. Legal Res: 13440 S.W. 80th Ave, Miami, Fla. 33156. Mailing Add: 7500 Red Rd. S, Miami, Fla. 33143.

RENNEKE, EARL WALLACE R
Minn. State Sen.
b. St. Peter, Minn, 3/10/28; s. John Gottfreid Renneke and Olga Strand R; m. 6/22/51 to Marjorie Elizabeth Eckberg; c. Rochelle, Lynnette and Kristin. Educ: Univ. Minn, Minneapolis, 1 year. Polit. & Govt. Pos: V.chmn, Sibley Co. Rep. Party, Minn, 66-67, chmn, 68-69; Minn. State Sen, Dist. 15, 69- Mem: Minn. Farm Bur. Fedn. Rel: Lutheran. Mailing Add: Route 2, Le Sueur, Minn. 56058.

RENNER, GLENN DELMAR R
b. Greeneville, Tenn, 11/18/25; s. Charles Dana Renner and Lula Hilton R; m. 6/30/45 to Gladys June Brooks; c. Glenna June and Joan Phyllis. Educ:

Tusculum Col, A.B, 46; Univ. Tenn, M.A, 50. Polit. & Govt. Pos: Tenn. State Rep, Greene Co, 64-67. Mil. Serv: Entered as A/S, Navy, 43, released as Seaman 1/C, 46. Mem: Soc. of Residential Appraisers; Nat. Asn. Real Estate Brokers; Nat. Asn. of Realtors; past pres, Greeneville Bd. of Realtors; reg. v.pres and chmn, educ. cmt, Tenn. Asn; of Real Estate Bds; Am. Legion; Mason; Shrine; Elks; Ruritan. Rel: United Methodist. Mailing Add: 315 Tusculum Blvd, Greeneville, Tenn. 37743.

RENNER, ROBERT G. Conservative
Minn. State Rep.
b. Hubbard Co, Minn, 1923; married; c. Five. Educ: B.A; LL.B. Polit. & Govt. Pos: Asst. co. attorney, Cass Co, Minn, 50-53; Minn. State Rep, 57- Bus. & Prof. Pos: Attorney-at-law. Mil. Serv: World War II. Mem: State, Dist. and Am. Bar Asns. Mailing Add: Walker, Minn. 56484.

RENNING, GEORGE R
S.Dak. State Rep.
b. Kadoka, S.Dak, 4/6/15; m. to Bertha Almen. Educ: High Sch. Polit. & Govt. Pos: S.Dak. State Rep, 58-; clerk on Twp. Bd; supvr, Soil Conserv. Bus. & Prof. Pos: Farmer; rancher. Mem: Mason; RAM. Rel: Lutheran. Mailing Add: Kadoka, S.Dak. 57543.

RENNINGER, JOHN S. R
Pa. State Rep.
b. Phila, Pa, 10/10/24; s. Francis Xavier Renninger and Mary Robinson R; m. to Katharine Steele; c. Ann, Molly, Sally and Patrick. Educ: Drexel Inst. Tech; Univ. Ore; Univ. Pa, B.A. and LL.B; assoc. ed, Law Rev. Polit. & Govt. Pos: Past pres, Bucks Co. Estate Planning Coun, Pa; Pa. State Rep, 64-, mem, Consumer Protection and Urban Affairs Cmts, Pa. State House of Rep, currently. Bus. & Prof. Pos: Attorney. Mil. Serv: Army Air Force, 42-46, Sgt; Ens, Naval Reserve; Asiatic Pac. Theater Serv. Medal with 1 Bronze Star. Mem: Bucks Co, Phila. and Pa. Bar Asns; Am. Legion. Rel: St. Luke's Church; Newton Diocesan Rep; Former Warden and Vestryman and chmn, Bldg. Fund. Dr. Mailing Add: 148 N. State St, Newton, Pa. 18940.

RENO, MAX E. D
b. Wapello Co, Iowa, 4/22/26; s. S.E. Reno and Evangeline Heady R; m. 1948 to Frances Hartzler; c. Stephen, Marcus, Heidi, William. Educ: Bloomfield Jr. Col. Polit. & Govt. Pos: Iowa State Sen, -66; former mayor, Bonaparte, Iowa. Bus. & Prof. Pos: Auctioneer and ins. agent. Mil. Serv: Navy, S. Pac. Mem: Masonic Lodge; Zerapath Consistory; Kaaba Shrine; Odd Fellows; Izaak Walton League; Elks; Am. Legion; Rotary; Farm Bur; Nat. and Iowa Asns. of Auctioneers. Rel: Baptist Church; deacon and Sunday Sch. Supt. Mailing Add: Bonaparte, Iowa. 52620. (1967)

RENO, OTTIE WAYNE D
Ohio Dem. State Cent. Committeeman
b. Pike Co, Ohio, 4/7/29; s. Eli Enos Reno and Arbannah Jones R; m. 5/22/47 to Janet Gay McCann; c. Ottie Wayne, II, Jennifer Lynn and Lorna Victoria. Educ: Franklin Univ, A.A. in bus. admin, 49, Col. Law, LL.B, 53; Capital Univ, J.D, 66. Polit. & Govt. Pos: Asst. prosecuting attorney, Pike Co, Ohio, 53-54, recorder, 56-; secy, Pike Co. Dem. Cent. Cmt, 56-; mem, Scioto Valley local bd. of educ, Pike Co, 62-66; Ohio Dem. State Cent. Committeeman, Sixth Cong. Dist, 69- Bus. & Prof. Pos: Cook, Mills Restaurants, Columbus, Ohio, 50-53; attorney-at-law, Pike Co. Bar Asn, 53- Mil. Serv: Entered as Recruit, Ohio Nat. Guard, 48, released as Pvt, 51, after serv. in Serv. Co, 166th Regt. Combat Team, Inf. Publ: The Story of Horseshoes, Vantage Press, Inc, 63; 'Horseshoe Pitching, a Perfect Farm Hobby,' Successful Farming Mag, 8/65; many articles on 'Sports in Pike County,' The Waverly Watchman, 55- Mem: Pike Co. Bar Asn; YMCA; Farm Bur; Nat. Farmers Orgn. Rel: Protestant. Mailing Add: Route 5, Box 305, Lucasville, Ohio 45648.

RENSTROM, DARRELL GEORGE D
Chmn, Weber Co. Dem, Utah
b. Ogden, Utah, 6/5/31; s. Arnold P. Renstrom and Ruby Salt R; single. Educ: Univ. Utah, B.S, 55; George Wash. Univ, J.S.D, 58; Phi Delta Phi. Polit. & Govt. Pos: Clerk, U.S. House of Rep, 55-56; asst. attorney, Weber Co, Utah, 59-63, chief prosecuting attorney, 63-66, fed. aid coordinator, 66-; chmn, Weber Co. Young Dem, 61-63; nat. committeeman, Young Dem. of Utah, 62-64; chmn, N.W. Young Dem, Young Dem. of Am, 63-65; chmn, Weber Co. Dem, 65- Bus. & Prof. Pos: Teacher, Arlington Co. Pub. Schs, 56-58; legal counsel, Nat. Educ. Asn, 67-69. Mil. Serv: Entered as Pvt, Marine Corps, 52, released as Sgt, 54, after serv. in Korean Theater of War; UN, Korean Theater of War and Overseas Ribbons. Mem: Secy, Weber Co. Bar Asn, 60; Utah State and Am. Bar Asns; Kiwanis Serv. Club. Outstanding Young Dem. of Utah, Outstanding Nat. Young Dem, 65. Rel: Latter-day Saint; Master M-Man Award. Legal Res: 259 24th St, Ogden, Utah 84401. Mailing Add: 1001 Third St. S.W, Apt. 404, Washington, D.C. 20024.

RENSVOLD, ROGER FREDERIC R
State Committeeman, Stephens Co. Rep. Cmt, Okla.
b. Madison, S.Dak, 12/2/21; s. Philip Matthew Rensvold and Amanda Theodora Rogne R; m. 5/21/44 to Charlotte Maurine Bury; c. Roger B. and Sue Ann. Educ: Univ. S.Dak, B.A, 43, M.A, 48; Sigma Pi Sigma. Polit. & Govt. Pos: Mem, Okla. Rep. State Cmt, 61; chmn, Stephens Co. Rep. Cmt, 60-69, state committeeman, 69-; mem, Rep. State Exec. Cmt, 61-67; mem, State Exec. Cmt, Oklahomans for Goldwater, 63-64; del-at-lg, Rep. Nat. Conv, 64; treas, Third Cong. Dist. Rep. Cmt, 67- Mil. Serv: Entered as Pvt, Army, 44, released as T/Sgt, 46, after serv. in 92nd Evacuation Hosp, I Corps, Southwest Pac; Southwest Pac. Ribbon with 2 Campaign Stars, Philippine Liberation Ribbon with 1 Star; Army of Occup, Victory and Good Conduct Medals. Mem: bd. dirs, N.Tex. Soc. Petroleum Engrs, 57; nat. membership cmt, Soc. Petroleum Engrs; Am. Inst. Mining, Metallurgy and Petroleum Eng, 59; ed. v.pres, Duncan Toastmasters, 66, pres, 67; Am. Chem. Soc; Am. Petroleum Inst; Stephens Co. Rifle and Pistol Club; Nat. Rifle Asn. Holder, U.S. Patents on tools and processes for petroleum prod. Rel: Methodist. Mailing Add: 1308 Spruce, Duncan, Okla. 73533.

RENTSCHLER, THOMAS BECKETT R
Ohio State Rep.
b. Hamilton, Ohio, 8/23/32; s. Walter Anthony Rentschler and Edith Beckett R; m. 1/28/54 to Dorothy Grevey; c. Thomas B, Jr. and Mark G. Educ: Haverford Col, B.S, 54. Polit. & Govt. Pos: Co. chmn, Ohio Rep. Finance Cmt, 63-66; mem, Young Rep, 63-; precinct committeeman, Butler Co. Rep. Party, 64-; Ohio State Rep, 40th Dist, 67- Bus. & Prof. Pos: Employee, Fifth Third Union Trust Co, Cincinnati, Ohio, 56-58; v.pres, Citizens Bank, Hamilton, 58-68, dir, 66-68, pres, 68- Mil. Serv: Entered as A/S, Navy, 54, released as Personnelman 3/C, 56, after serv. in U.S. Naval Training Center, Bainbridge, Md, 54-56; Naval Res, 53-59. Publ: Three articles in American Rifleman, Nat. Rifle Asn, 63, 64 & 65. Mem: Ohio, Butler Co. and Am. Bankers Asns; Am. Inst. of Banking; Manuscript Soc; Hamilton Asn. of Trade & Indust; Ohio Hist. Soc; Rotary; past bd. mem, Commun. Chest; bd. mem, Salvation Army; past pres. and bd. mem, Boy's Club; Nat. Muzzle Loading Rifle Asn; Isaac Walton League; Antique Automobile Club of Am; chmn. gen. div, United Appeals; adv. mem, Girl Scouts; Newcomen Soc. of N.Am; Nat. Rifle Asn; Ohio Gun Collectors Asn. Medallion Award, Boy's Club of Am, 64; Outstanding Young Man of Ohio, 68. Rel: Lutheran. Legal Res: 1030 New London Rd, Hamilton, Ohio 45013. Mailing Add: P.O. Box 387, Hamilton, Ohio 45012.

RENTSCHLER, WILLIAM HENRY R
Mem, Exec. Cmt, United Rep. Fund of Ill.
b. Hamilton, Ohio, 5/11/25; s. Peter Earl Rentschler and Barbara Schlosser P; m. to Martha G. Snowdon; c. Sarah Y, Peter F, Mary A. and Phoebe M. Educ: Princeton University, B.A. in history. Polit. & Govt. Pos: Pres, Ill. Young Rep, 57-59; mem, Rep. Cmt. on Prog. and Progress, 59; campaign chmn, Nat. Young Rep. Fedn, 59-60; cand, U.S. Sen, Ill, 60; Ill. chmn, Win with Nixon-Lodge Campaign, 60 and Registrn. & Get-Out-Vote Dr, 62; del, Rep. Nat. Conv, 64; chmn. selection cmt, Rep. Blue Ribbon Legis. Cand, Ill, 64; chmn. polit. strategy cmt, Percy for U.S. Sen. Campaign, 66; chmn, United Rep. Forum of Ill; mem, exec. cmt, United Rep. Fund of Ill; Ill. chmn, Nixon/Agnew Campaign, 68; spec. adv, President Nixon's Nat. Prog. for Vol. Action, 69- Bus. & Prof. Pos: Reporter and asst. to exec. ed, Minneapolis Star & Tribune, 49-52; 2nd v.pres, North. Trust Co, 53-56; pres, Stevens Candy Kitchens, Inc, 57-66; pres, Martha Washington Kitchens, Inc, Ill, 66-68; pres. and founder Corp. Mid-Am, Inc, 69. Mil. Serv: Entered as A/S, Navy, 43, released as PO 3/C, 46, after serv. in U.S. Publ: Weekly Syndicated Column, 'Politics: Viewpoint from Mid-American,' 80 newspapers; various articles for periodicals. Mem: Colonial Club of Princeton; Econ. and Exec. Clubs of Chicago; Polit. Responsibility Cmt, Ill. State C. of C; Young Pres. Orgn; trustee, Rockford Col; dir, Chicago Coun. on For. Rels; dir, Better Boys Found; dir, Int. Christian Relief Found, Luxembourg; chmn, Annual Nat. Football League Player Awards Dinner, 67-68; chmn, first annual conf, Strategy for the New City, 69; Tavern Club; Racquet Club; Onwentsia Club. Legal Res: 479 Washington Rd, Lake Forest, Ill. 60045. Mailing Add: 105 W. Adams, Suite 3000, Chicago, Ill. 60603.

RENWICK, WILLIAM F. D
Pa. State Rep.
b. St. Marys, Pa, 12/30/15; Lawson Renwick and Julia Bucheit R; m. to Aurelia O'Donnell; c. Kathleen, Jack and Joe. Educ: St. Marys Cent. Catholic High Sch, 34. Polit. & Govt. Pos: Mem, St. Marys Borough Coun, 45-49; Pa. State Rep, 54- Mil. Serv: Marine Corps, World War II. Mailing Add: 130 Straub Ave, St. Marys, Pa. 15857. (1967)

REPICCI, FRANCIS C. D
Chmn, Genesee Co. Dem. Party, N.Y.
b. Batavia, N.Y, 8/9/44; s. John Repicci, Jr. and Clara DiPiazza R; single. Educ: St. Bonaventure Univ, B.A, 66. Polit. & Govt. Pos: Secy-treas, Genesee Co. Dem. Party, N.Y, 67-69, chmn, 69-; cand. for del, Dem. Nat. Conv, 68; asst. to State Chmn. for Upstate N.Y, 68- Bus. & Prof. Pos: Proprietor, Bel-Air Motel, Batavia, N.Y, 66-; soc. studies teacher, Elba Cent. Sch, 67-68; proprietor, Tekee's Motel and Concord Inn Restaurant, 68- Mem: Nat. Educ. Asn; Lions Int. Rel: Catholic. Legal Res: 119 Jackson St, Batavia, N.Y. 14020. Mailing Add: 3922 W. Main Rd, Batavia, N.Y. 14020.

REPKO, ANDREW R
Chmn, Willington Rep. Town Cmt, Conn.
Polit. & Govt. Pos: Chmn, Willington Rep. Town Cmt, Conn, currently; Conn. State Rep, 55-66; Conn. State Sen, 67-68. Mailing Add: West Willington, Conn. 06279. (1967)

REPPE, LILLIAN LENORA R
V.Chmn, Clark Co. Rep. Cent. Cmt, S.Dak.
b. Crocker, S.Dak; d. Henry A. Obermeier and Annie Saur O; m. 1/14/44 to Einar Reppe; c. Lyle O. Educ: Northern State Teachers Col, 4 years; Nat. Sch. of Cosmotology, Affiliated with DeGuile, Minneapolis. Polit. & Govt. Pos: Precinct Committeewoman, Spring Valley, Clark Co. Rep. Party, S.Dak, 46-64; v.chmn, Clark Co. Rep. Cent. Cmt, 64- Bus. & Prof. Pos: Beauty Operator. Mem: Chmn, Sch. Bd, 9 years. Rel: Lutheran; Treas, Lutheran Church. Mailing Add: Lily, S.Dak. 57250.

REPPERT, HOWARD C, JR.
Iowa State Sen.
b. Des Moines, Iowa, 1/24/18; m. 5/3/41 to Helen Keller; c. Suzanne. Educ: Drake Univ; State Univ. Iowa; Indust. Col. Armed Forces; Phi Delta Theta. Polit. & Govt. Pos: Iowa State Rep, 55-61 & 63-65; Iowa State Sen, 27th Dist, 65-, chmn, Govt. Subdiv. Cmt, banking mem, Ways and Means Cmt. and Mem, Commerce and Transportation Cmts, Iowa State Senate. Bus. & Prof. Pos: Pres, Reppert Investment Co, Inc, Retail Merchants Delivery, Ads on Wheels and Lido Beach Investment Co; exec. v.pres, Reppert Transfer and Storage Co, Inc. Mil. Serv: Army and Air Force, 42-46; Distinguished Flying Cross; 6 Air Medals; 2 Presidential Citations; 5 Battle Stars. Mem: Nat. bd. mgr, Coun. State Govt, 59-61 & 67-; Advert. Club; Mfrs. Rep. Asn; Res. Officers Asn; Air Force Asn.(past wing comdr); bd. dirs, Nat. Arthritis Found; chmn, Iowa Arthritis Found; Iowa Welfare Asn; Am. Legion; VFW; Mason; Scottish Rite; Shrine; C. of C; Sojourners. Rel: Lutheran. Legal Res: 4108 Oak Forest Dr, Des Moines, Iowa 50312. Mailing Add: Senate Bldg, Iowa State House, Des Moines, Iowa 50312.

RESCIA, GEORGE FRANK R
Chmn, Ludlow Rep. Town Cmt, Mass.
b. Springfield, Mass, 2/18/30; s. Frank Rescia and Lydia Lora R; m. 4/14/51

to Elizabeth Grace Nedeau; c. Daniel George, Lynda May, Cynda May and Elizabeth Lora. Educ: Springfield Tech. High, 45-47. Polit. & Govt. Pos: Chmn, Ludlow Elem. Sch. Surv, Mass, 62-65; dist. coordinator, Edward W. Brooke for Attorney Gen, 64 & 66 and U.S. Sen, 68; chmn, Ludlow Elem. Sch. Bldg. Cmt, 64-; mem, Ludlow Finance Cmt, 67-; chmn, Ludlow Rep. Town Cmt, 68- Bus. & Prof. Pos: Dept. mgr. and salesman, Sears Roebuck & Co, 53-63; agent, Prudential Ins, 64-67; mgr. and owner, Frank Realty, 66-; investigator, Dept. Labor & Indust, 67- Mem: K. of C; Mass. State Employees Asn; Ludlow Jaycees (dir); Boys Club (dir); Chicopee Country Club. Rel: Catholic. Mailing Add: Marion Circle, Ludlow, Mass. 01056.

RESNICK, ALAN MARVIN D
Md. State Del.
b. Baltimore, Md, 5/14/28; s. Benjamin Harry Resnick and Dorothy Goldman R; m. 12/29/57 to Dorlee Meyers; c. Marcy Lynn and Leslie Ann. Educ: Univ. Md, A.B, 50, Sch. of Law, LL.B, 52; Pi Sigma Alpha; Phi Alpha; pres. of Hillel, Univ. of Md. Polit. & Govt. Pos: Md. State Del, Fifth Dist, 58-, chmn, Ins. Subcmt, Md. State House of Del, currently. Mil. Serv: Entered as Pvt, Army, 52, released as Sgt, 54, after serv. as Judge Adv. & Hq. Comdr. Mem: Bd. mem, Md. Asn. for The Day Care of Children. Appointed by the Gov. to Cmn. on Ment. Hygiene. Rel: Chizuk Amuno Congregation. Legal Res: 6320 Ivy Mount Rd, Baltimore, Md. 21209. Mailing Add: 303 E. Fayette St, Baltimore, Md. 21202.

RESNICK, GEORGE J. R
b. Manchester, 5/6/25; married; c. 1. Educ: Bus. Col. Polit. & Govt. Pos: N.H. State Rep, -67; coun. mem, N.H. Vets. Coun; former selectman. Bus. & Prof. Pos: Pres-treas, Globe Office Equip. Co. Mil. Serv: Marine Corps, S. and Cent. Pac. Mem: Elks; Masons; Shrine; Am. Legion; Jewish War Vets. of Am; presently dept. comdr. of Jewish War Vets. of N.H. Rel: Am. Jewish. Mailing Add: Globe Office Equipment Co, Manchester, N.H. 03101. (1967)

RESNICK, JAMES D. D
Chmn, City Dem. Party, Davenport, Iowa
b. Davenport, Iowa, 5/29/31; m. 1956 to Joan Marie McNamara; c. 4 boys, 1 girl. Educ: St. Ambrose Col, B.A; Iowa State Univ, M.S. Polit. & Govt. Pos: Mem, Am. Asn. for the UN; mem. staff, Pub. Health Serv, 55-57; former Iowa State Rep; chmn, City Dem. Party, Davenport, Iowa; del, Dem. Nat. Conv, 68. Bus. & Prof. Pos: Asst. Prof. chem, St. Ambrose Col. Mem: Am. Chem. Soc; Iowa Acad. of Sci; Holy Name Soc; Parish Cana Conf. chmn. Mailing Add: 2024 Gaines St, Davenport, Iowa 52804. (1967)

RESOR, STANLEY R. R
Secy. of the Army
b. N.Y.C, 12/5/17; m. to Jane Lawler Pillsbury; c. Seven. Educ: Yale, B.A. in Govt, 39; Yale Law Sch, LL.B, 46. Polit. & Govt. Pos: Under Secy. of the Army, 65, Secy. of the Army, 65- Bus. & Prof. Pos: Assoc, Debevoise, Plimpton, Lyons & Gates, Attorneys, 46-55, parter, 55- Mil. Serv: Entered as 2nd Lt, Army, 42, released in 46, after serv. with the 10th Armored Div, ETO, 44-45, participating in the defense of Bastogne during the Battle of the Bulge; Silver Star; Bronze Star; Purple Heart; Distinguished Unit Citation. Mem: Am. and N.Y. State Bar Asns; Asn. of the Bar of N.Y.C; Coun. of For. Rels, Inc; Metrop, Chevy Chase, Yale, Links, New Canaan Country and New Canaan Winter Clubs. Mailing Add: Dept. of the Army, Pentagon, Washington, D.C. 20310.

RESTER, JAMES AUSBON D
b. Picayune, Miss, 9/10/29; married. Polit. & Govt. Pos: Former Miss. State Sen. Bus. & Prof. Pos: Dairy farmer. Mem: Am. Legion; Farm Bur; PTA; Gulf Milk Dairy Asn. Rel: Baptist. Mailing Add: Route 3, P.O. Box 254-A, Picayune, Miss. 39466. (1967)

RETTGERS, FORREST ITHAMAR D
b. Reading, Pa, 11/20/21; s. Ithamar B. Rettgers and Laura Hartenstine R; m. 4/3/43 to Virginia Mae Felix; c. Robin (Mrs. Harry W. Stone, III), Pamela (Mrs. John Vandervort) and Bonnie Jean. Educ: Univ. Md, B.A; George Wash. Univ, M.A; Am. Univ, Ph.D. cand. Polit. & Govt. Pos: Asst. to dir. U.S. Mil. Assistance Prog, Dept. of Defense, 64-65, dept. asst. to secy. of defense for legis. affairs, int. security affairs, 65-66 and spec. asst. to asst. secy. of defense, 66; admin. asst, U.S. Sen. H.F. Byrd, Jr, Va, 66- Mil. Serv: Entered as Pvt, Army, 40, released as Col, 66; Legion of Merit; Bronze Star W/V Device; Dept. of Defense Commendation Medal; Dept. of Army Commendation Medal with Two Oak Leaf Clusters; Purple Heart; European Theater Ribbon with Five Battle Stars. Mem: Asn. of Admin. Asst. and Secy, U.S. Senate; Asn. of U.S. Army; Army Aviation Asn; VFW; F&AM. Rel: Protestant. Mailing Add: 8414 Camden St, Alexandria, Va. 22308.

REUSS, FREDERICK M, JR. R
Mem, Queens Co. Rep. Cmt, N.Y.
b. Richmond Hill, N.Y, 12/4/32; s. Frederick M. Reuss and Elizabeth R. Sullivan R; m. 11/30/68 to Tria Gaffikin. Educ: Fordham Col, B.S; Univ. Pa. Law Sch, LL.B. Polit. & Govt. Pos: Nat. chmn, Col. Cmt. for Taft, 52; chmn. col. div, N.Y. State Young Rep, 52-53; admin.asst. to Cmnr. of Corrections, N.Y.C, 57-58; chmn, Parents and Taxpayers, 63-; asst. to Chmn. of Ways and Means Cmt, N.Y. State Assembly, 64-65; mem, Queens Co. Rep. Cmt, 64-; Rep. cand, N.Y. State Assemblyman, 29th Assembly Dist, 65; pres, Midland Rep. Club, Queens Village, 65-68; chmn, Citizens Crime Cmn, Queens Co, 65-; cand, Del. to Constitutional Conv, N.Y, 66; alternate del, Rep. State Conv, 66; chmn, Citizens Cmt. for Nixon-Agnew, Sixth Cong. Dist, N.Y, 68; del, Rep. Nat. Conv, 68. Bus. & Prof. Pos: Private practice of law, N.Y.C, 57-63 , Hollis, N.Y, 63- Mem: N.Y. State and Queens Co. Bar Asns; Cath. Lawyers Guild; Am. Judicature Soc; K. of C; Order of Lafayette; Lions; Midland Rep. Club; Queens Village Rep. Club; Queens Braddock Civic Asn; Hollis Civic Asn; Bell-Ville Civic Asn; Parents and Taxpayers; Young Am. for Freedom; Am. Conservative Union; Animal Haven, Inc; Nat. Rifle Asn. Numerous awards by civic and other orgns, for work in fields of Educ. and Commun. Crime Control. Rel: Roman Catholic. Mailing Add: 93-31 239th St, Bellerose, N.Y. 11426.

REUSS, HENRY S. D
U.S. Rep, Wis.
b. Milwaukee, Wis, 2/22/12; m. 1942 to Margaret Magrath; c. Christopher, Michael, Jacqueline and Anne. Educ: Cornell Univ, B.A; Harvard Law Sch, LL.B; v.pres, Chi Psi Alumni Asn; past pres, Cornell Alumni Asn. of Wis; bd. of alumni visitors, Harvard Law Sch, 57-60; bd. of visitors, Cornell Univ. Polit. & Govt. Pos: Asst. corp. counsel, Milwaukee Co, Wis, 39-40; asst. gen. counsel, Off. Price Admin, Wash, D.C, 41-42; dep. gen. counsel, Marshal Plan, Paris, France, 49; spec. prosecutor, Milwaukee Co. Grand Jury, Wis, 50; personal counsel to Secy. of State Fred Zimmerman in Reapportionment Case, Wis. Supreme Court, 53; mem, Milwaukee Sch. Bd, 53-55; U.S. Rep, Wis, 54-; del, Dem. Nat. Conv, 68. Bus. & Prof. Pos: Lawyer; lectr; writer; former pres, White Elm Nursery Co, Hartland, Wis; former dir, Marshall and Ilsley Bank, Milwaukee and Niagara Share Corp, Buffalo, N.Y. Mil. Serv: 2nd Lt, Army, 43-45, served in 63rd and 75th Inf. Div; chief, Price Control Br, Off. of Mil. Govt. for Germany, 45; Awarded Bronze Star Medal for action at crossing of Rhine and Bronze Stars for Normandy, North. France and Cent. Germany. Publ: The Critical Decade, 64. Mem: V.chmn, Jr. Bar Asn; chmn, Constitution and Citizenship Cmt, Milwaukee Co. Bar Asn; v.chmn, For Policy Asn; former mem, Legal Adv. Cmt. Nat. Resources Bd, Wash, D.C; dir, Children's Serv. Soc; Milwaukee City Club; Milwaukee Chap, Nat. Inst. for Infantile Paralysis; nat. bd, Youth Hostel Asn. Legal Res: Milwaukee, Wis. 53200. Mailing Add: 2159 Rayburn House Office Bldg, Washington, D.C. 20515.

REUTER, CLIFFORD SILVA, III. R
Fla. State Sen.
b. Scarsdale, N.Y, 11/15/27; s. Clifford Silva Reuter, Jr. and Louise Hull R; m. 4/6/57 to Marilyn O. Byard; c. Sara Louise, Clifford S, IV, Carolyn Culver and George, II. Educ: Univ. N.H, B.S, 51; Psi Epsilon. Polit. & Govt. Pos: Dist. committeeman, Dade Co. Rep. Cmt, Fla, 60-61; pres, S.Brevard Co. Rep. Cmt, 62-; precinct committeeman, Brevard Co. Rep. Cmt, 62-; organizer, Atlantic Coast Rep. League, 65; past chmn, Brevard Co. Rep. Exec. Cmt; Fla. State Sen, 67- Bus. & Prof. Pos: Gen. mgr, Missile Eng. Prod. Co, 58-59; from asst. to pres, Barfield Inst. Co, 59-62; analyst, Pan Am. Airways, 62- Mil. Serv: Entered as Pvt, Army, 46; released as Pfc, 47. Mem: Soc. Adv. Mgt; Fla. Cattleman's Asn; Am. Legion. Rel: Protestant. Mailing Add: P.O. Box 162, Sharpes, Fla. 32959.

REVELES, ROBERT APODACA D
b. Miami, Ariz, 11/25/32; m. 7/11/59 to Carlotta Norris; c. Robert Gregory, Rachel Antonia, Rebecca Maria, Sara Christina and Ruth Elizabeth. Educ: Univ. of Md, Overseas Prog, 53-54; Georgetown Univ. Sch. of For. Serv, B.S.F.S, 62. Polit. & Govt. Pos: Secy. to U.S. Rep. Stewart L. Udall, Ariz, 56 & 58-61; secy. to U.S. Rep. Morris K. Udall, Ariz, 61-63 and spec. asst, 66-68; legis. asst. to U.S. Rep. George F. Senner, Jr, Ariz, 63-64; admin. asst. to U.S. Rep. Paul J. Krebs, N.J, 64-66; exec. secy. to U.S. Rep. Frank Thompson, Jr, N.J, 69- Mil. Serv: Entered as Pvt, Air Force, 52, released as Airman 1/C, 55, after serv. in Hq, Allied Air Forces South. Europe NATO. Mem: VFW; Am. GI Forum; Nat. Orgn. for Mexican-Am. Serv. Rel: Catholic. Legal Res: Miami, Ariz. Mailing Add: 7621 Kingsbury Rd, Alexandria, Va. 22310.

REVENS, JOHN COSGROVE, JR. D
R.I. State Rep.
b. Providence, R.I, 1/29/47; s. John C. Revens and Rita M. Williams R; single. Educ: R.I. Jr. Col, A.A, 66; Providence Col, B.A, 69; Suffolk Univ. Law Sch, 69-; Dillon Club; St. Thomas More Club (secy); Political Union (pres, Dem. Caucus). Polit. & Govt. Pos: Page, R.I. House of Rep, 65-66, asst. head page, 67, head page, 68; R.I. State Rep, 69- Mem: K. of C; R.I. Jr. Col. Alumni Asn; Providence Col. Alumni Asn. Bishop Hendricken High Sch Letterman's Club Alumni Man of the Year, 69. Rel: Roman Catholic. Mailing Add: 572 Main Ave, Warwick, R.I. 02886.

REVERCOMB, CHAPMAN R
b. Covington, Va, 7/20/95; s. George A. Revercomb and Elizabeth Chapman R; m. 6/9/26 to Sara Venable Hughes; c. William, George, Anne R.(Mrs. Graney) and James. Educ: Wash. and Lee Univ, 14-16; Univ. Va, LL.B, 19; Omicron Delta Kappa; Phi Delta Phi; Delta Sigma Rho; Raven Soc; Phi Kappa Sigma. Polit. & Govt. Pos: Mem, W.Va. State Rep. Cmt, 33-34; pres, Young Rep. League, 35-36; chmn, W.Va. State Rep. Judicial Conv, 36; U.S. Sen, W.Va, 43-49 & 56-59; del, Rep. Nat. Conv, 68. Mil. Serv: Entered as Pvt, Army, 17, released as Cpl, 18, after serv. in Battery A, 35th Regt, CAC, U.S.A. Mem: Pres, Charleston Bar Asn, 35; v.pres, W.Va. State Bar Asn, 38; Am, W.Va. and Kanawha Co. Bar Asns; Judicial Conf, Fourth U.S. Judicial Circuit; Va. State Bar; Am. Legion; Elks; Rotary; hon. mem, Amvets. Rel: Presbyterian. Legal Res: 917 Edgewood Dr, Charleston, W.Va. 25302. Mailing Add: 821 Kanawha Valley Bldg, Charleston, W.Va. 25301.

REVERCOMB, GEORGE H. R
Assoc. Dep. Attorney Gen, Dept. of Justice
Mailing Add: Constitution Ave. & Tenth St. N.W, Washington, D.C. 20530.

REVERCOMB, WILLIAM C, JR. R
b. Charleston, W.Va, 12/2/27; s. Chapman Revercomb and Sara Hughes R; m. 2/19/52 to Marjorie Boston; c. William C, III, Stephen B. and Carolyn H. Educ: Princeton Univ, A.B, 48; Col. Physicians & Surgeons, Columbia Univ, M.D, 51; Internship and Residencies in Internal Med, 51-53 & 55-57; Univ. Hosps, Cleveland Ohio; Parkland Hosp, Dallas, Tex, 56-57. Polit. & Govt. Pos: Alternate del, Rep. Nat. Conv, 68. Bus. & Prof. Pos: Private practice, internal med, 57-; dir, Cardiac Work Classification Unit, Institute, W.Va, 59-68. Mil. Serv: Entered as 1st Lt, Air Force, 53, released as Capt, 55, after serv. in Strategic Air Command, 53-55; Capt. inactive Res. Mem: Dipl. Am. Bd. Internal Med; Am. Col. Physicians; Am. Soc. Internal Med; Am. Med. Asn; Am. Heart Asn; Rotary. Rel: Episcopal. Legal Res: 1726 Louden Heights Rd, Charleston, W.Va. 25314. Mailing Add: 806 Atlas Bldg, Charleston, W.Va. 25301.

REX, CLYDE R
Iowa State Rep.
b. Webster City, Iowa, 9/8/22; s. Clyde Judson Rex and Alice Wilson R; m. 6/6/44 to Eleanor Grace Liming; c. Clydene (Mrs. Dick Evans), Le Ann, Debra and Jill. Educ: Ellsworth High Sch, grad. Polit. & Govt. Pos: Co. Supvr, Hamilton Co, Iowa, 60-68; Iowa State Rep, 69- Bus. & Prof. Pos: Farmer, 47- Mil. Serv: Entered as Pvt, Army, 46, released as Pfc, 46. Mem: Am. Legion; Farm Bur; Jewell Country Club. Rel: Methodist. Mailing Add: Ellsworth, Iowa 50075.

REYNOLDS, ADRIAN WALL D
Wyo. State Rep.
b. Sedan, Kans, 8/30/00; s. Adrian Reynolds, Jr. and Rhoda May Wall R; m. 3/16/24 to Helen Lancaster; c. Mary Ruth (Mrs. George W. Layton), Rhoda (Mrs. M.L. Hallacy), Adrian K. and George L. Educ: Colo. Col; Univ. Kans, 19-23; Sigma Delta Chi; Owl Soc. Polit. & Govt. Pos: Supvry. acct, Works Prog. Admin, Rock Springs, Wyo, 33-36; dep. co. clerk, Sweetwater Co, 37-42; precinct committeeman and exec. committeeman, Sweetwater Co. Dem. Cent. Cmt, 54- and west. co. area chmn, 68-; Wyo. State Rep, 61-65 & 66-; del. and mem. resolutions cmt, Dem. State Conv, 64, 66 & 68. Bus. & Prof. Pos: Reporter and advert. mgr, various newspapers, 24-33; ed, Daily Reminder, Rock Springs, Wyo, 36-37; ticket clerk, Union Pac. R.R, Green River, Wyo, 42-45 and chief clerk to asst. supt, 45-51; publisher and ed, Green River Star, 51- Mil. Serv: Pvt, Army Inf, 18. Publ: Continuously published feature material for newspapers and press serv. for 40 years, recently specializing in hist. Mem: Am. Legion (past comdr); Odd Fellows; Int. Typographical Union; Lions (past pres, Green River Chap); C. of C.(past pres); past pres, Wyo. Press Asn. and Wyo. State Hist. Asn; chmn, Southwest Wyo. Develop. Cmt; past v.pres, Wyo. Indust. Develop. Coun; state chmn, Wyo. Powell Centennial Cmt. and Observance; Wyo. mem, Cmn. of Intergovt. Coop, Coun. of States. Various Press Asn. Awards. Rel: Congregational. Legal Res: 192 N. First West, Green River, Wyo. 82935. Mailing Add: P.O. Box 592, Green River, Wyo. 82935.

REYNOLDS, ALMA EBRIGHT R
b. Osborne Co, Kans, 12/25/99; d. Elmer Ebright and Dorcas Loomis E; m. 2/22/19 to Eugene T. Reynolds; c. Francis Drake and Vance Leroy. Polit. & Govt. Pos: Precinct committeeman, Bellingham, Wash, 45-57; pres, Bellingham Rep. Women's Club, 55-56 and Camano Island Rep. Women's Club, 59-60; second dist. dir, Wash. Federated Rep. Women, 60-61; v.chmn, Island Co. Rep. Party, Wash, 63-66; alternate del, second cong. dist, Rep. Nat. Conv, 64. Mem: Women's Soc. Christian Serv; organist, Eastern Star; Fire Sirens. Rel: Methodist. Mailing Add: Route 4, Box 180, Camano Island, Wash. 98292.

REYNOLDS, BENJAMIN J. R
Pa. State Rep.
b. W. Grove, 1/29/27; s. S. Evan Reynolds and Carsye Bower R; m. to Eleanor Marshall; c. three. Educ: Kennett Consol. Sch. Polit. & Govt. Pos: Former pres, South. Chester Co. Young Rep, Pa; chmn, Mason Dixon Task Force, Pa-Md-Del. Water Proposal; dir, Chester Co. Develop. Coun, Pa; New Garden Twp. supvr, 60-65; Chester Co. Rep. committeeman, 62-; Pa. State Rep, 62- Bus. & Prof. Pos: Dairy farmer and retailer. Mem: Chester Co. Hist. Soc.(dir); Nat. Soc. State Legislators; Health and Welfare Coun; Civic Asn.(past pres); Pa. and Chester Co. Farmers Asn; Avondale Fire Co; Chester Co. Fireman's Asn; assoc, Fraternal Order of Police; C. of C. Collects colonial currency and early Pa. maps; active in restoration of hist. houses. Mailing Add: R.D. 1, Avondale, Pa. 19311.

REYNOLDS, EDWARD HARRIS D
b. Notasulga, Ala, 10/7/18; s. Edward Harris Reynolds and Vivian Wise R; m. 5/30/48 to Sarah Elizabeth Avant; c. Edward Harris, Jr, and Jeanne. Educ: Ala. Polytech. Inst, B.S, 40; Univ. Ala, LL.B, 43; Phi Gamma Delta. Polit. & Govt. Pos: Ala. State Sen. until 66; asst. attorney gen, Ala, 66-, chief, State Lands Div, 67- Mil. Serv: World War II; served in Pac. Area, Philippine Islands, Japan and Hawaii; was in War Crimes Div, Tokyo, 1 year. Mem: Mason. Rel: Methodist. Mailing Add: Notasulga, Ala. 36866.

REYNOLDS, HOBSON RICHMAN R
b. Winton, N.C; s. Reuben Reynolds and Julia Belle R; m. 1926 to Evelyn Crawford. Educ: Waters Normal Inst. and N.C. Bus. Col. Hon. LL.D, Bethune-Cookman Col, 48 and Allen Univ, 63. Polit. & Govt. Pos: Pa. State Rep, 34 & 38; selected by President Franklin D. Roosevelt as an observer at formation of UN Orgn; referee in workmen's compensation, Pa. Labor Cmn, 50-55; Consul of Liberia; del. and seconded nomination of Dwight D. Eisenhower, Rep. Nat. Conv, 52, del, 56, and alternate del-at-lg, 68; appointed by President Eisenhower as asst. to Comnr. Fed. Housing; mem, Pa. Constitutional Conv, 68. Mem: F&AM (past Grand Master, Prince Hall Affil. of Pa); bd. mem, Nat. Urban League; trustee, Bethune-Cookman Col, Fla; chmn. bd. trustees, Cheyney State Col, Pa; Elks (Grand Dir, Dept. Civil Liberties, 39-60; Grand Exalted Ruler, 60). Distinguished and outstanding pub. serv. selected by AFRO-American newspaper, placed on its honor roll, 49-50. Rel: Baptist; Chmn. trustee bd, Wayland Temple Baptist Church, Pa. Mailing Add: 1522 N. 16th St, Philadelphia, Pa. 19121.

REYNOLDS, JAMES JOSEPH D
b. Brooklyn, N.Y, 1/8/07; s. James J. Reynolds and Katherine Mahoney R; m. 7/22/65 to Helen May. Educ: Columbia Univ, A.B, 28. Polit. & Govt. Pos: Former Under Secy. of Labor. Bus. & Prof. Pos: Pres, Am. Inst. Merchant Shipping, currently. Mailing Add: 1120 Connecticut Ave. N.W, Washington, D.C. 20036.

REYNOLDS, JERRY LEE R
Asst. Exec. Asst. to the Postmaster Gen.
b. Salamanca, N.Y, 11/20/28; s. Gerald Alfred Reynolds and Virginia Ewings R; m. 6/9/51 to Frances Utley; c. Marlene (Mrs. Hahn) and Patricia (Mrs. Banks). Educ: Pa. State Univ, 47-48. Polit. & Govt. Pos: Press asst, Nixon for Gov, 62; press secy, Don H. Clausen for U.S. Rep, 62-63; admin. asst, U.S. Rep. Don H. Clausen, M.C, 63-69; asst. exec. asst. to the Postmaster Gen, 69- Bus. & Prof. Pos: Sports Ed, Warren Times-Mirror, Warren, Pa, 46-47; staff correspondent, United Press Int, Sacramento, Calif, 52-62. Mil. Serv: Entered as A/S, Navy, 48, released as Journalist, 2/C, 52, after serv. as Ed. of Daily and weekly newspapers and a magazine, Great Lakes, Ill. and Philippine Islands. Mem: Bull Elephants; Tantallon Country Club. Rel: Lutheran. Legal Res: Sacramento, Calif. Mailing Add: 9211 Reid Lane, Washington, D.C. 20022.

REYNOLDS, JOHN W. D
b. Green Bay, Wis, 4/4/21; s. John W. Reynolds and Madge Flatley R; m. 5/26/42 to Patricia Ann Brody; c. Kate M, Molly and Jimmy. Educ: Univ. of Wis, B.S, 46, LL.B, 49. Polit. & Govt. Pos: Attorney Gen, Wis, 59-63; del, Dem. Nat. Conv, 60 & 64, v.chmn, 64; Gov, Wis, 63-65; U.S. Dist. Judge, East. Dist, Wis, 65- Bus. & Prof. Pos: Admitted to Wis. Bar, 49; attorney-at-law, Green Bay, Wis, 49- Mem: Am, Wis. and Brown Co. Bar Asns. Mailing Add: 4654 N. Woodburn, Milwaukee, Wis. 53211. (1967)

REYNOLDS, JULIAN ALEXANDER D
S.C. State Rep.
b. Bishopville, S.C, 1/31/15; s. Purley H. Reynolds and Lou M. Alexander R; m. 6/4/40 to Edith Floride Josey; c. Edith F, J.A, Jr, Chris and Rebecca. Educ: Clemson Col, 34-36; Univ. S.C, 36-38. Polit. & Govt. Pos: Mem. city coun, Andrews, S.C, 53-57 & 59-62, mayor-pro-tem, 58-63; S.C. State Rep, 63- Bus. & Prof. Pos: Former R.R. locomotive engr; druggist and owner, Reynolds Drug Store, Andres and Seaboard. Mem: Mason; Shrine. Rel: Presbyterian; Ruling Elder. Mailing Add: 7 S. Morgan Ave, Andrews, S.C. 29570.

REYNOLDS, JULIAN SARGEANT D
Va. State Sen.
b. New York, N.Y, 6/30/36; m. to Elizabeth Weir Venneman. Educ: Wharton Sch. of Finance, Univ. of Pa, B.S. in econ. Polit. & Govt. Pos: Mem. exec. cmt, Young Dem. Clubs of Va; pres, Young Dem. Club of Richmond; Va. State Del, 66-68; Va. State Sen, 69- Bus. & Prof. Pos: Asst. treas, Reynolds Metals Co; bd. of dirs, Bank of Va. Mem: Country Club of Va; Commonwealth Club; Metrop. Club of Wash; Surf Club in Miami; bd. of dirs. and exec. cmt, Boys' Club of Richmond; bd. of dirs, Robert E. Lee Coun. of Boy Scouts, Tuckahoe Br. of YMCA and Gills Country Day Sch. Rel: Presbyterian. Mailing Add: 5621 Cary St. Rd, Richmond, Va. 23226. (1967)

REYNOLDS, LOUISE ELLIOTT R
Alderman, Louisville, Ky.
b. Lewisburg, Tenn, 5/4/16; d. William Thomas Elliott and Carrie Mae Taylor E; m. 5/11/37 to James Elwood Reynolds, Sr; c. Linda Louise. Educ: Louisville Munic. Col, 39-40 & 47-48; Univ. of Louisville, 50-51 & 54-56. Polit. & Govt. Pos: Secy, Jefferson Co. Rep. Orgn, Ky, 46-53; committeewoman, 11th Ward Rep. Orgn, 52-; secy. to U.S. Rep. John M. Robesen, Ky, 53-58; mem, Task Force Cmt. on Human Rights and Responsibilities, currently; alderman, 11th Ward, Louisville, Ky, 61- Bus. & Prof. Pos: Pres, Reynolds Realty Co, Inc, currently. Mem: Pres, Louisville Real Estate Brokers Asn, 58-60; Nat. Asn. of Real Estate Brokers; bd. dirs, Plymouth Settlement House; YWCA; NAACP; South. Christian Leadership Coun; Moles, Inc; ONO; Lincoln Club; 3rd Dist. Women's Rep. Club. Rel: Methodist. Mailing Add: 3310 Dumesnil, Louisville, Ky. 40211. (1967)

REYNOLDS, MARTHA M. R
Mem, Calif. Rep. State Cent. Cmt.
b. Clinton, Ill, 1/31/31; d. Frank Dow Moots and Grace Riddle M; m. 2/11/51 to George Maurice Reynolds; c. Greg Ingham, Mark Franklin, Bart Andrew, Doug Maurice and Keith Martin. Educ: Univ. Ill, Champaign, 49-51; Milliken Univ, 54-56; Pi Beta Phi. Polit. & Govt. Pos: Vol, Rep. precinct work, 54-; pres, Malibu Federated Rep. Women, 67-69; mem, Los Angeles Co. Rep. Cent. Cmt, 67-69; mem, Calif. Rep. State Cent. Cmt, 68- Mem: Jr. Ebell; Santa Ana Panhellenic (pres, 61-62); S. Coast Alumnae of Pi Beta Phi (pres, 61-62 & 63-64); PTA (various cmts); C. of C. Rel: Protestant. Mailing Add: 6223 Frondosa Dr, Malibu, Calif. 90265.

REYNOLDS, MERLE C, JR. D
Chmn, Middlefield Dem. City Cmt, Conn.
b. New Bedford, Mass, 6/13/20; s. Merle C. Reynolds and Elsie L. Reca R; m. 6/2/45 to Carmelina M. Aresco; c. Merle Co, III and Marie A. Educ: Univ. Vt, 2½ years. Polit. & Govt. Pos: Registr. of voters, Middlefield, Conn, 46-54; chmn, Middlefield Dem. City Cmt, 62-; Conn. State Rep, 54-56; assessor, Middlefield, 54-; justice of peace, Conn, 54- Bus. & Prof. Pos: Design engr, Emhart Mfg. Co, 45-56 and Aceomatic Eng. Co, 56-60; agent, Prudential Ins. Co. Am, 60-65, asst. mgr, 65- Mem: K. of C; Lions Int; PTA; Conn. Asn. Life Underwriters; Middlefield Volunteer Fire Dept. Rel: Roman Catholic. Mailing Add: Valley View Dr, Middlefield, Conn. 06455.

REYNOLDS, NEWTON LUTHER D
b. Toney, Madison Co, Ala, 6/20/11; s. John Elias Reynolds and Eula Leona Dickey R; m. 2/13/42 to Christine Wattenbarger; c. Cheryl Sue, Steven Milburn. Educ: David Lipscomb Col, Nashville, Tenn. Polit. & Govt. Pos: Ala. State Rep, 51-66. Bus. & Prof. Pos: Merchant; farmer; cotton ginner. Mil. Serv: Army Air Force, sgt, 42-45. Mem: Elks; Eagles; Am. Legion; 40 et 8. Rel: Church of Christ. 1967 Legal Res: 2225 Calif. St, Huntsville, Ala. No mailing address available. (1967)

REYNOLDS, RICHARD L. D
b. Saugus, Conn; m. to Barbara Smith; c. Three. Educ: Univ. of Miami, B.S, Civil Eng; Suffolk Law Sch, LL.B, 1963. Saugus Selectmen, 3 terms. Bus. & Prof. Pos: Practicing Lawyer; Civil Engr. Mil. Serv: WW II. Mem: Mass. Bar Asn. Mailing Add: 12 Henry St, Saugus, Mass. 01906. (1967)

REYNOLDS, ROBERT CHARLES R
Mass. State Rep.
b. Rochester, N.H, 11/6/34; s. Everett Leon Reynolds and Anne Eckles R; m. 12/19/52 to Carol Everlens Norris; c. Robert C, Jr, Raymond Scott, Ralph Alan and Richard Leon. Educ: Boston Univ; Suffolk Law Sch. Polit. & Govt. Pos: Town moderator, Northborough, Mass; Mass. State Rep, Worcester's 23rd Dist, 69- Bus. & Prof. Pos: Practicing attorney, R.R. Reynolds, Northborough, Mass, currently; pres, Renco Ins, 62-, Renco Realty, Westboro, 65- Mil. Serv: Airman 1/C, Air Force, 52-56. Mem: Worcester Co. and Mass. Bar Asns; Am. Trial Lawyers Asn; Lions; Am. Legion; Aleppo Temple Lodge. Rel: Protestant. Legal Res: 20 Solomon Pond Rd, Northborough, Mass. 01532. Mailing Add: 5 W. Main St, Northborough, Mass. 01532.

REYNOLDS, ROBERT JACKSON D
Chmn, Montgomery Co. Dem. Exec. Cmt, Ky.
b. Joplin, Mo, 5/5/10; s. Roy Randolph Reynolds and Roberta Katherine Taulbee R; m. 7/2/31 to Anne Kenney Prewitt; c. Elizabeth (Mrs. Carr) and Robert Jackson, Jr. Educ: Univ. Mo, 2 years; Sigma Nu. Polit. & Govt. Pos:

Mem, Ky. Tuberc. Sanatoria Cmn, 48-50; Ky. State Sen, 50-58; Dem. precinct committeeman, Montgomery Co, Ky, 56-; chmn, Montgomery Co. Dem. Exec. Cmt, 60- Bus. & Prof. Pos: Owner, R.J. Reynolds, Gen. Contractor, 45-; pres, Hwy. Concrete Pipe, Inc, 49-, Hwy. Drainage Pipe, Inc, 54- and Mt. Sterling Broadcasting Corp, 56-; v.pres, Capitol Broadcasting Corp, 62- and Del-Marysville Broadcasting Corp, 64- Mem: Assoc. mem, Am. Soc. Civil Engrs; life mem, Ky. Sheriff's Asn; hon. mem, Ky. Hwy Employees Ten-To-Forty Club; assoc. mem, Islamorada Fishing Guides Asn, Fla. Rel: Christian Church. Legal Res: Route 2, Mt, Sterling, Ky. 40353. Mailing Add: P.O. Box 373, Mt. Sterling, Ky. 40353.

REYNOLDS, ROBERT LEONARD, JR. D
Mem. Bd, Dane Co. Dem. Party, Wis.
b. Madison, Wis, 6/11/30; s. Robert Leonard Reynolds and Sarah Chickering R; m. 8/23/52 to Marjorie Jill Bump; c. Ann T. and Robert L, III. Educ: Univ. Wis, Madison, B.A, 53, LL.B, 60. Polit. & Govt. Pos: Alderman, Madison, Wis, 64-68; del, Dem. Nat. Conv, 68; mem. bd, Dane Co. Dem. Party, 68- Bus. & Prof. Pos: Trust officer, Security State Bank, Madison, 62-68; practicing attorney, Madison, 68- Mil. Serv: Entered as Lt, Army, 53, released as 1st Lt, 55; Army Res, 55-60, Capt. Mem: Wis. State Bar Asn; Dane Co. Bar Asn. Rel: Episcopal. Mailing Add: 2327 Eton Ridge, Madison, Wis. 53705.

REYNOLDS, RUSSELL C. D
Ky. State Rep.
b. Leeco, Ky, 7/30/21; s. Porter Reynolds and Myrtle Gabbard R; div; c. Sharon Sue and Russella Rhea. Educ: Lees Jr. Col, Ky, 2 years; Georgetown Col, 7 hours; East. Ky. State Col, 7 hours. Polit. & Govt. Pos: Ky. State Rep, 78th Dist, 54- Bus. & Prof. Pos: Sch. teacher, 38-42; merchant, 42-69. Legal Res: Armory Dr, Jackson, Ky. 41339. Mailing Add: 329 Broadway, Jackson, Ky. 41339.

REYNOLDS, STEVE D
Ga. State Sen.
b. Jackson Co, Ga, 6/6/20; s. Waldo Bryant Reynolds (deceased) and Lalyer Evans Crowe R; m. 11/19/39 to Rebecca Harper; c. David W. Educ: South. Bus. Col, 1 year; LaSalle Exten. Univ, 3 years. Polit. & Govt. Pos: Ga. State Sen, Dist. 48, currently. Bus. & Prof. Pos: Former pres. and gen. mgr, Cent. Containers Co, Inc; pres. and gen. mgr, Reynolds Oil Co, currently. Mil. Serv: Entered as Pvt, Army, 44, released as T-5, 46, after serv. in Army Inf, U.S. Mem: Am. Legion; Kiwanis; PTA; Farm Bur. Rel: Presbyterian; Elder. Legal Res: 297 Craig Dr, Lawrenceville, Ga. 30245. Mailing Add: P.O. Box 303, Lawrenceville, Ga. 30245.

REYNOLDS, W. J, JR. 'BILL' D
Ky. State Rep.
b. 1920. Educ: Univ. of Ky; Morehead State Col. Polit. & Govt. Pos: Ky. State Rep, 64-; alternate del, Dem. Nat. Conv, 68. Bus. & Prof. Pos: Right-of-Way Supvr, United Fuel Gas Co. Mil. Serv: Army Air Force. Mem: Am. Legion; VFW; Mason; PTA; Big Sandy Develop. Corp. Rel: Christian. Mailing Add: Allen, Ky. 41601. (1967)

REYNOLDS, WARREN G. R
Chmn, Peoria Co. Bd. Supvr, Ill.
b. Tazewell Co, Ill, 1931; s. P.J. Reynolds and Lura Black R; m. 1961 to Carol Ackerman; c. Lorie Rose and Charles Warren. Educ: Bradley Univ, B.S, 53 and M.A, 66; Pi Kappa Delta; Omicron Delta Kappa; Lambda Chi Alpha. Polit. & Govt. Pos: Secy, Peoria Co. Rep. Cent. Cmt, Ill, 62-; mem, Peoria Co. Bd. Supvr, 64-, chmn, 69- Bus. & Prof. Pos: Asst. advert. mgr, Keystone Consol. Industs, Inc, 64-66, exec. staff asst. to pres, 66-68, corporate secy, 68- Mem: Pres, Jr. C. of C. Distinguished Serv. Award, Jaycees; Honor Cert, Freedoms Found. Mailing Add: 1626 W. Christine Ave, Peoria, Ill. 61614.

RHIAN, ALVIN J. R
S.Dak. State Sen.
b. 1/31/07; m. 10/23/34 to Marion M. Rice. Educ: Yankton High Sch. Polit. & Govt. Pos: Former S.Dak. State Rep; S.Dak. State Sen, 67- Bus. & Prof. Pos: Owner-mgr, Petroleum bus. and automobile-truck sales. Mil. Serv: Lt, Corps of Engrs, Army, World War II, with serv. overseas, 26 months. Mem: Elks; Moose; VFW; Am. Legion; Mason; Shrine; past pres, Yankton C. of C. and S.Dak. Independent Oil Mens Asn; dir, S.Dak. Auto Dealers Asn; mem. lay bd, Sacred Heart Hosp; v.chmn, bd. of trustees, Yankton Col. Rel: Church of Christ Congregational. Mailing Add: 1009 Douglas, Yankton, S.Dak. 57078.

RHINEHART, SHELBY AARON D
Mayor, Spencer, Tenn.
b. Monterey, Tenn, 5/5/27; s. Shelby A. Rhinehart and Laura Underwood R; m. 9/20/52 to Margret Wrenn; c. Shelby Porter and James Barney. Educ: Tenn. Tech. Univ; Stanford Univ; Rho Chi. Polit. & Govt. Pos: Mem, Bd. of Educ, Spencer, Tenn, 56-; chmn, Van Buren Co. Dem. Exec. Cmt, 58-; Tenn. State Rep, 59-63; Mayor, Spencer, 63- Bus. & Prof. Pos: Owner, Spencer Drug Co, 56- Mil. Serv: Entered as Pvt, Army, 44, released as Sgt, 51, after serv. in Army Ord, Pac, 46 and 51; South West Pac. and Good Conduct Medals; World War II and Korean Victory Medals; Korean Serv. Medal. Mem: Mason; VFW; Am. Legion; Civitan; Am. and Tenn. State Pharmaceutical Asns. Rel: Baptist. Mailing Add: Box 128, Spencer, Tenn. 38585. (1967)

RHOADES, ANNA ROSA R
V.chmn, Ocean Co. Rep. Exec. Cmt, N.J.
b. Basel, Switz, 10/9/13; d. Jacob Hirschbiegel and Mary Steiner H; div; c. Linda (Mrs. Robert Pitman) and Judith. Educ: Lakewood High Sch, N.J, 4 years. Polit. & Govt. Pos: Prin. clerk, Ocean Co. Court House, N.J, 40-; secy, Lakewood Rep. Munic. Cmt, 58-; mem. exec. bd, N.J. V.Chmn. Asn, 65-66; V.chmn, Ocean Co. Rep. Exec. Cmt, 65- Bus. & Prof. Pos: Receptionist, Madison Agency, Inc, 53- Mem: Bd. dirs, Ocean Co. Sheltered Workshop; Toms River Bus. and Prfnl. Women's Club; bd. dirs, Ocean Co. Employees Fed. Credit Union; Lakewood Regular Rep. Club; bd. dirs, Ocean Co. Hist. Soc. Rel: Lutheran. Mailing Add: 5 S. Oakland St, Lakewood, N.J. 08701.

RHOADS, WILLARD C. R
Wyo. State Rep.
b. Kansas City, Kans, 8/20/07; m. to Elaine; c. Two. Educ: Ore. State Univ, B.S. Polit. & Govt. Pos: Del. to President Eisenhower's Conf. on Educ. Probs; past v.pres, Wyo. Sch. Trustees Asn; past pres, Big Horn Basin Sch. Trustees Asn; mem. sch. bd, 12 years; Wyo. State Rep. and Wyo. Legis. Rep, West. States Water Coun, currently. Bus. & Prof. Pos: Treas. and mgr, North Fork Valley Ditch Co; cattle rancher. Mem: Elks; past dir, Park Co. Fair Bd. and S.C.S. Bd; past co. pres, Farm Bur; Wyo. Stockgrowers Asn, chmn, exec. cmt. and pub. lands cmt; Shoshone Nat. Forest Adv. Bd. Rel: Methodist. Mailing Add: North Fork Route, Cody, Wyo. 82414.

RHODEN, LOUIS ALLEN R
b. Conroe, Tex, 2/24/43; s. Louis S. Rhoden and Minnie Tipton R; m. 12/22/62 to Bettye L. Vestal; c. Louis Allen, II. Educ: Sam Houston State Col, B.S, 65. Polit. & Govt. Pos: Former chmn, Liberty Co. Rep. Party, Tex. Mem: Tex. State Teachers Asn; Cleveland Class Room Teachers Asn; Optimists. Rel: Baptist. Mailing Add: Box 632, Cleveland, Tex. 77327.

RHODES, ALFRED HENRY, JR. D
Chmn, Hinds Co. Dem. Exec. Cmt, Miss.
b. Midnight, Miss, 3/16/41; s. Alfred Henry Rhodes and Willie Mae Hall R; m. 3/21/63 to Lottie Mary William; c. William Wyatt. Educ: Utica Jr. Col, Miss, 59-61; Tougaloo Col, B.A, 64; Jackson State Col, cand. for M.S; Omega Psi Phi. Polit. & Govt. Pos: v.chmn, Third Cong. Dist. Dem. Party, Miss, currently; secy, State Exec. Cmt, Miss. Freedom Dem. Party, currently; mem, State Exec. Cmt, Young Dem. Clubs of Miss, currently; del, Dem. Nat. Conv, 68; chmn, Hinds Co. Dem. Exec. Cmt, 69- Bus. & Prof. Pos: Dir, Miss. Proj, Nat. Fedn. of Settlements and Neighborhood Centers, currently; commun. organizer, Child Develop. Group, 65-66; teacher, Hinds Co. Pub. Schs, 65-66; consult, Miss. Med. and Surg. Asn, 67; consult, Michael Schwerner Mem. Fund, 68-69; consult, Nat. Coun. Negro Women, 69. Mem: Bd. of Jackson Urban League; bd. of Bethlehem Ctr; bd. of Syst. Training & Redevelopment; YMCA; Hinds Co. Farmer's Asn. Rel: Baptist. Mailing Add: 1557 Reddix St, Jackson, Miss. 39209.

RHODES, BEN S. R
b. Saunemin, Ill, 4/11/89; m. to Julia O'Neill R. Educ: Ill. Wesleyan U. Law Sch; Phi Gamma Delta; Delta Phi. Polit. & Gov. Pos: Ill. State Rep, 38-62; Asst. to the Co. Judge of McLean Co; Chief clerk, Bloomington City Elec. Cmn; Private Secy. to Frank Funk of Ill. Pub. Utilities Cmn; Supvr. of McLean Co; Mayor of Bloomington, 3 terms; former Secy. and Chmn. of the McLean Co. Rep. Central Cmt; Majority leader, 67th Gen. Assembly. Mem: A founder of Am. Legion (St. Louis caucas); past post Comdr, Dist. Comdr, grand correspondent of the 40 et 8; Trustee, Masonic bodies. Rel: First Christian Church of Bloomington. Mailing Add: 1211 Broadway St, Normal, Ill. 61761. (1967)

RHODES, ELDRIDGE C. D
b. Stokes Bridge, Lee Co, 8/29/95; s. William Henry Rhodes and Ella Cornellia Woodham R; m. 12/22/22 to Mary Maxwell. Educ: Florence High Sch. Polit. & Govt. Pos: Mem, State Budget and Control Bd. and State Bd. of Health, S.C; exec. secy. and treas, State Rural Electrification Authority; Comptroller Gen, S.C. 42-68. Mailing Add: State Capitol, Charleston, S.C. 29202. (1967)

RHODES, FRED BURNETT R
Dep. Adminstr, Vet. Affairs
b. Washington, D.C, 12/17/13; s. Fred B. Rhodes and Florence Shuffle R; m. 12/25/56 to Winona Henderson. Educ: Colgate Univ, A.B, 36; Univ. Md, LL.B, 41; Simga Nu. Polit. & Govt. Pos: Exec. dir, Joint Cmt. on Atomic Energy, 47-49; chief counsel, Cmt. on Armed Serv, U.S. Senate, 53-55; gen. counsel, Vet Admin, 60-61; minority counsel, Cmt. on Appropriations, U.S. Senate, 62-64, secy. and staff dir, Policy Cmt, 64-69; Dep. Adminstr. Vet. Affairs, 69- Bus. & Prof. Pos: Private law practice, 55-60. Mil. Serv: Entered as Pvt, Army, 41, released as Maj, 47, after serv. in Manhattan Eng. Dist; recalled, Army, 51-53; Commendation Ribbon and other awards for Atomic Bomb Proj; Col, Army Res, 64. Mem: Am, Fed. and D.C. Bar Asns; Nat. Lawyers Club; Potomac Appalachian Trail Club; Army Navy Country Club; Exec. Cmt, South. Baptist Conv. Rel: Baptist. Legal Res: 3101 N. Peary St, Arlington, Va. 22207. Mailing Add: Veterans Administration Bldg, Suite 1001, 801 Vermont Ave. N.W, Washington, D.C. 20420.

RHODES, GEORGE FRED D
Chmn, Calhoun Co. Dem. Exec. Cmt, Tex.
b. San Antonio, Tex, 8/2/25; s. George E. Rhodes and Clara Stutzenbecker R; m. 11/24/51 to Marion Kathleen Athey; c. George Fred, Jr, Kathleen and Lisa. Educ: Tex. Col. of Arts and Industries, B.S, 50; S. Tex. Col. Law, LL.B, 54; Alpha Chi; Phi Kappa Delta; Debate Team, 3 years; pres, Student Body Sr. Year. Polit. & Govt. Pos: Chmn, Calhoun Co. Dem. Exec. Cmt, Tex, 56-; committeeman, 18th Sen. Dist, Tex. State Dem. Exec. Cmt, 68- Mil. Serv: Entered as Aviation Cadet, Air Force, 43, released as Sgt, 46. Mem: Pres, Calhoun Co. Bar Asn, 61-62 and secy-treas, 62-65; chmn, Salvation Army Serv. Unit, Calhoun Co, Tex, 58-; pres, Rotary, 64-65; Elks Lodge 729 Victoria, Tex. Rel: Methodist. Legal Res: Route 1, Box 80, Port Lavaca, Tex. 77979. Mailing Add: P.O. Box 986, Port Lavaca, Tex. 77979.

RHODES, GEORGE MILTON D
b. Reading, Pa, 2/24/98; m. 1921 to Margie Seiverling. Educ: Reading Pub. Schs. Polit. & Govt. Pos: Mem. Rationing Bd, War Manpower Cmt; U.S. Rep, Pa, 48-68. Bus. & Prof. Pos: Printer; bus. mgr; labor ed. and labor rep; pres, Reading and Berks Co. Cent. Labor Union, AFL, 22 years; bd. mem, Reading Housing Authority. Mil. Serv: Vet. of World War I. Mem: Coun. of Soc. Agencies; Commun. Gen. Hosp; YMCA. Mailing Add: 505 Brighton Ave, Reading, Pa. 19606.

RHODES, JAMES ALLEN R
Gov, Ohio
b. Coalton, Ohio, 9/13/09; s. James Llewellyn Rhodes and Susan Howe R; m. 12/18/41 to Helen Rawlins; c. Susan, Saundra and Sharon. Educ: Ohio State Univ. Polit. & Govt. Pos: Auditor, Columbus, Ohio, 39-42, mayor, 42-53; state auditor, Ohio, 53-63, Gov, 63- Publ: Johnny Shiloh, Bobbs-Mer-

rill Co, 58; The Trial of Mary Todd Lincoln, 59; The Court-Martial of Commodore Perry, 60. Mem: Past pres, Amateur Athletic Union; former chmn, U.S. Olympic Cmt; founder, Pan-Am. Games. Recipient of the Silver Keystone Award by Boys Clubs of Am. and the Helms Found. Award. Rel: Presbyterian. Mailing Add: Governor's Office, Columbus, Ohio 43215. (1967)

RHODES, J(AMES) R(OBERT), JR. 'JIMMY' D
b. Albany, Ga, 2/20/39; s. James Robert Rhodes and Annie Hall R; single. Educ: Univ. Miss, B.A, 62; Sigma Nu. Polit. & Govt. Pos: Ga. State Rep, 63-66. Bus. & Prof. Pos: Farmer. Mem: Mason. Rel: Baptist. Mailing Add: Newton, Ga. 31770. (1967)

RHODES, JOE EDD D
b. Gifford, Ark, 9/13/97; s. James Wesley Rhodes and Susan Giles R; m. 1/13/18 to Vada Winnie Harrison; c. Vada-Joe (Mrs. Barron). Educ: Traskwood High Sch, Ark, 11-15. Polit. & Govt. Pos: Court reporter-law clerk, Little Rock, Ark, 28-66; circuit judge, Sixth Judicial Circuit of Ark, 66 & 17th Judicial Circuit, 68-; del, Dem. Nat. Conv, 68. Mem: Ark. Bar Asn; Mason; Shrine. Rel: Christian Scientist. Mailing Add: Riceland Hotel, Stuttgart, Ark. 72160.

RHODES, JOHN J. R
U.S. Rep, Ariz.
b. Council Grove, Kans, 9/18/16; s. J. J. Rhodes and Gladys Thomas R; m. 5/24/42 to Mary Elizabeth (Betty) Harvey; c. John J, III, Thomas H, Elizabeth Campbell and James Scott. Educ: Kans. State Col, B.S, 38; Harvard Law Sch, LL.B, 41; Blue Key; Beta Theta Pi. Polit. & Govt. Pos: V.chmn, Ariz. Bd. of Pub. Welfare, 51-52; U.S. Rep, First Dist, Ariz, 52- Bus. & Prof. Pos: Partner, Rhodes, Killian & Legg, law firm, Mesa, Ariz, 46-52; v.pres, Farm & Home Life Ins. Co, Phoenix, 51- Mil. Serv: Entered as 1st Lt, Army Air Force, 41, released as Lt. Col, 46, after serv. in Air Force Training Command; Col.(Ret), Judge Adv. Gen. Corps, Army Res. Mem: Ariz, Kans, D.C. and Am. Bar Asns; Scottish Rite (33°); SAR; Burning Tree; Rotary; Elks; Moose; Am. Legion (past sr. v.comdr); Ariz. Club; Jaycees; C. of C.(past pres, Mesa Chap); Mesa Country Club; Cong. Country Club. Rel: Methodist. Legal Res: 926 W. Mountain View Dr, Mesa, Ariz. 85201. Mailing Add: 2312 Rayburn House Office Bldg, Washington, D.C. 20515.

RHODES, NINA D
b. Brooklyn, N.Y, 1/8/34; d. Jack Fried and Clare Forman F; m. 6/4/61 to Michael Rhodes; c. Ross Benett and Laura Raven. Educ: Hollywood High Sch, Calif, grad. Polit. & Govt. Pos: Chmn. fund raising, Young Prfnl. for Kennedy, Calif, 68, committeewoman, Gala Finance Cmt. for Kennedy under Warschaws, 68; del, Dem. Nat. Conv, 68; mem. bd. dirs, Dem. Womens Forum, Calif, 68- Bus. & Prof. Pos: Actress, NBC and Screen Gems, currently. Mem: Screen Actors Guild; Am. Fedn. TV and Radio Artists. Rel: Jewish. Mailing Add: 4342 Nogales Dr, Tarzana, Calif. 91356.

RHODES, WILMA MELISSA R
Mem, Alaska Rep. State Cent. Cmt.
b. Loogootee, Ind, 9/9/07; d. Joseph Lish Crays and Ida Jane Montgomery C; m. 3/3/42 to Merle Frank Rhodes; c. Richard, Donald, Robert, Joan and Janette. Educ: Night sch, high sch. and bus. sch. subjects, hotel and motel mgt. and col. course in acct. Polit. & Govt. Pos: Pres, Gastineau Channel Rep. Women's Club, 59-61; secy, S.E. Alaska Sen. Dist. Cmt, 60-61, chmn, 62-63; mem, Alaska Rep. State Cent. Cmt, 62-63 & 66-; fourth dist. campaign chmn, Lowell Thomas, Jr. for Cong, 64; del, Rep. Nat. Conv, 64; Rep. Committeewoman for S.E. Alaska, 66-; precinct committeewoman, Alaska Rep. Party, currently. Bus. & Prof. Pos: Owner-mgr, Apt. House, Alaska. Mem: Bus. & Prfnl. Women's Club; Women of Moose; C. of C; Rep. Women's Club; Juneau Methodist Women; Pioneers of Alaska Auxiliary; Gastineau Channel Rep. Club; Alaska Comprehensive Health Adv. Coun. Rel: Methodist. Mailing Add: 336 E. Third St, Juneau, Alaska 99801.

RIBICOFF, ABRAHAM A. D
U.S. Sen, Conn.
b. New Britain, Conn, 4/9/10; m. to Ruth Siegel; c. Peter and Jane. Educ: N.Y. Univ; Univ. Chicago Law Sch, LL.B, 33. Hon. degrees from 20 cols. and univs. Polit. & Govt. Pos: Conn. State Rep, 38-42; munic. judge, Hartford, 41-43 & 45-47; U.S. Rep, Conn, 48-52; Gov, Conn, 54-61; Secy. of Health, Educ. and Welfare, 61-62; U.S. Sen, Conn, 62- Bus. & Prof. Pos: Lawyer, Hartford, Conn. Legal Res: Hartford, Conn. Mailing Add: 321 Old Senate Office Bldg, Washington, D.C. 20510. (1967)

RICCI, HUGO L. D
b. Providence, R.I, 3/2/12. Educ: Providence Col, 34; Boston Univ. Law Sch, LL.B, 37, LL.M, 42. Polit. & Govt. Pos: R.I. State Rep, 59-69; mem, Gov. Refugee Relief Cmt; mem, Korean Vet. Bonus Bd; del, State Constitutional Conv, 64. Bus. & Prof. Pos: Attorney-at-Law; bd. of adv, St. Francis Col, Biddeford, Maine. Mil. Serv: U.S. Army, 989th F.A. Bn, 42-45 in Ireland, Eng, France, Germany and Austria. Mem: Bigelow Asn. Awarded Star of Solidarity, Repub. of Italy. Mailing Add: 78 Commodore St, Providence, R.I. 02904. (1967)

RICE, CARL VENTON D
b. Lovilla, Iowa, 3/27/98; s. Walter S. Rice and Ida Isabelle Chamberlain R; wid; c. Ruth Isabelle (Mrs. Jefferson Mitchell), Carlene Virginia (Mrs. George Lind), Mary Elizabeth (Mrs. Samuel Wells) and Grace Lucille (Mrs. John A. Muder, Jr). Educ: Kans.Univ, LL.B. and L.D, 18; Delta Theta Phi. Polit. & Govt. Pos: Chmn, Labette Co. Dem. Party, Kans, 22-34; chmn, Dem. Cong. Dist, 26-28; chmn. platform cmt, State Dem. Conv, 28, 30, 32 & 38; mem, Kans. State Hwy. Cmn, 31-33; del, Dem. Nat. Conv, 32, 40, 44, 48, 52 & 60, mem. platform cmt, 32 & 60, mem. credentials cmt, 56, alternate del, 36, 64 & 68; counsel, Reconstruction Finance Corp, Kans, 33-49 and State Bank Dept, 37-39; Dem. Nat. Committeeman for Kans, 44-52; dir, Kans. Emergency Resources Mgt. Plan, 67-; mem, Urban Renewal Cmt. Cmn, Kansas City, 67- Mil. Serv: Entered as Pvt, Army, 18, released as Sgt. Maj, 19 after serv. in Field Artil. Mem: Am, State and local Bar Asns; Am. Legion; C. of C; Kans. City Club; Univ. Club; Indian Hills Country Club. Rel: Protestant. Mailing Add: 2108 Washington Blvd, Kansas City, Kans. 66102.

RICE, CHARLES E.
b. New York, N.Y, 8/7/31; s. Laurence J. Rice and Mary Convey R; m. 8/25/56 to Mary E. Mannix; c. John Laurence, Mary Frances, Anne Patricia, Joseph Patrick, Charles Peter, Jeanne Elizabeth, Teresa Helen and Kathleen Bernadette. Educ: Col. Holy Cross, A.B, 53; Boston Col. Law Sch, LL.B, 56; N.Y. Univ, LL.M, 59 and J.S.D, 62. Polit. & Govt. Pos: State v.chmn, Conservative Party, N.Y, 62-69. Bus. & Prof. Pos: Lectr. hist. & polit. sci, C.W. Post Col, 59-62; lectr. and vis. asst. prof, N.Y. Univ. Sch. of Law, 59-62; prof. law, Fordham Univ. Sch. of Law, 60-69; prof. law, Univ. Notre Dame Sch. of Law, 69- Mil. Serv: Entered as 2nd Lt, Marine Corps, 56, released as 1st Lt, 58, after serv. at Air Sta, Quantico, Va, 57-58; Maj, Marine Corps Res, currently. Publ: Freedom of Association, N.Y. Univ. Press, 62; The Supreme Court and Public Prayer, Fordham Univ. Pres, 64; The Vanishing Right to Live, Doubleday & Co, 69. Mem: Am. and N.Y. State Bar Asns; K. of C. Rel: Roman Catholic. Mailing Add: 820 Cavanaugh Dr, South Bend, Ind. 46617.

RICE, DALE HARVEY R
Chmn, Benton Co. Rep. Cmt, Ark.
b. Bentonville Ark, 6/3/17; s. Sidney Lee Rice and Maude Piercy R; m. 3/17/46 to Dorothy Arlene Enewold; c. Darrel Alan and Gary Dale. Educ: Vaughn High School, grad. Polit. & Govt. Pos: Chmn, Benton Co. Rep. Cmt, Ark, 66- Mil. Serv: Entered as Pvt, Air Force, 41, released as S/Sgt, 46, after serv. as Instr. in Bombsight Tech. Sch. Mem: Farm Bur.(pres, Benton Co. Chap, 61-64). Rel: Protestant. Mailing Add: Route 4, Box 266, Bentonville, Ark. 72712.

RICE, DORIS ELIZABETH R
b. Searsburg, Vt, 11/16/03; m. to Gordon R. Rice; c. Two. Educ: Brattleboro Mem. Hosp. Nursing Sch, 25. Polit. & Govt. Pos: Mem, Sch. Bd, Wilmington, Vt, 54- and former chmn; town auditor, Wilmington; Vt. State Rep, 59-67. Bus. & Prof. Pos: Housewife; nurse. Rel: Baptist. Mailing Add: Wilmington, Vt. 05363. (1967)

RICE, EDWARD W. D
Chmn, Uncasville Dem. Town Cmt, Conn.
b. Haverhill, Mass, 10/15/11; s. William H. Rice and Elizabeth Donahue R; m. 1/19/29 to Ethel M. Staubley; c. Marjorie (Mrs. Rousseau) and Dorothy (Mrs. Gorra). Educ: Palmer Mem. Sch, Montville, Conn, 8 years. Polit. & Govt. Pos: Mem. and chmn, sch. bd, Uncasville, Conn, 44-54, mem, 64-; Conn. State Rep, 45-47; judge, Montville Justice Court, 60-62; chmn, Uncasville Dem. Town Cmt, 64-; presidential elector, Conn, 68. Bus. & Prof. Pos: Bus. agent, Local No. 671, Teamsters Union, 40-43, former pres, Joint Coun. 64, Conn, 43-53, secy-treas, Local No. 493, 43-, chmn. two arbit. cmts, Conn. Cmt, 45-, E. Coast, 63-, trustee, two pension funds and two health and welfare funds, 53-; former mem, Conn. State Bd. of Arbit, 67. Mem: Mason (32°); Teamsters Union. Received Citation for Life Saving, Boy Scouts, 26; McAuliffe Medal Award, Diocesan Labor Inst. of the Archdiocese of Hartford for outstanding leadership in labor rels, 67. Rel: American Baptist. Mailing Add: 19 Red Cedar Ave, Uncasville, Conn. 06382.

RICE, FRED R
Chmn, Jackson Co. Rep. Exec. Cmt, Ohio
b. Wellston, Ohio, 8/8/11; s. Fred Rice and Margaret Mae Halterman R; m. July 24 to Virginia Riley; c. Fred Winsor and John Thomas. Educ: Kent State Univ, B.S, 33. Polit. & Govt. Pos: Ohio State Rep, Jackson Co, 59-62; chmn, Jackson Co. Rep. Exec. Cmt, Ohio, 59-; fire marshall, State of Ohio, 63-65; registr, Bur. Motor Vehicles, 65- Bus. & Prof. Pos: Sales rep, Goodyear Tire & Rubber Co, 33-46; pres, Buckeye Mill & Lumber Co, Jackson, Ohio, 47-65. Mil. Serv: Entered as Pvt, Air Force, 42, released as Capt, 46, after serv. in China-India-Burma, Okinawa and Philippine Islands, 42-46; Res, 46-68, Maj.(Ret). Mem: Elks; Kent State Univ. Varsity Club; United Commercial Travelers; Automobile Club; Am. and Ohio Farm Bur Fedns; Mason; Shrine; Eagles; Farmer Sportsman; Ohio Forestry Asn; Am. Legion; Farm Bur; Moose; Rotary (past pres); twice chmn, Jackson Co. Apple Festival; chmn, Agr. Soc. and Co. Fair Bd. Rel: Methodist. Legal Res: Route 2, Wellston, Ohio 45692. Mailing Add: 1578 Penworth Dr, Columbus, Ohio 43229.

RICE, JOHN S. D
b. Adams Co, Pa, 1/28/99; m. to Luene Rogers; c. Ellen F. Educ: Gettysburg Col, B.S, 21. Hon. LL.D, Temple Univ. Polit. & Govt. Pos: Pa. State Sen, 32-40, Majority Floor Leader, Pa. State Senate, 37, Pres. Pro Tempore, 38; first chmn, Pa. Salvage Dr, 41; Dem. nominee for Gov, Pa, 46; secy. Dept. Property and Supplies, 56-57; secy, Commonwealth of Pa, 58-61; Ambassador to Netherlands, 61-64; chmn, Pa. State Dem. Cent. Cmt, 59-61 & 65-66; del, Dem. Nat. Conv, 68. Bus. & Prof. Pos: Former dir, Gettysburg Nat. Bank; pres, Rice, Trew and Rice Co, Biglerville, Pa, 29-55; trustee, Gettysburg Col, 39-, chmn. bd. trustees, 55-61; trustee, Gettysburg Lutheran Theol. Sem, 41-55; pres, State Container Co, 47-55. Mil. Serv: Entered as Pvt, Army, World War I, re-entered Army Air Force, 42, released as Col, 45; Col.(Ret), Army Res; Legion of Merit. Mem: Am. Legion; VFW; Mason; Elks. Rel: Lutheran. Mailing Add: 60 W. Broadway, Gettysburg, Pa. 17325.

RICE, MICHAEL G. D
b. Astoria, N.Y, 8/26/24; m. to Irene Reis; c. Michael G, IV. Educ: E. Sch. for Physicians Aides; Columbia Univ. Col. of Pharm. Polit. & Govt Pos: N. Y. State Assemblyman, 64-66; exec. bd, Columbia Dem. Club. Bus. & Prof. Pos: Admin. dir, owner, Flushing Labs. Mil. Serv: Army, Sgt, 43-46; Soldiers Medal for Valor; 4 Battle Stars; Conspicuous Serv. Medal, State of N.Y. Mem: P. v.comdr, chmn, Americanism Cmt, Am. Legion; founder, adminstr, Whitestone Mobile Med. Serv. Unit of Civil Defense; p. v.pres, Div. 15, Ancient Order of Hibernians; publicity chmn, Francis Lewis Mem. Comm; p. state v.pres, Soc. of Am. Technologists; Holy Name Soc; K. of C; Whitestone Commun. Post 4787, VFW; Whitestone Lions; chmn, Francis Lewis Mem. Civic and Commun. Asn; Blood Brother, Matimacok Indian Tribe of Flushing; Hon, Gerbina Asn, Corona; life mem, Vet. of Nat. Guard and Naval Militia; 1st Friday Club; DAV; Boy Scouts; exec. bd, Dist. chmn, instr, Jr. Rifle Club; exec. officer, Matinocok Rifle Club; Rifle Marksmanship instr, Nat. Rifle Asn. Rel: Catholic; p. pres, 21 Club. Mailing Add: 18-09 Murray St, Whitestone, N.Y. 11357. (1967)

RICE, ROBERT CLIFFORD R
Chmn, Langlade Co. Rep. Orgn, Wis.
b. Fargo, N.Dak, 9/11/20; s. Clifford Lewis Rice and Maren Paulsen R; m. 6/19/49 to Winifred Mabel Graupman; c. John Robert, Andrew Paulsen and Jerry Albert. Educ: St. Thomas Military Acad; Univ. Minn, B.Ch.E. Polit. & Govt. Pos: Secy-treas, Langlade Co. Rep. Orgn, Wis, 54-64, chmn, 64- Bus. & Prof. Pos: Registered prfnl. engr, Wis; pres, Master Gas Serv. Co, 49-, City Gas Co, Antigo, Wis, 56- and Antigo Area Ind. Corp, 64-; v.pres, Gas Masters, Inc, 50- Mil. Serv: Entered as 2nd Lt, Army, 40, released as Capt, 46, after serv. in Coast Artillery and Signal Corps, ETO. Mem: Kiwanis; Elks; Am. Legion; C. of C; City Plan Cmn; Wis. Soc. of Prfnl. Engrs. Rel: Protestant. Legal Res: 1231 N. Superior St, Antigo, Wis. 54409. Mailing Add: 733 Fifth Ave, Antigo, Wis. 54409. (1967)

RICE, VILAS C. R
Secy, Hancock Co. Rep. Cent. Cmt, Ill.
Polit. & Govt. Pos: Secy, Hancock Co. Rep. Cent. Cmt, Ill, 67- Mailing Add: R.R. 3, Carthage, Ill. 62321.

RICE, V(IRGIL) THOMAS R
Chmn, Rep. Party of Hawaii
b. La Harpe, Ill, 6/29/20; s. Vilas E. Rice and Jane N. Robertson R; m. 2/14/69 to Phyllis Ann Carpenter; c. Lesley Jean, Sharon Leilan and Clayton Taylor. Educ: Univ. Ill, B.A, 41; Univ. Ill. Col. of Law, J.D, 48; Phi Sigma Kappa; Phi Delta Phi. Polit. & Govt. Pos: V.pres, 37th Precinct, Fourth Rep. Dist, Hawaii, 53-55; del, Hawaii State Rep. Conv, 53-69; chmn, 17th Rep. Dist. Cmt, Hawaii, 55-60; mem, Honolulu Co. Rep. Cmt, 56-60, chmn, 69; mem, Hawaii Homes Cmn, 60; mem, chmn, and secy, State Transportation Adv. Cmn, 60-64; v. chmn, various precincts in Hawaii, 60-69; chmn, Rep. Party of Hawaii, 69- Bus. & Prof. Pos: Assoc, Law off. of James P. Blaisdell, 48-50, assoc. and partner, Blaisdell & Moore Attorneys, 53-61, partner, Moore, Torkildson & Rice, 61-64, Quinn and Moore, 64, Rice and Lee, 64- Mil. Serv: Entered as Leading Aircraftsman, Royal Can. Air Force, 41, transfered to U.S. Army Air Corps, 43, released as Capt, 45, after serv. in 415th Squadron Royal Can. Air Force, 43-44 and Air Transport Command, 44-45, ETO; Capt, U.S. Air Force, 50, released as Maj, 53, after serv. in Pac. Div, Hawaii; Lt. Col.(Ret), Air Force Res, 69; Distinguished Flying Cross; Air Medal with 3 Oak Leaf Clusters; Nat. Serv. Defense Medal; Can. Vol. Serv. Medal with Maple Leaf Clasp; Res. Medal. Mem: Am, Hawaii and Ill. Bar Asns; Air Force Asn; Judge Advocates Asn; life mem, Child and Family Serv; charter mem, Hawaii Planned Parenthood; mem. bd. and treas, Health and Commun. Serv. Coun. of Hawaii; Am. Legion. Rel: Protestant. Legal Res: Apt. 707, 2877 Kalakaua Ave, Honolulu, Hawaii 96815. Mailing Add: Suite 410, 735 Bishop St, Honolulu, Hawaii 96813.

RICE, WALTER LYMAN R
U.S. Ambassador to Australia
b. Peever, S.Dak, 7/29/03; s. Carl J. Rice and Milda Orfield R; m. 7/6/60 to Inger Vestergaard; c. Lisa Milda. Educ: Univ. Minn, B.A, 25; Harvard Law Sch, LL.B, 28; Phi Beta Kappa; Sigma Delta Chi; Chi Phi. Polit. & Govt. Pos: Spec. asst. to the U.S. Attorney Gen, 30-41; U.S. Ambassador to Australia, 69- Bus. & Prof. Pos: Prosecuting attorney, U.S. Dist. Court, N.Y, 28-30; gen. counsel, Reynolds Metals Co, 41, v.pres. and dir, 42, pres, Reynolds Mining Corp, 43; pres, Caribbean Steamship Co, Reynolds Haitian Mines, Guianan Mines and Lydford Enterprises, Inc, 44-68; chmn. policy cmt, U.S. C. of C, 65-66, dir, 56-69, v.pres, 67-69. Publ: Drafted Fed. Anti-Racketeering Act for Cong, 34. Mem: Country Club of Va; Harvard Club; Cong. Country Club. Mailing Add: American Embassy, Canberra, Australia.

RICE, WILLIAM GORHAM D
b. Albany, N.Y, 12/30/92; s. William Gorham Rice and Harriet Langdon Pruyn R; m. 6/29/20 to Rosamond Eliot; c. Andrew Eliot, Pamela (Mrs. Christian F. Rendeiro) and Timothy Eliot. Educ: Harvard Univ, A.B, 14, A.M, 15, Law Sch, LL.B, 20, S.J.D, 21. Polit. & Govt. Pos: Mem, Madison Bd. of Educ, Wis, 29-32; asst. gen. counsel, Nat. Labor Bd, Wash, D.C, 34 and UN Relief and Rehabilitation Admin, 45; asst. gen. counsel and gen. counsel, Nat. Labor Rels. Bd, 34; labor cmnr, U.S. Labor Dept, Geneva, Switz. 35-36; mem, Nat. Defense Mediation Bd, Wash, D.C, 41-42; cmt. chmn, Nat. War Labor Bd, 42-45; del, Dem. Nat. Conv, 48 & 68. Bus. & Prof. Pos: Law clerk with Justice Louis D. Brandeis, Wash, D.C, 21-22; from asst. prof. to prof. of law, Univ. of Wis, 22-63, emer. prof, 63-; faculty mem, Salzburg Seminar on Am. Studies, Salzburg, Austria, 48; lectr. on Am. law, India and Pakistan, 59; assoc, law firm of Anderson, Bylsma and Eisenberg, Madison, Wis, 63-68; attorney at law, 68- Mil. Serv: Am. Field Serv. with French Army, 15-17; U.S. Army, 17-19, 2nd Lt, serv. in Am. Ambulance Field Serv, in field and Gen. Hq, France; Croix de guerre (three citations). Publ: Law Among States in Federacy, 59; A Tale of Two Courts, 67; Vietnam and International Law, 67; plus others. Mem: Am. Law Inst; Nat. Lawyers Guild; Am. Soc. of Int. Law; World Peace Through Law Center; Am. Fedn. of Teachers; Am. Asn. of Univ. Prof. Rel: Unitarian-Universalist. Mailing Add: 2212 Hillington Green, Madison, Wis. 53705.

RICH, CARL W. R
b. Cincinnati, Ohio, 9/12/98; s. David William Rich and Rosa West R. Educ: Univ. Cincinnati, A.B, 22, LL.B, 24; Tau Kappa Alpha; Lambda Chi Alpha; Phi Alpha Delta; Omicron Delta Kappa. Hon. LL.D, Univ. Cincinnati, 59. Polit. & Govt. Pos: City councilman, Cincinnati, Ohio, mayor; judge, Common Pleas Court of Hamilton Co; asst. city prosecutor, Cincinnati, asst. city solicitor; U.S. Rep, Ohio, 63-64; prosecuting attorney, Hamilton Co. Bus. & Prof. Pos: Chmn. bd, Cincinnati Royals prof. basketball team; chmn. bd. and pres, Kennedy Savings and Loan Co; v.pres, Cent. Hyde Park Savings & Loan Co; chmn. bd, First Nat. Bank, Morrow, Ohio; dir, Grand Cent. Savings & Loan Co; Home State Savings & Loan Co; Hamilton Mutual Ins. Co; legal counsel, Bldg. & Loan Co. Mil. Serv: Army, World War I; served to Col, CWS, AUS, World War II. Mem: Mason (33°); Shrine; Moose; Eagles; Cincinnati Club (past v.pres); adv. bd, Gr. Cincinnati unit, Salvation Army. Recipient, Nat. Distinguished Alumni Award, Tau Kappa Alpha, 61. Legal Res: Cincinnati Club, Cincinnati, Ohio 45202. Mailing Add: 2220 Kroger Bldg, Cincinnati, Ohio 45202.

RICH, JACK W. D
Mem, Ark. State Banking Bd.
b. Colt, Ark, 2/4/05; s. Walter R. Rich and Allie Gatten R; m. 6/14/28 to Lois Wallin; c. Sara (Mrs. J. Everett Norfleet) and Mary (Mrs. Duke B. Clement). Educ: Emory Univ, 24; Alpha Tau Omega. Polit. & Govt. Pos: Mem, State Forestry Cmn, Ark, 44; del, Dem. Nat. Conv, 64 & 68; mem, Ark. State Banking Bd, currently. Bus. & Prof. Pos: Pres, Rich Industries Inc, 30-; chmn, Guaranty Loan & Real Estate Co, Tex, 38-; chmn, Bank of West Memphis, 48- Mem: Former pres, Home Builders Asn. of Memphis; former pres, Ark. Lumber Dealers Asn; West Memphis Meadowbrook Country Club; Memphis Country Club. Rel: Methodist. Legal Res: 1701 N. Avalon, West Memphis, Ark. 72301. Mailing Add: 506 E. Broadway, West Memphis, Ark. 72301.

RICH, JOE LYNN D
Chmn, Dallas Co. Dem. Party, Tex.
b. Wellington, Tex, 5/12/24; s. Otto Brian Rich and Allie Green R; m. 12/20/45 to Linda Margaret McGee; c. Mark William, Lynn Brian, Alison and Jody. Educ: North Tex. State Univ, 40-42; Univ. Tex, Austin, B.S. in Archit, 51. Polit. & Govt. Pos: Dem. precinct chmn, Dallas Co, Tex, 56-66; city councilman, Irving, 57-59; chmn, Dallas Co. Dem. Party, 66-; del, Dem. Nat. Conv, 68. Bus. & Prof. Pos: Partner, Wright-Rich & Assoc, Architects, 54- Mil. Serv: Entered as Aviation Cadet, Navy, 42, released as Lt. Comdr, 54, after serv. in 211, 201 and 48 Patrol Squadron, S. Am. and Korea, 42-54. Mem: Am. Inst. of Architects; Construction Specifications Inst.(pres, Dallas Chap, 63). Rel: Presbyterian. Legal Res: 1500 Colony Dr, Irving, Tex. 75060. Mailing Add: 2727 Cedar Springs, Dallas Tex. 75201.

RICHARD, ELMO D
Secy-treas, Henry Co. Dem. Party, Ohio
b. 4/16/06; s. Daniel L. Richard and Myrtle Pearson R; m. 9/5/36 to Violet Franz. Educ: Bowling Green State Univ, 2 years. Polit. & Govt. Pos: Dep, Henry Co. Auditor's Off, Ohio, 30-38; committeeman and mem. exec. cmt, Henry Co. Dem. Party, 32-, secy-treas, 51-; dir, Henry Co. Bd. Elec, 42- Bus. & Prof. Pos: Sch. teacher, Grand Rapids, Ohio, 28-29; off. mgr, Production Credit, 41-57; Life Ins. Agent, Lincoln Life Ins. Co, 57- Mil. Serv: Air Force, 43, Pvt.(medical discharge) 63 days. Mem: Am. Legion; hon. life mem. Elks (adv. coun, Past Exalted Ruler); K. of P; Fraternal Order of Police; Ohio Elec. Off; Twp. Trustee's Asn. Rel: Protestant. Legal Res: Route 1, Napoleon, Ohio 43545. Mailing Add: P.O. Box 346, Napoleon, Ohio 43545.

RICHARDS, ELIZABETH MILLER D
b. Providence, R.I, 3/27/12; d. Dr. Albert Heircy Miller and Ada Holding M; m. 10/1/35 to Jonathan Barlow Richards; c. Jonathan B, II, Kathleen, Victoria (Mrs. Bastron) and Charles Emery. Educ: Radcliffe Col, A.B, 34. Polit. & Govt. Pos: Secy. and Seventh Dist. committeewoman, Dem. State Cent. Cmt, Iowa, 60-64; alternate del-at-lg, Dem. Nat. Conv, 60, del. and secy. to the Iowa Del, 64; chmn, Iowa State, Operation Support, Dem. Nat. Cmt, 61-68; co-ed. and co-organizer, Iowa Dem. Womens Activities, 63-64; mem, Women's Adv. Cmt, John R. Hansen for Cong, 64 & 66; staff, Iowa Humphrey-Muskie Hq, 68. Mem: Pres, SW Iowa Progress Inc. CAP, 65-67; chmn, Low Rent Housing Agency of Red Oak, Iowa, 66-68; coun. pres, Nishabotna Girl Scout Coun, SW Iowa, Inc, 54-56; past pres, Red Oak PTA Coun; Red Oak Chap, Am. Asn. of Univ. Women; v.pres, Iowa UNA-USA. Rel: Congregational. Mailing Add: 1112 Boundary St, Red Oak, Iowa 51566.

RICHARDS, GEORGE HOWE D
b. Tyler, Tex, 11/24/12; s. George Louis Richards and Susie Gainey R; m. 5/30/40 to Mary Jo West. Educ: Tex. A&M Univ, B.S, 35. Polit. & Govt. Pos: Tex. State Rep, Dist. 17, 59-67. Bus. & Prof. Pos: Co. agr. agent, Tex. A&M Agr. Exten. Serv, 35-48; Huntsville Nat. Bank, 48-60; gen. ins. agency, 54-66. Mem: Ex-Students Asn, Tex. A&M Univ; Rotary; Farm Bur; Local, Regional and Nat. C. of C; Tex. Asn. of Independent Ins. Agents. Rel: Presbyterian. Legal Res: 1528 Ave. P, Huntsville, Tex. 77340. Mailing Add: P.O. Box 168, Huntsville, Tex. 77340.

RICHARDS, HAROLD LELAND D
Chmn, Huron Co. Dem. Party, Mich.
b. Port Hope, Mich, 3/7/08; s. Lewis James Richards and Emma Anderson R; m. 10/16/30 to Blanche McNair; c. Robert R, Donald B, Mary Lou (Mrs. Lively) and Marjorie Ann (Mrs. Nilsen). Educ: Port Hope High Sch, 23-27. Polit. & Govt. Pos: Former cand. for Co. Register of Deeds, 77th Dist. Mich. State Rep. and Huron Co. Clerk, Mich; chmn, Huron Co. Econ. Opportunity Agency; mem, Huron Co. Planning Cmn; membership chmn, Huron Co. Dem. Party, 53-64, chmn, 65-; councilman and city cmnr, Harbor Beach, 64-66; del, Ohio State Dem. Conv, 65, 67 & 68. Bus. & Prof. Pos: Crew leader, Hercules, Inc, currently. Mem: Pres, UAW Local 812, 20 years; pres, Harbor Beach Commun. Fed. Credit Union, 68-; secy, Huron AFL-CIO Coun, 66-; pres, Huron Co. Hist. Soc. Community Leader of Am. Award, 68; Huron Co. Dem. Party Award, 68. Rel: Reorganized Latter-day Saint; Presiding minister, Harbor Beach Reorganized Church of Jesus Christ of Latter-day Saints. Mailing Add: 233 S. Third St, Harbor Beach, Mich. 48441.

RICHARDS, PAUL AUGUSTINE D
b. Oakland, Calif, 5/27/27; s. Donnell Charles Richards and Theresa Pasquale R; m. 3/20/48 to Ann Morgans; c. Paul Morgans. Educ: Col. of Pac, B.A, 50; Univ. San Francisco, LL.B, 53. Polit. & Govt. Pos: Mem, Nev. Dem. State Cent. Cmt, 60-66, v.chmn, 66-68; chmn, Washoe Co. Dem. Cent. Cmt, 64-66; del, Dem. Nat. Conv, 68. Bus. & Prof. Pos: Attorney-at-Law, Reno, Nev, 53-; mem. bd. dirs, Pig 'n Whistle Corp, currently, v.pres. west. div, currently. Mil. Serv: Seaman 1/C, Navy. Mem: Am, Nev, and Washoe Co. Bar Asns; Am. and North. Nev. Trial Lawyers Asns; bd. of govs, Asn. of Ins. Attorneys; Elks; Nat. Trustee, Ducks Unlimited; Int. Acad. of Law & Sci. Rel: Catholic. Legal Res: 1018 La Rue St, Reno, Nev. 89502. Mailing Add: P.O. Box 3018, Reno, Nev. 89505.

RICHARDS, RICHARD R
Mem, Rep. Nat. Cmt.
b. Ogden, Utah, 5/14/32; s. Blaine Boyden Richards and Violet G. Williams R; m. 1/15/54 to Annette Bott; c. Julie, Albert and Jan. Educ: Univ. Utah, LL.B.

Polit. & Govt. Pos: Chmn, Utah Young Rep, 60-61; admin. asst. to U.S. Rep. Laurance J. Burton, Utah, 63-64; former chmn, Utah Rep. State Cent. Cmt; mem, Rep. Nat. Cmt, currently, dir. polit. div, currently; del, Rep. Nat. Conv, 68. Mil. Serv: Entered as Pvt, Army, 52, released as 2nd Lt, 55. Mem: Am. Bar Asn. Rel: Latter-day Saint. Legal Res: 529 44th St, Ogden, Utah 84403. Mailing Add: 13305 Collingwood Terr, Silver Spring, Md. 20904.

RICHARDS, WILLIAM SIDNEY R
Mem, Marin Co. Rep. Cent. Cmt, Calif.
b. San Jose, Calif, 11/22/10; s. Charles M. Richards, M.D. and Alice Rodgers R; m. 10/11/47 to Emily White; c. William S, III, James E, John R. and Cynthia A. Educ: Stanford Univ, A.B, 31, M.B.A, 38; Kappa Alpha. Polit. & Govt. Pos: Mem, Marin Co. Rep. Cent. Cmt, Calif, 67-; mem, Calif. Rep. State Cent. Cmt, 69- Mil. Serv: Army, 31-61, Col.(Ret), after serv. in ETO, 45, Far East Command, 52-55, and U.S, 31-44, 46-52 & 55-61; Bronze Star Medal; Army Commendation Medal with Oak Leaf Cluster. Mem: Asn. of the U.S. Army. Rel: Protestant. Mailing Add: 118 Linden Lane, San Rafael, Calif. 94901.

RICHARDSON, ARTHUR HARRIS D
Va. State Del.
b. Dinwiddie, Va, 8/24/99; m. to Nora Chambliss Edmunds. Educ: Randolph-Macon Col; Kappa Alpha. Polit. & Govt. Pos: Past pres, Young Dem. Club of Dinwiddie, Va; Va. State Del, 46-; mem. Ft. Lee adv. bd, Va. Adv. Legis. Coun; del, Dem. Nat. Conv, 56. Bus. & Prof. Pos: Lumber dealer, farmer, warehouseman; pres, Va. Tobacco Warehouse Co, Petersburg, Va; dir, Petersburg Savings and Am. Trust Co. Mil. Serv: World War I. Mem: Mason; Elks; Princess Anne Country Club; Rotunda Club of Richmond; Downtown Club of Richmond; Ruritans; Am. Legion (Past Comdr). Rel: Methodist. Mailing Add: Dinwiddie, Va. 23841. (1967)

RICHARDSON, ELLIOT LEE R
Under Secy. of State
b. Boston, Mass, 7/20/20; s. Edward P. Richardson (deceased) and Clara Shattuck R.(deceased); m. 8/2/52 to Anne Francis Hazard; c. Henry Shattuck, Anne Hazard and Michael Elliot. Educ: Harvard Col, A.B. cum laude, 41; Harvard Law Sch, LL.B. cum laude, 47. Polit. & Govt. Pos: Asst. to Sen. Leverett Saltonstall, Mass, 53-54; asst. to Gov. Christian A. Herter, 55-56; asst. secy. for legis, U.S. Dept. Health, Educ. and Welfare, 57-59, acting secy, 58; U.S. Attorney for Mass, 59-61; spec. asst. to the Attorney Gen, U.S, 61; Lt. Gov, Mass, 65-67; attorney gen, Mass, 67-69; Under Secy. of State, 69- Bus. & Prof. Pos: Assoc, Ropes, Gray, Best, Coolidge and Rugg, Law Firm, 49-53 & 54-56; lectr. law, Harvard Law Sch, 52; partner, Ropes & Gray, 61-62 & 63-64. Mil. Serv: Entered as Pvt, Army, 42, released as 1st Lt, 45, after serv. in Fourth Inf. Div, ETO; Bronze Star Medal; Purple Heart with Oak Leaf Cluster; Combat Med. Badge; ETO Medal with Five Battle Stars. Publ: 'Freedom of Speech and the Function of Courts,' Harvard Law Rev, 52; 'Poisoned Politics,' Atlantic Monthly, 61; 'Judicial Intervention in the Civil Rights Movement,' Boston Univ. Law Rev, 66. Mem: Boston, Fed, Mass. and Am. Bar Asns; mem. bd. of overseers, Harvard Col, 68-; Am. Acad. Arts & Sci; adv. coun, Sch. of Law, Northeast. Univ; Ad Hoc Cmt. on Harvard Law Sch. Faculty Appointments; Harvard Overseers' Cmt. to visit Harvard Univ. Press and Grad. Sch. of Pub. Admin; dir, Civic Educ. Found, Tufts. Rel: Unitarian. Legal Res: Brookline, Mass. Mailing Add: Department of State, Washington, D.C. 20520.

RICHARDSON, EUGENE ALLISON R
Co. Cmnr, Linn Co, Ore.
b. Turpin, Okla, 5/9/24; s. C. Lester Richardson and Evelyn Tina Solano R; m. 12/5/54 to Elizabeth Ann Workman; c. Cindy Ann, Lori Carol and Cheri Lynn. Educ: Herbert Hoover High Sch, Glendale, Calif. Polit. & Govt. Pos: Mem, Rep. Party Precinct Cmt, Ore, 62-64; co. cmnr, Linn Co, 69- Mil. Serv: Entered as MM 3/C, Navy, 42, released as MM 2/C, 46, after serv. in 98th Construct. Bn, S.Pac; reenlisted CD 2/C, 50-51, Korea. Mem: Officer, Elks; Mason; past comdr, Post 10, Am. Legion, Albany, Ore; Beaver Boys State Chmn. for Albany; DeMolay (Dad Adv); Sch. Bd. Dist. 5; C. of C.(dir); charter mem, Linn Co. Juvenile Adv; Shrine. Rel: Presbyterian. Mailing Add: 1615 S. Sherman, Albany, Ore. 97321.

RICHARDSON, GORDON W. R
Wash. State Rep.
Married; c. three. Educ: West. Wash. Col; Univ. of Wash. Polit. & Govt. Pos: Mem, Co. and State Rep. Platform Cmts, Wash; pres, W. Valley Sch. Bd. and mem, 3 terms; Wash. State Rep, 67- Bus. & Prof. Pos: Real estate; food distribution bus. Mem: C. of C; Kiwanis; chmn, Spokane Valley Commun Col. Cmt; Boy Scouts. Mailing Add: N. 2314 Coleman Rd, Spokane, Wash. 99206. (1967)

RICHARDSON, H. L. 'BILL' R
Calif. State Sen.
b. 1927; married; c. Three. Educ: Olympic Col; Cornish Conserv, Seattle, Advert. Degree. Polit. & Govt. Pos: Mem, Arcadia Young Rep. and Rep. State Cent. Cmt, Calif; Calif. State Sen, 67- Bus. & Prof. Pos: Graphic Arts and Advert. Bus. Mil. Serv: Naval Air Force, 46. Publ: Slightly to the Right; produced 3 films on communism and a film on marijuana. Legal Res: 463 Fairview Ave, Arcadia, Calif. 91006. Mailing Add: 735 W. Duarte Rd, Arcadia, Calif. 91006.

RICHARDSON, HARRISON LAMBERT R
Majority Floor Leader, Maine House of Rep.
b. Bangor, Maine, 1/26/30; s. Harrison L. Richardson and Janet Lovejoy R; m. 6/15/57 to Elsa Bartholomay Chapin; c. Janet L, Harrison L, III and James Brooks. Educ: Univ. Maine, A.B, 53; Univ. Calif, Hastings Col. of Law, LL.B, 59. Polit. & Govt. Pos: Legis. asst, Chicago Crime Cmn, 62-63; Maine State Rep. and Majority Leader, Maine House of Rep, currently; del, Rep. Nat. Conv, 68. Mil. Serv: Entered as 2nd Lt, Marine Corps, 53, released as Capt, 56; Letter of Commendation; Korean, UN Defense and Am. Defense Ribbons. Mem: Am, Maine State and Cumberland Bar Asns; Portland Club; Cumberland Club. Rel: Congregational. Legal Res: 250 Blanchard Rd, Cumberland Center, Maine 04021. Mailing Add: 103 Exchange St, Portland, Maine 04111.

RICHARDSON, HENRY BURCHILL D
S.C. State Sen.
b. 10/15/16; s. Richard C. Richardson and Margaret Sullivan R; m. 5/30/42 to Thelma Lucile Seigler. Educ: Univ. of S.C, LL.B, 47. Polit. & Govt. Pos: Magistrate, Sumter City Dist, S.C, 48-52; S.C. State Sen, 55- Bus. & Prof. Pos: Lawyer. Mil. Serv: 41-45. Mem: Am. Legion; DAV; Co, S.C, and Am. Bar Asns; Am. Judicature Soc; Past Exalted Ruler, Elks 855, 52. Mailing Add: 120 N. Main St, Sumter, S.C. 29150. (1967)

RICHARDSON, JEFF ROLAND, JR. R
Mem, S.C. Rep. State Exec. Cmt.
b. Greenville, S.C, 5/2/29; s. Jeff Roland Richardson and Maude Blakely R; m. 6/16/51 to Florence McKenzie; c. Lyn, Katherine and Caroline. Educ: Furman Univ, B.A, 50. Polit. & Govt. Pos: Chmn, Greenville Co. Rep. Party, S.C, 63-66; mem, S.C. Rep. State Exec. Cmt, 66- Bus. & Prof. Pos: Pres, Jeff Richardson Co, 50-66. Mil. Serv: Entered as Pvt, Army, 51, released as Sgt, 53. Mem: S.C. and Nat. Real Estate Bds; C. of C; Jr. C. of C. Rel: Methodist. Legal Res: N. Laurens Rd, Simpsonville, S.C. 29681. Mailing Add: Box 553, Simpsonville, S.C. 29681. (1967)

RICHARDSON, JOHN, JR. R
Asst. Secy. for Educ. and Cultural Affairs, Dept. of State
b. Boston, Mass, 2/4/21; s. John Richardson and Hope Hemenway R; m. to Thelma Ingram; c. Eva (Mrs. Karoly Selek Teleki), Teren, Hope H, Bonnie Catherine and Hetty L. Educ: Harvard Col, B.A. cum laude, 43; Harvard Law Sch, LL.B, 49. Polit. & Govt. Pos: Asst. Secy. for Educ. and Cultural Affairs, Dept. of State, 69- Bus. & Prof. Pos: Attorney-at-law, Sullivan & Cromwell, 49-55; partner, Paine, Webber, Jackson & Curtis, 55-61; pres, Free Europe, Inc, N.Y.C, 61-68. Mil. Serv: Entered as Lt, Army, 43, released as Capt, after serv. in 17th Airborne Div, Parachute Artil, ETO, 43-46; Bronze Star with Combat Victory Medal. Publ: Chap. in Peace and War in the Modern Age, Doubleday & Co, 65. Mem: Am. and N.Y.C. Bar Asns; Coun. on For. Rels; bd, Int. Rescue Cmt, 57-61 & 68-69; bd, For. Policy Asn, 58-68; bd, Freedom House, 63-69; NAACP. Legal Res: McLean, Va. Mailing Add: Room 6218, Dept. of State, Washington, D.C. 20520.

RICHARDSON, LLOYD CLIFFORD, JR. R
b. Dell Rapids, S.Dak, 2/9/24; s. Lloyd C. Richardson and Leonora Thompson R; m. to Caroline O. Jackus; c. Sarah, Paul and James. Educ: Univ. S.Dak, 2 years; Univ. Minn, Minneapolis, B.S.L. and LL.B; Eta Sigma Phi; Lambda Chi Alpha; Phi Delta Phi. Polit. & Govt. Pos: Chmn, Brown Co. Rep. Party, S.Dak, 52-54; del, Rep. State Conv, 64 & 66; del, Rep. Nat. Conv, 68. Bus. & Prof. Pos: Law partner, Voas, Richardson, Groseclose & Kornmann, 54-; solicitor, Chicago, Milwaukee, St. Paul and Pac. R.R. Co, N. & S.Dak, 64-; chmn, S.Dak. R.R. Asn, Aberdeen, 64- Mil. Serv: Entered as Pvt, Army, 42, released as T/Sgt, 46, after serv. in Inf, 1st Army Div. Mem: State Bar Cmnr, S.Dak. State Bar Asn, 67-; Am. Bar Asn; Nat. Asn. of R.R. Trial Counsel; Fedn. of Ins. Attorneys; S.Dak. State dir, Asn. of Ins. Attorneys; pres, Aberdeen C. of C, 69- Rel: Lutheran. Legal Res: 1324 N. Fourth St, Aberdeen, S.Dak. 57401. Mailing Add: P.O. Box 489, Aberdeen, S.Dak. 57401.

RICHARDSON, MABEL LOWE R
N.H. State Rep.
b. Randolph, N.H; d. Thaddeus Sobiesky Lowe and Frances Hinds Jenkins L; m. to Herbert Randall Richardson; c. Edwin H. and Dwight B. Educ: Univ. N.H, summer credits; Keene State Col, summer credits. Polit. & Govt. Pos: N.H. State Rep, 47-; chairwoman, Rep. Party of N.H, 50-69. Bus. & Prof. Pos: Pub. rels. consult, 36-69. Mem: Grange; Am. Legion Auxiliary; Rebekah (past state pres, Rebekah Assembly of N.H); past pres, PTA; past dir, 4-H Club. Rel: Protestant. Mailing Add: Randolph, N.H. 03593.

RICHARDSON, MARYCLAIRE S. R
b. Montrose, Minn; d. Ernest Winfield Swanson and Claire Miller S; m. to Herbert Cavanaugh Richardson, Wid; c. Nancy and J. Michael. Educ: Univ. Minn, B.B.A; Minn. Sch. Bus, dipl. Polit. & Govt. Pos: Precinct chmn. Precinct Two, Ward 13, Fifth Dist. Rep. Party, Minn, 59, chmn, Ward 13, 60-62, NTN chmn, 63-64, v.chmn, 64 and chmn, 65-69; v.chmn, Hennepin Co. Rep. Party, Minn, 63; mem, Minn. Rep. State Exec. Coun. and Minn. Rep. State Cent. Cmt, 65-69; del, Rep. Nat. Conv, 68. Bus. & Prof. Pos: Real estate saleswoman, Eberhardt Co, 69. Mem: Am. Asn. Univ. Women; Minn. Bd. Realtors; Univ. Minn. Alumni Asn.(asst. mgr, 67); Wine and Food Soc; Woman's Club of Minn; Southwest Commun. Coun; Southwest Homeowners Asn; Citizen's League; Area Orgn. of Girl Scouts. Rel: Presbyterian. Mailing Add: 410 Groveland Ave, Apt. 1504, Minneapolis, Minn. 55403.

RICHARDSON, REDMOND RODGERS D
Secy-Treas, San Diego Co. Labor Coun, Calif.
b. Koshkonong, Mo, 3/22/09; s. Thomas Jefferson Richardson and Madelene Rodgers R; m. 9/2/34 to Avis Isabelle Wilcox; c. Ronald Dale, Marsha Ann, Carolyn Sue, Gordon Lynn, Sharon Kay and Sandy Lou. Educ: Koshkonong High Sch, grad. Polit. & Govt. Pos: Mem, Selective Serv. Appeals Bd, Dist.1, San Diego and Imperial Co, Calif; mem, Selective Serv. Draft Bd. 139, San Diego; dir, 22nd Dist. Agr. Asn, 60-68, pres. bd. dirs, 65-66; mem, Cmn. of the Californias, 64; mem, Gov. Statewide Non-Partisan Voter Registrn. Cmt; mem, Mayor's Cmt. for Master Plan of San Diego, Mayor's Full Employment Coord. Cmt. and Mayor's Cmt. for Jobs, Inc; mem, Citizens Interracial Cmt. of San Diego; mem, Citizens Adv. Cmt. on Sch. Fianance; mem, San Diego Urban Coalition Steering Cmt; mem, Task Force Employment Cmt. of San Diego Urban Coalition; head bus. rep, Laborers Local 89; v.pres, San Diego Co. Bldg. and Construction Trades Coun; v.pres, Calif. State Bldg. and Construction Trades Coun; secy-treas, San Diego Co. Labor Coun, 63-; mem. exec. bd. and secy-treas, South. Dist. Coun. of Laborers; mem. bd. trustees, San Diego Plaster Tenders Group Ins. Trust; mem. bd. trustees, San Diego Construction Laborers Group Ins. Pension and Vacation Trust; chmn. bd. trustees, Off. Employees Int. Union Local 139 Pension Plan; pres. and v.pres, Int. Labor Affairs Coord. Cmt; mem, AFL-CIO-CTM Border Cmt; secy-treas, San Diego Labor Scholarship Fund; pres, San Diego Gen. Apprenticeship Cmt. Bus. & Prof. Pos: Stock boy, checker, produce mgr, asst. mgr. and mgr, Atlantic and Pac. Tea Co, 29-38; employee and self-employed, grocery and filling sta. bus, 39-46; laborer, brick tender and plaster tender, Laborers Local 89, 46-50, mem. exec. bd. and appt. asst. bus. rep. for the Oceanside, Calif. Br. Off,

50, head bus. rep, 51-63. Mem: Adv. bd, Salvation Army; adv. bd, San Diego Urban League, Inc; dir, United Commun. Serv. of San Diego Co; v.chmn, United Crusade; dir, San Diego Convention and Visitors Bur; dir, United Serv. Orgn, Inc; dir, Better Jobs Thru Training, Inc; dir, San Diego 200th Anniversary, Inc; adv. bd, Univ. Calif, San Diego. Rel: Protestant. Legal Res: 7825 El Paso St, La Mesa, Calif. 92041. Mailing Add: 339 W. Broadway, San Diego, Calif. 92101.

RICHARDSON, ROBERT R
Mich. State Sen.
b. Saginaw, Mich, 4/20/26; married; c. Robert L. III, Thomas Matthew and Charles Cummings. Educ: Univ. Mich, A.B, 50, LL.B, 51. Polit. & Govt. Pos: Cmnr, Circuit Court, Mich, 52; admin. asst. to U.S. Rep. Alvin Bentley, 53-56; Asst. U.S. Attorney, 57-58; prosecuting attorney, Saginaw Co, Mich, 59-63, civil counsel, 63-64; Mich. State Sen, 64-, chmn, Judiciary Cmt, Mich. State Senate. Bus. & Prof. Pos: Attorney-at-Law. Mil. Serv: Army, 44-46. Mem: Mich. and Saginaw Co. Bar Asns; State Bar Mich; D.C. and U.S. Supreme Court Bar Asns; F&AM; Kiwanis; VFW; Am. Legion. Rel: Methodist. Mailing Add: 210 Stoneham Rd, Saginaw, Mich. 48603.

RICHARDSON, ROBERT LLOYD R
Mem, Calif. State Rep. Cent. Cmt.
b. Glendale, Calif. 9/7/25; s. Louis Michael Richardson and Agnes F. Jones; m. 4/8/49 to Elizabeth M. McCall; c. Susan C. and Steven M. Educ: Westminster Col.(Mo), 43-44; Univ. South. Calif, B.S. in Naval Sci. and Tactics, 45, B.E. in Petroleum Eng, 48; founder, Univ. South. Calif. Chap, Phi Delta Theta. Polit. & Govt. Pos: Mem, Ventura Co. Rep. Cent. Cmt, Calif, 62-; v.chmn, 65-66, chmn, 67-68; chmn, Goldwater for President Campaign, Ventura City, 64; mem, Calif. State Rep. Cent. Cmt, 64- Bus. & Prof. Pos: Engr, Rocky Mt. Drilling Co, Los Angeles, 48-49, Dean H. Sheldon, Consult, South Pasadena, 50-53 and Douglas Oil Co. of Calif, Lobitos, Peru, 54-56; consult. petroleum engr, Ventura, 57- Mil. Serv: Entered as A/S, Navy, 43, released as Ens, 47, after serv. as Exec. Officer on PCE 895, Pac-Hawaiian Sea Frontier, 45-46; Naval Res, 46-65, Lt. Ret; World War II Victory, Am. Theater and Asiatic-Pac. Theater Medals. Publ: 'Field Performance Multicell Linear,' J. Petroleum Tech, 61. Mem: Soc. Petroleum Engrs; Am. Inst. Mining, Metallurgical and Petroleum Engrs.(chmn. local sect, 59 and chmn, Calif. Regional Fall Meeting, 62); Am. Petroleum Inst; assoc. mem, Am. Asn. Petroleum Geologists; Registered Prfnl. Engr. Petroleum Eng, Calif; YMCA (mem. bd. dirs, Ventura Co. Br). Rel: Presbyterian. Mailing Add: 644 Via Arroyo, Ventura, Calif. 93003.

RICHARDSON, SAM D
b. Bowie, Tex, 11/14/98; s. Andrew Ramesy Richardson and Alabama Prestwood R; m. 9/6/21 to Silvia Dell Mills; c. Geraldine (Mrs. Meyer), Doni (Mrs. Woodson) and Doris (Mrs. May). Educ: Bowie Commercial Col; Decatur Baptist Col. Polit. & Govt. Pos: Dem. chmn, 30th Tex. Sen. Dist, 34-38; Mayor, Lamesa, Tex, 45-50. Bus. & Prof. Pos: Dir, Can. River Munic. Water Authority; owner, Richardson Mercantile Co, Lamesa, Tex, 24-46; pres, Lamesa Fed. Savings & Loan Asn, 55- Mil. Serv: Entered as Pvt, Army, 17, released as Sgt, 19, after serv. in Evacuation Hosp. 17, A.E.F. Siberia; Siberian Campaign Ribbon. Mem: Rotary; Am. Legion; Vet. World War I; C. of C; Mason (32°), Shrine. World Traveler, all countries of Europe and the USSR and all Provinces of Canada; Hudson Bay explorer. Legal Res: 312 N. Ave F, Lamesa, Tex. 79331. Mailing Add: P.O. Box 239, Lamesa, Tex. 79331.

RICHARDSON, TRUMAN D
b. Ardmore, Okla, 2/10/27; s. J.W. Richardson and Pauline Hendricks. Educ: Univ. Okla, B.A, M.A; George Washington Univ; Phi Beta Kappa; Phi Eta Sigma; Sigma Delta Chi. Polit. & Govt. Pos: Admin. asst. to U.S. Rep. Tom Steed, Okla, currently. Bus. & Prof. Pos: Former city ed, Shawnee News-Star; instr. hist. and jour, Okla. Baptist Univ, 53-54; spec. lectr. hist, 63. Legal Res: Shawnee, Okla. Mailing Add: 2037 N. Kensington, Arlington, Va. 22205.

RICHARDSON, WILLIS JENKINS, JR.
b. Cincinnati, Ohio, 10/28/23; s. Willis Jenkins Richardson and Mildred Chambliss R; m. 7/2/48 to Elizabeth Pope Head; c. Willis J, III and Scott. H. Educ: Univ. of Ga, J.D, 49; Delta Theta Phi; Sigma Alpha Epsilon; Gridiron Club; G. Club. Polit. & Govt. Pos: Spec. agent, Fed. Bur. Invest, 50-54; Ga. State Rep, 116th Dist, 63-69. Mil. Serv: Entered as Aviation Cadet, Army Air Force, 43, released as Lt, 46, after serv. in 99th Heavy Bombardment Group, 15th Air Force, Italy, 45-46; ETO Ribbon with Battle Star. Mem: Savannah Bar Asn.(pres, young lawyers sect, 58-59); Ga. Bar Asn. (pres, Young Lawyers Sect, 59-60, alternate del, bd. gov, 61-63); Am. Bar Asn; Am. Judicature Soc; Ga. Defense Lawyers Asn.(pres, 69-); Am. Arbitration Asn; Civitan; Am. Legion Post 135; Oglethorpe Club; Savannah Yacht and Country Club; Savannah Golf Club. Mem, Univ. Ga. Rose Bowl Team, 42 and Sugar Bowl Team, 46. Rel: Episcopal. Legal Res: 26 E. 56th St, Savannah, Ga. 31405. Mailing Add: P.O. Box 8837, Savannah, Ga. 31208.

RICHERSON, FRANCIS BUCKNER R
Mem, Ala. Rep. State Exec. Cmt.
b. Bagby, Va, 4/6/17; s. Frank Buckner Richerson and Mattie Sutton R; m. 1/23/43 to Dorothy Reed; c. Carolie (Mrs. Morgan Weed), Martha Gail and Bucky. Educ: Bluefield Col, B.S, 35; Va. Polytech. Inst, B.S. Ch.E, 38; Phi Lambda Upsilon. Polit. & Govt. Pos: Finance dir, Eighth Dist. Rep. Party, Ala, 65-67, chmn, 67-; mem, Ala. Rep. State Exec. Cmt, 65-; chmn, Morgan Co. Rep. Party, 67-; alternate del, Rep. Nat. Conv, 68. Bus. & Prof. Pos: Refrigeration engr, U.S. Dept. of Agr, Wash, D.C, 38-39; chem. engr, E.I. DuPont, Richmond, Va, 39-40; opers. engr, Chem. Warfare Serv, U.S. Army, Edgewood, Md, 40-42 and Pine Bluff, Ark, 42-45; div. engr, 3M Co, St. Paul, Minn, 45-62; plant engr. mgr, 3M Co, Decatur, Ala, 62- Mem: Am. Inst. of Chem. Engr; Am. Chem. Soc; Am. Inst. of Plant Eng; Rotary; Shrine; Mason; Ala. and Nat. Rep. Party; Metrop. Dinner Club. Recipient of Gold Key for Fund Raising, Ala. Rep. Party. Rel: Baptist. Mailing Add: 1807 Woodmont Dr, Southeast Decatur, Ala. 35601.

RICHESON, SAMUEL RANDOLPH, JR. D
Secy, New Castle Co. Dem. Cmt, Del.
b. Drumright, Okla, 6/15/23; s. Samuel R. Richeson and Velma E. Warner R; m. 10/26/43 to Elizabeth Otteni; c. Leslie (Mrs. Louis Winkler), Randolph P, Brenda C, Karl W, Michael Clark, Patricia Marie, Roger Allen and Barbara Robin. Educ: Univ. Del, 42-43; Muhlenberg Col, B.A, 43; Univ. Pa, 46-47; Alpha Kappa Alpha; Kappa Alpha Chap, Beta Epsilon. Polit. & Govt. Pos: Committeeman, Dem. Party, Del, 48-69; prothonotary, New Castle Co, 61-65; secy, New Castle Co. Dem. Cmt, 67-; alternate del, Dem. Nat. Conv, 68; title specialist, Del. Dept. of Justice, 69- Bus. & Prof. Pos: Pres, Equity Assocs, Inc, 59-69; secy-treas, Bldg. Maintenance Serv, Inc, 68- Mil. Serv: Entered as Pvt, Marine Corps, 42, released as 2nd Lt, 45, after serv. in King Battery, Second Marine Div, Asiatic Theater, 43-45. Mem: Del. Home Builders Asn; Del. Real Estate Asn; Edgemoor Gardens Civic Asn.(pres, 49); Pennyhill Dem. Club (pres, 64-67); Fedn. Dem. Clubs (parliamentarian, 67); Dem. of Brandywine Hundred (pres, 67-69); Coun. Civic Asn.(dir, 64-69); Civic League for New Castle Co.(pres, 69-70); v.pres, Pen-Jer-Del Open Space Cmt, 69-70; Marine Corps League; VFW; Am. Legion; Del. Vet. World War II. Mailing Add: 500 Ruxton Dr, Georgian Terr, Wilmington, Del. 19809.

RICHIE, RICHARD W. DFL
Minn. State Rep.
b. St. Paul, Minn, 1917; m. to Gladys; c. Faye Louise. Educ: St. Paul pub. schs. Polit. & Govt. Pos: Minn. State Rep, 58- Bus. & Prof. Pos: Truck driver. Mil. Serv: Marine Corps, 5 years. Mailing Add: 509 Fred St, St. Paul, Minn. 55101.

RICHMANY, JAMES M. D
b. 1934. Educ: Holy Cross Col; Boston Col. Law Sch. Polit. & Govt. Pos: Ward 5 city councilman. Bus. & Prof. Pos: pres, mgr, Richman Cafe, Inc. Mailing Add: Pittsfield, Mass. 01201. (1967)

RICHTER, ANNE THORBECK D
Mem. Co. Cmt, Wadena Co. Dem. Party
b. Churches Ferry, N.Dak, 6/15/11; d. George Thorbeck and Synneva Erie T; m. 12/28/40 to Paul Richter; c. Mary Ann, Paulette, Philip and Paul. Educ: Univ. Minnesota, St. Paul, B.S.Ed, 37; Gamma Omicron Beta; Home Econ. Asn. Polit. & Govt. Pos: Secy, Wadena Co. Dem. Party, Minn, 50-55, chairwoman, 55-65; mem. co. cmt, Wadena Co. Dem. Party, 50-; del, Dem. State Conv, 52-; v.chairwoman, Seventh Dist. Dem. Party, 64-68; chairwoman, Seventh Dist. Humphrey Campaign, 68; del, Dem. Nat. Conv, 68. Bus. & Prof. Pos: Teacher home econ, Barnesville, Minn, 37-38; home supvr, Farm Security Admin, Fergus Falls, Minn, 38-39; state 4-H staff, Univ. Minn. Exten. Serv, 39-40; dist. home mgt. supvr, Farm Security Admin, Brainerd, 40-42; spec. teacher, Wadena High Sch, 66-69. Mem: Am. Fedn. Teachers; Co. chmn. blood prog, Am. Red Cross; secy, Wadena Housing and Redevelop. Authority; secy, Wadena Recreation Bd; Univ. Minn. Alumni Asn; Wadena Hosp. Auxiliary. Girl Scout Thanks Badge, 52; Univ. Minn. Alumni Serv. Award, 63; Outstanding 4-H Alumni Award, Minn, 65. Rel: Catholic. Mailing Add: 415 Seventh St. S.W, Wadena, Minn. 56482.

RICKARD, ROBERT LEE, JR. R
Ind. State Rep.
b. Evansville, Ind, 10/3/23; s. Robert Lee Rickard, Sr. and Hazel Marie Snow R; m. 6/25/55 to Dolores Anne Ehrmann; c. Judith Ann (Mrs. Musser) and Terry Lee. Educ: Bosse High Sch, grad, 42. Polit. & Govt. Pos: Rep. precinct committeeman, Vanderburgh Co, Ind, 63-67; Ind. State Rep, Vanderburgh Co, 69- Bus. & Prof. Pos: Owner, Rickard Realty Co, 52- Mem: Mason; Scottish Rite; Shrine; Fraternal Order of Police; Sword of Bunker Hill; Ind. State Legislators Club; Brotherhood of Rwy. and Steamship Clerks (legis. rep, Local 860). Rel: Cumberland Presbyterian. Mailing Add: 2915 E. Walnut St, Evansville, Ind. 47714.

RICKENBACKER, WILLIAM FROST Conservative, N.Y.
Mem, State Exec. Cmt, Conservative Party, N.Y.
b. Beverly Hills, Calif, 3/16/28; s. Capt. Eddie Rickenbacker and Adelaide Frost R; m. 9/3/55 to Alexandra Harriman Leys; c. James Edward and Thomas. Educ: Harvard Univ, A.B. cum laude, 49. Polit. & Govt. Pos: Mem, State Exec. Cmt, Conservative Party, N.Y, 62- Bus. & Prof. Pos: Research analyst, Smith, Barney & Co, 55-58; invest. adv, 58-61; sr. ed, Nat. Rev, 61-; pres, Rickenbacker Report Corp. and Rickenbacker Enterprises, Inc, 69- Mil. Serv: Entered as Aviation Cadet, Air Force, 51, released as 1st Lt, 55, after serv. in various air transport units including continental U.S, Europe and Korea, 52-53; Air Medal with clusters; UN Theater Ribbon; Korean Ribbon. Publ: Wooden Nickels, 66 and Death of the Dollar, 68, Arlington House; The Free Man's Library (with Henry Hazlitt), D. van Nostrand, 66. Mem: Phila. Soc; Nockian Soc; Am. Inst. for Econ. Res; exec. secy, Spec. Interests; Stephen Decatur Soc; Ind. Iron Guard; Invisible Hand Soc; exec. secy, Power Brokers; Hardscrabble Asn; Am-African Affairs Asn; C. of C. 1st place, Nat. Steinway Piano Competition, 35; Westchester Jr. Champion, golf, 48-49; co-medalist, New England Intercollegiate Golf Championship, 49. Rel: Congregational. Mailing Add: Box 1000, Briarcliff Manor, N.Y. 10510.

RICKERT, DALE H. D
b. Luverne, Minn, 4/10/28; s. Herman Rickert and Ella R; m. 1950 to Esther Jamison; c. Claudia, Pamela and Jamie. Educ: Iowa State Univ, B.S, Animal Husbandry. Polit. & Govt. Pos: Iowa State Rep,-66. Bus. & Prof. Pos: Farmer. Mil. Serv: USAF, peacetime serv. Mem: Farm Bur; Farmers Union. Rel: Presbyterian. Mailing Add: Route 2, Wapello, Iowa. 52653. (1967)

RICKERT, JON EDWARD D
Ky. State Rep.
b. Louisville, Ky, 9/15/34; s. Harold Edward Rickert (deceased) and Dorothy Groves R; m. 7/10/65 to Roberta Gail Vincent; c. Jon Edward, Jr. Educ: Ind. Univ. Sch. of Bus, B.S; Vanderbilt Univ. Sch. of Law, LL.B; Phi Delta Theta. Polit. & Govt. Pos: Ky. State Rep, Dist. 25, 68- Bus. & Prof. Pos: Ornithology lab instr, Zoology Dept, Ind. Univ, Bloomington, 55-57; bus. law instr, Ind. Univ. Exten, Jeffersonville, 61-62; alumni rels. officer, Vanderbilt Univ, 61-62; asst. officer, Citizens Fidelity Bank & Trust Co, Louisville, Ky, 62-63; attorney-at-law, Rickert & Coyle, 63- Mil. Serv: Entered as Pvt, Air Force Nat. Guard, 53, released as Airman 1/C, 61, after serv. in Ind. and Tenn. Air Guard. Mem: Phi Delta Phi; Mason; Rotary; dir, Regional Ment. Health—Re-

tardation Bd. Voted by mem. of news media Most Outstanding Freshman in Ky. House of Rep, 68. Rel: Methodist. Legal Res: 709 Sunrise Lane, Elizabethtown, Ky. 42701. Mailing Add: 122 N. Main, Elizabethtown, Ky. 42701.

RICKERT, ROBERT TAYLOR DFL
Pres, Jackson Co. Dem-Farmer-Labor Party, Minn.
b. Rupert, Idaho, 2/13/16; s. Fred Rickert and Florence E. Taylor R; m. 6/29/41 to Hilda M. Ackermann; c. Judith Ann, Leslie Robert and Marvin LeRoy. Educ: Lakefield High Sch, 2 years. Polit. & Govt. Pos: Pres, Jackson Co. Dem-Farmer-Labor Party, Minn, 67- Bus. & Prof. Pos: Farmer, 40- Mem: Jackson Co. Farmers Union (pres); Farmers Exchange (past secy); Double H Local (past pres); Post Local (past pres); Lutheran Laymens League (dist. chmn). Rel: Lutheran. Mailing Add: R.F.D. 3, Okabena, Minn. 56161.

RICKETS, J. BEN D
Ind. State Rep.
Educ: Okla. State Univ; Sigma Nu. Polit. & Govt. Pos: Mem, Bd. of Sessions; chmn, Knox Co. Sch. Reorgn. Cmn. and Knox Co. Tax Adjust. Bd, Ind; trustee, Steen Twp, Knox Co, 55-62; Ind. State Rep, 63- Bus. & Prof. Pos: Farmer; ins. agent; owner, Wheatland Agency; dir, Citizens Bank & Trust Co, Wash. Mem: Mason; Elks; Rotary; Wabash Valley Asn; Wabash Valley Sugar Beet Asn; dir, Producers Livestock Asn. Rel: Presbyterian. Mailing Add: P.O. Box 38, Wheatland, Ind. 47597.

RICKETTS, MARVEL D
Single. Educ: Butler Univ; Ind. Univ. Exten; Delta Theta Tau. Polit. & Govt. Pos: Ind. State Rep, -66; precinct committeeman, 51-64; pres, Inter-Group Coun. of Women as Policy Makers; Marion Co. Dem. Women. Bus. & Prof. Pos: Acct. clerk. Mem: Mem. and former localpres, Commun. Workers of Am, AFL-CIO. Rel: Baptist. Mailing Add: 234 N. Delaware St, Apt. 405, Indianapolis, Ind. 46204. (1967)

RICKFORD, FRED E R
b. Griggs Co, N.Dak, 1898; married; c. Two. Educ: Interstate Bus. Col. Polit. & Govt. Pos: N.Dak. State Rep, 55-61; mem, LaMoure City Coun, 2 years, pres, 6 years. Bus. & Prof. Pos: Merchant and real estate. Mailing Add: LaMoure, N.Dak. 58458. (1967)

RICKMAN, GERALDINE R
Mem, Calif. Rep. State Cent. Cmt.
b. Champaign, Ill, 10/13/33; d. James T. Henry, Sr. and Vivian Snell H; div; c. Donald C, II, Donna Denise and Alan Vincent. Educ: Manhattanville Col. of the Sacred Heart, 51-54; Univ. San Diego Law Sch, 69- Polit. & Govt. Pos: V.chmn, Calif. Adv. Cmn. on Status of Women and chmn, Child Care Cmt, 67-; mem. bd. dirs, Calif. Coun. for Educ. Opportunity, currently; mem, Calif. Rep. State Cent. Cmt. and v.chmn, Commun. Action Cmt. of South. Calif, 69-; mem, Educ. Task Force, Urban Coalition, currently; mem. Steering Cmt, Urban Crisis and Higher Educ, sponsored by Univ. Calif, currently; mem. bd. dirs, Urban Affairs Inst, Los Angeles, currently. Bus. & Prof. Pos: First dir, Educ. Opportunities Prog, San Diego State Col; admin. serv. officer, Univ. Calif, San Diego, asst. to Provost, Muir Col, admin. asst. to Chancellor and mem, Chancellor's Urban Affairs Adv. Cmt, 69-; mat. cost analyst, Gen. Dynamics-Convair; secretarial asst. to Dir. of Placement and Alumni Affairs, Cent. State Univ, Wilberforce, Ohio; substitute teacher, St. Brigid High Sch, Xenia; pres, Commun. Opportunity Prog. in Educ. Found, 69-, dir, Commun. Opportunity Progs. in Educ. Consortium, San Diego, Calif, currently. Publ: Article on what the minority parent can do for his child, Calif. Parent-Teacher Mag, 12/66; 'The Community Gold Mine: Fool's Gold or the Real Stuff'? In: 'Some Who Dared,' Inst. for Local Self Govt, Berkeley, 6/69. Mem: Beach and Shoreline Cmt. of City Planning Dept, 67-68; co-chmn, YWCA Spec. Membership Drive, 67; Planning Cmt. for Proj. Summertime, 67; Planning Cmt. for Conf. on Effects of Discrimination on Youth, sponsored by PTA and Nat. Conf. of Christians and Jews, 67; Planning Cmt. for Intersession Workshop on Desegregating San Diego Schs, Area of Commun. Conflict, sponsored by San Diego State Col. Sch. of Soc. Welfare and Commun. Welfare Coun, summer 67, Planning Cmt. for Legis. Conf, sponsored by Commun. Welfare Conf, 67; consultations with Minority Group Admissions Subcmt, San Diego State Col, consultations with Col-High Sch. Rels. Subcmt. of Full Participation Cmt. and Planning Cmt. for Participant for Intergroup Rels. Workshop, San Diego State Col-Nat. Conf. of Christians and Jews, 68, bd. dirs, Nat. Conf. of Christians and Jews, currently; bd. dirs, San Diego Co. YWCA; Women, Inc; Women Extraordinaire; pres, Valencia Park PTA, 66-67; legis. chmn, Lincoln Coun, Ninth Dist. PTA, 66-67. Woman of Valor, Sisterhood of Temple Beth Israel, 67; Outstanding Young Women of Am. Award, 68; Nat. Sojourner Truth Award, Nat. Negro Bus. and Prfnl. Women's Clubs, 68. Rel: Catholic. Mailing Add: 6783 Alvarado Rd. 6, San Diego, Calif. 92120.

RICKMAN, HERBERT PAUL D
b. New York, N.Y, 7/31/31; s. Louis Rickman and Ida Greenfield R; single. Educ: N.Y. Univ, B.A, 51, LL.B, 54. Polit. & Govt. Pos: Spec, asst. to U.S. Attorney, South. Dist. N.Y, 61-62; exec. asst. to state chmn, N.Y. State Dem. Cmt, 63-66; exec. dir, N.Y. Citizens for McCarthy, 68; del, Dem. Nat. Conv, 68; dep. campaign mgr. for U.S. Rep. James H. Scheuer for mayor, 69. Bus. & Prof. Pos: Attorney, McLaughlin, Stickles, McKean and Hayden, 56-60; exec. dir, Am. for Permanent Peace in Mid.E, 67- Mil. Serv: Entered as Pvt, Army, 53, released as Pfc, 55. Publ: Contrib, 'Chicago 1968,' 10/68. Mem: Nat. Dem. Club; dir, Bronx-Nat. Conf. Christians & Jews. Rel: Hebrew. Mailing Add: 1060 Park Ave, New York, N.Y. 10028.

RIDDAGH, ROBERT W. R
Del. State Rep.
b. 1914. Polit. & Govt. Pos: Former Mayor, Smyrna Del; Del. State Rep, 67- Bus. & Prof. Pos: Welding supvr, Phila, Navy Yard; mgr, Am. Stores Co; owner, Towne Cleaners. Mem: Past Master, Harmony Lodge 13 AF&AM; treas, Smyrna-Clayton Bus. Develop. Asn. Rel: Methodist; Mem. Bd. Asbury Methodist. Church. Mailing Add: 24 Lake Drive, Smyrna, Del. 19977. (1967)

RIDDER, DANIEL HICKEY R
b. New York, N.Y, 5/3/22; s. Bernard Herman Ridder and Nell Hickey R; m. 2/7/49 to Betty Oppegard; c. Daniel Hickey, Randy, Richard J. Educ: Princeton, 43. Polit. & Govt. Pos: Trustee, Calif. State Col, currently. Bus. & Prof. Pos: Publisher, St. Paul Dispatch-Pioneer Press, 48-; co-pub, Long Beach Independent, Press, Telegram; v.pres, dir. Northwest Publs. Inc, Mid Continent Radio-TV, Inc; treas, dir. Midwest Radio-TV, Inc; secy, Aberdeen News Co; asst. treas, dir, Ridder Publs. Inc; dir, v.pres. Twin Coast Newspapers, Inc; treas, dir. Grand Forks Herald, Inc; pres, United Way, 65-66; Grand Forks Herald, 47-48; N.Y. J. of Commerce, 46-47. Mil. Serv: Naval Res, Lt.(jg), 43-46. Mem: Va. Country Club; El Dorado Country Club; Los Angeles Country Club. Mailing Add: 36 Portugese Bend Rd, Rolling Hills, Calif. 90274. (1967)

RIDDER, ROBERT CARL 'BOB' D
Wash. State Sen.
b. Bellingham, Wash, 2/25/27; s. Oscar William Ridder and Hilda Myrtle Brinkworth R; m. 3/18/50 to Ruthe Elvina Burmaster; c. Janet Louise, Robert Andrew, Susan Denise, David and William. Educ: Univ. Wash, B.A, 51 and grad. study, 52-56, 58, summer 68; Seattle Univ, grad. study, 62; Purple Shield; Men's Organized House Coun. Polit. & Govt. Pos: V.pres, 35th West Dem. Club, Wash, 64-65; alternate del, King Co. Cent. Dem. Cmt, 64-66; mem, Constitutional Reorgn. Meeting, King Co. Dem. Cent. Cmt, 64-66; precinct committeeman, Wash. State Dem. Party, 64-66; pres, Parkway Dem. Club, 65-66; del, Dist, State and Co. Dem. Conv, 66; Wash. State Sen, 35th Dist, 67-, chmn, Educ. Cmt, secy. Pub. Pension Cmt, secy, Joint Interim Cmt. on Educ. and mem, Gov. Planning Cmn. on Vocational Rehabilitation, Va. State Senate. Bus. & Prof. Pos: V.prin, Showalter Jr. High Sch, 59- Mil. Serv: Entered as Pvt, Army, 45, released as Sgt, 47, after serv. in Army Med. Corps, Pac. Theater, 24th Corps Korean Army of Occupation, 46-47; Pac. Theater Ribbon; 24th Corps Citation; Good Conduct Medal. Mem: Pres, South Cent. Educ. Asn. (54-55 & 66-67, and v.pres, 65-66); dir, Dept. of Classroom Teachers, Wash. Educ. Asn, 55-56; Nat. Educ. Asn; Greater Seattle Lutheran Coun; Asn. for Childhood Educ. Int; Riverton Post, Am. Legion; Munic. League; Parkway Dem. Club; 35th West Dem. Club; Metrop. Dem. Club; Boy Scouts; PTA; Kiwanis; S.Central Club; chmn, Renton Family Coun. Adv. Bd; v.pres, Rainier Boys Club. Received Golden Acorn Award for Service to Children, PTA. Rel: Lutheran; Sunday Sch. Teacher, 10 years. Mailing Add: 5809 S. Roxbury, Seattle, Wash. 98118.

RIDDLE, HARRY L, JR. D
b. Morganton, N.C, 9/13/14; s. H.L. Riddle and Helen Davis R; m. to Janie O. Hunt, 1933, deceased, 1956; m. 1/11/58 to Sally Sanborn Best; c. H.L, III, Herndon Hunt; Jerome Flora and stepchildren, Talbot Sanborn, James Marcellus and Catherine Street Best. Educ: Univ. N.C, A.B, 36; LL.B, 38. Polit. Pos: Liaison, N.C. Dem. Exec. Cmt. and Dem. Nat. Cmt, 60; pres, Burke Co. Young Dem, 43 and Univ. N.C. Young Dem, 35-36. Govt. Pos: Judge, N.C. Superior Court, 61-; N.C. Rep, Officer Chief Protocol, Dept. State, 61-; trustee, Univ. N.C, 48-; judge, Burke Co. Criminal Court, 43, solicitor, 40. Bus. & Prof. Pos: Dir, Morganton Savings & Loan Asn, N.C, 62- Mil. Serv: Entered as Ens, Naval Res, 43, released as Lt, 46, after serv. in Caribbean and Am. Theaters; Am. Defense Medal. Publn: North Carolina Law Review, 36-38. Marshal, 3rd Div, John F. Kennedy Inauguration. Rel: Episcopal. Mailing Add: 106 Terrace Place, Morganton, N.C. 28655. (1967)

RIDDLE, M. T. 'TOMMY' R
Ky. State Rep.
b. 1934. Educ: Bryant-Stratton Bus. Col, Ky. Polit. & Govt. Pos: Rep. Dist. Committeeman; Ky. State Rep, currently. Bus. & Prof. Pos: Real estate and ins. Mil. Serv: Air Nat. Guard. Mem: Lion's Eye Bank; Red Cross Blood Donors Gallon Club; Rotary; pres, charter mem. and past secy, Okolona Jaycees; pres, Okolona Commun. Coun; chmn, Libr. Dir; former mem, Okolona Vol. Fire Dept. Rel: Baptist. Mailing Add: 6307 Outer Loop, Louisville, Ky. 40219. (1967)

RIDDLEBERGER, JAMES W.
b. Washington, D.C, 9/21/04; m. to Amelie Otken; c. Three. Polit. & Govt. Pos: Reserach asst, Libr. of Cong, 24-27; U.S. Tariff Cmn, 27-29; career officer, U.S. Dept. of State For. Serv, 29-68; second secy, Geneva, 30-36, Berlin, 36-41 and London, 42-43; chief, Div. Cent. European Affairs, 44-47; counsr, Berlin, 47-49; dir, Off. of Polit. Affairs, Frankfort, 49-50, ECA, Paris, 50-52 and Bur. of German Affairs, 52-53; U.S. Ambassador to Yugoslavia, 53-58 and Greece, 58-59; dir, Int. Coop. Admin, 59-61; spec. asst. to Secy. of State, 61; chmn, Develop. Assistance Cmt. to Orgn. for Econ. Coop. and Develop, 61-62; U.S. Ambassador to Austria, 62-68; nat. chmn, Population Crisis Cmt, 69- Bus. & Prof. Pos: Asst. prof. int. rels, Georgetown Univ, 26-29. Legal Res: Woodstock, Va. 22664. Mailing Add: 1730 K St. N.W, Washington, D.C. 20006.

RIDER, HARRY DURBIN D
Pa. State Dem. Committeeman
b. Baltimore, Md, 12/15/05; s. Harry Durbin Rider and Amedia Whelan R; m. 9/1/28 to Catherine Antoinette Hulitt; c. Kathleen May, Dixie Gale (deceased), James Turner, Harry Durbin, Bonnie Lea, Marilyn Effie and Carletta Sylvia. Educ: Harford Seminary. Polit. & Govt. Pos: Secy, Pocono Mountain Dem. Club, 61-63, treas, 64-66; committeeman, Paradise Twp, Monroe Co, 62-; mem. exec. cmt, Monroe Co. Dem. Party, 63-66; del, Dem. Nat. Conv, 64; Pa. State Dem. Committeeman, 66- Bus. & Prof. Pos: Owner and mgr, Rider Decorating Co, 35-65; dir, Burnley Workshop, 64-66; dir, Camp Moll for Retarded, 66-; 1st v.pres, Pocono Mountain Joint Schs. Mem: Dir, Monroe Co. Asn. for Retarded Children; state bd. dirs, Pa. Asn. for Retarded Children; past dist. pres, Patriotic Order Sons of Am; cmnr, Boy Scouts; anti-poverty prog, Monroe Co, 66. Rel: Methodist. Mailing Add: Box 114, Cresco, Pa. 18326. (1967)

RIDER, JOSEPH ALFRED R
Mem, Calif. Rep. State Cent. Finance Cmt.
b. Chicago, Ill, 1/30/21; s. Dr. Dean L. Loller Rider and Dr. Jeannette L. Leszczynski R; m. 6/19/43 to Graclynn L. Rice; C. Charles and Dean. Educ: Univ. Chicago, S.B, 42, Ph.D. in Pharmacology, 51, Sch. of Med, M.D, 44; Sigma Xi. Polit. & Govt. Pos: Mem. pesticides and alternative study sect, Food and Drug Admin, 67-; mem, Calif. Rep. State Cent. Finance Cmt, currently. Bus. & Prof. Pos: Intern, Presby. Hosp, Chicago, Ill, 44-45; Resident in med, Univ. Tex, Galveston, 47-49 and Univ. Chicago, 49-50; fel. dept. of

med. and pharmacology, Univ. Chicago, 50-51, instr. in med, 51-52; asst. prof. med, Univ. Calif. Sch. of Med, San Francisco and asst. chief, Gastrointestinal Clin, 53-61 and asst. clin. prof. med, 61-66; dir, Gastrointestinal Research Lab, Franklin Hosp. Found, 63-; mem. of staff, St. Mary's Hosp. and Mary's Help Hosp, San Francisco. Mil. Serv: Capt, Army Med. Corps, 45-47, with serv. as Chief of Med, 172nd Sta. Hosp; Am. Theatre Medal; World War II Victory Medal; Army of Occup. Medal. Publ: Disturbances in Gastrointestinal Motility, Charles C. Thomas, 59; 'Gastric and Duodenal Ulcers, Encyclop. Britannica, 61; 'The Digestive System,' In: Better Homes and Gardens Family Medical Guide, Meredith Press, 64; plus others. Mem: Dipl, Am. Bd. Internal Med; dipl, Am. Bd. Gastroenterology; dipl, Nat. Bd. Med. Exam; fel, Am. Col. Physicians; fel, Am. Gastroenterological Asn; charter mem. med. bd, Myasthenia Gravis Found; Am. Asn. for Adv. of Sci; Am. Fedn. for Clin. Research; Am. Soc. Gastrointestinal Endoscopy; Am. Soc. for Pharmacology and Exp. Therapeutics; Am. and Calif. State Med. Asns; N.Y. Acad. Sci; San Francisco Co. Med. Soc; West. Soc. for Clin. Research; U.S. Cmt, World Med. Asn; Calif. Soc. Internal Med; Am. Med. Asn.(coun. pharm. and chem); West. Gastroenterology Research Club; Soc. for Exp. Biol. and Med; Am. Geriatrics Soc; Charles T. Stone Soc. Internal Med; Am. Therapeutic Soc; Gerontological Soc; West. Pharmacology Soc; hon. mem, Sexto Congreso Argentino de Gastroenterologia; Pan Am. Asn; Am. Soc. Pharmacology and Chemotherapy; Marin Co. Rep. Finance Cmt; Corinthian Yacht Club; San Francisco Press Club; Mill Valley Tennis Club. Cert. of Merit, Am. Col. Gastroenterology Sci. Exhibit, 57 & 58, Honorable Mention, 59, Second Prize, 59, 63 & 67; Billings Bronze Medal, 61, First Prize, 61 & 62 and Hull Gold Medal Award, 67. Rel: Methodist. Legal Res: 10 Charles-Dean Rd, Mill Valley, Calif. 94941. Mailing Add: 350 Parnassus Ave, Suite 900, San Francisco, Calif. 94117.

RIDER, LILA CATHERINE D
V.Chmn, Routt Co. Dem. Party, Colo.
b. Normal, Ky, 3/19/27; d. Mark L. William, Sr. and Lillian McNeal W; m. 10/26/52 to Ellsworth Wheeler Rider. Educ: Yampa Union High Sch, 3 years. Polit. & Govt. Pos: Dem. precinct committeewoman, Precinct 5, Phippsburg, Colo, 68-; v.chmn, Routt Co. Dem. Party, 69-; dep. tax assessor, Routt Co, currently. Publ: Columnist for Steamboat Pilot, Steamboat Springs, Colo, 20 years. Mem: Phippsburg Commun. Club (former pres); secy, Phippsburg TV Asn; Phippsburg Womans Club (past pres, v.pres, currently); Rebekah (secy, Lodge 84, Oak Creek); co. and local chmn, March of Dimes. Rel: Baptist. Mailing Add: Box 45, Phippsburg, Colo. 80469.

RIDER, ROBERT E, SR. D
b. Toledo, Iowa, 12/25/21; m. 1946 to Dorothy Wickersham; c. Patricia, Nancy, Robert Jr. and Ronald. Educ: Garwin High Sch. Polit. & Govt. Pos: Former Iowa State Rep. Bus. & Prof. Pos: Farmer; seed dealer; wool buyer; master lamb producer. Mem: Moose; Farm Bur.(former v.pres, Marshall Co. Farm Bur). Rel: Congregational. Mailing Add: Route 3, Marshalltown, Iowa 50158.

RIDGEWAY, WILLIAM GILBERT R
Committeeman, Ill. Rep. Cent. Cmt.
b. Coulterville, Ill, 3/6/27; s. William Clayton Ridgeway and Margaret Elizabeth Penrod R; m. 6/16/50 to Elizabeth Ann Greer; c. Carol Ann. Educ: South. Ill. Univ, B.A, 49; Univ. Ill, Col. Law, LL.B. and J.D, 68; Phi Alpha Delta. Polit. & Govt. Pos: State's attorney, Jackson Co, Ill, 56-64, pub. defender, 67-68, spec. asst. attorney gen, 69-; committeeman, Ill. Rep. Cent. Cmt, 66- Mil. Serv: Entered as Pvt, Army, 45, released as Pfc, 46, after serv. in Finance, Fifth Army, Ft. Sheridan, Ill. Mem: Jackson Co. Bar Asn. (pres); Ill. State and Am. Bar Asns; dir, C. of C, Murphysboro; Eagles; Elks; Lions; Mason; Shrine. Rel: Methodist. Legal Res: 712 N. Sixth St, Murphysboro, Ill. 62966. Mailing Add: 18½ S. Tenth St, Murphysboro, Ill. 62966.

RIDGLEY, ROBERT LOUIS R
b. Ft. Wayne, Ind, 3/4/34; s. C. Herbert Ridgley and Margaret Sparling R; m. 8/24/57 to Marilyn Hester; c. Gregory C. and Derek W. Educ: Cornell Univ, B.A, 56; Harvard Law Sch, LL.B, 59; Phi Beta Kappa; Sigma Phi; Chancery Club, Harvard. Polit. & Govt. Pos: Chmn, Packwood for Rep. Cmt. Ore. Campaign, 61-63; speakers chmn, Multnomah Co. Rep. Exec. Cmt, 62-65; asst. chmn, Ore. Rockefeller for Pres. Cmt, 64, chmn, 68; dir, Portland Sch. Bd, 66-68, chmn, 68-69; v.chmn, Myers for Secy. of State Campaign, 68. Bus. & Prof. Pos: Assoc, Davies, Biggs, Strayer, Stoel and Boley, 59-65 and partner, 65- Mil. Serv: Entered as 2nd Lt, Army, 59, released as 2nd Lt, 60, after serv. in Army Res, Fort Bliss, Tex; Distinguished Mil. Grad, Harvard Univ, 59. Mem: Am, Ore. and Multnomah Co. Bar Asns; World Peace Through Law Center. Portland Jr. First Citizen, Ore, 68. Rel: Protestant. Legal Res: 7116 S.E. 34th, Portland, Ore. 97202. Mailing Add: 1410 Yeon Bldg, Portland, Ore. 97204.

RIDINGS, CLARENCE OSBORNE D
b. Green Creek Twp, Polk Co, N.C, 11/9/92; s. James Isaac Ridings and Cora Gertrude Tanner R; m. 4/30/25 to Elizabeth Maude Carswell; c. Helen (Mrs. O.R. McKinney); grandson, Ronald Ridings McKinney. Educ: Fruitland Inst, Hendersonville, N.C, 12-16; Wake Forest Col. Sch. of Law, 21. Polit. & Govt. Pos: Chmn, Rutherford Co. Dem. Exec. Cmt, N.C, 28-30; former N.C. State Rep, Polk Co; co. attorney, Rutherford Co, 32-33; dist. solicitor, 18th Dist, 34-58; town attorney, Forest City, 45-46; mem, N.C. Dem. State Exec. Cmt; N.C. State Sen, 63-66. Bus. & Prof. Pos: Lawyer. Mil. Serv: Army, Pfc, 18-19. Mem: Pres, 18th Dist. Bar Asn; Rutherford Co. Bar Asn; N.C. State Bar; 29th Dist. Bar Asn; Mason; Am. Legion. Rel: Baptist. Mailing Add: 424 Arlington St, Forest City, N.C. 28043.

RIDLEY, WILLARD CLARENCE D
b. St. Paul, Minn, 3/7/35; s. Willard Clarence and Dorothy Horn C; m. 3/2/57 to Delores T. Starkey; c. Cindy, Steve, Lora and Stephanie. Educ: Wis. State Univ, River Falls; Eau Claire, 3 years, Econ. and speech; Univ. Minn, part-time; Augustana, part-time; spec. courses Alexander Hamilton Inst; Am. Mgt. Asn; Pi Kappa Delta, degree of spec. distinction; Col. Concert Bd; pres, Col. Club Young Dem; recording secy. and v.pres, Wis. Young Dem. Polit. & Govt. Pos: State pres, S.Dak. Young Dem, 62-64; del, Young Dem. Nat. Conv, 63; Great Plains Conf. Chmn, Young Dem. Am, 63-65; mem, U.S. Youth Coun, 64; del, Dem. Nat. Conv, 64; dir, Emergency Planning for U.S. Savings Bonds Div, Treasury Dept, state dir, 66, asst. to nat. dir, 68. Bus. & Prof. Pos: Sales rep, Procter & Gamble, 57-66. Mem: Toastmasters Int; U.S. Jr. C. of C; Fed. Businessmen's Asn; YMCA; Minneapolis Tribune Press Club. Pub. Speaking Awards; State Speak-Up Champion, S.Dak, 59; Sioux Falls Winner and Area Winner, Toastmasters Speech Contest; Nat. Chmn. of Combined Fed. Campaign for U.S. Savings Bonds Div. Rel: Methodist. Legal Res: Sioux Falls, S.Dak. Mailing Add: Room 351, Vanguard Building, 1111 20th St, N.W. Washington, D.C. 20226.

RIDLON, EDGAR M. R
b. Clarendon, Vt, 10/19/07; m. to Edna Bussino; c. Four. Educ: Shrewsbury Schs. Polit. & Govt. Pos: Rd. cmnr, Vt, 42-46; selectman, 50-65; Vt. State Rep, 65-67. Bus. & Prof. Pos: Farmer. Mem: Farm Bur; Bellows Falls Coop; past master Grange. Rel: Catholic. Mailing Add: Cuttingsville, Vt. 05738. (1967)

RIDLON, GEORGE HENRY R
Vt. State Rep.
b. Clarendon, Vt, 3/3/98; s. Merritt H. Ridlon and Etta Wesscott R; m. 6/14/30 to Esther E. Thomas; c. Joyce (deceased) and Barbara M. Educ: Clarendon Schs. Polit. & Govt. Pos: Lister and justice of the peace, Vt, 48-; chmn, Rutland Co. Rep. Party, 55-59; Vt. State Rep, 65-, mem, Agr. Stabilization and Conservation Cmt. Bus. & Prof. Pos: Former farmer and garageman; retired. Mem: Mason; Grange; Farm Bur. Rel: Congregational. Mailing Add: North Clarendon, Vt. 05759.

RIDOLFI, SIDO L. D
Pres, N.J. State Senate
married to Beatrice; c. Robert, Jane and Susan. Educ: Princeton Univ; Harvard Law Sch; spec. courses, N.Y. Univ; Seanman's Church Inst; U.S. Coast Guard Acad. Polit. & Govt. Pos: Secy. to the Sen. Minority Leader, 41; legal legis. adv, Gov. Charles Edison, 41-42; sheriff of Mercer Co, N.J, 47; city cmnr, Trenton, 51-57; N.J. State Sen, 53-, Minority Leader, N.J. State Senate, 56, past Majority Leader, pres, 66-; del, Dem. Nat. Conv, 68. Bus. & Prof. Pos: Attorney. Mil. Serv: Coast Guard, 3½ years. Mem: Mercer Co. Bar Asn.(pres, 52). Mailing Add: 383 W. State St, Trenton, N.J. 08618.

RIECHMANN, HOWARD CHRIST R
Chmn, Monroe Co. Rep. Cent. Cmt, Ill.
b. Valmeyer, Ill, 7/21/22; s. George Riechmann and Louise Kruse R; m. 11/23/44 to Melba Ida Ritzel; c. Jane Marie and John Howard. Polit. & Govt. Pos: Chmn, Monroe Co. Rep. Cent. Cmt, Ill, 66-; mem, Ill. Rep. State Cent. Cmt, currently. Bus. & Prof. Pos: Pres, Monroe Serv. Co, 61-64; dir, First Nat. Bank, Columbia, Ill, 66- Mem: Monroe Co. Farm Bur; Monroe Co. Tuberc. Asn; K. of C; pres, Ill. Polled Hereford Asn, 64; v.pres, Monroe Co. Fair Asn. Rel: Catholic. Mailing Add: R.F.D. 1, Valmeyer, Ill. 62295. (1967)

RIECKER, MARGARET ANN 'RANNY' R
First V.Chmn, Rep. State Cent. Cmt, Mich.
b. Ann Arbor, Mich, 11/9/33; d. Dr. Harry A. Towsley and Margaret Dow T; m. 7/30/55 to John E. Riecker; c. John Towsley and Margaret Elizabeth. Educ: Carleton Col, B.A, 54; Mt. Holyoke Col, 54-55. Polit. & Govt. Pos: V.chmn, Midland Co. Rep, Midland, Mich, 62-66; v.chmn, Tenth Cong. Dist. Rep. Party, Mich, 64-68; spec. asst. to State Chmn. for Women's Activities, 66-68; del, Rep. Nat. Conv, 68; first v.chmn, Rep. State Cent. Cmt, 69- Mem: Bd. Town and Campus, Northwood Inst; Women's bd, Northwood Inst. Rel: Protestant. Mailing Add: 3211 Valley Dr, Midland, Mich. 48640.

RIEGELMAN, ROSALIND D
Committeewoman, N.Y. State Dem. Party
b. New York, N.Y, 5/9/15; d. Harry S. Wolff and Ruth Bachrach W; m. 1/26/45 to William I. Riegelman; c. Mary Ann and Catherine. Educ: Hunter Col, 33-34. Polit. & Govt. Pos: Committeewoman, Westchester Co. Dem. Cmt, N.Y, 57- and mem, 60-; committeewoman, N.Y. State Dem. Party, 60-; del, Dem. Nat. Conv, 64. Bus. & Prof. Pos: Fund raiser, Am. Red Cross United Serv. Orgn, 41-43; dir. jr. div, United Jewish Appeal, 43-46; pub. rels, British War Relief and others. Mem: League of Women Voters; dir, Blythedale Children's Hosp; v.chmn, Westchester Women's Bd, Fedn. of Jewish Philanthropy. Rel: Jewish. Mailing Add: 68 Mamaroneck Rd, Scarsdale, N.Y. 10583. (1967)

RIEGLE, DONALD W, JR. R
U.S. Rep, Mich.
b. Flint, Mich, 2/4/38; s. Donald W. Riegle; m. 1957 to Nancy Brandt; c. Catherine Anne, Laurie Elizabeth and Donald W, III. Educ: Univ. Mich, B.A, 60; Mich. State Univ, M.B.A, 61; Harvard Univ. Bus. Sch, doctoral cand. Polit. & Govt. Pos: U.S. Rep, Mich, 66-, mem, Appropriations Cmt, U.S. House of Rep, currently. Bus. & Prof. Pos: Former col. teacher and faculty mem, Mich. State, Boston and Harvard Univs; former consult, Harvard-Mich. Inst. Tech. Joint Center on Urban Studies; financial specialist, Int. Bus. Mach. Corp, 61-64. Named one of the Ten Outstanding Young Men of the Nation in 1967, U.S. Jr. C. of C; one of the Two Best Congressmen of the Year 1967, The National mag. Legal Res: 425 Detroit St, Flint, Mich. 48502. Mailing Add: 1408 Longworth House Office Bldg, Washington, D.C. 20515.

RIEHLE, BEN A. D
b. Rietbrock, Wis, 5/15/97. Educ: Completed eighth grade. Polit. & Govt. Pos: Chmn, Local Soil Conserv. Cmt, Wis, 36-39; mem, Co. Bd, 41-42; Wis. State Assemblyman, 54-68. Bus. & Prof. Pos: Dairy farmer; logger; secy-treas. of coop milk plant; v.pres, Cheese Producers Coop & Coop Storage Co. Mil. Serv: Army, 18-19. Mem: Secy, Coop Livestock Shipping Asn; Union Coop Bd; Beef Producers Coop; Transport Coop; Sch. Treas, 25-40. Mailing Add: Route 3, Athens, Wis. 54411. (1967)

RIEHM, CURTIS GODFREY R
b. Britt, Iowa, 12/23/14; s. Fred Riehm and Jennie Manuel R; m. 2/23/43 to Mary Florine McDermott; c. Beverly, Charles and Carol. Educ: Univ. Iowa, B.A, 40, Law Sch, J.D, 42. Polit. & Govt. Pos: Hancock Co. attorney, Garner, Iowa, 47-51 and 65-; Iowa State Rep, Hancock Co, 54-58; chmn, Hancock Co. Rep. Cent. Cmt, Iowa, 12 years. Mil. Serv: Entered as Pvt, Army,

42, released as Capt, 46, after serv. in 30th Engrs, ETO and Pac. Mem: Mason; Consistory; Shrine; Rotary; VFW; Am. Legion. Rel: Methodist. Mailing Add: 440 W. Seventh St, Garner, Iowa 50438.

RIEMER, NEAL D
b. Freehold, N.J, 8/25/22; s. Elick Jacob Riemer and Elizabeth Krupnick R; m. 9/15/46 to Ruby Riemer; c. David Raphael, Jeremiah Michael and Seth Daniel. Educ: Clark Univ, B.A, 43; Harvard Univ, M.A, 48 and Ph.D, 49; Clark Univ. Scholarship Soc. Polit. & Govt. Pos: Alternate-del-at-lg, Dem. Nat. Conv, 68; del, Wis. State Dem. Conv, 69. Bus. & Prof. Pos: Teaching fel, Harvard Univ, 47-48; Prof. of polit. sci, Pa. State Univ, 48-64 and Univ. of Wis-Milwaukee, 64- Mil. Serv: Entered as Pvt, Army Air Force, 42, released as S/Sgt, 45, after serv. in USAIF, Base Air Depot 3, Great Britain, 43-45. Publ: The Revival of Democratic Theory, Appleton-Century-Crofts, 62; The Democratic Experiment, Van Nostrand, 67; James Madison, Wash. Sq. Press, 68. Mem: Am. Polit. Sci. Asn; Am. Civil Liberties Union. Rockefeller Fel. in Polit. Philos, 58-59; Fulbright Fel, 61-62; Outstanding Prof. Award, Univ. of Wis-Milwaukee, 67-68. Rel: Jewish. Mailing Add: 2726 E. Linnwood Ave, Milwaukee, Wis. 53211.

RIESNER, DANIEL J. R
b. New York, N.Y. 10/22/02; s. Henry Riesner and Lillian Wilson R; m. 12/24/26 to Ruth Gordon; c. Gordon and Sara Ann (Mrs. Friedman). Educ: Columbia Col, A.B, 25; Columbia Univ. Sch. Law, J.D, 27; mem. and v.chmn, Columbia Col. Fund, 65-67; Phi Sigma Delta. Polit. & Govt. Pos: Acting and asst. clerk, N.Y. State Gen. Assembly, 41-58; secy, N.Y. Rep. Co. Cmt, 41-59; del, Rep. Nat. Conv, 44, 48, 52 & 56, alternate del, 60 & 68; camping indust. mem, N.Y. State Wage Bd, 51-53; pres, Nat. Rep. Club, 54-59. Bus. & Prof. Pos: Sr. law partner, Riesner, Jawitz & Holland, 60-; pres. and dir, First Nat. Planning Corp, 64-; treas. and dir, Laser Link Corp, 65-; pres. and dir, Educasting Syst. Inc, 68-; treas. & dir, Comfax Communications Corp, 68-; treas. and dir, Computer Pix Corp, 69- Publ: Practical Politics, 50. Mem: Columbia Univ. Club; Old Oaks Country Club; Long Boat Key Golf and Country Club. Rel: Jewish. Legal Res: 920 Park Ave, New York, N.Y. 10028. Mailing Add: 770 Lexington Ave, New York, N.Y. 10021.

RIETZ, KEN R
b. Oshkosh, Wis, 5/3/41; s. Howard K. Rietz and Catherine Abbey R; single. Educ: George Wash. Univ, 60-64; pres, Phi Sigma Kappa. Polit. & Govt. Pos: Publicity dir, Wis. Young Rep, 65; mem, Sixth Dist. exec. cmt, Wis. Rep. Orgn, 66; campaign dir. for U.S. Rep. William Steiger, 66 & 68, legis. asst, 66-68; assoc, Treleaven Rep. Assocs, 68-; asst. commun. dir. and info. dir, Rep. Nat. Cmt, 69. Mil. Serv: Midn, U.S. Naval Acad. Rel: Methodist. Legal Res: 1447 W. Second St, Oshkosh, Wis. 54901. Mailing Add: 101 E St. S.E, Washington, D.C. 20003.

RIFFE, VERNAL G, JR. D
Ohio State Rep.
b. New Boston, Ohio, 6/26/25; s. Vernal G. Riffe, Sr. and Jewell Adkins R; m. 3/6/48 to Thelma Cooper; c. Kathy, Verna Kay, Mary Beth and Vernal G, III. Educ: Ohio Univ. Portsmouth, Ohio; Miami Univ, Ins. Agency Mgt. Sch. Polit. & Govt. Pos: Ohio State Rep, 22nd Dist, 59- Bus. & Prof. Pos: Pres, Sherman, Riffe & Bennett Ins. Agency, Inc; v.pres. and bd. mem, Merchants' and Mfrs' Mutual Ins. Co; bd. mem, Mark Man Investment Co. Mil. Serv: Entered as Pvt, Air Force, 43, released as S/Sgt, 45, after serv. in 15th Air Force, Italy, Mediterranean Theater, 44-45; Good Conduct Medal; Am. Campaign Medal; European-African-Middle East. Campaign Medal with 9 Bronze Stars; World War II Victory Medal. Mem: Mason (32°), Scottish Rite; Am. Legion; C. of C; Independent Ins. Agents Asn; Kiwanis; Bus. & Prfnl. Mens Asn; John K. Kennedy Club. Rel: Protestant. Mailing Add: 703 Lakeview Ave, New Boston, Ohio 45662.

RIFKIN, JULIE KAYE R
Mem, Calif. Rep. State Cent. Cmt.
b. Conn; m; c. Laurence A. Polit. & Govt. Pos: Mem, Cent. Calif. Educ. TV Corp, 52-, pres, North-Cent. Area; mem. Sacramento Appeals Rev. Bd; mem. cmt, Study Unification of City and Co. Health Dept; mem. exec. cmt, Betterment of Parking Conditions and Traffic Cmt, Sacramento; mem, Sacramento Regional Arts Coun, Calif; campaign chmn, Ivy Baker Priest for State Treas, 66; mem, Soc. Welfare and Marriage Counsr. Qualifications Bd, 69-; mem, Calif. Rep. State Cent. Cmt, currently; mem, Nat. Fedn. Rep. Women, currently. Bus. & Prof. Pos: Bank teller, 43-45; participant, Workshops for Youth, Mills and Claremont Cols. and Leadership Workshops, Stanford Univ; mem, C. of C. Study Conf. for Indust. Col. of Armed Forces Nat. Resources; participant progs. and workshops for Youth Welfare, Crime and Juvenile Justice, Soc. Welfare and Ment. Health; del, West. Cong. UNESCO, mem. bd. dirs, 1 year. Mem: PTA (chmn. ment. and soc. hyg. coun, leader discussion groups for parents, mem. film rev. bd, rev. and eval. current movies for children, Radio Sta. KROY 2 years, del. local and state conv); Red Cross (in charge clothing shipment to Europe prior to World War II, first vol. group, Women's Ambulance Corps, first aid demonstrator, State Fair, home serv. vol, soc. serv. worker, bd. dirs, Sacramento Co, chmn, residential dr, 51, Gray Lady, Mather and Travis Air Fields, participant, nat. conf); March of Dimes (Sacramento chmn, First Birthday Ball, chmn, Women's Div. Fund Dr); Women's Coun.(pres, 47-49); Rainbow Girls (mother adv); Am. Cancer Soc.(bd. dirs); Sacramento Soc. Crippled Children (bd. dirs); YWCA (bd. dirs, mem. adv. cmt, Capital Fund Dr, 57); Commun. Welfare Coun. bd. dirs, mem. cmt. aging and health); Commun. Chest (bd. dirs); Sacramento Co. Youth Cong. (planning cmt); Women's Cmt. Civic Repertory Theatre and Eaglet Theatre (chmn. and chmn. children's activities); Kiwani-Anns (pres); Guide Dogs for the Blind (chmn, Sacramento Br, 10 years, exec. bd, North. Calif, speakers bur); Pan Am. Soc.(v.pres); Sacramento Co. Vis. Nurses Asn.(pres. and v.pres, bd. dirs); charter mem, Sutter Hosp. Auxiliary (acting orientation chmn); Allied Arts Breakfast Club (bd. mem, parliamentarian); Saturday Club; Sacramento Women's Forum (music chmn); Mil. Manpower Cmt. Sacramento; Sacramento Symphony and Philharmonic Bd.(bd. dirs); Sacramento Freedom Train Cmt.(chmn); State Fair Awards for Women (chmn); Eastern Star (past matron); North Ridge Country Club (pres. soc. sect); Tuesday Club; Crocker Art Gallery; Opera Guild; Hist. Soc. Sacramento; Pilot Club Int.(pres, 64); Adv. Cmt. State Ment. Hygiene (chmn); Sacramento Friends of Libr.(v.pres); Soroptimist Club-North (chmn. serv. cmt, 67); Sacramento Chap. Nursing Homes (pres, 65); State Asn. Nursing Homes (v.chmn. legis. cmt); State Asn. Nursing Homes, Sanitariums, Rest Homes and Homes for the Aged (secy, 67 & 68-69, mem. exec. cmt); Am. Nursing Home Asn.(pub. rels. cmt); fel, Am. Col. Nursing Home Adminstr. Meritorious Serv. Award, Nat. Red Cross and Women of the Year Award Distinguished Commun. Serv, 66; judge, Miss Sacramento Contest. Mailing Add: 1206 43rd St, Sacramento, Calif. 95819.

RIGBY, JOSEPH P. R
b. Pittsburgh, Pa; s. Joseph Rigby and Anne Lavelle R; m. to Hilda Young; c. Joan. Educ: 3 years col. Polit. & Govt. Pos: Pa. State Rep, 50, 54-58 & 62-68; alderman and ward chmn, Seventh Ward, Pittsburgh. Bus. & Prof. Pos: Real Estate; ins; news reporter, 18 years, Pittsburgh. Mem: Alcoma Country Club; C. of C; YMCA; E. End Rod and Gun Club; Moose; Kiwanis. Mailing Add: 6028 Penn Center S, Pittsburgh, Pa. 15235. (1967)

RIGBY, RAY WENDELL D
Asst. Minority Leader, Idaho State Senate
b. Rexburg, Idaho, 4/16/23; s. Joseph Lester Rigby and Harriet Maria Lucas R; m. 12/8/44 to Lola Jean Cook; c. Laura Jean, Jerry, Natalie, Beverly, Blair, Joyce and Beth. Educ: Univ. Idaho, B.A. in letters and sci, LL.B; Phi Alpha Delta. Polit. & Govt. Pos: Prosecuting attorney, Madison Co, Idaho, 51-64; Idaho State Sen, Madison Co, 65-, asst. minority leader, currently. Bus. & Prof. Pos: Dir, Yellowstone Nat. Life Ins. Co, 61-63; dir, Idaho Bank of Commerce, 63-; dir. and secy, North Fork Reservoir Co, which administers Henry's Lake, currently. Mil. Serv: Entered as Pvt, Army Air Force, 44, released as Aviation Cadet, 45. Mem: Pres, 12th Dist. Bar Asn, 63-64; pres, Rexburg Rotary Club, 58-59; Am. Legion; Rexburg Golf Asn; Idaho Farm Bur. Named Outstanding Freshman Sen, Idaho Press Club, 65; KRXK Man of the Year, 66; Distinguished Serv. Award, U.S. Jr. C. of C, 52. Rel: Latter-day Saints; Bishop, Hibbard Ward, 58-67, mem, Ricks Col. Second Stake High Coun, 69- Mailing Add: Route 1, Rexburg, Idaho 83440.

RIGBY, VINCENT HERBERT R
Chmn, Clay Co. Rep. Cent. Cmt, Mo.
b. Joliet, Ill, 7/21/27; s. Vincent Lavern Rigby and Mildred Stutz R; m. 5/24/58 to Patricia Costello; c. Vincent Herbert, Jr, Scott Joseph, Marcella Mildred and Lisa Ann. Educ: Joliet Twp. High Sch, grad, 46. Polit. & Govt. Pos: Pres, Liberty Park Bd, Mo, 65 & 66; mem, tech. adv. group, Kans. City Planning Bd, 66 & 67; chmn, Clay Co. Rep. Cent. Cmt, 66-; dir, Liberty Hosp. Bd, 68- Bus. & Prof. Pos: New bus. rep, Gen. Finance Corp, Evanston, Ill, 49-69; partner, Rigby Realty, Liberty, Mo, 68- Mil. Serv: Entered as Pvt, Army, 46, released as Sgt, 48, after serv. in 19th Regiment, 24th Div, Far E. Command, Japan, 46-48. Mem: Optimist Club; Am. Legion. Rel: Presbyterian. Mailing Add: 313 Melrose Ave, Liberty, Mo. 64068.

RIGGIN, RICHARD E. R
Ind. State Rep.
b. Muncie, Ind, 5/16/34; s. Robert V. Riggin and Amelia Brinson R; m. 6/3/61 to Judith Ann Colip; c. Robert Wesley, Renee Diane (deceased), Ronald Delbert and Radelle Ann. Educ: Ball State Univ, B.S. in chem, 57; Ind. Univ, M.B.A, 58, Ph.D. in econ, 69; Pi Omega Pi; Alpha Kappa Psi; Lambda Chi Alpha. Polit. & Govt. Pos: Ind. State Rep, currently. Bus. & Prof. Pos: Asst. to pres, Riggin's Dairy, 55-57; mgt. consult, 62-; prof. of finance, Ball State Univ, 62- Mil. Serv: Entered as Pvt, Army, 53, released as Sgt, 55, after serv. in Korea, 45th Div. Mem: Mason; Scottish Rite; Elks; Am. Legion. Private Pilot. Rel: Presbyterian. Mailing Add: R.R. 5, Muncie, Ind. 47302.

RIGGS, L. ALTON D
b. St. David, Ariz, 1/14/03; s. John L. Riggs and Clara Pearl Richins R; m. 3/23/46 to Ruth Eutrelle; c. L. Alton, Robert, Sandra (Mrs. Earl Bleak), Patricia and Bettye. Educ: Ariz. State Teachers Col, 27; Univ. of Ariz, LL.B, 38. Polit. & Govt. Pos: Ariz. State Rep, 31-36 & 61-62; Dep. Maricopa Co. Attorney, 39-40, 52-53 & 59-60; mem, Tempe City Coun, 50-54 & 56-60; mem, Tempe Elem. Sch. Dist. Bd, 54-62; Spec. Asst. Attorney Gen, 55-59; supvr, Maricopa Co. Bd. of Supvr, 62-68, chmn, 65-68. Bus. & Prof. Pos: Teacher, Mesa, Ariz, 27-34; lawyer, 47- Mil. Serv: Lt. Col, Army, World War II. Mem: K. of P. Mailing Add: 315 Encanto Dr, Tempe, Ariz. 85281. (1967)

RIGGS, WARREN ELWOOD R
Chmn, Camden Co. Rep. Party, N.C.
b. Old Trap, N.C, 3/5/27; s. Charlie Sawyer Riggs and Ella Hubbard R; m. 7/21/48 to Jessie Mae Wright; c. Gale Raynette, Warren Curtis and Michael Cary. Educ: Shiloh High Sch, 11 years. Polit. & Govt. Pos: Treas. and secy, Camden Co. Rep. Party, N.C, 66-68 and chmn, 68- Bus. & Prof. Pos: Asst. Mgr, Freezer Locker Co, 48-56; Farmer & Merchant, self-employed, 56- Mil. Serv: Entered as A/S, Navy, 45, released as Seaman 1/C, 46, after serv. on U.S.S. Saidor CVE 117 and U.S.S. Amphion AR 13, Pac. Theatre and Atlantic Theatre. Mem: Mason; N.C. Farm Bur; Nat. Farmers Orgn. Rel: Methodist. Mailing Add: Old Trap, N.C. 27961.

RIGGS, WILLIAM ROBERT D
Fieldman, Nebr. Dem. Party
b. Nampa, Idaho, 8/5/42; s. Robert LeRoy Riggs and Ophal Jane Brietling R; single. Educ: Concordia Teachers Col, B.S.Ed, 64; Univ. Nebr, 64; Univ. Tex, Austin, 66-67; Int. Rels. Asn.(regional pres); campus govt; campus newspaper; dramatics and other activities. Polit. & Govt. Pos: Campaign worker, Frank Morrison Gov. Campaign, 62; organizer and founder, Concordia Teachers Col. Young Dem, 64; charter mem. and officer, Lancaster Co. Young Dem, Nebr, 64; campaign worker and off. staff, Sorensen for Lt. Gov, Nebr, 64; mem, Lafayette Co. Dem. Club, Mo, 64-67, pres, 67, mem. various cmts; committeeman, Freedom Twp. Dem. Party, 66-67; parliamentarian, Lafeyette Co. Dem. Cent. Cmt, 66-67; mem, Tex. Young Dem. and Univ. Tex. Young Dem, 66 & 67; del, Seward Co. Dem. Conv, Nebr, 68; del, Dem. State Conv, 68, alternate del, Dem. Nat. Conv, 68; coordinator, Kennedy Campaign, Seward Co, 68; co-chmn, Youth Coalition for Humphrey-Muskie, 68; Librarians for Humphrey-Muskie, 68; nat. committeeman, Nebr. Young Dem. Club, 68-, faculty adv. to local col. club, 68-; fieldman, Nebr. Dem. Party, 69- Bus. & Prof. Pos: Chmn, Concordia United Fund, Mo, 65-67; mem, Kansas City Int. Rels. Coun, 65-67; chmn, Libr-Media Cmt. Educ. Serv. Unit Six, Nebr, 67- Publ: Children's literature book review section, three articles, Lutheran

Educ, 68-69. Mem: Am. Libr. Asn; Orgn. Am. Historians; Seward Co. Educ. Asn.(legis. chmn, 68-); Nebr. Libr. Asn; Nebr. Educ. Asn.(chmn. dist. one libr-media cmt, 69); Nebr. Media Asn; Jaycees. Rel: Lutheran, Mo. Synod. Mailing Add: 10 Davisson Dr, Seward, Nebr. 68434.

RIGLER, ROBERT RAYMOND R
Iowa State Sen.
b. Great Falls, Mont, 1/5/23; s. John Pierce Rigler and Ferne Barr R; m. 11/15/47 to Virginia Eś Dorn; c. Nancy, Jane, John and Robert. Educ: State Univ. of Iowa, B.S. in commerce, 43; Univ. Wis. Sch. of Banking, 52; Beta Gamma Sigma; Order of Artus. Polit. & Govt. Pos: Co. chmn, Rep. Cent. Cmt, 52-53; Iowa State Sen, currently, majority leader, one session and minority leader, two sessions; chmn, Iowa Nixon for President Cmt. and alternate del, Rep. Nat. Conv, 68. Bus. & Prof. Pos: Securities analyst, Harris Trust & Savings Bank, Chicago, Ill, 46; exec. v.pres, Security State Bank, New Hampton, Iowa, 46- Mil. Serv: Entered as Pvt, Army, 43, released as M/Sgt, 46, after serv. in Qm. Supply Off, Hq, Calcutta, India, 44-46; China-Burma-India Theater Ribbon. Mem: Rotary; Am. Legion; Mason; Shrine. Rel: Congregational. Mailing Add: 251 S. Locust, New Hampton, Iowa 50659.

RILEY, BOB COWLEY D
Parliamentarian, Ark. House Rep.
b. Little Rock, Ark, 9/18/24; s. Columbus Allen Riley and Winnie Mae Craig R; m. 5/26/56 to Claudia Zimmerman; c. Megen. Educ: Univ. Ark, B.A, 50, M.A, 51, Ed.D, 57; Univ. Calif, Jr. Col. Credential, 56; Nat. Defense Educ. Act Inst, Univ. Nebr, 68; Phi Eta Sigma; Phi Alpha Theta; Phi Delta Kappa; Blue Key; Psi Chi; Alpha Phi Omega; Sigma Chi. Polit. & Govt. Pos: Ark. State Rep, 48-50, parliamentarian, Ark. House Rep, 69-; founder and first pres, Univ. Ark. Young Dem. Club; mem, Arkadelphia City Coun, 60-64; fire cmnr, Arkadelphia, mayor, 65-66; consult, Mitchellville Commun. Develop. Proj, 68; del, Dem. Nat. Conv, 68; solicitor fire and casualty ins, Ark. Ins. Dept. Bus. & Prof. Pos: Broker, Freeling Ins. Agency, Little Rock; instr, Little Rock Univ, 51-55; prof. hist. and polit. sci, Ouachita Baptist Univ, chmn. div. soc. sci, chmn. dept. polit. sci, 60- Mil. Serv: Entered as Pvt, Marines, 41, released as Cpl, 45, after serv. in Second and Third Div, Second and Ninth Regt, Pac. Theater, 42-45. Publ: They Never Came Back, Purdue Univ, 59; The Party That Almost Was, monograph, 60 and The Reorganization of the Arkansas State Legislature, monograph, 69, Pioneer. Mem: Am. Polit. Sci. Asn; Am. Asn. Univ. Prof; Nat. Coun. Soc. Studies; K. of P; Knights of Korassan; Eagles; Moose; Rotary; DAV; Blinded Vet. Asn. Blinded Vet. Asn. Nat. Achievement Award, 63; Distinguished Serv. Award, Ark. Munic. League. Rel: Baptist. Legal Res: 1076 N. Phelps Circle, Arkadelphia, Ark. 71923. Mailing Add: Dept. of Political Science, Ouachita Baptist University, Arkadelphia, Ark. 71923.

RILEY, EDWARD FRANCIS D
City Councilman, Seattle, Wash.
b. Seattle, Wash, 1898; m. to Freda R; c. four. Educ: Univ. Wash; Theta Delta Chi. Polit. & Govt. Pos: Wash. State Rep, 39-50; Wash. State Sen, 51-66; city councilman, Seattle, Wash, currently. Bus. & Prof. Pos: Partner, Palmer Supply Co, Seattle, Wash, 31- Mil. Serv: Army. Mem: Kiwanis; K. of C; Am. Legion; Elks. Mailing Add: 2320 Delmar Dr. E, Seattle, Wash. 98102.

RILEY, EDWARD PATTERSON D
b. Barnwell, S.C, 10/27/00; s. Richard Wilson Riley and Meta Dowling R; m. 10/31/27 to Martha Dixon; c. Edward Patterson, Jr, and Richard Wilson. Educ: Furman Univ, LL.B. Polit. & Govt. Pos: Co. chmn, Co. Dem. Party, S.C, 54-56; state exec. committeeman, Dem. Party, S.C, 58-60, state chmn, 60-64; co. attorney, Greenville Co, 58-69; del, Dem. Nat. Conv, 60. Mil. Serv: Entered as Lt, Navy, 42, released as Lt. Comdr, 45, after serv. in Pac. Theater; Asiatic Theater, Philippine Liberation, Victory and Am. Theater Medals. Mem: Am. Bar Asn; S.C. Bar Asn.(pres, 60); Greenville Co. Bar Asn.(pres, 56); Am. Judicature Soc; State Bar Presidents' Asn; Kiwanis (pres, 48); pres, Blue Ridge Coun, Boy Scouts, 48-50; Am. Legion (comdr, Post 3, 54); Mason; Elks; Ky. Col. Rel: Methodist. Legal Res: 314 E. Coffee St, Greenville, S.C. 29601. Mailing Add: P.O. Box 10355, Greenville, S.C. 29603.

RILEY, EMILY ODELL D
Mem, Calif. Dem. State Cent. Cmt.
b. Los Angeles, Calif, 8/25/04; d. Frank Eugene Odell and Mary Quirk O; wid; c. David Odell and Sidney Thornton. Educ: San Francisco State Col, B.A; Univ. South. Calif, M.S; Delta Phi Epsilon. Polit. & Govt. Pos: Co. committeeman, Los Angeles Co. Dem. Party, Calif, 40-44; city clerk, Hawthorne, 44-47; legis. chmn, Hawthorne Elem. Teachers Asn, 65; state assembly and sen. contact, Calif. Teachers Asn, 65-; pres, Hawthorne Dem. Club, 67-69; cong. contact, Calif. Teachers Asn. and Nat. Educ. Asn, 67-69; mem. bd. dirs, Asn. Better Citizenship, Calif. State Teachers Coun, 68-70; mem, Calif. Dem. State Cent. Cmt, 69- Bus. & Prof. Pos: Secy, Ore. State Pub. Welfare, 48-57; teacher, Hawthorne Elem. Sch. Dist, Calif, 59-68, counsr, 68-69, v.prin, 69- Mem: Asn. Am. Univ. Women; Bus. & Prfnl. Women's Club; Eastern Star; Oliver McCammon Scholarship Found; White Shrine; Hawthorne Coord. Coun; Southwest Commun. Health Clin. Auxiliary; Toastmistress Int; Beaver Club; Yukon PTA. Hon. life mem, PTA; resolution from Calif. Legis. Assembly Rules Cmt. Rel: Episcopal. Mailing Add: 13336 S. St. Andrews Place, Gardena, Calif. 90249.

RILEY, JAMES JOSEPH D
Mem, Ariz. Dem. State Exec. Cmt.
b. Binghamton, N.Y, 3/6/37; s. James Francis Riley and Anne Helen Kane R; m. 6/22/63 to Mary Josephine Maciulla; c. Christine Marie, Gabrielle Anne and Kara Maureen. Educ: Univ. of Ariz, B.S, 59, M.S, 63 and Ph.D, 68. Polit. & Govt. Pos: Pres, Kennedy for Pres. Club, and Univ. of Ariz. Campus Dem. Club, 60; youth coordinator, Morris Udall for Cong, 61; Dem. precinct committeeman, 24th precinct, Pima Co, Ariz, 63-; Pima Co. chmn, Youth for Johnson-Humphrey, 64; Dem. chmn, Sen. Dist. 7 E, Ariz, 66 & 68; mem, Ariz. Dem. State Exec. Cmt, 66- and Ariz. Dem. State Policy Cmt, 67; adv. Teen Dem, Tucson, 67; del, Dem. Nat. Conv, 68. Bus. & Prof. Pos: Research asst, Univ. of Ariz, 63-67, asst. dir, Water Resources Research Center, 68-69, project leader, Abu Dhabi Prog, Environ. Research Lab, 69- Publ: 'Heat Balance Class A Evaporation Pan,' Water Resources, 66; 'Physiological Responses of Plants to Salinity: Plant-Water Relations,' In: Physiological Systems in Semi Arid Environments, Univ. of N.Mex. Press, 69. Mem: Am. Asn. for the Adv. of Sci; Am. Soc. of Plant Physiol; Am. Geophys. Union; Am. Meteorol. Soc. Rel: Roman Catholic. Legal Res: 2230 E. 3rd St, Tucson, Ariz. 85719. Mailing Add: 2230 E. 9th St, Tucson, Ariz. 85719.

RILEY, JOHN JAMES D
Vt. State Rep.
b. Brooklyn, N.Y, 9/14/99; m. to Gladys Ruth Alexander. Educ: N.Y. Univ, commercial law and acct. Polit. & Govt. Pos: Lister, Panton, Vt, 6 years, auditor, 9 years formerly and 67-; zoning adminstr, 67- and town agent, 68-; dir, Fed. Land Bank Asn; Vt. State Rep, 65- Bus. & Prof. Pos: Auditor, Standard Oil Co, 18-26; secy. and gen. mgr, Schenectady Chem. Co, 26-34; dairy farmer, 34-63; retired. Mem: Vergennes Forest and Field Club; Addison Grand View Grange; secy. and pres, Addison Co. Farm Bur. Rel: Brethren. Mailing Add: R.D. 3, Vergennes, Vt. 05491.

RILEY, JOSEPH PATRICK, JR. D
S.C. State Rep.
b. Charleston, S.C, 1/19/43; s. Joseph P. Riley and Helen Schachte R; m. 8/20/66 to Charlotte Douglas de Loach; c. Joseph P, III. Educ: The Citadel, A.B, 64; Univ. S.C, J.D, 67; Omicron Delta Kappa; Phi Delta Phi. Polit. & Govt. Pos: S.C. State Rep, 69- Bus. & Prof. Pos: Mem. bd. dirs, Hibernian Mutual Ins. Co. and Charleston Home for Children, 68- Mem: S.C, Charleston Co. and Am. Bar Asns; S.C. and Am. Trial Lawyers Asns; Hibernian Soc; German Friends Soc; New Eng. Soc; Carolina Yacht Club; Alston Wilkes Soc. Rel: Catholic. Legal Res: 52 Logan St, Charleston, S.C. 29401. Mailing Add: 13-A Broad St, Charleston, S.C. 29401.

RILEY, LAKE R
Chmn, Marshall Co. Rep. Exec. Cmt, Ky.
b. Benton, Ky, 5/20/17; s. Lex G. Riley and Oma Johnston R; m. 1/1/35 to Leeoda Fooks; c. William M, Alevate (Mrs. Warren), Galon and James H. Educ: Freed-Hardeman Col. Polit. & Govt. Pos: Mem, Marshall Co. Bd. Educ, 64-; chmn, Marshall Co. Rep. Exec. Cmt, Ky, currently. Bus. & Prof. Pos: Dir, Ky. Coop. Coun, 62-66; pres, Marshall Co. Soil Improvement Asn. and Valley Cos, Ky. Coop, 62- Mem: Marshall Co. Farm Bur; United Asn. Plumbing and Pipe Fitting Local 184. Rel: Church of Christ; Minister. Mailing Add: Route 6, Benton, Ky. 42025.

RILEY, RICHARD D. D
b. Ayer, Mass, 6/7/30; m. to Doris Gosselin; c. 1 daughter. Educ: Deerfield, Epsom and Pembroke Acads. Polit. & Govt. Pos: Former N.H. State Sen. Bus. & Prof. Pos: Sport Shop and Motel Operator. Mil. Serv: N.H. Nat. Guard, 49-50. Mem: Hooksett Men's Club; Lions; life mem, Nat. Rifle Asn; Manchester Rifle and Pistol Club. Rel: Catholic. Mailing Add: Box 43, Daniel Webster Hwy, Hooksett, N.H. 03106. (1967)

RILEY, RICHARD WILSON D
S.C. State Sen.
b. Greenville, S.C, 1/2/33; s. Edward Patterson Riley and Martha Elizabeth Dixon R; m. 8/21/57 to Ann Osteen Yarborough; c. Richard W, Jr, Anne Y, Hubert D. and Theodore D. Educ: Furman Univ, A.B, 54; Univ. S.C. Law Sch, LL.B, 59; Blue Key; Phi Delta Phi; Sigma Alpha Epsilon. Polit. & Govt. Pos: Student page, S.C. State Senate and state v.pres, Young Dem, 58-59; S.C. State Rep, 63-66; S.C. State Sen, Greenville Co, 66- Bus. & Prof. Pos: V.pres, Young Lawyers Club, Greenville, 61. Mil. Serv: Entered as Ens, Navy, 54, released as Lt.(jg), 56, after serv. in Mine Force. Mem: Simpsonville and Mauldin Rotary Club; Jaycees; pres, Furman Univ. Alumni Asn, 68-69. Rel: Methodist. Mailing Add: 200 Sunset Dr, Greenville, S.C. 29605.

RILEY, TIMOTHY CROCKER R
Mem, Calif. Rep. State Cent. Cmt.
b. Wilmington, Del, 10/10/46; s. William Hale Riley and Mary Turner Brown R; m. 7/6/68 to Margaret Anne Marston. Educ: Loyola Univ, B.A, 68, teaching credential, 69; Delta Sigma Phi. Polit. & Govt. Pos: V.chmn, Westside Youth for Goldwater-Miller, Calif, 64; chmn, Loyolans for Reagan, 66; chmn, Loyola Student Coalition for Nixon-Agnew, 68; pres, Loyola Univ. Young Rep, 68; cand, Beverly Hills City Coun, 68; v.chmn, 59th Assembly Dist. Rep. Coord. Coun, 69; mem, Calif. Rep. State Cent. Cmt, 69- Bus. & Prof. Pos: Real estate salesman, William Riley Real Estate, Beverly Hills, Calif, 65-66; dir. research, Campaign Assocs, 67-68; teacher, Fowler High Sch, 69- Mem: Am. Polit. Sci. Asn; Am. Hist. Asn; Nat. Educ. Asn; Calif. Teachers Asn; Beverly Hills Munic. League; Friends of the Beverly Hills Pub. Libr. Rel: Episcopal. Mailing Add: 725 E. Buckingham Way, Fresno, Calif. 93704.

RILEY, TOM JOSEPH R
b. Cedar Rapids, Iowa, 1/9/29; s. Joseph W. Riley and Edna Kyle R; m. 1/1/52 to Nancy Evans; c. Pamela Jo, Peter Craig, Lisa Ann, Martha Sue, Sara Lynne and Heather Lee. Educ: State Univ. Iowa, Col. Liberal Arts, B.A, 50, Col. of Law, J.D, 52; Alpha Tau Omega; Delta Theta Phi. Polit. & Govt. Pos: Iowa State Rep, Linn Co, 61-65; chmn, Gov. Adv. Cmt. on the Aging, 64-65; Iowa State Sen, 65-68; Rep. cand. for U.S. Rep, Second Cong. Dist, Iowa, 68. Bus. & Prof. Pos: Practicing attorney, Simmons, Perrine, Albright & Ellwood, 54-; mem, bd. dirs, Iowa Surety Co, 65- Mil. Serv: 1st Lt, Air Force, 52-54, serv. in Judge Adv. Gen. Dept, Air Training Command. Publ: Response to Crisis, Basset Publ. Co, 68. Mem: Am, Iowa State and Linn Co. Bar Asns; Mason; Am. Legion; Eagles. Outstanding Freshman Legislator, Des Moines Press & Radio Club, 61. Rel: Presbyterian. Legal Res: 3610 Clark Rd, Cedar Rapids, Iowa 52403. Mailing Add: 1215 Merchants National Bank Bldg, Cedar Rapids, Iowa 52401.

RIMESTAD, IDAR
Dep. Under Secy. for Admin, Dept. of State
Legal Res: N.Dak. Mailing Add: Dept. of State, 2201 C St. N.W, Washington, D.C. 20520.

RIMM, BENJAMIN A. R
b. New York, N.Y, 8/25/06. Educ: Rutgers Univ. Law Sch, LL.B, 27. Polit. & Govt. Pos: Solicitor, Atlantic Co. Welfare Bd, 37-61, acting dir,

59-62; asst. city solicitor, Atlantic City, 43-44; mem, Atlantic City Fourth Ward Rep. Club; acting munic. court judge, Atlantic City; former N.J. State Assemblyman, secy. to three majority leaders, N.J. Gen. Assembly, parliamentarian, 46. Bus. & Prof. Pos: Attorney-at-law. Mil. Serv: Air Force, Troop Carrier Command, Legal Office. Mem: Past pres, Dist. 3, B'nai B'rith; pres, Atlantic City Jewish Commun. Center, 48-51; Quincy O'Gillmore Post, Am. Legion; Justice Lodge, F&AM; Atlantic Co. and State Bar Asns; N.J. Exec. Cmt, Anti-Defamation League. Rel: Jewish. Mailing Add: 442 Guarantee Trust Bldg, Atlantic City, N.J. 08401. (1967)

RINALDI, HERBERT M. R
N.J. State Assemblyman
b. Weehawken, N.J, 8/16/28; s. Frank J. Rinaldi and Margaret Felitti R; m. 2/9/57 to Diane Loprete; c. Georgia, Donna and Pamela. Educ: Princeton Univ, B.A, 49; Columbia Univ. Sch. of Law, LL.B, 52; Princeton Elm Club. Polit. & Govt. Pos: N.J. State Assemblyman, 68- Bus. & Prof. Pos: Attorney at law, 52- Mil. Serv: Officer Cand, Naval Res, 52, released as Lt.(jg), 55, after serv. in Naval Res. Fighter Squadron Sixty One, Air Force Atlantic Fleet, 53-55. Mem: Am, N.J, and Hudson Co. Bar Asns; legal cmt, N.J. Savings League. Rel: Roman Catholic. Mailing Add: 251 Forest Ave, Glen Ridge, N.J. 07028.

RINALDO, MATTHEW JOHN R
N.J. State Sen.
b. Elizabeth, N.J, 9/1/31; s. Matthew J. Rinaldo, Sr. and Ann Papaccio R; single. Educ: Rutgers Univ, B.Sc, 53; Seton Hall Univ, M.B.A, 59; N.Y. Univ, 64-69; Acct. Club; Finance Club; Mgt. Club. Polit. & Govt. Pos: Chmn, Young Rep, Union, N.J, 61-63; pres, bd. of Adjust, 62-64; freeholder, Union Co, 63-64; N.J. State Sen, Dist. 9, 68- Bus. & Prof. Pos: Asst. secy, Employers Asn, 62-; instr, Rutgers Univ, 63-; v.pres, Black, Little & Co, 68- Publ: 'The Businessmen's Responsibility in Politics,' The Enterprise, spring 68. Mem: Am. Soc. for Pub. Admin; Nat. Munic. League; bd. trustees, N.J. Heart Asn; bd. dir, Union Co. Heart Asn; bd. dir, Union Chap, Am. Red Cross; Rutgers Univ. Alumni Asn; Lions; Unico; K. of C; Union Co. Hist. Soc; Elks. Outstanding Young Man of the Year, Union C. of C, 65. Rel: Roman Catholic. Mailing Add: 142 Headley Terr, Union, N.J. 07083.

RINDEN, PAUL R
b. Foochow, China, 8/22/27; married; c. Three. Educ: Yale Col; Columbia Sch. of Law. Polit. & Govt. Pos: Legal counsel to N.H. Sen, 59; Merrimack Co. Attorney, N.H; former asst. U.S. Attorney; Civil Defense chmn. for Merrimack Co; N.H. State Sen. until 67. Bus. & Prof. Pos: Lawyer. Mailing Add: 50 Pleasant St, Concord, N.H. 03301.

RINEHART, D. ELDRED R
Rep. Nat. Committeeman, Md.
b. Smithsburg, Md, 11/13/03; s. John J. Rinehart and Carrie Needy R; m. 8/16/23 to Mary Edith Davis; c. John H, Mary Susan (Mrs. Harold L. Elgin); seven grandchildren. Educ: Pub. Schs. of Washington Co, Md. Polit. & Govt. Pos: Chmn, Washington Co. Rep. State Cent. Cmt, Md, 42-52; mem, Md. State Apple Cmn, 46-48; del. and mem. cmt. on agr, Rep. Nat. Conv, 48, alternate del, 52, del, 56, del. and chmn. of Del, 60, alternate del, 64 and del, mem. arrangements cmt. and chmn, subcmt. on transportation, 68; mem, Md. Racing Cmn, 51, chmn, 52-59 & 67-69; chmn, Md. Rep. State Cent. Cmt, 52-62; mem, Rep. Nat. Cmt, 52-62; Rep. Nat. Committeeman, Md, 64-; chmn, Md. Farm Phase-Out Cmt, 67-68; mem, Renegotiation Bd, 69- Bus. & Prof. Pos: Farmer operating Glen Afton Farms, currently; orchardist, pres. and treas, Rinehart Orchards, Inc, currently; dir, Citizens Nat. Bank and Trust Co, Waynesboro, Pa, currently. Mem: Pres, Nat. Asn. of State Racing Cmnr, 57; pres, Washington Co. Farm Bur, 42; pres. and gen. mgr, Hagerstown Fair and Racing Asn, 42-51; pres, Md. State Hort. Soc; mem. bd. mgr, Waynesboro Hosp, Pa; Agr. & Mech. Asn. Washington Co.(past pres); Md. Coop. Guernsey Breeders Asn; Interstate Milk Producers Asn; Mason (32°); Royal Order of Jesters; Shrine; Annapolis Yacht Club. Mailing Add: Glen Afton Farms, R.F.D. 2, Smithsburg, Md. 21783.

RINEY, JAMES E. 'JIM' D
Assessor, Marion Co, Mo.
b. Hannibal, Mo, 7/25/21; s. John Alexander Riney and Bess Rhodes R; m. 6/1/46 to Patricia Ann Dunn; c. James Michael, Paula Kay (Mrs. Jim Lyng), Dana Bruce, Jill Ann, Christopher Lynn, Lisa Kyle, Karen Leslie, Stephen Dean and Jonathon Scott. Polit. & Govt. Pos: Pres, Marion Co. Young Dem, Mo, 60-64; recording secy, Mo. Young Dem, 64-66, admin. v.pres, 66-68; pres, Marion Co. Dem. Club, 66-68; city assessor, Hannibal and co. assessor, Marion Co, currently. Mil. Serv: Entered as Pvt, U.S. Inf, 40, released as Sgt, 45, after serv. in 35th Div. and 66th Div, Pac. and European Theatres, 40-45; Combat Inf. Badge; Bronze Star Award. Mem: Secy, Marion Co. Ment. Health Soc; chmn, Marion Co. March of Dimes and Marion Co. Cancer Crusade; bd. dirs, Marion Co. Commun. Chest and Hannibal C. of C; bd. adv, Mo. Sch. of the Deaf (v.pres); Lions; Elks; Moose; Am. Legion; VFW; K. of C. Rel: Roman Catholic. Legal Res: 1421 Park Ave, Hannibal, Mo. 63401. Mailing Add: Court House, Hannibal, Mo. 63401.

RINEY, PATRICIA ANN D
b. Tulsa, Okla, 8/2/28; d. John Paul Dunn and Reba Dance D; m. 6/1/46 to James Edward Riney; c. James Michael, Paula (Mrs. James Lyng), Dana Bruce, Jill Ann, Christopher Lynn, Lisa Kyle, Karen Leslie, Stephen Dean and Jonathan Scott. Educ: Hannibal Sr. High Sch. Polit. & Govt. Pos: Secy. and v.pres, Marion Co. Young Dem, formerly; first v.pres, Marion Co. Women's Dem. Club; del, Dem. Nat. Conv, 68. Bus. & Prof. Pos: Behavior modifier, Hannibal Diagnostic Clin, currently. Rel: Roman Catholic. Mailing Add: 1421 Park Ave, Hannibal, Mo. 63401.

RING, CAROLYN LOUISE R
Chairwoman, Hennepin Co. Rep. Party, Minn.
b. Minneapolis, 8/12/26; d. Milford O. McLean and Bessy Martin M; m. 12/27/47 to Ward D. Ring; c. Linda, Peggy, Diane and Ward, Jr. Educ: Univ. Minn, 3 years; Pi Beta Phi. Polit. & Govt. Pos: Chairwoman, Rep. Party, Richfield, Minn, 60-62; secy, Third Dist. Rep. Party, 63-65, chairwoman, 65-67; chairwoman, Hennepin Co. Rep. Party, 67-; del, Rep. Nat. Conv, 68. Rel: Presbyterian. Mailing Add: 6304 Russell Ave. S, Richfield, Minn. 55423.

RING, ELEANOR REYNOLDS R
Rep. Nat. Committeewoman, Calif.
b. Tunkhannock, Pa, 8/19/05; d. Ziba Wells Reynolds and Belle Stewart R; m. to Stanhope Cotton Ring, wid; c. Stewart A. and Mrs. Robert Taylor Scott Keith, Jr. Educ: Univ. Calif. Polit. & Govt. Pos: Pres, Coronado Rep. Women Fedn, Calif, 58-59; v.chmn, Bob Wilson Campaign, 60; alternate del, Rep. Nat. Conv, 60, 64 & 68; pres, San Diego Co. Fedn, 61-62; mem, Coronado City Coun, 63-66; v.chmn, San Diego Co. Rep. Cent. Cmt, 65-66; Rep. Nat. Committeewoman, Calif, 68- Rel: Episcopal. Mailing Add: 801 Tolita Ave, Coronado, Calif. 92118.

RINGEN, WALTER EDWIN, JR. D
Chmn, Montclair Dem. City Cmt, N.J.
b. N.Y.C, 3/24/23; s. Walter Edwin Ringen and Marian Childs R; m. 3/11/45 to Shirley Macdonald; c. Walter E, III, Leland P, Alan R. and Constance M; Educ: Rutgers Univ, B.Sc. in Civil Eng, 49; Delta Kappa Epsilon. Polit. & Govt. Pos: Mem, Essex Co. Dem. Cmt, N.J, 65-69; chmn, Montclair Dem. City Cmt, 67-; del, Dem. Nat. Conv, 68; pres, Montclair Dem. Good Govt, 67, mem. exec. cmt, 67-68. Bus. & Prof. Pos: Engr, Factory Ins. Asn, Hartford, Conn, 49-53; engr, West. Elec. Co, N.Y.C, 53-57, dept. chmn. plant eng, 57- Mil. Serv: Entered as Pvt, Army Air Force, 43, released as T/Sgt, 45, after serv. in 303 Bomber Group, 359 Bomber Squadron, Eighth Air Force, ETO, 44-45; Air Medal with Five Clusters; ETO Ribbon with Two Battle Stars. Mem: Am. Legion; F&AM. Rel: Unitarian. Mailing Add: 169 Lorraine Ave, Upper Montclair, N.J. 07043.

RINGSAK, ELTON W. R
N.Dak. State Sen.
b. Grafton, N.Dak, 11/18/15; married; c. five. Educ: Univ. of N.Dak. Polit. & Govt. Pos: N.Dak. State Sen, 57- Bus. & Prof. Pos: Attorney-at-law. Mem: Am. Legion; DAV; Mason; Shrine; Eagles; Bar Asn. Mailing Add: Box 508, Grafton, N.Dak. 58237. (1967)

RINI, DOMINIC WILLIAM D
Mem. Exec. Bd, Will Co. Dem. Party, Ill.
b. New Orleans, La, 9/7/06; s. Louis Rini and Rose Vazzano R; m. 9/25/27 to Ann Seeni; c. Sarah (Mrs. Terry Aversa) and Louis V. Educ: Various classes and courses in bus. admin. and mgt; E.I. DuPont, U.S. Rubber and UniRoyal Supvry develop. training. Polit. & Govt. Pos: Committeeman, Will Co. Dem. Party, Ill, 49-69, mem. exec. bd, 59-; construction supvr, State of Ill, 60-65; rep. committeeman, 41st Dist. Dem. Party, 65- Bus. & Prof. Pos: Stock clerk, Int. Harvester, 24-25; shipping foreman, Bankers Thrift Corp, 25-30; mgr, Goldblatts, 32-34; gen. foreman, Stone & Webester, 40-41; road supvr, U.S. Rubber Co, 44-46; sales supvr, Electrolux Co, 46-51. Mem: Dem. Organizational Club. Rel: Catholic. Mailing Add: 2425 Erskine Rd, Joliet, Ill. 60432.

RINKER, DONALD KIRK R
Chmn, Co. Rep. Party, Pa.
b. Altoona, Pa, 3/3/18; s. Joseph S. Rinker and Helen Fraker R; m. 7/12/37 to Florence Gail Hetrick; c. Ronald, Max and Steve. Educ: Juniata Col, 36-37. Polit. & Govt. Pos: Committeeman, Co. Rep. Party, Pa, 56-66, chmn, 60- Bus. & Prof. Pos: Spec. agent, Selected Risks Indemnity Ga, 39-44; prod. planning mgr, Owens Corning Fiberglas, 44- Mem: Elks; Fire Co; Huntingdon Bus. & Indust. Asn. Rel: Evangelical United Brethren. Mailing Add: R.D. 1, Huntingdon, Pa. 16652.

RIOLO, MICHAEL A. D
Mem, Kent Co. Dem. Exec. Cmt, Mich.
b. Ludington, Mich, 4/2/20; s. Jack Riolo and Anna Nicosia R; m. 5/30/41 to Margaret S. Jones; c. Dr. Michael L. and Ricky L. Educ: Muskegon Jr. Col, 2 years; Mich. State Univ, B.A, 50; Sigma Delta Chi; Phi Theta Delta. Polit. & Govt. Pos: Mem, Kent Co. Dem. Cmt, Mich, 52-69; precinct del, Kent or Ottawa Co, Mich, 52-69; del, Dem. State Conv, since 54; chmn, Fifth Dist. Cong. Campaign Cmt, 58; mem, Kent. Co. Dem. Exec. Cmt, 64-; chmn, Fifth Dist. Dem. Cmt, 66-68; vol. dir. tutoring, Campeau Sch, Grand Rapids One-to-One tutoring, Commun. Action Prog, 66-; mem, Humphrey-Muskie Campaign Cmt, 68 and chmn. fifth dist. cmt, 68; del, Dem. Nat. Conv, 68. Bus. & Prof. Pos: Real estate broker & appraiser, Riolo Real Estate, 58- Mil Serv: Entered as Pvt, Air Force, 43, released as 1st Lt, 45, after serving in S.E. Training Command; Inactive Res, Capt. Mem: Elks; Am. Civil Liberties Union. Rel: Presbyterian. Mailing Add: 1437 Genesee St. S.E, Grand Rapids, Mich. 49506.

RIORDAN, (JUSTINE) KIM D
Educ: Mills Col, B.A. Polit. & Govt. Pos: Sacramento area chmn, Citizens for Kennedy, 67-68; del, Dem. Nat. Conv, 68. Bus. & Prof. Pos: Mgr. commercial real estate bus, 55- Mem: Women's Athletic Club, San Francisco; Sierra View Country Club, Roseville. Rel: Episcopal. Mailing Add: P.O. Box 214511, Sacramento, Calif. 95821.

RIOS, CARLOS M. D
b. Ponce, P.R, 3/5/14; m. to Candida Santos; c. Rose, Diana, Carlos Jr. Educ: San Juan Pub. Schs. Polit. & Govt. Pos: N.Y. State Assemblyman, 62-66; leader, 10th Assembly Dist, No, Regular Dem. Org; founder, E. Harlem Reform Dem; founder, P.R. Nat. Civil Rights Org. and Legion of Voters; bd, P.R. Forum. Bus. & Prof. Pos: Lay minister; labor rep, pres, United Independent Theatre Employees Union. Mem: Spanish Div, United Hatters and Millinery Workers Int. Union. Rel: Protestant. Mailing Add: 314 E. 105th St, New York, N.Y. 10029. (1967)

RIPPER, JACK DORLAND D
Ore. State Rep.
b. Bingen, Wash, 5/29/20; s. Percy Gilbert Ripper and Oris Loughary R; m. 6/27/42 to Nellie Christine Andersen; c. John Gilbert, Susan Kay (Mrs. Gary

Combs) and Richard William. Educ: Univ. Ore, 39-42; Portland State Col, B.S, 64; Delta Upsilon. Polit. & Govt. Pos: Mem, North Bend Planning Cmn, Ore, 59-60, chmn, 61; mem, gov. cmn. on youth, 69; Ore. State Rep, Dist. 16, Coos Co, 69- Bus. & Prof. Pos: Owner & operator of restaurants, North Bend, Ore, 43-60; educator hist. dept, North Bend Sch. Dist, 64-69. Mem: Ore. Educ. Asn; Nat. Educ. Asn; Elks; past pres, Lions Club; past pres, North Bend C. of C. Rel: Episcopal. Legal Res: Saunders Lake, North Bend, Ore. 97459. Mailing Add: Box 293, North Bend, Ore. 97459.

RISELING, BOB HENDERSON R
b. Columbus, Kans, 2/12/23; s. John William Riseling and Barbara Henderson R; m. 11/14/42 to Nila Fay Whitten; c. Mary Jane, Karen and Johnny. Educ: Howard Col, Ala, A.B, 49; Peabody Col, Tenn, M.A, 57. Polit. & Govt. Pos: Chmn, Marshall Co. Rep. Exec. Cmt, Ala, 60-68. Bus. & Prof. Pos: Ed. and publisher, Boaz Leader, Ala, 51-53; prof. of speech, Snead Col, Boaz, Ala, 58-59, dean of students, 59-65 and dir. of pub. rels, 65- Mil. Serv: Entered as Pvt, Air Force, 41, released as S/Sgt, 45. Mem: Ala. Educ. Asn; Am. Legion; Ala. Cattleman's Asn; Farm Bur; Am. Red Poll Breeders Asn; Nat. Geographic Soc; Methodist Men's Club. Rel: Methodist. Mailing Add: Route 5, Boaz, Ala. 35957. (1967)

RISHER, WILLIAM RHETT R
Chmn, Bamberg Co. Rep. Party, S.C.
b. Ehrhardt, S.C, 7/22/27; s. James F. Risher and Emma Jane Varn R; m. 11/27/48 to Marilyn McDill Hipps; c. Barbara Kay, Jane Wilkie and William Rhett, Jr. Educ: The Citadel, B.S; Univ. N.C; Sigma Pi Sigma. Polit. & Govt. Pos: Chmn, Bamberg Co. Rep. Party, S.C, currently; alternate del, Rep. Nat. Conv. Bus. & Prof. Pos: Headmaster, Carlisle Mil. Sch, 56- Mil. Serv: Army Res. Mem: Mason (past master); Shrine; S.C. Jaycees (pres); U.S. Jaycees (v.pres). Rel: Methodist. Legal Res: S. Carlisle St, Bamberg, S.C. 29003. Mailing Add: Carlisle Military School, Bamberg, S.C. 29003.

RISHWAIN, ROBERT JAMES D
Mem, San Joaquin Co. Dem. Cent. Cmt, Calif.
b. Stockton, Calif, 7/4/37; s. Ben T. Rishwain and Mary Romley R; m. 6/19/60 to Joan Elaine Strand; c. Mark, Scott and David. Educ: Stanford Univ; Univ. Santa Clara Law Sch. Polit. & Govt. Pos: Co. chmn, Pierre Salinger for Sen. Campaign, Calif, 64; chmn, Norb Schlei for Secy. of State Campaign, 66; co-chmn, San Joaquin Co. Brown for Gov. Campaign, 66; mem, San Joaquin Co. Dem. Cent. Cmt, currently, legal counsel, 66. Bus. & Prof. Pos: Dir. and secy, Hy-Lond Enterprises and v.pres, Senor Taco, Inc, 68- Mem: Pres, Santa Clara Co. Bar Asn; Am. and Calif. Bar Asns; Am. Trial Lawyers Asn; Pac. Dem. Club; Kiwanis; secy, Boys Clubs of Am; Crippled Children's Soc. Santa Clara Law Review Publns. Rel: Roman Catholic. Legal Res: 4140 Cliff Dr, Stockton, Calif. 94204. Mailing Add: 45 N. Hunter St, Stockton, Calif. 95204.

RISLEY, CHARLES E. D
b. Grasonville, Md, 6/9/20; married. Educ: Grasonville Schs. Polit. & Govt. Pos: Md. State Del, 55-67. Bus. & Prof. Pos: Waterman. Mil. Serv: Air Force, 41-45. Mem: Am. Legion; VFW; K. of P. Mailing Add: Grasonville, Md. 21638. (1967)

RISPOLI, MARCELLO D
Mem, Wilmington City Coun, Del.
b. Benevento, Italy, 3/27/14; s. Thomas Rispoli and Camille Parisi R; m. 12/3/35 to Anna Mary Grandell; c. Thomas Andrew, Mary Ellen and Anthony. Educ: High Sch. Polit. & Govt. Pos: Mem, Wilmington City Coun, Del, 60- Mem: Eagles; Fifth Ward Dem. Club; Bishop Curtis Coun; St. Anthony's Cath. Club; Fed. Hill Civic Asn; Hilltop Civic Asn. Rel: Catholic. Mailing Add: 1412 W. Seventh, Wilmington, Del. 19805. (1967)

RISSER, ANDREW WARNER D
Mem, Dem. Nat. Cmt.
b. Madison, Wis, 1/14/29; s. Fred E. Risser and Elizabeth Warner R; m. 6/16/57 to Judith Louise Mayer; c. Martha Kay, Laura Lee and Kathleen Ann. Educ: East. Wash. Col, B.A, 50; Wis. State Univ, Madison, LL.B, 58. Polit. & Govt. Pos: Mem. exec. bd, Eau Claire Co. Dem. Party, Wis, 59-65; del, State Dem. Conv, 59-65; alternate del, Dem. Nat. Conv, 60 & 64; Dem. precinct committeeman, Fall Creek, Eau Claire Co, 60-; cand, Wis. State Assembly, 62; mem, Dem. Nat. Cmt, Wis, 62- Mem: Am, Wis. and Eau Claire Co. Bar Asns; Lions; pres, Fall Creek Parents Club, 63-64. Rel: Protestant. Legal Res: 138 Wilson St, Fall Creek, Wis. 54742. Mailing Add: 4249 S. Pennsylvania Ave, Milwaukee, Wis. 53207.

RISSER, FRED A. D
Minority Leader, Wis. State Senate
b. Madison, Wis, 5/5/27; married; c. Three. Educ: Univ. Wis, B.A; Univ. Ore, LL.B, 52. Polit. & Govt. Pos: Wis. State Assemblyman, 56-62; del, Dem. Nat. Conv, 60 & 64, Presidential Elector and chmn, State Electoral Col, 64; Wis. State Sen, 62-, asst. minority leader, Wis. State Senate, 65-67, minority leader, 67-, chmn, Joint Cmt. on Finance and Bd. on Govt. Opers, v.chmn, Cmt. on Rules, mem, Taxation and State Affairs Cmts, State Bldg. Cmn, Emergency Bd, Ad hoc Cmt. on Tax Rev, Claims Cmn, Rev. of Assembly Rules Interim Cmt, Cmt. on Remedial Legis, Legis. Coun. and Election Laws Interim Cmt. Bus. & Prof. Pos: Attorney-at-law. Mil. Serv: World War II. Mem: Ore, Wis. and Dane Co. Bar Asns. Mailing Add: 15 W. Main St, Madison, Wis. 53703.

RISTUBEN, PETER J. D
b. Black River Falls, Wis, 10/4/33; s. Oliver T. Ristuben and Aleda Johnson R; m. 6/9/56 to Nina Christine Olson; c. Ann, Peter, Jr. and Erik. Educ: Concordia Col, Minn, B.A, 55; Univ. S.Dak, M.A, 57; Univ. Okla, Ph.D, 64; Sigma Tau Phi; Pi Gamma Mu. Polit. & Govt. Pos: Adv, Pac. Lutheran Univ. Young Dem, 60-; pres, 28th Dist. Dem. Club, 61-63; mem, Pierce Co. Dem. Cent. Cmt, 62-63, mem. exec. bd, 63; chmn, Pierce Co. Precinct Training Inst, 63; chmn, Sixth Cong. Dist. Dem. Orgn, Wash, 63-65; del. and mem, Credentials Cmt, Dem. Nat. Conv, 64; educ. adv, U.S. Peace Corps, North. Nigeria, 66-68. Bus. & Prof. Pos: Teacher, N.Y. Mills Pub. Schs, Minn, 55-56; assoc. prof. hist, Pac. Lutheran Univ, 60- Mem: Am. Asn. Univ. Prof; Orgn. of Am. Historians; chmn, Pac. Northwest Coun. on Regional Res; Rotary; Human Rights Chmn, UN Asn, Wash. State Coun; Wash. State Citizens Cmt, 64. One of 3 Outstanding Young Men of Year in Wash. State, Jr. C. of C, 64; Nat. Finalist, White House Fels. Competition, 65. Nat. Found. for the Humanities, summer research stipend, 69. Rel: Lutheran. Mailing Add: 12011 136th Ave. E, Puyallup, Wash. 98371.

RISTY, ALBERT R. R
S.Dak. State Rep.
b. Corson, S.Dak, 3/31/92; married; c. Two. Educ: State Col, Brookings. Polit. & Govt. Pos: Twp. and sch. bd. mem; dir, local farmers orgn; S.Dak. State Sen, 36-54; S.Dak. State Rep, 62- Bus. & Prof. Pos: Farmer and stock raiser. Rel: Am. Lutheran. Mailing Add: Corson, S.Dak. 57019.

RITCH, MARVIN LEE D
b. Vance Twp, Union Co, N.C, 3/7/89; s. William Capers Ritch and Martha Jane Lee R; m. to Lois Wilson; c. Three; grandchildren, Five. Educ: Univ. of N.C, 3 years; Georgetown Univ. Law Sch, LL.B, 14. Polit. & Govt. Pos: Personal clerk to U.S. Sen. John Hollis Bankhead, Ala, 14; clerk to Judge E.Y. Webb; N.C. State Rep, 39, 43 & 63-66. Bus. & Prof. Pos: Law practice, Charlotte, N.C, 14-; athletic dir. and coach, Student Army Training Corps, Univ. of N.C, 18. Mem: Excelsior Lodge of Mason, 261, 18-; York and Scottish Orders; Shrine. Set up and outlined exten. of educ. servs, Chapel Hill, autumn, 10; started basketball at Univ. of N.C, Capt. and Mgr. of first tean, 11; varsity football, Georgetown Univ, 12; All Star Atlantic Center. Rel: Methodist. Mailing Add: 1427 E. Seventh St, Charlotte, N.C. 28204. (1967)

RITNER, ROY R. D
b. Montesano, Wash, 3/16/11; s. Frank Ritner and Carrie C. Reed R; m. 11/2/35 to Phyllis C. Haburt; c. Gary R, Gail R. (Mrs. Gene Neuneke) and Roy R, Jr. Polit. & Govt. Pos: Wash. State Rep, 57-61; mem, Nat. Rivers and Harbor Cong, 60; state committeeman, Mason Co. Dem. Party, Wash, 60-64, chmn, 64; del, Dem. Nat. Conv, 60 & 64. Bus. & Prof. Pos: Restaurant owner, 42-59; real estate broker, Roy Ritner & Assocs, 60- Mem: Eagles; Elks; Kiwanis; Wash. Athletic Club. Rel: Methodist. Mailing Add: 2500 81st St. S.E, Mercer Island, Wash. 98040.

RITTER, GEORGE JOSEPH D
Conn. State Rep.
b. New York, N.Y, 3/26/20; s. Charles Joseph Ritter and Gertrude Sternberg R; m. 6/9/46 to Patricia Kingsley Sleezer; c. Martha Kingsley, Scott Robinson, Thomas Drummond, Penn Joseph and John Lathrop. Educ: Rutger Col. of Rutgers Univ, A.B, 41; Yale Univ. Law Sch, LL.B, 46, Sterling Fel, 46-47. Polit. & Govt. Pos: Corp. counsel, Hartford, Conn, 56-58, dep. mayor and mem. city coun, 59-69; mem, Hartford Charter Rev. Cmn, 53, 57 & 65; v.chmn, Gr. Hartford Mass Transit Dist, 63, chmn, 63-; mem. exec. cmt, Commun. Renewal Team, 64-; Conn. State Rep, 69- Bus. & Prof. Pos: Exec. dir. of Conn. Coun. 16, Am. Fedn. of State, Co. and Munic. Employees, AFL-CIO, 48-50; chmn, Cmt. on Admin. Law and Practices, Conn. State Bar Asn, 57; sr. partner, Ritter & Berman, Attorneys, currently. Mil. Serv: Entered as Pvt, Army, 43, released as S/Sgt, 45, after serv. in Eighth Army Hq, Far East; 3 Battle Stars; North. Solomons, Cebu in the Philippines and Leyte in the Philippines; Presidential Unit Citation. Mem: Civitan Club, 52-; VFW; Am. Vet. Cmt. Rel: Quaker. Legal Res: 248 N. Whitney St, Hartford, Conn. 06103. Mailing Add: 266 Pearl St, Hartford, Conn. 06103.

RITTER, JAMES PIERCE D
Pa. State Rep.
b. Allentown, Pa, 10/30/30; s. Pierce Albert Clairius Ritter and Rose Deutsch R; m. 11/16/51 to Faye Eilleen Morrissey; c. Karen Anne, Steven Pierce and David James. Educ: Allentown High Sch, grad, 48; Int. Correspondence Sch, 50. Polit. & Govt. Pos: Alderman, Allentown, Pa, 62-; Pa. State Rep, 65- Bus. & Prof. Pos: Draftsman, Pa. Power & Light Co, 54-58; design draftsman, Lehigh Struct. Steel Co, 58-63; designer and checker, F.W. Armitage Co, Inc, 63-64. Mil. Serv: Entered as Pvt, Army, 51, released as Sgt. 1/C, 54, after serv. in Army Security Agency, U.S. Mem: Pa. Magistrates Asn; Lehigh Valley Minor Judiciary Asns; Patriot Order, Sons of Am; bd. dirs, Police Athletic League; various fraternal orgns. and Dem. clubs. Rose grower, numerous ribbons. Rel: Lutheran. Mailing Add: 542 Mohawk St, Allentown, Pa. 18103.

RITTER, LUCY ELIZABETH D
b. Shanghai, China, 9/10/10; d. Ovid Herbert Ritter and Lucy Alma Corker D; single. Educ: Stanford Univ, A.B. cum laude, 30, M.A, 31; Pi Sigma Alpha. Polit. & Govt. Pos: Alternate del, Dem. Nat. Conv, 56 & 64; mem, Gov. Bus. Adv. Coun, 60; chmn, Citizens for Kennedy, 60; mem. bd. of admin, Calif. Pub. Employees Retirement Syst, Sacramento, 61-; chmn, Cmt. to Re-Elect Gov. Brown, 62 and Sacramento Women's Div, Johnson-Humphrey Campaign, 64; chmn, Cmt. on Status of Women, Sacramento Dem. Women's Club, 66-68. Bus. & Prof. Pos: Research secy, Calif. Taxpayers Asn, 31-34; security analyst, Securities Dept, 35-43, asst. treas. and mgr, 43-; second. v.pres, Calif-West. States Life Ins. Co, 54-68, first v.pres, 68- Publ: 'The Analysts' Need to be Objective Politically,' 7-8/65 and 'Common Stocks for Life Insurance Portfolios,' 1-2/66, Financial Analyst; plus others. Mem: Chartered Financial Analysts; Security Analysts of San Francisco; League of Women Voters; Crocker Art Gallery Asn; Sacramento Opera Guild; Kingsley Art Club; Sacramento Dem. Women's Club; Del Paso Country Club; Metrop. Club. Rel: Episcopal. Mailing Add: 1500 Seventh St, Apt. 14M, Sacramento, Calif. 95814.

RITTER, MABEL LOUISE R
Chmn, Perry Co. Rep. Party, Ark.
b. Houston, Ark, 11/9/29; d. Hubert Alderson Hill and Ruth Freeman H; m. 5/19/50 to Loren Eugene Ritter; c. Mickey Jean (Mrs. Danny Hill), Kathryn Louise, Ruth Leann, David Frank, John Alan, Jayne Alice, Loren Edward and Rita Gayle. Educ: Bigelow Sch, 4 years. Polit. & Govt. Pos: Secy, Perry Co. Rep. Party, Ark, 66-68, chmn, 68- Mem: St. Patricks Mothers Club; St.

Boniface Altar Soc; Union Exten. Homemakers Club; Perry Co. Exten. Homemakers Club. Rel: Catholic. Mailing Add: Route 1, Box 22, Bigelow, Ark. 72016.

RIVERA, AMOS D
Mem, Colo. Dem. State Cent. Cmt.
b. Taos, N.Mex, 10/1/33; s. Manuel C. Rivera and Estefanita Vigil R; m. 10/8/60 to Adina Rael; c. Thomas L, Amos T, Elizabeth E, Christine A. and Matthew M. Educ: Pueblo Jr. Col, 2 years; Adams State Col, 1 year; Univ. Md, B.A; Syracuse Col. of Mortuary Sci, Funeral Dir. Polit. & Govt. Pos: Coroner, Pueblo Co, Colo, 67-68; mem, Colo. Dem. State Cent. Cmt, 67-; del, Dem. State Conv, 69. Bus. & Prof. Pos: Pres. and gen. mgr, Rivera Funeral Home, 60- Mil. Serv: Entered Air Force, 52, released as Sgt. 1/C, 57, after serv. in Europe. Mem: Citizens Serv. Orgn.(pres, 69); Am. G.I. Forum; Alianza Hispana Americana; Spanish Am. Club; VFW. Rel: Protestant. Mailing Add: 1407 Constitution, Pueblo, Colo. 81001.

RIVERS, L. MENDEL D
U.S. Rep, S.C.
b. Berkeley Co, S.C, 9/28/05; m. 9/1/38 to Margaret Middleton; c. Margaret (Mrs. Robert G. Eastman), Lois Marion and Lucius Mendel, Jr. Educ: Col. of Charleston; Univ. S.C; Hon. LL.D, The Citadel, 59, Clemson Univ, 65 and Col. of Charleston, 68. Polit. & Govt. Pos: S.C. State Rep, 33-36; spec. attorney, U.S. Dept. Justice, 36-40; U.S. Rep, S.C, 40-, chmn, Cmt. on Armed Serv, U.S. House of Rep. Mem: Hon. mem, Am. and S.C. Dent. Asns; hon. mem, Fleet Res. Asn; Res. Officers Asn; Elks; Landmark Lodge 76; F&AM; life mem, Exchange Club. Minute Man Award, 65. Rel: Episcopal. Legal Res: Charleston, S.C. Mailing Add: 2205 Rayburn House Office Bldg, Washington, D.C. 20515.

RIVERS, RALPH JULIAN D
b. Seattle, Wash, 5/23/03; s. Julian Guy Rivers and Louisa Lavoy R; m. 12/21/28 to Lina Carol Caldwell; second m. 10/1/55 to Martha Marie Quehl; c. Julian Ralph and Joyce Carol (Mrs. Mansfield). Educ: Univ. Wash, LL.B, 29; Sigma Chi; Phi Alpha Delta. Polit. & Govt. Pos: U.S. Dist. Attorney, Fourth Judicial Div, Dist. of Alaska, 33-44; Attorney Gen, Alaska, 45-49; chmn, Employ. Security Cmn. of Alaska, 50-52; mayor, Fairbanks, 52-54; Sen, Alaska Territory, 55; second v.pres, Alaska Constitutional conv, 55-56; U.S. Rep. elect under Alaska-Tenn. Plan, 57-58; U.S. Rep, Alaska, 59-67; del, Dem. Nat. Conv, 68. Bus. & Prof. Pos: Attorney-at-law, Fairbanks, Alaska, 31-33 & 49- Mem: Pres, League of Alaskan Cities, 54; Elks; Pioneers of Alaska; SAR; Soc. Mayflower Descendants. Rel: Catholic. Legal Res: 308 Fifth Ave, Fairbanks, Alaska 99701. Mailing Add: P.O. Box 1951, Fairbanks, Alaska 99701.

RIVERS, ROBERT CAMPBELL, JR. D
b. Boone, N.C, 11/2/99; s. Robert Campbell Rivers, Sr. and Sarah Jurney R; m. 3/2/28 to Jean Lewis; c. Jane (Mrs. Krida) and Rachel (Mrs. Coffey). Educ: Appalachian Training Sch, 4 yrs. Polit. & Govt. Pos: Chmn, Watauga Co. Dem. Exec. Cmt, N.C, 40-42; del, Dem. Nat. Conv, 44, 52, 60 & 64. Bus. & Prof. Pos: Mem. bd. of dirs. and v-pres, Watauga Savings & Loan Asn, 33-; publisher, Watauga Dem, 33-; mem. bd. of dirs, Northwest. Bank, Boone, N.C, 63- Mem: N.C. Press Asn; Nat. Newspaper Asn; Mason; RAM, K.T; Lenoir Country Club; Blowing Rock Country Club; C. of C; Boone Merchants Asn. Rel: Methodist. Legal Res: 206 Rivers St, Boone, N.C. 28607. Mailing Add: 300 W. King St, Boone, N.C. 28607.

RIVET, EUGENE EDGAR D
R.I. State Rep.
b. Woonsocket, R.I, 5/20/19; s. Gasper Rivet and Ernestine Lorraine R; m. 5/24/47 to Lucy E. Archambault; c. Jeannine M. and Robert D. Educ: High sch. equivalency dipl, 46. Polit. & Govt. Pos: R.I. State Rep, Dist. 65, 67- Bus. & Prof. Pos: Sales rep, Costello Bros, 58- Mil. Serv: Entered as Pvt, Marine Corps, 42, released as Cpl, 46, after serv. in Second Marine Div, Fleet Marine Force, Pac. Theatre, 42-46. Mem: Elks; Favreau Bedford Amvets; IBT Local 64. Rel: Catholic. Mailing Add: 656 Bernon St, Woonsocket, R.I. 02895.

RIVIERE, RALPH LOUIS D
Coroner, Beaver Co, Pa.
b. Boston, Mass, 12/10/18; s. Lewis Riviere and Millicent Haynes R; m. to Gloria Laurie, wid; c. Gary J. Educ: Xavier Univ, B.S, 43; Meharry Med. Col, M.D, 46; Alpha Phi Alpha. Polit. & Govt. Pos: Alternate del, Dem. Nat. Conv, 68; coroner, Beaver Co, Pa, 68- Bus. & Prof. Pos: Pres, Piedmont Med. & Dent, 56. Mil. Serv: Pfc, Army Specialized Training Prog, 43. Mem: Am. and Nat. Med. Asns; Beaver Co. Med. Soc; Chi Soc; John H. Hale Surg. Soc; Elks; Mason (32°); Shrine. Top Hat Award, New Pittsburgh Courier, 69. Rel: Catholic. Mailing Add: 206 Woods Dr, New Brighton, Pa. 15066.

RIVKIN, WILLIAM R. D
b. Musastine, Iowa, 4/16/19; m. to Enid Hammerman; c. Laura, Julia, Robert and Charles. Educ: State Univ. Iowa, B.A, 41; Northwest. Univ, J.D, 48. Polit. & Govt. Pos: U.S. Ambassador to Luxembourg, 62-65 and Senegal and the Gambia, 66-68; consult, Bur. of Intel. and Research, Dept. of State, 65-66. Bus. & Prof. Pos: Lectr, Northwest. Univ, 48-50; attorney-at-law, Chicago, 48-; partner, Goldberg, Weigle, Mallin & Rivkin, Attorneys, 54- Mil. Serv: Entered Army, 41, released at Lt. Col, 46; Bronze Star. Mailing Add: c/o U.S. Dept. of State Foreign Service, Washington, D.C. 20521. (1967)

RIZLEY, ROSS R
b. Beaver, Okla, 7/5/92; s. Robert Martin Rizley and Arabella Narcissus McCown R; m. 6/8/16 to Ruby Elaine Seal; c. Merriam Elaine, Hortense (Mrs. Barrere), Roscoe Quentin, Robert Seal, Leota LaMoyne, Max Devon, Jerry Wallace. Educ: Univ. Kans. City, LL.B, 15. Polit. & Govt. Pos: Dist. judge, W. Dist, Okla; chmn, C.A. Board, 55; asst. secy. agr, 53-54; solicitor, P.O. Dept, 53; U.S. Rep, Okla, 41-49; state sen, 1st Okla. Dist, 31-35; co. attorney, Beaver Co, Okla, 19-20. Bus. & Prof. Pos: Actively practicing law since 15; admitted to Okla. Bar, 15. Mem: Am, Okla. Bar Asns; past dir, Guymon C. of C; Lions; Mason (32°); Shriner. Rel: Methodist. Mailing Add: 810 N.W. 15th St, Okla. City, Okla. 73106. (1967)

RIZZUTI, THERESA 'TESS' R
Committeewoman, Fourth Cong. Dist. Rep. Party, Okla.
b. Rome, N.Y, 11/9/18; d. Thomas Rossi and Angela Capponi R; m. 12/26/42 to Terigo 'Phil' Rizzuti; c. Terry Philip, Patrice Gail, Thea Lynn and Chris Andrew. Educ: Rome Free Acad, N.Y, secy. cert, 38; bus. courses, two years; pres. Gamma Zeta chap, Theta Chi Auxilliary, 47. Polit. & Govt. Pos; Mem, Okla. Co. Rep. Exec. Cmt, Okla, 67-; committeewoman, Fourth Cong. Dist. Rep. Party, 67 & 69-; v.pres, Cent. Okla. Rep. Women's Club, 68, pres, 69; precinct judge, Midwest City, 68; alternate del, Rep. Nat. Conv, 68; cand, Dist, 95, Okla. House of Rep, 68; youth activities chmn, Okla. State Fedn. Rep. Women, 68-; mem, Okla. Rep. State Exec. Cmt, 69- Bus. & Prof. Pos: Secy, U.S. Civil Serv, N.Y, 41-46, Okla. State Univ, 49-50, Rome, Civil Defense, N.Y, 54-55 and T. Phil. Rizzuti, Rome, 57-66. Mem: Newcomers Club, Midwest City, Okla; Acme Club Auxilliary, Rome, N.Y. Rel: Catholic. Mailing Add: 3004 Glenvalley Dr, Midwest City, Okla. 73110.

ROACH, CRISS WARREN D
Chmn, Andrew Co. Dem. Cmt, Mo.
b. Bolckow, Mo, 6/17/23; s. Walter P. Roach and Abbie Criss R; m. 2/27/44 to Doris Audrey Alkire; c. Phyllis E.(Mrs. Hendricks), Priscilla A.(Mrs. Stuart), Charles Randall and Gerald Wayne. Educ: High Sch, Maryville, Mo, 4 years. Polit. & Govt. Pos: Chmn, Andrew Co. Dem. Cmt, Mo, 52-; sales tax auditor, Mo. Dept. Revenue, 58-63; colonel, Gov. Hearnes Staff, 64; dairy inspector, Mo. Dept. Agr, 64-; chmn, Sixth Dist. Dem. Party, 66. Bus. & Prof. Pos: Farmer, Andrew Co, 41- Mil. Serv: Entered as Pvt, Army, 43, released as Sergeant, 46, after serv. in 755th Field Artil, Ninth Division, ETO, 44-45; Presidential Unit Citation; Purple Heart. Mem: Am. Legion; VFW; Mason. Rel: Protestant. Mailing Add: R. R. 1, Bolckow, Mo. 64427.

ROACH, RICHARD HOWARD R
Chmn, Bremer Co. Rep. Cent. Cmt, Iowa
b. Plainfield, Iowa, 4/19/29; s. Howard L. Roach and Freida Page R; m. 6/15/57 to Sandra Kay Smith; c. Peggy Anne, Michael R. and Shawn D. Educ: Wartburg Col, B.A, 50. Polit. & Govt. Pos: Committeeman, Local Cmt, Rep. Party, Iowa, 52-65; councilman, Plainfield Town Coun, 58-; chmn, Bremer Co. Rep. Cent. Cmt, 65-; mem, Bremer Co. Draft Bd, 67- Bus. & Prof. Pos: Treas, J. Roach Sons, Inc, 50-56; secy-treas, Roach Farms, Inc, 56-; pres, Plainfield Realty Co, 59-; v.pres, Plainfield Mills, Inc, 68- Mem: Am. Soc. Farm Mgr. and Rural Appraisers; Iowa Soc. Farm Mgr. and Rural Appraisers (past pres); Mason; Lions. Rel: Baptist. Mailing Add: Plainfield, Iowa 50666.

ROACH, WILLIAM NEALE D
Dir. Pub. Rels, Dem. Nat. Cong. Cmt.
b. Chevy Chase, Md, 12/29/12; married; c. Four. Polit. & Govt. Pos: Organizer of campaign and registrn. cmts. in many states and fund raising progs. in major cities for Dem. Party; serv. in admin, exec. and Cong. liaison positions with Dem. Nat. Cmt; mgr, Dem. Nat. Conv, 44, 48, 52 & 56; exec. dir, Dem. Sen. Campaign Cmt, 56; dir, Dem. Cong. Dinners, Wash, D.C, 60, 64 and 66-69; asst. chmn, Presidential Inaugural, 61; exec. dir, Presidential Inaugural Cmt, 65; dir. of pub. rels, Dem. Nat. Cong. Cmt, 65- Bus. & Prof. Pos: Consult, Neale Roach Assocs, 57- Mailing Add: Suite 609, 1725 K St. N.W, Washington, D.C. 20006.

ROARK, WILSON EUGENE R
Chmn, McCurtain Co. Rep. Party, Okla.
b. Plainview, Tex, 10/28/26; s. Cloyd E. Roark and Lucy Lagow R; m. 6/5/50 to Wanda Lu Hill; c. Jonathan Gene and Cynthia Lu. Educ: La. State Univ, Sch. of Med, M.D, 49. Polit. & Govt. Pos: Chmn, McCurtain Co. Rep. Party, Okla. Mil. Serv: Entered as 1st Lt, Air Force, 50, released as Capt, 53, after serv. in 307th Bomb Wing, Strategic Air Command; Maj, Air Force Res, 61. Mem: Lions; Okla. Med. Soc; Am. Med. Asn. Rel: Baptist. Mailing Add: 410 S. Park Dr, Broken Bow, Okla. 72748. (1967)

ROBBIE, JOSEPH, JR. D
b. Sisseton, S.Dak, 7/7/16; s. Joseph Robbie, Sr. and Jennie Ready R; m. 12/28/42 to Elizabeth Ann Lyle; c. Diane Elizabeth, David Lyle, Janet Lee, Joseph Michael, Kathleen Mary, Lynn Margaret, Deborah Ann, Timothy John, Brian Peter, Daniel Thomas and Kevin Patrick. Educ: North. State Teachers Col, 35-38; Univ. S.Dak, A.B, 43 and LL.B, 46; Degree of Spec. Distinction in Oratory and Debate, Pi Kappa Delta; Nat. Discussion Debate Champion, Tau Kappa Alpha; Sigma Tau Delta. Polit. & Govt. Pos: Dep. state attorney, Davison Co, S.Dak, 47-49; S.Dak. State Rep. and Minority Leader, S.Dak. House of Rep, 49-51; chmn, S.Dak. Dem. Cent. Cmt, 48-50; regional dir, Off. of Price Stabilization, 52-53; chmn, Minn. Adv. Cmt. to Dem. Nat. Cmt, 54-58; charter mem. and secy. treas, Twin Cities Metrop. Planning Cmn, Minn, 57-; chmn, Minn. Munic. Cmn, 59-65; campaign chmn, Humphrey for Pres, Charleston, W.Va, 60; fund raising rep, Humphrey for V.Pres, 64. Bus. & Prof. Pos: Attorney-at-law, 46-; instr. in econ, Dakota Wesleyan Univ, 46-51; debate coach and speech instr, Col. St. Catherine, 53-54; exec. secy. and dir, Minn. Candy & Tobacco Distributors Asn, 59-; pres. and managing gen. partner, Miami Dolphins, Ltd, 65- Mil. Serv: Entered as Seaman, Naval Res, 41, released as Lt.(jg), 45, after serv. with Comdr, Seventh Amphibious Force, Pac. Fleet, S.W. Pac, 45; Bronze Star and Leyte, Brunei Bay and Tarakan Invasion Ribbons; Intel. Officer, Naval Res, until 65. Publ: 'Report of Committee on Municipal Annexation and Consolidation,' 59 and 'Report of Commission on Municipal Laws,' 63, Minn. Legis. Research Cmt; 'Ethics in Government,' Va. Law Rev, 61. Mem: Am, S.Dak. and Minn. Bar Asns; Am. Judicature Soc; Nat. Munic. League; Minn. Planning Cmn; Am. Trial Lawyers Asn; K. of C; Citizens League of Minneapolis; Am. Legion; Lawyers Guild of Sir Thomas More; VFW; Elks; Moose; Minn. Planning Asn; admin. bd, Biscayne Col, Miami, 68-; adv. bd, Fla. Mem. Col, Miami, 67-; co-chmn, Notre Dame SUMMA fund raising campaign, 67; chmn, Biscayne Col. Challenge fund raising campaign, 68-69; Easter Seal Chmn, Miami, 69; bd. dirs, Crippled Childrens Soc. of Dade Co, 67- Received Charter J. Ernest O'Brien Award from Nat. Asn. of Tobacco Distributors as Outstanding Dir. of a State Asn, 66; Obtained Am.

Football League Franchise for Miami Dolphins, 65. Rel: Catholic. Legal Res: 339 W. Elmwood Place, Minneapolis, Minn. 55419. Mailing Add: 904 Cargill Bldg, Minneapolis, Minn. 55402.

ROBBINS, MRS. FLOYD T. R
b. Farmville, N.C, 4/26/11; s. William Seth Tyson and Lucy Odell Wingate T; m. 2/22/37 to Floyd Taft Robbins; c. William Tyson. Educ: Smithdeal-Massey Bus. Col, 32-33. Polit. & Govt. Pos: Clerk typist, Treas. Dept, Wash, D.C, 35-42 and Reconstruction Finance Corp, 43-44; secy, War Dept, 42-43; v.chmn, Wilson Co. Rep. Exec. Cmt, N.C, 56-60 and chmn, 60-68. Mem: Pres, Altrusa Club of Wilson, 63-64; dist. dir, Bus. & Prfnl. Women's Club, 59-60 and pres, 57-58; pres, Credit Women's Breakfast Club; jr. regent, Women of the Moose. Rel: Christian Science. Mailing Add: 707 Fleming St, Wilson, N.C. 27893. (1967)

ROBBINS, JESSE R
b. LaFayette, Ind, 10/17/17; s. Frank S. Robbins and Maybelle F. Clawson R; m. 7/17/41 to Virginia Margurite Whaley; c. Lydia E.(Mrs. Farris) and Debra Sue. Educ: Huntington Col; Elkhart Univ; Huntington Col. Alumni. Polit. & Govt. Pos: Precinct committeeman, Rep. Party, Ind, 48-60; field auditor, Ind. Dept. of State Revenue, 55-59; del, State Rep. Conv; committeeman, Fifth Cong. Dist, 60-66 and treas; former chmn, Huntington Co. Rep. Party. Mil. Serv: Entered as Seaman 1/C, Navy, 42, released as PO 1/C, 45, after serv. in Asiatic-Pac. Theater; ETO: Asiatic and Philippine Liberation Medals with Five Battle Stars; Good Conduct Medal. Mem: Optimist; VFW; Lincoln Club; Asn. of Ind. Off, Inc; Methodist Men. Rel: Methodist. Mailing Add: 649 First St, Huntington, Ind. 46750.

ROBBINS, PAUL D
Mem, Calif. Dem. State Cent. Cmt.
b. Buenos Aires, Argentina, 12/28/31; s. Harry Robbins and Celia Waingrod R; m. 8/26/56 to Phyllis Sosnick; c. Shelley Rhonda, Laura Meryl and Gregory Manolo. Educ: Univ. Calif, Berkeley, B.A, 53, J.D, 58; Sigma Alpha Mu; Pi Alpha Delta. Polit. & Govt. Pos: Mem, Calif. Dem. State Cent. Cmt, currently. Bus. & Prof. Pos: Self-employed attorney, 59-; pres, Cal Toy, Inc, 61- Mil. Serv: Entered as Pvt, Army, 53, released as Cpl, 55 after serv. in various Units, Caribbean, 54-55. Mem: Calif. State and Alameda Co. Bar Asns; bd. dirs, Lawyers Club of Alameda Co; bd. dirs, Dem. Lawyers Club of Alameda Co; former pres, Montclair Dem. Club; bd. dirs, Jewish Commun. Center, Oakland. Rel: Jewish. Legal Res: 109 Crocker, Piedmont, Calif. 94611. Mailing Add: 508 16th St, Oakland, Calif. 94612.

ROBBINS, RAY R
Dist. Chmn, Seventh Dist, Idaho State Rep. Cmt.
b. Preston, Idaho, 6/1/12; s. S.P. Robbins and Etta R; m. 6/10/41 to Elva Girardell; c. Paul, Susan and Nancy. Educ: Utah State Univ, grad, 1 year post-grad. study. Polit. & Govt. Pos: Co. chmn. and precinct committeeman, Rep. Party, Idaho; chmn, Idaho Rep. State Cmt, 58-61 and dist. chmn, Seventh Dist, 66-; del, State Rep. Conv, Idaho and Nat. Rep. Conv, 60 & 64. Mil. Serv: Entered as PO 1/C, Navy, 42, released as Lt, 46. Mem: Dir, Idaho Falls C. of C, 64-67; pres, Idaho Falls Automobile Dealers, 66; dir, Idaho Falls Kiwanis Club, 64; mem, Chrysler Corp. Regional Coun, Denver Region; Am. Legion; Elks. Rel: Protestant. Mailing Add: 2805 South Blvd, Idaho Falls, Idaho 83401. (1967)

ROBBINS, WILLIAM RAYMOND R
Chmn, Grundy Co. Rep. Cent. Cmt, Mo.
b. Spickard, Mo, 5/30/16; s. Albert Raymond Robbins and Agnes Nigh R; m. 5/4/50 to Marilyn Henderson; c. Meredith Nadine and Marsha Gail. Educ: Trenton Jr. Col, A.A; Univ. Mo, B.S. in Agr; Alpha Gamma Rho; QEBH. Polit. & Govt. Pos: Chmn, Grundy Co. Rep. Cent. Cmt, Mo, 60-; mem, Mo. State Rep. Cmt, 66-68. Bus. & Prof. Pos: Mem. pub. rels. staff, Fed. Land Bank of St. Louis, 39-42; mkt. news reporter, U.S. Dept. Agr, 42-46; dir. and v.pres, Farmers Mutual Windstorm Ins. Co, 46-59; secy-mgr. and treas, Farmers Mutual Ins. Co. of Grundy Co, 59- Mil. Serv: Entered as Pvt, Marine Corps, 42, released Capt, 51, after serv. in Marine Air Wing, Pac. Theater, 43-46, Res, Capt.(Ret). Mem: Mason; K.T; Shrine; Am. Legion; C. of C. Rel: Disciples of Christ. Mailing Add: 515 DeBolt, Trenton, Mo. 64683.

ROBE, EDWARD SCOTT R
Chmn, Athens Co. Rep. Exec. Cmt, Ohio
b. Cumberland, Ohio, 7/9/36; s. Thurlow Scott Robe and Alice McKibben R; m. 6/19/60 to Sally Ann Allen; c. Lisa Kathleen, Scott McKibben and Jennifer Allen. Educ: Ohio Univ, A.B, 59; Duke Univ, LL.B, 63; Phi Delta Phi. Polit. & Govt. Pos: Solicitor, Zaleski, Ohio, 64-; committeeman, Athens Co. Rep. Cent. Cmt, 64-66, chmn, 66-; chmn, Athens Co. Rep. Exec. Cmt, 69- Bus. & Prof. Pos: Partner in law firm, Rowland, Bridgewater & Robe, 65- Mil. Serv: 2nd Lt, Army, 59-60, serv. in Qm. Training Command; Capt, Ohio Army Nat. Guard, 63-69. Mem: Athens Co. Bar Asn.(pres); Ohio and Am. Bar Asns; Am. Judicature Soc; bd. trustees, Wesley Found, Ohio Univ. Distinguished Mil. Grad, Ohio Univ. ROTC, 59. Rel: Methodist. Mailing Add: 154 Morris Ave, Athens, Ohio 45701.

ROBERSON, DONALD W. D
b. Rutherfordton, N.C, 6/18/21; married. Educ: Grace Bus. Col. Polit. & Gov. Pos: Md. State House of Dels, 65-67; Co-chmn, Dem. Campaign, Prince George's Co, 62; 12th Precinct Dem. Club; past Pres, 9th Precinct Dem. Club; Lanham-Bowie Dem. Club; Prince George's Co. Bd. of License Cmnrs, 63-64. Bus. & Prof. Pos: Register Rep. and agent for investment and ins. co. Mil. Serv: Navy, 38-55. Mem: Masons; Am. Legion; past cubmaster, Pack 728, Boy Scouts; past Pres, Univ. Park Elem. Sch, PTA. Mailing Add: 13002 Ivy Dr, Beltsville, Md. 20705. (1967)

ROBERSON, JOHN R
Mem, N.Y. Rep. State Cmt.
b. New York, N.Y, 12/18/37; s. Earl Dewitt Roberson and Alaze Morris R; single. Polit. & Govt. Pos: Mem. and bd. of elec. inspector, Coliseum Rep. Club, petitions to draft Rockefeller for Pres, N.Y, 60; asst. mailing supv, Rep. City Cmt. and capt, Coliseum Rep. Club, N.Y.C, 61; chmn, Campaign Cmt. for 27th Sen. Dist, 62; mailing supvr, Rockefeller for Pres. Campaign, 64; mem, Co. Rep. Cmt. and mgr, Lindsay for Mayor Campaign, 78th Dist, 65; dist. leader, Key Rep. Club, 78th Dist, Bronx, 65-; del, State Rep. Conv, 66; cand, N.Y. State Constitutional Conv, 66; cand, N.Y. State Assemblyman, 78th Dist, 66; mem, N.Y. Rep. State Cmt, 66- Bus. & Prof. Pos: John Roberson, Assocs, Dance & Fashion Show Promotions. Mil. Serv: Entered as Seaman Recruit, Navy, 55, released as Airman, 56. Owns new and unused stamp collection, all issued in 1937 only. Rel: Catholic. Mailing Add: 1199 Boston Rd, Bronx, N.Y. 10456. (1967)

ROBERSON, PAT HOWELL D
Chmn, St. Clair Co. Dem. Exec. Cmt, Ala.
b. Cropwell, Ala, 3/29/83; s. James Russell Roberson and Adeline Jones R; wid. Educ: Univ. Ala; Lowell Textile Inst. Polit. & Govt. Pos: Chmn, St. Clair Co. Dem. Exec. Cmt, Ala, currently. Bus. & Prof. Pos: Retired pres, Union State Bank, Pell City, Ala. Mem: Mem. bd. educ, St. Clair Co; v.pres, Ala. Baptist State Conv; trustee, Baptist Found, Ala. Rel: Baptist. Legal Res: Cropwell, Ala. 35054. Mailing Add: Pell City, Ala. 35125.

ROBERSON, PAUL DAWSON D
b. Robersonville, N.C, 5/5/11; s. Orlando P. Roberson and Susan Carolyn Jenkins R; m. 10/21/39 to Mary Drusilla Elium; c. Mary Drew. Educ: Duke Univ, A.B, 32, M.A, 35; Duke Univ. Sch. of Law, LL.B, 36; pres, Martin-Beaufort, Washington-Hyde Duke Alumni Asn. Polit. & Govt. Pos: N.C. State Rep, 63-66; attorney, Town of Robersonville; Martin Co. Solicitor. Bus. & Prof. Pos: Lawyer; mem. bd. of mgrs, Robersonville Branch, Wachovia Bank & Trust Co; dir. and attorney, Peoples Savings & Loan Asn; dir, secy-treas, Mutual Tobacco Barn Fire Ins. Asn. Mil. Serv: Army, 43-45. Mem: Martin Co. Bar Asn; Second Judicial Bar Asn; N.C. State Bar; N.C. Bar Asn; dir. and secy, C. of C; pres, Robersonville PTA; dir, Robersonville Jaycees; formerly dir, B.H.M. Regional Libr. Asn; trustee, Jr. O.U.A.M. Children's Home; Mason (32°); Boy Scout Master; pres, Robersonville Rotary; Master, AF&FM Stonewall Lodge. Rel: Methodist, chmn, bd. of stewards; Sunday sch. supt. Mailing Add: Robersonville, N.C. 27871.

ROBERT, ERNEST R
Chmn, Granby Rep. Town Cmt, Mass.
b. Granby, Mass, 10/11/05; s. Ernest Robert and Angliana Pezrearlt R; m. 5/25/32 to Viola E. Theroux; c. Wilfred Robert. Educ: Granby schs, 14-18. Polit. & Govt. Pos: Chmn, Granby Rep. Town Cmt, Mass, 47- Rel: Catholic. Mailing Add: 104 South, Granby, Mass. 01033.

ROBERT, PARIS W. R
b. Whitehall, Mont, 1/25/23; s. Alex W. Robert and Rubie Maxwell R; m. 6/1/46 to Ruth Matheson; c. Art, Rita, Susan, Patrick and Alex. Educ: Kinman Bus. Univ. Polit. Pos: Chmn, Musselshell Co. Rep. Cent. Cmt, Mont, 64-65. Bus. & Prof. Pos: Pres. and v.pres, Miners & Merchants Bank, Roundup, Mont, 48-68; v.pres, Lincoln Security Bank, Libby, 64-66; v.pres, Security Bank, Butte, 64-68; pres, First Nat. Bank of Twin Bridges, currently. Mil. Serv: Entered as Pvt, Army, 43, released as Sgt, 45, after serv. in Engr. Corps, Philippines. Mem: Mont. Bankers Asn; Moose; VFW; Am. Legion; Elks. Rel: Catholic. Mailing Add: 810 E. Orr, Dillon, Mont. 59725.

ROBERTI, DAVID A. D
Calif. State Assemblyman
b. Los Angeles, Calif, 5/4/39; s. Emil Roberti and Elvira Ligrano R; married. Educ: Loyola Univ, Los Angeles, B.A, 61; Univ. South. Calif. Law Sch, J.D, 64; Univ. South. Calif. Law Rev. Polit. & Govt. Pos: Mem, Calif. Dem. Coun; chmn, Los Angeles Co. Young Dem, 65; dep. attorney gen, Calif, 65-66; chmn, 48th Assembly Dist. Dem. Coun, 66; Calif. State Assemblyman, 48th Dist, 67- Mem: Italian-Catholic Fedn; K. of C. Rel: Roman Catholic. Legal Res: 2912 Reservoir St, Los Angeles, Calif. 90026. Mailing Add: State Capitol, Sacramento, Calif. 95814.

ROBERTS, ANTHONY ALONGI R
Mem, Calif. Rep. State Cent. Cmt.
b. Rochester, N.Y, 7/17/24; s. Alfonso Alongi and Angela Farruggia A; m. 12/31/55 to Arlyn Kuhn; c. Dorian Lee and Stephen. Educ: La Salle Exten. Law Sch, currently. Polit. & Govt. Pos: Mem, Gt. Whittier Calif. Rep. Assembly, 69; unit chmn, United Rep. Calif, 69; mem, Los Angeles Rep. Cent. Cmt, 69-; mem, Calif. Rep. State Cent. Cmt, 69- Bus. & Prof. Pos: Exec. secy. and partner, Am. Land, Del Mar Village and Am. Cal. Corps, 62-65; v-pres. and gen. mgr, Niagara Invest. Co, Inc, 65- Mil. Serv: Entered as A/S, Naval Res, 43, released as HA 1/C, 65, after serv. in Pac. Theatre, 64-65. Mem: Town Hall of Calif; Rotary Int; Whittier C. of C; Calif. State C. of C; dist. finance chmn, Boy Scouts; bd. dirs, Whittier Boys Club; K. of C. Rel: Catholic. Legal Res: 7021 S. Friends, Whittier, Calif. 90602. Mailing Add: Box 548, Whittier, Calif. 90608.

ROBERTS, AUSTIN E. D
Educ: Univ. N.Mex, A.B, LL.B. Polit. & Govt. Pos: Spec. asst. attorney gen. assigned to N.Mex. State Hwy. Dept, 56-57; N.Mex. State Rep, 67, majority floor leader, N.Mex. House of Rep, 63-66. Bus. & Prof. Pos: Attorney. Mil. Serv: Naval Air Corps, 4 years. Mem: Past pres, Farmington Lions; past Exalted Ruler, Elks 1747, Farmington Lodge. Rel: Protestant. Mailing Add: 3317 Sunset Ave, Farmington, N.Mex. 87401.

ROBERTS, BETTY R. (MRS. KEITH D. SKELTON) D
Ore. State Sen.
b. Arkansas City, Kans, 2/5/23; d. David Murray Cantrell and Pearl Higgins C; m. 6/15/69 to Keith D. Skelton; c. Dian (Mrs. Odell), John, Jo and Randall Rice. Educ: Portland State Col, B.S; Univ. Ore, M.S; Northwest. Sch. Law, Lewis & Clark Col, LL.B. Polit. & Govt. Pos: Sch. bd. mem, Lynch Sch. Dist, Portland, Ore, 60-66; Ore. State Rep, Dist. 6, 65-68; del, Dem. Nat. Conv, 68; Ore. State Sen, 69- Bus. & Prof. Pos: Dean of girls, Reynolds High Sch, Troutdale, Ore, 58-60; teacher, Centennial High Sch, Gresham, 60-62; teacher, David Douglas High Sch, Portland, 62-66; teacher, Mt. Hood Commun. Col, Gresham, 67-; attorney-at-law, currently. Mem: Ore. and Nat. Educ. Asns; League of Women Voters. Legal Res: 319 S.E. Gilham, Portland, Ore. 97215. Mailing Add: 1220 S.W. Sixth, Portland, Ore. 97204.

ROBERTS, C. A. D
b. Lake Butler, Fla, 11/5/03; m. to Marjorie Lascola R; c. Elizabeth Ann, Barbara Jean, William Van, Avery Clarence. Educ: Union Co. Pub. schs. Polit. & Gov. Pos: Fla. State Rep, 50-66; Fla. State Bd. of Forestry, 52-56; Pres, 56; Draft Bd, 48-50; Bd. of Co. Cmnrs, Chmn, 40-48; Sch. trustee; City

Coun, 2 terms. Bus. & Prof. Pos: Naval stores and livestock. Mem: C. of C; Masons; Bd. of Am. Turpentine Farmers Asn, 64. Rel: Christian. Mailing Add: Route 1, Box 141, Lake Butler, Fla. 32054. (1967)

ROBERTS, CORBIN C. D
b. Jones Co, Ga, 1/26/13; s. Charlie R. Roberts and Sara Summers R; m. 4/24/36 to Sara Greene; c. Sara Faye, James Carlton. Educ: Jones Co. Schs. Polit. & Govt. Pos: Ga. State Rep, 61-66. Bus. & Prof. Pos: Restaurant owner and operator. Mem: Mason; Shriner; Kiwanian; Moose; W.O.W. Rel: Methodist. Mailing Add: Gray, Ga. 31032. (1967)

ROBERTS, DAN J. D
b. 1911. Polit. & Govt. Pos: Chmn, Walton-Boone Planning Cmn. and mem. exec. cmt, Ky. Planning League; mem. city coun, Walton, Ky, 46-50, mayor, 46-48; mem, Walton-Verona Bd. of Educ, 52-60; Ky. State Rep, 60-62 & 66-68. Bus. & Prof. Pos: Ins. agent. Mem: Lions; Boone Co. Asn. for Retarded Children; Boone Co. Dem. Club; Past Master and Dist. Dep. Grand Master, Masons. Rel: Methodist. Mailing Add: Walton, Ky. 41094. (1967)

ROBERTS, DONALD DUANE R
Chmn, Lincoln Parish Rep. Orgn, La.
b. Jamestown, N.Dak, 2/18/29; s. Calvin Boyd Roberts and Irma Roberts R; m. 6/28/52 to Ann Marie Valenti; c. Marie Therese, Marie Christine, Marie Kathleen, Susan Marie, Robert Joseph and Maribeth. Educ: Jamestown Col, B.S, 50; Loyola Univ, Ill, M.S, 57, Ph.D, 62. Polit. & Govt. Pos: Chmn, Lincoln Parish Rep. Orgn. and mem, Rep. State Cent. Cmt, La, 66- Bus. & Prof. Pos: Research chemist, Sherwin Williams, Chicago, Ill, 52-54; group leader, Borg Warner Corp, DesPlaines, 54-58; research chemist, Am. Oil Co, Whiting, Ind, 58-60. Mil. Serv: Entered as Cadet, Navy 48, released, 49 after serv. at Naval Flight Sch, Pensacola, Fla, 48-49. Publ: Auth. of 18 sci. papers in J. Org. Chem, 62- Mem: Sigma Xi; Am. Chem. Soc. Am. Chem. Soc. predoctoral research fel; research grants from Research Corp. Am. and Am. Chem. Soc. Petroleum Research Fund. Rel: Roman Catholic. Mailing Add: 2301 Cypress Springs Ave, Ruston, La. 71270.

ROBERTS, DONALD KEITH D
Constable, North Reading, Mass.
b. Winchester, Mass, 3/11/27; s. Harold L. Roberts and Ruth L. Elting R; m. 4/23/48 to Sally Ann McPartland; c. Ruth Ann, Lynee, Dawn, Donald Keith, Jr. and Todd Leonard. Educ: U.S. Air Force Tech. Schs, radar supvr, dipl, 50; City and Town Govt. Seminar, Boston, Mass, citation, 64. Polit. & Govt. Pos: Selectman, North Reading, Mass, 62-67, constable, 67- Bus. & Prof. Pos: Pres. and dir, North Reading Bd. of Trade, 62-63. Mil. Serv: Entered as Pvt, Army Air Force, 43, released as Corp, 50, after serv. in Mil. Air Transport Serv, U.S, 47-50. Mem: Am. Legion; Mass. Selectman's Asn; Dist. Cmnr, Boy Scouts. Rel: Protestant. Mailing Add: 171 Haverhill St, North Reading, Mass. 01864.

ROBERTS, EMMETT S. D
b. Clearwater, Fla, 6/23/13; m. to Jenlaura Geer R; c. Anna Maria, Patricia Jane. Educ: Univ. of Fla, B.S, 40; Sigma Phi Epsilon. Polit. & Gov. Pos: Fla. State Rep, 54-66; past Vice Chmn, Gov. Bd, Cent. and S. Fla. Flood Control. Bus. & Prof. Pos: Ins. agent; mortgage broker. Mil. Serv: Army qm. corps; Lt. Col, Active Army Res. Mem: Past pres, past dist. gov. of S. Fla. Lions; Am. Legion; VFW; past Dir, C. of C; area Chmn, March of Dimes; past Pres, Palm Beach Co. Resources Develop. Bd; past Exalted Ruler, Elks; Masons; Shriners; Res. Officers Asn. Rel: Episcopal, Vestry, Bd. of Trustees, past Sr. Warden. Mailing Add: 636 S.E. Second St, Belle Glade, Fla. 33430. (1967)

ROBERTS, FARRELL E. R
b. Salt Lake City, Utah, 3/29/22; m. 1948 to Phyllis E. Miller; c. Mark F. and Bruce E. Educ: U.S. Naval Acad, B.S; Univ. Mich, J.D, 49; Delta Sigma Phi; Delta Theta Phi. Polit. & Govt. Pos: Former asst. prosecuting attorney, Oakland Co, Mich; Mich. State Rep, 56-60; Mich. State Sen, 60-66; Circuit judge, Mich, currently. Bus. & Prof. Pos: Attorney-at-law. Mil. Serv: Combat vet; Comdr, Naval Res. Mem: Oakland Co, Mich. and Am. Bar Asns; Am. Judicature Soc; Amvets. Rel: Congregational. Legal Res: 1311 Porters Lane, Bloomfield Hills, Mich. 48013. Mailing Add: 1200 N. Telegraph Rd, Pontiac, Mich. 48053.

ROBERTS, FAY EDWIN D
b. Council Grove, Kans, 12/13/14; s. Eugene Alexander Roberts and Myrtle Eliza Eckert R; m. 2/10/50 to Edith Marie Cale; c. Donna June (Mrs. Fred Marvin Roberts). Educ: Kans. State Teachers Col, Emporia, B.S. in educ, 38; Pi Kappa Delta. Polit. & Govt. Pos: Chmn, Morris Co. Dem. Party, Kans, 58-65; postmaster, Council Grove, Kans, 65- Mil. Serv: Entered as Pvt, Army, 42, released as Sgt, 45, after serv. in Scotland, England, North Africa and Alaska; Good Conduct Medal; North African Invasion Ribbon; Expert Rifleman Medal. Mem: Am. Legion; VFW; AF&AM; Royal Arch and Royal and Select Mason; Knights Templar, AAONMS. Rel: Christian Church. Mailing Add: 221 Simcock, Council Grove, Kans. 66846.

ROBERTS, FRANK LIVEZEY D
Ore. State Rep.
b. Boise, Idaho, 12/28/15; s. Walter Scott Roberts and Mary Elizabeth Livezey R; div; c. Mary Linda and Leslie. Educ: Pac. Univ, Forest Grove, Ore, B.A, 38; Univ. Wis, Ph.M, 43; Stanford Univ, Ph.D, 54. Polit. & Govt. Pos: Chmn, Multnomah Co. Dem. Cent. Cmt, 60-63; mem, Portland Metrop. Study Cmn, 64-; mem, Mt. Hood Commun. Col. Bd, 65-; permanent chmn, Ore. Dem. State Conv, 66; Ore. State Rep, Sixth Dist, 67-; del, Dem. Nat. Conv, 68. Bus. & Prof. Pos: Prof. of speech, Portland State Univ, 46-, dean of undergrad. studies and assoc. dean of faculty, 63-66. Mil. Serv: Entered as Aviation Cadet, Army, 43, released as 1st Lt, 46, after serv. in Army Airways Commun. Serv, ETO, 46. Publ: Basic Parliamentary Procedure, Rigdon, 66. Mem: Portland City Club. Mailing Add: P.O. Box 751, Portland, Ore. 97207.

ROBERTS, GODFREY MEYER, JR. R
Mayor, Pierre, S.Dak.
b. Pierre, S.Dak, 8/30/23; s. Godfrey Meyer Roberts, Sr. and Bertha Brandhuber R; m. 8/9/52 to Henrietta Rudolph; c. Christine and Thomas. Educ: Univ. S.Dak, B.B.A; Beta Theta Pi. Polit. & Govt. Pos: Mayor, Pierre, S.Dak, 65- Bus. & Prof. Pos: Pres, State Publ. Co, 50-; dir, Pierre Nat. Bank, 60-; pres, S.Dak. Commercial Printers Asn, 62 & 63; pres, bd, St. Marys Sch. Practical Nursing, 64-; dir, Gr. S.Dak, Asn, 64-; chmn, S.Dak. Police & Munic. Retirement Bd, 67- Mil. Serv: Entered as Pvt, Army, 43, released as T/Sgt, 45, after serv. in Inf, ETO, 44-45; ETO Ribbon with 3 Stars; Bronze Star. Mem: Kiwanis; Elks; Izaak Walton League; Am. Legion; VFW. Alumnus of the Year Award, Univ. S.Dak. Sch. Bus, 66. Rel: Congregational. Legal Res: 303 E. Sioux, Pierre, S.Dak, 57501. Mailing Add: Box 100, Pierre, S.Dak. 57501.

ROBERTS, GRACE ESTER R
b. Rutland, Vt, 4/17/93; widow; c. Two. Educ: S. Royalton High Sch. Polit. & Govt. Pos: Vt. State Rep, 57-59; 63-65; Farm Bur. State Bd; Co. Bd; trustee, Pub. Libr, 8 years. Bus. & Prof. Pos: Homemaker. Mem: Windsor Co. Farm Bur. Woman's Chmn. and 4-H Club Leader. Rel: Methodist. Mailing Add: Bethel, Vt. 05032. (1967)

ROBERTS, HOUSTON W. D
b. Washington Co, Fla, 9/5/17; m. to Lillon Johnson R; c. Claude Delano, Houston Julian. Educ: pub. schs, Suwannee Co. Polit. & Gov. Pos: Fla. State Sen, 60-66; Fla. State Rep, 52-60; City Cmn. Bus. & Prof. Pos: farmer; hardware merchant. Mem: Lions; C. of C; Civil Air Patrol. Rel: Church of God. Mailing Add: Route 5, Box 262, Live Oak, Fla. 32060. (1967)

ROBERTS, JAMES ALLEN R
b. Ohio, 12/30/28; s. Dr. Harry Mark Roberts and Madge Allen R; m. 10/4/54 to Barbar Jane Schafer; c. Robyn Lynn, Stephen Allen, Holly Ann and Jamie Lee. Educ: Ohio State Univ, 48-50; Omaha Univ, 54; Journalism Soc. Polit. & Govt. Pos: Admin. asst. to U.S. Rep, Glenn Cunningham, Nebr, 63- Bus. & Prof. Pos: News dir, KMTV, Omaha, Nebr, 54-63; reporter, Ohio State Journal, Columbus, Ohio, 45-50. Mil. Serv: Entered as Pvt, Air Force, 50, released as S/Sgt, 54, after serv. in Info. Div, Strategic Air Command Hq; Nat. Defense Serv. Medal; Good Conduct Medal. Mem: Master Mason, Nebr. Lodge 1; Scottish Rite, Omaha Consistory; Am. Legion: Cong. Secy. Club; Omaha Press Club; Nat. Press Photographers. Rel: Episcopal. Mailing Add: 3105 S. 123rd St, Omaha, Nebr. 68144. (1967)

ROBERTS, JAMES HAZELTON R
Mem, Rep. State Exec. Cmt, W.Va.
b. Parkersburg, W.Va, 8/26/25; s. Leslie Van Dyke Roberts and Dorothy Folts R; m. 9/21/52 to Patricia Higgins; c. Sara Dorothy, Charlotte Ann and Christine Lee. Educ: Ohio State Univ, B.S; Univ. of Mich, M.S; Kappa Alpha; Phi Epsilon Kappa; Lettermans Club. Polit. & Govt. Pos: Chmn, Co. Rep. Exec. Cmt, W.Va, 57-; del, Rep. Nat. Conv, 60 & 68; mem, Rep. State Exec. Cmt, W.Va, 64- Mil. Serv: Entered as Seaman, Navy, 43, released as Athletic Specialist, 46; Good Conduct, Victory and Asian-Pac. Ribbons. Mem: Am. Legion; Lions; Moose; VFW; Farm Bur. Rel: Methodist. Mailing Add: Elizabeth, W.Va. 26143.

ROBERTS, JAMES WALKER D
b. Alexandria, Va, 12/2/91; m. to Elsie Palmer Brown R. Educ: Friends High Sch, Wash, D.C. Polit. & Govt. Pos: Va. State Del, 48-68; mem, Lay Bd. of De Paul Hosp, Norfolk; mem, Jamestown Corp. and Jamestown Found. Bus. & Prof. Pos: Mem. and retired chmn. bd, Henry B. Gilpin Co. Mil. Serv: Capt, Army Field Artil, 315th Regt, 80th Div, Blue Ridge; Lt. Col, commanded 1st Bn, Va. State Guard, 46. Mem: Lions (past pres. and past dep. dist. gov); C. of C; Am. Legion; YMCA (mem. bd. dir, Norfolk Navy Br). Norfolk First Citizen Cosmopolitan Club Medal, 43. Rel: Episcopal. Mailing Add: 6435 Tidewater Dr, Norfolk, Va. 23509.

ROBERTS, JOHN A. D
b. Lawrenceburg, Tenn, 3/9/04; s. Thomas W. Roberts and Tessie L. Marston R; m. 12/20/25 to Beatrice Estella Crowell; c. Johnny L, Kenneth, Charles M. and Mary E. Educ: Lawrence Co. High Sch, 4 years. Polit. & Govt. Pos: Campaign mgr, Local Campaigns, 24-; magistrate, Lawrence Co. Court, 33-42; campaign mgr, Sen. K.D. McKellar, Ross Bass for Cong. and Ross Bass for Sen; alternate del, Dem. Nat. Conv, 68. Bus. & Prof. Pos: Tie and lumber inspector, R.R, 22-29; self-employed, Milling Bus, 29-36 and Hardware Bus, 36-69. Mem: Mason; pres, Lions; pres, U.S. Hwy. 64 Improvement Asn. Rel: Methodist; Chmn. of Bd, First Methodist Church. Mailing Add: 324 Lafayette Ave, Lawrenceburg, Tenn. 38464.

ROBERTS, KENNETH ALLISON D
b. Piedmont, Ala, 11/1/12; s. John Franklin Roberts and Josephine Burton R; m. 9/22/53 to Margaret Hamilton McMillan; c. Margaret Hamilton and Allison McMillan. Educ: Samford Col, 29; Univ. Ala, LL.B, 35; Alpha Tau Omega; Phi Alpha Delta; Blue Key. Polit. & Govt. Pos: Mem, State Bd. Vets. Affairs; Ala. State Sen, 42; U.S. Rep, Ala, 51-65, mem, Interstate and For. Commerce Cmn, U.S. House of Rep; gen. counsel, Vehicle Equipment Cmn, D.C, 65-69; mem, Nat. Hwy. Safety Adv. Cmt, 67- Bus. & Prof. Pos: Attorney-at-law, Anniston, Ala, 35, 45-50, Talladega, 37-42; pres, Piedmont Develop. Co. Mil. Serv: Entered as Ens, Navy, 42, released as Lt, 46, after serv. in USS Micka, Atlantic and Pac. Theaters, 44-46; Lt. Comdr, Naval Res. (Ret); Atlantic and Pac. Theater Ribbons. Mem: Am, Ala. and D.C. Bar Asns; Nat. Press Club; Am. Legion; VFW; 40 et 8; Mason; Elks; past dist. gov, Lions; Cong. Country Club. Legal Res: 429 Belleville Ave, Brewton, Ala. 36426. Mailing Add: 1026 17th St. N.W, Washington, D.C. 20036.

ROBERTS, KENNETH LEWIS R
b. Dunganon, Va, 12/12/32; s. Clarence E. Roberts and Kathrine Osborne R; m. 9/10/55 to Anne Foster Cook; c. Stephen, Kenneth L, Jr. and Patrick. Educ: Vanderbilt Univ, B.A, 54; Vanderbilt Law Sch, LL.B, 59; pres, Phi Delta Phi; Order of the Coif; Omicron Delta Kappa; Student Christian Asn; Ace Club; V Club; pres, Sigma Chi; football scholarship, Vanderbilt Univ. Hon. LL.D, Steed Col. Polit. & Govt. Pos: Pres, Nashville Young Rep. Club, Tenn, 63; gen. counsel, Tenn. Fedn. Young Rep. Clubs, 63-65; mgr, State Rep. Campaign, 64; del, Rep. Nat. Conv, 64; chmn, Davidson Co. Rep. Party, 64-65; treas, Tenn. Rep. Party, 67. Bus. & Prof. Pos: Sales trainee, Eastman Chem. Prod, Inc, 54-55; asst. prof. law, Vanderbilt Univ. Law Sch, 59-60, lecturer-

in-law, 60; assoc, Waller, Lansden & Dortch Attorneys, 60-66; exec. v.pres, Commerce Union Bank, 66- Mil. Serv: Entered as 2nd Lt, Army, 55, released as Capt, 57, after serv. in Chem. Corps. Mem: Am, Tenn. and Nashville Bar Asns; Am. and Tenn. Bankers Asn; bd. gov, Nashville Area C. of C; YMCA; Mason; Jaycees; adv. bd, Salvation Army Bd. Dirs; Am. Red Cross; treas, Nashville Better Bus. Bur; bd. trustees, Cumberland Col; alumni bd. dirs, Vanderbilt Univ. Founder's Medalist, First in Class, Vanderbilt Law Sch. Rel: Presbyterian. Mailing Add: 2322 Golf Club Lane, Nashville, Tenn. 37215.

ROBERTS, KENNETH LLOYD R
S.Dak. State Sen.
b. Larchwood, Iowa, 6/30/07; s. Seymour J. Roberts and Beletha Celand R; second marriage 5/17/62 to Midred H. Lux; c. Marilyn I.(Mrs. Keith Williams). Educ: Grammar sch. Polit. & Govt. Pos: S.Dak. State Rep, 67- Bus. & Prof. Pos: Affil. with Rapid City Laundry & Dry Cleaners, S.Dak, 28-, pres. and prin. stockholder, currently; v.pres. and gen. mgr, D.T.W. Inc. and DBA Servall Towel & Linen Supply, 63- Mem: Am. Inst. Laundering (nat. dir, 59-67, pres, 64-65); Nat. Inst. Dry Cleaning; Linen Supply Asn. of Am; Elks (past exalted ruler and past state pres); Mason (32°); York Rite; Scottish Rite; Shrine. Rel: Episcopal. Legal Res: 312 Main, Rapid City, S.Dak. 55701. Mailing Add: P.O. Box 191, Rapid City, S.Dak. 57701.

ROBERTS, LEONA GRACE D
V.Chmn, Seward Co. Dem. Cmt, Kans.
b. Beaver Co, Okla, 7/20/09; d. Merton Clark Edgerly and Emma Marie Kruse E; m. 1/23/27 to Wiley Thomas Roberts; c. Thomas E. and Merle D. Educ: Emporia Teachers Col, 26. Polit. & Govt. Pos: Precinct committeewoman, Seward Co. Dem. Cmt, Kans, 52-, v.chmn, 56-62 & 68-, chmn, 62-68; first dist. v.pres, Woodrow Wilson Luncheon Club, 63-64; treas, Seward Co. Dem. Club, 67-; Dem. presidential elector, Kans, 68. Bus. & Prof. Pos: Off. mgr, Roberts Machine Shop, 29- Mem: Rebekah Lodge; former pres. and child welfare chmn, Am. Legion Auxiliary; pub. rels. chmn, Liberal Womans Club (former pres); Seward Co. chmn, Kans. Crippled Children Soc. Rel: First Christian. Legal Res: 805 N. Washington, Liberal, Kans. 67901. Mailing Add: P.O. Box 343, Liberal, Kans. 67901.

ROBERTS, MILBURN F. R
N.H. State Rep.
b. North Conway, 7/12/16; married; c. Three. Educ: Univ. N.H. Polit. & Govt. Pos: Trustee, North Conway Pub. Libr. Asn; cmnr, North Conway Water Precinct, 45-57; clerk bd. of selectmen, North Conway, 52-54; del, N.H. Rep. State Conv, 52-62; N.H. State Rep, 55- Bus. & Prof. Pos: Ins. and real estate. Mil. Serv: Army, 2nd Armored Div, African-Sicilian-European Campaign; Purple Heart. Mem: Am. Legion; F&AM. Rel: Episcopal. Mailing Add: North Conway, N.H. 03860.

ROBERTS, PHYLLIS ARENE D
Secy, Mesa Co. Dem. Cent. Cmt, Colo.
b. Aspen, Colo, 11/28/22; d. Jake Fred Lucksinger and Maybird Norris L; m. 4/26/41 to Robert Donald Roberts; c. John Douglas and Sue Ann. Educ: Basalt Union High Sch, 12 years. Polit. & Govt. Pos: Committeewoman, Mesa Co. Dem. Cent. Cmt, Colo, 64, v.chmn, 66 and secy, 69- Bus. & Prof. Pos: Bookkeeper, City Nat. Bank, Kansas City, Mo, 42-49; employee, Co. Clerks Off, Grand Junction, Colo, 67-69. Mem: Epsilon Sigma Alpha; Jane Jefferson Club. Rel: Congregational. Mailing Add: 1415 Houston St, Grand Junction, Colo. 81501.

ROBERTS, PRICE PARK R
Chmn, Leslie Co. Rep. Party, Ky.
b. Hyden, Ky, 7/22/27; s. Robert Roberts and Nancy Asher R; single. Educ: East. Ky. State Univ, B.S, 65. Polit. & Govt. Pos: Chmn, Leslie Co. Rep. Party, 65- Bus. & Prof. Pos: Teacher, Leslie Co. Bd. of Educ, Ky, 50-68; dir, Neighborhood Youth Corps, 68- Mil. Serv: Entered as Pvt, Army, 46, released as T/5, 47, after serv. in G.Hq, Tokyo, Japan, Far East Command. Mem: Ky. Educ. Asn; Leslie Co. Teacher's Asn; Leslie Co. Fish & Game Club; Leslie Co. Sports Club; Mason. Rel: Church of Christ. Mailing Add: Box 165, Hyden, Ky. 41749.

ROBERTS, RAY D
U.S. Rep, Tex.
b. Collin Co, Tex, 3/28/13; s. Roy C. Roberts (deceased) and Margaret Emma R; m. to Elizabeth Bush; c. Mrs. Tom Murray, III. Educ: Tex. A&M; N.Tex. State; Tex. Univ. Polit. & Govt. Pos: Former mem. staff of U.S. Rep. Sam Rayburn, Tex; Tex. State Sen, 55-62; U.S. Rep, Tex, 62- Mil. Serv: Navy; Capt, Naval Res. Legal Res: McKinney, Tex. 75069. Mailing Add: 2129 Cannon House Office Bldg, Washington, D.C. 20515.

ROBERTS, RAYMOND ROHRER D
b. Farmington, Mo, 7/20/33; s. Raymond Silas Roberts and Marguarite Rohrer R; m. 4/13/57 to Ruth Amanda McHaney; c. Raymond R, Jr, Ruth Amanda and Jonathan McHaney. Educ: Westminster Col, 51-53; Mo. Univ, LL.B, 57; Beta Theta Pi; Phi Alpha Delta. Polit. & Govt. Pos: Prosecuting attorney, St. Francois Co, Mo, 59-63; Mo. State Rep, 63-67. Bus. & Prof. Pos: Asst. secy-treas, Roberts-Lloyd Co, Inc, 59-63; secy-treas, Kewill Co, Inc, 63- Mil. Serv: Entered as Pvt, Army Nat. Guard, 57, released as S/Sgt, 62. Publ: 'Conflict of Laws—Family Law,' Mo. Law Rev, 64, 'Federal Tort Claims Act,' 56; various others. Mem: Am, Mo. and St. Francois Co. Bar Asns; Kiwanis; C. of C. Rel: Presbyterian. Mailing Add: 608 W. Columbia, Farmington, Mo. 63640. (1967)

ROBERTS, RONALD E. D
b. Abbott, Tex, 12/21/34; s. Thomas Roy Roberts (deceased) and Ethel Hargrove R; m. 8/27/65 to Carol Chernosky. Educ: N.Tex. State Univ, B.S, 57; Baylor Univ, M.S, 65; Pi Sigma Alpha; Phi Alpha Theta; pres, Chancery Club. Polit. Pos: Tex. State Rep, Dist. 42, Hill and Navarro Co, 60-66. Bus. & Prof. Pos: Instr, Polit. Sci, Houston Baptist Col, 66 and Hill Jr. Col, Summer, 63 and 64. Publns: 'Freedom to Teach and Learn,' Tex. Coun. of Soc. Studies, Fall, 63; Report of the House Textbook Investigating Committee of the 57th Legislature, State Of Tex, Spring, 63. Mem: Am. Polit. Sci. Asn; South. Polit. Sci. Asn; Southwest. Soc. Sci. Asn; Atlantic Coun. for the U.S; Acad. Polit. Sci; Jr. C. of C, Tex. Rel: Methodist. Mailing Add: 627 E. Elm St, Hillsboro, Tex. 76645. (1967)

ROBERTS, ROSCOE O. JR. D
b. Bon Air, Talladega Co, 6/30/23; s. Roscoe Owen Roberts and Louise Thayer R; m. to Jane Grote R; c. Roscoe Owen, III, Marion Grote, Ann Louise, William Barrier and Carl Thayer. Educ: Univ. of Ala. with degree in Bus. Admin. and LL.B. Phi Delta Phi; Phi Delta Theta. Polit. & Govt. Pos: Ala. State Sen, 62-66; Ala. State House of Rep, 2 terms, 54, 58. Mem: Kiwanis Club. Mailing Add: P.O. Box 287, Huntsville, Ala. 35804.

ROBERTS, THOMAS JEFFERSON D
b. Cleveland, Ohio, 4/8/41; s. Thomas Jefferson Roberts and Mary Nester R; m. to Lydia Adele Logwin; c. Beverly Carol and Shannon Adele. Educ: East. Ky. State Col; Univ. Ky. Col. of Law, J.D; Sigma Alpha; Debate Team; Track Team. Polit. & Govt. Pos: Dem. cand, U.S. Rep, Ky, 68. Mem: Am. and Ky. State Bar Asns; Bell Co. Bar Asn.(secy-treas, 67-69); Practicing Law Inst. of N.Y; Am. Judicature Soc; Jaycees. Rel: Presbyterian. Legal Res: 206 Summit Dr, Middlesboro, Ky. 40965. Mailing Add: P.O. Box J, Middlesboro, Ky. 40965.

ROBERTS, TREVOR CAROL R
b. Chicago, Ill, 7/4/31; s. Trevor Garfield Roberts and Helen R; m. 3/3/61 to Cynthia May Kaiser; c. Kathleen Celia, Elizabeth Carol and Cynthia Ann. Educ: Northwest. Univ, B.S. in Bus. Admin, 53; Chi Psi. Polit. & Govt. Pos: Mem, Reagan for Gov. Cmt, San Francisco, Calif, 66; cmnr, San Francisco Port Authority, 67-; alternate del, Rep. Nat. Conv, 68. Bus. & Prof. Pos: Pres, Hybrinetics, Inc, 67-69. Mil. Serv: Navy, 53-56, Lt.(jg), serv. in Comdesron Thirty, Atlantic Fleet, 54-56. Mem: Olympic Club, San Francisco; World Trade Club. Order of Maritime Merit. Rel: Methodist. Mailing Add: 190 Encinal, Atherton, Calif. 94025.

ROBERTS, VIRGIL H. R
Chmn, Schuyler Co. Rep. Party, Ill.
b. Augusta, Ill, 6/29/16; s. Herman Roberts and Iva Harris R; m. 11/12/38 to Mildred Kathryn Ayers; c. Mary Ruth (Mrs. John Phillips), Shirley Jean (Mrs. Kay Lord), Bettie Kathryn (Mrs. Keith White), Ronald Glenn and Paul Herman. Educ: Augusta High Sch, 4 years. Polit. & Govt. Pos: Secy, Augusta Bd. Educ, Ill, 46-51, pres, 61-64; supvr, Birmingham Twp, 50-; precinct committeeman, Birmingham Twp. Rep. Party, 50-; chmn, Schuyler Co. Rep. Party. 60- Bus. & Prof. Pos: Lifetime farmer. Mem: Mason; Consistory; Shrine; Farm Bur. Rel: Methodist. Mailing Add: Route 1, Augusta, Ill. 62311.

ROBERTS, WILBER EASTES D
Chmn, Dent Co. Dem. Party, Mo.
b. Salem, Mo, 10/7/09; s. Thomas Mattison Roberts and Alberta Hayes R; m. 5/30/30 to Bonnie Jewel Black; c. Ronald Dean and Lavonne Silva. Polit. & Govt. Pos: Mem, Dem. Cmt, 58-63; chmn, Dent Co. Dem. Party, Mo, 58- Bus. & Prof. Pos: Contractor. Mem: Odd Fellows. Rel: Southern Baptist. Mailing Add: Route 3, Salem, Mo. 65560.

ROBERTS, WILLIAM LOGAN D
Kans. State Rep.
b. Emporia, Kans, 1/23/30; s. William John Roberts and Irene Viola Logan R; single. Educ: Kans. State Teachers Col, B.S. in Educ, 51; Univ. Kans. Sch. Law, LL.B, 56; Phi Delta Phi; Sigma Tau Gamma. Polit. & Govt. Pos: Asst. attorney, State Hwy. Cmn, Kans, 57-61; asst. attorney, Wyandotte Co, 63-65; Kans. State Rep, Fifth Dist, 65- Mil. Serv: Entered as Pvt, Marine Corps Res, 51, released as 1st Lt, 53, after serv. in Ninth Staff Group, Kansas City; Lt. Col, Marine Corps Res, currently serv. as Exec. Officer, 24th Marine Regt, Kansas City. Mem: Kans. and Wyandotte Co. Bar Asns; Am. Trial Lawyers Asn; Marine Corps Res. Officers Asn; Mason; Scottish Rite; Am. Legion. Rel: Presbyterian. Mailing Add: 3800 Booth St, Kansas City, Kans. 66103.

ROBERTSON, A. WILLIS D
m. to Gladys Churchill; c. A. Willis, Jr. and Marion Gordon. Educ: Univ. Richmond, B.A. and LL.B; Wash. and Lee Univ; Phi Kappa Alpha; Omicron Delta Kappa; Phi Beta Kappa; Phi Alpha Delta. Hon. LL.D, Univ. Richmond and Col. William and Mary. Polit. & Govt. Pos: Va. State Sen, 16-22; commonwealth attorney, Rockbridge Co, Va, 22-28; chmn, Cmn. of Game and Inland Fisheries, 26-33; U.S. Rep, Va, 32-46; U.S. Sen, Va, 46-66. Mil. Serv: Army, 17-19. Mem: Jamestowne Soc; SAR; Soc. of the Cincinnati. Mailing Add: 502 Highland Rd, Lexington, Va. 24450.

ROBERTSON, C. DONALD D
b. Clarksburg, Harrison Co, W.Va, 6/9/26; s. Aubrey D. Robertson and Exie Mae Frame R; m. to Shirley Anne Stotler; c. April Lynn and C. Donald, Jr. Educ: Salem Col, A.B; W.Va. Univ, LL.B. Polit. & Govt. Pos: Past treas, Young Dem. Club of W.Va; past pres, Young Dem. Club of Harrison Co; city attorney for Salem, and acted as attorney for Harrison Co. Court in develop. of flood projs. and the co. airport; prosecuting attorney of Harrison Co, 52-56; W.Va. State Del, 56-58; attorney for Clarksburg Sanit. Bd, 56-60; W.Va. Attorney Gen, 60-68; secy. of Prosecuting Attorneys Asn. of W.Va, 61. Mil. Serv: Navy, World War II. Mem: Lions, Moose; Elks; Am. Legion; Jr. C. of C; Harrison Co. Bar Asn; W.Va. and Am. Bar Asns. Awarded the Jaycee (Jr.) 60 Distinguished Serv. Award for distinguished achievement, leadership and serv. to the commun. Rel: Presbyterian. Legal Res: 3504 Noyes Ave, S.E. Charleston, W.Va. 25304. Mailing Add: Capitol Bldg, Charleston, W.Va. 25305. (1967)

ROBERTSON, (ANNA) CAROL R
State Committeewoman, Okla. Rep. Party
b. Gage, Okla, 12/25/13; d. Lewis Hampton Long and Louis L. Geier L; m. 4/1/34 to Roma C. Robertson. Educ: High Sch, Shattuck, Okla. and exten. classes in Bible, bookkeeping, art and psychol, 35-36 & 52-61. Polit. & Govt. Pos: Precinct chmn, Wllis Co. Rep. Party, Okla, 59-60, v.chmn, 61-62, 63-64 & 65-66, chmn, 67-68; del, Rep. state and dist.conv, 61-; mem, Rep. State Cmt, 61-, mem, rules and order cmt, 62, resolutions cmt, 64 and resolutions cmt. in the dist, 68; mem, State Rep. Party Auditing Cmt, 67-68; alternate del-at-lg, Rep. Nat. Conv, 68; mem, Gov. Cmt. Children and Youth; State Committeewoman, Okla. Rep. Party, 69- Bus. & Prof. Pos: Merchant, music store, 46- Mem: Bus. and Prfnl. Women; Westerner Art Club; Missionary

Orgn; C. of C; Ellis Co. Sportsman Club. Rel: Christian; adult Bible teacher. Legal Res: 811 S. Locust, Shattuck, Okla. 73858. Mailing Add: P.O. Box 111, Shattuck, Okla. 73858.

ROBERTSON, DOUGLAS DUNCAN R
Chmn, Nashua City Rep. Cmt, N.H.
b. South Bend, Ind, 11/10/27; s. Norman T. Robertson (deceased) and Edna Mills R; m. 12/23/50 to Helen M. Palmer; c. Douglas D, Jr. and Janet R; Educ: Bowling Green State Univ, 49-50; Univ. Notre Dame, B.A, 52 and LL.B, 55; Phi Gamma Delta. Polit. & Govt. Pos: Chief trial attorney, Internal Revenue Serv, Boston, Mass, 56-63; chmn, Nashua Cleveland for Cong. Cmt, N.H, 64; chmn, Nashua City Rep. Cmt, N.H, 65-67. Bus. & Prof. Pos: Partner, Smith, Welts, & Robertson, 63- Mil. Serv: Entered as Seaman, Navy Air Corps, 45, released as PO 2/C, 48, after serv. in Antarctic Expedition, 46-47; Capt, Army Res, 62. Mem: Ind, Mass, N.H. and Nashua Bar Asns; Lions. Admitted to practice before U.S. Supreme Court, U.S. Dist. Courts for Mass. and N.H. and U.S. Tax Court. Rel: Congregational. Mailing Add: 42 Berkeley St, Nashua, N.H. 03060.

ROBERTSON, EDWARD D. D
Ala. State Rep.
b. Northport, Ala, 10/16/30; s. J.D. Robertson and Myra Marie Parsons R; m. 3/15/50 to Sarah Imogene Moore; c. Donna Marie. Educ: Gorgas High Sch, 12 years. Polit. & Govt. Pos: City councilman, Northport, Ala, 64-67; Ala. State Rep, 67- Bus. & Prof. Pos: V.pres, Local 351, United Rubber Workers, 65-67. Mem: United Rubber Workers. Rel: Baptist. Mailing Add: 13-A Northwood Lake, Northport, Ala. 35476.

ROBERTSON, EDWARD PEYTON, JR. R
Chmn, Stone Co. Rep. Party, Miss.
b. McComb, Miss, 12/25/39; s. Edward Peyton Robertson, Sr. and Delva Welch R; m. 6/11/62 to Barbara Ruth Davis; c. Tara Renee and Edward Peyton, III. Educ: Southwest Jr. Col, 1 year; Miss. South. Col, 2 years; Miss. Baptist Hosp, Med. Tech, 60; Phi Kappa Tau. Polit. & Govt. Pos: Radiological technician, Miss. Civil Defense Coun, 66-67; chmn, Stone Co. Rep. Party, 68- Bus. & Prof. Pos: Chmn, Nat. Found, Stone Co, Miss, 61-; adminstr, Azalea Gardens Nursing Center, Wiggins, 67- Mem: Nat. and Miss. Tech. Socs; Nat. Remotivation Rehabilitation Soc; Univ. South. Miss. Alumni Asn; Mason; Red Cross; Jr. C. of C.(pres, Stone Co. Chap, 62, v.pres, Miss. Chap, 69-); Miss. and Gulf Coast Athletic Activities Asns; v.pres, Stone Co. Little League Asn. Rel: Methodist. Mailing Add: 615 Baker St, Wiggins, Miss. 39577.

ROBERTSON, HAYES R
b. Chicago, Ill, 9/1/04; s. Robert Roy Robertson and Alice Warfield Hayes R; m. 8/1/31 to Louise Buckman; c. Kenneth Hayes and Dennis Birch. Educ: Wabash Col, A.B, 26; George Wash. Univ. LL.B, 31; Tau Kappa Alpha; Phi Delta Phi; Kappa Sigma. Polit. & Govt. Pos: Mem, Flossmoor Savings and Loan Asn, Ill, 47-51; alternate del, Rep. Nat. Conv, 52, del, 64 & 68, party elector, 56 & 64; committeeman, Rich Twp. Rep. Party, Ill, 54-66; Ill. State Sen, 56-60; mem, Atomic Energy Study Cmn, 57-60, Ill-Ind. Port Study Cmn, 58-60 and Twp. Govt. Cmn, Ill, 59-60; chmn, Cook Co. Rep. Cent. Cmt, 62-64. Bus. & Prof. Pos: Attorney-at-law, 32-40; pres, Hwy. Steel Prod. Co, 40-51; bd. chmn, Brummer Seal Co, 45-60; dir, Olympia State Bank, 61-; bd. chmn, Life Savings and Loan Asn, 63-; dir, Travco Corp, 64- Mem: Trustee, Ill. Masonic Hosp. and Am. Good Govt. Soc; bd. gov, Glenwood Sch. for Boys; Mason (32°), Medinah Shrine; Exec. Club of Chicago; SAR; Chicago Athletic Asn; Flossmoor Country Club. Rel: Presbyterian. Mailing Add: 1421 Braeburn Rd, Flossmoor, Ill. 60422. (1967)

ROBERTSON, JAMES ARTHUR, JR. D
Miss. State Rep.
b. Centreville, Miss, 12/8/39; s. James Arthur Robertson and Vera Parker R; m. 8/16/64 to Linda Lee McSwain; c. Margaret Estell. Educ: Hinds Jr. Col, 57-58 & 60-61; Univ. of South. Miss, B.S, 62 and M.S, 64; La. State Univ, 65-66; Pi Gamma Mu; Acacia. Polit. & Govt. Pos: Miss. State Rep, Amite, Franklin and Wilkinson Co, 68- Bus. & Prof. Pos: Instr. of Polit. Sci, Univ. of South. Miss, 64-67 and admissions counsr, 67-68. Mem: Mason; Lions. Rel: Methodist. Mailing Add: P.O. Box 222, Liberty, Miss. 39645.

ROBERTSON, JOHN ANDERSON R
Chmn, Baldwin Co. Rep. Exec. Cmt, Ala.
b. Cleveland, Ohio, 9/9/31; s. William Monroe Robertson and Pauline Slusher R; m. 4/23/54 to Faye Samford; c. John Anderson, Jr. and Polly Connor. Educ: Auburn Univ, B.S, 53; Sigma Alpha Epsilon. Polit. & Govt. Pos: Chmn, Indust. Develop. Bd. and mem, Aviation Bd, Fairhope, 65-; chmn, Baldwin Co. Rep. Exec. Cmt, Ala, mem, Ala. Rep. State Exec. Cmt. and v.chmn, Second Cong. Dist, Ala. Rep. Party, 66- Bus. & Prof. Pos: Brokerage consult, 60-62; dist. mgr, Conn. Gen. Life Ins. Co, 62-63; partner, Huffman-Robertson Ins. Agency, 64- Mil. Serv: Entered as Airman Basic, Air Force, 53, released as Airman, 2/C, 55. Mem: Past pres, Eastern Shore C. of C; past treas. & bd. mem, Eastern Shore Jr. C. of C. Rel: Methodist. Mailing Add: 556 Jan Dr, Fairhope, Ala. 36532. (1967)

ROBERTSON, JOHN HARTE R
Chmn, Norfolk City Rep. Cmt, Va.
b. Portsmouth, Va, 5/16/23; s. Augustus M. Robertson and Vivienne Wilson R; m. 1/26/46 to Mary Elizabeth Henderson; c. Alan Thomas and Claudia Susan. Polit. & Govt. Pos: Mem, Norfolk City Rep. Cmt, Va, 54-, chmn, 64-; cand, Va. House of Del, 65. Mil. Serv: Entered as Pvt, Air Force, 43, released as 2nd Lt, 45, after serv. in 15th Air Force, 98th Group, 415th Squadron; Capt, Air Force Res; ETO Ribbon with 4 Stars. Mem: Past pres, Norfolk Jr. C. of C; exec. cmt, Advance Norfolk. Rel: Presbyterian; past chmn, Bd. of Deacons, now Elder, Third Presby. Church. Mailing Add: 8356 Capeview Court, Norfolk, Va. 23518. (1967)

ROBERTSON, NEIL FREDERICK D
First V.Chmn, Bergen Co. New Dem. Coalition, N.J.
b. Weehawken, N.J; s. Neil Charles Robertson and Harriett Young R; m. 8/30/41 to Dorothy Tyrell; c. Neil Craig. Educ: Fairleigh Dickinson Univ, 48-51; N.Y. Univ, postgrad, 53-54. Polit. & Govt. Pos: Mem, Planning Bd, Paramus, N.J, 52-58; councilman, Boro of Paramus, 53-59; pres, Paramus Dem. Club, 58-60; del, Dem. Nat. Conv, 68; first v.chmn, Bergen Co. New Dem. Coalition, 69- Bus. & Prof. Pos: Asst. personnel dir, Jefferson Chem. Co, N.Y.C, 51-55; dir. of personnel, N.J. Hwy. Authority, Woodbridge, N.J, 55-62; personnel dir, Christ Hosp, Jersey City, N.J, 62-68 and Perth Amboy Gen. Hosp, Perth Amboy, N.J, 68- Mil. Serv: Entered as Pvt, Army, 42, released as 1st Lt, 46, after serv. in Signal Corps, Southwest Pac. Theatre, 44-45; Philippine Victory Ribbon; Southwest Pac. Campaign Ribbon; Four Battle Stars. Mem: N.J. Soc. for Hosp. Personnel Dirs.(past pres); Am. Soc. for Hosp. Personnel Dirs.(mem. labor rels. cmt); Am. Hosp. Asn; N.J. Hosp. Asn.(mem. coun. on mgt. practices, coun. on human resources and manpower and training dir. prog); N.J. Tele-Commun. Asn. Mailing Add: 53 Longview Court, Paramus, N.J. 07652.

ROBERTSON, RUTH ELIZABETH R
V.Chmn, 18th Cong. Dist. Rep. Party, Mich.
b. Kansas City, Mo, 4/10/17; d. Walter Ervin Maloy and Mary Baird M; m. 3/29/41 to Paul Corwin Robertson; c. Paul C, Jr, Mary Jane (Mrs. Bower); Martha Ruth; Julia Evelyn, David Wilson and John Baird. Educ: Kansas City Jr. Col, 35-36; Univ. Mich, A.B, 39. Polit. & Govt. Pos: Neighbor-to-neighbor worker, Rep. Party, Mich, 60-69; precinct del, Mich. Rep. Party, 63-65 & 68-; chmn, Oakland Co. High Sch. Prog, Mich, 64-65; pres, Beverly-Franklin Rep. Women, 65; pres, Oakland Co. Coun. Rep. Women's Clubs, 66-67; del, state and nat. fedn. conv, 67; mem. exec. cmt, Oakland Co. Rep. Cmt, 67-68; del, Rep. Nat. Conv. and Mich. del, Nat. Platform Cmt, 68; v.chmn, 18th Cong. Dist. Rep. Party, Mich, 69- Mem: Univ. Mich. Alumnae Club; League of Women Voters. Rel: Presbyterian. Mailing Add: 25665 River Dr, Franklin, Mich. 48025.

ROBERTSON, STOKES VERNON Independent
Assoc. Justice, Supreme Court of Miss.
b. Hattiesburg, Miss, 11/9/12; s. Stokes Vernon Robertson and Sudie Mason Burt R; m. 7/14/45 to Una Lurline Caldwell; c. Stokes V, III, David G. and Helen C. Educ: Millsaps Col, 29-32; Univ. Miss, B.A, 33 and LL.B, 35; Sigma Upsilon; Pi Kappa Delta; Omicron Delta Kappa; Phi Delta Phi; Kappa Alpha. Polit. & Govt. Pos: Chancery Judge, Fifth Chancery Court Dist, Miss, 55-66; assoc. justice, Supreme Court of Miss, 66- Mil. Serv: Entered as Capt, Army, 40, released as Lt. Col, 45, after serv. in 31st Inf. Div. and Mobile Qm. Bn, U.S. and S.W. Pac. Theatres; Col.(Ret) Army Res, Judge Adv. Gen. Corps, 60; Presidential Unit Citation; S.W. Pac. Theatre Medal with Three Battle Stars. Mem: Hinds Co. and Miss. State Bar Asns; Kiwanis; Am. Legion. Rel: Presbyterian. Mailing Add: 2246 N. Cheryl Dr, Jackson, Miss. 39211.

ROBIE, JOSEPH JEROME D
b. Pittsburgh, Pa, 10/4/23; s. Joseph H. Robie and Marion Mohr R; m. 7/24/46 to Shirley Fae Wagner; c. Thomas Charles, Jerome Joseph and Janet Ann. Educ: Norwich Univ; George Wash. Univ; Gannon Col, B.A; Am. Legion Medal Award; Theta Chi. Polit. & Govt. Pos: Treas, Redevelop. Authority, Erie, Pa, 62-63; councilman, Erie City Coun, 64-65, pres, 65; exec. asst. to Mayor, Erie, 66- Bus. & Prof. Pos: Teacher and coach, Cathedral Prep Sch, Erie, Pa, 49-55; secy, Mattis & Robie, Inc, Gen. Ins, 55- Mil. Serv: Entered as Pvt, Army, 43, released as Sgt, 46, after serv. in 467th Parachute Field Artil. Bn, ETO; Good Conduct Medal; European African Middle Eastern Theater Campaign Ribbon; Am. Theater Campaign Ribbon; Victory Medal. Mem: Munic. Finance Officers Asn. of the U.S. and Canada; dir, Independent Ins. Agents Asn. of Erie County, Inc; East Erie Turners; Foresters Beneficial Asn; Bus. and Prfnl. Men's Club; La Nuova Aurora Soc; Citizens Action Cmt. All-city and All-state football player. Rel: Roman Catholic. Mailing Add: 3423 Greengarden Blvd, Erie, Pa. 16508.

ROBILLARD, HERBERT BERNARD D
b. Gardner Twp, 5/22/20; s. Nelson Robillard and Anna Haase R; m. 6/20/42 to Doris Mary Jacquart; c. Clyde L, Reginald R. and Roderick B. Educ: La Salle Exten. Univ, Ill, 57. Polit. & Govt. Pos: Auditor and clerk, State Hwy. Cmn, Wis, 57-59; mem, Civil Serv. Cmt, Door Co, 59-62; precinct committeeman, Dem. Party; former chmn, Door Co. Dem. Party. Bus. & Prof. Pos: Ins. rep, Nat. Farmers Union, 56-; Income Tax Serv, 60-; pres. and mgr, Door Co. Dairy Co, 60-63 and secy, 66- Mem: Nat. Farmers Union. Rel: Roman Catholic; Holy Name del, St. Francis Xavier Cath. Church, Brussels, Wis. Mailing Add: Route 1, Brussels, Wis. 45204. (1967)

ROBINSON, ARTHUR ALEXANDER, JR. D
Committeeman, Calif. Dem. State Cent. Cmt.
b. Napoleonville, La, 2/20/28; s. Arthur Alexander Robinson, Sr. and Odessa Sophronia Noel R; m. 8/11/49 to Jeanette Wynne; c. Addrienne Antionette, Arthur Alexander, III, Anthony Ambrose, Angelique Avis, Anita White, John Mark White, Angelae Antionette and Andre Alexis. Educ: Xavier Univ, La, 50; Dillard Univ, B.A, 51; Atlanta Univ, 53; Gammon Theol. Sem, B.D, 54; South. Univ. Law Sch, 55; U.S. Army Chaplain Sch, Ft. Slocum, N.Y, grad, 60. The Evangelistic Ambassadors for Christ of the West Coast, hon. LL.D. Polit. & Govt. Pos: Secy, Interdenomination Ministers Alliance, Baton Rouge, La, 54-56, New Orleans, 56-60; pres, Scotlandville Br. NAACP, 54-56; pres, Pine Bluff Movement and Citizens Cmt, Ark, 62-65; commun. worker, Fed. Projs, Desert Sands Unified Sch. Dist, Indio, Calif, 66-69; mem. bd. dirs, Family Counseling Agency, Riverside Co, 66-; adv. committeeman, Indio of Tomorrow Adv. Cmt, 66-; mem. bd. dirs, Coachella Valley Title VI Proj, 67-; committeeman, Calif. Dem. State Cent. Cmt, 68- Bus. & Prof. Pos: Pastor, Boynton Methodist Church, Gretna, La, 47-51, Forsyth Charge, Ga, 51-54, Camphor Mem. Methodist Church, Baton Rouge, La, 54-57, Philips Mem. Methodist Church, New Orleans, 57-60, St. James Methodist Church, Pine Bluff, Ark, 62-64, Duncan Chapel Methodist Church, Little Rock, 64-65, Evergreen Baptist Church, Lake Charles, La, 65-66 and St. Mark United Methodist Church, Kingsport, Tenn, 69-; builder, Philips Mem. Methodist Church and Educ. Bldg, New Orleans, 58; pastor and builder, Mt. Calvary Baptist Church, Indio, Calif, 66-69; teacher, Martin Van Buren Elem. Sch, Indio, 66-67. Mil. Serv: Entered as STM 3/C, Navy, 43, released as STM 1/C, 46, after serv. in U.S.S. Tabberer D.E. 418, Asiatic Theatre, 44-46; entered as Pfc, Army Res, 49, released as Pvt. 2/C, 52, after serv. in SS-USAR; Chaplain 1st Lt, Army Res, 60-62, ETO; Navy Unit Commendation Award; Philippine Liberation Ribbon; Four Battle Stars for Invasion of Iwo Jima, Luzon in the Philippines, Okinawa and the Bombardment of Japan. Publ: 'Man's Responsibility to His Community,' Cent. Chris-

tian Advocate, 61. Mem: Calif. Teachers Asn; Calif. Sch. Employees Asn; Mexican-Am. Polit. Asn, Inc; asst. prog. secy, Butler St. Young Men's Bus. Asn, Atlanta, Ga, 52-53; hon. mem, New Orleans Police Dept, 57-69; Coachella Valley Improv. Asn.(pres, 66-69); Citation for Commun. Serv, United Way of Coachella Valley 1969 Campaign, 69; Cert. of Merit, Theodore Roosevelt Sch, 68. Rel: Methodist. Legal Res: 82-688 Crist Ave, Indio, Calif. 92201. Mailing Add: 921 Maple St, Kingsport, Tenn. 37660.

ROBINSON, BRANDON TERRY D
Chmn, Archuleta Co. Dem. Cent. Cmt, Colo.
b. Wichita Falls, Tex, 7/9/07; s. Benjamin Terry Robinson and Tommie White R; m. 8/5/34 to Ruth Dunlap. Educ: N.Mex. State Univ, 25-29; Phi Beta Theta. Polit. & Govt. Pos: Treas, De Baca Co, N.Mex, 37-40 and cmnr, 45-47; cmnr, Archuleta Co, Colo, 51-58; secy, Archuleta Co. Dem. Cent. Cmt, 59-66 and chmn, 67- Bus. & Prof. Pos: Rancher, 29- Publ: Articles published in periodicals. Mem: AF&AM; Eastern Star; Scottish Rite. Rel: Methodist. Mailing Add: Box 175, Pagosa Springs, Colo. 81147.

ROBINSON, CARL D
b. Richmond, Utah, 5/3/95; m. to Phyllis; c. 6. Educ: Utah and Star Valley Schs. Polit. & Govt. Pos: Wyo. State Sen, 1 1/2 terms; Wyo. State Rep, 4 terms -67; Speaker Wyo. State House 41; mem. Coun. of State Govt; Interstate Coop. Cmn. Bus. & Prof. Pos: Banker, businessman, rancher. Mem: Lions-charter mem, past pres, past dist. gov; holds 16 year perfect attendance record. Mailing Add: Box 8, Afton, Wyo. 83110. (1967)

ROBINSON, CARL D
Okla. State Rep.
b. Gould, Okla, 11/5/25; s. Earl Cooper Robinson and Sivilla Roberts R; m. 7/16/48 to Sue Carter; c. Gary Don, Eddie Ray and Roger Dee. Educ: Okla. Univ, 1 semester. Polit. & Govt. Pos: Okla. State Rep, 60th Dist, 68- Mil. Serv: Entered as Pvt, Air Force, 46, released as Cpl, 47, after serv. in Fifth Air Force, Pac. Theatre. Mem: Lions Int; Am. Legion; Okla. State Sch. Bd. Asn; Fraternal Order of the Red Red Rose; past pres, Hollis Sch. Bd; Gould Alumna (past pres). Valedictorian of Gould High Sch. Rel: Methodist; Pres. and chmn, Bd. of Stewards, First United Methodist Church. Mailing Add: 223 W. Versa, Hollis, Okla. 73550.

ROBINSON, CARLOS R. R
Chmn, Grant Co. Rep. Party, N.Mex.
b. Clovis, N.Mex, 3/20/30; s. Carlos R. Robinson and Iva B. Hymen R; m. m. 6/10/69 to Carol Lynn Nieburger; c. Gary Lee, Gregory Stephen, Frances Ann and Patrick Ashton. Educ: St. Michael's Col, N.Mex, 54; Univ. N.Mex, B.A. in Bus. Admin, 57; Sigma Chi. Polit. & Govt. Pos: Secy, Gov. N.Mex. Port of Entry Adv. Cmt, 67-; alternate del, Rep. Nat. Conv, 68; chmn, Grant Co. Rep. Party, N.Mex, 68- Mil. Serv: Entered as Pvt, Army, 51, released as 1st Lt, 53, after serving in Seventh Inf. Div, Artil, Korea, 52-53; Bronze Star Medal; Commendation Medal with Oak Leaf Cluster; Korean Serv. Medal with Two Battle Stars; UN Serv. Medal; Nat. Defense Serv. Medal. Mem: Jaycees; Elks. Rel: Methodist. Mailing Add: 1000 W. Seventh St, Silver City, N.Mex. 88061.

ROBINSON, CHARLES K. R
V.Chmn, Park Co. Rep. Party, Colo.
b. Uhrichsville, Ohio, 9/15/07; both parents deceased; m. 3/2/31 to Marge Welsh; c. Charles K, Jr. and John Welsh. Educ: Denison Univ, B.A. in Govt, 30; Sigma Alpha Epsilon. Polit. & Govt. Pos: V.chmn, Park Co. Rep. Party, Colo, currently. Mem: Lions Int. Mailing Add: Willo Wisp Route 1, Pine, Colo. 80470.

ROBINSON, CLYDE RAYFORD D
Chmn, Miller Co. Dem. Cmt, Mo.
b. Limn Creek, Mo, 3/29/10; s. Bertie Clyde Robinson and Lena Davis R; m. 9/29/32 to Pebble Wilma Hill. Educ: Bagnell High Sch, 4 years. Polit. & Govt. Pos: Chmn, Miller Co. Dem. Cmt, Mo, currently. Bus. & Prof. Pos: Bldg. contractor, currently. Mil. Serv: Entered as Pvt, Army, 43, released as T-5 after serv. in Corps Engrs, Asiatic-Pac. Theater, 44-45; Good Conduct Medal; Asiatic Pac. Medal. Mem: Mason (hon. mem. of all temples in Mo); Shrine. Rel: Baptist. Mailing Add: Lake Ozark, Mo. 65049.

ROBINSON, DAVE M. R
N.Dak. State Sen.
b. Bismarck, N.Dak, 8/1/18; s. George Marshall Robinson and Helen Clark R; m. 6/6/42 to Sheila Alice Crowley; c. Janet, Matthew and Stephen. Educ: N.Dak. State Univ, B.S. in Agr. Polit. & Govt. Pos: N.Dak. State Rep, McLean Co, 51; chmn, McClean Co. Rep. Party, 57-63; N.Dak. State Sen, Eighth Dist, 63- Mem: Pres, N.Dak. Stockmen's Asn, 64-66, Co. Agr. Improv. Asn. and Garrison Sportsmen's Club; Mason; Elks; Farm Bur. Soil Conserv. Award, Swift Tripper. Rel: Protestant. Mailing Add: Coal Harbor Stock Farm, Coleharbor, N.Dak. 58531.

ROBINSON, DONALD LOUIS D
b. Ottawa, Ill, 12/8/36; s. Arthur Robinson and Louise Freebury R; m. 8/4/62 to Sara Katharine Moore; c. Marshall Jackson. Educ: Northwest. Univ, B.A. in Hist, 58 and M.A. in Hist, 59; American Univ, Ph.D, 63; Alpha Phi Omega; Phi Mu Alpha; Phi Alpha Theta; Pi Gamma Mu; Pi Gamma Mu; Pi Sigma Alpha; Am. Univ. Hon. Soc. Polit. & Govt. Pos: Co-chmn, Speakers Bur, Young Citizens for Johnson-Humphrey Campaign, 64; admin. asst. to U.S. Rep. Henry S. Reuss, currently; co-chmn, Bi-Partisan Intern Prog, U.S. House of Rep, currently. Bus. & Prof. Pos: Assoc. prof. lectr, dept. of polit. sci, George Wash. Univ, currently. Mil. Serv: Entered as Ens, Navy, 59, released as Lt.(jg), 62, after serv. as Chief, Naval Opers. Mem: Am. Polit. Sci. Asn; Am. Civil Liberties Union; Americans for Dem. Action; chmn. bd. of dirs, St. Stephen's Enterprises, Inc. Rel: Episcopal; Lay Reader. Legal Res: 319 N. Kenosha Ave, Oglesby, Ill. 61348. Mailing Add: 1817 Kenyon St. N.W, Washington, D.C. 20010.

ROBINSON, DONITA GAIL R
Recording Secy, Chippewa Co. Rep. Party, Wis.
b. St. Croix Falls, Wis, 12/17/49; d. Neal W. Robinson and Deloris J. Andersen R; single. Educ: Wis. State Univ, Eau Clair, 68-69; Northwest and Wis. Fedn. Young Rep. Polit. & Govt. Pos: MORE chmn, Chippewa Co. Rep. Party, Wis, 68, recording secy, 69-; corresponding secy, Chippewa Co. Young Rep, 68-; recording secy, Northwest Fedn. Young Rep, 69, mem. exec. bd, 69-; secy, Cmt. Responsible and Effective Young Rep. Leadership, 69-; secy, Northwest Area Col. Young Rep, 69-; chmn, Tenth Dist. Young Rep, 69- Bus. & Prof. Pos: Advert. salesman, Spectator, Wis. State Univ, Eau Claire, 68, orgn. ed, 69; asst. secy, Eagle Point Mutual Ins. Co, Chippewa Falls, 69. Publ: 'Modern Math versus Traditional Math,' 3/68 and Books Are Most Nearly Universal Source of Pleasure,' 4/68, Chippewa Herald Tel; 'McLuhanism Discussed by Faculty Panel,' Spectator, 3/69. Mem: Chippewa Co. Rep. Party; Wis. and Northwest. Fedn. Young Rep. Miss Young Rep, Wis. Fedn. Young Rep, 69. Rel: Lutheran. Mailing Add: 765 Wilson St, Chippewa Falls, Wis. 54729.

ROBINSON, EDWARD J. D
b. Dearborn, Mich, 11/24/33; m. 1960 to Rose Marie Kirchner; c. Rachel Marie. Educ: Univ. of Notre Dame, B.A. in econs; Detroit Col. of Law, evening div, 60-64. Polit. & Govt. Pos: Mich. State Sen, 64-66; mem. 15th, 16th and 19th Dem. Cong. orgns; past officer and exec. bd. mem, Dearborn Dem. Club; Dearborn Heights and Redford Twp. Dem. Clubs; exec. bd. mem, Dearborn Commun. Col. Bus. & Prof. Pos: Personnel specialist. Mil. Serv: Marine Corps, 57-60. Rel: Roman Catholic. Mailing Add: 22835 Lodge Lane, Dearborn, Mich. 48128. (1967)

ROBINSON, ENID R
b. Thor, Iowa, 2/27/12; d. Knut J. Hanson and Gina J. H; m. 7/3/39 to William Lee Robinson, Jr; c. Jo Ella (Mrs. Helmers) and William Lee, III. Educ: Waldorf Jr. Col; St. Olaf Col; Phi Theta Kappa. Polit. & Govt. Pos: Mem, Iowa Rep. State Cent. Cmt, 52-58, v.chmn, 54-58; del. and mem. resolutions cmt, Rep. Nat. Conv, 56; cand. for Cong, 58; U.S. Del, Gen. Agreement on Tariff and Trade, Geneva, Switz, 58; U.S. Del, Atlantic Cong, London, Eng. and sponsor, Atlantic Coun, 59; women's chmn, Iowa Cmt. for Richard Nixon, 60; active Rep. precinct and state wide speaker; mem, State Judicial Nominating Cmn, Iowa, 69- Bus. & Prof. Pos: Owner-mgr, Enid's Fashion Fabrics, 65- Mem: PEO; Am. Asn. Univ. Women; Bus. & Prfnl. Womens Club; Nat. Fedn. Women's Clubs. Rel: Methodist. Mailing Add: R.R. 3, Hampton, Iowa 50441.

ROBINSON, ERROL WAYNE R
Mem, Ala. State Rep. Exec. Cmt.
b. Downey, Idaho, 11/23/23; s. Thomas Arnold Robinson and Nettie L. Johnson R; m. to Carla Ruth Harris; c. E. Wayne, Jr, Carla Rose, Rhea Ann and Helen Ruth. Educ: U.S. Naval Acad, Annapolis, B.S, 45; Univ. Wash, M.S, in Eng, 58. Polit. & Govt. Pos: Chmn, Madison Co. Rep. Exec. Cmt, Ala, 65-66; cand, Third Dist, Ala. State Senate; mem, Ala. Rep. State Exec. Cmt, currently. Bus. & Prof. Pos: Eng. supvr, The Boeing Co, 55- Mil. Serv: Entered as Midshipman, Navy, released as Lt, World War II and Korean Conflict; Air Medal with Gold Star; Presidential Unit Citation; Korean Serv, Asian Occup, Am. Theater, Pac. and Victory Medals. Mem: Former chmn. and mem, Co. Camping & Activities Cmt, Boy Scouts. Rel: Latter-day Saint. Mailing Add: 2903 Garth Rd. S.E, Huntsville, Ala. 35801. (1967)

ROBINSON, FRANK E. 'BUCK' D
b. Edina, Mo, 9/1/08; s. Frank Edward Robinson and Lillie Hunolt R; m. 3/29/50 to Betty Jo Luke. Educ: Northeast Mo. State Col, 4 years. Polit. & Govt. Pos: Mo. State Rep, 48-66; asst. dir, Mo. State Dept. of Revenue, 68- Bus. & Prof. Pos: Two years on construction of the Alaska Hwy; exec. v.pres, Mo. Motel Asn, 49-67; dir, Am. Motor Hotel Asn, Rockhill Construction Co, St. Louis, Mo. and Morrison-Knudson Co, Seattle, Wash. Mil. Serv: Pvt, Army 385th Tank Div, serv. in ETO, 43-45; 5 Battle Campaign Ribbons. Mem: Am. Soc. of Asn. Execs; Nat. Hwy. Users Cong; Conf. of Am. Small Bus. Orgn; First chmn, Nat. Motel Execs. Conf, 55; chmn, Gov. Task Force on Older Missourians; chmn, Miss. River Pkwy. Cmn; Lions; Meadow Lake Acres Country Club (pres); Am. Legion; VFW. Rel: Catholic. Mailing Add: P.O. Box 546, Jefferson City, Mo. 65101.

ROBINSON, HENRIETTA D
b. St. Petersburg, Fla, Nov. 1919; d. James Neal and Irene Smith N; div; c. Valrie Cynthia (Mrs. Simmons), Alexander and Charlotte Larua. Educ: Gibbs Trade and Business Sch, Practice Nurse, 52; Mumford Bus. Sch, Real Estate Law, 58. Polit. & Govt. Pos: Tenth Precinct Citizen Rep; mem, Women Pub. Affairs Cmt; charter mem, Coun. Precinct Del; Dem. Precinct Del, Dist. 22, Precinct 17, 60-; mem, Mich. Black Cacus, 68; alternate del, Dem. Nat. Conv, 68. Bus. & Prof. Pos: Supvr. of Danity Products, Detroit Area, 51-53; Real Estate Saleswoman, Gross Realty Co, 60- Mem: Nat. Counc. Negro Women; Escalator's Club; Am. Bridge Asn. Rel: Baptist. Mailing Add: 9320 Otsego, Detroit, Mich. 48204.

ROBINSON, HENRY M. R
b. South Hero, Vt, 8/5/94; married; c. One. Educ: Burlington Bus. Col. Polit. & Govt. Pos: Co. appraiser, mem. appeal bd, lister, several years and auditor, 6 years; selectman and overseer of the poor, 46-; former Vt. State Rep. Bus. & Prof. Pos: Farmer; dir, Grand Isle Creamery Asn, 50- Mil. Serv: Pvt, Inf, Army, World War I. Mem: Mason; Farm Bur. Rel: Congregational. Mailing Add: South Hero, Vt. 05486. (1967)

ROBINSON, JACK W. R
Kans. State Sen.
b. Arkansas City, Kans, 7/17/24; s. Earl Austin Robinson (deceased) and Merle Marie McGhlon R.(deceased); m. to Norma Klotz; c. Monte Charles, Melissa and Shelly. Educ: Kans. Univ, B.S, 49; Am. Univ, France, 1 year; Sigma Delta Chi; Lambda Chi Alpha. Polit. & Govt. Pos: Pub. relations dir, Colo. Goldwater Cmt, 63-64; Kans. State Sen, 69- Bus. & Prof. Pos: Statehouse reporter, Wichita Beacon, 49-54; city ed, Denver Post, 54-60; polit. reporter, Rocky Mountain News, 60-62; mem. staff, U.S. State Dept, Kabul, Afghanistan, 63; pub. relations dir, Lago-Whitehead, Inc, currently. Mil. Serv: Entered as Pvt, Army, 43, released as Pfc, 46, after serv. in 84th Inf. Div, 44-46; Three Battle Stars; Combat Infantry Badge. Mem: Elks; Am. Legion; VFW. Rel: Presbyterian. Mailing Add: 1945 Porter, Apt. A-54, Wichita, Kans. 67203.

ROBINSON, JAMES CARSON D
b. Rockhill, S.C, 7/19/22; m. to Elizabeth Thornton; c. Carson, Richard and Libby. Educ: Univ. Fla, B.A. and LL.B; Blue Key; Phi Delta Phi; pres, Phi Delta Theta. Polit. & Govt. Pos: Co. attorney, Orange Co, Fla, 58-68; Cand, U.S. House Rep, Fifth Dist, 68. Bus. & Prof. Pos: Attorney, 48-53; attorney, Giles, Hedrick & Robinson, 53-; dir, First Fed. Savings and Loan Asn. of Orlando, 54-; dir. and secy, Tradewinds Cafeterias, 59- Mil. Serv: Entered as Pvt, released as Lt, after serv. in Field Artil, ETO. Mem: Orange Co. and Am. Bar Asns; Cent. Fla. Develop. Cmt, 61-; sponsor, Cent. Fla. Coun. Alcoholism, 65-; dir, Cent. Fla. Civic Theater, 67-; Local Govt. Study Cmn. of Orange Co, 65 & 66; secy, Presby. Homes for Aging, 57-68; trustee, Fla. Presby. Col, 63-; pres, United Children's Serv, Inc; pres. Cent. Fla. Div, Children's Home Soc, 66, mem. bd. dirs, 69-; YMCA (mem, Century Club); counsr, Boy Scouts; mem. bd. dirs, Boy's Clubs of Orange Co, 69-; sponsored Cuban family, Cuban Relief Prog; Kiwanis; Orlando Area C. of C.(mem. bd. dirs, 66-68, v.pres. govt. affairs cmt, 68, mem. urban affairs cmt, 69-); East Orange C. of C; Fla. State C. of C.(mem. nat. affairs cmt, 69-); Univ. Clubs of Orlando and Winter Park; Fla. Asn. of the Amateur Atheletic Union (chmn. region two indust. cmt, 67); dir, Orlando Panthers Football Team, 68 & 69; Local Bd. 29, Selective Serv. Syst.(chmn, 62-69). Rel: Presbyterian; Elder and secy. bd. trustees, First Presbyterian Church of Orlando; mem. judicial cmn, Presbyterian Church of the U.S, 67. Mailing Add: 109 E. Church St, Orlando, Fla. 32801.

ROBINSON, JAMES KENNETH R
Va. State Sen.
b. Frederick Co, Va, 5/14/16; m. to Kathryn M. R. Educ: Va. Polytech. Inst, 37, B.S. in Hort. Polit. & Govt. Pos: Va. State Sen, 66- Bus. & Prof. Pos: Fruit grower, packer, farmer, and businessman. Mil. Serv: Infantry, 4 years, Maj. Mem: Rotary; Izaak Walton League; Am. Legion; Va. Farm Bur. Fedn; Elks; Exec. Bd, Boy Scouts; C. of C.(dir, Winchester-Frederick Co); Shenandoah Area Coun. Meritorious Serv. Award for serv. to Va. agr, Va. Polytech. Inst, 63; Man of the Year in Serv. to Va. Agr, Progressive Farmer Mag, 64. Rel: Quaker. Mailing Add: P.O. Box 668, Winchester, Va. 22601.

ROBINSON, JAMES LUTHER D
b. Raytown, Mo, 4/19/94; s. Samuel Green Robinson and Vyra Greene R; m. 6/6/17 to Anna Mae Dehoney; c. James Luther, Patricia Luann (Mrs. Reese) and Shirley Gene (Mrs. Latare). Educ: William Jewell Col, A.M; Lambda Chi Alpha. Polit. & Govt. Pos: Mo. State Rep, 13th Dist. Jackson Co, 61-66; Jackson Co. Planning Cmn. Bus. & Prof. Pos: Automobile dealer, Ford Motor Co, 19-54. Mil. Serv: Entered as Pvt, Army, 17, released as Lt, after serv. in Conserv. & Reclamation, U.S; several citations. Mem: Mason; Shrine; C. of C; Am. War Dads. Rel: Baptist. Mailing Add: 6412 Overton, Raytown, Mo. 64133.

ROBINSON, MRS. JOHN D. D
d. R. Murphy Williams; m. to Dr. John D. Robinson (deceased); c. Dr. John D, Jr. and Mrs. J.W. Doonan. Educ: Peace Col. Polit. & Govt. Pos: Mgr. women's div, Charles M. Johnson gubernatorial campaign, 48 and Gov. Dan Moore's campaign, 64; chmn, Gov. Cmt. on Beautification; mem, Dem. Exec. Cmt; former Dem. Nat. Committeewoman, N.C; del, Dem. Nat. Conv, 52 & 68. Bus. & Prof. Pos: Pres, Warner Hall Mfg. Co, Wallace, N.C; exec. dir. mkt. and pub. rels, Diners Fugazy Travel, Raleigh, N.C. Mem: Duplin Co. Med. Auxiliary; Wallace Women's Club; chmn, Duplin Co. Welfare Bd, 15 years; Colonial Dames of Am; Colonial Dames of XVII Century; DAR; Perennial Garden Club of Wallace; bd, Gen. Fedn. of Women's Clubs, 15 years. Named Tar Heel of Week, News & Observer, 64. Rel: Presbyterian; pres, Women of the Church, Wallace Presbyterian Church. Mailing Add: 3939 Glenwood Ave, Raleigh, N.C. 27609.

ROBINSON, KENNETH D
b. Panora, Iowa, 9/29/14; s. Albert M. Robinson and Ola Maynard R; m. 10/6/46 to Mary Louise Moulton. Educ: Drake Univ, A.B, 38; Sigma Delta Chi. Polit. & Govt. Pos: Past Seventh Dist. Chmn, Dem. Cent. Cmt, Iowa; State chmn, adv. cmt, Small Bus. Admin; co. chmn, Dem. Party; v.chmn, Gov. Cmt. to Employ the Handicapped; past pres, Gr. Guthrie Co. Develop. Asn; co. chmn, Nat. Found, 47-60; Iowa State Rep, until 66; mayor, Bayard, 53-64, and 68-; del-at-lg, Dem. Nat. Conv, 56, 60 & 64; mem, Iowa Develop. Cmn, 58-62; pres, League of Iowa Munic, 59. Bus. & Prof. Pos: Owner and publisher, Bagley, Iowa Gazette, 40-, Guthrie Co. Vedette, Panora, Iowa, 43-45, Stuart, Iowa Herald, 45-46 and Bayard, Iowa News. Mem: Hon. mem, Future Farmers of Am; past pres, Drake Nat. Alumni Asn; Lions; Iowa Press Asn; Nat. Educ. Asn; dir, Crippled Children's Soc. Recipient four First Place Award in Iowa Press Contests; Bayard News Second in Nation in Gen. Excellence, 1959. Mailing Add: Bayard, Iowa 50029.

ROBINSON, KENNETH WILLIAM D
b. Grand Rapids, Mich, 1/12/22; s. William Wesley Robinson and Margaret Schmidt R; m. 7/19/42 to Marguerite Anderson; c. James Kenneth, Phillip Terry, Richard Paul, Pamela Sue, Patti Ann and Sue Ann. Educ: Grand Rapids Cent. High Sch, grad. Polit. & Govt. Pos: Del, Co. and State Dem. Conv, Mich, 49-69 and Dem. Nat. Conv, 56, 60, 64 & 68; cmnr, Mich. Econ. Develop. Cmn, 57-60 and Mich. Civil Rights Cmn, 64-68; mem. bd. of control, Grand Valley State Col, currently. Bus. & Prof. Pos: Mgr, C. Thomas Stores, 40-42; aircraft assembler, Hayes Corp, 42-44. Mem: UAW (int. rep, 44-45, int. exec. bd. and regional dir, 55-). Rel: Protestant. Mailing Add: 1115 Keneberry E, Grand Rapids, Mich. 49506.

ROBINSON, LESLIE R
Nebr. State Sen.
b. Marquette, Mich, 12/28/06; s. Frank L. Robinson and Ema M. Chase R; m. 6/22/35 to Charlotte Agnes Shovlain; c. Frank E, Elizabeth E.(Mrs. Hinricks) and Jeanette E.(Mrs. Peterson). Educ: Univ. Nebr. Col. of Agr. Polit. & Govt. Pos: Twp. treas, Nebr, 42-48; Nebr. State Sen, 67- Bus. & Prof. Pos: Dir, Am. Polled Hereford Asn, Kansas City, Mo, 60-65. Mem: Elks; Farm Bur. Rel: Episcopal. Mailing Add: Route 2, Kearney, Nebr. 68847.

ROBINSON, RICHARD EARL R
b. Middleton, Mich, 7/31/16; s. William D. Robinson and Anne Schmalzried R; m. 9/28/41 to Jean Ellen Hahn; c. Ann, Patrick and Jane. Educ: Mich. State Univ, B.A, 39; Univ. of Mich, LL.B, 48. Polit. & Govt. Pos: Chmn, Eaton Co. Rep. Party, Mich, 64-66; circuit judge, Fifth Judicial Circuit, Mich, 67- Mil. Serv: Entered as 2nd Lt, Army, 41, released as Capt, 45, after serv. in 11th Airborne Div, Pac; Silver Star. Mem: Pres, Eaton Co. Bar Asn, 51; Mich. and Am. Bar Asns; Farm Bur; Kiwanis; VFW. Rel: Methodist. Mailing Add: Route 1, Eaton Rapids, Mich. 48827.

ROBINSON, ROBERT J. D
Chmn, Buncombe Co. Dem. Exec. Cmt, N.C.
b. Asheville, N.C, 11/7/36; s. Marvin C. Robinson (deceased) and Lucile Carmichael R; m. 6/18/53 to Anne Buchanan; c. Robert J, Jr, Jonathan Jay and Elizabeth Anne. Educ: Mars Hill Col, A.A, 56; Wake Forest Univ, B.A, 58; Wake Forest Univ. Law Sch, LL.B, 60; Kappa Alpha; Phi Delta Phi. Polit. & Govt. Pos: Law clerk to U.S. Dist. Judge Wilson Worlick, West. Dist. of N.C, Newton, N.C, 60-61; Asst. U.S. attorney, Asheville, N.C, 62-64; secy, Young Dem. Club of Buncombe Co, N.C, 67; chmn, Buncombe Co. Dem. Exec. Cmt, 67-; del, Dem. Nat. Conv, 68. Bus. & Prof. Pos: Partner, Patla, Straus, Robinson & Moore, Attorneys, Asheville, N.C, 64- Mem: Buncombe Co, N.C. and Am. Bar Asns; N.C. State Bar. Rel: Presbyterian. Mailing Add: 16 N. Kensington Rd, Asheville, N.C. 28804.

ROBINSON, SANKEY WRIGHT D
N.C. State Sen.
b. Columbus, N.C, 11/28/24; s. Jimsey L. Robinson and Mary Britt R; m. 8/9/47 to Elizabeth Wiseman; c. Mary Elizabeth. Educ: Wake Forest Col, B.S, 48; Wake Forest Sch. of Law, LL.B, 51; Phi Delta Phi; Alpha Sigma Phi. Polit. & Govt. Pos: Solicitor, Columbus Co. Court, N.C, 52-54, judge, 54-58; co. attorney, Columbus Co, 60-65; mem, Whiteville City Admin. Bd. of Educ, 63-68; N.C. State Sen, 15th Sen. Dist, 69- Mem: Columbus Co, N.C. and Am. Bar Asns; 13th Judicial Dist. Bar Asn.(pres, 63-64); N.C. State Bar; N.C. Acad. of Trial Attorneys; Am. Judicature Soc; Lions (dist. gov, 62-63); Mason (32°); Shrine. Rel: Baptist. Legal Res: 511 Bob White Lane, Whiteville, N.C. 28472. Mailing Add: Courthouse Square, Whiteville, N.C. 28472.

ROBINSON, SARA KATHARINE MOORE D
b. Chicago, Ill, 6/26/38; d. Herbert Jackson Moore and Margaret Emma Roberts M; m. 8/4/62 to Donald Louis Robinson; c. Marshall Jackson. Educ: Beloit Col, B.A, 59; Columbus Sch. of Law, Cath. Univ. of Am, J.D, 65; rush chmn, Kappa Alpha Theta; Young Dem; Kappa Beta Pi; assoc. ed. and ed-in-chief, Legal Issue. Polit. & Govt. Pos: Campaign secy, Wis. Humphrey for Pres. Cmt, 59; exec. secy. to U.S. Rep. Henry S. Reuss, 59-65, legal asst, 65- Publ: 'Legislative Reapportionment: In Court and Congress,' Kappa Beta Pi Quart. 12/64. Mem: Dean, Beta Gamma Chap, Kappa Beta Pi; Am. Civil Liberties Union; bd. dirs, Powerhouse, Inc; bd. dirs, Wash. Half-Way Home for Women. Rel: Episcopal; Mem. bd. dirs, St. Stephen's Enterprises, Inc; Jr. Warden, Church of St. Stephen and The Incarnation. Legal Res: 319 Kenosha Ave, Oglesby, Ill. 61348. Mailing Add: 1817 Kenyon St. N.W, Washington, D.C. 20010.

ROBINSON, SPOTTSWOOD WILLIAM, III
b. Richmond, Va, 7/26/16; s. Spottswood William Robinson, Jr. and Inez Clements R; m. 3/5/36 to Marian Bernice Wilkerson; c. Spottswood William, IV and Nina Cecelia (Mrs. Oswald G. Govan). Educ: Va. Union Univ, 32-34, 35-36, LL.D, 55; Howard Univ, LL.B, magna cum laude, 39. Polit. & Govt. Pos: Mem, U.S. Cmn. Civil Rights, 61-63; judge, U.S. Dist. Court D.C, 64-66, judge, U.S. Court Appeals for D.C. Circuit, 66- Bus. & Prof. Pos: Faculty, Howard Univ, 39-48, assoc. prof. law, 45-48, prof. and dean law sch, 60-63; admitted to Va. Bar, 43; mem. firm, Hill & Robinson, 43-44 and Hill, Martin & Robinson, 44-55; admitted to U.S. Supreme Court, 48; legal rep, Va. NAACP Legal Defense and Educ. Fund, 48-50, southeast regional counsel, 51-60; sole practitioner, 55-60; v.pres. and gen. counsel, Consolidated Bank & Trust Co, 63-64. Mem: Am, Nat. and Old Dominion Bar Asns; Va. State Bar; hon. mem. Bar Asn. D.C; hon. mem. Nat. Lawyers Club. Recipient Annual Alumni Award, Howard Univ, 51. Rel: Episcopal. Mailing Add: 5400 30th St. N.W, Washington, D.C. 20015.

ROBINSON, WILLARD JAMES R
Chmn, Calaveras Co. Rep. Cent. Cmt, Calif.
b. Lathrop, Calif, 11/20/92; s. William James Robinson and Helen Johnson R; m. 10/17/15 to Marie Barbara Holloway; c. Emery William and Evelyn Marie (Mrs. Olson). Educ: Univ. Calif, Berkeley, 1 year; Healds Bus. Col, 1 year. Polit. & Govt. Pos: Pres. bd. dirs, Woodbridge Irrigation Dist, Calif, 24-36; city councilman, Lodi, 52-60, mayor, 55-56; mem, Calaveras Co. Rep. Cent. Cmt, 66-, chmn, 69- Bus. & Prof. Pos: Mem, Robinsons Feed Fuel Warehousing Firm, Lodi, Calif, 14-19, owner, 36-47; farmer, 19-60. Mem: Odd Fellows; Farm Bur; Grange; Lions. Rel: Protestant. Legal Res: 27 Pine Dr, Arnold, Calif. 95223. Mailing Add: P.O. Box 414, Arnold, Calif. 95223.

ROBINSON, WILLIAM H. R
b. White Stone, Va, 5/11/09. Educ: Va. Union Univ, A.B; Univ. of Chicago Sch. of Soc. Serv. Admin, M.A; Omega Psi Phi. Polit. & Govt. Pos: Rep. committeeman, Second Ward, Chicago, Ill; mem, Adv. Cmt. of Cook Co. Dept. of Child Welfare; mem, Adv. Bd. Commun. Serv. Div. of Ill. Youth Cmn; parole officer, Ill. Dept. of Pub. Safety; dir, Cook Co. Dept. of Pub. Aid; Ill. State Rep, 55-65, chmn, Cmt. on Pub. Aid, Health and Welfare, 63-65; dir, Ill. Dept. of Registrn. and Educ, currently. Bus. & Prof. Pos: Field work instr, Univ. of Chicago Sch. of Soc. Serv. Admin; asst. exec. secy, Soc. Welfare Dept, Church Fedn. of Gr. Chicago, dir, Youth Serv. Bur; pres, Monumental Credit Union; lectr. and consult. on soc. welfare probs. and govt. progs. Mil. Serv: World War II. Mem: Bd. of dirs, Adult Educ. Coun. of Gr. Chicago, Am. Pub. Welfare Asn. and Central Baptist Children's Home; Inter-Agency Resources Adv. Coun, Chicago Alliance of Businessmen; exec. cmt, Chicago Cmt. on Urban Opportunity; v.pres, Chicago Urban League; Cmnr. on Pub. Welfare, Int. Elks; bd. dirs, Commun. Renewal Soc. and Family Serv. Asn. of Am; trustee bd, Garrett Theol. Sem; Ill. Cmn. for the 1970 White House Conf. on Children and Youth; Ill. State Coun. on Aging; Ill. Welfare Asn.(bd. dirs. and chmn, Membership Cmt); bd. dirs, Joint Negro Appeal; commun. adv. cmt, Jr. League of Chicago; v.chmn, Leadership Coun. of Metrop. Open Commun; Joint Welfare Cmt, Mayor's Cmn. on Youth Welfare; Nat. Assembly for Soc. Policy and Develop, Inc; Nat. Asn. of Soc. Workers (exec. bd, Chicago Chap); bd. of dirs, Nat. Conf. of Christians and Jews; chmn, Soc.

Welfare Cmt, Dept. of Soc. Justice, Nat. Coun. of Churches of Christ; Nat. Urban League (Personnel Develop. and Training Cmt, Commun. Resources Cmt. and Bus. Adv. Coun); Planned Parenthood Fedn. of Am.(exec. cmt, World Population); St. Leonard's House Adv. Bd; Ill. Off. of Pub. Instr. (Instructional TV and Radio and Adv. Coun); state adv. cmt, U.S. Cmn. on Civil Rights; Univ. of Chicago Sch. of Soc. Serv. Admin.(bd. of trustees, Alumni Asn. and mem, Vis. Cmt). Outstanding Freshman Legislator, Newspaper Correspondents in Springfield, 55; Layman of the Year, Gr. Chicago Churchmen, 58; Distinguished Serv. Award in Welfare and Govt, Frontiers Int, Chicago Chap, 58; Distinguished Serv. Award, Ill. Welfare Asn, 61; Serv. Recognition Award, Ill. Youth Cmn, 63; Ode to Excellence Award, Sigma Chap, Omega Psi Phi, 63; Dorothy Wigley Offield Award for Distinguished Leadership in Planned Parenthood, 64; Clarence Darrow Humanitarian Award, 65; Man of the Year, Beatrice Caffree Youth Serv, 66. Rel: Baptist; Deacon and Trustee, Monumental Baptist Church, supt. of Sunday Sch, 30 years. Mailing Add: 160 N. La Salle St, Chicago, Ill. 60601.

ROBINSON, WILLIAM HOBERT R
Chmn, Mercer Co. Rep. Party, Ky.
b. Washington Co, Ky, 7/3/10; s. J.H. Robinson and Martha Long R; m. 12/11/32 to Hestell Foster; c. Don W. Polit. & Govt. Pos: Mem, Purgation Bd. Rep. Party, Ky, 45-49; Rep. precinct committeeman, 45-57; elec. cmnr, Mercer Co. Rep. Party, 49-57, campaign chmn, 56 & 60 and chmn, 57- Bus. & Prof. Pos: Farmer, 30-43; grain dealer, 43- Mem: Mason; Modern Woodman of Am. Rel: Baptist. Mailing Add: 604 Greenwood St, Harrodsburg, Ky. 40330.

ROBINSON, WILLIAM INGRAHAM D
b. Kansas City, Mo, 9/20/09; s. Ernest Franklin Robinson and Mary Kip R; m. 9/05/42 to Virginia Burch; c. Mary Kip and William I, Jr. Educ: Univ. Mo, B.A, 31; Univ. Mich, J.D, 34; Phi Delta Phi; Phi Delta Theta. Polit. & Govt. Pos: Enforcement and acting regional attorney, Off. Price Admin, 41-42; Dem. precinct committeeman, Kans, 47-64; Dem. Cong. Cand, Fourth Dist, Kans, 60; hearing officer, Dept. of Justice, 62-; chmn, Sedgwick Co. Dem. Cent. Cmt, Kans, 62-66; del, Dem. Nat. Conv, 64 & 68; Dem. cand. for U.S. Senate, 68. Mil. Serv: Entered as 1st Lt, Army, 42, released as Maj, 45, after serv. in ETO, Third Army, 44-45; Lt. Col, Army Res; ETO Ribbon; 2 Bronze Stars. Mem: Am, Calif, Okla. and Kans. Bar Asns; Wichita Bar Asn.(mem. bd. dirs, 56-60); Am. Judicature Soc; Am. Legion; VFW. Rel: Episcopal. Legal Res: 3343 Country Club Place, Wichita, Kans. 67208. Mailing Add: American Savings Bldg, 201 N. Main, Wichita, Kans. 67202.

ROBINSON, WINTHROP LINCOLN R
Chmn, Taunton Rep. City Cmt, Mass.
b. Taunton, Mass, 9/11/05; s. Chester Winthrop Robinson (deceased) and Alice Maud Lincoln R.(deceased); m. 1/16/60 to Amy Mildred Cousins. Educ: High Sch, grad, 24; Int. Accounts Soc, Alexander Hamilton Inst, Chicago, Ill. Polit. & Govt. Pos: Mem, Selective Serv. Local Draft Bd, 54, Wards 5, 7 and 8, Taunton, Mass, 65-; Taunton Area coordinator for former U.S. Rep. Lawrence E. Curtis for U.S. Sen, Mass, 63; committeeman and treas, Taunton Ward 5; finance chmn, Taunton Area, Mass. State Rep. Cmt, 63-66; mem, Bristol Co. Rep. Club, 65-; chmn, Taunton Rep. City Cmt, currently; mem, Taunton Planning Bd, 68- Bus. & Prof. Pos: Bldg. contractor, Taunton, Mass, 35-66. Mem: Corp, Morton Hospital, Taunton and Bristol Co. Savings Bank; dir, Ment. Health Bargain Bazaar Thrift Shop and Taunton Area Ment. Health Clin; Mass. Rep. City Chmn. Asn. Rel: Baptist. Mailing Add: 5 Jefferson Ave, Taunton, Mass. 02780.

ROBISON, BLANCHARD GAILLARD, JR. D
b. Carrollton, Ala, 4/15/11; s. Blanchard Gaillard Robison and Virginia Kerr Hill R; m. 12/25/57 to Lois Esther Atkins Colvin. Educ: Univ. of Ala. Polit. & Govt. Pos: Ala. State Sen, until 66; mem, Tenn-Tombigbee Waterway Develop. Authority, 67- Mil. Serv: Navy. Rel: Presbyterian. Mailing Add: Carrollton, Ala. 35447.

ROBISON, HOWARD WINFIELD R
U.S. Rep, N.Y.
b. Owego, N.Y, 10/30/15; s. Addison J. Robison and Pluma Moe R; m. 11/1/46 to Gertrude L. Frederick; c. Howard W, Jr. and Douglas E. Educ: Cornell Univ, A.B, 37 and LL.B, 39; Phi Kappa Sigma. Polit. & Govt. Pos: Co. attorney, Tioga Co, N.Y, 46-58; Justice of Peace, Owego, 47-56, town attorney, 56-58; U.S. Rep, 33rd Dist, N.Y, 58- Mil. Serv: Entered as Pvt, Army, 42, released as Sgt, 46, after serv. in Counter-Intel. Corps. Mem: Pres, Sixth Judicial Dist. Bar Fedn, N.Y, 58 and Tioga Co. Bar Asn, 50; N.Y. State and Fed. Bar Asns; Kiwanis; Elks; Mason; Shrine; Am. Legion; Capitol Hill Club. Rel: Methodist. Legal Res: 333 Main St, Owego, N.Y. 13827. Mailing Add: 2436 Rayburn Office Bldg, Washington, D.C. 20515.

ROBISON, VAUGHAN HILL D
b. Montgomery, Ala, 3/17/18; s. Elbert Vaughan Robison and Laura Croom Hill R; m. 2/23/52 to Elizabeth Crommelin Robison. Educ: Univ. of Ala, B.A, 36; Univ. Law Sch, 38. Polit. & Govt. Pos: Ala. State Sen, 51-66. Bus. & Prof. Pos: Practicing law in firm of Hill, Robison & Belser. Mil. Serv: Army, Artil, Capt, ETO, 41-46. Mem: Mason; Shriner; Pythian; Elk; Am. Legion; VFW; past pres, Montgomery Co. Bar Asn. Rel: Presbyterian. Mailing Add: P.O. Box 901 or 36 S. Perry St, Montgomery, Ala. 36104. (1967)

ROBSION, JOHN MARSHALL, JR. R
b. Barbourville, Ky, 8/38/04; s. John Marshall Robsion and Lida Stansberry R; m. 7/15/49 to Laura Selinda Edwards. Educ: Union Col. Acad, Barbourville, 19; George Wash. Univ, J.D, 26; Georgetown Univ; Nat. War Col, 54. Hon. LL.D, Union Col, 69. Polit. & Govt. Pos: Cong. Secy, 20-26; Speaker of Little Cong, 26; chief of law div, U.S. Bur. Pensions, 29-32, mem, Bd. of Vets. Appeals, 32-35; gen. counsel, Rep. Party, Ky, 38-42; exec. secy, Young Rep. Nat. Fedn, 40-42; spec. circuit court judge, 46-52; U.S. Rep, Ky, 53-59, mem, Judiciary Cmt, 53-59 and Cmt. on Cmts, 55-59; del Interparliamentary Union Conf, Helsinki, 55, Bangkok, 56 and London, 57; del, Rep. Nat. Conv, 56 & 60; cand, Gov. of Ky, 59; chmn, Rep. Adv. Cmt, S.Fla, 66-68. Bus. & Prof. Pos: Attorney-at-law, Barbourville, 26-29, Louisville, 35-42, 46-52 & 59-; trustee, Ky. Jockey Club, 60-65. Mil. Serv: Army, 42-46; mem. staff Gen. Mark Clark, Italy and Austria. Mem: Trustee, Union Col; former chmn. and life mem. bd, Salvation Army, Louisville and bd, Ft. Lauderdale; Louisville Commun. Concert Series (pres, 60-63); Gt. Decisions Cmt, Ky.(chmn, 60-61); Louisville Amphitheater Prod.(pres, 61); past dist. comdr, Boy Scouts and VFW; Amvets; Am. Legion; DAV; past comdr, Mil. Order World Wars; past first v.pres, Louisville Bar Asn; past pres, Lincoln Club and Highlands Men's Club; Mason; Pendennis Club, Louisville. Rel: Christian Church. Mailing Add: 600 Lido Dr, Ft. Lauderdale, Fla 33301.

ROBSON, ROBERT MORGAN R
Chmn, Shoshone Co. Rep. Cent. Cmt, Idaho
b. Kellogg, Idaho, 11/28/21; s. Ira Allen Robson and Margaret Mary Morgan R; m. 8/28/44 to Catherine Penelope Agee; c. Catherine Lynn, James Allen, Margaret Leslie and Robert Agee. Educ: Univ. Idaho, LL.B, 49; Phi Delta Theta; Idaho Alpha. Polit. & Govt. Pos: Precinct committeeman, Grangeville, Idaho Co, 50-54, Kellogg, Shoshone Co, 58-62; prosecuting attorney, Idaho Co, 50-53; secy-treas, Idaho Co. Rep. Cent. Cmt, 52-54; dist. attorney, Trust Territory of the Pac. Islands, U.S. Dept. of Interior, 55-57; city attorney, Kellogg, Idaho, 58-64; chmn, Shoshone Co. Rep. Cent. Cmt, 62-; alternate del, Rep. Nat. and State Conv, 64, del, Rep. Nat. Conv, 68; attorney gen, Idaho, 69- Bus. & Prof. Pos: Attorney-at-law, Grangeville, 49-55, Kellogg, 60-; partner, Tuson & Robson, attorney, 57-60. Mil. Serv: Entered as Seaman 2/C, Navy, 42, released as Lt.(jg), 45, after serv. as Naval Aviator; Victory Medal; Am. and Pac. Theater Campaign Ribbons; Inactive Res. until 59. Mem: Am. Judicature Soc; Idaho State and Shoshone Bar Asns; Fed. Bar Asn, 55-57; Wardner Lodge 34, AF&AM; Elks Lodge 1847; Legion of Honor, DeMolay and Dad Adv, Kellogg Chapter; pres, Kellogg C. of C, 59-60 and Grengeville Jr. C. of C, 51-52; secy-treas, Grangeville C. of C, 50-53. Rel: Episcopal; Vestryman, Emmanuel Church of Kellogg; licensed lay reader for 17 years; trustee, Episcopal Diocese of Spokane; mem, Diocesan Coun. Legal Res: 605 Riverside Ave, Kellogg, Idaho 83837. Mailing Add: Box 539, Kellogg, Idaho 83837.

ROBY, ARTHUR E, SR. R
b. Concord, N.H, 6/3/91; married; c. Two. Educ: Concord Schs, N.H. Polit. & Govt. Pos: Pres. emer, N.H. City and Town Clerks Asn; city clerk, Concord, N.H, 44 years, now city clerk emer; former N.H. State Rep. Mem: Odd Fellows; Mason; Elks. Rel: Protestant. Mailing Add: 4 Donovan St, Concord, N.H. 03301. (1967)

ROCHA, GELBERT T. D
b. E. Providence, 10/17/31; m. to Joan K. Educ: Boston Col, B.S, 1954; Boston Col. Law Sch, LL.B, 1957; Boston Col. Varsity Club. Polit. Pos: R.I. State Sen, 59-66; Secy, Dem. State Cmt. Mem: R.I. Bar Asn; Lions; E. Providence Jr. C. of C; E. Providence Coun; K. of C; Int. Brewery Workers of Am, Local 114; Boston Col. Club of R.I; Bd. of Dir. Pre-Teen Football Asn. Mailing Add: 57 Tryon Ave, Rumford, R.I. 02916. (1967)

ROCHA, JAMES JOHN D
Chmn, Little Compton Dem. Town Cmt, R.I.
b. Little Compton, R.I, 11/18/39; s. Manuel B. Rocha and Alexandria Mello R; m. 11/24/63 to Anne P. McDonnell; c. James P. and Leslie M. Educ: J.F. Wilbur High Sch, 4 years. Polit. & Govt. Pos: Chmn, Little Compton Dem. Town Cmt, R.I, 66- Bus. & Prof. Pos: Salesman, R.J. Reynolds Tobacco Co. Mil. Serv: Entered as Pvt, Army, 58, released as SP-4, 60, after serv. in 23rd Transportation Bn; Eighth Army, First Cavalry Div, Korea, 58-59; Good Conduct Medal. Mem: K. of C. Rel: Catholic. Mailing Add: Long Pasture Rd, Little Compton, R.I. 02837.

ROCK, ISABEL K. R
b. Jersey City, N.J. Oct, 27; d. Arthur E. Kline and Carrie Birch K; m. 10/6/15 to P. Arthur Rock, wid; c. Philip Arthur and James Stoll. Educ: Goucher Col, A.B; Gamma Phi Beta. Polit. & Govt. Pos: Mem. exec. bd, Fairfield Co. Rep. Women's Asn, 54-, recording secy, 58-60; Conn. State Rep, 61-69; pres, past v.pres. and corresponding secy, Wilton Women's Rep. Club. Mem: Am. Asn. of Univ. Women; DAR; Garden Club; Hist. Soc; L. of W.V; Shore & Country Club. Rel: Congregational. Legal Res: 7 Kensett Ave, Wilton, Conn. 06897,

ROCK, ROBERT LEE D
b. Alexandria, Ind, 9/9/27; s. Walter Rock and Roseanna Scherer R; m. 6/23/56 to Mary Jo Ferguson; c. Kathy, Karen, Karel Jo and Robert. Educ: Ind. Univ, B.S; Sigma Chi. Polit. & Govt. Pos: Ind. State Rep, 57-63; Lt. Gov, Ind, 65-67; cand, Gov, 68. Bus. & Prof. Pos: Partner, The Rock Agency, Anderson, Ind, 49-65. Mil. Serv: Navy, 45-46. Mem: The Honorable Order of Ky. Colonels; The Coun. of the Sagamores of the Wabash; Elks; Indianapolis Athletic Club; Anderson Country Club. Rel: Presbyterian. Mailing Add: 1010 Atwood Lane, Anderson, Ind. 46011. (1967)

ROCKEFELLER, JOHN DAVISON, IV D
Secy. of State, W.Va.
b. New York, N.Y, 6/18/37; s. John Davison Rockefeller, III and Blanchette Hooker R; m. 4/1/67 to Sharon Percy. Educ: Harvard Univ, A.B, 61. Polit. & Govt. Pos: Philippine opers. officer, Peace Corps, Wash, D.C, 62-63; Indonesian Opers. officer, State Dept, 63-64; mem. staff commun. develop, Off. Econ. Opportunity, Charleston, W.Va, 64-66; W.Va. State Del, 66-68; Secy. of State, W.Va, 69- Publ: 'The Japanese Student', New York Times Mag, 6/60 and Life, 6/60. Rel: Presbyterian. Mailing Add: 1515 Barberry Lane, Charleston, W.Va. 25314.

ROCKEFELLER, NELSON ALDRICH R
Gov, N.Y.
b. Bar Harbor, Maine, 7/8/08; s. John D. Rockefeller, Jr. and Abby Aldrich R; m. 6/23/30 to Mary Todhunter Clark, div, 3/62; m. 5/4/63 to Margaretta Fitler Murphy; c. Rodman C, Ann (Mrs. Pierson); Steven C, Mary (Mrs. William J. Strawbridge, Jr), Michael C. (deceased), Nelson, Jr. and Mark F. Educ: Dartmouth Col, A.B. in Econ, 30; Phi Beta Kappa. Polit. & Govt. Pos: Coordinator Inter-Am. Affairs, 40-44; Asst. Secy. of State for Am. Repub. Affairs, 44-45; chmn, Int. Develop. Adv. Bd, 50-51; chmn, President's Adv. Cmt. on Govt. Orgn, 52-59; chmn, Spec. Cmt. on Reorgn. Defense Dept, 53; Under Secy, Dept. Health, Educ. and Welfare, 53-54; Spec. Asst. to the President for For. Affairs, 54-55; chmn. two studies, N.Y. State Constitution,

56-59; chmn, Gov. Conf. Cmt. on Civil Defense and Post Attack Recovery, 59-; Gov, N.Y, 59-; Presidential cand, 64 & 68; mem, Adv. Cmn. Intergovt. Rels, 65-; personal rep. of the President to Latin Am, 69. Rel: Baptist. Legal Res: Pocantico Hills, Tarrytown, N.Y. 10591. Mailing Add: Executive Chamber, State Capitol, Albany, N.Y. 12224.

ROCKEFELLER, WINTHROP R
Gov, Ark.
b. N.Y.C, 5/1/12; s. John D. Rockefeller, Jr. and Abby Aldrich R; m. 2/14/48 to Barbara Sears; div; m. 6/11/56 to Jeannette Edris; c. Winthrop Paul and stepchildren, Mrs. Salvatore Papa and Bruce Bartley. Educ: Yale Univ, 32-34; Delta Kappa Epsilon. Hon. LL.D, Univ. Ark, Hendrix Col, Col. William and Mary, Col. of the Ozarks and Southwest. at Memphis; hon. HH.D, N.Y. Univ. and Univ. San Francis Xavier. Polit. & Govt. Pos: Chmn, Ark. Indust. Develop. Cmn, 55-64; Gov, Ark, 67-; del, Rep. Nat. Conv, 68. Bus. & Prof. Pos: Trainee, Humble Oil & Refining Co, 34-37; with Chase Nat. Bank, 37-39; for. trade dept, Socony-Vacuum Oil Co, 39-41; producing dept, Socony Mobil Oil Co, 46-51; chmn, Ibec Housing Corp, 51-59; farming and invests, 53- Mil. Serv: Entered as Pvt, Army, 41, released as Lt. Col, 46, after serv. in 305th Inf. Regt, 77th Div, Pac. Theater, 42-46; Bronze Star with Oak Leaf Cluster; Purple Heart; Am. Defense, Am. Theater, Asiatic-Pac. Theater, Victory and Philippine Liberation Ribbons. Mem: Chmn. bd, Colonial Williamsburg, Inc. and Williamsburg Restoration, Inc; trustee, Loomis Sch, Conn. and Vanderbilt Univ, Tenn; director, Education Facilities Labs Inc, N.Y; chmn, Ark. Opportunity Fund and Rockwin Fund; Southwest. Adv. Cmt, Inst. of Int. Educ; trustee, Indust. Rels. Counsrs, Inc; dir, Rockefeller Bros, Inc; Santa Gertrudis Breeders Int; Delta Santa Gertrudis Breeders Asn; Am. Hereford Asn; Ark. Cattlemen's Asn; Am. Legion; hon. mem, Kappa Delta Pi. Rel: Baptist. Legal Res: Winrock Farms, Route 3, Morrilton, Ark. 72110. Mailing Add: State Capitol, Little Rock, Ark. 72201.

ROCKETT, J. HILARY R
Mass. State Rep.
b. Marblehead, Mass, 1/16/35; s. Richard H. Rockett and Irene McCrath R; m. 6/30/62 to Denise Hanlon; c. Hilary, Michael, Richard and Pamela. Educ: Tufts Univ, B.A, 57; New Eng. Sch. of Law, LL.B. cum laude, 67; Zeta Psi. Polit. & Govt. Pos: Selectman, Marblehead Bd. of Selectmen, 60-67; Mass. State Rep, 62- Bus. & Prof. Pos: Trustee, The Village Shopping Center Realty Trust, 68- Mil. Serv: Entered as Pvt, Army, released as Cpl, 59, after serv. in Signal Corps. Mem: Mass, Am. and Essex Co. Bar Asns; Elks; Marblehead Little League Asn. Named and given plaque as Hon. Citizen of the Town of Swampscott, Mass. for legis. work done on behalf of town, 68. Rel: Catholic. Legal Res: 59 Bayview Rd, Marblehead, Mass. 01945. Mailing Add: 39 School St, Marblehead, Mass. 01945.

ROCKWELL, GORDON R
Mich. State Sen.
b. Flint, Mich, 2/23/15; s. Harold C. Rockwell and Anna Lambert R; m. 1/12/41 to Bertha Protzman; c. Jan and Jill. Educ: Flint Jr. Col, 33-35. Polit. & Govt. Pos: Mem, Bd. Educ, Mt. Morris, Mich, 58-60; Mich. State Rep, 60-64; chmn, Twp. Zoning Bd, 62-64; appointee, State Sch. Reorgn. Bd, 65-66; mem, Rep. Co. Cmt; Mich. State Sen, 67- Mil. Serv: Entered as Pvt, Army, 43, released as M/Sgt, 46, after serv. in 14th Anti Aircraft Artil. Command, Southwest Pac, 44-46; Southwest Pac. Campaign Ribbons; Philippine Occup. Medal; 3 Battle Stars. Mem: Mason; Lions; Farm Bur. Rel: Methodist. Mailing Add: 9052 N. Saginaw St, Mt. Morris, Mich. 48458.

ROCKWELL, WILSON MILLER R
Colo. State Sen.
b. Bradford, Pa, 6/26/09; s. Robert Fay Rockwell and Aileen Miller R; m. 4/26/48 to Enid Wolverton; c. Daniel. Educ: Stanford Univ, B.A, 33; Denver Univ, M.A, 38; Phi Delta Phi. Polit. & Govt. Pos: Colo. State Sen, 62- Mil. Serv: Entered as Pvt, Air Force, 43, released as 1st Lt, 46. Publ: Sunset Slope, 56, Memoirs of a Lawman, 62 and Uncompahgre Country, 65, Sage Bks. Mem: Elks; Rotary Int; Am. Legion; Colo. Cattlemen's Asn; Colo. Author's League. Mailing Add: Maher, Colo. 81421.

RODBY, LEO BERNARD, JR. D
Dem. Nat. Committeeman, Hawaii
b. Wahiawa, Hawaii, 1/12/26; s. Leo R. Rodby and Carita Fisher R; m. 4/4/54 to Kuulei E. Directo; c. Leilani, Timothy, Leo III, Walter, and Peter. Educ: Va. Jr. Col, 2 years. Polit. & Govt. Pos: Various precinct and dist. off, Dem. Party, Hawaii, 54-65; mem, Hawaii Dem. State Cent. Cmt, 65-66, treas, 66-68; treas, Dem. State Campaign Cmt, 66; alternate del, Dem. Nat. Conv, 68; Dem. Nat. Committeeman, Hawaii, 68- Bus. & Prof. Pos: Pres. and gen. mgr, Wahiawa Distributors Ltd, Wahiawa, Hawaii, 48-; pres, Wahiawa Commun. Asn, 54; treas, Trinity Lutheran Church and Sch, 54-; pres, Wahiawa Hosp. Asn, 64-68. Mil. Serv: Entered as A/S, Navy, 43, released as Qm 2/C, 46, after serv. in Landing Craft, Pac, 44-46. Mem: Bishop Museum Asn; Honolulu Acad. of Arts; Hawaii Canoe Racing Asn; Lions. Named Jr. C. of C. Young Man of the Year, 54. Legal Res: 1828 Eames St, Wahiawa, Hawaii 96786. Mailing Add: P.O. Box 70, Wahiawa, Hawaii 96786.

RODD, PAT R
Asst. Supv, Jackson Co. Bd. of Supervisors, Ill.
b. Carbondale, Ill, 11/12/35; d. James Frank Dwyer and Clara Rogers D; div; c. Pamela Lynn. Educ: South. Ill. Univ, B.S, 66, South. Ill. Univ, Grad. Sch, 1½ years; St. Louis Univ. Sch. Law, 68-; Phi Kappa Delta. Polit. & Govt. Pos: Justice of the Peace, Carbondale Twp, Ill; mem, Carbondale Town Bd. of Auditors; asst. supv, Jackson Co. Bd. of Supvr, 64-; alternate del, Rep. Nat. Conv, 68. Mem: Pres, Jackson Co. Legal Secretaries, 68-69; bd. dirs, Carbondale C. of C, 67-; League of Women Voters. Legal Res: 607 W. Walnut, Carbondale, Ill. 62901. Mailing Add: P.O. Box 359, Carbondale, Ill. 62901.

RODDA, ALBERT S. D
Calif. State Sen.
b. Sacramento, Calif. Educ: Stanford Univ, Ph.D. in hist. Polit. & Govt. Pos: Mem, Sacramento Co. Dem. Cent. Cmt, Calif, 52-58; Calif. State Sen, 58- Bus. & Prof. Pos: Instr. econ. and hist, Sacramento City Col. Mil. Serv: Naval Res, World War II. Mailing Add: 4048 Capitol Bldg, Sacramento, Calif. 95814.

RODDENBERRY, ERNEST D
b. Sopchoppy, Fla, 12/6/05; m. to Lottie Stalnaker R; c. Robert Howard, Linda Gale, Ernest David. Educ: Jacksonville Bus. Col. Polit. & Gov. Pos: Fla. State Rep, 64-66; sch. trustee, 10 yrs. Bus. & Prof. Pos: retired merchant, real estate. Mem: Lions. Rel: Chmn, Off. Bd, Sopchoppy Methodist Church. Mailing Add: P.O. Box 96, Sopchoppy, Fla. 32358. (1967)

RODDEY, FRANK LANEY D
S.C. State Sen.
b. Lancaster, S.C, 2/3/27; s. Elliott B. Roddey and Beulah Mae Laney R; m. 11/16/47 to Ophelia Melbrae Taylor. Educ: Davidson Col, 44; Univ. S.C, 47-48. Polit. & Govt. Pos: Mem. city coun, Lancaster, S.C, 52-59; S.C. State Sen, 63- Bus. & Prof. Pos: Owner, Frank L. Roddey Ins. Mem: Mason; Jackson Lodge 53; Shriner Hejaz Temple; bd. of dir, C. of C. and United Fund; campaign chmn, United Fund, 61; pres, Jaycees, 56; pres, Jr. High Sch. PTA, 61-62; Chesterfield Ave. PTA, 58-60. Young Man of the Year, 56. Mailing Add: Box 129, Lancaster, S.C. 29720. (1967)

RODELL, MARTIN D
N.Y. State Assemblyman
b. N.Y.C, 8/14/15; m. to Sonya Bilmes. Educ: St. Johns Univ. and Law Sch. Polit. & Govt. Pos: Asst. dist. attorney, Queens Co, N.Y; N.Y. State Assemblyman, 64- Bus. & Prof. Pos: Lawyer. Mil. Serv: World War II. Mem: N.Y. State and Nat. Dist. Attorneys Asns; exec. bd, Martin Van Buren High Sch. Parents Asn; exec. bd, E. Queens Brotherhood Coun, Jewish War Vet; past chancellor, K. of P. Rel: Jewish. Mailing Add: 79-47 264th St, Queens Village, N.Y. 11004. (1967)

RODENBOUGH, GRACE TAYLOR D
b. Danbury, N.C, 10/5/99; d. James Spotswood Taylor and Nellie Pemberton Moon T; m. 8/4/47 to Stanley Leigh Rodenbough, Jr; stepchildren, Leigh and Charles. Educ: Guilford Col, A.B, 17; Woman's Col, Univ. N.C, M.A. Polit. & Govt. Pos: Mem, Gov. Cmn. for Study State Supported Insts. Higher Learning, 53- and N.C. Cmn. on Educ. and Employ. Women; N.C. State Rep, Stokes Co, 53-63; Stokes Co. Chmn, War Savings Bonds, 43-45; v.pres, N.C. Young Dem. Club, 38-39 and pres, Stokes Co. Young Dem. Club, 36-37. Bus. & Prof. Pos: Mem. bd. gov, Gov. Sch; mem. bd. trustees, Univ. N.C; supvr. instr, Stokes Co. Schs; agent, 3500 acre ancestral estate; mgr, several hundred acre farm; former teacher, Salem Col. Mem: Nat. Educ. Asn; secy, Stokes Co. Unit, N.C. Educ. Asn, 38-39, pres, 39-40; Asn. Supvr, Curriculum and Develop; Stokes Co. Sch. Masters Club; trustee, Northwest. Regional Libr; Delta Kappa Gamma; bd. dirs, Carolinas United; N.C. Cmn. to Study Cause and Cure of Cancer; pres, Hanging Rock Park Found; Stokes Co. Pres, Am. Red Cross, 42-43, exec. dir, Fla, 45-46, field rep, N.C, 46-47; DAR; United Daughters Confederacy; N.C. Literary and Hist. Asn; N.C. Soc. for Preservation Antiquities; Nat. Order Women Legislators; Am. Asn. Univ. Women. Distinguished Citizen's Award, Walnut Cove Rotary. Rel: Presbyterian; Sunday Sch. teacher. Mailing Add: Covington, Walnut Cove, N.C. 27052. (1967)

RODGERS, DAVID H. R
Mayor, Spokane, Wash.
b. New Albany, Ind, 8/10/23; s. Clarence Earl Rodgers and Gladys Hardy R; m. 7/17/65 to Naomi Fowle; c. Nancy (Mrs. Varnador) and Maureen Fowle and John T, Rebecca J, Brian A. and Janet P. Rodgers. Educ: Purdue Univ, B.S, 47; Sigma Alpha Epsilon. Polit. & Govt. Pos: Precinct committeeman, Rep. Party, Wash, 52-54; Rep. Dist. Leader, Spokane, Wash, 52-54; pres, Spokane Co. Rep. Club, 54-56; chmn, Spokane Co. Rep. Party, 56-58; mem, Wash. State Rep. Exec. Bd, 56-60; Rep. State Committeeman, Wash, 58-60; mayor, Spokane, 67- Bus. & Prof. Pos: Mgr. group and pension dept, Aetna Life Ins. Co, Spokane, 49- Mil. Serv: Navy, 45, Ens, serv. in Underwater Demolition Team. Mem: Boy Scouts (bd, Inland Empire Coun); Mason; Kiwanis; YMCA (pres. bd. dirs, 62). Rel: Presbyterian. Legal Res: 4511 S. Madelia, Spokane, Wash. 99203. Mailing Add: 654 City Hall, Spokane, Wash. 99201.

RODGERS, HENRY BENJAMIN D
b. Lofton, Fla, 8/08/03; s. James W. Rodgers and Kathleene Roddenberry R; m. 6/05/38 to Maggie Mason Stokes; c. Margaret Rose (Mrs. James Pitzer Gills), Henry Benjamin Jr, William Mason. Educ: Folkston High Sch. Polit. & Govt. Pos: Ga. State Rep, 55-66. Bus. & Prof. Pos: Naval stores operator. Rel: Baptist. Mailing Add: Folkston, Ga. 31537. (1967)

RODGERS, HENRY L. D
Justice, Supreme Court, Miss.
b. Phila, Miss, 4/6/03; s. Henry Herman Rodgers and Ettie Lee Brantley R; m. 5/18/29 to Leola Edwards. Educ: Miss. Col, 20-22; Cumberland Univ, B.A, 22; Univ. of Miss, LL.B, 27. Polit. & Govt. Pos: City attorney, Louisville, Miss, 45-46; dist. attorney, Fifth Judicial Dist, 46-51, circuit judge, 51-61; Justice, Supreme Court, Miss, 61- Mil. Serv: Miss. Nat. Guard, 29-35, Hq. Co, 155th Inf, 31st Div, Army, 43-44, 2nd Lt, 240 AAA East Coast Defense, Newport, R.I. Publ: 'Search and Seizure,' 12/56 and 'Process,' 8/59, Miss. Law J. Mem: Miss. Bar Asn; Inst. Judicial Admin, N.Y. Univ; Sons of Confederate Vets; Am. Legion; 40 et 8; Shrine; Moose; Lions, 36 years. Rel: Methodist. Legal Res: 431 N. Spring, Louisville, Miss. 39339. Mailing Add: Box 117, Jackson, Miss. 39205.

RODGERS, JOSEPH F, JR. D
R.I. State Sen.
b. Providence, R.I, 11/18/41; s. Joseph F. Rodgers and Gertrude Moan R; m. 2/19/66 to Donna Boudreau; c. Joseph F, III and Kristin E. Educ: Providence Col, B.A, 62; Boston Univ. Sch. of Law, LL.B, 66. Polit. & Govt. Pos: Treas, Young Dem. Club of R.I, 66-68, pres, 68-; R.I. State Sen, 68- Bus. & Prof. Pos: Attorney-at-law. Mem: Elks; Elmwood Civic Asn; Hibernians; R.I. Bar Asn; R.I. Bar. Rel: Roman Catholic. Mailing Add: 157 Atlantic Ave, Providence, R.I. 02907.

RODGERS, LOUISE V. D
Chmn. Women's Div, Madison Co. Dem. Party, Ala.
b. New Market, Ala, 5/4/20; d. William Roe Vandiver and Lillie Henshaw V; m. 9/28/38 to Walton White Rodgers; c. William Stanley, Kenneth White and

Augustus Donnell. Educ: New Market High Sch, grad, 38; Alverson-Draughon Bus. Col. Polit. & Govt. Pos: Co. off. mgr, DeGraffenried for Gov, Ala, 62 and co. mgr, 62-66; off. mgr, Glenn Hearn for Mayor, 64; co. off. mgr, Gilchrist for Gov. and Madison Co. Dem. Cand. Cmt, 66; v.chmn. women's div, Madison Co. Dem. Party, 67, chmn, 68-; alternate del, Dem. Nat. Conv, 68. Bus. & Prof. Pos: Bookkeeper and co-owner, Maple Ridge Hatchery, 45-62; free lance pub. rels. dir, 62- Mem: Press Club; Int. Concert Mgrs. Asn; Arts Coun, Inc; Phi Sigma Alpha; Civic Club Coun; Rocket City Toastmistress Club; Huntsville Bus. & Prfnl. Women's Club; adv. bd, Salvation Army; Altrusa Club of Huntsville; Madison Co. Heart Unit. Outstanding Serv. Awards from Salvation Army, United Givers Fund, Fantasy Playhouse, Civic Club Coun, Bus. & Prfnl. Women's Club, Cancer Soc, March of Dimes and Heart Asn; Good Neighbor Award. Rel: Presbyterian. Mailing Add: 208 White St. N.E, Huntsville, Ala. 35801.

RODINO, PETER WALLACE, JR. D
U.S. Rep, N.J.
b. Newark, N.J, 6/7/09; m. to Marianna Stango; c. Margaret Ann (Mrs. Charles Stanziale) and Peter III. Polit. & Govt. Pos: Past nat. chmn, Columbus Found, Inc; spearheaded dr. against Communism in April 1948 elec. in Italy; U.S. Del. to Intergovt. Cmt. for European Migration; del. to NATO Parliamentarians Conf; U.S. Rep, N.J, 48- Bus. & Prof. Pos: Attorney-at-law. Mil. Serv: One of first enlisted men to be commissioned overseas; First Armored Div. and Mil. Mission Ital. Army; discharged 46 as Capt; U.S. Bronze Star and other decorations. Holds knighthood in the Sovereign Mil. Order of Malta; Grand Officer, Order of Merit, Ital. Rep; Star of Solidarity, Ital. Rep; knighted by former King Umberto of Italy, Knight of the Order Crown of Italy, Knight of St. Maurizio Lazzaro; Ital. Cross of Merit and other for. decorations; awards and citations from VFW, Cath. War Vets, Jewish War Vets; Amvets Cong. Silver Helmet Award; recipient of 64 Bill of Rights Award for Distinguished Pub. Serv. in the field of govt; hon. life mem. of Unico. Legal Res: 205 Grafton Ave, Newark, N.J. 07104. Mailing Add: House Office Bldg, Washington, D.C. 20515.

RODINO, ROBERT JOSEPH D
Mem, Nassau Co. Dem. Cmt, N.Y.
b. Brooklyn, N.Y, 8/11/38; s. Dominick Joseph Rodino and Mary Rappa R; m. 7/3/65 to Elaine Ann Lamberti; c. Michelle Lyn. Educ: Manhattan Col, B.S, 59; Boston Univ, M.A, 65; N.Y. Univ, 66-, Ph.D. cand. Polit. & Govt. Pos: Mem, Nassau Co. Dem. Cmt, N.Y, 66-68 & 69-; treas, Gr. Roslyn Dem. Club, 67, second v.pres, 68 and first v.pres, 69; alternate del, Dem. Nat. Conv, 68; v.chmn, Roslyn Dem. Zone, 69. Bus. & Prof. Pos: Mathematician, Burroughs Corp, Paoli, Pa, 59-60; opers. analyst, Gen. Elec, Phila, 60-62; syst. analyst, strategic studies, Raytheon Corp, Bedford, Mass, 62-63; sr. syst. analyst, Airborne Instruments Labs, Deer Park, N.Y, 63-64 & 65-68; strategic planner, Westinghouse Learning Corp, N.Y.C, 68-69; proj. mgr, Urban Resources, Inc, 69- Mem: Am. Polit. Sci. Asn. Mailing Add: 308 Main St, Roslyn, N.Y. 11576.

RODRIGUEZ, ANTONIO F. R
b. San Antonio, Tex, 3/29/34; s. Antonio Rodriguez and Guadalupe Saldaña R; m. 3/19/58 to Angie Lerma; c. Tony, René and Carlos. Educ: Tex. Col. of Arts and Indust, B.S, 58; San Antonio Col, 2 years. Polit. & Govt. Pos: Precinct chmn, Rep. Party, Tex, 66-68; del, Rep. Nat. Conv, 68; asst. state chmn, Tex. Rep. Party, 68-69; cmnr. and dir, Cmn. for Border Develop. with Mex, 69- Mil. Serv: Entered as Pvt. E-1, Army, 55, released as E-4, 57, after serv. in Fourth Armored Div, 55-57. Mem: Life Underwriting Training Coun; K. of C; Optimist Int; Boy Scouts of Am. Rel: Catholic. Legal Res: 4103 Hillswind, San Antonio, Tex. 78217. Mailing Add: P.O. Box 10051, San Antonio, Tex. 78210.

RODRIGUEZ, DAVID D
Mem, Calif. Dem. State Cent. Cmt.
b. Holtville, Calif, 2/27/35; s. Bishan Sidhu and Simona Rodriguez; m. 10/21/56 to Seferina Magallanez; c. Monica Lynn, David Keith and Michael George. Educ: Am. River Col, 62. Polit. & Govt. Pos: Mem, Calif. Dem. State Cent. Cmt, Second Dist, 68-; mem, Overall Econ. Develop. Plan, Placer Co, 69. Bus. & Prof. Pos: With Aerojet-Gen. Corp, Sacramento, Calif, 58- Mil. Serv: Sgt. 1/C, Calif. Nat. Guard, 54-66. Mem: South Placer Comprehensive Med. Coun; Packmaster, Cub Scouts; K. of C. Coun; Placer Co. Ment. Retardation Asn; exec. bd. and secy, Local 946; Laws and Legis. Cmt.(past chmn). Rel: Catholic. Mailing Add: 511 Vine Way, Roseville, Calif. 95678.

RODRIGUEZ, EUGENE D
b. New York, N.Y, 6/4/29; m. to Carmen Garcia. Educ: Long Island Univ; Brooklyn Law Sch. Polit. & Govt. Pos: N.Y. State Assemblyman, 64-66; Pontiac Dem. Club. Bus. & Prof. Pos: Attorney. Mil. Serv: Counter-intelligence Corps, Army, Korean War. Mem: P.R. Forum; NAACP; Urban League of B'nai B'rith; P.R. Parade; Nat. Asn. for P.R. Affairs. Mailing Add: 568 W. 173rd, New York, N.Y. 10011. (1967)

RODRIGUEZ, JAY D
Mem, Calif. Dem. State Cent. Cmt.
b. La Verne, Calif, 1/15/28; s. Eliseo Rodriguez and Concha Estrada R; m. 8/26/61 to Patricia Ann McNab; c. Kate Louise, John Arthur, Paul Jay, David Alan and Steven Kent. Educ: Mt. San Antonio Col, A.A, 48; Univ. Calif, Riverside, 68-69. Polit. & Govt. Pos: Pres, Dem. Club, La Verne, Calif, 62, dist. del, 63-64; chmn, 49th Assembly Dist. Dem. Cent. Cmt, 66-68; del, Dem. Nat. Conv, 68; mem. exec. cmt. and chmn. 24th Cong. Dist. Del, Calif. Dem. State Cent. Cmt, 68- Bus. & Prof. Pos: Mem. advert. staff, Pomona Progress Bul, 47-63; restaurant owner, Casa de Mayo-The Barrister Pomona, 63-68; mem. staff pub. rels, Claremont, 68-69; mem. pub. rels. staff, KNBC, Los Angeles, 69- Mil. Serv: Entered as Pvt, Army, 49, released as Sgt, 52, after serv. in Tank Co, 40th Inf. Div, Japan and Korea, 51-52; Good Conduct Medal; Unit Citation. Mem: Navy League; Elks; Family Serv.(mem. bd); YMCA (mem. bd); Dem. Club. Named to All South. Calif. Football Team, 47; Menu of the Year, Nat. Restaurant Asn, 63, Promotion of the Year, 65; Young Man of the Year, Pomona, 63. Rel: Presbyterian. Mailing Add: 1447 Edgehill Dr, Pomona, Calif. 91767.

RODRIGUEZ, LYDIA T. D
V.Chmn, Conejos Co. Dem. Party, Colo.
b. La Jara, Colo, 5/25/29; d. Ismael Rodriguez and Mary B. Vigil R; div; c. Penny (Mrs. Sam Montoya). Educ: Centauri High Sch, 10 years; Gen. Educ. Develop. Diploma. Polit. & Govt. Pos: V.chmn, Conejos Co. Dem. Party, Colo, 67- Bus. & Prof. Pos: Clerk, Gen. Off, Trinidad Jr. Col, 9 years. Mem: Am. Legion Auxiliary. Rel: Catholic. Legal Res: 402 Walnut St, La Jara, Colo. 81140. Mailing Add: P.O. Box 205, La Jara, Colo. 81140.

ROE, CHARLES G. D
Chmn, Val Verde Co. Dem. Party, Tex.
b. Robert Lee, Tex, 7/9/15; s. Dan Roe and Sidney Martin R; m. 12/19/33 to Margarette Kiblinger; c. Neva Ann (Mrs. John Ferrera), Charles Jr. and James C. Educ: High sch. Polit. & Govt. Pos: Dem. precinct chmn, Del Rio, Tex, 58-65; chmn, Val Verde Co. Dem. Party, 65- Bus. & Prof. Pos: Mem. staff, Tex. Utilities Co, Del Rio, Tex, 32-39 and South. Pac. Co, 39- Mem: Odd Fellows; BRT (local chmn, 64-); United Transportation Union (local chmn, 69-). Rel: Methodist. Mailing Add: 504 Ave. E, Del Rio, Tex. 78840.

ROE, JERRY D. R
Exec. Dir, Mich. Rep. State Cent. Cmt.
b. Conrad, Montana, 5/18/36; s. Howard O. Roe and Ialene B. Freel R; m. 12/31/65 to Shirley Carol Hands. Educ: North. Mont. Col, 1 year; Col. Great Falls, B.A, 58; mem, Student Coun. Polit. & Govt. Pos: Chmn, Col. Great Falls Rep. Club, 56, Mont. Fedn. of Col. Rep. Clubs, 56-58 and Cascade Co. Young Rep, 57-58; exec. dir, Minn. Young Rep. League, 59-61 and Nat. Fedn. of Young Rep, 61-63; dir. of orgn, Mich. Rep. Party, 63-69; Rep. dist. rep. for U.S. Congressman Garry Brown, 67-69; exec. dir, Mich. Rep. State Cent. Cmt, 69- Mil. Serv: Mont. and Minn. Army Nat. Guards; Mont. Air Nat. Guard. Mem: Kiwanis; Toastmasters Int; AF&AM; Scottish Rite; Shrine; Teamsters Union; Soft Drink, Bakery and Brewers Union. Rel: Methodist. Mailing Add: 1005 W. Ottawa St, Lansing, Mich. 48915.

ROE, TEDDY W. D
b. Imperial, Nebr, 3/21/34; s. Wallace H. Roe and Coryelle Miller R; m. 11/11/67 to Marcie Rivin; c. Timothy. Educ: East. Mont. Col, 51-53; Mex. City Col, summer 58; Univ. Mont, B.A. in Journalism, 59; Univ. Buenos Aires, 60; Georgetown Univ, M.A. in Russian Area Studies, 65; Johns Hopkins Sch. of Adv. Int. Studies, 68-; Kappa Tau Alpha; Phi Kappa Phi. Polit. & Govt. Pos: Am. Polit. Sci. Asn. cong. fel, Off. U.S. Rep. Armistead Selden, Ala, 62 and Off. U.S. Sen. Mike Mansfield, Mont, 62; prfnl. staff man, U.S. Senate Dem. Policy Cmt, 62-65 and Secy. for the Majority, U.S. Senate, 65-69; asst. to the Majority Leader, U.S. Senate, 62- Bus. & Prof. Pos: Reporter and photographer, Great Falls Leader, Great Falls, Mont, summer 59; ed. writer, Des Moines Register, Des Moines, Iowa, 59-60. Mil. Serv: Entered as Pvt, Army, 57, released as Cpl, 59, after serv. in Seventh Inf. Regt, Third Div. Recipient of Inter-Am. Press Asn. Fel. Award for 1 year spent in Argentina; Am. Polit. Sci. Asn. Cong. Fel. Award, 61-62; Am. Polit. Sci. Asn. Cong. Staff Fel. Award, 68, for study and travel in Latin Am. and the Soviet Union. Rel: Protestant. Legal Res: Montana. Mailing Add: 140 N. Early St, Alexandria, Va. 22304.

ROE, THOMAS ANDERSON R
b. Greenville, S.C, 5/29/27; s. Thomas Anderson Roe and Leila Cunningham R; m. 12/12/50 to Bette Verner Bain; c. Thomas Anderson, III, Elizabeth Overton, Phillip Stradley and John Verner. Educ: Furman Univ, B.S, 48; Chi Beta Phi; Phi Sigma. Polit. & Govt. Pos: Former Greenville Co. committeeman, S.C; chmn, Greenville Co. Workman for Sen. Cmt; co-chmn. campaign publicity, Leon P. Crawford for U.S. Sen, Dan. H. Wallace for U.S. Rep. and James Threadgill for Mayor, Greenville; state committeeman from Greenville Co, and mem, State Budget and Orgn. Cmt. and Party Rules and Forms Cmt, S.C. Rep. Party, 62-64, state finance chmn, 63-64; mem, Nat. Rep. Finance Cmt, 63-64; hon. asst. sgt-at-arms, Rep. Nat. Conv, 60, del-at-lg, 64. Bus. & Prof. Pos: Research asst, cancer research prog, Furman Univ, 47-48; pres, Builder Marts of Am, Inc, 61- and subsidiaries, Colonial Co, Inc. and Citizens Builder Mart, Inc; chmn. of bd, First Piedmont Bank & Trust Co; v.pres, Am. Holdings, Inc, 66-; Compania De Fomento Las Palmas S.A. and Domaire, C por A. Publ: Co-auth, 'Carcinogenic Compounds,' Sci. Mag, 48. Mem: Pres, Carolina Lumber & Bldg. Material Dealer's Asn, 65; former v.pres, Greenville Home Builders Asn; bd. dirs, Greenville United Cerebral Palsy and Am. Red Cross Chap; Int. Housing Cmt, Nat. Asn. of Home Builders, 65-66; past pres, Players Club and Greenville Bldg. Materials Dealers Asn; former mem, Greenville Civil Defense Coun; pilot and past air inspector, Civil Air Patrol; v.pres, Gr. Greenville C. of C; bd. dirs, Altamont Club; Green Valley Country Club; Poinsett Club. One of 90 students from U.S. and Can. selected for for. rels. study in West. Europe, 48; Distinguished Serv. Award, 60 and Outstanding Leadership Award, 61, Greenville Sertoma Club; Guilder of the Year Award, Home Builders Asn. of Greenville, 62. Rel: Episcopal. Legal Res: R.F.D. 7, Paris Mountain, Greenville, S.C. 29609. Mailing Add: P.O. Box 2488, Greenville, S.C. 29602.

ROE, THOMAS S. D
b. Waukon, Iowa, 9/18/16; m. 1938 to Dolores Soride; c. Bonita (Mrs. Campbell), Karen (Mrs. Kruger), Thomas Jr, Steven, Lana and Lori. Educ: Waukon Jr. Col, 35. Polit. & Govt. Pos: Former Iowa State Rep. Bus. & Prof. Pos: Farmer; salesman. Rel: Lutheran. Mailing Add: First St. S.E, Waukon, Iowa 52172. (1967)

ROEHRIG, STANLEY HERBERT D
Hawaii State Rep.
b. Honolulu, Hawaii, 3/11/39; s. Kenneth William Roehrig and Ethel Seivers R; m. 6/18/65 to Janice Hodapp. Educ: Brown Univ, A.B. in Physics, 61; Univ. Wash. Law Sch, J.D, 65; Phi Gamma Delta. Polit. & Govt. Pos: Fund raising chmn, Co. Dem. Party, Hawaii, 66, co-chmn, rallies, 66, chmn, resolutions cmt, 68; pub. defender, Hawaii Co, 67-68; Hawaii State Rep, 69- Mem: Am, Hawaii State and Hawaii Co. Bar Asns; Civitan Club; Jaycees; Farm Bur; Big Island Cmt. on Alcoholism; Hawaii Island and Japanese C. of C; Cmt. on Aging. Rel: Christian. Legal Res: 25 Akepa St, Hilo, Hawaii 96720. Mailing Add: 159 C Keawe St, Hilo, Hawaii 96720.

ROEN, LELAND H. R
N.Dak. State Sen.
b. Bowman, N.Dak, 12/18/15; married; c. Two. Educ: Concordia Col. Polit.

& Govt. Pos: N.Dak. State Rep, 51-55; N.Dak. State Sen, 57- Bus. & Prof. Pos: Farmer, rancher. Mem: Pres, Co. Stockmen's Asn; bd. of dir, Old Four Eyes. Mailing Add: Bowman, N.Dak. 58623. (1967)

ROESLER, ALFRED D. R
b. Chicago, Ill, 9/3/92; m. to Edith Pascoe. Educ: Common sch. educ. Polit. & Govt. Pos: S.Dak. State Sen, 40-66; S.Dak. State Rep, 38; exec. bd. of Legis. Research Coun, 51-63; chmn. of bd, 57; majority leader of the Sen, 65; former pres. of Deadwood Sch. Bd. Bus. & Prof. Pos: Retired; ranched and farmed several years; foreman of Homestake Mining Co. Slime Plant. Mailing Add: 79 Forrest, Deadwood, S.Dak. 57732. (1967)

ROGALIN, WILMA CLARE R
V.Chmn, N.Y. State Rep. Cmt.
b. Minneapolis, Minn, 12/7/16; d. Ivar Sivertsen and Clare Wilmes S; m. 4/24/62 to John A. Rogalin. Educ: Univ. Minn, B.S, 37; Columbia Univ, M.A, 44; Kappa Alpha Theta. Polit. & Govt. Pos: Chmn. bd, Young Women's Rep. Club of N.Y.C, 47-48, pres, 48-50; v.pres, Asn. of N.Y. State Young Rep. Clubs, 50-52; temporary secy, N.Y. State Rep. Conv, 50 & 58; asst. to co-campaign Chmn, N.Y. State, 52, co-campaign chmn, 60 & 68; pres, Rep. Bus. Women, N.Y.C, 53-55 and v.pres, Region 2, Nat. Fedn. Young Rep. Clubs, 53-55; assoc. leader, Ninth Assembly Dist. Rep. Club, N.Y. Co, 53-59; mem. bd, Women's Nat. Rep. Club, 59-65 & 68-; v.chmn, N.Y. State Rep. Cmt, 59-, acting chmn, 63; del. and mem. platform cmt, Rep. Nat. Conv, 60, 64 & 68; mem, Women's Adv. Cmt, N.Y. State Exposition, 62-, N.Y. State Manpower Adv. Cmt, 63- and N.Y. State Women's Coun, currently. Bus. & Prof. Pos: Personnel mgr, Pan Am. World Airways, Inc, N.Y, 42- Mem: Vis. Nurse Serv. Cmt, N.Y.C; N.Y. Personnel Mgt. Asn; hospitality cmt, N.Y. State Pavilion, World's Fair, 64-65; chmn, Employee Contributions, Queens Salvation Army, 61-63; secy, N.Y. Airlines Personnel Mgrs. Asn, 58; pres, Univ. Minn. Alumni of N.Y, 53-54; Nat. Laywomen's Cmt, Nat. Coun. of Churches of Christ in U.S, 52-55; pres, Pan Am. World Airways' Skyline Club, 47-49; bd. mem, Queen's YWCA, 45-48. Rel: Presbyterian. Mailing Add: Cedar Hill Lane, Pound Ridge, N.Y. 10576.

ROGAN, RICHARD ROBERT D
b. Los Angeles, Calif, 5/6/14; s. James F. Rogan and Marie Lamer R; m. 11/7/42 to Judge Mary Goode; c. Patrick Goode, Michael D, Mary Frances, Brian J, Dennis A. and Richard Christopher. Educ: Univ. Calif, Los Angeles, A.B, 35; Univ. Paris, grad. work; Yale Sch. Law, LL.B, 39. Polit. & Govt. Pos: Mem, Los Angeles Co. Dem. Cent. Cmt, 48-64; nat. committeeman, Calif. Young Dem, 50; mem, Calif. Dem. State Cmt, 58-66; chief dep. attorney gen, Calif, 59-63; chmn, Calif. Lawyers for Kennedy, 60; chmn. spec. events, Dem. Nat. Conv, 60, del, 68. Bus. & Prof. Pos: Mem. ed. staff, State Bar J, 57-60; lectr, Harvard Law Sch, 61; dir, Providencia Bank, Burbank, 63- Mil. Serv: Entered as Ens, Naval Res, 43, released as Lt, 46, after serv. in European-African Theater. Mem: Lions; Am. Legion; Yale Law Sch. Alumni Asn; Am. Bd. Trial Advocates; Los Angeles Co, Calif. and Am. Bar Asns; pres, San Fernando Valley Bar Asn, 58 and Burbank Bar Asn, 59; past pres, Burbank Symphony Asn. and Burbank Commun. Concert Asn. Published 85 articles from Europe, 51; won 5 ribbons for oil paintings. Rel: Roman Catholic. Mailing Add: 301 E. Olive Ave, Burbank, Calif. 91502.

ROGERS, ANDREW JACOB 'ANDY' D
b. Ft. Worth, Tex, 12/24/24; s. Neal Dow Rogers and Guletta Fromm R; m. 7/27/50; c. Paula Ann, Andrea Jeanne and Andrew Jacob, Jr. Educ: Tex. A&M Col, grad; Univ. of Tex. Law Sch; pres, Bus. Hon. Soc; and Pre-Law Hon. Soc. Polit. & Govt. Pos: Tex. State Sen, 30th Sen. Dist, 52-67, Gov. for a Day and pres. pro-tem, Tex. State Senate, 58; Tex. State Rep, 48-52. Bus. & Prof. Pos: Mgr. and owner, Childress Ins. Agency, 58-; cattleman and stockman. Mil. Serv: Entered as Pvt, Army Air Force, released as Lt, after serv. as navigator and bombadier. Mem: Mason (32°), Scottish Rite, Grand RAM, RSM; Rotarian; Am. Legion; 40 et 8; Tex. and Southwest. Cattle Raisers Asn; Asn. of Former Students of Tex. A&M Univ; committeeman, Boy Scouts; Northwest Tex. Field and Stream Asn; dir, Childress Co. Unit, Am. Cancer Soc; Farm Bur; Elks. Rel: Baptist. Legal Res: 200 Main St, Childress, Tex. 79201. Mailing Add: Drawer 592, Childress, Tex. 79201. (1967)

ROGERS, BEN A. R
b. 1916; m. to Eileen Chaudoin; c. Janale and Judy. Educ: S.W. Mo. State Teachers' Col, B.S; Univ. Mo, M.E. Polit. & Govt. Pos: Mo. State Rep, 41-45; supt. of pub. schs, Sparta, Mo, one year, Eugene, Mo, six years; exec. secy, Mo. State Sch. Bd. Asn, five years; dir. of educ, State Reformatory for Boys at Algoa; Eugene Sch. Bd; chmn, Eugene Town Bd. Bus. & Prof. Pos: Financial consult. in planning, develop. pub. improv. and educ; farmer. Mem: Eastern Star; Mason. Rel: Christian Church; Elder. Mailing Add: Eugene, Mo. 65032.

ROGERS, BOBBY WAYNE D
b. Henderson, N.C, 6/19/34; s. Hartwell B. Rogers and Rena Gentry R; m. to Nancy Bell; c. Samuel J, Rena E, Michael F. and Matthew H. W. Educ: N.C. State Col, B.S.C.E; George Wash. Univ, LL.B. Polit. & Govt. Pos: Solicitor, Vance Co. Recorders Court, N.C, 64-68; asst. solicitor, Vance Co. Superior Court, 64-68; chmn, Vance Co. Dem. Exec. Cmt, 66-68. Bus. & Prof. Pos: Naval architect, Buships, Wash, D.C, 59-63; attorney-at-law, 63- Mil. Serv: Entered as Recruit, Navy, 52, released as AT-3, 55. Mailing Add: P.O. Box 696, Henderson, N.C. 27536.

ROGERS, BYRON GILES D
U.S. Rep, Colo.
b. Hunt Co, Tex, 8/1/00; s. Peter Rogers and Minnie M. Gentry R; married; c. Mrs. Hollis Martin and Byron Jr. Educ: Univ. Okla, 19-22; Univ. Colo, Univ. Denver, 23-25, LL.B; Phi Alpha Delta. Polit. & Govt. Pos: City attorney, Las Animas and co. attorney, Bent Co; Colo. State Rep, 31-35, Speaker, Colo. Gen. Assembly, 33; with Dept. of Agr. and Nat. Recovery Admin, Wash, D.C, 33-34; Asst. U.S. Attorney, Dist. of Colo, 34-36; appointed Attorney Gen. of Colo, 35, elected, 36-38; state chmn, Dem. State Cent. Cmt, Colo, 41-42; pub. mem, War Labor Bd, 42-45; co. chmn, Denver Dem. Cent. Cmt, 45-50; U.S. Rep, Colo, 50- Bus. & Prof. Pos: Practiced law, Las Animas, Colo, 25-33. Mil. Serv: Army, 18. Mem: Denver, Colo. and Am. Bar Asns; Lions Int; Mystic Shrine; Elks; Am. Legion; Odd Fellows; life mem, DAV. Rel: Baptist. Legal Res: Denver, Colo. 80206. Mailing Add: 2408 Rayburn House Office Bldg, Washington, D.C. 20515.

ROGERS, CHARLES McPHERSON ADUSTON, III Independent
b. Mobile, Ala, 11/10/32; s. Charles McPherson Aduston Rogers and Elisabeth Benson R; m. 6/19/54 to Gail Mildred Whitehurst; c. Anne Aduston, Charles McPherson, IV and Bradshaw. Educ: Williams Col, B.A, 54; Univ. Ala, LL.B, 59. Polit. & Govt. Pos: Ala. State Rep, 62-66; elected to vacancy in Mobile Legis. del. Bus. & Prof. Pos: Attorney-at-law; sr. v.pres. and trust officer, Am. Nat. Bank and Trust Co. of Mobile. Mil. Serv: Lt, Air Force, 2 years. Rel: Episcopal. Legal Res: 4010 Old Shell Rd, Mobile, Ala. 36608. Mailing Add: P.O. Box 1628, Mobile, Ala. 36601.

ROGERS, CHLOE D
Co. Recorder, Mineral Co, Colo.
b. Sanford, Colo, 8/23/18; d. George Ernest Wright and Fannie Jane Morgan W; wid; c. Lonnie Milton and Dannie Edward. Educ: Sanford High Sch, Colo. Polit. & Govt. Pos: Clerk and recorder, Mineral Co, Colo, 58-; v.chairwoman, Mineral Co. Dem. Party, 60- Colo. Dept. of Revenue Serv. Award. Rel: Latter-day Saint. Mailing Add: Creede, Colo. 81130.

ROGERS, DANIEL TOWNSEND R
b. Latta, S.C, 5/18/15; s. Luther Boyd Rogers and Janie Bethea R; m. 8/26/44 to Ethel McLaurin; c. Daniel T, Jr, Ethel Louise and Duncan McLaurin. Educ: High sch. Polit. & Govt. Pos: Chmn, Dillon Co. Rep. Party, S.C, 65-67. Bus. & Prof. Pos: From clerk to asst. mgr, S.C. Nat. Bank, 32-41; mgr, Peoples Loan Co, 62-65 and Rogers Co. Inc, 65- Mil. Serv: Entered as Aviation Cadet, Army Air Corps, 41, released as Lt. Col, 61 after serv. in 803rd Air Base Group, Tucson, Ariz; Air, Commendation and Am. Defense Medals; Asiatic-Pac. Theater Ribbon; Presidential Unit Citation. Mem: Farm Bur; Lions Int; Air Force Asn; Retired Officers Asn. Rel: Presbyterian. Mailing Add: 100 Richards St, Dillon, S.C. 29536. (1967)

ROGERS, DAVID D
Minority Leader, Ind. State Senate
b. Bloomington, Ind, 7/18/28; s. Donald A. Rogers and Marie Woolerig R; m. 11/24/56 to Virginia Hudelson. Educ: Ind. Univ, A.B, 50, Law Sch, J.D, 55; Phi Beta Kappa; Order of the Coif; Phi Delta Theta; Phi Delta Phi. Polit. & Govt. Pos: V.chmn, Ind. State Tax and Financing Policy Cmn, 59-; chmn, Ind. Judicial Study Cmn, 67-; Ind. State Sen, currently, majority caucus chmn, Ind. State Senate, mem, Legis. Adv. Cmn, 63-, minority leader, 69- Mil. Serv: Entered as 2nd Lt, Army, 51, released as 1st Lt, 53. Mem: Am. and Ind. State Bar Asns; Kiwanis; Mason. Rel: Disciples of Christ. Mailing Add: 1036 S. Jordan, Bloomington, Ind. 47401.

ROGERS, GEORGE D
Mass. State Rep.
b. New Bedford, Mass, 8/2/35; s. M. F. Rogers and Rose Soares R; single. Educ: Providence Col, A.B, 58; Bridgewater State Col, 59-60; Boston State Col, 65; New Bedford Club of Providence Col. Polit. & Govt. Pos: Mass. State Rep. and chmn, Cmt. on Educ, Mass. State House of Rep, currently. Bus. & Prof. Pos: Teacher, Fairhaven High Sch, Mass, 58-61; pub. rels. dir, Atlantic Ten Pin Lanes, Fairhaven, 59-61 and Holiday Lanes, South Dartmouth, 61-64; teacher-coach, New Bedford Voc. High Sch, 61-64. Mem: Nat. Educ. Asn; Mass. Teachers Asn; Mass. Coaches Asn; Mass. Track Coaches Asn; Nat. Soc. of State Legislators; Am. Voc. Asn; K. of C; Elks; Jr. C. of C; Holy Name Soc. Dean's List at Providence Col. Rel: Roman Catholic. Legal Res: 23 Robeson St, New Bedford, Mass. 02740. Mailing Add: State House, Boston, Mass. 02133.

ROGERS, GERALD R
b. Wellington, Kans, 4/19/29; s. Forrest Monroe Rogers and Josephine Holman R; m. 8/14/54 to Carol Ketcham; c. Jeffrey Alden, Kipp Alan, John David and Anne. Educ: Okla. State Univ, B.S, 53; Univ. Kans. Sch. Law, LL.B, 55; assoc. ed, Univ. Kans. Law Rev, 54-55; Alpha Phi Omega; Blue Key; Beta Theta Pi; Int. Rels. Club; Young Rep. Polit. & Govt. Pos: Pres, Young Rep. of Okla. State Univ, 50-52; del, Okla. Young Rep. Conv. and Nat. Young Rep. Conv, 52; sgt-at-arms, Rep. Nat. Conv, 52, alternate del, 68; co-chmn, Ferguson for Attorney Gen. Campaign, Kans, 62 and mem. exec. cmt, Ferguson for Gov. Campaign, 66; precinct committeeman, Wellington, Kans, 66-67. Bus. & Prof. Pos: Assoc, Rogers & Rogers, Attorneys and licensed abstractor, Rogers Abstract & Title Co, Wellington, Kans, 55- Mil. Serv: Entered as Pvt, Army, 47, released as Sgt, 48, after serv. in Armored Cavalry. Publ: 'Adverse Possession-Mistake as to Boundary,' 54 and 'Federal Estate Tax Marital Deduction-Widow's Statutory Share,' 54, Kans. Law Rev. Mem: Sumner Co. Bar Asn.(pres, 62); Kans. and Am. Bar Asns; Kans. Title Asn; Am. Land Title Asn; Lions Int; Elks; U.S. C. of C. Named Young Man of the Year, C. of C, 60. Rel: Baptist. Mailing Add: 24 Westborough, Wellington, Kans. 67152.

ROGERS, GLENN K. 'DOC' D
Wyo. State Sen.
b. Girard, Kans, 7/26/00; s. Benjamin Adelbert Rogers and Bell Britton R; m. 11/29/24 to Mary Ethola Read; c. Mary Lee (Mrs. Donald I. Meyer). Educ: Baker Univ, A.B, 24; Univ. Wyo, M.A, 37; Kans. Univ. and South. Methodist Univ, grad. study; Kappa Delta Pi; Sigma Phi Epsilon; B Club; Radio Club; letters in baseball, basketball and track. Polit. & Govt. Pos: Wyo. State Sen, Laramie Co, 67- Bus. & Prof. Pos: Coach and high sch. prin, Kanorado, Kans, 24-26; coach and sci. teacher, Wheatland, 27-38; high sch. sci. teacher, Cheyenne, Wyo, 38-66 and coach, 38-44; broker, Prudential Ins. Co. of Am, 43-; owner, lapidary shop, Doc's Rock's, Cheyenne. Publ: Book reviewer on physics and geol, Wyo. Libr. Roundup. Mem: Nat. and Wyo. Educ. Asns; Nat. and Wyo. Asn. Math. and Sci. Teachers; past pres, Cheyenne Classroom Teachers; Nat. Asn. Retired Teachers; former mem, Carpenters Union and Lions Club of Wheatland. Rel: Protestant. Mailing Add: 312 E. Pershing Blvd, Cheyenne, Wyo, 82001.

ROGERS, HAMILTON R
b. Englewood, Colo, 9/25/19; s. James Grafton Rogers and Cora Peabody R; m. 1/14/49 to Kate Raynolds; c. Toby Madison, Lark and Geoffrey Raynolds. Educ: Yale Univ, 39-40; Vt. Univ, 40-41; Denver Univ, 45-47. Polit.

& Govt. Pos: N.Mex. State Rep, 65-68. Bus. & Prof. Pos: Mem. staff, Mt. States Inspection Bur, 47-50; gen. agent, Hamilton Agency, 51-66; rep, Income Mgt, Inc, 69- Mil. Serv: Pvt, Army, 41-43. Mem: Elks; Optimists. Rel: Episcopal. Mailing Add: 3903 Aspen N.E, Albuquerque, N.Mex. 87110.

ROGERS, JACK R
b. 12/7/26; m. 9/21/49; c. Julie, Craig and Gary. Educ: S.Dak. State Univ, B.S. in Agr. Econ. and Animal Husbandry; S.Dak. State Univ. Alumni Asn. Polit. & Govt. Pos: S.Dak. State Rep, 64-68. Bus. & Prof. Pos: Real estate and ins. broker. Mil. Serv: Army, World War II, S.Pac. Theater and Korean War, 1 year. Mem: S.Dak. Asn. of Realtors; Asn. of Independent Ins. Agents; Nat. Asn. of Real Estate Brokers; Asn. of Farm Mgrs. and Rural Appraisers; Huron Rotary Club. Rel: Methodist; Off. Bd. of First Methodist.Church. Mailing Add: 551 Kansas Ave, Huron, S.Dak. 57350.

ROGERS, JACK HENRY D
Mammoth, Utah, 10/8/15; s. John Francis Rogers and Minnie Knotts R; m. 2/5/37 to Dorothy Grace Cole; c. Mary Ellen and Cathy Ann. Educ: Univ. Wash, 34-35. Polit. & Govt. Pos: Exec. secy, Wash. State Asn. of Counties, currently; Kitsap Co. cmnr, 66-69; Wash. State Rep, 63-67; Wash. State Sen, 44-56; co. coroner, Kitsap Co, 42-46; chmn, Kitsap Co. Rationing and Price Control Bd, 42-45. Mem: Elks. Rel: Episcopal. Mailing Add: 10838 Highway 3, Bremerton, Wash. 98310.

ROGERS, JAMES TRACY D
b. Binghamton, N.Y, 6/9/21; s. James Tracy Rogers and Ethel Coffin R; m. 9/15/46 to Janet Estabrook; c. Timothy Coffin, Nicole Helen and Karen Lacey. Educ: Harvard Col, B.S, 42. Polit. & Govt. Pos: Press secy, U.S. Sen. Irving M. Ives, 55-57; alternate del, Dem. Nat. Conv, 68. Bus. & Prof. Pos: Reporter, Gannett Newspapers, Binghamton, N.Y, 47-51 and Wash, D.C, 51-55; writer, news of week in rev, N.Y. Times, N.Y.C, 57-63; mem. bd. of ed, Sci. Am, 63-; trustee, Ridgewood Pub. Libr, Ridgewood, N.J, 66- Mil. Serv: Entered as 2nd Lt, Army, 42, released as Capt, 46, after serv. in 953rd Field Artil. Bn, ETO, 43-45; Bronze Star; Purple Heart. Publ: Story of Mathematics for Young People, Pantheon Books, 66; Four Tough Cases of the F.B.I, Holt, Rinehart & Winston, 69. Rel: Protestant. Mailing Add: 188 W. Glen Ave, Ridgewood, N.J. 07450.

ROGERS, JIMMIE FORT D
Ludowici, Ga, 1/25/14; s. John H. Rogers and Fannie Dunham R; m. 11/26/38 to Evelyn Elise Florie; c. Margaret S. (Mrs. Ray), James E, William D, Betty Jean (Mrs. Dubberly); grandchildren, Jimmie Darren Ray. Educ: Ludowici High Sch. Polit. & Govt. Pos: Ga. State Rep, 63-66; Long Co. bd. of educ, 58. Bus. & Prof. Pos: Ins; farmer; dist. mgr, Res. Life Ins. Co. Rel: Baptist. Mailing Add: Ludowici, Ga. 31316. (1967)

ROGERS, JOHN D
Secy. of State, Okla.
b. Clinton, Okla, 8/15/28; s. John M. Rogers and Annette Jaworsky R; div; c. John M, III and Mary Annette. Educ: Okla. City Univ. and Univ. Okla. Polit. & Govt. Pos: Nominated State Sen-at-lg, Okla, 64; Secy. of State, Okla, 67- Bus. & Prof. Pos: Partner, Rogers & Rogers, Accts, 50; exec. v.pres, Stemen Labs, 64. Mil. Serv: Entered as Pvt, Marine Corps, 46, released as Cpl, 48, after serv. in First Div, Japan; Re-entered as Pvt, Army, 53, released as Sgt. 1/C, 55, after serv. in 45th Inf. Div, Korean Conflict. Mem: Nat. Asn. Secy. of States; Pilots Int. Asn; Platform Speakers Asn. Rel: Disciples of Christ. Mailing Add: 211 State Capitol Bldg, Oklahoma City, Okla. 73105.

ROGERS, JOHN ISAAC R
W.Va. State Sen.
b. Keyser, W.Va, 7/10/10; s. Albin Isaac Rogers and Dessie Grace Alt R; m. 10/21/31 to Hazel V. Shumaker; c. Jane I.(Mrs. Nelson) and John I, II. Educ: Potomac State Col, W.Va. Univ, 28-32; Sigma Phi Omega; Phi Rho Pi. Polit. & Govt. Pos: Secy-treas, Mineral Co. Rep. Exec. Cmt, W.Va, 34-48, treas, 60-63, mem, 60-64; W.Va. State Del, 38-48 & 50-54; mem, W.Va. Cmn. to the Coun. of State Govts, 41-45; mem, Interstate Cmn. on Potomac River Basin, 41-58, chmn, 55-57; mem, Continuing Cmn. Northeast. Regional Conf. on Hwy. Safety and Motor Truck Probs, 42-45; W.Va. State Sen, 68- Bus. & Prof. Pos: Owner, Rogers Transfer Co, Keyser, 29-68, pres, 68-; farmer, Cabin Run Dist, Mineral Co, 56- Mem: Life mem, W.Va. Hort. Soc; W.Va. Motor Truck Asn; Farm Bur; Rotary; Odd Fellows; C. of C. Rel: Presbyterian. Legal Res: Route 1, Keyser, W.Va. 26726. Mailing Add: P.O. Box 385, Keyser, W.Va. 26726.

ROGERS, JOHN MARVIN D
State Exam. and Inspector, Okla.
b. Bessie, Okla, 4/24/00; s. John Layfayette Rogers and Martha Ellen Hatchett R; m. 9/2/22 to Annette Ann Jaworsky; c. Roberta Mae (Mrs. Henry R. Krueger) and John Marvin. Educ: Hills Bus. Col, Oklahoma City, Okla, 1 year; Univ. Okla, 2 years. Polit. & Govt. Pos: State exam. and inspector, Okla, 59- Mem: Okla. Soc. of CPA; Am. Inst. of CPA; Kiwanis. Rel: Christian. Legal Res: 3408 N.W. 60th St, Oklahoma City, Okla. 73112. Mailing Add: P.O. Box 53311, Oklahoma City, Okla. 73105.

ROGERS, JOHN RICHARD D
Mem, Ga. State Dem. Exec. Cmt.
b. Ashburn, Ga, 6/30/24; s. Edwin A. Rogers and Ella Mae Evans R; m. 8/6/53 to Reginald Ann Cox; c. Sylvia, Dawn and Starr. Educ: Univ. Ga, J.D, 49; Phi Eta Sigma; Blue Key; Phi Alpha Delta; Sigma Chi. Polit. & Govt. Pos: Chmn, Turner Co. Dem. Exec. Cmt, Ga, until 66. Bus. & Prof. Pos: V.pres, First Fed. Savings & Loan Asn, Turner Co, 62-; pres, Monroe Mall Corp, 65- Mil. Serv: Entered as 2nd Lt, Army, 44, released as 1st Lt, 46, after serv. in Marine Supply Depot, Manila, Philippine Islands. Mem: Am. Bar Asn; Ga. Bar Asn.(mem. bd. gov, 54-56); Tifton Circuit Bar Asn.(pres, 52-54); Am. Judicature Soc; Am. Trial Lawyers Asn; Mason; Shrine; Am. Legion; Farm Bur; C. of C.(pres, Turner Co, 57-58 & 69-). Rel: Methodist. Legal Res: E. Madison Ave, Ashburn, Ga. 31714. Mailing Add: P.O. Box 304, Ashburn, Ga. 31714.

ROGERS, JOSEPH OSCAR, JR. R
b. Mullins, S.C, 10/8/21; s. Joseph O. Rogers and Lila McDonald R. m. 8/26/49 to Kathleen Brown; c. Pamela, Joseph O, III and Timothy Julian. Educ: The Citadel, 3 years; Univ. S.C, LL.B. Polit. & Govt. Pos: S.C. State Rep, 55-66; Rep. cand. for Gov, S.C, 66; del, Rep. Nat. Conv, 68; U.S. Attorney for Dist. of S.C, 69- Bus. & Prof. Pos: Attorney at Law, 50- Mil. Serv: Entered as Pvt, Army Engrs, 43, released as Sgt, 46, after serv. in African and European Theaters. Mem: Mason; Civitan; Am. Legion; Farm Bur. Rel: Methodist; Lay Leader, Manning Methodist Church. Mailing Add: Horton St, Manning, S.C. 29102.

ROGERS, JUDITH D
Mem, Ark. Dem. State Cent. Cmt.
b. Newark, N.J, 1/14/32; d. Meyer Miles Marks and Florence M; m. 8/4/51 to Arthur Rogers; c. Meryl Debra, Steven Bruce and Alison Gail. Educ: Univ. of Fla, B.S.B.A, 52; La. State Univ, 54-55; Ind. Univ. Sch. of Law, J.D, 61; Beta Gamma Sigma; Phi Delta Delta. Polit. & Govt. Pos: Gen. counsel, Young Dem. of Ark, 64, v.pres, 65, and nat. committeewoman, 66-; mem, Pulaski Co. Dem. Cmt, 64-68; mem, Ark. Dem. State Cent. Cmt, 66-; chmn, Publ. Cmt, Ark. Dem. Party, 67-68; del, mem. credentials cmt. and secy, Ark. del, Dem. Nat. Conv, 68; mem, Gov. Cmn. on Status of Women, 68-; state lobbyist, Ark. Div. Am. Asn. Univ. Women, 69; mem, Attorney Gen. Consumer Protection Panel, 69. Bus. & Prof. Pos: Mem, Youth Jury Cmt, Pulaski Co, 67; bd. mem, Econ. Opportunity Agency Pulaski Co, 69. Publ: 'Women in American Politics,' Women Lawyer's J, 69. Mem: Am. Asn. Univ. Women (legis. chmn, Little Rock Branch, 65-69, implementation chmn. urban crisis, Ark. Div. and mem, state bd, 69-); Ark. Asn. Women Lawyers (pres, 66); Urban League (bd. mem, 66-); Nat. Asn. Women Lawyers (cmt. chmn, 67-69); Ark. Bar Asn.(chmn-elect of Family Law Security, and v.chmn, Domestic Rels. Rev, 69); Ark. Bus. Womens Asn; Bur. and Prfnl. Womens Asn; League of Women Voters; Am. and Pulaski Bar Asns; chmn, Pulaski Co. Cystic Fibrosis Drive, 69-; Women's C. of C; v.pres, Pulaski Co. Gen. Fedn. of Women's Club, 69-; Soroptomist Club (pres, 68-69); Young Dem. of Ark; Nat. Young Dem; Pulaski Co. Young Dem; Am. Civil Liberties Union bus. div. chmn, United Fund, 63-64, and mem, Budget Cmt, 64-66; Gr. Little Rock Fedn. of Womens Clubs (v.pres, 69-); Beta Gamma Sigma. Recipient of two-vol. Book Award, Ind. Univ. Sch. of Law; United Fund Comendation; Nat. Labor Rels. Bus. Div. Chmn, 64. Rel: Unitarian. Mailing Add: 3800 Pope Dr, North Little Rock, Ark. 72119.

ROGERS, LUTHER R
Chmn, Adams Co. Rep. Exec. Cmt, Ohio
b. West Union, Ohio, 9/16/30; s. Luther Rogers, Sr. and Mabel Vogler R; m. 11/24/50 to Mintie Florence Kimmerly; c. Janet Sue (Mrs. Boldman), Kimmy Ray and Carl Gene. Educ: Jefferson High Sch, Blue Creek, Ohio, grad. Polit. & Govt. Pos: Mem, Jefferson Local Sch. Bd, Blue Creek, Ohio, 54-61; dep. treas, Adams Co, West Union, 55-61, treas, 61-; chmn, Adams Co. Rep. Exec. Cmt, 58- Mem: Mason; Eastern Star; Peebles Royal Arch Mason. Rel: Baptist; Clerk, Cedar Grove Baptist Church. Mailing Add: Route 2, West Union, Ohio 45693.

ROGERS, MICHAEL K. R
Ind. State Rep.
b. Winchester, Ind, 6/14/41; s. Robert Emsley Rogers and Margaret Kennedy R; m. 5/17/64 to Nancy Ann Williams. Educ: Ind. Univ, B.S, 64; Ball State Univ, 67-; Kappa Tau Alpha; Sigma Pi. Polit. & Govt. Pos: Secy, Human Rights Cmn, New Castle, Ind, 64-67; Ind. State Rep, 66- Bus. & Prof. Pos: News dir, WCTW Radio, New Castle, Ind, 63-67; asst. to dir, Center for Radio and TV, Ball State Univ, 67- Mem: Sigma Delta Chi; Radio-TV News Dirs. Asn; Glass Blowers Asn. of U.S. and Can; Kiwanis. Rel: Soc. of Friends. Mailing Add: 2709 E. Fair Oaks Dr, New Castle, Ind. 47362.

ROGERS, PAUL GRANT D
U.S. Rep, Fla.
b. Ocilla, Ga, 6/4/21; s. Dwight L. Rogers and Florence Roberts R; m. to Rebecca Bell; c. Rebecca Laing. Educ: Univ. Fla, A.B, 42; George Wash. Univ, 46; Univ. Fla. Law Sch, LL.B, 48; pres, Fla. Blue Key; nat. debate champion, Tau Kappa Alpha. Polit. & Govt. Pos: U.S. Rep, Sixth Dist, Fla, 55-66, Ninth Dist, 66-, mem, Interstate and For. Commerce and Merchant Marine and Fisheries Cmts, U.S. House of Rep; del, Dem. Nat. Conv, 68. Bus. & Prof. Pos: Partner, Burns, Middleton, Rogers and Farrell, Attorneys, West Palm Beach, Fla. Mil. Serv: Entered Army, 42, released as Maj, 46, after serv. in Field Artil, ETO; Bronze Star Medal; 2 Battle Stars. Admitted to practice law before Fed. Courts and U.S. Supreme Court. Legal Res: West Palm Beach, Fla. 33401. Mailing Add: U.S. House Office Bldg, Washington, D.C. 20515.

ROGERS, RANDOLPH R
b. Cleveland, Ohio, 12/15/31; s. Winfield Heyser Rogers and Ruth Hawley R; m. 6/26/54 to Noreen Brown; c. Deborah, Peggy Ann, Kathleen, William, Brian and John. Educ: Yale Univ. Polit. & Govt. Pos: Mem, Bd. Rep, Stamford, Conn, 66- and chmn, Fiscal Cmt, 62-64; mem, Rep. Town Cmt, Stamford, 62. Bus. Pos: Asst. Mgr, Mutual of N.Y, 65-; agent, Am. Credit Indemnity, 62-65. Mil. Serv: Entered as Seaman Recruit, Navy, 52, released as Hospital Corpsman 3/C, 54. Rel: Catholic. Mailing Add: 66 Shady Lane, Stamford, Conn. 06903. (1967)

ROGERS, ROBERT DELWYN R
Conn. State Rep.
b. Boston, Mass, 10/19/26; s. William Francis Rogers, Jr. and Dolloretta Frances Coyle R; m. 10/22/55 to Dorothy J. Dannemiller; c. Laura Marie, Dorothy Jo, William Francis, III, Robert Delwyn, Jr. and Timothy John. Educ: Georgetown Univ. Sch. of For. Serv, B.S, 49; Georgetown Univ. Sch. of Law, LL.B, 55. Polit. & Govt. Pos: Mem, Representative Town Meeting, Greenwich, Conn, 64-68; chmn, Rep. Fund Drive, Greenwich, 67-68, v.chmn, Greenwich Rep. Finance Cmt, 67- and cmnr, Greenwich Housing Authority, 67-69; mem, Conn. Rep. State Finance Cmt, 69-; Conn. State Rep, 69- Bus. & Prof. Pos: Correspondent, Rogers & Rogers, Inc, N.Y.C, 55-58, v.pres, 58-63 and pres, 63- Mil. Serv: Midn, Maritime Serv, 44-46; 1st Lt, Air Force, 50-52. Publ: 'Financial Rehabilitation,' Boating Indust, 10/62. Mem: Bar of Conn, N.Y. and U.S. Supreme Court; Rotary, N.Y.C; Stanwich Club, Greenwich, Conn; Belle Haven Club; N.Y. Athletic Club, N.Y. Rel: Catholic. Mailing Add: MacKenzie Glen, Greenwich, Conn. 06830.

ROGERS, ROWENA EMERY R
b. Denver, Colo, 12/8/21; d. Roe Emery and Jeannette Carpenter E; m. 11/1/44 to Ranger Rogers; c. Susan, Jeannette, Roxana, Lorna, Robert Ranger and Sarah Blythe. Educ: Vassar Col, B.A, 43; Phi Beta Kappa. Polit. & Govt. Pos: Committeewoman, Arapahoe Co. Rep. Party, 52-60, mem, exec. cmt, various dates, v.chmn, 64-68; bonus mem, Colo. Rep. State Cent. Cmt, 56-58; v.chmn, Second Cong. Dist. Rep. Party, 57-58; pres, Littleton Rep. Women's Club, two terms; Second Dist. dir, Colo. Fedn. Rep. Women, 60. Rel: Episcopal. Mailing Add: 3011 Willamette Lane, Littleton, Colo. 80120.

ROGERS, STANLEY D
Mem, Los Angeles Co. Dem. Cent. Cmt, Calif.
b. Los Angeles, Calif, 2/28/34; s. Murray Harold Rogers and Rose Mednick R; m. 2/1/59 to Jane Hope Fegen; c. Susan Louise, John Stuart and Kenneth Andrew. Educ: Princeton, A.B, 56; Univ. Calif. Los Angeles Sch. Law, LL.B, 59; E.L.M. Club. Polit. & Govt. Pos: Pres, West Side Dem. Club, West Los Angeles, 62-63; chmn, 59th Assembly Dist. Coun, Calif, 64; mem, Los Angeles Co. Dem. Cent. Cmt, 67-; v.chmn, 26th Cong. Dist. Coun, 68; del, Dem. Nat. Conv, 68; chmn, 59th Assembly Dist. del, Los Angeles Co. Dem. Cent. Cmt, 68-; mem, State Dem. Cent. Cmt, 69. Bus. & Prof. Pos; Law clerk to Fed. Dist. Court Judge, Los Angeles, Calif, 59-60; assoc, Little, Curry & Hagen, Los Angeles, 60-63; partner, Rogers & Harris, Beverly Hills, 63-; arbitrator, Am. Arbit. Asn, 67- Mem: Los Angeles Co, Calif. State and Beverly Hills Bar Asns; Am. Judicature Asn; Friends of Santa Monica Park; PTA; Cmt. to Save Elysian Park; bd. dirs, Westdale Homeowners Asn; Cmt. for the City; Taxpayers Educ. Forum. Rel: Jewish. Mailing Add: 3133 Coolidge Ave, Los Angeles, Calif. 90066.

ROGERS, THELMA THARP R
Rep. Nat. Committeewoman, N.C.
b. Elkin, N.C; d. Noah W. Tharp and Alice Council T; m. 10/14/24 to Louis Godger Rogers; c. Catherine (Mrs. Buchanan) and Louis G, Jr. Educ: Winthrop Col. Polit. & Govt. Pos: V.chmn, Mecklenburg Co. Rep. Exec. Cmt, N.C, 46-53; organizer, Mecklenburg Co. Rep. Womens Club, 53; bd. mem, Mecklenburg Co. Soc. Planning Cmt, 56-60; del. and mem. platform cmt, Rep. Nat. Conv, 56, 60 & 64, mem. arrangements cmt, 64; mem, N.C. Rep. State Cent. Cmt, 56-; bd. mem, N.C. Fedn. Rep. Women; Rep. Nat. Committeewoman, N.C, 56-, mem, Site Selection Cmt, 59-60 and Cmt. on Conv. Reform, 66; mem, Nat. Adv. Cmt, White House Conf. on Aging, 58-59 and Gov. Coord. Cmt. on Aging, 59-60; mem, Cmt. on Oper. Dixie, 58-62; mem, Gov. Cmt. on Status of Women, 64. Publ: 'Mental Health Program in Mecklenburg County,' in History of Mecklinburg Co, 60. Mem: Past pres, Myers Park PTA and Mecklenburg Co. Ment. Health Asn; bd. mem, N.C. Ment. Health Asn; Charlotte City Club; Erosophian Book Club. Rel: Methodist; mem. off. bd, Myers Park Methodist Church, 62-65. Mailing Add: Route 3, Box 251 A, Charlotte, N.C. 28210.

ROGERS, VERDON LEE D
b. Eldorado, Okla, 8/21/23; s. Boney Woods Rogers and Media Ellen Brecheen R; married; c. Tony Allen, Rise Carmen, Kirk Arledge, Judd Enrique. Educ: Univ. Okla, B.A, 42-45; 46-47; Sigma Delta Chi. Polit. & Govt. Pos: Admin. asst. Rep. Walker, N.Mex, 65- Bus. & Prof. Pos: News dir, KDEF, Albuquerque, 62-63; asst. ed, Santa Fe, N.Mex. Mag, 61-62; news dir, KOB Albuquerque, 57-62; ed-owner, Eldorado Courier, Okla, 47-57. Mil. Serv: Army, Cpl, 46-47; official Army Correspondent; Received Army Commendation Medal; Army Res, Capt, 47-65. Rel: Catholic. Legal Res: Albuquerque, N.Mex. Mailing Add: 194 Easton S, Laurel, Md. 20810.

ROGERS, WALTER E. D
b. Texarkana, Ark, 7/19/08; s. Peter Gordon Rogers and Emma Gertrude Caperton R; m. 11/28/36 to Catherine R. Daly; c. John E, Thomas Kelly, Walter E, Jr, Robert Joseph, Susan Daly (Mrs. James C. Healey, Jr) and Mary Catherine. Educ: Austin Col; Univ. Tex. Polit. & Govt. Pos: City attorney, Pampa, Tex, 38-39; dist. attorney, 31st Judicial Dist, Tex, 41-45; U.S. Rep, 18th Dist, until 67. Mil. Serv: Entered as Maj, Army Res, 51, released as Lt. Col, after serv. in Judge Adv. Gen. Corps. Legal Res: P.O. Box 1699, Pampa, Tex. 79065. Mailing Add: 6219 Kennedy Dr, Chevy Chase, Md. 20015.

ROGERS, WILL I
b. Bessie, Okla, 12/12/98; s. John L. Rogers and Martha Ella Hatchett R; m. 8/18/45 to Ruby Thomas; c. Nell (Mrs. Sonnenfeld) and Kenneth Duggin. Educ: Cent. State Col, B.S, 26, A.B, 29; Okla. Univ, M.S, 30; Pi Kappa Alpha. Polit. & Govt. Pos: Hearing Examiner, U.S. Dept. Agr, 47-, asst. to secy. of agr, 46-47; asst. adminstr. solid fuels, Dept. Interior, 43-45; U.S. Rep, Okla, 33-43. Bus. & Prof. Pos: Supt. of Schs, Moore, Okla, 28-33, Chattanooga, 27-28, Rush Springs, 26-27; teacher, Okla. Pub. Schs, 17-24. Mem: Okla. Bar Asn; Fed. Trial Examiners Conf; Okla. Educ. Asn; life mem, Cent. State Col. and Okla. Univ. Alumni Asns; Mason, Shrine; Farmers Union; Civitan Club; Wash. Golf and Country Club. Rel: Baptist. Mailing Add: 2611 North Nelson, Arlington, Va. 22207. (1967)

ROGERS, WILLIAM JOSEPH D
Wis. State Assemblyman
b. Appleton, Wis, 12/9/30; s. Claude Joseph Rogers and Lucille Reichel R; m. Jan. 1955 to Kay Ludke; c. Michael, Steven, Patrick, Kevin, Scott, Laurie and Amy. Educ: St. Norbert Col, B.S. in Greek, 58; Mex. City Col, 1 year. Polit. & Govt. Pos: Councilman, Kaukauna City Coun, Wis, 60-; Wis. State Assemblyman, 62- Bus. & Prof. Pos: Teacher, Menasha, Wis, 58-62. Mil. Serv: Pvt, Army, 52-54, serv. in Mil. Police, Europe and Korean Conflict. Mem: VFW; K. of C; Am. Legion. Rel: Catholic. Legal Res: 1800 Peters Rd, Kaukauna, Wis. 54130. Mailing Add: 5-West, State Capitol, Madison, Wis. 53702.

ROGERS, WILLIAM PIERCE R
Secy. of State
b. Norfolk, N.Y, 6/23/13; s. Harrison A. Rogers and Myra Beswick R; m. 6/27/37 to Adele Langston; c. Dale Rogers (Mrs. Marshall), Anthony Wood, Jeffrey Langston and Douglas Langston. Educ: Colgate Univ, A.B, 34; Cornell Law Sch, LL.B, 37; Sigma Chi; Delta Theta Phi; Order of the Coif; Assoc. Ed, Cornell Law Quart. Polit. & Govt. Pos: Asst. Dist. Attorney, N.Y. Co, 38-42 & 46-47; chief counsel, Senate War Investigating Cmt, 47-48 and Senate Invests. Subcmt, Exec. Expenditures Cmt, 48-50; Dep. Attorney Gen, U.S, 53-57, Attorney Gen, 57-61; mem. U.S. Del, Twentieth Gen. Assembly of UN, 65; Secy. of State, 69- Bus. & Prof. Pos: Mem, N.Y. and Am. Stock Exchanges, 63-; Ltd. partner, Dreyfus & Co, 63- Mil. Serv: Entered as Lt.(jg), Naval Res, 42, released as Lt. Comdr, 46, after serv. in Air Group 10, Pac. Mem: Fed, Am. and D.C. Bar Asns; Bar Asn. of City of N.Y; Burning Tree Club; Racquett & Tennis Club; Recess Club; Sky Club; Metrop. Club. Rel: Presbyterian. Legal Res: 7007 Glenbrook Rd, Bethesda, Md. 20014. Mailing Add: Department of State, Washington, D.C. 20520.

ROGERSON, ROY HAROLD R
W.Va. State Del.
b. Wheeling, W.Va, 1/16/29; s. J. Russell Rogerson and Lilly Fisher R; m. 3/23/51 to LaVerne Yoho; c. Christine A, Marsha J, Lavon E. and Susan L. Educ: Wash. & Jefferson Univ, 46-47; W.Va. Univ, B.S.Ch.E, 51; Sigma Gamma Epsilon. Polit. & Govt. Pos: W.Va. State Del, currently. Bus. & Prof. Pos: Chem. engr, Corps of Engrs, U.S. Army, 51-55 and chem. div. Pittsburgh Plate Glass Co, 55- Mem: North. W.Va. Sect, Am. Inst. Chem. Engrs; Am. Inst. Chem. Engrs; local club orgn. leader, 4-H; Marshall Co. 4-H Leaders Orgn. Rel: Presbyterian. Mailing Add: R.D. 1, Moundsville, W.Va. 26041.

ROGOVIN, MITCHELL D
b. N.Y.C, 12/3/30; s. Max Shea Rogovin and Sayde Epstein R; m. 1/31/54 to Sheila Anne Ender; c. Lisa Shea, Wendy Meryl and John Andrew. Educ: Syracuse Univ, A.B, 52; Univ. Va. Law Sch, LL.B, 54; Georgetown Univ. Law Center, LL.M, 60; Phi Delta Phi. Polit. & Govt. Pos: Asst. to cmnr, Internal Revenue Serv, 61-65, chief counsel, 65-66; Asst. Attorney Gen, Dept. of Justice, 66-69. Bus. & Prof. Pos: Partner, Arnold and Porter, Wash, D.C, currently. Mil. Serv: Entered as Pvt, Marine Corps, 54, released as 1st Lt, 58; Capt, Marine Corps Res. Publ: The Charitable Enigma; Commercialism, Univ. South. Calif. Tax Inst, 64; 'The Four R's: Rulings, Regulations, Reliance & Retroactivity,' Taxes Mag, 12/65; 'Revenue Procedure 64-19,' The Practical Lawyer, 2/66. Mem: Chmn, Fed. Bar Asn. Cmt. on Taxation, 65-66; Va. and Am. Bar Asns; trustee, Lawyers' Electronic Legal Research Cmt; Joint Cmt, Standards of Tax Practice; Fed. Bar Asn. Rel: Hebrew. Legal Res: 4500 Klingle St. N.W, Washington, D.C. 20016. Mailing Add: 1229 19th St. N.W, Washington, D.C. 20036.

ROHLFING, FREDERICK W. R
Hawaii State Sen.
b. Honolulu, Hawaii, 11/2/28; s. R. R. Rohlfing and Kathryn Coe R; m. 7/15/52 to Joan Halford; c. Frederick W, III, Karl A. and Eric Bradford. Educ: Yale Univ, B.A, 50; George Wash. Univ. Law Sch, LL.B, 55; Phi Delta Phi; Beta Theta Pi. Polit. & Govt. Pos: Chmn, Oahu Young Rep, Hawaii, 57-58; dist. chmn, 17th Rep. Dist. Cmt, 58-59; Hawaii State Rep, 59-66, chmn, House Rep. Campaign Cmt, 62, minority floor leader, Hawaii House of Rep, 62-65, minority leader, 65-66; Hawaii State Sen, 66-, asst. minority leader, Hawaii State Senate, 66-68, minority policy leader, 69-; del, Rep. Nat. Conv, 68. Bus. & Prof. Pos: Assoc. attorney, Moore, Torkildson & Rice, 55-61; attorney-at-law, 61-63; partner, Rohlfing, Nakamura & Low, 63-68, Hughes, Steiner & Rohlfing, 68- Mil. Serv: Entered as Seaman Recruit, Navy, 51, released as Lt.(jg), 54; Comdr, Naval Res, 66. Mem: Am. and Hawaiian Bar Asns; Am. Trial Lawyers Asn; Naval Reserve Asn; Pac. Club; Hawaiian Govt. Employees Asn. Norman S. Hall Football Award, Yale, 50; William B. Stephenson Award, Outstanding Hawaii Naval Reservist, 68-69. Rel: Protestant. Mailing Add: 1409 Ohialoke St, Honolulu, Hawaii 96821.

ROHLFS, HARRY E. R
Mich. State Rep.
b. 7/15/02; married; c. Two daughters. Educ: Mich. State Univ, Bus. Sch. and Exten. Polit. & Govt. Pos: Former trustee, Fairgrove Twp; Mich. State Rep, 64- Bus. & Prof. Pos: Farmer; pres, R'n S Corp. of Akron and R'n S Chems, Inc, Bay City, mfrs. of commercial fertilizer; dir, Akron State Bank; pres, Mich. Elevator Exchange; mem, Akron Sch. Bd, 12 years. Mem: Mich. Coop. Bean Mkt. Asn; Mich. Bean Producers Asn; Mich. Wheat and Flour Inst; served on bd. of dirs, Mich. Elevator Exchange; mem, Nat. Bean Adv. Cmt; Tuscola Co. Fair Bd; adv. cmt, Tuscola Co. Agr. Exten. Dept; Rotary; Lions; Odd Fellows; Gateway Sportsman's Club. Rel: Presbyterian. Mailing Add: 2761 N. Merry Rd, Akron, Mich. 48701. (1967)

ROHMILLER, HAROLD C. D
Kans. State Rep.
b. Canton, Okla, 10/17/10; s. Nicholas Rohmiller and Martha Uhl R; m. 4/16/35 to D. Berniece Henson. Educ: Col. of Siskous; Pittsburg State Col, 3 years; Tahlequah State Col, B.S, 31. Polit. & Govt. Pos: Kans. State Rep, 67- Mil. Serv: Entered as Pvt, Army Air Corps, 36, released as S/Sgt, 39. Mem: Am. Legion (past comdr); C. of C.(past pres, 3 years); pres, LeCal Sch. Bd, 8 years; pres. bd. trustees, Labette Commun. Jr. Col. Rel: Catholic. Mailing Add: Chetopa, Kans. 37336.

ROLAND, PAUL GERALD D
b. Camden, N.J, 5/23/34; s. Francis C. Roland and Dorothy Carpen R; m. 10/28/67 to Sarah Frances Sweet. Educ: Univ. Pa, B.S. in econ, 57; Ind. Univ. Sch. Law, J.D, 64; Sphinx Sr. Soc; Univ. Pa; Phi Sigma Kappa; Phi Delta Phi. Polit. & Govt. Pos: Supvr, State Income Tax, Ind, 64; Ind. State Rep, Marion Co, 65-66; mem, Cmn. on State Tax and Financing Policy, Ind, Greater Indianapolis Progress Cmt, Senate-House Joint Cmt. on Taxation, Ind. and chmn, Death Tax Study Cmt, Ind, 65-; city attorney, Indianapolis. Mil. Serv: Entered as Pvt, Army, 57, released as Pfc, 57; Lt. Col, Ind. Guard Res, 65- Mem: Indianapolis, Ind. and Am. Bar Asns; Univ. Pa. Alumni Club, 57- Legal Res: 4515 N. Delaware St, Indianapolis, Ind. 46205. Mailing Add: Suite 1111, 129 E. Market St, Indianapolis, Ind. 46204.

ROLAPP, R. RICHARDS R
Spec. Asst. to the Dep. Attorney Gen, Dept. of Justice.
b. Los Angeles, Calif, 12/31/40; s. Ralph Thatcher Rolapp and Barbara Richards R; m. 8/30/63 to Marilyn Johnson; c. Todd Johnson and Juliane. Educ: Brigham Young Univ, B.S, 64; Harvard Law Sch, J.D, 67. Polit. & Govt. Pos: Chmn, Vol. for Ernest L. Wilkinson for U.S. Sen, Utah, 64; Spec.

counsel, Nixon Campaign, Wash, D.C, 68; assoc. gen. counsel, Presidential Inaugural Cmt, 69; spec. asst. to Dep. Attorney Gen, Dept. of Justice, 69- Bus. & Prof. Pos: Law clerk, Iverson and Hogoboom, Los Angeles, Calif, 66; assoc, Wilkinson, Cragun & Barker, Wash, D.C, 67-69. Publ: 'The Right of a Private College to Discipline its Students,' Brigham Young Univ. Bul, 7/69. Mem: Am, Fed. and D.C. Bar Asns. Student-Body Pres, Brigham Young Univ, 63-64. Rel: Latter-day Saint. Legal Res: Calif. Mailing Add: 2201 Shorefield Rd. Silver Spring. Md. 20902.

ROLDAN, ISRAEL BLAS R
b. Aguadilla, P.R, 11/24/23; s. Fidelio Roldan and Facunda Blas R; m. 6/27/42 to Rosario Gonzalez; c. Israel and Ernesto. Educ: Inter Am. Univ, P.R, B.A. Polit. & Govt. Pos: Rep, P.R. House of Rep, 62-68. Bus. & Prof. Pos: Prof, Spanish, Inter Am. Univ, until 62. Mil. Serv: Entered as Pvt, Army, 40, released as 2nd Lt, 45, after serv. in Inf, Caribbean; Good Conduct Medal; Overseas Award. Mem: Founder, Cultural & Civic Soc. of Aguadilla; Mason; Am. Legion. Rel: Catholic. Legal Res: 121 Betances St, Aguadilla, P.R. 00603. Mailing Add: P.O. Box 547, Aguadilla, P.R. 00603. (1967)

ROLDE, NEIL RICHARD D
b. Boston, Mass, 7/25/31; s. L. Robert Rolde and Lillian Lewis R; m. 3/12/60 to Carlotta Florsheim; c. Claudia Cathrene, Nicolette Adrienne and Andrea Jacqueline. Educ: Yale Univ, B.A; Columbia Univ. Sch. Journalism, M.S; Elizabethan Soc; Manuscript Soc. Polit. & Govt. Pos: Consult. to Maine Fed-State Coordinator, Augusta, 67-68; mem, Gov. Task Force on Oceanography, 67-; mem, Maine Cmn. on Arts and Humanities, 67-; co-chmn, Town of York Conserv. Cmt, 67-; del, Dem. Nat. Conv, 68; Dem. Cand, State Senate, dist. 1, 68; Maine trustee, New Eng. Aquarium, Boston, 68-; chmn, York Dem. Town Cmt, Maine, 68-; spec. asst. to Gov. Kenneth M. Curtis, 68-; mem, Gov. Task Force on Human Rights, 68- Bus. & Prof. Pos: Scriptwriter, Louis De Rochemont Assocs, N.Y.C, 56-; exec, R&S Construction Co, Boston, Mass, 58-60; free lance writer, currently. Mem: Pres. bd. trustees, Theatre by the Sea Portsmouth, N.H, 65-69; York Fish and Game Asn.(former secy-treas); mem. steering cmt, Seacoast Coun. Race & Relig, Portsmouth, N.H. Dean's prize, Yale, Univ. Mailing Add: Sewall's Hill, York, Maine 03909.

ROLFE, ERNEST L. R
N.H. State Rep.
b. Bridgton, Maine, 1/18/92; married. Educ: Bridgton High Sch. Polit. & Govt. Pos: Former councilman, N.H; N.H. State Rep, 43- Bus. & Prof. Pos: Proprietor, garage and filling sta, 25 years. Mil. Serv: World War I. Mem: Mason (32°). Rel: Methodist. Mailing Add: 82 Main St, East Rochester, N.H. 03867.

ROLFSRUD, HALVER D
b. Keene, N.Dak, 3/21/06; married; c. Four. Educ: Pub. Schs. Polit. & Govt. Pos: N.Dak. State Rep, 49-66; pres, McKenzie Co. Hosp. Asn; Twp. and Sch. Bds. Bus. & Prof. Pos: Farmer; v.pres, Baukol Noonan, Inc. Mailing Add: Watford City, N.Dak. 58854. (1967)

ROLLER, O. BEVERLEY R
Va. State Del.
b. Weyers Cave, Va, 5/6/24; m. to Dorothy Frances Stroop. Educ: Va. Polytech. Inst, B.A. in Agr. and grad. work; Madison Col, grad. work; Omicron Delta Kappa; Phi Kappa Phi; Alpha Zeta. Polit. & Govt. Pos: Past dist. gov, Woodrow Wilson Found; Va. State Del, 66- Bus. & Prof. Pos: Teacher. Mem: Ruritan; Nat. Educ. Asn; Augusta Co. Educ. Asn; past nat. officer, Future Farmers of Am. State Pub. Speaking Champion, Future Farmers of Am. Rel: Methodist. Mailing Add: Weyers Cave, Va. 24486. (1967)

ROLSTAD, BRUCE HOWARD D
Chaplain, N.Mex. State Legis.
b. Minneapolis, Minn, 1/29/36; s. Oscar Rolstad and Twyla Stansfield R; m. 6/14/58 to Jacqulyn Carol Rohwer; c. Krista Carol and Erik Bruce. Educ: Macalester Col, B.A, 58; Drake Univ, B.D, 61. Polit. & Govt. Pos: Chaplain, N.Mex. State Legis, 67-; co-chmn, McCarthy for Pres, Santa Fe Co, 68; del, Dem. Nat. Conv, 68; mem, N.Mex. State Dem. Cent. Cmt, 69- Bus. & Prof. Pos: V.pres, Christian Churches of N.Mex, 67-; secy. bd. trustees, St. Vincent Hosp, Santa Fe, 68- Mem: YMCA (v.pres, Santa Fe, 67-); Santa Fe Ministerial Asn.(pres, 66-67). Archbishop Lamy Award, 68. Rel: Disciples of Christ; Pastor, First Christian Church, Santa Fe, N.Mex. Mailing Add: 2270 Calle Cuesta, Santa Fe, N.Mex. 87501.

ROLVAAG, KARL FRITJOF DFL
b. Northfield, Minn, 7/18/13; s. Ole Edvart Rolvaag and Jennie Berdahl R; m. 8/28/43 to Florence Boedeker; c. Paul and Kristin. Educ: St. Olaf Col, B.A, 41; Univ. Minn. Grad. Sch, 46; Univ. Oslo, Am-Scandinavian Found. Fel, 47-48. Hon. LL.D, St. Mary's Col, 64. Polit. & Govt. Pos: Cand. for Cong, 46, 48 & 52; state chmn, Dem-Farmer-Labor Party, 50-54; del, Dem. Nat. Conv, 52, 60 & 64; Lt. Gov, Minn, 55-63, Gov, 63-67; exec. dir, Midwest Humphrey for President Cmt, 59-60; Ambassador to Iceland, 67-69. Bus. & Prof. Pos: V.pres, Group Health Mutual Ins. Co, 56-59. Mil. Serv: Entered as Pvt, Army, 41, released as Capt, 47, after serv. in 4th Armored Div, 3rd Army, ETO, France; Silver Star; Purple Heart; Presidential Unit Citation; Croix de Guerre. Publ: 'History of the Democrat-Farmer-Labor Party,' Minn. Heritage, 58. Mem: Norweg-Am. Hist. Soc; Minn. Hist. Soc; VFW; DAV; Am. Legion; Moose; Eagles; Purple Heart Vet; Nat. Grange. Distinguished Alumnus Award, St. Olaf Col, 59. Rel: Lutheran. Mailing Add: 311 Manitou St, Northfield, Minn. 55057.

ROLWING, FRANCIS DAVID D
b. Charleston, Mo, 7/23/34; s. F. D. Rolwing and Margaret Hunter R; m. 12/27/60 to Beverly Ruth Colliflower; c. Ruth Ellen and Laura Jane. Educ: St. Louis Univ, B.S, 56. Polit. & Govt. Pos: Pres, Miss. Co. Young Dem, Mo, 59-65; Mo. State Rep, 61-69. Bus. & Prof. Pos: Secy-treas, Rolwing-Moxley Co, 60-; owner, David Rolwing Ins. Agency, 62- Mil. Serv: Entered as Pvt, Army, 57, released as E-4, 59, after serv. in Hq. Troop, 1st Reconnaissance Squadron, 1st Cavalry Div, 1st Inf. Div, Ft. Riley, Kans, 59; Good Conduct Medal. Mem: Kiwanis; Farm Bur; C. of C. Named Outstanding Young Man of Am, 64. Rel: Roman Catholic. Mailing Add: 1305 E. Commercial, Charleston, Mo. 63834. (1967)

ROMANG, RICHARD EDWARD R
Okla. State Sen.
b. Breckinridge, Okla, 1/20/12; s. John Edward Romang and Sophia Berger R; div; c. Karen. Educ: Univ. Chicago, B.A, 34; Univ. Okla, LL.B, 36; Phi Alpha Delta. Polit. & Govt. Pos: Okla. State Rep, 48-60; Okla. State Sen, 60-, Rep. Caucus Chmn, Okla. State Senate, currently. Bus. & Prof. Pos: Attorney-at-law, Okla, 36-; mgr, Motion Picture Arbit. Off, Okla. City, 41-44. Mem: Okla. Bar Asn; Okla. and Am. Trial Lawyers Asns; Cong. Lit. Soc. Selected as One of the Five Outstanding Okla. State Sen. of the 1965 Session of the Okla. State Legis. Rel: Methodist. Legal Res: 1525 E. Randolph, Enid, Okla. 73701. Mailing Add: 121 W. Maine, Enid, Okla. 73701.

ROMANO, SAM D
Ill. State Sen.
b. Chicago, Ill; c. two; six grandchildren. Educ: Chicago pub. schs; eve. classes at Lewis Inst. and YMCA. Polit. & Govt. Pos: Ill. State Rep, 5 terms; Ill. State Sen, 66- Bus. & Prof. Pos: Practicing tax acct; sr. partner, Rapid Bus. Serv, a bookkeeping serv. and ins. firm. Mem: Civic and church activities. Mailing Add: 736 S. Claremont Ave, Chicago, Ill. 60612. (1967)

ROMANOS, GEORGE MARCUS, JR. R
b. Boston, Mass, 8/4/20; s. George M. Romanos and Marjorie Harris R; m. 9/25/43 to Ann Nowell Rowen; c. George David, Barbara (Mrs. Jean Yarrington, III), Joan (Mrs. James Houllahan), Elizabeth, Michael Peter, Suzanne and Stephanie Grace. Educ: Boston Latin High Sch. Polit. & Govt. Pos: V.chmn, Boston Rep. Cmt, Mass, 60-68; elec. cmnr, Boston, 61-; committeeman, Mass. Rep. State Cmt, 64-68; pres, Suffolk Co. Rep. Club, 64-69; mem, State Cmt. of Labor and Indust, 67-; del, several Rep. State Conv; del, Rep. Nat. Conv, 68. Mem: Dir, Gr. Boston Real Estate Bd, 60-; Youth Activities Cmt. Realtor of the Year for West. Dist, Boston Herald Traveler Newspaper, 64-66. Rel: Methodist. Mailing Add: 20 Spring Park Ave, Boston, Mass. 02130.

ROMANS, RONALD CHARLES R
Chmn, Young Rep. Nat. Fedn.
b. Ord, Nebr, 11/27/37; s. John Jack Romans and Glea Porter R; m. 6/13/59 to Phyllis Lee Jablonski; c. David Charles, Jeffrey John and Scott Martin. Educ: Hastings Col, 56-57; Omaha Univ, 67-68. Polit. & Govt. Pos: Nat. committeeman, Nebr. Fedn. of Young Rep, 63-64, state chmn, 65-66; alternate del, Rep. Nat. Conv, 64, del. and v.chmn, Nebr. Del, 68; chmn. state orgn. cmt, Young Rep. Nat. Fedn, 67-69, chmn, 69-; field dir, United Citizens for Nixon-Agnew, 68; del, Am. Coun. of Young Polit. Leaders, NATO Conf, Luxembourg, 68. Bus. & Prof. Pos: Treas, Omaha Transportation Coun, 67. Mil. Serv: Army Nat. Guard, 57-63. Mem: Nebr. Motor Carriers Asn; Omaha Traffic Club; Elks; Jaycees. Rel: Methodist. Mailing Add: 8113 Q St, Ralston, Nebr, 68127.

ROMELL, LOUIS C. R
b. Chicago, Ill, 4/7/99. Polit. & Govt. Pos: Wis. State Assemblyman, 60-66; Wis. State Assemblyman, 47-55; Town Supvr, 39-42; Adams Co. Bd. mem, 41. Bus. & Prof. Pos: Beef cattle raising; real estate dealer. Mem: Sch. Bd, 36-42. Mailing Add: Edgewood Dr, Rte. 1, Adams, Wis. 53910. (1967)

ROMER, HAROLD WILLIAM D
Chmn, Mercer Co. Dem. Exec. Cmt, Ohio
b. St. Henry, Ohio, 9/21/94; s. Joseph John Romer and Anna Hartings R; m. 9/23/22 to Anna Josephin Haas; c. Donald Edward and Joan (Mrs. Clarence Scott Braun). Educ: St. Henry Pub. Sch, Ohio, grad, 11. Polit. & Govt. Pos: City councilman, Coldwater, Ohio, 37-41; chmn, Mercer Co. Dem. Party, 51-56 & 59-69; chmn, Mercer Co. Dem. Exec. Cmt, 51-; Ohio State Rep, Mercer Co, 59-66; del, Dem. Nat. Conv, 68. Bus. & Prof. Pos: Mgr, Romer's Store, St. Henry, Ohio, 15-23; clerk in training, S.H. Kress Co, Nashville, Tenn, 23-24; mgr. and part owner, Romer Dry Goods Co, Coldwater, Ohio, 24-29; owner, Romer's Store, 29-55 and 66-69, mgr, 56-65. Mem: Elks; Moose; Eagles; K. of C. Honored as the outstanding polit. leader in Mercer Co, 66. Rel: Catholic. Legal Res: 803 W. Main St, Coldwater, Ohio 45828. Mailing Add: P.O. Box 83, Coldwater, Ohio 45828.

ROMER, ROY R. D
b. Garden City, Kans, 10/31/28; s. Irvine Rudolph Romer and Bessie Snieder R; m. 6/10/52 to Beatrice Miller; c. Mark, Paul, Mary Susan, Christopher, Timothy and Thomas. Educ: Colo. State Univ, B.S. in agr. econ, 50; Univ. Colo. Law Sch, LL.B, 52; Yale Univ, grad. study, 54-55. Polit. & Govt. Pos: Mem. agr. adv. cmt. to State Bd. Agr; chmn, Task Group on Post-High Sch. Educ. in Denver Metrop. Area, Colo; Colo. State Rep, 58-62, chmn, House Judiciary Cmt. and Joint House-Senate Cmt. on Educ. Beyond High Sch, v.chmn, House Appropriations Cmt. and mem, Joint Budget Cmt; mem, Gov. Cmn. on Aging, 60-62; Colo. State Sen, 62-66, asst. minority leader, Colo. State Senate, mem, Mining, Agr, Water and Vet. Affairs Cmts; cand for U.S. Senate, Colo, 66. Bus. & Prof. Pos: Former farmer, rancher and businessman; attorney-at-law, Denver, Colo, currently. Mil. Serv: Air Force, 52-54, serv. in ETO. Mem: Am. and Denver Bar Asns; past mem. bd. gov, Colo, 66. Asn; dir. and former v.pres, Denver Area Legal Aid Soc; former mem. bd. dirs, Colo. State Univ. Alumni; bd. trustees, Iliff Sch. Theol; Metrop. Coun. for Commun. Serv; charter mem, bd. trustees, Plains Conserv. Center; past bd. mem, Auraria Commun. Center, Denver Univ. YMCA and Denver Inner-City Protestant Parish. Mailing Add: 4600 Montview Blvd, Denver, Colo. 80207.

ROMERO, MOISES R
b. Cleveland, N.Mex, 3/27/00; s. David Romero and Cicilia Bernal R; m. 11/27/27 to Fidela Chacon (deceased), 11/15/39 to Sofia Padilla (deceased) and Carmelita Montoya; c. Antonia Cicilia, Barney, Pricilla, Henry, Freed Apodoca, Floraido Moises, Joe Christian, Jose F. Garcia (deceased), Videlita, Leanor Emilio, Luciano Petriolino, Maria Florida, Bertha Sorida and stepchildren, Maximinio Salazar, Maria Delfinia (Mrs. Bal Gonzales), Aurora (Mrs. Processo Chaves) and grandson, Jesse Roy Chavez. Educ: Adult educ. under the Works Prog. Admin. Polit. & Govt. Pos: Dep. co. clerk, N.Mex, 42-46; clerk, Bur. of Revenue, 51-62; chmn, Mora Co. Rep. Party, 57-58; counselor, Help Establish Lasting Peace, Mora Co, 68- Bus. & Prof. Pos:

Pub. sch. teacher, 20-34; farmer, Cleveland, N.Mex, 62- Rel: Catholic. Legal Res: Cleveland, N.Mex. 87715. Mailing Add: P.O. Box 63, Cleveland, N.Mex. 87715.

ROMINE, CHARLES EVERETT, JR. R
W.Va. State Del.
b. Spencer, W.Va, 1/16/36; s. Charles Everett Romine, Sr. and Shirley Reed R; m. 12/26/57 to Phyllis Cremeans; c. Charles E, III, David C, Bradley R. and Anne E. Educ: Marshall Univ, 4 years; Sigma Phi Epsilon. Polit. & Govt. Pos: W.Va. State Del, 69- Bus. & Prof. Pos: Local agent, State Farm Ins. Co, 58- Mem: Huntington Life Underwriters Asn; Cabell-Huntington Mental Health Asn.(past pres); Huntington Jaycees (past pres). Outstanding Young Man of 1968, Huntington, W.Va. Rel: United Methodist. Legal Res: 2745 N. Terrace, Huntington, W.Va. 25705. Mailing Add: P.O. Box 2225, Huntington, W.Va. 25723.

ROMINGER, JAMES CORRIDON R
Chmn, Stephens Co. Rep. Party, Tex.
b. Cisco, Tex, 4/27/20; s. C. V. Rominger and Myrtle Robinson R; m. 4/25/59 to Muriel Jean Henderson; c. James Whitney, Kurt Gideon, Jett Daniel and Stuart Robinson. Educ: Tex. A&M, B.A, 41. Polit. & Govt. Pos: Precinct chmn. and chmn, Stephens Co. Rep. Party, Tex, currently; pres, Sch. Bd, 63- Bus. & Prof. Pos: Acct, Chem. Process Co, 47-56, B.J. Serv, Borg Warner, 56-59 and Sheets & Walton Drilling Co, 59-65; v.pres, Citizens Nat. Bank, Tex, 65- Mil. Serv: Entered as 2nd Lt, Army, 41, released as Maj, 46, after serv. in 1st Armored Div, Africa and Italy, 42-45; Col, Army Res, 66; Bronze Star; Purple Heart; African and Italian Campaign Ribbons. Mem: Lions; Am. Legion; Elks. Rel: Roman Catholic. Mailing Add: 600 S. Mistletoe, Breckenridge, Tex. 76024.

ROMNEY, GEORGE WILCKEN R
Secy. of Housing and Urban Develop.
b. Chihuahua, Mex, 7/8/07; s. Gaskell Romney and Anna Amelia Pratt R; m. 7/2/31 to Lenore LaFount; c. Lynn (Mrs. Loren Keenan), Jane (Mrs. Bruce Robinson), Scott and Mitt. Educ: Univ. Utah; George Wash. Univ; more than a dozen hon. doctorates. Polit. & Govt. Pos: U.S. del, Int. Labor Conf, 46-; del. and v.pres, State Constitutional Conv, Mich, 61-62; Gov, Mich, 63-69; del, Rep. Nat. Conv, 68; Secy. of Housing and Urban Develop, 69- Bus. & Prof. Pos: Rep, Aluminum Co. of Am, 30-39; mgr, Automobile Mfrs. Asn, 39-48; asst. to pres. and v.pres, Nash-Kelvinator Corp, 48-54; bd. chmn. and pres, Am. Motors Corp, 54-62. Mem: Automobile Mfrs. Asn.(pres, 56-58); managing dir, Automotive Coun. for War Prod, 41-45; chmn, Citizens for Mich, 59-61. Rel: Latter-day Saint. Legal Res: Valley Rd, Bloomfield Hills, Mich. 48013. Mailing Add: HUD Bldg, Washington, D.C. 20410.

ROMNEY, JANICE CAHOON R
V.Chmn, Utah Rep, Party
b. Salt Lake City, Utah, 3/19/16; d. Leonard Cahoon and Matilda Rozella Watts C; m. 9/30/35 to Miles Pratt Romney; c. Miles Pratt, Jr, Leonard Cahoon, Wendy Virginia (Mrs. Hassibe), Rosanne and Hannah Hill. Educ: Univ. Utah, 35-37, B.S, 58, presently working on M.S; Kappa Kappa Gamma (pres). Polit. & Govt. Pos: Rep. dist. v.chmn, Precinct, Utah, 38-43, dist. chmn, 43-45; Rep. secy, Legis. Dist. 2, 38-45; co. and state del, Salt Lake Co. Rep. Party, 58-60; del, Utah Rep. State Conv, 64; chmn, women's div, Mitchell Melich for Gov. Campaign, 64; del, Utah Coun. for Improvement of Educ, 64; alternate del, Rep. Nat. Conv, 64, del, 68; del, West. States Conf, Rep. Party, 65; v.chmn, Utah Rep. Party, 65-; chmn, women's div, Utah Rep. Party and Rep. Fedn, 68; cmt. chmn, Gov. Inaugural, 68. Bus. & Prof. Pos: Psychol. teacher, Granger High Sch, 58-61, sch. counsr, 61-64; dist. counsr, Granite Sch. Dist, currently. Mem: Am. and Utah Personnel and Guidance Asns; Nat, Utah and Granite Educ. Asns; Women's State Legis. Coun. of Utah; Granite Counsr. Asn; Youth, Inc; pres, Am. Inst. of Mining, Metallurgical Engrs. Auxiliary; PTA. Rel: Latter-day Saint. Legal Res: 1930 Sheridan Rd, Salt Lake City, Utah 84108. Mailing Add: 340 E. 3540 S, Salt Lake City, Utah 84115.

ROMNEY, MILES D
Mont. State Rep.
b. Hamilton, Mont, 12/6/00; s. Miles Romney and Elizabeth Rosetta Robbins R; m. 2/18/25 to Ruth Gray. Educ: U.S. Mil. Acad, 18-19; George Wash. Univ, 19 & 20-21; Univ. Mont, B.A, 22; Kappa Sigma; Delta Sigma Chi. Polit. & Govt. Pos: Del, Mont. State Dem. Conv, 22-; committeeman, Ravalli Co. State Dem. Cent. Cmt, 40-; del, Dem. Nat. Conv, 56 & 60; Mont. State Rep, Dist. 25, 67-, mem, Mont. Dem. Legis. Coun, currently. Bus. & Prof. Pos: Worked on various newspapers; cmt. clerk, Pub. Lands Cmt. and clerk, Off. on Document Room, U.S. House of Rep, formerly; dir, Motor Vehicle Dept, Mont. R.R. Cmn, 36-37; ed. and publisher, West. News, Hamilton, Mont, 37- Mem: Mont. State Press Asn; AF&AM; Eagles; Elks; Ravalli Co. Fish & Wildlife Asn. Legal Res: 425 S. Third St, Hamilton, Mont. 59840. Mailing Add: P.O. Box 633, Hamilton, Mont. 59840.

ROMNEY, VERNON R
b. Colonia Juarez, Mex, 7/3/96; s. Miles Park Romney and Catherine Jane Cottam; m. 6/23/23 to Lois Bradford (deceased 4/19/57); c. Vernon B, Ralph Bradford, Rowena (Mrs. James D. Maher), Keith B, Beverly (Mrs. Robert Cutler), Geraldine (Mrs. Boyd Busath), Yvonne (Mrs. Grant Dixon) and John B; m. 11/6/64 to Helen Hackett Brown; stepchildren; Marilyn (Mrs. Benair Hansen), Jacqueline (Mrs. Darwin Anderson) and Thomas Vernon Brown. Educ: George Wash. Univ, J.D, 22, Phi Delta Phi; pres, Utah Legal Club of George Wash. Univ, 20-22. Polit. & Govt. Pos: Mem, Utah Rep. State Exec. Cmt, 36-62; chmn, Salt Lake Co. Rep. Cmt, 42-44; del, Rep. Nat. Conv, 44, 48 (seconded nomination of Sen. Robert A. Taft for President), 52, 60 & 64; Rep. Nat. Committeeman and Rep. State Chmn, Utah, 44-50 & 58-62; chmn, Rep. State Chmn. Orgn. Midwest and Rocky Mt. States, 49-50; mem. cent. campaign cmt, Sen. Robert Taft for President, campaign mgr. for Northwest. U.S; chmn, Cmn. Utah State Indian Affairs, 59; mem. civic cmt, Salt Lake City, 66- Bus. & Prof. Pos: Secy, Romney Lunt Land and Livestock Co, 14-24; West mgr, Nat. Wool Warehouse and Storage Co, 18-20; West rep, Am. Sheepbreeder, 18-20; admitted to Utah Bar, 22; attorney, Romney & Nelson, Salt Lake City, 22-; trustee, Robert A. Taft Mem. Found, 54-; v.pres, State Savings & Loan Asn, secy, Utah Cmt. for Int. Contact, 64-; mem, Nat. Lawyers' Cmt. John Marshall Mem. Bldg. Fund, Freedoms Found. at Valley Forge, 65- Mem: Am, Utah and Salt Lake Co. Bar Asns; governing bd, George Wash. Univ. Alumni Asn, 65-; George Wash. Law Asn; adv. cmt, John Foster Dulles Fund; U.S. Savings and Loan League; C. of C. Alumni Serv. Award, George Wash. Univ. Gen. Alumni Asn, 65. Rel: Latter-day Saint. Mailing Add: 404 Kearns Building, Salt Lake City, Utah 84101.

RONAN, BARBARA HUNT D
b. Washington, D.C, 7/19/26; d. Oscar P. Hunt and Elizabeth F. Mulloy H; m. to Matthias McDonald, 1947; John M. Ronan, 1953; c. Maureen E, Kathleen E, Sharon E, George Hunt and John Michael, Jr. Educ: Syracuse Univ, 44-47; Phi Mu. Polit. & Govt. Pos: Precinct Capt, Holly Precinct, Ariz, 66-; publicity coordinator, State Campaign Conf. for Dem. Women, 66; committeewoman, Ill. State Dem. Cent. Cmt, 62-65; precinct committeewoman, 62-65; alternate del-at-lg, Dem. Nat. Conv, 64; mgr, 12th Dist. Cong. Campaign, 64; mem, Lake Co. Registrn. Coun, 64. Bus. & Prof. Pos: Teacher practical politics, N. Chicago High Night Sch, Ill, 65; ed, Mundelein Libertyville News, 63-64; columnist, Independent Register, Libertyville, 61-62. Mem: Phoenix Alumnae of Phi Mu; Nat. Rifle Asn; St. Agnes Home and Sch. Asn; Xavier High Sch. Mothers' Club. Rel: Catholic. Mailing Add: 3301 E. Cypress St, Phoenix, Ariz. 85008. (1967)

RONAN, JAMES A. D
Ill. State Chmn, Dem. Party
b. Chicago, Ill, 7/2/04; s. James Ronan and Katherine McDonald; m. 7/2/29 to Margaret Mary Maloney; c. Margaret (Mrs. Stephen K. Healy), James, John, Martin. Educ: Univ. of Notre Dame, A.B, 26; Loyola Univ, J.D, 31. Polit. & Govt. Pos: Ill. Indust. Cmn, 49-53; del, Dem. Nat. Conv, 52, 56, 60, 64 & 68; Ill. State Chmn, Dem. Party, 52-; Dem. Committeeman, Ill, 60-; dir, Ill. State Finance, 61-69. Bus. & Prof. Pos: Pres, James Ronan Co, 26-; attorney-at-law, 32- Mem: Ill. Workmans Comp. Bar Asn, South Shore Country, K. of C, Notre Dame, Cath. Lawyers Guild. Rel: Catholic. Mailing 7115 S. Oglesby Ave, Chicago, Ill, 60649.

RONCALIO, TENO D
Dem. Nat. Committeeman, Wyo.
b. Rock Springs, Wyo, 3/23/16; s. Frank Roncalio and Ernestina Mussi R; m. 6/22/62 to Cecelia Waters Domenico; c. Teno Frank and John Waters; foster children, Carol, David, Joan and Louis. Educ: Univ. Wyo, LL.B, 47. Polit. & Govt. Pos: Mem. staff, U.S. Sen. O'Mahoney, 41; asst. clerk, U.S. Senate Libr, 41; dep. prosecuting attorney, Cheyenne, Wyo, 50-56; chmn, Wyo. State Dem. Cent. Cmt, 57-61; v.chmn, Wyo. del, Dem. Nat. Conv, 60, del, 64 & 68; mem, Interstate Cmn, Potomac River Basin, 61-63; chmn, U.S. Sect, Int. Joint Cmn, Wash, D.C, 61-63; U.S. Rep, Wyo, 65-66; Dem. Nat. Committeeman, Wyo, 69- Bus. & Prof. Pos: Ed, Wyo. Labor J, 49; law practice, Cheyenne, 49-; chmn. bd, Cheyenne Nat. Bank, 60-68. Mil. Serv: Army, Capt, World War II. Mem: Am. and Wyo. Bar Asns; Laramie Co. Bar Asn.(pres, 56); Lawyer-Pilots Asn. (area pres). Mailing Add: 3024 Capitol Ave, Cheyenne, Wyo. 82001.

RONCALLO, ANGELO D. R
Comptroller, Nassau Co, N.Y.
b. Port Chester, N.Y, 5/28/27; s. Anthony Roncallo and Connie Prochilo R; m. 5/31/52 to Priscille Pouliot; c. Marc, Paul, John, Jean and James. Educ: Manhattan Col, B.A, 50; Georgetown Univ, J.D, 53; Delta Theta Phi. Polit. & Govt. Pos: Dep. co. attorney, Nassau Co, N.Y, 58-60, comptroller, 67-; counsel, Joint Legis. Cmt, 61-63; councilman, Oyster Bay, L.I, 65-67; alternate del, Rep. Nat. Conv, 68; chmn, Oyster Bay Rep. Cmt, N.Y, 68- Mil. Serv: Entered as Pvt, Army, 44, released as Pfc, 46, after serv. in 130th Sta. Hosp. Mem: Nassau and N.Y. State Bar Asns; Catholic Lawyers Guild; K. of C; VFW; Exalted Ruler, Elks; Past Venerable, Sons of Italy; Massapequa C. of C; Roland Club; Am. Arbitration Asn. Rel: Catholic. Legal Res: 226 Toronto Ave, Massapequa, N.Y. 11758. Mailing Add: 240 Old Country Rd, Mineola, L.I, N.Y. 11501.

RONEY, JAMES ALBERT, JR. D
b. North East, Md, 7/22/13; s. James Albert Roney and Annie Wells R; m. 12/19/42 to Nancy Davis Smith; c. Sayre A. and James Albert, III. Educ: Univ. Md, A.B, 34, Law Sch, LL.B, 36. Polit. & Govt. Pos: State attorney, Md, 50-62; Md. State Sen, 62-66. Bus. & Prof. Pos: Trustee, West Nottingham Acad, 55-; dir, First Nat. Bank of North East, Md, 62-; dir, Union Hosp. of Cecil Co, 66. Mil. Serv: Entered as Pvt, Army, 42, released as Capt, 46, after serv. in 592nd Joint Assault Signal Co, Pac; Am. Theater, Pac. Theater and Philippine Liberation Ribbons with Arrowheads. Mem: Md. Bar Asn; pres, Cecil Co. and Second Judicial Circuit Md. Bar Asns; bd. mem, Coun. of State Govt; Mason; Rotary; Am. Legion. Rel: Methodist. Legal Res: R.D. 2, North East, Md. 21901. Mailing Add: 103 Court House Plaza, Elkton, Md. 21921.

RONIGER, PASCAL ALLEN R
Kans. State Rep.
b. Hymer, Kans, 11/10/14; s. Charles Roniger and Anna H. Allen R; m. 7/10/41 to Martha Sharer; c. Ann (Mrs. William A. Hussong) and John Charles. Educ: Kans. Univ, A.B, 39, grad work. in bact, 39-41; Phi. Chi. Polit. & Govt. Pos: Rep. precinct committeeman, Diamond Twp, Chase Co, Kans, 58 & 59, 69-; Kans. State Rep, 61st Dist, 69- Bus. & Prof. Pos: Serologist, N.Mex. State Bd. of Health, 41-42; Riley Co. sanitarian and milk inspector, Kans. State Bd. of Health, 42-51; farmer and stockman, Chase Co, 51- Mil. Serv: Entered as Ens, Navy, 44, released as Lt.(jg), 46, after serv. in Pac. Fleet; Lt, Naval Res, 46-51. Mem: Am. Legion; Farm Mgt. Asn; Chase Co. Soil Conserv; Diamond Creek Watershed. Banker's Award for Soil Conserv. Work. Rel: First Christian. Mailing Add: R.R. 1, Burdick, Kans. 66838.

ROODKOWSKY, ALICE MAY R
Secy, Mass. Rep. State Cmt.
b. New York, N.Y, 10/10/21; d. Otto Juenger and Mary M. Queenan J; m. 3/22/47 to Nikita D. Roodkowsky; c. Tatiana, Mary and Alexandra. Educ: Hunter Col; Packard Commercial Sch. Polit. & Govt. Pos: Del, Mass. Dem. State Conv, 66 and Worcester Conf, 67; campaign coordinator, Mass. State Sen. William I. Randall, 66; mem, Natick Rep. Town Cmt, 66- and secy, 66-68; mem, Mass. Rep. State Cmt, 68-, and secy, 68- Bus. & Prof. Pos: Secy. to Dean of the Col, Wellesley Col, Wellesley, Mass, currently. Rel: Roman Catholic. Mailing Add: 10 University Dr, Natick, Mass. 01760.

ROOK, DORIS MAE R
b. Washington, D.C, 6/22/21; d. Charles Willard Rook and Ruth Kelly R; single. Educ: George Wash. Univ, A.A, 48; Strayers Bus. Col, 1 year. Polit. & Govt. Pos: Secy, Dept. Army, 41-45; exec. secy, U.S. Rep. Carl T. Curtis, Nebr, 45-55, U.S. Sen. Carl T. Curtis, 55-63, admin. asst, 63- Mem: Eastern Star. Rel: Episcopal. Mailing Add: 103 Granville Dr, Silver Spring, Md. 20901.

ROOKS, JAMES ORVILLE R
Chmn, Henry Co. Rep. Cmt, Ga.
b. Jackson, Ga, 3/22/22; s. James Howard Rooks and Fannie Willard R; m. 12/27/45 to Peggy Marilyn Sanders; c. Denise (Mrs. Ricks), Anita and Melanie. Educ: Md. Inst. Fine Arts, Baltimore, 3 years. Polit. & Govt. Pos: V.chmn, Henry Co. Rep. Cmt, Ga, 66-68 and chmn, 68-; mem, Ga. Sixth Dist. Rep. Cmt, 67-; mem, Ga. Rep. State Cent. Cmt, 68- Bus. & Prof. Pos: Printer, Jackson Progress-Argus, Jackson, Ga, 46-49; engraver, Baltimore Type Corp, Md, 49-58; printer-pressman, Advertiser Printing Co, McDonough, Ga, 58-69. Mil. Serv: Entered as Pvt, Air Force, 42, released as T/5, 45, after serv. in Airborne Engrs, Fifth Air Force, Pac. Theatre, 43-45; Good Conduct Medal; Asiatic-Pac. Ribbon with Three Bronze Stars; Presidential Unit Citation; Among first 500 flown into Japan to make preparations for surrender and occup, 8/45. Publ: 'Republican Viewpoint,' weekly column, Weekly Advertiser. Mem: Kiwanis. Rel: Baptist. Mailing Add: 105 Carmichael St, McDonough, Ga. 30253.

ROONEY, FRED B. D
U.S. Rep, Pa.
b. Bethlehem, Pa, 11/6/25; s. Fred B. Rooney and Veronica K. McGreevy R; m. 12/14/63 to Evelyn Davis Lisle; c. Timothy Craig and Martha Lisle. Educ: Univ. Ga. at Athens, A.B. in bus. admin, 50. Polit. & Govt. Pos: Pres. and reorganizer, Young Dem. Club of Northampton Co, Pa, 56; Pa. State Sen, 58-63, mem, Bethlehem Housing Authority, 58-59; Pa. State Rep, 15th Dist, 63-66; U.S. Rep, Pa, currently. Mil. Serv: 515th Paratroop Inf. Regt, 13th Airborne Div, ETO. Publ: 'Power as Part of the Tocks Island Reservoir,' Pub. Utilities Fortnightly, 5/65, 'Europe Says: It (The Big Blackout) Couldn't Happen Here!' 5/66. Mem: Am. Legion; Amvets; VFW; CWV; past grand knight, K. of C. Rel: Catholic. Legal Res: 575 Brighton St, Bethlehem, Pa. 18015. Mailing Add: 3150 Highland Place N.W, Washington, D.C. 20008.

ROONEY, JOHN J. D
U.S. Rep, N.Y.
b. Brooklyn, N.Y, 11/29/03; m. to Catherine Kramm Curran; c. John James, Jr, Edward Patrick, Arthur Patrick Curran, William Edward and Mary Ann (Mrs. Farrell). Educ: St. Francis Col; Fordham Univ. Sch. of Law, 25. Polit. & Govt. Pos: Asst. dist. attorney, Kings Co, N.Y, 40-44; U.S. Rep, N.Y, 43-, chmn, Dem. Caucus U.S. House of Rep, 55-56; off. observer, First Bikini Atom Test; off. observer, Japanese Peace Conf, 51. Bus. & Prof. Pos: Attorney-at-law. Mem: Ecclesiastic Order of St. Gregory the Great (Knight Comdr. with Star); Elks (Past Exalted Ruler); Ancient Order of Hibernians in Am.(past N.Y. State v.pres); St. Patrick Soc. of Brooklyn (past pres); life mem, K. of C; hon. mem, VFW. Legal Res: Brooklyn, N.Y. Mailing Add: 2268 Rayburn House Office Bldg, Washington, D.C. 20515. (1967)

ROONEY, JOHN JOSEPH D
Wyo. State Rep.
b. Chadron, Nebr, 11/30/15; s. William Peter Rooney and Armena Broghamer R; m. 7/13/37 to Velma Kruse; c. Armena (Mrs. Taylor), Velma Ruth (Mrs. Yeargain), Margaret, Kathryn (Mrs. Cooper), Jean and John. Educ: Univ. of Minn; Univ. of Colo, A.B. and LL.B. Polit. & Govt. Pos: Spec. agent, Fed. Bur. of Invest, 41-58; precinct committeeman, Dem. Party, Wyo, 58-; mem. staff, U.S. Sen. J.J. Hickey, 61-63; Wyo. State Rep, 65-; mem, Statute Revision Cmn, 65-; chmn, Wyo. Dem. State Cent. Cmt, 65-; del, Dem. Nat. Conv, 68; city attorney, Cheyenne, 68- Rel: Catholic. Mailing Add: 420 W. 28th St, Cheyenne, Wyo. 82001.

ROORDA, NORMAN PAUL R
Iowa State Rep.
b. Pella, Iowa, 7/23/28; s. Isaac G. Roorda and Anna Terlouw R; m. 9/5/50 to Dorothy Ann Lawrence; c. Bruce Roger, Douglas Lawrence, Rebecca Ann, Marilyn Jean, Nancy Eileen and Dirk John. Educ: Cent. Col, 46-47; Iowa State Univ, B.S, 50. Polit. & Govt. Pos: Iowa State Rep, 67- Mil. Serv: Entered as Recruit, Army, 50, released as Cpl, 52, after serv. in 38th Field Artil, 2nd Div, Korea. Mem: Jasper Co. Commun. Action Cmt; Newton C. of C; past pres, Jasper Co. Farm Bureau; Am. Legion; Kiwanis. Rel: Presbyterian. Mailing Add: Route 1, Monroe, Iowa 50170.

ROORDA, WALTER JOHN R
Ind. State Rep.
b. De Motte, Ind, 9/20/30; s. Albert Frank Roorda and Gertrude Walstra R; m. 8/25/49 to Alberta Klemp; c. Kathleen Sue, Karen Louise, Marvin Allen, Milton Ryan, Mark Walter, Mitchell Albert and Krista Marie. Educ: De Motte Pub. Schs, grad. Polit. & Govt. Pos: Mem, Jasper Co. Young Rep, Ind, 58; precinct committeeman, Keener Twp. E, Jasper Co, 62-; pres, North. Jasper Co. Young Rep, 64-65; secy, Jasper Co. Rep. Cent. Cmt, 64-66, treas, 66-68; Ind. State Rep, Jasper, Porter and Pulaski Counties, 68- Bus. & Prof. Pos: Owner, Al's Upholstery Shop, 60, The Roorda Furniture Co, 65. Mem: Nat. Fedn. of Independent Bus; Nat. Retail Furniture Asn; De Motte C. of C. Rel: Christian Reformed Church. Mailing Add: R.R. 1, Box 6, De Motte, Ind. 46310.

ROOS, LAWRENCE K. R
Supvr, St. Louis Co, Mo.
b. St. Louis, Mo, 2/1/18; s. Sol Roos and Selma Kalter R; m. 4/30/55 to Mary Watson; c. Pamela, Mary Ellen, Jennifer and Lawrence K, Jr. Educ: Yale Univ, B.A, 40. Polit. & Govt. Pos: Mo. State Rep, 46-50; supvr, St. Louis Co, Mo, 62-; Rep. nominee for Gov, Mo, 68; app. by President Nixon to Adv. Cmn. on Intergovt. Rels. Bus. & Prof. Pos: Pres, Mound City Trust Co, St. Louis, Mo, 50-62; chmn. bd, First Security Bank of Kirkwood, 50-62. Mil. Serv: Entered as Pvt, Army, 41, released as Maj, 45, after serv. in ETO, 42-45; Five Battle Stars; Bronze Star Medal. Mem: Chmn, East-West Gateway Coord. Coun, 65-67; bd. dirs, Nat. Asn. of Counties; St. Louis Regional Indust. Develop. Corp.(exec. cmt); U.S. Assay Cmn, 55; Mo. chmn, Crusade for Freedom, 54. Hon. mem, Alpha Kappa Psi. Rel: Jewish. Mailing Add: 943 Tirrill Farms Rd, St. Louis, Mo. 63124.

ROOSEVELT, ELLIOTT D
b. N.Y.C, 9/23/10; s. Franklin Delano Roosevelt and Anna Eleanor R; m. 1960 to Patricia Whitehead; c. William Donner, Ruth Chandler, Elliott and David. Polit. & Govt. Pos: Mayor, Miami Beach, Fla, 65-69; del, Dem. Nat. Conv, 68; Dem. Nat. Committeeman, Fla. Bus. & Prof. Pos: Advert, editing and radio work, 29-40; pres, Elliott Roosevelt Int, Inc. Mil. Serv: Brig. Gen, Army Air Corps, 40-46; 2 Distinguished Flying Crosses; Legion of Merit; 12 Air Medals; Legion of Honor; Croix De Guerre with 2 Palms; Pre Pearl Harbour Medal with Star; Am. Theatre Medal; European Theatre Medal with 12 Battle Stars; Asiatic Theatre Medal; Victory Medal. Publ: Ed, F.D.R, His Personal Papers 1882-1945; author, As He Saw It, 46. Mem: La Gorce Country Club and Palm Bay Club, Miami Beach. Mailing Add: 2424 N. Bay Rd, Miami Beach, Fla. 33140. (1967)

ROOSEVELT, FRANKLIN DELANO, JR. D
b. Campobello Is, N.B, Can, 8/17/14; s. Franklin Delano Roosevelt and Eleanor Roosevelt R; m. 8/31/49 to Suzanne Perrin; c. Franklin Delano III, Christopher du Pont, Nancy S. and Laura D. Educ: Harvard, A.B, 37; Univ. Va, LL.B, 40. Polit. & Govt. Pos: U.S. Rep, N.Y, elected to fill unexpired term of Sol Bloom, deceased, 49, re-elected, 51-54; former Under Secy. Commerce; chmn, Equal Employ. Opportunity Cmn, 65- Bus. & Prof. Pos: Pres. and chmn, Roosevelt Automobile Co, 58- and Fiat-Roosevelt Motors, Inc, 65- Mil. Serv: Navy, 41-45; decorated Legion of Merit with Combat V; Silver Star; Purple Heart; Secy. Navy Commendation. Mem: Mason; Racquet and Tennis Club, N.Y.C; N.Y. Yacht Club. Rel: Episcopal. Legal Res: Clove Creek Farm, Poughquag, N.Y. 12570. Mailing Add: 532 Sylvan Ave, Englewood Cliffs, N.J. 07632.

ROOSEVELT, JAMES D
b. New York, N.Y, 12/23/07; s. Franklin Delano Roosevelt and Anna Eleanor R; m. 7/1/56 to Gladis Irene Kitchenmaster; c. Sara (Mrs. di Bonaventura), Kate (Mrs. Haddad), James, Jr, Michael, Anne (Mrs. Robert Johnston) and Hall Delano. Educ: Harvard Univ, 30; Boston Univ. Law Sch, 33. Polit. & Govt. Pos: Secy. to President of U.S, 37-38; chmn, Calif. Dem. State Cent. Cmt, 44-48; cand, Gov. of Calif, 50; U.S. Rep, Calif, 55-65; U.S. Rep, Econ. & Soc. Coun, UN, 65-67. Bus. & Prof. Pos: Exec. Roosevelt & Sargent, Inc, 30-38 & 46; motion picture exec, 39-41; pres, James Roosevelt & Co, Calif; pres, IOS Develop. Co, Ltd, Geneva, Switz, 67- Mil. Serv: Entered as Capt, Marine Corps, 40, released as Col, 45, after serv. as Exec. Officer, Second Raider Bn, Co. Fourth Raider Bn. and Intel. Officer, Fifth Amphibious Force, Brig. Gen.(Ret); Navy Cross; Silver Star. Publ: Affectionately, F.D.R.(co-author), George C. Harrap & Co, Ltd, 59. Mem: Am. Legion; VFW; Am. Vet. Cmt; Elks; Holland Soc. of N.Y; Harvard Club of N.Y. Rel: Episcopal. Mailing Add: 119 Rue de Lausanne, Geneva, Switz.

ROOT, CYRIL H. R
b. 5/23/96; m. 10/30/18 to Margaret Harvey; c. 2 daughters. Educ: Attended Mich. State Univ; received hon. master's degree in pub. admin. Polit. & Govt. Pos: Twp. supvr, Mich, 16 years; twp. treas, 2 years; dir, dist. sch, 30 years; Mich. State Rep, 50-68. Mem: Pres, State Asn. of Supvrs, 46; secy, Fairmount Hosp. Bd. of Trustees; treas, Kalamazoo Milk Producers Asn; secy and treas, Kalamazoo Co. Farm Bur; W. Oshtemo Grange; Kalamazoo Co. Pomona Grange; Mason; Eastern Star. Rel: Methodist. Mailing Add: 5401 W. H Ave, Kalamazoo, Mich. 49001. (1967)

ROOT, EDSON V, JR. R
Mich. State Rep.
b. Bangor, Mich, 8/27/03; m. 1937 to Frieda Shaefer. Educ: Olivet Col, B.A, 25. Polit. & Govt. Pos: Mem, Van Buren Co. Welfare Cmt, Mich, 50-52; Mich. State Rep, 52. Bus. & Prof. Pos: Fruit grower. Mem: Farm Bur; Paw Paw Lodge 25, F&AM; Paw Paw Chap. 34 RAM; DeWitt Clinton Consistory; Saladin Temple. Rel: Christian Church. Mailing Add: Arlington Rd, Bangor, Mich. 49013. (1967)

ROOT, HARMER F. R
Chmn, LaCrosse Co. Rep. Party, Wis.
b. Walla Walla, Wash, 11/4/14; s. Herbert D. Root and Hope Harmer R; m. 7/1/39 to Elsie D. Boudreau; c. Kathleen D. (Mrs. Weibel), Dennis M. and Mary Ellen. Educ: St. Thomas Col, B.A, 37; Univ. Minn. Grad. Sch, 38 & 39. Polit. & Govt. Pos: Chmn, LaCrosse Co. Rep. Party, Wis, 67- Bus. & Prof. Pos: Teacher, pub. schs, 37-; supvr, parochial schs, 46-48; assoc. prof, Wis. State Univ. Syst, 48-52; investment exec, N.Y. Stock Exchange-Am. Stock Exchange and all prin. exchanges, 59- Mem: Kiwanis; LaCrosse Country Club. Rel: Catholic. Legal Res: 520 South 11, LaCrosse, Wis. 54601. Mailing Add: Box 937, LaCrosse, Wis. 54601.

ROOT, MARV R
b. Caldwell, Idaho, 8/13/42; s. Lloyd Joseph Root and Rosabelle Huston R; single. Educ: Seattle Pac. Col, B.A. in Sociol, 64; West. Evangel. Sem, 64-67; Sigma Alpha Kappa. Polit. & Govt. Pos: Chmn, West. Fedn. Col. Rep, 65-67; del. and secy. Ore. del, Rep. Nat. Conv, 68; nominee, U.S. Rep, Second Dist, Ore, 68. Bus. & Prof. Pos: Free lance pub. rels. consult, 64-; dir. on-the-job manpower develop. and training prog, Ore. Automotive Wholesalers Asn, 67-68; radio commentator, Marv Root Legis. Report, 69-; sales rep, Motel Equip. Co, Bend, Ore, 69- Mem: Jaycees; Ore. Wheat Growers League; Ore. Farm Bur. Fedn; YMCA. named One of the Outstanding Young Men in Am, 67. Pres. and valedictorian, Madras High Sch, Ore; Rel: Free Methodist; Elder, Ore. Conf. of Free Methodist Church, 65- Legal Res: Rt. 1, Box 188, Madras, Ore. 97741. Mailing Add: P.O. Box 2203, Salem, Ore. 97308.

ROPA, MATT D
Ill. State Rep.
b. Chicago, Ill; c. Christine and Steven. Educ: Northwest. Univ. Polit. & Govt. Pos: Ill. State Rep, currently. Bus. & Prof. Pos: Ins. bus, 34; organizer and operator, fuel oil bus, 39; field rep, Pub. Savings and Loan Assoc. of Chicago and People's Fed. Savings Loan Asn, 47, dir, currently. Mil.

Serv: 42-45; Five Battle Stars. Mem: VFW; Am. Legion; Polish Roman Catholic Union; Moose; civic, soc. and athletic orgn. Mailing Add: 1710 W. 21st St, Chicago, Ill. 60608. (1967)

ROPER, ALLEN PAGE D
b. Canon, Ga, 4/20/13; s. King Samuel Roper and Carrie Blackwell R; m. 9/04/37 to Marian Hutcherson; c. Robert Allen, Kenneth Nelson, David Leon. Educ: Franklin Co. High Sch. Polit. & Govt. Pos: Ga. State Rep, 61-66; Ga. State Sen. (19th dist.), 59-60; 53-54. Bus. & Prof. Pos: Tree farmer and pulpwood dealer. Rel: Methodist. Mailing Add: Greensboro, Ga. 30642. (1967)

ROQUE, JOHN B. D
b. Grand Isle, Vt, 6/1/07; m. to Winifred C. Jewell; c. Three. Educ: Grand Isle and Alburg Schs; Navy Radio and Electronics Sch; Spec. Study Courses. Polit. & Govt. Pos: Former mem, Grand Isle Town and Co. Dem. Cmt, Vt, 24 years; former committeeman, Vt. State Dem. Cmt, 2 years; former chmn, Grand Isle Co. Dem. Cmt, 6 years; former dep. sheriff, justice of the peace, selectman and town moderator, Grand Isle; former chmn, Grand Isle Co. High Sch. Cmt; former dir, Grand Isle Co. Develop. Cmt; Vt. State Rep, 49 & 57-66. Bus. & Prof. Pos: Resort and serv. center operator and owner. Mil. Serv: Navy, Radioman. Mem: Vt. and Am. Hotel & Motel Asns. Rel: Catholic. Mailing Add: Grand Isle, Vt. 05458. (1967)

ROSA, PAUL JAMES, JR. R
Chmn, Ridgefield Rep. Town Cmt, Conn.
b. Stamford Conn, 8/11/27; s. Paul James Rosa and Anna Annunziato R; m. 5/25/57 to Kathryn Venus. Educ: Univ. of Conn, B.S. in mech. eng, 49; Kappa Sigma. Polit. & Govt. Pos: V.pres, New Canaan Young Rep. Club, Conn, 50-52; mem, Ridgefield Zoning Cmn, 61-65; mem, Ridgefield Rep. Town Cmt, 64-, chmn, 66-; v.chmn, Ridgefield Planning and Zoning Cmn, 65-66; chmn, 24th Sen. Dist. Conv, 66; v.chmn, Rep. Fifth Cong. Dist. Orgn, 67-68; del, Rep. State Conv, 68; alternate del, Fifth Cong. Dist. Conv, 68. Bus. & Prof. Pos: Mgr. of planning and control, Perkin-Elmer Corp, 51- Mil. Serv: Entered as Seaman, Navy, 45, released as Seaman 1/C, 46. Mem: Am. Soc. of Tool and Mfg. Eng; Am. Prod. and Inventory Control Soc; Indust. Mgt. Club; K. of C; Italian Am. Mutual Aid Soc; Univ. Conn. Club; Keeler Tavern Preservation Soc. Rel: Roman Catholic. Mailing Add: 10 Olmstead Lane, Ridgefield, Conn. 06877.

ROSA, VICTOR JOSEPH D
Mem, Calif. Dem. State Cent. Cmt.
b. San Francisco, Calif, 5/10/18; s. Victor J. Rosa (deceased) and May Ayers R; m. 3/30/45 to Elva Bech; c. Richard and Vicki Ann. Educ: Univ. Calif, Exten, sales, 49. Polit. & Govt. Pos: Recreation cmnr, South San Francisco, Calif, 53-54, planning cmnr, 55-57; campaign mgr. and adv. to Assemblyman Leo J. Ryan, 57-; mem, Calif. Dem. State Cent. Cmt, 58- Bus. & Prof. Pos: Salesman, L.D. Caulk Co, San Francisco, 47-51; salesman and owner, Brentwood Auto Sales, South San Francisco, 51-52; truck and fleet mgr, Smallcomb Chevrolet, San Bruno, 53-62; salesman, Les Vogel Chevrolet, San Francisco, 62- Mil. Serv: Entered as PO 3/C, Naval Res, 45, released as CPO, 45, after serv. in Pac. Fleet, 12th Naval Dist, S.Pac. Theater, 42-45; Am. Defense, Fleet, Asiatic Pac. Campaign and Am. Campaign Medals. Mem: Chevrolet Growth Prog; Legion of Leaders; Chevrolet Honor Club; Chevrolet Hall of Fame; Elks (past Exalted Ruler, past chmn. bd. trustees); Lions; Calif. Elks Asn.(chmn, Bay Area). Rel: Catholic. Mailing Add: 24 Werner Ave, Daly City, Calif. 94015.

ROSALES, JOHN A. D
Secy, Colo. Dem. State Cent. Cmt.
b. Pueblo, Colo, 8/29/26; s. Manuel Rosales (deceased) and María Magallanes R.(deceased); m. 11/9/46 to Patricia C. Gettler; c. Mike, John P, Marie A, Lizbeth A, Patty Jo, Suzanne, Charles F. and James C. Educ: Pueblo Jr. Col, 46-47; Colo. State Col, B.A, 50; Colo. Univ, 50-64; Colo. Col, M.A, 60; Loyola Univ, 56-57; Rice Univ, 65; Phi Sigma Iota. Polit. & Govt. Pos: Co, state and cong. del, Dem. Party, Colo; v.pres. and mem, Pueblo City Coun; pres, dist. six, Colo. Munic. League; del, Dem. Nat. Conv, 68; secy, Colo. Dem. State Cent. Cmt, currently; analyst, CRS, Dept. of Justice. Bus. & Prof. Pos: Rep. Pueblo Regional Planning Cmn; tech. adv. under Agency for Int. Develop. prog, Bi-Nat. Develop. Corp, Honduras. Mil. Serv: Entered as Recruit, Navy, 44, released as SM 3/C, 46, after serv. in Jasco Unit 19, Pac. Theater, 45-46; Asiatic-Pac. Star; Am. Defense Medal; Victory Bar. Publ: 'Problems of the Mexican-American Student,' Educ. Colo, 67; 'Las Voces Nuevas del Sudoeste,' Nat. Educ. Asn, 68. Mem: Phi Delta Kappa; Nat. Educ. Asn; Colo. Educ. Asn; Prfnl. Rights and Responsibilities Cmt, Cath. Educ. Asn; Human Rels. Cmt, GI Forum; Southwest Coun. of La Raza; Chi Alpha Sigma; Bishop's Adv. Coun; Am. Red Cross WSI Prog; Latin Am. Educ. Found; Colo. State Col. Alumni Asn. Outstanding Teacher Award, La Sertoma, 64; Outstanding Alumni Award, Colo. State Col, 66. Rel: Catholic. Mailing Add: 1804 Eden, Pueblo, Colo. 81004.

ROSE, ALEX Liberal
V.Chmn, N.Y. Liberal Party
b. Warsaw, Poland, 10/15/98; s. Hyman Royz and Faiga Halpern R; m. 8/7/20 to Elsie Shapiro; c. Mrs. Carmy Schwartz and Herbert. Polit. & Govt. Pos: V.chmn, N.Y. Liberal Party, currently; assisted in organizing Am. Labor Party, 36, state secy. and dir, 36-44; Presidential elector for Franklin D. Roosevelt, 40, Harry S. Truman, 48, Lyndon B. Johnson, 64 and Hubert H. Humphrey, 68; Liberal-Dem. del-at-lg, N.Y. State Constitutional Conv, 66. Bus. & Prof. Pos: Recording secy, Millinery Workers Union Local, 16, secy-treas, 24; v.pres, United Hatters, Cap and Millinery Workers Int. Union, 25, pres, 50-; headed the Appeals Cmt. of the AFL-CIO Conv. which expelled the IBT, 57. Mil. Serv: Brit. Army, 18-20. Mailing Add: 245 Fifth Ave, New York, N.Y. 10016.

ROSE, ARTHUR R
Chmn, Centre Co. Rep. Cmt, Pa.
b. Cincinnati, Ohio, 7/26/03; s. Erhardt Rose and Elizabeth Russell R; m. 7/7/28 to Elizabeth Gates; c. Arthur William, Eleanor Russell (Mrs. John Rowland) and Edward Gates. Educ: Univ. Cincinnati, B.A, 25, M.A, 26, Ph.D, 27; Phi Lamda Upsilon; Alpha Chi Sigma. Polit. & Govt. Pos: Chmn, Centre Co. Rep. Cmt, Pa, 66-; mem, Gov. Sci. Adv. Cmt, 68- Bus. & Prof. Pos: Instr. chem, Lehigh Univ. & Univ. Hawaii, 27-30; asst. prof. chem, Pa. State Univ, 30-41; tech. dir, Scioto Ord. Plant, 41-42; spec. asst. to U.S. Qm. Gen, 43; sr. chemist, U.S. Rubber Co, 44; prof. chem. eng, Pa. State Univ, 45-63; pres, Appl. Sci. Labs, Inc, 51-69. Publ: Auth, Condensed Chemical Dictionary, Reinhold, 4th, 5th, 6th and 7th ed, 50-68; Distillation Literature, Index and Abstracts, 41-45, 46-52 & 53-54. Mem: Am. Chem. Soc; Am. Inst. Chem. Engrs; fel, Am. Inst. Chemists; fel, Am. Asn. Adv. Sci; Am. Oil Chemists' Soc; N.Y. Acad. Sci; Am. Asn. Cost Engrs; Sigma Xi; Chemists Club, N.Y; Univ. Club, State College, Pa; Farmers Asn; C. of C.(dir. State Col. Area); Appalachian Thruway Asn.(dir). Oberly award, Am. Libr. Asn; Scroll of Honor, div. indust. and eng. chem, Am. Chem. Soc. Rel: Protestant. Legal Res: 525 S. Gill St, State College, Pa. 16801. Mailing Add: 135 N. Gill St, State College, Pa. 16801.

ROSE, CLINTON ELLSWORTH D
b. New Bedford, Mass, 5/12/18; s. Charles Henry Rose and Alice Fabio R; m. 2/7/53 to Bernice Mildred Kennedy. Educ: Layton Sch. Art, Milwaukee, Wis. Polit. & Govt. Pos: Mem, Gov. Cmn. on Human Rights, 52-65; dir, Voter Registrn. Hq, 58-63; mem, Milwaukee Co. Exec. Bd, 62-64; del, Dem. Nat. Conv, 64; chmn, 7 Ward Unit, Dem. Party, 65; mem. bd. supvr, First Dist, Milwaukee Co, 68- Bus. & Prof. Pos: Sr. steward, Everbrite Signs, 57-65; prod. mgr, Allison Signs Inc, 66- Mil. Serv: Entered as Pvt, Army, 42, released as S/Sgt, 45, after serv. in Qm. Corps, ETO, 43-45; European-African-Middle East. Theater Campaign Ribbon; Am. Theater Ribbon; Good Conduct and Victory Medals. Publ: Polit. editorials, Milwaukee Star, 65- Mem: Atkinson-Teutonia-Capitol Commun. Coun; First Ward Dem. Unit; NAACP; YMCA; We Milwaukeeans; Northtown Planning and Develop. Coun; Mason. Rel: Methodist. Legal Res: 2660 N. 18th St, Milwaukee, Wis. 53206. Mailing Add: Courthouse, Milwaukee, Wis. 53233.

ROSE, DOROTHY H. D
b. Buffalo, N.Y, 9/21/20; m. to Thomas A. Rose; wid. Educ: D'Youville Col, B.A; Geneseo State Teachers Col, B.S, Libr. Sci. Polit. & Govt. Pos: Mem, League of Women Voters of Hamburg, N.Y; pres, Dem. Bus. & Prfnl. Women's Club; v.chmn, Women's Div, Erie Co. Dem. Cmt; N.Y. State Assemblywoman, 65-69. Mem: Women's Asn. of Allied Beverage Indust, Buffalo Chap; Erie Co. Educ. Asn; Nat. Asn. of Parliamentarians; N.Y. State Teachers Asn; NEA; PTA; Women's Guild of Lake Shore Inter-Commun. Hosp; Women's Auxiliary, Evans Center, Vol. Fire Co; Evans Bus. and Prfnl. Women's Club; Asn. for Retarded Children; C. of C. Farm Bur; Evans Grange; Delta Kappa Gamma; Col. Club, Buffalo; Quota Club, Hamburg; Hamburg Women's Club. Rel: Catholic; Rosary and Altar Soc, Most Precious Blood Church. Mailing Add: 974 Gold St, Angola, N.Y. 14006.

ROSE, HOWARD VANCE, JR. D
b. Nashville, Tenn, 10/25/30; s. Howard Vance Rose, Sr. and Charlotte Jackson R; m. 6/24/54 to Patsy Patteson; c. Amanda, Howard Vance, III and Julie Gay. Educ: Tex. Christian Univ, 47-49; Univ. Tex, B.B.A, 52, LL.B, 53; Kappa Sigma. Polit. & Govt. Pos: Exec. asst. to Gov. John Connally, 63-64; rep. of Gov. Connally on Interstate Oil Compact Cmn, 63-68; chmn, Tex. Quality Water Bd, currently. Bus. & Prof. Pos: Assoc. and partner, Stubbeman, McRae, Sealy & Laughlin, Attorneys, Midland, Tex, 57-67; partner, Brown, Erwin, Maroney & Barber, Attorneys, Austin, 67- Mil. Serv: Entered as 1st Lt, Army, 54, released as Capt, 57, after serv. in Judge Adv. Gen. Corps. Mem: Phi Delta Phi. Rel: Presbyterian. Legal Res: 3401 Southhill Circle, Austin, Tex. 78703. Mailing Add: 900 Brown Bldg, Austin, Tex. 78701.

ROSE, IVAN W. D
Ark. State Rep.
b. Flippin, Ark, 11/26/25; s. W. E. Rose and Louisa Lee R; m. 2/9/44 to Betty Ruth Wood; c. Judy R. and Gary Lynn. Educ: St. Louis Col. of Pharm. Polit. & Govt. Pos: Ark. State Rep, 65- Mem: Coun, Ark. Pharmaceut. Asn, 61-67, pres, 65; Ark. State Bd. of Pharm, 57-62; Lions; Am. Pharmaceut. Asn; Nat. Asn. Retail Druggists. Rel: First Christian. Mailing Add: 124 W. Walnut, Rogers, Ark. 72756.

ROSE, JEROME C. D
Colo. State Rep.
b. Denver, Colo, 4/30/32; s. Paul L. Rose (deceased) and Fay Jones R.(deceased); m. 8/10/51 to Barbara Bryant; c. Gary, Duane, Diana and Jeffrey. Educ: Univ. Denver, B.S.B.A, 55, M.B.A, 65; Univ. Denver Col. Law, J.D, 69; Beta Gamma Sigma. Polit. & Govt. Pos: Committeeman, Rep. Party, Denver, Colo, 55-63, co-capt. dist. 15-B, 64-67; Colo. State Rep, 69- Bus. & Prof. Pos: Revenue receipts control auditor, City and Co, Denver, Colo, 55-63, dir, Motor Vehicle Div, 63- Mem: Am. Asn. Motor Vehicle Adminstr; Admin. Mgr. Soc; Colo. Co. Clerks Asn; Latin Am. Res. & Serv. Agency; Mile High United Fund; NAACP; Red Shield Commun. Center; Salvation Army; former dist. cmnr, Boy Scouts; chmn, United Way, 69. Rel: African Methodist Episcopal. Mailing Add: 3325 E. 26th Ave, Denver, Colo. 80205.

ROSE, JO ANN D
V.Chmn, Shawnee Co. Dem. Cent. Cmt.
b. Omaha, Nebr, 12/12/36; d. Robert Horace Brown and Lola Lucille Smith B; m. 3/30/57 to James Laurence Rose; c. Karen Lea, Susan Lynn, John Laurence and James Robert. Educ: Univ. Kans, B.S.Ed, with distinction, 59; Phi Lambda Theta; Alpha Chi Omega. Polit. & Govt. Pos: Precinct committeewoman, Kans. Dem. Cent. Cmt, June, 68-; v.chmn, Shawnee Co. Dem. Cent. Cmt, Aug, 68- Bus. & Prof. Pos: Teacher, Eudora Grade Sch, 59-62; legis. agent, Kans. Coun. of Churches, 69. Mem: Kans. State Teachers Asn. Rel: Congregational. Mailing Add: 3202 W. 33 Court, Topeka, Kans. 66614.

ROSE, JOE R
Chmn, Eddy Co. Rep. Cent. Cmt, N.Mex.
b. Carlsbad, N.Mex, 6/24/31; s. Jess Rose and Johnnie Nichols R; m. 12/23/54 to Anne Howard; c. Allen, Gregory and Melanie. Educ: Abilene Christian Col, 50-51; East. N.Mex. Univ, B.A, 57; Vet. Club; Geography Club; Bus. Assocs. Polit. & Govt. Pos: Alderman, Carlsbad City Coun, N.Mex, 62-66; campaign mgr, Eddy Co. Rep. Party, 62; mem, Eddy Co. Rep. Cent. Cmt, 62- and chmn, 67- Bus. & Prof. Pos: Pres, N.Mex. Sand and Gravel Asn, 60-

64; mem. bd, Nat. Ready Mix Concrete Asn, 66-68. Mil. Serv: Entered as Pvt, Army, 51, released as 1st Lt, 54, after serv. in Eighth Army Ord, Far East Command, Korea, 51-54; Commendation Medal; UN, Korean and Good Conduct Medals. Mem: Rotary; VFW; Boy Scouts (dist. chmn); C. of C.(bd. dirs, Carlsbad Chap, 62-66 & 68-). Rel: Church of Christ; Deacon. Mailing Add: 1308 S. Country Club, Carlsbad, N.Mex. 88220.

ROSE, KATHLEEN BLOUNT R
Exec. Secy, Rep. Party, Va.
b. Pine Beach, Va, 8/26/08; d. John Gardner Blount and Marye Alice Grubbs B; wid; c. Bettye Jean (Mrs. Marvin A. Moore) and Jeanette (Mrs. William Lloyd Pierce). Educ: Smithdeal-Massey Bus. Col; Richmond Prfnl. Inst, real estate appraisal; courses sponsored by Univ. Richmond. Polit. & Govt. Pos: Exec. secy, Rep. Party, Va, currently; freight classifier, Transportation Dept, Qm. Depot, 42-45; laison, Rep. Party, Va, 64-; in charge reservations and ticket sales, numerous state Rep. fund-raising dinners and projects, 65-; campaign materials coordinator, 66-68; conv. coordinator, Va. State Conv, 68; voter registration coordinator mem. and finance chmn, Hanover Co. Rep. Cmt; hon. Sgt-at-Arms, Rep. Nat. Conv, 68; del, Va. State Conv, 68, 69. Bus. & Prof. Pos: Notary pub, 48-; real estate broker, 52-; co-owner, Auto Machine Shop, 54-56; dealer, Paragon Homes, Inc, N.Y, 58-60; advert. counsr, Geiger Bros, Lewiston, Maine, 58- Mem: Charter mem, Real Estate Women Va, Inc. (secy, 63-64); Parliamentary Law Club Richmond; Christian Bus. & Prfnl. Women; Soroptimist Club Richmond; Eastern Star; Rebekahs; Royal Neighbors of Am.(recorder, 51-54); Daughters of Am.(state coun, 44-45, nat. dep, 50-52); Fraternal Cong.(pres, 56-57). Rel: Baptist; Sunday sch. teacher; deaconess, chmn. bd. deaconesses; choir leader, good will center vol; banquet and dinner vol. Mailing Add: 2315 W. Grace St, Richmond, Va. 23220.

ROSE, ROBERT EDGAR D
State Chmn, Nev. Dem. Party
b. Orange, N.J, 10/7/39; s. Edgar Oscar Rose and Loretta Kane R; m. 8/17/63 to Elizabeth Peterson. Educ: Juniata Col, Simpson Mem. Scholarship, 57-61 and B.A. with honors in hist, 61; N.Y. Univ. Sch. of Law, Root-Tilden Scholarship, 61-64 and LL.B, 64. Polit. & Govt. Pos: V.pres, Sierra Dem. Club, 65-66; pres, Young Dem. of Nev, 67-68 and west. regional dir, 68-; state chmn, Nev. Dem. Party, 68-; del, Dem. Nat. Conv, 68. Bus. & Prof. Pos: Law clerk, Nev. Supreme Court, 65; Partner, law firm, Goldwater, Taber, Hill & Mortimer, 65- Mem: Washoe Co. and Nev. State Bar Asns; YMCA; bd. dirs, Washoe Co. Cancer Soc. Rel: Episcopal. Legal Res: 16345 MacGregor, Reno, Nev. 89502. Mailing Add: P.O. Box 460, Reno, Nev. 89502.

ROSE, RUFUS CHAPPELL R
Conn. State Rep.
b. Waterford, Conn, 3/24/04; s. Frank B. Rose and Nellie Avery Chappell R; m. 6/30/30 to Margaret Skewis; c. James P, Rufus R. and Christopher S. Educ: Antioch Col, B.A, 29. Polit. & Govt. Pos: Mem. zoning and planning cmn, Waterford, Conn, 44-46, chmn. sch. bldg. cmt, 52-58, mem, 59-65; rep, Town Meeting, 58-63; Conn. State Rep, 69th Dist, 63- Bus. & Prof. Pos: Owner and producer, Rufus Rose Marionettes, 33-66; actor and puppeteer, Nat. Broadcasting Co. TV, 52-61; owner and producer, The Blue Fairy, TV series, 58; pres, Puppeteers of Am, 65; chmn. bd, Union Int. Marionette Artists, 67- Publ: Tech. articles, Puppetry J. of Am, 36-; article on puppetry, Book of Knowledge, Grolier Soc, Inc, 65-66. Rel: Unitarian. Mailing Add: 24 Avery Lane, Waterford, Conn. 06385.

ROSE, THOMAS CHAPIN R
Ill. State Rep.
b. White Hall, Ill, 12/8/32; s. George Lyndell Rose and Florence Chapin R; m. 6/12/54 to Harriet McLaughlin. Educ: Univ. Ill, A.B, 54; Univ. Mich, LL.B, 59; Phi Eta Sigma; Sachem; Ma Wan Da; Sigma Chi. Polit. & Govt. Pos: City Attorney, Jacksonville, Ill, 61-64; trustee, Oaklawn Tuberc. Sanatorium, 62-66; asst. states attorney, Morgan Co, 64-66; Ill. State Rep, currently, mem, Budgetary Cmn. and v.chmn, Appropriations Cmt, Ill. House of Rep; chmn, Rules Cmt. of the Nat. Legis. Conf. Bus. & Prof. Pos: Instr, Ill. Col, 65. Mil. Serv: Entered as 2nd Lt, Army, 54, released as 1st Lt, 56, after serv. in Security Agency. Mem: Am. and Ill. State Bar Asns; Morgan Co. Bar Asn, pres, 64; bd. dirs, Jacksonville Area Asn. for Retarded Children; Jacksonville Symphony Society; Visiting Nurses Asn; Kiwanis; United Fund; Morgan Co. Cancer Fund; trustee, Passavant Mem. Area Hosp. Rel: Presbyterian. Mailing Add: 307 W. State St, Jacksonville, Ill. 62650.

ROSEDALE, PETER KLAUS D
R.I. State Rep.
b. Germany, 7/14/31; s. Otto Julius Rosedale and Martha R; m. 5/4/69 to Beverly Ann Costantino. Educ: Col. Gen. Educ, Boston Univ, A.A, 51, sch. law, LL.B, 54. Polit. & Govt. Pos: City councilman, Providence, R.I, 59-62; judge, Providence Munic. Court, 62-67; mem, Providence Dem. Dist. Cmt, 62-69; R.I. State Rep, 69- Mil. Serv: Entered as Pvt, Army, 54, released as Specialist, 56, after serv. in Qm. Corp. Mem: B'nai B'rith; instnl. rep, Boy Scouts, Troop Ten. Rel: Jewish; bd. dir, Temple Beth-Israel. Legal Res: 127 Gallatin St, Providence, R.I. 02907. Mailing Add: 424 Hospital Trust Bldg, Providence, R.I. 02903.

ROSELEIP, GORDON W. R
Wis. State Sen.
b. Platteville, Wis, 7/30/12. Educ: High Sch, 34. Polit. & Govt. Pos: Mem, Co. Bd, Wis; serv. on Rep. campaign cmts, including Vet. for Eisenhower and for Nixon, Thomson for Gov. and for Cong; Wis. State Sen, 62- Bus. & Prof. Pos: Businessman. Mil. Serv: Nat. Guard, 28-33; vet, World War II, Korean Conflict. Mem: Vet. orgns; Elks; Eagles; Farm Bur; Kiwanis; Mason; Moose; Shrine; comdr, Wis. Dept. Am. Legion, 54. Valley Forge Award for Outstanding Americanism While State Comdr. of Am. Legion, Freedom's Found. Mailing Add: Box 167, Darlington, Wis. 53530. (1967)

ROSELL, ANTOINETTE FRASER R
Mont. State Sen.
b. Princeton, Ill, 9/18/26; d. Robert Berkely and Rosebel Walter Fraser; m. 3/29/57 to Earl Leonard Rosell,Jr; c. Rene Fraser. Educ: Mont. State Univ, B.A, Psychol, 48; Univ. Oslo, dipl, 51; Columbia Univ, M.A, Student Personnel Admin, 52. Polit. & Govt. Pos: Secy, Mont. Young Rep, 54-56, nat. committeewoman, 57-59; secy, Yellowstone Co. Young Rep, 57-58; by-laws chmn, Mont. Fedn. Rep. Women; Mont. State Rep, 57-58, 61-62 & 63-64, v.chmn, educ. cmt; Mont. State Sen, 67- Bus. & Prof. Pos: Dean of girls, Missoula Co. High Sch, 50-51; dir. student activities, East. Mont. Col. Educ, Billings, 54-56; girl counsr, Youth Guid. Coun, 58-59 & 61-67; partner, ET Ranch, 59-; guid. counsr, Lincoln Jr. High Sch, 67-; dir, R.B. Fraser, Inc; Fraser Land and Livestock Co; dean of girls, Billings Sr. High Sch. Mem: Billings Symphony Women's Cmt.(chmn, 57-58); pink lady, Deaconess Hosp; Billings Art Asn.(secy, 57-58); YWCA (bd. dirs, Billings); Nat. Order Women Legislators; Nat. Educ. Asn; Mont. Inst. Arts; League Women Voters; Am. Legion Auxiliary; Am. Asn. Univ. Women; Mont. Personnel and Guid. Asn; Bus. & Prfnl. Women's Club (first v.pres, Billings, 57-58); C. of C; Kappa Alpha Theta. One of Three Women of the Year, Mont. Fedn. Bus. & Prfnl. Women, 57, Woman of the Year, 67. Rel: Presbyterian. Mailing Add: 4200 Rimrock Rd, Billings, Mont. 59102.

ROSELLE, JOE L. D
b. Oklahoma City, Okla, 8/4/30; s. Joe L. Roselle and Pauline Vollers R; m. 3/25/54 to Lowery Bea Holland; c. Joe L, Sam S, Monica Lea and John David. Educ: Okla. Univ, pre-law; Okla. City Univ. Sch. Law, LL.B; Phi Delta Phi. Polit. & Govt. Pos: Okla. State Rep, Dist. 91, 65-66. Mil. Serv: Entered as Pvt, Air Force, 61, released as Cpl, 62, after serv. in 8th Air Force, 509th Bomb Wing, Eng. Mem: Okla. Co. and State Bar Asns; Trial Lawyers Asn; Nat. Soc. State Legis; Nat. Platform Conv; C. of C; past bd. dir, Jr. C. of C. Rel: Methodist. 1967 Legal Res: Oklahoma City, Okla. No mailing address available. (1967)

ROSELLINI, ALBERT D. D
b. Tacoma, Wash, 1/21/10; s. John Rosellini and Annunziata Pagni R; m. 6/1/37 to Ethel K. McNeil; c. John M, Janey (Mrs. Campbell), Sue, Lynn and Albert D, Jr. Educ: Univ. Wash; Phi Alpha Delta; Tau Kappa Epsilon. Polit. & Govt. Pos: Dep. prosecutor, King Co, Wash, 35-41; Wash. State Sen, 39-57; spec. asst. attorney gen, Wash, 41-46; Gov, Wash, 57-65; del, Dem. Nat. Conv, 68. Bus. & Prof. Pos: Lawyer, 33- Mem: Kiwanis; Moose; Eagles; Elks; K. of C; Sons of Italy. Rel: Catholic. Legal Res: 6320 N.E. 57th, Seattle, Wash. 98105. Mailing Add: 1429 Washington Bldg, Seattle, Wash. 98101.

ROSELLINI, EVELYN ELIZABETH D
Secy, Wash. State Dem. Cmt.
b. Sapulpa, Okla, 2/7/17; d. Victor Edwards and Ethel Gambill E; m. 4/8/39 to Dean Rosellini; c. Philip Edward and Deanne Marie. Educ: High Sch. Polit. & Govt. Pos: Adminstr, Dem. Polit. Campaigns, Hugh J. Rosellini for State Supreme Court Judge and Albert D. Rosellini for Gov, Wash, 56-64; secy, Wash. State Dem. Cmt, 61-; campaign coordinator, Warren G. Magnuson for Sen. Campaign, 68; del, Dem. Nat. Conv, 68. Bus. & Prof. Pos: Secy. legal dept, State Liquor Control Bd, 35-39. Rel: Catholic. Mailing Add: 5404 N.E. Windermere Rd, Seattle, Wash. 98105.

ROSEMOND, JOHN HENRY D
b. Jacksonville, Fla, 10/17/17; s. John H. Rosemond, Sr.(deceased) and Ida Belle Taylor R.(deceased); m. 3/15/43 to Rosalie Edge; c. John Henry, Jr, Janith Sheryl and Ronald Eliott. Educ: Fla. A&M Univ, B.S, 41; Howard Univ, M.D, 51; Omega Psi Phi. Polit. & Govt. Pos: Cand, Franklin Co. Coroner, Ohio, 64; alternate del, Dem. Nat. Conv, 68; Dem. nominee, City Coun, Columbus, Ohio, 69. Bus. & Prof. Pos: Civilian physician, U.S. Army Hosp, Ft. Belvoir, Va, 52-53; private practice med, Columbus, Ohio, 53-; staff mem, Mt. Carmel, Grant, St. Anthony, Mercy and Childrens Hosp, Columbus, Ohio. Mil. Serv: Entered as Pvt, Army Air Corps, 43, released as 1st Lt, 46, after serv. in 477th Composite Group, Navigator-Bombardier, U.S, 45-46. Mem: Columbus Acad. Med; Ohio State, Am. and Nat. Med. Asns; Franklin Co, Ohio and Am. Acads. of Gen. Practice; Flying Physicians Asn; Sigma Pi Phi; Cent. Ohio Coun, Boy Scouts; Develop. Cmt. for Gr. Columbus; Frontiers Int; life mem, NAACP; C. of C. Named Omega Man of the Year, 62 & 67; Columbus United Nations Day Award of Honor, 68. Rel: Presbyterian; Ruling Elder, Bethany Presby. Church. Mailing Add: 3300 E. Livingston Ave, Columbus, Ohio 43227.

ROSEN, HAROLD ELLIS R
b. Boston, Mass, 10/1/06; s. Samuel Rosen and Rebecca Cohen R; m. 6/16/52 to Marjorie Gillis. Educ: Boston Univ, B.B.A. Polit. & Govt. Pos: Mem: Dedham Sch. Cmt, 38-41 & 47-59; Mass. State Rep, 57- Mil. Serv: Entered as Pvt, Army, 42, released as 1st Lt, 45. Mem: Rotary; past comdr, Am. Legion Post 18, Dedham; treas, Nat. Soc. of State Legislators; v.pres, Mass. Legislators Asn. Rel: Hebrew. Mailing Add: 47 Greenlodge St, Dedham, Mass. 02026. (1967)

ROSEN, JUDITH MIRIAM D
b. N.Y.C, 7/27/35; d. Albert Loew and Sara Le Savoy L; m. 12/28/58 to Dr. Mervine Rosen; c. Sofia Anina and Daniel Jonathon. Educ: City Col. of N.Y, B.A, 57; Univ. of Minn, 3 years. Polit. & Govt. Pos: Precinct chmn, Fairfax Co. Dem. Cmt, Va, 67-; alternate del, Dem. Nat. Conv, 68. Mem: Bd. mem, North. Va. Fair Housing; New Dem. Coalition of North. Va; Va. Affiliate, Clergy and Lay Concerned About Viet-Nam. Rel: Jewish. Mailing Add: 5535 Hershey Lane, Alexandria, Va. 22312.

ROSEN, LESTER L. R
b. Wichita, Kans, 11/21/24; s. Herman Rosen and Dena Wishnuff R; m. 9/5/48 to Barbara Bernice Shustorman; c. Cynthia Kay, Sandra Ellen, Edward Howard. Educ: Univ. Wichita, A.B, 46-49; Pi Alpha Pi. Polit. & Govt. Pos: Admin. asst. Rep. Shriver, R-Kans. Mil. Serv: Amy, Tech. 5 Gr, 44-45. Mem: Wichita Advert. Club (v.pres. and pres.); Wichita Pub. Rel. Soc; Am. Col. Pub. Rel. Soc; Wichita-Sedgwick Co. Ment. Health Asn; Pub. rel. B'hai Israel Congregation. Rel: Jewish. Legal Res: 6504 E. Murdock, Wichita, Kans. Mailing Add: 7 Fulham Ct, Silver Spring, Md. 20902. (1967)

ROSEN, MEYER D
b. Georgetown, S.C, 11/17/19; s. Harry N. Rosen and Dora Lewenthal R; m. 9/19/48 to Lillian Rubin. Educ: Univ. of S.C, LL.B, 48; Blue Key Hon. Leadership Fraternity. Polit. & Govt. Pos: S.C. State Rep, 63-66. Bus. & Prof. Pos: Lawyer, firm of Rosen and Rosen. Mil. Serv: Army, Signal Corps, 41-

45; Pac. Theatre of Oper, 43-45. Mem: VFW; Am. Legion; Moose. Rel: Mem, formerly pres. Beth Elohim Congregation. Mailing Add: Box 583, Georgetown, S.C. 29440.

ROSEN, MILDRED PAFUNDI R
Councilman-at-large, N.Y.C. Coun.
b. Brooklyn, N.Y, 11/26/29; d. Michael Pafundi and Rose Sabina P; m. 3/15/63 to Nieson Hilton Rosen. Educ: St. John's Univ, B.B.A, 54; St. John's Law Sch, LL.B, 57; Phi Delta Delta. Polit. & Govt. Pos: V.chmn, Dewey-Warren Citizens Cmt, N.Y.C, 48; judicial dist. chmn, N.Y. State Young Rep, 59-61; asst. attorney gen, N.Y, 59-64; law asst. to Surrogate of Kings Co, 64-66; acting chief of adoption dept, Surrogate's Court, 65; councilman-at-large, N.Y.C. Coun, 66-; alternate del, Rep. Nat. Conv, 64 & 68; Kings Co. coordinator, New Yorkers for Nixon Agnew Campaign, 68. Bus. & Prof. Pos: Asst. to pub. rels. dir, Harriet Hubbard Ayer Div, Lever Bros, 47-49; promotional researcher, N.Y. Herald Tribune, 49-59. Mem: Women's City Club of N.Y; Brooklyn Heights Asn; Brooklyn Heights Jr. Cmt. Rel: Roman Catholic. Mailing Add: 242 Henry St, Brooklyn, N.Y. 11201.

ROSENAU, FRED W. D
Kans. State Rep.
b. Shawnee, Kans, 5/7/22; s. John W. Rosenau and Louise Stangle R; m. 8/2/52 to Betty M. Hines; c. Mark O, Ken F. and Rita L. Polit. & Govt. Pos: Mem. bd. educ, Turner Unified Dist. 202, 65-; Kans. State Rep, Dist. 35, Wyandotte Co, 66- Bus. & Prof. Pos: Excavating contractor, Kansas City, Kans, 27 years. Mil. Serv: Army Anti-Aircraft Training Bn, 42. Mem: Kans. State Sch. Bd. Asn; Lions; Mid-Co. Dem. Club, Wyandotte Co. Mailing Add: 3050 S. 65th, Kansas City, Kans. 66106.

ROSENBAUM, POLLY D
Ariz. State Rep.
m. 1939 to William George Rosenbaum, wid. Educ: Univ. Colo, B.A; Univ. South. Calif, M.Ed. Polit. & Govt. Pos: Ariz. State Rep, currently. Bus. & Prof. Pos: Former teacher; stenographer; gen. girl Fri. in copper and asbestos industs, law, real estate appraisal, savings and loan; co. clerk and recorder's offices; dent. receptionist. Mem: Globe Bus. & Prfnl. Women's Club; Zonta Int; Gila Co. Tuberc. Control Bd; past matron, Winkleman Chap, Eastern Star. Mailing Add: Box 609, Globe, Ariz. 85501.

ROSENBAUM, RICHARD MERRILL R
Chmn, Monroe Co. Rep. Party, N.Y.
b. Oswego, N.Y, 4/8/31; s. Jack M. Rosenbaum and Shirley Gover R; m. 6/1/58 to Judith Kanthor; c. Amy M, Jill M, Matthew A. and Julie F. Educ: Hobart Col, B.A, 52; Cornell Law Sch, LL.B, 55; Phi Phi Delta. Polit. & Govt. Pos: Town justice, Penfield, N.Y, 61-62; exec. committeeman, Penfield Rep. Party, 62-; legislator and asst. majority leader, Monroe Co. Legis, 67-68; del, Rep. Nat. Conv, 68; chmn, Monroe Co. Rep. Party, 68- Mem: Monroe Co, N.Y. State and Am. Bar Asns; Am. Arbit. Asn; N.Y. and Am. Trial Lawyers Asns; Phi Delta Phi; Rochester Touchdown Club (bd. dirs); F&AM. Named Man of the Year, City of Rochester Puerto Rican Soc, 69. Rel: Jewish. Mailing Add: 19 Denonville Ridge, Rochester, N.Y. 14625.

ROSENBAUM, WALTER ELIJAH D
b. Pratt Co, Kans, 1/16/93; s. John Casper Rosenbaum and Rose Etta Galbreath R; m. 1/9/65 to Merriel Stephenson Parker; c. Lawrence Walter, Evelyn Marie (Mrs. Kendall Crick) and stepchild, Aileen Marie (Mrs. Jerro Russo). Educ: Law Enforcement Officers Training Sch, Fed. Bur. Investigation; several courses of study with Kans. Bur. Invest. Polit. & Govt. Pos: Mem. sch. bd, Saratoga Twp, Kans, 24-34, trustee, 30-40; precinct committeeman, Saratoga Twp. Dem. Cmt, 30-35; sheriff, Pratt Co, 35-39 & 45-49, under sheriff, 39-40, 57-58 & 67-68; police patrol Pratt City, 40-42, & 45-49, chief of police, 49-52; Kans. State Rep, 74th Dist, 65-67, mem, Agr, Co. Lines and Co. Seats, Horticulture and R.R. Cmts, Kans. House of Rep. Bus. & Prof. Pos: Retired farmer, stockman and poultryman. Mil. Serv: Mil. Guard, Pratt Army Air Base, 42-43, serv. as fingerprint expert. Mem: Redman Lodge; secy. and treas, Farm Bur, 32-34; stockholder, Farmers Coop; Elks; charter mem, Nat. and Kans. Peace Officers Asns. Ex-wrestler and trainer. Rel: Methodist. Mailing Add: 516 South Hamilton St, Pratt, Kans. 67124.

ROSENBERG, ALEX JACOB D
Leader, 65 Assembly Dist. Dem. Party, N.Y.
b. N.Y.C, 5/25/19; s. Israel Rosenberg and Lena Zar R; m. 4/12/41 to Dorothy Hardy; c. Lawrence and Andrew. Educ: Albright Col, 36-38; Philadelphia Textile Col, 38-40; Sigma Phi Tau. Polit. & Govt. Pos: Leader, 65 Assembly Dist, Dem. Party, N.Y, 65-; del, cmt. for dem. voters, 65-, dem. Nat. Conv, 68 and cmt. for dem. alternatives, 68-69. Bus. & Prof. Pos: Pres, Anserphone, 59-65; partner, Northeast Management and Development Co, 66-69, v.pres, Starfax Corp, 69- Mil. Serv: Entered as Cadet, Air Force, 42, released as Lt, 45, after serv. in Fourth Photo Reconnaissance Squadron Hq, 43-45. Mem: Metropolitan Council; Am. Jewish Congress; trustee, New Lincoln Sch; exec. bd, Stephen Wise Free Synagogue. Legal Res: 277 West End Ave, New York, N.Y. 10023. Mailing Add: 630 Fifth Ave, New York, N.Y. 10020.

ROSENBERG, MARVIN D
b. New York, N.Y, 8/22/06; s. David Rosenberg and Annie Schwartz R; m. to Helene Feller R; c. Ellen (Mrs. Tovatt), David and Linda. Educ: City Col. of New York, B.S.S, 28; Harvard Univ. Law Sch, LL.B, 32. Polit. & Govt. Pos: Chmn, Nat. Exec. Cmt, Am. for Dem. Action, 57-58, nat. v.chmn, Am. for Dem. Action, 59-69; chmn, East. Div, Humphrey for President Cmt, 60; nat. treas, Humphrey for V.President Cmt, 64; del, Dem. Nat. Conv, 64 & 68; chmn. finance cmt, Citizens Cmt, O'Connor for Gov, N.Y, 66; mem, Nat. Adv. Cmt, Econ. Develop. Admin, 66-69; chmn, N.Y. State Humphrey-Muskie Campaign Cmt, 68. Bus. & Prof. Pos: Pres, Cameo Curtains Inc, 38-66. Mem: City Athletic Club; Fairview Country Club. Rel: Jewish. Legal Res: 2 West 67th St, New York, N.Y. 10023. Mailing Add: 260 Fifth Ave, New York, N.Y. 10001.

ROSENBERG, WILLIAM S. R
N.Y. State Assemblyman
b. Rochester, N.Y, 3/16/16; m. to Helen Daitz; c. two. Educ: Cornell Univ, 38; Albany Law Sch, 42. Polit. & Govt. Pos: Rep. committeeman, Brighton, N.Y; mem, Lincoln Rep. League; past pres, Brighton Men's Rep. Club; mem, Rep. Party Speakers Bur, Finance Cmt. and Rep. Forum, N.Y; incompetency referee, 48; N.Y. State Assemblyman, 60- Bus. & Prof. Pos: Attorney-at-law. Mil. Serv: Coast Guard, Lt.(jg), released 46, after serv. in Atlantic, exec. officer on LCI Pac. Mem: Rochester Bar Asn; Past Exalted Ruler, Elks; Rochester Track Officials; Civic Music Asn; mem. Art Gallery; JYMA Am. Legion; Cornell Club of Rochester. Rel: Jewish. Mailing Add: 1866 Clover St, Rochester, N.Y. 14618. (1967)

ROSENBLATT, JOSEPH B. D
Mem, N.Y. Co. Dem. Cmt, N.Y.
b. New York, N.Y, 8/28/22; s. Samson Rosenblatt and Jeannette Wacht R; m. 6/26/55 to Sheila Burger; c. Jill Marion, Sarah Jane and Samuel Wacht. Educ: Syracuse Univ, 40-43. Polit. & Govt. Pos: Pres, N.Y. Young Dem. Club, 55-56; chmn, Borough Pres. Planning Bd, 60-63; alternate del, Dem. Nat. Conv, 64; del, N.Y. State Dem. Cmt, 66; mem, exec. cmt, East Side Dem. Club, N.Y.C; mem, N.Y. Co. Dem. Cmt. Bus. & Prof. Pos: Pres, real estate cmt, Young Men's Bd. of Trade, 54; pres, Joseph B. Rosenblatt Assocs, 10 years; mem. housing cmt, Real Estate Bd. of N.Y, 62-; pres, Property Maintenance Co, 63- Mil. Serv: Entered as Pvt, Army, 43, released as Tech. 5th Grade, 45, after serv. in 5th Amphibious Force, Asiatic Theater; Bronze Battle Star; Navy Commendation Letter. Mem: Bd. dirs, Henry Kaufmann Campgrounds; leadership coun, United Jewish Appeal; Citizens Union; Coun. on Parks. Rel: Jewish. Mailing Add: 544 East 86th St, New York, N.Y. 10028. (1967)

ROSENBLATT, WILLIAM D
N.Y. State Sen.
b. New York, N.Y; s. Julius Rosenblatt and Tillie R; m. to Dorothy Richman; c. Jay Barry. Polit. & Govt. Pos: N.Y. State Sen, 44-; dir, James M. Power Regular Dem. Club. Bus. & Prof. Pos: Attorney-at-law. Mem: Pres, Brooklyn Div, Jewish Nat. Fund of Am; life pres, Coun. Hebrew Alliance; hon. mem, Beth Jacob Yeshiva; past chancellor, K. of C; N.Y. State Bar Asn; B'nai B'rith. Rel: Jewish. Mailing Add: 2519 E. 29th St, Brooklyn, N.Y. 11232. (1967)

ROSENCRANS, ARTHUR D
b. Brooklyn, N.Y, 3/12/95; s. Mathias L. Rosencrans and Cecelia Springer R; m. 7/30/17 to Mary E. Alper; c. Leslie, Janet (Mrs. Jacobs) and Edith (Mrs. Barnet). Educ: N.Y. Univ. Polit. Pos: Treas, Annual Dinner, Kings Co. Dem. Cmt, 56-; Dem. presidential elector, 64 and 60; del, Dem. Nat. Convs, 64, 60 and 52-56; del, several state convs. Govt. Pos: Mem. Bd. of Higher Educ, N.Y.C, 49- Bus. & Prof. Pos: Pres, Irvin Underwriting Co, Inc, Irvin Agency, Inc. and several real estate corps. Mem: Received Hon. Doctor of Humanities, Philathia Col. and Citation and Medal, Elroy Alfaro Found, Panama. Rel: Jewish. Mailing Add: 340 Shore Blvd, Brooklyn, N.Y. 11235. (1967)

ROSENFELD, MITCHELL ALLAN R
b. Phila, Pa, 11/24/28; s. Solomon C. Rosenfeld and Betty Shenkman R; m. 7/21/56 to E. Louise James; c. Erik J, Beth A. and Steven J. Educ: Temple Univ, B.S, 50; Armed Forces Info. Sch, Ft. Slocum, N.Y, 52; Beta Gamma Sigma; Pi Gamma Mu; Phi Alpha Theta; Sigma Delta Chi; ed. and managing ed, Temple Univ. News. Polit. & Govt. Pos: Pub. info. dir, Montgomery Co, Pa, 63-66; pub. rels. dir, Montgomery Co. Rep. Cmt, 63-69; admin. asst. to U.S. Rep. Lawrence Coughlin, Pa, 69- Bus. & Prof. Pos: Gen. mgr, Inter-Co. Publ. Co, Conshohocken, Pa; reporter and rewriteman, Delaware Co. Daily times, Phila. Daily News and Phila. Eve. and Sunday Bul; pub. rels. dir, World Mutual Health & Accident Ins. Co, King of Prussia, 66-68; Mil. Serv: Entered as Pvt, Army, 51, released as Pfc, 52, after serv. in 47th Inf. Div, Stateside. Mem: Montgomery Co. Ment. Health-Ment. Retardation Bd. Rel: Jewish. Legal Res: Montgomery Co, Pa. Mailing Add: 7111 Thrasher Rd, McLean, Va. 22101.

ROSENHEIM, ROBERT CHATWELL R
Mem, Colo. Rep. State Cent. Cmt.
b. Williamson, W.Va, 6/15/09; s. William Spiller Rosenheim and Frances Harris R; m. 11/25/32 to Frances Elizabeth Dillman; c. Jane Taylor. Educ: Marshall Col, A.B, 30; Harvard Bus. Sch, 43; Sigma Alpha Epsilon. Polit. & Govt. Pos: Chmn, Citizens for Eisenhower, Bonhomme Twp, St. Louis Co, Mo, 52; precinct committeeman, Denver, Colo, 57-59; mem, Colo. Rep. State Cent. Cmt, 59-63; bonus mem, currently; capt, 14th Dist. Denver Co. Rep. Cent. Cmt, 59-66; cmnr, Denver Urban Renewal Cmn, 61-; del, Rep. Nat. Conv, 68. Mil. Serv: Entered as Pvt, Army Air Force, 43, released as Capt, 46. Mem: Pres, Rocky Mt. Beverage Asn, 60; Kiwanis; Columbine Country Club; Lincoln Club. Rel: Episcopal. Mailing Add: 3203 S. Milwaukee, Denver, Colo. 80210. (1967)

ROSENMEIER, GORDEN Conservative
Minn. State Sen.
b. Royalton, Minn, 7/1/07. Educ: Univ. Minn; Leland Stanford Univ. Law Sch. Polit. & Govt. Pos: Minn. State Sen, 41-; pres. pro-tempore, Minn. State Senate, 63. Bus. & Prof. Pos: Lawyer. Mailing Add: 72 Broadway, Little Falls, Minn. 56345.

ROSENTHAL, BEATRICE HOLT D
Dem. Nat. Committeewoman
b. Brooklyn, N.Y, 6/7/00; d. Hamilton Holt and Alexina Smith H; m. 1950 to Joseph S. Rosenthal; c. William Holt, Joseph H. and Grace (Mrs. Johnson). Educ: Columbia Teachers Col, 17-18. Polit. & Govt. Pos: Past pres, Dem. Federated Clubs of Conn; chmn, Dem. Party of Waterford; mem, Dem. Nat. Adv. Cmt. on Polit. Orgn, 20th Sen. Dist. Dem. Cent. Cmt, Conn, Waterford Develop. Cmn. and Fedn. Dem. Women; Dem. Nat. Committeewoman, Conn, 56-; chmn; women's activities, Chester Bowles for Cong. Campaign, 58; del, Dem. Nat. Conv, 60 & 68. Mem: Trustee and secy, Mystic Oral Sch. for Deaf; trustee, Lesley Col. and Eugene O'Neill Theatre for Performing Arts; trustee and v.pres, Goodspeed Opera House; chmn, Hempsted House, New London; pres, auxiliary bd, Norwich State Hosp; corporator, Lawrence Mem. Hosp; pres, Antiquarian and Landmarks Soc, Conn. Named Woman of the Year by Niantic, Conn. News, 60. Mailing Add: Jordon Village, Waterford, Conn. 06385. (1967)

ROSENTHAL, BENJAMIN STANLEY D
U.S. Rep, N.Y.
b. New York, N.Y, 6/8/23; s. Joseph Rosenthal and Ceil Fischer R; m. 12/23/50 to Lila Moskowitz; c. Debra and Edward. Educ: Long Island Univ. and City Col; Brooklyn Law Sch, LL.B, 49; New York Univ, LL.M, 52. Polit. & Govt. Pos: U.S. Rep, N.Y, 62-, mem, Nat. Cmn. Food Mkt, 66, For. Affairs Cmt, Govt. Oper. Cmt, Spec. Inquiry on Invasion of Privacy, chmn, Spec. Inquiry on Comsumer Representation in Fed. Govt, mem, Steering Cmt, Mem. of Cong. for Peace Through Law, U.S. House of Rep. Bus. & Prof. Pos: Attorney-at-law, Peirez, Karmiol, Rosenthal & Ackerman, N.Y, currently. Mil. Serv: Entered as Pvt, Army, 43, released as Technician Fifth Grade, 46, after serv. in Iceland. Mem: Queens Co, N.Y. State and Am. Bar Asns; Rel: Jewish. Legal Res: 88-12 Elmhurst Ave, Elmhurst, L.I, N.Y. 11373. Mailing Add: House Office Bldg, Washington, D.C. 20515.

ROSENTHAL, JACOB D
b. Tel-Aviv, Palestine, 6/30/35; nat. U.S. citizen, 43; s. Manfred Rosenthal and Rachel Kaplan R; m. 4/6/63 to Marilyn Wayne Silver; c. John N. and Ann W. Educ: Harvard Univ, A.B, 56. Polit. & Govt. Pos: Asst. dir. pub. info, U.S. Dept. of Justice, 61-64, dir. pub. info, 64-66; exec. asst. to Under Secy. of State Nicholas Katzenbach, 66-67. Bus. & Prof. Pos: Sports reporter, Portland Oregonian, 50-57, news reporter and copy ed, 57-59; ed. writer and reporter, Portland Reporter, 59-61; fel, Inst. Polit, Harvard, 67-68; vis. assoc, Joint Center for Urban Studies, Harvard-Mass. Inst. Tech, 67-68; gen. ed, Kerner Cmn. Report 68; Nat. Urban Affairs Correspondent, Life, 68-69 and N.Y. Times, 69- Mil. Serv: Army, 58. Rel: Jewish. Mailing Add: 3704 Huntington St. N.W, Washington, D.C. 20015.

ROSENZWEIG, HARRY R
Chmn, Ariz. State Rep. Cmt.
b. Phoenix, Ariz, 7/8/07; s. Isaac Rosenzweig and Rosa Gross R; m. 6/20/58 to Sandy Pollack; c. Diane (Mrs. Jack Hardy), Harry, Jr. and Burke. Educ: Univs. Ariz. and Mich, 26 & 27. Polit. & Govt. Pos: City councilman, Phoenix, Ariz, 50-53; finance chmn, Maricopa Co. Rep. Cmt, 52; finance chmn, Ariz. State Rep. Cmt, 60-62, chmn, 65- Bus. & Prof. Pos: Partner, Rosenzweig's Jewelers, 28- Mem: Mason (32°); Thunderbirds; Sun Angel Found; Better Bus. Bur; Retail Jewelers of Am; Shrine; treas, Ariz. Retail Asn; Kiva Club; Phoenix Country Club. Rel: Jewish; Trustee, Temple Beth Israel. Legal Res: 512 W. Flynn Lane, Phoenix, Ariz. 85013. Mailing Add: 35 N. First Ave, Phoenix, Ariz. 85003.

ROSEWELL, EDWARD JOSEPH D
Pres, Young Dem. of Ill.
b. Chicago, Ill, 12/8/28; s. Andrew Rosewell and Edna M. Maguire R; single. Educ: De Paul Univ, Ph.B, 61; John Marshall Law Sch. Polit. & Govt. Pos: Mem, 29th Ward Dem. Orgn. and Capt, 51st Precinct Dem. Orgn, 59-; Young Dem. of Cook Co. and Ill. rep, State, Regional and Nat. Meetings, 59- and Dem. Nat. Conv, 60; 29th Ward rep, Young Dem. of Cook Co. Cent. Cmt, 59-; W. Area v.chmn, Young Dem. of Cook Co, 60-61, treas, 61-62 and chmn, 63-64; Sixth Cong. Dist. chmn, Young Dem. of Ill, 60- and state pres, 66-; campaign mgr, West Side-West Suburban for Marshall Korshak, 62; arrangements chmn, first nat. campaigns conf, Young Dem. of Am, 62, author of civil rights plank, nat. cmt. meeting, 62, nat. registrn. chmn, presidential campaign, 64 and 1st v.pres; mem. platform cmt, Ill. Dem. Party, 64; alternate del, Dem. Nat. Conv, 64 & 68; mem, Inaugural Cmt. for President Johnson and Vice President Humphrey, 65. Bus. & Prof. Pos: Dir. personnel and secy, Ill. State Toll Hwy. Cmn; chmn, personnel cmt, Int. Bridge, Tunnel and Turnpike Asn; narrator, relig. prog, Sta. WGES. Mil. Serv: Army, 2 years, released as Sgt-Maj. Mem: Founder and past pres, Garfield Park Improv. Asn; asst. dir, West Side Area Planning Bd; past pres, Our Lady of Sorrows Holy Name Soc; CWV of Ill; Am. Legion; K. of C. (3°); spec. correspondent, Commun. Publns. Rel: Catholic. Mailing Add: 3321 W. Gladys, Chicago, Ill. 60624. (1967)

ROSFELD, ARTHUR EDWARD D
Dep. Asst. Secy, Housing Assistance Admin, Dept. of Housing and Urban Develop.
b. Pittsburgh, Pa, 5/21/31; s. Norman C. Rosfeld and Florence Cassidy R; m. 8/15/53 to Natalie Eleanor; c. Leslie Roy E. and Carrie Lee. Educ: Pa. State Univ, B.A, 53; Phi Delta Theta. Polit. & Govt. Pos: Spec. asst. cmnr, Pub. Housing Admin, 61-63; dir, Oper. Serv. Div, Dept. of Housing and Urban Develop, 66-69, dep. asst. secy, Housing Assistance Admin, 68-69. Bus. & Prof. Pos: Mgr. commercial rels, Am-Standard, 58-60; dir. educ. activities, Action Inc, 60-61. Rel: Presbyterian. Mailing Add: 10201 Grosvenor Place, Rockville, Md. 20852.

ROSNER, HENRY GEORGE R
Chmn, Spencer Rep. Town Cmt, Mass.
b. Baltimore, Md, 8/17/02; s. George Rosner and Margaret Phaf R; m. Rose Rivers; c. Bernadette (Mrs. Ray Begin), Henry G, II, Austin L. and Jeanne Lee (Mrs. Richard Proto). Educ: Naval Radio Sch, Great Lakes, Ill, 19-20; Chicago Eng. Works, Elec. Eng, 27. Polit. & Govt. Pos: Vote teller, Mass, various years; ballot inspector, 50-; chmn, Spencer Rep. Town Cmt, 68-Bus. & Prof. Pos: Electrician, B. & D. R.R, Baltimore, Md, 22-23; wire-drawer, Wickwire Steel, Spencer, Mass, 24-26; electrician, Worcester-Elec. Light Co, 26, switch bd. operator, 28-38; load dispatcher, Mass. Elec. Co, Worcester, 38-67, retired, 67. Mil. Serv: Entered as A/S, Navy, 19, released as Radioman 3/C, 22, after serv. in Radio-Oper. and Maintenance, U.S.S. Utah, S.Am, Mediterranean and Europe, 20-22. Mem: Hon. citizen, Boystown, Nebr. Rel: Catholic. Mailing Add: 24 Highland St, Spencer, Mass. 01562.

ROSOW, JEROME MORRIS Independent
Asst. Secy. of Labor for Policy, Eval. and Research, Dept. of Labor
b. Chicago, Ill, 12/2/19; s. Morris Rosow and Mary Cornick R; m. 9/28/41 to Rosalyn Levin; c. Michael and Joel. Educ: Wright Jr. Col, A.A.B, 40; Univ. Chicago, B.A. cum laude, 42. Polit. & Govt. Pos: Position classification analyst, Dept. of the Army, Wash, D.C, 42-43; dir. compensation, orgn. and methods, War Assets Admin, 46-48; orgn. exam. and asst. mgr, Wage and Salary Div, Off. Secy. of Army, 48-51; dir. policy and salary, stabilization bd, Econ. Stabilization Agency, 52-53; Asst. Secy. of Labor for Policy, Eval. and Research, Dept. of Labor, 69- Bus. & Prof. Pos: Mem. staff, Creole Petroleum Corp, Standard Oil, Caracas, Venezuela, 53-55, various exec. pos, employee rels. dept, Standard Oil, N.J, 55-; mem. bus. adv. research cmt, Bur. Labor Statist, 58-65; mem. and chmn. coun. compensation, Nat. Indust. Conf. Bd, 59-66; assoc, Columbia Univ. Seminar on Labor, 61-; dir, Voc. Adv. Serv, N.Y.C, 61-, chmn. finance cmt, 62-65; consult, U.S. Bur. Budget and U.S. Civil Serv. Cmn, 64; mem. bd. trustees, Nat. Cmt. Employ. Youth, 65-68; mgr. employee rels. dept, ESSO Europe, Inc, London, Eng, 66-69. Mil. Serv: Entered as Pvt, Army, 43, released as Chief Warrant Officer, 46, after serv. in Qm. Corps. Publ: Ed, American Men in Government, Pub. Affairs Press, 49; numerous articles relating to industrial relations and compensation matters in prfnl. jour. including, Harvard Bus. Rev. and Nat. Indust. Conf. Bd. Record. Mem: Indust. Rels. Research Asn; Am. Mgt. Asn. Rel: Jewish. Legal Res: New York, N.Y. Mailing Add: 4201 Cathedral Ave. N.W, Washington, D.C. 20016.

ROSS, BETTY B. D
b. Hartford, Conn, 11/14/25; d. Harry H. Beckanstin and Frances Horowitz B; div; c. Elisabeth H. Educ: Smith Col, A.B. cum laude, 46. Polit. & Govt. Pos: Alternate del, Dem. Nat. Conv, 60, del, 64; publicity dir, Dem. Cent. Cmt, D.C, 60-64. Bus. & Prof. Pos: Free-lance writer and publicist, 50-62; dir. pub. rels, Shoreham Hotel, 62- Mem: Pub. Rels. Soc. Am; mem. bd, Woman's Nat. Dem. Club; secy, Soc. Am. Travel Writers; Am. Newspaper Women's Club; Am. Women in Radio & TV. Rel: Jewish. Mailing Add: 3516 Albemarle St. N.W, Washington, D.C. 20008.

ROSS, CHARLES ROBERT
b. Middlebury, Vt, 2/24/20; s. Jacob Johnson Ross and Hannah Elizabeth Holmes R; m. 8/28/48 to Charlotte Sells Hoyt; c. Jacqueline Hoyt, Peter Holmes and Charles Robert, Jr. Educ: Univ. Mich, A.B, 41, M.B.A. and LL.B, 48. Polit. & Govt. Pos: Mem, Burlington Bd. of Aldermen, Vt, 57-59; chmn, Vt. Pub. Serv. Cmn, 59-61; cmnr, Fed. Power Cmn, 61-68; cmnr, Int. Joint Cmn, 62- Bus. & Prof. Pos: Instr, Ore. State Col, 48-49; officer, Derby Construction Co, Inc, 49-53; attorney-at-law, 54-59; consult, New Eng. Regional Cmn, 68-; adjunct prof, Univ. Vt, Burlington, 69- Mil. Serv: Entered as Pvt, Air Force, 42, released as Capt, 46, after serv. in 94th Combat Wing, Eighth Air Force, ETO. Legal Res: Hinesburg, Vt. 05461. Mailing Add: R.F.D. 1, Shelburne, Vt. 05482.

ROSS, CLAUDE G.
U.S. Ambassador to Haiti
b. Chicago, Ill, 10/26/17; m. to Antigone Peterson; c. Two. Educ: Univ. South. Calif, B.A, 39. Polit. & Govt. Pos: Career officer, U.S. Dept. of State For. Serv, 40-; First secy, Mexico City, 40-41, Quito, Guayaquil, 41-45, Athens, 45-49 Noumea, 49-51 and Beirut, 54-56; Nat. War Col, 56-57; counselor, Cairo, 57-60, and Conakry, 60-62; dep. dir, Off. of African and Malagasy Union Affairs, 62-63; U.S. Ambassador to Cent. African Repub, 63-67 and Haiti, 67- Bus. & Prof. Pos: With Los Angeles Daily News, 34-35. Mailing Add: U.S. Dept. of State Foreign Service, Washington, D.C. 20521. (1967)

ROSS, DANIEL J. R
State Treas, Del.
b. Wilmington, Del, 1902; m. to Louise; c. Three. Polit. & Govt. Pos: Rep. committeeman, Del; cand. for Wilmington City Treas, 64; state treas, Del, 67- Bus. & Prof. Pos: DuPont Co.'s Gen. Serv. Dept, 24 years, foreman of cleaning sect, 61- Mem: Troop 15 Scoutmaster. Guard on Champion football team fielded in the 20's by Defiance Athletic Asn; later played for Hockessin & St. Anthony's; Archery trophy winner in interstate competition. Rel: Catholic. Mailing Add: 203 W. 35th St, Wilmington, Del. 19802.

ROSS, DONALD ROE R
V.Chmn, Rep. Nat. Cmt.
b. Orleans, Nebr, 6/8/22; s. Roe M. Ross and Leila Reed R; m. 8/29/43 to Janice Cook; c. Susan Jane, Sharon Kay, Rebecca Lynn, Joan Christine and Donald Dean. Educ: Univ. Nebr, LL.B, 48; Delta Theta Phi. Polit. & Govt. Pos: Mayor, Lexington, Nebr, 52-53; U.S. Dist. Attorney, Nebr, 53-56; chmn, Douglas Co. Rep. Party, 57-58; gen. counsel, Nebr. Rep. Party, 57-58; Rep. Nat. Committeeman, Nebr, 58-; mem, exec. cmt, Rep. Nat. Cmt, 64-, v.chmn, 65- Bus. & Prof. Pos: Partner, law firm, Cook & Ross, Lexington, Nebr, 48-53 and Swarr, May, Royce, Smith, Andersen & Ross, 56- Mil. Serv: Entered as Cadet, Air Force, 42, released as Maj, 46, after serv. in 306th Bomb Group, 8th Air Force, Eng, 43-45; Distinguished Flying Cross with Oak Leaf Cluster; Air Medal and 5 Clusters. Mem: Am, Nebr. and Omaha Bar Asns; Am. Legion; Mason. Rel: Congregational. Legal Res: 2233 South 85th Ave, Omaha, Nebr. 68124. Mailing Add: 3535 Harney St, Omaha, Nebr. 68131.

ROSS, EDNA GENEVIEVE R
V.chmn, Pima Co. Rep. Cmt, Ariz.
b. Wheeling, W.Va, 3/2/16; d. Eugene Edwin Reed and Stella May McConnaughy R; m. 6/30/34 to Andrew Wilson Ross; c. Kenneth Reed, Ellen Penelope and Carolyn Jennifer (Mrs. Mayhill). Educ: Univ. Ariz, 2 years and continuing. Polit. & Govt. Pos: Rep. precinct committeeman, Pima Co, 49-; ward committeeman, Tucson, 60-; secy. exec. cmt, Pima Co. Rep. Cmt, 63-66, v.chmn, 66-; mem, Ariz. State Rep. Cmt, 63- and secy, Tucson Trunk 'N Tusk Club, 67-; del. and secy. Credential's Cmt, Rep. Nat. Conv, 68; mem. bi-partisan elec. reform cmt, Pima Co, 69. Bus. & Prof. Pos: Bus. mgr, Tucson Ariz. Boys Chorus, 49-51. Mem: Suburban Women's Club; Tucson Women's Symphony; Ariz. Prfnl. Engrs. Auxiliary; Mrs. Wright's Pueblo Juniors; Pima Co. Rep. Women; Univ. Ariz. Faculty Wives; Sunday Eve. Forum. Rel: Episcopal. Mailing Add: 3117 E. 29th St, Tucson, Ariz. 85713.

ROSS, HENRY D
Mo. State Rep.
b. Kans. City, Mo, 8/22/25; m. 3/23/50 to Ora J. Ruffin Ross. Educ: R.T. Coles Voc. Sch. Polit. & Govt. Pos: Mem, Mo. State Dem. Club; mem, Motor Vehicle Unit, State Dept. of Revenue, 18 years; chmn, Cent. Coalition Polit. Club; Mo. State Rep. 64- Bus. & Prof. Pos: Co-owner, C.E. Davis Funeral Home; restaurant operator. Rel: Baptist. Mailing Add: 1415 Truman Rd, Kansas City, Mo. 64106. (1967)

ROSS, HOPE SNIDER D
b. Vonore, Tenn, 5/23/10; d. Henry Tipton Snider and Iris Ellis S; m. 6/4/31 to George T. Ross, M.D; c. Julia (Mrs. Douglas Grossman), Mary

Ruth (Mrs. Robert Allerton) and Gerald Henry. Educ: Tenn. Wesleyan Univ, 26-27; Maryville Col, A.B, 31; Univ. Okla. Sch. Med, M.D, 35; Crippled Children's Hosp, Okla. City, internship, 35-56; North Hudson Hosp, Weehawken, N.J, resident in med. and anesthesia; Commonwealth fel, Harvard Univ, 43. Polit. & Govt. Pos: Del, White House Conf. on Educ, 55; Hon. Col. on Gov. staff, 62; alternate del. and alternate asst. secy. of Okla. Del, Dem. Nat. Conv, 64; mem, Finance Adv. Cmt, Okla. Dem. Cent. Cmt, 65; med. consult, Cmt. on Physicians Participation, Medicare Adv. Cmt, 65 and Social Security Admin, currently; Presidential Elector, 68; mem, President's Cmt. on Employ. of Handicapped, 68-69; mem, Defense Adv. Coun. on Women in Serv, 68- Bus. & Prof. Pos: Sch. physician, Phillips Univ, 38-42; area consult, Okla. Voc. Rehabilitation, 64-; mem, Liaison Cmt, Okla. Acad. of Gen. Practice and Univ. Okla. Sch. Med, 65; state membership chmn, Asn. for the Gifted, Okla, 66; mem, Garfield Co. Health Bd, 66-; mem, Gov. Cmt. on Children and Youth, 69; mem, Southwest. Coop. Educ. Lab, Planning Cmt. of Okla. Regional Med. Progs, bd. dirs, St. Mary's Hosp. Sch. of Nursing and Gov. Adv. Cmt. for Statewide Planning for Voc. Rehabilitation Serv. and bd. mem, Okla. Rehabilitation Asn, currently. Publ: 'Problems of Deep Anesthesia,' South. Med. J, 6/41. Mem: Am. and Okla. State Med. Asn; Am. and Okla. Acad. of Gen. Practice; Am. Med. Women's Asn; staff mem, Enid Gen. Hosp. and St. Mary's Hosp; UN Asn. of the U.S; C. of C; hon. mem, Vance Air Force Base Officer's Wives Club, 68. Nominated for President Johnson's Nat. Talent Bank by Dem. Cent. Cmt, Okla, 65, Int. Hon. Mem, Beta Sigma Phi. Rel: Methodist; mem. off. bd, First Methodist Church of Enid. Legal Res: Box 28, Woodlands, Route 2, Enid, Okla. 73701. Mailing Add: 1101 E. Broadway, Enid, Okla. 73701.

ROSS, JAMES EUGENE D
b. Beaver Falls, Pa, 1/23/21; s. Philip Ross and Helen Syka R; m. 11/5/42 to Dorothy Moravec; c. Judith, Janice, Debborah, Rebecca, Helen, Dorothy, Barbra, Bernadette and James, Jr. Educ: Pa. State Univ, 50-58. Polit. & Govt. Pos: Workmans Compensation Referee, 55; committeeman, Beaver Co. Dem. Cmt, Pa, 57-59, treas, 58-60; Pa. Dept. of Labor and Indust, 60; chmn, Beaver Co. Bd. of Cmnr, 60-66; del, Dem. Nat. Conv, 68. Mil. Serv: Entered as Seaman, Coast Guard, 43, released as Watertender 3/C, 45, after serv. in South and North Pac. Theaters; Four Battle Stars. Publ: Care of Aged, Nat. Co. Cmt. Orgn, 6/66. Mem: Am. Legion; VFW; Sons of Italy. Rel: Catholic. Legal Res: 200 Fourth St, Beaver, Pa. 15009. Mailing Add: Courthouse, Beaver, Pa. 15009.

ROSS, JIM BUCK D
Cmnr. of Agr, Miss.
b. Pelahatchie, Miss, 8/14/17; s. E.N. Ross and Emma Jones R; m. 9/28/41 to Margaret Spann; c. James Hal and Mary Gwendolyn. Educ: Miss State Univ, 4 years; Jackson Sch. of Law, Admitted to Bar. Polit. & Govt. Pos: Mayor, Pelahatchie, Miss, 55-59; Miss. State Sen, 64-68; Cmnr. of Agr, Miss, 68- Bus. & Prof. Pos: Farm equip. dealer and cotton grower, Rankin Co, Miss, 45-57. Mil. Serv: Entered as Pvt, Army, 44, released as 1st Lt, 46, after serv. in S.Pac, 44-46. Mem: Nat. Asn. of State Dept. of Agr; South. Asn. of State Dept. of Agr; Gamma Sigma Delta; Miss. Econ. Coun. Rel: Methodist. Legal Res: Pelahatchie, Miss. 39145. Mailing Add: P.O. Box 1609, Jackson, Miss. 39205.

ROSS, JOHN RAYMOND R
b. Minneapolis, Minn, 3/27/23; s. Christopher Ross and Pearl La Bresh R; m. 1/13/68 to Mildred Elizabeth Conroy; c. John, Scott, Dennis, Michael and Timothy. Educ: Univ. South. Calif, B.Arch, 49; Alpha Rho Chi. Polit. & Govt. Pos: Mem, San Luis Obispo Co. Cent. Cmt, Calif, 65, chmn, 67; mem, Calif. Rep. State Cent. Cmt, 67, mem, exec. cmt, 68; area chmn, Calif. State Co. Chmn. Asn, 68; secy, Calif. State Bd. of Archit. Exam, 68- Bus. & Prof. Pos: Pres, John R. Ross & Assocs, Inc, San Luis Obispo, Calif, 56-; lectr. archit, Calif. State Polytech. Col, 57-68; pres, El Garro Corp, 60-; dir, Coastal Airlines, 66-; dir. and v.pres, Golden Tee Motel, Inc, Morro Bay, currently; dir, Swiftaire Air Lines, San Luis Obispo, 69. Mil. Serv: Entered as 2nd Lt, Army, 42, released as 1st Lt, 46, after serv. in 298th Inf, 25th Div, Cent. and S.Pac. Theatres, 42-46, reentered, 50, released as Capt, after serv. in 578th Engrs, 40th Div, Japan and Korea, 50-52; Capt.(Ret), Army Res, 65; theatre and campaign medals. Mem: Am. Inst. Architects; Am. Arbit. Asn; Rotary; Elks; Commonwealth Club; Caballeros of San Luis Obispo; Art Asn; ROA; Pilots Asn; Santa Maria Club; pres, La Fiesta Corp, 69. Rel: Catholic. Mailing Add: 580 Serrano Dr, San Luis Obispo, Calif. 93401.

ROSS, LEONARD WALTER D
Dep. Coroner, Rock Island Co, Ill.
b. Marathon, Iowa, 7/5/15; s. Robert G. Ross and Julia Johnson R; m. 7/7/34 to Sarah Dorthy Romine; c. Donna (Mrs. Gilbert Stormont) and Creel Leonard. Educ: Palmer Col, D.C, 49. Polit. & Govt. Pos: Mem, City Coun, Rock Island, Ill, 55-58; Ill. State Rep, 59-60; dep. coroner, Rock Island Co, 69- Mem: Pres, Prarie State Chiropractic Asn, 54-55; Shrine; Scottish Rite; Grotto; Mason. Chiropractor of the Year, 61. Rel: Methodist. Mailing Add: 3671 31st Ave, Rock Island, Ill. 61201.

ROSS, NEILL McKAY D
Chmn, Harnett Co. Dem. Exec. Cmt, N.C.
b. Lillington, N.C, 12/5/08; s. Charles Ross and Frances Reid McKay R; m. 2/23/41 to Lois Christine Ray; c. Frances Victoria (Mrs. Byrd), Lois Ray, Neill McKay, Jr, James Reid and Margaret Murchison. Educ: Davidson Col; Univ. of N.C. and Law Sch. Polit. & Govt. Pos: N.C. State Rep, 39-41; co. solicitor, Harnett Co, 47-52, co. tax attorney, 58-61 and co. attorney, 61; govt. appeal agent, Selective Serv, 47-66; chmn, Harnett Co. Dem. Exec. Cmt, N.C, 61- Mil. Serv: Entered as Pvt, Army, 44, released as S/Sgt, 46. Mem: Pres, 11th Judicial Dist. Bar Asn; Harnett Co. and N.C. Bar Asns; Nat. Asn. Co. Civil Attorneys; Am. Legion; Farm Bur. Rel: Presbyterian. Legal Res: R.R. 3, Lillington, N.C. 27546. Mailing Add: Box 186, Lillington, N.C. 27546. (1967)

ROSS, RAYMOND F. D
b. Springfield, Ohio, 10/28/12; s. Ernest Joshua Ross and Mary Haney R; m. 8/4/62 to Helen Delores Iacco; c. Richard R. Educ: Springfield Bus. Col. Polit. & Govt. Pos: Admin. Procurement Inspector, U.S. Air Force, 42-45; del, Dem. Nat. Conv, 68. Bus. & Prof. Pos: Dir, Region 2-A and mem, Int. Exec. Bd, UAW, 49-; pres, Ohio CIO Coun, 56-58; v.pres, Ohio AFL-CIO Coun, 58- Mem: UAW Local 402. Rel: Methodist. Mailing Add: 1010 Kenley Ave, Columbus, Ohio 43221. (1967)

ROSS, WILLIAM B.
Dep. Under Secy, Dept. of Housing & Urban Develop.
Legal Res: Va. Mailing Add: Dept. of Housing & Urban Development, 451 Seventh St. S.W, Washington, D.C. 20410.

ROSS, WILLIAM G, JR. R
b. Blackville, S.C, 10/5/32; s. William G. 'Red' Ross, Sr. and Azalee Miles R; m. 6/19/54 to Shirley Grace Dobbins; c. Christopher Eugene and William G, III. Educ: Univ. S.C, Econ. Polit. & Govt. Pos: Chmn, Berkeley Co. Rep. Party, S.C, 64-68. Bus. & Prof. Pos: Invest, Retail Credit Co, 61-67; appraiser, Charleston Co. Bd. of Assessment Control, 67- Mil. Serv: Entered as Pvt, Marine Corps, 52, released as Sgt, 55, after serv. in Hq. Co, First Marine Div, Korea, 53-54; Korean Presidential Unit Citation; UN Serv. Medal; Korean Serv. Medal with two Battle Stars; Nat. Def. Serv. Medal; Good Conduct Medal. Mem: S.C. Asn. of Assessing Off. Rel: Baptist. Mailing Add: 1202 Palm St, Apt. F, Hanahan, S.C. 29406.

ROSS, WILLIAM ROBERT D
b. Clarksburg, W.Va, 12/28/16; s. Harrison M.G. Ross and Mae Hedges R; m. 6/24/41 to Billy Colvin Jeffreys; c. William R, Jr.(deceased), Dixon J. and Susan Mae. Educ: W.Va. Univ, A.B, 38 and M.A, 39; Univ. Wis, 40-41; Columbia Univ, 47-48. Polit. & Govt. Pos: Econ. analyst, Off. of Price Admin, Wash, D.C, 42; consult, Legis. Interim Cmt, W.Va, 50-59; bill drafting serv, W.Va. State Legis, 51; alternate del, Dem. Nat. Conv, 52 & 68; mem, W.Va. Dem. State Exec. Cmt, 52-56; clerk, Judiciary Cmt, W.Va. House of Del, 53 & 57 and Finance Cmt, 55; mem, Morgantown City Coun, 59; mem. and v.chmn, Monongalia Co. Dem. Exec. Cmt, 60-64; mem, Emergency Resources Planning Cmt, 62-, W.Va. Cmn. on Constitutional Rev, 62- and State Elec. Cmn, 69- Bus. & Prof. Pos: Instr, Dept. of Polit. Sci, W.Va. Univ, 41-48, asst. prof, 48-62, assoc. prof, 63- and assoc. dir, Bur. for Govt. Research, 66-; exec. dir, W.Va. League of Munic, 66- Mil. Serv: Entered as Pvt, Army, 44, released as S/Sgt, 46, after serv. in 729th Mil. Police Bn, U.S. Publ: West Virginia Political Almanac, Bur. for Govt. Research, three eds, 56, 60 & 64; An Introduction to the Electoral Process in West Virginia, 62; West Virginia State and Local Government, co-auth, 63. Mem: Am. and South. Polit. Sci. Asns; Am. Asn. Univ. Prof. Rel: Protestant. Mailing Add: 425 Lawnview Dr, Morgantown, W.Va. 26505.

ROSSELOTT, HERMAN JOHN D
b. Buford, Ohio, 11/26/98; s. Charles F. Rosselott and Louie Moberly R; m. 5/26/26 to Bernice Boyd; c. Mary Lou (Mrs. David W. Steritz). Educ: Ohio Wesleyan Univ, A.B, 21; Ohio Wesleyan Union. Polit. & Govt. Pos: Mem, Highland Co. Bd. of Educ, Ohio, 46-66; del, Dem. Nat. Conv, 56, 60 & 68; mem, Ohio Cmn. on Aging, 61-62 & 66-; Presidential elector, Electoral Col, 64. Bus. & Prof. Pos: Supt. of schs, Buford, Ohio, 22-26; teacher, instrumental music, Highland Co. Schs, 26-37; owner and operator, Gen. Store, Buford, 26-36; pres, Farmers Exchange Bank, Lynchburg, 36-; dir, First Nat. Bank, Sardinia, 50-; owner and operator, farm, 50-; trustee, Tri-Co. Col, Macon, Ga, currently. Mil. Serv: Entered as Pvt, Army, 17-18, serv. in Student Army Training Corps, Ohio Wesleyan Univ. Mem: Mason; Shrine; Jesters; Eastern Star; Lions; Banking Orgns. Rel: Methodist. Mailing Add: 333 S. Main St, Lynchburg, Ohio 45142.

ROSSETTI, FRANK G. D
N.Y. State Assemblyman
Polit. & Govt. Pos: N.Y. State Assemblyman, 43-44 & 54-; exec. mem, Kanawha Club, Regular Dem. Orgn. of 16th Assembly Dist; del, Dem. Nat. Conv, 68; chmn, N.Y. Co. Dem. Party, currently. Bus. & Prof. Pos: V.pres, Oper. Plasterers and Cement Masons Int. Asn. Mem: Holy Name Soc; K. of C; Elks; Soc. of Tammany or Columbian Order. Mailing Add: 2253 First Ave, New York, N.Y. 10029. (1967)

ROSSI, ITALO AMRERICO R
b. Farmington, Ill, 4/21/20; s. Nello Rossi and Isolina Bonjean R; m. 8/19/41 to Norma Serangeli; c. Dianne Marie, Norma Jean and Italo, Jr. Educ: Purdue Univ, B.P.E, 42; P Men's Club, Delta Chi. Polit. Pos: Chmn, Tazewell Co. Rep. Party, Ill, 62-66 and secy, 52-66; precinct committeeman, Rep. Party, 48-66. Govt. Pos: Chief Down State Inspector, State Athletic Cmn, Rep. Party of Ill, 53-55. Mil. Serv: Entered as Seaman 1/C, Navy, 42, released as Chief PO, 45. Mem: Ill. Motel Asn; Am. Legion; Amvets; K. of C. (4°); Asn. of Commerce; Kiwanis; John Purdue Club. Football, wrestling and Mid-West Amateur Athletic Union; wrestling champion, 41. Rel: Catholic. Mailing Add: 332 S. 14th St, Pekin, Ill. 61554. (1967)

ROSSIDES, EUGENE TELEMACHUS R
Asst. Secy. of the Treas.
b. Brooklyn, N.Y, 10/23/27; s. Telemachus Rossides and Anna Maravel R; m. 12/30/61 to Aphrodite Macotsin; c. Gale Daphne, Michael Telemachus, Alexander Demetrius and Eleni Ariadne. Educ: Columbia Col, B.A; Columbia Law Sch, LL.B; Sigma Chi; Phi Delta Phi. Polit. & Govt. Pos: Criminal law investr, New York Co. Dist. Attorney's Off, N.Y, 52; asst. attorney gen, N.Y, 56-58; special asst. to Under Secy. of the Treas, 58-61, Asst. Secy. of Treas, 69- Bus. & Prof. Pos: Attorney-at-law, Royall, Koegel & Wells, N.Y.C, 54-56 & 61-69, partner, 66-69. Mil. Serv: 2nd Lt, Air Force, 52-53, with Air Materiel Command, Wright-Patterson Air Force Base; Capt, Air Force Res, 53- Mem: Acad. of Polit. Sci; Am, Fed. and N.Y. State Bar Asns; Am. Polit. Sci. Asn; N.Y. State Dist. Attorneys Asn; Int. Asn. of Chiefs of Police; Columbia Col. Coun; Columbia Col. Alumni Asn; Columbia Col. Varsity C Club; Ahepa; Nat. Football Found. and Hall of Fame; Touchdown Club of N.Y. Received Rolker Prize upon graduation from Columbia Col. Rel: Greek Orthodox; mem, Archdiocesan Coun, Greek Orthodox Church of N. and S. Am. Mailing Add: 4829 Drummond Ave, Chevy Chase, Md. 20015.

ROSSITER, MICHAEL ANTHONY D
Chmn, Yankton Co. Dem. Party, S.Dak.
b. Yankton, S.Dak, 8/25/35; s. Lawrence Rossiter and Florence Lase R; m. 8/4/62 to Theodora Horn; c. Cecilia Marie, Lawrence Dominic, Peter

Anthony and Rachel Mary. Educ: Creighton Univ, B.S. in B.A, 59; Delta Sigma Phi. Polit. & Govt. Pos: Chmn, Yankton Co. Dem. Party, S.Dak, 64-66 & 68-; area capt, S.Dak. Dem. Party, 69- Bus. & Prof. Pos: Salesman, Rossiter Ins, 59-62, Fuller Brush Co, 62 and Orchard & Wilhelmco, 62-63; owner, Rossiter Ins, 63-65; pres, Rossiter Agency, Inc, 65- Mil. Serv: Entered as E-1, Army, 56, released as E-4, 57, after serv. in 267th Field Artil, 5th Corps, Germany. Mem: K. of C; Yankton C. of C; Moose; Toastmasters; Jaycees. Rel: Catholic. Legal Res: 300 E. Fifth, Yankton, S.Dak. 57078. Mailing Add: Box 570, Yankton, S.Dak. 57078.

ROSSITER, THEODORA HORN D
State Committeewoman, S.Dak. Dem. Party
b. Omaha, Nebr, 2/27/37; d. Raymond Frederick Horn and Doris Viola Jamieson H; m. 8/4/62 to Michael Anthony Rossiter; c. Cecilia Marie, L. Dominic, Peter Anthony and Rachel Mary. Educ: Creighton Mem. St. Joseph's Hosp, Omaha, Nebr, R.N, 57; Creighton Univ, 60-62. Polit. & Govt. Pos: Precinct committeewoman, Dem. Party, Yankton, S.Dak, 66; co. chmn. for Robert Kennedy, Yankton Co, 68; del, Dem. Nat. Conv, 68; State committeewoman, S.Dak. Dem. Party, 68- Bus. & Prof. Pos: Staff nursing and nursing serv, St. Joseph's Hosp, Omaha, Nebr, 57-58 & 61-67; nursing-midwifery, Colombia, S.Am.(under auspices of Young Christian Movement, Chicago), 59-60. Mem: League Women Voters. Rel: Roman Catholic. Mailing Add: 300 E. Fifth, Yankton, S.Dak. 57078.

ROSSLEY, EILEEN G. D
b. Worcester, Mass, 2/6/15; wid; c. three. Educ: Mass. High Sch. of Commerce; New Woodland Prep. Sch. Polit. & Govt. Pos: N.H. State Rep, 64-68; clerk, House Exec. Dept. and Admin. Cmt, Gov. and Exec. Coun. appointee, N.H. Health and Welfare Cmn, 65-; mem, Portsmouth Dem. City Cmt; mem, Rockingham Co. Dem. Cmt; moderator, Rockingham Co. Dist. 29; justice of peace; city chmn, Portsmouth Women's Dem. Club; Dem. co-chmn. of Portsmouth Ward Six. Bus. & Prof. Pos: Saleswoman. Mem: Cath. Daughters of Am; K. of C. Auxiliary; bd. dirs, Rockingham Co. Commun. Action Prog. Rel: Roman Catholic. Mailing Add: 30 Gosling Rd, Portsmouth, N.H. 03801. (1967)

ROSSON, RENAL B. D
Tex. State Rep.
b. Stephens Co, Tex, 12/24/19; s. Oscar C. Rosson and Eula Prycilla Rutledge R; m. 7/11/45 to Dorothy Mae Murphree; c. Kyle Boyd. Educ: Tex. Tech. Col, B.B.A, 46; Univ. Tex, LL.B, 49. Polit. & Govt. Pos: Dist. attorney, 132nd Judicial Dist, Tex, 52-57; Tex. State Rep, 85th Legis. Dist, 59-, chmn, Representation Before Legis. Cmn. and v.chmn, Livestock and Stock Raising Cmn, 63-64, chmn, Tex. House Judiciary Cmt, 65-66 and Inland Salt Water Pollution Study Cmn, 66; mem, Tex. Civil Judicial Coun, 65-66. Bus. & Prof. Pos: Attorney and rancher raising Hereford Cattle. Mil. Serv: Entered as Pvt, 42, released as 1st Lt, 46, after serv. in Air Force as Bombardier and Observer in European Theater; Capt, Air Force Res, until 63; Air Medal with 3 Oak Leaf Clusters; Purple Heart; Distinguished Flying Cross; ETO Medal; 4 Invasion Medals including South. France Invasion Medal. Mem: Pres, United Fund Drive, Scurry Co, Tex, 59; pres, Scurry Co. Bar Asn, 61; Tex. Bar Asn; Lions; C. of C; Jr. C. of C; VFW; Am. Legion; Mason (32°), Scottish Rite and York Rite; Tex. Farm Bur; bd. dirs, Sweetwater and Tex. Hereford Asns. Rel: Baptist. Mailing Add: Box 217, Snyder, Tex. 79549. (1967)

ROSTAD, CARL R
Mont. State Sen.
b. Lennep, Mont, 6/26/07; s. Olaf Rostad and Marie Olson R; m. 1/24/39 to Helen Elizabeth Lepely. Educ: Mont. State Univ, Bozeman; Sigma Chi. Polit. & Govt. Pos: Co. comnr, Meagher Co, Mont, 50-60; Mont. State Sen, Meagher Co, 61- Bus. & Prof. Pos: Chmn. adv. bd, Lewis & Clark Forest, 58-; chmn. bd, Mt. View Mem. Hosp, White Sulphur Springs, Mont, currently. Mem: Mason, Scottish Rite, Shrine; Mont. Stockgrowers Asn; Farm Bur; Meagher Co. Livestock Asn. Rel: Lutheran. Mailing Add: Loweth Route, Martinsdale, Mont. 59053. (1967)

ROSTENKOWSKI, DAN D
U.S. Rep, Ill.
m. to LaVerne Pirkins; c. Four. Educ: Loyola Univ. Polit. & Govt. Pos: U.S. Rep, Ill, Nov, 58-, mem, Ways and Means Cmt, chmn, Dem. Caucus and mem, Dem. Steering Cmt, 67 & 69, U.S. House Rep; del, Dem. Nat. Conv, 60, 64 & 68; Ill. State Rep, 68th Gen. Assembly; Ill. State Sen. from 33rd sen. dist. in 69th and 70th Gen. Assemblies. Mil. Serv: Infantry in Korea, 2 years. Mem: K. of C; VFW; N.W. Town Kiwanis Club; Moose. Legal Res: Chicago, Ill. Mailing Add: U.S. House of Representatives, Washington, D.C. 20515.

ROSTOW, WALT WHITMAN D
b. N.Y.C, 10/7/16; s. Victor Aaron Rostow and Lillian Helman R; m. 6/26/47 to Elspeth Vaughan Davies; c. Peter Vaughan and Ann Larner. Educ: Yale, B.A, 36, Ph.D, 40; Balliol Col, Rhodes Scholar, 36-38. Polit. & Govt. Pos: Asst. chief, German-Austrian Econ. Div, Dept. of State, 45-46; dep. spec. asst. to President for nat. security affairs, 61; counsr. and chmn, Policy Planning Coun, Dept. of State, 61-66; U.S. rep. to Ambassador, Inter-Am. Cmt, Alliance for Progress, 64-66; spec. asst. to the President, 66-69. Bus. & Prof. Pos: Instr. econ, Columbia Univ, 40-41; Harmsworth prof. Am. hist, Oxford Univ, Eng, 46-47; asst. to exec. secy, Econ. Cmn. for Europe, 47-49; Pitt. prof. Am. hist, Cambridge Univ, Eng, 49-50; prof. econ. hist, Mass. Inst. Tech, 50-60; staff mem, Center Int. Studies, 51-60; prof. hist. and econ, Univ. Texas, Austin, 69- Mil. Serv: Maj, Off. Strategic Serv, Army, 42-45; Legion of Merit; Hon. Order Brit. Empire. Publ: Essays on the British Economy of the Nineteenth Century, 48; The United States in the World Arena, 60; The Stages of Economic Growth, 60; plus others. Mem: Cosmos Club, Wash, D.C; Elizabethan Club, New Haven. Medal of Freedom, with distinction, 69. Legal Res: 1506 W. Lake Dr, Austin, Tex. 78746. Mailing Add: Dept. of Economics, University of Texas, Austin, Tex. 78712.

ROTELLI, DELBERT LEROY R
b. Sonora, Calif, 9/8/34; s. Anelo Rotelli and Treana Pretto R; m. 9/20/58 to Kathleen Rohrman; c. Larry and Vickie. Educ: Col. San Mateo, A.A, 55; Idaho State Col, B.A, 57; Tau Kapa Epsilon; I Club. Polit. & Govt. Pos: Councilman, Sonora, Calif, 64-68; Mem, Calif. Rep. State Cent. Cmt, 68-69. Mem: Pres, Sonora Area Bus. Asn; exalted ruler, Sonora Elks Club; K. of C; pres, Italian Cath. Fedn; Sonora Volunteer Fireman. Rel: Catholic. Legal Res: 250 E. Pasadena Ave, Sonora Calif. 95370. Mailing Add: P.O. Box 297, Sonora, Calif. 95370.

ROTH, FRED M, JR. R
V.Chmn, Orleans Co. Rep. Cmt, N.Y.
b. Gaines, N.Y, 1/5/20; s. Fred M. Roth, Sr. and Lettie Miller R; m. 7/19/40 to Janet Irene Litchfield; c. William John and Linda Helena (Mrs. Zyne). Educ: Albion High Sch, grad. Polit. & Govt. Pos: Supt. of hwys, Ridgeway, N.Y, 52-; v.chmn, Orleans Co. Rep. Cmt, 60- Mil. Serv: Pvt, Army, 43-45, serv. in 28th Inf. Div, ETO, 44-45; Purple Heart; Three Battle Stars; Combat Inf. Badge. Mem: Ridgeway Volunteer Fire Co; Moose; VFW; Sacred Heart Soc, Medina; Medina Conservation Club. Rel: Protestant. Mailing Add: 11804 Ridge Rd, Medina, N.Y. 14103.

ROTH, GERALD IRWIN D
b. Allentown, Pa, 7/2/31; s. Eugene Roth and Juliet Weiss R; m. 8/30/53 to Selma Barbara Grossman; c. Judd K, Kyle R, Adam M, Douglas C. and Melissa B. Educ: Univ. Calif, Los Angeles, B.A, 52; Northwest. Univ. Sch. Law, J.D, 56; Phi Epsilon Pi. Polit. & Govt. Pos: Del, Dem. Nat. Conv, 68. Bus. & Prof. Pos: Spec. asst, Colo. River Bd, Calif. State Attorney Gen. Off, 55; prof, Univ. Calif. Sch. Law, Los Angeles, 56-57. Publ: 'Freedom from Arbitrary Removal in the Classified Civil Service—Real or Illusory,' 55 and 'Changes in Board Interpretation, Section 8(b) (4)(A) Taft-Hartley,' 55, Northwest. Univ. Law Rev. Mem: Order of the Coif; State Bars of Calif. and Pa; U.S. Supreme Court Bar; Lehigh Co. chmn, Cancer Crusade; spec. gifts cmt, Good Shepherd Home; bd. dirs, Allentown Jewish Commun. Center. Rel: Jewish. Mailing Add: 1048 N. 27th St, Allentown, Pa. 18104.

ROTH, STEPHEN J. D
b. Hungary, 4/21/08; s. Charles Roth and Johanna Zillai R; m. to Evelyn Gunner; c. Diane, Susan, Kayla, Charles and Bradford. Educ: Univ. Mich, LL.B; Univ. Notre Dame, Ph.B. Polit. & Govt. Pos: Asst. prosecuting attorney, Genesee Co, Mich, 37-38, prosecuting attorney, 41-42; chmn, Genesee Co. Dem. Cmt, 46-47; Attorney Gen, Mich, 49-50; Circuit Judge, Genesee Co, 52-62; U.S. Dist. Judge, East. Dist. Mich. and U.S. Courts, 62- Mil. Serv: Entered as Pfc, Army, 43, released as 2nd Lt, 45, after serv. in Criminal Invest. Div, Provost Marshal's Off; Am. and for. decorations. Legal Res: G-8458 S. Vassar Rd, Grand Blanc, Mich. 48439. Mailing Add: Federal Bldg, Flint, Mich. 48502.

ROTH, WILLIAM VICTOR, JR. R
U.S. Rep, Del.
b. Great Falls, Mont, 7/22/21; s. William V. Roth, Sr. and Clara Nelson R; m. 10/1/65 to Jane K. Richards; c. William V, III and Katharine Kellond. Educ: Univ. Ore, B.A, 44; Harvard Bus. Sch, I.A, 43 and M.B.A, 47; Harvard Law Sch, LL.B, 49. Polit. & Govt. Pos: Pres, State Fedn. of Young Rep. of Del, 56-58 and New Castle Co. Young Rep, Del, 59-60; chmn, Rep. State Cmt. and mem, Rep. Nat. Cmt, 61-64; chmn, Del. Cmn. on Modernization of State Laws, 61-67; U.S. Rep, Del, 67- Bus. & Prof. Pos: Sr. counsel, Hercules Inc, Wilmington, Del, 50-66. Mil. Serv: Entered as Pvt, Army, 43, released as Capt, 46, after serv. in Mil. Intel, Psychological Warfare Br. and Info. Chief, Japanese Radio in Hq, Supreme Command Allied Powers; Am. Theater Serv. Medal; Asiatic Pac. Serv. Medal with 3 Bronze Stars; Bronze Star Medal; Distinguished Unit Citation; World War II Victory Medal; Army of Occupation. Mem: Am. Bar Asn; Del. State Bar; State Bar of Calif; Am. Legion; VFW; Greenville and Wilmington Country Club; Harvard Club of N.Y.C; Univ. and Whist Club of Wilmington, Del. Rel: Episcopal. Legal Res: 2701 Centerville Rd, Wilmington, Del. 19808. Mailing Add: U.S. House of Representatives, Washington, D.C. 20515.

ROTHMAN, DAVID MICHAEL D
Mem, Calif. Dem. State Cent. Cmt.
b. Milwaukee, Wis, 5/23/37; s. Morris R. Rothman and Margaret Small R; m. 5/23/63 to Phyllis Levenstein; c. Sharon Donna. Educ: Univ. of Calif, Los Angeles, A.B, 59; Univ. of Chicago Law Sch, J.D, 62. Polit. & Govt. Pos: Dep. Attorney Gen, Calif, 63-67; mem, Calif. Dem. State Cent. Cmt, 66-; chmn, 59th Assembly Dist. Dem. Coun, 69- Bus. & Prof. Pos: Attorney-at-law, Los Angeles, Calif, 67- Publ: The Glass Menagerie (a book of drawings), Univ. of Chicago Press, 62. Mem: Los Angeles Co. Bar Asn; Univ. of Chicago Alumni Asn; Am. Civil Liberties Union (chmn, sub-cmt. on rights of privacy and mem. exec. cmt, lawyer's div, South. Calif. Chap); Univ. of Chicago Law Sch. Alumni Asn.(mem. bd. dirs, South. Calif. Chap); Sierra Club. Rel: Jewish. Legal Res: 1116 S. Shenandoah St, Los Angeles, Calif. 90035. Mailing Add: 4262 Wilshire Blvd, Los Angeles, Calif. 90005.

ROTHMAN, KENNETH J. D
Mo. State Rep.
b. St. Louis, Mo, 10/11/35; m. 4/10/65 to Geraldine Jaffe; c. David Haron. Educ: Washington Univ, St. Louis, A.B, LL.B; Sigma Alpha Mu; Phi Delta Phi; Eta Sigma Phi classical lang. hon. fraternity. Polit. & Govt. Pos: Asst. Prosecuting attorney, 59-61; pres, Hadley Twp. Dem. Club, 60-62; Mo. State Rep, 62- Bus. & Prof. Pos: Attorney, private practice of law, 59- Mil. Serv: Mo. Air Nat. Guard, 53-62; active duty, Berlin Crisis, 61-62. Mem: Mason. Rel: Jewish. Mailing Add: 90 Aberdeen Place, Clayton, Mo. 63105.

ROTHRAUFF, RICHARD M. D
Chmn, Blair Co. Dem. Cmt, Pa.
b. Pittsburgh, Pa, 1/3/31; s. Francis Wayne Rothrauff and Arvilla Kniseley R; m. 11/2/63 to Mary Jane Klevan. Educ: Pa. State Univ, spec. course in pub. rels, 1 1/2 years. Polit. & Govt. Pos: Chmn, Blair Co. Dem. Cmt, Pa, 64- Mil. Serv: Entered as Seaman, Navy, 48, released as A/S, 49, after serv. in U.S.A. Mem: Lions (past dir, Lakemount Chap); past state v.pres, and past state chmn, Commun. Develop. Pa. Jaycees; East. Paralyzed Vets. Asn, N.Y.C. Rel: Catholic. Mailing Add: Box 254 Sylvan Heights Dr, Hollidaysburg, Pa. 16648. (1967)

ROTHSTEIN, JAMES L. R
S.Dak. State Rep.
b. 4/10/14; m. 7/20/38 to Lucille A. Adkins; c. James, David, Michael and

John. Educ: Bus. Col. courses. Polit. & Govt. Pos: Chmn, Walworth Co. Bd. of Educ, S.Dak; bd. mem. and past pres, Mobridge Independent Sch. Dist; S.Dak. State Rep, 64-, Majority Leader, S.Dak. House Rep, 69-, chmn, State Affairs Cmt. Bus. & Prof. Pos: Ins. and motel bus. Mil. Serv: Radarman 3/C, Navy, 2 years. Mem: Dir. and secy, Mobridge Rodeo, 20 years; past pres. and bd. mem, Mobridge Commun. Hosp; past pres. and dir, Mobridge C. of C. and Mobridge Rotary Club; pres. and dir, Mobridge Country Club; Moose; Am. Legion; VFW; First Grand Knight, Mobridge Coun, K. of C, 3 terms; Gr. S.Dak. Asn.(dir, 69); exec. bd, Upper Midwest Research for S.Dak. Rel: Catholic. Mailing Add: 1414 Kennedy Dr, Mobridge, S.Dak. 57601.

ROTHSTEIN, JOSEPH MARVIN D

b. Wilmington, Del, 11/20/34; s. Abraham Rothstein and Celia Bobbins R; m. 2/2/59 to Adele Jo Baker; c. Steven W, Jeffrey D, Gregory R. and David B. Educ: El Camino Col, 52-54; Univ. of Calif, Los Angeles, B.A. in Int. Rels, 58, M.S. in Journalism, 59. Polit. & Govt. Pos: Spec. asst. to Gov. William A. Egan, Alaska, 61-64; statewide campaign mgr, Gravel for Senate, 68; del, Dem. Nat. Conv, 68; admin. asst. to Sen. Mike Gravel, Alaska, 69- Bus. & Prof. Pos: Exec. ed. and v.pres, Anchorage Daily News, 64-68. Mil. Serv: Entered as Pvt, Army, 54, released as Cpl, 56, after serv. in Transportation C, Europe. Recipient of various journalism awards for editing and writing, Alaska. Rel: Jewish. Legal Res: P.O. Box 2283, Anchorage, Alaska 99501. Mailing Add: 1018 Dead Run Dr, McLean, Va. 22101.

ROTHSTEIN, ROBERT N. D

Dist. Capt, Denver Co. Dem. Cent. Cmt, Colo.

b. Bronx, N.Y, 6/27/26; s. Isidor Rothstein and Netty Perlstein R; m. 6/27/48 to Natalie Cohen; c. Bonnie (Mrs. Keith Brewer) and Beth (Mrs. Steve Higinbotham). Educ: Univ. Colo, B.A, 48, M.A, 58; Phi Delta Kappa; Sigma Delta Chi; Phi Sigma Delta. Polit. & Govt. Pos: Campaign mgr. for Allegra Saunders for Denver Sch. Bd, 63 and Colo. State Sen, 66; del, Colo. State Dem. Conv, 64, 66 & 68; dist. capt, Denver Co. Dem. Cent. Cmt, 67-; alternate del, Dem. Nat. Conv, 68; chmn, Urban Affairs Cmt, Colo. Dem. Platform Cmt, 68. Bus. & Prof. Pos: Newspaper Reporter and Editor, Brooklyn Eagle, Brighton Blade, Idaho Falls Post Register and Denver Post, 48-53; teacher, Denver Pub. Schs, 53-66; prof, Temple Buell Col, 66- Mil. Serv: Pvt, Army, 43-44, serv. in Medical Corps, U.S. Publ: A Newspaper Bul, Columbia Scholastic Press Asn, 63; 'How Not to Communicate', KOA-Speech, 66; 'What College Students Think of Themselves', Empire, 67; plus others. Mem: Am. Asn. of Univ. Profs; Colo. Fedn. of Teachers (v.pres); pres, Denver Fedn. of Teachers, 63-65. Wall Street J. Fellow; Nat. Defense Educ. Act Scholarship; Outstanding Teacher Nominee. Rel: Jewish; Bd. mem, Temple Emanuel. Mailing Add: 875 S. Jersey, Denver, Colo. 80220.

ROTHWELL, ANGUS BERNARD

Exec. Dir, State Coordinating Coun. for Higher Educ, Wis.

b. Superior, Wis, 7/25/05; s. John Z. Rothwell and Eva C. Barton R; m. 8/8/27 to Florence M. Jones; c. William Stanley, Jean Ann (Mrs. Wm. Olson) and Marilyn Gail (Mrs. E. L. Geraldson). Educ: Wis. State Univ, B.A, 30; Columbia Univ, M.A, 32; Phi Delta Kappa. Hon. M.A, Lawrence Col, 45; LL.D, Carroll Col, 62. Polit. & Govt. Pos: State supt. of pub. instr, Wis, 61-66; exec. dir, State Coordinating Coun. for Higher Educ, currently. Bus. & Prof. Pos: Elem. sch. prin, Wausau, Wis, 26-34; curriculum dir, Superior, 34-35, high sch. prin, 35-41; supt. of schs, bd. of educ, Superior, 41-49, Manitowoc, 49-61. Mil. Serv: Entered as Lt, Navy, 43, released as Lt. Comdr, 46. Publ: Several articles in Wis. J. of Educ, Am. Sch. Bd. J. and Nations Schs, 35- Mem: Bd. of dirs, Coun. of Chief State Sch. Officers; pres, Wis. Asn. Sch. Admin, 57; pres, Wis. Educ. Asn, 55; chmn, Nat. Safety Cmn; Nat. Cmt. for Safety Educ; Nat. Educ. Asn; Mason; Shrine; v.chmn, Nat. Conf. of Christians and Jews. Rel: Presbyterian. Legal Res: 4429 Rolla Lane, Madison, Wis. 53711. Mailing Add: 732 N. Midvale Blvd, Madison, Wis. 53705.

ROTHWELL, ROBERT L. (LEE) D

V.Chmn, Grant Co. Dem. Cent. Cmt, Nebr.

b. Hyannis, Nebr, 6/15/19; s. George W. Rothwell and Gladys N. Crouch R; m. 2/27/43 to Ann T. Yockey; c. Robert G, John H, Rick T, George A. and Lynne Ann. Educ: Univ. Nebr, B.Sc. in Agr, 40; Kappa Sigma; Block and Bridle Club. Polit. & Govt. Pos: Co. cmnr, Nebr, 59-57; mem, Exten. Bd, 50 & 66; v.chmn, Grant Co. Dem. Cent. Cmt, 50-; pres, Sandhills Fire Protection Dist, 58-66; secy, Grant Co. Weed Dist, 66. Mil. Serv: Entered as Pvt, Army Air Corps, 42, released as 1st Lt, 45. Mem: Nebr. Stock Growers Asn; Grant Co. Agr. Stabilization & Conserv. Serv. Cmt, Educ. Serv. Unit 16; Mason; Elks; Am. Legion; Scottish Rite; Sandhills C. of C.(pres). Mailing Add: Hyannis, Nebr. 69350.

ROTONDO, JOHN LOUIS D

Co-Chmn, Second Dist. Dem. Cent. Cmt, Calif.

b. Hoboken, N.J, 10/2/13; s. Joseph Rotondo and Josephine Tabino R; m. 3/1/62 to Dora Mae Demorest; c. Gina Genelle. Educ: Lodi Sch. of Bus, N.J, 33-34. Polit. & Govt. Pos: Mem, Mariposa Co. Dem. Cent. Cmt, Calif, 65-67 and chmn, 67-; mem, Calif. State Dem. Cent. Cmt, 66; co-chmn, Second Dist. Dem. Cent. Cmt, 67- Bus. & Prof. Pos: Pres, Usona Develop. Corp, Mariposa, Calif, 59-61 & 62-; dir, Mariposa Co. Parks & Recreation Dept, 59- Mil. Serv: Entered as A/S, Navy, 42, released as MM 3/C, 45, after serv. in 95th C.B. Bn, Pac, Theatre, 43-45; Am. Theatre Victory Medal; Asiatic Pac. Medal with 3 Stars. Mem: Am. Park & Recreation Soc; Calif. Park & Recreation Soc.(v.pres, Dist. V, 69); Recreation Adv. Cmt, Calif. Supvrs. Asn; VFW; Am. Legion; Lions; C. of C. Rel: Catholic. Legal Res: Smith Rd, Mariposa, Calif. 95338. Mailing Add: P.O. Box 278, Mariposa, Calif. 95338.

ROUDEBUSH, RICHARD L. R

U.S. Rep, Ind.

b. Noblesville, Ind, 1/18/18; s. Roy L. Roudebush and Mae R; m. to Marjorie Elliott; c. Karen and Roy. Educ: Butler Univ, B.S. in bus. admin, 41; Sigma Chi. Polit. & Govt. Pos: U.S. Rep, Ind, 60-, mem, House Cmts. on Sci. and Astronaut. and Un-Am. Activities; chmn, Vet. Div, Rep. Nat. Cmt; mem, Ind. Rep. Speakers Bur. Bus. & Prof. Pos: Former partner, Roudebush Cmn. Co, Indianapolis, Ind. Mil. Serv: Army, 41-44, serv. in Mid. East, N.Africa and Italy; 5 Battle Stars. Mem: Nat. Comdr, VFW, 57-58, Nat. Chief of Staff, 54, State Comdr, 53-54, Dept. Serv, Officer, 8 years, State Legis. Chmn, 3 years. and State Poppy Chmn, 5 years; pres, Gr. D.C. area, Butler Univ. Alumni Club; Am. Legion; DAV; Amvets; Eagles; Mason; Scottish Rite; Shrine; Kiwanis; Farm Bur; Nat. Farm Orgn; Elks; past Nat. Comdr, 376th Bomb Group Vet. Asn. Cited by Fed. Bur. Invest. Dir. J. Edgar Hoover and numerous groups, including Am. for Constitutional Action and Civic Affairs Asn. Rel: Rufuge Christian Church. Mailing Add: R.R. 3, Box 23-A, Noblesville, Ind. 46060.

ROULIER, LEON 'PENNY' D

Secy-Treas, Thomas Co. Dem. Cent. Cmt, Kans.

b. Campbell, Nebr, 2/18/04; s. Dolor Roulier and Bernadette Choquette R; m. 1/19/35 to Margaret Grace Souders; c. Leon E, Robert R. and Jay C. Educ: Univ. Nebr, LL.B, 31; Phi Alpha Delta. Polit. & Govt. Pos: Dem. chmn, Sixth Dist, Kans; Thomas Co. attorney; Colby city attorney; chmn, Thomas Co. Dem. Cent. Cmt, 36-48, secy-treas, 48-; del, Dem. Nat. Conv, 44, 48, 52 & 64; mem, Kans. Bd. of Regents, 59-63. Mem: Dist. gov, Lions Int, 39-40; pres, Colby Lions, 37-38; pres, Colby C. of C; Colby Country Club; Goodland Elks. Rel: Catholic. Legal Res: 320 N. Garfield, Colby, Kans. 67701. Mailing Add: 145 W. Fifth St, Colby, Kans. 67701.

ROUNDS, EDWIN FREDERICK R

b. Sundance, Wyo, 5/9/87; s. Frederick Edwin Rounds and Florence Ballard R; m. 6/29/16 to Grace Gibson; c. Helen (Mrs. Hankins), Edwin Gibson and Donald Junior. Educ: Carney Nebr. Military Col; Episcopal Sch; Omaha Bus. Col. Polit. & Govt. Pos: Chmn, Crook Co. Rep. Cent. Cmt, Wyo, 26-66; U.S. Cmnr. for over 10 yrs; mem, Wyo. Bd. of Commerce and Indust. Bus. & Prof. Pos: Cashier, Sundance State Bank Inc. for 21 yrs; pres, Security Trust and Title Co, Sundance, 10 yrs; local agent for Continental Oil Co. for over 30 yrs; real estate broker for over 10 yrs; Ins. agent for over 50 yrs. Mem: Mason; Consistory, Shriner. Rel: Episcopal. Mailing Add: Sundance, Wyo. 82729.

ROUNDTREE, WILLIAM H. D

b. Waldo, Fla, 7/30/21; m. to Wanda Waggoner R; c. Wanda Sharon, William Steven, Dean Lea. Educ: George Washington Univ; Loyola Law Sch, LL.B; Phi Alpha Delta. Polit. & Govt. Pos: Fla. State Rep, 64-66; chmn, Brevard Co. Dem. Exec. Cmt, 62-64; Legal Asst. Off. of Attorney Gen, State of Calif. Bus. & Prof. Pos: Attorney. Mil. Serv: Navy, 41-53, A/S to Lt; Naval Aviator; Air Medal. Mem: Cocoa Elks Club; Dir, Acad. of Fla. Trial Lawyers. Rel: Baptist. Mailing Add: 7 Bellair Arcade, Box 1690, Cocoa, Fla. 32922 (1967)

ROUNTREE, HERBERT HORTON D

b. Farmville, N.C, 5/5/21; s. Charles Stanley Rountree and Madeline V. Horton R; m. 5/12/46 to Helen Elizabeth Lotz; c. Kathryn, Dorene, Charles S, III and Mary Helen. Educ: Univ. N.C, A.B, 43; Univ. N.C. Law Sch, LL.B, 50; Delta Theta Phi. Polit. & Govt. Pos: Solicitor, Pitt Co. Recorder's Court, N.C, 51-53; cmnr, Farmville, 55-57; mem. loan cmt, State Employers Credit Union, 58-62; asst. attorney gen, State of N.C, 59-62; mem, Gov. Indust. Financing Study Group and N.C. Judicial Coun, 61-62; N.C. State Rep, Pitt Co, 67-69, mem, Salvation Army Adv. Bd. and mem, N.C. Courts Cmn, 69. Mil. Serv: Entered as Aviation Cadet, Navy, 43, released as Lt.(jg), 46, after serv. in Pac, 45-46; Am. and Pac. Theater Ribbons. Mem: Farmville Masonic Lodge 517, New Bern Consistory 3, AASR, Sudan Temple, AAONMS of New Bern, N.C; Farmville Am. Legion Post 151; Greenville Lodge 885, Moose; Greenville Lodge 1645 Elks; Burnette-Rouse Post 9081, VFW; Pitt Co. Scottish Rite and Shrine Clubs. Rel: Episcopal. Mailing Add: 1209 Drexel Lane, Greenville, N.C. 27834.

ROUNTREE, WILLIAM M.

U.S. Ambassador to S.Africa

b. Swainsboro, Ga, 3/28/17; m. to Suzanne McDowall; c. Susan. Educ: Columbus Univ, LL.B, 41. Polit. & Govt. Pos: Acct-auditor, U.S. Treas. Dept, 35-41; budget officer, Off. of Lend-Lease Admin, 41-42; asst. to dir, Am. Econ. Opers, Mid. East, 42-45; Career officer, U.S. Dept. of State For. Serv, 46-, econ. adv. Bur. of Near East, S.Asian and African Affairs, 46-47; spec. asst. to Am. Ambassador to Greece, 47-49; dir. and dep. dir, Off. of Greek, Turkish and Iranian Affairs, 49-52; counselor, Ankara, 52-53; minister counselor, Tehran, 53-55; dep. asst. secy. for Near East, S.Asian and African Affairs, 55-56, asst. secy, 56-58; asst. secy. for Near East. and S.Asian Affairs, 58-59; U.S. Ambassador to Pakistan, 59-62, Sudan, 62-65 and S.Africa, 65- Superior Serv. Award, 52; Nat. Civil Serv. League Career Serv. Award, 57. Mailing Add: U.S. Embassy, Pretoria, S.Africa.

ROURKE, RUSSELL ARTHUR R

b. New York, N.Y. 12/30/31; s. Francis Xavier Rourke and Ethel Johnson R; m. 10/14/61 to Judith Anne Muller; c. Patricia Anne and Elizabeth. Educ: Univ. Md, B.A, 53; Georgetown Univ. Law Sch, LL.B, 59; Delta Theta Phi; Pi Sigma Alpha; Sigma Chi. Polit. & Govt. Pos: Admin. asst. to U.S. Rep. John R. Pillion, 61-64 and U.S. Rep. Henry P. Smith, III, 65- Bus. & Prof. Pos: Law clerk, Keogh, Carey and Costello, 59. Mil. Serv: Entered as Officer Cand, Marine Corps, 53, released as 1st Lt, 56, after serv. in 1st Marine Aircraft Wing, Korea, 55; Maj, Marine Corps Res, 55-; Nat. Defense Serv. Medal. Mem: D.C. Bar Asn; Ky. State Bar Asn; Capitol Hill Chap, Fed Bar Asn; Univ. of Md. Alumni Asn; Marine Corps Reserve Officers Asn;. Fifth Dist. Rep. Club, Md. Rel: Roman Catholic. Mailing Add: R.F.D. 6, 1629 Ridout Rd, Annapolis, Md. 21401.

ROUSE, ALLAN PRESTON R

Mem, Sacramento City Coun, Calif.

b. Sacramento, Calif, 12/27/20; s. Willard P. Rouse and Ruth Garrison R; m. 6/18/49 to Sue M. Ennis; c. Randolph, Russell, Margaret and Allison. Educ: Univ. Ore, B.S, 46; Alpha Delta Sigma; Alpha Tau Omega. Polit. & Govt. Pos: Mem, Sacramento City Coun, Calif, 66- Mil. Serv: Entered as Pvt, Air Force, 42, released as Cpl, 46, after serv. in ETO; Six Battle Stars. Mem: Nat. Asn. Real Estate Editors; Rotary; Univ. Club; Commonwealth Club; Mason. Rel: Protestant. Mailing Add: 6160 Fordham Way, Sacramento, Calif. 95831.

ROUSE, ELIENE WILHELMINA R

Mem. Exec. Cmt, Mich. State Rep. Cent. Cmt.

b. Traverse City, Mich, 10/20/18; d. John Oscar Lyon and Eleanora Elfofson L; m. 4/29/38 to Arthur Kennedy Rouse; c. Lavern Clark, Arthur Kennedy, Jr. and Kristin Kae (Mrs. Shassberger). Educ: Traverse City High Sch, grad.

Polit. & Govt. Pos: V.chmn, Charlevoix Co. Rep. Party, 57-63 and acting chmn, 62; mem. finance cmt, Mich. State Rep. Cent. Cmt, 62-63 and mem. exec. cmt, 63-; del, Rep. Nat. Conv, 64. Mem: PTA (secy, 57); mem. bd, Commun. Chest; secy, Child's Study Club, 54 and pres, 56; C. of C. (mem bd). Rel: Presbyterian. Mailing Add: 521 S. Park St, Boyne City, Mich. 49712. (1967)

ROUSE, FREDERICK OAKES R
Chmn, St. Clair Co. Rep. Cmt, Mich.
b. Bay City, Mich, 4/10/26; s. Frederick Oliver Rouse and Margaret Oakes R; m. 9/22/51 to Barbara Ellen Henry; c. Stephen, Mary and John. Educ: Port Huron Jr. Col, A.A, 48; Univ. Mich, 48-49; Olivet Col, B.A. in Econ, 51; Scabbard and Blade; pres, Phi Alpha Pi, 50. Polit. & Govt. Pos: Precinct worker and del, Co. Conv, 58-67; chmn, City of St. Clair Rep. Party, 60-63; mem, St. Clair Co. Bd. of Supvrs, Mich, 61-67; del, Rep. State Conv, 61-67 and chmn, 65; chmn, St. Clair Co. Rep. Cmt, Mich, 63-; del, Rep. Nat. Conv, 68; Mich. dep. co. chmn, currently. Bus. & Prof. Pos: Gen. sales mgr, Marysville Printing Co, 56-58; sales rep, Esterling Tri-Craft Press, Inc, 58-61; v.pres. sales and mem. bd. dirs, Gilson Press, 61-64; exec. v.pres, gen. mgr. and mem. bd. dirs, Indust. Printing Corp, 64- Mil. Serv: Entered as Pvt, Army Air Force, 44, released as Cpl, 46, after serv. in Ninth Air Force, ETO, 44-46; Good Conduct Medal; ETO and Am. Theatre Ribbons; Victory Medal; Army of Occup. Medal. Mem: Adcraft Club of Detroit; Graphic Arts Asn. of Mich; Rotary; Elks; Boy Scouts (chmn. coun. adv. cmt. and mem. exec. bd, Blue Water Coun); Eagle Scout; Am. Legion. Rel: Episcopal. Mailing Add: 729 N. Riverside Ave, St. Clair, Mich. 48079. (1967)

ROUSE, LeGRAND ARIAIL, II D
b. Spartanburg, S.C, 6/11/33; s. LeGrand Rouse and Virginia Ariail R; m. 8/23/58 to Patricia Adelle White; c. LeGrand Ariail, III, Laurie Adelle and Daniel Morris. Educ: Wofford Col, A.B. in hist, 54; Univ. S.C, LL.B, 59; Am. Univ, M.A. in govt, 69; Blue Key; Pi Gamma Mu; Sigma Alpha Epsilon; Phi Alpha Delta. Polit. & Govt. Pos: S.C. State Rep, 61-64; assoc. counsel, Sub Cmt. on Judicial Improv, U.S. Senate Judiciary Cmt, 63; prfnl. staff mem, U.S. Senate Post Off. & Civil Serv. Cmt, 64-68; regional v.pres, S.C. Young Dem. Clubs, 63-64; del, S.C. State Dem. Conv, 64; alternate del, Dem. Nat. Conv, 64. Bus. & Prof. Pos: Attorney, LeGrand A. Rouse, II, 60-64 & 68-; instr. bus. law, Univ. S.C, Spartanburg Br, 68; civics teacher, Woodruff Jr. High Sch, 68- Mil. Serv: Entered as 2nd Lt, Army, 55, released as 1st Lt, 57, after serv. in 36th Armored Inf. Bn, 3rd Armored Div, ETO; Capt, Army Res, 61-68. Mem: Spartanburg Co. and Am. Bar Asns; St. Johns Lodge 333 F&AM; SAR; WOW; Wofford Col. Alumni Asn; U.S. Senate Staff Club; Univ. S.C. Alumni Asn. Rel: Methodist. Mailing Add: 104 Monroe Rd, Spartanburg, S.C. 29302.

ROUSH, J. EDWARD D
b. Barnsdal, Okla, 9/12/20; s. Herman A. Roush and Eva B. Fisher R; m. 9/5/43 to Pauline Borton; c. David, Joel, Melody and Robin. Educ: Huntington Col, A.B, 42; Ind. Univ. Sch. Law, LL.B, 49; Phi Delta Phi. Polit. & Govt. Pos: Ind. State Rep, 49-50; prosecuting attorney, Huntington Co, 55-59; U.S. Rep, Fifth Dist, 59-68; del, Dem. Nat. Conv, 68. Bus. & Prof. Pos: Mem. bd. trustees, Huntington Col, 49- Mil. Serv: Entered as Pvt, Army, 42, released as Capt, 46, after serv. in combat in Europe with 99th Inf. Div; recalled to active duty, 50, released, 52; Maj, Army Res; Combat Inf. Badge; Bronze Star Medal; 2 Battle Stars; Am. Theater, European Theater, Victory and Army of Occupation Ribbons. Mem: Am. and Ind. Bar Asns; pres, Huntington Co. Bar Asn, 53; Am. Legion; VFW; Kiwanis. Rel: United Brethren in Christ. Mailing Add: 2340 College Ave, Huntington, Ind. 46750.

ROUSHAR, VICTOR THOMAS R
Secy, Montrose Co. Rep. Assembly, Colo.
b. Torrington, Wyo, 8/4/37; s. Joseph Manus Roushar and Ida Maurine Hooper R; m. 6/30/59 to Susan Jane Vetesk; c. Penny Patricia, Bradley Brian and Rodney Richard. Educ: Univ. Denver, B.S, 62, LL.B, 64; Phi Alpha Delta. Polit. & Govt. Pos: Secy, Montrose Co. Rep. Assembly, Colo, 69- Mem: Montrose Co, Colo, Seventh Judicial and Am. Bar Asns; Am. Trial Lawyers Asn; Elks. Rel: Episcopal. Legal Res: 111 Spruce Dr, Montrose, Colo. 81401. Mailing Add: P.O. Box 327, Montrose, Colo. 81401.

ROUSSE, JEANNE LAURA D
Secy. and Treas, Williamstown Dem. Town Cmt, Vt.
b. Williamstown, Vt, 2/7/16; d. Hormidas J. Rousse and Laura Longchamp R; single. Educ: Holy Ghost Convent, 30. Polit. & Govt. Pos: State committeeman, Vt. Dem. Party, 25 years; secy. to Secy. of State, Vt, 65 and Dep. Secy. of State, 65-69; secy. and treas, Williamstown Dem. Town Cmt, 68-; secy, State Legis. Coun, Vt, 69; asst, Coordinator title IV prog, Free Pub. Libr, 69- Bus. & Prof. Pos: Clerk, cert. div, Rock of Ages Corp, 42-65; local news reporter, Times-Argus, Barre, Vt, 12 years. Mem: Altrusa; Canadian Club; Red Cross vol, Cent. Vt. Hosp, Berlin. Good Neighbor Award, 55; Women Doers Award, Wash-Orange Co. Dem. Women's Club, 67; Bishop Fund Appeal Cert. for active participation in Diocesan prog. for charities and develop, 68. Rel: Catholic. Legal Res: Cogswell, Williamstown, Vt. 05654. Mailing Add: Graniteville, Vt. 05654.

ROUSSELOT, JOHN HARBIN R
b. Los Angeles, Calif, 11/1/27; s. Harbin Michon Rousselot and Mary Gibson R; m. 7/29/50 to Marilyn W. Cooper; c. Craig Nobel, Robin Lee and Wendy Gibson. Educ: Principia Col, B.A. in Polit. Sci. & Bus. Admin, 49. Polit. & Govt. Pos: Mem, Los Angeles Co. Rep. Cent. Cmt, Calif. and v.chmn, 55-58; del, Rep. Nat. Conv. and pres, Calif. Young Rep, 56; mem. exec. cmt, State Rep. Cent. Cmt, Calif, 56-57 & 60-61; U.S. Rep, 25th Dist, Calif, 61-63. Bus. & Prof. Pos: Owner and pub. rels. consult, John H. Rousselot & Assocs, 54-58; nat. dir. pub. info, Fed. Housing Admin, 58-60; nat. dir. pub. rels, John Birch Soc, 63-66; publisher, Am. Opinion Mag, 64-; mgt. consult, 67- Mem: Nat. Press Club; Capitol Hill Soc; Pub. Rels. Soc. of Am. Rel: Church of Christ, Scientist. Mailing Add: 1534 Wembley Rd, San Marino, Calif. 91108.

ROUTON, BONNIE ANTHONY R
Finance Chairwoman, Hempstead Co. Rep. Cmt, Ark.
b. Murfreesboro, Ark, 1/15/30; d. Graydon William Anthony and Nina Nelms A; m. 3/27/49 to William Ralph Routon; c. William Ralph, Stephen Anthony, Jane Marie and John Graydon Nelms. Educ: Monticello Col, 47-49; Henderson State Teachers Col, 49-51. Polit. & Govt. Pos: Charter mem, Hempstead Co. Rep. Women, Ark, 53; cmt. chmn, Hempstead Rep. Women, 60-69; finance chmn, Hempstead Co. Rep. Cmt, 66 & 69, campaign mgr, 66-68, finance chairwoman, 68-; alternate del, Rep. Nat. Conv, 68; sponsor, TAR, 69. Bus. & Prof. Pos: Reporter, Hope J, 49; asst. to coordinator, Hope Pub. Schs, 50-51. Mem: Ark. Arts Center; Hempstead Co. Rep. Women; Hope Country Club; Great Decisions; PTA; Daffodil Garden Club; Hope Duplicate Bridge; Nat. Asn. Jr. Auxiliaries. Rel: Methodist. Mailing Add: 601 E. 14th, Hope, Ark. 71801.

ROVANG, JOHN O. D
b. Bryant, S.Dak, 6/24/91; s. Ole Thompson Rovang and Thora Berg R; m. 8/19/17 to Anna Martha Knudtson; c. Mae Darline (Mrs. William Shortt), Lola Arline (Mrs. Kenneth Yeend), Dona Marie (Mrs. John Norton) and Shirley Rosemand (Mrs. Jim Rutledge). Educ: Brookings Col, 1 year. Polit. & Govt. Pos: Chmn, Hamlin Co. Dem. Party, S.Dak, 65-69; alternate del, Dem. Nat. Conv, 68. Bus. & Prof. Pos: Dir, Opdahl Fire & Lightning Ins. Co, 22-50, secy, 50-69; agent, Austin Mutual Ins. Co, Minneapolis, Minn, 25-69. Mem: Am. Automobile Asn; Farmers Union. Rel: Lutheran. Mailing Add: Bryant, S.Dak. 57221.

ROWAN, CARL THOMAS Independent
b. Ravenscroft, Tenn, 8/11/25; s. Thomas David Rowan and Johnnie Bradford R; m. 8/2/50 to Vivien Louise Murphy; c. Barbara, Carl Thomas and Geoffrey. Educ: Tenn. State Univ, 42-43; Washburn Univ, 43-44; Oberlin Col, A.B, 47; Univ. Minn, M.A, 48. Hon. Litt.D, Simpson Col, 57, Hamline Univ, 58, Oberlin Col, 62, Col. Wooster, 68 and Drexel Inst. Tech, 69; L.H.D, Washburn Univ, 64, Talledega Col, 65, St. Olaf Col. and Knoxville Col, 66; LL.D, Howard Univ, Alfred Univ. and Temple Univ, 64, Atlanta Univ, 65, Allegheny Col, 66 and Colby Col, 69; D.P.A, Morgan State Col, 64; Elijah P. Lovejoy Fel, Colby Col, 68. Polit. & Govt. Pos: Dep. asst. secy. of state for pub. affairs, Dept. of State, 61-63; U.S. Ambassador to Finland, 63-64; dir, U.S. Info. Agency, 64-65. Bus. & Prof. Pos: Copywriter, Minneapolis Tribune, 48-50; staff writer, 50-61; columnist, Chicago Daily News, Publ. Newspaper Syndicate, 65- Publ: South of Freedom, 52; The Pitiful and the Proud, 56; Go South to Sorrow, 57. Received Sidney Hillman award for best newspaper reporting, 52; citation for journalistic achievement, curators of Lincoln Univ, Mo, 52; selected one of ten outstanding young men of Am, U.S. Jr. C. of C, 54; award for best gen. reporting on segregation cases pending before U.S. Supreme Court, Sigma Delta Chi, 54; Am. Teamwork Award, Nat. Urban League, 55; for. correspondents medallion for articles on India, 55, for. correspondents medallion for articles on S.E. Asia, covering Bandung Conf, 56; Distinguished Achievement Award, Regents, Univ. Minn, 61; Golden Ruler award, Phila. Fel. Cmn, 61; commun. award in human rels, Antidefamation League, B'nai B'rith, 64; Contributions to Am. Democracy award, Roosevelt Univ, 64; Distinguished Serv. Award, Capital Press Club, 64; Nat. Brotherhood Award, Nat. Conf. Christians and Jews, 64; Am. South. Regional Press Inst. award, 65; Liberty Bell award, Howard Univ, 65. Mailing Add: 2832 Ellicott St. N.W, Washington, D.C. 20008.

ROWAN, ROBERT A. 'BOBBY' D
Ga. State Sen.
b. Nashville, Ga, 11/17/35; s. James Alvin Rowan and Lois Vickers R; m. 12/21/58 to Retha Amelia McMillan; c. Ferris Marie. Educ: Abraham Baldwin Agr. Col, 58; Univ. Ga, B.S, 58. Polit. & Govt. Pos: Ga. State Sen, Eighth Dist, 63- Bus. & Prof. Pos: Farmer; sch. teacher. Mil. Serv: Army, Sgt. 6 months active duty; Nat. Guard, 4½ years. Mem: Pres, Enigma Farm Bur. Rel: Baptist. Mailing Add: Enigma, Ga. 31749. (1967)

ROWE, EDMUND 'ED' R
b. Sherrodsville, Ohio, 12/20/92; s. William James and Phoebe Boulding J; m. to Mary Edna Wellen, wid; c. Mary Elizabeth, Edmund and Nell Ruth. Polit. & Govt. Pos: Mem. city coun, Akron, Ohio, 28-31, 34-35 & 38-42, pres, 42; U.S. Rep, Ohio, 43-44; Ohio State Rep, 55-58. Mem: Mason (32°), Consistory, Shriners, Grotto and other Masonic bodies. Rel: United Church of Christ. Mailing Add: 863 Delia Ave, Akron, Ohio 44320.

ROWE, HARRIS R
Chmn, Morgan Co. Rep. Cent. Cmt.
b. Jacksonville, Ill, 1923; m. to Alice Mary R; c. Sally, Mary and Millicent. Educ: Ill. Col; Northwest. Univ. Law Sch. Polit. & Govt. Pos: Alderman, Jacksonville, Ill, 8 years; Ill. State Rep, formerly; chmn, Morgan Co. Rep. Cent. Cmt. and mem, Ill. Rep. State Cent. Cmt, currently. Bus. & Prof. Pos: Attorney and ins. exec. Mem: Chmn, Morgan Co. Polio Found; past pres, Kiwanis; Mason; Elks; Am. Legion; Amvets. Rel: Presbyterian. Mailing Add: 110 N. East St, Jacksonville, Ill. 62650. (1967)

ROWE, HORTENSE C. MILLIGAN R
V.Chmn, Rep. Party, V.I.
b. Frederiksted, St. Croix, V.I, 10/21/38; d. Hugh Milligan and Marie Sackey M; div; c. Marc Alyn. Educ: Inter-Am. Univ, P.R, B.A, 62; Caribbean Orgn. Polit. & Govt. Pos: Acct, V.I. Corp, V.I. Dept. Interior, 62-64; v.chmn, Rep. Party, V.I, 68- Bus. & Prof. Pos: Acct. and off. mgr, Harvlan, Inc, 64-; acct, Andreas Esberg & Co, 68- Mem: Bus. and Prfnl. Women's Club (treas, 64-66, v.pres, 66-68, pres, 68-69); Fedn. Bus. & Prfnl. Women's Clubs (v.pres, 69-); Friends of Denmark Soc; St. Croix Commun. Theatre; Island Center. Rel: Roman Catholic. Legal Res: King St, Frederiksted, St. Croix, V.I. 00840. Mailing Add: P.O. Box 194, Frederiksted, St. Croix, V.I. 00840.

ROWE, MRS. JAMES HENRY, JR. D
b. Salisbury, Md, 1/12/12; d. Leon S. Ulman and Lilly Hawkins U; m. 9/6/37 to James Henry Rowe, Jr; c. Elizabeth, Clarissa, James Henry, III. Educ: Bryn Mawr Col, A.B, 33. Polit. & Govt. Pos: Chmn, Nat. Capital Planning Cmn, 61-, Mem, 61; Co-Chmn, Inaugural Parade, 61; Mem, D.C. Auditorium Cmn, 55-58; Campaign Aide, Dem. Nat. Cmt, 52-56, 40; Mem, Mrs. Johnson's Cmt. for More Beautiful Nat. Capital; Exec. Secy, Washington Br. ILO, 43-49; with Nat. Inst. Pub. Affairs, 34-35. Bus. & Prof. Pos: Women's Page Ed, United Mine Workers Jour, 35-37. Mem: Chatham Beach Clubs (Mass.); Tennis Club. Mailing Add: 3207 Highland Pl, Washington, D.C. 20008. (1967)

ROWE, JOHN L. D
b. Oconomowoc, Wis, 5/18/14; s. Alfred Augustus Rowe (deceased) and Abigail Erickson R.(deceased); single. Educ: Wis. State Univ, Whitewater, B.Ed, 35; State Univ. Iowa, M.A, 39; Teachers Col, Columbia Univ, Ed.D, 46; Sigma Tau Delta; Pi Omega Pi; Phi Delta Kappa; Kappa Delta Pi; Delta Pi Epsilon; Theta Chi. Polit. & Govt. Pos: Mem, Gov. Cmn. for Crippled Children, N.Dak, 66-69; del, Dem. Nat. Conv, 68; Rep. precinct committeeman, Grand Forks, N.Dak, 68-69; mem. adv. cmt, State Bd. of Voc. Educ, N.Dak, 69. Bus. & Prof. Pos: Regent, Mary Col, Bismarck, N.Dak, currently. Publ: World Economic Geography, Southwest. Pub. Co, 50; Gregg Typewriting for Colleges, 57, revised, 63 and Gregg Typing for High Schools, second ed, 58, revised 59 & 64, McGraw-Hill. Mem: Am. Voc. Asn; Nat. and Cath. Bus. Educ. Asns; Elks; Citizens Cmt. for Grand Forks Symphony Orchestra. Named Distinguished Univ. Prof; Recipient of Univ. N.Dak. Distinguished Serv. Award; Wis. Bus. Educ. Asn. Distinguished Alumnus, Wis. State Univ. Rel: Catholic. Mailing Add: 2515 Olson Dr, Grand Forks, N.Dak. 58201.

ROWE, MARIE RICH R
Pres, N.C. Fedn. of Rep. Women
b. Rock Hill, S.C, 5/19/08; d. William Thomas Rich and Ennis Culler R; m. 1/1/28 to Oliver Reagan Rowe; c. O. Reagan, Jr, Lynda (Mrs. Rankin) and Ralph Burnett (deceased). Educ: Univ. N.C, Greensboro, 25-28; Univ. N.C, Chapel Hill, B.S. in Pub. Admin, 34; Adelphian Soc. Polit. & Govt. Pos: Cand, N.C. State Rep, 58; pres, Mecklenburg Co. Rep. Women's Club, 58-60; precinct committeewoman, Mecklenburg Co. Rep. Party, 58-68 and v.chmn. for spec. events, 68 & 69; mem, Eisenhower's Cmt. of 44 on Prog. and Progress, 59; dist. rep, N.C. Fedn. of Rep. Women, 60-64, area v.pres, 64-68, pres-elect, 68 and pres, 69-; alternate del-at-lg, Rep. Nat. Conv, 68; mem, Mayor's Cmt. City Develop. of a Govt. Center, 68; mem, N.C. Rep. State Cent. Cmt, 68-69; N.C. state chmn, Nixon's Cultural and Fine Arts Cmt, 68-69. Mem: Pres, Mecklenburg Co. Alumnae Asn, Univ. N.C, Greensboro and chmn, Solicitation of Alumnae Funds; Mecklenburg Co. chmn, Teen-Age Summer Employ; Am. Asn. Univ. Women; YWCA; life mem, Charity League, Inc; League of Women Voters; Salvation Army Women's Auxiliary; life mem, Women's Soc. Christian Serv; United Church Women. Rel: Methodist; Bd. Dirs, Myers Park United Methodist Church. Mailing Add: 2823 Providence Rd, Charlotte, N.C. 28211.

ROWE, ROY D
b. Burgaw, N.C, 5/29/05; s. Nicholas Henry Rowe and Mary Belle King R; m. 2/22/29 to Nina Lavinia Worsley; c. Tonia and Roy, Jr. Educ: Univ. N.C; Carolina Indust. Sch, Pender Co; Vanceboro Farm Life Sch; Theatre Mgr. Sch, N.Y.C, 31. Polit. & Govt. Pos: N.C. State Sen, 37, 41, 45, 49, 57 & 63-66; N.C. State Rep, 43; chmn, N.C. Aeronaut. Cmn, 43-49; prin. clerk, N.C. Senate, 69- Bus. & Prof. Pos: Farmer; motel owner and operator; real estate. Mil. Serv: Maj, N.C. Wing, Civil Air Patrol, 44-47. Mem: Mason; King Solomon's Lodge 138; Burgaw; Rotary (past pres, Burgaw Club); pres, Theatre Owners of N. and S. Carolina, 34-44; pres, Carolina Aero Club, 42-44; pres, Asn. of Gov. Bd. of Univs. and Cols, 64. Rel: Unitarian Universalist. Mailing Add: Burgaw, N.C. 28425.

ROWELL, E. C. D
Fla. State Rep.
b. Oxford, Fla, 10/1/14; s. E. Cleveland Rowell and Edna Collier R; m. 11/15/43 to Marjorie Aylott; c. Barbara Catherine and Edna Diane. Educ: Univ. of Fla; Nat. Honor Soc. Polit. & Govt. Pos: Fla. State Rep, 56-, speaker, Fla. House of Rep, 64-66; dir, Fla. Govt, 69. Bus. & Prof. Pos: Owner, Sumter Finance, 58- Mil. Serv: Entered as Pvt, Air Force, 41, released as Sgt, 45, after serv. in 306th Bomb Wing, ETO. Mem: Mason; Scottish Rite; Bahia Temple Shrine; Am. Legion (past comdr); Lions; C. of C; pres, Sumter Co. Farm Bur; state dir, Fla. Farm Bur; chmn, Sumter Co. Polio Chap; Cattlemen's Asn. Rel: Baptist. Mailing Add: P.O. Box 191, Wildwood, Fla. 32785.

ROWELL, JAMES VICTOR R
S.C. State Rep.
b. Trio, S.C, 9/18/39; s. Ervin Robert Rowell and Hallie Boykin R; m. 7/27/63 to Pearl Casselman; c. Linda Karen. Educ: Univ. S.C, 3 years. Polit. & Govt. Pos: S.C. State Rep, 69- Bus. & Prof. Pos: Mgr, Rowell Bros, Trio, 62-66, owner, 66- Mem: Mason; Jr. C. of C. Rel: Methodist. Legal Res: Trio, S.C. 29595. Mailing Add: P.O. Box 55, Trio, S.C. 29595.

ROWEN, ELIZABETH GORE R
Women's V.Chmn, Marin Co. Rep. Cent. Cmt, Calif.
b. Marks, Miss, 1/30/20; d. Weaver Ellis Gore and Bessie Griffin G; m. 8/22/42 to James Alan Rowen; c. Diane (Mrs. Stephen R. Adams) and Patricia L. Educ: Hinds Jr. Col, Raymond, Miss, 2 years. Polit. & Govt. Pos: First Cong. Dist. dir, Calif. Rep. Assembly, 65 & 66 and dir-at-lg, 69; assoc. mem, Calif. State Rep. Cent. Cmt, 67 and mem, 68-69; precinct chmn, Marin Co. Rep. Cent. Cmt, 67-68 and women's v.chmn, 69- Mem: Am. Bus. Women's Asn; Eastern Star; Girl Scouts. Cert. of Appreciation, Girl Scouts, 61; Grand Cross of Colors, Order of Rainbow for Girls, 63; Selected as Woman of Year, Marin Charter Chap, Am. Bus. Women's Asn, 65. Rel: Protestant. Mailing Add: 360 Johnstone Dr, San Rafael, Calif. 94903.

ROWETT, ROBERT MELLEN R
Idaho State Sen.
b. Mountain Home, Idaho, 7/14/31; s. Victor Charles Rowett and Lottie Mellen R; m. 12/28/52 to Maxine Louise Miller; c. Victor Charles, Robert Mellen, Jr, Patricia Joann Rosemary. Educ: Univ. Idaho, B.S, 53, LL.B, 59; Delta Chi; Phi Alpha Delta. Polit. & Govt. Pos: V.chmn, Elmore Co. Rep. Cent. Cmt, 61; Idaho State Sen, Dist. 19, 66- Mil. Serv: Entered as 2nd Lt, Air Force, 54, released as 1st Lt, 56, after serv. in Alaskan Air Command; Capt, Air Force Res. Mem: Am. and Idaho Bar Asns; C. of C; Am. Legion; Mason; Shrine; Toastmasters. Distinguished Serv. Award, Mountain Home Jaycees. Rel: Episcopal. Mailing Add: 480 E. 6 N, Mountain Home, Idaho 83647.

ROWLAND, EMORY L. D
Ga. State Rep.
b. Wrightsville, Ga, 5/20/02; s. Willis David Rowland and Louanna Ivey R; m. 12/22/26 to Mary Hodges; c. Mary Virginia and Emory Hodges. Educ: Ga. Mil. Col. Polit. & Govt. Pos: Ordinary, Johnson Co, 31-36; Ga. State Rep, 41, 43-44 & 49-; solicitor, City Court of Wrightsville, 45-49. Bus. & Prof. Pos: Attorney, began practice 32. Mem: Mason. Rel: Methodist. Mailing Add: College St, Wrightsville, Ga. 31096. (1967)

ROWLAND, JOHN PATRICK R
b. El Monte, Calif, 7/12/37; s. Thomas A. Rowland and Erma M. Cole R; m. 6/3/61 to Virginia Annette Patton; c. Thomas A, Carrie A. and Colleen V. Educ: Univ. South. Calif, B.S, 59 and M.B.A, 60; Beta Gamma Sigma; Tau Kappa Epsilon; Pi Sigma Epsilon. Polit. & Govt. Pos: Admin. asst. to U.S. Rep. Charles E. Wiggins, Calif, 69- Bus. & Prof. Pos: Reporter, El Monte Herald, Calif, 58-60 and advert. prom. mgr, 60-61; mgr, El Monte-South El Monte C. of C, 61-67; dir. of cong. action, U.S. C. of C, Wash, D.C, 67-69. Mil. Serv: M/Sgt, PIO, Calif. Nat. Guard, 55-63. Mem: Cong. Secy. Club; K. of C; Boys Club San Gabriel Valley. Tom May Mkt. Award; Am. Mkt. Award; Young Man of the Year Award, El Monte, 63. Rel: Catholic. Mailing Add: 2315 Jackson Pkwy, Vienna, Va. 22180.

ROWLANDS, DAVID D.
b. Pittsburgh, Pa, 3/22/15; s. Charles Wilson Rowlands and Laura Isabelle Dickson R; m. 5/25/43 to Sarah B. Hamilton; c. David D, Jean Louise, Margaret Jane and John Hamilton. Educ: Westminster Col, A.B, 37; Univ. Chicago, M.A, 40. Polit. & Govt. Pos: Planning dir. and asst. to city mgr, Wichita, Kans, 45-48; city mgr, Mt. Lebannon, Pa, 49-52 and Eau Claire, Wis, 52-56; instr. tech. munic. admin, Inst. Training Munic. Adminstrs; mem, Gov. Retirement Study Cmn, 55 and Gov. Adv. Expenditure Coun, Wash, 58; city mgr, Tacoma, Wash, 56-; mem. cmn. nat. cmt. fire defense, Nat. League Cities, 59-62; Munic. Fire Defense Inst, 61-62; mem. exec. cmt, Puget Sound Govt. Conf; chmn, Gov. Commun. Serv. Adv. Cmt. on Title I Funds, 68-69. Mil. Serv: Capt, Army, World War II. Mem: Int. City Mgrs. Asn. (pres, 67); Am. Soc. Planning Officials; Munic. Finance Officers Asn; Rotary. Legal Res: 807 N. Yakima Ave, Tacoma, Wash. 98403. Mailing Add: County-City Bldg, Tacoma, Wash. 98402.

ROWLEY, EVELYN FISH R
Chmn, Morris Rep. Town Cmt, Conn.
b. Southington, Conn, 3/15/27; d. J. Hamilton Fish and Hazel Shepard F; m. 5/5/56 to James William Rowley; c. James E, 'Jed,' Eileen Harriet and Corinne Elizabeth. Educ: Univ. Conn, B.S, 49; Block & Bridle Club. Polit. & Govt. Pos: V.chmn, Morris Rep. Town Cmt, Conn, 64-66, chmn, 66-; del. or alternate del, cong, sen. or assembly dist. conv, 65, 66, 67 & 68; del, Conn. Rep. State Conv, 66, 67 & 68; mem, Litchfield Co. Rep. Orgn, currently. Mem: Pres, Morris Friendly Serv; secy, Morris Serv. Unit, Salvation Army; PTA; Episcopal Church Women; Univ. Conn. Alumni Asn; Sixth Cong. Dist. W. Rep. Women; Bethlehem Rep. Women's Club. Rel: Episcopal. Mailing Add: Straits Turnpike Lane, Morris, Conn. 06763.

ROY, CATHERINE H. R
V.Chmn, Pitkin Co. Rep. Party, Colo.
b. Springfield, Ill, 7/23/27; d. Ottis C. Moore and Catherine Hickox M; m. 10/24/47 to Robert Oliver Roy; c. Rob, Cynthia L, Barbara and Douglas. Educ: Mary Wash. Col, Univ. Va, 44; Lindenwood Col, 45-46; Univ. Illinois, cand, B.A. and M.A. Polit. & Govt. Pos: Rep. precinct committeewoman, Urbana, Ill, 49-50, Boulder, Colo, 53 and Aspen, 56-66; v.chmn, Pitkin Co. Rep. Party, Colo, 57-60 & 67-; v.chmn, Colo. Rep. State Cent. Cmt, 67-; chmn, Cmt. for Reorganization of Sch. Dists, 68-69. Bus. & Prof. Pos: Co-owner, Teenage Night Club, Aspen, 66-67. Mem: Past pres, Hosp. Benfit; PTA (past pres); League of Women Voters (co-founder, Aspen Chap); Citizens Adv. Cmt. for Schs; Aspen Ski Club; Aspen Chamber Visitors Bur. Rel: Episcopal. Legal Res: Castle Creek, Aspen, Colo. 81611. Mailing Add: Box 9, Aspen, Colo. 81611.

ROY, EDGAR J. D
N.H. State Rep.
b. 7/28/96; married; c. Eleven. Educ: Berlin High Sch, N.H. Polit. & Govt. Pos: Ward moderator, 10 years; councilman, 38-40; chief registr, 40; N.H. State Rep, 55-57 & 61- Bus. & Prof. Pos: Oil dealer. Mem: Charter mem, Joliette Club; Joliette Snow Shoe Club. Rel: Catholic. Mailing Add: 115 Madigan St, Berlin, N.H. 03570. (1967)

ROY, WENDELL P. D
b. East Barnet, Vt, 7/26/07; m. to Alice Blaisdell, wid. Educ: Univ. Vt, B.S. in elec. eng, 28. Polit. & Govt. Pos: Civil defense chmn, Barnet, Vt, several years, mem, town budget cmt, sch. dir, 3 years and town moderator, 63-; Vt. State Rep, 65-67. Bus. & Prof. Pos: Engr. Mil. Serv: Entered as Lt, Army Res, 28, released as Maj, 62, after active duty, 42-46. Mem: Odd Fellows; Grange; Reserve Officers Asn; VFW; Am. Legion. Rel: Protestant. Mailing Add: Barnet, Vt. 05821.

ROYALL, KENNETH CLAIBORNE D
b. Goldsboro, N.C, 7/24/94; s. George Royall and Clara Howard Jones R; m. 8/8/17 to Margaret Best; c. Kenneth Claiborne Jr. and Margaret (Mrs. James Evans Davis). Educ: Univ. N.C, A.B, 14; Harvard, LL.D, 17; Phi Beta Kappa. Polit. & Govt. Pos: N.C. State Sen. and author, N.C. Bank Liquidation Statute, 27; Presidential Elector, N.C, 40; counsel in saboteur case before spec. session, U.S. Supreme Court, 42; spec. asst. to Secy. of War, Serv. Overseas, 44-45; Undersecy. of War, 45, Secy. of War, 47; Secy. of Army, 47-49; mem, Presidential Racial Cmt, Birmingham, 63; del-at-lg, Dem. Nat. Conv, 64. Bus. & Prof. Pos: Assoc. ed, Harvard Law Rev, 15-17; admitted to N.C. Bar, 16; attorney-at-law, 19-31; law practice Raleigh and Goldsboro, N.C, 31-42; assoc, Dwight, Royall, Harris, Koegel & Caskey, 49-57, Royall, Koegel, Harris & Caskey, 58-61, Royall, Koegel & Rogers, 61-; trustee, John F. Kennedy Libr. Mil. Serv: 2nd Lt, Field Artil, 17-18, 1st Lt, overseas, 18-19, Col, Army, 42-43, Brig. Gen, 43-45; Distinguished Serv. Medal. Mem: Gen. Alumni Asn. of Univ. N.C, pres, 59-60; Am. and N.Y. Bar Asns; N.C. Bar Asn, pres, 29-30; Am. Law Inst; Delta Kappa Epsilon, hon. nat. pres, 48; Links, Blind Brook, Econ, Chevy Chase Burning Tree and Army-Navy Country Clubs. Rel: Episcopal. Mailing Add: 1040 Fifth Ave, New York, N.Y. 10028. (1967)

ROYALL, KENNETH CLAIBORNE, JR. D
N.C. State Rep.
b. Warsaw, N.C, 9/2/18; s. Kenneth Claiborne Royall and Margaret Pierce

Best R; m. 2/10/45 to Julia Bryan Zollicoffer; c. Kenneth C, III, Jere Zollicoffer and Julia Bryan. Educ: Univ. N.C, A.B, 40; Univ. Va. Law Sch, 40-41; Wake Forest Col. Law Sch, 41-42; Delta Kappa Epsilon. Polit. & Govt. Pos: Mem, Durham Co. Sch. Bd, 57-66, chmn, 59-66; N.C. State Rep, 67- Mil. Serv: Entered as Pvt, Marine Corps, 42, released as Maj, 45, after serv. in 2nd Bn, 3rd Marine Div, 21st Marine Corps, S.Pac; Bronze Star with V. Mem: Pres, Sales & Mkt. Execs, 59 and Durham Merchants Asn, 65; bd. of dirs, Durham C. of C, 62-64 & 65-67 and N.C. Merchants Asn, 66-67; South. Retail Furniture Asn; Rotary; Elks. Rel: Episcopal. Legal Res: 64 Beverly Dr, Durham, N.C. 27707. Mailing Add: P.O. Box 8766 F.H. Station, Durham, N.C. 27707.

ROYBAL, EDWARD R. D
U.S. Rep, Calif.
b. Albuquerque, N.Mex, 2/10/16; m. 9/27/40 to Lucille Beserra; c. Lucille, Lillian and Edward R, Jr. Educ: Univ. of Calif, Los Angeles; Southwest. Univ. Hon. LL.D, Pac. States Univ. Polit. & Govt. Pos: Mem, Los Angeles City Coun, Calif, 49-62, pres. pro tempore, 61-62; U.S. Rep, Calif, 62- Bus. & Prof. Pos: With Civilian Conserv. Corps until 35; dir. of health educ, Los Angeles Co. Tuberc. and Health Asn, 42-49; social worker and pub. health educator, Calif. Tuberc. Asn; pres, Eastland Savings & Loan Asn. Mil. Serv: Army, 44-45. Mem: K. of C; Am. Legion. Rel: Catholic. Legal Res: Los Angeles, Calif. Mailing Add: 11728 Auth Lane, Silver Spring, Md. 20902.

ROYER, BAKER R
b. Ephrata, 1/9/94; s. L.E. Royer and Ida L. Baker R; m. to Rosanna Cooper. Educ: F. & M. Acad, 11; Franklin & Marshall Col, 15; Pa. State Col, B.S. 16; Grad. Sch, Univ. of Pa, 17; Chi Phi. Polit. & Govt. Pos: Pa. State Rep, 36-67; mem, Rep. Co. Cmt, Pa; chmn, Joint State Govt. Cmn, 49-60 & 63-66; mem, Gov. Interdepartmental Cmt. on Migrant Labor, 52-60; mem, Gov. Adv. Cmt. on Pub. Assistance, 61-62. Bus. & Prof. Pos: Dir, Farmers Nat. Bank. Mil. Serv: World War I, 17-19, AEF, 15 months, Hq. 2nd Army Corps, brigaded with BEF, Somme Sector, 3/18-12/18. Mem: Am. Legion, past comdr; VFW; F&AM; Lions; Odd Fellows. Rel: Lutheran. Mailing Add: 1157 W. Main St, Ephrata, Pa. 17522.

ROYSTER, FRED S. D
b. Dabney, Vance Co, N.C, 12/31/08; m. 1/4/42 to Launah Parker. Educ: Duke Univ. Polit. & Govt. Pos: N.C. State Sen, 53-66; N.C. State Rep, 45-51; chmn, State of N.C. Personnel Coun, 49-; chmn, Cmt. of Growers of U.S. Tobacco, 64; Nat. Tobacco Indust. Adv. Cmt, USDA, 62-; exec. cmt, Tobacco Growers Info. Cmt, 59-; bd. of dirs, Tobacco Assocs, Inc, 47-; bd. of dirs, Coun. for Tobacco Research, USA, 54- Bus. & Prof. Pos: Pres, Tobacco Tax Coun, 61-; managing dir, Bright Belt Warehouse Asn, Inc, 57-; pres, Bright Belt Warehouse Asn, Inc, 45-57; operator, tobacco warehouses, 38-57; engaged in farming and employed in tobacco warehouses, 27-37. Rel: Methodist; teacher, Men's Bible Class, 39- Mailing Add: Henderson, N.C. 27536. (1967)

ROYSTER, WILLIAM REID D
Mo. State Rep.
b. Independence, Mo, 12/30/14; s. William Edgar Royster and Berenice Swinney Scarritt R; div; c. William Edward. Educ: Mo. Univ, A.B, 42; Sigma Chi. Polit. & Govt. Pos: Mo. State Rep, at present; city councilman, Kansas City, Mo, 59-63. Mil. Serv: Entered as Ens, Navy, 42, released as Lt. Comdr, 54, after serv. in Surface Craft, Atlantic and Pac. Theaters and Korea; Lt. Comdr. (Ret), Naval Res; Atlantic, Pac. and Korean Medal with Five Stars; UN, Expert Rifle and Victory Medals. Mem: VFW; Am. Legion. Rel: Methodist. Mailing Add: 3500 Gladstone, Blvd, Kansas City, Mo. 64123. (1967)

ROZELL, FRANKLIN RUSSELL R
Chmn, Medina Co. Rep. Party, Tex.
b. Livingston, Tex, 2/24/33; s. Walter Leon Rozell and Berniece Gillespie R; m. 5/24/57 to Sylvia Stubblefield; c. Tracie Karen, Russell Carlton and Jason Randall. Educ: Lamar State Col. of Tech, B.S, 53; Univ. Tex. Dental Br, D.D.S, 57; Xi Psi Phi. Polit. & Govt. Pos: Chmn, Medina Co. Rep. Party, 67- Publ: 'Case Report', Tex. Dental J, 11/68; 'Dentistry, A Changing Profession', San Antonio Dist. J, 3/69. Mem: Am, Tex. and San Antonio Dental Asns; Lions Int; C. of C; Hondo Golf Asn. Rel: Baptist. Mailing Add: 1107 28th St, Hondo, Tex. 78861.

ROZYCKI, STANLEY F. D
Mich. State Sen.
b. Detroit, Mich, 4/12/08; married; c. Four sons. Educ: Attended Wayne State Univ. and the Univ. of Detroit. Polit. & Govt. Pos: Former chmn, First Cong. Dem. Party Org, Mich; Mich. State Sen, 55- Bus. & Prof. Pos: Gen. mgr, Fireside Printing and Pub. Co, 38-; assoc. with his father, Rozycki Brothers Co, Detroit. Mem: K. of C; Polish Nat. Alliance; Detroit Typographical Union. Rel: Catholic. Mailing Add: 2389 E. Outer Dr, Detroit, Mich. 48234

ROZZI, DOLORES LOUISE D
Pres, Wash. Co. Young Dem, Pa.
b. Charleroi, Pa, 4/3/41; d. Ralph Rozzi and Victoria Ducato R; single. Educ: Chaffey Col, 60-61; Calif. State Col, B.S, 64; Zeta Tau Alpha; pres, Col. Young Dem. and Econs. Club; v.chmn, Inter-Collegiate Conf. on Govt; UN Club; Col. Coordinator for West. Pa. Young Dem; Newman Club; Hist. and Int. Rels. Club. Polit. & Govt. Pos: Mem. personal staff, Genevieve Blatt for U.S. Senate Campaign, 64; alternate del, Dem. Nat. Conv, 64; acct, Corp. Tax, Pa. Dept. of Revenue, 64; soc. worker, Wash. Col. Child Welfare Serv, Pa. Dept. of Welfare, 64-66; justice of peace, Pa, 64-; pres, Wash. Co. Young Dem, Pa, 65-; secy, Dem. Action Force, 66- Bus. & Prof. Pos: Guid. counsr, Ringgold Sch. Dist, Pa, 66- Mem: Bus. & Prfnl. Women of Am; Wash. Co. Minor Judiciary and Constables Asn; Pa. Magistrates Asn; chmn, Stockdale March of Dimes and Cancer Drive; YWCA; Cath. Col. Women. James Finnigan Fel. Award, 64. Rel: Catholic. Mailing Add: 230 Bow St, Stockdale, Pa. 15483. (1967)

RUANE, PAUL G. R
Pa. State Rep.
b. Carbondale, Pa, 7/31/33; s. Joseph Ruane and Mary Burke R; m. 6/22/63 to Anita Ellen Barni; c. Paul Patrick and Susan. Educ: E. Stroudsburg State Col, B.S. in educ, 55; Bucknell Univ, M.S. in educ, 59. Polit. & Govt. Pos: Pa. State Rep, currently. Mil. Serv: Entered as Pvt, Army, 55, released as Cpl, after serv. in Nike Guided Missile Ban, Milwaukee, Wis, 57; Sgt, Army Res, 59; Good Conduct Medal. Mem: Pa. State and Nat. Educ. Asns; Pa. Asn. of Safety Educ; Elks; Keystone Fish and Game Asn; CWV; K. of C; Pa. Asn. for Retarded Children. Rel: Roman Catholic. Mailing Add: 1021 E. Sunbury St, Shamokin, Pa. 17872.

RUBEL, DONALD CLARKE R
Chmn, Phila. Rep. Policy Cmt, Pa.
b. Cincinnati, Ohio, 10/1/00; s. Henry M. Rubel and Gretchen E. Scott R; m. 10/10/25 to Julia Davis Lee; c. Julia Lee (Mrs. O'Brien) and Walter Lee. Educ: Brown Univ, A.B, 23. Polit. & Govt. Pos: Mem, Health and Welfare Coun. Phila, Pa; chmn, Phila. Cmt. on Pub. Affairs; registrn. cmnr, Phila; city councilman, Phila, 54-58; del, Rep. Nat. Conv, 60 & 64; mem. exec. cmt. and chmn. Phila. Rep. Policy Cmt, 60- Bus. & Prof. Pos: Treas, Frederick Douglas Mem. Hosp, bd. mem, Lincoln Univ. and pres, bd. trustees, East. Pa. Psychiat. Inst, formerly; v.pres. and former chmn, bd. corporators, Woman's Med. Col; pres. bd. dirs, City Trusts; gen. partner, Parrish and Co; mem. N.Y. Stock Exchange. Mil. Serv: Marine Corps, World War I. Mem: Bond Club Phila; Union League; Phila. Cricket Club; Anglers Club; Egypt Mills Club; Phila. Chap, Security Analysts Asn; Penn Club; former mem. adv. cmt, W. Mt. Airy Neighbors; former chmn, S. Broad St. United Serv. Orgn. and Cmt. of 70; former v.chmn, Citizens' Charter Cmt; former exec. bd. mem, Pub. Charities Asn. and Big Brother Asn; former mem, Citizens for Commun. Col. Rel: Unitarian; past pres, bd. trustees, Germantown Unitarian Church. Mailing Add: 606 Westview St, Philadelphia, Pa. 19119.

RUBENDALL, KAY R
V.Chairwoman, Davison Co. Rep. Party, S.Dak.
b. Lincoln, Nebr, 12/6/41; d. Paul Boyd McKibben and Frances Farrens M; m. 6/6/64 to Jerome Patrick Rubendall; c. Patrick and Ann Margaret. Educ: Univ. Nebr, B.S, 63; Speech Therapy Hon; Pi Beta Phi. Polit. & Govt. Pos: Rep. precinct committeewoman, Mitchell, S.Dak, 67-; secy, Davison Co. Young Rep, 67-; v.chairwoman, Davison Co. Rep. Party, 68-; nominated to Gov. Cmt. on Outdoor Recreation, 69. Bus. & Prof. Pos: Speech therapist, Dr. Lord's Crippled Children's Sch, Omaha, Nebr, 63-64 and Mitchell Pub. Schs, Number 45, S.Dak, 64-66. Mem: Am. and S.Dak. Speech and Hearing Asns; Coun. for Exceptional Children; Beta Sigma Phi (treas, Mitchell Chap); pres-elect, St. Joseph Hosp. Auxiliary; Cath. Daughters of Am. Girl of the Year Award, Beta Sigma Phi. Rel: Catholic; Div. leader, Holy Family Church. Mailing Add: 1413 E. Fourth Ave, Mitchell, S.Dak. 57301.

RUBENSTEIN, LEON A. D
Mem, Baltimore City Coun, Md.
b. Poland, 2/26/06; s. Eli S. Rubenstein and Anna Schwartz R; m. to Carolyn Strauss; c. Arthur Michael and Elinor Louise (Mrs. Edenbaum). Educ: Univ. Md, LL.B, 29. Polit. & Govt. Pos: Md. State Del, 39-47; mem. city coun, Baltimore, 55-, mem, Mayor's Cmt. on Probs. of Aging and Cmt. for Estab. Marriage Conciliation Serv; dir, Dept. of Legis. Reference, Baltimore, 67- Bus. & Prof. Pos: Mem. exec. bd, Talmudical Acad. of Baltimore; pres, Linwood Children's Center, 54-; secy. Jewish Family and Children's Serv, 55- Mem: Pres, Nat. Asn. Hebrew Day Sch. PTA, 55-58 and Baltimore Jewish Nat. Fund Coun, 57-60; mem. bd, Health and Welfare Coun, Bais Yaakov Sch. for Girls; Amicable Lodge 25, AF&AM. Rel: Jewish. Mailing Add: 6018 Clover Rd, Baltimore, Md. 21215.

RUBIN, A. MICHAEL D
Chief Counsel, Passaic Co. Rep. League, N.J.
b. Paterson, N.J, 5/27/38; s. Louis Rubin and Anna Lefkowitz R; m. 1/26/63 to Marilyn Marks; c. Jennifer and David. Educ: Rutgers Univ, A.B, 59; Fordham Law Sch, LL.B, 62; Beta Sigma Rho. Polit. & Govt. Pos: Chmn, Rutgers Young Rep, N.J, 58-59 and Col. Young Rep, N.J, 59-60; treas, Passaic Co. Young Rep, 62-64, chmn, 63-64; alternate del, Rep. Nat. Conv, 64; asst. gen. counsel, N.J. Young Rep, 64-65, gen. counsel, 65-66; former city prosecutor, Paterson, N.J; chief counsel, Passaic Co. Rep. League, 69- Bus. & Prof. Pos: Partner, Rowinski, Gavenda & Rubin, Esquires, 66- Mil. Serv: S/Sgt, Army Res. Mem: Am. and Passaic Co. Bar Asns; N.J. Inst. Muniv. Attorneys; bd. dirs. N.J. br, Human Soc. U.S; pres, Humane Soc. Passaic Co; Jr. C. of C; Audubon Soc; Wilderness Soc; Defenders of Wildlife. Rel: Jewish. Mailing Add: 295 Linden Rd, Wayne, N.J. 07470.

RUBIN, ARTHUR D
b. Phila, Pa, 2/6/08; s. Abraham Rubin and Rebecca Gordon R. Educ: Phila. pub. schs. Polit. & Govt. Pos: Pa. State Rep, 50-54, 60-68. Bus. & Prof. Pos: Traffic court admin. Mil. Serv: Marine Corps, Pac. Theatre, World War II. Mem: Am. Legion. Mailing Add: 612 Wood St, Philadelphia, Pa. 19106. (1967)

RUBIN, GEORGE ALLEN R
Ind. State Sen.
b. Michigan City, Ind, 6/11/32; s. Maurice Rubin and Laura Wilson R; m. 6/23/63 to Jan Holtz; c. Kristine and Sara Beth. Educ: Ind. Univ, B.S, 54; Northwest. Univ. Law Sch, J.D, 59; Zeta Beta Tau. Polit. & Govt. Pos: Law clerk, Supreme Court of Ind, 59-60; dep. attorney gen, Ind, 60-61; Ind. State Sen, 69- Mil. Serv: Entered as 2nd Lt, Air Force, 55, released as 1st Lt, 67, after serv. in Officer's Preflight Training, San Antonio, Tex, 55-57. Mem: Indianapolis, Ind. and Am. Bar Asns; Phi Delta Phi; Indianapolis Jewish Commun. Rels. Coun. Rel: Jewish. Legal Res: 926 Oakwood Trail, Indianapolis, Ind. 46260. Mailing Add: 500 Union Federal Bldg, Indianapolis, Ind. 46204.

RUBIN, HYMAN D
S.C. State Sen.
b. Charleston, S.C, 1/21/13; s. Joseph Rubin and Bessie Peskin R; m. 3/29/40 to Rose Rudnick; c. Jane and Hyman, Jr. Educ: Univ. of N.C, 2 years; Univ. of S.C, A.B, 35; Phi Beta Kappa; Tau Epsilon Phi. Polit. & Govt. Pos: City councilman, Columbia, S.C, 52-66 and mayor pro tempore, 56-66; S.C. State Sen, 66- Bus. & Prof. Pos: Partner, J. Rubin & Son Co, wholesale textiles and apparel, 35- Mem: Nat. Asn. Textile and Apparel Wholesalers; C. of C;

past pres, Columbia Civitan Club; Elks; WOW; B'nai B'rith (past pres. S.C. Asn. Lodges, past pres, Dist. Grand Lodge 5); Shrine; Mason; Univ. S.C. Alumni Asn; bds, S.C. Ment. Health Asn; past pres, Commun. Center for Retarded Children; Bethlehem Youth Center; Historic Columbia Found; United Fund; adv. bd, Aurora Center for Blind; past pres, Columbia Travelers Aid Soc. Rel: Jewish. Legal Res: 2428 Wheat St, Columbia, S.C. 29205. Mailing Add: 1742 Blanding St, Box 5506, Columbia, S.C. 29205.

RUBIN, ISRAEL D
b. N.Y.C, 12/14/26; s. Oscar Rubin and Rose Begun R; m. 6/27/59 to Roslyn Gelber; c. Lisa Merrill, Janet Lynne and Gail Roberta. Educ: St. John's Univ, B.B.A, 49; St. John's Univ. Sch. of Law, J.D, 50. Polit. & Govt. Pos: Exec. mem, Bronx Pelham Dem. Club, N.Y, 66; v.pres, Benjamin Franklin Reform Dem. Club, N.Y, 67-69; first dept. judicial del, Dem. Party, 67-69; del, Dem. Nat. Conv, 68; counsel to the minority, N.Y. State Assembly, 69. Bus. & Prof. Pos: Attorney, Mokotoff, Rubin & Mondshine, 63-69; arbitrator, Civil Court of the City of New York and Am. Arbit. Asn, 64-69. Publ: 'Wiretapping in the State Constitution,' Dem. Voice, 67. Mem: Am, N.Y. State and Bronx Co. Bar Asns; N.Y. Co. Lawyers Asn; Am. Judicature Soc; Nat. Lawyers Club; Commun. Planning Bd. 11; Mizrachi; Boy Scouts of Am; Parent's Asn. P.S. 96; B'nai B'rith; Jewish Center of Williamsbridge; Mason. Recipient of Cert. of Appreciation, N.Y.C; Cert. of Appreciation, Boy Scouts of Am; Year of the Negev Award, State of Israel. Rel: Jewish. Mailing Add: 610 Waring Ave, Bronx, N.Y. 10467.

RUBINO, THEODORE SALVATORE A. R
Chmn, Chester Co. Rep. Cmt, Pa.
b. Malvern, Pa, 11/27/11; s. Joseph Rubino and Raphaela Modano R; single. Educ: Pa. State Univ. Polit. & Govt. Pos: Clerk, bd. elecs, Malvern, Pa, 41; pres, Malvern Coun, 52; sheriff, Chester Co, 63; chmn, Chester Co. Rep. Cmt, 64-; cmnr, 4 years, chmn, bd. comnrs, currently. Bus. & Prof. Pos: Supvr. stone prod, Warner Co, Pa; owner-operator, Knickerbocker Sanit. Landfill, 52-; dir, Paoli Savings & Loan, 56- and Upper Main Line Bank, 64- Mem: Malvern Civic Asn; Lions; Malvern Fire Co; K. of C; Paoli Massacre; assoc. capt, Chester Co. Group of Layman's Week-End Retreat League; trustee, Am. Inst. for Italian Culture. Rel: Roman Catholic. Mailing Add: P.O. Box 484, Malvern, Pa. 19355.

RUBINS, GLENNA H. D
b. Gonic, N.H, 5/15/26; married; c. two. Educ: N.H. and Bellevue Sch. of Nursing, N.Y.C. Polit. & Govt. Pos: N.H. State Rep, 63-68; mem, Legis. Coun; clerk of Substantive Law Subcmt; former selectman. Bus. & Prof. Pos: Registered nurse. Mem: St. Margaret's Altar Guild; Gonic PTA, Leader Brownie Troop 428. Rel: Episcopal. Mailing Add: Oak St, Gonic Sta, Rochester, N.H. 03867.

RUBLE, JAMES D, JR. D
Chmn, Douglas Co. Dem. Cent. Cmt, Wash.
b. Mountain View, Ark, 1/29/14; s. James D. Ruble, Sr. and Amy Elvesa Wade R; m; div; m. 4/8/50 to Ina Lorraine Coffy; c. Amy Lee (Mrs. Wright). Educ: Bellefonte Grade and High Sch, Ark, 9 years; Houston High Sch, Mo, grad. Polit. & Govt. Pos: Precinct committeeman, Douglas Co. Dem. Cent. Cmt, Wash, 62 & 64, precinct committeeman capt, 65 & 66, treas, 68, chmn, 66 & 68-; del, Dem. Nat. Conv, 68. Mem: Switchmen's Union of N.Am, AFL-CIO (v.pres. and local chmn); United Transportation Union (local union legis. rep); pres, Douglas Co. Unit, Am. Cancer Soc. Mailing Add: 940 N. Baker Ave, East Wenatchee, Wash. 98801.

RUBY, ELLIS SCOTT R
Chmn, Garden Co. Rep. Party, Nebr.
b. Broadwater, Nebr, 6/15/21; s. Clarke Ellis Ruby and Audra Scott R; m. 12/21/51 to Irple Gibson; c. Barbara Ann, Susanna Jo and James Ellis. Educ: Univ. Nebr, B.S, 47, M.Sc, 48; Texas A&M Col, Ph.D, 51. Polit. & Govt. Pos: Chmn, Garden Co. Rep. Party, Nebr, 68- Bus. & Prof. Pos: Asst. prof, Univ. Ark, 51-53; mgr, Rushcreek Land & Livestoct Co. Arabian Horse Div, 53- Mem: Sigma Xi. Rel: Presbyterian. Mailing Add: Lisco, Nebr. 69148.

RUBY, JOHN ALLEN D
Patronage Asst. to Chmn, Ind. State Dem. Cent. Cmt.
b. Indianapolis, Ind, 10/21/35; s. Harold Allen Ruby and Helen Siler R; single. Educ: Purdue Univ, B.S, 57; Ind. Univ, M.B.A, 59; Pi Kappa Phi. Polit. & Govt. Pos: Asst. exec. secy, Pub. Employees Retirement Fund, 61-63; mgt. analyst, Dept. of Admin, Ind, 63-65; pres, 10th Dist. Young Dem, 63-65; Ind. State Rep, 65-66; patronage asst. to chmn, Ind. State Dem. Cent. Cmt. and pres, Ind. Young Dem, currently. Bus. & Prof. Pos: Acct, Gen. Motors Corp, 57; asst. to pres, Rushville Nat. Bank, 59-61. Mem: Elks. Rel: Christian Church. Legal Res: 510 N. Main St, Carthage, Ind. 46115. Mailing Add: Sheraton-Lincoln Hotel, Indianapolis, Ind. 46204. (1967)

RUCHALA, JOSEPH F. R
Mem, Queens Co. Rep. Cmt, N.Y.
b. N.Y.C, 12/10/44; s. Joseph Ruchala and Frances R; m. 7/6/68 to Lorraine Nowicki. Educ: Adelphi Univ, A.B; Fordham Univ. Sch. of Law, LL.B. Polit. & Govt. Pos: Mem, Queens Co. Rep. Cmt, N.Y, 65-; v.pres, Midland Rep. Club, 65-; v.chmn, Parents and Taxpayers, N.Y.C, 65- and Citizens Cmt. Against Civilian Rev. Bd, 66; del, N.Y. Rep. State Conv, 66; alternate del, Rep. Nat. Conv, 68; co-chmn, Citizens for Nixon-Agnew, Sixth Cong. Dist, N.Y, 68. Mem: K. of C; Lions; Hollis Civic Asn. Rel: Roman Catholic. Mailing Add: 93-25 Hollis Court Blvd, Queens Village, N.Y. 11428.

RUCKELSHAUS, WILLIAM DOYLE R
Asst. Attorney Gen, Civil Div, Dept. of Justice
b. Indianapolis, Ind, 7/24/32; s. John K. Ruckelshaus and Marion Doyle R; m. 5/12/62 to Jill Elizabeth Strickland; c. Catherine, Mary, Jennifer, William and Robin. Educ: Princeton Univ, A.B. cum laude, 57; Harvard Law Sch, LL.B, 60; Cottage Club, Princeton Univ. Polit. & Govt. Pos: Dep. attorney gen, Ind, 60-63; chief counsel, attorney gen. off, Ind, 63-65; minority attorney, Ind. State Sen, 67-69; Ind. State Rep, 67-69, majority leader, Ind. House of Rep, 67-69; Rep. nominee, U.S. Sen, Ind, 68; Asst. Attorney Gen, Civil Div, Dept. of Justice, 69- Bus. & Prof. Pos: Attorney-at-law, Ruckelshaus, Bobbit & O'Connor, 60-68. Mil. Serv: Entered as Pvt, Army, 53, released as Sgt, 55, after serv. in U.S. Publ: 'Reapportionment—A Continuing Problem', Res Gestae, 63. Mem: Indianapolis, Ind. and Am. Bar Asns; Am. Polit. Sci. Asn; Indianapolis Coun. of For. Rels; Columbia Club, Indianapolis. Named Outstanding Rep. Legislator in Ind. House of Rep. by the Working Press, 67; Ind. Broadcastors Asn. Award for Outstanding First Year Legislator in the House, 67; named Man of the Year, Indianapolis Jaycees. Rel: Roman Catholic. Legal Res: 4320 N. Meridian, Indianapolis, Ind. 46208. Mailing Add: 11124 Luxmanor Rd, Rockville, Md. 20852.

RUCKMAN, CLARENCE AUGUSTUS D
Chmn, Pleasants Co. Dem. Exec. Cmt, W.Va.
b. St. Marys, W.Va, 2/17/00; s. John Ruckman, Jr. and Ida Bircher R; m. 11/16/18 to Edna Leona Hart; c. Ruth Eloise (Mrs. Charles D. Horner) and Robert Blaine. Educ: Received 8th grade diploma, 14 and passed W.Va. Teacher's Exam. Polit. & Govt. Pos: Chmn, Pleasants Co. Dem. Exec. Cmt, W.Va, 63- Bus. & Prof. Pos: Teacher, rural sch, 17-19; with Quaker State Oil Refinery, St. Marys, 21-25 and Monongahela Power Co, 25-65; retired. Mem: AF&AM; Odd Fellows (past grand patriarch of Grand Encampment); Kiwanis (past pres, St. Marys Club); Farming for Better Living Coun. Rel: Church of Christ. Legal Res: 607 Fourth St. St. Marys, W.Va. 26170. Mailing Add: P.O. Box 222, St. Marys, W.Va. 26170.

RUDD, JOHN ALLISON D
Prosecuting Attorney, Leon Co, Fla.
b. Tallahassee, Fla, 4/18/23; s. S.O. Rudd, Sr. and Media Sanders R; m. 7/28/65 to Geraldine Collins; c. John A, Jr, William S. and David E. Rudd; stepchildren, Charles L, Jr, Dianne (Mrs. Ashmore) and Linton B. Eason. Educ: Fla. State Univ, 52-56; Univ. Fla, LL.B, 59. Polit. & Govt. Pos: Munic. judge, Tallahassee, Fla, 53-65, city cmnr, 66-69, mayor, 68; prosecuting attorney, Leon Co, 69- Mil. Serv: Entered as A/S, Navy, 43, released as GM 2/C, 45, after serv. in Armed Guard, Am. and Pac. Theatres, 43-45; Three Bronze Stars. Mem: Am. Judicature Soc; Tallahassee Bar Asn.(dir); State Munic. Judges Asn.(pres); Elks; Am. Legion; VFW; C. of C. State Jaycee Good Govt. Award, Mayor City of Tallahassee. Rel: Baptist. Legal Res: 117½ S. Monroe St, Tallahassee, Fla. 32301. Mailing Add: P.O. Box 587, Tallahassee, Fla. 32302.

RUDDY, CLARENCE JOHN D
b. Batavia, Ill, 6/20/05; s. Clarence S. Ruddy and Mary Behan R; m. 4/20/40 to Dorothy Culkin; c. Philip Culkin, Clarence John, Jr. and Mary Margaret. Educ: Univ. Notre Dame, J.D, 27. Polit. & Govt. Pos: Precinct committeeman, Dem. Party, 42-; del, Dem. Nat. Conv, 15th Ill. Cong. Dist, 64 and alternate del, 56 and 52; chmn, Kane Co. Dem. Cent. Cmt, 42-46; asst. Attorney Gen, State of Ill, 33-42. Bus. & Prof. Pos: Spec. asst. attorney gen, State of Ill, 61-69; gen. counsel, Supreme Lodge of the World, Loyal Order of Moose, 61-; partner, Ruddy & Myler, 63-, Ruddy & Brown, 51-63 and Putnam, Johnson, Alschuler & Ruddy, 39-51; assoc. in practice of law, 27-39. Mem: Moose; Elks; K. of C; Kane Co, Ill. and Am. Bar Asns; Aurora Country Club; Union League Club of Aurora; Phoenix Club. Rel: Roman Catholic. Legal Res: 164 S. Elmwood Dr, Aurora, Ill. 60505. Mailing Add: 111 W. Downer Place, Aurora, Ill. 60504.

RUDDY, MACHAEL A. R
b. Chicago, Ill, 9/2/00; c. two. Educ: Parochial & Pub. Schs, Chicago. Polit. & Gov. Pos: Ill. State Rep, 56-73 Gen. Assemblies. Bus. & Prof. Pos: Mfr. and retailer. Mailing Add: 1700 W. Garfield Blvd, Chicago, Ill. 60636. (1967)

RUDE, ARTHUR HERMAN R
Fla. State Rep.
b. Chicago, Ill, 7/27/26; s. Arthur William Rude and Mildred Chott R; m. 11/24/52 to Catherine Boyd Erskine; c. Sharyn Elizabeth, Leisa Beth and John Arthur. Educ: Univ. Ill, B.S. in archit, 50. Polit. & Govt. Pos: Precinct committeeman, Rep. Exec. Cmn, Broward Co, Fla, 62-; mem, Ft. Lauderdale Bd. of Rules and Appeals, 64-; Fla. State Rep, 67- Bus. & Prof. Pos: Architect, 57- Mil. Serv: Entered as A/S, Navy, 44, released as Qm. 2/C, 46, after serv. in U.S.S. LCI (L) 871, Asiatic-Pac. Theater, 44-46; also serv. in U.S.S. Boxer CV-21 in Korean Conflict, 51-53; Lt. Comdr, Construction Bn, Civil Eng. Corps, Naval Res; Letter of Commendation; Presidential Unit Citation and Korean Presidential Unit Citation; Good Conduct, Am. Defense, Victory and Japanese Occupation Medals; Asiatic-Pac. and Korean Theater Campaign Medals; Korean, China and UN Serv. Medals; Philippine Liberation Medal. Mem: Am. Inst. Architects; Fla. Asn. of Am. Inst. Architects; Ill. Alumni Asn; Christian Bus. Men's Cmt, Int; Navy League, Navy Acad. Found; Reserve Officers Asn; Am. Legion; VFW; Amvets; C. of C; PTA; Toastmasters Int; former mem, Jaycees; Audubon Soc. Rel: Grace Brethren Church. Mailing Add: 630 N.E. 14th Ave, Ft. Lauderdale, Fla. 33304.

RUDERIAN, HARVEY LEE D
b. Los Angeles, Calif, 5/13/47; s. Max Jack Ruderian and Armen Mary Kalfaian R; single. Educ: Univ. of Calif, Los Angeles, 3 years; Univ. of Calif, Santa Barbara, 1 year; Beta Theta Pi. Polit. & Govt. Pos: Finance chmn. and treas, South. Calif. Students for Kennedy, 68; del, Dem. Nat. Conv, 68; treas, Calif. Dem. Student Alliance, 68; del. from Univ. of Calif. to Nat. Student Asn. Cong, 68; co-founder and co-chmn, Calif. Kennedy Action Corps, 68-69; founder and pres, Inst. for Soc. Adv, 68-69; pres, Newer World Young Dem, 69. Rel: Unitarian. Mailing Add: 545 Hanley Ave, Los Angeles, Calif. 90049.

RUDICEL, CHANDLER CLIFTON D
Chmn, Reno Co. Dem. Party, Kans.
b. Rush Center, Kans, 11/15/05; s. Thomas Clifton Rudicel and Laura McClintock R; m. 5/25/58 to Velma Jewel Hanselman. Educ: High Sch, La Crosse, Kans, 20-24; G.E.D. & 2CX, 51. Polit. & Govt. Pos: Exec. secy, Reno Co. Cent. Cmt, Kans, 66-68; precinct committeeman, S. Reno Twp, Hutchinson, 66-; presidential elector, 68; chmn, Reno Co. Dem. Party, 68- Mil. Serv: Entered as Pvt, Army, 26, released as Lt. Col, 60, after serv. in Army and Air Force, Australia, New Guinea, Korea, China, Japan, Okinawa and France, 41-60. Mem: Lions Int; VFW; Retired Officers Asn; Reserve Officers Asn; Am. Legion. Mailing Add: 15 Glass Manor Lane, Hutchinson, Kans. 67501.

RUDOLF, JACOB PAUL R
b. South Norwalk, Conn, 2/18/26; s. David Rudolf and Rachel Levak R; m. 1/12/55 to Barbara Anne Burke. Educ: Norwalk High Sch, grad, 43; Acad. Traffic & Transportation, 6 months. Polit. & Govt. Pos: Mem, Norwalk Common Coun, Conn, 59-67, Majority Leader, 63 and pres, 64, 66 & 67; mem, Norwalk Rep. City Cmts, 59-67; Conn. State Sen, 67-69. Bus. & Prof. Pos: Gen. mgr, Rudolf Motor Lines Inc, 46-58; sales mgr, Williamson Transportation, Inc, 59-; bd. dir, Louv & Co. Yacht Sales, currently. Mil. Serv: Entered as A/S, Navy, 44, released as Seaman 1/C, 46, after serv. in Navy Armed Guard, European and N. Atlantic Convoy Duty. Mem: Am. Legion; U.S. Power Squadron; Moose. Rel: Hebrew. Mailing Add: Jarvis St, Norwalk, Conn. 06851.

RUDOLPH, JOSEPH H. MILNOR R
Educ: Highlands Univ, B.A, post B.A. Polit. & Govt. Pos: N.Mex. State Rep, 63-68; alternate del, Rep. Nat. Conv, 68. Bus. & Prof. Pos: Rancher. Mil. Serv: Navy, 4 years. Mem: Lions; Elks. Rel: Catholic. Mailing Add: P.O. Box 266, Mora, N.Mex. 87732. (1967)

RUEHLMANN, EUGENE P. R
Mayor, Cincinnati, Ohio
b. Cincinnati, Ohio, 2/23/25; s. John F. Ruehlmann and Hattie Mehrckens R; m. 8/30/47 to Virginia M. Juergens; c. Virginia, Peter, Margaret, Andrea, Gregory, James, Mark and Richard. Educ: Univ. Cincinnati, B.A. with honors in polit. sci, 48; Harvard Law Sch, LL.B, 50; Phi Beta Kappa; Omicron Delta Kappa; Beta Theta Pi. Polit. & Govt. Pos: City councilman, Cincinnati, Ohio, 59-, chmn, Capital Improv. Cmt. and Finance Cmt, and v.chmn, Urban Develop. and Pub. Utilities Cmt, Cincinnati City Coun, 61-; v.mayor, Cincinnati, 63-67, mayor, 68-; chmn, Ohio Mayors for Nixon Campaign, 68. Bus. & Prof. Pos: Partner, Law Firm of Strauss, Troy & Ruehlmann, 52- Mil. Serv: Marine Corps, 43. Publ: 'State Taxation of Radio and TV,' Univ. Cincinnati Law Rev, 1/51. Mem: Am, Ohio and Cincinnati Bar Asns; West. Hills Country Club; Cincinnatus Asn; Lions; Univ. Cincinnati Alumni Asn; Hamilton Co. Rep. Club; Boys' Week Cmt, Robert E. Bentley Post 50, Am. Legion. McKibbon Medal Award Winner, Univ. Cincinnati, 47; Cincinnati's Outstanding Young Man of the Year, 60; Distinguished Am. Award for serv. in connection with the new stadium in Cincinnati, Nat. Football Found. and Hall of Fame. Rel: Presbyterian. Legal Res: 4966 Cleves Warsaw Pike, Cincinnati, Ohio 45238. Mailing Add: 1800 First National Bank Bldg, Cincinnati, Ohio 45202.

RUFFE, DORIS IRENE D
Secy, San Miguel Co. Dem. Cent. Cmt.
b. Montrose, Colo, 11/29/31; d. Glenn Ruffe and Hazel McKeever R; single. Educ: Montrose Co. High Sch, 4 years. Polit. & Govt. Pos: Treas, Placerville Commun. Asn, Colo, 61-68; secy-treas, Placerville TV Asn, 62-69; Dem. committeewoman, San Miguel Co, 62-69; secy, San Miguel Dem. Cent. Cmt, 64- Bus. & Prof. Pos: Acct, San Miguel Motor Co, 50-69. Mem: Life mem, Chrysler-Plymouth Div, Honor Soc. Acct. Mailing Add: P.O. Box 94, Placerville, Colo. 81430.

RUFFIN, JAMES EDWARD D
b. Tipton Co, Tenn, 7/24/93; s. John Brahan Ruffin and Mary Culbreath R; m. 7/29/33 to Grace Gresham. Educ: Drury Col, A.B, 16; Cumberland Univ, LL.B, 20; Lambda Chi Alpha; All-Mo. Valley Tackle, football and record-holder, Mo. Inter-collegiate discus throw, 15. Polit. & Govt. Pos: U.S. Rep, Mo, 33-35; spec. asst. attorney gen. of U.S, 35-53. Mil. Serv: 1st Lt, Army, 17-19, serv. as Comdr, Co. M, 53rd Pioneer Inf, France, also serv. as Capt, Judge Adv. Gen. Dept, Army Res, 24-26. Mem: Mo. Bar Asn; Mil. Order of World Wars; Mo. State Hist. Soc; 40 et 8; Am. Legion. Rel: Methodist. Mailing Add: 820 S. McCann Ave, Springfield, Mo. 65804.

RUFFIN, SUSIE BOLDEN D
Parliamentarian, Miss. Freedom Dem. State Exec. Cmt.
b. York, Ala, 5/25/08; d. Rev. Henry Bolden (deceased) and Bettye Davis B.(deceased); m. Sanders Ruffin (deceased); c. Bettye Davis (Mrs. John Earl Walton), Babe Ruth Sanders, Mildred (Mrs. Walker), Patrick Essie Sanders, Waydeen (Mrs. Green) and foster son, Lloyd D. Jones. Educ: Kemper Co. Sch, Laurel City Schs, 10 years. Polit. & Govt. Pos: Committeewoman, Jones Co. Dem. Freedom Party, Miss, 64-68; newsletter ed, State Freedom Dem, 65; del, Dem. State and Nat. Conv, 68; parliamentarian, Miss. Freedom Dem. State Exec. Cmt, 69- Bus. & Prof. Pos: Home food bus, 56-59. Mem: Headstart Commun. Cmt; NAACP; citizenship teacher, South. Christian Leadership Conf. Prog. Cert, Completion of Training in Commun. Develop, Pa. Commun. Conf. Center; Cert, Citizenship Prog, South. Christian Leadership Conf. Rel: Baptist. Mailing Add: 905 Amaranth Ave, Laurel, Miss. 39440.

RUFFIN, WILLIAM HAYWOOD Independent
b. Louisburg, N.C, 2/8/99; s. William Haywood Ruffin and Sally Johnson White R; m. 10/30/29 to Josephine Craige Kluttz; c. William H, Jr. and Josephine R. (Mrs. Adamson). Educ: Univ. of N.C, B.S, 21; Omicron Delta Kappa; Alpha Kappa Psi; Beta Gamma Sigma; Phi Psi; Kappa Sigma; Order of the Gimghoul. Bus. & Prof. Pos: Secy. and treas, Erwin Mills, Inc, 32-42, v.pres. and treas, 42-48, pres, 48-64, chmn. of the bd, 64-; v.pres, Burlington Industs, Inc, 64- Mil. Serv: Entered as 1st Sgt, Army, released as 2nd Lt, 19. Mem: Pres, Nat. Asn. Mfrs, 51 and Am. Textile Mfrs. Inst, 62; Univ. Club, NYC; Augusta Nat. Golf Club; Country Club of N.C, Pinehurst. Rel: Episcopal. Legal Res: 25 Oak Dr, Forest Hills, Durham, N.C. 27707. Mailing Add: P.O. Box 2656, West Durham Station, Durham, N.C. 27705.

RUFO, PASQUALE V. R
b. Concord, N.H, 8/18/22; married; c. three. Educ: Colby Col. Polit. & Govt. Pos: N.H. State Rep, 57-68; mem, Concord Planning Bd; chmn, Ward Nine Rep. Cmt; former v.chmn. and chmn, Merrimack Co. Rep. Cmt; chmn, Merrimack Co, Del; chmn. exec. cmt, Merrimack Co. Bus. & Prof. Pos: Florist. Mil. Serv: Marine Corps. Mem: Elks (past exalted ruler); VFW; K. of C; Eagles; Moose; Farm Bur. Rel: Catholic. Mailing Add: 119 Rumford St, Concord, N.H. 03301. (1967)

RUGG, GLEN THOMAS R
Mont. State Sen.
b. Walsh, Colo, 4/24/24; s. James Tisdale Rugg and Ada Land R; m. 12/22/51 to Elaine Grace Crawford; c. Kathy, Patricia, Pamela, Glena and Duane. Educ: High sch, Walsh, Colo, 12 years. Polit. & Govt. Pos: State committeeman, Mont. Rep. Party, 60-62; chmn, Fallon Co. Rep. Club, 62-66; Mont. State Sen, First Dist, 67- Bus. & Prof. Pos: Rancher, Fallon Co, Mont, 52-69. Mil. Serv: Merchant Marine, 43-46, released as Jr. Engr. Mem: RAM; Farm Bur; Am. Nat. Cattlemens Asn. Rel: Protestant. Mailing Add: P.O. Box 188, Plevna, Mont. 59344.

RUGGIERO, PHILIP S. D
Pa. State Rep.
b. Washington Twp, Pa, 3/4/28; s. Stephen Ruggiero and Angeline Natalizio R; single. Educ: Temple Univ, Col. Liberal Arts, 50, Sch. Law, LL.B, 53. Polit. & Govt. Pos: Hearing examiner, Bur. Traffic Safety, Pa, 55-61; chmn, Northampton Co. Area Three Dem. Party, 60-; asst. dist. attorney, Northampton Co, 64-; Pa. State Rep, 137th Dist, currently. Mem: Northampton Co. and Pa. Bar Asns. Rel: Catholic. Legal Res: 920 North Main St, Bangor, Pa. 18013. Mailing Add: 31 S. First St, Bangor, Pa. 18013.

RUGGLES, DANIEL B, III R
b. Salem, Mass, 11/28/24; s. Daniel Blaisdell Ruggles, Jr. and Dorothy Johnson R; m. 10/12/49 to Elaine Parsons. Educ: Dartmouth Col, 42; Denver Univ, Army Specialized Traning Prog, 43; Babson Inst, 45. Polit. & Govt. Pos: Vt. State Sen, Washington Co, until 68. Bus. & Prof. Pos: Pres, radio stas, WSKI and WMRC in Montpelier, Vt. and Milford, Mass, currently. Mil. Serv: Entered as Pvt, Air Force, 43, released as Sgt, 46, after serv. in Fifth Air Force, Pac. Mem: C. of C. (pres, Montpelier Chap, 60); Lions (pres, Barre Club, 66); Elks; Vt. Farm Bur; Am. Legion. Rel: Protestant. Mailing Add: Box 364, Montpelier, Vt. 05602.

RUHNKE, ARNOLD J. R
b. Plymouth, Nebr, 8/26/08; m. 2/10/33 to Elizabeth Mahloch. c. Three. Educ: Plymouth High Sch. Polit. & Govt. Pos: Chmn. AAA Cmt, Jefferson Co, Nebr, mem. sch. reorgn. cmt, mem. sch. bd. and supvr. soil conserv. dist; Nebr. State Sen, 55-69; exec. dir, Nebr. Asn. Co. Off, currently. Bus. & Prof. Pos: Farmer. Mem: Jefferson Co. Farmers Union. Rel: United Church of Christ. Mailing Add: Plymouth, Nebr. 68424.

RULE, CHARLES H. D
Chmn, Saline Co. Dem. Orgn, Nebr.
b. Friend, Nebr, 4/11/21; s. Harvey F. Rule and Grace A. Smith R; m. 9/5/48 to Harriett J. Baum. Educ: Friend High Sch, 4 years. Polit. & Govt. Pos: Dem. precinct worker, Friend, Nebr, 54-64; secy, Saline Co. Dem. Orgn, 64-66, chmn, 66- Bus. & Prof. Pos: Owner, livestock trucking co, 47-60; farmer, 48-; owner, dump truck and construction co, 60- Mil. Serv: Pvt, Army, 42-43, released after serv. in Air Force Engrs, U.S.A. Mem: Am. Legion; DAV; Mason; Elks. Rel: Protestant. Legal Res: 904 Fifth, Friend, Nebr. 68359. Mailing Add: Box 185, Friend, Nebr. 68359.

RULE, HERBERT CHARLES, III D
Ark. State Rep.
b. Little Rock, Ark, 11/21/37; s. Herbert C. Rule and Dora Stafford R; m. 8/24/61 to Elizabeth Dolbey; c. Herbert C.N. and James Christopher. Educ: Yale, B.A, 59; Univ. Ark, LL.B; Beta Theta Pi; Torch Honor Soc. Polit. & Govt. Pos: Ark. State Rep, 22nd Dist, 67- Bus. & Prof. Pos: Partner, Rose, Meek, House, Barron, Nash & Williamson, 66- Mil. Serv: Entered as 1st Lt, Marine Corps Res, 59, released 61, after serv. in Third Marine Div, 60-61. Mailing Add: 720 W. Third St, Little Rock, Ark. 72201.

RUMAN, HELEN ANNE D
Dem. State Committeewoman, Ariz.
b. Corning, N.Y, 7/20/26; d. Roy L. Albertson and Helen Ryan A; m. 8/27/43 to Robert Paul Ruman; c. Diane, Nora and Mary Anne. Educ: Univ. Ariz, B.S, 44; Alpha Chi Omega; Newman Club. Polit. & Govt. Pos: Dist, chmn, 60-66; precinct committeewoman 60-68 and state committeewoman, 62-; co. v.chairwoman, 62-64; mem, Co. Welfare Bd, 66-; soc. worker. Mem: Cath. Daughters of Am; Nat. Coun. Cath. Women; St. Joseph's Auxiliary, Good Shepherd Guild. Rel: Catholic. Mailing Add: 5615 N. 11th Ave, Phoenix, Ariz. 85013. (1967)

RUMFORD, WILLIAM BYRON D
b. Courtland, Ariz, 2/2/08; s. Chauncey Goodrich Rumford and Margaret Lee Johnson R; m. 10/8/32 to Elsie Rebecca Carrington; c. William B. and Elsie Rebecca, II. Educ: Univ. Calif. Col. Pharmacy, Berkeley, Ph.G, 31, Univ. Calif, Berkeley, A.B. in polit. sci, 48, M.A. in pub. admin, 59; Alpha Phi Alpha; Sigma Pi Phi. Polit. & Govt. Pos: Calif. State Assemblyman, 48-66, chmn, Pub. Health Cmn, Calif. State Assembly, 15 years; mem, Comprehensive Health Planning Adv. Coun, Region 9, Dept. Health, Educ. and Welfare, San Francisco, currently. Bus. & Prof. Pos: Owner, Rumford's Pharmacy, Berkeley, Calif; chmn, House of Del, Am. Pharmaceutical Asn, 67-68; pres, Beneficial Develop. Group, presently. Publ: 'Housing and Health,' Calif. Health, 60. Mem: Mason; Shrine; Am. Polit. Sci. Asn; adv. bd, Stiles Hall YMCA; Commonwealth Club of Calif; Berkeley Commons Club; adv. agr. coun, Univ. Calif; trustee, John F. Kennedy Univ, Martinez, Calif. and Alta Bates Hosp. Named one of Univ. of Calif. most distinguished grads, Calif. Monthly Mag, 3/68; Pharmacy Col. Alumni of the Year, 65. Rel: Methodist. Mailing Add: 1500 Stuart St, Berkeley, Calif. 94703.

RUMMAGE, FREDERICK CHARLES D
Md. State Del.
b. Hunlock Creek, Pa, 3/27/31; s. Walter Eugene Rummage and Hilda Croop R; m. 9/12/53 to Loretta Cecilia Formulak; c. Kama Croop. Educ: Bloomsburg State Col, B.S; Univ. Miami, J.D; Kappa Delta Pi; Phi Sigma Pi; Delta Theta Phi. Polit. & Govt. Pos: Md. State Del, 67- Bus. & Prof. Pos: Exec. dir, Nat. Found, Wash. D.C, 59-62; house counsel, Nat. Asn. of Elec. Co, 62-65; exec. secy. and counsel, Educators' Asn, Prince George, Md, 65- Mil. Serv: Entered as Pvt, Army, 56, released as Lt, 58, after serv. in Army Intel, Metrop. Dist, Wash, D.C, 56-58. Mem: Fla. and Wash, D.C. Bars; Dem. Clubs; Rotary. Rel: Protestant. Legal Res: 5700 George Washington Dr, Camp Springs, Md. 20031. Mailing Add: 8008 Old Marlboro Pike, Forestville, Md. 20028.

RUMMLER, JOSEPH MANIG Constitution
Mem. Exec. Coun, Constitution Party, Tex.
b. Chicago, Ill, 7/12/06; s. William Richard Rummler and Susan Harding R; m. 5/27/39 to Dixie Kennedy; c. David Clark, Lt, U.S. Navy and Susan (Mrs. Downman). Educ: Cornell Univ, B.A, 30; Am. Tech. Soc. Chicago, Ill, bus. admin, 36-37; DePaul Univ, mgt. eng, 44-45; Pi Delta Epsilon; Quill and Dagger; Delta Phi. Polit. & Govt. Pos: Chmn. exec. cmt, Constitution Party, Harris Co, Tex, 56; chmn. exec. cmt, Constitution Party, Tex, 56, mem. exec. coun, 58-, secy, 63, pres, 64 & 69; cand. for R.R. Cmnr, 56, Tex. State Sen, Sixth Dist, 58, Comptroller of Pub. Acct, 60 & 62 and Lt. Gov, 64. Bus. & Prof. Pos: Sales rep, Wagstaff Corp, Houston, Tex, 52-58; sales mgr, Gr. Houston Advert. Specialty Co, 59-60; sales rep, Advert. Specialty Co, 60-61; mgr, and owner, Bus. Incentives & Sales Aids, 62-67; sales agent and life underwriter, Occidental Life Ins. Co. of Calif, 68- Mem: Cornell Club of Houston. Rel: Protestant. Legal Res: 5000 Mimosa Lane, Bellaire, Tex. 77401. Mailing Add: P.O. Box 26, Bellaire, Tex. 77401.

RUMSFELD, DONALD R
Dir, Off. of Econ. Opportunity
b. Evanston, Ill, 7/9/32; s. George Rumsfeld and Jeannette Husted R; m. 12/27/54 to Joyce Pierson; c. Valerie and Marcy. Educ: Princeton Univ, A.B, 54. Polit. & Govt. Pos: Admin. asst. to U.S. Rep. David Dennison, Ohio, 58; staff asst. to U.S. Rep. Robert Griffin, Mich, 59; U.S. Rep, Ill, 63-69, former mem, Sci. and Astronaut. Cmt, Govt. Opers. Cmt. and Joint Econ. Cmt, U.S. House of Rep; dir, Off. of Econ. Opportunity, 69- Bus. & Prof. Pos: Registered rep, A.G. Becker & Co, Inc, 60-62. Mil. Serv: Entered as Ens, Navy, 54, released as Lt.(jg), 57, after serv. as Naval Aviator; Lt. Comdr, Naval Res, currently. Mem: Jaycees; Assocs. Chicago Presby-St. Luke's Hosp; dir, Clearbrook Sch. for Retarded Children, Arlington Heights; adv. coun, Dept. Politics, Princeton Univ; hon. mem, Glenview Rotary. All Navy Wrestling Champion, 56. Rel: Protestant. Legal Res: 1373 Ashland Lane, Wilmette, Ill. 60091. Mailing Add: Office of Economic Opportunity, 1200 19th St. N.W, Washington, D.C. 20036. (1967)

RUNDLE, EARL CLIFFORD R
N.Dak. State Rep.
b. Dickinson, N.Dak, 5/9/06; s. Philip Henry Rundle and Rachel Thompson R; m. 10/23/33 to Elinor Aird; c. Rachel (Mrs. Hoovestol), Don Philip and Lynne (Mrs. Carlson). Educ: Univ. Mont, 24-26; Dickinson State Col. and N.Dak. State Univ, 28-29; N.Dak. State, 28-29; Sigma Delta Chi. Polit. & Govt. Pos: Supvr, Dovre Twp, N.Dak, 28-37; mem. sch. bd, Dovre Consol. Dist, 33-37; committeeman, AAA Co, 34-36; mem, Co. Selective Serv. Bd, 6 years and Co. Rationing Bd, 2 years; city auditor, Marmarth, 40-45; city auditor. and pres. sch. bd, New England, N.Dak, 49-59; del, many N.Dak. State Conv; precinct committeeman and co. secy, Rep. Party; N.Dak. State Rep, 39th Dist, 65- Bus. & Prof. Pos: Teacher, country schs, 27-29; owner and operator, Rundle Ranch, New England, 27-; ed. and publisher, Slope Messenger, Marmarth, 37-59; pres, Register Publ. Co, Chamberlain, S.Dak, 58-60. Mil. Serv: Pvt, Army, 44-45. Mem: Pres, N.Dak. Press Asn, 53; pres, Slope Co. Sch. Officers Asn, 35 and Hettinger Co. Asn, 56; Mo. Slope Sch. Officers Asn, pres, 57; Mason, Shrine; Royal Order of Jesters; Lions, zone chmn, 55; Am. Legion, state v.cmnr, 46. Rel: Congregational. Mailing Add: Rundle Ranch, New England, N.Dak. 58647.

RUNGE, GILBERT ANDY R
Chmn, Audrain Co. Rep. Cent. Cmt, Mo.
b. Springfield, Mo, 7/31/30; s. Rev. A.C. Runge (deceased) and Astrid Glidden R; m. 11/16/52 to Winifred Rosalie Yoes; c. Louesa Schell, Frederic Andrew and Russell Glidden. Educ: Cent. Methodist Col, A.B, 52; Univ. Mo, Columbia, J.D, 57. Polit. & Govt. Pos: Chmn, Audrain Co. Rep. Cent. Cmt, Mo, 62-; chmn, Mo. State Legis. Redistricting Cmn, 66. Bus. & Prof. Pos: With Law Firm of Edwards, Wright & Seigfreid, Mexico, Mo, 57; mem. law firm of Edwards, Seigfreid & Runge. Mil. Serv: Entered Army, served in Korea, 52-54. Mem: Mo, Audrain Co. and Am. Bar Asns; AF&AM; RAM; K.T; Shrine; Jaycees; Kiwanis; C. of C.(v.pres, Mexico, Mo. Chap); Farm Bur. Rel: Methodist. Legal Res: 1318 Webster Dr, Mexico, Mo. 65265. Mailing Add: 123 E. Jackson St, Mexico, Mo. 65265.

RUNKLE, JERRY CHLOYD R
Chmn, Decatur Co. Rep. Cent. Cmt, Iowa
b. Pisgah, Iowa, 9/27/15; s. Jerry Franklin Runkle and Chloie Scherer R; m. 8/19/38 to Wilma Irene Michael; c. Jane Catherine and Jerry Michael. Educ: Univ. North. Iowa, B.S, 38; Univ. Iowa, M.A, 42; Univ. Calif, Berkeley, 48-50; summers, Northwest. Univ, 45, Univ. Minn, 58, Univ. Va, 64 and Univ. Calif, Los Angeles, 67. Polit. & Govt. Pos: Chmn, Decatur Co. Rep. Cent. Cmt, Iowa, 68- Bus. & Prof. Pos: Teacher, Clarence Pub. Sch, Iowa, 38-42 and DeWitt Pub. Sch, Iowa, 42-43; prof. econ, Graceland Col, 42- Mem: Am. Econ. and Midwest Econ. Asns; Am. Asn. Univ. Prof. Rel: Reorganized Latter-day Saint; Evangelist. Mailing Add: 202 N. Silver St, Lamoni, Iowa 50140.

RUNNELS, HAROLD LOWELL D
N.Mex. State Sen.
b. Dallas, Tex, 3/17/24; s. Elbert Dewey Runnels and Stella McCutcheon R; m. 3/25/44 to Dorothy Francis Gilland; c. Michael Lowell, Phillip Harold, Dewey Mathew and Eydie Francis. Educ: Cameron State Agr. Col, Lawton, Okla, 43. Polit. & Govt. Pos: N.Mex. State Sen, 60-, chmn, Senate Finance Cmt, chmn, legis. finance cmt. Bus. & Prof. Pos: Owner and mgr, Runnels Mud Co. and Runco Acidizing and Fracturing Co. Mil. Serv: Pvt, Air Corp. Res. Mem: Mason (32°); Shrine; Am. Legion; Am. Petroleum Inst. Rel: Baptist. Legal Res: 218 S. 7th, Lovington, N.Mex. 88260. Mailing Add: P.O. Box 937, Lovington, N.Mex. 88260.

RUNNING, JOHN MARK D
b. Merrill, Wis, 8/10/23; s. Mark A. Running and Amanda Allison R; m. 8/24/44 to Ethel Shields; c. Joan and Mary. Educ: Univ. Wis, Madison, 40-46; Rutgers Law Sch, LL.B, 52. Polit. & Govt. Pos: Asst. to state chmn, Kefauver for Pres, 52; borough attorney, Ringwood, N.J, 66-; borough leader, Ringwood Dem. Party, 67-68; alternate del, Dem. Nat. Conv, 68. Bus. & Prof. Pos: Attorney-at-law, 53- Mil. Serv: Entered as Pvt, Air Corps, 43, released as 1st Lt, 45, after serv. in 14th Air Force, Italy, 44-45; Air Medal with 5 Stars; ETO Medal with Stars. Mem: Am, State and Co. Bar Asns; Lions; Moose. Rel: Catholic. Mailing Add: 35 Cupsaw Dr, Ringwood, N.J. 07456.

RUNYON, FRANK JASPER, II D
Tenn. State Rep.
b. Clarksville, Tenn, 3/18/28; s. Charles Vineyard Runyon and Dorothy Lardner R; m. 4/3/61 to Sheila Bowman; c. Mary Neill, Frank Jasper, III, Markley Preston and Dorothy Donnelly. Educ: Univ. Va, B.A. in econ, 50; Vanderbilt Univ, Law Sch, LL.B, 57; Phi Delta Phi; Sigma Alpha Epsilon. Polit. & Govt. Pos: Tenn. State Rep, Floterial Rep, 67-69, Dir. Rep, 69- Mil. Serv: Navy, 50-54. Mem: Bd. dirs, Clarksville C. of C; Kiwanis; United Givers Fund. Rel: Catholic. Mailing Add: 201 Cherokee Lane, Clarksville, Tenn. 37040.

RUPERT, EMERSON R
b. Pittsburgh, Pa, 7/20/15; s. John H. Rupert and Edith Ellen Woolever R; m. 2/14/41 to Eleanor Dowdell Graybill; c. Emerson H, II, John G. and Frank R.R. Educ: Univ. of Pittsburgh; Pa. State Univ, B.A, 40; Am. Univ; Alpha Delta Sigma; Alpha Phi Omega; InterCollegiate Int. Rels. Club; Pa. State Players; Thespians; Pa. State Club; Independent Polit. Party; Elected mem. of Student Council. Polit. Pos: Del, Rep. Nat. Conv, San Francisco, 64; Rep. nominee, U.S. Sen, 62; Rep. cand, Gov. of Fla, 60. Govt. Pos: Chief, Industrial News Off, Off. Secy. of Defense, Wash, D.C, 50-52 and 42-44; dir of information, Nat. Blood Prog, Exec. Off. of the President, Wash, D.C. Bus. & Prof. Pos: Consult. engr. in mgt, bus. develop. and indust. design. Mil. Serv: Spec. Assignment, Mil. Intel. Serv. Mem: Am. Legion; Elks; C. of C. Rel: Protestant. Legal Res: 519 27th Ave. N, St. Petersburg, Fla. 33704. Mailing Add: P.O. Box 690, St. Petersburg, Fla. 33704.

RUPPE, PHILIP E. R
U.S. Rep, Mich.
b. Laurium, Mich, 9/29/26; m. to Miller; c. Five. Educ: Cent. Mich. Univ; Univ. Mich; Yale Univ, 48. Polit. & Govt. Pos: Mich. Indust. Ambassador, 2 years; U.S. Rep, Mich, 67- Bus. & Prof. Pos: Pres. and gen. mgr, Bosch Brewing Co, 55-65; dir, Commercial Nat. Bank of L'Anse, 62- Mil. Serv: Ens, Naval Res, 48; Navy, 52, Japan and Korea. Mem: Am. Legion; VFW; Houghton Rotary Club, v.pres. Legal Res: Woodland Rd, Houghton, Mich. 49931. Mailing Add: House Office Bldg, Washington, D.C. 20515.

RUS, WILLIAM P. R
b. Evansville, Ind, 5/24/20; s. William P. Rus, Sr. and Frances Alice Fuller R; m. 12/24/53 to Scharlott E. Schultz; c. Helen Ann, William Eric, Robert Mark and Janet Marie. Educ: Univ. Calif, Berkeley, B.S. in Civil Eng, 48, B.S. in Bus. Admin, 50; Tau Kappa Epsilon. Polit. & Govt. Pos: Mem. planning cmn, Palo Alto, Calif, 57-61, city councilman, 61-67, former vice mayor; pres, San Mateo Chap. Rep. Alliance, 65; pres, Santa Clara Co. Rep. Alliance, secy, Bay Area Rep. Alliance and assoc. mem, Calif. State Rep. Cent. Cmt, currently. Bus. & Prof. Pos: Res. engr, Utah Construct. Co, 50-58; pres, Wm. P. Rus, Inc, 58- Mil. Serv: Entered as Pvt, Army, released as 1st Sgt, after serv. in Corps of Engrs, Pac. Theater. Mem: Am. Soc. Civil Engrs; Am. Soc. Mil. Engrs; F&AM; Scottish Rite, Shrine; Elks. Rel: Congregational. Mailing Add: 263 Fairfield Court, Palo Alto, Calif. 94306.

RUSH, CAROLYN SUE R
V.Chairwoman, Ark. Rep. Party
b. Russellville, Ark, 10/9/33; d. Modie Daniel Morgan and Ora May Morgan M; m. 8/8/53 to Marshall Neil Rush; c. Stephanie Ann, Kathryn Sue and Allison Lee. Educ: Tex. Univ. for Women, 2½years; Singing Stars. Polit. & Govt. Pos: Mem, Young Rep. Club of Jefferson Co. and Jefferson Co. Rep. Womens Club; second v.chairwoman, Jefferson Co. Rep. Cent. Cmt, 51-65; nat. committeewoman, Young Rep. Ark, 62-63; secy, Fourth Cong. Dist, 63; pres, Jefferson Co. Rep. Women's Orgn, 63-64; v.chairwoman, Ark. Rep. Party, 64-; del, Rep. Nat. Conv, 68. Mem: PTA (bd. mem, Lakeside Sch. Chap); Time Club; League of Women Voters; Jaycee Auxiliary (secy). Rel: Baptist. Mailing Add: 209 W. Harding, Pine Bluff, Ark. 71601. (1967)

RUSH, DEWEY DAVENT D
Ga. State Rep.
b. Glennville, Ga, 5/16/16; s. Lewie Leroy Rush and Amy Porcell R; m. 1/15/38 to Una Mae Weathers; c. Derrel D, Quinton S, Aris Dianne (Mrs. Wilson), Lynn Gail and David Roy. Educ: Glennville High Sch. Polit. & Govt. Pos: Ga. State Rep, 75th Dist, Tattnall and Long Cos, 65- Mem: Masons; Lions; Farm Bur. Rel: Missionary Baptist. Mailing Add: R.R. 4 Box 262, Glennville, Ga, 30427. (1967)

RUSH, FRANCIS J. D
Pa. State Rep.
b. Philadelphia, Pa, 5/25/21; s. Lawrence Rush and Mary Ann Kilfeather R; m. 7/3/43 to Eleanore F. Flood; c. Christina E. Educ: LaSalle Col; St. Joseph's Col. Polit. & Govt. Pos: Chief real estate appraiser, Inheritance Tax Div, Pa, 55-63; Pa. State Rep, 201st Dist, 67-; del, Dem. Nat. Conv, 68. Bus. & Prof. Pos: Self-employed, real estate and ins, 62- Mil. Serv: Entered as A/S, Navy, 42, released as Tel Man 2/C, 46; also serv. in Korea, 50-53, and in Naval Res; 5 Campaign and Am. Theater Ribbons; World War II Victory Medal; Good Conduct Medal; Nation Defense and Reserve Ribbons. Mem: Nat. Bd. of Realtors; Friendly Sons of St. Patrick; Germantown Business Men's Asn; K. of C. Rel: Roman Catholic. Mailing Add: 5300 Chew Ave, Philadelphia, Pa. 19138.

RUSH, KENNETH
U.S. Ambassador to Germany
b. Walla Walla, Wash, 1/17/10; s. David Campbell Rush and Emma Kate Kidwell R; m. 6/12/37 to Jane Gilbert Smith; c. George Gilbert (deceased), David (deceased), Malcolm, Cynthia Shepherd, John Randall and Kenneth. Educ: Univ. Tenn, A.B, 30; Yale, LL.B, 32. Hon. LL.D, Tusculum Col, 61. Polit. & Govt. Pos: Mem, President Johnson's Cmt. on For. Trade Policy, 68-69; mem, Secy. of Commerce's Cmt. on For. Direct Investment, 69; U.S. Ambassador to Germany, 69- Bus. & Prof. Pos: Assoc, Chadbourne, Stanchfield & Levy, 32-36; asst. prof, Duke Univ. Law Sch, 36-37; mem. staff, Union Carbide Corp, 36-, v.pres, 49-61, dir, 58-, chmn. gen. operating cmt, 65- and pres. and mem. exec. cmt, 66-69; dir, Bankers Trust Co, 66-69 and Am. Sugar Co, 61-69; chmn. bd. and mem. exec. cmt, Mfg. Chemists Asn, 66-67. Mem: Industs. cmt, Advert. Coun, 66-69; Am. Judicature Soc; exec. cmt, Yale

Law Sch. Asn, 52-62; develop. coun, Univ. Tenn, 63-; secy-treas. and trustee, Grand Cent. Art Galleries, 50-69; trustee, Taft Sch, 57-62; dir. and mem. Cmt. on For. Investment and Econ. Develop, U.S. Coun, Int. C. of C, 55-69; trustee, For. Policy Asn, 64-69; Coun. For. Rels; Apawamis Club; Univ. Club; Pine Valley Golf Club; Royal and Ancient Golf Club; Blind Brook Club; Ekwanok Country Club; Lyford Cay Club; Links Club. Rel: Episcopal; formerly Vestryman and Sr. Warden. Legal Res: North Manursing Island, Rye, N.Y. Mailing Add: U.S. Embassy, Bonn, Germany.

RUSH, SAMUEL LEE R
Committeeman, La. Rep. State Cent. Cmt.
b. Alexandria, La, 4/27/92; s. William Slade Rush and Betty Harwell R; m. 4/20/12 to Fannie Winfree; c. Stanley, Florine (Mrs. Blount), Juanita (Mrs. Reynolds), R. L. and Vanelda (Mrs. Elliott). Polit. & Govt. Pos: Mem, Electoral Col, 52; committeeman, La. Rep. State Cent. Cmt, 52- Bus. & Prof. Pos: Sawmill supt, Hillyer Deutsch Edwards, Inc, 27-57. Rel: Methodist. Mailing Add: 403 Maple St, Oakdale, La. 71463.

RUSH, WILLIAM D
Md. State Del.
b. Belfast, North. Ireland, 11/3/19; married. Educ: Pub. schs, Belfast and Baltimore Co. Polit. & Govt. Pos: Md. State Del, 63- Mil. Serv: Army. Mem: Mason; Pitman Masonic Club; Am. Legion; VFW; Ancient and Hon. Nobles of the Hardshells; Parkville Golf Club; Sportsman Club. Mailing Add: 3307 E. Putty Hill Ave, Baltimore, Md. 21234. (1967)

RUSH, WILLIAM VAN, JR. R
Exec. Dir, Rep. State Cmt, Ark.
b. Dover, Ark, 12/16/27; s. William Van Rush, Sr. and Martha Adeline Ross R; m. 8/3/56 to Mary Christine Bridges. Educ: Ark. Polytech. Col, 48-49. Polit. & Govt. Pos: Staff writer, Winthrop Rockefeller for Gov. Campaign, Ark, 65-66; ed. and pub. rels. dir, Ark. Rep. State Cmt, 66-68 and exec. dir, 68-; campaign dir, Rep. Constitutional Cands, Ark, 68. Bus. & Prof. Pos: Reporter and copy ed, Ark. Dem, Little Rock, Ark, 50-51 & 60-63; mem. pub. rels. staff, Southwest. Bell, Little Rock and St. Louis, 51-59; free-lance writing and pub. rels, Little Rock, 63-65. Mil. Serv: Entered as Pvt, Marines, 46, released as Cpl, 47, after serv. in Second Div, Pub. Information, Camp Lejeune, N.C, 47. Mem: Advertising Club of Little Rock; Mason; Ark. Pvt. Pilots Asn; Kiwanis. Rel: Protestant. Mailing Add: 1728 N. Spruce, Little Rock, Ark. 72207.

RUSHING, JOHN SLATON R
b. Claxton, Ga, 10/15/11; s. Charles M. Rushing (deceased) and Agnes Waters Rushing (deceased); 1st m. 7/9/38 to Leaneda Huff, wid; 2nd m. 8/18/62 to Alice Bent Culbertson; c. Lynda L. and Judith A. and step daughters, Joan Abendroth (Mrs. Robert H. Pratt), Jean Abendroth (Mrs. John L. Dickson) and Mary A. Abendroth. Educ: Ga. South. Col; Univ. Md. Polit. & Govt. Pos: V.chmn. and treas, Orange Co. Goldwater for President Cmt, Fla, 64; chmn, Orange Co. Rep. Exec. Cmt, 65-68. Bus. & Prof. Pos: Auditing clerk, Courts & Co, Atlanta, Ga, 35-40; account exec, Goodbody & Co, Orlando, Fla, 61-62; exec. dir, Orlando-Orange Co. Expressway Authority, 68. Mil. Serv: Entered as 2nd Lt, Army, 40, released as Col, 60, after serv. as Comdr, 3505th Air Base Group, Air Training Command, Greenville Base, Miss; Am. Defense, Am. Theater, World War II, Nat. Defense and Air Force Res. Ribbons. Mem: C. of C. and Univ. Club, Orlando, Fla. Rel: Episcopal. Mailing Add: Whispering Waters 1-G, Winter Park, Fla. 32789.

RUSK, DEAN D
b. Cherokee Co, Ga, 2/9/09; s. Robert Hugh Rusk and Frances Elizabeth Clotfelter R; m. 6/19/37 to Virginia Foisie; c. David Patrick, Richard Geary and Margaret Elizabeth. Educ: Davidson Col, B.A, 31; St. John's Col, Oxford, Rhodes Scholarship, 33 and M.A, 34; Phi Beta Kappa; Kappa Alpha. Polit. & Govt. Pos: Spec. asst. to Secy. of War Patterson, 46-47; dir, Off. UN Affairs, Dept. of State, 47-49, Asst. Secy. of State, 49, Dep. Under Secy. of State, 49-50, Asst. Secy. of State for Far East. Affairs, 50-51, Secy. of State, 61-68. Bus. & Prof. Pos: Asst. prof. govt, Mills Col, 34-38, dean of faculty, 38-40; pres, Rockefeller Found, N.Y.C, 52-61. Mil. Serv: Entered as Capt, Army, 40, released as Col, 46, after serv. in Inf. and Gen. Staff; Legion of Merit with Oak Leaf Cluster; Hon. Col, Army Res. Rel: Presbyterian. Mailing Add: 4980 Quebec St. N.W, Washington, D.C. 20016. (1967)

RUSMISEL, JACK RAYMOND R
Mem, Calif. Rep. State Cent. Cmt.
b. Scottsbluff, Nebr, 8/17/28; s. John Raymond Rusmisel and Irene Ekberg R; m. 8/31/52 to Sallie Fortner; c. John, Roger, Steven, Jana Elaine and Sara Leigh. Educ: Scottsbluff Col, 48-49; Univ. Denver, B.S.B.A, 52; Golden Gate Col, 53-55; Beta Alpha Psi; Sigma Chi. Polit. & Govt. Pos: Chmn, Fremont, Calif. Capital Improv. Cmt, 64-66; mem, Calif. Rep. State Cent. Cmt, 68- Bus. & Prof. Pos: Staff acct, Arthur Young & Co. CPA, San Francisco, Calif, 52-53; partner, Carl W. Flegal & Co. CPA, Fremont, 55-63; controller, Besco Builders & Developers, San Leandro, 63- Mil. Serv: Entered as A/S, Navy, 46, released as Aviation Electronics Tech. 3, 48, after serv. in Fleet Aircraft Serv. Squadron Seven. Mem: Calif. Soc. CPA; Nat. Asn. Acct; Fremont C. of C.(dir); Boy Scouts (troop cmt); Tri-Cities Rep. League; Fremont Rep. Assembly; life mem, Fremont Jr. C. of C. Rel: Protestant. Mailing Add: 38202 Ashford Way, Fremont, Calif. 94536.

RUSS, JOSEPH, IV R
Finance Chmn, Humboldt Co. Rep. Cent. Cmt, Calif.
b. Eureka, Calif, 7/25/36; s. Joseph Russ and Annette Tamboury R; m. 11/16/63 to Karen Lane; c. Reneé and J. Lane. Educ: Univ. of Calif, Berkeley, B.S, 59. Polit. & Govt. Pos: Mem, Calif. Rep. State Cent. Cmt, 64-68; v.chmn, First Cong. Dist. Rep. Cmt, 64-; chmn, Humboldt Co. Rep. Cent. Cmt, 66-68 and finance chmn, 68-; del, Rep. Nat. Conv, 68. Bus. & Prof. Pos: Dir. Bank of Coleta, 64-; v.chmn, Humboldt Co. Planning Cmt, 66-69. Mil. Serv: Entered as Pvt, Marine Corps Air Reserve, 59, released as Cpl, 64, after serv. in HMR 769; Honor man of Platoon. Mem: State pres, Calif. Asn. Future Farmers of Am, 54-56; pres, Humboldt Co. Cattlemen's Asn, 62-64; v.pres, Humboldt Co. Farm Bur, 66-69; Native Sons of Golden West; Commonwealth Club of Calif; Rotary. Am. Farmer Award. Rel: Catholic. Mailing Add: Bunker Hill Ranch, Ferndale, Calif. 95536.

RUSSELL, ALLEN E. R
Ky. State Rep.
b. 1928. Educ: South. Ill. Univ; Univ. of Louisville. Polit. & Govt. Pos: Ky. State Rep, 64-; mem, Rep. Fiscal Affairs Cmt. Bus. & Prof. Pos: Bus. syst. analyst. Mil. Serv: Army Nat. Guard. Mem: Int. dir. and past pres, Data Processing Mgt. Asn. Recipient of DPMA Individual Performance Award, 56; Awarded Cert. in Data Processing (CDP); Named One of Outstanding Young Men in Am, 64. Rel: Methodist. Mailing Add: 3031 Dale Ann Dr, Louisville, Ky. 40220. (1967)

RUSSELL, C. E. D
b. Apalachicola, Fla, 9/11/21; m. to Rosalie Priest R; c. Van Priest, Rosalie Ann. Educ: Univ. of Ga; Utah State Univ, 42. Polit. & Gov. Pos: Fla. State Rep, 62-66; past Chmn, Madison Co. Dem. Exec. Cmt; Suwanee River Develop. Authority. Bus. & Prof. Pos: Regional mgr, Am. Family Life Ins. Co. Mil. Serv: Air Force, Coast Artillery Co. M, 346th Regt, 87th Inf. Div. Mem: Past Pres, Bd. of Dir, Madison Rotary; past Comdr, VFW, Colin Kelly Post No. 4364; past Cub Scout Master. Rel: Church of Jesus Christ of Latter Day Saints; Elder, Supt, Sunday Sch. Mailing Add: P.O. Box 592, Madison, Fla. 32340. (1967)

RUSSELL, CHARLES HINTON R
b. Lovelock, Nev, 12/27/03; s. Robert James Russell and Ellen Daisy Ernst R; m. 3/19/39 to Marjorie Ann Guild; c. Clark George, Virginia Ellen, Craig Robert, Charles David and James Todd. Educ: Univ. Nev, A.B, 26. Polit. & Govt. Pos: Nev. State Assemblyman, 35-40; Nev. State Sen, 41-46, pres. pro tem, Nev. State Senate, 43; U.S. Rep, Nev, 47-49; mem, Cmn. on For. Econ. Coop, 49-50; Gov, Nev, 50-58; dir, U.S. Operations Mission, Asunción, Paraguay, 59-63. Bus. & Prof. Pos: Teacher, 26-27; mine office, Ruth, Nev, 28-29; ed, The Ely Record, 29-46; dir. develop. and asst. to pres, Univ. Nev, Reno, 63-69. Mem: Mason; Shrine. Rel: Episcopal. Mailing Add: 302 N. Minnesota St, Carson City, Nev. 89701.

RUSSELL, DONALD STUART D
b. Lafayette Springs, Miss, 2/22/06; s. Jesse L. Russell and Lula R; m. 6/15/29 to Virginia Utsey; c. Donald Stuart, Mildred Pendleton, Walker Scott and John Richardson. Educ: Univ. of S.C, B.A, 25, LL.B, 28; Univ. of Mich, grad. work in law, 29; Phi Beta Kappa. Polit. & Govt. Pos: Mem, Price Adjust. Bd, War Dept, Wash, D.C, 42; asst. to Dir. of Econ. Stabilization, 42; asst. to Dir. of War Mobilization, 43; dep. dir, Off. War Mobilization and Reconversion, 45; Asst. Secy. of State for Admin, 45-47; mem, S.C. Pub. Sch. Curricula Cmt; mem, Hoover Cmn. on Govt. Reorg; mem, Wriston Cmn. on Reorgn. For. Serv, 54; Gov, S.C, 63-65; U.S. Sen, S.C, 65-66; U.S. Dist. Judge, S.C, 67- Bus. & Prof. Pos: Lawyer; pres, Univ. of S.C, 52-57. Mil. Serv: Army, Maj, 44, SHAEF. Mem: Chmn. bd. of trustees, Spartanburg Gen. Hosp, 58-61; bd. trustees, Converse Col, Emory Univ, Spartanburg Jr. Col, Benedict Col. and Christ Sch; Mason; Rotary; Am. Legion; head, March of Dimes and Easter Seal Drives in S.C. Rel: Methodist. Legal Res: 716 Otis Blvd, Spartanburg, S.C. 29302. Mailing Add: Federal Bldg, Spartanburg, S.C. 29301.

RUSSELL, EDWARD WESLEY R
First Selectman, Weston, Conn.
b. New York, N.Y, 5/14/10; s. Frank Edward Russell and Antoinette Parisette R; m. 8/1/36 to Ruth Utz. Educ: Ohio Wesleyan Univ, B.A, 32; Harvard Univ, 32-33; West. Res. Univ. Law Sch, 33-35; Phi Delta Phi; Alpha Tau Omega. Polit. & Govt. Pos: Prosecuting grand juror, Conn, 56-61; mem, Weston Bd. Finance, 61-63; Conn. State Rep, 63-65; del, Gubernatorial Conv, 63-66; trustee, Weston Rep. Club and mem, Weston Town Rep. Cmt, 66-69; first selectman, Weston, 69- Bus. & Prof. Pos: Attorney, Travelers Ins. Co, Cleveland Br, 35-36; asst. claims mgr, Am. Auto Ins. Co, 36-42; attorney mgr, Am. Assoc. Ins. Co, Br, Buffalo, N.Y, 45-52; pres. and treas, Crown Founds, Inc, 52- Mil. Serv: Entered as Lt.(jg), Navy, 42, released as Lt, Comdr, 57, after serv. in 5th Amphibious Force, South and Southwest Pac, 42-45; Naval Res; Pac. Theater Ribbon with 6 Stars; Philippine Liberation Medal with 2 Stars; Victory Medal; Am. Theater Ribbon. Mem: Am. and N.Y. Bar Asns; Bar of Ohio; Bar of N.Y; Brooklawn Country Club. Rel: Episcopal. Legal Res: Kettle Creek Rd, Weston, Conn. 06880. Mailing Add: 225 Federal St, Bridgeport, Conn. 06609.

RUSSELL, FRED J. R
Dep. Dir, Off. of Emergency Preparedness, Exec. Off. of the President
b. Edmonton, Alta, Can, 6/9/16; s. Fred H. Russell and Agnes Maye Clements R. (deceased); div; c. Terry Lee (Mrs. Benjamin F. Hayes) and Fred B. Educ: Univ. Calif, Los Angeles Exten. Div, 37-41. Polit. & Govt. Pos: Dep. dir, Off. of Emergency Preparedness, Exec. Off. of the President, 69- Bus. & Prof. Pos: Asst. to asst. gen. mgr. prod. control, material, Douglas Aircraft Co, Santa Monica, Calif, 36-42; asst. works mgr, Timm Aircraft Corp, Van Nuys, 42-45; pres. & gen. mgr, Weiser Co, South Gate, 45-68; pres, Russell Properties Co, Los Angeles, 64-69. Mil. Serv: Entered as Pvt, Marine Corps Res, 35-39 with serv. in 13th Bn. Mem: Los Angeles Country Club; Calif. Club. Legal Res: 143 N. Arnaz Dr, Beverly Hills, Calif. 90211. Mailing Add: 2650 Virginia Ave, N.W, Washington, D.C. 20037.

RUSSELL, GEORGE EDWARD R
Pres, Stamford Bd. of Rep, Conn.
b. Brooklyn, N.Y, 11/28/15; s. Edward Joseph Russell and Mary Elizabeth Bonser R; m. 9/21/40 to Helen Elizabeth Kearns; c. Donna M. (Mrs. Knight), George Edward, Jr. and Wayne Michael. Educ: Drexel Inst. of Tech. Polit. & Govt. Pos: Mem, Stamford Bd. of Rep, Conn, 51- and pres, 65-; dep. acting mayor, Stamford, Conn, 64-65 and acting mayor, 65- Bus. & Prof. Pos: Supvr, Machlett Labs, Div. Raytheon, 36- Mem: K. of C; Hibernians; Stamford Rural Men's Rep. Club; Kiwanis; Am. Soc. for Metals; Conn. Indust. Mgt. Clubs; Stamford Police Asn. Rel: Roman Catholic. Mailing Add: 18 Sleepy Hollow Lane, Springdale, Stamford, Conn. 06879. (1967)

RUSSELL, HARVEY POTTER R
b. Monkton, Vt, 7/10/90; m. to Celia J. Sprague; c. one. Educ: Burlington Bus. Col. Polit. & Govt. Pos: Town auditor, 24-34; selectman, 45-51 & 54-; chmn, Town Rep. Cmt; Vt. State Rep, 63-66. Bus. & Prof. Pos: Retired farmer. Rel: Friends. Mailing Add: R.D, N. Ferrisburg, Vt. 05456. (1967)

RUSSELL, HENRY PHILLIP, JR. D
Ga. State Rep.
b. Milledgeville, Ga, 7/14/16; s. Henry Phillip Russell, Sr. and Lelia Harris R; m. 5/2/37 to Myrtis Wynnette Dekle; c. Henry Phillip, III and Sally Wynnette. Educ: Thomasville High Sch, 34. Polit. & Govt. Pos: Thomas Co. Cmnr, Roads and Revenue, Ga, 57-65; Ga. State Rep, 63- Bus. & Prof. Pos: Owner, Russell Dairy Farm. Mil. Serv: Entered as Seaman 2/C, Navy, 44, released as Radarman 2/C, 46, after serv. in Amphibious Corps, Pac, 44-46; Asiatic-Pac. Ribbon with 2 stars. Mem: Moose; Elks; VFW (Comdr, 48-50); Am. Legion; Farm Bur; Am. Jersey Cattle Club; Ga. Livestock Asn; Thomas Co. Livestock Asn.(pres, 56). Rel: Presbyterian. Mailing Add: Route 1, Boston, Ga. 31626.

RUSSELL, HOWARD EDWIN, JR. R
Chmn, Rep. State Cent. Cmt, R.I.
b. Providence, R.I, 2/15/21; s. Howard Edwin Russell and Grace Williams Chase R; m. to Bessie Crabtree; c. Sally Arlin, Polly Jeanne and Heidi Elizabeth. Educ: Brown Univ, A.B, 43; Theta Delta Chi. Polit. & Govt. Pos: Chmn, E. Greenwich Rep. Town Cmt, 59-65; admin. asst. for legis affairs, Gov. of R.I, 63-65; chmn, Rep. State Cent. Cmt, R.I, 65-; nominee, U.S. House of Rep, 68; del, Rep. Nat. Conv, 68. Bus. & Prof. Pos: Pres, Howard Russell, Inc, 54- Mil. Serv: Pvt, Marine Corps, 42-46 & 50-52; various mil. awards and decorations; Lt. Col, Res. Mem: R.I. Asn. Ins. Agents; Legion of Honor, DeMolay; Am. Legion; Varnum Continentals; Mil. Order For. Wars; Rotary; Big Bros. Rel: Baptist. Legal Res: 240 Division St, East Greenwich, R.I. 02818. Mailing Add: 87 Weybosset St, Providence, R.I. 02903. (1967)

RUSSELL, J. A. R
Chmn, Jerome Co. Rep. Cent. Cmt, Idaho
b. Roy, Utah, 8/31/03; s. John Patterson Russell and Rosaline Anderson R; m. 5/31/24 to Minnie Burgoyne; c. Kenneth W. and Geraldine. Educ: High Sch; Bus. Col. Polit. & Govt. Pos: Precinct committeeman, Rep. Party, Idaho, 61-62; chmn, Jerome Co. Rep. Cent. Cmt, 62- Mem: Charter mem, Elks; Jerome C. of C; Zone chmn, dep. dist. gov. and dist. gov, Jerome Lions Club. Rel: Methodist. Mailing Add: 613 Second Ave. E, Jerome, Idaho 83338.

RUSSELL, JAMES 'JAY' D
Mo. State Rep.
b. St. Louis, Mo, 11/4/28; m. 6/11/55 to Delphie Mann; c. Jeanne and Jim. Educ: Univ. Mo, Columbia. Polit. & Govt. Pos: Mo. State Rep, 62- Bus. & Prof. Pos: Restaurant owner. Mil. Serv: Marine Corps. Mem: K. of C. Rel: Catholic. Mailing Add: 700 Bellarmine Lane, Florissant, Mo. 63031. (1967)

RUSSELL, JEAN ALBACH R
V.Chmn, Routt Co. Rep. Party, Colo.
b. Omaha, Nebr, 3/8/34; d. John Solon Albach and Beatrice Leighton A; m. 7/5/58 to Richard W. Russell; c. Clayton, Elizabeth and David. Educ: State Univ. Iowa, M.A, 56; Kappa Kappa Gamma. Polit. & Govt. Pos: V.chmn, Routt Co. Rep. Party, Colo, 69- Mem: Jr. League of Des Moines, Iowa. Rel: Episcopal. Mailing Add: Box W, Steamboat Springs, Colo. 80477.

RUSSELL, JOE W. D
Mem, Ill. Dem. State Cent. Cmt.
b. Roberts, Ill, 7/29/00. Educ: Univ. Ill. Col. of Agr. Polit. & Govt. Pos: Ill. State Rep, 32-44, 54 & 60-68; mem, State Fair Adv. Bd. under Gov. Horner and chmn. of same bd. under Gov. Stevenson; mem, Ill. Dem. State Cent. Cmt, 68-69; alternate del, Dem. Nat. Conv, 68. Bus. & Prof. Pos: Farming and IHC implement dealer. Mailing Add: 22 E. Chestnut St, Piper City, Ill. 60959. (1967)

RUSSELL, JOHN THOMAS R
Minority Whip, Mo. House of Rep.
b. Lebanon, Mo, 9/22/31; s. Aubrey F. Russell and Velma F. Johnson R; m. 12/29/51 to Margaret Ann Carr; c. John Douglas and Georgia Jeanette. Educ: Drury Col, Springfield, Mo, 3½ years. Polit. & Govt. Pos: Finance chmn, Laclede Co. Rep. Cent. Cmt, Mo, 60; Mo. State Rep, Laclede Co, 62-66, 125th Dist, 67-, minority whip, Mo. House of Rep, 67- Bus. & Prof. Pos: Dir, and officer, Laclede Metal Prod. Co. and Detroit Tool & Eng. Co, Lebanon, 57- and Gen. Aluminum Supply Co, Kansas City, 59-; So-Mo Transportation Co, Lebanon, 60; partner, Faith Leasing Co, Lebanon, 69- Mil. Serv: Entered Air Force, 51, released as Airman 1/C, 54. Mem: Kiwanis; Am. Legion; Mason; past mem. bd. dirs, Jaycees. Rel: Southern Baptist. Legal Res: W. City Route 66, Lebanon, Mo. 65536. Mailing Add: Box 93, Lebanon, Mo. 65536.

RUSSELL, LLOYD A. R
N.Y. State Assemblyman
b. East Otto, N.Y, 7/4/21; s. Lester W. Russell and Ada Dreier R; m. 3/19/43 to Margaret Bailey; c. Cheryl Jean. Educ: Agr. Tech, Alfred, N.Y, 38-39. Polit. & Govt. Pos: Justice of Peace, East Otto, N.Y, 59-64; town Committeeman, East Otto, 62; Cattaraugus Co. Rep. Committeeman, N.Y, 62-; mem, Cattaraugus Co. Civil Serv. Cmn, 64-, chmn, 66-; N.Y. State Assemblyman, 66- Mil. Serv: Entered as Pvt, Air Corps, 42, released as Flight Officer, Glider Pilot, 45, after serv. in 1st Provisional Glider Group, Asiatic Theatre, 44. Mem: Am. Legion; Farm Bur; Dairymens League; Grange; Cattaraugus Co. Magistrates Asn; Vol. Fireman; Mason. Rel: Methodist. Mailing Add: East Otto, N.Y. 14729.

RUSSELL, MARGARET A. D
b. Keene, N.H, 8/7/29; married; c. 1 daughter. Educ: Keene High Sch. Polit. & Govt. Pos: N.H. State Rep, -67; clerk, Ward 5, Keene. Bus. & Prof. Pos: Housewife. Mem: Cath. Daughters of Am, grand regent; O.W.L; League of Women Voters. Rel: Catholic. Mailing Add: 573 West St, Keene, N.H. 03431. (1967)

RUSSELL, NEWTON R. R
Calif. State Assemblyman
b. Los Angeles, Calif, 6/25/27; s. John Russell and Amy Requa R; m. 2/12/53 to Diane Henderson; c. Steve, Sherry and Julie. Educ: Univ. South. Calif, B.S. in bus. admin; Univ. Calif, Los Angeles and Georgetown Univ, postgrad. study; Squires; Delta Tau Delta; Alpha Kappa Psi. Polit. & Govt. Pos: Former precinct chmn; Calif. State Assemblyman, 62nd Dist, Los Angeles Co, 64-, mem, Educ, Revenue and Taxation and Urban Affairs and Housing Cmts. and the Joint Cmt. on Pub. Domain, currently and former mem, Rules Cmt, Calif. State Assembly; mem. credentials cmt, Calif. Rep. State Cent. Cmt. and mem, Los Angeles Co. Rep. Cent. Cmt, 62nd Dist, currently; alternate del, Rep. Nat. Conv, 68. Bus. & Prof. Pos: Spec. agent, Northwest. Mutual Life Ins. Co, 54- Mil. Serv: Entered as A/S, Navy, World War II, released as Seaman 1/C. Mem: Nat. Asn. of Life Underwriters; chmn, Tujunga United Way Residential Campaign, 63; bus. solicitor, Commun. Chest; Rotary; Am. Legion Post 250; C. of C; mem-at-lg, Boy Scouts; Masters Men. Skiing, Swimming and Tennis. Rel: Presbyterian. Legal Res: 6407 Chaffee St, Tujunga, Calif. 91042. Mailing Add: 3507 W. Magnolia Blvd, Burbank, Calif. 91505.

RUSSELL, PATRICIA BROWN R
Chmn, Wayne Co. Rep. Party, Mo.
b. Poplar Bluff, Mo, 2/7/32; d. William Leo Brown, Sr. and Ella Pauline Stack B; m. 2/2/48 to Robert Sidney Russell; c. Aaron Lynn (Mrs. Talley), Sidney Madison, Michael Earl and Dallas Brown. Educ: Poplar Bluff High Sch. Polit. & Govt. Pos: Chmn, Wayne Co. Rep. Party, Mo, 68- Bus. & Prof. Pos: Owner and Mgr, Holliday Landing Resort, 62- Mem: Eastern Star; Rep. Women's Club. Rel: Baptist. Mailing Add: Holliday Landing, Greenville, Mo. 63944.

RUSSELL, RICHARD BREVARD D
U.S. Sen, Ga.
b. Winder, Ga, 11/2/97; s. Richard Brevard Russell and Ina Dillard R. Educ: Univ. of Ga, B.L, 18; Sigma Alpha Epsilon. Hon. LL.D, Mercer Univ, 57 and The Citadel. Polit. & Govt. Pos: Former attorney, Barrow Co, Ga; Ga. State Rep, 21-31, Speaker, Ga. House of Rep, 27-31; Gov, Ga, 31-33; U.S.Sen, Ga, 33-, President Pro-Tem, U.S. Senate, 69-; mem, Presidential Cmn. to Investigate Assassination of President Kennedy. Mil. Serv: Naval Res, 18. Mem: Am. and Ga. Bar Asns; Am. Legion; 40 et 8; Mason; Kiwanis; Odd Fellows; Shrine; Elks; Burns Club of Atlanta; Sphinx Hon. Soc. of Univ. of Ga. Recipient, Minute Man of Year in Nat. Defense Award, Reserve Officers Asn, 59. Legal Res: Winder, Ga. 30680. Mailing Add: 205 Old Senate Office Bldg, Washington, D.C. 20510. (1967)

RUSSELL, RUTH D
Mem, Dem. Nat. Cmt, Tenn.
b. Gallatin, Tenn, 2/28/08; d. Frank Bernard Seay and Nancy Jackson S; m. 6/4/27 to Oscar Alexander Russell. Educ: Gallatin Private Inst, 25-27. Polit. & Govt. Pos: Court reporter, Sumner, Trousdale, Wilson and Macon Co, Tenn, 28-58; dep. clerk, Chancery Ct, Sumner Co, Tenn, 46-59; mem, Tenn. Dem. Exec. Cmt, 46-59 and chmn, 56-59; mem, Dem. Nat. Cmt, Tenn, 57-; del, Dem. Nat. Conv, 68. Bus. & Prof. Pos: Dir, First Mortgage Co. Mem: A.R.C. (registrn. chmn, Sumner Co); Tenn. Clerks Asn. (chmn, Middle Tenn. Div, 58-59); Eastern Star (past matron); Gallatin Bus. and Prof. Women's Club (past pres. and chmn, career adv). Named Bus. Woman of the Year, 56. Legal Res: Gallatin, Tenn. 37066. Mailing Add: Court House, Gallatin, Tenn. 37066. (1967)

RUSSELL, THEODORE HENRY D
Chmn, Kennebec Co. Dem. Cmt, Maine
b. Waterville, Maine, 11/6/25; s. Clyde E. Russell and Doris Garland R; m. 6/8/48 to Ethelyn Bradstreet; c. Bonnie Ellen, Franklin Arthur, Andrew Nelson, Mark Theodore, Lucinda Ethel, Steven Clyde, Barbara Lynne, Beth Ann and Doreen Doris. Educ: Colby Col, A.B, 47; Bates Col, Navy V-12 Prog, 3 semesters; Univ. Notre Dame, Naval Midshipman Sch, 1 semester; Delta Upsilon. Polit. & Govt. Pos: State committeeman, Maine Dem. State Cmt, 62-66; chmn, Kennebec Co. Dem. Cmt, 67-; del, Dem. Nat. Conv, 68. Bus. & Prof. Pos: Local rep, East. States Farmers Exchange, Winslow, Maine, 53-58; agent, State Farm Ins. Co, Waterville, 59-61 and agency mgr, Augusta, 61- Mil. Serv: Entered as A/S, Navy, 44, released as Lt, 53 after serving on U.S.S. N.K. Perry, ComDesPac, 45-46 and Sixth Fleet, 51-53; World War II Victory, Am. Theater and Asiatic-Pac. Theater Medals. Mem: Kennebec Valley Life Underwriters Asn; Maine Dairymen's Asn.(past pres); Maine Breeding Coop.(past dir); Winslow Grange (past master); Maine State and Nat. Grange; VFW (past Comdr, Ernest A. Rutter Post); AF&AM. Recipient of awards for ins. and farm work. Rel: United Church of Christ. Legal Res: R.F.D. 5, Augusta, Maine 04330. Mailing Add: 8 Green St, Augusta, Maine 04330.

RUSSELL, WALLACE CLAYTON, SR. R
b. Montgomery, Vt, 2/8/99; m. to Eva Pearl Govro; c. two sons and three daughters. Educ: Montgomery, Albany and Craftsbury schs. Polit. & Govt. Pos: Vt. State Rep, 61-66. Bus. & Prof. Pos: Farmer. Mem: Mason; Eastern Star; Farm Bur; Nat, State and Crystal Lake Grange. Rel: Congregational. Mailing Add: Barton, Vt. 05822. (1967)

RUSSILLO, MICHAEL P.
b. New Rochelle, N.Y, 10/24/05; m. 2/5/28 to Christine A. Gallagher; c. Anne C, Julie E, Michael P. Jr. Educ: U.S. Naval Acad, Annapolis, Md, 1927. Polit. & Govt. Pos: Nebr. Unicameral Legis, 59-66. Bus. & Prof. Pos: Mgr, Omaha C. of C. Hwy. Develop. Dept. Mil. Serv: Retired Rear Adm. of the U.S. Navy. Mem: Omaha Club; Omaha C. of C; Am. Legion. Mailing Add: 673 N. 59th St, Omaha, Nebr. 68132. (1967)

RUSSO, GAETANO ARTHUR, JR. R
Alderman, Waterbury, Conn.
b. Waterbury, Conn, 8/31/18; s. Gaetano Arthur Russo, Sr. and Carmela Luella R; m. to Edith Barbieri; c. Gaetano Arthur, III, Christopher Robert and Gregory Jon. Educ: Holy Cross Col, B.A, 40; Univ. Conn. Law Sch, LL.B, 48. Polit. & Govt. Pos: Alderman, Waterbury, Conn, 67-; Rep. nominee, U.S. Rep, 68. Mil. Serv: Entered as Pvt, Army, 42, released as 1st Lt, 46, after serv. in ETO, 44-46; Lt. Col, Conn. Nat. Guard, currently; Bronze Star; ETO Ribbon with Two Battle Stars. Mem: Cadets Athletic Club; life mem, VFW; Am. Legion. Rel: Catholic. Mailing Add: 101 Birchwood St, Waterbury, Conn. 06708.

RUSSO, JOSEPH R
R.I. State Rep.
b. Brooklyn, N.Y, 9/3/07. Educ: N.Y. City Schs. Polit. & Govt. Pos: R.I.

State Rep, 62- Bus. & Prof. Pos: Poultry husbandry. Mem: Former pres, Chariho Lions and Poultry Producers Asn. of R.I; dir, East. States Farmers Exchange. Mailing Add: Woodville, R.D, Hope Valley, R.I. 02832. (1967)

RUSSO, LUCIO F. R
N.Y. State Assemblyman
b. New Castle, Pa; m. to Tina Iarossi; c. Thomas, Anthony. Educ: Fordham Col. and Law Sch. Polit. & Govt. Pos: Mem, Richmond Co. Rep. Exec. Cmt; referee, Workmens Compensation Bd, N.Y, 49-52; N.Y. State Assemblyman, 52- Bus. & Prof. Pos: Lawyer. Mem: Richmond Co. Bar Asn; Eagles; Staten Island War Mem. Soc; Staten Island Hist. Soc; (4°) K. of C; Ital. Club of Staten Island; Conf. House Asn; Staten Island Little League; Boy Scouts; Kiwanis; Stapleton Athletic Club (bd. dirs); Visiting Nurse Asn; Dongan Hills Commun. Asn. Mailing Add: 82 Romer Rd, Dongan Hills, Staten Island, N.Y. 10304. (1967)

RUSSO, MARIUS THOMAS D
Chmn, East Lansdowne Town Dem. Cmt, Pa.
b. N.Y.C, 1/1/22; s. Rocco Russo and Carmella Romano R; m. 4/27/46 to Irene D. Durant; c. Irene S, Beth Ann and Thomas R. Educ: U.S. Army Sig. Corps Radio Sch, 42. Polit. & Govt. Pos: Coun. mem, East Lansdowne Borough, Pa, 54-, pres. of coun, 62-; chmn, East Lansdowne Town Dem. Cmt, 60-; del, Dem. Nat. Conv, 64. Bus. & Prof. Pos: V.pres, E.B. Krausen Inc, 61- Mil. Serv: Entered as Pvt, Army, 42, released as T-5, 45, after serv. in 1373rd Sig. Unit, ETO; ETO, Rhineland and Cent. Europe Serv. Medals; World War II Medal; Am. Serv. Medal; Europe-Africa-Mid. East Serv. Medal; Good Conduct Medal. Mem: Chaplain, George Wash. Post, Am. Legion. Rel: Catholic. Mailing Add: 111 Beverly Ave. E, Lansdowne, Pa. 19050.

RUSSUM, JULIUS FRANKLIN D
Chmn, DeSoto Co. Dem. Cmt, Miss.
b. Flora, Miss, 2/18/95; s. Wilson Frank Russum and Cornelia Hospon R; m. 12/20/22 to Beatrice Brunson; c. Lawrence Brunson and Betty (Mrs. Manning). Educ: Miss. State Univ, B.S, 21; George Peabody Col, M.A, 28; Phi Delta Kappa. Polit. & Govt. Pos: Chmn, DeSoto Co. Dem. Cmt, Miss, 48- Bus. & Prof. Pos: Supt. Hernando Schs, Miss, 36-45; co. supt. of educ, DeSoto Co, Miss, 48-56. Mil. Serv: Entered as Pvt, Army, 18, released as Wagoner, 19, after serv. in 304th Am. Tr, 79th Div, Argonne Forest, France. Mem: Miss. and Nat. Educ. Asns; Miss. and Nat. Dept. of Supt; Mason; Rotary (past pres); Farm Bur; VFW (past comdr); Am. Legion (past comdr). Rel: Baptist; Deacon, Hernando Baptist Church. Mailing Add: 138 East St, Hernando, Miss. 38632.

RUST, ROBERT WARREN R
U.S. Attorney Designate, South. Dist. Fla.
b. Long Island, N.Y, 8/16/28; s. A.H. Rust and Helen Dauth R; m. 1/28/53 to Mary Ruth Duncan; c. Benjamin D, Lani L, Debra D, Bonnie L, Randall D, Wendy E. Educ: St. Lawrence Univ; Univ. Miami Law Sch, J.D; Marine C. Command & Staff Col; Marine C. Amphib. Warfare Sch; Tank Leaders Sch; Sigma Alpha Epsilon; Phi Delta Phi. Polit. & Govt. Pos: Patrolman, Miami Police Dept, Fla, 53-54; asst. U.S. Attorney, Dept. Justice, 58-61; city prosecutor, North Bay, 62-63; chief asst. solicitor, Palm Beach Co, 64-66; cand. for Fla. State Rep; Fla. State Rep, 66-68; Palm Beach Co. Rep. Committeeman, 66-; mem, Fla. Law Rev. Cmt, 67-; del, Rep. Nat. Conv, 68; legal counsel, Crime & Law Enforcement Cmt, Fla. House Rep, 69; U.S. Attorney designate, South Dist, Fla, 69. Bus. & Prof. Pos: Asst. auditor, First Nat. Bank Miami, 54-56; assoc. attorney, Smathers, Thompson & Dyer, 56-58 & Shutts & Bowen, 61-63; attorney, 66- Mil. Serv: Entered as Pvt, Marine Corps Res, 47, released as Lt. Col, after serv. in C Co, 2nd Amphib. Tractor Bn, 2nd Marine Div, 50-52 and Commanding Off, C Co, 4th Amphib. Tractor Bn, 4th Marine Div, 64-66; Nat. Defense Serv. Medal; Marine Corps Res. Ribbon; Expert Rifleman Badge. Mem: Fed, Inter-Am, Am, Fla. Dade & Palm Beach Co. Bar Asns; Fla. Prosecuting Attorneys Asn; Palm Beach Co. Police Chiefs Asn; Nat. Dist. Attorneys Asn; Am. Legion; Kiwanis; Mil. Order World Wars; Res. Officers Asn; Marine Corps Res. Officers Asn; Nat. Rifle Asn; Navy League; Boys Club Palm Beach Co; Rod and Reel Club. Fla. Khoury League Coun. Oscar, 58; Award of Merit from Secy. Treas, Douglas Dillon & Chief of U.S. Secret Serv, James Rowley, for assisting in protecting from harm the President-Elect of U.S, John F. Kennedy, 60; Legis. Award, Fla. State Lodge Fraternal Order of Police for outstanding effort on behalf law enforcement off, 67; Named One of Outstanding Mem. of 1967 Fla. Legis. for Efforts in the Anti-Crime and Pub. Safety Fields, Capital Press Corps Poll. Rel: Presbyterian. Mailing Add: 132 Royal Palm Way, Palm Beach, Fla. 33480.

RUSTAD, ELMER LEWIS R
Nat. Dir, U.S. Savings Bonds Div.
b. Wakonda, S.Dak, 8/11/08; s. John Rustad and Hannah Forsethlien R; m. 8/8/32 to Berniece Elizabeth Hillery; c. Patricia (Mrs. W.J. Herrmann) and Robert L. Educ: Sioux Falls Col, B.A. cum laude, 29; Univ. Minn, M.A, 37. Polit. & Govt. Pos: State dir, U.S. Savings Bonds Div, S.Dak, 41-52; dir. of sales, Wash, D.C, 52-66; asst. nat. dir, 66-69; nat. dir, 69- Bus. & Prof. Pos: Supt. of schs, Egan, S.Dak, 29-34; prin, jr. high schs, Aberdeen, 34-41. Mil. Serv: Entered as Lt.(jg), Navy, 43, released as Lt. Comdr, 46, after serv. in Navy Air Training, Pac. Theatre. Meritorious Serv. Award, U.S. Treas. Dept. Rel: Baptist. Mailing Add: 2019 Lorraine Ave, McLean, Va. 22101.

RUSTOM, R. M. R
b. Devils Lake, N.Dak, 1910; m. to Ruby R. Educ: Received educ. Devils Lake, N.Dak. Schs. Polit. & Gov. Pos: Precinct committeeman; Vice Pres, 28th Dist; Rep. Club; Vice Pres, and acting chmn, 29th Dist. Club. Bus. & Prof. Pos: Carpenter and Builder; Operated Rudy's Serv. & Grocery, Spanaway, 51-52; Farmed; Mechanic work during 30's; operated Tveten's Serv, 34-35; Newspaper work; arbitrator for farmers in civil cases; apartment owner; logger; machinist. Mil. Serv: Vet. Mailing Add: 7441 S. Tacoma Ave, Tacoma, Wash. 98408. (1967)

RUSTON, BERNICE LORIS R
Mem, Calif. Rep. State Cent. Cmt.
b. El Centro, Calif, 10/24/19; d. Edward Leonidas Bridgers and Loris Phillips B; m. 11/6/38 to Newton Joseph Ruston; c. Sally Rae (Mrs. Deleenheer) and Barbara Sue (Mrs. Oswald). Educ: Woodbury Col. of Art, 36-38; Sigma Iota Chi; Woodbury Art Soc; Woodbury Photographers. Polit. & Govt. Pos: Mem, Calif. Rep. State Cent. Cmt, 69-; mem, San Bernardino Co. Rep. Cent. Cmt, 69- Bus. & Prof. Pos: Milinery and costume designer, Campbell, Marks, Hollywood, Calif, 38-39; dispatcher, Lockheed Air Craft Corp, 41-43. Mem: Arrowhead and San Bernardino Co. Rep. Women; Lake Arrowhead Womens Club; Lake Arrowhead Country Club Auxilary (past pres); Pioneers Mem. Hosp. Auxilary (past pres); Lake Arrowhead Yacht Club; DAR. Rel: Presbyterian. Legal Res: 28411 N. Shore Rd, Lake Arrowhead, Calif. 92352. Mailing Add: P.O. Box 937, Lake Arrowhead, Calif. 92352.

RUTH, EARL BAKER R
U.S. Rep, N.C.
b. Spencer, N.C, 2/7/16; s. Earl Monroe Ruth and Amon M. Butler R; m. 12/27/38 to Jane Wiley; c. Billie Jane (Mrs. Frank Foil), Earl Wiley, Marian Ann (Mrs. Joe Reber) and Jacqueline Dell (Mrs. Clay Burleson). Educ: Univ. of N.C, A.B, 38, M.A, 42 and Ph.D, 55. Polit. & Govt. Pos: City councilman, Salisbury, N.C; U.S. Rep, Eighth Dist, N.C, 69- Bus. & Prof. Pos: Teacher and coach, Chapel Hill High Sch, Chapel Hill, N.C, 38-39 and Piedmont Jr. High Sch, Charlotte, N.C, 39-40; shipping dept, McCrary Mills, Asheboro, N.C, 40; asst. supt, N.C. State Parks, 41; grad. asst, Dept. of Phys. Educ, Univ. of N.C, 41-42; dir. of recreation, Kings Mountain, N.C, 45; asst. football coach, baseball coach, basketball coach, athletic dir, chmn, Dept. of Phys. Educ. and dean of students, Catawba Col, 46. Mil. Serv: Entered as Ens, Navy, 42, released as Lt, 45, after serv. in U.S.S. St. George. Mem: Nat. Sportscasters and Sportswriters Awards Prog.(mem. of original cmt. and past pres); Am. Legion; Civitan; Elks; YMCA (past bd. mem). Rel: Presbyterian. Legal Res: Salisbury, N.C. Mailing Add: U.S. House Office Bldg, Washington, D.C. 20515.

RUTHER, WILLIAM RICHARD R
b. Clarence, Iowa, 7/17/27; s. Elmore William Ruther and Selma Hulse R; m. 6/25/50 to Maxine Lenore Blake; c. Virginia Rae, Blake William and Brent Richard. Educ: State Univ. of Iowa, B.A, 48 and J.D, 50; Order of the Coif; Alpha Tau Omega; Phi Delta Phi. Polit. & Govt. Pos: Secy. and precinct committeeman, Des Moines Co. Rep. Cent. Cmt, Iowa, 52-56, treas, 57-61, finance chmn, 62-65; co. attorney, Des Moines Co, 55; dist. chmn, Young Rep. of Iowa, 56; del, Rep. Nat. Conv, 64. Bus. & Prof. Pos: Attorney-at-law, Burlington and Clarence, Iowa, 50-57; v.pres. and trust officer, Nat. Bank of Burlington, 57-65 and Nat. Bank of Appleton, 65-66; partner, Dailey, Dailey, Ruther & Bauer, Attorneys, 66- Mil. Serv: Entered as A/S, Navy, 45, released as Yeoman 3/C, 46. Publ: 'Statutory Trends Toward Legalization of Gambling,' Iowa Law Rev, 50; 'Planning the Medium-Sized, Modern Estate,' Trusts and Estates, 1/66. Mem: Am. and Iowa State Bar Asns; State Bar of Wis; Rotary Int; Elks. Rel: Protestant. Mailing Add: 17 Cascade Terr, Burlington, Iowa 52601.

RUTHERFORD, CLARA BERYL R
Mem, Calif. Rep. State Cent. Cmt.
b. Porterville, Calif, 3/2/12; d. Harry Abbey Wilcox and Jessie Jefford W; m. 4/29/33 to Kenneth Carr Rutherford; c. Jane (Mrs. Barry V. Smith), Anne and Alan. Educ: Porterville Jr. Col, A.A, 31. Polit. & Govt. Pos: Asst. clerk, Selective Serv. Bd, Porterville, Calif, 41-42; secy, Calif. Rep. Assembly, Porterville Area, 65-66, v.pres, 67, pres, 68; mem, Tulare Co. Rep. Cent. Cmt, 67-; mem, Calif. Rep. State Cent. Cmt, 67- Bus. & Prof. Pos: Bookkeeper, Claubes Prescription Pharmacy, Porterville, Calif, 48-60. Mem: Farm Bur; Am. Nat, Tulare Co. and Calif. CowBelles; Calif. Cattlemen's Asn. Rel: Protestant. Mailing Add: 33195 Success Valley Dr, Porterville, Calif. 93257.

RUTHERFURD, DOUGLAS R
b. Vernon, N.J, 5/23/00. Educ: Princeton Univ. Polit. & Govt. Pos: Mem, Vernon Twp. Rep. Cmt, N.J, 49-57, chmn, 51 & 53-55; former N.J. State Assemblyman. Bus. & Prof. Pos: Dir, Sussex Co. Trust Co; retired. Mem: Rotary; past pres, Sussex Co. Peace Officers Asn; Mason; trustee, Franklin Hosp. Mailing Add: Sparta, N.J. 07871. (1967)

RUTHRAUFF, WILLIAM EDGAR, JR. R
b. Phila, Pa, 4/7/11; s. William Edgar Ruthrauff, Sr. and Millicent Cook R; m. 7/7/30 to Elsie Lillian Haas; c. Phyliss Gale (Mrs. Ronald R. Hamilton) and Raymond W. Educ: West Phila. High Sch, 3 years. Polit. & Govt. Pos: Mayor, Collingdale, Pa, 61-66; chmn, Collingdale Rep. Party, 61-; clerk, Delaware Co. Courts, 63-; mem, Delaware Co. Bd. Supvr, 67-; del, Rep. Nat. Conv, 68; mem, Delaware Co. Airport Authority, 68- Bus. & Prof. Pos: Mgr, Am. Stores Co, Delaware Co, 29-35; asst. br. mgr, Pillsbury Mills, Inc, Phila, 35-45; sales rep, J.A. Sexauer, N.Y.C, 45-47; v.pres. and secy, Daniel P. Creed Co, Collingdale, Pa, 47-58, pres. and owner, 58- Mem: F&AM; Shrine; Del-Hi Grotto; Delco Lambskin Club; Hi-Twelve Club; Lions; Havertown Stamp Club; Collingdale Fire Co. 1 and 2; Sheriff's State Asn; Fraternal Order of Police; Collingdale Businessmen's Asn; YMCA; exec. bd, Nat. Found; Prothonotary Clerk of Courts; Asn. of Pa. Ky. Col; Bachelor of Goodwill, Louisville, Ky; Cert. of Appreciation, Borough of Collingdale; Tenn. Squire; Boy Scout Award; Explorer Scout Award; Nat. Found. Award. Rel: Lutheran. Mailing Add: 350 MacDade Blvd, Collingdale, Pa. 19023.

RUTKOWSKI, WALTER ALEXANDER D
Ohio State Rep.
b. Cleveland, Ohio, 3/28/17; s. Frank Walter Rutkowski and Henrietta J. Bobrowska R; single. Educ: Cleveland Col, B.B.A, 41; West. Reserve Univ. Grad. Bus. Sch, M.B.A, 57. Polit. & Govt. Pos: Mem, Cuyahoga Co. Dem. Exec. Cmt, Ohio; Dem. precinct committeeman, Cleveland and Maple Heights, 48-; mem, Maple Heights Bd. of Educ, 58-63, v.pres, 60 and pres, 61-63; mayor, Maple Heights, 64-67; Ohio State Rep, 69- Bus. & Prof. Pos: Cost analyst, Standard Oil Co, Cleveland, Ohio, 42-65. Mil. Serv: Entered as Pvt, Army Air Corps, 42, released as Sgt. Maj, 46, after serv. in 402nd Base Air Dept, ETO, 43-46. Mem: Nat. Soc. of State Legislators; Nat. Munic. League; Am. Soc. of Pub. Adminstr; Cuyahoga Co. Mayors and City Mgr. Asn; VFW (past post comdr); Cath. War Vet; Amvets; Fraternal Order of Police Assocs; K. of C; Polish Legion of Am. Vet; Cleveland Soc; Lions; Polish-Americans, Inc; Maple Heights Dem. Club; Maple Heights Boosters Club; Citizens' League of Gr. Cleveland. Cath. War Vet. Civic Award, 67. Rel: Roman Catholic. Mailing Add: 6110 Dunham Rd, Maple Heights, Ohio 44137.

RUTLEDGE, CATHERINE ANNE D
b. New Britain, Conn, 1/31/02; d. James Joseph Rutledge and Elizabeth A. Flemming R; single. Educ: Col. of New Rochelle, B.L, 23. Polit. & Govt. Pos: Founder and first pres, Stamford Dem. Women's Club, 60-63; Conn. State Dem. Cent. Committeewoman, 60-66; mem, Conn. State Platform Cmt, 62 & 64; del. from Stamford and mem, Credential Cmt, Dem. Nat. Conv, 64; dir, Fairfield Co. Federated Women's Clubs, 65; mem, Conn. State Teacher's Cert. Adv. Bd, 68- Bus. & Prof. Pos: Teacher, Stamford Pub. Schs, 25-32; treas, Flemming Rutledge Inc, 30-59, pres, 55-59, dir, Flemming Rutledge Oil Corp, 59-66. Mem: Col. of New Rochelle Alumnae Asn; first v.pres. exec. bd, Cath. Charities, 59-65; bd. mem, Women's Auxiliary, St. Joseph's Hosp, Stamford; Woodway Country Club; Soroptimist Int. Asn. Rel: Roman Catholic. Mailing Add: 65 Glenbrook Rd, Stamford, Conn. 06902.

RUTLEDGE, PHYLLIS J. D
W.Va. State Del.
b. Charleston, W.Va, 3/11/32; d. Roger Carlton Lewis and Inez May Snodgrass L; m. 9/1/51 to Ralph J. Rutledge; c. Jeannie and James Roger. Polit. & Govt. Pos: Secy, Kanawha Co. Dem. Exec. Cmt, W.Va, 64-68, committeewoman, 68-; W.Va. State Del, Kanawha Co, 68- Mem: Kanawha Co. and S.Charleston Woman's Clubs; Kanawha Co. Young Dem. Club. Rel: Baptist. Mailing Add: 1332 Frame St, Charleston, W.Va. 25302.

RUTTER, LOREN STANLEY DFL
b. Sandstone, Minn, 8/9/05; s. Philip Earl Rutter and Valerie Maye Fairbanks R; m. 3/26/27 to Irene Kallio; c. Loren Stanley (deceased), Betty Lou (Mrs. Betty Dicklich) and John Fayne. Educ: Martin Hughes High Sch, grad, 25; awarded Am. Legion Medal for outstanding work in athletics and scholarship. Polit. & Govt. Pos: Justice of peace, Kinney, Minn, 35-38, mayor, 39-41, trustee, 46-48; Minn. State Rep, 63rd Dist, 49-69, mem, Cmts. on Appropriations, Commerce, Mfg. and Retail Trade, Engrossment and Enrollment, Forestry and Pub. Domain, Game and Fish Munic. Affairs, Rules and Welfare, Minn. House Rep; del, Dem. Nat. Conv, 52. Bus. & Prof. Pos: Agent-Telegrapher, Great North. Rwy, 37- Publ: Many articles in local newspapers. Mem: Mason (32°); Elks; Moose; Moose Legion; Chisholm, Mt. Iron and Bush Country Sportsmens Clubs; Hibbing Chap, Izaak Walton League; Order of R.R. Telegraphers; hon. mem, United Steelworkers Local 1663; Va. C. of C; Hibbing C. of C. Author of bill in Minn. House of Rep. naming the Loon the state bird for Minn; has won a number of awards as an outstanding curler. Rel: Methodist. Mailing Add: 225 Main St, Kinney, Minn. 55758.

RUWE, L. NICHOLAS R
Asst. Chief of Protocol, Dept. of State
b. Detroit, Mich, 9/22/33; s. Lester Frederick Ruwe and Ruth Maude Devoy R; single. Educ: Brown Univ, B.A, 55; Univ. Mich, Grad. Sch. of Bus. Admin, 56; Psi Upsilon. Polit. & Govt. Pos: Mem, presidential campaign staff and nat. adv. staff, Nixon-Lodge, Wash, D.C, 60; dir, scheduling and itinerary, John G. Tower for Sen. Campaign, Tex, 61; co-campaign dir. for John W. Goode, Jr, 20th Cong. Dist, Tex, 61; mem, Gubernatorial Campaign Staff of Richard Nixon, Los Angeles, Calif, 62; campaign mgr, Mayoralty Race, Houston, Tex, 63; scheduling and itinerary, Charles Percy Gubernatorial Campaign, Ill, 64; dir, scheduling and itinerary for Richard Nixon, Presidential Campaign, 64; mem, Advance Staff of Richard Nixon, N.Y.C, 66 and Campaign Staff of Richard Nixon, 68; asst. chief of protocol, Dept. of State, 69- Rel: Roman Catholic. Legal Res: 217 Touraine Rd, Grosse Pointe Farms, Mich. 48236. Mailing Add: Department of State, Washington, D.C. 20520.

RUYLE, LYDIA M. D
V.Chairwoman, Weld Co. Dem. Cent. Cmt, Colo.
b. Denver, Colo, 8/4/35; d. David J. Miller and Lydia A. M; m. 9/15/57 to Robert A. Ruyle; c. Stephen Robert, Margaret Lee and Robin Lee. Educ: Univ. Colo, B.A. magna cum laude, 57; Colo. State Col, 68-; Phi Beta Kappa; Pi Gamma Mu; Delta Phi Delta; Gamma Phi Beta. Polit. & Govt. Pos: Past chmn, Greeley High Sch. Young Dem, Colo; chmn, Univ. Colo. Young Dem, 56-57; prog. chmn, Weld Co. Jane Jeffersons, 65-67; co-chmn, Kennedy for Pres, 68; chmn, Weld Co. Monfort for Senate, 68; v.chairwoman Weld Co. Dem. Cent. Cmt, 69-; chmn, Weld Co. Equal Rights Cmn, currently. Bus. & Prof. Pos: Research assoc, Univ. Colo. Bur. of Govt. Research, 57-59; legal probate asst, Miller & Ruyle Law Off, currently. Mem: Am. Asn. Univ. Women; sch. bd. rep, Jackson Sch. Parent Teacher Coun; bd. and art teacher, Greeley Commun. Center for Creative Arts; residential chmn, Greeley United Fund; ticket chmn, Greeley Concerts Asn; pre-sch. chmn, Parents Cmt. Second Place, Am. Asn. Univ. Women Art Exhib, 69; Exhib. Award, Poudre Valley Art League, 69. Rel: United Church of Christ; bazaar chmn, First Congregational United Church of Christ. Mailing Add: 2101 24th St, Greeley, Colo. 80631.

RYAN, A. J, JR. D
b. Dania, Fla, 5/20/27; m. to Johanna Rasch R; c. Archie, Michael, Timothy, Jeffrey, Christopher, Elizabeth. Educ: Univ. of Fla, LL.B, 55; Sigma Alpha Epsilon; Fla. Blue Key; ed, Law Rev; Order of the Coif. Polit. & Govt. Pos: Spec. Asst. Attorney Gen, Fla, 55; Fla. State Rep, 56-62; Fla. State Sen, 62-66. Bus. & Prof. Pos: Attorney. Mil. Serv: Navy and Army. Mem: Fla. and Am. Bar Asns; dir, Dania C. of C; Am. Legion; K. of C; Elks; Moose; W.O.W. Rel: Catholic. Mailing Add: 269 S.W. Ninth St, Dania, Fla. 33004. (1967)

RYAN, AILEEN BARLOW D
b. Bronx, N.Y; m. to E. Gerard Ryan; wid; c. Gerald, Alanna, Francis X. Educ: Hunter Col; N.Y. Law Sch. Polit. & Govt. Pos: Mem, N.Y.C. City Coun, 66-; N.Y. State Assemblywoman, 58-66; N.Y. State Dem. Women; unit mgr, N.Y.C. Census Bur; v.pres, Siwanoy Dem. Clubs, Inc. Bus. & Prof. Pos: Teacher, supvr. of Educ, Mus. of the City of N.Y. Mem: Bronx Chap. Red Cross; Bus. & Prfnl. Women's Club; League of Women Voters; Ladies of Charity; charter mem. Bronx Hist. Soc; exec. cmt, Ladies Auxiliary Misericordia Hosp. and Bronx Munic. Hosp; Bronx Women's Club; Columbiettes; Auxiliary Stratton Pk. Little League; Bronx Div, Cancer Cmt. of N.Y.C; Auxiliary, Dominican Sisters of Sick Poor; former den mother, Cub Scouts, Boy Scouts; Coord. Coun, PAL; Ancient Order of Hibernians Auxiliary: Soroptimists, Bronx Coord, Arthritis and Rheumatism Found; Legis. Cmt, Bronx Ment. Health Asn; Bronx chmn, Comm. of 500 to Combat Juvenile Narcotics Addiction. Outstanding Woman of the Year, Am. Women's Club Asn. Mailing Add: 1129 Beach Ave, Bronx, N.Y. 10472.

RYAN, ANDREW W, JR. R
N.Y. State Assemblyman
b. Plattsburgh, N.Y, 6/13/31; s. Andrew W. Ryan, Sr. and Lillian MacDougal R; m. 8/31/57 to Dorothy Larabee, c. Maura Ann and Andrew W, III. Educ: Georgetown Univ, B.S.S.S; Albany Law Sch, LL.B. Polit. & Govt. Pos: Confidential Supreme Court Clerk, N.Y, 59-63; N.Y. State Assemblyman, 108th Dist, 69-; secy, Clinton Co. Rep. Cmt. Bus. & Prof. Pos: Attorney-at-law, 60-69; assoc. with Fitzpatrick, Bennett and Trombley, 65-69. Mil. Serv: Entered as 2nd Lt, Army Artil, 55, released as 1st Lt, 56, after serv. in 760th Bn. Artil, Germany, 56-57. Mem: N.Y. State Bar Asn; Clinton Co. Bar Asn; N.Y. State Trial Lawyers Asn; Elks; Rod and Gun Club; K. of C; Kiwanis; past dir. bd. of trustees, Am. Red Cross. Rel: Catholic. Legal Res: 48 Grace Ave, Plattsburgh, N.Y. 12901. Mailing Add: 48 Court St, Plattsburgh, N.Y. 12901.

RYAN, DONALD NEIL D
b. Springfield, Mass, 1/27/30; s. Charles Vincent Ryan, Jr. and Josephine MacDonald R; m. 10/21/52 to Ann Elizabeth Larkin; c. John Francis, Ann Josephine, Mary Spencer, Donald Neil, Jr. and Edward Larkin. Educ: Fordham Univ, B.S. in Pharm, 51; Varsity baseball team. Polit. & Govt. Pos: Ward 8 committeeman, Springfield Dem. City Cmt, Mass, 63-; committeeman, Mass. Dem. State Cmt, 63-; Mass. State Sen, First Dist, 67-68. Bus. & Prof. Pos: Registered pharmacist, Ryan Drug Co, Inc, 54- and pres, 56- Mil. Serv: Entered as Pvt, Army, 52, released as Cpl, 54, after serv. in ETO. Mem: Nat. Asn. of Retail Druggists; Joint Civic Agencies, Springfield; dir, Springfield Hobby Club; Tuesday Club. Rel: Catholic. Mailing Add: 15 Puritan Circle, Springfield, Mass. 01119. (1967)

RYAN, ELLA MARICE D
b. Westernport, Md; d. James Michael Ryan and Catherine Cosgrove R; single. Educ: Potomac State Col; Wash. Sch. for Secretaries; Berlitz Sch. of Lang. Polit. & Govt. Pos: Admin. asst. to U.S. Rep. Thomas G. Morris, N.Mex, 63-68; mem. staff, U.S. Rep. George Mahon, Tex, 69- Rel: Roman Catholic. Legal Res: 2701 Arlington, Lawton, Okla. 73501. Mailing Add: 2314 Rayburn House Office Bldg, Washington, D.C. 20515.

RYAN, HAROLD L. R
b. Weiser, Idaho, 6/17/23; s. Frank D. Ryan and Luella Neibling R; m. 2/17/61 to Ann Dagres; c. Michael C, Timothy F. and Thomas P. Educ: Univ. Idaho, LL.B, 50; Phi Gamma Delta. Polit. & Govt. Pos: Prosecuting attorney, Wash. Co, Idaho, 51-52; Idaho State Sen, 62-66. Bus. & Prof. Pos: Cmnr, Idaho State Bar Asn, 67-, pres, 68- Mil. Serv: Entered as A/S, Navy, 43, released as Lt.(jg), 46, after serv. in S.Pac. Mem: Am. and Idaho Bar Asns; Idaho Defense Attorney Asn; AF&AM; Shrine; Elks. Rel: Episcopal. Mailing Add: Box 587, Weiser, Idaho 83672.

RYAN, HAROLD MARTIN D
b. Detroit, Mich, 2/6/11; s. Matt Ryan and Ida Schultz R; m. 9/2/44 to Lillian A. Wargonier; c. Kathleen, Nancy, Harold Martin, John and Theresa Marie. Educ: Mich. State Univ, 30-31; Univ. Detroit, J.D, 35; Gamma Eta Gamma. Polit. & Govt. Pos: Prosecuting attorney, Wayne Co, Mich, 45-46; Mich. State Sen, 49-62, Dem. Leader, Mich. State Senate, 56-62; del, Dem. Nat. Conv, 52, 56, 60 & 64; U.S. Rep, Mich, 61-64; state coordinator, Marquette Tercentenary Cmn. Bus. & Prof. Pos: Attorney-at-Law. Mem: Steuben Soc; Kolping Soc; Friendly Sons of St. Patrick; Lions; K. of C; D Club, Univ. Detroit. Mailing Add: 3610 Bedford Ave, Detroit, Mich. 48224.

RYAN, JOHN C. R
Mo. State Sen.
married; c. two daughters; two grandchildren. Polit. & Govt. Pos: Chmn, Pettis Co. Rep. Cmt, Mo; mem. bd. regents, Cent. Mo. State Col; Mo. State Sen, 67- Bus. & Prof. Pos: Mem. bd. dirs, Mo. State Bank; v-pres, Bryant Motor Co; farmer, Pettis Co. and bus. in Sedalia. Mem: Mason; Shrine; Kiwanis (lt. gov); Elks; Black Angus Asn; Lake of the Ozarks Coun. Boy Scouts; chmn, Pettis Co. Commun. Chest Dr. and Am. Red Cross Fund Dr; past pres, Sedalia Civic Club and Coun. Rel: Methodist; chmn. bd. trustees, Wesley Methodist Church. Mailing Add: Walnut Hills, Route 3, Sedalia, Mo. 65301.

RYAN, JOHN M. R
Ind. State Sen.
b. Mahonoy City, Pa, 7/3/20; s. Michael J. Ryan and Veronica Sommers R; m. 4/30/45 to Mary Ellen Kennedy; c. John M, Jr. and Kathryn E. Educ: Univ. Notre Dame, A.B, 41; Ind. Univ, J.D, 48; Sigma Alpha Epsilon; Phi Delta Phi. Polit. & Govt. Pos: City prosecutor, Indianapolis, Ind, 51-55; judge, Superior Court of Marion Co, Ind, 57-59 and Appellate Court of Ind, 59-65; Rep. nominee, Lt. Gov, Ind, 64; Ind. State Sen, 69- Bus. & Prof. Pos: V.pres. and counsel, Am. Fletcher Nat. Bank, 65- Mil. Serv: Entered as Aviation Cadet, Navy, 43, released as Lt.(jg), 45, after serv. as Navy Pilot, Am. Theatre, 44-45. Mem: Indianapolis, Ind. and Am. Bars; Am. Arbit. Asn; Indianapolis Athletic Club; Columbia Club; Country Club of Indianapolis; Am. Legion. Rel: Roman Catholic. Legal Res: 5640 Washington Blvd, Indianapolis, Ind. 46220. Mailing Add: 101 Monument Circle, Indianapolis, Ind. 46204.

RYAN, LEO JOSEPH D
Calif. State Assemblyman
b. Lincoln, Nebr, 5/5/25; s. Leo Joseph Ryan and Autumn Mead R; m. 1948 to Margaret Mary Casson; c. Christopher, Shannon, Patricia, Kevin and Erin. Educ: Creighton Univ, B.S, 49, M.S, 51. Polit. & Govt. Pos: City councilman, South San Francisco, 56-62, mayor, 62; Calif. State Assemblyman, 63-, mem, Assembly Rules, Ways and Means and Educ. Cmts; adv, Compensatory Educ. Cmn, Calif, 66; del, Dem. Nat. Conv, 68. Bus. & Prof. Pos: Exec. v.pres, Pension Investment Corp, 66. Mil. Serv: Entered as A/S, Navy, 43, released as Seaman 1/C, 46, after serv. in Submarine Force, Pac. Fleet, 44-45. Publ: Understanding California Government & Politics, Fearon Publ, 66. Mem: Elks; Moose; Commonwealth Club. Rel: Roman Catholic. Mailing Add: 308 Linden Ave, South San Francisco, Calif. 94080.

RYAN, MARGARET MARY D
Secy, Lake Co. Dem. Exec. and Cent. Cmts, Ohio
b. Painesville, Ohio, 1/15/25; d. Francis Patrick Ryan and Irene Dowling Ryan; single. Educ: Ursuline Col. for Women, Cleveland, Ohio, A.B, 46.

Polit. & Govt. Pos: Mem, Lake Co. Dem. Cent. Cmt, Ohio, 60-; mem, Lake Co. Dem. Exec. Cmt, 62-; trustee, Morley Libr. Bd, Lake Co, 65-; secy, Lake Co. Dem. Exec. and Cent. Cmts, 68-; trustee, East. Lake Co. Dem. Club, 69; trustee, Lake Co. Dem. Women's Club, 69. Bus. & Prof. Pos: Teacher, St. Mary Sch, Painesville, Ohio, 46-; secy, St. Mary Church, Painesville, 46- Mem: Northeast. Ohio Teachers Asn; Nat. Cath. Educ. Asn; Nat. Music Educ. Asn; Ursuline Col. Alumnae Asn; East. Lake Co. Dem. Club (past secy); Lake Co. Dem. Women's Club; W.Lake Co. Dem. Club; Ohio Libr. trustees Asn; Federated Dem. Women of Ohio. Rel: Roman Catholic. Mailing Add: 311 Rockwood Dr, Painesville, Ohio 44077.

RYAN, MATTHEW J. R
Pa. State Rep.
b. Phila, Pa, 4/27/32; s. Thomas F. Ryan and Kathleen Mullin R; m. to Mary Jane Mullray; c. three. Educ: Villanova Univ, B.S, LL.B. Polit. & Govt. Pos: Mem, Newtown Twp. Rep. Finance Cmt; mem, Citizens for Nixon-Lodge; chmn, Newtown Twp. Rep. Party; Pa. State Rep, 62- Bus. & Prof. Pos: Attorney; dir, Gr. Del. Valley Savings and Loan Asn. Mil. Serv: 1st Lt, Marines, 54-56; Marine Corps Res, 52-60. Mem: Marine Corps Res. Officers Asn. Mailing Add: 29 Dunminning Rd, Newtown Square, Pa. 19073. (1967)

RYAN, ROBERT JOSEPH
b. Hatfield, Mass, 7/11/14; m. to Mary Frances O'Leary; c. Robert James and Thomas. Educ: Univ. Mass, 32-34; Columbus Univ, LL.B, 40. Polit. & Govt. Pos: Career officer, U.S. Dept. of State For. Serv, 37-; clerk, 37-42; asst. chief, div. of dept. personnel, 42-50 and div. of for. serv. personnel, 50-53; chief, personnel opers. div, 53-55; exec. dir, Bur. of Near East, S.Asian and African Affairs, 55-58; Nat. War Col, 58-59; counsr, Paris, 59-64; U.S. Ambassador to Niger, 64-68; Dep. Asst. Secy. State, 68-69; Dir. Mgt. Sci, UN, 69- Mem: D.C. Bar Asn. Superior Serv. Award, 54, Dept. of State; Commendable Serv. Award, 50. Legal Res: Washington, D.C. Mailing Add: 340 E. 64th St, New York, N.Y. 10021.

RYAN, THEODORE S R
b. Suffern, N.Y, 6/30/05; m. 1940 to Ruth Robinson; c. Randolph, Saville and Sharon. Educ: Yale Univ, grad. 27; studied law at Yale and Cornell Univs. Polit. & Govt. Pos: Conn. State Sen, 53-57, Minority Leader, Conn. State Senate, 55, pres. pro tempore, 57; co-chmn, Conn. Del, Rep. Nat. Conv, 64; former mem, Rep. Nat. Cmt, Conn. Mil. Serv: Civilian, Off. Strategic Serv, 42-45. Mem: Headed Disaster Fund in Winsted after floods of 55; incorporator trustee and past pres, St. Thomas More Corp. which built Catholic Chapel for Yale Univ; former trustee and past pres, Sharon Hosp. Mailing Add: Sharon, Conn. 06069.

RYAN, THOMAS Liberal
Married; c. Eight. Polit. & Govt. Pos: Cand, Minn. State Sen, 66; former Minn. State Rep; former spec. asst. U.S. Dist. Attorney; spec. asst. Attorney Gen, State of Minn. Bus. & Prof. Pos: Attorney. Mil. Serv: Navy. Mailing Add: Pine City, Minn. 55063.

RYAN, THOMAS F. D
Mo. State Rep.
b. Hartford, Conn, 7/31/09; m. 5/12/36 to Thelma Scholl; c. four. Educ: Conn. schs. Polit. & Govt. Pos: Mo. State Rep, 64-; hon. dir. of Rockhurst Col; mem, Old Westport Dem. Club. Bus. & Prof. Pos: Indust. engr; has been employed in eng. dept. of Pratt & Whitney Aircraft, Ford, Bacon & Davis, Engrs. and Builders Cut Stone Co. Mil. Serv: Naval Res. Mem: Optimist Club; K. of C; Hibernians. Rel: Roman Catholic. Mailing Add: 8702 Hiawatha, Kansas City, Mo. 64114. (1967)

RYAN, WILLIAM A. D
Mich. State Rep.
b. Morgantown, W.Va, 5/2/19. Educ: High sch. grad. Polit. & Govt. Pos: Mich. State Rep, 58-; del, Dem. Nat. Conv, 68. Bus. & Prof. Pos: Former ed, The Wage Earner; former pres, financial secy, Local 104, UAW. Mil. Serv: Marines. Mem: Pres, Cath. Interracial Coun, 53-55; former pres, Nat. Cath. Soc. Action Conf. Rel: Roman Catholic. Mailing Add: 1582 Defer Place, Detroit, Mich. 48214. (1967)

RYAN, WILLIAM FITTS D
U.S. Rep, N.Y.
b. Albion, N.Y, 6/28/22; s. Bernard Ryan and Harriet Fitts R; m. to Priscilla Marbury Ryan; c. William, Priscilla, Virginia and Catherine. Educ: Princeton Univ, A.B, 44; Columbia Univ, LL.B, 49. Polit. & Govt. Pos: Dist. attorney, New York Co, N.Y, 50-57; pres, N.Y. Young Dem, 55-56; founding mem, Riverside Dem; founder, N.Y. Dem. Reform Movement; Dem. Leader, Seventh Assembly Dist, N.Y. Co, 57-61; U.S. Rep, N.Y, 60-; Reform Dem. Cand. for Mayor of N.Y.C, 65; del, Dem. Nat. Conv, 68. Bus. & Prof. Pos: Attorney-at-Law. Mil. Serv: World War II, 1st Lt, Field Artil, Japanese and Philippine Campaigns and Japanese Occup, 32nd Inf. Div. Mailing Add: 1040 St. Nicholas Ave, New York, N.Y. 10032.

RYAN, WILLIAM HERBERT R
Mass. State Rep.
b. Rochester, N.H, 7/17/38; s. Herbert L. Ryan and Mary A. Sullivan R; m. 5/5/68 to Maureen E. Ryan. Educ: Haverhill Schs, Mass. Polit. & Govt. Pos: Registrn. chmn, Haverhill Rep. City Cmt, Mass, 64-69; del, Mass. Rep. State Conv, 66; pres, Merrimack Valley Young GOP Club, 68-69; Mass. State Rep, 69-, mem, Cmt. on Soc. Welfare, Mass. House of Rep. Bus. & Prof. Pos: Lab. technician, Oxford Paper Co, Lawrence, Mass. Mil. Serv: Entered as A/B, Air Force, 55, released as Airman 1/C, 59; Air Force Res, 64-68. Mem: Haverhill Young Rep. Club; Elks; Jaycees; bd. dirs, Essex Club, Mass, 65-69; St. James Men's Club; North. Essex Asn. for Retarded Children; Men. of Merrimack; St. James Convent Asn; Div. 14, Hibernians. Mailing Add: 1073 Main St, Haverhill, Mass. 01830.

RYAN, WILLIAM JOSEPH D
b. Montpelier, Vt, 9/13/13; s. Patrick H. Ryan and Mary Ann Magee R; m. 9/12/51 to Anastasia McEvoy; c. Julie Ann and Michael J. Educ: Univ. Vt, B.S, 34. Polit. & Govt. Pos: Sheriff, Montpelier, Vt, 37-40; chmn, Vt. Dem. State Cent. Cmt, 50-56; mem, Dem. Nat. Cmt, Vt, 64-68; del, Dem. Nat. Conv, 68. Bus. & Prof. Pos: Newspaper reporter, Montpelier Argus and secy, Montpelier C. of C, 35-37; engaged in private bus, 46-50 & 52-55; admitted to Vt. Bar, 55; mem, Ryan & Ryan, Attorneys, 55-; trustee, Middlesex Col, 64-65. Mil. Serv: Army, 41-46, 50-52; Bronze Star; Medal of War, Brazil. Mem: Vt. Bar Asn.(treas, 55-56); Am. and Wash. Co. Bar Asns; Am. Trial Lawyers Asn; Am. Legion; VFW; 43rd Inf. Div. Vet. Asn; K. of C.(4°); Elks. Rel: Roman Catholic. Legal Res: 52 Terrace St, Montpelier, Vt. 05601. Mailing Add: 38 State St, Montpelier, Vt. 05601. (1967)

RYAN, WILLIAM MURRAY R
N.Mex. State Rep.
b. Central, N.Mex, 7/22/22; s. James Stanton Ryan and Lyda Murray R; m. 8/25/45 to Marian E. Buchella; c. William Murray, Jr, Kathleen Mary, Robin Patricia and twins, Kerry Frank and Kevin Frank. Educ: N.Mex. State Teachers Col, 40-42; U.S. Mil. Acad, B.S, 45. Polit. & Govt. Pos: Mem. and chmn, Silver City Sch. Bd. Educ, N.Mex, 59-65; N.Mex. State Rep, Grant Co, 69- Mil. Serv: Entered as Cadet, U.S. Mil. Acad, 42, released as 1st Lt, 49. Mem: Am. Inst. of Mining Engrs; K. of C; VFW; Am. Legion. Rel: Catholic. Legal Res: 1709 W. Sixth St, Silver City, N.Mex. 88061. Mailing Add: Box 110, Silver City, N.Mex. 88061.

RYBACKI, RAY J. D
Mem, Cook Co. Dem. Cent. Cmt, Ill.
b. Chicago, Ill, 5/19/31; s. Anton Rybacki and Lottie Wisowaty R; m. 6/13/53 to Jacqueline Mary Murphy; c. Charlotte, Pamela and Jacqueline. Educ: Wilson Jr. Col, Chicago, Ill, 50-51; Bradley Univ, 52-53; Roosevelt Univ, B.S, 53. Polit. & Govt. Pos: Pres, Palos Twp. Young Dem, Ill, 61-63; v.chmn, Cook Co. Young Dem, 61-63; v.pres. Palos Twp. Dem. Orgn, 62-65; Dem. cand. for Cong, Fourth Cong. Dist, 64-66; Dem. committeeman, Palos Twp, 65-; alternate del, Dem. Nat. Conv, 68; mem, Cook Co. Dem. Cent. Cmt, currently. Bus. & Prof. Pos: Indust. salesman, Fullerton Metals, Chicago, Ill, 56-57, Kasle Steel Corp, 57-60, Croname, Inc, 60-63 and U.S. Steel Supply, Div. of U.S. Steel, 63-65; arbitrator, Ill. Indust. Cmn, 65- Mil. Serv: Entered as Pvt, Army, 53, released as Pfc, 55, after serv. in First Specially Organized Electronic Warfare Counter-Measures Unit, Ft. Bliss, Tex, 54-55. Mem: K. of C. Rel: Catholic. Mailing Add: 11917 Timber Lane Dr, Palos Park, Ill. 60464.

RYBAK, WILLIAM C. D
Pa. State Rep.
b. New York, N.Y, 3/2/21; s. John Rybak and Katie Revotski R; m. 4/28/56 to Louise D. Golab; c. John William, Mary Louise, Margaret Anne, Susan Jane, Lucy Anne and Anthony Edward. Educ: Temple Univ, B.S. in commerce, 45; Univ. Miss. Sch. Law, J.D, 49; Phi Delta Phi; Newman Club; Wilson Club. Polit. & Govt. Pos: Attorney adv, U.S. Rent Control, Lehigh Valley Area, Pa, 50-51; dir, Bethlehem Sch. Bd, 53-58, v.pres, 55-56, pres, 57-59; Pa. State Rep, 135th Dist, 66- Bus. & Prof. Pos: Attorney-at-law, Bethlehem, Pa, 50- Mem: Northampton Co, Pa. and Miss. Bar Asns; Gr. Bethlehem Area Cmt. for Employ. of the Handicapped; Bethlehem Sr. Citizens Coun; Eagles; K. of C; Young Dem. Club, S. Bethlehem; Home of Good Samaritans. Pa. Handicapped Citizen of the Year, 66; Benjamin Rush Award, 67; Citizen of the Decade, 68. Rel: St. Josephats Ukranian Catholic. Legal Res: 1337 Easton Ave, Bethlehem, Pa. 18018. Mailing Add: 12 E. Fourth St, Bethlehem, Pa. 18015.

RYBOLT, GERALD W. R
Educ: Lambda Chi Alpha. Polit. & Govt. Pos: Ind. State Sen, 61-66; Kokomo City attorney, 60; Judge of Superior Court, Howard Co, 53-58. Bus. & Prof. Pos: Lawyer. Mem: past pres, Scottish Rite Club; Shrine; Howard Co. Bar Asn; State Bar Asn; Elks; YMCA; dir. and treas. of Ment. Health Asn, 4 years; chmn, Howard Co. Chap. of Red Cross, 8 years. Rel: Methodist; Main St. Methodist Church trustee. Mailing Add: 304 Armstrong-Landon Bldg, Kokomo, Ind. 46901. (1967)

RYBURN, BENNIE, JR. D
Ark. State Rep.
b. Rison, Ark, 7/26/34; s. Bennie Ryburn, Sr. and Virginia Morrison R; m. 7/28/61 to Judith McKenney; c. Bennie, III, Angelia Dawn and Ray Morrison. Educ: Univ. Ark. and Ark. A&M Col, 52-57. Polit. & Govt. Pos: Ark. State Rep, currently. Bus. & Prof. Pos: Owner and gen. mgr, Ryburn Motor Co, 58-; pres, Ryburn Ins. Inc, 61-; pres, First State Savings and Loan, 66-; mem. bd. dirs, Commercial Bank and Trust Co, 69- Rel: Baptist. Legal Res: 1 Westood Lane, Monticello, Ark. 71655. Mailing Add: Box 390, Monticello, Ark. 71655.

RYDER, JOHN N. R
Wash. State Sen.
b. Seattle, Wash, 3/15/07; s. Heman Ryder and Flora Linton R; m. to Margaret Dyer; c. Lynn, Anne (Mrs. Zimmerman) and John K. Educ: Rutgers Univ, Grad. Sch. of Banking. Polit. & Govt. Pos: Formerly Wash. State Rep, term; Wash. State Sen, 55-; del, Rep. Nat. Conv, 68. Bus. & Prof. Pos: Banker. Mem: Rainer Club; F&AM. Mailing Add: 6811 55th N.E, Seattle, Wash. 98115.

RYGG, MAYNARD STERLING R
Mont. State Rep.
b. Warren, Minn, 12/26/14; s. Peder Theodore Rygg and Etta Oakland R; m. 10/29/42 to Inga Johnson; c. Thomas Sterling, Philip John and Mary Ingrid. Educ: Concordia Col, Moorhead, Minn. Polit. & Govt. Pos: Mont. State Rep, 61- Mil. Serv: Entered as Storekeeper 3/C, Navy, 42, released as Lt.(sg), after serv. in Mediterranean Theatre. Mem: Pres, Whitefish C. of C, 59; Rotary; Am. Legion. Rel: Lutheran. Legal Res: 37 7th St. E, Kalispell, Mont. 59901. Mailing Add: Box 429, Kalispell, Mont. 59901.

RYHERD JAMES MICHAEL 'MIKE' D
Chmn, King Co. Dem. Cent. Cmt, Wash.
b. Portland, Ore, 1/16/39; s. Andrew Jackson Ryherd (deceased) and Marie Daniels Ryherd Main; m. 6/24/61 to Lynn Wilcox; c. Soren Leigh and Majken Kai. Educ: Portland State Univ, B.A, 63; Univ. Wash. Grad. Sch, 64. Polit. & Govt. Pos: Anthropologist, field research, Nat. Sci. Found, 63; del, Dem.

Nat. Conv, 68; chmn, King Co. Dem. Cent. Cmt, Wash, 68- Bus. & Prof. Pos: Account exec, Xerox Corp, Seattle, Wash, 64-66; br. mgr, Royfax Div, Litton Indust, 66-67; Northwest. rep, Kalman Floor Co, Ore, Wash, Idaho, Mont, Wyo, Brit. Columbia and Alaska, 67-68. Mil. Serv: Entered as E-1, Army, 56, released as E-5, 59, after serv. in ETO Hq, Heidleberg, Germany, 57-59. Mem: Wash. Dem. Coun; New Dem. Coalition; Jr. C. of C. Rel: Unitarian. Mailing Add: 13022 N.E. 87th St, Kirkland, Wash. 98033.

RYND, RICHARD D
Md. State Del.
b. Bronx, N.Y, 8/1/31; s. Abraham Rynd and Rebecca Presalsky R; m. 10/24/54 to Selma Boritzer; c. Marcy, Sonia and Alan. Educ: William & Mary College; N.Y. Univ. Polit. & Govt. Pos: Mem, Baltimore Co. Cmn. on Aging, Md, 65-67; Md. State Del, Second Dist, 67-, v.chmn, Econ. Matters and Capitol Budget Cmts, Md. House of Del. Bus. & Prof. Pos: V.pres, Md. Nursing Home Asn, 65, mem. legis. cmt, 65-67, chmn, 65- Mil. Serv: Seaman, Navy, 50-52. Mem: Mason, Yedz Grotto; Boy Scouts; Safety First Club; Towson and Baltimore C. of C; Aircraft Owners & Pilots Asn; B'nai B'rith; Citizens Housing and Planning Cmt. Rel: Jewish. Mailing Add: 3222 Midfield Rd, Baltimore, Md. 21208.

RYSKIND, MARY HOUSE R
V.Chmn, Los Angeles Co. Rep. Cent. Cmt, Calif.
b. Oklahoma City, Okla, 5/28/04; d. Julius Temple House and Flora Smith H; m. 12/19/29 to Morrie Ryskind; c. Ruth (Mrs. Ohman) and Allan H. Educ: Univ. Chicago, Ph.B, 23; Columbia Teachers Col, post-grad. work, 27; Phi Upsilon. Polit. & Govt. Pos: Mem, Calif. Rep. State Cent. Cmt, 52-56 & 66-; mem, Los Angeles Co. Rep. Cent. Cmt, 59th Assembly Dist, Calif, 67-, v.chmn, 69- Mailing Add: 605 N. Hillcrest Rd, Beverly Hills, Calif. 90210.

S

SAAL, GEORGE L. D
b. Pekin, Ill, 12/2/18; m. to Jane Allen S; c. four sons, one daughter. Educ: Pekin pub. schs. Polit. & Govt. Pos: Tazwell Co. sheriff, Ill, 50-54 & 58-62; pres, Ill. Sheriff's Asn, 53-54; Ill. State Rep, 69th and 70th Gen. Assemblies and 62-68; del, Dem. Nat. Conv, 68. Bus. & Prof. Pos: Operator, George L. Saal Ins. Agency, Pekin, Ill. Mil. Serv: Marines, Southwest Pac, 4 years; Purple Heart. Mem: Am. Legion; 40 et 8; Marine Corps League; Amvets; Elks; Moose; Eagles. Mailing Add: 910 Washington St, Pekin, Ill. 61554. (1967)

SAARI, RUTH DESIREE D
b. Berlin, Germany, 7/29/29; d. Manfred Simon and Margot Goldsmith S; m. 3/22/51 to Leonard W. Saari; c. Neilton Jared. Educ: Univ. Wash, B.A, 51; Theta Sigma Phi. Polit. & Govt. Pos: Mem, Pierce Co. Adv. Coun. to Wash. State Bd. Against Discrimination, 54-56; Dem. precinct committeeman, 31st Dist, Wash, 60-64, secy, 62-64; del, Wash. State Dem. Conv, 62, 64, 66 & 68; Dem. precinct committeeman, 35th Dist, Wash, 66-; voter registr, King Co, 67-; founding mem, Nat. Citizens for Humphrey, 68; mem, Wash. State Dem. Cmn. on Party Struct. and Del. Selection, currently; del, Dem. Nat. Conv. and hon. secy. of Wash. del, 68. Bus. & Prof. Pos: Copy writer, KBKW Radio, Aberdeen, Wash, 51-52; reporter, Upper Valley Rev, Naches, 52; copy writer, KTNT-TV & Radio, Tacoma, 53-54; pub. info. specialist, Pierce Co. Civil Defense, 54-56 and Heart Asn, Wash, D.C, 65-66. Mem: Univ. Wash. Alumni Asn; Theta Sigma Phi Prfnl. Chap; PTA; Nat. Asn. Blackfeet Indians. Several awards for poetry. Legal Res: 6203 S. 117th St, Seattle, Wash. 98178. Mailing Add: 605 N. Overlook Dr, Alexandria, Va. 22305.

SABATINI, FREDERICK ANTHONY R
Chmn, Cass Co. Rep. Party, Ind.
b. Chicago, Ill, 10/16/37; s. Fausto J. Sabatini and Josephine Marocco S. (deceased); single. Educ: Ind. Univ, A.B, 60, J.D, 64; Phi Delta Phi; Blue Key; Sigma Nu. Polit. & Govt. Pos: Mem. staff, U.S. Rep. Charles A. Halleck, 62-65; chmn, Cass Co. Young Rep, Ind, 65-66; del, Ind. State Rep. Conv, 66 & 68; chmn, Cass Co. Rep. Party, 66-; co. attorney, Cass Co, 69-; exec. comdr, Ind. State Chmn. of Nat. Rep. of Italian Descent; mem, Ind. Legis. Local Govt. Study Cmn. Bus. & Prof. Pos: Attorney, Hanna, Small, Sabatini and Becker, 65- Mil. Serv: Pvt, Army, 60; Army Res. Mem: Am, Ind. and Cass Co. Bar Asns; Elks; bd. of dirs, Logansport Jr. Achievement; Fraternal Order of Police; bd. of dirs, Red Cross and Am. Cancer Soc; Boy Scouts; Eagles; Am. Legion; bd. dirs, Sangralea Valley Boys Home. Logansport Outstanding Young Man, 67-68. Rel: Catholic. Legal Res: 1129 Erie Ave, Logansport, Ind. 46947. Mailing Add: 208 Fourth St, Logansport, Ind. 46947.

SABBATINO, JULES G. D
N.Y. State Assemblyman
b. Manhattan, N.Y; m. to Nancy Albarino; c. Jules J, Theresa-Ann. Educ: De Witt Clinton High Sch; St. John's Univ. Sch. of Acct, grad. in Commerce and Finance. Polit. & Govt. Pos: Mem, Queens Dem. Co. Cmt, N.Y; v.pres, Taminent Regular Dem. Club; chief economist, N.Y.C. Dept. of Commerce, 51-53; marshall, N.Y.C, 54-58; N.Y. State Assemblyman, 58- Bus. & Prof. Pos: Pub. acct, Long Island City, N.Y. Mem: Nat. Soc. of Pub. Accts; former pres, Knickerbocker Civic League; Queensboro Lodge, Elks; Lincoln Coun. 312, K. of C; Holy Name Soc, Immaculate Conception of Astoria. Rel: Catholic. Mailing Add: 23-06 21st St, Astoria, Long Island City, N.Y. 11105. (1967)

SABENS, MARSHALL T. R
Treas, Vt. Rep. State Cmt.
b. Burlington, Vt, 5/1/26; s. Harold T. Sabens and Freda Bliss S; m. 4/24/54 to Joan Coffman; c. Elizabeth and George. Educ: Univ. Vt, B.A, 51; Sigma Alpha Epsilon. Polit. & Govt. Pos: Treas, Vt. Rep. State Cmt, 66- Mil. Serv: Army, 45-47. Mem: Rotary; treas, Vt. State Chap, March of Dimes. Rel: Episcopal. Mailing Add: 4 Highland Ave, Montpelier, Vt. 05601.

SABLAN, JAMES TAITANO D
Sen, Guam Legis.
b. Agana, Guam, 6/11/12; s. Ramon Diaz Sablan and Dolores Taitano S; m. 4/14/37 to Rosalia Lujan Pangelinan; c. Rita (Mrs. Fejarang), James Taitano, Jr, Patricia (Mrs. Cruz), John Pangelinan, Dolores Pangelinan, William Pangelinan, Joseph Pangelinan, Juanita Pangelinan and Lolita Pangelinan. Educ: Guam Normal Sch. for Teachers, 34-46. Polit. & Govt. Pos: Assemblyman, Guam Assembly, 48-50; Sen, Guam Legis, 51-61 & 69-, Legis. secy, 69-; dir. of pub. safety, Govt. of Guam, 61-68; v.pres, Pac. Conf. of Legislators, 69- Bus. & Prof. Pos: Sch. Teacher, Guam, 34-47. Mil. Serv: Entered as Pvt, Guam Mil, 28, released as Maj, 52, after serv. as Bn. oper. and Training Officer. Mem: Int. Asn. of Chiefs of Police; Marianas Asn. of Law Enforcement; Mason; Scottish Rite. Commun. Leader, 68. Rel: Baptist. Legal Add: Agana Heights, Guam 96910. Mailing Add: P.O. Box 363, Agana, Guam 96910.

SABLUSKI, FRANK CHARLES D
b. Nashua, 3/26/05. Educ: Univ. of N.H; studied law Suffolk and Northeast. Law Schs; Weaver Sch. of Real Estate. Polit. & Govt. Pos: N.H. State Rep, 57-67; chmn. of the City Planning Bd; past chmn. of the Nashua del. to the Gen. Court; presently v.chmn, Nashua Del; past chmn, Hillsborough Co. del. to the Gen. Court, 61-62; mem, Hillsborough Co. Exec. Cmt, 3 terms; mem, Govt. Reorganization Cmt. of the 62 Dem. Issues Conf. Bus. & Prof. Pos: Real estate broker. Mil. Serv: Air Force (Ord.), 3 years, European, African, Middle-E, Asiatic and Pac. Theatres; awarded six service stars. Mem: Am. Legion; VFW; Elks. Mailing Add: 80 Linwood St, Nashua, N.H. 03060. (1967)

SABO, MARTIN OLAV DFL
Minority Leader, Minn. State House of Rep.
b. Crosby, N.Dak, 2/28/38; m. 6/30/63 to Sylvia Ann Lee; c. Karin Margaret and Julie Ann. Educ: Augsburg Col, B.A, cum laude, 59. Polit. & Govt. Pos: Minn. State Rep, 61-, Minority Leader, Minn. State House of Rep, 69- Bus. & Prof. Pos: Life ins. salesman, Aetna Life Ins. Co. Rel: Lutheran. Mailing Add: 3129 E. 22nd St, Minneapolis, Minn. 55406.

SABOL, JOSEPH, JR. R
b. Stefanovce, Austria-Hungary, 4/11/09; s. Joseph Sabol and Anna Bonko S; m. 2/18/34 to Mary Stefanik. Educ: St. Procopius Col-Sem, 26-29; Robert Morris Jr. Col, 37-38; Duquesne Univ, B.A, 39; Polit. & Govt. Pos: Chmn, Planning Cmn, Duquesne, Pa, 51-59, mayor, 62-66; third class cities rep, Allegheny Conf. on Commun. Develop. and Southwest Regional Planning Cmn, 62-66; southwest. v.chmn, League of Cities, State of Pa, 62-66; mem, Blue Ribbon Ins. Cmn, 68-; Rep. nominee for U.S. Rep, 68. Bus. & Prof. Pos: Expediter, real estate dept, U.S. Steel Corp, Pittsburgh, Pa, 40-41; real estate-ins. broker, Duquesne, 40-; admin. asst, Standard Steel Spring Co, N.Am. Rockwell Corp, Pittsburgh, 41-46. Publ: Wage-Salary Stabilization Proceedure, Standard Steel Spring Co, 43. Mem: St. Procopius Col. Develop. Cmt; Duquesne Univ. Develop. Fund; C. of C; exec. cmt, Boy Scouts; Byzantine Serra Club; Greek Cath. Union of the U.S.A.(pres, gymnastic br, Pittsburgh, Pa, 48-64); First Cath. Slovak Union of the U.S.A; United Socs. of the U.S.A; Croatian Fraternal Union; Polish Nat. Alliance; Greater Beneficial Union; Elks; Eagles; Moose; Carpathian Russian Club; Slovak Club; Serbian Club; Croatian Club; K. of C.(4°). Rel: Byzantine Catholic. Mailing Add: 15 S. Second St, Duquesne, Pa. 15110.

SABONJIAN, ROBERT V. R
Mayor, Waukegan, Ill.
b. Waukegan, Ill, 1/4/16; s. Lazurus Sabonjian and Zaruhey Mooradian S; m. 6/7/47 to Lorene Terrill; c. Dana Jo and Robert Glen. Educ: High Sch. Polit. & Govt. Pos: Alderman, Second Ward, Waukegan, Ill, 51-52 & 55-57, mayor, 57-; acting postmaster, U.S. Post Off, Waukegan, 52-54. Bus. & Prof. Pos: Owner, Dutch Mill Dry Cleaners, 48-57; dir, Bank of Waukegan, 63-66. Mil. Serv: Entered as A/S, Coast Guard, released as Boatswain Mate 2/C, 45, after serv. in S. Pac; Asiatic Pac. Medal; Good Conduct Medal; Pearl Harbor Medal; Am. Theater Medal; Victory Medal. Mem: Eagles; Moose; DAV; Am. Legion; VFW; Amvets; Mason (32°); Scottish Rite, Shrine; Waukegan City Club; Waukegan and N. Chicago C. of C. Rel: Disciples of Christ. Legal Res: 410 Flossmoor, Waukegan, Ill. 60085. Mailing Add: City Hall, 106 N. Utica St, Waukegan, Ill. 60085.

SABOTA, FRANCIS ROBERT D
Mem, Wallingford Dem. City Cmt, Conn.
b. Wallingford, Conn, 1/23/19; s. John Bartholomew Sabota and Katherine Sczerba S; single. Educ: Yale Univ, B.S. in indust. eng, 48; Univ. Conn, LL.B, 58; Tau Beta Pi. Polit. & Govt. Pos: Mem, Planning and Zoning Cmn, 53-65, chmn, 58-60; mem, Wallingford Dem. City Cmt, Conn, 55-; prosecutor, Munic. Court, 59-60; mem, Bd. of Finance, 61; Conn. State Rep, 63-66; judge of probate, 67- Bus. & Prof. Pos: Attorney-at-law, 58- Mil. Serv: Entered as 2nd Lt, Army, 41, released as Capt, 46, after serv. in Pac. Theater. Mem: Elks; Am. Legion; K. of C. Rel: Catholic. Mailing Add: 12 Lake St, Wallingford, Conn. 06492.

SACCHETTI, DOMINIC VINCENT R
Chmn, Boston Rep. City Cmt, Mass.
b. Boston, Mass, 8/11/43; s. James Vincent Sacchetti and Martha Scimemi S; m. 6/8/64 to Sylvia Garmendia; c. Sylvia. Educ: Burdett Col, Assoc. Degree, 66; Curry Col, B.A. in Bus, 68; Boston State Col, 68- Polit. & Govt. Pos: Chmn. Ward Three and exec. mem, Boston Rep. City Cmt, Mass, 68- Bus. & Prof. Pos: Salesman, Boston Printing Firm, 65-68; printing broker, 68-; teacher, Boston Pub. Schs, 68- Mem: East. Bus. Teachers Asn; Boston Teachers Union; North End Athletic Asn.(bd. dirs); Gr. Boston Jr. C. of C; Gr. Boston Young Rep. Club. Citation, Mass. Dept. Jewish War Vet; Human Rels. Brotherhood Prog. Rel: Catholic. Mailing Add: 150 Salem St, Boston, Mass. 02113.

SACCO, GEORGE LAWRENCE, JR. D
Mass. State Rep.
b. Boston, Mass, 7/19/36; s. George Lawrence Sacco and Margaret T. Zamparelli S; m. 12/9/67 to Elaine Denise Golden. Educ: Northeast. Univ; Suffolk Univ, B.A, 59, Law Sch, LL.B, 62. Polit. & Govt. Pos: Mem. and v.chmn, Medford Sch. Cmt, Mass, 58-62; Mass. State Rep, 62-, mem. cmt. on educ, Mass. House of Rep, 62-63, mem. and clerk cmt. on the Judiciary, mem. cmt. on legal affairs and mem. spec. cmns. on racing and wiretapping, 62-63, asst. majority leader, 64-65, mem. cmt. on rules, 64-65, chmn. cmt. on fed. financial assistance, 66-67, mem. cmt. on ways and means, 68-, v.chmn, 69- Mem: Mass. and Middlesex Bar Asns; Mass. Asn. Sch. Cmts; Mass. Legisla-

tors Asn; Elks; Sons of Italy; Malden Irish-Am. Club; Holy Name Soc; Medford Ment. Health Center; Gr. Boston Asn. for Retarded Children; Wakefield Drug Action Cmt; chmn, Medford Cancer Crusade, 69; United Fund. Man of the Year, Ital. War Vet. Asn, Mass, 69; commendations from various pub. and private orgn. Rel: Roman Catholic. Mailing Add: 10 High St, Medford, Mass. 02155.

SACHS, ALICE D
Leader, 66th Assembly Dist, Dem. Party, Manhattan, N.Y.
b. Kansas City, Mo, Dec. 18; d. Charles Sachs and Flora Weil; single. Educ: Wellesley Col, B.A; Sorbonne, Cert. d'Etudes Francaises; Durant Scholar; Phi Beta Kappa. Polit. & Govt. Pos: Founder, Lexington Dem. Club, N.Y, 49, mem. exec. cmt, 50-; leader, 66th Assembly Dist. Dem. Party, Manhattan, 53-; cand, N.Y. State Assembly, 56, 58 & 60; mem. gen. cmt, N.Y. Cmt. Dem. Voters, 59-; mem. adv. coun, N.Y. Young Dem. Club, 59-65; cand, N.Y. State Senate, 62; chmn, Dem. Human Rels. Cmt, N.Y. Co, 62-63; mem, State Dem. Platform Cmt, 64. Bus. & Prof. Pos: Ed, Crown Pub, Inc, 39- Mem: Commun. Planning Bd. Eight; Women's City Club; League of Women Voters; Citizens Union; Americans for Dem. Action; Am. Civil Liberties Union; Urban League; NAACP; B'nai B'rith. Mailing Add: 140 E. 63rd St, New York, N.Y. 10021.

SACHS, HERBERT D
b. N.Y.C, 2/22/29; m. to Sheila; c. Three. Educ: L.I. Univ, Graduated; Brooklyn Law Sch, LL.B, 1951; LL.M, 1953. Polit. & Govt. Pos: N.Y. State Assemblyman, 64-66. Bus. & Prof. Pos: Attorney; Offices, 254 Pettit Ave, Bellmore, N.Y. Mem: Organizer and Past Pres, Lawrence Lawns Civic Asn; Nassau Co, Am, and Criminal Courts Bar Asn; Chmn, Fund Raising Drives for Various Orgns; Pres, Temple Beth-El Men's Club; B'nai B'rith Anti Defamation League; Aircraft Owners and Flyers Asn. Mailing Add: 1127 Huckleberry Rd, N. Bellmore, N.Y. 11710. (1967)

SACK, FLOYD M. R
Colo. State Rep.
b. Logan Co, Colo, 2/22/31; s. Roy Sack and Hazel Cole S; m. 5/9/57 to Dorothy Ann Nelson; c. Mark Melvin, David Paul, Mary Ann and Rebecca Lisa. Educ: Midwest Christian Col, B.A, 52; Tex. Christian Univ, B.A, 53, M.A, 55. Polit. & Govt. Pos: Rep. committeeman, Arapahoe Co. Rep. Party, Colo, 64 & 65; Rep. finance capt, Jefferson Co. Rep. Party, 66; Colo. State Rep, 67- Bus. & Prof. Pos: Minister, Christian Churches, 49-69; area mgr, Vita Craft Corp, 49- Mem: Kiwanis; Denver Area Christian Ministers. Rel: Christian Church of N.Am. Mailing Add: 415 Lamar, Lakewood, Colo. 80226.

SACKETT, WALTER W, JR. D
Fla. State Rep.
b. Bridgeport, Conn, 11/20/05; s. Walter Wallace Sackett, Sr. and Hermine Archambault S; m. 5/31/49 to Mary Millos, separated; c. Monica Ann, Walter Wallace III, John A.(deceased) and Charles A. Dunn, stepson. Educ: Harvard, 22-23; Univ. Miami, B.A, 32; Univ. Ala, post grad, 32-34; Rush Med. Col, M.D, 38. Polit. & Govt. Pos: Fla. State Rep, 67- Bus. & Prof. Pos: Instr. anat, Univ. Ala, 34-36; prof. anat, Col. Mortuary Sci, St. Louis, 36-37; intern, Berwyn Hosp, Ill, 37-38; resident, St. Lukes Hosp, St. Louis, 38-39; instr. obstetrics, student health phys, Univ. Ala, 39-40; resident, Charity Hosp, Natchez, Miss, 40-41; gen. practice med, 41-; mem, Med. Research Found, Univ. Miami, 50-53; pioneer, oral polio vaccine in newborns, 60-61; adv. cmt, Poliomyelitis, diabetes and arthritis, U.S. Pub. Health Serv, 61-62. Publ: Bringing Up Babies, 62; plus various articles. Mem: Bd. of trustees, Univ. of Miami, 61-63; Asn. Am. Physicians and Surgeons; pres. and chmn. bd. trustees, Dade Co. Med. Asn; Am. Cancer Soc: Am. Soc. Abdominal Surgeons; Univ. Miami Alumni Asn.(former dir, v.pres, pres). Recipient Outstanding Alumni Award, Univ. Miami, 57. Rel: Catholic. Mailing Add: 3911 Crawford Ave, Coconut Grove, Miami, Fla. 33133.

SACKETT, WAYNE B. R
Mich. State Rep.
b. Gobles, Mich, 7/16/07; s. Fred Sackett and Bessie M. Olmstead S; m. 7/29/33 to Zelma Irene Roberts; c. Nancy (Mrs. Kaiser), Diane (Mrs. Bumpus) and Ruthann (Mrs. Solomon). Educ: Wolf Point High Sch, Mont, Dipl. Polit. & Govt. Pos: Pres. and founder, Portage Rep. Orgn, 64-67; Mich. State Rep, 69- Bus. & Prof. Pos: Decorating contractor, 20 years. Mem: Westwood Vol. Fire Dept, 25 years; F&AM; Metrop. Club of Am; Lakes Area and Kalamazoo Co. Conserv. Clubs; Cmt. on Land Use of the Kalamazoo Co. Planning Cmn; Mich. United Conserv. Club (dir, 8 years); Kiwanis (pres); Mason; Grange; Farm Bur; Chmn, Portage Park and Recreation Bd. Rel: Presbyterian. Mailing Add: 515 Larkspur, Portage, Mich. 49081.

SACKS, ALEXANDER R
b. N.Y.C, 11/11/09; s. Barnett Sacks and Eva Molloy S; m. 8/16/41 to Vera Peskin; c. Nina Flora (Mrs. Ramos d'Acevedo). Educ: City Col. of N.Y, 27-29; Brooklyn Law Sch, LL.B, 32; New Sch. Soc. Research, 39-40; N.Y. Univ. Grad. Sch. Pub. Admin, 41-42. Polit. & Govt. Pos: Spec. attorney, Dept. Justice, Wash. and N.Y, 42-47; financial consult, Supreme Hq, London, on assignment by Attorney Gen. of U.S, 45; attorney and sr. economist, Off. Mil. Govt, Berlin and Frankfurt, 47-49; Rep-Conservative Cand. for U.S. Rep, 23rd Cong. Dist, N.Y, 68; mem, Bronx Co. Rep. Law Cmt, 69- Bus. & Prof. Pos: Attorney, consult. economist and pub. affairs specialist, private practice, 50- Publ: Numerous articles and monographs on domestic and foreign banking, industrial and political problems. Mem: Admitted to N.Y. State Bar and U.S. Supreme Court Bar; Fed. Bar Asn; Nat. Economists Club; Nat. Asn. Bus. Economists; Soc. Int. Develop; Am. Conservative Union. Rel: Jewish. Mailing Add: 200 W. 57th St, New York, N.Y. 10019.

SACKS, LEON D
b. Phila, Pa, 10/7/02; s. Morris Sacks and Dora Clayman S; m. 6/22/38 to Shirley Kimelman; c. Estelle Myra (Mrs. Sidney A. Chivian) and Fredlyn Jeri (Mrs. Martin D. Brown). Educ: Univ. Pa, Wharton Sch. of Admin. & Bus, Law Sch, 26; McKean Club. Polit. & Govt. Pos: Dep. Attorney Gen, Pa, 35-36; U.S. Rep, Pa, 36-42; mem, Registrn. Cmn, Phila, 51-53, chmn, 53-65; c.chmn, State Vet. Cmt, Pa, 50-62, chmn, 62-; Off. Chief Counsel, U.S. Customs, currently. Mil. Serv: Entered as Capt, Army Air Force, 42, released as Lt. Col, Judge Adv. Gen. Corps, 45, Legion of Merit. Mem: Am. Legion; Jewish War Vets; F&AM; Mason. Rel: Hebrew. Mailing Add: B 101 Bromley House, 6901 Old York Rd, Philadelphia, Pa. 19126.

SACKS, STANLEY ELLIOTT D
Va. State Del.
b. Norfolk, Va, 5/27/22; s. Herman Abraham Sacks and Sallie F. Feldman S; m. 7/22/53 to Carole Freedman; c. Andrew Michael and Betty Ann. Educ: Wash. and Lee Univ, A.B, 46, Law Sch, LL.B, 48; Phi Beta Kappa; Order of the Coif; Zeta Beta Tau. Polit. & Govt. Pos: Mem, Dem. City Cmt, precinct committeeman, Precinct 23; mem, Norfolk City Dem. Steering Cmt, Kennedy Campaign, 60; mem, speaker's cmt, Dem. Campaign Cmt. for Presidential Elec, 64; del, Va. State Dem. Conv, 64; alternate del, Dem. Nat. Conv, 64, del, 68; Va. State Del, 65- Mil. Serv: Entered as Pvt, Air Force, released as Sgt, after serv. in Pac. Theater. Publ: 'Preservation of the Civil Jury,' Wash. & Lee Law Rev, 'Uninsured Motorist Law,' Trials and Tort Trends and 'Effective Use of Pleadings in Opening Statement,' Personal Injury Annual, 64. Mem: Bar Found. Cmt, Va. State Bar; chmn, Continuing Legal Educ. Cmt, Norfolk-Portsmouth Bar Asn; fel, Int. Acad. Trial Lawyers; pres, Va. Trial Lawyers Asn, 64. Rel: Jewish. Legal Res: 6058 Newport Crescent, Norfolk, Va. 23505. Mailing Add: 915 Virginia National Bank Bldg, Norfolk, Va. 23510.

SADDLEMIRE, CARL LEWIS R
Chmn, Tioga Co. Rep. Cmt, N.Y.
b. Owego, N.Y, 9/7/14; s. Dalton F. Saddlemire and May Signor S; m. 9/4/37 to Lucille Bogart; c. Ann, Ruth and Richard D. Educ: Univ. Mich, A.B, 35; Cornell Univ, M.A, 36; Pi Delta Phi. Polit. & Govt. Pos: Clerk, bd. supvrs, Tioga Co, N.Y, 47-57, treas, 58-; chmn, Tioga Co. Rep. Cmt, 64- Publ: Chmn, ed. cmt, Manual for Clerks of Bd. of Supvrs, published in conjunction with Cornell Univ. Mem: Past exalted ruler, Owego Lodge 1039, Elks; dir, Tioga Co. Hist. Soc; dir, Paget-Price Home for Retired Presby. Ministers; treas. & mgr, Tioga Co. Soil & Water Conserv. Dist; Dist. Forest Practice Bd. Rel: Presbyterian. Mailing Add: Treasurer's Office, Owego, N.Y. 13827. (1967)

SADLAK, ANTONI NICHOLAS R
b. Rockville, Conn, 6/13/08; s. Stanislaw W. Sadlak and Julia Krukierek S; m. 5/30/39 to Alfreda Janina Zalewska; c. Antoni N, Jr. and Alita. Educ: Georgetown Univ. Sch. Law, LL.B, 31. Hon. LL.D, Georgetown Univ, 58. Polit. & Govt. Pos: Exec. secy. to Conn. State Rep-at-lg, B. J. Monkiewicz, 39-41 & 43-44; spec. inspector, U.S. Dept. of Justice, 41-43; Conn. State Rep-at-lg, 47-59; asst. mgr, Vet. Admin. Regional Off, Hartford, 59-60; Judge of Probate, Ellington Probate Dist, Conn, 66- Bus. & Prof. Pos: Exec. secy, Rockville Area C. of C, 63-66. Mil. Serv: Entered as Lt.(jg), Naval Res, 44, released as Lt.(sg), Top Secret Officer, Staff Adm. Kincaid, Comdr. 7th Fleet, Southwest Pac, 45-46. Mem: Moose; K. of C; Polish-Am. Citizens Club; Am. Legion; VFW; dir, Hockanum Valley YMCA. John Carroll Award, Georgetown Univ. Rel: Roman Catholic. Mailing Add: 105 Grove St, Rockville, Conn. 06066.

SADLER, JAMES KENNETH, JR, 'KEN' R
b. New Orleans, La, 10/25/35; s. James Kenneth Sadler and Letitia Wood S; m. 6/12/58 to Sarah Blair Smethurst; c. Christopher Knox, Gordon Wood, Stevens Moore. Educ: Washington & Lee, B.A, 58; Sigma Alpha Epsilon. Polit. & Govt. Pos: Mem, Jefferson Parish Polit. Action Coun, Rep. Club, 67-; mem, Rep. Exec. Cmt, Gulfport, Miss. and Harrison Co. Rep. Exec. Cmt, until 67; chmn, Harrison Co. Young Reps, 63-65; del, Nat. Rep. Conv, 64 and Miss. Rep. Conv, 64. Bus. & Prof. Pos: Chartered Life Underwriter, 65. Mil. Serv: Entered as Ensign, Navy, 58, released as Lt.(jg), 61, after serv. with U.S.S. Des Moines, CA 134, Mediterranean, U.S. 6th Fleet; Lt, Naval Res. Mem; Am. Soc. Chartered Life Underwriters; Rotary; Jaycees. Rel: Methodist. 1967 Legal Res: Metairie, La. No mailing address available. (1967)

SADLER, RICHARD SHERMAN D
b. Hawarden, Iowa, 9/10/28; s. Edward Anthony Sadler and Elsie June Sherman S; m. 2/2/52 to Mary Aliene Dusterhoft; c. Edward Allen, Richard Paul and Connie Louise. Educ: St. Marys High Sch, Clinton, Iowa. Polit. & Govt. Pos: Financial secy, Clinton Co. Young Dem, Iowa, 52-53; Dem. precinct committeeman, Natrona Co, Wyo, 66-; del, Dem. Nat. Conv, 68; chmn, Natrona Co. Dem. Party, Wyo, 68, mem. exec. bd, 69. Bus. & Prof. Pos: Round house foreman, Chicago & North West. Rwy. Co, 54- Mil. Serv: Seaman, Navy, 46-49, U.S. Navy-Pac. Fleet; World War Victory Medal; Good Conduct Medal. Mem: IBEW. Rel: Catholic. Mailing Add: 2626 Bonnie Brae, Casper, Wyo. 82601.

SADOWSKY, EDWARD L. D
City Councilman, N.Y.C.
b. Brooklyn, N.Y, 2/6/29; s. David Sadowsky and Bina Greenberg S; m. 12/20/53 to Jean T. Fishkin; c. Richard, Nina and Jonathan. Educ: N.Y. Univ, A.B, 50; Columbia Univ, LL.B, 53. Polit. & Govt. Pos: City councilman, N.Y.C, 62-; alternate del, Dem. Nat. Conv, 68. Bus. & Prof. Pos: Partner, Tenzer, Greenblatt, Fallon and Kaplan, Attorneys, N.Y.C, currently. Mil. Serv: Entered as Pvt, Army, 53, released as SP-4, 55. Rel: Jewish. Mailing Add: 13-15 160th St, Beechhurst, N.Y. 11357.

SAFFARRANS, MAURICE D
Chmn, Marion Co. Dem. Cent. Cmt, Mo.
b. Palmyra, Mo, 12/3/14; s. George Verdner Saffarrans and Mary Brooks S; m. 10/30/37 to Marjorie Morton; c. Maurie (Mrs. Robertson) and Maurice, Jr. Educ: Kirksville State Teachers Col, 1 year. Polit. & Govt. Pos: Co. committeeman, Agr. Stabilization & Conserv, Mo, 62; chmn, Marion Co. Dem. Cent. Cmt, 66- Bus. & Prof. Pos: Pres, Marion Co. Jersey Cattle Club, Mo, 43, Sch. Bd, Palmyra, 45 and Mo. Jersey Cattle Club, 55. Publ: Several articles on Pasture Improvement and on the raising of dairy cattle published in the Jersey Bulletin and Missouri Ruralist. Mem: Mo. Farmers Asn; Am. Jersey Cattle Club (judge, and mem. nat. show cmt); committeeman, Mo. Agr. Farmers; Co. and State Dem. Clubs; Farm Bur; Nat. Farmers Orgn; Odd Fellows. Constructive Breeders Award and numerous awards in the cattle bus. and pasture improve, Univ. Mo. Exten. Serv. Rel: Baptist. Mailing Add: Route 2, Box 29, Palmyra, Mo. 63461.

SAFFELS, WINONA R. D
V.Chmn, First Dist. Dem. Party, Kans.
b. Clay Center, Kans, 11/20/21; d. Herman A. Vahsholtz and Agatha L. Weerts V; m. 2/20/43 to Dale Emerson Saffels; c. Suzanne (Mrs. Gravitt), Deborah Lynn and James Bradford. Educ: Emporia Bus. Col; Menninger Bible Course, 4 years. Polit. & Govt. Pos: Dem. precinct committeewoman, Garden City, Kans, 56-60; assisted in planning husbands gubernatorial campaign, Kans, 62; v.chmn, First Dist. Dem. Party, 66-; del, Dem. Nat. Conv, 68. Mem: Belles of St. Catherine Hosp. Auxilary (chmn); Grey Lady; Red Cross Blood Mobile; Woodrow Wilson Woman's Club (v.chmn, first dist); Southwest Art Asn; Kappa Alpha Theta; Mother's Club; Logepedic's Auxilary; Commun. Concert Asn; Monday Club; PTA; Fortnightly Club; Women's Golf Asn; C. of C. Auxiliary. Selected One of Ten best dressed women in community. Rel: Lutheran. Mailing Add: 802 Pat's Dr, Garden City, Kans. 67846.

SAFIAN, A. CHESTER D
State Committeeman, N.Y. State Dem. Party
b. N.Y.C, 3/23/34; s. Felix Safian and Ruth Weiner S; m. 1/20/61 to Lois Jacobs; c. Judith, Robert and Thomas. Educ: Princeton Univ, A.B, 55; Harvard Law Sch, LL.B, 58. Polit. & Govt. Pos: Co. committeeman, Westchester Dem. Party, N.Y, 61-69; chmn, Westchester Young Dem, 63-65; del, Dem. Nat. Conv, 68; state committeeman, N.Y. State Dem. Party, 68- Bus. & Prof. Pos: Attorney, various firms, 59-67; stockbroker, A.G. Becker, 67-69. Mil. Serv: Entered as Pvt, N.Y. Nat. Guard, 58, released as Sgt, 64. Publ: 'Joint Accounts,' N.Y. Law J, 62. Mem: Urban League (mem, bd. of dirs, Westchester Chap); Anti-Defamation League (mem, regional bd); Family Consultation Serv. of Eastchester (pres). Mailing Add: 23 Anpell Dr, Scarsdale, N.Y. 10583.

SAFRAN, DANIEL D
b. N.Y.C, 2/3/39; s. Saul Safran and Hannah Israel S; m. 6/4/61 to Barbara Ann Karfunkel; c. Lisa and Debra. Educ: Queens Col, B.A, 60; Univ. Pa. Grad. Sch. Arts and Sci, 1 year; Bryn Mawr Col. Grad. Dept. Soc. Work, M.S.S. 63. Polit. & Govt. Pos: Del, Dem. Nat. Conv, 68. Bus. & Prof. Pos: Consult, Off. Econ. Opportunity, 65-; dir. div. training and educ, Inst. for Resource Mgt, Bethesda, Md, 68-69; v.pres, HUMANICS, Inc, Wash, D.C, 69-; asst. prof, grad. sch. soc. work, Univ. Md, 69- Mem: Nat. Asn. for Commun. Develop; Commun. Develop. Soc; Soc. for Int. Develop; Adult Educ. Asn; Am. Soc. for Training and Develop; PTA (pres. Takoma Elem. Sch). Queens Col. Departmental Honors, 60; Jewish Settlement House Found. Award, 61. Rel: Jewish. Mailing Add: 219 Whittier St. N.W, Washington, D.C. 20012.

SAFRAN, HUBERT MAYER D
Asst. Minority Leader, Colo. State House of Rep.
b. Salt Lake City, Utah, 12/25/30; s. Joseph Jacob Safran and Idalla Aaron S; m. 8/10/58 to Anita Elaine Shankman; c. Howard Daniel and Michelle Lynn. Educ: Colo. Univ, J.D, 54. Polit. & Govt. Pos: Mem, Small Bus. Cmt, West. States Dem. Conf, 63, coordinator, Colo. Del, 63; Colo. State Rep, 65-, Asst. Minority Leader, currently; mem, Steering Cmt, Dem. Platform Cmt, Colo, 66; chmn, Colo. State Dem. Platform Cmt, 68. Mem: Colo. and Denver Bar Asns; Am. and Colo. Trial Lawyers Bar Asns; Harvey Park Brentwood Lions Club (pres, 64-65); v.pres, Southwest Denver Serv. Asn, 64-65; Abraham Lincoln Jaycees; Anti-Defamation League Coun; B'nai B'rith. Rel: Jewish. Mailing Add: 4790 Lakeridge Rd, Denver, Colo. 80219.

SAGARDIA SANCHEZ, ANTONIO Popular Dem, P.R.
Rep, P.R. House of Rep.
b. San Sebastian, P.R, 9/13/13; s. Antonio Sagardia Torrens and Damasa Sanchez S; m. 7/17/32 to Emma Perez Cancio; c. Emma (Mrs. Mercedes), Antonio, José M. and Reinaldo. Educ: High Sch, grad, 32; Grad. of Commerce, 36. Polit. & Govt. Pos: Mem, Munic. Assembly, San Sebastian, P.R, 60-64; Rep, P.R. House of Rep, 64- Mem: Pres, San Sebastian High Sch. Teachers and Fathers Asn, 50-54; pres, Cancer Soc, San Sebastian, P.R, 50-63; pres, Am. Red Cross, San Sebastian, P.R, 56-64; Rotary (pres, San Sebastian Club, 56). Rel: Roman Catholic. Legal Res: 28 Muñoz Rivera St, San Sebastián, P.R. 00755. Mailing Add: P.O. Box 753, San Sebastian, P.R. 00755.

SAGGIOTES, SOTERIOS ARTHUR D
b. Newport, N.H, 2/17/22; s. Arthur G. Saggiotes and Georgia Canelos S; m. 10/27/46 to Evelyn Karras; c. Arthur S, Georgia S. and Charles S. Educ: Towle High Sch, Newport, N.H, 4 years. Polit. & Govt. Pos: Dem. town secy, 47, chmn, 48 and treas, 49; treas, Young Dem. of N.H, 48, nat. committeeman, 59-61; mem, N.H. Dem. State Cmt, formerly; chmn, Sullivan Co. Dem. Party, 63-65; mem, Sullivan Co. Exec. Cmt, 68; mem, N.H. Aeronaut. Cmn, 68- Bus. & Prof. Pos: Trustee and pres. of bd, Newport Hosp, N.H, 56-65; dir, First Nat. Bank, 63-69; chmn, Newport Planning Bd, 68-69; airport cmnr, 69. Mil. Serv: Entered as Pvt, Marines, 42, released as S/Sgt, 46, after serv. in 29th Marines, Sixth Marine Div, Pac. Theatre, 44-46. Mem: Am. Legion; Mason. Rel: Greek Orthodox. Legal Res: 25 Summit Rd, Newport, N.H. 03773. Mailing Add: 59 Main St, Newport, N.H. 03773.

SAHAGIAN, HERMAN D. R
Maine State Rep.
b. Kasrig Harpout, Armenia, 1/1/00; s. Sahag Sahagian and Sarig Yagjian S; m. 9/5/20 to Stella Der Derian; c. Virginia (Mrs. King), Anita (Mrs. Cook), Dorothy (Mrs. Silvano) and Herman D, Jr. Polit. & Govt. Pos: Appointee, Inter-Govt. Cmt; mem, Natural Resources Cmt; Maine State Rep, 60- Bus. & Prof. Pos: Founder and past pres, Fairview Wine Co, Cardiner, Maine. Mem: Cardiner Rotary; Mason, Shrine. Speeches Published in Cong. Records; lecturer. Rel: Episcopal. Mailing Add: Belgrade, Maine 04918.

SAHR, WILLIAM K. R
b. Pierre, S.Dak, 7/21/24; m. to Carla Aplan; c. James, Marquerite, Elizabeth, David, John. Educ: Northwest. Univ, LL.B. Polit. & Govt. Pos: S.Dak. State Rep, 62-66; State's attorney, Hughes Co, 59-62. Bus. & Prof. Pos: Owns law firm in Pierre. Mil. Serv: Army, 42-46. Mem: Am. Legion; Izaak Walton League; K. of C; bd. of trustees, Carnegie Libr; adv. bd. St. Mary's Hosp. Rel: Catholic. Mailing Add: 366 1/2 S. Pierre St, Pierre, S.Dak. 57501. (1967)

SAIA, DAVID JOSEPH 'JOE' D
Cmnr, Crawford Co, Kans.
b. Chicopee, Kans, 5/2/04; s. Phillip Saia and Elizabeth Piraro S; m. 10/12/57 to Olga Emma Leon; c. Philip J. and Betty Jo (Mrs. Sol Hammons). Educ: Frontenac pub. sch, 8 years. Polit. & Govt. Pos: Cmnr, Crawford Co, Kans, 38- Bus. & Prof. Pos: Saia Appliance & Furniture, Frontenac, Kans, 40-; Saia Explosives Co, Inc, 62- Mem: Eagles; Elks; Lions; Frontenac Civic Club. Rel: Catholic. Mailing Add: 611 W. Harris, Frontenac, Kans. 66762.

SAIKI, PATRICIA R
Hawaii State Rep.
b. Hilo, Hawaii, 5/28/30; d. Kazuo Fukuda and Shizue Inoue F; m. 6/19/54 to Stanley Mitsuo Saiki; c. Stanley M, Jr, Sandra S, Margaret C, Stuart K. and Laura H. Educ: Univ. Hawaii, B.S. Polit. & Govt. Pos: State Secy, Rep. Party of Hawaii, 64-66 and State V.Chmn, 66-68; Research Asst, State Senate Rep, 66-68; del, Hawaii Constitutional Conv, 68; alternate del, Rep. Nat. Conv, 68; Hawaii State Rep, 68- Bus. & Prof. Pos: Sch. teacher, Dept. Educ, Hawaii, 59-66. Mem: Oahu Prfnl. Educators Chap, Hawaiian Govt. Employees Asn; League of Women Voters; Fedn. of Rep. Women; Kapiolani Hosp. Auxiliary. Rel: Episcopal. Mailing Add: 784 Elepaio St, Honolulu, Hawaii 96816.

ST. ANGELO, GORDON D
Chmn, Ind. State Dem. Cent. Cmt.
b. Huntingburg, Ind, 6/20/27; s. George St. Angelo and Lillian N. S; m. 1952 to Beatrice Larsen; c. Paul, Kurt and John. Educ: N.Cent. Col, B.A. in Polit. Sci, 50. Polit. & Govt. Pos: Precinct committeeman, Dubois Co, Ind, 53-56; chmn, Dubois Co. Dem. Party, 56-64; chmn, Eighth Dist. Dem. Party, 60-65; pres, Eighth Dist. Young Dem, 2 years; state campaign chmn, Branigin for Gov, 64; chmn, Ind. State Dem. Cent. Cmt, 65-; mem. field staff for Congressman Winfield Denton, Favorite Son Primary, 68; mem, Branigin for Pres. Campaign and nat. v.chmn, Humphrey for Pres, 68; del, Dem. Nat. Conv, 68. Bus. & Prof. Pos: Pres. and gen. mgr, St. Angelo's Inc, Huntingburg, Ind, 52-64; bd. mem, Jackson Standard Life Ins. Corp, currently. Mil. Serv: Entered as Seaman, Navy, 45, released as Yeoman 3/C, 46, after serv. in Am. Theater; Victory Medal; Am. Theater Ribbon. Mem: Elks; Jaycees; Am. Legion; Kiwanis; Huntingburg Country Club; Indianapolis, Exec. Club and Athletic Club; bd. overseers, St. Meinrad Col. and St. Meinrad Theol. Sem; bd. dir, Flanner House of Indianapolis; Hon. Order of Ky. Col; Sagamore of the Wabash; Indianapolis 500 Assocs; Dem. News. Rel: Presbyterian. Mailing Add: 7604 N. Meridian St, Indianapolis, Ind. 46204.

ST. CYR, JOHN F. R
Mass. State Rep.
b. 1936. Polit. & Govt. Pos: Legal asst. to former Attorney Gen. Edward W. Brooke; Mass. State Rep, 67- Bus. & Prof. Pos: Former teacher; attorney. Mailing Add: 138 Pleasant St, Millis, Mass. 02054. (1967)

ST. GEORGE, KATHARINE R
b. England; m. to George Baker St. George; c. One. Polit. & Govt. Pos: Dir. and mem. bd. gov, Women's Nat. Rep. Club; chmn, Orange Co. Rep. Cmt, N.Y; former pres, bd. educ, Tuxedo, N.Y. and mem. town bd, 15 years; del, Rep. Nat. Conv, 44; U.S. Rep, N.Y, 47-64. Bus. & Prof. Pos: Former dir, Tuxedo Hosp. Mem: Past pres, Tuxedo Rep. Club; Orange Co. Fedn. Women's Rep. Clubs; Tuxedo Chap. A.R.C; N.Y. State Agr. Soc; Orange Co. Home Bur. Rel: Episcopal. Mailing Add: Tuxedo Park, N.Y. 10987. (1967)

ST. GERMAIN, FERNAND JOSEPH D
U.S. Rep, R.I.
b. Blackstone, Mass, 1/9/28; m. to Rachel O'Neill; c. Two. Educ: Providence Col, B. Philos, 48; Boston Univ. Law Sch, LL.B, 55. Hon. LL.D, Providence Col, 65. Polit. & Govt. Pos: R.I. State Rep, 52-60; mem, Young Dem. of R.I; del, R.I. Constitutional Conv, 55; pres, Woonsocket Young Dem; mem, Nationalities Div, Dem. Nat. Cmt; mem, First Rep. Dist. Cmt. of Woonsocket; U.S. Rep, R.I, 60-; del, Dem. Nat. Conv, 68. Bus. & Prof. Pos: Lawyer. Mil. Serv: Army, 49-52. Mem: R.I. and Woonsocket Bar Asns; Am. Legion. Legal Res: Woonsocket, R.I. Mailing Add: 1201 Longworth House Office Bldg, Washington, D.C. 20515.

ST. LAWRENCE, JOSEPH THOMAS D
b. Sayville, N.Y, 8/9/13; s. John St. Lawrence and Winifred McTernan S; m. 6/22/41 to Marguerite Clinton Downey; c. Joseph, George, Timothy and Christopher. Educ: Cortland State Teachers Col, B.S; N.Y. Univ, M.A; Col. of William & Mary, Univ. of Ariz. and Harvard Univ, grad. work. Polit. & Govt. Pos: Councilman, Ramapo Town Coun, N.Y, 61-64; N.Y. State Assemblyman, 64-68. Bus. & Prof. Pos: Fulbright prof, U.S. State Dept, 53-54; dir, phys. educ, Suffern High Sch, 45-64. Mil. Serv: Entered as Seaman, Navy, 42, released as Lt.(jg), 45, after serv. in Third Fleet, Pac. Theatre; Presidential Citation; seven Campaign Medals and Six Battle Stars. Mem: Ramapo Dem. Club; K. of C; Holy Name Soc; Parents Club of Sacred Heart Sch; Am.Legion; VFW; Cath. Inter-Racial Coun; N.Y. State Teachers' Asn. Established six collegiate track and field records. Rel: Roman Catholic. Mailing Add: 5 Campbell Ave, Suffern, N.Y. 10901. (1967)

ST. LOUIS, GEORGE D
Mem. Exec. Bd, Delta Co. Dem. Cmt, Mich.
b. Escanaba, Mich, 2/22/05; s. Joseph St. Louis and Maria Margaret Hjort S; single. Educ: Univ. Mich, 1 year; Univ. Md, 1 year; Georgetown Univ, 1 year. Polit. & Govt. Pos: Cong. secy, U.S. House Rep, 37-39; mem. staff, U.S. Dept. Interior, 39, U.S. Dept. Agr, 39-44, UN, Italy, Egypt, Greece, 44-46, U.S. Dept. State, Philippines and China, 46-50, U.S. Mutual Security Admin, Taipeh, Taiwan and Rangoon, Burma, 50-54, U.S. For. Aid. Admin, Seoul, Korea, 55-57 and U.S. Agency for Int. Develop, Karachi, Pakistan, 57-59, New Delhi, India, 59-62 and Bogota, Columbia, 62-65; chmn, Delta Co. Dem. Cmt, Mich, 66-69, mem. exec. bd, 69- Bus. & Prof. Pos: Lectr. for. affairs, Mich. State Univ, 67-68. Mem: Golf Club Ohio; Yacht Club, Mich; Univ. Club, Ohio; El Gezira Club, Egypt; Circle Sportif, Am. Club, Jewish Club and For. Correspondents Club, Shanghai, China; For. Correspondents Club, Hong Kong; Delta Coun. Health Coun, Mich; Akron Country Club; Univ. Mich. Alumni Asn. Rel: Presbyterian. Mailing Add: Route 2, Box 145, Escanaba, Mich. 49829.

ST. ONGE, WILLIAM LEON D
U.S. Rep, Conn.
b. Putnam, Conn, 10/9/14; m. Sept. 1945 to Dorothy R. Hughes; c. William

H, Susanne, Anne, Mary and Constance. Educ: St. Thomas Sem, Bloomfield, 32-34; Grand Sem, St. Brieuc, France and L'Ecole des Sciences Politiques, Paris, 34-37; Tufts Col, B.A, 41; Univ. Conn. Law Sch, LL.B, 48. Hon. Doctor of Law and Culture, Mexican Acad. of Int. Law; hon. LL.D, St. Michael's Col. Polit. & Govt. Pos: Mem, Bd. Educ, Putnam, Conn, 40; Conn. State Rep, 41; probate judge, Putnam, 48, prosecuting attorney, 49-51, judge, 55; chmn, Putnam Housing Authority, 48-56; dir, Putnam Redevelop. Agency, 56-58; dir. and v.pres, Conn. Urban Renewal Asn, 59-61; mayor, Putnam, 61-62; U.S. Rep, Second Cong. Dist, Conn, 63-, mem, Judiciary Cmt, Subcmt. on Patents, Trademarks, Copyrights and Rev. of Laws, Spec. Subcmt. on Submerged Lands, Merchant Marine and Fisheries Cmt, Subcmts. on Merchant Marine, Coast Guard, Coast and Geodetic Surv. and Navigation, Oceanography, and Bd. of Visitors to U.S. Coast Guard Acad; del, Dem. Nat. Conv, 68. Mil. Serv: Army Air Corps, 42-45, served 19 months overseas, received Flight Engrs. Wings, served as instr, Aircraft maintenance; 5 Battle Stars. Mem: Am, Conn. and Windham Co. Bar Asns; trustee, Univ. Conn. Law Sch. Alumni Asn; adv-trustee, Annhurst Col, S.Woodstock, Conn; Am. Legion; VFW; K. of C. Received Friends Award, Nat. Info. Bur. for Jewish Life, 64, and many honors and awards from other groups. Rel: Catholic. Legal Res: 88 Mechanics St, Putnam, Conn. 06260. Mailing Add: 405 Cannon House Office Bldg, Washington, D.C. 20515.

ST. PETER, GEORGE T. R
b. Abilene, Kans; m. 8/4/17 to Marie Loe; c. Billie Marie (Mrs. L.C. Lindsay); 4 grandchildren. Educ: N. West. Bus. Col; Tillison Sch. of Music. Polit. & Govt. Pos: Mo. State Rep, 58-66; twp. committeeman, 10 years. Bus. & Prof. Pos: Taught music in Tex. Pub. Schs. 10 years; Ark. Pub. Schs. 4 years; Stockman-farmer 20 years; own and operate 900 acre Linwood Hereford Farm at Modena, Mo; band leader on USS George Washington (This was the honor band for President Wilson and Peace Conf. to and from France, 18-19). Mil. Serv: Navy, WWI; Tex. Nat. Guard, 144th Inf, 36th Div, Warrant Officer, 27-34. Mem: Mason; York Rite Bodies; Legion of Honor, Shrine Moila Temple; Rotary Club; Am. Legion; Ellis-Casteel Post 22, charter mem, past pres, Mercer Co. Farm Bur. Winner of St. Louis Globe-Dem. Meritorious Award for House mem. showing greatest growth in leadership and ability in the 72nd Gen. Assembly, 64. Rel: Methodist. Mailing Add: Mill Grove, Mo. 64662. (1967)

SAJOR, EDMUND CASIMER R
b. Brooklyn, N.Y, 9/17/30; s. Kasimer Sajor and Sophie Nowak S; m. 10/31/53 to Edith Wasmuth; c. William E. and Donald J. Educ: Walter Hervey Jr. Col, A.A, 50; N.Y. Univ, 51-52; Univ. Calif, Los Angeles, B.A, 55; Coro Found, 55-56. Polit. & Govt. Pos: Asst. to the Speaker, Calif. State Legis, 56-59; asst. to the gen. mgr, Bay Area Rapid Transit Dist, 64- Mil. Serv: Entered as Pvt, Army, 52, released as Electronics Specialist, 54, after serv. in 532nd Signal Bn, Europe, 53-54. Mem: Am. and West. Polit. Sci. Asns; West. Govt. Research Asn; Nat. Capitol Hist. Soc; mgr, govt. affairs dept, Oakland C. of C, 59-64. Rel: Protestant. Legal Res: 2617 Lancaster Rd, Hayward, Calif. 94542. Mailing Add: 814 Mission St, San Francisco, Calif. 94103.

SALA, ROGER ANDREW D
b. North Adams, Mass, 8/8/93; s. L. Victor Sala and Valentina Andreotta S; single. Educ: Suffolk Law Sch, LL.B, 32. Polit. & Govt. Pos: Mem, Bd. of Appeals, North Adams, Mass, 39-43, Sch. Cmt, 39-47, Housing Authority, 42-65 and Draft Bd, 49-55; trustee, Soldier's Home, Holyoke, 48; Mass. State Rep, 53-68. Bus. & Prof. Pos: Lawyer, 32- Mil. Serv: Entered as Pvt, Army, 17, released as Cpl, 19, after serv. in 82nd Div, France. Mem: Berkshire Bar Asn; Elks; Eagles; K. of C; VFW. Rel: Roman Catholic. Mailing Add: 1 Pebble St, North Adams, Mass. 01247.

SALAMONE, THOMAS CARMEN D
Conn. State Rep.
b. Waterbury, Conn, 3/28/27; s. Rosario Salamone and Antonette Marinelli S; m. 5/30/53 to Margaret Sullivan; c. Lisa, Linda and Margaret 'Meg'. Educ: Post Jr. Col; Life Ins. Sch. of N.Y; Two Billion Life Serv; Nationwide Challenger Club; Casualty Key Club. Polit. & Govt. Pos: 1st v.pres, Wolcott Dem. Men's Club, Conn, 61-62; mem. Zoning Bd. of Appeals, 61-63; adv, Wolcott Ins. Cmt, 61-; mem, State Legis. Cmt. Ins, 62-66; Conn. State Rep, 62- Bus. & Prof. Pos: Owner, ins. agency, 61. Mil. Serv: Entered as A/S, Navy, 45, released as Seaman 1/C, 46, after serv. in PT Boats, S.Pac; Am. Area Medal; Victory Medal. Mem: K. of C; Lions; VFW; Farview Commun. Club; St. Pius Men's Club; Capitol Hill Jockey Club. Rel: Roman Catholic. Mailing Add: 10 Woodland Dr, Wolcott, Conn. 06716. (1967)

SALAS, G. RICARDO R
Rep. Nat. Committeeman, Guam
b. Agana, Guam, 11/14/23; s. Jose Salas and Clotilde San Nicolas Santos S; m. 11/26/51 to Rosa Teresita Leon Guerrero Perez; c. Richard Conrad Perez. Educ: San Francisco City Col, 46-47; Doane Col, B.A, 49; Univ. Chicago Col. Law and Hastings Col. Law, 57-58; Delta Kappa Pi. Polit. & Govt. Pos: Asst. Budget Officer, Govt. of Guam, Agana, Guam, 52; Internal Revenue Agent, Acct, and Dep. Cmnr. of Revenue & Taxation, 52-57, Dep. Cmnr. of Ins, Dep. Adminstr. of Securities, and Cmnr of Licenses and Registration, 61-63; Sen, Guam Legis, 64-66, chmn, Rules Cmt, mem, Cmt. Econ. Develop, Cmt. Finance and Taxation and Cmt. on Govt. Affairs; Second v.pres, Rep. Party Guam, 68-; Rep. Nat. Committeeman, Guam, currently. Bus. & Prof. Pos: Chief clerk and asst. oper. officer, Bank of Am, Guam Branch, Agana, 50; acct. and off. mgr, Standard-Vacuum Oil Co, 51-52; purchasing agent, Pac. Constr. Co, Inc, Los Angeles Off, Calif, 60; asst. mgr, Operations Officer and Acct, Bank of Hawaii, Guam Br, 63-66; owner, gen. mgr, Real Estate Broker, Property Mgr. and Appraiser, Salas Agency Corp, Guam, 66- Mil. Serv: Prisoner of War, Guam, 41-44. Mem: Lions; Young Men's League of Guam; Am. Red Cross. Rel: Catholic. Mailing Add: P.O. Box 1697, Agana, Guam 96910.

SALCHERT, JOHN JOSEPH DFL
Minn. State Rep.
b. Minneapolis, Minn, 8/9/36; s. Hubert Salchert (deceased) and Helen Mary Ley S. (deceased); m. 8/31/57 to Dolores Elsie DeMars; c. Michael, Mark, Anna Marie, Julie and Stephen. Educ: Col. of St. Thomas, 54-57; Univ. Minn, B.S, 57, M.D, 61; Phi Beta Pi. Polit. & Govt. Pos: V.Chmn, Hennepin Co. Dem-Farmer-Labor Party, Minn, 62-64; Dem-Farmer-Labor chmn, Third Ward, Minneapolis, 62-64; mem, Minn. State Cmn. Against Discrimination, 63-66; mem, Hennepin Co. Park Bd, 65-66; Minn. State Rep, 66-; mem, Minn. State Dem-Farmer-Labor Cent. Cmt, 67-; mem. bd. dir, Hennepin Co. Daytime Activity Care Center, currently; del, Dem. Nat. Conv, 68. Mil. Serv: 1st Lt, Army Nat. Guard, 62, Maj, 204th Med. Bdn, 62- Mem: Am. Acad. Gen. Practice (cmt. med. educ, 67, alternate del, 69); Am. Med. Asn; Am. Asn. Col. Physicians; cmt. med. educ, Minn. Med. Asn, 67. Rel: Roman Catholic. Mailing Add: 1015 Washburn Ave. N, Minneapolis, Minn. 55411.

SALEEBY, THAD ELI D
b. Hartsville, S.C, 7/7/29; s. Elias A. Saleeby and Creola Stokes S; m. 8/11/56 to Eloise McLain; c. Carl, Bryan and Rosemary. Educ: Univ. of S.C, A.B. and LL.B, 55; Lamba Chi Alpha; Delta Sigma Phi. Polit. & Govt. Pos: S.C. State Rep, 59-60 & 63-66; dist. cmnr, State Hwy. Dept, 68- Bus. & Prof. Pos: Attorney, Saleeby, Saleeby & Herring, 55- Mem: Scholarship Fund, Univ. of S.C; Jolly Jeepsters; Mason; Moose; Omar Temple. Rel: Episcopal. Legal Res: 2713 W. Carolina Ave, Hartsville, S.C. 29550. Mailing Add: Box 519, Hartsville, S.C. 29550.

SALEM, JOSEPH JOHN D
Tex. State Rep.
b. Corpus Christi, Tex, 12/29/20; both parents deceased; m. 2/19/43 to Christine Louise Aboud. Polit. & Govt. Pos: Tex. State Rep, 69- Mil. Serv: Entered as Pvt, Air Force, 41, released as 1st Lt, 45, after serv. as acting Capt. Legal Res: 350 Cape Hatteras Dr, Corpus Christi, Tex. 78412. Mailing Add: 64 Parkdale Plaza, Corpus Christi, Tex. 78411.

SALERNO, ROBERT D
b. Medford, Mass; s. Joseph Salerno and Mary S. Educ: Tufts Univ, B.A. in econ; Boston Col. Law Sch, LL.B; Northeast. Univ; State Col. at Boston. Polit. & Govt. Pos: Mem, Medford Ward and City Cmt, Mass; cand. for Mass. State Rep. Bus. & Prof. Pos: Attorney-at-law; formerly with Internal Revenue Serv; former corporate attorney. Mil. Serv: Air Force Res, active duty in 62. Mem: Elks; Sons of Italy; Boston Bar Asn. Mailing Add: 91 Princeton St, Medford, Mass. 02155.

SALIBA, ALFRED J. R
Chmn, Houston Co. Rep. Exec. Cmt, Ala.
b. Dothan, Ala, 2/22/30; s. Joseph E. Saliba and Maria Accawie S; m. 8/20/55 to Henrietta Carpenter; c. Annamarie, Alfred, Jr. and James Mark. Educ: Dothan High Sch, grad; Univ. Ala, B.S. in Civil Eng; pres, Eng. Sch; pres, Sigma Phi Epsilon; Omicron Delta Kappa; Jasons; Chi Epsilon; Alpha Phi Omega; Pershing Rifles; Cotillion Club. Polit. & Govt. Pos: Orgn. dir, Houston Co. Rep. Exec. Cmt, Ala, 62-65, chmn, 65-; mem, Ala. Rep. State Exec. Cmt, 66- Bus. & Prof. Pos: Owner and mgr, Alfred Saliba Homes Inc, 55- Mil. Serv: Entered as 2nd Lt, Air Force, 53, released as 1st Lt, 65, after serv. in 1503rd Air Installations Squadron, Japan; Korean Serv. Medal; UN Serv. Medal; Nat. Defense Serv. Medal; Capt, Air Force Res, at present. Mem: Pres, Dothan Home Builders Asn, 61 & 66; pres, Dothan Jr. C. of C, 60; bd. dir, United Fund, 62-65. Rel: Presbyterian; Elder. Mailing Add: Saliba Homes Inc, Dothan, Ala. 36302.

SALIN, WILLIAM N. R
Secy. of State, Ind.
b. Anderson, Ind, 10/23/31; s. Nathan Salin and Sophia McGillen S; m. 6/5/55 to Jane Robertson; c. William, II, Sherri and Susan. Educ: Ind. Univ. Sch. Bus, B.S, 54; Ind. Univ. Law Sch, J.D, 59. Polit. & Govt. Pos: City attorney and mem. bd. works and safety, Kendallville, Ind, 60-62; Secy. of State, Ind, 68- Bus. & Prof. Pos: Staff mem, Argonout Realty Div, Gen. Motors, Detroit, Mich, 54; v.pres. and trust officer, Ind. Bank & Trust Co, Ft. Wayne, Ind, 62-68. Mil. Serv: Entered as Pvt, Army, 54, released in 56, after serv. in Guided Missile Unit. Mem: Lions, Ft. Wayne; Orchard Ridge Country Club. Rel: Methodist. Mailing Add: 7744 Brookview Lane, Indianapolis, Ind. 46250.

SALING, GERALD L. R
Wash. State Rep.
b. Spokane, Wash, 4/11/28; s. James H. Saling (deceased) and Isla Womack S; m. 6/4/49 to Dee A. Bender; c. Susan E. and Ronald L. Educ: East. Wash. State Col, B.A, 51, Ed.M, 56; Wash. State Univ, 67-68; Phi Delta Kappa. Polit. & Govt. Pos: Served in Sierra Leone, W. Africa for Agency for Int. Develop, summer 63; Wash. State Rep, 65- Bus. & Prof. Pos: Educator, prin, Hutton Elem. Sch, Spokane. Mil. Serv: Entered as A/S, Navy, 45, released as MOMM 3/C, 47, after serv. in U.S.S. LSM-455, China, Korea and Japan, 46-47. Mem: Spokane, Wash. and Nat. Elem. Prin. Asns; Spokane Educ. Asn.(pres, 61-62); Wash. Educ. Asn.(dist. dir, 64-66); Nat. Educ. Asn. (state dir, 66-); Mason; Brotherhood of Friends; Rotary Int. Distinguished Alumnus Award, East. Wash. State Col, 69; Educator-Citizen of the Year, 69. Rel: Presbyterian. Mailing Add: W. 320 Nebraska, Spokane, Wash. 99208.

SALINGER, PIERRE EMIL GEORGE D
Mem, Calif. Dem. State Cent. Cmt.
b. San Francisco, Calif, 6/14/25; s. Herbert Salinger (deceased) and Jehanne Bietry S; m. 6/18/65 to Nicole Helene Gillmann; c. Marc, Suzanne, Stephen and Gregory. Educ: Univ. San Francisco, B.S. in Hist, 47. Polit. & Govt. Pos: Investr, Senate Select Cmt. on Improper Activities in the Labor Mgt. Field, 57-59; press secy. to U.S. Sen. Kennedy, Mass, 59-60; press secy. to the President of the United States, 61-64; U.S. Sen, Calif, 64; mem, Calif. Dem. State Cent. Cmt, currently; del, Dem. Nat. Conv, 68. Bus. & Prof. Pos: Reporter, San Francisco Chronicle, 46-55; guest lect. journalism, Mills Col, 50-55; contrib. ed, Colliers Mag, 55-56; v.pres. int. affairs, Continental Airlines and v.pres. and dir, Continental Air Serv, Inc, 65-69; chmn. bd, Gramco Int, 68-69; sr. v.pres, Amprop Inc; 69- Mil. Serv: Entered as A/S, Navy, 43, released as Lt.(jg), 46, after serv. in Pac. Area; Navy and Marine Corps Medal. Publ: With Kennedy, Doubleday & Co, 66. Mem: Nat. Press Club; Am. Newspaper Guild, 42-56. Mailing Add: 9101 Hazen Dr, Beverly Hills, Calif. 90210.

SALITERMAN, JOEL A. DFL
Educ: Univ. Minn. Polit. & Govt. Pos: Sgt-at-arms, state conv. Mailing Add: 2205 S. Hill Lane, St. Louis Park, Minn. 55416. (1967)

SALLADE, GEORGE WAHR D
Mem, Second Dist. Dem. Cmt, Mich.
b. Ann Arbor, Mich, 11/16/22; s. James A. Sallade and Nathalie Wahr S; m. 8/25/45 to Charlotte Haas; c. Natalie Ann, Elizabeth Lee, James Edward and Barbara Jean. Educ: Univ. Mich, A.B, 43, LL.B, 61; Phi Alpha Delta; Sigma Delta Chi; Sigma Phi. Polit. & Govt. Pos: Councilman, Ann Arbor, Mich, 50-52, pres, coun, 53-55; Mich. State Rep, 55-60; chmn, Washtenaw Co. Dem. Cmt, 65-69; Dem. cand. for Mich. State Sen, 66; dem. cand. for Mich. State Rep, 68; mem, Second Cong. Dist. Dem. Cmt, 69- Mem: Washtenaw Co, Mich. and Am. Bar Asns; Am. Trial Lawyers Asn; Mason; Moose; Rotary. Rel: Episcopal. Mailing Add: 2307 Hill St, Ann Arbor, Mich. 48104.

SALLEY, GUSS C. R
Mo. State Rep.
b. Benton Co, Mo, 4/3/98; m. 5/29/26 to Laura Lee Williams; c. Phillip C. Educ: Cent. Mo. State Col, Warrensburg; Kansas City Col. of Osteopathy and Surg, D.O, 24; charter mem, Atlas Club. Polit. & Govt. Pos: Mem, Benton Co. Rep. Cmt, Mo; coroner, Benton Co; former mayor, Warsaw; Mo. State Rep, 63- Bus. & Prof. Pos: Practice of osteopathic med, 25- Mil. Serv: World War I, Students' Army Training Corps. Mem: Lions (charter mem, Warsaw Club; Past Mo. Dist. Gov; Int. Counsr); active in estab. of the Eye Tissue Bank Prog, Univ. Mo, Columbia; founder, first pres. and chmn, Mo. Coroners' Asn; Mo. Asn. of Osteopathic Physicians and Surgeons; life mem, Am. Osteopathic Asn; C. of C; Am. Legion; Elks; Mason (32°); Scottish Rite; K.T; Soc. Am. Magicians; Int. Brotherhood of Magicians. Distinguished Serv. Award, Mo. Asn. of Osteopathic Physicians and Surgeons, 66; Mo. State House of Rep. Citations: App. House Physician by Speaker Thomas D. Graham, 63, Named Magician of the Year from Mo, 63, Honored for Serv. as House Physician, 65, Recognition as Esteemed Mem, Physician, Magician and Politician, 67, and declared Hon. House Physician. Well-known amateur at magic and sleight of hand. Mailing Add: Warsaw, Mo. 65355.

SALMON, THOMAS P. D
Minority Leader, Vt. House of Rep.
b. Cleveland, Ohio, 8/19/32; married; c. four. Educ: Boston Col, A.B, 54, Boston Col. Law Sch, LL.B, 57; N.Y. Univ. Law Sch, LL.M, Taxation, 58. Polit. & Govt. Pos: Justice of the peace, Rockingham, Vt, 59, mem. town coun, 59-, mem, Temporary Adv. Cmn. on Sch. Dist. Reorgn; munic. judge, Bellows Falls, 63-65; del, Dem. Nat. Conv, 64 & 68; Vt. State Rep, 65-, minority leader and chmn, Judiciary and Criminal Code Rev. Cmns, Vt. House of Rep, 69-; chmn, Windham Co. Dem. Party, 67- Bus. & Prof. Pos: Attorney-at-law; pres, Bellows Falls Area Develop. Corp; dir, Vt. Nat. Bank. Mem: Elks; Moose; K. of C; C. of C; Am, Vt. and Windham Co. Bar Asns; Rotary; trustee, Rockingham Mem. Hosp. and Steamtown Found. Rel: Catholic. Mailing Add: 24 Atkinson St, Bellows Falls, Vt. 05101.

SALMONSEN, LYMAN STANLEY R
Ward Chmn, Worcester Rep. City Cmt, Mass.
b. Worcester, Mass, 10/27/08; s. Peter Salmonsen and Marian Bach S; m. 4/18/33 to Veronica Mary Couming; c. Peter C. and Mark R. Educ: Worcester Polytech. and Clark Univ, evening classes. Polit. & Govt. Pos: Ward Chmn, Worcester Rep. City Cmt, Mass, 63-; chmn. trustee, Worcester State Hosp, 67. Bus. & Prof. Pos: Engr, New Eng. Power Serv. Co, 67. Publ: Design and Construction of Electric Rubber Glove Tester, 58 and Antique Meter Museum, 60, Elec. World. Mem: Inst. Elec. and Electronic Engrs; Columbus Park Soc.(chmn); Mason. Rel: Episcopal. Mailing Add: 18 Columbus St, Worcester, Mass. 01603.

SALMORE, RAPHAEL F. DFL
Married; c. Four. Polit. & Govt. Pos: Minn. State Sen, 51-66; lib. cand. for Pres. Pro Tem of Sen, 65; secy. of Lib. Group, 63; del, Dem. Nat. Conv, 60. Bus. & Prof. Pos: Real estate broker; secy-treas, Greenbrier, Inc. Mil. Serv: World War II. Mailing Add: 731 W. Orleans, Stillwater, Minn. 55082.

SALOME, J. M. 'JOE' D
b. Atlanta, Ga, 3/5/28; s. Dave A. Salome and Rosa Kaliphy S; m. 6/12/51 to Jeanne Boackle; c. Loretta, Ann Marie, David Joseph, Jean Marie, Joseph Michael. Educ: Ga. Tech, B.S; Emory Univ. Polit. & Govt. Pos: Ga. State Sen, 63-66. Bus. & Prof. Pos: Attorney. Mil. Serv: Army, T/Sgt, 1 1/2 years; 1st Lt, AAF Inactive Res. Rel: Catholic. Mailing Add: 946 Underwood Ave, S.E, Atlanta, Ga. 30316. (1967)

SALOMON, SIDNEY, JR. D
Dem. Nat. Committeeman, Mo.
b. N.Y.C, 4/20/10; s. Sidney Salomon and Mollie Jesselson S; m. 11/19/36 to Jean Korach; c. Sid and Susan. Educ: Culver Mil. Acad, 29. Polit. & Govt. Pos: Exec. Asst. to Postmaster Gen, Wash, D.C, 45; mem. col's staff, Gov. Forrest Smith, 49-52; treas, Dem. Nat. Cmt, 50-51; mem. staff, Gov. Phil M. Donnelly, 53-56; finance dir, Dem. Sen. Campaign Cmt, 54, hon. finance dir, 56; del-at-lg, Dem. Nat. Conv, 56, 60, 64 & 68; chmn, Finance Cmt. Dem. City Campaign, 59; mem, Appellate Judicial Cmn, 59-64; nat. finance chmn, Kennedy-Johnson Campaign, 60; mem. staff, Gov. John L. Dalton, 60-64; mem staff, Gov. Warren E. Hearnes, 64-68; mem. adv. cmt, 750 Club of Dem. Nat. Cmt; Dem. Nat. Committeeman, Mo, 68- Bus. & Prof. Pos: Mem. bd. trustees, Harry S Truman Libr, Inc; bd. trustees, John F. Kennedy Libr; pres, St. Louis Blues Hockey Club, Inc; gov, Nat. Hockey League, Inc; former exec. v.pres. and mem. bd, St. Louis Browns Am. League Baseball Club; former mem. bd. and part owner, St. Louis Cardinals Nat. League Baseball Club, Inc; former pres. and founder, Miami Marlins Baseball Club of Int. League; former pres. and founder, Hampton Gardens, St. Louis, Mo; mem. bd. develop. coun, St. Louis Univ; dir, River Center Redevelop. Corp; bd. dir, St. Louis and St. Louis Co. Chap, Nat. Found. of Infantile Paralysis, Inc; mem. bd. dir, Nat. Jewish Hosp. and Research Center; mem. bd. dir, Lovelace Clin, Lovelace, Tex; mem. bd. dir, Am. Med. Center, Denver, Colo. Mem: Elected mem, Mo. Squires, 66; Am. Battle Monuments Cmn, 61; St. Louis Life Underwriters Asn; chmn. adv. coun, East. Mo. Prfnl. Golfers Asn; adv. coun, Prfnl. Golfers Asn. of Am; life mem, Mil. Order of World Wars; life mem, Navy League; life mem, Culver Legion; Westwood and Meadowbrook Country Clubs; St. Louis Club, St. Louis, Mo; Chicago Standard Club; Scarsdale Quaker Ridge Country Club, N.Y; Miami Beach Country Club; Westview Country Club, Miami Beach, Fla; Woodmont Country Club, Wash, D.C; Jewish War Vet; Am. Legion; B'nai B'rith; St. Louis C. of C; Clayton C. of C; bd, St. Anthony Hosp, St. Louis, Mo; State of Mo. Cancer Bd. Received Michael Angelo Award for Distinguished Serv. to Children, Boy's Town of Italy, 59; Miami Advert. Club Award, Miami, Fla, 56; Recipient of Bruce Campbell Award, 68. Legal Res: 10 Vouga Lane, Frontenac, Mo. 63131. Mailing Add: 7820 Maryland Ave, St. Louis, Mo. 63105.

SALOMONE, MICHAEL JOHN D
b. Brooklyn, N.Y, 2/15/34; s. Michael John Salomone and Leah Spadofora S; m. 8/2/59 to Amelia Ciullo; c. Michael B, Kenneth L. and David. Educ: N.Y. Univ, B.S, 56; Brooklyn Law Sch, LL.B, 58, LL.M. cum laude, 63; Alpha Delta Sigma; Delta Sigma Phi. Polit. & Govt. Pos: Admin. asst, U.S. Rep. Lester L. Wolff, N.Y, 66-; Dem. committeeman, 18th Assembly Dist, Nassau Co, N.Y, 69- Bus. & Prof. Pos: Partner, Kimball, Salomone & Lally, 68- Mil. Serv: Entered as Pvt, N.Y. Nat. Guard, 58, released as E-5, 67, after serv. in 369th Artil. Mem: N.Y. State Bar Asn; Asn. Immigration & Nationality Lawyers; Nassau Co. Lawyers Asn; Kiwanis; Order of Sons of Italy in Am; K. of C; L.I. Athletic Club; Sky Island Club. Rel: Catholic. Mailing Add: 200 Middle Neck Rd, Port Washington, N.Y. 11050.

SALOOM, EUGENE GEORGE R
Pa. State Rep.
b. Mount Pleasant, Pa, 9/22/34; s. George Saloom and Isabell Karfelt S; m. 12/28/58 to Nancy Lou Newill. Educ: Elon Col, 55-57; Pittsburgh Inst. Mortuary Sci, Grad, 55; Alpha Pi Delta. Polit. & Govt. Pos: Pa. State Rep, 67- Bus. & Prof. Pos: Owner, Eugene G. Saloom Funeral Home, Mt. Pleasant, Pa, 60- Mil. Serv: Entered as Pvt, Army, 58, released as SP-4, 60, after serv. as Qm; Good Conduct Award. Mem: Westmoreland Co, Pa. and Nat. Funeral Dirs. Asns; Elks; Odd Fellows; Moose; Grange. Rel: Protestant. Mailing Add: 730 W. Main St, Mt. Pleasant, Pa. 15666.

SALTER, WILEY D
b. Monroeville, 7/6/26; s. Mack Crimon Salter and Fannie Mae Allison S; m. 5/27/56 to Fannie Louise Salter, wid; c. Elizabeth Ann, Rebecca Louise. Educ: Troy State Col, B.S; Ala. Polytech. Inst. (Auburn Univ.), M.A. Polit. & Govt. Pos: Ala. State Rep, 59-66. Bus. & Prof. Pos: Salesman connected with Chilean Nitrate Sales Corp. at Montgomery. Mil. Serv: Army, 3rd Cavalry, 45-46. Mem: Mason. Rel: Protestant. Mailing Add: Evergreen, Ala. 36401. (1967)

SALTONSTALL, LEVERETT R
b. Newton, Mass, 9/1/92; s. Richard Middlecott Saltonstall and Eleanor Brooks S; m. 6/27/16 to Alice Wesselhoeft; c. Leverett, Jr. (deceased), Rosalie (deceased), Emily (Mrs. Byrd), Peter Brooks (deceased), William Lawrence and Susan. Educ: Harvard Univ, B.A, 14, LL.B, 17; hon. mem, Phi Beta Kappa; Hasty Pudding; Porcellian Club; Delta Kappa Epsilon; Sigma Kappa. Polit. & Govt. Pos: Alderman, Newton, Mass, 20-22; asst. dist. attorney, Middlesex Co, 21-22; Mass. State Rep, 23-37, Speaker, Mass. State House of Rep, 8 years; Gov, Mass, 38-44; U.S. Sen, Mass, 44-67; del, Rep. Nat. Conv, 68. Bus. & Prof. Pos: Former dir, Nat. Shawmut Bank of Boston and Boston Safe Deposit & Trust Co, Mass; lawyer, Gaston, Snow, Saltonstall and Hunt, Boston, 19-28; v.chmn, MBUF, 67-; trustee of IVEST. Mil. Serv: 1st Lt, Army, 17-19, serv. in Field Artil. Mem: Former mem, Boston, Middlesex Co. and Mass. Bar Asns; Mason (32°); Elks; Am. Legion; Ancient and Hon. Artil. Co; hon. mem, Rotary, Kiwanis and Grange. Capt, Harvard Second Crew, which won the Grand Challenge Cup at Henley, 14; mem, Harvard Hockey Team; riding, golf and sailing. Rel: Unitarian. Mailing Add: Smith St, Dover, Mass. 02030.

SALTONSTALL, SALLY BROOKS R
b. Boston, Mass, 8/29/40; s. Richard Saltonstall and Mary Rogers S; single. Educ: Bradford Jr. Col, A.A. Polit. & Govt. Pos: Mem. staff, Sen. Edward W. Brooke, 67-; youth coordinator, Brooke for U.S. Sen, Mass, 66; campaign secy, Rep. Gov. Asn, 65-66; mem, Draft Lodge Movement, 64; secy. and youth coordinator, George C. Lodge for U.S. Sen, 61-62. Bus. & Prof. Pos: Secy, NBC-TV, Wash, 64-65. Rel: Episcopal. Legal Res: Farm Rd, Sherborn, Mass. 01770. Mailing Add: 1251 New Senate Office Bldg, Washington, D.C. 20510. (1967)

SALTONSTALL, WILLIAM LAWRENCE R
Mass. State Sen.
b. Newton, Mass, 5/14/27; s. Sen. Leverett Saltonstall and Alice Wesselhoeft S; m. 4/18/53 to Jane Chandler; c. William L, Jr, Claire and Abigail. Educ: Harvard Col, A.B, 50; Harvard Bus. Sch, M.B.A, 52. Polit. & Govt. Pos: Campaign worker, Saltonstall for Sen, 54 & 60 and Whittier for Gov, 56; mem. staff, Sen. L. Saltonstall, 59-60, admin. asst, 61-66; Mass. State Sen, 66- Bus. & Prof. Pos: Security Analyst, New Eng. Mutual Life Ins. Co, Boston, Mass, 52-58. Mil. Serv: Entered as A/S, Navy, 45, released as Qm. 3/C, 46. Rel: Protestant. Mailing Add: 388 Summer St, Manchester, Mass. 01944.

SALTZ, THOMAS LEON R
Chmn, Henderson Co. Rep. Party, N.C.
b. Hendersonville, N.C, 9/1/30; s. Roy F. Saltz and Dora Shipman S; m. 6/27/54 to Doris Eleanor Balch; c. Dwight Earl, Donald Edwin, Richard Lee and Barry Glenn. Educ: Blanton's Bus. Col, 3 years. Polit. & Govt. Pos: Secy, Henderson Co. Young Rep. Club, 56-60; secy. south east precinct, Henderson Co. Rep. Party, 60-64, treas, 63-69, chmn, 69-; co. campaign mgr, cong. cand, 64; campaign mgr, clerk court cand, 66; alternate del, Rep. Nat. Conv, 68; mem, Henderson Co. Bd. Elec, 68- Bus. & Prof. Pos: Mail carrier, U.S. Post Off, Hendersonville, N.C, 54; prod. scheduler, Gen. Elec. Co, 55-56, foreman, 56-58, data processing technician, 58-63, prog. specialist, 63-65; gen. acct. specialist, 65-68; mgr, acct. payable and gen. acct, 68- Mil. Serv: Entered as Pvt, Army, 51, released as Cpl, 53, after serv. in 9352 TSU Ord, Third Army, 52-53; Nat. Defense Medal. Mem: WOW; Am. Legion. Outstanding Woodman, 66. Rel: Baptist. Mailing Add: 307 Fairground Ave, Hendersonville, N.C. 28739.

SALTZMAN, EDWARD HAROLD D
b. Paterson, 2/22/07; s. Abraham Saltzman and Anna Schoen S; m. 6/21/36 to Frances Bornstein; c. Michael Ira and Allan Waganett. Educ: Rutgers Univ, LL.B, 29; Alpha Phi Pi. Polit. & Govt. Pos: Alderman, Paterson, N.J, 34-35; Asst. Prosecutor, Passaic Co, 35-44; alternate del, Dem. Nat. Conv, 68. Mem: New Jersey and Fed. Bar Asns; Passaic Co. Bar Asn.(pres); YMHA (pres); YWHA (pres); Preakness Hills Country Club (pres). Rel: Hebrew. Legal Res: 400 12th Ave, Paterson, N.J. 07514. Mailing Add: 64 Hamilton St, Paterson, N.J. 07505.

SALVETER, TED C. D
Mo. State Rep.
b. Washington, Mo, 5/5/36; s. Theodore C. Salveter and Nelda Oberhauz S; m. 8/30/57 to Sharon Lee Downen; c. Ted C, IV, Phillip A. and Paige A. Educ: Drury Col, B.A, 59; St. Louis Univ. Sch. of Law, J.D, 60; Sigma Phi Epsilon. Polit. & Govt. Pos: Mo. State Rep, 69- Bus. & Prof. Pos: Attorney-at-law, Springfield, Mo, 60-; instr. polit. sci, Southwest Mo. State Col, 65-66. Mil. Serv: Entered as Pvt, Marine Corps Res, 55, released as Pfc, 61, after serv. in 12th Rifle Co, 55-61; Range Medals. Mem: Greene Co, Mo. and Am. Bar Asns; Jr. C. of C; C. of C. Rel: Baptist. Mailing Add: 1333 E. Delmar, Springfield, Mo. 65804.

SALVETTI, LLOYD DONALD R
b. Weymouth, Mass, 10/19/41; s. Peter C. Salvetti and Olga Marcucci S; m. 6/13/64 to Gail Patricia Sheehan; c. J. Michael, Lisa Marie and Matthew Lloyd. Educ: Tufts Univ, B.A, 63; George Wash. Univ, 1 year; Westfield State Col, 1 year; Sigma Nu. Polit. & Govt. Pos: Admin. asst. to U.S. Rep. Hastings Keith, Mass, 69- Bus. & Prof. Pos: Intel. officer, Cent. Intel. Agency, 67-68. Mil. Serv: Entered as 2nd Lt, Air Force, 63, released as Capt, 67, after serv. in Calif, Vietnam and Mass; Capt, Air Force Res; Bronze Star; Air Medal; Vietnamese Honor Medal. Rel: Roman Catholic. Mailing Add: 1446 Greenmont Court, Reston, Va. 22070.

SAMARDICH, GEORGE R. DFL
Educ: Wis. State Univ, B.A, 55, M.A, 60; Univ. Minn, studied teaching mentally retarded. Polit. & Govt. Pos: Mem, Brooklyn Park Coun, Minn, 63-; mem, Gov. Cmn. for Mentally Retarded, 66-; former Minn. State Rep. Bus. & Prof. Pos: Rep, Text Book Publ. Co; switchman, Great North. R.R, 54-55; teacher, Va. Pub. Schs, 57-59 and Robinsdale Pub. Schs, 59-65. Mil. Serv: Navy, 2 years. Mem: Minn. Fedn. of Teachers; Minn. Educ. Asn, 57-58; state chmn, Cmt. on Polit. Educ, 59-65; Brooklyn Park Jaycees, 56- Mailing Add: 7032 Carey Lane, Osseo, Minn. 55369. (1967)

SAMMONS, JAMES BLAINE R
b. San Angelo, Tex, 1/31/31; s. James Blaine Sammons and Bernice Estelle Jones S; m. 10/21/51 to Fredda Joan Wyche; c. James Blaine, III, Ann and Sue. Educ: Tex. A&M Univ. Polit. & Govt. Pos: Chmn, Culberson Co. Rep. Party, Tex, 64-67. Rel: Presbyterian. Mailing Add: 601 Goliad, Van Horn, Tex. 79855. (1967)

SAMP, ROLLYN H. R
b. Chester, S.Dak, 9/20/43; s. Elden B. Samp and Ardyce Habegar S; m. 6/29/64 to Karen Moore. Educ: Augustana Col, B.S. in polit. sci, 65; Univ. S.Dak. Law Sch, J.D, 68; Zeta Chi Omega; Phi Kappa Delta. Polit. & Govt. Pos: Chmn, Augustana Col. Young Rep, 62-63; treas, S.Dak. Col. Young Rep, 62-63, conv. chmn, 65; govt. field rep, U.S. Rep. Ben Reifel, S.Dak, 62-67; campaign mgr, Frank L. Farrar for Gov, 68; admin. asst. to Gov. Frank L. Farrar, 69- Mem: Am. Law Student Bar Asn; Univ. of S.Dak. Student Bar Asn; S.Dak. Young Rep. Fedn; S.Dak. and Am. Bar Asns; cabinet, Augustana Col. Fels, 68- Sen. Francis Case leadership award, Outstanding Young Rep. in S.Dak, 65. Rel: Lutheran. Mailing Add: 304 S. Jefferson, Pierre, S.Dak. 57501.

SAMPLE, ALEX K, JR. R
m. to Joyce Dory; c. Martha, Barbara, Alexander III. Educ: Univ. of Minn; Grad. Sch. of Banking, Univ. Wis. Polit. & Govt. Pos: Trustee, Flathead Educ. Found; mem, Pres. Coun. of the Am. Inst. of Mgt; past mem, Gov. Space Cmt, Mont; adv. coun, State Planning Bd; mem. and past chmn, Adv. Coun. of Sch. of Bus. Admin, Univ. Mont; pres, Kalispell C. of C, 63; Mont. State Sen, 66-68. Bus. & Prof. Pos: Dir, Mont. Power Co; nat. bank exam, 8 years; pres. and chmn. bd, Conrad Nat. Bank. Mil. Serv: Navy, World War II, S.Pac. Mem: Elks; Am. Legion. Mailing Add: 404 Ashley Court, Kalispell, Mont. 59901. (1967)

SAMPSON, CURTIS ALLEN R
b. Hector, Minn, 7/6/33; s. Selmer B. Sampson and Sophie Sjogren S; m. 9/18/54 to Marian Arlys Walter; c. Paul Curtis, Randall David, Russell Steven and Susan Joy. Educ: Univ. Minn, B.B.A. with distinction, 55; pres, Beta Alpha Psi, 54-55; All Univ. Cong. Polit. & Govt. Pos: Co. chmn, John Zwach Campaign, 67; chmn, Renville Co. Rep. Party, Minn, 67-69; site cmt. mem, Rep. State Conv, 68; co. dir, Doug Head for U.S. Sen, 69; conv. chmn, Sixth Cong. Dist. Rep. Conv, 69. Bus. & Prof. Pos: Various mgt. and financial pos, N.Am. Commun. Corp. and predecessor co, 55-68, exec. v.pres. and treas, N.Am. Commun. Corp, 68- Mem: Ins. cmt, Minn. Telephone Asn, 64-; U.S. Telephone Asn; Independent Telephone Pioneer Asn; Mason (past master); Civic and Commerce Asn.(former pres); Kiwanis (past pres, Hector Club). Rel: Lutheran. Mailing Add: Hector, Minn. 55342.

SAMUEL, HOWARD DAVID D
V.Chmn, Westchester Co. Dem. Cmt, N.Y.
b. New York, N.Y, 11/16/24; s. Ralph E. Samuel and Florence Weingarten S; m. 4/15/48 to Ruth H. Zamkin; c. Robert Harry, Donald Franklin and William Howard. Educ: Dartmouth Col, B.A, 48; Phi Beta Kappa. Polit. & Govt. Pos: Chmn, White Plains City Dem. Cmt, N.Y, 60-64; alternate del, Dem. Nat. Conv, 64; v.chmn, Westchester Co. Dem. Cmt, 59-, registration chmn, 64, campaign chmn, 65; mem, N.Y. State Dem. Adv. Cmn, 69- Bus. & Prof. Pos: V.pres, Amalgamated Clothing Workers Am, AFL-CIO, 49-64 & 66-; v.pres, New Sch. Soc. Research, 65. Mil. Serv: Entered as Pvt, Army, 43, released as Sgt, 46. Publ: Co-auth, Congress at Work, 52 and Government in America, 57, Henry Holt & Co; ed, Toward a Better America, MacMillan, 68. Mailing Add: 7 Sherman Ave, White Plains, N.Y. 10605.

SAMUEL, RICHARD IRVING D
b. Brooklyn, N.Y, 2/21/40; s. Alexander Samuel and Mollie Fleischer S; m. 8/27/61 to Ellen Ruth Sherman; c. Miriam Sharon and Joanne Marsha. Educ: Rensselaer Polytechnic Inst, B.E.E, June, 61; Boston Col. Law Sch, LL.B, June, 65; Geo. Wash. Univ. Law Sch; Alpha Epsilon Pi. Polit. & Govt. Pos: Alternate del, Dem. Nat. Conv, 68;chmn, Volunteers for McCarthy, 12th Cong. Dist, N.J, 68; New Jersey's Temporary Rep, Nat. Steering Cmt. of New Dem. Coalition, 69- Bus. & Prof. Pos: Electrical Eng, Raytheon Co, Lexington, Mass, 61-63; electrical engr, Harvard Univ, 63-65; mem, Patent Staff, Bell Telephone Laboratories, Inc, Murray Hill, N.J, 66- Mem: Dist. of Columbia Bar Asn. Rel: Jewish. Mailing Add: 534 E. Broad St, Westfield, N.J. 07090.

SAMUELS, HOWARD JOSEPH D
b. Rochester, N.Y, 12/3/19; s. Harry L. Samuels; m. 2/22/42 to Barbara J. Christie; c. William Christie, Susan Carey, Catherine Christie, Victoria, Howard Christie, II, Barbara Christie, Jacqueline and Janine. Educ: Mass. Inst. of Tech, B.S. in Bus. Eng. Admin, 41. Polit. & Govt. Pos: Chmn, admin. cmt, N.Y. State Dem. Adv. Coun, 63-66; chmn, Citizen's Cmt. for an Effective Constitution, 65-66; Dem. nominee for Lt. Gov, N.Y, 66; leader, Campaign to Convene N.Y. State Constitutional Conv, Apr. 67; Under-Secy of Commerce, Wash, 67-68; del, Dem. Nat. Conv, 68; nat. adminstr, Small Bus. Admin, Wash, 68-69. Bus. & Prof. Pos: Vis. lectr, New Sch. for Soc. Res, spring, 69; v.pres, Mobil Chem. Corp. and gen. mgr, plastics div, Macedon and New York, N.Y; founder, Kordite Corp, Macedon, N.Y. Mil. Serv: Entered as 2nd Lt, Army, 41, released as Lt. Col, 45, after serv. on staff of Gen. George S. Patton, Third Army, Europe; cited as an outstanding officer on the staff of Gen. George S. Patton. Publ: An Insufficient House, 65; numerous articles and essays in periodicals and mag. on finance, Black econ. develop. and educ. Mem: N.Y. State Bus. Adv. Cmt, 54-58; chmn, N.Y. State Cancer Crusade, Am. Cancer Soc, 63-64; appointed by President Johnson to Nat. Citizens' Cmt. for Commun. Rels, 64; U.S. Employment Serv. Task Force, 65; Pub. Educ. Asn; Am. Histadrut Cultural Exchange Inst; exec. cmt, Am-Israel Pub. Arrairs Cmt; sponsor, Ad Hoc Cmt. of New Yorkers Against Anti-Ballistic Missles; trustee, Keuka Col. and Franklin Pierce Col; sponsor, Fund for New Priorities in Am. Award for serv. as N.Y. State Chmn, Nat. Found. March of Dimes, 64; Citizenship Day Award, Citizen's Forum of City and State of N.Y, 65; Herbert H. Lehman Mem. Citation, Nat. Info. Bur. for Jewish Life, 66; fel, Brandeis Univ. Rel: Jewish. Legal Res: Smith Rd, Canandaigua, N.Y. 14424. Mailing Add: 40 Central Park S, New York, N.Y. 10019.

SAMUELS, NATHANIEL R
Dep. Under Secy, Dept. of State
Legal Res: N.Y. Mailing Add: Dept. of State, 2201 C St. N.W, Washington, D.C. 20520.

SAMUELSON, DON W. R
Gov, Idaho
b. Woodhull, Ill, 7/27/13; s. Fred W. Samuelson and Nellie Johnson S; m. 2/22/36 to Ruby A. Mayo; c. Steve and Donna. Educ: Knox Col. Polit. & Govt. Pos: Idaho State Sen, 60-66; Gov, Idaho, 67-; del, Rep. Nat. Conv, 68. Mil. Serv: Entered as Seaman 1/C, Naval Res, 44, released as Gunners Mate 1/C, 46, after serv. in Am. Theater. Mem: Am. Legion; Elks; Kiwanis; Nat. Rifleman's Asn; Pend Oreille Gem Club and several sportsmen's orgn. Rel: Methodist. Legal Res: 1805 N. 21st, Boise, Idaho 83702. Mailing Add: State House, Boise, Idaho 83701.

SAMUELSON, DONALD B. DFL
Minn. State Rep.
b. Brainerd, Minn, 8/23/32; s. Walter H. Samuelson and Ellen Gallagher S; m. 5/17/52 to Nancy O'Brien; c. Stephen, Laura, Paula and Christine. Educ: Wash. High Sch, Brainerd, Minn. Polit. & Govt. Pos: Chmn, Sixth Dist. Cmt. on Polit. Educ, Minn, 60-66; mem, State Cent. Cmt, Dem-Farmer-Labor Party, 64-66; chmn, Crow Wing Co. Dem-Farmer-Labor Party, 64-; Minn. State Rep, 68- Bus. & Prof. Pos: Construct. foreman, Bor-Son Construct. Co. Mem: Elks; Eagles; Moose; YMCA; secy, Bricklayers Union; v.pres, Minn. AFL-CIO; Housing and Redevelop. Authority; pres, Brainerd Trades and Labor. Rel: Catholic. Mailing Add: 1018 Portland Ave, Brainerd, Minn. 56401.

SAMUELSON, JEAN MARGARET D
b. Marion, N.Dak, 11/11/09; d. Wesley C. McDowell and Mercy Anna Pushor M; m. 4/19/35 to John Elmer Samuelson; c. John McDowell and Mercy Ann (Mrs. Strom). Educ: Moorhead State Teacher's Col, 27; Valley City State Col, B.S. in Educ, 65. Polit. & Govt. Pos: Dem. precinct committeewoman, Burleigh Co, Bismarck, N.Dak, 62-66 & 69-; cand, N.Dak. State Sen, 66; pres, N.Dak. Dem. Non-Partisan League Women, Burleigh Co, N.Dak, 67; chmn, N.Dak. State Educators for Humphrey, 68; del, Dem. Nat. Conv. and mem. platform cmt, 68. Bus. & Prof. Pos: Elem. teacher, Lenten Dist, Jamestown, N.Dak, 29-30, Buffalo, 31-33. Velva, 33-35, Underwood, 48-51 and Bismarck, 55-; del, Nat. Educ. Asn, Minneapolis, Minn, 66; N.Dak. del, Teachers in Polit. Conv, St. Louis, Mo, 67. Mem: N.Dak. Educ. Asn; Bismarck Educ. Asn.(chmn. legis. cmt, 66-67, mem. legis. cmt, 68); Am. Asn. Univ. Women; Delta Kappa Gamma; DAR. Rel: Congregational. Mailing Add: 1242 S. Highland Acres Rd, Bismarck, N.Dak. 58501.

SANASARIAN, HAROUT O. D
Wis. State Assemblyman
b. Baghdad, Iraq, 3/29/29; s. Onnig Sanasarian and Julia Ibrahim S; m. 4/17/64 to Joy Anne Draak. Educ: Univ. Wis, Milwaukee, B.A. in Polit. Sci, 61. Polit. & Govt. Pos: Chmn, Armenians for Proxmire, Wis, 64; chmn, Third Ward Dem. Unit Credentials Cmt, 66; mem, Wis. State Dem. Conv, 66; prog. chmn, Fourth Ward Dem. Unit, 68; Wis. State Assemblyman, Fourth Dist, 69-; del, 5 Wis. State Dem. Conv; mem. platform cmt, Milwaukee Co. and Wis. Dem. Parties, several years. Bus. & Prof. Pos: Coordinator, export work, Allis Chalmers Mfg. Co, 61-65; teacher, high sch. civics, Milwaukee Pub. Schs, 67-68. Publ: 'Analysis of Middle East Political Picture,' Milwaukee J, 65. Mem: Am. Acad. Polit. and Soc. Sci; Milwaukee Teachers Educ. Asn; Milwaukee Teachers Union; Milwaukee Art Center. Rel: Armenian. Mailing Add: 1111 N. Astor, Milwaukee, Wis. 53202.

SANBORN, BLAKE PAUL R
City Councilman, Whittier, Calif.
b. Pomona, Calif, 10/7/24; s. Carl H. Sanborn and Sallie Dossett S; m. 7/29/49 to Mae Louise Moore; c. Jennifer and Shelley. Educ: Pomona Col. B.A, 49; Kappa Delta. Polit. & Govt. Pos: Town chmn, Ramsay for Congress, 62; pres, Whittier Young Rep, 63; del, Los Angeles Co. Young Rep, 63; victory squad chmn, 66th Assembly Dist. Goldwater Campaign, 64; town chmn, Wiggins for Congress, 66 & 68; city councilman, Whittier, Calif, 68-; mem. bd. dirs, Whittier Rep. Club, 69; chmn, Lincoln Club and Nixon Homecoming, 69; city of Whittier del, President Nixon's Inauguration, 69. Bus. & Prof. Pos: Dist. mgr, Farmers Ins. Group, 56-69; pres, Capital Leasing Corp, 69- Mil. Serv: Entered as Seaman, Navy, 42, released as Lt. Naval Aviator, 53, after serv. in VB-14 World War II, Fasron Seven, Korean Action (recalled), 42-47 & 52-53; Naval Res, 53-56; Designated Naval Aviator. Mem: President's Coun; pres, Whittier Exchange Club and C. of C. Rel: Lutheran. Mailing Add: 8607 LaTremolina Lane, Whittier, Calif. 90605.

SANBORN, BURT D. R
b. Greeley, Colo, 9/19/40; s. Philo Houston Sanborn and Lorraine Elizabeth Howe S; single. Educ: Univ. Denver, B.A, 62; N.Mex. State Univ, 63-66; Tau Kappa Epsilon. Polit. & Govt. Pos: Pres, Univ. Denver Young Rep, Colo, 60-62; v.pres, N.Mex. Young Rep, 63-65; coordinator, Ed Foreman for Congress Campaign, 68; admin. asst. to U.S. Rep. Ed Foreman, N.Mex, 69- Legal Res: Box 373 Mesilla Park, N.Mex. 88047. Mailing Add: 702 S. Fairfax, Alexandria, Va. 22314.

SANCHEZ, CORDELIA C. D
Committeeman, Bernalillo Co. Dem. Cent. Cmt, N.Mex.
b. Albuquerque, N.Mex, 3/22/26; d. Elfido Chavez and Gregorita Martinez C; m. 6/5/51 to John J. Sanchez; c. Kenneth John and Margaret Marie. Educ: Univ. N.Mex, B.A. in Educ; 46; pres. sub-chap, Phrateres; pres, Girl Scout Leader's Club. Polit. & Govt. Pos: Chairwoman, Citizens for Kennedy, Cent. N.Mex, 68; alternate del, Dem. Nat. Conv, 68; del, N.Mex. State Dem. Conv, 68; committeeman, Bernalillo Co. Dem. Cent. Cmt, N.Mex, currently. Bus. & Prof. Pos: Rep, Legis. Cmn. of Classroom Teachers, 66-67 & 68-69. Mem: Alternate del, N.Mex. Classroom Teachers Asn, 67-68; rep, Albuquerque Classroom Teachers Asn, 68-69. Rel: Presbyterian. Mailing Add: 6500 Rio Grande N.W, Albuquerque, N.Mex. 87107.

SANCHEZ, J. CHRIS D
b. Duran, N.Mex, 4/20/12; s. Trancito Sanchez and Erinea Duran S; m. 6/2/34 to Irene Werdna Waylie; c. Frieda and J. Larry; 4 grandchildren. Educ: N.Mex. Highlands Univ. Polit. & Govt. Pos: Auditor, State Bur. of Revenue, N.Mex, 43-50; Asst. Secy. of State, N.Mex, 51-54, Dep. State Treas, 55-66. Bus. & Prof. Pos: Sch. teacher, Torrance Co. Schs, N.Mex, 31-43; bookkeeper, Southwest Dist. Co, 68- Mem: Moose. Rel: Catholic. Mailing Add: 1207 Vitalia St, Santa Fe, N.Mex. 87501.

SANCHEZ, MAURICE D
b. Lemitar, N.Mex, 5/27/12; s. John Francis Sanchez and Mariana Miera S; m. 3/25/40 to Violet Lurba; c. Eileen Marie and Philip Charles. Educ: Univ. of N. Mex, A.B, 36; Northwest, B.S. in law, 37, LL.B, 39; Phi Kappa Phi; Pi Sigma Alpha; Delta Theta Phi. Polit. & Govt. Pos: Asst. U.S. Attorney, 42-51; U.S. Attorney, Dist. N.Mex, 51-53; mayor, ex-officio, Albuquerque, N.Mex, 54-62, chmn, City Cmn. Bus. & Prof. Pos: Law practice in Albuquerque, N.Mex, 39- Mem: Am. and N.Mex, Bar Asns; Am. Judicature Soc; K. of C. Rel: Catholic. Legal Res: 933 McDuffie Circle N.E, Albuquerque, N.Mex. 87110. Mailing Add: Bank of N.Mex. Bldg, Albuquerque, N.Mex. 87101.

SANCHEZ, PACO D
Colo. State Rep.
b. Guadalajara, Jalisco, Mex, 12/9/15; s. Rafael Sanchez and Juana Valadez S; div; c. Ralph, Francisco, Veronica (Mrs. Zegarra), Rose Marie (Mrs. Cespedes) and Yolanda. Educ: Col, Guadalajara, Jalis, Mex, 3 years. Polit. & Govt. Pos: Chmn, Wyatt Sch. Cmt; adv, Model Cities; gov, Denver Urban Coalition; cmnr, Denver Urban Renewal Authority; Colo. State Rep, 68- Bus. & Prof. Pos: Owner, Radio Sta. KFSC, 54-; founder, Good Am. Orgn, 54-, Good Am. Orgn. Fed. Credit Union, 55- and Good Am. Orgn. Homes Inc. Mem: HUD; Footprinters. Rel: Catholic. Mailing Add: 2185 Broadway, Denver, Colo, 80205.

SANCHEZ-VILELLA, ROBERTO People's Party, P.R.
Pres, People's Party, P.R.
b. Mayaguez, P.R, 2/19/13; s. Luis Sánchez-Frasqueri and Angela Vilella-Vélez; m. 7/10/36 to Conchita Dapena-Quiñones; c. Evelyn (Mrs. Salomón Monserrate) and Vilma (Mrs. Salvador Márquez); m. 9/30/67 to Jeannette Ramos-Buonomo; c. Robert José. Educ: Ohio State Univ, B.C.E, 34; Tau Beta Pi; Theta Xi. Polit. & Govt. Pos: Sub-cmnr. of the interior, P.R, 41-42; dir. Transportation Authority, 42-45; admin, Capital of P.R, 45-46; spec. asst. to Pres, P.R. Sen, 46-47; exec. secy, Govt. or P.R, 49-51; secy. of pub. works, 51-59; Secy. of State, P.R, 52-64; Gov, P.R, 64-68; pres, People's Party, P.R, currently. Bus. & Prof. Pos: Resident engr, Caribe Hilton Hotel, 47-48. Publ: Función y Acción de la Rama Ejecutiva. Mem: P.R. Col. Engrs; Am. Soc. for Pub. Admin. Annual Award, Am. Soc. Pub. Admin, 63. Rel: Catholic. Legal Res: 128 F, Paris St, Hato Rey, P.R. 00919. Mailing Add: 156 F.D. Roosevelt Ave, Hato Rey, P.R. 00919.

SANCKEN, GEORGE A, JR. Independent
Mayor, Augusta, Ga.
b. Augusta, Ga, 3/3/19; s. George A. Sancken and Sarah O'Farrell S; m. 1/4/47 to Ulainee Drawdy; c. George, III. Educ: Acad. Richmond Co, grad; Va. Mil. Inst, B.S. in chem, 41. Polit. & Govt. Pos: Mem, City Coun, Augusta, Ga, 56-61,mayor, 64- Bus. & Prof. Pos: Regional dir, Borden Co, 51-56; v.chmn. of bd, First of Ga. Ins. Group, 56- Mil. Serv: Entered as 2nd Lt, Army, 41, released as 1st Lt, 44, after serv. in 4th Inf. Div, ETO; Silver Star; Bronze Star; ETO Ribbon with 5 Battle Stars. Mem: Elks; VFW; Am. Legion; Rotary. Rel: Episcopal. Mailing Add: 2926 Bransford Rd, Augusta, Ga. 30904.

SANDACK, A. WALLY D
b. Chicago, Ill, 6/26/13; s. Jack M. Sandack and Ethel Grossman S; m. 11/12/40 to Helen Frank; c. Nancy (Mrs. Borgenicht), Roger D, Richard P, Arthur F. and Susan. Educ: Univ. Utah, LL.B. Polit. & Govt. Pos: Chmn, Salt Lake Co. Dem. Cmt, Utah, 54-57; del, Dem. Nat. Conv, 56, 60 & 68; mem. Utah State Legis. Coun, 65-66; chmn, Utah State Dem. Cmt, 67-68; regent, Univ. Utah, 69. Bus. & Prof. Pos: Attorney, Draper, Sandack & Saperstein, 37- Mil. Serv: Entered as A/S, Navy, 42, released as Lt, 45, after serv. in Pac. Theatre. Rel: Jewish. Mailing Add: 26 N. Wolcott St, Salt Lake City, Utah 84103.

SANDBERG, CHESTER C. R
Educ: Billerica Schs. Polit. & Govt. Pos: Billerica Planning Bd, 51-55; secy. of bd, 1 year; chmn, 1 year; dir. of Vets. Servs. for Town of Billerica; Town Meeting Rep. Bus. & Prof. Pos: Mgt. of Sandys Potato Chips; owning and managing Sandy's Restaurant 10 years. Mil. Serv: WWII, S. Pac. Mem: Charter mem, Billerica Elks, 2071; Am. Legion Post 116; Solomon Post VFW 8819; Mass. Vets. Serv. Agent Asn. Mailing Add: 405 Middlesex Turnpike, Billerica, Mass. 02114. (1967)

SANDBERG, JOHN CECIL D
Idaho State Sen.
b. Manti, Utah, 11/7/01; s. John Christian Sandberg and Agnes Hoggan S; m. 1/9/29 to Grace A. Anderson; c. John Cecil, Jr. and Shirley Ann (Mrs. Richard Merrill). Educ: Ricks Col, 23; Latter-day Saints Bus. Col, 29. Polit. & Govt. Pos: Coroner, Bingham Co, Idaho, 30's; mayor, Blackfoot, 45-47; Idaho State Sen, 60-; mem. bd, Idaho State Parks, 65-67; mem, Gov. Comprehensive Health Planning Cmt, 68- Bus. & Prof. Pos: Chmn, War Finance Cmt, Bingham Co, 42-50. Mem: Pres, Blackfoot C. of C, 43 & 57-58, Tendoy Coun, Boy Scouts, 51-53, Idaho Funeral Serv. Asn, 46-47, Bingham Co. Chap, Am. Red Cross, 56-60 and Blackfoot Rotary, 42-43; Rotary Int; Elks Lodge 1416. Achievements; Sponsored bill in past 2 spec. sessions of State Legis. after doing spec. research on reapportionment, 35-70 Senate-House ratio passed by legis, upheld by Fed. Courts; Silver Beaver Award, Boy Scouts. Rel: Latter-day Saint. Mailing Add: 9 North Shilling Ave, Blackfoot, Idaho 83221.

SANDE, KERMIT ANDREW D
Exec. Secy, S.Dak. Dem. Party
b. Huron, S.Dak, 2/23/43; s. Andrew Hanson Sande and Helen Busch; single. Educ: Augustana Col, B.A, 65; George Washington Univ, summer 65; Univ. S.Dak, J.D, 68; Kappa Theta Phi. Polit. & Govt. Pos: Mem. staff, Sen. George McGovern, Wash. D.C, summer 65; cand. for Cmnr. of Sch. and Pub. Lands, 68; del, Dem. Nat. Conv, 68; legis. counsel, S.Dak. Dem. Party, 68 and exec. secy, 69- Bus. & Prof. Pos: Practicing attorney, 68- Mil. Serv: Naval Res. Publ: Loyalty Oaths, The U.S. Supreme Court and South Dakota's Loyalty Oath Requirement, spring 67 and South Dakota's Bad Check Statutes, winter 68, S.Dak. Law Rev. Mem: Am. and S.Dak. Bar Asns; Phi Delta Phi; life mem, S.Dak. Law Rev. Asn. Nat. Honor Soc; S.Dak. Boys State. Rel: Lutheran. Legal Res: 718 Beach Ave, S.E, Huron, S.Dak. 57350. Mailing Add: Box 807, Huron, S.Dak. 57350.

SANDEL, JERRY WAYNE D
b. Woodson, Tex, 5/25/42; s. Wayne Sandel and Sally Martin S; m. 11/27/64 to Nancy Potts; c. Michelle 'Mlle'. Educ: Tex. Tech. Col, B.A, 65; Univ. Tex. Sch. of Prod. Rig Oper, 1 year; Soc. for Adv. of Mgt; Circle K. Polit. & Govt. Pos: Alternate del, Dem. Nat. Conv, 68; pres, Young Dem, Farmington, N.Mex, 68- Bus. & Prof. Pos: Pres, Totah Rental & Equipment Co. Inc, Aztec, N.Mex. and v.pres, Aztec Well Servicing Co, currently. Mem: Am. Petroleum Inst; N.Mex. Lawman Asn; Mason; Elks. Participant, Presidents Council Youth Orgn; participant in Project Gasbuggy, first nuclear detonation for industrial application. Rel: Christian Church N.Am. Mailing Add: 107 West 32nd St, Farmington, N.Mex. 87401.

SANDERS, ALEXANDER MULLINGS, JR. 'ALEX' D
S.C. State Rep.
b. Columbia, S.C, 9/29/39; s. Alexander Mullings Sanders and Henrietta Thomas S; m. 12/19/64 to Zoe Dutrow. Educ: Univ. S.C, B.S, 59, LL.B, 62; Phi Delta Phi; Sigma Alpha Epsilon. Polit. & Govt. Pos: Town judge, Forest Acres, S.C, 66; S.C. State Rep, 67- Mil. Serv: Pvt, Army, 57; Army Res. Mem: Am. Bar Asn; Am. Trial Lawyers Asn; pres, S.C. Trial Lawyers Asn; secy. and treas, Richland Co. Bar Asn, 66. Rel: Episcopal. Mailing Add: Barringer Bldg, Columbia, S.C. 29201.

SANDERS, CARL EDWARD D
b. Augusta, Ga, 5/15/25; s. Carl T. Sanders and Roberta Jones S; m. 9/6/47 to Betty Bird Foy; c. Betty Foy and Carl E, Jr. Educ: Univ. Ga, LL.B, 47; Chi Phi; Phi Delta Phi. Polit. & Govt. Pos: Ga. State Rep, 54-56; Ga. State Sen, 56-62, Pres. Pro Tem, Ga. State Senate, 60-62; Gov, Ga, until 67. Bus. & Prof. Pos: Sr. Mem, Law Firm of Sanders, Thurmond, Hester & Jolles, Augusta, Ga, 47-62. Mil. Serv: Entered Air Force, released as 1st Lt, after serv. as 1st pilot of a B-17 heavy bomber. Mem: Official positions in the YMCA; Ga-Carolina Council, Boy Scouts; Am. Red. Cross; Jr. C. of C; Am, Ga. and Augusta Bar Asns; Am. Legion; Mason; Moose; Elks; Exchange Club. Selected Young Man of the Year, Augusta Jaycees, 55; honored by Ga. Jaycees as one of five outstanding young Georgians, 59. Rel: Baptist. Mailing Add: 2212 Morningside Dr, Augusta, Ga. 30904.

SANDERS, CECIL CARLTON D
Mem, Ky. State Dem. Cent. Cmt.
b. Garrard Co, Ky, 3/2/14; s. James Blythe Sanders and Suella Jones S; m. 10/10/40 to Nancy Viola Layton; c. Jerry Sue (Mrs. Johnson) and James Stephen. Educ: Transylvania Col, A.B; Univ. Ky, LL.B; Phi Alpha Delta. Polit. & Govt. Pos: City attorney, Lancaster, Ky, 49-; Ky. State Rep, 53-57; Ky. State Sen, 57-59; mem, Ky. State Dem. Cent. Cmt, currently. Bus. & Prof. Pos: Mem, bd. regents, East. Ky. State Col, 53-59; chmn. bd, Midway Jr. Col, currently. Mil. Serv: Entered as Ens, Navy, 42, released as Lt, 46, after serv. in M.T.B's ETO and Pac; Am, Pac, Mediterranean and European Ribbons; Navy and Marine Corps Medal; Bronze Star; Presidential Unit Citation. Mem: Am. and Ky. Bar Asns; Am. Judicature Soc; Am. Acad. Polit. Sci; Mason; Am. Legion. Civilian Pilot, Golf and Tennis. Rel: Disciples of Christ; Elder and Sunday Sch. Teacher. Legal Res: Maple Ave, Lancaster, Ky. 40444. Mailing Add: 100 Paulding St, Lancaster, Ky. 40444.

SANDERS, DONALD GILBERT D
b. St. Louis, Mo, 4/26/30; s. Howard W. Sanders and Ann M. Schmitz S; m. 8/31/52 to Dolores L. Henderson; c. Deborah Ann, Michael Steven and Matthew Henderson. Educ: Univ. Mo, 47-49 and LL.B, 54; Wash. Univ, 50-51; Alpha Gamma Rho; Phi Alpha Delta. Polit. & Govt. Pos: City attorney, Columbia, Mo, 56-58; asst. prosecuting attorney, Boone Co, Mo, 59; spec. agent, Fed. Bur. of Invest, Birmingham, Ala. and Miami, Fla, 59-64 and supvry. spec. agent, Wash, D.C, 64-69; chief counsel, U.S. House of Rep. Cmt. on Internal Security, 69- Bus. & Prof. Pos: Pvt. practice of law, Columbia, Mo, 56-59. Mil. Serv: Entered as 2nd Lt, Marine Corps, 54, released as 1st Lt, 56, after serv. in Legal Off, Camp Pendleton, Calif, 55-56. Mem: Am. and Mo. Bar Asns; admitted to practice before U.S. Supreme Court; Soc. Former Spec. Agents Fed. Bur. of Invest; Am. Legion. Rel: Methodist. Legal Res: 6423 Rotunda Court, Springfield, Va. 22150. Mailing Add: 309 Cannon Bldg, Washington, D.C. 20515.

SANDERS, FRANK D
Asst. Secy. of the Navy for Installations and Logistics
b. Tarboro, N.C, 7/30/19; m. to Mary Ellen Gilbert; c. Douglas and Frank, Jr. Educ: Armstrong Jr. Col, Savannah, Ga, grad; George Wash. Univ. Law Sch, grad; Univ. Md, Govt. and Polit. Polit. & Govt. Pos: Mem. staff, Cmt. on Appropriations, U.S. House of Rep, 19 years, staff asst, Subcmt. on Mil. Construction and Subcmt. on Defense Dept; Asst. Secy. of the Navy for Installations and Logistics, 69- Mil. Serv: Entered as Pvt, Army, 41, released as Capt, 45, after serv. in Intel. and Surv. Sect. of div. artil. staffs of the 85th and 34th Inf. Div; Lt. Col, Army Officer Res. Corps; Bronze Star; European Theater Ribbon with Three Battle Stars. Mem: Trustee and past pres, Gospel Mission, D.C; former trustee, Wash. Bible Col; adv. bd, Pinwheel Jr. Rifle Club; assoc. mem, Inst. for Strategic Studies, London; Psi Sigma Alpha. Rel: Presbyterian; Elder, Fourth Presby. Church. Legal Res: Bethesda, Md. 20014. Mailing Add: Dept. of the Navy, Pentagon, Washington, D.C. 20350.

SANDERS, GUYNELL R. D
b. Leesville, La, 6/17/23; d. Guy Van Russell and Leola Cecelia Parker V; m. 1/8/44 to Joseph Durwood Sanders; c. Carolyn (Mrs. Carter), JoAnne, Joseph Durwood, Jr, Stephen Cullen and Jean Marie. Educ: Port Arthur Tex. Bus. & Radio Col, 39. Polit. & Govt. Pos: Participant, Dem. Campaigns, Tenn, 56-; chmn. campaign for Metrop. Charter Cmn, 61 and chmn, Women's Div, Campaign for Metrop. Govt, 62; chmn, Women's Activities, Campaign of Mayor Beverly Briley, 62 & 66; admin. asst. to Mayor, Metrop. Govt, Nashville and Davidson Co, 63-; del, Dem. Nat. Conv, 64; coordinator, Dem. Nat. Elecs, Davidson Co, 64, 66 & 68 and Women's Activities, Davidson Co. Dem. Primaries, 64, 66 & 68. Bus. & Prof. Pos: Jr. clerk, Qm. Corps, Tenth Civil Serv. Dist, 40-41; secy. to Dir. Pub. Rels. and Assoc. Ed, Co. Mag, Timm Aircraft Corp, Van Nuys, Calif, 42-44; asst. to Ed, Madison Commun. News, Tenn, 57-60; exec. secy, Madison C. of C, 61-63. Mem: League Women Voters; bd. dirs, Tenn. Fedn. Dem. Women; proj. chmn, Dem. Women's Club of Davidson Co; charter mem, Madison-Old Hickory Bus. & Prfnl. Women's Club; chmn, Women's Div, Citizens for Better Govt, Nashville; Civic Cmt. on Pub. Educ; past pres, Madison Dem. Women's Club; bd. dir, Relig. Heritage of Am; March of Dimes Area Chmn. Rel: Catholic. Legal Res: 1110 Fernbank Dr, Madison, Tenn. 37115. Mailing Add: 107 Metropolitan Court House, Nashville, Tenn. 37201.

SANDERS, H. E. 'GENE' R
b. W. Frankfort, Ill, 5/10/28; s. Holden Julius Sanders and Lora Absher S; m. 12/8/55 to Mary L. Newsom; c. Mary Leigh, John K, and William McDonald. Educ: Univ. Miami, B.A, 56, LL.B, 59; Omicron Delta Kappa. Polit. & Govt. Pos: Ga. State Sen, 41st Dist, 65-66; staff attorney, Fed. Commun. Cmn, 62 and Fed. Trade Cmn, 60-61. Mil. Serv: Entered as Pvt, Air Force, 49, released as Sgt, 53, after serv. in 435th Troop Carrier Wing. Publ: Articles in Univ. of Miami Law Review, 59 and Fla. Law Review, 60. Mem: Am. Bar Asn; Fla. and Georgia Bars; Clarkston 492, F&AM; Am. Radio Relay League. Rel: Methodist. Mailing Add: 3223 Buford Highway N.E, Atlanta, Ga. 30329. (1967)

SANDERS, HAROLD BAREFOOT, JR. D
b. Dallas, Tex, 2/5/25; s. Harold Barefoot Sanders and May Elizabeth Forester S; m. 6/6/52 to Jan Scurlock; c. Janet Lea, Martha Kay, Mary Frances, Harold Barefoot III. Educ: Univ. Tex, B.A, 49, LL.B, 50; Phi Delta Phi; Phi Delta Theta. Polit. & Govt. Pos: Tex. State Rep, 52-58; Dem. cand, U.S. Rep, Tex, 58; U.S. Attorney, North. Dist, Tex, 61-65; Asst. Dept. U.S. Attorney Gen, 65-66; Asst. Attorney Gen, U.S, 66-67; legis. counsel to President Lyndon B. Johnson, 67-69. Bus. & Prof. Pos: Assoc, Storey, Sanders, Sherrill & Armstrong, Dallas, 50-52; partner, Sanders & Sanders, 51-61; partner, Clark, West, Keller, Sanders & Ginsberg, Dallas, Tex. and Wash, D.C, 69- Mil. Serv: Lt.(jg), Naval Res, World War II. Mem: Am. and Dallas Bar Asns; Fed. Bar Asn.(bd. dirs, Nat. Coun, 63-66); State Bar Tex; Tex. Ex-Students Asn.(pres, Dallas Chap, 55-56); Blue Key; Mason; Chaparral Club; pres, Wash, D.C. Tex-Exes, 68-69. Distinguished Serv. Award, Dallas Fed. Bar Asn, 64. Rel: Methodist. Legal Res: 7326 Malabar, Dallas, Tex. 75230. Mailing Add: First National Bank Bldg, Dallas, Tex. 75202.

SANDERS, HORACE W. R
N.H. State Rep.
b. Concord, N.H, 10/1/90; wid; c. 1. Educ: Concord Pub. Schs. Polit. & Govt. Pos: N.H. State Rep, 61- Bus. & Prof. Pos: Retired, U.S. Post Office Dept. Mem: Masons; Odd Fellows; Nat. Asn. of Letter Carriers; Nat. Asn. Retired Civil Employees. Rel: Protestant. Mailing Add: 50 Monroe St, Concord, N.H. 03301.

SANDERS, JAMES WILLIS R
Chmn, Williamson Co. Rep. Party, Ill.
b. Marion, Ill, 9/30/23; s. Lawrence A. Sanders and Minnie Harris S; m. 5/4/47 to Myrla Leach; c. Jane, Larry, John, Gail and Ann. Educ: Univ. Ill, B.S, 48; John Marshall Law Sch, 51. Polit. & Govt. Pos: Chmn, Williamson Co. Rep. Party, Ill, currently; mem, Ill. Rep. State Cent. Cmt, currently. Mil. Serv: Entered as Pvt, Army, 42, released as T/Sgt, 47, after serv. in 310th Inf, 78th Div, ETO, 44; Purple Heart. Mem: Pres, Williamson Co. Bar Asn, 64; Am. Legion; DAV; VFW; Rotary. Rel: Methodist. Mailing Add: 208 N. Market St, Marion, Ill. 62959. (1967)

SANDERS, JOE WILLIAM D
Assoc. Justice, Supreme Court of La.
b. Pleasant Hill, La, 5/31/15; s. Oliver Lud Sanders and Ozie Allen S; m. 10/26/40 to Marie Sistrunk. Educ: La. State Univ, B.A, 35; LL.B, 38; Phi Kappa Phi; Omicron Delta Kappa; Gamma Eta Gamma; Pi Sigma Alpha; Pi Gamma Mu; Theta Xi. Polit. & Govt. Pos: La. State Rep, 40-44; del, Dem. Conv, 52; chmn, East Baton Rouge Parish Juvenile Cmn, 51-54; judge family court, East Baton Rouge Parish, 54-60; mem. adv. coun. judges, Nat. Coun. Crime and Delinquency, 55-; assoc. justice, Supreme Court of La, 60- Bus. & Prof. Pos: Attorney-at-law, Many, La, 38-42, Baton Rouge, 46-54; chmn, Blue Ridge Training Inst. of South. Juvenile Court Judges, 57. Mil. Serv: Capt, Army, 42-46. Mem: Bd. dirs, Baton Rouge YMCA, 58-61, 52-55; Am. and La. Bar Asns; Am. Judicature Soc; Nat. Coun. Juvenile Court Judges; Coun. La. State Law Inst; Am. Law Inst; Am. Legion; Amvets, past post comdr; VFW; Order of the Coif; Mason; WOW. Legal Res: 209 Lovers Lane Dr, Baton Rouge, La. 70806. Mailing Add: 301 Loyola Ave, New Orleans, La. 70112.

SANDERS, ROBERT R. R
State Printer, Kans.
b. Mulvane, Kans, 1/4/03; s. William Bernard Sanders and Marietta Clark S; m. 6/16/22 to Letha Gwendolyn King; c. Dona Jeanne (Mrs. Ralph H. Woertendyke) and Robert Dana. Educ: Plainville and Manhattan High Schs, Kans. Polit. & Govt. Pos: State printer, Kans, 65- Bus. & Prof. Pos: Owner, Globe-Sun Printing Co, Salina, Kans, 44-65. Mem: Kiwanis; Mason (32°); Shrine; Elks; Int. Typographic Union; Kans. Typographical Union (pres, 4 years). Rel: Methodist. Legal Res: 944 Highland, Salina, Kans. 67401. Mailing Add: 201 W. 10th, Topeka, Kans. 66612.

SANDERS, ROY D
b. Dorton, Ky, 4/9/95; s. Adam Sanders and Martha E. Bumgardner S; m. 12/29/49 to Josephine Vanovier. Educ: East. State Col, B.S; Kans. Univ, M.D. Polit. & Govt. Pos: Ky. State Rep, 63-66 and 49-52. Bus. & Prof. Pos: Operates Small Hosp, 46-66; private practice, Medicine, 38-66. Mil. Serv: 1st Lt, Army, 16-19; Capt, Army Res, 39. Mem: Pike Co. Med. Soc; Ky. State Med. Soc; Am. Medical Asn; Acad. Practice and Southern Medical Soc; Mason, Shrine; Am. Legion. Baseball. Mailing Add: Dorton, Ky. 41520. (1967)

SANDERS, WILFRED LEROY, JR. D
Coordinator, First Cong. Dist. Dem. Cmt, N.H.
b. Marlboro, Mass, 11/20/35; s. Wilfred L. Sanders, Sr. and Rose A. Harper S; m. 8/22/59 to Mary Jo; c. Elizabeth Rose and Jonathan Lee. Educ: Univ. N.H, B.A, 59; Boston Col. Sch. Law, LL.B, 62; Sigma Alpha Epsilon (pres); Newman Club (v.pres); Class Pres, Univ. N.H. Polit. & Govt. Pos: Secy, N.H. Constitutional Conv, 65; chmn, Rockingham Co. Dem. Cmt, 65-68; chmn, N.H. State Dem. Conv, 66 & 68; del, Dem. Nat. Conv, 68; coordinator, First Cong. Dist. Dem. Cmt, 68- Mil. Serv: Entered as Pvt, N.H. Nat. Guard, 58-66. Mem: Am. Trial Lawyers Asn; Am, N.H. and Rockingham Co. Bar Asns; Jaycees (pres, Hampton Chap, 64); C. of C.(dir, Hampton Beach Chap); Child & Family Serv.(pres, 69). Rel: Roman Catholic. Mailing Add: 21 Exeter Rd, Hampton, N.H. 03842.

SANDERSON, GAINES MILFRED 'RAB' D
Miss. State Rep.
b. Wayne Co, Miss, 1/3/11; married. Polit. & Govt. Pos: Miss. State Rep, currently. Bus. & Prof. Pos: Farmer and livestock. Mem: C. of C; Royal Moose; Farm Bur; Mason. Rel: Methodist. Mailing Add: 806 Wayne St, Waynesboro, Miss. 39367. (1967)

SANDERSON, GLADYS LOUISE R
Mem, Calif. Rep. State Cent. Cmt.
b. San Luis Obispo, Calif, 9/7/12; d. Frank F. Benton (deceased) and Frances Kennedy B. (deceased); m. 8/29/42 to Herbert Carlyle Sanderson; c. James Carlyle, Stephen Dempster and Cynthia Louise. Educ: San Diego State Col, Bus. Admin, 28-34; Economics and Psychology Nat. Hon. Socs; Alpha Chi. Polit. & Govt. Pos: Supt, Juvenile Hall Detention Home, San Diego Co, Calif, 34-42; dep. sheriff, 34-42; mem. Nat. Off. Price Admin. and head War Price-Ration Bd. Consol, San Francisco, 42-47, head, Price Control Bd, 45-47; mem. Nixon Campaign, Sacramento, 62; mem, Goldwater Campaign, Sacramento, 64; co-chmn, Reagan Campaign, Sacramento, 66; mem, Calif. Rep. State Cent. Cmt, 66-; mem. Reagan Citizens Trust Fund and Reagan Favorite Son Cmt, 67; vol. chmn, Milton Marks Campaign, Calif. State Sen, Sacramento and San Francisco, 68, John Nejedly Campaign, Calif. State Sen, Sacramento and Contra Costa, 69, Clare Berryhill Campaign, Calif. State Assemblyman, Sacramento and Monterey, 69; chmn, vol. orgn. for Gov. Reagan, currently; mem, United Rep. Calif, currently; mem, Calif. Rep. Assembly, currently. Bus. & Prof. Pos: Mem. bd. dirs, and pres. two years, Childrens Receiving Home, 50-56. Mem: Women's Medical Auxiliary of Calif; Calif. Thoroughbred Breeders Asn; Calif. Athletic Int. Cult. Exchange; Commun. Chest United Crusade (vol, 53). Rel: Episcopal. Mailing Add: 3949 Park Rd, Sacramento, Calif. 95841.

SANDISON, GORDON D
Wash. State Sen.
b. Auburn, 1919; m. to Muriel S; c. Five. Educ: U. Grad; Post Grad. Work; Alpha Tau Omega. Polit. & Govt. Pos: Wash. State Rep, 5 terms; mem. West. Interstate Cmn. for Higher Educ, 59-, exec. bd. mem, 63-68, chmn, 68-69; chmn, Wash. State Legis. Coun. on Higher Educ, 65-69; Wash. Cmnr, Educ. Cmn. of the States, 67-; Wash. State Sen, currently. Bus. & Prof. Pos: Ins. agent; real estate bus. Mil. Serv: Marines. Mem: Elks; Eagles; VFW; Grange; Am. Legion. Mailing Add: P.O. Box 967, Port Angeles, Wash. 98362.

SANDLIN, HUGH MARTIN D
Okla. State Rep.
b. Mt. Pleasant, Miss, 8/4/04; s. James G. Sandlin and Dora Karl Hays S; m. 8/22/34 to Rena Jo Livingston; c. Rena Jo (Mrs. Fudge), Martha Fay (Mrs. Bowles) and Dora Dell (Mrs. Roberts). Educ: Univ. Okla, A.B, 27; Cumberland Univ, LL.B, and J.G, 28. Polit. & Govt. Pos: Chmn, Hughes Co. Dem. Party, Okla, 40-42; chmn, Fourth Dist. Dem. Party, 42-46; del, Dem. Nat. Conv, 46, 56 & 68; Okla. State Rep, 52-56 & 64-; Okla. State Sen, 56-60. Mem:

State, Local and Am. Bar Asns; Mason (32°); Shrine; Elks; pres, Holdenville Kiwanis, 46, lt. gov, Dist. 10 Kiwanis, 48, dist. gov, Tex-Okla. Kiwanis, 50. House received Cert. of Awards for Legis. Work in Soil Conserv, Cattleman's Asn, Chickasaw Indian Nation, Creek Nation and State Peace Officers Asn. Rel: Methodist. Legal Res: 1124 N. Gulf, Holdenville, Okla. 74848. Mailing Add: P.O. Box 152, Holdenville, Okla. 74848.

SANDMAN, CHARLES W, JR. R
U.S. Rep, N.J.
b. Phila, Pa, 10/23/21; s. Charles W. Sandman and Rose Frasch S; m. 4/3/48 to Marion Louise Cooney; c. Carol, William, Marion, Robert, Charles and Richard. Educ: Temple Univ, 40-42; Rutgers Law Sch, 45-48; Theta Kappa Phi. Polit. & Govt. Pos: Del, Rep. Nat. Conv, 56, 60, 64 & 68; N.J. State Sen, 56-66, Majority Leader, Senate, 62 & 63, pres, 64 & 65; U.S. Rep, N.J, 67- Bus. & Prof. Pos: Solicitor, West Cape May, N.J, 50-66, Lower Twp, 51-61, First Nat. Bank of Stone Harbor, 57- and Cape May, 57 & 64- Mil. Serv: Entered as Aviation Cadet, Air Force, 42, released as Flight Officer, 45, after serv. in 483rd Bomb Group, 840th Bomb Squadron, 15th Air Force, ETO, 44; ETO Ribbon; Air Medal with 2 Gold Crosses. Mem: Rotary Int; Am, N.J. and Cape May Co. Bar Asns; VFW; Am. Legion. Rel: Catholic. Legal Res: 1 Crescent Dr, Erma Park, N.J. 08204. Mailing Add: 421 Washington St, Cape May, N.J. 08204.

SANDOVAL, ALICE CATHERINE D
Mem, Calif. Dem. State Cent. Cmt.
b. Glendale, Calif, 5/2/43; d. Crescent D. Sandoval and Lucy S. Sauceda S; single. Educ: Immaculate Heart Col, 61-64; Univ. Calif, Los Angeles, B.A, 66; Univ. South. Calif, Doctoral cand; Theta Iota Pi. Polit. & Govt. Pos: Orgn. chmn, Dem. South. Calif; San Fernando Valley Chmn, Cmt. to elect Pierre Salinger to U.S. Senate, 64; San Fernando Valley chmn, Cmt. to Re-elect Gov. Pat Brown, 66; secy, Educators Cmt. to elect Humphrey, S. Calif, 68; mem, Calif. Dem. State Cent. Cmt, 68- Bus. & Prof. Pos: Teacher, Eng, Roosevelt High Sch, Los Angeles, 67-69, asst. girls vice principal, currently; supv. of Eng. instr, San Fernando Valley State Col, Educ. Opportunities Prog, summer session, 69. Mem: Am. Fedn. of Teachers; Cmt. Advocating Reform in Educ; Assoc. of Mexican-Am. Educators; Educ. Issues Coord. Cmt; Latin-Am. Civic Asn; Mexican-Am. Polit. Asn; Van Nuys Dem. Club (recording secy); Dem. of South. Calif.(orgn. chmn). Hon. panelist with Vice-President Humphrey, 'Press Conference', TV show, summer 68. Rel: Catholic. Mailing Add: 916 N. Frederic St, Burbank, Calif. 91505.

SANDOVAL, HILARY JOSEPH, JR. R
Adminstr, Small Bus. Admin.
b. El Paso, Tex, 1/29/30; s. Hilary Joseph Sandoval, Sr. and Theodora Aguirre S; m. 8/11/51 to Dolores B. Morales; c. Mary Dolores, Irene Roberta, Hilary Joseph, III, George Edward and Anthony F. Educ: Univ. Ariz, B.A; Univ. Mex; Tex. Tech. Col. Polit. & Govt. Pos: Chmn, El Paso Co. Rep. Exec. Cmt, Tex, 62; asst. chmn, Tex. Rep. Party, 66; adminstr, Small Bus. Admin, 69- Bus. & Prof. Pos: Pres, Sandoval News Serv, Inc, 53- Mil. Serv: Entered as Pvt, Army, 51, released as Capt, 53; Capt, Army Res, currently. Mem: Past pres, El Paso Club, Sales and Mkt. Execs. Int; past pres, Mid-Am. Periodicals Distributors Asn; former co-chmn, Bur. of Independent Publ. and Distributors; past pres, League of United Latin Am. Citizens Coun. 8; dir, El Paso Rotary Club, 66; C. of C. Sales Exec. of the Year Award, El Paso Club, Sales and Mkt. Execs. Int, chosen Most Valuable Mem. of the Lulac Dist. 4, 66-67; Tex. State Man of the Year, Air Force Asn, 68. Rel: Catholic. Legal Res: 9917 Fenway, El Paso, Tex. 79925. Mailing Add: 1441 L St. N.W, Room 1000, Washington, D.C. 20416.

SANDS, ERNEST MONROE R
N.Dak. State Sen.
b. Pincher Creek, Alberta, Can, 4/30/22; s. Monreoe Edwin Sands and Anna Catherine Barr S; m. 5/8/44 to Hazel Ione Yeager; c. Nancy Rae and William Ernest. Educ: Univ. N.Dak, B.S, 43; Phi Delta Theta. Polit. & Govt. Pos: City cmnr, Velva, N.Dak, 60-62; mayor, Velva, 62-; pres, N.Dak. League of Cities, 65; N.Dak. State Sen, Seventh Dist, 66- Mil. Serv: Entered as Pvt, Army Air Force, 43, released as 1st Lt, 45, after serv. in 458th Heavy Bombardment Group, Eighth Air Force, Eng, 44-45; Air Medal. Mem: Mason (Past Master); Elks; Lions; Am. Legion; C. of C.(pres, 50). Rel: Methodist. Mailing Add: 301 N. Main, Velva, N.Dak. 58790.

SANDSTROM, ELSA R
State V.Pres, Calif. Fedn. of Rep. Women
b. Chicago, Ill; m. Polit. & Govt. Pos: Women's Chmn, Nixon-for-Gov. Cmt, Santa Clara Co, Calif, 62, women's chmn, Goldwater for President Cmt, 64; del, Rep. Nat. Conv, 64; Rep. Elector, Tenth Cong. Dist, 64; mem, Calif. Rep. State Cent. Cmt, currently; state v.pres, Calif. Fedn. of Rep. Women, currently; plus numerous offices and chairmanships in vol. polit. Mailing Add: P.O. Box 977, Los Altos, Calif. 94022.

SANDSTROM, THEODORE FREDERICK, JR. D
b. Wilmington, Del, 3/29/31; s. Theodore Frederick Sandstrom and Marian Pedersen S; m. 12/22/56 to Jewell Kathleen Ott; c. Christine and Alicia. Educ: Univ. Del, B.A, 53; Dickinson Sch. Law, LL.B, 60; Omicron Delta Kappa; Delta Tau Delta. Polit. & Govt. Pos: Admin. asst. to Gov. of Del, 66-67; parliamentarian and chmn. platform cmt, Del. State Dem. Conv, 68; del, Dem. Nat. Conv, 68. Bus. & Prof. Pos: Law clerk for Judges of Superior and Court of Chancery, Wilmington, Del, 60-61; attorney-at-law, Killoran & Van Brunt, 61- Mil. Serv: Entered as 2nd Lt, Army, 53, released as 1st Lt, 57, after serv. in U.S. for $2\frac{1}{2}$ years and Greenland, 56-57, Army Res, 57- Mem: Am. and Del. Bar Asns; Am. Judicature Soc; Bi-racial coord. cmt. of Gr. Wilmington; Newark Kiwanis; v.pres, PTA. Rel: Episcopal. Mailing Add: 420 Lark Dr, Newark, Del. 19711.

SANDQUIST, ELROY C. R
Ill. State Rep.
b. Chicago, Ill, 2/28/99; c. four. Educ: Lane Tech. High Sch. Polit. & Govt. Pos: Park cmnr, former River Park Dist, 28-34; Ill. State Rep, currently. Bus. & Prof. Pos: Automobile Salesman, 22- Mil. Serv: Marines. Mailing Add: 2762 W. Wilson Ave, Chicago, Ill. 60625. (1967)

SANFORD, BERNARD H. R
Chmn, Dickinson Co. Rep. Party, Mich.
b. Oshkosh, Wis, 9/29/01; m. 9/30/24 to Sarah Rostagno; c. Helen June and Donna Marie. Polit. & Govt. Pos: Mem, Bd. of Canvassers and chmn, Dickinson Co. Rep. Party, Mich, currently. Bus. & Prof. Pos: Dist. mgr; ins. counsr; speaker at high schs. Mem: Mason; Eastern Star and others. Legal Res: Hamilton Lakes, Vulcan, Mich. 49892. Mailing Add: Box 26, Norway, Mich. 49870.

SANFORD, I. S. D
b. Jones Co, Miss, 6/28/10; married. Polit. & Govt. Pos: Mem, Pub. Serv. Cmn; chancery clerk; Miss. State Rep, 40-44; former Miss. State Sen. Bus. & Prof. Pos: Farmer. Mem: VFW; Mason; Shrine; Am. Legion. Rel: Baptist. Mailing Add: P.O. Box 55, Collins, Miss. 39428. (1967)

SANFORD, JOHN L, Jr. D
b. Baltimore, Md, 11/13/10; married. Educ: Mt. Wash. Sem. and Loyola High Sch, Baltimore; Georgetown Univ; Wash. Col, A.B, 32; Univ. of Md. Law Sch, LL.B, 35; Order of the Coif. Polit. & Govt. Pos: Md. State Sen, 59-67; State's Attorney, Worcester Co, 67- and 51-55. Bus. & Prof. Pos: Attorney. Mem: Am. and Md. Bar Asns. Mailing Add: Berlin, Md. 21811. (1967)

SANFORD, LOREN WILLIAM R
Chmn, Eighth Cong. Dist. Rep. Party, Minn.
b. Milaca, Minn, 8/8/31; s. Clement E. Sanford and Mabel Telander S; m. August, 1956 to Paula Cranston; c. Laura K, James A. and Matthew W. Educ: Univ. Minn, Minneapolis, B.A, 55, J.D, 57; Alpha Delta Phi; Phi Delta Phi; Phoenix; Iron Wedge. Polit. & Govt. Pos: Precinct chmn, Rep. Party of Minn, 59-60; v.chmn, 61st Legis. Dist. Rep. Party, 61-65; v.chmn, Eighth Cong. Dist. Rep. Party, 63-67, chmn, 67-; del, Rep. Nat. Conv, 68. Bus. & Prof. Pos: Assoc, Wheeler, Burns & Buchanan, 56-61, partner, 62- Mil. Serv: Entered as Pfc, Minn. Nat. Guard, Army, 48, released as Sgt, 52, after serv. in 47th Div, Camp Rucker, Alabama, 50-52; School Medal, Fort Belvoir, Va. Mem: 11th Dist, Minn. State and Am. Bar Asns; C. of C; YMCA. Rel: Protestant. Mailing Add: 17 S. 28th Ave. East, Duluth, Minn. 55812.

SANFORD, TERRY D
b. Laurinburg, N.C, 8/20/17; s. Cecil L. Sanford and Elizabeth Martin S; m. 7/4/42 to Margaret Rose Knight; c. Elizabeth Knight and James Terry. Educ: Univ. N.C, A.B, 39, Univ. N.C. Law Sch, LL.B, 46. Polit. & Govt. Pos: N.C. State Sen, 53; del, Dem. Nat. Conv, 56, 60, 64 & 68; Gov, N.C, 61-65; nat. chmn, Citizens for Humphrey-Muskie, 68. Bus. & Prof. Pos: Lawyer, Sanford, Cannon, Adams and McCullough, 65- and dir, A Study of Am. States, Duke Univ, 65-67; pres, Urban Am, Inc, 68- Mil. Serv: Entered as Pvt, Army, 42, released as 1st Lt, 45, after serv. in 517th Parachute Combat Team, ETO, 43-45. Publ: But What About the People?, Harper & Row, 66; Storm Over the States, McGraw-Hill, 67. Rel: Methodist. Mailing Add: 307 Sylvan Rd, Fayetteville, N.C. 28305.

SANGER, RICHARD CALVIN R
Chmn, Canton Rep. Town Cmt, Conn.
b. N.Y.C, 8/12/30; s. Edmund P. Sanger and Clara Wilde S; m. 12/29/54 to Eleanor Matejcek; c. Robert Calvin. Educ: Trinity Col, B.A, 52; Univ. Conn. Sch. Law, LL.B, 61; Delta Kappa Epsilon. Polit. & Govt. Pos: Chmn, Canton Rep. Town Cmt, Conn, 67- Mil. Serv: Entered as 2nd Lt, Air Force, 52, released as Capt, 58, after serv. in 28th SRW, Strategic Air Command, 53-58; Res, 58-69, Maj; Commendation Ribbon. Mem: Am, Conn. and Hartford Co. Bar Asns; Lions Int. Rel: Congregational. Mailing Add: Mohawk Dr, Canton, Conn. 06019.

SANGSTER, THOMAS I. D
b. Vienna, Ga, 7/25/31; s. Homer Lloyd Sangster and Faustine Britt S; m. 12/18/60 to Linda Lou Burnley. Educ: Ga. State Col, B.B.A, 60; outstanding sr. and pres. student body; Sigma Nu; Alpha Kappa Psi. Polit. & Govt. Pos: Mem, State Young Dem; Ga. State Rep, 61-63, mem, House Appropriations Cmt; dir, Property and Intangible Tax Div, Ga, 63- Bus. & Prof. Pos: Timber; livestock; mem. bd. dirs, DeJournette Mfg. Co, Atlanta. Mil. Serv: Army, Engr, 54-55. Mem: Am. Legion; Mason; Ga. Tax Assessing Orgn; state chmn, Int. Asn. of Assessing Officers; chmn, Southeast. Tax Cmt. on Pub. Utilities; bd. trustees, Ga. State Col. Found; bd. dirs, Ga. State Col. Alumni Asn. Selected as One of the Outstanding Young Men of the Year by the Jr. C. of C; Commun. Leader of Am. Award, 68. Rel: Baptist. Mailing Add: 6600 Bridgewood Valley Rd. N.W, Atlanta, Ga. 30328.

SANGUIN, WAYNE CURTIS D
Okla. State Rep.
b. Hugo, Okla, 1/28/20; s. Thomas Edward Sanguin and Cledith Collins S; m. 8/19/38 to Frances Elisabeth Williams; c. Polly (Mrs. Joe H. Patrick); Kay (Mrs. Bill R. Medley) and Judy (Mrs. Bob R. Long). Educ: Murray State Col, 1 year; Okla. City Univ, 1 year; Okla. Univ, 1 year. Polit. & Govt. Pos: Okla. State Rep, Choctaw Co, 60-62; Okla. State Rep, Dist. 19, 64- Bus. & Prof. Pos: Aircraft welder, Phila, Pa, 40-43; machine shop owner, Hugo, Okla, 43-57; rancher, Hugo, Okla, 57- Mil. Serv: Entered as Pfc, Army, 44, released as M/Sgt, 45. Mem: Mason; Shrine; Elks; Rotary; Eastern Star; Okla. Polled Hereford Asn; Am. Quarterhorse Asn; Hugo Rodeo and Quarterhorse Asn; Farm Bur; Farmers Union; Choctaw Co. Fair Bd; Draft Bd; C. of C. Hon. Chap. Farmer of Future Farmers of Am, Hugo and Grant, Okla; Citizen of the Year Award, Choctaw Co. C. of C. Rel: Baptist. Mailing Add: P.O. Box 608, Hugo, Okla. 74743.

SANSBURY, PAUL ANDREWS D
S.C. State Rep.
b. Darlington, S.C, 6/22/20; s. P. A. Sansbury and Margaret McGirt S; m. to Mary Anne Harris; c. Clevie, Andy, Danny and Susan. Educ: Univ. S.C, A.B, 41; LL.B, 43; Omicron Delta Kappa. Polit. & Govt. Pos: Attorney, Darlington Co, S.C, 50-53; chmn, Darlington Co. Dem. Party, 50-56; state exec. committeeman, S.C. Dem. Party, Darlington Co, 58-66; city attorney, Darlington, 62-; S.C. State Rep, currently. Mil. Serv: Entered as Pvt, Air Force, 42, released as Sgt, 45, after serv. in Army Air Communications System, British Guiana, Trinidad, 43-45. Mem: Exec. cmt, S.C. Bar Asn, 64-66, chmn, 66-67; pres,

Univ. S.C. Alumni Asn, 55-56; Kiwanis; Am. Legion; VFW. Rel: Presbyterian. Legal Res: 107 Greenway Dr, Darlington, S.C. 29532. Mailing Add: Box 502, Darlington, S.C. 29532.

SANSOM, ERNEST SAMUEL D
b. Austin, Tex, 2/15/22; s. Ernest Swenson Sansom and Elizabeth Gribble S; m. 3/13/43 to Imo Heacock; c. Andrew and Jeanne. Educ: Sam Houston State Col, B.S, 42; S.Tex. Col. Law, LL.B, 54; Kappa Delta Pi; Alpha Chi; Alpha Chi Sigma. Polit. & Govt. Pos: City secy, Lake Jackson, Tex; Dem. precinct chmn, Precinct 22; del, Dem. Nat. Conv, 68. Bus. & Prof. Pos: Patent attorney, Dow Chem. Co. Mil. Serv: Entered as A/S, Navy, 42, released as Lt. Comdr, 68, after serv. in U.S. Area, S.W. Pac. Area, Naval Res. Law Co, 42-68, Retired. Mem: State Bar of Tex; Brazoria Co. and Am. Bar Asns; Am. Chem. Soc; ROA. Rel: Presbyterian. Mailing Add: 304 Oak Dr, Lake Jackson, Tex. 77566.

SANSTEAD, WAYNE GODFREY D
N.Dak. State Rep.
b. Hot Springs, Ark, 4/16/35; s. Godfrey A. Sanstead and Clara Buen S; m. 6/16/57 to Mary Jane Bober; c. Timothy Wayne. Educ: St. Olaf Col, B.A. in speech and polit. sci, 57; Northwest. Univ, M.A. in pub. address and group communication, 66. Polit. & Govt. Pos: N.Dak. State Rep, 5th Legis. Dist, 64- Bus. & Prof. Pos: Dir. debate, Luverne High Sch, Minn, 59-60; dir. forensics, Minot Sr. High Sch, 60-69. Mil. Serv: Entered as Pvt, Army Res, 57, released as Pfc, 59, after serv. in Intel. Center, Baltimore, Md. Mem: Past pres, Am. Fedn. of Teachers, Local 302; Speech Asn. of Am; pres, N.Dak. Speech Asn; Am. Forensic Asn; Am. Civil Liberties Union; Sons of Norway; Nat, N.Dak. and Minot Educ. Asns; Toastmasters Int; Elks; Nat. Youth Fel. of the YMCA. Degree of Distinction, Pi Kappa Delta Minn. Beta Chap, 57; Degree of Distinction, Nat. Forensic League, 62; Outstanding Young Speech Teacher Award, Cent. States Speech Asn, 63; Minot and N.Dak. Jaycees Outstanding Young Educator Awards, 67. Rel: Lutheran; Chmn, West. N.Dak. Research and Social Action Cmt, American Lutheran Church. Mailing Add: 823 Ninth Ave. N.E, Minot, N.Dak. 58701.

SANTARELLI, DONALD EUGENE R
Assoc. Dep. Attorney Gen, Dept. of Justice
b. Hershey, Pa, 7/22/37; s. Ambrose Santarelli and Ercolina Altobelli S; m. 6/28/66 to Anne Constance Dunlap. Educ: Mount St. Mary's Col, 55-59; Va. Law Sch, LL.B, 62; Univ. Va. Grad. Sch, 62-64; Elibanana; Delta Kappa Epsilon; Pi Delta Epsilon. Polit. & Govt. Pos: Asst. Corp. coun, D.C, 65-66, asst. U.S. attorney, 66-67; minority counsel, Cmt. on Judiciary, U.S. House Rep, 67-69; spec. counsel, Subcmt. on Constitutional Rights, Cmt. on Judiciary, U.S. Senate, 69; Assoc. Dep. Attorney Gen, Dept. of Justice, 69- Bus. & Prof. Pos: Law Clerk, U.S. Dist. Judge Thomas J. Michie, Fourth Circuit Court, 64-65. Mem: Va. State, D.C. and Am. Bar Asns; Judicial Conf. of D.C; Univ. Va. Alumni Asn; Univ. Va. Club Wash.(exec. cmt); Farmington Country Club; Charlottesville, Va; Univ. Club of Wash. Rel: Roman Catholic. Mailing Add: 503 Queen St, Alexandria, Va. 22314.

SANTIESTEBAN, HUMBERTO TATI D
Tex. State Rep.
b. El Paso, Tex, 11/3/34; s. Ricardo Santiesteban Jr. and Carmen Leyva S; m. 12/26/56 to Ruby Sue McMillen; c. Valori Lynn, Stephanie Diane and Ricardo Tati. Educ: N.Mex. Mil. Inst, B.A. with honors, 56; Univ. Tex. Sch. of Law, Austin, LL.B, 62; Spanish honor soc; Letterman's Club; pres. and chmn. bd. gov, Student Bar Asn; Praetor. Polit. & Govt. Pos: Mem, El Paso Zoning Bd. of Adjust, Tex, 63-65; Tex. State Rep, Dist. 67-1, 67-, mem, criminal jurisp, judicial dist, judiciary, liquor regulation and sch. dist. cmts, Tex. House of Rep, 60th Legis, v.chmn. fed. regulations, appropriations, pub. health, criminal jurisprudence and liquor regulation cmts, 61st Legis. Bus. & Prof. Pos: Partner, law firm, Paxson & Santiesteban, 62- Mil. Serv: Entered as 2nd Lt, Army, 56, released as 1st Lt, 59, after serv. in Airborne Inf. and Mil. Police, 56-59; Jungle Warfare and Ranger Airborne Badge. Mem: Am. and Tex. State Bar Asns; Am. and Tex. Trial Lawyers Asns; El Paso Jr. Bar Asn.(dir); El Paso Bar Asn.(dir); C. of C; Am. Arbit. Asn.(nat. panel of arbitrators); League of United Latin Am. Citizens; Southeast Optimist Club. Distinguished Mil. Student; Cadet Col; Univ. Tex. Law Sch. Dean's List; recognition for work on State Legis. Criminal Jurisprudence Cmt, Tex. Bar Asn. Rel: Roman Catholic. Legal Res: 601 La Cruz, El Paso, Tex. 79902. Mailing Add: 500 El Paso International Bldg, El Paso, Tex. 79901.

SANTORO, THOMAS D. D
b. Westerly, R.I, 11/17/22. Educ: Westerly High Sch. Polit. & Govt. Pos: R.I. State Sen, 51-57 & 64-66; R.I. State Rep, 61-64. Bus. & Prof. Pos: Gen. ins. and hotel owner. Mailing Add: 168 High St, Westerly, R.I. 02891. (1967)

SANTOS, CARLOS MESA D
Treas, Dem. Party, Guam
b. Agana, Guam, 11/4/25; s. Joaquin Taimanglo Santos and Maria M. Mesa S; m. 8/30/48 to Brigida Benavente Naputi; c. Joaquin N, Ann Ruth, Dora N, Richard N, Eve Marie, Pauline Jane, Alfred Anthony, Carolyn June and Charles Glenn. Educ: George Wash. Jr. High, 3 years. Polit. & Govt. Pos: Dem. precinct chmn, Barrigada Village, Guam, 52-69; mem, Land Transfer Bd, Govt. of Guam, 61-69; treas, Dem. Party of Guam, 67-; alternate del, Dem. Nat. Conv, 68. Bus. & Prof. Pos: Mgr, J & G Motor Co, Inc, Guam, 46-58, J & G Surplus Store and J & G Bldg. Material & Supply, 58-69. Mem: PTA (pres, Barrigada Jr. High Sch, 63-64 & 68-69, Carbullido Elem. Sch, 63-66); adv, Explorer Post 34, Boy Scouts, Guam, 51-56, asst. scout master, Barrigada, 54-56. Rel: Catholic. Legal Res: Barrigada Village, Guam 96910. Mailing Add: P.O. 3388, Agana, Guam 96910.

SAOBENTO, AUGUSTO W. D
b. Pawtucket, R.I, 7/10/26. Educ: Providence Col, A.B, 1950; Boston Univ. Law Sch, LL.B, 1952. Polit. Pos: R.I. State Rep, 57-66; Chmn, Third Representative Dist. Cmt; Mem, E. Providence Dem. Town Cmt; Chmn, Portuguese Sect. of For. Lang. Prog. for Dem. Party, 1956; Del, Constitutional Conv, 1955 and 1964. Bus. & Prof. Pos: Attorney-at-Law. Mil. Serv: U.S. Army, 44-46. Mem: DAV; I.B.E.S. of R.I; Am. Bar Asn; R.I. Bar Asn; Fed. Bar Asn; E. Providence Coun, K. of C; P.A.D.C. of E. Providence. Mailing Add: 685 Warren Ave, E. Providence, R.I. 02914. (1967)

SAPERSTEIN, ESTHER D
Ill. State Sen.
b. Chicago, Ill; wid; c. Sidney and Natalie. Educ: Northwest. Univ. Polit. & Govt. Pos: Mem, Mayor's Juvenile Welfare Cmt. and Cmt. on Human Rels, Chicago, Ill; Ill. State Rep, 62-66; Ill. State Sen, 66- Mem: Former pres, Chicago Region, PTA; former secy, Juvenile Protective Asn; adv. bd, Citizens Sch. Cmt; pub. affairs chmn, Hadassah, Nat. Coun. of Jewish Women; citizens adv. cmt, Welfare Coun. of Metrop. Chicago; bd. dir, Jewish Commun. Center, Rogers Park; bd. dir, Little City; bd. dir, Chicago Sch. for Retarded Children; bd. dir, Dr. Gen. Hosp; bd, Women's Auxiliary, Bernard Horwich Center; bd. dir, Chicago Area Proj; exec. cmt, Zionist Orgn; one of the founders of City of Hope; League of Women Voters; Pub. Affairs of Metrop. YWCA. Rel: Jewish; North Shore B'nai B'rith. Mailing Add: 1432 W. Rosemont Ave, Chicago, Ill. 60626. (1967)

SARAPO, DONATO FRANK R
Treas, Lenawee Co. Rep. Party, Mich.
b. N.Y.C, 7/2/25; s. Donato Frank Sarapo, Sr. and Teresa Miglionico S; m. 12/20/47 to Lois Marie Miller; c. Terry Lee (Mrs. Merle Humphrey), Nora Lynn, Guy Donato and David Wayne. Educ: Columbia Col, Columbia Univ, B.A, 49; N.Y. State Med. Col. at N.Y.C, M.D, 52. Polit. & Govt. Pos: Rep. precinct leader, Eighth Precinct, Adrian, Mich, 58-61; del, Mich. State Rep. Conv, 59-68; chmn, Adrian City Rep. Party, 61-62; chmn, Adrian Twp, Lenawee Co. Rep. Party, 63-69; mem. exec. cmt, Lenawee Co. Rep. Party, 64-, treas, 67-; mem. platform cmt, Second Cong. Dist. Rep. Party, 66, mem. exec. cmt, 68-69; alternate del, Rep. Nat. Conv, 68. Mil. Serv: Entered as Pvt, Army, 43, released as Pfc, 46 after serving in Army Specialized Training Prog, 346 Inf. Div, ETO and Pac. Theater of Opers, 43-46; Good Conduct Medal; Combat Infantry Badge. Mem: Am, Mich. State and Lenawee Co. Med. Asns; Mich. Asn. of Professions; Am. Col. of Physicians; Am. and Mich. Asns. of Internists; chmn lay adv. bd, Siena Heights Col, 68; Rotary. Rel: Catholic. Legal Res: 4314 Evergreen Dr, Adrian, Mich. 49221. Mailing Add: Mill St. Professional Bldg, Adrian, Mich. 49221.

SARASIN, RONALD A. R
Conn. State Rep.
b. Fall River, Mass, 12/31/34; s. Joseph A. Sarasin and Mary D. Pereira S; m. 8/9/58 to Marjorie Ann Grazio; c. Michael A. Educ: Univ. Conn, B.S. in Bus. Admin, 60; Univ. Conn. Sch. of Law, LL.B, 63. Polit. & Govt. Pos: Corp. counsel, Beacon Falls, Conn, 63-, Justice of the Peace, 65-; Conn. State Rep, 95th Assembly Dist, 69- Bus. & Prof. Pos: Asst. prof. law, New Haven Col, 64-67; admitted to practice before U.S. Supreme Court, Fed. and Conn. Bar. Mil. Serv: Entered as Seaman Recruit, Navy, 52, released as PO 2/C, 56, after serv. in Mediterranean; Good Conduct Medal; European Theater Medal; Korean Theater Medal. Mem: Am, Conn. and New Haven Co. Bar Asns; Valley Bar Asn.(secy, 68-); Conn. Asns. of Munic. Attorneys; Am. Trial Lawyers Asn; Lions Int. Distinguished Serv. Award, Lions Club of Beacon Falls, 69. Rel: Roman Catholic. Legal Res: 155 Munson Rd, Beacon Falls, Conn. 06403. Mailing Add: 135 Main St, Seymour, Conn. 06483.

SARBACHER, GEORGE WILLIAM, JR. R
b. Phila, Pa, 9/30/19; s. George William Sarbacher and Martha H. Cathcart S; m. 8/15/42 to Florence W. Forsyth; c. Susan F, Sandra A. and George W, III. Educ: Temple Univ, B.S. in commerce, 42. Polit. & Govt. Pos: U.S. Rep, Pa, 47-49; advisor, Young Rep, 47-50; dep. dir. revenue, Commonwealth of Pa, 49-50. Bus. & Prof. Pos: Secy. and assoc, Nat. Scientific Labs, Inc, 50-54, v.pres. and secy, 54-56 and pres. and chmn. bd, 56-69; v.pres, Bowser, Inc, 62-69; v.pres, Int. Systs. Eng. Corp, 69- Mil. Serv: Entered as Officer Cand, Marine Corps, 42, released as Capt, 47, after serv. in 2nd Marine Div, 1st Marine Brigade, Pac. Theater, 42-45; Lt. Col.(Ret), Marine Corps Res, 65; Presidential Unit Citation; Navy Unit Citation; Asiatic Pac. Ribbon with 3 Battle Stars. Mem: Inst. of Elec. & Electronics Engrs; Navy League of the U.S; Mason (32°); Shrine; Army and Navy Club. Rel: Methodist. Mailing Add: 3211 Leland St, Chevy Chase, Md. 20015.

SARBANES, PAUL SPYROS D
Md. State Del.
b. Salisbury, Md, 2/3/33; s. Spyros P. Sarbanes and Matina Tsigounis S; m. 6/11/60 to Christine Dunbar; c. John Peter, Michael and Janet. Educ: Princeton Univ, A.B, 54; Oxford Univ, Eng, B.A, 57; Harvard Law Sch, LL.B, 60; Phi Beta Kappa; Rhodes Scholarship. Polit. & Govt. Pos: Asst. to chmn, Coun. Econ. Adv, Wash, D.C, 62-63; exec. dir, City Charter Revision Cmn, Baltimore, Md, 63-64; exec. dir, Md. Citizens for Johnson-Humphrey, 64; Md. State Del, 67-; state coordinator, Md. Kennedy for Pres. Cmt, 68. Bus. & Prof. Pos: Assoc, Baltimore Law Firm of Venable, Baetjer and Howard, 65- Mem: Am, Md. and Baltimore City Bar Asns. Rel: Greek Orthodox. Mailing Add: 1704 Bolton St, Baltimore, Md. 21217.

SARGEANT, MARION TAYLOR R
b. Whiting, Vt, 10/23/00; widow; c. One. Educ: Brandon High Sch, 18; Castleton Normal Sch, Summer Session, 19. Polit. & Govt. Pos: Vt. State Rep, -66; secy, Town Rep. Club; past master, Moss Glen Grange; Pub. Health Cmn; town auditor, 22-24, 37-40, 47-50; sch. dir, 33-35; asst. town clerk; treas, 34-35. Bus. & Prof. Pos: Homemaker; formerly sch. teacher. Mem: Grange; Eastern Star; Am. Legion Auxiliary; Women's Soc. of Christian Serv; Franville Ladies Club; libr. trustee. Rel: Methodist; Granville Methodist Church treas. and treas. of WSCS. Mailing Add: Granville, Vt. 05747. (1967)

SARGENT, FRANCIS W. R
Gov, Mass.
b. Hamilton, Mass, 1915; s. Mrs. Charles Adams, father deceased; m. to Jessie Fay; c. Fay, Francis W, Jr. and Jessie. Educ: Mass. Inst. Tech. Polit. & Govt. Pos: Chmn, Atlantic States Marine Fisheries Cmn. and Mass. Water Resources Cmn, dir, Marine Fisheries and cmnr, Mass. Dept. of Natural Resources, 56-59; exec. dir, U.S. Outdoor Recreation Resources Rev. Cmt, D.C, 59-62; adv. to Calif. Park and Recreation Dept, 64-; panel chmn. for President's White House Conf. on Natural Beauty; cmnr, Mass. Dept. of Pub. Works, 65-66; Lt. Gov, Mass, 67-68, Gov, 68- Bus. & Prof. Pos: Founder and owner, Goose, Hummock Shop Inc, Orleans, Mass. Mil. Serv: Capt, Army Inf, 10th Mt. Div, World War II; Bronze Star; Purple Heart with Oak Leaf Cluster. Mem: Chmn, state campaign for Mass. Ment. Health Fund; Mass. state employ-

ees chmn, Heart Fund; govt. chmn, Mass. Bay United Fund; dir, Boston Patriots Football Club; Corp. of Boston Mus. of Sci; trustee, New Eng. Aquarium; adv. bd, Cape Cod Commun. Col; state employees chmn, Savings Bond Drive; dir, Mass. Soc. Prev. Cruelty to Animals. Rel: Protestant. Mailing Add: Farm St, Dover, Mass. 02030.

SARGENT, STAN R
b. McPherson, Kans, 8/2/28; s. Paul E. Sargent and Rowena Vaniman S; m. to Barbara York; c. Andrew Paul, Peter Randol and Mary. Educ: McPherson Col, B.S, 50; Kans. Univ, M.B.A, 56. Polit. & Govt. Pos: Chmn, McPherson Co. Rep. Cent. Cmt, Kans, 64-68. Bus. & Prof. Pos: Cashier, Peoples State Bank, 53-66; asst. gen. mgr, Thompson Transport Co. Inc, 58-63. Mil. Serv: Entered as Pvt, Air Force, 50, released as S/Sgt, 53. Mem: Rotary. Rel: Brethren. Legal Res: 202 Eastmoor Dr, McPherson, Kans. 67460. Mailing Add: Box 436, McPherson, Kans. 67460.

SARK, GUY O. R
Chmn, Pickaway Co. Rep. Exec. Cmt, Ohio
b. Ashville, Ohio, 10/21/02; s. John H. Sark and Anna Markwood S; m. 1923 to Leona Wright; c. Ruth Ann (Mrs. Swisher), Eleanor (Mrs. Foreman) and Virginia Lee (Mrs. Bowers). Polit. & Govt. Pos: Chmn, Pickaway Co. Rep. Exec. Cmt, Ohio, 68- Bus. & Prof. Pos: Asst. cashier, City Nat. Bank & Trust Co, Columbus, Ohio, 20-67. Mem: Mason; RAM (past Grand Marshal). Knight of the York Cross of Honour; Grand Encampment K.T. Cross of Honor. Rel: Protestant. Mailing Add: 215 E. Main St, Ashville, Ohio 43103.

SARTIN, FRANK COMER R
Ky. State Rep.
b. Tompkinsville, Ky, 10/22/95; s. John Westley Sartin and Polly Jane Williams S; m. 1/20/25 to Flossie Mae Branham; c. Selma (Mrs. Leslie Smith), Ruth I.(Mrs. Joe Gordon Rogers) and Jean. Educ: Correspondence Schs; Bus. Course, Wichita Falls, Tex, 23. Polit. & Govt. Pos: Mem, Ky. Hwy. Dept, 25-33; supt. of WPA, Green and Taylor Co. Rds, 43-65; Ky. State Rep, Green and Adair Co, 66-; cand, Ky. State Senate, 16th Dist, 69. Bus. & Prof. Pos: Teacher, Ky, 18-32; real estate dealer, farmer and surveyor, 65- Mem: Mason. Ky. Col. Rel: Church of Christ. Mailing Add: 107 Hodges St, Greensburg, Ky. 42743.

SASINE, ROBERT GALE R
b. Los Angeles, Calif, 4/18/34; s. Emil George Sasine and Jennie Gale S; m. 9/6/55 to Caroline Lucy Spencer; c. Jacqueline, Diane, Judith, John and Ronald. Educ: Brigham Young Univ, 52-56; West. State Col. of Law, 67-; Athenian. Polit. & Govt. Pos: Chmn, Cmt. to Re-elect Congressman Del Clawson, Downey, Calif, 64; region chmn, Cmt. to Elect Ronald Reagan Gov, 66; mem, Calif. Rep. State Cent. Cmt, 67-69; South. Calif. chmn, Friends of Gov. Reagan, 67-; alternate del, Rep. Nat. Conv, 68. Bus. & Prof. Pos: Mgr, Sav-On Drugs, Inc, Downey, Calif, 58-67, dist. supvr, Los Angeles, 67- Mem: South. Calif. Pharmaceutical Asn; Aircraft Owners and Pilots Asn; Optimist; C. of C.(pres, Downey, Calif. Chap, 64-65); Chmn, Downey United Crusade, 65-66; Cougar Club-Brigham Young Univ. Alumni Asn. Outstanding Commun. Serv. Award, N.Am. Aviation Mgt. Club, Downey, Calif. Rel: Latter-day Saint. Mailing Add: 600 Elinor Dr, Fullerton, Calif. 92632.

SASLOW, MICHAEL GEORGE D
b. Rochester, N.Y, 4/8/37; s. George Saslow and Julia Ipcar S; m. 6/19/59 to Carol Ann Griffiths. Educ: Harvard Col, A.B, 60; Univ. Calif, Berkeley, Ph.D, 66; U.S. Pub. Health Serv. fel. Polit. & Govt. Pos: Vol. work, Dem. Party, St. Louis, Mo, Cambridge, Mass. and Albany, Calif, 48-65; Dem. committeeman, Precincts 46-83, Seattle, Wash, 65-69; v.chmn, 46th Legis. Dist, 66; cand. Wash. State Senate, 46th Legis. Dist, 66; dist. chmn, 46th Legis. Dist, 67-68; consult, Seattle-King Co. Econ. Opportunity Bd, 67-68; educ. dir, Young Dem. of Wash. State, 67-68; first cong. dist. coordinator, McCarthy for Pres, 68; chmn, First Cong. Dist. Dem. Caucus, 68; mem. grievance cmt, Wash. State Dem. Conv, 68; del, Dem. Nat. Conv, 68; del, King Co. Dem. Exec. Bd, Wash, 69. Bus. & Prof. Pos: Lectr. and research asst. prof. psychol, Univ. Wash, Seattle, 65-67; asst. dir, Wash-Alaska Regional Med. Prog, Seattle, 68-69; asst. prof. teaching research div, Ore. State Syst. of Higher Educ, Monmouth, 69- Publ: Washington Democratic Council Precinct Committeeman's Campaign Handbook (w. Carol A. Saslow), Mimeographed, 68; plus others. Mem: West. Psychol. Asn; Asn. Am. Historians; Acoustical Soc. Am; Seattle Urban League; North Cascades Conserv. Coun; Wash. Dem. Coun. Pres. Youth Opportunity Award, 68. Mailing Add: Route 2, Box 111 B, Philomath, Ore. 97370.

SATHRE, HARVEY B. Conservative
Minn. State Rep.
b. Austin, Minn, 1920; married; c. seven. Educ: Austin High Sch. Polit. & Govt. Pos: Minn. State Rep, 62- Bus. & Prof. Pos: Dairy farmer. Mil. Serv: Army, 41-48, China-Burma-India Theatre. Mem: Mason; Am. Legion; VFW; Adams Grange; past pres, Mower Co. Farm Bur; treas, Adams Conserv. Club; dir, Mower Co. Agr. Soc, 58-; State Bd. of Educ. Cmn. on Sch. Dist. Reorganization, 65-; Minn. Educ. Coun, 68- Rel: Lutheran. Mailing Add: Box 225, Adams, Minn. 55909.

SATRIALE, JOHN T. D
Mem, N.Y. State Dem. Adv. Coun.
b. Fordham-Pelham Pkwy. Sect, Bronx Co, N.Y. Educ: De Witt Clinton High Sch; Fordham Col; Brooklyn Law Sch, LL.B. Polit. & Govt. Pos: N.Y. State Assemblyman, 48-65, chmn, Ways and Means Cmt; mem, N.Y. State Dem. Adv. Coun; Dem. Dist. Leader; mem, Cmn. on State and Local Fiscal Rels. Bus. & Prof. Pos: Attorney-at-Law, Bronx, N.Y; mem. bd. dirs, North N.Y. Savings & Loan Asn; counsel to Victorian Soc. in Am. Publ: N.Y. State Budget and You. Mem: Bd. of Dir, Adult Educ. Centers, Columbus and De Witt Clinton High Schs; Hon. Chmn, Belmont Sr. Citizens Center; Mayor's Cmt. on Scholastic Achievement, Six Years; E. Tremont Neighborhood Asn; Pelham-Pkwy. Citizens Coun; N.Y. Zool. Soc; N.Y. Chap, Am. Soc. for Pub. Admin; Am. Acad. of Polit. Sci; Chmn, Co. Cmt, Seventh Assembly Dist; Del. to Many State and Judicial Convs. Mailing Add: 2488 Grand Concourse, Bronx, N.Y. 10458.

SATTER, ROBERT D
Gen. Counsel, Dem. Majority, Conn. State Legis.
b. Chicago, Ill, 8/19/19; s. Henry Satter and Patty Salvin S; m. 11/27/46 to Ruth Lyttle; c. Richard, Mini, Susan and Jane. Educ: Rutgers Univ, A.B, 41; Columbia Univ. Law Sch, LL.B, 47; Phi Beta Kappa. Polit. & Govt. Pos: Mem, Newington Develop. Cmt, Conn, 58-, chmn, 67; mem, Newington Charter Cmt, 59, 61 & 68; Conn. State Rep, 59-65; mem, bd. of Finance, Newington, 61-66; gen. counsel, Dem. Majority, Conn. State Legis, currently. Bus. & Prof. Pos: Mem, bd. of ed, Conn. Bar Jour, 62-; mem, bd. of dirs, numerous corps. Mil. Serv: Entered as Midn, Naval Res, 42, released as Lt.(sg), 46, after serv. in Pac, 42-46; Lt.(sg), Naval Res; Pac. Theater Campaign Ribbon and 7 Battle Stars. Publ: 'Social-Legal Counselling,' 58 and 'Lawyer as Lobbyist,' 60, Conn. Bar Jour; 'How to Pass Your Law,' Progressive Mag, 59. Mem: Ethics Cmt, Hartford Co. Bar Asn; pres, Hartford Commun. Coun, 62-64; bd. dirs, Family Serv. Soc; counsel, Hartford Cmn. Renewal Team; Urban Coalition. Doubles tennis champion, Newington, 59- and singles tennis champion, 2 times. Mailing Add: 75 Brookside Rd, Newington, Conn. 06111.

SATTERFIELD, DAVID E, III D
U.S. Rep, Va.
b. Richmond, Va, 12/2/20; s. David E. Satterfield, Jr. and Blanche Kidd S; m. 12/27/43 to Anne Elizabeth Powell; c. David E, IV and John B. Educ: Univ. Richmond, 39-42; Univ. Va, LL.B, 47; Phi Gamma Delta; Phi Alpha Delta. Polit. & Govt. Pos: Asst. U.S. Attorney, 50-53; city councilman, Richmond, Va, 54-56; Va. State Del, 60-64; U.S. Rep, Va, 64- Bus. & Prof. Pos: Attorney, Firm of Satterfield, Haw, Anderson, Parkerson & Beazley, currently. Mil. Serv: Entered as Seaman 2/C, V-5, Navy, 42, released as Lt, 45, after serv. as Fighter Pilot; Capt, Naval Res, 46-; Air Medal with Three Gold Stars; Purple Heart. Mem: Kiwanis, Reserve Officers Asn; Naval Reserve Asn; Navy League; Am. Legion; Richmond and Va. Bar Asns; Mason (32°); Shrine; former pres. and dir, Richmond Area Heart Asn. and of the Consultation and Evaluation Clinic; former dir, Thalhimer-Va. Wildlife Exhibit; former counsel and dir, Boys Club of Richmond; former civilian adv. to the Nat. Health Serv. Rel: Episcopal. Legal Res: 511 St. Christopher's Rd, Richmond, Va. 23226. Mailing Add: 324 Cannon Office Building, Washington, D.C. 20515.

SATTERFIELD, FRANCES GIBSON D
b. Maxton, N.C, 3/30/08; d. Dr. Milton R. Gibson and Elizabeth McLean G; m. 9/21/28 to Merrill Boydston Satterfield; c. Lenore, Neil Boydston and Karen (Mrs. Brand). Educ: Univ. N.C, Greensboro, A.B, 28; Columbia Univ. Sch. of Journalism, 29. Polit. & Govt. Pos: Volunteer and staff mem, Dem. Nat. Cmt, D.C, 36-41, dir. res, women's div, 43-46; res. chmn, Dem. Forum, Fulton Co, Ga, 56; chmn, speakers bur, Fulton Co. Dem. Party, res. chmn, 60; former mem, Fulton Co. Dem. Exec. Cmt. Bus. & Prof. Pos: Trade jour. writer; free lance; feature writer articles and columnist. Publ: There's a Job for You in Georgia, Charles Duncan McIver Brochures. Mem: Am. Asn. for UN; N.W. Ga. Girl Scout Coun; Ga. Writers Asn; Dixee Coun. Authors and Journalists; nat. bd. dir, Girl Scouts U.S, 60-69; Am. Asn. Univ. Woman; League Women Voters; United Church Women; nat. pres, Alumnae of Univ. N.C, Greensboro, 48-50; bd. dir, Atlanta Girls Club, 63-66. Rel: Methodist. Mailing Add: 2900 Nancy Creek Rd. N.W, Atlanta, Ga. 30327.

SATTERTHWAITE, CAMERON B. D
b. Salem, Ohio, 7/26/20; s. William David Satterthwaite and Mabel Cameron S; m. 12/23/50 to Helen Elizabeth Foster; c. Mark Cameron, Tod Foster, Tracy Lynn, Keith Alan and Craig Evan. Educ: Col. of Wooster, B.A; Ohio State Univ, 2 years; Univ. Pittsburgh, Ph.D; Sigma Xi; Sigma Pi Sigma. Polit. & Govt. Pos: Sch. dir, Monroeville, Pa, 59-61; Dem. nominee, U.S. House Rep, 22nd Dist, Ill, 66; del, Dem. Nat. Conv, 68; chmn, Independent Dem. Coalition, 69. Publ: 15 articles in scientific journals. Mem: Am. Phys. Soc; Am. Asn. for the Adv. Sci; Fedn. Am. Scientists (dir, 64-65, v.chmn, 67, chmn, 68); Urban League; Am. Civil Liberties Union. Rel: Soc. of Friends. Mailing Add: 101 E. Florida Ave, Urbana, Ill. 61801.

SATZ, ARNOLD R
Chmn, Lawrence Co. Rep. Cmt, Pa.
b. Minneapolis, Minn. 12/30/20; s. Samuel Satz and Bertha Shulman S; m. 1/28/45 to Marjorie Fisher; c. Karen Rita and David Lawrence. Educ: Univ. Minn, B. Metallurgy Eng, 43; Tau Beta Pi; Sigma Alpha Sigma. Polit. & Govt. Pos: Bd. mem, New Castle Area Sch. Bd, Pa, 64-68; chmn, Lawrence Co. Rep. Cmt, 66- Bus. & Prof. Pos: Pres, New Castle Foundry Co, 47-; v.pres, Gallagher Bros, Inc, 58-; bd. mem, Peoples Bank of West. Pa, 64-; v.pres, Am. Clay Machinery, Inc, 68- Mem: Am. Foundrymen's Asn; bd. mem, Jameson Mem. Hosp; chmn, Lawrence Co. U.S. Savings Bond Prog. Rel: Jewish. Mailing Add: 311 Sumner Ave, New Castle, Pa. 16105.

SAUCIER, EMILY M. D
b. Providence, R.I, 8/30/26; d. Rep. Thomas P. McHugh (deceased). Educ: Central High Sch. Polit. & Gov. Pos: R.I. State Rep, 63-66. Bus. & Prof. Pos: Housewife. Mailing Add: 95 Newark St, Providence, R.I. 02908. (1967)

SAUER, WALTER CHARLES
First V.Pres. and V.Chmn, Export-Import Bank of U.S.
b. Jersey City, N.J, 3/5/05. Educ: Princeton Univ, A.B, 28; Yale Univ, LL.B, 31. Polit. & Govt. Pos: First v.pres. and v.chmn, Export-Import Bank of the U.S, currently. Bus. & Prof. Pos: Attorney-at-law. Legal Res: University Club, 1135 16th N.W, Washington, D.C. 20036. Mailing Add: Export-Import Bank of the U.S, Lafayette Bldg, 811 Vermont Ave. N.W, Washington, D.C. 20571. (1967)

SAUERBREY, ELLEN RICHMOND R
V.chmn, Baltimore Co. Rep. Cent. Cmt, Md.
b. Baltimore, Md, 9/9/37; d. Edgar Arthur Richmond and Ethel Landgraf R; m. 6/27/59 to Wilmer John Emil Sauerbrey. Educ: West. Md. Col, B.A. Summa Cum Laude, 59; Sigma Sigma Tau; Beta Beta Beta. Polit. & Govt. Pos: V.chmn, Baltimore Co. Rep. Cent. Cmt, Md, 66-; del, Rep. Nat. Conv, 68. Bus. & Prof. Pos: Biol. teacher, Baltimore Co. Sch. Syst, 59-64, chmn. dept. sci, 60-64. Publ: Columnist, 'Congressional Rollcall,' The Jeffersonian, 65-66. Mem: Md. Fedn. Rep. Women; Nat. Multiple Sclerosis Soc.(secy. Md. chap). Rel: Methodist. Mailing Add: 1303 Providence Rd, Towson, Md. 21204.

SAUGSTAD, STANLEY R
N.Dak. State Rep.
b. Minot, N.Dak, 1/27/08; married; c. four. Educ: Minot State Teachers Col;

N.Dak. State Univ. Polit. & Govt. Pos: N.Dak. State Rep, 53-, Asst. Majority Floor Leader, N.Dak. State House of Rep, 61, Speaker, 63; mem, sch. bd. Bus. & Prof. Pos: Farmer and appraiser. Mailing Add: Minot, N.Dak. 58701.

SAULNIER, JOSEPH DOUGLAS R
Mass. State Rep.
b. New Bedford, Mass, 4/14/06; s. Ovila Saulnier and Victoria Gauthier S; m. 4/25/32 to Pauline Strahoska; c. Ralph Joseph, Donald James and Jeanne Claire. Polit. & Govt. Pos: Del, Mass. Rep. State Conv, 40-; mem, New Bedford City Coun, 42-50, pres, 45; Mass. State Rep, 51-; mem, credentials cmt, Rep. Nat. Conv, 56, mem, rules cmt, 58, del, 60 & 68; v.pres, Mass. Franco-Am. Rep. Civic League, 58-; mem, Benjamin Franklin Found. Cmt, 60; 2nd v.pres, Mass. Legislators Asn, 65, 1st v.pres, 66, pres, 67. Bus. & Prof. Pos: Owner and gen. mgr, New Bedford Auto Wrecking Co, 30-50. Mem: K. of C. (4°); Elks; Moose; Eagles; pres, Club Richelieu of New Bedford, 63. Rel: Roman Catholic. Mailing Add: 122 Fern St, New Bedford, Mass. 02744. (1967)

SAUMUR, GEORGE R
b. Grand Forks, N.Dak, 5/5/92; married; c. 6. Educ: Pub. schs. Polit. & Govt. Pos: N.Dak. State Sen, 57-66; N.Dak. State Rep, 35-55. Bus. & Prof. Pos: Retired farmer. Mem: C. of C; K. of C; Elks. Mailing Add: Grand Forks, N.Dak. 58201. (1967)

SAUNDERS, ALLEGRA D
Colo. State Sen.
m. to George E. Saunders; c. Two. Polit. & Govt. Pos: Mem, Colo. State Bd. of Educ, 2 terms; Denver Sch. Bd, 66-; Colo. State Sen, 66-, mem, Agr. and Livestock, Natural Resources, Health,and Welfare, Educ. and Water Cmts. Mem: Pres. elect, Kidney Found. Auxiliary Bd; Hemophelia Bd; St. Anthony's Hosp. Lay Adv. Bd. Mailing Add: 4840 Tennyson St, Denver, Colo. 80212.

SAUNDERS, CHARLES BASKERVILLE, JR. R
Dep. Asst. Secy. for Legis, Dept. of Health, Educ. and Welfare
b. Boston, Mass, 12/26/28; s. Charles B. Saunders and Lucy Carmichael S; m. 9/9/50 to Margaret Shafer; c. Charles B, III, George C, Margaret K, Lucy C. and John R. Educ: Princeton Univ, A.B, 50; Univ. Cottage Club. Polit. & Govt. Pos: Legis. asst. to U.S. Sen. H. Alexander Smith, N.J, 57-58; spec. asst. to Asst. Secy. for Legis. Elliot L. Richardson, Dept. of Health, Educ. and Welfare, 58-59, admin. asst. to Secy. Arthur S. Flemming, 59-60, Dep. Asst. Secy. for Legis, 69-; mem, Montgomery Co. Bd. of Educ, Md, 66-; mem. bd. trustees, Montgomery Jr. Col, 69- Bus. & Prof. Pos: Newspaper reporter, Ogdensburg J, N.Y. and Hartford Times, Conn, 50-53; asst. dir. pub. rels, Trinity Col, 53-55; asst. dir. pub. info, Princeton Univ, 53-57; asst. to the pres, Brookings Inst, Wash, D.C, 61-69. Publ: The Brookings Institution: A Fifty-Year History, Brookings Inst, 66. Mem: Nat. Sch. Bd. Asn; Md. Asn. of Bd. of Educ. Rel: Presbyterian. Mailing Add: 7622 Winterberry Place, Bethesda, Md. 20034.

SAUNDERS, ROBERT L, JR. 'BOB' D
Fla. State Sen.
b. Quitman, Ga, 1/22/29; s. Robert L. Saunders, Sr. and Lois Patrick S; m. 6/15/51 to Millicent Johns; c. Sandra Lynn and Robert L, III. Educ: Univ. of Fla. A.A, 51. Polit. & Govt. Pos: Fla. State Sen, Seventh Dist, 68- Bus. & Prof. Pos: Pres, Fla. Petroleum Marketers Asn. Mem: C. of C.(dir, Gainesville area); dir, Alachua Co. United Fund; Rotary. Runner-up for the Outstanding First Termer in the Fla. State Senate. Rel: Episcopal. Legal Res: 1705 N.W. 26th Way, Gainesville, Fla. 32601. Mailing Add: P.O. Box 849, Gainesville, Fla. 32601.

SAUTE, GERMAIN R
Mem, R.I. State Rep. Cent. Cmt.
b. Laiche, Belgium, 6/19/07; s. J. Emile Sauté and Rosalie Collignon S; m. 11/11/33 to Barbara E. Newell; c. Mrs. J. F. McEnroe and Mrs. David W. Dumas. Educ: Harvard Col, S.B, 28; Pierian Sodality of 1808. Polit. & Govt. Pos: Cand. for R.I. State Sen, 60 & 62; cand. for R.I. State Rep, 64; alternate del, Rep. Nat. Conv, 64, del, 68; pres, Coventry Town Coun, R.I, 66-68; chmn, Coventry Rep. City Cmt, currently; mem, R.I. State Rep. Cent. Cmt, currently. Bus. & Prof. Pos: Pres. & treas, What Cheer Garage, Inc, 47- Mem: Treas, Harvard Club of R.I; v.pres, Assoc. Harvard Clubs; Past Master, Manchester Lodge 12 F&AM; former trustee and secy. of corp, Rocky Hill Country Day Sch. Rel: Congregational; Former trustee and treasurer, Riverpoint Congregational Church. Mailing Add: 2 Potter Court, Coventry, R.I. 02816.

SAVAGE, CARL PRESTON, SR. D
b. Duplin Co, N.C, 1/16/00; s. John James Savage and Mary Idella Knowles S; m. 8/19/24 to Josie Bodeker Shea; c. Carl Preston, Jr, John Bodeker, Virginia Elizabeth (Mrs. A. J. Morris) and Richard David. Educ: Univ. N.C, Chapel Hill; Med. Col. of Ga; Theta Kappa Psi. Polit. & Govt. Pos: City councilman, Montezuma, Ga, 25 years, mayor, 57-65; former Ga. State Rep, 58th Dist. Bus. & Prof. Pos: Intern, Greenwood City Hosp, S.C; resident, Lee Mem. Hosp, Ft. Myers, Fla; physician and surgeon, 25-66; hosp. adminstr, Riverside Sanatorium, Ga, 38-66. Mil. Serv: Pvt, Army, 18. Mem: Sumter Co. Med. Soc; Ga. and Am. Med. Asns; past pres, South. Med. Asn; past v.pres, Ga. Munic. Asn; C. of C; Farm Bur; Mason, Shrine; Eastern Star; past pres, Kiwanis. Rel: Baptist; Deacon and chmn. bd. Mailing Add: 511 S. Dooly St, Montezuma, Ga. 31063. (1967)

SAVAGE, CHARLES R. D
Wash. State Rep.
b. La Farge, Wis, 1906; m. to Helen S; c. two. Educ: High sch; some spec. training. Polit. & Govt. Pos: U.S. Rep, Wash, 1 term; Wash. State Rep, currently. Bus. & Prof. Pos: Logger. Mailing Add: 2011 King St, Shelton, Wash. 98584. (1967)

SAVAGE, EMILY GIERASCH R
b. Concord, Mass, 10/31/30; d. Walter Gierasch and Mary Hellen G; m. 10/24/53 to John M. Savage; c. Karyn, Adrianne and Janet. Educ: Wheaton Col, Norton,Mass, B.A, 51. Polit. & Govt. Pos: Held various positions, Rep. Party, 58-65; del, Dist. and State Conv, 59-64; secy, Rep. Hq, Anchorage, Alaska, 62-64 and Lowell Thomas, Jr. for U.S. Rep, 64; del, Rep. Nat. Conv, 64; mem, Alaska Comprehensive Health Adv. Coun, 68. Bus. & Prof. Pos: Secy, Harvard Bus. Sch, 57-58. Mem: Pres, Anchor Park Kindergarten Asn, 65-66; Alaska Del, Nat. Asn. Women. Hwy. Safety Leader, 67-68. Rel: Protestant. Mailing Add: 1954 Stanford Dr, Anchorage, Alaska 99504.

SAVAGE, JOHN J. R
Fla. State Rep.
b. Louisville, Ky, 12/6/10; s. Patrick Henry Savage and Henrietta Holtman S; m. 1/2/42 to Mary Francis Walsh. Educ: Jefferson Sch. Law, LL.B, 32; Univ. Louisville, LL.B, 50. Polit. & Govt. Pos: Precinct worker, dist. worker and various cmt, assignments, Rep. Co. Exec. Cmt, Louisville, Ky, 32-41; Ky. State Rep, 39-41; spec. agent, Fed. Bur. of Invest, 42-49; precinct worker, dist. worker and various cmt. assignments, Pinellas Co. Rep. Exec. Cmt, Fla, 55-; mem. and chmn, Pinellas Co. Bd. of Adjustment and Appeal, 61-64; Fla. State Rep, 64- Bus. & Prof. Pos: Attorney-at-law, 32-41; spec. agent, Am. Ins. Asn, 49- Publ: Police publ. and various University's publ. on law enforcement, 49-65. Mem: Ky. Bar Asn; Fla. State Bar Asn; others. Rel: Roman Catholic. Legal Res: 16919 First St. E, North Redington Beach, Fla. 33708. Mailing Add: P.O. Box 8063, St. Petersburg, Fla. 33738.

SAVAGE, JOSEPH A. D
b. Newport, R.I, 1/28/15; m. to Lillian C. Educ: Naval Torpedo Sta. Apprentice Machinist Sch. Polit. Pos: R.I. State Sen, 57-66; R.I. State Rep, 51-56; Newport Coun. Number 256. Bus. & Prof. Pos: Mfrs. Rep. Mem: K. of C; Elks; Friendly Sons of St. Patrick; St. Joseph's Holy Name Soc; Ancient Order of Hibernians; Kiwanis; W.T. Bull Mem. Sportsmen's Club; Irish-Am. Athletic Club; Rogers High Alumni Asn; Hon. Mem, Int. Asn. of Machinists, A.F. of L. Mailing Add: 10 Friendship St, Newport, R.I. 02840. (1967)

SAVAGE, LEON H. R
Utah State Rep.
b. Hyrum, Utah, 5/23/35; s. Gordon C. Savage and Phyllis Hansen S; m. 11/26/58 to Paula Fluckiger; c. Ralph, Janet, Kent, Bruce, Blake and Roy. Educ: Utah State Univ, 55; Univ. Utah, 59; Latter-day Saints Bus. Col, 58. Polit. & Govt. Pos: Utah State Rep, Dist. 25, currently. Bus. & Prof. Pos: Owner, apartments, 63- Rel: Latter-day Saint. Mailing Add: 4123 W. 4990 S, Kearns, Utah, 84118.

SAVAGE, STELLA RAMSAY R
b. Bloomfield, 8/15/98; married; c. five. Educ: Stratford, N.H. High Sch. Polit. & Govt. Pos: Asst. town clerk, N.H, 28, town clerk, 28-; N.H. State Rep, 39-45 & 61-66. Bus. & Prof. Pos: Motel and restaurant bus. Mem: Past pres, Am. Legion Auxiliary; Pythian Sisters. Rel: Episcopal. Mailing Add: North Stratford, N.H. 03590. (1967)

SAVAGE, WALLACE HAMILTON D
b. Houston, Tex, 11/21/12; s. Homer H. Savage and Mary Wallace S; m. 10/12/40 to Dorothy Harris; c. Virginia Wallace and Dorothy Harris. Educ: Univ. Va, B.S, 33; Harvard, LL.B, 36; fel, Univ. Colo, 36-37. Polit. & Govt. Pos: Mayor-pro-tem, Dallas, Tex, 47-49, mayor, 49-51; chmn, Dallas Co. Dem. Party, and State Dem. Party, 52-54; Dallas Co. chmn. and nat. v.chmn, Citizen's Cmn, Hoover Report, 52-54; mem, Dir. Citizen's Cmt. Reorgn. Exec. Br. Govt, 54-59. Bus. & Prof. Pos: Partner, Lane, Savage, Counts, & Winn and dir, Lakewood Bank and Trust Co, currently. Mil. Serv: Comdr, Naval Res, 41-45. Mem: Tex, Am. and Dallas Bar Asns; Dallas Country Club; Idlewood Club; Terpischorean Club. Rel: Episcopal; parish chancellor and church vestryman. Legal Res: 5703 Swiss Ave, Dallas, Tex. 75204. Mailing Add: Republic Bank Bldg, Dallas, Tex. 75201.

SAVELKOUL, DONALD CHARLES 'DON' D
b. Minneapolis, Minn, 7/29/17; s. Theodore Charles Savelkoul and Edith Lindgren S; m. 5/17/41 to Mary Joan Holland; c. Jeffrey Charles, Jean Marie and Edward Joseph. Educ: Univ. Minn, B.A, 39; Minneapolis-Minn. Col. Law, B.S. in law, 50 and LL.B, 51; Phi Beta Kappa; Delta Theta Phi. Polit. & Govt. Pos: Various admin. pos, U.S. Dept. of Commerce, War and Labor, 40-51; exec. asst, Wage Stabilization Bd, 51; munic. judge, Fridley, Minn, 52-53; Minn. State Rep, 67-68. Bus. & Prof. Pos: Attorney-at-law, 52-; chmn. bd, Fridley State Bank, 62-66. Mil. Serv: Entered as Pvt, Army, 43, released as 1st Lt, 46, after serv. in Signal Corps, Pac, 44-46; Bronze Star. Mem: Am, Minn. and Hennepin Co. Bar Asns; K. of C; C. of C; Am. Legion. Rel: Catholic. Legal Res: 916 W. Moore Lake Dr, Fridley, Minn. 55421. Mailing Add: 1020 Plymouth Bldg, Minneapolis, Minn. 55402. (1967)

SAVELKOUL, HENRY JEROME R
Minn. State Rep.
b. Lansford, N.Dak, 7/1/40; s. Harry N. Savelkoul and Mary Davis S; m. 6/25/64 to Margaret Ann Sykes; c. Patricia Ann and Donald Wayne. Educ: St. Thomas Col, lib. arts, 4 years; Univ. Minn. Law Sch, J.D, 65; Alpha Kappa Psi; Delta Theta Phi. Polit. & Govt. Pos: Secy, Freeborn Co. Rep. Party, Minn, formerly; Minn. State Rep, currently. Bus. & Prof. Pos: Counsel, Christian, Slen, Savelkoul, Johnson & Broberg, Albert Lea, Minn, 65- Mem: Am. and Minn. Bar Asns. Bush Found. Fel. Award. Rel: Roman Catholic. Mailing Add: 1100 Cedar, Albert Lea, Minn. 56007.

SAVICKAS, FRANK DAVID D
Ill. State Rep.
b. Chicago, Ill, 5/14/35; s. Frank L. Savickas and Estelle Ivaskevich S; m. 6/26/54 to Adrienne C. Shenoha; c. Michael David, Linda Diane and Sharon Eileen. Educ: Wildon Jr. Col, 2 years. Polit. & Govt. Pos: Ill. State Rep, 27th Dist, 66- Mem: K. of C. (4°); Lithuanian C. of C; Chicago Journeyman Plumbers Local Union 130; Moose; Riano Soc. Club. Rel: Catholic. Legal Res: 6940 S. Artesian Ave, Chicago, Ill. 60629. Mailing Add: 3455½ W. 63rd St, Chicago, Ill. 60629.

SAWICKI, JOHN GERALD R
Mem, Calif. Rep. State Cent. Cmt.
b. Denver, Colo, 1/10/43; s. Walter J. Sawicki, Jr. and Mary K. Christensen S; m. 11/16/68 to Jo Ann Sloan Miller. Educ: Big Bend Commun. Col, Moses Lake, Wash, A.A, 64; Gonzaga Univ, 64-65; East. Wash. State Col, B.A, 66.

Polit. & Govt. Pos: Campaign mgr, Douglas A. McKee, 61st Assembly Dist, 68; campaign mgr, Dr. William Vickrey, Douglas McKee Culver City Sch. Bd, 69; campaign field dir, Robert Dornan, 28th Cong. Dist, currently; third v.pres, Los Angeles Co. Young Rep, 69-; mem, Calif. Rep. State Cent. Cmt, mem, 61st Calif. Assembly Dist. Cent. Cmt. and alternate, Los Angeles Co. Rep. Cent. Cmt, currently. Mil. Serv: Entered as Airman 3/C, Air Force, 61, released as Airman 1/C, 64, after serv. in 568th Strategic Missile Squadron, Strategic Air Command, 61-64; Good Conduct Medal; Outstanding Airman of the Year Award. Mem: Los Angeles World Affairs Coun; Los Angeles World Trade Asn. Rel: Catholic. Legal Res: 2391 Paloma Ave, Pasadena, Calif. 91104. Mailing Add: 10006 Palms Blvd, Los Angeles, Calif. 90034.

SAWYER, CHARLES D
b. Cincinnati, Ohio, 2/10/87; s. Edward Milton Sawyer and Caroline Butler S; m. to Margaret Johnston (deceased); m. 6/10/42 to Elizabeth L. de Veyrac; c. Anne Sawyer Greene (Mrs. John Bradley), Charles (deceased), Jean Johnston (Mrs. John J. Weaver), John and Edward. Educ: Oberlin Col, A.B, 08; Univ. Cincinnati, LL.B, 11. Hon. LL.D, Univ. Cincinnati, 50. Polit. & Govt. Pos: Mem, Cincinnati City Coun, Ohio, 11-15; Lt. Gov, Ohio, 33-35; mem, Dem. Nat. Cmt, Ohio, 36-44; Dem. cand. for Gov, Ohio, 38; Ambassador to Belgium, Minister to Luxembourg, 44-46; Secy. of Commerce, 48-53; mem, Cmn. on Money and Credit, 59-60. Bus. & Prof. Pos: Sr. partner law firm, Taft, Stettinius & Hollister, Cincinnati; dir, numerous corps; chmn, Cincinnati Commun. Chest, 54; chmn, Cincinnati United Appeal, 55-60; Citizens Develop. Cmt, Cincinnati; hon. trustee, Oberlin Col. Mil. Serv: Entered Army, 17, released as Maj, 19, after serv. in Inf, AEF, 18-19. Mem: Am, Fed. and Ohio Bar Asns; Mason; Queen City Club; Commercial Club; Commonwealth Club; Cincinnati Country Club; Nat. Press Club; Everglades Club; Bath and Tennis Club. Rel: Episcopal. Legal Res: 95 E. Fountain Ave, Glendale, Ohio 45246. Mailing Add: 2513 Central Trust Tower, Cincinnati, Ohio 45202.

SAWYER, DONALD RAYMOND R
City Councilman, South Gate, Calif.
b. Dakota City, Iowa, 3/26/11; s. Thomas Sawyer and Julia Bergeson S; m. 8/29/34 to Gladys Marie Breed; c. Sonya Marie and Ramona Gene. Educ: Drake Univ; Coyle Sch. Law. Polit. & Govt. Pos: Pres. and mem, sch. bd, Dakota City, Iowa, 34-43; justice of the peace, Humboldt Co, 34-43; planning cmnr, South Gate, Calif, 58-62, city councilman, 62-; mayor, 63-64. Bus. & Prof. Pos: Dir, State Escrow, Inc, 51- Mem: Dir, Southeast Bd. Realtors, 52-62, pres, 60; state dir, Calif. Real Estate Asn, 65-66; Mason; Eagles; Rotary; C. of C. Rel: Lutheran; Pres, Peace Lutheran Church of South Gate, 58-59. Legal Res: 9630 Annetta Ave, South Gate, Calif. 90280. Mailing Add: 4313 Tweedy Blvd, South Gate, Calif. 90280. (1967)

SAWYER, E. P. R
b. Beaumont, Ky, 11/18/15; s. James G. Sawyer and Nettie Hay S; m. 4/29/39 to Jean Dunagan; c. Linda (Mrs. David French) and Diane. Educ: West. Ky. Univ, A.B, 40; Univ. Louisville, LL.B, 47. Polit. & Govt. Pos: Asst. Commonwealth's attorney, Jefferson Co, Ky, 47-52, co. attorney, 62-68, co. judge, 68-; del, Rep. Nat. Conv, 68. Bus. & Prof. Pos: Attorney, Louisville, Ky, 43- Mil. Serv: Entered as Ens, Navy, 43, released as Lt, 44, after serv. in Atlantic and Pac. Theatres, Lt; Naval Res. Mem: Am, Ky. and Louisville Bar Asns; Mason (32°); Kiwanis. Rel: Methodist. Mailing Add: 29 Sterling Rd, Louisville, Ky. 40220.

SAWYER, EUGENE, JR. D
Committeeman, Sixth Ward Dem. Orgn, Ill.
b. Greensboro, Ala, 9/3/34; s. Eugene Sawyer, Sr. and Bernice Mauldin S; m. 8/28/55 to Celeste Cavalier Banks; c. Shedrick Eugene, Sheryl Celeste and Roderick Terrence. Educ: Ala. State Col, B.S, 56; Alpha Phi Alpha. Polit. & Govt. Pos: Area chmn, Young Dem. of Cook Co, Ill, 61-62; chmn, registrn, Young Dem. of Ill, 64-65; committeeman, Sixth Ward Dem. Orgn, 68- Mem: Miss. State Teachers Asn; bd. dirs, Woodlawn Boys Club; Wisdom Lodge 102; bd. dirs, Pkwy. Commun. Center; Plumbers Union; bd. trustees, Hull House Asn; NAACP. Rel: Methodist. Legal Res: 7406 S. Wabash Ave, Chicago, Ill. 60619. Mailing Add: 435 E. 71st St, Chicago, Ill. 60619.

SAWYER, F. GRANT D
Dem. Nat. Committeeman, Nev.
b. Twin Falls, Idaho, 12/14/18; s. Harry W. Sawyer and Bula Cameron S; m. 8/1/46 to Bette Norene Hoge; c. Gail. Educ: Linfield Col, 38-39; Univ. Nev, B.A, 41; George Wash. Univ. Law Sch, 41-42; Georgetown Univ. Law Sch, LL.B, 48; LL.D, Univ. Nev. and Linfield Col; pres, Alpha Tau Omega. Polit. & Govt. Pos: Former chmn, Elko Co. Dem. Cmt; former presiding officer, Dem. State Conv, Nev; dist. attorney, Elko Co, Nev, 50-58; chmn, Nev. Dem. Cmt, 55; del, Dem. Nat. Conv, 56, 60, 64 & 68; mem, Nat. Dem. Platform Cmt, 58-60, 64 & 68; mem. bd. regents, Univ. Nev, 57; Gov, Nev, 59-67; chmn, Nat. Gov. Conf. and pres, Coun. State Govt, 64-65; chmn, West. Gov. Conf, 65-66; Spec. U.S. Ambassador to Paraguay, 68; Dem. national committeeman, Nev, 68- Bus. & Prof. Pos: Bd. of Trustees, John F. Kennedy Libr. Mil. Serv: Entered as Pvt, Army, 42, released as 1st Lt, 46, after serv. in Pac. Theater. Mem: Dir, Nat. Dist. Attorneys Asn; pres, Nev. Dist. Attorneys Asn. and Elko Co. Bar Asn; Am. Bar. Asn; Am. Judicature Soc; Mason; Shrine; C. of C; VFW; Amvets; Am. Legion; Lions; PTA; Am. Cancer Soc; Boy Scouts. Outstanding Young Dem. of Nev, 55; Elko Young Man of Year, 52. Rel: Baptist. Mailing Add: 6985 Mira Vista, Las Vegas, Nev. 89109.

SAWYER, FERN D
Chmn, Lincoln Co. Dem. Party, N.Mex.
b. Buchannen, N.Mex, 5/17/17; d. Uyless Devoe Sawyer and Dessie Leivis S; div. Educ: Texas Tech. Col, $2\frac{1}{2}$ years; Univ. N.Mex, 1 year; Alpha Delta Pi. Polit. & Govt. Pos: Co. chairwoman, Lincoln Co. Dem. Party, N.Mex, 62-66, chmn, 66-; alternate del, Dem. Nat. Conv, 68. Bus. & Prof. Pos: Prfnl. rodeo performer, 20 years; Hereford Cattle rancher. Mem: Rodeo Cowboys Asn. Won World's Championship for riding cutting horses and Girl's All Around World Championship of 47. Rel: Episcopal. Mailing Add: Nogal, N.Mex. 88341.

SAWYER, FRANK N. R
N.H. State Rep.
b. Weare, N.H, 12/25/96; married; c. two. Educ: LaSalle Univ. Polit. & Govt. Pos: Del, Constitutional Conv; N.H. State Rep, currently. Bus. & Prof. Pos: Retired exec. Mil. Serv: Army, World War I, 325th Motor Trans. Co; World War II, Lt. Col, 385th Bn, Anti-Aircraft Artil. Mem: Mason (32°); Am. Legion; Vet. of World War I. Rel: Congregational. Mailing Add: R.F.D. 1, Weare, N.H. 03281. (1967)

SAWYER, LEONARD ALSON D
b. Puyallup, Wash, 5/18/25; s. Alson L. Sawyer and Velma MacDonald S; m. 12/17/50 to Beverly M. Farrell; c. Carla, Colleen, Cynthia, L. Clark and Craig. Educ: Univ. Puget Sound, B.A, 48; Univ. Wash, law degree, 51; Kappa Sigma. Polit. & Govt. Pos: Dep. prosecuting attorney, Prosecutor's Off, Wash, 52-55; Wash. State Rep, 55-66, Majority Whip, Wash. State House of Rep. and chmn, Joint Interim Cmt. on Hwys, Wash. Legis, 65-66; mem, Seattle World's Fair Cmn, 58-62; mem, exec. bd, West. Conf. State Gov, 65-66. Mil. Serv: Entered as A/S, Navy 43, released as Ens, 46, after serv. as Port Dir, Post Off, Pac. and China, 45-46; Pac. and China Campaign Ribbons. Mem: Wash. and Am. Bar Asns; Elks; VFW; Am. Legion. Rel: Presbyterian. Mailing Add: Route 3, Box 1990, Sumner, Wash. 98390.

SAWYER, MILBURN ERCELL D
b. Powells Point, N.C, 12/3/14; s. Norris Baum Sawyer and Selma Harrison S; m. 10/22/44 to Norma Maxine Banks; c. Carol Ann, Brenda Sue, Milburn Brent, Kathy Arlene. Educ: Poplar Branch High Sch, 34. Polit. & Govt. Pos: N.C. State Rep, 63-66; precinct chmn, past 15 years; Co. Cmnr, 55-56, 61-62. Bus. & Prof. Pos: Farmer and fertilizer salesman. Mil. Serv: Coast Guard, Machinist Mate, 38-41. Mem: Poplar Branch Ruritan Club; Lower Currituck Vol. Fire Dept. Rel: Christian Church. Mailing Add: Powells Point, N.C. 27966. (1967)

SAWYER, MRS. U. D. 'DESSIE' D
Dem. Nat. Committeewoman, N.Mex.
b. Tex; wid; c. Fern and Merle (Mrs. Jeff Good). Polit. & Govt. Pos: Precinct chmn, Dem. Party, N.Mex; co. chmn, mem. co. cent. Dem. cmt. and Dem. state chairwoman; Dem. Nat. Committeewoman, N.Mex, 48-; del, Dem. Nat. Conv, 68. Mem: Chmn, March of Dimes, 27 years; chmn. restoration cmt, Old Lincoln Co, 18 years. Mailing Add: Crossroads, N.Mex. 88114.

SAWYER, WAYNE ROBERT R
Mem, San Joaquin Co. Rep. Cent. Cmt, Calif.
b. San Francisco, Calif, 9/17/31; s. Albert Pierce Sawyer and Margaret Bird S; m. 6/30/57 to Anne Laudig; c. Robert Garrett and Allan Thomas. Educ: Santa Rosa Jr. Col, A.A, 51; Univ. Calif, Berkeley, A.B, 53; Univ. Calif. Med. Sch, San Francisco, M.D, 56; Phi Beta Kappa; Sigma Xi; Alpha Kappa Kappa. Polit. & Govt. Pos: Chmn, San Joaquin Co. Goldwater for Pres. Cmt, Calif, 64; alternate del, Rep. Nat. Conv, 64; cong. dist. dir, Calif. Rep. Assembly, 65; finance chmn, San Joaquin Co. Reagan for Gov. Cmt, 66; assoc. bd, Calif. State Rep. Cent. Cmt, 68, 69; mem, San Joaquin Co. Rep. Cent. Cmt, 69- Bus. & Prof. Pos: Dir. lab, Dameron Hosp, Stockton, Calif. and El Dorado Clin. Lab, 64- and Lodi Commun. Hosp, 66-; chmn, Dept. Nuclear Med, Dameron Hosp, 69- Mil. Serv: Capt, Army, 57-59; serv. in Tenth Gen. Dispensary, ETO. Publ: Several articles relating to pathology. Mem: San Joaquin Co. Med. Soc; Calif. and Am. Med. Asns; fel. Col. Am. Pathologists; fel. Am. Soc. Clin. Pathologists; Soc. Nuclear Med; dipl. Am. Bd. Path. Rel: Episcopal. Mailing Add: 1937 Lincoln Rd, Stockton, Calif. 95207.

SAWYERS, RAY EARL D
W.Va. State Sen.
b. Smoot, W.Va, 11/16/08; s. James Lewis Sawyers and Maude Samples S; m. 12/26/45 to Jaunita Josephine Williams. Polit. & Govt. Pos: W.Va. State Del, 63-66; W.Va. State Sen, currently. Bus. & Prof. Pos: Chief clerk to supt, C&O Rwy. Co, 45- Mem: Elks; Moose; Mason; Toastmasters; Brotherhood of Rwy. Clerks; Willowwood Country Club. Rel: Protestant. Mailing Add: 502 Miller Ave, Hinton, W.Va. 25951.

SAX, SARAH ELLEN R
b. Colville, Wash, 10/7/25; d. Lester Cohrs and Nora Sturman C; m. 3/30/47 to Philip Arthur Sax; c. Nancy Ellen, Linda Jane, Richard Philip and William Sturman. Educ: Gonzaga Univ; St. Luke's Hosp. Sch. of Nursing. Polit. & Govt. Pos: Chmn, Stevens Co. Rep, Cent. Cmt, Wash, 64-67. Mem: Wash. State Nurses Asn: Eastern Star; PEO; Am. Cancer Soc, Wash. Div. Rel: Episcopal. Mailing Add: 1195 Garden Homes Dr, Colville, Wash. 99114. (1967)

SAXBE, WILLIAM B. R
U.S. Sen, Ohio
b. Mechanicsburg, Ohio, 6/24/16; s. Bart Saxbe and Faye Carey S; m. Sept, 1940 to Ardath Kleinhans; c. Juli (Mrs. Sam Lopeman), Bart and Rocky. Educ: Ohio State Univ, A.B, LL.B; Chi Phi; Phi Delta Phi. Polit. & Govt. Pos: Ohio State Rep, 47-54, Majority Leader, Ohio State House of Rep, 51-52 and Speaker House, 53-54; Attorney Gen, Ohio, 63-69; chmn, Ohio Crime Cmn, 67-; U.S. Sen, Ohio, 69- Mil. Serv: Entered as Pvt, Ohio Nat. Guard, 37, released as Col, 66, after serv. in Inf, Air Force; active duty, World War II and Korean Conflict. Mem: Local, state and nat. Bar Asns; Am. Judicature Soc; Am. Legion; Amvets; Ohio Grange; Masonic Bodies; other fraternal, service and civic groups. Rel: Episcopal. Legal Res: Route 2, Mechanicsburg, Ohio 43044. Mailing Add: Senate Office Bldg, Washington, D.C. 20510.

SAXON, JAMES J. D
b. Toledo, Ohio, 4/13/14; s. Samuel Joseph Saxon and Catherine Ann Mulhanney S; m. 12/30/44 to Dorothy Stewart Bell; c. James J, Jr, Stephen, Dorea, Kevin, Catherine and Lucy. Educ: St. John's Col, A.B; Georgetown Univ. Law Sch, LL.B; Cath. Univ. Am, post-grad. work in econ. and finance; Delta Theta Phi. Polit. & Govt. Pos: Treas. attaché, Treas. Dept, 41-42, economist and spec. asst. to dir, div. of monetary res, Off. of Int. Finance, 42-45, asst. to Secy. of Treas, 45-50, spec. asst, dept, 50-52, comptroller of currency, 61-68. Bus. & Prof. Pos: Gen. counsel, Am. Bankers Asn, 52-56; attorney, First Nat. Bank of Chicago, 56-61. Mem: D.C. and Ill. Bars; Am. and Fed. Bar Asns; Nat. Tax Asn; Tax Exec. Inst; Coun. of Profit Sharing Indust; Chicago Athletic Club; Navy League of the U.S. Rel: Catholic. Mailing Add: 6024 Western Ave, Chevy Chase, Md. 20015. (1967)

SAYERS, NANCY J. D
b. Waco, Tex, 4/21/30; d. Brian Marsh deGraffenried and Lucille Bowman deGraffenried Goode; m. 9/5/50 to Scott Philen Sayers, wid; c. Scott P, Jr. and Brian Sam. Educ: Univ. Tex, B.A, 51; Kappa Alpha Theta. Polit. & Govt. Pos: Committeewoman, Dem. Party, Tex, 65-68; chmn, Dem. Woman's Day, 67; mem, Gov. Inaugural Cmt, 67 & 69; del, Dem. Nat. Conv, 68; chmn. and exec. dir, Tex. Employ. Cmn, 69- Mem: Tex. Pub. Employees Asn; Int. Asn. Personnel in Employ. Security; Jr. Leagues of Austin and Ft. Worth, Tex. Rel: Methodist. Legal Res: 2322 Townes Lane, Austin, Tex. 78703. Mailing Add: 624 Texas Employment Commission Bldg, Austin, Tex. 78701.

SAYLER, HENRY B, JR. R
Fla. State Sen.
b. Savannah, Ga, 1/16/21; s. Henry B. Sayler and Jessie Dixon S; m. 3/22/47 to Wyline Chapman; c. Lee, Alan, Robin and Van. Educ: U.S. Mil. Acad, B.S, 43. Polit. & Govt. Pos: Fla. State Sen, currently. Bus. & Prof. Pos: Dir, Bank of Seminole, 60-; dir, R.W. Page Corp, 61-; secy-treas, Skyline Prod, Inc, 62-; pres, Security Planning of Fla, Inc, 62-; dir, Founders Life Assurance Co, 63- Mil. Serv: Entered as 2nd Lt, Air Force, 43, released as Lt. Col, 55, after serv. in 8th Air Force, Eng. as fighter pilot, final assignment, Air Force Missile Test Center; Distinguished Flying Cross; Air Medal with 6 Clusters; Am. Theater Ribbon; European Theater Ribbon; Am. Defense and Victory Medals. Mem: Chartered Life Underwriter, 63; Nat. Asn. Life Underwriters; Kiwanis. Fla. Badminton Champion, Doubles. Rel: Methodist. Mailing Add: 220 Rafael Blvd. N.E, St. Petersburg, Fla. 33704.

SAYLOR, JOHN PHILLIPS R
U.S. Rep, Pa.
b. Conemaugh, Pa, 7/23/08; s. Tillman Kulp Saylor, Sr. and Minerva Phillips S; m. to Grace Doertsler; c. J. Phillips and Susan Kathleen. Educ: Franklin and Marshall Col, B.A; Dickinson Law Sch, LL.B; Chi Phi. Hon. LL.D, St. Francis Col. Polit. & Govt. Pos: U.S. Rep, 22nd Dist, Pa, 49-, ranking minority mem, Cmt. on Interior and Insular Affairs, U.S. House of Rep, mem, Vet. Affairs Cmt, mem, Steering Cmt, Pa. Cong. Del, mem, Exec. Cmt, Rep. Cong. Cmt. Bus. & Prof. Pos: Former co-partner, law firm, Spence, Custer & Saylor; pres. and mem. bd. dirs, Johnstown Fed. Savings and Loan Asn. Mil. Serv: Navy, World War II; Capt, Naval Res. Mem: Cambria Co, Pa. State and Am. Bar Asns; Am. Legion; VFW; Amvets; Elks; Mason; Shrine; President Eisenhower's Outdoor Recreation Resources Rev. Cmn; Nat. Forest Reservation Cmn; Pub. Land Law Rev. Cmn; Am. Revolution Bicentennial Cmn; former lay mem, Synodical Coun, Pittsburgh Synod, E & R Church; former mem, Cmn. on Christian Soc. Action; del, Nat. Study Conf. on Church and Econ. Life of Fed. Coun. of Churches, 50; lay del, Conv. for Merger of Evangel. and Reformed Church with Congregational Christian Church, 57; bd. trustees, Massunutten Acad; bd. regents, Mercersburg Acad; exec. bd, Adm. Robert E. Peary Coun, Inc; Boy Scouts; assoc. mem, Boone and Crockett Club, 64. Nat. Parks Asn. Award for Distinguished Serv. on Behalf of Nat. Parks and Monuments, 54; Nat. Conserv. Award Presented by the Six Leading Conserv. Orgn. in U.S, 58; Conservationist of the Year Award, Pa. Outdoor Writers Asn, 65; Conservationist of the Year Award, Nat. Wildlife Fedn, 64; Gold Medal of Pa. State Fish and Game Protective Asn. for Distinguished Leadership in Preservation of Nation's Natural and Wildlife Resources, 67; Trout Conserv. Award, 67; Bernard M. Baruch Conserv. Award, 67. Rel: Protestant. Legal Res: 411 Orchard St, Johnstown, Pa. 15905. Mailing Add: Room 2354 Rayburn Bldg, Washington, D.C. 20515.

SAYLOR, JOHN THOMAS D
Secy, Centre Co. Dem. Cmt, Pa.
b. Bellefonte, Pa, 11/24/31; s. Philip P. Saylor and Kathryn M. Hoy S; single. Educ: N.W. Mo. State Col, 51; Univ. Scranton, 55; Pa. State Univ, B.A, 58, M.Ed, 59. Polit. & Govt. Pos: Dem. committeeman, Bellefonte Borough, Pa, 61-62; treas, Centre Co. Dem. Cmt, 62-68, secy, 68-; treas, Young Dem. Club of Centre Co, 64-; inspector of elections, Bellefonte Borough N. Ward, 65-; secy, 34th Pa. Dist. Dem. Constitutional Del. Nominating Conv, 67; alternate del, Dem. Nat. Conv, 68. Bus. & Prof. Pos: Rehabilitation counselor, Pa. Bur. Voc. Rehabilitation, Pittsburgh, Pa, 59-60; teacher, Bellefonte Sch. Dist, 60; tech. writer, HRB-Singer, Inc, State College, Pa, 61- Mil. Serv: Entered as Pvt, Air Force, 51, released as S/Sgt, 55, after serv. in Strategic Air Command, Strategic Air Command Hq, Omaha, Nebr, 51-54; Nat. Defense Serv. Medal. Mem: Toastmasters Int; Am. Legion. Rel: Catholic. Mailing Add: 238 N. Penn St, Bellefonte, Pa. 16823.

SAYLOR, STANLEY RAYMOND R
Chmn, Snyder Co. Rep. Cmt, Pa.
b. Beavertown, Pa, 12/17/16; s. William H. Saylor and Ida Doebler S; m. 10/25/47 to Beatrice E. Lepley. Educ: High Sch. Polit. & Govt. Pos: Pres, Beavertown Borough Coun, Pa, 47-61; mem, Pa. State Rep. Cmt, 58-60; chmn, Snyder Co. Rep. Cmt, 60- Bus. & Prof. Pos: Pres, Beavertown Develop. Co. Mil. Serv: Entered as Pvt, Army, 42, released as S/Sgt, 45, after serv. in ETO, 44; European Theater Ribbon with 4 Battle Stars; Bronze Star. Mem: Past master, F&AM, 53; Harrisburg Consistory; Zembo Temple; VFW; Am. Legion; Moose; dir, Snyder Co. Chapter Am. Red Cross; past pres, West Snyder Rotary; Spring Twp. Planning Cmn; Union Co. Sportsmen Club. Rel: Lutheran. Mailing Add: Beavertown, Pa. 17813.

SAYRE, ROBERT MARION
U.S. Ambassador to Panama
b. Hillsboro, Ore, 8/18/24; s. William Octavius Sayre and Mary Brozka S; m. 12/29/51 to Elora Amanda Moyhihan; c. Marian Amanda, Robert Marion and Daniel Humphrey. Educ: Willamette Univ, B.A. summa cum laude, 49; George Wash. Univ, J.D, and Alexander Wellborn Weddell Peace Prize, 56; Stanford Univ, M.A, 60. Hon. LL.D, Willamette Univ, 65. Polit. & Govt. Pos: Career officer, Dept. of State For. Serv, 49-; econ. adv. on Latin Am, 50-52, mil. adv, 52-57; officer in charge, Inter-Am. Security Affairs, 57; chief of polit. sect, Embassy, Lima, Peru, 58-59; financial adv, Embassy, Havana, Cuba, 60; exec. secy, Task Force on Latin Am, State Dept, 61; officer in charge, Mexican Affairs, 61-63, dir. and officer, 64; dep. dir, Off. of Caribbean and Mexican Affairs, 63-64; sr. staff mem, White House, 64-65; dep, asst. secy, Bur. of Inter-Am. Affairs, 65-69; U.S. Ambassador to Uruguay, 68-69 & Panama, 69- Mil. Serv: Capt, Army, World War II; Col, Army Res. Mem: Admitted to D.C. Bar, 56 and U.S. Supreme Court, 62; Am. Econ. Asn; Blue Key; Phi Delta Theta; Phi Eta Sigma; Tau Kappa Alpha. Rel: Methodist. Legal Res: 3714 Bent Branch Rd, Falls Church, Va. 22041. Mailing Add: U.S. Embassy Panama, P.O. Box 2016, Balboa, C.Z.

SCAGLIA, PHILLIP P. D
Mo. State Rep.
b. Pueblo, Colo, 10/6/18; m. 6/6/64 to Patricia Lee Lyons; c. Phillip Patrick. Educ: Univ. Mo, Kansas City. Polit. & Govt. Pos: Mo. State Rep, 64-; chmn. and one of the organizers of Dem. Citizens Asn. Jackson Co, Inc. Bus. & Prof. Pos: Merchant, 39-57; prin. underwriter, United Funds Inc, Kansas City; real estate and ins. broker, Waddell & Reed, Inc. Mem: K. of C; Elks; St. Vincent DePaul Soc; Rockhurst Hon. Dirs. Asn. Rel: Catholic. Mailing Add: 5101 Brookwood, Kansas City, Mo. 64128. (1967)

SCALIA, ROBERT CHARLES R
Gen. Dep, Dept. of Housing and Urban Develop.
b. Dansville, N.Y, 8/28/34; s. Charles Scalia and Anna Walker S; m. 1/18/55 to Bonnie Elaine Anderson; c. Michael and Russell Mark. Educ: Monterey Peninsula Col, A.A, 60; Calif. State Col. at Fresno, B.A, 63; Univ. Calif, Santa Barbara, 67-68; Artus Hon. Econ. Soc. Polit. & Govt. Pos: Labor policy asn. trainee, Redevelop. Agency, Fresno, Calif, 62-63, relocation finance officer, Seaside, 63-64, exec. dir, Crescent City, 64-65 and Santa Maria, 65-69; gen. dep, Dept. of Housing and Urban Develop, 69- Bus. & Prof. Pos: Br. mgr, Sequoia Mortgage, San Jose, Calif, 64. Mil. Serv: Entered as Pvt, Army, 55, released as SP-3, 57, after serv. in Adj. Gen. Corps, Calif. and Alaska. Mem: Nat. Asn. of Housing and Redevelop. Off; steering cmt, Santa Maria Retarded Children's Coun; World Affairs Coun. Legal Res: 521 N. Ranch St, Santa Maria, Calif. 93454. Mailing Add: 2121 Paul Spring Rd, Alexandria, Va. 22307.

SCALISE, LAWRENCE F. D
b. Des Moines, Iowa, 4/25/33; m. 1961 to Joanne L. Bradley; c. Tamara. Educ: Univ. San Francisco; Univ. Iowa, B.A, 55; Univ. Iowa Law Sch, LL.B, 58; Delta Upsilon; Phi Delta Phi. Polit. & Govt. Pos: Mem, Consumer and Investor Protection Cmt, Nat. Asn. of Attorneys Gen; former chmn, Legis. Subcmt, Iowa Workmen's Compensation Adv. Cmt; asst. co. attorney, Polk Co, Iowa, 59-60; dir. law enforcement div, Iowa Liquor Control Cmn, 63-64; Iowa Attorney Gen, 64-66; del, Dem. Nat. Conv, 68. Bus. & Prof. Pos: Attorney-at-law, Des Moines, Iowa, 58 & 61-63. Mem: Iowa and Polk Co. Bar Asns; Int. Acad. of Law and Sci. Mailing Add: R.R. 1, Carlisle, Iowa 50047. (1967)

SCAMMAN, W. DOUGLAS R
N.H. State Rep.
b. Biddeford, Maine, 9/23/15; s. Walter A. Scamman and Elizabeth Hirst S; m. 9/14/38 to Frances Gile; c. Beatrice, W. Douglas, Jr. and Marlene. Educ: High Sch. Polit. & Govt. Pos: Chmn, Rockingham Co. Rep. Cmt, N.H, 65-67; mem, State Adv. Cmt; Town Chmn; mem, Sch. Bd, N.H, trustee, trust funds; N.H. State Rep. and Speaker of House. Bus. & Prof. Pos: Dairy farm owner and operator. Mem: Grange; Mason; DeMolay (Legion of Honor). Rel: Episcopal. Mailing Add: Stratham, N.H. 03885. (1967)

SCAMMAN, WALTER DOUGLAS, JR. R
N.H. State Rep.
b. Concord, N.H, 11/26/41; s. Walter Douglas Scamman and Frances Gile S; m. 4/13/63 to Stella Emanuel; c. Twins, Karl Michael and Kirk Quentin. Educ: Univ. N.H, B.A. in Polit. Sci, 64; Phi Mu Delta. Polit. & Govt. Pos: Auditor, Stratham Sch. Dist, N.H, 64-65; town auditor, Stratham, 65-67; chmn, Stratham Rep. Party, 65-69; mem, sch. bd, Stratham, 67-; N.H. State Rep, 69- Bus. & Prof. Pos: Owner and operator, Dairy Farm, Stratham, 64- Mem: Univ. N.H. Alumni Asn. Outstanding Young Farmer in N.H, 69. Rel: Congregational. Mailing Add: River Rd, Stratham, N.H. 03885.

SCAMMON, RICHARD MONTGOMERY
Dir. Elec. Research Center, Govt. Affairs Inst.
b. Minneapolis, Minn, 7/17/15; s. Richard Everingham Scammon and Julia Simms S; m. 2/20/52 to Mary Stark Allen; c. Anne Valerie. Educ: Univ. Minn, A.B, 35; Univ. Mich, M.A, 38; London Sch. Econ, cert, 36. Polit. & Govt. Pos: Dep. mil. gov, U.S. Off. Mil. Govt, Kreis Mergentheim, Württemberg, Germany, 45, polit. officer, Land Baden-Württemberg, 45-46, chief polit. activities br, Civil Admin. Div, Germany, 46-48; chief, Div. Research for West. Europe, Dept. of State, 48-55; dir, Elec. Research Center, Govt. Affairs Inst, 55-; chmn, U.S. Del. to Observe Elec. in U.S.S.R, 58; dir, Bur. Census, Dept. Commerce, 61-65; chmn, President's Cmn. on Registrn. and Voting Participation, 63 and Select Cmn. on West. Hemisphere Immigration, 66-68. Bus. & Prof. Pos: Asst. in polit. sci, Univ. Mich, 37-38; research secy, radio off, Univ. Chicago and assoc. producer, Univ. Chicago-NBC Round Table, 39-41. Mil. Serv: Army, 41-46, released as Capt. Publ: America at the Polls; ed, America Votes, vols. 1-7; contrib. to jour. Mem: Am. Polit. Sci. Asn; Am. Acad. Polit. and Soc. Sci; Acad. Polit. Sci; Can. Polit. Sci. Asn; Cosmos Club; mem. adv. cmt, Who's Who in Am. Polit, 67 & 69. Legal Res: 5508 Greystone St, Chevy Chase, Md. 20015. Mailing Add: 1619 Massachusetts Ave. N.W, Washington, D.C. 20036.

SCANLAN, ROBERT JOSEPH R
b. Miles City, Mont, 1/30/20; s. Joseph Dominic Scanlan and Sarah M. McDougal S; m. 1/27/43 to Florence Irene Boyd; c. R. Joseph, Salli P. (Mrs. Bennett) and Allan M. Educ: Custer Co. Jr. Col, 40-41. Polit. & Govt. Pos: Publicity chmn, Custer Co. Rep. Party, Mont, 60-65, finance chmn, 63-64; del, Mont. Rep. Conv, 64; del, Rep. Nat. Conv, 64; aide to U.S. Rep. John J. Rhodes, First Cong. Dist, Ariz, 66- Bus. & Prof. Pos: Publisher, Miles City Star, Miles City, Mont, 51-65; gen. mgr, Star Printing Co, Inc, 51-65, pres, 61-65. Mil. Serv: Entered as PO 3/C, Navy, 41, released as PO 1/C, 45, after serv. in Pac. Theater; Admiral's Commendation Medal; Pac. Theater Campaign Ribbon; Good Conduct Medal. Publ: Weekly personal column, Scanning the News With Scanlan, Miles City Daily Star, Mont, 60-65. Mem: Pres, Miles City C. of C, 65, Rotary, 56, Mont. Daily Newspaper Asn, 56-65 and Mont. Press Asn, 55; Am. Legion; DAV; Elks; Nat. Cowboy Hall of Fame. Rel: Catholic. Mailing Add: P.O. Box 1874, Scottsdale, Ariz. 85252.

SCANLON, EUGENE FRANCIS D
Pa. State Rep.
b. Pittsburgh, Pa, 12/19/24; s. William E. Scanlon and Marie A. Garrity S; m.

1/11/47 to Ann Boyle; c. Eugene F, II and Mary Barbara. Educ: Univ. Pittsburgh, B.A, 50, law sch, J.D, 53. Polit. & Govt. Pos: Pa. State Rep, 67- Bus. & Prof. Pos: Attorney-at-law, Pittsburgh, Pa, 53-; case ed, Pitt Law Rev. Mil. Serv: Entered as Pvt, Army, 43 released as 1st Lt, 46, after serv. in 86th Div, Philippine Islands, 45-46. Publ: 'Sex offender and Law', Pitt Law Rev, 49. Mem: Allegheny Co, Pa. and Am. Bar Asns; K. of C; Knights of Equity; Elks. Rel: Roman Catholic. Mailing Add: 1431 Termon Ave, Pittsburgh, Pa. 15212.

SCANLON, LEO JOHN D
Chmn, Crawford Co. Dem. Exec. Cmt, Ohio
b. Galion, Ohio, 2/22/03; s. Michael Edward Scanlon and Marie E. Dougherty S; wid; c. Maureen (Mrs. Robert Sharrock), Patricia (Mrs. Patrick McKeever) and Sheila (Mrs. Michael Brewer). Educ: Notre Dame Univ, Hoynes Col. of Law, J.D, 30. Polit. & Govt. Pos: City solicitor, New Washington, Ohio, 33-; spec. counsel, New Washington, 34-39; attorney, Home Owners Loan Corp, Crawford Co, 34-; prosecuting attorney, Crawford Co, Ohio, 35-53; chmn, Crawford Co. Dem. Exec. Cmt, 48-; city solicitor, Ontario, 58. Bus. & Prof. Pos: Attorney, Cath. Knights of Ohio. Mem: Crawford Co, Ohio State and Am. Bar Asns; Judicature Soc; Bucyrus Elks; Am. Legion; Crestline; Eagles; K. of C; Cath. Knights of Ohio; Crestline Dem. Club; Bucyrus Moose Club. Rel: Catholic. Mailing Add: 121 Pearl St, Crestline, Ohio 44827.

SCANLON, TERENCE J. D
b. St. Joseph, Mo, 7/26/31; s. Byron B. Scanlon and Margaret S. Zirkle S; m. 3/8/69 to Doris J. Blasdel; c. Kerry O'Connell. Educ: Wichita State Univ, B.A, 56. Polit. & Govt. Pos: Admin. asst, Water Dept, City of Wichita, Kans, 56-58, admin. asst. to City Mgr, 58-59, Budget Dir, 59-62, exec. asst. to City Mgr, 62-63 and dir. of Admin, 63-66; exec. dir, Dept. of Admin, State of Kans, 67-; del, Dem. Nat. Conv, 68; mem, Kans. Cmn. on Interstate Coop, currently; secy, Kans. State Finance Coun, currently; mem, Kans. Turnpike Authority, currently. Mil. Serv: Entered as Pvt, Army, 53, released as Cpl, 55, after serv. in Artil, U.S. Mem: K. of C; Elks. Rel: Catholic. Mailing Add: 1320 W. 27th, A-4, Topeka, Kans. 66611.

SCANNELL, JOSEPH JOHN D
b. Wilmington, Del, 4/2/15; s. Joseph Cornelius Scannell and Eva Eckrich S; m. 9/23/38 to Anne Curlett; c. Eva Judith, Kathleen, Joseph, Susanna and Teresa. Educ: Univ. Del, B.A, 37. Polit. & Govt. Pos: Claims exam, Unemploy. Compensation Cmn, Del, 38-46, off. mgr, 46, chief of placement, 47-52; mem, Gov. Aid to the Physically Handicapped Cmt, 46-50; adj. gen, Del, 50-; cand, U.S. House of Rep, 52. Bus. & Prof. Pos: Instr. bus. law and Eng, Beacon Col, Wilmington, 37-38. Mil. Serv: 2nd Lt, Army Res, 37; Capt, Army, 41-45, 198th C.A.C. Regt, S.W. Pac, 41-43, instr, Anti-aircraft Artil. Sch, 43-44; Mil. Govt, Tinian, Philippines, Japan and Korea, 45; 1st Lt. to Maj. Gen, Del. Nat. Guard. Mem: Am. Legion; VFW; K. of C. Mailing Add: 2010 Monroe Place, Wilmington, Del. 19802. (1967)

SCANNELL, WILLIAM FRANCIS R
Secy, Ill. Rep. State Cent. Cmt.
b. Chicago, Ill, 11/23/23; s. Albert Terrence Scannell and Florence O'Connor S; m. to Louise Bouchard; c. Frances and Terrence. Educ: Kenyon Col, 45; Univ. Va. Law Sch, LL.B, 49; Sigma Phi Epsilon. Polit. & Govt. Pos: Committeeman, Ill. Rep. State Cent. Cmt, 62 and secy, 69-; engr, agreements div. and admin. asst, right-of-way div, Cook Co. Hwy. Dept, Ill, 68; mem, Med. Center Cmn. and spec. asst. to attorney gen, State of Ill, 69- Bus. & Prof. Pos: Lawyer, gen. practice, Va, 48 and Ill, 49-; pres, Archer Iron Works, Inc, Chicago, Ill, 50-67. Mil. Serv: Entered as Pvt, Army, 43, released as Lt.(jg), after serv. in Engrs. Corps, ETO; Lt.(jg), (Ret), Naval Res. Mem: Am, Va, Ill. and Chicago Bar Asns; Am. Legion. Mailing Add: 7216 S. Shore Dr, Chicago, Ill. 60649.

SCARBOROUGH, DAN IRVING D
Fla. State Sen.
b. Hortense, Ga, 2/6/33; s. Robert H. Scarborough and Vivian Strickland S; m. 12/21/52 to Virginia Louise Zipperer; c. John Robert, Vicki Elizabeth, Lynn and Karen. Educ: Univ. Fla, 52-53. Polit. & Govt. Pos: Fla. State Rep, 66-68; Fla. State Sen, Tenth Dist, 68- Bus. & Prof. Pos: Owner-pres, Answer Phone of Jacksonville, St. Augustine, currently. Mil. Serv: Sgt, Marine Corps Res, 52-59. Mem: Jr. C. of C; Masons; Scottish Rite; Shrine; Fla-Ga. High Sch. Football Off. Asn; St. Johns Flying Club. Rel: Methodist. Legal Res: 4538 Ortega Farms Circle, Jacksonville, Fla. 32210. Mailing Add: 404 West Monroe St, Jacksonville, Fla. 32202.

SCARBOROUGH, HOMER M, JR. D
Ga. State Rep.
b. Macon, Ga, 7/20/41; s. Homer M. Scarborough, Sr. and Mrs. Vivian Keeling Tew; single. Educ: Univ. Ga, J.D, 66. Polit. & Govt. Pos: Ga. State Rep, 69- Bus. & Prof. Pos: Attorney-at-law, Macon, Ga, 66- Mem: Am, Ga. and Macon Bar Asns; Am. Trial Lawyer's Asn; Phi Alpha Delta; Elks; Moose; Eagles; Macon Morning Optimist Club; Macon's Young Movers. Rel: Methodist. Mailing Add: 418 American Federal Bldg, Macon, Ga. 31201.

SCARBOROUGH, JOHN C, JR. D
b. Pinehurst, Ga, 9/14/29; s. John C. Scarborough and Mary Wilkes S; m. 10/6/51 to Marion Elizabeth Bartlett; c. Richard Wilson and Teresa Michelle. Educ: N.Ga. Col; Mercer Univ; Univ. Ga, LL.B, 53; Phi Alpha Delta; Omicron Delta Kappa; Blue Key; Gridiron; Scabbard & Blade. Polit. & Govt. Pos: City attorney, 59- and co. attorney, 60-; Ga. State Rep, 61-66. Bus. & Prof. Pos: Attorney. Mil. Serv: Cpl, Marine Corps, 46-48; 1st Lt, Army, Korea, 53-56. Mem: Jr. C. of C; Moose; Kiwanis. Rel: Baptist. Mailing Add: Roberta, Ga. 31078. (1967)

SCARBOROUGH, ROBERT BOWMAN D
S.C. State Sen.
b. Charleston, S.C, 6/28/28; s. Yancey Wilcox Scarborough and Lillie Thomas S; m. 1/10/53 to Elizabeth Martin; c. Wallace Berry and Robert Bowman, Jr. Educ: The Citadel, A.B, 50. Polit. & Govt. Pos: Mem, President's Traffic Safety Cmt, 56 and S.C. State Safety Cmt, 63; S.C. State Rep, 63-66, first v.chmn, Educ. and Pub. Works Cmt, S.C. House of Rep; S.C. State Sen, 66- Bus. & Prof. Pos: Agent, Cosmopolitan Life Ins. Co, 50-53, spec. agent, 54; secy-treas, Atlantic Coast Life Ins. Co. Mil. Serv: Entered as 2nd Lt, Nat. Guard, 50, released as Capt, 63. Mem: Bd. gov, Nat. Red Cross, 66-69, Cmt. of Resolutions for Nat. Conv, 65, Cmt. on Conv. Orgn, 63, Southeast. Area Adv. Coun, 62-65, chmn, S.Atlantic Blood Adv. Cmt, 60-63 and Home Serv. Cmt, 60-62, Blood Procurement Study Panel, 61, chmn, Charleston Co. Chap, 58-59, v.chmn, 56-57, Disaster Chmn, 53-55; chmn, West Ashley Bus. Group, United Fund, 56; secy. and wearer Honor Ring, Sumter Guards; bd. dirs, Cancer Soc, 56-59, crusade chmn, 52; Charleston Citadel Club; bd. dirs, Asn. Citadel Men, 58-59, v.pres, 67, pres, 68, athletic adv. cmt, 61-64, for dist. at large, 65-66; v.pres, Charleston Navy League, 59-62, pres, 62-64; Mason (32°), Landmark Lodge 76 F&AM, Scottish Rite, Omar Temple Shrine; bd. mem, Salvation Army, 61-67; chmn, Episcopal Church Warden Asn, 62; Charleston Country Club; pres, Coastal Carolina Fair, 57-61; Carolina Yacht Club; Hibernians; v.pres, Charleston C. of C, 62, v.pres. for commun. betterment, 64; pres, Charleston Exchange Club, 57; secy, S.C. State Exchange Club, 58, v.pres, 59, pres, 60; bd. dirs, Nat. Exchange Club, 62-67, v.pres, 68, pres, 69, Citizenship Study Panel, 58, chmn, Fed. Youth Rehabilitation Study Panel, 59; Charleston Alert, 61-62. Man of Year, Exchange Club, 55, 58 and 59; Distinguished Serv. Award, Jr. C. of C, 62. Rel: Episcopal. Legal Res: 26 Broughton Rd, Charleston, S.C. 29407. Mailing Add: P.O. Box 855, Charleston, S.C. 29402.

SCARCELLI, VINCENT F. D
b. Phila, 6/16/14; s. Frank Scarcelli and Rose Dodara S; m. to Nancy Sue Russo; c. Vincent Jr, Philomena, Patricia. Educ: Secretarial Sch. of Phila; Mastbaum Voc. Sch. Polit. & Govt. Pos: Pa. State Rep, 54-67; 48th Ward Dem. Exec. Cmt. Bus. & Prof. Pos: Owner, mgr, confectionery bus; operated a butter and egg route; supervised receiving and shipping depts, Edward Tailoring Co, 14 yrs. Mem: Shop Steward, Int. Brotherhood of Teamsters, Local 830 AFL; Bartenders and Hotel Workers Union, AFL; worker for St. Mary's Orphanage; Ambler; Order of Brotherly Love; Hon, mem, VFW, Post 3094. Rel: Catholic; League of the Sacred Heart of Jesus; Holy Name Soc. Mailing Add: 2103 S. Lambert St, Philadelphia, Pa. 19145. (1967)

SCARFF, ROSS WILSON R
Md. State Del.
b. Fallston, Md, 6/15/26; s. George Ross Scarff and Addie Wilson S; single. Polit. & Govt. Pos: Md. State Del, 62- Bus. & Prof. Pos: Owner, grocery store, 53-66. Mil. Serv: Entered as Pvt, 51, released as Cpl, 53. Mem: Lions; Ruritan; Farm Bur; Tuberc. Asn. of Md. Rel: Methodist. Mailing Add: Upper Cross Rds, Fallston, Md. 21047. (1967)

SCARIANO, ANTHONY D
Ill. State Rep.
c. three. Educ: George Wash. Univ; Georgetown Univ. Law Sch. Polit. & Govt. Pos: Mem, Wash. staff, U.S. Sen. Scott W. Lucas; asst. U.S. dist. attorney under Otto Kerner, U.S. Dist. Attorney for North. Dist, 5 years; spec. counsel, Chicago Heights bd. dir, Immigrants' Serv. League and exec. bd; attorney, Sch. Dist. 169; Ill. State Rep, currently. Bus. & Prof. Pos: Pvt. law practice. Mil. Serv: Army Officer, Allied Mil. Govt, O.S.S. unit in Italy. Mem: Boy Scouts. Voted one of the outstanding freshmen of the Gen. Assembly by Ill. Legis. Correspondents Asn, 57; named one of Ill. Best Legislators, 59th session, by Independent Voters of Ill, 61, hon. mention all other terms; James M. Yard Brotherhood Award, Nat. Coun. of Christians and Jews. Mailing Add: 38 W. Rocket Circle, Park Forest, Ill. 60466.

SCHABARUM, PETER F. R
Calif. State Assemblyman
b. Los Angeles, Calif, 1929; married; c. Three. Educ: Univ. Calif, Berkeley, B.S. in Bus. Admin. Polit. & Govt. Pos: Calif. State Assemblyman, 67-; mem, Calif. Rep. State Cent. Cmt, currently. Bus. & Prof. Pos: Pres. and owner of real estate and investment co. Mem: Int. Coun. of Shopping Centers; former mem. Covina Rotary. Former mem. San Francisco 49'er Pro-Football Team; former All-Coast Football Player. Mailing Add: 573 S. Barranca Ave, Covina, Calif. 91722.

SCHACHTER, MARVIN D
Mem, Calif. Dem. State Cent. Cmt.
b. N.Y.C, 5/17/24; s. Max Schachter and Fanny Javits S; m. 5/26/56 to Esther Adler; c. Pamela and Amanda. Educ: Univ. Chicago, Cert. in Russian Studies, 43; Univ. Minn, Cert. in German Studies, 44; Brooklyn Col, B.A; Univ. Colo, M.A, 50; Cambridge Univ, Econ. Research, 51-52; Phi Gamma Mu. Polit. & Govt. Pos: State issues chmn, Calif. Dem. Coun, 58-59, state legis. chmn, 67-68; mem, Kennedy Campaign Cmt, 60; chmn, 42nd Assembly Dist. Dem. Party, 60-61; mem, McCarthy Campaign Cmt, 68; mem, Cranston Campaign Cmt, 68; mem, Bradley Campaign cmt, 69; mem, Calif. Dem. State Cent. Cmt, 69- Bus. & Prof. Pos: Buyer, May Co, 55-62; merchandise mgr, Shoe Corp. of Am, 62-63; v.pres, R.B. Mfg, Co, 63-64 and Vol. Merchandise, Inc, 64- Mil. Serv: Entered as Pvt, Army, 43, released Pfc, 46, after serv. in Mil. Intel. Mem: Am. Econ. Asn; Am. Civil Liberties Union of S. Calif. (bd. dirs); Los Angeles Town Hall. Rel: Jewish. Mailing Add: 300 California Terrace, Pasadena, Calif. 91105.

SCHACKMANN, GEORGE SEVERINE D
b. Newton, Ill, 12/30/09; s. John Charles Schackmann and Sophia Mary Speasl S; m. 3/5/48 to Lucile June Danner; c. Cinda Lu and George Severine, Jr. Polit. & Govt. Pos: Former Mayor, Danville, Ill. Mil. Serv: Entered as Pvt, Army, 42, released as S/Sgt, 46, after serv. in S.Pac; S.Pac. Bronze Star. Mem: Painters Local 398 (pres, 48-50); Am. Legion (comdr, 47-49); Ill. Vets. Cmn; del, Trades and Labor Coun, 48-50; adv. counsel, Ill. Munic. League, 63-67; Moose; K. of C; Kiwanis; Vermilion Co. Museum Soc; Wabash Valley Asn; VFW; Cent. Ill. Mayors Asn; exec. cmt, Route 1 Developing Asn. Rel: Catholic. Mailing Add: 513 N. Hazel St, Danville, Ill. 61832.

SCHADEBERG, HENRY CARL R
U.S. Rep, Wis.
b. Manitowoc, Wis, 10/12/13; s. George Schadeberg, Sr. and Rosa Brockhoff S; m. 6/18/38 to Ruth Eleanor Hamilton; c. Kenwood Dudley, Nancy Jo, Christine Rose and Ramona Rae. Educ: Carroll Col, B.A, 38; Garrett Biblical Sem, B.D, 41; Pioneer Club of Carroll Col. Polit. & Govt. Pos: U.S. Rep, First Cong. Dist, Wis, 61-65 & 67- Bus. & Prof. Pos: Pastor, Lyons Circuit, Wis,

38-40, Oconto Circuit, 40-42, Evansville Methodist Church, 42-43 and Plymouth Congregational Church, Burlington, 46-60; pres, Res. and Pub. Affairs, Serv. Inc, 65-67. Mil. Serv: Entered as Lt.(jg), Navy, 43, released as Lt. Comdr, 46, after serv. as Sr. Chaplain, U.S. Naval Hosp, Bainbridge, Md, 52-53; Capt, Naval Res.(Ret); 2 Battle Stars, Asian Theater for Philippine Area; Letter of Commendation. Mem: YMCA; Mil. Chaplain's Asn; Reserve Officer's Asn; Rotary; Kiwanis; VFW Post 2823; Post 79, Racine Co, First Dist. and Dept. of Wis. Chaplain, Am. Legion; Chaplain, Dept. of Racine Co. Coun, Boy Scouts, Wis. Rel: Congregational; Clergyman. Mailing Add: 333 Emerson St, Burlington, Wis. 53105.

SCHAEFER, HARRY H. D
b. Weld Co, Colo, 12/28/14; m. to Nettie; c. Two. Educ: High Sch. Polit. & Govt. Pos: Former Wyo. State Rep; Brotherhood of Locomotive Engrs. Legis. Rep; chmn, Wyo. Citizens Cmt. for Reapportionment. Bus. & Prof. Pos: Locomotive Engr, UP. Mem: former mem, Toastmaster Int. Rel: Lutheran. Mailing Add: 1612 E. 18th St, Cheyenne, Wyo. 82001. (1967)

SCHAEFER, MIKE R
City Councilman, San Diego, Calif.
b. San Diego, Calif, 3/25/38; s. Bert J. Schaefer (deceased) and Mary Alice Downes S; single. Educ: Univ. Notre Dame, 56-57; Univ. Calif, Berkeley, B.S. in Acct, 60; Georgetown Univ. Law Center, J.D, 63; Alpha Phi Omega; Alpha Kappa Psi. Polit. & Govt. Pos: Chmn, Univ. Calif. Young Rep, 60; financial analyst, U.S. Securities & Exchange Cmn, 62; dep. city attorney, San Diego, Calif, 64-65, city councilman, 65-; dir, City-Co. Camp Cmn. and mem, Pub. Bd. of Health; cand, U.S. House of Rep, 37th Dist, Calif, 68. Bus. & Prof. Pos: Partner, Ludecke & Schaefer, Attorneys, San Diego, 65- Publ: 'You are Before the Council,' Dicta, 67. Mem: Am. and San Diego Co. Bar Asns; Am. Juridical Soc; Kiwanis; State Bar of Calif. Am. Jurisprudence Award for Excellence in Tax Studies, 62. Rel: Catholic. Legal Res: 2350 Sixth Ave, San Diego, Calif. 92101. Mailing Add: 1450 Fourth Ave, San Diego, Calif. 92101.

SCHAEFER, MRS. ORVILLE TYLER D
V.Chmn, Ga. Dem. State Exec. Cmt.
b. Atlanta, 9/2/08; d. Orville Ernest Tyler and Hattie Isabel Horne T; m. 10/7/34 to William Bruce Schaefer; c. William Bruce and Tyler. Educ: Brenau Col, Gainsville, Ga, A.B, 30; Delta Kappa Gamma; Delta Delta Delta; Zeta Phi Eta, award for outstanding contribution in chosen field, 52. Polit. & Govt. Pos: Charter mem, Ga. Cmt, Nat. Coun. Crime and Delinquency; dramatic platform reader, Dem. Nat. Conv, 32; Ga. chmn, Mid-Century White House Conf. Children and Youth, 50; sponsored and presided at first Ga. Conf. of Handicapped Children, 55; del, Dem. Nat. Conv, 56 & 60; participant, Nat. Health Forum, N.Y.C, 57-58; mem, Ga. Bd. of Educ, 57-; chmn, Gov. of Ga. Conf. on Recreation and Leisure Time, 58; v.chmn, Ga. Dem. State Exec. Cmt, 58-; mem, Dem. Nat. Cmt. for Ga. and mem. exec. cmt, 60-63; Cmnr. of Welfare, Ga, 63- Bus. & Prof. Pos: Trustee, Brenau Col; summer instr, Univ. Ga, 30; instr. speech, Gordon Mil. Col, 30-31. Publ: 'Volunteers at Work' and 'Volunteers Manual,' 57. Mem: DAR; UDC; PTA; v.pres. and trustee, Nat. Soc. Crippled Children and Adults; Ga. Fedn. Womens Clubs; chmn. legis. cmt, Am. Med. Asn. Auxiliary; nat. pres, Alumnae Asn. of Brenau Col; Cushman Club, Brenau Col; Garden Club; Women's Libr. Club, Toccoa. Named Woman of the Year, Toccoa C. of C, 56; The Great Georgian Award, WSB. Radio, Atlanta, Ga, 69. Legal Res: Hillcrest, Point View, Lakemont, Ga. 30552. Mailing Add: 930 18th Ave. S, Naples, Fla. 33940.

SCHAEFER, ROBERT 'BOB' D
b. Seattle, Wash, 1930; m. to Sally S; c. three. Educ: Willamette U. Law Sch; Phi Delta Phi; Phi Delta Theta. Polit. & Gov. Pos: Wash. State Rep, 4th term, until 66; Speaker of the House elect, 65. Bus. & Prof. Pos: Attorney. Mil. Serv: Army; Res. for 7 yrs. Mailing Add: 122 N. Devine, Vancouver, Wash. 98661. (1967)

SCHAEFFER, FRANK E, JR. D
b. Milwaukee, Wis, 2/1/05. Educ: Milwaukee Voc. Sch. Polit. & Govt. Pos: Del, Dem. State Conv, 38, 44-52 & 58-62; del, Federated Trade Coun; Wis. State Assemblyman, 44-54 & 58-68. Bus. & Prof. Pos: Employee, Milwaukee Brewing Co; bldg. supt, 20 years; painting contractor, 18 years. Mem: Brewery Workers Union; Red Cross; Civil Defense Coun; Bldg. Serv. Union (past v.pres). Mailing Add: 1623 W. Wisconsin Ave, Milwaukee, Wis. 53233. (1967)

SCHAETZEL, J. ROBERT
Ambassador to European Commun.
b. Holtville, Calif, 1/28/17; m. to Imogen Spencer; c. Ann Hathaway and Wendy. Educ: Pomona Col, B.A, 39, hon. LL.D, 66; Univ. Mexico, 40; Harvard Univ, 40-42. Polit. & Govt. Pos: Admin. analyst, Bur. of the Budget, 42-45; spec. asst. to dir, Off. of Int. Trade Policy, 45-50; spec. asst. to Asst. Secy. of State for Econ. Affairs, 50-55; student, Nat. War Col, 54-55; head, Peaceful Uses Sect, Off. of Spec. Asst. to Secy. of State for Atomic Energy and Outer Space, 55-59 & 60; task forces for President Elect Kennedy, 60-61; sr. asst. to Under Secy. for Econ. Affairs, 61; spec. asst. to Under Secy. of State, 61-62; Dep. Asst. Secy. of State for Atlantic Affairs, 62-66; ambassador to European Commun, 66- Recipient Rockefeller Pub. Serv. Award, study of European integration movement, Brussels, 59-60. Mailing Add: U.S. Mission to European Communties, APO New York 09667.

SCHAFER, ALAN HELLER D
Chmn, Dillon Co. Dem. Party, S.C.
b. Baltimore, Md, 1/12/14; s. Samuel I. Schafer and Wilhelmina Heller S; m. to Helen Swinson (deceased); c. William H, Richard H. and Frederic R. Educ: Univ. S.C, A.B. in Journalism, 34; Sigma Delta Chi; Pi Lambda Phi; Clariosophic Soc. Polit. & Govt. Pos: Chmn, Dillon Co. Dem. Party, S.C. and Exec. Cmt, 60-; del, Dem. Nat. Conv, 68. Bus. & Prof. Pos: Chmn and pres, Schafer Distributing Co, Inc, 35-, Palmetto Properties, Inc. and Modern Music Co, 46-69, South of the Border Co, 50- and Ace-Hi Advertising Corp, 60- Mil. Serv: Entered as Pvt, Army, 43, released as Pfc, 45, after serving in Fourth Serv. Command, Atlanta, Ga, 43-45. Mem: Am. Legion; VFW; Mason; Shrine(Bd. Gov. and Shrine Bowl, Greenville Crippled Children's Hosp). Rel: Jewish. Legal Res: Hwy. 57, Dillon, S.C. 29536. Mailing Add: South of the Border, Dillon, S.C. 29536.

SCHAFER, ERNEST ELMER R
Minn. State Rep.
b. Martin Co, 1/13/14; s. John D. Schafer and Dora Finke S; m. 8/24/37 to Evelyn Boeck; c. Gary, Darrel, Nancy, Janet (Mrs. Senst), Kathleen, Louise and Bill. Educ: Buffalo High Lake Sch, 4 years. Polit. & Govt. Pos: Rep. Chmn, Renville Co, Minn, 56-62; Minn. State Rep, Renville Co, 62- Bus. & Prof. Pos: Farmer. Mem: Farm Bur; pres, Buffalo Lake Livestock Asn; dir, Fed. Land Bank of Redwood Falls. Rel: United Methodist. Mailing Add: Buffalo Lake, Minn. 55314.

SCHAFER, JOHN ROBERT 'BOB' R
Colo. State Rep.
b. Denver, Colo, 7/8/12; s. John George Schafer and Zena Kulp S; m. 8/23/36 to Erma I. Garlick; c. John Keith and Robert Gary. Educ: Colo. State Univ, 30-31; Sigma Phi Epsilon. Polit. & Govt. Pos: Pres, Hugo Sch. Bd, Colo, 59-61; Colo. State Rep, 61- Bus. & Prof. Pos: Dir, First Nat. Bank, Hugo, Colo, 54-; pres, State and Local Cattlemen's, 57-58; dir, Nat. West. Stock Show, Denver, 58- Rel: Methodist. Mailing Add: Boyero, Colo. 80806. (1967)

SCHAFER, MRS. MARIAN N. See BERTSCH, MARIAN N.

SCHAFER, NEAL EDWIN R
Chmn, Belmont Co. Exec. and Cent. Cmts, Ohio
b. Marietta, Ohio, 1/23/12; s. William Schafer and Jessie McCullick S; m. 3/4/38 to Evelyn Lucille Lewis; c. Elaina (Mrs. McClarin) and Neal E, Jr. Educ: Bridgeport Schs. Polit. & Govt. Pos: Mem, Village Coun, Bridgeport, Ohio, 48-52, mayor, 52-54; chmn, Belmont Co. Exec. and Cent. Cmts, Ohio, currently. Mem: Eagles; F&AM; Scottish Rite; Shrine; Rotary. Rel: Presbyterian. Mailing Add: 707 Howard St, Bridgeport, Ohio 43912.

SCHAFFER, LARRY D. R
Chmn, Holt Co. Rep. Party, Nebr.
b. Emmet, Nebr, 10/12/28; s. Dewey Cramer Schaffer and Elizabeth Gribble S; m. 10/23/48 to Lois Cole; c. Elizabeth and Dewey, II. Educ: Univ. Nebr, 46-47; Sigma Nu. Polit. & Govt. Pos: Chmn, Holt Co. Rep. Party, Nebr, 66- Mem: Boy Scouts (dist. chmn, Sandhills Dist); Mason; Shrine; Am. Quarter Horse Asn; Nebr. Stockgrowers; Sandhills Cattle Asn; Am. Nat. Cattleman's Asn. Rel: Presbyterian. Mailing Add: Box 587, O'Neill, Nebr, 68763.

SCHALLER, BARRY RAYMOND R
Chmn, Branford Rep. Town Cmt, Conn.
b. Hartford, Conn, 11/23/38; s. Raymond T. Schaller and Mildred McCollum S; m. 9/1/62 to Deborah Douglas; c. Katherine Deborah, Jane Elizabeth and Peter Douglas. Educ: Yale Col, B.A, 60, Law Sch, LL.B, 63; Phi Delta Phi. Polit. & Govt. Pos: State Youth Chmn, Conn. Alsop for Gov. Cmt, 62; coord, Stelio Selmona for Cong, 66; chmn, Branford Rep. Town Cmt, 67-; counsel to Minority Leader, Conn. House of Rep, 69- Bus. & Prof. Pos: Partner, Bronson & Rice, Attorneys, New Haven, 63- Mem: New Haven Co, Conn. and Am. Bar Asns; Conn, U.S. Dist. and U.S. Supreme Courts; U.S. Court of Appeals, Second Circuit; Graduates Club; C. of C; Yale Club; Lions. Rel: Episcopal. Mailing Add: 114 Flax Mill Rd, Branford, Conn. 06405.

SCHALLER, JEROME DONALD D
b. St. Paul, Minn, 6/27/25; s. David A. Schaller and Gertrude Lack S; m. 10/23/48 to Helen Marie Hanelt; c. Stephanie and Sandra Jean. Educ: St. Thomas Col, B.A, 49. Polit. & Govt. Pos: Exec. asst. to Mayor, St. Paul, Minn, 50-53; alternate del, Dem. Nat. Conv, 56, del, 60 & 64; admin. asst. to U.S. Rep. J.Karth, 58-64; Fourth Dist. Chmn, Dem-Farmer-Labor Party, Minn, 60, mem. exec. cmt, 60-61; admin. asst. to Sen. Walter Mondale, 64-66; consultant for V.Pres. H.H. Humphrey, 67. Bus. & Prof. Pos: Asst. to advert. mgr, Weyerhaeuser Sales Co, 48-50; pub. rels. dir, Minn. AFL-CIO Fedn. of Labor, 53-58; v.pres, Walter Butler Co, St. Paul, Minn, 60; mgr, Govt. Rels. 3M Co, Wash, D.C, 67-; mem. bd. dir, Universal Syst. Inc, currently. Mil. Serv: Entered as Pvt, Army Air Force, 43, released as Sgt, 46. Mem: Int. Pub. Rels. Asn; Nat. Defense Exec. Reserve; Wash, D.C. Georgetown Club; St. Paul Athletic Club; Wash, D.C. Nat. Capital Dem. Club. Rel: Catholic. Mailing Add: 5020 37th Place, Washington, D.C. 20023.

SCHAPELER, RUBEN D
b. Bates Co, Mo, 12/28/20; m. 5/21/43 to Norma Clutter; c. Judith and Kenneth. Educ: Fort Scott Jr. Col, Kans. Polit. & Govt. Pos: Chmn, Butler Co. Dem. Party, Mo, 58-60; Butler City Clerk; Mo. State Rep, 62-66. Bus. & Prof. Pos: Farming; licensed rep. with Waddell & Reed, Inc; farm implement bus, 45-62. Mil. Serv: Navy, 42-45. Mem: Mason; Am. Legion; C. of C. Rel: Presbyterian. Mailing Add: 607 W. Dakota St, Butler, Mo. 64730. (1967)

SCHATZ, HAROLD H. R
b. Brooklyn, N.Y, 5/20/11; married; c. Two. Educ: N.Y.C. City Schs. Polit. & Govt. Pos: N.H. State Rep, -67. Bus. & Prof. Pos: Retired Bn. Chief New York Fire Dept; statistician, Pan Am. World Airways, N.Y.C, 66- Mem: Brooklyn F&AM; N.Y.C. Fire Chiefs'Asn; N.Y.C. Uniformed Firemen's Asn. Rel: Lutheran. Mailing Add: 600 Hylan Boulevard, Staten Island, N.Y. 10305.

SCHAUFELE, WILLIAM EVERETT, JR.
b. Lakewood, Ohio, 12/7/23; s. William Elias Schaufele and Lillian Bergen S; m. 2/1/50 to Heather Moon; c. Steven William and Peter Henry. Educ: Yale, B.A, 48; Columbia Univ, M.I.A, 50. Polit. & Govt. Pos: Career officer, Dept. of State For. Serv, 50-; resident officer, Pfaffenhefen an der Ilm, Germany, 50-52 and Augsburg, 52; v.consul, Duesseldorf, 52-53 and Munich, 53-56; State Dept, 56-59; consul, Casablanca, 59-63 & Bukavu, 63-64; off. in charge Congolese Affairs, 64-65; dep. dir. Cent. African Affairs, 65-67; dir, Cent.W. African Affairs, 67-69; appointed by President, U.S. Ambassador to Upper Volta, 69. Mil. Serv: Army, 43-46, ETO. Legal Res: 32150 Lake Rd, Avon Lake, Ohio 44012. Mailing Add: Ouagadougou, Dept. of State, Washington, D.C. 20521.

SCHAUS, THOMAS MARTIN D
b. Milwaukee, Wis, 6/7/37; s. Thomas R. Schaus and Alice O. LeBlanc S; single. Educ: Marquette Univ, B.S, 59; Wis. Univ, Madison, LL.B, 62. Polit. & Govt. Pos: Wis. State Assemblyman, Milwaukee, 5th Dist, 65-66. Mil. Serv: Entered as Pvt, Marine Corps Res, 53, released as Pfc, 61, after

serv. in 5th SP Inf. Bn, Milwaukee. Mem: Brotherhood of R.R. Trainmen; K. of C. Rel: Catholic. Mailing Add: 2666 N. 36th St, Milwaukee, Wis. 53404. (1967)

SCHAW, WALTER A. R
Committeeman, Ill. Rep. Cent. Cmt.
b. E.Chicago, Ind, 11/2/34; s. Walter H. Schaw and Mary Barkal S; m. 9/14/68 to Kathleen McConnell; c. Debra Lynne. Educ: Valparaiso Univ, B.A, 59; Theta Chi; Capt, Football Team, 57; Sigma Delta Chi. Polit. & Govt. Pos: Mem. Bd. Supvr, Kane Co, Ill, 65-66; committeeman, Ill. Rep. Cent. Cmt, 67-; Presidential elector, 13th Cong. Dist. Rep. Party, Ill, 68. Bus. & Prof. Pos: Managing Ed, Journal Newspapers, Lansing, Ill, 59-61; copy ed, Chicago's American, 62; book ed, American Foundrymen's Soc, Des Plaines, Ill, 63, admin. asst. and asst. secy, 64-68, secy, 68- Mil. Serv: Entered as Pvt, Army, 54, released as S/Sgt, 62, after serv. in 395th Evacuation Hosp, Army Res, 61-62; Citation from Hospital Comdr, Beaumont General Hosp, El Paso, Tex, as Chief Medical NCO, Surgical Sect, 395th Evacuation Hosp. Mem: Asn. of Indust. Advertiser; Honorary mem, National Thespian Soc; Ill. Newspaper Asn; Rep. clubs of Palatine Twp. and Dundee Twp; Lions, Lansing. Rel: Lutheran. Mailing Add: 214 N. Haman Rd, Barrington, Ill. 60010.

SCHECHTER, MAURICE D
Mo. State Sen.
b. St. Louis, Mo, 6/27/07; m. 6/28/31 to Bess Ragin Schechter; c. Stanley I, Judith Kay (Mrs. Siegel); grandchildren, Debora Jean and Elizabeth Ellen Schechter and Nancee Hope and Stephen Siegel. Educ: Wash. Univ; City Col. of Law and Finance, LL.B. Polit. & Govt. Pos: Charter mem. and first pres, Creve Coeur Twp. Dem. Club, St. Louis Co; Mo. State Rep, 34-38; Mo. State Sen, 60- Bus. & Prof. Pos: Practicing attorney, 28- Mem: Scottish Rite; Mason; Shrine; Am, Mo. and St. Louis Bar Asns; B'nai B'rith; Lawyers Asn. of St. Louis. Rel: B'nai Amoona Congregation. Mailing Add: 41 Country Fair Lane, Creve Coeur, Mo. 63141. (1967)

SCHECTER, SHELDON DALE D
Co-Chmn, Ohio New Dem. Coalition
b. Cleveland, Ohio, 12/1/26; s. Morris Schecter and Betty Romanoff S; m. 9/29/63 to Renee Louise Fried; c. Mark Byron, David Michael and Cynthia Elise. Educ: West. Reserve Univ, B.A, 50 and LL.B, 53; Pi Sigma Alpha; Omicron Sigma Alpha; Tau Epsilon Rho. Polit. & Govt. Pos: V.chmn, Cleveland Am. for Dem. Action, Ohio, 67-68; Ohio and Cleveland Co-chmn, McCarthy for Pres. Cmt, 68; alternate del, Dem. Nat. Conv, 68; co-chmn, Ohio New Dem. Coalition, currently. Mil. Serv: Pvt, Army, 45-46, with serv. in Mil. Police, Italy; Good Conduct Medal; Mediterranean Theatre Medal. Mem: Ohio, Cleveland, Cuyahoga and Vet. Bar Asns; Citizen League; City Club. Rel: Jewish. Mailing Add: 3605 Ingleside Rd, Shaker Heights, Ohio 44122.

SCHEDLER, SPENCER JAIME R
Asst. Secy. of the Air Force for Financial Mgt.
b. Manila, Philippine Islands, 10/23/33; s. Edmund W. Schedler; m. 8/30/69 to Judy Hamilton. Educ: Univ. Tulsa, B.S. in Petroleum Eng, 55; Harvard Bus. Sch, M.B.A, 62; Phi Kappa Gamma; Sword and Key. Polit. & Govt. Pos: Asst. Secy. of the Air Force for Financial Mgt, 69- Bus. & Prof. Pos: Petroleum engr, Humble Oil & Refining Co, Tulsa, 58-60; cost analyst and asst. to chmn. of the bd, Houston Oil Field Material Co, Tex, 62; financial analyst, Sinclair Oil Corp, Tulsa, Okla, 63, asst. dir. of budgets, N.Y.C, 65, mgr, budgets and financial analysis, 66, mgr, budgets and analysis, 67. Mil. Serv: Entered as 2nd Lt, Air Force, 55, released as 1st Lt, 58, after serv. in 41st Fighter-Interceptor Squadron, Guam, 57-58; Capt, Air Force Res. Mailing Add: SAFFM, Room 4E 978, Pentagon, Washington, D.C. 20330.

SCHEER, GEORGE M. D
Chmn, Putnam Co. Dem. Exec. Cmt, Ga.
b. Richmond, Va, 7/27/93; s. John Scheer and Rosa Jarmulowsky S; m. 7/21/18 to Florence J; c. Gloria (Mrs. Leder), George M, Jr, Frederick O. and Frieda S. Educ: Univ. of Ga, B.S. in Sci, 18; Gridiron Secret Soc; Phi Epsilon Pi. Polit. & Govt. Pos: Mem, Tenth Cong. Dist. Family and Children Serv, Ga; presidential elector, Sixth Dist, Cong. Dist, Ga; chmn, Putnam Co. Dem. Exec. Cmt, currently. Mil. Serv: Entered as Pvt, Army, 17, released as Capt, 19, after serv. in Qm. Corps, 82nd Div. Mem: Am. Legion; Mason; Kiwanis; chmn, Putnam Co. chap, Am. Nat. Red Cross. Rel: Jewish. Mailing Add: Box 8, Eatonton, Ga. 31024.

SCHEFFNER, RICHARD F. D
City Councilman, Erie, Pa.
b. Erie, Pa, 5/23/27; s. Frank A. Scheffner and Hattie Kohler S; m. 11/3/48 to Audrey Ann Dolan; c. Judith, Janet, Joanne, Jean, Jacqueline and Mark. Educ: Va. Mil. Acad; Gannon Col. Polit. & Govt. Pos: Committeeman, First Ward Dem. Party, Pa, 50-52, ward chmn, 52-56; committeeman, Sixth Ward Dem. Party, 56-62; city councilman, Erie, 62- Bus. & Prof. Pos: Self employed, Tavern-Restaurant, 51- Mil. Serv: Pvt, Air Force, 45. Hobbies; Football and Boxing. Rel: Roman Catholic. Mailing Add: 938 W. 31st St, Erie, Pa. 16508.

SCHEIDLE, HARRY F. R
Co. Supvr, San Diego Co, Calif.
b. San Diego, Calif, 8/16/22; s. Fred A. Scheidle and Gladys Weitzel S; m. 10/4/41 to Joy Virginia Simmons; c. Jeffrey C. and Michael F. Polit. & Govt. Pos: Councilman, Third Dist, San Diego, Calif, 68-69; co. supvr, third dist, San Diego Co, 69- Bus. & Prof. Pos: Pres, Waldorf House of TV, 46- Mil. Serv: Entered as A/S, Navy, 44, released as AMM 2/C, 46. Mem: F&AM; Shrine. Mailing Add: 5091 Cliff Place, San Diego, Calif. 92116.

SCHEIDT, VIRGIL D. R
Chmn, Ninth Dist. Rep. Cent. Cmt, Ind.
b. Columbus, Ind, 9/23/28; s. Harry Scheidt and Mildred Armuth S; m. 2/20/49 to Bettie L. Todd; c. Don Randall, Deborah Diane, Warren Ray and Christie Cheryl. Polit. & Govt. Pos: Treas, Bartholomew Co, Ind, 62-; chmn, Bartholomew Co. Rep. Cent. Cmt, 65-; state chmn. co. off, 65 & 66; nat. dir. co. off, 65 & 66; chmn, Ninth Dist. Rep. Cent. Cmt, 66-; del, Rep. Nat. Conv, 68. Jr. C. of C. Good Govt. Award, 62; First runner-up Outstanding Co. Treas, U.S, 65. Rel: Lutheran. Legal Res: R.R. 2, Columbus, Ind. 47201. Mailing Add: County Treasurer, Bartholomew County Court House, Columbus, Ind. 47201.

SCHEIERMAN, MABEL M. R
Secy, Third Cong. Dist. Rep. Party, Colo.
b. Stratton, Colo, 2/27/19; d. Joseph W. Garner and Sarah S. Hampton G; m. 3/4/52 to Kenneth Scheierman. Educ: Blair's Bus. Col, Colorado Springs, 36-37; Anderson Col, 44-45. Polit. & Govt. Pos: V.chmn, Kit Carson Co. Rep. Party, Colo, 60-; secy, Third Cong. Dist. Rep. Party, 64- Mem: Bd, Keep Colo. Beautiful; adv. bd, High Plains Libr. Syst; M.S.A. Club; Am. Nat. Cowbelle; Colo. Cowbelle; Kit Carson Co. Cowbelle. Rel: Church of God; Woman's Missionary Soc.(state secy). Mailing Add: Stratton, Colo. 80836.

SCHENCK, JOSEPH SAMUEL R
b. Canton, N.C, 10/15/17; s. Adrian Sereno Schenck and Ellen Cathey S; m. 5/28/50 to Elaine Pehota; c. Mary Ellen. Educ: George Wash. Univ, A.A, 46, Law Sch, LL.B, 51; Phi Sigma Kappa. Polit. & Govt. Pos: Chmn, and mem. exec. cmt, Haywood Co. Rep. Party, N.C, 66-68. Mil. Serv: Entered as Pvt, Army, 42, released as Pfc, 43, after serv. in Qm. Corps. Mem: N.C, D.C, Haywood Co. and Buncombe Co. Bar Asns; Dist. Court of Appeals, Kiwanis; Civitan. Mailing Add: 112 Skyland Terrace, Canton, N.C. 28716. (1967)

SCHENK, CHARLES H. D
Polit. & Govt. Pos: Ind. State Sen, 63-66; Ind. State Rep, 55-62. Bus. & Prof. Pos: Retired farmer; dir, Am. Nat. Bank of Vincennes. Mem: Pres, Wabash Valley Sugar Beet Asn; Farm Bur; Elks; Harmony Soc; dir, Wabash Valley Asn. Rel: Catholic. Mailing Add: R.R. 4, Vincennes, Ind. 47951. (1967)

SCHERER, GORDON HARRY R
Mem, Ohio Rep. State Cent. and Exec. Cmts.
b. Cincinnati, Ohio, 12/26/06; s. John E. Scherer and Minnie Kuehnle S; m. 2/18/33 to Virginia Mottern; c. Gordon Mottern and Suzanne (Mrs. Louiso). Educ: Univ. Cincinnati, Salmon P. Chase Col. of Law, LL.B, 29; Order of Curia; Phi Alpha Delta. Hon. LL.D, Institutum Divi Thomae, 62. Polit. & Govt. Pos: Pres, Young Rep. Club of Hamilton Co, Ohio, 33-34; asst. prosecuting attorney, Cincinnati City Coun, 33-40, dir. of safety, 43-44, mem, coun, 45-49; v.pres, Hamilton Co. Rep. Club, 38-42; U.S. Rep, Ohio, 53-62; chmn, Hamilton Co. Rep. Party, 62-68; mem, Ohio Rep. State Cent. and Exec. Cmts, 62-; mem, Hamilton Co. Bd. of Elec, Ohio and Task Force on Crime and Delinquency, Rep. Nat. Cmt, currently; del, Rep. Nat. Conv, 64 & 68, mem. platform cmt, and Nixon floor mgr. for Ohio del, 68. Bus. & Prof. Pos: Mem, bd. of dirs, Universal Guaranty Life Ins. Co. of Ohio, 63- Publ: 'Key Targets of the Communists,' Am. Legion Mag, 8/62; 'Are Americans Aware?' Vital Speeches, 8/58; 'I Was A Target,' Readers Digest, 7/54. Mem: DeMolay Legion of Honor; Mason (33°); Shrine; Grotto; Eastern Star; Royal Order of Jesters; trustee, Cincinnati South. Railway; bd. of trustees, Am. for Constitutional Action. Recipient, Patriotic Serv. Awards from Am. Coalition of Patriotic Soc, Am. Legion and DAR. Rel: Protestant. Legal Res: 2101 Highland Towers, Cincinnati, Ohio 45202. Mailing Add: 1717 Carew Tower, Cincinnati, Ohio 45202.

SCHERER, GORDON M. R
Ohio State Rep.
b. Cincinnati, Ohio, 8/1/38; s. Gordon Harry Scherer and Virginia Mottern S; m. 12/30/61 to Judith Marjorie Myers; c. Gordon W. and Steven M. Educ: Univ. Cincinnati, B.A. in polit. sci, 61; Salmon P. Chase Col. Law, J.D, 66; Phi Alpha Delta; Sigma Alpha Epsilon. Polit. & Govt. Pos: Ohio State Rep, currently. Bus. & Prof. Pos: Mem, Govt. Affairs Br, Cincinnati Real Estate Bd, Ohio, 62-66; assoc, P.G. Graves Inc, Indust. Realtors, 62-66; attorney-at-law, Scherer and Scherer, currently. Mem: Mason (32°); Scottish Rite; Shrine. Rel: Presbyterian. Mailing Add: 2857 Springwood Court, Cincinnati, Ohio 45211.

SCHERER, ROGER H. R
Minn. State Rep.
b. Minneapolis, Minn, 7/31/35; s. Clarence Scherer and Julia Rudolph S; m. 8/1/59 to Irma Marie Gentilini; c. Rachael, Lisa Ann, Peter, Kristopher and Mark. Educ: St. John's Univ, B.S. in polit. sci, 58; William Mitchell Col. of Law, LL.B, 64; Delta Theta Phi. Polit. & Govt. Pos: Chmn, Minn. Fedn. Col. Rep. Club, 56-57; chmn, Brooklyn Center Rep. Party, 59-60; Minn. State Rep, 67- Bus. & Prof. Pos: Secy, Scherer Bros. Lumber Co, 63- Mil. Serv: 2nd Lt, Army, 59; Army Res. ROTC Prog; 1st Lt, Army Res. Outstanding Young Man of Brooklyn Center, 67; Outstanding Young Man of Minnesota, 67; J.C. Distinguished Serv. Award. Mem: Hoo Hoo; Lumberman's Fraternal. Rel: Roman Catholic. Mailing Add: 7118 N. Willow Lane, Minneapolis, Minn. 55430.

SCHERESKY, LAURENCE THEODORE R
Chmn, Fourth Dist. Rep. Party, N.Dak.
b. Max N.Dak, 2/5/29; s. Joseph J. Scheresky and Dorothy Dassenko S; m. 6/24/53 to Lenore Irene Hines; c. Katherine, Kari Lynn, Kimberly Ann and Barry Jay. Educ: Minot State Col, 2 years; N.Dak. State Univ, 1 year. Polit. & Govt. Pos: Agr. Stabilization and Conserv. Serv. Committeeman, Ward Co. N.Dak, 59-61, chmn, 61-62; chmn, Fourth Dist. Rep. Party, 67- Mem: N.Dak. Farm Bur; Am. Farm Bur. Fedn; Toastmasters Int. Named Outstanding Young Farmer, Ward Co. N.Dak, 60 & 65; Runnerup for Outstanding Young Farmer, N.Dak, 65. Rel: Seventh Day Adventist. Mailing Add: Des Lacs, N.Dak. 58733.

SCHERFF, JUDITH SUE R
b. Pittsburg, Kans, 10/2/39; d. Albert Wood Scherff and Flora Tomasi S; single. Educ: Kans. State Col, B.A. in polit. sci. and M.S. in soc. sci; Nat. Honor Soc; Organ Guild of Am. Polit. & Govt. Pos: State chmn, Youth for Nixon, Kans, 59-60; secy, Third Dist. Rep. Party, 60; co-chmn, Col. Rep. Nat. Cmt, 60-63; personal secy. to Attorney Gen, Kans, 63-65; nat. committeewoman, Kans. Young Rep, 63-65; exec. asst. Kans. State Rep. Cmt, 66-68; mem, adv. bd, Nat. Cmt, Travel Agents-United Citizens for Nixon-Agnew, 68. Bus. & Prof. Pos: Instr. polit. sci, Washburn Univ, 63-; travel agent, Club Serv. Travel, Inc, 68- Rel: Methodist. Legal Res: Arma, Kans. 66712. Mailing Add: 3513 W. 29th St. Terr, Topeka, Kans. 66614.

SCHERLE, WILLIAM J. R
U.S. Rep, Iowa
b. Little Falls, N.C, 3/14/23; m. 6/7/47 to Jane Goldapp; c. William David and John Robert. Educ: South. Methodist Univ, Bus, Admin. Polit. & Govt. Pos: Mem, Legis. Research Cmt, Iowa; Col. on Mil. Staff Interim Cmt. of Gov. Norman Erbe, 63-65; Young Rep. precinct committeeman; chmn, Mills Co. Rep. Cent. Cmt, 3 terms; Iowa State Rep, until 66; chmn, Senate and House Hwy. Study Cmt; U.S. Rep, Seventh Dist, Iowa, 66-, mem. educ. and labor cmt. and cmt. on internal security, U.S. House of Rep; mem, Rep. Task Force on Agr. and Nat. Rivers and Harbors Cong. Bus. & Prof. Pos: Grain and livestock farmer; asst. div. mgr, Geo D. Barnard Co, Dallas, Tex. Mil. Serv: Vet. of World War II; Naval Res. Mem: Nat. Livestock Feeders Asn; Am. Legion; VFW. Named Outstanding Legislator by Iowa Press Corps; Award of Merit, Iowa Good Roads Asn, 64; Watchdog of the Treasury Award, Nat. Assoc. Businessmen, 68; Distinguished Serv. Award, Nat. Educ. Asn, 68. Rel: Catholic. Legal Res: R.F.D, Henderson, Iowa 51541. Mailing Add: 512 Cannon House Office Bldg, Washington, D.C. 20515.

SCHERTZER, SILAS DEAN R
Secy, Henry Co. Rep. Cent. Cmt, Ill.
b. Roll, Okla. Territory, 11/2/07; s. Harry F. Schertzer and Bertha Durflinger S; m. 12/15/32 to Hildegard Roselund; c. Berndt D. and Thomas L. Educ: Kewanee Bus. Col, Ill, 30. Polit. & Govt. Pos: Sales tax inspector, State of Ill, 59-61; secy, Henry Co. Rep. Cent. Cmt, 60- Mem: AF&AM (Master Lodge 1944). Rel: Lutheran. Mailing Add: 214 E. Second St, Kewanee, Ill. 61443.

SCHEUER, JAMES H. D
U.S. Rep, N.Y.
b. New York, N.Y, 2/6/20; m. to Emily. Educ: Swarthmore Col, A.B; Columbia Law Sch, LL.B; Harvard Grad. Sch. of Bus. Admin, degree in indust. admin. Polit. & Govt. Pos: Mem, Nat. Panel of Arbitrators, Am. Arbit. Asn; developer of residential commun. in eight cities under the Fed. Urban Renewal prog; del. to four UN Conf. on housing and urban probs. and human rights; economist, U.S. For. Econ. Admin, 45-46; mem. of legal staff, Off. of Price Stabilization, 51-52; U.S. Rep, N.Y, 64-; del, Dem. Nat. Conv, 68. Bus. & Prof. Pos: Writer and lecturer. Mil. Serv: Flight instr, Army, 43-45. Publ: To Walk the Streets Safely, Doubleday, 69. Mem: Bar Asn. of N.Y.C; pres, Citizens' Housing and Planning Coun. of N.Y.C; bd. mem, Nat. Housing Conf; dir, Bronx Boys Club; mem, bd. of dirs, Bronx Chap, Nat. Conf. of Christians and Jews. Hon. mem, Am. Inst. of Architects, 68. Legal Res: Bronx, N.Y. Mailing Add: 3238 R St. N.W, Washington, D.C. 20007.

SCHICK, JOHN JOSEPH, JR. D
Chmn, Ulster Co. Dem. Exec. Cmt, N.Y.
b. Connelly, N.Y, 6/13/20; s. John Joseph Schick and Marie Whalen S; m. 1/9/55 to Elizabeth Gill; c. Christopher J, Shawn O, Malcolm D, Julia V. and Holly M. Educ: Siena Col, A.B, 50; Albany Law Sch, LL.B, 52. Polit. & Govt. Pos: Asst. dist. attorney, Ulster Co, N.Y, 53-56; spec. city judge, Kingston, N.Y, 58; dir, Ulster Co. Bd. of Health, 61-; mem, N.Y. State Dem. Cmt, 99th Assembly Dist, currently; chmn, Ulster Co. Dem. Exec. Cmt, currently. Bus. & Prof. Pos: Partner, Schick & Klein, Esq, 57-; dir, St. Cabrini Sch, West Park, 63- Mem: N.Y. State and Ulster Co. Bar Asns; N.Y. State Dist. Attorney's Asn; Elks; Am. Legion; Town of Esopus, Port Ewen, N.Y; W. Esopus Land Asn; Kiwanis; La. Societe Des Four Hommes et 8 Chevaux; United Commercial Travelers; Twallfskill Country Club; Hudson Valley Flying Club. Rel: Roman Catholic. Legal Res: 263 Albany Ave, Kingston, N.Y. 12401. Mailing Add: 259 Fair St, Kingston, N.Y. 12401.

SCHIEFFELIN, JOSEPH B. R
Colo. State Sen.
b. New York, N.Y, 1/18/27; married; c. three. Polit. & Govt. Pos: Colo. State Sen, 67-; Colo. State Rep, one term; former precinct committeeman, 6 yrs. Bus. & Prof. Pos: Ins. agent. Mailing Add: 11674 Applewood Knolls Dr, Lakewood, Colo. 80215. (1967)

SCHIFFLER, ANDREW CHARLES R
b. Wheeling, W.Va, 8/10/89; s. Andrew J. Schiffler and Emma Frantz S; m. 8/28/59 to Margaret C. McCluskey; c. Robert A. Polit. & Govt. Pos: Referee in bankruptcy, U.S. Dist. Court, 18-22; prosecuting attorney, Ohio Co, W.Va, 25-33; U.S. Rep, First Dist, W.Va, 39-45; Cmnr. of Accounts, Ohio Co. Court, W.Va, 56-63. Mem: Am, W.Va. and Ohio Co. Bar Asns; Mason; Shrine; Odd Fellows; K. of P; Elks; Eagles. Mailing Add: 1531 Atlas Rd, Wheeling, W.Va. 26003.

SCHIFTER, RICHARD D
Chmn, Montgomery Co. Dem. Cent. Cmt, Md.
b. Vienna, Austria, 7/31/23; s. Paul Schifter and Balbina Blass S; m. 7/3/48 to Lilo Krueger; c. Judith L, Deborah E, Richard P, Barbara F. and Karen E. Educ: City Col. N.Y, B.S. Soc. Sci, summa cum laude, 43; Yale Law Sch, LL.B, 51; Phi Beta Kappa. Polit. & Govt. Pos: Mem, Md. State Bd. Educ, 59-, v.pres, 67-; mem. bd. visitors, Md. Sch. Deaf, 60-; chmn, Montgomery Co. Dem. Cent. Cmt, 66-; v.chmn, Md. Dem. State Cent. Cmt, 67-; del, Dem. Nat. Conv, 68. Bus. & Prof. Pos: Assoc, Strasser, Spiegelberg, Fried, Frank & Kampelman, 51-57, partner, 57- Mil. Serv: Entered as Pvt, Army, 43, released as T/Sgt, 46, after serv. in T-Force, 12th Army Group, ETO, 44-45. Mem: Am. Bar Asn. Rel: Jewish. Mailing Add: 6907 Crail Dr, Bethesda, Md. 20034.

SCHILFFARTH, RICHARD ALLEN R
b. Milwaukee, Wis, 4/24/31; s. Herman T. Schilffarth and Elizabeth Rausch S; m. 7/21/53 to Marlene Thiele; c. Christine Lynn and Richard Allen. Educ: Univ. Wis, B.B.A, 53; Delta Tau Delta. Polit. & Govt. Pos: Del, Wis. State Rep. Conv, 61-69; del, Rep. Nat. Conv, 68; chmn, Wis. State Get-Out-The-Vote, 68. Bus. & Prof. Pos: Pres, Dataforms, Inc, Milwaukee, Wis, 68- Mil. Serv: Entered as 2nd Lt, Army, 53, released as 1st Lt, 55 after serv. in 4th Armored Div. Mem: V.pres, Printing Indust. of Wis; mem. exec. cmt, Int. Bus. Forms Industs; dir, Dominican Col; mem. bd, Friends of Art-Milwaukee; Delta Tau Delta Alumni Club of Milwaukee; mem, Printing Adv. Cmt, State of Wis. Rel: Lutheran. Mailing Add: 15025 Cascade Dr, Elm Grove, Wis. 53122.

SCHILKE, DONALD LEE R
b. Oak Park, Ill, 6/24/30; s. Clarence W. Schilke and Florence V. S; m. 4/14/56 to Margaret A. Chernals; c. Carole, Peter and Paul. Educ: Univ. Ill, B.S, 56. Polit. & Govt. Pos: Committeeman, Oak Park Twp. Rep. Party, Ill, 66-; state adminstr. of promotion, 69- Bus. & Prof. Pos: Advert. rep, Field Enterprises, Chicago, Ill, 56-69. Mil. Serv: Entered as Seaman Recruit, Navy, 48, released as Aviation Electricians Mate 1/C, 52, after serv. in Air Anti-Submarine Squadron 21, Korea, 50-52; Korean Theatre Medal. Mem: Oak Park Club. Rel: Protestant. Mailing Add: 1126 Miller, Oak Park, Ill. 60302.

SCHILLER, CHARLOTTE D
Mem, Calif. Dem. State Cent. Cmt.
b. Germany, 5/25/20; d. Alfred Bernheim and Ilse Michalowski B; m. 9/24/40 to Hans J. Schiller; c. Ian, Peter and Anita. Educ: Teachers Col. for Women, Tel Aviv, Israel, 40. Polit. & Govt. Pos: Assembly dist. rep, Calif. Dem. Coun, 66-; mem, Calif. Dem. State Cent. Cmt, 68-; pres, Mill Valley Dem. Club, 69- Bus. & Prof. Pos: Part time teaching, Israel, 40-46. Mem: PTA. Rel: Jewish. Mailing Add: 22 Madrone Park Circle, Mill Valley, Calif. 94941.

SCHILLER, MILTON JOE D
b. Rogers, Tex, 8/6/17; s. Joe S. Schiller and Wmilie Haisler S; m. 2/7/37 to Vivian Donaho; c. Linda Ann, Peggy Jo and Nancy Kay. Polit. & Govt. Pos: Mem. city coun, Cameron, Tex, 48-54; mem. Cameron Bd. Educ, 58-62; Tex. State Rep, until 68. Mem: Mason (32°); Shrine; Rotary; Farm Bur; Farmers Union; Cameron Country Club. Rel: Southern Baptist. Legal Res: 711 E. 11th, Cameron, Tex. 76520. Mailing Add: P.O. Box 108, Cameron, Tex. 76520. (1967)

SCHILSON, DONALD LEE D
b. Carthage, Ill, 8/11/28; s. Erwin Donald Schilson (deceased) and Hattie Ellen Boyer S; m. 7/20/68 to Elizabeth Warnebold Allan; c. stepdaughters, Elizabeth and Kathryn. Educ: Carthage Col, A.B, 50; Western Ill. Univ, M.S, 53; State Univ. of Iowa, Ph.D, 62; Alpha Mu Gamma; Beta Beta Beta; Phi Delta Kappa. Polit. & Govt. Pos: Dem. cand. for U.S. Rep, 20th Cong. Dist, Ill, 68; precinct committeeman, Hancock Co, 68-69; legis. aide to Illinois State Legislature, 69. Bus. & Prof. Pos: Pub. sch. adminstr, Fulton Co. Ill, 53-60; asst. prof, Fla. State Univ, 62-64, Ohio Univ, 64-67; special adv. in Viet Nam, U.S. Agency of Int. Develop, 66; assoc. prof, Univ. of Ark, 67-68; prof. and dept. head, Univ. North Dakota, 69- Publ: 'The Elementary Principal: Selection and Training,' American School Board Journal, 4/65; 'Finance and Education,' Duquesne Review, 65; 'School Self Study: Initiation and Functions, Clearing House, 67. Mem: Life mem, Nat. Educ. Asn; Farm Bur; Aircraft Owners and Pilots Asn; Nat. Rifle Asn. Writing award in col; music awards; athletic awards. Rel: Christian Church. Legal Res: Carthage, Ill. 62321. Mailing Add: 3206 Chestnut, Grand Forks, N.Dak. 58201.

SCHIMEK, HERBERT H. D
Chmn, Adams Co. Dem. Party, Nebr.
b. Elba, Nebr, 9/20/38; s. Henry J. Schimek and Clara A. Ingerle S; m. 6/1/63 to Di Anna Ruth Rebman; c. Samuel Wolfgang. Educ: Nebr. State Col, Kearney, A.B. in Educ, 62; Colo. State Univ, 63; Univ. Nebr, 65; Young Dem; pres, Campus Independents; mem, Kennedy for Pres. Col. Campaign, 59-60. Polit. & Govt. Pos: Mem, Robert F. Kennedy for Pres. Campaign, Adams Co. Nebr, 68; chmn, Adams Co. Dem. Party, 68-; mem, Nebr. State Dem. Cent. Cmt, Dist. 33, currently. Mem: Nat. Educ. Asn; Nebr. State Educ. Asn.(bd. dir, 69-72); Hastings Educ. Asn.(pres, 67-68, del, nat. conv, 67); Am. Hist. Asn; Jaycees. Rel: Catholic. Mailing Add: 1325 Apache, Hastings, Nebr. 68901.

SCHIMMEL, ALLAN D. R
b. Sioux Center, Iowa, 6/18/40; s. A. Arie Schimmel and Magdelena Scheffer S; single. Educ: Northwest. Col, B.A, 62; Univ. Iowa, M.A, 66. Polit. & Govt. Pos: Legis. asst. U.S. Rep. Fred Schwengel, Iowa, 63-64, admin. asst, 67- Mem: Am. Polit. Sci. Asn. Rel: Protestant. Legal Res: 1920 Le Claire, Davenport, Iowa 52800. Mailing Add: 512½ D St. S.E, Washington, D.C. 20003.

SCHINNERER, MARK CHRISTOPHER R
Ohio State Rep.
b. Riley, Ind, 6/3/99; s. John Schinnerer and Mayme Swinda S; m. 5/31/24 to Alma Katinka Shanks; c. Gretel (Mrs. Robinson). Educ: Ind. State Univ, A.B, 20; Columbia Univ, A.M, 23; West. Reserve Univ, Ph.D, 43; Phi Delta Kappa; Acacia. Polit. & Govt. Pos: Ohio State Rep, 63-64 & 67- Bus. & Prof. Pos: Teacher, prin. and asst. supt, Cleveland Pub. Schs, Ohio, 23-47 and supt. of schs, 47-61; educ. consult, N.Y.C, Los Angeles, U.S. Off. of Educ, 61-64; v.pres. and dir, Shaker Savings Asn, 61- Mil. Serv: Entered as Pvt, Army, 18, released as Sgt. Mem: Trustee, YMCA, Cleveland Zoo, Martha Holden Jennings Found. Adv. Cmt. Received Distinguished Serv. Award, Am. Asn. of Sch. Adminstrs, 63. Legal Res: 1489 Bunts Rd, Lakewood, Ohio 44107. Mailing Add: Shaker Savings Asn, 1010 Euclid Ave, Cleveland, Ohio 44115.

SCHIRGER, WILLIAM EDWARD D
Chmn, Winnebago Co. Dem. Party, Ill.
b. Somerville, N.J, 7/13/35; s. Joseph Charles Schirger and Veronica Jakubick S; m. 5/12/62 to Carolyn Ann Collins; c. Suzanne, Kathleen and John. Educ: St. Peter's Col, N.J, B.S. in Govt, 58; Univ. Notre Dame, J.D, 63. Polit. & Govt. Pos: Campaign coordinator for Adlai Stevenson III, 66; asst. attorney gen, State Ill, 66-69; chmn, Winnebago Co. Dem. Party, 68-; assoc. judge, Winnebago Co, 69- Bus. & Prof. Pos: Chmn. bd, Northwest Publ. Co. 67- Mil. Serv: Entered as 2nd Lt, Army, 58, released as Capt, 65, after serv. in Inf; Capt, Army Standby Res. Publ: Guide to Estate Planning, 63; Economic Rebirth of Germany, Pavaun, 57. Mem: Winnebago Co. and Ill. State Bar Asns; Am. Trial Lawyers Asn; Cmt. Ill. Govt.(bd. dirs); Elks (Tiller, 69); Rockford Notre Dame Club (pres, 69). Rel: Catholic. Legal Res: 1321 Camp Ave, Rockford, Ill. 61103. Mailing Add: 401 W. State, Rockford, Ill. 61101.

SCHIRO, VICTOR HUGO D
Mayor, New Orleans, La.
b. Chicago, Ill, 5/28/04; s. Andrew E. Schiro and Mary Pizatti S; m. 11/10/32

to Margaret Mary Gibbes. Educ: Santa Clara Univ; Tulane Univ, 24; Alpha Delta Gamma; Tau Kappa Epsilon. Hon. D.Sc, Nat. Col, Can, 59; hon, D.Litt, Am. Int. Acad, 57. Polit. & Govt. Pos: Cmnr. of Pub. Bldg. and Parks, New Orleans, La, 50-54, councilman-at-lg, 54-61, mayor, 61-, pres, New Orleans Pub. Belt R.R, and Sewerage and Water Bd. of New Orleans, cmnr, Orleans Parish Levee Bd, mem, Bd. of Liquidation City Dept; del, Dem. Nat. Conv, 68. Bus. & Prof. Pos: Import-export businessman; advertising man; radio announcer; exec, Metrop. Life Ins. Co, 31-48; pres, Vic Schiro Ins. Agency, 48- Mil. Serv: U.S. Coast Guard, 42-45. Mem: Adv. bd, Bank of New Orleans and Salvation Army; bd, Nat. Cerebral Palsy Asn; dir, Mt. Carmel Acad, Int. House; exec. bd, New Orleans Spring Fiesta Asn; La. Munic Asn; Am. Legion; past pres, Young Men's Bus. Club; exec. bd, La. Police Jury Asn; hon. mem, Daughters of Confederacy and New Orleans Honduran Asn; Italo-Am. Soc. of La; VFW; hon. int. pres, Am. Int. Acad; dir, Gr. New Orleans C. of C; lt, U.S. Power Sq; La. Landmarks Asn; bd. govs, Tulane Univ; World Trade Develop. Cmt. and Membership Cmt, Int. House; exec. bd, Police Jury Asn. of La; bd, New Orleans Oprea House Asn; Wine and Foods Soc; chmn, Civil Defense Cmt, Nat. League of Cities; Soc. of Bacchus, Pub. Officials Adv. Coun, 66; Citizens Adv. Cmt, Intercultural Educ, Southwest Educ. Develop. Lab; Inst. of Culture of Spain; U.S. Rep, exec. cmt, Inter-Am. Munic. Asn; Optimist Club; pres, Inter-Am. Munic. Orgn, 69- Carlos Cespedes Order of Merit of Cuba; Solidarity Medal of Honor, Italy; Ami de Paris, France; Distinguished Serv, DAV; Companion Order of Aran, Italy; Order of Civil Merit, Spain; Medal of Honor, San Miguel, El Salvador; Grand Cross, Andorra; Commendation of Merit, Italy; Amitie Florimontaine, Belgium; Order of Civil Merit, Higher Rank, Spain; La Grande Medaille de Verneil, France; Diploma de Gascogne, France; Eloy Alfaro Award, Panama; Boswell Inst. Award; Spanish Gold Medal of Madrid; Grand Cross of Justice, Knights of Malta; officer, Legion d'Honneur, France; Rank Knight Comdr, Isabel la Catholica, Spain; Knight, Order of St. Brigette; Man of the Year, Delgado Col, 69. Legal Res: 24 Tern St, New Orleans, La. 70124. Mailing Add: Mayor's Office, City Hall, New Orleans, La. 70112.

SCHISLER, D. GALE D
Ill. State Rep.
b. Knox Co, Ill, 3/2/33; s. D. Claire Schisler and Doris Jacobs S; m. 12/30/57 to Carolyn K. Cochran; c. Kimberley Joy, Pamela Jill and Kurt Jeffrey. Educ: West. Ill. Univ, B.S. in Educ, 59; N.E. Mo. State Teachers Col, M.A. in sch. admin, 62; West Ill. Univ. Alumni Asn. Polit. & Govt. Pos: U.S. Rep, Ill, currently. Bus. & Prof. Pos: Teacher and coach, Elem. and Jr. High Schs, London Mills, Ill, 59-60, prin, 60-64. Mil. Serv: Entered as A/B, Air Force, 52, released as Airman 1/C, 55; Good Conduct Medal. Mem: Ill. and Nat. Educ. Asns; Jr. High Sch. Prin. Asn; Spoon River Valley Teachers Asn; Mason, Shrine, Mohammed Temple; Am. Legion; life mem, Amvets. Mem. European Serv. Volleyball Championship Team; France All Star Football Team. Rel: Protestant. Mailing Add: London Mills, Ill. 61544 (1967)

SCHLAFLY, PHYLLIS R
b. St. Louis, Mo, 8/15/24; d. John Bruce Stewart and Odile Dodge S; m. 10/20/49 to John Fred Schlafly; c. John F, Bruce S, Roger S, Phyllis D, Andrew L. and Anne V. Educ: Wash. Univ, A.B, 44; Radcliffe Col, M.A, 45; Phi Beta Kappa; Pi Sigma Alpha. Polit. & Govt. Pos: Ill. Rep. State Cent. Committeewoman, 56-58; del, Rep. Nat. Conv, 56, 64 & 68, alternate del, 60; pres, Ill. Fedn. Rep. Women, 60-64; precinct committeewoman, 64-; first v.pres, Nat. Fedn. Rep. Women, 65-67. Bus. & Prof. Pos: Research librn, First Nat. Bank and St. Louis Union Trust Co, 46-49; radio commentator, weekly radio prog, Am. Wake Up, 62-66; author and lectr, currently. Publ: A Choice Not An Echo, 64, The Gravediggers, 64, Strike From Space, 65, Safe—Not Sorry, 67 and The Betrayers (with Rear Admiral Chester Ward, Ret), 68, Pere Marquette Press. Mem: DAR, Nat. chmn, Am. Hist. Month Cmt, 65-68 and Bicentennial Cmt, 68-; Jr. League of St. Louis; Authors Guild; Am. Legion Auxiliary. Woman of Achievement in Pub. Affairs, St. Louis Globe-Dem, 63. Mailing Add: Fairmount, Alton, Ill. 62002.

SCHLEI, NORBERT ANTHONY D
Mem, Calif. Dem. State Cent. Cmt.
b. Dayton, Ohio, 6/14/29; s. William Frank Schlei and Norma Lindsley S; m. 8/26/50 to Jane Moore, div. Jan. 64, m. 3/7/65 to Barbara Lindemann; c. Anne, William, Andrew, Bradford L. and Graham. Educ: Ohio State Univ, B.A, 50; Yale, LL.B, magna cum laude, 56; Benjamin N. Cardozo Prize, 54; Edward S. Robbins Mem. Prize, 56; ed, law jour, 55-56; Phi Alpha Delta; Phi Kappa Sigma; Phi Eta Sigma. Polit. & Govt. Pos: Law clerk to U.S. Justice Harlan, 56-57; Dem. cand. for Calif. State Assemblyman, 62; mem, Los Angeles Co. Dem. Cmt, 62-64; mem, Calif. Dem. State Cent. Cmt, 62-64 & 66-; Asst. U.S. Attorney Gen, Wash, D.C, 62-66; Dem. cand. for Secy. of State, Calif, 66; chmn, task force on human rels, Calif. Dem. State Assembly, 67-; del, Dem. Nat. Conv, 68. Bus. & Prof. Pos: Assoc. of firm O'Melveny & Myers, Los Angeles, Calif, 57-59; mem. of firm Greenberg, Shafton & Schlei, 59-62; George H. Leatherbee lectr, Harvard Grad. Sch. Bus. Admin, 61; lectr. law, Univ. South Calif. Sch. Law, 61-62; mem. of firm, Munger, Tolles, Hills & Rickershauser, Los Angeles, Calif, 67-; mem. of firm, Kane, Shulman & Schlei, Wash, D.C, 67- Mil. Serv: Naval Res, Lt.(jg), 50-53. Publ: Studies in World Public Order, McDougal & Assocs, 61; State Regulation of Corporate Financial Practices: The California Experience, 62; plus others. Mem: Am, Calif, Los Angeles and Fed. Bar Asns; Am. Judicature Soc; Am. Soc. of Int. Law; Order of Coif; Fed. City Club, Wash, D.C. Co-recipient Annual Award, Am. Soc. Int. Law, 62. Legal Res: 1021 Stone Canyon Rd, Los Angeles, Calif. 90024. Mailing Add: 606 S. Hill, Los Angeles, Calif. 90014.

SCHLEICHER, BEN T. R
Mayor, Rockford, Ill.
b. Rockford, Ill, 10/10/16; m. 5/1/36 to Evelyn Waltz; c. Ben K. and Sally Jo (Mrs. Ross). Educ: Rockford Cent. High Sch, dipl, 34. Polit. & Govt. Pos: Supv. for Gov. Woodward, Rockford, Ill, 37-57; alderman, Seventh Ward, Rockford, Ill, 48-57, mayor, 57- Rel: Lutheran. Mailing Add: 1811 W. State St, Rockford, Ill. 61103.

SCHLEICKER, JAMES GERARD D
b. Erie, Pa, 5/18/37; s. Edward Schleicker and Christine Kiehlmeier S; m. 9/18/65 to Patricia Ann Stinneford. Educ: Gannon Col, B.A, 59; Univ. Pa, LL.B, 65; Tau Kappa Epsilon. Polit. & Govt. Pos: Admin. asst. Rep. Vigorito, D-Pa; admin. asst. Erie Co. Dem. Com, 61-64; press asst. Gov. Lawrence, Pa, 59. Publ: Author Metrop. Govt. 1967 Legal Res: 1521 N. 12th St, Arlington, Va. No mailing address available. (1967)

SCHLENKER, GERALD D
Mem, Calif. Dem. State Cent. Cmt.
b. Buffalo, N.Y, 12/6/36; s. Elmer C. Schlenker and Marie Lexner S; m. 9/22/57 to Elizabeth Bye; c. Sandra. Educ: N.Y. Univ. Col, Buffalo, B.S, 62; San Diego State Col, M.A, 68; Kappa Delta Pi; Phi Alpha Theta. Polit. & Govt. Pos: Nominee for Calif. State Assemblyman, 76th Assembly Dist, 68; mem, San Diego Co. Dem. Cent. Cmt, Calif, 68-; mem, Calif. Dem. State Cent. Cmt, 68-; pres, Downtown Dem. of San Diego, Calif, 69- Bus. & Prof. Pos: Bd. Dirs, Combined Health Agencies, San Diego, 69- Mil. Serv: Entered as Airman Basic, Air Force, 54, released as Airman 2/C, 58, after serv. in 30th Air Transport Squadron, Mil. Air Transport Serv; Good Conduct Medal; Air Crew Members Badge. Publ: 'The Internment of the Japanese,' Star News 5/68. Mem: Am. Fedn. of Teachers; bd. dirs, Multiple Sclerosis Soc, San Diego, 69-; Econ. Educ. Coun; San Diego Co. Coun. of Soc. Studies (bd. dirs, 67-68); Conf. of Calif. Hist. Socs.(state coordinator, Young Historians, 66-68); South Bay Hist. Soc; Jaycees, San Diego; Amvets; Serv. Employees Union Local 102. One of San Diego's Ten Outstanding Young Men, 68. Rel: United Church of Christ. Mailing Add: 6564 Jackson Dr, San Diego, Calif. 92119.

SCHLEPPEGRELL, JOHN DANIEL R
Chmn, North Star Borough Rep. Party, Alaska
b. Park Rapids, Minn, 2/15/26; s. Thorald William Schleppegrell and Harriet Weyhrauch S; single. Educ: Col. of St. Thomas; Univ. Minn. Polit. & Govt. Pos: Rep. precinct committeeman, Alaska, 58-60; treas, 16th Legis. Dist. Rep. Party, 60-62; committeeman, Rep. State Cent. Cmt, 62-; chmn, North Star Borough Rep. Party, 64- Bus. & Prof. Pos: Pres, NGA Stores. Mil. Serv: Entered as Pvt, Army, 44, released as Sgt, 46, after serv. in Army Engr, ETO; ETO Campaign Ribbon and Bronze Star. Mem: Am. Legion; VFW; Kiwanis; C. of C. Mailing Add: Box 697, Fairbanks, Alaska 99701. (1967)

SCHLESINGER, ARTHUR MEIER, JR. D
b. Columbus, Ohio, 10/15/17; s. Arthur M. Schlesinger and Elizabeth Bancroft S; m. 8/10/40 to Marion Cannon; c. Stephen Cannon, Katharine Bancroft, Christina and Andrew Bancroft. Educ: Harvard Univ, A.B. summa cum laude, 38, mem, Soc. of Fellows, 39-42; Muhlenberg Col, D.Litt, 50; Bethany Col, LL.D, 56; Univ. N.B, D.C.L, 60; Phi Beta Kappa. Polit. & Govt. Pos: Consult, Off. of War Info, 42-43, Off. of Strategic Serv, 43-45, Econ. Coop. Admin, 48 and Mutual Security Admin, 51-52; mem, Adlai Stevenson Campaign, 52 & 56; spec. asst. to President of U.S, 61-64. Bus. & Prof. Pos: Assoc. prof. hist, Harvard, 46-54, prof, 54-61; Schweitzer prof. humanities, City Univ. New York, 66- Mil. Serv: Army, 45. Publ: Politics of Upheaval, 60; Kennedy or Nixon, 60; Politics of Hope, 63; A Thousand Days: John F. Kennedy in the White House, 65; plus many others. Mem: Mass. Hist. Soc; Colonial Soc. Mass; Am. Hist. Asn; Am. Vet. Cmt; Nat. Inst. Arts & Letters; v.chmn, Am. Dem. Action; Century Club; Harvard Club, N.Y.C. Pulitzer Prize in Hist, 45; Guggenheim fel, 46; Am. Acad. Arts & Letters grant, 46; Francis Parkman Prize, 57; Bancroft Prize, 58. Legal Res: 166 E. 61st St, New York, N.Y. 10021. Mailing Add: 33 W. 42nd St, New York, N.Y. 10036. (1967)

SCHLESINGER, JAMES RODNEY R
Asst. Dir, Bur. of the Budget
b. N.Y.C, 2/15/29; s. Julius Schlesinger and Rhea Rogen S; m. 6/19/54 to Rachel Mellinger; c. Cora K, Charles L, Ann R, William F, Emily, Thomas S. and Clara. Educ: Harvard Univ, A.B. in Econ. summa cum laude, 50, Frederick Sheldon Prize fel, 50-51, A.M. in Econ, 52, Ph.D. in Econ, 56; Phi Beta Kappa. Polit. & Govt. Pos: Acad. consult, Naval War Col, 57, consult, bd. gov, Fed. Reserve Bd, 62-63; consult, Bur. of the Budget, 65-69, asst. dir, 69- Bus. & Prof. Pos: Asst. prof. econ, Univ. Va, 55-58, assoc. prof, 58-63; sr. staff mem, Rand Corp, Santa Monica, Calif, 63-67, dir, strategic studies, 67-69. Publ: The Political Economy of National Security, Frederick A. Praeger, 60; Organizational Structures and Planning, Nat. Bur. of Econ. Research, 67, reprint from Issues in Defense Economics distributed by Columbia Univ. Press; 'Systems Analysis and the Political Process', J. Law and Econ, 10/68. Rel: Lutheran. Mailing Add: 3601 N. 26th St, Arlington, Va. 22207.

SCHLICKMAN, EUGENE F. R
Ill. State Rep.
b. Dubuque, Iowa, 12/17/29; s. Leander L. Schlickman and Helen Juergens S; m. 6/9/51 to Margaret M. Muraski; c. J. Andrew, Stephen E, Mary Elizabeth and Monica Ann. Educ: Loras Col, Dubuque, Iowa, B.A, 51; Georgetown Univ. Law Center, LL.B, 56. Polit. & Govt. Pos: Statistician, Dept. of Labor, 52-53; trustee, Arlington Heights, Ill, 59-64; Ill. State Rep, 65-; Wheeling Twp. Rep. Committeeman, 66-; v.pres, Nat. Coun. for Rev. of State Constitutions, Phila, Pa, 69. Bus. & Prof. Pos: Asst. to exec. v.pres, Corn Indust. Research Found, 53-56; research dir, Nat. Foundry Asn, 56-60; labor rels. specialist, Ekco Prod. Co, 60-64; partner, Burfeind & Schlickman, 64- Publ: 'Labor Relations in Foundry Industries,' Labor Law J, 7/57; Suburban Cook County Politics, New City, 11/65. Mem: Am, Ill. and Northwest Suburban Bar Asns; K. of C. John Howard Asn. Award, 67; Outstanding Legislator Award, Rutgers Univ, 66; Jaycee Man of the Year, Arlington Heights, Ill, 60. Rel: Roman Catholic. Mailing Add: 1219 E. Clarendon, Arlington Heights, Ill. 60004.

SCHLOSSER, JACK A. D
b. Bronx, N.Y, 3/3/30; single. Educ: Cornell Univ, B.A; N.Y. Univ, grad. work in pub. admin. Polit. & Govt. Pos: Supvr, Wallkill, N.Y, 62-64; N.Y. State Assemblyman, 65-67; del, Dem. Nat. Conv, 68. Bus. & Prof. Pos: Landscape contractor, Middletown. Mem: Mid-Orange United C. of C; Circleville Fire Dept; Bullville Rod and Gun Club; Middletown Lions Club. Mailing Add: R.D. 3, Midland Lake Rd, Middletown, N.Y. 10018. (1967)

SCHLOSSER, JAMES DOUGLAS R
b. Jamestown, N.Dak, 8/13/37; s. Reynold Martin Schlosser and Marie Huilk S; m. 1/27/62 to Sharon Jean Martin; c. Leslie Anne and Lynne Marie.

Educ: Marquette Univ, Milwaukee, Wis, 55-56; St. John's Univ, Minn, B.A. in polit. sci, 59; Univ. N.Dak. Sch. Law, J.D, 62; Law Rev. Staff; Phi Alpha Delta. Polit. & Govt. Pos: Chmn, Univ. N.Dak. Young Rep, 59-61; Rep. campaign dir, Stutsman Co, 60; mem. exec. cmt, Midwest Col. Fedn. Young Rep, 60-62; mem. exec. cmt, N.Dak. Young Rep, 60-68, chmn, 61-63 and v.chmn, 62-64; asst. state attorney, Stutsman Co, 62-63; exec. secy, N.Dak. Rep. Party, 63-65; ed, N.Dak. Young Rep. Spokesman, 65-67; asst. attorney gen, N.Dak, 65-; campaign dir, Rep. Tom Kleppe, Second Dist, N.Dak, 66 & 68. Publ: Assoc. ed, The Campus Conscience Magazine, 61; 'Eminent Domain and Land Condemnation in Notrh Dakota,' N.Dak. Law Rev, 1/62. Mem: Am. and Burleigh Co. Bar Asns; secy-treas, N.Dak. Bar Asn, 66-68; bd. dirs, YMCA, 68-; trustee, Mary Col, Bismarck, N.Dak, 69-; Elks; Eagles; K. of C. Gov, Boys State, 54; King, Univ. N.Dak. Law Sch, 62; Outstanding Sr. Award, 62; Little All-Am. Football, 54; prin. research asst, Agr. Law Inst, 61-62; Chosen Outstanding Young Man, Bismarck, N.Dak. and N.Dak, 69. Rel: Catholic. Legal Res: 609 Capitol Ave, Bismarck, N.Dak. 55801. Mailing Add: Box 1762, Bismarck, N.Dak. 58501.

SCHLOTH, WILLIAM JOHN R
Gen. Counsel, Muscogee Co. Rep. Exec. Cmt, Ga.
b. Portland, Ore, 8/23/14; s. Michael Rudolph Schloth and Maud Dolan S; m. 10/8/41 to Maude Williams; c. Jeanette S.(Mrs. Dan Snavely) and Lucile M.(Mrs. Leon Jordan, Jr). Educ: Univ. Ore; Cath. Univ. of Am; Friars; Chi Psi; Alpha Delta Sigma; Scabbard & Blade. Polit. & Govt. Pos: Mem. exec. cmt, Ga. State Rep. Cent. Cmt, 56-64, exec. officer, 60-64, mem, 66-; del, Rep. Nat. Conv, 60, alternate del, 64 & 68; chmn, Muscogee Co. Rep. Party, 60-64; mem, Elec. Laws Study Cmt, Ga, 62-64; Presidential Elector, Ga, 64; chmn, Third Cong. Dist. Rep. Party, 64-66; gen. counsel, Muscogee Co. and Third Dist. Rep. Exec. Cmts, Ga, 66- Bus. & Prof. Pos: Partner, Swinson, Elliott & Schloth, Attorneys, 50-62 and Foley, Chappell, Hollis & Schloth, 62-69. Mil. Serv: Entered as Lt, Army, 40, released as Maj, 46, after serv. in 11th Airborne Div, Pac. Theater and ETO; Bronze Star; Air Medal; N.African Campaign Ribbon; 3rd Zuave, France; Philippines Liberation Medal; Combat Infantryman's Badge; 2 Invasion and 6 Battle Stars; Parachutist's Badge; Air Force Qualified Observer. Mem: Am. Bar Asn; Cmt. on Judiciary and chmn, Publ. Cmt, State Bar Ga; bd. dirs, Am. Judicature Soc; Kiwanis; judge, Am. Horse Show Asn. Rel: Presbyterian. Legal Res: Green Island Hills, Columbus, Ga. 31904. Mailing Add: P.O. Box 196, Columbus, Ga. 31902.

SCHLUTER, WILLIAM EVERETT R
N.J. State Assemblyman
b. Bronxville, N.Y, 11/5/27; s. Fredric E. Schluter and Charlotte Mueller S; m. 7/3/50 to Nancy Hurd; c. William E, Jr, Nancy C, Sally R, Peter L. and Stephen A. Educ: Princeton Univ, B.A, 50. Polit. & Govt. Pos: Pres. and co-founder, Hopewell Valley Young Rep. Club, N.J, 55; committeeman, Mercer Co. Rep. Party, 58-63; munic. Rep. capt, Pennington Borough, N.J, 59-63; councilman, Borough of Pennington, N.J, 63-, coun. pres, 66; del, Rep. Nat. Conv, 64; Rep. cand, N.J. State Senate, Sixth Dist, 65; N.J. State Assemblyman, currently. Bus. & Prof. Pos: V.pres, Garden State Forge Co, 56- Rel: Presbyterian. Mailing Add: 205 S. Main St, Pennington, N.J. 08534. (1967)

SCHMA, DONALD WILLIAM R
Chmn, Monterey Co. Rep. Cent. Cmt, Calif.
b. Evanston, Ill, 7/16/32; s. John William Schma and Suzanne Kremer S; m. 12/27/56 to Marjorie Bray Cohen; c. Douglas, Kathryn, Jennifer, Peter, Elizabeth and Sarah. Educ: Purdue Univ, Lib. Arts, 53; Northwest. Univ, D.D.S, 57; Univ. Calif, San Francisco, postgrad. work, 58; Phi Gamma Delta; Delta Sigma Delta. Polit. & Govt. Pos: Mem, Calif. Rep. State Cent. Cmt, 68-; mem, Monterey Co. Rep. Cent. Cmt, 68-69 and chmn, 69-; mem, Calif. Co. Chmn. Asn; chmn, 34th Assembly Rep. Cmt. Bus. & Prof. Pos: Dentist, self employed, 57- Mil. Serv: Entered as Ens, Navy, 56, released as Lt, 60, after serv. in Fleet Activities, Sasebo, Japan. Mem: Calif. and Am. Dent. Asns; Commonwealth Club, Calif; exec. bd, Anti-Poverty Coord. Coun; Lions (past dir); Commun. Chest. Rel: Roman Catholic. Legal Res: Ronda Rd, Pebble Beach, Calif. 93953. Mailing Add: 400 Pacific, Monterey, Calif. 93940.

SCHMALZL, KURT CHARLES R
Cmt. Secy, Logan Co. Rep. Cent. Cmt, Ill.
b. Lincoln, Ill, 3/21/06; s. Johann C. Schmalzl and Anna Louise Ziegler S; m. 6/1/28 to Lois Naoma McKinney. Educ: High Sch, class 25. Polit. & Govt. Pos: Justice of the Peace, East Lincoln Twp, Ill, 46-50; town auditor, East Lincoln 60-; v.chmn, Logan Co. Rep. Cent. Cmt, 48-52, committee secy, 52- Mem: Nat. Asn. Independent Ins. Agents; Nat. Asn. Mutual Ins. Agents. Rel: Evangelical Lutheran Church Mo. Synod. Mailing Add: 503 N. Sherman St, Lincoln, Ill. 62656.

SCHMARJE, CLARENCE F. R
Iowa State Rep.
b. Muscatine, Iowa, 7/30/11; s. Claus H. Schmarje and Emma Silberhorn S; m. 6/15/33 to Doris I. De Camp; c. David P, Ronald R. and Diane S. (Mrs. Wood). Educ: Univ. Iowa, B.S. in mech. eng, 32, M.S, 34 and Ph.D.(mech. eng), 35; Tau Beta Pi; Sigma Xi. Polit. & Govt. Pos: Iowa State Rep, 67- Bus. & Prof. Pos: Pres. and founder, Schmarje Tool Co, 42- Publ: Radiation in Boiler Furnaces, Am. Soc. Mech. Engrs, 34. Mem: Am. Soc. Mech. Engrs; Iowa Eng. Soc; Am. Soc. Tool & Mfg. Engrs; Elks; Mason; Consistory; K.T; Shrine. Rel: Methodist. Legal Res: 2015 Mulberry Ave, Muscatine, Iowa 52761. Mailing Add: P.O. Box 16, Muscatine, Iowa 52761.

SCHMIDHAUSER, JOHN RICHARD D
b. Bronx, N.Y, 1/3/22; married; c. Steven, Paul, Thomas, John Christopher, Martha, Sarah and Susan. Educ: Univ. Del, B.A, 1949; Univ. Va, M.A, 1952, Ph.D, 1954; Phi Beta Phi; Phi Beta Kappa. Polit. & Govt. Pos: Precinct committeeman and chmn, Johnson Co. Dem. Party, Iowa; U.S. Rep, Iowa, 64-66; mem, Nat. Cmt. on Tax Justice, currently. Bus. & Prof. Pos: Prof. polit. sci, Univ. Iowa, 54- Mil. Serv: Enlisted man in U.S. Navy including duty on the aircraft carrier U.S.S. Bon Homme Richard, Philippine campaign, the Battle of Okinawa, and final assault on Japan under Adm. Halsey, Aug. 1941 to Dec. 1945. Publ: The Supreme Court as Arbiter in Federal State Relations, Univ. N.C. Press, 58; The Supreme Court; Its Politics, Personalities and Procedures, Holt, Rinehart and Winston, 60; Constitutional Law in the Political Process, Rand McNally, 63. Mem: Am. Asn. of Univ. Profs; Am. Polit. Sci. Asn; Izaak Walton League; Am. Asn. for the Adv. of Sci. Rel: Unitarian Church. Mailing Add: 1112 E. Court St, Iowa City, Iowa 52240.

SCHMIDT, ADOLPH WILLIAM R
U.S. Ambassador to Can.
b. McKeesport, Pa, 9/13/04; s. Adolph Schmidt and Louise S; m. 6/27/36 to Helen S. Mellon; c. Helen S.M.(Mrs. Bidwell) and Thomas M. Educ: Princeton Univ, A.B, 26; Harvard Univ, M.B.A, 29; Univ. Dijon, Univ. Berlin and Univ. Paris, Cert, 26-27. Hon. LL.D, Univ. Pittsburgh, 54; hon. L.H.D, Chatham Col, 65. Polit. & Govt. Pos: Chmn, Pa. State Planning Bd, 55-67; U.S. Ambassador to Can, 69- Bus. & Prof. Pos: Officer, Mellon Nat. Bank and affiliated orgns, Pittsburgh, Pa, 29-42; pres. and trustee, A.W. Mellon Educ. and Charitable Trust, 40-65; v.pres. and gov, T. Mellon & Sons, Pittsburgh, 46-69; trustee, Old Dominion Found, currently; Carnegie Inst, currently. Mil. Serv: Entered as Capt, Army, 42, released as Lt. Col, 46, after serv. in Inf, Off. Strategic Serv, African and European Theatres and Allied Control Cmn, Berlin; Bronze Star; two Battle Stars. Mem: Pres. and chmn, Allegheny Conf. on Commun. Develop, Pittsburgh, Pa; chmn, Southwest. Pa. Regional Planning Cmn; dir, Pittsburgh Regional Planning Asn; v.chmn, Urban Redevelop. Authority; Atlantic Coun. of the U.S, Wash, D.C; Atlantic Inst, Paris; Coun. on For. Rels, N.Y; Mil. Order of the World Wars. David Glick Award, World Affairs Coun, 64. Rel: Presbyterian. Legal Res: Star Route S, Ligonier, Pa. 15658. Mailing Add: U.S. Embassy, 100 Wellington St, Ottawa 4, Ontario, Can.

SCHMIDT, ARTHUR LOUIS R
Ky. State Rep.
b. Cold Spring, Ky, 5/1/27; s. Joseph Edwin Schmidt and Elizabeth Bertsch S; m. 4/28/51 to Marian Seibert; c. Karen Ann and Marianne. Educ: Univ. Ky, '57-58. Polit. & Govt. Pos: Treas, Campbell Co. Young Rep. Party, 57; co. chmn, Campbell Co. Young Rep, 58 & 59; state chmn, Young Rep. Clubs of Ky, 59 & 60; mem, Ky. State Rep. Cent. Cmt, 60-; city Coun, Cold Spring, 62 & 63; Ky. State Rep, 64, 65 & 68-; del, Rep. Nat. Conv, 64 & 68; mem, Tax Appeal Bd, Cold Spring, 66. Bus. & Prof. Pos: Plant dept, Cincinnati & Sub. Bell Tel. Co, 46-55, communication consult, 55-58, eng. tech, 58-62 and mkt. develop. supvr, 62; mem. bd. dir, Lakeside Place Home for the Aged, 62 & 63; mem. bd. dir, Bank of Alexandria, 67-; mem. bd. dir, North. Ky. C. of C, currently. Mil. Serv: Entered as A/S, Navy, 45, released as Seaman 1/C, 46, after serv. in Asiatic Pac. Area, 45-46; Victory Medal; Am. Area Campaign Medal; Asiatic Pac. Area Campaign Medal; Japan Occupation Medal. Mem: K. of C; Holy Name Soc; YMCA; Lakeside Place Asn; chmn, United Appeal; past mem, AFL-CIO; CWA. Rel: Catholic. Mailing Add: 134 Winters Lane, Cold Spring, Ky. 41076.

SCHMIDT, ERIC WILLIAM R
Colo. State Rep.
b. Newark, N.J. 5/31/33; s. Erich Herman Schmidt and Elfriede Böhm S; m. Feb. 1955 to LaKay Gottier; c. Deborah, Eric Thomas, Laura and Jennifer. Educ: Norwich Univ, 51-53; Univ. Colo, B.S, 55; Maroon Key; Lambda Chi Alpha. Polit. & Govt. Pos: Colo. State Rep, Dist. 42, 69- Mem: Jaycees (bd. dirs. & internal v.pres, Denver Chap, state pres, Colo. Chap, nat. v.pres); sen, Jr. Chamber Int; bd. dirs, Colo. C. of C; bd. dirs, Colo. Univ. Alumni; mem, Gov. 100 Man Cmn. on Local Govt; mem, Gov. Indust. Develop. Adv. Coun; mem, Colo. Tech. Serv. Adv. Coun; trustee, Boulder Tomorrow. Outstanding Dir. Award, Key Man Award, Paul West Award and Clayton Frost Award, Jaycees; Named One of Five Outstanding Jaycee State Pres. in the U.S; Named Boulder's Outstanding Young Man, 69; Named One of Three Outstanding Young Men of Colorado, 69. Rel: Lutheran. Mailing Add: 2670 Iliff, Boulder, Colo. 80302.

SCHMIDT, FREDERICK D. D
N.Y. State Assemblyman
b. Queens, N.Y, 6/30/32; m. to Julia Casassa; c. Four. Educ: Holy Trinity High Sch; St. John's Col. Polit. & Govt. Pos: N.Y. State Assemblyman, 64- Bus. & Prof. Pos: Trial attorney, firm of Terhune, Gibbons, and Muluehill. Mil. Serv: 1st Lt, Marine Corps. Mem: N.Y. State Bar Asn; Fordham Law Alumni, St. Thomas Holy Name Soc; Moose; Am. Legion; Steben Soc; hon. mem, Richhaven Little League; chmn, Interfaith Christmas Procession. Mailing Add: 94-39 Park Lane, South Woodhaven, N.Y. 11421. (1967)

SCHMIDT, LOUIS EDWARD R
b. Saginaw, Mich, 6/25/09; s. Edward John Schmidt and Mary Louisa Pratt S; m. 3/27/34 to Frances Ann Baumgarten; c. Barbara J. and Betty J. Educ: Cent. Mich. Univ, A.B, 31; Univ. Mich, M.A, 37; grad. study, Mich. State Univ. and Wayne State Univ; Phi Delta Kappa. Polit. & Govt. Pos: Mem, Livonia Traffic Cmn, Mich, 51-62; v.chmn, Livonia Youth Cmn, 63-66; Mich. State Rep, 35th Dist, 67-68. Bus. & Prof. Pos: Prin, Kalkaska High Sch, Mich, 31-37, Onaway Sch, 37-42, Eaton Rapids Sch, 42-44 and Plymouth High Sch, 46-48; supt, Clarenceville Sch. Dist, 48-66. Mil. Serv: Entered as Lt.(jg), Navy, 44, released as Lt, 46, after serv. in Asiatic-Pac. Theater; Asiatic-Pac. Theater Ribbon with Three Stars; Philippine Liberation Medal; Am. Theater Ribbon. Mem: Mich. and Nat. Educ. Asns; Mich. and Am. Asn. Sch. Adminstrs; Optimist (past pres. and secy); VFW; F&AM (past master). Rel: Presbyterian. Mailing Add: 20405 Antago, Livonia, Mich. 48152. (1967)

SCHMIDT, RICHARD HUESTIS D
b. Burlington, Vt, 11/8/31; m. to Joan Sampson. Educ: Middlebury Col, B.A, 54; George Wash. Univ. Law Sch, LL.B, 59. Polit. & Govt. Pos: Vt. State Rep, 63-66. Bus. & Prof. Pos: Lawyer. Mil. Serv: Army, Pfc, 54-56, Germany. Mem: Am, Vt. and Chittenden Co. Bar Asns; Legal Aid Soc. Rel: Episcopal. 1967 Legal Res: Burlington, Vt. No mailing address available. (1967)

SCHMIDT, RICHARD MARTEN, JR. D
b. Winfield, Kans, 8/2/24; s. Richard M. Schmidt and Ida Marten S; m. 1/2/48 to Ann Downing; c. Eric, Gregory, Rolf and Heidi. Educ: Univ. Denver, A.B, 45, Col. Law, LL.B, 48; Omicron Delta Kappa; Lambda Chi Alpha; Phi Delta Phi. Polit. & Govt. Pos: Dep. dist. attorney, dist. attorney, Denver, Colo, 49-50; mem. finance cmt, Colo. Dem. State Cmt, 54-64; spec. counsel, U.S. Senate Spec. Agr. Invest. Subcmt, 59-60; mem, Dem. State Adv. Cmt, Colo, 62-65; del-at-lg, Dem. Nat. Conv, 64; mem, Colo. Cmn. on Higher Educ,

65; gen. counsel and cong. liaison, U.S. Info. Agency, D.C, 65-68. Bus. & Prof. Pos: Partner, Schmidt, Van Cise, Freeman & Tooley, Attorneys, Denver, Colo, 54-65; partner, Cohn & Marks, D.C, 69- Mem: Am. and Colo. Bar Asns; pres, Denver Bar Asn, 63-64; Fed. Commun. Bar Asn; Univ. Club; bd. trustees, Univ. Denver; Fed. City Club; Denver and Nat. Press Club. Distinguished Honor Award, U.S. Info. Agency, 68. Mailing Add: 1920 L St. N.W, Washington, D.C. 20036.

SCHMIDT, ROBERT D
b. Kenosha Co, Wis, 8/2/13; s. Jacob Schmidt and Elizabeth Riechel S; m. 5/25/35 to Virginia Marie Hembrook; c. Robert Allen, Dorian Lee and Dolores Mae. Polit. & Govt. Pos: Town supvr, Greenfield, Wis, 52-54; supvr, Milwaukee Co, 56-60; Wis. State Assemblyman, 23rd Assembly Dist, 52-54. Mem: West Allis Blue Lodge 291, AF&AM; Chap, Consistory, Shrine; Union pres, Local 335, UAW, CIO; YMCA; Hy. 41 Advancement Asn. Rel: Lutheran. Mailing Add: 4017 S. 104th St, Greenfield, Wis. 53328.

SCHMIDT, ROBIN R
b. Santa Barbara, Calif, 3/31/28; m. 1953 to Gretchen Reinke; c. Bridget, Michael and Prudence. Educ: Univ. Calif, Santa Barbara, 4 years. Polit. & Govt. Pos: Admin. asst, U.S. Rep. Pete McCloskey, Calif, 68- Bus. & Prof. Pos: Newspaper reporter, Los Angeles Times and Alhambra Post-Advocate, Calif, 50-55; mgr, News Bur, Pac. Finance Corp, Los Angeles, 55-57; dir. advert. and pub. rels, Solar, subsidiary of Int. Harvester, San Diego, 57-63; v.pres, Phillips-Ramsey Inc, San Diego, Calif, 63-68. Mil. Serv: Entered as A/S, Naval Res, 45, released as Seaman 1/C, 46, after serv. in Pac. Theatre; World War II Victory and Pac. Theatre Medals. Mem: Pub. Rels. Soc. Am; San Diego Pub. Rels. Club; pub. rels. adv. cmt, Aerospace Industs. Asn; pub. rels. cmt, San Diego Zool. Soc; Bearcats-Wildcats Asn. of San Diego; La. Jolla Beach and Volleyball Club. George Washington Honor Medal, Freedoms Found; First prize for best publ, Calif. State Fair; numerous pub. rels. awards. Legal Res: 4425 Casitas St, San Diego, Calif. 92107. Mailing Add: 1511 Longworth House Office Bldg, Washington, D.C. 20515.

SCHMIT, LORAN R
Nebr. State Sen.
b. Butler Co, Nebr, 8/14/29; m. 8/5/50 to Irene JoAnn Squire; c. Marcia, Steven, Mary, Julie, John, Michele, Susan, Jeanie, Lori and Mike. Educ: Univ. Nebr, B.S, 50. Polit. & Govt. Pos: Chmn, Butler Co. Rep. Party, Nebr, currently; Nebr. State Sen, Dist. 23, 69- Bus. & Prof. Pos: Pres, Mid-Am. Helicopter Serv, Inc, currently; Owner, Farm, Butler Co, Nebr, currently. Rel: Catholic. Legal Res: R.R. 3, David City, Nebr. 68632. Mailing Add: State Capitol, Lincoln, Nebr. 68509.

SCHMIT, NICHOLAS MATTHEW 'NICK' D
Chmn, 26th Dist. Dem. Non-Partisan League Exec. Cmt, N.Dak.
b. Wyndmere, N.Dak, Mar. 15; s. Nicholas Schmit Sr. and Rose Woodle S; m. 5/16/42 to Eleanore Klosterman; c. Kairouan (Mrs. Moffett), Mary, Nicholas M, III, Anthony and Patricia. Educ: Wyndmere Public Schools. Polit. & Govt. Pos: N.Dak. State Sen, 53-55; city councilman, Wyndmere, N.Dak, 54-56; mem. adv. cmt, N.Dak. Dem. Non-Partisan League Legis. Group, 66-; mem. exec. cmt, N.Dak. Dem. Non-Partisan League Century Club, 67-; alternate del, Dem. Nat. Conv, 68; campaign cmt. mem, U.S. Senate Cmt, 68; mem, N.Dak. Dem. Non-Partisan League Exec. Cmt, 68-; chmn, 26th Dist. Dem. Non-Partisan League Exec. Cmt, currently. Bus. & Prof. Pos: Pres, Schmit Inc, Wyndmere, N.Dak, 61- Mil. Serv: Qm.C, Army, 42-45; Marksmanship Medal. Mem: N.Dak. Bldg. Mover's Asn; Elks; Am. Legion; K. of C; Wyndmere Commercial Club. Rel: Roman Catholic. Mailing Add: Wyndmere, N.Dak. 58081.

SCHMITT, C. L. D
Pa. State Rep.
b. Pittsburgh, Pa, 5/8/12; s. Ludwig Schmitt and Hattie Primbs S; m. 5/6/35 to Sally Lou Byers; c. Patty Lou (Mrs. Martini), James P, Susan J. and David L. Educ: Univ. Pittsburgh. Polit. & Govt. Pos: Mem. city coun, New Kensington, Pa, 50-54; Pa. State Rep, 64- Bus. & Prof. Pos: Owner, C.L. Schmitt Real Estate and Ins, 44- Mem: Soc. Real Estate Appraisers (S.R.A. Degree); Am. Col. Real Estate Appraisers; New Kensington Bd. Realtors (past pres); Pa. Realtors Asn.(past state v.pres); Nat. Asn. Real Estate Bd; Int. Brotherhood of Magicians (Int. pres, 61-62); Lions Int.(Int. counsr, 44-); Lower Burrell C. of C.(charter pres, 59-60); Lions Club of New Kensington (charter pres, 39-40); K. of C; Moose; Holy Name Soc; Vol. for Good Govt. Rel: Catholic. Legal Res: 1015 Edgewood Rd, New Kensington, Pa. 15068. Mailing Add: 96 Craigdell Rd, Lower Burrell, Pa. 15068. (1967)

SCHMITT, JOHN WILLIAM D
b. Milwaukee, Wis, 2/3/20; s. Joseph Charles Schmitt and Margaret Nowak S; m. 5/4/46 to Gertrude Mary Strelka; c. James John, Jane Catherine, Jeffrey Robert and John Joseph. Educ: Univ. Wis. Exten, 39-40. Polit. & Govt. Pos: Alternate del, Dem. Nat. Conv, 68. Bus. & Prof. Pos: Corresponding and recording secy, Brewery Workers AFL-CIO, 52-60; exec. v.pres, Wis. State AFL-CIO, 60-66, pres, 66- Mil. Serv: Entered as Pvt, Army, 42, released as Sgt, 45, after serv. in Hq. Fifth Army, Africa-Italy Theatre, 43-45. Good Conduct medal; Two Battle Stars; Am. Theatre Ribbon; Europe-Africa-Middle East Theatre Ribbon; Four Overseas Serv. Bars; One Serv. Stripe, Victory Medal. Mem: Policy bd, State Bd. Voc, Tech. and Adult Educ. Rehabilitation Div; state adv. cmt, Title III, Elem. and Sec. Educ. Act. 1965; state apprenticeship cmt, Adv. Cmt. Sch. Workers, Univ. Wis; bd. visitors, Stout State Univ; City of Milwaukee; Audit and Surv. Cmt; World Festival Cmt; Milwaukee Co. Planning Cmn; Wis. Adv. Cmt. Unemploy. Compensation and Workmen's Compensation; Wis. Equal Employ. Opportunity Asn; Nat. Conf. Christian & Jews; Cath. Interracial Coun. Rel: Catholic. Legal Res: 3326 N. 79th St, Milwaukee, Wis. 53222. Mailing Add: 6333 W. Bluemound Rd, Milwaukee, Wis. 53213.

SCHMITZ, JOHN G. R
Calif. State Sen.
b. Milwaukee, Wis, 8/12/30; m. to Mary E. Suehr; c. John, Joseph, Jerome, Mary Kay, Theresa Ann and Elizabeth Louise. Educ: Marquette Univ, B.S, 52; Long Beach State Col, M.A, 60; Claremont Grad. Sch; Phi Alpha Theta. Polit. & Govt. Pos: Former mem. bd. dirs, Orange Co. Conserv. Coord. Coun; former faculty adv, Santa Ana Col. Young Rep; chmn, Orange Co. Coord. Rep. Assembly, twice; mem, Calif. Rep. Assembly, United Rep. of Calif. and Calif. Young Rep; Calif. State Sen, Orange Co, 64-66, 34th Sen. Dist, 66-, chmn, Local Gov. Cmt, mem, Finance Cmt, past chmn. and mem, Mil. and Vet. Affairs Cmt, mem, Educ. Cmt. and Elec. and Reapportionment Cmt, Calif. State Senate; mem, Joint Cmt. on Higher Educ. and Calif. Delinquency Prev. Cmn. Bus. & Prof. Pos: Instr. philos, hist. and polit. sci, Santa Ana Col, 60- Mil. Serv: Aviator, Marine Corps, 52-60; Lt. Col. Marine Corps Res. Mem: Am. Legion; Mil. Order of World Wars; K. of C; Order of the Alhambra; John Birch Soc; Phi Alpha Theta; Nat. Rifle Asn; Calif. Rifle and Pistol Asn; Marine Corps Reserve Officers Asn; Marine Corps League; adv. bd, Boys Club of Tustin; charter mem, Nat. Soc. State Legislators. Mailing Add: 18002 Irvine Blvd, Tustin, Calif. 92680.

SCHMITZ, ROBERT JOSEPH DFL
b. Jordan, Minn, 4/23/21; s. Jacob Schmitz and Mary Lambrecht S; m. 11/22/47 to Grace Savage; c. Susan, Murray, Kristine, Robin and Karen. Educ: Jordan High Sch, grad. Polit. Pos: Chmn, Scott Co. Dem-Farmer-Labor Party, Minn, 63-66. Bus. & Prof. Pos: Chmn, Scott Co. Farmers Union, 60-64. Rel: Catholic. Mailing Add: Jordan, Minn. 55352. (1967)

SCHMUTZLER, EMIL HERMANN, JR. R
Ind. State Sen.
b. Huntingburg, Ind, 9/26/23; s. Emil H. Schmutzler, Sr. and Lovina Reutepohler S; m. 5/8/49 to Wanda Faye Giesler; c. Kurt William, Mark Stephen, John Scott and Ann Margaret. Educ: Ind. Univ. Sch. Mortuary Sci, grad, 48. Polit. & Govt. Pos: Coroner, Dubois Co, Ind, 56-64; Ind. State Sen, 66- Bus. & Prof. Pos: Owner, Schmutzler Funeral Homes, 46- and Schmutzler Apt, 56-; mem. bd. dirs, World Life & Accident Asn, 58- and Tyler Fiberglass, Inc, 60- Mil. Serv: Entered as A/S, Navy, 42, commissioned as Naval Aviator, 43, with serv. as fighter pilot aboard aircraft carrier, World War II and jet pilot, Korea; Comdr, Naval Aviation Res. and commanding officer, Res. Navy Jet Squadron, currently; Silver Star; Three Distinguished Flying Crosses; eleven Air Medals; Presidential Unit, Pac. Fleet and Korean Presidential Unit Citations; eleven other area and battle citations. Publ: 'Abortion in Indiana', Newsweek, 67; 'Capitol Punishment—Yes or No', Indianapolis J, 69. Mem: Nat. Soc. of State Legislators; Nat. and Ind. Funeral Dirs. Asns; Nat. Asn. of Jet Fighter Pilots; Nat. Asn. of United Serv. Orgn; Mason; Shrine; Am. Legion; VFW; 40 et 8; Navy Club of the U.S.A; Elks; Moose; Eagles; past pres, Dist. PTA. Named one of three outstanding Freshmen Senators, 67; Outstanding Award, Dist. PTA; Legionnaire Outstanding Award, 68. Rel: United Church of Christ. Legal Res: 1427 Newton St, Jasper, Ind. 47546. Mailing Add: P.O. Box 378, Jasper, Ind. 47546.

SCHNEEBELI, HERMAN THEODORE R
U.S. Rep, Pa.
b. Lancaster, Pa, 7/7/07; s. Alfred Schneebeli and Barbara Schneider S; m. 9/21/39 to Mary Louise Meyer; c. Marta and Susan. Educ: Dartmouth Col, A.B, 30; Amos Tuck Sch, Dartmouth Grad. Sch, M.C.S. in Bus. Admin, 31; Theta Delta Chi. Polit. & Govt. Pos: Former mem, Williamsport Sch. Bd, Pa; U.S. Rep, Pa, 60- Bus. & Prof. Pos: Cmn. distributor, Gulf Oil Corp, 39-; Buick automobile dealer, Muncy Motor Co, 48-65; dir, Fidelity Nat. Bank of Williamsport. Mil. Serv: Entered as Lt, Army, 42, released as Capt, 46, after serv. in Ord. Dept. as Exec. and Commanding Officer, 3 different high explosive plants, U.S. Mem: Past pres, bd. trustees, YWCA; bd. mgrs, Williamsport Hosp; past v.pres, Williamsport Indust. Cmt; past pres, Williamsport Commun. Chest; Am. Legion; Elks; Kiwanis; past bd. mem, Williamsport Coun. of Churches. Recipient Meritorious Commun. Serv. Award presented by Grit. Rel: Episcopal; Vestryman. Legal Res: 870 Hollywood Circle, Williamsport, Pa. 17701. Mailing Add: 1336 Longworth House Office Bldg, Washington, D.C. 20515.

SCHNEEBERG, ERVIN F. R
Wis. State Assemblyman
b. Brown Deer, Wis, 4/7/19; s. Charles Schneeberg and Alma S; m. 11/23/51 to Georgia Karrns; c. Becky and Kirk. Educ: Univ. Wis-Milwaukee, 2 years. Polit. & Govt. Pos: Mem. sch. bd, Brown Deer Sch, Wis, 45-50; town clerk, Twp. of Granville, 50-55; village clerk, Brown Deer, 55-57, village mgr, 57-60; Wis. State Assemblyman, 69- Bus. & Prof. Pos: Owner, Erv Schneeberg Agency, 49- Mem: Brown Deer Businessmen's Asn. Rel: Lutheran. Mailing Add: 8540 N. 42nd, Brown Deer, Wis. 53209.

SCHNEIDER, ALLAN IVAN R
Co. Chmn. Rep. Party, Tex.
b. Scotland, 11/15/29; s. Ivan Earp Schneider and Jean Simpson S; m. 7/18/63 to Margaret Varner; c. David, Sandra, Bruce and Laura. Educ: Baylor Univ, LL.B, 58; Phi Delta Phi. Polit. & Govt. Pos: Co. Chmn, Rep. Party, Tex, currently. Bus. & Prof. Pos: Attorney-at-law, 58-66. Mil. Serv: Entered as Pvt, Air Force, 47, released as T/Sgt. Mem: Tex. State Bar Asn; Rotary; C. of C. Rel: Methodist. Legal Res: 489 Schneider, Giddings, Tex. 78942. Mailing Add: Box 87, Giddings, Tex. 78942.

SCHNEIDER, EDWARD R
b. Chicago, Ill. Polit. & Govt. Pos: Ill. State Rep, 65th-73rd Gen. Assemblies; pres, Eighth Ward Rep. Orgn. Bus. & Prof. Pos: Assoc. with Robert E. L. Brooks, Inc. Mil. Serv: Infantry, in France, as Lt. Mem: Ill. Fedn. of Sportsmen's Club; 40 et 8; Ava Cross Chatham Post No. 27-05; VFW; Builders' Tee Club; Elks; Past Master of Aaron Masonic Lodge; Grand Crossing Chap. No. 219; RAM; Englewood Commandery, K.T; AASR, Valley of Chicago and Medinah Temple. Mailing Add: 8638 S. Euclid Ave, Chicago, Ill. 60617.

SCHNEIDER, JOHN DURBIN D
Mo. State Rep.
b. St. Louis, Mo, 3/1/37; s. F. John Schneider and Kathleen Durbin; m. 11/4/61 to Mary Jo Steppan; c. Anne Marie, John Steppan and Robert Durbin. Educ: St. Louis Univ, 54-60, B.S. and J.D; Phi Delta Phi. Polit. & Govt. Pos: Mo. State Rep, 26th Dist, 69- Bus. & Prof. Pos: Attorney, Transit Casualty Co, 60-65, Chief Trial Attorney, 66-68 and Assoc. Gen. Counsel, 68- Mil. Serv: Army, 61, released as Pfc. Rel: Catholic. Mailing Add: 1185 Penhurst, Florissant, Mo. 63033.

SCHNEIDER, LOUIS JACOB, JR. R
Judge, Ohio Supreme Court
b. Cincinnati, Ohio, 9/26/21; s. Louis J. Schneider and Florence Hinnenkamp S; m. 9/5/47 to Ruth Ann Kirkendall; c. Thomas, Carol and Nancy. Educ: Princeton Univ; Univ. Cincinnati, A.B, 47, LL.B, 49; Order of the Coif; Phi Delta Phi; Beta Theta Pi. Polit. & Govt. Pos: Ohio State Rep, 51-59; co. cmnr, Hamilton Co, Ohio, 59-63; tax cmnr, Ohio, 63-64; judge, Ohio Supreme Court, 65- Bus. & Prof. Pos: Attorney-at-law, Cors, Scherer & Hair, 49-53; partner, law firm Cors, Hair, Hartsock & Schneider, 53-61; attorney-at-law, private practice, Cincinnati, 61-64. Mil. Serv: Entered as Pvt, Army, 43, released as 1st Lt, 46, after serv. in Inf, Alaska. Publ: Co-auth, Schneider's Criminal Code, W. H. Anderson Co, 51. Mem: Cincinnati, Ohio State and Am. Bar Asns; Cincinnatus Asn; F&AM; Scottish Rite; Shrine; Am. Legion; Sons of Union Vet. of the Civil War; The Athletic Club of Columbus; The Univ. Club of Columbus. Rel: Mariemont Community Church. Mailing Add: 6932 Maimi Bluff Dr, Mariemont, Ohio 45227.

SCHNEIDER, MILTON EDWARD D
b. Milwaukee, Wis, 9/2/10; s. Harry Schneider and Sarah Borenstein S; m. 1/31/42 to Gloria Bocaner; c. Stephen, Thomas, Gerald and Laurie. Educ: Marquette Univ, Bus. Admin. Polit. & Govt. Pos: Chmn, Wood Co. Dem. Party, Wis, 50-52; mem-at-lg, Admin. Cmt, Dem. Party, Wis, 51-57 & 69-; del, Dem. Nat. Conv, 52, 56, 64 & 68; pres, Proxmire for Gov. Clubs of Wis, 56; pres, Area PTA, 58-60; chmn, Commun. Coun. Higher Educ. Cmt, 60-66; v.chmn, Univ. Wis. Bd. of Visitors, 63-65, chmn, 65-67. Bus. & Prof. Pos: Partner, Bocaner Schneider Enterprises, 47-; pres, Gen. Distributing Corp, 58- Mil. Serv: Entered as Pvt, Army, 43, released as 1st Lt, 46, after serv. in Adj. Gen. Corps, Am. Theater; Army Commendation Medal. Mem: Rotary; C. of C; Commun. Coun. Received Wisconsin Rapids Citizen of Year Award, 62. Mailing Add: 447 Mead Circle, Wisconsin Rapids, Wis. 54494.

SCHNEIDER, MORRIS H. D
Mem, Nassau Co. Dem. Cmt, N.Y.
b. New York, N.Y, 8/15/10; s. Philip Schneider and Bessie Haas S; m. 2/7/37 to Estelle I. Simon; c. Alan and Betsy. Educ: St. John's Univ, B.S, 32, Sch. Law, J.D, 36; past pres, Sigma Lambda Tau. Polit. & Govt. Pos: Pres, Rockville Centre Dem. Club, N.Y, 55-57; committeeman, Rockville Centre Zone, Dem. Party, 55-; mem, Affiliated Young Dem, N.Y, 55-; trustee and mem, Citizens Party, Rockville Centre, 60-; mem, Nassau Co. Cmt. for Aged, 64, Nassau Co. Off. Econ. Opportunity and Nassau Co. Youth Bds, 65-, Nassau Co. Crime Coun, 67-, Nassau Co. Health and Welfare Coun. and Nassau Co. Supreme Court Libr. Bd, chmn. and mem, Nassau Co. Traffic Safety Coun. and mem, Nassau-Suffolk Comprehensive Health Planning Coun; co. attorney, Nassau Co, 65-; mem, Nassau Co. Dem. Cmt. and leader, Rockville Centre Dem. Orgn, currently. Bus. & Prof. Pos: Exec. secy. and counsel, Metrop. Contractors Asn, 41-62 and Nat. Refrigeration and Air Conditioning Contractors Asn, 48-50. Mem: Unlawful Practice Cmt, Brooklyn Bar Asn, 40-, Ethics Cmt, 52- and Arbitration Cmt; Ment. Hygiene Cmt, N.Y. State Bar Asn, 60- and Cmt. to Establish a Law Center and sch. in Nassau Co. and Suffolk; chmn, Nassau Co. Bar Asn. Publ, Nassau Lawyer, 63-65; Nassau Co. Bar Asn, Grievance and Labor Cmts, 68-; past chancellor, Herzl Lodge K. of P; Mason; past pres, Rockville Centre Jewish Commun. Coun; past pres. and trustee, Cent. Synagogue Men's Club; pres. and trustee, Cent. Synagogue Nassau; Chautaugua Soc; trustee, Nat. Fedn. Temple Brotherhoods, Metrop. Conf, Mid Village Civic Asn. and Cmt. for Better Educ, Rockville Centre Sch. Dist; v.pres, Lawyers Div, Fedn. Jewish Philanthropies; Gen. Coun, Nassau Commun. Col; bd. dirs, Nassau Co. Law Serv. Cmt, Inc; dir, Nat. Asn. Co. Civil Attorneys, 67-; Nat. Inst. Munic. Law Officers. Rel: Hebrew. Mailing Add: 386 Raymond St, Rockville Centre, N.Y. 11570.

SCHNEIDER, NELSON MYRON D
V.Chmn, Prince Georges Co. New Dem. Coalition, Md.
b. Brooklyn, N.Y, 3/24/39; s. Mullen S. Schneider and Anne Barnett S; m. 2/10/62 to Marilyn Siegel; c. Craig David and Glenn Russell. Educ: Brooklyn Polytech. Inst, 56-58; Brooklyn Col, 58-61; Ed-in-chief, Brooklyn Col. Newspaper; KEN. Polit. & Govt. Pos: Publicity chmn, Kings Co. Dem. and Independents for Johnson, Humphrey & Kennedy, N.Y, 64 and Kings Co. Reform Dem. for Lindsay, 65; coordinator, Ryan for Mayor Primary Campaign, 13th Cong. Dist, 65; treas, Roosevelt Reform Dem. Club, 65-67; finance chmn, Mel Dubin for Cong, primary campaign, 66 and spec. elec. campaign, 68; press secy, McCarthy for Pres, Ga. State Campaign, 68; alternate del, Dem. Nat. Conv, 68; asst. press secy, Paul O'Dwyer for U.S. Senate Campaign, 68; v.chmn, Prince Georges Co. New Dem. Coalition, Md, 69- Bus. & Prof. Pos: Assoc. ed, Weekly Bond Buyer, N.Y.C, 61-64; asst. financial ed, N.Y. World-Tel. & Sun, 64-66; v.pres, Wyle Assocs, Inc, 66-68; ed, J. of the Nat. League of Insured Savings Asns, 68-69; chmn. bd, Schumacher-Schneider, Inc, Pub. Rels, 69- Publ: Various newspaper and mag. articles on finance. Mem: N.Y. Financial Writers Asn; K. of P. Rel: Jewish. Mailing Add: 12225 Shadetree Lane, Laurel, Md. 20810.

SCHNEIDER, ROBERT ALLEN R
b. San Antonio, Tex, 8/27/37; s. Theodore Schneider, Sr. and Viola Singer S; m. 12/20/67 to Jacoba Johanna Hoogenkamp. Educ: Univ. Tex, Austin, B.A, 61; Mass. Inst. of Tech, 61-62 & spring 64 & 65; Free Univ. Berlin, 62-63; Phi Beta Kappa. Polit. & Govt. Pos: Rep. nominee, U.S. House of Rep, 20th Dist, Tex, 68. Bus. & Prof. Pos: Pres, Nat. Employers Dir. Serv, Inc, 68- Mil. Serv: Entered as Pvt. E-1, Army, 55, released as Specialist E-4, 58, after serv. in U.S. Army Med. Lab, Landstuhl, Germany, ETO, 56-58. Rel: Methodist. Mailing Add: 1407 W. Woodlawn, San Antonio, Tex. 78201.

SCHNEIDER, RUSSELL EDWARD D
Mem, Ashland Co. Dem. Exec. Cmt, Ohio
b. Greer, Ohio, 11/3/10; s. E.G. Schneider and Francis Weaver S; m. 9/3/31 to Irma Louise Bell; c. Sue (Mrs. Richardson), Mary Alice (Mrs. Staman) and Elisabeth (Mrs. Keneth L. Swinson). Polit. & Govt. Pos: Alternate del, Dem. Nat. Conv, 64; mem, Ashland Co. Dem. Exec. Cmt, Ohio, currently. Bus. & Prof. Pos: Design engr, Flexible Co, 36- Mem: Mason; Nat. Asn. Invest. Club 1135. Rel: Lutheran. Mailing Add: Maple Heights, Loudonville, Ohio 44842.

SCHNEIDER, WILLIAM R
Chmn, Franklin Co. Rep. Exec. Cmt, Ohio
b. Columbus, Ohio, 12/7/92; s. Henry Schneider and Christine Deibert S; m. 9/17/23 to Frieda Heimann; c. William H, Herbert H. and Richard R. Educ: Ohio State Univ. Col. Law, LL.B, 17. Polit. & Govt. Pos: Secy, Franklin Co. Rep. Exec. Cmt, Ohio, 20-35, chmn, 35-; chmn, Ohio Rep. State Speakers Cmt, 36-46; mem, Franklin Co. Bd. of Elec, 38-66, chmn, 40-48; del, Rep. Nat. Conv, 40-68. Bus. & Prof. Pos: Attorney-at-law, Columbus, Ohio, 17-; mem, Graham, Ley & Schneider, Attorneys, 31-45. Mil. Serv: Pvt, Army, 18-19, serv. in Co.B, 309th Ammunition Train, 84th Div, ETO. Mem: Columbus Bar Asn; Mason; Scottish Rite (33°); Shrine; Eastern Star; Am. Legion; Columbus Athletic Club; Columbus Maennerchor; Columbus Automobile Club. Rel: United Church of Christ. Mailing Add: 3816 Norbrook Dr, Columbus, Ohio 43221. (1967)

SCHNEPP, PAULINE HELEN R
V.Chmn, Fremont Co. Rep. Cent. Cmt, Iowa
b. Sidney, Iowa 3/14/12; d. Clinton J. Sanderson and Martha Jane Barrett S; m. 5/21/32 to Verbyl L. Schnepp; c. Danny Lee Schnepp (deceased). Educ: Riverton High Sch, grad, 30; Teachers Col, 3 summers, Teacher's Cert, Cedar Falls. Polit. & Govt. Pos: Rep. precinct committeewoman, Prairie Twp, Fremont Co, Iowa, 41-; pres, Fremont Co. Rep. Women, 64-66; v.chmn, Fremont Co. Rep. Cent. Cmt, 64-; membership chmn, Iowa Fedn. of Rep. Women, Seventh Dist, 65-66, pres, 67-69; del, Rep. Nat. Conv, 68. Bus. & Prof. Pos: Sch. teacher, Fremont Co. Schs, Iowa, 30-32, substitute teaching, 33-58; secy, bookkeeper and agent, Schnepp Ins. Agency, Sidney, Iowa, 50-; secy. and bookkeeper, Schnepp Motor Co, 58-61. Mem: Local, civic and community clubs and organizations. Rel: Protestant; Held off. in church and women's orgn, taught Sunday Sch. and directed church progs, Farragut Congregational Church. Mailing Add: Box 155, Sidney, Iowa 51652.

SCHNITTKER, JOHN ALVIN D
b. Nashville, Kans, 9/22/24; s. John Schnittker and Dorothea Steffan S; m. 5/20/50 to Catherine Patricia Conroy; c. Joseph P, John M, Martin T, Daniel T. and Ann Marie. Educ: Kans. State Univ, B.S. and M.S; Iowa State Univ, Ph.D. Polit. & Govt. Pos: Sr. Staff Econ, Coun. of Econ. Adv, 58-59; dir, agr. econ, U.S. Dept. of Agr, 64-65; undersecy, U.S. Dept. Agr, 65-69. Bus. & Prof. Pos: Asst. prof, Kans. State Univ, 56-58, assoc. prof, 59-61, prof, 69- Mil. Serv: Entered as 2nd Lt, Army, 51, released as 1st Lt, 52; Korean Campaign Ribbon; Bronze Star. Legal Res: Manhattan, Kans. 66502. Mailing Add: Dept. of Economics, Kansas State University, Manhattan, Kans. 66502.

SCHOEBERLEIN, ALLEN L. 'AL' R
Ill. State Rep.
b. Aurora, Ill. Educ: Bus. Col. Polit. & Govt. Pos: Chmn. and mem. Kane Co. Bd. Supvr, Ill, 4 years; alderman, First Ward; mayor pro tem, 18 years; v.pres, Ill. Munic. League, 16 years; Rep. precinct committeeman, 26 years; chmn. precinct orgn, 4 years; Ill. State Rep, 62- Bus. & Prof. Pos: Owner, All-Steel Equip. Inc. Mem: Moose (fel. degree); YMCA; Elks; Aurora Sportsmen's Club; Am. Turners; active mem. in numerous other civic and soc. orgn. Mailing Add: 1543 Downer Place, Aurora, Ill. 60506. (1967)

SCHOECK, (VIOLA) JEAN D
Secy, Wyo. Dem. State Cent. Cmt.
b. Rosiclare, Ill, 10/14/23; d. Charles Leonard Schoeck and Viola Wilson S; single. Polit. & Govt. Pos: Secy. to Mayors Ben Nelson and Ed Warren, 48-52; alternate del, Dem. Nat. Conv, 52 & 56, del. and mem, Cmt. on Selection of Chmn, for Nat. Conv, 60; secy. to Sen. Joseph C. O'Mahoney, 54; secy. to co. attoreny Walter B. Phelan, 54-57; secy, Laramie Co. Dem. Cent. Cmt, 54-57, second v.chairwoman, 57-59; secy, Wyo. Dem. State Cent. Cmt, 57-61 & 62-; mem, Gov. Adv. Cmt. on Civil Defense, 59-60; secy. to Theodore C. Sorensen, spec. counsel to President John F. Kennedy, 60-61. Bus. & Prof. Pos: Secy. to Teno Roncalio, state chmn, attorney and banker, 57-60; owner, Jeanne's Secretariat, Cheyenne, Wyo, 62- Publ: 'I've Got 35,000 Bosses,' The Denver Post, 50; 'East Meets West,' Tavern Talk, 53; 'Out Where the West Begins,' Seydell Quart, Belgium, 51. Mem: Eastern Star, Oak Leaf Chap; past pres, Beta Sigma Phi Epsilon Chap; past mem, Cerebral Palsy Asn. and legal secy, Nat. Asn; v.pres, Cheyenne Kennel Club, 68-Named Community Leader of Am, 68. Rel: Protestant. Legal Res: 3315 Cribbon Ave, Cheyenne, Wyo. 82001. Mailing Add: 240 Plains Hotel, Cheyenne, Wyo. 82001.

SCHOEL, RICHARD GEORGE R
Chmn, Union Co. Rep. Party, N.J.
b. Chicago, Ill, 11/4/20; s. Richard George Schoel and Marguerite Mendenhall S; m. 3/18/44 to Helen Shirley Cathcart; c. Marguerite Lynn (Mrs. Conn) and Kenneth Richard. Educ: Univ. Mich, B.S.E, 43; Scabbard and Blade; Delta Tau Delta; Alpha Phi Omega. Polit. & Govt. Pos: Mem, Bd. of Educ, Hicksville, N.Y, 53-55; mem, Union Co. Rep. Cmt, N.J, 61-64, mem. exec. cmt, 62-64; chmn, Goldwater Campaign, Westfield, 64; chmn, Union Co. Rep. Citizens Cmt, 65-66; chmn, Union Co. Rep. Party, 68- Bus. & Prof. Pos: Asst. sales mgr, Solventol Chem. Prod, Detroit, Mich, 46-48; asst. to gen. mgr, John Robert Powers Prod, New York, N.Y, 48-49; asst. sales mgr, Clairol, Inc, 49-50; brand mgr, Lever Bros. Co, 50-55; prod. group dir, Johnson & Johnson, New Brunswick, N.J, 55- Mil. Serv: Entered as Sgt, Army, 43, released as Capt, 46, after serv. in 13th Ord. Bomb Disposal Squad, Mediterranean Theatre of Opers, 45-46; Soldiers Medal. Mem: F&AM. Rel: Orthodox Presbyterian. Mailing Add: 26 Fair Hill Rd, Westfield, N.J. 07090.

SCHOELLKOPF, PAUL A, JR. R
Mem, Nat. Rep. Finance Cmt.
b. Niagara Falls, N.Y, 11/20/16; s. Paul A. Schoellkopf, Sr. and Mattie Irwin Penn S; m. 5/24/41 to Jane Farron Murray; c. Ann Farron, Jane Penn and Susan Beatrice. Educ: Cornell Univ, grad, 41; Kappa Alpha. Polit. & Govt. Pos: Mem, Nat. Rep. Finance Cmt, currently. Bus. & Prof. Pos: Mgr, Gluck Realty Co, 38-46, dir. and pres, 45-46; asst. to chmn. bd, Buffalo Niagara Elec. Co, 45-48; pres. and dir, Pine Ave. Corp, Niagara Falls, 45-; mem, Marine Midland Trust Co, 46-, dir, 53 and chmn. adv. bd, Power City Off, 54-; dir, Niagara Falls Power Co, 48-51 and Niagara Wall Paper Co, Niagara Falls, 48-52; limited partner, Schoellkopf and Co, Buffalo, 48-52; dir, Niagara Falls Hotel Corp, 48-55, v.pres, 49-55; dir, Cornell Aeronaut. Lab, Williamsville, 48- and Trico Prod. Corp, 50-; v.pres, Niagara Share Corp, Buffalo, 51-61, dir, 51- and chmn. exec. cmt, 61-; dir, Genesee Motoramp Garage, Inc, 51-62; dir, Spirella Int, Inc, Niagara Falls, N.Y, 52-58, v.chmn, 53-54, chmn.

bd, 54-58; dir, Mohawk Airlines, Inc, Utica, 52-; dir, Spirella Co. Gt. Brit, Ltd, Herts, Eng, 53-57; v.chmn. bd. and dir, Spirella Co, Inc, Niagara Falls, N.Y. and Spirella Co, Ltd, Niagara Falls, Ont, Can, 53-57; treas. and dir, Niagara Frontier Amusement Corp, 53-54; treas, WGR Corp, 54-56, dir, 54-57 and chmn. exec. cmt, 56-57; chmn. bd. and dir, Int. Breweries, Inc, Detroit, Mich, 55-62, Transcontinent Facilities, Inc, 59-64 and Civic Broadcasters, Inc, 62; v.pres. and dir, Buffalo Niagara Investors, Inc, 56-58 and Chautauqua Broadcasting Corp, Buffalo, 59-61; dir. and chmn. bd. and trustee in liquidation, Transcontinent TV Corp, 56-; v.pres. and dir, Seventy Niagara Serv, Inc, Buffalo, 56-; dir, N.Am. Electronics, Inc, Lynn, Mass, 58-61; chmn. exec. cmt. and dir, Buffalo Sintering Corp. Div, Chicago, Ill, 58-60; dir, Northeast. Pa. Broadcasting Inc, Scranton, Pa, 58, chmn. bd, 64-; asst. secy. and dir, Marietta Broadcasting, Inc, San Diego, Calif, 59-61; dir, Schoellkopf, Hutton and Pomeroy, Inc, 60; pres. and dir, Schoell-Penn Corp, 60-; chmn. bd. and dir, Crescent Niagara Corp, 60-; v.pres. and dir, Ontario Marine, Inc, 61-; dir, Golding Wave Clip Co. Inc, Buffalo, 62-66; dir, Del. Mohawk Garage, Inc, Buffalo, 62-; trustee, Crescent Niagara Found, 63-; chmn. bd. and dir, Bridgeport Hardware Mfg. Corp, 64-65; dir, Baseball Holding Corp, 64- and H.D. Taylor Co, Buffalo, N.Y, 65- Mil. Serv: Entered Army, 40, released as Lt. Col, 46, after serv. in 209th Coast Artil, N.Africa and ETO, 43-44. Mem: Cmn, Niagara Frontier State Park Cmn; trustee, Cornell Univ; v.pres. and dir, SPUR, Niagara Falls; treas. and trustee, DeVeaux Sch. and Niagara Falls Mem. Hosp; Med. Found. Buffalo, Inc; Buffalo Coun. on World Affairs; bd. dir, Gr. Buffalo Develop. Found; dir. and nat. assoc, Boys' Clubs Am; trustee, Niagara Falls YMCA; Buffalo Area Coun, Boy Scouts; dir, 4-H Develop. Fund; chmn. bd, Buffalo Chap, Am. Red Cross; trustee, United Fund Buffalo and Erie Co; bd. mgr, Buffalo and Erie Co. Hist. Soc; Niagara Falls and Buffalo Hist. Socs; former mem, Univ. Buffalo Coun; former trustee, Elmwood-Franklin Sch, Inc. and Bennett Col; Buffalo and Niagara Falls C. of C; Country Club, Niagara Falls; Niagara Club; Youngstown Yacht Club; Cornell Clubs, Buffalo and Niagara Falls; Country Club, Buffalo; Buffalo Club; Buffalo Athletic Club; Buffalo Tennis and Squash Club; Bond Club, Buffalo; Mid-Day Club, Buffalo; Cult of White Buffalo; West Side Rowing Club; Buffalo Automobile Club; Pack Club, Buffalo; dir, Buffalo Saddle and Bridle Club; Buffalo Mus. Sci; Buffalo Ornithological Soc; life mem, Albright-Knox Art Gallery; Am. Water Ski Asn; Fifth Ave. Club; Genesee Valley Hunt, Inc; Capitol Hill Club. Rel: Episcopal. Legal Res: Lewiston Heights, Lewiston, N.Y. 14092. Mailing Add: 70 Niagara St, Buffalo, N.Y. 14202.

SCHOEN, KENNETH BERNARD D

b. Louisville, Ky, 2/2/21; s. William Joseph Schoen and Virginia Key; m. 10/14/44 to Gloria Ann Catignani; c. Michael Joseph and Patrick Edward. Educ: Univ. Notre Dame, Arts and Letters, 43; N.Y. Inst. of Finance, N.Y.C, Cert, 46. Polit. & Govt. Pos: Chmn, Tenn. State Alcoholic Beverage Study Cmn, 45-47; del, Dem. Nat. Conv, 68. Bus. & Prof. Pos: Partner, J.C. Bradford & Co, Investment Bankers, Nashville, Tenn, 45-; allied mem, N.Y. Stock Exchange, 65-; financial v.pres, secy, treas. and bd. mem, Aurora Publishers, Inc, Nashville, Tenn, 69- Mil. Serv: Entered as A/S, Coast Guard Res, 41, released as PO 2/C, 45, after serv. in Seventh and Ninth Naval Dist; Good Conduct Medal. Publ: Sixty Years of Columbianism in Tennesee, Scott Printing Co, 62; Report of the Tennessee Alcoholic Beverage Study Commission, Rich Printing Co, 67. Mem: Nat. Asn. of Security Dealers; Nashville Security Traders Asn; bd, Aquinas Jr. Col; adv. cmt, Nat. Coun. of Cath. Men; K. of C.(Grand Knight, Nashville Coun. 544, 51, dist. dep. for Mid. Tenn, 52-54, Faithful Navigator, Bishop Adrian Gen. Assembly, 53-55, state dep, 60-62, State Master 4°, 62-66); Elks; Ky. Club; Richland Country Club; Nashville City Club; Town Club; pres, Nashville Area Coun. on Alcoholism and Proj. Equality; hon. mem. bd, Cumberland Heights; founder and mem. bd, Samaritans Anonymous; state mem, John F. Kennedy Mem. Libr. Cmt; bd, Cath. Charities of Tenn. and Diocesan Lay Adv. Cmt; Cath. Youth Orgn.(mem. bd, 15 years, currently treas. bd); St. Thomas Hosp. Sch. Nursing (mem. bd, 11 years, chmn. bd, 4 years); Serra Int.(mem. bd, 3 years, past v.pres. and secy); Travelers Aid Soc.(mem. bd. and first v.pres, currently and past treas); United Serv. Orgn.(Nashville exec. cmt, 15 years, former chmn, Davidson Co); Nat. Cath. Commun. Serv. App. Knight of St. Gregory by Pope Paul VI, 66; Selected as Man of Year, Notre Dame, 67. Rel: Catholic. Legal Res: 2303 Golf Club Lane, Nashville, Tenn. 37215. Mailing Add: J.C. Bradford & Co, 170 Fourth Ave. N, Nashville, Tenn. 37219.

SCHOENBERGER, CHARLOTTE SALLY R

Secy, Boulder Co. Rep. Cent. Cmt, Colo.

b. Lehighton, Pa, 12/21/17; d. Hubert Hager and Margaret Laury H; m. 7/30/40 to Morton W. Schoenberger; c. Susan (Mrs. Bruce MacQueen). Educ: Mt. Sinai Hosp. Nurses Training Sch, R.N, 40. Polit. & Govt. Pos: Blockworker, Tioga Co. Rep. Party, N.Y, 59-63, committeewoman, 62-66; financial secy, Boulder Co. Rep. Party, Colo, 67-68; secy, Boulder Co. Rep. Cent. Cmt, 68- Bus. & Prof. Pos: Gen. duty nurse, Mt. Sinai Hosp, Phila, Pa, 40; vis. nurse, Commun. Nurse Asn, Lehighton, 40-47; med. secy, Gnaden Huetten Hosp, Lehighton, 47-52; off. nurse, Dr. Irving Dolsky, Linden, N.J, 52-59. Mem: Eastern Star; Boulder Woman's Club. Rel: Protestant. Mailing Add: 7660 Ferris Way, Boulder, Colo. 80302.

SCHOENBERGER, MARALYN MORTON D

State Committeewoman, Maine Dem. Party

b. Pittsburgh, Pa, 10/1/29; d. Stanley Francis Morton and Eleanor Birdetta Hill M; m. 2/2/52 to Dr. Walter Smith Schoenberger; c. Karen. Educ: Gimbel Bros. Scholarship, Bellefield Sch, Pittsburgh, Pa, 47-48, retailing post grad. cert; Univ. Maine Col. Arts & Sci, 67-68. Polit. & Govt. Pos: Dem. cand. Maine House Rep, 66 & 68; mem, Bd. Voter Registrn, Orono, 66-68; justice of the peace, Penobscot Co, 67-; mem. finance cmt, 500 Club, Dem. Party Maine, 68 & 69; state committeewoman, Maine Dem. Party, Penobscot Co, 68-; chmn, Penobscot Co. Registrn. Cmt, 68-; mem. platform cmt, Dem. State Cmt, 68-; lobbyist, Maine Chiropractic Asn, 69. Bus. & Prof. Pos: Bookkeeper, Mellon Nat. Bank and Trust Co, 48-50; receptionist and secy, Harbison Walker Refractories, 50-53; libr. asst, Fletcher Sch. Law & Diplomacy, 53-54, proctor, 54-56; secy. and admin. asst, registr. office, Univ. Maine, 61 64. Mem: League of Women Voters U.S; Thursday Wives Club; YWCA. Rel: Presbyterian. Mailing Add: 25 College Heights, Orono, Maine 04473.

SCHOENBERGER, WALTER SMITH D

Secy, Orono Dem. Town Cmt, Maine

b. Pittsburgh, Pa, 11/19/20; s. Homer Schoenberger and Alice May Smith S; m. 2/2/52 to Maralyn Morton; c. Karen. Educ: Univ. Pittsburgh, A.B, 50, M.A, 53; Fletcher Sch. Law and Diplomacy, Medford, Mass, M.A, 54, Ph.D, 63; Pi Sigma Alpha. Polit. & Govt. Pos: Del, Maine Dem. Conv, 62, 64, 66 & 68; mem, Penobscot Co. Dem. Cmt, 64-; alternate del, Dem. Nat. Conv, 68; Maine state chmn, UN Day, 68 & 69; mem, Gov. Task Force on Taxation, 68-69; secy, Orono Dem. Town Cmt, currently; mem, Dem. Cmn. on Party Reform, 69. Bus. & Prof. Pos: Clerk, Gulf Oil Corp, Pittsburgh, Pa, 39-42; lectr. polit. sci, Univ. Pittsburgh, 51-53; teaching asst, Tufts Univ, 54-56; research asst, Assocs. for Int. Research, Cambridge, Mass, 55-56; prof. polit. sci, Univ. Maine, 56- Mil. Serv: Entered as Aviation Cadet, Navy, 42, released as Lt.(jg), 46, after serv. in Bombing-Fighting Aircraft 20, Fighter Squadron 46, Pac. Theatre, 44-45; Lt, Naval Res, 69; two Air Medals. Publ: Decision of Destiny, Ohio Univ. Press, 69. Mem: Am. Asn. Univ. Prof; Am. Polit. Sci. Asn; Int. Studies Asn. Distinguished Faculty Award, Univ. Maine, 63. Rel: Swedenborgian. Mailing Add: 25 College Heights, Orono, Maine 04473.

SCHOENECK, CHARLES A. R

Chmn, N.Y. State Rep. Cmt.

b. Syracuse, N.Y, 2/3/12; s. Charles A. Schoeneck and Louise E. Kappesser S; m. 10/11/46 to Elizabeth Ellen Brandt; c. Charles A, III and Elisabeth N. Educ: Syracuse Univ, A.B, 33; Harvard Univ. Law Sch, LL.B, 36; Sigma Alpha Epsilon. Polit. & Govt. Pos: Mem, N.Y. State Rep. Cmt, 52-, chmn, 67-; N.Y. State Assemblyman, 55-60, Majority Leader, N.Y. State Assembly, 59-60; del. and chmn. N.Y. del, Rep. Nat. Conv, 68. Bus. & Prof. Pos: Attorney-at-law, Bond, Schoeneck & King, 36- Mil. Serv: Entered as Pvt, Army, 42, released as Capt, 45, after serv. in 37th Inf. Div, Asian Pac, 43-45; Combat Inf. Badge; Bronze Star Medal. Mem: Onondaga Co, N.Y. State and Am. Bar Asns; Am. Legion. Rel: Episcopal. Mailing Add: 110 Juneway Rd, Syracuse, N.Y. 13215.

SCHOLES, WILLIAM LEON D

Tenn. State Rep.

b. Paris, Tenn, 9/16/26; s. Med Hooper Scholes and Myrtle Petty S; m. 9/19/47 to Marie Porter; c. Peggy Lynn, Terry Porter, Donald Lee and Cynthia Jane. Educ: Univ. Tenn, D.D.S, 52; Delta Sigma Delta. Polit. & Govt. Pos: Tenn. State Rep, 67-68 & 69- Mil. Serv: Entered as Pvt, Army, 44, released as Sgt, 46, after serv. in 305th Bomb GP, ETO, 45-46; Maj, Army Res, 62. Mem: Lions; Mason; PTA. Rel: Baptist. Mailing Add: 3203 Southlake Dr, Nashville, Tenn. 37211.

SCHOLLE, AUGUST D

b. Creighton, Pa, 5/23/04; s. Henry Scholle and Elizabeth Danner S; m. 10/23/42 to Kathleen Beatrice Jones; c. Susan A. (Mrs. Connor) and Kathleen E. Educ: Rossford High Sch,1 year. Polit. & Govt. Pos: Dem. Nat. Committeeman, Mich, 48-52, 56-60 & 64-68; chmn, Mich. Natural Resources Cmn, currently; del, Dem. Nat. Conv, 68. Bus. & Prof. Pos: Pres, Glass Workers Local Union Nine, Toledo, Ohio, 33-37; regional dir, CIO, Ohio, Ill, Mich, 37-54; pres, Mich. State CIO Coun, 40-58; pres, Mich. State Coun, AFL-CIO, 58- Mil. Serv: Army, 43-45. Mem: Mich. Workmen's Compensation Study Cmn; Unemploy. Compensation Study Cmn; Mich. Econ. Develop. Cmn; Mich. Civil Defense Adv. Coun; Mich. Week Cmt; Mich United Fund.(past pres. and chmn. bd, exec. bd. mem. currently); United Found. Adv. Bd; Relig. and Labor Found. Nat. Exec. Bd; Natural Resources Cmn.(chmn); Freedom from Hunger Coun; Gr. Mich. Found; Hosp. Research and Educ. Reserve Mich. (exec. bd); Labor Adv. Cmt, Inst. Indust. Rels, Univ. Mich. and Wayne State Univ; Gov. Cmt. Legis. Compensation; Manpower Adv. Cmt, U.S. Dept. Labor (N.Cent. Region); Traffic Safety Mich. Exec. Bd; Wayne Co. Commun. Col. Study Cmt; adv. cmt, Mich. Sch. Finance Study, State Bd. Educ; Mich. United Conservations Clubs; Oakland Commun. Col. Adv. Cmt; Mich. Asn. Regional Med. Prog; Mich. Crime and Delinquency Coun; Cmt. Mich. Econ. Future; Mich. Indust. Ambassador; NAACP; Am. Civil Liberties Union; Family Serv. Cmt; Constitutional Conv. Preparatory Cmn. Legal Res: 2710 Vinsetta, Royal Oak, Mich. 48073. Mailing Add: 716 Lothrop, Detroit, Mich. 48202.

SCHOLZ, FREDERICK JAMES R

b. Jersey City, N.J, 9/1/11; s. Frederick Joseph Scholz and Florence Galvin S; m. 6/8/35 to Beatrice M. Lavach; c. Barbara (Mrs. Heymann), Joan (Mrs. Gallagher), Robert P. and William. Educ: Am. Inst. Banking, grad. and post grad. certificates. Polit. & Govt. Pos: N.J. State Sen, Camden Co, 64-68; cmn, N.J. Legis. Reapportionment Cmt, currently. Bus. & Prof. Pos: Pres, The Midland Bank, Paramus, N.H, 69- Rel: Roman Catholic; Papal Knight of St. Gregory, 67. Legal Res: Dundee Court, Mahwah, N.J. 07430. Mailing Add: The Midland Bank, E. Ridgewood Ave, Paramus, N.J. 07652.

SCHOON, WARREN EUGENE R

Chmn, Rock Co. Rep. Cmt, Minn.

b. Ash Creek, Minn, 10/3/21; s. Jacob Schoon and Viola Hansen S; m. 12/25/43 to Elizabeth Johnson; c. Steven Warren, Susan Elizabeth, Christian John, Peter Marshall and Robert Hansen. Educ: Univ. Minn, B.A, 43; Phi Beta Kappa; Phi Delta Theta. Polit. & Govt. Pos: Chmn, Rock Co. Rep. Cmt, Minn, 54-57 & 60-; mayor, Luverne, 55-57, former chmn, Planning Cmt. Bus. & Prof. Pos: Partner and gen. mgr, Two Auto Dealerships, 50-57; mgr, Charlotte Zone, Pontiac Motor Div, Gen. Motors Corp, 57 and N.Y. Zone, 59-60, advert. mgr, 58-59; pres, Schoon Motor Sales, Inc, Luverne, Minn, Schoon Motor Co, Rochester and Oxford St. Motors, Inc, Worthington, 60-66. Mil. Serv: Entered as A/S, Navy, 43, released as Lt.(jg), 46, after serv. in Amphibious Forces, Cent. Pac. and Naval Air Corps, Tex; Invasion of Marshall Islands Ribbon. Mem: Nat. Auto Dealers Asn; Mason; Shrine; Rotary; Am. Legion; VFW; Farm Bur; Elks; C. of C; Luverne and Minnehaha Sioux Falls Country Clubs. Rel: Presbyterian. Mailing Add: Box 40, Luverne, Minn. 56156.

SCHOONMAKER, NEILL WEISS, JR. R

b. Ware, Mass, 10/25/35; s. Neill Weiss Schoonmaker and Cleone Oostdyke S; m. 3/24/56 to Sandra Lee Sattler; c. John Neill, Deborah Sue and Jeffrey Hall. Educ: Yale Univ, B.A, 57; Boston Univ. Law Sch, LL.B. Polit. & Govt. Pos: Chmn, Ware Town Rep. Cmt, Mass, 64-66. Bus. & Prof. Pos: Attorney-at-law, self-employed, 60- Mem: Am. Bar Asn; Rotary (secy, Ware Club, 60-65 & 69-, v.pres, 65-66, pres, 66-67). Rel: Protestant. Legal Res: Williston Dr, Ware, Mass. 01082. Mailing Add: 16 Bank St, Ware, Mass. 01082.

SCHOONOVER, LELAND HOWARD D
Mont. State Rep.
b. Philipsburg, Mont, 6/16/09; s. James Samuel Schoonover and Charlotte Elizabeth Friend S; m. 11/29/33 to Dorothy Marion Daugherty; c. Joann (Mrs. Sagmiller) and Carol (Mrs. Plouffe). Educ: West. Mont. Col, B.E, 37; Univ. Mont, MAE, 55; Phi Delta Kappa. Polit. & Govt. Pos: Precinct committeeman, Mont, 30; Mont. State Sen, Lake Co, 61-64; Mont. State Rep, Dist. 28, Lake Co, 69-, mem, State Land Law Rev. Cmt. and Subcmt. on Pesticide Study, Mont. House of Rep, 69-; chmn, Lake Co. Dem. Cent. Cmt, currently. Bus. & Prof. Pos: Farmer, Moiese, Mont, 30-35; teacher, Armington, Harlem, Fort Shaw, Augusta and Ronan, 37-47; supt, Fort Shaw, Mont, 43; high sch. prin, Augusta, Mont, 45-46; teacher, Polson, Mont, 47- Mil. Serv: Entered as Pvt, Army, 44, released as Sgt, 45, after serv. in Signal Corps. Publ: A Positive Approach to Teaching Democracy in the Local Community, Univ. Press, Univ. Mont, 56. Mem: Mont. and Nat. Educ. Asns; Lower Flathead School Masters Asn; AF&AM; Elks; Am. Legion; Lake Co. Productions, Inc; Polson Outdoors, Inc; Mont. and Nat. Wildlife Fedn; Lions. Gov. Award as Montana's Outstanding Conservationist, 66. Rel: Presbyterian. Legal Res: 105 Sixth Ave. W, Polson, Mont. 59860. Mailing Add: P.O. Box 941, Polson, Mont. 59860.

SCHORGL, JAMES JOSEPH 'JOE' D
Mo. State Rep.
b. Kansas City, Mo, 9/13/22; s. James Joseph Schorgl (deceased) and Catherine Burns S.(deceased); m. 4/23/48 to Helen Marie Rice; c. Patricia, Denise and Elizabeth. Educ: N.E. High Sch, Kansas City, Mo, grad, 39. Polit. & Govt. Pos: Mo. State Rep, Ninth Dist, 69- Bus. & Prof. Pos: Switchman, Mo. Pac. R.R, Kansas City, Mo, 46-69; partner, J & L Elec, 54-69. Mil. Serv: Entered as Pvt, Army, 42, released as Pfc, 45, after serv. in Third Inf. Div, ETO, 42-45. Mem: Dem. Good Govt. Asn; K. of C; Am. Legion; Northeast Commun. Coun; East Side Commun. Coun. Rel: Catholic. Mailing Add: 126 N. Quincy, Kansas City, Mo. 64123.

SCHOSBERG, PAUL ALAN D
b. New York, N.Y, 4/6/37; s. Eugene Louis Schosberg and Thelma Siegel S; m. 12/21/58 to Jane Mindlin; c. Jill Ernestine and Richard Eugene. Educ: Middlebury Col, B.A, 59; Columbia Law Sch, 59-61. Polit. & Govt. Pos: Admin. asst. to U.S. Rep, Richard L. Ottinger, 65-; campaign coordinator, Ottinger for Cong, 64 and campaign dir, 66 & 68. Bus. & Prof. Pos: Bur. mgr, Westchester Co. Publishers, 63-64, night city ed, 62-63 and reporter, 61-62. Publ: See How They Run, Chilton, 64. Breeder and exhibitor of German Shepherd Dogs. Legal Res: 3 Claremont Rd, Scarsdale, N.Y. 10583. Mailing Add: 11600 Virgate Lane, Reston, Va. 22070.

SCHOUWEILER, BART McCLAIN R
Nev. State Assemblyman
b. Wendell, Idaho, 8/11/34; s. LeRoy Schouweiler and Dora L. Murphy S; single. Educ: Menlo Col, A.A, 54; Stanford Univ, B.A, 56; Georgetown Univ. Law Center, LL.B, 59; Delta Kappa Epsilon. Polit. & Govt. Pos: Asst. city attorney, Reno, Nev, 63-64, munic. judge pro tem, 65; pres, Reno Young Rep. Club, 65-66; Nev. State Assemblyman, 67-; alternate del, Rep. Nat. Conv, 68. Bus. & Prof. Pos: Attorney-at-law, Bart M. Schouweiler, Reno, Nev, 64- Mil. Serv: Entered as 1st Lt, Air Force, 60, released as Capt, 63, after serv. in Judge Adv. Gen. Dept, Strategic Air Command, 60-63; Capt, Air Force Res. Mem: Am. and Washoe Co. Bar Asns; State Bar of Nev. Rel: Episcopal. Legal Res: 2510 Eastshore Dr, Reno, Nev. 89502. Mailing Add: 1 E. First St, Reno, Nev. 89501.

SCHOWALTER, HERBERT JOSEPH R
Wis. State Assemblyman
b. Milwaukee, Wis, 3/30/27; s. Herbert Schowalter and Henrietta Gilberg S; m. 5/28/49 to Geraldine Sinnen; c. Christine, Lynne and Jan. Educ: De Vry Tech. Inst, Elec. Eng. dipl, 51. Polit. & Govt. Pos: Village trustee, Saukville, Wis, 61-65 & 68-69; precinct committeeman, Ozaukee Co. Rep. Party, 62-, chmn, statuatory cmt, 66-68; Wis. State Assemblyman, Ozaukee Co, 69- Bus. & Prof. Pos: Field Serv. supvr, Sq. D Co, Milwaukee, 63-65, supvr, eng. syst. serv, 65- Mil. Serv: Entered as A/S, Navy, 45, released as Hospitalman, 46, after serv. in Hosp. Corps, Am. Theater, 45-46; recalled as Hospitalman, 51-52; Am. Theater and Victory Medals. Mem: Nat. Soc. State Legislators; Am. Legion; Am. Legion Past Comdr. Club, Wis. Rel: Roman Catholic. Mailing Add: 642 S. Main St, Saukville, Wis. 53080.

SCHRADE, JACK R
Calif. State Sen.
b. Williamsport, Pa, 5/25/02; Educ: Pa. and N.Y. Schs. Polit. & Govt. Pos: El Cajon Police Posse; v.pres. and dir, Helix Irrigation Dist, 12 years; Calif. State Sen, 62- Bus. & Prof. Pos: Retired rancher and businessman; dir, Southland Savings and Loan Asn. Mem: Rotary; Eagles; Elks; Moose; El Cajon Valley Club; Farm Bur; Hwy. 94 Club; Hwy. 80 Asn; C. of C; Mother Goose Parade Assoc; YMCA; Lions; Kiwanis. Mailing Add: 1904 Hotel Circle, San Diego, Calif. 92110.

SCHRADER, LEO W. D
Mo. State Rep.
b. Joplin, Mo, 10/25/38; s. Leo Ray Schrader and Helen Marguerite Woodford S; m. 8/26/60 to Cean G. Carter; c. Kara Lee and Marady Lynn. Educ: Southwest Mo. State Col, 56-57; Univ. Ark, B.S.B.A, 60; Univ. Mo. Sch. Law, LL.B, 63. Polit. & Govt. Pos: Asst. prosecuting attorney, Jasper Co, Mo, 65-66; Mo. State Rep, 69- Mil. Serv: Army, 64-65, 1st Lt, serv. in 69 Signal Bn; Capt. Res. Mem: Optimist. Rel: Protestant. Mailing Add: 2829 Kentucky, Joplin, Mo. 64801.

SCHRAEDER, FRED JOSEPH D
Chmn, Peoria Co. Dem. Cent. Cmt, Ill.
b. Iroquois Twp, Ill, 12/26/23; s. Fred A. Schraeder and Iva Marie Roth S; m. 3/2/46 to Helen Ruth Wilson; c. Ivan L, Fred M. and Kevin H. Educ: High Sch, special courses at higher level. Polit. & Govt. Pos: V.chmn, Peoria Co. Dem. Cent. Cmt, Ill, 57-63, chmn, 63-, Ill. State rep-at-lg, 65-; arbitrator, Indust. Cmn, Ill, 61-64. Bus. & Prof. Pos: Chmn, Peoria-Tazewell Indust. Union Coun, AFL-CIO, 54-57, v.chmn. and chmn, Peoria-Tazewell Labor Coun, 57-61; bus. rep. and pres, Int. Union of United Brewery Workers of Am, Local 77, 54-61; restaurant owner, 65- Mil. Serv: Pvt, Army, serv. in Amphibious Engrs, Asian Theater; Asian and Pac. Theater Ribbons. Mem: Budget cmt, Commun. Chest & Coun. Rel: Roman Catholic; past chmn, Christian Family Movement, Peoria Diocese. Mailing Add: 205 E. Arcadia Ave, Peoria, Ill. 61603.

SCHRAEDER, VERNON VIRGIL D
Cmnr, Hodgeman Co, Kans.
b. Burdett, Kans, 12/24/17; s. Frank Schraeder and Clara Pivonka S; m. 2/26/47 to Mildred Rice; c. James J. and Jo Lana. Educ: Ft. Hays, Kans. State Col, A.B, 40; Phi Sigma Epsilon. Polit. & Govt. Pos: Co. cmnr, Hodgeman Co, Kans, 57-; pres, Co. Cmnrs. Asn, 62; mem. gov. cmn. on criminal admin, 69. Bus. & Prof. Pos: Rancher, 47- Mil. Serv: Entered as Aviation Cadet, Army Air Force, 40, released as Capt, 45, after serv. in Eighth Air Force, ETO, 43-44; Unit Citation; Air Medal with Three Oak Leaf Clusters; Distinguished Flying Cross. Mem: Am. Legion; Lions. Rel: Methodist. Mailing Add: Jetmore, Kans. 67854.

SCHRAG, LLOYD R
S.Dak. State Sen.
b. Marion, S.Dak, 1/10/15; m. 8/2/39 to Lorraine Miller; c. Lois Kay and Larry James. Educ: High Sch. Polit. & Govt. Pos: Co. cmnr, 52-56; Turner Co. Crop Improv. Asn; S.Dak. State Sen, 58- Bus. & Prof. Pos: Farming. Rel: Mennonite. Mailing Add: Marion, S.Dak. 57043. (1967)

SCHRAMM, JACK JOSEPH D
Mo. State Rep.
b. St. Louis, Mo, 1/21/32; s. Ben J. Schramm and Frieda Goruch S; m. 2/12/57 to Rebecca June McHale; c. Lori Brooke and Adam Curtis. Educ: Colgate Univ, A.B, 53; Wash. Univ. Sch. of Law, J.D, 59; Alpha Tau Omega; Phi Delta Phi. Polit. & Govt. Pos: Exec. v.pres, and dir, United Young Dem. of St. Louis Co, Mo, 60-64, mem, 60-; mem, Creve Coeur Twp. Regular Dem. Club, 61-, dir, 65-; mem, University City Traffic Cmn, 63-66; Mo. State Rep, 37th Dist, 65- Bus. & Prof. Pos: Attorney, Zimbalist, Sachs, Schramm & Branom, 66- Mil. Serv: Entered as Pvt.(E-1), Army, 54, released as Spec. 4 (E-4), 56, after serv. in Div. Hq, 82nd Airborne Div, 55-56; Parachutist's Badge. Mem: St. Louis Co, Mo. and Am. Bar Asns; Am. Judicature Soc; past pres, Gr. St. Louis Chap, United Nations Asn; past pres, Clayton Jr. C. of C; past v.pres, Mo. B'nai B'rith; dir, Mo. Epilepsy Fedn; past munic. chmn, Muscular Dystrophy Dr; Colgate Alumni Club of St. Louis; Am. Jewish Cong; University City Charter Asn; Jewish War Vets. Carter-Tedrow Mem. Award, Wash. Univ. Sch. of Law; Clayton Jr. C. of C, Outstanding Mem, 60-61; St. Louis Bar Asn, Cert. of Distinction; Mo. House of Rep, Speakers Award for The Outstanding First-Term Dem; Colgate Univ. Alumni Corp, Maroon Citation; Mo. Bar Asn, Spec. Serv. Award; Cited by President's Cmt. on Employment of the Handicapped and the St. Louis Co. Suburban Teachers Asn. for Legis. Leadership. Rel: Jewish. Mailing Add: 7529 Gannon Ave, University City, Mo. 63130.

SCHREIBER, ANN F. D
b. Maywood, Ill; d. Emil A. Schreiber and Pauline Winkler S; single. Educ: Proviso High Sch, Maywood, Ill, 4 years. Polit. & Govt. Pos: Admin. asst. to U.S. Rep. Edgar A. Jones, 49-54; admin. asst. to U.S. Rep. John F. Baldwin, 54-66; exec. secy. to U.S. Rep. Jerome R. Waldie, Calif, 66- Bus. & Prof. Pos: Secy. to dir, Eng. Dept, Fred S. James Co, Inc, Chicago, Ill, 37-40; passenger dept. rep, Santa Fe R.R, 40-44; secy. to assoc. dir, Nat. Physicians Cmt, 44-49. Mem: Cong. Secy. Club. Rel: Protestant. Mailing Add: 2700 Virginia Ave. N.W, Apt. 1009, Washington, D.C. 20037.

SCHREIBER, JOHN PAUL R
Chmn, Archer Co. Rep. Party, Tex.
b. Windthorst, Tex, 9/13/13; s. T.A. Schreiber and Clara Hoff S; m. 10/20/38 to Gertrude Mary Zotz; c. Jo-Ann (Mrs. Gilbert Murillo), Ronald J, David A, Raymond J, John P, Jr, Margaret (Mrs. James Baumhadt) and Janie H. Polit. & Govt. Pos: Mem. sch. bd, Windthorst Pub. Schs, Tex, 56-58; chmn, Archer Co. Rep. Party, 63- Mem: K. of C; Farm Bur. Rel: Catholic. Mailing Add: Route 1, Box 34, Windthorst, Tex. 76389.

SCHREIBER, MARTIN JAMES D
Wis. State Sen.
b. Milwaukee, Wis, 4/8/39; s. Martin Eugene Schreiber and Emeline Kurz S; m. 6/3/61 to Elaine Ruth Thaney; c. Katherine, Martin and Kristine. Educ: Valparaiso Univ; Marquette Univ, LL.B; Univ. Wis-Milwaukee, grad. student in urban affairs. Polit. & Govt. Pos: Mem, Seventh Ward Dem. Unit, Wis; Wis. State Sen, 63-, mem, Senate Conserv. Cmt, Senate Pub. Welfare Cmt, Legis. Coun. Judiciary Cmt. and v.chmn, State Fiscal Policy Cmt, 63-64, mem, Legis. Coun. Children's Court Center Cmt, 65-66, mem, Senate, Labor, Taxation, Ins. and Banking Cmt, Gov. Cmt. on Eminent Domain and chmn, Legis. Coun. Ins. Laws Revision, 65-69; Senate Dem. Caucus chmn. and mem, Bd. of Govt. Opers Educ. Cmt, Ford Found. Study Cmt. and Joint Cmt. on Legis. Orgn, 67-69; cand. for Lt. Gov, Wis, 66; mem, pub. policy cmt, Wis. Asn. for Ment. Health, 67-68. Bus. & Prof. Pos: Attorney-at-law. Mem: Am. Coun. to Improve our Neighborhoods; 13th Ward Commun. Coun; AFL-CIO Locals 9 and 113; Midtown Neighborhood Improv. Asn; Coop. West Side; Wis. League of Sr. Citizens; Milwaukee Jr. and Milwaukee Bar Asns. Rel: Lutheran. Mailing Add: 3128 N. 50th St, Milwaukee, Wis. 53216.

SCHRETTE, ROLAND DONALD R
Mem, Calif. State Rep. Cent. Cmt.
b. Renton, Wash, 4/25/29; s. Almond Donald Schrette and Ruby Beaudry S; m. 3/7/54 to Hildegard Grete Duser; c. Kristi Lynn and Thomas Henry. Educ: Napa Col, A.A, 51. Polit. & Govt. Pos: Mem, finance cmt, Napa Co. Rep. Cent. Cmt, Calif, 67-68, chmn. cand. cmt, 68-69; mem, Calif. State Rep. Cent. Cmt, 69- Bus. & Prof. Pos: Sales mgr and secy-treas, Henry Duser Co. Inc, Napa, Calif, 53-66; owner, Paine's Cocktail Lounge, 66- Mil. Serv: Entered as Pvt. E-1, Army, 51, released as Cpt, 53, after serv. in 508th Airborne, Ft. Benning, Ga, 3rd Army, 52-53. Mem: Active 20-30 Club Int; Elks. Dist. Gov, Northern Calif; Active 20-30 Clubs Outstanding Governor Award, 64-65. Rel: Catholic. Mailing Add: 2516 Linda Vista Ave, Napa, Calif. 94558.

SCHREURS, WAYNE LeROY R
Nebr. State Sen.
b. Lincoln, Nebr, 8/17/28; s. John Schreurs and Cona Emry S; m. 8/29/48 to Caltha Nora Rhoads; c. Gregory Wayne, Leslie Dean and Anita Marie. Educ: Westmar Col, B.A, 49; Evangel. Theol, B.D, 53; Concordia Col, Teachers Cert, 65. Polit. & Govt. Pos: Secy, Seward Co. Rep. Conv, Nebr, 68; Nebr. State Sen, 69- Bus. & Prof. Pos: Minister, Evangel. United Brethren Churches, 53-66; teacher, Seward Pub. High Sch, 66-69. Mem: Nebr. State and Nat. Educ. Asns; Scoutmaster, Troop 257, Boy Scouts. Rel: Methodist. Mailing Add: 194 E. Seward St, Seward, Nebr. 68434.

SCHRIEFER, ROGER BERNARD D
Mem, Calif. Dem. State Cent. Cmt.
b. Gilman, Ill, 9/8/29; s. Bernard Schriefer and Verna Heersema S; m. 8/28/49 to Viola Fay Sharpe; c. Kathy Sue and Kim Diane. Educ: Ill. State Univ, B.S, 50; Univ. Ill, M.Ed, 54. Polit. & Govt. Pos: Mem, Calif. Dem. State Cent. Cmt, 68-; mem. exec. bd, Dem. Vol. of Calif, 46th Assembly Dist, 69. Bus. & Prof. Pos: Soc. sci. instr, Onarga High Sch, Ill, 50-54 and Redondo Union High Sch, Calif, 54- Mil. Serv: Entered as Pvt, Marine Corps Res, 49, released 50, after serv. in Inactive Res. Mem: Calif. Teachers Asn; South Bay Union High Sch. Dist. Faculty Asn; Calif. Coun. for Soc. Studies. Rel: United Church of Christ. Mailing Add: 5021 Emerald St, Torrance, Calif. 90503.

SCHRIEVER, WILLIAM W.
b. Norman, Okla, 8/19/26; s. William Schriever and Lucille Weisenbach S; m. 10/10/53 to Barbara Dwight. Educ: Univ. Okla, B.S, 47; Univ. Ill, M.S, 49; Harvard Univ, 54-61; Tau Beta Pi; Sigma Tau; Sigma Pi Sigma; Eta Kappa Nu; Pe-et; Gamma Alpha. Polit. & Govt. Pos: Chmn, Dem. Campaign, Southold, N.Y, 63 & 64; chief, Civil Defense Rescue, Town of Southold, 63-; del, Dem. Nat. Conv, 64; mem, Suffolk Co. Dem. Cmt, N.Y, 64-68; v.chmn, Southold Dem. Town Cmt, 64-69. Bus. & Prof. Pos: Research engr, Black, Sivalls & Bryson, summer 47; teaching asst, physics dept, Univ. Ill, 47-50, research asst, 50-52; reservoir engr, research lab, Atlantic Refining Co, summers 48 & 49; research physicist, prod. research lab, Carter Oil Co, 53-54. Mil. Serv: Entered as A/S Naval Res, 44, released as Ens, 46, after serv. in V-12 Unit, Norman, Okla, Am. Theater, Eighth Naval Dist; Victory and Am. Campaign Medals; Lt.(jg) (Ret), Naval Res, 59. Publ: 'A Double Seal Vacuum Coupling,' The Rev. of Sci. Instruments, 5/53; U.S. Patent 2,902,667, Vertical Velocity Dynamic Geophone, 9/59. Mem: Am. Phys. Soc; Am. Asn. of Physics Teachers; Am. Asn. for the Adv. of Sci; nat. coun. rep, scoutmaster and former dist. chmn, Boy Scouts; dir, Commun. Action Southold Town; secy, Orient Fire Dept; Suffolk Co. Civil Defense; U.S. Power Squadrons; Orient Yacht Club; Orient Commun. Activities; Orient Gun Club; Oysterponds Hist. Soc; Southold Town Dem. Club. Rel: Protestant. Mailing Add: Main Rd, Orient, N.Y. 11957.

SCHRIVER, HENRY HALEY R
b. Elyria, Ohio, 10/13/14; s. Frank Emory Schriver and Sarah Haley S; m. 6/14/38 to Dorothy Ellen Langshaw; c. Carol (Mrs. Carpenter), Sally (Mrs. Kocher), Ellen Joy, James, William, Donald, Paul, Larry, Randy, Ted and Kenneth. Educ: Ohio State Univ, B.S, 37; Gamma Sigma Delta; Buckeye Club. Polit. & Govt. Pos: Ohio State Rep, 75th Dist, 67-68; mem, Lorain Co. Regional Planning Cmn. Bus. & Prof. Pos: Farmer, philosopher and nat. lectr. Film: Cows, Kids, Co-ops, Am. Inst. of Coop, 65. Mem: Future Farmers of Am; Co, State and Nat. Farm Burs; Prod. Credit Asn; Ohio State Hort. Soc; Int. Platform Asn; Milk Producer's Asn; North Ohio Breeders Asn. Received Nat. Award for Serv. to Youth, for Outstanding Contribution to Youth and Farm Bus. Prog. from Am. Inst. of Coop. and Olin Mathiesen Award from Nat. 4-H Alumni Asn. Rel: Methodist. Legal Res: Mennel Rd, R.R. 2, Grafton, Ohio 44044. Mailing Add: R.R. 2, Grafton, Ohio 44044. (1967)

SCHROCK, CLYDE W. D
b. Rock Lake, N.Dak, 9/12/01; married; c. 3. Educ: Palmer Sch. of Chiropractic. Polit. & Govt. Pos: N.Dak. State Sen, 43-61; pres, New Rockford City Cmn, 37-48. Mailing Add: New Rockford, N.Dak. 58356. (1967)

SCHROEDER, ALFRED GUSTAV R
Justice, Kans. Supreme Court.
b. Newton, Kans, 6/5/16; s. Gustav D. Schroeder and Grete Janzen S; m. 8/8/42 to Katheryn Marie Diel; c. John Scott, Hedy Marie and Marilyn Sue. Educ: Bethel Col, 2 years; Kans. State Col, B.S. in Agr. with high honors, 37; Harvard Law Sch, LL.B, 40; Phi Kappa Phi; Alpha Zeta; Farm House. Polit. & Govt. Pos: Probate and co. judge, Harvey Co, Kans, 47-53; dist. judge, Ninth Judicial Dist, Harvey and McPherson Co, 53-57; Justice, Kans. Supreme Court, 57- Bus. & Prof. Pos: Law practice, Newton, Kans, 40-42. Mil. Serv: Entered as Pvt, Air Force, 42, released as 1st Lt, 46, after serv. in Hq. Off, Lake Charles Army Air Force Base, 42-46; Res, 46-50, Capt; Good Conduct Medal. Publ: Opinions written in Kans. Off. Supreme Court Reports from 1/57 to present. Mem: Am. and Kans. Bar Asns; hon. mem. Phi Alpha Delta. Winner State Coop. Mkt. Exam, 4-H, 35. Rel: Protestant. Mailing Add: 825 Buchanan, Topeka, Kans. 66606.

SCHROEDER, ARTHUR E. D
b. Big Rapids, Mich, 2/24/13; s. Edward John Schroeder and Helena W. Mehl S; m. 5/24/33 to Nina Marie Rhoades; c. Arthur L. Polit. & Govt. Pos: Secy, Mecosta Co. State Dem. Conv, Mich, 52-63; del, Mecosta Co. Dem. Conv, 52-; mem. zoning bd, Big Rapids, Mich, 54-60, mem. planning bd, 54-64, chmn, 62 & 63 and mem. bd. of cavassers, 66-; chmn, Mecosta Co. Dem. Cmt, 63-69; chmn, Mecosta Co. State Dem. Conv, 63-; Tenth Dist. Dem. Steering Cmt, 63-, adv. cmt, 64- Bus. & Prof. Pos: Recording secy, Local 389, UAW(AFL-CIO), 43-46, Bargaining Cmt, 43-65, financial secy-treas, 46-52 and pres, 52-65; shipping clerk, Hanchett Mfg. Co, Big Rapids, 65- Rel: Lutheran. Mailing Add: 1003 N. State St, Big Rapids, Mich. 49307.

SCHROEDER, CLARENCE HENRY R
Chmn, Duval Co. Rep. Party, Tex.
b. San Antonio, Tex, 6/1/18; s. Frederick Nathaniel Schroeder and Theresa Manka S; single. Educ: Tex. Col. of Arts & Indust, 1 year; Univ. of Tex, 3 years. Polit. & Govt. Pos: Chmn, Duval Co. Rep. Party, Tex, 59- Bus. & Prof. Pos: Cmn. agent, Mobil Oil Corp, 45- Mil. Serv: Entered as Pvt, Army, 40, released as T/3, 45, after serv. in Div. Surg. Off, 2nd Inf. Div, ETO. Mem: Rotary; K. of C; VFW; Curcillos; Univ. Tex. Alumni Asn; former mem, Am. Legion. Rel: Catholic. Legal Res: Box 246, San Diego, Tex. 78384. Mailing Add: Gravis St, San Diego, Tex. 78384.

SCHROEDER, FLORENCE PARKS R
Chmn, Dorchester Co. Rep. Cent. Cmt, Md.
b. Cambridge, Md, 2/2/07; d. Elijah James Parks and Rachel Mellott P; m. 4/8/30 to David Frank Schroeder; c. Anna R.(Mrs. Harris) and David C. Educ: Cambridge High Sch; additional courses, Sears, Roebuck & Co. Polit. & Govt. Pos: Pres, Rep. Womens Club, Dorchester Co, Md, 52-56; chmn, Dorchester Co. Rep. Cent. Cmt, 66-; chmn, First Cong. Dist. Rep. Cmt, 67- Bus. & Prof. Pos: Mem. staff, inventory investment control, Sears, Roebuck & Co, 36-45; retail grocer, 45-; mem, Bd. of Educ, Dorchester Co, Md, 52-61; in charge of 1960 Fed. Census. Rel: Protestant. Mailing Add: 1002 Locust St, Cambridge, Md. 21613.

SCHROEDER, FREDERICK CARL R
Wis. State Assemblyman
b. West Bend, Wis, 1/19/10; s. Herbert Schroeder and Minnie Gumm S; m. 9/26/31 to Molly Weddig; c. William Carl. Educ: High Sch, West Bend. Polit. & Govt. Pos: Wis. State Assemblyman, currently, chmn, Cmt. on Commerce and Mfrs. and mem, Cmt. on Agr, Cmt. on Excise and Fees and Cmt. on State Inst, Wis. State Assembly. Bus. & Prof. Pos: Farmer and dairy operator. Mem: Bd. dirs, Wash. Co. Holstein Asn; mem, E.Cent. Breeders Coop, Waupun, 55-67, pres, 2 years, secy-treas, 3 years; mem, Wash. Co. Agr. Stabilization and Conserv. Serv. Cmt, 54-64, chmn, 3 years; rep, Nat. Coun. of Churches, 61; bd. dirs, Wash. Co. Dairy Herd Improv. Asn; Lions; Moose. Progressive Breeder Award of the Holstein-Friesian Asn. of Am; 4-H Alumni Award, Wis, 67. Rel: United Church of Christ. Legal Res: Route 1, Box 150, West Bend, Wis. 53095. Mailing Add: Wisconsin State Capitol, Room 35 S, Madison, Wis. 53702.

SCHROEDER, JACK
b. Davenport, Iowa, 8/21/25; s. Walter Frederick Schroeder and Flora M. Clausen S; m. 4/30/46 to Virginia M. Posateri; c. Sandra Cangilosi and Walter. Educ: St. Ambrose Col, Davenport, Iowa, B.S, 49; Drake Univ, Des Moines, Iowa, J.D, 52; Delta Theta Phi; Waukonda Club; Des Moines Golf and Country Club. Polit. & Govt. Pos: Iowa State Sen, 54-67, majority leader, 58th Gen. Assembly, Iowa State Senate, 2 terms; Iowa State Rep, 2 terms; mem, Iowa Develop. Cmn, 67; alternate del, Rep. Nat. Conv, 68. Bus. & Prof. Pos: Chmn, bd dir. and chief exec. officer, Gen. Life of Iowa Investment Co. and Gen. Life of Iowa Ins. Co, 62; pres, chmn. bd. dir. and chief exec. officer, Gen. United Group, Inc, Gen. United Life Ins. Co . and Gen. United Serv, Inc, currently. Mil. Serv: Navy Air Forces, $3\frac{1}{2}$ years. Mem: Mason; Zerapath Consistory; Kaaba Shrine; Elks; Am. Legion. Rel: Lutheran. Legal Res: 3117 Park Plaza Dr, Des Moines, Iowa 50315. Mailing Add: 2015 Grand Ave, Des Moines, Iowa 50312.

SCHROEDER, LAVERNE W. R
Iowa State Rep.
b. 1933; married. Polit. & Govt. Pos: Hardin Twp. Bd. of Trustees, Iowa, 64-66; Iowa State Rep, 67- Bus. & Prof. Pos: Farmer. Mil. Serv: Army, Korean War, 53-55. Mem: Farm Bur, 2nd V.Comdr, Am. Legion Post 725. Mailing Add: Treynor, Iowa 51575.

SCHROEDER, MARTHA K. D
Chmn, Hot Springs Co. Dem. Cent. Cmt, Wyo.
b. Donnybrook, N.Dak, 5/7/03; d. Edward M. King (deceased) and Anna M. Powers K.(deceased); m. 5/17/27 to Lawrence John Schroeder; c. Shirley Ann (Mrs. Crawford). Educ: Donnybrook High Sch, grad, 21; Minot State Normal Sch, Teachers Cert, 23. Polit. & Govt. Pos: Committeewoman, Hot Springs Co. Dem. Cent. Cmt, Wyo, 60-63, chmn, 66- Bus. & Prof. Pos: Teacher, N.Dak. and Mont, 22-27; bookkeeper, Maytag Co. and J.C. Penny Co, 27-35. Mem: Toastmistress Club; Altar Soc; Hot Springs Co. Women's Dem. Club; proj. dir, Big Horn Basin, Women in Commun. Serv; Beta Sigma Phi (dir, Tau chap, 67-). Outstanding Toastmistress in Thermopolis Club. Rel: Catholic. Mailing Add: 1136 Amoretti, Thermopolis, Wyo. 82443.

SCHROEDER, WILLIAM H. D
S.Dak. State Rep.
b. Lane, S.Dak, 3/24/13; s. George Schroeder and Anna Boelts S; m. 12/24/41 to Lora M. Reiner; c. Bruce and Colleen. Educ: Lane Independent High Sch, 31. Polit. & Govt. Pos: Chmn, Lane Independent Sch. Dist, S.Dak, 49-66; chmn, Co. Bd. of Educ, 56-64; chmn, State Cmt. Co. Bd. of Educ, 58; S.Dak. State Rep, 65- Mem: Farmers Union; Lutheran Brotherhood; chmn, S.Dak. Egg Coun. Rel: Lutheran. Mailing Add: Wessington Springs, S.Dak. 57382.

SCHROM, EDWARD JOSEPH D
b. Albany, Minn, 3/17/11; s. John H. Schrom and Julia Grausam S; m. 8/26/36 to Dorothy Eva Beumel; c. Kenneth (deceased), Donald and Eileen (Mrs. William Nathe). Polit. & Govt. Pos: Del-at-lg, Dem. Nat. Conv, 68. Mem: K. of C; Albany Sportsman's Club; Albany Golf Club; Farmers Union; Township Treasurer, Rocky Mountain JimBeam Bottle and Specialty Club. Rel: Catholic. Mailing Add: Albany, Minn. 56307.

SCHROTE, JOHN E. R
b. Findlay, Ohio, 5/6/36; s. Millard L. Schrote and Alberta Ellis S; m. 3/2/57 to Rachel Daly; c. James D. and Gretchen L. Educ: Ohio State Univ, B.S, 58; Univ. Cincinnati, 58-59; Miami Univ, 59-60; Xavier Univ, M.B.A, 64; Tower Club; Saddle & Sirloin Club; Intramurals. Polit. & Govt. Pos: Page, Ohio House Rep, spec. session, 57; mem, Warren Co. Goldwater for President Cmt, 64; secy, Warren Co. Young Rep, 65; regional dir, Lukens for Cong. Cmt, 66; mem. Warren Co. Rep. Cent. Cmt, 65-68; Warren Co. chmn, Herbert for State Treas. Cmt, 66; del, Ohio Young Rep. State Conv, 66, 67 & 68; alternate del, Rep. State Conv, 66; mem, Franklin City Recreation Bd, 66; admin. asst, U.S. Rep, D.E. 'Buz' Lukens, 67-; advance man and hotel chmn, Citizens for Reagan Cmt, Rep. Nat. Conv, 68; asst. to exec. dir, Inaugural Ball Cmt, 69. Bus. & Prof. Pos: Buyer and expediter, McGraw Construction Co, Middletown, Ohio, 58-59; buyer, Armco Steel Corp, 59-66. Mem: The

Bull Elephants Club; Congression Secy. Club; trustee, Warren Co. Youth Coun; Poky Griffith Dist. Cmt. Boy Scouts. Rel: Episcopal. Legal Res: 540 Alvin Ct, Franklin, Ohio 45005. Mailing Add: 2301 Cheshire Lane, Alexandria, Va. 22307.

SCHRUNK, TERRY DOYLE D
Mayor, Portland, Ore.
b. Stayton, Ore, 3/10/13; s. James F. Schrunk and Pearl Margaret Doyle S; m. 5/17/36 to Virginia Dorothy Price; c. Michael, Judy Ann and Patrick. Educ: Univ. Portland, 33-35; Univ. Ore, B.A. in econ. and polit. sci, 42; Tau Kappa Epsilon. Polit. & Govt. Pos: Sheriff, Multnomah Co, Ore, 49-57; chmn, Ore. Del. to Dem. Nat. Conv, 52; Mayor, Portland, Ore, 57- Bus. & Prof. Pos: Firefighter, Portland Fire Bur, Ore, 35-42, Capt, 45-49; ed, Ore. State Fire Fighters Monthly Mag, 48-49. Mil. Serv: Entered as Ens, Navy, 42, released as Lt, 45, after serv. in USS Ticonderoga C.V. 14, S.Pac, Third and Fifth Fleet, 44-45; Purple Heart; Silver Star; Asiatic-Pac. Theater Ribbon with Four Stars; Philippine Liberation Medal with Star; Am. Theater Ribbon; Victory Medal. Mem: Chmn. Am. Exec. Cmt. of Japan-Am. Conf. of Mayors and C. of C. Pres; Host-Mayor to Sixth Japan-Am. Conf. of Mayors and C. of C. Pres; past pres, U.S. Conf. Mayors; past pres, League of Ore. Cities; past exec. secy. of Ore. State Firefighters Asn; past del, Portland Cent. Labor Coun, AFL; past pres, Ore. State Sheriffs' Asn; past gov, Nat. Sheriffs' Asn; VFW; Am. Legion; Order of Purple Heart; Elks; Eagles; Mt. Hood Masonic Lodge, Scottish Rite, Shrine; PTA; Ore. State Grange; past pres, Boys Clubs of Portland, Inc. and Local 43, Int. Firefighters Asn. Active in various youth programs. Rel: Presbyterian. Legal Res: 5407 N. Houghton, Portland, Ore. 97203. Mailing Add: 303 City Hall, Portland, Ore. 97204.

SCHUBERT, THEODORE R. R
Colo. State Rep.
b. Crowley Co, Colo, 1/29/24; m. to Beverly Bresser; c. Five. Polit. & Govt. Pos: Colo. State Rep, currently. Bus. & Prof. Pos: Ranch owner; farm and ranch salesman, Walker and Co. Mil. Serv: Army, World War II. Mem: Pikes Peak and Colo. Cattlemen's Asns. Mailing Add: Route 2, Box 37, Calhan, Colo. 80808. (1967)

SCHUCHMAN, WINIFRED GUTHRIE D
V.Chmn, Kittitas Co. Dem. Cent. Cmt, Wash.
b. St. Louis, Mo, 11/15/06; d. James Guthrie and Hattie Bates G; wid; c. James, Mary (Mrs. Elmer Lofstrom), Charles, Ann (Mrs. Larry Young), Harry and Calvin M. Educ: Hardin Col, 1 year; Univ. of Mo, B.A, 23. Polit. & Govt. Pos: Secy, Kittitas Co. Dem. Cent. Cmt, 10 years, v.chmn, 66-67, 68-, chmn, 67-68. Mem: C. of C; Womens Federated Club; Wash. State and Nat. Press Asns. Mailing Add: 817 E. Second St, Cle Elum, Wash. 98922.

SCHUCK, JAROLD RAYMOND R
Pub. Rels. Dir, Wis. Rep. Party
b. Marinette, Wis, 7/16/36; s. Raymond William Schuck and Kathryn Scherer S; m. 9/5/59 to Susan Jennifer Rouse; c. Christopher Raymond, Gregory Karl, Stephen Elliott and Daniel Jason. Educ: Univ. Wis, B.S, 60. Polit. & Govt. Pos: Mem, Dane Co. Rep. Party, Wis; pub. rels. dir, Wis. Rep. Party, currently, dir, Radio and TV, 60-62; admin. asst. to Lt. Gov. Jack B. Olson, 64-65; staff mem, Gov. Warren P. Knowles, 65. Bus. & Prof. Pos: Pub. rels. dir, GEX Milwaukee Corp, 62-64. Mil. Serv: Entered as Pvt, Army, 54, released as Specialist 3/C, 56, after serv. as Teletype Operator, Army Commun. Center, Germany; Expert Carbine; Good Conduct Medal; Nat. Defense Serv. and Army Occupation Medals. Mem: Madison Press Club; Wis. Alumni Club of Madison; Wis. Alumni Asn; Holy Name Soc. Rel: Roman Catholic. Mailing Add: 2222 Ravenswood Rd, Madison, Wis. 53711.

SCHUCKER, ALBERT EDWIN R
Councilman, Reading, Pa.
b. Reading, Pa, 9/1/22; s. Edwin A. Schucker and Lizzie R. Knoll S; m. 12/25/49 to Lillian A; c. Suzanne M. and Nancy A. Educ: Chicago Tech, Specialized Construction, 41; Wharton Sch, Univ. Pa. Polit. & Govt. Pos: Councilman and dir. streets and pub. improvs, Reading, Pa, 63- Bus. & Prof. Pos: Gen. mgr, Edwin A. Schucker Construction Co, 54-; owner, Schucker Construction Co, 59- Mil. Serv: Entered as Pvt, Army, 42, released as Cpl, 43, after serv. in 305th Ord. Regt. Mem: Mason; Shrine; Am. Pub. Works Asn; building construction orgns; many civic groups. Rel: Protestant. Legal Res: 1510 Greenview Ave, Reading, Pa. 19601. Mailing Add: Luzerne and Warren Sts, Reading, Pa. 19601.

SCHUELE, WILFRED D
Wis. State Sen.
b. Hales Corners, Wis, 5/15/06. Educ: Marquette Univ. Polit. & Govt. Pos: Wis. State Assemblyman, 58; Wis. State Sen, 64- Bus. & Prof. Pos: V.pres, water softener mfg. co; bus. investment counselor; State WPA adminstr; disbursement off. RFC, War Assets Admin. and U.S. Treas. Dept. Mailing Add: 3036 N. 84th St, Milwaukee, Wis. 53222.

SCHUETZ, JACK R
Exec. V.Chmn. and Finance Dir, Nebr. Rep. State Cent. Cmt.
b. Hawarden, Iowa, 3/31/12; s. Orange N. Schuetz and Mary Topp S; m. 7/20/33 to Lucille Balkema; c. Terry and Dianne (Mrs. Howard). Educ: Bus. Col. Polit. & Govt. Pos: Exec. Secy, Nebr. Rep. State Cent. Cmt, 58-; Nebr. representative, U.S. Rep. Ralph Beerman, 61-64; Nebr. representative, U.S. Sen. Roman L. Hruska, 68- Bus. & Prof. Pos: Owner-operator, Finance & Ins. Bus, 34-54. Mil. Serv: Entered as PO 3/C, Navy, 44, released as PO 2/C, 46. Mem: Am. Legion, K. of P; Cosmopolitan; Farm Bur. Rel: Presbyterian. Mailing Add: R.R. 8, Lincoln, Nebr. 68526.

SCHULER, JOHN HAMILTON R
Mem, State Rep. Exec. Cmt, Ala.
b. Birmingham, Ala, 10/15/26; s. Robert Eustace Schuler and Doris Moughon S; m. 12/14/54 to Elizabeth Ann Locke Mattison; c. George A. Mattison, IV, Elizabeth Locke, John Hamilton, Jr. and Robert Eustace, II. Educ: Auburn Univ, B.S. Indust. Mgt, 52; Sigma Alpha Epsilon. Polit. & Govt. Pos: Del, Rep. Nat. Conv, 64 & 68; state finance chmn, Rep. Party, Ala, 64-66; mem, State Rep. Exec. Cmt, 64-; campaign mgr, Nixon-Agnew Cmt, 67-68; mem, Rep. Nat. Finance Cmt, 64- Bus. & Prof. Pos: Admin. v.pres, Anderson Elec Corp, 56-57, v.pres. opers, 57-58, exec. v.pres. and gen. mgr, 58-66, pres. and treas, 66-69 and chmn. and chief exec. officer, 69- Mil. Serv: Entered as Seaman, Coast Guard, 44, released as Seaman 1/C, 46, after serv. in Pac. Theatre, 44-46. Mem: Auburn Alumni Eng. Coun; Nat. Elec. Mfrs. Asn; Nat. Asn. Mfrs; Assoc. Indust. of Ala; past pres. and past chmn, Birmingham Area C. of C; exec. cmt, Jr. Achievement of Jefferson Co; v.pres. finance, Salvation Army Adv. Bd; Better Bus. Bur; Samford Univ. Pres. Develop. Coun; Birmingham Symphony Asn.(past pres. and present chmn); Ala. Opera Asn. (pres). Rel: Episcopal. Legal Res: 2964 Cherokee Rd, Birmingham, Ala. 35223. Mailing Add: P.O. Box 455, Leeds, Ala. 35094.

SCHULER, LOUIS EUGENE R
Chmn, Cerro Gordo Co. Rep. Cent. Cmt, Iowa
b. Griswold, Iowa, 2/9/22; s. George A. Schuler and Iona Kreamer S; m. 6/4/48 to Mildred Hines; c. George Richard, Louis Eugene, Jr, Herbert Theodore, Mark Luther and Helen Elisabeth. Educ: Grinnell Col, B.A, 43; Drake Univ, summer 43; State Univ. Iowa, J.D, 49; Friars; pres, Gamma Eta Gamma, Univ. Iowa, 49. Polit. & Govt. Pos: City attorney, Clear Lake, Iowa, 56-, city attorney, Ventura, 60- and Thornton, 68-; chmn, Cerro Gordo Co. Rep. Cent. Cmt, 68- Bus. & Prof. Pos: Partner, Boyle, Schuler & Oltrogge, 49- Mil. Serv: Entered as Pvt, Air Force, 43, released as S/Sgt, 46, after serv. in 20th Air Force, Asiatic Theatre, 45-46; Good Conduct Medal and Asiatic Theatre Medal. Publ: Articles in Iowa Law Rev, 49. Mem: Am. Judicature Soc; Iowa State Bar Asn; Am. Trial Lawyers Asn; 12th Judicial Dist. Bar Asn.(pres, 69); Cerro Gordo Co. Bar Asn.(v.pres, 69); Clear Lake Lions Club (pres, 49); Am. Legion (Comdr, 50); VFW; 40 et 8; Farm Bur. Boss of the Year, Clear Lake, Iowa, 67. Rel: Lutheran. Mailing Add: 408 N. Shore Dr, Clear Lake, Iowa 50428.

SCHULER, T. E. R
b. Streeter, N. Dak; Single. Educ: Pub. Schs. Polit. & Govt. Pos: N. Dak. State Rep, 47-61. Bus. & Prof. Pos: Farmer. Mil: WW II. Mem: Am. Legion; Comdr, Legion Post, 49. Mailing Add: Streeter, N.Dak. 58483. (1967)

SCHULTZ, FREDERICK HENRY D
Speaker, Fla. House of Rep.
b. Jacksonville, Fla, 1/16/29; s. Clifford G. Schultz and Mae Wangler S; m. 8/11/51 to Nancy Jane Reilly; c. Catherine G, Frederick H, Jr, Clifford G, II and John Reilly. Educ: Princeton Univ, A.B, 51; Univ. Fla. Law Sch, 54-56; Phi Delta Phi. Polit. & Govt. Pos: Fla. State Rep, Duval Co, 63-, speaker, Fla. House of Rep, 69- Bus. & Prof. Pos: Investor, Personal and Family Investments, 57- Mil. Serv: Entered as 2nd Lt, Army, released as 1st Lt, 54, after serv. in Artil, Korea; Aide-de-camp, Brig. Gen. Ralph C. Cooper, 9 months; Army Res, 54-60; Bronze Star and Korean Serv. Medal; UN Medal. Rel: Roman Catholic. Legal Res: 4314 Ortega Forest Dr, Jacksonville, Fla. 32210. Mailing Add: Suite 3B, 118 W. Adams St, Jacksonville, Fla. 32202.

SCHULTZ, MIKE R
Mem, Imperial Co. Rep. Cent. Cmt, Calif.
b. Chicago, Ill, 6/19/20; s. Phillip Schultz and Mollie Krohn S; m. 8/8/43 to Ruth Litrov; c. Laura Jean and Michael Alan. Educ: Univ. Calif, Berkeley, 3 years. Polit. & Govt. Pos: Mem, Imperial Co. Rep. Cent. Cmt, Calif, 64-; State agr. chmn. to Ronald Reagan, Campaign, 66; mem, For. Trade Cmn. and Local Appln. Adv. Bd, 66-; del, Rep. Nat. Conv, 68. Bus. & Prof. Pos: Pres, Mike Schultz & Son, El Centro, Calif, 51-, Fitz-Gerald & Litrov, 68- Mil. Serv: Entered as Pvt, Army, 41, released as Capt, 46, after serv. in Hawaiian Artillery Command-Staff, Pac. Theatre, 44-46; Pac. Theatre Medal. Mem: West. Growers Asn; Elks. Rel: Jewish. Legal Res: 935 Vine St, El Centro, Calif. 92244. Mailing Add: 2930 Corda Lane, Los Angeles, Calif. 90049.

SCHULTZ, WALDEMAR HERBERT D
Secy, Milwaukee Co. Dem. Statutory Cmt, Wis.
b. Milwaukee, Wis, 12/3/21; s. Walter J. Schultz and Emma L. Sievert S; single. Educ: St. Olaf Col; Univ. Wis. Polit. & Govt. Pos: Membership chmn, West Allis-West Milwaukee Unit Dem. Party, 46-, treas, 49 & 55-; mem, state and co. platform cmts. and Dem. Constitution Cmt, 48; Dem. committeeman, Fourth Ward, 50-64, Second Ward, 64-; chmn, Eighth Sen. Dist. Dem. Party, 50 & 65; secy, Milwaukee Co. Dem. Statutory Cmt, Wis, 52-; treas, Milwaukee Co. Dem. Party, 60-63; alternate del, Dem. Nat. Conv, 64; asst. to chmn, Dem. State Conv; state legis. chmn, Wis. Conf. of Br, NAACP, 68- Mil. Serv: A/S, Navy, 43-44. Publ: Why I Am a Democrat—The Creed of Your U.S. Senator, Congressman and Assemblyman, Artcraft Press; 'A Democratic Profile—Waldemar Schultz—Christian,' Milwaukee Sentinel Press. Mem: West Allis NAACP; second v.pres, Milwaukee Conf. of the Am. Lutheran Churchmen, 69- Rel: Lutheran. Mailing Add: 1968 S. 72nd St, West Allis, Wis. 53219.

SCHULTZE, CHARLES LOUIS D
b. Alexandria, Va, 12/12/24; s. Richard Lee Scultze and Nora Woolls Baggett S; m. 9/6/47 to Rita Irene Hertzog; c. Karen M, Kevin C, Helen L, Kathleen E, Carol R. and Mary G. Educ: Georgetown Univ, A.B, 48, M.A, 50; Univ Md, Ph.D, 60. Polit. & Govt. Pos: Research analyst, Army Security Agency, 48-49; mem. staff, President's Coun. Econ. Adv, 52-58; asst. dir, Bur. of Budget, 62-65, chief, 65-67. Bus & Prof. Pos: Assoc. prof. econ, Ind. Univ, 59-61; prof, Univ. Md, 61- Mil. Serv: Entered as Pvt, Army, 43, released as Pfc, 46, after serv. in Inf, ETO, 44-45; Purple Heart; Bronze Star. Publ: National Income Analysis, Prentice Hall, 64; 'Recent Inflation in the United States,' Joint Econ. Cmt, U.S. Cong, 59; 'Prices, Costs and Output in the Postwar Decade,' Cmt. for Econ. Develop. Mem: Am. Econ. Asn; Royal Econ. Soc. of Eng; Am. Asn. of Univ. Prof. Rel: Catholic. Mailing Add: 5826 Nevada Ave. N.W, Washington, D.C. 20015. (1967)

SCHULZ, HARRY JOHN D
b. Falls City, Tex, 3/27/13; s. John Gottlieb Schulz and Catherine Sheehy S; m. 12/21/38 to Virginia Swett; c. Mary Virginia, Betty, Harriet Ann, Peggy and Harry J, Jr. Educ: St. Mary's Univ, 30-32; Univ. Tex, LL.B, 32-35; Newman Club. Polit. & Govt. Pos: Co. attorney, Live Oak Co, Tex, 36-40; city attorney, Three Rivers, 45-; trustee, Three Rivers Independent Sch. Dist, 57-; presidential elector, 60; del, Dem. Nat. Conv, 64, alternate del, 68; dir, Nueces River Reclamation and Conserv. Dist, 64-; committeeman, State Dem.

Exec. Cmt, 65-69. Bus. & Prof. Pos: Dir, First State Bank, Three Rivers, Tex, 64- Mem: Am. Bar Asn; chmn, Grievance Cmt, 14B Dist, Tex. Bar Asn, 50-68; Rotary; K. of C; Farm Bur; Beeville Co. Club; C. of C. Papal Knight, Knight of St. Gregory. Rel: Roman Catholic. Legal Res: 623 Harborth, Three Rivers, Tex. 78071. Mailing Add: P.O. Drawer 580, Three Rivers, Tex. 78071.

SCHUMACHER, ANITA M. A. R
V.Chmn, S.Dak. Rep. State Cent. Cmt.
b. Douglas Co, S.Dak, 9/7/14; d. William C. Wenzel and Johanna Mattheis W; m. 6/17/34 to Herbert J. Schumacher; c. Darleen Anne (Mrs. James Kautz) and Harold H. Educ: Grad. of Dale Carnegie; Epsilon Sigma Alpha. Polit. & Govt. Pos: Precinct woman, Rep. Party, Hutchinson Co, S.Dak, 48-; committeewoman, S.Dak. Rep. State Cent. Cmt, 58-65, v.chmn, 65-; chmn, Hutchinson Co. Rep. Finance Cmt, 58-65; organizer and chmn, Parkston Rep. Women's Fedn, 59-65; del. and hon. chmn. S.Dak. del, Rep. Nat. Conv, 60; area chmn, Rep. Campaign, 60; mem, Gov. Gubbrud Steering Cmt, 60; mem, S.Dak. State Fair Bd, 61-, v.pres, 63-64; mem, State Rep. Adv. Cmt, 65-; exec. mem, S.Dak. Rep. Women's Fedn, 65- Bus. & Prof. Pos: Acct, Parkston Automobile Agency, 48-; pres, Bus. Mgt. Coun, Omaha Zone, 62-63. Cert. of Award for Outstanding Achievement in Acct; Award, Dale Carnegie Best Prepared Speech; Citizen of the Week, Sioux Falls Argus Leader Newspaper. Rel: Am. Lutheran. Mailing Add: Parkston, S.Dak. 57366.

SCHUMACHER, LEO WILLIAM D
Committeeman, Ill. Dem. Cent. Cmt.
b. LaRose, Ill, 5/7/00; s. Charles F. Schumacher and Margaret Hahn S; m. 5/10/28 to LaVon West; c. Barbara (Mrs. Seggerman) and Roger. Educ: High sch. Polit. & Govt. Pos: Twp. clerk, LaRose, Ill, 5 terms, twp. assessor, 1 term and twp. supvr, 5 terms; field investr, Dept. Agr, 61-; committeeman, Ill. Dem. Cent. Cmt, currently. Bus. & Prof. Pos: Farmer. Mem: Farm Bur. Rel: Lutheran, Mo. Synod. Mailing Add: LaRose, Ill. 61541.

SCHUMACHER, ROBERT J. R
S.Dak. State Rep.
b. Mitchell, S.Dak, 2/10/29; m. to Carole L. Laws; c. Mary Ann, R.C. and Jane Louise. Educ: Univ. S.Dak, LL.B, 53. Polit. & Govt. Pos: Mem, S.Dak. Code Compilation Cmn. and S.Dak. Indian Affairs Cmn; spec. city attorney, Rapid City; dep. states attorney, Pennington Co; S.Dak. State Rep, 62-68. Bus. & Prof. Pos: Law practice; ranching. Mem: Mason; Consistory; Elks; United Commercial Travelers; C. of C. Rel: Congregational. Mailing Add: 618 Sixth, Rapid City, S.Dak. 57701. (1967)

SCHUMACHER, SNEAD D
S.C. State Sen.
b. Walhalla, S.C, 3/8/24; s. George D. Schumacher and Clara Snead S; m. 4/27/45 to Jimmie Crofford; c. Susan. Educ: Tex. A&M, ASTP, 43-44; Clemson Col, B.S.C.E, 47. Polit. & Govt. Pos: Councilman, Walhalla, S.C, 50-59 & 62-64, mayor pro tempore, 64; dir, Oconee Co. Planning Bd, 58; S.C. State Rep, 65-66; S.C. State Sen, Dist. One, 67- Bus. & Prof. Pos: Registered prfnl. engr, S.C. and Ga; contractor, 50-58; sch. teacher, 58-65; civil engr, owner, Schumacher Eng. Serv. and Land Surveyor. Mil. Serv: S/Sgt, Army, 42-45, Co. C, 393rd Inf, 99th Div, served in ETO; Combat Inf. Badge, 2 Battle Stars. Mem: Master, Blue Ridge Masonic Lodge, 56; pres, Lions Club, 54; VFW; Hejaz Shrine; charter mem, Sertoma; Sons of Confederate Vet; chmn, Oconee Co. Christmas Seal Campaign, 64-65; adv. cmt, Tri-Co. TEC Eng. Curriculum; bd. dirs, Oconee Mem.Hosp, 67- Commun. Leader of Am, 69. Rel: Lutheran; Supt. Sunday Sch, St. John's Lutheran Church, 50-59, councilman, 50-68, financial secy, 62. Mailing Add: Box 512, Walhalla, S.C. 29691.

SCHUMANN, ALFRED OSCAR R
Minn. State Rep.
b. Eyota, Minn, 3/27/24; s. Frederick William Schumann and Christina Pries S; m. 2/2/52 to Helen Marie Strike; c. Robert, Glen, Nancy, Donna, Wayne and Vicki. Educ: Rochester Jr. Col, pre-law, 42-43. Polit. & Govt. Pos: V.chmn, Co. Rep. Party, Minn, 61; Minn. State Rep, currently. Mem: Mason; Farm Bur. Rel: United Church of Christ. Mailing Add: Eyota, Minn. 55934.

SCHUMANN, MARVIN C. Conservative
b. Benton Co, Minn. Educ: Univ. Minn. Sch. of Agr. Polit. & Govt. Pos: Mem, Bd. of Co. Cmnrs, Benton, Minn, 44-54; Minn. State Rep, 54-68. Bus. & Prof. Pos: Livestock farmer, breeder of registered Aberdeen Angus cattle. Mailing Add: Rice, Minn. 56367. (1967)

SCHUMANN, MERRITT J. R
Committeeman, Rep. Party of Tex.
b. New Braunfels, Tex, 6/16/28; s. Herbert O. Schumann and Meta Krause S.(deceased); m. 6/4/50 to Iris Timmermann; c. Sharon Lynn, Sandra Kay, Susan Jeannine, Sara Christine and Sheila Anne. Educ: Univ. of Tex, B.B.A, 50. Polit. & Govt. Pos: Mem. and treas, bd. of trustees, New Braunfels Independent Sch. Dist, 56-59; chmn, Comal Co. Rep. Party, Tex, 62-66 & 68-; mem, Elected Charter Cmn, New Braunfels, 66; chmn, Good Govt. League of New Braunfels, 66 & 67; mem, Rep. Task Force on Educ, 67; committeeman, Rep. Party of Tex, 68- Bus. & Prof. Pos: Pres, New Braunfels Indust. Found, 67-; co-chmn. steering cmt, Comal Co. Jr. Col, currently Mil. Serv: Entered as Ens, Navy, 50, released as Lt, 53, after serv. in Sea Duty, USS Pritchett DD561, Korean Theatre; UN and Korean Medals; Admirals Commendation, Outstanding Supply Dept. in DesLant Atlantic Fleet. Mem: Pres, New Braunfels Jr. C. of C, 59-60, Comal Co. Community Fund, 61-62, New Braunfels Lions Club, 63-64, Comal Co. C. of C, 64-65 and Univ. of Tex. Exes, Comal Co, 63-64; dir. and treas, San Antonio Chap, Chartered Life Underwriters, currently; San Antonio, Tex. and Nat. Asns. of Life Underwriters; San Antonio Chap, Col of Life Underwriters; Longhorn Club. Named Outstanding Jaycee of the Year, 59-60; Besserung Award, 66. Rel: United Church of Christ; pres, United Church of Christ, New Braunfels. Mailing Add: 1079 Fredricksberg Rd, New Braunfels, Tex. 78130.

SCHURMAN, BEATRICE REDFIELD PARKER D
b. Coventry, Vt, 1/18/98; d. John Isaac Parker and Mary Agnes Elder P; m. 9/24/24 to Dr. Charles Good Schurman (deceased); c. Dr. Charles G, Jr. and Mary Louise Margaret (Mrs. James Palin). Educ: Beebe Acad; Stanstead Col; Macdonald Col; Montreal Gen. Hosp, Nurses Training, 20-24; Sigma Alpha Epsilon. Polit. & Govt. Pos: Mem, Newport City Dem. Cmt, Vt, 33-69 and Vt. State Dem. Cmt, 35-69; Dem. nat. committeewoman, Vt, 44-68; del, Dem. Nat. Conv, 48-, mem, Speakers Cmt, 48, Platform Cmt, 48 & 52, Credentials Cmt, 57 & 64 and Site Cmt, 60; Dem. nominee for Lt. Gov, Vt, 50; chmn, Orleans-Essex and Caledonia Co. Campaign Hq. Stevenson for Pres, 56; mem, Women's Exec. Dem. Cmt. for India Edwards for V.pres, 56; chmn, Vt. State Dem. Women's Club, 56-69; mem, Vt. Dem. Finance Cmt, Vt. Adv. Cmt, 57; chmn, Orleans-Essex Co. Campaigns Hq. Kennedy for Pres, 60, Hoff for Gov, 62, 64 & 66 and Lyndon B. Johnson for Pres, 64. Bus. & Prof. Pos: Sch. teacher, 16-20; Med. secy, nurse and receptionist, husband's off, Vt, 24-68. Mem: Organizer and past pres, Vt. State Dem. Club; mem, exec. cmt, Vt. Dem. Fedn. Womens Club; Mothers Club; Vt. Gov. Club; 100 Club; chmn, Orleans Co. Dem. Women's Club; treas, Vt. War Chest; chmn. women's div, Newport War Bond and Stamp Sale; finance cmt, Orleans Co. Chap, Am. Red Cross; Women's Auxiliary, State Med. Soc; DAR; Acad. Polit. Sci; life mem, Vt. Hist. Soc; Dist. Dep. Grand Matron, Eastern Star, 42-45; pres, Past Matrons Asn, 52-53; Newport Country Club. Achievements: On honor list of King George V as chmn, Jr. Red Cross, 14-48; rose and orchid gardening; golf, Ladies Championship, Newport Country Club, 33, 35 and 36. Rel: Episcopal. Mailing Add: 8 Prospect St, Newport, Vt. 05855.

SCHURTER, MARION EVELINE R
V.Chmn, Fifth Cong. Dist. Rep. Party, Kans.
b. Redford, N.Y, 9/23/16; d. Edgar John Haley and Esther Ada Hanlon H; m. 3/7/42 to Roy William Schurter. Educ: Midwest Inst, 65-66; Kans. State Teachers Col, summers 66 & 67; correspondence sch, Univ. Kans, 68. Polit. & Govt. Pos: Precinct committeewoman, Rep. Party, 58-; v.chmn, Co. Rep. Cent. Cmt, Kans, 58-64, chmn, 64-; v.chmn, Fifth Cong. Dist. Rep. Party, Kans, 62- Mem: Kans. Fedn. Rep. Women. Rel: Catholic. Mailing Add: R.D. 3, Eureka, Kans. 67045.

SCHUTZER, JEROME D
b. Bronx, N. Y; m. to Harriet Mohr; c. Steven, Mitchell, Hillary. Educ: Stuyvesant High Sch; Col. of the City of N. Y; Brooklyn Law Sch, LL.B. Polit. & Govt. Pos: N. Y. State Assemblyman, 60-66; officer, Sedgwick Dem. Club, Regular Dem. Orgn, Third Assembly Dist. Bus. & Prof. Pos: Mem, law firm of Schutzer and Mohr. Mem: Bronx Co. Bar Asn; and an active mem. of several local and nat. relig, civic, and philanthropic orgns. Mailing Add: 1740 Grand Ave, Bronx, N.Y. 10453. (1967)

SCHWAB, C. B. R
Chmn, Jefferson Co. Rep. Cmt, Nebr.
b. Morrowville, Kans, 1/22/22; s. John Benjamin Schwab and Jessie Mallery S; m. 8/28/40 to Mildred I. Stewart; c. Ronald L. and Lana A.(Mrs. Criner). Educ: Kans. State Univ, D.V.M, 44; Block and Bridle; Jr. Am. Vet. Med. Asn. Polit. & Govt. Pos: Second precinct committeeman, 48-58 & 63-64; mem. city coun, Fairbury, Nebr, 50-52, mem. sch. bd, 52-55, mayor, 69-; chmn, Jefferson Co. Rep. Cmt, 64- Mil. Serv: Entered as Pvt, Army, 45, released as Cpl, 46, after serv. in 970 Counter Intel. Corps, ETO; ETO Serv. Medal. Mem: Pres, Fairbury Lect. Club, 68-69 and Pioneer Shrine, 64-65, Fairbury Lions, 60 and Nebr. Vet. Med. Asn, 60; v.pres, Nebr. Vet. Med. Asn, 59; Shrine; Mason; Elks; VFW; C. of C; Am. Vet. Med. Asn. Silver Beaver Scout Leaders Award. Rel: Presbyterian. Mailing Add: 1210 B, Fairbury, Nebr. 68352.

SCHWAB, MERLE EDWIN R
Chmn, Riley Co. Cent. Cmt, Kans.
b. Morganville, Kans, 1/31/26; s. Edwin N. Schwab and Ruth Bodine S; m. 6/1/50 to Florence Hope Oberg; c. Linda, Melodie and Scott. Educ: Kans. State Univ, B.S. in civil eng, 49; Theta Xi. Polit. & Govt. Pos: Chmn, Riley Co. Young Rep, Kans, 60-62; dist. chmn, Kans. Young Rep, 62-64; chmn, Riley Co. Cent. Cmt, 65-; mem, State Bd. Eng. Exam, 65-; del, Rep. Nat. Conv, 68. Bus. & Prof. Pos: Owner, Merle E. Schwab, Civil Engrs, 55-57; partner, Schwab, Eaton & Assocs, 57-66; pres, Schwab & Eaton, 66- Mil. Serv: Entered as Seaman 2/C, Navy, 44, released as Aviation Cadet, 47. Mem: Nat. Soc. Prfnl. Engrs; Am. Soc. Civil Engrs; Elks; Manhattan Country Club. Rel: Methodist. Mailing Add: 354 N. 15th, Manhattan, Kans. 66502.

SCHWABE, MAX R
b. Columbia, Mo, 12/6/05; s. Dr. George W. Schwabe and Lulu M. Stotts S; m. 7/12/30 to Georgia May Ashlock; c. June and Maxine Lusk. Educ: Univ. Mo. Polit. & Govt. Pos: U.S. Rep, Mo, 43-48; state dir, Farmers Home Admin, U.S. Dept. Agr, 54-61; former mem, Boone Co. Rep. Cmt, Mo. Bus. & Prof. Pos: Underwriting supvr, MFA Mutual Ins. Co, Columbia, Mo, 62- Rel: Christian Church. Mailing Add: 2105 S. Country Club Dr, Columbia, Mo. 65201. (1967)

SCHWADER, FERDINAND D
b. Howard, 5/11/07; m. to Violet Hagermann; c. 2. Polit. & Govt. Pos: S.Dak. State Rep, 54-66; sch. bd. mem; twp. bd, 20 years. Bus. & Prof. Pos: Farming. Mem: Triple A chmn; helped organize Sportsman's Club. Rel: Lutheran. Mailing Add: Howard, S.Dak. 57104. (1967)

SCHWAMM, JOHN A. D
Alaska State Rep.
b. Sitka, Alaska, 8/25/43; s. George S. 'Tony' Schwamm (deceased) and Kathryn H. Schilstra S; m. 6/28/68 to Beverly K. Vance; c. Anthony Christopher. Educ: Alaska Methodist Univ, B.A, 67. Polit. & Govt. Pos: Alaska State Rep, 69- Bus. & Prof. Pos: Off. mgr, Tyonek Mgt. Corp, 67-68; real estate develop. mgr, Carr-Gottstein & Co, 69- Mem: Jaycees. Rel: Catholic. Mailing Add: 3008 W. 32nd, Anchorage, Alaska 99503.

SCHWANER, ANNIE MAE R
N.H. State Rep.
b. Carnesville, Ga, 4/24/12; d. Charles Holman Ginn and Mary Elizabeth Terrell G; m. to Nelson Marshall Schwaner (deceased); c. Audrey M.(Mrs. David L. Barker), Susan A.(Mrs. Anthony D. Iannuccillo), Marsha M.(Mrs. Walter E. Karbowsky), Gordon W. and N. Marshall. Educ: Ga, S.C. and Va. Schs. Polit. & Govt. Pos: N.H. State Rep, 63-; past pres, Plaistow Rep. Women's Club; mem, Rep. Town Club; mem, State Security Task Force and Price Stabilization Bd; mem, Constitutional Conv, 64. Bus. & Prof. Pos: Former Va. news-

paper reporter and columnist. Mem: Founder and pres, Plaistow Civic Orgn; former chmn. of vols, Gr. Haverhill Chap. of Am. Red Cross, exec. bd. mem, nat. del. and br. chmn; town chmn. for a number of Red Cross, Boy Scout and Heart Fund Drives; former PTA Coun. Cmt. Chmn; N.H. Diocesan Sch. Bd. and Speaker's Bur; bd. dir, Seacoast Regional Develop. Asn; bd. dir, Citizens for Educ. Freedom; N.H. Coun. on World Affairs; N.H. Coun. for Better Schs; N.H. Mother's Cmt; N.H. Regional Women's Rep. Club; bd. dir, N.H. Heart Asn; 2nd v.pres, State Order of Women Legislator's. Cert. of Merit, Am. Mother's Cmt, 60; Bronze Medallion, N.H. Heart Asn. Rel: Catholic. Legal Res: Elm St, Plaistow, N.H. 03865. Mailing Add: Box 236, Plaistow, N.H. 03865.

SCHWARTZ, AARON ROBERT D
Tex. State Sen.
b. Galveston, Tex, 7/17/26; s. Joseph Schwartz and Clara Bulbe S; m. 7/14/51 to Marilyn Ruth Cohn; c. Robert A, Richard A, John R. and Thomas L. Educ: Tex. A&M, pre-law, 44, 46-47; Univ. Tex, LL.B, 51; Delta Sigma Rho. Polit. & Govt. Pos: Asst. attorney, Galveston Co, Tex, 51-54; Tex. State Rep, 54-58; Tex. State Sen, 60-, pres. pro-tem, Tex. State Senate, 66, chmn, Rules Cmt, 69; acting gov. for a day, Tex, 66. Mil. Serv: Seaman 1/C, Naval Res, 44-46, serv. in Pac, 45-46; 2nd Lt, Air Force Res, 48-53. Rel: Jewish. Legal Res: Galveston, Tex. Mailing Add: Room 307, Cotton Exchange Bldg, Galveston, Tex. 77550.

SCHWARTZ, EDNA BARBARA D
Mem, Weston Dem. Town Cmt, Mass.
b. Boston, Mass, 5/19/09; d. Abram Smith and Louise Halter S; m. 7/31/41 to Edward Lester Schwartz; c. Andrea (Mrs. Saiet). Educ: Emerson Col, B.Lit, 34; Portia Law Sch, LL.B, 39. Polit. & Govt. Pos: Del, Mass. State Dem. Conv, 32; mem, Brookline Dem. Town Cmt, 32-38; mem, exec. Cmt, Newton Dem. City Cmt, 60-65; pres, Dem. Women on Wheels, 62-64; state chmn, Operation Support, 62-68; mem. adv. coun, Mass. State Small Bus. Admin, 64-66; mem, Weston Dem. Town Cmt, 66-; del, Dem. Nat. Conv, 68. Publ: Personality Improvement, Barnes & Noble, 40; The Best I Know, Waverly, 41. Mem: Nat. Coun. Jewish Women (pres. Gr. Boston Sect, v.pres. New Eng. Regional Div); Brandeis Women's Auxiliary; Beth Israel Hosp. Women's Auxiliary; Jewish Children and Family Serv.(women's cmt). Mailing Add: 17 Ledgewood Rd, Weston, Mass. 02193.

SCHWARTZ, GEORGE X. D
City Councilman, Philadelphia, Pa.
b. N.Y.C, 1/28/15; s. Max Schwartz and Ida Ochroch S; m. 8/8/37 to Jerre Davidov; c. William G, Marjorie (Mrs. Richard Dilsheimer) and Susan. Educ: Temple Univ, B.S, 36, Law Sch, LL.B, 40; Pyramid; Alpha Epsilon Pi. Polit. & Govt. Pos: Legal consult, Redevelop. Authority, Phila, Pa, 52-60; Pa. State Rep, 53-60; city councilman, Phila, 60-, Majority Floor Leader and chmn, Finance Cmt, City Coun, 62-; committeeman, 34th Ward Dem. Exec. Cmt, Phila. Dem. City Exec. Cmt, 62-; del, Dem. Nat. Conv, 64 & 68. Bus. & Prof. Pos: Partner, Blank, Rome, Klaus & Comisky, Attorneys, 62-; mem. bd, Old Phila. Develop. Corp. and Food Distribution Center, 62- Mem: Phila, Pa. and Am. Bar Asns; mem. of bd, Fedn. of Jewish Agencies of Gr. Phila; Phila. 1976 Bicentennial Corp; Phila. Grand Opera Co; Phila. Lyric Opera; Phila. Conv. and Tourists Bur; Franklin Inst.(city rep); Brith Sholom Found; Independent order of Brith Sholom; B'nai B'rith; Locust Club of Phila; Green Valley Country Club; adv. cmt, Task Force, Eminent Domain Law, Joint State Govt. Cmn, Pa. Rel: Jewish. Mailing Add: 7015 Greenhill Rd, Philadelphia, Pa. 19151.

SCHWARTZ, HARRY F. D
Chmn, Sheridan Co. Dem. Party, Wyo.
b. Washington, D.C, 2/1/15; m. to Lee; c. Five. Educ: Univ. Colo, B.A; Univ. Wyo, LL.B. Polit. & Govt. Pos: Wyo. State Rep. until 67; chmn, Sheridan Co. Dem. Party, currently. Bus. & Prof. Pos: Lawyer. Mem: Mason; Shrine; Elks; Am. Legion; Kiwanis Club. Rel: Protestant. Mailing Add: 50 E. Loucks, Sheridan, Wyo. 82801. (1967)

SCHWARTZ, HOWARD LELAND R
Mem, Calif. Rep. State Cent. Cmt.
b. San Francisco, Calif, 9/23/33; s. Morris Schwartz and Hannah Harband S; m. 11/20/60 to Marion F. Schmerl; c. Michael, Randall and Bryan. Educ: Stanford Univ, B.A, 55; Stanford Law Sch, LL.B, 59; Delta Tau Delta; Phi Delta Phi. Polit. & Govt. Pos: Dep. dist. attorney, Alameda Co, Calif, 59-61; pres, Piedmont Young Rep, 64; chmn, 16th Assembly Dist. Rep. Precinct Orgn, 68; alternate mem, Alameda Co. Rep. Cent. Cmt, 68 & 69; mem, Calif. Rep. State Cent. Cmt, 68-; mem. bd, East Bay Rep. Alliance, 69. Bus. & Prof. Pos: Assoc. and partner, Gross, Gross, Rose & Schwartz, Oakland, Calif, 61- Mil. Serv: Entered as Ens, Navy, 55, released as Lt.(jg), 57, after serv. on U.S.S. Princeton, 55-57; Lt, Naval Res, 57- Mem: Alameda Co. and Criminal Courts Bar Asns; Barristers Club; Lions; East Bay Stanford Men's Club; mem. bd, Am. Jewish Cmt. and Jewish Commun. Rels. Coun. Elected Attorney Gen, Calif. Boys State, 50; mem, Moot Court Bd, Stanford Law Sch. Rel: Jewish. Mailing Add: 5 Scenic Ave, Piedmont, Calif. 94611.

SCHWARTZ, MURRAY M. D
V.Chmn, N.Y. State Dem. Law Cmt.
b. N.Y.C, 8/8/25; s. Abraham Schwartz and Edith Kosakofsky S; m. 9/19/48 to Gladys Lucille Rubin; c. Karen Patricia, Robert David, Stephen Murray and Richard Peter. Educ: Syracuse Univ. Col. Liberal Educ, B.A, 49; Col. Law, LL.B, 52; Phi Delta Phi; Scabbard and Blade. Polit. & Govt. Pos: Del, N.Y. State Judicial Conv, 52-64; chmn, law cmt, Onondaga Co. Dem. Cmt, 56-66; v.chmn, N.Y. State Dem. Law Cmt, 63-; alternate del-at-lg, Dem. Nat. Conv, 64. Bus. & Prof. Pos: Attorney, Schwartz & Taylor, 55-59 and Hayman, Amrose, Schwartz & Schlesinger, 60-; attorney-at-law, 62-66; confidential clerk to Justice of State Supreme Court, 65- Mil. Serv: Entered as Pvt, Air Force, 43, released as Sgt, 46, after serv. in Airways Communication Syst, India-Burma-China Theater; Am. Theater Ribbon; India-Burma-China Theater Ribbon with Two Battle Stars; Presidential Citation; Unit Citation; others; 1st Lt, Air Force Res, 61. Mem: Onondaga Co, N.Y. State and Am. Bar Asns; Jewish War Vets; Mason; N.Y. State Hist. Asn; Syracuse Press Club and various local groups. Rel: Jewish. Mailing Add: 203 Scott Ave, Syracuse, N.Y. 13224. (1967)

SCHWARTZ, RAMON, JR. D
S.C. State Rep.
b. Sumter, S.C, 5/25/25; s. Raymon Schwartz and Madge Grossman S; m. 6/24/50 to Rosa Weinberg; c. Barbara, Ramon, III, Milton and Bill. Educ: Univ. S.C, A.B. and LL.B; Omicron Delta Kappa; Kappa Sigma Kappa. Polit. & Govt. Pos: Judge, Munic. Court, Sumter, S.C, 53-57 & 60-64; chmn, Sumter Co. Libr. Bd, 61-68; chmn, Sumter Housing Authority, 65-68; S.C. State Rep, 69- Mil. Serv: Entered as Pvt, Army, 43, released as Pfc, 46, after serv. in ETO. Mem: Life trustee, Tuomey Hosp. and Solomon's Home for the Aged; Jaycees (pres, Sumter Chap, 56-57, pres, S.C. Chap, 59-60); pres, Sumter C. of C, 62-63 and Sumter Rotary Club, 68-69; Am. Legion; VFW; Elks. Outstanding Young Man of Year Award, Sumter, S.C, 57. Rel: Jewish. Legal Res: 214 Haynsworth St, Sumter, S.C. 29150. Mailing Add: Law Range, Sumter, S.C. 29150.

SCHWARTZ, RONALD M. R
b. Stamford, Conn, 2/7/33; s. Paul Schwartz and Kathlyn Satin S; single. Educ: Duke Univ, A.B, 53, Sch. Law, LL.B, 56; Phi Delta Phi; Zeta Beta Tau. Polit. & Govt. Pos: Asst. Corp. Counsel, City of Stamford, Conn, 66-, pres, bd. of rep, 63-64 and minority leader, 61-63, alternate mem, zoning bd, 65-66, mem, charter revision cmn, 62; ed-in-chief, State Young Rep. Newspaper, 57; pres, Stamford Young Rep. Club, 58. Bus. & Prof. Pos: Private Gen. Practice, 64-; partner, Law Firm of Macrides, Zezima & Schwartz, 56-64. Publn: 'The Availability of Federal Forums in Non Diversity Litigation Under Section 301 (a) of Taft-Hartley,' Conn. Bar J, 9/57; 'Federal Court Application of the 'Doing Business' Test in Diversity Cases,' Duke Bar J, 56. Mem: Am, Conn. and Stamford Bar Asns; Am. Trial Lawyers Asn; pres, Fairfield Co. Alumni Asn. of Duke Univ, 57-; Metropolitan Alumni Asn. of Duke Univ, N.Y, 56-; Alumni Admissions Cmt, Duke Univ, 64-; v.pres, Lions Club of N. Stamford, Conn, 66; Belltown Volunteer Fire Dept; Stamford Jewish Center; B'nai B'rith; Zionist Orgn. of Am; Temple Beth El; C. of C. Rel: Jewish. Legal Res: 65 Glenbrook Rd, Stamford, Conn. 06905. Mailing Add: 19 River St, Stamford, Conn. 06901.

SCHWARTZMAN, SARAH D
b. Kletzk, Poland, 12/25/24; d. Aaron Kotler and Channa Meltzer K; div; c. Jacob, Shalva, William, Eta, Miriam and Isser. Educ: Brooklyn Col, B.A, 62; Columbia Univ, M.A, 66, Ph.D. cand; Phi Beta Kappa; journalism and Dem. clubs. Polit. & Govt. Pos: Proj. research dir, Robert F. Kennedy Sen. Campaign, 64; research assoc, Joint Legis. Cmt. for Higher Educ, N.Y, 67-68; del, Dem. Nat. Conv, 68; dir. spec. projs, James Scheuer Mayoralty Campaign, N.Y, 69. Bus. & Prof. Pos: Research asst, Columbia Univ. Sch. of Int. Affairs, summer 65; consult, Univ. Notre Dame Study of the Effect of Soc. Serv. on the Poor in N.Y.C, Chicago and Wash, D.C, 66; instr, New Sch. for Soc. Research, 67-68; instr, Rutgers Univ, 68. Mem: Am. for Dem. Action (co-chmn, N.Y. State Bd); N.Y. State New Dem. Coalition (for. policy cmt); Lexington Dem. Club; Park Slope Independent Dem; New Horizons Reform Dem. Club. Rel: Jewish. Mailing Add: 4701 15th Ave, Brooklyn, N.Y. 11219.

SCHWARTZMILLER, FRIDOLIN D
Mem, Seneca Co. Dem. Exec. Cmt, Ohio
b. Tiffin, Ohio, 10/26/99; s. John M. Schwartzmiller and Rose Buchman S; m. 4/30/27 to Marie A. Gillig; c. Dorothy (Mrs. Arnold), Martha (Mrs. Finsel) and Ruth (Mrs. Lucius). Educ: Ohio State Univ. Polit. & Govt. Pos: Mem, Seneca Co. Dem. Exec. Cmt, Ohio, currently, chmn, 56-62; del, Dem. Nat. Conv, 64. Bus. & Prof. Pos: Former pres, New Riegel Tel. Co; owner and operator, Brookdale Turkey Farm, 28-63; dir, 1st Nat. Bank of Tiffin, 37- Mem: K. of C.(4°); Lions; Farm Bur. Farmer of the Year award, Cleveland C. of C, 56. Rel: Roman Catholic. Mailing Add: Route 2, Tiffin, Ohio 44883.

SCHWARZ, ADOLPH C. R
Pres, Bloomingdale Twp. Regular Rep. Orgn, Ill.
b. Chicago, Ill, 8/25/35; s. Adolph O. Schwarz and Margaret Michalik S; m. 7/9/59 to Barbara Ann Latham; c. Melody Ann and Brenda Marie. Educ: Univ. Ill, 56; Trane Air Conditioning Inst, 60; I.B.R. Hydronic Heating Inst, 62. Polit. & Govt. Pos: Precinct capt. and dir, 23rd Ward Rep. Orgn, Ill, 58-64; pres, 23rd Ward Young Rep. Club, 60-61; pres, Clear-Ridge Rep. Club, 61-65; officer, Cook Co. Young Rep. Orgn, 62-64; notary pub, Ill, 62-; admin. asst. to pres, Ill. Young Rep. Orgn, 63-65; del, Rep. Nat. Conv, 64; chmn, Coburn for State Auditor Campaign, Ill, 64; pres, Bloomingdale Twp. Regular Rep. Orgn. and Rep. Committeeman, 65-; police cmnr, Glendale Heights, 65-; mem, Plan & Indust. Develop. Cmn. and spec. dep. sheriff, DuPage Co, 65- Bus. & Prof. Pos: Treas, Waner Heating & Air Conditioning Corp, 59-62, v.pres, 62- Mil. Serv: Entered as Seaman Recruit, Navy, 52, released as Seaman, 55, after serv. in Pac; Good Conduct and Sharpshooter Medals; Korean Campaign Ribbon. Publ: We The People, Clear-Ridge Rep. Club, 60. Mem: Kiwanis Int; Schwaben Verein; Polish Nat. Alliance; Sheet Metal Workers Union. Named Outstanding Young Rep. of Year, 61 and Outstanding Rep. of Year, 63, Cook Co, Ill. Rel: Roman Catholic. Mailing Add: 66 East Armitage Ave, Glendale Heights, Ill. 60137. (1967)

SCHWARZKOPF, LYALL ARTHUR R
Minn. State Rep.
b. Waupaca, Wis, 6/10/31; s. Arthur Charles Schwarzkopf and Dora Venem S; m. 9/6/58 to Inez Minerva Olson; c. Erik Arthur, Kurt Ian and Dana Marit. Educ: Univ. Minn, B.A, 53. Polit. & Govt. Pos: Mem, Mayor's Youth Welfare Cmn, Minneapolis, Minn, 47-48; mem, Gov. Youth Welfare Cmn, 47-48; state secy-treas, Minn. Young Rep. League, 58-60, state chmn, 61 & 62, nat. committeeman, 63 & 64; mem, Rep. Exec. Cmt. and State Cent. Cmt, Minn, 61-62 & 65-; Minn. State Rep, 63-; chmn, Hennepin Co. Rep. Cmt, 65-; del, Rep. Nat. Conv, 68; mem, Gov. Cmn. on Aging, 68- Bus. & Prof. Pos: Field secy, Minn. State Med. Asn, 56-65. Mil. Serv: Entered as Pvt, Army, 54, released as Sp. 3/C, 56; Commanding Gen. Citation; Letters of Commendation. Mem: Univ. Minn. Alumni Asn; Exchange Club; AF&AM; Odd Fellows; YMCA. Rel: Lutheran. Mailing Add: 4840 Bloomington Ave, Minneapolis, Minn. 55417.

SCHWEDER, WARREN DICKENS R
Exec. Dir, Ky. State Rep. Cent. Cmt.
b. Chicago, Ill, 9/25/21; s. Edmund Woland Schweder and Leela Dickens S; m. 4/25/46 to Eve Maurice; c. Warren Maurice, John Woland and Daniell Dickens. Educ: Univ. Ky. Polit. & Govt. Pos: Exec. dir, Ky. State Rep. Cent.

Cmt, 64- Bus. & Prof. Pos: Polit. writer, Lexington Leader, Ky, 46-53 & 63-64; managing ed, The Blood-Horse, 53-63. Mil. Serv: Entered as Pvt, Army, 43, released as Cpl, 45, after serv. in Signal Corps (Radar), ETO; ETO Ribbon with 5 Battle Stars. Edited annual edition, American Race Horses, 56-62. Rel: Presbyterian. Legal Res: 700 Albany Rd, Lexington, Ky. 40502. Mailing Add: 1619 Heyburn Bldg, Louisville, Ky. 40202.

SCHWEFEL, WILLIAM S. R
Wis. State Assemblyman
b. Oakfield, Wis, 10/5/02. Educ: Wis. Univ. Polit. & Govt. Pos: Town assessor, Oakfield, Wis, 40-46, town chmn, 51-69; mem, Fond du Lac Co. Bd. of Supvr, 51-68; Wis. State Assemblyman, 64- Bus. & Prof. Pos: Retired farmer. Mem: Former mem, Exchange Club; mgr, Fond du Lac Agr. Soc, 55-66. Mailing Add: Route 1, Oakfield, Wis. 53065.

SCHWEIGERT, THOMAS F. R
Pres, Mich. State Senate
b. Detroit, Mich, 9/29/17; s. Thomas H. Schweigert and Marie Martinek S; m. 7/3/43 to Margaret Chapman; c. Frank Thomas, Ralph Fred and Charles James. Educ: Mich. State Univ, B.S. in forestry, 39; Xi Sigma Pi; Phi Delta Theta. Polit. & Govt. Pos: Forester, U.S. Forest Serv, 39-43 & 46-48; supvr, Emmet Co, Mich, 55-61; Mich. State Sen, 37th Dist, 61-, former minority leader and pres. pro tempore, Mich. State Senate, now pres; acting Lt. Gov, Mich, currently. Bus. & Prof. Pos: Consulting Forester and land surveyor, self-employed, 48- Mil. Serv: Entered as Pvt, Army, 43, released as 1st Lt, 46, after serv. in Inf. and 17th Major Port, U.S. and ETO, 45-46; U.S. Theater, ETO, Occupation and Victory Ribbons. Mem: Soc. Am. Foresters; Am. Cong. on Surv. & Mapping; Asn. of Consult. Foresters; Mich. Soc. Registered Land Surveyors; Mich. Forestry & Park Asn; Kiwanis; Elks; Mason, K.T, Shrine; VFW. Award, Distinguished Serv. to Agr. Rel: Christian Science. Mailing Add: 920 East Mitchell, Petoskey, Mich. 49770.

SCHWEIKER, RICHARD SCHULTZ R
U.S. Sen, Pa.
b. Norristown, Pa, 6/1/26; s. Malcolm Alderfer Schweiker and Blanche Schultz S; m. 9/10/55 to Claire Joan Coleman; c. Malcolm C, Lani L, Kyle C. and Richard S, Jr. Educ: Pa. State Univ, B.A, 50; Phi Beta Kappa. Hon. LL.D, Ursinus Col, 63. Polit. & Govt. Pos: Founder and 2 term pres, Montgomery Co. Young Rep, 52-54; committeeman, Montgomery Co. Rep. Cmt, Worcester-East, 52-55; alternate del, Rep. Nat. Conv, 52 & 56; fund-raiser, Rep. Finance Cmt, Pa, 52-60; dir, Pa. State Young Rep, 53-55; chmn, Montgomery Co. Rep. Campaign, 58; mem, Pa. Rep. State Exec. Cmt; secy, Pa. Rep. Cong. Del; U.S. Rep, 13th Dist, Pa, 61-69, mem, House Armed Serv. and Govt. Opers. Cmts; U.S. Sen, Pa, 69-, mem, Armed Serv. and Labor and Pub. Welfare Cmts, U.S. Senate. Mil. Serv: Enlisted in Navy, World War II, served aboard aircraft carrier. Mem: Hon. life mem, Lansdale Jr. C. of C. and VFW Post 32; Kiwanis; bd. dirs, Schwenkfelder Libr; past secy-treas, Worcester Lions; Am. Legion; U.S. Navy League; SAR; Pa. Soc; Nat. Captive Nations Cmt. Named Outstanding Young Man of Lansdale, 54; Outstanding Young Man of Pa, Pa. Jaycees, 61; Citizenship Citation for Meritorious Serv, B'nai B'rith, 61; Liberty Bell Award, Pa. Jr. Bar Asn, 65; Appreciation Award, JFK Coun, K. of C, 66; Spec. Appreciation Award, Nat. Coun. Sr. Citizens, 66; Gr. Del. Valley Citizenship Award, 21 Jewel Square Club, 67. Rel: Schwenkfelder Church. Legal Res: Worcester, Pa. Mailing Add: New Senate Office Bldg, Washington, D.C. 20510.

SCHWEND, RENATO TIMOTHY R
Chmn, Thompson Rep. Town Cmt, Conn.
b. Bronx, N.Y, 7/31/23; s. Henry A. Schwend and Lillian F. Marchetti S; m. 11/25/48 to Marjorie E. Raymond; c. Keith Renato, Jeffrey Stephen, David Michael, Elaine Susan, Robert Timothy and Roberta Marjorie. Educ: Nichols Col, A.B.A, 48. Polit. & Govt. Pos: Tax collector, Thompson, Conn, 63-; chmn, Thompson Rep. Town Cmt, 67- Bus. & Prof. Pos: Supt, Am. Optical Co, 58- Mil. Serv: Entered as Pvt, Army, 43, released as Sgt, 46, after serv. in 20th A.F, China-Burma-India, Okinawa, 44-46; China-Burma-India Ribbons. Mem: VFW; Am. Legion; Civil Defense coordinator; Little League pres; charter mem, East. Conn. Police Asn; charter mem, Thompson Boy Scouts. Rel: Catholic. Legal Res: 52 Route 12, Grosvenordale, Conn. 06255. Mailing Add: Box 265, North Grosvenordale, Conn. 06255.

SCHWENGEL, FRED R
U.S. Rep, Iowa
b. Franklin Co, Iowa, 5/28/07; s. Gerhardt Schwengel and Margaret Stover S; m. 8/15/31 to Clara Ethel Cassity; c. Frank and Dorothy (Mrs. Cosby). Educ: Northeast Mo. State Teachers Col, B.S, 30; State Univ. Iowa, grad. work, 35-36; Lincoln Mem. Univ, Sullivan Award. L.H.D, Lincoln Col; LL.D, Parsons Col, 59. Polit. & Govt. Pos: Chmn, Adair Co. Young Rep, Mo, 35-36 and Scott Co. Young Rep, 38-39; Cong. Rep. committeeman, Scott Co, Iowa, 38-55; dist. chmn, Iowa Young Rep, 39-40; Iowa State Rep, Scott Co, 44-54; U.S. Rep, First Cong. Dist, Iowa, 66- Bus. & Prof. Pos: Gen. agent, Am. Mutual Life Ins. Co, 38-55. Mil. Serv: Entered as Pvt, Nat. Guard, 33, released as Sgt, 37. Mem: Pres, U.S. Capitol Hist. Soc; pres, Rep. Heritage Found; Lincoln Group, Wash, D.C, 56-62; life coun. Phi Sigma Epsilon. Rel: Baptist. Legal Res: 3311 W. Locust St, Davenport, Iowa 52804. Mailing Add: 404 Union Arcade Bldg, Davenport, Iowa 52801.

SCHWENK, EDWIN MILLER R
Chmn, Suffolk Co. Rep. Cmt, N.Y.
b. Southampton, N.Y, 12/5/23; s. Edwin Schwenk and Rosalind Miller S; m. 4/12/47 to Diana Barnes; c. Diana B, Jr, Christopher and Kathryn. Educ: Colgate Univ, B.A, 47; Phi Kappa Psi. Polit. & Govt. Pos: Chmn, Suffolk Co. Rep. Cmt, 67-; del, Rep. Nat. Conv, 68; mem. exec. cmt, N.Y. Rep. State Cmt, 68- Bus. & Prof. Pos: Pres, E. Schwenk's Dairy, Inc, 46-; pres, Katrinka Dairy Stores, 61-; v.pres, Tinker Nat. Bank, 63-67. Mil. Serv: Entered as A/S, Navy, 43, released as Lt.(jg), 46, after serv. in Atlantic Fleet, 43-45. Mem: Elks; Mason; Rotary: VFW; Goodfellow's; Colgate Univ. Maroon Coun; Am. Legion; Southampton Meadow Club; founder and mem, Southampton Golf Club; Southampton Bath and Tennis Club; Gov. Club of N.Y. State. Rel: Methodist. Legal Res: Hampton Park, Southampton, N.Y. 11968. Mailing Add: Edge of the Woods Rd, Southampton, N.Y. 11968.

SCHWESINGER, CHESTER ROBERT R
b. Trout Lake, Mich, 12/10/16; s. Karl A. Schwesinger and Veronica Weber S; m. 11/23/64 to Virginia G. Wulf. Educ: Marquette Univ; Univ. Detroit, LL.B, 38. Polit. & Govt. Pos: Asst. prosecuting attorney, Genesee Co, Mich, 47-48, prosecuting attorney, 51-54; chmn, Genesee Co. Rep. Cmt, 60-62; del, Rep. Nat. Conv, 64; chmn, Crime Study Cmn, Flint, 64-65. Mil. Serv: Entered as Sgt, Army, 42, released as M/Sgt, 45, after serv. in 186th Ord. Corps, ETO; ETO Ribbon with Five Battle Stars. Mem: Am, Mich. State and Genesee Co. Bar Asns; Am. Legion; VFW; Elks. Legal Res: 426 E. Court St, Flint, Mich. 48503. Mailing Add: 307 E. Court St, Flint, Mich. 48503.

SCHWETHELM, A. C. D
Chmn, Kendall Co. Dem. Cmt, Tex.
b. Comfort, Tex, 8/6/31; s. Chester A. Schwethelm and Julia Seidensticker S; m. 6/3/51 to Marilyn Fortner; c. Julia May and Otto Chester. Educ: Draughon's Bus. Col, bus. degree, 48; San Antonio Col, night sch, 57- Polit. & Govt. Pos: Precinct chmn, Dem. Party, Tex, 52-60; chmn, Kendall Co. Dem. Cmt, Tex, 60- Mem: Tex. and Nat. Asns. Ins. Agents; Nat. and Tex. Real Estate Asns; Kendall Co. Bd. of Realtors; Mensa; Comfort C. of C.(pres, 56, chmn. indust. cmt, 62-); Lions (dist. gov, Dist. 2 A 2, 61-62); Hermann Sons Lodge. Named Man of the Year, Comfort C. of C, 58. Rel: Baptist. Legal Res: 221 Manor Drive, Comfort, Tex. 78013. Mailing Add: Box 248, Comfort, Tex. 78013.

SCHWIEGER, YVONNE OCEA R
Recording Secy, Iowa Fedn. Rep. Women
b. Hampton, Iowa, 4/27/13; d. Mark Richard Kempthorne and Ocea Myers K; m. 6/24/34 to Howard William Schwieger; c. John Richard, Carlyn Bryce and Barton Lee. Educ: Ellsworth Jr. Col, 2 years. Polit. & Govt. Pos: Rep. committeewoman, Morgan Precinct, Iowa, 55-69; pres, Franklin Co. Rep. Women's Club, 58-60; pres, Third Dist. Rep. Women's Fedn, 61-62; state flag chmn, Iowa Fedn. of Rep. Women, 61, pub. rels. chmn, 62-64, chaplain, 64-66, historian, 66-67 and recording secy, 67-; mem, Community Action Bd, Franklin Co, Hampton, 65-69; alternate del, Rep. Nat. Conv, 68. Bus. & Prof. Pos: Secy, Schwieger Farms, Inc, Dows, Iowa, 61- Mem: Farm Bureau (former co. women's chmn, 65). Rel: United Methodist. Mailing Add: R.R. 1, Box 70, Dows, Iowa 50071.

SCHWINN, TOM LOMAX R
b. Portland, Ore, 6/5/22; s. W.H. Schwinn and Cecile Lomax S; m. 12/28/68 to Jane Dillon; c. Tom F, Joseph H, Trilby Ann, Hadyn C. and Brooke. Educ: U.S. Mil. Acad, grad; Univ. Kans. Sch. Law, grad; Beta Theta Pi; Phi Delta Phi; staff of Law Rev. Polit. & Govt. Pos: Numerous co. & dist. offices, Rep. Party, 50-57; asst. city attorney, Wellington, Kans, 54-57, city attorney, 57-59; Kans. State Rep, Sumner Co, 57-58; alternate del, Rep. Nat. Conv, 64; mem, Gov. Oil and Gas Adv. Cmt, currently. Bus. & Prof. Pos: Partner, Law Firm of Schwinn & Schwinn, 52-66 and Schwinn, Ferguson, Schwinn & Doctor, 66; secy, Liaison Cmt, Coop. Oil & Gas Asns, 63-65. Mil. Serv: Entered as Pvt, Army, 42, released as 1st Lt, 49, after serv. in Airborne Div, Far East; Lt. Col, (Ret), Kans. Army Res. Nat. Guard. Publ: Articles in Kans. Bar Asn. J. and Univ. Va. Law Rev. Mem: Am. and Kans. Bar Asns; pres, Sumner Co. Bar Asn, 54; Post Comdr, Am. Legion, 55; Elks; VFW; Petroleum Club Wichita; exec. v.pres, Kans. Independent Oil and Gas Asn; East. Kans. Oil and Gas Asn; Import Policy Cmt, Independent Petroleum Asn. Am; Farm Bur. Rel: Protestant. Legal Res: 1308 N. Washington Ave, Wellington, Kans. 67152. Mailing Add: Box 549, Wellington, Kans. 67152.

SCIRO, FRANK JOSEPH R
N.J. State Sen.
b. Serino, Italy, 3/16/10; s. Angelo Sciro and Anna Franzesa S; m. 6/25/40 to Emma Fiorentino; c. Theodora and Frank, Jr. Educ: Rutgers Law Sch, LL.B. Polit. & Govt. Pos: Naturalization clerk, Passaic Co, N.J, 39-40; mayor's secy, Paterson, 40-42, city clerk, 42-; Magistrate, West Paterson, 63-68; N.J. State Sen, Passaic Co, 68- Mem: Passaic Co. and N.J. Bar Asns; Italian Circle; North Jersey Country Club; YMCA. Rel: Catholic. Legal Res: 322 E. 40th St, Paterson, N.J. 07504. Mailing Add: 152 Market St, Paterson, N.J. 07505.

SCOBEE, BARRY D
Chmn, Jeff Davis Co. Dem. Cmt, Tex.
b. Pollock, Mo, 5/2/85; s. James Wesley Scobee and Sarah Ann Mason S; m. 11/24/11 to Katherine Delphina Ford. Educ: State Teachers Col, Kirksville, Mo. Polit. & Govt. Pos: Chmn, Jeff Davis Co. Dem. Cmt, Tex, 39-; Justice of the Peace, Jeff Davis Co, Tex, 39- Bus. & Prof. Pos: Reporter, daily newspapers, Kans, Tex, Wash. State, intermittently, 11-18; fiction writer, 14-50. Mil. Serv: Entered as Pvt, Mo. Militia, 01; Pvt, Army, 07, serv. in Philippines, 09; Tex. State Guard, 42-45, released as 1st Lt, after serv. as commercial ship's clerk, Caribbean, S.Am. Publ: Old Fort Davis, Naylor, San Antonio, Tex, 47; Fort Davis Texas, privately publ, 63; Nick Mersfelder: A Remarkable Man, Anchor Publ. Co, San Angelo, Tex, 69. Mem: Mason; W.Tex. Hist. and Sci. Soc, Alpine, Tex; Fort Davis Hist. Soc, Tex. Awarded 50 year membership cert. and emblem, Masonic Lodge. Rel: Protestant. Mailing Add: Box 803, Ft. Davis, Tex. 79734.

SCOGGINS, RALPH WILLIAM D
Tex. State Rep.
b. El Paso, Tex, 9/2/31; s. Ralph W. Scoggins and Celia Weir S; m. 6/24/55 to Sandra L. Rodehaver; c. Valorie Lynn, Julie Ann, Melanie Lou and Blake William. Educ: Tex. West. Col; Univ. Tex. Sch. Law; Phi Alpha Theta. Polit. & Govt. Pos: Tex. State Rep, Place Five, 65- Bus. & Prof. Pos: Right-of-way attorney, Tex. Hwy. Dept, 62-63; Attorney, self-employed, 63- Mil. Serv: Entered as Pvt, Air Force, 51, released as Airman 1/C, 54. Mem: C. of C; Jaycees; State and Local Bar Asns; Rel: Episcopal. Mailing Add: 2909 Aurora, El Paso, Tex. 79930.

SCOLNIK, LOUIS D
b. Lewiston, Maine, 2/14/23; s. Julius Scolnik and Bessie Picker S; m. 7/30/51 to Paula Revitz; c. Nina, Donna and Julie. Educ: Bates Col, A.B, 47; Georgetown Law Center, LL.B, 52. Polit. & Govt. Pos: Corp. counsel, City of Lewiston, Maine, 57-62; mem. platform cmt, Dem. Party, Maine, 60 & 68;

chmn. Maine adv. cmt, U.S. Cmn. Civil Rights, 64-69; del, Dem. Nat. Conv, 68; mem, Gov. Task Force Human Rights, 68-69. Mil. Serv: Entered as A/S, Navy, 43, released as Lt.(jg), 46, after serv. in C.O. LCI(L) 776, Pac. Theatre, 45-46; Unit Citation. Mem: Am. and Maine Bar Asns; Androscoggin Co. Bar Asn.(v.pres, 69); Am. Trial Lawyers Asn; Maine Trial Lawyers Asn. (educ. cmt, 67); Am. Judicature Soc; Lewiston-Androscoggin Rotary Club (dir); Am. Civil Liberties Union (mem. nat. bd. dirs); Androscoggin Ment. Health Asn.(first pres); Maine Civil Liberties Union (pres, 68-69, dir. and exec. cmt); NAACP (legal counsel and dir, Cent. Maine Br, 62-69); Lewiston-Androscoggin Jewish Fedn.(past pres). Commun. Serv. Award, 62. Rel: Judaism; Dir, Beth Jacob Synagogue, 68-69. Mailing Add: 10 Mountain Ave, Lewiston, Maine 04740.

SCORESBY, CLIFFORD NORMAN R
Idaho State Rep.
b. Queensland, Australia, 2/26/01; s. William Scoresby and Jessie Ann Higgs S; m. 2/6/24 to Johanna L. Horman; c. Fern (Mrs. Lynn Benson), Clifford William, Leah (Mrs. Harry Thacker), Charles, Mary Lou (Mrs. Doyle Rilndsbaker), Mary-lin (Mrs. Niel Sargent), Fred, Harold and John F. Educ: Idaho Falls High Sch, 2 years. Polit. & Govt. Pos: Mem, Iona Village Bd, Idaho, 30-46; sch. trustee, Independent Sch. Dist. Five, 34-48; dir, Progressive Irrigation Dist, 44-69; mem. selective serv. bd. number ten, Bonneville Co, 53-69; Idaho State Rep, 67- Mem: Farm Bur. Rel: Latter-day Saint. Mailing Add: Iona, Idaho 83427.

SCOTT, ALPHONSE A. R
Chmn, Ward 21 Rep. Cmt, Boston, Mass.
b. Boston, Mass, 7/28/19; s. Frank Scott and Lillian Malatesta S; m. 8/20/45 to Margaret Capobianco; c. John, Marguerite and Judith. Educ: St. John's Univ. Polit. & Govt. Pos: Mem, Gov. Finance Cmt. and Gov. Appointment Staff, Mass, currently; mem, Suffolk Co. Rep. Club, currently; chmn, Rep. Club of Boston, currently; chmn, Ward 21 Rep. Cmt, Boston, 68- Bus. & Prof. Pos: Dir, construction co, 55; v.pres, develop. corp, 60; trustee, real estate corp, 67; gen. mgr, Whitehead Realty Corp, 69. Mil. Serv: Entered as Pvt, Army, 42, released as Sgt, 45, after serv. in 536th Ord. Tank Co; Army Res, 45. Publ: Articles for YMCA jour. Mem: Treas, Allston and Brighton Mental Health Bd; chmn, bd. dir, Brighton YMCA; Engrs. Club; past chaplin, Elks; past grand knight, K. of C; bd. gov, Health and Exec. Club. Rel: Roman Catholic. Mailing Add: 129 Chiswick Rd, Brighton, Mass. 02135.

SCOTT, BEATRICE NORMADINE R
b. Gentry, Ark, 7/25/30; d. Glenn Oliver Beckwith and Velma Lee Hardy B; m. 5/1/59 to Buford Scott; c. Harold Leon, Glenn Arthur, Buford Lee, Rebecca Lynne, James Kent (deceased), Raymond Buell, Richard Landon and Cynthia Ann (Mrs. Wilken). Polit. & Govt. Pos: Past chmn. for many Rep. cand; pres, Stanton Co. Women Rep. Club, 60 & 62; co-dir, First Dist. and Fifth Dist, Kans. Fedn. Rep. Women, 62, dir, First Dist, 62-66; first alternate del, Rep. Nat. Conv, 64; exec. mem. bd, Rep. Assocs. of Southwest Kans; precinct committeewoman; co-chmn. for gubernatorial cand. Rick Harman, First Dist; secy-treas, Stanton Co. Taxpayers Fedn; Rep. State Subdist. Finance Chmn. Bus. & Prof. Pos: Asst. buyer, Corset Dept, Crosby Bros, Topeka, Kans, 58-59. Mem: Pres, Cosmos Club; secy-treas, Hellou Leborium Club; Methodist Women Soc; Kans. Flying Farmers; Sweet Adalines, Inc; Womens Kans. Day Club; Native Sons & Daughters; Aircraft Owners & Pilots Asn. Named included on the Rep. Mem. at Gettysburg, Pa. Rel: Methodist; Sunday Sch. instr. Mailing Add: Box 388, Nipp St, Johnson, Kans. 67855.

SCOTT, BURL E. D
b. Macedonia, Iowa, 8/23/28; s. Richard F. Scott and Bernice M; m. 1952 to Lois Gustafsen; c. Debra, Randy, Cynthia, Ken and Daniel. Educ: Voc. Agr. Training under the G.I. Bill of Rights, 36 months; Spec. Elec. Training. Polit. & Govt. Pos: Former chmn, Agr. Stabilization and Conserv. Cmt, Macedonia Twp; Iowa State Rep. until 66. Bus. & Prof. Pos: Elec. Contractor. Mil. Serv: Korean War. Mem: V.pres, Shelby Bus. Club; Past Comdr, Macedonia and Shelby Am. Legion posts; Mason. Rel: Congregational. Mailing Add: 802 Walnut St, Avoca, Iowa 51521.

SCOTT, C. FRANK MRS. D
Tenn. State Cmnr. of Employ. Security
b. Obion Co, 8/14/03; m. to C. Frank Scott; c. Dorothyann. Educ: Univ. Okla. Polit. & Govt. Pos: Mgr, women's div, Ellington for Gov. Campaign Tenn; original mem, Legis. Coun. Cmt, secy, 4 years; Tenn. State Sen, 1 term; del, White House Conf. on Children and Youth, 50-60 and White House Conf. on Aging, 61; Tenn. State Rep, 51-56; cmnr, Pub. Welfare, 58; Tenn. State Cmnr. of Employ. Security, 63- Mem: Past pres, Idlewild PTA, Memphis Coun. of Parents and Teachers, exec. bd, Tenn. Cong. of Parents and Teachers; adv. bd, Cong. of Parents and Teachers; exec. cmt, Memphis chap, Nat. Found. for Infantile Paralysis; serv. cmt, Am. Cancer Soc; legis. chmn, Tenn. Fedn. of Women's Clubs; dir, emergency welfare serv, Civil Defense; welfare policy cmt, Am. Pub. Welfare Asn. Tenn. Mother of the Year, 52. Rel: Baptist. Mailing Add: 4237 Chanwil Place, Memphis, Tenn. 38117. (1967)

SCOTT, CARL G. D
b. Montgomery, Vt, 9/15/06; m. to Irene Chase; c. One. Educ: Montgomery Jr. High Sch. Polit. & Govt. Pos: Selectman, Vt, 10 years; constable, 40-54; town overseer of the poor; v.pres, Vt. Elec. Coop; v.pres, Border Town Develop; Vt. State Rep, 61-67. Bus. & Prof. Pos: Farmer, secondhand and antique store operator; carpenter; auctioneer. Mem: Mason; Grange (7°). Rel: Methodist. Mailing Add: Montgomery Center, Vt. 05471. (1967)

SCOTT, CATHERINE DOROTHY R
Mem. Bd. Dirs, League of Rep. Women, D.C.
b. Washington, D.C, 6/21/27; d. Leroy Stearns Scott and Agnes Meade S; single Educ: Cath. Univ. Am, B.A, 50, M.S. in L.S, 55; Triamond Club; mem. staff, The Tower; Cath. Univ. Am. Yearbook Staff, 50. Polit. & Govt. Pos: Mem. bd. dirs, Young Rep. Club, D.C, 52-59, nat. committeewoman, 56-57, first v.pres, 58-59; del, Young Rep. Nat. Conv, 55 & 57; v.pres, Eisenhower-Nixon Club, 56; co-chmn, Region III, Col. Fedn. Young Rep; v.chmn, Eisenhower Inaugural Cmt. and co-chmn, Prog. Cmt, Inaugural Ball, 57; mem. bd. dirs, League of Rep. Women, D.C, 56-, elected dir, 59-63, polit. study group dir, 62-63, campaign chmn, 65-66, roster chmn, 67-68; mem, D.C. Rep. Cmt, 59-68, v.chmn, 60-68; v.pres, Nixon-Lodge Club, 60; D.C. Precinct Campaign Coordinator, 60 & 64; del, Rep. Nat. Conv, 64 & 68, secy, Platform Cmt, 64, mem, 68; co-chmn, D.C. Goldwater-Miller Campaign, 64; exec. secy, Women for Nixon-Agnew Nat. Adv. Coun. and prog. chmn, D.C. Women for Nixon-Agnew, 68; mem, Inaugural Cmt, Gov. Reception Press Cmt, 69; liaison to Nat. Fedn. of Rep. Women, 69- Bus. & Prof. Pos: Asst. librn, Export-Import Bank of U.S, 53-55; reference and asst. librn, Nat. Asn. of Home Builders, 55-62; chief librn, Bellcomm, Inc, 62- Mem: Bd. dirs, Wash. Chap, Spec. Libr. Asn, corresponding secy, 66-67, chmn. sci-tech. group, 67-69, secy. aerospace div, Nat. Spec. Libr. Asn, 68-69; D.C. Libr. Asn; Int. Fedn. for Documentation; D.C. Cmt. for Nat. Libr. Week; League of Rep. Women of D.C; coordinator, United Givers Fund; Women of St. Dominic's Holy Cross Guild; Cath. Univ. of Am. Alumni Asn. Rel: Roman Catholic. Mailing Add: 700 Seventh St. S.W, Washington, D.C. 20024.

SCOTT, DAVID ALAN R
Md. State Del.
b. New York, N.Y, 5/20/16; s. George T. Scott and Ruth Cowing; m. to Barbara Wing; c. Alison and Ann. Educ: Princeton Univ, A.B, 38; Columbia Univ, M.A, 46; George Wash. Univ, LL.B, 49. Polit. & Govt. Pos: Md. State Del, currently. Mil. Serv: Entered as Midn, Navy, 40, released as Lt. Comdr, 46. Rel: Presbyterian. Mailing Add: 5800 Midhill St, Bethesda, Md. 20034.

SCOTT, DONALD LEE R
Treas, D.C. Rep. Cmt.
b. Pioche, Nev, 2/11/22; s. Albert Louis Scott and Mona Bowling S; c. Terri Phillips. Educ: Rutgers Univ, Stonier Grad. Sch. Banking, dipl, 58; Univ. Va, Sch. Consumer Banking, dipl, 64. Polit. & Govt. Pos: Treas, D.C. Rep. Cmt, currently. Bus. & Prof. Pos: V.pres, Nat. Savings and Trust Co, 63- Mil. Serv: Entered as Aviation Cadet, Army Air Corps, 42, released as 1st Lt, 46, after serv. in 23rd Fighter Group, China-Burma-India Theater, 44-45; Presidential Unit Citation; Am. Theater Ribbon; Asiatic-Pac. Theater Ribbon with 4 Battle Stars; World War II Victory and Air Medals. Mem: Metrop. Wash. Bd. of Trade; Bond Club of Wash, D.C; Wash. Chap, Am. Inst. of Banking; Mortgage Bankers Asn; Robert Morris Assocs; dir, Boys' Club of Greater Wash, D.C; treas, Bowers Family Found; Retail Credit Asn, Wash, D.C; Nat. Aviation Club, Wash, D.C; Columbia Country Club, Chevy Chase, Md. Rel: Episcopal. Mailing Add: 719 15th St. N.W, Washington, D.C. 20005.

SCOTT, EDWARD SMITH R
Secy, Arapahoe Co. Rep. Party, Colo.
b. Denver, Colo, 8/4/28; s. Jesse Carl Smith and Iola Verne Steveson S; m. 10/17/48 to Dorothy Edna Schmid; c. Christopher, Bradford, Wendy, Rebecca, Cynthia and Jonathan. Educ: Univ. Denver and Univ. Wash, 45. Polit. & Govt. Pos: Councilman, Englewood, Colo, 55-57, mayor, 57-60; cmnr, Arapahoe Co, 61-65; Colo. State Sen, 65-69; secy, Arapahoe Co. Rep. Party, 69- Bus. & Prof. Pos: Staff announcer, KLZ Radio, Denver, 47-49; staff performer, CBS-WBBM, 49-53; free lance performer, Chicago, Ill, 53; free lance Radio-TV performer, Denver, Colo, 53-61; pres, KLAK Radio, 61- Mem: Pres, Advert. Club of Denver, 66-67; dir, Colo. Broadcasters Asn, 64-67; Denver Press Club; Pinehurst Country Club. Selected as Colo. Young Man of the Year, 1959. Rel: Lutheran, Missouri Synod. Mailing Add: 2750 S. Grant, Englewood, Colo. 80110.

SCOTT, FRANK, JR. R
Mem, N.J. Rep. Finance Cmt.
b. Port Richmond, N.Y, 7/2/97; s. Frank Scott and Julia Mills S; m. 1/9/23 to Helen Mae Morey; c. Patricia Ann and Mahlon Morey. Educ: Union Bus. Col; Miller Bus. Col; Pace and Pace, N.Y; N.Y. Univ. Sch. of Finance. Polit. & Govt. Pos: Chmn, Union Co. Savings Bonds Div, U.S. Treas, 39-62; del, Rep. Nat. Conv, 56, 60 & 68, alternate del-at-lg, 64; cmnr, Union Co. Park Cmn, 63, treas, 64, pres, currently; mem, N.J. Rep. Finance Cmt, currently; chmn, Union Co. Rep. Cmt, 8 years, former chmn. of finance cmt; mem, Commun. Welfare Coun. of East. Union Co, former gen. chmn; trustee, N.J. Citizens Transportation Coun; mem, Nat. Rivers and Harbors Cong; v.pres, Union Co. Safety Coun; mem, Cmt. on Govt. Expenditures, U.S. C. of C; mem, N.J. Regional Planning Cmn. Bus. & Prof. Pos: Asst. statistician, Elec. Bond & Share Co, N.Y, 15-17; bond salesman, Nat. City Co. of N.Y, 19-23; v.pres, Morey LaRue Laundry Co, Elizabeth, N.J, 23-41, pres, 41-; mem. adv. bd, Elizabeth Gen. Hosp, asst. treas. and treas, 10-15 years; mem, N.J. Metropolitan Rapid Transit Cmn; dir, Nat. Jewish Hosp, Denver, Colo; dir. and mem. exec. cmt, Union Co. Trust Co, Elizabeth, N.J; v.pres. and trustee, Union Co. Savings Bank, Elizabeth; trustee, Evergreen Cemetery, Hillside, N.J. Mil. Serv: Pvt, Army, 17-19, with serv. in Essex Troop Cavalry. Mem: Bd. of fels, Union Col; Police Athletic League (trustee, Elizabeth Chap); trustee, Pingrey Sch; Rotary (pres, 35); YMCA (pres, Elizabeth Chap, 40, trustee, currently, mem. Atlantic Area Bd); C. of C, (dir, East. Union Co, 22 years, pres, 16 years, mem, adv. cmt, currently); Elks; Essex Club, Newark; Baltusrol Golf Club, Springfield; Maskenozha and Shawnee Country Club, Stroudsberg, Pa; Suburban Club, Union; YWCA (trustee, Elizabeth Chap); Union Co. Jr. Achievement (adv. bd); bd. of mgrs, Union Co. Chap, Am. Cancer Soc; Boxwood Hall Mem. Asn; Nat. Conf. of Christians and Jews (dir. and mem. bd. of dirs); trustee, Commun. Chest of East. Union Co; Boy Scouts of Am. (corporate trustee, Union Coun); spec. gifts cmt, N.J. Chap, Arthritis and Rheumatism Found; Mason; S.P.R.S; AAONMS. Rel: Presbyterian; Elder, Westminster Presbyterian Church. Legal Res: 572 Westminster Ave, Elizabeth, N.J. 07208. Mailing Add: Morey LaRue Laundry Co, Elizabeth, N.J. 07207.

SCOTT, FRED L. D
b. Nashville, Tenn, 11/16/07; s. Harbert Lee Scott and Tommie Ann Horn S; m. 12/31/47 to Lucille Moore; c. Thomas Lee, Phyllis Jean, Charles Hooper, Edgar Allen and Patricia Ann. Educ: David Lipscomb Col; Harding Col; U.S. Navy Materiel Sch. Polit. & Govt. Pos: W.Va. State Del, 64-66. Bus. & Prof. Pos: Radio announcer, 36-50; owner and operator, appliance and TV bus. Mil. Serv: Navy. Mem: Nat. Appliance and Radio-TV Dealers Asn; former mem. bd. of dirs, Am. Fedn. of Radio Artists, Cincinnati, Ohio. Rel: Church of Christ. Mailing Add: 3910 Noyes Ave, Charleston, W.Va. 25304.

SCOTT, GEORGE WILLIAM R
Maine State Rep.
b. Old Town, Maine, 3/29/10; s. Clarence Scott and Folsom S; m. 12/22/39 to

Jean Elizabeth Keddie; c. David F. and Timothy G. Educ: Univ. Maine, B.S. in Elec. Eng, 36; Kappa Sigma. Polit. & Govt. Pos: Chmn, Aroostook Co. Rep. Party, Maine, 62-63; mem, Maine State Rep. Cmt, 64-65; Maine State Rep, 67-68 & 69- Bus. & Prof. Pos: Secy-treas, Maine Mutual Group of Ins. Co, 40-69; v.pres, Aroostook Co. Fed. Savings & Loan Asn, Caribou, Maine, 54-69. Mil. Serv: Entered as Ens, Navy, 40, released as Lt.(sg), 45, after serv. in Bombing-Patrol Squadron, Pac. Theatre, 42-45. Mem: Kiwanis; Mason; Am. Legion. Rel: Methodist. Mailing Add: 32 Wislon St, Presque Isle, Maine 04769.

SCOTT, GEORGE WILLIAM R
Wash. State Rep.
b. Seattle, Wash, 7/9/37; s. Arthur Pausette Scott and Eleanor Irene Bleasdale S; m. 10/16/65 to Carol Susan Rogel. Educ: Whitworth Col, B.A, 59; Univ. Wash, M.A, 66; Phi Alpha Theta. Polit. & Govt. Pos: Wash. State Rep, 46th Dist, 69- Mil. Serv: Entered as 2nd Lt, Marines, 59, released as Capt, 66, after serv. in Third Marine Div, Okinawa. Mem: Am. Legion; Mason; City Coun; Ripon Soc. Mailing Add: 2530 N.E. 105th Place, Seattle, Wash. 98125.

SCOTT, HENRY D
b. Woonsocket, R.I, 11/23/18; m. to Irene S. Educ: Schs. of Woonsocket. Polit. & Gov. Pos: R.I. State Rep, 61-66. Bus. & Prof. Pos: Rubber Worker. Mailing Add: 158 Arnold St, Woonsocket, R.I. 02895. (1967)

SCOTT, HUGH R
Minority Leader, U.S. Senate
b. Fredericksburg, Va, 11/11/00; s. Hugh D. Scott and Jane Lee Lewis S; m. 4/12/24 to Marian Huntington Chase; c. Marian (Mrs. Concannon) and seven grandchildren. Educ: Univ. Pa, 18; Randolph-Macon Col, A.B, 19; Univ. Va, LL.B, 22; Phi Beta Kappa; Tau Kappa Alpha; Phi Alpha Delta; Alpha Chi Rho. Hon. LL.D, Randolph-Macon Col, 55, Temple Univ. and Dickinson Col, 59, Phila. Textile Inst. and Ursinus Col, 60, Wash. and Jefferson Col, 61, Lebanon Valley Col, 62, Lincoln Univ, 63 and Westminster Col, 64; L.H.D, La Salle Col, 55; D.P.A, Suffolk Univ, 59; Litt.D, Phila. Col. Osteopathy, 60; Sc.D, Del. Valley Col, 63. Polit. & Govt. Pos: Asst. dist. attorney, Phila, Pa, 26-41; U.S. Rep, Pa, 41-58, mem, Cmts. on Rules, Interstate and For. Commerce and Judiciary, U.S. House of Rep; nat. chmn, Rep. Party, 48-49; mem, Bd. Visitors, Naval Acad, 48, chmn, Bd. Visitors, Merchant Marine Acad, 59, Coast Guard Acad, 63; chmn, Eisenhower Hq. Cmt, mem, personal staff and chmn. regional orgn, Eisenhower Campaign, 52; gen. counsel, Rep. Nat. Cmt, 55-60; U.S. Sen, Pa, 58-, mem, Cmts. on Commerce, Judiciary, Rules and Rep. Policy, U.S. Senate, U.S. del, Int. Orgn. meetings in Uruguay, India, Switz, Australia, Can, Germany, France and Gt. Brit, v.pres, Rep. Sen. Campaign Cmt, Asst. Floor Leader, 69, Minority Leader, 69-, mem, Joint Cmt. on Printing, Rep. Coord. Cmt. and Joint House-Seante Rep. Leadership Cmt, currently; mem. Bd. of Regents, Smithsonian Inst, currently; Nat. Visitor Facilities Adv. Cmn, Interparliamentary Union, currently; del, Rep. Nat. Conv, 68. Bus. & Prof. Pos: Counsel to firm of Obermayer, Rebmann, Maxwell and Hippel, Phila. Mil. Serv: Entered as Lt, Naval Res, 42, released, 46, after serv. with N.Atlantic Patrol, Occup. of Iceland, Pac. Theater and Occup. of Japan with Third Amphibious Force, also served temporary duty aboard carrier Valley Forge and at Naktong in Korean War, 50; Capt.(Ret), Naval Res; Navy Commendation Ribbon; Philippine Liberation Medal; Atlantic Convoy Medal. Publ: The Golden Age of Chinese Art: The Lively T'ang Dynasty, Charles E. Tuttle Co, 66; How to Run for Public Office and Win, The Nat. Press, Inc, 68; Come to the Party, Prentice-Hall, Inc, 68; plus 3 others and numerous mag. articles. Mem: Am, Pa. and Phila. Bar Asns; Am. Soc. Int. Law; hon. fel, Am. Bar Found; bd, Georgetown Center for Strategic Studies; Am. Legion; VFW; Amvets; SAR; Soc. of Cincinnati; Friendly Sons of St. Patrick; Phila. Cricket Club; Germantown Lions; Pa. Soc. of N.Y; Chinese Art Soc. of Am; Oriental Ceramic Soc. Comdr, Royal Order of Phoenix, Greece; Grand Cross, Order of El Quetzal, Guatemala; Order of Serv. Merit, First Class, Repub. of Korea; First Annual For. Trade Award for Outstanding Serv. to the Port and City of Phila; Gr. Phila. Mag. 50th Anniversary Award; Pa. Asn. Broadcasters' Award, 63; numerous civic and Man of Year awards. Rel: Episcopal. Legal Res: 44 Hillcrest Ave, Chestnut Hill, Philadelphia, Pa. 19118. Mailing Add: 260 Senate Office Bldg, Washington, D.C. 20510.

SCOTT, J. W. 'BILL' D
b. McLean Co, Ill, 4/18/15; c. three. Educ: Ill. State Normal Univ. Polit. & Govt. Pos: Former Ill. State Rep. Bus. & Prof. Pos: Engaged in bus, 25 years Mem: Co. athletic officer for the Jr. Legion Baseball prog. and 17th dist. athletic officer; Past Comdr, Am. Legion; 40 et 8; Arrowsmith Masonic Lodge No. 737; Bloomington Consistory; Bloomington Shrine; Mohammed Temple. Mailing Add: 730 Towanda St, Bloomington, Ill. 61701. (1967)

SCOTT, JEFFREY J. R
Mont. State Rep.
b. Chicago, Ill, 3/7/39; s. Ernest J. Scott and Aurelia Peter S; m. 6/7/62 to Valerie Weeks; c. Matthew Henry. Educ: Yale Col, B.A, 61, law sch, LL.B, 64. Polit. & Govt. Pos: Committeeman, Yellowstone Co, Mont; founding dir, Yellowstone Co. Rep. Club; Mont. State Rep, 69- Bus. & Prof. Pos: Partner, Scott, Scott & Baugh, Attorneys. Publ: 'The Dual Citizenship of Corporations and their Principal Place of Business,' Fed. Bar J, Spring, 63. Mem: Yellowstone Co, Mont. and Am. Bar Asns; AF&AM; Lions. Mailing Add: First Citizens Bank Bldg, Billings, Mont. 59101.

SCOTT, JEREMIAH RONALD, JR. R
Chmn, Humboldt Co. Rep. Cent. Cmt, Calif.
b. Fortuna, Calif, 9/18/36; s. Jeremiah R. Scott and Faye Townsend S; m. 6/25/61 to Mary Griswold; c. McGregor W, Stuart J. and Catherine A. Educ: Westminster Col, A.B, 58; Univ. Santa Clara, J.D, 63; Scabbard and Blade Mil. Soc; Beta Theta Pi. Polit. & Govt. Pos: Mem. bd. of trustees, Eureka Bd. of Educ, Calif, 68-; chmn, Humboldt Co. Rep. Cent. Cmt, 69- Bus. & Prof. Pos: Attorney, Eureka, Calif, 64- Mil. Serv: Entered as 2nd Lt, Army, 59, released as Lt, 60; Capt, Army Res, 60-68. Mem: Calif. and Am. Bar Asns; F&AM; Kiwanis. Rel: Protestant. Mailing Add: 4945 Myers St, Eureka, Calif. 95501.

SCOTT, JOHN L. R
b. Minersville, Pa, 10/28/92; married; c. Two. Educ: Bliss Elec. Sch, Wash, D.C. Polit. & Govt. Pos: N.H. State Rep, 61-63; former mem, Derry Zoning Bd. Bus. & Prof. Pos: Retired dist.mgr, Pub. Utility. Mil. Serv: WWI. Mem: Kiwanis; Am. Legion. Rel: Protestant. Mailing Add: RFD 2, Derry, N.H. 03038. (1967)

SCOTT, JOSEPH ALEXANDER 'JOE' D
b. Dallas, Tex, 1/31/29; s. Joseph Alexander Scott, Sr. and Thelma B. Jones S; m. 12/29/50 to Cecilia Arvis Brooks; c. Joseph A, III, James A, Cynthia Ann and Cecily Arvis. Educ: Prairie View A&M Col, B.A, 50; Our Lady of the Lake Col, M.E, 54; Omega Psi Phi; Courtiers Social Club; The Dukes. Polit. & Govt. Pos: Del, Dem. Nat. Conv, 64, alternate del, 68. Bus. & Prof. Pos: Pres, Scott Ins, pres, Joe Scott Co. and owner and operator, Hotel Poco, currently. Mil. Serv: 1st Lt, Army, 50-52, serv. in 410th Mil. Govt. Unit, ETO. Mem: Bd. dirs. and secy, Tex. South. Univ; bd. dirs, Alamo City C. of C; St. Joseph's AF&AM; dir, Good Govt. League; dir, United Polit. Orgn. of Tex; NAACP. Track, Prairie View A&M Col, 49. Rel: Catholic. Legal Res: 3415 Chateau Dr, San Antonio, Tex. 78219. Mailing Add: 122 Heimann St, San Antonio, Tex. 78205.

SCOTT, JOSEPH HAROLD 'JOE' R
Mem, Calif. Rep. State Cent. Cmt.
b. St. Louis, Mo, 7/1/07; s. James Walter Scott and Marie Viola Rice S; m. to Virgie Kathryn Carmody; c. Jean Louraine (Mrs. Brame). Educ: Los Angeles Polytech. Law Sch, 26. Polit. & Govt. Pos: Cand, co. recorder, Kern Co, Calif; cand, Calif. State Sen, Dist. 18; mem, Calif. Rep. State Cent. Cmt, currently. Mil. Serv: Entered Marine Corps, 42, released as S/Sgt, 45, after serv. in Admin, 42-45. Mem: Bakersfield Independent Ins. Agent Asn.(past pres); Nat. and Calif. Asns. Independent Ins. Agents; Soc. Residential Appraisers (past pres, 57); chaplain, Elks; Eagles (past pres, twice, past dep, Grand Aerie Order); Am. Legion (former officer); Marine Corps League; 40 et 8; Marine Mem. Club. Testimonial plaque for Valuable Serv. and Contribution, Soc. Residential Appraisers. Rel: Catholic. Legal Res: 1701 Elm St, Bakersfield, Calif. 93301. Mailing Add: 700 18th St, Bakersfield, Calif. 93301.

SCOTT, LEONARD A. R
Chmn, Somerville Rep. City Cmt, Mass.
b. Boston, Mass, 1/5/16; s. Frank Squillacciotti and Teresa Malatesta S; m. 4/24/54 to Louise Kathrine Scarabino; c. David John, Ralph Francis and Paula Marie. Educ: Mass. State Teachers Col. Boston, B.S. in Educ; Calvin Coolidge Col, M.A; Boston Univ. Sch. of Educ, 2 years. Polit. & Govt. Pos: Mem, Somerville Rep. Ward and City Cmt, Mass, 50-, treas, 64-68, chmn, 68-; alderman, Somerville, Mass, 54-56; mem, Mayor's Adv. Group Educ, 62-68; committeeman, Somerville Sch. Cmt, 60-68, v.chmn, 63, chmn, 64-65. Bus. & Prof. Pos: V.chmn, New Eng. Tel. Engrs. Asn, 67- Mil. Serv: Entered as Pvt, Army Air Corps, 41, released as M/Sgt, 46, after serv. in 501st Group, Am, European and Asiatic Theatres, 42-46; Theatre Citations; Good Conduct Medal. Mem: Ital-Am. War Vet.(state comdr, 60); VFW; Am. Legion; Amvets; Sons of Italy. Sta. WHIL Outstanding Citizen Award. Rel: Roman Catholic. Mailing Add: 99 Pearson Ave, Somerville, Mass. 02144.

SCOTT, MILFORD A. D
b. Springfield, Ga, 12/19/24; s. James Anderson Scott and Christine Wells S; m. 9/14/46 to Mary Margaret Knight; c. Sandra Margaret, Milford Anderson Jr, Carolyn Geneva and Richard Raburn. Educ: James L. Fleming Sch, 37; Richmond Acad, 40. Polit. & Govt. Pos: Ga. State Sen, 63-66. Bus. & Prof. Pos: Meat packer; realtor. Mil. Serv: Navy, Seaman 1st Class. Mem: Mason; Scottish Rite; Alee Temple; Augusta Optimistic Club; Am. Bus. Club. Rel: Methodist. Mailing Add: 2003 Scott Rd, Augusta, Ga. 30906.

SCOTT, NORMA KATHLEEN D
b. Seattle, Wash, 4/28/20; d. Guy Satterlee and Mamie Makonen S; m. 12/31/46 to Robert F. Scott. Educ: Lincoln High Sch, grad. Polit. & Govt. Pos: Postmaster, Nome, Alaska, 62-63. Mem: Am. Legion Auxiliary; Arctic Club. Rel: Presbyterian. Mailing Add: Box 714, Nome, Alaska 99762. (1967)

SCOTT, RALPH R
b. Stutsman Co, N. Dak, 1/19/09; Single. Educ: Pub. Schs. Polit. & Govt. Pos: N. Dak. State Rep, 53-61. Bus. & Prof. Pos: Farmer; Farm Columnist. Mem: 4-H Club leader, 15 yrs; Pres, N. Dak. 4-H Club. Mailing Add: Jamestown, N. Dak. 58401. (1967)

SCOTT, RALPH H. D
N.C. State Sen.
b. Haw River, N.C, 12/12/03; s. Robert Walter Scott and Elizabeth Hughes S; m. 11/11/25 to Hazeleene Tate; c. Miriam (Mrs. C.W. Mayo, III), Ralph Henderson, Jr. and William Clevenger. Educ: N.C. State Col, B.S, 24. Polit. & Govt. Pos: N.C. State Sen, 51-56 & 61-, mem, Cmt. Penal Insts, Agr, Pub. Welfare, Ins, Univ. Trustees and Educ, v.chmn, Cmt. Interstate and Fedn. Rels, Pub. Roads, Appropriations, 67, finance chmn, 67, Cong. Redistricting, Mfg, Labor & Commerce, Pub. Utilities, Banking, Salaries & Fees, Wildlife, past chmn, Propositions and Grievances, past pres, Cmt. on Agr, mem, Adv. Budget Cmn, 61-62, 63-64 & 68, author, Haw River Stream Pollution Legis, Pres-Pro-Tem, 63, chmn, Rules Cmt, 63, chmn, Higher Educ, 63, chmn, Gov. Cmn. Ment. Retardation and State Farmers Home Admin. Adv. Cmt, N.C. State Senate; del, Dem. Nat. Conv, 68. Bus. & Prof. Pos: Pres. and mgr, Melville Dairy, Inc; pres. and treas, Alamance Frozen Foods, Inc; dir, Carolina Casualty Ins. Co, First Fed. Saving & Loan Asn, Copland Fabrics and Copland, Inc, Burlington Commun. Cent, Inc. and Mid State Tile Co; past pres. and dir, N.C. R.R; v.pres. and dir, Alamance Broadcasting Co; pres. and dir, Alamance Dairy Foods, Inc. Mem: N.C. Dairy Prod. Asn.(pres, 47); Nat. Dairy Coun, Raleigh, Durham-Burlington Unit,(pres, 39 & 45-46); N.C. Jersey Breeders Asn.(past pres); dir, Farm Bur; N.C. State Grange; Burlington Kiwanis Club (pres, 42); Burlington C. of C.(pres, 44-56); Burlington Optimist Club; Alamance Co. Tuberc. Asn.(pres, 42 & 53-54, past chmn); N.C. Tuberc. Asn; trustee, May Mem. Libr; Alamance Co. Commun. Coun; Burlington Merchants Asn; dir, N.C. Conf. Soc. Serv; dir, N.C. Div. Am. Cancer Soc; dir, Commun. YMCA; Athletic Coun, N.C. State Univ; pres, N.C. State Univ. Alumni Asn, 62; dir, Mem. Hosp. Alamance; trustee, Elon Col. and Univ. N.C, Chapel Hill; bd. visitors, St. Andrews Presby. Col; AF&AM; Elks; K.T; RAM; Moose. Nat. Distinguished Legis. Serv. Award, Nat. Educ. Asn. Dept. Rural Educ, 66. Rel: Presbyterian; chmn, Cmt. Christian Educ, teacher, Young Married Couples Class, trustee, Orange Presbytery Sch, Glade Valley, chmn.

bd. and trustee, Orange Presbytery Camp New Hope, mem. exec. cmt, Church Exten, Synod of N.C, chmn. Bd. Deacons, 38-50 and Elder, 50. Mailing Add: Box 909, Burlington, N.C. 27215.

SCOTT, RALPH JAMES D
Chmn, Stakes Co. Dem. Exec. Cmt, N.C.
b. Pinnacle, N.C, 10/15/05; s. Samuel Martin Scott and Daisy Cook S; m. 11/30/29 to Verna Denny; c. Patricia Ann Southern, W.F. Southern, Nancy Ellen Shumate and Grady C. Shumate. Educ: Wake Forest Col, LL.B, 30. Polit. & Govt. Pos: N.C. State Rep, 36-37; chmn, Stakes Co. Dem. Exec. Cmt, N.C, 36-; dist. solicitor, 38-56; U.S. Rep, N.C, 56-66. Bus. & Prof. Pos: Attorney-at-law, 30- Mem: N.C. Bar Asn; N.C. State Bar, Inc; Mason; Shrine; Elks; Moose. Rel: Baptist. Mailing Add: Box 97, Seven Island Rd, Danbury, N.C. 27016.

SCOTT, ROBERT F. D
Mem, N.W. Alaska Dist. Dem. Cmt.
b. Nome, Alaska, 6/29/22; s. Tolbert P. Scott and Vallie M. Wilson S; m. 12/31/46 to Norma K. Satterlee. Educ: Am. Acad. Dramatic Arts, N.Y.C, 41-42; Pasadena Playhouse, 48. Polit. & Govt. Pos: Chief dep. clerk, U.S. Courts, Nome, Alaska, 50-57; mem, N.W. Alaska Dist. Dem. Cmt, 56-; city clerk, Nome, 57-66; alternate del, Dem. Nat. Conv, 60, del, 64; chmn, Nome Precincts 1 and 2 Dem. Cmts, 66- Mil. Serv: Entered as Pvt, Army Air Force, 43, released as 1st Lt, 46, after serv. as navigator, 321st Sq, 90th Bomb Group, 5th Air Force, S.Pac. Theater; South. Philippines, Luzon, West. Pac, New Guinea and China Offensive and Defensive Ribbons; Air Medal with 2 Oak Leaf Clusters; Am. and Asiatic Pac. Theater Campaign Medals; Philippines Liberation and Victory Medals. Mem: Past pres. and life mem, Igloo 1, Pioneers of Alaska; past comdr, Am. Legion; VFW. George Washington Honor Medal Award for Editorial in Nome Nugget Newspaper, Freedom Found. at Valley Forge, 67. Rel: Protestant. Mailing Add: P.O. Box 714, Nome, Alaska. 99762.

SCOTT, ROBERT WALTER D
Gov, N.C.
b. Haw River, Alamance Co, N.C, 6/13/29; s. W. Kerr Scott and Mary Elizabeth White S; m. 9/1/51 to Jessie Rae Osborne; c. Mary Ella, Margaret Rose, Susan Rae, W. Kerr and Janet Louise. Educ: Duke Univ, 47-49; N.C. State Col, B.S, Animal Indust, 50-52. Polit. & Govt. Pos: Dem. Precinct Chmn; Co. V.Chmn. and State Solicitorial Dist. Exec. Cmt, 60-64; Lt. Gov, N.C, 65-69, Gov, 69-; del, Dem. Nat. Conv, 68. Bus. & Prof. Pos: Dairy Farmer. Mil. Serv: Spec. Agent Counter Intel. Corps, Army, 53-55. Mem: N.C. Farm Bur, Fedn; N.C. State Grange (Master, 61-63); past chmn, United Forces for Educ. in N.C; pres, N.C. Soc. of Farm Mgr. and Rural Appraisers; Burlington-Alamance Co. C. of C; Haw River Jr. C. of C; Soil Conserv. Soc. of Am; N.C. Lit. and Hist. Asn. Nat. Grange Young Couple of the Year, 59; Alamance Co. Young Farmer of the Year, 57. Rel: Presbyterian; Deacon, Hawfields Presbyterian Church, 59-63, Elder, 63- Legal Res: 1, Haw River, N.C. 27258. Mailing Add: Capitol, Raleigh, N.C. 27602.

SCOTT, ROGER WILLIAM D
b. Lake View, 6/19/02; s. Nathans T. Scott and Myrtle Miller S; m. 8/25/37 to Ruby McKenzie. Educ: Kemper High Hill and Chadbourn, N.C. Polit. & Govt. Pos: S.C. State Rep, 41-44 & 47-48; S.C. State Sen, 63-66. Bus. & Prof. Pos: Farmer. Mailing Add: Route 1, Lake View, S.C. 29563. (1967)

SCOTT, TASSO HAROLD D
b. Natoma, Kans, 1/25/05; s. Paul Dawson Scott and Sadie Velzetta Kroh; m. 12/5/42 to Kathryn Marie Terhune; c. Watson Terhune, Thomas Harold and Douglas Bennett. Educ: Univ. Colo, A.B, 31; Georgetown Univ, M.S, 33; George Wash. Univ, J.D, 40; Phi Kappa Tau. Polit. & Govt. Pos: Legis. asst. to late U.S. Sen. Alva B. Adams, Colo, 34-41; attorney, Fed. Trade Cmn, 41-60; assoc. cmnr, Indian Claims Cmn, 60-69. Bus. & Prof. Pos: Mem, Rhyne & Rhyne, Attorneys, 69- Publ: 'Export Trade Activities Under the FTC,' 53, 'Injunctions For and Against the Federal Trade Commission,' 54 and 'How the Federal Trade Commission Keeps Up With TV Commercials,' 57, Trade Practice Annual. Mem: Fed, Inter-Am, Am. and D.C. Bar Asns; Am. Judicature Soc; Nat. Lawyers Club; World Peace Through Law Center; past pres, Colo. State Soc; Kenwood Club. Admitted to practice law before Fed. Courts, including U.S. Supreme Court; mem, Univ. Colo. wrestling team 3 years, capt, 1 year and Rocky Mt. Champion in his weight div. Rel: Methodist. Legal Res: Boulder, Colo. Mailing Add: 4125 Leland St, Chevy Chase, Md. 20015.

SCOTT, WILLIAM J. R
Attorney Gen, Ill.
b. Chicago, Ill, 11/11/26; s. William Earl Scott and Edith Swanson S; m. 5/27/50 to Dorothy Lorraine Johnson; c. Elizabeth Ann and William Gregory, Educ: Bucknell Univ, 45; Univ. Pa, 46; Chicago-Kent Col. of Law, LL.B, 50. Polit. & Govt. Pos: Rep. precinct Committeeman, Ill, 17 years; first v.pres, Ill. Young Rep. Orgn, Ill, 49, exec. dir, 50; chmn, Cook Co. Young Rep. Orgn, 50; spec. asst. to U.S. Attorney, North. Dist. of Ill, 59; state treas, Ill, 63-67; attorney gen, Ill, 69- Bus. & Prof. Pos: Lawyer; officer, Am. Nat. Bank; v.pres, commercial div. and mem, mgt. cmt, Nat. Blvd. Bank of Chicago, 59-62. Mil. Serv: Navy, 45-46. Mem: Ill. Bankers Asn; Ill. Bar Asn; Chicago Asn. of Commerce; Ill. C. of C; trustee, MacMurray Col. Rel: Presbyterian; Elder. Legal Res: 652 Sheridan Rd, Evanston, Ill. 60202. Mailing Add: State House, Springfield, Ill. 62706. (1967)

SCOTT, WILLIAM L. R
U.S. Rep, Va.
b. Williamsburg, Va, 7/1/15; m. to Inez Hoffman; c. Gail Ann, Bill Jr. and Paul. Educ: Nat. Univ. Sch. of Econ. and Govt, 2 yrs; George Wash. Univ. Sch. of Govt, 1 1/2 yrs; Nat. Univ. Sch. of Law, LL.B. and LL.M; past chancellor, Sigma Nu Phi. Polit. & Govt. Pos: U.S. Rep, Va, 67-; del, Rep. Nat. Conv, 68. Bus. & Prof. Pos: Attorney-at-law; under-clerk, sr. clerk, Govt. Printing Off, 34-39; jr. attorney, prin. attorney, Dept. of Justice, 21 years; spec. asst. to solicitor of Dept. of Interior, 61. Mil. Serv: U.S. Army, World War II. Mem: Fairfax Co, Va. State and Am. Bar Asns; Lions; Am. Legion; 40 et 8; Mason; Shrine. Rel: Methodist; former chmn, off. lay-leader del. to annual conf; lay speaker; adult class teacher. Mailing Add: 3930 W. Ox Rd, Fairfax, Va. 22030.

SCOTT, WILLIAM Z. R
b. Lansford, Pa, 7/4/16; s. Dr. William C. Scott and Mellie Zimmerman S; m. to Marion Sampson; c. Carol S. and William Z, Jr. Educ: Lafayette Col, B.A; Univ. Pa, Law Sch, LL.B; Maroon Key Club; Knights of the Round Table; Phi Kappa Psi. Polit. & Govt. Pos: Pa. State Rep, 46-54; Pa. State Sen, 54-67; mem, Pa. Liquor Control Bd, 66, chmn, 67- Bus. & Prof. Pos: Attorney. Mil. Serv: Burma Campaign, World War II, Capt, Merrill's Marauders; Purple Heart; Inf. Combatmen's Badge; Presidential Citation; Bronze Star. Mem: Carbon Co. Bar; Amvets; P.O.S. of A; Elks; Mason; Four Co. Firemen's Asn. Rel: Episcopal. Legal Res: Box 121, Pocono Manor, Pa. 18349. Mailing Add: Scott & Lazokchick, Attorneys-at-Law, Lansford, Pa. 18232.

SCOTT-CRAIG, MARY M. D
b. Ithaca, N.Y, 12/25/06; married; c. Three. Educ: Cornell Univ. B.A. and M.A. Polit. & Govt. Pos: Supvr. of the check lists and N.H. State Rep, formerly. Bus. & Prof. Pos: Former teacher and dean, William Smith Col, Geneva, N.Y. Mem: N.H. League of Women Voters. Rel: Roman Catholic. Mailing Add: 2 Chase Rd, Hanover, N.H. 03755.

SCRANTON, WILLIAM WARREN R
b. Madison, Conn, 7/19/17; s. Worthington Scranton and Marion Margery S; m. 7/6/42 to Mary L. Chamberlin; c. Susan, William W, Joseph C. and Peter K. Educ: Yale Univ, B.A, 39, Yale Law Sch, LL.B, 46. Polit. & Govt. Pos: Spec. asst. to Secy. of State Christian A. Herter, administering the secy. private off. and interpreting U.S. for. policy for the press; U.S. rep, conf. in Latin Am, NATO and UN; U.S. Rep, Pa, 61-63; Gov, Pa, 63-67; del, Rep. Nat. Conv, 64 & 68; made two fact-finding missions for President Nixon to West. Europe and the Mid. East, 68; U.S. rep, Int. Conf. on Commun. by Earth Satellite Syst, 69; U.S. Ambassador, 69; mem, President's Arms Limitation Cmn, currently. Mailing Add: Box 116, Dalton, Pa. 18414.

SCREVANE, PAUL R. D
b. Woodcliff, N.J, Aug. 1914; s. Joseph Screvane and Anne Reordon S; m. 1942 to Bridie McKessey; c. Paul Owen, Sara Anne, Christopher and Brian. Educ: Miss. State Col. Polit. & Govt. Pos: Chmn, Munic. Cmt, Heart Fund, N.Y.C; dir. opers, Sanitation, 53-57, cmnr, 57-61; dep. mayor, N.Y.C, 61; pres, city coun, 62-65; coordinator, Anti-Poverty Prog, 64-; mem. exec. cmt, United Serv. Orgn. Bus. & Prof. Pos: With dept. of sanitation, N.Y.C, 36-53. Mil. Serv: Entered Field Artil, Army, 41, released as Maj, 45, after serv. in ETO; Silver Star; Bronze Star; decorations from Govt. of Greece and Italy; named Knight of Order of Merit, Italy. Mem: Am. Pub. Works Asn. (pres, 64); Gr. Fund of World's Fair, N.Y, 64-65. Mailing Add: 10 E. 40th, New York, N.Y. 10016. (1967)

SCRIBNER, DUANE C. DFL
b. Lewisville, Minn, 10/16/31; s. Dewey Dean Scribner and Loretta Herrgott S; m. 6/14/53 to Marcheta Jeanine Lund; c. Kirsten, Lisa, Kathleen, Maria and Emily. Educ: Moorhead State Col, B.S, 53; Univ. Minn, M.A, 61; Kappa Delta Pi; Sigma Tau Delta. Polit. & Govt. Pos: Admin. asst. to U.S. Sen. Walter F. Mondale, Minn, 67- Bus. & Prof. Pos: Instr, Henning Pub. Schs, Minn, 55-56, Mounds View Schs, St. Paul, 56-61, Moorhead State Col, 61-65, Univ. Minn, 65-67. Publ: 'Teaching or Preaching?,' Minn. J. Educ, 12/63; 'Hierarchies of Learning & Literary Sequence,' Eng. J, 3/67. Mem: Phi Delta Kappa; Nat. and Minn. Educ. Asns; Asn. Higher Educ; Nat. and Minn. Coun. Teachers Eng; Conf. Eng. Educ. Rel: Protestant. Legal Res: 188 Arthur Ave. S.E, Minneapolis, Minn. 55414. Mailing Add: 10127 Ranger Rd, Fairfax, Va. 22030.

SCRIBNER, FRED CLARK, JR. R
Gen. Counsel, Rep. Nat. Cmt.
b. Bath, Maine, 2/14/08; s. Fred Clark Scribner and Emma Adelaide Cheltra S; m. 8/24/35 to Barbara Curtis Merrill; c. Fred, Clark, III, Curtis Merrill and Charles Dewey. Educ: Dartmouth Col, A.B, 30; Harvard Col, LL.B, 33; Phi Beta Kappa; Delta Sigma Rho; Alpha Chi Rho. Hon. LL.D, Univ. Maine, 58, Dartmouth, Colby and Bowdoin, 59, Univ. of Vt, 60. Polit. & Govt. Pos: Chmn, Portland City Rep. Cmt, Maine, 36-40; chmn, Maine Coun. Young Rep. Clubs, 38-40; mem. exec. cmt, Maine State Rep. Cmt, 40-50, chmn, 44-50; Rep. nat. committeeman, Maine, 48-56; del, Rep. Nat. Conv, 40, 44, 56, 60, 64 & 68, gen. counsel, Arrangements Cmt. 56, 64 & 68; gen. counsel, Rep. Nat. Cmt, 52-55 & 61-; gen. counsel, Dept. Treas, 55-57, asst. secy. treas, 57, under secy. treas, 57-61; pres, Maine Constitutional Cmt, 62-63. Bus. & Prof. Pos: Partner, law firm Pierce, Atwood, Scribner, Allen & McKusick, Portland, Maine and Scribner, Hall, Casey, Thornburg & Thompson, Wash, D.C; dir, gen. counsel, v.pres. and treas, Bates Mfg. Co, Lewiston, Maine, 46-55; chmn. bd. of dirs, Rockland-Rockport Lime Co, Inc. and Coordinated Apparel, Inc. Mem: Mason (33°); pres. of trustees, Bradford Jr. Col; dir, Maine Med. Center; mem. of Corp, Cardigan Mt. Sch; Capitol Hill Club; Portland Club; Woodfords Club; Kiwanis; Settlers Club; Boy Scouts (mem. regional exec. cmt, Region I); dir, Am. Coun. Nationalities Serv. Alexander Hamilton Award. Rel: Episcopal; Mem. of Standing Cmt, Diocese of Maine; del, Gen. Conv. P.E. Church, 43, 48, 52, 61, 64 & 68. Legal Res: 335 Foreside Rd, Falmouth, Maine 04105. Mailing Add: Rm. 902, 465 Congress St, Portland, Maine 04111.

SCRIBNER, G. E. (CASEY) R
S.Dak. State Rep.
b. Eddyville, Iowa, 1906; m. to Sylvia Whitaker; c. Kent and Bruce. Educ: Univ. Iowa, 26-28. Polit. & Govt. Pos: S.Dak. State Rep, 61- Bus. & Prof. Pos: Mem. staff, Cessna Aircraft Co, 5 years; retail hardware bus, 8 years; operator, children's amusement park. Mem: United Commercial Travelers; C. of C; High Twelve Club; Cosmopolitan Club; Knife and Fork Club; Unity Lodge No. 130 AF&AM Cyrene Commandry No. 2; Chap. No. 2 RAM; El Raid Shrine. Rel: Methodist. Mailing Add: 2716 S. Duluth, Sioux Falls, S.Dak. 57105. (1967)

SCRIBNER, RODNEY LATHAM D
b. Rumford, Maine, 5/6/35; s. Dwight Latham Scribner and Evaline May House S; m. 2/28/63 to Evelyn Jean Sanborn. Educ: Maine Maritime Acad, B.S, 56. Polit. & Govt. Pos: V.chmn, Oxford Co. Dem. Cmt, Maine, 61-62; chmn, Ward 3, Precinct 2, 64-66; asst. legis. finance officer, Maine Legis, 65; treas, Portland Dem. City Cmt, 66-68; Maine State Rep, 67-68; dep. cmnr, Maine Dept. of Finance and Admin, 68-; acting cmnr, Maine Dept. of

Indian Affairs, 69- Bus. & Prof. Pos: Certified Pub. Acct, Staples & Boyce, Portland, Maine, 62-68. Mil. Serv: Entered as Ensign, Navy, 56, released as Lt.(jg), 58; Lt.(jg), Naval Res, 56-; Third Mate, Merchant Marine, 58-62. Publ: 'Raising State and Local Revenues: Emerging Patterns in Revenue Syst,' Nat. Gov. Conf, 7/68. Mem: Am. Inst. of Certified Pub. Accts; Maine Soc. of Pub. Accts; K. of P; Dramatic Order Knights of Khorassan. Rel: Baptist. Mailing Add: 190 Alton Rd, Augusta, Maine 04330.

SCROGHEM, ALPHEUS M. D
Chmn, Dade Co. Dem. Cent. Cmt, Mo.
b. Westfield, Tex, 11/14/96; s. Thomas Daniel Scroghem and Annie Martin S; m. 7/3/19 to Nell A. Dixon; c. Hazel Nell and Margaret Gene. Educ: Nev. Bus. Col, Mo. Polit. & Govt. Pos: Inspector, Mo. State Dept. of Revenue, 47-59; chmn, Dade Co. Dem. Cent. Cmt, Mo, 64- Bus. & Prof. Pos: Farmer, 31- Mil. Serv: Entered as Pvt, Army Nat. Guard, 13, released as Sgt, 19, after serv. in 2nd Mo. Inf, Mex. Border, 16, 128th MG. Bn, AEF, 17-19; reentered as Capt, Army, 41, released as Lt. Col, 45, after serv. in Caribbean Defense Command; Army Res.(Ret), 56; Mex. Border Ribbon; World War I Victory Medal; Am. Defense and Am. Theater Ribbons. Mem: Am. Legion; Res. Officers Asn. Rel: Presbyterian; Elder. Mailing Add: P.O. Box 142, Greenfield, Mo. 65661.

SCRUGGS, CLESTON D
b. Iuka, Miss, 1/23/13; married. Educ: Miss. State Univ. Polit. & Govt. Pos: Former Miss. State Rep. Bus. & Prof. Pos: Teacher; farmer; former supt. of educ. Mem: Mason; MEA; PTA; Farm Bur. Rel: Methodist. Mailing Add: Route 3, Iuka, Miss. 38852. (1967)

SCULLY, LEO P. D
b. Denver, 3/14/24; s. State Sen. Pat Scully; single. Educ: Don Martin Sch. of Radio and TV, Hollywood, Calif; Univ. of Wyo. Polit. & Govt. Pos: Wyo. State Rep, first term -67. Bus. & Prof. Pos: Sta. mgr, KOWB Radio. Mil. Serv: Korean War. Mem: VFW; Am. Legion; Sertoma. Rel: Catholic. Mailing Add: c/o Radio Station KOWB, Laramie, Wyo. 82070. (1967)

SCULLY, PAT D
b. Lincoln, N.H, 10/16/05; m. Annette; c. 2. Educ: N.H. Acct. Sch. Polit. & Govt. Pos: Wyo. State Sen, 2 terms, -67; Wyo. State Rep, 4 terms; House Majority Floor Leader, 59; House Minority Floor Leader, 61. Bus. & Prof. Pos: Supv, Union Pac. R.R. Co. Mem: VFW, past comdr, Laramie Post 2221; Am. Legion; Elks; Moose; K. of C. Rel: Catholic. Mailing Add: c/o Veterans of Foreign Wars Post 2221, Laramie, Wyo. 82070. (1967)

SCULLY, WILLIAM JAMES, JR. D
Conn. State Rep.
b. Waterbury, Conn, 12/11/39; s. William James Scully, Sr. and Alice Doyle S; m. 11/25/65 to Ellyn Bergin; c. Mary Margaret, Kathleen Elizabeth and William James, III. Educ: Univ. of Conn, B.A; Fairfield Univ, 1 year; Sherman House; Newman Club; Young Dem. Polit. & Govt. Pos: Mem, local exec. bd, State Young Dem, Conn, 62-68, treas, 63-65 and v.pres, 65-66; del, Young Dem. State Conv, 63-68; del, Young Dem. Nat. Conv, 65; Conn. State Rep, 91st Dist, 69- Mem: Toast Masters Int; K. of C; Hiberians; Eagles. Rel: Catholic. Mailing Add: 278 E. Main St, Waterbury, Conn. 06702.

SCURLOCK, LOUIE M. D
b. Walker Co, 3/3/27; married; c. 2. Educ: Walker Co. Pub. Schs. Polit. & Govt. Pos: Ala. State Rep, 63-66; Mayor and alderman in Sumiton; Young Dems. Mil. Serv: Navy Seabees, served overseas. Mem: Lions; VFW; Am. Legion. Mailing Add: Gen. Delivery, Sumiton, Ala. 35148. (1967)

SCURRY, FREDERICK G. D
b. Saluda, Hickory Grove Commun, S.C, 8/26/23; s. Frederick Grant, Sr. and Hallie Sineath S; m. 7/20/47 to Margaret Collins; c. Ralph, Janice, Grant. Educ: Sptbg. Jr. Col; Newberry Col, B.S, Bus. Admin, 49. Polit. & Govt. Pos: S.C. State Sen, 57-66. Bus. & Prof. Pos: Farmer; beef cattle. Mil. Serv: Army, 44-45, Co. I, 36th Armored Inf. Regt, 3rd Armored Div; wounded in action. Mem: Mason; Lions Club; Am. Legion; Grange; pres, S.C. Advent Christian Conf, 58-60, 62, 64; pres, South. Advent Christian Asn, 63-64; v. pres, Advent Christian Gen. Conf. of Am, 63-65; chmn, Cancer Crusade Saluda Co, 58-59; 64; chmn, Handicapped Prog. Saluda Co, 59. Rel: Advent Christian Church. Mailing Add: RFD 1, Saluda, S.C. 29138. (1967)

SEABORG, GLENN T. D
Chmn, U.S. Atomic Energy Cmn.
b. Ishpeming, Mich, 4/19/12; s. H. Theodore Seaborg and Selma Erickson S; m. 6/6/42 to Helen L. Griggs; c. Peter, Lynne (Mrs. William B. Cobb), David, Stephen, Eric and Dianne. Educ: Univ. Calif, Los Angeles, A.B, 34; Univ. Calif, Berkeley, Ph.D. in Chem, 37; Phi Beta Kappa; Alpha Chi Sigma; Phi Lambda Upsilon; Pi Mu Epsilon; Sigma Xi. Polit. & Govt. Pos: Mem, First Gen. Adv. Cmt, U.S. Atomic Energy Cmn, Wash, D.C, 46-50, mem, Hist. Adv. Cmt, 58-61, chmn, Cmn, 61-; consult, Argonne Nat. Lab, 46-51; consult, Tech Adv. Panel on Atomic Energy, Research and Develop. Bd, Dept. of Defense, 50-55; mem, Adv. Cmt. for Chem, Oak Ridge Nat. Lab, 54-61; mem. vis. cmt, Dept. Chem, Brookhaven Nat. Lab, 55-58; mem, Adv. Cmt. on New Educ. Media, U.S. Off. Educ, 58-60; mem, President's Sci. Adv. Cmt, 59-61; mem, Nat. Sci. Bd, Nat. Sci. Found, 60-61, mem, Adv. Coun. on Col. Chem, 62-67; mem, Educ. Serv. Inc, 61-67; U.S. Rep, 5th thru 13th Gen. Conf, Int. Atomic Energy Agency, Vienna, 61-69; mem, Fed. Radiation Coun, 61-; mem, Fed. Coun. for Sci. and Tech, 61-; mem, Nat. Aeronaut. and Space Coun, 61-; chmn, U.S. del. to USSR for signing of Memorandum on Coop. in Field of Utilization of Atomic Energy for Peaceful Purposes, 63; mem, Secy. of State Rusk's del. to USSR for signing of Limited Test Ban Treaty, 63; mem, Sci. Adv. Cmt, Pac. Sci. Center Found, Seattle, 63-; chmn, U.S. del, Third Int. Conf. on Peaceful Uses of Atomic Energy, Geneva, 64; mem, Am. Heritage Dictionary Panel of Usage Consult, 64-68; trustee, Sci. Serv, 65-, pres, 66-; mem, Sci. Adv. Group, Nat. Selective Serv, 65-; mem, Corp. of Educ. Develop. Center, Newton, Mass, 67- Bus. & Prof. Pos: Research assoc. with Prof. Gilbert N. Lewis, Univ. Calif, Berkeley, 37-39, instr. chem, 39-41, asst. prof, 41-45, prof, 45-,(on leave of absence, 61-), dir. nuclear chem. research, Lawrence Radiation Lab, 46-58, assoc. dir. lab, 54-61, chancellor, Univ, 58-61; dir. plutonium work, Manhattan Proj, Univ. Chicago Metallurgical Lab, 42-46. Publ: The Transuranium Elements, Yale Univ. Press, 58; The Chemistry of the Actinide Elements (with J.J. Katz), John Wiley and Sons, 58; Elements of the Universe (with E.G. Valens, won Thomas Alva Edison Found. Award for Best Sci. Book for Youth), E.P. Dutton & Co, 58; Man-Made Transuranium Elements, 63 and The Nuclear Properties of the Heavy Elements (with E.K. Hyde and I. Perlman), 64, Prentice-Hall; Education and the Atom (with D.M. Wilkes), McGraw-Hill, 64; Oppenheimer (with I.I. Rabi, R. Serber, V.F. Weisskopf and A. Pais), Charles Scribner's Sons, 69. Mem: Am. Acad. of Arts and Sci; fel, Am. Asn. for Adv. of Sci; fel, Am. Nuclear Soc; fel, Am. Phys. Soc; fel, Calif. Acad. of Sci; fel, N.Y. Acad. of Sci; fel, Royal Soc. of Arts, Eng; Am. Chem. Soc.(cmt. on chem. and pub. affairs, 65-70); hon. mem, Am. Inst. Chemists; life mem, Am. Ord. Asn; Am. Philos. Soc; hon. fel, Chem. Soc, London; hon. fel, Royal Soc. of Edinburgh; Coun. on For. Rels; Nat. Acad. of Sci; for. mem, Royal Swedish Acad. of Eng. Sci; Soc. Nuclear Med; assoc. mem, Am. Scandinavian Found.(trustee, 68-); hon. mem, Chemists Club of N.Y; hon. mem, Swedish Club of Los Angeles; Am. Swedish Hist. Found; Bavarian Acad. of Sci; Argentine Nat. Acad. of Sci; Spanish Royal Acad. of Sci; Nat. Cmt. on America's Goals and Resources, Nat. Planning Asn, 62-64; Cmn. on Humanities, Am. Coun. of Learned Socs, Coun. of Grad. Schs. and United Chap. of Phi Beta Kappa, 62-65; Coun. on Educ. of Teachers in Sci, Nat. Sci. Teachers Asn, 63-; mem-at-lg, Coun, Asn. of Col. Honor Socs, 65-66; bd. gov, Int. Platform Asn, 67-, pres, 68-69; adv. bd, Nova Univ, Ft. Lauderdale, Fla, 68-; Electoral Col, Hall of Fame for Great Americans, N.Y. Univ, 69-; Bohemian Club and Commonwealth Club of San Francisco; Chevy Chase Club; Claremont Country Club; Contra Costa Golf Club; Cosmos Club; Faculty Club, Univ. Calif, Berkeley; Metrop. Club; Univ. Club; Vasa Order of Am. Outstanding Young Man of Chicago Award, 46; One of America's Ten Outstanding Young Men, 47; Award in Pure Chem, Am. Chem. Soc, 47; William H. Nichols Medal, N.Y. Sect, Am. Chem. Soc, 48; John Ericsson Gold Medal, Am. Soc. Swedish Engrs, 48; co-recipient, Nobel Prize for Chem, 51; Perkin Medal, Am. Sect, Soc. Chem. Indust, 57; Enrico Fermi Award, U.S. Atomic Energy Cmn, 59; Sci. and Eng. Award, Fedn. Eng. Soc, Drexel Inst. Tech, 62; Charles Lathrop Parsons Award, Am. Chem. Soc, 64; Wash. Award, West. Soc. Engrs, 65; Willard Gibbs Medal, Chicago Sect, Am. Chem. Soc, 66; Arches of Sci. Award, Pac. Sci. Center, Seattle, 68; plus numerous other awards and more than 35 hon. degrees; co-discoverer of Elements 94 through 102. Rel: Protestant. Legal Res: 3825 Harrison St. N.W, Washington, D.C. 20015. Mailing Add: U.S. Atomic Energy Commission, Washington, D.C. 20545

SEABRIGHT, JOHN L. D
b. Wheeling, 6/4/27; s. Walter W. Seabright and Clara J. Becker S; m. 6/11/51 to Joan A. Schadel; c. Jeff, Mark, Mike and Leslie. Educ: Oberlin Col, B.A. Polit. & Govt. Pos: Mem, Ohio Co. Airport Authority, W.Va; mem, City Budge Cmt, Wheeling; W.Va. State Del, 64-66. Bus. & Prof. Pos: Sand, gravel and concrete bus. Mil. Serv: Navy. Mailing Add: 45 Barrows Rd, Wheeling, W.Va. 26003. (1967)

SEABROOK, CORDES GAILLARD, JR. R
Second V.Chmn, S.C. Rep. Party
b. Anderson, S.C, 3/12/27; s. Cordes Gaillard Seabrook and Ruth Brownlee S; m. 11/24/51 to Araluen Clinkscales; c. Cordes C, III, Araluen Louise, Eleanor Brownlee and March Edings. Educ: Citadel, Charleston, S.C, B.S, 48; Mass. Inst. Tech, S.M, 60. Polit. & Govt. Pos: Chmn, Anderson Co. Rep. Party, S.C, 60-64, finance chmn, 62-66; finance chmn, Third Cong. Dist. Rep. Party, 66-69; second.v.chmn, S.C. Rep. Party, 66-; alternate del, Rep. Nat. Conv, 68. Bus. & Prof. Pos: Partner, Seabrook Transmission Co, 50-64; treas, Seabrook Inc, 64-66, pres, 66-; treas, E.E. Smith & Sons Inc, 61- Mil. Serv: Army, 48-49, 2nd Lt, serv. in Third Div, Third Army. Mem: Anderson C. of C.(pres, 69). Rel: Episcopal. Legal Res: 1202 Rutledge Way, Anderson, S.C. 29621. Mailing Add: P.O. Box 6, Anderson, S.C, 29621.

SEABROOK, STERLING WITHERS D
Miss. State Rep.
b. Memphis, Tenn, 10/13/23. Polit. & Govt. Pos: Miss. State Rep, 60- Bus. & Prof. Pos: Farmer. Mem: Rotary. Rel: Episcopal. Mailing Add: Route 1, Tunica, Miss. 38676. (1967)

SEAGROVES, JESSIE RUTH D
Third V.Chmn, Chatham Co. Dem. Exec. Cmt, N.C.
b. Siler City, N.C, 2/6/22; d. Jesse Anderson Crutchfield and Emma Richardson C; div; c. Joel Brent, James Keith and John David. Educ: Silk Hope Sch, N.C, grad, 39. Polit. & Govt. Pos: Area chmn. women, Terry Sanford for Gov. Campaign, N.C, 60; v.pres, Young Dem. Chatham Co, 61; mem, Albright Twp. Dem. Precinct Cmt, 61-69; co-organizer, Chatham Co. Dem. Women, 62; mem, N.C. Centennial Cmn, 62; mem. exec. cmt, Chatham Co. Dem. Women, 62-68; pres, Chatham Co. Dem. Women, 64-68; alternate del, Dem. Nat. Conv, 68; chmn, Chatham Co. Bob Scott for Gov. Campaign, 68; third v.chmn, Chatham Co. Dem. Exec. Cmt, 68- Bus. & Prof. Pos: Merchant, Crutchfield's Store, N.C. Publ: Newspaper columnist, Chatham News, N.C, 15 years. Mem: N.C. Food Dealers Asn; charter mem, Chatham Co. Hist. Soc; N.C. Lit. and Hist. Soc; adv, Jr. Hist. Club, Silk Hope Sch; charter mem, Albright Home Demonstration Club; Chatham Co. Farm Bur; United Daughters Confederacy; Am. Legion Auxiliary; 81st Wildcat Div. Auxiliary; co-organizer, Albright 4-H Club, 62, mem. sponsoring cmt, 4-H Clubs, 64-69 and Chatham Co. Del. to Leadership Conf, Nat. 4-H Club Cong, D.C, 67. Chatham Co. Dem. Woman of Year, 62. Rel: Baptist. Mailing Add: Route 1, Box 79, Siler City, N.C. 27344.

SEALE, THOMAS GRISWOLD R
Chmn, Culberson Co. Rep. Party, Tex.
b. Abilene, Tex, 6/3/35; s. Dr. William Hubert Seale and Lena V. Griswold S; m. 7/20/57 to Rebecca Louise Willingham; c. Stacey Elizabeth, Steven Culver and Shelley Kay. Educ: Univ. Tex, Austin, 1 year; McMurray Col, 2 years; Tex. Tech. Col, B.S, 58; Alpha Zeta. Polit. & Govt. Pos: Chmn, Culberson Co. Rep. Party, Tex, 65- Bus. & Prof. Pos: Soil scientist, Soil Conserv. Serv, 58; pub. sch. teacher, Van Horn Pub. Schs, 65- Mil. Serv: Naval Res, 53-61. Rel: Methodist. Mailing Add: Box 515, Van Horn, Tex. 79855.

SEALY, ALBERT HENRY R
b. Columbus, Ohio, 10/23/17; s. Albert Henry Sealy and Lillian Stock S; m. 8/23/47 to Flora Kinkel; c. Catherine A, Thomas P. and Joan D. Educ: Ohio State Univ, B.A, 38; Harvard Law Sch, LL.B, 41; Phi Beta Kappa; Pi

Sigma Alpha; Sigma Chi. Polit. & Govt. Pos: Mem, Zoning Bd. Appeals, Bedford, N.Y, 53-55, mem, Bd. Educ, 53-55; chmn, housing adv. cmt, Dayton City Cmn, Ohio, 64-66; Ohio State Rep, 67-68; cand. for Rep. nomination for Gov, Ohio, 68. Mil. Serv: Entered as Ens, Navy, 43, released as Lt, 46, after serv. in Off. Gen. Coun, Navy Dept. Publ: 'Acquisitions & Mergers,' Bus. Lawyer, Am. Bar Asn, 11/60; 'The Functions of Spin-Offs and Partial Liquidations,' Proceedings of 20th Annual Inst. on Fed. Taxation of N.Y. Univ, 62; 'Formation of An Ohio Corp,' Ohio Bar of Ohio Bar Asn, 9/62. Mem: Am. and N.Y. State Bar Asns; Asn. of the Bar of the City of New York; chmn, Corp. Law Cmt, Ohio State Bar Asn, 62-67; Commun. Develop. Cmt, Dayton Area C. of C; chmn, Urban Renewal Cmt, Dayton Bar Asn, 63- Rel: Presbyterian. Mailing Add: 236 W. Schantz Ave, Dayton, Ohio 45409.

SEAMAN, ROGER GEORGE D
b. Chicago, Ill, 5/17/26; s. Anthony George Seaman and Elizabeth Smith S; wid; m. 1/8/66 to Marilyn Rose Wasyluka; c. David, Joanne, Gail, Paul, Mary Beth and Carolyn Patrice. Educ: Wilson Jr. Col, 46-48; John Marshall Law Sch, LL.B, 48-51; Delta Theta Phi. Polit. & Govt. Pos: Precinct capt, 16th Ward Regular Dem. Orgn, Ill, 46-; asst. state attorney, Cook Co, 52-57; asst. corp. counsel, Chicago, 57-65; v.pres, Young Dem, Cook Co, 58-60; 1st v.pres, Young Dem, Ill, 60-62, pres, 62-64; admin. aide to pres. of Metrop. Sanitary Dist, 65- Bus. & Prof. Pos: Attorney-at-law, Seaman & Seaman, 51- Mil. Serv: Entered as A/S, Navy, 44, released as Radar Operator One, 46, after serv. in Atlantic and Pac, 45-46; Atlantic and Pac. Theatre Ribbons; Peace Ribbon. Publ: Water and Air Pollution—What Do You Control First? Ill. Munic. League, 68. Mem: Air Pollution Control Asn; Am. Pub. Works Asn; Groundhog Club; Chicago Bar Asn; CWV; Catholic Lawyers Guild. Named Outstanding Young Dem. of the Young Dem. Clubs of Am, 1964; Award of Merit, CWV, 69. Rel: Roman Catholic. Legal Res: 2642 W. 86th St, Chicago, Ill. 60652. Mailing Add: 100 E. Erie, Chicago, Ill. 60611.

SEAMANS, ROBERT CHANNING, JR. R
Secy. of the Air Force
b. Salem, Mass, 10/30/18; m. to Eugenia A. Merrill; c. Katherine (Mrs. Padulo), Robert C, III, Joseph, May and Daniel. Educ: Harvard Univ, B.Sc. in Eng, 39; Mass. Inst. Tech, M.Sc. in Aeronaut, 42 and D.Sc. in Instrumentation, 51. Hon. D.Sc, Rollins Col. and N.Y. Univ. Polit. & Govt. Pos: Mem. tech. cmts, Nat. Adv. Cmt. for Aeronaut, 48-58; consult, Sci. Adv. Bd. of the Air Force, 57-59, mem, 59-62 and assoc. adv, 62-67; assoc. adminstr, NASA, 60-65, dep. adminstr, 65-68, consult. to adminstr, 68; Secy. of the Air Force, 69- Bus. & Prof. Pos: Asst. prof. and assoc. prof, Dept. of Aeronaut. Eng, proj. engr, Instrumentation Lab, chief engr. of Proj. Meteor and dir, Flight Control Lab, Mass. Inst. Tech, 41-55; mgr, Airborne Systs. Lab and chief systs. engr, Airborne Systs. Dept, Radio Corp. of Am, 55-58, chief engr, Missile Electronics and Controls Div, Burlington, Mass, 58-60; Jerome Clarke Hunsaker vis. prof, Mass. Inst. Tech, 68. Mem: Nat. del, Adv. Group for Aerospace Research and Develop, NATO; Int. Acad. Astronaut; bd. overseers, Harvard Univ; Am. Asn. for Adv. of Sci; Am. Astronaut. Soc; Am. Soc. for Pub. Admin; Am. Acad. of Arts and Sci; Nat. Space Club; For. Policy Asn; Nat. Acad. of Eng; Sigma Xi. Naval Ord. Develop. Award, 45; Sperry Award, Am. Inst. of Aeronaut. and Astronaut, 51; Godfrey L. Cabot Aviation Award, 65; NASA Distinguished Serv. Medal, 65; Goddard Trophy, 68. Mailing Add: Dept. of the Air Force, Pentagon, Washington, D.C. 20330.

SEARCEY, WILLIAM A. D
Ga. State Sen.
b. Savannah, Ga, 9/2/21; s. William B. Searcey and Effie Brown S; m. 11/22/52 to Lorise Virginia Rakal; c. William A, Jr. Educ: Univ. Ga. Law Sch, LL.B, 49. Polit. & Govt. Pos: Ga. State Sen, 63- Bus. & Prof. Pos: Attorney-at-law. Mil. Serv: Savannah Vol. Guards; Sgt. Nat. Guard, 37-40; Fed. Serv, 40-42; commissioned 2nd Lt, anti-aircraft Artil. Platoon Comdr, 42; 1st Lt, 43-45; Ga. Nat. Guard, 50-61; presently, Maj. in U.S. Army Res; Salerno Invasion. Rel: Episcopal. Mailing Add: 408 Georgia State Bldg, Savannah, Ga. 31402. (1967)

SEARCY, NELSON DONALD D
b. Lincoln, Nebr, 9/1/33; s. Harry Nelson Searcy and Blanche Novak S; m. 12/18/54 to Gwendolyn Marie Reich; c. Jeffrey Nelson, Daniel Kent and Kathleen Betty Marie. Educ: Univ. Nebr, B.S, 55, M.A, 57 and grad. work, 60-61 & 65-66; Sigma Xi; Gamma Theta Upsilon; Pi Gamma Mu. Polit. & Govt. Pos: Pres, Univ. Young Dem, 54-55; del, Dem. Nat. Conv, 68. Bus. & Prof. Pos: Assoc. Prof. of Geog, Kearney State Col, 57- Mil. Serv: Yeoman 1/C, Navy, 51-58. Publ: Nebraska Atlas, Nebr. Atlas Publ. Co, 64; 'Nebraska' in Book of Knowledge, Groliers, 63; 'Nebraska' in Colliers Encyclop, Collier-Macmillan, 65. Mem: Asn. of Am. Geogr; Geog. Soc. of Am; Nat. Coun. for Geog. Educ; Nat. Educ. Asn; Elks. Named Outstanding Young Man. Rel: Lutheran. Mailing Add: 724 W. 22nd St, Kearney, Nebr. 68847.

SEARL, TOM R
Wyo. State Sen.
Educ: Bus. Col. Polit. & Govt. Pos: Wyo. State Rep, 4 terms; Wyo. State Sen, 67- Bus. & Prof. Pos: Real estate; pres, Tom Searl-Frank McCue Inc. Mailing Add: 104 E. 30th St, Cheyenne, Wyo. 82001.

SEARLE, RODNEY N. Conservative
Minn. State Rep.
Married to Janette; c. R. Newell, Jr, Alan J. and Linda. Educ: Rutgers Univ; Mankato State Col. Polit. & Govt. Pos: Minn. State Rep, currently. Bus. & Prof. Pos: Life ins. underwriter. Mailing Add: R.R. 1, Waseca, Minn. 56093.

SEARS, BETTY JEAN R
V.Chairwoman, Gunnison Co. Rep. Cent. Cmt, Colo.
b. Canon City, Colo, 11/27/18; d. Wesley Luther Weller and Mae Williams W; m. 4/5/42 to Arthur Marsden Sears; c. Arthur Welsey and David Alden. Educ: West. State Col, 37 & 69. Polit. & Govt. Pos: Pres, Thursday Rep. Women's Club, Colo, 62; capt, Boulder Co. Rep. Cent. Cmt, 63; v.pres, Colo. Fedn. Rep. Women, 63; v.chairwoman, Gunnison Co. Rep. Cent. Cmt, 64-; pres, Gunnison Co. Rep. Womens Club, 65-66; presidential elector, Colo, 69. Mem: Eastern Star; DeMolay; Mothers Club; Gunnison Golf Club, Inc. (tournament chmn. ladies golf); mem, Den Mothers Training Recognition Plan, Nat. Coun. Boy Scouts. Commendation for work with youth. Rel: Episcopal. Mailing Add: 518 N. Spruce, Gunnison, Colo. 81230.

SEARS, FRED N. D
Co. Chmn, Thomas Co. Dem. Party, Kans.
b. Ashland, Nebr, 10/3/05; s. Charles Edgar Sears and Mabel Brewster S; m. 1/2/28 to Elsie Ann Graber; c. John N. Polit. & Govt. Pos: Co. Chmn, Thomas Co. Dem. Party, Kans, 62-; del, Dem. Nat. Conv, 68; Forestry, Fish and Game Cmnr, 69- Mem: Mason; Shrine; Northwest Kans. Med. Planning Bd; Kans. Century Club; Colby Country Club; Hi Plains Shrine Club. Rel: Presbyterian. Legal Res: 220 N. Garfield, Colby, Kans. 67701. Mailing Add: Box 232, Colby, Kans. 67701.

SEARS, HARRY L. R
N.J. State Sen.
b. Butler, N.J, 1920; m. to Emma Sehulster; c. Ralph, Mary Ann, Barbara, Judy and Donna. Educ: Tusculum Co, B.A, 42; Rutgers Law Sch, LL.B, 48. Polit. & Govt. Pos: Munic. and sch. bd. attorney, 49-, Borough of Butler, Hanover Twp, Hanover Sewerage Authority, Mt. Lakes Bd. Educ, Twp. Randolph, Twp. Montville and Montville Twp. Munic. Utilities Authority, currently; counsel, N.J. Fedn. Off. Planning Bds, 57-58 & 65; mem, Rep. Co. Cmt, Mountain Lakes, 54-60; past counsel, Morris Co. Rep. Cmt; N.J. State Assemblyman, 61-66, mem, Cmt. Pub. Safety Defense and Vet. Affairs, Ins. Law Revision Cmn, Cmn. Interstate Coop, chmn, Cmt. Interstate Coop, Co. and Munic. Govt. Cmt, chmn, Subcmt. on Pensions, Judiciary Cmt. and Rules Cmt, chmn, 64, N.J. State Assembly; alternate del-at-lg, Rep. Nat. Conv, 64, & 68; chmn, N.J. Speakers Bur. Nixon for Pres. Campaign Cmt, 68; N.J. State Sen, 68-, mem, Appropriations Cmt, Interstate Coop. Cmt, Rules and Order Cmt, Liaison Cmt, State Libr. Cmt, v.chmn, Ways and Means Cmt. and Fed. Aid Study Cmn, Asst. Majority Leader, 69-, N.J. State Senate. Bus. & Prof. Pos: Legal clerkship, David Young, III Law Off, 49; attorney, Young and Sears, 54-; dir, State Bank N.J. Mil. Serv: Entered as Commissioned Officer, Naval Res, 42, released as Lt.(sg), 46, after serv. in Atlantic, Mediterranean and Pac. Theatres of Opers. Mem: N.J. and Am. Bar Asns; Morris Co. Bar Asn. (past chmn. Supreme Court Ethics and Grievance Cmt); N.J. Inst. Munic. Attorneys (trustee of Inst, 62-, pres, 67-68); N.J. State League Munic.(mem. Legis. and Resolutions Cmt); Nat. Inst. Munic. Law Officers; Am. Judicature Soc; past mem. bd. trustees, Legal Aid Soc. Morris Co; Cmt. Munic. and Sch. Law, State Bar Asn; Rockaway River Country Club (past mem. bd. gov. secy); Mountain Lakes Club; VFW, Butler and Boonton; bd. dirs, Morris Co. Ment. Health Asn.(co. fund raising chmn, 62); bd. trustees, Wilson Sch, Mountain Lakes. Rel: Community Church; Past Trustee, Mountain Lakes, N.J. Mailing Add: 22 Larchdell Way, Mountain Lakes, N.J. 07046.

SEARS, JOHN RAYMOND, JR. D
Va. State Del.
b. Norfolk, Va, 6/15/21; s. John R. Sears and Ethel Towe S; m. 1/14/51 to Jean Barnacascel; c. Jane T. and John R, III. Educ: Univ. N.C, B.S, 44; Univ. Va, LL.B, 49; Delta Theta Phi; Sigma Nu. Polit. & Govt. Pos: Chmn, Mayor's Adv. Cmt, Norfolk, 44-45, mem, City Planning Cmn, 45-46; Va. State Del, 66- Bus. & Prof. Pos: Mem. adv. bd, Va. Nat. Bank; past pres, Tidewater Group Savings & Loans, Va. Savings & Loan League, Norfolk C. of C. and Norfolk Better Bus. Bur; pres, Home Fed. Savings & Loan Asn, currently. Mil. Serv: Entered as Ens, Navy, 44, released as Lt, 50, after serv. as Command Officer in U.S.S. YMS-8, S. Pac. Theater, from 44-46; Lt.(Ret), Navy; Navy Unit Citation. Mem: Norfolk Portsmouth Bar Asn; bd. mem, Urban Coalition; past pres, Norfolk Girl's Club; Sertoma Club; Harbor Club; AF&AM; Scottish Rites and Khedive Temple; Norfolk Yacht and Country Club; exec. cmt, United Commun. Fund; chmn, Int. Azalea Festival, 65. Officer in Order of the Crown, decreed by King Baudouin I of Belgium. Rel: Methodist. Legal Res: 1320 Harmott Ave, Norfolk, Va. 23509. Mailing Add: 700 Boush St, Norfolk, Va. 23510.

SEARS, JOHN WINTHROP R
b. Boston, Mass, 12/18/30; s. Richard Dudley Sears and Frederica Fulton Leser S.(Deceased); m. 5/29/65 to Catherine Coolidge. Educ: Harvard, A.B. in govt, 52; Oxford, B.Litt, 57; Harvard Law, LL.B, 59; Phi Beta Kappa; SPEE; Signet Soc; Varsity Club; Hasty Pudding-Inst. of 1770. Polit. & Govt. Pos: Mass. State Rep, 65-68; del, Rep. Nat. Conv, 68; sheriff, Suffolk Co, 68-69. Bus. & Prof. Pos: Brown Brothers, Harriman & Co, 59-65. Mil. Serv: Entered as Ens, Naval Res, 52, released as Lt.(jg), 54, reentered Naval Res. as Lt, 61, released as Lt. Comdr, 62, after serv. in Atlantic Theater. Mem: U.S. Naval Inst; Mass. and Boston Bar Asns; Mass. Legislator's Asn; Rep. Club of Mass; Beacon Hill Civic Asn; Back Bay Neighborhood Asn; State Club; Boston Study Group; trustee, Boys Club of Boston, Thompson's Acad, St. Mark's Sch, Boston Zoological Soc; Boston Tuberc. Asn. and Penobscot Marine Mus; Ward 5 Rep. Cmt. Rel: Episcopal. Mailing Add: 56 Branch St, Boston, Mass. 02108.

SEARS, PHILIP MASON R
Boston, Mass, 12/29/99; s. Philip Shelton Sears and Mary Cabot Higginson, S; m. 12/29/24 to Zilla MacDougall; c. Philip Mason, Charlotte MacDougall (deceased). Educ: Harvard, A.B, 22. Polit. & Govt. Pos: U.S. Rep, Trusteeship Coun, UN, 53-60 (pres, 55-56); spec. U.S. ambassador Independence Celebration Cameroun, W. Africa, 60; U.S. ambassador, chmn. UN Vis. Mission to E. Africa, 60; Ambassador, Independence Celebration of Ghana, 57; U.S. Del. Silver Jubilee, Emperor of Ethiopia, Addis Ababa, 55; alt. rep. of U.S. to 13th Gen. Assembly, UN; del. Rep. Nat. Convs, 52, 48; chmn. Mass. Rep. St. Com, 49-50; mem. Mass. Legis, 35-48. Mil. Serv: Army, Pvt, WWI; USNR, Capt, 41-46; with Third Fleet at Guadalcanal and Bougainville. Mem: Am. Legion; Mason. Rel: Episcopalian. Mailing Add: West St , Dedham, Mass. 02026. (1967)

SEARS, RUTH PARKER R
Chmn, Worthington Rep. Town Cmt, Mass.
b. Northampton, Mass, 3/31/31; d. Leston Eugene Parker and Beulah Griffin P; m. 8/6/49 to Raymond H. Sears; c. Donna (Mrs. Richard Thayer), Susan (Mrs. David Stone), Lawrence and Ronald. Educ: Northfield Sch. for Girls. Polit. & Govt. Pos: Secy, Sch. Cmt, Worthington, Mass, 60-63, finance secy, 64-67; secy. to clerk, Worthington Bd. Assessors, 60-67; coordinator for polit. campaigns, State Rep. John Barrus, 62-64, Pres. Cand, Barry Goldwater,

64, State Rep. Donald Madsen, 66 & 68; Gov. Coun, Raymond Fontana, 66, Gov. John Volpe, 66, Dist. Attorney Oscar Grife, 68 and President Richard Nixon, 68; membership chmn, Hampshire City Rep. Club, 64-66, recording secy, 66-67; secy, Worthington Rep. Town Cmt, 64-68, chmn, 68-; clerk typist, Mass. Registry of Motor Vehicles, 66-; dep. sheriff, Hampshire Co, 68- Bus. & Prof. Pos: Secy-bookkeeper, Worthington Garage, Mass, 49-58; secy-bookkeeper, Cummington Garage, Mass, 55-; demonstrator and dealer, Stanley Home Prod, 61-63; salesgirl and dealer Avon Prod, Williamsburg, 63; bookkeeper and salesgirl, Kinne Brook Kitchens, Pittsfield, 63; secy, Prestape, Inc, Northampton, 64-66. Mem: Eastern Star; Am. Legion Auxiliary; Dep. Sheriffs Asn; Hampshire Co. Rep. Club; PTA; N.Am. Family Campers Asn. First woman to serv. on Town Finance Cmt; First Woman to serv. as Chmn, Rep. Town Cmt. Rel: Protestant. Mailing Add: Huntington Rd, Worthington, Mass. 01098.

SEARS, WILLIAM R. R
N.Y. State Assemblyman
b. Utica, N.Y, 5/25/28; s. Edward J. Sears (deceased) and Gladys Waldron S; m. 1/9/54 to Anne M. Miller; c. William J. Educ: Utica Col, 60. Polit. & Govt. Pos: Town councilman, Forestport, N.Y, 61-65; Rep. committeeman, Forestport Rep. Party, 62-; chmn, Forestport Rep. Town Cmt, 62-; Rep. chmn, north. towns, Oneida Co, 63-65; N.Y. State Assemblyman, 115th Dist, 66- Mil. Serv: Entered as Pvt, Army, 50, released as Sgt. 1/C, 52, after serv. in 140th AAA, 40th Div, Korea, 51-52; Korean Conflict Medal; Occup. of Japan, Distinguished Serv. and Sharpshooter Expert Medals. Mem: K. of C; Elks; Moose; Am. Legion; VFW; life mem, DAV; numerous rod and gun clubs; Nat. Rifle Asn. Rel: Catholic. Mailing Add: Bear Creek Rd, Woodgate, N.Y. 13494.

SEATON, FREDERICK ANDREW R
V.Chmn, Rep. Nat. Finance Cmt, Region 11
b. Washington, D.C, 12/11/09; s. Fay Noble Seaton and Dorothea Elizabeth Schmidt S; m. 1/23/31 to Gladys Hope Dowd; c. Donald Richard, Christine (Mrs. Epp), Monica (Mrs. Robert Snodgrass) and Alfred. Educ: Kans. State Col, 27-31; Beta Theta Pi; Sigma Delta Chi; Pi Kappa Delta; Newcomen Soc. Hon. LL.D, Kans. State Univ, 55, Univ. Alaska, 58, Miami Univ, Gettysburg Col, Univ. Hawaii and Univ. Redlands, 59, Univ. Md, John Carroll Univ. and Rose Polytech. Inst, 60; L.H.D, Maryville Col, 55; Dr. Eng, Worcester Polytech. Inst, 59 and Colo. Sch. Mines, 60. Polit. & Govt. Pos: V.chmn, Young Rep. Club Kans, 32-34, chmn, 34-37; v.chmn, Kans. State Rep. Cmt, 34-37; chmn, Adams Co. Rep. Party, Nebr; Nat. Committeeman, Young Rep. Kans, 35; Secy. to Alfred M. Landon, Nat. Campaign, 36; del. and v.chmn, Kans. Del, Rep. Nat. Conv, 36, del, 68; Nebr. State Sen, 45-49; U.S. Sen, Nebr, 51-52; personal adv. to Gen. Eisenhower, Presidential Campaign, 52; Asst. Secy. of Defense, 53-55; admin. asst. to President Eisenhower, 55, dep. asst, 55-56; Secy. of Interior, 56-61; v.chmn, Rep. Nat. Finance Cmt, Region 11, 62-; mem, Rep. Finance Cmt, 69- Bus. & Prof. Pos: Publisher, Hastings Daily Tribune, 37-; mem. bd. trustees, Univ. Nebr. Found. and Hastings Col, 41-; corporate officer in Seaton Group, including newspapers, farm mag. and radio and TV sta; mem. bd. dir, First Nat. Bank, Hastings, Nebr, 61- and Life Investers of Nebr, Omaha, 65-; Nebr. State Chmn, Radio Free Europe Fund, 65-66; mem. bd. trustees, Wash. Journalism Center, D.C, 65-; mem. bd. dir, Investors Growth, Inc, Omaha, 68-; mem. nat. corp, Radio Free Europe, N.Y.C, 68-; mem. bd. adv, Nat. Trust for Historic Preservation, currently; mem, Presidential Cmt. to Commemorate Bi-Centennial Anniversary of Revolutionary War, currently. Mem: Hon. mem, Innocents Soc, Univ. Nebr. and Nat Coun. Boy Scouts; bd. trustees, J.N. Darling Found, Des Moines, Iowa; Mason (32°); Scottish Rite; Shrine; Elks; Rotary; St. Andrew's Soc; Lochland Club; Hastings Club; Univ. Club; Lincoln Club; Nat. Press Club. Recipient, Medal of Freedom; Hon. Ky. Col. Rel: Episcopal. Legal Res: 1820 W. 12th St, Hastings, Nebr. 68901. Mailing Add: 209 Tribune Bldg, Hastings, Nebr. 68901.

SEAY, THOMAS WALLER, JR. D
b. Salisbury, N.C, 4/14/26; s. Dr. Thomas W. Seay and Inez May Marks S; m. 9/3/49 to Martha Jane Zimmerman; c. Carolyn Jane and Linda Ann. Educ: Duke Univ, B.A, 49; Duke Univ. Law Sch, LL.B, 52; Pi Kappa Phi; Delta Theta Phi. Polit. & Govt. Pos: Prosecuting attorney, Rowan Co. Court, N.C, 56-58 and Judge, 58-60; N.C. State Sen, 63-66. Bus. & Prof. Pos: Lawyer; mem, Kesler & Seay, Salisbury, N.C. Mil. Serv: Army, 44-46. Mem: Am, N.C, Rowan Co. and N.C. State Bar Asns; Kiwanis; Spencer Lodge 543, F&AM; York Rite, Oasis Temple; Jack A. Hutchins Post 241; Shrine; Am. Legion. Rel: Methodist. Mailing Add: 400 Carolina Ave, Spencer, N.C. 28159. (1967)

SEAY, WILLIAM E. D
b. Salem, Mo, 12/13/21; m. 5/7/50 to Shirley Anderson; c. Jefferson, Elizabeth, Anderson, William Camm. Educ: Cent. Col, Fayette, Mo, 39-40; Univ. of Mo, LL.B, 49; Single Engine Flying Sch, Mission, Tex; Phi Delta Phi. Polit. and Govt. Pos: Mo. State Rep, 64-66; past pres. Dent Co. Young Dem. Club; prosecuting attorney of Dent Co, 50-64. Bus. & Prof. Pos: Private practice of law in Salem. Mil. Serv: Air Force, Capt, WWII; instr. fighter plane gunnery, 1 year and served in combat as P-47 pilot in Pac. Theater. Rel: Methodist. Mailing Add: Salem, Mo. 65560. (1967)

SEBELIUS, KEITH GEORGE R
U.S. Rep, Kans.
b. Almena, Kans, 9/10/16; s. Dr. Carl Elstrom Sebelius and Minnie Peak S; m. 3/5/49 to Bette A. Roberts; c. Gary and Douglas. Educ: Ft. Hays Kans. State Col, A.B; George Wash. Univ. Law Sch, LL.B; Pi Kappa Delta; Pi Gamma Mu; Phi Kappa Phi. Polit. & Govt. Pos: Attorney, Norton Co, Kans, 46-51; mayor and city councilman, Almena, Kans, 47-50; cmnr, Kans. Indust. Develop. Cmt, 61-62; Kans. State Sen, 62-68; U.S. Rep, First Dist, Kans, 69- Mil. Serv: Entered as Pvt, Army, 41, released as Maj, 66, after serv. in Korean Conflict and Res. Mem: Comdr, Am. Legion Dept. Kans, 54-55; pres, Ft. Hays Kans. State Col. Alumni Asn, 54; v.pres, Kans. Reclamation Asn, 59-; Mason; Shrine; Lions; Am. Legion; DAV; VFW; Odd Fellows. Rel: Methodist. Legal Res: 602 W. Wilberforce, Norton, Kans. 67654. Mailing Add: 1117 Longworth House Office Bldg, Washington, D.C. 20515.

SEBENS, RAYMOND WILLARD D
b. Milnor, N.Dak, 10/9/25; s. William P. Sebens and Mildred Bunnell S; m. 8/14/64 to Janet Benedict; c. Mark, Todd and Karen. Educ: Univ. Calif, Los Angeles, B.A, 49. Polit. & Govt. Pos: Admin. asst. to U.S. Rep. George A. Kasem, 59-60; admin. asst. to Calif. State Assemblyman George Brown, 61-62; admin. asst. to U.S. Rep. George E. Brown, Jr, Calif, 63- Bus. & Prof. Pos: Ed, El Monte Press, Calif, 53-54; self-employed, lettershop, pub. rels, 55-58. Mil. Serv: Entered as Aviation Cadet, Army Air Corps, 43, released as 2nd Lt, 45. Legal Res: Calif. Mailing Add: 2927 Lawrence Dr, Falls Church, Va. 22042.

SEBO, WALTER J. R
Chmn, Fulton Co. Rep. Cent. Cmt, Ill.
b. Chicago, Ill, 12/8/18; s. Louis Sebo and Anna Pavco S; m. 11/22/42 to Doris O. Schuette; c. Renee L, Adele E. and Thomas J. Educ: Univ. Ill, B.S, 47; Univ. Ill. Law Sch, J.D, 50. Polit. & Govt. Pos: Clerk, Third Appellate Dist, Ill, 56-58; Asst. States Attorney, Fulton Co, 57-60, Pub. Defender, 60-; mem. sch. bd, Canton Union Sch. Dist. 66, 64-, pres. sch. bd, 68-69; chmn, Fulton Co. Rep. Cent. Cmt, 67- Bus. & Prof. Pos: Practicing attorney, 50- Mil. Serv: Entered as Pvt, Air Force, 41, released as 1st Lt, 45, after serv. in ETO, 44; Distinguished Flying Cross; Air Medal with Three Oak Leaf Clusters. Mem: Am. and Ill. State Bar Asns; Trial Lawyers Asn; Pub. Defenders Asn; Dist. Attorneys Asn; Am. Legion; Elks. Rel: Lutheran. Legal Res: 980 N. Main, Canton, Ill. 61520. Mailing Add: 122 N. Ave. A, Canton, Ill. 61520.

SEBREE, WILLIAM T. D
Polit. & Govt. Pos: Ind. State Rep, 61-66. Bus. & Prof. Pos: Teacher. Mil. Serv: Army. Mem: Exchange Club; Am. Legion; Amvets; Am. Fedn. of Teachers. Rel: Church of God. 1967 Legal Res: 332 W. Eighth St, Anderson, Ind. No mailing address available. (1967)

SEBRELL, LORIN B. R
Del. State Rep.
Educ: Mt. Union Col, B.S; Univ. Wis, M.S; Ohio State Univ, Ph.D. Polit. & Govt. Pos: Del. State Rep, 67- Bus. & Prof. Pos: Research consultant; research dir, Int. Latex Corp. and Goodyear Tire & Rubber Co, Akron, Ohio. Mailing Add: 229 N. State St, Dover, Del. 19901. (1967)

SECREST, ROBERT THOMPSON D
Ohio State Sen.
b. Senecaville, Ohio, 1/22/04. Educ: Muskingum Col, A.B, 26; Wash, D.C. Col. of Law, LL.B, 40; Columbia Univ, M.A. in polit. sci, 43; Naval Sch. of Mil. Govt. Columbia Univ, grad, 43; Brit. Sch. of Civil Affairs, Wimbledon, Eng, 43. Hon. LL.D, Muskingum Col, 55; hon. Bachelor of Commerce, Bliss Col, 63. Polit. & Govt. Pos: Mem, Ohio Legis, 31-32; U.S. Rep, Ohio, 33-42, 48-54 & 63-66; mem, Fed. Trade Cmn, 54-61; dir. of commerce, Ohio, 62; Ohio State Sen, 69- Bus. & Prof. Pos: Prin, Senecaville High Sch, 26-31; supt. of schs, Murray City, Ohio, 31-32. Mil. Serv: Navy, Comdr, 42-46; served in Eng, Africa, Italy and 1 year on Adm. Nimitz's staff in Pac. as mil. govt. officer. Mem: Former Past Comdr. and life mem, Senecaville Am. Legion Post 747; life mem, Amvets, VFW, and Regular Vet. Asn; 40 et 8. Mailing Add: Route 1, Cambridge, Ohio 43725.

SECREST, T. L. R
Chmn, N.Dak. Rep. State Cmt.
b. Paris, Tex, 3/16/27; m. 6/3/51 to Barbara; c. Bruce and Brenda. Educ: Dickinson State Col, three years; Univ. N.Dak, Ph.B. and J.D, 56. Polit. & Govt. Pos: Chmn, N.Dak. Rep. State Cmt, 65- Bus. & Prof. Pos: Attorney-at-law. Rel: Congregational. Legal Res: Hettinger, N.Dak. 58639.

SEDGWICK, HAROLD THOMAS R
b. Lincoln, Nebr, 5/9/99; m. to Bessie; c. two. Educ: Univ. of Nebr. Polit. & Govt. Pos: Mem, Elem. Sch. Bd, 16 years; mem, adv. bd, Chico State Col, Calif, 50-; mayor, Oroville, 8 years; Calif. State Sen, 55-66. Bus. & Prof. Pos: Operates a group of retail stores in North. Calif. Mil. Serv: Army, World War I. Mem: Rotary Club; Elks; Fellows Club; Mason; Shrine; Eagles; C. of C. Mailing Add: 1015 F St, Marysville, Calif. 95901.

SEDILLO, FILO M. D
Chief Asst. Dist. Attorney, Valencia Co, N.Mex.
b. Albuquerque, N.Mex, 12/14/08; s. Antonio A. Sedillo and Tula Vigil S; m. 6/15/34 to Emily Page; c. Filo M, Jr, Raul Abad and Sonia (Mrs. Tony James). Educ: St. Louis Univ, 2 years; Univ. Va, 1 year; Nat. Law Sch, LL.B, 33; Beta Theta Pi. Polit. & Govt. Pos: Mem, N.Mex. Dem. State Cent. Cmt, 35-; Attorney Gen, N.Mex, 39-40; city attorney, Belen, 42-48; chmn, Valencia Co. Dem. Party, 42-; attorney and chief clerk, U.S. Senate Pub. Works Cmt, 55-59; chief asst. dist. attorney, Valencia Co, N.Mex, 61-; del, Dem. Nat. Conv, 68. Bus. & Prof. Pos: Dir, Belen Savings & Loan Asn, 64- Mem: Elks. Legal Res: 402 N. Fifth St, Belen, N.Mex. 87002. Mailing Add: P.O. Box 495, Belen, N.Mex. 87002.

SEDITA, FRANK A. D
Mayor, Buffalo, N.Y.
b. New Orleans, La, 6/20/07; m. to Sarah; c. Paulette and Frank Jr. Educ: Canisius Col; Univ. of Buffalo Law Sch, LL.B, 31. Polit. & Govt. Pos: Asst, Corp. Counsel, Buffalo, N.Y, 35-38; secy, Buffalo Div. of Water, 38-41; clerk, Buffalo City Court, 41-47; first dep, Erie Co. Surrogate's Court, 47-49; Buffalo City Court, 49-57; mayor, Buffalo, 58-61 & 66-; del, Dem. Nat. Conv, 68. Mailing Add: 20 Colonial Circle, Buffalo, N.Y. 11209.

SEE, CHARLES MELBERTH R
b. Cumberland, Md, 5/12/02; s. Amos E. See and Bessie Keller S; m. 9/3/41 to Margielea Stonestreet. Educ: Md. Sch. for the Blind, 24. Polit. & Govt. Pos: Md. State Del, 39-54 & 62-67; Md. State Sen, 55-62. Bus. & Prof. Pos: Former piano tuner and repairer; employee, Md. Workshop for the Blind, West. Md. Br, since 39, dir, currently. Mem: Elks; Eagles; Knights of Malta; Lions; S. Cumberland Bus. & Civic Asn; Tuberc. Asn; Friends Aware of Handicapped Children; Cmn. on the Aging; bd. trustees, Md. Workshop for the Blind; Md. Poetry Soc, Inc. Rel: Episcopal. Mailing Add: 508 Forster Ave, Cumberland, Md. 21502.

SEELY, ROBERT D. R
Chmn, Goodhue Co. Rep. Party, Minn.
b. Decatur, Ill, 10/8/26; s. Kenneth Dwight Seely and Audrian Fisher S; m.

8/26/46 to Irene Davidson; c. Christina (Mrs. Gilfillan), Joe and Trisha. Educ: S.Dak. State Univ, 1 year; Univ. Minn, 1 year; Sigma Nu. Polit. & Govt. Pos: Co. chmn, Goldwater Cmt, Goodhue Co, Minn, 64; chmn, Goodhue Co. Rep. Party, 64-; dist. chmn, Pillsbury Cmt, 66; Goodhue Co. del, Minn. State Rep. Cent. Cmt, 69. Bus. & Prof. Pos: Pres, Bob Seely Ford Co, 54- Mil. Serv: Pvt, Army, 44-45. Mem: Nat. Automobile Dealers Asn; Mason; Zumbrota Commercial Club; Toastmasters. Rel: Lutheran. Mailing Add: 643 Second Ave, Zumbrota, Minn. 55992.

SEER, EDNA ELEANOR D
Exec. Secy, Milwaukee Co. Dem. Party, Wis.
b. Milwaukee, Wis, 2/21/09; d. Mannie Kloth and Nelda Bub K; wid; c. Nelda (Mrs. Madison) and Donald M. Stahl. Educ: Bus. Admn, 2 years. Polit. & Govt. Pos: Chmn, Ward Unit Dem. Party, 51-54; exec. secy, Milwaukee Co. Dem. Party, Wis, 53-; chmn, Sen. Dist, Dem. Party, 54-56; del, Dem. Nat. Conv, 60, 64 & 68. Mem: Office Workers and Prfnl. Int. Local 9, AFL-CIO. Rel: Baptist and Disciples of Christ. Mailing Add: 1767 N. Cambridge Ave, Apt. 11, Milwaukee, Wis. 53202.

SEERGY, EDMUND GEORGE R
Leader, 49th Assembly Dist. Regular Rep. Club, Inc, Brooklyn, N.Y.
b. New York, N.Y, 6/2/21; s. Elias Seergy and Afifee Janan S; m. 6/30/56 to Jean Marie Hines; c. Joan Marie, Barbara and Carolyn. Educ: Thermo Air Conditioning Inst, 40; Army Air Force Cent. Instrs. Sch, 44. Polit. & Govt. Pos: Leader, 49th Assembly Dist. Regular Rep. Club, Inc, Brooklyn, N.Y, 54-; del, Rep. Nat. Conv, 64, alternate del, 68. Bus. & Prof. Pos: Dist. mgr, nat. account, Frigidaire Div, Gen. Motors Corp, 48-56; v.pres. sales, Typhoon Air Conditioning Div, Hupp Corp, 56- Mil. Serv: Entered as Aviation Cadet, Army Air Force, released as 1st Lt, 44, after serv. in 460th Bomb Group, ETO; Distinguished Flying Cross with Oak Leaf Cluster; Air Medal with 3 Oak Leaf Clusters; Purple Heart; European Theater Ribbon with 3 Battle Stars; Presidential Citation; Conspicuous Serv. Cross of N.Y. State. Mem: Am. Soc. of Heating, Refrigerating & Air Conditioning Engrs; Ft. Hamilton Officers Club; K. of C; Archbishop John Hughes Coun; Am. Legion; CWV. Stamp and coin collector; recipient of 6 medals for track in the Air Force and High Sch. Rel: Roman Catholic. Mailing Add: 34 Colonial Court, Brooklyn, N.Y. 11209.

SEGURA, PERRY D
Committeeman, La. Dem. State Cmt.
b. New Iberia, La, 12/14/29; s. Paul F. Segura and Levie Broussard S; m. 12/26/50 to Emma Lou Dauant; c. Perry James, II, Christopher Antony, Thérèse Mary, David Charles and Coleen Mary. Educ: Univ. Southwest. La, 47-50; La. State Univ, B.S, 54; Ta Beta Pi. Polit. & Govt. Pos: Committeeman, Iberia Parish Dem. Cmt, La, 62-; del, Dem. Nat. Conv, 68; committeeman, La. Dem. State Cmt, Dist. Seven, 68- Bus. & Prof. Pos: Architect, Perry Segura & Assoc, 56-; farmer, Angel Acres Breeding Farm, 62- Mil. Serv: Entered as Pvt, La. Nat. Guard, 48, released as S/Sgt, 52. Mem: Am. Inst. of Architects; La. Architects Asn; Kiwanis; K. of C; Farm Bur. Rel: Catholic. Mailing Add: P.O. Box 1300, New Iberia, La. 70560.

SEIBEL, ALBERT EDGAR R
N.Dak. State Rep.
b. Harvey, N.Dak, 6/16/16; s. Christ J. Seibel and Matilda Schmidt S; m. 8/21/38 to Lorraine Schmidt; c. Sharon Rae (Mrs. Larry Womble), Kirby, Myrna and David. Educ: Minot State Col, 45-46; Polit. & Govt. Pos: Mem, sch. bd, Martin Sch, N.Dak, 48-56; alderman, Martin, N.Dak, 65-; N.Dak. State Rep, Dist, 14, 66- Mem: Gideons Int. Rel: Protestant. Mailing Add: Martin, N.Dak. 58758.

SEIBEL, MARION IRMA R
Del. State Rep.
b. Fond Du Lac, Wis, 1/31/22; d. Simon Albert Arthur and Irma W. Spielberg A; m. 9/11/43 to John Parshall Seibel; c. Susan M, John Henry and Richard James. Educ: Fond Du Lac Senior High Sch, grad. Polit. & Govt. Pos: Committeewoman, Delaware Rep. Party, 59-; pres, Suburban Rep. Womens Club, 60-64; campaign coordinator for Snowden for Congress, 64; mgr, Second Dist. Rep. Cmt, 65-68; mem. Exec. Bd, Del. Federation of Rep. Women, 66; Del. State Rep, 68- Mem: League of Women Voters; YWCA; PTA. Rel: United Methodist. Mailing Add: 20 Knickerbocker Dr, Newark, Del. 19711.

SEIBERT, GEORGE H. R
Minority Leader, W.Va. House of Del.
b. Wheeling, W.Va, 2/27/13; s. George H. Seibert and Grace C. Smith S; m. 7/18/39 to Janice Boone; c. Nancy Sue, James Edward and Sally Ann. Educ: W.Va. Univ, A.B. and LL.B; Phi Sigma Kappa; Phi Alpha. Polit. & Govt. Pos: Former munic. judge and former mem. bd. of gov, Wheeling, W.Va; W.Va. State Del, 52-, Minority Leader, W.Va. House of Del, 57- Bus. & Prof. Pos: Lawyer. Mil. Serv: 39 months in armed forces. Mem: Ohio Co, W.Va. and Am. Bar Asns; W.Va. State Bar; Mason (32°); Shrine; Am. Legion. Rel: Presbyterian. Mailing Add: 1684 National Rd, Wheeling, W.Va. 26003. (1967)

SEINER, JAMES CALVIN D
Chmn, Polk Co. Dem. Cmt, Mo.
b. Aldrich, Mo, 6/1/01; s. George Lee Seiner and Eliza Waggoner S; m. 2/22/40 to Mary Ernestine Parsons. Educ: High sch. Polit. & Govt. Pos: Chmn, Polk Co. Dem. Cmt, Mo, 53- Mem: Former mem. bd. of dirs, Am. Angus Asn; pres, Southwest Mo. Angus Breeders Asn, 53; pres, Ozark Empire Angus Breeders Asn, 54 and dir, 54- Rel: Christian Church. Mailing Add: Route 2, Bolivar, Mo. 65613. (1967)

SEITER, ROBERT FRANKLIN D
Chmn, Cent. Cmt, Greene Co. Dem. Party, Ohio
b. Connersville, Ind, 9/2/23; s. Franklin A. Seiter and Winifred Casey S; m. 7/7/45 to Jeannette Marie Hibbert; c. Joseph Vincent, Jeffrey Christopher, Robert Franklin, Jr, Matthew Gerard, Timothy Francis and Mary Jeannette. Educ: Univ. Dayton, B.A, 51; Upsilon Delta Sigma. Polit. & Govt. Pos: Chmn, Cent. Cmt, Greene Co. Dem. Party, Ohio, 69- Bus. & Prof. Pos: Owner, Ins. Assocs, Xenia, Ohio, 49- Mil. Serv: Entered as Pvt, Army, 43, released as Capt, 47, after serv. in 76th Inf. Div, Co. A, 417th Inf. and others, Am-European-Asiatic Theatres, 43-47; Capt, Ohio Nat. Guard, 51-52; Bronze Star with V; Oak Leaf Cluster; Combat Infantryman Badge; Theater Awards; Battle Stars. Mem: Nat. and Ohio Asns. of Ins. Agents; Am. Legion; K. of C. Outstanding Young Man, Xenia, Ohio, 56; One of Five Outstanding Young Men in Ohio, 57; Paul Revere Award, Ohio Asn. Ins. Agents, 65. Rel: Roman Catholic. Mailing Add: 1096 Woodland Dr, Xenia, Ohio 45385.

SELBY, MARY N. D
Mem, Calif. Dem. State Cent. Cmt.
b. Childress, Tex, 5/18/28; d. Edward D. Morris and Georgia E. DeShazo M. div. Educ: West Texas State Univ, 46-48. Polit. & Govt. Pos: Mem, Calif. Dem. State Cent. Cmt, 68- Mem: VFW Auxiliary (pres. and secy, 3 years); Am. Legion Auxiliary (pres, secy. and dist. secy); USW (grievance Rep. and secy, clerical & tech. local). Rel: Baptist. Mailing Add: 9910 Juniper St, Fontana, Calif. 92335.

SELDEN, ARMISTEAD I, JR. D
b. Greensboro, Ala, 2/20/21; m. 1948 to Mary Jane Wright; c. Martee Graham, Armistead I, III, Jack Wright, Edith Cobbs and Thomas Lawson. Educ: Univ. of the South, A.B, 42; Univ. of Ala, LL.B, 48; Phi Delta Phi; Blue Key; Omicron Delta Kappa; Sigma Alpha Epsilon. Polit. & Govt. Pos: Ala. State Rep, 50-52; U.S. Rep, Ala, 53-69. Bus. & Prof. Pos: Lawyer; sr. partner, Boykin, De Francis & Selden, Wash, D.C, 69- Mil. Serv: Navy, Lt, 42-46; served 31 months aboard ship, primarily in N. Atlantic; Capt, Naval Res. Mem: Ala. and Am. Bar Asns; Am. Legion; VFW; Rotary Int; v.chmn, Cmt. on Inter-Am. Bar Rels, Bar Asn. of D.C. Rel: Episcopal. Legal Res: Greensboro, Ala. Mailing Add: 2600 Virginia Ave. N.W, Suite 812, Washington, D.C. 20037.

SELDIN, ABE R
b. N.Y.C, 6/15/23; married; c. four. Educ: Queens Col, N.Y, 41; Princeton Univ, spec. courses, 42; Phi Epsilon Pi. Polit. & Govt. Pos: New Hyde Park exec. area chmn, Nassau Co. Rep. Finance Cmt, N.Y, 52-; Rep. committeeman, 16th Elec. Dist, North Hempstead, 53-; del. and alternate del, Rep. State Conv, 54, 58, 62 & 66; New Hyde Park chmn and v.chmn, North Hempstead Rep. Year Book Cmt, 54-; mem, Bd. of Zoning and Appeals, North Hempstead, 58-65; co. and town exec. committeeman, New Hyde Park Exec. Area, 64-; del, Judicial Conf, 66; N.Y. State Assemblyman, 17th Dist, 66, mem, pensions, pub. serv. and taxation cmts; N.Y. State Assembly; North Hempstead chmn, Nassau Co. Rep. Victory Reception, 66 & 67; v.chmn, North Hempstead Rep. Cmt, 67; fifth sen. dist. del, N.Y. State Constitutional Conv, mem, cmts. on legis. and health, housing and soc. serv; chmn, Study Cmt. for Revision of Discrimination Clause in New York State Constitution, 68; Rep. cand, U.S. House of Rep, third dist, 68; mem, North New Hyde Park Rep. Club; mem. and chmn, various cmts, New Hyde Park Rep. Club; appointed by Nassau Co. Rep. Conf. to study water resources and anti-pollution measures and to review the problems of mental retardation; appointed by the minority leader to develop Rep. position on welfare problems in the state of N.Y; mem, adv. coun, Joint Legis. Cmt. on Consumer Protection, N.Y. State Legis; mem, adv. cmt, Constitutional Changes for Fifth Sen. Dist. Bus. & Prof. Pos: Co-owner, Gen. Ins. Agency, Mineola, N.Y, 46-; organizer and dir, State Bank of L.I. Mil. Serv: Army Air Force, ETO. Mem: Various ins. and other bus. orgn; Comdr, Post 90, Jewish War Veterans, 50, N.Y. state exec. committeeman and Nat. Americanism Cmn; Queens Co. brotherhood chmn, all veterans organizations; Am. Legion; B'nai B'rith; Elks; L.I. Athletic Club, Inc; chmn, fund raising drives, Fedn. of Jewish Philanthropies, Israel Bonds, Reformed Judaism Appeal and United Jewish Appeal; New Hyde Park chmn, fund raising drives, Asn. for the Help of Retarded Children, Red Cross, Cancer and commun. leader for cerebral palsy fund drives; active in drives for Boy Scouts, Girl Scouts, Heart Fund, Cath. Charities and Maryhaven Sch. for Exceptional Children; pres, Hillside Heights Civic Asn, 53; chmn, youth cmt, New Hyde Park Kiwanis; coached Merrillon Little League; Cub Scout Pack committeeman and Boy Scout committeeman-at-lg; Boy Scout Neighborhood cmnr, 65. Cited by Fedn. of Jewish Philanthropies, Israel Bonds, Reformed Judaism Appeal, United Jewish Appeal and Nat. Conf. of Christians and Jews for brotherhood activities. Rel: Jewish; Trustee and past pres. and v.pres, Temple Emanuel, New Hyde Park, N.Y. Mailing Add: 46 Camden Place, New Hyde Park, N.Y. 11040.

SELF, EARL BURDELL D
b. Subligna, Ga, 11/19/23; s. Eric Basil Self and Cora Manning S; m. 4/22/60 to Bertha M. Kellett. Educ: Berry Col, 41-43; Univ. Ga, LL.B, 49; Phi Kappa Phi; Delta Theta Phi. Polit. & Govt. Pos: City recorder, Summerville, Ga, 50-52 and city attorney, 55-60; chmn, Chattooga Co. Dem. Cmt, 50-; solicitor gen, Lookout Mountain Judicial Circuit, 52- Bus. & Prof. Pos: Attorney-at-Law, Summerville, Ga, 49- Mil. Serv: Entered as A/S, Navy, 43, released as Aviation Fire Controlman 1/C, 46. Mem: Lookout Mountain and Ga. Bar Asns; pres, Solicitor General's Asn. of Ga, 62-63; Nat. Dist. Attorney's Asn; Am. Legion; VFW; Lions; Elks; Mason; Farm Bur. Rel: Baptist. Legal Res: Route 2, Summerville, Ga. 30747. Mailing Add: Box 192, Summerville, Ga. 30747.

SELF, JOHN SPENCER D
b. Greene Co, Ill, 3/2/21; s. Marion Spencer Self and Mary Z. Talkington S; m. 12/24/45 to Mary Jane Goeins; c. Kathy Ann (Mrs. Hart) and Michael G. Educ: Ill. Col, B.A, 43; Wash. Univ, LL.B, 48, J.D, 68; Phi Delta Phi; Sigma Pi. Polit. & Govt. Pos: City attorney, Jerseyville, Ill, 50-52; judge, Jersey Co, 52-62; asst. attorney gen, 66-69. Mil. Serv: Entered as Pvt, Army, 42, released as Sgt, 46, after serv. in Ninth Weather Group, Air Force, Am. Theatre. Mem: Jersey Co, Ill. State and TRL Co. Bar Asns; Mason; Consistory; Shrine; Am. Legion; 40 et 8; VFW; Elks; C. of C. DeMolay Legion of Honor, 61. Rel: Baptist. Mailing Add: 400 Harrison, Jerseyville, Ill. 62052.

SELIGMAN, HOWARD L. R
Mem, Calif. Rep. State Cent. Cmt.
b. Washington, D.C, 7/30/36; s. Arthur Seligman and Ida Buxbaum S; m. 11/29/64 to Cyrildean Stone; c. Kathryn Ann and Brian Arthur. Educ: Univ. Calif, Berkeley, A.B, 57, Boalt Law Sch, J.D, 60; Phi Alpha Delta. Polit. & Govt. Pos: Chmn, San Joaquin Young Rep, Calif, 61; asst. counsel, Calif. State Young Rep, 62; mem. bd. dirs, Calif. Rep. Assembly, 63-; mem, Calif.

Rep. State Cent. Cmt, 63-; mem. city coun, Stockton, Calif, 63-67 and Charter Rev. Cmn, 68-69. Bus. & Prof. Pos: Attorney with John Wilson, 61 and William H. Dick, 62-64; attorney-at-law, 64-; teacher polit. sci, night sch, Delta Jr. Col, currently. Mil. Serv: SP6, Army Res, 55-63. Mem: Kiwanis; Jr. C. of C; 20-30 Club; W. Lane Tennis Club; Univ. Calif. Alumni Asn; Stockton Symphony Asn; Commonwealth Club of Calif. Rel: Jewish. Mailing Add: 1676 W. Poplar, Stockton, Calif. 95203.

SELIN, IVAN

Acting Asst. Secy. of Defense for Systs. Anal.
b. New York City, N.Y, 3/11/37; s. Saul Selin and Freida Kuhlman S; m. 6/8/57 to Nina Evvie Cantor; c. Douglas Scott and Jessica Beth. Educ: Yale Univ, B.E, 57, M.E, 58, Ph.D, 60; Fulbright Scholar, Univ. Paris, Ph.D, 62; Sigma Xi; Tau Beta Pi. Polit. & Govt. Pos: Radar and space defense analyst, systs. anal, Off. of Secy. of Defense, 65, dir. strategic retaliatory div, 65-67, Dep. Asst. Secy. of Defense for Systs. Anal, 67-69, Acting Asst. Secy. of Defense for Systs. Anal, 69- Bus. & Prof. Pos: Engr, Melpar Inc, Calif, 59-60; research engr, Rand Corp, Santa Monica, 60-65. Publ: Detection Theory, Princeton Univ. Press, 65. Mem: Inst. Elec. and Electronics Eng.(Ed, Group on Info. Theory Abstracts). Rel: Jewish. Mailing Add: 518 G. St. S.W, Washington, D.C. 20024.

SELIN, VIRGINIA MAE D

Chmn, Marquette Co. Dem. Party, Mich.
b. Lewiston, Mich, 6/18/20; d. John G. Golden and Goldie Lasker G; m. 4/12/63 to Leslie H. Selin; c. Judy Spelman, Jill (Mrs. David Prosten), Marcy (Mrs. Stuart Steinberg), Karen and Wendy. Educ: Univ. of Mich, B.A, 41. Polit. & Govt. Pos: Trainee clerk, War Food Admin, Dept. of Agr, Wash, D.C, 42; off. mgr, Tenth Cong. Dist. Va. Campaign, 58; secy. to Sen. Richard Neuberger, Ore, 59; exec. secy. to Sen. Harrison Williams, N.J, 60-63; chmn, Marquette Co. Dem. Cmt, Mich, 67-; del, Dem. Nat. Conv, 68; v.chmn, Mich. Polit. Reform Cmn, 69. Rel: Jewish. Mailing Add: 8 Marquette Dr, Marquette, Mich. 49855.

SELKIRK, RUSSELL R

b. Selkirk, N.Y, 10/20/05; m. to Mildred Boughton; c. John, Robert and Anne (Mrs. William R. Tauzel, Jr). Educ: Albany High Sch. Polit. & Govt. Pos: Chmn, Schoharie Co. Soil Conserv. Dist, N.Y, 4 years; supvr, Cobleskill, 40-47; N.Y. State Assemblyman, 58-66. Bus. & Prof. Pos: With N.Y. Power and Light Corp, 29-35; pres, Selkirk Hardware Inc, which he establ. in 1935; dir, Cobleskill Savings & Loan Asn; dir. and v.pres, Sterling Ins. Co. Mem: Bd. of gov. and pres, Nat. Retail Hardware Asn; former pres, N.Y. State Retail Hardware Asn; adv. cmt, Bus. Tech. Div, State Univ. Agr. and Tech. Inst, Cobleskill; bd. dirs, Hosp. Educ. and Research Fund, Inc; former pres, N.Y. State Coun. of Retail Merchants; Asn. of Towns, N.Y; former Small Bus. Adv. Coun. to Legis; Cobleskill State Sch; Grange; Schoharie Co. Farm Bur; former pres, Cobleskill C. of C; Commun. Hosp. of Schoharie Co; Cobleskill Rotary; Cobleskill Golf and Country Club; F&AM; Elks. Rel: Methodist; Trustee, Cobleskill Methodist Church. Mailing Add: 8 Washington Ave, Cobleskill, N.Y. 12043. (1967)

SELLARS, RICHARD B. R

b. Worcester, Mass, 9/9/15; s. Frank H. Sellars, Jr. and Ruth Miller S; m. to Doris Sophia Johnson; c. Richard B, Jr, Peter Carl, Christine and Carolyn. Educ: Am. Int. Col, Springfield, Mass, 33-34; Maryville Col, Maryville, Tenn, 34-35. Polit. & Govt. Pos: Rep. Nat. Committeeman, N.J. and treas, Rep. Nat. Cmt, 62-64. Bus. & Prof. Pos: Bd. of dirs, Johnson & Johnson. Mem: Young Presidents Orgn; Somerset Co. Park Cmt; U.S. Cmt. of World Med. Asn. Mailing Add: Brady Dr, Peapack, N.J. 07977. (1967)

SELLECK, HAROLD C. R

b. Sudbury, Vt, 6/28/93; m. to Stella L. Jones; c. One son (deceased); two daughters. Educ: Brandon High Sch. Polit. & Govt. Pos: Asst. town clerk, Brandon, Vt, 40-; Justice of Peace; Vt. State Rep, 53-55 & 65-67. Bus. & Prof. Pos: Retired farmer. Mem: Mason; St. Paul's 25, Brandon; Marble Chap. 80, Eastern Star. Mailing Add: R.F.D. 1, Brandon, Vt. 05733. (1967)

SELLERS, JOHN DEWEY R

Chmn, Brunswick Co. Rep. Party, N.C.
b. Supply, N.C, 7/20/12; s. John Winslow Sellers and Milie S; m. 12/23/39 to Reba Myra Evans. Educ: Shallotte High Sch, 3 years. Polit. & Govt. Pos: Precinct chmn, Rep. Party, Brunswick, N.C, 64-68; chmn, Brunswick Co. Rep. Party, 68- Bus. & Prof. Pos: Rwy. car inspector, Wilmington Transportation Dept, 40- Mem: BRCA; Farm Bur. Orgn. Rel: Baptist. Mailing Add: Route 1, Box 9, Supply, N.C. 28462.

SELLIE, JOHN MARTIN R

Chmn, 14th Legis. Dist. Rep. Party, N.Dak.
b. Fessenden, N.Dak, 5/15/27; s. Con Sellie and Oline Ingvaldson S; m. 6/9/52 to Carol Joan Wammer; c. Karen and Peter John. Educ: Fessenden High Sch, N.Dak, 41-45. Polit. & Govt. Pos: Charter mem, Wells Co. Young Rep. Exec. Cmt, N.Dak, 58-62; chmn, Wells Co. Rep. Party, 62-67; mem. bd, Hamburg Twp, 62-68, chmn. bd, 67-68; chmn, 14th Legis. Dist. Rep. Party, 67-; mem. exec. cmt, N.Dak. Rep. Party, 68- Bus. & Prof. Pos: Farmer and rancher. Mil. Serv: Seaman Recruit, Navy, 52-54. Mem: New Rockford Toastmasters (past pres); N.Dak. Farm Bur; N.Dak. Stockmans Asn; U.S. Durum Growers Asn; C-400 Club, Concordia Col, Moorhead, Minn. Second Place Award in Wells Co. Soil Conserv. Contest, 64. Rel: Lutheran; Secy. of Stewardship Cmt, East. N.Dak. Dist. of Am. Lutheran Church. Mailing Add: R.R, Cathay, N.Dak. 58422.

SELMAN, EDWIN WILLIAM, JR. D

Chmn, Steuben Co. Dem. Party, Ind.
b. Ames, Iowa, 6/9/33; s. Edwin W. Selman, Sr. and Francis Rea S; m. 1960 to Betty Ann Tolly; c. Edwin W, III and Thomas Hugh. Educ: St. Ambrose Col, $2\frac{1}{2}$ years; Gov. Club. Polit. & Govt. Pos: Chmn, Steuben Co. Dem. Party, Ind, 65-; treas, Fourth Dist. Dem. Party, 67; field rep, Ind. Dem. State Cmt. Bus. & Prof. Pos: Partner, Selman Heating & Plumbing, 60- Mil. Serv: Entered as Pfc, Army, 53, released 55, after serv. in 11th Airborne Div; Parachute Badge. Mem: Jr. C. of C. Mailing Add: 515 E. Gale St, Angola, Ind. 46703.

SELSTAD, TOM AARON R

Mont. State Sen.
b. Dutton, Mont, 3/8/27; s. Thomas Selstad and Esther Aamodt S; m. 6/11/50 to Elnore Marie Smith; c. Scott, Spencer and Sherman. Educ: Univ. Mont, B.A. in educ, 50; Univ. Wash, grad. work, 52; Phi Delta Theta. Polit. & Govt. Pos: Mont. State Rep, 62-66; Mont. State Sen, 67-; Rep. nominee for Lt. Gov, 68. Bus. & Prof. Pos: Pres, Selstad Soil Serv. and Triple S Ranch, currently. Mem: Optimists; Farm Bur; dir, YMCA; Am. Legion. Rel: Lutheran. Mailing Add: 133 29th Ave. N.W, Great Falls, Mont. 59401.

SELTZER, H. JACK R

Pa. State Rep.
b. Phila, Pa, 8/12/22; s. Harvey L. Seltzer and Jennie Behmer S; m. to Geneva Shepherd; c. Four. Educ: Palmyra Schs; Harrisburg Acad; Mercersburg Acad. Polit. & Govt. Pos: Former chmn, Lebanon Co. Rep. Finance Cmt, Pa; mem, Lebanon Co. Rep. Exec. Cmt; mem, Palmyra Borough Coun, 7 years, pres, 5 years; Pa. State Rep, 56- Bus. & Prof. Pos: Mfr. Mil. Serv: Navy, 42-46, S.Pac. Mem: VFW; Am. Legion. Mailing Add: 229 S. Forage Rd, Palmyra, Pa. 17078. (1967)

SELYA, BRUCE MARSHALL R

Mem. Exec. Cmt, R.I. Rep. State Cent. Cmt.
b. Providence, R.I, 5/27/34; s. Herman Charles Selya and Betty Brier S; m. 2/24/65 to Ellen Barnes; c. Dawn Meredith and Lori Ann. Educ: Harvard Col, A.B. magna cum laude, 55; Harvard Law Sch, LL.B, 58; John Harvard Scholar; Young Rep; UN Coun; Eliot House. Polit. & Govt. Pos: Law clerk, U.S. Dist. Court, R.I, 58-60; mem, Providence Rep. City Cmt, 60-65; mem, Providence Rep. Second Ward Cmt, 60-65; secy, R.I. Judicial Coun, 64-; legal counsel, R.I. Rep. State Cent. Cmt, 65-68, mem. and mem. exec. cmt, 65-; mem, Lincoln Rep. Town Cmt, 65-; judge, Probate Court, 66-; mem, R.I. Crime Cmn, 67-68; chmn, 58th Rep. Dist. Cmt, 67-; del, Rep. Nat. Conv, 68. Bus. & Prof. Pos: Attorney and partner, Gunning & La Fazia, 60- Publ: Various articles for legal periodicals. Mem: Am. and R.I. Bar Asns; R.I. Defense Counsel Asn; Am. Jurisp. Soc. Rel: Jewish. Legal Res: 19 Kirkbrae Dr, Lincoln, R.I. 02865. Mailing Add: 533 Industrial Bank Bldg, Providence, R.I. 02903.

SEMANS, MARY DUKE BIDDLE TRENT D

b. New York, N.Y, 2/21/20; d. Joseph Drexel Bibble and Mary Lillian Duke B; m. 10/17/52 to Dr. James Hustead Semans; c. Mary Duke, Sarah Elizabeth, Rebecca Grey, Barbara Biddle, Jenny Lillian, James Duke Biddle, Trent and Elizabeth Gotham. Educ: Duke Univ, A.B, 51; Kappa Alpha Theta. Polit. & Govt. Pos: Mem, City Coun, Durham, N.C, 51-55, mayor pro tem, 53-55; mem, N.C. Dem. State Exec. Cmt, 55-58; alternate del, Dem. Nat. Conv, 56; mem, Human Rels. Cmt, 57-; chmn, Cmt. on Living Arrangements, Gov. N.C. Conf. on Aging, 60; Educ. White House Conf. on Aging, 61; mem, Nat. Adv. Coun. on Voc Rehabilitation, 61-; chmn, Exec. Mansion Fine Arts Cmt, 65-; chmn, Gov. Study Cmn. on Voc. Rehabilitation, 67-69. Bus. & Prof. Pos: Chmn, Duke Univ. Friends of the Libr, Mary Duke Biddle Found; trustee, Duke Endowment, N.Y.C, Duke Univ. and Shaw Univ; mem, N.C. Libr. Bd, 58-61; mem. bd. dirs, N.C. Mus. of Art, 61- and N.C. Nat. Bank, Durham, 62-; pres, Durham Homes, Inc, 69- Mem: Durham Chap, Hadasah, 60; League of Women Voters; Bus. & Prfnl. Clubs; Altrusa Club; Durham Woman's Club; chmn, Durham Commun. Chest, 52; pres, Durham United Fund, 53. Mother of the Year Award, Durham, 52; Citizen of the Year Award, Durham C. of C, 58; Humanitarian-Freedom Award (with husband), Durham Chap, Hadassah, 60. Rel: Methodist; mem. bd. trustees. Legal Res: Durham, N.C. Mailing Add: The Duke Endowment, 30 Rockefeller Plaza, New York, N.Y. 10020.

SEMENSI, JOSEPH JOHN D

Mass. State Rep.
b. Randolph, Mass, 3/6/23; s. Lawrence Semensi and Louise Cicolari S; m. 1/12/46 to Lillian Josephine Lola; c. Linda Louise, Joseph John, Jr. and Valerie Jean. Polit. & Govt. Pos: Mem, Sch. Cmt, Randolph, Mass, 48-50, town clerk, selectman, town treas. and mem. Dem. Town Cmt, 51-66; Mass. State Rep, 67- Mil. Serv: Entered as Pvt, Army, 43, released as 2nd Lt, 46; Capt, Army Res. Mem: Elks; Lions; K. of C; Amvets; Am. Legion; Mass. Selectmens Asn. Rel: Roman Catholic. Mailing Add: 22 Tileston Rd, Randolph, Mass. 02368. (1967)

SEMOS, CHRIS VICTOR D

Tex. State Rep.
b. Dallas, Tex, 6/2/36; s. Victor H. Semos and Evelyn Tassos S; m. 2/25/67 to Anastasia Canella Kontos. Educ: Ecole Hotelier, Lausanne, Switz, 54-55; South. Methodist Univ, 56-62. Polit. & Govt. Pos: Mem, Dallas Action Cmt. for Commun. Improv, City of Dallas Bd, 65-66; Tex. State Rep, 67- Bus. & Prof. Pos: Owner, Torch Restaurant, Dallas; co-owner, Semos Coffee and Tea Co, Dallas. Publ: Series of articles on Greece, Dallas Morning News, 50. Mem: Dallas Restaurant Asn.(past dir); Tex. Restaurant Asn; Lions; Mason (32°); Shrine (Ambassador); Dallas Coun. World Affairs (bd. mem); Gr. Dallas Coun. Churches (exec. cmt). Key Mem: Award, Lions Int. Rel: Greek Orthodox. Legal Res: 327-V N. Gilpin, Dallas, Tex. 75211. Mailing Add: 3620 W. Davis St, Dallas, Tex. 75211.

SEMPLE, FLORENCE EMMA R

b. Exline, Iowa, 9/7/88; d. Charles Fullerton and Anna Jane Huff F; m. 4/17/38 to Carl Y. Semple, wid; c. George Raymond (deceased), Barbara (Mrs. Meek), Elizabeth (Mrs. Hayes). Educ: Hill's Bus. Univ, Oklahoma City. Polit. & Govt. Pos: Precinct Committeewoman; Past Mem, Rep. Nat. Com, Kans. Bus. & Prof. Pos: Mem, Endowment Bd, Kans. State Col; Grain Exporter, Okla. City; lead, zinc, coal mining, Baxter Springs, Kans, 18-; Mgr, Semple Mining & Investment Co; Real Estate & Investments Counselor; Mem, Bd, Baxter Springs Hosp; Chmn, Baxter Springs Youth Center. Mem: Nat. Fedn. Rep. Women; Cherokee Co. Fedn. Rep. Women; DAR; Kans. State & Baxter Springs C. of C; Dames of Court of Honor; Daughters of Am. Colonists Clubs: Baxter Springs Women's; Kans. Day (V.Pres, 50). Rel: Presbyterian. Mailing Add: Box 390, Baxter Springs, Kans. 66713. (1967)

SENDAK, THEODORE LORRAINE R

Attorney Gen, Ind.
b. Chicago, Ill, 3/16/18; s. Jack Sendak and Annette Frankel S; m. 9/13/42 to

Tennessee Elisabeth Read; c. Theodore Tipton, Timothy Read and Cynthia Louise. Educ: Harvard Univ, A.B. cum laude in polit. sci, 40; Valparaiso Univ. Sch. Law, LL.B, 58. Polit. & Govt. Pos: Pub. rels. dir, Ind. Dept. of Vet. Affairs, 46-48; cand. for U.S. Rep, First Dist, Ind, 48; dist. supvr, U.S. Census, Dept. of Commerce, 60; chmn, Lake Co. Rep. Cent Cmt; mem, Ind. Rep. State Cent. Cmt. and chmn, First Cong. Dist. Rep. Cmt, 62-66; Rep. mem, Gov. Cmn. on Voting and Registrn, 64; del, Rep. Nat. Conv, 64; attorney gen, Ind, 69- Bus. & Prof. Pos: Chief ed, writer, Times, Hammond, Ind, 40-41; gen. mgr, Gary Elec. Co, 49-57, pres, 57-59; attorney-at-law, 59- Mil. Serv: Entered as Pvt, Army, 41, released as Capt, 46, after serv. in Philippine Civil Affairs Unit, Southwest Pac. and Asiatic Theaters, 44-45; Asiatic-Pac. Theater Ribbon with 3 Battle Stars; Am. Defense Ribbon; Am. Theater Ribbon; Victory Medal; Philippine Liberation Ribbon with 1 Star; Philippine Presidential Unit Citation; Res. Serv. Medal; Col, Gen. Staff, Army Res, Dep. Comdr, 5073 Logistical Command, Gary, Ind, 67- Publ: Daily editorials, Times, Hammond, Ind, 40-41, weekly mil. columns, 41-46; occasional articles and features, Post-Tribune, Gary, 55-60. Mem: Am. and Ind. State Bar Asns; pres, Crown Point-Lowell Bar Asn, 62-63; pres, Valparaiso Univ. Law Sch. Alumni Asn, 63-64; dir, Crown Point Rotary; Reserve Officers Asn; Am. Legion Post 369; Elks Lodge 981; Indianapolis Press Club; Youche Country Club; Roosevelt Lodge 716, F&AM; Scottish Rite; Orak Shrine. Rel: Methodist. Legal Res: R.R. 4, Box 30, Crown Point, Ind. 46307. Mailing Add: Office of the Attorney General, 219 State House, Indianapolis, Ind. 46204.

SENNER, GEORGE FREDERICK, JR. D
b. Miami, Ariz, 11/24/21; m. to Willodene Waldon; c. George, III and Gregg. Educ: Ariz. State Univ; Univ. Ariz. Law Sch, 52. Polit. & Govt. Pos: Asst. town attorney, Miami, Ariz, 52-54; Gila Co. Attorney, 54-56; Ariz. Dept. Comdr, VFW, 56-57; mem, Ariz. Corp. Cmn, 57-63 and chmn, 58-63; U.S. Rep, Ariz, 66-68. Bus. & Prof. Pos: Private law practice, Senner and Senner until 54. Mil. Serv: Marine Corps, 42-45, S.Pac. Mem: Elks; Lions; Mason; Shrine; VFW; Am. Legion; State Bar of Ariz; Gila Co. and Am. Bar Asns. Rel: Lutheran. 1967 Legal Res: Miami, Ariz. No mailing address available. (1967)

SENNETT, WILLIAM C. R
Attorney Gen, Pa.
Mailing Add: Capitol Bldg, Harrisburg, Pa. 17120. (see addenda).

SENSENBRENNER, FRANK JAMES, JR. R
Wis. State Assemblyman
b. Chicago, Ill, 6/14/43; s. Frank James Sensenbrenner and Margaret Luedke S; single. Educ: Stanford Univ, A.B. in polit. sci, 65, Univ. Wis. Law Sch, J.D, 68; Phi Alpha Delta. Polit. & Govt. Pos: V.chmn, Wis. Youth for Nixon, 60; exec. secy, San Mateo Co. Young Repub, 62, treas, 63-65; dir. region 10, Col. Rep. Nat. Cmt, 63-65, chmn, Cmt. on Rules, 65, del, Col. Rep. Nat. Conv, 63 & 65; mem, Nat. Steering Cmt, Youth for Goldwater-Miller, 64; staff asst. to U.S. Rep. J. Arthur Younger, 65; admin. asst. to majority leader Sen. Jerris Leonard, Wis. State Senate, 67-68; Wis. State Assemblyman, 25th Dist, Milwaukee Co, 69-, chmn, Joint Cmt. on Rev, Repeals and Uniform Laws, v.chmn, Cmt. on Elec. and mem, Cmt. on Judiciary, Wis. State Assembly. Bus. & Prof. Pos: Attorney-at-law, Milwaukee, 68- Mem: Milwaukee, Wis. and Am. Bar Asns; State Hist. Soc. of Wis; Am. Inst. of Parliamentarians; Commonwealth Club of Calif; North Shore Jaycees; Shorewood Men's Club. Named Outstanding Young Rep. in Midwest, 69. Rel: Episcopal. Legal Res: 1601 E. Lake Bluff Blvd, Shorewood, Wis. 53211. Mailing Add: P.O. Box 5471, Shorewood, Wis. 53211.

SENSENBRENNER, MAYNARD E. D
Mayor, Columbus, Ohio
b. Circleville, Ohio, 9/18/02; s. Edward Sensenbrenner and Anna Lama S; m. 10/8/27 to Mildred Sexauer; c. Edward and Richard. Educ: Pub. Schs, Circleville, Ohio. Polit. & Govt. Pos: Investr. and clerk, Ohio Civil Serv. Cmn, 34-53; mayor, Columbus, Ohio, 54-59 & 64- Mem: V.pres, Boy Scouts, 20 years, mem, Cent. Ohio area bd; v.pres, Camp Fire Girls, 10 years; YMCA; Goodwill Industs; dir, Columbus Jets Prfnl. Baseball Club; Big Brother Asn; Police Asn; past pres, Kiwanis; Moose; Elks; Eagles. Recipient, Silver Beaver Award, Boy Scouts; Betsy Ross Award; Fiorella La Guardia Award; Award for Distinguished Commun. Serv, Columbus Area C. of C; Commun. Serv. Award, Hilltop Lions; Outstanding Citizen's Award, Elks; Good Neighbor's Award, Eagles, Lancaster, Ohio; Ludwig Hoge Mem. Award. Rel: Presbyterian; Elder. Legal Res: 4665 Scenic Dr, Columbus, Ohio 43214. Mailing Add: City Hall, 90 W. Broad, Columbus, Ohio 43215.

SENTER, HARRY LEE D
b. Bristol, Tenn, 2/16/11; s. William Wiley Senter and Nina Cornett S; m. 6/10/39 to Mary Anna Stone; c. Harry Lee, Jr, Anna Celeste, Riley Stone and Mary Cheryl. Educ: Univ. of Tenn, LL.B, 34; Tenn. Law Review; Phi Delta Phi; Kappa Alpha. Polit. & Govt. Pos: Tenn. State Rep, Sullivan Co, 50-54, 56-64 & 66-68. Mil. Serv: Entered as 1st Lt, Army, 41, released as Maj, 45, after serv. in S.W. Pac. Area, 43-45; Am. Defense Serv. and Asiatic Pac. Campaign Medals; Four Overseas Serv. Bars; Am. Victory Medal; Philippine Liberation Ribbon and One Bronze Star; Army Res. Medal and One Bronze Star for New Guinea Campaign; Meritorious Achievement Unit Citation; Maj.(Ret), Army Res. Mem: VFW; Am. Legion; Kiwanis Int; Travelers' Protective Asn. Rel: Methodist. Mailing Add: 100 Knollwood Rd, Bristol, Tenn. 37620. (1967)

SENTER, KENNETH LEE R
N.H. State Rep.
b. Boston, Mass, 9/8/01; s. E. Lee Senter and Nellie P. Coulter S; m. 5/16/21 to Beatrice Campbell; c. Kenneth Lee, Patricia (Mrs. Levandowski), Roger Campbell, Sandra (Mrs. Mack) and Brenda. Educ: Pub. Schs, Boston, Mass; Pinkerton Acad, Derry, N.H. Polit. & Govt. Pos: Mem, Sch. Bd, Derry, N.H, asst. Moderator, Town Auditor, Auditor, Fire Dept, dir, Hood Park Recreation, Chmn, Rationing Bd, Chmn, State Lay Prfnl. Coun, Chmn, Supvry. Sch. Union 10 and Chmn, Bldg. Cmt; del, Rockingham Co. Rep. Conv; N.H. State Rep, 69-, mem, Constitutional Rev. Cmt, Labor, Human Resources and Rehabilitation Cmt, N.H. House of Rep, currently. Bus. & Prof. Pos: Merchant, 26-55; Gen. Ins. Adjuster and Appraiser, Gen. Adjust. Bur, N.Y, 55-67. Mem: Chmn, Derry Businessmen's Asn; trustee, Red Cross. Rel: Methodist; Trustee, St. Luke's Methodist Church, Derry, N.H. Mailing Add: 19 Boyd Rd, Derry, N.H. 03038.

SEPE, MICHAEL D
b. Cranston, 12/1/15; m. to Nora. Educ: New Eng. Eng. and Financing; Johnson and Wales Bus. Sch, 37; Exten. Courses, Bryant Col. and Providence Col. Polit. & Govt. Pos: Former treas, R.I. Dem. State Cmt. and former chmn, Cranston Dem. City Cmt; R.I. State Rep, 45-66, second dep. speaker, R.I. House of Rep, 65-66. Bus. & Prof. Pos: Accountant. Mem: Pres, Franklin D. Roosevelt Club of Cranston; pres, Order Sons of Italy; K. of C; Providence Aerie 99, Eagles; AFL; City Hall Athletic Club. Mailing Add: 18 Casino Ave, Cranston, R.I. 02920. (1967)

SERAFIN, MARY WALUS D
b. Sayreville, N.J, 4/20/10; d. Martin Michael Walus and Agnes Cygan; m. 11/23/39 to Edmund Joseph Serafin; c. Ralph Robert and Gail (Mrs.James). Educ: Drakes Secretarial Sch, Secretarial Arts Course. Polit. & Govt. Pos: Mem. and v.pres, Sayreville Bd. of Educ, N.J, 37-40; mem, Middlesex Co. Welfare Bd, 65-, chmn, 69-; munic. v.chmn, Borough of South River, 67-69, munic. chmn, 69-; alternate del, Dem. Nat. Conv, 68. Bus. & Prof. Pos: Secy, Provident Mutual Life Ins. Co. of Phila, New Brunswick, N.J, 30-41; self-employed in gen. ins, 41- Publ: Compiled two recipe books, 56 & 65. Mem: V.pres. of N.J, Union of Polish Women in Am, Phila, Pa; past pres, St. Mary's PTA, South River, N.J; organizer and first pres, South River Columbiettes, Auxiliary to K. of C, first pres, South. Chap. Columbiettes; first treas, N.J. State Columbiettes and past dir, State Supreme Columbiettes; mem, Pastoral Coun, Trenton Diocese, Roman Catholic Church. Outstanding Citizen Award, 65. Rel: Roman Catholic. Mailing Add: 22 Raritan Ave, South River, N.J. 08882.

SERLIN, I. EDWARD D
Mass. State Rep.
b. Chicago, Ill, 8/21/12; s. Benjamin Serlin and Dora S; m. to Edith. Educ: Suffolk Law Sch, LL.B, 34. Polit. & Govt. Pos: Asst. dist. attorney, Suffolk Co, Mass, 62; Mass. State Rep, currently. Mem: Mass. Trial Lawyers. Mailing Add: 606 Harvard St, Mattapan, Mass. 02126.

SERMONS, WAYLAND JAMES D
b. Winterville, N.C; s. Matthew C. Sermons and Mimie Jacson S; m. 6/28/52 to Marilyn Stokes; c. (Mrs. Harry Roberts, Jr), Lois, Anne, Sue, Wayland J, Jr, Carol and Carl Winston. Educ: E. Carolina Teachers Col, 1 year. Polit. & Govt. Pos: Chmn, N.C. Motorboat Study Cmn, 58; N.C. State Rep, 59-66. Bus. & Prof. Pos: Operator of tobacco auction warehouse; pres, Carolinian Hotel Corp; Phillips Petroleum jobber for Beaufort Co. Mem: Jaycee DSA, 50, lifetime Jaycee; F&AM, Orr Lodge 104; Sudan Temple; Wash. Lodge 822 Elks(Esteemed Lecturing Knight 57, Esteemed Loyal Knight, 58, Leading Knight, 59, Exalted Ruler, 60). Rel: Christian Church; Bd. of Stewards, First Christian Church of Washington, N.C. Mailing Add: Washington, N.C. 27889. (1967)

SEROTKIN, DAVID M. R
Mich. State Rep.
b. Pittsburgh, Pa, 12/9/38; s. Harry N. Serotkin and Dorothea M. Moist S; single. Educ: Princeton Univ, A.B. cum laude, 60; Univ. Mich. Law Sch, J.D, 63; Princeton Campus Club; Barrister Soc. Polit. & Govt. Pos: Chmn, Macomb Co. Young Rep, Mich, 66-67; mem, Macomb Co. Rep. Exec. Cmt, 66-; mem, St. Clair Co. Rep. Exec. Cmt, 67-; Mich. State Rep, 75th Dist, 67-; campaign cmt. v.chmn, Rep. State Cent. Cmt. Mich, 69- Bus. & Prof. Pos: Attorney, Matthews, Nonk & Spier, Mt. Clemens, Mich, 63- Mem: State Bar of Mich; Macomb Co. Bar Asn; Air Force Asn; Metrop. Club Am; Kiwanis; Gr. Mt. Clemens Jaycees; Big Bros. Macomb Co. Distinguished Serv. to Educ, Warren Educ. Asn, 69. Mailing Add: 86 Lincoln Ave, Mt. Clemens, Mich. 48043.

SERRANO, FRANCISCO ADROVER R
Mem, Munic. City Coun, Jayuya, P.R.
b. Jayuya, P.R, 3/17/18; s. Damian Adrover Planas Serrano and Juana Maria S; m. 6/9/56 to Ena Elba Nivera Medina; c. Francisco Javier Adrover. Educ: Jayuya, P.R, 33. Polit. & Govt. Pos: Mem, Munic. City Coun, Jayuyo, P.R, currently. Rel: Catholic. Mailing Add: P.O. Box 7, Jayuya, P.R. 00664.

SERWER, ARNOLD D
b. N.Y.C, 4/6/11; s. Isidor Serwer and Mary Gordon S; m. 6/20/37 to Dora Shulman; c. David and Cathy. Educ: Univ. Wis, Madison, B.A. in Journalism, 33. Polit. & Govt. Pos: Info. specialist, Fed. Emergency Relief Admin. and Works Progress Admin, Wash, D.C, 34-36 and War Prod. Bd, 42-43; labor rels. specialist, War Manpower Cmn, 43-44; dir, press sect, War Relocation Authority, 44-46; chmn, Stevenson Vol, New Hyde Park, N.Y, 52 & 56; mem. exec. cmt, Nassau Co. Stevenson Vol, L.I, N.Y, 60; state orgn. dir, McCarthy for Pres. Cmt, Wis, 68; del-at-lg, Dem. Nat. Conv, 68. Bus. & Prof. Pos: Proprietor, Indust. Adv. Serv, pub. rels, N.Y.C, 49-62; assoc. ed, The Progressive Mag, Madison, Wis, 62- Mil. Serv: Entered as Pvt, Army Air Force, 41, released as Spec 5/C, after serv. in 126th Obsn. Squadron, U.S; Air Force Res, 41-43. Publ: 'McCarthy's Winning of Wisconsin,' The Progressive, 6/68; plus others. Mem: Madison, Wash, D.C. and N.Y. Newspaper Guilds. Rel: Jewish. Mailing Add: 1014 Forster Dr, Madison, Wis. 53704.

SESLER, WILLIAM G. D
Pa. State Sen.
b. Uniontown, Pa, 4/18/28; s. Frederick Allen Sesler and Pauline Dixson S; m. 4/26/58 to Cecily Ann Parke; c. Gregory Parke, Douglas William and Elizabeth Ann. Educ: Kenyon Col, A.B. cum laude, 50; Univ. Mich. Law Sch, LL.B, 56; Tau Kappa Alpha; Sigma Pi. Polit. & Govt. Pos: Pa. State Sen, 60-; alternate del, Dem. Nat. Conv, 64 & 68. Bus. & Prof. Pos: Attorney, Law Firm of Dunn, Wolford and Sesler, 68- Mil. Serv: 1st Lt, Air Force, 50-53, serv. in Combined Command Rec. Activities, Korea, 52-53; Bronze Star. Mem: Courts of Erie Co, Pa, Superior and Supreme Courts of Pa, and U.S. Dist. Court for West. Dist. of Pa; Am. Legion; VFW; Air Force Asn; dir, Erie Co. Tuberc. Asn. and Booker T. Washington Center. Selected Young

Man of the Year, Erie Jr. C. of C, 64. Rel: Presbyterian. Legal Res: 24 East 37th St, Erie, Pa. 16504. Mailing Add: 1111 G. Daniel Baldwin Bldg, Erie, Pa. 16501.

SESSIONS, PAUL TRAMMELL D
Ala. State Rep.
b. Marietta, Ga, 11/17/98; s. Walter Lee Sessions and Alice T; m. 1/28/21 to Ann Elizabeth Quarles; c. Paul Trammell, Jr, Margaret Lamont (Mrs. Bulloch). Educ: Univ. Ala; Sigma Alpha Epsilon. Polit. & Govt. Pos: Ala. State Rep, 58 & 62- Bus. & Prof. Pos: Assoc. gen. agent, Mass. Mutual Life Ins. Co, 22 years; Liberty Nat. Life Ins. Co, 42- Rel: Methodist. Mailing Add: Box 2612, Birmingham, Ala. 35202. (1967)

SESSIONS, WILLIAM STEELE R
City Councilman, Waco, Tex.
b. Ft. Smith, Ark, 5/27/30; s. Will Anderson Sessions, Jr. and Edith Steele S; m. 10/5/52 to Alice June Lewis; c. William Lewis, Peter Anderson and Mark Gregory. Educ: Univ. Kans, 48-51; Baylor Univ, B.A, 56, LL.B, 58, J.D, 69; Pi Sigma Alpha; Delta Chi; Phi Delta Phi. Polit. & Govt. Pos: Campaign mgr, Sen. John Tower, McLennan Co, Tex, 66 and for Carl McIntosh, 67; alternate del, Rep. Nat. Conv, 68; city councilman, Waco, Tex, 69- Bus. & Prof. Pos: Partner, Haley, Fulbright, Winniford, Sessions & Bice, 62- Mil. Serv: Entered as Pvt, Air Force, 51, released as 1st Lt, 55, after serving in 3565th Observer Training Sq, Air Training Command, 52-55; Res, 55-58, Capt. Mem: Waco, McLennan Co. and Tex. Bar Asns; Am. Judicature Soc; Lions; dir, Waco YMCA; mem, McLennan Coun. on Alcoholism and Freeman House, Inc. Outstanding Young Layman, Jr. C. of C, 65. Rel: Methodist. Mailing Add: 2200 Gorman, Waco, Tex. 76706.

SESSUMS, THOMAS TERRELL D
Speaker Pro Tem, Fla. House of Rep.
b. Daytona Beach, Fla, 6/11/30; s. Thomas Little Sessums and Dorothy Cornwall S; m. 8/16/58 to Neva Ann Steeves; c. Thomas T, Jr, Richard H. and Sandra Lynn. Educ: Univ. Fla, B.A, 52, LL.B, 58; Fla. Blue Key; Hall of Fame; Student-Body Pres, Phi Eta Sigma; Phi Alpha Delta; Alpha Tau Omega; Tau Kappa Alpha. Polit. & Govt. Pos: Fla. State Rep, 65th Dist, 63-, speaker pro tem, Fla. House of Rep, 68- Bus. & Prof. Pos: Partner, Albritton, Sessums & Ryder, Attorneys, 61- Mil. Serv: Entered as 2nd Lt, Air Force, 54, released as Capt, 56, after serv. in 3813th Air Police Sq, Air Univ. Command, Maxwell AFB, Ala; Nat. Defense Serv. Ribbons; Korea War Ribbon. Mem: Acad. of Fla. Trial Lawyers; Am. Trial Lawyers Asn; City, Co, State and Am. Bar Asns; Gr. Tampa C. of C; Cmt. of 100; Univ. Club; Davis Islands Yacht Club; bd. dirs, Kiwanis. Received St. Petersburg Times Award, Most Valuable Mem. of the House for the 1967 Session and Dixie Prod. News Award For Outstanding Debate on the Floor of the House During 1969 Session. Rel: Methodist. Legal Res: 1113 Dunbar Ave, Tampa, Fla. 33609. Mailing Add: 925 First Federal Bank Bldg, Tampa, Fla. 33602.

SETHER, VIRGINIA HILL R
Alternate Del, Rep. State Cent. Cmt, Minn.
b. Albert Lea, Minn, 5/15/17; d. Charles Fredrick Hill and Violet Lanetta Ruble H; m. 10/5/36 to Russell Ranvig Sether; c. JoAnne (Mrs. Menard), Kristin and Lisa. Polit. & Govt. Pos: Co. chairwoman, Freeborn Co. Rep. Party, Minn, 59-61; v.chmn, 1st Dist. Rep. Party, 61-63 and chairwoman, 63-65; mem, Legis. Search Cmt, 62; del, Rep. Nat. Conv, 64; alternate del, Minn. Rep. State Cent. Cmt, 65- Rel: Presbyterian. Mailing Add: 634 E. Park Ave, Albert Lea, Minn. 56007. (1967)

SEVERSON, STANLEY RAYMOND R
Chmn, Adams Co. Rep. Cent. Cmt, N.Dak.
b. Hettinger, N.Dak, 12/29/23; s. Ernest James Severson and Ida Marie Pariseau S; m. 4/7/45 to Ruth P. Austad; c. Diane L, Barbara J. and Pat J. Educ: Hettinger Pub. Schs. Polit. & Govt. Pos: Chmn, Adams Co. Rep. Cent. Cmt, N.Dak. and treas, 39th Legis. Dist, N.Dak, 62-; precinct committeeman 62- Bus. & Prof. Pos: Mgr, Carl J. Austad & Son, Inc, 46- Mil. Serv: Entered as A/S, Navy, 42, released as MoMM 2/C, 45, after serv. in Pac. Theater. Mem: Pres, Hettinger C. of C, 57; Mo. Valley Councilman, Boy Scouts, 59-66, dist. chmn, Saxvick Dist, 60-61; Nat. Americanism Committeeman, Am. Legion, 65 and dist. oratorical chmn, 66-67; Hettinger Country Club; Elks; 40 et 8. Rel: Catholic. Legal Res: 255 S. Seventh, Hettinger, N.Dak. 58639. Mailing Add: Box 568, Hettinger, N.Dak. 58639. (1967)

SEVITS, WILLIS LEE R
Chmn, Macon Co. Rep. Party, Mo.
b. Greentop, Mo, 12/8/21; s. Sherman Harrison Sevits and Maude Mae Willis S; m. 10/3/46 to Eva Dean Helton; c. Jerry Lee and Tom G. Educ: Mo. State Col, Kirksville, B.S, 54; Phi Omega Pi; Phi Sigma Epsilon. Polit. & Govt. Pos: City alderman and clerk, Elmer, Mo, 53-60; mem. and treas, Macon Co. Sch. Bd, 64-69; chmn, Macon Co. Rep. Party, 68- Bus. & Prof. Pos: Acct. and salesman, Chevrolet Dealership, LaPlata, Mo, 54-61; controller, Kirksville Col. Osteopathy and Surgery, 63- Mil. Serv: Entered as A/S, Navy, 42, released as Motor Machinist's Mate 3/C, 46, after serv. in Amphibious Force, ETO, 43-45; 5 Bronze Stars, Africa, Sicily, Salerno, Anzio and Normandy. Mem: Mo. Hist. Soc; K.T.(chmn, Educ. Found. Cmt, Kirksville); AF&AM; Am. Legion; Shrine; Moose; RAM. Rel: Protestant. Mailing Add: Elmer, Mo. 63538.

SEWALL, F. ALBERT D
N.H. State Rep.
b. Newmarket, N.H, 8/21/98; married; c. Eleven. Educ: Univ. N.H. Polit. & Govt. Pos: Selectman, N.H, 14 years; del, Constitutional Conv, 56; N.H. State Rep, currently. Mil. Serv: ROTC. Rel: Protestant. Mailing Add: R.F.D. 1, Newmarket, N.H. 03857. (1967)

SEWARD, GEORGE HORTON D
b. East Orange, N.J, 11/7/04; s. John Seward and Florence Horton S; m. 12/3/40 to Nola Marie Purkiss; c. Richard Leddel, Sherry (Mrs. Hart) and John Craig. Educ: Strayer Col. of Accountancy, B.C.S; Columbus Law Sch. Polit. & Govt. Pos: Secy. to U.S. Sen. Key Pittman, 33-40; dep. dir, Can. Div, War Prod. Bd, 41-48; area supvr, Census Bur, 48-51; secy. to U.S. Rep. Walter S. Baring, Nev, 52, admin. asst, 57-69. Awarded the Newel Perry Award for distinguished public service to blind welfare, 58. Legal Res: 609 Burton St, Henderson, Nev. 89015. Mailing Add: 432 Sorrento Dr, Sorrento Shores, Osprey, Fla. 33559.

SEWARD, ROLAND QUINCY R
Finance Chmn, Vt. Rep. State Cmt.
b. East Wallingford, Vt, 3/4/17; s. Arthur B. Seward and Ella Quincy Bunker S; m. 9/17/38 to Dorothy Catherine Poloske; c. Roland Q, Jr, Thomas R. and John B. Educ: Rutland Bus. Col, Vt, grad, 35. Polit. & Govt. Pos: Mem, Vt. Develop. Cmn, 53-59; chmn, Rutland Co. Rep. Party, 59-61; chmn, Vt. Develop. Bd, 61-63; mem, Vt. Indust. Bldg. Authority, 61-63; chmn, Vt. Rep. State Cmt, 61-63, finance chmn, 67-; mem, Vt. Gov. Coun. of Econ. Adv, 69- Bus. & Prof. Pos: Proprietor, Valley View Creamery, East Wallingford, 36-; pres. and treas, Sewards Dairy, Inc, Rutland, 47-; trustee, Vt. Found. of Independent Cols, 53-; mem. bd, Vt. Develop. Credit Corp, 58-, pres, 59-63; pres, New Industs, Inc, Rutland, 59-; mem. bd. dirs, Proctor Trust Co, 61-; pres, The Seward Family, Inc, 63-; pres, Sewards Restaurant of Burlington, 63-; pres, Seward Foods, Inc, Rutland, 64-; trustee, Col. of St. Joseph the Provider, 67- Mem: Mason (32°); Shrine; Elks; Odd Fellows; United Commercial Travelers. Rel: Congregational. Mailing Add: R.D, East Wallingford, Vt. 05742.

SEWELL, J. RICHARD D
b. Orlando, Fla, 1/3/35; s. A. James Sewell and Bertie Johns S; m. 8/27/66 to Margaret M. Mahon. Educ: Univ. Fla, B.S.J, 59; Pi Kappa Alpha. Polit. & Govt. Pos: Asst, Secy. of State, Fla, 60; admin. asst. to U.S. Rep. Charles E. Bennett, Fla, 63-; staff coordinator, House Select Cmt. on Standards and Conduct, 65-66. Bus. & Prof. Pos: Sports ed, Orlando Star, 57 & 58; writer, Atlanta Constitution, 59; advert. and pub. rels, Jacksonville, Fla, 61-63. Mil. Serv: Army Res, 57. Mem: Fla. Pub. Rels. Asn; Nat. Press, Seminole and Ponte Vedra Clubs; Nat. Capitol Dem. Club; pres, Burro Club of U.S, 67-68, Univ. Fla. Alumni Club, Wash, D.C, 68 and Fla. State Soc, 69-70. Rel: Baptist. Legal Res: Jacksonville, Fla. Mailing Add: 2501 Calvert St. N.W, Apt. 709, Washington, D.C. 20008.

SEWELL, JOHN WILLIAM D
b. Newnan, Ga, 7/17/14; s. Richard Clarence Sewell and Ruth Lane S; m. 6/17/39 to Martha Teague Johns; c. John William, Ruth Lane, Martha Ann, James Wesley, Charles Ross. Educ: Clayton High Sch, 32. Polit. & Govt. Pos: Ga. State Rep, 63-66. Bus. & Prof. Pos: Farmer; merchant; lumberman. Mem: Moose; Elk; pres, Plains Lions Club, 54-55; pres. Plains High Sch. PTA, 60; Plains Charge Methodist Mens Club, pres, 60; pres. Americus Sub-Dist. Methodist Laymen, 61. Rel: Methodist. Mailing Add: Plains, Ga, 31780. (1967)

SEXNER, SIDNEY JAY D
b. Chicago, Ill, 3/26/34; s. Leonard Louis Sexner and Anna Newman S; m. 12/28/65 to Rosalind Zisook; c. Mitchell Scott and Richard Edward. Educ: Northwest. Univ, B.S, 56; Northwest. Law Sch, LL.B, 58; Phi Epsilon Pi; Phi Alpha Delta. Polit. & Govt. Pos: Del, Young Dem. of Am. Conv, 61-63 & 65-67; pres, Seventh Ward Young Dem, Ill, 62; Disaster Fee Attorney, Small Bus. Admin, 62; arbitrator, Ill. Indust. Cmn, 65; alternate del, Dem. Nat. Conv, 68; del, Platform Cmt, Dem. Party of Ill, 68; pres, Young Dem. of Ill, 68, nat. committeeman, 69- Mil. Serv: Entered as Pvt, Air Force Reserve, 58, released as Airman 3/C, 64, Mem: Am. and Ill. Bar Asns; Chicago Bar Asn. (div, Younger Mem. Cmt, 63-64); Am. and Ill. Trial Lawyers Asns; Pres, B'nai B'rith Council of Greater Chicago. Young Democrats Man of the Year, 68. Rel: Jewish. Legal Res: 1054 Williamsburg, Northbrook, Ill. 60062. Mailing Add: 7 S. Dearborn, Chicago, Ill. 60603.

SEXTON, CLARENCE D, JR. D
Chmn, Lexington Co. Dem. Party, S.C.
b. Columbia, S.C, 2/5/27; s. Clarence D. Sexton, Sr. and Ada Smith S; m. 7/14/51 to Mary Irene Tenk; c. Margaret, Mary, Jenny, Terry and Betty Ann. Educ: Univ. S.C, B.S.C.E, 48; Sigma Phi Epsilon. Polit. & Govt. Pos: Chmn, Lexington Co. Dem. Party, S.C, 67-; del, Dem. Nat. Conv, 68. Bus. & Prof. Pos: Proj. engr, Standard Oil Co, N.J, Aruba, 48-55; v.pres, Repub. Contracting Corp, Columbia, S.C, 55- Mil. Serv: Entered as Pvt, Army, 41, released as Sgt, 47, after serv. in Third Inf. Div; Army Res, 2nd Lt. Mem: Am. Soc. Civil Engrs; Lions; Moose; WOW; C. of C; Alumni of Univ. S.C. Rel: Presbyterian. Mailing Add: 1428 Redwood Dr, West Columbia, S.C. 29169.

SEYBERT, MYRON SILVER R
Chmn, Madison Co. Rep. Party, Ind.
b. Anderson, Ind, 12/28/08; s. Fred A. Seybert and Lottie G. S; m. 3/15/35 to Georgia Helen Wantz; c. Sharon L. (Mrs. Stinson) and Shirley A. (Mrs. Aubrey). Polit. & Govt. Pos: Chmn, Madison Co. Rep. Party, Ind, currently; alternate del, Rep. Nat. Conv, 68. Mailing Add: 1331½ Main St, Anderson, Ind. 46016.

SGAMBATO, FRANK D
R.I. State Sen.
b. N.Y.C, 8/24/00; m. to Juliet C. Educ: Pub. sch, N.Y.C. Polit. & Govt. Pos: Mem, North Providence Town Cmt, 35-40; R.I. State Sen, 41-, Dep. Majority Leader, R.I. State Senate, 59-62, Majority Leader, 63- Bus. & Prof. Pos: Int. v.pres, United Textile Workers of Am, AFL-CIO. Mil. Serv: Navy. Mem: Elks; officer, Centredale Fire Dept. Mailing Add: 581 Woonasquatucket Ave, North Providence, R.I. 02911.

SGAMBELLURI, RALPH CAMACHO D
Sen, Guam Legis.
b. Agana, Guam, 4/28/28; s. Marcelo Sgambelluri and Joaquina Desa Camacho S; m. 8/16/50 to Irene Perez Ploke; c. Darleen Bernadine, Jennifer Jeanette, Pamela Susette and Raffaeli Marcelli John. Educ: Belmont Abby Col, Prep. Sch, Belmont, N.C, 46-48. Polit. & Govt. Pos: Sen, 10th Guam Legis, 67-, chmn, Cmt. Housing and Urban Develop, 69-, v.chmn, Cmt. Health, Educ. and Welfare, 67-68, mem, Cmt. Govt. Opers, 67-, Cmt. Labor and Indust. Rels, 67-, Cmt. Pub. Safety and Vets. and Mil. Affairs, 67-, Cmt. Orgn. Labor, 67- and Select Cmt. Parks and Monuments, 67- Bus. & Prof. Pos: Pres, Sgamby's Gen.

Serv, 66-; v.pres, Guam/Tokyo Hotel, 68-; v.pres, Guam/Tokyo Ltd, Inc, 67- Mem: Guam Farm and Ranch Club; Boys Scout; Holy Name Soc; Tuberc. Asn. Spec. Cmt; Young Men's League of Guam; Dem. Party of Mongmong-Maite-Toto (chmn); adv. chmn, Mongmong, Toto & Maite Headstart Center, Guam. Rel: Catholic. Legal Res: Mongmong-Toto-Maite, Guam USA 96910. Mailing Add: P.O. Box 2818, Agana, Guam USA 96910.

SHABAZ, JOHN C. R
Wis. State Assemblyman
b. Milwaukee, Wis, 6/25/31. Educ: Wis. Univ, 53; Marquette Univ, LL.B, 57. Polit. & Govt. Pos: Wis. State Assemblyman, 64- Bus. & Prof. Pos: Attorney; farming; sales; machine operation. Mil. Serv: Army, 54-56. Mem: Bar Asns; U.S. Jaycees, past nat. dir. pres. coun, Metrop. Jaycees; past chmn, N.Berlin Rep. Br. Outstanding W. Allis Jr. C. of C, 63-64. Mailing Add: 21425 W. Glengarry Dr, North Berlin, Wis. 53151. (1967)

SHABLOW, FRANK S. D
b. Lancaster, Minn, 10/15/09; married; c. two. Educ: Pub. Schs. Polit. & Govt. Pos: N. Dak. State Rep, 61-66. Bus. & Prof. Pos: Farmer and implement dealer. Mem: Elks; Commercial Club; Curling Club; Gun Club. Mailing Add: Langdon, N. Dak. 58249. (1967)

SHACKLE, H. GENE D
Cent. Committeeman, Stark Co. Dem. Cent. Cmt, Ohio
b. Canton, Ohio, 8/13/29; s. Harold L. Shackle and Margaret Smith S; m. to Marylou Beaumont; c. Sheryl, Susan, David, Mary Katheryn, Eric, Linda, Kathleen and James. Educ: Kent State Univ, 48-50; Wm. McKinley Sch. of Law, 50-54, LL.B, 54. Polit. & Govt. Pos: Cent. Committeeman, Stark Co. Dem. Cent. Cmt, Ohio, 62-; alternate del, Dem. Nat. Conv, 68; mem, Stark Co. Dem. Exec. Cmt, 68- Bus. & Prof. Pos: Credit correspondent, Diebold Inc, Ohio, 51-52, field off. mgr, Robert Carter Co, 52-54; asst. to the secy, Nat. Can Corp, Ill, 54-56; employee rels. mgr, Argonne Nat. Lab, 56-57; secy. and gen. counsel, E.W. Bliss Co, 57-68, v.pres. admin. and dir, 68- Mil. Serv: Entered as Pvt, Army, 46, released as Sgt, 48, after serv. in Armored Sch. Mem: Am, Ohio and Stark Co. Bar Asns; Corp. Secretaries Soc. Am; Am. Mgt. Asn; Canton Club; Canton Annexation Cmn; Canton Welfare Fedn.(bd. trustees); Canton C. of C.(bd. dirs); adv. bd, Mercy-Timken Mercy Hosps, bd. trustees, Seven Co. Exten. of Regional Planning Bd; YMCA (bd. trustees); Brookside Country Club. Rel: Lutheran. Mailing Add: 934 Raff Rd. S.W, Canton, Ohio 44710.

SHACKLEFORD, ROBERT MITCHELL, JR. R
Chmn, Clarke Co. Rep. Exec. Cmt, Ala.
b. Mobile, Ala, 6/7/20; s. Robert M. Shackleford, Sr. and Myrtice Christine Brannon S; m. 10/1/47 to Mary Frances Stimpson; c. Robert M, III, Mary Katherine and Christine S. Educ: Ill. Col. of Optom, O.D; Omega Epsilon Phi. Polit. & Govt. Pos: Chmn, Clarke Co. Rep. Exec. Cmt, Ala, 62- Mil. Serv: Entered as Pvt, Army, 39, released as Sgt, 45, after serv. in 569 Signal HDG. Bn, ETO, 42-45. Mem: Ala. Optom. Asn.(pres, 54); Rotary; Am. Legion. Rel: Methodist. Mailing Add: 501 N. Portis Ave, Jackson, Ala. 36545.

SHACKLETON, POLLY D
Mem, D.C. City Coun.
b. Brookline, Mass; d. Adolph Ehrlich and Marion E; m. 7/1/46 to Robert W. Shackleton. Educ: Simmons Sch. Social Work; Boston Univ; Mass. Inst. Tech; New Sch. Social Research. Polit. & Govt. Pos: Mem, D.C. Dem. Cent. Cmt, 54-67; del, Dem. Nat. Conv, 56, 60 & 64, mem. Platform Cmt, 56 & 64; alternate nat. committeewoman, D.C, 56-60, Dem. nat. committeewoman, D.C, 61-67; mem, Women's Nat. Dem. Club; mem, D.C. City Coun, 67- Bus. & Prof. Pos: Ed. reference books Am. Fedn. Arts; info. specialist, picture ed, OWI, Dept. State, Dept. Army, 42-48; ed. biweekly newsletter, pub. rels. activities as mem. hq. staff, A.I.A, Wash, D.C, 50-63. Mailing Add: 3232 Reservoir Rd. N.W, Washington, D.C. 20007.

SHADDUCK, LOUISE R
b. Coeur d'Alene, Idaho, 10/14/15; d. Lester Carson Shadduck and Mary Jeannette Furgason S; single. Educ: Coeur d'Alene High Sch, Idaho, 4 years. Univ. Idaho, hon. J.D, 69. Polit. & Govt. Pos: Admin. asst, Gov. and Lt. Gov, Idaho; exec. secy, U.S. Sen, Idaho; dir, Dept. of Commerce and Develop, Idaho; admin. asst, U.S. Rep. Orval Hansen, Idaho, 69- Bus. & Prof. Pos: Reporter, Coeur d'Alene (Idaho) Press and Spokesman-Rev, Spokane, Wash, 10 years. Publ: Ed, Centennial Year Idaho Almanac; auth, articles, leaflets and brochures. Mem: First v.pres, Nat. Fedn. of Press Women, Region One (past dir); Am. Indust. Develop. Asn; Altrusa; Beta Sigma Phi; Theta Sigma Phi; life mem, Quill and Scroll Soc, Idaho Press Asn. and Idaho Advert. Club, Boise; Idaho Press Women (past pres). Women's Sugar Plum Award, Wash. State Press; Citation for journalistic works and pub. serv, Univ. Idaho. Rel: Presbyterian. Legal Res: Boise, Idaho. Mailing Add: 1321 Longworth House Office Bldg, Washington, D.C. 20515.

SHAEFFER, JOHN ALLEN R
Chmn, Moody Co. Rep. Party, S.Dak.
b. Sioux Falls, S.Dak, 8/10/40; s. Dr. James H. Shaeffer and Maylou Reidesal S; m. 12/8/67 to Cheryl Dott. Educ: Loyola Univ, 59-62; Univ. S.Dak, LL.B, 65. Polit. & Govt. Pos: Chmn, Moody Co. Rep. Party, S.Dak, 66- Mem: S.Dak. Bar Asn; secy-treas, Tri-Co. Bar Asn, 66; mem. Bd. Dirs, Flandreau Jr. C. of C, 66; K. of C. Coaching 10 and 11 yr. old youngsters in basketball and baseball in the community. Rel: Catholic. Mailing Add: Flandreau, S.Dak. 57028.

SHAFER, EARL T. R
Chmn, Stark Co. Rep. Cent. Cmt, Ill.
b. Stark Co, Ill, 4/1/12; s. Frank Shafer and Nellie Ingram S; single. Educ: Wyo. Commun. High Sch, grad, 29. Polit. & Govt. Pos: Supvr, Stark Co. Bd. of Supvrs, Ill, 55-63; precinct committeeman, Stark Co. Rep. Party, 55-; chmn, Stark Co. Rep. Cent. Cmt, 60-; chmn, Ill. Soil and Water Conserv. Bd, 69- Bus. & Prof. Pos: Owner and operator, Shafer Reconditioned Cylinder Head Co, 29-42; flight instr, Govt. Flying Schs, 42-44; owner and mgr, Farms in Stark, Bureau & Lee Counties, Ill, 46- Mil. Serv: Entered as Flight Officer, Army Air Corps, Atlantic, N.Africa and China-Burma-India, 44-45; N. Africa and China-Burma-India Theatre Ribbons. Mem: Mason; Scottish Rite; Shrine; Am. Legion; Retired Officers Asn; Ill. Farm Bur. Rel: Protestant. Mailing Add: P.O. Box 105, Wyoming, Ill. 61491.

SHAFER, ESTHER VIRGINIA R
b. Painesville, Ohio, 6/25/21; d. Ralph Widgren and Anna Ladvala W; m. 1/21/45 to Jack Frankin Shafer. Educ: High Sch. Grad. Polit. & Govt. Pos: V.chairwoman, Laramie Co. Rep. Cent. Cmt, Wyo, 60-64; del, Rep. Nat. Conv, 64; Wyo. State Rep. Committeewoman, Laramie Co, 64-69; del, Wyo. State Rep. Conv, 68; del, State Rep. Women's Conv, 68 Mem: Former mem, Cheyenne Women's Civic League, Laramie Co. Cowbelles, Airport Golf Club, Mem. Hosp. Auxiliary and Laramie Co. Home Demonstration Club; life mem, Jayshees; Honolulu Rep. Women's Club; Honolulu Salvation Army Women's Auxiliary. Rel: Presbyterian. Mailing Add: Mooring 40, 6370 Hawaii Kai Dr, Honolulu, Hawaii 96821.

SHAFER, RAYMOND PHILIP R
Gov, Pa.
b. New Castle, Pa, 3/5/17; s. David Paul Shafer and Mina Belle Miller S; m. 7/5/41 to Jane Harris Davies; c. Raymond Philip, Diane Elizabeth and Jane Ellen. Educ: Allegheny Col, B.A. in hist. and polit. sci, 33; Yale Univ. Law Sch, LL.B, 41; Phi Beta Kappa; dir, Moot Court, Barrister's Union. Polit. & Govt. Pos: Lt. Gov, Pa, 62-67; chmn, Gov. Select Cmt. on Educ, 63; chmn, Admin. Legis. Policy Cmt, 63-65; pres, Pa. State Senate; chmn, Bd. of Pardons, Commun, Affairs Adv. Coun. and Coun. on Human Serv; hon. chmn, Gov. Cmn. on Constitutional Revision; mem, Sch. Finance Surv. Cmt, Gov. Tax Study Cmt. and Cmn. on Inter-State Coop; Gov, Pa, 67-; del, Rep. Nat. Conv, 68. Bus. & Prof. Pos: Secy. and dir, Meadville City Hosp. Mil. Serv: Entered Navy, 42, released as Comdr. of PT Boat, 45, after serv. in S.Pac; Bronze Star; Purple Heart; Philippine Liberation Medal. Mem: Am, Pa. and Crawford Co. Bar Asns; pres, Western Crawford Co. Commun. Chest and Allegheny Col. Alumni Asn; chmn, Red Cross Chap; trustee, Hosp. Asn. of Pa; Grange; Rotary; Am. Legion; VFW. Legal Res: 660 Seminole Rd, Meadville, Pa. 16335. Mailing Add: Governor's Office, Main Capitol, Harrisburg, Pa. 17120.

SHAFER, ROBERT LeROY R
b. Amery, Wis, 5/10/32; s. William Charles Enoch Shafer and Gertrude Porter S. Educ: St. John's Univ, Collegeville, Minn, B.A; Georgetown Univ, LL.B; Named One of Ten Outstanding Srs. on Basis of Scholarship and Extra-Curricular Activities. Polit. & Govt. Pos: Admin. asst. to Rep. Alvin E. O'Konski (R), Wis; State chmn, Students for Stevenson, 52. Bus. & Prof. Pos: Secy-treas, Mercer Industs, Mercer, Wis. Mil. Serv: Army, Artil, Pfc, 55-56. Mem: St. John's Debate Team; Orchestra and Men's Chorus; Wis. Bar Asn; pres, St. John's Col. Student Coun; State v.chmn. Nat. Students Asn; pres, D.C. Chap, St. John's Alumni Asn. Publn: Assoc-ed. Sketchbook. Legal Res: Amery, Wis. Mailing Add: 109 Seventh St. N.E, Washington, D.C. 20002. (1967)

SHAFF, DAVID O. R
b. Clinton, Iowa, 2/18/24; m. 1953 to Lissi Cornell; c. Karen, Martha and Jay. Educ: Univ. Iowa, B.A. and J.D. Polit. & Govt. Pos: Iowa State Sen, 54-66; Iowa State Rep, 55th Gen. Assembly; del, Rep. Nat. Conv, 68. Bus. & Prof. Pos: Partner, Shaff and Farwell, Attorneys, Clinton, Iowa. Mil. Serv: Air Force, World War II, China-Burma-India- Theater. Mailing Add: 246 Woodlawn Court, Clinton, Iowa 52732. (1967)

SHAFFER, BUTLER DeLANE R
b. Lincoln, Nebr, 1/12/35; s. Marvin E. Shaffer and Sarah J. Robinson S; m. 12/28/57 to Jane Ellen Conger; c. Bretigne Anne, Heidi Leigh and Gretchen Liesl. Educ: Univ. Nebr, B.Sc, 58 and B.A. in arts and sci, 59; Univ. Chicago Law Sch, J.D, 61; Delta Theta Phi. Polit. & Govt. Pos: Exec. secy, Rep. Party of Nebr, 61-63; secy, Nebr. State Rep. Finance Cmt, 61-63; secy, Rep. Founders Day, 61-63; alternate del, Rep. Nat. Conv, 64; mem, Nebr. Young Rep. Exec. Cmt, 64-65; mem, Nebr. State Rep. Cent. Cmt, 64-65. Bus. & Prof. Pos: Lincoln mgr, Midwest Employers Coun, 63-66; columnist, Colorado Springs Gazette Telegraph, 64-; columnist, Santa Ana Register, Calif, Odessa American, Tex, and Whitehall, White Laker, Mich, 65-; teaching asst, The Freedom Sch, 66-; partner, Law Firm of Swoboda and Shaffer, Omaha, Nebr, currently. Mil. Serv: Served as enlisted man in Nebr. and Ill. Air Nat. Guards. Publ: 'Unionism and Economic Stagnation,' Fall 66 and 'Analysis of Conflict,' Spring 68, Rampart J. Mem: Bd. Gov, Independent Bar Asn; Nebr. State Bar Asn; Univ. Chicago Alumni Asn. Mailing Add: 1031 N. 90th, Omaha, Nebr. 68114.

SHAFFER, CHARLES RAYMOND R
W.Va. State Del.
b. Rupert, W.Va, 3/29/27; s. Charles Henry Shaffer and Constance Black S; m. 4/17/49 to Vivian Yvonne Ruger; c. Mark Steven, Charles Roger and Laura Yvonne. Educ: W.Va. Wesleyan Col, B.S, 50. Polit. & Govt. Pos: W.Va. State Del, Upshur Co, 69- Mil. Serv: Entered as A/S, Navy, 45, released as Seaman 2/C, 46, after serv. in Naval Res, U.S; Am. Campaign and Victory Medals. Mem: Mason; Am. Legion; Lions; Christian Bus. Men's Cmt; United Commercial Travelers; W.Va. Educ. Asn; exec. cmt, Co. Educ. Asn. Rel: United Methodist. Mailing Add: Route 4, Box 35, Buckhannon, W.Va. 26201.

SHAFFER, ROBERT EDWIN D
Supvr, Schoharie Co. Bd. of Supvr, N.Y.
b. Gilboa, N.Y, 1/1/16; s. Robert Edwin Shaffer and Edna Van Tyle Mattice S; m. 2/2/46 to Marion G. Gallagher; c. Gail Susan and Edwin Robert. Educ: Chicago Acad. Fine Arts, 39-40. Polit. & Govt. Pos: Supvr, Schoharie Co. Bd. Supvr, N.Y, 51-, chmn, 65-67. Mil. Serv: Entered as Pvt, Army, 41, released as T-5, 42, after serv. in Hq. Battery, 867 AAA (AW) Bn, Cent. Pac, Theatre, 42-45; Am. Defense Medal; Asiatic-Pac. Serv. Medal; Good Conduct Medal. Mem: Am. Legion; F&AM; RAM. Rel: Protestant. Mailing Add: North Blenheim, N.Y. 12131.

SHAFFREY, INA THERESA D
V.Chmn, Mo. State Dem. Cmt.
b. Nashville, Tenn, 10/26/11; d. P.S. Smith and Martha E. Garrett S; m. 5/12/27 to George C. Shaffrey; c. Leola G. (Mrs. Meifert), Patricia D. (Mrs. Morard) and George C, Jr. Polit. & Govt. Pos: Committeewoman, 24th Ward,

Mo, 44-; state Dem. Committeewoman, Third Cong. Dist, 60; v.chmn, Mo. State Dem. Cmt. and secy, City Dem. Cent. Cmt, 66- Rel: Catholic. Mailing Add: 6314 W. Park Ave, St. Louis, Mo. 63139.

SHAKER, MITCHELL FRANCIS D
Exec. secy, Trumbull Co. Dem. Exec. Cmt, Ohio
b. Niles, Ohio, 1/3/22; s. Isaac Shaker (deceased) and Sophia Joseph S; m. 7/26/45 to Mary K. Christopher; c. Mary Alice (Mrs. Weiss), Margaret Ann, Mitchell F, Jr, Kathryn T, Thomas J, Patricia L, Christopher J. and Robert I. Educ: John Carroll Univ, B.A, magna cum laude, 43; West. Reserve Univ. Sch. of Law, J.D, 48; Alpha Sigma Nu; Order of the Coif, Delta Theta Phi. Polit. & Govt. Pos: City solicitor, Niles, Ohio, 50-55, 62-63 & 66-; exec. secy, Trumbull Co. Dem. Exec. Cmt, 63-; mem. bd. elec, Trumbull Co, 66-67. Bus. & Prof. Pos: Attorney-at-law, 48- Mil. Serv: Entered as Midn, Navy, 43, released as Lt.(jg), 45, after serv. in Fifth Fleet, S.Pac, 44-45. Mem: Niles Area C. of C; Am. Legion; K. of C; Elks. Rel: Roman Catholic. Legal Res: 403 Hogarth Ave, Niles, Ohio 44446. Mailing Add: 502-3 Niles Bank Bldg, Niles, Ohio 44446.

SHAKESPEARE, FRANK R
Dir, U.S. Info. Agency
b. N.Y.C, 4/9/25; s. Francis J. Shakespeare and Frances Hughes S; m. 10/9/54 to Deborah Anne Spaeth; c. Andrea, Fredricka and Mark. Educ: Holy Cross Col, B.A, 46. Polit. & Govt. Pos: Dir, U.S. Info. Agency, 69- Bus. & Prof. Pos: With Liberty Mutual Ins. Co, Wash, D.C, 47-49, Proctor & Gamble Co, 49-50, Radio Sta. WOR, N.Y, 50, WOIC TV Sta, Wash, 50 and Columbia Broadcasting Syst, N.Y, 50-57, gen. mgr, WXIX-TV, Milwaukee, Wis, 57-59; v.pres. and gen. mgr, WCBS-TV, N.Y, 59-63; v.pres, CBS-TV Network, 63-65, sr. v.pres, 65, exec. v.pres, CBS-TV Stas, 65-67, pres, CBS/TV Serv, 68-69. Mil. Serv: Lt.(jg), Navy. Mem: Stanwich Club, Greenwich, Conn. Young Man of the Year, N.Y, 60. Rel: Catholic. Legal Res: Cliff Rd, Greenwich, Conn. 06830. Mailing Add: 1750 Pennsylvania Ave. N.W, Washington, D.C. 20547.

SHANAHAN, ELWILL M. R
Secy. of State, Kans.
b. Salina, Kans, 9/22/12; d. August G. Mattson and Adine O. Peterson M; m. 10/13/51 to Paul R. Shanahan; wid. Educ: Grad. and registered nurse, Swedish Covenant Hosp, Chicago, Ill, 34. Polit. & Govt. Pos: Secy. of State, Kans, 66- Mem: Nat. Asn. of Secy. of States; Kans. Fedn. Rep. Women's Clubs; Topeka Soroptomist Club; Am. Bus. Women's Asn; bd. dirs, Kans. Chap, Am. Soc. for Pub. Adminstrs; hon. chmn, Sunflower Chap, Nat. Cystic Fibrosis Found; Shawnee and Wabaunsee Sportsman Asns; past mem, Beta Sigma Phi, Bus. & Prfnl Women's Club and Nat. State Nurses Asn. Rel: Protestant. Legal Res: 1320 W. 27th St, Apt. J-62, Topeka, Kans. 66611. Mailing Add: Secretary of State Office, Topeka, Kans. 66612.

SHANAHAN, FRANK EDWARD, JR. D
b. Vicksburg, Miss, 8/20/23. Educ: Univ. Miss, B.B.A. and LL.B, 48, J.D, 68; Sigma Nu; Delta Sigma Pi. Polit. & Govt. Pos: Former secy, Workmen's Compensation Cmn, Miss; Miss. State Rep, 56-68. Bus. & Prof. Pos: Lawyer. Mem: Miss. State Bar Asn; Am. Bar Asn; Scribes; VFW; Am. Legion; K. of P; Am. Judicature Soc. Rel: Methodist. Mailing Add: Box 75, Vicksburg, Miss. 39180.

SHANK, CLARE BROWN WILLIAMS R
Life Mem, Pinellas Co. Rep. Exec. Cmt, Fla.
b. Syracuse, N.Y, 9/19/09; d. Curtiss Crofoot Brown and Clara Irene Shoudy B; m. 2/18/40 to Frank Eugene Williams (deceased 2/13/57); m. 12/28/63 to Seth Carl Shank. Educ: Syracuse Univ, B.A. in oral eng, 31; Zeta Phi Eta; Pi Beta Phi. Polit. & Govt. Pos: Mem. exec. cmt, Fla. Fedn. Rep. Women, 52-64; life mem, Pinellas Co. Rep. Exec. Cmt, 52-; mem, Pinellas Co. State Rep. Cmt, 54-58; mem, Fla. State Rep. Exec. Cmt, 54-; mem. exec. cmt, Rep. Nat. Cmt, 56-64, asst. chmn, and dir. women's activities, 58-64; mem. adv. bd, U.S. Civil War Centennial Cmn; mem, Defense Adv. Cmn. on Women in Serv, 59-65; alternate del, and mem. exec. arrangements cmt, Rep. Nat. Conv, 60; del. and mem. prog. and arrangements cmts, 64. Bus. & Prof. Pos: Teacher, 31-33; merchandising exec, 33-42. Mem: Bus. & Prfnl. Women's Club; Am. Asn. Univ. Women; Am. Newspaper Women's Club; Gen. Fedn. Women's Clubs; DAR; Colonial Dames; 17th Century Club; Capitol Hill Club; pres, Women's Rep. Club, 55-57; Woman's Club; Yacht Club; Bath Club. Recipient, George Arents Award, Syracuse Univ. Rel: Presbyterian. Mailing Add: 7200 34th St. S, Apt. 6A, St. Petersburg, Fla. 33711.

SHANK, MARY ELLEN D
V.Pres, Kans. Fedn. Women's Dem. Clubs
b. St. John, Kans, 12/24/35; d. Harry Judah Waters and Cora Helen Long W; m. 3/17/57 to Robert Henry Shank; c. Theryne Kay and Kevyn Ray. Educ: McPherson Col, Elem. Sch. Teaching Cert, 56. Polit. & Govt. Pos: Dem. precinct committeewoman, Rose Valley Twp, Stafford Co, Kans, 59-; charter pres, Stafford Co. Federated Women's Dem. Club, St. John, 61-65; secy, Stafford Co. Dem. Cent. Cmt, 62-64, v.chmn, 64-68, chmn, 68-; First S.Dist. dir, Kans. Fedn. Dem. Women's Club, 65-69, v.pres, 69-; mem. Pvt. and Govt. Employ. Cmt, Gov. Cmn. on Status of Women, 68- Bus. & Prof. Pos: Elem. sch. teacher, Johnson, Kans, 56-58; co-owner and operator of farm, 57- Publ: 'Protests Inaugural', Hutchinson News, Kans, 1/69. Mem: Jr. Golden Circle (served in every off. during last ten years, presently pres). Rel: Church of the Brethren; chorister, Eden Valley Church of the Brethren, St. John, Kans, 62-67, Women's Work V.Pres, 66-68. Mailing Add: R.R. 2, Box 126, St. John, Kans. 67576.

SHANK, RICHARD EUGENE R
Ind. State Rep.
b. North Lima, Ohio, 10/26/32; s. Lauren J. Shank and Mary Yoder S.(deceased); m. 2/24/57 to Eileen A; c.Larry J, David L. and Sharon K. Educ: Hesston Col, 50-51. Polit. & Govt. Pos: Secy, Concord Twp. Adv. Bd, Ind, 64-66; Ind. State Rep, Elkhart, Noble and Lagrange Co, 66-; mem, Gov. Traffic Safety Adv. Cmt, 67-; chmn. pub. safety, Fed. Safety Prog, 68-; chmn, Local Transportation Study Cmt, currently. Mem: Pres, Elkhart Co. Homebuilders; Goshen Realtors; Moose; Farm Bur; Jaycees (pres, 60); C. of C; Boy Scouts; Red Cross; Toastmasters. Nominee, Distinguished Serv. Award, 3 times. Rel: Protestant. Mailing Add: R.R. 1, Box 337-L, Elkhart, Ind. 46514.

SHANKEL, BUFORD L. D
Chmn, Johnson Co. Dem. Cmt, Kans.
b. Hiattville, Kans, 11/16/26; s. Elmer D. Shankel and Lola Mae Neil S; m. 6/5/55 to Carolyn M. Ramsey. Educ: Fort Scott Jr. Col, A.A, 48; Wichita Univ, B.A, 51; Washburn Univ, LL.B, 53; Phi Alpha Delta. Polit. & Govt. Pos: Chmn, Bourbon Co. Dem. Cmt, Kans, 57-60; exam, State Workmen's Compensation Cmn, 58-61; co. attorney, Bourbon Co, 55-57; chmn, Johnson Co. Dem. Cmt, 66- Mil. Serv: Entered as Pvt, army, 45, released as S/Sgt, 46, after serv. in Pac. Theatre, 45-46. Mem: Johnson Co. Kans. Bar Asn; Am. Trial Lawyer Asn; VFW; Elks; Am. Legion; Mason. Rel: Protestant. Mailing Add: 6010 Reinhardt Dr, Shawnee Mission, Kans. 66205.

SHANLEY, BERNARD MICHAEL R
Rep. Nat. Committeeman, N.J.
b. Newark, N.J, 1903; s. Bernard Michael Shanley and Regina Ryan S; m. 8/1/30 to Maureen Virginia Smith; c. Maureen Virginia, Seton, Kevin, Brigid and Brendan. Educ: Columbia Univ, 25; Fordham Univ. Law Sch, 28. Polit. & Govt. Pos: Adv. on Eisenhower's Campaign Staff, 52; spec. counsel to the President, 53-55, secy, 55-57; counsel and chmn, N.J. Rep. State Cmt; former mem. exec. cmt, Rep. Nat. Cmt; Rep. Nat. Committeeman, N.J, currently. Bus. & Prof. Pos: Law practice, Shanley & Fisher, Newark, 52-; also Shanley, Fisher & Kuykendall, Wash, on leave of absence, 53-55; trustee, Victoria Found. Mil. Serv: Army, 42-45; War Dept. Citation. Mem: Am, N.J, Essex Co. and Somerset Co. Bar Asns; K. of M; Somerset Hills Country Club, Bernardsville; Essex Club, Newark; Metrop, Capitol Hill and Union Clubs; Nat. Golf Links of Am. Club, Southhampton. Rel: Roman Catholic. Mailing Add: Dryden Rd, Bernardsville, N.J. 07924. (1967)

SHANNAHAN, JOHN D
b. Sioux City; c. one son. Educ: Sioux City High Sch. Polit. & Govt. Pos: Iowa State Rep -66; Secy. and Lobbyist for Iowa Truckers Asn; 2 years Fed. Govt, Supvry. capacity as a Transportation Spec. Bus. & Prof. Pos: Ed, The Truckers Farm Mkt. News, Publisher 17 years; Sold motor trucks 10 years. Rel: Catholic. Mailing Add: 905 Cornelia St, Sioux City, Iowa 51105. (1967)

SHANNON, JANET LORETTA D
b. San Rafael, Calif, 12/17/37; d. H. W. Laster and Flora Rogers L; m. 2/7/58 to Larry R. Shannon; c. Careen and Patrick. Educ: Univ. Calif, Davis, 1½ years; San Francisco State Col, 1½ years; Alpha Phi Gamma. Polit. & Govt. Pos: Alameda Co. Press Aide, Salinger for Sen. Campaign, Calif, 64; alternate del, Dem. Nat. Conv, 68; mem, N.Y. State New Dem. Coalition, 68-69, del, 69; mem, Concerned Dem. for New Polit, 68-69, exec. bd, 69. Bus. & Prof. Pos: Freelance, Pub. Relations, Fremont, Calif, 63-64; Reporter, Fremont News Register, 64-66. Mem: Fremont Dem. Women's Forum, 63-66. Mailing Add: 98-40 57th Ave, Rego Park, N.Y. 11368.

SHANNON, JOE, JR. D
Tex. State Rep.
b. Fort Worth, Tex, 11/9/40; s. Joe Shannon and Juanita Elizabeth Milliorn S; m. 8/10/68 to Carol Tinsley; c. Kelly Jane and Joseph Patrick. Educ: Univ. Tex, B.A, 62 and LL.B, 63; Phi Alpha Delta; Silver Spurs. Polit. & Govt. Pos: Tex. State Rep, Dist. 52-2, 64- Bus. & Prof. Pos: Attorney-at-law, 63- Mem: Mason; State and Local Bar Asns; Jr. C. of C. Rel: Presbyterian. Legal Res: 4416 Tamworth, Fort Worth, Tex. 76116. Mailing Add: 306 Union Bank Bldg, Ft. Worth, Tex. 76102.

SHAPIRO, DAVID CHARLES R
Ill. State Rep.
b. Mendota, Ill, 2/16/25; s. Hymen Shapiro and Minnie Sprizer S; m. 9/15/47 to Norma Jean Hall; c. Sarah Beth, Deborah Leah, Margaret Sue, Edward Henry 'Ned,' Michael Andrew, Elizabeth Ann and Daniel Hall. Educ: Stanford Univ, ASTP, 43-44; Univ. Ill, B.S, 48; Univ. Ill, Col. of Dent, D.D.S, 52. Polit. & Govt. Pos: Pres, Lee Co. Bd. Health, 60-69; pres, Ill. Asn. Bd. Health, 63-64; mem, Amboy Unit Dist. 272 Sch. Bd, 61-69; alderman, Amboy, Ill, 61-69; Ill. State Rep, 35th Dist, 69- Bus. & Prof. Pos: Pres, Amboy Pub. Hosp, 53-59. Mil. Serv: Entered as Pvt, Army, 43, released as Pfc, 46, after serv. in 289th Inf, ETO, 44-46; Bronze Star; Combat Infantryman's Badge; Three Battle Stars. Mem: Whiteside-Lee Dent. Soc.(pres, 63); Ill. State Dent. Soc. (prog. chmn, 65); Am. Dent. Asn.(del, annual conv, 62); Amboy Lions Club (pres, 56); Elks; Am. Legion; AF&AM; Consistory; Shrine. Rel: Jewish. Mailing Add: 32 N. Jefferson, Amboy, Ill. 61310.

SHAPIRO, MARVIN S. D
Legal Counsel, Calif. Dem. Party
b. New York, N.Y, 10/26/36; s. Benjamin Shapiro and Sally Book S; m. 7/12/59 to Natalie Kover; c. Donna and Meryl. Educ: Columbia Col, N.Y.C, A.B, 57; Columbia Law Sch, N.Y.C, LL.B, 59. Polit. & Govt. Pos: alternate del, Dem. Nat. Conv, 68; Legal counsel, Calif. Dem. Party, 68- Bus. & Prof. Pos: Trial Attorney, Civil Div, U.S. Dept. of Justice, 59-61; assoc, Law Firm of Irell & Manella, 62-66, partner, 66- Mil. Serv: Entered as E-1, Army, 60, released as E-3, 63, after serv. in 311th Logistical Command. Publ: Personal Holding Companies Under the 1964 Revenue Act, Univ. of South. Calif. Tax Inst, 65; 'Incipient Tax Benefits in Widow's Election Wills: the Vardell and Gregory Cases' (with E.M. Kaufman), Calif. State Bar J. and Taxes Mag, 63. Mem: Am, Calif. and Los Angeles Bar Asns; bd. of gov, Beverly Hills Bar Asn, 69-; pres, Beverly Hills Barristers, 70. Rel: Jewish. Legal Res: 432 N. Cliffwood Ave, Los Angeles, Calif. 90049. Mailing Add: 900 Gateway East Bldg, Century City, Los Angeles, Calif. 90067.

SHAPIRO, SAMUEL H. D
m. 5/21/39 to Gertrude Adelman. Educ: St. Viator Col; Univ. Ill, J.D, 29. Polit. & Govt. Pos: Past secy. and treas, Young Dem. Ill; city attorney, Kankakee, 33; state's attorney, Kankakee Co, 36; Ill. State Rep, 46-60, chmn, Pub. Aid, Health, Welfare and Safety Cmt, Ill. House of Rep, 59, mem, Judiciary, Appropriations and Exec. Cmts; chmn, Gov. Adv. Coun. on Ment. Retardation; mem, Intergovt. Cmn. and Legis. Coun; chmn, Ment. Health Cmn, 61; Lt. Gov, Ill, 61-68 and Gov, 68-69; del, Dem. Nat. Conv, 68. Mil. Serv: Navy, World War II, serv. in antisubmarine warfare unit. Mem: Chmn, Nat. Conf. Lt. Gov, 62; Coun. on Improv. Econ. and Soc. Status Older People; Narcotics Cmn; Am, Ill, Kankakee Co. and Chicago Bar Asns; Decalogue Soc. Lawyers; C. of C; Country Club; Kiwanis; Moose; Past Exalted Ruler,

Elks; Covenant Club Ill; B'nai B'rith; Am. Legion; Amvets; Temple B'nai Israel; past pres, Musician's Union and Kankakee Fedn. Labor; past nat. pres, Alpha Epsilon Pi; Nat. Civil Rights Cmt, Anti-Defamation League. Rel: Jewish. Legal Res: 208 S. La Salle St, Chicago, Ill. 60604. Mailing Add: City Nat. Bank Bldg, Kankakee, Ill. 60901.

SHAPIRO, STANLEY LESTER R
b. New York, N.Y, 3/8/40; s. Harry Shapiro and Rose Morgenstern S; m. 5/31/64 to Natalie Laura Bernstein; c. Carolyn Gail and Andrea Ruth. Educ: City Col, N.Y.C, B.B.A, 61; N.Y. Univ. Sch. Law, LL.B, 66; Carolan Guard, Student Houses at City Col. Polit. & Govt. Pos: Cong. intern, Congressman J. V. Lindsay, N.Y, 61; with Off. of Probation, City of New York, 64-65, asst. to cmnr, Dept. Water Supply, Gas and Elec, 65-66; area coordinator, Lindsay for Mayor, 65; Rep. nominee for U.S. Rep, N.Y, 68; law chmn, Morrissania Rep. Club, Bronx, 68- Bus. & Prof. Pos: Attorney, Law Off. of Thomas J. Manton, 67-68; partner, Shapiro & Marks, Attorneys at law, 68-69; attorney, Law Off. of Stanley L. Shapiro, 68-69. Mil. Serv: Entered as 2nd Lt, Army, 61, released as 1st Lt, 63, after serv. in Second Brigade, Fifth Div, Ft. Devans, Mass; Two Letters of Commendations. Mem: Morrissania Rep. Club. Rel: Jewish. Legal Res: 6 Thornwood Way, Setauket, N.Y. 11733. Mailing Add: 401 Broadway, New York, N.Y. 10013.

SHAPP, MILTON J. D
b. Cleveland, Ohio, 6/25/12; s. Aaron Shapiro Shapp and Eva Smelsey S; m. 5/19/47 to Muriel Matzkin; c. Dolores (Mrs. Gary Graham), Richard and Joanne. Educ: Case Inst. of Tech, B.S.E.E, 33; Tau Beta Pi; Sigma Alpha Mu. Polit. & Govt. Pos: Consult, Peace Corps, 61-63; consult, U.S. Dept. of Commerce for Econ. Develop, 61-63; v.chmn, Nat. Pub. Adv. Cmt. on Area Redevelop, 61-64; former chmn, Phila. Peace Corps Serv. Orgn, Pa; former chmn, Manpower Utilization Cmn, Phila; former mem, Gov. Cmt. of 100 for Better Educ; del, Dem. Nat. Conv, 68. Bus. & Prof. Pos: Pres. and chmn. bd, Jerrold Corp, Phila, 47-66; pres, Shapp Corp, 67- Mil. Serv: Entered as 2nd Lt, Army, 42, released as Capt, 46, after serv. in Signal Corps, Mediterranean and Austrian Occup, 43-46. Publ: 'Report of the Delaware Valley Committee on New Growth and New Jobs'; 'New Growth: New Jobs for Pennsylvania'; 'The Shapp Report', (2 issues), 65. Mem: Jewish Commun. Rels. Coun; Am. Jewish Coun; United World Federalists; Nat. Coun. on Aging; Phila. Asn. for Retarded Children, Inc; VFW; Jewish War Vet; B'nai B'rith; Am. Legion. Humanitarian Award, Pa. State Baptist Conv, 66; Good Neighbor Award, Sherwood Cobbs Creek Citizens for Commun. Improv, 66; Man of the Year Award, Nat. Coun. of Indust. Mgt. Clubs, 65-66; Distinguished Serv. Award, North City Cong, 65; B'nai B'rith Youth Serv. Award, 65, Rueben J. Miller B'nai B'rith Youth Award, 64, William Penn Lodge B'nai B'rith Youth Award, 64; Phila. Chap. Unico Man-of-the-Year Award, 64; Achievement Award, Bright Hope Baptist Church, 63; Annual Award for Good Citizenship, Pa. AFL-CIO, 63; People-to-People Award, Phila. Zionist Orgn, 63; Brotherhood Award, Frontiers Int, Inc, 61 & 63; Women's Am. Citation for Meritorious Serv, Orgn. for Rehabilitation Through Training, Phila, 63; Case Inst. of Tech. Alumni Award, 63; Greater W.Oak Lane Coord. Coun. Award, 63; Humanitarian Award, Nat. Bus. League, Phila, 62; Phila. Fel. Cmn. Award, 62; Allied Jewish Appeal Award, Fedn. of Jewish Agencies for Greater Phila, 62; Citizenship Award, Salem Baptist Church, Jenkintown, 62; Citation, Nat. Pub. Adv. Cmt. on Redevelop, 61. Rel: Jewish. Legal Res: 626 S. Bowman Ave, Merion, Pa. 19066. Mailing Add: 1425 Walnut St, Philadelphia, Pa. 19102.

SHARATZ, MARGUERITE THERESA R
Mem, Calif. Rep. State Cent. Cmt.
b. Shreveport, La, 6/9/15; d. George Lee Church and Marie O'Dwyer C; m. 6/26/48 to Nick Sharatz; c. Joan (Mrs. Antonacci); grandchildren, Angelia, Pamela and Donald. Educ: Amarillo High Sch, Tex, 4 years. Polit. & Govt. Pos: Mem, Calif. Rep. State Cent. Cmt, 67- Bus. & Prof. Pos: Patents for inventing Outside Safety Toe and Method for Displaying Minute Man Pennants, 53. Mem: Eastern Star; Wednesday Club; Nat. Fedn. Rep. Women. Rel: Catholic. Mailing Add: 2148 Tipton Way, Fairfield, Calif. 94533.

SHARFSIN, JOSEPH D
b. Allendale, S.C; s. Moses Sharfsin and Rebecca Hepner S; single. Educ: Dickinson Sch. Law, LL.B, 20; Phi Epsilon Pi; Friendly Sons of St. Patrick. Polit. & Govt. Pos: City solicitor, Phila, Pa, 36-40; spec. counsel, Fed. Works Admin, 40-41; mem, Pa. Pub. Utility Cmn, 56-65, chmn, 61-65; alternate del, Dem. Nat. Conv, 64, del, 68. Mil. Serv: Entered as Pvt, Army, 18, released as Sgt, 19, after serv. in Students Army Training Corps. Publ: 'Capitalizing Future Income to Meet Depression Needs,' Pa. Bar Asn. Quart, 4/40; 'The Lawyer's Role in Regulation,' Pub. Utilities Fortnightly, 11/8/62. Mem: Phila. Bar Asn; Lawyers Club of Phil; exec. cmt, Nat. Asn. of R.R. and Utility Cmnrs; mem. of bd, Phila. Housing Authority, 68-69. Capt, Tennis Team, Dickinson Col; Jr. Championship Doubles of Pa. Rel: Jewish. Mailing Add: Philadelphia National Bank Bldg, Broad & Chestnut Sts, Philadelphia, Pa. 19106.

SHARKEY, GEORGE EDWARD D
Chmn, Alger Co. Dem. Party, Mich.
b. Munising, Mich, 6/16/29; s. Edward James Sharkey and Beatrice Miron S; m. 11/21/53 to Rita Ann Dauzy; c. Steven. Educ: Mather High Sch, Munising, Mich, 12 years. Polit. & Govt. Pos: Chmn, Alger Co. Dem. Party, Mich, currently. Mil. Serv: Entered as Pvt, Army, 51, released as Sgt, 52, after serv. in 24th Inf. Div, Japan. Mem: Am. Legion (past vice comdr); K. of C; Catholic Order of Foresters; Union Steward, Local 87, United Paper Workers of Am; secy, Pictured Rocks Golf and Country Club; Munising City Cmn. Rel: Catholic. Mailing Add: 212 Lynn St, Munising, Mich. 49862.

SHAROOD, RICHARD NEWELL R
b. Fargo, N.Dak, 4/27/35; s. Robert A. Sharood and Catewood Hoy S; m. 7/9/60 to Barbara Hammes; c. John N, Julia M. and Mary C. Educ: Georgetown Univ, B.S, 58, LL.B. and J.D, 63; Delta Theta Phi. Polit. & Govt. Pos: Exam, Fed. Maritime Cmn, Va, 59-64; mem, Arlington Co. Rep. Cmt, Va, 64-67; admin. asst. to U.S. Rep. William L. Scott, Va, 68-69; minority counsel, House Cmt. on Merchant Marine and Fisheries, 69- Bus. & Prof. Pos: Attorney-at-law, Alexandria, Va, 64-68. Mil. Serv: Entered as Pvt, Army, 58, released as Sp-4, 59; Res, 59-64. Mem: Am. Bar Asn; U.S. Naval Inst; Va. Trial Lawyers Asn; Civitan Int. Rel: Catholic. Mailing Add: 7600 Mahoney Dr, Lorton, Va. 22079.

SHARP, ANTHONY GRAY R
Chmn, Pottawatomie Co. Rep. Party, Okla.
b. Sacred Heart, Okla, 3/7/23; s. William Rouss Sharp and Aimee Jean Butts S; m. 12/14/52 to Sara Sue Slagle; c. Sara Lyn, Toni Gay and Amy Beth. Educ: Univ. Okla, B.S. in geology, 51. Polit. & Govt. Pos: Campaign mgr, Okla. State Sen, Pottawatomie Co, 64; chmn, Pottawatomie Co. Rep. Party, 65- Mil. Serv: Entered as Pvt, Air Force, 43, released as Cpl, 46, after serv. in 397th Bomb Group; hon. discharge. Mem: Am. Legion; Mason; Farm Bur. Rel: Church of Christ. Mailing Add: 714 West Wood, Shawnee, Okla. 74801.

SHARP, DUDLEY CRAWFORD R
b. Houston, Tex, 3/16/05; s. Walter Benona Sharp and Estelle Boughton S; m. 1/8/29 to Tina Cleveland; c. Dudley C, Jr. and Julia May Vergara (Mrs. Jose). Educ: Princeton Univ, B.S, 28; Tiger Inn Club. Polit. & Govt. Pos: Asst. secy. of Air Force, 55-59, undersecy, 59 and secy, 59-61; chmn, Tex. Rep. Finance Cmt, 64 & 65; finance chmn, Sen. Tower's Campaign, 66; del, Rep. Nat. Conv, 68. Bus. & Prof. Pos: V.pres, Mission Mfg. Co, 28-46, pres, 46-55, v.chmn. of bd, 61-64, chmn. bd, 64- Mil. Serv: Entered as Lt.(jg), Navy, released as Lt. Comdr, 45, after serv. in Anti-Submarine Warfare, Atlantic and Pac. Areas; Exceptional Civilian Serv. Award; Defense Medal of Freedom. Mem: Chmn. bd, Houston Lighthouse for the Blind; dir, Houston C. of C; Houston Country Club; Petroleum Club; Ramada Club; Tejas Club. Rel: Episcopal. Mailing Add: 109 N. Post Oak Lane, Houston, Tex. 77024.

SHARP, JOSEPH LESSIL R
Chmn, Custer Co. Rep. Cent. Cmt, Idaho
b. Logan, Utah, 10/8/14; s. Joseph Lessil Sharp, Sr. and Helga Elisa Larsen S; m. 2/16/41 to Elsie Joyce Fox; c. William Derrell and Jacqueline Elsie (Mrs. Richards). Educ: Univ. Idaho, South. Br, 37-38; Utah State Col, B.S. in Educ, 41. Polit. & Govt. Pos: Co. Supt. Pub. Instr, Custer Co, Idaho, 49-51; justice of the peace, Challis Precinct, Custer Co, 51-53; probate judge, Custer Co, 54-; finance chmn, Custer Co. Rep. Cent. Cmt, 56-64, chmn, 66-; Rep. committeeman, Challis Precinct, 64- Bus. & Prof. Pos: Teacher and prin, Idaho High Schs, 40-50; pres, Custer Co. Abstract Co. Ltd, Challis, 47-61; owner-mgr, Challis Ins. Agency, 47-69; pres, Custer Co. Title Inc, 61- Publ: Numerous letters on various subjects, Post Register and Idaho Daily Statesman. Mem: Idaho Probate Judges Asn.(secy, 60 & 61, v.pres, 62, pres, 62-64); AF&AM; RAM (Grand Chap); K.T.(Grand Commandry); AAONMS; Cent. Idaho Rod and Gun Club; Lions (pres, Challis Chap, 65); C. of C. Hagerman High Sch. Scholarship Hon. Plaque, 33; Boxing Letter, Univ. Idaho, 37-38. Rel: Latter-day Saint. Legal Res: 100 N. Main, Challis, Idaho 83226. Mailing Add: Box 37, Challis, Idaho 83226.

SHARP, JOHN MALCOLM R
Treas, Pine Co. Rep. Cmt, Minn.
b. St. Paul, Minn, 6/27/19; s. Arthur Benjamin Sharp and Jessie D. Parshall S; m. 3/23/43 to Susan Jane Peterson; c. John M, Jr, Susan Marion and James Arthur. Educ: Univ. of Minn, B.S.L, 40, LL.B, 47; Iron Wedge. Polit. & Govt. Pos: Spec. asst. attorney gen, Minn, 48-55; secy, Pine Co. Rep. Cmt, 62-65, chmn, 65-68, treas, 68-; chmn, Pine Co. Redevelop. Cmn, 62- Bus. & Prof. Pos: Attorney-at-law, 55- Mil. Serv: Entered as Ens, Naval Res, 41, released as Lt. Comdr, 45, after serv. in Patrol Squadron 74, Pac. and Atlantic Theatres; Presidential Unit Citation; Am, Asiatic and Atlantic Theatre Ribbons. Mem: Minn. State Bar Asn.(mem. coun, real estate sect, 56-60); Am. Judicature Soc; Past Master, Mason; VFW; State Youth Activities Cmt; mem. exec. cmt, Lake Superior Coun, Boy Scouts, mem, Nat. Coun; Lions; Wilderness Soc; Sierra Club. Nat. Aide-de-camp, VFW, 68. Rel: Presbyterian. Legal Res: 105 Third Ave. N.E, Pine City, Minn. 55063. Mailing Add: 243 Sixth St, Pine City, Minn. 55063.

SHARP, JOSHUA P. R
Chmn, Whitley Co. Rep. Party, Ky.
b. Williamsburg, Ky, 4/23/09; s. James W. Sharp and Lula Belle Ellis S; m. 8/11/53 to Emma Patrick; c. Jolly Kay. Educ: Cumberland Col, 29-31; London Sch. of Bus. Polit. & Govt. Pos: Campaign chmn, Whitley Co. Rep. Party, Ky, 56, 60 & 62, chmn, 64-; field secy to U.S. Rep. Tim Lee Carter, Fifth Dist, Ky, 69- Bus. & Prof. Pos: Teacher, Whitley Co. Bd. of Educ, various years since 32; tax consult, Williamsburg, Ky, 46-; off. mgr, Steely Ins. Agency, 53-63. Publ: Polit. Advert. Writing in various local papers, 51- Mem: Optimists. Legal Res: Florence St, Williamsburg, Ky. 40769. Mailing Add: P.O. Box 36, Williamsburg, Ky. 40769.

SHARP, MRS. THELMA P. D
Mem, Dem. Nat. Cmt. for N.J.
b. Vineland, N.J, 5/12/98; d. James Casper Parkinson and Ina Fenton P; m. 6/28/41 to William Howard Sharp, wid. 12/17/57. Educ: Smith Col, A.B, 21. Polit. & Govt. Pos: Dem. state committeewoman, Cumberland Co, N.J, 22-; mem, Cumberland Co. Bd. Taxes, 23-36, pres, 26-29; del-at-lg, Dem. Nat. Conv, 24-56, mem, Platform Cmt, 52, co-chmn, 56 and del, 68; del, White House Conf. on Educ; mem, N.J. Bd. Tax Appeals, 32-34; mem, Assay Cmn, 36; v.chmn, Cumberland Co. Dem. Party, 48-56; mem, Dem. Nat. Cmt, N.J, 54- and mem. Nat. Exec. Cmt. Adv. Cmt, 56-; del, White House Conf. on Educ; pres, Civil Serv. Cmn, N.J; mem, Women's Adv. Cmt, World's Fair, N.Y. Bus. & Prof. Pos: Pres. bd. visitors, Vineland Training Sch; v.pres. bd. dirs, Roosevelt Park Colony for Aged; trustee, Methodist Home for Aged, N.J. Welfare Coun; adv. coun, Grad. Sch. Soc. Studies, Rutgers Univ; teacher, Vineland High Sch, 22. Mem: Women's Soc. Christian Serv.(past pres.); Am. Asn. UN (trustee N.J. Br.); Am. Asn. Univ. Women (past pres, Cumberland Br; past state div. 2nd v.pres; state legis. chmn.); United Coun. Church Women (past regional v.pres); Acad. Polit. & Soc. Scis; Am. Legion Auxiliary; Newcomb Hosp. Auxiliary; N.J, Cumberland Hist. Asns; N.J. Art League Vineland Little Theater; N.Y. State Grange; N.J. Welfare Coun. Mailing Add: 702 Wood St, Vineland, N.J. 08360. (1967)

SHARPE, JOHN GEORGE R
Chmn, Columbia Co. Rep. Cmt, N.Y.
b. Bronx, N.Y, 3/24/30; s. John Sharpe and Ada Crawford S; m. 10/29/50 to Joan Marie Sherman; c. Elizabeth Ann, Barbara Jean and Susan Marie. Educ: N.Y. Univ, 2 years; Russell Sage Col, 1 year. Polit. & Govt. Pos: Committeeman, Columbia Co. Rep. Party, N.Y, 58-; del, N.Y. State Rep. Conv, 66; chmn, Columbia Co. Rep. Cmt, 69- Bus. & Prof. Pos: Ins. claimsman, Nationwide

Ins, 54-57; ins. broker, Sharpe Agency Inc, Hudson, N.Y, 57- Mil. Serv: Pvt, Army Nat. Guard, 48; Capt, Res, currently; State of N.Y. Long and Faithful Serv. Medal. Mem: Militia Asn. of the U.S; Elks; Jr. C. of C. Int.(lifetime fel). Recipient of Distinguished Serv. Award, Jr. C. of C. Rel: Dutch Reform. Mailing Add: East Camp Rd, Germantown, N.Y. 12526.

SHARPE, T. MALONE D
Mem, Ga. State Dem. Exec. Cmt.
b. Atlanta, Ga, 2/23/33; m. to Conni Loy; c. Marcia and Sterling. Educ: Mid. Ga. Col, grad, 52; Walter F. George Sch. Law, Mercer Univ, grad, 55. Polit. & Govt. Pos: Aide to Lt. Gov. Garland T. Byrd, Ga, 59-62; aide to Lt. Gov. Peter Zack Geer, 63-66; one of four campaign mgr. for Gov. Marvin Griffin, 62; worked in candidacies of Lt. Gov. Peter Zack Geer and Gov. Lester Maddox, 67; mem, Cong. Dist. Dem. Orgn, 69-; mem, Ga. State Dem. Exec. Cmt, 69-; mem. finance cmt, Dem. Party of Ga, 69-; chmn, Toombs Co. Dem. Exec. Cmt, Ga, 69- Bus. & Prof. Pos: Partner, Law Firm of Sharpe, Sharpe, Hartley & Newton, Lyons, Ga, currently. Mem: Circuit, Ga. and Am. Bar Asns; mem. gen. practice and ins. and negligence counsel sect, Am. Bar Asn; past v.chmn, sect. of workmen's compensation and secy. sect. on ins, Ga. Bar Asn; Defense Counsel Asn; dir, Peoples Bank of Lyons; mem. adv. bd, Atlanta Muscular Dystrophy Asn; past ex-officio mem. of bd. dir, Ga. Soc. for Prevention of Blindness; former dir, Ga. Asn. Mental Health; Bulldog Booster Club, Lyons, Ga; Bulldog Club, Univ. Ga; mem. bd. dir, State C. of C; mem, Lyons Elem. PTA; Jaycees. Rel: Methodist; former teacher of Young Adult Class and mem, Bd. Stewards and chmn, Finance and Stewardship Cmt, First Methodist Church of Lyons; cert. lay speaker. Mailing Add: Lyons, Ga. 30436.

SHARPE, THOMAS G. R
Mich. State Rep.
b. Fowlerville, 4/6/17; m. 1936 to Esther Cornell; c. Thomas, Ronald, Diana, Linda. Educ: Detroit Bus. Univ. Polit. & Govt. Pos: Del, Constitutional Conv; Mich. State Rep, 62- Bus. & Prof. Pos: Farmer and real estate salesman. Mem: Lions Club; past pres, Livingston Co. Farm Bur; former 4-H Club leader. Rel: Nazarene Church. Mailing Add: 4603 Argentine Rd, Howell, Mich. 48843. (1967)

SHARPE, WILLIAM R, JR. D
W.Va. State Sen.
b. Clarksburg, 10/28/28; s. William R. Sharpe and Helen Whitwam S; m. 7/3/53 to Pauline Lester. Educ: W.Va. Univ; Salem Col; Bliss Eng. Sch, Wash, D.C. Polit. & Govt. Pos: W.Va. State Sen, 60- Bus. & Prof. Pos: Elec. engr. and contractor. Mem: Mason; Shrine; Elks; Moose; Int. Brotherhood of Elec. Workers. Rel: Methodist. Mailing Add: State Senate, State Capitol Bldg, Charleston, W.Va. 25305. (1967)

SHARROW, CLEMENT CHARLES D
b. St. Albans, Vt, 6/20/04; m. to Mary Loretta Wry; c. five. Educ: St Albans High Sch. Polit. & Govt. Pos: Dep. sheriff, Vt; sch. cmnr, 54-; Vt. State Rep, 59-63; Vt. State Sen, 65-66. Bus. & Prof. Pos: Transportation acct. for C. V. Rwy, 20 years; customs brokerage. Mem: K. of C; Brotherhood of Rwy. Clerks. Rel: Catholic; Holy Name Soc. Mailing Add: 12 Stowell St, Albans, Vt. 05478.

SHATTUCK, FAY B. R
b. Huntington, Vt, 3/13/00; m. to Maude Wright; c. Two. Educ: Huntington Schs, Vt. Sch. dir, Huntington Center, Vt, 24-26, road cmnr, 34-, fire warden, 35-50 and justice of the peace, 18 years; Vt. State Rep, 57-59 & 65-69. Bus. & Prof. Pos: State patrolman, 10 years. Mem: Dir, Cemetery Asn. Rel: Baptist; trustee. Mailing Add: Huntington Center, Vt. 05462.

SHATTUCK, GEORGE WILLIAM R
Mass. State Rep.
b. Hollis, N.H, 7/17/16; s. George Arthur Shattuck and Grace Smith S; m. 6/12/37 to Martha Elizabeth Duley; c. William Arthur and George Michael. Educ: Bowdoin Col; Univ. N.H. Polit. & Govt. Pos: Committeeman, Schs, Danville, N.H, 45-51, selectman, 45-57; N.H. State Rep, 55-57; mem, Finance Cmt, Pepperell, Mass, 59-; Mass. State Rep, 65-, Minority Whip, Mass. State House of Rep. Bus. & Prof. Pos: Owner, Shattuck Poultry Farms, 39-57; treas, G.A. Shattuck, Inc, 58-66. Mem: Rotary; Mason; Groton Rotary Club; Gidean Lodge. Rel: Protestant. Mailing Add: Mt. Lebanon St, Pepperell, Mass. 01463.

SHATTUCK, PAUL HOWARD R
b. Danville, 9/18/94; m. to Melissa Gill. Educ: Danville. Polit. & Govt. Pos: Vt. State Rep, 61-66; chmn, Rep. Town Cmt. Bus. & Prof. Pos: Ins. agent and farmer. Mem: Grange; Farm Bur; Men's Club. Rel: Congregational. Mailing Add: RFD 1, Concord, Vt. 05824. (1967)

SHAUBAH, JOSE M. R
Mem, V.I. State Rep. Cent. Cmt.
b. Viequez, Puerto Rico, 12/29/19; s. Jose S. Shaubah and Petra Roman de S; single; c. Elena L. Shaubah and Simon J. Shaubah Gill. Educ: High Sch. Polit. & Govt. Pos: Del, Rep. Nat. Conv, 48, 60 & 64, alternate del, 68, mem, platform cmt, 60 & 64; state v.chmn, V.I. Rep. Party, 52-56, state chmn, 56-60; secy, 60-64; Rep. Nat. Committeeman, 57 & 59; mem, V.I. State Rep. Cent. Cmt, 66- Bus. & Prof. Pos: Self employed cattle raiser. Mem: Rotary; V.I. Cattlemen Asn. Rel: Roman Catholic. Mailing Add: P.O. Box 614, Christiansted, St. Croix, Virgin Islands 00820. (1967)

SHAUGHNESSY, EDWARD PAUL D
b. Warren, Ohio, 8/25/40 to Edward Joseph Shaughnessy and Geniveve Giemza S; m. 9/2/61 to Mary Delores Boos; c. Edward Phillip and Michael Paul. Educ: Rockhurst Col, A.B, 61; Dartmouth Col, M.A, 63; Lehigh Univ, Ph.D, 69; Alpha Sigma Nu. Polit. & Govt. Pos: Alternate del, Dem. Nat. Conv, 15th Cong. Dist, Pa, 68. Bus. & Prof. Pos: Asst. prof, math, Lafayette Col, 63- Mem: Am. Math. Soc; Am. Math. Asn. Rel: Roman Catholic. Mailing Add: 305 Monroe St, Easton, Pa. 18042.

SHAUGHNESSY, JOSEPH, JR. R
Ariz. State Rep.
b. Phoenix, Ariz, 6/24/32; s. Joseph Shaughnessy and Kathryn E. Davis S; single. Educ: Ariz. State Univ, B.S, 54; Phi Sigma Kappa. Polit. & Govt. Pos: Precinct Committeeman, Maricopa Dist. 8L, Westwood Rep. Party, 66-; Ariz. State Rep, 66- Mil. Serv: Entered as 2nd Lt, Air Force, 54, released as 1st Lt, 56, after serv. in Hq, Edwards Air Force Base, Calif, Air Research and Develop. Command; Capt, Air Force Res, at present. Mem: Nat. Asn. of Accountants; F&AM. Rel: Protestant. Mailing Add: 2118 W. Heatherbrae Dr, Phoenix, Ariz. 85015.

SHAVER, GERALD DEAN D
Mo. State Rep.
b. Anderson, Mo, 7/22/15; s. Richard Elmer Shaver and Effie Hollis S; m. 11/1/37 to Virginia Lee Lewis; c. Carolyn Kay, Marolyn Fay and Jackie Dean. Polit. & Govt. Pos: Committeeman, Dem. Co. Cmt, 60-64; Mo. State Rep, 65- Bus. & Prof. Pos: Owner, operator, Shaver Bros. Gen. Store, 47-60. Mil. Serv: Pvt, Marine Corps, 45. Mem: Am. Legion. Rel: Baptist. Mailing Add: R.R. 1, Anderson, Mo. 64831. (1967)

SHAVER, JAMES L, JR. D
Ark. State Rep.
b. Wynne, Ark, 11/23/27; s. James Levesque Shaver and Louise Davis S; m. 7/17/49 to Bonnie Wood; c. James Levesque, III and Bonnie Sue. Educ: Univ. Ark, J.D, 51; Delta Theta Phi. Polit. & Govt. Pos: Ark. State Rep, Cross Co, Ark, 55- Mil. Serv: Navy. Mem: N.E. Ark. Develop; Cross Co. Bar Asn. (secy-treas); Ark. and Am. Bar Asns; Rotary; 100 Club; Cross Co. Wildlife Asn; Crowley's Ridge Country Club; Gaslite Club. Rel: Presbyterian. Mailing Add: 568 N. Killough Rd, Wynne, Ark. 72396.

SHAW, EDWARD J. D
Ill. State Rep.
b. Chicago, Ill; c. Edward J, Jr. Educ: Loyola Univ. Polit. & Govt. Pos: Ill. State Rep, currently; mem, 26th Ward Regular Dem. Orgn. Bus. & Prof. Pos: Asst. supt, Bur. of Parking, City of Chicago; Served as adult probation officer for 13 years. Mil. Serv: World War I, 42nd Rainbow Div, France; Purple Heart. Mem: Am. Legion; Rainbow Div. Vets; VFW; Chicago Soc. of Polish Nat. Alliance; Polish Roman Catholic Union of Am; Moose. Rel: Catholic. Mailing Add: 2208 W. Walton St, Chicago, Ill. 60622. (1967)

SHAW, EDWARD WALTER Socialist Workers Party
Nat. Orgn. Secy, Socialist Workers Party
b. Lake County, Ill, 7/13/23; m. 3/2/49 to Rita Roth; c. Two. Polit. & Govt. Pos: Nat. Orgn. secy, Socialist Workers Party, 64- Mil. Serv: Merchant Marine, 42-48. Mem: Int. Typographical Union. Mailing Add: 873 Broadway, New York, N.Y. 10003.

SHAW, ELIZABETH ORR R
Iowa State Rep.
b. Monona, Iowa, 10/2/23; d. Harold Topliff Orr and Hazel Kean O; m. 8/16/46 to Donald Hardy Shaw; c. Elizabeth Ann, Andrew Hardy and Anthony Orr. Educ: Drake Univ, A.B, 45; Univ. Minn, grad. study polit. sci, 46; Univ. Iowa, J.D, 48; Phi Beta Kappa; Order of the Coif; Kappa Kappa Gamma. Polit. & Govt. Pos: Mem, Scott Co. Rep. Women's Club; Iowa State Rep, currently. Bus. & Prof. Pos: Attorney-at-Law, Arlington Heights, Ill, 48-50, Lord Bissel & Brook, Chicago, 50-52 and attorney-at-law, 66- Mem: Iowa and Ill. Bars; PEO Sisterhood; League of Women Voters, Scott Co. Rel: Congregational. Mailing Add: 29 Hillcrest Ave, Davenport, Iowa 52803.

SHAW, JOSEPH TYRON SR. D
b. Ludowici, Ga, 7/16/09; s. Dan Shaw and Laura McGowan S; m. 7/16/39 to Martha Rimes; c. Laura Helen, Joseph Tyron Jr. Educ: Grad. Ludowici High Sch. Polit. & Govt. Pos: Ga. State Rep, 63-64, resigned 63; Ga. State Sen, 59-60; town coun, 49-; co. com, 57, 58. Bus. & Prof. Pos: Civil Engr. Rel: Baptist. Mailing Add: Ludowici, Ga. 31316. (1967)

SHAW, LUTHER WALLACE D
b. Ithaca, N.Y, 11/9/32; s. Dr. Luther Shaw and Lowell Lewis S; m. 12/23/56 to Carolina Georgia Kallquist; c. Luther W and Susan C. Educ: West. Carolina Col, B.S, honors. Polit. & Govt. Pos: Admin. asst. Rep. Roy A. Taylor, 60- Bus. & Prof. Pos: Writer, Asheville Citizens-Times, N.C. Mil. Serv: Spec. 4/C, Army Engrs, 54-56; 1st Lt, Army Res. Legal Res: Waynesville, N.C. 28786. Mailing Add: 5504 Margate St, Springfield, Va. 22151.

SHAW, ROBERT ERNEST R
Chmn, Columbia Co. Rep. Orgn, Wis.
b. Pratt, Kans, 6/27/16; s. Cedric Hadaway Shaw and Harriet Elizabeth Garnett S; m. 2/7/46 to Betty Buck; c. Ann Elizabeth, Jane Luise, Marta Grace and Elizabeth Buck. Educ: Univ. Okla, B.S, 38; Delta Tau Delta. Polit. & Govt. Pos: Spec. Agent, Fed. Bur. Invest, U.S. Dept. Justice, 41-46; Investigative staff mem, House Govt. Opers. Cmt, House Appropriations Cmt, Senate Agr. Cmt. and Senate Judiciary Cmt, 46-55; chmn, Columbia Co. Rep. Orgn, Wis, 67- Bus. & Prof. Pos: Personnel and pub. rels. dir, C.J. Berst & Co, Portage, Wis, 55-60; acct. exec, Marshall Co, Madison and Portage, Wis, 60- Rel: Episcopal. Legal Res: 929 W. Conant, Portage, Wis. 53901. Mailing Add: Box 338, Portage, Wis. 53901.

SHAW, ROBERT JENNINGS R
Chmn, Fulton Co. Rep. Party, Ga.
b. Bronwood, Ga, 8/21/29; s. Robert Edward Shaw and Vesta Jennings S; m. 12/25/50 to Mary Elaine Smith; c. Maria Elena, Melanie Dawn, Susan June and Bobbie Elizabeth Ann. Educ: Ga. Inst. Tech, 47; Univ. Ga, Atlanta Div, 48-50. Polit. & Govt. Pos: V.chmn. finance cmt, Fulton Co. Rep. Party, Ga, 63, chmn. speaker's bur, 64, house dist. chmn. and campaign mgr, cand. for Ga. State Rep, 65, first v.chmn. and chmn. cand. cmt, 66, chmn, 68-; cand, Ga. State Sen, 64; mem. exec. cmt, Fifth Cong. Dist. Rep. Party, 65-; mem, Ga. State Rep. Cent. Cmt, 66- Bus. & Prof. Pos: Gen. agent, Pan-Am. Life Ins. Co, 61-; mem. bd. dir, Atlanta Hosp, 68- Mil. Serv: Entered as Pvt, Air Force, 50, released as S/Sgt, 52, after serv. in 116th Fighter Wing, Far E. Theatre, 51-52. Mem: Atlanta Asn. of Life Underwriters; Gen. Agents and Mgr. Asn. of Atlanta; hon. lifetime mem, South Cobb Jaycees; hon. mem, Phi Sigma Epsilon; pres, Bolton Civic Asn, 66-; v.pres, Bolton Grammar Sch.

PTA, 69. Rel: Baptist; Pres, Brotherhood, 1st Baptist Church of Chattahoochee, 69. Legal Res: 2152 Collins Dr. N.W, Atlanta, Ga. 30318. Mailing Add: 1819 Peachtree St. N.E, Atlanta, Ga. 30309.

SHAW, STANLEY F. R
Maine State Rep.
b. Augusta, Maine, 9/26/17; s. Frederick W. Shaw, Sr. and Abby Carleson S; m. 4/8/44 to Esther L. Zoschka. Educ: St. Paul's Episcopal Sch, grad, 37; Univ. Toledo, Ohio, 43; Univ. Maine. Polit. & Govt. Pos: Mem, Kennebec Co. and First Dist. Cmts; former chmn, Rep. Town Cmt, Chelsea and active mem, 20 years, mem, Area Planning Bd, 2 years, Budget Cmt, 2 years, dir. of Civil Defense, 4 years, truant officer, 9 years, health officer, 9 years, dep. forest fire warden, 13 years, selectman, 11 years and chmn. of bd, 5 years; co. sheriff, Kennebec Co, 8 years; Maine State Rep, 67-, chmn, House Vet. Affairs Cmt. Bus. & Prof. Pos: Lumberman, self-employed. Mil. Serv: Entered as Pvt, Air Force, 43, released as 1st Lt, 46, after serv. in 8th Air Force as B-17 Pilot, ETO; Maj, Air Force Res.(Ret), 66. Mem: Past pres, Kennebec Co. Sheriff's Asn. and Chelsea Volunteer Fire Dept; past master, Chelsea Grange; E. Kennebec Pomona; Maine State and Nat. Grange; Gardiner Lions Club; Fitzgerald Commings Post, Am. Legion; Nat. Guard Asn; dir, Gardiner Gen. Hosp. Rel: Protestant. Legal Res: Chelsea, Maine. Mailing Add: R.R. 2, Gardiner, Maine 04345.

SHAWAN, JACOB ALBRIGHT, III R
b. Columbus, Ohio, 6/11/17; s. Jacob A. Shawan, Jr. and Marie Fahl S, div; c. Cynthia Ann (Mrs. Choate), Jacob A, IV and R. Scott. Educ: Ohio State Univ, B.Sc. in agr, 40; Am. Col. Life Underwriters, C.L.U, 58; Delta Tau Delta. Polit. & Govt. Pos: Councilman, Marble Cliff, Ohio, 42-54, mayor, 54-60; Ohio State Rep, 60-66; co. cmnr, Franklin Co, 68-69; app. by Gov. Rhodes as chmn, Ohio Retirement Study Cmn. Team, 68- Bus. & Prof. Pos: Mem. bd, World Neighbors Inc, Oklahoma City, Okla, 53- and Repub. Franklin Life Ins. Co, 61-; pres, Columbus Life Underwriters, 64-65; v.pres, Cent. Warehouse Distributors Inc, 66- and First Ohio Securities Corp, 68- Mil. Serv: Entered as Pvt, Army, 41, released as Capt, 46, after serv. in 5th Armored Div, ETO, 44-45; 5 Campaign Ribbons; Bronze Star. Mem: Chartered Life Underwriters; life and qualifying mem, Million Dollar Round Table; Mason (32°); Kiwanis; Am. Legion; past pres, Columbus Jr. C. of C. Rel: Protestant. Legal Res: 2350 Neil Ave, Columbus, Ohio 43201. Mailing Add: 1429 King Ave, Columbus, Ohio 43212.

SHAY, SHIRLEY ANN R
Pres, Ore. Fedn. of Rep. Women
b. Williston, N. Dak, 12/25/31; d. Edward B. George and Ann Farris G; m. 9/9/52 to Theodore Lucien Shay; c. Ted, Cammy, Jed and Kim. Educ: Northwest. Univ, 49-52; Willamette Univ, B.A, 67; Alpha Xi Delta. Polit. & Govt. Pos: Pres, Petticoat Pollys Rep. Women's Club, Ore, 63 & 64; v.chmn, Marion Co. Rep. Cent. Cmt, 64-66, chmn, 66-68; legis. chmn, Ore. Fedn. of Rep. Women, 65, second v.pres, 65-67, first v.pres, 67-69, pres, 69-; secy, Ore. Rep. State Cent. Cmt, 66-69; elector, Ore. Electoral Col, 68. Mem: Salem Art Asn; Salem Mem. Hosp. Auxiliary; City Club. Rel: Episcopal. Mailing Add: 3190 Mulberry Dr. S, Salem, Ore. 97302.

SHEA, BART E. D
b. Savannah, Ga, 10/4/27; s. Barth E. Shea, Jr. and Ernestine Ray S; m. 9/12/53 to Nancy C. Morrissey; c. David P, M. Kevin, Theresa M, Sandra P, Gary M, Francis S. and Robert B. Educ: Univ. Ala, B.S, 51; Emory Univ. Law Sch, LL.B, 53. Polit. & Govt. Pos: Ga. State Rep, 63-66; Ga. State Sen, 67-69. Bus. & Prof. Pos: Attorney, Savannah. Mil. Serv: U.S. Inf, 2nd Lt, 46-48; Discharged 1st Lt, U.S. Signal Corps. Mem: K. of C; Savannah Jr. C. of C. (pres, 60-61); bd. dirs, Family Serv-Travelers Aid; Legal Aid Soc. of Savannah; Savannah C. of C; Coastal Empire Coun; Boy Scouts; Whitemarsh Island Commun. Club (past pres). Named Outstanding Young Man of the Year for Savannah, 56. Rel: Catholic. Mailing Add: 31 W. Congress St, Savannah, Ga. 31401. (1967)

SHEA, DONALD F. D
b. Pawtucket, R.I, 9/14/25; m. June, 1950 to Ursula S. Rafferty; c. Donald, Michaela, Christopher, Sarah and Elizabeth. Educ: Providence Col, 50; Georgetown Law Sch, LL.B, 54. Polit. & Govt. Pos: R.I. State Rep, 61-68; campaign chmn. for Frank Licht, 68; exec. asst. to Gov. of R.I, 69- Bus. & Prof. Pos: Attorney-at-law. Mil. Serv: Navy, 43-46. Rel: Roman Catholic. Mailing Add: 26 Fenwick Rd, East Providence, R.I. 02914.

SHEA, GERALD W. D
Ill. State Rep.
b. Oak Park, Ill, 7/25/31; s. John W. Shea and Gertrude Gearen S; m. 6/15/59 to Joanne Sevcik; c. Courtney Claire. Educ: Univ. Ill. Sch. Commerce, B.S. in finance, 57; DePaul Univ. Col. Law, LL.B, 60. Polit. & Govt. Pos: Ill. State Rep, Seventh Dist, currently. Mil. Serv: Entered as Pvt, Army, 54, released as Cpl, 56. Rel: Catholic. Mailing Add: 141 Herrick Rd, Riverside, Ill. 60546.

SHEA, H. JAMES, JR. D
Mass. State Rep.
b. Boston, Mass, 12/10/39; s. Herman James Shea, Jr. and Eileen Curtin S. Educ: Tufts Univ, B.A, 61, study, 67-68; Univ. Va. Law Sch, 61-64; Northeast. Univ, 68-69; pres, Univ. Va. Young Dem. Club. Polit. & Govt. Pos: Alderman, Newton, Mass, 66-; Mass. State Rep, 69- Mem: Am. Polit. Sci. Asn; Mass. Cerebral Palsy (bd. dirs); Newton Citizens for Educ. Rel: Roman Catholic. Mailing Add: 53 Princess Rd, West Newton, Mass. 02165.

SHEA, JAMES D. D
Vt. State Rep.
b. Chester, Pa, 10/7/19; m. to Emelda M. LeBlanc; c. Four. Educ: Chester, Pa. High Sch; St. Michaels Col. Polit. & Govt. Pos: Supvr, Unorganized towns, Chittenden Co, Vt; justice of peace; overseer of poor; mayor; councilman, 3 terms; chmn, Planning Cmn; city grand juror; treas, Chittenden Co. Dem. Cmt; chmn, Winooski Dem. City Cmt; mem, State Judicial Coun; Vt. State Rep, 65-, v.chmn, House Banking and Corp. Cmt, 3 years, House Commerce Cmt, 1 year and House Gen. and Mil. Affairs Cmt, 1 year, Vt. State House of Rep; mem, State Legis. Coun; alternate del, Dem. Nat. Conv, 68. Bus. & Prof. Pos: Admin. asst; salesman. Mil. Serv: Army, Lt, Ord. Dept, 41-45. Mem: K. of C; VFW; Eagles. Rel: Catholic. Mailing Add: 36 LeClair St, Winooski, Vt. 05404.

SHEA, JOHN A. D
b. Cincinnati, Ohio, 11/20/17; s. John A. Shea and Luscia Lively S; m. 11/29/40 to Rebecca L. Thomas; c. John Raymond and Jerry Stephen. Polit. & Govt. Pos: Ind. State Rep, 64-66; treas, Miami Co. Dem. Cent. Cmt, 60-64; justice of peace, 56-62; precinct committeeman, 52-62. Mem: K. of C; Steelworkers, Local 1054. Rel: Roman Catholic. Mailing Add: Amboy, Ind. 46911. (1967)

SHEA, JOHN DANA D
b. Keene, N.H, 8/21/35; s. James Patrick Shea and Ruth White McQuesten S; single. Educ: Burdett Col, 53-55; Delta Nu Omega. Polit. & Govt. Pos: Del. and v.chmn. Cheshire Co. Del, N.H. Dem. Conv, 62-64; city councilman, Keene, N.H, 62-65; N.H. State Rep, 63-64; del, Dem. Nat. Conv, 64. Bus. & Prof. Pos: Bond underwriter, Peerless Ins. Co, 55- Mil. Serv: Entered as Pvt, Army, 58, released as SP-4, 60; Res, 966th Ord. Co. Mem: K. of C; scoutmaster, Boy Scouts; mem. state cmt. and chief counsellor, Local Circle 1619, Columbian Squires. Rel: Roman Catholic. Mailing Add: 90 Adams St, Keene, N.H. 03431. (1967)

SHEA, JOHN FRANCIS D
Chmn, Sonoma Co. Dem. Cent. Cmt, Calif.
b. Winfield, Kans, 12/19/30; s. Perry M. Shea and Anna Fiebiger S; m. 1/18/64 to Dorothy Kennedy Jones; c. Jennifer Marie. Educ: Santa Rosa Jr. Col, A.A, 51; Stanford Univ, B.A, 53; Univ. Calif, Berkeley, J.D, 58; Phi Delta Phi. Polit. & Govt. Pos: Chmn, Sonoma Co. Dem. Cent. Cmt, Calif, 68- Bus. & Prof. Pos: Trial attorney, Dorr, Cooper & Hayes, San Francisco, Calif, 61-62; partner, gen. practice, Geary, Geary & Shea, 63- Rel: Roman Catholic. Legal Res: 3715 Montecito Ave, Santa Rosa, Calif. 95405. Mailing Add: 37 Old Courthouse Sq, Santa Rosa, Calif. 95404.

SHEA, JOSEPH W, JR. D
Mayor, Norwood, Ohio
b. Cincinnati, Ohio, 7/6/18; s. Joseph W. Shea, Sr. and Ada A. Mooar S; m. 4/24/41 to Gertrude M. Reardon; c. Mary C. (Mrs. Heckman), Joseph W, III, Patricia M. and Dennis M. Educ: Xavier Univ. and Chase Col. of Law, Ohio. Polit. & Govt. Pos: City solicitor, Norwood, Ohio, 48-57, mayor, 58-67 & 69-; del, Dem. Nat. Conv, 68. Bus. & Prof. Pos: Lawyer, Shea & MacKay, 46- Mil. Serv: Entered as 2nd Lt, Army, 43, released as Capt, 46, after serv. in China-Burma-India; China-Burma-India Campaign Ribbon. Mem: Many Dem. Clubs; Cincinnati Bar Asn. Swimming and Golf. Rel: Catholic. Legal Res: 2216 Cathedral Ave, Norwood, Ohio 45212. Mailing Add: 4000 Montgomery Rd, Norwood, Ohio 45212.

SHEA, ROBERTA TOLMAN R
b. Hampton, N.H, 5/6/19; d. Robert Eben Tolman and Alice Bemis T; div; c. Robert Jonathan. Educ: Northfield Sch. for Girls, Mass, 34; Nashua High Sch, N.H, 35-37; Margaret's N.H. Sch. of Beauty. Polit. & Govt. Pos: Chmn, Keene Young Rep. Club, N.H, mem. finance cmt, Keene Bus. and Prfnl. Women's Club and Keene Woman's Club, formerly; membership chmn, Cheshire Rep. Women's Club; ballot inspector and moderator, Ward II, Keene; N.H. State Rep, 63-64, 65-66 & 67-68. Bus. & Prof. Pos: Instr, Keene Beauty Acad, 66; dir, Concord Col. Cosmetology, 67 and La Baron Hairdressing Acad, 68- Mem: Nat. Order of Women Legislators; Cheshire Rep. Women's Club; Northfield Alumnae Asn. Rel: Baptist. Legal Res: Nelson, N.H. Mailing Add: 97 E. Broadway, Derry, N.H. 03038.

SHEA, WILLIAM T. D
s. Charles E. Shea; m. to Janice E. Weigand; c. Mary Louise, William T, Jr, Ellen and Kathleen Marie. Educ: Wharton Sch. of Finance and Commerce, Univ. Pa, B.S. in Econ; Univ. Pa. Law Sch, LL.B. Polit. & Govt. Pos: Pres, Meriden Young Dem, Conn, 57-59; mem. bd. of tax rev, Meriden, 2 terms; mayor, Meriden, 63; Conn. State Rep. and minority leader, Conn. House of Rep. until 67; del, Dem. Nat. Conv, 68. Bus. & Prof. Pos: Sr. mem, Shea & Kramer, Attorneys. Mem: Organized the Meriden Cmt. of the Nat. Multiple Sclerosis Soc. Outstanding Young Man of the Year Award by the Meriden C. of C, 63; One of the Outstanding Young Men of Conn, Conn. State Jr. C. of C, 64. Mailing Add: 264 Bradley Ave, Meriden, Conn. 06450. (1967)

SHEALY, WILSON OTTO R
Chmn, Lexington Co. Rep. Party, S.C.
b. Pelion, S.C, 8/16/26; s. Wilson Frank Shealy and Vera Sturkie S; m. 10/26/47 to Edythe Louise Long; c. Wilson O, Jr, Phillip Lee and Barry Dwayne. Educ: Univ. S.C. Polit. & Govt. Pos: Chmn, Lexington Co. Rep. Party, S.C, 66-; pres, Swansea Precinct Rep. Party; co-chmn, Marshal Parker for Sen, Lexington Co. Bus. & Prof. Pos: Salesman, Champion Spark Plug Co, 52-; secy-treas, Johnson Auto Parts Inc, Mt. Pleasant, S.C, currently. Mil. Serv: Entered as Seaman, Navy, 43, released as ADE 3, 47, recalled, 50; Am. Theater Ribbon. Mem: Mason (32°); Shriner; VFW; Toastmasters; Boy Scouts; Nat. Asn. for Stock Car Auto Racing; trustee, Lexington Co. Hosp. and mem, Opers. and Finance Cmt; chmn. bd. of trustees, Sandy Run Acad, Private Sch, Swansea, S.C. Rel: Methodist. Mailing Add: P.O. Box 337, Swansea, S.C. 29160.

SHEAR, DAPHFINE D
Dem. Nat. Committeewoman, Okla.
b. Davis, Okla, 5/15/19; d. Benjamin Franklin Lundy and Eula Boyles L; m. 8/29/40 to Warren Shear; c. Ken-Sue (Mrs. J.S. Doerfel), Lynn, Sloane and David Lundy. Educ: Stephens Col, 37; South. Methodist Univ, 38; Dallas Little Theater Sch, 39; St. Louis Little Theater Sch, 40. Polit. & Govt. Pos: Co-chmn, Dem. Precinct Cmt, Okla, 60-62; co-chmn, Dem. Dist. Cmt, 62-64; del, Dem. Nat. Conv, 64 & 68, mem, Dem. Nat. Platform Cmt, 64 & 68; Dem. Nat. Committeewoman, Okla, 64- Rel: Episcopal. Legal Res: Plato Rd, Duncan, Okla. 73533. Mailing Add: P.O. Box 807, Duncan, Okla. 73533.

SHEAR, WILLIAM MERRILL R
b. Muncie, Ind, 3/11/29; s. Robert Joseph Shear and Ruth McCreery S; single. Educ: Ball State Teachers Col, B.A, 50; Duke Univ, M.A, 51; Syracuse

Univ, D.S.S, 59. Polit. & Govt. Pos: Prog. assoc, Off. of Gov. Nelson Rockefeller, 60-61; campaign mgr, Rep. cand. for U.S. Senate, Alaska, 62; pres, Greater Anchorage Borough Assembly, 63-64; chmn, Rep. Party, Polit. Educ. and Orgn, S. Cent. Alaska, 63-65; chmn, Rockefeller for Pres, Cent. Alaska, 64; alternate del, Rep. Nat. Conv, 64; campaign mgr, 14th Assembly Dist, Calif, 66. Bus. & Prof. Pos: Asst. prof, polit. sci, Alaska Methodist Univ, 61-65; assoc. prof, Armstrong Col, 65- Mil. Serv: Entered as Seaman Recruit, Navy, 51, released as Lt.(jg), 55. Mem: Am. Polit. Sci. Asn. Elected as Young Man of the Year, Jaycees, Anchorage, 63. Rel: Methodist. Mailing Add: 1255 Post St, Suite 609, San Francisco, Calif. 94109.

SHEEHAN, CHARLES A. D
Mo. State Rep.
b. New York, N.Y, 1/31/15; m. 7/2/58 to Anna M. Finn; c. Charles Finn and Michael Thomas. Educ: St. Josephs Sem. and Col, N.Y; St. Louis Univ, B.A; Fordham Univ. Sch. of Law, LL.B. Polit. & Govt. Pos: Admin. asst, U.S. War Dept; asst. clerk to Learned Hand; Asst. U.S. Attorney; asst. prosecuting attorney, Jefferson Co, Mo; Mo. State Rep, 62- Bus. & Prof. Pos: Attorney; prof. polit. sci, Marymount Col, Tarrytown, N.Y; prof. law, St. Louis Univ. Law Sch. Mil. Serv: Army, Corps of Engrs. Mem: Holy Name Soc; K. of C; Elks; Lions; Am. Legion. Rel: Catholic. Mailing Add: RFD 1, Box 434, House Springs, Mo. 63051. (1967)

SHEEHAN, GUS, JR. D
Ky. State Rep.
b. 1917. Educ: Xavier Univ; Univ. Hawaii; Univ. Cincinnati; Chase Law Sch, LL.B. Polit. & Govt. Pos: Past pres, Kenton Co. Dem. Club, Ky; trial cmnr, Kenton Co, 52-58; commonwealth attorney, 58; dep. sheriff, Kenton Co, 59-61; Ky. State Rep, 50, 52, 63, 64 & 66- Bus. & Prof. Pos: Attorney-at-law. Mil. Serv: Army Air Force, World War II. Mem: Crusaders Club; Am. Legion; VFW; K. of C; Commercial Travelers of Am. Mailing Add: 612 Altamont Rd, Covington, Ky. 41016.

SHEEHAN, JOHN FRANCIS D
b. Quincy, Mass, 4/12/31; s. Fred M. Sheehan and Mary Keaveny S; m. 6/22/57 to Barbara Ann Frazier; c. Mary Ellen, James Dennis, Ann Marie and Eileen. Educ: Bridgewater State Col, B.S. in Ed, 58, M.S. in Ed, 61; Phi Delta Kappa; Alpha Upsilon. Polit. & Govt. Pos: Del, Mass. Dem. State Conv, 54, 56, 58, 60 & 62; mem, Weymouth Dem. Town Cmt, 54-68, v.chmn, 64-68; mem, Gov. Staff, 57-60; trustee, Norfolk Co. Agr. Sch, 60-65; orgn. coordinator, Dem. State Cmt, 64-65, mem, 64-68; exec. dir, Quincy Coun. on Aging, 67- Bus. & Prof. Pos: Teacher, Weymouth Sch. Syst, Mass, 58-64; youth supvr, John F. Kennedy Serv. Center, 65-67. Mil. Serv: Entered as SN, Coast Guard, 51, released as SK-2, 54, after serv. in N. Atlantic, 52-54; Korean War Bar; Good Conduct Medal. Mem: Dir, Quincy Commun. Action Prog; K. of C. Rel: Catholic. Mailing Add: 521 Union St, South Weymouth, Mass. 02190.

SHEEHAN, JOHN J, JR. D
b. Providence, R.I, 5/2/27; m. to Delores Montecalva S. Educ: LaSalle Acad; exten. courses, Bryant Col; Univ. R.I. Polit. & Govt. Pos: R.I. State Rep, 63-66. Bus. & Prof. Pos: Ins. sales mgr. Mil. Serv: Armed Forces. Rel: St. Pius Church. Mailing Add: 15 Pinehurst Ave, Providence, R.I. 02879. (1967)

SHEEHAN, JOHN JOSEPH D
b. Manchester, N.H, 4/28/99; s. Daniel C. Sheehan and Mary Sullivan S; m. 1/08/43 to Ellinor Nielson; c. Karen Ann, Susan Mary, Mary Ellinor. Educ: Georgetown Univ; admitted to N.H. Bar, 23. Polit. & Govt. Pos: Del. Dem. Nat. Conv, 60, 48, 40, 36; Mem. Spec. Adv. Com. on Rules, Dem. Nat. Conv, 56; U.S. Attorney, Dist. N.H, 49-53; Del. N.H. Constl. Convs, 48, 41, 38, 30; Co. Solicitor, Hillsborough Co, 33-37; N.H. Sen, 31; Mem. N.H. House of Reps, 25-28. Bus. & Prof. Pos: Mem, Sheehan, Phinney, Bass and Green and predecessor firms, Manchester, N.H, 46-; Chmn, Bd. Trustees, Carpenter Mem. Libr, Manchester. Mil. Serv: Served from Capt. to Maj. USAAF, 42-45; stationed with 8th and 9th Air Forces overseas. Mem: Am, N.H. (V.pres.), Manchester (Pres, 40-41) Bar Asns; Am. Legion; VFW; Am. Judicature Soc; Nat. Asn. R.R. Trial Counsel; K. of C. Mailing Add: 875 Elm St, Manchester, N.H. 03101. (1967)

SHEEHAN, PATRICIA QUEENAN D
Mayor, New Brunswick, N.J.
b. Newark, N.J, 2/22/34; d. Michael Queenan and Sarah McAfee Q; m. to Daniel Martin Sheehan (deceased); c. Elizabeth, Daniel and Michael. Educ: Trinity Col, A.B, 55; George Wash. Univ. Grad. Sch, 56; Rutgers Univ. Grad. Sch. Educ, 62-67; Pi Gamma Mu. Polit. & Govt. Pos: State committeewoman, Citizens for Kennedy & Johnson, 60; mem. women's div, N.J. Dem. Orgn, 67-, mem. task force for women, 68-69, mem. reform cmt, 69; mayor, New Brunswick, 67-; mem, Mayors For Humphrey, 68; chmn, Women's Activities for Humphrey-Muskie, N.J, 68; alternate del, Dem. Nat. Conv, 68. Bus. & Prof. Pos: Jr. economist, Personnel Rels. Conf, Air Transport Asn, Wash, D.C, 56-57; research asst, Educ. Testing Serv, Princeton, N.J, 57-58; compensation analyst, Johnson & Johnson, New Brunswick, 63- Mem: St. Peter's PTA; St. Peter's Hosp. Auxiliary; Trinity Col. Alumnae Asn.(secy, 67-69); Middlesex Lay Adv. Bd, Diocese of Trenton (past pres); hon. mem, New Brunswick Br, Am. Asn. Univ. Women, YWCA and New Brunswick Woman's Club; Roosevelt Hosp. Auxiliary; N.J. and U.S. Conf. of Mayors; N.J. Conf. Mayors; N.J. League Munic. Rel: Roman Catholic. Mailing Add: 5 Llewellyn Place, New Brunswick, N.J. 08902.

SHEEHAN, TIMOTHY P. R
b. Chicago, Ill, 2/9/09; s. Timothy P. Sheehan and Catherine Harris S; m. to Mary Celeste McNearney (deceased), m. 9/6/56 to Marilyn D. Muehl; c. Mary (Mrs. Eugene Plunkett), Kathleen (Mrs. Edward Bertany), Eileen, Timmy, and Sheila. Educ: Northwest. Univ, B.S.C, 31; Beta Gamma Sigma; Delta Sigma Pi. Polit. & Govt. Pos: Ward committeeman, 41st Ward Rep. Orgn, 34-66; U.S. Rep, Ill, 51-58; chmn, Cook Co. Rep. Cent. Cmt, 64-68; del, Rep. Nat. Conv, 68; secy, Ill. Racing Bd, 68- Bus. & Prof. Pos: Pres, Silver Brook Beverage Co, 45-66; owner, Swedish Food Prods, 56-66; treas. and dir, Peerless Fed. Savings & Loan, 61-66. Publ: Reflections with Edmund Burke, Vantage Press, 1960. Mem: St. Paul of Cross; K. of C. Rel: Roman Catholic. Mailing Add: 7439 W. Lunt Ave, Chicago, Ill. 60631.

SHEEHY, EDWARD DRISCOLL D
Mem, Mass. Dem. State Cmt.
b. Richmond, Va, 7/9/38; s. Eugene Morgan Sheehy and Cathrine Driscoll S; m. 9/6/58 to Paula S. Shea; c. Timothy Edward, Erin Maura and John Driscoll. Educ: Hartford Col, 1 year; Harvard Univ, 2 years. Polit. & Govt. Pos: Mem, North Attleborough Dem. City Cmt, 59-, chmn, 67-69; chmn, North Attleborough Waterways Cmt, 62-64 and Commun. Action Cmt, 65-66; chmn, Head Start, 65-66; mem, North Attleborough Cmt. on Fed. Funds, 66-68; mem, Mass. Dem. State Cmt, 68- Bus. & Prof. Pos: Salesman, Dieges & Clust, Providence, R.I, 62-69. Mem: Providence C. of C. Sales and Contact Clubs, R.I; Kiwanis. Rel: Catholic. Mailing Add: 22 Prince St, North Attleborough, Mass. 02760.

SHEEKS, BROOKS D
Chmn, Clay Co. Dem. Cent. Cmt, Ark.
b. Corning, Ark, 1/17/02; s. Edgar Van Buren Sheeks and Willie Brooks; m. 36 to Rubye McCarroll; c. Emily, Willie and Winnie. Educ: Wash. Univ, St. Louis, 21; Univ. Mo, 22. Polit. & Govt. Pos: Mayor, Corning, Ark, 24; chmn, Clay Co. Dem. Cent. Cmt, Ark, 54- Mil. Serv: Entered as Pvt, Army, released as Capt. Mem: Mason. Rel: Christian Church. Mailing Add: 910 W. Hazel St, Corning, Ark. 72422.

SHEELY, KATHERINE BASKERVILL R
Chmn, Americanizon Miss. Rep. Women
b. Rankin Co, Miss, 1/4/06; d. William Hunt Baskervill and Kate Allen Taylor B; m. 9/3/30 to Clyde Quitman Sheely; c. Clyde Quitman, Jr, William Baskervill and Robert Allen. Educ: Whitworth Col, B.A, 25; George Peabody Col, B.S. and M.S, 29; Philomathean Soc. Polit. & Govt. Pos: Platform del, Rep. Nat. Conv, 64; pres, Oktibbeha Co. Rep. Women's Club, Miss, 63-68; v.pres, Miss. Rep. Women, 65-67; chmn, Americanizon Miss. Rep. Women, currently. Bus. & Prof. Pos: Teacher Eng, Pelahatchie, Miss, 26-28 and Birmingham High Sch, Ala, 29-30. Mem: Starkville Br, Am. Asn. Univ. Women (pres, 34-36); Sorosis Club; Commun. Youth Coun. Rel: Methodist. Mailing Add: Drawer CQ, State College, Miss. 39762.

SHEERIN, GARY ASHER D
Chmn, Ormsby Co. Dem. Cent. Cmt, Nev.
b. Elko, Nev, 10/7/38; s. Chris H. Sheerin and Evelyn Asher S; m. 8/26/61 to Jo Ann Hartman; c. Christopher Hartman, Jennifer Lynn and Howard Hartman. Educ: Loyola Univ. of Los Angeles, B.S. in Eng, 61; Hastings Col. of Law, LL.B, 64; Tau Kappa Epsilon. Polit. & Govt. Pos: Admin. asst. to Gov. Grant Sawyer, Carson City, Nev, 64-65; chmn, Ormsby Co. Dem. Cent. Cmt, 67-; del, Dem. Nat. Conv, 68. Bus. & Prof. Pos: Attorney-at-law, Carson City, Nev, 66- Mem: Am. Judicature Soc; Nev. State Bar Asn; North. Nev. Trial Lawyers Asn. Rel: Catholic. Legal Res: 549 Ruby Lane, Carson City, Nev. 89701. Mailing Add: Box 606, Carson City, Nev. 89701.

SHEETS, JAMES LEE R
b. Arkansas City, Kans, 3/29/31; s. June Palmer Sheets and Mae Robinson S; m. 5/24/54 to Martha Lou Hamlin; c. Kimberly Ann and Mark Randall. Educ: John Brown Univ, B.A, 53. Polit. & Govt. Pos: Ark. State Rep, 67-68. Bus. & Prof. Pos: Commercial mgr, Radio Sta. KUOA, 53-55; dir. pub. rels, John Brown Univ, 58- Mil. Serv: Entered as Pvt, E-1, Army, 55, released as Cpl, E-4, 58, after serv. in Joint Task Force 7, assigned to Atomic Energy Cmn, Naval Supply Center, Oakland, Calif. Mem: Past dir, Mid South Dist, Am. Col. Pub. Rels. Asn; past gov, Kiwanis Int, Mo-Ark. Dist. Rel: Baptist. Legal Res: 720 W. Jefferson, Siloam Springs, Ark. 72761. Mailing Add: John Brown University, Box 1270, Siloam Springs, Ark. 72761.

SHEFFELS, PATRICIA O. R
b. Riverside, Calif, 2/14/37; d. John Ohmen and Waneta DeForest O; m. 9/1/56 to John Henry Sheffels; c. Eric Brian and Kristin Claire. Educ: Univ. Colo, B.A, 58; Nat. Geogr. Hon; Delta Delta Delta; Orchesis. Polit. & Govt. Pos: Legis. chmn, Cascade Co. Rep. Women's Club, Mont, 62-63, v.pres, 64-65, pres, 66-67 and participant in campaign activities, 69; mem, Cascade Co. Rep. Cent. Cmt, 66-67; alternate del, Rep. Nat. Conv, 68. Mem: Great Falls Jr. League. Rel: Protestant. Mailing Add: 39 Prospect Dr, Great Falls, Mont. 59401.

SHEFFIELD, HORACE LINDSEY D
b. Vienna, Ga, 2/22/16; s. Horace Lindsey Sheffield, Sr. and Georgie Brown S; m. 1/7/50 to Mary Katherine Otto; c. Corliss Amelia, Horace Lindsey, III, Kathryn Rose and LaVonne Marie. Educ: Detroit Inst. Tech, Wayne State Univ, Univ. Calif, Los Angeles. Polit. & Govt. Pos: Mem, Mayor's Spec. Youth Employ. Proj, Active Commun. Teams, Mich. Human Resources Cmt, Adv. Cmt, Apprenticeship Info. Center, Mich. Manpower Develop. and Training. Bus. & Prof. Pos: Wrote column for Detroit News, formerly; write weekly column for the Mich. Chronicle, presently. Mem: United Foundation; Tuberc. and Health Soc; Fedn. of Settlements; Neighborhood Service Orgn; Boulevard Gen. Hospital. Rel: Lutheran. Legal Res: 2101 Bryanston Crescent, Detroit, Mich. 48207. Mailing Add: 8000 E. Jefferson, Detroit, Mich. 48214.

SHEFFIELD, WILLIAM J. D
Committeeman, Wash. State Dem. Party
b. Idaho, 6/2/97; both parents deceased; m. to Hazel L; c. Harold and William J, Jr. Polit. & Govt. Pos: Committeeman, Wash. State Dem. Party and precinct committeeman, 64- Bus. & Prof. Pos: Gen. Agent, Life Ins, retired. Mil. Serv: Pvt, Army, 18. Mem: Elks; Am. Legion. Mailing Add: 11, 111 Hwy. 21, Bremerton, Wash. 98310.

SHEINBAUM, STANLEY K. D
Calif. State Dem. Cent. Cmt.
b. New York, N.Y, 6/12/20; s. Herman H. Sheinbaum and Selma Klimberg S; m. 5/29/64 to Betty Warner. Educ: Stanford Univ, A.B, 49; Phi Beta Kappa; Phi Eta Sigma. Polit. & Govt. Pos: Dir, Calif. Dem. Coun, 66-; Dem. cand, U.S. House Rep, 13th Cong. Dist, 68; del, Dem. Nat. Conv, 68; mem, Calif. State Dem. Cent. Cmt, 69- Bus. & Prof. Pos: Mem. econ. faculty, Stanford Univ, 52; mem. econ. faculty, Mich. State Univ, 55-60 and coordinator, Vietnam Proj, 57-59; economist, Center Study Dem. Insts, Santa Barbara, 60-; dir, Presidio Savings & Loan Asn, 64-; dir, Warner Ranch Co. Inc, Los An-

geles, 65-; v.pres, Warner Indust, 68- Mil. Serv: Entered as Pvt, Army, 42, released as T/Sgt, 46, after serv. in 30th Engrs. and 650th Engrs, West. Pac, 45-46. Mem: Am. Econ. Asn; Soc. Int. Develop. Fulbright fel, Paris, 2 years. Rel: Jewish. Mailing Add: 819 San Ysidro Lane, Santa Barbara, Calif. 93103.

SHELDON, CLARENCE E. D
b. Flathead, Mont; m. to Alyce W. Gunderson; c. John L, Ann Sellen. Polit. & Govt. Pos: Mont. State Rep, 59-61; cand. for Mont. State Rep, 66; former dep. field assessor, Flathead Co; former mem, Weed Bd. Bus. & Prof. Pos: Farmer. Mem: Farmer's Union Exchange (bd. dir); Eagles. Mailing Add: Kalispell, Mont. 59901.

SHELDON, GEORGIANA H. R
Educ: Keuka Col, A.B; Cornell Univ, M.S; Alpha Psi Omega. Polit. & Govt. Pos: Exec. Asst. to chmn, Rep. Party of Va, 56-61; exec. asst, South. Chmn. Asn, 58-61; exec. secy, Found. for Spec. Group Housing, 61-62; Speaker's Bur, Rep. Nat. Cmt, 62; former exec. secy, U.S. Rep. Rogers C. B. Morton, Md; asst. to dir. and spec. recruiter, Peace Corps, 69- Bus. & Prof. Pos: Instr, Avon Cent. Sch. and Caledonia Cent. Sch, 45-48; assoc. dir. of admissions, Keuka Col, 49-53; personnel dir, Boca Raton Hotel and Club, Fla, 53-54; dir. of admissions and registr, Stetson Univ. Col. of Law, 54-56; v.pres, Sorin Hall, Inc, Wash, D.C, 61. Mem: Indust. Mgt. Team. Mailing Add: 4201 Massachusetts Ave. N.W, Washington, D.C. 20016.

SHELDON, JOE S, JR R
Chmn, Orleans Parish Rep. Party, La.
b. San Antonio, Tex, 4/15/26; s. Joe S. Sheldon and Julia Burns S; m. 8/30/59 to Kay Lilley; c. Barbara Lynn and James Edward. Educ: Univ. Tex, Austin, B.S, 49; Phi Gamma Delta. Polit. & Govt. Pos: Mem, La. State Rep. Cent. Cmt, 64-; mem, Orleans Parish Rep. Exec. Cmt, 64-; chmn, Orleans Parish Rep. Party, 68-; del, Rep. Nat. Conv, 68. Bus. & Prof. Pos: Geologist, Humble Oil & Ref. Co, 49-52; partner, Petroleum Geol. Consult, 52-58, owner, 58- Mil. Serv: Entered as A/S, Naval Res, 43, released as Signalman 3/C, 46, after serving in Pac. Theater, 44-46. Mem: Am. Asn. Petroleum Geologists; New Orleans Geol. Soc; Independent Petroleum Asn. Am; Petroleum Club New Orleans; C. of C; New Orleans Country Club; Int. House. Legal Res: 1624 Charlton Dr, New Orleans, La. 70122. Mailing Add: Suite 1401, 225 Baronne St, New Orleans, La. 70112.

SHELDON, ROBERT EDWARDS D
b. Snohomish, Wash, 6/3/83; s. Robert E. Sheldon, Sr. and Flora McCallum S; m. 8/20/21 to Ann J. Bergman; c. Frances S.(Mrs. Erickson). Educ: Int. Correspondence Sch, marine eng; LaSalle Inst, acct. Polit. & Govt. Pos: Alaska Territorial Rep, Fourth Judicial Div, 25 & 27; postmaster, Fairbanks, Alaska, 33-40; Alaska State Rep, 59-60 & 65-66. Bus. & Prof. Pos: V.pres. and gen. mgr, Richardson Hwy. Transportation Co, 15-25 and McKinley T. & T. Co, 26-33; dir. emer, First Fed. Savings and Loan Asn, Fairbanks, 69- Mem: Mason; past pres, Igloo 4, Pioneers of Alaska; Tanana Hist. Soc. Award from Gov. of Alaska as mem. of appeals bd, World War II. Rel: Protestant. Legal Res: 1205 Tenth, Fairbanks, Alaska 99701. Mailing Add: c/o Claremont Hotel, Seattle, Wash. 98121.

SHELHAMER, KENT D. D
Pa. State Rep.
b. Orangeville, 11/30/24; s. Lester S. Shelhamer and Bertha E. Howell S; m. to Mary J. Holmes; c. Five. Educ: Pa. State Univ. Polit. & Govt. Pos: Pa. State Rep, 64-; sch. dir. Bus. & Prof. Pos: Fruit grower; auditor. Mil. Serv: Army Engrs. Corps, Sgt, ETO. Mem: Oriental Lodge; Caldwell Consistory; Irem Temple; Columbia Co. Exten. Serv; dist. chmn, Iroquois Dist. Boy Scouts; capt, United Fund Drive, 64; pres. and dir, Columbia Co. Farmers Asn. Rel: Evangelical United Brethren; Lay leader. Mailing Add: R.D. 2, Berwick, Pa. 18603. (1967)

SHELL, JOSEPH C. R
b. La Conner, Wash, 9/7/18; m. 6/12/40 to Barbara Morton; c. Barbara, Joseph, Jr, David, Harold and Diane. Educ: Univ. South. Calif, B.S. in Bus. Admin; Sigma Alpha Epsilon; Skull and Dagger. Polit. & Govt. Pos: Calif. State Assemblyman, 53-66 and minority leader, Calif. State Assembly. Bus. & Prof. Pos: Oil Bus, 21 years. Mil. Serv: Pilot, Navy Air Corps, World War II; Naval Res. Mem: Am. Legion; Mil. Order of World Wars. Capt, 1939 Rose Bowl Championship Football Team. Mailing Add: 400 Burnside, Los Angeles, Calif. 90036. (1967)

SHELL, ROGER MAX D
Del. Exec. Bd, King Co. Dem. Cent. Cmt, Wash.
b. Seattle, Wash, 5/8/42; s. Max Henry Shell and Marguerite Judd S; m. 1/18/69 to Linda Rae Graves. Educ: Univ. Wash, B.A. in Music Composition. Polit. & Govt. Pos: 32nd Legis. Dist. caucus chmn, Gene McCarthy Del, Wash, 68; del. to Legis. Dist, Co. and State Dem. Conv, 68; alternate del, Dem. Nat. Conv, 68; Dem. precinct committeeman, 32nd Legis. Dist, King Co, Wash, 68; 32nd Legis. Dist. Club chmn. and First Cong. Dist. coordinator, Wash. Dem. Coun, 68-; del. exec. bd, King Co. Dem. Cent. Cmt, Wash, 69-, King Co. Dem. Cent. Cmt. rep. to Cmt. for Agr. Workers Legis. Bd, 69- Mem: Individuals Against the Crime of Silence. Rel: Christian. Mailing Add: 4722 15th Ave. N.E, Seattle, Wash. 98105.

SHELLEY, JAMES ERNEST R
Ariz. State Rep.
b. Rensselaer, Ind, 3/18/23; s. James Augustine Shelley and Mary Abbott S; m. to Lavona Fern Bennett; c. Theresa Anne, Cheryl Ann, James Augustine, John Bryon, Joseph Daniel and Robert Allen. Educ: St. Joseph's Col; Ariz. State Univ. Polit. & Govt. Pos: Ariz. State Rep, currently. Mil. Serv: Entered as Pvt, Air Corps, 42, released as S/Sgt, 46. Mem: Elks; Am. Legion; VFW. Rel: Catholic. Mailing Add: 409 Mill Ave, Tempe, Ariz. 85281.

SHELLEY, JOHN FRANCIS D
b. San Francisco, Calif, 9/3/05; m. Genevieve Giles, deceased; m. 1953 to Thelma Smith; c. Joan-Marie, Kathleen Patricia and Kevin Francis. Educ: Univ. San Francisco Law Sch, LL.B, 32. Polit. & Govt. Pos: Calif. State Sen. 38-46, Dem. Floor Leader, Calif. State Senate, 42; U.S. Rep, Calif, Fifth Dist, 49-62, mem. appropriations cmt, U.S. House Rep; mayor, San Francisco, 64-68. Bus. & Prof. Pos: Pres, San Francisco Cent. Labor Coun, AFL, 37-48; pres, Calif. State Fedn. of Labor, 47-50. Mailing Add: 70 Everson, San Francisco, Calif. 94131. (1967)

SHELLY, ALICE E. R
Dep. Chmn, Honolulu Co. Rep. Cmt, Hawaii
b. Roseville, Ohio, 1/1/36; d. Lewis A. Shelly and Lois Wilcox S; single. Educ: Baldwin-Wallace Col, A.B, 58; Delta Zeta. Polit. & Govt. Pos: State membership chmn, Hawaii Young Rep, 62, nat. committeewoman, 65-67; precinct secy, Rep. Party, 12th Precinct, 15th Dist, Hawaii, 62, dist. committeewoman, 63, precinct pres, 64; del, Rep. State Conv, 62-69; del, Young Rep. State Conv, 62-69; secy, Oahu Young Rep, 63, first v.chmn, 64-65; dist. secy, Rep. Party, 15th Dist, 65; dir, State TAR, 65; del, Young Rep. Nat. Fedn. Conv, 65 & 67; v.chmn, Honolulu Co. Rep. Cmt, 65-68, chmn, 68-69, dep. chmn, 69-; co. committeewoman, Rep. Party, 16th Dist, 67-68. Bus. & Prof. Pos: Personnel asst, Research Center, Standard Oil Co. Ohio, Cleveland, 58-60, patent secy, 60-62; secretarial, gen. off, Manpower, Inc, Honolulu, Hawaii, 63-64; tech. asst, Lemmon, Freeth, Haines & Jones, Honolulu, 64-65; archit. specifications writer, currently. Mem: Construction Specifications Inst; Delta Zeta Alumna; Bus. & Prfnl. Club. Outstanding Young Rep, Oahu Young Rep, 64; Outstanding Young Rep, Hawaii Young Rep, 64; Outstanding Serv. Award, Bus. & Prfnl. Club, 67; Bronze Hard Chargers Award, Young Rep. Nat. Fedn, 68. Mailing Add: 3824 Leahi Ave, Apt. 215, Honolulu, Hawaii 96815.

SHELTON, ALLEN CLIFTON D
b. York, Sumter Co, Ala, 10/12/95; s. Robert J. Shelton and Sallie P. 'Hattie' McDonald S; m. 5/19/26 to Mary G. Pullen; c. Allen Clifton, Jr. Thomas Robert and Mary Ann (Mrs. O'Brian). Educ: State Teachers Col, Livingston, 17; George Peabody Col, B.S, 23, M.S, 29. Polit. & Govt. Pos: Mem, City Coun, Jacksonville, Ala, 12 years; mem, Dem. State Exec. Cmt, 36-40; Ala. State Sen, 54-66. Bus. & Prof. Pos: Prin. of schs, Yantley and Flomaton, Ala; prin, Waverly Hall, Ga; head math. dept, Columbus, Ga. city schs, 1 year; supt. of schs, Woodburg, Ga, 1 year; dir. of exten, State Teachers Col, Jacksonville, Ala, 21 years; supt, Calhoun Co. Schs, Anniston, 8 years. Rel: Methodist. Mailing Add: 302 S. Pelham Rd, Jacksonville, Ala. 36265.

SHELTON, CLARA KATHRYN 'KATHY' D
b. Medford, Ore, 11/26/44; d. Joseph Winfred Shelton and Clara Schenk S; single. Educ: Idaho State Univ, 64; Whitman Col, B.A, 67; Patterson Sch. Diplomacy, Univ. Ky, M.A, 68, Ph.D. studies, currently; William A. Patterson grad. fel, 67-; Pi Kappa Delta; Pi Sigma Alpha; Motar Bd; Alpha Phi (pres); grad. mem, Univ. Ky. Latin Am. Steering Cmt. Polit. & Govt. Pos: Pres, Minidoka Co. Young Dem, Idaho, 62; v.pres, Young Dem. Club of Idaho, 64-66, Dem. nat. committeewoman, 65-; pres, Whitman Col. Young Dem, 66-67; del, Dem. Nat. Conv, 68- Am. Field Serv. Exchange Student to Argentina, 63; Chester C. Maxey Forensic Award, 66; Maxey Outstanding Young Polit. Scientist, 67. Rel: Methodist. Legal Res: Route 1, Rupert, Idaho 83350. Mailing Add: Cooperstown F-322, Lexington, Ky. 40508.

SHELTON, JAMES HUSTON D
Dist. Attorney, 19th Judicial Dist, Colo.
b. Wayne Co, Iowa, 11/13/16; s. Oliver T. Shelton and Hazel Huston S; m. 5/28/43 to Virginia Marie Gore; c. Judith, John and Mary. Educ: Iowa State Univ, B.S, 39; State Univ. Iowa, J.D, 48. Polit. & Govt. Pos: Chmn, Weld Co, Colo, 58-65; dist. attorney, 19th Judicial Dist, Colo, 65- Bus. & Prof. Pos: Attorney-at-law, 49-66. Mil. Serv: Entered as 2nd Lt, Army, 39, released as Maj, 46, after serv. in 223rd Field Artil. Group, S.Pac. Mem: Elks; Mason; Shrine; Rotary. Rel: Episcopal. Legal Res: 2108 14th St. Rd, Greeley, Colo. 80631. Mailing Add: First National Bank Bldg, Greeley, Colo. 80631. (1967)

SHELTON, TRAVIS DUANE D
b. Tahoka, Tex, 1/30/21; s. Sanford Lane Shelton and Lena Mae Ansley S; m. 4/14/46 to Mary Lou Metcalf; c. Shelly, Christy and Steve. Educ: Texas Tech. Col, 40-42; Univ. Tex, LL.B, 49; Phi Alpha Delta; Centaurs Social Club. Polit. & Govt. Pos: Dist. Attorney, Lubbock Co, Tex, 51-57; co-chmn. for Kennedy-Johnson Ticket, Lubbock Co, 60; committeeman, Tex. State Dem. Exec. Cmt, 28th Sen. Dist, 60-64; dist. coordinator for Johnson-Humphry Ticket, 19th Cong. Dist, 64; alternate del, Dem. Nat. Conv, 68. Bus. & Prof. Pos: Mem, committee to revise penal code for State of Texas, 65- Mil. Serv: A/S, Coast Guard, 42, released as Lt.(jg), 46, after serv. in Sea Duty Pacific Theatre, 44-46; Decorations for Pacific Theatre. Mem: State Bar of Tex. (dir, 65-68); Lubbock Co. Bar Asn.(pres, 52-53); Tex. Bar Found.(charter mem); Lubbock Lions (pres, 58-59). Rel: Presbyterian. Mailing Add: 3810 27th St, Lubbock, Tex. 79410

SHELTON, ULYSSES D
Pa. State Rep.
b. St. Petersburg, Fla, 7/1/17; s. Wright Shelton and Lela Arline S; m. to Pearl A. Daniels; c. Two. Educ: Mastbaum Voc. Sch. Polit. & Govt. Pos: Mem, 20th Ward Dem. Exec. Cmt; former writ server, Phila. Traffic Court; former clerk, Dept. of Records, Phila; former aide, U.S. Rep. Michael Bradley; former magistrate's clerk, Court 13; Pa. State Rep, 60- Bus. & Prof. Pos: Real estate mgr. Mil. Serv: Air Force, S/Sgt, $3\frac{1}{2}$ years; Flight Chief at Westover Field, Mass. Mem: N. Phila. Civic League. Mailing Add: 717 W. Berks St, Philadelphia, Pa. 19122

SHENKER, MORRIS A. D
b. Russia, 1/10/07; s. Abraham Shenker and Tzipora Meshurith S; m. 12/23/39 to Lillian Rose Koplar; c. Morris Arthur, Jr. and Patricia Ann. Educ: Wash. Univ, A.B. and LL.B, 32; Nu Beta Epsilon. Polit. & Govt. Pos: Chmn, 18th Ward Dem. Orgn, 35-45; provisional judge, St. Louis City Court, 37-41 and St. Louis Court of Criminal Correction, Mo, 44-50; mem, Mo. State Dem. Cmt, 44-48; chmn, 23rd Ward Dem. Orgn, 44-50; del, Dem. Nat. Conv, 48 & 52, del-at-lg, 64, del, 68; chmn, 25th Ward Dem. Orgn, 50-52, committeeman, 52-54; chmn. finance cmt, City Dem. Campaign Cmt, 62; chmn. exec. cmt, Citizens for Re-Election of Sen. Stuart Symington, 64; Mo. Coordinator for Nat. Dem. Campaign, Johnson-Humphrey, 64. Publ: 'How to Try a Criminal Tax Case,' Criminal Law Bul, 7-8/65 and Criminal Law

Rev, 11/65; 'The Impact of the Post Escobedo Decisions on Defense Counsel,' Mo. Bar J, 11/66; 'Freedom of Press versus Fair Trial,' St. Louis Univ. Law J, 12/66. Mem: Hon. mem, Alpha Kappa Psi, St. Louis Univ, 62; Mo. and St. Louis Bar Asns; pres, Nat. Asn. of Defense Lawyers in Criminal Cases, 64-65; coun. mem. and Mo. State membership chmn, Criminal Law Sect, Am. Bar Asn, 64; exec. cmt, Lawyers Asn. of St. Louis, 64, v.pres, 58-59; pres, Jewish Fedn. of St. Louis; trustee, United Israel Appeal, Inc; adv. bd, Am. Jewish Cong; exec. cmt, Am. Jewish Cmt; Wash. Univ. Planning and Develop. Coun; bd. dirs, Am. Friends of Hebrew Univ; bd. overseers, Jewish Theol. Sem. of Am; B'nai B'rith. Rel: Jewish. Legal Res: 220 North Kingshighway Blvd, St. Louis, Mo. 63108. Mailing Add: 408 Olive St, St. Louis, Mo. 63102. (1967)

SHEPARD, ALLAN G. R
Justice, Idaho Supreme Court
b. Gardnear, Mass, 12/18/22; s. Guy H. Shepard and May Kendall S; m. 6/30/46 to Beverly Davis; c. Lynn Kendall, Paul Vernon and Ann Kendall. Educ: Boston Univ; Univ. Wash, B.S. and LL.B; Delta Theta Phi. Polit. & Govt. Pos: Asst. attorney gen, Idaho, 51-57; Idaho State Rep, 58-63; attorney gen, Idaho, 63-68; chmn, West. Asn. of Attorneys Gen, 65-66; v.pres, Nat. Asn. of Attorneys Gen, 67-68, pres, 68-69; Justice, Idaho Supreme Court, 69- Bus. & Prof. Pos: Admitted to practice in Idaho, Fed. Dist. Court, Fed. Circuit Court and United States Supreme Court. Mil. Serv: Army Air Corps, 43-46. Rel: Episcopal. Legal Res: 4208 Edgemont Rd, Boise, Idaho 83704. Mailing Add: State House, Boise, Idaho 83707.

SHEPARD, JULIUS JACK 'SKIP' D
b. Chelsea, Mass, 6/14/12; s. Samuel Shepard and Annie Stone S; m. 8/17/41 to Selma Dratler; c. John. Educ: Delehanty Inst, grad. in mech. eng. and drawing prog. planning. Polit. & Govt. Pos: Chmn, Spec. Events for President John F. Kennedy, 60-61; chmn, Visitors Rels. Cmt, Miami-Dade Co. C. of C, Fla, 60-61; mem, Citizens Rating Bd, Fourth Cong. Dist, Fla, 60-61; admin. asst. to Sen. George Hollahan, 63; state advance and consult, L.B. Johnson Campaign, 64; del, Dem. Nat. Conv, 64, alternate del, 68; mem, Fla. Cmn. on Aging, 66. Bus. & Prof. Pos: Owner, Leamington and Ponce de Leon Hotels, 45-; off. greeter, Miami, 55; owner, Capri Hotel, Havana, Cuba, 58; fed. receiver, Caribbean Towers, Miami Beach, Fla, 64 and Bay Terr. Apts, Miami Beach, 65-; gen. mgr, Du Pont Plaza Hotel, Miami, 65-; registered mortgage broker, 66. Mil. Serv: Entered as Pvt, Army, 42, released as Sgt, 44, after serv. in Third Army, Tenth Armored Div, 796th Bn; Purple Heart. Mem: Past v.pres, Coral Gables Optimists; chmn, Spec. Gifts Cmt, Div. 1, Dade Co. United Fund, 62; Master Mason, Ambassador, Mahai Temple, Horse Patrol, Mahai Shrine; Am. Legion; Cancer Soc; Elks; Int. Stewards and Caterers Asn; Tropical Audubon Soc; Am. Soc. Travel Agents; pres, Gr. Miami Hotel Asn, 54-55; South. Fla. Hotel & Motel Asn; Hotel Greeters of Am; Am. Hotel & Motel Asn; President's Club Nat. Dem. Party; Navy League of U.S; Dade Co. C. of C. Rel: Jewish. Mailing Add: 300 Biscayne Bay Blvd, Du Pont Plaza Hotel, Miami, Fla. 33131 (1967)

SHEPHERD, MARGARET BRAUN D
b. Mellette, S.Dak, 7/16/13; d. Arnold Braun and Sophia Elizabeth Schmitz B; m. 6/2/38 to Harry C. Shepherd; c. Mary Elizabeth and Thomas Arnold. Educ: Los Angeles Jr. Col, 2 years; Univ. Calif, Los Angeles, B.E. Polit. & Govt. Pos: Cmnr. recreation, Montebello, Calif, 58-62; campaign mgr, Councilman Harry C. Shepherd, Montebello, 60, 64 & 68; v.chmn, 19th Cong. Dist. Dem. Exec. Cmt, Calif. Dem. State Cent. Cmt, 64-66; asst. campaign mgr, Assemblyman J.R. Fenton, 51st Dist, 64, campaign worker, 66 & 68. Mem: Am. Asn. Univ. Women; charter mem, Montebello Beverly Commun. Hosp. Guild; charter mem, Rio Hondo Regional Friends of Libr; Los Angeles Co. Optom. Auxiliary (former pres); Calif. Optom. Auxiliary (former treas); Euterpe Opera Club of Los Angeles. Rel: Catholic. Mailing Add: 3000 Via Breve, Montebello, Calif. 90640.

SHEPHERD, RINEHART S. D
Chmn, Greenup Co. Dem. Party, Ky.
b. Fullerton, Ky, 10/10/11; s. Jerome Shepherd and Mary Holcomb S; m. Jan, 1935 to Lucille Voiers; c. Celia J, Sarah A. and Jerome. Educ: Univ. Ky, LL.B; Phi Delta Phi. Polit. & Govt. Pos: Chmn, Greenup Co. Dem. Party, Ky, currently, campaign chmn, 64-; city attorney, South Shore, Ky, 64- Mem: Elks; Farm Bur. Rel: Christian. Mailing Add: South Shore, Ky. 41175.

SHEPPARD, BAZEL BUNYAN D
b. Orangeburg Co, S.C, 9/4/03; s. John Bunyan Sheppard and Lena Fickling S; m. 7/18/33 to Marie Tindall; c. John Bunyan, II, Michael Bazel and William Macon, II. Educ: The Citadel, B.S, 23. Polit. & Govt. Pos: Dem. precinct officer, Orangeburg Co, S.C, 46-66; chmn, Orangeburg Co. Dem. Party, 66-68. Bus. & Prof. Pos: Teacher, Staunton Mil. Acad, Va, 23-27; Neeses High Sch, Orangeburg Co, S.C, 28-36; chief dep. sheriff, 37-42; vet. serv. officer, 46- Mil. Serv: Entered as 1st Lt, Army, 42, released as Capt, 45, after serv. in Army Ground Forces, European and Asiatic-Pac. Theatres; Maj.(Ret), Army Res, 63; Army Commendation Medal; Asiatic-Pac. Serv. Medal; European-African-Mid. East. Serv. Medal. Mem: Past exalted ruler, Elks Lodge 897; Master Mason; Retired Officers Asn; Asn. of Citadel Men; past comdr, Am. Legion Post 4; past comdr, 40 et 8 Voiture 1282; VFW. Rel: Baptist. Mailing Add: 705 Carolina N.E, Orangeburg, S.C. 29115.

SHEPPARD, ELEANOR PARKER D
Va. State Del.
b. Pelham, Ga, 7/24/07; d. John William Parker and Irwin Baggs W; m. 2/23/28 to Thomas Edward Sheppard; c. Edith (Mrs. Matthew Nelson Ott, Jr) and Sally (Mrs. Robert Earl Dunnington). Educ: Limestone Col, 3 years. Polit. & Govt. Pos: City councilman, Richmond, Va, 54-68, v.mayor, 60-62 and mayor, 62-64; coun. rep, Richmond Libr. Bd. and Regional Planning and Econ. Develop. Cmn, 60-62 and Richmond City Planning Cmn, 64-66; chmn, Coun. Agencies Cmt, 60-62, mem, 64-66; mem, Coun. Legis. Cmt, 64-; Va. State Del, 68-; mem, Defense Adv. Cmt. on Women in the Serv, 68-; mem, Adv. Cmt. of U.S. Surgeon Gen. on Air Pollution, Gov. Cmn. on Status of Women, Va. Adv. Legis. Coun. on Grants in Aid to Localities, Sr. Center Adv. Bd, Nat. Cmt. on Uniform Traffic Code, Richmond Int. Coun. Bd, Va. Wildlife Exhibit Bd, Cent. Va. Educ. TV Bd, Gov. Cmn. to Study Estab. of State Univ. in Richmond Metrop. Area, Steering Cmt, Richmond Area Community Coun. Recreation Task Force and Cmt. on Continuing Educ. of Med. Col. Va. Sch. of Nursing; chmn, Adv. Cmt. on Practical Nurse Educ; trustee, Richmond Forward. Mem: Dir, Richmond Dist. PTA, 51-54; bd. mem, Va. Cong. PTA, 51-54, Christmas mother, 53; pres, Ginter Park PTA and Richmond Fedn. PTA, 52-53; Colony Club; mem. bd. and treas, Lewis Ginter Commun. Bldg; bd. mem. and chmn, membership nominating cmt, Richmond Coun. Girl Scouts; bd. mem, YWCA and United Serv. Orgn; adv. bd, Inst. for Bus. and Commun. Develop, Univ. Richmond and Camp Ruther Glen; v.chmn, Coun. on Ment. Health Serv; chmn, Adv. Coun. on Proj. Head Start and Early Childhood Educ; Va. Citizens Planning Asn; Nat. and Va. Munic. Leagues; hon. mem, Richmond Symphony Dirs, Kappa Delta Epsilon, Treble Clef and Book Lovers Club; Bus. & Prfnl. Women's Club; Soroptimist Int; 2300 Club; Ginter Park Woman's Club. Richmond First Club Good Govt. Award, 64; Jaycee's Gold Feather Award, 68; Bus. & Prfnl. Women's Woman of Achievement Award, 68. Rel: Baptist. Mailing Add: 1601 Princeton Rd, Richmond, Va. 23227.

SHEPPARD, HARRY RICHARD D
b. Mobile, Ala, 1/10/85; m. 5/24/33 to Kay O'Keefe Olson. Polit. & Govt. Pos: U.S. Rep, Calif, 37-62; Dean, Calif. Cong. Del; del, Appropriations Com; chmn, sub cmt, Mil. Construction. 1967 Legal Res: Yucaipa, Calif. No mailing address available. (1967)

SHEPPARD, L. E, JR. R
Chmn, Bexar Co. Rep. Party, Tex.
b. Beaumont, Tex, 2/28/36; Leighlus Erman Sheppard, Sr. and Florence G. Lumbley S. (deceased); stepmother, Jessie E. Miller S; m. 7/5/58 to Wanda Lee Deaton; c. Joanna Leigh and Malinda Kaye. Educ: A&M Col. Tex, B.S, Agr. Eng, 57; Phi Eta Sigma; Tau Beta Pi; Alpha Zeta; Students Asn. Polit. & Govt. Pos: Precinct leader, Rep. Party, Nueces Co, Tex, 60; Rep. chmn, Precinct 15, Jim Wells Co. Rep. Party, 61-63; exec. dir, Bexar Co. Rep. Party, 63-67, chmn, 68- Bus. & Prof. Pos: Agr. engr, Cent. Power & Light Co, Corpus Christi and Alice, Tex, 57-63; pavilion mgr. HemisFair 68, Int. Bus. Machines Corp. San Antonio, 68, sales rep, 68-69; plant mgr, DPD Co, San Antonio, 69- Mil. Serv: Entered as 2nd Lt, Army, 57, released 58, after serv. in Co. A, Third Bn, Basic Training Regt; Army Nat. Guard, 58-69, Maj; Grad. Ord. Officer's Adv. Course, Aberdeen Proving Ground, Md, 67. Mem: Am. Soc. Agr. Engr; Tex. Soc. Prfnl. Engr; Tex. and U.S. Nat. Guard Asns; Bexar Co. Young Adult Rep. Club. Rel: Baptist. Mailing Add: 407 Sprucewood Lane, San Antonio, Tex. 78216.

SHERER, ALBERT WILLIAM, JR.
U.S. Ambassador to Togo and to the Repub. of Equatorial Guinea
b. Wheaton, Ill, 1/16/16; s. Albert William Sherer and Linda Van Nostran S; m. 10/24/44 to Carroll Russell; c. Peter, Susan and Anthony. Educ: Yale Univ, A.B, 38; Harvard Univ, LL.B, 41. Polit. & Govt. Pos: For. serv. officer, Tangier, Morocco, 46-49 and Budapest, Hungary, 49-51; assigned to Off. East. European Affairs, Dept. of State, 51-54 & 57-61; first secy, Prague, Czech, 55-57; dep. chief of mission, Warsaw, Poland, 61-66; for. serv. inspector, Dept. of State, 66-69; U.S. Ambassador to Togo, 67- and to the Repub. of Equatorial Guinea, 69- Bus. & Prof. Pos: Admitted to Ill. Bar, 51. Mil. Serv: Army Air Force, 41-45. Mailing Add: U.S. Embassy, Lome, Togo.

SHERIDAN, ALFRED A. D
Mich. State Rep.
b. Detroit, Mich, 10/28/28; m. 1953 to Irene Marek; c. Kathy, Tom, Mike and John Patrick. Educ: High sch. grad. Polit. & Govt. Pos: Former admin. asst. to supvr, Taylor Twp, Mich; precinct del, Dem. Party; Mich. State Rep, 64- Mil. Serv: Armed Forces, 50-52. Mem: Dem. Party Cmt; Lions; Moose; Little League; Amvets; VFW; Boy Scouts. Rel: Catholic. Mailing Add: 8272 Weddel, Taylor, Mich. 48180.

SHERIDAN, GEORGE P. D
b. Marietta, Wash, 1914; wid; c. Four. Educ: Bus. Col. Polit. & Govt. Pos: Former Wash. State Rep. Bus. & Prof. Pos: Pub. rels. work. Mem: Dir, Tacoma Athletic Cmn; dir, Sportsmen's Club. Mailing Add: 1510 S. Seventh St, Tacoma, Wash. 98405. (1967)

SHERMAN, JOHN HAYES, JR. R
Ga. State Rep.
b. Augusta, Ga, 3/2/28; s. John Hayes Sherman and Katherine Card S; m. 4/24/54 to Anne Eve Carmichael; c. Ernest L, II, John H, III and James C. Educ: Univ. of the South, B.S, 49; Univ. Ga, 49-50; Sigma Nu. Polit. & Govt. Pos: Ga. State Rep, 66- Bus. & Prof. Pos: Pres, Augusta Bd. of Independent Ins. Agents, 59; mem. bd. trustees, Univ. of the South. 62- Mil. Serv: Entered as Recruit, Army, 50, released as Pfc, 52, after serv. in Chem. Corps. Rel: Episcopal. Legal Res: 728 Oberlin Rd, Augusta, Ga. 30904. Mailing Add: P.O. Box 1063, Augusta, Ga. 30903.

SHERMAN, KENNETH LELAND R
N.H. State Rep.
b. Monson, Mass, 12/4/98; s. Frank James Sherman and Grace Allen S; m. 6/9/23 to Ila Gray; c. John Allen. Educ: U.S. Naval Acad, 3 years; Boston Univ, B.S. in Educ. Polit. & Govt. Pos: Mem. sch. bd, Newbury, N.H, 57; N.H. State Rep, 67-; selectman, Newbury, 68- Bus. & Prof. Pos: Prin, Dedham Jr. High Sch, 26-34 and Andover Jr. High Sch, 34-35; supt. schs, Andover, Mass, 35-55 and Laconia, N.H, 57-66. Mil. Serv: Entered as Midn, Navy, 17, released as Comdr, 45, after serv. in Lion I and Air Sea Rescue, S.Pac, New Hebrides and Solomons, 42-45; various theatre decorations; Presidential Citation. Mem: Nat. Educ. Asn; Am. Legion; Rotary; Mason. Rel: Protestant. Mailing Add: Morse Hill, South Newbury, N.H. 03856.

SHERMAN, LEWIS FRANK R
Calif. State Sen.
b. Glasgow, Mont, 2/10/17; s. Frank Laurence Sherman (deceased) and Margery Jones S.(deceased); m. 12/27/44 to Mary Lois Maxwell; c. Janet Margery and Frank Garth. Educ: Univ. Calif, A.B, 46, J.D, 49; Order of the Coif. Polit. & Govt. Pos: Chmn, Alameda Co. Rep. Cent. Cmt, Calif, 61-66; Calif. State Sen, Eighth Dist, Alameda Co, 67- Mil. Serv: Entered as Pvt, Air Corps, 41, released as Capt, 44, after serv. in 358th Fighter Group, ETO, 43-44; Distinguished Flying Cross; Air Medal with 15 Oak Leaf Clusters; Croix

de Guerre. Mem: Berkeley-Albany Bar Asn.(pres, 55); Alameda Co, Calif. State and Am. Bar Asns; Alameda Co. Lawyers Club; Mason; Elks; Kiwanis; Am. Legion; VFW. Rel: Protestant. Legal Res: 670 Colusa Ave, Berkeley, Calif. 94707. Mailing Add: 1111 Jackson St, Oakland, Calif. 94607.

SHERMAN, LLOYD G. R
b. Littleton, N.H, 10/2/11; married. Educ: Univ. N.H; Harvard Sch. of Police Sci; Harvard Assocs. in Polit. Sci. Polit. & Govt. Pos: N.H. State Rep, 63-66; chmn, Lancaster Rep. Cmt; treas, Coos Co. Rep. Cmt. Bus. & Prof. Pos: Sgt, N.H. State Police (Retired). Mem: Past pres, White Mt. Shrine Club; Mason (32°); Shrine; N.H. Police Asn. Rel: Protestant. Mailing Add: 4 Prospect Park, Lancaster, N.H. 03584. (1967)

SHERMAN, LOUIS D
Pa. State Rep.
b. N.Y.C, 3/8/07; m; c. One. Educ: T.E.R. Polit. & Govt. Pos: Chief Investr, City Collection Income Tax Dept; acting chief, Consumer Goods Sect, O.P.S. during World War II; formerly Naturalization Exam, Immigration and Naturalization, Dept. of Justice; mem, Dem. Ward Exec. Cmt, 38-; Pa. State Rep, 54-Bus. & Prof. Pos: Attorney-at-Law, 32. Mem: Phila. and Pa. Bar Asns; Pannonia Beneficial Asn; Lions; former pres, Big Four Fathers Asn; vol. defender, Feltonville and Olney Dist. of Phila. Writes a weekly neighborhood newspaper column. Mailing Add: 4805 B St, Philadelphia, Pa. 19120.

SHERMAN, NORMAN D
b. Richmond, Va, 10/19/27; m. to Evelyn S. Educ: Univ. Minn, B.A, 50, grad. study; Univ. Conn, grad. study. Polit. & Govt. Pos: Former press secy. to V.Pres. Hubert Humphrey; polit. asst. for Orville Freeman, Eugene McCarthy, Karl Rolvaag, Chester Bowles. Bus. & Prof. Pos: Teaching asst, instr. in humanities, Univ. Minn; tech. and sci. writer, Gen. Dynamics, Minneapolis-Honeywell, Univac. Mailing Add: 3801 Jenifer St. N.W, Washington, D.C. 20015. (1967)

SHERNOFF, WILLIAM M. D
Mem, Calif. Dem. State Cent. Cmt.
b. Chicago, Ill, 10/26/37; s. Harry Shernoff and Arlene Sher S; m. 6/5/60 to Joann Ruth Ruggero; c. Howard Stephen and David Jordan. Educ: Univ. of Miami, B.B.A, 59; Univ, of Wis, J.D, 62; Phi Delta Phi. Polit. & Govt. Pos: Trial lawyer, Nat. Labor Rels. bd, 65-66; pres, Pomona Valley Dem. Club, 68; mem, Los Angeles Co. Dem. Cmt, 68-; mem, Calif. Dem. State Cent. Cmt, 68- Mil. Serv: Entered as Lt, Army, 62, released as Capt, 65, after serv. in Judge Adv. Gen. Corps. Mem: Calif. Trial Lawyers Asn; Am. and Calif. Bar Asns. Mailing Add: 1788 Danbury Rd, Claremont, Calif. 91711.

SHERRER, WAYMAN G. R
Mem, State Rep. Exec. Cmt, Ala.
b. Birmingham, Ala, 11/15/27; s. Claude Wayman Sherrer and Rosalee Garner S; m. 8/13/60 to Betty Lou Rodgers; c. Elizabeth Ann and William Jefferson. Educ: Samford Univ, A.B; Univ. of Ala, LL.B; Omicron Delta Kappa; Pi Gamma Mu; Sigma Nu; Alpha Kappa Psi. Polit. & Govt. Pos: Co. solicitor, Blount Co, Ala, 65-69; Rep. Party Attorney, Blount Co, currently; del, Rep. Nat. Conv, 68; mem, State Rep. Exec. Cmt, Ala, 68- Bus. & Prof. Pos: Spec. agent, Fed. Bur. of Invest, 56-62; attorney-at-law, presently. Mil. Serv: Entered as Pvt, Marine Corps, 46, released as Cpl, 48. Mem: Past pres, Blount Co. Bar Asn; Ala. Bar Asn; past pres, Oneonta Rotary Club; C. of C; past chmn, Soc. of Former Fed. Bur. of Invest. Agents, Birmingham, Ala. Chap. Rel: Methodist; assoc. lay leader, Albertville Dist, United Methodist Church; steward, Lester Mem. United Methodist Church. Mailing Add: 107 Redbud Rd, Oneonta, Ala. 35121.

SHERROD, HENRY FLOYD D
b. Florence, Ala, 12/6/90; s. John Henry Sherrod and Rosalee Sherrod S; wid; c. Estalee (Mrs. Sandlin) and Henry Floyd, II. Educ: Florence State Teacher's Col, Dipl; George Peabody Col, B.S; Univ. Ala; Kappa Delta Pi. Polit. & Govt. Pos: Chmn, Morgan Co. Govt. Price Control Bd, Ala, 42-46; del, Dem. Nat. Conv, 52 & 68; campaign mgr, State Sen. Jim Allen for Gov. Ala. and Judge B.L. Malone for Cong. Ala. Bus. & Prof. Pos: Teacher, elem. sch, Colbert Co, Ala, prin. Rogersville High Sch, Lauderdale Co, high sch, Lawrence Co, Eva High Sch, Morgan Co, Woodville High Sch, Jackson Co. and high sch, Paden, Miss, 22-69; realtor, Decatur, Ala, 69. Mil. Serv: Pvt, Army, 18-19, with serv. in Inf, Camp Pike, Ark; App. Capt, State Guard Inf. Militia, Ala, 41. Mem: Morgan Co. Tuberc. Asn.(pres); Am. Legion (comdr, Decatur Chap); charter mem, Civitans (Lt. Gov, Ala. Dist, 51-52; bd. dirs; v.pres. and prog. chmn, Decatur Chap, del, Civitan Int. Conv. six times, organized first club, Courtland, Ala); Salvation Army (bd. dirs); Boy Scouts (organized first club, Courtland, Ala; mem. nat. coun); Mason; WOW; charter mem, Decatur Country Club; charter mem, Decatur Exec. Club; Metrop. Dinner Club of Gr. Decatur; Morgan Co. Farm Bur; Ala. Hist. Soc; Decatur Commun. Concert Asn. Recipient of Citation for Serv. Rendered, Boy Scouts. Rel: Church of Christ. Mailing Add: 509 Eighth Ave. S.E, Decatur, Ala. 35601.

SHEVIN, ROBERT LEWIS D
Fla. State Sen.
b. Miami, Fla, 1/19/34; s. Aaron Shevin and Pauline Bott S; m. 1/27/57 to Myrna Bressack; c. Laura Dawn and Hilary Beth. Educ: Univ. Fla, B.A, 55; Univ. Miami, LL.B, magna cum laude, 57; South. Collegiate Debate Champion; secy, Men's Affairs and Relig. Affairs; Fla. Blue Key; Hall of Fame; pres, Pi Lambda Phi; scholastic award for highest male grad, Univ. Miami; ed, Miami Law Quart; pres, Student Bar Asn. and Bar and Gavel; State Moot Court Champion. Polit. & Govt. Pos: State Speakers chmn, Citizens for Johnson, Fla, 64; Fla. State Rep, 65-66, mem, State Cmt. on Law Enforcement and Admin. of Justice, del, Conf. Pres. Cmn. on Law Enforcement, Fla. State House of Rep; speaker's chmn, Oper. Pub. Conscience, Dade Co, 66; Fla. State Sen, 43rd Dist, 67-, chmn, Miami Econ. Adv. Bd, Fla. Fair Share Cmt. for Roads and Representation and Courts Budget Cmt. of Dade Co, Fla. State Senate; legal counsel, Dade Co. Legis. Del; mem, Local Mkt. Develop. Cmt, Govt. Research Coun. and Indust. Develop. Coun, Dade Co; Miami Beach Dem. Club; Dade Co. Young Dem. Club. Bus. & Prof. Pos: Attorney-at-law, Shevin, Goodman & Holtzman, 57-; instr, Law Rev. Inst; bank dir. Mil. Serv: Capt, Active Army Res, 8 years. Mem: Am, Fla. and Dade Co. Bar Asns; bd. dirs. Dade Co, Fla. Trial Lawyers Asn; Nat. Panel, Am. Arbit. Asn; Miami-Dade Co. C. of C; pres, Gr. Miami Pi Lambda Phi Alumni Asn; Univ. Miami Alumni Asn; bd. dirs, Univ. Fla. Alumni Asn, S.Fla. Epilepsy Found, Youth Employ. Serv. of Dade Co, Miami Youth Symphony and Tiger Bay Club; bldg. chmn, United Fund Drive; pres. and chmn. bd, Sertoma Club of Miami; Dade Co. Chap, Nat. Multiple Sclerosis Soc; Men's Club of Children's Cardiac Hosp; YMCA; YMHA; Fla. Regional Bd. Anti-Defamation League of B'nai B'rith; Dade Co. Ment. Health Soc; Jewish Family and Children's Serv; discussion leader, Univ. Miami Adult Educ. Prog. Recipient Allen Morris Award for outstanding first term of freshman mem, Fla. State Legis, 65; selected one of top ten most valuable mem. of Fla. State Legis. by Capitol Press Corps and Fla. newspaper editors. Rel: Jewish; mem, bd. dirs, Beth David Synagogue. Mailing Add: 4901 S.W. 87th Court, Miami, Fla. 33132. (1967)

SHIELDS, CHARLIE D. D
Chmn, Lauderdale Co. Dem. Exec. Cmt, Miss.
b. Center, Miss, 3/26/09; s. Charlie Walter Shields and Nadie Mary Price S; m. 9/2/34 to Vivian Beatrice Williams; c. Camille (Mrs. Key) and Sharlynn (Mrs. Baltzell). Educ: Bus. Col; Am. Law Sch, Chicago, LL.B. Polit. & Govt. Pos: Chmn, Lauderdale Co. Dem. Exec. Cmt, Miss, 51-; City councilman, Meridian, 52-56. Bus. & Prof. Pos: Attorney-at-law, 30-; partner, Security Ins, 50-; pres, First Savings & Loan Asn, 52- Mil. Serv: Pvt, Army Air Corps, 28-29. Mem: Masonic Lodges from the Blue Lodge through the Shrine, including Eastern Star; Lions; Lauderdale and Miss. Bar Asns. Rel: Baptist. Legal Res: 2715 28th St, Meridian, Miss. 39301. Mailing Add: P.O. Box 367, Meridian, Miss. 39301.

SHIELDS, I. LAWRENCE D
b. Thomson, Ga, 7/1/94; s. Wiley Octavius Shields and Georgia Hall S; m. 9/7/30 to Reba Meadows; c. Reba June and Sylvia Lillian. Educ: High Sch. Polit. & Govt. Pos: Ga. State Rep, 45-49 & 66-68; cmnr, Columbus, Ga. 52-53 and mayor, 53; chmn, Columbus Bd. Pub, Safety, 65. Mil. Serv: Pvt, Army, 18, serv. in Co. E, 304th Ammunition Train; Meuse-Argonne Offensive France Ribbon; also served as Capt, Muscogee Co. State Guard, 41-44. Mem: Rotary; Moose; Elks; Mason; Am. Legion; VFW. Rel: Baptist. Mailing Add: 2506 Techwood Dr, Columbus, Ga. 31906.

SHIELDS, WILLIAM HENRY R
Gen. Counsel, Rep. State Cmt, Fla.
b. Walland, Tenn, 4/11/29; s. John E. Shields and Belle Williams S; m. 10/12/52 to Jean Ione Pelton; c. David William and Kathy Jean. Educ: Maryville Col, B.A, 50; Univ. Tenn. Col. Law, J.D, 53; Pi Kappa Delta; Phi Delta Phi. Polit. & Govt. Pos: Precinct committeeman, Blount Co. Rep. Party, Tenn, 55-63, v.chmn, 59-63; chmn, Rep. Primary Bd, Blount Co, 56-60; secy, Young Rep. State Cmt, 59-63; chmn, Tenn. Young Rep. Fedn, 61-62; chmn, Young Rep. Trust Fund, Fla, 64-65; gen. counsel, Rep. State Cmt, 66- Bus. & Prof. Pos: Attorney, self-employed, Blount Co, Tenn, 55-63; attorney, Pavese, Waldorf, Shields & D'Alessandro, Ft. Myers, Fla, 63- Mil. Serv: Entered as Pvt, Army, 53, released as Cpl, 55, after serv. in Judge Adv. Sect, Third Army Area Command, 53-55, Cpl, Res, 6 years; Cert. of Achievement. Publ: 'Let's Do Something About the Trial Bar,' Fla. Bar J, spring 69; 'Don't Call Me Doctor,' Am. Bar Asn. J, 69. Mem: Tenn. Bar Asn; Blount Co. Bar Asn.(pres, 61-62); various other bar asns; Mason (32°); Scottish Rite. Merit Award, Blount Co. and Tenn. Bar Asns. for work done during term as pres. Rel: Presbyterian. Legal Res: 5027 Northampton Dr, Ft. Myers, Fla. 33901. Mailing Add: P.O. Box 1611, Ft. Myers, Fla. 33902.

SHIFLET, WILLIAM MARION D
W.Va. State Del.
b. Monroe, Co, W.Va, 6/12/27; s. Rev. Alvin B. Shiflet and Grace Givens S; m. 10/9/54 to Katherine Hancock; c. Katherine Hancock and Marian Hopkins. Educ: Va. Polytech. Inst. Polit. & Govt. Pos: Mayor, Union, W.Va, 54-62; W.Va. State Del, 64- Bus. & Prof. Pos: Ins. Agency and mgr, Finance Co; pres, Monroe Develop. Corp; v.pres, Big 8 Develop. Corp. Mil. Serv: World War II. Mem: Monroe Co. Farm Bur; pres, Monroe Co. C. of C; Mason; Bluegrass Ruritan Club; Am. Legion; Monroe Co. Game Protection Asn: Mercer Anglers Club; pres, Union Fire Dept; secy, former pres, Union Rotary Club. Rel: Presbyterian; Elder. Mailing Add: Union, W.Va. 24983. (1967)

SHILLITO, BARRY JAMES D
Asst. Secy. of Defense for Installations and Logistics
b. Dayton, Ohio, 1/1/21; s. Lucian W. Shillito and Mary Ellen O'Connor S; m. 12/2/42 to Eileen Elizabeth Cottman; c. Barry, Jr, Elaine, Daniel, James and Colleen. Educ: Univ. Dayton, B.S, 49; Univ. Calif, Los Angeles, Adv. Mgt. Prog. Polit. & Govt. Pos: Sect. chief and contracting officer procurement div. and chmn, fighter fire control systs. planning group, Air Force Hq, Air Materiel Command, Wright-Patterson Air Force Base, 49-54; Asst. Secy. of the Navy for Installations and Logistics, 68-69; Asst. Secy. of Defense for Installations and Logistics, 69- Bus. & Prof. Pos: Gen. mgr, Harris-Lincoln Supply Co, Dayton, Ohio, 45-49; dir. of materiel, Hughes Aircraft Co, Culver City, Calif, 54-58, dir. of sales, 58-59; exec. v.pres, Houston Fearless Co, 59-60, pres, 60-62; pres, Logistics Mgt. Inst, 62-68. Mil. Serv: Entered Army Air Corps, 42, completed pilot training, 43, prisoner of war in Germany, 43-46. Mem: Armed Forces Mgt. Asn; Young Pres. Orgn; fel. Soc. of Logistics Engrs; Alumni Asns. of Univ. Dayton and Univ. Calif, Los Angeles; hon. life mem, Nat. Contract Mgt. Asn.(adv. bd); Am. Legion; K. of C; Kenwood Country Club, D.C. and Moraine Country Club, Dayton, Ohio. Legal Res: 5004 Baltan Rd, Sumner, Md. Mailing Add: Dept. of Defense, Pentagon, Washington, D.C. 20301.

SHILTS, WILLIAM WINSTON R
Committeeman, Summit Co. Rep. Exec. Cmt, Ohio
b. Akron, Ohio 4/15/10; s. William Delbert Shilts and Edna Robens S; m. 7/3/35 to Martha Weimer; c. William Weimer, Winifred Weimer and Rebecca Weimer. Educ: Mt. Union Col, B.A, 31; N.Y. Univ, 34-35; Akron Univ, 36-37; Cleveland Col, 38-39; Sigma Nu. Polit. & Govt. Pos: Councilman, Hudson, Ohio, 39-41, village clerk, 41-57; precinct committeeman, Rep. Cent. Cmt, 40-; committeeman, Summit Co. Rep. Exec. Cmt, 60-; area dir, N.Summit Co. Rep. Exec. Cmt, 62-; alternate del, Rep. State Conv, 64, 66 & 68; del, Rep. Nat. Conv, 68. Bus. & Prof. Pos: Ed-mgr, Hudson Times, Ohio, 32-34; salesman, Austin Print Works Co, Akron, 35-39 and Bellows-Claude Neon Co,

40-41; mfgs. sales rep, Goodyear Tire & Rubber Co, 41-69. Mem: F&AM (worthy master, 42-43); Goodyear 25 Year Club. Rel: Congregational. Mailing Add: 422 N. Main St, P.O. Box 534, Hudson, Ohio 44236.

SHINALL, ROBERT PHILLIP, JR. R
Mem, Ga. State Rep. Cent. Cmt.
b. White, Ga, 11/25/23; s. Robert Phillip Shinall and Maurine Parsons S; m. 3/24/45 to Alice W. Clements; c. Robert Phillip, III, Mary Alice and Myrick Clements. Educ: Emory Univ, B.S. and Med. Sch, M.D; Sigma Alpha Epsilon; Phi Chi. Polit. & Govt. Pos: Treas, Dekalb Co. Rep. Party, Ga, 64-66; mem, Exec. Cmt, Dekalb Co, Fourth Cong. Dist. and chmn, 64-66; mem, Ga. State Rep. Cent. Cmt, currently. Mil. Serv: Entered as Pvt, Army, 41, released as Capt, 49, after serv. in Med. Corps. Mem: Bd. of dirs, Dekalb Co. C. of C, 59; pres, Decatur Kiwanis, 57; Gridiron; Am. Med. Asn; Fulton Co. Med. Asn; Am. Acad. of Dermatology. Rel: Methodist. Mailing Add: 927 Artwood Rd. N.E, Atlanta, Ga. 30307.

SHINBERG, AARON M. I. D
b. Boston, Mass, 5/27/40; s. Jacob W. Shinberg and Rose Nathan; m. 12/6/68 to Rosita Cuan-Perez. Educ: Brooks Sch, North Andover, Mass, 54-58; Cornell Univ, 58-61; Boston Univ, B.S, 63; Tau Delta Phi. Polit. & Govt. Pos: V.pres, Cornell Univ. Young Dem, 60-61; Mass. State Rep, 17th Essex Dist, 65-68, asst. majority leader, Mass. House of Rep, 68; assoc. mem, Haverhill Dem. City Cmn, 65- Bus. & Prof. Pos: Market research dir, Statistical Research, Boston, Mass, 67-; treas. and dir, Interspec Corp, Boston, 67-; treas. and dir, Merrimack Valley Communications, Inc, Boston, WXPO-TV, 68-; treas. and dir, Ultra-Casting, Inc, Newark, N.J, 68- Pub. Serv. Award from Senior Citizens and Assoc. of Am, May, 66. Rel: Jewish. Legal Res: 102 Lakeview Ave, Haverhill, Mass. 01830. Mailing Add: 22 Chestnut Place, Brookline, Mass. 02146.

SHINBERG, ROSE RUTH D
Committeewoman, Mass. Dem. State Cmt.
b. Amsterdam, N.Y; d. Abram M. Nathan and Ethel B. Swelten N; m. Jacob W. Shinberg (deceased); c. Aaron M. I. Polit. & Govt. Pos: Committeewoman, Mass. Dem. State Cmt, 44-; del, Dem. Nat. Conv, 68. Bus. & Prof. Pos: Real estate broker, currently. Recipient of gold pin for being chmn. of the Protestant Guild for the Blind, Haverhill, Mass; recipient of a gold pin for being pres. of Haverhill Chap, Hadassah. Rel: Jewish. Mailing Add: 102 Lakeview Ave, Haverhill, Mass. 01830.

SHINE, HENRY MARTIN, JR. R
b. Lincoln, Maine, 6/7/21; s. Henry Martin Shine and Mary Ann Carter S; m. 9/30/61 to Marguerite Ann Timlin; c. Mari Marguerite and Christianna Jean. Educ: Harvard Col, A.B, 48; Notre Dame Law Sch, LL.B. cum laude, 51; South. Methodist Univ. Law Sch, grad. fel, 51-52; Sigma Alpha Epsilon; Hasty Pudding Club, Harvard Col; Alpha Phi Omega; Phi Alpha Delta. Polit. & Govt. Pos: Asst. to cmnr, Cmn. on Orgn. of the Exec. Br. of the Fed. Govt, 53-55; asst. staff dir, Cmn. on Civil Rights, 58-59; exec. dir. and counsel, U.S. sci. exhibit, Dept. of Commerce, 60-61; dir, Calif. State Dept. of Prfnl. and Voc. Standards, 65-69; asst. to the secy. and dir. of cong. liaison, Dept. of the Interior, 69; exec. dir, President's Coun. on Youth Opportunity, 69- Bus. & Prof. Pos: Admin. ed, Notre Dame Lawyer; admin. ed, Oil and Gas Reporter, Southwest. Legal Found, Dallas, Tex, 52; attorney-at-law, Dresser Industs, Dallas, Tex, 55-57, Wash. rep, D.C, 57-58; from legis. dir. to dir, Nat. Housing Center, Nat. Asn. of Home Builders, 61-65. Mil. Serv: Entered as A/S, Navy, 42, released as Ens, 43; Lt. Comdr, Naval Res. Publ: 'A JAG Corps for the Navy', Fed. Bar J, 55; articles in Notre Dame Lawyer, 50. Mem: Fed. and Am. Bar Asns.(nat.off); admitted to practice before the U.S. Supreme Court, U.S. Court of Appeals, D.C. circuit, U.S. Court of Claims, U.S. Court of Customs and Patent Appeals, U.S. Dist. Court, D.C, U.S. Court of Mil. Appeals and Tex. Supreme Court; chmn, first Fed. Conf. on State Occupational Licensing; initiator, first Calif. Conf. on Allied Health; Metrop. Club; Capitol Hill Club; Nat. Lawyers Club. Rel: Roman Catholic. Legal Res: Sacramento, Calif. Mailing Add: Box 12, Metropolitan Club, 1700 H St. N.W, Washington, D.C. 20006.

SHIPLEY, CARL L. R
Chmn, Dist. of Columbia Rep. Cmt.
b. Washington, D.C, 12/16/19; s. Edmund D. Shipley and Inez Beale S; m. 9/8/48 to Nancy Kane; c. Zachary Kane and Joshua Beale. Educ: Georgetown Univ, B.S, 42; Foreign Serv. Sch; Harvard Law Sch, LL.B, 48. Polit. & Govt. Pos: Spec. asst. to U.S. Attorney Gen, 53-56; mem, D.C. Urban Renewal Coun, 58-61; chmn, Dist. of Columbia Rep. Cmt, 58- Mil. Serv: Entered as Ens, Naval Res, released as Lt. Rel: Protestant. Mailing Add: 3740 Fordham Rd. N.W, Washington, D.C. 20016.

SHIPLEY, GEORGE EDWARD D
U.S. Rep, Ill.
b. Richland Co, Ill, 4/21/27; m. to Ann Watson; c. Five. Educ: Georgetown Univ. Polit. & Govt. Pos: Chief Dep. Sheriff, Richland Co, Ill, 50-54; Sheriff of Richland Co, 54-58; U.S. Rep, Ill, 58- Bus. & Prof. Pos: Restaurant owner Mil. Serv: Marine Corps, 3 years, discharged 47, serv. in S.Pac. Legal Res: Olney, Ill. 62450. Mailing Add: 237 Cannon Building, Wash, D.C. 20515.

SHIPMAN, GORDON D
b. Manawa, Wis, 4/19/01; s. Harry Shipman and Margaret Niven S; m. 7/28/28 to Agnes Vanneman; c. Margaret (Mrs. Robert S. Cooper), Anne (Mrs. Kurt Pasch) and Eleanor (Mrs. John W. Lucas). Educ: Univ. Wis, Madison, B.A, 26, M.A, 27, Ph.D, 32; Univ. Nebr, Lincoln, 27-28; Columbia Univ, 31-32; Pi Sigma Alpha. Polit. & Govt. Pos: Chmn, Citizens for McCarthy, Portage Co, Wis, 68; del, Dem. Nat. Conv, 68; del, Wis. State Dem. Conv, 68 & 69; del, Dist. Dem. Conv, Wis, 69. Bus. & Prof. Pos: State probation-parole agent, Div. of Corrections, Wis, 34-46; head dept. soc. sci, Shurtleff Col, 46-49; instr. sociol, Wis. State Col, Milwaukee, 49-56, prof. sociol, Univ. Wis-Milaukee, 56-66, chmn. dept. sociol, 56-61; chmn. dept. sociol, Wis. State Univ, Stevens Point, 66-69. Publ: 'Speech Thresholds and Voice Tolerance in Marital Interaction', Marriage and Family Living', 11/62; 'A Proposal for Revising Marriage License Procedure', J. of Marriage and the Family', 5/65; 'The Psychodynamics of Sex Education', Family Coordinator, 1/68. Mem: Fel, Am. Sociol. Asn; Mid-W. and Wis. Sociol. Asns; Nat. Coun. on Family Rels; Nat. Coun. on Crime and Delinquency; Soc. for Sci. Study of Sex; Soc. for Study of Soc. Probs; past pres. of Local 79, Am. Fedn. of Teachers, Milwaukee, 55-57; chmn, Wis. Family Life Asn, 65; mem. exec. bd, Planned Parenthood, Milwaukee, 64-66. Mailing Add: 2536 Peck St, Stevens Point, Wis. 54481.

SHIPPEE, WILEY WRIGHT D
b. Lena, Ill, 6/13/20; s. Leon Wright Shippee and Eliza May Wiley S; m. 2/26/47 to Laurel Elizabeth Fenton; c. Lynne Ellen, Steven Leon, Randall Craig and Donna Jo. Polit. & Govt. Pos: Precinct committeeman, Dem. Party, Ill, 48-; chmn, Stephenson Co. Dem. Cent. Cmt, 64-68. Mil. Serv: Entered as Pvt, Marine Corps Res, 42, released as Cpl, 46, after serv. in First Assault Signal Co, First Marine Div, Pac; Presidential Unit Citation with two stars; Good Conduct, Am. Campaign and China Serv. Medals; Asiatic-Pac. Campaign Medal with two Stars; Victory Medal World War II; Navy Occup. Serv. Medal with Asia Clasp. Mem: Am. Legion; AF&AM; Freeport Consistory. Rel: Methodist. Mailing Add: Lena, Ill. 61048.

SHIRAH, ROSS PATRICK R
Mem, La. Rep. State Cent. Cmt.
b. Beaumont, Tex, 8/6/40; s. Ross Jefferson Shirah and Mary L.E. Gandy S; single. Educ: Northeast La. State Col, B.A, 68, grad. study, currently; chmn, Young Rep; Conservative Club. Polit. & Govt. Pos: Fifth Cong. Dist. chmn, La. Young Rep. Fedn, 65-67; alternate del, Rep. Nat. Conv, 68; mem, Rep. Exec. Cmt, Ouachita Parish, La, 68-; mem, La. Rep. State Cent. Cmt, 49th Representative Dist, 68- Bus. & Prof. Pos: Reporter, Monroe News-Star, Monroe, La, currently. Mil. Serv: Entered as E-1, Army, 59, released as Specialist-4, 61, after serv. in Intel. Div, Heidelberg, Germany and 95th Civil Affairs Group, Ft. Gordon, Ga; Good Conduct Medal. Rel: Church of Christ. Legal Res: 1202 S. Third St, Monroe, La. 71201. Mailing Add: P.O. Box 2713, Louisville Sta, Monroe, La. 71201.

SHIRK, KENELM LAWRENCE, JR. R
Chmn, Lancaster Co. Rep. Cmt, Pa.
b. Lancaster, Pa, 6/26/22; s. Kenelm Lawrence Shirk, Sr. and Beatrice Marie S; m. 11/10/45 to Romaine Sensenig; c. Kenelm Lawrence, III, Kathie Romaine Sensenig and Kraig Leofric. Educ: Franklin and Marshall Col, 40 & 42; Wash. and Lee Univ, A.B, 43; Dickinson Sch. Law, J.D, 48; Phi Beta Kappa; Sigma Delta Chi; Lambda Chi Alpha. Polit. & Govt. Pos: Mem, Rep. State Platform Cmt, Pa, 50; chmn, Pa. Fedn. Young Rep. Clubs, 50-51 & 56-58; mem, Rep. State Exec. Cmt, 50-51; co. cmt. mem, Lancaster, Pa, 50-54; chmn. exec. cmt, Lancaster Co. Rep. Cmt, 54; chmn. registrn. cmt, Pa. State Rep. Cmt, 58; asst. to chmn, Co. Rep. Cmt, 58-60, counsel to, 60-64; chmn, Lancaster Co. Rep. Cmt, 64- Bus. & Prof. Pos: Pres, R.U. Fassnacht Ins. Agency, Inc, 50-; dir. and solicitor, Farmers Nat. Bank of Ephrata, 59-; dir. and secy, Gehman Feed Mill Inc. Mil. Serv: Entered as Pvt, Army Air Force, 43, released as 1st Lt, 46, after serv. in ETO in Italy as navigator with Fifth Air Force, 45; Capt, Air Force Res, 51-53; Air Medal with Clusters; European Theatre Medal. Mem: Am, Lancaster and Pa. Bar Asns; mem. planning cmt, World Peace Thru Law Center; past gen. legal counsel, Jr. Chamber Int. and U.S. Jaycees; Elks (past Exalted Ruler); Lancaster Commun. Coun.(past pres); Lancaster Jr. C. of C.(past pres). Jaycee of the World; Elk of the Year. Rel: Presbyterian, Elder, First Presbyterian Church, Lancaster. Legal Res: 211 S. Seventh St, Akron, Pa. 17501. Mailing Add: 33 N. Duke St, Lancaster, Pa. 17602.

SHIRLEY, EDWIN ALAN D
Iowa State Sen.
b. Des Moines, Iowa, 11/17/37; s. Donald J. Shirley and Winnifred McArthur S; m. 8/30/59 to ViiviAnn Aarma; c. Elise and Jill. Educ: State Univ. of Iowa, 57-60; Drake Univ, LL.B, 63; Delta Tau Delta. Polit. & Govt. Pos: Iowa State Sen, 65- Bus. & Prof. Pos: Mem, Iowa State Bar Asn. Cmt. on Legis, 65- Mil. Serv: Sp-4, Army Res. Mem: Iowa State Bar Asn; Elks. Mailing Add: 1602 Warford, Perry, Iowa 50220.

SHIRLEY, MARVIN SCOTT D
b. Minburn, Iowa, 9/16/37; s. Slocum Scott Shirley and Alma Cole S; m. 2/25/61 to Janice Denison; c. Kim and Lori. Educ: Iowa State Univ, B.S, 59; Alpha Gamma Rho. Polit. & Govt. Pos: Secy, Iowa Young Dem, 57-95; committeeman, Wash. Twp, 62-66; Iowa State Rep, 65-66. Bus. & Prof. Pos: V.pres, Dallas Co. Farmers Union, 64- Mil. Serv: Entered as Pvt, Iowa Nat. Guard, 60, released as S/Sgt, 66. Mem: Iowa Farmers Union. Rel: Methodist. Mailing Add: RFD, Minburn, Iowa 50167. (1967)

SHIRO, BURTON GRANT D
b. Newtonville, Mass, 7/26/23; s. Louis J. Shiro and Celia C. Wasser S; m. 10/28/51 to Phyllis Anne Kovner; c. Louis Jay, Brian Charles and Leslie Rose. Educ: Colby Col, B.A, 47; Boston Univ. Sch. Law, LL.B, 50 and LL.M, 51; Murray Prize Debating Team; hon. mention, Little All Am. Polit. & Govt. Pos: Maine State Sen, 64-66, chmn, Legal Affairs Cmt. and Interim Study Cmt. on Domestic Rels, mem, Interim Study Cmn. on Transportation, secy, Transportation Cmt, Maine State Senate; city solicitor, Waterville, Maine, 66. Bus. & Prof. Pos: Attorney-at-law, 51- Mil. Serv: Entered as Pvt, Army, 43, released 46, after serv. in 43rd Inf. Div, 103rd Regt, S.Pac; Purple Heart; New Guinea and Philippines Campaign Ribbons. Mem: Bd. gov, Maine Trial Lawyers Asn; Maine State Bar Asn; Am. Trial Lawyers Asn; Commercial Law League of Am; Mason. Rel: Jewish. Mailing Add: 167 First Rangeway, Waterville, Maine 04902. (1967)

SHIRPSER, CLARA D
b. San Francisco, Calif, 8/25/01; d. Leo Garfinkle and Alexandra Shragge G; m. 11/10/40 to Adolph Shirpser; c. Barbara (Mrs. Robert De Liban). Educ: Univ. of Calif, 19-21. Polit. & Govt. Pos: Mem, Franchise, Taxation, Charter Amendment Cmts, Berkeley City Coun, 48-50; Dem. nominee for Calif. State Assemblyman, 50; mem, Alameda Co. and Calif. State Dem. Cmts, 50-56; mem, Dem. Nat. Cmt, 52-56; del, Dem. Nat. Conv, 52, 56 & 60; co-chmn, Nat. Exec. Cmt, Stevenson-Kefauver Pres. Campaign, 56; v.chmn, Nat. & Calif. Kefauver Primary Campaign for Pres, 56; Calif. Campaign Cmt, Brown for Gov, 59-66; mem, Gov. Adv. Cmt. to Calif. Consumers Coun, 59-; mem, Nat. Inauguration Cmt, 61; chmn, Alameda Co. Women for Johnson & Humphrey, 64; mem, N.Calif. exec. campaign cmt, Alan Cranston for U.S.

Sen, Calif, 68; mem, exec. campaign cmt, Jeffery Cohelanfor Cong, 68. Bus. & Prof. Pos: Owner and mgr, retail bus, Berkeley, Calif, 25-45; mem, Berkeley Soc. Welfare Cmt, Grey Lady, Navy Oak Knoll Hosp, Blood Bank, 46-49; chmn. women's div, Herrick Mem. Hosp, 51; Nat. Bd. Atlantic Union; mem, Menninger Found; pres, Arch Herrick Hosp. Guild, 57-; chmn, E. Bay Rehabilitation Center, Women's Div, 58-61 (mem. adv. coun); bd. of dirs, Calif. Heritage Coun, 59-; v.pres, Brandeis Univ. Women's Div, 69- Mem: League of Women Voters (pres, Berkeley Chap, 48-49, town meeting chmn, 49-50); Coun. for Soc. Planning, Alameda Co, 65-; Nat. Population Crisis Cmt, 67-; bd. of dirs, Planned Parenthood of Alameda Co, 68-; Children's Hosp. Asn; Univ. of Calif. Alliance, World Affairs Counsel; dir, UN Orgn. Mailing Add: 2515 Hilgard Ave, Berkeley, Calif. 94709.

SHIVERS, ALLAN D
b. Lufkin, Tex, 10/5/07; s. Robert A. Shivers and Easter Creasy S; m. 10/5/37 to Marialice Shary; c. John, Allan, Jr, Marialice Sue, Brian McGee. Educ: Univ. Tex, A.B, 31, LL.B, 33. Polit. & Govt. Pos: State Sen, Tex, 35-46; Lt. Gov, Tex, 47-49; Gov, Tex, 49-57; del, Dem. Nat. Conv, 68. Bus. & Prof. Pos: Dir, Tex. Gulf Sulphur Co, Champlin Petrol. Co, Dresser Industs; Tex. Nat. Bank of Commerce, Houston, Citizens State Bank of Woodville, Chem. Bank and Trust Co, Global Marine, Inc, Capital Nat. Bank, Houston, Celanese Corp, Frontier Airlines, Lone Star Cement Corp. and Tex. Good Roads Asn; Houston First Savings Asn; chmn. bd, West. Pipe Line, Inc, 57-63 and Austin Nat. Bank, currently; chmn. adv. cmt, Export-Import Bank U.S. Mem: Past pres, U.S. C. of C; Mason (33°); Shrine. Rel: Baptist. Legal Res: 6 Niles Rd, Austin, Tex. 78703. Mailing Add: 300 Austin National Bank Bldg, Austin, Tex. 78701.

SHOCKLEY, PAUL E. D
b. 1907. Polit. & Govt. Pos: Del. State Rep, 53-68. Bus. & Prof. Pos: Allied Kid Co, 35 years; city clerk, Wilmington, Del. Mailing Add: 731 W. Fourth St, Wilmington, Del. 19801. (1967)

SHOCKNESSY, JAMES WHITE D
b. Springfield, Ohio, 11/26/06; s. James A. Shocknessy and Margaret White S; single. Educ: Notre Dame Univ, A.B, 28; Harvard Law Sch, LL.B, 31. Hon. LL.D, Wilberforce Univ, 57. Polit. Pos: Chmn, Ohio Turnpike Cmn, 49-; del, Dem. Nat. Conv, 64; presidential elector, 48-64; del. and mem. platform cmt, Dem. Nat. Conv, 60; v.chmn, Ohio Dem. State Exec. Cmt, 48-58; mem, Ohio Adv. Cmt, U.S. Cmn. on Civil Rights, 58; mem, Ohio Post War Planning Cmn, 46-47; bd. trustees, Sinking Fund and Bd. Tax Cmnrs, City of Columbus, 41-42. Govt. Pos: Mem. Bd. Trustees, Ohio State Univ, 65-; mem. and chmn, Ohio Turnpike Cmn, 49-; mem, Cmt. Bar Examiners, Supreme Court of Ohio, 47-52 and chmn, 51-52; regional counsel, Home Owners' Loan Corp, Ohio and W.Va, 37-39; state counsel, Home Owners' Loan Corp, Ohio, 35-37; asst. state counsel, Home Owners' Loan Corp, 33-35. Prof. Pos: Private practice of law, 39- Mil. Serv: Entered as Lt, Army Air Force, 42, released as Major, 45. Mem: Am, Ohio and Columbus Bar Asns; Columbus Club; Columbus Athletic Club; Country Club; Harvard Club of Cent. Ohio; President's Club. Kappa Alpha Psi citation for humanitarian policy of non-discrimination in administering Ohio Turnpike Cmn, 55; Gov. award for excellent work as spec. consult. & expediter for construct. Interstate Hwy. 1-71, Ohio Sen. Resolution of Commendation, 65. Rel: Roman Catholic. Legal Res: 136 Broad St, Columbus, Ohio 43215. Mailing Add: 17 S. High St, Columbus, Ohio 43215. (1967)

SHOEMAKER, LEWIS EDGAR R
b. Quarryville, Pa, 1/30/98; s. Leandrew Shoemaker and Leora Kent S; m. 11/25/20 to Bertha E. De Long; c. Lewis Ellsworth, Kenneth Evan, Richard Kent, Jean Muriel (deceased) and Faye DeLong (Mrs. Wade). Educ: Millers State Teachers Col, 16-17; Paige Soc. Polit. & Govt. Pos: Clerk, Quarter Session, Lancaster, Pa. Court of Oyer and Terminer, 48-52; Rep. committeeman, Colerain Twp; alternate del, Rep. Nat. Conv, 64. Bus. & Prof. Pos: V.pres, Oxford Grain & Hay Co; dir, Farmers Nat. Bank, Quarryville; owner and mgr, White Plain Dairy Farms. Mil. Serv: Pvt, Army, 17. Mem: Trustee, Millersville State Teachers Col, 54-60; Masonic Lodge 156, Wash; Mason (32°), Ground Hog Lodge, Friends of the Land, Chap. Oxford, Pa, Am. Legions; Lions, Quarryville; Sportsman Club, Quarryville. Big Game Hunter, N.Am; Varsity Team, Millersville State Teachers Col. Rel: Presbyterian; Trustee, Union, Pa. for 12 years. Mailing Add: R.D, Kirkwood, Pa. 17536.

SHOEMAKER, MYRL HOWARD D
Ohio State Rep.
b. Chillicothe, Ohio, 4/14/13; s. Royal Shoemaker and Sadie Mick S; m. 2/23/35 to Dorothy Ruth Cook; c. Ronald Jerome, Keith Alan, Myrl Howard, Jr, Michael Cook, Kevin Lee, Deborah Lou, Kathy Ann and Brenda Susan. Educ: Bliss Col, 30-32. Polit. & Govt. Pos: Mem. sch. bd, Twin Sch. Dist, Ohio, 37-59; sch. bd. clerk, Paint Valley Sch. Dist, 58-60; Ohio State Rep, Ross Co, 58- Bus. & Prof. Pos: Owner, Twin Construction Co, until 66. Mem: Paint Valley Foxhunters; Farmers Union Farm Bur; YMCA. Prfnl. Baseball, Cardinal Orgn. Rel: Christian Union. Legal Res: Bourneville, Ohio 45617. Mailing Add: State Capitol Bldg, Columbus, Ohio 43215. (1967)

SHOEMAKER, PHILIP RAY D
b. Upper Strasburg, Pa, 5/29/93; s. Luther Calvin Shoemaker and Lillie May Kearns S; m. 1/31/14 to Francis Henry; m. 2/17/45 to Eliza Mayes Soult; c. Marcella Irene, Jay Elwood, Philip R, Jr, Betty Louise, Wilbur Luther and Glen R. Educ: Pa. State Univ, courses in shop mgt; Lasalle Univ, Accountant, 34. Polit. & Govt. Pos: Engr, Works Progress Admin, Pa, 36-40; alternate del, Dem. Nat. Conv, 36 & 64; mem, Pa. State Dem. Cmt, 52-54; chmn, Mifflin Co. Dem. Cmt, 54-64; supt. hwys, Pa, 55-56, maintenance engr, Pa. Hwy. Dept, 56-62; auditor, Auditor Gen. Dept, Pa, 62-65; jury cmnr, Mifflin Co; chmn, Mifflin Co. Dem. Exec. Cmt, 64-69. Mem: Am. Soc. Hwy. Engrs. Rel: Protestant. Mailing Add: R.R. 2, Lewiston, Pa. 17044. (1967)

SHOEMAKER, WINFIELD ALLEN D
Exec. Dir, South. Div. Calif. Dem. Party
b. Santa Barbara, Calif, 4/18/30; s. Rexford Irving Shoemaker and Dorothy Smith S; m. 11/7/59 to Elizabeth Ann McFadden; c. Matthew Brian and Jennifer Ellen. Educ: San Francisco State Col, A.B, 55; Univ. Calif, Berkeley, 54; Phi Delta Kappa. Polit. & Govt. Pos: Mem, Prog. Adv. Cmt. to Consumer Coun, Calif, 62-65; chmn, Santa Barbara Co. Dem. Cent. Cmt, 63-64; Calif. State Assemblyman, 65-69, chmn, Assembly Majority Caucus, 67-69; mem, Gov. Cmn. on Ocean Resources, Calif, 65-69 and Constitution Rev. Cmn, 66-69; del, Dem. Nat. Conv, 68; exec. dir, South. Div. Calif. Dem. Party, 69- Bus. & Prof. Pos: Int. rep, Investors Overseas Serv, Geneva, Switz, 59-61; chmn, Soc. Studies dept, Lompoc High Sch, Calif, 61-64; assoc. prof, Calif. State Col, at Los Angeles, 69- Mil. Serv: Entered as Pvt, Army, 48, released as Pvt. E-2, 49, after serv. in 2nd Armored Div, Tex. Mem: YMCA; PTA; VFW; Calif. Teachers Asn; Marine Tech. Soc; trustee, John F. Kennedy Mem. Scholarship Fund. Award for Outstanding Legis. Serv, Calif. Asn. of Adult Sch. Adminstrs. Legal Res: 12138 Maxwellton Rd, North Hollywood, Calif. 91604. Mailing Add: Democratic Headquarters, 3440 W. Eighth St, Los Angeles, Calif. 90005.

SHOEMAN, JOHN D. R
b. Waukee, Iowa, 9/12/02; m. 6/6/28 to Dan Oberwetter; c. two. Educ: Vet. Med, Kansas State Col, 28. Polit. & Govt. Pos: Iowa State Sen, -66; Atlantic City Coun, 4 yrs; Co. Rep. Finance Chmn, 6 yrs. Bus. & Prof. Pos: Vet. Research Dir, Walnut Grove Prods. Co, Sept. 57-; praticed vet. med. 9 yrs. at Dallas Center, Iowa; 17 yrs. at Atlantic; 3 yrs, U.S. Bur. of Animal Indust. Mem: Masonic, Elks Lodges; Za-Ga-Zig Temple Shrine, Des Moines. 1967 Legal Res: 1315 Birch St, Atlantic, Iowa. No mailing address available. (1967)

SHOFNER, AUSTIN WILLIAMS R
Hon. Chmn. for Life, Bedford Co. Rep. Exec. Cmt, Tenn.
b. Shelbyville, Tenn, 7/13/88; s. Monroe Shofner and Mattie Williams S; m. 9/6/11 to Rachel Conner; c. Brig. Gen. Austin C. and Lt. Col. Emory M. (deceased). Educ: Peabody Col, Teachers Degree, 07; Univ. Tenn, B.S, 09; Phi Kappa Phi. Polit. & Govt. Pos: Co. agr. agent, U.S. Dept. Agr, 17-21, Bankhead Cotton Agent, 34-37; mem, Bedford Co. Bd. of Educ, Tenn, 21-23; mem, Bedford Co. Elec. Cmn, 49-69; chmn, Bedford Co. Rep. Exec. Cmt, Tenn, 50-65, hon. chmn. for life, currently; state elector, Rep. Ticket, 64, Nat. Elec, 64. Bus. & Prof. Pos: Principal, Pleasant Grove High Sch, Bedford Co, 35-41, Bell Buckle High Sch, 32-35 and Tullahoma High Sch, 28-32; high sch. teacher, Bedford Co. Central High, 22-27; high sch. teacher and coach, Hamilton Co. High Sch, 09-17. Mem: Tenn. Teachers Asn; Nat. Retired Teachers Asn; past master, F&AM, Mason Lodge 601; co. secy, Farmers Union; co. secy, Farm Bur. Rel: Lutheran. Mailing Add: Route 5, Shelbyville, Tenn. 37160.

SHOLES, RUSSELL GEORGE R
Vt. State Rep.
b. Sherburne, N.Y, 6/5/98; s. George Leon Sholes and Sara R. Palmer S; m. 9/9/22 to Faith Elizabeth Nickell; c. George N, Nancy (Mrs. Edwin J. Harper) and Susan (Mrs. Roger H. Cox). Educ: Rensselaer Polytech. Inst, 17-18; Syracuse Univ, 18-20; Wash. Univ, A.B, 22, M.A, 23; Univ. Ill, Minn. and Chicago, grad. work, 27-37; Pi Gamma Mu; Theta Chi. Polit. & Govt. Pos: Clin. psychologist, N.Y. State Prison Cmn. Surv, 22, Child Guid. Clin, St. Louis, 22-24; prin. and asst. supt, Bur. of Educ, War Dept, Philippines, 24-27; mem. bd. and cmns, six Gov, Vt, 27-69, Bd. of Insts, 60-68, Bd. of Parole, 60-69, Gov. Cmn. on Voc. Rehabilitation, 67-, Bd. of Corrections, 68; trustee, Middlebury, 66-67; Vt. State Rep, 15th Dist, 69- Bus. & Prof. Pos: Prof. and chmn, Sociol-Anthrop. and Div. of Soc. Sci, Middlebury Col, 27-63. Mil. Serv: Pvt, SATC, Syracuse Univ, 17. Mem: Vt. Conf. of Soc. Concerns (past pres; mem. bd, Vt. Childrens Aid; Asn. of Paroling Authorities (charter mem, and past dir); Am. Correctional Asn; Nat. Coun. on Crime & Delinquency; East. Sociol. Soc; Nat. Rehabilitation Asn; Mason; Shrine. Prof. Emer, Middlebury Col; Citation by Vt Conf. of Soc. Concerns. Rel: Congregational. Mailing Add: 10 Adirondack View, Middlebury, Vt. 05753.

SHOLLENBARGER, JOSEPH HIRAM 'JOE' R
Chmn, Deaf Smith Co, Rep. Party, Tex.
b. Tucumcari, N.Mex, 12/11/39; s. Joseph Kenneth Shollenbarger and Helen Goats S; m. 9/3/60 to Janice Carol Biles; c. Joseph Randall and James Scott. Educ: Abilene Christian Col, B.S, 61; Tex. A&M Univ, 61-62; Phi Delta Psi. Polit. & Govt. Pos: Chmn, Deaf Smith Co. Rep. Party, Tex, 68- Bus. & Prof. Pos: Secy. and mem. bd. dirs, Arrowhead Mills, Inc, 66-; secy. and mem. bd. dirs, Her-Tex Milling Co, Inc, 67- Mem: Am. Inst. CPA; Tex. Soc. CPA; Panhandle Chap, Tex. Soc. CPA; Lions; bd. dirs, United Fund. Rel: Church of Christ. Legal Res: 243 Beach, Hereford, Tex. 79045. Mailing Add: 614 E. Park Ave, Hereford, Tex. 79045.

SHOOK, ROBERT H. R
Chmn, Wash. Co. Rep. Party, Colo.
b. Akron, Colo, 9/13/14; s. Dillon Leroy Shook and Osa M. Salley S; m. 6/6/34 to Sylvia E. Jackson; c. Robert Dillon, Ronald Leroy, Lynn Jackson, David Jame and Sylvia Ann. Educ: Akron High Sch. Polit. & Govt. Pos: Rep. precinct committeeman, Colo, 50; co-founder, Rep. 1200 Club, 65; chmn, Wash. Co. Rep. Party, 65- Bus. & Prof. Pos: Farmer, 50. Mil. Serv: Entered Army, 44, released as Pfc, 108 Reg, 40th Div, 46; Combat Inf. Badges; Asiatic Pac. Service Medal; Victory Medal; Philippine Liberation Ribbon; Good Conduct Medal. Mem: Farm Bur. Rel: Baptist. Mailing Add: Burdett Route, Akron, Colo. 80720. (1967)

SHORES, ARTHUR DAVIS D
City councilman, Birmingham, Ala.
b. Birmingham, Ala, 9/25/04; s. Richard Shores and Pauline McGhee S; m. 8/5/38 to Theodora Helen Warren; c. Helen (Mrs. Robert Lee) and Barbara. Educ: Talladega Col, A.B, 27; Univ. Kans, 34; LaSalle Exten. Univ, LL.B, 35; Alpha Phi Alpha. Polit. & Govt. Pos: Mem. exec. cmt, Jefferson Co. Dem. Party, Ala, 62; del, Dem. Nat. Conv, 68; city councilman, Birmingham, Ala, 68- Bus. & Prof. Pos: Secy-dir, Brown-Belle Bottling Co, 41-47; secy-treas, Hollins & Shores Realty Co, 43-49; pres, Jones Valley Finance Co, 45-62; v.pres and gen. counsel, Citizens Fed. Savings & Loan Asn, 57-; dir, Am. Nat. Bank, 64-66; cmnr, Birmingham Housing Authority, 66-68; Mem: Nat, Am. and Ala. Bar Asns; F&AM (33°); Shrine; K. of P; Birmingham Press Club; chmn. bd. trustees, Talladega Col. Alpha Medal of Honor, Alpha Phi Alpha, 56; Recipient of awards from South. Beauty Cong, Inc, 49, Alpha Chi Chap, Omega Psi Phi, 54, Nat. Bar Asn, 60, and Cook Co. Bar Asn, 65; Russwurm

Award, Nat. Newspapers Publishers Asn, 69. Rel: Congregational. Legal Res: 1021 N. Center St, Birmingham, Ala. 35204. Mailing Add: P.O. Box 1668, Birmingham, Ala. 35201.

SHOREY, GREGORY DAY, JR. R
Chmn, Fourth Cong. Dist. Rep. Party, S.C.
b. Belmont, Mass, 6/27/24; s. Gregory Day Shorey and Lucille McNamara S; m. 3/6/46 to Betty Jane Young; c. Pamela Grace, Gregory Day, III, Cynthia Ann and Amy Jeanne. Educ: Boston Univ, B.S, 48; Intercollegiate Debating Soc; Soc. Student Couns. Polit. & Govt. Pos: Pres, Col. Young Rep, S.C, 45-48; Young Rep. Nat. Committeeman, 49-54; co. committeeman, Rep. Party, S.C, 52-68, chmn, 54-56; del, Rep. Nat. Conv, 56, 60 & 64; chmn, S.C. State Rep. Cmt, 56-61; hon. v.chmn. and life committeeman, S.C. State Rep. Cmt; Fed. Jury Cmnr, U.S. Justice Dept, 58-; chmn, Fourth Cong. Dist. Rep. Party, 68- Bus. & Prof. Pos: Pres. and gen. mgr, Style-Crafters, Inc, Div. Microtron Corp, currently; dir, Am. Field Serv. and pres, Greenville Hi Chap, currently. Mil. Serv: Entered as A/S, Navy, 43, released as Ens, 45, after serv. in Navy Armed Guard and Amphibious Fleet, Atlantic and Mediterranean Theaters, 43-45; All Theater Ribbons and Five Battle Stars; Presidential Citation; Atlantic Aerial Gunnery Citations; Purple Heart. Publ: 'Selling A Profit,' Sporting Goods Dealer, 62; 'Market Outlook,' Selling Sporting Goods, 64-66. Mem: Nat. Sporting Goods Asn; pres, Marine Mfr. Safety Equipment Asn, 62-66; bd. gov, Nat. Asn. Engine and Boat Mfrs, 62-66; Pub. Rels. Inst, Asn. Fishing Tackle Mfrs; bd. dirs, YMCA; Nat. Asn. Mfrs; Local and State C. of C; Carolinas Golf Asn; Greenville Country Club; Episcopal Church Lay Orgns. Brand Name Mfg. of 1966, Marine. Rel: Episcopal. Mailing Add: 711 Crescent Ave, Greenville, S.C. 29601.

SHORT, ALAN D
Calif. State Sen.
b. San Francisco, Calif. Educ: Col. of the Pac; Hastings Col. of Law, Univ. Calif. Polit. & Govt. Pos: Past pres, San Joaquin Co. Coun. of Dem. Clubs; Young Dem. of Calif; dep. dist. attorney of San Joaquin Co, 4 years; Calif. State Sen, Sixth Sen. Dist, 54-, chmn, Senate Transportation Cmt. and mem, Finance, Ins. and Financial Inst. and Govt. Efficiency Cmts, currently, chmn, Senate Interim Cmt, on Ment. Illness, formerly; del, Dem. Nat. Conv, 68. Bus. & Prof. Pos: Attorney-at-law. Mil. Serv: Navy, World War II. Mem: Native Sons; Elks; Grange; Mason. Joseph P. Kennedy, Jr. Found. Award, 62. Legal Res: Stockton, Calif. 95205. Mailing Add: State Capitol, Sacramento, Calif. 95814.

SHORT, DON L. R
b. Le Mars, Iowa, 6/22/03; s. Hugh Connorran Short and Anne Otley Corkery S; m. 2/26/31 to Edith E. Whittemore; c. Anne Whittemore (Mrs. Kendall Johnson), Connie (Mrs. K. Paul McDonald), Arthur and Susan. Educ: Mont. State Col, 18-19; Pillsbury Mil. Acad, Owatonna, Minn, 21; Univ. Minn, 22-26. Polit. & Govt. Pos: Co. supvr, Farm Security Admin, 37-38; N.Dak. State Rep, 57; U.S. Rep, N.Dak, 59-64. Bus. & Prof. Pos: Small feed crop producer, Medora, N.Dak; wheat farmer; cattle rancher; dir, Mandan Prod. Credit Asn, 45-58; mem, N.Dak. Sanit. Livestock Bd, 46-56; pres, Nat. Beef Coun, 56-57; chmn, N.Dak. Beef Coun, 46-48. Mem: Theodore Roosevelt State Cent. Cmn, 58; Am. Nat. Cattlemen's Asn.(v.pres, 54-55); N.Dak. Stockman's Asn.(pres, 43-45); Medora Grazing Asn.(pres, 38-39). Rel: Episcopal. Mailing Add: Medora, N.Dak. 58645.

SHORT, E. RUSSELL R
b. Moscow, Idaho, 11/19/25; s. Howard R. Short and Margaret MaKelheney S; m. 8/4/68 to Judy Jo Wicks; c. Barbara Ann and Howard R. Educ: 3 years of col. Polit. & Govt. Pos: Chmn, Latah Co. Rep. Party, Idaho, 58-69. Bus. & Prof. Pos: State pres, Idaho Funeral Serv, 60; v.pres, News-Rev. Publ. Co, Inc. and pres. bd. dirs, Gritman Hosp, currently. Mil. Serv: Entered as Seaman 3/C, Navy, released as Seaman 1/C, after 4 years serv. in S.Pac. Mem: Past dep. comdr, Am. Legion; VFW; Lions; C. of C. Rel: Protestant. Mailing Add: 713 East E St, Moscow, Idaho 83843.

SHORT, JACK MARWOOD R
Okla. State Sen.
b. Mangum, Okla, 10/28/24; s. William Frank Short (deceased) and Jewel Jeanette Scott B. and step-father Z.A. Benson; m. 2/7/48 to Julia Anne Jones; c. Stephanie Lucinda, Sharon Gayle and Sabrina Jeanette. Educ: Cameron Jr. Col, 42-43; Tulane Univ, B.A, 50; Univ. of Okla, LL.B, 58; Phi Theta Kappa; Delta Theta Phi; Sigma Chi. Polit. & Govt. Pos: Temporary co. judge, Stephens Co, Okla, 59; mem, ad hoc, Rules Study Cmt; precinct chmn, Okla. Co. Rep. Cmt, 62-63, area leader, 63-64 and ward chmn, 64-66; mem, Okla. Rep. State Cmt, 65-66; Okla. State Sen, 66-; del, Rep. Nat. Conv, 68. Bus. & Prof. Pos: Attorney-at-Law. Mil. Serv: A/S, V-12, Navy, 43-46. Mem: Okla, Am. and Oklahoma Co. Bar Asns; YMCA; Oklahoma City C. of C. Rel: Presbyterian; Elder, Presbyterian Church. Mailing Add: 2015 N.W. 21st St, Oklahoma City, Okla. 73106.

SHORT, PAUL R
b. 1923. Educ: Knoxville Bus. Col. Polit. & Govt. Pos: Former Ky. State Rep. Bus. & Prof. Pos: Gen. mgr, automotive parts and machine shop. Mil. Serv: Army. Rel: Church of God. Mailing Add: Harlan, Ky. 40831. (1967)

SHORT, ROBERT E. D
married; c. Seven. Educ: Col. of St. Thomas; Georgetown Law Sch; Univ. Minn; Harvard Sch. of Bus. Admin. Polit. & Govt. Pos: Nat. chmn, Pres. Discover Am. travel prog; regional adv. to Fed. Small Bus. Admin; chmn, State Adv. Cmt. on Manpower Develop. and Training; active in Humphrey and McCarthy campaigns; involved in Dem. activities since 40; asst. U.S. Attorney for Minn; asst. U.S. Attorney for D.C; former treas, Dem. Nat. Cmt; del, Dem. Nat. Conv, 68. Bus. & Prof. Pos: Attorney; owns a truck line and a hotel. Mailing Add: Leamington Hotel, Minneapolis, Minn. 55436. (1967)

SHORT, SAMUEL JAMES R
b. Moulton, Iowa, 12/23/91; s. James Short and Cora Jennings S; m. 6/8/38 to Violet Dimmick; c. Samuel James, Jr, Jane Marie (Mrs. Wortz) and Judith Sandra (Mrs. Underwood). Educ: Kans. State Dent. Col. Polit. & Govt. Pos: Chmn, Cedar Co. Rep. Cmt, Mo, 60-69; chmn, El Dorado Springs City Rep. Cmt; particitating Dent, Vets. Admin. Bus. & Prof. Pos: Participating Dent, Div. Welfare, Cedar Co. Mem. Hosp. Mem: Mason; Lions; v.pres, S.W. Mo. Dent. Soc. Hon. Alumnus, Kans. City Dent. Col. Rel: Methodist. Mailing Add: 112 W. Martin, El Dorado Springs, Mo. 64744. (1967)

SHORT, W. MARCUS D
N.C. State Rep.
b. Greensboro, N.C, 8/4/30; s. George A. Short and Blanche Futrell S; m. 2/16/52 to Dorothy Mangum; c. Nancy Elizabeth. Educ: Univ. N.C, B.S. in bus. admin, LL.B, 58. Polit. & Govt. Pos: N.C. State Rep, 65- Mil. Serv: Entered as Pvt, Air Force, 50, released as S/Sgt, 53. Mem: Am, State, N.C, Greensboro and 18th Judicial Dist. Bar Asns; past pres, Sumner PTA and Sumner Civitan Club; past gov, Greensboro Moose Lodge; Buena Vista Odd Fellows; YMCA; Sedgefield Country Club; C. of C. Played in Greensboro Gr. Open Pro-Amateur Golf Tournament, 64-69. Rel: Methodist. Legal Res: 2004 Kylemore Dr, Greensboro, N.C. 27406. Mailing Add: 228 Southeastern Bldg, Greensboro, N.C. 27401.

SHOTT, JOHN CARY R
Tenth Sen. Dist. Mem, Rep. State Exec. Cmt, W.Va.
b. Bluefield, W.Va, 2/17/24; s. James Howard Shott and Martha Easley S; m. 12/27/46 to Bonnie Reark; c. John Headley and Michael Reark. Educ: W.Va. Univ, B.S. in Bus. Admin, 48; Phi Kappa Psi. Polit. & Govt. Pos: Tenth Sen. Dist. Mem, Rep. State Exec. Cmt, W.Va, 57-, chmn, 65-68; alternate del, Rep. Nat. Conv, 68. Bus. & Prof. Pos: Salesman, Paper Supply Co, 48-54 and WHIS, 54-55; sales mgr, WHIS-TV, 55-58, sta. mgr, 58-63; gen. mgr, WHIS-AM-FM-TV, 63-68; v.pres. and gen. mgr, WHIS-AM-FM-TV and WBTW-TV, 68- Mil. Serv: Entered as Aviation Cadet, Navy, 43, released as Ens, 45, after serv. as Flight Instr. Mem: Broadcast Pioneers; Mercer Co. Tuberc. and Health Asn.(former pres. and drive chmn); Mercer Co. Heart Asn.(former drive chmn); United Fund of Gr. Bluefield (former drive chmn); W.Va. Broadcasters Asn;(former pres); W.Va. State Indust. Adv. Cmt. (former chmn). Rel: Presbyterian. Mailing Add: 208 Springdale Ave, Bluefield, W.Va. 24701.

SHOULDERS, BILLY JOE D
b. Westmoreland, Tenn, 10/31/25; s. Roey Dewey Shoulders and Minnie Harris S; m. 8/23/46 to Doris Jean Krisle; c. Suzanne. Educ: YMCA Law Sch, LL.B, 50. Polit. & Govt. Pos: Advisement and guidance clerk, Veterans Admin, Nashville, Tenn, 46-51; exec. admin. asst. to Gov. Frank G. Clement, Tenn. 63-66; admin. asst. to U.S. Rep, Ray Blanton, Tenn, 69- Bus. & Prof. Pos: Admin. asst, Base Detachment Comdr, Tenn, 53-55; asst. adj. gen. Tenn. Air Nat. Guard, 55-68. Mil. Serv: Entered as Pvt, Army, 44, released as S/Sgt, 46, after serv. in Signal Corps, Asiatic-Pac. Theatre, transferred to Air Force, 48; Brig. Gen, Tenn. Air Nat. Guard, 68-; World War II Victory Medal; Good Conduct Medal; Asiatic Pac. Medal with Three Stars; Philippine Liberation Medal with One Star; Philippine Presidential Unit Citation Medal; Air Force Outstanding Unit Award (Off. of Spec. Investigation); Am. Campaign Medal; Nat. Defense Serv. Medal; Air Force Res. Medal with HGD; Air Force Longevity Serv. Award; Tenn. Nat. Guard Distinguished Serv. Medal; Tenn. Nat. Guard Commendation Medal; Tenn. Nat. Guard Serv. Ribbon with One Bronze Serv. Star and Three Bronze Oak Leaf Clusters; Meritorious Unit Commendation. Mem: YMCA Law Sch. Alumni Asn; Quiet Birdmen; VFW; Am. Legion; Burro Club. Rel: Church of Christ. Mailing Add: 131 Rivera Dr, Hendersonville, Tenn. 37075.

SHOUSE, JOUETT D
b. Woodford Co, Ky, 12/10/79; s. John Samuel Shouse and Anna Armstrong S; m. 12/2/32 to Catherine Filene Dodd; c. Elizabeth and Marion. Educ: Univ. Mo; Univ. Miami, Ohio. Polit. & Govt. Pos: Kans. State Sen, 13-15; U.S. Rep, Kans, 15-19; Asst. Secy, Treas, Kans, 19-20; del-at-lg, Dem. Nat. Conv, 20, 24 & 32; chmn, Dem. Nat. Exec. Cmt, 28-32; pres, Asn. Against Prohibition Amend, 32-33; pres, Am. Liberty League, 34-40. Bus. & Prof. Pos: Newspaper work and bus. enterprises, Lexington, Ky, 98-11; farming and stock raising, Kinsley, Kans, 66; lawyer, Wash, D.C, 40-; past chmn, bd, Kinsley Bank, Kans; dir. MSL Industs, Inc; trustee, Nat. Realty Trust. Mem: Phi Delta Theta; Metrop. Club, Wash, D.C; Jockey Club; Am. Boxer (del, Am. Kennel Club). Rel: Christian Disciples Church. Mailing Add: 1916 F St, Washington, D.C. 20006. (1967)

SHOVELL, WILLIAM LEE, III D
b. Missoula, Mont, 10/27/23; s. William L. Shovell and Josephine Mann S; m. to Mildred I. Wickhurst; c. W. Lee, IV and Jo Ann. Educ: Macalester Col, grad. Polit. & Govt. Pos: State chmn, Young Dem-Farmer-Labor Party, 48-50; Minn. State Rep, 52-62, chmn, Pub. Insts. Cmt, 55-58 and House Appropriations Cmt, 58-62; chmn, Fourth Dist. Dem-Farmer-Labor Party, 60; exec. asst, Pres. Cmt. on Juvenile Delinquency and Youth Crime, 61-62. Mil. Serv: Entered as Pvt, Air Force, 43, released as Sgt, 46, after serv. in ETO; ETO and Am. Theater Ribbons; Good Conduct Medal. Publ: Minnesota Work Release Plan. Mem: Pub. Admin. Asn; Minn. Corrections Asn; Am. Legion; VFW. Rel: Congregational. Mailing Add: 4550 Warwick Blvd, Apt. 509, Kansas City, Mo. 64111.

SHOWALTER, CARL EDWARD R
Colo. State Rep.
b. Harrisonburg, Va, 11/29/13; s. Earl E. Showalter and Mary Heatwole S; m. 11/25/34 to Ruby Lela Yoder; c. Gearldine Lee (Mrs. Mellon), Karla Jean (Mrs. Romero) and George E. Educ: Goshen Col, 2 years. Polit. & Govt. Pos: Mayor, Johnston, Colo, 58-; Colo. State Rep, Dist. 44, 69- Bus. & Prof. Pos: Farm operator, La Junta, Colo, 35-37; automobile bus, Lamar, 37-41; local mgr, Nat. Dehydrating & Milling Co, Johnstown, 41-51; owner and mgr, Colo. Alfalfa Milling & Prod. Co, Milliken, 51-68. Mem: Am. Dehydrators Asn; Aircraft Owners & Pilots Asn; life mem, Elks; Rotary; Weld Co. Farm Bur; Colo. Cattle Feeders Asn. Rel: United Methodist. Legal Res: 5 Madden, Johnstown, Colo. 80534. Mailing Add: Box K, Johnstown, Colo. 80534.

SHOWALTER, MYRTLE MAY R
V.Chmn, Moffat Co. Rep. Party, Colo.
b. Strang, Nebr, 1/28/97; d. John Thomas Rathbun and Cora Johnson R; m. 2/28/17 to Lee C. Showalter; c. Robert, Donald and Eileen (Mrs. Schrader). Educ: Jefferson Co. Pub. Schs, Nebr, grad; music from private teacher, 8 years; Delphian Course, 4 years. Polit. & Govt. Pos: Hq. Secy, Moffat Co.

Rep. Party, Colo, 52, v.chmn, 53-; mem. various cmts. in Dist. and State Rep. Orgn. Mem: Eastern Star (Past Matron, Anita Chap); adult mem, Order of Rainbow for Girls (founder, Craig Assembly); charter mem, Craig Woman's Club (past pres); Rep. Woman's Club of Moffat Co. Woman of the Year, Daily Press, 67; mgr. of Thrift Shop manned by vol. workers of Rep. Woman's Club. Rel: Congregational. Legal Res: 848 Taylor St, Craig, Colo. 81625. Mailing Add: Box 1062, Craig, Colo. 81625.

SHRECENGOST, WILLIAM G. R

Educ: Pi Kappa Alpha Alumni. Polit. & Govt. Pos: N.Mex. State Rep, 61-69, former Minority Whip, N.Mex. State House of Rep. Bus. & Prof. Pos: Apple orchardist, livestock. Mil. Serv: Air Corps, 38 months active duty; Maj, N.Mex. Nat. Guard, assigned 111th Brigade Hq. Mem: Past pres, N.Mex. Apple Coun; pres, West Apple Growers of Am; Optimist Int; Am. Legion Post 79; Mason. Rel: Episcopal; Lay Reader. Mailing Add: P.O. Box 68, Lincoln, N.Mex. 88338.

SHREWDER, ROY VALENTINE R

b. Ft. Worth, Tex, 2/14/99; s. William Fred Shrewder and Sarah Blanche Hamilton S; m. 4/25/29 to Dorothy Berryman; c. Sarah (Mrs. Paul J. Tracy) and Susan (Mrs. R.E. Wescott). Educ: Hon. LL.D, Col. Emporia. Polit. & Govt. Pos: Mem, Ashland City Coun, Kans, 46-52; Kans. State Rep, 95th Dist, 60-66; former finance chmn, Kans. State Rep. Party; alternate del, Rep. Nat. Conv, 68. Bus. & Prof. Pos: Auditor, Home Lumber & Supply Co, Ashland, Kans, 29-48, gen. mgr, 48-61, pres, 50- Mil. Serv: World War I. Mem: Mason; Shrine; Wichita Club; life mem. Kans. Peace Officers Asn; Nat. Mgt. Inst; Capitol Hill Club, Wash, D.C. Lapidary and Silver Smith. Rel: Presbyterian. Mailing Add: Box 506, Ashland, Kans. 67831.

SHRIVER, DONALD WOODS, JR. D

b. Norfolk, Va, 12/20/27; s. Donald W. Shriver and Gladys Roberts S; m. 8/9/53 to Peggy Ann Leu; c. Gregory, Margaret Ann and Timothy. Educ: Davidson Col, A.B, 51; Union Theol. Sem, B.D, 55; Yale Univ, S.T.M, 56; Rockefeller fel, Harvard Univ, 59-62, Ph.D, 62; Phi Beta Kappa; Omicron Delta Kappa; Sigma Pi. Polit. & Govt. Pos: Dem. committeeman, Second Precinct, Wake Co, N.C, 63-64 and Dem. chmn, 64-68; del, Dem. State Conv, 64, 66 & 68; mem. and chmn. subcmt. housing, Raleigh Commun. Rel. Cmt, 66-; alternate del, Dem. Nat. Conv, 68. Bus. & Prof. Pos: Presby. minister, N.C. State Univ, Raleigh, 62-67 and assoc. prof. relig. and dir. Univ. Prog. on Sci. and Soc, 68- Mil. Serv: Entered as Pvt, Army, 46, released as T-5, 47, after serv. in Signal Corps, Am. Theatre, 46-47. Publ: The Unsilent South: Prophetic Preaching In Racial Crisis, John Knox, 65; How Do You Do—And Why?: An Introduction To Christian Ethics for Young People, Covenant Life Curriculum, 66; Religious Ethics and Business Ethics, Relig. In Life, fall 68. Mem: Am. Soc. Christian Ethics; Am. Sociol. Asn; Soc. Sci. Study Relig; Soc. Relig. in Higher Educ. "Tar Heel of the Week," May 10, 64, The Raleigh News and Observer, 64. Rel: Presbyterian. Legal Res: 3608 Dade St, Raleigh, N.C. 27609. Mailing Add: P.O. Box 5666, State College Sta, Raleigh, N.C. 27607.

SHRIVER, GARNER E. R

U.S. Rep, Kans.

b. Towanda, Kans, 7/6/12; s. Ed Arthur Shriver and Olive M. Glass S; m. 6/4/41 to Martha Jane Currier; c. Kay (Mrs. Leroux), David and Linda. Educ: Wichita State Univ, A.B, 34; Univ. South. Calif, Los Angeles, Grad. Sch, 36; Washburn Law Sch, LL.B, 40; Phi Alpha Delta; Kappa Delta Pi; Phi Delta Theta. Polit. & Govt. Pos: Kans. State Rep, 47-51; Kans. State Sen, 53-60; U.S. Rep, Kans, 61- Bus. & Prof. Pos: Trustee, Roland P. Murdock Art Collection, 57-; legal counsel, Wichita Bd. of Educ, 51-60. Mil. Serv: Entered as A/S, Navy, released as Lt.(sg), 46, after serv. in Pac. Theater. Mem: Am, Kans. and Wichita Bar Asns; VFW; Am. Legion; Nat. Sojourners; ROA; Mason; Scottish Rite; York Rite Bodies; DeMolay Legion of Honor; Kiwanis. Univ. Wichita Alumni Achievement Award, 1961. Rel: Methodist. Legal Res: 5051 East Lincoln, Wichita, Kans. 67218. Mailing Add: 2439 Rayburn House Office Bldg, Washington, D.C. 20515.

SHRIVER, ROBERT SARGENT, JR. D

U.S. Ambassador to France

b. Westminster, Md, 11/9/15; s. Robert Sargent Shriver and Hilda S; m. 5/23/53 to Eunice Mary Kennedy; c. Robert Sargent III, Maria Owings, Timothy Perry, Mark Kennedy and Anthony Paul Kennedy. Educ: Yale Univ, B.A. cum laude, 38, LL.B, 41; Delta Kappa Epsilon. Hon. LL.D, St. Procopius Col, 59, Notre Dame Univ, DePauw Univ, Seton Hall Col, 61, St. Louis Univ, Kans. State Univ, Brandeis Univ, 62, St. Michael's Col. Vt, Fordham Univ, 63, Boston Col, Yale Univ, Dusquesne Univ, Georgetown Univ, N.Y. Univ. and Wesleyan Univ; D.C.L, Univ. Liberia, 63; H.H.D, Salem Col, 63; L.H.D, Bowling Green State Univ, Springfield Col, 63, Univ. Scranton and Providence Col; Dr. Polit. Sci, Chulalongkorn Univ, Bangkok. Polit. & Govt. Pos: Pres, Chicago Bd. Educ, 55-60; dir, Peace Corps, 61-66; dir, Off. Econ. Opportunity, 64-68; spec. asst. to the President, 64-68; U.S. Ambassador to France, 68- Bus. & Prof. Pos: With Winthrop, Stimson, Putnam & Roberts, 40-41; assoc. ed, Newsweek, 45-46; assoc, Joseph P. Kennedy Enterprises, 46-48; asst. gen. mgr, Merchandise Mart, Chicago, 48-60; pres, Cath. Interracial Coun, Chicago, 55-60; exec. dir, Joseph P. Kennedy, Jr. Found. Mil. Serv: Lt. Comdr, Naval Res, 40-45. Publ: Point of the Lance, 64. Mem: Mem-at-lg, Nat. Coun. Boy Scouts; dir, Yale Art Gallery Asn; mem. pres. coun, St. Xavier Col; exec. cmt, Yale Law Sch. Asn; life mem. Navy League; dir, Chicago Coun. For. Rels; Serra Club; Econ. Club; Racquet Club; Exec. Club, Chicago; Onwentsia Club, Lake Forest, Ill; Yale Club, N.Y.C; Univ. Club, D.C; Chevy Chase Club. Yale Medal, 47; Chicago Medal Merit, 57; James J. Hoey Award, Cath. Interracial N.Y, 58; Lay Churchman of the Year, Relig. Heritage Am, 63; Golden Heart Pres. Award, Philippines, 64. Rel: Catholic. Legal Res: 140 E. Walton Pl, Chicago, Ill. 60611. Mailing Add: American Embassy Paris, APO New York 09777.

SHRUM, WILLIAM PAUL R

b. Carnegie, Pa, 11/3/24; s. Amos A. Shrum and Theressa Mattes S; m. 12/26/50 to Eleanor Hall; c. Deirdre and Heidi. Educ: Carnegie Inst. of Tech, B.S. in Mech. Eng, 46; Univ. of Buffalo, M.D, 54; Pi Tau Sigma; Kappa Sigma. Polit. & Govt. Pos: Chmn, Kootenai Co. Rep. Cent. Cmt, Idaho and Rep. Dist. Chmn, 66; regional med. adv, S. Asia and U.S. sci. attaché, Pakistan, U.S. Dept. of State, Karachi, Pakistan, 67-69. Bus. & Prof. Pos: Physician and surgeon, 55-57 & 69- Mil. Serv: Entered as Seaman 1/C, Navy, 44, released as Petty Off, 3/C, 45. Mem: Am. Med. Asn; Am. Asn. of Physicians & Surgeons; Am. Acad. Gen. Practice; Idaho State Med. Asn; Am. Legion; C. of C. Rel: Independent Presbyterian. Mailing Add: Morton Medical Center, Morton, Wash. 98356.

SHUEE, CHARLES EDWARD D

Chmn, Putnam Co. Dem. Party, Ind.

b. Bainbridge, Ind, 9/23/16; s. Austin Shuee and Stella Everesole S; m. 9/22/33 to Rosalie Eileen Shoaf; c. Robert Kieth, Claude Austin and Donald Wayne (deceased). Polit. & Govt. Pos: Dem. precinct committeeman, Putnam Co, Ind, 39-57; chmn, Putnam Co. Dem. Party, 57-; coordinator, Seventh Dist. Dem. Party, 65-66, chmn, 68-; mem, Exec. Cmt. to the Gov, 68; del, Dem. Nat. Conv, 68. Bus. & Prof. Pos: Dist. mgr, Massey Ferguson Corp, 12 years; real estate broker, 62-; ins. agent, 64- Mem: Mason; Scottish Rite; Shrine; Elks; Moose; v.commodore, Catract Yacht Club; Windy Hill Country Club. Rel: Protestant. Mailing Add: R.R. 1, Greencastle, Ind. 46135.

SHUEY, DON E. D

b. Lucerne, Mo, 4/3/10; m. 12/5/35 to Frances M. Bramhall; c. Shirley Ann, Donna L. Educ: Univ. of Mo, Columbia, B.S, Agr. Polit. & Govt. Pos: Mo. State Rep, 64-66; mem. bd. of dirs. of Nat, Mo. Alumni Asn. Bus. & Prof. Pos: Farmer; ins. bus; formerly with U.S. Dept. of Agr. Mil. Serv: Air Force, World War II. Mem: People to People; Int. Platform Asn; AF&AM; Eastern Star. Rel: Christian Church. Mailing Add: 2208 Main St, Unionville, Mo. 63565.

SHUEY, JOHN ARTHUR R

Del, Calif. Rep. State Cent. Cmt.

b. Penninsulia, Ohio, 2/23/33; s. Arthur Edward Shuey and Lois Rose Fisher S; m. 3/31/63 to Diane Enid Roulier; c. Jay Arthur. Educ: Union High Sch, Vacaville, Calif, 2 years; Beall High Sch, Frostburg, Md, 2 years. Polit. & Govt. Pos: Del, Calif. Rep. State Cent. Cmt, 69- Bus. & Prof. Pos: Machinist, Space Craft, Venice, Calif, 60-63; pres, Shuey Aircraft Inc, Gardena, Calif, 63- Rel: Protestant. Mailing Add: 13605 S. Van Ness, Gardena, Calif. 90249.

SHUEY, RUTH MURPHY D

b. Vienna, Ill, 2/21/10; d. William Thomas Murphy and Pernolia Mitchell M; m. 5/2/34 to Walter Ayers Shuey; c. Walter Harmon (deceased). Educ: South. Ill. Univ, 28-30. Polit. & Govt. Pos: Del, Va. State Dem. Conv, 64; former organizer and conductor, women's polit. cmt, drive for voter registrations; mem. local cmt, Johnson-Humphrey Campaign, 64; mem. campaign cmt, Hopewell-Prince George Co. Rep. to Va. House of Del; campaign mem, Sixth Sen. Dist. Contest, 65; former mem, Hopewell Dem. Cmt. and Women's Cmt, Va; mem. cmt, Hopewell Dem. Dinner, 66. Bus. & Prof. Pos: Women's ed, Hopewell News, Va, 56-64, managing ed, 64-; v.pres, Hopewell Publ. Co, Inc. Mem: Int. hon. mem, Beta Sigma Phi; bd. dirs, Va. Press Women, 58-66, pres, 60-62; regional dir, Nat. Fedn. Press Women, 62-66; Richmond Br, Nat. League Am. Pen Women; Women's Club Hopewell; bd. dirs, Southside Area Chap, Va. Soc. for Crippled Children and Adults and Hopewell United Fund; James River Br, Asn. for Preservation Va. Antiquities; Va. Press Asn; hon. mem, Future Bus. Leaders Am, Xi Psi Chap, Beta Sigma Phi and Prince George High Sch. Band; bd. dirs, Hopewell Unit, Am. Cancer Soc, 67- Numerous Awards, Nat. Fedn. Press Women's contests for writing and photog. and Va. Press Women writing and photog. contests; awards for Excellency of Front Page in daily and for promotion of Nat. Newspaper Week, Va. Press Asn; Optimist Int. Newspaper Commendation Award; Hats Off Award, DeMolay, twice; Citation for Commun. Serv, Hopewell Jaycees, 65; Meritorious Serv. Award, Am. Legion, 65; Boy Scout Commun. Serv. Award, 68; Outstanding Serv. to Commun. Plaque, VFW, 68; Woman of Distinction, Va. Press Women, 68; Woman of Achievement, Bus. & Prfnl. Women Club, 68; Nike Statuette Representing the Triumph of Womanhood; Friend of Girlhood Award Girl Scout, 68. Rel: Methodist. Mailing Add: 615 E. Poythress St, Hopewell, Va. 23860.

SHUFFLEBARGER, THOMAS GARNETT D

b. Cove Creek, Va, 3/22/10; s. Thomas Lockhart Shufflebarger and Pauline Belle Gregory S; single. Educ: Univ. Va, Du Pont Scholarship and LL.B, 36; Delta Sigma Phi; Delta Sigma Rho; Jefferson Soc; Va. Players; Univ. Debating Team. Polit. & Govt. Pos: Adminstr, Civil Works Admin, Tazewell Co, Va, 33-34; secy, Tazewell Co. Dem. Cmt, 36-40, chmn, 40-42 & 60-65 and v.chmn, 65-69; substitute Judge, Tazewell Co. Court and Juvenile & Domestic Rels. Court, 60-; mem, Va. State Dem. Cent. Cmt. and v.chmn, Ninth Cong. Dist. Dem. Cmt, 65-69. Mil. Serv: Entered as Pvt, Army, 42, released as 1st Sgt, 45, after serv. in 79th Inf. Div. and Judge Adv. Gen. Dept. Combat Infantryman's Badge; Presidential Unit Citation Badge; Europe-Africa-Middle East Medal with Silver Star; Bronze Star Medal with Oak Leaf Cluster; Croix de Guerre with Palm. Mem: Am. Bar Asn; Coun, Va. State Bar Asn, 60-66; pres, Tazewell Co. Bar Asn, 49-50; Nat. Lawyers' Club; Univ. Club; Tazewell Co. Country Club; Rotary; Am. Legion; VFW; nat. secy, 315th Inf. Asn, 48-65; C. of C; dir, Bluefield Automobile Club, 37-42 & 60-; hon. fel. Harry S. Truman Libr. Inst. Rel: Methodist. Legal Res: 1429 Farmer St, Richlands, Va. 24641. Mailing Add: P.O. Drawer 728, Richlands, Va. 24641.

SHUFORD, ADRIAN LAFAYETTE, JR. D

N.C. State Sen.

b. Hickory, N.C, 12/23/10; s. Adrian Lafayette Shuford, Sr. and Annie Warlick S; m. 6/16/32 to Dorothy Winter Cilley; c. Adrian L, III and Dorothy Anna. Educ: Cornell Univ, 28-29; Univ. N.C, 29-31; Pi Kappa Alpha. Polit. & Govt. Pos: Past chmn, Catawba Co. Bd. of Cmnrs, N.C; former mayor, Conover; N.C. State Sen, 65- Bus. & Prof. Pos: Pres, Conover Knitting Co, N.C, 32-; dir, First Nat. Bank of Catawba Co; dir, Riegel Textile Corp; pres, Jackson Buff Corp, 59-; past chmn. bd, Nat. Asn. of Hosiery Mfrs. Mil. Serv: Navy, 43, released as Lt, 45, serv. in Pac. Theater. Mem: Chmn. bd. of trustees, Catawaba Col, Salisbury, N.C; pres, Newton-Conover Rotary Club; past pres, Eastern Catawba Co. United Fund. Rel: Evangelical & Reformed Church. Legal Res: First Avenue Place, N.E, Conover, N.C. 28613. Mailing Add: P.O. Box 398, Conover, N.C. 28613.

SHULER, LEWIS HAYNE D
b. Bowman, 11/5/10; s. John D. Shuler and Julia Albergotti S; m. 9/20/34 to Frances Fair; c. John A, Julia Francena. Educ: Bowman High Sch, 27. Polit. & Govt. Pos: Mem, Orangeburg Co. Hwy. Cmn, S.C, 49-52; S.C. State Rep, 53-69. Bus. & Prof. Pos: Farmer and businessman. Mem: Past patron, Agsaloma Chap. Order of the Eastern Star; past master Bowman Masonic Lodge 290; past pres. Bowman Ruritan Club. Rel: Methodist; bd. of stewards, Wightman Methodist Church, Bowman; dist. steward, Orangeburg Dist. Methodist Church. Mailing Add: Route 1, Bowman, S.C. 29018. (1967)

SHULL, LEON
b. Phila, Pa, 11/8/13; s. Samuel Shull and Yetta S; m. 12/29/38 to Anne Wollod; c. Jane Ellen and Susan Deborah. Polit. & Govt. Pos: Dir. several polit. campaign cmts. in Pa, 51-63; mem. staff, Americans for Dem. Action, 51-63, nat. dir, 64- Bus. & Prof. Pos: Owner, Logan Furniture Co; dir, Jewish Labor Cmt. Mil. Serv: Army, 42-46. Rel: Jewish. Legal Res: 6417 Western Ave. N.W, Washington, D.C. 20015. Mailing Add: 1424 16th St. N.W, Washington, D.C. 20036.

SHULTZ, GEORGE P.
Secy. of Labor
b. N.Y.C, 12/13/20; s. Birl E. Shultz and Margaret Pratt S; m. 1946 to Helena Marie O'Brien; c. Margaret, Kathleen, Peter, Barbara and Alex. Educ: Princeton, B.A, 42; Mass. Inst. Tech, Ph.D. in Indust. Econ, 49. Polit. & Govt. Pos: Sr. staff economist, President's Coun. of Econ. Adv, 55-56; consult. to Off. of the Secy, Dept. of Labor, 59-60; mem, Steering Cmt, Study of Collective Bargaining in the Basic Steel Indust, 60; dir, Pub. Interest in Nat. Labor Policy, 61; consult, President's Adv. Cmt. on Labor-Mgt. Policy, 61-62; co-chmn, Automation Fund Cmt, 62-68; mem. exec. bd, Indust. Rels. Research Asn, 63-66; mem, Gov. Cmt. on Job Vacancies, Ill, 63-64; mem, Research Adv. Bd, Cmt. for Econ. Develop, 65-67; Secy. of Labor, 69- Bus. & Prof. Pos: Acting dir, Indust. Rels. Sect, Dept. of Econ, Mass. Inst. of Tech, 54-55, assoc. prof, 55-57; prof. indust. rels, Grad. Sch. Bus, Univ. Chicago, 57-68, dean, Grad. Sch. Bus, 62-68. Mil. Serv: Entered Marine Corps, 42, released as Maj, 55. Mem: Bd. dirs, Borg-Warner Corp, 64-69, J.I. Case Corp, 64-68 and Stein, Roe & Farnham Stock and Balanced Funds, 66-69; vis. cmt, Dept. of Econ, Mass. Inst. Tech, 66-; bd. visitors, U.S. Naval Acad, 66-69; bd. dirs, Gen. Am. Transportation Corp, 66-69; Cmt. on Honors and Awards, Am. Econ. Asn, 67-; Indust. Rels. Research Asn.(pres, 68); fel, Center for Adv. Study in Behav. Sci, 68. Mailing Add: 2735 Ft. Scott Dr, Arlington, Va. 22202.

SHULTZ, MARGARET HAMPTON D
Chmn, Bingham Co. Dem. Cent. Cmt, Idaho
b. Blackfoot, Idaho, 10/10/16; d. George Victor Hampton and Josephine Mathewson H; m. 6/3/44 to Donald Earl Shultz; c. George Hampton and Sally Jane (Mrs. Nelson). Educ: Idaho State Univ, B.A, 61; Beta Sigma Phi. Polit. & Govt. Pos: Committeewoman, Thomas Precinct, Dem. Cent. Cmt, 60-; chmn, Bingham Co. Dem. Cent. Cmt, Idaho, 63-; del-at-lg. and mem, Credentials Cmt, Dem. Nat. Conv, 64 & 68; del. and chmn, Nominating Conv, Idaho State Dem. Assembly, 64 and del. and chmn, Credentials Cmt, 68; co. rep, Southeast. Idaho Co. Orgn, 65-66; mem, Idaho Dem. Cmt. on Party Structure and Del. Selection, 69- Bus. & Prof. Pos: Teacher, Elem. grades, 38-44 and Jr. High Sch, 54-60. Mem: Pres, Blackfoot Teachers Asn, 42; Idaho Educ. Asn; Nat. Educ. Asn. Rel: Methodist. Mailing Add: Route 5, Box 189, Blackfoot, Idaho 83221.

SHUMAN, CHARLES B. D
b. Sullivan, Ill, 4/27/07; s. Bliss Shuman and Grace Baker S; m. 6/24/33 to Ida Wilson, wid, 54; m. 5/5/56 to Mabel Ervin; c. Charles W, Janet (Mrs. Roger Roney), George E. and twins, Paul E. and John L. Educ: Univ. of Ill, B.S, 28 and M.S, 29; Sigma Xi; Alpha Zeta; Gamma Sigma Delta; Phi Eta Sigma. Hon. Ph.D, Millikin Univ, Wesleyan Univ, DePauw Univ, Ill. Col. and Mo. Valley Col. Bus. & Prof. Pos: Farmer, Sullivan, Ill, 29-; dir, Moultrie Co. Farm Bur, Ill, 31-33 and pres, 34-39; mem. bd. of dirs, Ill. Agr. Asn, 41 and pres, 45-55; former pres, Country Life Ins. Co, Country Mutual Casualty Co, Ill. Agr. Holding Co. and Ill. Agr. Serv. Co; dir. and secy, Livestock Shipping Asn; dir, Nat. Livestock and Meat Bd; dir, Am. Farm Bur. Fedn, 45-54 and pres, 54-; dir, Ill. State Fair Adv. Bd, 46-55; dir, Nat. Livestock Producers Asn, 48-55; dir, Am. Agr. Mutual Ins. Co, 49 and pres, 54- Mem: Transportation Asn. Am; pres, Am. Agr. Mkt. Asn; Am. Inst. Coop; trustee, Nat. Safety Coun; Farm House; bd. of trustees, Millikin Univ, Found. for Econ. Educ. and Freedom Found. Distinguished Alumnus, Univ. Ill. Rel: Methodist. Mailing Add: R.F.D. 1, Sullivan, Ill. 61951.

SHUMAN, HAROLD EUGENE R
Chmn, Wyandot Co. Rep. Exec. and Cent. Cmt, Ohio
b. Carey, Ohio, 8/15/22; s. Carlton C. Shuman and Hazel Long S; m. 9/8/57 to Donna Marcile Led; c. David E. and Barbara V. Educ: Findlay Col, one year. Polit. & Govt. Pos: Co. Cmnr, Wyandot Co, Ohio, 57-65; chmn, Wyandot Co. Rep. Exec. and Cent. Cmt, 68- Mil. Serv: Entered as Pvt, Army, 46, released as Pfc, 47, after serv. in Signal Corps. Mem: Mason; Odd Fellows. Rel: United Methodist. Mailing Add: 527 N. Warpole St, Upper Sandusky, Ohio 43351.

SHUMAN, HOWARD E. D
b. Atwood, Ill, 2/23/24; s. Frank Hamilton Shuman and Doris King S; m. 9/5/53 to Betty Ellen Hoigard; c. Ellen, Scott Howard and Barbara Ann. Educ: Univ. Ill, B.A, 43 and M.A, 48; Univ. Mich, B.B.A, 49; Harvard Bus. Sch, 44; Oxford Univ, Eng, Litt.B, 52. Polit. & Govt. Pos: Legis. asst. to U.S. Sen. Paul H. Douglas, Ill, 55-61 and admin. asst, 61-67; exec. dir, Nat. Cmn. on Urban Probs, Wash, D.C, 67-68; Admin. Asst. to U.S. Sen. William Proxmire, Wis, 69- Bus. & Prof. Pos: Instr. econ, Univ. Ill, 53-54. Mil. Serv: Entered as A/S, Navy, 43, released as Lt.(jg), 46, after serv. in Naval Ammunition Depot, Oahu, Pac. Theatre, 45-46; Am. and Pac. Theatre Ribbons; Good Conduct Medal; World War II Victory Medal. Publ: 'Civil Rights and the Rules of the Senate,' Am. Polit. Sci. Asn. Rev, 1/58; 'The Large Poor Family,' a Housing Gap,' (with Walter Rybeck and Walter Smart), Nat. Cmn. on Urban Probs. Research Report, Number 5, 68; 'Behind the Scenes and Under the Rug,' Wash. Monthly, 7/69. Mem: Pres, Oxford Union Soc. Rel: Protestant. Mailing Add: 2433 N. Kenmore St, Arlington, Va. 22207.

SHUMAN, JACK W. D
b. Pembroke, Ga, 8/20/22; s. Robert M. Shuman and Myrtle Davis S; m. 5/20/41 to Gloria Jane Mauney; c. Richard Douglas, Jack W. Jr, Martha Jane. Educ: Bryan Co. High Sch, 41. Polit. & Govt. Pos: Ga. State Rep, 59-66. Bus. & Prof. Pos: Distributor-building materials; pres. of 20 corps. in Ga, Tenn, Ala, Fla, S.C. Mil. Serv: 44-45. Mem: Elk; Am. Legion; Farm Bur; App. Millionaires Club. Rel: Baptist. Mailing Add: Pembroke, Ga. 31321. (1967)

SHUMAN, WILLIAM O. D
Pa. State Rep.
b. Antrim Twp, 7/23/21; s. Grover C. Shuman and Iva Adele Graham S. Educ: Exten. courses at several col. Polit. & Govt. Pos: Past pres, Greencastle-Antrim Dem. Club, Pa; former co. chmn, dinners, registrn. drives; dep. chief, Franklin Co. Cmnrs, 57; treas, Franklin Co. Dem. Party, 58-61; Pa. State Rep, 64-, chmn, Joint Vet. Coun, dep. comdr, Adams, Franklin and York Co. Cmts, mem, Nat. Counter Subversive Activities Cmt. and Mason Dixon Coun, Pa. State House of Rep. Bus. & Prof. Pos: Asst. ed, bus. mgr, weekly newspaper. Mil. Serv: Army, World War II, serv. as Sgt, 83rd Div. Artil; Bronze Star. Mem: Sr. v.comdr, VFW, post chaplain and state chaplain; past chaplain, Am. Legion; DAV; nat. chaplain, 83rd Inf. Div. Asn; chmn, Am. Red Cross; Salvation Army. Mailing Add: 162 E. Madison St, Greencastle, Pa. 17225. (1967)

SHUMWAY, BOYD ALBERT D
Ariz. State Rep.
b. Shumway, Ariz, 7/12/17; s. Albert Minerly Shumway and May Denham S; m. 11/16/42 to Elizabeth Widen; c. Boyd Robert, Karin Elizabeth (Mrs. Rex W. Foster, Jr) and William Widen. Educ: Ariz. State Univ, B.A. in Educ, 40. Polit. & Govt. Pos: Precinct committeeman, Dem. Party, Winslow, Ariz, 54-69; Ariz. State Rep, 69- Mil. Serv: Entered as Aviation Cadet, Army, 42, released as 1st Lt, 45, after serv. in 14th Air Force, China-Burma-India Theatre, 44; Distinguished Flying Cross; Air Medal. Mailing Add: 619 W. Maple, Winslow, Ariz. 86047.

SHUMWAY, DREW R
b. 1932; m. 1959 to Joan Randall; c. Four daughters and two sons. Educ: Brigham Young Univ, 57. Polit. & Govt. Pos: Precinct committeeman, Holbrook, Ariz; former chmn, Navajo Co. Rep. Party. Bus. & Prof. Pos: Formerly in farming; pres, Shumway-Broadbent Ins. Agency, Inc, currently. Mem: Rotary; C. of C. Rel: Latter-day Saint; Served two year mission. Mailing Add: Box 426, Holbrook, Ariz. 86025.

SHUMWAY, JAMES McBRIDE R
b. Edinburg, Ill, 8/6/21; s. Dorice Dwight Shumway and Marcella McBride S; m. 12/18/43 to Berte Alden Scovel; c. James McBride and Ralph Scovel. Educ: Univ. Ill, B.S; Stanford Univ, LL.B; Alpha Kappa Psi; Phi Delta Phi. Polit. & Govt. Pos: Counsel, Solano Co, Calif, 56-67; chmn, Planning Cmn, Fairfield, 58-62; asst. adminstr, Calif. Health and Welfare Agency, 67-68; mem, Calif. Unemployment Ins. Appeals Bd, 68; Rep. cand. for U.S. Rep, 68; chmn, Calif. Alcoholic Beverage Control Appeals Bd, currently. Bus. & Prof. Pos: Attorney-at-law, 52- Mil. Serv: Entered as Seaman 2/C, Navy, 42, released as Lt. Comdr, 45, after serv. as carrier pilot, Dive Bomber Squadron, S.Pac. Theatre, 43-44; Comdr.(Ret), Naval Res; Navy Cross; Silver Star; Two Distinguished Flying Crosses. Mem: Dir, Nat. Asn. of Co. Counsels; first v.pres. and dir, Dist. Attorney Asn. Calif; State Bd. of Calif; Solano Co. Bar Asn; Legal Aid Soc. Rel: Protestant. Legal Res: 19 Willotta Dr, Suisun, Calif. 94585. Mailing Add: P.O. Box 154, Fairfield, Calif. 94533.

SHUNN, MAXINE FAYE D
V.Chmn, Cloud Co. Dem. Orgn, Kans.
b. Clyde, Kans, 8/20/17; d. Charles Leroy Hose and Carrie Lewellen H; m. 11/6/38 to Herman Joyce Shunn; c. Charlene (Mrs. Garzillo) and Marvin. Educ: Concordia Pub. Schs, grad. Polit. & Govt. Pos: V.chmn, Cloud Co. Women's Dem. Club, Kans, 61-65; Dem. committeewoman, Ward 3, Cloud Co, 61-; treas, Cloud Co. Dem. Party, 61-65 & 69-, dep. treas, 65-69; v.chmn, Cloud Co. Dem. Orgn, 65- Mem: Concordia Bus. & Prfnl. Women of Am. (off. holder, 61-); pres, Concordia Grade Sch. PTA. Rel: Christian Church. Mailing Add: 1156 E. Ninth St, Box 164, Concordia, Kans. 66901.

SHUPNIK, FRED JOSEPH D
Pa. State Rep.
b. Swoyersville, Pa, 11/18/16; s. Joseph Shupnik and Helen Lostrick S; m. 8/13/46 to Margaret Hutsko; c. Margaret Ann and Susan. Educ: Scranton Univ, B.A, 40; N.Y. Univ, M.A, 42. Polit. & Govt. Pos: Pa. State Rep, 59- Mil. Serv: Entered as Seaman, Navy, 43, released as Lt.(jg), 46, after serv. in Navy Minesweeper, Pac, 44-46. Mem: Nat. Educ. Asn; Pa. State Educ. Asn; Am. Legion; Kiwanis; VFW; K. of C. Rel: Catholic. Mailing Add: 550 Charles St, Luzerne, Pa. 18709.

SHURBERT, FLOYD E. R
b. Winnebago Co, 10/30/00.
Mem, Co. Bd, Oshkosh, Wis, 54-; Wis. State Assemblyman, 58-68. Bus. & Prof. Pos: Retired; wholesale-retail meat bus, 25-45; owned mink farm, 36-54. Mem: Active in conserv. groups. Mailing Add: 2904 Oakwood Lane, Oshkosh, Wis. 54901. (1967)

SHUTE, ELDEN H, JR. R
Dep. Secy. of State, Maine
b. Sebec, Maine, 5/6/16; s. Elden H. Shute, Sr. and Lucretia Howe Flanders S; m. 11/8/40 to Jane A. Rafnell; c. Gary H. and Judith L. Educ: Boston Univ, 36-37. Polit. & Govt. Pos: Sch. Bd. mem, Auburn, Maine, 52-56; chmn, bd. of dirs, Sch. Admin. Dist. 9, 62-65; Maine State Rep, 67-68; dep. secy. of state, Maine, 69- Mil. Serv: Entered as Pvt, Marine Corps, 44, released as Cpl, 46, after serv. in Asiatic-Pac. Theater; Presidential Unit Citation; Asiatic-Pac. Theater and China Serv. Ribbons. Mem: Pres, Maine Asn. of Broadcasters, 57-58; F&AM; RAM and Commandery; Shrine; Rotary; VFW; Am. Legion. Rel: Unitarian-Universalist. Legal Res: 63 Perham St, Farmington, Maine 04938. Mailing Add: P.O. Box 590, Farmington, Maine 04938.

SHUTE, RALPH D. R
N.H. State Rep.
b. Whitefield, N.H, 1/12/87; married; c. Three. Educ: Whitefield and Lancaster Pub. Schs. Polit. & Govt. Pos: Mem. sch. bd, Lancaster, N.H; N.H. State Rep, 61- Bus. & Prof. Pos: Farmer. Mem: Grange P. of H. Rel: Baptist. Mailing Add: Route 1, Whitefield, N.H. 03060. (1967)

SIBAL, ABNER WOODRUFF R
b. New York, N.Y, 4/11/21; s. Charles L. Sibal and Elizabeth Buckett S; m. 7/2/44 to Mary Ellen Igou; c. Susan Wells and John Woodruff. Educ: Wesleyan Univ, A.B, 43; St. John's Univ, LL.B, 49; Psi Upsilon. Polit. & Govt. Pos: Conn. State Sen, 57-61, minority leader, Conn. State Senate, 59-61; U.S. Rep, Conn, 61-65. Mil. Serv: Entered as Pvt, Army, 43, released as 1st Lt, 46, after serv. in ETO and Asiatic Pac, 44-46. Rel: Congregational. Mailing Add: Kettle Creek Rd, Weston, Conn. 06880.

SIBLEY, HARPER, JR. D
b. Rochester, N.Y, 5/2/27; s. Harper Sibley and Georgiana Farr S; m. 2/19/49 to Virginia Beatrice Blair; c. Elizabeth, Harper, III, Montgomery Blair and John Durbin. Educ: Princeton Univ. Polit. & Govt. Pos: Civilian Adv. to the Secy. of the Army, 65-; pub. safety cmnr, Rochester, N.Y, 65-66; chmn, Monroe Co. Dem. Campaign Cmt, Rochester, N.Y, 66. Bus. & Prof. Pos: Pres, Dietrich-Sibley Agency, Inc, 51- and Sibley Corp, 55-; dir, West. Union Tel. Co, N.Y, Cent. Trust Co, Rochester, N.Y, Republic Nat. Bank, N.Y, Norwalk Truck Lines, Inc, Norwalk, Ohio and Automatic Sprinkler Corp, Cleveland, Ohio. Mil. Serv: Entered as Pvt, Army, 49, released as 2nd Lt, 53. Mem: Trustee, Genesee Hosp, Rochester, N.Y; Am. Found. on Automation and Employ, N.Y.C. Rel: Episcopal. Legal Res: 129 Ambassador Dr, Rochester, N.Y. 14610. Mailing Add: 550 E. Main St, Rochester, N.Y. 14604.

SICILIANO, MARION ELIZABETH R
Committeewoman, N.Y. State Rep. Orgn.
b. N.Y.C, 2/2/20; d. Edward P. Eaton and Clara Collins E; m. 2/4/40 to Carmin T. Siciliano; c. Sherry (Mrs. John Cole, Jr) and Ronald; grandson, John Cole, III. Educ: Syracuse Univ, 1 year; Hunter Col, 1 year. Polit. & Govt. Pos: Committeewoman, 26th Elec. Dist, Town of Greenburgh, Westchester Co, N.Y, 15 years; coordinator, Town of Greenburgh Rep. Elec, past 10 years; founder and past pres, Elmsford Women's Rep. Club; founder, Asn. of Rep. Clubs, Town of Greenburgh; chmn, Housewives for Rockefeller, Westchester Co, 66; rep, N.Y. State Lottery, 67-; chmn, Nixon-Agnew Campaign Cmt, Town of Greenburgh, 68; alternate del, Rep. Nat. Conv, 68; chmn, Village of Elmsford Rep. Orgn, N.Y, currently; v.chmn, Town of Greenburgh Rep. Orgn, currently; committeewoman, N.Y. State Rep. Orgn, currently. Bus. & Prof. Pos: Clerk, Union Free Sch. Dist. 9, Town of Greenburgh; asst. mgr. personnel, Alexander's Dept. Stores, White Plains. Mem: Chmn, United Fund and State Agencies, Westchester Co; Bus. & Prfnl. Women's Clubs; League Women Voters; Phelps Mem. Hosp. Asn. Tendered Rep. Testimonial Dinner, 69. Rel: Catholic. Mailing Add: 7 Locust St, Elmsford, N.Y. 10523.

SICILIANO, ROCCO C. R
Under Secy, Dept. of Commerce
b. Salt Lake City, Utah, 3/4/22; s. Joseph Vincent Siciliano and Mary Arnone S; m. 11/8/47 to Marion Leonore Stiebel; c. Loretta, Albert Vincent, Fred Rocco, John Carmine and Maria. Educ: Univ. Utah, B.A, 44; Georgetown Univ, LL.B, 48. Polit. & Govt. Pos: Legal Asst, Nat. Labor Rel. Bd, 48-50; asst. secy, Dept. of Labor, 53-57; spec. asst. to President for personnel mgt, 57-59; under secy, Dept. of Commerce, 69- Bus. & Prof. Pos: Legal adv. and exec, Procon Inc, Universal Oil Products, Des Plaines and Chicago, Ill, 50-53; partner, Wilkinson, Cragun & Barker, Wash, D.C, 59-69; pres, Pac. Maritime Asn, San Francisco, Calif, 65-69. Mil. Serv: Entered Army, 43, released as 1st Lt, 46, after serv. as Inf. Platoon Leader, Tenth Mt. Div. in Italy and Personnel Staff Officers, Hq, U.S. Forces, Austria; Bronze Star for Valor; Combat Infantryman's Badge; awarded Spec. Commendation Ribbon by General Mark Clark, 45-46. Mem: Fed. and Am. Bar Asns; Nat. Adv. Coun, Univ. of Utah; Trustee, Fed. Women's Award. Rel: Roman Catholic. Legal Res: San Francisco, Calif. Mailing Add: 2923 45th St, N.W, Washington, D.C. 20016.

SICKLES, CARLTON R. D
b. Hamden, Conn, 6/15/21; m. to Simone Shornick; c. one. Educ: Georgetown Col. of Arts and Sci, B.S.S, cum laude, 43; Georgetown Law Sch, J.D, 48. Polit. & Govt. Pos: Md. State Del, 55-62; U.S. Rep, Md, 62-66; del, Dem. Nat. Conv, 64 & 68; cmnr, Wash. Suburban Transit Cmn, 69-; v.chmn, Wash. Metrop. Area Transit Authority, 69-; cmnr, Md. State Planning Cmn, 69- Bus. & Prof. Pos: Lawyer, 49; adjunct prof, Georgetown Univ. Law Sch; officer, Carday Assocs, Inc; partner, Sickles, Goldberg & Sickles, Law Firm. Mil. Serv: Army, Inf, 43-46, serv. in U.S, India, China; Korean War, 51-52, Air Force, Off. of Spec. Invests. Mem: Am. Bar; D.C. Bar; Prince Georges Bar; Md. Bar Asn. Mailing Add: Lanham, Md. 20801.

SICULA, PAUL EDWARD D
Wis. State Assemblyman
b. Milwaukee, Wis, 1/31/39; s. Harry Sidney Sicula and Lillian Rosenthal S; m. 6/30/63 to Marna Jane Koshakow; c. Howard Steven and Michelle Lee. Educ: Univ. Wis, B.S, 62, Law Sch, LL.B, 64; Pi Lamba Phi; Phi Delta Phi; res. ed, Wis. Law Review. Polit. & Govt. Pos: Wis. State Assemblyman, 5th Dist, 67- Bus. & Prof. Pos: Attorney, Atinsky, Kahn & Sicula, 64- Mil. Serv: Entered as Pvt. E-1, Army, 59, released as Specialist, E-5, 65; Army Res, 5½ years. Publ: 'Rule of Early Vesting,' Wis. Law Review, May, 63. Mem: Am. Trial Lawyer's Asn; Wis, Milwaukee and Milwaukee Jr. Bar Asns; B'nai B'rith Century Lodge; Milwaukee Jewish Commun. Center; Anshe Sfard Congregation; Old Time Ballplayers Asn. Rel: Jewish. Mailing Add: 3287 N. 48th St, Milwaukee, Wis. 53216.

SIDD, ALLAN D
Treas, Mass. Dem. State Cmt.
b. Boston, Mass, 8/14/23; s. David Sidlosky and Sara Kerrch S; m. 2/9/47 to Shirley Liberman; c. Diane. Educ: Boston Univ, 40-42. Polit. & Govt. Pos: Dem. State Committeeman, Norfolk-Suffolk Dist, Mass, 64-; alternate del, Dem. Nat. Conv, 68; treas, Mass. Dem. State Cmt, 68- Bus. & Prof. Pos: Prod. mgr, Century of Boston, Inc. Mil. Serv: Entered as Pvt, Air Force, 43, released as Tech. Fifth Grade, 45, after serv. in 12th Air Force, ETO. Rel: Agnostic. Mailing Add: 148 Mason Terr, Brookline, Mass. 02146.

SIDERIUS, GEORGE E. D
Mont. State Sen.
b. Moders, Mich, 11/18/07; s. Everett Siderius and Gertrude deBoer S; m. 6/9/34 to Ella J. Arth; c. Richard. Educ: West. Mont. Col, grad, 34. Polit. & Govt. Pos: Mont. State Sen, currently, Pres. Pro Tem. Ad Interim, Mont. State Senate, 69- Mem: Eagles; Farmers Union. Rel: Presbyterian. Mailing Add: Somers Stage, Kalispell, Mont. 59901.

SIDES, JULIAN EARL, JR. R
Chmn, Tunica Co. Rep. Exec. Cmt, Miss.
b. Dundee, Miss, 8/7/25; s. Julian Earl Sides and Kathryn Willingham S; m. 2/16/46 to Mary Jane Williams; c. Thomas Earl, Mary K. and Julianne. Educ: Ga. Inst. of Tech. Polit. & Govt. Pos: Chmn, Tunica Co. Rep. Exec. Cmt, Miss, 60-; mem, Miss. State Rep. Exec. Cmt, 68- Mil. Serv: Entered as A/S, Navy, 43, released as Lt.(jg), 46. Mem: Rotary; Farm Bur. Rel: Presbyterian. Mailing Add: Box 37, Dundee, Miss. 38626.

SIDI, JACQUES ALBERT R
Wyo. State Rep.
b. Marseille, France, 10/29/28; s. Albert Sidi and Irene Smadja S; m. 1/15/55 to Bernadette Mary Weisenberger; c. Veronica and Michael. Educ: Academie de Grenoble, France, B.A, 47; Northwest. Univ, M.A, 51. Polit. & Govt. Pos: Mem-at-lg, Natrona Co. Rep. Exec. Cmt, Wyo, 68-69; Wyo. State Rep, 69- Bus. & Prof. Pos: Teacher, Cherry Lawn Sch, Darien, Conn, 47-50; teacher, eighth grade U.S. Hist, Morgan Jr. High Sch, Casper, Wyo, 55- Mil. Serv: Entered as Pvt, Air Force, 51, released as S/Sgt, 55, after serv. in Ground Observer Corps, Wyo, Air Force Post Off. Serv, Alaska and Off. of Spec. Invest, France and French Morocco, 51-55. Mem: Wyo. Taxpayers Asn; Casper Country Club. Mailing Add: 433 W. 15th, Casper, Wyo. 82601.

SIDLE, CHARLES LLOYD D
Chmn, Ind. Stream Pollution Control Bd.
b. South Milford, Ind, 8/7/99; s. Cyrus Sidle and Cora Blanchard S; m. 3/17/45 to Anne Nesta Benson; c. Malcolm Charles. Educ: Valparaiso Univ; Sorbonne Univ. Polit. & Govt. Pos: Mem, Bd. Pub. Works, Ft. Wayne, Ind, 62-64; chmn, Ind. Stream Pollution Control Bd, presently. Bus. & Prof. Pos: Gen.mgr, Wayne Tank & Pump Co, 21-24; gen. mgr, Paige & Jones Chem. Co, 25-27; pres, Miracle Chem. & Solvent Corp, 28-41. Mil. Serv: Entered as Pvt, Army, 16, released as Col, 46, after serv. in Eng, ETO; Mex. Border Medal; Victory Medal with Battle Star; ETO Ribbon with 2 Battle Stars and Arrow Head; Croix De Guerre with Palms; Purple Heart. Publ: Hand Book of Water Treatment Data. Mem: Ind. Soc. Prfnl. Engrs; Nat. Asn. Prfnl. Engrs; Scottish Rite, Shrine; Am. Legion; DAV; Retired Officers Asn. Rel: Methodist. Mailing Add: 2615 Terrace Rd, Ft. Wayne, Ind. 46805.

SIDWELL, GEORGE C. R
Chmn, Clermont Co. Rep. Cent. Cmt, Ohio
b. Loveland, Ohio, 7/19/07; s. Edwin H. Sidwell and Martha Louise Bonnell S; m. 9/4/37 to Doris Marie Lake; c. Judith Ann (Mrs. George Anderson) and Edwin S. Educ: Univ. Cincinnati, Eve. Col, 2 years. Polit. & Govt. Pos: Rep. committeeman, Milford Village Precinct B, Ohio, 53-; chmn, Clermont Co. Rep. Exec. Cmt, 59-65; investigator, Pub. Utilities Cmn. of Ohio, 64-; chmn, Clermont Co. Rep. Cent. Cmt, 66- Bus. & Prof. Pos: Customer contact and term. mgr, Sewell Motor Express, 46-51; owner and operator, Sidwell Furnace Co, 41-49; salesman, William F. Smysor Co, 49-51; mfg. eng. and quality control auditor, Gen. Elec. Co, 51-63. Mem: F&AM; Soc. of Am. Magicians; Royal Arch Masons; Scottish Rite. Rel: Methodist. Mailing Add: 645 Wallace Ave, Milford, Ohio 45150.

SIEGEL, GERALD D
b. Baltimore, Md, 7/20/26; married. Educ: Univ. of Baltimore; Univ. of Baltimore Law Sch, LL.B, 51. Polit. & Gov. Pos: Md. State Del, 63-67; Police Magistrate Northwest. Dist, 59-61; Baltimore City Bldg. Code Enforcement Officer, 56-59. Mil. Serv: Army. Mem: Trial Magistrates Asn; Am, Md, Baltimore City, Md. Plaintiffs Bar Asns; Md. Law Enforcement Officers Asn; Grotto; Masons; Am. Legion. Mailing Add: 6315 Green Meadow Pkwy, Baltimore, Md. 21209. (1967)

SIEGEL, NORMA KAIDEN D
b. N.Y.C, 12/19/26; d. Sidney B. Kaiden and Frances Glantz K; m. 6/24/49 to Robert Siegel; c. Joanne and Peter. Educ: Antioch Col, B.A, 48; N.Y. Univ. Grad. Sch. Soc. Work, currently. Polit. & Govt. Pos: Committeewoman, Mt. Pleasant Dem. Party, N.Y, 64-; alternate del, Dem. Nat. Conv, 68; v.chmn, Mt. Pleasant Dem. Cmt, 69- Mem: Women for Peace, Westchester; Women's Int. League for Peace and Freedom. Mailing Add: 17 Usonia Rd, Pleasantville, N.Y. 10570.

SIEGRIST, ROBERT RYAN R
b. Lansing, Mich, 4/14/19; s. William E. Siegrist (deceased) and Clara Mary Ryan S.(deceased); m. 9/19/42 to Mary Jean Wright; c. Anne Marie, Mark William, Mary Roberta and Linda Michelle. Educ: Mich. State Univ, class of 40. Polit. & Govt. Pos: Rep. nominee, U.S. House Rep, Ninth Dist, Ill, 52; chmn. publicity and host cmt, Rep. Nat. Conv, 52; chmn publicity, Inaugural Ball, 69; asst. press-pub. rels, U.S. Rep. William H. Harsha, Ohio, 69; admin. asst. to U.S. Rep. Laurence G. Williams, Pa, 69- Bus. & Prof. Pos: Radio news commentator and journalist, WGN, Chicago and Mutual Broadcasting Syst, Hearst Corp, 46-56; chief ed. writers, Milwaukee Sentinel; commentator, WISN; owner, Siegrist Enterprises, 56-66; contract commentator, Mutual Broadcasting Syst, Wash, D.C, 66-68. Mil. Serv: Entered as Info. Specialist, Army, Pub. Rels. Troop Orientation, 42, released as T-w, 46, after serv. in ASF, Sixth Serv. Command, Chicago. Eight Freedoms Found. Awards; Christopher Award; Celtic Cross, Cath. War Vet; Spec. Award, Wis. State Cath. War Vet; Resolution of Commendation for Broadcast Efforts, Am. Legion Ill. State and Nat. Conv; Four Vigilant Patriot Awards, All Am. Conf. to Combat Communism; DAR Award; VFW Award. Rel: Roman Catholic. Mailing Add: 4751 Whitehaven Pkwy. N.W, Washington, D.C. 20007.

SIEMENS, GEORGE R. D
Ky. State Rep.
b. 1926. Polit. & Govt. Pos: Mem, Shively Dem. Club, Ky; councilman, Shively; dir. civil Defense, Shively; Ky. State Rep, currently. Bus. & Prof. Pos: Plumbing and heating contractor. Mil. Serv: Navy, World War II. Mem: K. of C; Am. Legion; C Dist. Club; 40th Dist. Club. Rel: Catholic. Legal Res: Shively, Ky. 40216. Mailing Add: 1701 Marlow Rd, Louisville, Ky. 40216. (1967)

SIEMINSKI, ALFRED D. D
b. Jersey City, N.J, 8/23/11; s. William Sieminski and Helen Fiston S; m. 5/30/47 to Countess Marie Felice Czarkowska-Golejewska; c. step daughters, Christine Elizabeth (Mrs. John G. Hunt) and Isabella (Mrs. James H. Noyes). Educ: Hamburg Univ, Germany, summer 30; Univ. Warsaw, Poland, summer, 33; Princeton Univ, B.A. in polit. sci, 34; Harvard Law Sch, 38; pres, Princeton Boxing Club, 32; Alpha Chi Sigma; Tiger Inn Club, Princeton; Lincoln's Inn and Marshall Club, Harvard. Polit. & Govt. Pos: Mem. staff, U.S. Mil. Govt. Austria, 45-46; U.S. Rep, 51-59; alternate del, Dem. Nat. Conv, 52; mem. staff, Med. and Gen. Reference Libr, Vet. Admin, D.C, 62- Bus. & Prof. Pos: Controller and v.pres, Brunswick Laundry, 37-51; admin. v.pres, Hun Sch, Princeton, 59. Mil. Serv: Entered as Pvt, Army, 42, released as Lt. Col, Army Res, 63; Bronze Star; ETO Ribbon; Legion of Merit; Korean Serv. Ribbon with 3 Battle Stars; Italian Campaign Ribbon with 3 Battle Stars; life mem, 7th Regt, N.Y. Nat. Guard. Mem: Kiwanis; Rotary; pres, St. Agnes Episcopal Sch. PTA, Alexandria, Va, 58-59; F St. Club, Princeton Club and Am-Austrian Soc, D.C; dir, McLean Horse Show Asn, Va. Mem: Princeton 150 Lb. Crew, Royal Henley Regatta, Eng, 33; pinch-hitter, Dem. Championship Baseball Team, U.S. House of Rep, 51-55; Fairfax Hunt Club, Fairfax Co, Va. Rel: Episcopal. Mailing Add: 9430 Lakeside Dr, Vienna, Va. 22180.

SIENA, JAMES VINCENT D
Dep. Under Secy. of the Army for Int. Affairs
b. Cleveland, Ohio, 9/25/32; s. Vincent James Siena and Virginia Catherine Johnson S; m. 8/21/54 to June Elizabeth Harvey; c. Katherine June, James Harvey and Margaret Johnson. Educ: Miami Univ, 51-52; West. Reserve Univ, B.A, 55; Stanford Law Sch, LL.B, 61; Order of the Coif; pres, Stanford Law Rev, 60-61. Polit. & Govt. Pos: Consult, Off. of Econ. Opportunity, Wash. D.C, 64-65; Dep. Under Secy. of the Army for Int. Affairs, 67- Bus. & Prof. Pos: Assoc, Covington & Burling, Wash, D.C, 61-67. Mil. Serv: Entered as 2nd Lt, Marines, 55, released as Capt, after serv. in First and Third Marine Div, Japan and Calif, 55-58. Mem: D.C. Bar Asn. Mailing Add: 6351 Utah Ave. N.W, Washington, D.C. 20015.

SIEROTY, ALAN GERALD D
Calif. State Assemblyman
b. Los Angeles, Calif, 12/13/30; s. Julian M. Sieroty and Jean Sommer S; single. Educ: Stanford Univ, B.A. in econ, 52; Univ. of Southern Calif. Sch. of Law, LL.B, 56; Phi Beta Kappa; Breakers. Polit. & Govt. Pos: Mem, Los Angeles Co. Dem. Cent. Cmt, 58- and Calif. State Dem. Cent. Cmt, 62-; pres, Beverly Hills Dem. Club, 59-60; admin. asst. to Lt. Gov, 61-62; exec. secy, Calif. Cmn. on Interstate Coop, 62-65; exec. secy. to Lt. Gov. Glenn M. Anderson, 62-65; dep. dir, Chile-Calif. Prog, 65-66; Calif. State Assemblyman, 67-; del, Dem. Nat. Conv, 68. Bus. & Prof. Pos: Partner, Neiman & Sieroty, Law Firm, 60- Mem: Calif. and Los Angeles Co. Bar Asns; World Peace Through World Law Asn; Am. Friends of Africa; Am. Civil Liberties Union; Am. Jewish Cmt; Am. Jewish Cong; B'nai B'rith; United Nations Asn; Anytown, U.S.A. Rel: Jewish. Legal Res: 1002 N. Rexford Dr, Beverly Hills, Calif. 90210. Mailing Add: 849 S. Broadway, Los Angeles, Calif. 90014.

SIETSEMA, GEORGE D
b. Grundy Center, Iowa, 4/1/18; married; c. Georgia Kay, Carmen Eillen, Deborah Ann. Polit. & Govt. Pos: Mich. State Rep, 64-66; former supvr, treas, munic. judge in Wyo. Twp; mem. Kent Co. Bd. of Supvrs. Bus. & Prof. Pos: Owner, Mich. Private Invest. Bur. Mil. Serv: Vet. Mailing Add: 1501 Lee St, S.W, Wyoming, Mich. 49509. (1967)

SIGMUND, HELEN NICOLAI D
Chmn, Portage Co. Dem. Party, Wis.
b. Milwaukee, Wis, 9/20/25; d. Fred E.G. Nicolai and Edna Ritzi N; m. 8/28/48 to Elwin W. Sigmund; c. Lise and Glenn. Educ: Milwaukee State Teachers Col, 47; Univ. Cincinnati, 47-48; Univ. Ill, summer 52; pres, Alpha Chap. of Kappa Delta Pi, Univ. Ill, 52-53; Honor Ten; Commonwealth student body pres; Sports Feature Page Ed, Echo Weekly. Polit. & Govt. Pos: Secy-treas, Seventh Dist. Dem. Party, Wis, 57-61; secy, Portage Co. Dem. Party, 65-66 and chmn, 67-; chmn. and mgr, Dahl for Cong. Cmt, 68; mem-at-lg, State Admin. Cmt, Dem. Party of Wis, 69- Bus. & Prof. Pos: Chmn. faculty, Champaign Jr. High, Ill, 52-53; v.chmn, art teachers, Pub. Schs, Springfield, 55-56. Mem: Delta Kappa Gamma (treas, 68-); Wis. Educ. Asn; Am. Asn. for Health, Phys. Educ. and Recreation; Am. Asn. Univ. Women; Portage Co. Asn. Ment. Health (secy. & pres, 57-60); Univ. Women. Ment. Health Award, Portage Co. Asn. Ment. Health, 60. Rel: Presbyterian; Past pres. Women's Asn, Frame Memorial Presbyterian Church. Mailing Add: 624 Soo Marie Ave, Stevens Point, Wis. 54481.

SIGOURNEY, ANDRE R. D
Mass. State Rep.
Educ: Grad. Harvard Univ. and Harvard Law Sch. Polit. & Govt. Pos: Acting town counsel of Nahant, Mass; Mass. State Rep, currently. Bus. & Prof. Pos: Former law assoc. of late Gov. Joseph B. Ely; trial attorney, currently. Mil. Serv: Marine Corps Vet. Mem: Active in United Fund, Retarded Children Fund, Cancer Fund, Cystic Fibrosis; judge advocate Post 215, Am. Legion; former advocate K. of C; Nahant Recreation Comm; Elks. Publ: 'Writ Revision, Boston Bar J, 3/66; 'Free Press and Fair Trial Legislation,' Mass. Law Quart, 6/66; 'The Crime of Chapter 229: The Wrongs of Our Wrongful Death Statute,' The Legalite, 6/20/66; plus one other. Mailing Add: 2 Vernon St, Nahant, Mass. 01908.

SIKES, ROBERT L. F. D
U.S. Rep, Fla.
b. Isabella, Ga, 6/3/06; s. Ben F. Sikes and Clara Ford S; m. to Inez Tyner; c. Bobbye S.(Mrs. Wicke) and Robert K. Educ: Univ. Ga, B.S, 27; Univ. Fla, M.A, 29; Phi Kappa Phi; Alpha Zeta; Sigma Delta Chi; Phi Sigma; Blue Key; Alpha Gamma Rho. Hon. LL.D, Stetson Univ, 69; hon. D.H.L, St. Leo Col, 69. Polit. & Govt. Pos: Chmn, Co. Planning Cmt, Fla, 34; chmn, Co. Dem. Exec. Cmt, 34; Fla. State Rep, 36 & 38; asst. to treas, Dem. Nat. Cmt, 36, 40 & 44; U.S. Rep, First Dist, Fla, 40-; del, Pan Am. Roads Conf, Caracas, Venezuela, 54; del. and chmn. Fla. Del, Dem. Nat. Conv, 56 & 60; del, Inter-Parliamentary Conf, Warsaw, Poland, 59 and Sixth World Forestry Cong, Madrid, Spain, 66. Bus. & Prof. Pos: Publisher, Okaloosa News J, 40. Mil. Serv: Entered as Maj, Army, 44, released as Lt. Col, 46, after serv. in Supreme Hq, Allied Expeditionary Forces; Maj. Gen.(Ret), Army Res; European-African-Mid. East. Campaign Ribbon; Am. Campaign Ribbon; World War II Victory Ribbon; Legion of Merit Award. Mem: Retired Officers Asn; Nat. Asn. of Supvrs; Am. Fedn. of Gov. Employees; United Fedn. of Postal Clerks, Local 551; Pensacola Chap, Nat. Asn. of Master Mechanics and Foremen Asn; pres, Fla. Press Asn, 37; Scottish Rite; Mason (33°) (grand orator, Fla. Masonic Grand Lodge, 68-69); Red Cross of Constantine; York Rite of Free Masonry; KCCH; Grotto; K.T; Shrine; K. of P; Rotary; Lions; Civitan; Moose; Elks; VFW; Am. Legion; 40 et 8; Mil. Order of World War; Kiwanis; Fleet Reserve Asn; Am. Soc. of Arms Collectors; life mem, Nat. Rifle Asn; Res. Officers Asn; bd. trustees, Naval Aviation Mus. Asn; bd. dir, Fla. Hist Soc; v.pres. and dir, Nat. Rivers and Harbors Cong, 59-69. Sr. mem, Fla. Del, U.S. House of Rep; Hon. Faculty Chair in Govt. Designated in Honor of Robert L.F. Sikes, Okaloosa-Walton Jr. Col, Niceville, Fla; Recipient of Nat. Affairs League's Leadership Award, 51; Distinguished Serv. Award, Res. Officers Asn, 58; Am. Gun Dealers Leadership Award, 59; Gov. Conserv. Award, 60; Guatemalan Order of Merit, 61; Fla. Young Dem. Clubs' Award, 61; Am. Legion Distinguished Serv. Award, 62; Navy Times Good Neighbor Award, 62; Humanitarian Award, Children's Asthma Research Inst, 63; Fla. Nat. Guard Outstanding Serv. Award, 63; Res. Officers Asn. Minute Man Hall of Fame Award, 64; Distinguished Serv. Award, Retired Officers Asn, 66; George Wash. Mem. Award, Nat. Rivers and Harbors Cong, 66; Good Govt. Award, Pensacola Realty Bd, 66; Defender of Free Enterprise Award, Life Underwriters, 66; Reserve Officers Asn. Man of the Year Award for Contributions to Nat. Defense, 67; Hon. State Farmer Award, Fla. Asn. of Future Farmers of Am, 67; Alpha Gamma Rho Alumni Award, 68; UPI'S Fla. Pub. Serv. Award, 68; Order of Ahepa Award, 69. Rel: Methodist. Legal Res: Route 1, Crestview, Fla. 32536. Mailing Add: 2269 Rayburn Bldg, Washington, D.C. 20515.

SILBERMAN, LAURENCE HIRSCH R
Solicitor of Labor, Dept. of Labor
b. York, Pa, 10/12/35; s. William Silberman and Anna Hirsch S; m. 1/5/57 to Rosalie Gaull; c. Robert, Katherine and Anne. Educ: Dartmouth Col, B.A, 57; Harvard Law Sch, LL.B, 61. Polit. & Govt. Pos: Solicitor of Labor, Dept. of Labor, 69- Bus. & Prof. Pos: Assoc, Moore, Torkildson & Rice and Quinn & Moore, 61-64; law partner, Moore, Silberman & Schulze, Honolulu, Hawaii, 64-67; attorney, Nat. Labor Rels. Bd, 67-69. Mil. Serv: Entered as Pvt, Army Res, 57, released as Cpl, 63, after serv. at Ft. Dix, N.J, 6 months. Mem: Hawaii and Am. Bar Asns. Mailing Add: 12436 OverRidge Rd, Potomac, Md. 20854.

SILER, EUGENE R
b. Williamsburg, Ky, 6/26/00; s. Adam Siler and Minnie Chandler S; m. 10/17/25 to Lowell Jones; c. Dorothy, Annette, Carolyn and Eugene. Educ: Cumberland Col, Williamsburg, Ky, A.A, 20; Univ. Ky, A.B, 22; Columbia, 22 Univ. Ky, 23-24; trustee, Cumberland Col. Polit. & Govt. Pos: Judge, Court of Appeals, Ky, Seventh Appellate Dist, 45; U.S. Rep, Ky, 55-63; alternate del, Rep. Nat. Conv, 68. Bus. & Prof. Pos: Admitted to Ky. Bar, 23; dir, Bank of Williamsburg, Ky; lawyer, Firm Tye, Siler, Gillis & Siler, 25-38; lawyer, Firm Tye & Siler, 38-42; attorney-at-law, 45- Mil. Serv: Navy, World War I; Army, Capt, 42-45. Mem: Am. Legion, past dist. comdr. in Ky; Jr. O.U.A.M, past state coun. of Ky, 33; Ky. Bar Asn; Sigma Alpha Epsilon; Phi Alpha Delta; Mason; Odd Fellow. Rel: Baptist; Ky. moderator, 52-53. Mailing Add: Walnut St, Williamsburg, Ky. 40769.

SILK, JAMES J. D
Md. State Del.
b. Baltimore, Md, 1/2/11; married. Educ: Mt. St. Joseph Col. Polit. & Govt. Pos: Md. State Del, 47- Bus. & Prof. Pos: Investr. and Income Tax Consult. Mailing Add: 2641 Hudson St, Baltimore, Md. 21224. (1967)

SILK, ROBERT H. D
b. Detroit, Mich, 12/23/25; s. Herbert Silk and Gertrude Nurko S; m. 7/16/55 to Susan Thumin; c. Nina and Caroline. Educ: Univ. Mich, LL.B, 51; Inter-Cooperative Coun. Polit. & Govt. Pos: Alternate del, Dem. Nat. Conv, 68; v.pres, Franklin Delano Roosevelt-Woodrow Wilson Dem, N.Y. 67th Assembly Dist, 69; del, Dem. Judicial Conv, First Dept, 69. Bus. & Prof. Pos: Partner, Merbaum, Bunks & Silk, Law firm, N.Y.C, 65- Mil. Serv: Seaman, Merchant Marine, World War II. Mem: Am. and N.Y. State Trial Lawyers Asns; N.Y. Co. Lawyers Asn; Nat. Lawyers Guild; Nt. Maritime Union (retired); UAW (inactive). Rel: Jewish. Mailing Add: 201 W. 85th St, New York, N.Y. 10024.

SILLERS, DOUGLAS HUGH R
b. Calvin, N.Dak, 2/9/15; s. Archie Sillers and Mabel Betrice Tuthill S; m. 8/2/41 to Margaret Rose Baller; c. Jean Margaret, Douglas Hal, Cynthia Betrice and Hether Phillis. Educ: Concordia Col, B.A, 39; Univ. Minn, 40; N.Dak. State, 57. Polit. & Govt. Pos: Minn. State Rep, Clay Co, 63-67. Bus. & Prof. Pos: High sch. instr, Menahga, Minn, 39-41; fieldman, Fed. Land Bank, Washburn, N.Dak, 41-42; mgr. and owner, farm, 45- Mil. Serv: Entered as Yeoman 3/C, Navy, 43, released as Lt.(jg), 45, after serv. in Navy Electronics Vol, Fargo, N.Dak, 8 months, Europe, 18 months; Am. Zone, European Zone, European Invasion D Day Ribbons. Mem: Am. Legion; VFW; Mason; Farm Bur; C. of C; Crop Improv. Asn. Minn. State Soil Conserv. Winner, 56. Rel: Presbyterian. Mailing Add: R.R. 2, Moorhead, Minn. 56560

SILLIMAN, NEVELLE I. R
First V.Pres, North. Div, Calif. Fedn. Rep. Women
b. Aromas, Calif, 11/5/06; d. Floyd Huston Hawkins and Alice Wehrley H; m. 3/26/34 to James W. Silliman; c. Karen, Floyd James and Thomas Leland.

Educ: Heald's Bus. Col, 2 years. Polit. & Govt. Pos: Mem, Calif. Rep. State Cent. Cmt, 58-; chmn. cong. campaign, Monterey Co, 62; mem, Monterey Co. Rep. Cent. Cmt, 62-69, secy, 68-69; mem, 12th Cong. Dist. Rep. Cmt, 62-; chmn, Women for Reagan for Gov. Campaign, Monterey Co, 66; chmn, Women for Nixon, West. Div. North. Calif, 68; first v.pres. North Div, Calif. Fedn. Rep. Women, 68- Publ: So What Now, Pageant Press, 65. Mem: Eastern Star; Pals Club of Sacramento, Legis. Ladies Club (v.pres, 58); Grange. Rel: Protestant. Mailing Add: 246 Hawthorne St, Salinas, Calif. 93901.

SILLS, ARTHUR JACK D
Attorney Gen, N.J.
b. Brooklyn, N.Y, 10/19/17; s. Herman Silverman and Ida Rosenweig S; m. to Mina Minzer; c. Hedy Erna. Educ: Rutgers Univ, B.A, 38; Harvard Law Sch, LL.B, 41; Phi Beta Kappa; Kirkpatrick Scholarship, Harvard Law Sch. Hon. LL.D, Rutgers Univ, 66; D.L.H, Newark State Col, 67. Polit. & Govt. Pos: Rate counsel, N.J, 58-60; Attorney Gen, N.J, 62-; mem, State Supreme Court Cmt. on Press Rels, 65-66; chmn, Gov. Cmt. on Poverty and Law, Gov. Interdepartmental Cmt. on Equal Opportunity, State Coord. Coun. on Traffic Safety, Police Training Cmn, State Law Enforcement Planning Agency, Gov. Coun. Against Crime and Adv. Cmt. to Attorney Gen. on Govt. Immunity; mem. exec. bd, Nat. Conf. on Bail and Criminal Justice; cmnr, State Narcotics Adv. Coun; mem, N.J. Cmn. on Interstate Coop, Cmn. on Status of Women, Gov. Cmn. on Pub. Broadcasting, N.J. Housing Finance Agency and State Atomic Energy Coun. Bus. & Prof. Pos: Attorney-at-law, David T. Willentz Off, 41-50; counsr-lectr, Rutgers Univ, until 57; partner, Wilentz, Goldman, Spitzer and Sills, 50-62; bd. dirs, WHYY-TV; mem. bd. trustees, WNDT-TV, 68- Publ: 'The Imbroglio of Constitutional Revision—Another By-Product of Reapportionment,' Rutgers Law Rev, fall 65; 'Automated Data Processing and the Issue of Privacy,' State Govt, spring 67; 'The Supreme Court and Police Morale,' N.J. League of Munic, 4/67; plus nine others. Mem: State chmn, March of Dimes, 63; Nat. Asn. of Attorneys Gen.(pres, 68-, chmn, Miranda Study Cmt. and Habeas Corpus and Bail Cmt, mem. exec. bd, mem, Cmt. on Off. of the Attorney Gen, Research and Adv. Cmt. and Fed-State Tax Probs. Cmt); Nat. Dist. Attorneys Asn; Am. Bar Asn.(mem, house of del, mem, sect. cmt. on the rights of the accused and of the pub); N.J, Middlesex Co. and Perth Amboy Bar Asns; Am. Judicature Soc; chmn, N.J. Cmt. for Comeback, Inc; East. region chmn, Nat. Asn. for State Info. Syst; cmt. on info. syst, Coun. State Govt; UN Asn.(mem. adv. coun, N.J. Br); pres, B'nai B'rith Hillel Bldg. Fund; dir, N.J. Soc. for Crippled Children and Adults; Int. Platform Asn; trustee, Garden State Ballet, John Marshall Inst. of Taxation and Opera Theatre of N.J. Pope Paul VI Humanitarian Award, 68; Louis Brownlow Mem. Prize, 68. Rel: Jewish. Legal Res: 204 Dellwood Rd, Metuchen, N.J. 08840. Mailing Add: State House Annex, Trenton, N.J. 08625.

SILSBY, FANNIE J. R
b. Lemington, Vt, 6/19/87; m. to David W. Silsby; c. Three. Educ: Lyndon Normal Sch, 30; refresher course, 46; U.V.M, summer sessions, 22, 35, 41. Polit. & Govt. Pos: Vt. State Rep, 57-66; chmn, Rep. Town Cmt, 59 & 63-64. Bus. & Prof. Pos: Retired teacher, homemaker. Mem: Subordinate, Pomona, State and Nat. Granges; PTA; Vt. Hist. Soc; Northeast. Develop. Asn; WSCS. Rel: Congregational. Mailing Add: South Lunenburg, Vt. 05906. (1967)

SILVA, ALEXANDER A, JR. D
b. New Bedford, Mass, 10/1/29; s. Alexander A. Silva and Rose S. Educ: St. Polytech. Col, B.S. magna cum laude, 61. Polit. & Govt. Pos: Former admin. asst. to U.S. Rep. Cameron, Calif. Bus. & Prof. Pos: Staffwriter, San Gabriel Valley Daily Tribune, 59-61 and Covina Sentinel, 62; pub. affairs, Coro Found, 62. Mil. Serv: PO 1/C, Navy, 42-56, ETO. Legal Res: Pomona, Calif. Mailing Add: 3829 Taft Ave, Alexandria, Va. 22304. (1967)

SILVA, SANTIAGO IGLESIAS R
b. San Lorenzo, P.R, 3/21/02; s. Ramóm Iglesias and Angela Silva I; m. 7/25/18 to Cruz Rodríguez; c. Graciela, Gladys and Santiago. Polit. & Govt. Pos: Mem, Munic. Assembly, San Lorenzo, P.R, 24; pres, Liberal Party, P.R, 48; hon. pres, San Lorenzo Statehood Rep. Party; Rep, P.R. Legis, 56-69. Bus. & Prof. Pos: Chief, P.R. Leaf Tobacco Co, 22-28; owner tobacco bus. Mem: Mason. Rel: Catholic. Mailing Add: Muñoz Rivera 7, San Lorenzo, P.R. 00754. (1967)

SILVER, EDGAR P. D
b. Baltimore, Md, 7/1/23; married. Educ: Talmudical Acad; Baltimore City Col; Univ. of Baltimore; Mt. Vernon Law Sch, LL.B, 53. Polit. & Gov. Pos: Md. State Del, 55-65. Mil. Serv: Maritime Serv, 43-45. Mem: Vice chmn, Mayor's Cmt. Traffic Safety; Nat. Cmn. on Uniform Traffic Laws & Ordinances; Assoc. mem, Pres. Cmt. on Traffic Safety; Am. Jewish Cong; Bd, Baltimore Safety Coun; Citizens Planning and Housing; K. of P. Mailing Add: 2405 Rockwood Ave, Baltimore, Md. 21209. (1967)

SILVER, ETHEL MARIE R
Mem, Calif. Rep. State Cent. Cmt.
b. Hemet, Calif, 6/25/26; d. George Andrew Gruber and Myrtle Johnson G; m. 4/17/48 to Harrison Edward Silver; c. Jeffrey and Jennifer. Educ: Los Angeles Gen. Hosp. Sch. of Nursing, R.N, 47. Polit. & Govt. Pos: Hq. chmn, 38th Cong. Rep. Campaign, Calif, 64; mem, Calif. Rep. State Cent. Cmt, 64-66 & 69-; pres, Riverside Rep. Women Fedn, Calif, 66-68, bd. mem, 68-; area precinct chmn, Riverside, 68; mem, 74th Assembly Rep. Campaign Cmt, 68; mem, Nixon Campaign Cmt, 68; chmn, Riverside Co. Rep. Cent. Cmt, Third Supervisorial Dist, 69- Mem: Woman's Auxiliary, Riverside Co. Med. Asn; Riverside Opera Asn; Jr. League; Riverside Commun. Planning Coun; Nat. Charity League. Rel: Lutheran. Mailing Add: 5841 Grand Ave, Riverside, Calif. 92504.

SILVER, PAUL D
b. Brooklyn, N.Y, 5/14/05; s. Michael Silver and Anna Feldman S; m. 1/10/32 to Molly Chanenko; c. Simon David and Merle Isbelle. Educ: Detroit City Col, 25-26. Polit. & Govt. Pos: Committeeman, 17th Dist, Dem. State Cent. Cmt, Mich, 52-69; treas, Wayne Co. Dem. Orgn, 53-69; mem, Wayne Co. Bd. Supvrs, 56-69; mem, Mich. Adv. Hosp. Coun, 62. Bus. & Prof. Pos: Pres, Local 351, UAW, 41-63, rep, Commun. and Membership Rels, Regional, 63-; mem. exec. bd, Mich. State AFL-CIO, 58-64 & 66. Mem: UAW; B'nai B'rith; Mich. Asn. Emotionally Disturbed Children; Detroit Old Timers. Legal Res: 19777 Rutherford, Detroit, Mich. 48235. Mailing Add: 8000 E. Jefferson, Detroit, Mich. 48214. (1967)

SILVERMAN, LEONARD D
N.Y. State Assemblyman
b. Brooklyn, N.Y, 11/10/30; s. Frank E. Silverman and Rose Worona S; single. Educ: N.Y. Univ, B.A, 52; Brooklyn Law Sch, LL.B, 54; Iota Theta. Polit. & Govt. Pos: N.Y. State Assemblyman, 48th Assembly Dist, 69- Bus. & Prof. Pos: Attorney, Silverman & Lifschitz, currently. Mem: Brooklyn Bar Asn; Brooklyn Criminal Bar Asn; Mason; Kiwanis; Moose; B'nai B'rith; United Jewish Appeal; Fedn. Jewish Philanthropies; Roosevelt Dem. Club (66th precinct commun. coun). Handicapped Children Award. Rel: Hebrew. Mailing Add: 1250 Ocean Pkwy, Brooklyn, N.Y. 11230.

SILVERSTEIN, LAWRENCE G. D
Chmn, Midland Co. Dem. Party, Mich.
b. Binghamton, N.Y, 3/19/29; m. to Betsey; c. Deborah, Mary Jo, Susan, Barbara, William and Jeffrey. Educ: Harpur Col. of State Univ. N.Y; Univ. Rochester. Polit. & Govt. Pos: Chmn, Humphrey-Muskie Cmt, Mich, 68; chmn, Midland Co. Dem. Party, 69- Bus. & Prof. Pos: Indust. hygienist, Dow Chem. Co, currently. Big Bros. Award, 65. Mailing Add: 2312 E. Sugnet Rd, Midland, Mich. 48640.

SILVIS, JOHN MARSHALL R
b. Greensburg, Pa, 4/25/40; s. J.H. Silvis, Jr. and Lydia Wilkinson S; m. 3/31/67 to Mary Jo Pagnanelli; c. Kathleen Michelle. Educ: Pa. State Univ, B.S, 63; Delta Theta Sigma. Polit. & Govt. Pos: Treas, Westmoreland Co. Young Rep, Pa, 64-65 and pres, 65-67; del, Young Rep. Nat. Conv, 67; del, Rep. Nat. Conv, 68; chmn, Youngwood Rep. Party, Pa, 67- Bus. & Prof. Pos: Sales rep, Silvis Farms Inc, 63-67; sales mgr, Encyclop. Britannica, 67-68; territorial salesman, Allied Mills, Inc, 68- Mil. Serv: Pfc, Army Res, 63; 1st Lt, Army Res. Mem: Jr. C. of C. Master of Sales, Encyclop. Britannica Sales Masters Club. Rel: Lutheran. Mailing Add: 103 N. Fifth St, Youngwood, Pa. 15697.

SIMAS, JEAN LENORE R
Mem, Calif. Rep. State Cent. Cmt.
b. Santa Cruz, Calif, 10/9/13; d. Leslie Oliver Ward and Berenice Nitchings W; m. 5/18/41 to Walter Simas; c. Edward Thomas. Educ: Univ. Calif. Exten, 3 years; Blake Col, 1 year. Polit. & Govt. Pos: Auditor head off, Local, North. Div. and State Rep. Women's Clubs, Calif, 30-; Alameda Co. campaign chmn. women's div. for Assemblyman Mulford for Gov, Nixon for Gov, Calif. and President U.S; state treas, Calif. Rep. Women, 3 years; Alameda Co. campaign chmn. women's div. for U.S. Sen. Kuchel, 58, U.S. Sen. Knowland, 60 and Ivy Baker Priest, 66; mem, Calif. Rep. State Cent. Cmt, currently; dir. Citizen Cmt. on Urban Renewal, 60- Bus. & Prof. Pos: Dir-secy, Highland Improv. & Bus. Club, 42-66; mem. bd. dirs, Vol. of Am, Calif, 64- Mem: Toastmistress Club; Opera League; Oakland Symphony; Soroptimist Club; Bus. & Prfnl. Womens Club; Oakland Federated Womens City Club; Recipient of Testimonial Dinner with Civic Group, Oakland, Calif, 58. Rel: Episcopal. Legal Res: 15 La Salle Court, Piedmont, Calif. 94611. Mailing Add: 1436 14th Ave, Oakland, Calif. 94606.

SIMCOE, BERNARD (DOC) D
b. Calwood, Mo, 11/27/19; m. 8/9/41 to Mildred May Harris; c. Donald Lee. Sidney Bruce, Roy Wayne, Rebecca Faye. Educ: Fulton High Sch. Polit. & Govt. Pos: Mo. State Rep, 50-66. Bus. & Prof. Pos: Operates a Grade A dairy farm; former employee of the Int. Shoe Co. Mem: Odd Fellows, Lodge 105, Fulton, Mo; Adv. Bd. of Credit Production Asn. Rel: Baptist. Mailing Add: RFD 1, Fulton, Mo. 65251. (1967)

SIMCOX, EDWIN JESSE R
b. LaPorte, Ind, 1/12/45; s. Willard J. Simcox and Rachel L. Gibbs S; single Educ: Ind. Univ, Bloomington, A.B. in Govt. and Econ; Ind. Univ. Sch. Law, Bloomington 1 year; Ind. Univ. Sch. Law, Indianapolis, currently; Ind. Univ. Young Rep. Polit. & Govt. Pos: Del, Ind. Rep. Conv, 66; advance man, Third Cong. Dist, Rep. Cong. Campaign, 66; del, Young Rep. Nat. Conv, 67; exec. secy, Ind. Collegiate Young Rep, 67; advance man, Whitcomb for Gov. Cmt, 68; exec. secy, Ind. State Hwy. Cmn, 69- Mem: Young Rep. Club of LaPorte Co.(past temporary chmn); bd. mem, State House Young Rep. Rel: Methodist. Legal Res: Route 4, Box 16, LaPorte, Ind. 46350. Mailing Add: 3800 W. Michigan St, Apt. 2210, Indianapolis, Ind. 46222.

SIMKIN, WILLIAM E. D
b. Merrifield, N.Y, 1/13/07; s. Alfred E. Simkin and Florence Manchester S; m. 8/31/29 to Ruth Helen Commons; c. Thomas E. and Peter A. Educ: Earlham Col, B.S, 27 and LL.D, 63; Columbia Univ, part time, 28-31; Univ. Pa, 37-39. Polit. & Govt. Pos: Spec. mediation rep, Nat. War Labor Bd, 42-43, chmn. shipbuilding cmn. and assoc. pub. mem, 43-45, co-chmn. steel cmn, 45-47; dir, Fed. Mediation and Conciliation Serv, 61-69. Bus. & Prof. Pos: Prin, Sherwood Cent. Sch, 28-30; sci. teacher, Brooklyn Friends Sch, 30-32; field rep, Am. Friends Serv. Cmt, W.Va, 32-37; instr, indust, Wharton Sch. Finance and Commerce, Univ. of Pa, 37-39; labor arbitrator, self-employed, 39-61 & 69-; lectr, Harvard Sch. of Bus. Admin, 69- Publ: Arbitration of Grievances (w. Van D. Kennedy), U.S. Dept. of Labor, 48; Acceptability as a Factor in Arbitration Under an Existing Agreement, Univ. Pa. Press, 52. Mem: Pres, Nat. Acad. of Arbitrators, 50; Indust. Rels. Res. Asn. Rel: Society of Friends. Mailing Add: 9 Tavern Lane, Lexington, Mass. 02173.

SIMKINS, LEROY HAMPTON, JR. R
Ga. State Rep.
b. Augusta, Ga, 9/30/33; s. Leroy Hampton Simkins and Sarah Rebecca Bryan S; m. 7/28/56 to Sarah Burney Turner; c. Martha Turner, L. Hampton III and Nathaniel Turner. Educ: Wash. & Lee Univ, A.B, 55; Sigma Delta Psi; Kappa Alpha Sigma. Polit. & Govt. Pos: Mem, State Exec. Cmt, Young Rep, Ga, 63-64; mem, Exec. Cmt, Richmond Co. Rep. Party, 63-66; del, Rep. Nat. Conv, 64, alternate del, 68; Ga. State Rep, 65-66 & 69-, House Minority Leader, Ga. Legis, 66; mem, State Rep. Cmt, 68- Bus. & Prof. Pos: V.pres, Sherman Hemstreet, Inc, 65-66; real estate broker. Mil. Serv: Entered as 2nd Lt, Army, 55, released as 1st Lt, 57, after serv. in Transportation Corps, U.S.

and Germany, 57. Mem: Nat. Inst. of Farm and Land Brokers; Augusta Real Estate Bd; dir, Kiwanis; YMCA; U.S. Navy League; Asn. U.S. Army; Nat. Rifle Asn. Rel: Presbyterian. Mailing Add: 2815 Lombardy Ct, Augusta, Ga. 30904.

SIMMONS, ARTHUR E. R
Ill. State Rep.
b. Lake Co, Ill, 1/25/05; m. to Elizabeth Richter S; c. George S, Roberta G. Educ: Walton Sch. of Comm, Chicago; Wis. Univ; Northwest. Univ. Polit. & Govt. Pos: Rep. Committeeman, Niles Twp, Ill, 6 years; clerk, Niles Twp; Mayor, Skokie; Ill. State Rep, currently. Bus. & Prof. Pos: Pres, Arthur E. Simmons, Inc, a real estate and ins. brokerage off. Mil. Serv: Sgt, Ill. Res. Militia. Mem: Past Pres, Lions; charter mem, Eagles; Morton Grove Lodge 1146; AF&AM; Medinah Shrine; life mem, St. Colletta's Guild of Chicago. Rel: Methodist. Mailing Add: 9421 LeClaire Ave, Skokie, Ill. 60076.

SIMMONS, JOHN GROVER D
b. Baldwin, Ga, 2/12/21; s. Cleveland Simmons and Martha Broome S; m. 1/19/47 to Novella Emmett; c. Joyce Marie, Wanda Gayle and Martha Renee. Educ: Baldwin High Sch, 40. Polit. & Govt. Pos: Ga. State Rep, 61-66. Bus. & Prof. Pos: Chicopee Mfg. Corp. Mil. Serv: Army, S/Sgt, 43-45; Bronze Star; Good Conduct Medal. Mem: Mason. Rel: Baptist. Mailing Add: RFD 1, Baldwin, Ga. 30511.

SIMMONS, RALPH TERRELL R
Chmn, Jones Co. Rep. Party, Miss.
b. Laurel, Miss, 1/27/33; s. Colby D. Simmons and Linnie Cockrell S; single. Educ: Univ. South. Miss, B.S, 54; Birmingham Sch. Law; Kappa Alpha. Polit. & Govt. Pos: Del. and chmn, Miss. Rep. Conv, 68; chmn, Jones Co. Rep. Party, 68-; dir, Fifth Cong. TAR. Bus. & Prof. Pos: Don Drennen Motor Co, Birmingham, Ala, 58-63; credit mgr, North. Elec. Co, Laurel, 63- Mil. Serv: Entered as 2nd Lt, Army, 54, released as 1st Lt, 58, after serv. in Finance Corps, U.S. and Europe, 54-58; Maj, Army Nat. Guard, 63- Mem: Kiwanis; Nat. Guard Asn; Univ. South. Miss. Alumni Asn; v.pres, Jones Co. Heart Asn; AOPA. Rel: Baptist. Mailing Add: 1808 Seventh Ave, Laurel, Miss. 39440.

SIMMONS, RAY CLIFFORD R
b. Washington, D.C, 8/17/25; s. Robert Glenmore Simmons and Gladyce Weil S; m. 7/13/57 to Marianne Kelley; c. Michael K. and Elizabeth L. Educ: Univ. Nebr, B.A, 49, LL.B, 50; Phi Beta Kappa; Order of Coif; Phi Delta Phi; Alpha Tau Omega. Polit. & Govt. Pos: Law clerk to Assoc. Justice Harold H. Burton, U.S. Supreme Court, 50-51; chmn, Nebr. Young Rep, 57; Nebr. State Sen. and chmn, Judiciary Cmt, Nebr. State Senate, 57-61; del, Rep. Nat. Conv, 64; former mem, Nebr. State Rep. Cent. Cmt. Mil. Serv: Entered as A/S, Naval Res, 43, released as Lt, 53, after serv. in Pac. during World War II and as Comdr. of destroyer forces, Atlantic staff, Korea; Comdr, Naval Res, 53-64: Campaign Ribbons. Publ: Nebraska Automobile Negligence Law, Thomas Law Book Co, 57. Mem: VFW; Am. Legion; Mason; Shrine; Eagles; Izaak Walton League. Rel: Presbyterian. Mailing Add: 525 W. 19th St, Fremont, Nebr. 68025.

SIMMONS, RAYMOND HEDELIUS R
Mem, Calif. Rep. State Cent. Cmt.
b. San Francisco, Calif, 9/27/30; s. Raymond John Simmons and Aurella Rose Stephen S; m. 8/3/57 to Antoinette Catherine Lynch; c. Raymond H, Jr, John L, Molly E. and Peter A. Educ: City Col. of San Francisco, A.A, 50; Univ. San Francisco Law Sch, J.D, 55; Phi Alpha Delta. Polit. & Govt. Pos: Dep. dist. attorney, Monterey Co, Calif, 60-62; mem, Monterey Co. Water Recreation Adv. Cmn, 62-68; mem, Calif. Rep. State Cent. Cmt, 68- Bus. & Prof. Pos: Partner, Muller, Pia & Simmons, Attorneys at Law, Salinas, Calif, 62- Mil. Serv: Entered as Pvt, Marines, 48, released as Cpl, 52, after serv. in 1st Tank Bn, 1st Marine Div, Korea, 50-51; several unit and theatre citations; Good Conduct. Mem: Calif. and Monterey Bar Asns; Calif. Trial Lawyers Asn.(mem. exec. coun. Conf. of Barristers of Calif. Bar Asn, 60-64); Elks; K. of C. Rel: Catholic. Mailing Add: 503 W. Acacia St, Salinas, Calif. 93901.

SIMMONS, SAMUEL J. D
Asst. Secy. for Equal Opportunity, Dept. of Housing and Urban Develop.
b. Flint, Mich, 4/13/27; m. to Barbara Lett; c. David Clay and Robert Allen. Educ: West. Mich. Univ, A.B. in Soc. Sci, 49; adv. work, Univ. Mich. Sch. of Soc. Work and Dept. of Pub. Admin, Wayne State Univ. Polit. & Govt. Pos: Former placement officer, Mich. Employ. Security Cmn, Detroit; with the Fair Employ. Practices Cmn, Detroit, Regional Dir, 56; formerly exec. secy, Mich. Labor Mediation Bd, Detroit; mem. bd. of appeals and rev, Post Off. Dept, 62-64; dir, Field Serv. Div, U.S. Cmn. on Civil Rights, 64-69; Asst. Secy. for Equal Opportunity, Dept. of Housing and Urban Develop, 69- Bus. & Prof. Pos: Formerly student sociologist, State Prison of South. Mich, Jackson, boy's worker, Sophie Wright Settlement, Detroit and admin. asst, Detroit Br, NAACP. Mem: Former secy-treas, Nat. Asn. of State Labor Rels. Agencies; former chmn, Cmt. on Uniform Activity Reporting, Nat. Asn. of State Mediation Agencies; NAACP (life mem. and former bd. mem, Detroit Br, v.pres. two terms, Mich. State Conf. of Branches); Am. Soc. Pub. Admin. Meritorious Serv. Award, Post Off. Dept. Legal Res: Detroit, Mich. Mailing Add: Dept. of Housing and Urban Development, 451 Seventh St. S.W, Washington, D.C. 20410.

SIMON, PAUL D
Lt. Gov, Ill.
b. Eugene, Ore, 11/29/28; s. Martin P. Simon and Ruth Troemel S; m. 4/21/60 to Jeanne Hurley; c. Sheila and Martin. Educ: Univ. Ore; Dana Col; Sigma Delta Chi. Polit. & Govt. Pos: Ill. State Rep, 54-62; Ill. State Sen, 62-69; del, Dem. Nat. Conv, 68; Lt. Gov, Ill, 69- Bus. & Prof. Pos: Writer of books and mag. articles, started as newspaper publisher at 19; gradually expanded newspaper holdings until 14 newspapers published in Ill, sold newspaper interests, 65. Mil. Serv: Entered as Pvt, Army, 51-53, served in Counter Intel. Corps as Spec. Agent along the Iron Curtain in Cent. Europe. Publ: 'Lincoln's Preparation for Greatness,' Univ. Okla. Press, 66; A Hungry World, Concordia Publ. House, 66; Protestant-Catholic Marriages Can Succeed, Asn. Press, 67. Mem: Am. Polit. Sci. Asn; Lions; Am. Legion; VFW; NAACP; Urban League. Received Award for Distinguished Reporting of State and Local Govt, Am. Polit. Sci. Asn, 57. Rel: Lutheran. Mailing Add: 306 E. Market St, Troy, Ill. 62294.

SIMON, RAYMOND CLARK R
City Councilman, Modesto, Calif.
b. Conrad, Mont, 5/4/31; s. David Lawrence Simon and Etta May Bruce S; m. 8/31/57 to Joan Ellen Pedego; c. Jeffrey Stephen and Julie Ann. Educ: Modesto Jr. Col, A.A, 55; Univ. Calif, Berkeley, A.B. in Criminology, 58; Sigma Nu. Polit. & Govt. Pos: Mem, Calif. Rep. State Cent. Cmt, 64-, area precinct v.chmn, 64; planning cmnr, Modesto, 65-67, city councilman, 67-; Rep. cand, Calif. State Assembly, 30th Dist, 69. Bus. & Prof. Pos: Asst. security agent, Seattle Pub. Schs, Wash, 59-60; secy-treas, Freese and Gianelli Ins. Adjusters Inc, Modesto, Calif, 60- Mil. Serv: Entered as Pvt, Air Force, 49, released as S/Sgt, 53, after serv. in Strategic Air Command; Good Conduct and Nat. Serv. Defense Medals. Mem: Nat. Asn. Arson Investr; Calif. State and Nat. Asns. Independent Ins. Adjusters; Am. Legion; Modesto Swim and Racquet Club; pres, Modesto Jr. Col. Found. Outstanding Young Man of Modesto, 65. Rel: Lutheran. Mailing Add: 2816 Hampshire Lane, Modesto, Calif. 95350.

SIMON, RAYMOND F. D
Corp. Counsel, Chicago, Ill.
b. Chicago, Ill, 11/7/32; s. Peter Simon and Mary Doody S; m. 10/6/56 to Mary Cassaretto; c. Raymond Matthew, Mark Thomas, John Anthony, Gregory Joseph, David, Kevin and Maria. Educ: Loyola Univ, B.S, 53, Sch. Law, J.D, 56; Blue Key; Phi Alpha Delta; Sigma Pi Alpha. Polit. & Govt. Pos: Admin. asst. to mayor, Chicago, Ill, 56-61, admin. officer, 62-64, corp. counsel, 65-; alternate del, Dem. Nat. Conv, 68. Mil. Serv: Lt, Army, 55-56, serv. in Mil. Intelligence. Mem: Chicago, Ill. and Am. Bar Asns. Rel: Roman Catholic. Legal Res: 1255 W. Hood Ave, Chicago, Ill. 60626. Mailing Add: Room 511, City Hall, Chicago, Ill. 60602.

SIMON, SEYMOUR FRANK D
Alderman, Chicago, Ill.
b. Chicago, Ill, 8/10/15; s. Benjamin Simon and Gertrude Rusky S; m. 5/26/54 to Roslyn Schultz Biel; c. Anthony H. Biel, Nancy (Mrs. Harris) and John B. Educ: Northwest. Univ, LL.B, 35, Sch. of Law, J.D, 38; Phi Beta Kappa; Order of the Coif. Polit. & Govt. Pos: Spec. attorney, Anti-Trust Div, Dept. of Justice, Wash, D.C, 38-42; alderman, 40th Ward, Chicago, Ill, 55-61, 67-; Dem. committeeman, 40th Ward, Chicago, 60-; mem, exec. cmt, Dem. Party Cook Co, 60-; mem. and pres, Bd. of Cmnr, Cook Co, 62-66; pres, Forest Preserve Dist. of Cook Co, 62-66; del, Dem. Nat. Conv, 68. Bus. & Prof. Pos: Attorney-at-law, 46- Mil. Serv: Entered as Ens, Navy, 42, released as Lt, 45, after serv. in Serv. Squadron, Tenth Pac; Legion of Merit. Mem: Ill. and Chicago Bar Asns; Am. Legion; Am. Vet. Cmt; VFW; B'nai B'rith. Rel: Jewish. Legal Res: 5900 N. Christiana, Chicago, Ill. 60645. Mailing Add: 39 S. LaSalle St, Chicago, Ill. 60603.

SIMON, WARREN JOSEPH D
La. State Rep.
b. Kaplan, La, 8/15/19; s. L. V. Simon and Rena LeBlanc S; div; c. Cordell (Mrs. Hebert), Michael J, Claudette M. and Christine Ann. Educ: Kaplan High Sch, La, 12 years. Polit. & Govt. Pos: La. State Rep, Vermilion Parish, 60-68, Vermilion and Acadia Parishes, 35th Dist, 68- Bus. & Prof. Pos: Co-owner and mgr, Bourque Simon Ins. Agency, Kaplan, 51-; secy-treas, Kaplan Loan & Investment Co, 57-; pres, Ropel Chem. Co, 60-; secy-treas, Roi-Tex, Inc, 67- Mem: Lions; K. of C. Named Outstanding Legislator in Conservation, by Nat. and La. Wildlife Fedns, 66. Rel: Catholic. Legal Res: 502 N. Irving Ave, Kaplan, La. 70548. Mailing Add: P.O. Box 156, Kaplan, La. 70548.

SIMONS, CHARLES E, JR. D
b. Johnston, S.C, 8/17/16; s. Charles E. Simons, Sr. and Frances Rhoden S; m. 10/18/41 to Jean Brewster Knapp; c. Charles E, III, Paul Knapp, Richard Brewster and Jean Brewster. Educ: Univ. of S.C, A.B, 37, LL.B, 39; Phi Beta Kappa; chmn, Hon. Coun; mem, Debating Team; Blue Key and Clariosophic Literary Soc. Polit. & Govt. Pos: S.C. State Rep, Aiken Co, 42, 47-48 & 60-64, mem, Ways and Means Cmt, S.C. State House of Rep; mem, S.C. Constitutional Rev. Cmt, 48; U.S. Dist. Judge, Dist.of S.C, 64- Bus. & Prof. Pos: Attorney, Lybrand, Simons & Rich, Aiken, S.C, 39-64; mem, Bd. of Discipline and Grievance, S.C. Bar Asn, 3 years and mem, Exec. Cmt. Mil. Serv: Entered Navy, 42, released as Lt, Naval Res, 46, after serv. in Atlantic and Pac. Theaters. Mem: Am. Bar Asn; Am. Judicature Soc; mem. and past v.pres, Aiken C. of C, past pres, Aiken Jr. C. of C; adv. cmt, Aiken Co. Retarded Children's Asn; dir, United Fund for Aiken Co; Lions; past comdr, Am. Legion Post 26; VFW; 40 et 8; mem. and past pres, Aiken Bus. Men's Club; pres, Univ. of S.C. Alumni Asn, 61-62, mem, Univ. S.C. Develop. and Adv. Coun. Recipient, Algernon Sidney Sullivan Award during College and again as an alumnus in 64. Rel: Baptist. Legal Res: 910 Valley Green Dr, S.W, Aiken, S.C. 29802. Mailing Add: P.O. Box 2185, Aiken, S.C. 29802.

SIMONS, HERBERT EDWIN D
b. Riverton, Ill, 12/8/19; s. Charles Arthur Simons and Ellen Margaret Dailey S; m. 6/25/43 to Avis Irene Draper; c. Timothy Herbert, Pamela Irene, Jayne Merl and Melissa Avis. Educ: McKendree Col, Lebanon, Ill, 38-40; Wash. Univ, St. Louis, Mo, 41-42; Univ. Nebr, B.S. in Chem. Eng, 46-47; Student Chap, Am. Inst. of Chem. Engrs; Sigma Tau; Alpha Chi Sigma; Alpha Mu Omega. Polit. & Govt. Pos: Chmn, Morton Co. Dem. Non-Partisan League, N.Dak; former chmn, 34th Dist. Dem. Non-Partisan League, Bus. & Prof. Pos: Chem. engr, Tech. Serv, Whiting Refinery, Standard Oil Co, Ind, 47-52, asst. gen. foreman, 52-54; operating foreman, Mandan Refinery, Am. Oil Co, 54-66, tech. supvr, 66- Mil. Serv: Entered as Pvt, Army, 42, released as 1st Lt, 46, after serv. in L Co, 417th Inf. Regt, 76th Div, ETO, 45; Lt. Col, Army Res, currently; Ardennes, Rhineland & Cent. Europe Campaign Ribbons; Combat Inf. Badge; Purple Heart; Bronze Star; Am. Theater Ribbon; Armed Forces Res. Medal. Mem: PTA; Lions; Toastmasters Club. Rel: Episcopal. Mailing Add: 1400 Monte Dr, Mandan, N.Dak. 58554.

SIMONS, JOHN C. D
b. Salem, Utah, 2/23/21; m. to Ora; c. Five. Educ: Colo. State Univ, D.V.M. Polit. & Govt. Pos: Wyo. State Sen. until 67. Bus. & Prof. Pos: Veterinarian, L.D.S. Mem: Am. Vet. Med. Asn; Wyo. Vet. Med. Asn. Mailing Add: 2525 Main, Torrington, Wyo. 82240.

SIMONS, WILLIAM HENRY D
V.Chmn, D.C. Dem. Cent. Cmt.
b. Washington, D.C, 6/1/24; s. Alfred Edgar Simons, Sr. and Mattie Garrett

S; m. 12/19/48 to Elaine Davis; c. Sheryl Patrice and Wilma Lorraine. Educ: Miner Teachers Col, B.S, 47; N.Y. Univ, M.A, 49; Am. Univ, 51-57. Polit. & Govt. Pos: Del, Dem. Nat. Conv, 68; v.chmn, D.C. Dem. Cent. Cmt, 68- Bus. & Prof. Pos: Teacher, Banneker Jr. High Sch, Wash, D.C, 47-65. Mil. Serv: Entered as Pvt, Army, 43, released as M/Sgt, 45, after serving in 262 Qm. Bn, ETO, 43-45; Good Conduct Medal; Bronze Star; Croix de Guerre. Publ: 'Who Should Control the Public Schools? ' Coun. Woman, spring 69. Mem: Pres, Wash. Teachers' Union Local 6, Am. Fedn. Teachers, 64-; bd. dirs, Wash. Urban League, 68-; Woodridge Civic Asn. Mailing Add: 1917 Randolph St. N.E, Washington, D.C. 20018.

SIMONSON, HAROLD JAMES DFL
Chmn, Pope Co. Dem-Farmer-Labor Party, Minn.
b. Glenwood, Minn, 10/7/12; s. Christ Simonson and Celia Kopitzke S; m. 6/28/36 to Luverne Thorstad; c. Janice, Mary and Nancy. Polit. & Govt. Pos: Mem. exec. cmt, Pope Co. Dem-Farmer-Labor Party, Minn, 60-66, chmn, 65-; del, Dist. and State Conv, 60-66. Bus. & Prof. Pos: Chmn. credit cmt, Minneapolis, St. Paul & Sault Sainte Marie Credit Union, 61-66. Mem: Mason; RAM; Brotherhood of Locomotive Firemen, 41, Local Organizer, 52. Rel: Lutheran. Mailing Add: 711 E. Minnesota Ave, Glenwood, Minn. 56334. (1967)

SIMPKINS, LLOYD L. D
Secy. of State, Md.
b. Mt. Vernon, Md, 6/6/22; m. to Betty Wilson; c. one daughter. Educ: Univ. of Md, B.S, 47; Univ. of Md. Law Sch, LL.B, 52. Polit. & Govt. Pos: Md. State Del, 51-59; exec. asst. to Gov. Md, 59-61; Secy. of State, Md, 61- Bus. & Prof. Pos: Former attorney to the town of Princess Anne; former attorney to Co. Liquor Bd; seafood bus; partner, Simpkins & Simpkins, Princess Anne, Md; attorney-at-law. Mil. Serv: Seaman, USN, 41, discharged as Ens, 46 after serv. in S. Pac. Mem: State Bar Asn. Cmt. on Admissions, 60- Mailing Add: Princess Anne, Md. 21853.

SIMPKINS, ROBERT LEE D
W.Va. State Del.
b. Mingo Co, W.Va, 1/6/18; s. Wayne Simpkins and Lottie Staten S; m. 11/16/40 to Helen Irene Adkins; c. Robert Lee, Jr. and Mabel Ann. Educ: Marshall Univ, B.A, M.A. Polit. & Govt. Pos: W.Va. State Del, 64- Bus. & Prof. Pos: Secy. sch. prin. Mil. Serv: Navy, 43-46, S.Pac. Theatre. Mem: Moose; Hugh C. Boyd Lodge No. 119, Matewan AF&AM; Nat. State and Co. Educ. Asns; W.Va. Sec. Prin. Asn; scoutmaster, Izaak Walton League of Am. Rel: Protestant. Mailing Add: P.O. Box 130, Meador, W.Va. 25682.

SIMPSON, ALAN K. R
Wyo. State Rep.
b. Denver, Colo, 9/2/31; m. to Ann; c. Three. Educ: Univ. Wyo, B.S. & J.D. Polit. & Govt. Pos: Asst. Attorney Gen. of Wyo, 59; Cody City Attorney, 59-69; U.S. Cmnr, 59-69; Wyo. State Rep, currently; chmn, Standing Legis. Cmt, Corporations and Pub. Utilities and mem, Judiciary Cmt, Wyo. House of Rep; mem, Wyo. Compilation Cmn. and Wyo. Higher Educ. Coun, currently. Bus. & Prof. Pos: Attorney-at-Law. Mem: Rotary; Elks; Mason; Shrine; VFW; Park Co, Fifth Judicial, Wyo. and Am. Bar Asns; former mem. bd. dir, Wyo. Asn. of Munic; former dir, Univ. Wyo. Alumni Asn. (pres, 62-63); admitted to practice, U.S. Supreme Court; bd. trustees, Buffalo Bill Mem. Asn. and Whitney Gallery of West. Art; trustee, Northwest Commun. Col, Powell. Rel: Episcopal. Mailing Add: Box 470, Cody, Wyo. 82414.

SIMPSON, BRYAN D
b. Near Kissimmee, Fla, 5/30/03; s. Arthur Allen Simpson and Mary Elizabeth Bryan S; m. 2/15/41 to Sarah George Hall Hixon, wid. 1/6/67; c. Bryan Simpson, Jr. and stepsons, John Hall, George Cooley and Joseph Morris Hixon, III; m. 3/1/68 to Sally Peel Thompson Jones; stepdaughter, Eve Dunbar Jones and stepson, Isaac Franklin Jones, III. Educ: Univ. of Fla, LL.B, 26; Phi Delta Phi; Kappa Alpha Order. Hon. LL.D, John B. Stetson University, 58. Polit. & Govt. Pos: U.S. Circuit Judge, Fifth Circuit, 66-; Chief Judge, U.S. District Court, Middle District of Florida, 62-66; Southern District, 60-62, U.S. Dist. Judge, 50-60; circuit judge, Fourth Fla. Circuit, 46-50; judge, Criminal Court of Record, Duval Co, 39-46; asst. state attorney, Fourth Fla. Circuit, 33-37. Bus. & Prof. Pos: Jr. partner, Knight, Adair, Cooper and Osborne, Jacksonville, Fla, 28-33, law clerk, Cooper, Knight, Adair, Cooper and Osborne, 26-27; miscellaneous summer employ. during col. Mil. Serv: 1st Lt, Army, 43-45, serv. in ETO, 44 and U.S; Good Conduct Medal; Am. Serv. Ribbon; ETO Campaign Ribbon with 2 Battle Stars; Army Res, until 53. Mem: Am, Fla. and Jacksonville Bar Asns; Am. Judicature Soc; hon. mem, Lawyers Club, D.C; Nat. Exec. Cmt, Boy Scouts; bd. mem, Bolles Sch, Jacksonville; state bd, Children's Home Soc. Fla; trustee, Cummer Gallery of Art, Rotary and Rotary Int; Timuquana Country Club; Pontevedra Club; former mem, Am. Legion, VFW, Moose and Elks. Awarded citation, Univ. Fla. Centennial, 53. Rel: Protestant Episcopal. Legal Res: 4157 Ortega Blvd, Jacksonville, Fla. 32210. Mailing Add: P.O. Box 4940, Jacksonville, Fla. 32201.

SIMPSON, CLYDE WAGNER D
b. Jacksonville, Fla, 10/13/20; s. Clyde Hendrix Simpson and E. Ruthe Wagner S; m. 8/25/45 to Dorothy Anne Banks; c. Clyde Banks, Amy DeVries and Rae McMillan. Educ: Gordon Mil. Col, 37-38; Univ. of Fla, A.A, A.B. and 1 year of law sch, 38-43; Alpha Phi Omega; Pi Kappa Alpha. Polit. & Govt. Pos: Fla. State Rep, 64-66; city utilities cmnr, Jacksonville, 67-68; cmnr. mem, Jacksonville Port Authority, 67- Bus. & Prof. Pos: Life and health ins. agent, Pac. Mutual Life, 49-, gen. ins. agent, 52-; pres, Clyde W. Simpson & Co, Jacksonville, Fla, 57- Mil. Serv: Entered as Ens, Navy Res, 43, released as Lt.(jg), 46, after serv. in Squadrons 9, 10 and 28, torpedo boats, Southwest Pac. Theatre; Comdr, Naval Air Res; Torpedo Boat Unit Citation; VR 741 Unit Safety Award. Mem: Jacksonville and Fla. Realtors Asns; Life Underwriters Ins. Asn; Nat. Asn. of Appraisers and Realtors; Mason; Shrine; Jaycees (past pres. and life mem, Jacksonville Chap, past state v.pres, past nat. dir); bd. of dirs, Boy Scouts and Cub Scouts; Univ. of Fla. Alumni Asn; Jacksonville Univ. Alumni Asn; assoc. mem, Young Dem; United Serv. Orgn; Dads Clubs; PTA. Good Govt. Award, C. of C; Distinguished Serv. Award, Fla. Voc. Asn; Good Govt. Award, Federated Dads Clubs. Rel: Episcopal. Legal Res: 1620 Charon Rd, Jacksonville, Fla. 32205. Mailing Add: 608 Atlantic Bank Bldg, Jacksonville, Fla. 32202.

SIMPSON, HAROLD DWAINE R
Nebr. State Sen.
b. Harlan, Iowa, 6/1/26; s. Harold W. Simpson and Esther Elizabeth Michelson S; m. 1/11/46 to Clara Salome Hitz; c. Roger Allen, Harold Dwaine, Jr, John William, Marjorie Ann, Thomas Edwin and James Edward. Educ: High Sch. Polit. & Govt. Pos: Nebr. State Sen, 46th Dist, currently. Bus. & Prof. Pos: Bus. Agent, Grainmillers Local 31, 54-69; with Gooch Milling and Elevator Co. Mil. Serv: Entered as Pvt, Air Force, 44, released as Pfc, 47, after serv. in U.S. Mem: WOW; Boy Scouts; Am. Fedn. of Grain Millers; PTA. Rel: Methodist. Mailing Add: 1805 North 30th St, Lincoln, Nebr. 68503.

SIMPSON, JACK RAYMOND R
b. Condon, Ore, 12/18/09; s. Cass Andrew Simpson and Helen Parman S; m. 7/18/36 to Nova Hedin; c. Erik and Mark. Educ: Willamette Univ, 31-36; Westminster Law Sch, LL.B, 39. Polit. & Govt. Pos: Pres, Anchorage Rep. Club, Alaska, 57-58; finance chmn, South. Cent. Dist. Rep. Party, 59-63, chmn, 63-65; finance chmn, Alaska State Rep. Cent. Cmt, 65-66; former Alaska State Rep; alternate del, Rep. Nat. Conv, 68. Mem: Lions. Rel: Presbyterian. Mailing Add: 710 M St, Anchorage, Alaska 99501. (1967)

SIMPSON, JAMES CHARLES 'JIM' D
Miss. State Rep.
b. Gulport, Miss, 5/18/30; married. Educ: Phi Kappa Tau. Polit. & Govt. Pos: Miss. State Rep, currently. Bus. & Prof. Pos: Seafood canner. Mem: C. of C; VFW; Pass Christian Yacht Club. Rel: Catholic. Mailing Add: 706 W. Beach Blvd, Pass Christian, Miss. 39571. (1967)

SIMPSON, MACKIE D
b. Glenwood, Ga, 8/16/25; s. Bob Simpson and Minky McDaniel S; m. 11/28/46 to Mary Stone; c. Marybeth. Educ: Glenwood High Sch, 42; attended Abraham Baldwin Col. Polit. & Govt. Pos: Ga. State Rep, 61-66. Bus. & Prof. Pos: Clerk, sup. ct. Mil. Serv: USMC, Cpl, 43-46; S. Pac. Mem: Mason. Rel: Methodist. Mailing Add: Glenwood, Ga. 30428. (1967)

SIMPSON, MILWARD L. R
b. Jackson, Wyo, 11/12/97; s. William L. Simpson and Margaret Burnett S; m. 6/29/29 to Lorna Kooi; c. Peter Kooi and Alan Kooi. Educ: Tome Prep. Sch, Port Deposit, Md; Univ. Wyo, B.S, 21; Harvard Univ. Law Sch, LL.B, 25; Alpha Tau Omega. Hon. LL.D, Univ. Wyo, 55. Polit. & Govt. Pos: Wyo. State Rep, 26-27; Gov, Wyo, 55-59; former mem, Exec. Cmt. of Gov. Conf; U.S. Sen, Wyo, 62-66. Bus. & Prof. Pos: Attorney-at-law, 26-55 & 59; partner, Simpson & Simpson, 59-60; partner, Simpson, Kepler & Simpson, 60- Mil. Serv: 2nd Lt, Army Inf, 18. Mem: Am, Wyo, Fifth Judicial Dist. and Park Co. Bar Asns; Cmt. on Integration of Wyo. Bar; Nat. Coun. Boy Scouts; Mason (33°); Am. Legion; 40 et 8; Rotary Int; Elks; Eagles; Moose; past potentate, Kalif Temple, AAONMS; pres, Park Co. Asn. Ment. Health and v.pres, Wyo. Asn. Ment. Health, 60-61; v.pres, Region V, Nat. Asn. for Ment. Health, 61 and mem. nat. exec. cmt. and bd. dirs, 59; chmn, Coun. Ment. Health and Research West. Interstate Cmn. for Higher Educ; chmn, Interstate Oil Compact Cmn, 57-58. Rel: Episcopal; Vestryman. Mailing Add: 901 Simpson Ave, Cody, Wyo. 82414.

SIMPSON, PAUL LEE D
Chmn, McNairy Co. Dem. Exec. Cmt, Tenn.
b. Lambert, Miss, 9/22/36; s. Bret E. Keeter and Minnie Riley K; m. 8/17/68 to Jackie D. Matlock. Educ: Univ. Tenn, B.S, 59, LL.B, 62; Delta Sigma Phi; Phi Alpha Delta; Delta Sigma Pi. Polit. & Govt. Pos: Del, Dem. Nat. Conv, 68; chmn, McNairy Co. Dem. Exec. Cmt, Tenn, 68- Bus. & Prof. Pos: Assoc, Galloway & Clinton, Attorneys, 62-63; adjustor, State Farm Mutual, Jackson, 63-65; attorney, Selmer, 65- Mem: Am, Tenn. and McNairy Co. Bar Asns; Am. Trial Lawyers Asn; Rotary; Mason; Jaycees (pres); Moose. Rel: Primitive Baptist. Legal Res: 244 N. Third, Selmer, Tenn. 38375. Mailing Add: 165 W. Court, Selmer, Tenn. 38375.

SIMPSON, RAY CHAPMAN D
Committeeman-at-Lg, Pulaski Co. Dem. Cmt, Va.
b. Pulaski Co, Va, 8/16/06; s. Essa William Simpson and Jennie Turner S; m. 10/11/35 to Blenna Mae Anderson; c. Thelma (Mrs. Thomas H. Pifer), Ronald Clay, William Anderson and John Ray. Polit. & Govt. Pos: V.chmn, Precinct Cmt, Dem. Party, Va, 47-53; committeeman-at-lg, Pulaski Co. Dem. Cmt, 53-; mem, Dist. Dem. Finance Cmt, 59-61; del, Dem. Nat. Conv, 64; mem, New River Valley Indust. Authority, Selective Serv. Bd, Pulaski Co. and Sewerage Authority of Pulaski Co, currently. Bus. & Prof. Pos: Founder and owner, Ray C. Simpson Trucking Co, 35-58; pres. and treas, Ray C. Simpson Corp, 58-64. Mem: Ruritan; Mason (32°); Shrine. Rel: Presbyterian; Deacon and Trustee, Fairlawn Presbyterian Church. Mailing Add: Box 280, Dublin, Va. 24084.

SIMPSON, ROBERT FOSTER Conservative, N.Y.
Mem, State Cmt, Conservative Party, N.Y.
b. Fulton, N.Y, 3/22/28; s. Leigh Arthur Simpson, M.D. and Marion S. Edgarton S; m. 6/19/54 to Ann Watrous Lines; c. Susan Leigh, Leigh Ann, Robert Foster, Jr, Elizabeth Joan, Jean Virginia and William Harold. Educ: Syracuse Univ, A.B, 51; Sigma Chi; Varsity Club. Polit. & Govt. Pos: Mem, State Cmt. and chmn, Ontario Co. Cmt, Conservative Party, N.Y, presently. Bus. & Prof. Pos: Mem. sales dept, Union Carbide Corp, 52-54 and Genesee Heating Serv, Rochester, 54-62; owner, Pennysaver Printing and Specialty Co, The Robert Simpson Co. and Naples Pennysaver, N.Y, 62- Mil. Serv: Entered as A/S, Navy, 46, released as Pharmacist Mate 3/C, 48. Rel: Protestant. Mailing Add: R.R. 3, Short Rd, Canandaigua, N.Y. 14424.

SIMPSON, ROBERT LEWIS R
Chmn, Imperial Co. Rep. Cent. Cmt, Calif.
b. Hinton, Okla, 10/2/21; s. Francis M. Simpson and Clinnie Chitsey S; m. 3/15/44 to Barbara Mae Barrett; c. Sandra Lou, Robert Michael, Barbara Mae and Polly Dee. Educ: Okla. City Univ. Polit. & Govt. Pos: Mem, Young Rep, Calif, 49; mem, Imperial Co. Rep. Cent. Cmt, 59, chmn, 61-; pres, Asn. of Rep. Co. Cent. Cmt. Chmn. of Calif, 65-; alternate del, Rep. Nat. Conv, 68. Bus. & Prof. Pos: Bldg. contractor, 47-48; farm supply salesman, Ralston Purina Co, 49-52; farmer, 52-58; real estate broker, Calif, 58. Mil. Serv: Entered as Aviation Cadet, Air Force, 43, released as 1st Lt, 46, after serv.

in Am. Theater. Mem: Mason; Elks. Rel: Methodist. Legal Res: 510 Marilyn St, Brawley, Calif. 92227. Mailing Add: P.O. Box 456, Brawley, Calif. 92227.

SIMPSON, ROBERT TENNENT D
Assoc. Justice, Supreme Court, Ala.
b. Florence, Ala; s. Robert Tennent Simpson and Nellie Moody S; wid; 2nd m. 12/28/58 to Sally Sewell Bodiford (deceased); 3rd m. 7/3/68 to Ann Moses Parham; c. Robert T. and William F. Educ: Florence State Col, 12; Univ. Ala, A.B, 15, LL.B, 17; Phi Beta Kappa; Sigma Alpha Epsilon; Sigma Delta Kappa. Polit. & Govt. Pos: Solicitor, 11th Judicial Circuit, 19-40; judge, Ala. Court of Appeals, 40-44; assoc. justice, Supreme Court of Ala, 44- Bus. & Prof. Pos: Lawyer, Simpson & Simpson, 19-29. Mil. Serv: Entered as 1st Lt, Army, 17, released as Capt, 19, after serv. as Comdr, 1st Bn, 327th Inf. Meuse-Argonne, Flirey Sector, Lucey, Marbache and St. Mihiel; Brigade Citation; Silver Star. Mem: Ala. and Am. Bar Asns; past pres, Jr. C. of C; Mason; Elks; WOW; Odd Fellows; K. of P; Am. Legion; 40 et 8; VFW; DAV; Nat. Sojourners; Mil. Order of World Wars; SAR; Sons of Confederate Vets; Unity Literary Club; Knife & Fork Club; Montgomery Country Club. Awarded Cross of Mil. Serv, United Daughters of Confederacy, 63. Rel: Presbyterian. Legal Res: 35 W. Ogden Rd, Montgomery, Ala. 36105. Mailing Add: P.O. Box 171, Montgomery, Ala. 36101.

SIMPSON, RUSSELL G. R
b. Springfield, Mass, 5/22/27; s. Archer R. Simpson and Ethel Gordon S; m. 9/11/54 to Bickley S. Flower; c. Barbara, Elisabeth and Helen Blair. Educ: Yale Univ, B.A, 51; Boston Univ. Sch. Law, LL.B, 56. Polit. & Govt. Pos: Del, Mass. State Rep. Conv, 60, 62, 64, 66 & 67; mem, Spec. Adv. Cmt. to Mass. Secy. of State for Revision of Corrupt Practices Act, 61-62; alternate del-at-lg, Rep. Nat. Conv, 64, exec. chmn. Mass. Delegation to Rep. Nat. Conv, 68; mem, Sherborn Rep. Town Cmt, 56-67; dist. finance chmn, Mass. Rep. State Cmt, 57-59, state committeeman, 59-67, chmn. exec. cmt, 62-67. Bus. & Prof. Pos: Advert. mgr, Burden Bryant Co, Springfield, Mass, 51-53; assoc, Goodwin, Procter & Hoar, Attorneys, 56-64, partner, 65- Mil. Serv: Entered as A/S, Navy, 45, released as PO 3/C, 46. Mem: Boston, Mass, Am. and Inter-Am. Bar Asns; mem, Panel Corporate Law Ed. Prog. and of For. and Int. Bus. Law Cmt. of Am. Bar Asn; hon. consul, Boston for Republic of Bolivia. Named Outstanding Young Man of Greater Boston by Jr. C. of C, 63. Rel: Protestant. Legal Res: 76 Brook Hill Rd, Milton, Mass. 02187. Mailing Add: 28 State St, Boston, Mass. 02109.

SIMPSON, STANLEY R. R
Chmn, Boone Co. Rep. Cent. Cmt, Iowa.
b. Des Moines, Iowa, 11/3/27; s. James W. Simpson and Helen Joy S; m. 11/11/53 to Avonell Zener; c. Candice, Stanley and Kelly. Educ: Univ. Wyo, 45; Drake Univ, J.D, 51; Delta Theta Phi. Polit. & Govt. Pos: Mayor, Ogden, Iowa, 57-59; co. attorney, Boone, 59-; chmn, Boone Co. Rep. Cent. Cmt, 64- Mil. Serv: Pvt, Army, 45-46. Mem: Nat. Dist. Attorneys Asn; Iowa and Am. Bar Asns; Am. Judicature Soc; Shrine; Elks; Lions; Mason; Odd Fellow. Rel: Protestant. Legal Res: Ogden, Iowa 50212. Mailing Add: Lippert Bldg, Boone, Iowa 50036.

SIMPSON, WILDER ARTHUR R
b. Lyndon, Vt, 6/22/87; m. to Ruth E.C. Hoffman; c. Four. Educ: Lyndon Inst, 05. Polit. & Govt. Pos: Sch. dir, Lyndonville, Vt, 14-20, selectman, 21-35; Vt. State Rep, 23, 47 & 63-69; town moderator, Lyndonville, 26-; Vt. State Sen, 27; mem, State Hwy. Bd, 27-33; mem, Old Age Assistance Cmn, 35-44; cmnr, Social Welfare, 47-59. Bus. & Prof. Pos: Farming. Mailing Add: Lyndonville, Vt. 05851. (1967)

SIMPSON, WILLIAM WALTON D
b. Washington, D.C, 5/3/14; s. William Simpson and Elizabeth Walton S; m. 4/10/57 to Edith Berkley; c. Betty (Mrs. Cornish). Educ: Miner Teachers Col, 34-35. Polit. & Govt. Pos: Del, Dem. Nat. Conv, 68. Bus. & Prof. Pos: Pres, Billy Simpson's, Inc, 56-; pres, Pioneer Sale & Distribution Co, 57-60; pres, Brookland Enterprises, Inc, 66- Mil. Serv: Entered as Seaman 3/C, Navy, 43, released as Motor Machinist 2/C, 46, after serv. in Logistic Support, Eniwetok and Hawaii, 45-46. Mem: Mason (32°); Shrine (bd. gov, Mecca Temple 10); Mayor's Cmn. for Employ. Handicapped; Urban Coalition; YMCA (mem. bd); Pigskin Club of Washington, Inc; Student Enterprises, Fisk Univ. (mem. bd). Outstanding Citizen of D.C, Nat. Educ. Asn, 66; cmnr, Youth Coun, 66; YMCA Achievement award, 68. Rel: Baptist. Mailing Add: 4507 Iowa Ave. N.W, Washington, D.C. 20011.

SIMS, JOHN THAXTER D
b. Mt. Olivet, Ky, 10/10/04; s. John Morgan Sims and Sallie McCracken S; m. 6/20/32 to Sallie Asbury Worthington. Educ: Univ. Ky, LL.B; Phi Delta Phi. Polit. & Govt. Pos: Co. Attorney, Ky, 30-34; del, Dem. Nat. Conv, 68. Mem: Ky. and Am. Bar Asns; life mem, Sixth Circuit Court of Appeals Judicial Conf; Rotary. Rel: Christian Church. Legal Res: East Pike St, Cynthiana, Ky. 41031. Mailing Add: Box 244, Cynthiana, Ky. 41031.

SIMS, P. D. D
b. Chattanooga, Tenn, 1/16/93; s. Minos P. Sims and Hettie Gordon S; m. 6/27/27 to Eva Dorothy Ramskill; c. Graham D, Marian (Mrs. John Werner) and Ann Louise (Mrs. Jimmie Gist). Educ: Dixie Col, 2 years. Polit. & Govt. Pos: State committeeman, Big Horn Co. Dem. Party, Wyo, 28-30; postmaster, Lovell, 34-61; alternate del, Dem. Nat. Conv, 68. Mil. Serv: Entered as Pvt, Army, 18, released as Pfc, 20, after serv. in 45th Inf, Ninth Div. Mem: Am. Legion; Vet. of World War I; AF&AM; Odd Fellows; C. of C. Rel: Baptist. Legal Res: 241 Park, Lovell, Wyo. 82431. Mailing Add: Box 397, Lovell, Wyo. 82431.

SIMS, ROYDON E. D
b. Hannibal, Mo, 1/8/27; m. 10/1/47 to Mary L. Dryden; c. Susan Kaye, Jayne Lynn, Karen Leslie, Gregg. Educ: Am. Landscape Sch, Des Moines, Iowa. Polit. & Govt. Pos: Mo. State Rep, 64-66; Ralls Co. Dem. Party. Bus. & Prof. Pos: Farmer, nurseryman and orchardist in Ralls Co; operates orchards in Dunklin Co. and owns and operates a Garden Center and Nursery at Hannibal. Mil. Serv: Army, 45-46, served Hq. over Hq, Allied Forces, Naples, Italy; Recipient of Army Occup. Medal, German, and Victory Medal, European-African-Middle East. Theater. Mem: Past pres. of Ralls Co. U. Exten. Coun; past pres. Ralls Co. Farm Bur; Hannibal Masonic Lodge 188; Knignt Templar; Moolah Shrine; Hannibal C. of C; Nemo Shrine. Rel: Baptist. Mailing Add: RFD 3, Hannibal, Mo. 63401. (1967)

SINCLAIR, DONALD Conservative
Minn. State Sen.
b. 1/9/99; married; c. Three. Educ: Univ. of Minn, 24. Polit. & Govt. Pos: Minn. State Sen, 47-, Pres-Pro Tem, Minn. State Senate, 65. Bus. & Prof. Pos: Farmer. Mil. Serv: Navy, World War I. Mailing Add: Stephen, Minn. 56757. (1967)

SINCLAIR, IVAN BENJAMIN 'BEN' R
b. Pittsburgh, Pa, 6/19/33; s. Ivan Benjamin Sinclair, Jr. and Emily Armstrong S; m. 4/16/66 to Patricia Ann Meredith. Educ: Pa. State Univ, B.S, 55; Dickinson Sch. Law, LL.B, 48; Omicron Delta Kappa; mgr, Men's Debate Team; chmn. bd, Dramatics and Forensics; chmn, Lion Party; chmn, Pa. Interstate Debaters' Cong; regional dir, Intercol. Conf. Govt; mem, Gymnastics Team and All Univ. Cabinet. Polit. & Govt. Pos: Chmn, Pa. State Univ. Young Rep. Club, 51-53; chmn, Am. for Eisenhower, 52; pres, Centre Co. Young Rep. Club, 53-54; chmn, Pa. Youth for Eisenhower-Nixon, 56; chmn, Youth for Scott-McGonigle, 58; pres, Cent. Delaware Co. Young Rep. Club, 62-63 & 64-66; Delaware Co. chmn, Win with Scott, 64; mem. exec. bd, Delaware Co. Young Rep, 64-68; asst. legal counsel, Young Rep. Pa, 64-66, chmn, 66-68; treas. region II, Mid-Atlantic Coun. Young Rep. Clubs, 65-66; mem. adv. bd, Rep. State Cmt, 66-68; mem. exec. cmt. and chmn. spec. groups cmt, Young Rep. Nat. Fedn, 67-69; mem. exec. cmt, Citizens for Richard S. Schweiker, 68; Delaware Co. chmn, Lawyers Cmt. to Elect Judge Hannum to a Full Term, 68; alternate del, Rep. Nat. Conv, 68. Bus. & Prof. Pos: Mem. bd. dirs, Chester Savings & Loan Asn; assoc, Bell, Pugh, Sinclair & Prodoehl, Media, Pa, currently. Mil. Serv: Pvt, Pa. Nat. Guard, 58-64, with serv. as Chief Opers. and Legal Asst, Off. Staff Judge Adv, Ft. Knox, Ky; Capt. and Asst. Legal Officer, 446th Civil Affairs Co, Army Res, 64-67. Mem: Pa. Bar Asn. (bd. gov. and chmn, young lawyers sect, 65-66); Delaware Co. Bar Asn. (v.chmn. and secy, past chmn, v.chmn. and secy. young lawyers sect, former chmn. legal serv. cmt, past chmn. speakers cmt. and court house tour cmt); former pres, Pa. State Alumni Club of Delaware Co; exec. bd, Pa. Coun. Abolish the Penalty of Death; SAR (secy, Phila-Continental Chap); chmn, Upper Providence Twp. March of Dimes, 65-66; Am. Civil Liberties Union; Ripon Soc; Citizens Coun. of Delaware Co; Delaware Co. Hist. Soc. Admitted to practice before the U.S. Supreme Court. Rel: Methodist. Legal Res: 1221 Robin Hill, Rose Tree Rd, Media, Pa. 19063. Mailing Add: Court House Sq. N, Media, Pa. 19063.

SINCLAIR, JAMES MONCRIEFF D
b. Nashville, Tenn, 5/20/03; s. William Moncrieff Sinclair and Della Heaston S; m. 4/5/34 to Rose Beniche; c. James M, Jr, Joan (Mrs. McCullough) and William Joseph. Educ: Univ. Calif, Berkeley, A.B, 24; Gamma Eta Gamma. Polit. & Govt. Pos: Mem, Los Angeles Co. Gen. Hosp. Adv. Cmn, 59-60; Presidential elector, 64. Mem: Pres, N.E. Los Angeles Bar Asn; 56; pres, Highland Park Optimists, 59; Bd. of Gov, YMCA; Calif. Bar Asn; Elks. Rel: Presbyterian. Mailing Add: 3749 Aguilar St, Los Angeles, Calif. 90065.

SINCLAIR, JOHN PAUL D
b. Ellerslie, Ga, 7/20/17; s. George Lott Sinclair and Stella Ridenhour S; m. 5/11/41 to Ernestine Woodson; c. Stella Carol, Paula Ava and John Paul Jr. Educ: Waverly Hall High Sch, 34; W. Ga. Col. Polit. & Govt. Pos: Mem, Macon Co. Bd. of Educ, Ga, 55-; Ga. State Rep, 61-66. Bus. & Prof. Pos: Bldg. material dealer. Mil. Serv: Vet, 42-46; World War II Victory Medal; Am. Serv. Medal; Good Conduct Medal; Asiatic Pac. Medal. Mem: Mason; Kiwanis. Rel: Methodist. Mailing Add: P.O. Box 470, Montezuma, Ga. 31063.

SINCLAIR, JOHN RICHLEY R
b. Detroit, Mich, 3/11/35; s. C. Gordon Sinclair and Kathryn Richley S; single. Educ: Wayne State Univ, B.S. in Journalism, 58. Polit. & Govt. Pos: Admin. Asst. to U.S. Rep. William S. Broomfield, Mich, 67- Mil. Serv: Entered as Pvt, Army, 58, released as SP-4, 58. Rel: Protestant. Legal Res: Royal Oak, Mich. Mailing Add: 1400 S. Joyce St, C 1605, Arlington, Va. 22202.

SINCLAIR, ORRIETTE COINER R
First V.Chmn, Idaho Rep. Party
b. Twin Falls, Idaho, 9/17/21; d. Walter A. Coiner and Marietta Hunsberger Detweiler C; m. 4/21/46 to James Alfred Sinclair; c. Rose Ann, Jan, Judy and James Walter. Educ: Univ. Utah, 39-40; Univ. Idaho, B.S. in Bus, 43; Kappa Kappa Gamma. Polit. & Govt. Pos: Secy. to Twin Falls Co. Rep. Party chmn, Idaho, 44; dep. clerk of the dist. court, Twin Falls Co, 44-45; pres, Twin Falls Co. Young Women Rep. Club, 'Pettycoat Pollys,' 45, 63 & 64, secy, 66; state committeewoman, Twin Falls Co. Rep. Cent. Cmt, 64, 66 & 68-, secy, 66; del, Idaho State Rep. Assembly, 64, 66 & 68, permanent secy, 66; v.chmn, Appreciation Day Cmt. honoring Representative George Hansen, 66; secy, Fifth Region of Idaho Rep, 68; first v.chmn, Idaho Rep. Party, 68- Bus. & Prof. Pos: Secy, Bur. of Entomology & Plant Quarantine, 43-44; secy, E.W. McRoberts & Co, 45-46. Mem: Kappa Kappa Alumnae Club; Pan Hellenic; Am. Legion Auxiliary; PEO; Int. Toastmistress Clubs; state and local Rep. orgns. Rel: Presbyterian. Legal Res: 262 Lincoln, Twin Falls, Idaho 83301. Mailing Add: P.O. Box 249, Twin Falls, Idaho 83301.

SINDELAR, CHARLES D
b. Manitowoc, Wis, 1/30/17; s. Charles Sindelar Sr. and Anna Benes S; m. 9/7/40 to Janet Zima; c. Michael, Peter, Barbara and Anna Marie. Educ: La Salle Exten. Univ; Milwaukee Sch. Eng. Polit. & Govt. Pos: Pres, City Coun, Manitowoc, Wis, 63, alderman, 57-64; secy-treas, Eighth Cong. Dist. Dem. Party, 63-69. Bus. & Prof. Pos: Owner, Sindelar's Wallcleaning Serv, 51- Mil. Serv: Entered as Pvt, Army, 45, released as S/Sgt, 46, after serv. in Pac; Asiatic-Pac. Theater Ribbon; Victory Medal; Army of Occupation Medal. Mem: K. of C; Sierra; Musicians Union; Manitowoc Symphony Orchestra. Rel: Catholic; choir dir. Mailing Add: 708 Chicago St, Manitowoc, Wis. 54220.

SINES, THELMA L. D
b. Creek, Tenn, 8/31/18; d. Walter L. Galloway and Recie M. Cole G; m. 6/18/38 to Ralph K. Sines; c. Barbara Jolene, Leton Earl and Vicki Jewel. Educ: Delphi High Sch, grad, 37; Nat. Honor Soc. Polit. & Govt. Pos: Precinct vice committeewoman, Dem. Party, Ind, 40-56; v.chmn, Carroll Co. Dem. Cent. Cmt, Ind, 56-66; mgr, Auto License Br, 61-66. Bus. & Prof. Pos: Clerk, Co. Auditors Off, Ind, 58-60. Mem: Am. Legion Auxiliary; Carroll Co. Dem. Women's Club; Bus. Prfnl. Women's Club; Modern Homemaker's Demonstration Club. Rel: Protestant. Mailing Add: R.R. 4, Box 89, Delphi, Ind. 46923.

SINGER, JAMES MILFORD D
Mem, Santa Cruz Co. Dem. Cent. Cmt, Calif.
b. Leavenworth, Kans, 7/24/04; s. James Jones Singer and Mary Ida Coon S; m. 5/19/28 to Martha Sewall Barnes; c. James Milford, Jr, John Alfred and Frances Dawn (Mrs. Dorbin). Educ: Gardena High Sch, Calif. Polit. & Govt. Pos: Supt. of mails, Gardena, Calif, asst. postmaster, until 59; mem, Santa Cruz Co. Dem. Cent. Cmt, 68-; pres, Sr. Citizens Dem. Club, Santa Cruz, currently; treas, Santa Cruz Co. Dem. Club, currently. Mem: DeMolay. Legion of Honor. Rel: Protestant. Legal Res: 3701 Glen Haven Rd, Soquel, Calif. 95073. Mailing Add: P.O. Box 422, Soquel, Calif. 95073.

SINGER, M. KEITH R
Colo. State Rep.
b. Colorado Springs, Colo, 12/4/27; married; c. five. Educ: Univ. of Colo, B.A. in polit. sci; Univ. Denver, LL.B. Polit. & Govt. Pos: Chmn, drafting cmt, Arvado City Charter; mem, Rep. Party Cmt, for Legis. Recruitment and Training; presently; Colo. State Rep, presently. Bus. & Prof. Pos: Attorney-at-law. Mailing Add: 8830 W. 66th Ave, Arvado, Colo. 80002.

SINGER, RUTH D
b. Andover, Hants, Eng, 3/12/41; d. Philip Singer and Betty Segal S; single. Polit. & Govt. Pos: Secy. to U.S. Rep. Joseph Y. Resnick, 28th Dist, N.Y, 65-68. Rel: Jewish. Mailing Add: 1300 Army-Navy Dr, Arlington, Va. 22202. (1967)

SINGER, SAM S. D
b. Plains, Ga, 10/29/28; s. Julian H. Singer and Lucille Sumner S; m. 6/21/51 to Ann Jennings; c. Sam S, Susan McKay. Educ: Grad. Webb Sch, Bell Buckle, Tenn; attended Ga. Tech, 3 years; Alpha Tau Omega. Polit. & Govt. Pos: Ga. State Rep, 55-66; mayor, Lumpkin, 52-55; Lumpkin city coun, 50-51. Bus. & Prof. Pos: Merchant; v.pres, Lumpkin Develop. Corp. Mem: Mason; Shriner; Lion. Rel: Methodist. Mailing Add: Lumpkin, Ga. 31815. (1967)

SINGLETON, ERNEST D
La. State Rep.
b. Amite, La, 9/3/11; s. Fred Singleton and Annie Thompson S; m. 6/1/35 to Evelyn Caro McCoy; c. Ernest Lynn. Educ: High Sch. Polit. & Govt. Pos: Pres, St. Helena Parish Sch. Bd, La, 46-64; pres, St. Helena Parish Bd. of Supvrs. of Elecs, 52-60; La. State Rep, 64- Bus. & Prof. Pos: Foreman, St. Helena Parish Police Jury, 31-35; supt. of shipyards, Equitable Equipment Co, 39-41 and Allen Boat Co, 41-45; dairy farmer, 45-59; pres, Ernest Singleton, Inc, 58- Mem: Bd. dirs, Forest Festival Asn; Int. Operating Engrs. Rel: Catholic. Mailing Add: Greensburg, La. 70441.

SINGLETON, SAMUEL MORRIS R
Chmn, Emery Co. Rep. Party, Utah
b. Ferron, Utah, 10/19/27; s. Morris Samuel Singleton and Mary Elva Huntsman S; m. 10/13/55 to Alta Mae Brown; c. Morris Wayne, Kyle Jay and Myron Bruce. Educ: Brigham Young Univ, B.S, 52; Univ. Utah, Grad. Work, 62-64; Kent State Univ, Grad. Work, 65; Utah State Univ, Master of Educ, 69. Polit. & Govt. Pos: Chmn, Ferron Precinct Rep. Party, Utah, 55-60; chmn, Emery Co. Rep. Party, 60- Bus. & Prof. Pos: Secy, Emery Co. Teachers Asn, 58-60. Mil. Serv: Entered as Pvt, Army, 50, released as Cpl, 52, after serv. in 5th AAA Bn. Mem: Life mem, Nat. Educ. Asn; Utah Educ. Asn; Utah Library Asn; Am. Legion; Farm Bur. Coin collecting. Rel: Latter-day Saint. Mailing Add: Ferron, Utah 84523.

SINGLEY, VASCO MONETT D
Miss. State Rep.
b. Columbia, Miss, 2/2/18; s. Monett Malachi Singley and Agnes Thornhill S; m. 12/6/37 to Edna Earl Coward; c. Julie (Mrs. Pinkston), Mary (Mrs. A. Sandt) and Sime. Educ: Forest Co. Agr. Sch, 34-36. Polit. & Govt. Pos: Miss. State Rep, Marion-Walthal Co, 68- Mailing Add: Rt. 2 Box 71E, Columbia, Miss. 39429.

SINK, JOSEPH STANFORD D
b. Lexington, N.C, 1/12/11; s. Fred O. Sink and Mary Cecil S; m. 12/3/36 to Dorothea Dorsett; c. Joe Jr. and Wood D. Educ: Duke Univ, 29-33. Polit. & Govt. Pos: N.C. State Sen, 63-66. Bus. & Prof. Pos: Newspaper publisher. Mem: Red Men; POSA; Jr. OUAM; WOW; Mason; Shriner. Rel: Methodist; bd. of stewards, Methodist Church. Mailing Add: 400 Duke Dr, Lexington, N.C. 27292. (1967)

SINKS, JOHN R. R
Ind. State Rep.
Educ: Ind. Univ, A.M; Ball State Teacher's Col. Polit. & Govt. Pos: Ind. State Rep, currently. Bus. & Prof. Pos: Teacher govt, Elmhurst High Sch, Fort Wayne, Ind. Mil. Serv: Air Force, Korea. Mem: Nat. Educ. Asn; Ind. State Teachers Asn. Rel: Episcopal. Mailing Add: 13311 W. Hamilton Lane, Ft. Wayne, Ind. 46804. (1967)

SINNER, GEORGE ALBERT D
b. Fargo, N.Dak, 5/29/28; s. Albert F. Sinner and Katherine Wild S; m. 8/10/51 to Elizabeth Jane Baute; c. Robert, Martha, James, George, Paula, Gerard, Elizabeth, Mary Jo and Joseph. Educ: St. John's Univ, B.A, 50. Polit. & Govt. Pos: N.Dak. State Sen, 62-66; mem. platform cmt, Dem. Nat. Party, 64; cand. for U.S. Rep, First Dist, N.Dak, 64; regional chmn. state educ. policy cmt, Fourth Dist. Dem. Party; chmn, S.E. Regional Ment. Health Center, 66-67; del, Dem. Nat. Conv, 64 & 68; v.pres, N.Dak. Bd. of Higher Educ, currently. Bus. & Prof. Pos: Partner, Sinner Bros. & Bresnahan, Beef & Pure Seed Farm, 53- Mil. Serv: Enlisted in N.Dak. Air Nat. Guard, 50, released as Airman 1/C, 52, after active duty in Air Force Strategic Air Command, U.S. Mem: Dir, S.E. N.Dak. Ment. Health and Retardation Serv. Unit, Inc; legis. adv, N.Dak. Cattle Feeders Asn; chmn, N.Dak. Gov. Adv. Cmt. on Sugar Beets; Am. Legion; N.Dak. Ment. Health Asn. Rel: Catholic. Mailing Add: Box 458, Casselton, N.Dak. 58012.

SIPLE, RANDOLPH EDWARD R
b. Glendale, Calif, 6/5/33; s. Edward Randolph Siple and Sadie Bradford S; m. 6/1/63 to Ann Brady; c. Shaun Derek. Educ: Stanford Univ, A.B, 55; Univ. South. Calif, LL.B, 61; Delta Upsilon; Phi Delta Phi. Polit. & Govt. Pos: Rep. cand, Calif. State Assembly, 68; mem, Ventura Co. Rep. Cent. Cmt. and Calif. Rep. State Cent. Cmt, 68-69. Mil. Serv: Entered as 2nd Lt, Army, 56, released as 1st Lt, 58, after serv. in 14th Armored Cavalry Regt, Seventh Army, Germany; Lt, Naval Res, 64- Mem: Am. and Calif. State Bar Asns; Elks; Navy League. Rel: Protestant. Mailing Add: 305 Mariposa Dr, Ventura, Calif. 93001.

SIRIANNI, CARMEL A. R
b. Carbondale, Pa, 9/14/22; d. John Sirianni (deceased) and Amelia Pascoe S; single. Educ: Bloomsburg State Col, Bloomsburg, B.S, 44; Buchnell Univ, Lewisburg, M.S. in Educ, 52; Marywood Col, Scranton, M.S. in Guid, 59. Polit. & Govt. Pos: Committeewoman, Susquehanna Co. Rep. Cmt, 54-66, secy, 56-60, finance chmn, 62; del, Rep. Nat. Conv, 64; former pres, Susquehanna Co. Rep. Woman, 6 years and former v.chmn, 8 years. Bus. & Prof. Pos: Teacher, Hop Bottom High Sch, Pa, 45-58; guid. dir, Mt. View High Sch, Kingsley, 59-66. Mem: Delta Kappa Gamma; Pa Counselors Asn; Pa. Deans and Counselors Asn; APAG; Montrose Country Club; Elkview Country Club; Hop Bottom Women's Club; pres, Susquehanna, Wyoming Deanery of Cath. Women, 2 years; St. Patrick Altar and Rosary Soc, Nicholson, Pa. Rel: Catholic. Mailing Add: Hop Bottom, Pa. 18824. (1967)

SIROIS, LEO O. R
N.H. State Rep.
b. Lesle Verte, Can, 10/20/97; s. Simon Sirois and Eugenie Chenard S; m. 4/6/19 to Lillian M. Rousseau. Educ: St. Louis High Sch, Nashua, N.H, grad, 14. Polit. & Govt. Pos: Clerk, Parks and Recreation Cmn, N.H, 34-59; N.H. State Rep, 69- Bus. & Prof. Pos: Owner and operator, Clothing store, 30-59; Retired. Mil. Serv: Entered as Pvt, Air Force, 17, released as Sgt, 19, after serv. in 836th Squadron, Overseas, 17-19. Mem: Charter mem, life mem. Am. Legion (post comdr, del, 50th Anniversary Conv, 69); VFW; Cath. War Vet; Moose (gov. 2 years, fel. degree); participant, 200th year Hillsborough Co. Celebration and 150 years State House Celebration, 69. Awards from Am. Legion and Moose. Rel: Catholic. Mailing Add: 28 Park Ave, Nashua, N.H. 03060.

SISCO, EDWARD R
N.J. State Sen.
b. Paterson, N.J, 7/3/23; s. George Edward Sisco and Jessie Steele S; m. 12/7/46 to Evelyn Youngster; c. Nancy, Mark and Lori. Educ: Paterson High Sch, N.J, grad; Travel Mgr. Int, grad, 49. Polit. & Govt. Pos: Councilman, Wayne, N.J, 61-64, coun. pres, 62-63 and mayor, 64 & 66-; N.J. State Sen, Passaic Co, 68- Bus. & Prof. Pos: Secy-treas, Horizons Travel Serv, 63-68; pres, T-Bow Inn Int, 64-69; dir, Ramapo Bank, 68-69; pres, Willowbrook Inn Inc, 69. Mil. Serv: T/Sgt, Army, 43-46, serv. in Army Ord, ETO. Mem: Lions; C. of C; Am. Legion. Rel: Protestant. Legal Res: 756 Black Oak Ridge Rd, Wayne, N.J. 07470. Mailing Add: P.O. Box 744, Wayne, N.J. 07470.

SISCO, FRIEDMAN R
Chmn, Washington Co. Rep. Cmt, Ark.
b. Delmar, Ark, 8/11/13; s. C.P. Sisco and Lucy Sims S; m. 4/1/38 to Helen Lucille Vierheller; c. Charles Paul and Kenneth. Educ: Ark. Med. Sch, M.D, 37. Polit. & Govt. Pos: Chmn, Wash. Co. Rep. Cmt, Ark, currently. Mem: Rotary; Wash. Co. Rep. Club; VFW; Farm Bur; various med. socs. Legal Res: 700 N. Mill, Springdale, Ark. 72764. Mailing Add: P.O. Box 65, Springdale, Ark. 72764.

SISCO, JOSEPH JOHN
Asst. Secy. of State for Near East. and S. Asian Affairs
b. Chicago, Ill, 10/31/19; m. 3/26/46 to Jean Head; c. Carol and Jane. Educ: Knox Col, B.A, 41; Univ. Chicago, M.A, 47, Ph.D, 50. Polit. & Govt. Pos: Mem. staff, Dept. of State, 51-, polit. adv, U.S. dels. to UN Gen. Assembly, 51-, dep. dir, Off. of UN Polit. Affairs, 58-61, dir, 61-63, Dep. Asst. Secy. of State for Int. Orgn. Affairs, 63-65, Asst. Secy. of State for Int. Orgn. Affairs, 65-69, Asst. Secy. of State for Near East. and S.Asian Affairs, 69- Mil. Serv: 1st Lt, Inf, Army, 41-45. Publ: Numerous articles on int. orgn. and for. affairs. Mem: Am. Polit. Sci. Asn; Am. Soc. Int. Law; Am. For. Serv. Asn; Phi Beta Kappa; Tau Kappa Epsilon. State Dept. Superior Serv. Award, 60. Mailing Add: 5334 Falmouth Rd, Washington, D.C. 20016.

SISITSKY, ALAN DAVID D
Mass. State Rep.
b. Springfield, Mass, 6/4/42; s. Eli Joseph Sisitsky and Dorothy Dietz S; single. Educ: Cornell Univ, B.A, 64; Yale Law Sch, LL.B, 67; Phi Beta Kappa; Phi Alpha Delta. Polit. & Govt. Pos: Mass. State Rep, 69- Bus. & Prof. Pos: Attorney, Choate, Hall & Stewart, Boston, 68-69. Mil. Serv: Lt.(jg), Navy. Mem: Am, Boston, Hampden Co. and Mass. Bar Asns; Elks. Rel: Jewish. Mailing Add: 54 Draper St, Springfield, Mass. 01108.

SISK, ARTHUR C, SR. R
Chmn, Lee Co. Rep. Party, Ark.
b. Mountianview, Ark, 3/18/11; s. Arthur Stephen Sisk and Amanda Bell Freeman S; m. 3/19/38 to Delphia Ethel Farris; c. Jimmie Dee (Mrs. Millard) and A.C, Jr. Educ: Big Flat and Marianna High Schs, Ark. Polit. & Govt. Pos: Chmn, Lee Co. Rep. Party, Ark, 62-; elec. cmnr, Lee Co, 64-; alternate del, Rep. Nat. Conv, 68; mem, Ark. Soil and Water Conserv. Cmn. Bus. & Prof. Pos: Pres, Sisk Farms Inc, Lee Co, Ark, v.pres, Lee Co. Co-op Gin, Marianna, dir, Lee Co. Farm Co-op Store and v.pres, S&W Housing Develop. Co, currently. Mem: Lee Co. Farm Bur. (past pres. and currently dir); past

dir, Lee Co, Marianna C. of C. Farm Family of the Year, 62. Rel: Church of God of Prophecy. Legal Res: Route 3, Marianna, Ark, 72360. Mailing Add: Route 3, Box 243, Marianna, Ark. 72360.

SISK, B. F. D
U.S. Rep, Calif.
b. Montague, Tex, 12/14/10; s. Arthur Lee Sisk and Lavina Thomas S; m. 4/20/31 to Reta Mitchell; c. Mrs. J. Martin Temple and Mrs. John H. Pittenger. Educ: Abilene Christian Col, Abilene, Tex. Polit. & Govt. Pos: U.S. Rep, Calif, 54- Legal Res: Fresno, Calif. Mailing Add: 129 6th St. N.E, Washington, D.C. 20002.

SISLER, GEORGE FREDERICK R
b. Andrew, Iowa, 11/25/96; s. Charles Napolean Sisler and Sarah Marie Glade S; single. Educ: Univ. Dubuque, Iowa, A.B, 19; Univ. Chicago, M.A, 21. Polit. & Govt. Pos: Former Ill. State Rep. Bus. & Prof. Pos: V.pres, 1st Nat. Bank of Chicago, 31-61; George Sisler & Assocs, 62- Mil. Serv: Entered as Sgt, Army, 18, serv. in Students Army Training Corps, Black Horse Troop, 106th Cavalry, in 1930's. Mem: Past pres, Rotary Club 1, Chicago; Chicago Exec. Club; past pres, Church Fedn. of Greater Chicago; co-sponsor, The 1st Nat. Interfaith Conv. of Catholics, Jews and Protestants. Distinguished Achievement Award, Univ. of Chicago Alumni; Distinguished Serv. Citation, Chicago Cmn. on Human Rels. Rel: Presbyterian; Elder. Legal Res: Hancock Bldg, Chicago, Ill. 60611. Mailing Add: 38 S. Dearborn St, Chicago, Ill. 60603.

SITTLER, EDWARD LEWIS, JR. R
Co. Cmnr, Fayette Co, Pa.
b. Greensburg, Pa, 4/21/08; s. Edward Lewis Sittler and Stella Sheldrake S; m. 1936 to Harriet J. Long; c. Jane Ann and Richard E. Educ: Brown Univ, A.B, 30; Am. Col. Life Underwriters, C.L.U, 40; Phi Beta Kappa; Phi Delta Theta. Polit. & Govt. Pos: Judge of elec, Fifth Ward, Uniontown, Pa, 32-33; mayor, Uniontown, 48-50; U.S. Rep, Pa, 50; Pa. Rep. State Committeeman, 60-; co. cmnr, Fayette Co, 68- Mil. Serv: Entered as Pvt, Army, 43, released as Capt, 46, after serv. as Capt. of Ord, ETO. Mem: Rotary; Am. Soc. of C.L.U; Fraternal Order of Police; Uniontown Country Club; pres, Pa. State YMCA, 62-65; pres, Fayette Co. Develop. Coun; Uniontown C. of C; former dist. coun-dir, Pa. State C. of C; Pa. Econ. League. Rel: Disciples of Christ. Legal Res: Adams Lane, Uniontown, Pa. 15401. Mailing Add: P.O. Box 516, Uniontown, Pa. 15401.

SIZEMORE, JAMES MIDDLETON, JR. R
Chmn, Talladega Co. Rep. Party, Ala.
b. Mobile, Ala, 5/25/42; s. James Middleton Sizemore, Sr. and Margaret Davidson S; m. 8/6/66 to Stephenie Freeman; Educ: Howard Col, A.B, 63; Va. Sch. Law, LL.B, 66. Polit. & Govt. Pos: Exec. secy, Ala. Young Rep, 62-63 and Nat. Committeeman, 63-65; Dir, Region Six, Young Rep. Nat. Fedn, 65-67; chmn, Talladega Co. Rep. Party, Ala, currently. Bus. & Prof. Pos: Attorney-at-law, Bolton and Sizemore, Sylacauga, Ala, 67- Mem: Va, Ala. and Am. Bar Asns. Rel: Presbyterian. Legal Res: 208-A E. Fort Williams St, Sylacauga, Ala. 35150. Mailing Add: P.O. Box 227, Sylacauga, Ala. 35150.

SKAAR, ANDREW ORDEEN
Minn. State Rep.
b. Thief River Falls, 1/3/22; s. Ole Andrew Skaar and Olga Nelson S; single. Educ: Northwest Sch. of Agr, Univ. Minn, Crookston, 37-40. Polit. & Govt. Pos: Minn. State Rep, currently. Mem: Rotary. Rel: Lutheran. Mailing Add: Route 1, Thief River Falls, Minn. 56701.

SKAAR, HAROLD GEORGE D
b. Hannaford, N.Dak, 7/25/04; s. John Larson Skaar and Gertrude Hakastad S; m. 9/16/33 to Selma Louisa Larson; c. Ardis (Mrs. Detienne), Joyce (Mrs. Risan) and Marlys (Mrs. Nordquist). Educ: Pub. Schs. Polit. & Govt. Pos: Twp. supvr. and chmn, N.Dak, 44-58; treas, Sch. Bd, 46-59; Dem. committeeman, 56-69; N.Dak. State Rep, 57-69. Bus. & Prof. Pos: Farmer, 69- Mem: Bd. of dirs, Grain Terminal Asn; v.chmn, Co. Farmers Union; WOW. Rel: Lutheran. Mailing Add: New Town, N.Dak. 58763.

SKAGGS, JAMES CORDELL D
Mo. State Rep.
b. Ruble, Mo, 9/29/21; m. 3/17/39 to Ollie Gore; c. Shirley Jean, James Dale, Betty Jane, Donald Wayne, Lindell Paul, Chester Orville, Bertha Ann, Wanda Mae, Sandra Kay and David Leo. Educ: Reynolds Co. Pub. Schs. Polit. & Govt. Pos: Mem, Reynolds Co. Courts, Mo, 52-56; Mo. State Rep, 56- Bus. & Prof. Pos: Farmer and automobile salesman. Mil. Serv: S.Pac, 44-45. Mem: Odd Fellows; Am. Legion; VFW. Mailing Add: R.R. 2, Ellington, Mo. 63638. (1967)

SKAGGS, JOEL HENRY R
Chmn, LaRue Co. Rep. Cmt, Ky.
b. Buffalo, Ky, 1/20/12; s. Henry Blaine Skaggs and Viola Ferrill S; first wife deceased; m. 6/27/64 to Lucille Vocook; c. Marvin R, Carolyn K. and Steven R. Educ: High Sch. Polit. & Govt. Pos: Hwy. patrol, Ky. State Hwy. Dept, 44-48, with dept, 68-; co. elec. cmnr, 49-51; investr, U.S. Dept. of Agr, 54-62; chmn, LaRue Co. Rep. Cmt, Ky, presently and campaign chmn, 63. Bus. & Prof. Pos: Owner and operator of farm, 48- Mem: Mason; Lions; Nat. Farmers Orgn. Rel: Baptist. Mailing Add: R.F.D. 1, Buffalo, Ky. 42716.

SKAGGS, RAYMOND LEO R
Mo. State Rep.
b. Fredericktown, Mo, 10/25/33; s. Paul Skaggs and Ruth Schulte S; m. 9/25/57 to Martha Ann Walden; c. Cydney Rae and Whitney Ann. Educ: Univ. Mo, Columbia, B.S. in Agriculture, 55. Polit. & Govt. Pos: Pres, Madison Co. Rep. Club, Mo, 66-69; Mo. State Rep, 150th Dist, 69- Mil. Serv: Entered as Seaman Recruit, Navy, 55, released as PO 2/C, 57. Mem: Elks; Jr. C. of C; C. of C; Farm Bur. Outstanding Young Farmer, 66; Outstanding Young Man, 69. Rel: Catholic. Mailing Add: P.O. Box 346, Fredericktown, Mo. 63645.

SKARDA, WILLIAM R, JR. R
Nebr. State Sen.
b. Omaha, Nebr; m. 1943; c. Cheryl, Christine. Educ: South High Sch. Polit. & Govt. Pos: Nebr. State Sen, 59- Bus. & Prof. Pos: Pub. Rels. Man. Mem: Rep. to Assoc. Civic Clubs of Omaha and Douglas Co; past pres, Better Omaha Club; Czech Civic Alliance; S. 13th St. Merchants; Eagles Club; Polish-American Civic Club; Nebr. Game and Hunt Club; Omaha Traffic Club; S.E. Improvement Club; Old Timers Baseball Asn. Mailing Add: 1720 Monroe St, Omaha, Nebr. 68107. (1967)

SKEATE, JOHN P. DFL
b. Manannah, Minn, 3/23/11; s. Charles Skeate and Fanny Koch S; wid; c. John E. and Thomas. Educ: Pub. High Sch; Minn. Sch. of Bus. Polit. & Govt. Pos: Precinct chmn, Minneapolis First Ward, Dem-Farmer-Labor Party, 47-48, ward chmn, 48-58, state del, 48-58, chmn, Third Cong. Dist, 54-56; Minn. State Rep, 52-69. Bus. & Prof. Pos: Bus. assoc, Cent. Ave. Commercial Asn; polit. dir, T.S.C. 32, P.E.C, 59-60; bus. mgr, Local Union 664, 61-69. Mil. Serv: Entered as Pvt, Minn. State Guard, 46, released as Sgt, 47; Good Conduct Medal. Mem: Eagles; Moose; K. of C; United Appeal; Mothers March on Polio; March of Dimes; M.A.R.C; YMCA; PTA; Local Union 664. Awards from March of Dimes and United Appeal. Rel: Catholic. Mailing Add: 1814 Ulysses St. N.E, Minneapolis, Minn. 55418.

SKEEN, JOSEPH RICHARD R
Minority Leader, N.Mex. State Sen.
m. 11/17/45 to Mary Helen Jones; c. Mary Elisa and Mikell Lee. Educ: Tex. A&M, B.S. in Eng. Polit. & Govt. Pos: Chmn, N.Mex. Rep. Cent. Cmt, 61-65; N.Mex. State Sen, 61-, Minority Leader, N.Mex. State Sen, 65- Bus. & Prof. Pos: Owner, Buckhorn Ranch, Picacho, N.Mex, 54-; owner and pres, Brown Flying Serv, Inc, 67- Mil. Serv: Navy, World War II, Air Force. Mem: N.Mex. Livestock Bur; N.Mex. Wool Growers; N.Mex. Cattle Growers. Mailing Add: Picacho, N.Mex. 88343.

SKELTON, ARCH MASON D
b. Higginsville, Mo, 4/23/32; s. Arch Mason Skelton and Harriett Frances Oglesby S; m. 8/7/57 to Lee Ann Hill; c. Samuel Arch, Melinda Lee and Susan Hill. Educ: William Jewel Col, 50-52; Mo. Univ, A.B, 57; Mo. Univ. Sch. Law, J.D, 58; Phi Delta Phi; Kappa Alpha Order. Polit. & Govt. Pos: Pres, Green Co. Young Dem, Mo, 61-62; chmn, Greene Co. Dem. Cent. Cmt, 62-66; gen. chmn, Jackson Day Banquet, 67-69; del, Dem. Nat. Conv, 68. Bus. & Prof. Pos: Assoc, Mann, Walter, Powell, Burkart & Weathers, 58-59, Chinn and White, 59-61 and Chinn, White & Dickey, 61-63; partner, White, Dickey & Skelton, 63-65 and Skelton and Bonacker, 65-68; Attorney, Arch M. Skelton, 68- Mil. Serv: Entered as Pvt, Army, 53, released as Pfc, 55. Mem: Greene Co, Mo. State and Am. Bar Asns; Am. Col. Trial Lawyers; Mo. Asn. of Claimant Attorneys; Masons; AF&AM; Elks; U.S. Jr. C. of C; Springfield C. of C; Springfield Speech & Hearing Asn; Ozark Empire Coun, Boy Scouts; Scottish Rite Bodies; Shrine. Recipient, Outstanding Young Man of the Year Award, 65. Rel: Methodist. Legal Res: 2714 E. Pythian, Springfield, Mo. 65802. Mailing Add: 306 W. Court, Springfield, Mo. 65803.

SKELTON, BYRON GEORGE D
b. Florence, Tex, 9/1/05; s. Clarence Edgar Skelton and Avis Ione Bowmer S; m. 11/28/31 to Ruth Alice Thomas; c. Sue Helen (Mrs. Jerry Dwain Ramsey) and Sandra Ruth (Mrs. Robert Terrance Farrell). Educ: Univ. Tex, B.A, 27, M.A, 28 and LL.B, 31; Phi Beta Kappa; Pi Sigma Alpha; Sigma Delta Pi; Tejas Club; pres, Students' Asn; Cowboys; Students' Assembly; permanent pres, Acad. Class of 27. Polit. & Govt. Pos: Co. attorney, Bell Co, Tex, 34-38; spec. asst. to U.S. Ambassador to Argentina, 42-45; city attorney, Temple, Tex, 45-60; del, Dem. State Conv, 46-64; del, Dem. Nat. Conv, 48, 56, 60 & 64, mem. site cmt, 64; exec. cmt. chmn, Tex. Dem. Adv. Cmt, 54-55, chmn, 55-56; Dem. Nat. Committeeman, Tex. and mem. credentials cmt, Dem. Nat. Cmt, 56-64; mem, Nat. Inaugural Cmt, 61; judge, U.S. Court of Claims, 66- Bus. & Prof. Pos: Attorney-at-law, Temple, Tex, 31-34, 38-42 and 45-; dir, First Nat. Bank, Temple, 46-; pres, Temple Indust. Found, 66-; partner, Skelton, Bowmer and Courtney, Temple, Tex. and Pehle, Lesser, Mann, Riemer and Luxford, Wash, D.C. Mem: Am. Bar Asn; legis. cmt. and admin. justice cmt, State Bar of Tex, 62-, grievance cmt, 60-62; past pres, Bell-Lampasas-Mills Co. Bar Asn, 60; Am. Law Inst; Am. Judicature Soc; pres, Temple Kiwanis, 33 and 38; dir. and past pres, Temple C. of C, 46-47; past worshipful master and past dist. dep. grand master, Temple Masonic Lodge, Shrine; past pres, YMCA, United Serv. Orgn. Coun. and Univ. Tex. Ex-Students Asn; hon. mem, Delta Theta Phi, D.C. Bar Asn. and Nat. Lawyers Club. Admitted to practice law before U.S. Circuit Court Appeals, 37, U.S. Supreme Court, 46, Fed. Commun. Cmn, 50, Tax Court U.S, 52, U.S. Treas. Dept, 52 and Interstate Commerce Cmn, 53. Rel: Methodist. Legal Res: 819 N. 11th St, Temple, Tex. 76501. Mailing Add: Watergate East, Apt. 708-S, 2500 Virginia Ave. N.W, Washington, D.C. 20037.

SKELTON, DARRELL J. D
b. Pratt, Kans, 5/4/24; married; c. six. Educ: Acct. and Law. Polit. & Gov. Pos: Colo. State Rep; serv. as precinct committeeman, dist. Capt. for his party. Bus. & Prof. Pos: Attorney; operates own bus. Mailing Add: 1869 Glen Gyle Dr, Lakewood, Colo. 80215. (1967)

SKELTON, IKE N, JR. D
b. Lexington, Mo. 12/20/31; s. Ike N. Skelton and Carolyn Boone S; m. 7/22/61 to Susan Anding; c. Ike N, V, James A. and Harry Page. Educ: Lexington High Sch, grad, 49; Wentworth Mil. Acad, grad, 51; Univ. Mo, A.B, 53, LL.B, 56; Univ. Edinburgh, Scotland, summer 53; Phi Beta Kappa; Phi Delta Phi; Sigma Chi. Polit. & Govt. Pos: Prosecuting attorney, Lafayette Co, Mo, 57-60; spec. asst. to Attorney Gen, 61-63; chmn, Lafayette Co. Cent. Dem. Cmt, 62-66. Bus. & Prof. Pos: Attorney-at-Law, Bradley, Skelton & Schelp, 56-; dir. and secy, Wellington Bank, 69. Mem: Lafayette Co, Am. and Mo. Bar Asns; Am. Trial Lawyers Asn; dir, Lions Club; Mason; Elks. Rel: Christian Church. Mailing Add: 712 Highland Ave, Lexington, Mo. 64067.

SKELTON, JOHN BOONE D
b. Jacksonville, Fla, 10/22/39; s. Isaac Newton Skelton and Carolyn Marie Boone S; m. 8/20/65 to Kathryn Susan Barnard. Educ: Univ. Mo-Columbia, B.S, 65; Sigma Chi. Polit. & Govt. Pos: Chmn, Lafayette Co. Dem. Cent. Cmt, Mo, 66-68; del, Nat. Dem. Conv, 68. Bus. & Prof. Pos: Asst. cashier, Bank of Odessa, Mo, 66-68; pres, Wellington Bank, 68- Mil. Serv; Seaman, Coast Guard, 59, released as Storekeeper 2/C, 63, after serv. in Mediterranean

Sect. Mem: Mo. Banker's Asn; VFW; Lions; Elks. Rel: Christian Church. Legal Res: Wellington, Mo. 64097. Mailing Add: Box 116, Wellington, Mo. 64097.

SKELTON, KEITH D. D
Ore. State Rep.
b. Cambridge Springs, Pa, 5/6/18; s. Benjamin E. Skelton and Anna K. Kahrl S; div; c. Carol Jane, Ann Elizabeth, K. Douglas and Thomas Blake; m. to Betty Roberts. Educ: Edinboro State Col, B.S; Univ. Mich. Grad. Sch; Syracuse Univ. and Univ. Wash. at Seattle Law Sch, J.D, Univ. Ore Grad. Sch; Pi Sigma Alpha. Polit. & Govt. Pos: Ore. State Rep, 57-61 & 66-; mem, Lane Co. Planning Cmn, 63-65; del, Dem. Nat. Conv, 68. Bus. & Prof. Pos: Attorney, private practice, 49-; assoc. prof. law, Univ. Ore, 63-68; Portland State Univ, 68- Mil. Serv: Entered as Aviation Cadet, Army Air Force, 43, released as Capt, 45, after serv. as bomber pilot, Southwest Pac. Theater; Six Theater of War Ribbons; Air Medals with Five Clusters and others. Publ: Author, 'Legislative Interim Committees Created by Resolution,' 2/59 and 'The 1965 Oregon Workmen's Compensation Law: a Model for the States,' 12/65, Ore. Law Rev; ed, 'Workmen's Compensation in Oregon: A Symposium,' Univ. Ohio, 66. Mem: Am, Wash. State and Ore. State Bar Asns; Am. Judicature Soc; bd. mem, Am. Civil Liberties Union and others. Rel: Congregational. Mailing Add: 319 S.E. Gilham, Portland, Ore. 97215.

SKERRY, PATRICK JOSEPH D
Mayor, Medford, Mass.
b. Medford, Mass, 4/10/12; s. Patrick Joseph Skerry and Nora T. Fannon S; m. to Dorothy Bennett; c. Judith Ann (Mrs. Moniz), David Paul and Patricia Marie. Educ: Medford High Sch. Polit. & Govt. Pos: Del, Dem. Nat. Conv, 68; chmn. sch. cmt, Medford, Mass, ward alderman and city coun; mayor, Medford, 68- Mem: K. of C; St. Francis Holy Name Soc.(past pres). Rel: Catholic. Mailing Add: 92 Circuit Rd, Medford, Mass. 02155.

SKEVIN, JOHN M. D
N.J. State Assemblyman
Married; c. Five. Educ: St. John's Univ. Schs. of Commerce and Law, grad; Phi Delta Phi Int. Legal Fraternity. Polit. & Govt. Pos: N.J. State Assemblyman, currently; chmn, Bergen Co. Dem. Cmt. for Fair Elec. Rates, 62. Bus. & Prof. Pos: Practicing attorney, N.J. Mil. Serv: Army Vet. Mem: Chmn, Oradell Mental Health Fund Dr, 62; Bergen Co, N.J. and Am. Bar Asns; Am. Judicature Soc; chmn, Oradell Girl Scout Fund Dr, 64-65; Cubmaster, 64-65; K. of C; Holy Name Soc, St. Joseph's Roman Cath. Church; Nat. Coun. of Cath. Men. Rel: Roman Catholic. Mailing Add: 476 Bergen Blvd, Oradell, N.J. 07649.

SKIFFINGTON, JOHN JOSEPH, JR. D
R.I. State Rep.
b. Woonsocket, R.I, 7/28/18; m. to Helen Ann S. Educ: Woonsocket sch; La Salle Acad. Polit. & Govt. Pos: R.I. State Rep, 51-; del, Dem. Nat. Conv, 68; chmn, Woonsocket City Dem. Party, R.I, currently. Bus. & Prof. Pos: Rubber worker. Mil. Serv: Aviation Mech. 2/C. Mem: Pres. and former treas, Local 224, United Rubber Workers, AFL-CIO; exec. bd, Fairmount Post, Am. Legion No. 85; former mem, exec. bd, State CIO. Mailing Add: 394 Third Ave, Woonsocket, R.I. 02895. (1967)

SKINNER, ELLIOTT PERCIVAL D
b. Port-of-Spain, Trinidad, 6/20/24; m. to Thelma Garvin; c. Victor, Gale, Sagha and Touray. Educ: N.Y. Univ, B.A, 51; Columbia Univ, M.A, 52, Ph.D, 55. Polit. & Govt. Pos: Guest lectr, For. Serv. Inst; U.S. Ambassador, Upper Volta, 66-69. Bus. & Prof. Pos: Lectr. anthrop, Columbia Univ, 54-59 and N.Y. Univ, 59-63; prof. Columbia Univ, 63-66. Mil. Serv: Army, World War II. Publ: The Mossi of Upper Volta, 64; several publ. on Upper Volta. Legal Res: N.Y. Mailing Add: c/o U.S. Dept. of State Foreign Service, Washington, D.C. 20521. (1967)

SKINNER, ELMER L. D
b. 1919. Educ: Courses in bus. admin, cost acct, bus. econs. Polit. & Govt. Pos: N.Mex. State Rep, 61-67; Carlsbad City Coun. 4 years; Mayor of Carlsbad 1 year. Bus. & Prof. Pos: Pres, The Mine Supply Co. and Southwest Bearing Co; v.pres, San Mateo Bearings. Mem: First v.pres. Carlsbad C. of C; Kiwanis. Rel: Baptist. Mailing Add: P.O. Box 1330, Carlsbad, N.Mex. 88220. (1967)

SKIPTON, JOHN ALLEN R
Chmn, Ohio State Rep. Finance Cmt.
b. Marietta, Ohio, 2/21/19; s. Robert A. Skipton and Hazel Preston S; m. 7/14/42 to Edith Virginia Gardner; c. Craig Allen and Eileen. Educ: Ohio State Univ, LL.B, 48, B.Sc. in bus. admin, 46. Polit. & Govt. Pos: Dir. of research, Ohio Rep. State Cmt, 50-52; claims cmnr, Ohio Attorney Gen, 52; dir, Ohio Legis. Serv. Cmn, 53-57; dir. of finance, Ohio, 57-59; mem, Findlay City Sch. Bd, 61-63; mem, Hancock Co. Rep. Exec. Cmt, 61-; chmn, Ohio State Rep. Finance Cmt, Hancock Co, 61-; v.chmn. bd. trustees, Toledo State Col. of Medicine, 64-; secy-mem, Ohio Tax Study Cmn, 65-67. Bus. & Prof. Pos: Personnel officer, Remington-Rand, Inc, Marietta, Ohio, 41-42; attorney-at-law, Columbus, 49-50; asst. to v.pres, Marathon Oil Co, 59-63, mgr. pub. affairs, 63- Mil. Serv: Entered as Pvt, Air Force, 42, released as Capt, 46, after serv. in Statistical Control, Air Technical Servs. Mem: Bd. Dirs, Effective Citizens Orgn; Findlay Bar Asn; Rotary; Pub. Affairs Research Coun, Nat. Indust. Conf. Bd; pres, Hancock Ohio State Univ. Alumni Asn; Findlay Country Club; pub. affairs cmt, U.S. C. of C; Ohio and Findlay C. of C; Univ. Club, Columbus, Ohio; F&AM. Rel: Presbyterian. Legal Res: 943 Breezewood Court, Findlay, Ohio 45840. Mailing Add: 539 S. Main St, Findlay, Ohio 45840.

SKJERVOLD, PAUL ARNOLD DFL
Del, Dem-Farmer-Labor State Cent. Cmt, Minn.
b. Westbrook, Minn, 9/1/26; s. Hjalmar Saul Skjervold and Lillian Hedvig Osterberg S; m. 4/2/52 to June Elizabeth Lobdell; c. Kristafer Erik, Nathan Paul, Peter Alan and Sara Rose. Educ: Worthington Jr. Col; Univ. of Minn; William Mitchell Col. Law. Polit. & Govt. Pos: Spec. asst. attorney gen, Minn, 57-58, dep. attorney gen, 58-60; del, Dem-Farmer-Labor State Cent. Cmt, 66- Bus. & Prof. Pos: Attorney-at-Law. Mil. Serv: Entered as A/S, Navy, 45, released as Seaman, 46. Publ: Two Volumes of literature. Mem: Am. and Minn. Bar Asns; Am. Judicature Soc; Sons of Norway; NAACP; Am. Legion. Rel: Protestant. Mailing Add: Excelsior, Minn. 55331.

SKUBITZ, JOE R
U.S. Rep, Kans.
b. Frontenac, Kans; s. Joe Skubitz and Mary Youvan S; m. 9/27/30 to Mary Jess McClellan; c. Dan Joseph. Educ: Grad, Kans. State Col, B.S, M.S; George Wash. Univ; Spec. Citation from Kans. State Col. Polit. & Govt. Pos: Admin. asst. to Sen. Clyde M. Reed and Sen. Andrew F. Schoeppel; U.S. Rep, Kans, currently. Bus. & Prof. Pos: Licensed to Practice Law in Kans. and Wash, D.C. Legal Res: Pittsburg, Kans. 66762. Mailing Add: 7704 Glennon Dr, Bethesda, Md. 20034.

SLACK, C. TIMOTHY R
Pa. State Rep.
b. Coatesville, Pa, 4/11/13; s. Samuel M. Slack and Annie Watson S; m. 9/27/40 to Louise Gibney; c. C. Timothy and Wynann (Mrs. Ronald Moore). Educ: Lafayette Col, C.E, 35. Polit. & Govt. Pos: Chief of party surveys, Pa. Dept. of Hwys, 35-39; chief of party surveys, Pa. Turnpike Cmn, 40-42, dist. engr, 48-52; city councilman, Coatesville, 48-52 and 53-56; city engr, 56-58; Pa. State Rep, 61- Bus. & Prof. Pos: Consult. Engr. and surveyor, self-employed, 52-60. Mil. Serv: Entered as C.C.M, Seabees, 42, released as C.C.M. Perm, 46, after serv. in ETO, 43; European and Am. Theater Ribbons with Battle Citation. Mem: Pa. and Nat. Socs. Prfnl. Engrs; Am. Water Works Asn; Am. Mil. Engrs; Elks; Eagles; Moose; Lions; Pa. Aeronaut. Cmn. Rel: Presbyterian. Mailing Add: 129 S. Fifth Ave, Coatesville, Pa. 19320.

SLACK, JOHN M, JR. D
U.S. Rep, W.Va.
b. Charleston, W.Va, 3/18/15; married; c. One son. Educ: Va. Mil. Inst. Polit. & Govt. Pos: Former mem, Kanawha Co. Court, W.Va; U.S. Rep, W.Va, 58-, mem, House Cmt. on Appropriations, U.S. House of Rep; mem, James Madison Mem. Cmn, 60-; del, Dem. Nat. Conv, 60, 64 & 68; mem, U.S-Can. Interparliamentary Conf, 62, 64 & 68. Mem: Scottish Rite; York Rite; Mason; Shrine; Exchange Club; Elks. Rel: Presbyterian. Legal Res: Charleston, W.Va. Mailing Add: 2230 Rayburn House Office Bldg, Washington, D.C. 20515.

SLADE, ARTHUR ROY, SR. D
Committeeman, Ill. Dem. State Cent. Cmt.
b. Urbana, Ill, 4/10/10; s. William Henry Slade and Minnie May McGraw S; m. 4/10/28 to Ruby Bernice Smalley; c. Barbara (Mrs. Thomas Marshky), Arthur Roy, Jr. and Naomi (Mrs. John Hawn). Educ: Urbana Pub. Schs, Ill, 11 years. Polit. & Govt. Pos: Precinct committeeman, Ill. Dem. State Orgn, 48-; treas, Co. Dem. Reform Orgn, 58-62; Alderman, Urbana, Ill, 61-65; chmn, Urbana Dem. Cmt, 63-65; v.chmn, Cunningham Twp. Dem. Cmt, Ill, 65-; chmn, Urbana Dem. Picnic Grounds, 65-; representative committeeman, 48th Dist. Dem. State Orgn, 68-; committeeman, Ill. Dem. State Cent. Cmt, currently. Bus. & Prof. Pos: Owner, grocery bus, 49-56 and Concrete Construction Co, 53-68. Mil. Serv: Pvt, Army, 30-34. Rel: Protestant. Mailing Add: 806 E. Park St, Urbana, Ill. 61801.

SLADE, ROBERT HENRY D
b. Jersey City, N.J, 5/22/28; s. Bozy Slade and Geraldine Phillips Farrall S; m. 3/25/67 to Phoebe J. Williams; c. Robert H, Jr. Educ: Seton Hall Univ, 53-54. Polit. & Govt. Pos: Dem. committeeman, Bergen-Lafayette Ward, Jersey City, N.J, 60-64; dep. register mortgages and deeds, Hudson Co, N.J, 62-; del, Dem. Nat. Conv, 68; campaign mgr, Councilmanic Elec, Jersey City, 69. Bus. & Prof. Pos: Counsr, Newark Youth House, 52-54; park patrolman, Jersey City Police Dept, 55-57; spec. investr, Hudson Co. Surrogate Court, 58-62. Mil. Serv: Entered as Pvt, Air Force, 45, released as S/Sgt, 48, after serv. in Aviation Engrs, Alaska, 46-47; Recalled as Airman 1/C, 50-52. Publ: 'A Fair Share of America for Everyone,' Jersey J, 12/67. Mem: Chmn, Bergen Neighborhood Organizational Coun, 68; co-chmn, Cando Antipoverty Camp Prog, 68; bd. dirs, Cando Antipoverty Prog, 68; Mayor's Coun. on Youth Opportunity; Brotherhood and Action Cmt; Upward Bound Proj, Montclair State Col; planning cmt, Hudson Co. Fed. Shelter Prog. Man of the Year, Ballentine Brewery, 61; Cert. of Award, Oper. Step-Up, 68; Jersey City Housing Authority. Rel: Catholic. Mailing Add: 12 McDougal St, Jersey City, N.J. 07304.

SLADE, THOMAS HOWELL R
Fla. State Sen.
b. Albany, Ga, 3/13/36; s. Thomas Howell Slade, Sr. and Flora B. Jackson S; m. 5/5/55 to Judith Ann Griggs, div; c. Tom, Jack and Jeff. Educ: Emory at Oxford, 53-55; South. Inst. Tech, A.S. in gas fuel tech, 57. Polit. & Govt. Pos: Fla. State Rep, 62-64; Fla. State Sen, Dist. Nine, presently; alternate del, Rep. Nat. Conv, 68. Bus. & Prof. Pos: Pres, Slade Gas Co, 57-, Slade Petroleum Co, 62- and Slade Heating & Air Conditioning Co, 64- Mem: YMCA; Sales and Mkt. Execs; Traffic Club; Home Builders Asn; Rotary; Navy League. Rel: Presbyterian. Mailing Add: 6565 Beach Blvd, Jacksonville, Fla. 32216.

SLADEK, HENRY ROBERT R
Chmn, Wayne Co. Rep. Cmt, Mich.
b. Cicero, Ill, 5/7/22; s. Henry Joseph Sladek and Augusta Weisenborn S; m. 12/31/42 to Gloria Kleiber; c. Arthur Edward (deceased), Larry Alan, Susan Janis, Marianne Katherin and Steven Henry. Educ: Univ. Mich, 2 years. Polit. & Govt. Pos: Chmn, Wayne Co. Rep. Party, 19th Dist, Mich, 65-66; charter cmnr, Livonia, 66-67; chmn, Wayne Co. Rep. Cmt, 66- Bus. & Prof. Pos: Installer, West. Elec. Co, Inc, 40-47, supvr, 47-53, dept. head, 53-60 and dist. mgr, 60- Mil. Serv: Entered as Pvt, Army, 43, released as M/Sgt, 46, after serv. in 82nd Signal Bn, Pac, 45-46; Philippine Theatre Ribbon; Okinawa Ribbon; Battle Star; Spec. Citation, Island Comdg. Gen, Ie Shima. Mem: Rotary; Burton Hollow Civic Asn; PTA, NAACP. Rel: Lutheran. Mailing Add: 17410 Loveland, Livonia, Mich. 48152.

SLAGLE, FRANK D
b. Kettle Falls, Wash, 21; s. Jefferson H. Slagle and Lucile Brooks S; m. 5/26/46 to Elizabeth A. Hoeft; c. Frank J, Richard M. and Carmen R. Educ:

Wash. State Univ, B.S, 51. Polit. & Govt. Pos: Wash. State Rep, 65-66. Bus. & Prof. Pos: Self-employed druggist. Mil. Serv: Entered as Pvt, Army Air Force, released as S/Sgt, 3 years. Mem: Mason; Shrine; Eagles; Lions; former Elk. Rel: Protestant. Legal Res: 1198 N. Main, Colville, Wash. 99114. Mailing Add: P.O. Box 8, Colville, Wash. 99114.

SLAGLE, GENE D
b. Bucyrus, Ohio, 11/20/14; s. Milford G. Slagle and Olive C. Ballou S; m. 12/24/37 to Emily F. Weber; c. Nelson E, Bonnie J. (Mrs. Shaffstall), Betty J. (Mrs. Huckaba), James W. and John W. Educ: Ohio State Univ, B.S. in Agr, 36; pres, Delta Theta Sigma; mem. Student Senate, Inter-Fraternity Pres. Coun; All Agr. Coun. Polit. & Govt. Pos: Dist. supvr, Farm Security Admin, U.S. Dept. Agr, 37-42; mem, Auctioneers Cmn, Ohio, 63-65; mem. platform cmt, State Dem. Conv, 64 & 68; Ohio State Rep, Marion Co, 65-66. Bus. & Prof. Pos: Auctioneer in ten states and Can; instr, Reppert Sch, Auctioneering, Decatur, Ind, 55- Mem: Nat. Auctioneers Asn; dir, Ohio Auctioneers Asn, pres, 63; Nat, State & Local Real Estate Bds; trustee, Ohio Asn. Real Estate Bds, 64; pres, Marion Bd. Realtors, 63; master, Marion Pamona Grange, 62 and 63; master, United Grange, 57-59; pres, Pearl St. PTA, 64; Kiwanis; C. of C; pres, Salvation Army Bd, 69. Rel: Methodist. Legal Res: 1350 Bucyrus Rd, Galion, Ohio 44833. Mailing Add: 463 E. Center St, P.O. Box 5, Marion, Ohio 43302.

SLATE, HAROLD EDWIN R
Chmn, Patrick Co. Rep. Party, Va.
b. Claudville, Va, 3/26/44; s. Murray Owen Slate and Etta Anderson S; m. 10/3/65 to Ann Puckett. Educ: Patrick Henry Br, Univ. Va, 63; Nat. Bus. Col, Roanoke, 63-64; Alpha Kappa Phi. Polit. & Govt. Pos: Assoc. chmn, Patrick Co. Rep. Party, Va, 67 and chmn, 68- Bus. & Prof. Pos: Supvr, modernized yarn, E.I. DuPont de Nemours & Co, Inc, 65- Mem: AF&AM; Eastern Star; Patrick Co. Jaycees; bd. dirs, Patrick Co. United Fund, Inc; Red Bank Ruritan Club. Rel: Presbyterian; chmn. bd. deacons; youth adv. Mailing Add: Route 1, Claudville, Va. 24076.

SLATE, RALPH E. D
Ala. State Rep.
b. 1/11/27; m. to Ann Vinsant; c. Two daughters. Educ: Univ. Ala, LL.B. Polit. & Govt. Pos: Ala. State Rep, currently; Co. Solicitor, 2 terms. Bus. & Prof. Pos: Practicing attorney. Mil. Serv: Capt, Army, World War II and Korea. Mem: Ala. Bar Asn; K. of P; VFW; Am. Legion. Rel: Baptist. Mailing Add: Box 1344, Decatur, Ala. 35601. (1967)

SLATER, ELEANOR FRANCES D
b. Jersey City, N.J, 10/16/08; d. Francis Patrick Boland and Eleanor Krieg B; m. 10/15/34 to William Richard Slater; c. William Richard, Jr. and Thomas Francis. Educ: Montclair State Col, 29. Polit. & Govt. Pos: Mem, Warwick Sch. Cmt, R.I, 54-58; del, Dem. Nat. Conv, 56, 60, 64 & 68; mem, Cmn. for Higher Educ, R.I, 57-58; R.I. State Rep, 58-66; v.chmn, Dem. State Cmt, R.I, 58-69; mem, President Kennedy's Cmn. for Youth Employ, 61-62; chmn, R.I. Cmn. to Study Feasibility of a Long Island Sound Bridge, 64-65; R.I. State Sen, 67-68; coordinator, Dept. of Community Affairs, R.I, 69-; mem, R.I. Women's Dem. Club and Warwick Women's Dem. League, currently. Mem: Potowomut Golf Club. Selected Outstanding Woman of Achievement, R.I. Fedn. of Bus. & Prfnl. Women's Clubs, 68. Mailing Add: 202 Narragansett Bay Ave, Warwick, R.I. 02889.

SLATTERY, FRANK D
b. Wilkes-Barre, Pa, 9/28/04; s. Frank P. Slattery and Mary Rutledge S; m. 4/13/35 to Marguerite Goebel; c. Frank P, IV and Joseph A, II. Educ: St. Vincents Prep. Acad, Latrobe, Pa, 22; Princeton Univ, 26; Univ. Pa. Law Sch, 29, Elm Club. Polit. & Govt. Pos: Former mayor, Wilkes-Barre, Pa; asst. dist. attorney, Luzerne Co, Pa, 35-37; dep. attorney gen, Pa, 49-52; solicitor, Twps. and Boroughs. Bus. & Prof. Pos: Attorney-at-law, 30-; proj. adminstr, Concentrated Employ. Prog, currently. Mil. Serv: Entered as 2nd Lt, Army, 42, released as Maj, 46, after serv. in Austria; Mediterranean-African, Am. and European Occupation Ribbons. Mem: Luzerne Co, Pa. State and Am. Bar Asns; Elks; Eagles; K. of C; Am. Legion. Rel: Roman Catholic. Mailing Add: 164 N. Franklin, Wilkes-Barre, Pa. 18701.

SLAUGHTER, DANIEL FRENCH, JR. D
Va. State Del.
b. Culpeper Co, Va, 5/20/25; m. to Kathleen Wilson Rowe. Educ: Va. Mil. Inst. and Univ. of Va, B.A, LL.B; Omicron Delta Kappa; Raven Soc; Delta Psi; pres, Univ. Va. Alumni Asn, 69-70. Polit. & Govt. Pos: Va. State Del, 58-; v.chmn, Cmn. on Pub. Educ, 58-62; chmn, Cmn. on Voc. Educ, 63-64; chmn, Income Tax Study Cmn, 66-68; Culpeper Co. Dem. Cmn. Bus. & Prof. Pos: Lawyer. Mil. Serv: Army, combat infantry. Mem: Ruritans; C. of C; Am. Legion; VFW; Farm Bur; Am, Va, and local Bar Asns; Rotary. Recipient of Distinguished Serv. Award for Culpeper Co, 60. Rel: Episcopal. Mailing Add: 139 W. Davis St, Culpeper, Va. 22701.

SLAY, FRANCIS R. D
Mo. State Rep.
b. St. Louis, Mo, 10/28/27; s. Joseph K. Slay and Marie Elias S; m. 10/6/51 to Ann Sobocinski; c. Gerard, Francis, Sharron, Michael, Brenda, Raymond, Ann, Maria, Leo and Thomas. Educ: High Sch. Polit. & Govt. Pos: Mo. State Rep, 64th Dist, currently; committeeman, Dem. 23rd Ward, 67; del, Dem. Nat. Conv, 68. Bus. & Prof. Pos: Pres, Slays Food, Inc. Mil. Serv: Army, 45-47. Mem: K. of C; Maronite Soc; Kiwanis; St. Jude Alsac; bd. trustees, Health Welfare of Restaurants, St. Louis. Rel: Catholic. Mailing Add: 6532 Scanlan Ave, St. Louis, Mo. 63139. (1967)

SLAYDEN, GLADYS D
Miss. State Rep.
b. Marshall Co, Miss; m. to Everett Slayden (deceased). Polit. & Govt. Pos: Miss. State Rep, currently. Bus. & Prof. Pos: Farmer. Mem: Life mem, Nat. Garden clubs; life mem. and past pres, Garden Clubs of Miss; Farm Bur; DAR; UDC; past pres. and pilgrimage chmn, Holly Springs Garden Club. Rel: Baptist. Mailing Add: The Magnolias, Holly Springs, Miss. 38635. (1967)

SLEAR, JOHN KLUMP D
b. Williamsport, Pa, 3/15/91; s. Henry Gutelius Slear and Hettie Elizabeth Clark S; m. 4/3/20 to Julia Ramsay McNinch. Educ: Va. Polytech. Inst; Nat. Univ. Law Sch, LL.B, M.P.L, 37. Polit. & Govt. Pos: Secy. to U.S. Rep. Alfred L. Bulwinkle, N.C, 31-43; mem, Mecklenburg Co. Dem. Cmt; exec. officer of Green Pastures Rally honoring President Franklin D. Roosevelt, Charlotte, N.C, 36; del, N.C. Young Dem. Conv, 40; secy. to U.S. Rep. Cameron A. Morrison, N.C, 43-45; charter mem, Nat. Burro Club, Wash, D.C, 45; secy. to U.S. Rep. Robert L. Doughton, N.C, 46-47; secy. to U.S. Rep. Hamilton C. Jones, N.C, 47-50; adv, Dem. Nat. Conv, 48; admin. asst. to U.S. Sen. Willis Smith, N.C, 51-53; admin. asst. to U.S. Sen. Alton A. Lennon, N.C, 53-54; chief counsel to Subcmt. on Govt. Employees Security under U.S. Sen. Olin D. Johnston, S.C, 55-56; admin. asst. to U.S. Rep. Alton A. Lennon, N.C, 57- Bus. & Prof. Pos: Trustee in bankruptcy and receiver, Charlotte, N.C, 29-31; night sch. instr. math, Mecklenburg Co. Pub. Schs, 30; erected first tel. line from Black Mt. to Mt. Mitchell, N.C. Mil. Serv: Entered as 2nd Lt, Coast Artil. Corps, 17, released as 1st Lt, 19, after serv. in France. Mem: Fed. and N.C. State Bar Asns; N.C. Dem. Club of Wash, D.C; N.C. State Soc, Wash, D.C.(pres, 9 years); Am. Legion (treas, Hornet's Nest Post 9, 29; founder and publisher, newspaper); del, Am. Legion Nat. Conv. in Paris, France, 27; aide to Comdr-in-Chief of 39th Annual Reunion of United Confederate Vet, Charlotte, 29; organized Nat. Cherry Blossom Pageant, Wash, D.C, 48; Nat. Conf. of State Soc, Wash, D.C.(charter pres, 52, mem. adv. cmt. to pres); mem, past pres. Conf. of State Soc; VFW; DAV; N.C. Cong. Secretaries Club; Wash, D.C; Senate Admin. Assistants and Secretaries Asn; Capital Hill Burro Club; Capital Hill Fed. Bar; English Speaking Union; U.S. Cong. Little Cong; Roanoke Island Hist. Asn; N.C. Soc. for Preservation of Antiquities; Nat. Capital Dem. Club; organized Maid of Cotton Fashion Show, Wash, D.C, 49; Nat. Lawyers Club; SAR; N.C. Literary and Hist. Asn; N.C. State Art Soc; N.C. Folklore Soc. Rel: Methodist; Helped organize First Methodist Church, Charlotte, N.C, 23-27, steward; steward and supt, Intermediate Dept. of Sunday Sch, Tryon Street Methodist Church, 24-27; helped to organize and establish Uptown Methodist Church. Legal Res: 511 N. Church St, Charlotte, N.C. 28202. Mailing Add: 100 Maryland Ave. N.E, Apt. 403, Washington, D.C. 20002.

SLEET, THOMAS PRESTON D
b. Perryville, Ky, 8/28/21; s. Lot Sleet and Cora Golden S; m. 5/2/42 to Anna Louise Peebles; c. Gyjuan L. Educ: Butler Univ, B.S; Ind. Univ, M.S. Polit. & Govt. Pos: City Councilman, Indianapolis, Ind, 66- Bus. & Prof. Pos: Teacher, Pub. Sch. Syst, 48-; Sch. Dist. 17 and Crispus Attucks High Sch, 18 years; basileus, Omega Psi Phi. Mil. Serv: Entered Army, 43, released as Sgt, 45; Battle of the Bulge Medal. Mem: Ind. Teachers Asn; Indianapolis Supper Club; Dem. Club; Oak Hill Civic Asn. Omega Man of Year, Zeta Phi Chap, Omega Psi Phi, 64; Crispus Attucks B Mens Award, Butler Univ; honors, Bates High Sch, Danville, Ky. Rel: Methodist. Mailing Add: 2703 Ralston, Indianapolis, Ind. 46218.

SLENKER, GLENN R. R
Ind. State Rep.
Polit. & Govt. Pos: Ind. State Sen, 29-33; Ind. State Rep, 35-, Majority Leader, 61 and Dean State Legislators, Ind. State House of Rep; former prosecuting attorney, Carroll and White Co. and former pub. counsellor; former mem, Pub. Serv. Cmn. Bus. & Prof. Pos: Lawyer. Mem: Ind. State and Am. Bar Asns; Am. Legion. Mailing Add: Box 181, Monticello, Ind. 47960. (1967)

SLINGERLEND, ROBERT J. D
b. Mecosta Co, 5/4/15; married; c. Glenn, Malcolm James. Educ: Grad. of Cent. Mich. Univ, B.S, cum laude; degree, Wayne State Univ. Polit. & Govt. Pos: Mich. State Rep, 64-66; chem, biol. and radiological civil defense officer. Bus. & Prof. Pos: Chem. engr. Mem: Active leader in Boy Scouts; 4-H Club; Jr. Farm Bur; Jr. Achievement; pres, Rochester area br, UN Asn. of the U.S; steering cmt, Rochester area Human Rels. Coun; adv. Paint Creek Conserv. Proj; vol. policeman; Apple Blossom Club, Cent. Mich. Univ; Soc. of Automotive Engrs; Am. Soc. for Testing Materials; Detroit Rubber and Plastics Group, Inc; Mich. Christmas Tree Growers Asn; chmn, Legis. Cmt, Detroit Sportsmen Cong, Mich. United Conserv. Clubs; Nat. Soc. of State Legislators. Rel: Unitarian. Mailing Add: 3201 Lake George Rd, Lake Orion, Mich. 48035. (1967)

SLOAN, CHESTER WESLEY R
Chmn, Lee Co. Rep. Cent. Cmt, Iowa
b. Oakville, Iowa, 10/7/15; s. John Leslie Sloan and Echo Jaren S; m. 10/13/51 to Joan Harriman; c. Margaret Humble and Elizabeth Mary. Educ: Ft. Madison High Sch, Iowa, Grad. Polit. & Govt. Pos: Dist. campaign mgr. for cand. in primaries for Gov. of Iowa, 57; mem, Great River Rd. Cmt, Iowa, 58-62; chmn, Lee Co. Rep. Cent. Cmt, 59-; mem, Gov. Cmt. for Employ. of Physically Handicapped, 61-62. Bus. & Prof. Pos: Officer and dir, Iowa State Indust. Safety Asn, 56-62; dir, Iowa Good Rd. Asn, 58-; mem, Iowa Mfrs. Asn. Safety Cmt, 67-69. Mil. Serv: Entered as Pvt, Army, 42, released as T/Sgt, 45, after serving in 822nd Tank Destroyers, Am. and European African Mid. East.Theaters, 42-45; Bronze Star. Publ: Three or four articles in ins. and safety publ. Mem: C. of C; Elks; Rotary; Ft. Madison Country Club. Rel: Episcopal. Mailing Add: 712 Ave. E, Ft. Madison, Iowa 52627.

SLOAN, DEAN R
Mem, Calif. Rep. State Cent. Cmt.
b. Dalhart, Tex, 11/13/33; s. Ira B. Sloan and Ola Dixon S; m. 6/23/56 to Karen Thomson; c. Steven, Julie and Gary. Educ: Woodbury Bus. Col, 1 year; El Camino Col, 1 year; Univ. of Calif, Los Angeles, 1 semester. Polit. & Govt. Pos: Cand. research and develop, 65th Rep. Assembly Cent. Cmt, Calif, 67; Campaign mgr, Merle Mergell for Inglewood Coun, 67 and Veregge for State Assembly, 68; mem, Calif. Rep. State Cent. Cmt, 69- Bus. & Prof. Pos: Cost analyst, Douglas Aircraft, 55-61; sales eng, Hitco, Gardena, Calif, 61-62; v.pres, Sloan's Stationers, Inglewood, 62- Mil. Serv: Entered as Pvt, Army, 53, released as Sgt, 55, after serv. in Seventh Inf. Div, Korea 54-55; Korean Serv. Medal; UN Serv. Medal; Nat. Defense Serv. Medal. Mem: Douglas Aircraft Mgt. Club; Inglewood Commun. Stabilization Bd; C. of C; Rotary Int. past pres, Inglewood Chap, 20-30. Key Man Award, Jr. C. of C. Rel: Methodist. Mailing Add: 11836 Christopher, Inglewood, Calif. 90303.

SLOAN, DONALD RICHARD R
b. Des Moines, Iowa, 3/15/33; s. Morris Sloan and Alma R. Ewert S; m. 11/25/53 to Jean Wells; c. Kathleen Lynn and Julie Ann. Educ: Drake Univ,

B.S, 51-55; Alpha Kappa Psi. Polit. & Govt. Pos: Councilman and pres, Overland Park City Coun, Kans, 60-62; chmn, Overland Park Rep. City Cmt, 60-68; mem. exec. cmt. and campaign chmn, Johnson Co. Rep. Cent. Cmt, 62-68; alternate del, Rep. Nat. Conv, 64, del, 68. Bus. & Prof. Pos: CPA, partner, Peat, Marwick, Mitchell & Co, 55- Mem: Am. Inst. of CPA's; Mo. and Iowa Socs. of CPA's; Nat. Asn. of Accts; C. of C; dir, Des Moines United Campaign. Rel: Methodist. Mailing Add: 2000 Willowmere Dr, Des Moines, Iowa 50321.

SLOAN, FRANK KEENAN D
Exec. Committeeman, Richland Co. Dem. Party, S.C.
b. Johnson City, Tenn, 10/11/21; s. Z. Frank Sloan and Maria Witten S; m. 2/23/46 to Helen Rhett Yobs; c. Richard O, Christine, Lewis W. and Frank K. Jr. Educ: Univ. S.C, A.B, 43, LL.B, 48; Phi Beta Kappa; Omicron Delta Kappa; Order Wig & Robe; Sigma Chi; Kappa Sigma Kappa. Polit. & Govt. Pos: Co. and ward officer, Richland Co. and Columbia, S.C. Dem. Party, 48-69; reporter, S.C. Judicial Coun, 56-60; mem, S.C. Alcohol Cmn, 58-62; S.C. Campaign Mgr. for Pres. John F. Kennedy, 60; S.C. chmn, Citizens for Kennedy-Johnson, 60; state orgn. chmn, S.C. Dem. Party, 61-62, secy-treas, 64-65; dep. asst. secy. defense, Dept. of Defense, D.C, 62-64; regional dir, U.S. Off. Econ. Opportunity, Atlanta, Ga, 65-67; Dem. nominee, U.S. House Rep, Second Dist, S.C, 68; exec. committeeman, Richland Co. Dem. Party, 69- Bus. & Prof. Pos: Assoc. and partner, Cooper & Gary, Attorneys, Columbia, S.C, 48-65; assoc. prof. law, Univ. S.C, 55-65; v.pres, Inst. Polit. and Planning, Wash, D.C, 67-; attorney at law, Sloan & Gardner, Attorneys, Columbia, S.C, 68- Mil. Serv: Entered as Ens, Navy 43, released as Lt(jg), 46, after serv. in Atlantic and Pac. Theatres, recalled, 51-52, Lt, U.S.S. Salem, Sixth Fleet, 51-52; Capt, Res, 65-; Presidential Unit Citation with Star; Naval Res. Medal; World War II Serv. Medal; Atlantic Theatre Medal; Pac. Theatre Medal with Five Battle Stars; Korean Serv. Medal; Philippine Victory Medal with Star. Publ: Number of articles in professional legal journals, 49- Mem: Am. Law Inst; Am. Judicature Soc; Am. Bar Asn; S.C. Bar Asn.(chmn. cmt, procedure & law reform, 56-62); Richland Co. Bar Asn; Am. Legion; VFW; Rotary; Am. Fedn. Musicians; Palmetto Club; Forest Lake Club; Naval Res. Asn; Int. Asn. Ins. Counsel. Rel: Lutheran. Mailing Add: 3320 Devereaux Rd, Columbia, S.C. 29205.

SLOAN, GRACE McCALMONT D
Mem, Pa. State Dem. Policy Cmt.
b. Dayton, Pa, d. Charles Plumer McCalmont and Minnie Boals Elwinger M; m. to John E. Sloan, wid; c. Mary Kathryn (Mrs. Buckley) and Jacqueline (Mrs. Ketner). Polit. & Govt. Pos: Mem, Pa. State Dem. Exec. Cmt, 44-50; mem, Pa. State Dem. Cmt, 44-60; mem, Clarion Co. Dem. Women's Club; mem, Clarion Co. Exec. Cmt, Pa, 46-; reg. dir, Pa. Fedn. of Dem. Women, 49-53, mem, 49-, pres, 57-61; mem, State Employees' Retirement Bd, 57-65 & 69-; mem, Pa. State Dem. Policy Cmt, 57-; co-chmn, Dem. Statewide Registrn. Cmt, 60-; state treas, Pa, 61-65 & 69-, auditor gen, 65-69. Bus. & Prof. Pos: Treas, Gen. State Authority, State Hwy. and Bridge Authority and State Pub. Sch. Bldg. Authority, 61-; mem, Bd. of Finance and Revenue, 61-; Bd. of Cmnrs. of Ground and Bldge, 61-, del, River Port Authority, 61-; treas, Pa. Higher Educ. Facilities Authority, 68-; treas, Pa. Transportation Assistance Authority, 69- Mem: Defense Adv. Cmt, Women in the Armed Serv, 66-69; Nat. Asn. of State Auditors; Comptrollers and Treasurers; chmn, Florence Dornblaser Mem. Scholarship Cmt; Fedn. of Bus. & Prfnl. Women; Am. Legion Auxiliary; Ambassadors Club. of Trans World Airlines; Nat. Women's Party; Clarion Civic Club; Eagles Nest. Rel: Presbyterian. Legal Res: 1104 Main St, Clarion, Pa. 16214. Mailing Add: Grayco Apartments, Harrisburg, Pa. 17101.

SLOAN, JAMES WENDELL D
b. Hoxie, Kans, 12/30/27; s. Floyd A. Sloan and Wilburma Gallogly S. Educ: Washburn Univ, A.B, 50, LL.B, 52; Delta Theta Phi; Alpha Delta; Washburn Players; Young Dems. Polit. & Govt. Pos: Asst. co. attorney, Shawnee Co, Kans, 59-61; chmn, Shawnee Co. Dem. Party, 61-66. Bus. & Prof. Pos: Attorney-at-law, 52-69. Mil. Serv: Entered as Pvt, Army, 46, released as T/5, 47, after serv. in 706 Ord. L.M.Co. Mem: Am, Kans. and Topeka Bar Asns; VFW. Post 1650. Rel: Presbyterian. Mailing Add: 349 Woodbury Ct. N, Topeka, Kans. 66606.

SLOAN, PAUL CROSIER R
Committeeman, Ill. Rep. Cent. Cmt.
b. Rushville, Ill, 7/24/00; s. George Crosier Sloan and Fannie Florence Moore S; m. 2/14/23 to Nina Mildred York; c. Patricia Jeanne (Mrs. Richard Hamm). Educ: Gem City Bus. Col, Quincy, Ill, 1 year. Polit. & Govt. Pos: Mayor, Rushville, Ill, 48-64; committeeman, Ill. Rep. Cent. Cmt, currently. Bus. & Prof. Pos: Ed, Schuyler News, Rushville, Ill, 34-40; news reporter, advert. layout and sales, Rushville, Ill. Times, 40-47; driver license exam, Secy. of State, Ill, 54-64; owner and operator, restaurant, 42-47; area pres, Ill. Munic. League, 54-62. Mem: Odd Fellows (Past Noble Grand, 34-45); Optimist Club (pres, 47-52); Moose; Ill. Police Asn; Twin Oaks Rep. Club. Rel: Christian Church of N.Am. Legal Res: 209 S. Liberty, Rushville, Ill. 62681. Mailing Add: P.O. Box 296, Rushville, Ill. 62681.

SLOCOMBE, LAWRENCE DAVIS R
Kans. State Rep.
b. Peabody, Kans, 5/10/05; s. Edgar William Slocombe and Katie Pearl Davis S; m. 6/10/28 to Florence Kittell Slocombe; c. Lavonne and Janet. Educ: Kans. State Univ. Polit. & Govt. Pos: Kans. State Rep, 57-, chmn, Assessment and Taxation Cmt; chmn, Nursing Hosp. Bd, 64- Mem: Mason, Shrine; C. of C; Kiwanis; Farm Bur; Livestock Asn; Peabody Golf Club. Rel: Methodist. Mailing Add: 507 Sycamore, Peabody, Kans. 66866.

SLONAKER, WILLIAM B. D
b. Capon Bridge, W.Va, 11/4/21; s. Arthur B. Slonaker and Carrie Shanholtzer S; m. 11/4/42 to Ila Stickley; c. Steve and Shirley. Educ: Potomac State Col. Polit. & Govt. Pos: W.Va. State Del, 58-66; former co. supvr, Potomac Valley Dist. Bus. & Prof. Pos: Breeder of Angus cattle; orchardist. Mem: Dir, Farm Bur; dir, Capon Bridge Fire Dept; secy, Capon Bridge Ruritan Club. Hampshire Co. Conserv. Farmer, 57. Rel: Methodist. Mailing Add: Capon Bridge, W.Va. 26711. (1967)

SLUDDEN, CHARLES JOSEPH D
b. Belfast, Ireland, 9/12/13; s. John J. Sludden and Elizabeth McMullen S; m. Sept. 1941 to Margaret Francis Flaherty; c. Margaret (Mrs. David Charles Frey), Mary Ann, Charles J, Jr. and Elizabeth Ann. Educ: High Sch. grad. Polit. & Govt. Pos: Del, Dem. Nat. Conv, 68. Bus. & Prof. Pos: Gen. chmn, BRT, 45-49 and Pa. state legis. rep, 49-69; v.pres, Pa. AFL-CIO, 60-; Pa. state legis. dir, United Transportation Union, 69- Rel: Roman Catholic. Legal Res: 413 Alta Vista Ave, Harrisburg, Pa. 17109. Mailing Add: 2107-09 N. Sixth, Harrisburg, Pa. 17110.

SMABY, ALPHA SUNDE DFL
b. Sacred Heart, Minn, 2/11/10; d. Alfred T. Sunde and Mathilda Hovde S; m. 9/2/39 to Arthur J. Smaby; c. Marit Ragnhild, Karlin Bergetta and Jan Ingrid. Educ: Univ. Minn, B.A, magna cum laude. Polit. & Govt. Pos: Chmn, Minn. Vols. for Stevenson, 56; Minn. State Rep, 41st Dist, 64-69; U.S. del. to Women's Adv. Coun. of Int. Coop. Alliance; mem, Gov. Cmn. on Status of Women; exec. cmt. mem, Dem-Farmer-Labor 2nd Ward Club; del, Dem. Nat. Conv, 68. Publ: 'The Lutheran Voter and the Catholic Candidate,' and 'The Christian and the Federal Income Tax,' Am. Lutheran Church, 60. Mem: League of Women Voters; Am. Civil Liberties Union; Foreign Policy Asn; Girl Scouts. Rel: Lutheran. Mailing Add: 1531 E. River Rd, Minneapolis, Minn. 55414. (1967)

SMAIL, JOHN RICHARD WHARTON D
b. Cairo, Egypt, 2/14/30; s. George Sommerville Smail and Kathryn Wharton S; m. 8/2/58 to Laura Woolsey Lord; c. John Lord and Daniel Lord. Educ: Harvard Col, A.B, 51, Harvard Univ, M.A, 52; Cornell Univ, Ph.D, 64; Signet Soc. Polit. & Govt. Pos: Del, Dem. State Conv, Wis, 68 & 69; alternate del, Dem. Nat. Conv, 68. Bus. & Prof. Pos: From instr. to assoc. prof, S.E. Asian Hist,.Univ. Wis, Madison, 62- Mil. Serv: Entered as Pvt, Army, 53, released as Cpl, 55, after serv. in First Cavalry Div, Japan, 53-55. Publ: Bandung in the Early Revolution, 1945-6, Cornell Modern Indonesia Proj, 64. Mem: Asn. Asian Studies; Cmt. Concerned Citizens, 19th Ward; Am. Fedn. Teachers. Mailing Add: 5059 Marathon Dr, Madison, Wis. 53705.

SMALL, ROY CURTIS D
b. Harrisburg, Ill, 6/12/32; s. Curtis Glen Small and Margaret Helen Hamby S; m. 2/4/56 to Bonnie Elaine Thomas; c. Leta Ann. Educ: Univ. Ill, B.S. in Journalism, 55; Sigma Delta Chi; Beta Theta Pi. Polit. & Govt. Pos: V.chmn, 59th Dem. Dist. Citizens for Powell, Ill, 64; pres, Saline Co. Young Dem. Orgn, 65-66; state committeeman, Ill. Young Dem. Orgn, 65-69; mem, Ill. Sesquicentennial Cmn, 66-69; former Ill. State Rep; chmn, State of Ill. Cmn. on Compensation of State and Local Govt. Off, 68- Bus. & Prof. Pos: Off. mgr, Harrisburg, Daily Register, Ill, 57-; pres, Shawnee Hills Medalists; 60-69; v.pres, Gallatin Co. Publishers, 65-68, pres, 69-; v.pres, Spacecraft Medals, 66-68, pres. and chmn, bd, 68- Publ: Articles on medallic art and numismatics various professional journals. Mem: All Masonic Bodies including 32° and Shrine; Harrisburg Jaycees; twice past president, Rotary Club; University of Illinois Citizens Committee and Coun. of Area Rep. Society of Medalists; Ill, Ind. and Ky. Numismatic Asns; Token and Medal Soc. Rel: Protestant. Legal Res: 1121 South Roosevelt St, Harrisburg, Ill. 62946. Mailing Add: P.O. Box 342, Harrisburg, Ill. 62946.

SMALLEY, I. M. D
N.Mex. State Sen.
b. 1906. Educ: Univ. of Pa, B.S. in Econ; South. Methodist Univ. Law Sch, LL.B. Polit. & Govt. Pos: N.Mex. State Rep, 47-52; N.Mex. State Sen, 57- Bus. & Prof. Pos: Attorney. Mem: Rotary; Mason. Rel: Protestant. Mailing Add: Box 879, Deming, N.Mex. 88030. (1967)

SMALLEY, K. MAXINE R
Mem, Calif. Rep. State Cent. Cmt.
b. Ft. Wayne, Ind, 9/27/20; d. George Lee Morrison and Cora Ellen Waggoner M; m. 10/16/48 to Benjamin Franklin Smalley. Educ: Ind. Univ, Bloomington, 39-41. Polit. & Govt. Pos: Alternate mem, Los Angeles Co. Rep. Cent. Cmt, 39th and 44th assembly dist, Long Beach, Calif, 65-68, mem, 44th assembly dist, 69-; legis. chmn, 32nd Dist. Rep. Women, Long Beach, 65, treas, 67, and first v.pres, 69; precinct chmn, 32nd dist, 65-69; mem, Calif. Rep. State Cent. Cmt, 66-; rep. for poor of Long Beach, v.chmn, Downtown Neighborhood Coun, mem. bd, Commun. Action Agency, Off. of Econ. Opportunity. Bus. & Prof. Pos: Prod. control and acct. clerk, Gen. Elec. Co, Ft. Wayne, Ind, 42-45; payroll supvr, U.S. Navy Finance Off, Long Beach, Calif, 45-60. Mem: Eastern Star; finance chmn, The Ebell of Long Beach. Outstanding Performance Award, U.S. Navy Finance Off. Recognized as one of ten in state for precinct leadership by Gov. Reagan and Rep. State Cent. Cmt; Merit Award, Los Angeles Co. Rep. Cent. Cmt. Rel: Methodist. Mailing Add: 436 Cedar Ave, Long Beach, Calif. 90812.

SMALLEY, PHIL D
Majority Whip, Okla. State Sen.
b. Norman, Okla, 9/4/37; s. Joseph A. Smalley and Virginia Coleman S; m. 4/15/61 to Anna Beth Halverson; c. Joseph Alexander and Sarah Beth. Educ: Okla. Univ, LL.B, 62; Phi Alpha Delta. Polit. & Govt. Pos: Okla. State Rep, 64-66; Okla. State Sen, 67-, Majority Whip, Okla. State Sen, 69- Bus. & Prof. Pos: Law Partner, Vaughan and Smalley, Attorneys, 62- Mil. Serv: ROTC, 55-56. Mem: Bd. dirs, C. of C, 66-, Kiwanis, 66, Planned Parenthood, 65-66 and chmn, Cleveland Co. Chapter Nat. Found, 64-67. Rel: Baptist. Legal Res: 535 E. Boyd, Norman, Okla. 73069. Mailing Add: 124 E. Main St, Norman, Okla. 73069.

SMALLEY, ROBERT HARRIS, JR. D
Ga. State Sen.
b. Hartwell, Ga, 8/1/29; s. Robert Harris Smalley and Evelyn Carr S; m. Jane Cumming (deceased), m. 4/3/65 to Mary Matilda King; c. Jane Cumming 'Janet' and Robert Harris, III. Educ: Univ. Ga, B.B.A, 49, LL.B. cum laude, 51; Phi Beta Kappa; Phi Delta Phi; Beta Gamma Sigma. Polit. & Govt. Pos: Del, Dem. Nat. Conv, 60; Ga. State Sen, 61-, mem, Sen. Appropriations Cmt, Ga. State Sen, 61-, mem, Legis. Servs. Cmt, 63-, chmn, Sen. Judiciary Cmt, 63- Bus. & Prof. Pos: Partner, Beck, Goddard, Owen, & Smalley, Attorneys, 54- Mil. Serv: Entered as 2nd Lt, Army, 51, released as 1st Lt, 53, after serv. in 72nd Tank Bn, 2nd Inf. Div, Korea; Bronze Star Medal. Mem: Ki-

wanis; Elks; Moose; Am. Bar Asn; State Bar of Ga; Am. Trial Lawyers Asn; Nat. Asn. of R.R. Trial Counsel. Rel: Episcopal. Legal Res: 945 Maple Dr, Griffin, Ga. 30223. Mailing Add: P.O. Box 116, Griffin, Ga. 30233.

SMALLEY, ROBERT MANNING R
Spec. Asst. to Secy. for Pub. Affairs, Dept. Commerce
b. Los Angeles, Calif, 11/14/25; s. William Denny Smalley and Helen McConnell S; m. 1/4/57 to Rosemary Sumner; c. Leslie Estelle and David Christian. Educ: Univ. Calif, Los Angeles, 46-47. Polit. & Govt. Pos: Pres, Westward Young Rep, Los Angeles, Calif, 54; confidential secy. to mayor, San Francisco, 61-64; press secy. to William F. Miller, Rep. Nat. Cmt, 64, asst. dir. pub. rels,Rep. Nat. Cmt, 64, dir. pub. rels, 64-65; campaign mgr, U.S. Sen. Robert P. Griffin, Mich, 66; consult, Cmt. for Govt. of the People and Allegheny Co. Rep. Exec. Cmt, Pa, 67; asst. press secy, Gov. Spiro T. Agnew, cand for Vice President, 68; spec. asst. to Secy. for Pub. Affairs, Dept. Commerce, 69- Bus. & Prof. Pos: Partner, Whitaker & Baxter, San Francisco, Calif, 65-69. Mil. Serv: Entered as A/S, Navy, 44, released as Yeoman 2/C, 46, after serv. in ACORN & AFRS, Pac. Theatre; S.Pac. Serv. and Combat Zone Ribbons. Publ: 'White Australia,' Plain Talk, 5/50; weekly column, 'USA Today,' Calif. Feature Serv, 68-69. Mem: Nat. Press Club; San Francisco Press and Union League Club, until 60; Gr. Los Angeles Press Club, 52-55; assoc. mem, U.S. Naval Inst, Annapolis, Md; Capitol Hill Club. Ephebian Soc. and Calif. Scholarship Fedn, 43. Rel: Protestant. Legal Res: 4518 N. 35th St, Arlington, Va. 22207. Mailing Add: Room 5418, U.S. Dept. of Commerce, Washington, D.C. 20230.

SMALLWOOD, RICHARD BURTON D
Mo. State Rep.
b. St. James, Mo, 9/2/37; s. Charles Smallwood and Alice Burton S; single. Educ: Univ. Mo. Col. Agr, B.S. in agr, 59 and M.S. in agr. econs, 63; Gamma Sigma Delta; Alpha Zeta. Polit. & Govt. Pos: Committeeman, Phelps Co. Dem. Cmt, 64-66; Mo. State Rep, 67- Bus. & Prof. Pos: Ins. and real estate agent, Smallwood Ins. Agency, 63- Mil. Serv: Entered as 2nd Lt, Army, 60, released as 1st Lt, 62, after serv. in 7th Bn, 11th Artil, 25th Inf. Div, Hawaii, 62; also served as 1st Lt, Mo. Nat. Guard, 128th Artil, 62-65; Capt. Army Res, 67. Mem: Mo. Asn. of Independent Ind. Agents; C. of C; Jr. C. of C; Lions. Rel: Catholic. Legal Res: 568 S. Jefferson, St. James, Mo. 65559. Mailing Add: 102 N. Jefferson, St. James, Mo. 65559.

SMART, CLIFFORD H. R
Mich. State Rep.
b. Sault Ste. Marie, Mich, 1/14/05; married; c. Marybeth, William and Robert. Educ: Grad. of Wayne State Univ, B.S, M.A. Polit. & Govt. Pos: Mich. State Rep, 64- Bus. & Prof. Pos: Supt. of schs. for 35 years. Mem: Past pres, Mich. Educ. Asn. and Mich. Asn. of Sch. Adminstrs; past mem. of bd. of mgrs, legis. chmn. and state treas, Mich. Cong. of Parents and Teachers; elected in 64 to Bd. of Trustees, Oakland Co. Commun. Col; Rotary Club; past pres, C. of C; F&AM 528; United Fund (area chmn.); Am. Acad. of Soc. Sci; active in local PTA's. Rel: Episcopal. Mailing Add: 555 W. Walled Lake Dr, Walled Lake, Mich. 48088.

SMART, WILLIAM HOWARD R
b. Milwaukee, Wis, 9/30/09; s. Charles Henry Smart and Marie Troyer S; m. 1/9/47 to Helen Carson. Educ: Univ. Ill, 29-33; Phi Sigma Kappa. Polit. & Govt. Pos: Councilman, Washington, Iowa, 51-53, mayor, 54-58; chmn, Washington Co. Rep. Party, 52-56, finance chmn, 68-69; Rep. committeeman, third ward, Washington, 63-69; alternate del, Rep. Nat. Conv, 68. Mil. Serv: Entered Army, 42, released as Sgt, 43, after serv. in 809 Ord. Co. Mem: Mason; Am. Legion; Eastern Star; Kiwanis. Rel: Christian Science. Mailing Add: Box 487, Mt. Pleasant, Iowa 52641.

SMATHERS, GEORGE ARMISTEAD D
b. Atlantic City, N.J, 11/14/13; s. Frank Smathers and Lura Jones S; m. 1939 to Rosemary Townley; c. John and Bruce. Educ: Univ. of Fla, B.A; Col. of Law, Univ. of Fla, LL.B. Polit. & Govt. Pos: Asst. U.S. Dist. Attorney, 40-42; asst. to Attorney Gen, 45-46; U.S. Rep, Fla, 47-50; U.S. Sen, Fla, 51-68; del, Dem. Nat. Conv, 68. Mil. Serv: Marine Corps, 42-45; Col, Marine Corps Res. Mem: Fla. Bar Asn. Legal Res: Miami, Fla. Mailing Add: Smathers, Merrigan and O'Keefe, Suite 1001, 1700 Pennsylvania Ave, N.W, Washington, D.C. 20006.

SMAZAL, VINCENT AUGUST D
Chmn, Twin Falls Co. Dem. Party, Idaho
b. Papillion, Nebr, 6/3/13; s. Charles Frank Smazal and Elizabeth Klein S; m. 2/16/53 to Mabel M. Buchanan; c. William Charles. Educ: High sch, 3 years. Polit. & Govt. Pos: Dem. committeeman, 15th Precinct, Twin Falls, Idaho, 46-48, Fourth Precinct, 48-62; pres, Young Dem. Club, Twin Falls Co, 46-48; state coordinator, Dist. Dem. Cmt, 60-62; del, Dem. State Cmt, 66 & 68; chmn, Twin Falls Co. Dem. Party, 66-; del, Dem. Nat. Conv, 68; mem, Idaho State Dem. Cent. Cmt, currently. Bus. & Prof. Pos: Farmer, 28-39; mechanic, wrecker serv. body, fender and painting, 40-45; partner, Off. Equip. Sales & Serv, 45-63, owner, 63- Mem: C. of C; Elks; Idaho Tax Equality Asn. Rel: Catholic. Mailing Add: 530 Main Ave. S, Twin Falls, Idaho 83301.

SMEED, RALPH E. R
b. Caldwell, Idaho, 12/30/21; s. John W. Smeed and Florence Beckmann S; single. Educ: Col. of Idaho, 40-41, 47-48; Orion; Intercollegiate Knights. Polit. & Govt. Pos: Former dist. chmn, State Rep. Exec. Cmt, Idaho; del, Rep. Nat. Conv, 64; pres, Idaho Compass. Bus. & Prof. Pos: Bd. of Dir, C. of C, 55-57. Mil. Serv: Entered as Pvt, Army, released as Sgt, after serv. in Signal Corps, Pacific. Mem: Elks; Am. Legion; Farm Bur; Salvation Army Bds; Rep. Boosters Club. Rel: Presbyterian. Mailing Add: 1617 Idaho St, Caldwell, Idaho 83605.

SMELSER, CHARLES HAROLD D
Md. State Sen.
b. Uniontown, Md, 7/4/20; s. Charles Harold Smelser and Grace Ann Devilbiss S; m. 5/11/46 to Betty Marie Krueger; c. Barbara Ann and Bernard Charles. Educ: Univ. Md, B.S, 42; Omicron Delta Kappa; Alpha Tau Omega. Polit. & Govt. Pos: Md. State Del, Frederick Co, 55-63; Md. State Sen, Dist. Two, 67- Bus. & Prof. Pos: Trustee, Frederick Mem. Hosp, Frederick, Md, 57-; dir, New Windsor State Bank, New Windsor, 57-; pres, Capitol Milk Producers Asn, Frederick, 68- Mil. Serv: Entered as Cadet, Army Air Corps, 43, released as 1st Lt, 45, after serv. in 490th Bomb Group, Eighth Air Force, Europe, 44-45; Res, 45-58; Distinguished Flying Cross; Air Medal with Five Clusters. Mem: Lions Int; Elks; Moose; Amvets; Farm Bur. Legislator of the Year, 60. Rel: Methodist. Mailing Add: R.F.D. 2, Union Bridge, Md. 21791.

SMILEY, RICHARD DURHAM R
b. Louisville, Ky, 8/16/26; s. John Samuel Smiley and Camille Overstreet S; m. 11/2/45 to Eloise Westlake; c. Richard Glen, James Dee and Ann. Educ: Gallatin Co. High Sch, Bozeman, Mont; Grantham Radio Sch. Polit. & Govt. Pos: Mont. State Rep, Gallatin Co, 63-66, mem, Educ, Bus. and Indust. and Ways and Means Cmts, Mont. House of Rep; mem. sub-cmt. sch. law rev, Cmts, Mont. House of Rep; Mont. Legis. Coun; cand, U.S. House of Rep, Mont, 68. Bus. & Prof. Pos: Owner and operator, Radio Sta KXXL, Bozeman, Mont. Mem: Elks; Rotary; Nat. Assoc. Press, Radio and TV Bd; former pres, Mont. State Univ. Athletic Scholarship Asn. and Mont. Broadcasters' Asn. Bozeman Jaycee Distinguished Serv. Award, 60. Rel: Christian Church. Mailing Add: Route 2, Box 149, Bozeman, Mont. 59715. (1967)

SMIRL, JODY GUTHRIE R
W.Va. State Del.
b. Mobile, Ala, 8/30/33; d. Raymond Booth Guthrie and Emmajean Cole G; m. 12/17/55 to Daniel Warren Smirl; c. Thomas Booth and Daniel Marvin. Educ: Auburn Univ, 54; Owls; Oracles; WSGA; Alpha Gamma Delta; sponsor, Alpha Tau Omega Fraternity. Polit. & Govt. Pos: Mem, W.Va. Rep. Coord. Cmt, 65; v.pres, Cabell-Huntington Rep. Women, 65 & 66; cmt. chmn, Rep. Women's Serv. League, 66; 1st Woman pres, Cabell Co. Young Rep, 66; mem, W.Va. Fedn. Rep. Women, W.Va. Young Rep. League; W.Va. State Del, Cabell Co, 67- Mem: W.Va. Cong. of Parents & Teachers; W.Va. Fedn. Women's Clubs; YWCA; Jr. Dept. Woman's Club of Huntington; Gallaher PTA and Cabell Co. PTA Coun; League of Women Voters; Friends of the Huntington Libr; Isaac Walton League; Youth Bd. of YMCA; W.Va. Del, Ohio Basin Seminar, 68; chosen by Rep. Nat. Cmt. as Speaker of 15th Annual Women's Conf, Chicago, 67. Awarded Plaque for Outstanding Commun. Serv, Huntington Jaycees, 66 & 67; Platform Cmt. of Rep. State Conv, 68; Chosen Most Outstanding Jr. Woman, 69. Rel: Presbyterian. Mailing Add: 507 Forest Rd, Huntington, W.Va. 25705.

SMISSON, WILLIAM HOWARD R
Chmn, Comanche Co. Rep. Party, Okla.
b. Ft. Valley, Ga. 4/22/29; s. Roy Clayton Smisson and Mary Smith S; m. 8/6/66 to Carolyn Faye Burchett. Educ: Univ. Ga, B.S, 49; Sigma Alpha Epsilon. Polit. & Govt. Pos: Chmn, U.S. Savings Bonds, Lawton, Okla, 60-; chmn, Right-To-Work Petition Campaign, Comanche Co, summer 67; co. finance chmn, Congressman Jim Smith, 68; chmn, Comanche Co. Rep. Party, 69- Bus. & Prof. Pos: Salesman, Minn. Mining & Mfg. Co, Atlanta, Ga, 50-53; ins. agent, New Eng. Life, Albany, 53-54, Bill Smisson Agency, Lawton, Okla, 57-68; registered rep, Westamerica Securities, 68- Mil. Serv: Entered as 2nd Lt, Army, 55, released as 1st Lt, 57, after serv. in 602nd FA Bn, Ft. Sill, Okla. Mem: Treas, mem. exec. cmt. and div. gen, United Fund; Mason; Rotary. Rel: Episcopal. Legal Res: 4635 Gore Blvd, Lawton, Okla. 73501. Mailing Add: P.O. Box 185, Lawton, Okla. 73501.

SMIT, RAYMOND J. R
Mich. State Rep.
b. Detroit, Mich, 9/21/28; s. Maurice J. Smit and Myrtle Cassity S; m. 2/10/51 to Patricia Jones O'Donaghey; c. Deborah, Edward and Norman. Educ: Univ. Mich, B.S. and M.S. in civil eng. Polit. & Govt. Pos: City chmn, Ann Arbor Rep. Party, Mich, 63-65; mem, Gov. Romney's Task Force on Water Rights, Use & Pollution Control, 64-; Mich. State Rep, 53rd Dist, 67- Bus. & Prof. Pos: Partner, Ayers, Lewis, Norris & May, consulting engrs, 50- Mil. Serv: Entered as Pvt, Army, 51, released as Pfc, after serv. in Artil. Sch, Ft. Sill, Okla. Publ: Technical papers. Mem: Am. Soc. Civil Engrs; Nat. Soc. Prfnl. Engrs; Am. Water Works Asn; Am. Water Pollution Control Fedn; Mich. Asn. of Professions; Kiwanis; People to People. Mailing Add: 330 Hazelwood, Ann Arbor, Mich. 48103.

SMITH, A. LEDYARD, JR. R
Chmn, Bolton Rep. Town Cmt, Mass.
b. Milwaukee, Wis, 9/27/32; s. A. Ledyard Smith and Nancy Sawyer Falk S; m. 12/17/55 to Jacqueline Walker; c. Katharine Marquand, Margaret Falk, A. Ledyard, III and Robert Eliot, II. Educ: Harvard Univ, 2 years; Bentley Sch. Acct. and Finance, Boston, Mass, grad, 61; Fly Club. Polit. & Govt. Pos: Mem. Bd. of Registrars, Bolton, Mass, 67-68, mem. Planning Bd, Bolton, Mass, 68-69; chmn, Bolton Rep. Town Cmt, 68- Mil. Serv: Entered as Pvt, Marines, 52, released as Lance Cpl, 60, after serv. in HMR 161, Korean Theatre, 53-54. Mem: Lions. Rel: Protestant. Mailing Add: Century Mill Rd, Bolton, Mass. 01740.

SMITH, ABNEY ALEXANDER D
S.C. State Rep.
b. Columbia, S.C, 7/19/10; s. Ernest Smith and Vera Abney S; m. 8/16/41 to Louise Prichard. Educ: Univ. of S.C, B.A, 32. Polit. & Govt. Pos: S.C. State Rep, currently. Bus. & Prof. Pos: Owner Smith Indust. Parts and Repair Co. and A.A. Smith Co. Mil. Serv: Maj, Army, 41-46; Col, Army Res. Mem: Past chmn, Camping Cmt, Coastal Carolina Boy Scouts; past finance chmn. and charter mem, North Charleston Rotary Club; Cooper River Parks and Playground Cmt, 49-64; A&FM; Elks; Am. Legion; ROA; Citadel Educ. Found. Rel: Methodist; mem. Bd. of Stewards. Mailing Add: Box 5286, North Charleston, S.C. 29406. (1967)

SMITH, ALBERT F. R
Chmn, Rural New Castle Rep. Cmt, Del.
b. Mulhall, Okla, 6/16/13; s. Mary A. Wall; m. 11/30/60 to Beryl B. Baumgardner; c. Patricia and James. Educ: Okla. State Univ, B.S. in chem. eng, 32; Univ. Ill, Ph.D. in chem, 36; Phi Beta Kappa; Phi Kappa Phi; Phi Lambda Upsilon; Sigma Tau; Sigma Xi; Blue Key. Polit. & Govt. Pos: Chmn, Brandywine Hundred Rep. Cmt, Del, 56-60, acting state chmn, Mar, 60; del, Rep. Nat. Conv, 56, 60, 64 and 68; mem, Del. Rep. State Cmt, 58-; chmn, Rural New

Castle Rep. Cmt, Del, 60-; mem, Del. River and Bay Authority, 69- Bus. & Prof. Pos: Res. chemist, Du Pont Co, 36-39, res. supvr, 39-64, lab. dir, 52-54, res. dir, 54- Mem: Am. Chem. Soc; Soc. of Rheology; Am. Phys. Soc; N.Y. Acad. of Sci; Am. Inst. of Physics; Cmt. of 39. Several Technical Articles and Patents. Rel: Northern Baptist. Mailing Add: 4609 Bedford Blvd, Wilmington, Del. 19803.

SMITH, ALBERT S. R
N.J. State Assemblyman
b. Reading, Pa, 7/7/04. Educ: Perkiomen Sch, Pennsburg, Pa, 26; West. Md. Col. Polit. & Govt. Pos: Postmaster, Brigantine, N.J, 28-42, tax assessor, 37-42; mem, Brigantine Bd. Educ, 34-42, pres, 37-42; mem, Atlantic Co. Bd. Freeholders, 43-60; undersheriff, Atlantic Co, 50-53; pres, Atlantic Co. Bd. Taxation, 54; N.J. State Assemblyman, currently. Bus. & Prof. Pos: Assoc, Hotel Belvidere and The Seaview-Bouvier, 32-52. Mailing Add: 201 Dolphin Ave, Northfield, N.J. 08225. (1967)

SMITH, ARTHUR C. D
b. Cumming, Ga, 8/26/23; s. Arthur C. Smith, Sr. and Estie Pirkle S; m. 12/29/45 to Claudia Ellorie Vaughn; c. Terry Jack, Judith Ann, Philip Arthur. Educ: Cumming High Sch, 41; N. Ga. Col, 42. Polit. & Govt. Pos: Ga. State Rep, 63-66; 57-58; past chmn, Hosp. Authority. Bus. & Prof. Pos: Hatchery, feed bus; poultry processor; v.pres, Forsyth Co. Bank. Mil. Serv: Air Force, 43-45. Mem: Mason; Shriner; Elk; Kiwanis; Gridiron; bd. of dirs, Southeast. Poultry and Egg; past pres, Ga. Poultry Fedn. Rel: Concord Baptist Church, mem, bd. of deacons. Mailing Add: Cumming, Ga. 30130. (1967)

SMITH, BERNARD C. R
N.Y. State Sen.
b. Barnesboro, Pa, 7/29/23; s. Charles Smith and Mary DePaepe S; m. 12/29/49 to Elizabeth Ann Reynolds; c. Bernard C, Terry Ross, Craig Lawrence and Timothy Blythe. Educ: Cornell Univ, A.B, 44 and LL.B, 49; Phi Delta Phi; Kappa Delta Rho. Polit. & Govt. Pos: N.Y. State Sen, 66-; dist. attorney, Suffolk Co, Riverhead, N.Y. Mil. Serv: Army, Pac. Theater. Mem: Adv. bd, Sch. Polit. Sci, State Univ. of N.Y; bd. mgrs, St. Johns Hosp; Rotarian, past pres. Rel: Episcopal. Mailing Add: Franklin St, Northport, N.Y. 11768. (1967)

SMITH, BERNARD CHESTER R
Committeeman, White Co. Rep. Party, Ark.
b. Bradford, Ark, 12/15/24; s. George D. Smith and Mae Beatrice Ransom S; m, 51; remarried 64 to Frances M. Williams; c. David Bruce. Educ: Univ. Ark, B.S, 45, Sch. Med, M.D, 49, internship and res. Obstetrics-Gynecology, 49-51. Polit. & Govt. Pos: Committeeman, White Co. Rep. Party, Ark, 64- Bus. & Prof. Pos: Gen. practice, Smith Hosp, Bradford, Ark, 51- Mil. Serv: Lt.(jg), Navy, 49-50, serv. in Naval Hosp, Pensacola, Fla; Nat. Guard, 51-59, Maj. Mem: Am. Med. Asn; Ark. and White Co. Med. Socs; F&AM; Shrine. Rel: Protestant. Mailing Add: Bradford, Ark. 72020.

SMITH, BETTE BELLE R
Mem, Calif. Rep. State Cent. Cmt.
b. Modesto, Calif, 1/17/21; d. James Alfred Anderson and Maysel Hughes A; m. 5/4/45 to Jean Talbott Smith; c. Talbott Anderson, Timothy Melton and Mary Margaret. Educ: Modesto Jr. Col, A.A, 39; Univ. Calif, Los Angeles, 2 years; Kappa Delta. Polit. & Govt. Pos: Mem. and secy, Modesto Jr. Col. Rep. Youth, Calif, 38-39; second v.pres, Rep. Women of Modesto, 66-67, first v.pres, 67-68 and mem, 68-69; Modesto Womens chmn, Ronald Reagan for Gov, primary elec, 67, co-chmn, Richard Lying for Sen, gen. elec, 67; co-chmn, Stanislaus Co. Women for Nixon-Agnew, 68; mem, Calif. Rep. State Cent. Cmt, 69- Bus. & Prof. Pos: Music and dancing teacher, 34-39. Mem: Vol. dist. rep, Am. Field Serv. Int. Scholarships; Modesto Jr. Col. Found; Modesto Jr. Col. Alumni Asn.(exec. cmt); life mem, Omega Nu Sorority; Guide Dogs for the Blind; hon. life mem, Enslen Sch. PTA; past pres, Roosevelt PTA; bd. dirs, United Crusade; People to People; Girl Scouts (bd. mem. and troop leader). Named Woman of the Year, Soroptimist Club, Modesto, Calif, 66. Rel: Christian Science. Mailing Add: 415 Sycamore Ave, Modesto, Calif. 95354.

SMITH, BETTY DENNY R
Chmn, 29th Cong. Dist, Rep. Cent. Cmt, Calif.
b. Centralia, Ill, 11/12/32; d. Otto Hasenfuss and Elizabeth Ferne Beier H; m. to Judge Peter S. Smith; c. Carla Kip and Bruce Kimball. Educ: Univ. Ill, Bus. Admin, 50-52; Pi Phi Theta; Delta Gamma. Polit. & Govt. Pos: Chmn, Rousselot for Cong, Monterey Park, Calif, 60; v.pres, Monterey Park Young Rep, 63; chmn, Goldwater for Pres, Monterey Park, 64; mem, Calif. Rep. State Cent. Cmt, 64-; Rep. chmn, 29th Cong. Dist. Precinct Orgn, Calif, 65; mem. organizing cmt, Bob Finch for Lt. Gov, 66; Los Angeles coordinator, Williams for Attorney Gen, 66; mem. exec. cmt, Los Angeles Co. Rep. Cent. Cmt, 66-, v.chmn, 67-; mem, Cand. Research and Develop. Cmt. for Los Angeles Co, 67-; chmn, 29th Cong. Dist. Rep. Cent. Cmt, 69- Bus. & Prof. Pos: Loan officer, N.Park Finance, San Diego, Calif, 52; free lance fashion coordinator, Los Angeles Co, 53-60; prod. mgr, Mo Nadler Fashions, 61-64; show room dir, Jean of Calif, 65. Mem: Mannequins Asn. of Los Angeles; legis. chmn, Pet Assistance Found; bd. dirs, San Gabriel Valley Lawyers Wives; Mayor's Vol. Corps, Las Angelenas; Los Angeles Opera Assocs; Los Angeles Athletic Club; United Rep. of Calif. Mannequin of the Month, 67; Cert. of Merit Award, Los Angeles Rep. Cent. Cmt, 68. Rel: Christian. Mailing Add: 1766 Bluffhill Dr, Monterey Park, Calif. 91754.

SMITH, BILL D
b. Muskogee, Okla, 3/2/31; s. Roy Hildred Smith and Mary E. Peek S; div; c. Chyrll Marie. Educ: Okla. Univ. Col. of Continuing Educ, 65. Polit. & Govt. Pos: Staff asst, Okla. Dem. State Cent. Cmt, 64; secy-treas, Dem. Cent. Cmt, 64, chmn, 64-65; pres, Okla. Dem. Coun, 65-66. Mil. Serv: Entered as Pvt, Marines, 48, released as T/Sgt, 57; Nat. Defense Medal. Mem: Mason, York Rite; Okla. State Jr. C. of C.(former state v.pres); former nat. dir, U.S. Jr. C. of C. Mailing Add: 2427 N.W. 13th, Oklahoma City, Okla. 73107. (1967)

SMITH, BOYD KEITH D
b. McGill, Nev, 11/15/20; s. James Ross Smith and Ada Fawcett S; m. 7/5/42 to Lois Hannah Christopherson; c. David Scott, Cathryn Ann and Stephen Boyd. Educ: Univ. Nev. Polit. & Govt. Pos: Asst. postmaster, Postal Dept, Nev, 47-52; chief dep. assessor, White Pine Co, 52-59, clerk, 59-; former chmn. and mem. exec. bd, White Pine Co. Dem. Cent. Cmt. Mil. Serv: Entered as Seaman, Navy, 42, released as Radioman 1/C, 46, after serv. in Asiatic Seventh Fleet; Asiatic Pac. and Am. Campaign Ribbons; Good Conduct Medal; Tarawa, Kwajalein and Saipan Campaign Ribbons. Mem: Past Exalted Ruler, Elks; past v.pres, Nev. Fiscal Off. Asn; trustee, Nev. Soc. for Crippled Children and Adults; C. of C. Mgr. Pony Express Days Celebration, White Pine Co, 12 years. Rel: Latter-day Saint. Legal Res: 751 Lyons Ave, Ely, Nev. 89301. Mailing Add: P.O. Box 659, Ely, Nev. 89301. (1967)

SMITH, CATHLEEN WINSOR Independent
b. Providence, R.I, 5/28/05; m. to Earl S. Smith; c. 2 sons, 2 daughters. Educ: Tabbut-Hubbard Bus. Sch, Pawtucket, R.I. Polit. & Govt. Pos: Mem, Norton Sch. Bd, Vt, 59-61; Vt. State Rep, 65-67. Bus. & Prof. Pos: Co-owner & mgr, vacation camp on Norton Lake. Rel: Protestant. Mailing Add: Norton Lake, Norton, Vt. 05907. (1967)

SMITH, CHARLES COURTLAND D
b. Eldorado, Ga, 11/21/07; s. William Ritchie Smith and Elizabeth McQuarrie S; m. 6/19/43 to Nell Martin; c. Charles C. Jr, Susan, Linda. Educ: Martha Berry Schs; Ga. Sch. of Commerce. Polit. & Govt. Pos: Ga. State Rep, 63-66; Ga. State Sen. (4th dist.), 59-60. Bus. & Prof. Pos: Pres, Peoples Bank, St. Marys, Ga, 55-; exec. officer, State Bank of Kingsland, Ga, 47; Fla. Nat. Bank, 26-47. Mil. Serv: WWII, Capt, Chem. Warfare, 4 years. Mem: Mason; Shriner. Rel: Methodist. Mailing Add: St. Marys, Ga. 31558. (1967)

SMITH, CHARLES F, JR. R
b. Rinelander, Wis, 7/16/18; s. Charles F. Smith, Sr. and Jeanette S; m. 2/7/48 to Joan Sampson; c. Nancy, Kathryn, Charles and Richard. Educ: Wis. Univ, B.A, 41, LL.B, 48; Sigma Alpha Epsilon. Polit. & Govt. Pos: Chmn, Marathon Co. Bd, Wis, Wausau alderman and co. bd. mem, 50-60; co. chmn, Rep. Party, 59-62; Wis. State Sen, 62-66, majority caucus secy, Wis. State Senate, 63, caucus chmn, 65. Bus. & Prof. Pos: Pres, Marathon Co. Bar Asn, 69-; partner, Tinkham, Smith, Bliss & Patterson, currently. Mil. Serv: Entered as Pvt, Army, 42, released as 1st Lt, 46, after serv. in Pac. Theatre, 45-46. Mem: Int. Asn. of Ins. Counsel; Marathon Co, Wis. and Am. Bar Asns; Elks; Am. Legion; C. of C; pres. and mem. local Rotary Club and Cancer Soc; Wis. State Coun. for Home and Family; v.chmn, Wis. Natural Beauty Coun. Legal Res: 910 Fulton St, Wausau, Wis. 54401. Mailing Add: 630 Fourth St, Wausau, Wis. 54401.

SMITH, CHARLES FRANKLIN, SR. 'CHARLIE' R
Chmn, Douglas Co. Rep. Party, Ga.
b. Atlanta, Ga, 8/22/38; s. Grady A. Smith, Sr. and Helen Nelson O'Kelley S; m. 10/17/63 to Estelle Carroll; c. Charles Franklin, Jr. 'Chuck.' Educ: Univ. Md. (Correspondence), 57; Univ. Calif, Berkeley, 60-61. Polit. & Govt. Pos: Chmn, Douglas Co. Rep. Party, Ga, 68- Bus. & Prof. Pos: Chem. process engr, Standard Oil Co, Richmond, Calif, 60-62; ins. salesman, James B. Porter & Assocs, 62-67, Robert J. Shaw & Assocs, currently. Mil. Serv: Entered as Airman Basic, Air Force, 56, released as Airman 2/C, 60, after serv. in Mil. Air Transport, 3753rd Mil. Air Transport Serv; Good Conduct Medal. Publ: 'The How & Why,' (Feature Section), Nat. Ins. Salesman, 68. Mem: Lithia Springs Jaycees (past dir, v.pres, present parliamentarian). Sales Awards. Rel: Baptist. Mailing Add: 3997 Janet Leigh St, Lithia Springs, Ga. 30057.

SMITH, CHARLES O, JR. R
b. Russellville, Ala, 4/5/23; s. Charles O. Smith, Sr. and Ida Lee Pace S; m. 12/25/41 to Faye Louise McClung; c. Charles S. and Carol F. Educ: Florence State Col, 40-41. Polit. & Govt. Pos: Alternate del, Rep. Nat. Conv, 56; cand. for probate judge, Franklin Co, Ala, 58; served in all positions, Co. Rep. Politics; former area coordinator and chmn. cand. recruitment, N.Ala. State Rep. Cmt; v.chmn, Ala. State Rep. Cmt, 62-69. Bus. & Prof. Pos: Former owner, local hardward bus, 4 years; mgr, Ira A. Watson Co, 48-55; dist. mgr, Victor Lipchin Co, Life Ins. Co, 62- Mil. Serv: Entered as Pvt, Army, 45, released as S/Sgt, 46, after serv. in 824th Antiaircraft Artil. Bn, Pac. Theater. Mem: Ala. Life Underwriters Asn; Farm Bur; Mason; Lions; VFW; Am. Legion. Rel: Baptist. Legal Res: 1300 N. Jackson, Russellville, Ala. 35635. Mailing Add: P.O. Box 218, Russellville, Ala. 35635. (1967)

SMITH, CHARLOTTE WESTBROOK R
V.Chmn, Calhoun Co. Rep. Exec. Cmt, Mich.
b. Battle Creek, Mich, 8/3/29; m. to John W. Smith; c. Deborah, Todd, Kim and Ruth Ellen. Polit. & Govt. Pos: Co. supvr, 11th Dist; v.chmn, Calhoun Co. Rep. Exec. Cmt, Mich, currently; del, Calhoun Co. Rep. Conv. Bus. & Prof. Pos: Farmer. Rel: Christian Science; Sunday Sch. Teacher. Mailing Add: R.R. 1, Homer, Mich. 49245.

SMITH, CHRISTY KNUT R
b. Horton, Wyo, 11/27/16; s. Nels H. Smith and Marie S. Christensen S; m. 12/20/43 to Bethel Muir; c. Kristy Kay, Colleen and Michele. Educ: Univ. Wyo. Polit. & Govt. Pos: Committeeman, Wyo. State Rep. Party, 55-66; del, Rep. Nat. Conv, 64. Bus. & Prof. Pos: Dir, Nat. Bank of Newcastle, 64-; dir, Tri-Co. REA Bd, 65- Mem: Mason (32°); Farm Bur; Am. Hereford Asn; Shrine; Stock Growers. Rel: Methodist. Mailing Add: 19 N. Summit Ave, Newcastle, Wyo. 82701.

SMITH, CLARK A. D
b. Pine Bluffs, Wyo, 1/8/25; m. to Ann; c. 6. Educ: Beloit Col; Univ. of Wyo. Polit. & Govt. Pos: Wyo. State Rep, -67. Bus. & Prof. Pos: Real estate and ins. Mem: Nat. Asn. of Realtors; Cheyenne Bd. of Realtors; Kiwanis Club; C. of C; Bd. of Trustees of Cole Shopping Ctr. Merchants Asn. Rel: Catholic. 1967 Legal Res: 1222 W. 32nd St, Cheyenne, Wyo. No mailing address available. (1967)

SMITH, CLARY HOOD D
b. Spartanburg, S.C, 9/20/28; s. M.B. Smith, Jr. and Maude Hood S; m. 7/8/50 to Betty Ruth Blanchard; c. Clary, Jr, Ricky, Mark and Joy. Educ: Clemson Col, 50. Polit. & Govt. Pos: Former S.C. State Rep. Bus. & Prof.

Pos: Fuel oil dealer; owner, Clary Smith Oil Co; serv. sta. operator, Smiths' Esso Servicenter, partner. Mil. Serv: 1st Lt, Army, 51-52; 25th Inf. Div, Korea. Mem: Teacher Intermediate Boys; Brotherhood pres, Cedar Springs Baptist Church; Jaycees; Lions Club. Rel: Baptist. Mailing Add: RFD 4, Dairy Ridge Rd, Spartanburg, S.C. 29302. (1967)

SMITH, CLAUDE HARMAN R
Chmn, Culpeper Co. Rep. Cmt, Va.
b. Winston, Va, 11/3/08; s. James Wilbur Smith and Mary E. Biedler S; m. 6/17/33 to Genevieve Grace Wright (deceased); m. 4/2/54 to Dorothy Mae Neal; c. Elaine Joy (Mrs. Dazey), Claude Harman, Jr. and John Calvin Wright. Educ: Univ. Md, A.B, 32;Southeast. Univ, LL.B, 36; Command and Gen. Staff Sch, U.S. Army, 44; Phi Kappa Phi; Omicron Delta Kappa; Beta Pi Theta; Scabbard & Blade; pres, Student Govt. Asn, Coun. of Debate and Religions Work Coun; M Club. Polit. & Govt. Pos: Dist. supvr, U.S. Treas. Dept, 33-41; Chief Int. Civil Aviation Orgn. Officer, U.S. Civil Aeronaut. Admin, 46-49, chief, Int. Civil Aviation Orgn. Div, 52-59; mem. or chmn, numerous U.S. Govt. Del. to Int. Aviation Conv; alternate U.S. Rep. to Int. Civil Aviation Orgn, 49-52, U.S. Rep. to Air Navig. Cmn, Int. Civil Aviation Orgn, 49-52 & 59-60; chief, Int. Orgn. Div, U.S. Fed. Aviation Agency, 60-64; chmn, Culpeper Co. Rep. Cmt, Va, 66- Mil. Serv: Entered as 1st Lt, Army, 41, released as Lt. Col, 46, after serv. in Hq. Air Force; Legion of Merit; Am. Theater and Pre-Pearl Harbor Ribbons. Mem: Mason (32°); Am. Legion; Culpeper and Va. Hist. Socs; SAR, pres, Va. Soc, 65-66, chmn, Cmt. on Americanism, Nat. Soc. bd. of dirs, Culpeper Farm Bur, 67-, Culpeper Country Club, 67-, Culpeper Mem. Hosp, 68- and Culpeper C. of C, 67- Rel: Protestant. Mailing Add: Savilla Manor, Route 4, Box 153A, Culpeper, Va. 22701.

SMITH, CLIFFORD EDWIN, JR. D
b. Frankfort, Ky, 1/22/37; s. Clifford Edwin Smith, Sr. and Anita Sower S; single. Educ: Wash. and Lee Univ. B.A, 58; Univ. Ky, LL.B, 64; Omicron Delta Kappa (pres, Alpha Circle, 57-58); Phi Delta Phi; Kappa Alpha Order. Polit. & Govt. Pos: V.chmn, Sixth Cong. Dist. Young Dem. Clubs of Ky, 62-63, chmn, 63-64; State Youths Speakers chmn, Dem. Gubernatorial Campaign, 63; Young Citizens Coordinator, Presidential Campaign, Ky, 64; pres, Young Dem. Clubs of Ky, 66-69. Bus. & Prof. Pos: Univ. Ky. Law Alumni Chmn, Univ. Ky, Law Alumni Day Cmt, 66. Mil. Serv: Entered as Ens, Naval Res, 58, released as Lt.(jg), 61, after serv. as Legal Officer, aircraft carrier U.S.S. Intrepid, Second and Sixth Fleets, Atlantic and Mediterranean, 58-61; Lt, Naval Res, currently; Commendation by Capt. Paul Masterton, Commanding Officer, U.S.S. Intrepid. Mem: Am, Ky. and Franklin Co. Bar Asns; Am. Trial Lawyers Asn; Jaycees; Franklin Co. and State Farm Bur; Rotary; bd. of dirs, Ky. Angus Asn. Represented Ky. at Am. Law Students Asn. Conv. before grad. from law sch. Rel: Baptist. Legal Res: 118 W. Campbell St, Frankfort, Ky. 40601. Mailing Add: P.O. Box 457, Frankfort, Ky. 40601.

SMITH, COY D
Ala. State Rep.
b. Baxtorville, Miss, 11/21/33; m; c. five. Educ: E. Miss. Jr. Col; Univ. of Tenn. Polit. & Govt. Pos: Mem, town coun, Ala; Ala. State Rep, currently. Bus. & Prof. Pos: Gasoline bus. Mem: Kiwanis Club. Rel: Baptist. Mailing Add: Citronelle, Ala. 36522. (1967)

SMITH, DALE AUGUSTUS R
Chmn, Switzerland Co. Rep. Cent. Cmt, Ind.
b. Vevay, Ind, 2/18/03; s. Charles Wesley Smith and Minnie Farrell S; m. 5/4/29 to Helen Marie Adams; c. Rosemary (Mrs. Clifford). Educ: Vevay High Sch. Polit. & Govt. Pos: Mem, Welfare Bd, Ind, 46-54; trustee, Pleasant Twp, 46-54; chmn, Switzerland Co. Rep. Cent. Cmt, 52-; Ind. Gross Income Tax Div, 53-61. Bus. & Prof. Pos: Owner and operator of a farm. Rel: Methodist. Mailing Add: R.R. 1, Vevay, Ind. 47043.

SMITH, DARRELL FENWICK R
b. Provo, Utah, 2/13/27; s. Walter F. Smith and Eleanor Seegmiller S; m. 8/27/51 to Marjorie Hill; c. Wendy Jean, Rebecca Ann, Kevin Fenwick, Karen Kay and Teresa Lynne. Educ: George Wash. Univ, 50-53; Am. Univ. LL.B, 56. Polit. & Govt. Pos: Co. attorney, Maricopa Co, Ariz, 59-61; Asst. Attorney Gen, Ariz, 61, Attorney Gen, 65-68. Bus. & Prof. Pos: Former dir, Mesa Credit Union; with legal dept, Vet. Admin, Phoenix, Ariz, 59; mem, Wade & Smith Attorneys, Mesa, Ariz, 61-64; pres, San Tan Br, Gila River Indian Reservation, 64- Mem: Am, Ariz, D.C. Bar Asns, Am. Trial Lawyers Asn, Nat. Asn. Attorneys Gen; Mesa C. of C; Mesa Sertoma Club. Rel: Latter-day Saint; Former Stake Mission Pres. Mailing Add: 703 W. Sixth Ave, Mesa, Ariz. 85201. (1967)

SMITH, DEAN CONRAD R
b. Seattle, Wash, 9/5/29; s. T.J. Smith and Pearl Wellwood S; m. 12/16/50 to Julia J. Smithwick; c. Tremaine John, II and Jeanine. Educ: Whitman Col, 47-48; Univ. Wash, B.S. and LL.B; mem. ed. bd, Wash. Law Rev; Tau Kappa Epsilon; Phi Alpha Delta. Polit. & Govt. Pos: Munic. judge, Wapato, Wash, 57-62; Rep. precinct committeeman, Wapato, Wash, 61-62; chmn, City Planning Cmn, Wapato, 62-69; state committeeman, Wash. Rep. Party, 67-68; chmn, Yakima Co. Rep. Cent. Cmt, 68; U.S. attorney, East. Dist. of Wash, 69- Bus. & Prof. Pos: Dep. prosecuting attorney, Yakima Co, Wash, 55-56; partner, Smith & Smith, Wapato, Wash, 56-69. Mil. Serv: Entered as Pvt, Army, 53, released as 1st Lt, 55, after serv. in 6006 ASU, Judge Adv. Gen. Corps, Ft. Lewis, Wash. Publ: 'Law Review Comment,' Wash. Law Rev, 51. Mem: Yakima Co, Wash. State and Am. Bar Asns; Am. Trial Lawyers Asn; Lions; Am. Legion; Elks; Univ. Wash. Alumni Asn. Rel: Presbyterian. Mailing Add: 309 Southpark Dr, Wapato, Wash. 98951.

SMITH, DENNIS A. D
b. Boston, Mass, 1939. Educ: Grad. Stonehill Col; Boston Col. Grad. Sch. of Soc. Work. Polit. & Govt. Pos: Rsch. dir. for Sen. Pres; Assoc. dir. of the Commonwealth Serv. Corps; del. to State Convs. in 62 and 64; Dem. Town Cmt. Mailing Add: 8 Holborn St, Milton, Mass. 02168. (1967)

SMITH, DONALD ALBERT R
b. Yonkers, N.Y, 11/19/31; s. Albert Henry Smith and Ruth Joudrey S.(deceased); m. 12/27/57 to Barbara Eleanor Atkeson; c. Jean Marie, David Andrew and Carolyn Rene. Educ: Columbia Col, B.A, 53; Union Theol. Sem, B.D, 56; Teachers Col, Columbia Univ, M.A, 59, Ed.D, 65; Phi Delta Kappa; Kappa Delta Pi; Curtis Medal for Excellence in Pub. Speaking; Sigma Chi; Yearbook and Newspaper Staff; German Club. Polit. & Govt. Pos: Chmn, Barbour Co. Rep. Exec. Cmt, W.Va, 64-67. Bus. & Prof. Pos: Asst. minister, Demarest Baptist Church, Flemington, N.J, 53-56; Instr. of Eng, Kanto Gakuin Univ, Yokohama, Japan, 56-57; asst, Off. of Registr, Teachers Col, Columbia Univ, 57-58, asst. placement officer, Grad. Sch. Bus, 58-60; assoc. dean of students and dir. of Student Union, Alderson-Broaddus Col, 60-64, dir, Off-Campus Educ, 64- Mem: Am. Asn. of Univ. Prof; Student Union Asn; Mid-Atlantic Placement Asn; Coop. Educ. Asn; W.Va. Student Personnel Asn; Am. Personnel and Guid. Asn; W.Va. Acad. of Sci, Lions Int; Barbour Co. Fair Asn; Barbour Co. Improv. Asn. Rel: Baptist. Mailing Add: Alderson-Broaddus Col, Philippi, W.Va. 26416.

SMITH, DONALD EDWIN D
b. Huntington, W.Va, 3/9/25; s. Cline H. Smith and Pearl May S; m. 1/16/42 to Mary Faye Withers; c. Jeanette Ann and Connie Sue (Mrs. Michael Kuhn). Educ: Marshall Univ; Huntington Sch of Bus; Spring Arbor Col; Winona Lake Sch. of Theol. Polit. & Govt. Pos: Chaplain of House of Del, W.Va, 57th Session; W.Va. State Del, 64-66. Bus. & Prof. Pos: Minister and businessman; pres, First Nat. Ins; Huntington Motor Sales and Uptown Motors, Inc, presently. Mem: Mason (32°); Shrine; 100F; Lions Club; Huntington C. of C; Huntington Christian Businessmen's Asn; W.Va. Automobile Dealers Asn. Rel: Methodist. Mailing Add: 4210 16th St, Huntington, W.Va. 25705.

SMITH, DONALD EUGENE R
Chmn, Lake Co. Rep. Exec. Cmt, Fla.
b. Sanford, Maine, 7/17/24; s. Harold Ernest Smith and Ruth Elizabeth Garland S.(deceased); m. 12/31/57 to Mary Jo Richardson; c. stepsons, Edgar Jerome and Lamar Eugene Elton. Polit. & Govt. Pos: Del, Rep. Nat. Conv, 64; precinct committeeman; chmn, Lake Co. Rep. Exec. Cmt, Fla, currently. Bus. & Prof. Pos: Inspector, Retail Credit Co, 46-; sports correspondent, Tampa Tribune, Orlando Sentinel, Leesburg Daily Commercial and Jacksonville J. Times Union. Mil. Serv: Entered as A/S, Naval Res, 43, released as Aviation Ordnanceman 2/C, 45; Chief Personnelman, Naval Air Res, 68-; World War II Victory Medal; Am. and Asiatic-Pac. Theater Ribbons; Naval Res. Medal; Meritorious Serv. Ribbon. Publ: Feature Story in all Fla. Mag, 65. Mem: Life mem, U.S. Jr. C. of C; Girl Scouts; Elks; past state v.pres. and nat. dir, Jaycees. Rel: Baptist. Legal Res: 2513 Winona Ave, Leesburg, Fla. 32748. Mailing Add: P.O. Box 692, Leesburg, Fla. 32748.

SMITH, DONALD HOUSTON D
Exec. Committeeman, Ark. Dem. Cent. Cmt.
b. Peach Orchard, Ark, 3/18/30; s. Harmon Smith and Mary Ellen Cox S; m. 8/31/57 to Rose Mary Albano; c. Donald Houston, Jr, Mary Ann and Brian Davis. Educ: Ark. State Univ, B.A, 53; Univ. Ark, LL.B, 59; Blue Key; Phi Kappa Alpha; Phi Alpha Delta. Polit. & Govt. Pos: Chmn, Jefferson Co. Dem. Cent. Cmt, Ark, 64-; chmn, Jefferson Co. Elec. Cmn, 64-; exec. committeeman, Ark. Dem. Cent. Cmt, 69- Bus. & Prof. Pos: Chmn, Jefferson Co. Commun. Action Proj, 66-67, Southeast Ark. Econ. Develop. Dist, 67- Mil. Serv: Entered as 2nd Lt, Army, 53, released as 1st Lt, 56, after serv. in 17th Field Artil. Bn. and First Cavalry Artil, Far East Command, 54-56. Mem: Am. and Jefferson Co. Bar Asns; Judicature Soc. of Am. Bar Asn; Ark. Bar Asn.(chmn, Family Law Sect, 69-); Pine Bluff C. of C; Pine Bluff Jr. C. of C.(past pres); Ark. Jr. C. of C.(past pres). Pine Bluff Jr. C. of C. Distinguished Serv. Award, 63; Lawyer's Citizen Award, Ark. Bar Asn, 67. Rel: Baptist. Mailing Add: 718 W. Harding, Pine Bluff, Ark. 71601.

SMITH, DONALD L. R
Vt. State Sen.
b. Barre, Vt, 5/20/24; s. Donald W. Smith and Freda Ladd S; m. Oct, 1947 to Ruth Reynolds; c. Donald R. and Rebecca Ruth. Educ: Mass. State Col, B.S, 46. Polit, & Govt. Pos: Vt. State Sen, 55-59 & 65-; fed. housing dir, Vt, 59-61. Bus. & Prof. Pos: Life ins. broker. Mem: Rotary; Elks; Mason; Farm Bur; Grange. Rel: Congregational. Mailing Add: R.R. 1, Barre, Vt. 05641.

SMITH, DONALD L. R
b. Anchorage, Alaska, 3/14/39; s. Eugene C. Smith and Ingaborg E. Swanson S; m. 6/9/59 to Nancy L. Knight; c. Donald L, Jr, Kollette E. and Laura Lee. Educ: Univ. Alaska, 58-62; Alpha Kappa Psi; Epsilon Psi. Polit. & Govt. Pos: Former Alaska State Rep; Assemblyman, Gr. Anchorage Area Borough, 65-66. Bus. & Prof. Pos: Internal auditor, Radio Corp. Am, 63; sales rep, Int. Bus. Mach, 63- Mil. Serv: Pfc, Alaska Nat. Guard, 56-65. Mem: Elks. Rel: Episcopal. Legal Res: 10920 Timberline Trail, Anchorage, Alaska 99501. Mailing Add: P.O. Box 3516, Anchorage, Alaska 99501. (1967)

SMITH, DOYLE JACKSON, JR. D
Tenn. State Rep.
b. Chillicothe, Mo, 5/26/38; s. Doyle Jackson Smith and Christine Cain S; m. 8/15/59 to Barbara Reid; c. Nelle Christine and Doyle Jackson, III. Educ: Vanderbilt Univ, B.A, 59; Harvard Law Sch, LL.B, 62; Phi Eta Sigma. Polit. & Govt. Pos: Del, Dem. State Conv, 64; Tenn. State Rep, 65-; Tenn. membership chmn. and charter mem, Nat. Soc. of State Legis, presently. Bus. & Prof. Pos: Attorney-at-law, partner in firm of Rickey, Shankman, Agee, Harpster & Smith, Memphis, Tenn, presently. Mem: Harvard Club of Memphis; Bd. of Dirs, Memphis Heart Asn; Memphis and Shelby Co. Safety Coun, Traffic Safety Cmt; Jr. C. of C; Tenn. Hist. Soc; Memphis Country Club; W. Tenn. Sportsmen's Asn; Memphis and Shelby Co, Tenn. and Am. Bar Asns; Memphis Trial Lawyers Asn; Citizen's Asn. Selected as Outstanding Young Man in Memphis by Memphis Jaycees, 64; Selected as One of the Outstanding Young Men of Am, 66. Rel: Episcopal. Legal Res: 522 Adrian Dr, Memphis, Tenn. 38122. Mailing Add: 32nd Floor, 100 North Main Bldg, Memphis, Tenn. 38103.

SMITH, DUANE E. R
b. Havre, Mont, 6/16/30; s. Edmond I. Smith and Lucy M. Marlow S; m. 8/24/57 to Aureta McMenomey. Educ: Univ. Mont. Polit. & Govt. Pos: Precinct committeeman, Mont, 60-; alderman, Billings City Coun, 63-, pres, 69-; chmn, Yellowstone Co. Rep. Cent. Cmt, 64. Bus. & Prof. Pos: Partner, CPA firms, McCann & Smith, 54-61, Janke & Smith, 61-67 and Smith & Mangis, 67- Mil. Serv: Entered as 2nd Lt, Air Force, 52, released as 1st

Lt, 54, after serv. in Auditor Gen. Dept. Mem: Am. Inst. of CPA's; Mont. Soc. of CPA's; Mont. and Billings C. of C; Elks. Rel: Protestant. Legal Res: 2008 Colton Blvd, Billings, Mont. 59102. Mailing Add: 450 Mutual Benefit Life Bldg, Billings, Mont. 59101.

SMITH, E. ARNOLD D
Chmn, Montgomery Co. Dem. Party, Tex.
b. Willis, Tex, 9/6/13; s. E. Arnold Smith, Sr. and Allie D. Spiller S; m. 2/12/41 to Allene Marie Hopkins; c. Laura Elizabeth (deceased). Educ: Rice Univ, B.A, 37; Univ. Tex, LL.B, 40; Sigma Nu Phi. Polit. & Govt. Pos: Co. attorney, Montgomery Co, Tex, 41-45, co. judge, 45-49; chmn, Montgomery Co. Dem. Party, currently. Bus. & Prof. Pos: Partner, Smith & Simpson, Attorneys, Conroe, Tex. Mem: AF&AM, Conroe Lodge 748, Scottish Rite, Houston Consistory; Tex. and Montgomery Co. Bar Asns. Rel: Methodist. Legal Res: 202 Pine Shadows, Conroe, Tex. 77301. Mailing Add: P.O. Box 523, Conroe, Tex. 77301.

SMITH, EARL VICTOR, SR. D
b. New Orleans, La, 5/7/02; s. George Smith and Pheobia Welch S; m. 8/5/25 to Lilly Waldo; c. Earl V, Jr. and Earnest C. Educ: High Sch, 16. Polit. & Govt. Pos: Pres, Smithsonian Dem. Club, Calif, 61-; admin. asst. to U.S. Rep. Carley V. Porter, 38th Dist, Calif, 63-65. Bus. & Prof. Pos: Nurses asst, Vet. Hosp, 25-59; assoc. mem, pres. and chmn, Local 625, Nat. Fedn. Fed. Employees, 45-57; pres, Smith & Sons, Enterprises, 62-64. Mem: Mason (32°); West. Compton Civic League. Rel: Methodist. Mailing Add: 1716 W. 163rd St, Compton, Calif. 90220. (1967)

SMITH, EDGAR B, JR. D
b. Chauncey, Ga, 3/28/08; s. Edgar Bayard Smith and Eva Bussey S; m. 9/07/40; Nellie Clare Woodle; c. Edgar B, III, Mary Elizabeth. Educ: Emory Univ; Pi Kappa Phi. Polit. & Govt. Pos: Ga. State Rep, 63-66; City Coun, 62-63; Mayor Pro Tem, McRae, 62; Bd. of Educ, McRae, 52- Bus. & Prof. Pos: Real estate; farmer; timber; naval stores bus, 28-53. Mem: Mason; Rotary; Pres, McRae Club, 45; Pres, McRae C. of C, 59. Rel: Methodist. Mailing Add: Box 6, McRae, Ga. 31055. (1967)

SMITH, EDWARD BRUCE R
Mont. State Rep.
b. Dagmar, Mont, 5/7/20; s. Bruce Albert Smith and Johanna Grelong S; m. 9/29/45 to Juliet Ellevold; c. Gary, Douglas, Bruce and Rodney. Polit. & Govt. Pos: Mem, Co. Fair Bd, Mont, 60-; Mont. State Rep, Sheridan Co, 67- Mem: Mont. Wool Growers (pres); N.E. Mont. Wool Growers; Mont. Grain Growers (dir); Sheridan Co. Grain Growers Asn; Elks; Moose; 4-H Leader. Rel: Lutheran. Mailing Add: Dagmar, Mont. 59219.

SMITH, EDWARD HENRY R
Chmn, Cleveland Co. Rep. Exec. Cmt, N.C.
b. Charlotte, N.C, 10/8/25; s. Edward Arthur Smith, Jr. and Winifred Eloise Moss S; single. Educ: Riverside Mil. Acad, Gainesville, Ga, 42-43; Univ. N.C, Chapel Hill, 45-49; Phi Kappa Sigma; Dialectic Senate. Polit. & Govt. Pos: Mem, N.C. Citizens for Eisenhower Cmt, 52; Rep. precinct chmn, Kings Mountain, N.C, 60-66; chmn, Cleveland Co. Young Rep. Club, 64-66; mem, N.C. Rep. State Exec. Cmt, 64-; chmn, Cleveland Co. Rep. Exec. Cmt, 66-; Tenth Dist. Rep. presidential elector, 68. Bus. & Prof. Pos: V.pres, Edward A. Smith & Sons, Kings Mountain, N.C, 50-; radio newscaster, Cyanamid Textile News, WBIG and WFBC Greenville and WBT, Charlotte, currently. Publ: A History of the Battle of Kings Mountain, Kings Mountain Hist. Drama Asn, 53; series of newspaper articles, 'The Republican Party in North Carolina on its 100th Anniversary,' Shelby Daily Star and other papers, 4/67; weekly columnist, 'This Week in North Carolina History,' Kings Mountain Herald and other papers. Mem: Bd. dir, Cleveland Co. Hist. Soc; N.C. Lit. and Hist. Soc; Brotherhood of St. Andrew; Charlotte Textile Club. Author of TV documentary 'Signers for Liberty' for which WBT-V, Charlotte, N.C. received a George Washington Awards Medal from Freedoms Found, 67. Rel: Episcopal; mem, Church Vestry, Trinity Episcopal Church, Kings Mountain, N.C. Mailing Add: 303 Battleground Ave, Kings Mountain, N.C. 28086.

SMITH, EDWARD J. H. DFL
Mem, Minn. State Dem-Farmer-Labor Cent. Cmt.
Polit. & Govt. Pos: App. CLIC Parks Task Force, 63-69; former cand, Minn. State Rep; mem, Minn. State Dem-Farmer-Labor Cent. Cmt, currently. Bus. & Prof. Pos: Lubrication engr, Kerr McGee Oil Industs, Inc, 59; brokerage salesman, West. Oil & Fuel Co, 59-64; real estate sales and rentals, currently. Mil. Serv: Army, 1 year. Mem: Minn. Hist. Soc; Ft. Snelling State Park Asn; Miss. Gorge Asn; Keep Minn. Clean and Scenic; Gov. Cmn. on Air Resources. Mailing Add: 3518 Edmund Blvd, Minneapolis, Minn. 55406.

SMITH, EDWARD JACK D
S.C. State Rep.
b. Chesterfield, S.C, 7/18/18; s. Jackson Calhoun Smith and Mary Katherine McDougald S; m. 2/11/39 to Louella Gandy; c. Jacquelyn (Mrs. John Laney Melton) and Dowell Jack. Educ: Chesterfield High Sch, grad. Polit. & Govt. Pos: S.C. State Rep, 66- Bus. & Prof. Pos: Ins. agent, Nationwide Ins. Co, 53; r.r. fireman engr, Seaboard R.R, 42. Mil. Serv: Entered as Pfc, Army, 44, released as Sgt, 45, after serv. in R.R. Detachment. Mem: Mason; York Rite Shrine; Eastern Star; Am. Legion; Lions; C. of C; Nationwide Ins. Agent; R.R. Fireman Engr. Man of the Month, Ins. Agents S.C. Rel: Baptist; Chmn. Bd. Deacons, Emmanuel Baptist Church, several years; Chmn. Bldg. Cmt. Legal Res: Hwy. 15 N, Hartsville, S.C. 29550. Mailing Add: P.O. Drawer 458, Hartsville, S.C. 29550.

SMITH, EDWIN ANGUS R
b. Anaconda, Mont, 4/16/02; m. to Clara Ellen Carpenter; c. 2 sons, 1 daughter. Educ: Cabot High Sch, 20. Polit. & Govt. Pos: Former Vt. State Rep. Bus. & Prof. Pos: Farmer; dir, Cabot Farmers Coop. Creamery, 4 years. Mem: Wash. Co. Farm Bur; F&AM; RAM; Mt. Sinai Temple; Mt. Zion Commandery. Rel: Congregational. Mailing Add: Cabot, Vt. 05647. (1967)

SMITH, EDWIN STEEVES R
Chmn, Davison Co. Rep. Cent. Cmt, S.Dak.
b. Rochester, Minn, 6/24/38; s. John W. Smith and Florence Steeves S; m. 8/3/63 to Louise J. Blair; c. Andrea Louise. Educ: Carleton Col, B.A, 60; Univ. Minn. Law Sch, LL.B, 63; Gamma Eta Gamma. Polit. & Govt. Pos: Researcher, Legis. Reference Serv, Library of Cong, 58; chmn, Carleton Col. Rep. Club, S.Dak, 58-59; asst. to Rep. Albert H. Quie, 59; chmn, Minn. Fedn. Col. Rep, 59-60; chmn, Midwest Fedn. Col. Rep. Clubs, 60-61; chmn, First and Second Ward, Hennepin City, Minn. Young Rep, 61-63; chmn, Davison Co. Rep. Cent. Cmt, S.Dak, 66-; dep. states attorney, Mitchell, 68- Bus. & Prof. Pos: Asst. to Elmer L. Andersen, Cand. for Gov. of Minn, 60; trust off, Aberdeen Nat. Bank, 63-65; attorney, Tinan, Carlson, Padrnos and Smith, Mitchell, 65- Publ: Estate Planning for Farmers, series of 12 articles, Dak. Farmer, 64-65. Mem: S.Dak. Bar Asn, secy-treas, Young Lawyers Sect. and state chmn, Law Day USA, 66-68; pres. elect, Mitchell Kiwanis; Jaycees, trustee, Methodist Hosp; co-ordinator for judicial activities, S.Dak. Girls State; dir, S.Dak. Children's Aid. Rel: Methodist. Legal Res: 500 W. Fourth, Mitchell, S.Dak. 57301. Mailing Add: Box 488, Mitchell, S.Dak. 57301.

SMITH, ELBERT BENJAMIN, JR. D
b. Benham, Ky, 5/1/20; s. Elbert Benjamin Smith and Gladys Huffaker S; m. 12/26/44 to Jean Frances; c. Randall E, Henry Scott, Stephen A, Robert O. and Amy J. Educ: Maryville Col, A.B, 40; Univ. Chicago, A.M, 47, Ph.D, 49; Kappa Delta Pi; varsity football. Polit. & Govt. Pos: Participant, Summer Seminar, U.S. Dept. of State, 51, dir, 52; chmn. exec. cmt, Mahoning Co. Young Dem, Ohio, 53-54; pres, Story Co. Dem. Club, Iowa, 59-61; Dem. precinct committeeman, Iowa, 59-61; cand. for U.S. Sen, Iowa, 62 & 66; Dem. coordinator, Presidential Campaign, Iowa, 64; del, Dem. Nat. Conv, 64. Bus. & Prof. Pos: Assoc. prof. hist, Youngstown Univ, 49-57; Fulbright visiting prof, Univ. of Tokyo, 54-55; assoc. prof. hist, Iowa State Univ, 57-63, prof, 63-67; vis. prof. hist, Univ. of Wis, Madison, 67-68; prof. hist, Univ. of Md, 68- Mil. Serv: Entered as Hospital Apprentice 1/C, Navy, 42, released as Lt.(jg), 46, after serv. in Destroyer Escorts Brough and Oswald, Atlantic and European Command, 43-45; European and Atlantic Theater Campaign Ribbons. Publ: Making of American Foreign Policy, U.S. Info. Serv, 55; Magnificent Missourian, J.B. Lippincott Co, 58; The Death of Slavery: the United States, 1837-65, Univ. of Chicago Press, 67; plus one other. Mem: Am. Asn. for UN; Am. Hist. Asn; Soc. Am. Historians; Am. Civil Liberties Union; NAACP. Rel: Presbyterian. Mailing Add: 5904 Chestnut Hill Rd, College Park, Md. 20740.

SMITH, ELDON L. R
Chmn, Potter Co. Rep. Party, S.Dak.
b. Gettysburg, S. Dak, 2/11/28; s. Raymond C. Smith and Elda M. Rausch S; 10/28/49 to Billie C. Smith; c. Pamela N, Craig E, Kelly C. and Paula J. Educ: S. Dak. State Col, 1 year; Black Hills State Teachers Col, 1 year. Polit. & Govt. Pos: Chmn, Potter Co. Rep. Party, S.Dak, currently. Mem: Mason; Shrine; C. of C.(pres, Gettysburg Chap, 65). Rel: Episcopal. Mailing Add: 308 S. Park St, Gettysburg, S.Dak. 57442.

SMITH, ELMER EUGENE R
Chmn, Mo. State Rep. Cmt.
b. Wayne Co, Mo, 8/23/26; s. Ira D. Smith and Mabel Turnbough S; m. 9/21/46 to Bessie M. Thompson; c. Nancy (Mrs. Babel), Sandra Sue and Donald Eugene. Educ: St. Louis Univ, B.S, 51. Polit. & Govt. Pos: Dir, R-2 Sch. Dist, Mo, 61-63; dir. of revenue, St. Louis Co. Govt, 63-; mem, Mo. State Rep. Cmt, 66-, chmn, 68- Bus. & Prof. Pos: Purchasing mgr, Natkin & Co, St. Louis, Mo, 54-59, asst. mgr, 59-61. Mil. Serv: Entered as A/S, Navy, 44, released as Aviation Radio Man 2/C, 51, after serv. aboard several ships, Pac. Theatre, 45-46; Three Battle Stars; Pac. Theater Ribbon; Japanese Occup. Ribbon; Am. Theater Ribbon; Presidential Unit Citation. Mem: Int. Asn. Assessing Officers; Nat. Tax Asn; Mo. Hist. Soc; White Conf. on Educ. Cmt, St. Louis Co, Mo; Am. Legion. Mo. Rep. of the Year, by the Mo. Asn. Rep, 67. Rel: Methodist. Legal Res: 822 Gerald Place, Ferguson, Mo. 63135. Mailing Add: St. Louis County Courthouse, 7900 Forsyth, Clayton, Mo. 63105.

SMITH, EMMA E. R
b. Waimea, Kauai, Hawaii, 3/21/18; d. Samuel L. Smith and Alexandrine K. Peahu S; single. Educ: Univ. Hawaii, 39-41. Polit. Pos: Exec. secy, Rep. Party, Kauai, Hawaii, 65-66; pres, Kauai League of Rep. Women, 63-65; del, State and Co. Convs, 63, 64, 65 and 66; del, Nat. Rep. Conv, San Francisco, 64; pres, Kekaha Rep. Precinct Club, 62-64. Govt. Pos: Personnel clerk, Air Force, 44-46; chief clerk, U.S. Navy-901, 44; plotter, U.S. Army (Ward), 42-44. Bus. & Prof. Pos: Indust. rels. secy, Kekaha Sugar Co, Ltd, 46- Mem: Pres, Kekaha Commun. Asn, Kauai, Hawaii; Kauai League of Rep. Women; Kekaha Rep. Precinct Club. Rel: Protestant. Mailing Add: P.O. Box 301, Kekaha, Kauai, Hawaii 96752. (1967)

SMITH, ERNEST HENRY D
Chmn, St. Tammany Parish Dem. Exec. Cmt, La.
b. Union City, N.J, 4/24/18; s. Henry A. Smith and Elsie Drinkhaus S; m. 8/16/39 to Frances Johnson; c. Diane. Educ: Univ. Ala. Polit. & Govt. Pos: Mem, St. Tammany Parish Dem. Exec. Cmt, La, 60-64, chmn, 64- Bus. & Prof. Pos: Master and chief officer, U.S. Merchant Marine, 35-49; South Dist. Mgr, Whitlock Cordage Co, 49-60 and Cating Rope Works, 60- Mil. Serv: Entered as Ensign, Maritime Serv, 41, released as Comdr, 45; North Atlantic, Mid. E, Pac, Far East and Mediterranean Theater Ribbons. Mem: Propeller Club of the U.S; Int. House, New Orleans, La; Lacombe Civic Club. Rel: Lutheran. Mailing Add: P.O. Box, 38, Lacombe, La. 70445.

SMITH, EUGENE LINN R
b. Elk City, Kans, 8/5/29; s. Eugene H. Smith and Helen Linn S; m. 12/18/55 to Elizabeth M. Davis; c. Tracey Linn, Daric Scott and Porter Davis. Educ: Kans. State Col, B.S. in mech. eng, 51; Washburn Univ, LL.B, 57; Pi Tau Sigma; Sigma Tau; Scabbard & Blade; assoc. mem, Law Rev. Bd. Polit. & Govt. Pos: Co. and dist. chmn, Young Rep, Kans, 59-63; precinct committeeman, Rep. Party, 61-65; state chmn, Kans. Young Rep. Fedn, 63-65; asst. co. attorney, Seward Co, 64; del, Rep. Dist. and State Conv, 64; alternate del, Rep. Nat. Conv, 64; mem, bd. of dirs, Rep. Assoc, S.W. Kans, 64-66; del, Young Rep. Nat. Conv, 65; ex-officio mem, Kans. Young Rep. State Exec. Cmt, 65- Bus. & Prof. Pos: Trial attorney, Fed. Power Cmn, 57-59; pres, Reserve Pipeline, Inc, 60-66; partner, Smith & Greenleaf, Attorneys, 61- Mil. Serv: Entered as 2nd Lt, Air Force, 51, released as

1st Lt, 53. Mem: Rotary; Kansas and S.W. Kans. Bar Asns; bd. of dirs, Yucca Girl Scout Coun. Legal Res: 1006 Harrison Circle, Liberal, Kans. 67901. Mailing Add: Box 296, Liberal, Kans. 67901.

SMITH, EWING, JR. D
Tenn. State Rep.
b. Murfreesboro, Tenn, 1/3/33; s. Ewing Smith and Mozelle McCullough S; m. 12/30/52 to Angelyn Jenkins; c. Sheryl Lynn and Sandra Lee. Educ: Univ. Tenn, J.D, 55; Phi Delta Phi; Sigma Chi. Polit. & Govt. Pos: City councilman, Murfreesboro, Tenn, 64-, chmn, Water and Sewer Bd, 65, v.mayor, 68-; Tenn. State Rep, 69- Mem: Am, Tenn, Murfreesboro Bar Asns; Am. Pub. Works Asn; Am. Water Works Asn; Rotary; Moose. Rel: Baptist. Legal Res: 1003 Walton Dr, Murfreesboro, Tenn. 37130. Mailing Add: P.O. Box 1159, Murfreesboro, Tenn. 37130.

SMITH, FOREST BOWLEY D
b. Capon Bridge, W.Va, 12/17/92; s. Albert Thomas Smith and Annie Miller S; div; c. Jack, Dr. J.A, Forest, Jr, Geraldine (Mrs. Turnbow), Tommy, Johnny, Emory, Bobby and Sally. Educ: Porter Mil. Acad; Med. Col. of W.Va. Polit. & Govt. Pos: Chmn, Andrews Co. Dem. Party, Tex, 60-69. Bus. & Prof. Pos: Pharmacist, Independent, 14- Mem: Elks; Moose; Nat. Asn. of Retail Druggists; Tex. Pharmaceutical Asn. Rel: Episcopal. Mailing Add: 1105 N.W. Ave. C, Andrews, Tex. 79714. (1967)

SMITH, FRANCIS P. D
R.I. State Sen.
b. Blackstone, Mass, 1/27/03; m. to Matilda R. S. Educ: Holy Cross Col, 25; Boston Univ. Law Sch, LL.B, 28. Polit. & Govt. Pos: R.I. State Sen, 51-; mem, Woonsocket Sch. Cmt; Pres. Pro Tempore of the Sen, 59; del, Dem. Nat. Conv, 68. Bus. & Prof. Pos: Attorney-at-Law. Mailing Add: 219 Prospect St, Woonsocket, R.I. 02895.

SMITH, FRANK E. D
b. Sidon, Miss, 2/21/18; s. Frank Smith and Sadie Ellis S. (Mrs. L.C. Spencer, Sr); m. 12/15/45 to Helen Ashley McPhaul; c. Kathleen and Frederick. Educ: Sunflower Jr. Col, Miss, grad, 36; Univ. Miss, B.A, 41; American Univ, 46; Beta Theta Pi. Polit. & Govt. Pos: Legis. asst. to U.S. Sen. John Stennis, 47-49; Miss. State Sen, 48-50; U.S. Rep, Third Dist, Miss, 51-62; dir, Tenn. Valley Authority, 62- Bus. & Prof. Pos: Managing ed, Greenwood Morning Star, Greenwood, Miss, 46-47. Mil. Serv: Entered as Pvt, Army, 42, released as Maj, 46, after serv. in 243rd Field Artil. Bn, 3rd Army, ETO; Bronze Star. Publ: Congressman From Mississippi, Pantheon, 64; Look Away from Dixie, La. State Univ. Press, 65; The Politics of Conservation, Pantheon, 66; plus others. Mem: Dir, Southern Regional Coun; sponsor, Atlantic Coun; Southern Hist. Asn. Rel: Methodist. Mailing Add: 204 Suburban Rd, Knoxville, Tenn. 37919.

SMITH, FRANK J. D
Ill. State Rep.
b. Chicago, Ill, 4/7/92; m. to Mary Johnston S; c. Lucille, Frank J. Jr, Edward, William R, Dorothy, Ruth and Laverne (Mrs. Scavuzzo). Educ: Pub. and Parochial schs. Polit. & Govt. Pos: Chief engr, Chicago, Ill; supvr. utilities, Chicago Dist, Ill; chmn, Bd. Exam. Engrs, Chicago, 39-48; alternate del, Dem. Nat. Conv, 68; mem, Ill. Dem. State Cent. Cmt, 68-; Ill. State Rep, currently. Bus. & Prof. Pos: Gen. supt, J.S. Wylie Construction Co. Mem: K. of C; Steam and Oper. Engrs. Local 150, AFL. Rel: Catholic. Mailing Add: 4549 S. Emerald Ave, Chicago, Ill. 60609. (1967)

SMITH, FRANK LESTER, SR. R
Treas, Tenth Cong. Dist, N.C.
b. Caldwell Co, N.C, 11/1/93; s. Marcus Columbus Smith and Amanda E. Rector S; m. 6/27/17 to Lucy Ann Amos; c. Frank L, Jr. and Marcy Nash (Mrs. Lyn E. Pollard). Educ: Rutherford Col, Appalachian State Teachers Col, Univ. N.C, A.B. Polit. & Govt. Pos: Chmn, Caldwell Co. Rep. Party, N.C, 42-69; secy-treas, Ninth Cong. Dist. Rep. Party, 43-60; mem, State Exec. Rep. Cmt, 52-69; treas, Tenth Cong. Dist. Rep. Party, 69- Bus. & Prof. Pos: Pres, Smith Printing Co, Inc, Lenoir; v.pres. and chmn. bd. dirs, Nashlyn's, Inc; on bd. of several smaller co. Publ: History of Baptist in Burke and Caldwell Counties, 60. Mem: Mason; K. of P; Moose; Exec. Club; WOW; C. of C; Merchants Asn; Kiwanis; Lenoir Country Club; Athletic Club of Caldwell. Awards from, Co. and dist. Rep. Parties, WOW Life Soc; K. of P. and Kiwanis. Rel: Baptist. Legal Res: 317 Pennton Ave, Lenoir, N.C. 28645. Mailing Add: P.O. Box 618, Lenoir, N.C. 28645.

SMITH, FRED J. D
Ill. State Sen.
b. Chattanooga, Tenn, 7/4/99; m. to Margaret S; c. Raymond and Frank. Educ: Christian Inst; Roger-Williams and Fisk Univ. Polit. & Govt. Pos: Former Ill. State Rep, 6 terms; dep. clerk, Munic. Court, Chicago, 30-; Ill. State Sen, currently. Rel: Catholic. Mailing Add: 4949 S. Martin L. King Dr, Chicago, Ill. 60607. (1967)

SMITH, FREDERICK ORVILLE, II R
Finance Chmn, Franklin Co. Rep. Cmt, Maine
b. Cambridge, Mass, 7/17/34; s. Harry Francis Smith and Dorothy Zeller S; m. 6/6/65 to Mabel Roxie Moore; c. Sarah Zeller and Jennifer Joy. Educ: Bowdoin Col, B.A, 56; Sigma Nu, Delta Psi Chap. Polit. & Govt. Pos: Nat. committeeman, Maine Fedn. Young Rep, 60-62, chmn, 62-64; pres, New Eng. Coun. Young Rep, 62-64; finance chmn, Franklin Co. Rep. Cmt, 66-; alternate del, Rep. Nat. Conv, 68; New Vineyard Sch. Admin. Dist. Nine Rep, Bd. Dirs. Bus. & Prof. Pos: Corp. secy. and sales rep, Fred O. Smith Mfg. Co, Inc, 60-66, v.pres. and clerk, 66- Mil. Serv: Entered as Ens, Naval Res, 56, released as Lt.(jg), 60, after serv. in U.S.S. Sullivans, Atlantic Fleet, 56-58 and Naval Sta, Adak, Alaska, 59-60; Res, 65-, Lt. Comdr; Am. Expeditionary Medal. Mem: Rotary Int; Woodturners and Shapers Asn; Maine Hardwood Asn; AF&AM; New Vineyard Vol. Fire Dept; dir, Civil Defense; Sugarloaf Ski Asn; Porter Lake Fish & Game Asn.(pres). Rel: Congregational. Mailing Add: High Street, New Vineyard, Maine 04956.

SMITH, FURMAN BEASLEY D
b. Gilbert, S.C, 8/27/06; s. J. Luther Smith and Mary Elizabeth Roof S; m. 1/18/30 to Ruth Geraldine Shealy. Educ: Wofford Col, A.B, 27. Polit. & Govt. Pos: Former S.C. State Rep. Bus. & Prof. Pos: Educator (retired teacher) and farmer; trustee of Pond Br. Elem. Sch, 30. Mil. Serv: 2nd Lt, Army Res, 27-32. Mem: Pres, Mid-Carolina Elect. Coop, 52-64; past pres. and now dir, Lexington Co. Farm Bur; pres. Lexington Co. Educ. Asn, 54; mem. Coun. of Del, S.C. Educ. Asn, 59-61; Gilbert Young Farmers, 59-64; pres. Gilbert Ruritan Club, 63; vol. worker with Boy Scouts. Mailing Add: Box 6, Gilbert, S.C. 29054. (1967)

SMITH, GEORGE LEON, II D
Ga. State Rep.
b. Stittmore, Ga, 11/27/12; s. Dr. DeSaussaure Dugas Smith and Sarah Wilder S; m. 12/29/37 to Frances McWhorter Mobley; c. Sally. Educ: Univ. Ga; Delta Tau Delta. Polit. & Govt. Pos: Solicitor, City Court, Swainsboro, Ga, 37-44; city attorney, 41-; exec. mem, Ga. State Dem. Exec. Cmt, 40-41 & 59-61; Ga. State Rep, 45-, Speaker-Pro-Tem, 47-54 and Speaker, 59-62, Ga. State House of Rep; mem. exec. cmt, Nat. Conf. State Legis. Leaders, 60-, pres, 63-64. Bus. & Prof. Pos: Attorney. Mem: Ga. Bar Asn. (mem. bd. gov, 58-62); Mason; Shrine; Exchange Club; Jr. C. of C. (state pres, 41-42); Gridiron Club. Rel: Methodist. Mailing Add: Louisville Rd, Swainsboro, Ga. 30401. (1967)

SMITH, GEORGE PAYNE, JR. D
Chmn, Fluvanna Co. Dem. Cmt, Va.
b. Clifton Forge, Va, 1/11/18; s. George Payne Smith and Hallie Haden Harlowe S; m. 9/6/52 to Shirley Gray Black. Educ: Univ. Va, B.S, 39, LL.B, 41; Delta Upsilon; Sigma Nu Phi. Polit. & Govt. Pos: Commonwealth's attorney, Fluvanna Co, Va, 51-55 & 59-; chmn, Fluvanna Co. Dem. Cmt, 58- Bus. & Prof. Pos: Ed-in-chief, Michie Publ. Co, Charlottesville, Va, 48-50; attorney-at-law, Palmyra, 50- Mil. Serv: Entered as Pvt, Army, 42, released as Capt, 46. Publ: Harrison on Wills and Administration (Smith's Ed), Michie, 60. Mem: Va. State Bar; Va. State Bar Asn; Am. Bar Asn; AF&AM. Rel: Baptist. Mailing Add: Palmyra, Va. 22963.

SMITH, GEORGE ROSE D
b. Little Rock, Ark, 7/26/11; s. Hay Watson Smith and Jessie Rose S; m. 12/3/38 to Peg B. Newton; c. Laurinda H. Educ: Wash. & Lee Univ, 28-31; Univ. Ark, LL.B, 31-33; Phi Delta Phi; Sigma Alpha Epsilon. Polit. & Govt. Pos: Assoc. Justice, Supreme Court of Ark, 49- Mil. Serv: Entered as 2nd Lt, Air Force, 42, released as Major, 46. Publ: Ark. Annotations of Restatement of Trusts, Am. Law Inst, 38; Ark. Mining and Mineral Law, Conway Printing Co, 42; The Current Opinions of the Supreme Court of Ark, 1 Ark. Law Rev. 89, 47. Mem: Inst. of Judicial Admin; Am. and Ark. Bar Asns. Rel: Presbyterian. Legal Res: 2 Cantrell Rd, Little Rock, Ark. 72207. Mailing Add: Justice Bldg, Little Rock, Ark. 72201.

SMITH, GEORGE THORNEWELL D
Lt. Gov. of Ga.
b. Camilla, Ga, 10/15/16; s. George Cleveland Smith and Rosa Grady S; m. 9/1/43 to Eloise Taylor. Educ: Middle Ga. Col; Abraham Baldwin Agr. Col, 40; Univ. of Ga, LL.B, 47. Polit. & Govt. Pos: Former city attorney, Cairo, Ga; former co. attorney, Grady Co; solicitor, city court of cairo, 51-59; Ga. State Rep, 59-66, Speaker, Ga. House of Rep, 63-66; Lt. Gov. of Ga, presently. Bus. & Prof. Pos: Lawyer, 47- Mil. Serv: U.S. Navy, Lt. Comdr; recieved Secy. Navy citation, all war theatre ribbons, Victory medal and Fatherland of War, 2nd Class (Russian). Mem: Past gov, Ga. Dist, Kiwanis; Cairo, Am, Ga. and Southwest. Judicial Bar Asns; VFW; Am. Legion. Key Citizen Award for Outstanding Serv. to Cities and Citizens of Ga, Ga. Munic. Asn, 68; Award for Outstanding Serv. in Health and Welfare, Med. Asn. of Ga, 68. Rel: Baptist. Mailing Add: Box 156, Cairo, Ga. 31728.

SMITH, GEORGE WILLIAM R
Chmn, Saline Co. Rep. Cmt, Ark.
b. E. St. Louis, Ill, 4/11/17; s. William Robert Smith and Chloe McCormick S; m. 1/28/40 to Lottie Verniece Comer; c. Philip George, Carolee Ann (Mrs. Dunn) and David Curtis. Polit. & Govt. Pos: Chmn, Saline Co. Rep. Cmt, Ark, 64- Bus. & Prof. Pos: Dept. Foreman, Alcoa Aluminum, 58-66. Mem: E. St. Louis, Ill, Lodge 504, AF&AM. Rel: Methodist. Mailing Add: 1224 Jameson, Benton, Ark. 72015.

SMITH, GERARD COAD R
Dir, U.S. Arms Control and Disarmament Agency
b. N.Y.C, 5/4/14; s. John T. Smith and Mary A. S; m. 8/9/41 to Bernice L. Maguire; c. John Thomas, Sheila (Mrs. Richard B. Griffin, Jr), Gerard L. and Hugh M. Educ: Yale Col, B.A, 35; Yale Law Sch, LL.B, 38. Polit. & Govt. Pos: Spec. asst, Atomic Energy Cmn, 50-54; spec. asst. to Secy. of State for Atomic Affairs, Dept. of State, 54-57, dep. chief, U.S. del. negotiating Int. Atomic Energy Agency Treaty, 55-56, liaison officer to for. rels. cmt. on disarmament affairs, 57, chief aide to Secy. of State, London Disarmament Conf, 57, Asst. Secy. of State and dir, policy planning staff, 57-61, consult, policy planning coun, 61, spec. adv. to Secy. of State for Multilateral Force Negotiations, 62 & 64; chief polit. adv, first Atoms-for-Peace Conf, 55; chief polit. adv, Tech. Talks with Soviet Union on Safeguards Against Diversion of Nuclear Materials to Weaponry, 55; dir, U.S. Arms Control and Disarmament Agency, 69- Bus. & Prof. Pos: Mem, legal dept, Gen. Motors Corp, 39-41; mem, John Thomas Smith & Son, N.Y.C, 46-47; partner, Smith & McInerney, 47-49; owner, Gerard Smith Law Firm, 49-50; for. policy consult, Wash. Center For. Policy Research, 61; mem, Coun. on For. Rels, 61; mem, exec. cmt, Yale Law Sch. Asn, 62; mem, law cmt, Yale Univ. Coun, 64; dir, Am. Security & Trust Co, 64; trustee, Sheridan Sch. & Canterbury Sch, 67; dir, Atlantic Coun, 67; publisher, Interplay Mag, 67. Mil. Serv: Entered as Ens, Navy, 41, released as Lt, 45; Letter of Commendation from Secy. of Navy. Publ: 'The Steadfast Warrior', (book rev), 5/68, 'The Future of Two Foreign Policies: II The U.S', 11/68 and 'The French Temptation,' 2/69, Interplay Mag. Mem: Racquet and Tennis Club, N.Y.C; Nat. Golf Links, Southampton, L.I; Chesapeake Bay Yacht Club, Easton, Md; Metrop. Club, Wash, D.C. Rel: Roman Catholic. Legal Res: 2425 Tracy Place, Washington, D.C. 20008. Mailing Add: 5930 Department of State, Washington, D.C. 20451.

SMITH, GLEE SIDNEY, JR. R
Kans. State Sen.
b. Rozel, Kans, 4/29/21; s. Glee Sidney Smith and Bernice Augustine S; m. 12/14/43 to Geraldine Buhler; c. Glee Sidney, III, Stephen B. and Susan Kay.

Educ: Univ. Kans, A.B, 43 and LL.B, 47; Phi Delta Phi; Order of Coif; Sigma Delta Chi; Delta Tau Delta. Polit. & Govt. Pos: Attorney, Pawnee Co, Kans, 49-53; mem. bd. educ, Larned, 51-63, pres, 53 & 61; Fifth Dist. Chmn, Young Rep, 52-53; v.chmn, Rep. State Cent. Cmt, 53; state chmn, Young Rep, 53-54; mem, Judicial Coun, 63-64; mem, Legis. Coun. Kans. and Finance Coun, 63-; legis. campaign chmn, Rep. Legislators, 64; Kans. State Sen, 57- and pres. pro tem. Mil. Serv: Entered as Pvt, Army Air Force, 42, released as 1st Lt, 45, after serv. in 1st Air Force, Training Command. Publ: 'Laws of the 1965 Legislature,' Kans. Bar J, 65. Mem: Cmnr, Nat. Coun. of Cmnrs. on Uniform State Laws; Am. Asn. of Defense Attorneys; pres, State Co. Attorneys' Asn, 51; pres, Southwest Kans. Bar Asn, 65-66 and v.pres, 64-65; dist. comdr, Am. Legion, 54-55, state legis. chmn, 57-65 and state and dist. judge adv, 65-66; pres, Kiwanis Club, 50, lt. gov, 56; pres, C. of C, 53; State Taxation Coun, State C. of C, 59-; Mason, Blue Lodge Consistory, Shrine, Chapter, Commandery, Master, Masonic Lodge, 56; Eastern Star; Farm Bur; State Grange; Elks; Eagles. Awarded Silver Beaver for work in Kanza Coun, Boy Scouts. Rel: Presbyterian; Elder and Trustee. Mailing Add: 616 West Fourth, Larned, Kans. 67550.

SMITH, GLENN E. D
Co. Chmn, Dem. Party, Pa.
b. Loysville, Pa, 4/13/17; s. Roy E. Smith and Sarah Kretzing S; m. 2/14/38 to Anna Amelia Rudy; c. Nancy and John. Polit. & Govt. Pos: Sch. dir, Saville Twp, Pa, 40-46; cmnr, Perry Co, 52-63; dir, Pa. State Soil Conserv. Cmn, 54-63; del, Dem. Nat. Conv, 60 & 64; co. chmn, Dep. Dem. Party, Pa, 64- Bus. & Prof. Pos: Farmer, 38-54; salesman, Ins. agent, Nationwide Ins. Co, 54- Mem: Mason; Lions; Moose; Owls; VFW; Am. Legion. Rel: Lutheran. Mailing Add: R.D. 1, Loysville, Pa. 17047.

SMITH, GORDON BENNIS D
Chmn, 12th Legis. Dist. Dem. Party, N.Dak.
b. Maddock, N.Dak, 8/1/26; s. Albin Smith and Gerda Toso S; m. 10/17/54 to Helen Arlene Hansen; c. Renee, Gary, Joann, Roger and Paula. Educ: Benson Co. Agr. and Training Sch, 42-44. Polit. & Govt. Pos: Precinct Committeeman, Dem. Party, N.Dak, 54; twp. supvr, Isabel Twp, 57-; secy, 20th Legis. Dist. Dem. Party, 59-65; mem. sch. bd, Maddock Sch. Dist. Nine, 64-; chmn, 12th Legis. Dist. Dem. Party, 68- Bus. & Prof. Pos: Dir, Farmer Union Oil Co, Maddock, 58-64; chmn, Benson Co. Rain, Inc, Weather Modification, 66- Mil. Serv: Entered as A/S, Navy, 44, released as Ship Fitter 3/C, 46, after serv. in Aircraft Carrier, Asian Theater, 44-45. Mem: VFW; N.Dak. Farmer Union; Toastmasters. Rel: Lutheran. Mailing Add: R.R, Maddock, N.Dak. 58348.

SMITH, GRACCHUS LATTIMORE D
Chmn, Cedar Co. Dem. Cent. Cmt, Mo.
b. Newport, Ark, 10/28/16; s. Gracchus Lattimore Smith and Nora Hunter S; m. 7/7/45 to Zella Lee Simrell; c. Hunter, Pam and Pat. Educ: Tuckerman High Sch, Ark; Draughon's Bus. Col, Springfield, Mo. Polit. Pos: Chmn, Cedar Co. Dem. Cent. Cmt, Mo, 64- Mil. Serv: Entered as Pvt, Army, 41, released as Sgt, 123rd Field Artil, 43, after serv. in Am. Expeditionary Forces, S.Pac. and Australia, 42-43; Asiatic Pac. Serv. Ribbon; Am. Defense Serv. Medal; Good Conduct Ribbon. Mem: Mason; Lions; Am. Legion; VFW; 40 et 8; past comdr, Stockton Am. Legion Post, 1966. Rel: Presbyterian. Mailing Add: 1009 South St, Stockton, Mo. 65785. (1967)

SMITH, H. ALLEN R
U.S. Rep, Calif.
b. Dixon, Ill, 10/8/09; s. Allen N. Smith and Mayme English S; m. 6/25/34 to Elizabeth McKay; c. Stephen and Lauren. Educ: Univ. Calif, Los Angeles, A.B, 31; Univ. South. Calif, LL.B, 33; Alpha Tau Omega; Alpha Kappa Psi. Polit. & Govt. Pos: Calif. State Assemblyman, 43rd Dist, 48-56; U.S. Rep, 20th Dist, Calif, 57- Bus. & Prof. Pos: Attorney-at-Law, 34-; spec. agent, Fed. Bur. Invest, 35-42. Mem: Masons, Shrine. Rel: Methodist. Legal Res: 1818 Verdugo Loma Dr, Glendale, Calif. 91208. Mailing Add: House of Representatives, Washington, D.C. 20515.

SMITH, HAROLD KENNETH 'BUD' D
Mem. State Adv. Cmt, Dem. Party, Fla.
b. Columbus, Ohio, 10/16/19; s. Harold Kenneth Smith and Mildred Worthington S; m. to Wilma Price; c. John A. (deceased); grandson, Harold Kenneth III. Educ: Duke Univ, B.A, 41; Omicron Delta Kappa; Theta Alpha Phi; Delta Sigma Phi. Polit. & Govt. Pos: Chmn, Duval Co. Dem. Exec. Cmt, Fla, 65-66, precinct committeeman, currently; committeeman, Duval Co. Dem. Party, 65-; chmn, Third Cong. Dist. Dem. Party, 65-; mem. adv. cmt, Dem. Party, Fla, 65-; del, Dem. Nat. Conv, 68. Bus. & Prof. Pos: V.pres, Mkt. Info. Jno. H. Swisher & Son, Inc, Jacksonville, Fla, currently; dir, Am. Maize Prod. Co, N.Y.C, Out Island Inn, Georgetown, Bahamas, Flavesco Inc, Jacksonville, and King Edward Tobacco Co, Quincy, currently. Mil. Serv: Entered as Pvt, Air Force, 42, released as Lt, 46, after serv. in Army Med. Corps. Mem: Jacksonville Rotary Club (dir); Fla. Yacht Club (dir); Jacksonville Symphony Asn.(dir); Am. Constitutional Action (dir); Eng. Speaking Union (dir); St. Johns Dinner Club; Revellers; USLTA; Timuquana Country Club; River Club; Pontevedra Club; Free Soc. Asn; Dem. Club. Rel: Episcopal. Legal Res: 5061 Pirates Cove Rd, Jacksonville, Fla. 32210. Mailing Add: Box 2230, Jacksonville, Fla. 32203.

SMITH, HARRIS PAGE D
S.C. State Rep.
b. Easley, S.C, 7/19/28; s. of Lloyd H. Smith and Phyllis Page S; m. 4/18/52 to Nell Whitley; c. Sam, Susan, Hugh, and Phyllis. Educ: Davidson Col, B.S, 49; Univ. S.C, LL.B, 52; ODK, cum laude, Wig and Robe; Assoc. Ed. of S.C. Law Quarterly. Polit. & Govt. Pos: S.C. State Rep, 63- Bus. & Prof. Pos: Lawyer. Mil. Serv: U.S. Army, 2/12/52-8/30/54, 1st Lt, Judge Advocate Gen. Corps; Maj, USAR. Mem: Am. and S.C. Bar Asns; Secy-treas, Pickens Co. Libr. Asn, 55-59; v.pres, Easley Jaycees, 56; secy-treas, Pickens Co. United Fund, 56-60; chmn, Pickens Co. Chap, Am. Red Cross, 57-58, presently v.chmn; pres, Easley Rotary Club, 58-59, secy-treas, 59-62; secy-treas, YMCA of Easley and Pickens Co, 58-63, pres, 63-64; v.pres, Pickens Co. Bar Asn, 58-; exec. bd, Blue Ridge Coun, Boy Scouts, 59-63, dist. chmn, Keowee Dist, 61-62; U.S. Comnr, West. Dist. of S.C, 60-62. Young Man of the Year, 57. Rel: Presbyterian, Secy, Bd. of Deacons, 56-62. Mailing Add: Box 68, Easley, S.C. 29640.

SMITH, HARRY CLINTON D
b. Sanger, Tex, 10/13/12; s. Joseph Ernest Smith and Mary Stover S; m. 10/17/41 to Emily Claire Ferguson. Educ: Tex. A&M Univ, B.A. Polit. & Govt. Pos: Mem, Gregg Co. Dem. Exec. Cmt, Tex, 38-41 and Dallas Co. Dem. Exec. Cmt, 52-66; mem, Tex. State Dem. Exec. Cmt, 66-68. Bus. & Prof. Pos: Tax agent, Ad Valorem Tax Dept, SW Area, Mobile Oil Corp, 46-63 and asst. mgr, 63- Mil. Serv: Entered as 1st Lt, Army, 41, released as Maj, 45, after serv. in 12th Corps, ETO; Campaign ribbon for N.African Theater, Sicilian-Italian Theater and ETO; Bronze Star; Purple Heart. Mem: Mason; Scottish Rite. Rel: Methodist. 1967 Legal Res: Dallas, Tex. No mailing address available. (1967)

SMITH, HENRY A. JR. R
Chmn. Sully Co. Rep. Cent. Cmt, S.Dak.
b. Fosters, Ala, 7/11/17; s. H. Albert Smith, Sr. and Anna Card S; m. 7/31/43 to Patricia Nelson; c. Patricia, Henry, III, Pamela and Penelope. Educ: Univ. Ala, 36-40; Theta Tau. Polit. & Govt. Pos: Finance chmn, Sully Co. Rep. Cent. Cmt, S.Dak, 62; chmn, Sully Co. Rep. Cent. Cmt, presently. Mil. Serv: Entered as Pvt, Army, 40, released as Lt. Col, 46, after serv. in 97th Inf. Div, Europe and Far East Theaters; Bronze Star with Cluster; European and Pac. Theater Ribbons; German and Japanese Occup. Ribbon; Brig. Gen, Army. Nat. Guard, 64. Mem: Nat. Guard Asn. of U.S; Asn. of U.S. Army; Am. Legion; VFW. Mailing Add: Box 525, Onida, S.Dak. 57564.

SMITH, HENRY P, III R
U.S. Rep, N.Y.
b. N. Tonawanda, N.Y, 9/29/11; s. Henry Perkins Smith and Ida Hale Hubbell S; m. 4/3/37 to Helen Elliott Belding; c. Susan Choate (Mrs. Walter B. McConnell), Lucinda Belding (Mrs. Gavin D. Lee) and Christiana Long. Educ: Dartmouth, A.B, 33; Cornell, LL.B, 36; Theta Delta Chi; Phi Delta Phi. Polit. & Govt. Pos: Mem, Local Bd. Selective Serv. Syst; mayor, North Tonawanda, N.Y, 62; Niagara Co. Judge, Surrogate and Family Court Judge, 63-; U.S. Rep, N.Y, 65- Bus. & Prof. Pos: Bd. dir, Beeman Found; attorney-at-law, Ithaca, N.Y, 36-41 and North Tonawanda, 41-64. Mem: Pres. dir. chmn, trustee United Commun. Fund Tonawandas; Am, N.Y. State and Tonawandas Bar Asns; past pres, Tonawandas C. of C; past pres, Rotary. Named Citizen of the Year, Tonawandas C. of C, 63. Rel: Presbyterian; elder. Legal Res: 253 Christiana St, North Tonawanda, N.Y. 14120. Mailing Add: 3126 Ordway St. N.W, Washington, D.C. 20008.

SMITH, HOMER ALBERT D
Chmn, Shannon Co. Dem. Cent. Cmt, Mo.
b. Summersville, Mo, 10/28/05; s. Robert Newton Smith and Fannie Jane Davis S; m. 6/21/25 to Ethel Winnie Belew; c. Lawrence H, Beulah E.(Mrs. George Bryant), Earnest P, Wayne E, Wanda Lee (Mrs. Don McNeall), Merle D, Harold G. and Ronnie J. Polit. & Govt. Pos: P.M.A. twp. committeeman, Summersville, Mo, 39-46; P.M.A. co. chmn, 46-48; chmn, Shannon Co. Dem. Cent. Cmt, 64- Bus. & Prof. Pos: Farmer and auctioneer, 43; owner and operator, livestock auction, 45-; adv. cmt, Health Center, 69- Mem: C. of C; Summersville Saddle Club; Future Farmers of Am. Rel: Baptist; Deacon. Mailing Add: Summersville, Mo. 65571.

SMITH, HORACE CARROLL D
S.C. State Sen.
b. Gray Court, S.C, 6/11/22; s. John Harley Smith and Josephine Kesler S; m. 7/21/42 to Dorothy Williams; c. David Carroll, Stephen Harley and Cynthia Lynn. Educ: Spartanburg Jr. Col, 38-40; Wofford Col, B.S, 42; Duke Univ. Law Sch, 46-48; Phi Delta Phi. Polit. & Govt. Pos: S.C. State Rep, Spartanburg Co, 50-56 & 58-60; col. solicitor, Spartanburg Co, 60-66; S.C. State Sen, Spartanburg Co, 66- Bus. & Prof. Pos: Attorney-at-law, Spartanburg, S.C, 48- Mil. Serv: Entered as Pvt, Air Force, 42, released as S/Sgt, 45, after serv. in 2nd Air Force, U.S.A. Mem: Spartanburg and S.C. Bar Asns; S.C. Trial Lawyers Asn; Lions; Mason. Rel: Baptist. Legal Res: 224 Beechwood Dr, Spartanburg, S.C. 29301. Mailing Add: Box 1144, Spartanburg, S.C. 29301.

SMITH, HOWARD WORTH D
b. Broad Run, Va, 2/2/83; s. William Worth Smith and Lucinda Lewis S; m. 6/27/23 to Annie Corcoran; c. Howard W, Jr. and Violett (Mrs. Tonahill). Educ: Bethel Mil. Acad; Univ. Va. Polit. & Govt. Pos: Judge, Corp. Court, 22-28 and 16th Judicial Dist, Va, 28-30; U.S. Rep, Eighth Dist, Va, and chmn, House Rules Cmt, 31-67. Bus. & Prof. Pos: Chmn. Bd, Alexandria Nat. Bank, Va. Mem: Elks; Masons; Odd Fellows. Rel: Episcopal. Legal Res: Broad Run, Va. 22014. Mailing Add: 204 W. Walnut St, Alexandria, Va. 22313.

SMITH, HULETT CARLSON D
Dem. Nat. Committeeman, W.Va.
b. Beckley, W.Va, 10/21/18; s. Joe L. Smith (deceased) and Christine Carlson S; m. 7/25/42 to Mary Alice Tieche; c. Carolyn Tieche (Mrs. Paul Hutchinson, Jr), Alice Christine McCulloch, Paul Luther Updyke, Mark Weston, Susan Elaine Chapman and Hulett Carlson, Jr. (deceased). Educ: Univ. Pa, Wharton Sch, B.S. in econ, 34; Beckley Col; Beta Gamma Sigma; Phi Delta Theta. Hon. LL.D, Beckley Col, Concord Col, W.Va. Univ, Marshall Univ, Davis and Elkins Col, W.Va. Wesleyan Col. and W.Va. Inst. Tech; Hon. Dr. Pub. Affairs, Bethany Col; Hon. L.H.D, W.Va. State Col. Polit. & Govt. Pos: Chmn, Beckley City Dem. Cmt, 47-51; chmn. and mem, W.Va. State Aeronaut. Cmn, 47-59; chmn, W.Va. Dem. Exec. Cmt, 56-61; cmnr, W.Va. Dept. of Commerce, 61-63; Gov, W.Va, 65-69; del, Dem. Nat. Conv, 68; Dem. Nat. Committeeman, 68-; mem. bd, President's Air Quality Adv. Bd, Wash, D.C, 68- Bus. & Prof. Pos: Pres, Home Ins. Agency, 46-65 and currently; pres, Investment Securities, Inc, 48-65 and currently; v.pres, First Beckley Corp, 48-65; v.pres, Beckley Col, 50-65; dir. and treas, Beckley & Oak Hill Hosps, 53-65 and currently; dir, Bank of Raleigh, 53-65 and currently; pres, Nat. Coun. for Revision of State Constitutions, Inc, Harrisburg, Pa, currently. Mil. Serv: Entered as Ens, Navy, 42, released as Lt, 46, after serv. in Am. Theater, West. Sea Frontier and Navy Dept; Lt. Comdr.(Ret), Naval Res. Mem: Soc. of Property and Casualty Underwriters; Chartered and Casualty Underwriters; co-organizer of Beckley Area Rural Develop. Coun, Beckley Bus. Develop. Corp. and W.Va. Hist. Drama Asn; hon. life mem, W.Va. Jr. C. of C. (pres, 49-50); charter mem. and first W.Va. Jr. Chamber Int. Sen; v.pres, U.S. Jr. C. of C, 52-53; Am. Legion; Eagles; Moose; Elks; Mason. Is Li-

censed Private Pilot; Named Outstanding Young Man of Year, W.Va. Jr. C. of C, 48. Rel: Presbyterian. Legal Res: 2105 Harper Rd, Beckley, W.Va. 25801. Mailing Add: 1578 Kanawha Blvd. E, Charleston, W.Va. 25311.

SMITH, IRENE M. D
b. Belvidere, N.J, 4/9/10; d. Winfield Scott Mackey and Ruth Hayes M; m. 7/2/32 to Harold J. Smith; c. Gary W. and Julianne (Mrs. Tieff); grandchildren, Dona Lynn Tieff and Brett Mackey Smith. Educ: E. Stroudsburg State Col, 27-29. Polit. & Govt. Pos: Motor vehicle agent, Oxford, N.J, 54; gen. agent, N.J. Div. Motor Vehicles, 60, field supvr, 67-; Dem. cand, N.J. State Sen, Tenth Dist, 65; mem, Women's Task Force, N.J. State Dem. Cmt, 24 years, acting chmn, 7 times; co-chmn, N.J. Women's Div. State Cmt; chmn, N.J. Forum Dem. Women; moderator and panel mem, Women's State Conv; mem, State Speakers Bur; conducted over 100 schs. for politics; alternate del, Dem. Nat. Conv, 68. Bus. & Prof. Pos: Teacher, 5 years, Asst. Co. Supt. Sch, Northampton Co, 2 years; mem. nat. staff, Am. Red Cross, 3½ years, mem. disaster staff; credit mgr, retail chain stores, Phila; Radio Show, Sta. WCRU, Washington, N.J, 67- Publ: Author of short stories, papers on travel, history, autobiographies and anecdotes. Mem: Belvidere High Sch. Alumni Asn.(past pres); E. Stroudsburg Col. Alumni Asn; White Shrine of Jerusalem (past officer); N.J. Soc. Crippled Children (bd. gov); Eastern Star; DAR; Daughters Am. Colonists; Am. Red Cross. Testimonial, 60. Rel: Episcopal; Vestry, St. Mary's Episcopal Church. Mailing Add: 628 Third St, Belvidere, N.J. 07823.

SMITH, JAMES F. R
Mich. State Rep.
b. 1923. Educ: Mich. State Univ, 2 yrs; Amherst Col, 1 yr. Polit. & Govt. Pos: Mich. State Rep, 67-; Mayor of Davison; Mem, Davison City Coun; Mem, Genesee Co. Bd. of Supvrs. Bus. & Prof. Pos: Owner & operator of Smith Finance. Mil. Serv: WW II. Mailing Add: 408 E. Flint St, Davison, Mich. 48423. (1967)

SMITH, JAMES HAROLD D
Chmn, Cape and Plymouth Dem. Cmt, Mass.
b. Fall River, Mass, 6/1/29; s. James Francis Smith and Ada Quigley S; m. 7/19/52 to Margaret Joan Ross; c. Terrence J, Kevin R, Brendan M, Shaun, Tracy M, Timothy G. and Kelly Ann. Educ: Boston Col, B.S, 52; Portia Law Sch, LL.B, 57. Polit. & Govt. Pos: Chmn. Dem. Town Cmt, Falmouth, Mass, 61-65; chmn, Woods Hole Martha's Vineyard Nantucket Steamship Authority, Mass, 61-; del, Dem. State Conv, 62 & 64 and monitor, 62; alternate del, Dem. Nat. Conv, 64 & 68; chmn, Cape and Plymouth Dem. Cmt, currently. Bus. & Prof. Pos: Master and chancery, Barnstable Co, 64-69; dir. and counsel, Bay Colony Fed. Savings and Loan Asn, South Yarmouth. Mil. Serv: Entered as Seaman, Naval Res, 47, released as Lt, 54, after serv. in Sixth and Seventh Fleet, 52-54; Lt, Naval Res; Naval Res. Ribbon; European, Am. and United Nations Serv. Ribbons; Korean Campaign Ribbon with Battle Star; Korean Presidential Unit Citation. Mem: Woods Hole Golf Club; Barnstable Co. Nat. Found. Infantile Paralysis; Cross Cup Pishon Post 281; Am. Legion; VFW Hooper Post. Rel: Roman Catholic. Mailing Add: 207 Shore St, Falmouth, Mass. 02540. (1967)

SMITH, JAMES K. K. R
b. Glasgow, Scotland, 6/9/98; s. James Kelpatrick Smith and Isabella S; m. to Charlotte; c. one son. Educ: Pittsburgh schs. Polit. & Govt. Pos: Pa. State Rep, 64-67; served Allegheny C. for over 22 yrs; clerk, Bd. of Judges, Common Pleas Court, assigned to Criminal Court, ret. 64; pres, v.pres, mem. of exec. bd. and intergovt. com. of Allegheny Boroughs Asn; organized the Allegheny Co. Mayors of Boroughs Asn, pres, mem; organized, Asn. of Mayors of the Boroughs of Pa, pres, 15 yrs; Dormont Borough Constable, 30-38; Councilman, 38-42, pres, 40-41; Burgess, 42-65; Young Rep. Club. Mem: former secy-treas, Order of Rwy. Conductors, Pullman Div. No. 711, Pittsburgh; Rep. Citizens League. Rel: Presbyterian. Mailing Add: 1710 Hillsdale Ave, Pittsburgh, Pa. 15216. (1967)

SMITH, JAMES McCORMICK R
Assoc. mem, Adams Rep. Town Cmt, Mass.
b. Adams, Mass, 2/13/17; s. Gustave A. Smith and Ann McCormick S; m. 7/3/41 to Ruth Esther Carpenter; c. Melanie Ann and Jason William. Polit. & Govt. Pos: Former mem, Mt. Greylock Tramway Authority, Mass; pres, Adams Rep. Town Cmt, Mass, until 68, assoc. mem, 68- Bus. & Prof. Pos: Owner, Smith Studio Adams, Mass, 45-; pres, Photronics, 61-; trustee, Tri-S Realty Co, 65- Mem: Pres, Adams C. of C; past pres, Adams Lions Club; AF&AM; Elks. Rel: Congregational. Mailing Add: 6 B Street, Adams, Mass. 01220.

SMITH, JAMES P. D
La. State Rep.
b. Marion, La, 9/6/25; s. J. Duff Smith and Sallie Turner S; m. 11/2/45 to Foye Nolan; c. James Bradly, Danny Allen, Max Graham, Roslyn Ann and Jayne Ellen. Educ: N. Cent. Area Vocational Sch; Northeast State Col, speech and pub. rels. Polit. & Govt. Pos: La. State Rep, 66- Bus. & Prof. Pos: Mem, Union Parish Sch. Bd, Transportation, 45-66. Mil. Serv: Entered as Pvt, Army, 43, released as Pfc, 45, after serv. in 106th Inf. Div, ETO; Combat Inf. Badge with 2 Battle Stars; Bronze Star. Mem: Am. Legion; Union Fraternal Lodge 53; Woodman of the World; Farmerville Industrial Develop. Orgn; Mason (32°). Rel: Baptist. Mailing Add: Box 135, Farmerville, La. 71241. (1967)

SMITH, JAMES ROSWELL R
Asst. Secy. for Water and Power Develop, Dept. of the Interior
b. Sioux Falls, S.Dak, 5/10/17; s. Dick R. Smith and Ednah Woodruff S; m. 10/1/41 to Arlene Skredsvig; c. Dick R, Douglas J. and Robert M. Educ: Sioux Falls Col, A.A, 37; Univ. S.Dak, LL.B, 40; Beta Theta Pi. Polit. & Govt. Pos: Asst. Secy. for Water and Power Develop, Dept. of the Interior, 69- Bus. & Prof. Pos: Attorney-at-law, Sioux Falls, S.Dak, 41-42; mem, C. of C. Admin, Pierre and Yankton, 42-53; v.pres. and counsel, Miss. Valley Asn, Omaha, Nebr, 53-65; mgr, mkt. rels, North. Natural Gas Co, 65-69. Mem: S.Dak. Bar Asn; Mason (32°); Shrine; dir, Nebr. Resources Found; dir, Nebr. Asn. of Commerce; former pres, Omaha Zool. Soc; trustee, Nebr. Humane Soc; chmn, econ. develop. coun, Nebr. Asn. of Commerce and Indust; chmn, water resources cmt, Omaha C. of C; v.chmn, Omaha Red Feather-Red Cross United Appeal; Rotary; envoy, Nebr. Diplomats. Distinguished Civilian Serv. Award, Dept. of the Army. Rel: Protestant. Legal Res: 701 Hackberry Rd, Omaha, Nebr. 68132. Mailing Add: 6171 Leesburg Pike, Apt. 325, Falls Church, Va. 22044.

SMITH, JAMES VERNON R
Adminstr, Farmers Home Admin, U.S. Dept. Agr.
b. Oklahoma City, Okla, 7/23/26; s. Fred Smith and Josephine Meder S; m. 8/26/46 to Mary Belle Couch; c. James Vernon, Jr, Sarah Eileen and Lee Ann. Educ: Okla. Col. of Lib. Arts, 65. Polit. & Govt. Pos: Mem, Four Year State Cols. Bd. of Regents; chmn, Grady Co. Rep. Party, Okla, 62-66; U.S. Rep, Sixth Dist, Okla, 67-69; del, Rep. Nat. Conv, 68; adminstr, Farmers Home Admin, U.S. Dept. Agr, 69-; mem. bd. trustees, Intercollegiate Studies Inst. Inc; mem. bd. dirs, Am. Heritage Center, Okla. Christian Col. Mem: Hon. mem, Chickasha Jr. C. of C; C. of C; mem, Farm Bur. and past dir; Farmers Home Admin. Rel: Church of Christ. Legal Res: Chickasha, Okla. 73018. Mailing Add: 7506 Wellesley Dr, College Park, Md. 20740.

SMITH, JANET MARGARET 'JAN' D
Mem. Exec. Bd, Nev. State Dem. Cent. Cmt.
b. Los Angeles, Calif, 4/26/28; d. Thomas Franklin Curtis and Catharine Collins C; m. 11/3/46 to Prince Lyle Smith, Jr; c. Cathleen Elizabeth (Mrs. Jeffery L. Skillman), Christene Evelyn (Mrs. Douglas A. Skillman), James Richard, Margaret Mary Corrine, Marie Daniell and John Lyle. Educ: Chaffey Jr. Col, 46-47. Polit. & Govt. Pos: Mem, Clark Co. Dem. Cent. Cmt, Nev, 62-; del, Co. and State Dem. Conv, 62-; secy, Henderson Dem. Club, 63-64, treas, 64-65 and v.pres, 65-66; legal research and extradition clerk, Dist. Attorney's Off, Clark Co, 63-65; fed. court clerk, Fed. Dist. of Nev, 65-66; judicial secy. to Hon. Thomas J. O'Donnell, Dist. Court Judge, 66-; secy, Las Vegas Womens Dem. Club W, 66-; mem. exec. bd, Nev. State Dem. Cent. Cmt. currently. Mem: Jr. Womens Improv. Club, Bishop, Calif; vol, Am. Red Cross, Las Vegas and Clark Co. Med. Health Team; secy, Neighborhood Coun, Henderson; President Kennedy's Legis. Prog; Nev. bd. dirs. and chmn. housing cmt, NAACP; Toastmistress; Nev. Exec. Cmt. on Alcoholism. Commendation for Sen. Cannons Recourt, 64; Presidential Commendation for Party Activities; Gov. Commendations for Party Endeavor. Rel: Catholic; Mem. Coun, St. James Parish; Secy, St. Peter's Parish Coun. Mailing Add: 31 Jade Circle, Las Vegas, Nev. 89106.

SMITH, JANICE MARY R
Mem, Calif. Rep. State Cent. Cmt.
b. Sioux City, Iowa, 11/2/36; d. Herman Carl Wulf and Phyllis Thelma Cram W; m. 4/23/60 to Louis Edward Smith. Educ: Danbury Pub. Sch, Iowa, 12 years. Polit. & Govt. Pos: Dep. registr, Los Angeles Co, Calif, 65-; precinct chmn, 48th assembly dist, Los Angeles Co. Rep. Cent. Cmt, 68-; mem, Calif. Rep. State Cent. Cmt, 69- Bus. & Prof. Pos: Long distance operator, Bell Syst, 56-57, supvr, 57-66 and customer instr, 66-68. Publ: Contrib, 48th Precinct Informer. Mem: Rep. Women's Federated Club; Parkside Rep. Action Club. Attendance and music awards; Top Five Musicians Medal; three Iowa State Solo Medals. Rel: Christian. Mailing Add: 4607 Jessica Dr, Los Angeles, Calif. 90065.

SMITH, JOHN B. D
Dist. Attorney, Twelfth Judicial Dist. of Colo.
b. Madison, Mo, 9/16/29; s. Victor B. Smith and Gladys Dowdy S; m. 8/25/51 to Edna Pauline Vinci; c. Lorella A, Victor P, John S. and Nickie. Educ: Univ. Colo, B.A, Univ. Denver, LL.B; Sigma Nu; Lambda Phi Beta; Phi Delta Phi. Polit. & Govt. Pos: Dist. attorney, Twelfth Judicial Dist. of Colo; Co. attorney, Alamosa Co, Colo, 59- Bus. & Prof. Pos: Law partner, Smith and Smith Attorneys, 62- and pres, San Luis Valley Bar Asn. Mem: Elks; Am, Colo. and San Luis Valley Bar Asns; Meatcutters Union. Rel: Catholic. Legal Res: 305 Edgemont, Alamosa, Colo. 81101. Mailing Add: 915 Fourth St, Box 58, Alamosa, Colo. 81101.

SMITH, JOHN E. D
Utah State Rep.
b. Grantsville, Utah, 2/28/21; s. Frank Smith and Nellie Barrus S; m. 12/2/45 to Lorna Diekmann; c. Nola and Susan. Educ: Grantsville High Sch, grad. Polit. & Govt. Pos: City councilman, Grantsville City, Utah, 56-60 & 65-69; chmn, Grantsville Citizen's Improv. Asn, 58-69; chmn, Grantsville Credit Union, 65-67; chmn, Dist. Three Dem. Party, 65-69; Utah State Rep, Tooele Co, 67-; West. Interstate appointment on Aeronaut, 69. Mil. Serv: Entered as A/S, Navy, 42, released as PO, 45, after serv. in Atlantic and Pac. Theatres, 42-45. Publ: 'Letters of John,' 66, 'Politics of John,' 68 and 'Journal Anecdotes,' 69, Smith's Secretarial Serv. Mem: DAV. Rel: Latter-day Saint. Mailing Add: 107 S. Hale St, Grantsville, Utah 84029.

SMITH, JOHN ELBERT R
b. Rhea Springs, Tenn, 9/13/98; both parents deceased; m. 2/2/65 to Cordia Ann Collins; c. Billy Frank and Clyde T. Educ: 2 years col. Polit. Pos: Asst. mgr. of Bill Brocks Campaign, Rhea Co, Tenn; chmn, Rep. Party, Rhea Co, Tenn, 62-64. Bus. & Prof. Pos: Teacher, Rhea Co. Schs, 21-52; asst. agr. teacher, G.I. Training. Mem: Odd Fellows; WOW. Rel: Baptist. Mailing Add: P.O. Box 1, Evensville, Tenn. 37332. (1967)

SMITH, JOHN GREGORY R
Chmn, White Pine Co. Rep. Orgn, Nev.
b. St. Albans, Vt, 9/25/23; s. James Gregory Smith and Genevieve C. Babbitt S; m. 3/3/60 to Margaret A. Gulley Wilcox; c. Rebecca Wilcox (Mrs. William Staunton), M. Kathleen Wilcox, James W. Wilcox, John S. Wilcox and Genevieve E. Educ: Yale Univ, 42-43; Colo. Sch. Mines, E.M, 50; Tau Beta Pi; Blue Key; Alpha Tau Omega; Letter Club; Press Club. Polit. & Govt. Pos: Treas, White Pine Co. Rep. Orgn, Nev, 67-68 and chmn, 68-; del, State Rep. Conv, several times. Bus. & Prof. Pos: Underground shift boss, Braden Copper Co, Sewell, Chile, S.Am, 50-53; surveyor, U.S. Vanadium Co, Uravan, Colo, 53-54; indust. safety engr, several maintenance engr. and jobs planning foreman, Kennecott Copper Corp, Ruth, Nev, 54- Mil. Serv: Entered as Pvt, Army Air Corps, 43, released as Cpl, 45, after serv. in 769th Bomb Squadron VN, Far East China-Burma-India, 44-45; Theatre Awards; Battle Stars; Good Conduct Medal. Mem: Am. Inst. of Mining, Metallurgical and Petroleum

Engrs; Elks; Am. Legion; Nat. Rifle Asn; Nat. Muzzle Loading Rifle Asn. Rel: Congregational. Legal Res: 1195 Ave. M, E. Ely, Nev. 89315. Mailing Add: Box 856, Ely, Nev. 89301.

SMITH, JOHN KERWIN D
Mayor, Hayward, Calif.
b. Hayward, Calif, 10/18/26; s. May Kerwin; m. 9/4/53 to Lottie Verzic; c. Cynthia Jame. Educ: Stanford Univ. and Hastings Col. Law. Polit. & Govt. Pos: Parks cmnr, Hayward, Calif, 56-61, councilman, 61-66, mayor, 66- Bus. & Prof. Pos: Partner, Law Firm of Haley, Schenone, Tucker, Birchfield & Smith, 53- Mil. Serv: Entered as Pvt, Army, 44, released as 2nd Lt, 46; re-entered, Korean Conflict, 51-53. Mem: Am, Calif, Alameda Co. and South. Alameda Co. Bar Asns; Native Sons. Rel: Roman Catholic. Legal Res: 22237 Prospect St, Hayward, Calif. 94541. Mailing Add: P.O. Box 450, 1331 B. St, Hayward, Calif. 94543.

SMITH, JOHN MALCOLM DFL
b. Owatonna, Minn, 4/2/22; s. Wilber J. Smith and Anne Foran S; m. 7/29/50 to Therese Frances Martin; c. Bernard Patrick, Stephen John, Robert Martin, Anne Therese, Mary Louise, Tracy Marie and Kathleen Bridget. Educ: St. Mary's Col, Minn, 46-47; Creighton Univ, Omaha, Nebr, LL.B, 50; Delta Theta Phi. Polit. & Govt. Pos: Co. attorney, Steele Co, Minn, 58-62; first v.chmn, Steele Co. Dem-Farmer-Labor Exec. Cmt, Minn, 56-57, mem, 59-69; del, Minn. State Dem-Farmer-Labor Conv, 60, 62, 64 & 66; alternate del, Dem. Nat. Conv, 68. Mil. Serv: Entered as Aviation Cadet, Navy, 42, released as Lt.(jg), 45, after serv. in VF-17 and VF 84 in S.Pac. Area, 43-45; recalled to serv. as Lt, Navy, 51, released as Lt. Comdr, 54, after serv. at U.S. Naval Air Sta, Minneapolis, Minn; Capt, Naval Res, 63-; 8 Distinguished Flying Crosses; Navy Commendation Ribbon; Asiatic Pac. Theater with 4 Battle Stars; 7 Air Medals; Am. Defense Theater, World War II Victory and U.S. Naval Res. Ribbons; Presidential Unit Citation; Navy Unit Citation. Mem: Pres, Steele Co. Bar Asn, 56-64; Minn. Bar Asn; Am. Trial Lawyers Asn; Minn. Co. Attorneys Asn; Nat. Dist. Attorneys Asn; K. of C; Elks; Am. Legion; VFW; Am. Fighter Aces Asn; Res. Officers Asn; Naval Res. Asn. Rel: Roman Catholic. Mailing Add: 1131 Lilac, Owatonna, Minn. 55060. (1967)

SMITH, JOHN NEIL D
Miss. State Rep.
b. Tylertown, Miss, 1/11/20; s. Newell Booker Smith and Bessie Hall S; m. 5/24/66 to Donis Luter; c. Wayne Nettles (stepson) and Jay Neil. Educ: Univ. South. Miss, B.A, 49. Polit. & Govt. Pos: Miss. State Rep, 44th Dist, 68- Mil. Serv: Entered as Aviation Cadet, Army Air Corps, 42, released as Lt. Col, 68, after serv. in 36th Fighter Group ETO, 44-45; Lt. Col.(ret), Air Force Res, 68; Air Medal with 12 Oak Leaf Clusters; Distinguished Flying Cross; Presidential Unit Citation with Oak Leak Cluster. Mem: Mason; Royal Arch Mason; Knights Templar; Shine. Rel: Baptist. Mailing Add: 806 Oak Dr, Tylertown, Miss. 39667.

SMITH, JOSEPH W. D
b. Girard, Russell City, Ala; s. E.C. Smith and Essie Baker S; m. 7/17/43 to Lenora West Coghlan; c. Sydney Bowen, Lenora West, Joseph W. Jr, Walter C. II. Educ: Univ. of Ala, LL.B, 41. Polit. & Govt. Pos: Ala. State Sen, until 67; Ala. State Rep, 59-63; Ala. Educ. Cmn, 57-58. Bus. & Prof. Pos: Lawyer, 41- Mil. Serv: Army, Maj, Corps of Mil. Police, 41-47. Mem: Phenix City Lions Club; Am. Legion; Ala. Bar Asn; Am. Bar Asn. Rel: Methodist. Mailing Add: Box 519, Phenix City, Ala. 36867. (1967)

SMITH, KEN D
Fla. State Rep.
b. Clanton, Ala, 10/19/26; m. to Betsy Jones; c. K. Bruce, Jr, W. Crit and Susan. Educ: Auburn Univ; Fla. State Univ, B.S, 52, M.S, 54. Polit. & Govt. Pos: Fla. State Rep, 60- Bus. & Prof. Pos: Teacher. Mil. Serv: Air Force. Rel: Baptist, Sunday Sch. Teacher; Young People's Dir; Adult Training Union Dir. Mailing Add: 110 W. Main St, Perry, Fla. 32347. (1967)

SMITH, KENT NEPHI D
b. Central, Ariz, 8/26/21; s. James Martin Smith and Winnie Elizabeth Bigler S; m. 9/17/40 to Geraldine LaRue Ballard; c. Ross Kent, Michael Wayne, Gary Noel and Karen Elizabeth. Educ: Gila Jr. Col, cert. in bus, 40. Polit. & Govt. Pos: Mem, Sch. Bd, Mohave Co, Ariz, 51-52; precinct committeeman, Dem. Party, Mohave Co, 57-58; Ariz. State Rep, Mohave Co, 65-67. Bus. & Prof. Pos: Partner-mgr, Cane Springs Ranch, Mohave Co, Ariz, 46- Mil. Serv: Entered as Pvt, Army, 44, released as S/Sgt, 46, after serv. in Japan; Asiatic-Pac. Campaign and Victory Medals; Philippine Liberation Ribbon; Good Conduct Medal with Clasp. Rel: Latter-day Saint. Mailing Add: Cane Springs Ranch, Sandy Route, Kingman, Ariz. 86401.

SMITH, L. EUGENE R
Pa. State Rep.
b. Punxsutawney, Pa, 9/3/21; s. Charles Smith and Olive Curry S; m. to Jean Hue; c. three. Educ: Army Air Force Pilot Training Sch. Polit. & Govt. Pos: Pa. State Rep, 63-; mayor, Punxsutawney, 1 term. Mil. Serv: Air Force, World War II, serv. in 306th Bomb Group, ETO. Mem: Former mem, bd. of dir, YMCA; Mason; VFW; Am. Legion. Rel: Methodist; Trustee, First Methodist Church. Mailing Add: RD 1, Box 180, Punxsutawney, Pa. 15767. (1967)

SMITH, LARRY GILBERT D
Ohio State Rep.
b. Uniontown, Pa, 11/11/14; s. Lonnie Smith (deceased) and Eva B. S; wid; c. Larry G, Jr, Karin L. and Lillie G; five grandchildren. Educ: Diamond Bus. Col; Fenn Col. Polit. & Govt. Pos: Personnel officer, Co. Recorder's Off, Cleveland, Ohio; mem, Cuyahoga Co. Dem. Exec. Cmt; mem, 20th Ward Dem. Club and leader, 62-66; Ohio State Rep, 67-; alternate del, Dem. Nat. Conv, 68; mem, Ohio State Dem. Exec. Cmt. Bus. & Prof. Pos: Trucking bus, formerly; licensed real estate broker, Ohio; notary pub; multiple line ins. agent. Mem: Hough Commun. Coun.(past pres); Hough Sch. PTA; bd. mem, Bell Center Neighborhood House and League Park Neighborhood Center; Plus Club; Real Estate Brokers Asn; Cleveland Bus. League; Fair Housing Cmt; United Freedom Movement; Midwest. Christian Leadership Conf; pres, Negro Am. Labor Coun; Champs Inc.(past pres, trustee, currently); pres, Univ. Euclid Redevelop. Adv. Coun; pres, Commun. Opportunity Bd; Mewton Street Club(past pres); Street Club Pres. League (cmt. chmn); trustee, Cleveland Develop. Hough House Bd; bd. mem, Citizens for Better Housing; Area Coun. Asn; Boy Scout Cmnr; bd. mem, NAACP, Nat. Soc. of State Legislators, Fairhill Psychatric Hosp. and Gr. Cleveland Neighborhood Centers Asn; Elected Pub. Officials of Ohio; Fedrick Douglas Civic Club; Mason (32°); Shrine. Rel: Baptist. Mailing Add: 1871 E. 97th St, Cleveland, Ohio 44106.

SMITH, LAWRENCE PETER D
Chmn, Ottawa Co. Dem. Cmt, Mich.
b. Holland, Mich, 8/27/16; s. Peter Smith and Nellie King S; m. 2/27/40 to Clara Jane Overbeek; c. Martha Ann. Educ: Minneapolis-Honeywell Sch. of Aeronaut. Electronics & Electronic Equipment, Univ. Minn, 43; LaSalle Exten. Univ, Ill. Polit. & Govt. Pos: Del, every Mich. State Dem. Conv, 46-, v.chmn, Fifth Dist. Del, 54; secy, Ottawa Co. Dem. Cmt, 54-67, chmn, 67-; v.chmn, Ottawa Co. Bd. of Elec. Canvassers, 63-65, chmn, 65-67; del, Dem. Nat. Conv, 64; mem, Ninth Cong. Dist. Dem. Exec. Cmt, 67-; mem, Ottawa Co. Re-apportionment Cmn, 67- Bus. & Prof. Pos: Tech. rep, Aeronaut. Div, Minneapolis-Honeywell Regulator Co, 43-45, assigned to various Air Force Bases within 1st and 2nd U.S. Air Forces, U.S. and 2nd Air Div, U.S. 8th Air Force, Eng, 44-45; sales engr, Radio Electronic Supply Co, 47-49; v.pres, Radio Parts, Inc, 49-50; Electronic logistics engr, Instrument Div, Lear Siegler, Inc, 51- Mem: Elks; Eagles; Am. Radio Relay League, Newington, Conn; Radio Soc. of Gt. Brit. Amateur Radio Operator, with Sta. Call Sign W8SKI. Rel: Roman Catholic. Mailing Add: 1718 Summit St, Holland, Mich. 49423.

SMITH, LEE CREECY D
b. Biltmore, N.C, 7/15/26; s. Willis Smith and Anna Lee S; m. 7/24/54 to Mary Adele Hardison; c. Lee Creecy, Jr. and Willis, II. Educ: Duke Univ, A.B, 50, Sch. of Law, LL.B, 53; Kappa Alpha Order; Delta Theta Phi. Polit. & Govt. Pos: Chmn, N.C. State Bd. of Elec, 66-; del, Dem. Nat. Conv, 68. Bus. & Prof. Pos: Dir, various corporations; asst. secy, Occidental Life Ins. Co. of N.C, 58-; trustee, W.W. Holding Tech. Inst, 65-66 and Wake Co. Blood Procurement Plan, 66- Mil. Serv: Navy, 44-46. Mem: Am, N.C. and Wake Co. Bar Asns; Lions; Rel: Episcopal. Legal Res: 3301 Dryden Court, Raleigh, N.C. 27609. Mailing Add: P.O. Box 750, Raleigh, N.C. 27602.

SMITH, LeROY WILBUR D
b. Monmouth, Ill, 9/10/21; s. Grant B. Smith and Berniece S. Educ: Univ. Tex, B.B.A, 49; Am. Col. Life Underwriters, C.L.U; Delta Sigma Pi. Polit. & Govt. Pos: Del, Dem. State Conv, Tex, 48-; chmn, Zoning Bd. of Adjustment, San Antonio, 61-66; dir, Nueces River Reclamation Dist, 63-; del, Dem. Nat. Conv, 64 & 68; coordinator, South. Portion Bexar Co, Tex. for Gov. John Connally. Bus. & Prof. Pos: Branch mgr, Ralston Purina, 50-58; life ins. agent, Great South. Life, 58- Mil. Serv: Entered as Pvt, Army, 41, released as Capt, 46, after serv. in ETO; Bronze Star; North. Europe, Am. Theater and 3 Campaign Ribbons; Good Conduct Medal. Mem: Lions; past comdr, Post 10, Am. Legion; C. of C. Rel: Protestant. Mailing Add: P.O. Box 12408, San Antonio, Tex. 78212.

SMITH, LYMAN ROBERT D
Chmn, Ventura Co. Dem. Cent. Cmt, Calif.
b. Pocatello, Idaho, 4/7/36; s. Lyman Jones Smith and Wilma B. Shappart S; m. 1/22/56 to Marjorie Louise Donald; c. Jennifer Carol, Lyman Jay and Matthew G. Educ: Univ. Calif, Berkeley, B.S, 58; Univ. Calif, Berkeley, Boalt Hall, LL.B, 61; Alpha Chi Rho; Phi Delta Phi. Polit. & Govt. Pos: Mem, Ventura Co. Dem. Cent. Cmt, 64- and chmn, 66- Mem: Secy, Ventura Co. Bar Asn, 64; State Bar of Calif; Am. Bar Asn; Mason; Rotary. Rel: Protestant. Mailing Add: 600 Teague Dr, Santa Paula, Calif. 93060.

SMITH, LYNN, JR. D
Chmn, Gonzales Co. Dem. Party, Tex.
b. Luling, Tex, 11/22/27; s. Lynn Smith and Sallie Davis S; m. 6/21/48 to Ruth Janet Laurence; c. Loy Elizabeth and Lynnette. Educ: Baylor Univ; Southwest. Tex. State Col; grad. Inf. course at Ft. Benning, Ga. Polit. & Govt. Pos: Chmn, Gonzales Co. Dem. Party, Tex, presently. Bus. & Prof. Pos: Owner of theaters and ranching interests. Mil. Serv: Entered as Pvt, Tex. Nat. Guard, 48, released as Maj, 66; Tex. Nat. Guard Res, released as Lt. Col, 69. Mem: Southwest. Cattle Raisers Asn; hon. life mem, Future Farmers Am. Rel: Presbyterian. Mailing Add: Gonzales, Tex. 78629.

SMITH, MANSON BOWLES R
N.H. State Rep.
b. Hebron, N.H, 1/1/01; s. George Samuel Smith and Florence Bowles S; m. 10/25/21 to Evelyn Scott; c. Manson Parker, Dorcas S. (Mrs. VanSchaick) and Sara S. (Mrs. Chisholm). Educ: Phillips Exeter Acad, 4 years. Polit. & Govt. Pos: Town Moderator, Hebron, N.H, 27-69; N.H. State Rep, Grafton Dist. Ten, 69- Bus. & Prof. Pos: Owner, Hillside Inn, 40-65. Mem: Mason; Grange. Rel: Congregational. Legal Res: Hebron, N.H. 03232. Mailing Add: East Hebron, N.H. 03232.

SMITH, MARGARET CHASE R
U.S. Sen, Maine
b. Skowhegan, Maine, 12/14/97; d. George Emery Chase and Carrie Murray C; m. 5/14/30 to Clyde H. Smith, wid, 40. Educ: Colby Col, A.M, 43; Pi Sigma Alpha; Delta Kappa Gamma; Sigma Kappa; Beta Sigma Phi. Hon. LL.D, Wilson Col, 45, Coe Col, Ala. Col, Univ. Maine and Smith Col, 49, Syracuse Univ. and Bowdoin Col, 52, Univ. New Brunswick, Columbia Univ, Univ. N.C, Tufts Col, Wesleyan Univ. and Drexel Inst, 55, West. Col. for Women, Russell Sage Col. and Univ. R.I, 56, Mills Col. and Wash. Col, 57, George Wash. Univ. and Gettysburg Col, 58, Park Col. and Bryant Col, 59, Lindenwood Col, Beaver Col, East. Mich. Univ. and Ursinus Col, 61, Mt. Holyoke Col, 62, Brandeis Univ, 63, Georgian Court Col. and Skidmore Col, 64, Kenyon Col, Whittier Col. and Lake Erie Col, 65, Am. Int. Col, 66, Bates Col, 67, Notre Dame Col, 68 and Nasson Col, 69; L.H.D, Hood Col, 51, Hamilton Col. and Lafayette Col, 55, Rollins Col, 56, Keuka Col, 57, Woman's Med. Col. of Pa, 59 and Hahnemann Med. Col. and Hosp, 64; Litt.D, Temple Univ, 55; D.C.L, Pace Col, 56; J.S.D, Portia Law Sch, 57; Ed.D, Lesley Col, 59; D.S, Muskingum Col, 63; D.P.A, Northeast. Univ, 64 and Southeast. Mass. Tech. Inst,

67; D.S, Hartwick Col, 65. Polit. & Govt. Pos: Mem, Maine State Rep. Cmt, 30-36; secy. to U.S. Rep. Clyde H. Smith, 37-40; U.S. Rep, Second Dist, Maine, 40-49, mem, House Naval Affairs and Armed Serv. Cmts; U.S. Sen, Maine, 49-, mem, Appropriations, Armed Serv, Space, Govt. Opers, Rules, D.C. and Rep. Policy Cmts, former chmn, Ammunition Shortage Investigating Subcmt. and Reorgn. Subcmt, currently mem, Appropriations, Armed Serv, Space, Preparedness Investigating Subcmt. and the C.I.A, Subcmt; Presidential nominee, Rep. Nat. Conv, 64; chmn, Conf. of all Rep. Sen, 67. Bus. & Prof. Pos: Teacher; tel, newspaper and woolen co. exec; nationally syndicated columnist. Mil. Serv: Lt. Col, Air Force Res. Mem: Am. Acad. Arts and Sci; Pi Sigma Alpha; Delta Kappa Gamma; Sigma Kappa; Beta Sigma Phi. Politics Achievement Award, Women's Nat. Press Club, 48; Woman of the Year, 48 & 54 and Woman of the Year in Polit, 49, 50 & 57, Assoc. Press; Woman of the Year, United Press Radio Ed, 49 & 64; Named one of Ten Americans Doing Most for Nation, Mutual Broadcasting Syst, 49; Freedom Award for Americanism, Freedom's Found, 50; Designated Econ. Champion in Senate, Coun. of State C. of C, 51 & 52; Honest Politician Award, Liberty Mag, 51; Designated Most Charming Woman in Govt, Charm Inst, 52; Rated Sixth Best Sen. of 96 in Poll of 50 Leading Polit. Scientists in U.S, 52; Voice of Democracy Award, 53; Woman of Year, NBC Jinx's Jury, 54; VFW Medal for Americanism, 54; Nat. Achievement Award, Chi Omega, 54; Distinguished Serv. Award, Nat. Fed. of Bus. & Prfnl. Women's Clubs, 55; Distinguished Serv. Award on Nat. Defense, 55 and Minute Man Award for Individual Making Greatest Contribution to Nat. Security, 64, Res. Officers Asn; Lord and Taylor Award, 56; Americanism Citation, Calif. State Legis, 56; Int. Achievement Award, Soroptimist Int, 56; Achievement Award, Beta Sigma Phi, 57; Woman of Achievement Award, Soroptimists, 58; Number One Favorite, Women Ed. Nat. Poll. for V.Pres, 59; Multiple Awards for Nat. Health Leadership, 60; Most Valuable Senator Rating, Newsweek Press Gallery Poll, 60; Gold Medal Award for Humanitarianism, Inst. Soc. Sci, 64; Women's Twentieth Century Hall of Fame, 65; Nat. Leadership Award, Four Chaplains, 66; Rated One of Ten Most Influential Women in World, U.P.I. Poll, 67. Legal Res: Norridgewock Ave, Skowhegan, Maine 04976. Mailing Add: Senate Office Bldg, Washington, D.C. 20510.

SMITH, MARGARET KEANE D
Committeewoman, Conn. State Dem. Cent. Cmt.
b. Hartford, Conn; d. James Joseph Keane and Susan Ann Fanning K; m. 5/1/42 to Herbert Knox Smith; c. Susanne Barbara, Herbert Knox, Jr, William Warren and Robert David. Educ: High Sch. Polit. & Govt. Pos: Pres, Newgate Young Dem, 50; nat. committeewoman, Conn. Young Dem, 52-54; chmn, East Granby Dem. Town Cmt, 54-60, v.chmn, 60-66; Justice of Peace, East Granby, 54-69; secy, East Granby Planning & Zoning Cmt, 55-56; del, Dem. Nat. Conv, 56 & 60, alternate del, 64 & 68; publicity chmn, East Granby Centennial, Conn, 58; committeewoman, Conn. State Dem. Cent. Cmt, 58-; consult, Conn. State Pub. Works, 61-64; v.pres, Seventh Dist. Dem. Cmt, 63-66; Field rep, Conn. State Cmn. on Serv. for the Elderly, 64-65; Sixth Cong. Dist. mem, Subcmt. on Conn. Dem. Party Rules, 68; mem, Conn. State Fedn. Dem. Women, presently. Mem: Chmn, East Granby, March of Dimes, 52 & 53; chmn, East Granby, Hartford Heart Asn, 66; leader, 4-H; St. Francis Hospital Auxiliary. Rel: Roman Catholic. Mailing Add: Spoonville Rd, East Granby, Conn. 06026.

SMITH, MARILU CRAFTON R
Rep. Nat. Committeewoman, Ga.
b. Dublin, Ga, 12/15/13; d. John Claxton Crafton and Mattie Julia Adkins C; m. 3/5/31 to Albert Edward Smith, wid; c. twins, Edwina Crafton and Marilyn Crafton. Educ: Kaigler Bus. Col, Macon, Ga, grad, 31. Polit. & Govt. Pos: Mem, Muscogee Rep. Women and Ga. and Nat. Fedn. Rep. Women, 54-; mem, Muscogee Co. Rep. Exec. Cmt, 62-66; mem, Third Dist. Rep. Cmt, 63-66; chmn, Third Dist. Goldwater Campaign and Third Dist. Draft Goldwater Campaign, 64; mem, Ga. Rep. Exec. Cmt, 64-; Rep. Nat. Committeewoman, 64-; mem, Ga. State Cmt. to Make Uniform Consumer Credit Code Study, 69- Mem: Adv. bd, Muscogee Co. Juvenile Court; organizer, Columbus Lawyer's Auxiliary, 59, pres, 60-61; pres, Columbus Area Tuberc. Asn, 61-63, bd. dirs. and exec. cmt, 61-66; bd. dirs. and exec. cmt, Patient Serv. Cmt, Ga. Tuberc. Asn; Ga. Litter Bug Cmt; Pintree Garden Club; Columbus Symphony Orchestra, 62-66; vol, Girl Scouts, 13 years; exec. cmt, mem. and publicity dir, Commun. Counseling Center; adv. coun, Southeast. Area, Am. Red Cross and Gray Lady, World War II; Ga. Heart Asn; Columbus Country Club. Named Woman of Year, Columbus. Rel: Methodist; mem, Wynnton Study Club. Mailing Add: 801 Peachtree Dr, Columbus, Ga. 31906.

SMITH, MARTHA ALEENE R
Secy, U.S. Rep. George Bush
b. Bay City, Tex, 7/30/09; d. Joseph Simpson Reed (deceased) and Mamie Anselin R.(deceased); m. 9/8/31 to Hargrove Smith; c. Don Hargrove and Alen Reed. Educ: Univ. Tex, Austin, 39. Polit. & Govt. Pos: Co-chmn, Eisenhower-Nixon Campaign Cmt, Colorado Co, Tex, 52; precinct chmn, Rep. Party, Colorado Co, Tex, 52-60; mem, Tex. Rep. State Exec. Cmt, 52-60; alternate del, Rep. Nat. Conv, 56; exec. secy, Harris Co. Rep. Party, 61-63; precinct chmn, Rep. Party, Harris Co, 66-; secy, U.S. Rep. George Bush, Seventh Dist, Tex, 66- Bus. & Prof. Pos: Stenographer, Southwest. Bell Tel. Co, Houston, 28-31; secy. and acct, First Nat. Bank, Beaumont, Austin Nat. Bank and Mercantile Nat. Bank, 43-47; ed, Eagle Lake Headlight, 47-50; acct, Lehrer Interests, Garwood, 50-59; admin. asst, Tex. Heart Asn, 59-60; exec. secy, Rep. Party Houston, 61-63; secy, George Bush Campaign for U.S. Sen, 64, George Bush Zapata Off-Shore Co, 65, George Bush Campaign for U.S. House Rep, 66. Mem: Rep. Women of Capitol Hill; Cong. Secretaries Club; Cent. Federated Rep. Women's Club. Rel: Episcopal. Legal Res: 2016 Main St, Houston, Tex. 77002. Mailing Add: 2525 N. Tenth St, Arlington, Va. 22201.

SMITH, MARVIN W. R
Iowa State Rep.
b. Near Ireton, Iowa, 2/25/01; m. 6/6/25 to Mabel Brown; c. Helen (Mrs. Lynford Pauling), Frances (Mrs. Don Burgess) and Margaret Ann (Mrs. E. Brian McGregor). Educ: Iowa State Univ, B.S, 23; Delta Chi. Polit. & Govt Pos: Iowa State Rep, currently; Speaker-Pro-Tem, Iowa State House of Rep; mem, Co. Sch. Bd; alternate del, Rep. Nat. Conv, 56. Bus. & Prof. Pos: Farmer and Purebred Shorthorn Cattle Breeder, 38 years; Inst. of Vets. on-the-Farm Training, 3 years. Mem: Mgr, Interstate Shorthorn Breeders Asn, 10 years; Lions. Rel: Presbyterian. Mailing Add: 502 S. Willow, Paullina, Iowa 51046. (1967)

SMITH, MARY LOUISE R
Mem, Rep. Nat. Cmt, Iowa
b. Eddyville, Iowa, 10/6/14; d. Frank Epperson and Louise Jager E; m. 10/7/34 to Elmer Milton Smith; c. Robert Charles, Margaret Louise and James Edward. Educ: Univ. Iowa, Iowa City, B.A, 35; Kappa Alpha Theta. Polit. & Govt. Pos: Mem. bd. educ, Eagle Grove Commun. Schs, Iowa, 55-60; mem, Gov. Cmn. on Aging, 61-62; mem, Iowa Cmn. for Blind, 61-62, chmn, 62-63; mem. state adv. bd, Iowa Fedn. Rep. Women, 61-; v.chmn, Wright Co. Rep. Cent. Cmt, 62-63; state v.chmn, Iowa Rep. Presidential Campaign, alternate del-at-lg, Rep. Nat. Conv, 64, del-at-lg, mem. cmt. on arrangements and platform cmt, 68; mem, Rep. Nat. Cmt, Iowa, 64-, mem. exec. cmt, 69-; mem, Rep. Nat. Subcmt. on Conv. Reform, 66-; v.chmn, Mid-West Region Rep. Conf, 69. Bus. & Prof. Pos: Pres, Eagle Grove Commun. Chest, Iowa, 53-54; mem. bd. dir, Ment. Health Center, N.Iowa, 61-63. Mem: PEO; Woman's Auxiliary, Am. Med. Asn. Rel: Protestant. Mailing Add: 654 59th St, Des Moines, Iowa 50312.

SMITH, NEAL D
U.S. Rep, Iowa
b. Hedrick, Iowa, 3/23/20; m. to Beatrix Havens; c. Douglas and Sharon. Educ: Drake Univ. Law Sch, grad; Mo. Univ. Col. of Lib. Arts; Syracuse Univ. Schs. of Pub. and Bus. Admin. Polit. & Govt. Pos: Nat. pres, Young Dem. Clubs of Am, 53-55; former asst. co. attorney, Polk Co, Iowa; U.S.Rep, Iowa, 58- Bus. & Prof. Pos: Farmer and lawyer. Mil. Serv: Vet, World War II; Nine Battle Stars; Air Medal; 4 Oak Leaf Clusters; Purple Heart. Mem: 4-H Club mem. and leader, 10 years; former chmn, Polk Co. Bd. of Soc. Welfare; DAV; Mason; various farm, sch. and serv. orgn. Legal Res: Altoona, Iowa 50009. Mailing Add: 2458 Rayburn House Office Bldg, Washington, D.C. 20515.

SMITH, NELS JENSEN R
Wyo. State Rep.
b. Newcastle, Wyo, 1/29/39; s. Peter Franklin Smith and Helen Jensen S; m. 12/21/68 to Jeanette Keener Vannoy. Educ: Univ. Wyo, B.S, 61; Phi Epsilon Phi; Alpha Zeta; Sigma Alpha Epsilon; Young Rep. Polit. & Govt. Pos: Wyo. State Rep, 62- Bus. & Prof. Pos: Owner and operator, Cattle Ranch, Sundance, Wyo, 61-, part-time mgr, before 61. Mem: Sundance 9, AF&AM; Farm Bur; Mem, Exec. Cmt, Wyo. Stockgrowers Asn, 65-; pres, Crook Co. Wildlife Asn; pres, Crook Co. Animal Disease Bd; Sundance Rod & Gun Club. Rel: Protestant. Mailing Add: Sundance, Wyo. 82729.

SMITH, NORMAN A. D
Okla. State Rep.
b. Santa Barbara, Calif, 7/28/31; s. Tower G. Smith and Anna Norman S; m. 3/19/54 to Nancy Kathryn Kennedy; c. Norman, Jr, Julie Kathryn and Amanda Jane. Educ: Univ. Okla, B.A, 54, M.A, 56 and LL.B, 59; fel, Rockefeller Brothers Theological Prog, Yale Divinity Sch, 56-57; Phi Eta Sigma; Phi Alpha Delta. Polit. & Govt. Pos: Okla. State Rep, McClain Co, 61- Bus. & Prof. Pos: Attorney-at-Law, 59- Mil. Serv: Entered as 2nd Lt, Air Force, 54, released as 1st Lt, 56, serv. as Intel. Officer. Mem: Okla. and Am. Bar Asns; Mason (32°). Rel: Methodist. Mailing Add: 319 W. Washington, Purcell, Okla. 73080. (1967)

SMITH, ODIS ODELL D
b. Jackson, Tenn, 8/30/04; s. Samuel Thomas Smith and Anna Burton Taylor S; wid. Educ: West Side High Sch, 15-16; Univ. Ark. Spec. Labor Course. Polit. & Govt. Pos: Del, Dem. Nat. Conv, 68. Mem: Pres.and bus. mgr, Chauffeurs, Teamsters and Helpers Local 878, 31 years; mem, Laborer's Local Union 490, Hot Springs; past pres, Ark. State Fedn. of Labor; first pres, Ark. State AFL-CIO; past pres, Little Rock Cent. Trades Coun. and Little Rock Bldg. Trades Coun; IBT, Nat. Negotiations Cmt. for Nat. Area Freight Agreements; policy cmt, South. Conf. of Teamsters; trustee mem, South. Conf. Pension Fund and Cent. States, Southeast and Southwest Areas Pension Fund; pres, Ark-Okla. Teamsters Joint Coun. 92, bd. rev. for State of Ark; bd. mem. and other pos. on Pulaski Co. United Fund, 30 years. Received award for selling War Bonds during World War II; award from Gov. Orval E. Faubus for sincere dedication as a mem. of the Faubus Off. Family from 55-67. Rel: Baptist. Mailing Add: 2616 Chester St, Little Rock, Ark. 72206.

SMITH, ORVILLE D
b. 6/28/09; m. 10/26/35 to Luevern Meyer; c. Darlene Jorgensen. Polit. & Govt. Pos: Twp. bd. mem; State Rep, -66. Mem: Elks; Izaak Walton League. Soil Conserv. Award Winner in Hamill Dist, 64; second place winner, 62. Rel: Catholic. Mailing Add: Witten, S.Dak. 57584.

SMITH, PAUL BRUCE R
Mem, Calif. Rep. State Cent. Cmt.
b. Long Beach, Calif, 9/3/37; s. Philip Wallace Smith and Emily M. Grundy S; m. 8/27/60 to Meredith Susan Bolton; c. Cameron Bruce and Brandon Paul. Educ: Univ. Calif, B.A, 60, Hasting Col. Law, J.D, 65; Beta Theta Pi. Polit. & Govt. Pos: Rep. nominee, State Bd. Equalization, First Dist, Calif, 66; mem, Calif. Rep. State Cent. Cmt, 67-; pres, Los Altos Chap, Calif. Rep. League, 67-; mem. steering Cmt, Assemblyman George Milias, 67-; Santa Clara Co. chmn, Sen. Thomas Kuchel, 68; mem, Santa Clara Co. Rep. Cent. Cmt, 68- Mem: Am, Calif. Santa Clara Co. and Palo Alto Area Bar Asns; Attorneys for Legal Aid Soc.(panel mem).San Mateo and Santa Clara Co); Rotary; Commonwealth Club Calif; Sierra Club; Cmt. Green Foothills (dir); C. of C; Save San Francisco Bay Asn. Rel: Unitarian. Legal Res: 677 Benvenue, Los Altos, Calif. 94022. Mailing Add: 660 W. Dana St, Mountain View, Calif. 94040.

SMITH, PAUL THOMPSON D
Chmn, Mont. Railroad and Pub. Serv. Cmn.
b. Boulder, Mont, 5/2/04; s. Cornelius Smith and Sarah Maguire S; m. 6/4/38 to Vivian F. Flaherty; c. Tresa and Paul B. Educ: High sch. Polit. & Govt. Pos: Co. Treas, Jefferson Co, Boulder, Mont, 32-36; cmnr, 38-; chmn, Mont. R.R. and Pub. Serv. Cmn, 38-; del, Dem. Nat. Conv, 68. Mem: Eagles. Rel: Catholic. Mailing Add: Box 27, Boulder, Mont. 59632.

SMITH, PERRY ROWAN D
Chmn, Bexar Co. Dem. Exec. Cmt, Tex.
b. Jena, La, 1/6/26; s. James Allen Smith and Mattie Jane S; m. 2/10/51 to

Norma Webb Dalehite; c. Perry Rowan, Jr, James Allen, Terry Bruce, Jason Alexander and Darlene Angwen. Educ: Southwest. La. Inst, 44; Rice Univ, B.A, 48; Univ. Tex. Law Sch, LL.B, 51. Polit. & Govt. Pos: Asst. dist. attorney, Bexar Co, Tex, 53-54, asst. city attorney, San Antonio, Tex, 55; chmn, Bexar Co. Dem. Exec. Cmt, 68- Bus. & Prof. Pos: Partner, Green, Smith & Wiley, Law Off, 56-59; partner, Glosserman, Alter, Smith & Rosenheim, 59- Mil. Serv: Entered as Seaman, Navy, 44, released as Ens, 47, after serv. in U.S.A. Wilke, Caribbean and D.E. Officer Training, Naval Res. Officer Training Corps, 44-47. Mem: San Antonio, Tex. and Am. Bar Asns; Am. Judicature Soc. Rel: Methodist. Legal Res: 202 Shannon Lee, San Antonio, Tex. 78216. Mailing Add: 504 Petroleum Commerce Bldg, San Antonio, Tex. 78205.

SMITH, PHILIP HARDY D
Ala. State Rep.
b. Talladega, Ala, 5/28/31; s. Philip Smith and Florence Riddle S; m. 12/28/51 to Catherine Elizabeth Wellbaum; c. Hardy, Cay, Barbara and Peggy. Educ: Auburn Univ, 50; Univ. of the South, B.S, 51; Univ. Rochester, M.S, 53; Univ. Ala, LL.B, 58; Phi Beta Kappa; Sigma Delta Kappa; Omicron Delta Kappa. Polit. & Govt. Pos: Alternate del, Dem. Nat. Conv, 56; pres, Univ. Ala. Young Dem, 57; pres, Talladega Co. Young Dem, 62-66; secy-treas, Talladega Co. Dem. Exec. Cmt, 66-; Ala. State Rep, Talladega Co, 67-; chmn, Ala. Legis. Coun, 69- Bus. & Prof. Pos: Lawyer, Talladega, Ala, 58- Mem: Talladega Co, Ala. and Am. Bar Asns; Southeast. Sect, Am. Phys. Soc; Am. Asn. for the Adv. of Sci; Ala. Archaeol. Soc; Am. Soc. for Legal Hist; The Selden Soc; Kiwanis; Ala. Farm Bur; Ala. Cattlemen's Asn. Rel: Methodist. Mailing Add: P.O. Box 15, Talladega, Ala. 35160.

SMITH, PHILIP LAWRENCE R
b. Kingston, Mass, 11/1/91; m. to Rachel McAllister; c. 3 sons. Educ: Schs. in Mass, Vt, Colo, Scotland. Polit. & Govt. Pos: Former Vt. State Rep. Bus. & Prof. Pos: Retired teacher. Mil. Serv: Army, Second Cavalry, 17-19; Sgt. in Machine Gun Troop. Mailing Add: Johnson, Vt. 05656. (1967)

SMITH, PRESTON EARNEST D
Gov, Tex.
b. Williamson Co, Tex, 3/8/12; s. Charles Kirby Smith and Effie Mae Strickland S; m. 6/20/35 to Ima Mae Smith; c. Preston Michael and Jan Lauren (Mrs. Conrad Schmid). Educ: Tex. Tech. Col, B.B.A, 34. Polit. & Govt. Pos: Tex. State Rep, 44-50; Tex. State Sen, 57-63; Lt. Gov, Tex, 63-67; del, Dem. Nat. Conv, 68; Gov, Tex, 69- Bus. & Prof. Pos: Owner, Tex. movie theaters, 36- Mem: Lubbock C. of C; Kiwanis; Mason (33°); United Fund; Salvation Army; Am. Red Cross. Rel: Methodist. Legal Res: Governor's Mansion, Austin, Tex. 78701. Mailing Add: Governor's Office, State Capitol, Austin, Tex. 78711.

SMITH, PRISCILLA B. R
V.Chairwoman, Fulton Co. Rep. Party, Ga.
b. Melrose, Mass, 4/2/17; d. Charles Everett Baker (deceased) and Mollie Lopaus B.(deceased); m. 7/27/40 to William Armstrong Smith; c. Johannah, Baker Armstrong and Deborah. Educ: Melrose Hosp. Sch. Nursing, R.N, 39. Polit. & Govt. Pos: Pres, South Fulton Fedn. Rep. Women, Ga, 64-68; legis. chmn, Ga. Fedn. Rep. Women, 65-68; del, Rep. Nat. Conv, 68; v.chairwoman, Fulton Co. Rep. Party, 68- Rel: Presbyterian. Mailing Add: 1405 DeLowe Dr. S.W, Atlanta, Ga. 30311.

SMITH, QUINTIN MILLER D
Chmn, Rutherford Co. Dem. Exec. Cmt, Tenn.
b. Buffalo, Tenn, 5/11/91; s. Edward Jerome Smith and Nancy Elizabeth Miller S; m. 8/17/38 to Laura Marie Simmons; c. Quintin M, Jr, Nancy Jean and William E. Educ: Peabody Col, B.S. and M.A, 17; Kappa Delta Pi; Phi Delta Kappa. Polit. & Govt. Pos: Chmn, Rutherford Co. Dem. Exec. Cmt, Tenn, presently. Bus. & Prof. Pos: Pres, Tenn. Polytechnic Inst, 20-38; pres, Mid. Tenn. State Col, 38-58; v.pres, Nat. Bank of Murfreesboro, 58-; chmn, Rutherford Co. Planning Cmn, presently. Mil. Serv: Entered as A/S, Navy, 18, released as Ens, 19; Major, Army Res, 23-42. Mem: Pres, Tenn. Educ. Asn, 37; Nat. Educ. Asn; pres, Tenn. Col. Asn, 38; Tenn. Bar Asn; Mason, Shrine; Am. Legion; Rotary; Farm Bureau; Stones River Country Club. Rel: Church of Christ. Legal Res: Rt. 3, Box 356, Murfreesboro, Tenn. 37130. Mailing Add: 129 E. Main St, Murfreesboro, Tenn. 37130.

SMITH, RALPH TYLER R
U.S. Sen, Ill.
b. Granite City, Ill, 10/6/15; s. Alfred Thomas Smith and Clara Slattery S; m. 10/23/42 to Mary Elizabeth Anderson; c. Sharon Lynne. Educ: Ill. Col, A.B, 37; Wash. Univ, J.D, 40; Phi Delta Phi. Polit. & Govt. Pos: Del, Ill. State Rep. Conv, 54-69; Ill. State Rep, 55-69, Majority Whip, Ill. House of Rep, 63, Speaker of the House, 67-69; del. and parliamentarian, Ill. State Rep. Conf, 66; del, Rep. Nat. Conv, 68; downstate campaign mgr, Carpentier for Gov, Ill, 64 and Ogilvie for Gov, 68; U.S. Sen, Ill, 69- Bus. & Prof. Pos: Dir, Greater Alton Asn. of Commerce, 64-66; chmn. of bd, Bank of Alton, 69- Mil. Serv: Entered as A/S, Naval Res, 42, released as Lt.(sg), 66, after serv. in Europe and Pac; Am, European and Pac. Theater Ribbons; Japanese Occupation Medal. Mem: Alton, Wood River, Madison Co, Ill. and Am. Bar Asns; VFW; Am. Legion; Elks; Eagles; Moose; Mason, Consistory, Shrine; Optimist. Rel: Presbyterian. Legal Res: 1 Signal Dr, Alton, Ill. 62002. Mailing Add: 604 E. Broadway, Alton, Ill. 62002.

SMITH, RAY ALLEN R
Committeeman, Grady Co. Rep. Party, Okla.
b. Tuttle, Okla, 7/17/43; s. Homer Ezra Smith (deceased) and Rhoda Brown S; m. 6/1/62 to Donna Louise Troop; c. Mark Alan and Shawnda Kay. Educ: Tuttle Pub. Schs, 12 years. Polit. & Govt. Pos: Rep. precinct chmn, Tuttle, Okla, 65-67; coordinator, Smith For Cong, Tuttle, 67-68; chmn, Bellmon For Senate, Grady Co, 68; chmn, Grady Co. Rep. Party, 68 and committeeman, 69- Mem: Baptist Brotherhood; Young Rep; Am. Red Cross; Outstanding Citizens Award, Ford Motor Co, 68. Rel: Baptist. Mailing Add: R.R. 2, Tuttle, Okla. 73089.

SMITH, RAYMOND FELIX D
Chmn, Putnam Co. Dem. Exec. Cmt, Fla.
b. Palatka, Fla. 10/31/19; s. Charles Calvin Smith and Lucy Couver S; m. 6/19/49 to Clara Belle Whitaker; c. Raymond Caca, John T. and Lucy Kay. Educ: Palatka High Sch, grad, 37. Polit. & Govt. Pos: Chmn, Putnam Co. Dem. Exec. Cmt, Fla, 48-; mayor, Palatka, 58-61. Mil. Serv: Entered as Pvt, Army Air Force, 42, released as Sgt, 45, after serv. in 43rd Bomb Squadron. Mem: Am. Legion; Elks. Good Govt. Award, 61; Good Citizenship Award, 59. Rel: Episcopal. Legal Res: 105 Cedar St, Palatka, Fla. 32077. Mailing Add: P.O. Box 569, Palatka, Fla. 32077.

SMITH, RAYMOND K. D
Mayor, South Corning, N.Y.
b. Corning, N.Y, 7/27/23; s. Walter Kneale Smith and Edith Canfield S; m. 5/24/47 to Eileen Kelly; c. Jeffrey Kneale, Timothy Lee and Corinne Ann. Educ: Am. Inst. Banking, part-time, 10 years; Rutgers Univ. Grad. Sch. Banking, Commercial Banking Cert, 55. Polit. & Govt. Pos: Village trustee, South Corning, N.Y, 50-69, mayor, 69-; alternate del, Dem. Nat. Conv, 68. Bus. & Prof. Pos: Pres, First Nat. Bank and Trust Co, Corning, N.Y, currently. Mil. Serv: Entered as Pvt, Army, 43, released as T/Sgt, 45, after serving in First Army Europe, 43-45; Bronze Star. Publ: 'Truth in Lending Testimony', U.S. Senate Banking Cmt, 4/19/67. Mem: Steuben Co. Bankers Asn.(chmn, 53); N.Y. State Bankers Asn.(coun. admin, 55 and chmn. group III, 66); Independent Bankers Asn. Am.(resolutions cmt, 68, govt. fiscal policy cmt, 69); Rotary Int; Am. Legion; Elks. Rel: Catholic. Mailing Add: 22 S. Elm, Corning, N.Y. 14830.

SMITH, RICHARD MACLIN D
Va. State Del.
b. Brunswick Co, Va, 1/14/06; m. to Annie Elizabeth Gee. Educ: Univ. Richmond; Med. Col. of Va; Phi Delta Chi. Polit. & Govt. Pos: Va. State Del, 54-; Kenbridge Town Coun, 10 years. Bus. & Prof. Pos: Druggist, farmer; mem. bd. dirs, Lunenburg Bank; pres, Imperial Brickett Corp. Mem: Va. Pharmaceutical Asn; bd. dirs, Va. Aberdeen Angus Asn; Mason; Kiwanis (past pres). Rel: Methodist; Lay Leader. Mailing Add: Kenbridge, Va. 23944. (1967)

SMITH, RICHARD PARKER R
Chmn, West Hartford Rep. Party, Conn.
b. New Britain, Conn, 7/24/14; s. David C. Smith and Bertha Allen S; m. 10/25/44 to Elizabeth Taylor; c. Marilyn and Carolyn. Educ: Wesleyan Univ, B.A, 36; Univ. Conn. Law Sch, LL.B, 40; Alpha Chi Rho. Polit. & Govt. Pos: Alderman-at-lg, Hartford, Conn, 41-42; councilman, West Hartford, 55-61, mayor, 59-61; chmn, West Hartford Rep. Party, 68- Bus. & Prof. Pos: Attorney, Phoenix Mutual Life Ins. Co, 40-, second v.pres. and counsel, 65- Mil. Serv: Entered as Pvt, Army, 42, released as Capt, 46, after serv. in 71st Inf. Div. and Ninth Inf. Div, ETO, 45-46. Publ: 'Trusts as Beneficiaries or Assignees of Life Insurance Policies,' Asn. Life Ins. Counsel, 5/56. Mem: Am, Conn. and Hartford Co. Bar Asns; Asn. Life Ins. Counsel; Civitan Int.(past int. judge advocate). New Eng. Dist. Honor Key of Civitan Int. Rel: Protestant. Mailing Add: 53 Hillsboro Dr, West Hartford, Conn. 06107.

SMITH, RICHARD R. R
b. Fall River, Mass, 9/21/21; s. John Smith and Jennie Twigg S; m. 7/24/53 to Marilyn Joanne Stafne; c. Jay Bradford, Randi, Bradley Wade and Wade Stafne. Educ: Univ. Mass, B.S.(chem), 42; Columbia Univ, M.A.(chem), 50, Ph.D.(chem), 53; Phi Lamda Upsilon; Sigma Xi; Alpha Gamma Rho. Polit. & Govt. Pos: Chmn, Bonneville Co. Rep. Cent. Cmt, Idaho, 64-69. Bus. & Prof. Pos: Chemist, Phillips Petrol. Co, Idaho Falls, Idaho, 53-55; Knolls Atomic Power Lab, 55-56; staff scientist, Argonne Nat. Lab, 56- Mil. Serv: Entered as Aviation Cadet, Army Air Force, 42, released as 1st Lt, 47, after serv. in N.Africa, ATC, Alaska, 49 Recon. Squadron; ETO Service Ribbon. Mem: Am. Nuclear Soc. Rel: Presbyterian. Mailing Add: 915 S. Higbee, Idaho Falls, Idaho 83401.

SMITH, RICHARD RACINE R
Chmn, 63rd Legis. Dist. Rep. Party, Minn.
b. Ft. Benning, Ga, 9/8/28; s. Thomas Scott Smith and Esther Racine S; m. 8/25/51 to Virginia Ann Miller; c. Elizabeth Racine and Douglas Scott. Educ: Mich. Tech. Univ, B.S. in mining eng, 49, B.S. in metall. eng. & M.S. in mining engr, 50; Tau Beta Pi; Blue Key; Delta Sigma Phi. Polit. & Govt. Pos: Del, Dickinson Co. & Mich. State Conv; secy. and precinct leader, Dickinson Co. Rep. Party, Mich, 61, chmn, 62; gen. chmn, Upper Peninsula Inauguration, 64; finance chmn, St. Louis Co. Dist. Rep. Party, Minn, 66-67; chmn, 63rd Legis. Dist. Rep. Party, 67-; del, St. Louis Co. Conv, 67-; del, Eighth Dist. and Minn. State Conv, 68-69. Bus. & Prof. Pos: Operating engr, Cleveland Cliffs Iron Co, 51-59; mill Supt, Hanna Mining Co, 59-63, plant supt, 63-65 and gen. supt, 65- Mem: Am. Inst. of Mining Engrs; Am. Soc. for Testing & Materials; Mesaba Country Club; Algonquin Club. Rel: Presbyterian. Mailing Add: 2122 Tenth Ave. E, Hibbing, Minn. 55746.

SMITH, RICHARD RUSSELL D
b. Clarkesville, Ga, 10/7/32; s. Olin Smith; Madge McCrackin S; m. 6/16/63 to Laura Edwards. Educ: Piedmont Col, 49-51; Univ. Ga, B.S, 54; West. Carolina Col, M.A.Ed, 68; Gridiron Club. Polit. & Govt. Pos: Tax assessor, Clarkesville, Ga, 54 & 56; Ga. State Rep, 61-65. Bus. & Prof. Pos: Teacher, Habersham Co. Schs, 54-56; part-time teacher, Piedmont Col, 56-59; barber, 48-63; restaurant operator, 63-64; teacher, Habersham Co. Schs, 64-67 and Tallulah Falls Sch, 67- Mem: Nat. Sci. Teachers Asn; Ga. Educ. Asn; WOW; Mason; Lions. Star Teacher, Tallulah Falls Sch, 69. Rel: Baptist. Mailing Add: Route 2, Clarkesville, Ga. 30523.

SMITH, RICHARD WADDELL R
Pub. Rels. Dir, Rep. Party Fla.
b. Charleston, W.Va, 2/2/40; s. Everett C. Smith, Jr. and Edith Waddell S; m. 3/22/69 to Marialice Durgin. Educ: Univ. Miami, B.A, 63; Kappa Alpha Order, Young Am. for Freedom, Young Rep. Polit. & Govt. Pos: V.chmn, Univ. Miami Young Am. Freedom, 62; dep. chmn, Dade Co. Citizens for Goldwater, Fla, 64; pub. rels. dir, Fla. Fedn. Young Rep, 65-67; v.pres, Dade Co. Young Rep, 66; campaign mgr, Thompson for Congress, 66; ed, Fla. Rep. Challenger, 66-68; regional dir, Young Rep. Nat. Fedn, 67-69, nat. v.chmn, 69-; pub. rels. dir, Rep. Party Fla, 67-; host cmt. staff, Rep. Nat. Conv, 68. Bus. & Prof. Pos: Pres, Jan-Allen/Burgess, Advert, Miami, 66-67. Mil.

Serv: Entered as Pfc, Army Nat. Guard, 64, released as SP-4, 66, after serv. in 35th Surg. Hosp, North Miami, Fla. Rel: Protestant. Mailing Add: 325 S.E. Sixth St, Ft. Lauderdale, Fla. 33301.

SMITH, ROBERT CHARLES D
Chmn, Boone Co. Dem. Cmt, Mo.
b. Fulton, Mo, 8/16/23; s. Robert Carter Smith and Agnes Thompson S; m. 6/2/45 to Jean Isabell; c. Robert Durant, Laura Penney; Jeanne Marie and Haden Douglas. Educ: Univ. Mo, Columbia, A.B, 48 and LL.B, 49; Omega Delta Kappa; Phi Delta Theta; Phi Delta Phi. Polit. & Govt. Pos: Mo. State Rep, 56-60 and Speaker Pro-Tem, Mo. House of Rep, 58-60; mayor, Columbia, Mo, 64-65; chmn, Boone Co. Dem. Cmt, Mo, 66- Mil. Serv: Entered as Pvt, Army, 43, released as 1st Lt, 46, after serv. in First Div, ETO, 45-46; recalled, 50-52, serv. in Korea; Bronze Star; Air Medal with Three Clusters; UN Ribbon. Mem: Boone Co. Bar Asn.(pres, 68); Jaycees (pres, Columbia Chap, 49); Kiwanis (pres, Columbia Chap, 60-61). Rel: Baptist. Mailing Add: 709 Russell, Columbia, Mo. 65201.

SMITH, ROBERT FLECK R
Chmn, Dauphin Co. Rep. Cmt, Pa.
b. Harrisburg, Pa, 7/4/34; s. Paul J. Smith and Ruth Fleck S; m. 8/10/59 to Gabrielle Walker; c. Lisa Rose, Robert Fleck, Jr. and Lydia Ruth. Educ: Dickinson Col, A.B, 56; Theta Chi. Polit. & Govt. Pos: Chmn, Dauphin Co. Rep. Cmt, Pa, 66-; del, Rep. Nat. Conv, 68. Bus. & Prof. Pos: Gen. agent, Columbus Mutual Life Ins. Co, 66-; pres, Robert F. Smith, Inc, 67- Mil. Serv: Entered as 2nd Lt, Army, 56, released as 1st Lt, 63, after serv. in Third and 79th Inf. Div; 1st Lt, Res. Publ: 'Urban Problems & Peaceful Integration,' Cong. Record 10/67. Mem: Pa. Asn. Life Underwriters; Harrisburg Asn. Life Underwriters (pres, 67-68); Tri-Co. Ment. Health Asn.(dir, 65-69); Pa. Soc; Kiwanis; Dauphin Co. Negro Rep. Coun; Mason; Harrisburg Area C. of C; Young Rep; Gov. Blue Ribbon Cmt. Rel: Presbyterian. Legal Res: 1188 Twin Lakes Dr, Harrisburg, Pa. 17111. Mailing Add: 1337 N. Front St, Harrisburg, Pa. 17102.

SMITH, ROBERT FRANKLIN D
Chmn, Saratoga Co. Dem. Cmt, N.Y.
b. Tenn, 7/14/25; s. Elbert B. Smith and Margaret G. Huffaker S; m. 6/26/50 to Barbara Leigh Eggleston; c. Michael and Kevin. Educ: Maryville Col, B.A, 48; Univ. Tenn, M.A, 51; Univ. Chicago, Ph.D, 55. Polit. & Govt. Pos: Mem. exec. cmt, Saratoga Co. Dem. Cmt, N.Y, 63-, chmn, 68- Bus. & Prof. Pos: Instr, Univ. Tenn, 49-51, Idaho State Col, 54-55; lectr, Northwest. Univ, 53; asst. prof. and assoc. prof, South. Methodist Univ, 55-60; assoc. prof. and prof, Skidmore Col, 60-69. Mil. Serv: Entered as A/S, Navy, 43, released as PhM 2/C, 46, after serv. in Sea Duty, USS Wis, BB64, ETO and Caribbean, 44-46. Publ: Philosophical Approach to International Relations, State Univ. of Iowa Press, 57; 'The New York State Farm Bureau and the Legislative Process,' J. Farm Econ, 67. Mem: Am. and N.Y. Polit. Sci. Asns; Am. Asn. of Univ. Prof. Grants, Ford Found, 56 and N.Y. State Legis. Internship, 65. Rel: Protestant. Mailing Add: Loughberry Rd, Saratoga Springs, N.Y. 12866.

SMITH, ROBERT GENE R
b. Broken Arrow, Okla, 8/16/34; s. Roy Fredrick Smith and Beulah Dean Smith Bradley; single. Educ: Univ. Okla, B.S, 56; Wash. Univ. Sch. Med, M.D, 59; Harvard Univ, LL.B, 63, M.P.H, 64; Phi Eta Sigma; Omicron Delta Kappa; Phi Beta Pi; Lincoln's Inn Soc; Jackson Johnson Regional Scholarship, Wash. Univ. Sch. Med, 55-59. Polit. & Govt. Pos: Rep. cand, U.S. House Rep, Second Dist, Okla, 68. Bus. & Prof. Pos: Partner, law firm, Ellison, Smith, Morrel & Manke, Tulsa, Okla, 68- Mil. Serv: Lt. Comdr, 66-68, Navy Med. Corps, with serv. in Hq, U.S. Mil. Assistance Command, Vietnam and Nat. Naval Med. Center, Bethesda, Md, 66-68; Lt. Comdr, Naval Res, 68-; Navy Commendation Medal; Vietnamese Tech. Serv. Honor Medal First Class. Publ: Co-auth, 'The Chilean Agrarian Reform,' Inter-Am. Law Rev, 1/64-7/64 and 'The Senile Testator: Medico-Legal Aspects of Competency,' Cleveland-Marshall Law Rev, 9/64. Mem: Boston, Mass, Am. and Okla. Bar Asns; Am. Med. Asn; Am. Soc. Int. Law; Am. Asn. Mil. Surgeons; Am. Asn. Univ. Prof; Am. Soc. Tropical Med. and Hygiene; VFW. Named Most Outstanding Young Tulsan for 65-66, Tulsa Jr. C. of C. Rel: Christian Church of N.Am. Mailing Add: R.F.D. 3, Broken Arrow, Okla. 74105.

SMITH, ROBERT HALLOCK R
b. Mitchell, S.Dak, 2/9/17; s. Robert Loyd Smith and Grace Anderson S; m. 6/1/40 to Bettina R. Ball; c. Victoria Susan (Mrs. Colin M. Holman), Peter Hallock and Christy Owen. Educ: Pasadena City Col, A.A, 35; Calif. Inst. Tech, B.S, 37; Polit. & Govt. Pos: Nev. State Assemblyman, Third Dist, 67-69; mem, Civil Serv. Bd, Henderson, Nev. Bus. & Prof. Pos: Supt, Harlow Aircraft Co, 37-40; instr, Pasadena City Col, 40-41; owner, Smith Bldg. Co, Inc, 46-51; construct-maintenance, DASA Lake Mead Base, 54-63; partner-mgr, Henderson Builders Supply, 63- Mil. Serv: Entered as Ens, Navy, 42, released as Comdr, 46; also served 51-53; Capt, Naval Res, 60. Mem: F&AM; VFW. Rel: Presbyterian. Mailing Add: 431 Blackridge Rd, Henderson, Nev. 89015. (1967)

SMITH, ROBERT HAROLD D
Chmn, Benton Co. Dem. Party, Iowa
b. Walker, Iowa, 8/5/33; s. John Ferdinand Smith and Christina May Kramer S; single. Educ: Urbana Consol. Schs, Iowa, grad. Polit. & Govt. Pos: Committeeman, Polk Twp, Iowa, 64-67; chmn, Benton Co. Dem. Party, 67- Bus. & Prof. Pos: Steno-clerk Wabash R.R, Omaha, Nebr, 57-60; owner, Bobs Kountry Kitchen, 62- Mil. Serv: Entered as Pvt-E-1, Army, 54, released as Sp-3, 56, after serv. in 11th Field Artil. Bn, 24th Inf. Div, Korea, 55-56. Mem: Pres, Urbana Businessman's Club; K. of C; hon. mem, Am. Legion. Rel: Catholic. Mailing Add: Box 305, Urbana, Iowa 52345.

SMITH, ROBERT LEE D
b. Waycross, Ga, 11/5/18; s. Doat Smith and Lula Hargrove S; m. 6/22/41 to Betty Barbour; c. Robert Lee, Jr. and Barbara B. Educ: Morehouse Col, B.S, 42; Howard Univ, D.D.S, 46; Alpha Phi Alpha. Polit. & Govt. Pos: Mem, Palm Beach Co. Dem. Exec. Cmt, Fla; chmn, Mayor's Cmt. on Commun, Rels, West Palm Beach, 58, Mayor's Cmt. on Slum Clearance, 59, cand. for City Cmnr, 66, chmn, Zoning Bd. of Appeals, 67, v.chmn, 68 and mem, 68-; del-at-lg, Dem. Nat. Conv, 68. Bus. & Prof. Pos: State dir, Alpha Phi Alpha, 69. Mil. Serv: Pfc, Army Res, 42-44, served as Guard Police, War Dept; Cert. for Good Character. Mem: Nat. Dent. Asn.(chmn. budget cmt, 66-67, chmn. exec. bd. and secy, 67, publicity dir, 67-69); Am. and Fla. Dent. Asns; Fla. Med, Dent. & Pharmaceutical Asn.(exec. secy, 58-69); Am. Legion; Vanguard Club; United Fund of Palm Beach Co; K. of P; Palm Beach Co. Referral Bd; Comprehensive Commun. Ment. Health Center. Spec. Serv. Award, Nat. Dent. Asn; award, United Negro Col. Fund; trophy, Palm Beach Co. Referral Bd; several awards and cert. for Outstanding Serv. in local commun. Rel: Baptist. Legal Res: 825 3rd St, West Palm Beach, Fla. 33401. Mailing Add: 431 Rosemary Ave, West Palm Beach, Fla. 33401.

SMITH, ROBERT LEONARD D
b. Portland, Ind, 2/14/04; s. John M. Smith and Margaretta Leonard S; m. 10/6/50 to Evelyn L. Swhier; c. Carolyn E. Educ: Earlham Col, Richmond, Ind, A.B, 26. Polit. Pos: Ind. State Rep, Jay and Randolph Cos, 41-42, 61-66. Bus. & Prof. Pos: Lawyer. Mem: Am. Judicature Soc; Elks; Eagles; Moose. Rel: Roman Catholic. Mailing Add: 1004 S. Meridian, P.O. Box 1002, Portland, Ind. 47371. (1967)

SMITH, ROBERT LOUIS D
Committeeman, Ill. Dem. Cent. Cmt.
b. Chicago, Ill, 7/13/34; s. Robert L. Smith, Sr. and Margaret B. Warchol S; m. 7/19/58 to Laura Jean Frodyma; c. Robert John. Educ: Univ. Ill, 52-53; North. Ill. Univ, 53-54; Northwest. Univ, D.D.S, 58; Psi Omega. Polit. & Govt. Pos: Twp. supvr, Stickney Twp, Ill, 61-69; pres, bd. pub. health, Stickney Pub. Health Dist, Ill, 61-69; committeeman, Ill. Dem. Cent. Cmt, 66- Bus. & Prof. Pos: Dentist, Chicago, Ill, 58-62; owner, The Old Barn, Oak Lawn, Ill, 66- Mem: Am. Dent. Asn; Ill. Asn. of Bd. of Health; Twp. Off. of Ill; Cook Co. Supvr. Asn; Nat. Restaurant Asn; Rotary; Northwest. Alumni Asn; YMCA (mem. bd. dirs, Southwest Chap); Moose. Outstanding Student Class of 58, Psi Omega; Leadership Award, Independent Voters of Ill, 62; Guy E. Reed Mem. Award, Citizens of Gr. Chicago, 63; Young Man of the Year, State of Ill, 67. Rel: Catholic. Mailing Add: 8100 S. Parkside Ave, Oak Lawn, Ill. 60459.

SMITH, ROGER A. R
N.H. State Rep.
b. Concord, N.H, 6/6/32; married; c. one. Educ: Concord High Sch. Polit. & Govt. Pos: N.H. State Rep, currently; supvr, Fifth Ward Checklist; mem, Concord Rep. City Cmt; chmn, Fifth Ward Rep. Cmt. Bus. & Prof. Pos: Plant dept, N.E. Tel. & Tel. Co. Mil. Serv: Army, Korea; 981st F.A. Bn, 49th Inf. Div. Mem: Int. Brotherhood of Tel. Workers, Local 20. Mailing Add: 95 Center St, Concord, N.H. 03301. (1967)

SMITH, ROGER HOLLINGSHEAD R
b. Bayonne, N.J, 1/7/31; s. Harry William Smith and Mary Hollingshead S; m. 6/16/56 to Patricia Ann Blossom; c. Britt, Anne, Craig and June. Educ: Ind. Univ, B.S. in bus, 52, Sch. of Law, J.D, 58; Phi Delta Phi; Flame Club; Tomahawk. Polit. & Govt. Pos: Chmn, Franklin Co. Young Rep, Ind, 60-62; chmn, Franklin Co. Rep. Cent. Cmt, 62-67; chmn, Brookville Town Rep. Cent. Cmt, 63-67; del, Ind. State Rep. Conv, 65 & 68; co. attorney, Franklin Co, 68- Bus. & Prof. Pos: Partner, C.C. Tague, Sr, 59-62, Tague & Smith, 63-67 & Roger H. Smith, 68-; dir, World Life Cent. Agency and World Life and Accident Asn, 64-; mem, bd. dirs, Farquhar Co, 67- Mil. Serv: Entered as Pvt, Army, 52, released as Sp-2, 55, after serv. in Army Security Agency, Pac, 54-55; Korean Campaign Ribbon; Pac. Theater Ribbon. Mem: Am. and Ind. Bar Asns; 37th Judicial Circuit Bar Asn.(pres, 69-); Am. Legion; dir. and pres, Franklin Co. C. of C; Liberty Country Club; Masons, Knights, York Rite Cross of Honor; chmn, bd. dirs, Franklin Co. United Fund; dir, Riverview Heights Homeowner's Asn; Cent. Ind. Unit, Wally Byam Caravan Club Int. Rel: Methodist. Mailing Add: R.R. 4, Brookville, Ind. 47012.

SMITH, S. C. D
b. Arcadia, Fla, 1/13/96; m. to Mary Lee Taylor; c. Marjorie (Mrs. Charles E. Mundell, Jr.). Educ: Col. of Pharm, Ga. Polit. & Govt. Pos: Fla. State Rep, 50-66; Mayor of Arcadia; Chmn, Arcadia City Coun. Bus. & Prof. Pos: Retail Pharmacist and Citrus Grower. Mil. Serv: Mexican Border, 1917; WWI, WWII; Fla. Nat. Guard, 23-47; Bronze Star; Retired as Brig. Gen. of Artil. Mem: Am. Legion; VFW, Kiwanis; Elks; DeSoto Co. Cattlemen's Asn; Masons; Shrine; Fla. State Pharmacists Asn; Farm Bur. Rel: Presbyterian. Mailing Add: P.O. Box 150, Arcadia, Fla. 33821. (1967)

SMITH, SAMUEL J. D
b. Gibsland, La, 7/21/22; s. The Rev. Stephen Kelly Smith and Berniece C. Bailey S; m. 1/29/47 to Marion King; c. Amelia I, Aldwin Carl, Anthony, Donald C, Ronald C. and Stephen Kelly, II. Educ: Seattle Univ, B.S.S, 51; Univ. Wash, B.A. in Econ, 52, grad. work in econ. and polit. sci, 52-53; Phi Beta Sigma. Polit. & Govt. Pos: Clerk typist regional off, U.S. Vet. Admin. Br. 11, 46-47, fiscal accts. clerk, 47-51; Dem. precinct committeeman, Seattle, Wash; Wash. State Rep, 37th Dist, 58-69. Bus. & Prof. Pos: Printing and advert. salesman, self-employed, 46-50; expediter, Boeing Co, Seattle, Wash, 51-; publisher and ed, Commun. Newspaper, 52-54. Mil. Serv: Entered as Pvt, Army, 42, released as Warrant Officer (jg), 46, after serv. in Qm. Corps and Transportation Corps, Asiatic Pac. Theater, New Guinea, Philippine Islands, 44-46; Good Conduct Medal; Asiatic Pac. Theater and New Guinea Campaign Ribbons; Philippines Liberation Medal; 2 Bronze Stars; World War II Vets. Medal. Mem: Past Comdr, VFW Post 289; Aero Mechanics Lodge 751; Seattle Automobile Asn. Am. Played semi-pro baseball for 8 years; sponsored semi-pro team. Rel: Baptist; Pres. of Fellowship, Mt. Zion Baptist Church. Mailing Add: 1814 31st Ave, Seattle, Wash. 98122. (1967)

SMITH, SAMUEL LAMONT D
Asst. Secy, Ga. State Senate
b. Glennville, Ga, 6/07/09; s. Dr. Samuel F. Smith and Bertha Gross S; m. 11/23/49 to Corrine Kirkland. Educ: Univ. Ga; Univ. N.C. Polit. & Govt. Pos: Mem, Glennville City Coun, Ga, 34-42; asst. secy, Ga. State Senate, 43-44 & 47- Bus. & Prof. Pos: Former newspaper editor & publisher; bus. mgr, Ga. State Prison, currently. Mem: Elks; Mason; Shrine. Rel: Baptist. Mailing Add: Reidsville, Ga. 30453. (1967)

SMITH, SHELDON B. R
Chmn, 19th Cong. Dist. Rep. Cmt, Mich.
b. Pontiac, Mich, 1/21/39; s. Rolfe H. Smith and Ruth E. Annett S; m. 8/9/68 to Sharon Wilkes Applegate; c. Kevin J. Applegate. Educ: Univ. Mich, 56-58. Polit. & Govt. Pos: Membership chmn, Oakland Co. Young Rep, Mich, 66-67; membership chmn, Mich. Fedn. Young Rep, 67-68; chmn, 19th Cong. Dist. Rep. Cmt, 69- Bus. & Prof. Pos: Prog. dir, Radio Sta. KMAN, Manhattan, Kans, 58-60; realtor, Rolfe H. Smith Co, Pontiac, Mich, 65- Mil. Serv: Entered as Pvt, Army, 62 released as Sgt, 64, after serv. in Am. Forces Network, Europe, 62-64. Mem: Pontiac Area Bd. Realtors; Mich. Real Estate Asn; Nat. Inst. Real Estate Brokers of Nat. Asn. Real Estate Bd; Pontiac Area C. of C; Downtown Pontiac Kiwanis; Pontiac City Club; Am. Fedn. TV and Radio Artists; Screen Actors Guild. Rel: Methodist. Mailing Add: 502 Shoreview Dr, Pontiac, Mich. 48054.

SMITH, SIEGMUND WILSON R
b. Philippine Islands, 4/7/10; s. Fine Wilson Smith and Mildred Whiting S; m. 9/21/45 to Frances Dorothea O'Connor; c. Donald Wilson, Brian Richard and Patricia Christine. Educ: Univ. Ky, 1 year. Polit. & Govt. Pos: Admin. asst. to U.S. Rep. Lionel Van Deerlin, Calif, 63- Bus. & Prof. Pos: Sports dir, Radio Sta. WGR, Buffalo, N.Y, 36-52; news ed, KFSD-TV, San Diego, Calif, 53-60; sports dir, XETV-TV, 60-63. Mil. Serv: Entered as Pvt, Army, 42, released as Sgt, 45, after serv. in Mil. Intel, ETO, 44-45. Mem: Wash. Contract Bridge League; Nat. Capitol Swimming Asn. Rel: Episcopal. Legal Res: San Diego, Calif. Mailing Add: 8002 Park Crest Dr, Silver Spring, Md. 20910.

SMITH, STANLEY EUGENE, JR. D
Ga. State Sen.
b. Liberly, Mo, 9/7/19; s. Stanley Eugene Smith and Della Thurston S; m. 7/17/43 to Carolyn Coleman; c. Carol Lynn and Susan Christine. Educ: William Jewell Col; Wagner Col; St. Lawrence Univ, Brooklyn Law Sch, 1 year. Polit. & Govt. Pos: Mayor, Perry, Ga, 54-60; chmn, Houston Co. Hosp. Authority, 58; former chmn, Perry Planning and Zoning Cmn; Ga. State Sen, 18th Dist, currently. Bus. & Prof. Pos: Pres, Perry Indust. Develop. Corp, Ga, 55-; v.pres, Travel Host of Am, Inc, 60-; dir, First Nat. Bank of Perry, 64- Mil. Serv: Entered as Pvt, Army, 41, released as Capt. 45, after serv. as Exec. Officer, Maintenance Div, Warner Robins Air Material Area. Mem: Pres, Perry C. of C; Am. Legion; Mason; Salvation Army Bd; Kiwanis. Selected Man of Year, Kiwanis, 58 and Citizen of Year, Civitan, 64. Rel: Methodist. Mailing Add: 101 Marshallville Rd, Perry, Ga. 31069.

SMITH, STEPHEN WELLS R
Gov. Coun, N.H.
b. Chicago, Ill, 6/11/30; s. George Dresser Smith and Eleanor Wells S; m. 11/15/58 to Dorothy Louise Merris; c. S. Wells, Donald Merris, Matthew Doyle and Jennifer Ann. Educ: Kenyon Col, A.B, 52; Alpha Delta Phi. Polit. & Govt. Pos: Chmn, Grafton Co. Rep. Cmt, N.H, 60-64; treas, Plymouth, N.H, 61-62; cmnr, Plymouth Village Fire Dist, 61-; N.H. State Rep, 63-67, mem, Cmt. on Exec. Depts. and Admin, 63-65, chmn, Transportation Cmt, 65-67; chmn, N.H. Uniform Vehicle Code Study Cmt, 66-68; chmn, Plymouth Rep. Town Cmt, 67-; Gov. Coun, N.H, 69- Mem: Rotary; Elks. Rel: Protestant. Legal Res: 115 Highland St, Plymouth, N.H. 03264. Mailing Add: 71 Main St, Plymouth, N.H. 03264.

SMITH, STEVEN EARL D
b. Torrance, Calif, 2/17/37; s. Lyman M. Smith and Verna Hoskins S; m. 11/17/62 to Helena Catherine Robinson; c. Steven Earl, Jr, Jennifer Alison, Catherine Kimberly and James Robinson. Educ: Los Angeles State Col, B.A, 59; Phi Rho Pi. Polit. & Govt. Pos: South. Calif. chmn, Calif. Fedn. of Young Dem, 58-60; Young Dem. Nat. committeeman, 60-61; mem, Calif. State Dem. Cent. Cmt, 59-61; first v.pres, Young Dem. Clubs of Am, 61-63; Assembly-Sen. liaison officer, Calif. State Assembly, Sacramento, 61, consult, Cmt. on Revenue and Taxation, 61-62, Assembly chief admin. officer, 62-64, consult, Cmt. on Elec. and Reapportionment, 65-66; South. Calif. campaign mgr, Johnson-Humphrey Campaign, 64; cand, Calif. State Sen, 31st Dist, 66; South. Calif. campaign mgr, Sen. Robert F. Kennedy, 68; del, Dem. Nat. Conv, 68. Bus. & Prof. Pos: Prin. assoc, Econ. Consult. Inc, Los Angeles, 66-67; owner, Pac. Mgt. Assocs. and The Pac. Poll, 67- Publ: '1963 Final Report of the Assembly Interim Committee on Revenue and Taxation,' State of Calif, 1/63. Mem: Union of State Employees, AFL-CIO, 62-66. Resolution of Commendation Unanimously adopted by Calif. State Assembly, 64. Rel: Protestant. Mailing Add: 13584 Cheltenham Dr, Sherman Oaks, Calif. 91403.

SMITH, THOMAS EARLE, JR. D
S.C. State Rep.
b. Oxford, N.C, 7/22/38; s. Thomas Earle Smith and Margaret Louise Osterhout S; m. 6/23/61 to Elizabeth Eulalia Munn; c. Mary Dresden and Amy Louise. Educ: Davidson Col, A.B, 60; Univ. S.C, LL.B, 63; Chief Justice; Phi Alpha Delta; Phi Delta Theta; Co-capt, Davidson Col. Swimming Team and v.chmn, Student Coun. of YMCA, 59-60. Polit. & Govt. Pos: Pres, S.C. Young Dem. Club, 67-69; S.C. State Rep, Florence Co, 67-, mem, Judiciary Cmt, 67-, mem, Agr. and Conservation Cmt, 69-; del, Dem. Nat. Conv, 68. Bus. & Prof. Pos: Mem. bd. dir, Pamplico Bank and Trust Co. and Johnsonville State Bank, 65-; pres, Pamplico Devlop. Co, Inc, 66. Mem: Lions; Mason; Shrine; Omar Imps; Jaycees (pres, Pamplico Jaycees, 65-66, legal counsel and parliamentarian, S.C. Jaycees, 66-67). Rel: Methodist; secy, official bd, Pamplico Methodist Church, 65- Legal Res: Trade St, Pamplico, S.C. 29583. Mailing Add: P.O. Box 308, Pamplico, S.C. 29583.

SMITH, THOMAS G. D
Chmn, McClain Co. Dem. Cent. Cmt, Okla.
b. Santa Barbara, Calif,7/25/29; s. Tower G. Smith and Anna J. Norman S; m. 2/28/52 to Barbara J. Smith; c. Tommy, Terry, Jan, Natalie and Nickie. Educ: Univ. Okla, B.A. and LL.B; Phi Eta Sigma; Phi Beta Kappa; Sigma Alpha Epsilon. Polit. & Govt. Pos: Secy-treas, McClain Co. Dem. Cent. Cmt, Okla, 52-56, chmn, 60-; co. attorney, McClain Co, 55-56; admin. asst. to Congressman John Jarman, Okla, 56-59; chmn, McClain Co. Commun. Action Prog, 67-69; chmn, Delta Community Action Prog, 69; city attorney, Purcell, Okla, 69- Mailing Add: Box 146, Purcell, Okla. 73080.

SMITH, V. MAURICE (MAURY) R
Married; c. 1 daughter; 2 grandchildren. Polit. & Govt. Pos: Alaska State Rep, 63-64; Alaska State Sen, 67-69. Bus. & Prof. Pos: Radio and TV newscasting. Mailing Add: 229 Well St, Fairbanks, Alaska 99701. (1967)

SMITH, VICTOR L. R
Chmn, Ill. Rep. Party
b. Crawford Co, Ill. Educ: Univ. Ill. Polit. & Govt. Pos: State organizer of first Young Rep. Orgn, Ill; former pres, Robinson Young Rep. Club and Crawford Co. Fedn. of Young Rep. Clubs; precinct committeeman, Rep. Party, 32 years; chmn, Crawford Co. Rep. Party, several years; mem, Ill. Rep. State Cent. Cmt, 6 years; former Rep. Nat. Committeeman; chmn, Ill. Rep. Party, 60-; del, Rep. Nat. Conv, 68. Bus. & Prof. Pos: Publisher, Robinson Argus, Ill, currently. Mailing Add: 205 S. Franklin, Robinson, Ill. 62454.

SMITH, VIRGIL T. D
Ga. State Rep.
b. Dalton, Ga, 10/04/23; s. Roy Virgil Smith and Anna Painter S; m. 5/02/47 to Betty Jo Holloway; c. Timothy Virmal, Donna Jo. Educ: Herrin Sch. of Bus, 47-49; Tenn. Temple Col, 51-54; Univ. of Chattanooga, B.S, 56. Polit. & Govt. Pos: Ga. State Rep, 57- Bus. & Prof. Pos: Owner, Virgil T. Smith Ins. Agency. Mil. Serv: Navy, 43-46; Presidential Citation; Asiatic-Pac. Medal with Six Stars; Philippine Liberation Ribbon; Victory Medal. Rel: Baptist; Minister. Mailing Add: 609 Murray Hill Dr, Dalton, Ga. 30720. (1967)

SMITH, VIRGIL WALTER D
Chmn, Rusk Co. Dem. Party, Wis.
b. Brooks, Minn, 4/5/14; s. Earl Melvine Smith and Eva Whittish S; m. 10/2/37 to Coramay Flom; c. Carol Ann, Ronald Earl, Virginia Rae, Bonnie Lou and Walter Martin. Educ: Madison Voc. Sch, 2 years; Univ. Wis, 2 Semesters. Polit. & Govt. Pos: Secy-treas, Tavern League of Rusk Co, Inc, 49-; village clerk, Ingram, Wis, 50-; mem, Sect. Redevelop. of Ingram, 58-; v.chmn, Rusk Co. Dem. Party, 62-63, chmn, 63-; third v.pres, Tavern League of Wis, Inc, 65- Mem: Eagles, Madison; Gregg Club; jr. and sr. leader, 4 H Club; Sportsman Club, Ladysmith, Wis. Rel: Catholic. Mailing Add: Box 175, Ingram, Wis. 54535. (1967)

SMITH, W. MURRAY R
Chmn, Clay Co. Rep. Exec. Cmt, W.Va.
b. Uler, W.Va, 12/20/08; s. William Cary Smith and Ida Boggs S; m. 11/10/28 to Ethel A. Pierson; c. Elizabeth Ann. Educ: New River State Col. Polit. & Govt. Pos: City councilman, Clay, W.Va, 34-38; chmn, Clay Co. Rep. Exec. Cmt, 62- Bus. & Prof. Pos: Teacher and prin, Clay Co, W.Va, 30-36; pres, Clay Citizens Tel. Co, 32-58, dir. and regional mgr, W.Va. Tel. Co, 58-; mem. staff, Clay Co. Bank, 36-, pres, currently; pres, Elk Develop. Co, 54- Mem: Lions; Farm Bur; Co. and State Hon. Future Farmer. W.Va. 4-H Alumni award, 55. Rel: Methodist. Mailing Add: 1 Carr St, Clay, W.Va. 25043.

SMITH, W. R. D
b. 1901. Educ: East. Ky. State Col. Polit. & Govt. Pos: Presidential elector, 32; Del, Dem. Nat. Conv, 40, 44 & 68; former Ky. State Rep. Bus. & Prof. Pos: Bank pres. Mem: Mason. Rel: Methodist. Mailing Add: Hindman, Ky. 41822. (1967)

SMITH, WADE ORCHIN D
b. Poplarville, Miss, 2/16/11; married. Polit. & Govt. Pos: Former Miss. State Rep; former dir, Pearl River Co. Dem. Party. Bus. & Prof. Pos: Farmer. Mem: Pres, Farm Bur; Wolf River Wildlife Coun. Rel: Baptist. Mailing Add: Route 2, Box 168, Poplarville, Miss. 39470. (1967)

SMITH, WALTER L, JR. R
N.J. State Assemblyman
b. E. Riverton, N.J, 12/17/17; married; c. Three. Educ: Am. Inst. of Banking; Drexel Inst. of Tech; S. Jersey Law Sch; Rutgers Law Sch. Polit. & Govt. Pos: N.J. State Assemblyman, 64- Bus. & Prof. Pos: Attorney-at-Law, 53- Mem: Burlington Co. Bar Asn; Am. Right-of-way Asn. Mailing Add: 1403 Riverton Rd, Cinnaminson Twp, Riverton, N.J. 08077.

SMITH, WILBURN R
Chmn, Fayette Co. Rep. Cmt, Ala.
b. Bankston, Ala, 6/26/03; s. James Howell Smith and Dessie Johnson S; m. 5/14/32 to Jalia Blanche Sawyer; c. June (Mrs. Aldridge). Educ: Univ. Ala, B.Ed. Polit. & Govt. Pos: Rep. precinct worker, Bankston, Ala, 36 and mem. dist. Rep. Orgn, 52-; v.chmn, Fayette Co. Rep. Cmt, 56-62, chmn, 62- Bus. & Prof. Pos: Teacher elem. sch, 29-31 & 48-; prin. jr. high sch, 31-41 & 46-48; patrolman defense plant, 41-45. Mem: Fayette Co. Teachers Asn; Am. and Nat. Educ. Asns; AFL; 4-H Club; Farm Bur. Rel: Missionary Baptist. Mailing Add: R.R. 1, Bankston, Ala. 35542.

SMITH, WILL L. D
Dean, Tex. House of Rep.
b. De Ridder, La, 10/29/17; s. Will L. Smith, Sr. and Lillian Williams S; single. Educ: Lamar State Col. Tech; Tex. A&M Col. Polit. & Govt. Pos: Dean, Tex. House of Rep, Tex. State Rep, 43-47 & 52- Bus. & Prof. Pos: Pres, Smith Ward Jewelry Co, 46- Publ: Co-author, The Texas Legislature since 1846. Rel: Baptist. Legal Res: 644 Ave. C, Beaumont, Tex. 77705. Mailing Add: 336 Bowie, Beaumont, Tex. 77701.

SMITH, WILLIAM ARMSTRONG R
Ga. State Sen.
b. Brookline, Mass, 3/30/14; s. William Henry Smith and Josephine MacIntosh S; m. 7/27/40 to Priscilla Baker; c. Johannah, Baker Armstrong and Deborah. Educ: Northeast. Univ, B.S. in Chem. Engr, 36; Tau Beta Pi. Polit. & Govt. Pos: Chmn, 96th Dist. Rep. Party, Fulton Co, Ga. and v.chmn, Fifth Cong. Dist. Rep. Party, 66; Ga. State Sen, 34th Dist, 67- Bus. & Prof. Pos: Trustee, Arlington Schs; pres, DeKalb Christian Acad, 60-67. Mil. Serv: Naval Air Corps, 36. Mem: Pres. and dir, Ga. Bus. & Indust. Asn; Ga. C. of C; South Fulton Co. C. of C; past pres, South. Soc. for Paint Tech. and Saint Simons Island C. of C; South Fulton Cattlemens Asn; Cedar Grove Civic Club. Distinguished Engr, Tau Beta Pi, 68. Rel: Presbyterian; Elder. Mailing Add: 1405 DeLowe Dr. S.W, Atlanta, Ga. 30311.

SMITH, WILLIAM FORREST D
b. Beaumont, Tex, 1/6/29; s. William Enoch Smith and Mary Bray S; m. 1/22/51 to Martha McCarley; c. Sherry Roxann, Jill Ann and Lori Ann. Educ: Lon Morris Jr. Col, Jacksonville, Tex, 45-47; Southwest. Univ.(Tex), B.A, 49; South. Methodist Univ. Sch. of Law, 49-51, J.D, 57, LL.M, 63; Kappa Sigma. Polit. & Govt. Pos: Dem. precinct chmn, Dallas Co, Tex, 66-; mem, Dallas Co. Dem. Exec. Cmt, 66-; alternate del, Dem. Nat. Conv, 68; mem, Bd. of Dallas Dem, 68-69. Bus. & Prof. Pos: Acct, Magnolia Petroleum Co, 52-54, tax acct, 54-58; attorney, Mobil Oil Corp, 58- Mil. Serv: 1st Lt, Tex. Nat. Guard, Judge Advocate Gen. Sect, 49th Armored Div, 11 years. Publ: State Taxation of the Oil and Gas Industry as Limited by the Interstate Commerce Clause, South. Methodist Univ. Sch. of Law, 63; Pollution Problems in the Petroleum—Construction of and Compliance with Federal and State Laws, Matthew Bender, 68. Mem: Tex. Mid-Continent Oil and Gas Asn. (chmn. soc. security cmt); Mid-Continent Oil and Gas Asn.(chmn. cmt); Mobil Mgt. Asn.(past pres); Mobil Fed. Credit Union (v.pres); Dallas Bar; Tex. and Am. Bar Asns; Richardson Parents League Asn.(founder and past pres); C. of C; solicitor, United Fund; South. Methodist Univ. Sustentation Fund. Vernon Law Book Award, South. Methodist Univ. Rel: Methodist. Legal Res: 7509 Stonecrest, Dallas, Tex. 75240. Mailing Add: P.O. Box 900, Dallas, Tex. 75221.

SMITH, WILLIAM FRENCH R
b. Wilton, N.H, 8/26/17; s. William French Smith and Margaret Dawson S; m. to Jean Webb; c. William French, III, Stephanie Oakes, Scott Cameron and Gregory Hale. Educ: Univ. Calif, Los Angeles, A.B, 39; Harvard Law Sch, LL.B, 42; Phi Beta Kappa; Pi Gamma Mu; Pi Sigma Alpha. Polit. & Govt. Pos: Chmn. Speakers Bur, Calif. Rep. State Cent. Cmt, 54-56; v.chmn. bd. trustees, Rep. Assocs, Los Angeles Co, 67-; del. and chmn. Calif. Del, Rep. Nat. Conv, 68; v.chmn, Nixon-Agnew Finance Cmt, Calif, 68. Bus. & Prof. Pos: Attorney-at-law, partner, Gibson, Dunn & Crutcher, Los Angeles, Calif, currently; mem. bd. dirs, Pac. Lighting Corp, 67- and Pac. Tel. & Tel. Co, 69- Mem: Calif. Cong. Recognition Coun.(chmn, 57-60 & 64-66); nat. v.pres. and chmn, Harvard Law Sch. Asn. South. Calif, 62-64; bd. dirs, Legal Aid Found, Los Angeles, 63-, Calif. State C. of C, 63- and Independent Cols. South. Calif, Inc, 69-; Los Angeles Co. Bar Asn.(chmn, cmt. on admin. agencies, 64-65); State Bar of Calif.(mem, disciplinary appeals bd, 66-, chmn, 68); bd. trustees, Claremont Men's Col, 67-; bd. regents, Univ. Calif, 68-; adv. bd, Calif. State Col, Los Angeles, 68-; Los Angeles Coun. on For. Rels; fel, Am. Bar Inst; Am. Judicature Soc; Am. Bar Asn; Newcomen Soc. N.Am; Chancery Club; Calif. Club; Valley Hunt Club; Annandale Golf Club. Rel: Episcopal. Legal Res: 1256 Oak Grove Ave, San Marino, Calif. 91108. Mailing Add: 634 S. Spring St, Los Angeles, Calif. 90014.

SMITH, WILLIAM MARION D
Miss. State Sen.
b. Natchez, Miss, 2/2/32; s. Frank Levon Smith and Alice Kaiser S; m. 8/19/67 to Carolyn Vance; c. Emily Mitchell. Educ: Univ. of Miss, B.A, 53, LL.B. and J.D, 55; Omicron Delta Kappa; Phi Eta Sigma; Phi Delta Phi; Phi Delta Theta. Polit. & Govt. Pos: Miss. State Sen, 60- Bus. & Prof. Pos: Assoc. prof. law, Univ. Miss, 58-59; lawyer, presently. Mem: Jr. C. of C; Adams Co, Miss. and Am. Bar Asns. Rel: Episcopal. Mailing Add: 205 Glenwood Dr. Natchez, Miss. 39120.

SMITH, WILLIAM R. D
b. 1912; married; c. ten. Educ: High sch. grad. Polit. & Govt. Pos: Iowa State Rep. until 67. Bus. & Prof. Pos: Tool grinder, Allis Chalmers Mfg. Co. Mem: UAW Local 1316, v.pres, Linn Co. UAW Citizenship Coun; exec. bd, Cedar Rapids Labor Assembly; pres, Second Cong. Dist. C.O.P.E; mem. and past pres, Wildlife and Outdoor Club; exec. bd. and past treas, Iowa Wildlife Fedn; assoc. mem, Nat. Wildlife Fedn. Rel: Presbyterian. Mailing Add: 1601 E Ave. N.E, Cedar Rapids, Iowa 52402. (1967)

SMITH, WILLIAM ROY D
Va. State Del.
b. Petersburg, Va, 7/8/20; s. Robert Blackwell Smith (deceased) and Mary Ridout S; m. 6/8/46 to Virginia Lee Brown Nunnally; c. Robert W.N, Virginia, Lee and Robert Blackwell, II. Educ: Sch. of Pharmacy, Med. Col. of Va, B.S, 41; Rho Chi; Alpha Sigma Chi; Sigma Zeta; Kappa Psi. Polit. & Govt. Pos: Chmn, Petersburg Dem. Cmt, Va, 46-52; Va. State Del, 52-, mem, Gov. Adv. Cmt. on the Budget, 55; Chmn, Joint Dem. Caucus, Va. House of Del, 62-66. Bus. & Prof. Pos: Secy, Phys. Prod. Co, Inc. Div. of Int. Latex Corp. 47-51, pres, 51-52 & 62-66; pres, William R. Smith Co, 62- Mem: Past legis. chmn, Am. Pharmaceutical Asn; past pres, Va. Pharmaceutical Asn; AF&AM; Elks; Commonwealth Club; Lions. Rel: Episcopal. Legal Res: 1750 Westover Ave, Petersburg, Va. 23803. Mailing Add: P.O. Box 1270, Petersburg, Va. 23805.

SMITH, WILLIAM T, II R
N.Y. State Sen.
b. Corning, N.Y, 1/25/16; s. Maynard Smith and Carrie Shriver S; m. to Dorothy Nowak; c. William T, III, Mary Judith, Bonnifer, Deborah and Michael. Educ: Corning Free Acad, grad; N.Y. State Col. Agr, Cornell Univ, grad, 38. Polit. & Govt. Pos: Mem, Chemung Co. Planning Bd, N.Y, 58-62; mem, Big Flats Rep. Town Cmt. and Big Flats Park Cmn; N.Y. State Sen, 49th Dist, 62-, chmn, Standing Cmt. on Taxation and mem, Agr. and Mkts, Conserv. and Recreation, Pub. Utilities, Villages, Finance, Ins. and Motor Vehicles and Transportation Cmts, 66. Bus. & Prof. Pos: Farm owner, Smithome Farms, Big Flats, N.Y; operator, dairy bar and restaurant; interests in retail bldg. materials and fiberglass fabrication plant. Mem: Past pres, Chemung Co. Farm Bur, N.Y. State Poultry and Hatchery Fedn. and Big Flats Vol. Fire Co; past v.chmn, Chemung Co. Agr. Stabilization and Conserv. Cmt; Rotary; Fur, Fin and Feather; Coldbrook Club; Corning Country Club; C. of C. Rel: Presbyterian; Trustee, Big Flats Presby. Church. Mailing Add: R.R. 1, Elmira, N.Y. 14903.

SMITH, WILLIAM WARREN, III DFL
First V.Chmn, Hennepin Co. Dem-Farmer-Labor Party, Minn.
b. Charlottesville, Va, 8/29/37; s. William Warren Smith, Jr. and Hattie Williams S; m. 9/1/56 to Florestine Bogar; c. Cynthia Vernice, Terrence Eugene, Timothy Stephen, Marcus Aaron and William Warren, IV. Educ: Jackson P. Burley High Sch, Charlottesville, Va, 49-54. Polit. & Govt. Pos: Chief precinct organizer, Coun. for Racial Justice, Minn, 61; mem. exec. bd, Minn. Chap, Am. for Dem. Action, 68; mem. exec. cmt. and Minn. chmn, Nat. Cmt. of Inquiry, 68; mem. constitutional cmt, acts of constitutional reform cmt, Minn. State Dem-Farmer-Labor Party, 68; cmnr, Minneapolis Cmn. on Human Rels, 68; del, Dem. Nat. Conv, 68; first v.chmn, Hennepin Co. Dem-Farmer-Labor Party, 68. Bus. & Prof. Pos: Dir. field opers, Crusade for Opportunity, Syracuse, N.Y, 66-67; exec. dir, Black Star, Inc, Minneapolis, 68; asst. adminstr, Pilot City Health Center, Minneapolis, currently; instr, polit. and soc. sci. dept, Augsburg Col, currently. Mil. Serv: Entered as Airman Basic, Air Force, 54, released as AC, 58, after serv. in 674 AC and W Squadron, Air Defense Command. Publ: 'Black Tide,' 62 and 'Analysis of Minneapolis Elections,' 69, Spokesman. Mem: AF&M Prince Hall Affil; Minn. Coun. of Racial Justice; NAACP. Rel: Baptist. Mailing Add: 1659 Sheridan Ave. N, Minneapolis, Minn. 55411.

SMITH, WILLIE CONLY D
b. Wiggens, Miss, 8/21/00; married. Polit. & Govt. Pos: Former Miss. State Sen; former mem, Citizens Coun, Kokomo, Miss. Bus. & Prof. Pos: Teacher; farmer. Mem: Miss. Educ. Asn; Farm Bur. Rel: Baptist. Mailing Add: Kokomo, Miss. 39643. (1967)

SMITH, WINI R
Chmn, Wilson Co. Rep. Party, Tex.
b. Cairo, Ga, 1/2/22; d. Vester Stokes and Clyde Gray S; m. 8/14/44 to William Allen Smith; c. William Stephan. Educ: Georgia Col. Milledgeville, B.S, 42. Polit. & Govt. Pos: Chmn, Wilson Co. Rep. Party, Tex, 65-; del, Rep. Nat. Conv, 68. Rel: Baptist. Mailing Add: 1202 G St, Floresville, Tex. 78114.

SMITHER, CHARLES GABRIEL D
La. State Sen.
b. New Orleans, La, 11/28/14; s. James William Smither and Louise Person S; m. 10/17/39 to Charlotte Mary Hardie; c. Charles Hardie, Louise Person and Charlotte Sanders. Educ: Tulane Univ, B.A, 36; Beta Theta Phi. Polit. & Govt. Pos: La. State Rep, 62-68; La. State Sen, 68- Bus. & Prof. Pos: Dir, Arrow Food Distributors, Inc, 47- and Jefferson Cold Storage, Inc, 53-; mgr, New Orleans Agency, Union Cent. Life Ins. Co; v.pres. and treas, Ferd, Marks-Smither & Co, Ltd; chmn. of bd, Kalvar Corp. Mil. Serv: Entered as Pvt, Army, 42, released as Maj, 45, after serv. in S3 119th Inf, 30th Inf. Div, ETO; Silver Star; Bronze Star; Purple Heart; ETO Campaign Ribbon with 5 Battle Stars; Victory Medal; Croix de Guerre, France. Mem: Mil. Order of World Wars Asn; C. of C, Int. Horse; New Orleans Country Club; Stratford Club; Boston Club; Nat. Asn. of Life Underwriters; Am. Soc. of Chartered Life Underwriters; Plimsoll Club; Pickwick Club; bd. visitors, Tulane Univ; v.pres, Tulane Alumni Asn; bd. trustees, Episcopal Diocese of La; Tulane Univ. Bd. of Adminstr; pres, New Orleans Buccaneers. Mem, Tulane Univ. football team, 34, played 53 minutes in first Sugar Bowl game. Rel: Episcopal. Legal Res: 440 Audubon St, New Orleans, La. 70118. Mailing Add: Suite 300, Adeco Bldg, 1600 Canal St, New Orleans, La. 70112.

SMITHERMAN, JACK N. R
Ind. State Rep.
Educ: Purdue Univ; Alpha Gamma Rho. Polit. & Govt. Pos: Ind. State Rep, currently. Bus. & Prof. Pos: V.pres, Smitherman Hatcheries, Inc. Mem: Past pres, Lions; dir, C. of C; past dir, State Poultry Asn; Columbia Club; Brown Co. Hist. Soc. Rel: White Lick Friends Soc. Mailing Add: R.R. 4, Mooresville, Ind. 46138. (1967)

SMITHERMAN, WILLIAM C. R
b. Calvert, Tex, 1/22/32; s. William W. Smitherman and Margaret Merchant S; m. 9/3/55 to Alice L. Leyland; c. Stephen and Paul. Educ: Baylor Univ, B.B.A, in Acct. and LL.B; Phi Alpha Delta. Polit. & Govt. Pos: V.chmn, Ariz. State Hosp, Bd, 63-; chmn, Cochise Co. Rep. Cmt, Ariz, 64-69. Mil. Serv: Entered as Airman, Air Force, 52, released as 1st Lt, 57, after serv. in 43rd Bomb Wing Strategic Air Command. Mem: Cochise Co, Ariz. State and Tex. State Bar Asns; Ariz. Cattle Growers Asn; Am. Legion; Rotary; Salvation Army. Rel: Episcopal. Legal Res: 119 San Jose Dr, Rt. I, Warren, Ariz. 85642. Mailing Add: Box 450, Bisbee, Ariz. 85603. (1967)

SMOAK, D. FRANK D
b. Savannah, Ga, 7/17/18; m. to Euteva Best; c. Dan F, III and Judee V. Educ: Univ. Fla, B.S.B.A, 41, LL.B, 47. Polit. & Govt. Pos: Fla. State Rep, 62-66; former mayor, Punta Gorda, Fla. Bus. & Prof. Pos: Lawyer; former spec. agent, Fed. Bur. Invest. Mil. Serv: Army, serv. as Commanding Officer Battery, Field Artil, N.Africa, Italy, Germany and South. France, 5 years, World War II and Judge Adv. Gen. Corps, Pentagon, 2 years; Bronze Star. Mem: Past pres, Kiwanis; Mason (32°). Rel: Presbyterian; Deacon. Mailing Add: 161 Ott Circle, Port Charlotte, Fla. 33950. (1967)

SMOAK, MARION H. R
Asst. Chief of Protocol to the President
b. Aiken, S.C, 7/8/16; s. William M. Smoak and Marion Hartzog S; m. to Mary Frances Meister; c. Elmore Fitzpatrick, Frederic Meister and Mary Frances. Educ: The Citadel, B.A, 38; Univ. S.C. Law Sch, LL.B, 41; Alpha Tau Omega. Polit. & Govt. Pos: S.C. State Sen, 66-68; alternate del, Rep. Nat. Conv, 68; asst. chief of protocol to the President, Dept. of State, 69- Mil. Serv: Entered as 1st Lt, Army, 41, released as Lt. Col, 61 after serv. in ETO and S.W. Pac. as Staff Judge Adv. of the 82nd and 11th Airborne Div. and Berlin Command, Germany and Instr. at U.S. Marine Acad, West Point. Mem: Am. Bar Asn; S.C. Bar Asn. Legal Res: Aiken, S.C. 29801. Mailing Add: Box 50, Aiken, S.C. 29801.

SMOTHERS, JOHN MADISON D
b. Willisburg, Ky, 11/9/98; s. Edward A. Smothers and Pearlie Carney S; m. 12/22/25 to Margie Lillian Perkins; c. Robert M. and Carolyn. Educ: High Sch. Polit. & Govt. Pos: Wash. Co. Court Clerk, 22-56; assoc. cmnr, Ky. Dept. Revenue, 56-60; Ky. State Rep, 64-66; mem. staff, Frankfort Co. Court Clerk's Off, 67-68. Mem: Mason; Farm Bur; past secy-treas, v.pres. and pres, Co. Court Clerks Asn, Ky. Rel: Baptist. Legal Res: Springfield, Ky. 40069. Mailing Add: 1040 Sioux Trail, Frankfort, Ky. 40601.

SMRCKA, THOMAS CAROL R
b. Little Falls, N.Y, 10/15/31; s. Thomas Joseph Smrcka and Irene Bandre S; single. Educ: Wartburg Col, Iowa, B.A, 53; Wartburg Theol. Sem, B.D, 57; Luther Theol. Sem, Minn, adv. study; Beta Beta Beta. Polit. & Govt. Pos: Precinct chmn, Cosmos Village, 64-65; chmn, Meeker Co. Rep. Party, Minn, 65-67. Bus. & Prof. Pos: Asst. pastor, St. John Lutheran Church, Owatonna, Minn, 57-59; pastor, Peace-Trinity Lutheran Parish, Cosmos, Minn, 60-67; regional dir. of parish educ, The Am. Lutheran Church, Midwest Region, 67- Mem: Southwest. Minn. Dist. Bd. of Parish Educ. Cmt, The Am. Lutheran Church; secy, Kandiyohi Conf, The Am. Lutheran Church; former chmn, South Cent. Minn. Migrant Cmt; former chmn, Cosmos Commercial Club; Lions; bd, Cosmos Sch. Syst. Wrestling. Letterman, Wartburg Col. Rel: Lutheran. Legal Res: 5909 N. Kenmore, Apt. 209, Chicago, Ill. 60626. Mailing Add: 327 S. LaSalle, Room 929, Chicago, Ill. 60604.

SMYKOWSKI, JAMES GEORGE R
Chmn, 26th Dist. Rep. Party, N.Dak.
b. Cayuga, N.Dak, 7/9/34; s. George Walter Smykowski and Kathrine Kaczynski S; m. 5/3/56 to Annette Elizebeth Olson; c. Kenneth John, Kevin James, Dennis Michael, Robert Allan, Candia Marie, Anthony George and Patricia Lynn. Educ: Lidgerwood Pub. High Sch, grad, 52. Polit. & Govt. Pos: Rep. committeeman, Herman Precinct, N.Dak; chmn, 25th Dist. Rep. Party; pres, Lidgerwood Sch. Bd, 62-68; mem, Personal Property Tax Cmn, N.Dak, 67-69; chmn, 26th Dist. Rep. Party, currently. Bus. & Prof. Pos: Farming, currently; auctioneering, 58-; real estate broker, 69- Mem: K. of C; Farm Bur. Rel: Catholic. Mailing Add: R.R, Cayuga, N.Dak. 58013.

SMYLIE, ROBERT E. R
b. Cherokee Co, Iowa, 10/31/14; s. Lorne F. Smylie and Ida May Stevens S; m. 12/4/43 to Lucille C. Irwin; c. William R. and Steven S. Educ: Col. Idaho, A.B, 38; George Wash. Univ, J.D, 42, LL.D, 60; Phi Alpha Delta; Order of the Coif. Polit. & Govt. Pos: Asst. Attorney Gen, Idaho, 47, Attorney Gen, 47-55, Gov, 55-67; former co-chmn, Pres. Fed-State Rels. Cmt; mem, Rep. Coord. Cmt. and Adv. Cmn. on Intergovt. Rels; chmn, Rep. Gov. Conf, 63- Bus. & Prof. Pos: Assoc. mem, Law Firm of Covington & Burling, Wash, D.C, 40-42 & 46; sr. partner, law firm, Langroise, Clark, Sullivan and Smylie. Mil. Serv: Entered as A/S, Coast Guard Res, 42, released as Lt, 46, after serv. in Atlantic and Pac. Theaters, Philippines & New Guinea; Lt, Coast Guard Res, until 54; Atlantic and Pac. Theater Ribbons; Philippine Liberation Medal with Star. Publ: 'The Constitutionality of Federal Airport Zoning,' George Wash. Law Rev, 43; 'Federal State Relations,' George Wash. Univ. Mag, 66. Mem: Chmn, Fed-State Rels. Cmt, Nat. Gov. Asn; Adv. Cmt, Who's Who in Am. Politics; Am. Legion; AF&AM; VFW; 40 et 8; Elks; Moose. Rel: Methodist Episcopal. Legal Res: 117 Locust St, Boise, Idaho. 83702. Mailing Add: P.O. Box 1466, Boise, Idaho 83701.

SMYTH, HENRY DEWOLF
U.S. Rep, Int. Atomic Energy Agency
b. Clinton, N.Y, 5/1/98; m. to Mary de Coningh. Educ: Princeton Univ, A.B, 18, A.M, 20, Ph.D, 21; Cambridge Univ, Ph.D, 23. Hon. D.Sc, Drexel Inst, 50, Case Inst. Tech, 53 and Hamilton Col, 65; hon. LL.D, Rutgers Univ, 68. Polit. & Govt. Pos: Consult, Nat. Research Coun. and Off. of Sci. Research and Develop, World War II; consult, Manhattan Dist. Proj, 43-45; mem, U.S. Atomic Energy Cmn, 49-54, consult, 54-; consult, Joint Cong. Cmt. on Atomic Energy, 58-; U.S. Rep, Int. Atomic Energy Agency, 61- Bus. & Prof. Pos: Prof. physics, Princeton Univ, 36-66, chmn. dept, 35-48, chmn, bd. sci. and eng. research, 54-59, chmn, Univ. Research Bd, 59-66, emer. prof, 66- Publ: Books and articles on the phys. sci. and atomic energy. Mem: Chmn. bd. of trustees, Univ. Research Assocs, 68-; trustee, Assoc. Univ. Brookhaven Nat. Lab, 46-49; fel, Am. Phys. Soc.(past pres); fel, Am. Acad. of Arts and Sci; Am. Philos. Soc; ed. bd, Princeton Univ. Press. Atoms for Peace Award, 68. Legal Res: 5 Lafayette Rd. W, Princeton, N.J. 08540. Mailing Add: American Embassy, Vienna, Austria.

SMYTH, JOHN R. R
Chmn, Lunenburg Co. Rep. Cent. Cmt, Va.
b. Pittsburgh, Pa, 7/3/18; s. Victor R. Smyth and Marie Brumbaugh S; m. 6/8/46 to Susan Hite Neblett; c. John L, Sidney M. and Sterling M. Educ: Pa. State Univ, grad, 40; Theta Delta Chi. Polit. & Govt. Pos: Chmn, Lunenburg Co. Rep. Cent. Cmt, Va. and finance chmn, Fourth Dist. Rep. Party. Bus. & Prof. Pos: Pres. and owner, Smyth's Frozen Foods Co. Mil. Serv: Entered as Pvt, Army, 41, released as Capt, 46, after serv. in 155th Inf, 31st Div, Pac. Theater; Bronze Star. Mem: Mason; Lions; Am. Legion; VFW; pres, PTA. Rel: Episcopal. Mailing Add: Kenbridge, Va. 23944.

SMYTH, JOHN RICHARD D
b. Rawlins, Wyo, 10/6/32; s. Sarah Frances Murphy S; m. to Elizabeth Blanchard; c. Suzanne, Dianne, Carolyn and Teresa. Educ: Univ. of Santa Clara, B.S, 54; Univ. Wyo. Law Sch, LL.B, 59. Polit. & Govt. Pos: Spec. asst. attorney gen, State Bd. Equalization and Pub. Serv. Cmn, Wyo, 59-60; justice of the peace, Carbon Co, 61; dep. co. attorney, Carbon Co, 62; Wyo. State Rep, Laramie Co, 67-69; Cheyenne munic. juvenile judge, 68-69. Mil. Serv: Entered as 2nd Lt, Army, 54, released as 1st Lt, 56, after serv. in 594th Field Artil. & 597th Armored Field Artil, 11th Army, Germany. Mem: Am. and Laramie Co. Bar Asns; Cheyenne Quarterback Club; Elks; Lions; VFW. Rel: Catholic. Mailing Add: 3631 Dover Rd, Cheyenne, Wyo. 82001.

SMYTHE, HUGH HEYNE
b. Pittsburgh, Pa, 8/19/13; s. William Henry Smythe (deceased) and Mary Elizabeth Barnhardt S.(deceased); m. 7/26/39 to Mabel H. Murphy; c. Karen Pamela. Educ: Va. State Col, B.A, 36; Atlanta Univ, M.A, 37; Northwest Univ, Ph.D, 45. Hon. LL.D, Va. State Col, 68. Polit. & Govt. Pos: Dir. of research, N.Y. State Senate Finance Cmt. Eval. Proj. of State Cmn. Against Discrimination, 56; spec. lectr, For. Serv. Inst, Dept. State, Wash, D.C, 60; sr. adv. on econ. and soc. affairs, U.S. Mission to UN and mem. U.S.del, to 16th Session, UN Gen. Assembly, 61-62, mem, Conf. on Elimination of Statelessness, 61, UNICEF Prog. Cmt. and Exec. Bd. Meeting, 61-62, Int. Coffee Conf, 62, Develop. Fund, 62, Spec. Fund Governing Coun, 62, Statist. Cmt, 62, Soc. Cmt, 62, Status of Women Cmt, 62, Human Rights Cmt, 62, Sub Cmn. on Prev. of Discrimination and Protection of Minorities, 62, First Int. Cong. of Africanist, Accra, Ghana, 62; Ambassador to Syrian Arab Repub, 65-67; consult, Dept. of State, 67; Ambassador to Malta, 67-69. Bus. & Prof. Pos: Researcher and admin. asst, Am. Youth Cmn. of Am. Coun. on Educ, Wash, D.C, 37-38; research asst. and instr, Fisk Univ, 38-39; research assoc, Atlanta Univ, 42; asst. dir. of research, Negro Land Grant Col. Coop. Soc. Studies Proj, 44; prof. sociol, Morris Brown Univ, 44 and Tenn. State Agr. and Indust. Univ, 45-46; dep. dir. of spec. research, NAACP, N.Y.C, 47-49; dir. of research, W.B. Graham & Assoc, 49-50; vis. prof. sociol. and anthrop, Yamaguchi Nat. Univ, Japan, 51-53; prof. sociol, Brooklyn Col, 53-61 & 62-65; Fulbright prof, Chulalongkorn Univ. and sr. adv, Nat. Research Coun. Thailand, 63-64; lectr, Spec. Forces, Army, Ft. Bragg, N.C, 64; UN correspondent, East. World and Africa Trade and Develop, London, 64; chief consult, Youth in Action, Poverty Prog. in Brooklyn, N.Y, 65. Mil. Serv: Army, World War II. Publ: Co-auth, Negro Land Grant Colleges Social Studies Project, 44, New Nigerian Elite, 60 and Educating the Culturally Disadvantaged Child, 66; plus others. Mem: Fel. of African Studies Asn, Soc. of Appl. Anthrop. and Am. Anthrop. Asn; East. Sociol. Soc; Asn. Asian Studies; Japan Soc; Am. Asn. Teachers Chinese Lang. and Culture; Inst. Race Rels. Gt. Brit; Siam Soc; Opers. Crossroads Africa; Sociol. Soc. Japan; Am. Asn. Univ. Prof; Am. Cmt. Africa; Cmt. World Develop. and World Disarmament; Mid. East Inst; Am. Civil Liberties Union; NAACP; Nat. Urban League; Am. For. Serv. Asn; Cmt. Dem. Insts; Malta C. of C; Unitarian Serv. Cmt; Mus. African Art; Am. Negro Leadership Conf. Africa; Recreation Asn. of State; USIA; AID; United Serv. Orgn. of Malta; Malta Union Club; Lions Club of Malta; Malta-U.S. Alumni Asn; Alpha Phi Alpha. Brit. Colonial Off. Award, 48; Am. Friends Serv. Cmt. Grantee, 50; Ford Found. Fel, 57-58; Soc. Sci. Research Coun. Award, 60; Distinguished Alumni, Va. State Col, 57; Delta Tau Kappa Award for Distinquished Work in Soc. Sci, 67; dipl, Int. Inst. JVEK of Germany for Contributions to Better Human Rels. and World Peace, 68; Knight of the Grand Cross of the Royal Crown of Crete, 68. Rel: Protestant. Mailing Add: 345 Eighth Ave, New York, N.Y. 10001.

SNARE, ORVILLE E. R
Pa. State Rep.
b. McConnellstown, Pa, 7/3/18. Educ: Pub. schs, Huntingdon Co. Polit. & Govt. Pos: Pa. State Rep, 56- Bus. & Prof. Pos: Partner in grocery store bus; passenger brakeman, Pa. RR; project engr, Pa. Dept. of Hwys. Mil. Serv: World War II, 41-45. Mailing Add: 609 Mt. Vernon Ave, Huntingdon, Pa. 16652.

SNEAD, EDWARD CLEO D
N.C. State Rep.
b. Hope Mills, N.C, 2/25/04; s. Edward White Snead and Lincey Lee S; m. 7/25/27 to Sarah Ruby Davis; c. Jo Anne (Mrs. Dennison) and Nancy (Mrs. Kelsch). Educ: Wilmington Law Sch, 40-41. Polit. & Govt. Pos: With U.S. Customs Serv, Wilmington, N.C, Charleston, S.C. and Wash, D.C, 30-59; pub. admin. adv, Monrovia, Liberia, 63-66; N.C. State Rep, currently. Bus. & Prof. Pos: Exec. v.pres, Waters Shipping Co, Wilmington, N.C, 60- Mil. Serv: Entered as A/S, Navy, 23-26, re-entered, 43, released as Comdr, 46, after serv. in Atlantic, Pac. and Korean Theatres, Navy Res, 46-64; Atlantic and Pac. Theatre Medals; Philippines Occup. Victory Medal; World War II, Korean War and Naval Res. Medals. Publ: Liberian Customs Code and Liberian Customs Regulations, 63-66. Mem: Mason; Elks; Am. Legion; VFW. Rel: Methodist. Mailing Add: 1239 Columbus Circle, Wilmington, N.C. 28401.

SNEDEGAR, VIOLET COX D
Dem. Nat. Committeewoman, W.Va.
b. Clarksburg, W.Va, 3/5/18; d. Porter L. Cox (deceased) and Emma Carter C; m. 7/23/38 to Nunley Beard Snedegar; c. William Nunley, Suzanne Marie, Barbara Lee and Jean Houghton. Educ: W.Va. Univ, B.A. Polit. & Govt. Pos: Mem, W.Va. State Dem. Exec. Cmt, 56-; Dem. Nat. committeewoman, 56-60 & 64-; del, Dem. Nat. Conv, 68. Mem: Bd. dirs, Gen. Fedn. of Women's Clubs, 50-56 and jr. dir, 50-52; jr. dir, W.Va. Fedn. of Women's Clubs, 48-50; Elkins Women's Club; Am. Asn. of Univ. Women; Worthy Matron, Eastern Star, 50-51. Rel: First Methodist. Mailing Add: 106 High St, Elkins, W.Va. 26241. (1967)

SNELL, CHARLES SHERMAN D
Ala. State Rep.
b. Langdale, Ala, 8/20/20; s. Charles Raymond Snell and Mary Ethel Foster S; m. to Marabel Clifford; c. Shirley Ann and Dorothy Lee. Educ: Ala. Polytech. Inst, B.S, 48, M.S, 52. Polit. & Govt. Pos: Ala. State Rep, currently. Bus. & Prof. Pos: Teacher, Valley High Sch, Fairfax, Ala. Mil. Serv: Lt. Col, commanding officer, 231st Armor Group, Ala. Nat. Guard. Legal Res: Fairfax, Ala. 36854. Mailing Add: Citizens National Bank, Shawmut, Ala. 36876. (1967)

SNELL, EDWARD LOUIS R
Secy-Treas, Park Co. Rep. Cent. Cmt, Colo.
b. Alma, Colo, 10/13/04; s. Edward Daniel Snell and Hannah Hoffman S; m. 12/4/37 to Mary Katherine Horine; c. Emily and Mary Helen. Educ: Blair's Bus. Col, 1 year. Polit. & Govt. Pos: Councilman, Alma, Colo, 37 and Fairplay, Colo, 62-; secy-treas, Park Co. Rep. Cent. Cmt, Colo, 69- Bus. & Prof. Pos: Mill foreman, Climax Molybdenum Co, Colo, 23-27; mill wright and metallurgist, Molybdenum Corp. of Am, Yucca, Ariz, 27-28, mech. engr, Questa, N.Mex, 28-35 and mill supt, 37-46; mine mgt, several firms, Alma, Colo, 47-62. Publ: Metallurgical and geol. reports. Mem: N.Mex. and Colo. Mining Asns; Mason; Doric Lodge; Colo. Consistory. Rel: Christian Church of N.Am. Legal Res: Front St, Fairplay, Colo. 80440. Mailing Add: P.O. Box 171, Fairplay, Colo. 80440.

SNELL, HILARY FRED R
Chmn, Fifth Cong. Dist. Rep. Party, Mich.
b. Grand Rapids, Mich, 7/17/34; s. Frank Y. Snell and Edna Westfall S; m. 10/26/63 to Constance Mae Zick; c. Hilary E. Educ: Colgate Univ, A.B, 56; Univ. Mich, J.D, 59; Phi Beta Kappa; Delta Upsilon. Polit. & Govt. Pos: Precinct del, Kent Co. Rep. Party, Mich, 61-63, asst. chmn, 62-66 and chmn, 66-68; del, Rep. Nat. Conv, 68; chmn, Fifth Cong. Dist. Rep. Party, Mich, 69- Bus. & Prof. Pos: Assoc, McCobb & Heaney Attorneys, Mich, 59-65, partner, 65-68; partner, Wheeler, Upham, Bryant & Uhl Attorneys, 68- Mil. Serv: Entered as Recruit, Army Res, 59, released as Sgt, 65. Mem: Grand Rapids

Bar Asn.(prog. cmt, 62, Americanism cmt, 63, legis. cmt, 64-65 and chmn. civil liberties cmt, 66-68); Am. Bar and Mich. Bar Asns; dir, Grand Rapids Child Guid. Clin, 59-60, secy, 61-62, exec. cmt, 61-66, v.pres, 63-64 and pres, 65-66; Colgate Univ. Alumni Club (secy-treas, 61-63, treas, 65-66 and chmn. fund campaign, 67); Jr. C. of C.(parliamentarian, Grand Rapids Chap, 60, dir, 61-62, v.pres, 62-63, pres, 64 and chmn. bd, 65); Peninsular Club. Named Outstanding Young Man of the Year, Grand Rapids Jr. C. of C, 66. Rel: Protestant. Mailing Add: 1065 Plymouth Rd. S.E, Grand Rapids, Mich. 49506.

SNELLING, RICHARD ARKWRIGHT R
Mem, Chittenden Co. Rep. Cmt, Vt.
b. Allentown, Pa, 2/18/27; s. Dr. Walter Otheman Snelling and Marjorie Gahring S; m. 6/7/47 to Barbara Weil; c. Jacqueline Taylor, Mark Hornor, Diane Bryant and Andrew Preston. Educ: Lehigh Univ, 43; Univ. Havana, Cuba, summer 43; Harvard Col, A.B. cum laude, 48. Polit. & Govt. Pos: Mem, Chittenden Co. Rep. Cmt, Vt, 56-, chmn, 63-66; Vt. State Rep, 59-60; mem, Vt. Develop. Cmn, 59-61; del, Rep. Nat. Conv, 60 & 68; mem, Vt. Rep. State Cmt, 63-66; Rep. nominee for Lt. Gov. of Vt, 64, Rep. nominee for Gov, 66; chmn, Vt. Aeronaut. Bd, 69- Bus. & Prof. Pos: Pres, Shelburne Industs, Inc, Shelburne, Vt, 59-; pres. and chmn. exec. cmt, Gr. Burlington Indust. Corp, 61-64; pres, Miller & VanWinkle Spring Co, Inc, Paterson, N.J, 63-, Wessel Hardware Co, Inc, Phila, Pa, 67- and Barrecrafter Ski Prod. Co, Shelburne, Vt, 68- Mil. Serv: Entered as Pvt, Army, 44, released as T/5, 46, after serv. in Inf, ETO, Army of Occup, 45-46. Mem: Young Pres. Orgn; U.S. C. of C; Mason; Am. Legion; Rotary. Rel: Unitarian. Mailing Add: Harbor Rd, Shelburne, Vt. 05482.

SNELLINGS, WILLIAM ROSS D
Ga. State Rep.
b. Columbus, Ga, 10/29/16; s. Samuel Daughtry Snellings and Julia Schley S; m. 8/9/47 to Elizabeth Tedards; c. William Ross, Jr, Alexande Mitchell, Kirkley Elizabeth and Ross Schley. Educ: Auburn Univ, B.S. in agr. eng, 41. Polit. & Govt. Pos: Ga. State Rep, presently. Mil. Serv: Entered as 2nd Lt, Army, 41, released as Major, 47, after serv. in Europeon Normandy Invasion, 44; Silver Star; 2 Purple Hearts; Major, Hon. Res. Mem: Nat. Real Estate Bd; dir, Augusta Real Estate Bd, 58-59; dir, Augusta C. of C, 54-66, v.pres, 65; Lions; Am. Legion; Richmond Co. Game and Fish Conserv. Club; Augusta Country Club. Rel: Episcopal. Mailing Add: 3006 Lake Forest Dr, Augusta, Ga. 30904.

SNELSON, W. E. 'PETE' D
Tex. State Sen.
b. Grandfalls, Tex, 3/28/23; s. Luke R. Snelson and Maggie Beaty S; m. 5/30/59 to Susan Mae Sutton; c. Wallace Eugene, II, Sandra Susan, Stephen Sutton and Stanley Shane. Educ: Tex. West. Col, B.A, 46; Univ. Nebr, Army Spec. Prog; Northwest. Univ, M.S, 50; Sigma Alpha Epsilon. Polit. & Govt. Pos: Tex. State Rep, 60-62; Tex. State Sen, 64- Bus. & Prof. Pos: Pres, Tex. Jr. C. of C, 57-58. Mil. Serv: Entered as Pvt, Army, 43, released as T/Sgt, 46, after serv. as Spec. Agent. Counter Intel. Corps, ETO; ETO Ribbon with 3 Battle Stars; Bronze Star; Purple Heart; 1st Lt, Army Res, 48-54. Mem: Mason (32°); Scottish Rite; Lions Club. Rel: Presbyterian. Mailing Add: 2406 Shell St, Midland, Tex. 79701.

SNIDER, D. DWAIN D
b. Lakenan, Mo, 9/4/32; m. 12/24/54 to Muriel J. Winkler; c. Delline, Sherard and Eilayne. Educ: Gem City Bus. Col, Quincy, Ill. Polit. & Govt. Pos: Mem, Shelbina City Coun, three terms; Mo. State Rep, 64-66. Bus. & Prof. Pos: Formerly employed by the Marley Co, Kansas City, Mo, 51-53; owner, implement bus, Shelbina, Mo, presently. Mil. Serv: Army, 113th Counterintelligence Corps Detail, 5th Army Hq, Chicago, Ill, 53-54. Mem: Mem. and past adjutant of Am. Legion Post 376 of Shelbina. Rel: Methodist. Mailing Add: 109 S. Cramer, Shelbina, Mo. 63468.

SNIDER, FREDDIE REMBERT R
Chmn, Schley Co. Rep. Party, Ga.
b. Ellaville, Ga, 4/15/40; s. James Walter Snider and Velma Florette Watson S; m. 8/28/59 to Earlene Willis; c. Gregory Earl and Sandra Kay. Educ: Schley Co. Consol. Schs, 12 years. Polit. & Govt. Pos: Chmn, Schley Co. Rep. Party, Ga, 68- Bus. & Prof. Pos: Assembly worker, Champion Mobile Home Builders, Ellaville, Ga, 59-64; owner and mgr, Standard Oil Serv. Sta, 64-68; ins. agent, Ga. Farm Bur. Ins. Co, Macon, 67-68; ins. agent, South. Trust Ins. Co, 68-; owner and pres, Snider-Gordon Distributing Co, Ellaville, 68- Mem: Lions; F&AM; Tri-County Country Club. Rel: Methodist. Legal Res: Buena Vista Rd, Ellaville, Ga. 31806. Mailing Add: P.O. Box 334, Ellaville, Ga. 31806.

SNIPES, AL M. R
Okla. Rep. State Committeeman
b. Cameron, N.C, 4/11/21; s. Alfred Marshall Snipes and Bassie McLaurin S; m. 11/30/47 to H. Rebecca Davis; c. Alfred M, Jr, William R. and Rebecca L. Educ: Spec. courses, Columbia Tech, Geneva Col. and Okla. Univ. Polit. & Govt. Pos: V.pres, Okla. City Young Rep, 52-58; Ward Four chmn, Okla. Co. Rep. Cmt, 52-60, co. campaign chmn, 58-60, co. chmn, 60-67; chmn, Fifth Cong. Rep. Dist. of Okla, 63-69; del, Rep. Nat. Conv, 64, alternate del, 68; mem, Okla. State Rep. Exec. Cmt, 65-69; Okla. Rep. State Committeeman, 67- Bus. & Prof. Pos: Mgr, super mkt, 46-48; owner, Al's Super Mkt, 48-55; owner, Al M. Snipes Gen. Ins. Agency, 55-67; pres, Al M. Snipes Inc, 67-69; real estate; investment; dir, Grant Square Bank. Mil. Serv: Entered as Pvt, Army Air Force, 43, released as Cpl, 46. Mem: Rotary; Mason; Am. Legion; bd. mem. and past chmn. of bd, Capitol Hill YMCA; chmn, Nat. Affairs Cmt, Capitol Hill C. of C. Rel: Baptist. Legal Res: 2405 S.W. 80, Oklahoma City, Okla. 73159. Mailing Add: 3215 S. Western, Oklahoma City, Okla. 73109.

SNITOW, VIRGINIA L. D
b. New York, N.Y; d. Dr. Louis Levitt and Tillie Rosenberg L; m. 11/2/35 to Charles Snitow; c. Ann B. and Alan M. Educ: Hunter Col, B.A, 31; Columbia Univ, post-grad. study, 31-32; Phi Sigma Sigma. Polit. & Govt. Pos: Del, Dem. Nat. Conv, 68; del-at-lg, Concerned Dem. of Westchester Co, N.Y, 68- Bus. & Prof. Pos: Teacher of Eng, Wadleigh High Sch, 32-42; v.pres, U.S. World Trade Fair, N.Y.C, 57-66; Nat. Pres, Women's Div, Am. Jewish Cong, 65- and v.pres, Gen. Div, 66-; secy-treas, Leadership Conf. of Jewish Women's Orgn, 69- Publ: 'The Mushroom Cloud' West. Polit. Quart; 'I Teach Negro Girls' New Repub; a series of short pieces on children, Family Circle Mag. Mem: past mem, The Teachers Union and Eng. Teachers Asn; Pan Pac. South East Asia Women's Asn; League of Women Voters; Nat. Woman's Party; United Nations Asn; Rep. to United Nations Non-Govt. Coun. Received Am. Jewish Cong. Serv. Citation. Rel: Jewish. Mailing Add: 81 Walworth Ave, Scarsdale, N.Y. 10583.

SNODDY, CAROL NADINE R
b. Great Falls, Mont, 2/27/38; d. Guy Leon Maberry and Muriel Robertson M; m. 6/28/57 to David Lee Snoddy; c. Deborah Layne, Judith Renee, Rebecca Diane and Nancy Carol. Educ: Macalester Col, 56-57; Macalester Col. Young Rep. Polit. Pos: State chmn, Mont. Young Rep, 64-65, state v.chmn, 63-64, mem, Speakers Bur, 63-65, State Teen-age Rep. Adv, 63-64; Liaison, Mont. Young Rep. and Mont. Fedn. of Rep. Women, 63-65; mem, Mont. State Cent. Cmt, 64-65; mem, Mont. Rep. Women's Adv. Cmt, 63-65; region co-dir, Goldwater Couples Canvass, 64; del. and mem. Rules Cmt, Rep. Nat. Conv, 64; precinct committeewoman, Hill Co, 62-64; del. and mem. Rules Cmt, Nat. Young Rep. Conv, 63; Liaison for Women's Rep. Club. and Young Rep, 61-63; charter mem. and secy, Hill Co. Young Rep, 61-63, Teen-Age Rep. adv, 61-62; active worker, local and state campaigns. Bus. & Prof. Pos: Bookkeeper and secy, N. Mont. Chinchilla Ranch; head, Accts. Payable Dept, Brada Trucking Co, 59-60 and head, Billing Dept, Flexonics Corp, 57-58. Mem: Eastern Star; Rainbow Girls (mother adv, 68-); Brownie-Girl Scout Leader. Rel: Christian Church. Mailing Add: Star Route 36, Havre, Mont. 59501.

SNODGRASS, WILLIAM R. D
Comptroller, Tenn. Gen. Assembly
b. Sparta, White Co, Tenn, 9/15/22; s. Robert J. Snodgrass and Nannie Lee S; m. 12/28/68 to Faye Birdwell Bailey; c. Emily Faye and Sarah Elizabeth. Educ: David Lipscomb Col, Nashville, Tenn, grad, 42; Univ. of Pa, 43; Univ. of Tenn. Col. of Bus. Admin, B.S, 47; Univ. of Tenn, grad. work in accounting. Polit. & Govt. Pos: Comptroller, Tenn. Gen. Assembly, presently. Bus. & Prof. Pos: Research asst, Bur. of Bus. Research, Univ. of Tenn, 47; consult. on munic. accounting and finance, Munic. Tech. Adv. Serv, Univ. of Tenn, 51; dir. of the budget and dir. of local finance, Univ. of Tenn, 53. Mil. Serv: 43-46. Mem: Am. Legion; Nashville Exchange Club; Nat. Asn. of State Auditors, Comptrollers and Treas; Nat. Asn. of Tax Adminstrs; Coun. of State Gov; Tenn. Cmn. on Inter-govt. Coop. Rel: Church of Christ. Mailing Add: State Capitol Bldg, Nashville, Tenn. 37219.

SNOW, HAROLD R
Asst. Majority Leader, Idaho State House of Rep.
b. Moscow, Idaho, 12/23/10; s. Arthur Sherman Snow and Lella Driskill S; m. to Vivian Wilson; c. Sherman Arthur and Susan Mary (Mrs. Flock). Educ: Univ. Idaho, 29-30; Sigma Nu. Polit. & Govt. Pos: Idaho State Rep, 52-, Asst. Majority Leader, Idaho State House of Rep, 60-, chmn, Ways and Means Cmt. and v.chmn, State Affairs Cmt, 65-67. Mem: Latah Co. Cattlemen's Asn.(past pres); Latah Co. Wheat Growers' Asn.(past pres); state dir. and chmn, Soil Conserv. Dist; secy. of Agr. Adv. Cmt. on Soil and Water, 48-50; Shrine; Elks; Mason. Rel: Methodist. Mailing Add: 211 N. Blaine, Moscow, Idaho 83843.

SNOW, PARIS JOHN R
Maine State Rep.
b. Caribou, Maine, 8/2/18; s. Thomas K. Snow and Theresa Pierce S; m. 12/25/42 to Willetta McGrath; c. Jane Elizabeth and Constance. Educ: Aroostook State Teachers Col, 40. Polit. & Govt. Pos: Mem. and past chmn, Caribou, Town Coun, 52-; mem, Maine Water Improv. Cmn, 66; mem, exec. bd, Maine Munic. Asn, presently; Maine State Rep, Caribou, 67- Bus. & Prof. Pos: Sch. teacher, Maine, 40-41; seed & potato grower and shipper, 41-62; sales rep, Bancroft & Martin, 62-; farm owner, presently. Mem: Maine Good Roads Asn; Maine Chap. Am. Pub. Works; Rotary; Mason, Shrine; Odd Fellows. Rel: Universalist. Mailing Add: Grimes Rd, Caribou, Maine. 04736.

SNOW, WAYNE, JR. D
Ga. State Rep.
b. Old Hickory, Tenn, 1/10/36; s. Thomas Wayne Snow, Jr. and Johnnie Haffine S; single. Educ: Univ. Ga, A.B, 58, LL.B, 60; Phi Delta Phi; Sigma Chi. Polit. & Govt. Pos: Ga. State Rep, 63- Bus. & Prof. Pos: Attorney-at-Law, 60- Mil. Serv: Tenn. Nat. Guard, Pfc, 54-56; 56-58, Control Group; Specialist 5, Army Res, Garrison, 58-62. Mem: Ga. Bar & Lookout Mt. Judicial Bar Asns; Campaign Dir, Walker Co. March of Dimes, 63-64; Am. Judicature Soc; Rossville Jaycees (pres, 68-69); Rossville Exchange Club; LaFayette Elks; pres, Seventh Dist. Legis. Asn, 68. Rel: Methodist; Lay leader Chmn. & Chmn, Cmns. on Missions. Mailing Add: R.F.D. 2, Chickamauga, Ga. 30707.

SNOWDEN, GENE E. R
Ind. State Sen.
b. Huntington, Ind, 4/7/28; s. Ben W. Snowden and Anna L. Orr S; m. 8/26/49 to Carol J. Replogle; c. Connie J, twins Barbara J. and Beverly J. and Jodi A. Educ: Olivet Col, Kankakee, Ill, 48-49; Int. Accounting Sch, Chicago, 50: Polit. & Govt. Pos: Ind. State Sen, 66-; pres. elect, Nat. Soc. State Legislators, 68-69; mem. bd. trustees, Olivet Col, 68-; charter v.pres, Huntington Med. Mem. Found, 68- Bus. & Prof. Pos: Mem. bd. of trustees, Huntington Col, 65. Mem: Nat. Asn. Life Underwriters; Nat. Soc. State Legislators; Ind. Ins. Leaders Club; life mem, Optimist Club. Distinguished Serv. Award, U.S. Jr. C. of C, 60, One of the Outstanding Young Men of Am, 64; Master Life Underwriter Award, 65. Rel: Nazarene. Legal Res: 1433 Cherry St, Huntington, Ind. 46750. Mailing Add: Box 2, Huntington, Ind. 46750.

SNOWDEN, PHILIP HUGH 'PHIL' D
Mo. State Rep.
b. St. Joseph, Mo, 10/14/38; s. Leonard A. Snowden and Lillian Pauline Phillips S; m. 9/2/61 to Jane Ellen Armstrong; c. Sharon Lyn, Kristen Gai and Stephanie Mill. Educ: Univ. of Mo, Columbia, B.A, 60, LL.B, 64; The Mystic 7; Phi Delta Theta; quarterback, Univ. of Mo. football team. Polit. & Govt. Pos: Mo. State Rep, 86th Dist, 67- Bus. & Prof. Pos: Attorney-at-law, Dietrich, Tyler, Davis, Burrell & Dicus, 64-67; Snowden & Crain, 67- Mem:

Lawyers Asn. of Kansas City; Clay Co. and Mo. Bar Asns; trustee, Univ. of Mo. Alumni Asn; chmn, Univ. of Mo. Alumni Develop. Fund; Gladstone Optimist Club; Gr. Kansas City Sports Cmn; bd. of trustees, YMCA; adv. bd, Fel. Christian Athletes. Rel: Methodist; pres, Bd. of Trustees. Mailing Add: 6218 N. Bales, North Kansas City, Mo. 64119.

SNOWE, PETER TRAFTON R
State Committeeman, Maine Rep. Party
b. Lewiston, Maine, 1/16/43; s. Guy Carlton Snowe and Barbara Dillingham S; single. Educ: Bentley Col; Univ. Maine. Polit. & Govt. Pos: Maine State Rep, 103rd Legis. Dist, 67-69; del, Rep. Nat. Conv, 68; chmn, Auburn Rep. City Cmt, 68-; state committeeman, Maine Rep. Party, 68- Bus. & Prof. Pos: Gen. mgr, Maine Am. Vault Co, Inc, Bangor, 63-64, v.pres, 64-66; pres, Superior Concrete Co, Inc, Auburn, 66- Mil. Serv: Maine Army Nat. Guard, 64-69, Pfc. Mem: Auburn-Lewiston Lions Club (pres, currently); Androscoggin Valley Sq. & Compass Club; Mason; Jaycees; Auburn Businessman's Asn; Lewiston-Auburn Go Getters Club. Rel: Methodist. Mailing Add: 114 Nottingham Rd, Auburn, Maine 04210.

SNYDER, ARTHUR KRESS R
City Councilman, Los Angeles, Calif.
b. Los Angeles, Calif, 11/10/32; s. Arthur Snyder and Ella Keck S; m. 3/5/54 to Mary Frances Neely; c. Neely Arthur and Miles John. Educ: Los Angeles City Col, A.A, 51; Pepperdine Col, B.A, 53; Univ. South. Calif. Sch. Law, J.D, 58; Pi Kappa Delta; Phi Delta Phi. Polit. & Govt. Pos: Councilmanic field dep, Los Angeles, Calif, 59-67, city councilman, 67- Bus. & Prof. Pos: Attorney-at-law, 59- Mil. Serv: Entered as Sgt, Marine Corps, 53, released as Capt, 55, after serv. in Air Fleet Marine Force, Pac. Theatre, 54-55; Maj, Res, 55- Mem: Am, Calif. State and Los Angeles Co. Bar Asns; Am. Judicature Soc. Rel: Am. Baptist; Bd. Dirs, Los Angeles Baptist City Soc. Legal Res: 2832 Lawndale Dr, Los Angeles, Calif. 90065. Mailing Add: 333 City Hall, Los Angeles, Calif. 90012.

SNYDER, CECIL VERNON D
b. Richland Co, Ohio, 3/26/11; s. Gustave Leroy Snyder and Tessie Peterson S; m. 8/23/45 to Leona Blanch Prosser. Educ: High Sch, Lexington, Ohio, 12 years. Polit. & Govt. Pos: Chmn, Troy Twp. Bd. of Trustees, 53-65; chmn, Morrow Co. Dem. Exec. Bd, 60-62, 65 & 69; mem, Co. Elec. Bd, 65- Bus. & Prof. Pos: Owner, Farm, Ohio, 39-69; pres, Galion Tire Shop, Inc, 62- Mem: Mason (32°). Rel: Methodist; Chmn, Bd. of Trustees, Steam Corners United Methodist Church. Mailing Add: R.F.D. 8, Lexington, Ohio 44904.

SNYDER, D. W. D
Pub. Serv. Cmnr, Miss.
b. Cumberland, Miss, 7/29/15; s. William Frank Snyder and Wilmuth Doss S; m. 1/8/42 to Estelle Arnold; c. Edwin Arnold and William Don. Educ: Miss. State Univ, B.S, 39. Polit. & Govt. Pos: Sheriff, Webster Co, Miss, 48-52 & 56-60; fire Marshall, State of Miss, 52-56; Info. and Educ. Officer, Miss. Forestry Cmn, 56-60; Pub. Serv. Cmnr, State of Miss. North. Dist, 64- Bus. & Prof. Pos: Teacher and coach, Eupora and Charleston Schs, 39-42; mgr, Doss Oil Co, Eupora, 46-48. Mil. Serv: Entered as Pvt, Army, 42, released as Capt, 45, after serv. in 99th Inf. Div, ETO, 43-45; Bronze Star; Silver Star. Mem: Miss. Law Enforcement Asn; Tenn-Miss. Sheriffs' and Peace Officers Asn; Nat. Sheriffs' Asn; FBI Nat. Acad; VFW; Am. Legion; Farm Bur; Miss. State Col. Alumni; Mason; Shrine. Rel: Church of Christ. Legal Res: Dunn St, Eupora, Miss. 39744. Mailing Add: P.O. Box 134, Eupora, Miss. 39744.

SNYDER, ELMER ANDREW R
b. Cowansville, Pa, 10/4/15; s. Clarence Reese Snyder and Margaret Maude Stouffer S; m. 6/7/41 to Annabelle Claypoole; c. Thomas Clarence, David Elmer and Mark Andrew. Educ: Kittanning Sr. High Sch, grad. Polit. & Govt. Pos: Del, Rep. Nat. Conv, 68. Bus. & Prof. Pos: Pres, Snyder Bros. Inc, Kittanning, Pa, 45-, Glacial Sand & Gravel Co, 52- and Hwy. Equip. and Supply Co, Orlando, Fla, 55-; v.pres, C.H. Snyder Co, 60- and Allegheny Mineral Corp, Pa, 65- Mem: Mason; Shrine; Elks. Rel: Protestant. Mailing Add: P.O. Box 126, Cowansville, Pa. 16218.

SNYDER, EVELYN BOYCE D
Mem, Ark. State Dem. Cmt.
b. Dardanelle, Ark, 11/10/15; d. Ruben Thomas Boyce and Lillian Hearn B; m. 8/24/41 to Harold Snyder; c. Betsy (Mrs. Harris). Educ: High sch. grad. Polit. & Govt. Pos: Mem,Yell Co. Womens Dem. Cmt, 58-; mem, Ark. State Dem. Cmt, 66-; del. and mem. platform cmt, Dem. Nat. Conv, 68. Mem: Bus. & Prfnl. Womens Club; Garden Club; PTA (past pres); Cancer Soc.(past pres. and mem. state bd); Good Citizen and Founders Award, Girl Scouts Am. Rel: Presbyterian. Mailing Add: 815 Second St, Dardanelle, Ark. 72834.

SNYDER, F. TRIGG, JR. R
b. Shattuck, Okla, 5/31/41; s. Francis Trigg Snyder, Sr. and Elsie Welch S; m. 11/5/60 to Delila Ann Christensen; c. Kecia Deneen and Ayreann. Educ: High Sch, 4 years. Polit. & Govt. Pos: Chmn, Dewey Co. Young Rep, Okla, 64-65; Chmn, Dewey Co. Rep. Party, 67-69. Bus. & Prof. Pos: Salesman, Pierson Chevrolet Co, Vici, Okla, 64- Mil. Serv: Entered as Recruit E-1, Army Nat. Guard, 60, released as Sgt, 64. Mem: Chevrolet Legion of Leaders; Chevrolet Truck Sales Hall of Fame; F&AM; C. of C. Rel: Christian. Mailing Add: R.R. 2, Vici, Okla. 73859.

SNYDER, FLOYD FRANCIS, JR. R
S.Dak. State Rep.
b. Flandreau, S.Dak, 10/11/20; s. Floyd Francis Snyder and Dora Weatherford S; m. 2/27/43 to Phyllis Evangeline Weber; c. James Martin. Educ: Nettleton Commercial Col, Sioux Falls, S.Dak, 39-40; Grad. Sch. of Savings and Loan, Univ. Ind, Bloomington, Grad. Key, 61. Polit. & Govt. Pos: S.Dak. State Rep, 68- Bus. & Prof. Pos: Contact Rep, Veterans Admin, 46-49; Revenue Agent, Dept. of Internal Revenue, 49-54; Dir, First Fed. Savings and Loan Asn. of Watertown, 54-, exec. v.pres, 62- Mil. Serv: Entered as Pvt, Army, 43, released as S/Sgt, 46, after serv. in Signal Corps, Pac. Theatre. Mem; Am. Legion (Past Comdr); C. of C. (Past pres); Watertown Area Bus. Corp (Past pres); Memorial Hospital Bd. of Dirs; Cosmopolitan Club. Rel: Methodist. Mailing Add: 1217 Second St. N.W, Watertown, S.Dak. 57201.

SNYDER, GEORGE ELMER D
Md. State Sen.
b. Hagerstown, Md, 1/12/29; s. George Merlin Snyder and Janet Miller S; m. 6/30/50 to Helen Hite; c. George E, Jr, Laura Jean, Rebecca H. and Paige E. Educ: Univ. Md; Alpha Phi Omega. Polit. & Govt. Pos: Founder and First pres, Wash. Co. Young Dem, 50; Md. State Sen, currently; del, Dem. Nat. Conv, 68. Bus. & Prof. Pos: Founder and pres, Snyder Prods. Corp, wholesale ice cream and soft pretzel distributorship, sixteen states. Mem: Past local pres, state pres, nat. bd. mem. and nat. membership chmn, Jaycees; C. of C; Kiwanis; United Commercial Travelers; Elks; Nat. Soc. State Legis; Int. Asn. Ice Cream Mfg's. Rel: Lutheran. Mailing Add: 810 Oak Hill Ave, Hagerstown, Md. 21740.

SNYDER, JAMES EUGENE R
N.C. State Rep.
b. Lexington, N.C, 9/9/11; s. C.A. Snyder and Sallie Frances Myers S; m. 6/7/41 to Sarah Frances Olive; c. Jean Olive; James Eugene Jr. Educ: Wake Forest Col, B.S, 32; Wake Forest Col. Law Sch, LL.B, 38; Gamma Eta Gamma. Polit. & Govt. Pos: N.C. State Rep, 47 & 63-; mem. State Bd. of Elec, 50-54. Bus. & Prof. Pos: Attorney, firm of Leonard and Snyder. Mem: N.C. and Davidson Co. Bar Asns; past pres, Lexington Civitan Club; one of the organizers and pres. for two years of Lexington Parents' League. Rel: Baptist; Deacon; Sunday Sch. teacher. Mailing Add: 402 Park St, Lexington, N.C. 27292. (1967)

SNYDER, JOHN PARR D
b. Indianapolis, Ind, 4/12/26; s. Ralph Wadsworth Snyder and Freda Parr S; m. 5/3/52 to Jeanne Marie Kallmeyer; c. Barbara and Carolyn. Educ: Purdue Univ, B.S.Ch.E, 48; Mass. Inst. Tech, S.M.Ch.E.P, 49; Tau Beta Pi. Omega Chi Epsilon, Sigma Xi. Polit. & Govt. Pos: Dem. co. committeeman, Morris Co. Dem. Party, N.J, 61-65; v.chmn, Madison Dem. Cmt, 64-65; cand. for Borough Coun, Madison, 65 & 66; del, Dem. Nat. Conv, 68; cand. for mayor, Madison, 69. Bus. & Prof. Pos: Chem. engr, Procter & Gamble Co, Cincinnati, Ohio, 49-53; chem. engr, Congoleum-Nairn, Inc, Kearny, N.J, 53-56; prof. engr, CIBA Pharmaceutical Co, Summit, 56- Mil. Serv: Entered as S 1/C, Naval Res, 44, released as AETM 3/C, 46. Publ: The Story of N.J.'s Civil Boundaries, 1606-1968, State of N.J, 69; Chemical Resistance of Construction Materials, Mooney Bros. Corp, 61; 'The Bounds of Newark-Tract, Township and City,' N.J. Hist, 68. Mem: Licensed Prfnl. Eng, N.J. and Ohio; Am. Inst. Chem. Eng; N.J. Hist. Soc; Human Rels. Coun. Madison; NAACP. Rel: Quaker. Mailing Add: 32 Sherwood Ave, Madison, N.J. 07940.

SNYDER, JOHN WESLEY
b. Jonesboro, Ark, 6/21/95; s. Jere Hartwell Snyder and Ellen Hatcher S; m. 1/5/20 to Evlyn Cook, wid. 5/56; c. Edith Cook (Mrs. John E. Horton). Educ: Vanderbilt Univ, 14-15; Omicron Delta Kappa. Polit. & Govt. Pos: Nat. bank receiver, Off. Comptroller of Currency, 31-37; v.pres. and dir, Defense Plant Corp, Wash, D.C, 40-43; asst. to dirs, Reconstruction Finance Corp, 40-44; Fed. loan adminstr, 45; dir, Off. War Mobilization and Reconversion, 45; Secy. of Treas, 46-53, del, Int. Financial Conf, Mexico City, 45-52, Rio de Janeiro, 47, London, 47, Paris, 50-52, Ottawa, 51, Rome, 51 and Lisbon, 52. Bus. & Prof. Pos: Banker, Ark. and Mo, 19-30; mgr, St. Louis Loan Agency, Reconstruction Finance Corp, 37-43; v.pres, First Nat. Bank, St. Louis, 43-45; pres. and dir, Overland Corp, currently. Mil. Serv: Served as Capt, Field Artil, 57th Brigade, World War I; Col.(Ret), Army, 55. Mem: Am. Legion; Res. Officers' Asn.(past pres, Mo. Dept); Alpha Tau Omega; Mo. Athletic Club, St. Louis; Chevy Chase Club; Alfalfa Club, Wash; Toledo Club. Rel: Episcopal. Legal Res: 8109 Kerry Lane, Chevy Chase, Md. 20015. Mailing Add: Overland Corp, Security Bldg, Toledo, Ohio 43604.

SNYDER, JOSEPH M. D
Mich. State Rep.
b. Barberton, Ohio, 3/18/15; m. 1942 to Rita Kanthak; c. Donna, Michael and Ronald. Polit. & Govt. Pos: Mich. State Rep, 62-, Dem. Caucus Chmn, Mich. House of Rep, 67-; councilman, St. Clair Shores; Macomb Co. Supvr; del. to the Constitutional Conv. Bus. & Prof. Pos: Int. rep, UAW. Mem: Chmn, St. Clair Shores Planning Cmn; dir. Macomb chap, Mich. Soc. for Ment. Health; chmn. St. Clair Shores Pub. Safety Cmt. Mailing Add: 22912 Rosedale Ave, St. Clair Shores, Mich. 48080.

SNYDER, MARION GENE R
U.S. Rep, Ky.
b. Louisville, Ky, 1/26/28; s. M.G. Snyder and Lois Berg S; m. 3/23/51 to Louise Hodges; c. Mark. Educ: Univ. Louisville; Jefferson Sch. Law, LL.B. cum laude, 50. Polit. & Govt. Pos: Mem, S. End Rep. Club; mem, Young Rep. Club Louisville and Jefferson Co; mem, First Magisterial Dist. Rep. Club; past pres, Lincoln Rep. Club; city attorney, Jeffersontown, 54-58; magistrate, First Dist, Jefferson Co, 57-61; v.pres, Ky. Magistrates and Cmnr, 58; U.S. Rep, Ky, 63-65 & 67-; del, Rep. Nat. Conv, 68. Bus. & Prof. Pos: Attorney-at-law; Louisville, Ky, 50-; farming, 57-; residential construction bus, 58-66. Mem: Past v.pres, Jefferson Civic Center; Ky. Bar Asn; Farm Bur; Optimists. Legal Res: 2308 Blankerbaker Lane, Jeffersontown, Ky. 40299. Mailing Add: 516 Cannon House Office Bldg, Washington, D.C. 20515. (1967)

SNYDER, MELVIN CLAUD R
b. Albright, W.Va, 10/28/98; s. Allison Wirt Snyder and Laura Jenkins S; m. 7/13/25 to Mabel Price; c. Melvin C, Jr, Melita (Mrs. Sokolowski) and Laurella (Mrs. Constante). Educ: W.Va. Univ, LL.B, 23, J.D, 69; Theta Chi; Phi Delta Phi. Polit. & Govt. Pos: Mayor, Kingwood, W.Va, 26-27; prosecuting attorney, Preston Co, 28-42; surplus property officer for Aleutian Islands, 46; U.S. Rep, Second Cong. Dist, W.Va, 47-48; judge, 18th Judicial Circuit, W.Va, 53- Bus. & Prof. Pos: Mem, W.Va. Judicial Coun, 56-; dir, Albright Nat. Bank, 62- Mil. Serv: Pvt, Army, 18; Col, Nat. Guard, 101st Inf, Alaska Defense Command, 41-46; Col.(Ret), Army, 60; Bronze Star; Legion of Merit. Mem: W.Va, Preston Co. and Am. Bar Asns; W.Va. Judicial Conf; Am. Legion; VFW; Mason; K. of P; Moose; Rotary Int.(Past Dist. Gov). Rel: Baptist. Mailing Add: 307 Tunnelton St, Kingwood, W.Va. 26537.

SNYDER, NORMAN GENE R
Chmn, 49th Assembly Dist, Los Angeles Co. Rep. Cent. Cmt, Calif.
b. Adel, Iowa, 4/28/23; s. Milo Myran Snyder and Phoebe Crouse S; m.

8/13/50 to Delphia Gertrude Norman; c. Michael Dean, David Neil, Catherine Ann and Jonathan Scott. Educ: Drake Univ, 40-42; Iowa State Univ, 46-47; Univ. Iowa Col. of Med, M.D, 51; Nu Sigma Nu. Polit. & Govt. Pos: City councilman, West Covina, Calif, 60-64, mayor, 64-65; chmn, 49th Assembly Dist, Los Angeles Co. Rep. Cent. Cmt, 64-, committeeman, 62-64; co-chmn, West Covina Mayor's Blue Ribbon Cmt. on Drug Abuse, 68- Mil. Serv: Entered as Seaman, Navy, 43, released as Electronics Technician 1/C, 46, after serv. in Asiatic area, Philippines, and Japan, 44-45; Philippine Liberation Ribbon; Asiatic Theater Ribbon with Seven Battle Stars; Lt.(jg), Med. Corps Res. until 60. Mem: Town Hall, Los Angeles, Calif; Los Angeles World Affairs Coun; Los Angeles Co. Dist. Attorney Adv. Coun. Named Man of the Year for the Greatest Contribution to Human Rights by Govt, Covina, West Covina and La Puente Human Rights Cmn, 65. Rel: Protestant. Mailing Add: 2042 Daniels Ave, West Covina, Calif. 91790.

SNYDER, RICHARD A. R
Pa. State Sen.
b. Lititz, Pa, 3/26/10; s. Paris F. Snyder and Barbara Ziegler S; m. to Toylee McClinton. Educ: Moravian Col; Franklin and Marshall Col, B.A; Temple Law Sch, LL.B; assoc. ed, Temple Univ. Law Review. Polit. & Govt. Pos: Lancaster Co. Rep. Chmn, 58-64; admitted to Lancaster Co. Courts, Pa. Supreme and Superior Courts; Pa. State Sen, 62- Bus. & Prof. Pos: Mem. of staff Lancaster New Era, 31-34 & 35-42; attorney-at-law. Mil. Serv: Army, 42-45, 18 months, ETO; spec. agent, Counter Intel. Corps and Capt, Army Res, 48-54. Mem: Am, Pa, Lancaster Co. Bar Asns; former dir, Lancaster C. of C; past comdr, Lancaster Am. Legion Post 34; Mason; Elks; Am. Bus. Club; staff mem, Assoc. Press, 34-35; former mem, Pa. Legis. Correspondents Asn, 35-41. Occasional Contrib. to N.Y. Times Travel Sect. Mailing Add: 27 Orchard Rd, Lancaster, Pa. 17601.

SNYDER, ROBERT O. R
b. Lima, Ohio, 7/25/17; s. Karl O. Snyder and Ruth Stuff S; m. 2/8/41 to Margaret Elizabeth Beaton; c. John Gregory, Elizabeth Ann and Margaret Ruth. Educ: Ohio Univ, B.S, 39; St. Louis Univ, LL.B, 51; Delta Tau Delta; Phi Alpha Delta. Polit. & Govt. Pos: Mo. State Rep, 9th Dist, 61-62, 11th Dist, 63-64 and 45th Dist, 67-68. Bus. & Prof. Pos: Dist. rep, Gen. Elec. Co, 46-52, sales mgr, 52-55; attorney-at-law, 55-56; partner, Henderson, Heagney & Snyder, 56- Mil. Serv: Entered as Ens, Navy, 43, released as Lt.(jg), 46, after serv. in U.S.S. Kendrick, DD612, invasion of South. France, 44, Mediterranean and Atlantic, 44-45. Mem: Am, Mo. and St. Louis Bar Asns; Lawyers Asn. of St. Louis; Mason; Kiwanis; Am. Legion; United Cerebral Palsy Asn. Rel: Presbyterian. Mailing Add: 420 Claybrook Lane, Kirkwood, Mo. 63122.

SNYDER, SIDNEY R. D
Secy, Wash. State Senate
b. Kelso, Wash, 7/30/26; s. Alfonso Snyder and Adah Beeman S; m. 6/30/51 to Bette Anne Kennedy; c. Sidney R, Jr, Karen Jo and Sally Elaine. Educ: Longview Jr. Col, 1 year. Polit. & Govt. Pos: Legis. employee, Olympia, Wash, 49-53; precinct committeeman, Long Beach Dem. Party, 49-69; asst. chief clerk, Long Beach, Wash, 57-69; state committeeman, Wash. Dem. Party, 61-65; del. and mem. Rules Cmt, Dem. Nat. Conv, 68; secy, Wash. State Senate, 69- Bus. & Prof. Pos: Owner-operator, supermkt, 53- Mil. Serv: Aviation Cadet, Army Air Force, 44-45. Mem: Elks; Lions Int; Am. Legion; C. of C. Rel: Protestant. Legal Res: 16th Blvd, Long Beach, Wash. 98631. Mailing Add: Box 531, Long Beach, Wash. 98631.

SNYDER, WILLIAM V. D
Polit. & Govt. Pos: Dems. for Progress Org; Dems. for Better Govt; State Rep, -66. Bus. & Prof. Pos: Gen. supt. of material and transportation, Whirlpool Corp, Evansville Div. Mil. Serv: Marine Corps. Mem: C. of C; Indust. Traffic and Transportation Asn. of Ind; Vanderburgh Cty. Air Bd, 58-60. Rel: Church of God, Forest Hills. 1967 Legal Res: 9911 Petersburg Rd, Evansville, Ind. No mailing address available. (1967)

SOARES, WILFRED 'BUDDY' R
Hawaii State Rep.
b. Honolulu, Hawaii, 9/4/29; s. Jack A. Soares (deceased) and Alice Pamenta S; m. 11/19/50 to Lorraine R. Perry; c. Kevin, Kirk, Kelly Ann and Kyle. Educ: Univ. Hawaii, 49-50. Polit. & Govt. Pos: Pres, Rep. Precinct Club, Hawaii, 66; Hawaii State Rep, 17th Dist. and minority leader, currently. Bus. & Prof. Pos: Acct. exec, Pan Am Airlines, 56-69 & 60-65; gen. sales mgr, West. Dairy Prods, 59-60; commun. affairs dir, AMFAC, 69. Mem: Sales and Mkt. Execs. of Hawaii; Allied Mem, Am. Soc. Travel Agents; Hawaii Kai Commun. Asn; Punahou O'Men's Club; Holy Trinity Holy Name Soc; St. Louis Alumni Asn; Interscholastic League. Rel: Catholic. Legal Res: 674 Pepeekeo St, Honolulu, Hawaii 96821. Mailing Add: P.O. Box 3230, Honolulu, Hawaii 96801.

SOASH, RICHARD MORTON D
Chmn, Routt Co. Dem. Cent. Cmt, Colo.
b. Steamboat Springs, Colo, 8/3/41; s. Irvin Elwood Soash and Nellie Elizabeth Gray S; m. 5/21/60 to Kathleen Diane Pluta; c. Curtis John, William Irvin; Richard Morton, Jr. and Josephine Anne. Educ: Colo. State Col, 59-60; Colo. State Univ, B.A. with high distinction, 64; Sigma Tau Delta; Pi Gamma Mu. Polit. & Govt. Pos: Dem. committeeman, 12th Precinct, Routt Co, Colo, 66-68 and Seventh precinct, 68-69; chmn, Routt Co. Dem. Cent. Cmt, 69- Bus. & Prof. Pos: Rancher, 65- Mem: Colo. State Grange. Rel: Catholic. Mailing Add: Mystic Route, Steamboat Springs, Colo. 80477.

SOCHOWSKI, CLARY S. D
b. Chicago, 3/28/25; s. Stanley Joseph Sochowski and Agnes Glovacki S; m. 9/11/65 to Gloria D. Bozich; c. Stephen C, Lynda M. and Thomas A. Educ: Chicago Schs. Polit. & Govt. Pos: Salesman, Boyle-Midway Prods, Chicago, Ill, 48-55; salesman, Midwest Prods, Chicago, 54-55; dist. sales mgr, Skilsaw Corp, Chicago, 55-58; admin. asst, Rep. Daniel Rostenkowski, 59-; state dir, Ill. U.S. Treasury Dept. Savings Bonds Div, 68- Bus. & Prof. Pos: Sales engr, Cleco Air Tools, Chicago, Ill, 58. Mil. Serv: Army, Inf, European Theatre, 86th Inf. Div; Combat Infantryman Badge; Good Conduct Medal; Victory Medal. Mem: Am. Legion; Polish-Am. Club of Chicago; Holy Name Soc; Catholic War Vets; pres, Cong. Secys. Club; v.pres. and bd, Cong. Fed. Employees Credit Union; Polish Roman Catholic Union. Named Cong. Secy. of Year, 65. Golf, Basketball, Softball and Bowling. Rel: Catholic. Mailing Add: 2100 Eastview Dr, Des Plaines, Ill. 60018.

SODEN, IRVING HENRY R
b. Worcester, Mass, 1/10/19; s. William H. Soden and Mabel Teasdale S; m. 7/18/48 to Evelyn Leslie Kimball; c. Richard K, Marsha J, Janet E. and Barbara J. Educ: Harvard Col, B.S, 39; Harvard Law Sch, LL.B, 43; Harvard Varsity Club. Polit. & Govt. Pos: Mem. and chmn, Concord Sch. Bd, N.H, 57-63; del, Rep. Nat. Conv, 64. Bus. & Prof. Pos: Chmn, Prfnl. Conduct Cmt, N.H. Bar Asn, 62-65. Mem: N.Y. and N.H. Bars; Am, N.H. and Merrimack Co. Bar Asns; Fedn. of Ins. Counsel; Am. Col. Trial Lawyers; Concord Country Club; Harvard Club of N.H. and Boston. Rel: Congregational. Legal Res: 16 Kensington Rd, Concord, N.H. 03301. Mailing Add: 9 Capitol St, Concord, N.H. 03301.

SODERSTROM, CARL W. R
Ill. State Rep.
b. Streator, Ill, 12/14/15; m. to Virginia Merriner S; c. Carl, Jr, Virginia Jean, Robert, Jane Ann and Reuben. Educ: Univ. Ill, B.S, 37; Univ. Ill. Law Sch, 43. Polit. & Govt. Pos: Ill. State Rep, currently. Bus. & Prof. Pos: Lawyer. Mem: Ill. State Bar; State Bar Asn; Boilermakers and Musicians Unions; Odd Fellows; Royal Neighbors; Jr. C. of C; Elks; Lions. Rel: Presbyterian. Mailing Add: 1001 Riverside Ave, Streator, Ill. 61364. (1967)

SODERSTROM, CHARLES WALLACE R
Mem. Exec. Cmt, Calif. Rep. State Cent. Cmt.
b. Seattle, Wash, 2/14/13; s. Charles Wallace Soderstrom and Clare Eloise Kimball S; m. 4/15/46 to Dolore Lorraine Petersen; c. Maya Eloise, Mona Lee and Charles Wallace, Jr. Educ: Univ. Calif, Los Angeles, 3 years; U.S. Coast Guard Acad, commission, 45; Blue Key; Phi Kappa Sigma, Capt, Univ. Calif. Rowing Team. Polit. & Govt. Pos: Chmn, Co. Cent. Cmt, 17th Cong. Dist, 55-63; finance chmn, United Rep. Finance Cmt, 17th Cong. Dist, 54; mem, exec. cmt. and v.chmn, Los Angeles Co. Rep. Cent. Cmt. several years, past chmn. budget cmt, chmn, 66-69; v.chmn, Los Angeles Co. United Rep. Finance Cmt, 57; chmn, United Rep. Finance Cmt. Los Angeles Co, 59; treas, Los Angeles Co. Rep. Cmt, 60-66; past chmn, Los Angeles Co. Rep. Almanac Cmt; del, Rep. Nat. Conv, 68; mem, Calif. Rep. State Cent. Cmt, 69-, mem. exec. cmt, currently; South area chmn, Asn. Rep. Co. Cent. Cmt. Chmn, Calif. Bus. & Prof. Pos: Private pilot, 36 years; Ford Dealer; San Pedro, Calif, 36 years; Lincoln-Mercury Dealer, 10 years; pres, Triple AAA Water Co, South. Calif. and West Ariz; pres, Bastanchury Water Co. Orange Co; pres, Charles Soderstrom, Inc, real estate property mgt. and develop; pres. and one of founders, Hacienda Hotel and Golf Course; pres, Soderstrom Leasing and Rental Co. Mil. Serv: Coast Guard, Serv. in destroyer escorts, N.Atlantic; Asiatic and European Theater Combat Ribbons. Mem: Kiwanis; Am. Legion; 40 et 8; C. of C.(past dir, San Pedro Chap); Los Angeles Citizens Cmt. Parks and Recreation Bond Issue (past v.chmn); past mem, Los Angeles Cmt. to bring Rep. and Dem. Conv. to Los Angeles; past campaign chmn. to raise $65,000 for physically handicapped children in Harbor Area; pres. and dir. Am. Bottled Water Asn; Motor Car Dealers Asn. South Calif.(past pres. and dir, past chmn. legis. cmt); Gr. Los Angeles Zoo Asn.(bd. trustees, treas); Los Angeles Co. Hotel Legis. Cmt.(past chmn). Mailing Add: 1553 S. Pacific Ave, San Pedro, Calif. 90731.

SOIK, NILE WARREN R
Wis. State Sen.
b. Milwaukee, Wis, 5/2/23. Educ: West Point, B.S. 45; Wis. Univ, M.B.A, 51; postgrad. study, Cornell. Polit. & Govt. Pos: Mem, N.Shore Rep. Club; v.chmn, Milwaukee Co. Rep. Party; Wis. State Assemblyman, 60-69; Wis. State Sen, 69- Bus. & Prof. Pos: Personnel Mgt; instr. bus. admin, Marquette Univ. Mil. Serv: Army Corps of Engrs. Mem: Am. Soc. of Training Dir; Commun. Chest; YMCA, Northside Bldg. and Branch Sites Campaign; Arthritis and Rheumatism Found; Jr. Achievement. Mailing Add: 6266 N. Santa Monica Blvd, Whitefish Bay, Wis. 53217.

SOKOL, WILLIAM D
b. Denver, Colo, 1/9/21; s. Alex Sokol and Martha Wysowatcky S; m. 5/24/51 to Rosetta Marie Frank; c. Linda M, Richard A. and Sandra L. Educ: Denver Univ; Barnes Sch. Commerce; Westminster Law Sch; Delta Sigma Pi. Polit. & Govt. Pos: Asst. to U.S. Rep. John A. Carroll, 47; councilman and mayor pro tem, Westminster, Colo, 56-61; secy, Adams Co. Dem. Party, 57-59, chmn, 59-61; mem, Colo. State Dem. Cent. Cmt, 57-66; mem, Colo. State Dem. Exec. Bd, 59-61; co. campaign mgr, McVicker for Cong, 64-65, asst. to U.S. Rep. Roy L. McVicker, 65-69. Bus. & Prof. Pos: Asst. Pub. Admin, 52-63; real estate owner, 62-65; real estate broker, Dunton Realty, 65-66. Mil. Serv: Entered as A/S, Navy, 42, released as Chief Yeoman, 46, after serv. in Alaska; Am. Theater and Asia Theater Ribbons. Mem: Elks; Kiwanis; Westminster Civic Asn. Rel: Catholic. Mailing Add: 8550 Cedar Lane, Westminster, Colo. 80030. (1967)

SOLARZ, STEPHEN J. D
N.Y. State Assemblyman
b. N.Y.C, 9/12/40; s. Sanford Solarz and Ruth Fertig S; m. 2/5/67 to Nina Koldin. Educ: Brandeis Univ, A.B, 62; Columbia Univ, M.A. in Pub. Law & Govt, 67. Polit. & Govt. Pos: N.Y. State Assemblyman, 69- Bus. & Prof. Pos: Instr, Brooklyn Col, 67-68 & 69- and N.Y.C. Commun. Col, 68-69. Publ: Numerous articles published in Greater Philadelphia and Newsfront. Mem: Am. Polit. Sci. Asn; Am. Jewish Cong; B'nai B'rith; Am. for Dem. Action; Am. Civil Liberties Union; Zionist Orgn. of Am; bd. dirs, League Sch. for Seriously Disturbed Children. Rel: Jewish. Mailing Add: 241 Dover St, Brooklyn, N.Y. 11235.

SOLBERG, IVER D
N.Dak. State Rep.
b. Buxton, N.Dak, 9/18/04; s. John O. Solberg and Christine Hodnefield S; m. 6/19/29 to Jennie Foss; c. Dorvan. Educ: Concordia Col, Moorhead, Minn, 2 years. Polit. & Govt. Pos: N.Dak. State Rep, 37-39 & 67-; N.Dak. State Sen, 41-43, 49-55 & 59-66. Mem: Farmers Union; bd. of dirs, Ray Farmers Union Elevator Co, 41-47. Rel: Lutheran. Mailing Add: 123 Third Ave. E, Ray, N.Dak. 58849.

SOLBERG, NELS LEROY D
Idaho State Sen.
b. Lewiston, Idaho, 12/4/30; s. Nels Solberg and Mabel Storholt S; m. 6/12/53

to Mary Ann McNair; c. Janet Ann, Julie Lynne, Jill Kaye and Nels Don. Educ: Univ. of Idaho, B.S, in bus. admin, 52; Alpha Tau Omega. Polit. & Govt. Pos: v.chmn, Idaho Co. Dem. Cent. Cmt, 59 and precinct committeeman, 58; Idaho State Sen, Eighth Dist, 66- Bus. & Prof. Pos: Mgr, Solberg Agency, Inc, at present. Mil. Serv: Entered as 2nd Lt, Air Force, 52, released as 1st Lt, 54. Mem: Grangeville C. of C; Elks. Rel: Protestant. Mailing Add: 200 South College, Grangeville, Idaho 83530

SOLBERG, OSCAR D
N.Dak. State Rep.
b. Mylo, N.Dak, 5/16/11; married; c. One daughter. Educ: Pub. Schs. Polit. & Govt. Pos: N.Dak. State Rep, 49-61 and currently. Bus. & Prof. Pos: Farmer. Mem: Agate Farm Club; Farmers Union; Co. A.A. Cmt; Mylo PTA. Mailing Add: Rolla, N.Dak. 58367. (1967)

SOLDINI, JOHN LOUIS D
Committeeman, Richmond Co. Dem. Cmt, N.Y.
b. Staten Island, N.Y, 11/7/35; s. Bernard Soldini and Mary Morris S; m. 6/13/59 to Dina Marie Frega; c. Donna and David. Educ: Staten Island Commun. Col, AAS, 59; City Col. N.Y, B.A. and M.A. cum laude, 61; Phi Beta Kappa. Polit. & Govt. Pos: Committeeman, Richmond Co. Dem. Cmt, N.Y, 65-; pres, Staten Island Reform Dem. Asn, 67-68; del, Dem. Nat. Conv, 68; del, New Dem. Coalition, 68- Bus. & Prof. Pos: Teacher soc. studies, Tottenville High Sch, 61- Mil. Serv: Entered as SR, Navy, 53, released as SK 3, 56, after serv. in Atlantic, 53-56. Mem: Nat. Soc. Social Studies; Orgn. Am. Historians; Staten Island and South Shore Ment. Health Asns; United Fedn. Teachers; Am. Civil Liberties Union; South. Christian Leadership Coun; Mensa. Rel: Roman Catholic. Mailing Add: 51 Van Brunt St, Staten Island, N.Y. 10312.

SOLER-FAVALE, SANTIAGO C. New Progressive, P.R.
Attorney Gen, P.R.
b. Yauco, P.R, 3/24/32; s. Victoriano Soler and Emilia Favale de S; m. 6/11/55 to Ivette Agostini; c. Marie Ivette, Jeannette Emile, Santiago César, Lizzette and Jackeline. Educ: Univ. P.R, B.A, 52, B.L. cum laude, 57. Polit. & Govt. Pos: Mem. exec. cmt, New Progressive Party, P.R. 68; Attorney Gen, P.R, 69- Bus. & Prof. Pos: Attorney-at-law, 57-68. Mil. Serv: Entered as 2nd Lt, Army, 52, released as 1st Lt, 54, after serv. in 101st Airborne Div, Camp Breckinridge, Ky, 53-54. Mem: P.R. Bar Asn.(former v.pres); Am. Bar Asn; Interam. Bar Asn.(former P.R. rep); Rotary; Lions. Distinguished Mil. Student and Grad; Most Outstanding Law Student. Rel: Catholic. Mailing Add: 65 Santiago Iglesias St, Condado, San Juan, P.R. 00907.

SOLES, ROBERT CHARLES, JR. D
N.C. State Rep.
b. Tabor City, N.C, 12/17/34; s. Robert C. Soles and Myrtle Norris S; single. Educ: Wake Forest Univ, B.S, 56; Univ. N.C. Sch. Law, LL.B, 59; Phi Alpha Delta. Polit. & Govt. Pos: Chmn, Seventh Cong. Dist. Young Dem. Club, N.C; city attorney, Tabor City, N.C; co. attorney, Columbus Co; chmn, Columbus Co. Dem. Exec. Cmt; N.C. State Rep, 69- Mil. Serv: Entered as 2nd Lt, Army Res, 56, released as Capt, 68, after serv. in various res. units. Publ: 'Interpretation of the Term Gross Income as Used in North Carolina Alimony Without Divorce Award' N.C. Law Rev, 59. Mem: N.C. and Am. Bar Asns; Am. Trial Lawyers Asn; N.C. Acad. of Trial Lawyers; Rotary (past pres); Red Cross (bd. dirs); Econ. Develop. Cmn; Cmt. of 100; Tobacco Bd. of Trade. Rel: Baptist. Mailing Add: P.O. Box 275, Tabor City, N.C. 28463.

SOLÍS, HILARIO GARCÍA 'LALO' D
b. San Antonio, Tex, 10/21/02; s. Juan Morales Solís and Francisca García S; m. 8/19/31 to Teresa Sotelo; c. Francisca S. (Mrs. Alvarado), Sister Felipa Solís, M.C.M, Florencia (Mrs. Casarez), Hilario, Jr, Teresa, Juan and Benigno. Educ: San Antonio Pub. Schs, 10-16. Polit. & Govt. Pos: Del, Tex. State Dem. Conv, 6 times, mem. resolutions cmt, 68; Dem. committeeman, Precinct 204, Bexar Co, Tex, 52-66 & 68-; state campaign mgr, Henry B. Gonzalez for Gov, 58, state coordinator, Henry B. Gonzalez for U.S. Sen, 61 and Don Yarborough for Gov, 62; asst. foreman, Precinct 1, Bexar Co, 60-62, co. patrolman, Precinct 2, 66-68; del, Dem. Nat. Conv, 68. Bus. & Prof. Pos: With Maintenance Dept, San Antonio Independent Sch. Dist, 35-60. Mil. Serv: Army, 20-21 & 42-43. Mem: St. Vincent de Paul. Rel: Roman Catholic. Mailing Add: 615 Gould St, San Antonio, Tex. 78207.

SOLOMON, ANTHONY JOSEPH D
R.I. State Rep.
b. Providence, R.I, 4/1/32; s. Joseph Solomon and Naza Simon S; m. 6/20/54 to Sarah Rachael Symia; c. Donna Marie, Michael Anthony, Sharon Ann and Anthony Elias. Educ: Providence Col, 52-53; R.I. Col. Pharm, B.S, 56; Kappa Psi. Polit. & Govt. Pos: R.I. State Rep, 11th Dist, 67-; chmn, Spec. Cmn. Studying Entire Field of Day Care, 67-; v.chmn, R.I. Narcotics Cmn, 69- Bus. & Prof. Pos: Owner and operator, Anthony Rexall Drugs, 57- Rel: Catholic. Mailing Add: 115 Joslin St, Providence, R.I. 02909.

SOLOMON, BERNARD D
Mem, Brookline Dem. Town Cmt, Mass.
b. Boston, Mass, 3/17/23; s. Samuel Solomon and Lillian Eisenberg S; m. 2/17/57 to Jolane Baumgarten; c. Sue, Samuel and Sarah Leslie. Educ: Northeast. Univ, 41-42; Univ. Ill, 42-43. Polit. & Govt. Pos: Asst. to Gov, Commonwealth of Mass, 57; cmnr. of Purchasing, 57-60, chmn, Emergency Finance Bd, 60-; del, Dem. Nat. Conv, 60, 64 & 68; mem, Brookline Dem. Town Cmt, 68-; secy-treas. Univ. Mass. Bldg. Authority, currently. Bus. & Prof. Pos: V.pres. civic and govt. rels, Stop & Shop, Inc, dir, Garden City Trust and dir, Grove Hall Savings Bank, currently. Mil. Serv: Entered as Pvt, Army, 42, released as Pfc, 46, after serv. in Eighth Armored Div, ETO, 44-46; Good Conduct Medal; ETO Medal with Three Battle Stars. Rel: Jewish. Mailing Add: 295 Reservoir Rd, Chestnut Hill, Mass. 02167.

SOLOMON, VICKI M. D
Chmn, Red Willow Co. Dem. Party, Nebr.
b. Holyoke, Colo, 10/21/23; d. Elmo L. Neiman and Esther V. Williams N; m. 4/10/48 to John R. Solomon; c. Debby Sue, Deanna Jane, Rex Douglas and John Bruce. Educ: Barnes Bus. Col, grad, 42; McCook Jr. Col, 45; summer sch. and off campus courses, Colo. Univ. and Nebr. Univ. Polit. & Govt. Pos: Precinct cmt, Red. Willow Co. Dem. Party, Nebr, 65-66, v.chmn, 67, chmn, 68- Bus. & Prof. Pos: Teacher, Eustis, Nebr. Rural Sch, 40 and Stockville, Nebr, 41; instr. photog, Lowry Field Army Base, 42-43; projection chief of photo lab, 36th St. Airport, Miami, Fla, 44; elem. teacher, Dist. Eight, McCook, Nebr, 46 and Holyoke, Colo, 47. Rel: Congregational. Mailing Add: Route 1, McCook, Nebr. 69001.

SOLTESZ, ANDREW, JR. D
Chmn, Burlington Co. Dem. Party, N.J.
b. Hungary, 1/29/21; s. Andrew Soltesz and Barbara S; m. 2/20/44 to Elizabeth Bartha; c. Andrea (Mrs. Henry Liszewski) and David A. Educ: Trenton High Sch, grad, 38. Polit. & Govt. Pos: Committeeman, Burlington Co. Dem. Party, N.J, 49-67 and chmn, 68-; del, Dem. Nat. Conv, 52 & 68; chmn, Dem. Fund Raising Dinners, N.J, 52-69; twp. committeeman, Bordentown Twp, 53-59 and Mayor, 55-57; confidential aide, N.J. Motor Vehicle Dept, 58-60; pres, Dem. Club of Burlington Co; clerk, Bd. of Freeholders, Burlington Co, 60-67 and undersheriff, 67-69; chmn. exec. cmt, Dem. Club, 69; pres, Edgewater Park Dem. Club, 69. Mil. Serv: Seaman 1/C, Coast Guard, 42, released 44, serv. in U.S. Theatre of Operation. Mem: Am. Legion; F&AM; Mason. Rel: Hungarian Reformed. Mailing Add: 442 Cottage Ave, Edgewater Park, N.J. 08010.

SOMERS, ROBERT VANCE R
b. Iredell Co, N.C, 11/21/37; s. Walter Vance Somers and Ethel Owens S; m. 7/27/68 to June Blalock. Educ: East Tenn. State Univ, B.S, 60; Univ. N.C, Chapel Hill, LL.B, 63. Polit. & Govt. Pos: Solicitor, Randolph Co, Asheboro, N.C, 64; judge, Randolph Co, 65-66; prosecuting attorney, Rowan Co. Court, Salisbury, N.C, 67-68; Rep. nominee, U.S. Sen, 68. Bus. & Prof. Pos: Attorney, 63- Mem: Am. and N.C. Bar Asns; N.C. Asn. Munic. and Co. Court Judges; Am. Conservative Union; Jr. C. of C; C. of C; YMCA; Optimist Club; Salisbury Country Club. Mailing Add: 201 Law Bldg, Salisbury, N.C. 28144.

SOMERVILLE, RONALD L. R
Mo. State Sen.
b. Hopkins, Mo, 2/1/21; m. 1/27/48 to Kathleen A. Marley; c. Kimberly, Peter, Brynell and Shelly. Educ: Westminster Col; Univ. Mo, LL.B, 49; Delta Tau Delta; Phi Delta Phi. Polit. & Govt. Pos: Prosecuting attorney, Livingston Co, Mo, 51-53; Mo. State Sen, 65- Bus. & Prof. Pos: Sr. partner law firm, Somerville & Cleaveland; farm owner, Livingston Co, Mo. Mil. Serv: Lt.(sg), Navy, 42-46; serv. as Aviator. Mem: Am. Legion; 40 et 8. Rel: Episcopal. Mailing Add: 1424 Forest Dr, Chillicothe, Mo. 64601. (1967)

SOMMER, CLIFFORD CARL R
Minn. State Sen.
b. Minneapolis, Minn, 5/25/08; s. Carl Henry Sommer and Anna Mathilda Petersen S; m. 9/14/35 to Eleanore Gurney; c. Margaret (Mrs. William Anderson) and Gayle (Mrs. Stanley Gaffin). Educ: Univ. Minn, B.B.A; Grad. Sch. Banking, Rutgers Univ, 3 years; Minn. Col. Law Night Sch, 2 years; Am. Inst. Banking Night Sch, 6 years; Phi Delta Theta. Polit. & Govt. Pos: Mem, City Bd. of Park Cmnrs, Minneapolis, Minn, 52-55; chmn, Minn. Rep. $100 Dinner, Jan. 60 & Feb. 66; mem, Minn. Rep. State Finance Cmt, 60-66; chmn, Gov. Bus. Adv. Cmt, 61-63; chmn, Steele Co. Rep. Finance Cmt, 63; Minn. State Sen, 66-; chmn, $1,000 a Plate Nixon-Agnew Dinner, Sept. 68; chmn, numerous local Rep. finance dr. Bus. & Prof. Pos: V.pres, Midland Nat. Bank of Minneapolis, Minn, 49-55; pres. and dir, Security Bank and Trust Co. of Owatonna, 55-; mem. bd. dirs, Lutheran Mutual Life Ins. Co, 56-; chmn, 69- Mil. Serv: Entered as Lt.(jg), Navy, 43, released as Lt, 45, after serv. in Armed Guard and Amphibious Units, Pac. Theatre, 44-45; Lt. Comdr.(Ret), Naval Res. Mem: Am. Legion; Navy League; Owatonna Country Club; Elks; Minneapolis Athletic Club; Minneapolis Club. Rel: Lutheran. Mailing Add: 1021 Kellford Place, Owatonna, Minn. 55060.

SOMMERDORF, VERNON L. DFL
Minn. State Rep.
b. McLeod Co, Minn, 21; s. Lester W. Sommerdorf and Luella Laugeson S; m. 12/31/46 to Norma Jean Seaquist; c. Jean (Mrs. Thomas Battey), Marianne, Delores and Philip. Educ: Univ. Minn, M.D, 53; Phi Beta Pi. Polit. & Govt. Pos: Mem, Gov. Cmn. on Health and Rehabilitation and Gov. Cmn. on Status of Women, Minn; Minn. State Rep, 64-, mem, Appropriations, Higher Educ, Financial Inst, Health and Welfare and Educ. Cmts, Minn. House Rep. Bus. & Prof. Pos: Physician. Mil. Serv: Entered as Hosp. Apprentice, 2/C, Navy, 42, released as Pharmist Mate 1/C, 46 after serv. in Submarine Serv. Mem: Past pres, Ramsey Co. Acad. of Gen. Practice. Rel: American Baptist. Mailing Add: 1 Kennard Court, St. Paul, Minn. 55106.

SONG, ALFRED H. D
Calif. State Sen.
b. Hawaii, 2/16/19; s. C.K. Song and C.Y. Kim S; m. 2/20/40 to Florence Eva Kim; c. Leslie Rose, Marsha Alane, Mark Elliott and Frances Jean. Educ: Univ. South. Calif, B.S, 42, J.D, 49, LL.M, 57 and LL.D. Polit. & Govt. Pos: City councilman, Monterey Park, Calif, 60-62; Calif. State Assemblyman, 62-65; former chmn, South. Calif. Dem. State Cmt; Calif. State Sen, 67- Bus. & Prof. Pos: Former sr. partner, Lemaire, Mohi, Morales, Dumas & Song, 50- Mailing Add: 2337 S. Garfield Ave, Monterey Park, Calif. 91754.

SONGER, JACK DOUGLAS R
Chmn, Vermilion Co. Rep. Cent. Cmt, Ill.
b. Danville, Ill, 10/23/21; s. Herman F. Songer 'Lee' and Lela Morris S; m. 4/28/43 to Henrietta Barkman 'Pat'; c. Sandra Sue, Stephen Jay and Deborah Lee. Educ: Mo. Mil. Acad. Polit. & Govt. Pos: Precinct committeeman, Rep. Party, Ill, 60-66; mem, Vermilion Co. Rep. Exec. Cmt, 62-66; del, State Rep. Conv, 64; chmn, Vermilion Co. Rep. Cent, Cmt, Ill, 66-; mem, bd. of dirs, Ill. Co. Chmn. Orgn, 66. Bus. & Prof. Pos: Pres, Songer Chevrolet Sales Inc, 46- Mil. Serv: Entered as Pvt, Army Air Force, 42, released as Capt, 46, after serv. in 20th Air Force, Pac. Theater, 45; Lt. Col, Air Force Res; Distinguished Flying Cross; Air Medal; Air Force Commendation; Distinguished Unit Citation; Pac. Defense Medal; Reserve 10 year Medal. Mem: Gen. Motors Chevrolet Dealer Planning Cmt; v.pres, Res. Officers Asn, Scott Southwestern Chap; bd. dirs, Vermilion Co. Chap, Red Cross; Mason (32); Elks; Am. Legion; Vermilion Co. Farm Bur; dir, Boy Scouts; Vermilion Hills Country Club. Rel: Methodist; Lay Speaker. Mailing Add: Dolan Rd, Catlin, Ill. 61817.

SONNENBERG, LOWELL ERNEST R
Colo. State Rep.
b. Sterling, Colo, 9/6/28; s. Ernest Albert Sonnenberg and S. Luella Heist S; m. 9/16/51 to Elizabeth Ann Duncan; c. Dean Eugene, Roberta Ann, Marilyn Jo and Gregory Scott. Educ: Westmar Col, 46-47; Colo. State Univ, B.S, 53. Polit. & Govt. Pos: Colo. State Sen, 65-67; Colo. State Rep, 67- Bus. & Prof. Pos: Operator, Farming Enterprise, 46-56, owner-operator, 56- Mil. Serv: Serv. as Recruit, Colo. Nat. Guard, 48-49; also 1st Lt, Air Force, 56; serv. in 7534th Squadron and 7568th Squadron, 3rd Air Force, Eng, 54-56. Mem: Policeman's Protective Asn; Mason (32°); Logan Co. Farm Bur; Rotary Int; Colo. Craftmen; Eastern Star; AFAAA. Rel: Leroy United Methodist. Mailing Add: Route 2, Fleming, Colo. 80728.

SONNEVELDT, CHRIS H.
Mayor, Grand Rapids, Mich.
b. Grand Rapids, Mich, 10/10/11; s. Christian Sonneveldt; m. 8/14/37 to Doris L; c. Christian H, III, Richard G, Robert B, Roger S. and Terry B. Educ: Grand Rapids Jr. Col; West. Mich. Univ. Polit. & Govt. Pos: Mayor, Grand Rapids, Mich, 64- Bus. & Prof. Pos: Teacher music, pub. schs, Rockford, Mich, 34-38, Fremont, 38-40; partner, Sonneveldt Co, Grand Rapids, 40- Mem: Grand Rapids Symphony Orchestra, 43-51; membership cmt, U.S. C. of C, 61-62; v.chmn. bd, Grace Bible Col, 61-, chmn, exec. cmt, 62-; pres, Grand Rapids Jr. Achievement, 62 and now bd. dirs; bd. dirs, Nat. Jr. Achievement; trustee, Mich. Munic. League (pres, 67-68); Gr. Grand Rapids C. of C.(pres, 63-64). Legal Res: 1560 Seminole Rd. S.E, Grand Rapids, Mich. 49506. Mailing Add: 435 Ionia Ave. S.W, Grand Rapids, Mich. 49502.

SONNICHSEN, JOHN WILLIAM R
b. Madison, Conn, 1/12/13; s. Christian L. Sonnichsen and Augusta Wendt S; m. 6/29/65 to Shirley Cotton; c. Cris and stepdaughter, Cindy. Educ: Roanoke Col. Polit. & Govt. Pos: Pres, Madison Young Rep, Conn, 36-37; mem, Madison Rep. Town Cmt, 36-66, chmn, 66-68; chmn, Madison Planning and Zoning Cmn, 53-59; chmn, Pub. Land, Study and Acquisition Cmt, 58-66. Bus. & Prof. Pos: Owner, Bldg. & Land Develop. Co, 50- Mil. Serv: Entered as PO 2/C, Navy, 42, released as PO 1/C, 46, after serv. in S.Pac. Mem: Am. Legion; Exchange Club. Volunteer Fireman, Madison Hose Co. 1. Rel: Protestant. Legal Res: 153 Wildwood Ave, Madison, Conn. 06433. Mailing Add: P.O. Box 417, Madison, Conn. 06433.

SORENSEN, EMIL S. R
V.Chmn, Sussex Co. Rep. Cmt, N.J.
b. Jersey City, N.J, 1/30/20; s. Emil S. Sorensen, Sr. and Helga Beyer S; m. 4/24/48 to Valnette Rowley; c. Maren, Paul and Mark. Educ: Upsala Col, B.A, 41; Rutgers Univ. Law Sch, LL.B, 48. Polit. & Govt. Pos: Mem, Bd. Educ, Sparta, N.J, 57-60, councilman, 60-68, mayor, 63-68; pres, Sparta Rep. Club, 57-59; co. campaign mgr, Mitchell for Gov, 61; chmn, Sparta Rep. Party, 67-; v.chmn. and committeeman, Sussex Co. Rep. Party, 67-; v.chmn, Sussex Co. Rep. Cmt, 67-; chmn, Sussex Co. Bd. Elec, 68-; mem, Sparta Bd. Adjust, 68- Bus. & Prof. Pos: Asst. sales mgr, Mennen Co, Morristown, 49-62; asst. sales mgr, A.W. Faber Pencil Co, Newark, 62-63; owner and operator of own bus, Sparta, 63- Mil. Serv: Entered as Pvt, Army, 42, released as S/Sgt, 46, after serv. in Counter Intel. Corps, Germany, 45-46. Mem: Rotary; Elks; C. of C; VFW. Rel: Lutheran. Mailing Add: 8 Glenside Trail, Sparta, N.J. 07871.

SORENSEN, PHILIP CHAIKIN D
b. Lincoln, Nebr, 8/31/33; s. Christian Abraham Sorensen and Annis Chaikin S; m. 12/20/58 to Janice Jo Lichtenberger; c. Rebecca Chaikin, Allan Philip and Karen Maria. Educ: Univ. Nebr. Col. Arts & Sci, 50-51 and 54-55; Univ. Nebr. Col. Law, B.S, 57, LL.B. cum laude, 59; Order of the Coif; ed-in-chief, Nebr. Law Rev, 57-58. Polit. & Govt. Pos: Mem, Nebr. State Dem. Cent. Cmt, 64; chmn, State Cmt. on Ment. Retardation; state coordinator, Civil Rights Activities; mem, Gov. Cmn. Human Rights; Lt. Gov, Nebr, 65-67; chmn, Cmn. on Exec. Reorganization, Ind, 68-69. Bus. & Prof. Pos: Law clerk, U.S. Dist. Judge, Robert Van Pelt, 59-60; part-time instr, Univ. of Nebr. Col. of Law, 60-61 and Univ. of Omaha, 65-66; partner, law firm, Flansburg, Mattson, Field, Ricketts, Sorensen & Gourlay, 60-65; exec. dir, Cummins Engine Found, Irwin-Sweeney-Miller Found. and Irwin Union Found, 67-; bd. dirs, Tougaloo Col, Jackson, Miss, 68-, Coun. on Founds, N.Y.C, 68- and Center for Community Change, Wash, D.C, 69. Mil. Serv: Entered as Seaman Recruit, Coast Guard, 51, released as PO 2/C, 54; Korean Theater Campaign Ribbon; UN Serv. Ribbon. Mem: Am, Nebr. and Ind. Bar Asns; C. of C; VFW; Am. Legion. Rel: Unitarian. Legal Res: 3719 Waycross Dr, Columbus, Ind. 47201. Mailing Add: 301 Washington St, Columbus, Ind. 47201.

SORENSEN, THEODORE CHAIKIN D
Chmn, Adv. Cmt, N.Y. State Dem. Cmt.
b. Lincoln, Nebr, 5/8/28; s. C.A. Sorensen and Annis Chaikin S; m. 6/28/69 to Gillian Martin; c. Eric, Stephen and Philip. Educ: Univ. Nebr, B.S.L, 49, Sch. Law, LL.B, 51; Phi Beta Kappa; Order of the Coif; Ed. in Chief, Law Rev. Hon. LL.D, Univ. Canterbury, 66. Polit. & Govt. Pos: Attorney, Fed. Security Agency, 51-52; staff mem, Joint Cmt. on R.R. Retirement, 52; asst. to U.S. Sen. John F. Kennedy, Mass, 53-61; secy, New Eng. Senators' Conf, 54-59; spec. counsel to the President, 61-64; mem, Temporary State Cmn. on Constitutional Conv, N.Y, currently; chmn, adv. cmt, N.Y. State Dem. Cmt; del, Dem. Nat. Conv, 68. Bus. & Prof. Pos: Lectr, foreign countries and 27 states; vis. lectr. in pub. and int. affairs, Woodrow Wilson Sch, Princeton Univ, 66-68; ed-at-lg, Sat. Rev, currently; partner, Law Firm of Paul, Weiss, Goldberg, Rifkind, Wharton & Garrison, N.Y, currently; trustee, Robert F. Kennedy Mem, 69- Publ: Decision-Making in the White House, 63; Kennedy, 65; The Kennedy Legacy, Macmillan, 69. Mem: Bar of U.S. Supreme Court, State of N.Y. and State of Nebr; bd, Lawyers Cmt. for Civil Rights Under Law; bd, John F. Kennedy Mem. Libr. and Inst; bd, Sat. Rev. Corp. Selected one of Ten Outstanding Men of Year, U.S. Jr. C. of C, 61; winner, Brotherhood Award, Mass. Cmt. of Catholics, Protestants and Jews, 65. Mailing Add: 345 Park Ave, New York, N.Y. 10022.

SORENSON, ED. C. D
b. Tyler, Minn, 12/13/08; m. to Florence; c. John. Educ: Univ. of Minn. Polit. & Govt. Pos: S.Dak. State Sen, 62-66; mayor of Chamberlain. Bus. & Prof. Pos: Theater owner and operator. Mem: Pres. of the C. of C; pres. of the Kiwanis Club; Masonic Lodge. Rel: United Church of Christ. Mailing Add: Chamberlain, S.Dak. 57325. (1967)

SORG, NATHAN F. R
Iowa State Rep.
b. Hawkeye, Iowa, 1910; married; c. two daughters. Educ: State Col. of Iowa, B.S; Univ. of Iowa, B.S, M.A. Polit. & Govt. Pos: Iowa State Rep, 67- Bus. & Prof. Pos: Pharmacist, Sorg Pharmacy. Rel: Methodist. Mailing Add: 1204 Washington Dr, Marion, Iowa 52302. (1967)

SORLIE, OSCAR J. R
N.Dak. State Sen.
b. Buxton, N.Dak, 7/11/07; married; c. one. Educ: Pub. schs. Polit. & Govt. Pos: N.Dak. State Rep, 49-61; N.Dak. State Sen, currently. Bus. & Prof. Pos: Farmer. Mem: Mason; Elks; Boy Scouts. Rel: Lutheran. Mailing Add: Buxton, N.Dak. 58218. (1967)

SORRELLS, MARVIN WILLIAMS D
Ga. State Rep.
b. Walton Co, Ga, 12/7/36; s. Charles James Sorrells and Ruth Williams S; m. 12/15/62 to Mary Kathryn Floyd; c. Laura Karrell. Educ: Univ. Ga, B.B.A, 59; Univ. Ga. Lumpkin Sch. Law, LL.B, 62; Sigma Nu. Polit. & Govt. Pos: Sheriff, Walton Co, Ga, 62; dep. sheriff, 62-63; probation officer, Juvenile Court, Walton Co, 64-; Ga. State Rep, 69- Bus. & Prof. Pos: Mem. law firm, Pollock, Sorrells & Hearn, currently. Publ: Column in the Walton Tribune. Mem: State Bar of Ga; West. Bar Asn; Walton Co. Bar Asn.(secy-treas, 67-); Rotary (dir, Monroe Club, currently). Most Outstanding Young Man Award, Walton Co. Jaycees, 68. Rel: Baptist. Legal Res: 514 Breedlove Dr, Monroe, Ga. 30655. Mailing Add: 116 Court St, Monroe, Ga. 30655.

SORRELS, CYRIL PERSHING R
b. Bismarck, N.Dak, 5/2/19; s. C.R.O. Sorrels and Selma Johnson S; m. 10/15/46 to Dolores Elaine Luedke; c. Cheryl, Beverly, Stephen and Douglas. Educ: Northwest Sch. of Agr, 3 years; Univ. Minn, 3 months. Polit. & Govt. Pos: Mem. and clerk, Williams Sch. Bd, Minn, 55-62; chmn, Iron Co. Rep. Orgn, Wis, 67-68. Bus. & Prof. Pos: Farmer, C.R.O. Sorrels & Sons, Williams, Minn, 46-62; farm mgr, Swanee Spud Farm, Gurney, Wis, 62- Mil. Serv: Entered as Pvt, Army, 42, released as Maj, 52, after serv. in 36th Inf. Div, ETO, 43-45; Purple Heart. Mem: Wis. Potato Growers Asn; Am. Legion. Rel: Lutheran. Mailing Add: Gurney, Wis. 54528.

SOSSAMAN, JAMES J. R
Ariz. State Rep.
b. Phoenix, Ariz, 7/17/32; s. Jasper Harvey Sossaman and Faith Mather S; m. 12/20/53 to Carolyn Sue Peters; c. Kimberlee Ann, Stephen James and Scott Harvey. Educ: Ariz. State Univ, 50-52. Polit. & Govt. Pos: Precinct committeeman, Queen Creek Precinct, Ariz, 62-69; Ariz. State Rep, Dist. 8A, 69- Bus. & Prof. Pos: Owner, Sossaman Farms, 56- Mil. Serv: Entered as Cadet, Navy, 52, released as Lt.(jg), 56, after serv. in Patrol Plane, 47 and Fleet Aircraft Serv. Squadron, Far East, 53-56; Korean Serv. Medal; Nat. Defense Medal. Mem: Sch. Bd. Trustee; Maricopa Co. Farm Bur.(past pres. and dir); Chandler Hosp. Dist. 1 (past pres); Ariz. Flying Farmers (past pres); dir, Ariz. Cotton Growers Asn; United Dairymen of Ariz. Winner of Dist. 3, Ariz. High Yield of Short Staple Cotton, 65; Arizona's Outstanding Young Farmer, Jr. C. of C, 66; Flying Farmer of the Year, Ariz. Flying Farmers, 69. Rel: United Methodist. Mailing Add: Route 1, Box 80, Higley, Ariz. 85236.

SOUCY, EMILE J. R
N.H. State Rep.
b. Manchester, N.H, 8/5/00; married. Polit. & Govt. Pos: N.H. State Rep, 47, 53-57 & 61- Bus. & Prof. Pos: Ins. and pub. rels. Mailing Add: 2146 Elm St, Manchester, N.H. 03104. (1967)

SOURS, HUDSON RALPH R
Ill. State Sen.
b. Peoria, Ill, 10/29/09; m. to Priscilla Kelly S; c. Hudson Ralph Jr. and Linda Laurel. Educ: Wabash Col, B.A, 31; Yale Law Sch, LL.B, 35; Phi Beta Kappa; Phi Gamma Delta. Polit. & Govt. Pos: Secy, Peoria Co. Cent. Cmt, Ill, 54-58; Ill. State Sen, 60- Bus. & Prof. Pos: Attorney, Law Firm of Sours, Newell and Nicol. Mil. Serv: Army Air Force, 42-46, Maj. Mem: Pres, Peoria Bar, 60; trustee, Peoria Pub. Libr; Am, Ill. and Peoria Bar Asns; Miss. Valley Hist. Asn; Peoria Hist. Soc; v.chmn, Ill. Sesquicentennial Cmn, 65-; chmn, Ill. Civil War Centennial Cmn, 61-65. Received Open Door Award, 62, presented by Chicago Cmt. on Alcoholism. Rel: Presbyterian. Mailing Add: 2623 W. Moss Ave, Madison Manor, Peoria, Ill. 61602.

SOUTER, SYDNEY SCULL R
b. Trenton, N.J, 6/17/31; s. Sydney H. Souter, Jr.(deceased) and Josephine Scull S; m. 8/16/58 to Deborah Grierson; c. Gifford MacLeod; Julia Elizabeth and Matthew Thomas. Educ: Yale Univ, B.A, 54; Yale Law Sch, LL.B, 59; Book and Gavel; Phi Alpha Delta. Polit. & Govt. Pos: Campaign mgr, Lawrence Twp, N.J, 60, Rep. Club pres, 61-62 and Rep. munic. chmn, 63; cand. for N.J. State Assembly, Mercer Co, 64; staff aid, Dumont for Gov. Campaign, N.J, 65; Munic. Judge, Montgomery Twp, 66-67; cand. for U.S. Rep. Fourth Cong. List, N.J, 68; mem. finance cmt, Cahill for Gov. Campaign, 69. Bus. & Prof. Pos: Salesman and statistician, Overseas Serv. Corp, Frankfurt, Germany, 49-50; asst. dean of Freshmen, Yale Univ, 58-59; assoc, Minton, Dinsmore & Bohlinger, Princeton, N.J, 60-63; McCarthy, Bacsik & Hicks, 63-66; dir, Ewing Bank & Trust Co, 63-; partner, Souter, Scozzari & Steffens, Attorneys, 66-; pres, Hamilton State Bank, 69. Mil. Serv: Entered as 2nd Lt, Marine Corps, 54, released as 1st Lt, 56, after serv. in Second Marine Div, Continental U.S. and Caribbean; Maj, Marine Res, currently. Mem: Am. N.J. State, Mercer Co. and Princeton Bar Asns; Am. Arbit. Asn; Marine Corps Reserve Officers Asn; Kiwanis; Am. Legion; bd. gov, Helene Fuld Hosp. Commun. Leader Award, 69. Rel: Presbyterian; Trustee, Lawrenceville Church. Legal Res: 106 Carson Rd, Lawrenceville, N.J. 08648. Mailing Add: Province Line Rd, R.D. 3-88, Princeton, N.J. 08540.

SOUTH, STEPHEN E. D
b. Rock Island, Ill, 11/25/42; s. Chester P. South and Marquerite V. Braem S; m. 9/11/65 to Sharon Kay Goettsch. Educ: Univ. Notre Dame, B.S. in Eng.

Sci, 64; Grad. Sch. of Indust. Admin, Carnegie Mellon Univ, M.S. in Indust. Admin, 66; London Sch. of Econ. and Polit. Sci, 66; Tau Beta Pi; ed-in-chief, Notre Dame Tech. Rev. Polit. & Govt. Pos: Admin. asst. to U.S. Rep. James W. Symington, Mo, 69- Bus. & Prof. Pos: Mgt. consult, NATO For. Exchange Prog, 66-67; corporate planner, McDonnell-Douglas Corp, St. Louis, Mo, 67-69. Mem: St. Louis Coun. on World Affairs. Bausch and Lomb Award; Outstanding Sci. Student of Grad. Class, 60. Rel: Roman Catholic. Legal Res: Clayton, Mo. 63105. Mailing Add: 201 Eye St. S.W, Washington, D.C. 20024.

SOUTHALL, MARK T. D
N.Y. State Assemblyman
b. Norfolk, Va, 6/1/11; s. George Edward Southall and Bertha Shiver S; m. 1/5/63 to Joanne Fletcher; c. Joanne F. Educ: Collegiate Inst; Henry George Sch. of Social Sci; Poh's Inst. of Ins. Polit. & Govt. Pos: Confidential aide to Judge, Gen. Session and Supreme Courts, 60-62, del, Dem. Nat. Conv, 68; N.Y. State Assemblyman, 69- and chmn, Adv. Cmt. on Crime and Safety in the Streets, N.Y. State Assembly; co. and state committeeman, judicial del. and dist. leader, N.Y. Co. Dem. Orgn, chmn, N.Y. Co. Dem. Cmt. and N.Y. Dem. State Cmt. on Crime, currently. Bus. & Prof. Pos: Licensed Ins. and Real Estate Broker, self-employed, 47-; v.pres. and dir, Mocho Industs, currently. Mem: Exec. mem, New Horizons Dem. Club. Legal Res: 345 W. 145th St, New York, N.Y. 10031. Mailing Add: 274 W. 145th St, New York, N.Y. 10039.

SOUTHERLAND, JAMES F. D
b. Pender Co, N.C, 2/8/27; s. Daniel Patron Southerland and Annie Laura Page S; m. 4/30/53 to Beverly Townsend; c. Mark Townsend and Laura Page. Educ: N.C. State Col, 43-44; Univ. N.C, A.B. in Journalism, 50. Polit. & Govt. Pos: Admin. asst, Gov. Fla, 59-60; confidential asst, U.S. Secy. Commerce, 61-65; admin. asst, U.S. Rep. Claude Pepper, Fla, 65- Bus. & Prof. Pos: Reporter, Parker Bros. Newspapers, Ahoskie, N.C, 50-51; reporter, Greensboro Daily News, 51-53; reporter and feature writer, Winston-Salem Jour, 53-54; assoc. ed, Fla. Times-Union, Jacksonville, 54-56; ed. writer, Daytona Beach Jour, 56-59. Mil. Serv: Entered as Seaman 1/C, Navy, 45, released as EM 2/C, 47, after serv. in Bikini Atomic Bomb Tests, Pac, 47; Ens, Naval Res, 51-65. Mem: Nat. Capital Dem. Club. Rel: Unitarian. Legal Res: 8300 Crespi Blvd, Miami Beach, Fla. 33141. Mailing Add: 6310 Ft. Hunt Dr, Alexandria, Va. 23307.

SOUTHERN, RICHARD EARL D
Mo. State Sen.
b. Madison, Mo, 9/9/36; s. Earl Robert Southern and Lillie Belle Crosswhite S; m. 6/15/57 to Nancy Blanche Youngs; c. Earl Richard, Jr, Deborah Lynn and Todd Andrew. Educ: Moberly Jr. Col, cert, 56; Univ. Mo, B.A, 58, LL.B, 60; Phi Alpha Delta. Polit. & Govt. Pos: Clerk, Off. Budget & Comptroller, Mo, 57; auditor, Mo, 57-59; attorney, Mo. Revenue Dept, 59-61; mem, Ninth Dist. Young Dem, 61; Mo. State Rep, 61-67; parliamentarian, State Young Dem, 62; Mo. State Sen, 18th Dist, 67-; del, Dem. Nat. Conv, 68. Bus. & Prof. Pos: Attorney-at-law, 60; realtor, 64- Mem: Mo. Bar Asn. Rel: Christian Church. Mailing Add: 511 N. Chestnut, Monroe City, Mo. 63456.

SOUZA, JAMES STANLEY R
b. Pepeekeo, Hawaii, 6/16/29; s. Manuel Calafat Souza and Adelia Morris S; m. 10/23/54 to Janet Hisano Osaki; c. Geri Ann and James Stanley, Jr. Educ: Hilo High Sch, 47. Polit. & Govt. Pos: Mem, Hawaii State Bd. of Paroles and Pardons, 62-64; chmn, Second Dist. Co. Rep. Party, 63-66; mem, Hawaii State Rep. Exec. Cmt, 63-66; del, Rep. Nat. Conv, 64; cand. for Hawaii State Rep, 66; councilman, Hilo Dist, Hawaii Co, 69- Bus. & Prof. Pos: Repair dept. mgr, Hilo Motors, Ltd, 54-66, sales rep, 66-; pres, Realty Invest. Fed. Credit Union, 58-63 & 67-68; dir, Kurohara's Shop for Men, 61; trustee, Mauna Kea Mem. Park, 68-69. Mem: Pres, Hilo Jaycees, 63-64 and South Hilo Rotary, 64-65; chmn, Hawaii Co. Fair, 64; dir, Hawaii Unit, Am. Cancer Soc; past secy, Papaikou Holy Name Soc; committeeman, Troup 58, Boy Scouts; past pres, Francis Coun. and past state pres, Young Men's Inst. Man of the Year Award, Young Men's Inst, 61; Outstanding Man of Year and Distinguished Serv. Award, Jaycees, 65. Rel: Catholic. Legal Res: Kaapoko Homesteads, Papaikou, Hawaii 96781. Mailing Add: P.O. Box 385, Papaikou, Hawaii 96781.

SOVIK, LAURENCE D
b. Johnstown, N.Y, 1/27/04; s. Stephen Sovik and Mary Hladik S; m. 4/25/31 to Gladys Michaels; c. Laurence F, Alicia S.(Mrs. Socia), Ann (Mrs. Weeks), Janet and William S. Educ: Syracuse Univ, LL.B, 26; Phi Delta Phi; Newman Club. Bus. & Prof. Pos: Mem. of law firm, Smith, Sovik, Terry, Kendrick, McAuliffe & Schwarzer, 46- Mil. Serv: Selective Service Medal of Honor. Mem: Am. and N.Y. Bar Asns; Fed. Commun. Bar; 200 Club; Onondaga Golf & Country Club; Sleepy Hollow Golf & Country Club. Local golf championships. Rel: Catholic. Mailing Add: 805 Demong Dr, Syracuse, N.Y. 13214.

SOWARDS, GLADE MILTON R
Utah State Rep.
b. Vernal, Utah, 9/9/29; s. Harmon Silas Sowards and Ida Rebecca Jensen S; m. 5/29/52 to Rachel Elizabeth Farley; c. Rebecca Jane, Olivia, Harmon Scott, John Farley, Paula, Allen Henderson, Samuel Layne and Trinadad Madge Ben. Educ: Univ. Utah, B.S; Phi Kappa Phi; Sigma Chi. Polit. & Govt. Pos: Councilman, Vernal City, Utah, 61-69; Utah State Rep, 69- Bus. & Prof. Pos: Mgr, H.S. Sowards & Sons, Inc, 54-69; pres, Uqueahgut,Inc, 66-69. Publ: 'And the Desert Shall Blossom as the Rose,' Improv. Era, 65. Mem: Pres, Vernal Lions Club and C. of C. Acct. Award, Univ. Utah Bus. Dept; Master M Man Award (church). Rel: Latter-day Saint. Mailing Add: 380 West First S, Vernal, Utah 84078.

SOWELL, J. RALPH, JR. D
Miss. State Rep.
b. Canton, Miss, 7/3/40; s. James Ralph Sowell and Hazel Darby; m. to Gloria Winstead. Educ: Millsaps Col, B.A, 62; Miss. Col, 62-64, cand. for M.A; Jackson Sch. Law, grad, 69; Omicron Delta Kappa; Alpha Psi Omega; Kit Kat; Int. Rels. Club; Kappa Alpha. Polit. & Govt. Pos: Campaign mgr, cand. for Lt. Gov, Miss, 63; Miss. State Rep, Hinds Co, 68- Bus. & Prof. Pos: Acct. exec, Lawrence E. Davis & Assoc. adv. and pub. rels, 62-63; owner, Capital City Adv. and Pub. Rels, 63-64; pub. rels. dir, Hinds Jr. Col, 64-69; pres, Franklin Printers, Inc, 69- Mem: Pub. Rels. Asn. of Miss; pres, Jackson Jr. C. of C, 66. Selected as Outstanding Young Man of Jackson and Outstanding Young Man of Miss, 67. Rel: Baptist. Mailing Add: 5221 Wayneland Dr, Jackson, Miss. 39211.

SOWELL, POLLY ROLLINS R
Dep. V.Chmn, Rep. Party of Tex.
b. Charlottesville, Va, 11/3/27; d. Wiley Jackson Rollins and Maury Coleman R; m. 10/1/49 to Richard Maurice Sowell; c. Susan Channing. Educ: Sweet Briar Col, A.B, 48. Polit. & Govt. Pos: Campaign chmn, Nixon-Lodge, Hidalgo Co. Rep. Party, Tex, 60, co. v.chmn, 61; mem, Tex. State Rep. Exec. Cmt, Sen. Dist. 27, 62-66; dep. v.chmn, Rep. Party of Tex, 66-; del, Rep. Nat. Conv, 68. Mem: McAllen Libr. Bd.(pres); McAllen Jr. Serv. League (former pres); McAllen Citizen's League Bd. Dirs; Rio Grande Valley Int. Music Festival Bd; McAllen Coun. for Better Educ.(past pres). Mailing Add: 401 Wichita, McAllen, Tex. 78501.

SOWER, FRANK WILLIAM D
Mayor, Frankfort, Ky.
b. Frankfort, Ky, 12/10/10; s. John Rodman Sower and Rose Elma Edwards S; m. 8/22/37 to Minnie Lynn Evans; c. Frank William, Jr, Lynn (Mrs. Michael E. Bufkin) and John Rodman. Educ: Northwest. Univ, B.S, 33; Sigma Nu. Polit. & Govt. Pos: Pres, Ky. Hist. Soc, 66-68; mayor, Frankfort, Ky, 68- Bus. & Prof. Pos: Dir, Farmers Bank & Capital Trust Co, 66. Mil. Serv: Entered as Lt.(jg), Navy, 44, released as Lt, 46, after serv. in Naval Res, Southwest Pac. Theatre. Mem: Am. Legion; VFW; former pres, Rotary, Frankfort C. of C, Ky. Merchants' and Ky. Retail Hardware Asns. Rel: Catholic. Legal Res: 112 Wilkinson St, Frankfort, Ky. 40601. Mailing Add: P.O. Box 453, Frankfort, Ky. 40601.

SOWERS, ROY GERODD, JR. D
b. Sanford, N.C, 9/9/28; s. Dr. Roy G. Sowers and Evelyn Bazemore S; m. 10/16/49 to Joyce Howell; c. Roy G, III and Joyce Lynn. Educ: Wake Forest Col, B.S, 49; Kappa Sigma. Polit. & Govt. Pos: Aide de camp to Gov. Terry Sanford, N.C, 61-65; mem, N.C. State Dem. Exec. Cmt, 61-69; mem, Sanford Bd. of Aldermen, 61-; del, Dem. Nat. Conv, 64; mem, N.C. Rural Elec. Authority, 64; v.pres, N.C. Young Dem. Club, 66. Bus. & Prof. Pos: Adjustor, First Citizens Bank & Trust, 49-52; owner real estate firm, 56-62; asst. to pres, Roberts, Co, 62- Mil. Serv: Lt. Col, Army Res. Mem: Elks; Moose; Am. Legion; Mason; MWA. Rel: Methodist. Legal Res: 816 Gulf St. E, Sanford, N.C. 27330. Mailing Add: P.O. Box 85, Sanford, N.C. 27330. (1967)

SPADANUTA, BARBARA BELVEK D
b. Chicago, Ill, 5/29/32; d. R. Robert Belvek and Helen Smith B; m. 8/23/52 to Andrew Long Spadanuta; c. Louis Robert, Kathi Alyn and Susan Lee. Educ: Univ. Dubuque, 2 years. Polit. & Govt. Pos: Alternate del, Dem. Nat. Conv, 68; coordinator, McCarthy-O'Dwyer-Lowenstein Campaigns, Oceanside, N.Y, 68; secy, Long Island New Dem. Coalition, N.Y, currently; secy, Oceanside Dem. Club, currently; co-chmn, Oceanside New Dem. Coalition, currently. Bus. & Prof. Pos: Owner, Place in Back, Cedarhurst, N.Y, 67-68. Mem: Oceanside Cmt. for Human Rights; Cath. Inter-Racial Coun; Women's Strike for Peace; Another Mother for Peace. Rel: Christian. Mailing Add: 265 Foxhurst Rd, Oceanside, N.Y. 11572.

SPAFFORD, ENVAL AINSWORTH D
Secy, Ashtabula Co. Dem. Party, Ohio
b. Footville, Ohio, 6/29/02; s. Eddie A. Spafford and Cynthia Hyneman S; div; c. Kay (Mrs. McMahan) and Robert. Educ: Ohio State Univ, B.S. in Agr, 25; West. Reserve Univ, Master of Ed, 33; Delta Theta Sigma. Polit. & Govt. Pos: Chmn, Ashtabula Co. Dem. Party, Ohio, 56-62; secy, 62-; secy, Ashtabula Co. Dem. Cent. and Exec. Cmt, 10 years; mem. Ashtabula Co. Bd. Elec, 12 years. Mailing Add: Route #1, Rock Creek, Ohio 44084.

SPAHR, WILLIAM EDWARD D
Mont. State Rep.
b. Newville, Pa, 3/31/16; s. Wilbur Edward Spahr and Myrtle Mae Heller Neidigh S; div; c. Kathy Irene and Keri Louise. Educ: West. Mont. Col, B.S, 49; Univ. Wash, 50; Univ. Mont, M.A, 55; Univ. Colo, 60. Polit. & Govt. Pos: Mont. State Rep, Dist. 18, Cascade Co, 61-; mem, Great Falls City Coun, 63-65. Bus. & Prof. Pos: Journalism instr. and publ. dir, Great Falls High Sch, 58- Mil. Serv: Entered as Pvt, Army Air Force, 41, released as Capt, 46, after serv. in ATC, African Theatre; Capt, Res; African Campaign Ribbon with One Battle Star; Am. Theatre and World War II Medals; Letter of Commendation. Mem: Mason (32°); Scottish Rite; Shrine. Gold Key, Univ. Mont. Rel: Presbyterian. Legal Res: 1411 Third Ave. S, Great Falls, Mont. 59401. Mailing Add: Box 1010, Great Falls, Mont. 59401.

SPAIN, JACK D
b. Greenville, N.C, 5/9/03; s. John Sidney Spain and Olivia Johnston S; m. 12/14/29 to Marie Hardee; c. Frances Hardee, Jack Jr. Educ: Univ. of N.C, A.B; Rocky Mt. Law Sch.(passed State Bar). Polit. & Govt. Pos: Admin. asst, Sen. Samuel J. Ervin, Jr, N.C, currently; admin. asst. to late Sen. Hoey, 45-54; secy, Rep Bonner, 1-N.C, 40-45; mayor, Greenville, N.C, 39-40; alderman, Greenville, 37-39; prosecuting attorney, Greenville, 32-36. Mem: Phi Gamma Delta; Phi Assembly U.N.C; German Club; pres, U.N.C. Alumni Asn, Wash; Christian Church, Greenville, N.C; N.C. Farm Bur; pres, Sen. Secys. Asn, 56; pres, Cong. Secys. Club, 62; pres, N.C. Dems. Club of D.C; pres, Conf. of State Secys. of D.C; pres, N.C. State Secy. of D.C. Legal Res: Greenville, N.C. Mailing Add: 6607 Burlington Place, Springfield, Va. 22150. (1967)

SPAIN, JAMES EARL D
Mo. State Rep.
b. Clarksville, Tex, 12/15/34; s. Elbert Earl Spain and Wilma Waters S; m. 2/11/56 to Jo Anne Prather; c. Cynthia Lynn, Melinda Anne and Samuel Prather. Educ: Ark. State Col, 52-53; Southeast Mo. State, A.B, 55; Univ. Mo, LL.B, 60; Phi Alpha Theta; Phi Alpha Delta; Sigma Phi Epsilon; Varsity Club. Polit. & Govt. Pos: Secy, Bd. Educ, Mo, 63-66; Mo. State Rep, 151st Dist, 67-; del, Dem. Nat. Conv, 68. Bus. & Prof. Pos: Lawyer, Hearnes & Spain, 60-62; lawyer, Briney, Welborn & Spain, 62- Mil. Serv: Entered as

Pvt, Army, 55, released as Specialist 4/C, 57, after serv. in 2nd Inf. Div, Alaska, 56-57. Publ: 'Implied Warranty of Food and Drink in Missouri,' Mo. Law Review, 60. Mem: Mo. and Am. Bar Asns. Rel: Methodist. Mailing Add: Spring St, Bloomfield, Mo. 63825.

SPAINHOWER, JAMES I. D
Mo. State Rep.
b. Stanberry, Mo, 8/3/28; m. 6/10/50 to Joanne Steanson; c. Janet Dovell, James Jeffrey. Educ: Phillips Univ; Lexington Theol. Assembly; Univ. of Ark; Pacific Sch. of Rel; B.A, B.Div. Polit. & Govt. Pos: Mo. State Rep, 62- Bus. & Prof. Pos: Minister, First Christian Church, Fayetteville, Ark, 53-58; Minister, First Christian Church, Marshall, Mo, 58-64. Rel: First Christian Church. Mailing Add: 516 S. Drive, Marshall, Mo. 65340. (1967)

SPALDING, KENNETH WOODMAN, JR. R
N.H. State Rep.
b. Southbridge, Mass, 11/26/34; s. Kenneth W. Spalding, Sr. and Hilda Luce S; m. 8/10/57 to Audred A. Ide; c. Scott Woods, David Ide, Kenneth Woodman, III and Martha Dorothy. Educ: St. Lawrence Univ, B.A, 56; Sigma Pi. Polit. & Govt. Pos: Mem, Amherst Bd. of Adjust, N.H, formerly; supvr. of checklist, formerly; past treas, Hillsborough Co. Rep. Cmt; past pres, Souhegan Young Rep. Club; past recording secy, N.H. Fedn. of Young Rep. Clubs; N.H. State Rep, 69- Bus. & Prof. Pos: Sales engr, New Eng. Homes, formerly; dir, Yankee Develop. Corp, currently. Mil. Serv: Entered as 2nd Lt, Army, 57, released as 1st Lt, 59, after serv. in Armed Serv. Police Detachment, Boston, Mass. Mem: Charter mem, Souhegan Valley Jaycees; Mason; trustee, New Hampton Sch. Rel: Protestant. Legal Res: Green Rd, Amherst, N.H. 03031. Mailing Add: Box 184, Amherst, N.H. 03031.

SPALDING, LESTER HELM D
b. Lebanon, Ky, 6/16/20; s. Bennie G. Spalding and Hazel Helm S; m. 9/12/42 to Nell Terry; c. Larry Helm, Susan Terry and Steven Lynn. Educ: West. Ky. Univ, B.A, 41; Univ. Louisville Sch. Law, LL.B, 48; Omicron Delta Kappa; Phi Alpha Delta. Polit. & Govt. Pos: Co. Attorney and Judge, Marion Co, Ky, several occasions prior to 56; City Attorney, Lebanon, 56-58; Commonwealth's Attorney, Eleventh Judicial Dist. of Ky, 58-; mem, Ky. Disabled Ex-Servicemen's Bd, 59-61; del, Dem. Nat. Conv, 68; mem, Lincoln Trail Regional Crime Coun, 69-, Bus. & Prof. Pos: Attorney, Bd. Educ, Marion Co, Ky, 56-; dir, Marion Nat. Bank, Lebanon, 65-; asst. attorney, Marion Co. Savings and Bldg. Asn, 67-; adv, Marion-Wash. Co. Voc. Sch, 68- Mil. Serv: Entered as 2nd Lt, Air Force, 42, released as Maj. after serv. in Judge Adv, 123rd Fighter-Interceptor Wing, Maj.(Ret), Air Force Res, 61. Mem: Ky. Bar Asn; Commonwealth's Attorneys Asn; Mason (pres, Masonic Temple Co); VFW (Past Dept. Judge Advocate); Am. Legion (Past Comdr, Marion Post 49); lay speaker, Campbellsville Dist, United Methodist Church; Kiwanis (Past v.pres, Lebanon Club); dir. and secy, Marion Co. Pub. Libr. Serv. Corp. Rel: Methodist; Pres, Methodist Men and mem, Off. Bd, Lebanon United Methodist Church. Legal Res: Park Heights, Lebanon, Ky. 40033. Mailing Add: 7 Court Sq, Lebanon, Ky. 40033.

SPALDING, PHILIP EDMUNDS, JR. R
b. Honolulu, Hawaii, 7/21/18; s. Philip Edmunds Spalding and Alice Cooke S; m. 11/21/52 to Phyllis Hume; c. Philip Edmunds, III, Alfred Tozzer, Anne Margaret, Philip Hume, Michael Scott and Joan (Mrs. Steven Milo Peterson). Educ: Princeton Univ, 2 years; Colonial Club. Polit. & Govt. Pos: Finance Chmn, Rep. Party of Hawaii, 46 and treas, 48; alternate del, Rep. Nat. Conv, 68. Bus. & Prof. Pos: Pres, Hawaiian West. Steel Limited, 58; Dir, Bank of Hawaii, 63-, Dillingham Corp, 67- and Hawaiian Elec. Co, Inc, 69- Mil. Serv: Ens, Navy, 46. Mem: Hawaii Acad. of Sci; Pac. Club; Oahu Country Club. Legal Res: 2377 Makiki Heights Dr, Honolulu, Hawaii 96822. Mailing Add: 91-150 Hanua St, Ewa, Hawaii 96706.

SPANAGEL, HARRY BORMAN D
Ind. State Rep.
b. Lawrenceburg, Ind, 5/27/11; s. Albert Spanagel and Jeannette Emerson S; m. 8/17/40 to Helen Marcella Greive; c. Sondra (Mrs. A.Wallace Field). Educ: Miami Univ, Oxford, Ohio, degree in bus. admin, 33; Sigma Nu. Polit. & Govt. Pos: Pres, Ind. State Bd. Pub. Welfare, 63-64; mem, Town Bd. Greendale, 64; Ind. State Rep, 65- Bus. & Prof. Pos: Pres, Kiwanis, 40; dir. and Former pres, Dearborn Co. Mental Health Asn; dir, Dearborn Co. United Fund and Dearborn-Ohio Co. Am. Red Cross, 64-; dir, budget chmn. and mem. exec. cmt, Community Mental Health Clinic, Inc, 67- Mem: Mason; Eastern Star. Rel: Episcopal. Mailing Add: 231 Oakey Ave, Lawrenceburg, Ind. 47025.

SPANOS, CHARLES VAIOS D
b. Newport, 9/14/28; s. Vaios S; Spanos and Mary Stasso S; m. 6/17/56 to Joy Cynthia Ashley; c. Kassandra Leah, Theo Carol and Alexis Katherine. Educ: Univ. N.H, B.A, 57; Boston Univ. Law Sch, LL.B, 60; Pi Gamma Mu; Kappa Sigma. Polit. & Govt. Pos: Secy, Sullivan Co. Dem. Party, N.H, 63-65, chmn, 65-67; co. attorney, Sullivan Co, 64- Bus. & Prof. Pos: Assoc. mem, Spanos & Spanos Law Off, 60-67; trustee, Univ. N.H, 67- Mil. Serv: Entered as Pvt, Army, 51, released as Cpl, 53. Mem: N.H. Bar Asn, exec. dir, 66-67; Sullivan Co. Bar Asn; dir, Nat. Dist. Attorneys' Asn, 68-; pres, N.H. Co. Attorneys Asn, 69- Rel: Greek Orthodox. Legal Res: 7 Bellevue Ave, Claremont, N.H. 03743. Mailing Add: 137 Broad St, Claremont, N.H. 03743.

SPANOS, HARRY V. D
N.H. State Sen.
b. Newport, N.H, 5/8/26; married; c. Three. Educ: Harvard Col; Harvard Law Sch. Polit. & Govt. Pos: N.H. State Rep, 63-67; N.H. State Sen, 67-; moderator, Newport, N.H, former town attorney, former mem, Sch. Bd. and former chmn, Planning Bd; Assoc. Judge, Newport Munic. Court. Bus. & Prof. Pos: Attorney. Rel: Greek Orthodox. Mailing Add: P.O. Box 132, Newport, N.H. 03773.

SPARACINO, ANTHONY JOSEPH D
W.Va. State Del.
b. Mabscott, W.Va, 12/25/16; s. Joseph Sparacino, Sr. and Conchetta Briguglio S; m. 7/17/49 to Joeann Robertson; c. Catherine Grace and Anthony J, Jr. Educ: Catholic Univ. Am, A.B, 39; W.Va. Univ. Col. Law, LL.B, 42; Blue Key Soc; Sen. Club. Polit. & Govt. Pos: City Police Judge, Beckley, W.Va, 49-52; Prosecuting Attorney, Raleigh Co, 53-64; W.Va. State del, Raleigh Co, 69- Bus. & Prof. Pos: Pres, Raleigh Co. Bar Asn, 66. Mil. Serv: Entered as Ens, Navy Res, 42, released as Lt.(sg), 46, after serv. in Landing Craft Flotilla, European and Pac. Theatres, 43-46; Three Battle Stars. Mem: Raleigh Co, W.Va. and Am. Bar Asns; Mem, W.Va. State Bar; Lions; Elks; Black Knight Country Club. Rel: Catholic. Legal Res: 901 S. Oakwood Ave, Beckley, W.Va. 25801. Mailing Add: Box 1663, Beckley, W.Va. 25801.

SPARKMAN, JOHN J. D
U.S. Sen, Ala.
b. Hartselle, Ala, 12/20/99; s. Whitten J. Sparkman and Julia Mitchell Kent S; m. 6/2/23 to Ivo Hall; c. Julia Ann (Mrs. Tazewell Shepard, Jr). Educ: Univ. Ala, A.B, 21, LL.B, 23, A.M, 24, LL.D, 58. LL.D, Spring Hill Col, 56, Auburn Univ, 60. Polit. & Govt. Pos: U.S. Cmnr, 30-31; U.S. Del, Fifth Session UN Gen. Assembly; U.S. Rep, Ala, 37-46; U.S. Sen, Ala, 46-; Dem. cand. for Vice President, U.S, 52. Bus. & Prof. Pos: Instr, Huntsville Col, 25-28; attorney, 25-30; partner, Taylor, Richardson & Sparkman, 30-36; trustee, Am. Univ. and Athens Col. Mil. Serv: Army, World War I, Col, Organized Res. Mem: Huntsville C. of C; Mason; Eastern Star; WOW; Kiwanis. Rel: Methodist. Mailing Add: Senate Office Bldg, Washington, D.C. 20510.

SPARKS, BILLY SCHLEY D
b. Marshall, Mo, 10/1/23; s. John Sparks and Clarinda Schley S; m. 5/14/46 to Dorothy Stone; c. Stephen Stone, Susan Lee and John David. Educ: Mass. Inst. Tech, 43-44; Harvard Col, A.B, 45 and Harvard Law Sch, LL.B, 49. Polit. & Govt. Pos: Mem, Mission Planning Cmn, Mission, Kans, 56-63; precinct committeeman, Johnson Co. Dem. Party, 56-; mem, Sch. Bd, Dist. 110, Shawnee-Mission, Kans, 63-69, pres. and v.pres; mem, Sch. Bd. Dist, 512, Shawnee-Mission, 69-; mem. legis. coun, Nat. Asn. of Sch. Bd, 69- Bus. & Prof. Pos: Attorney and partner, Linde, Thomson, Van Dyke, Fairchild & Langworty, 58- Mil. Serv: Entered as Pvt, Army Air Force, 43, released as Lt, 66, after serv. in China-India-Burma Theater; China-India-Burma Campaign Ribbon with 4 Battle Stars. Publ: Various Legal Articles. Mem: Am, Mo. and Kansas City Bar Asns; Lawyers Asn. of Kansas City; Harvard Sch. & Scholarship Cmt; Legis. Cmt, Kansas City C. of C, 58- Rel: Christian Church. Legal Res: 8517 W. 90th Terr, Shawnee-Mission, Kans. 66212. Mailing Add: Union National Bank Bldg, Kansas City, Mo. 64106.

SPARKS, DONN EVERETT R
b. Marion, Ind, 8/19/29; s. Mainel E. Sparks and Juanita M. Hudson S; m. 1/3/54 to Mary Lou Gorman; c. Douglas Lee, Robert Ray, Jeffrey Dean, Mark Everett, Todd Allan and Jill Marie. Educ: Purdue Univ, B.S, 58; pres, Indust. Econ. Club. Polit. & Govt. Pos: Rep. precinct committeeman, Clark Co, Wash, 62-; co. co-chmn, Dan Evans for Gov, 64; regional coordinator, Nixon for pres, 68; del, Rep. Nat. Conv, 68. Bus. & Prof. Pos: Br. mgr, First Fed. Savings & Loan Asn, Vancouver, 60-63; mgr, Columbia Savings & Loan Asn, 63-64; v.pres, Equitable Savings & Loan Asn, Portland, Ore, 68- Mil. Serv: Entered as Pvt, Air Force, 50, released as S/Sgt, 54, after serv. in Air Police Squadron, Strategic Air Command, 50-54; UN Serv. Ribbon; Korean Serv. Ribbon; Good Conduct Medal; Nat. Defense Ribbon. Mem: Am. Savings & Loan Inst; U.S. Savings & Loan League; sen, Jr. Chamber Int; Portland C. of C; Ore. Advert. Club. Jr. First Citizen, Vancouver, 61. Rel: Quaker. Mailing Add: 9711 S.E. Boulder Ave, Vancouver, Wash. 98664.

SPARKS, E. CLYDE D
Chmn, Kent Co. Dem. Cent. Cmt, Md.
b. Chestertown, Md, 1/9/17; s. H. Finley Sparks and Rachael V. Vansant S; m. 2/26/62 to Anna Mae Gsell; c. Rachael Virginia, Charlotte Ann and Christine Cecilia. Educ: Chestertown High Sch, Md. Polit. & Govt. Pos: Substitute and temporary rural mail carrier, U.S. Post Off, Chestertown, Md, 47-55; substitute elec. supvr, Kent Co. Dem. Party, 50-54; chmn, Kent. Co. Dem. Cent. Cmt, 54- Bus. & Prof. Pos: Farmer, Chestertown, Md, 37-61; dist. sales mgr, Pioneer Corn Co, 54-66. Mem: Kent Co. Farm Bur. Rel: Roman Catholic. Mailing Add: R.D. 2, Chestertown, Md. 21620. (1967)

SPARKS, HARRY MAGEE D
b. Livingston, Ky, 7/27/07; s. Robert Absalom Sparks and Lena Bentley S; m. 6/4/34 to Lois Ogden Stiles; c. Harry M, Jr, Phillip Stiles and Susan Nunnelley. Educ: Univ. Ky, Ed.D, 54 and M.A, 41; Transylvania Col, A.B, 30; Phi Delta Kappa; Kappa Delta Pi; Kappa Alpha. Polit. & Govt. Pos: Supt. Pub. Instr, Ky, 64-68. Bus. & Prof. Pos: Adv. to Cmnr. of Educ, P.L. 89-10, Title III, 65-66; educ. consult, W. German Govt, 64; pres, Murray State Univ, 68- Mil. Serv: Entered as Lt.(jg), Navy, 44, released as Lt. Comdr, 46. Mem: Pres, Ky. Asn. of Cols. and Sec. Schs, 54; past pres. and life mem, Ky. Educ. Asn. Rel: Methodist. Legal Res: 1510 W. Main St, Murray, Ky. 42071. Mailing Add: President's Office, Murray State University, Murray, Ky. 42071.

SPARKS, JOHN DUDLEY, JR. R
Chmn, Md. Rep. State Cent. Cmt.
b. Chester, Md, 2/7/34; s. John Dudley Sparks, Sr. and Audrey Harris S; m. 11/24/55 to Mary Jane Golt; c. Lauren Jane and Dudley Golt. Educ: Wash. Col, A.B, 56; Lambda Chi Alpha. Polit. & Govt. Pos: Chmn, Md. Rep. State Cent. Cmt, 68- Bus. & Prof. Pos: Owner and operator, Tastee Freez Drive-in, 58-68; teacher, Queen Anne's Co, Md, 56-69. Mil. Serv: Entered as Pvt, Army Nat. Guard, 57, released as SP-3, 68. Mem: Nat. Educ. Asn; Md. State and Queen Anne Co. Teachers Asns; Lions; VFW; Kent Island Methodist Men. Rel: Methodist. Mailing Add: Harbor View, Chester, Md. 21619.

SPARKS, SHERMAN PAUL R
Chmn, Rockwall Co. Rep. Party, Tex.
b. Toledo, Ill, 1/23/09; s. Ernest Melvin Sparks and Nancy Jane Keller S; m. 1/23/65 to Joyce Marie Patterson; c. James Earl, Randal Paul, Robert Dale and Paul David. Educ: Univ. Ill, B.S, 32, M.S, 38; Kirksville Col. of Osteopathy & Surgery, D.O, 45; Psi Sigma Alpha; Atlas Club; Alpha Phi Omega. Polit. & Govt. Pos: Rockwall Co. Coordinator, Civil Defense, Tex, 50-66; chmn, Rockwall Co. Rep. Party, 63- Mem: V.pres, Tex. Asn. of Osteopathic Physicians & Surgeons, 53-54, trustee, 51-53, pres, Dist. 5, 50 and pres, Dallas Co. Div, 47; Am. Osteopathic Asn; Hella Shrine; past pres, Rockwall C. of C, PTA, Band Boosters and Centennial Celebration. Inventor of Photoeletric Turbidimeter for bacterial determinations. Rel: Methodist. Mailing Add: 106 N. Second, Rockwall, Tex. 75087.

SPARKS, THOMAS EVERETT D
Ark. State Rep.
b. Crossett, Ark, 8/15/11; s. Albert Theodore Sparks and Clara Morton S; m. 6/29/40 to Julia Benton; c. Thomas Everett, Jr, Julianna (Mrs. Joseph T. Dickey) and Helen Benton. Educ: Hendrix Col, B.A, 32; Wash. and Lee Univ, LL.B, 35. Polit. & Govt. Pos: Ark. State Rep, 67- Bus. & Prof. Pos: Gen. practice of law, Fordyce, Ark, 35-; secy-treas, Benton Realty Co, Inc, Benton Furniture Co, Inc, Benton Hardware Co, Inc. and Benton Casket Mfg. Co, Inc, 47-60, pres, 60-; owner, Morton Abstract Co, Fordyce, Ark. Mil. Serv: Entered as Lt.(jg), Navy, 43, released as Lt, 46, after serv. in West. Pac, 43-45. Mem: Ark. and Am. Bar Asns; Ark. Trial Lawyers Asn; C. of C; Rotary; Fordyce Country Club; Dallas Co. Indust. Develop. Corp; Country Club Little Rock; The Capital Club. Rel: Methodist. Mailing Add: R.F.D. 2, Fordyce, Ark. 71742.

SPARLING, JAMES M, JR. R
b. Saginaw, Mich, 8/8/28; s. James Sparling and Mystle Hashbarger; m. 6/3/50 to Esther Mary Haar; c. James M, III, Jana Sue, Tamra Lynn. Educ: Alma Col. Polit. & Govt. Pos: Admin. Asst, U.S. Rep, James Harvey, Mich, 61- Mil. Serv: Journ. 3/C, USN, 46-48; Victory, Am, N. Atlantic Ribbons. Mem: Elks; pres, Mich. State Soc, 66; Zeta Sigma. Col. basketball. Legal Res: Saginaw, Mich. Mailing Add: 6104 Sherborn Lane, Springfield, Va. 22150.

SPARROW, DAVID JOHN D
b. Detroit, Mich, 7/5/27; James Percy Sparrow and Elizabeth Stuart Robb S; m. 8/27/49 to Dona Patricia Waters; c. Susan Patricia, Nancy Ann and Joanne Elizabeth. Educ: Highland Park Community Col, 47-48; Detroit Col. of Law, LL.B, 51, J.D, 68; Delta Theta Phi. Polit. & Govt. Pos: Del, Dem. Nat. Conv, 68; mem, Bd. of Educ, Oakland Schs, Mich, 69- Bus. & Prof. Pos: Partner, Rowin & Sparrow, Attorneys, 51-; pres, Plaza Investment Co, 62- Mil. Serv: Entered as Pvt, Army Air Force, 45, released as Cpl, 47. Mem: State Bar of Mich; Detroit and Am. Bar Asns; Nat. Asn. of Real Estate Boards; Bloomfield Open Hunt Club. Rel: Episcopal. Mailing Add: 5080 Tootmoor, Bloomfield Hills, Mich. 48013.

SPATT, MOSES R
V.Chmn, Kings Co. Rep. Cmt, N.Y.
b. Brooklyn, N.Y, 2/21/96; s. Jacob Spatt and Esther Kapner S; m. 12/24/19 to Rena Silverstein; c. Milton E. and Irene E. (Mrs. Morse). Educ: N.Y. Univ, D.D.S, 16. Polit. & Govt. Pos: V.chmn. and chmn. finance Cmt, Kings Co. Rep. Cmt, N.Y, currently; cmnr, Interstate Sanitation Cmn, 45- Bus. & Prof. Pos: Past pres, Brooklyn Jewish Center, N.Y; pres, Comet Operating Corp, currently; Jewish Hosp. and Med. Center, currently. Mil. Serv: Entered as Pvt, Army, 18, released as Pfc. Mem: Past pres. and founder, Brooklyn Jewish Commun. Coun; Mason; Unity Club; Nonpareil Club. Rel: Jewish. Legal Res: 505 East. Parkway, Brooklyn, N.Y. 11216. Mailing Add: 16 Court St, Brooklyn, N.Y. 11201.

SPAULDING, EMERSON O. R
b. Cambridge, Vt, 2/15/78; wid; c. three sons and four daughters. Educ: Fletcher dist. sch. Polit. & Govt. Pos: Road cmnr, Fairfield, Vt, 28-30, selectman, 38-41; Vt. State Rep, 53-66. Bus. & Prof. Pos: Farmer. Rel: Methodist; Trustee, Binghamville Church. Mailing Add: R.D. 2, East Fairfield, Vt. 05455. (1967)

SPAULDING, JOSIAH A. R
Chmn, Mass. Rep. State Cmt.
b. Worcester, Mass, 1923; m. to Helen Bowdoin. Educ: Yale Univ, B.A; Columbia Univ. Law Sch, LL.B. Polit. & Govt. Pos: Chmn, Mass. Rep. State Cmt, 67-; del, Rep. Nat. Conv, 68. Bus. & Prof. Pos: Partner, Bingham, Dana & Gould, Boston, 58- Mil. Serv: 2nd Lt, Marines, World War II, Capt, Korea, serv. as Naval Aviator; Distinguished Flying Cross; four Air Medals; Squadron Citation. Legal Res: Gale's Point, Manchester, Mass. 01944. Mailing Add: 73 Tremont St, Boston, Mass. 02108.

SPAULDING, ROMA ALMA R
N.H. State Rep.
b. Woodstock, Vt, 10/16/14; d. John Wilhelm Magnusson and Eveline Bourdon M; m. 12/24/37 to Bedford Thomas Spaulding; c. Diane and Cynthia (Mrs. Douglas Dutilley). Educ: High sch. Polit. & Govt. Pos: Supvr. checklist, Rep. Party, Claremont, N.H, 63-, city chairwoman, 65-; N.H. State Rep, Ward Two, 67-, v.chmn, pub. health and welfare cmt, N.H. House Rep, 69-; mem, N.H. State Rep. Cmt, 69- Mem: Claremont Women's Rep. Club; Claremont Hist. Soc. Rel: Methodist. Mailing Add: 8 Maple Ave, Claremont, N.H. 03743.

SPEARE, WILLIAM JAMES D
Mont. State Rep.
b. Sioux City, Iowa, 2/14/29; s. Edwin C. Speare and Henrietta Troup S; m. 10/2/54 to Shirley Ruth Mutbach; c. Margaurete Ann and Heather Joy. Educ: Mont. State Univ, 47-49; Univ. Mont, LL.B, 52; Phi Delta Phi. Polit. & Govt. Pos: Co. attorney, Yellowstone Co, Mont, 59-65; Mont. State Rep, Dist. Nine, 69- Bus. & Prof. Pos: Partner, Felt, Speare, & Thompson, 65- Mil. Serv: Entered as 2nd Lt, Air Force, 52, released as Capt, 56. Mem: Am, Mont. and Yellowstone Co. Bar Asns; Elks; Mason. Rel: Episcopal. Legal Res: 2436 Teton Ave, Billings, Mont. 59102. Mailing Add: 117 N. 27th St, Billings, Mont. 59101.

SPEARMAN, CRAWFORD HENRY, JR. D
Okla. State Rep.
b. Oklahoma City, Okla, 4/27/30; s. Crawford Henry Spearman and Freda Stewart S; m. 2/10/59 to Shirley Ann Landon; c. Mark Landon, Tina Suzzette and John Paul. Educ: Cent. State Col, B.A, 52; Univ. Okla. Law Sch, LL.B, 55; Arena Club. Polit. & Govt. Pos: City judge, Edmond, Okla, 64; Okla. State Rep, currently. Mem: Okla. and Am. Bar Asns. Nat. Debate Champion, 51; Nat. Extemporaneous Champion, 52. Rel: Presbyterian. Mailing Add: 333 Memory Lane, Edmond, Okla. 73034.

SPEARS, FRANKLIN SCOTT D
b. San Antonio, Tex, 8/20/31; s. J. Franklin Spears and Lois Louise Harkey S; m. 9/6/52 to Jo Ann Hyltin; c. Franklin Scott, Jr, Carleton Blaise and John Adrian Lucius. Educ: South. Methodist Univ, 48-50; Univ. of Tex, B.B.A. and LL.B, 54; Friars Soc; Phi Alpha Delta; pres, Students' Asn, 53-54; Silver Spurs; Kappa Alpha. Polit. & Govt. Pos: Tex. State Rep, 59-61; Tex. State Sen, 61-67; Judge, 57th Judicial Dist. Court of Tex, 68- Bus. & Prof. Pos: Attorney-at-law, 54-68. Mil. Serv: Entered as 2nd Lt, Army, 55, released as 1st Lt, 56, after serv. in Tenth Inf. Div, Germany. Mem: San Antonio, Tex. and Am. Bar Asns; VFW; Farm Bur; Boy Scouts; YMCA; Jaycees. Barbershop Quartet, SPEBSQSA, Int. Champion, 69; Selected Outstanding Young Man in San Antonio, San Antonio Jaycees, 62. Rel: Protestant. Legal Res: 11406 Destiny, San Antonio, Tex. 78216. Mailing Add: Bexar Co. Courthouse, San Antonio, Tex. 78204.

SPEARS, LaVERNE H. R
Kans. State Rep.
b. Wamego, Kans, 9/20/06; s. Herbert Spears and Flora S; m. 12/3/27 to Edna Iona Vilven; c. Helen L. (Mrs. Eugene Seigel) and Ruth E. (Mrs. William Larson). Educ: Kans. State Univ, B.S, 36; Lambda Chi Alpha. Polit. & Govt. Pos: Mayor, Rossville, Kans, 55-65; mem. bd. dir, Cross Creek Watershed Dist, 59-69; pres, League Kans. Munic, 62-63; chmn, Capitol Area Planning Cmn, 65-69; Kans. State Rep, 49th Dist, 65- Bus. & Prof. Pos: Agency mgr, Farm Bur. Mgt. Ins. Serv, 39-69; owner and operator, livestock and grain farm, owner Rossville Implement Co, and builder subdivisions, Rossville, 48-69. Mem: Mason (Past Master, Hesperian Lodge); Eastern Star (Past Patron, Amaryllis 321, Past Grand Patron, Kans, 62-63); Lions; Scottish Rite; Shrine; dir, Topeka C. of C, 69. Rel: Methodist; Trustee, Rossville United Methodist Church. Mailing Add: Rossville, Kans. 66533.

SPECKMAN, GEORGE RAYMOND D
Chmn, Clinton Co. Dem. Cmt, Mo.
b. Hannibal, Mo, 5/9/38; s. George William Speckman and Edith Geneva Inlow S; m. 8/25/57 to Eleanor Louise Kennedy; c. Cynthia Louise and George Raymond, Jr. Educ: Univ. Mo, Columbia, B.S, 59, LL.B, 63; Ruf Nex (pres); Agr. Econ. Club. Polit. & Govt. Pos: Mem, Clinton Co. Dem. Cmt, Mo, 64-; chmn, 65-; mem. Sixth Cong. Dist. Dem. Cmt, 65-; chmn. youth activities, Mo. State Dem. Cmt, 68; del, Dem. Nat. Conv, 68. Mem: Mo. and Clinton Co. Bar Asns; Bar U.S. Supreme Court; Elks; Mason. Rel: Christian Church of N.Am; Deacon, First Christian Church. Mailing Add: Route 1, Plattsburg, Mo. 64477.

SPECKMAN, LEON GEORGE R
Chmn, Massac Co. Rep. Cent. Cmt, Ill.
b. Metropolis, Ill, 9/23/09; s. Wm. G. Speckman and Jessie Cooper S; m. 7/26/42 to Marjorie Inez Ward. Educ: Metropolis Commun. High Sch. Polit. & Govt. Pos: Chmn, Massac Co. Rep. Cent. Cmt, Ill. Mil. Serv: Entered as Pvt, Army, 43, released as S/Sgt, 83 Inf, after serv. in European Theater, 46. Mem: Elks; VFW; Am. Legion. Rel: Catholic. Mailing Add: 510 E. Sixth St, Metropolis, Ill. 62960. (1967)

SPECKNER, ROBERT F. D
Polit. & Govt. Pos: Vet's. serv. officer for Jackson City, 49-50; Ind. State Rep, until 66. Bus. & Prof. Pos: Sales rep, Al-Jax Chem. Co. Mil. Serv: Navy. Mem: Rotary; Am. Legion; Elks; K. of C. Rel: Catholic. Mailing Add: R.R. 3, Seymour, Ind. 47274. (1967)

SPECTER, ARLEN R
b. Wichita, Kans, 2/12/30; s. Harry Specter and Lillie Shanin S; m. 6/14/53 to Joan Lois Levy; c. Stephen and Shanin. Educ: Univ. Okla, 47-48; Univ. Pa, B.A, 51; Yale Univ. Law Sch, LL.B, 56; Phi Beta Kappa; Delta Sigma Rho; Phi Alpha Theta; Phi Alpha Delta. Hon. LL.D, Phila. Col. of Textiles and Sci, 68. Polit. & Govt. Pos: Asst. dist. attorney, Phila, Pa, 59-63 and dist. attorney, 66-; asst. counsel, Warren Cmn, Wash, D.C, 64; spec. asst. Attorney Gen, Pa. Dept. Justice, 64-65; del, Rep. Nat. Conv, 68. Mil. Serv: Entered Air Force 51, released as 1st Lt, 53, after serv. in Off. of Spec. Invests. Publ: 'Mapp v. Ohio: Pandora's Problems for the Prosecutor,' Univ. Pa. Law Rev, 62; 'Free Press and Free Trial,' Villanova Law Rev, 66; 'Review of Conviction,' Yale Law J, 67; plus two others. Mem: Am, Pa. and Phila. Bar Asns; exec. bd. mem, Boy Scouts; bd. dirs, YMHA, YWHA, Police Athletic League and Nat. Coun. on Alcoholism, Del. Valley Area; Mason. Named Outstanding Young Man of the Year, Jr. C. of C, 64; Commun. Serv. Award, Drexel Inst, Sigma Alpha Mu, 65; B'nai B'rith Youth Serv. Award, 66; Brith Sholom Man of the Year, 67; Sons of Italy Award, Alessandroni Lodge, 68; Commun. Humanitarian Award, Morris Chapel Baptist Church, 69. Rel: Jewish. Legal Res: 3417 Warden Dr, Philadelphia, Pa. 19129. Mailing Add: Room 666, City Hall, Philadelphia, Pa. 19107.

SPECTOR, ALLEN BERNARD D
Md. State Del.
b. Baltimore, Md, 1/17/34; s. Albert Morris Spector and Jean Apple S; m. 12/25/54 to Rochelle Lichter; c. Bruce Sheldon, Stephen Lowell and Ira Ross. Educ: East. Col, A.A, 60; Mt. Vernon Sch. Law, LL.B, 62; Phi Sigma Beta; Outstanding Scholarship Award; Tau Epsilon Phi. Polit. & Govt. Pos: Dep. sheriff, Baltimore, Md, 62-63; gen. attorney, recovery br, U.S. Army Claims Serv, 62-63; Md. State Del, 66-, sponsor, Successful Abortion Law Reform, Md, 67-68. Bus. & Prof. Pos: Mgr, Spector's Retail Credit; attorney-at-law, 62-63; partner, Friedman, Friedman & Spector, 63-64; gen. partner, Friedman, Spector & Brotman, 64-65; partner, Steinberg, Spector, Brotman & Zerwitz, 65- Mil. Serv: Entered as Pvt, Army, 54, released as Pfc, 55, after serv. in Corps of Engrs; Capt, Judge Adv. Gen. Corps, Army Res, 63-; Good Conduct Medal; Overseas Serv. and European Serv. Medals. Mem: Am, Md. State and Baltimore Bar Asns; Fed. Bar Asn.(bd. mem. and chmn, cmt. law observance); East. Col. Alumni Asn; Jefferson Lodge 9, Odd Fellows; Amicable Lodge 25, AF&AM; Yedz Grotto B'rith Sholom; B'nai B'rith; Safety First Club of Md; Am. Legion; Cancer Fund; Heart Fund; Asn. Jewish Charities. Named Man of Year, Brotherhood. Rel: Jewish. Legal Res: 5740 Jonquil Ave, Baltimore, Md. 21215. Mailing Add: 10 South St, Baltimore, Md. 21202.

SPEED, JAMES DAVIS D
N.C. State Rep.
b. Louisburg, N.C, 1/30/15; s. Henry Plummer Speed and Addie Jeffreys S; m. 1947 to Martha Matthews; c. Claudia and Robert Thomas. Educ: Gold Sand High Sch, Franklin City, N.C, grad, 34. Polit. & Govt. Pos: Chmn, Franklin City Dem. Exec. Cmt, 60-64; N.C. State Rep, 61- Bus. & Prof. Pos:

Supvr. of sales, Henderson Tobacco Mkt, 48-60; farmer, tobacco warehouseman, presently. Mem: Master, Louisburg Masonic Lodge, 44-45; pres, Franklin Farm Bur, 48-49; Franklin City Bd. of Health, 48-; bd. of trustees, Franklin Mem. Hosp, 48-; v.pres, Louisburg Prod. Credit Asn; Sudan Temple Shrine. Mailing Add: Route 3, Louisburg, N.C. 27549.

SPEER, ALFRED ALTEN R
b. St. Louis, Mo, 4/12/31; s. Boyd A. Speer and Lena Lee Hoberecht S; m. 9/18/54 to Mary Anne Hedley. Educ: Wash. Univ, A.B. and J.D, 57; Phi Delta Phi; Sigma Nu. Polit. & Govt. Pos: Mo. State Rep, 12th Dist, 60-66; mem, Tech. and Adv. Rev. Cmt, St. Louis Co. Planning Cmt, 66- Bus. & Prof. Pos: Gen. practice of law, 57-; partner, Speer & Speer. Mil. Serv: Entered as 2nd Lt, Army, 54, released as 1st Lt, 56, after serv. in 1st Armored Div, U.S; Nat. Defense Ribbon. Mem: St. Louis, St. Louis Co, Mo. and Am. Bar Asns; Mo. Asn. of Trial Attorneys. Speakers Award for Outstanding Rep. in Debate, Mo. State House of Rep, 64 & 66. Rel: United Presbyterian. Mailing Add: 840 Alexandria Ave, St. Louis, Mo. 63122.

SPEER, KEITH DEMPSEY D
b. Cumberland, Ky, 11/9/26; m. to Mary Ruth Belcher. Educ: Va. Polytech. Inst; Univ. Tenn; East. Tenn. State Univ, B.S; Med. Col. of Va, D.D.S. Polit. & Govt. Pos: Va. State Del, 64-69. Bus. & Prof. Pos: Dentist. Mil. Serv: Navy, 2 years. Mem: Buchanan-Dickenson Med. Soc; S.W. Va. Dent. Soc; Va. State Dent. Asn; Am. Dent. Asn; mem. bd. dirs, Breaks Interstate Park Asn; Past Worthy Patron Eastern Star; Mason; Shrine; Buchanan C. of C. (past pres); Grundy Lions (past pres). Rel: Christian Church. Mailing Add: Box JJ, Grundy, Va. 24614. (1967)

SPEERS, FREDERIC WARDEN R
Mem, Calif. Rep. State Cent. Cmt.
b. Davenport, Iowa, 7/26/06; s. Dr. Will Frederic Speers (deceased) and Agnes Petersen S.(deceased); m. 10/12/35 to Victoria Rountree. Educ: Stanford Univ, A.B, 28; Denver Univ. Law Sch, 34-35; Sigma Delta Chi; Delta Lambda Sigma; Phi Gamma Delta. Polit. & Govt. Pos: Secy, San Diego Co. Rep. Cent. Cmt, Calif, 50-55; mem, Calif. Hwy. Cmn, 55-59; Presidential elector for Calif, 60; mem, Calif. Rep. State Cent. Cmt, 60-; mem, Nixon Finance Cmt. of San Diego Co, Calif, 68; mem, Postmaster Gen. Stamp Adv. Cmt, 69- Bus. & Prof. Pos: Reporter, Denver Post, Colo, 28-36; managing ed, Wyo. State-Tribune, Cheyenne, 36-37; publisher, North Platte Daily Bulletin, Nebr, 37-47, Daily Times-Advocate, Escondido, Calif, 47-65; bd. chmn, Palomar Savings and Loan, 50- Mil. Serv: Entered as 1st Lt, Air Force, 42, released as Maj, 46, after serv. in Sixth Bomb Group (VH), Pacific Theater, 44-46; Bronze Star; Air Medal; Two Presidential Unit Citations; Four Battle Stars. Publ: 'Behind the Datelines', 54 and 'Datelines of Trouble,' 1956, Escondido Times-Advocate; 'The Zemstvo Gazetteer' in Vol. 30 of Billig's Philatelic Handbook, 1964 (Publ. by Fritz Billig). Mem: The Royal Philatelic Society, London; Military Order of the World Wars; Am. Legion; VFW; Rotary; Elks. Commander, Northern San Diego Co. Chap, Mil. Order of the World Wars which in 68, received the Nat. Order's designation as Chapter of the Year. Rel: Presbyterian. Mailing Add: 118 N. Caroline Way, Escondido, Calif. 92025.

SPEERS, JERROLD BOND R
b. Cambridge, Mass, 6/5/41; s. Ronald Thomas Speers and Shirley Bond S; single. Educ: Colby Col, B.A, 63; Georgetown Univ, LL.B, 66; Phi Delta Theta. Polit. & Govt. Pos: Col. chmn, Maine Coun. Young Rep, 61-62, Rep. nat. committeeman, 62-63; nat. auditor, Young Rep. Nat. Fedn, 63-65; asst. to exec. secy, Maine Cmn. on Intergovt. Rels, summers 64 & 65; alternate del, Rep. Nat. Conv, 64, del, 68; secy, Maine State Senate, 67- Mem: Maine Bar Asn. Rel: Congregational. Mailing Add: Memorial Dr, Winthrop, Maine 04364. (1967)

SPEETH, HENRY WILLIAM D
b. Cleveland, Ohio, 1/9/08; s. Henry Speeth and Marie Dauster S; m. 6/30/32 to Nada Checie; c. Dr. Sheridan D, Henry Q, Christopher E. and Jeffrey J. Educ: John Marshall Sch. of Law, LL.B, 30; Delta Theta Phi. Polit. & Govt. Pos: Pres, Bd. of Co. Cmnrs, Cuyahoga Co, Ohio, 66 and Co. Cmnr, 49-; city councilman, Cleveland, 30-49. Prof. Pos: Attorney at Law, 30- Mem: Mason. Rel: Protestant. Mailing Add: 10411 Lake Ave, Cleveland, Ohio 44102. (1967)

SPENCE, FLOYD DAVIDSON R
S.C. State Sen.
b. 4/9/28; s. James William Wilson Spence and Addie Lucas S; m. 12/22/52 to Lula Hancock Drake; c. Floyd D, Jr, Zack W, Benjamin D. and Caldwell D. Educ: Univ. S.C, A.B. in eng, Law Sch, LL.B; Nat. War Col, grad. of Defense Strategy Seminar; pres, S.C. Asn. Student Govt, Student Body and Jr. Class; Omicron Delta Kappa; Kappa Sigma Kappa; Kappa Alpha Order; German Club; Compass and Chart Soc; Dean's List; YMCA and Cabinet; Block C Club; ed, S.C. Law Quarterly; chief justice, Phi Alpha Delta; v.pres, Law Fedn. and mem, Cabinet. Polit. & Govt. Pos: S.C. State Rep, Lexington Co, 56-62, mem, Judiciary Cmt, 2 terms, mem. Ways and Means Cmt, 1 term; S.C. State Sen, Dist. 22, 67-; exec. committeeman, Lexington Co. Rep. Party; del, Rep. Nat. Conv, 68. Bus. & Prof. Pos: Attorney-at-law, Callison and Spence, West Columbia, S.C. Mil. Serv: Comdr, Naval Res. Mem: Lexington Co, S.C. and Am. Bar Asns; Am. Trial Lawyers Asn; Am. Judicature Soc; Farm Bur; former dir, West Columbia-Cayce C. of C; Lexington and S.C. C. of C; former mem, Lexington Jr. C. of C; former chmn, Granby Dist. and former scoutmaster and exec. bd. mem, Cent. S.C. Coun, Boy Scouts; former v.pres, 11th Circuit and former coun-at-lg, Univ. S.C. Alumni Asn; Lexington Voiture, 40 et 8; 1st. pres, Lexington Co. Hist. Soc; S.C. Hist. Soc; co. chmn, S.C. Ment. Health Asn, 59; adv. cmt, Confederate Centennial Cmt, 59-66; S. Caroliniana Soc; Sons Confederate Vet; bd. dirs, Columbia Carillon; Naval Res. Asn; charter mem, Univ. S.C. Asn. Lettermen; Nat. Geog. Soc; Counter-Subversive Activities Cmt, S.C. Dept, Am. Legion; chmn, Joint Legis. Cmt. to Promote Am. Way of Life, 61-62; exec. cmt, Columbia Alert. Outstanding Sr, capt. track team and state record holder in mile relay event, mem. football and basketball teams and Algernon-Sydney Sullivan Award, 52, Univ. S.C; participant, numerous Anti-Communist Seminars; author and speaker on communism. Rel: Lutheran; Mem. Church Coun. and Adult Sunday Sch. Teacher, St. Peter's Lutheran Church. Mailing Add: Box 387, Lexington, S.C. 29072.

SPENCE, FOSTER HOYT R
b. Pikeville, Ky, 2/23/22; s. Vernon Roland Spence and Fonna Mae Justice S; m. 1/19/50 to Irene Johnson; c. Foster Hoyt, II and Susan Elizabeth. Educ: Ashland Jr. Col, 41-43; Univ. of Ky, B.S, 43; Univ. of Louisville, D.M.D; Delta Sigma Delta; K-Club. Polit. & Govt. Pos: Ky. State Sen, Dist. 31, 64-69. Bus. & Prof. Pos: Self employed. Mil. Serv: Entered as Pvt, Army, 43, released as Sgt, 46, after serv. in 78th Inf. Div, Co. C, First Bn, 310th Inf, ETO, 44-46; Bronze Star; Combat Inf. Badge; ETO Ribbon with 3 Battle Stars; Unit Citation Award. Mem: Ky. Col; Fraternal Order of Police, Ky; Ky. Mountain Dent. Asn; Ky. Dent. Asn; C. of C; dir, Breaks Interstate Park; Kiwanis; Mason; Pikeville Country Club; dir. Wheelwright Golf Club; Ky. Mountain Club. Rel: Presbyterian. Legal Res: 105 Cedar Lane, Pikeville, Ky. 41501. Mailing Add: Box 987, Pikeville, Ky. 41501. (1967)

SPENCE, ROBERT NOEL R
b. Hagerstown, Md, 2/19/34; s. Kenneth F. Spence and Mary Noel S; m. 11/22/56 to Connie Ann Padian; c. Robert Noel, Jr. and William Padian. Educ: Wash. & Lee Univ, B.A, 56; Univ. Md. Law Sch, LL.B, 58. Polit. & Govt. Pos: Md. State Del, 63-66. Bus. & Prof. Pos: Attorney-at-Law, 58-; spec. agent, Fed. Bur. Invest, 59-60. Mem: United Fund, Budget & Admissions Cmt. Rel: Presbyterian. Mailing Add: 107 Windsor Circle, Hagerstown, Md. 21741. (1967)

SPENCE, WILLIAM JAMES D
Mass. State Rep.
b. Brockton, Mass, 5/4/30; s. John Frederick Spence and Grace Joyce S; m. 6/13/53 to Wilma Ellen Collins; c. Jay William, Darcie Ellen, Jeffrey O'Connell and Kerry Lee. Educ: Harvard Col, A.B, 52, Grad. Sch. of Bus. Admin, M.B.A, 56; Pi Eta Club. Polit. & Govt. Pos: Mass. State Rep, 69- Bus. & Prof. Pos: Pres, The Surf Inc, Hull, 57-; mem, bd. dirs, Rockland Trust Co, Rockland, 65-; pres, Mass. Bay Lines, Inc, 67-. Mil. Serv: Ens, Navy, 52, released as Lt.(jg), 54. Mailing Add: 14 Amber Rd, Hingham, Mass. 02043.

SPENCER, ALVIE GLENN, JR. R
Chmn, Carroll Co. Rep. State Cent. Cmt, Md.
b. Patapsco, Md, 2/19/33; s. Alvie G. Spencer and Myrtle Shamer S; m. 9/17/60 to Phyllis Beaver; c. Alan Craig. Educ: Gettysburg Col, B.A, 59; Johns Hopkins Univ, B.S, 66; Sigma Pi Sigma; Sigma Chi. Polit. & Govt. Pos: Mem. precinct cmt, Rep. Party, Md, 56-; chmn, Carroll Co. Rep. State Cent. Cmt, 62-; app. by Gov. Spiro Agnew to Coun. of Higher Educ. for Md; app. by co. cmnr. to Govt. Study Cmn. for Carroll Co, 68; del, Rep. Nat. Conv, 68. Bus. & Prof. Pos: Engr, Bendix Corp, 59-62; account exec, Merrill Lynch Inc, 62- Mil. Serv: Navy, 53-55, after serv. in U.S.S. Glynn APA 239, Atlantic Fleet; hon. discharge. Mem: Baltimore Bond Club; VFW; Rotary Int; Jr. C. of C. Rel: Methodist. Mailing Add: 265 Smith Ave, Westminster, Md. 21157.

SPENCER, ANN L. R
Women's V.Chmn, Calif. Rep. State Cent. Cmt.
b. San Pedro, Calif, 9/4/14; d. William A. Lohmann and Irene Waters L; m. 7/9/65 to William Lee Spencer; c. Mary and John S. Gallagher. Educ: Univ. Calif. at Los Angeles. Polit. & Govt. Pos: Precinct chmn, Calif. Fedn. Rep. Women, Cong. Dist. 35, 58-62, Orange Co, 60-65, South. Div, 62-65 and Calif. Fedn, 63-65; alternate mem, Orange Co. Rep. Cent. Cmt, 58-66; women's v.chmn, Calif. Rep. State Cent. Cmt, 64- Mem: PTA; Property Owners Asn; Girl Scout Leader; Cub Scout Den; PTO; Job's Daughters, Red Hill Tennis Club; Irvine Coast Racquet Club. Rel: Protestant. Mailing Add: 718½ Marigold Ave, Corona del Mar, Calif. 92625. (1967)

SPENCER, ANNE H. D
b. Lynn,Mass, 5/20/19; d. Francis Michael Foley and Catherine J. Keane F; m. 2/20/41 to Lloyd J. Spencer; c. Michael John, Kathleen, Robert Lloyd and Timothy P. Educ: Classical High Sch, grad; Gen. Electric Vestibule Engr. Sch, course in Eng. Polit. & Govt. Pos: Mem. exec. bd, Essex Co. Dem. Club, Mass, 51-69; mem, Lynn City Dem. Cmt, 56-69; Gubernatorial coordinator for Mass, 62-66; mem, Mass. Dem. State Cmt, 64-68; mem, Platform Cmt. and Rules Cmt, Mass. State Dem. Conv, 66; State Forum coordinator for Essex Co, 66; del. & secy, Mass. Del, Dem. Nat. Conv, 68. Bus. & Prof. Pos: Housewife, 25 years; secy, Co. Cmnrs, Superior Court House, Salem, 66-69. Mem: Past secy, K. of C. Women's Orgn; D. of Isabella; St. Mary's Sodality. Rel: Roman Catholic. Mailing Add: 243 Linwood St, Lynn, Mass. 01905.

SPENCER, ARTHUR CONOVER R
Exec. dir, N.J. Rep. State Cmt.
b. Orange, N.J, 9/30/27; s. Arthur Wilson Spencer and Jean A. Burns S; m. 1/26/57 to Marie D. Barnes; c. Elaine, Michael and Kevin. Educ: Wooster Sch, Danbury Conn.(Prep), 1 year; Columbia Univ, 2 years. Polit. & Govt. Pos: Dir. and v.chmn, N.J. Young Rep. Bd. Dirs, 66-69; exec. dir, N.J. Rep. State Cmt, 66-; dir, N.J. Nixon-Agnew Campaign Cmt, 68; secy. to majority, N.Y. State Assembly, 68-; cmnr, Somerset Co. Libr, 68-; dep. sheriff, Somerset Co, 68- Mil. Serv: Entered as Pvt, Marines, 45, released as Pfc, 46; Area Serv. Ribbon. Mem: Nat. Press Club; pres, N.J. Legis. and State House correspondents Club, 66. Rel: Roman Catholic. Mailing Add: Sunset Lake, R.D. 1, Basking Ridge, N.J. 07920.

SPENCER, EDWARD L, JR. R
Chmn, Lee Co. Rep. Exec. Cmt, Ala.
b. Loachapoka, Ala. 9/8/30; s. Edward L. Spencer and Florence Rowell S; m. 9/8/53 to Ruth Priester; c. Edward Lee, III, Bruce Steven and Sandra Jean. Educ: Auburn Univ, B.S, 52; Univ. Col. of North Staffordshire, Fulbright Scholar, 53. Polit. & Govt. Pos: Chmn, Lee Co. Rep. Exec. Cmt, Ala, currently. Bus. & Prof. Pos: Owner, E.L. Spencer Lumber Co. Mil. Serv: Entered as 2nd Lt, Air Force, 52, released as 1st Lt, after serv. in 406 Fighter Wing, USAFE, 56. Mem: Fraternal, Civic Clubs. Rel: Presbyterian. Legal Res: Magnolia Ave, Auburn, Ala. Mailing Add: Box 190, Auburn, Ala. 36830. (1967)

SPENCER, GEORGE LLOYD D
b. Sarcoxie, Mo, 3/27/93; s. George Spencer and Luella Riley S; m. 11/26/19 to Bun Hays; c. Hilda Kim (deceased). Educ: Henderson Col, Ark.

Polit. & Govt. Pos: U.S. Sen, Ark, 41-43; dir, Southwest Ark. Water Dist, 58- Bus. & Prof. Pos: Cashier, First Nat. Bank, Hope, Ark, 24-38, pres, 38-65 and chmn. bd, 65- Mil. Serv: Seaman 2/C, Navy 18; Lt. Comdr.(Ret), Naval Res. Mem: Mason; Am. Legion; Ark. Farm. Bur. Rel: Methodist. Legal Res: 401 S. Spruce St, Hope, Ark. 71801. Mailing Add: c/o First National Bank, Hope, Ark. 71801.

SPENCER, HARRY A. R
Justice, Supreme Court of Nebr.
b. Bishops Walton, Eng, 9/16/03; s. Richard Spencer and Mary Ellen Richardson S; m. 6/28/25 to Leone Eggenberg; c. Pagean (Mrs. Hugh Carter), Harry A, Jr, Marlene D.(Mrs. Kenneth Mansfield), Leone (Mrs. Neal Harlan), Terry L. and Victor R. Educ: Univ. Nebr, A.B, 29; Univ. Nebr. Sch. Law, LL.B. cum laude, 30, J.D, 68; Order of the Coif; Acacia; Delta Theta Phi. Polit. & Govt. Pos: Del, Rep. Nat. Conv, 36 & 40; co. judge, Lancaster Co, Nebr, 45-52; dist. judge, 52-61; justice, Supreme Court of Nebr, 61- Mem: Lincoln Bar Asn.(pres, 46); Nebr. State Bar Asn.(v.pres, 46-47, exec. coun, 50-60); Am. Bar Asn.(resolutions cmt, exec. cmt. and coun, sect. judicial admin, adv. cmt, fair trial and free press, exec. cmt, appellate judges' asn); Lincoln Traffic Cmn.(chmn); Lincoln Coun. Churches (pres); Elks (Justice Subordinate Forum); Lincoln Univ. Club; AF&AM (Past Grand Master); RAM (Past Grand High Priest); Shrine (Potentate); Bd. Nebr. Masonic Home; Mason (33°); DeMolay; Job's Daughters (Assoc. Grand Guardian); Nebr-Iowa Dist. Kiwanis (past gov); Kiwanis Int.(chmn. resolutions cmt. and cmt. achievement). Good Govt. Award, Lincoln Jr. C. of C; Cross of Honor and Hon. Legion Honor, DeMolay. Rel: Methodist. Legal Res: 1500 Crestview Dr, Lincoln, Nebr. 68506. Mailing Add: State House, Lincoln, Nebr. 68509.

SPENCER, ROY L. R
Mich. State Rep.
b. Attica, Mich, 9/10/19; m. 8/8/42 to Irene Joan Nagy; c. Linda, Richard, Darlene and Rodger. Polit. & Govt. Pos: Mich. State Rep, 60-; former twp. clerk and supvr, Attica, Mich; former v.chmn, Lapeer Co. Rep. Cmt. Bus. & Prof. Pos: Poultry farmer. Mil. Serv: Capt, Army, 41-46; serv. in 104th Inf. Div, 413th Inf. Regt, Germany, France, Belgium and Holland. Mem: F&AM; Eastern Star; Mason. Rel: Methodist. Mailing Add: 3355 Newark Rd, Attica, Mich. 48412. (1967)

SPENCER, W. THOMAS D
b. Crawfordsville, Ind, 8/6/28; s. Walter White Spencer and Jean Springer S; single. Educ: Wabash Col, 46-47; Univ. Miami, A.B, 50, LL.B, 56; Pi Kappa Delta; Omicron Delta Kappa; Iron Arrow; Beta Theta Pi; Alpha Phi Omega; Phi Delta Phi; pres, student body govt, Univ. Miami, 56-57. Polit. & Govt. Pos: Mem. bd. dirs, Dade Co. Young Dem, Fla, 60-61; Fla. State Rep, 63-66; Fla. State Sen, 66-68. Bus. & Prof. Pos: Assoc, Dean, Adams & Fischer, Miami, Fla, 57-63; attorney-at-law, Spencer & Taylor, 63- Mil. Serv: Entered as OSSICEA cand, Navy, 52, released as Lt.(jg), 55, after serv. as Exec. Officer on U.S.S. Kishwaukee, 53-55; Lt, Navy Res, currently. Mem: Dade Co, Am. and Fla. Bar Asns; Am. Judicature Soc; C. of C; Crime Cmn. Gr. Miami; Coral Gables Country Club. Rel: Presbyterian. Legal Res: 2472 Inagua Ave, Miami, Fla. 33133. Mailing Add: 1105 Biscayne Bldg, Miami, Fla. 33130.

SPENCER, WARREN H. R
Pa. State Rep.
b. Wellsboro, Pa, 8/22/21; s. Stacey S. Spencer and Mildred Emberger S; m. to Julia Thomas; c. one. Educ: Dickinson Col, A.B; Dickinson Sch. of Law, LL.B; basketball; Phi Delta Theta; Omicron Delta Kappa. Polit. & Govt. Pos: Pa. State Rep, 62- Bus. & Prof. Pos: Attorney. Mil. Serv: Sgt, 502nd Parachute Inf, 101st Airborne Div, 41-45. Mem: Superior and Supreme Courts of Pa; Tioga Co. Bar Asn; Am. Legion. Mailing Add: 54 Walnut St, Wellsboro, Pa. 16901. (1967)

SPENO, EDWARD J. R
N.Y. State Sen.
b. Syracuse, N.Y, 9/23/20; m. to Audrey Bernichon; c. four. Educ: Niagara Univ; Cornell Law Sch, LL.B. Polit. & Govt. Pos: N.Y. State Sen, 54-; Rep. committeeman for Seventeenth Elec. Dist. of Nassau; exec. cmt. of Nassau Co. East Meadow Rep. Club. Bus. & Prof. Pos: Attorney; partner of Speno, Goldberg, Moore and Margules. Mem: Kiwanis; C. of C; Am. Legion; VFW; K. of C; Elks; Interfaith Coun; Nassau Co. Boy Scout Coun; past dir, Nassau Co. Bar Asn; Nassau Co. Cerebral Palsy Asn; Cent. Island Ment. Health Bd; hon. chmn. of bd. of Nassau Co. Cancer Soc; chmn, Hofstra Univ. Coun; trustee, Niagara Univ. Mailing Add: 863 Richmond Rd, East Meadow, N.Y. 11554.

SPERAT, GUY JOSEPH, JR. D
b. Pottstown, Pa, 2/11/27; s. Guy Sperat and Concetta Morello S; m. 4/23/49 to Gloria Marie Wagg; c. Donna Jean and Marie Elena. Educ: Pierce Sch. Bus. Admin, Admin. Acct. Cert, 51; Sigma Gamma Omega. Polit. & Govt. Pos: Mem, Pottstown Borough Coun, Pa, 54-66, pres, 66; justice of the peace, Borough of Pottstown, 56-62, ward committeeman, 56-64, tax collector, 66- Bus. & Prof. Pos: Mgr, Doehler-Jarvis Pottstown, 51-66; acct, self-employed, 51- Mil. Serv: Entered as Seaman 2/C, Navy, 44, released as RM 3/C, 46, after serv. in European and Pac. Theaters, 45-46; Pac. and Am. Theater Ribbons; Victory Medal. Mem: Elks; Am. Legion; K. of C.(4°); Arch. Ryan Gen. Assembly, Phila, Pa; Maria Assunta & St. Gabriel Lodges, Pottstown, Pa. Rel: Roman Catholic. Mailing Add: 103 S. Franklin St, Pottstown, Pa. 19464.

SPERLING, JACK IRVING R
Alderman, Chicago, Ill.
b. N.Y.C, 6/1/11; s. Louis Sperling and Dora Fialkoff S; m. 12/29/35 to Dorothy Weiss; c. Judith (Mrs. Filler), Suzanne (Mrs. Schiller) and Robert. Educ: Crane Jr. Col, 2½ years; DePaul Univ. Sch. Law, 1½ years; Chicago-Kent Col. Law, LL.B. Polit. & Govt. Pos: Alderman, 50th Ward, Chicago, Ill, 55-; del, Rep. Nat. Conv, 68. Bus. & Prof. Pos: Practice of law, 33- Mil. Serv: Entered as Lt.(jg), Naval Res, 43, released as Lt.(sg), 46, after serv. in Pac. and European Theatres; Lt. Comdr, Navy Res.(Ret); Combat Star; Mediterranean-Pac. Theatre Ribbon. Mem: Chicago, Am. and Ill. Bar Asns; B'nai B'rith; Am. Legion. Rel: Hebrew. Legal Res: 2616 W. Jarvis, Chicago, Ill. 60645. Mailing Add: 33 N. Dearborn, Chicago, Ill. 60602.

SPEROS, GUS D
N.C. State Rep.
b. Maxton, N.C, 10/6/23; s. Thomas Speros and Mary Aftanas S; m. 1/17/47 to Christine Lee; c. Thomas Lee, Michael Gus, Steven Eugene and Catherine Anne. Educ: Maxton High Sch, N.C, grad, 40. Polit. & Govt. Pos: Cmnr, Maxton, N.C, 51-53; mem, N.C. Adv. Coun. Small Bus. Admin, 64-68; N.C. State Rep, 24th Dist, 69- Bus. & Prof. Pos: Pres, Speros Construction Co, Inc, 46-; owner, Speros Supply, 53; v.pres, First Realty Corp, 62; pres, Jackson Serv. Co, 67; pres, Defiance of the Carolinax, Inc, 67; mem. bd. dirs, Quehele Corp, 67; pres, Maxton Indust. Develop. Corp. Mil. Serv: Entered as Pvt, Army, 43, released as Sgt, 46, after serv. in 870th Signal Combat Unit. Mem: Asn. Gen. Contractors of Am; Nat. Bd. Realtors; C. of C, Laurinburg and Lumberton; Civitan Club, Maxton. Selected to testify before U.S. Sen, 87th and 88th Cong. for Small Bus. Set-Aside in Construction, 62 & 63. Rel: Presbyterian. Legal Res: 322 Shoe Heel St, Maxton, N.C. 28364. Mailing Add: P.O. Drawer 878, Maxton, N.C. 28364.

SPERRAZZO, V. JAMES D
Mem, Calif. Dem. State Cent. Cmt.
b. Enfield, Conn, 2/15/25; s. Thomas Sperrazzo and Maria S; m. 2/2/52 to Kathryn Shaker; c. Monica, Maria and Luisa. Educ: Ill. Inst. of Tech, B.S.E.E, 45; Univ. Ill, Urbana, M.S. in E.E, 47; Univ. Calif, Los Angeles, 2 years. Polit. & Govt. Pos: Pres, Downey Dem. Club, 65 & 66; treas, 23rd Cong. Dist. Dem. Coord. Coun, 66; bd. dirs. and mem, 52nd Assembly Dist. Dem. Coord. Coun, 67-69; Dem. cand, U.S. House Rep, 23rd Cong. Dist, 68; mem, Calif. Dem. State Cent. Cmt, 68- Bus. & Prof. Pos: Proj. mgr, Autonetics, Downey, Calif, 54-60; mkt. mgr, Hughes Aircraft Co, Culver City, 66-69, opers. mgr, 69- Mil. Serv: Entered as A/S, Navy, 43, released as Seaman 2/C, 45. Publ: Electronic Equivalent of Lattice Network, private publisher, 47. Mem: Inst. Electronic & Elec. Engrs; Am. Legion. Commendation for 'Proj. Engr, Navigation Equip. for Hist. North Pole Voyages of Nautilus Submarine. Rel: Catholic. Mailing Add: 10309 Downey Ave, Downey, Calif. 90241.

SPERRY, ALLEN R. D
S.Dak. State Sen.
b. Langford, S.Dak, 7/13/02; s. Allen Harry Sperry and Ida Steffen S; m. to Marjorie Jones; c. James and Marian (Mrs. Miller). Educ: North. State Col, 3 years; Pi Kappa Delta. Polit. & Govt. Pos: Former mem, sch. bd, twp. bd. and Brown City Exten. Bd; S.Dak. State Sen, 65-66 & 69- Bus. & Prof. Pos: Farmer, presently. Mem: Pres, S.Dak. Wheat Growers Asn, Aberdeen. Rel: Methodist. Mailing Add: Bath, S.Dak. 57427.

SPERRY, KENNETH C. R
Chmn, Edwards Co. Rep. Party, Ill.
b. West Salem, Ill, 1/9/06; s. M. Lee Sperry and Minerva I. Shelby S; m. 10/10/31 to Goldie M. Copley. Educ: West Salem Commun. High Sch, grad, 24. Polit. & Govt. Pos: Hwy. equip. operator, State of Ill, 41-46; field investr, State Ill. Dept. Finance, 55-61; chmn, Edwards Co. Rep. Party, 58- Bus. & Prof. Pos: Owner, Grocery Store, 50-55 and mgr, 62-67. Mil. Serv: Entered as A/S, Navy, 43, released as Specialist-X, 45, after serv. in Norfolk, Va. Mem: AF&AM; Am. Legion Post 658; Rotary. Rel: Protestant. Mailing Add: 110 S. Broadway, West Salem, Ill. 62476.

SPERRY, RALPH RUSSELL D
b. Owosso, Mich, 3/15/28; s. Frank Sperry and Gertrude Watson S; m. 9/18/54 to Clarice Louise Watson; c. Anne Marie, Jo Ellen, Guy Gordon, Lee Richard, Lyn S, Tim A. and Thom M. Educ: Mich. State Univ, B.A, 54; Detroit Col. of Law, LL.B, 58; Sigma Nu Phi. Polit. & Govt. Pos: Pub. adminstr, Ogemaw Co, Mich, 60-; closing attorney, Ogemaw Co. Farmers Home Admin, 61-; chmn, Ogemaw Co. Dem. Cmt, 62-66; mem, Sch. Reorganization Cmt, Ogemaw Co, 65; Bd. of Control, Norcap, 65; pres, 7-Cap, Inc, 66. Bus. & Prof. Pos: Pres, 34th Judicial Bar Asn, 63-64. Mil. Serv: Entered as Pvt, Marine Corps, 46, released as Sgt, 49, after serv. in 1st Marine Div. Mem: Mich. State Bar Asn. Rel: Protestant. Mailing Add: 105 N. Burgess, West Branch, Mich. 48661.

SPESSARD, ROBERT WOODS D
Va. State Del.
b. Roanoke, Va, 12/11/15; m. to Esther Brame Proffit. Educ: Wash. and Lee Univ, LL.B. Polit. & Govt. Pos: Va. State Del, 66-; mem, Va. State Water Control Bd, 68- Bus. & Prof. Pos: Lawyer. Mem: Roanoke Country Club. Chosen Boss of the Year, 64, by the Nat. Secy. Asn.(Int), Roanoke Chap. Rel: Presbyterian; Elder, Salem Presbyterian Church; mem, Men's Work, Montgomery Presbytery. Mailing Add: 404 Shenandoah Bldg, Roanoke, Va. 24001.

SPICER, DON L. R
Mayor, St. Petersburg, Fla.
b. Harrisonville, Mo, 1/3/28; s. Francis Marion Spicer and Helen Martin S; m. 6/10/50 to Dorothy L. Hirst; c. Ann Hirst and Don L, Jr. Educ: Univ. Mo, B.S. in Civil Eng, 50; Tau Beta Phi; Omicron Delta Kappa; Phi Mu Epsilon; Chi Epsilon; Phi Delta Theta. Polit. & Govt. Pos: Mem, Commun. Rels Cmn, Fla, 66-67; mem, Fla. Develop. Cmn, 67-69; Mayor, St. Petersburg, Fla, 69- Bus. & Prof. Pos: Pres, DFS, Inc, St. Petersburg, Fla, 62-68 and chmn. bd, 68-69. Mil. Serv: Entered as Pvt, Army, 45, released as Cpl, 47; reentered as Cpl, Air Force, 51, released as 1st Lt, 53. Mem: Assoc. Gen. Contractors; Am. Mgt. Asn; C. of C; Cmt. of 100; Suncoasters, Inc. Rel: Protestant. Mailing Add: 416 Brightwaters Blvd. N.E, St. Petersburg, Fla. 33704.

SPICER, THOMAS T. D
b. Golden Hill, Md, 1/19/11; single. Educ: Strayer Bus. Col. Polit. & Gov. Pos: Md. State Del, 43-47, 63-67. Bus. & Prof. Pos: Farmer; timber bus. Mailing Add: Golden Hill Rd, Church Creek, Md. 21622. (1967)

SPICOLA, GUY WILLIAM D
Fla. State Rep.
b. Tampa, Fla, 2/27/38; s. Joseph G. Spicola and Alma Norona S; m. 8/19/61 to Bonnie Sharon Wallace; c. Brandon Sean and Betsy Sue. Educ: Univ. Fla, B.A, 60, LL.B, 62; Phi Delta Phi; Alpha Tau Omega; Circle K, Pre-Law Club. Polit. & Govt. Pos: Attorney, Finance and Taxation Cmts, Fla. State

House of Rep, 63; city attorney, Temple Terrace, 63-66; Fla. State Rep, 67-, mem, Finance and Taxation Cmt, Game and Fresh Water Fish Cmt, Labor Cmt, Ment. Health Cmt, State Govt. Orgn. and Efficiency Cmt, House Select Cmt. on Mass Transportation, Interim Cmt. on Mass Transportation and Interim Cmt. on Ways and Means, Fla. State House of Rep, mem, Dem. Steering Cmt, 67, Majority Whip, 69-, chmn, Subcmt. on Natural Resources and Agr, State Govt. Orgn. and Efficiency Cmt; notary pub; alternate del, Dem. Nat. Conv, 68. Mem: Tampa-Hillsborough Co, Fla. and Am. Bar Asns; Acad. of Fla. Trial Lawyers; Bay Area and Am. Trial Lawyers Asns; Am. Judicature Soc; C. of C; Jr. C. of C; Big Bros; Merrymakers Club; pres. and mem. bd. dirs, Young Dem. of Hillsborough Co, 65-66; Nat. Soc. State Legislators. Rel: Catholic. Mailing Add: 7802 53rd St, Tampa, Fla. 33610.

SPIELMAN, ALOIS B. R

Chmn, Ashland Co. Rep. Party, Wis.

b. Mandan, N.Dak, 1/29/21; s. George Henry Spielman, M.D. and Helen Berrier S; m. 11/17/53 to Dorothy Jean Swanberg; c. Thomas Karl, James Peter and Margaret Ann. Educ: Minneapolis Sch. Art, grad, 51; Univ. Minn. Exten. Div, 3 years. Polit. & Govt. Pos: Finance chmn, Morrison Co. Rep. Party, Minn, 56, treas, 57, v.chmn, 58; del, Dist. and State Rep. Conv, 58; sixth dist. mem, Minn. State Rep. Cent. Cmt, 58-60; mem, Small Bus. Admin. Regional Bd, 60; v.chmn, Anoka Co. Rep. Party, 61-66; chmn, Rep. City Conv, Anoka, 62 & 63; del, Dist. and State Rep. Conv, Wis, 66-68; v.chmn, Ashland Co. Rep. Party, 66-68, chmn, 68- Bus. & Prof. Pos: Dept. mgr, Munsingwear, Inc, Minneapolis, 51, plant mgr, Albert Lea, 53 and Little Falls, 54; dist. sales mgr, Crestliner, Inc, 60; indust. engr, Munsingwear, Inc, Minneapolis, 62, div. mgr. bowling shirts, 63, dept. mgr, 65, plant mgr, Ashland, Wis, 66- Mil. Serv: Entered as Pvt, Army, 41, released as T-5, 45, after serv. in 150th Ord. Bn. Med. Detachment, ETO, 44-45; Am. Defense Am. Theater Opers. Medal; ETO Ribbon with Five Battle Stars; Presidential Unit Citation; Good Conduct Medal; German Occup. Medal; Victory Medal. Mem: Mason; Royal Arch Mason; K.T; Shrine; Elks; Rotary Int; City Planning Cmn; mem. bd, Trinity Lutheran Hosp. amd Mem. Med. Center. Rel: Lutheran. Mailing Add: 810 MacArthur Ave, Ashland, Wis. 54806.

SPIELMAN, GORDON L. DFL

Mem, Second Cong. Dist. and Martin Co. Cmt, Dem-Farmer-Labor Party Minn.

b. New York, N.Y, 10/21/17; s. Maximillian H.B. Spielman and Agnes Michaelis S; m. 7/5/41 to Phyllis R. Posivio; c. Joseph, Gordon, Jr, Robert, Suzanne and Rose. Educ: City Col. of N.Y, evenings, 34-39. Polit. & Govt. Pos: Past dist. chmn. and mem. state exec. cmt, Affiliated Young Dem, N.Y, 36-40; v.chmn, Martin Co. Dem-Farmer-Labor Party, Minn, 48-56; mem, Gov. Coun. on Aging, 52-60; secy, Dist. Dem-Farmer-Labor Candidates Cmt, 54-60; mem, Minn. State Dem-Farmer-Labor Exec. Cmt, 56-60; dist. v.chmn, Second Cong. Dist, Dem-Farmer-Labor Party, 56-60, chmn, 60-68; chmn, State Conv. Platform Cmt, 56; del, Dem. Nat. Conv, 64; mem, Second Cong. Dist. and Martin Co. Cmt, Dem-Farmer-Labor Party, 68- Bus. & Prof. Pos: Ed. and publisher, Trimont Progress & Ceylon Herald, 47-; pres, Cent. Publ, Inc, presently. Mil. Serv: Entered as Pvt, Army Air Force, 42, released as 1st Lt, 46, after serv. in Artil, S.Pac. and Philippine Theaters; Asiatic Pac. Ribbon with 2 Battles Stars; Philippine Liberation Ribbon; Victory Medal; Army Res, 46-52. Mem: Nat. Press Photographers Asn; Nat. and Minn. Newspaper Asns; Am. Legion; former dir, Martin Co. Agr. Asn; dir, Trimont United Fund Inc; v.pres, South. Minn. Newspaper, Inc; Sigma Delta Chi. Sweepstakes award for best news picture of year, 1959, Minn. Newspaper Asn. Rel: Methodist. Mailing Add: Trimont, Minn. 56176.

SPIKES, HARRY RUSSELL D

b. LaGrange, Ga, 2/15/97; s. Lewis Edward Spikes and Lottie Rowe S; m. 4/30/23 to Eunice Lucille Moore; c. Iris (Spikes) Kilgore. Educ: South. Shorthand & Bus. Col; Am. Inst. of Banking. Polit. & Govt. Pos: Ga. State Rep, 63-66. Bus. & Prof. Pos: Banker, retired; various offs. in banking, 20-54; Pres, C & S Bank of LaGrange, 54-3/1/62, retired; Dir, C & S Bank of LaGrange; V.pres, LaGrange Industs. Inc. Mem: Lions, Pres, 6/39-6/40; Dir, 6/30/62; Trustee-Treas, LaGrange Col, 10/1/54; Treas, United Fund Appeal, 5/1/62; Secy.-Treas, Highland Country Club. Rel: Baptist; Treas. Mailing Add: LaGrange, Ga. 30240.

SPINGARN, NATALIE DAVIS D

b. N.Y.C, 5/26/22; d. Aaron W. Davis and Helen Miller D; m. 6/14/44 to Jerome H. Spingarn; c. Jeremy Davis and Jonathan Edward. Educ: Vassar Col, B.A, 43. Polit. & Govt. Pos: Feature writer, Off. of War Info, 45; asst. to pub. rel, dir, Women's Div, Dem. Nat. Cmt, 48 and publicity dir, 60; asst. to dir, pub rels, Volunteers for Stevenson-Kefauver, 56; del, Dem. Nat. Conv, 60, alternate del, 64; staff asst. to Secy. Ribicoff, Dept. of Health, Educ. & Welfare, 61-62; exec. asst. to Sen. Ribicoff, 63-67; mem. staff of Mrs. Hubert H. Humphrey, Dem. Campaign, 64; asst. dir, Center for Commun. Planning, Dept. Health, Educ. and Welfare, 67-69. Bus. & Prof. Pos: Reporter, The Newspaper PM, 43-44; free lance writer, 45-61. Publ: To Save Your Life, Little Brown, 1963; several magazine articles. Mem: Woman's Nat. Press Club; Women's Nat. Dem. Club; Bd. mem, Family and Child Servs, Wash, D.C. Rel: Jewish. Mailing Add: 3212 McKinley St. N.W, Washington, D.C. 20015.

SPINGARN, STEPHEN J. D

b. Bedford, N.Y, 9/1/08; s. J.E. Spingarn and Amy Judith S; single. Educ: Yale Univ; Univ. Grenoble, France; Rollins Col; Stanford Univ; Univ. Ariz, A.B, 30 and LL.B, 34; v.pres, law sch. student body; managing ed, Univ. Humor Mag; pres, lit. soc; v.justice, Phi Alpha Delta. Polit. & Govt. Pos: Attorney and spec. asst. to gen. counsel, Treas. Dept, 34-42; spec. asst. to attorney gen, 37-38; mem. working cmt, Truman Loyalty Prog, 46-47; asst. gen. counsel and legis. counsel, Treas. Dept, dep. dir, Contract Settlement, legal counsel, Secret Serv. and coordinator, Treas. enforcement agencies, legal mem, Treas. Loyalty Bd, 46-49; Treas. rep, Int. Conf, Lima, Peru, 47; admin. asst. to President, 49-50; v.chmn, White House Loyalty Bd, 50; cmnr. and frequently acting chmn, Fed. Trade Cmn, 50-53; nat. dir, Spec. Activities for V.Pres. Campaign, 56; mem, Small Bus. Adv. Cmt, Dem. Nat. Cmt, 56-57. Bus. & Prof. Pos: Attorney, self-employed. Mil. Serv: Entered as Capt, Army, 42, released as Lt. Col, 46, after serv. in Counter-Intel. Corps, Mediterranean Theater and ETO; Combat Legion of Merit; Bronze Star Medal with Valor Emblem; Invasion Arrowhead, and five battle stars. Publ: Articles on counter-espionage, law and other subjects. Mem: Ariz. State Bar; Bars of U.S. Dist. Court and Court of Appeals for D.C; Am. Bar Asn; former nat. officer, Fed. Bar Asn; SAR; former mem, Bd. Gov, Nat. Counter Intel. Corps Asn; Am. Polit. Sci. Asn. sponsor, Nat. Capital Dem. Club; Nat. Press Club. Mailing Add: 2801 New Mexico Ave. N.W, Washington, D.C. 20007.

SPINGLER, WILLIAM ANTHONY D

b. Phila, Pa, 9/9/41; s. Anthony F. Spingler and Rose McCafferty S; m. 8/25/62 to Phyllis A. Diaddezio; c. William A, Jr. and Marybeth.. Educ: Villanova Univ, B.S. in Econ. and Finance, 63; Delta Pi Epsilon; Finance Soc. Polit. & Govt. Pos: Committeeman, Radnor Twp, Delaware Co, 62-68, treas, 65-; del, Dem. Nat. Conv, 68; chmn, Humphrey-Muskie Campaign Cmt, Delaware Co, Pa, 68. Mem: Ital. Am. Club. Rotary Club Leader of Tomorrow, Wayne, Pa, 58. Rel: Roman Catholic. Mailing Add: 20 Longwood Dr, Wayne, Pa. 19087.

SPINKS, FORD BELMONT D

Ga. State Sen.

b. Tifton, Ga, 4/5/27; s. Durward Belmont Spinks and Jewel Lillybelle Ford S; m. 1950 to Ruby Lee Pritchard; c. Monty, Suzanne and Michael. Educ: Norman Jr. Col, 2 yrs. Polit. & Govt. Pos: Ga. State Sen, 63-; mem, Ga. State Dem. Exec. Cmt, presently. Bus. & Prof. Pos: Pres, Tifton Tractor Co; chmn. bd, Dealers Equip. Credit Corp; dir, The Bank of Tifton, Ga. Mil. Serv: Entered as Pvt, Army, 45, released as S/Sgt, 47, after serv. in 10th Constabulary, Germany; Victory and Good Conduct Medals. Mem: Dir, C. of C; chmn, Surge Govt. Cmt; chmn, Coastal Plain Area Tourism Coun. Rel: Baptist. Mailing Add: R.R. 1, Tifton, Ga. 31794.

SPIRY, ARTHUR WILLIAM R

S.Dak. State Sen.

b. Bangor, S.Dak, 3/6/05; s. Philip Spiry, Sr. and Rosina Oster S; m. 8/17/30 to Erna C. Kunz; c. Joyce (Mrs. Gale Hankins) and A. William. Educ: Univ. S.Dak, B.Sc, 29; Creighton Univ. Sch. Med, M.D, 31. Polit. & Govt. Pos: S.Dak. State Sen, Campbell, Corson and Walworth Co, 68- Bus. & Prof. Pos: Mem. clin. faculty, Univ. S.Dak. Sch. Med, currently; med. dir. and bus. mgr, Mobridge Hosp, 38-59; dist. and local surgeon, Chicago, Milwaukee, St. Paul and Pac. R.R, 38- Mil. Serv: Army Med. Corps, 41. Mem: Am. Med. Asn; N.W. Dist. Med. Soc.(past pres); S.Dak. State Med. Soc.(past pres); Am. Asn. Rwy. Surgeons; Int. Acad. of Proctology; Am. Acad. Gen. Practice; Rotary (past pres, Mobridge Club); Mason; Shrine; Elks; Moose; Am. Legion; Mobridge C. of C.(past dir); Mobridge Rodeo Asn.(past pres); Tex. Citrus Asn; Mobridge Sportsman's Club. Hon. mem, Ecuadorian Acad. Med. Rel: Lutheran. Mailing Add: 108 Seventh St. E, Mobridge, S.Dak, 57601.

SPITLER, RAYMOND RUFFNER D

b. Pleasantville, Ohio, 3/14/06; s. Ira C. Spitler and Viola Ruffner S; m. 5/26/37 to Grace Barrow. Educ: Ohio State Univ, 23-26; Alpha Gamma Rho. Polit. & Govt. Pos: Dem. precinct committeeman, Pleasantville, Ohio, 46; chmn, Fairfield Co. Dem. Exec. Cmt, 54-69; mem, Fairfield Co. Bd. of Elec, 56-; alternate del, Dem. Nat. Conv, 68. Bus. & Prof. Pos: Trustee, South Cent. Power Co, 56- Mem: Mason; York Rite; Scottish Rite; Shrine; Farm Bur; Nat. Farmers Union; Nat. Farmers Orgn; Dem. Clubs. Mailing Add: Route 1, Pleasantville, Ohio 43148. (1967)

SPITZER, ROBERT R. R

b. Waukesha Co, Wis, 5/4/22; s. John Spitzer and Ruth St George S; m. 6/22/46 to Marie Woerfel; c. John, Jeffrey and Susan. Educ: Univ. Wis, B.S, 43, M.Sc, 43, Ph.D, animal nutrition , 47. Polit. & Govt. Pos: Alternate del, Rep. Nat. Conv, 64, del, 68; former finance chmn, Dist. Rep. Party, Wis; chmn, Rep. Cong. Campaigns, two elections; former chmn, Nat. Nixon Food and Agr. Cmt; chmn, Commodity Adv. Cmt, currently; organizer and leader, Agr. Effort for Richard Nixon, 68. Bus. & Prof. Pos: Dir. research, Murphy Prod. Co, 47-53, v.pres. research and promotion, Murphey Products Co, Inc, 53-57, exec. v.pres, 57-58, pres, 58-60, pres. and gen. mgr, 60-; lectr. and radio and TV. appearances. Publ: Articles on Americanism, opportunity, education and freedom. Mem: Nat. chmn, Am. Feed Mfg. Asn, 68; v.pres, Wis. Mfg. Asn, 69-; pres, Int. Univ. Wis. Alumni Asn.(gov. bd. econ. develop); pres, Rotary Club; pres, Burlington Mem. Hosp. Bd. Sales and Mkt. Exec. of the Year, Sales and Mkt. Exec. Milwaukee; Wis. Small Businessman of the Year; Farm Mkt. Man of the Year; Nat. Agr. Advert. and Mkt. Asn. Award; honors from Am. Legion, 4-H Club, VFW, Freedoms Found. Valley Forge and industry and agricultural orgn. Rel: Episcopal; Church warden. Legal Res: 448 Westridge Ave, Burlington, Wis. 53105. Mailing Add: Murphy Products Co, Inc, 124 S. Dodge St, Burlington, Wis. 53105.

SPIVA, ULRIC WINSTON R

Chmn, Union Co. Rep. Party, Ga.

b. Blairsville, Ga, 2/14/25; s. Guy Cook Spiva and Bessie Lee Duckworth S; m. 1/14/45 to Mary Lawanda Reece; c. Walter Eugene, James Fred, Robert Jerry, Linda Rose, Donald Ulric, Eva Ruth, Debra Louise and Peggy Ann. Educ: Blairsville High Sch, Blairsville Ga, 3 years. Polit. & Govt. Pos: Chmn, Union Co. Rep. Party, Ga, 66- Bus. & Prof. Pos: V.pres, Hunter Construction Co, Inc, 68- Mem: F&AM; Royal Arch Mason. Rel: Methodist. Mailing Add: Route 1, Blairsville, Ga. 30512.

SPIVAK, ALVIN A. D

b. Phila, Pa, 11/30/27; s. Herman Spivak and Bella Haimovitz S; m. 11/26/65 to Martha Barry; c. Denise. Educ: Temple Univ, B.S, 49. Polit. & Govt. Pos: Former dir. of info, Nat. Adv. Cmn. on Civil Disorders; dir. of pub. info, United Dem. for Humphrey, 68; dir. of pub. affairs, Dem. Nat. Cmt, 68- Bus. & Prof. Pos: With Int. News Serv, 49-58, Senate reporter and mem. gen. staff, Wash, 51-58; with United Press Int. Serv, 58-68, White House reporter, 60-68. Mil. Serv: Army Air Force, 46-47. Mem: Sigma Delta Chi; Beta Gamma Sigma; Nat. Press & Fed. City Clubs, Wash. Legal Res: 11516 Links Dr, Reston, Va. 22070. Mailing Add: Suite 612, 2600 Virginia Ave. N.W, Washington, D.C. 20037.

SPLAIN, MAURICE DANIEL, JR. D

b. Oil City, Pa, 8/8/12; s. Maurice Splain, Sr. and Mary Agnes Lawler S; m. 7/9/46 to Teresa Eileen Billigan; c. Daniel, Sheila and Maureen. Educ: St. Joseph High Sch, Oil City, Pa. Polit. & Govt. Pos: State chmn, Dem.

Party, Pa, 49-54. Mem: State Secy, Pa. State Aerie, Eagles, 46-, Int. Membership dir, 53- and Int. Pres, 55-56; Moose; Elks; K. of C. Rel: Roman Catholic. Mailing Add: 1928 Spring Valley Rd, Pittsburgh, Pa. 15243.

SPLAINE, JAMES RAYMOND D
N.H. State Rep.
b. Portsmouth, N.H, 8/7/47; s. John E. Splaine, Sr. and Althea Duval S; single. Educ: Univ. N.H, 66- Polit. & Govt. Pos: Pres, Portsmouth Young Dem, N.H, 67-68, mem. exec. cmt, 68-69; mem. exec. cmt, Univ. N.H. Young Dem, 68-69; sen, Univ. N.H. Student Senate, 68-69; mem. exec. cmt, N.H. Young Dem, 68-69; N.H. State Rep, Ward Five, Portsmouth, 69- Mem: Portsmouth and N.H. Young Dem. Legal Res: 256 Deer St, Portsmouth, N.H. 03801. Mailing Add: 83 Willard Ave, Portsmouth, N.H. 03801.

SPOCK, BENJAMIN D
b. New Haven, Conn, 5/2/03; s. Benjamin Ives Spock and Mildred Louise Stoughton S; m. 6/25/27 to Jane Davenport Cheney; c. Michael and John Cheney. Educ: Yale Univ, B.A, 25; Yale Med. Sch, 25-27; Col. Physicians and Surgeons, Columbia Univ, M.D, 29. Polit. & Govt. Pos: Co-chmn, Nat. Cmt. for Sane Nuclear Policy, 67- Bus. & Prof. Pos: Instr. pediatrics, Cornell Med. Col, 33-47, Inst. on Personality Develop, 38-47; assoc. prof. psychiat, Mayo Found, Univ. Minn. and consult. psychiat, Mayo Clin, 47-51; prof. child develop, Univ. Pittsburgh, 51-55, West. Reserve Univ, 55- Mil. Serv: Lt. Comdr, Naval Res, Med. Corps, 44-46. Publ: Baby—Child Care, 46; Feeding Your Baby and Child (with M. Lowenberg), 55; Dr. Spock Talks With Mothers, 61; Problems of Parents, 62 (Family Life Book Award, 63); Dr. Spock on Vietnam (with M. Zimmerman), 68; plus others. Legal Res: Lagoon Marina, Red Hook, St. Thomas, V.I. Mailing Add: 538 Madison Ave, New York, N.Y. 10022.

SPOLLETT, DORIS M. R
N.H. State Rep.
b. Hampstead, N.H, 9/12/97. Educ: Hampstead and Keene and Plymouth Teachers' Cols. Polit. & Govt. Pos: Former N.H. State Sen; selectman, currently; N.H. State Rep, currently. Bus. & Prof. Pos: Mail carrier and farmer. Mem: Farm Bur; Grange. Rel: Protestant. Mailing Add: Hampstead, N.H. 03842.

SPONBERG, RAYMOND LINDELL R
Chmn, Garvin Co. Rep. Party, Okla.
b. Manor, Tex, 10/28/20; s. Charles William Sponberg and Freda Lindell S; m. 9/14/47 to Catherine Ann Brassell; c. Deborah Catherine and Phyllis Ann. Educ: Univ. Tex, Austin, B.S. in Mech. Eng, 42; Pi Tau Sigma; Tau Beta Pi; Phi Kappa Tau. Polit. & Govt. Pos: Chmn, Garvin Co. Rep. Party, Okla, 67- Bus. & Prof. Pos: Field engr, Texas Co, Salem, Ill, 46-48; prod. engr, Sohio Petroleum Co, Edmond, Okla, 48-51, dist. engr, Russell, Kans, 51-56, sr. engr, Oklahoma City, Okla, 56-58 and prod. foreman, Pauls Valley, 58- Mil. Serv: Entered as Ens, Navy, 42, released as Lt, 46, after serv. in Naval Aviation, Pac. Theatre and Jacksonville, Fla, 43-45. Mem: Golden Trend Chap, Am. Petroleum Inst. Rel: Catholic. Mailing Add: 605 S. Paul, Pauls Valley, Okla. 73075.

SPONG, WILLIAM BELSER, JR. D
U.S. Sen, Va.
b. Portsmouth, Va, 9/29/20; m. to Virginia Galliford. Educ: Hampden-Sydney Col; Univ. of Va, LL.B, 47; Univ. of Edinburgh, Scotland; Pi Kappa Alpha; Omicron Delta Kappa. Polit. & Govt. Pos: Va. State Del, 54-55; Va. State Sen, 56-66; chmn, Va. Cmn. on Pub. Educ, 58-62; U.S. Sen, Va, 66-; del, Dem. Nat. Conv, 68. Bus. & Prof. Pos: Lawyer; lectr. law and govt, Col. of William and Mary, 48-49. Mil. Serv: Army Air Force, 42-45. Mem: Pres-elect, Va. State Bar Asn, 65-66; trustee, Hampden-Sydney Col. Rel: Methodist. Legal Res: 403 Court St, Portsmouth, Va. 23704. Mailing Add: 5327 New Senate Office Bldg, Washington, D.C. 20510.

SPONSLER, EARL L. D
Mo. State Rep.
b. Texas City, Mo, 4/13/13; m. 7/8/34 to Lois Flowers; c. Dale Lloyd and Vivian Earlene. Educ: S.W. Mo. State Col. Polit. & Govt. Pos: Chmn, Dem. Co. Cmt, Mo, 6 years; Mo. State Rep, 60- Bus. & Prof. Pos: Former teacher; presently dairy and livestock farmer. Rel: Protestant; Chmn. Bd. of Trustees, Bado Community Church. Mailing Add: RFD 2, Cabool, Mo. 65689.

SPOTTS, OSCAR DONALD 'DON' R
Kans. State Rep.
b. South Haven, Kans, 5/22/07; s. Oscar Lyle Spotts and Laura Mae Blue S; m. 8/7/27 to Carol J. Broadie; c. Betty Joan (Mrs. Arnspiger) and Donna Jean (Mrs. Blackburn). Educ: Kans. State Univ, 26-27; Chillicothe Bus. Col, Mo. Polit. & Govt. Pos: City coun, Ashland, Kans, 50's; Kans. State Rep, 120th Dist, 68- Bus. & Prof. Pos: Store mgr, Kroger Grocery & Baking Co, Kansas City, 31-32; owner grocery, 32-39; mem. staff, Panhandle Lumber Co, Amarillo, Tex, 39-43; mem. staff, Amsden Lumber Co, Wichita, Kans, 43-46; owner, Don Spotts Lumber Co, 47- Mem: Kiwanis; Mason; Consistory; Shrine. Rel: Presbyterian; Elder. Mailing Add: Box 248, Ashland, Kans. 67831.

SPOTTSWOOD, JOHN MALONEY D
Fla. State Sen.
b. Key West, Fla, 6/17/20; s. Robert Fleming Spottswood and Florence Cathcart Maloney S; m. 3/13/49 to Mary Myrtle Sellers; c. John M, Jr, William B, Florence G. and Robert A. Educ: Riverside Mil. Acad, Eng. dip, 38. Polti. & Govt. Pos: Asst. sgt-at-arms, Dem. Nat. Conv, 48, 52 & 56; sheriff, Monroe Co, Fla, 52-63; dir, Monroe Co. Civil Defense, 59-62; mem, Fla. State Indust. Adv. Coun. and Fla. Dem. State Exec. Cmt; Fla. State Sen, 63- Bus. & Prof. Pos: Purchasing agent, U.S. Naval Sta, 40-42; owner and gen. mgr, Radio Sta. WKWF, 45-; pres. and gen. mgr, Cable-Vision, Inc, Key West, Fla, 59-, Casa Marina Hotel and La Concha Motor Inn, 66- Mil. Serv: Entered as 2nd Lt, Army, 42, released as Capt, 44, after serv. as Paratrooper, Aide to a Gen, Officer-in-Charge Secret and Top Secret Procurement, 124th Inf. Regt. and Qm. Gen; Capt. Army Res. Mem: Nat. and Fla. Asns. of Broadcasters; Nat. Commun. TV Asn.(past dir); Fla. CATV Asn; Am. and Fla. Hotel and Motel Asns; Mason; Shrine; Jesters; Legion of Honor, DeMolay; Elks; Moose; Am. Legion; Jr. and Sr. C. of C.(past mgr); Fla. Sheriffs Asn.(past pres); Navy League of the U.S.(pres, Key West Coun); Nat. Capital Dem. Club; Key West Country Club; Capital City Country Club, Tallahassee; Key West Yacht Club; Miami Club; Fraternal Order of Police; Sombrero Country Club; Marathon. Grad, U.S. Naval Sch. Underwater Swimmers, 64. Rel: Episcopal. Legal Res: 531 Caroline St, Key West, Fla. 33040. Mailing Add: P.O. Box 1300, Key West, Fla. 33040.

SPRACHER, DWIGHT D
Chmn, Wash. Dem. Party
Mailing Add: 320 Alaska Bldg, Seattle, Wash. 98104.

SPRADLING, ALBERT M, JR. D
Mo. State Sen.
b. Cape Girardeau, Mo, 3/13/20; s. A.M. Spradling; m. 7/9/43 to Margaret Whyman; c. Albert M, II and Robert Whyman. Educ: Southeast Mo. State Col; Univ. Mo, LL.B. Polit. & Govt. Pos: City attorney, Cape Girardeau, Mo, 48-52; first chmn, Mo. Atomic Energy Cmn, 59; v.chmn, Coun. State Govt, former chmn. bd; Mo. State Sen, 52-, Pres.-Pro Tem, Seventy-First and Seventy-Second Gen. Assemblies. Bus. & Prof. Pos: Lawyer, Spradling & Spradling, 42; spec. agent, Fed. Bur. Invest, 42-45; lawyer, Spradling & Bradshaw, currently; pres, Town Plaza Shopping Center, Inc, lectr, Wash. Univ. St. Louis and chmn. bd, Farmers and Merchants Bank, currently. Mem: AF&AM; RAM; RSM; K.T. Received St. Louis Globe-Dem. award as mem. of Legis. showing greatest growth in leadership, 57-58; award as second most valuable mem. of the Legis, 59-60. Rel: Baptist. Mailing Add: 225 Keller Ave, Cape Girardeau, Mo. 63701.

SPRADLING, GRADY R. D
b. Huntsville, Ark, 10/23/18; s. Fred M. Spradling and Winnie R. Ray S; m. 7/9/40 to Helen A. Neumann; c. Joyce. Educ: Castleford High Sch, Idaho; Chevrolet Merchandising Sch. Polit. & Govt. Pos: Secy, Legis. Dist. 24, Twin Falls Co. Dem. Cent. Cmt, Idaho, 61-64, v.chmn, 64-65, chmn, 65-66 and dist. chmn, 66-69. Bus. & Prof. Pos: V.pres, Magic Valley Motors Inc, 60-65, pres, 65- Mil. Serv: Entered as Pvt, Army, 43, released as S/Sgt, 46, after serv. in 24th Div. Pac. Theater; Pac. Theater Medal; 24th Div. Unit Citation; Good Conduct Medal. Mem: VFW; Mason (32°), Scottish Rite; Kiwanis; Auto Dealers Nat. Safety Coun; secy, Buhl Country Club. Rel: Methodist. Legal Res: 617 Broadway N, Buhl, Idaho 83316. Mailing Add: P.O. Box 424, Buhl, Idaho 83316. (1967)

SPRADLING, SHERMAN D
b. Hollis, Okla, 11/5/12; s. William Carroll Spradling and Nancy Christian S; m. 8/29/35 to Billy Burke Hendrick; c. Sandra Sue (Mrs. Terry Byrd), John William and Betty Ann (Mrs. James A. Roberts). Educ: Cent. State Col, B.S, 38; Lettermans Club. Polit. & Govt. Pos: Chmn, Harmon Co. Dem. Party, Okla, 57-69. Bus. & Prof. Pos: High sch. football, basketball and track coach, Marlow, Okla, 38-43; construction supt, Walco Eng. & Construction Co, Tulsa, 43-49; owner and mgr, Tri-Co. Butane Co, Hollis, Gould, Duke, Mangum, Vinson and Eldorado, 49-60; farmer-rancher, Hollis, 60- Mem: Okla. Athletic Asn; Okla. and Tex. Liquified Petroleum Gas Asns; Okla. Sch. Bd. Mem. Asn; Mason (32°); Kiwanis; Southwest Water Resource Bd; Nat. Farm Orgn, Harmon Co. Chmn, Nat. Found; Scottish Rite. Rel: Baptist. Legal Res: 307 E. Walnut St, Hollis, Okla. 73550. Mailing Add: P.O. Box 588, Hollis, Okla. 73550.

SPRAGENS, THOMAS ARTHUR D
Committeeman, Boyle Co. Dem. Party, Ky.
b. Lebanon, Ky, 4/25/17; s. William Henry Spragens and Lillian Brewer S; m. 5/24/41 to Catharine Smallwood; c. Thomas Arthur, Jr, Barbara Allen and David William. Educ: Univ. Ky, A.B, 38; Syracuse Univ, 39-40; hon. LL.D, Univ. Ky. and Westminster Col; Hon. Litt.D, Univ. Ala. Polit. & Govt. Pos: Admin. analyst, U.S. Bur. Budget, Wash, D.C, 40-41, sr. analyst, 42-45; admin. asst. to cmnr, Ky. Dept. Revenue, 41-42; asst. chief food allocation, For. Econ. Admin, Wash, D.C, 45; del, Dem. Nat. Conv, 68; committeeman, Boyle Co. Dem. Party, Ky. 69- Bus. & Prof. Pos: Asst. to the pres, Stanford Univ, 45-51; secy. and treas, fund for adv. educ, Ford Found, 51-52; pres, Stephens Col, 53-57; pres, Centre Col, 57- Mem: Am. Coun. Educ.(dir); South. Asn. Cols. and Schs.(cmn. cols); South. Univ. Conf.(dir); Ky. Independent Col. Found.(dir); Am. Asn. Cols.(chmn. col. finance and legis); Univ. Club; Pendennis Club; Rotary. Rel: Presbyterian; Bd. Dirs, Bd. Christian Educ. Mailing Add: 763 W. Main St, Danville, Ky. 40422.

SPRAGUE, ARTHUR W. R
b. La Grange, Ill, 8/2/02; c. two sons, three daughters. Educ: Dartmouth Col; U. Ill. and Northwestern Law Schs, LL.B; U. of Ill, Order of Coif. Polit. & Gov. Pos: Ill. State Sen; Ill. State Rep, 5 terms. Bus. & Prof. Pos: Partner, law firm, Sprague and Jerstrom, Chicago. Mil. Serv: Navy. Mem: Am. Legion, past Comdr, Post 1941, Ill; Mason; Shrine. Rel: Episcopal Church, La Grange. 1967 Legal Res: 345 S. Spring Ave, La Grange, Ill. No mailing address available. (1967)

SPRAGUE, DAVID GORTON D
Wash. State Rep.
b. North Cohocton, N.Y, 6/11/20; s. Lloyd Drummond Sprague and Iva Gorton S; m. to Bette Henriksen; c. Robert, William, Judith, Thomas, Mark and Paul. Educ: Wesleyan Univ, B.A, 41; Fletcher Sch. of Law and Diplomacy, M.A, 42; Am. Univ. of Cairo, Egypt, 37-38; Phi Beta Kappa; Delta Sigma Rho; Alpha Chi Rho. Polit. & Govt. Pos: Intel. analyst, U.S. Dept. State, 46-48; chmn, King Co. Finance Cmt, Wash, 54-58; chmn. bd, West. Wash. State Col, 57-; chmn, Citizens Cmt. on Urban Area Govt, Adv. to State Legis, 62-63; chmn, Metrop. Dem. Club, 62-64; Wash. State Rep, 37th Dist, 67- Bus. & Prof. Pos: Acct. exec, Fred S. James and Co, 48-58; pres, Sprague-Israel; Inc, 58- Mil. Serv: Entered as Aviation Cadet, Navy, 42, released as Lt. (sg), 45, after serv. in Squadron VC 69 as a Pilot; Atlantic- European-North Africa, 43-45; Air Medal; Presidential Unit Citation. Mem: Chmn, Polit. Participation Cmt, Seattle C. of C; bd, Seattle Munic. League; bd, Seattle World Affairs Coun; chmn, Seattle Cmt. on For. Rels; chmn, Mayor's Cmt. on UN Day; Seattle Tennis Club. Rel: Episcopal. Mailing Add: 806 35th Ave, Seattle, Wash. 98122.

SPRAGUE, IRVINE H. D
b. San Francisco, Calif, 7/4/21; s. Irvine Henry Sprague and Claire Kelly S; m. 11/3/40 to Margie Craw; c. Michael, Terry and Kristine. Educ: Col. of

the Pacific, B.A, 47; Univ. Ind; George Wash. Univ. Polit. & Govt. Pos: Admin. asst. to U.S. Rep, McFall, 57-63; dep. dir. of finance, Calif, assigned as Wash. Rep. for Gov. Edmund G. Brown, Calif, 63-66; mem, San Joaquin Co. Cent. Cmt; del, Dem. Nat. Conv, 64; White House Staff, Aide to President Johnson for Cong. Rels, 67-68; dir, Fed. Deposit Ins. Corp, 69- Mil. Serv: Entered as Pvt, Army, 43, released as 1st Lt, 46, after serv. in Rifle Inf. Platoon, 41st Inf. Div, South. Philippines; Two Bronze Stars; Purple Heart; Combat Infantryman's Badge; Lt. Col, Army Res, at present. Rel: Catholic. Legal Res: Stockton, Calif. Mailing Add: 7514 Wellesley Dr, College Park, Md. 20740.

SPRAUL, THOMAS C. D
b. Cincinnati, Ohio, 1/13/25; s. Clarence E. Spraul and Mary Buddeke S; m. to Elizabeth Conaty; c. Nancy, Judy, Steve, Don, Mary and Elizabeth. Educ: Xavier Univ, Ph.B; Univ. Cincinnati, LL.B. Polit. & Govt. Pos: Asst. Attorney Gen, Ohio, 58-60; councilman, Cincinnati, 60-63; former treas, Hamilton Co. Dem. Exec. Cmt; del, Dem. Nat. Conv, 68. Bus. & Prof. Pos: Lawyer. Mil. Serv: Entered as Pvt, Army, 44, released as Sgt, after serv. in European Theater, 46; ETO; Victory and Occup. Ribbons. Mem: K. of C; Am. and Ohio State Bar Asns; Am. Trial Lawyers Asn; Soc. of Plymouth Men. Rel: Roman Catholic. Mailing Add: 2690 Fleetwood, Cincinnati, Ohio 45211. (1967)

SPRING, LEWIS N. R
b. Orangeville, N.Y, 5/27/96; s. Burt Spring and Helen Nesbitt S; m. 6/21/16 to Anna Crane; c. Avis M. (Mrs. I. Fred Pattridge) and Raymond L. Educ: Warsaw High Sch. Polit. & Govt. Pos: Chief of Police, Warsaw, N.Y, 20-33; Under-Sheriff, Wyoming Co, 33-36; Sheriff, 36-51; mem, Wyoming Co. Rep. Cmt, 36-69, v.chmn, 63-69; mem, N.Y. State Rep. Cmt, 6 years. Mem: N.Y. State Sheriffs Asn.(pres, 43-44); F&AM; Shrine; Commandery; Odd Fellows. Rel: Baptist. Mailing Add: Route 1, Box 205S, Frostproof, Fla. 33843.

SPRINGER, CHARLES EDWARD D
b. Reno, Nev, 2/20/28; s. Edwin Springer and Rose Mary Kelley S; m. 3/17/51 to Jacqueline Dora Sirkegian; c. Kelli Ann. Educ: Univ. Nev, B.A, 50; Georgetown Univ. Law Center, LL.B, 53; Phi Delta Phi. Polit. & Govt. Pos: Co. del. chmn, Washoe Co. Dem. Cent. Cmt, Nev, 60; state v.chmn, Dem. Party, 60-61 & 64-65, state chmn, 61-64, Nat. Committeeman, 64; attorney gen, Nev, 62-63; exec. committeeman, West. States Dem. Conv, 63-64. Bus. & Prof. Pos: Legis. legal adv. to Gov, Nev, 59-65; mem, Nat. Small Bus. Adv. Coun, 62-; chmn, State Apprenticeship Coun, 64-66. Mil. Serv: Entered as Pvt, Army, 45, released as 2nd Lt, 51, after serv. in 11th Airborne Div, Japan. Mem: V.pres, Int. Acad. of Law and Sci; Elks; VFW; Am. Legion; state pres, Am. Cancer Soc; v.pres, North. Nev. Ment. Health Asn. Recipient, Outstanding Young Dem. in the U.S. Award, Nat. Young Dem. Conv, 65. Rel: Catholic. Mailing Add: 1001 Dartmouth Dr, Reno, Nev. 89502.

SPRINGER, ERCHAL JOHN DFL
Chmn, Lincoln Co. Dem-Farmer-Labor Party, Minn.
b. Judith Gap, Mont, 5/22/17; s. John Springer and Mary Herchowski S; m. 1/29/62 to Eldora Stringer; c. Jo Ann (Mrs. Adrain Lanners), Sharon (Mrs. Richard De' Pestal), Marylou and Erchal Eldo. Educ: Mandato State Teachers Col. Polit. & Govt. Pos: Chmn, Lincoln Co. Dem-Farmer-Labor Party, Minn, 50-, twp. assessor, 50-57, cmnr, 58-62. Mem: Chmn, March of Dimes, 17 Yrs; committeeman, Agr Soil Conserv. Twp; Farm Union; Red Cross; K. of C; Welfare Bd; Holy Name Soc. Rel: Catholic. Mailing Add: Porter, Minn. 56280.

SPRINGER, ERIC W. D
b. N.Y.C, 5/17/29; s. Owen Winston Springer and Maida Stewart S; m. 10/25/58 to Cecile Marie Kennedy; c. Brian and Christina. Educ: Rutgers Univ, A.B, 50; N.Y. Univ. Sch. of Law, LL.B, 53; Alpha Phi Alpha. Polit. & Govt. Pos: Cmnr, Cmn. on Human Rels, Pittsburgh, Pa, 61-69, chmn, 64-69; dir. of compliance, U.S. Equal Employ. Opportunity Cmn, 67; alternate del, Dem. Nat. Conv, 68. Bus. & Prof. Pos: Assoc. research prof, Sch. of Pub. Health and Sch. of Law, Univ. Pittsburgh, 56-68, adj. assoc. research prof, Sch. of Pub. Health, 68-; dir. publ, Aspen Systs. Corp, 68- Mil. Serv: Entered as Pvt, Army, 53, released as Cpl, 55, after serv. in 2053rd S.U.P.C, Ft. George G. Meade, Md, 54-55; Good Conduct Medal. Publ: Hospital Law Manual, (joint author), Health Law Center, 59; 'The Unconquerable Prejudice of Caste,' Duquesne Univ. Law Rev, 66; 'Automation and Health Records,' Med. Record News, 68. Mem: Am. and Nat. Bar Asns; Am. Pub. Health Asn. (fel). Mailing Add: 5665 Bartlett St, Pittsburgh, Pa. 15217.

SPRINGER, WILLIAM LEE R
U.S. Rep, Ill.
b. Sullivan, Ind, 4/12/09; s. Otha L. Springer and Daisy Ellen Tucker S; m. 5/9/42 to Elsie Mattis; c. Katherine Curtis, Ann Tucker and Georgia Mattis. Educ: DePauw Univ, A.B, 31; Univ. Ill. Law Sch, LL.B, 35; Phi Delta Theta; Phi Delta Phi. Hon. LL.D, Millikin Univ, 53 and Lincoln Col, 66. Polit. & Govt. Pos: State's attorney, Ill, 40-42; Judge, Champaign Co, 46-50; U.S. Rep, Ill, 51- Bus. & Prof. Pos: Assoc, law firm, Busch & Harrington, Champaign, Ill, 36- Mil. Serv: Entered as Lt.(jg), Navy, 42, released as Lt, 45. Mem: Ill. State, Am. and Champaign Co. Bar Asns; Am. Judicial Soc; Champaign Country Club. Received The Nat. Collegiate Athletic Asn. Award, 66. Rel: Presbyterian. Legal Res: 900 W. Park Ave, Champaign, Ill. 61820. Mailing Add: 16 W. Lenox St, Chevy Chase, Md. 20015.

SPRINKEL, WARREN REED R
Mem, Calif. Rep. State Cent. Cmt.
b. Los Angeles, Calif, 6/30/22; s. Walter Reed Sprinkel and Florence Werdin S; m. 10/7/48 to Edna Louise Boyle; c. Steven, Annette and Susan. Educ: Univ. South. Calif, B.S. in Bus. Admin, 46; Kappa Alpha; Blue Key; Alpha Kappa Psi; Skull and Dagger. Polit. & Govt. Pos: Mem, President's Adv. Cmt. Int. Trade, Dept. Commerce, 58-60; chmn, San Bernardino Co, Richard Nixon for Pres, 60; mem. and finance chmn, San Bernardino Co. Rep. Cent. Cmt, 60-; mem, Calif. Rep. State Cent. Cmt, 64-; chmn, San Bernardino Co. Ronald Reagan for Gov, 66; app. mem, Contractors' State License Bd, 67-, chmn, 69-; del, Rep. Nat. Conv, 68. Bus. & Prof. Pos: Pres, Fontana Paving, Inc, 56-; dir. and officer, Vernon Asphalt Constructors, Los Angeles, Calif, 66- Mil. Serv: Entered as Air Cadet, Air Force, 43, released as Maj, 52, after serv. in 484th Bomb Group, 15th Air Force, ETO, 44-45; Recalled, 51-52, serv. in Fifth Air Force, Korea; Distinguished Flying Cross; Air Medal with Six Oak Leaf Clusters; Presidential Unit Citation. Mem: Am. Rd. Builders Asn.(pres, contractors div, 69); Calif. and Nat. Asphalt Pavement Asns; Eng. Grading Contractors Asn.(pres, San Bernardino-Riverside Chap, 63); Rotary; Fontana Club; C. of C.(pres, 53). Rel: Presbyterian. Legal Res: 7706 Calle Casino, Cucamonga, Calif. 91730. Mailing Add: P.O. Box 847, Fontana, Calif. 92335.

SPURRIER, MARGARET NORVELL R
Mem, Rep. Nat. Cmt, Tenn.
b. Nashville, Tenn, 4/7/19; d. Richard Norvell and Margaret Parker N; m. 6/26/40 to Keith McCauley Spurrier; c. Lucia Parker and Irene LeJau. Educ: Wellesley Col; Vanderbilt Univ; Kappa Alpha Theta; Chi Delta Phi; Mortar Bd. Polit. & Govt. Pos: Co-chmn, Shelby Co. Rep. Party, Tenn, 62-66; mem, Tenn. State Rep. Exec. Cmt, 66-; mem, Rep. Nat. Cmt, Tenn, currently. Mem: Nat. Fedn. of Rep. Women; Nat. Cong. of Parents and Teachers; Memphis Jr. League; Memphis Symphony League; bd. mem, Shelby United Neighbors (United Fund); bd, Tenn. Botanical Gardens and Fine Arts Center, Inc. Rel: Episcopal. Mailing Add: 89 Goodwyn, Memphis, Tenn. 38111.

SQUIRE, LOREN D. D
b. Manti, Utah, 1/2/98; s. John P. Squire and Christene Kenney S; m. 10/22/18 to Amelia Sanders; c. DeLance, Phil, Don, DuWayne, Jerald, Adrien, Scott, LoRene and Sandra. Educ: Manti High Sch. Polit. & Govt. Pos: Justice of Peace for 10 years; former Utah State Rep. and Town Bd. Pres; Utah State Sen. until 67. Bus. & Prof. Pos: Trooper, Utah Hwy. Patrol, 33-45, sgt, 45-50, Lt, 50-58. Publ: A Genealogy; Observations of Life. Rel: Latter-day Saint; Bishop. Mailing Add: 165 S. Main St, LaVerkin, Utah 84745.

SQUIRES, JAMES DUANE R
b. Grand Forks, N.Dak, 11/9/04; s. Vernon Purinton Squires and Ethel Claire Wood S; m. 9/5/28 to Catherine Emily Tuttle; c. Vernon Tuttle and James Wood. Educ: Univ. N.Dak, A.B, 25; Univ. Minn, M.A, 27; Harvard Univ, Ph.D, 33; Phi Beta Kappa; Delta Sigma Rho; Sigma Nu. Hon. LL.D, Univ. N.Dak, 58. Polit. & Govt. Pos: Mem, Cmt. of Historians for Gen. H. H. Arnold, Wash, D.C, 43-44; del, Rep. Nat. Conv, 52, 56 & 64; del, N.H. State Rep. Conv, 58 & 62; mem, citizens adv. cmn, U.S. Cmn. on Govt. Security, 57; chmn, N.H. Civil War Centennial Cmn, 59-65; mem, Rep. State Platform Cmt, rep. of Gov. Walter Peterson to Golden Spike Centennial, 69. Bus. & Prof. Pos: Prof. hist, N.Dak. State Col, 27-33; chmn, Dept. soc. studies, Colby Jr. Col, 33- Publ: Mirror to America, Concord, N.H, 52; The Granite State of the United States, New York, N.Y, 56; The Story of New Hampshire, Princeton, N.J, 64. Mem: Soc. of Am. Historians; N.H. Hist. Soc; Newcomen Soc; N.H. SAR; N.H. Old Home Week Asn; United Baptist Conv. of N.H; Old Number Four Assocs; pres, Am. Baptist Hist. Soc, 69- Citation of Merit for serv. with Gen. Arnold in a civilian adv. capacity, U.S. Army Air Force; Univ. N.H. Distinguished Serv. Citation, 52; Andover Newton Theological Sch. Citation, 52; Freedoms' Found. Award, 56. Rel: Am. Baptist Convention. Mailing Add: 10 Burpee Lane, New London, N.H. 03257.

STAATS, ELMER BOYD
Comptroller Gen. of U.S.
b. Richfield, Kans, 6/6/14; s. Wesley F. Staats and Maude Goodall S; m. 9/14/40 to Margaret S. Rich; c. David Rich, Deborah Rich and Catharine Jane Rich. Educ: McPherson Col, B.A, 35; Univ. Kans, M.A, 36; Univ. Minn, Ph.D, 39; Phi Beta Kappa; Pi Sigma Alpha. Hon. LL.D, McPherson Col, 66. Polit. & Govt. Pos: Research asst, Kans. Legis. Coun, 36; staff, Pub. Admin. Serv, Chicago, Ill, 37-38; asst. dir. charge of legis. reference, U.S. Bur. of Budget, 47-49, exec. asst. dir, 49-50, dep. dir, 50-53 & 58-66; exec. officer, Operations Coordinating Bd, Nat. Security Coun, 54-58; Comptroller Gen. of U.S, 66- Bus. & Prof. Pos: Teaching asst, Univ. Minn, 36-38; prof. lectr. pub. admin, George Wash. Univ, 44-49; research dir, Marshall Field & Co, 53. Publ: Personnel Standards in the Social Security Program, 39; contrib, Am. Econ. Rev, Pub. Personnel Rev. and Am. Polit. Sci. Rev. Mem: Bd. trustees, William A. Jump Mem. Award; Am. Polit. Sci. Asn; Am. Soc. Pub. Admin; Cosmos and Chevy Chase Clubs; bd. dir, Am. Acad. Polit. & Soc. Sci, 66-; Research Adv. Cmt. of the Coun. of State Govt, 66-; Fed. Govt. Acct. Asn, 66-; President's Cmn. on Budget Concepts, 67; bd. trustees, Pub. Admin. Serv, Chicago, 67-; Nat. Acad. Pub. Admin, 68-; bd. trustees, Nat. Inst. Pub. Affairs, 69; bd. trustees, Am. Univ, 69- Rockefeller Pub. Serv. Award, 61; Alumni Achievement Award, Univ. Minn, 64; Distinguished Serv. Citation, Univ. Kans, 66. Rel: Methodist. Mailing Add: 5011 Overlook Rd. N.W, Washington, D.C. 20016.

STABILE, JOSEPH ANTHONY D
b. Brooklyn, N.Y, 3/26/30; s. Joseph A. Stabile and Sarah Malvica S; m. 3/2/58 to Maria Gallucci; c. Sarah Ann, Gina and Marilisa. Educ: City Col. New York, B.S, in Soc. Studies; Brooklyn Law Sch, LL.B. and LL.M. Polit. & Govt. Pos: Econ. analyst, Port of Authority, N.Y, 51-54; Dep. State Attorney Gen, N.Y, 56; hearing cmnr, N.Y. State Supreme Court, 61; cand. for Dist. Court Judge, Suffolk Co, 63 & 65; Dem. committeeman, 79th E.D, Babylon, Suffolk Co, 63-; alternate del, Dem. Nat. Conv, 64; pres, North Babylon Dem. Club, 65-66; del, Second Dist. Judicial Conv, 66; town campaign mgr, Babylon Dem. Party, 66; former v.chmn, Suffolk Co. Dem. Cmt. Bus. & Prof. Pos: Attorney-at-law, Scalzi & Stabile, 58- Mil. Serv: Entered as Pvt, Army, 54, released as Cpl, 56, after serv. in Pub. Info. Off, Sixth Army. Mem: N.Y. State and Queens Co. Bar Asns; Catholic Lawyers Guild; Columbian Lawyers Asn; L.I. Columbia Asn; DAV; Lions Int; Catholic Charities. Rel: Catholic. Mailing Add: 224 W. Seventh St, Deer Park, N.Y. 11729. (1967)

STABLER, W. LAIRD, JR. R
Del. State Rep.
b. 1930. Educ: Princeton, B.A; Univ. of Va. Law Sch, LL.B. Polit. & Govt. Pos: Past Dep. Attorney Gen, Del; Del. State Rep, 67, majority leader, Del. House of Rep, 69. Bus. & Prof. Pos: Attorney-at-Law; past pres, Children's Home Inc; trustee, Univ. of Del. Libr. Asn; pres, Scottish Games Asn. of Del. Inc; trustee, Del. Sch. Auxiliary Asn; ex-master, The Family Court of New Castle Co. Mailing Add: Montchanin, Del. 19710.

STACHOWSKI, STANLEY JOSEPH D
b. Buffalo, N.Y, 4/10/16; s. Joseph V. Stachowski and Martha Kaszprzyk S; m. 2/17/45 to Pearl Wojcik; c. Michael J. and William T. Polit. & Govt. Pos: Sgt. at Arms, Buffalo Common Coun, N.Y, 48-52; Cmnr. of Parks, Buffalo, 66-; alternate del, Dem. Nat. Conv, 68. Bus. & Prof. Pos: Dir. Prfnl. Businessmen's Asn, 48-52. Mil. Serv: Entered as Pvt, Army, 42, released as M/Sgt, 45, after serv. in 339th Serv. Squadron, ETO; Five Battle Stars; various unit citations; Bronze Star. Mem: Am. Legion; Polish League of Am. Vet; Polish Roman Catholic Union. Rel: Catholic. Mailing Add: 2030 Clinton St, Buffalo, N.Y. 14206.

STACK, AMOS MOREHEAD R
b. Robeson Co, N.C, 12/8/26; s. Amos Morehead Stack and Hannah McNeill S; m. 9/15/63 to Gillian Rose Scaturro; c. Elizabeth McNeill. Educ: The Citadel, 43-44; Univ. N.C, A.B. in Am. Hist, 49; Alpha Tau Omega. Polit. & Govt. Pos: Precinct chmn, Cumberland Co. Rep. Exec. Cmt, N.C, 62-68, mem, 66-68; del, Nat. Fedn. of Young Rep. Conv, 63; orgn. chmn, N.C. Fedn. of Young Rep, 63-64; del, Rep. Nat. Conv, 64 & 68; mem, N.C. State Rep. Exec. Cmt, 66-68. Bus. & Prof. Pos: Employ. mgr, McLean Trucking Co, 49-54; pres. and founder, Hercules Steel Co, 54-; pres. and bd. chmn, Brachen Steel Co, Sanford, N.C. and Jarratt, Va, 67- Mil. Serv: Entered as A/S, Navy, 44, released as Radarman 3/C, 46, after serv. in N.Atlantic; Am, European and China-Burma-India Theater Ribbons. Mem: Am. Inst. of Steel Construction; U.S. C. of C; Nat. Fedn. of Independent Bus, Inc; AF&AM; Young Americans for Freedom. Sailboat racing, foxhunting and thoroughbred horses. Rel: Presbyterian. Legal Res: Box 66, Route 6, Fayetteville, N.C. 28301. Mailing Add: P.O. Box 5205, Fayetteville, N.C. 28301.

STACK, EDWARD J. R
Sheriff, Broward Co, Fla.
b. Bayonne, N.J, 4/29/10; s. William J. Stack and Hannah S; m. 1954 to Jean Pierce; c. Kathleen and William. Educ: Lehigh Univ, B.A, 31; Univ. Pa. Law Sch, LL.B, 34; Columbia Univ, M.A, 38; Beta Theta Pi. Polit. & Govt. Pos: City cmnr, Pompano Beach, Fla, 65-69 and mayor, 67-69; North Broward Campaign chmn, Claude R. Kirk for Gov, Fla, 65; mem, Pompano Beach Rep. Club, 65-; mem, Rep. State and Nat. Finance Cmt; mem. and dir, Rep. Citation Cmt. of Broward Co, Fla; mem, Fla. Develop. Cmn, 67-; Fla. State Chmn, Nixon for Pres. Campaign, 68; mem, Gov. Adv. Cmt. for Broward Co; alternate del, Rep. Nat. Conv, 68; sheriff, Broward Co, 69- Bus. & Prof. Pos: New York Bar, 34-; owner and mgr, Silver Thatch Inn, Pompano Beach, Fla, 55-; dir, First Nat. Bank, Ft. Lauderdale, 69- Mil. Serv: Entered as Ens, Coast Guard, 42, released as Lt.(sg), 46. Mem: Am. Legion; Elks; Izaak Walton League; Fraternal Order of Police; dir, Navy League; Kiwanis; Emerald Soc; Boys Club of Broward Co; United Fund Appeal. Rel: Catholic. Legal Res: 518 N. Riverside Dr, Pompano Beach, Fla. 33062. Mailing Add: P.O. Box 8069, Ft. Lauderdale, Fla. 33310.

STACK, GERALD ALPHONSUS D
Co. Attorney, Hot Springs Co, Wyo.
b. Denver, Colo, 6/10/18; s. Gerald Alphonsus Stack and Louise Frances Werlen S; m. 11/22/54 to Anne Kathryn Gustin; c. Louise Marie and Anne Kathryn. Educ: Univ. Colo, 35-39; Univ. Wyo, LL.B, 41; Phi Delta Phi; Sigma Nu. Polit. & Govt. Pos: Chmn, Fremont Co. Dem. Party, Wyo, 44-45; dist. enforcement attorney, Off. Price Admin, Wyo, 45; state committeeman, Hot Springs Co. Dem. Party, 46-52, chmn, 52-58; city attorney, Thermopolis, 48-56; mem. exec. cmt, Wyo. State Dem. Cent. Cmt, 50-52; co. and prosecuting attorney, Hot Springs Co, Wyo, 59-; del, Dem. Nat. Conv, 68. Mem: Nat. Dist. Attorney's Asn. (dir); Wyo. Co. Attorney's Asn; Wyo. State Bar (past cmnr); Elks; C. of C; Country Club. Rel: Roman Catholic. Legal Res: 103 Sunset Dr, Thermopolis, Wyo. 82443. Mailing Add: First National Bank Bldg, Thermopolis, Wyo. 82443.

STACK, JACK MICHAEL R
Rep. Finance Dir, Mich. Tenth Cong. Dist.
b. Cadillac, Mich, 3/1/38; s. Jack Martin Stack and Ruth Foster S; m. to Carol Anderson; c. Molly, Matthew, Michael and Martin. Educ: Mich. State Univ, B.S, 59; Univ. Mich, M.D, 63. Polit. & Govt. Pos: Del, Mich. State Rep. Convs, 66-69; Rep. finance chmn, Gratiot Co. Rep. Party, 66-69; alternate del, Rep. Nat. Conv, 68; Rep. finance dir, Tenth Cong. Dist, 68- Bus. & Prof. Pos: Chmn, Gratiot Co. Ment. Health Bd, Mich, 66-69; bd. dirs, Alma C. of C, 67-69; chmn, Alma Arts & Crafts Center, 68-69; v.pres, Mich. Coun. Study Abortion, 68-69; mem, bd, Mich. Soc. for Ment. Health, 69- Mem: Mich. State Med. Soc; Am. Med. Asn; Am. Acad. Gen. Practice; Am. Soc. Anesthesiologists. One of Five Outstanding Young Men in Mich, Mich. Jaycees, 67. Rel: Lutheran. Mailing Add: 4313 Birmingham Rd, Alma, Mich. 48801.

STACY, ESTELLE MABRY R
Mem. Exec. Cmt, Rep. Nat. Cmt, Wyo.
b. Grimes Co, Tex, 9/3/13; d. David Dixon Mabry and Rosa Miller M; m. 12/24/33 to Jack Leonard Stacy, wid. 5/26/63; c. Richard A. Polit. & Govt. Pos: Pres, Converse Co. Rep. Women's Club, Wyo, 59-61; pres, Wyo. Fedn. Rep. Women, 60-62; v.chmn, Wyo. Rep. State Cmt, 60-66; precinct committeewoman, Southeast Precinct, Douglas, 64-; Rep. nat. committeewoman, Wyo, 66-, mem. exec. cmt, Rep. Nat. Cmt, 69-; mem, Site Selection Cmt, Rep. Nat. Conv, 68 and mem. Arrangements Cmt, Chmn. Cmt. Permanent Orgn. and del, 68. Bus. & Prof. Pos: V.pres, Stacy Drilling Co, 47-63, pres, 63-; secy. and v.pres, Teno United, 58-63, pres, 63- Publ: 'Women in Politics,' Wyo. on Review, 62. Mem: Wyo. Drilling Asn; pres, Converse Co. Libr. Bd. Trustees, 65-; Wyo. Taxpayers Asn; mem. bd. dirs, Wyo. Safety Coun, 67-; Douglas Country Club; C. of C; past Matron, Woodbine Chapter 18, Eastern Star; Daughters of the Nile; Ladies of Oriental Shrine; past pres, Douglas Civic Club; Epsilon Sigma Alpha; Wyo. Fedn. of Women's Clubs, advert. mgr. for state magazine, 2 years; treas, Converse Co. Found, mem. bd. of trustees, 52- Rel: Episcopal. Legal Res: 3 Hilltop Rd, Douglas, Wyo. 82633. Mailing Add: P.O. Box 96, Douglas, Wyo. 82633.

STACY, JOHN RAYMOND R
Mem, Okla. State Rep. Cmt.
b. Spokane, Wash, 6/15/14; s. William Kellogg Stacy and Mary May Raymond S; m. 8/21/43 to Barbara Baley; c. William Kellogg, II, James Bradford, Thomas Wood, Susan Ellen, Mary Jane and Barbara Ann. Educ: Oberlin Col, B.S, 37; West. Res; Univ. Sch. Med, M.D, 42. Polit. & Govt. Pos: Doorkeeper, Rep. Nat. Conv, 36, alternate del, 64; designated physician, U.S. Dept. of Labor, 53-; precinct chmn, Okla. City Rep. Party, 61-; mem, Okla. State Rep. Cmt. and Okla. Co. Exec. Cmt, 63- Bus. & Prof. Pos: Attending physician, Will Rogers Vet. Hosp, 48-; clinical prof, orthopaedic and traumatic surgery, Okla. Univ. Sch. Med, 49- Mil. Serv: Entered as 2nd Lt, Army, 38, released as 1st Lt, 43, after serv. in Medical Corps. Mem: Fel, Int. Col. Surgeons, Am. Col. Surgeons and Am. Acad. Orthopaedic Surgeons; Econ. Club. of Okla; chmn, pub. rels. cound, Okla. State Med. Asn, 61; secy. and treas, Oklahomans for Right to Work, 61-64, pres, 64-67; pres, Okla. Co. Med. Soc, 62; bd. dirs, Okla. City C. of C, 62-; speaker, House of Dels, Am. Asn. Physicians and Surgeons, 63; Men's Dinner Club; Univ. Okla. Sch. Med. Faculty Club; Am. Bd. Orthopaedic Surgery; U.S. C. of C; Free Soc. Asn; South. States Indust. Coun. Rel: Congregational. Legal Res: 3100 N.W. 24th, Oklahoma City, Okla. 73107. Mailing Add: 415 N.W. 12th, Oklahoma City, Okla. 73103.

STACY, TED THEODORE D
W.Va. State Del.
b. Grundy, Va, 3/10/23; s. Samuel Mathew Stacy and Eleventha Smith S; m. 3/27/60 to Elizabeth Ann Barnette; c. Larry Ted. Educ: Beckley Col, A.B.A, 52; Morris Harvey Col, 68; LaSalle Exten. Univ, LL.B, 69. Polit. & Govt. Pos: W.Va. State Del, 58-60 & 68- Bus. & Prof. Pos: Owner, General Ins. Agency, Beckley, W.Va, 48- Mil. Serv: Entered as Pvt, Army, 40, released as Cpl, 45, after serv. in Coast Artil, Spec. Serv. Entertainment Sect, S. Pac, 41-45. Mem: Mason (Master, High Priest Chap); Shrine; Lions; Odd Fellows. Rel: Baptist. Legal Res: 600 Northwestern Ave, Beckley, W.Va. 25801. Mailing Add: Box 929, Beckley, W.Va. 25801.

STADELMAN, GEORGE PETER R
Rep. Nat. Committeeman, Ore.
b. The Dalles, Ore, 6/1/08; s. Peter J. Stadelman and May Kelly S; m. 1/26/31 to Lorraine Pierce; c. Sally (Mrs. Dougherty) and George Pierce. Educ: Univ. Ore; Sigma Nu; Alpha Kappa Psi; Friars; Order of O. Polit. & Govt. Pos: Mayor, The Dalles, Ore, 41-44; chmn, Ore. Cmt, Lodge for President; del, Rep. Nat. Conv, 56, 64 & 68; mem, Ore. State Rep. Exec. Cmt, 60-64; former treas, Ore. State Rep. Cmt; Rep. Nat. Committeeman, Ore, 67- Bus. & Prof. Pos: Pres, Cherry Lane Orchards, 66-; v.pres, Stadelman Fruit, Inc, 66-; dir, First Nat. Bank of Ore, 66- Mem: Elks; Kiwanis; pres, C. of C, 60-64; bd. overseers, Lewis & Clarke Col. Rel: Christian. Mailing Add: 605 Pentland St, The Dalles, Ore. 97058.

STADELMAN, GEORGE PIERCE R
b. The Dalles, Ore, 5/30/36; s. George Peter Stadelman and Lorraine Pierce S; m. 8/17/58 to Mary Lou Glass; c. Julie and Carol. Educ: Univ. Ore, B.B.A, 58; Theta Chi. Polit. & Govt. Pos: Chmn, Wasco Co. Young Rep. Club, 64-65; alternate del, Rep. Nat. Conv, 64 & 68. Bus. & Prof. Pos: V.pres, Stadelman Fruit Inc, The Dalles, Ore, 68-; mem. exec. cmt, Northwest Cherry Briners, 68-; dir, Nat. Cherry Growers & Industs, 69. Mil. Serv: Entered as 2nd Lt, Army, 58, released as 1st Lt, 60, after serv. in 53rd Qm. Co, Fort Ord, Calif. Mem: Elks; Lions(past pres); C. of C.(dir); Farm Bur. Distinguished Serv. Award, The Dalles, Ore, 68; Young Man of the Year. Rel: Protestant. Mailing Add: 2214 Bridge St, The Dalles, Ore. 97058.

STADER, VICTOR BERNARD, JR. D
b. Latrobe, Pa, 7/25/08; s. Victor Bernard Stader, Sr. and Mary Ruffner S; m. 9/12/33 to Mary Ellen Thurston; c. Miriam Ann (Mrs. Martin E. Fontaine) and Virginia Lee (Mrs. Donald E. Harvey). Educ: Georgetown Univ, 27-28; Univ. Pittsburgh, B.S, 31; Edward White Debating Soc. Polit. & Govt. Pos: Mayor and dir. civil defense, Latrobe, Pa, 50-61; v.pres, Westmoreland Co. Dem. Mayors & Off. Holders Asn, 54-61; v.chmn. and mem, Tri-City Airport Authority, Westmoreland Co, 56-66; mem. exec. bd, Gr. Latrobe Dem. Club, 63-66; del, Dem. Nat. Conv, 64; city Auditor, Latrobe, Pa, 66-69. Bus. & Prof. Pos: Asst. secy-treas, Kingston Brick Co, 31-38; owner, Stader Furniture Co, Latrobe, Pa, 31-62; chmn. exec. sch. bd, Greensburg Cent. Cath. High Sch, 68-69. Mem: Pres, Latrobe Rotary Club, 43; v.pres, Westmoreland Catholic Welfare Asn, 46-50; pres, Gr. Latrobe C. of C, 48; dir, Latrobe Commun. Nursing Serv, 49-50; pres, Westmoreland Co. Mayor's Asn, 52; exec. cmt, Pa. State Mayors' Asn, 54-61; adv. bd, Practical Nurse Asn, 54-64; dir, Latrobe Chap, Am. Red Cross. Numismatist; Amateur Oil Painter, Six Art Shows; Writer, Local Hist. Rel: Roman Catholic. Mailing Add: 827 Walnut St, Latrobe, Pa. 15650.

STADLER, GLEN M. D
Ore. State Sen.
b. Woodburn, Ind, 8/17/11; s. Clarence Walter Stadler (deceased) and Ellen Wilson S. (deceased); m. 7/24/48 to Helene Nielsen. Educ: Toledo Univ, 30-32; Ind. Univ, 32-33; Evansville Col, B.A, 47; Univ. Ore, M.A. in Jour, 50. Polit. & Govt. Pos: Ore. State Rep, Lane Co, 57-59; Ore. State Sen, Lane Co, 63- Bus. & Prof. Pos: Chief bur, United Press, Paris, 40-41; chief correspondent, Columbia Broadcasting Syst, Madrid, 43-44; pres, KEED, Ind, 54-65; pres, Radio Wonderful Willametteland, Inc, 63- Publ: This Is The Enemy, Little, 42. Mem: Sigma Delta Chi; Broadcast Pioneers; Elks; Kiwanis. Co-recipient, Pulitzer Award, 41; Ore. Press Club Award, 51 & 52. Rel: Methodist. Mailing Add: 303 Fairway Loop, Eugene, Ore. 97401.

STADLER, ROBERT FRY R
b. Iola, Kans, 7/29/20; s. John George Stadler and Barbara R. Fry S; single. Educ: Univ. Kans, A.B, 41 and LL.B, 48; Scabbard & Blade; Phi Delta Phi; Beta Theta Pi. Polit. & Govt. Pos: Mem, bd. trustees, Iola Pub. Libr, Kans, 59-69; Kans. State Rep, Tenth Dist, 67-68; judge, Div. 2, Fourth Judicial Dist, Kans, 69- Bus. & Prof. Pos: Partner, Cannon & Stadler, Attorneys, Humboldt, 52-68. Mil. Serv: Entered as 2nt Lt, Army, 41, released as 1st Lt, 45, after serv. in Asiatic-Pac. and Mediterranean Theaters; Maj, Mil. Intel, Army Res, 56-; Asiatic-Pac. Theater and ETO Ribbons; Distinguished Unit Citation. Mem: Am, Kans. State and Allen Co. Bar Asns; Rotary Int; Elks. Rel: Presbyterian. Legal Res: 302 S. Cottonwood St, Iola, Kans. 66749. Mailing Add: Courthouse, Iola, Kans. 66748.

STAEBLER, NEIL D
Assoc. Committeeman, Dem. Nat. Cmt, Mich.
b. Ann Arbor, Mich, 7/11/05; s. Edward W. Staebler and Magdalena Dold S;

m. 2/8/35 to Burnette Bradley; c. Michael B. and Elizabeth. Educ: Univ. Mich, A.B, 26, LL.D, 62; Theta Chi. Polit. & Govt. Pos: Chief bldg. materials br, price div, Off. Price Admin, Wash, D.C, 42-43; Mich. finance dir, Dem. Nat. Cmt, 49-50; chmn, Dem. State Cent. Cmt, 50-61; del, Dem. Nat. Conv, 56, 60, 64 & 68; mem, Pres. Cmn. Campaign Costs, 61-62; Dem. nat. committeeman, Mich, 61-68; U.S. Rep, Mich, 63-64; assoc. committeeman, Dem. Nat. Cmt, Mich, 68-, adv. on orgn. to chmn. Fred Harris, currently. Bus. & Prof. Pos: Partner, Staebler & Son, Ann Arbor, Mich, 26-; treas, Staebler-Kempf Oil Co, 26-51; vis. prof. practical politics, Univ. Mass, spring, 62; mem. bd. dirs, Citizens Research Found. and Detroit Area Coun. World Affairs Inc. Mil. Serv: Lt, Navy, 43-45. Publ: How to Argue with a Conservative, Grossman Publishers, Inc, N.Y.C, 2/66; 'Management of State Political Parties,' In: Practical Politics in the United States, 67. Mem: Am. Polit. Sci. Asn; Am. Econ. Asn; dir-at-lg, Nat. Bd, Nat. Training Labs, Nat. Educ. Asn, 64-69; Am. Vets. Cmt. Rel: Unitarian. Legal Res: 601 Huron View Blvd, Ann Arbor, Mich. 48103. Mailing Add: 408 Wolverine Bldg, Ann Arbor, Mich. 48108.

STAFFORD, CHESTER JEFFERSON D
Chmn, Giles Co. Dem. Cmt, Va.
b. Giles Co, Va, Apr; s. Chester Jefferson Stafford and Elizabeth Painter S; single. Educ: Col. William and Mary, B.A; Univ. Va. Law Sch, LL.B. Polit. & Govt. Pos: Chmn, Giles Co. Dem. Cmt, Va, 67-; alternate del, Dem. Nat. Conv, 68. Bus. & Prof. Pos: Lawyer, Dillow & Andrews, Pearisburg, Va, 66-Mil. Serv: Entered as 1st Lt, Army, 64, released as Capt, 66, after serv. in Seventh Inf. Div, Korea, 65-66; Capt. Army Res, 66-; Cert. of Achievement, Seventh Inf. Div; Cert. of Achievement, USALMC. Mem: AF&AM; Moose; Jaycees. Rel: Methodist. Mailing Add: Wenonah Ave, Pearisburg, Va. 24134.

STAFFORD, DON H. R
Fla. State Rep.
b. Madison Co, Ala, 1/12/38; s. H.H. Stafford and Lucille Blackwell S; m. 10/1/65 to Donna Hall. Educ: Univ. Ala, 59-60; St. Petersburg Jr. Col, 61-62 and 64-65; Univ. of Tampa, 63. Polit. & Govt. Pos: Chmn, Ins. Cmt, Largo, Fla, 66; Fla. State Rep, presently. Mil. Serv: Entered as Seaman Recruit, Navy, 55, released as Air Controlman 2/C, 59, after serv. in Pac. and Atlantic. Mem: Dir, St. Petersburg Jr. Col. Alumni Asn; pres, Largo Jr. C. of C; Largo C. of C; Greater Pinellas Co. Young Rep. Club; former mem, Civitan and Amvets. Rel: Lutheran. Legal Res: 1568 Oak Lane, Clearwater, Fla. 33516. Mailing Add: P.O. Box 865, Largo, Fla. 33540.

STAFFORD, EDWIN SAMUEL D
Committeeman of Ninth Dist, Blount Co, Tenn.
b. Maryville, Tenn, 5/5/14; s. John Nuebert Stafford and Bertha Elizabeth Henry S; m. 4/26/34 to Dorothy Verna McCammon; c. Max(deceased), Edwin Don, John Leon, Bertha Kay and Robert Dale. Educ: High Sch, 32. Polit. & Govt. Pos: Chmn, Blount Co. Dem. Exec. Cmt, Tenn, 58-60 & 62-64; mgr, Pres. John F. Kennedy's Blount Co. Campaign, 60-62; mgr, Sen. Ross Bass' Blount Co. Dem. Cmt, 64-66; Committeeman of Ninth Dist, Blount Co, currently. Bus. & Prof. Pos: V.pres, Local 309 USW, 52-56. Mem: Local 309 USW; Am. Angus Asn; Hampshire Swine Registry. Rel: Methodist. Mailing Add: Route 3, Maryville, Tenn. 37801.

STAFFORD, GEORGE WALTER R
Majority Whip, N.H. State House of Rep.
b. Laconia, N.H, 7/23/37; s. Walter George Stafford and Deloria Lesveque S; m. 1/24/68 to Margarete M. Brummerloh; c. George W, II and stepsons, Clifford H. and Kenneth M. Educ: Georgetown Univ, B.S. in Pub. Admin, 61. Polit. & Govt. Pos: Chmn, Laconia City Del, N.H, 63-66; v.chmn, Cmt. on Exec. Dept. & Admin, 63-64; clerk, N.H. Legis. Coun, 65-66; N.H. State Rep, 65-, chmn, N.H. Pub. Works Cmt, N.H. House of Rep, 65-, chmn, N.H. Non-Pub. Sch. Study Cmn, 69- and Majority Whip, N.H. House of Rep, 69-; chmn, Belknap Co. Del, 67-68. Bus. & Prof. Pos: Pub. rels. officer, Stafford Enterprises, 61-68; pres, Stafford Rentals, Inc, Laconia, N.H, 68. Mil. Serv: Pvt, N.H. Nat. Guard, 62-63, serv. in Battery C, Laconia, N.H. Mem: Nat. Soc. State Legislators (past nat. pres); Int. Brotherhood of Magicians; Soc. Am. Magicians; Elks (Past Exalted Ruler Laconia Lodge 876); K. of C; Eagles; Snowshoe Club; Nat. Coun. Catholic Men. Hon. Citizen, States of Pa, Ark, N.C. and S.Dak. and Cities of New Orleans, La. and Magnolia, Ark; Lt. Col. on Staff, Gov. of La. Rel: Roman Catholic. Legal Res: Pendleton Beach, Laconia, N.H. 03246. Mailing Add: P.O. Box 94, Lakeport, N.H. 03246.

STAFFORD, HENRY ALEXANDER R
b. Orleans, Vt, 11/1/91; married; c. two daughters. Educ: Tufts Col, B.S, 16; 3 years night sch. at Phila. Textile. Polit. & Govt. Pos: Town selectman, Bethel, Vt; mem, Windsor Co. Draft Bd. and served on Local War Rationing Bd; supvr, White River Soil Conserv. Dist, 43-; Vt. State Rep, 59-67. Bus. & Prof. Pos: Formerly in textile indust, dairy and cattle breeding; former dir, Bethel Coop. Creamery and Vt. Coop. Coun; retired. Mil. Serv: Chem. Warfare Serv. Mem: Vt, Jersey and New Eng. Breeders Asn; White River Rod and Gun Club; Rotary; Am. Legion. Rel: Universalist. Mailing Add: R.F.D. 3, Bethel, Vt. 05077. (1967)

STAFFORD, JACK DWAYNE R
b. Princeton, W.Va, 4/19/36; s. Elbert Luther Stafford and Willie Waddell S; m. 9/30/61 to Carol Blevins; c. Staci Lynne and John Phillip. Educ: Bluefield Col, 54-55; N.C. State Univ, B.S, 59; Concord Col, B.S, 59; Am. Inst. of Chem. Engrs; Am. Inst. of Physics; Lambda Chi Alpha. Polit. & Govt. Pos: Mem, Mercer Co. Exec. Cmt, W.Va, 68; pres, Mercer Co. Rep. Club, 68-69; v.chmn, W.Va. Rep. Party, 68-69; mem, campaign staff, U.S. Rep. Arch A. Moore, Jr, 69; asst. to Gov. Arch A. Moore, Jr, 69; asst. state rd. cmnr, 69-Bus. & Prof. Pos: Research engr, Celanese Corp. of Am, Narrows, Va, 59-62; chief of quality assurance, N.Am. Rockwell Corp, Princeton, W.Va, 62-68. Publ: Three books in field of synthetic fibers, 60-62. Mem: Am. Soc. for Quality Control; Am. Mgt. Asn; Nat. Gov. Conf. Cmt. on Transportation, Commerce and Tech; dir, W.Va. Heart Asn; Elks; v.pres, Melrose Lions Club; past pres, Princeton Jaycees; AF&AM; Bluefield Commandery; Knights Templar; Shrine; Mercer Co. Horsemans Asn; N.C. State Univ. Alumni Asn. Rel: Methodist; mem, off. bd. and lay personal cmt, First Methodist Church, Princeton, W.Va. Mailing Add: Box 277, Athens Star Route, Princeton, W.Va. 24740.

STAFFORD, RALPH E. R
Vt. State Rep.
b. South Wallingford, Vt, 3/2/05; m. to Mabel A. Rice. Educ: Wallingford High Sch. Polit. & Govt. Pos: Former Rep. town committeeman, South Wallingford, selectman and overseer of poor, 40-47; Vt. State Rep, 47 & 63-; Vt. State Sen, 49-55. Bus. & Prof. Pos: Ins. agent; farmer. Mem: Mason; Eastern Star (Past Dep); Grange (Past Dep); Farm Bur; Shrine; Vt. Sugar Maker's Asn. Rel: Congregational. Mailing Add: South Wallingford, Vt. 05771.

STAFFORD, ROBERT T. R
U.S. Rep, Vt.
b. Rutland, Vt, 8/8/13; s. Bert L. Stafford and Mabel Stratton S; m. 10/15/38 to Helen Kelley; c. Madelyn Ann, Susan Britton, Barbara Jean and Dianne Louise. Educ: Middlebury Col, B.S, 35; Univ. Mich; Boston Univ. Law Sch, LL.B, 38; Delta Epsilon. Hon. LL.D, Middlebury Col, 60, Norwich Univ, 60, Boston Univ, 59 and St. Michels Col, 68. Polit. & Govt. Pos: State attorney, Rutland Co, Vt, 47-51; dep. attorney gen, Vt, 53-55, attorney gen, 55-57, lt. gov, 57-59 and gov, 59-61; del, Rep. Nat. Conv, 60 & 68; U.S. Rep, Vt, 61-Mil. Serv: Entered as Ens, Navy, 42, released as Lt. Comdr, 46, after serv. in Am, European and Southwest Pac. Theaters; various campaign ribbons; Capt, Naval Res, 62- Mem: Vt. Bar Asn; Am. Legion; VFW; Lions; Eagles; Elks; Mason. Private pilot. Rel: Protestant. Legal Res: 64 Litchfield Ave, Rutland, Vt. 05701. Mailing Add: 3541 Devon Dr, Falls Church, Va. 22042.

STAGG, TOM R
Nat. Committeeman, La. Rep. Exec. Cmt.
b. Shreveport, La, 1/19/23; s. Thomas Eaton Stagg and Beulah Meyer S; m. 8/21/46 to Margaret Mary O'Brien; c. Julie and Margaret. Educ: La. State Univ, B.A, 43; La. State Univ. Law Sch, J.D, 49. Polit. & Govt. Pos: Chmn, Fourth Cong. Dist. Rep. Party, La, 53-63; chmn, Caddo Parish Rep. Exec. Cmt, 53-60; del, Rep. Nat. Conv, 56, 60, 64 & 68; chmn, Platform Cmt, Rep. Party of La, 62-; nat. committeeman, La. Rep. Exec. Cmt, 64-; mem, Shreveport Airport Authority, 67- Bus. & Prof. Pos: V.pres, King Hardware Co, Inc, 55-; sr. partner, Stagg, Cady & Beard, 58-; pres, Abe Meyer Corp, Real Estate, 60-; managing partner, Pierremont Mall Shopping Center, 63-; pres, Stagg Investments, Inc, 64- Mil. Serv: Entered as 2nd Lt, Army, 43, released as Capt, 46, after serv. in 411th Inf, ETO; Bronze Star; Purple Heart with Oak Leaf Cluster. Mem: Shreveport, La. and Am. Bar Asns; C. of C; Int. Coun. of Shopping Centers. Legal Res: 4847 Camellia Lane, Shreveport, La. 71106. Mailing Add: 406 Petroleum Tower, Shreveport, La. 71101.

STAGGERS, HARLEY ORRIN D
U.S. Rep, W.Va.
b. Keyser, W.Va, 8/3/07; s. Jacob Kinsey Staggers and Frances Cumberledge S; m. 10/4/43 to Mary Casey; c. Margaret Anne, Mary Katherine, Frances Susan, Elizabeth Ellen, Harley Orrin, Jr. and Daniel Casey. Educ: Emory and Henry Col, A.B. Hon. LL.D, Emory and Henry Col, 53 and Davis and Elkins Col, 69. Polit. & Govt. Pos: U.S. Rep, W.Va, 48-; del, Dem. Nat. Conv, 68. Mil. Serv: Navy, 42-46. Mem: Am. Legion; VFW; DAV; Amvets; Moose; Lions; Elks; K. of P; W.Va. Farm Bur. Rel: Methodist. Legal Res: New Creek Dr, Keyser, W.Va. 26726. Mailing Add: 2366 Rayburn House Office Bldg, Washington, D.C. 20515.

STAGGS, RALPH EUGENE R
b. Phoenix, Ariz, 1/9/22; s. Clyde S. Staggs and Susie Dale S; m. 7/9/47 to Patricia Pell; c. Clyde, Jeff, Jimmy and Cindy. Polit. & Govt. Pos: Rep. precinct committeeman, Ariz, 52-; finance chmn, Maricopa Co. Rep. Party, 58-61, chmn, 61-64; chmn. fund raising dinner for Pres. Eisenhower, 59 and Sen. Goldwater, 60 & 61; cand, Ariz. State Sen, 66. Bus. & Prof. Pos: Regional v.pres, Nat. Asn. Home Builders, 53 & 55, nat. dir, 56-66; pres, Phoenix Asn. Home Builders, 54. Mem: Ariz. Develop. Bd, 61-64; v.pres, Roosevelt Coun. Boy Scouts, 65 and 66; Rotary; Moose; Boys Club Am; Paradise Valley Country Club; Nat. Asn. Home Builders Spike Club; Realtors. Spec. award, Boys Club Am; Cert. of Appreciation, House and Home Finance Agency, 61; citation, Phoenix Symphony Youth Orchestra, 62; Good Citizenship Medal, SAR; hon. citizen, Mazatlan, Sinaloa, Mex. Rel: Methodist. Mailing Add: 4801 E. Palomino Rd, Phoenix, Ariz. 85018.

STAHL, DAVID EDWARD D
Dep. Mayor, Chicago, Ill.
b. Chicago, Ill, 4/10/34; s. Archie Edward Stahl and Dorothy Berning S; m. 6/23/56 to Carol Downs; c. Stephen D, Michael J, Kurt E. and Thomas A. Educ: Miami Univ, B.S, 56; Phi Beta Kappa; Beta Gamma Sigma; Omicron Delta Kappa; Delta Upsilon. Polit. & Govt. Pos: Dir. land disposition, Dept. Urban Renewal, City of Chicago, Ill, 61-63, spec. asst. to mayor for housing, 66-68; dep. mayor, 68-; del, Dem. Nat. Conv, 68. Bus. & Prof. Pos: Exec. v.pres, Republic Realty Mortgage Corp, Chicago, Ill, 63-66. Mil. Serv: Entered as 2nd Lt, Air Force, 56, released as 1st Lt, 59, after serv. in 316th Air Division, ETO; Capt. Res. Mem: Nat. Asn. Housing & Redevelop. Off. (past pres, Chicago Chap); Nat. Housing Conf.(dir); Boy Scouts (mem. bd. Chicago Area Coun); bd. assocs, Mercy Hosp and Med. Center; bd, Adler Planetarium; Econ. Club. Chicago; Sauganash Commun. Asn; Lambda Alpha. Ten Outstanding Young Men Award, Chicago Jr. Asn. Commerce and Indust, 68. Rel: Roman Catholic. Legal Res: 5951 N. Kenneth Ave, Chicago, Ill. 60646. Mailing Add: Room 507, City Hall, Chicago, Ill. 60602.

STAHL, JACK L. R
N.Mex. State Rep.
b. Lincoln, Ill, 6/28/34; s. Edwin R. Stahl and Edna Burns S; m. 6/23/56 to Carol Anne Townsend; c. Cheryl, Nancy and Kellea. Educ: Univ. N.Mex, B.S, 56; Sigma Alpha Epsilon. Polit. & Govt. Pos: N.Mex. State Rep, Dist. 11, 69-Bus. & Prof. Pos: Teacher, Albuquerque Pub. Schs, 56-59; Proprietor, Jack Stahl Realtor, 60-67; partner, Hooten-Stahl Realtors, 67- Mem: dir, Albuquerque Bd. of Realtors. Rel: Protestant. Legal Res: 1517 Arizona N.E, Albuquerque, N.Mex. 87110. Mailing Add: 2051 Wyoming Blvd. N.E, Albuquerque, N.Mex. 87112.

STAHL, THOMAS BURTON R
Treas, Sandusky Co. Rep. Cent. Cmt, Ohio
b. Fremont, Ohio, 4/5/04; s. John Burton Stahl and Florence Fisher S; m.

11/4/36 to Harriett May Beatty; c. John Thomas and James Philip. Educ: Miami Univ, 22-23; Univ. Toledo, 23-24; Ohio State Univ, LL.B, 27; Delta Theta Phi. Polit. & Govt. Pos: Mem, Sandusky Co. Rep. Cent. Cmt, Ohio, 29-, treas, 65-; pres, Sandusky Co. Law Libr. Asn, 35-; common pleas judge, Sandusky Co, 36-37; alternate del, Rep. Nat. Conv, 68. Bus. & Prof. Pos: Mem, bd. dir, Fremont Savings Bank Co, Ohio, 57- Mem: Am, Ohio and Sandusky Co. Bar Asns; Am. Judicature Soc; Mason (32°); Elks(past exalted ruler, Fremont Post 169); Shrine; Fremont Country Club; Catawba Island Club. Rel: Protestant. Legal Res: 720 Garrison St, Fremont, Ohio 43420. Mailing Add: 615 Croghan St, Fremont, Ohio 43420.

STAHLER, HERBERT H. R
b. Boston, Mass, 11/22/95; wid; c. three sons, two daughters. Educ: Lyndonville Schs. Polit. & Govt. Pos: Overseer of the poor, Lyndon Center, Vt, 12 years, sch. dir, ten years, town selectman, ten years and justice of the peace, 53-; Vt. State Rep, 51 & 65-67. Bus. & Prof. Pos: Retired, Fairbanks Morse Co, 61. Mil. Serv: Mex. Border Serv; sgt, World War I. Mem: F&AM. Rel: Baptist. Mailing Add: Star Route, Lyndon Center, Vt. 05850. (1967)

STAHLIN, JOHN HENRY R
Mem, Mich. State Rep. Cent. Cmt.
b. Belding, Mich, 4/6/14; s. Edward M. Stahlin and Sadie Mayor S; m. 11/15/35 to Pauline Mary Underwood; c. John M, Susan M, Paul F. and Edward W. Educ: Ferris State Col, 33-34. Polit. & Govt. Pos: Mich. State Sen, 25th Dist, 58-62; mem, Mich. State Rep. Cent. Cmt, 62-; finance chmn, Ionia Co. Rep. Party, 64-65; mem, Fifth Dist. Rep. Finance Cmt, 64-; mem, Higher Educ. Facility Cmn. and Econ. Develop. Cmn, Mich, 65-; spec. asst. polit. affairs for Gov. William G. Milliken, Mich, 65-; del,Rep. Nat. Conv, 68. Bus. & Prof. Pos: Pres, Stahlin Bros. Fibre Works, Inc, 36-; v.pres, J.P. Carter Co, 49-; secy-treas, Gulf View, Inc, 52- Mem: Mason; Mich. C. of C; Belding C. of C; Detroit Athletic Club; Lansing City Club; Detroit Econ. Club. Rel: Christian Scientist. Mailing Add: 222 S. Broas St, Belding, Mich. 48809.

STAISEY, LEONARD CLIFTON D
b. Duquesne, Pa, 11/10/21; s. Daniel Leonard Staisey and Anna Kostelac S; m. 9/21/46 to Emilie Consuelo Sylvester; c. Consuelo Emilie and Nancy Lora. Educ: Northwest. Univ, B.S.S, 44, Law Sch, J.D, 47; Phi Eta Sigma; Phi Alpha Delta; Theta Xi; Purple Key; Deru, Northwest. Univ. Polit. & Govt. Pos: Campaign chmn, polit. analyst, writer and speaker; mem, Duquesne Bd. of Educ, Pa, 49-59; asst. dist. attorney, Allegheny Co, 50-65; mem, Adv. Coun. for the Blind, Pa, 55-66; Duquesne Dem. chmn, 58-; mem, Duquesne City Coun, 59-60; mem, Adv. Coun. for Educ. TV, 60-66; Pa. State Sen, 45th Dist, 60-66; del, Dem. Nat. Conv, 68; chmn, Bd. of Co. Cmnr, Allegheny Co, 68- Mem: Am, Pa. and Allegheny Co. Bar Asns; Am. Trial Lawyers Asn; Moose; Eagles; Elks. Awards in Conserv; Student Scholarships; Help to the Handicapped and Self Achievement. Rel: Episcopal. Legal Res: 500 Commonwealth Ave, Duquesne, Pa. 15110. Mailing Add: 1009 Duquesne Blvd, Duquesne, Pa. 15110.

STALBAUM, LYNN E. D
b. Waterford, Wis, 5/15/20; m. to Alice Gunderson; c. Two daughters, two sons. Educ: Racine Co. Agr. Sch, grad, 36. Polit. & Govt. Pos: Wis. State Sen, 54, 58 & 62, caucus chmn, Wis. State Senate, 57, 59 & 61, asst. minority leader, 63; U.S. Rep, Wis, 64-66. Bus. & Prof. Pos: With U.S. Dept. of Agr, Racine Co, 36-44, admin. officer, 39-44; feed salesman, 46-51; secy-treas, Racine Milk Producers Coop. Asn. and mgr. of the Harmony Dairy Co, 51-64; asst. to gen. mgr, Assoc. Dairymen, Inc, 69- Mil. Serv: Navy, destroyer, 44-46. Mem: Am. Legion, past comdr, Waterford Post; VFW, charter mem, Wind Lake Post. Mailing Add: 6311 Blackwood Rd, Bethesda, Md. 20034.

STALBAUM, MERRILL R
Wis. State Assemblyman
b. Norway, Racine Co, Wis, 4/24/11. Educ: Waterford High Sch. Polit. & Govt. Pos: Clerk, Norway, Wis, 37-67; mem, Racine Co. Sch. Cmt, 49-60; Wis. State Assemblyman, 60- Bus. & Prof. Pos: Surveyor and farmer. Mailing Add: Route 1, Waterford, Wis. 53185.

STALDER, LLOYD W. R
b. Humboldt, Nebr, 2/23/88; m. 1/22/13 to Louise Power. Educ: Univ. of Nebr. Polit. & Govt. Pos: Secy, Richardson Co. Soil Conserv. Dist, Nebr, 20 years; past mem, Bd. of Rural Sch. Dist; past councilman, Humboldt; former Nebr. State Sen. Bus. & Prof. Pos: Former farmer and grain elevator operator; livestock feeder, currently. Mem: Past pres, Humboldt C. of C; Richardson Co. Fair Bd. for 25 years, pres. for past 3 years; charter pres, Humboldt Rotary Club; Mason; Scottish Rite; Shrine. Mailing Add: Humboldt, Nebr. 68376.

STALHEIM, LARRY L. R
S.Dak. State Rep.
b. Kranzburg, S.Dak; s. Henry O. Stalheim and Ellen Nelson S; m. 10/1/49 to Laverne Bockelmen; c. Cindy, Connie, Mark and Mary. Educ: Kans. State Univ, B.S, 47. Polit. & Govt. Pos: S.Dak. State Rep, 69- Bus. & Prof. Pos: Pres, Stalheim Inc, 20 years. Mil. Serv: Entered as Seaman, Navy, 41, released as PO, 45, after serv. in U.S. Bennington, Pac. Theatre. Mem: VFW; Am. Legion; Mason; Kiwanis. Rel: Protestant. Mailing Add: Hwy. 14 W, Desmet, S.Dak. 57231.

STALLINGS, GEORGE B, JR. D
b. Jacksonville, Fla, 5/12/18; m. to Marguerite Hamilton; c. Ann Frances (Mrs. Lucas), Margo Hamilton and Deborah Brooks. Educ: Univ. Va; Univ. Fla, LL.B, 49. Polit. & Govt. Pos: Fla. State Rep, 58-67. Bus. & Prof. Pos: Attorney. Mil. Serv: Army Air Corps. Mem: Gr. Riverside Bus. Asn; past pres, Bolles Sch. Alumni Asn. Rel: Presbyterian. Mailing Add: 5127 Pirates Cove Rd, Jacksonville, Fla. 32210. (1967)

STALLMAN, THOMAS R. D
b. Beardsley, Minn, 4/10/23; married; c. five. Educ: State Sch. of Sci. Polit. & Govt. Pos: N. Dak. State Rep, 59-66. Bus. & Prof. Pos: Farmer. Mil: WW II vet. Mem: Am. Legion; VFW. Mailing Add: Barney, N. Dak. 58008. (1967)

STALLWORTH, JOHN ROBERT, III D
b. Tuscaloosa, Ala, 1/6/28; s. John Robert Stallworth, Jr. and Gladys Sizemore S; div; c. Mary Elizabeth, Nancy Ann, John Edward and William Robert. Educ: Trevecca Nazarene Col, A.B; Livingston State Col, M.A. Polit. & Govt. Pos: Del, Dem. Nat. Conv, 64. Mil. Serv: Army, 51-52. Mem: Farm Bur; Lions; Am. Legion. Rel: Nazarene. Mailing Add: 1406 22nd Ave, Tuscaloosa, Ala. 35401. (1967)

STALNAKER, EARL H. D
W.Va. State Del.
b. Elkins, W.Va, 6/22/20; s. James G. Stalnaker and Inez Marie Duckworth S; m. 7/27/41 to Vetla R. Perry; c. Phillip E. Educ: Pub. Schs, Randolph Co. Polit. & Govt. Pos: W.Va. State Del, 54-56 & 64- Bus. & Prof. Pos: X-ray technician. Mil. Serv: Air Corps, World War II. Mem: Elks; Moose; Am. Legion; 40 et 8. Rel: Methodist. Mailing Add: 1736 S. Gate Rd, Elkins, W.Va. 26241. (1967)

STALNAKER, PAUL D
b. Wellston, Ga, 12/12/27; s. Joseph P. Stalnaker and Alma Hartley S; m. 2/27/47 to Margaret Tharpe; c. Virginia K, Robert M. and Rusell P. Educ: Bonaire High Sch. Polit. & Govt. Pos: Ga. State Rep, 63-68. Bus. & Prof. Pos: Mfr; Pres, Rol-O-Valve Co. Inc. Mil. Serv: Navy, World War II, European, African and Mid. East Theatres; Good Conduct Medal; Commendation from President Harry S Truman; Victory Medal. Rel: Baptist. Mailing Add: 112 Pattie Dr, Warner Robins, Ga. 31093. (1967)

STAMLER, NELSON F. R
b. Elizabeth, N.J, 5/4/09; single. Educ: W.Va. Univ; Rutgers Law Sch. Polit. & Govt. Pos: Dep. Attorney Gen, N.J, 47-53; N.J. State Assemblyman, 60-62; N.J. State Sen, 62-67. Bus. & Prof. Pos: Lawyer. Mem: Nat. cmnr. of Anti-Defamation League of B'nai B'rith; v.chmn. of Adv. Bd. of Salvation Army; pres, Union Co. Bar Asn; gen. coun, State Bar Asn. Mailing Add: 29 Broad St, Elizabeth, N.J. 07201. (1967)

STAMM, ANTHONY R
Mich. State Sen.
b. Kalamazoo, Mich, 7/3/12; s. John Stamm and Stella Berghuis S; m. 11/4/55 to Miriam Jean Wise. Educ: Western Mich. Univ, B.S, 46 and M.A, 60. Polit. & Govt. Pos: Co. clerk, Kalamazoo Co, Mich, 41-67; alternate del-at-lg, Rep. Nat. Conv, 48; del, Rep. State Conv; state chmn, Mich. Fedn. Young Rep, 48-49; second legis. dist. del, Mich. Constitutional Conv, 61-62; Mich. State Sen, currently. Mem: Pres, Western Mich. Chap, Am. Soc. of Pub. Administration; Kalamazoo Rep. Cmt; Elks; del, Am. Kennel Club; Kalamazoo Kennel Club. Rel: Presbyterian. Mailing Add: 2097 S. Fourth St, Kalamazoo, Mich. 49001.

STAMP, FREDERICK P, JR. R
W.Va. State Del.
b. 1934. Educ: Linsly Mil. Inst; Taft Sch; Wash. and Lee Univ; Univ. of Richmond. Polit. & Govt. Pos: W.Va. State Del, 67-; chmn, Ohio Co. Rep. Finance Cmt. and mem, State Rep. Finance Cmt, presently. Bus. & Prof. Pos: Partner, Schmidt, Laas, Schrader and Miller Law Firm, presently; secy. and mem. of bd. of dirs, Ohio Valley Indust. and Bus. Develop. Corp, presently. Mem: Exec. cmt. and bd, Wheeling Symphony Soc; secy, Salvation Army Adv. Bd; bd. of trustees, Davis and Elkins Col; secy, Ohio Co. Bar Asn, 61; chmn, Legal Aid Cmt, Ohio Co. Bar Asn, 65. Rel: Presbyterian. Mailing Add: R.D. 1, Wheeling, W.Va. 26003.

STAMPS, HAL BURTON D
Secy-treas, Third Cong. Dist. Dem. Party, Okla.
b. Wapanucka, Okla, 7/6/21; s. Hal Stamps and Velma Trotter S; m. 1/9/41 to Louise Alsup; c. Susan Lyn (Mrs. Forguson) and Bob Hal. Educ: Murray State Agr. Col, Okla, 1 year. Polit. & Govt. Pos: Chmn, Johnston Co. Dem. Cent. Cmt, Okla, 62-69; secy-treas, Third Cong. Dist. Dem. Party, currently. Bus. & Prof. Pos: Owner, Stamps 5 & 10, 47-62; co-owner, Stamps Dry Goods, 62- Mem: Past pres, Tishomingo Rotary Club. Rel: Methodist. Mailing Add: 706 E. 18th, Tishomingo, Okla. 73460.

STANCIL, JOAN M. R
Mem, Calif. Rep. State Cent. Cmt.
b. Orient, S.Dak, 7/3/21; d. Frederick Lorenzo Dow Sweetland and Rose-Margaret Anglin S; m. 6/22/46 to Joseph Elijah Stancil; c. Lisa (Mrs. Ronald Rohrer), Joseph E, Jr. and Edward Sean. Educ: Presentation Sch. of Nursing, Aberdeen, S.Dak, R.N, 42; Sacramento State Col, B.A. in Psychol, 70. Polit. & Govt. Pos: Secy, Federated Rep. Women, El Dorado Co, Calif, 62-63, pres, 63-64; mem, Calif. Rep. State Cent. Cmt, 65-; mem, adv. bd, El Dorado Mental Health Prog, Calif, 68- Mil. Serv: Entered as 2nd Lt, Army Nurse Corps, 42, released as 1st Lt, 46, after serv. in 16th Evacuation Hosp. Unit, Mediterranean Theatre, 5th Army, 43-45; 2 Battle Stars, Naples-Foggia and Rome-Arno Campaigns; 2 Bronze Service Stars, North Appenines Campaign and Po Valley Campaign; Battle Participation Awards. Mem: Calif. State Nurses' Asn. Rel: Roman Catholic. Legal Res: Chili Bar Rd, Placerville, Calif. 95667. Mailing Add: 659 Main Street, Placerville, Calif. 95667.

STANDAFER, DARYL LLOYD R
Dist. Del, Minn. State Rep. Cent. Cmt.
b. Adrian, Minn, 7/14/42; s. Lloyd L. Standafer and Eunice Maree Kellam S; m. 9/8/62 to Janice Marie Zimmerman; c. Philip Daryl, Jeffrey Lloyd and Gregory Robert. Educ: McPherson Col, Kans, B.A, 64. Polit. & Govt. Pos: Fieldman, Minn. Rep. Party, 64; chmn, Nobles Co. Rep. Cmt, 64-67; alternate del, State Cent. Cmt, 67-69; chmn, Dist. Nixon Cmt, 68; alternate del, Rep. Nat. Conv, 68; dist. del, Minn. State Rep. Cent. Cmt, 69- Mem: Minn. and Am. Farm Bur; Holstein-Friesian Asn. Am; Minn. Holstein Asn; secy, Worthington Jaycees; U.S. Jaycees. Winner Second Prize, Nat. Farm Bur. Speech Contest, 59. Rel: Church of the Brethren. Mailing Add: R.R. 1, Worthington, Minn. 56187.

STANDLEY, FRED M. D
b. Boyd, Tex, 4/2/23; s. Fred M. Standley and Belfa Redford S; m. 9/26/45 to Ann Leonard; c. Kim, Lynn and Reed L. Educ: W.Tex. State Col, 41-42 & 46-47; Univ. Utah, B.S, 47, J.D, 50; Phi Alpha Delta. Polit. & Govt. Pos:

Asst. Attorney Gen, N.Mex, 53-55, Chief Asst. Attorney Gen, 55-56 and Attorney Gen, 58; campaign mgr, Joseph M. Montoya for U.S. Rep, N.Mex, 57-62 and for N.Mex. State Sen, 64; chief attorney for N.Mex. State Senate, 59 and for N.Mex. Hwy. Dept, 60; state campaign mgr, Lyndon Johnson Campaign, 60; acting Dem. state chmn, 61-62; del, Dem. Nat. Conv, 56, 64 & 68. Mil. Serv: Entered as Pvt, Air Force, 42, released as 1st Lt, 45, after serv. in 487th Bombardment Group, Eighth Air Force, Eng, 44-45; Air Medal with 4 Clusters; Distinguished Flying Cross; ETO Campaign Ribbon with 4 Clusters. Mem: Am. and Santa Fe Co. Bar Asns; Bar Asns. of State of N.Mex. and Utah; Supreme Court of U.S, 57; Elks; VFW; Am. Legion; Phi Alpha Delta Alumni. Rel: Methodist. Mailing Add: P.O. Drawer A, Santa Fe, N.Mex. 87501.

STANFORD, DONALD McIVER D
N.C. State Rep.
b. Orange City, N.C, 5/7/26; s. Charles Whitson Stanford Sr. and Mary Willcox McIver S; m. 6/30/49 to Patricia Denning Stanford; c. Donald, Randolph Lewis, Charles Ashley and James Cooper. Educ: N.C. State Univ, 42-43; Univ. N.C, Chapel Hill, A.B, 50. Polit. & Govt. Pos: Cmnr, Orange, N.C, 56-64, chmn, 60-64; pres, Young Dem. Club, Orange City, 58; dir, N.C. Asn. City Cmnrs, 59; organizer, Sixth Dist. Dem. Party, 59 and col. orgn, 60; mem, Dist. Bd. Health and Exec. Cmt, Research Triangle Planning Cmn, 60-64; N.C. State Rep, 65- Bus. & Prof. Pos: Dairy farmer. Mem: N.C. Dairy Found.(pres); Am. Dairy Asn. N.C.(secy-treas); C. of C; Rotary Int; Chapel Hill Rotary (secy, 60); Jaycees. Young Man of the Year, Chapel Hill, 58; O. Max Gardner Award, N.C. Young Dem. Rel: Presbyterian; Deacon, 56-63; Sunday Sch. Supt, 59. Mailing Add: 420 Whitehead Circle, Chapel Hill, N.C. 27514.

STANGELAND, ARLAN INGHART R
Minn. State Rep.
b. Fargo, N.Dak, 2/8/30; s. Inghart Stangeland and Pearle Olson S; m. 6/24/50 to Virginia Grace Trowbridge; c. David Arlan, Beth Ann, Brian Kent, Jean Gail, Todd Scott, Jeffrey Craig and Stuart Glen. Educ: Moorhead High Sch, grad, 48; Nat. Honor Soc. Polit. & Govt. Pos: Secy, Wilkin Co. Rep. Cmt, Minn, 59-65, chmn, 65-66; Minn. State Rep, 66- Mem: Farm Bur; Minn Shorthorn Asn; Red River Valley Shorthorn Asn; Red River Valley Livestock Asn; PTA. Rel: Lutheran. Mailing Add: R.R. 2, Barnesville, Minn. 56514.

STANHAGEN, JOHN FRANKLIN R
Chmn, Fairfield Co. Rep. Cmt, Ohio
b. Monongah, W.Va, 11/24/96; s. John Franklin Stanhagen and Amelia Horchler S; m. 12/23/19 to Mary Grace Rice; c. John Franklin, III and Mary Louise. Educ: W.Va. Univ. Exten. Polit. & Govt. Pos: Chmn, Fairfield Co. Rep. Cmt, Ohio, presently; mem, Bd. Elec, Ohio, presently. Bus. & Prof. Pos: Traffic mgr, Lancaster Glass Corp, retired 64. Mil. Serv: Entered as Pvt, Army, released as Sgt, after serv. in 30th Co, 155th Depot Brigade. Mem: Am. Legion. Rel: Lutheran. Mailing Add: Amanda, Ohio 43102.

STANISH, PAUL JOSEPH D
Ind. State Sen.
b. East Chicago, Ind, 8/11/37; s. Joseph John Stanish and Bertha B. Wasieleski S; m. 2/23/63 to Marilynn Jane Fuss; c. Paul Joseph, Philip John, Marla Joan and Tanya Jo. Educ: St. Joseph's Col, Calumet Campus; Ind. Univ, Northwest Campus. Polit. & Govt. Pos: Ind. State Sen, 64- Bus. & Prof. Pos: Pres, Paul Joseph's, Inc, 63-; pres, Just, Inc, 68- Mil. Serv: Entered as Pvt, Army, 60, released as Pfc, 66. Mem: Local 208 AFL-CIO; Vet. in Polit; Elks; C. of C; Optimists; Woodrow Wilson Club. Rel: Roman Catholic. Legal Res: 6340 Forest Ave, Hammond, Ind. 46324. Mailing Add: 2712 169th St, Hammond, Ind. 46323.

STANISLAUS, DOROTHY JEANNE R
Rep. Nat. Committeewoman, Okla.
b. Sand Springs, Okla, 9/8/25; d. Van Dolph Herrington and Sibly Schuler H; m. 6/2/45 to O. Doyle Stanislaus. Educ: Stephens Col, 43; Okla. Univ, 44-45; Delta Delta Delta. Polit. & Govt. Pos: Co. v.chmn, Okla. State Rep. Party, 62-63, co. chmn, 64 and v.chmn, 65-; del. and mem. platform cmt, Rep. Nat. Conv, 64, alternate del, 68; Rep. nat. committeewoman, Okla, 68- Rel: Episcopal. 1967 Legal Res: Pryor, Okla. No mailing address available. (1967)

STANLEY, DAVID R
Iowa State Sen.
b. Dubuque, Iowa, 1928; s. C.M. Stanley and Elizabeth Holthues S; m. 1948 to Jean Leu; c. Lincoln, Rebecca, Nathan and Elizabeth. Educ: Univ. Iowa Col. of Law, grad, 53, ranked 1st in grad. class; Phi Beta Kappa. Polit. & Govt. Pos: Secy, Muscatine Rep. Club, Iowa; former orgn. chmn, Iowa Young Rep; former Iowa State Rep; Iowa State Sen, 64-; nominee for U.S. Sen, Iowa, 68. Bus. & Prof. Pos: Sr. partner in Muscatine Law Firm. Mil. Serv: Air Force, 46-54. Mem: Iowa State Bar Asn; legis. chmn, Iowa Jr. C. of C; dir, Muscatine United Fund; v.pres, Muscatine City Tuberc. and Health Asn; Rotary; Toastmasters; Farm Bur; Mason; Moose; Muscatine Develop. Corp. Rel: Methodist. Mailing Add: 814 Iowa Ave, Muscatine, Iowa 52761. (1967)

STANLEY, ELIOT HUNGERFORD D
b. Baton Rouge, La, 1/4/42; s. Dr. Allan John Stanley and Ruth Moore S.(deceased); m. 8/27/66 to Nancy Elizabeth Schmid. Educ: Harvard Univ, B.A. cum laude in Hist, 63. Polit. & Govt. Pos: Asst. to dir, Okla. City Urban Renewal Authority, 63-64; legis. asst, U.S. Sen. Fred R. Harris, Okla, 64-65; spec. asst. legis, Off. Secy. Housing and Urban Develop, 65-66; admin. asst, U.S. Rep. B.S. Farnum 66-67 and U.S. Rep. Chet Holifield, 67-; adv. staff, Dem. Presidential nominee, 68. Publ: 'Academic Freedom in the South,' The Harvard Rev, 63. Mem: Am. Polit. Sci. Asn. Rel: Unitarian. Mailing Add: 1014 E. Capitol St, Apt. 3, Washington, D.C. 20003.

STANLEY, LEROY R. R
Chmn, Holmes Co. Rep. Cmt, Fla.
b. Ponce de Leon, Fla, 3/14/14; s. Jesse S. Stanley and Abbie Whitton S; m. 1/25/47 to Roma A. Shelneyt. Polit. & Govt. Pos: Chmn, Holmes Co. Rep. Cmt, Fla, 68- Rel: Baptist. Legal Res: Route 2, Box 6, Ponce de Leon, Fla. 32455.

STANLEY, MARY T. R
Mem, Calif. Rep. State Cent. Cmt.
b. Grand Forks, N.Dak, 10/7/27; s. Al Kimble and Geraldine Sabourin K; m. 11/6/53 to Jay E. Stanley; c. Gerald A, Cheryl A.(Mrs. John Peters) and Judith M. Educ: Cathedral High Sch, N.Y.C, 2 years; Messmer High Sch, Milwaukee, Wis, dipl, 44. Polit. & Govt. Pos: Rep. precinct capt, Goldwater for Pres, Calif, 64; campaign coordinator, 32nd Assembly Dist. Cand, 64; mem. exec. cmt, Friends of Reagan, Fresno, 65; assoc. mem, Calif. Rep. State Cent. Cmt, 65-66, mem, 66-; chmn. 32nd Assembly Dist, United Rep. of Calif, 65-67; mem. bd. dirs, Fresno and City Federated Rep. Women, 65-68; dir, 16th Cong. Dist. Calif. Rep. Assembly, 66; Fresno Co. Rep. precinct chmn, Reagan for Gov, 66; state v.pres, Calif. Rep. Assembly, 66-67; dir-at-lg, Calif. Rep. Assembly Precinct and Polit. Strategy Cmt, 66-67 & 69-; precinct chmn, Fresno Co. Rep. Cent. Cmt, 67-68, mem. exec. bd, 69-; five co. area chmn, Max Rafferty for U.S. Senate, 68. Bus. & Prof. Pos: V.pres, J-M.A.R. Enterprises Inc, 53-60; secy-treas, Zero Foods Inc, 61- Mem: Nat. Asn. of Food and Freezer Provisioners; Calif. State Asn. of Food and Freezer Provisioners; C. of C; March of Dimes; Fresno Luncheon Toastmistress Club. Rel: Protestant. Legal Res: 1361 N. Del Mar, Fresno, Calif. 93728. Mailing Add: 225 E. McKinley, Fresno, Calif. 93728.

STANLEY, MILES CLARK D
b. Dunbar, W.Va, 10/2/24; s. Worthy Carson Stanley and Opal E. Clark S; m. 4/2/43 to Romaleda E. Smith; c. Brenda Joyce (Mrs. Stanley Elliott), Penelope Lynne and Teresa Lea. Educ: Pub. schs. and Armed Forces Inst. Hon. L.H.D, Marshall Univ, 63 and W.Va. Inst. Tech, 66; Hon. LL.D, W.Va. Col, 67. Polit. & Govt. Pos: Alternate del, Dem. Nat. Conv, 68. Bus. & Prof. Pos: Pres, Steelworkers Union Local, Dunbar, W.Va, 47-56; exec. secy-treas, W.Va. Indust. Union Coun, CIO, Charleston, 56-57; pres, W.Va. Labor Fedn, AFL-CIO, 57-; asst. to pres, AFL-CIO, Wash, D.C, 65-67. Mil. Serv: Entered as Pvt, Army, 43, released as Pfc, 45, after serv. in ETO, 44-45; Five Combat Battle Stars; One Invasion Arrowhead. Mem: USW, AFL-CIO. Distinguished Laymans Award, Evangel. United Brethren Church, 62. Rel: United Methodist. Mailing Add: 1700 Kanawha Ave, Dunbar, W.Va. 25064.

STANS, MAURICE H. R
Secy. of Commerce
b. Shakopee, Minn, 3/22/08; s. J. Hubert Stans and Mathilda Nyssen S; m. 9/7/33 to Kathleen Carmody; c. Steven, Theodore, Maureen (Mrs. Walter Helmick) and Terrell (Mrs. William Manley). Educ: Northwest. Univ, 25-28; Columbia Univ, 28-30. Hon. LL.D, Grove City Col, St. Anselm's Col, Northwest. Univ, Ill. Wesleyan Univ. and DePaul Univ; D.P.A, Parsons Col. Polit. & Govt. Pos: Financial consult. to the Postmaster Gen, Post Off. Dept, 53-55, Dep. Postmaster Gen, 55-57; dep. dir, Bur. of the Budget, 57-58, dir, 58-61; chmn, Nixon for Pres. Cmt, 68; chmn, Rep. Nat. Finance Cmt, 68-69; Secy. of Commerce, 69- Bus. & Prof. Pos: Mem. and exec. partner, Alexander Grant & Co, Chicago, Ill, 28-55; treas. and dir, Moore Corp, Joliet, Ill, 38-45, chmn. bd, 42-45; dir. and mem. exec. cmt, James Talcott, Inc, N.Y.C, 41-55; pres, West. Bancorp, Los Angeles, Calif, 61-62; pres, Glore Forgan, William R. Staats, Inc, N.Y.C, 63-68. Mem: Am. Inst. of CPA; Nat. Asn. of Postmasters; Am. Soc. Pub. Admin; Fed. Govt. Acct. Asn; Econ. Club and Union League Club, Chicago; Capitol Hill Club and Safari Club, Wash, D.C; Calif. Club, Los Angeles; Recess Club and Metrop. Club, N.Y.C; Adventurers Club; Explorers Club; hon. mem, E.African Prfnl. Hunters Asn; Shikar-Safari Club. Am. Acct. Asn. Annual Award, 52; Am. Inst. of CPA Annual Award, 54; elected to Acct. Hall of Fame, 60; Tax Found. Award for Distinguished Pub. Serv, 59; Great Living Am. Award, U.S. C. of C, 61. Mailing Add: 2500 Virginia Ave. N.W, Washington, D.C. 20037.

STANSBERRY, RICHARD DONALD R
Okla. State Sen.
b. Oklahoma City, Okla, 10/8/28; s. Cecil Roy Stansberry and Lillian Smith S; m. 10/2/54 to Billie Jo Hogue; c. Richard Donald, Jr. Educ: Oklahoma City Univ, B.A, 50; George Wash. Sch. of Med, M.D, 58; Lambda Chi Alpha. Polit. & Govt. Pos: Okla. State Sen, Dist. 40, 65-; del, Rep. Nat. Conv, 68. Bus. & Prof. Pos: Physician, 58- Mil. Serv: Entered as Pvt, Air Force, 50, released as 1st Lt, 53, after serv. in Spec. Duty with the State Dept, Wash, D.C, 52-53. Publ: Med. articles. Mem: Am, Okla. State and Co. Med. Asns; Oklahoma City Obstetrics and Gynecology Soc; Oklahoma City Chem. Soc; Kiwanis; C. of C. Rel: Methodist. Mailing Add: 4120 N.W. 45th St, Oklahoma City, Okla. 73112. (1967)

STANT, FREDERICK THOMAS, JR. 'BINGO' D
b. Norfolk, Va, 4/21/18; s. Frederick Thomas Stant and Christine Schall S; m. 6/5/43 to Bette Cassidy; c. Frederick T, III, Jennifer C, Peter C, Charles M, J. Tyler and Gregory K. Educ: Cath. Univ, B.A. in Econ, 40; Georgetown Univ. Law Sch, LL.B, 49; Phi Delta Phi. Polit. & Govt. Pos: Chmn, Norfolk City Dem. Cmt, Va, 61-64; chmn, Second Dist. Dem. Cmt, 64-68; nominee for U.S. Rep, Va, 68. Mil. Serv: Entered as Navy Air Cadet, Navy, 42, released as Lt.(sg), 45. Mem: Am. and Va. Bar Asns; Am. Trial Lawyers. Nat. Intercollegiate Boxing Champion, 39. Rel: Roman Catholic. Mailing Add: 428 Mowbray Arch, Norfolk, Va. 23510. (1967)

STANTON, HUGH W, JR. D
b. Memphis, Tenn, 3/2/28; s. Hugh W. Stanton and Virginia Wills S; m. 10/4/53 to Marion Ward; c. Milner Marion. Educ: Southwest. at Memphis, B.A; Vanderbilt Univ, LL.B; Kappa Sigma. Polit. & Govt. Pos: Tenn. State Rep, 64-66; Tenn. State Sen, 66-68. Bus. & Prof. Pos: Asst. Pub. Defender, Appellate Work. Mil. Serv: Entered as Pvt, Marine Corps, 46-48; reentered as Lt, Marine Corps Res, 52, released as Capt, 53, after serv. in Engr. Bn, Korea; Korean Serv. Medal; Presidential Unit Citation; Korean Unit Citation; Victory Medal. Mem: Memphis and Shelby Co. Bar Asns; Am. Legion. Rel: Episcopal. Legal Res: 323 Fernway Rd, Memphis, Tenn. 38117. Mailing Add: Lincoln American Tower, Memphis, Tenn. 38103.

STANTON, JOHN WILLIAM R
U.S. Rep, Ohio
b. Painesville, Ohio, 2/20/24; s. Frank M. Stanton and Mary Callinan S; m. 12/3/66 to Peggy Smeeton; c. Kelly Marie. Educ: Georgetown Univ, B.S, 49; pres, Int. Rels. Club; pres, Sr. Class. Polit. & Govt. Pos: Cmnr, Lake Co, Ohio, 56-64; U.S. Rep, Ohio, 65- Bus. & Prof. Pos: Owner, J.W. Stanton

Motors, Inc, 49-62; pres. and co-owner, Stanton-Leonard Motors, Inc, 62-65. Mil. Serv: Entered as 2nd Lt, Army, 42, released as Capt, 46, after serv. in New Guinea, Netherlands, E. Indies and Philippines; Bronze Star with Oak Leaf Cluster; Purple Heart; Presidential Unit Citation and three major campaign ribbons. Mem: Past pres, Painesville C. of C; charter mem, Jr. C. of C; Moose; Past Exalted Ruler, Painesville Elks; past pres, Painesville Exchange Club; Am. Legion; K. of C.(4°); Irish-Am. Club of Lake Co. Rel: Catholic. Legal Res: 7 North Park Place, Painesville, Ohio 44077. Mailing Add: 132 Cannon House Office Bldg, Washington, D.C. 20515.

STANTON, RALPH CALVIN, JR. R
Chmn, Richland Co. Rep. Cent. Cmt, Ohio
b. Pittsburgh, Pa, 6/22/24; s. Ralph C. Stanton, Sr. and Eloise Robinson S; m. 9/17/52 to Ida Louise Guadaynino; c. Crisella, Michael David, Lee Ann and Robert Charles. Educ: Ohio State Univ, 42-43, B.S, 48; Baldwin Wallace Col, 43-44; Pi Kappa Alpha. Polit. & Govt. Pos: Councilman, Mansfield City Coun, Ohio, 59-63; v.chmn, Richland Co. Cent. Cmt, 63-68, chmn, 68- Bus. & Prof. Pos: Pres, Stanton-Long Ins. Agency Inc, 61-; dir, Mansfield Bldg. & Loan Asn, 63- Mil. Serv: Entered as A/S, Navy, 43, released as Lt.(jg), after serv. in 7th Amphibious Force, Pac. Theatre, 44-46; Res, Lt; Theatre Decorations; 1 Battle Star. Mem: Ohio and Nat. Asns. of Ins. Agents; Am. Legion; Univ. Club; YMCA; Ohio Rep. Club; Sheriff's Adv. Cmt. Outstanding Civic Serv. Award, C. of C, 63. Rel: Protestant. Legal Res: 602 Crescent Rd, Mansfield, Ohio 44907. Mailing Add: P.O. Box 397, Mansfield, Ohio 44901.

STAPLETON, ARLEY, JR. D
Chmn, Hancock Co. Dem. Exec. Cmt, Tenn.
b. Sneedville, Tenn, 10/5/29; s. Arley Stapleton and Daisy Greene S; m. 8/29/52 to Deloris Fern Trent; c. Dale Evan, Kathy Sharon and Tammie. Educ: East Tenn. State Univ, 2 years. Polit. & Govt. Pos: Chmn, Good Government Party, Hancock Co, Tenn, 66-; chmn, Hancock Co. Dem. Exec. Cmt, 67- Bus. & Prof. Pos: Parts mgr, Sneedville Motor Co, 52-; service officer, Hancock Co, Tenn, 60-68 and registr, 68- Mil. Serv: Entered as Pvt. E-1, Army, 50, released as Cpl, 52, after serv. in 194th Engr. Combat Bn, FECOM, Korea; Korean Service Medal; Good Conduct Medal with Three Bronze Serv. Stars. Mem: Asst. Chief, Sneedville Fire Dept; Pres, Hancock Co. Rescue Squad; F&AM; VFW; Am. Legion; dir, Tenn. Library Asn, Sneedville. Rel: Protestant. Mailing Add: Box 154, Sneedville, Tenn. 37869.

STAPP, ROBERT R. D
b. Columbus Junction, Iowa, 8/10/14; s. Jay Stapp and Margaret Donovan S; m. 2/15/41 to Maureen Shay; c. Steven J. Educ: Notre Dame Univ, A.B; Am. Press Inst. Polit. & Govt. Pos: Admin. asst. to U.S. Rep. Roy H. McVicker, Colo, 65-66 and U.S. Rep. Byron G. Rogers, Colo, 67-68. Mil. Serv: Entered as Ens, Navy, 42, released as Lt. Naval Aviator, 45. Rel: Catholic. Legal Res: 2401 Grape St, Denver, Colo. 80207. Mailing Add: Apt. 517, 1900 S. Eads St, Arlington, Va. 22202. (1967)

STARBIRD, SEAWARD GLENN, JR. D
Maine State Rep.
b. Bangor, Maine, 4/12/29; s. Seaward Glenn Starbird and Nina M. Dobson S; m. 10/3/53 to Louise Evelyn Ames; c. S. Glenn, III, Charles Ames and Deborah Ann. Educ: Lee Acad, grad, 47; Univ. Maine. Polit. & Govt. Pos: Local mail carrier, Maine, 51-54; Maine State Rep, currently. Hobbies: Amateur Genealogist. Rel: Methodist. Mailing Add: P.O. Box 736, Kingman, Maine 04451. (1967)

STARK, ABE D
Pres, Borough of Brooklyn, N.Y.
m. to Lilyan; c. one son. Educ: Pub. Sch; hon. LL.D, L.I. Univ. and Pratt Inst. Polit. & Govt. Pos: Pres, N.Y.C. Coun, N.Y, 54-61; pres, Borough of Brooklyn, 61- Bus. & Prof. Pos: Businessman. Mem: Cerebral Palsy Unit of Brownsville; Indust. Home for Blind Prog; founder, Brownsville Boys Club. Urban League of Brooklyn Award; Brooklyn Col. Gold Medal. Mailing Add: 21 Borough Hall, Brooklyn, N.Y. 11201. (1967)

STARK, ALEXANDER D
b. Baltimore, Md, 1/19/17; s. Samuel S. Stark and Esther M. Hecker S; m. 10/9/45 to Frances Astrachan; c. Jonathan Samuel. Educ: Univ. Baltimore, LL.B, 37. Polit. & Govt. Pos: Former Md. State Del, asst. state's attorney and asst. city solicitor. Bus. & Prof. Pos: Lawyer, 38- Mil. Serv: Entered as Seaman, Navy, 42, released as CPO, 45, after serv. in Combat Intel. Mem: City, State and Am. Bar Asns; Am. Soc. for Pub. Admin. Rel: Jewish. Legal Res: 5809 Berkeley Ave, Baltimore, Md. 21215. Mailing Add: 36 Equitable Bldg, Baltimore, Md. 21202.

STARK, CARROLL JOSEPH D
b. Paterson, N.J; s. Joseph Stark and Helena S; m. 1932 to Helen Hurd; c. Nancy (Mrs. Lawrence Fette) and James C. Educ: Rutgers Univ, J.D. Polit. & Govt. Pos: N.J. State Assemblyman, Passaic Co, N.J, 37-38; surrogate, Passaic Co, N.J, 57-67; alternate del, Dem. Nat. Conv, 68. Mem: Am, N.J. and Passaic Co. Bar Asns; K. of C.(Grand Knight). Mailing Add: 30 Jefferson Place, Hawthorne, N.J. 07506.

STARK, LLOYD CROW D
b. Louisiana, Mo, 11/28/86; s. Clarence McDowell Stark and Lilly Crow S; m. 11/11/08 to Margaret Pearson Stickney (deceased); c. Lloyd Stickney and John Wingate; m. 11/23/31 to Katherine Lemoine Perkins; c. Mary (Mrs. Richard Strassner) and Katherine (Mrs. Richard Clark Bull). Educ: U.S. Naval Acad, B.S, 08. Hon. LL.D, Westminster Col. of Univ. Mo, 37, Cent. Col, Fayette, Mo, 39, Beloit Col. and Wash. Univ, 41. Polit. & Govt. Pos: Gov, Mo, 37-41; chmn, Gov. Conf. of U.S. and pres, Coun. of State Govt, 39; mem, Bd. of Mgrs. of State Govt, 41-47; mem. adv. coun, Nat. Arboretum, D.C, 46-; chmn, Mo. Cmt. for Nixon, 68. Bus. & Prof. Pos: Gen. mgr, Stark Bros. Nurseries, 12-17 & 19-35; discovered the Stark Golden Delicious Apple, 13; v.pres. and dir, Mo. State C. of C, 25-29; chmn. bd, Stark Bros. Nurseries, 35-37 & 41-; mem. exec. coun. and bd, Mo. Boy Scouts, 41; trustee, U.S. Naval Acad. Alumni Bd, 41-47. Mil. Serv: Naval Off, 04-12, serv. in Turkey, 09; S. Am. waters, 10; submarines, 11; served as Maj, batt. comdr. & acting asst. div. chief of staff, 80th Div. & Commanded 315th Field Artil, A.E.F. in Argonne, France, 17-19; awarded Victory Medal & two Battle Clasps. Mem: Hon. life membership, Am. Asn. Nurserymen (pres, 17, 20); Fedn. Garden Clubs of Mo; Naval Inst. Mo; Garden Clubs of Am; Am. Saddle Horse Breeders Asn.(past dir.); Naval Acad. Grads. Asn; Navy Athletic Asn; Navy League of U.S. (v.pres. and dir, 41-46); Pan-Am. Soc. (St.Louis Com, 41); Rotary; St. Louis Country Club; Univ. Club, St. Louis; Army and Navy Club, D.C. Appreciation Award, Nixon Inaugural Medal. Rel: Episcopal. Mailing Add: Stark Bros. Nurseries & Orchards Co, Louisiana, Mo. 63353.

STARK, ROBERT L. R
Secy. of State, N.H.
b. Goffstown, N.H, 6/5/11; s. Frederick L. Stark and Caroline L. Morgrage S; m. 11/11/38 to Emmy Lou Flanders; c. Elizabeth A, Rodney L. and Marilyn F. Educ: Univ. N.H, B.A, 33; Theta Upsilon Omega. Polit. & Govt. Pos: Asst. clerk, N.H. House of Rep, 41-53, clerk, 55-57; asst. secy, N.H. Constitutional Conv, 48-56; dep. secy. of state, N.H, 57-60, acting secy. of state, 60-61, Secy. of State, 61- Mailing Add: 33 High St, Goffstown, N.H. 03045.

STARNES, JOHN WALLACE D
Ala. State Rep.
b. Albertville, Ala, 5/11/39; s. Eugene Hendrix Starnes and Lucille Bishop S; m. 3/11/61 to Dottie Little; c. Melissa Blair 'Missy' and Dorothy Lucille 'Lucy'. Educ: Snead Jr. Col, 59; Univ. Ala, B.S. in Commerce and Bus. Admin, 63, LL.B, 65; Sigma Chi. Polit. & Govt. Pos: Ala. State Rep, Seventh Dist, 67- Bus. & Prof. Pos: Attorney-at-law, pvt. practice, 65- Mem: Am, Ala. and Marshall Co. Bar Asns; Jaycees; C. of C; Marshall Co. Cattleman's Asn Rel: Baptist. Legal Res: Wyeth Dr, Guntersville, Ala. 35976. Mailing Add: P.O. Box 262, Guntersville, Ala. 35976.

STARNES, RICHARD L, JR. D
b. Emory University, Ga, 6/15/36; s. Richard L. Starnes, Sr. and Mildred Williamson S; single. Educ: Darlington Sch, 47-54; Shorter Col, A.B, 58; Mercer Univ. Law Sch, LL.B, 61; Phi Sigma Alpha; Alpha Tau Omega. Polit. & Govt. Pos: Ga. State Rep, 13th Dist, 66-69; Judge, City Court, Floyd Co, Ga, 69- Mem: Am. and Rome Bar Asns; State Bar Asn. Ga; Jaycees; Elks. Alumnus of the Year, Ga. Warm Springs Found, 68. Rel: Baptist. Legal Res: 1001 Terrace Dr, Rome, Ga. 30161. Mailing Add: P.O. Box 1348, Rome,Ga. 30161.

STARR, GEORGE EDDIE D
b. Jay, Vt, 1/1/90; m. to Hazel Merle Hardy; c. four sons, three daughters. Educ: Island Pond High Sch; private tutoring. Polit. & Govt. Pos: Fire warden, Troy, Vt, 36-, lister, 44- and town agent, 52-; Vt. State Rep, 57-66. Bus. & Prof. Pos: Retired rural mail carrier; farmer. Mem: F&AM; Kiwanis (past pres); hon. mem, Future Farmers of Am. Rel: Protestant. Mailing Add: Highland Ave, North Troy, Vt. 05868. (1967)

STASSEN, HAROLD EDWARD R
b. West St. Paul, Minn, 4/13/07; s. William Stassen and Elsie Mueller S; m. 11/14/29 to Esther G. Glewwe; c. Glen, Harold and Kathleen Esther. Educ: Univ. Minn, B.A, 27 and Col. Law, LL.B, 29; Sigma Alpha Epsilon; Delta Sigma Rho; Gamma Eta Gamma; Grey Friars. Hon. LL.D, Hamline Univ, 39, Univ. Pa, 48 and Princeton Univ, 50; L.H.D, Temple Univ, 49. Polit. & Govt. Pos: Co. attorney, Dakota Co, Minn, 30-38; pres, Minn. Young Rep, 36; del, Rep. Nat. Conv, 36; Gov, Minn, 38-42; temporary chmn. and keynoter, Rep. Nat. Conv, 40; mem, Coun. State Govt, 40-41; chmn, Nat. Gov. Conf, 40-42; U.S. Del. to San Francisco Conf. and one of original U.S. signers of UN Charter, 45; mutual security adminstr, 53; dir, For. Opers. Admin, 53-55; spec. asst. to President with cabinet rank to direct studies of U.S. on world arms limitation and control, 55-58. Bus. & Prof. Pos: Admitted to Minn. Bar, 29; Godkind lectr. human rights, Harvard Univ, 46; pres, Univ. Pa, 48-53; partner, Stassen and Kephart, 58- Mil. Serv: Navy, Mem. staff of Adm. W.F. Halsey, S.Pac, 43-45, Asst. Chief of Staff, 44; Legion of Merit; Bronze Star; Citation Medal; Six Battle Stars. Publ: Where I Stand, 47; Man Was Meant To Be Free, 51. Mem: Pres, Int. Coun. Rel. Educ, 42-50; nat. chmn, Brotherhood Week, Nat. Conf. Christians and Jews, 46; nat. chmn, Am. Heart Campaign, 49; v.pres, Nat. Coun. Churches, 50-52, original charter signer, 50 and pres, Div. Christian Educ, 52; pres, Am. Baptist Conv, 63-64; Mason; Shrine. Selected Outstanding Young Man, Nat. Jr. C. of C, 39; chmn, World Law Day, Geneva, Switz, 67. Rel: Baptist. Legal Res: Penn Towers, Philadelphia, Pa. 19103. Mailing Add: 1020 Fidelity Bldg, Philadelphia, Pa. 19109.

STASSEN, RICHARD J. R
b. St. Paul, Minn, 1909; married; c. Two. Educ: Univ. Minn; St. Paul Col. of Law. Polit. & Govt. Pos: Block and precinct worker, state Rep. party since 37; original mem. of party's Paul Revere Riders. Bus. & Prof. Pos: Field auditor, Rock Island Lumber Co; asst. east. div. credit mgr, Allied Bldg. Credit Corp; regional credit mgr, Interstate Accounts Serv; mgr, Lustrasilk, Inc; real estate broker, now retired. Mil. Serv: Army. Mailing Add: 744 Winslow Ave, St. Paul, Minn. 55107. (1967)

STASTNY, GEORGE F. R
b. Jersey City, N. J. Educ: DePaul U, Col. of Comm, B.S, 49; DePaul U, Col. of Law. Polit. & Govt. Pos: Ill. State Rep, 4 terms; Vice Pres, Young Rep. Orgn. of Ill; former Vice Chmn of the Young Rep. Orgn. of Cook Co; past Pres. of the 19th Ward Young Rep. Club, Inc. Bus. & Prof. Pos: Acct. Mailing Add: 11130 S. Western, Chicago, Ill. 60643. (1967)

STATEN, ROY NEVILLE D
Md. State Sen.
b. Sandidges, Va, 6/20/13; married. Educ: Va. Commercial Col. Polit. & Govt. Pos: Md. State Del, 53-67; Md. State Sen, 67-; del, Dem. Nat. Conv, 68. Bus. & Prof. Pos: Acct, Div. Chief, Bethlehem Shipbuilding. Mil. Serv: Army. Mem: Lions; Moose. Mailing Add: 3012 Dunglow Rd, Baltimore, Md. 21222. (1967)

STATHAKIS, JAMES JOHN D
b. Gastonia, N.C, 12/12/30; s. John Pete Stathakis and Alexandria Matalas S; m. 11/3/57 to Despo Plumpides; c. John James and William James. Educ: Anderson Pub. Schs, 12 years. Polit. & Govt. Pos: Del, Anderson Co. Dem.

Conv, S.C, 58,60,62,64,66 & 68; councilman, Anderson City Coun, 62-64; pres. Ward Four Precinct, 62-; del, S.C. State Dem. Conv, 66 & 68; del, Dem. Nat. Conv, 68. Bus. & Prof. Pos: Owner, J.J. Stathakis Package Shop; v.pres and treas, Valley Bldg. Co, Inc, River Heights Builders, Inc, and Dostak, Inc; co-owner, Stathakis Bros. Enterprizes. Mil. Serv: Entered as Pvt, Army, 51, released as Cpl, 53, after serv. in 796 Hqs. and Hqs. Co, Vienna, Austria, 52-53; Good Conduct Medal; European Theater Medal. Mem: Anderson C. of C; K. of P; Am. Legion; life mem, VFW; Sertoma Club; Elks; assoc. mem, Jaycees (dir, 60-61, pres, 61-62); assoc. mem, YMCA; PTA (pres, 66, coun. pres, 67); cubmaster, Pack 117, St. Johns Methodist Church; Cmt. of 100, Dem. Party S.C, 68. Jaycee Outstanding Local Pres, S.C, 61-62, Six, Jaycee of Month Awards, Three, Pres. Awards; Outstanding Young Man, Anderson, S.C, 64. Rel: Greek Orthodox. Mailing Add: 1001 E. River St, Anderson, S.C. 29621.

STATHOS, DONALD L. R
Ore. State Rep.
b. Portland, Ore, 4/7/24; s. Harry L. Stathos and Sylvia Davis S; m. 7/2/55 to Barbara B. Brown; c. Jenny L. and Holly A. Educ: Ore. State Univ, B.A, 50; Sigma Nu. Polit. & Govt. Pos: Chmn, Youth for Eisenhower-Nixon, Ore, 56; chmn, Young Rep, Ore, 57 and chmn, Jackson Co. Rep. Cent. Cmt, 58-59; secy, Ore. State Rep. Cent. Cmt, 60-61; Ore. State Rep, Jackson Co, 69- Bus. & Prof. Pos: Pres, Don Stathos, Insuror, Inc, 60-68. Mil. Serv: Entered as Seaman, Navy, 42, released as PO 2/C, 45, after serv. in Armed Guard, S.Pac, 42-45; 2nd Lt, Res, 45-50. Mem: Ins. Agents Asn; Lions; Keep Ore. Green Asn. Rel: Methodist. Mailing Add: 40 Coachman Dr, Jacksonville, Ore. 97530.

STATON, ROBERT HOWARD D
Chmn, Hamilton Co. Dem. Party, Ind.
b. Indianapolis, Ind, 4/4/25; s. William H. Staton and Pearl Edwards S; m. 6/28/58 to Jane Ellen Cox; c. Jennifer Lee and Elizabeth Ashley. Educ: Ind. Univ, A.B, 52; Ind. Univ. Sch. Law, LL.B, 55; Alpha Tau Omega. Polit. & Govt. Pos: Dep. prosecuting attorney, 19th Judicial Dist, Ind, 58-62; Dem. precinct committeeman, Third Precinct, 27th Ward, Marion Co, 58-64; dep. elec. cmnr, Marion Co, 64; hearing exam, Pub. Serv. Cmn, 64-67; Dem. precinct committeeman, Clay-center Precinct, Hamilton Co, 64-69; Dem. cand. for U.S. Rep, Tenth Cong. Dist, 66; del, Dem. Nat. Conv, 68; chmn, Hamilton Co. Dem. Party, 68- Bus. & Prof. Pos: Partner, Staton and Collignon, 55-59, Staton, Ward and Rice, 59-61, Staton, Ward and Magnuson, 61-66 and Williamson, Colvin, Liggitt, Sargent and Staton, 66-69. Mil. Serv: Entered as Pvt, Army, 43, released as Sgt, 46, after serv. in 91st Inf, Fifth Army, ETO, 44-46; Meritorious Unit Award; Good Conduct, Am. Theater Serv, Victory and European Theater Medals. Publ: 'The Case Against McCarthyism', Armenian Rev, winter 54; 'Indiana's Underpaid Judges', Res Gestae, 57; plus others. Mem: Sigma Delta Kappa (Ind. alumni pres. and grand nat. trustee); Indianapolis, Am. and Seventh Circuit Fed. Bar Asn; Ind. State Bar Asn. (past article ed, Res Gestae and first and organizing ed); Judicature Soc; Indianapolis Cmt. on For. Affairs; Am. Legion; VFW; Mason; Scottish Rite; Shrine; Deerfield Civic Asn.(past pres. and chmn. bd). Rel: Society of Friends. Legal Res: 9706 Deerfield Mall, R.R. 2, Carmel, Ind. 46032. Mailing Add: 1005 First Federal Bldg, Indianapolis, Ind. 46204.

STATON, WILLIAM WAYNE D
N.C. State Sen.
b. Marshville, N.C, 10/11/16; s. Oscar M. Staton and May Young S; m. 6/28/47 to Ellen Douglas Boone; c. William Wayne, Jr. and Allyn Moore. Educ: Wake Forest Col; Wake Forest Law Sch; Univ. N.C; Judge Adv. Gen. Sch, U.S. Army; Omicron Delta Kappa. Polit. & Govt. Pos: Pres, Young Dem. Clubs of N.C, 52-53; personal campaign mgr. for Gov. Terry Sanford; del, Dem. Nat. Conv, 52, 60 & 64; co. attorney, Lee Co, N.C, 60-62; mem, N.C. State Dem. Cmt, 60-64; committeeman, Dem. Nat. Exec. Cmt, N.C, 60-64; city attorney, Sanford, N.C, 63-65; N.C. State Rep, 22nd Dist, formerly; N.C. State Sen, presently. Mil. Serv: Entered as Pvt, Army, 42, released as Capt, 46, after serv. in Hq. 78th Inf. Div, Berlin Mil. Dist, Germany; ETO Ribbon with 5 Battle Stars; Bronze Star Medal; Purple Heart; Col, Judge Adv. Gen. Corps, N.C. Army Nat. Guard, at present. Mem: Pres, Sanford C. of C, 58-59; Fourth Dist. Bar Asn, 65-66; Lee Co, N.C. State and Am. Bar Asns; Elks; Moose; Am. Legion; VFW; WOW; bd. of trustees, Wake Forest Col. Rel: Baptist. Legal Res: 636 Palmer Dr, Sanford, N.C. 27330. Mailing Add: P.O. Box 1009, Sanford, N.C. 27330.

STAUFFACHER, MADELINE JEANNE R
b. Freeport, Ill, 8/16/13; d. Michael Stephan Rigney and Goldie Clara Sachtjen R; m. 5/10/41 to Marvin William Stauffacher; c. Michael Stephan and Marsha Lynn. Educ: Freeport High Sch, Ill, grad, 31; post-grad. high sch. bus. course, 32. Polit. & Govt. Pos: V.chmn, Green Co. Rep. Party, Wis, 8 years and fund raising chmn, 5 years; del, Rep. State Conv, 15 years; mem, Wis. Rep. State Exec. Cmt, 4 years; mem, Second Dist. Rep. Exec. Cmt, 7 years; alternate del, Rep. Nat. Conv, 68; spec. events chmn, Federated Rep. Women, 69. Bus. & Prof. Pos: Secy, Alliance Life Ins. Co, Freeport, Ill, 33-35; lab. technician, Kraft Cheese, 35-36; sales, women's ready to wear store, Madison, Wis, 37-40 and Monroe, Wis, 41; owner, tavern, 42-66; worker, Defense Plant, 43-45; Swiss Colony Cheese Off, 45-51; owner, Coryell Nursery, 67-69. Mem: VFW Auxiliary; Am. Legion Auxiliary; Cancer Soc.(mem. bd, 54-, co. chmn, 65-66); former chmn, Browntown Heart Drive; 94th Div. Auxiliary; Polio and March of Dimes Chap, 54-, spec. events chmn, 60- Mailing Add: Route 1, Browntown, Wis. 53522.

STAUFFER, JOHN R
Pa. State Rep.
b. Phoenixville, Pa, 5/28/25; s. John Stauffer and Alice Funk S; m. to Mary Elizabeth Bergantz; c. three. Educ: Phoenixville High Sch. Polit. & Govt. Pos: Pres, Borough Coun, Phoenixville, Pa, 62-64; Pa. State Rep, 64-; mem, Pa. State Planning Bd, 68- Bus. & Prof. Pos: Merchant. Mem: Nat. Asn. Retail Clothiers and Furnishers; founder and first chmn, Schuylkill Valley Hwy. Asn. Mailing Add: 1215 Dorothy Ave, Phoenixville, Pa. 19460.

STAUFFER, ROBERT EDWARD R
Mem. Exec. Cmt, Winnebago Co. Rep. Party, Wis.
b. Oshkosh, Wis, 5/23/24; s. Adolph F. Stauffer and Viola Eulrich S; m. 8/23/47 to Shirley L. Wrasse; c. Robert E, Jr. and Scott W. Educ: Univ. Chicago, 1 year; Yale Univ, 6 months; Northwest. Univ, B.S, 48. Polit. & Govt. Pos: City councilman, Oshkosh, Wis, 57-59, v.pres. coun, 59-60, pres. coun, 60-63, mem. planning comn, 63-65; v.chmn, Winnebago Co. Rep. Party, 65-67, chmn, 67-69; mem. exec. cmt, Sixth Dist. Rep. Party, 67- Mil. Serv: Entered as Pvt, Air Force, 43, released as 1st Lt, 46, after serv. in ETO. Mem: Wis. Soc. CPA(secy. and treas, North. chap, 52-53, v.chmn, 60-61, chmn, 61-62 and state bd. dirs, 61-62); Am. Inst. and Ill. Soc. CPA; Elks; Lions; Am. Legion; Oshkosh Area C. of C.(v.pres. econ. develop, 65-66, pres, 67, exec. cmt, 68); chmn, auditing cmt, budget dir. and v.pres, Oshkosh Area United Fund, 63- Rel: United Church of Christ. Mailing Add: 317 W. 15th Ave, Oshkosh, Wis. 54901.

STAUFFER, SARAH ANN R
Rep. Nat. Committeewoman, Pa.
b. Lancaster, Pa, 6/13/15; d. Charles F. Stauffer and Gertrude Frantz S; single. Educ: Lancaster Bus. Col; Franklin and Marshall Col; Univ. Pa, Wharton Sch. Bus. Admin. Polit. & Govt. Pos: Participant in formation local group, Young Rep, Pa, 36, state asst. ed, magazine, 37, participant in reformation of local group, 46, Pa. jr. nat. committeewoman, 48-50 and mem. state bd, 48-50; mem, legis, resolutions, nominating and prog. cmts, Pa. Coun. Rep. Women, 47-56, jr. publicity chmn, 48 and mem. bd, 58-62; co-chmn. and organizer jr. group, Rep. Party, 48-51; pres, Women's Rep. Club Lancaster Co, 58-60; formed nat. cmt. of civic leaders to support Nixon, Nat. Fedn. Rep. Women, 60; del, White House Conf. on Children and Youth, 60; del, pres. meeting nat. orgn. rep. on prevention of juvenile delinquency and Wash. Pres. Conf. on Voice of America; Rep. Nat. committeewoman, Pa, 64- and mem. Rep. Nat. Exec. Cmt, 64-; del, Rep. Nat. Conv, 68. Bus. & Prof. Pos: Off. mgr. and admin. asst, Aircraft Dept, Munitions Div, Armstrong Cork Co, 42-44. Mil. Serv: Entered as Lt, Motor Corps, Am. Red Cross, released as Capt, 46, after serv. with 45th Inf. Div, Mediterranean and European Theaters Opers; also dir, personnel and opers, Clubmobile Dept, U.S. Occupied Territory, ETO, 46; Sicilian, Rome Arno, Ardennes-Alsace, South. France, Naples-Foggia, Anzio, Rhineland and Cent. European Campaign Ribbons. Mem: Am. Acad. Polit. and Soc. Sci; Women's Nat. Rep. Club; finance cmt, YMCA, 35; chmn, Christmas Cheer Toy Shop, Lancaster Co. Family Serv, 34-36, dir, 51-55, treas, 55-57; Asn. of Jr. Leagues Am, Inc; del-at-lg, Commun. Chest Coun, 58-60; exec. cmt. and del-at-lg, Lancaster Co. Commun. Coun, 63-; co-organizer and v.pres, Homemaker Serv. of Lancaster Co; hon. mem, Lancaster Soroptimists; chmn, Jr. Red Cross, 37-39, home serv. cmt, 47-53, mem. bd, 47-51, treas, Lancaster Co. Red Cross, 49-51, co-chmn, House-to-House Campaign Drive, 51. Named Distinguished Daughter of Pa, 66. Rel: Lutheran. Mailing Add: Rohrerstown, Pa. 17571.

STAUM, ROBERT MARION R
b. Boaz, Wis, 6/13/22; s. Lewis Staum and Nellie Hanson S; m. 2/9/46 to Rita I. Ewers; c. Peggy Jo, Debra and Mark. Educ: Madison Bus. Col, Wis, M.A, 42. Polit. & Govt. Pos: Treas, Richland Co. Rep. Exec. Cmt, Wis, 63-65; former chmn, Richland Co. Rep. Cmt; with State Civil Serv, currently. Bus. & Prof. Pos: Asst. v.pres, Richland Co. Bank, 63-69; bus. mgr, Wis. State Univ-Richland Campus, currently. Mil. Serv: Entered as Pvt, Air Force, 42, released as 1st Lt, 45, after serv. as Navigator, 95th Bomb Group, 93rd Combat Bomb Wing, 8th Air Force, ETO Command, 43-45; Maj, Air Force Res, 62; Distinguished Flying Cross; Air Medal with 3 Oak Leaf Clusters; 8th Air Force Distinguished Unit Citation; Europe-African-Middle East. Medal with 6 Bronze Stars for Normandy, North. France, Rhineland, Ardennes, Cent. Europe and Air Warfare Europe Campaigns. Mem: C. of C.(v.pres. and dir, 64, pres, 65); VFW; Am. Bowling Cong. Rel: Evangelical United Brethren. Mailing Add: 765 S. James St, Richland Center, Wis. 53581.

STAVES, MARION COLE D
Admin. Coordinator, Chester Co. Dem. Cmt, Pa.
b. Bellingham, Wash, 4/17/27; s. Marion Cole Staves and Edith Krayer S; m. 7/30/54 to Monique Kennell; c. George van Rensselaer and Elizabeth Jean. Educ: Am. Univ, B.S, 52; Georgetown Univ, M.S, 54, LL.B, 59. Polit. & Govt. Pos: Co. campaign chmn, for Genevieve Blatt, Chester Co, Pa, 64; del, Dem. Nat. Conv, 64 & 68; chmn. citizens for Johnson-Humphrey-Blatt, Chester Co, 64; admin. coordinator, Chester Co. Dem. Cmt, 68- Bus. & Prof. Pos: Patent attorney, Hercules Inc, Wilmington, Del, 59- Mil. Serv: Entered as Seaman 3/C, Navy, 45, released as Seaman 1/C, 46, after serv. in Seabees, Pac. Mem: Phila. Patent Law Asn. Rel: Episcopal. Mailing Add: R.D. 2, Kennett Square, Pa. 19348.

STEADMAN, HOYT GAY D
b. Sheffield, Ala, 10/4/22; married. Polit. & Govt. Pos: Former Miss. State Rep. Bus. & Prof. Pos: Minister; cattle farmer. Mem: C. of C; Mason; Am. Legion. Rel: Baptist. Mailing Add: Route 5, Louisville, Miss. 39339. (1967)

STEAGALL, HENRY II D
Ala. State Rep.
b. Abbeville, Ala, 9/4/22; s. O.M. Steagall and Susie Koonce S; m. to Frances Rector; c. Henry B, Susan Frances and Fred Rector. Educ: Ala. Polytech. Inst, grad; Univ. Ala. Law Sch; Kappa Sigma, Phi Delta Phi. Polit. & Govt. Pos: Ala. State Rep, 55- Bus. & Prof. Pos: Lawyer. Mil. Serv: Navy, World War II. Mem: Am. Legion; VFW. Rel: Methodist. Mailing Add: 315 S. Union Ave, Ozark, Ala. 36360.

STEAKLEY, ZOLLIE COFFER, JR. D
Justice, Supreme Court of Tex.
b. Rotan, Tex, 8/29/08; s. Zollie Coffer Steakley and Frances Elizabeth McGlasson S; m. 6/3/39 to Ruth Butler. Educ: Hardin-Simmons Univ, B.A, 29, Univ. of Tex, LL.B, 32. Hon. LL.D, Univ. of Corpus Christi, 58 and Hardin-Simmons Univ, 59. Polit. & Govt. Pos: Asst. attorney gen, Tex, 39-42; secy. of state, Tex, 57-60; justice, Supreme Court of Tex, 61- Bus. & Prof. Pos: Attorney-at-law, 32-39 & 46-57. Mil. Serv: Naval Res, 42-46. Mem: Am. Bar Asn; Am. Judicature Soc; State Bar of Tex; Philos. Soc; Mason; Shrine; Lions (dist. gov, 52-53). Legal Res: 3302 Mt. Bonnell Dr, Austin, Tex. 78731. Mailing Add: Supreme Court Bldg, Austin, Tex. 78711.

STEAR, DAVID SPRING R
Committeeman, La. Rep. State Cent. Cmt.
b. Chambersburg, Pa, 7/17/25; s. Jacob Ray Stear and Freda Hallie Spring; m. 11/6/54 to Marjorie Belle Matherne; c. Freda Anne, Susan Spring, Joan Elizabeth, Ruth Allison and Margaret Frances. Educ: Washington and Jefferson Col, B.A; Univ. of Tulsa, BSPE; Alpha Tau Omega. Polit. & Govt. Pos: Co-treas, Dem. for Nixon Cmt, La, 60; co-chmn, Goldwater for Pres. Cmt, 64; committeeman, Iberia Parish Rep. Exec. Cmt, 64- and chmn, 68-; committeeman, La. Rep. State Cent. Cmt, 64- Bus. & Prof. Pos: Petroleum engr. trainee, The Texas Co, Golden Meadow, La, 50-51, Houma, La, 51, Petroleum engr, 51-54, Golden Meadow, La, 54-57; Petroleum engr, TEXACO Inc, New Iberia, La, 57- Mil. Serv: Entered as Pvt, Army, 44, released as Pfc, 45, after serv. in 75th Div. Co. A, 289th Inf. Regt, ETO, 45; Combat Infantryman Badge, Purple Heart; ETO Ribbon with Battle Star. Publ: 'Elements of Dynamometer Tests' World Oil, 2/1/51. Mem: Am Inst. of Mining, Metallurgical and Petroleum Engrs; Evangeline Chap. of Am. Petroleum Inst; Nat. Asn. of Corrosion Engrs. Rel: Methodist. Mailing Add: 616 Dodson St, New Iberia, La. 70560.

STEARN, SUE SMITH R
Mem, State Rep. Exec. Cmt, Wis.
b. Chicago, Ill, 4/24/28; d. Leathem Daley Smith and Alva Fredrickson S; m. 12/14/46 to Richard Andrus Stearn; c. Leathem Smith, Margaret Frost, Eric Andru and Jonathan Daley. Educ: Conn. Col. for Women, 46. Polit. & Govt. Pos: V.chmn, Door Co. Rep. Party, Wis, 59-63; alternate del, Rep. Nat. Conv, 64 & 68; v.chmn, Eighth Dist. Rep. Party, 65-; mem, State Rep. Exec. Cmt, 65-; mem, State Campaign Cmt, 67-68; State Budget and Finance Cmt, 67-68 and Wis. Gov. Cmt. Youth and Children, 69- Rel: Moravian. Mailing Add: 1106 Pennsylvania St, Sturgeon Bay, Wis. 54235.

STEARNS, CLIFFORD DWIGHT R
b. Hinsdale, N.H, 3/23/92; married; c. three. Educ: Univ. N.H. Polit. & Govt. Pos: Selectman, N.H, 21 years; former N.H. State Rep. Bus. & Prof. Pos: Employee, Agr. Stabilization & Conserv. Prog, U.S. Dept. Agr, 16 years; retired. Rel: Protestant. Mailing Add: Hinsdale, N.H. 03451. (1967)

STEARNS, RAYMOND MILTON R
Committeeman, Ill. Rep. Cent. Cmt.
b. Hallidayboro, Ill, 3/19/15; s. George Washington Stearns and Sarah Margaret Lane S; m. 10/19/32 to Violet Evelyn Johns; c. Billy Ray and Joanna Joy (Mrs. Carl Jack Jones). Educ: Goreville Commun. High, Ill, 1 year; Elkville Commun. High, 1 year. Polit. & Govt. Pos: Precinct committeeman, Goreville Twp, Ill, 66; committeeman, Ill. Rep. Cent. Cmt, 68- Bus. & Prof. Pos: Farmer, Goreville, Ill, 32-; automotive machinist and engine rebuilder, 37-66; cabinet and custom furniture mill worker, 68- Mem: Eagles; Goreville Commun. Saddle Club; United Brotherhood of Carpenters and Joiners of Am. Local Union 508. Gr. Chicago Safety Coun, Silver Plaque, 41 & 42. Rel: Freewill Baptist. Mailing Add: R.F.D. 1, Goreville, Ill. 62939.

STEBBINS, MARGUERITE ANN D
Secy, Vt. Dem. Cmt.
b. Vergennes, Vt, 9/11/41; d. Albert Francis Abair and Beatrice LeBeau A; m. 8/22/59 to Robert Warren Stebbins; c. Robert W, II, Thomas Addison and Audrey Jean. Educ: Vergennes High Sch, grad, 59. Polit. & Govt. Pos: Chmn. Addison City Voter Serv, Vt. Fedn. Dem. Women, 66, secy, 67-69; secy, Middlebury Dem. Cmt, 66-; secy-treas, Addison Co. Dem. Cmt, 66-; Addison Co. committeewoman, Vt. Dem. Cmt, 66-, secy, 68- Mem: St. Mary's Parish Soc; League of Women Voters; Vergennes High Sch. Alumni Asn. Rel: Catholic. Legal Res: Happy Valley Rd, Middlebury, Vt. 05753. Mailing Add: P.O. Box 211, Middlebury, Vt. 05753.

STECKER, RUSSELL LEE R
Conn. State Rep.
b. Barron, Wis, 8/7/24; s. George Willard Stecker and Ingaborg Lee S; m. 9/8/46 to Flora Burch; c. Susan L, Kris L, George R, Paul S. and Steven R. Educ: Augustana Col, Ill, 42-43; U.S. Mil. Acad, 45; Cornell Univ, B.Arch, 49; Tau Beta Pi; Delta Phi; Gargoyle; Logive. Polit. & Govt. Pos: Mem, Simsbury Charter Revision Cmn, Conn, 62-63; secy, Simsbury Town Plan Cmn, 63-66; chmn, Tri-Town Talcott Mt. Cmt, 64-65; mem, Capitol Region Planning Agency, 65-, chmn, Transportation Cmt, 69-; Conn. State Rep, 39th Assembly Dist, 67-; chmn, Simsbury Commun. Develop. Action Plan Coord. Cmt, 68- Bus. & Prof. Pos: Partner, Wilkins & Stecker, Architects, 56-64, Stecker and Colavecchio, Architects, 64- Mil. Serv: Entered as Pvt, Air Force, 43, released as Cadet, 45, after serv. in Ninth Air Force, ETO, 44-45. Mem: Am. Inst. Architects (nat. committeeman); Conn. Bldg. Cong.(past pres); Rotary. Charles Goodwin Sands Medal for Archit Design; Edlitz Fel. for Travel to Advance Archit. Educ. Rel: Protestant. Mailing Add: 25 Rosewood Dr, Simsbury, Conn. 06070.

STEDELIN, HAROLD DAVID D
Ill. State Rep.
b. Sparta, Ill, 11/8/02; s. John William Stedelin and Margaret Martsloff S; wid; c. David E. and Carolyn (Mrs. Gierten). Educ: Centralia High Sch, Ill. Polit. & Govt. Pos: Mem, Centralia Sch. Bd, Ill, 12 years; mem, Marion Co. Bd. of Supvr; Ill. State Rep, 58th Dist, currently. Bus. & Prof. Pos: Pres, Centralia Eng. and Machine Corp, 32- Mem: AF&AM; Consistory; Shrine; Elks; Moose; Kiwanis; past pres. and past lt. gov, United Commercial Travelers of Am; past grand counsr, State of Ill. Rel: Methodist. Mailing Add: 711 S. Elm, Centralia, Ill. 62801.

STEED, CARL D
b. Saratoga, Ind, 5/31/26; s. Carl Steed, Sr. and Opal Dakin S; m. 3/15/48 to Mona Marie Robbins; c. Angela Sue and Robert Willis. Educ: Ind. Cent. Col, grad, 48; Col. Training Prog, Gen. Motors Corp, Sr. Acct, 53-55; Col. Sch. Real Estate, grad, 66. Polit. & Govt. Pos: Secy, Jay Co. Dem. Cent. Cmt, Ind, 50-51; treas, Jay Co, 51-52, precinct committeeman, 59-; del, Ind. State Dem. Conv, 59-; dist. mgr. and corp. auditor, Ind. Dept. Revenue, 65-66; alternate del, Dem. Nat. Conv, 68; citizens mem, Portland City Planning Cmn, Ind, 69- Bus. & Prof. Pos: Owner, Steed Realty Co. and Steed Bus. Serv. Tax Acct, 49- Mil. Serv: Entered as A/S, Naval Construction Bn, 44, released as Machinist's Mate 2/C, 46, after serv. in 61st Naval Seabee Bn, Atlantic and S.Pac. Theatres, 45-46; Philippines Liberation Ribbon; Asiatic-Pac. Ribbon; Am. Theatre Ribbon; Victory World War II Medal. Mem: Chmn, Jay Co. March of Dimes, 5 years; Mason (32°); Shrine; Elks; Odd Fellows; Moose; Am. Legion; DAV; VFW; Country Club, Portland. Commendation, Nat. March of Dimes. Rel: Methodist. Legal Res: 1422 S. Meridian St, Portland, Ind. 47371. Mailing Add: P.O. Box 1066, Portland, Ind. 47371.

STEED, TOM D
U.S. Rep, Okla.
b. Rising Star, Tex, 3/2/04; m. 2/26 /23 to Hazel Bennett; c. Richard N. and Roger (deceased). Polit. & Govt. Pos: U.S. Rep, Okla, 48-; del, Dem. Nat. Conv, 68. Bus. & Prof. Pos: Newspaperman, Okla. dailies, 20 years; managing ed, Shawnee News and Star, 4 years. Mil. Serv: Entered as Pvt, Army, 42, released as 2nd Lt, 45, after serv. in India-Burma Theater and Off. of War Info. Legal Res: Shawnee, Okla. 74801. Mailing Add: Congressional Hotel, Washington, D.C. 20003.

STEEH, VICTOR R. D
b. Mt. Clemens, Mich, 5/8/23; married; c. Vickie Mae, Karin. Educ: Attended East. Mich. Univ; Castle Heights Mil. Acad; West. Mich. Univ; grad. of Wayne State Univ, B.S, bus. admin. Polit. & Govt. Pos: Mich. State Rep, 64. Bus. & Prof. Pos: Ins. salesman. Mil. Serv: Vet. Mem: Amvets; DAV; Macomb Co. Dem. Club; Club 53. Rel: Episcopalian. Mailing Add: 65 Lodewyck Ave, Mt. Clemens, Mich. 48043. (1967)

STEELE, DEAN C. R
Del. State Sen.
b. 1905. Polit. & Govt. Pos: Del. State Sen, 67-, chmn, Finance Cmt, Del. State Senate; past chmn, State Unified Sch. Legis. Cmt; past dir, Del. Safety Coun. Bus. & Prof. Pos: Control mgr, Pigments Dept, DuPont, 42-; past pres, Gen. Gas and Elec. Corp; acct.(finance, tax); bus. mgt; pub. utility acct; officer and dir. of numerous pub. utilities co. Mem: Financial Execs. Inst; past pres, Del. Chap, Nat. Asn. Accts; life mem. and past pres, legis. chmn. and chmn. of study Cmt. on State Finances of Del. Cong. of PTA. Mailing Add: 128 Rockingham Dr, Windsor Hills, Wilmington, Del. 19803.

STEELE, G. FRED, JR. R
Mem, N.C. State Rep. Exec. Cmt.
b. Columbus, Ga, 10/27/29; s. Garland Fredrick Steele and Elizabeth Jenkins S; m. 9/9/49 to Elizabeth Eugenia Sherwood; c. Robert Cary, Gregory Wayne Brian Sherwood and Carol Elizabeth. Educ: North Ga. Col; Ga. Inst. Tech. Polit. & Govt. Pos: Treas, Durham Co. Young Rep. Exec. Cmt, N.C, 63, mem, 63-64; alternate del, Rep. Nat. Conv, 64; chmn, Durham Co. Rep. Exec. Cmt, 64 & 65; mem, N.C. State Rep. Exec. Cmt, 64-, mem, Election Laws Revision Cmn, 65-67; Rep. nominee for U.S. Rep, Fifth Dist, N.C, 66 and Fourth Dist, N.C, 68; fed. co-chmn, Coastal Plains Regional Cmn, 69- Mem: Pres, Durham Asn. of Ins. Agents, 64-65, chmn, exec. cmt, 65-66. Rel: Methodist. Mailing Add: 3928 Nottaway Rd, Durham, N.C. 27707.

STEELE, NEWTON J. D
b. Elk City, Okla, 7/21/31; s. John Albert Steele, Sr. and Dixie Pickett S; m. 7/20/57 to Nancy Rodman; c. John Rodman. Educ: Univ. Tex, B.A, 52, LL.B, 57; Texas Cowboys. Polit. & Govt. Pos: Co. campaign chmn, Midland Co, Tex, 60, chmn, Midland Co. Dem. Cmt, 64-66. Bus. & Prof. Pos: Landman, Humble Oil & Refining Co, 57-58; partner, Turpin, Smith, Dyer and Hardie, 58-65; lawyer, 65-; independent oil operator, 65- Mil. Serv: Entered as Pvt, Army, 52, released as Sgt, 54; Nat. Defense and Good Conduct Medals. Mem: Midland Co, Tex. and Am. Bar Asns. Rel: Presbyterian. Mailing Add: 2000 Humble, Midland, Tex. 79701.

STEELE, PHILIP REED D
b. Plymouth, Maine, 4/16/33; s. Joseph Daniel Steele and Doris Eulilia Mcatee S; single. Educ: Freedom Acad; Thomas Bus. Col; Colby Col. Polit. & Govt. Pos: Town treas, Troy, Maine, 58-59, town secy. and tax collector, 60-61, Justice of the Peace and Notary Pub, 60-69 and chmn, Town Cmt, 62-; del, Maine State Dem. Conv, 58, 60, 62, 64, 66 & 68; mem, Waldo Co. Dem. Cmt, Maine, 64-69, v.chmn, 68-69; del, Dem. Nat. Conv, 64 & 68, mem. rules cmt, 68; mem, First Dist. Dem. Cmt, Maine, 64-65 & 68-69; Dedimus Justice, Augusta, 64- Bus. & Prof. Pos: Acct, Border Express, 55-60; off. mgr, Kennebec Cooler Co, Inc, 60-66, Quinn Freight Lines Inc, 66-69; credit mgr. and acct, Barrows Transfer & Storage Co, 69- Mem: Secy, Troy Grange, 57-58; Maine State Grange; Mason (Star, West Lodge, Unity); AASR, Consistory; Order of Amaranth; Fish & Game Club, Unity; Blue Chip Club, Waterville; Winnecook Jaycees; Eastern Star; Boy Scout leader, 58-59; 4-H Club leader, 58-59. Rel: Methodist. Mailing Add: Troy, Maine 04987.

STEELE, ROBERT HOWE R
Mem, San Francisco Co. Cent. Cmt, Calif.
b. Hartville, Mo, 12/28/13; s. Howe Steele and Linnie Robertson S; m. 11/25/49 to Jean Welborn; c. Frederick Howe and Marjorie Ann. Educ: Drury Col, A.B; Harvard Grad Sch. Bus. Admin, M.B.A. Polit. & Govt. Pos: Pres, San Francisco Young Rep, Calif, 49-51; nat. committeeman, Calif. Young Rep, 50; mem, San Francisco Co. Cent. Cmt, Calif, 52-, chmn, 54-60; presidential elector, 56 & 60; pres, Asn. Calif. Co. Chmn, 56-60; del, Rep. Nat. Conv, 60 & 64. Mil. Serv: Entered as Pvt, Army Signal Corps, 42, released as Capt, 55; World War II Victory, Good Conduct, Am. Theater and Armed Forced Res. Medals. Rel: Episcopal. Mailing Add: 2450 Francisco St, San Francisco, Calif. 94123.

STEELMAN, DORMAN LLOYD R
b. Cedar Grove, Mo, 2/17/27; s. Reamy Aaron Steelman and Erma Kell S; m. 11/21/51 to Maxine Livesay; c. David Lloyd, Deborah Lynne and Donald Alan. Educ: Univ. Mo, LL.B, 52, J.D, 69. Polit. & Govt. Pos: City attorney, Salem, Mo, 56-57; Mo. State Rep, Dent Co, 57-64, floor leader, Mo. House of Rep, 60-64; chmn, Mo. Rep. State Cmt, 66-68; del, Rep. Nat. Conv, 68. Bus. & Prof. Pos: Attorney-at-law, 52- Mil. Serv, Navy, 44-46. Mem: Odd Fellows; Mason; Am. Legion; VFW. Rel: Methodist. Legal Res: Elmer Bldg, Salem, Mo. 65560. Mailing Add: 204 E. Fourth, Salem, Mo. 65560.

STEEN, CURTIS W. D
b. Dagsboro, Del, 1906; s. Arlie C. Steen and Anna C. Hickman S; m. to Mattie Atkins; c. Eleanor Ann, Curtis W, Amanda A. and Edward. Polit. &

Govt. Pos: Del. State Sen, 50-66. Bus. & Prof. Pos: Farming, feed mercantile bus. Mem: AF&AM; Shriner; Tall Cedars of Lebanon; Mason. Rel: Methodist. Mailing Add: Dagsboro, Del. 19939. (1967)

STEEN, DONALD MARINER R
Mem. Exec. Cmt, State Rep. Party, Nebr.
b. Scottsbluff, Nebr, 3/25/24; s. Dr. Clarence G. Steen and Jean Whipple S; m. 11/30/46 to Bonnie Jeanne Jirdon; c. John Robert and William Gary; Educ: Univ. Nebr, 41-42; U.S. Merchant Marine Acad, 43-45; Univ. Denver, 46; Sigma Alpha Epsilon. Polit. & Govt. Pos: Cmt. mem, Scottsbluff Co. Rep. Party, Nebr, 48-, v.chmn, 63-65 and chmn, 65-; mem. finance cmt, State Rep. Party, 68-, founders day cmt, 68- and exec. cmt, 69- Bus. & Prof. Pos: Exec. v.pres, John R. Jirdon Ind, Inc, Morrill, 47-; v.pres, Blue J Feeds, Inc, Gering, 50-; pres, Cody Feed, Inc, Wyo, 65-; consult, Allied Chem. Corp, New York, N.Y, 66- Mil. Serv: Entered as Midn, Navy, 43, released as Lt.(jg), 46, after serv. as Chief Eng, U.S.S. Rushmore, Pac, 45-46. Mem: Am. Soc. Naval Eng; past comdr, Am. Legion; Rotary; Elks; Mason; Scottish Rite; Morrill C. of C; N. Platte Valley C. of C; local chmn, Salvation Army; Nebr. Stock Growers Asn. Rel: Presbyterian. Mailing Add: P.O. Box 295, Morrill, Nebr. 69358.

STEERS, EDWIN KEMP
b. Indianapolis, Ind, 1/19/15; s. Edwin M. Steers and Leila E. Kemp S; m. 6/15/39 to Dorothy Hamilton; c. Susan Jane, Sandra Lynn. Educ: Ind. Univ, A.B, 35, LL.B, 37. Polit. & Govt. Pos: Dep. prosecuting attorney, Marion Co, Ind, 40-49; Attorney Gen, Ind, 52-64. Bus. & Prof. Pos: Mem, Steers, Klee, Jay & Sullivan; dir, State Auto Ins. Asn; Meal-A-Minute, Inc. Mil. Serv: Naval Res, 42-46, 51-53; Naval representative Army-Navy War Crimes Dept, 45, spec. prosecutor, Off. U.S. Chief Counsel for Prosecution Axis Criminality, 45-46; defense counsel, Gen. Court Martial, Great Lakes, Ill, 51-53. Mem: Am, Ind. and Indianapolis Bar Asns; Indianapolis Lawyers Asn; Indianapolis Men's Asn; Am. Legion; VFW; Marion Co. Rep. Vets. of World War II; Mason (33°); Shrine (Imperial Coun. Rep, 52-57). Legal Res: 3808 Devon Dr, Indianapolis, Ind. 46226. Mailing Add: 45 N. Pennsylvania 312, Indianapolis, Ind. 46204.

STEERS, NEWTON IVAN, JR. R
b. Glen Ridge, N.J, 1/13/17; s. Newton Ivan Steers and Claire Louise Herder S; m. 6/8/57 to Nina Gore Auchincloss; c. Newton I, III, Hugh Auchincloss and Burr Gore. Educ: Yale Col, B.A, 39; Yale Law Sch, LL.B, 48; Zeta Psi. Polit. & Govt. Pos: Rep. cand, U.S. Rep, Md, 62; chmn, Md. Del, Rep. Nat. Conv, 64; state chmn, Rep. Party, Md, 64-66; Md. State Ins. Cmnr, 67- Bus. & Prof. Pos: Pres, Shares in Am. Indust, Inc, 53-65; pres, Atomics, Physics and Sci. Fund. Mil. Serv: Entered as Pvt, Army Air Force, 42, released as Capt, 46, after serv. in 368th Fighter Group, ETO; Presidential Unit Citation; Capt, Air Force Res. Rel: Methodist. Mailing Add: 6601 River Rd, Bethesda, Md. 20034.

STEEVES, JOHN M.
Dir-Gen, For. Serv, U.S. State Dept.
b. Brinsmade, N.Dak, 5/6/05; m. to Jean Bergstresser; c. Mrs. R. H. Bergstrom. Educ: Walla Walla Col, B.A, 27; Univ. Wash, M.A, 36. Polit. & Govt. Pos: With Off. of War Info, China-Burma-India Theatre, 43-45; career officer, For. Serv, U.S. State Dept, 45-, 1st secy, New Delhi, 48-50, counsr, Nat. War Col, 50-51, Tokyo, 51-53 & 55-57, Djakarta, 53-55, for. rels. consult to High Cmnr. of Ryuku Islands and consul gen. In Naha, 55-57, polit. adv. to Comdr. in Chief, Pac, 57-59, consul gen, Hong Kong and Macao, 59-60, Dep. Asst. Secy. of State for Far East. Affairs, 60-62, U.S. Ambassador to Afghanistan, 62-66 and Dir-Gen, For. Serv, U.S. State Dept, 66- Bus. & Prof. Pos: Educ. work in India, 27-35 & 36-43. Mailing Add: 4620 Reservoir Rd. N.W, Washington, D.C. 20007. (1967)

STEFANELLI, JOSEPH CHARLES D
Chmn, Jefferson Co. Dem. Cmt, Pa.
b. Reynoldsville, Pa, 2/11/11; s. Domenic Stefanelli and Mary Frabeni S; m. 9/29/32 to Jessie Katherine Garofalo; c. Joseph J. and Donald W. Polit. & Govt. Pos: Secy-treas, Jefferson Co. Dem. Cmt, Pa, 55-65, chmn, 65- Bus. & Prof. Pos: Salesman, Damus Bros, Inc, 45-50; field rep, United Construction Workers, 50-52; salesman, A. Ferraro & Co, 52-65; field auditor, Auditor Gen, Commonwealth of Pa, 65-66. Mem: Eagles (secy, Reynoldsville Aerie, 43-, state trustee, Pa. State Aerie, 61-67); Elks; Sons of Italy. Rel: Catholic. Mailing Add: 300 Bradford St, Reynoldsville, Pa. 15851. (1967)

STEFANI, J. ROBERT D
Mem, Calif. Dem. State Cent. Cmt.
b. Merced, Calif, 9/7/41; s. Joseph R. Stefani and Mary Gonella S; m. 5/1/66 to Bonnie R. Stewart; c. Mary Kathleen. Educ: Univ. Notre Dame, 59-60; Univ. Calif, 60; Univ. San Francisco, A.B, 64. Polit. & Govt. Pos: Co. chmn, North. Calif. Youth for Kennedy-Citizens for Kennedy, 60; v pres, Univ. San Francisco Dem. Club, 63-64; mem, Calif. Dem. State Cent. Cmt, 68- Bus. & Prof. Pos: Merchandise mgr, Stefani's Mens & Boys Clothiers, 67; exec. v.pres, Stefani's On the Mall, 69. Mem: K. of C.(4°); Ital-Am. Lodge. Rel: Catholic. Mailing Add: 55 E. 20th St, Merced, Calif. 95340.

STEFFEN, VINCENT B. D
b. Dunkerton, Iowa, 4/29/28; s. Joseph Steffen and Mathilda S; married. Educ: Dunkerton Pub. High Sch, grad, 45. Polit. & Govt. Pos: Iowa State Rep, 61-68, Speaker, Iowa State House of Rep, 65-66. Bus. & Prof. Pos: Founder and pres. of Harvestall Indust, Inc, New Hampton, Iowa. Mil. Serv: U.S. Corps of Engrs. Mem: Am. Soc. of Agr. Engrs; Am. Legion; K. of C; Iowa Develop. Cmn. Selected by U.S. Jr. C. of C. as One of the Nation's Outstanding Young Men, 64. Rel: Catholic. Mailing Add: 321 E. Hamilton, New Hampton, Iowa 50659.

STEFFEY, JOHN W. R
Md. State Sen.
b. Baltimore, Md, 5/29/25; married. Educ: U.S. Coast Guard Acad, B.S, 46; Mass. Inst. Tech; Johns Hopkins Univ. Polit. & Govt. Pos: Former mem, Anne Arundel Co. Rep. Cent. Cmt, Md. and former dist. chmn. and mem, Rep. State Cent. Cmt; Md. State Sen, 65-, mem, Finance Cmt. and Econ. Affairs Cmt, Md. State Senate; mem, Gov. Adv. Cmt. Patuxent River Watershed. Bus. & Prof. Pos: Real estate broker; builder. Mil. Serv: Coast Guard, 43-49. Mem: Charter cmn, Baltimore; past pres, Md. Real Estate Asn; officer and dir, Md. Home Builders Asn; real estate bd, Gr. Baltimore and Anne Arundel Co; Gr. Baltimore Cmt. Citizens Planning & Housing Asn; Elks; Anne Arundel Co. Trad Coun, Ind; Historic Annapolis, Inc; C. of C, Gr. Annapolis, Inc; Md. Rep. Founder Club; Navy League; U.S. Power Sq. YMCA; Annapolis Yacht Club; Baltimore Country Club; Center Club. Mailing Add: 18 E. Lexington St, Baltimore, Md. 21202.

STEGALL, WHITNEY D
b. Rockvale, Tenn, 2/17/16; s. Benjamin Duggan Stegall and Nannie Mai Love S; m. 12/29/56 to Orene Cowan; c. Whitney, Jr. and Amy. Educ: Mid. Tenn. State Col, B.S, 37; Vanderbilt Univ, LL.B, 50. Polit. & Govt. Pos: Educ. adv. and admin. officer, Civilian Conserv. Corps, 39-42; Tenn. State Sen, 65-66. Bus. & Prof. Pos: Teacher, Rutherford Co. Sch. Bd, 37-39; practice of law, Stegall & LaRoche, Murfreesboro, Tenn, 50-; trustee, Mid. Tenn. State Univ. Loan, Scholarship & Develop. Found, presently. Mil. Serv: Entered as Pvt, Army, 42, released as Maj, 47, after serv. in 4025th Signal Serv. Group, Southwest, Pac; Soldiers Medal; Asiatic-Pac. Serv. Medal with 3 Battle Stars; Victory Medal; Am. Campaign Medal; Philippine Liberation Ribbon with Bronze Star. Mem: Tenn. and Am. Bar Asns; past lt. gov, Kiwanis. Rel: Methodist. Legal Res: 132 Park Circle, Murfreesboro, Tenn. 37130. Mailing Add: 106 E. College St, Murfreesboro, Tenn. 37130.

STEGEMANN, JOHN DIETRICH D
Chmn, Sioux Co. Dem. Cent. Cmt, Iowa
b. Boyden, Iowa, 10/18/03; s. Herman Stegemann and Katherine Winter S; m. 2/18/44 to Anna Laura Schedtler; c. Esther. Educ: Boyden High Sch, Iowa, grad. Polit. & Govt. Pos: Chmn, Sioux Co. Dem. Cent. Cmt, Iowa, 66- Bus. & Prof. Pos: V.pres, Int. Luther League of Am. Lutheran Church, Columbus, Ohio, 33-35, pres, 35-43. Publ: 'The Federal Farm Program,' Des Moines Register, 7/23/67. Mem: National Farmers Union. Rel: Lutheran. Mailing Add: R.R. 1, Boyden, Iowa 51234.

STEGER, WILLIAM MERRITT R
State Chmn, Rep. Party of Tex.
b. Dallas, Tex, 8/22/20; s. Merritt Steger and Lottie Reese S; m. 2/14/48 to Ann Hollandsworth; c. Reed . Educ: Baylor Univ, 38-41; South. Methodist Univ, LL.B, 50; Delta Theta Phi. Polit. & Govt. Pos: U.S. Attorney, Eastern Dist. of Tex, 53-59; state committeeman, Repub. Party of Tex, 66-69 and state chmn, 69-; del, Rep. Nat. Conv, 68. Bus. & Prof. Pos: V.pres, Texas Rose Festival Asn, 67; chmn, Grievance Cmt. State Bar of Tex, 67-68. Mil. Serv: Entered as Aviation Cadet, Air Force, 42, released as Capt, 47, after serv. in 31st Fighter Group North African, Tunisian, Sicilian and Italian Campaign, 42-44; Air Medal with Four Oak Leaf Clusters. Rel: Baptist. Mailing Add: 3710 Bain Place, Tyler, Tex. 75701.

STEHLING, ARTHUR D
Chmn, Gillespie Co. Dem. Exec. Cmt, Tex.
b. Fredericksburg, Tex, 10/10/04; s. John Stehling and Mary Lewis S; m. 2/14/27 to Beatrice Deen; c. Beatrice Helen, Jack A. and Elaine (Mrs. Wallendorf). Educ: St. Edwards Univ, LL.B, 31; LaSalle Exten. Univ. Polit. & Govt. Pos: Chmn, Gillespie Co. Dem. Exec. Cmt, Tex, currently. Bus. & Prof. Pos: Attorney; pres, Security State Bank & Trust, Brady Mills, Brady, Tex, Radio Sta. KNAF and Fredericksburg Cable Corp, Fredericksburg, Tex; v.pres, Allen Keller Co; secy, Mkt. Produce Co; Indust. Projs. Corp. Mem: Charter mem, Fredericksburg Lions Club; Fed. Legis. Cmt, Am. Bar Asn. Rel: Catholic. Legal Res: 118 W. Main, Fredericksburg, Tex. 78624. Mailing Add: Box 272, Fredericksburg, Tex. 78624.

STEIFF, IRMA S. D
V.Chmn, Hancock Co. Dem. Cent. Cmt, Iowa
b. Everly, Iowa, 5/30/18; d. Max A. Jensen and Helena Feddersen J; m. 12/22/45 to Paul Walter Steiff; c. Renee, Judy, Lorene and Dennis. Educ: St. Cloud State Teachers Col, 36-37; Am. Bus. Col, 37-38. Polit. & Govt. Pos: V.chmn, Hancock Co. Dem. Cent. Cmt, Iowa, 66- Rel: Methodist; past Lay Leader, United Methodist Church, Forest City. Mailing Add: Route 2, Forest City, Iowa 50436.

STEIFF, PAUL WALTER D
b. Forest City, Iowa, 10/9/20; s. Semon Steiff and Bessie Enderson S; m. 12/22/45 to Irma Sophia Jensen; c. Renee, Judy, Lorene and Dennis. Polit. & Govt. Pos: Chmn, Hancock Co. Dem. Cent. Cmt, Iowa, 54-68 and former co. committeeman. Bus. & Prof. Pos: Farming. Mem: Mason; Nat. Farmers Orgn; Farmer's Union. Rel: Methodist. Mailing Add: Route 2, Forest City, Iowa 50436.

STEIGER, SAM R
U.S. Rep, Ariz.
b. New York, N.Y, 3/10/29; s. Lewis Steiger and Rebecca Klein S; m. c. twins, Lewis and Gail and Delia Rebecca. Educ: Cornell Univ, 46-48; Colo. Agr. and Mech. Univ, 48-50. Polit. & Govt. Pos: Ariz. State Sen, 61-64; U.S. Rep, Ariz, 67- Bus. & Prof. Pos: Rancher. Mil. Serv: 1st Lt, Army, 51-53; Silver Star; Purple Heart. Mem: Yavapai Co. Sheriff's Posse; Elks; Am. Legion; Mason; Kiwanis. Legal Res: Prescott, Ariz. 86301. Mailing Add: 126 Cannon House Office Bldg, Washington, D.C. 20515.

STEIGER, WILLIAM ALBERT R
U.S. Rep, Wis.
b. Oshkosh, Wis, 5/15/38; m. 1963 to Janet Dempsey. Educ: Univ. of Wis, B.S, 60. Polit. & Govt. Pos: Nat. chmn, Col. Young Rep, 59-61, mem, Practices Cmt, 60; chmn, for. affairs cmt, Young Rep. Nat. Fedn, 61-63; Wis. State Assemblyman, 61-66; permanent chmn, Young Rep. State Conv, 66; U.S. Rep, Wis, 67-, mem, House Cmt. on Educ. and Labor, 67- and House Rep. Planning and Research Cmt, 69-, U.S. House of Rep; del, Rep. Nat. Conv, 68. Bus. & Prof. Pos: Pres, Steiger-Rathke Develop. Co, 62-66; mem. bd. of dirs, Oshkosh Motor Lodge, Inc, presently. Publ: 'Form or Substance?,' Nat. Civic Rev, 4/64. Mem: Bd. dirs, Lutheran Home of Oshkosh, Inc; v.gen. chmn, Bethel Home Fund Dr; Elks; Madison Club; Nat. Rep. Club; Wis. Rep. Party; Wis. Fedn. of Young Rep; Jr. C. of C; bd. of dirs, Wis. Asn. of Chi Psi; C. of C; chmn, YMCA Youth in Govt. Cmt. Young Am. Medal for Serv,

presented by President Eisenhower, White House, 55; Selected One of Five Outstanding Young Men of Wis, Wis. Jr. C. of C, 64; Distinguished Serv. Award, OshkoshJaycees, 65; Selected Outstanding Young Rep. of Wis, Wis. Fedn. of Young Rep, 66; Selected One of Ten Outstanding Young Men in Am, U.S. Jaycees, 68. Rel: Episcopal. Mailing Add: P.O. Box 1279, Oshkosh, Wis. 54901.

STEIN, ANDREW JAY D
N.Y. State Assemblyman
b. N.Y.C, 1/10/45; s. Jerry Finkelstein and Shirley Marks F; div; c. Paige Amber. Educ: Southampton Col, B.A, 68. Polit. & Govt. Pos: Adv. to Dep. Under Secy. for Admin, Dept. of State, N.Y, 68; N.Y. State Assemblyman, 69-, chmn, Minority Cmt. on Malnutrition and Human Needs, N.Y. State Assembly, mem, Cmt. on Housing and Cmt. on Health; mem, N.Y. State Joint Legis. Cmt. on Consumer Affairs. Bus. & Prof. Pos: V.pres, N.Y. Law J, 68. Mem: City Club of N.Y; judicial and city coun. cmts, Citizens Union; Am. Jewish Cmt; B'nai B'rith. Rel: Jewish. Legal Res: 205 Third Ave, New York, N.Y. 10003. Mailing Add: 150 E. 39th St, New York, N.Y. 10016.

STEIN, IVAN C. R
b. South Haven, Mich, 12/21/08; s. Charles Frederick Stein and Mary Underwood S; m. 5/3/32 to Ruth Dilley; c. Charles Ross and Julie Ann (Mrs. Taylor) and 4 Grandchildren. Polit. & Govt. Pos: Chmn, Van Buren Co. Rep. Party, Mich, 62-69; mem, Mich. State Apple Cmn, 63-, chmn, 66; del, Rep. Nat. Conv, 64. Bus. & Prof. Pos: Owner, Ross-Ann Orchards, 44-; pres-mgr, Triple S-Produce, 60- Mem: Rotary Club; Mich. State Hort. Soc; South Haven Commun. Hosp. Bd; Elks; Farm Bur; Van Buren Co. Road Cmn. Mailing Add: R.R. 5, South Haven, Mich. 49090.

STEIN, ROBERT D
b. New York, N.Y, 3/4/24; s. Isidor Stein and Gertrude Bohrer S; m. 3/31/56 to Dorothy Weichel; c. Gregory Matthew, Keith Haywood and Clifford Braden. Educ: City Col, N.Y, B.A, 47; Columbia Univ, 47-48. Polit. & Govt. Pos: Chmn, Fed. Woman's Award, 66; alternate del, Dem. Nat. Conv, 68; mem, Gov. Cmt. on Minority Hiring in Mass Media, 68-69. Bus. & Prof. Pos: Ed, Redbook Mag, 58-65, McCall's Mag, 65-67; v.pres, McCall Publ. Co, 68- Mil. Serv: Entered as Pvt, Army, 43, released as T-5, 46, after serv. in 80th Div, ETO, 45-46; Purple Heart; Combat Infantryman's Badge, ETO Ribbon with two Battle Stars. Publ: Articles in Reader's Digest, Saturday Rev. and others, 49-68. Mem: Exec. cmt, Am. Soc. Mag. Ed; Overseas Press Club. Richard Neuberger Award, Am. Soc. Mag. Ed, 61; Citizen Diplomacy Award, Citizen Exchange Corps, 68. Mailing Add: McCall Publishing Co, 230 Park Ave, New York, N.Y. 10017.

STEINBERG, LIONEL SANFORD D
V.Pres, Calif. State Bd. of Agr.
b. Fresno, Calif, 4/20/19; s. William Steinberg and Selma S; m. 4/10/49 to Mary Louise Endfield; c. William E, Barbara Dee and Mary Frances. Educ: Fresno State Col, grad. with highest honors, 40; Am. Univ. Grad Sch, Wash, D.C, fel. grad. work in agr. and econ. and soils, 41; Harvard Grad Sch. Bus, 42-43. Polit. & Govt. Pos: Pres, Calif. State Fedn. Young Dem, 49-52; chmn, Fresno Co. Dem. Cent. Cmt, 52-58; mem, farm platform cmt, Dem. Party, 52-; del, Dem. Nat. Conv, 56-64; rep, World Farmers Conv, Israel, 59; v.pres, Calif. State Bd. Agr, 59-; treas, Nat. Exec. Cmt, Farmers for Kennedy-Johnson, 60; mem, Chile-Calif. Adv. Cmt, 63; co-chmn, Calif. Farmers for Johnson-Humphrey and mem. exec. cmt, Rural Americans for Johnson-Humphrey, 64; mem, U.S. Dept. Agr, Citizens Adv. Cmt. on Civil Rights, 65-68; former v.chmn, Dem. State Cent. Cmt. and former state chmn, Calif. Freedom from Hunger Coun. Bus. & Prof. Pos: Pres, David Freedman & Co, Inc. Mil. Serv: Lt, Navy, 42-46. Mem: Dir, Calif. Grape & Tree Fruit League, 52-64; West Growers Asn; Am. Farm Econ. Asn; Calif. Farm Bur; Grange; Racquet Club; Int. Platform Asn; Am. Food for Peace Coun. Leader, People-to-People Farmers' Group West. and East. Europe, 62 and 63. Rel: Jewish. Legal Res: 797 Via Vadera, Palm Springs, Calif. 92262. Mailing Add: P.O. Box 501, Thermal, Calif. 92274.

STEINBERG, MELVIN ALLEN D
Md. State Sen.
b. Baltimore, Md, 10/4/33; s. Irvin Steinberg and Julia Levenson S; m. 3/23/58 to Anita Akman; c. Edward Bryan, Susan Renee and Barbara Ellen. Educ: Univ. Baltimore, A.A, 52; Univ. Baltimore Sch. Law, LL.B, 55; Nu Beta Epsilon. Polit. & Govt. Pos: Md. State Sen, Baltimore Co, 67-; del, Dem. Nat. Conv, 68. Mil. Serv: Entered as Seaman Recruit, Navy, 55, released as Storekeeper 3/C, 57, after serv. in U.S.S. R.K. Huntington DD781. Mem: Am, Md. State and Baltimore City Bar Asns; Md. Plaintiff's Bar Asn; Judicature Soc; Safety First Club of Md; Nat. Soc. of State Legislators; AF&AM; Yedz Grotto; Jr. C. of C; B'nai B'rith; Histadrut; Md. Asn. for Retarded Children, Inc. Distinguished Serv. Award, Jr. C. of C, Randallstown Chap. Rel: Jewish. Legal Res: 3412 Maryvale Rd, Baltimore, Md. 21207. Mailing Add: 202 Loyola Federal Bldg, Towson, Md. 21204.

STEINEGER, JOHN FRANCIS, JR. D
Kans. State Sen.
b. Kansas City, Kans, 9/13/24; s. John F. Steineger and June Wear S; m. 12/1/49 to Margaret Leisy; c. John, III, Cynthia, Mellissa and Christian. Educ: Univ. South. Calif; Kans. Univ; George Wash. Univ; Phi Delta Phi; Phi Delta Theta. Polit. & Govt. Pos: Cultural attaché, U.S. Dept. of State, Europe and Near East, 50-58; local chmn, Kennedy for President Cmt. and Johnson for President Cmt; Kans. State Sen, 64-; chmn, Third Cong. Dist. Dem. Cmt, presently; del, Dem. Nat. Conv, 68. Bus. & Prof. Pos: Attorney, Finnigen, Poizner, Tucker, Steineger & Reid, at present. Mil. Serv: Entered as A/S, Navy, 43, released as Lt.(jg), 46, after serv. in Pac. Mem: Chmn, Kansas City, Kans. People-to-People Chap; Kiwanis; Century Club; pres, Kansas City Ballet Asn. Rel: Episcopal. Legal Res: 6400 Valley View Rd, Muncie, Kans. 66057. Mailing Add: 645 Ann Ave, Kansas City, Kans. 66101.

STEINFELD, SAMUEL S. R
Justice, Court of Appeals, Ky.
b. Louisville, Ky, 2/15/06; s. Emile Steinfeld and Florence Simons S; m. 7/24/29 to Flora Loebenberg; c. Helane (Mrs. Howard B. Grossman); James F. Steinfeld; five grandchildren. Educ: Univ. Louisville, LL.B, 28. Polit. & Govt. Pos: Co. attorney, Jefferson Co, Ky, 46-49; mem, Co. Rep. Exec. Cmt, Ky, 46-66; mem, Jefferson Co. Elec. Cmn, 55-66; justice, Court of Appeals, Ky, Frankfort, 67- Bus. & Prof. Pos: Dir. and secy, various corp; assoc, Gifford & Steinfeld, 28-35; partner, Steinfeld and Steinfeld, 35-66; chmn, Judicial Coun. Ky, 69- Mem: Am, Ky. and Louisville Bar Asns; Am. Judicature Soc; Commercial Law League Am; Lincoln Club Ky; L Club, Univ. Louisville; Ky. Hist. Soc; Commanding Officers Club; B'nai B'rith; Adath Israel Mens Club. Distinguished Law Alumni Award, Univ. Louisville, 66. Rel: Jewish. Mailing Add: 3512 St. Germaine Court, Louisville, Ky. 40207.

STEINGASZNER, ELFRIDA HELEN R
Mem, State Rep. Cent. Cmt, Md.
b. Vienna, Austria, 5/11/34; d. Karl Kainz and Maria Pawelka K; m. 4/29/61 to Dr. Laszlo Steingaszner; c. Beatrice. Educ: Univ. Cambridge, Cert. Eng, 54; Univ. Paris, cert. French, 55. Polit. & Govt. Pos: Pres, Fedn. Rep. Women, Md, 67-69; alternate del, Rep. Nat. Conv, 68; mem, State Rep. Cent. Cmt, 68- Bus. & Prof. Pos: Secy, Canadian Embassy, Vienna, Austria, 56-59; secy, UN High Cmnr. for Refugees, 59-60; secy, Indian Embassy, Wash, D.C, 60-62. Publ: 'How A Conservative Government Could Benefit Me,' Polit, 3/68. Mem: Women's Auxiliary, Baltimore City Med. Asn. and Baltimore Co. Med. Asn; Cosmopolitan Club. Rel: Roman Catholic. Mailing Add: 805 Stags Head Rd, Baltimore, Md. 21204.

STEINGLASS, STEVEN HENRY D
b. N.Y.C, 11/15/42; s. Sam Steinglass and Rose Feldbrill S; single. Educ: Univ. Pa, B.S, 64; Columbia Univ. Law Sch, LL.B, 67; Univ. Wis, Madison, 68-69. Polit. & Govt. Pos: Del, Dem. Nat. Conv, 68. Bus. & Prof. Pos: Asst. prof. polit. sci, Wis. State Univ, Platteville, 67-69; attorney, Freedom Through Equality, 69- Publ: 'County Home Rule in New York State,' In: Essays on the New York Constitution, 66. Mem: Wis. Bar Asn; Am. Polit. Sci. Asn; Am. Asn. Univ. Prof; Wis. Civil Liberties Union. Mailing Add: 2724 N. Murray, Milwaukee, Wis. 53211.

STEINGUT, STANLEY D
N.Y. State Assemblyman
b. Brooklyn, N.Y, 5/20/20; m. to Madeline Fellerman; c. Robert Ted and Ilene. Educ: Union Col, St. John's Univ. Law Sch. Polit. & Govt. Pos: Exec. mem, Madison Club, 18th Assembly Dist, N.Y; N.Y. State Assemblyman, 52-; chmn, Kings Co. Dem. Party, N.Y, currently; del, Dem. Nat. Conv, 68. Bus. & Prof. Pos: Attorney. Mem: Unity Club, Brooklyn; Nat. Dem. Club; Jewish War Vet; Kings Co. Bar Asn; Brooklyn Jewish Center. Mailing Add: 1298 President St, Brooklyn, N.Y. 11213. (1967)

STEINHAUER, JOHN MATHIAS, JR. D
b. Nashville, Tenn, 7/23/25; s. John Mathias Steinhauer and Gertrude Garretty S; m. 6/21/52 to Betty Jane Hagewood; c. Joni, John M, III, Janet, Steven Harold and Julie. Educ: Univ. Tenn, 46 & 47. Polit. & Govt. Pos: Former Tenn. State Rep. Bus. & Prof. Pos: Pub. rels. dir, Bill Hudson & Assocs, 65; pres, B.A.T, Inc. and Hendersonville Optical Dispensary, 66. Mem: Sertoma; Mason (32°); Scottish Rite; Shrine. Rel: Lutheran. Legal Res: 124 Circle Dr, Hendersonville, Tenn. 37075. Mailing Add: 327 Main St, Hendersonville, Tenn. 37075. (1967)

STEINHILBER, JACK DANIEL R
Wis. State Assemblyman
b. Oshkosh, Wis, 9/14/31; s. Elmer G. Steinhilber and Rose Wingeier S; m. 2/22/64 to Sandra B. Guest; c. Jennifer and Leslie. Educ: Univ. of Wis, B.S, 53 and LL.B, 55; Artus; Phi Alpha Delta; Kappa Sigma. Polit. & Govt. Pos: Chmn, Univ. of Wis. Young Rep. Club, 52-53; exec. cmt. positions, Co, Dist. and State Rep. Orgn, 53-63; mem, State Exec. Cmt, Rep. Party of Wis, 55-57; state committeeman, Wis. Young Rep, 55-57, Nat. Committeeman, 61-63; asst. dist. attorney, Winnebago Co, 56, dist. attorney, 57-64; Wis. State Assemblyman, 67- Mem: Secy-treas, Wis. Dist. Attorneys Asn, 63 and pres, 64; Am. Bar Asn; Nat. Dist. Attorneys Asn; Elks; Kiwanis; Jaycees; C. of C. Rel: Lutheran. Legal Res: 1748 Southland Ave, Oshkosh, Wis. 54901. Mailing Add: 302 N. Main St, Oshkosh, Wis. 54901.

STEIS, WILLIAM BURTON D
Chmn, Harris Co. Dem. Exec. Cmt, Ga.
b. Elbon, Pa, 3/3/07; s. John Burton Steis and Harriet Eggleston S; m. 5/12/33 to Helen Cecilia Rosenkrans; c. Marjorie Helen (Mrs. Beard) and Kathryn Faye (Mrs. Pace). Educ: Univ. Notre Dame, Pre-law, 28; Duquesne Univ. Law Sch, 31; John Marshall Law Sch, 47; Sigma Nu Phi. Polit. & Govt. Pos: Chmn, Harris Co. Dem. Exec. Cmt, Ga, 49-; Ga. State Sen, 25th Dist, 55-56; Ga. State Rep, 59-68. Bus. & Prof. Pos: Attorney. Mil. Serv: Pa. Nat. Guard, 33-41; entered as 1st Sgt, Army, 41, released as Maj, 47; Victory Medal. Mem: Patrons of Husbandry; Eagles; Red Men; Am. Legion; C. of C.(past cmt. mem); organizer, Health Found; PTA (chmn. and pres). Rel: Catholic. Mailing Add: Pine Mt. Valley, Ga. 31823. (1967)

STELLA, ANTHONY JOSEPH D
N.Y. State Assemblyman
b. Bronx, N.Y, 6/19/28; s. Otino Stella and Jennie Merola S; m. 8/28/54 to Rose Marie Colella; c. Marc, Valerie and Carla. Educ: City Col. N.Y, B.B.A, 50; St. John's Sch. Law, LL.B, 55; Circolo Dante Alighieri and Newman Soc. City Col. N.Y. Polit. & Govt. Pos: Law secy, Civil Court, 61; mem, Bronx Co. Dem. Cmt, N.Y, 62 & 65-66; N.Y. State Assemblyman, 92nd Assembly Dist, 66 and 86th Assembly Dist, 69-, aide to speaker, N.Y. State Assembly, 67-68. Bus. & Prof. Pos: Mem, joint bd, ILGWU, 50-61; attorney-at-law, Bronx, N.Y, 61- Mil. Serv: Pvt. E-1, Army, 51, serv. in basic training. Mem: Bronx Bar Asn; Police Athletic League; Boy Scouts; Columbus-Esca Alliance; K. of C; Wakefield and Williams Bridge Taxpayer and Civic Asns; NAACP; Hillside Little League; Father's Club; Holy Name Soc; Wakefield-Woodlawn Baseball League. Honored by St. Burbmia Aid Soc, Brooklyn, N.Y, 69. Rel: Catholic. Legal Res: 2527 Radcliff Ave, Bronx, N.Y. 10469. Mailing Add: 2488 Grand Concourse, Bronx, N.Y. 10458.

STEMBRIDGE, BOB JONES D
Ala. State Rep.
b. Newton, Ala, 10/17/18; s. William Grady Stembridge and Pearl Beasley S; single. Educ: Troy State Col; Mercer Univ, B.A, 52. Polit. & Govt. Pos:

Former tax collector, Houston Co, Ala; Ala. State Rep, 55- Bus. & Prof. Pos: Farming and cattle raising. Mil. Serv: Army, World War II. Mem: Mason; Shriner; Elks; WOW. Rel: Methodist. Mailing Add: Box 712, Dothan, Ala. 36301. (1967)

STEMMER, JAY A. R
Treas, Union Co, N.J.
b. Wilkes-Barre, Pa, 10/29/15; s. Jay A. Stemmer and Nell Quigley S; m. 7/2/38 to Mary Kearney, wid. 9/5/68; c. Jay, Wayne and Susan. Educ: Univ. Pa, Wharton Sch. of Finance. Polit. & Govt. Pos: Town clerk, Clark, N.J, 49-51, cmnr, 51-59, mayor, 52-59; mem, Union Co. Rep. Cmt, 52-, chmn, 63-67; city chmn, Clark, N.J. Rep. Cmt, 56-64; freeholder, Union Co, 60-65; treas, Union Co, 69- Bus. & Prof. Pos: Pres, Stemmer Realty; mem. adv. bd, Summit & Elizabeth Trust Co. Mil. Serv: Pvt, Air Force, 45. Mem: V.pres. and dir, Kiwanis. Rel: Roman Catholic. Mailing Add: 990 Raritan Rd, Clark, N.J. 07066.

STEMMLER, GUST L. D
Pa. State Rep.
b. 12/10/99; s.Julius Stemmler and Pauline BergerS; m. to Irene Schrum; c. five. Educ: Derry Twp. Schs. Polit. & Govt. Pos: Mem, Derry Twp. Sch. Bd, Pa, 45-51; Pa. State Rep, 62- Bus. & Prof. Pos: Self-employed merchant. Mem: Derry Bus. & Prfnl. Men's Asn.(charter mem. and past pres); Derry Commun. Develop. and Recreation Corp.(charter mem); Lions (charter mem. and former officer); Derry Vol. Fire Dept; former dir. Chestnut Ridge Chap, Am. Red Cross; Price Panel Bd, World War II; sponsor and pres, Oaklawn Sandlot Baseball Team; charter mem, Salem Beagle Club and other area Sportsman Clubs; Eagles; Elks; Moose. Mailing Add: R.D. 1, Box 34, Derry, Pa. 15627. (1967)

STEMPIEN, MARVIN R. D
Mich. State Rep.
b. Detroit, Mich, 7/26/33; m. 1955 to Corinne J. Lotowski; c. Lynn, Christine and Sharon. Educ: Univ. of Mich, B.B.A; Detroit Col. of Law, LL.B; Walsh Inst. of Accountancy. Polit. & Govt. Pos: Mich. State Rep, 64-66 & 68-; Northville City Attorney, 67-68. Bus. & Prof. Pos: Attorney; part-time mem. faculty, Walsh Inst. of Accountancy. Mil. Serv: Air Force, 3 years; res. duty for 7 years. Mem: Jr. C. of C; Teachers Club of Metrop. Detroit; Former Lord Coun, K. of C; Polish Legion of Am. Vets; Mich. and Livonia Bar Asns. Rel: Roman Catholic. Mailing Add: House of Representatives, Capitol Bldg, Third Floor, Room N, Lansing, Mich. 48933.

STEMPIEN, RONALD ROBERT D
b. Detroit, Mich, 1/13/29; s. Vincent S. Stempien and Martha C. Pisula S; m. 12/27/52 to Geraldine M. Kosal; c. Karen, David, Denise, Ronald, Tamra and Timothy. Educ: Univ. Mich, B.A, 52; Detroit Col. of Law, LL.B, 56, J.D, 68. Polit. & Govt. Pos: Councilman, Lincoln Park, Mich, 59-61, mayor, 61-67, city attorney, 67-69; mem. bd. supvrs, Wayne Co, 61-67. Mil. Serv: Entered as A/S, Navy, 46, released as S.N, Pac, 48. Mem: Mich. and Downriver Bar Asns; Catholic Lawyers Soc; Jaycees; C. of C; Kiwanis; K. of C; Polish Legion Am. Vet; Catholic War Vet; Holy Name Soc; St. Vincent DePaul Soc. Rel: Catholic. Legal Res: 25490 East River Rd, Grosse Ile, Mich. 48138. Mailing Add: 3858 Fort St, Lincoln Park, Mich. 48146.

STENDER, JOHN H. R
Wash. State Sen.
b. Ismay, Mont, 7/16/16; m. to Ida; c. two sons and two daughters. Educ: Rocky Mt. Col. Polit. & Govt. Pos: Mem, Wash. State Legis. Coun; mem. sub-cmt. job opportunities, Nat. Rep. Coord. Cmt; v.chmn, Wash. State Spec. Cmt, Indust. Ins. Appeals; mem. exec. bd, King Co. Young Men's Rep. Club, Wash; mem, Nat. Cmt, Prog. and Progress, Percy Cmt, 59 and Nat. Big Cities Cmt, Bliss Cmt, 60; Rep. cand. for Cong, 60; Wash. State Sen, currently. Bus. & Prof. Pos: Int. v.pres, Int. Brotherhood Boilermakers, Iron Ship Builders, Blacksmiths, Forgers and Helpers, AFL-CIO Northwest Sect, mem, Boilermakers Exec. Coun. and 12 years bus. mgr and secy, Boilermakers Welders' Local 541, Seattle, Wash. Mem: Eagles; Lions. Elected, King Co. Rep. Man of Year, 61. Rel: Presbyterian. Mailing Add: 27420 Military Rd, Auburn, Wash. 98002. (1967)

STENGEL, JAMES LOWELL R
b. Milbank, S.Dak, 4/1/26; s. Ezra G. Stengel and Helen Bury S; m. 8/21/49 to Dorthey Mavis Fudge; c. Debbie, Cindy, Jimmy and Mark. Educ: N.Cent. Col, B.S. in Bus. Admin, 50. Polit. & Govt. Pos: Chmn, Grant Co. Rep. Party, S.Dak, 58-66. Bus. & Prof. Pos: Pres, Dakota Granite Co, 52-; dir, Otter Tail Power Co, 65-;Dakota State Bank, 65- Mil. Serv: Entered as Seaman 3/C, Navy, 44, released as PO 3/C, 45, after serv. in U.S.S. Stribling. Mem: Pres, Am. Monument Asn, 62-64; pres, Milbank Kiwanis Club; AF&AM. Rel: United Church of Christ. Mailing Add: 803 S. Fifth St, Milbank, S.Dak. 57252.

STENNIS, JOHN CORNELIUS D
U.S. Sen, Miss.
b. Kemper Co, Miss, 8/3/01; s. Hampton Howell Stennis and Cornelia Adams S; m. 1929 to Coy Hines; c. John Hampton and Mrs. Samuel Syme. Educ: Miss. State Univ, B.S, 23; Univ. of Va. Law Sch, LL.B, 28; Phi Beta Kappa; Phi Alpha Delta; Alpha Chi Rho. Hon. LL.D, Millsaps Col, 57, Univ. Wyo, 62 and Miss. Col, 69. Polit. & Govt. Pos: Miss. State Rep, 28-32; prosecuting attorney, 16th Judicial Dist, 31-37; circuit judge, 37-47; U.S. Sen, Miss, 47- Mem: Mason; Lions; Farm Bur; Miss. and Am. Bar Asns; past pres, State 4H Club Adv. Coun. Rel: Presbyterian. Legal Res: De Kalb, Miss. Mailing Add: 3609 Cumberland St, Washington, D.C. 20008.

STENVIG, CHARLES Independent
Mayor, Minneapolis, Minn.
b. Minneapolis, Minn, 1/16/28; s. Selmer Stenvig and Myrtle Lee S; m. 8/6/51 to Audrey L. Thompson; c. Terri, Tracy, Todd and Thomas. Educ: Augsburg Col, B.A. in Sociol, 51; Univ. Minn, Juvenile Officers Inst, 60. Polit. & Govt. Pos: Detective, Minneapolis Police Dept, Minn, 56-69; mayor, Minneapolis, 69- Mil. Serv: Entered as Pvt, Army, 46, released, 47, after serv. in S.Pac; Lt, Air Force Nat. Guard, 52-53; Cpl, Army Res; S/Sgt, Air Force Res; Lt, Air Nat. Guard Res. Publ: Originator, The Law Officer Mag, Minneapolis, 67- Mem: Minn. Police and Peace Officers Asn; pres, Police Officers Fedn. of Minneapolis, 65-69; co.chmn, Minneapolis Fire and Police Joint Coun, 65-67; Minneapolis United Labor Cmt, 65-69; v.pres, Int. Conf. of Police Asn, 66-69, chmn, Int. Mag. Cmt, 67-69; Minn. Citizens Conf. on Courts and Minn. Gov. Cmn. on Law Enforcement, 66; City Coun. Cmn. on Human Develop. and Minneapolis Citizens League on Taxation, 67; VFW; PTA; Minneapolis Police Band; Minnehaha Lodge; Mason; K.T; Shrine; Lions Int; NAACP; Augsburg Col. Alumni Club. Reverence for Law Award, Fraternal Order of Eagles, 69. Rel: Methodist. Legal Res: 5604 35th Ave S, Minneapolis, Minn. 55417. Mailing Add: 127 City Hall, Minneapolis, Minn. 55415.

STEPHEN, JAMES BARNETT D
S.C. State Sen.
b. Spartanburg, S.C, 5/17/25; s. James Littlejohn Stephen and Annie Barnett S; m. 8/23/67 to Sara Goodwin; c. Susan, Kathy and James G. Educ: Univ. S.C, A.B, 45; Duke Univ, LL.B, 49; Phi Delta Phi; Pi Kappa Alpha. Polit. & Govt. Pos: S.C. State Rep, 61-68; S.C. State Sen, 69- Bus. & Prof. Pos: Attorney-at-law. Mil. Serv: Entered as Cadet, Navy, 42, released as Ens, 46, after. serv. aboard cargo vessel, Pac. Theatre, 45; Lt. Comdr.(Ret), Res. Mem: S.C. and Spartanburg Co. Bar Asns; Mason; Shrine; K. of P; VFW; Am. Legion; Optimist. Rel: Presbyterian. Legal Res: 220 Saratoga Ave, Spartanburg, S.C. 29303. Mailing Add: Cleveland Law Range, Spartanburg, S.C. 29301.

STEPHENS, CAROLYN KAY R
Nat. Committeewoman, Ohio League of Young Rep. Clubs
b. Dayton, Ohio, 9/3/36; d. Charles Donald Stephens and Florence Thornhill S; single. Educ: Ohio Univ, A.A, 56; Zeta Tau Alpha. Polit. & Govt. Pos: Del, Ohio Young Rep. Conv, 60-; mem, Montgomery Co. Young Rep. Exec. Cmt, 61-; secy, Montgomery Co. Young Rep, 62-63, second v.pres, 63-64; mem, Ohio Young Rep. Exec. Cmt, 62-; state dir, Teen-Age Rep. Clubs, 63-64; state co-chmn, Ohio Young Rep. Clubs, 63-64; Ohio del, Nat. Young Rep. Fedn. Conv, 63, 65, 67 & 69 and mem, Nat. Cmt, 65-; del, Ohio State Rep. Conv, 64, 66 & 68; alternate del, Rep. Nat. Conv, 64 & 68; mem, Montgomery Co. Rep. Exec. Cmt, 64-, adv. cmt, 69-; state chmn, Ohio League Young Rep. Clubs, 66-67, nat. committeewoman, 67- Bus. & Prof. Pos: Secy, to Adding Machine Sales Dir, The Nat. Cash Register Co, 56- Mem: Barney Children's Hosp. Serv. Cmt; Dayton City Panhellenic Asn; Montgomery Co. Rep. Bus. Women; Ohio Univ. Alumnae; Zeta Tau Alpha Alumnae. Rel: Protestant. Mailing Add: 120 Cambridge Ave, Dayton, Ohio 45406.

STEPHENS, EDGAR J. JR. D
Miss. State Rep.
b. New Albany, Miss, 5/26/16; single. Educ: Univ. Miss, B.A, 38, LL.B, 40; Sigma Chi; Phi Delta Phi. Polit. & Govt. Pos: Prosecuting attorney, Union Co, Miss, 47-51; Miss. State Rep, 52-, chmn, Appropriations Cmt, Miss. State House of Rep, 67- Bus. & Prof. Pos: Attorney-at-law; real estate broker. Mil. Serv: Naval Res, 41-54; on staff of Adm. Wm. F. Halsey, 43-44. Mem: Miss. Bar Asn; Am. Legion; Rotary; Farm Bur. Rel: Assoc. Reformed Presbyterian. Mailing Add: Box 330, New Albany, Union Co, Miss. 38652.

STEPHENS, JACK LeROL D
Ga. State Sen.
b. Atlanta, Ga, 7/26/27; s. Ben Davis Stephens, Sr. and Ruth Epperson S; m. 12/6/46 to Betty Mae Norman; c. Jack, Jr. and Christopher Robert. Educ: N.Y. Univ, 49; John Marshall Law Sch, LL.B, 50, LL.M, 54; Univ. Ga, 61; Sigma Delta Kappa. Polit. & Govt. Pos: Mem, Dem. Exec. Cmt, Atlanta, Ga, 65; Ga. State Sen, 36th Dist, currently. Mil. Serv: Entered as Seaman, Naval Res, 45, released as Seaman 1/C, 46. Rel: Baptist. Mailing Add: 2484 Macon Dr. S.E, Atlanta, Ga. 30315. (1967)

STEPHENS, JOHN RANDOL D
b. Haleyville, Ala, 9/12/16; s. George Thomas Stephens and Ada Parrish S; m. 3/1/44 to Beatrice Ann Johnson; c. Ann R, Sarah Holmes. Polit. & Govt. Pos: Admin. asst. to U.S. Sen. Ross Bass, Tenn, 64-69. Bus. & Prof. Pos: Owner, Stephens Supply Co, 46-54; owner radio sta, WKSR, 52-63; publisher, Giles Free Press, 60-63. Mil. Serv: Lt, Army, 41-46; serv. in Qm. and Med. Serv. Corps. Rel: Episcopal. Mailing Add: R.F.D. 5, Pulaski, Tenn. 38478.

STEPHENS, MERLE LEON R
Chmn, Southeast Dist. Three Rep. Orgn, Alaska
b. Coeur D'Alene, Idaho, 11/22/08; s. Charles P. Stephens and Florence Rhodes S; m. 7/7/59 to Mildred Head Miller. Educ: Harrison High Sch, Idaho, 4 years. Polit. & Govt. Pos: Chmn, Southeast Dist. Three Rep. Orgn, Alaska, 68- Mil. Serv: Entered as Pvt, Army Air Force, 42, released as Sgt, 45, after serv. in 600th Air Engr. Squadron, Pac. Theatre, 45; Good Conduct Medal; Victory Medal; Am. Theatre Serv. Medal; Asiatic-Pac. Serv. Medal; Philippine Liberation Medal with One Bronze Star. Mem: Secy, Sitka Rotary Club, Alaska, 66- Rel: Christian Scientist. Legal Res: 201 New Archangel St, Sitka, Alaska 99835. Mailing Add: P.O. Box 979, Sitka, Alaska 99835.

STEPHENS, RICHARD L. R
Iowa State Sen.
b. Wash. City, Iowa, 2/8/04; s. D. D. Stephens and Blanche Cocklin S; m. 8/28/26 to Florence Krause; c. Richard Allan and Boyd. Educ: Iowa State Univ. Polit. & Govt. Pos: Mem, Sch. Bd, Ainsworth, Iowa; former Iowa State Rep; Iowa State Sen, currently. Bus. & Prof. Pos: Farming and livestock prod. Mem: V.pres, Iowa Farm Bur. Fed, 8 years; trustee, Iowa State Univ. Farm Found; treas, Iowa Swine Producers Asn; bd. of Iowa Farm Security Admin; Nat. Planning Asn; trustee, Iowa 4-H Club Found. and Wesley Acres; pres, Iowa Master Farmers' Club; Mason; Shrine. Chosen Master Corn Grower and Mast Swine Producer. Rel: Methodist. Mailing Add: Ainsworth, Iowa 52201. (1967)

STEPHENS, ROBERT GRIER, JR. D
U.S. Rep, Ga.
b. Atlanta, Ga, 8/14/13; s. Dr. Robert Grier and Martha Lucy Evans S; m. 1938 to Grace Winston; c. Grace Winston (Mrs. D.R. Bianchi), Robert Grier, III, Mary

Winston and Lawton Evans. Educ: Univ. Ga, B.A, 35; Univ. Hamburg, Germany, exchange student scholarship; M.A, 37; law degree, cum laude, 41; Phi Beta Kappa; Phi Kappa Phi; Phi Delta Phi; Kappa Alpha Order. Polit. & Govt. Pos: City attorney, Athens, Ga, 47-50; Ga. State Sen, 51-53; Ga. State Rep, 53-59; U.S. Rep, Ga, 60- Bus. & Prof. Pos: Taught hist. and polit. sci, Univ. of Ga, 36-40; practicing lawyer, 46-61. Mil. Serv: Army, World War II; last assignment before separation was on the legal staff of Mr. Justice Robert Jackson at Nuremberg trials. Mem: Am. Legion; VFW; Elks; Kiwanis (Lt. Gov); WOW; Omicron Delta Kappa. Rel: Presbyterian; Elder. Legal Res: Athens, Ga. Mailing Add: Cannon House Office Bldg, Washington, D.C. 20515.

STEPHENS, RONALD LeMOYNE R
Chmn, Fifth Cong. Dist. Rep. Fedn, Wash.
b. Butler, Pa, 11/28/33; s. Howard A. Stephens and Carolene Cross S; div; c. Mark LeMoyne and Cathy Ann. Educ: Univ. Denver, B.S; Univ. Mont. Law Sch, 67-68; Kappa Sigma. Polit. & Govt. Pos: Precinct committeeman, Rep. Party, Chester, Mont, 60-62; Rep. nominee, Mont. State Sen, 64; nat. committeeman, Mont. Young Rep, 65; nat. committee, Young Rep. Nat. Fedn, 65-66, nat. exec. bd, 66-67, v.chmn-at-lg, 66-67; del, Young Rep. Nat. Conv, 65; del. chmn, Young Rep. Nat. Fedn. Conv, 67; chmn, Mont. Young Rep. Fedn, 67; admin. asst. to speaker of the house, Mont. House Rep, 67; mem. exec. cmt, Mont. Rep. Party, 67-68; alternate del, Rep. Nat. Conv, 68; chmn, Fifth Cong. Dist. Rep. Fedn, Wash, 69- Bus. & Prof. Pos: Owner, Stephens Farm, Chester, Mont, 59-67; owner, Stephens Agency, 60-67; invest. exec, Goodbody & Co, Spokane, Wash, 68- Mil. Serv: Entered as Pvt, Army, 54, released as Cpl, 55, after serv. in 11th Signal Bn, Ft. Huachuca, Ariz; Good Conduct and Nat. Defense Serv. Medals. Mem: Farm Bur; Mont. Grain Producers Asn; life mem. Nat. Rifle Asn; AF&AM; Shrine. Rel: Lutheran. Legal Res: N. 6411 Stevens, Spokane, Wash. 99208. Mailing Add: W. 525 Sprague Ave, Spokane, Wash. 99210.

STEPHENS, STANLEY GRAHAM R
Mont. State Sen.
b. Calgary, Alberta, Can, 9/16/29; s. Joseph Stephens and Margaret Farrelly S; m. 6/15/54 to Ann Hanson; c. Alana and Carol Ann. Educ: West Can. High Sch, Calgary, 44-47. Polit. & Govt. Pos: Mont. State Sen, Dist. 19, 69- Bus. & Prof. Pos: V.pres and secy, Radio Sta. KOJM, Havre, Mont, 65-; pres, Big Sky TV Cable Inc, Sidney, 68-; pres, Glasgow TV Cable Inc, 68-; pres, Commun. TV Inc, Havre, 68- Mil. Serv: Entered as Pvt, Army, 51, released as S/Sgt, 53, after serv. in Armed Forces Radio Serv, Korea, 51-53; U.S. Commendation Ribbon with Pendant. Mem: Nat. Asn. Broadcasters; Broadcast Pioneers of Am; Nat. Cable TV Asn; Mason; Shrine; Am. Legion; Elks; Eagles. Outstanding Young Man of Havre, 62; Mont. Assoc. Press Radio Ed. Award, 63-68. Rel: Lutheran. Mailing Add: 33 Beaver Creek Blvd, Havre, Mont. 59501.

STEPHENS, VERN R
b. Portland, Ore, 11/12/22; s. Loyd M. Stephens and Esther C. Steiner S; m. 9/17/50 to Lucille M. Hanmula; c. Robert O, Peter C, Dennis P, William L. and Ann M. Educ: Wash. State Univ, A.B. in Polit. Sci, 49; Beta Theta Pi. Polit. & Govt. Pos: Exec. secy, Rep. State Cent. Cmt. Ore, 56; asst. dir. territories, U.S. Dept. Interior, 57-59, asst. cmnr. Indian affairs, 59-61; spec. asst. to Sen. Milton R. Young, Rep, N.Dak, 61; pub. rels. dir, Sen. Campaign, Ala, 62; dir, Berks Co. Rep. Campaign, Pa, 63; personal asst. to Sen. Barry Goldwater, 64; campaign dir. for Congressman Wendell Wyatt, Rep, Ore, 64; admin. asst. to Congressman Henry Schadeberg, Rep, Wis, 67-68; dir. pub. affairs, Govt. Serv. Admin, 69- Bus. & Prof. Pos: Textile mfr, 49-56. Mil. Serv: Entered as Pvt, Air Force, 42, released as Sgt, 46. Rel: Protestant. Mailing Add: 2611 Schooley Dr, Alexandria, Va. 22306.

STEPHENS, WILLIS H. R
N.Y. State Assemblyman
b. Patterson, N.Y, 6/7/25; m. Daphne Dunbar; c. four. Educ: Princeton Univ. Polit. & Govt. Pos: N.Y. State Assemblyman, 52-; mem, N.Y. State Rep. Cmt, 66- Bus. & Prof. Pos: Coal bus; dir, Nat. Bank of N.Am, presently. Mil. Serv: U.S. Air Force. Mem: Am. Legion; Mason (32°); Elks; dir, Putnam Community Hosp. Mailing Add: Indian Well Farm, Brewster, N.Y. 10509.

STEPHENSON, GEORGE EDWARD D
Polit. & Govt. Pos: Mem, Sch. Bd; Mem, Twp. Adv. Bd, two years; State Rep, -66. Bus. & Prof. Pos: Machine operator. Mil. Serv: Air Force. Mem: Am. Legion; 40 et 8; Masonic Lodge; United Auto Workers Local 287; Co. Farm Bur. Rel: Cammack Methodist Church. Mailing Add: R.R. 2, Yorktown, Ind. 47396. (1967)

STEPHENSON, MARGUERITE D
b. Weleetka, Okla, 11/16/19; d. John Butler Thomas and Mary Potter T; m. 5/30/37 to Clem H. Stephenson; c. John H, Judy K. and Mary S. Educ: High Sch. and Stauffers Bus. Col. Polit. & Govt. Pos: Alternate Del, Dem. Nat. Conv, 64; co-chmn, 4th Dist. Dem. Party, Okla, 64; co-chmn, Seminole Co. Dem. Cmt, 61-64; mgr, John F. Kennedy Presidential Campaign, Seminole Co, 60; mem, Seminole Co. Women's Dem. Club. Mem: Chmn, Legis. Cmt, Bus. & Prfnl. Women's Club, Seminole, Okla; Eastern Star; Jefferson Bryan Club. Rel: Southern Baptist. Legal Res: 901 McKinley, Seminole, Okla. 74868. Mailing Add: 316 E. Oak, Seminole, Okla. 74868. (1967)

STEPOVICH, MICHAEL A. R
b. Fairbanks, Alaska, 3/12/19; s. Mike Stepovich and Olga Barta S; m. 11/27/47 to Matilda Baricevic; c. 13. Educ: Gonzaga Univ, B.A; Univ. Notre Dame, LL.B. Hon. LL.D, Carroll Col. Polit. & Govt. Pos: Formerly mem, Alaska Territorial House of Rep, and Senate; Gov, Alaska, 57-59; mem, Judiciary Coun, currently. Bus. & Prof. Pos: Lawyer; city attorney, Fairbanks. Mil. Serv: Naval Res, World War II. Admitted to bar, Territory of Alaska. De Smet Medal, Gonzaga Univ, 66. Rel: Catholic. Legal Res: 323 Charles St, Fairbanks, Alaska 99701.

STEPP, MARC D
V.Chmn, First Dist. Dem. Orgn, Mich.
b. Versailles, Ky, 1/31/23; s. Ulyses Grant Stepp and Elizabeth Buford S; m. 10/31/55 to Eleanor Hardy. Educ: Wolerine Trades Sch, 48-49; Lewis Bus. Col, 51; Univ. Detroit, B.B.A, 63. Polit. & Govt. Pos: Precinct del, Dem. Party of Mich, 52; chmn, First Dist. Dem. Orgn, Mich, 64-67, v.chmn, 69-; v.chmn, Wayne Co. Dem. Cmt, 64-67, trustee, 69-; del, Dem. Nat. Conv, 68; mem, Wayne Co. Bd. of Supvr, 68-69. Bus. & Prof. Pos: Asst. Dir. Community Relations, C/h/a, 61-67; Int. Representative UAW Union, 67. Mil. Serv: Entered as Pvt, Army, 43, released as Cpl, 46, after serv. in 1903 Ordnance-AF, Pac. Theatre, 44-46. Mem: NAACP. Rel: Protestant. Legal Res: 4329 W. Grand Ave, Detroit, Mich. 48238. Mailing Add: 8000 E. Jefferson, Detroit, Mich. 48214.

STEPTOE, ROBERT M. D
b. Clarksburg, W.Va, 5/15/20; s. Phillip P. Steptoe and Mary Lou Wetherell S; m. 4/2/42 to Sarah Virginia Duff; c. Robert M, Jr, Phillip P, Sally W. and James Duff. Educ: Haverford Col; Shepherd Col; Univ. of Va, LL.B. Polit. & Govt. Pos: Asst. Prosecuting Attorney, Berkeley Co, W.Va; W.Va. State Del, 62-69. Bus. & Prof. Pos: Lawyer. Mil. Serv: Lt. Comdr, Navy, 41-46, serv. in European and Pac. Theatres, 45. Mem: Elks; Rotary; Am, W.Va. and Berkeley Co. Bar Asns. Rel: Episcopal. Mailing Add: Martinsburg, W.Va. 25401. (1967)

STERBENK, WILLIAM D. R
Chmn, Lake Co. Rep. Cent. Cmt, Calif.
b. Oakland, Calif, 5/7/31; s. Frank R. Sterbenk and Edna T. Williams S; m. 12/29/50 to Beverly Ann Hage; c. Melodee Kae and Mark William. Educ: Kelseyville Union High Sch, grad, 49. Polit. & Govt. Pos: Mem, Calif. Rep. State Cent. Cmt, 67-; dir, 49th Dist. Agr. Asn, 68; chmn, Lake Co. Rep. Cent. Cmt, 69- Mil. Serv: Entered as Airman, Navy, 49, released as Aviation Ordinanceman 2/C, 53, after serv. in Fighter Squadron 74, Korea, 52-53; Korean Serv, U.S. Serv. and Good Conduct Medals. Mem: Calif. Rep. chmn. Asn; VFW; Lakeport Volunteer Fire Dept; Konocti Rod & Gun Club. Rel: Catholic. Legal Res: 320 Lakeshore Blvd, Lakeport, Calif. 95453. Mailing Add: P.O. Box 412, Lakeport, Calif. 95453.

STERLING, BARRY H. D
b. Los Angeles, Calif, 10/25/29; s. J. David Sterling and Sara Elizabeth Abramson S; m. 8/30/52 to Audrey M. Shapiro; c. Joy Anne and Laurence Garrett. Educ: Stanford Univ, A.B, 50; Stanford Univ. Law Sch, LL.B, 52; Phi Alpha Delta; El Toro Eating Club. Polit. & Govt. Pos: Del, Dem. Nat. Conv, 64; mem, South. Calif. Dem. Finance Cmt, 64-68; mem, Calif. State Dem. Cent. Cmt, 65-68; treas, Dem. Nat. Cmt, Calif, 65-68; comptroller, Cmt. to Reelect Gov. Brown, Calif, 66. Bus. & Prof. Pos: Exec. v.pres, Acme Eagle Corps, 58-62; dir, Home Bank, 60-66; partner, Hindin, Sterling, McKithick and Powsner, Attorneys at Law, 60-; dir, Columbia Savings & Loan, 63-65; secy-dir, Allied Prod. Corp, 65-; gen. counsel, I.O.S. Mgt. Co, Geneva, Switz, 67- Mil. Serv: Entered as 1st Lt, Army, 52, released as Capt, 54, after serv. in Judge Adv. Gen. Corps, Pentagon, Wash, D.C. Mem: Am. and Calif. Bar Asns; charter mem. and treas, Golden Bear Club; bd. of trustees, City of Hope; Presidents Club; founder, Los Angeles Music Center and Los Angeles Art Mus. Rel: Jewish. 1967 Legal Res: Los Angeles, Calif. No mailing address available. (1967)

STERLING, ERNST HIRAM D
Chmn, Douglas Co. Dem. Cent. Cmt, Colo.
b. Jeanesville, Pa, 1/28/97; s. John Emory Sterling and Nellie Ernst S; m. 6/6/20 to Elizabeth Merle Ditty, wid. 9/18/66. Educ: Pomona Jr. Col, Calif, 1 year. Polit. & Govt. Pos: Cand. for State Auditor, Colo, 44; state supvr. farm census, Dept. Commerce, 45; cand. for State Treas, 46; mem, Dem. State Cent. Cmt. and Exec. Cmt, 56-59; cand. for Colo. State Sen, 58 & 66; chmn, Douglas Co. Dem. Cent. Cmt, 65- Bus. & Prof. Pos: Former secy-treas, Dayton-Goose Creek Rwy, Dayton, Tex; acct. and statistician, Union Pac. R.R. Co, Los Angeles, 23-28; wheat and cattle rancher, 33- Mil.Serv: Army, 18. Mem: Mason; Consistory; Shrine; Farmers Union. Rel: Presbyterian. Mailing Add: Route 1, Box 76, Littleton, Colo. 80120.

STERN, EDWARD D
b. Bangor, Maine, 1/31/08; s. Hyman Stern and Mamie Lipsky S; m. 3/27/38 to Mollie Rubin; c. Marshall A. and Howard D. Educ: Univ. Maine, A.B, 30; Harvard Law Sch, 30-31. Polit. & Govt. Pos: Recorder and acting judge, Bangor Munic. Court, Maine, 35-39; pub. adminstr, Penobscot Co, 58-62; former Maine State Sen, chmn, State Govt. Cmt. and Judiciary Cmt, 65-66. Mem: B'nai Brith; Am. and Maine Trial Lawyers; Am, Maine and Penobscot Co. Bar Asns; Zionists. Rel: Jewish. Legal Res: 28 Bellevue Ave, Bangor, Maine 04401. Mailing Add: 15 Columbia St, Bangor, Maine 04401.

STERN, HARRY L R
b. Chicago, Ill, 6/10/30; s. Gardner H. Stern and Hanchen Strauss S; div; c. Harry L, Nicolas Denison and Carla. Educ: Yale Univ, B.A, 52; Univ. Geneva, 54-55; Univ. Chicago, 57-60; Phi Gamma Delta. Polit. & Govt. Pos: Rep. precinct capt, 43rd Ward, Chicago, Ill, 58-; pres, 43rd Ward Young Rep. Orgn, 59-60; treas, 43rd Ward Regular Rep. Orgn, 62-63; alternate del, Rep. Nat. Conv, 68. Bus. & Prof. Pos: Businessman, 55- Mil. Serv: Entered as Pvt, Army, 52, released as Pfc, 54, after serv. in 101st Airborne Div. and Hq. Co, Ft. Myer, Va. Rel: Jewish. Mailing Add: 1440 Lake Shore Dr, Chicago, Ill. 60610.

STERN, HERBERT LYMAN, JR. D
Chmn, Lake Co. Dem. Cent. Cmt, Ill.
b. Chicago, Ill, 4/10/15; s. Herbert Lyman Stern and Lucille Rosenberg S; m. to Grace Mary Dain; c. Gwen Louise, Herbert Lyman, III and Robert Phillips; step c, Ann Nason Suber, Peter Dain Suber, Thomas Merritt Suber and John McLellan Suber. Educ: Yale Univ, B.A, 36; Yale Law Sch, LL.B, 39. Polit. & Govt. Pos: Dem. precinct committeeman, Deerfield Twp, Lake Co, Ill, 64-; del, Dem. Nat. Conv, 68; chmn, Lake Co. Dem. Cent. Cmt, 68- Bus. & Prof. Pos: Partner, Law Firm of Gottlieb & Schwartz, Chicago, Ill, 48-; secy-dir. and gen. counsel, EZ Paintr Corp, Milwaukee, Wis, 48-; secy. and dir, LaMere Industs, Walworth, Wis, 60-; secy. and dir, Norwood Mills, Inc, Janesville, 60-; secy. and dir, Rayburn Prod, Inc, Wheeling, Ill, 62-; chmn. bd. dirs, Tapecoat Corp, Evanston, 69- Mil. Serv: Entered as 1st Lt, Army Air Force, 41, released as Lt. Col, 46, after serv. in India-Burma Theater and Mil. Intel. Serv, War Dept. Gen. Staff; 12th Air Force Res; Bronze Star plus Serv. Ribbons. Publ: Series of articles on rural develop. in E. and S.E. Asia, various

newspapers, 67-68. Mem: Ill. State, Chicago and Lake Co. Bar Asns; VFW; Am. Legion; Standard Club; Midday Club; Downtown Club; Lake Shore Country Club; secy. and treas, Found. for Hearing & Speech Rehabilitation; trustee, Highland Park Hosp. Found. Mailing Add: 1128 Green Bay Rd, Highland Park, Ill. 60035.

STERN, HOWARD MORRIS R
Mem, Calif. Rep. State Cent. Cmt.
b. San Jose, Calif, 4/11/30; s. Harold K. Stern and Elizabeth McDougall S; m. 2/21/54 to Gloria Louise Dillon; c. Holly L, Jeffrey H, Bradford W. and Clayton H. Educ: Stanford Univ, 46-48; Alpha Tau Omega. Polit. & Govt. Pos: Mem. and chmn, various cmts, Santa Clara Co. Rep. Cent. Cmt, Calif, 56-; regional chmn, Santa Clara Co. Rep. Precinct, 60-66; pres, San Jose Rep. Assembly, 63-64; mem, bd. dir, Santa Clara Co. Rep. League, 64-66; mem, Calif. Rep. State Cent. Cmt, 64-; chmn, Congressman's Gubser Co. Cmt, 67- Bus. & Prof. Pos: Owner, Stern's Luggage, San Jose, Calif, 48- Mil. Serv: Entered as Pvt, Army, 51, released as Sgt, 53, after serv. in Counterintel, Korea; Korean Serv. Medal with Two Bronze Serv. Stars; UN. Serv. Medal; Commendation Medal. Mem: Pres, San Jose 20-30 Club, 57; Rotary; Elks; bd. dir, Santa Clara Co. Nat. Conf. Christians and Jews; bd. dir, Asn. of Metrop. San Jose, 69. Rel: Episcopal. Mailing Add: 1176 Janis Way, San Jose, Calif. 95125.

STERN, JERE BART D
Committeeman, Morris Co. Dem. Party, N.J.
b. Baltimore, Md, 12/18/32; s. Samuel Maurice Stern and Kathryn Sinskey S; m. 6/5/60 to Carol Ann Parodneck; c. Emily Beth. Educ: George Wash. Univ, B.S, 54, Sch. Med, M.D, 58; Phi Beta Kappa. Polit. & Govt. Pos: Alternate del, Dem. Nat. Conv, 68; committeeman, Morris Co. Dem. Party, N.J, 68-; mem. exec. cmt, Morris. Co. New Dem. Coalition, 69- Bus. & Prof. Pos: Chief pathologist, Riverside Hosp, Boonton, N.J, 66- Publ: Several scientific publ. in med. jour. Mem: Col. Am. Pathologists; Am. Soc. Clin. Pathologists; N.J. Soc. Pathologists; Am. Med. Asn; Med. Soc. N.J; Morris Co. Med. Soc; Mountain Lakes Human Rels. Coun. Mailing Add: 30 Valley Rd, Mountain Lakes, N.J. 07046.

STERN, OTTO R
S.Dak. State Rep.
b. Freeman, S.Dak, 9/2/09; m. to Vernell Fischer; c. Roger and Margaret. Educ: Common Sch; Correspondence Course. Polit. & Govt. Pos: Rep. precinct committeeman, Freeman, S.Dak, 8 years, Twp. Supvr, 3 years and mem, Sch. Bd, 9 years; Fed. Crop Ins. Agent, 2 years; mem, P.M.A. and A.S.C. City Cmt, 7 years; S.Dak. State Rep, 56- Bus. & Prof. Pos: Farmer. Mem: 4-H Leader, 6 years; secy-treas, Farmers Coop. Grain Asn, 9 years; City Exten. Bd. and pres, City Crop Improv. Asn. Rel: Lutheran; Treas, Unity Lutheran Church, 9 years. Mailing Add: Freeman, S.Dak. 57029. (1967)

STERNER, E. DONALD R
b. Belmar, N.J, 1/3/94; s. Willard J. Sterner and Jennie Disbrow S; m. 1/2/43 to Dorothy Smock; c. Dorothy (Mrs. Braly), George W. and John N. Educ: Asbury Park High Sch, grad, 13; hon. LL.D, Monmouth Col. Polit. & Govt. Pos: Mem, Bd. Educ, Belmar, N.J, 24-27; N.J. State Assemblyman, Monmouth Co, 28-29; N.J. State Sen, 30-32; mem, Monmouth Co. Rep. Cmt, 32-35; chmn, N.J. State Rep. Cmt, 34-35; N.J. State Hwy. Cmnr, 35-42; chmn, Monmouth Co. Planning Bd, Freehold, 53-; alternate del, Rep. Nat. Conv, 68. Bus. & Prof. Pos: V.pres, Sterner Coal and Lumber Co, Belmar, N.J, 19-42; pres, 42-; v.pres, Belmar Savings and Loan Asn, 26-; dir, Belmar-Wall Nat. Bank, Belmar, N.J, 33-, N.Y. and Long Branch R.R, 35-, First Merchants Nat. Bank, Asbury Park, 43- and Monmouth Elec. Co, Neptune, 59-; pres, Sterners Inc, 50- Mil. Serv: Entered as Pvt, Army, 17, released as 1st Lt, 19, after serv. in Second Dist. AEF, First Army, Aisne, Marne, St. Mihiel, Champagne, Meuse and Argonne, 18-19. Mem: Boy Scouts (pres, Monmouth Coun, 38-); Am. Legion (post comdr, 19-20, co. comdr, 25-27); Mason; Kiwanis; VFW; Grange; Red Men. Rel: Presbyterian. Legal Res: R.D. 1, Colts Neck, N.J. 07722. Mailing Add: P.O. Box 120, Belmar, N.J. 07719.

STETIN, SOL D
b. Poland, 4/2/10; U.S. citizen; s. Hyman Joseph Stetin (deceased) and Fannie Balzen S.(deceased); m. 3/15/34 to Frieda Goldstein; c. Sondra Regina (Mrs. Cash) and Myra Irene (Mrs. Levine) and four grandchildren. Educ: Hon. L.H.D, Rutgers Univ, 61. Polit. & Govt. Pos: Del-at-lg, Dem. Nat. Conv, 64. Bus. & Prof. Pos: Former mem, N.J. Mediation Bd; int. v.pres, Textile Workers Union of Am, AFL-CIO; 44-67, gen. secy-treas, 68-, mem. exec. bd, Indust. Union Dept, AFL-CIO, currently; labor mem, Rutgers Inst. Labor and Mgt. Rels, 47-51; mem, Bd. dirs, N.J. Group Health Ins. and trustee Paterson State Col, currently. Mem: B'nai B'rith; Jewish Labor Cmt; Rutgers Labor Alumni; Americans for Dem. Action. Legal Res: 39 E. 39th St, Paterson, N.J. 07514. Mailing Add: Textile Workers Union of America, 99 University Place, New York, N.Y. 10003.

STEVENS, CHANDLER HARRISON, JR. Independent
b. Trenton, N.J, 1/3/35; s. Chandler Harrison Stevens, Sr. and Margaret Cheyney S; m. 8/18/56 to Joann Gail Orcutt; c. Emily Joan. Educ: Duke Univ, 52-53; Ga. Inst. Tech, B.E.E, 56; Am. Univ, 57-59; Mass. Inst. Tech, Ph.D, 66; Tau Beta Pi; Phi Kappa Phi; Alpha Tau Omega. Polit. & Govt. Pos: Selectman, Bedford, Mass, 62-65; Mass. State Rep, 35th Middlesex Dist, 65-68; dir, Gov. Adv. Coun. for the Develop. of Govt. Progs, P.R, 69- Bus. & Prof. Pos: Data processing sales, Int. Bus. Machines, Atlanta, 56-57; teacher and research asst, Mass. Inst. Tech, 60-63, vis. soc. scientist, Center for Int. Studies, 67-68 and sr. lectr, Sloan Sch. of Mgt, 69-; mgt. consult, Adams Assocs, Bedford, 60-64; adj. asst. prof, econ. dept, Brandeis Univ, 66-67. Mil. Serv: Entered as 2nd Lt, Air Force, 57, released as 1st Lt, 60, after serv. in Air Force Computer Center, Pentagon; Air Force Res, 60-64, Capt; Commendation Medal. Publ: 'Tapping Citizen Resources,' Mass. Selectman, 63; 'Truth-in-Legislating,' Boston Sunday Globe Mag, 10/66. Rel: Protestant. Legal Res: 148 Hubbard St, Concord, Mass. 01742. Mailing Add: 1156 Magdalena Ave, Santurce, P.R. 00915.

STEVENS, EDWIN WALTER R
Cong. Committeeman, Madison Co. Rep. Cent. Cmt, Mont.
b. Monore, Wash, 6/7/08; s. Erdmand J. Stevens and Elizabeth Horning S; m. 10/21/35 to Lucille Barrett; c. Diane Barrett. Educ: Mont. Sch. Mines, 44; Theta Tau. Polit. & Govt. Pos: Rep. precinct committeeman, Mont, 60-66, co. chmn, Rep. Party, 66; cong. committeeman, Madison Co. Rep. Cent. Cmt, 66- Bus. & Prof. Pos: Consult. engr; mine supt, United Sierra Div, Cyprus Mines Corp, 51- Mem: Am. Inst. Mining Engrs; Mont. Soc. Prfnl. Engrs; Northwest Mining Asn; Elks; AF&AM; Scottish Rite; AAONMS; Eastern Star. Mailing Add: Yellowstone Mine, Cameron, Mont. 59720.

STEVENS, GERALD FAIRLIE R
Conn. State Rep.
b. New Haven, Conn, 3/17/38; s. George Stevens, Jr. and Edith Barringer S; m. 4/18/64 to Judith Anne Stedman; c. Karen Anne and Laurie Jean. Educ: Univ. Conn, B.A, 60; George Wash. Univ, LL.B, 63; Phi Alpha Theta; Phi Delta Phi; Theta Xi. Polit. & Govt. Pos: V.pres, Milford Young Rep. Club, Conn, 64-65, pres, 65-66; campaign mgr, Mayoralty Elec, Milford, 65; secy. and mem, Milford Charter Revision Cmn, 65-66; mem, Rep. Town Cmt, 65-; Conn. State Rep, 122nd Dist, 67-, co-chmn, Legis. Intern Cmt, Conn. State House of Rep, 69-, Ranking Rep, Judiciary and Governmental Functions Cmt. and mem, Pub. Health and Safety Cmt. Mem: Conn, New Haven Co. and Milford Bar Asns; Conn. Bar; U.S. Dist. Court, Conn; Court of Appeals; Jr. C. of C; Mason; AF&AM; dir, Milford YMCA, 64-66; sgt-at-arms, Milford Rotary Club, 66-67. Admitted to practice before, U.S. Supreme Court; Man of the Year Award, Milford Jr. C. of C; One of the Three Outstanding Young Men in Conn, State Jr. C. of C, 68. Rel: Congregational. Mailing Add: 26 Woodhead Dr, Milford, Conn. 06460.

STEVENS, HENRY L. R
b. Salisbury, N.H, 4/25/90; married; c. 1 son. Educ: Univ. N.H; Acacia. Polit. & Govt. Pos: N.H. State Rep, 61-67; town moderator; auditor; budget committeeman; moderator, sch. dist; former ward clerk. Bus. & Prof. Pos: Poultry bus. and ins; dir. and v.pres, Farm Bur. Mutual Ins. Co. Mil. Serv: Mexican Border; WWI; WWII, 5 year mem. of Bd. 9, Selective Serv; chmn, Merri. Co. War Bd. Mem: Masons (32°); Odd Fellows; Grange; Jr. O.U.A.M; past master of Masons and Grange; Agr. Club of N.H; dir. and past pres, N.H. Poultry Growers Asn; secy, Northeastern Poultry Producers Coun; trustee, Pittsfield Savings Bank. Rel: Baptist. Mailing Add: Box 36, Gossville, N.H. 03239. (1967)

STEVENS, J. HAROLD R
b. Lansing, Mich, 3/21/95; married; c. Thomas H. and Janet (Mrs. Robert Papworth); six grandchildren. Educ: Hillsdale Col, A.B; Univ. of Mich, M.A; Detroit Col. of Law, J.D; Alpha Tau Omega; Sigma Nu Phi. Polit. & Govt. Pos: Mich. State Rep, 64-68; del. to the Constitutional Conv. Bus. & Prof. Pos: Attorney; retired teacher of govt. Mil. Serv: Vet, res. army officer for 17 years. Mem: Mason; Consistory; Shrine; Hiawatha Sportsman's Club; Northwest Detroit Rep. Club; State Bar of Mich; Hist. Soc. of Mich; Am. Legion; several educ. orgn. Rel: Congregational. Mailing Add: 16826 Huntington, Detroit, Mich. 48219.

STEVENS, JAMES PRICE D
S.C. State Sen.
b. Loris, S.C, 4/4/20; s. M.D. Stevens and Lalla McQueen S; m. to Madeleine Zabelicky; c. James Price, Jr, Randle McQueen, Douglas Yancey and Victoria Joy. Educ: Univ. S.C, LL.B, 52; pres, Law Sch. student body, 52; Phi Alpha Delta; Law Sch. Honor Coun. Debate Team, 51-52; Wig and Robe. Polit. & Govt. Pos: S.C. State Sen, 56- Bus. & Prof. Pos: Lawyer. Mil. Serv: Coast Guard, 40-46. Mem: VFW; Am. Legion; Mason. Rel: Methodist; Teacher of men's Bible class, Loris Methodist Church. Mailing Add: 3995 Walnut St, Loris, S.C. 29569.

STEVENS, JEAN M. R
b. Turtle Creek, Pa. 12/9/21; d. Donald Harold DeForrest, Sr. and Kathryn McCune D; m. 9/28/46 to Vincent A. Stevens; c. Linda, Susan, Vincent A, II and Ann. Educ: Huntingdon High Sch, grad. Polit. & Govt. Pos: Committeewoman, Penn Hills Rep. Cmt, Pa, 60-, secy, 62-66, v.chmn, 66-; alternate del, Rep. Nat. Conv, 68. Mem: PTA; Penn Hills Young Rep; Coun. Rep. Women; Girl Scouts; Eastmont Civic Asn. Mailing Add: 388 Princeton Dr, Penn Hills, Pa. 15235.

STEVENS, ROBERT S. R
Calif. State Sen.
b. 1916; married; c. Four. Educ: Univ. of Utah; Stanford, B.S; Stanford Law Sch, LL.B. Polit. & Govt. Pos: Mem, Los Angeles Co. Rep. Cent. Cmt, 52-; Calif. State Assemblyman, 62-67; Calif. State Sen, 67- Bus. & Prof. Pos: Bd. of Mgrs, W. Los Angeles YMCA; Dir, Los Angeles Commun. Concert Asn. Mem: past pres, Westwood Jr. C. of C; past pres, Westwood Village Bar Asn; past chmn, Westwood Village & Los Angeles W. Area Commun. Chests; former Exec. Cmt, Crescent Bay Coun. Boy Scouts. Pres, Mormon Choir of Calif. Mailing Add: 1245 Glendon Ave, Los Angeles, Calif. 90024.

STEVENS, ROGER L. D
b. Detroit, Mich, 3/12/10; s. Stanley Stevens and Florence Jackson S; m. 1/1/38 to Christine Gesell; c. Christabel. Educ: Univ. of Mich, 28-30; Phi Gamma Delta. Hon. H.H.D, Wayne State Univ, 60 and Tulane Univ, 61; hon. D.H.L, Univ. of Mich, 64, Amherst Col, 68 and Skidmore Col, 69. Polit. & Govt. Pos: Chmn, Finance Cmt, Dem. Party, 56; asst. to President on the Arts, 64-68; chmn, Nat. Coun. of the Arts, 65-69. Bus. & Prof. Pos: Real estate broker specializing in hotels and investment properties, 24-60; co-producer in over 100 Broadway Shows, including, West Side Story, Cat on a Hot Tin Roof, Bus Stop, Tea and Sympathy and Mary, Mary; chmn. bd. trustees, John F. Kennedy Center Performing Arts, currently. Mem: Trustee, Am. Shakespeare Theater and Acad; dir, Metrop. Opera Asn; chmn, Am. Film Inst; fel, Royal Soc. of Arts; chmn, Nat. Book Awards Adv. Cmt; adv. bd, Partisan Rev; dir, Assoc. Coun. of the Arts; dir, Nat. Opera Inst; Bohemian, San Francisco, Racquet and Tennis, Century Asn, N.Y.C. and Pilgrims, N.Y.C. Clubs. Legal Res: 3410 Q St. N.W, Washington, D.C. 20007. Mailing Add: John F. Kennedy Center for Performing Arts, 726 Jackson Place N.W, Washington, D.C. 20566.

STEVENS, THEODORE FULTON 'TED' R
U.S. Sen, Alaska
b. Indianapolis, Ind, 11/18/23; s. George A. Stevens (deceased) and Gertrude

Chancellor S; m. 3/29/52 to Ann May Cherrington; c. Susan, Walter, Ben, Beth and Ted, Jr. Educ: Ore. State Col; Mont. State Col; Univ. Calif. Los Angeles; Harvard Law Sch; Delta Kappa Epsilon. Polit. & Govt. Pos: U.S. attorney, Fairbanks, Alaska, 53-56; legis. counsel, Dept. Interior, Wash, D.C, 56-58, asst. to Secy. Interior, 59 and solicitor, Dept. Interior, 60; cand. for U.S. Sen, Alaska, 62; state chmn, Rockefeller for Pres. Cmt, 64; Alaska State Rep, 65-68; U.S. Sen, Alaska, 68- Bus. & Prof. Pos: Attorney, Law Off, Northcutt Ely, Wash, D.C, 50-52 and Collins and Clasby, Fairbanks, Alaska, 53; partner, Stevens and Roderick, 61-63, Stevens and Stringer, 64 and Stevens, Savage, Holland, Erwin & Edwards, 64- Mil. Serv: Entered as Pvt, Army, 43, released as 1st Lt, 46, after serv. in 14th Air Force, China; Air Medal with Cluster; Distinguished Flying Cross with Cluster; China-Burma-India Ribbon; Yuan Hai Medal from Chinese Nationalist Govt, 46. Mem: Anchorage, Fed. Alaska, Am, Calif. and D.C. Bar Asns; Am. Legion; VFW; Petrol. Club. of Anchorage; Rotary. Named Alaska 49'er, one of 49 Alaskans chosen by Alaska Press Club for outstanding serv. to Alaska, 63. Rel: Episcopal. Legal Res: 1435 12th Ave, Anchorage, Alaska 99501. Mailing Add: Box 879, Anchorage, Alaska 99501.

STEVENS, TOM D
Fla. State Rep.
b. Dade City, Fla, 5/20/31; div; c. Tommy, Jr, Warren, Mary Lou, Nancy and Laura. Educ: Univ. of Fla, 49-50; St. Leo Jr. Col, 61; Univ. of S. Fla. Polit. & Govt. Pos: Fla. State Rep, 62-, chmn, Banks and Loans Cmt, Fla. State House of Rep, currently. Bus. & Prof. Pos: Ins. agent, State Farm Ins. Co. Mil. Serv: Nat. Guard. Rel: Assembly of God. Mailing Add: 405 E. Church Ave, Dade City, Fla. 33525.

STEVENS, WILLIAM ARNALD D
Miss. State Rep.
b. Alcorn Co, Miss, 7/20/21; s. George B. Stevens and Ernestine Haynie S; m. 7/8/51 to Ruth Moore. Educ: Farmington High Sch, 4 years. Polit. & Govt. Pos: Miss. State Rep, Dist. One, 68- Bus. & Prof. Pos: Shipping and receiving clerk, Weaver Pants Corp, 45- Mil. Serv: Entered as Pvt, Army Air Corp, 42, released as T/Sgt, 45, after serv. in 15th Air Force, ETO, 44-45; Good Conduct Medal; Air Medal with 4 Battle Stars. Mem: Am. Legion; VFW; Farm Bur; Amalgamated Clothing Workers Am. Rel: Christian Church of N.Am. Mailing Add: Route 6, Corinth, Miss. 38834.

STEVENSON, ADLAI EWING, III D
State Treas, Ill.
b. Chicago, Ill, 10/10/30; s. Adlai Ewing Stevenson and Ellen Borden S; m. 6/25/55 to Nancy Anderson; c. Adlai E, IV, Lucy Wallace, Katherine Randolph and Warwick Lewis. Educ: Harvard Col, A.B, 52; Harvard Law Sch, LL.B, 57. Hon. LL.D, Elmhurst Col, 68; Hon. L.H.D, Chicago Theol. Sem, 68. Polit. & Govt. Pos: Past Chmn, Gov. Cmt, for Distinguished For. Guests; bd. dir, Asn. for UN, Ill; past dir. and treas, Cmt. on Ill. Govt; Chicago Crime Cmn; Ill. State Rep, 65-67; state treas, Ill, 67-; del, Dem. Nat. Conv, 68. Bus. & Prof. Pos: Law clerk to Ill. State Supreme Court Justice, Chicago & Springfield, 57-58; assoc, Law Firm of Mayer, Friedlich, Spiess, Tierney, Brown & Platt, Chicago, 58-66, partner, 66-67. Mil. Serv: Entered as Pvt, Marine Corps, 52, released as 1st Lt, 54, after serv. in Third Marine Div, Japan and First Marine Div, Korea, 52-54; Capt, Marine Corps Res, 61. Mem: Past dir, Lincoln Park Conserv. Asn. and North Side Boys Club. Legal Res: 1519 N. Dearborn St, Chicago, Ill. 60610. Mailing Add: 160 N. LaSalle St, Chicago, Ill. 60601.

STEVENSON, BILL D
Ore. State Rep.
b. Portland, Ore, 1/22/40; s. William H. Stevenson and Louise R. Lamb S; m. 10/10/64 to Kerry Charlene Gatherer. Educ: Portland State Col, B.A. in polit. sci, 62; Theta Delta Phi. Polit. & Govt. Pos: Staff asst. to U.S. Rep. Edith Green, 61-63; Ore. State Rep, currently. Bus. & Prof. Pos: Staff asst, Ore. AFL-CIO, 64-66. Mil. Serv: Seaman, Coast Guard Res, 63- Mem: Paint and Brush Makers Local Union 523, AFL-CIO. Rel: Protestant. Mailing Add: 11 N.E. Buffalo St, Portland, Ore. 97211.

STEVENSON, EDWARD A. D
N.Y. State Assemblyman
b. Jamaica, W.I, 11/9/07; s. William Alexander Stevenson and Emma Newton S; m. 1934 to Katy Haskins; c. Edward A, Jr. Educ: Harlem Evening High Sch, grad; N.Y. Univ, 56-59. Polit. & Govt. Pos: N.Y. State Assemblyman, 66-; Dist. Leader, 78th Assembly Dist. Dem. Party, Bronx, 69- Bus. & Prof. Pos: Food serv. dir, N.Y.C. Dept. of Correction, 34 years. Mem: N.Y.C. Prfnl. Employees; NAACP (bd. of dir, Bronx Br). Named Outstanding Civil Serv. Employee, 65. Rel: Protestant. Mailing Add: 1136 Jackson Ave, Bronx, N.Y. 10456.

STEVENSON, HARRY D
Mayor, Irvington, N.J.
b. Newark, N.J. 9/22/14; s. Thomas Henry Stevenson and Ellen Smith S; m. 11/12/44 to Audrey Louise Lackner; c. Janet L. Educ: N.Y. Univ, Sch. of Commerce, B.C.S, 40; Beta Gamma Sigma; Phi Beta Kappa. Polit. & Govt. Pos: Cmnr, Fed. Housing Authority, 53-54; pres, Bd. of Educ, Irvington, N.J. 54-60; pres, Munic. Coun, Irvington, 62-64, councilman, 64-66; mayor, Irvington, 66-; alternate del, Dem Nat. Conv, 68. Bus. & Prof. Pos: Acct, Parr Elec. Co, Inc, 33-38; export mgr, Parr Elec. Export Corp, 38-41; head, elec. sect, Distributors Div, War Prod. Bd, 41-42; self-employed, CPA, 46- Mil. Serv: Entered as Pvt, Army, 42, released as 1st Lt, 46, after serv. in 7th Major Port, Japan. Mem: Am. Inst. CPA; N.J. Soc. CPA; Nat. Asn. Acct; Am. Legion; VFW; Optimist Club; Elks; Moose; Eagles. Rel: Protestant. Mailing Add: 34 Clinton Terr, Irvington, N.J. 07111.

STEVENSON, JAMES W, JR. R
b. McKeesport, Pa, 9/9/18; s. Dr. James W. Stevenson and Margaret Asche S; m. 11/2/40 to Frances McConnell; c. James W, III and Thomas Lee. Educ: Univ. Pittsburgh, B.S, 40. Polit. & Govt. Pos: Del, Rep. Nat. Conv, 68. Bus. & Prof. Pos: Pres, Stevenson, Williams Co, 40-41, St. Clair Investment Co, 46-; Forest Lawn Gardens, 54-60. Mem: Inst. Real Estate Mgt; Nat. Asn. Real Estate Bd; Greater Mt. Lebanon Multilist Realty Bd.(pres, 62-63); F&AM; Duquesne Commandery; Shrine; C. of C.(pres, Mt. Lebanon chap, 67-). Rel: Presbyterian. Mailing Add: 131 Markhan Dr, Pittsburgh, Pa. 15228.

STEVENSON, LESLIE R. D
b. Marinette, Wis, 7/31/15. Educ: Jordan Col; Wis. Univ. Polit. & Govt. Pos: Alderman and pres, City Coun, Marinette, Wis, 58-61; supt, Pub. Works; Wis. State Assemblyman, 65-68. Bus. & Prof. Pos: Former upholsterer. Mil. Serv: Army Corps of Engrs, ETO, 44-46. Mem: Am. Pub. Works Asn; Elks; pres, UAW local, 57-60; pres, Marinette and Menominee Labor Coun, 58-61. Mailing Add: 603 Ogden St, Marinette, Wis. 54143. (1967)

STEVENSON, M. ROSS D
b. Howard City, Iowa, 9/1/06; m. 1928 to Laura L Larsen; c. Mildred, Harlan, Eugene, Hollis, Lyle, Norman, four grand c. Educ: Cresco High Sch. Polit. & Govt. Pos: Iowa State Rep, -66; served on Howard City Ext. Coun, 5 yrs. Bus. & Prof. Pos: Owns and operates 280 acre farm. Mem: Iowa Farmers Union; past dir, rural sch. and Lime Springs Ind. sch; former dir. and chmn, Farmers Co-op Feed Co. of Lime Springs; dir, Iowa State Farmers Union Bd; 4-H club work. Rel: Methodist. Mailing Add: RFD 3, Lime Springs, Iowa. 52155. (1967)

STEVENSON, MARY H. R
Secy, Wash. State Rep. Cent. Cmt.
b. Spokane, Wash, 4/13/20; d. Dr. John E. Hoyt and Ethel Case H; m. 3/27/43 to Bruce McCornack Stevenson; c. Laura Jean, Anne and Leslie. Educ: Univ. Wash, B.A, 41; Phi Mu Gamma; Zeta Phi Eta; Delta Gamma. Polit. & Govt. Pos: Pres, Klickitat Co. Womens Rep. Club, Wash, 65-67; pres, W. Klickitat Co. Womens Rep. Club, 68; v.chmn, Klickitat Co. Rep. Cent. Cmt, 68; del, Wash. State Rep. Conv, 68; alternate del, Rep. Nat. Conv, 68; state committeewoman, Klickitat Co. Rep. Cent. Cmt, 69-; secy, Wash. State Rep. Cent. Cmt, 69- Rel: Episcopal. Mailing Add: P.O. Box 487, White Salmon, Wash. 98672.

STEVENSON, ROBERT D. D
b. Seattle, Wash, 12/13/19; s. William D. Stevenson and Ava Dodson S; m. 7/25/48 to Elsie Barber; c. William R, James D. and Robert D. Educ: Univ. Wash, B.A, 43; Beta Alpha Psi; Sigma Nu. Polit. & Govt. Pos: Collection agent, U.S. Internal Revenue Serv, 46-53; dep. cmnr, Dept. of Taxation, Territory of Alaska, 53-57, cmnr, 57-59; dep. cmnr, Dept. of Revenue, Alaska, 59-62, cmnr, 62-69 and chief excise tax div, 69- Mil. Serv: Army Signal Corps, 42-45. Mem: Am. Legion; VFW; Nat. Tax Asn; Nat. Asn. Tax Adminstr; Nat. Asn. of State Auditors, Comptrollers and Treasurers. Rel: Congregational. Mailing Add: State Dept. of Revenue, Pouch S, Juneau, Alaska 99801. (1967)

STEVENSON, RUSSELL E, JR. R
Chmn, Tolland Rep. Town Cmt, Conn.
b. Hartford, Conn, 11/7/37; s. Russell E. Stevenson, Sr. and Anna Waters S. (deceased); m. 6/14/62 to Maryalis Truehart; c. Jennifer and Robert. Educ: Morse Col, B.A; Am. Col. Life Underwriters, C.L.U. Polit. & Govt. Pos: Chmn, Manchester Co. Young Rep, 60, Tolland Young Rep, 65-66; Tolland Co. Young Rep, 67 and Citizens for Nixon-Agnew, 68; chmn, Tolland Rep. Town Cmt, 68-; Justice of the Peace, Tolland, Conn. and chmn, Salary Study Cmt, currently. Bus. & Prof. Pos: Dir, Mass. Mutual Life Asn. of Chartered Life Underwriters, currently. Mil. Serv: Entered as E-1, Coast Guard Res, 58, released as E-6, 66. Mem: Hartford and Nat. Asns. Life Underwriters; Hartford Chap, Chartered Life Underwriters; Am. Soc. Chartered Life Underwriters; AF&AM; Commerce Club Norwich. Rel: Episcopal. Mailing Add: Sherry Circle, Tolland, Conn. 06084.

STEVENSON, WILLIAM HENRY R
b. Kenosha, Wis, 9/23/91; s. Maj. John Henry Stevenson and Minna Fenske S; m. 9/4/13 to Lulu Belle Bucklin; c. Phyllis Belle (Mrs. Grams), James Stephen and Claudia. Educ: La Crosse State Teachers Col; Univ. Wis. Col. of Law; Phi Alpha Delta. Polit. & Govt. Pos: Dist. attorney, Richland Co, Wis, 26-30; divorce counsel, Richland Co, 28-30; cmnr, Circuit Court, Richland Co, 30-31; dist. attorney, La Crosse Co, 34-40; U.S. Rep, Wis, 41-49. Bus. & Prof. Pos: Attorney-at-law, Richland Center, Wis, 21-31, La Crosse, 31-41 and Onalaska, 50- Mem: La Crosse Bar Asn; State Bar of Wis; La Crosse Co. Hist. Soc. (pres, 66-); Mason (32°); Shrine; Scottish Rite; K. of P; Dramatic Order Knights of Korazan; Richland Center, Wis. and La Cross Kiwanis. Rel: Methodist. Mailing Add: 502 S. Third Ave, Onalaska, Wis. 54650.

STEWARD, WILLIAM ROBERT D
Chmn, Haskell Co. Dem. Party, Okla.
b. Edgewood, Tex, 8/9/06; s. Robert Lee Steward and Nellie Brandon S; m. 2/10/45 to Veda Mae Heckman; c. Bobby Mac. Educ: Northeast. State Teachers College, Tahlequah, Okla, B.S. Polit. & Govt. Pos: Chmn, Haskell Co. Dem. Party, Okla, 62- Bus. & Prof. Pos: Teaching Prin. Educ, 32-66; ranching, 59-66. Mem: Odd Fellows; v.pres, Farmers Union, Haskell Co. Rel: Methodist. Mailing Add: R.R. 1, McCurtain, Okla. 74944.

STEWART, BRICE HORACE R
Chmn, Nev. Co. Rep. Cmt, Ark.
b. Prescott, Ark, 7/2/11; s. Lewis Edward Stewart and Ella Waddle S; m. 10/18/47 to Della Mae Duke. Educ: Bluff Springs, Ark. Pub. Schs. Polit. & Govt. Pos: Pres, Nev. Co. Rep. Club, Ark, 63; chmn, Nev. Co. Rep. Cmt, 64- Mil. Serv: Entered as Pvt, Army, 40, released as Pfc, 44, after serv. in Co. C, 153rd Inf, Alaska, 41-44; Good Conduct Medal. Mem: Nev. Co. Serv. chmn, Am. Cancer Soc, 61-; Nev. Co. Chap. chmn, Am. Red Cross and Blood Bank chmn, Am. Red Cross, 60-65; Mason; Am. Legion. Served unofficially as Chaplain during World War II. Rel: Presbyterian. Mailing Add: 605 Oak St, Prescott, Ark. 71857.

STEWART, CARLYLE VEEDER, JR. R
b. Springfield, Ohio, 9/12/27; s. Carlyle Veeder Stewart and Delma Fahnestock S; m. 11/23/57 to Virginia Burgess Ellington. Educ: Univ. Mich, Ann Arbor, A.B, 50; Lambda Chi Alpha. Polit. & Govt. Pos: Vol, Eisenhower and Nixon Campaign, 52, 56 & 60; precinct chmn, D.C. State Rep. Cmt, 61-65; mem. bd. dirs, D.C. Young Rep, 61-65 and treas, 63-64; hon. asst. sgt-at-arms, Rep. Nat. Conv, 64; nat. fieldman ballot security, Oper. Eagle Eye, Citizen's for Goldwater-Miller, 64; mem. finance cmt, Young Rep. Nat. Fedn, 64-65; dir. spec. projs, United Citizens Cmt. for Nixon-Agnew, 68. Bus. & Prof. Pos: Salesman, Johns-Manville, Kaiser Aluminum, United Clay Prods. Co. and Real Estate Sales, 53-64; consult, Data Processing and Field Orgn,

64-; exec. dir, Research Serv. Inst, 67 & 68; pres, Smart, Inc, Wash, D.C, 68- Mil. Serv: Midn, Merchant Marine, 45-47; Navigator, Air Force, 50-53; Mediterranean and Atlantic Theatre Ribbons. Mem: Civil War Round Table of D.C. Rel: Presbyterian. Mailing Add: Smart, Inc, 627 National Press Bldg, Washington, D.C. 20004.

STEWART, CHARLES WESLEY, JR. D
Ark. State Rep.
b. El Dorado, Ark, 9/25/27; s. Charles Wesley Stewart and Mettie Adams S; m. 7/16/55 to Joanne Dee Rogers; c. Charles Wesley, IV and Thomas Rogers. Educ: Univ. Ark, J.D, 51; Alpha Kappa Psi; Sigma Nu; Alpha Phi Omega. Polit. & Govt. Pos: Ark. State Rep, Dist. Seven, Washington Co, 55- Bus. & Prof. Pos: Secy-Treas, Ozark Steel Co, Fayetteville, Ark, 51-69; Gen. Mgr, Stewart & Sons, 60-69. Mil. Serv: Entered as A/S, Navy, 45, released as Seaman 1/C, 46, after serv. in several ships, Am. Theatre. Publ: 'Case Comment Arkansas Uniform Securities Law' Arkansas Law Review, 59. Mem: Washington Co. Asn; Ark. Bar; First v.pres, Fayetteville C. of C, 69; Exchange Club; Elks; Am. Legion; Fayetteville Country Club; Bella Vista Country Club. Outstanding Young Man Award, Fayetteville Jr. C. of C. Rel: Baptist. Legal Res: Township Rd. & Jimmy Dr, Fayetteville, Ark. 72701. Mailing Add: P.O. Drawer 1167, Fayetteville, Ark. 72701.

STEWART, DAN, JR. D
b. Knox Co, Ky, 7/2/29; s. D.D. Stewart and Mary Gilbert S; m. 12/23/49 to Betsy Royalty; c. Dan, III. Educ: Centre Col, B.A, 51; Phi Delta Theta. Polit. Pos: Ky. del, Dem. Nat. Conv, 64. Govt. Pos: Mem, Gov. Cmn. on Status of Women. Bus. & Prof. Pos: Regional v.pres, Ky. C. of C, 62-66; int. dir, Jr. C. of C, 64, U.S. v.pres, 62-63, Ky. pres, 61-62, nat. dir, 2 times. Mem: V.pres, Bluegrass Coun, Boy Scouts, 64-66; pres, Centre Col. Alumni Asn, 65; v.pres, Culver Mil. Schs. Alumni Asn, 62-; board mgr, United Christian Missionary Soc, 64-66; bd. dirs, Ky. Mil. Inst. Alumni Asn. and Friends of Ky. Libr. Asn; chmn, Ky. Nat. Libr. Week, 63; bd. trustees, Ky. Travel Coun, 65-68; v.chmn, Ky. Higher Educ. Assistance Authority. Silver and Gold Key Man Awards and Clayton Frost Mem. Award, Jr. C. of C; 1 of 3 Outstanding Young Men in Ky, 62; Ky. Mil. Inst. Humanitarian Award, 63; Allstate Ins. Co. Safety Crusader Cert. of Commendation, 63. Rel: First Christian Church of Pineville, Elder. Legal Res: Summit Dr, Pineville, Ky. 40977. Mailing Add: Box 758, Lexington, Ky. 41001. (1967)

STEWART, DAVID WALLACE R
b. New Concord, Ohio, 1/22/87; s. Wilson Stewart and Mary Ann Wallace S; m. 9/15/20 to Helen E. Struble; c. Robert Bruce. Educ: Geneva Col, Beaver Falls, Pa, A.B, 11; Univ. Chicago, J.D, 17; pres. of trustees of Morningside Col. Polit. & Govt. Pos: U.S. Sen, Iowa, 26-27. Bus. & Prof. Pos: Admitted to Iowa Bar, 17, lawyer, firm of Stewart and Hatfield, 17- Mil. Serv: Marine Corps. Mem: Sioux City Boy Scouts; Am, Iowa State and Woodbury Co. Bar Asns; trustee, Sioux City YMCA; Sioux City C. of C, pres. 25-26; Am. Legion; Mason. Rel: Presbyterian. Legal Res: 3827 Country Club Blvd, Sioux City, Iowa 51104. Mailing Add: 830-838 Frances Bldg, Sioux City, Iowa 51103. (1967)

STEWART, DONOVAN R
Ariz. State Rep.
b. Seattle, Wash, 3/5/03; s. Horatio A. Stewart and Bessie E. Sandison S; m. 7/29/28 to Blanche I. Robinson; c. Nancy (Mrs. Belian) and Sandra (Mrs. Karolczyk). Educ: Ore. State Univ, B.S. Polit. & Govt. Pos: Precinct committeeman, Rep. Party, Ariz, 66-; Ariz. State Rep, 69- Bus. & Prof. Pos: Livestock appraiser, Bank of Am, Los Angeles, Calif, 46-48; livestock loan adv, First Nat. Bank, Phoenix, Ariz, 48-68. Mil. Serv: Entered as 2nd Lt, Army, 42, released 1st Lt, 44; Commendation by Gen. McNair, 44; mem, ROTC Rifleteam from 11 West. States, 27. Mem: Ariz. State Univ. Found. Bd. (one of six incorporators); appointed to Ariz. State Fair Cmn, 51,52 & 53; Mason; Am. Legion. Given plaques for serv. to Future Farmers of Am. and 4-H Club Mem. by both orgn. and Ariz. State Univ, 68. Rel: Protestant. Mailing Add: 4002 W. Keim Dr, Phoenix, Ariz. 85019.

STEWART, E.L, JR. 'BUD' R
b. Ft. Benning, Ga, 6/7/28; s. Elam L. Stewart and Angie Lateer S; m. 4/7/51 to Katharine Sherman; c. Matthew Sherman. Educ: Univ. Ill, 46; DePauw Univ, A.B, 50; Sigma Chi; v.pres, DePauw Rep. Club. Polit. & Govt. Pos: Rep. precinct chmn, Precinct, 4, Ward 1, Shawnee, Okla, 61; chmn, Pottawatomie Co. Rep. Party, 63-65; del, Rep. Nat. Conv, 64; chmn, Okla. Rep. State Cmt, 65-69; alternate del, Rep. Nat. Conv, 68; Fed. co-chmn, Ozark Regional Cmn, 69. Bus. & Prof. Pos: Landman, Humble Oil & Refining Co, 51-61; partner, Sigma Oil & Gas Co, 61-68, owner, 68- Mil. Serv: Capt, Army Res. Transportation Corps. Mem: Am. Asn. Petroleum Landmen. Mailing Add: 1627 N. Pennsylvania, Shawnee, Okla. 74801.

STEWART, EARL C. D
Chmn, Putnam Co. Dem. Exec. Cmt, W.Va.
b. Charleston, W.Va, 3/3/25; s. London S. Stewart and Izora Cavender S; m. 3/19/46 to Lee Powell; c. Laberta Sue and Dorinda Jean. Educ: Hurricane High Sch, W.Va. Polit. & Govt. Pos: Mem, Putnam Co. Young Dem. Club, W.Va; councilman, Hurricane, 58-62; bd. mem, Hurricane Water Works, 62-65; state chmn, Citizens for Hulett Smith for Gov, 64; chmn, Putnam Co. Dem. Exec. Cmt, currently. Bus. & Prof. Pos: Owner, Stewart Motors, 56-65; asst. dist. mgr, Standard Coffee Co, 65-66; asst. state fire marshal, W.Va, 66. Mil. Serv: Entered as Pvt, Army, 44, released as Pfc, 45, after serv. in 37th Inf. Div, Pac. Area; Combat Infantrymans Badge; Asiatic-Pac. Theater Ribbon with 2 Bronze Stars; Philippine Liberation Ribbon with 1 Bronze Star; Good Conduct Medal. Mem: Am. Legion; JOUAM; Odd Fellows; Mountain Lodge of W.Va. Legal Res: 1 Catherine Dr, Hurricane, W.Va. 25526. Mailing Add: P.O. Box 235, Hurricane, W.Va. 25526. (1967)

STEWART, ELLIS CAMERON D
b. Columbus, Ohio, 10/27/01; s. Elmer Darius Stewart and Henrietta Peden S; m. 5/24/24 to Vannie Lamar; c. Ellis Cameron, Jr. Educ: North Augusta High Sch, grad, 18. Polit. & Govt. Pos: Dir, Ala. Div. Records and Reports, 47; chmn, Gov. Cmt. Employ. Physically Handicapped, 47-51; dir. consumer prices, Off. Price Stabilization Ala, 51-53; chmn, Ala. UN Cmt, 55; exec. secy, Ala. River Develop. Authority, 58-59; staff asst, Off. Emergency Planning, Wash, D.C, 62-63; staff asst, Senate Select Cmt. Small Bus, 64-65; staff asst, U.S. Sen. John Sparkman, Ala, 65-66, exec. secy, 67-68, admin. asst, 69- Bus. & Prof. Pos: Partner, Levysteins, Montgomery, Ala, 42-47, Stewarts, 47-58; ed. writer, Montgomery Advertiser, 44-46. Rel: Methodist. Legal Res: 337 Boyce St, Montgomery, Ala. 36107. Mailing Add: 417 A St, S.E, Washington, D.C. 20003.

STEWART, FLOSSIE KLEDITH D
Finance Chmn, Dem. Womans Club, Lebanon, Ind.
b. Whitestown, Ind, 1/24/02; d. Quince A. Ford and Millie Wolf F; m. 6/23/27 to Forrest Russell Stewart. Educ: High Sch. Polit. & Govt. Pos: Precinct committeewoman, Dem. Party of Ind, 45-; v.chmn, Boone Co. Dem. Cmt, Ind, 56-66; former treas, Dem. Womans Club, Lebanon, 10 years, finance chmn, currently. Mem: Red Cross; Civil Defense; finance chmn, Bus. & Prfnl. Women's Club; Kappa Delta Phi; Grey Lady and Blood Prog. Rel: Methodist. Mailing Add: 422½ E. Main St, Lebanon, Ind. 46052. (1967)

STEWART, GEORGE DANIEL D
b. Willacoochee, Ga, 5/14/13; s. Charles E. Stewart and Helen Burns S; m. 9/10/66 to Frances Stanford; c. Suzanne and George D, Jr. Educ: S.Ga. Col; Univ. Ga; Sigma Nu. Polit. & Govt. Pos: Dir, Milk Control Bd, Ga, 45-47; mem, Ga. Turnpike Authority, 53-56; spec. asst. Attorney Gen, Ga, 50; mem, Ga. Turnpike Authority, 53-56; secy, Ga. State Dem. Exec. Cmt. and Ga. Senate, 49-66. Bus. & Prof. Pos: Attorney-at-Law, Atlanta, Ga, 37- Rel: Baptist. Mailing Add: 701 Hurt Bldg, Atlanta, Ga. 30303.

STEWART, HAROLD W. D
Polit. & Govt. Pos: Mayor of Greencastle, Ind, 48-52; State Rep, -66. Bus. & Prof. Pos: Teacher, Greencastle High Sch. Mem: Past pres, Ind. Indust. Educ. Asn; Ind. State Teachers Asn; Nat. Educ. Asn; Am. Voc. Asn; Ind. Voc. and Practical Arts Asn. Rel: First Christian Church. Mailing Add: 812 Gardenside Dr, Greencastle, Ind. 46135. (1967)

STEWART, JOE WILLIAM D
b. Jackson, Mo, 5/9/28; s. William Stewart and Mabel Porter S; m. 11/20/62 to Marie Thayer. Educ: Mo. Univ, B.J, 59; Univ. Wyo, M.A, 64. Polit. & Govt. Pos: Wyo. State Rep, 67-68; del, Dem. Nat. Conv, 68. Mil. Serv: Entered as A/S, Navy, 46, released as Yeoman 3/C, 48, after serv. in Pac. Theater. Mem: Wyo. Educ. Asn; Mason; Elks; VFW. Rel: Methodist. Mailing Add: 1320 Ivy Lane, Casper, Wyo. 82601. (1967)

STEWART, JOHN GEORGE
b. Wilmington, Del, 6/2/90; s. Hamilton Stewart and Marie Schaefer S; wid; c. Frank Hamilton and Irene Taber. Educ: Univ. Del, 09-11; Sigma Nu. Polit. & Govt. Pos: Architect, U.S. Capitol, 54-; eng. consult. lands div, Dept. of Justice, Wash. Corps of Engrs, 51-54. Bus. & Prof. Pos: Engr; pres, Stewart & Donohue, Inc, Gen. Contractors, Wilmington. Mem: Am. Inst. Architects; Del. State Athletic Cmn. Mailing Add: 2939 Van Ness St. N.W, Washington, D.C. 20008. (1967)

STEWART, JOSEPH ALEXANDER 'JOE' R
State Committeeman, Idaho Rep. Party
b. Burnt Prairie, Ill, 1/28/88; s. Alexander Stewart and Sybby Book S; wid; c. Vaughan Alexander. Polit. & Govt. Pos: State committeeman, Idaho Rep. Party, 45 years; in charge of campaigns for govs, congressmen and U.S. Sen; del, Rep. Nat. Conv, 68. Bus. & Prof. Pos: Rancher, real estate broker, loan agency and ins. agency. Mem: Elks. Rel: Protestant. Legal Res: 392 E. Court, Blackfoot, Idaho 83221. Mailing Add: P.O. Box 8, Blackfoot, Idaho 83221.

STEWART, MARY RUTH R
Secy, Nebr. Rep. Cent. and Exec. Cmts.
b. Los Angeles, Calif, 2/17/29; d. Joseph L. Ryons and Norma Heine R; m. 6/14/51 to William Alexander Stewart, Jr; c. Leslie Jane, William A, III, Courtney Ann and Lisa Kyle. Educ: Univ. Nebr, B.S. in Educ, 51; Kappa Kappa Gamma. Polit. & Govt. Pos: V.chmn, Dawson Co. Young Rep, Nebr, 57-58, Dawson Co. Rep, 60-62 and Nebr. Young Rep, 61-62; secy, Nebr. Rep. Cent. and Exec. Cmts, 65- Bus. & Prof. Pos: Third grade teacher, Lexington Pub. Sch, Nebr, 67- Mem: Nat. and Nebr. Educ. Asns; Coun. for Exception Children; Girl Scouts (leader); Am. Legion Auxiliary. Rel: Episcopal. Mailing Add: R.R. 1, Lexington, Nebr. 68850.

STEWART, MELVIN JAMES D
Chmn, Tuscola Co. Dem. Cmt, Mich.
b. Vassar, Mich, 12/22/07; s. Lee Roy Stewart and Jennie E. Arnold S; m. 5/5/37 to Ursula S. Schnell; c. Luther James and Bervaine Ann (Mrs. Daniel K. Pratt). Educ: Vassar High Sch, grad, 29. Polit. & Govt. Pos: Chmn, Vasser Dem. Club, Mich, 60-61; v.chmn, Seventh Cong. Dist, 61-65; chmn, Tuscola Co. Dem. Cmt, 61-; alternate del, Dem. Nat. Conv, 64. Bus. & Prof. Pos: Gen. serviceman, The Detroit Edison Co, 37-66. Mem: Mason; Dem. Cmt. on Agr; regional rep, 66 Party Develop. Cmt, Mich. Dem. Party. Rel: American Lutheran. Mailing Add: 312 N. Cass Ave, Vassar, Mich. 48768.

STEWART, POTTER
Assoc. Justice, U.S. Supreme Court
b. Jackson, Mich, 1/23/15: s. James Garfield Stewart and Harrier Loomis Potter S; m. 4/24/43 to Mary Ann Bertles; c. Harriet Potter (Mrs. Richard R. Virkstis), Potter, Jr. and David Bertles. Educ: Yale Col, B.A. cum laude, 37; Cambridge Univ, fel, 37-38; Yale Law Sch, LL.B. cum laude, 41; Phi Beta Kappa; Delta Kappa Epsilon; Phi Delta Phi. Polit. & Govt. Pos: City councilman, Cincinnati, Ohio, 50-53, v.mayor, 52-53; U.S. Judge, Court of Appeals, Sixth Circuit, 54-58; assoc. justice, U.S. Supreme Court, 58- Bus. & Prof. Pos: Attorney-at-law, N.Y.C, 41-42 & 45-47, Cincinnati, Ohio, 47-54. Mil. Serv: Lt, Naval Res, 42-45. Mem: Am, Ohio, Cincinnati and N.Y.C. Bar Asns; Yale Law Sch. Asn; Order of the Coif; Am. Law Inst; Camargo, Commonwealth, Commercial and Univ. Clubs, Cincinnati; Univ. and Chevy Chase Clubs, Wash;

Century Club, N.Y.C. Rel: Episcopal. Legal Res: Cincinnati, Ohio. Mailing Add: 5136 Palisade Lane N.W, Washington, D.C. 20016.

STEWART, RICHARD OLIN R
Chmn, Denton Co. Rep. Cmt, Tex.
b. New Philadelphia, Ohio, 6/14/22; s. Walter Kenna Stewart and Florence Newton S; m. 2/10/46 to Susanne Sharp; c. Richard Olin, Jr, Barbara Lois, Allen Kenna and Laura Susanne. Educ: Univ. Calif, Los Angeles, A.A, 47, B.S, 49. Polit. & Govt. Pos: Rep. precinct chmn, Tulsa, Okla, 57-60 and Denton, Tex, 60-64; chmn, Denton Co. Rep. Cmt, Tex, 64-; campaign pilot for Spiro T. Agnew, 68. Bus. & Prof. Pos: Airline Pilot, Am. Airlines, Inc, 49- Mil. Serv: Entered as Pvt, Army, 42, released as Capt, 45, after serv. in 13th Air Force, S.Pac. Theater, 43-45; reentered serv. as Capt, Air Force, 51, released as Maj, 53, after serv. in Korea; Col, Air Force Res; Air Medal with 5 Oak Leaf Clusters; Am. Theater Medal; Asiatic-Pac. Theater Ribbon with 4 Battle Stars; World War II Victory Medal; Korean Serv. and Air Force Res. Medals; Armed Serv. Medal with Hour Glass; Philippine Liberation Medal with 2 Battle Stars. Mem: Bd. Dirs, Airlines Pilots Asn, 58-60; v.pres, Night Fighter Asn, 52-53; Allied Pilots Asn; Optimist (mem. bd. dirs, pres, 68-69, lt. gov, 69-); C. of C; bd. dirs, Girl Scouts; v.pres, Boys Club, Denton; Air Force Asn; Am. Econ. Found; Am. Conserv. Union. Golden Gloves Boxing; Univ. Calif, Los Angeles, Boxing Team. Rel: Church of Christ. Mailing Add: 2710 Crestwood Place, Denton, Tex. 76201.

STEWART, ROBERT F. D
b. Benwood, W.Va, 4/25/12; s. Bruce A. Stewart and Henrietta McCombs S; m. 7/28/35 to Julia Marcissin; c. Mrs. William Howard, Betsy Ann, Bruce. Educ: Pub. Schs. of Marshall City. Polit. & Govt. Pos: W.Va. State Del, 64-66. Bus. & Prof. Pos: Supervisor, steel corp. Mem: Marshall Union Lodge No. 8, AF & AM; 32° Scottish Rite; Wheeling Commandery No. 1; Knights Templar; Elks; Marshall City Park and Recreation Bd; Nat. Mgt. Asn; W.Va. Arts and Crafts Asn; Pres, Glen Dale Lions; Marshall City Watershed Asn. Rel: Methodist. Mailing Add: Moundsville, W.Va. 26041. (1967)

STEWART, ROBERT POTTER D
b. Kans, 10/10/29; s. Jack Francis Stewart and Jennie Potter S; m. 6/2/50 to Wilma P; c. Michael Robert, Pauline, Shawn Jay, Blake Douglas, Raun David and Naunie. Educ: Weber State Col; Utah State Univ; Colo. Col; Phi Delta Kappa. Polit. & Govt. Pos: Utah State Rep, Weber Co, 63-66. Bus. & Prof. Pos: Elem. sch. prin, Weber Co. Schs, 57- Mil. Serv: Serv. as Cpl, Army, 47-48 and S/Sgt, Air Force, 51-52. Mem: Dist. Sci. Chmn, Sci. Fair, Weber Co, 57; pres, Roy Jr. C. of C, 56-57; pres, Ogden Squadron Air Force Asn; chmn, Weber Valley Air Fair; Utah Jr. C. of C. State Awards Chmn; State Sci. Text Book Adoption Cmt; Nat. and Utah Educ. Asns; Air Force Asn; pres, Weber Educ. Asn; pres, Ogden Field Chap, Phi Delta Kappa; trustee, Col. of South. Utah. Received Outstanding State Chmn. Trophy, Utah Jaycees, 56; Roy and Utah Distinguished Serv. Awards, 59; Air Force Asn. Exceptional Serv. Award, 60; Named Man of Year, Air Force Asn, 61. Rel: Latter-day Saint. Mailing Add: 5408 South 2375 West, Roy, Utah 84067.

STEWART, ROBERT WENDELL D
Treas, Ind. Dem. State Cent. Cmt.
b. Daleville, Ind, 4/17/25; s. Archiebald Henry Stewart and Pearl Pugsley S; m. 4/29/44 to Barbara Ellen Ulmer; c. Robert A. and Carol Ann. Educ: Wofford Col, 6 months; Ball State Univ, B.S, 48. Polit. & Govt. Pos: Precinct committeeman, Dem. Party, Daleville, Ind, 52-; co. assessor, Delaware Co, 59-67; chmn, Delaware Co. Dem. Party, 64-; del, Dem. Nat. Conv, 68; treas, Ind. Dem. State Cent. Cmt, 68- Bus. & Prof. Pos: Gen. ins. agency, Daleville, Ind, 52-; real estate, 69. Mil. Serv: Entered as Pvt, Army Air Force, 43, released as Sgt, 46, after serv. in Ninth Air Force, ETO, 45-46; Air Medal; Presidential Citation; ETO Ribbon; Good Conduct Medal. Mem: Mason; Am. Legion; Amvets; VFW; Elks; Moose. Rel: Christian Church of N.Am. Mailing Add: 909 River Rd, Box 327, Daleville, Ind. 47334.

STEWART, TRAVIS BURNS D
b. East Point, Ga, 3/2/29; s. Jack Thomas Stewart and Lillie R. Hemperley S; m. 7/24/54 to Rachel Alicia Cosby; c. Rebekah and Reneé. Educ: Univ. Ga, Atlanta Div, 47-50; Ga. State Col, B.B.A, 56; Woodrow Wilson Law Sch, LL.B, 62; Sigma Nu. Polit. & Govt. Pos: Dir. info, State Vet. Serv. Dept, Ga, 49-51; exec. asst, Exec. Dept, 56-58; dir, Ga. Young Dem, 56-58; dir, State Bd. of Probation, 58-63; exec. dir, Dem. Party of Ga, 63-68; secy, Dem. Nat. Conv, 64. Mil. Serv: Entered as Pvt, Marine Corps, 51, released as Sgt, 54, after serv. in Third and First Marine Air Wings, 52-53, Korean Theater, 52; several awards. Mem: Pres, Ga. Probation and Parole Asn, 61; Cong. of Corrections, 58-62; Am. Legion; VFW; The Gridiron Soc; Druid Hills Golf Club; Navy League; adv. coun, Naval Affairs. Rel: Baptist. Mailing Add: 1405 Cornell Rd, Atlanta, Ga. 30301. (1967)

STEWART, WALDABA HAMILTON, JR. D
N.Y. State Sen.
b. Ancon, Canal Zone, 1/15/36; s. Waldaba Hamilton Stewart and Ruby Sealey S; m. 1/18/69 to Marjorie Cooper. Educ: Balboa Jr. Col, Canal Zone, A.A; Pace Col, B.A; Hunter Col, M.A. Polit. & Govt. Pos: N.Y. State Sen, 18th Senatorial Dist, 69- Bus. & Prof. Pos: Teacher, Bd. of Educ, 56-66; Associate Dir, Commun. Corp, 67-68. Mem: Independent United Order of Mechanics; Mason; Better Govt. Dem. Orgn; Unity Dem. Club; Commerce Labor Indust. Corp of Kings; Brooklyn Model Cities Cmt; Brooklyn Local Economic Development Corp; Bicycle Racing Asn. Community Corp, Acceptance of Serv; Boy Scouts Century Club Award. Rel: Protestant. Mailing Add: 715 St. Marks Ave, Brooklyn, N.Y. 11216.

STEWART, WILLIAM A, JR. R
b. Lexington, Nebr, 5/14/29; s. William A. Stewart and Margaret Jeffrey S; m. 6/14/51 to Mary Ruth Ryons; c. Leslie, William, Courtney and Lisa. Educ: Univ. Nebr, B.S, 51, LL.B, 55; Phi Delta Phi; Phi Delta Theta. Polit. & Govt. Pos: Mem, Nebr. Young Rep. Exec. Cmt, 56-59; mem, Nebr. State Rep. Exec. Cmt, 57-59; co. attorney, Dawson Co, Nebr, 58-66; chmn, Dawson Co. Rep. Cmt, 63-68. Bus. & Prof. Pos: Del, Nebr. State Bar Asn, House of Dels, 65-67. Mil. Serv: Entered as 2nd Lt, Army, 51, released as 1st Lt, 53, after serv. in First Cavalry Div, Korea, 52-53; Korean Serv. and UN Serv. Medals. Mem: Am. and Nebr. State Bar Asns; VFW; Am. Legion; Mason; pres, West. Nebr. Bar Asn, 67-69. Rel: Presbyterian. Mailing Add: R.R. 1, Lexington, Nebr. 68850.

STEWART, WILLIAM F. R
b. Fairfield, Idaho, 6/1/27; s. Carroll Wright Stewart and Metta Fern Lee S; m. 9/6/47 to Opal Louise Tritthart; c. Steven Francis, Terrill Wright, William Alan, Mark Wayne and Reed Lee. Educ: Univ. Idaho, 47-48. Polit. & Govt. Pos: Chmn, Camas Co. Rep. Cent. Cmt, Idaho, 62-68. Bus. & Prof. Pos: Co. mgr. and sales mgr, Wendell Mill & Lumber Co. Inc, 58-65; owner, The Mkt. Basket, 65-66. Mil. Serv: Entered as A/S, Navy, 45, released as Carpenters Mate 3/C, 46. Mem: Camas Prairie Lions; Am. Legion. Rel: Latter-day Saint. Mailing Add: Box 25, Fairfield, Idaho 83327. (1967)

STEWART, WILLIAM O. R
V.Chmn, Ill. Rep. State Cent. Cmt.
b. Chicago, Ill, 2/8/25; s. James Stewart and Marvella Brewer S; single. Educ: Tenn. State Univ, B.S, 50; DePaul Univ, M.E, 67; Kappa Alpha Psi; Polit. & Govt. Pos: Pres, Third Ward Young Rep, 56; v.chmn, Cook Co. Young Rep, 57; v.pres, Ill. Young Rep, 58; committeeman, Ill. Rep. State Cent. Cmt, 66-, v.chmn, 67-; pres, Third Ward Rep. Orgn, 67- Bus. & Prof. Pos: Teacher, Chicago Bd. Educ, 51-; dist. supvr, Chicago Teachers Union, 68- Mem: Am. Fedn. Teachers; Am. Asn. Health, Phys. Educ. and Recreation; Chicago Teachers Union; life mem. U.S. Jaycees; Urban League; NAACP; Toastmasters Int. Good Guy Award, WGRT Radio Sta; Outstanding Alumnus Award, Tenn. State Univ, 63. Rel: Methodist. Mailing Add: 219 E. 45th St, Chicago, Ill. 60653.

STICKNEY, CHARLES WILLIAM DFL
Chmn, Sherburne Co. Dem-Farmer-Labor Party, Minn.
b. Clear Lake, Minn, 2/3/96; s. Charles Abner Stickney and Adah White S; m. 12/8/20 to Rhea Marguerite Head. Educ: Univ. Minn, farm. Exten, 3 years. Polit. & Govt. Pos: Chmn. State Cmt, AAA PMA, Agr. Prog, Minn, 36-52; chmn, Sherburne Co. Dem-Farmer-Labor Party, 53- Bus. & Prof. Pos: Farmer. Mil. Serv: Entered as Pvt, Army, 17, released as Sgt. 1/C, 19, after serv. in First Field Signal Bn, Second Div, all Major Battles, 17; Silver Star Gallantry in Action. Mem: Mason; VFW; Farmers Union. Rel: Methodist. Legal Res: R.F.D. 1, Clear Lake, Minn. 55319.

STICKNEY, HAROLD DEAN R
b. Edgemont, S.Dak, 11/8/25; s. Guy Harold Stickney and Blanche Mickelsen S; m. 8/3/47 to Creta Dawn Boschma; c. Elayne Rae, Randall Guy, Renee L, Leigh Ann, Carl Leonard and Jeff Dean. Educ: Univ. of Nebr, B.S in Bus. Admin, 49; Alpha Kappa Psi. Polit. & Govt. Pos: Chmn, Sall River Co. Young Rep, S.Dak, 51-56; precinct committeeman, Rep. Party, 56-68; committeeman, S.Dak. Rep. State Cent. Cmt, 61; chmn, S.Dak. State Police Civil Serv. Cmn, 61-; alternate del, Rep. Nat. Conv, 68; mem, Gov. Adv. Coun, S.Dak, 68-69. Bus. & Prof. Pos: Mem, Zone Dealer Council Ford Motor Co, 59 & 62; Pres, Greater Edgemont Move. Inc, 62-68; Regional Rep, Dealer Council Int. Harvester Co, 66-68. Mil. Serv: Entered as Pvt, Air Force, 43, released as T/Sgt, 45, after serv. in 90th Bomb Group S. Pac. Theatre, 44-45; Air Force Res, 45-48, 1st Lt; Asiatic Pacific Medal with Seven Battle Stars, Air Medal with Two Oak Leaf Clusters, Philippine Liberation Medal. Mem: Lions (pres, 51); C. of C. (pres, 59); Elks; Am. Legion; Odd Fellows. Named Outstanding Businessman, Soil Conserv. Dist, 63; Named Man of the Year, Jaycees, 64. Rel: Congregational. Mailing Add: 903 F St, Edgemont, S.Dak. 57735.

STICKROD, DON PERRY R
b. Quincy, Ill, 9/23/29; s. Warren William Stickrod (deceased) and Eunice Echo Shultz S; m. 9/19/53 to Edith Ruth Searcy; c. Warren W, Anne L. and Janet A. Educ: Kans. Univ, B.S, 51; Beta Theta Pi. Polit. & Govt. Pos: Chmn, Pottawatomie Co. Rep. Party, Okla, 61-63; mem, Okla. State Rep. Cmt, 61-69; chmn, Fourth Cong. Dist. Rep. Party, 64-69; mem, Okla. State Rep. Exec. Cmt, 67-69; del, Rep. Nat. Conv, 68. Bus. & Prof. Pos: Sales Mgr, Shawnee Steel Co, Shawnee, Okla, 55-69. Mil. Serv: Entered as Aviation Cadet, Air Force, 52, released as 2nd Lt, 55, after serv. in MATS. Rel: Presbyterian. Mailing Add: 3 Hughes Circle, Shawnee, Okla. 74801.

STIDGER, RUBY JANE D
Mem, Calif. Dem. State Cent. Cmt.
b. Catossa, Okla, 12/8/11; d. Willis Ervan Brown and Alice Kelly B; m. 3/22/30 to Burwell Colquitt Stidger; c. Donal Ray, Jimmy Odel, Beverly Jane (Mrs. McCormick), John Ervan and Linda Sue (Mrs. Smith). Educ: Amarillo High Sch, Tex, grad, 1930. Polit. & Govt. Pos: Treas, 25th Cong. Dist. Dem. Party, Calif, 57-63; mem, Co. Dem. Cmt, 50th Assembly Dist, 58-60, 58th Assembly Dist, 62-64; 58th Assembly Dist. dir, Calif. Dem. Coun, 62; mem, Calif. Dem. State Cent. Cmt, 58th Assembly Dist, 64-; mem, Lynch Presidential del, 68. Mem: San Gabriel Valley Womens Dem. Club; West Covina Emblem Club. Rel: Methodist. Mailing Add: 4915 N. Peck Rd, Elmonte, Calif. 91732.

STIDHAM, JEANNE R
Mem, Calif. Rep. State Cent. Cmt.
b. Tulsa, Okla, 3/16/26; d. Arden Enoch Polston and Dora MacPherson Hedgecock P; div; c. Dennis Keith, Marna Kathleen and Dana Wayne Knauber. Educ: Bakersfield Col, 51-53; Valley Col, 57-58. Polit. & Govt. Pos: Commun. chmn, Reinecke for Cong, Newhall-Saugus, Calif, 64; mgr, Newhall-Saugus-Valencia C. of C, 64-68; assoc. mem. labor cmt, Calif. Rep. State Cent. Cmt, 65-66, mem, 66-; chmn, Los Angeles Co. Rd. Cmt, 65-68; local coordinator, Rep. vol. orgn, Rep. Coun, 66-69; mem, Los Angeles Co. Castaic Recreation Cmt, Supvr, Warren Dorn, 67-68; commun. chmn, Jack Lindsey for Cong, 27th Cong. Dist, 69. Bus. & Prof. Pos: Owner, Standby Employ. Agency, 62-67; leasing agent, properties, Newhall Land and Farming, Valencia, 69- Mem: Calif. Employ. Agencies; Prfnl. Personnel Agencies; South. Calif. C. of C. Exec; Int. Toastmistress Club; Bus. & Prfnl. Women Federated; United Rep. Calif; mem. exec. bd. and youth cmt. bd, Pleasantview Opportunity Center; Soledad Twp. Coord. Coun. (Christmas basket chmn). Award of Merit, Los Angeles Co. Bd. Supvr; Appreciation Awards, Newhall-

Saugus-Valencia C. of C. Rel: Protestant. Mailing Add: 35600 San Francisquito Canyon Rd, Saugus, Calif. 91350.

STIEGHORST, LEWIS EARL R

Bonus Mem, Colo. Rep. State Cent. Cmt.

b. Sheboygan, Wis, 9/26/26; s. Alfred W. Stieghorst and Marie S. Strassburger S; m. 9/15/50 to Marion D. Doylen; c. Kent D. and Kim D. Educ: Univ. Wis, Madison, B.S.E.E, 50; Denver Univ, 1 year; Phi Kappa Phi; Eta Kappa Nu; Delta Epsilon; pres, Mens Halls Asn; Iron Cross. Polit. & Govt. Pos: Precinct committeeman, Rep. Party, Jefferson Co, Colo, 62-, dist. capt, 63-65; pres, Columbine Hills Civic Asn, 63-65; campaign mgr. various local cand, Jefferson Co, 64, 66 & 68; mem, Jefferson Co. Planning Cmn, 65-; v.chmn, Colo. Rep. Workshops, 67; mem, Jefferson Co. R-1 Sch. Bd, 67-; chmn, Citizens for Jefferson Co. Law Enforcement Authority, 69; bonus mem, Colo. Rep. State Cent. Cmt, 69- Bus. & Prof. Pos: Engr, Allen-Bradley Co, 51-58; systs. engr, Martin-Marietta Corp, 58-65; sales engr, Westinghouse Elec. Corp, 65- Mil. Serv: Entered as Pvt, Army, 44, released as Cpl, 46, after serv. in 84th Inf. Div, Germany, 45-46. Mem: Inst. Elec. and Electronic Engrs; Inst. Aeronaut. and Astronaut, C. of C; Columbine Hills Civic Asn.(ed, Columbine Hills Newsletter, 63-65). Man of Year Award and Five Year Distinguished Serv. Plaque, Columbine Hills Civic Asn. Rel: Methodist. Mailing Add: 7752 S. Ames Way, Littleton, Colo. 80120.

STIEHL, WILLIAM D. R

Treas, Ill. Rep. State Cent. Cmt.

b. Belleville, Ill, 12/3/25; s. Clarence G. Stiehl and Florence H. Stoffel S; m. 6/3/47 to Celeste M. Sullivan; c. William D. and Susan M. Educ: Univ. N.C, 43-45; St. Louis Univ. Sch. of Law, LL.B, 46-49; Sigma Alpha Epsilon. Polit. & Govt. Pos: Mem, Bd. of Educ, Belleville Twp. High Sch. and Jr. Col, Ill, 49-50 & 54-56, pres, 56-57; pres, St. Clair Co. Young Rep. Club, 54-55; v.pres, Ill. Young Rep. Orgn, 55-57; co. civil attorney, St. Clair Co, 56-60; chmn, St. Clair Co. Rep. Cent. Cmt, 60-66; mem, exec. cmt, Ill. Rep. Co. Chmn. Asn, 60-66; mem, Bd. of Gov, Ill. Rep. Citizens League, 61-; Rep. Voter Registration chmn, Ill, 64; state cent. committeeman, 24th Cong. Dist, 66-; treas, Ill. Rep. State Cent. Cmt, 66-; presidential elector, 68. Bus. & Prof. Pos: Attorney-at-law, 49-50 & 52-; pres, Belle Valley Coal Co, Inc, 59- Mil. Serv: Entered as A/S, Navy, 43, released as Ens, 46, after serv. on U.S.S. Charlevoix and staff Comdr. Marianas, Pac. Theater; recalled as Lt.(jg), Navy, 50, released as Lt, 52, after serv. on Staff Comdr. Cruiser Div. 5 and legal adv. to the Naval Delegate at the Korean Armistice Conf, Korean Theater; Comdr, Naval Res; Navy Commendation Medal; Korean Presidential Unit Citation; Navy Res. and Armed Forces Res. Medals; Am. and Asiatic-Pac Theater Ribbons; Victory Medal; Korean Campaign Ribbon with 4 Battle Stars; UNC Campaign Ribbon. Mem: Pres, Belleville Bar Asn, 57-58; St. Clair Co, St. Louis, Ill. State and Am. Bar Asns; Am. Trial Lawyers Asn; Mo. Athletic Club; VFW. Rel: Methodist. Legal Res: 406 McKinley Dr, Belleville, Ill. 62221. Mailing Add: 23 S. First St, Belleville, Ill. 62220.

STIENEKE, DONALD JUNIOR D

Chmn, Buena Vista Dem. Cent. Cmt, Iowa

b. Quimby, Iowa, 8/18/27; s. Victor Fed Stieneke and Venis Viola Hollingshead S; m. 4/24/49 to Helen Lydia Grieme; c. Daniel Luther, Patricia Ann and Charles Phillip. Educ: Quimby High Sch, 4 years. Polit. & Govt. Pos: Twp. trustee, Nokomis, Iowa 56-68; chmn, Buena Vista Dem. Cent. Cmt, 64- Mil. Serv: Entered as Seaman, Navy, 44, released as Seaman 1/C, 46. Rel: Lutheran. Mailing Add: R.R. 2, Alta, Iowa 51002.

STIENMIER, HAROLD R

Chmn, Eagle Co. Rep. Cmt, Colo.

b. Canon City, Colo, 7/4/10; s. John G. Stienmier and Caroline Watts S; m. 8/27/35 to Agnes Madeline Hannah; c. Richard H, Carol (Mrs. Johnson) and Roy L. Educ: Colo. State Univ, B.S.M.E, 35; Commoners Club. Polit. & Govt. Pos: Chmn, Eagle Co. Rep. Cmt, Colo, 69- Bus. & Prof. Pos: Engr, N.J. Zinc Co, 38-47, plant engr, 47-50, plant chief, 50-67, asst. mgr, 67- Mil. Serv: Entered as Pvt, Army Nat. Guard, 34, released as Lt. Col, 46, after serv. in ETO, 44-46, Lt. Col, Res.(Ret). Mem: Am. Inst. Mining Engr; ROA; Soc. Commissioned Officers; Mason; Colo. Consistory. Rel: Episcopal. Legal Res: House 642, Gilman, Colo. 81634. Mailing Add: P.O. Box 117, Gilman, Colo. 81634.

STIERN, WALTER W. D

Calif. State Sen.

b. San Diego, Calif, 1914; m. 1938 to Alysjune Dunning; c. two daughters. Educ: Bakersfield Col; State Col. of Wash, B.S, 37; State Col. of Wash. Sch. of Vet. Med, D.V.M, 38. Polit. & Govt. Pos: Calif. State Sen, 58-; mem, Calif. Dem. State Cent. Cmt, 68- Bus. & Prof. Pos: Practicing vet, 16 years. Mil. Serv: Maj, Air Force Res, 42-46, serv. in China-Burma-India Theatre. Mem: Nat. Calif. State and Kern Co. Vet. Med. Asns; Am. Asn. for the UN; Rotary; Kern Co. Libr. Asns; Child Guid. Clin; Family Serv. Agency; Kern Co. Hist. Soc; Horseless Carriage Club. Mailing Add: 2901 Skyline Blvd, Bakersfield, Calif. 93305.

STIERWALT, LOTUS H. R

Chmn, Washakie Co, Rep. Party, Wyo.

b. Galatia, Ill, 3/8/16; m. 4/25/37; c. William C. and Barbara A. Polit. & Govt. Pos: Chmn, Washakie Co. Rep. Party, Wyo, 66- Rel: Methodist. Legal Res: 900 Obie Sue, Worland, Wyo. 82401. Mailing Add: Box 472, Worland, Wyo. 82401.

STILES, ANNIE LOVINA R

b. West Hawley, Mass, 9/12/07; d. George Edwin Sears and Carrie E. Snyder S; m. 8/15/32 to Philip L. Stiles; c. Mary Esther (Mrs. Streeter). Educ: North Adams Normal, 26-28. Polit. & Govt. Pos: Chmn, Hawley Rep. Town Cmt, Mass, 52-68. Bus. & Prof. Pos: Elem. teacher, Mass, 28-33 & 44-45, substitute teacher, 55-66. Mem: Charlemont Woman's Club and Reading Club; Bridge of Flowers Art Guild. Rel: Congregational. Legal Res: Hawley, Mass. Mailing Add: West Hawley Rd, Charlemont, Mass. 01339.

STILES, BARBARA JEAN R

Mem, Calif. Rep. State Cent. Cmt.

b. Long Beach, Calif, 4/28/32; d. Mertroe Wenn Hollinger and Ethel Chace H; m. 5/26/51 to Lawrance Lee Stiles; c. Catherine Lee, William Mertroe, Tracey Lynn and Matthew Lawrance. Educ: Various Colleges, 50-69. Polit. & Govt. Pos: Mem. Elec. Bd, San Luis Obispo, Calif, 58; block chmn. and precinct worker, Livermore Rep. Party, 62; campaign worker, Shell for Gov, 62; fundraiser, Cologne for Cong, 66; v.pres, Yucaipa Valley Nat. Fedn. of Rep. Women, 66-68; chmn, Reagan for Gov. Campaign, 66; co-chmn, Pettis for Cong. Cmt, 68; mem, Calif. Rep. State Cent. Cmt, 69- Mem: Yucaipa Valley Nat. Fedn. Rep. Women; PTA; Yucaipa Flying Fish Swim Club. Rel: Protestant. Mailing Add: 11485 Acropolis Dr, Yucaipa, Calif. 92399.

STILES, BEATRICE MAY R

V.Chmn, Bloomfield Rep. Town Cmt, N.J.

b. Newark, N.J, 8/19/06; d. Joseph W. Raymond and Stella Mathews R; m. 5/11/22 to Raymond Bell Stiles; c. Le Roy Francis. Educ: Cent. High Sch, 2 years; Col. Bus. Col, 1 year. Polit. & Govt. Pos: Mem, Essex Co. Rep. Cmt, 27-29 & 35-, v.chmn, 54-59; cmt. clerk, N.J. Gen. Assembly, 52-55, jour. clerk, 54 & 55, asst. jour. clerk, 56 & 57; N.J. State Assemblyman, 60-61; v.chmn, Bloomfield Rep. Town Cmt, 65-; del, N.J. Constitutional Conv, 66; alternate del, Rep. Nat. Conv, 68. Bus. & Prof. Pos: Clerk, H.R. Wilson Co, 40-41; clerk transportation dept, West. Elec, Kearney, 43-45. Mem: Nat. Order Women Legislators; N.J. Fedn. Rep. Women; Essex Co. Women's Rep. Club; Bloomfield Rep. Club; Brookdale Second Ward Rep. Club; Am. Nat. Red Cross (chmn. serv. mil. families and mem. bd. dirs, Bloomfield Dist); Am. Red Cross (mem. Essex Chap. serv. to mil. families steering cmt); League Assocs. League Family Serv; DVA; Brookdale Womens Club. Rel: Protestant. Mailing Add: 702 Broad St, Bloomfield, N.J. 07003.

STILES, FRANK O. R

b. Johnson, Vt, 9/10/01; m. to Grace E. Prisbie; c. three sons; one daughter. Educ: Univ. Vt, B.S, 23; Ed.M, 39. Polit. & Govt. Pos: Vt. State Rep, 65-68. Bus. & Prof. Pos: Supt. of schs, ret. Mil. Serv: Army ROTC, U.V.M, 19-21. Mem: Waterman Lodge 83, F&AM; Nat. Educ. Asn; Am. Asn. of Sch. Adminstrs; Vt. Retired Teachers Asn, pres; Fair Haven Commun. Camp, bd. of trustees; Vt. Cong. of Parents and Teachers; chmn. rural educ. bd. of dir; Fair Haven Fish & Game Club, past pres. Rel: Methodist. Mailing Add: Johnson, Vt. 05656.

STILL, EUGENE FONTAINE D

Ark. State Rep.

b. Lookahoma, Miss, 8/30/03; s. James Albert Still and Minnie Murphy S; m. 5/25/29 to Eva Ruth Stevens; c. Eugene F, II and Dianne (Mrs. Green). Educ: Univ. Miss, 21-23. Polit. & Govt. Pos: Mayor, Plymouth, N.C, 45-47; Ark. State Rep, 67- Bus. & Prof. Pos: Pres, Plymouth Box & Panel Co, N.C, 33-45; E.F. Still Co, 47-; v.pres, Sewell Motor Co, Kennett, Mo, 48-; dir, First Nat. Bank, Blythville, Ark, 52-; pres, Caldwell & Still Gin Co, 53-; Osceola Prod. Co, Osceola, 62-; v.pres, Quality Coach Co, Blytheville, 69- Rel: Methodist. Legal Res: 1130 Chickasaw Lane, Blytheville, Ark. 72315. Mailing Add: P.O. Box 1257, Blytheville, Ark. 72315.

STILLINGS, RICHARD WALLACE R

Maine State Rep.

b. Berwick, Maine, 9/5/28; s. Maurice Burleigh Stillings and Doris Allen S; single. Educ: Univ. of Maine, B.A, 52; Univ. of N.H, 64-65; Gorham State Col, Univ. of Maine, 66-69; Scabbard & Blade; Theta Chi. Polit. & Govt. Pos: Moderator, Town Meeting, Berwick, Maine, 56-, chief of police, 58-59 & 67-, dir, civil defense and pub. safety, 58-68 and chmn, planning bd, 65-; Maine State Rep, 69- Bus. & Prof. Pos: Adjuster, N.H. Finance Corp, 54-57; Proprietor, Richard W. Stillings Insurance, 57-59; Exec. Dir, Greater Somersworth C. of C, N.H, 59-62; Teacher, Berwick High Sch, Berwick, Maine, 63- Mil. Serv: Entered as Pvt, Regular Army, 46, released as Lt, 53, after serv. in U.S. Constabulary Forces, Germany 47-48 and 40th Inf. Div, Korea 52-53; Army Res, 53-66, Major; Bronze Star Medal with V Device; Korean Serv. Medal with Battle Star; World War II Victory Medal; Army of Occupational Medal; Nat. Defense Serv. Medal; Armed Forces Reserve Medal; UN Serv. Medal; ROK Presidential Citation; Combat Infantryman Badge. Mem: Nat. Educ. Asn; Maine Teachers Asn; Maine Law Enforcement Asn; Masons (Blue Lodge, Chapter, Council, Comdr); Am. Legion (past comdr); Knights of Pythias (past chancellor comdr & deputy grand chancellor). Rel: Protestant. Mailing Add: 90 Sullivan St, Berwick, Maine 03901.

STILLMAN, GUY D

Dem. Nat. Committeeman, Ariz.

b. N.Y.C, 11/7/18; s. James A. Stillman (deceased) and Mrs. Fowler McCormick; m. to Carolyn Weyand; c. Alexandra (Mrs. Jon Bernard Carlin), Victoria (Mrs. Richard C. Withers), Sharee (Mrs. Ted Brookhard), Charles, Christopher and Guy H. Stillman, Frank C. Teal, III, and John W. Teal. Educ: Rensselaer Polytech. Inst, B.I.E, 41; Am. Inst. for For. Trade, B.F.T, 62. Polit. & Govt. Pos: Mem, Ariz. Dem. State Finance Cmt, 53-63; chmn, Maricopa Co. Dem. Party, 54-58; exec. secy. and treas, Ariz. Citizens for Johnson, 64; coordinator, President's Club and co-chmn, Maricopa Co. Dem. Finance Cmt, 64-65; Dem. Nat. Committeeman, Ariz, currently. Bus. & Prof. Pos: Vending machine bus, Ariz. Cent. Machine Co, Phoenix, 46-49; asst. mgr. and prod. develop. engr, Int. Harvester Proving Grounds, Chandler, 49-50; farm implement dealer, Maricopa Equipment Co, Glendale and Buckeye, 50-60; local consult. engr, Skidmore, Owings and Merrill of San Francisco, Calif. and dir. and mem. exec. cmt, South. Ariz. Bank and Trust Co, currently. Mil. Serv: Entered as Ens, Naval Res, 41, released to inactive duty as Lt. Comdr, 45, after serv. in Naval Gun Factory, D.C, 41, post grad. course, Cornell Univ. Sch. of Eng, 42, Eng. Officer, Motor Torpedo Boat Serv, serv. in all New Guinea and Philippine Campaigns, 42-45, sr. instr. and Eng. Officer, Motor Boat Squadrons Training Center, Melville, R.I; Commanding Officer, Naval Res, Div. 11-1, Phoenix, 46-48. Mem: Pres, Reserve Officers Naval Serv, Phoenix, 46-49 and Reserve Officers Asn, Dept. of Ariz, 48; nat. v.pres, Navy, Reserve Officers Asn. of U.S, 49; chmn, Gr. Phoenix Planning Cmt, 46-48; co-chmn, Phoenix Charter Rev. Cmt, 47-48; dir, Glendale C. of C, 51-53; pres, Paradise Valley Improv. Asn, 52-54; dir, Valley Beautiful Cmt,

Phoenix Metrop. Area Beautification and Adv. Community Planning; Ariz. State Univ. Cmt. to Establish a Col. of Eng, 59-62; dir, Arabian Horse Asn. of Ariz.(pres, 62-63); Maricopa Co. mem, Nat. Cmt. on Crime and Juvenile Delinquency; chmn, Scottsdale City Adv. Cmt; Scottsdale Rotary; chmn, Small Bus. Admin. Adv. Coun. for Ariz; Navy League of Phoenix; Ariz. Cmt. for Econ. Develop, 65; chmn, Cystic Fibrosis Campaign in Maricopa Co, 64-65; trustee, Phoenix Country Day Sch, Orme Ranch Sch. and Am. Inst. for For. Trade; bd. visitors, U.S. Naval Acad, 61-63, chmn. bd. of visitors, 65; educ. consult, Navy of S.Viet Nam, Jan. 69. Legal Res: 7303 N. Scottsdale Rd, Scottsdale, Ariz. 85251. Mailing Add: 300 W. Osborn Rd, Phoenix, Ariz. 85013.

STILLMAN, JOHN STERLING D
Committeeman, Orange Co. Dem. Cmt, N.Y.
b. N.Y.C, 9/6/18; s. Ernest Goodrich Stillman and Mildred M. Whitney S; m. 9/15/67 to Amelia Pasquint Jackson; c. Nathaniel, Linda B. and John Whitney Stillman and stepchildren John H, Philipp Y. and Mark C. Jackson. Educ: Harvard Col, S.B, 40; Yale Law Sch, 40-41; Columbia Law Sch, J.D, 47; Hasty Pudding; D.U. Club; Phi Delta Phi; Corby Court. Polit. & Govt. Pos: Capt, Grover Cleveland Dem. Club, Ninth Assembly Dist, N.Y, 46-48; founder, secy. and dir, N.Y. Young Dem. Club, 47-50 & 53-55; del, N.Y. State Dem. Conv, 50, 52 & 54; attorney adv, Div. Counsel, Nat. Prod. Authority, Wash, D.C, 51; legis. asst. U.S. Rep. F.D. Roosevelt, Jr, 52; regional enforcement cmnr, wage and salary stabilization, Nat. Enforcement Cmn, 52-53; chmn, Orange Co. Dem. Cmt, 54-61, committeeman, currently; del, Dem. Nat. Conv, 56 & 60, alternate del-at-lg, 68; mem, N.Y. State Bridge Authority, 56-61, chmn, 57-60; N.Y. State Del. Liaison and Hudson Valley Campaign Coordinator, J.F. Kennedy for Pres, 60; dep. under secy, U.S. Dept. Commerce, 61-62, dep. secy. for cong. rels, 63-65; del. coordinator, Nat. Citizens for Johnson-Humphrey, 64; dir, U.S. Investment and Indust. Develop. Mission to India, 65; dir. urban renewal, Newburgh Urban Renewal Agency, 67; coordinator 27th and 28th Cong. Dist, Robert F. Kennedy for Pres. Pre-Primary Campaign, 68. Bus. & Prof. Pos: Assoc, Dow and Symmers, 47-48; attorney-at-law, 49-50 & 55-60; assoc, Paul, Weiss, Rifkind, Wharton and Garrison, 53-54; dir. and treas, Planned Commun, Inc, 65-; partner, Gilinsky, Stillman and Mishkin, 65-; dir, Great Am. Mgt. & Research Co, Ltd, 66- Mil. Serv: Entered as Ens, Naval Res, 41, released as Lt. Comdr, 46, after serv. in Off. Comdr-in-Chief, Wash, D.C. 1 year and in U.S.S. Montpelier, S. and S.W. Pac, 42-45; Res, 45-61, Lt. Comdr.(Ret); Naval Res. Medal; Pac. Area Ribbon with 13 Battle Stars; Navy Unit Commendation, Philippine Liberation and Victory Medals. Mem: N.Y.C, N.Y. State, Fed. and Orange Co. Bar Asns; dir, Patterns for Progress; Citizens Housing and Planning Coun; Regional Plan Asn; Orange Co. Ment. Health Asn; Nat. Serv. Secretariat Inc; Am. Legion; Am. Vet. Cmt.(nat. chmn, 65-67); Nat. Capital Dem. Club; Fed. City Club; City Club N.Y; trustee, Storm King Sch. and Mt. St. Mary Col; Asia Soc; N.Y. Urban Coalition; F&AM. Rel: Unitarian; Former Bd. Mem, Newborgh Unitarian-Universalist Church. Legal Res: 72 Maple Rd, Cornwall-on-Hudson, N.Y. 12520. Mailing Add: 277 Park Ave, New York, N.Y. 10017.

STILLMAN, SAUL G. R
Chmn, Cuyahoga Co. Rep. Cent. Cmt, Ohio
b. Cleveland, Ohio, 1/27/10; both parents deceased; m. 12/11/33 to Cecelia P. Huberman; c. Arthur, Jean (Mrs. Lewis Wolff) and Barbara (Mrs. Larry Meister). Educ: Harvard Col, B.A, 30; Law Sch, LL.B, 33; Phi Beta Kappa. Polit. & Govt. Pos: Mem, Rep. State Cent. and Exec. Cmt, Ohio, 62-; mem, Cuyahoga Co. Bd. Elec, 64-; alternate del, Rep. Nat. Conv, 68; chmn, Cuyahoga Co. Rep. Cent. Cmt, 68- Mem: Cleveland, Cuyahoga Co. and Ohio Bar Asns. Rel: Jewish. Mailing Add: 3619 Blanche Rd, Cleveland Heights, Ohio 44118.

STIMMEL, DON PERRY D
Mem, Colo. Dem. State Cent. Cmt.
b. Ft. Collins, Colo, 8/13/38; s. Lester Hendren Stimmel and Margaret Perry S; m. 8/4/67 to Mary Elizabeth Kirk. Educ: Univ. N.Mex, 57-58; Colo. State Univ, B.A, 60; Univ. Wis, Madison, M.S, 62; Univ. Colo, J.D, 64; Omicron Delta Kappa; Phi Kappa Phi; Pi Gamma Mu. Polit. & Govt. Pos: Pres, Colo. State Univ. Young Dem, 58-59, publicity chmn, 59-60; col. coordinator, Young Dem. of Colo, 61-63, col. dir, 63-64, dist. dir, First Dist, 66-67; pres, Boulder Co. Young Dem, 68-; precinct committeeman, Boulder Co. Dem. Party, 68-; mem, Colo. Dem. State Cent. Cmt, 69- Bus. & Prof. Pos: Asst. prof. law, Washburn Univ, 64-65; attorney, assoc. with different firms, Denver, Colo, 65-66, Stevens & Koeberle, Boulder, 66-68 and Martin & Riggs, 68- Publ: 'Case note on 1962 Colorado Reapportionment Amendment,' 5/63, 'Colorado Wage and Hour Law: Analysis and Suggestions,' 4/64 and 'Criminality of Voluntary Sexual Acts in Colorado,' 5/68, Univ. Colo. Law Rev. Am. Trial Lawyers Asn; Colo. and Boulder Co. Bar Asns; Boulder Tennis Asn. Rel: Unitarian. Mailing Add: 2685 28th, Apt. 16, Boulder, Colo. 80302.

STINNETT, RONALD F. D
b. Cleveland, Tenn, 10/16/29; s. Owen E. Stinnett (deceased) and Lillian McNeely S; m. 6/9/56 to Betty Jane Burleson; c. Barbara Dean, Debora Jean and Ronald F. and Sean Lee. Educ: Cortland State Univ, B.S. magna cum laude, 52; Univ. Minn, M.A, 56, grad. fel, 59, Tozer Found. grant for individual research, 60, Ph.D, 61. Polit. & Govt. Pos: Exec. dir, Minn. Citizens for Kennedy-Johnson, 60; campaign mgr, Arthur Nafalin for Mayor, Minneapolis, 61 & 63; campaign mgr, researcher, coordinator, Minn. Dem-Farmer-Labor Legis. Cand. and registrn. and voter turnout progs, 62; research dir, Dem. Senate Campaign Cmt, 63-64; asst. coordinator, V.Pres. Campaign, 64; asst. to Vice President, Hubert Humphrey, 65-67. Bus. & Prof. Pos: Teacher Eng. and Soc. Studies, High Sch, N.Y. State, 6 years; teacher, Univ. Minn, 1 year; asst. teach. dir, Univ. Minn. Theater; specialist in recounts, 62-; pres, Wash. Group, Inc, currently. Publ: Recount; Democrats, Dinners and Dollars. Mailing Add: 1101 17th St. N.W, Washington, D.C. 20036.

STINSON, BESS B. R
Ariz. State Rep.
single. Educ: Okla. Univ; classes in practical polit. offered by U.S. C. of C. Polit. & Govt. Pos: First pres, Metrop. Rep. Women of Phoenix, Ariz; mem, Nat. Fedn. of Rep. Women; Ariz. State Rep, 67- Bus. & Prof. Pos: Asst. v.pres. and dir. spec. serv, First Nat. Bank of Ariz, 52-; teacher practical polit, U.S. C. of C; home serv. adv, Dist-State Pub. Serv. Co. Mil. Serv: Women's Army Corps. Mem: League of Bus. & Prfnl. Women; dept. and nat. Americanism Cmts; Nat. Asn. of Bank Women; State women's chmn, U.S. Savings Bonds; Goodwill Auxiliary; Assoc. Women for Pepperdine Col; Women's Med. Col, Phila. Miss Stinson's Have Flag-Will Fly Prog, now nationwide, was initiated through the Ariz. Fedn. of Woman's Clubs. Mailing Add: 1919 W. Earll Dr, Phoenix, Ariz. 85015. (1967)

STINSON, DEAN KING R
b. Athens, Ind, 4/5/06; s. Arthur Eugene Stinson and Grace King S; m. 10/2/45 to La Vonna Jeanette Bailey; c. Nancy (Mrs. Shaffer), Dean K, Jr, Anne (Mrs. Clay), Barbara (Mrs. McGee), Mrs. Tom Trosin and Steven A. Educ: Ind. Univ, B.S, 27, M.D, 29; Theta Kappa Psi. Polit. & Govt. Pos: Chmn, Fulton Co. Rep. Cent. Cmt, Ind, 52-64; del, Rep. Nat. Conv. and Rep. State Conv, 64; Rep. party worker and contributor. Bus. & Prof. Pos: Physician and surgeon, 30-; Fulton Co. Coroner, 34-56. Mem: Am. Asn. of Rwy. Surgeons; Am. Acad. Gen. Practice; Fulton Co. and Ind. State Med. Socs; Am. Med. Asn; Mason; York Rite; Scottish Rite; Shrine; Grotto; Elks; Moose; Odd Fellows. Legal Res: 1318 Main St, Rochester, Ind. 46975. Mailing Add: 816 Main St, Rochester, Ind. 46975.

STINSON, FORD EDWARDS D
La. State Rep.
b. Benton, La, 8/24/14; s. Robert Tidwell Stinson, Sr. and Mamie Edwards S; m. 2/2/46 to Edna Earle Richardson; c. Mary Carol, Janet and Ford E, Jr. Educ: La. State Univ, LL.B; Phi Delta Phi; Kappa Alpha. Polit. & Govt. Pos: Mem, Benton Town Coun, La, 36-40; mem, Bossier Parish Dem. Exec. Cmt, 36-; La. State Rep, Bossier Parish, 40-44 & 52- Bus. & Prof. Pos: Attorney, Nat. Bank of Bossier City, La, 48- Mil. Serv: Entered as 1st Lt, Army, 41, released as Lt. Col, Air Force, 46; Bronze Star; Campaign Ribbons for Africa, Mediterranean, Am. and Europe. Mem: Lions; Bossier Parish and La. State Bar Asns; VFW; Am. Legion; 40 et 8; Am. Trial Lawyers Asn. Rel: Methodist. Legal Res: Oak Ridge Dr, Benton, La. 71006. Mailing Add: P.O. Box 276, Benton, La. 71006. (1967)

STITES, ALBERT KARL D
Committeeman, Ill. Dem. State Cent. Cmt.
b. Rockford, Ill, 6/17/31; s. Arthur Joseph Stites, Sr. and Caroline Kappen S; single. Educ: Rockford West Senior High Sch, 3 years. Polit. & Govt. Pos: V.pres, Winnebago Co. Young Democrats, Ill, 63-64, pres, 64-65, secy, 66-67; committeeman, Ill. Dem. State Cent. Cmt, 66- Mem: UAW; CIO. Rel: Lutheran, Missouri Synod. Mailing Add: 801 Daisyfield Rd, Rockford, Ill. 61102.

STITES, ROBERT CLARE R
Mich. State Rep.
b. Hudson, Mich, 1/7/15; s. Clair Stites and Ellalie Knapp S; m. 11/22/39 to Virginia May Haines; c. David W, Douglas W. and Diane W. Polit. & Govt. Pos: Cmnr, Pub. Safety, Mich, 51-53; chief of police, Adrian and supvr, Lenawee Co, 51-53; sheriff, Lenawee Co, 57-64; Mich. State Rep, 67- Mil. Serv: Entered as Pvt, Army, 43, released as S/Sgt, criminal investr, 46; Am. Theater Serv. Medal; Meritorious Unit Award; Good Conduct and Victory Medals. Mem: Am. Legion; 40 et 8; Mason; Odd Fellows; Elks; exec. secy. and lobbyist, Mich. Sheriffs Asn, 64-65; Nat. Sheriffs Asn. Rel: Presbyterian. Mailing Add: 2399 Round Lake Hwy, Manitou Beach, Mich. 49253. (1967)

STITT, NANCY CATHERINE R
b. Portland, Ore, 8/20/26; d. Ben Harrison Whitmer and Pearl Henry W; m. 7/5/52 to Harry Lee Stitt; c. David, Paul and John. Educ: Ore. State Univ, B.S, 48; Kappa Kappa Gamma. Polit. & Govt. Pos: Mem, Calif. Rep. State Cent. Cmt, until 69. Bus. & Prof. Pos: Teacher, Astoria Jr. High, Ore, 48-51 and Sequoia Sr. High, Redwood City, Calif, 51-53. Mem: Antioch Rep. Women's Club. Rel: Lutheran. Legal Res: Blossom Dr, Antioch, Calif. 94509. Mailing Add: Route 1, Box 257, Antioch, Calif. 94509.

STIVERS, OLIVER CHARLES R
Mem, Calif. Rep. State Cent. Cmt.
b. Superior, Wis, 11/15/16; s. Charles Oscar Stivers and Emma Amorde S; m. 9/17/36 to Evva Beatrice Bitney; c. John Earl. Educ: San Francisco Law Sch, 51-52. Polit. & Govt. Pos: Mem, Visitors and Tourism Cmn, Calif, 67-; Alameda Co. chmn, Cmt. to Elect George Murphy to U.S. Senate and to Elect Ronald Reagan Gov. of Calif; S.Alameda Co. chmn, Cmt. to Elect Richard Nixon Pres. of the U.S; adv, numerous local, state and nat. campaigns; mem, Calif. Rep. State Cent. Cmt, currently; mem, Alameda Co. Rep. Finance Cmt, currently. Bus. & Prof. Pos: Owner and adminstr, Stivers' Pvt. Schs, Hayward, Calif, 51- Mil. Serv: Entered as Pvt, Army, 40, released as S/Sgt, 45, after serv. in 34th Div, 151st Field Artil. Bn, ETO, 42-45. Publ: Victory 1966, privately publ, 67. Mem: Am. Legion; Rep. Bus. and Prfnl. Men's Club; Arabian Horse Asn. Rel: Protestant. Mailing Add: 21465 Tanglewood Dr, Castro Valley, Calif. 94546.

STOCK, SHERMAN EDWARD D
b. Milwaukee, Wis, 4/26/28; s. William J. Stock and Ann E. Semrau S; m. 6/19/51 to Sally Ann; c. Anne, Christopher and Kathryn. Educ: Marquette Univ, B.S. in bus. admin, 51; Marquette Univ. Law Sch, LL.B, 58; Alpha Kappa Psi; Delta Theta Phi. Polit. & Govt. Pos: Chmn, Dem. Unit, Wis, 63; legal counsel to U.S. Sen. Gaylord Nelson, Wis, 63-; del, Dem. Co. Coun. and State Dem. Conv, 5 years; del, Dem. Nat. Conv, 64; secy, State Campaign, Lyndon B. Johnson, 64. Bus. & Prof. Pos: Lawyer, 58- Mil. Serv: Entered as E-1, Army, 51, released as 1st Lt, 53, after serv. in 278th Regimental Combat Team; Capt, Army Res, 65. Mem: Wis. Bar Asn. Rel: Episcopal. Legal Res: 11229 Bridget Lane, Hales Corners, Wis. 53130. Mailing Add: Room 570, Federal Bldg, 517 E. Wisconsin Ave, Milwaukee, Wis. 53202.

STOCKDALE, ROBERT EDMONDS R
Ohio State Sen.
b. Defur, Ore, 8/6/16; s. Harry C. Stockdale and Garnett Hamilton S; m. 8/16/41 to Helen Gray; c. Susan, Robert and Ann. Educ: Kent State Univ, B.S. in educ, 40, M.A, 50; West. Res. Univ, grad. work, 50-53. Hon. LL.D, Heidelberg Col, 69. Polit. & Govt. Pos: Mem, city coun, Ravenna, Ohio,

39-41; sheriff, Portage Co, 52-56; Ohio State Rep, 60-62; Ohio State Sen, 62- Bus. & Prof. Pos: Teacher, Paris Twp. High Sch, Ohio, 39-41, Ravenna High Sch, 46-50 and Newton Falls High Sch, 48-50; asst. prof, speech and govt, Kent State Univ, 50-52, polit. sci, 64- Mil. Serv: Entered as Pvt, Marine Corps Res, released as Capt, after serv. in S.Pac, Fleet Marine Force, 43-45. Mem: Am. Asn. of Univ. Prof; Mason; Am. Legion; Elks. Rel: Methodist. Mailing Add: 1485 South Blvd, Kent, Ohio 44240.

STOCKEBRAND, MAYNARD LEON R
Chmn, Woodson Co. Rep. Cent. Cmt, Kans.
b. Yates Center, Kans 12/10/16; s. Edward W. Stockebrand and Edith Weide S; m. 5/25/43 to Lottie Lucille Mabe; c. Henri Lucille, David, H.H. and Sandra. Educ: Yates Cent. High Sch, grad. Polit. & Govt. Pos: Rep. precinct committeeman, Kans, 46-66; chmn, Woodson Co. Rep. Cent. Cmt, 62- Bus. & Prof. Pos: Chmn, Cemetery Bd, Owl Creek Cent. Dist, 48-62. Mil. Serv: Entered as A/S, Navy, 41, released as PO 1/C, 45; Pac, Atlantic and Caribbean Theater Ribbons. Mem: Pres, Kans. Farm Bur, 52-; Kans. Livestock Asn; Kans. Grange. Rel: United Methodist. Mailing Add: R.R. 3, Yates Center, Kans. 66783.

STOCKER, LUELLA HEINE R
Chairwoman, Minn. State Rep. Cmt.
b. Ellendale, N.Dak, 7/24/24; d. Robert Heine and Laura Schwarze H; m. 1/20/46 to Philip Frank Stocker; c. Paul and Tedd. Educ: N.Dak. State Univ, 41-42; Univ. Minnesota, Degree in Nursing, 46; Alpha Gamma Delta. Polit. & Govt. Pos: Precinct chairwoman, Falcon Heights Rep. Cmt, Minn, 61-63 and legis.chairwoman, 63--65; chairwoman, Ramsey Co. Rep. Cmt, 65-67; vice chairwoman, Minn. State Rep. Cmt, 67-69 and chairwoman, 69-; alternate del, Rep. Nat. Conv, 68. Bus. & Prof. Pos: Head Nurse, Medical Floor, Bethesda Hosp, St. Paul, Minn, 47-49. Mem: League of Women Voters. Rel: Lutheran. Mailing Add: 1463 W. Iowa, St. Paul, Minn. 55108.

STOCKMAN, JACQUE R
b. Alamo, N.Dak, 9/21/23; married; c. three. Educ: N.Dak. State Univ; Univ. N.Dak. Polit. & Govt. Pos: N.Dak. State Rep, 55-66; former young Rep. nat. committeeman. Bus. & Prof. Pos: Lawyer and farmer. Mil. Serv: World War II. Rel: Lutheran. Mailing Add: 1215 14th Ave. N, Fargo, N.Dak. 58102.

STOCKMEISTER, CHARLES F. D
N.Y. State Assemblyman
b. Rochester, N.Y, 8/12/14; m. to Ruth Marie Weaver; c. Charlotte and Franklin. Educ: Aquinas Inst. Polit. & Govt. Pos: Mem, Monroe Co. Dem. Cmt, N.Y; party leader, First Ward Dem. Greek Cmt; secy-treas, Greek Dem. Cmt; N.Y. State Assemblyman, 49-50 & 60-, chmn, Cmt. on Conserv. and Joint Legis. Cmt. on Conserv, Natural Resources and Scenic Beauty; secy, Northwest. N.Y. Water Cmn, 50; cmnr, Monroe Co. ABC Bd, 57-59. Bus. & Prof. Pos: Inspection facilities controller, Eastman Kodak. Mem: Pres, Braddock Heights Fire Dept; Lakeview Fire Dept; Liars Club; Greek K. of C; Elks; Barnard Exempts; Steuben Soc. Rel: Pres, St. Mark's Church Men's Club. Mailing Add: 74 Second Ave, Braddock Heights, Rochester, N.Y. 14612. (1967)

STOCKMEYER, NORMAN OTTO R
b. Caseville, Mich, 7/17/07; s. C. August Stockmeyer and Bertha Singleton S; m. 9/16/33 to Lillian R. Hitchman; c. Norman Otto, Paul Kelly, Lona (Mrs. Harris) and Carol Ann. Educ: Wayne State Univ, A.B, 29; Harvard Univ, M.B.A, 32; hon. mem, Omicron Delta Kappa; Beta Eta Circle. Polit. & Govt. Pos: Mem, Wayne Commun. Sch. Bd, Mich, 46-61; treas, 16th Dist. Rep. Party, 54-56; secy, Rep. State Cent. Cmt, 57-65; chmn, Rep. Co. Cmt, 58-62; mem, Wayne Co. Sch. Bd, 61-; Rep. nominee, Secy. State, Mich, 62; bd. gov, Wayne State Univ, 64-67, chmn, 67- Bus. & Prof. Pos: Accountant, A&P Tea Co, 32-35; pres, Wayne Investment Co, Detroit, Mich, 50- Mil. Serv: Entered as Lt.(jg), Navy, 44, released as Lt.(sg), 46, Lt.(Ret), Naval Res; Pre-Pearl Harbor and Atlantic Theatre Ribbons. Mem: Mich. Real Estate Asn.(pres, 60); Detroit Real Estate Bd.(pres, 52); Detroit Athletic Club; Detroit Econ. Club; Detroit Press Club; pres, Mich. Assembly for Ombudsman; NAACP; Am. Civil Liberties Union; trustee, Detroit Tech. Distinguished Alumnus Award, Wayne State Univ, 51; Hon. Alumnus, Univ. Mich. Rel: Congregational. Legal Res: 38042 Glenwood Rd, Westland, Mich. 48185. Mailing Add: 1409 Ford Bldg, Detroit, Mich. 48226.

STOCKSDALE, RUSSELL HORNER D
b. Phila, Pa, 9/17/13; s. Albert Horner Stocksdale and Ann May Knorr S; m. 3/12/49 to Ruth Ellen Bronson; c. Rebecca Ellen, Sally Ann, Mary Elizabeth and David Horner. Educ: Chillicothe Bus. Col, Mo, grad, 33; Harvard Grad. Sch, Seminar for Bank Pres, 62; Am. Inst. Banking. Polit. & Govt. Pos: V.pres, Cole Co. Young Dem, Jefferson City, Mo, 38-40; 25th Ward elec. judge, City of St. Louis, 44-46; councilman, City of Bucklin, 54-56; v.chmn, Mo. State Park Bd, 65; mem, Mo. European Trade Mission, 65; Clay Co. del, Mo. State Dem. Conv, 68; del, Dem. Nat. Conv, 68; pres, Cent. Clay Co. Dem. Club, Mo, 68- Bus. & Prof. Pos: Pres. and dir, Bucklin State Bank, 50-, Nat. Commercial Bank, Liberty, 61- and Farmers Bank, Polo, 64-; dir, Liberty Hills Develop. Corp, Liberty, 66-; pres, Multnomah Investment Co, 67- Mem: Am, Mo. and Clay Co. Bankers Asns; Independent Bankers Asn.(state dir); charter mem, Liberty Hills Country Club; Rotary; Shrine; Odd Fellow; pres, Mo. State Jr. C. of C, 44. Outstanding Boss, Liberty, 64, Mr. Civic Responsibility, 65. Rel: Methodist. Legal Res: 2 S. Fairview, Liberty, Mo. 64068. Mailing Add: National Commercial Bank, Liberty, Mo. 64068.

STOCKSDALE, VAUGHN FRANKLIN D
b. Union City, Ohio, 10/27/39; s. Glen Wagner Stocksdale (deceased) and Ethel Barnhart S; m. 7/20/63 to Barbara Jo. Erbaugh; c. Margaret Ann and Catherine Renee. Educ: Manchester Col, B.A. in polit. sci, 63; Alpha Psi Omega; Dramatics, Debate and Hist. Clubs. Polit. & Govt. Pos: Precinct committeeman; Ohio State Rep, Darke Co, 65-66. Mem: Jr. C. of C; Grange; Farm Bur; Elks; YMCA; Leader, Boy Scouts. Named one of Outstanding Young Men of U.S, U.S. Jaycees. Rel: Church of the Brethren. Mailing Add: R.R. 1, Rossburg, Ohio 45362. (1967)

STOCKSETH, JOSEPH O. D
b. Salt Lake City, Utah, 1/14/19; s. Rudolph Martinus Stockseth and Oline Stephenson S; m. 2/21/47 to Emma Loa Jacobson Hallman; c. Gayle Loa, Dana Lynne, Joel Davis and Michael Chad. Educ: Univ. of Utah; bus. and trade schs. Polit. & Govt. Pos: Precinct chmn, Dem. Party, 56-; Utah State Rep, until 67; chmn, Davis Co. Dem. Party, 62-64; co. pres, Young Dems, 58-60. Mil. Serv: Entered as Pvt, Army Air Force, 41, released as Sgt, 45, after serv. in Eng. Corps and Alaska Defense Command. Mem: Ogden Typographical Union. Rel: Latter-day Saint. Mailing Add: 525 East 400 South, Clearfield, Utah 84015. (1967)

STOCKTON, RUTH S. R
Colo. State Sen.
b. Ridgefield Park, N.J, 6/6/16; d. Arthur Everett Small and Mary Rose Hart S; m. 11/1/37 to Truman Alex Stockton, Jr; c. Alexe R. Educ: Vassar Col, ex 37; Columbia Univ; Colo. Univ. Polit. & Govt. Pos: Co-chmn, 11 West. States Coun. of Young Rep, 46-47; nat. co-chmn, Young Rep, 47-49; nat. committeewoman, Rep. Party, Colo, 54-56; Colo. State Rep, 61-65; Colo. State Sen, 65-; mem, Gov. Cmn. on Ment. Health and Ment. Retardation and Gov. Cmn. on Voc. Rehabilitation, Colo, 66. Mem: Pres. bd. dirs, United Fund, 65 & 66; Bus. & Prfnl. Women; bd, Child Welfare Coun; bd, Hemophila Found; East Jefferson C. of C. Woman of the Year Award, Golden Bus. & Prfnl. Women, 66. Rel:Methodist. Mailing Add: 1765 Glen Dale Dr, Lakewood, Colo. 80215.

STOESSEL, WALTER JOHN, JR.
U.S. Ambassador to Poland
b. Manhattan, Kans, 1/24/20; s. Walter John Stoessel and Katherine Haston S; m. 6/20/46 to Mary Ann Ferrandou; c. Katherine F, Suzanne P. and Christine M. Educ: Stanford Univ, B.A, 41; Russian Inst, Columbia Univ, 49-50; Center of Int. Affairs, Harvard Univ, 59-60; Phi Delta Theta. Polit. & Govt. Pos: Third secy, v.consul, Caracas, Venezuela, 42-44, second secy, v.consul, Moscow, U.S.S.R, 47-49; polit. officer, Bad Nauheim, Germany, 50-52; officer in charge Russian Affairs, Dept. of State, 52-56, dir, exec. secretariat, 60-61, dep. asst. secy. for European Affairs, 65-68; mem. staff, White House, 56; first secy, consul, Paris, France, 56-59; counsr. of embassy, Paris, France, 61-63; minister-counsr, Moscow, U.S.S.R, 63-65; U.S. Ambassador to Poland, 68- Mil. Serv: Ens, Naval Res, 44-46. Mem: Chevy Chase Club. Legal Res: 302 20th St, Santa Monica, Calif. 90402. Mailing Add: c/o American Consulate General, APO N.Y. 09757.

STOIA, VIOREL G. R
State Finance Chmn, S.Dak. Rep. Party
b. Aberdeen, S.Dak, 2/13/24; s. John Stoia and Seana Biliboca S; m. 9/10/49 to Donna Marie Maurseth; c. Marsha Jo, Nancy Kay, Gregory Allen, Thomas John and James Vincent. Educ: Univ. Minn, B.B.A, 49; Am. Col. Life Underwriters, C.L.U, 57. Polit. & Govt. Pos: Campaign mgr. for Congressman Ben Reifel, 60; finance chmn, Brown Co. Rep. Cent. Cmt, S.Dak, 60-63, precinct committeeman, 62-65, co. chmn, 66-; del, S.Dak. State Conv, 62 & 64; Presidential elector, S.Dak. Rep. Party, 68, state finance chmn, 69- Bus. & Prof. Pos: Spec. agent, Northwest. Mutual Life Ins. Co, 50-60, dist. agent, 60-; broker, Aetna Life & Casualty, Prudential Ins. Co, Mass. Mutual Life Ins. Co, Manhattan Life Ins. Co. and Continental Assurance Co, currently. Mil. Serv: Entered as A/S, Navy, 42, released as Chief PO, 46, after serv. in Amphibious Force, Pac. Theatre, 42, 46; Am. Theater Ribbon; Pac. Theater Ribbon; Good Conduct Medal; Philippine Liberation Ribbon. Mem: Nat. Asn. Life Underwriters; Am. Soc. Chartered Life Underwriters; Aberdeen Dist. Life Underwriters Asn; Am. Legion YMCA; C. of C. Distinguished Serv. Award, Aberdeen Jr. C. of C, 55; Nat. Qual. Award, Nat. Asn. Life Underwriters, 54-69, Nat. Sales Achievement Award, 66; Life Underwriter of the Year of S.Dak, S.Dak. Asn. Life Underwriters, 63; Qualifying Mem, Million Dollar Round Table, 65-67 & 69. Legal Res: 1022 N. Main St, Aberdeen, S.Dak. 57401. Mailing Add: P.O. Box 98, Aberdeen, S.Dak. 57401.

STOKES, CARL BURTON D
Mayor, Cleveland, Ohio
b. Cleveland, Ohio, 6/21/27; s. Charles Stokes and Louise Stone S; m. Jan, 1958 to Shirley Edwards; c. Carl, Jr, Cordi and Cordell Edwards. Educ: Univ. Minn, B.S. in Law, 56; Cleveland-Marshall Law Sch, LL.B, 58. Hon. degrees, Cleveland-Marshall Law Sch, Wilberforce Univ, Cent. State Univ, Tufts Univ, Univ. Cincinnati, St. Francis Col.(Maine), Lincoln Univ, Union Col. and Livingston Col; Chubb fel, Yale Univ, 69. Polit. & Govt. Pos: Asst. prosecutor, Cleveland, Ohio, 4 years; mem, Nat. Citizens Cmt. for Commun. Rels; mem, Ohio and Cleveland Bd, Am. for Dem. Action; charter mem, Federated Co. Dem. of Ohio; mem. exec. cmt, Cuyahoga Co. Dem. Party and adv. cmt, Cuyahoga Co. Young Dem; Ohio State Rep, 62-67, mem, Judiciary, Indust. and Labor and Pub. Welfare Cmts, Ohio House of Rep; cand. for Mayor of Cleveland, 65; Mayor, Cleveland, 67-; del, Dem. Nat. Conv, 68. Bus. & Prof. Pos: Attorney, Stokes & Stokes, 58-67. Mil. Serv: Entered as Pvt, Army, 45, released as Cpl, 46, after serv. in ETO. Mem: Cleveland, Cuyahoga and Ohio Bar Asns; Kappa Alpha Psi; Gamma Eta Gamma; Elks; Citizens Adv. Cmt. to Fairhill Psychiat. Hosp; v.pres, bd. trustees and exec. cmt, Cleveland Urban League; exec. cmt, Cleveland Br, NAACP; Mt. Pleasant Commun. Coun, Cleveland Negro Am. Labor Coun. and Cent. Planning Bd. and Group Work Coun, Cleveland Welfare Fedn; Center-City Dist. bd. dirs, Boy Scouts; bd. trustees, Cleveland Legal Aid Soc; Children's Serv. and Cleveland Commun. Fund; bd. dirs, Fair Housing, Inc; U.S. Conf. of Mayors; Nat. League of Cities; Ohio Munic. League. Shavego Serv. Award, Cuyahoga Co. Young Dem; Biennial Citation, ed. of Who's Who in Midwest, 66. Rel: Methodist. Legal Res: 13508 Larchmere Rd, Cleveland, Ohio 44120. Mailing Add: City Hall, Cleveland, Ohio 44114.

STOKES, A. GORDON R
Iowa State Rep.
b. Plymouth City, Iowa, 2/16/98; m. to Laura Bixby. Educ: High Sch. grad. Polit. & Govt. Pos: Iowa State Rep, currently. Bus. & Prof. Pos: Farmer; pres, Oyens Coop. Elevator Co. Mem: Past pres, Co. Farm Bur; charter mem, N.W. Iowa Farm Bur. Asn; dir, First Nat. Bank of LeMars; Mason; Shrine; Eastern Star; Rotary. Rel: Presbyterian; Elder. Mailing Add: Route 1, LeMars, Iowa 51031. (1967)

STOKES, DIANA JOHNSON R
b. New Brunswick, N.J, 1/26/32; d. John Seward Johnson and Ruth Dill J; m. 2/14/59 to Richard Gaines Stokes; c. Lorna Douglass Johnson and Richard

Christopher. Educ: Bennett Jr. Col, Millbrook, N.Y, 52. Polit. & Govt. Pos: Mem, Rep. Women's Club, Loudoun Co. Chap, Va, 60; chmn, Loudoun Co. Rep. Cmt, 64-68. Mem: V.pres, Loudoun Country Day Schs; v.pres. and bd. dirs, Loudoun Hunt. Training thoroughbred horses for track and horse shows. Rel: Episcopal. Mailing Add: Shenstone Farm, Route 1, Box 43, Leesburg, Va. 22075. (1967)

STOKES, J. EMERY R
Co. Chmn, Rep. Party, Pa.
b. Blain, Pa, 2/25/13; s. Warren I. Stokes and Sarah J. Weibley S; m. 12/3/32 to Martha Harper Richter; c. James W. and John W. Educ: Pa. State Univ, 30-31. Polit. & Govt. Pos: Borough concilman, Marysville, Pa, 52-58, tax collector, 58-; co. chmn, Rep. Party, Pa, 60- Mem: Mason; Blue Lodge Consistory; Shrine. Mailing Add: R.D. 1, Box 273, Marysville, Pa. 17053.

STOKES, JOHN MYERS R
Exec. Dir, Rep. Party of Tex.
b. Lufkin, Tex, 9/4/39; s. Carol Myers Stokes and Evelyn Brister S; m. 7/1/61 to Nancy Joan Baldwin; c. John Myers, Jr. Educ: Tex. Tech. Univ, A.B, 61; George Wash. Univ. Law Sch, J.D, 64; Phi Delta Phi; Delta Tau Delta. Polit. & Govt. Pos: Law clerk to Chief Judge Wilson Cowen, U.S. Court Claims, Wash, D.C, 64-66; legis. research dir, Rep. Party of Tex, 68, exec. dir. and spec. counsel, 68- Bus. & Prof. Pos: Assoc. attorney, Cleary, Gottlieb, Steen & Hamilton, Wash, D.C, 66-68. Publ: 'Discovery in the FCC,' 12/63 and 'A Few Irreverent Comments about Antitrust, Agency and Regulation Primary Jurisdiction,' 12/64, George Wash. Law Rev. Mem: Am, Fed. and D.C. Bar Asns. Rel: Lutheran, Mo. Synod. Legal Res: 1514 Forest Trail, Austin, Tex. 78703. Mailing Add: 310 Littlefield Bldg, Austin, Tex. 78701.

STOKES, LOUIS D
U.S. Rep, Ohio
b. Cleveland, Ohio, 2/23/25; s. Louis Charles Stokes and Louise Stone S; m. 8/21/60 to Jeanette Francis; c. Shelley Denise, Angela Rochelle, Louis C. and Lorene Allison. Educ: Cleveland Col. of West. Reserve Univ, 46-48; Cleveland Marshall Law Sch, J.D, 53; Kappa Alpha Psi. Hon. LL.D, Wilburforce Univ, 69. Polit. & Govt. Pos: Mem, Ohio State Adv. Cmt, U.S. Cmn. on Civil Rights, v.chmn, Cleveland Subcmt, 66; U.S. Rep, 21st Dist, Ohio, 69-, mem, Educ. and Labor Cmt. and House Cmt. on Internal Security, U.S. House of Rep, currently. Bus. & Prof. Pos: Private law practice, Cleveland, Ohio, 14 years; mem, Law Firm of Stokes, Character, Terry and Perry; guest lectr, Ashland Col, Kent State Univ, Oberlin Col, Cuyahoga Co. Bar Asn. Seminar, 66, Ohio Acad. of Trial Lawyers Conv, Cleveland, 68, Ohio State Bar Asn. Conv, Toledo, Ohio, 68, Univ. Mich, 68, Conv. of Nat. Asn. of Defense Lawyers in Criminal Cases, Greenbrier, W.Va, 68 and Law Enforcement Seminar, Columbus, Ohio, 68. Mil. Serv: Entered as Pvt, Army, 43, released as Technician 4/C, 46, after serv. in Army Engr. Corp, Am. Theatre, 43-46; Am. Theatre Ribbon; Good Conduct and World War II Victory Medals. Publ: Criminal Law, Cuyahoga Co. Bar Asn, 66. Mem: United Appeal (sect. chmn, 59-61); NAACP (chmn, legal redress cmt, Cleveland Br, 60-65, v.pres, 65-66, exec. bd, currently); Cuyahoga Co. Bar Asn. (chmn, criminal courts cmt, 64-68, past mem. bd. trustees); Boy Scouts (dist. chmn, Center City Dist, 65); YMCA (dist. chmn, Cedar Br, past mem. bd. mgrs, membership dr, 68); bd. mgrs, Rainey Inst; Cleveland Bar Asn. (exec. cmt); manpower planning and develop. cmn, Welfare Fedn; Ohio State Bar Asn.(chmn, criminal justice cmt, bd. dirs); bd. dirs, Nat. Asn. of Defense Lawyers in Criminal Cases, Fair Housing, Inc, Urban League, Citizens League, Am. Bar Asn, John Harlan Law Club, Am. Civil Liberties Union and The Plus Club; bd. dirs. and life mem, Kappa Alpha Psi. Recipient of Distinguished Serv. Award, Cleveland Br, NAACP, 63; Man of the Year Award in Civil Rights, Khayyams Klyb, 63; Cert. of Appreciation, U.S. Cmn. on Civil Rights, 67; Cert. of Award for Serv. Rendered in Behalf of the Annual Scholarship Fund, Champs, Inc, 68; Cert. of Award of Outstanding Commun. Serv, Metrop. Civic Club, 68; YMCA Award for being Gen. Chmn. of Cedar Br. Membership Dr, 68; Man of the Year Award, 27th Ward Civic League, 68; Citizen Award, Bel-Air Civic Club, 68; Champs Citizen of the Year Award, 68; Achievement Award, Cleveland Alumni Chap, Kappa Alpha Psi, 68. Rel: Methodist; V.chmn. and mem. bd. trustees, St. Paul A.M.E. Zion Church. Legal Res: 3130 Albion Rd, Shaker Heights, Ohio 44120. Mailing Add: 1229 Longworth Bldg, Washington, D.C. 20515.

STOKES, MARIAN R
Secy, Sandusky Co. Rep. Cent. and Exec. Cmt, Ohio
b. Woodville, Ohio 4/10/26; d. William Moellman and Freda Myerholtz M; m. 2/1/49 to Dan Stokes; c. Cliff C. II. Educ: High Sch. Grad. Polit. & Govt. Pos: Chairwoman, Sandusky Co. Rep. Women, 63-; pres, Sandusky Co. Women's Rep. Club, 63-; dir, Sandusky Co. Bd. Elec, 66-; precinct committeeman, Rep. Party, Ohio, 66-; second v.pres, Ohio Asn. Elec. Officals, 68-; secy, Sandusky Co. Rep. Cent. and Exec. Cmt, 68- Bus. & Prof. Pos: Prfnl. Flower Arranger, 56-64. Mem: Nat. Soc. DAR; Hayes Garden Club; Garden Club Ohio; Fremont Fedn. Women; Ohio Fedn. Rep. Women; Shrine. Best of Show and Blue Ribbons in Flower and Art Shows. Rel: Episcopal. Legal Res: Route 1, County Rd. 122, Fremont, Ohio 43420. Mailing Add: Board of Elections, Court House, Fremont, Ohio 43420.

STOKLEY, ROBERT W.
b. Denver, 4/13/18; s. Cecil Inlow Stokley and Mary Louise Willson S; m. 12/18/40 to Dorothy Hannah Phillips; c. John Robert, Nancy Louise and Katherine Dorothy. Educ: Univ. Chicago, A.B, 40, grad. study, 41; Indust. Col. Armed Forces, 58-59; Phi Beta Kappa. Polit. & Govt. Pos: With estimates div, U.S. Bur. Budget, 41 & 43-54; planning officer, Fed. Civil Defense Admin, 54-58; dep. dir. prog. and policy officer, Off. Civil & Defense Mobilization, 58-61; dir. prog. develop, Off. Emergency Planning, 61-69; chief-of-party, Pub. Admin. Serv, Bangkok, Thailand, 69- Mem: Pres, Emergency Cmt. for Preservation of Potomac Palisades, 65-67. Legal Res: 4617 Clark Place N.W, Washington, D.C. 20007. Mailing Add: PAS USOM/PA, APO, San Francisco, Calif. 96346.

STOLBERG, IRVING JULES D
b. Phila, Pa, 9/24/36; s. Ralph B. Stolberg and Lillian Blank S; single. Educ: Univ. Calif, Los Angeles, B.A, 58; Boston Univ, M.A, 66. Polit. & Govt. Pos: Pres, W.Los Angeles Young Dem, 57-58; mem. exec. cmt. and chmn. nominating cmt, New Haven McCarthy for Pres, 68; del, Conn. Dem. State Conv, 68; alternate del, Dem. Nat. Conv, 68; founder and mem. exec. cmt, New Haven Dem. Reform Movement, 68-69; founding mem, Caucus of Conn. Dem, 68-69; justice of the peace, New Haven, 68- Bus. & Prof. Pos: Int. campus adminstr, U.S. Nat. Student Asn, 58-59; prog. dir, Boston Int. Student Center, 59-60; midwest dir, World Univ. Serv, 60-63; leader, Experiment in Int. Living, Austria, 61, Turkey, 64 and Tanzania, 65; participant, World Univ. Serv. Seminar, Asia, 62, leader, World Univ. Serv. Team, Latin Am, 63; teaching fel, Boston Univ, 64-66; asst. prof. geog. South. Conn. State Col, 66-; participant, U.S. Off. Educ. African Seminar, Ethiopia, 67. Publ: 'Campus International Awareness,' In: The Idea of a Student, 59; 'Asian Students,' Intercollegian, 1/63; 'Geography and Peace Research,' Prfnl. Geogr, 7/65. Mem: Asn. Am. Geogr; Peace Research Cmt; Am. Geog. Soc; African Studies Asn; Conn. coordinator, Nat. Coun. Geog. Educ; Am. Asn. Univ. Prof.(chap. pres, 67-68). Mailing Add: 325 Mansfield St, New Haven, Conn. 06511.

STOLDT, ROBERT JAMES R
Chmn, Seneca Co. Rep. Exec. Cmt, Ohio
b. Attica, Ohio, 8/11/25; s. Joseph T. Stoldt and Sheila Glasgow S; m. 5/10/48 to Myrial Sheerer; c. Linda, Barbara and Robert. Educ: Heidelberg Col, B.A, 49; Pi Kappa Delta; Heidelberg Young Rep. Polit. & Govt. Pos: Precinct Committeeman, Rep. Party, Ohio, 50-; mem, Seneca Co. Rep. Exec. Cmt, 52-, secy, 58-60, chmn, 60-; chmn, Seneca Co. Rep. Cent. Cmt, 64-; alternate del, Rep. Nat. Conv, 64, del, 68. Bus. & Prof. Pos: Partner, Sheerer & Stoldt, Inc, 50- Mil. Serv: Entered as Pvt, Marine Corps, 43, released as Cpl, 46, after serv. in 2nd Marine Div, Pac. Area, 44-46; Okinawa Ribbon; Occupation of Japan Medal; Good Conduct Medal. Mem: Ohio Farm and Power Equipment Asn; Shrine; Scottish Rite; F&AM; Am. Legion; Elks; Rotary. Rel: Lutheran. Mailing Add: 207 N. Liberty St, Attica, Ohio 44807.

STOLL, NORMAN ADOLPH D
Mem, Dem. Nat. Cmt, Ore.
b. Milwaukee, Wis, 11/18/12; s. Herman Fred Stoll and Frieda Scharpf S; m. 6/7/41 to Helen V. Nicholas; c. Norman Robert and Julia Hart. Educ: Univ. Wis, Ph.B, 32, LL.B, 34; Theta Chi. Polit. & Govt. Pos: Legal research asst. and attorney, Wash, D.C, 34-35; attorney, Securities and Exchange Cmn, 35-42, Bd. Econ. Warfare, 42-43; chief legis. secy. and asst. solicitor, Dept. of Commerce, 46-48; gen. counsel, Bonneville Power Admin, 48-54; consult, President's Water Resources Policy Cmn, 50; legal consult. water policy, U.S. Bur. Budget, 51-52; consult. to solicitor, Dept. of Interior, 54-55; spec. asst. to Attorney Gen, Ore, 57-61; alternate chmn, Multnomah Co. Dem. Cent. Cmt, 59-; del, Ore. State Dem. Platform Conv, 60; mem, Dem. Nat. Cmt, Ore, currently; del, Dem. Nat. Conv, 68. Bus. & Prof. Pos: Lawyer, Reinhardt, Coblens & Stoll, 54-; mem. faculty law, Univ. Ore, 55, Northwest. Col. of Law, 56-60. Mil. Serv: Army, 43-46, released as Capt, after serv. in war plans div, Judge Adv. Gen. Off, 44, War Crimes Off, 45-46 and prosecution staff, Nuremburg Trials, 45. Mem: V.chmn, Ore. State Law Improv. Cmt, 63-; Am, Fed. and Ore. State Bar Asns; Am. Soc. Int. Law; Am. Judicature Soc; Judge Adv. Asn; Am. Vet. Cmt; City Club of Portland. Mailing Add: 11000 S.W. Collina Ave, Portland, Ore. 97219. (1967)

STOLL, RICHARD PHILIP D
Chmn, Sainte Genevieve Co. Dem. Cmt, Mo.
b. Festus, Mo, 5/27/24; s. Philip Stoll and Agnes Kreitler S; m. 1/17/47 to Betty June Hamilton; c. Philip Brad, Clay Richard and Sarah Leigh. Educ: Univ. Mo, Columbia, $1\frac{1}{2}$ years. Polit. & Govt. Pos: Chmn, Ste. Genevieve Co. Draft Bd, Mo, 15 years; chmn, Ste. Genevieve Co. Dem. Cmt, 63- Bus. & Prof. Pos: Ins. Agent, Prudential Ins. Co, Ste. Genevieve, 57. Mil. Serv: Entered as Seaman, Navy, 43, released as Yeoman 2/C, 46, after serv. in Aleutian Islands, N.Pac. Theater, 43-46; N.Pac. Ribbon; Am. Theater Ribbon; Good Conduct Medal. Mem: Life Underwriters; VFW; Am. Legion; K. of C; Lions; C. of C; Jaycees; Leader Club. Rel: Catholic. Mailing Add: 218 St. Jude, Ste. Genevieve, Mo. 63670.

STOLLE, HELLMUT W. R
Ill. State Rep.
b. Berlin, Germany; c. four. Educ: Voc. Sch. Polit. & Govt. Pos: Ill. State Rep, 62-64 & 66- Bus. & Prof. Pos: Self-employed bakery, delicatessen and catering bus, 44- Mem: C. of C.(former pres, secy. and treas); Retail Bakers Gr. Chicago (mem. bd. dirs, 47-, treas, 3 years, pres, 3 years); Am. Bakers Asn. Conv.(chmn. retail session, 61-); Lions (dir. and chmn, Boys and Girls Cmn. Higgins-Norwood Lions Club, 66-); Pan-Am. Cycling Cmt; past dir, Amateur Bicycle League Am; chmn, Norwood Park Golden Wheel Bicycle Derby, 18 years. Mailing Add: 6111 Northwest Hwy, Chicago, Ill. 60631.

STOLLER, MURRAY ARTHUR D
b. N.Y.C, 3/16/19; s. A.H.L. Stoller (deceased) and Anna Sugar S. (deceased); m. 12/24/41 to Arlene B. Witt; c. Judith (Mrs. Carl T. Curtis, Jr) and Laurel A. (deceased). Educ: Univ. Va. Col. Law, LL.B, 41; Va. South. Col, 47-52; Univ. Richmond, cert. of achievement in Christian educ, 63. Polit. & Govt. Pos: City councilman, Roanoke, Va, 62-66, mayor, 62-64; Dem. nominee for Sixth Cong. Dist, 66. Bus. & Prof. Pos: Assoc, Law Firm of Jesse, Phillips, Klinge & Kendrick, Arlington, Va, 41-42; practice of law, Roanoke, 45- Mil. Serv: Entered as Pvt, Army, 42, released as Sgt, 44, after serv. in Pub. Rels. Off, Ft. Monroe, Va, Inf. Instr. and Platoon Sgt, New Cumberland, Pa, Mil. Police Sgt, Ft. Benning, Ga, 42-44; Am. Theater Ribbon; Good Conduct and Victory Medals. Publ: Ed, Am. Legion Bul, Roanoke, Va, 45- Mem: Va. and Am. Bar Asns; past dir, Roanoke Bar Asn; past comdr, Am. Legion; past chef de gare, 40 et 8; past dir, Jr. C. of C. Authorized to perform marriages, 47-, married over 1000 couples. Rel: Baptist; Deacon and Clerk, Calvary Baptist Church, Roanoke, Va. Legal Res: 2907 Oak Crest Ave. S.W, Roanoke, Va. 24015. Mailing Add: 709 Colonial Bank Bldg, Roanoke, Va. 24011.

STOLZ, MABEL SMITH D
Mem. Shiawasse Co. Dem. Exec. Cmt, Mich.
b. Alpena, Mich, 3/15/11; d. Thomas J. Smith and Susan Hazelgrove S; m. 7/6/31 to Armond J. Stolz; c. Dr. Benjamin and Joseph W. Educ: Cent. Mich.

Univ, A.B, 38. Polit. & Govt. Pos: Secy, Shiawassee Co. Dem. Cmt, Mich, 60, chmn, 63-67; mem, Credentials Cmt, Dem. Nat. Conv, 64 and Platform Cmt, 68; mem, Shiawassee Co. Dem. Exec. Cmt, 69- Bus. & Prof. Pos: Teacher, Owosso Pub. Schs, Mich, 45- Mem: Owosso Educ, Asn.(pres, 53-56); League Women Voters Owosso (mem. bd. dirs); del, Regional Coun. Owosso Educ. Asn, Mich. Educ. Asn. Rel: Unitarian. Mailing Add: 202 W. North, Owosso, Mich. 48867.

STONE, CHARLES D. D
Pa. State Rep.
b. Beaver, Pa, 4/11/20; s. Charles H. Stone and Emily Claire S; m. to Virginia M. Smith; c. Three sons. Educ: Grove City Col, A.B; Univ. Pittsburgh Law Sch, LL.B, Geneva Col; Varsity Letters in Football, Swimming and Track; Pi Gamma Mu. Polit. & Govt. Pos: Mem, Beaver Co. Munic. Authority, Pa; sheriff, Beaver Co; mem, Parking Authority, Aliquippa; solicitor, Hopewell Twp; Pa. State Rep, 52- Bus. & Prof. Pos: Attorney; admitted to practice before Supreme and Superior Courts of Pa. and Beaver Co. Courts. Mil. Serv: Entered as Pvt, Army, 42, released as Capt, 46, after serv. overseas in N.Africa and Italy, 2 years. Mem: Bd. dirs, Aliquippa Hosp. Asn; Citizens' Adv. Cmt. to Juvenile Court of Beaver Co; Beaver Co. Hist. Soc; SAR; VFW. Rel: Presbyterian. Mailing Add: 100 N. Brodhead Rd, Aliquippa, Pa. 15001. (1967)

STONE, CHARLES L. D
V.Chmn, Orange Co. Cent. Cmt, Calif.
b. South Bend, Ind, 1/1/36; s. Charles P. Stone and Angela C. Wagner S; m. 1/15/55 to Joyce E. Stitz; c. Sonie L, Charles J. and Lynda M. Educ: San Diego Jr. Col, 56-59. Polit. & Govt. Pos: V.pres, Calif. Fedn. Young Dem, 60-61; mem, Huntington Beach Unified High Sch. Dist. Adv. Bd, Calif, 66-67; del, Dem. Nat. Conv, 68; v.chmn, Orange Co. Cent. Cmt, Calif, 68- Bus. & Prof. Pos: Mgr, N.Am. Rockwell, 66-69. Mil. Serv: Entered as Basic Airman, Ind. Air Nat. Guard, 53, released as Airman 2/C, 56, after serv. in Res. Mailing Add: 17271 Avalon Lane, Huntington Beach, Calif. 92647.

STONE, CLARENCE F. D
Chmn, Lander Co. Dem. Party, Neb.
b. Rockland, Idaho, 9/7/04; s. Friend Stone and Josephine Johnson S; m. 12/27/26 to Leolo Larsen; c. Keith L, Jeraldine (Mrs. Wirthlin) and Bruce W; Polit. & Govt. Pos: Chmn, Lander Co. Dem. Party, Nev, 45- Bus. & Prof. Pos: Gen. Construction Supt, S.Pac. R.R. Co, 27-45; Gen. Contractor, 45- Mem: Free & Accepted Masons. Rel: Protestant. Legal Res: Battle Mountain, Nev. 89820. Mailing Add: Box 514, Battle Mountain, Nev. 89820.

STONE, DAVID BONESTEEL R
Ariz. State Rep.
b. Ft. MacPherson, Ga, 6/1/13; s. Charles Bertody Stone and Katharine Bonesteel S; m. 5/22/37 to Isabella Scott Roby; c. Mary Isabella, David Bonesteel, Jr, Susan Eleanor, Katharine Alexandra and Peter Edward. Educ: U.S. Mil. Acad, West Point, B.S, 35. Polit. & Govt. Pos: Ariz. State Rep, Pima Co, 67- Bus. & Prof. Pos: Research analysis, Hughes Aircraft, Tucson, 62-64; sales mgr, Prickett Realty, 64- Mil. Serv: Entered as 2nd Lt, Army, 35, released as Col, 66, after serv. in Armor Unit, Iceland and Third Armored Cavalry Regt, Panama, 35-60; Bronze Star; Various Theater Ribbons. Mem: West Point Soc. South. Ariz.(pres, 68-). Rel: Catholic. Mailing Add: 85 Calle Primorosa, Tucson, Ariz. 85716.

STONE, DELBERT JAMES R
b. Rupert, Vt, 7/18/84; s. John Mark Stone and Eloya Shaw S; m. 12/24/41 to Florence Emery; c. Ruth Ann (Mrs. Clayton W. Pearce). Educ: Burr and Burtom Sem, Manchester, Vt. Polit. & Govt. Pos: Vt. State Rep, 61-65. Mil. Serv: Vt. Nat. Guard, 20 years. Mem: Odd Fellows. Rel: Congregational. Mailing Add: Westminster, Vt. 05158.

STONE, ERNEST D
State Supt. Educ, Ala.
b. Crossville, Ala, 12/24/12; s. Samuel Washington Stone and Belinda K. McDaniel S; m. 8/18/34 to Katherine Gann; c. William Ernest. Educ: Jacksonville State Univ, B.S, 33; Univ. Ala, B.A, 38, M.A, 39; Samford Univ, LL.D, 62; grad. study, Mich. State Univ. and Columbia Univ; Phi Delta Kappa; Kappa Phi Kappa; Kappa Delta Pi; Delta Chi. Polit. & Govt. Pos: Del, Dem. Nat. Conv, 56; State Supt. Educ, Ala, 67- Bus. & Prof. Pos: Prin, Kilpatrick Jr. High Sch, Crossville, Ala, 33-36, Crossville High Sch, 36-42; supt, DeKalb Co. Schs, Ft. Payne, Ala, 42-43; dir, Lab. Schs. and supt, Jacksonville City Schs, Ala, 46-67; Govt. Study Educ, Marshall Aid Countries, 50; mem, Lacky-Edwards Cmt. Sch. Finance, 58; Ala. rep, Exploring Educ. Needs for Sci. Future, 60. Mil. Serv: Entered as Seaman, Navy, 43, released as Lt. Comdr, 46, after serv. in Am. and Pac. Theatres. Publ: Eighty-Three Case Studies, Univ. Ala. Press, 39; 'Preventive Medicine,' Sch. Exec, 38; 'Mr. Stone Goes to Europe,' Ala. Sch. J, 50. Mem: Ala. and Nat. Educ. Asns; Ala. Asn. Sec. Sch. Prin; Nat. Coun. Chief State Sch. Officers; Rotary; Mason; Am. Legion; Shrine. Ala. Most Promising Young Educator's Award, 38. Rel: Baptist; Deacon. Legal Res: 403 Edgewood Dr, Jacksonville, Ala, 36265. Mailing Add: State Dept. of Education, Montgomery, Ala. 36104.

STONE, FLOYD N. R
b. Halifax, Vt, 8/20/97; m. to Kathryn Moxley; c. Two sons and two daughters. Educ: Clawson Hamilton Bus. Col, Brattleboro. Polit. & Govt. Pos: Lister, selectman and sch. dir, Vt, several years; Vt. State Rep, 65-67. Bus. & Prof. Pos: Dairy farmer. Rel: Community Church. Mailing Add: Jacksonville, Vt. 05342. (1967)

STONE, GEORGE WILLIAM D
Mayor, Choctaw, Okla.
b. Byars, Okla, 4/17/19; s. William Alexander Stone and Martha Jones S; m. 5/15/37 to Maskell L. Weed; c. George W, Jr, Chester L, David M. and Richard E. Educ: Okla. Baptist Univ, A.B, 48. Polit. & Govt. Pos: Dem. precinct chmn, Oklahoma City, Okla; alternate del, Dem. Nat. Conv, 60, 64 & 68; trustee and mayor, Choctaw, Okla, 67- Mailing Add: 1141 W. Sheridan, Oklahoma City, Okla. 73106.

STONE, GORDON EARL R
Chmn, Reno Co. Rep. Party, Kans.
b. Andover, S.Dak, 11/27/09; s. Earl L. Stone and Frances Smith S; m. 10/18/58 to Helen Weeks; c. Robert, Allen and Richard. Educ: Univ. S.Dak, B.S; Wash. Univ, M.D; Alpha Omega Alpha; Phi Chi. Polit. & Govt. Pos: Chmn, Reno Co. Rep. Party, Kans, 67- Bus. & Prof. Pos: On the staff, Grace Hosp. and St. Elizebeth Hosp. Mil. Serv: Maj, Army, 42-46, Fourth Serv. Co, U.S. Army. Mem: Am. Med. Asn; Kans. Med. Soc. Rel: Protestant. Legal Res: 226 Curtis, Hutchinson, Kans. 67501. Mailing Add: 519 Wiley Bldg, Hutchinson, Kans. 67501.

STONE, HARRIET REED R
b. Danby, Vt, 9/2/02; m. to Howard L. Stone; c. Three sons, one daughter. Educ: Burr and Burton Sem, Manchester. Polit. & Govt. Pos: Town agent and grand juror, E. Arlington, Vt, town treas, 9 years, town clerk, 14 years; cemetery cmnr, 9 years; overseer of the poor, 7 years; auditor, 8 years and justice of the peace, 12 years; Vt. State Rep, 59-67. Bus. & Prof. Pos: Housewife. Mailing Add: Box 144, East Arlington, Vt. 05250. (1967)

STONE, IVAN Conservative
Minn. State Rep.
b. Brown Co, 1907; married; c. Seven. Educ: Univ. Minn. Col. of Agr. Polit. & Govt. Pos: Minn. State Rep, 60- Bus. & Prof. Pos: Farmer and hatcheryman. Mil. Serv: World War II; Bronze Star. Mailing Add: 614 N. Jefferson St, New Ulm, Minn. 56073. (1967)

STONE, J. W. R
Mem, Mo. State Rep. Cmt.
b. Fortescue, Mo, 11/6/27; s. Perry Allen Stone and May Murrah S; single. Educ: Northwest Mo. State Col, B.S. in sec. educ; Univ. Mo, Kans. City, M.A. in educ. admin. and post grad. work; Kappa Delta Pi; Pi Omega Pi. Polit. & Govt. Pos: Committeeman, Minton Twp. Rep. Party, Mo, 52-; mem, Sixth Cong. Dist. Rep. Cmt, 58- and Judicial Cmt; chmn, Holt Co. Rep. Cent. Cmt, 58-; mem, Town Coun, Fortescue, 62-; mem, Mo. State Rep. Cmt, 64-; mem. bd, Northwest Mo. Econ. Opportunity Corp, secy. and treas, 65-; regional bd. dir, Voc. Rehabilitation, Mo, 67-; del. representing Mo. State Rep. Cmt. at the Presidential Inauguration, 69. Bus. & Prof. Pos: Farmer, Fortescue, Mo, 44-; instr, bus. dept, Region III Sch. Dist, Craig, 57-59; supt. of schs, Holt Co, 59-61; supt. of schs, Region III, Craig, 61- Mil. Serv: Entered as Pvt, Army, 50, released as Sgr. 1/C, 52, after serv. in 1905th Engr. Aviation Bn. Mem: Nat. Educ. Asn; Am. Asn. of Sch. Adminstr; Mo. State Teachers Asn; Mo. Sch. Adminstr. Asn; Holt Co. Teachers Asn; past v.pres, Mo. Coun. of Churches; Am. Legion; Mason; York Rite; Scottish Rite; Shrine; Farm Bur; Red Cross; Heart Found; Cancer Soc; Tau Kappa Epsilon; Eastern Star; official del. representing U.S. and Methodist Church, World Conf. on Christian Educ, Tokyo, Japan, 58; off. del, World Methodist Coun, Oslo, Norway, 61; bd. mem. and v.pres, Welsey Found, Northwest Mo. State Col, 68-; del. representing U.S. to Russia, Hungary and Denmark for the Research Center for the Study of Socialist Educ. and the Annual Comparative Educ. Society's Seminar and Field Study. Basketball letterman, 5 years, track, 2 years. Rel: Methodist; Church sch. supt, adult Bible instr; lay leader, Maryville Dist, United Methodist Church, 68- Legal Res: Fortescue, Mo. 64452. Mailing Add: Craig R-III School District, Craig, Mo. 64437.

STONE, NORMA WALSH R
Mem, N.Y. State Rep. Cmt.
b. Marcellus, N.Y, 8/24/95; d. Thomas F. Walsh and Luella Spingler W; m. 6/14/16 to Horace M. Stone, wid; c. Norma Suzann, Nan S. (Mrs. James Farrell), Horace M, Jr. and Marguerite S. (Mrs. John M. Mead). Polit. & Govt. Pos: Del, Rep. State Conv, 50, 54 & 56; v.chmn, Onondaga Co. Rep. Cmt, 50-65; del, Rep. Nat. Conv, 52, 56, 60 & 64; del, Judicial Conv, 55; mem, N.Y. State Rep. Cmt, currently. Woman of the Year in Politics Award, Bus. & Prfnl. Women, Syracuse, N.Y. Rel: Presbyterian. Mailing Add: 2 North St, Marcellus, N.Y. 13108.

STONE, PAUL D
Ill. State Rep.
b. Newton, Ill, 9/21/15; s. Claude L. Stone and Ruth Stewart S; m. 2/7/39 to Thelma Lucille Jones; c. Elaine, Paul L, Michael L. and Marsha R. Educ: Univ. Ill, B.S, 40, Law Sch, LL.B, 42. Polit. & Govt. Pos: Appeal agent, Ill. Selective Serv. Syst, 48-; Ill. State Rep, 51-52 & 67- Bus. & Prof. Pos: Past pres, Moultrie Co. Bar Asn; chmn, Teachers Col. Bd, Ill. and Bd. of Gov, State Col. & Univ; mem, Univ. Civil Serv. Merit Syst, West. Ill. Univ. Found. and Ill. State Univ; Found. Mem: Moultrie Co. and Am. Bar Asns; Am. Judicature Soc; Am. Acad. Polit. and Soc. Sci; Mason; Kiwanis; Elks; Moose. Rel: Methodist. Mailing Add: 16 S. Washington, Sullivan, Ill. 61951.

STONE, RICHARD BERNARD D
Fla. State Sen.
b. N.Y.C, 9/22/28; s. Alfred Stone and Lily Abbey S; m. to Marlene Singer; c. Nancy, Amy and Elliott. Educ: Harvard Univ, B.A. cum laude, 49; Columbia Univ. Law Sch, LL.B, 54; Varsity Swimming Team, Harvard Univ. Polit. & Govt. Pos: City attorney, Miami, Fla, 66-67; Fla. State Sen, 48th Dist, 67- Bus. & Prof. Pos: Former secy, Royal Castle Syst, Inc; former mem. bd. dirs, Army Eagle Navy, Inc; partner, Stone, Bittell, Langer, Blass & Corrigan, currently. Mem: Dade Co, Am. and Inter-Am. Bar Asns; Corp. Banking and Bus. Law Cmt; Fla. State Bar; Am. Judicature Soc; Tiger Bay Club; Dade Family Opera; S.Fla. Coun, Boy Scouts; Moose; Elks; K. of P; Rotary. Acad. Awards at Harvard Univ; Best Freshman Sen. Rel: Jewish. Legal Res: 11880 S.W, 63rd Ave, South Miami, Fla. 33143. Mailing Add: 28 W. Flagler St, Miami, Fla. 33130.

STONE, THOMAS MITCHELL D
Miss. State Rep.
b. Holly Springs, Miss, 1/24/15; s. Thomas Calvin Stone and Lillie Caviness S; m. 8/21/40 to Annie Ruth Holley; c. Tommye Ann (Mrs. Gale Goode), Mitch, Jr, Cherri Marke and Merri Holley 'Pebble'. Educ: Sunflower Jr. Col, 37-38; Univ. Ala, 38-40. Polit. & Govt. Pos: Miss. State Rep, Benton, Desoto and Marshall Counties, Dist. 4, 68- Bus. & Prof. Pos: Sch. teacher & coach, 40-43 & 45-63. Mil. Serv: Entered as Pvt, Navy, 43, released as Radar 2/C, 45, after serv. in U.S.S. ATR 21. Mem: VFW; Am. Legion; Lions. Rel: Methodist. Mailing Add: P.O. Box 6, Potts Camp, Miss. 38659.

STONE, WILLIAM CLEMENT R
b. Chicago, Ill, 5/4/02; s. Louis Stone and Anna M. Gunn S; m. 6/16/23 to Jessie V. Tarson; c. Wendell Clement, Donna (Mrs. David Bradshaw) and Nor-

man. Educ: Detroit Col. of Law, 20; Northwest. Univ, 30-32; hon. J.D, Monmouth Col, Ill, 63; hon. L.H.D, Interlochen Center for Arts, Mich, 64; hon. Litt.D, Nat. Col. of Chiropractic, Lombard, Ill, 69; Alpha Kappa Psi. Polit. & Govt. Pos: Alternate del, Rep. Nat. Conv, 68. Bus. & Prof. Pos: Pres. and dir, Combined Am. Ins. Co, Dallas, Tex, 45-, Combined Ins. Co. of Am, Chicago, Ill, 47-, Hearthstone Ins. Co. of Mass, Boston, 49- and First Nat. Casualty Co, Fond du Lac, Wis, 54-; ed. and publisher, Success Unlimited Mag, Chicago, Ill, 54- Publ: Success Through a Positive Mental Attitude (w. Napoleon Hill), 60, Success System That Never Fails, 62 and The Other Side of the Mind (w. Norma Lee Browning), 64, Prentice-Hall. Mem: Chicago Asn. Health Underwriters; Am. Mgt. Asn; Am. Risk and Ins. Asn; Chicago Asn. Commerce and Indust; Exec. Club, Chicago; Ill. State C. of C; Ins. Fedn. Ill; Int. Asn. Health Underwriters; Sales Mkt. Execs, Chicago; Sales Mkt. Execs. Int, Inc; Soc. Midland Authors; United Shareholders of Am; Am. Life Conv; Art Inst, Chicago; Center for Adv. Intercultural Studies; Chicago Hist. Soc; Chicago Planetarium Soc; Int. Soc. Gen. Semantics; Lyric Opera, Chicago; Auditorium Theater Coun; Ravinia Festival Asn; Am-Scandinavian Found; Ancient Accepted Scottish Rite; Mason (33°); Chicago Press Club; Kiwanis, North Shore; Mich. Shores Country Club; Travelers' Clubs Int; Univ. Ill. Pres. Club. Layman of the Year, Relig. Heritage of Am, 62; Horatio Alger Award, 63; Church Layman of the Year, Church Fedn. Gr. Chicago, 68; Daniel A. Lord Award, Loyola Acad, 68; Boys' Club Golden Keystone Award, Boys' Clubs of Am, 68. Rel: Presbyterian. Legal Res: 8 Milburn Park, Evanston, Ill. 60201. Mailing Add: 5050 Broadway, Chicago, Ill. 60640.

STONE, WILLIAM FRANCIS D
Va. State Sen.
b. Stoneville, N.C, 9/29/09; m. to M. Ivey Courtney. Educ: Wash. and Lee Univ, LL.B, 33; Atlanta Law Sch, LL.M, 35. Polit. & Govt. Pos: Va. State Del, 54-56; Va. State Sen, 58- Bus. & Prof. Pos: Lawyer. Mailing Add: Box 1432, Martinsville, Va. 24112. (1967)

STONER, RICHARD BURKETT D
Dem. Nat. Committeeman, Ind.
b. Ladoga, Ind, 5/15/20; s. Edward Norris Stoner and Florence Burkett S; m. 2/22/42 to Virginia Austin; c. Pamela, Richard B, Jr, Benjamin, Janet, Rebecca and Joanne. Educ: Ind. Univ, B.S, 41; Harward Law Sch, LL.B, 47; Beta Gamma Sigma; Blue Key; Sigma Nu. Polit. & Govt. Pos: Del, Dem. State Conv, Ind, 52, 54, 56, 58, 60 and 62; precinct committeeman, Bartholomew Co, Ind, 52-58; del, Dem. Nat. Conv, 56, 60, 64 & 68; treas, Bartholomew Co. Dem. Cent. Cmt, 58, chmn, 58-60; dir, Ind. Employ. Security Bd, 61-69, pres, 64; chmn, Ninth Dist. Dem. Cmt, 62-66; Dem. nat. committeeman, Ind, 66-; mem, Ind. Adv. Cmn. on Academic Facilities, currently. Bus. & Prof. Pos: Dir. personnel, Cummins Engine Co, 53-55, v.pres. personnel and mfg, 55-57; v.pres. opers, 57-60, exec. v.pres. opers, 60-64 and Corp. exec. v.pres. and gen. mgr, 64-69, v.chmn. bd, 69-; dir, Am. Fletcher Nat. Bank and Trust Co, currently; mem. exec. cmt, West. Hwy. Inst. and Machinery and Allied Prod. Inst, currently. Mil. Serv: Entered as Pvt, Army, released as Capt, Finance Dept. Mem: Am. Mgt. Asn; Indianapolis Athletic Club; bd. dir, Columbus Chap, NAACP. Rel: Christian Church. Mailing Add: 2770 Franklin Dr, Columbus, Ind. 47201.

STONUM, ELIZABETH ANN R
Mem, Calif. State Rep. Cent. Cmt.
b. Bowling Green, Ohio, 8/23/26; d. Glen Drum Greek and Florence Evelyn Utter G; m. 6/23/46 to Robert Gale Stonum; c. Gayle Kathleen and Neil Allan. Educ: Modesto Jr. Col, A.A. Polit. & Govt. Pos: Mem, Calif. State Rep. Cent. Cmt, 68- Mem: Eastern Star; Calif. Cong. Parents and Teachers; Modesto Commun. Concert Asn. Hon. life mem, Calif. Cong. Parents and Teachers. Rel: Protestant. Legal Res: 1905 Devonshire Ave, Modesto, Calif. 95353. Mailing Add: P.O. Box 748, Modesto, Calif. 95353.

STOPCZYNSKI, STEPHEN D
Mich. State Rep.
b. Detroit, Mich, 1/1/11; married; c. Steven, Jr, Stanley and Thaddeus. Educ: St. Stanislaus High Sch; Highland Park Ford Trade Sch; Northeast. High Sch. Polit. & Govt. Pos: Precinct del, Mich; del. to Constitutional Conv; Mich. State Rep, 64- Bus. & Prof. Pos: Machinist. Mem: Holy Name Soc; Dem. State Cent. Cmt; Wayne Co. AFL-CIO Coun; N.Detroit Dom Polski Asn; v.pres, Pulaski Dem. Club of N. Detroit; v.pres. Polish Am. Polit. Club; Polish Roman Cath. Union, Polish Cent. Citizens Cmt. Rel: Roman Catholic. Mailing Add: 13463 Eureka, Detroit, Mich. 48212.

STOPKA, JOHN P. D
b. 1928. Educ: Univ. Minn. Polit. & Govt. Pos: Elected Mayor of Columbia Hts, 51, served 4 terms; honored 52 Nat. Dem. Conv. as youngest mayor; del. to 56 Nat. Conv. Bus. & Prof. Pos: Printer. Mil. Serv: Army occupation forces in Korea, 47-48. Mailing Add: 4338 McLeod St. N.E, Columbia Heights, Minn. 55421.

STOPYRA, AGNES THERESA D
V.Chmn, Cayuga Co. Dem. Party, N.Y.
b. Auburn, N.Y, 12/18/19; d. Sam DeLuca and Teresa Luciano D; m. 6/14/39 to Walter Joseph Stopyra; c. Thomas Patrick and Mark A. Educ: Auburn East. High Sch, N.Y, grad, 38. Polit. & Govt. Pos: V.chmn, Cayuga Co. Dem. Party, N.Y, 63- Bus. & Prof. Pos: Legal secy, Thomas Stopyra Law Off, Auburn, N.Y, 65-67. Mem: Past co. chmn, Am. Legion Auxiliary, Christopher Columbus Commemorative Cmt. and Cayuga Co. Dem. Ladies Club; secy. to bd. dirs, Nat. Found. March of Dimes. Young Cayugan Appreciation Award, Auburn Jr. C. of C, 60; Commun. Serv. Award, Auburn Serv. League, 61. Rel: Roman Catholic. Mailing Add: 97 Perrine St, Auburn, N.Y. 13021.

STOREY, BOB WILSON R
Kans. State Sen.
b. Siloam Springs, Ark, 9/5/34; s. Jess Burl Storey and Gertrude Feaster S; m. 8/2/58 to Patricia Lou Moon; c. Bradley Lewis and Jennifer Kay. Educ: Independence Jr. Col, 2 years; Washburn Univ, B.B.A, 60; Washburn Law Sch, LL.B, 63; Phi Delta Theta. Polit. & Govt. Pos: Asst. gen. counsel, Kans. Corp. Cmn, 63-66; Kans. State Sen, 68- Bus. & Prof. Pos: Attorney-at-law, Tilton & Storey, Topeka, Kans, 63-; motor carrier exam, Kans. Corp. Cmn, 66-68. Mil. Serv: Entered as E-2, Army, 57, released as Pfc, 57, after serv. in Army Signal Corps. Mem: Am. Kans. and Topeka Bar Asns; Am. and Kans. Trial Lawyers Asns; Phi Alpha Delta; C. of C; Elks. Rel: Methodist. Mailing Add: 3241 College, Topeka, Kans. 66611.

STOREY, WALLACE L. D
b. Boardman, Fla, 2/14/28; m. to E. Patricia Parker; c. Wallace Lee, Jr. and John Parker. Educ: Fla. South. Col, B.S, 58; Stetson Univ. Col. of Law, LL. B, 59. Polit. & Govt. Pos: Mem, Bd. of Overseers, Stetson Univ. Col. of Law, Fla; asst. attorney, Polk Co; past city judge, Ft. Meade; first asst, Polk Co. Solicitor; chmn, Polk Co. Planning Bd; asst. city attorney, Bartow; city attorney, Mulberry; Fla. State Rep, 64-67, research asst, Fla. Legis. Cmt. on Finance and Taxation, Fla. House of Rep. Bus. & Prof. Pos: Asst. prof. law, Stetson Univ. Col. of Law, 59-60; attorney. Mil. Serv: Marine Corps, 46-47; Army Res, 50-53. Mem: Phi Delta Phi; Lions (past secy. and pres, Bartow Club; Stetson Lawyer's Asn.(past pres). Rel: First Baptist. Mailing Add: P.O. Box 796, Bartow, Fla. 33830. (1967)

STORKE, THOMAS MORE D
b. Santa Barbara, Calif, 11/23/76; s. Charles Albert Storke and Martha More S; m. 1920 to Marion Day; c. (Mrs. Jean Isabel Menzies), (Mrs. Elsie Margaret Cox), Charles Albert and Thomas More. Educ: Stanford, A.B, 98. Hon. LL.D, Univ. Calif, 60 and Colby Col, 63. Polit. & Govt. Pos: Postmaster, Santa Barbara, Calif, 14-21; U.S. Sen, Calif, 38-39; mem, Calif. Crime Cmn, 51-52; bd. regents, Univ. Calif, 55-60. Bus. & Prof. Pos: Ed, publ. and owner, Santa Barbara News-Press, 01-64, emer. ed. and publ, 64-; founder and pres, Thomas More Storke Found. Publ: California Editor, 59; I Write for Freedom, 62. Mem: Santa Barbara City, Univ. and Valley of Montecito Clubs. Lauterbach Award, 61; Pulitzer Prize Ed. Writing, 62; Lovejoy Award, 62. Legal Res: 1716 Santa Barbara St, Santa Barbara, Calif. 93101. Mailing Add: News-Press Publishing Co, Santa Barbara, Calif. 93101.

STORY, CLIFTON MARTIN R
b. Jericho, Vt, 12/11/92; m. to Grace Little; c. One daughter. Educ: Univ. of Vt, B. S, 14. Polit. & Govt. Pos: Mem, Zoning Cmn, Vt; Lister; Vt. State Rep, 63-67. Bus. & Prof. Pos: Inspector of milk and ice cream, State Dept. of Agr, retired. Mem: Mason; Odd Fellows; Windsor Co. Adv. Coun. Rel: Congregational. Mailing Add: Box 21, Reading, Vt. 05062. (1967)

STORY, EARL P. D
b. Leah, Ga, 9/14/06; s. Wm. Harvey Story and Hester Bohler, S; m. 7/24/33 to Addie Pharr; c. Carol Pharr. Educ: Univ. Ga, B.S.A, 31; grad. work Univ. of Fla. Polit. & Govt. Pos: Ga. State Rep, 57-66. Bus. & Prof. Pos: Merchant. Mem: Mason; Past Pres, Lawrenceville Merchants Asn; Past Pres, Gwinnett Co. C. of C; Past Pres, Lawrenceville Kiwanis Club; Past Lt-Gov, 10th Div. of Kiwanis Int. Rel: Methodist; Sunday Sch. teacher. Mailing Add: Lawrenceville, Ga. 30245. (1967)

STORY, HARRY G. D
b. Jacksonville, Ill, 5/5/17; s. Charles H. Story and Martha A. Spencer S; m. 8/24/51 to Marian Wright. Educ: Ill. Col, A.B, 39; St. Louis Univ. Col. of Law, LL.B, 42; Phi Delta Phi. Bus. & Prof. Pos: Attorney, 46- Mil. Serv: Entered as Pvt, Army, 42, released as Capt, 45 after serv. in ETO. Mem: Am, Ill. State and Morgan Co. Bar Asns; Nat. Trial Lawyers. Rel: Protestant. Mailing Add: 1227 West State St, Jacksonville, Ill. 62650. (1967)

STORY, MELVIN EMMETT R
b. Farmington, Iowa, 7/7/06; s. James William Story and Linnie Petrie S; m. 9/17/32 to Martha B. Buchanan; c. William R. and David J. Educ: Farmington High Sch, 2 years. Polit. & Govt. Pos: Iowa State Rep, 67. Bus. & Prof. Pos: Lineman, N.W. Bell Tel. Co, 26-29, construct. foreman, 29-44, engr, 44-53 and independent co. rels. rep, 53-66. Mil. Serv: Entered as 2nd Lt, Air Force, 42, released as 1st Lt, 44, after serv. in Signal Corps, Am. Theatre. Mem: Mason; Consistory; Shrine. Rel: Protestant. Mailing Add: R.R. 2, North English, Iowa 52316.

STORY, PATRICIA JORDAN R
b. Hood River, Ore, 3/6/27; d. Leonard Beck Jordan and Grace Edgington J; m. 7/1/51 to Charles F. Story, Jr; c. Tamara Ann, Karen Marea and Jordan Charles. Educ: Whitman Col, 45-46; Univ. Idaho, B.S, 50; Kappa Kappa Gamma. Polit. & Govt. Pos: Campaign worker and organizer for many cand. in Wash. and Idaho, 51-62; officer, Federated Rep. Women, Marin and San Joaquin Co, Calif, 63-68; coordinator, Goldwater for Pres, Marin Co, fall 64; Marin Co. finance co-chmn, Reagan for Gov, 66; precinct chmn, San Joaquin Co. Rep. Cent. Cmt, 67-68 & 69; alternate mem, Calif. Rep. State Cent. Cmt, 67-69. Bus. & Prof. Pos: Various short term jobs in pub. rels, mostly connected with the Rep. Party, 51- Mem: Nat. Assistance League; Kappa Kappa Gamma Alumni Asn; PTA Bd. Ronald Reagan Award as one of the outstanding precinct leaders in Calif, 68. Rel: Episcopal. Mailing Add: 1638 Greeley Way, Stockton, Calif. 95207.

STORY, PAUL JACKSON D
b. Sparta, N.C, 10/21/04; s. Rev. J.C. Story and Hida Reynolds S; m. 8/7/35 to Helen Virginia Goldsmith; c. Jane Cameron and Paul Jackson, Jr. Educ: Davidson Col, A.B, 24; Univ. of N.C, LL.B, 31; Phi Delta Theta; Phi Alpha Delta. Polit. & Govt. Pos: Judge, McDowell City Criminal Court, N.C, 38-49; pres, 18th Judicial Dist. Bar, 48-49; mem, N.C. Bar Coun, representing 29th Judicial Dist, 52-62; N.C. State Rep, 63-66. Bus. & Prof. Pos: Lawyer. Mem: N.C. Bar Asn; Mason; AF&AM; Dist. Dep. Grand Master of Grand Lodge of N.C. for the 52nd Masonic Dist, 48-50. Rel: Presbyterian; Deacon, 6 years; Supt. of Sunday Sch, 48-54; Elder, 54. Mailing Add: Montevista Ave, Marion, N.C. 28752.

STORY, STEVE BIXLER D
Chmn, Fayette Co. Dem. Cent. Cmt, Iowa
b. Monticello, Iowa, 12/3/32; s. Dillon Wells Story and Clarice Isabelle Bixler S; m. 6/7/53 to Donna Ketchum; c. Karen Diane, Janet Kay, Linda Jeane and Steven Paul (deceased). Educ: Coe Col, B.A, 54; State Univ. Iowa, M.A, 58; Mo. Univ. Polit. & Govt. Pos: Chmn, Fayette Co. Dem. Cent. Cmt, Iowa, currently; del, Dem. Nat. Conv, 64. Bus. & Prof. Pos: High sch. athletic coach, basketball and baseball, 54-66; high sch. prin, North High Sch, 66-; pres,

West Union Jr. C. of C, 62-64. Mem: Nat. and Iowa State Educ. Asns; Mason. Rel: Methodist; Lay Leader, 1st Methodist Church, 63- Mailing Add: 401 Smith, West Union, Iowa 52715.

STOTTS, KEITH HORACE R
Mo. State Rep.
b. Stotts City, Mo, 7/22/14; s. Horace Green Stotts and Hannah Enright S; m. 10/14/36 to Helen Mae Abram; c. Bill Keith and Susan Elaine. Polit. & Govt. Pos: Former mem, Pierce City Sch. Bd, Lawrence Co. Draft Bd. and Welfare Bd, Mo; mayor, Pierce City, 46-56; Mo. State Rep, Lawrence Co, currently. Bus. & Prof. Pos: Owner, Stotts Pharm, 44- Mem: Nat. Asn. of Retail Druggists; Mo. Pharmaceutical Asn; Mo. State C. of C; Pierce City C. of C; Red Cross; charter mem, Pierce City Kiwanis. Mailing Add: 506 Walnut St, Pierce City, Mo. 65723. (1967)

STOUT, CARMEN LEE D
Chmn, Vernon Co. Dem. Party, Wis.
b. LaFarge, Wis, 11/27/39; s. John Joe Stout and Garnet Campbell S; m. 7/11/64 to Shirley Rosol; c. Sherri Lee. Educ: LaCrosse Univ, B.E; Vernon Co. Teacher Col, teaching cert, 59. Polit. & Govt. Pos: Mem. exec. cmt, Vernon Co. Dem. Party, Wis, 60-65, chmn, 65-; del, Wis. Dem. Conv, 61 & 65; sr. adv, Vernon Co. Young Dem. Clubs, 62-63; precinct committeeman, LaFarge and Webster, Wis, 63-66. Bus. & Prof. Pos: Teacher and prin, Bloomingdale Sch, 59-66; area rep, Lincoln Libr. Reference Books, 65-66; legis. dist. chmn, Vernon-Crawford Assembly Dist. for Wis. Educ. Asn. and bd. of dirs, Coulee Region Community Action Prog, presently. Mem: Secy, Westby Area Educ. Asn, 63-64 and treas, 65-66; Nat. Wis. and Northwest. Wis. Educ. Asns; K. of P; LaFarge Trapshooters Asn; Mt. Sianai, LaFarge and Valley Rod and Gun Clubs; bd. of dirs, Citizens for Better State Govt. Cmn; Wis. Farmers Union; secy, West Fork Sportsmen Club, presently. Interested in juvenile behavior; research on revamping Wis. Juvenile Code. Rel: Protestant. Mailing Add: R.R. Three, Westby, Wis. 54467.

STOUT, GEORGE R. D
b. Tipton, Ind, 7/7/22; Frank Stout and Edna League S; m. 3/21/50 to Betty Jane Guerin; c. Vicky and Laurie Ellen. Educ: Univ. Ore, B.S. in Polit. Sci, 50; East. Ore. Col. Educ, B.S; Univ. North. Ill, 62. Polit. & Govt. Pos: Chmn, Thurston Co. Dem. Party, Wash, 67-68, precinct committeeman, 68- Bus. & Prof. Pos: Elem. sch. teacher, Lincoln Co. Sch. Dist, Ore, 51-54; Teacher, Creswell Sch. Dist, 54-57; North Thurston Sch. Dist, Wash, 57-69. Mil. Serv: Entered as Pvt, Air Force, 42, released as Cpl, 45, after serv. in 96th Fighter Squadron, ETO. Mem: Am. Polit. Sci. Asn; Nat. Educ. Asn; Nat. Cong. of Parents and Teachers. Rel: Unitarian. Mailing Add: Route 8, Box 326, Olympia, Wash. 98501.

STOUT, HELEN LARSON D
b. Minneapolis, Minn; d. Harold Chester Larson and Albie Solem L; m. 12/25/49 to William Job Stout; c. Craig William, Tobias Jonathan and Leslie Ann. Educ: Univ. Minn, 3 years. Polit. & Govt. Pos: Del, Dem. Nat. Conv, 68. Rel: Agnostic. Mailing Add: 1125 San Ysidro Dr, Beverly Hills, Calif. 90210.

STOUT, JUNE WINDLE R
Chmn, Linn Co. Rep. Cent. Cmt, Ore.
b. Salt Lake City, Utah, 9/19/19; d. James Edgar Windle and Mary Myrl Skelton W: m. 10/19/46 to Lermond E. Stout; c. Mary Kathleen and Gary Lee. Educ: Northwest. Bus. Col, Portland, Ore, 38-39. Polit. & Govt. Pos: Mem. various Rep. supplemental groups and Rep. Women's Fedn; precinct committeewoman, Linn Co. Rep. Cent. Cmt, Ore, 52-, precinct chmn, 62-68 and co. chmn, 68-; second dist. v.chmn, Ore. State Rep. Cent. and Exec. Cmts, 68- Bus. & Prof. Pos: Secy. and staff claims adjuster, Northwest. Mutual Fire & Casualty Co, 41-49; co-owner, Marco Polo Motel, Albany, Ore, 51-59 and Waverly Plaza Apts, 56-62. Mem: Albany Citizens Adv. Cmt; Springhill Country Club; PTA. Rel: Presbyterian. Mailing Add: 1207 W. 26th, Albany, Ore. 97321.

STOUT, RICHARD RALSTON R
N.J. State Sen.
b. Ocean Grove, N.J, 9/21/12; s. Richard Weslord Stout and Lillian Nevin Ralston S; m. 1/18/47 to Nancy Tucker; c. Penelope (Mrs. Nachman), Mary Elizabeth, Margaret Tucker, Richard Ralston, Jr, Susan Nichols and Nancy Tucker. Educ: Princeton Univ, A.B, 35; Rutgers Law Sch, LL.B, 39; Tiger Inn; Delta Theta Phi. Polit. & Govt. Pos: Pres, Monmouth Co. Young Rep, N.J, 49; N.J. State Sen, Monmouth Co, 52-; del, N.J. Constitutional Conv, 66; del, Rep. Nat. Conv, 68. Mil. Serv: Entered as 1st Lt, Army, 40, released as Col, 46, after serv. in Mid. East, 42-44; Col, Army Res.(Ret); Legion of Merit; Army Commendation Medal. Mem: Am, N.J. and Monmouth Co. Bar Asns; Mason; Elks; Lions; VFW; Am. Legion. Rel: Methodist. Legal Res: Wickspecko Dr. W, Allenhurst, N.J. 07711. Mailing Add: 301 Main St, Allenhurst, N.J. 07711.

STOUTZ, EDWIN A, JR. D
Chmn, Second Cong. Dem. Exec. Cmt, La.
b. New Orleans, La, 9/13/41; s. Edwin A. Stoutz, Sr. and Isabelle Taaffe S; m. 2/24/68 to Catherine Michie McHardy; c. W. Clifton. Educ: Georgetown Univ, B.S. and B.A, 63; Tulane Univ, LL.B, 67; Phi Delta Phi. Polit. & Govt. Pos: Mem, La. State Dem. Cent. Cmt, 29th Rep. Dist, 67-; del, Dem. Nat. Conv, 68; chmn, Second Cong. Dem. Exec. Cmt, La, 68- Mem: La. State and Am. Bar Asns; Young Men's Bus. Club; New Orleans Mid-winter Sports Asn; Alliance for Good Govt. Youngest mem. of the La. Del, Dem. Nat. Conv, 68. Rel: Catholic. Legal Res: 1801 Pine St, New Orleans, La. 70118. Mailing Add: 1746 National Bank of Commerce Bldg, New Orleans, La. 70130.

STOVALL, REGINALD MORRIS R
Mayor, Ft. Worth, Tex.
b. Tupelo, Okla, 8/1/16; s. William Dudley Stovall (deceased) and Grace Allen S.(deceased); m. 9/9/39 to Amelia Zich; c. Linda (Mrs. Robert Neal Meredith), Marsha, Peggy and Nancy. Educ: Tex. Christian Univ, 36. Polit. & Govt. Pos: Councilman, Ft. Worth, Tex, 63-68; mayor, 69- Bus. & Prof. Pos: Pres, Panther City Off. Supply Co, 44-; v.pres, Bell Reproduction Co, 50- Mem: Mason (32°); DeMolay; Shrine (Potentate). Rel: Episcopal. Mailing Add: 2428 Medford Court E, Ft. Worth, Tex. 76109.

STOVALL, THELMA LOYACE D
State Treas, Ky.
b. Munfordville, Ky, 4/1/19; d. Samuel Dewey Hawkins and Addie Mae H; m. 9/30/36 to Lonnie Raymond Stovall. Educ: LaSalle Exten. Univ, law, 2 years; Univ. Ky, 2 summers; East. State Col, 1 summer. Polit. & Govt. Pos: Ky. State Rep, 38th Legis. Dist, 50-56; nat. committeewoman, Young Dem. Clubs of Ky, 52-56, pres, 56-58; Secy. of State, Ky, 56-60 & 64-68; State Treas, Ky, 60-64 & 68- Bus. & Prof. Pos: Secy, Tobacco Workers Int. Union, Local 185, 11 years; bd. dirs. of educ. dept, Ky. State Fedn. of Labor, 8 years; recording secy, Nat. Asn. of Secys. of State, 67, secy, 68; chmn, Cmt. on Employment of the Governor's Cmn. on the Status of Women, 66. Mem: Woman of the Moose; Eastern Star; Young Dem; Bus. & Prfnl. Womens' Club. Rel: Baptist. Legal Res: 104 Valley Rd, Louisville, Ky. 40204. Mailing Add: Capitol Annex Bldg, Frankfort, Ky. 40601.

STOWELL, EDWARD ALLEN D
b. Cleveland, Ohio, 7/26/24; s. G. Paul Stowell and Lydia Jones S; m. 6/26/48 to Janice Elizabeth Young; c. Susan Elizabeth, Richard Paul and David Edward. Educ: Oberlin Col, A.B, 47; Univ. Toledo Col. Law, LL.B, 51; Delta Theta Phi. Polit. & Govt. Pos: Pres, Lucas Co. Young Dem, Ohio, 57; ins. cmnr, Ohio, 59-61; asst. to Gov. Michael V. DiSalle, 61-62; del, Dem. Nat. Conv, 64; secy, Lucas Co. Dem. Exec. Cmt, 64-66. Bus. & Prof. Pos: Partner law firm, Finkbeiner, Ide & Stowell, Toledo, Ohio, 63-66; asst. secy. and asst. gen. attorney, Allstate Ins. Co, Ill, 66- Mil. Serv: Entered as A/S, Naval Res, 43, released as Ens, 46. Mem: Am, Ohio and Toledo Bar Asns. Rel: Congregational. Mailing Add: 242 Poplar Rd, Highland Park, Ill. 60035.

STRAHAN, ERNEST WESLEY R
Kans. State Sen.
b. Williamsburg, Kans, 3/1/01; s. Marion Ernest Strahan and Naomi Santee S; m. 2/17/38 to Helen Dillingham; c. John W. Educ: Ottawa Univ. Polit. & Govt. Pos: Mem. agr. and hwy. safety and transportation cmts, Mid-West Coun. State Govt, currently; mem. cmt. and exec. cmt, Nat. Cmt. Uniform Traffic Laws and Ord, currently; mem, Nat. Legis. Cmt. Hwy. Safety and Transportation, Kans. Turnpike Authority and Kans. Cmn. Reciprocity and Proration, currently; Kans. State Sen, 57-, chmn. cmt. transportation and Utilities, Kans. State Senate, currently. Bus. & Prof. Pos: Retired mfr. Rel: Protestant. Legal Res: 835 S. Sante Fe, Salina, Kans. 67401. Mailing Add: State Capitol, Topeka, Kans. 66612.

STRAIGHT, JOHN LESLIE R
b. San Pedro, Calif, 5/7/34; s. Charles Leslie Straight and Jean McWhirter S; m. 3/21/59 to Mary Artelle Smith. Educ: Palos Verdes Col; Harbor Col; Pasadena Playhouse. Polit. & Govt. Pos: Rep. nominee to U.S. Presidential Electoral Col, 64; mem, Los Angeles Co. Rep. Cent. Cmt, Calif, 64-68. Bus. & Prof. Pos: Trustee, Int. Longshoremen's & Warehousemen's Union, 63-64, secy-treas, 64-66 and bus. agent, 64-66. Mil. Serv: Naval Recruit, Naval Res. Mem: Chem-Allied and Off. Workers Union; Int. Longshoremen's & Warehousemen's Local 20; Nat. Rifle Asn; Nat. Forensic League; Nat. Thespian Soc; Am. Temperance Soc; Relig. Liberty Asn. Rel: Seventh-day Adventist. Mailing Add: 2029 Averill Ave, San Pedro, Calif. 90732. (1967)

STRAIT, DONALD E. D
b. Canon City, Colo, 5/14/27. Polit. & Gov. Pos: Colo. State Rep, 64-66. Bus. & Prof. Pos: Real estate broker; owns advertising agency. Mailing Add: 1164 Emporia St, Aurora, Colo. 80010. (1967)

STRANAHAN, CLINTON GOODWIN D
b. Helena, Mont, 10/28/96; s. Farrand Ebenezer Stranahan and Sarah Ellen Goodwin S; m. 12/15/22 to Marie Ethel Schultz; c. Lorene (Mrs. A.C. Parsons, Jr.) and Anne (Mrs. Wm. A. Shaw). Educ: Mont. State Col, B.S. in Animal Husb, 18. Polit. & Govt. Pos: Mont. State Rep, Chouteau Co, 63-65. Bus. & Prof. Pos: Pres, Fort Benton Powerline, 39-44. Mil. Serv: Entered as Pvt, Army, 18, released as 2nd Lt, after serv. in Field Artillery Res. Corps. Mem: Mason; Farm Bur; Mont. Libr. Asn; Mo. Headwaters Asn; Am. Legion; Eastern Star. Rel: Episcopal. Mailing Add: P.O. Box 25, Fort Benton, Mont. 59442. (1967)

STRAND, CLAIR R
Iowa State Rep.
b. Grinnell, Iowa, 8/21/09; married; c. Two daughters. Educ: Gilman High Sch. Polit. & Govt. Pos: Past mem, Grinnell Sch. Bd, Libr. Bd. and City Planning Bd, Iowa; mem, City Develop. Cmn; Iowa State Rep, 67- Bus. & Prof. Pos: Owner of laundromats and farms; former grocer; bd. mem, Grinnell Fed. Savings and Loan Asn. Mem: Past chmn, United Fund Dr; Red Cross Campaign Mgr. Rel: Baptist; Bd. of Deacons. Mailing Add: Grinnell, Iowa 50112.

STRAND, NEAL A. R
Treas, S.Dak.
b. Canton, S.Dak, 3/25/24; s. Henry N. Strand and Alma A. Ekle S; single. Educ: S.Dak. State Univ; Sears Club. Polit. & Govt. Pos: Sch. clerk, Sch. Dist, S.Dak, 52-55; co. auditor, 61-62; S.Dak. State Sen, 62-69; treas, S.Dak, 69- Bus. & Prof. Pos: Farmer and livestock feeder, 48- Mil. Serv: Entered as Pvt, Army, 44, released as Sgt, 46, after serv. in Signal Corps, Pac. Mem: Mason; Am. Legion; VFW; Farm Bur; Rotary; Elks. Rel: Lutheran. Legal Res: Rural Route 1, Canton, S.Dak. 57013. Mailing Add: State Capitol, Pierre, S.Dak. 57501.

STRANEY, MARTIN LOUIS Independent
b. New Stithton, Ky, 1/5/26; s. Arthur Goble Straney and Hassie Stivers S; m. 8/4/44 to Mary Bernice Leonard; c. Louis Lee and Debra Sue. Educ: Vine Grove High Sch, grad. Polit. & Govt. Pos: Inspector, Dept. Motor Transportation, Ky. 56-60; Ky. State Rep, 64-66. Bus. & Prof. Pos: Real estate broker; home builder; investments. Mil. Serv: Cpl, Army, 45-46; serv. in Hq. Serv. Co, America Theatre. Mem: C. of C; Mason; Scottish Rite; Shrine. Rel: Baptist. Mailing Add: Route 6, Pear Orchard Rd, Elizabethtown, Ky. 42701.

STRASSER, GEORGE LOUIS, JR. D
Chmn, City Coun, Hamburg, N.Y.
b. Buffalo, N.Y, 9/11/12; s. George L. Strasser and Mary Hupf S; m. 6/21/37

to Laura V. Barry; c. George L, III. Educ: Bennett High Sch. Polit. & Govt. Pos: Chmn, City Coun, Hamburg, N.Y, currently; mem, exec. cmt, Erie Co. Dem. Cmt; v.chmn, Town Chmns. Asn. Rel: Catholic. Mailing Add: 4752 S. Park, Hamburg, N.Y. 14075.

STRATTON, HARRY O, SR. D
b. Tellico-Plains, Tenn, 3/23/12; m. to Paula Kickliter; c. Harry, Jr, Mike, Mary, Paula S, Lisa Michelle, Joel Mark. Educ: Univ. of Tenn. Polit. & Govt. Pos: Fla. State Sen, 54-67; Pres, pro-tem, 63; Fla. State Rep, 52-54. Bus. & Prof. Pos: Gen. Ins. Agency; Mem, Fla. Medication Serv. Mem: Mason; C. of C; Shriner; Past Pres, Fla. Fair Asn; Chmn, March of Dimes; Pres, N.E. Fla. Fair. Rel: Baptist. Mailing Add: P.O. Box 268, Callahan, Fla. 32011. (1967)

STRATTON, ROBERT J. R
b. Jaffrey, N.H; married; c. two. Educ: Becker Col, Worcester, Mass. Polit. & Govt. Pos: Former N.H. State Rep. and Rep. Town Chmn, two terms. Bus. & Prof. Pos: Ins. agent. Mil. Serv: Navy, 2 years. Mem: Kiwanis; Mason; Shrine; VFW; Eagles. Rel: Protestant. Mailing Add: E. Broadway, Derry, N.H. 03038.

STRATTON, SAMUEL STUDDIFORD D
U.S. Rep, N.Y.
b. Yonkers, N.Y, 9/27/16; s. Rev. Paul Stratton and Ethel Irene Russell S; m. 12/17/47 to Joan H. Wolfe; c. Lisa, Debra, Kevin, Kim and Brian. Educ: Univ. Rochester, A.B, 37; Harvard, M.A, 40; Phi Beta Kappa; Psi Upsilon. Polit. & Govt. Pos: Exec. secy. to U.S. Rep. Thomas E. Eliot, Mass, 41-42; dep. secy. gen, Far East. Cmn, Wash, D.C, 46-48; councilman, Schenectady, N.Y, 50-56, mayor, 56-59; U.S. Rep, N.Y, 59- Bus. & Prof. Pos: Lectr, Union Col. and Rennsselaer Polytech. Inst, 48-54; TV and radio news commentator, Schenectady, 50-56; registered rep, First Albany Corp, 57- Mil. Serv: Entered as Ens, Naval Res, 42, released,46; re-entered in 51, released in 53 after serv. in Korea; Capt, Res, currently. Mem: ROA; Navy League; Am. Legion; VFW; Amvets; Mason. Rel: Presbyterian. Legal Res: Amsterdam, N.Y. Mailing Add: Rayburn House Office Bldg, Washington, D.C. 20515.

STRATTON, SCOTT B. R
Mont. State Rep.
b. Wing, N.Dak, 6/24/13; s. Charles A. Stratton and Dorothy Artz S; m. 7/3/35 to Virginia E. Connolly; c. Rev. James, C.S.S.R, Jon D. and Virginia Ann. Educ: Univ. Mont, 34; Univ. Wash, Am. Banking Inst, grad, 56; Phi Sigma Kappa. Polit. & Govt. Pos: Mont. State Rep, Cascade Co, 66- Bus. & Prof. Pos: V.pres, 1st Nat. Bank, Mont. Mil. Serv: Seaman 1/C, Navy, 46. Mem: Am. Inst. of Banking; Am. Legion; C. of C; Serra Club; Rotary. Rel: Catholic. Legal Res: 502 22nd St. N, Great Falls, Mont. 59401. Mailing Add: Holiday Motel, Helena, Mont. 59101. (1967)

STRATTON, WILLIAM GRANT R
b. Ingleside, Ill, 2/26/14; s. William J. Stratton and Zula Van Wormer S; m. 12/27/50 to Shirley Breckenridge; c. Nancy Helen, Sandra Gardner and Diana Weiskopf. Educ: Univ. Ariz; Delta Chi. Hon. degrees, Univ. Ariz, Bradley Univ, Lincoln Mem. Univ, Elmhurst, N.Cent. and Shurtleff Col, John Marshal Law Sch. and South, Ill. Univ. Polit. & Govt. Pos: U.S. Rep, Ill, 41-43 & 47-49; state treas, Ill, 43-45 & 51-53; Gov, Ill, 53-61; chmn, Interstate Oil Compact, 55; chmn, Ill. Del, Rep. Nat. Conv, 56 & 60; chmn, Nat. Gov. Conf, 57; mem, Lincoln Sesquicentennial Cmn, 58; mem, Fed. Adv. Cmn. on Intergovt. Rels, 59. Bus. & Prof. Pos: Operator, Black Angus Cattle Farm; v.pres, Canteen Corp, 68- Mil. Serv: Lt.(jg), Navy, 45-46; serv. in Pac. Mem: Mason (33°); Shrine; Lions; Eagles; Elks; Am. Legion; Amvets; VFW. Rel: Methodist. Legal Res: 3260 Lake Shore Dr, Chicago, Ill. Mailing Add: Canteen Corp, Merchandise Mart, Chicago, Ill. 60654.

STRAUB, CHESTER JOHN D
N.Y. State Assemblyman
b. Brooklyn, N.Y, 5/12/37; m. to Patricia Morrissey; c. Chester John, Jr, Michael Joseph and Christopher James. Educ: St. Peter's Col, B.A. in Arts and Sci; Univ. Va, LL.D. Polit. & Govt. Pos: Mem, Pioneer, White Eagle, Polonia and Consolidated Dem. Clubs; former counsel, N.Y. State Coun. of Polish Dem. Clubs; former exec. mem, Univ. Va. Young Dem; personal aide to Sen. Robert Kennedy during sen. campaign; former liaison officer, N.Y. State Dem. Cmt. for Young Citizens for Johnson and Humphrey; N.Y. State Assemblyman, 35th Dist, currently, mem, Claims, Internal Affairs, Penal Insts, Pensions, Pub. Printing and Taxation Standing Cmts. and Joint Legis. Cmt. on Matrimonial and Family Laws, N.Y. State Assembly. Bus. & Prof. Pos: Former legal adv, Pulaski Bus. and Prof. Men's Asn, Inc; attorney-at-law, N.Y, currently. Mil. Serv: 1st Lt, Army Intel. and Security Corps, grad. from Inf. Sch, Intel. Sch. and Audio-Visual Spanish Lang. Sch; additional serv. during Berlin and Cuban Missile Crises; Cert. of Achievement from Commanding Gen. of the Second U.S. Army. Publ: Co-auth, Legal Institutions of New York City, Asn. of the Bar of City of New York. Mem: Former v.chmn. and parks cmt. chmn, Brooklyn Borough Pres. Stark's Commun. Dist. Planning Bd. for Greenpoint and Williamsburg; former mem, Lexington Coun. K. of C; del, advocate, gen. legis. rep. and chancellor, Greenpoint Civic Coun; charter mem, Greenpoint-Williamsburg Health Coun; past diocesan del, Holy Name Soc, St. Stanislaus Kostka Parish; bd. dir, N.Y. League for Histadrut; Kosciuszko Found; Sons of Poland; Polish Nat. Alliance; St. Aloysius Young Men's Cath. Club. Rel: Catholic. Legal Res: Greenpoint, N.Y. 11222. Mailing Add: 678 Manhattan Ave, Brooklyn, N.Y. 11222.

STRAUB, JOSEPH J. D
Chmn, Kossuth Co. Dem. Cent. Cmt, Iowa
b. New York, N.Y, 1/5/30; s. Joseph J. Straub and Catherine R. Walsh S; m. 8/25/51 to Mary C. Cash; c. Catherine, Joseph, Donald, Lisa, Mary Ellan, Robert, Peter, Thomas, James and Monica. Educ: Univ. Notre Dame, B.A, 52, LL.B, 55. Polit. & Govt. Pos: Chmn, Kossuth Co. Dem. Cent. Cmt, Iowa, 64-; chmn, Kossuth Co. adv. bd, Off. Econ. Opportunity, 67-69; city attorney, Bancroft, 68-; co. attorney, Kossuth Co, 69- Mem: Kossuth Co, Iowa and Am. Bar Asns; Grand Knight, Algona K. of C, 59-60; Notre Dame Alumni Asn. Rel: Roman Catholic. Mailing Add: 200 S. Durant St, Algona, Iowa 50511.

STRAUB, PEARL ANN D
Secy, Clear Creek Co. Dem. Cent. Cmt, Colo.
b. Idaho Springs, Colo, 10/14/00; d. John Joseph Hoban and Kathryn M. Murphy H; m. 8/7/21 to C. Irving Straub; c. John Raymond, Maxine Evelyn (deceased), Louis Irving, Jacquelynn Ann (Mrs. Norman H. Buckley), Ronald D. and twins, Glen F. and Leonard F. Educ: Idaho Springs High Sch, 12 years. Polit. & Govt. Pos: Pres, Clear Creek Co. Jane Jefferson Club, Colo, 45-47, 56-57 & 63-65; committeewoman, Precinct Six, Colo, 52-; secy, Clear Creek Co. Dem. Cent. Cmt, 54- Bus. & Prof. Pos: Newspaper Reporter, Idaho Springs Mining J, 63- Mem: Bus. and Prfnl. Womans Club, 60-65. Rel: Catholic. Mailing Add: 147 Colorado Blvd, Idaho Springs, Colo. 80452.

STRAUB, ROBERT W. D
State Treas, Ore.
b. San Francisco, Calif, 5/6/20; m. to Pat; c. six. Educ: Dartmouth Col, B.A, M.B.A. Polit. & Govt. Pos: Cmnr, Lane Co, Ore, 55-59; Ore. State Sen, 59-63; state treas, Ore, 64-; del, Dem. Nat. Conv, 68. Bus. & Prof. Pos: Land developer; farmer; rancher. Mil. Serv: World War II. Mailing Add: Office of the State Treasurer, State Capitol, Salem, Ore. 97310.

STRAUGHAN, NILE R
b. Ansted, W.Va, 7/10/09; s. Edward Thomas Straughan and Carrie Lee Reynolds S. Polit. & Govt. Pos: Mem, Rep. Nat. Cmt. for Va, 61-68. Bus. & Prof. Pos: Pres, Janney-Marshall Co, Inc, Fredericksburg, Va, 44-, Germania Mills Co, 44-; pres, and owner, Idlewild Farms, 50-; pres, Va. Research Co, 51-, Whittaker Grocery Co, Inc, Terra Alta, 58-, Wholesale Builders Supply Co, 58-, Double Discount Stamp Co, Fredericksburg, 61- and South. Indust. Loan Corp, Covington, 62- Mailing Add: Drawer 59, Fredericksburg, Va. 22401. (1967)

STRAUS, R. PETER D
b. New York, N.Y, 2/15/23; s. Nathan Straus and Helen Sachs S; m. 2/6/50 to Ellen Louise Sulzberger; c. Diane Ellen, Katherine Louise, Jeanne Helen and Eric Peter. Educ: Yale Univ, B.A, 40-43; Yale Club. Polit. & Govt. Pos: Chief secy, Manpower Div, Off. Mil. Govt, Germany, 46-47; mem, admin. cmt, N.Y. Citizens Cmt. for Kennedy-Johnson, 60; del, Dem. Nat. Conv, 60 & 64; chmn, N.Y. State Dem. Campaign Cmt, 64; co-chmn, N.Y. Cmt. Constitutional Issues, 67; asst. adminstr. Africa, Agency Int. Develop, 67-68. Bus. & Prof. Pos: Exec. asst. to Dir. Gen, Int. Labor Orgn, Geneva, Switzerland, 50-55; dir, Int. Labor Orgn, Wash. Br, 55-58; exec. v.pres, Sta. WMCA, 58-59; pres, Straus Broadcasting Group, 59- Mil. Serv: Entered as Air Cadet, Army Air Corps, 42, released as 1st Lt, 45; Air Medal and 5 Oak Leaf Clusters. Mem: Young Pres. Orgn; Coun. on For. Rels; N.Y. Exec. Cmt, Anti-Defamation League; U.S. Cmt. for the UN; United Jewish Appeal, Radio-TV Div; Yale Club; Century Country Club; Nat. Press Club; Fed. City Club; mem. exec. cmt, Interracial Coun. Bus. Opportunity. Rel: Jewish. Mailing Add: 415 Madison Ave, New York, N.Y. 10017.

STRAUSS, LEWIS LICHTENSTEIN R
b. Charleston, W.Va, 1/31/96; s. Lewis Strauss and Rosa Lichtenstein S; m. 3/5/23 to Alice Hanauer; c. Lewis H. Polit. & Govt. Pos: Secy. to Herbert Hoover, 17-19; mem, Atomic Energy Cmn, 46-50; asst. to pres. on Atomic Energy Matters, 53, chmn, cmn, 53-58; Secy. of Commerce, 58-59. Bus. & Prof. Pos: Staff mem, Kuhn, Loeb & Co, 19-46, partner, 29-47; mem, Cancer Hosp, N.Y; trustee, Inst. for Crippled and Disabled, George Wash. Univ, Jewish Theol. Sem, Hebrew Union Col, Inst. for Adv. Study and Sloan-Kettering Inst; consult. and financial adv. to Messrs. Rockefeller, 50-53; dir, Kirkeby-Natus Corp, Gen. Am. Transportation Co, Inland Steel Co, Nat. Broadcasting Co. and Radio Corp. of Am. Mil. Serv: Lt. Comdr, Naval Res, 26, adv. to Rear Adm, 45; Distinguished Serv. Medal; Legion of Merit; Gold Star; Oak Leaf Cluster; Commendation Ribbon; Officer, Legion of Honor, France; Medal of Freedom, U.S; Grand Officer, Order of Leopold, Belgium. Publ: Men and Decisions, 62. Mem: Belgian Educ. Found; Metrop. Opera; Va. Mus. Fine Art Clubs; Century Asn, N.Y.C; Metrop. Club, D.C. Rel: Jewish. Mailing Add: Brandy Station, Va. 22714. (1967)

STRAUSS, ROBERT S. D
Dem. Nat. Committeeman, Tex.
b. Lockhart, Tex, 10/9/18; s. Charles H. Strauss and Edith V. S; m. 5/27/41 to Helen Jacobs; c. Robert A, Richard C. and Susan. Educ: Univ. Tex, LL.B, 41. Polit. & Govt. Pos: Mem, Bank Bd, State of Tex, 63-; Dem. Nat. Committeeman, Tex, 68-; mem, exec. cmt, Dem. Nat. Cmt, 69- Bus. & Prof. Pos: Attorney, Akin, Gump, Strauss, Hauer & Feld, Attorneys, Dallas, 45-; pres, Strauss Broadcasting Co, 64- Mil. Serv: Spec. agent, FBI, 41-45. Mem: Tex. and Am. Bar Asns. Rel: Jewish. Legal Res: 6223 De Loache, Dallas, Tex. 75225. Mailing Add: 2800 Republic National Bank Bldg, Dallas, Tex. 75201.

STRAUSS, RONALD I. R
b. Phila, Pa, 4/5/40; s. Jacob Strauss and Elizabeth Krasner S; m. 4/19/68 tc Nancy K. Allis; c. Kim Allison. Educ: Univ. Miami, B.A, 62; Univ. Miami Sch. of Law, J.D, 65; Bar and Gavel; Alpha Epsilon Phi; Tau Epsilon Rho; Int. Law Club. Polit. & Govt. Pos: Nominee for U.S. Rep, Fla, 68. Bus. & Prof. Pos: Sr. partner, Strauss & McCormick Law Firm, 67-; v.pres, dir. and secy, Ketria, Inc, Fla, 67-; secy, treas. and dir, Seaferro Inc, 68- Mil. Serv: Entered as Pvt, Marines, 60, released as Cpl, 66, after serv. in Anglco, Miami, Fourth Div. Mem: Am. and Fla. Bar Asns; Criminal Defense Lawyers Asn; Fed. Bar; Am. Judicature Soc; Supreme Court, State of Fla; Elks; Jr. C. of C. of Gr. Miami. Cert. of Appreciation, Lions Int. Rel: Jewish. Legal Res: 7960 S.W. 144th St, Miami, Fla. 33158. Mailing Add: 66 W. Flagler St, Miami, Fla. 33130.

STRAUSS, TEOFIL NICK R
b. San Antonio, Tex, 1/4/37; s. Fred Eugene Strauss and Gladys Mauritz S; m. 9/2/59 to Sandra McLaughlin; c. Marshall Fred, Teofil Nick and Philip Hoch. Educ: Tex. A&M. Polit. & Govt. Pos: Chmn, Guadalupe Co. Rep. Party, Tex, 61-68. Bus. & Prof. Pos: Owner, Strauss Construction Co, 63- Mil. Serv: Entered as Pvt, Army, 57, released as 1st Lt, 64, after serv. in 144th Inf, 36th Div. Mem: Elks; Kiwanis; C. of C. Rel: Lutheran. Legal Res: 1704 Rosewood St, Seguin, Tex. 78155. Mailing Add: 313 E. Court St, Seguin, Tex. 78155. (1967)

STRAUSZ-HUPE, ROBERT
b. Vienna, Austria, 3/25/03; s. Rudolph Strausz-Hupé and Doris Hedwig Strausz-H; naturalized, 38; m. 4/26/38 to Eleanor deGraff Cuyler. Educ:

Univ. Pa, A.M. and Ph.D, 44. Polit. & Govt. Pos: Appointed U.S. Ambassador to Morocco by the President, 69. Bus. & Prof. Pos: Investment banker, 27-37; assoc. ed, Current Hist, 39-41; spec. lectr, 40-46; assoc. prof. polit. sci, Univ. Pa, 46-52, prof, 52-, dir. For. Policy Research Inst, 55-; lectr, Air War Col, 53. Mil. Serv: Lt. Col.(Ret), Army. Publ: International Relations, 50; The Zone of Indifference, 52; Power and Community, 56; plus others. Mem: Fel. Royal Geog. Soc; Am. Polit. Sci. Asn; Coun. For. Rels; Research Coun. of Atlantic Inst; dir, Atlantic Coun. of the U.S; Merion Cricket Club, Haverford, Pa; Cosmos Club, Wash; Brook Club, N.Y.C. Rel: Lutheran. Legal Res: White Horse Farms, Newtown Square, Pa. 19073. Mailing Add: U.S. Dept. of State Foreign Service, Washington, D.C. 20521.

STRAUT, CHARLES H, JR. D
b. Pearl River, N.Y, 1/9/36; s. Charles Herbert Straut and Ida Hammond S; m. 8/23/58 to Judith Hawkins; c. David Charles, Amy Beth and Susan Judith. Educ: Drew Univ, A.B, 58, B.D, 62. Polit. & Govt. Pos: Alternate del, Dem. Nat. Conv, 68; mem, Citizens Adv. Cmt, East Rutherford, N.J, 68-; del, N.J. New Dem. Coalition Conv, 69; chmn, Minority Housing Subcmt, East Rutherford, 69- Bus. & Prof. Pos: Pastor, Colesville Circuit Methodist Churches, N.J, 59-62; organizing pastor, Methodist Church, Kinnelon, 62-65; Pastor, Christ United Methodist Church, East Rutherford, 65- Mem: Bd. Christian Social Concerns, North. N.J. Annual Conf, United Methodist Church; Racial & Cultural Rels. Cmt. and Urban Crisis Task Force, Social Educ. & Action Dept,N.J. Coun. Churches; N.J. Clergy Consultation Serv. on Abortion; S. Bergen Human Rights Cmt; Bergen Co. Health & Welfare Coun; Clergy & Layman Concerned About Vietnam; Bergen Co. Peace Coun; Am. Civil Liberties Union; United World Federalists; Nat. Cmt. for a Sane Nuclear Policy. Rel: United Methodist. Mailing Add: 228 Main St, East Rutherford, N.J. 07073.

STRAVA, JOHN F. D
b. Thompson, Ohio, 9/18/18; s. John Strava and Victoria Cadar S; m. 7/3/65 to Virginia Bork; c. Burt, Sharon, Linda and Joanne Bork. Educ: Ohio State Univ, 37-41. Polit. & Govt. Pos: Employee, Ledgemont Bd. of Educ, Ohio, 42-66; precinct committeeman, Geauga Co. Dem. Cmt, 15 years, treas, 52-56, second v.chmn, 56-58,first v.chmn, 58-60 and chmn, 60-64 & 66; mem, Geauga Co. Bd. of Visitors, 56-66; mem, Geauga Co. Bd. of Elec, 56-66; chmn, 64-66; mem. adv. bd, Geauga Co. Planning Cmn, 60-61; del, Dem. Nat. Conv, 64; area supvr, Bur. of Census, Ohio, 64-65; cand. for co. cmnr, Geauga Co, 66; exec. secy, Geauga Co. Dem. Exec. Cmt, 66-68. Bus. & Prof. Pos: Licensed real estate salesman and real estate appraiser; v.pres, Lake Erie Acad. of Cosmetology, 56-66; field rep, Kingwood Oil Co, 63-64. Mem: Pres. Geauga Co. Chap, Ohio State Alumni Asn, 65; past v.pres. N.C. Dist, Ohio Asn. Pub. Sch. Employees; Ohio Elec. Off; past dir, Geauga Co. Farm Bur; PTA; past v.pres, Ohio Grape Inst; Eagles. Attended by invitation, inaugurations of President Kennedy, 61 and President Johnson, 65. Rel: Catholic. Mailing Add: 15746 Thompson Rd, Thompson, Ohio 44086. (1967)

STRAW, EZEKIEL A. R
Treas, N.H. Rep. Party
b. Manchester, N.H, 6/23/25; s. Ezekiel A. Straw and Virginia Slayton S; m. 9/4/48 to Margaret McCracken; c. William P, Jeffrey S, Sarah S. and Ezekiel A. Educ: Dartmouth Col, A.B, 49. Polit. & Govt. Pos: Treas, N.H. Rep. Party, 69- Bus. & Prof. Pos: Various banking titles and jobs; pres. and chmn. exec. off, Manchester Savings Bank, 67- Mil. Serv: Entered as Pvt, Air Force, 43, released as 1st Lt, 45, after serv. in Eighth Air Force, ETO, 44-45; Air Medal with Five Oak Leaf Clusters. Rel: Protestant. Mailing Add: 1311 Chestnut St, Manchester, N.H. 03104.

STRAYHORN, EARL EDWARD D
b. Columbus, Miss, 4/24/18; s. Earl Edward Strayhorn and Minnie Lee Davis S; m. 8/17/41 to Lygia Jackson; c. Donald R. and Earlene E. Educ: Univ. Ill, A.B, 41; DePaul Univ. Col. of Law, J.D, 48; Kappa Alpha Psi. Polit. & Govt. Pos: Asst. State's attorney, Criminal Trial Div, Cook Co, Ill, 48-52; former mem, 20th Ward Regular Dem. Orgn; mem, Second Ward Regular Dem. Orgn, 54; mem, Civil Serv. Cmn, Chicago, 59-63; mem, Subcmt. on Correction and former mem, Subcmt. on Budget, Welfare Coun. Metrop. Chicago; v.pres, Metrop. Sanit. Dist, Gr. Chicago, 63-; alternate del, Dem. Nat. Conv, 68. Bus. & Prof. Pos: Trial lawyer, criminal court and sr. partner, Evins, Pincham, Fowlke and Strayhorn, 67- Mil. Serv: Entered as Pvt, Army, 41, released as 1st Lt, 46, after serv. in 600th Field Artil. Bn, 94th Inf. Div; Lt. Col. and Comdr, 1st Bn, 178th Inf, Ill. Army Nat. Guard, 68-; European-African-Middle East. Theater Ribbon with 2 Battle Stars; Victory Medal; Am. Theater Ribbon; Italian Croix de Guerra. Publ: Municipal Employees and the Law, Law Forum Vol. 3, Col. Law, Univ. Ill, fall 61. Mem: Nat., Am. and Cook Co. Bar Asns; Bar U.S. Supreme Court, U.S. Court of Appeals and 7th and 6th Circuit Courts of Appeals; 3rd v.pres. and mem, bd. mgr, Asn. Defense Lawyers; consult. and former v.pres. and bd. mem, Chicago Urban League; bd. dirs, Wash. Park Dept. YMCA, 54-59; NAACP; Nat. Guard Asn; Cmn. on Race and Relig, Presbytery of Chicago, United Presbyterian Church. Rel: Presbyterian; chmn, Wills and Investment Cmt, treas, Bldg. Fund and former mem, bd. trustees, Sixth-Grace United Presbyterian Church. Legal Res: 401 E. 32nd St, Chicago, Ill. 60616. Mailing Add: 100 E. Erie St, Chicago, Ill. 60611.

STREET, J. D. R
b. Bakersville, N.C, 1/1/08; s. W.C. Street and Sarah Elizabeth S; m. 7/28/28; c. Seven. Educ: Yancey Collegiate Inst; Appalachian State; E. Tenn. State Univ; Appalachian State Teachers Col; E. Tenn. State Teachers Col. Polit. & Govt. Pos: Acting postmaster, U.S. Post Off, Bakersville, N.C, 53-54, treas, Mid. Dist, 59-60; tax supvr. and city acct, Bakersville, 15 years; N.C. State Rep, 63-67. Bus. & Prof. Pos: Teacher, 14 years; farmer. Mem: Mason. Rel: Baptist. Mailing Add: Route 2, Box 113, Bakersville, N.C. 28705. (1967)

STREET, TOMMY H. D
Chmn, Buchanan Co. Dem. Cmt, Va.
b. Davenport, Va, 5/1/30; s. Robert Lee Street and Susie Rasnake S; m. 10/2/54 to Eva June Vaughn; c. Karen Leigh, Gary Wayne, Barbara June and Audrey Catherine. Educ: Hiwassee Col, A.A, 55; E. Tenn. State Univ, B.S, 58. Polit. & Govt. Pos: Treas, Young Dem. of Va, 64, v.pres, 65; chmn, Buchanan Co. Dem. Cmt, Va, currently. Bus. & Prof. Pos: Asst. prin, Haysi High Sch, 58-61; prin, Buchanan Voc. Sch, 60- Mil. Serv: Entered as Pvt, Air Force, 47, released as Pfc, 49, after serv. in 20th Air Force, Marianis, 47-49; Good Conduct Medal. Mem: V.pres, Hiwassee Alumni Asn, 59-60; Nat. and Va. Educ. Asns; Moose. Mailing Add: R.R. A Box 99, Davenport, Va. 24239. (1967)

STREETER, BERNARD A, JR. R
Mem. Gov. Coun, N.H.
b. Keene, N.H, 2/6/35; s. Bernard A. Streeter and Isabella Crane S; m. 8/31/58 to Janice Bowman; c. Shannon Lea and Christopher Bowman. Educ: Boston Univ, B.S, 57; grad. work at Boston Univ. and Keene State Col; Kappa Phi Alpha; Boston Univ. Young Rep. Club. Polit. & Govt. Pos: Pres, Gr. Nashua Young Rep. Club, 65-66; v.chmn, N.H. Fedn. Young Rep. Clubs, 66-; ward chmn, Nashua City Rep. Cmt, 67-68; mem, N.H. State Rep. Cmt, 68-; alternate del, Rep. Nat. Conv, 68; mem. Gov. Coun, Dist. 4, N.H, 69- Mil. Serv: Entered as Pvt, Army, 57, released as S/Sgt; Res, 7 years. Publ: Short stories and feature articles in various state and regional publ. Mem: Am. Hosp. Asn; Mass. Hosp. Asn; pres, Gt. Nashua Jaycees, 65-66; pres, N.H. Multiple Sclerosis Soc, 66-68; v.pres, Merrimack Valley Region Asn, 67-70; chmn. educ, N.Eng. Hosp. Pub. Rels. Asn, 68-70; v.pres, Nashua, N.H. Dollars for Scholars, 68-70; trustee, N.H. State Prison Trustees; Nashua Citizens Adv. Cmt; Club Nat; Rotary; Elks. Nashua Outstanding Young Man of the Year, 65; N.H. Outstanding Young Man of the Year, 66. Rel: Methodist. Mailing Add: 26 Indiana Dr, Nashua, N.H. 03060.

STREETER, JOYCE KATHERINE R
b. Decatur, Ill, 12/9/38; s. Harry Winton Streeter and Helen Paige S; single. Educ: Wheaton Col, Mass, 56-58; Katharine Gibbs Sch, Boston, Mass, 59. Polit. & Govt. Pos: Secy, Rep. Nat. Cmt, 59-61, Rep. John Rousselot, Calif, 61-62, Rep. Edward Gurney, Fla, 63, D.C. Young Rep. Club, 63-65 and Walton for Cong. Cmt, 64; admin. secy, Young Rep. Nat. Fedn, 64 & 66, nat. v.chmn, 65-67, secy, 67-69; secy, Rep. Glenn Andrews, Ala, 65; exec. secy, Rep. Donald Lukens, Ohio, 67-; del, Rep. Nat. Conv, 68; v.pres, Southwest Rep. Club, D.C, 68-69. Mem: Bd. dirs, D.C. Young Rep. Club, 63-67, Nat. Young Rep. Leadership Training Inst, Inc, 65-69 and Am. Coun. of Young Polit. Leaders, 69; del, Atlantic Asn. of Young Polit. Leaders, Luxemborg, 68. Rel: Protestant. Mailing Add: 283 G St. S.W, Washington, D.C. 20024.

STREETT, JULIAN DuVALL D
Ark. State Rep.
b. Camden, Ark, 2/3/37; s. Johnson Bruce Streett and Gertrude Sanderson S; m. to Mary Burns; c. Rebecca Louise, Katherine Sanderson and David Julian. Educ: Univ. Ark, B.A, 58 and LL.B, 61. Polit. & Govt. Pos: City attorney, Camden, Ark, 62-64; Ark. State Rep, Dist. 40, 69- Mil. Serv: Entered as E-2, Army Res, 59, released as Sgt. E-6, 65. Mem: Am. and Ark. Bar Asns; Ouachita Co. Bar Asn.(pres, 68-69); Am. and Ark. Trial Lawyers Asns; Kiwanis; pres, Whiteside PTA, currently. Legal Res: 922 Woodcrest, Camden, Ark. 71701. Mailing Add: 139 Jackson St, Camden, Ark. 71701.

STREHLOW, ARTHUR FRANK R
b. Omaha, Nebr, 2/21/99; s. Robert Carl Strehlow and Ann Rau S; m. 10/15/36 to Drusilla Kathryn Farwell; c. Frederick A. and James H. Educ: Univ. Wis; Phi Gamma Delta. Polit. & Govt. Pos: Mem, Alameda Co. Rep. Cent. Cmt, Calif, 32-54; state pres, Calif. Rep. Assembly, 47-48; del, Rep. Nat. Conv, 48 & 56 and alternate del, 64. Mil. Serv: Entered as Pvt, Army, 18, released as 2nd Lt, 18, after serv. at Camp Mabry, Tex. Mem: Past Master, Oak Grove Lodge 215 F&AM, Alameda, 42; Lt. Gov, Kiwanis, Calif. Dist. 2, and pres, 31; Alameda Lodge Elks 1015; Calif. Asn. Ins. Agents; Castlewood Country Club. Rel: Lutheran. Mailing Add: 3122 Gibbons Dr, Alameda, Calif. 94501.

STRELZIN, HARVEY LLOYD D
N.Y. State Assemblyman
b. N.Y.C, 7/19/07; s. Abraham Strelzin and Dora Garber S; m. 7/5/45 to Marie C. Warren; c. Paul J, Lynn S.(Mrs. Steinberg), Janyce C. and Adrienne M. Educ: Brooklyn Law Sch, LL.B, 27; N.Y. Law Sch, LL.M. summa cum laude, 62 and J.S.D, 67. Polit. & Govt. Pos: Asst. Attorney Gen, N.Y, 33-39; chmn, Bd. of Assessors, N.Y.C, 55-57; del, State Constitutional Conv, 67; N.Y. State Assemblyman, 69- Bus. & Prof. Pos: Legal ed, Beverage Times, 44-49; lectr, Brooklyn Col, 56; prof. law, N.Y. Law Sch, 65-67; prof. medico-jurisp, Col. Ins, 68-69; columnist, weekly newspaper, Williamsburg News and Coney Island Times, 68-, counsel, Spencer Mem. Church, Brooklyn Heights, N.Y, currently. Mem: Brooklyn Bar Asn; N.Y. Co. Lawyers Asn; pres, YMHA and YWHA, Williamsburg; bd. trustees, Fedn. Jewish Philanthropies. Rel: Hebrew. Legal Res: 59 Penn St, Brooklyn, N.Y. 11211. Mailing Add: 253 Broadway, New York, N.Y. 10007.

STREMEL, NICK A. D
V.chmn, Ford Co. Dem. Cent. Cmt, Kans.
b. Bison, Kans, 8/26/16; s. Anton J. Stremel and Anna Sauer S; m. 9/1/42 to LaVona Maria Peintner; c. Gary R, Janice (Mrs. Larry Penka), Mary Darlene, Linda Marie and Roger J. Educ: Otis High Sch, 35. Polit. & Govt. Pos: Committeeman, Dodge City, Kans, 55-; treas, Ford Co. Dem. Cent. Cmt, Kans, 62- Bus. & Prof. Pos: Car dealer, Stremel Motor Co, 44-50; owner & operator, Nick Stremel Ins. Agency, 50- Rel: Catholic. Mailing Add: 1211-A, Dodge City, Kans. 67801.

STREMLAU, JOSEPH P. D
b. Peru, Ill, 3/24/92; m. 1/30/13 to Catherine Sondgeroth St; c. eight sons, two daughters; 45 grandchildren. Educ: Parochial Schs. Polit. & Govt. Pos: Ill. State Rep, -66; Mem, Toll Rd. Adv. Bd, 4 yrs; Dep. Sheriff of LaSalle Co; 4 yrs, Oil Insp. Div; over 5 yrs. Dep. Collector, Treas. Dept. Bur. of Internal Revenue. Bus. & Prof. Pos: Owns and operates farm with son; Mgr, Peterstown Farmers Elevator Co, 13 yrs. Mem: Farm Bur; Farmers Union; Starved Rock Gen. Assembly; 4th Degree K. of C; Past Faithful Navigator; Elks; Moose, past Gov; Nat. Farmers Orgn. Mailing Add: R.R. 2, Box 170, Mendota, Ill. 61342. (1967)

STRETCH, D. ALLEN, JR. D
b. Bridgeton, N.J, 6/6/22; s. David A. Stretch and Rebecca Johnson S; m. 4/5/48 to Marie C. Ruggero; c. Katherine. Educ: Pratt Inst. Tech, 3 years.

Polit. & Govt. Pos: Agent, N.J. Motor Vehicle Div, 56-58; city leader, Ocean City, N.J, 57-, mem. cmt. pub. safety and cmt. pub. affairs, 59-67; mem, Beach Erosion Cmt, State N.J, 58-; alternate del, Dem. Nat. Conv, 68; mem, Cape May Co. Bd. Elec, 68- Bus. & Prof. Pos: Pres, Bd. Realtors, 58, Cape May Co. Ins, 59 and Shore Mem. Hosp, 68-69; v.pres, Independent Free Appraisers, 69, state dep. dir, 69. Mil. Serv: Entered as Pvt, Army, 42, released as Sgt, 45, after serv. in Second Inf. Div, ETO, 44-45; Bronze Star; Combat Inf. Badge; ETO Ribbon with Three Battle Stars; Colmar Colors. Mem: Am. Soc. Appraisers, sr. mem, Independent Fee Appraisers (appraiser-counsr. mem); F&AM; Tall Cedars of Lebanon; Shrine; Am. Legion; VFW. Rel: Baptist. Legal Res: 9 E. Edinburgh Rd, Ocean City, N.J. 08226. Mailing Add: 800 Ocean Ave, Ocean City, N.J. 08226.

STRICKLAND, ALLISON R. D
b. Chassahowitzka, Fla, 5/26/26; m. to Eloise Dumas; c. Edith Rose and Arthur. Educ: Pub. Schs. Polit. & Govt. Pos: Fla. State Rep, 56-67. Bus. & Prof. Pos: Commercial fisherman and guide. Mil. Serv: Army, Second Inf. Div, ETO, World War II. Mem: Am. Legion; VFW; Mason. Rel: Presbyterian. Mailing Add: Star Route 1, Box 38, Inverness, Fla. 32650. (1967)

STRICKLAND, ERNEST WILLIE D
b. Daisy, Ga, 12/26/08; s. Dempsey Marvin Strickland; Lennie Hodges S; m. 12/20/31 to Rubye Durrence; c. Lex W, Gerald L, James E, Daniel M. Educ: Daisy High Sch. Polit. & Govt. Pos: Ga. State Rep, 59-62 & 63-66. Bus. & Prof. Pos: Farmer; wholesale petroleum prods. distributor. Elected Ga. State Rep. to fill vacancy caused by death of G. Ed Percy, 63. Rel: Methodist. Mailing Add: Claxton, Ga. 30417. (1967)

STRICKLAND, ROY BEDFORD D
b. Perry City, Miss, 9/28/33; married. Polit. & Govt. Pos: Miss. State Rep, 60-66; chancery judge, Eighth Chancery Dist, Div. II, Miss, 66- Bus. & Prof. Pos: Lawyer. Mem: Mason; Shrine; Odd Fellows; Am. Legion; Elks; Miss. and Am. Bar Asn. Rel: Methodist. Mailing Add: Box 156, Wiggins, Stone City, Miss. 39577.

STRICKLAND, TED L. R
Colo. State Sen.
b. Austin, Tex, 9/17/32; married. Polit. & Govt. Pos: Blockworker, Adams Co. Rep. Party, Colo, Rep. precinct committeeman; pres, Adams Co. Young Rep; former Colo. State Rep; Colo. State Sen, currently. Bus. & Prof. Pos: Mgr, Rocky Mt. Well Logistics Serv, Water Conserv. and Water Resources. Mailing Add: 9361 Knox Court, Westminster, Colo. 81089. (1967)

STRICKLAND, THOMAS EDWARD D
N.C. State Rep.
b. Goldsboro, N.C, 6/16/30; s. Willie Strickland and Weltha Dail S; m. 12/25/53 to Shirley T. Lancaster; c. Larry Thomas and Ruth Ann. Educ: Univ. of N.C, A.B. in Polit. Sci, 52; Wake Forest Law Sch, LL.B, 55; Phi Delta Phi. Polit. & Govt. Pos: Chmn, Sch. Adv. Cmt, New Hope, N.C, 62-66; mem, Wayne Co. Dem. Exec. Cmt, 62-66; Dem. precinct chmn, Saulston Twp, 62-66; mem, Judiciary Cmt, Dem. Party, 64-66; N.C. State Rep, 66-Mil. Serv: Entered as Cpl, Marine Corps, 55, released as 1st Lt, 57. Mem: Am, N.C. and Wayne Co. Bar Asns; Mason; Elk; New Hope Ruritan Club; Civitan; Wayne Co. Wildlife Club; Saulston Grange; Odd Fellows; WOW. Rel: Methodist. Mailing Add: Route 2, Goldsboro, N.C. 27530.

STRIDER, HENRY CLARENCE, SR. D
Miss. State Sen.
b. Cascilla, Miss, 6/27/04; married. Polit. & Govt. Pos: Former chmn, State Game and Fish Cmn, Miss; Miss. State Sen, currently. Bus. & Prof. Pos: Merchant; planter; cattleman and Flying Serv. Mem: Sheriffs and Peace Off. Asn; Farm Bur; Nat. Cotton Coun; Delta Coun; MEC; Cotton Producers Inst. Rel: Methodist. Mailing Add: R.F.D. 2, Charleston, Miss. 38921. (1967)

STRIKE, JOHN LOUIS R
Salt Lake City, Utah, 5/6/23; s. Louis N. Strike and Christina Chipian S; m. 10/29/50 to Norma Leston; c. Chrysse, Alice, Julie. Educ: Westminster Col, 41-43; Univ. Utah, B.S, 48; Northwestern Univ, M.B.A, 50; Alpha Kappa Psi. Polit. & Govt. Pos: Mem. Gov. Utah Com. Employ. Physically Handicapped, 60-; bd. dir, Indust. Rels. Coun; regent Univ. Utah. Bus. & Prof. Pos: Co-mgr, Ajax Presses, div. mgr. apparel equip. sales, 65-; asst. mgr, Ajax Presses, div. Am. Laundry Machinery Industs, div. McGraw Edison Co, 55-65; asst. prof, lectr. dept. mgt, Northwestern Univ, 53-55; factory mgr. Ajax Pressing Machine Co, 51-52. Mem: Mason; Shriner; Rotary; Alta Club. Rel: Greek Orthodox. Mailing Add: 5600 Holladay Blvd, Salt Lake City, Utah. 84117. (1967)

STRIKER, MABEL D. D
b. Jay Co, Ind, 4/8/07; d. James William Stewart and Catherine Rebecca Elliott S; m. 4/25/26 to Fred D. Striker; c. Gloria Charlyne (Mrs. John T. Doyle), Karen Stewart (Mrs. James E. Dragge, Jr) and Mara Dee (Mrs. Ronald Lee Vetter). Polit. & Govt. Pos: Recorder, Adams Co, Ind, 53-60, dep. recorder, 61; state v.chmn, Ind. Dem. Cent. Cmt, 61-65; dir, Women and Children's Bur, Ind. Div. of Labor, 65-; 1st v.pres, Ind. Women's Dem. Club, 66-67. Mem: Pres, Riley Club; Ind. Chap. 127, Eastern Star; Pythian Sisters of K. of P. Chap. 39, Decatur, Ind; Ind, Adams Co, Marian Co, Wayne Twp. and East Side Dem. Women's Clubs; Indianapolis Civic Theatre; Int. Toastmistress Club; Riley Toastmistress Club of Indianapolis; adv. bd, Fort Wayne Sch. for Retarded Children; Women for Better Govt; Gov. Status of Women Cmn. of Ind. Rel: Evangelical United Brethren. Legal Res: 402 Mercer Ave, Decatur, Ind. 46733. Mailing Add: 6003 W. 25th St, Indianapolis, Ind. 46224.

STRINDEN, EARL STANFORD R
N.Dak. State Rep.
b. Litchville, N.Dak, 11/28/31; s. Teddie Isaac Strinden and Martha Eidsvig S; m. 9/27/53 to Janice Semmens; c. Ronda Marie, Jon Earl, Karen Ann, Thomas Isaac and Elizabeth Joy. Educ: Concordia Col, Moorhead, Minn, B.A, 53; Univ. N.Dak, M.A, 57. Polit. & Govt. Pos: Mem, City Coun. of Grand Forks, N.Dak, 62-, pres, 66-68; N.Dak. State Rep, 67-, Asst. Majority Floor Leader, N.Dak. House Rep, 69- Bus. & Prof. Pos: Teacher, Thief River Falls, Minn, 58-59; retail mgr, Strinden's Hardware, 59-69; Asst. Alumni Dir, Univ. N.Dak, 69. Mil. Serv: Entered as Pvt, Marines, 53, released as 1st Lt, 55, after serv. in 3rd marines, Far East, 54-55. Mem: Rotary; VFW; Am. Legion; Elks; Retarded Children. Jaycees Outstanding Young Man of Year, Grand Forks. Rel: Lutheran. Mailing Add: 2812 Chestnut, Grand Forks, N.Dak. 58201.

STRINGER, CLARENCE MAINE R
Mem, Calif. Rep. State Cent. Cmt.
b. Park City, Utah, 6/11/19; s. Myron M. Stringer and Alva Barton S; m. 6/21/47 to Lolita Keating; c. Clay M. and Victoria Ann. Educ: Golden Gate Col, Bus, 4 years, Mgt. Develop, 1 year; Am. Sch. of Law, LL.B. Polit. & Govt. Pos: Rep. precinct chmn, Fifth Dist, Calif, 62-69; mem, Calif. Rep. State Cent. Cmt, 62-; pres. N.Peninsula Chap, Calif. Rep. Assembly, 63-65, pres, Daly City, Colma Chap, 66-67; mem, San Mateo Co. Rep. Cent. Cmt, 63-; foreman, Grand Jury, San Mateo Co, 64; mem, United Rep. Finance Cmt, 66-69. Bus. & Prof. Pos: Sr. right-of-way agent, Pac. Gas and Elec. Co, 55-62, supvr, spec. assignments, 62-65, supvr, fee and spec. acquisition, 65-68 & 69-, supv. off. engr, 68-69. Mil. Serv: Entered as Pvt, Army, 43, released as 1st Lt, 46, after serv. in Amphibious Corps, First Brigade, E.B.&S.R, Pac. Theatre, 43-45; Asiatic Campaign Medal; Philippine Liberation Medal; Bronze Arrowhead with one Silver and two Bronze Stars; World War II Victory Medal. Mem: Pac. Coast Elec. Asn; Pac. Coast Gas Asn; Licensed Real Estate Broker, State of Calif; Westlake Cath. Mens Club; St. Francis Retreat League. Rel: Catholic. Mailing Add: 80 Parkwood Dr, Daly City, Calif. 94015.

STRIPP, JANE DEARBORN R
Dir, First Dist, Wash. State Fedn. Womens Rep. Clubs
b. Seattle, Wash, 5/21/23; d. Frank Wilbur Dearborn and Gertrude Lunbeck D; m. 6/22/44 to William Clayton Stripp, Jr; c. Michael William and Rebecca Jane. Educ: Univ. Wash, 41-44; Delta Delta Delta. Polit. & Govt. Pos: Pres, Assoc. Rep. Women, 62-64; legis. chmn, First Dist, Wash. State Fedn. Womens Rep. Clubs, 62-66, dir, 65-; v.chmn, King Co. Cent. Cmt, Wash, 64; campaign coordinator, Sen. Campaign, 64; alternate del, Rep. Nat. Conv, 64. Bus. & Prof. Pos: Partner, Wedding Consultants, 68- Mem: PTA; Overlake Hospital Asn; Orthopedic Hospital Asn; Delta Delta Delta Alumnae Asn. Rel: Presbyterian. Mailing Add: 1626 98th N.E, Bellevue, Wash. 98004.

STROBURG, ELDON LEONARD D
Iowa State Rep.
b. Blockton, Iowa, 11/4/27; s. Clark Emil Stroburg and Sola Straight S; m. 1/18/48 to Mary Aelene Johnston; c. Suzane, Jeffery, Monica and Peggy. Educ: Northwest. Mo. State, 2 quarters. Polit. & Govt. Pos: Mem, Clayton Twp. Sch. Bd, Bedford, Iowa, 53; clerk, Jefferson Twp, Blockton, 65-69; Iowa State Rep, 69- Bus. & Prof. Pos: Farmer, Bedford, Iowa, 48-56 & 57-68; machine parts inspection, Seattle, Wash, 57; bd. dirs, Clearfield, Iowa. Mil. Serv: Entered as Seaman 3/C, Navy, 45, released as Seaman 1/C, 46, after serv. in 90th Construction Bn, Pac. Theater, 45-46. Mem: Am. Legion; Mason; Consistory; Shrine; Lions; Wildlife Conserv. Club. Rel: Methodist. Legal Res: R.R. 2, Blockton, Iowa 50836. Mailing Add: State House, Des Moines, Iowa 50139.

STROFFOLINO, LOUIS JOSEPH R
Conn. State Rep.
b. Derby, Conn, 1/1/08; s. Joseph Stroffolino (deceased) and Louise S; m. 1/27/30 to Theresa Valiante; c. Louise (Mrs. Esposito) and Josep. Educ: Conn. Col. Pharm, New Haven, 26. Polit. & Govt. Pos: Asst. Prosecutor, Westport, Conn, 29-41; Conn. State Rep, 67- Bus. & Prof. Pos: Pharmacist, 28- Mem: Conn. Pharmaceutical Asn; chmn, Southwest. Pharmaceutical Asn; K. of C; Elks; Alhambra. Rel: Catholic. Mailing Add: 11 Sachem Trail, Westport, Conn. 06880.

STROGER, JOHN HERMAN, JR. D
b. Helena, Ark, 5/19/29; s. John Stroger and Ella Jones S; m. 8/29/69 to Yonnie Rita Batchelor; c. Hans Eric, Todd Herman and Yonnie Lynn. Educ: Xavier Univ, B.S. in Bus. Admin, 52; DePaul Univ. Law Sch, LL.B, 65; Alpha Phi Alpha; Phi Alpha Delta. Polit. & Govt. Pos: Pres, Third Ward Young Dem. Orgn, Ill, 54-55; personnel dir, Cook Co. Jail, 55-59; secy, Cook Co. Young Dem, 59-60; chief exam, Sales Finance Agency Div, Ill. Dept. Financial Insts, 67-68; committeeman, Eighth Ward Dem. Orgn, 68- Bus. & Prof. Pos: Attorney-at-law, Rogers, Garnett, Harth, Vital & Stroger, Chicago, Ill, 68- Mem: Chicago, Ill, Cook Co. and Am. Bar Asns; S.Avalon Commun. Orgn; Holy Name Soc; Knights of St. Peter Claver. Rel: Catholic. Mailing Add: 8534 S. Blackstone, Chicago, Ill. 60619.

STROM, CLYDE FRANKLIN D
S.C. State Rep.
b. Edgefield Co, S.C, 3/9/25; s. James Harrison Strom and Lucy Green S; m. 2/13/57 to Vennie Moseley; c. Lewis Ivey Haigler, stepson. Educ: Univ. S.C, B.S. in Bus. Admin, 50. Polit. & Govt. Pos: S.C. State Rep, Aiken Co, 68- Bus. & Prof. Pos: Dept. Overseer, Graniteville Co, 52-64; Dist. Rep, Int. Correspondence Schs, 65-68; Distributor, Allstates Safety Control, 69-Mil. Serv: Entered as A/S, Naval Res, 43, released as PhM 2/C, 45. Mem: Mason (Past Master Star Lodge 99, Past Dist. Dep. Grand Master); Graniteville Exchange Club; Am. Legion. Rel: Baptist. Mailing Add: 501 Trolley Line Rd, Graniteville, S.C. 29829.

STROMBERG, VERNON S. R
R.I. State Rep.
b. Seekonk, Mass, 1/23/16; m. to Josephine M. DeCedric; c. Vernon, Jr. Educ: E.Providence Pub. Sch. Polit. & Govt. Pos: R.I. State Rep, 65-, mem, Standing Cmt, spec. legis. Cmn. to Study R.I. Temporary Disability Ins. Fund, R.I. State House of Rep; mem, Rep. State Cent. Cmt, 66- Bus. & Prof. Pos: With Bird and Sons. Mem: Audubon Soc. R.I; bd. mem, Big Brothers of R.I, Inc; United Fund Budget Panel; trustee, Local 878 United Papermakers and Paperworkers AFL-CIO; mem. adv. bd, 3-Rs Rehabilitation and adv. bd. educ. cmt. Mailing Add: 6 Leahy St, Rumfrod, R.I. 02916.

STROMER, DELWYN DEAN R
Iowa State Rep.
b. Garner, Iowa, 4/22/30; s. Aaron Aurthur Stromer and Ruby Goll S; m.

8/26/50 to Harriet June Ostendorf; c. Linda, Randall, Pamela and David. Educ: High Sch. grad. Polit. & Govt. Pos: Iowa State Rep, 67- Mil. Serv: Entered as Pvt, Army, 53, released as Sgt. 1/C, 55, after serv. in 538th Field Artil. Bn, Camp Carson, Colo; Good Conduct Medal; Nat. Serv. Ribbon. Mem: Am. Legion; Farm Bur; Boy's 4-H Leader. Rel: United Church of Christ. Mailing Add: R.R. 3, Garner, Iowa 50438.

STROMER, MARVIN E. R
b. Hastings, Nebr, 11/22/33; m. 4/8/56 to Peggy Larson. Educ: Univ. Nebr, B.A, 55 and M.A, 62; Pi Kappa Phi. Polit. & Govt. Pos: Nebr. State Sen, 61-66; cong. liaison on staff of Fred A. Seaton, former secy. of interior, Wash, D.C; past exec. secy, Nebr. Rep. State Cent. Cmt; alternate del, Rep. Nat. Conv, 68. Bus. & Prof. Pos: Visiting instr. in Polit. Sci, Nebr. Wesleyan Univ. Mil. Serv: Army, 1st Lt, Counterintelligence Corps, 55-57. Mem: Past pres, Innocents Soc, Univ. Nebr, 54-55; pres. bd. dirs, Lincoln Commun. Playhouse; Mason; Scottish Rite; Shrine. Awarded Outstanding Nebraskan, Univ. Nebr, 55. Mailing Add: 613 E. 26th St, Scottsbluff, Nebr. 69361. (1967)

STRONG, JACK BOYNTON D
Tex. State Sen.
b. Carthage, Tex, 2/18/30; s. James Garrison Strong and Willie Belle Boynton S; m. to Rose Nanda Otts; c. Charlotte, Greg, Joe and Steve. Educ: Lon Morris Jr. Col, 1 year; Stephen F. Austin Col, 1 semester; Univ. Tex, B.A. and LL.B, 52. Polit. & Govt. Pos: Tex. State Sen, 2nd Dist, 62-, chmn, Privileges and Elect. Cmt, v.chmn, Ins, mem. Finance, State Affairs, Jurisprudence, Oil and Gas, Redistricting, Nominations and Water and Conserv. Cmts. and chmn, Drug Abuse and Educ. Study Cmn. and Slum Clearance Evaluation Cmn, Tex. State Senate; alternate del, Dem. Nat. Conv, 68. Bus. & Prof. Pos: Attorney-at-law, Tex, currently; dir, Am. Bank, Longview, Tex. Mem: Tex. Bar Asn; Am. Judicature Soc; Tex. Independent Producers & Royalty Owners; Mason; Shrine; Scottish Rite; Elks; charter mem, Henderson Rotary; Jr. C. of C. Elected one of Five Outstanding Young Texans, Tex. Jaycees, 65. Rel: Methodist. Legal Res: 605 Noel, Longview, Tex. 75601. Mailing Add: 312 Petroleum Bldg, Longview, Tex. 75601.

STRONG, JEANETTE B. D
First Dist. V.Chmn, Ind. Dem. State Cent. Cmt.
b. Gary, Ind, 5/5/20; d. Edward Buchanan and Virginia Thomas B; m. 9/26/58 to Curtis R. Strong; c. Lawrence, Penelope (Mrs. A. Johnson) and Curtidean (Mrs. R. Haynes). Educ: Ind. Univ, 3 years; Hammond Bus. Col, 2 years; La Salle Bus. Col, 1 year. Polit. & Govt. Pos: First dist. v.chmn, Ind. Dem. State Cent. Cmt, 62-64, 68-; election worker, Humphrey for President and Get Out the Vote, Nat. Dem. Cmt, 68; del, Dem. Nat. Conv, 68. Bus. & Prof. Pos: Asst. to financial secy, USW, AFL-CIO-1014, 50- Mem: Life mem. NAACP; Ind. Dem. Women's Orgn; Cent. Dem. Women's Orgn (C'de-Modes); Nat. Hosp. Vol. Asn; Eastern Star; League of Women Voters; VFW. Jenny Award for outstanding work in Dem. Party, Ind. Dem. Women; named Citizen of the Year by two local and one Indianapolis, Ind. paper; Loren Henry Award for outstanding service in field of civil rights, Ind. State Conf. NAACP; Distinguished Serv. Award, Gary-East Chicago Chap. of Frontiers Int; Mary White Ovington Award for Outstanding leadership in field of human rights, Gary Branch NAACP; Citizens Award in the fields of civil rights and politics, Lake Co. Educ. & Polit. Asn. Rel: Baptist. Mailing Add: 1987 Harrison St, Gary, Ind. 46407.

STRONG, ROBERT CAMPBELL
b. Chicago, Ill, 9/29/15; m. to Betty Jane Burton; c. Three. Educ: Beloit Col, A.B. magna cum laude, 38; Univ. Wis, 38-39; Phi Beta Kappa. Hon. LL.D, Beloit Col, 67. Polit. & Govt. Pos: Career officer, U.S. Dept. of State For. Serv, 39-; v.consul, Frankfurt, 39, Prague, 39-40, Durban, 40-44 and Sofia, 44-46; Naval War Col, 46-47; consul, Tsingtao, 47-49; first secy, Canton, Chunking, 49 and Taipei, 49-50; spec. asst. to dir, Off. of Chinese Affairs, 51-53; mem, Policy Planning Staff, 53-54; consul and counsr, Damascus, 54-58; Army War Col, 58-61; dir, Off. of Near East. Affairs, 61-63; U.S. Ambassador to Iraq, 63-67. Bus. & Prof. Pos: Diplomat-in-residence and prof. polit. sci. and hist, Univ. Okla, 67-68. Received State Dept. Superior Serv. Award, 59 and Nat. Civil Serv. League Award, 65. Mailing Add: 826 W. Cresta Loma Dr, Tucson, Ariz. 85704.

STROOCK, THOMAS F. R
Wyo. State Sen.
b. N.Y.C, 10/10/25; s. Samuel Stroock and Dorothy Frank S; m. 6/14/49 to Marta Freyre de Andrade; c. Margaret, Sandra, Betty and Anne. Educ: Yale Univ, B.A, 48; York Hall. Polit. & Govt. Pos: V.pres, Wyo. State Young Rep, 52; alternate del, Rep. Nat. Conv, 56; chmn, Casper City Parks Cmn, 58-60; precinct committeeman, 60-62; mem, Natrona Co. Rep. Cent. Cmt, 62; pres, Natrona Co. High Sch. Dist. and Dist. 2, 63 & 66; mem, Wyo. State Rep. Cent. Cmt, 64; finance chmn, Gov. Cmt. on Educ, 64-66; pres, Wyo. Sch. Bd. Asns, 65-66; Wyo. State Sen, Natrona Co. 67- Bus. & Prof. Pos: Sr. partner, Stroock and Rogers, Oil & Gas Properties Brokers, 52-66; dir, Great Plains Life Ins. Co, 65-; dir, Security Bank & Trust Co, 66- Mil. Serv: Entered as Pvt, Marine Corps, 43, released as Sgt, 46, after serv. in Continental U.S. and Pac. Theater of Operations; Marine Corps Res. Mem: V.pres, Rocky Mountain Oil and Gas Asn, 65-; Elks; Kiwanis; Casper Petrol. Club; Casper Country Club; Denver Club. Rel: Unitarian. Legal Res: 714 W. 19th St, Casper, Wyo. 82601. Mailing Add: P.O. Box 66, Casper, Wyo. 82601.

STROTHMAN, CHARLES F. R
Iowa State Rep.
b. Near Danville, Iowa, 1901; s. Charles Strothman and Parma Oberman S; m. 1929 to Doris Maxwell; c. Carol (Mrs. Messer), Charlotte (Mrs. Young), Charlene (Mrs. Larson), Charles M, Frederic, John and 16 grandchildren. Educ: Iowa State Univ, Awarded Scholarship. Polit. & Govt. Pos: Iowa State Rep, currently; pres, sch. bd; Rep. precinct and cong. committeeman. Bus. & Prof. Pos: Farming, livestock feeding and breeding of registered polled Hereford cattle with sons Frederic, John and son-in-law. Mem: New London Farmers Coop; City Farm Bur; City 4-H Club Cmt; bank, church and livestock bds; pres, Southeast Iowa Hereford Asn. and Henry City Taxpayers' Asn; Farm Bur; Am. and Am. Polled Hereford Asn; Nat. Livestock Feeders; Iowa Taxpayers Asn. Rel: Methodist. Mailing Add: R.R, New London, Iowa 52645. (1967)

STROUD, GARNER RAMSEY R
b. Salem, Ark, 10/22/26; s. William Owen Stroud and Elsie Garner S; m. 9/8/49 to Rena Luttrell; c. John Robert, Sally Ann and Eric Garner. Educ: Harding Col; Ark. State Univ, B.S.E; George Peabody Col, grad. Polit. & Govt. Pos: Ward chmn, Shriver for Cong, 60-62; exec. secy, Kans. State Rep. Cmt, 65-68. Bus. & Prof. Pos: Prin, Manila Pub. Sch. Syst, Ark, 50-51; supt, Biggers-Reyno Sch. Syst, Ark, 51-52; landman, Gulf Oil Corp, Wichita, Kans, 53-65. Mil. Serv: Entered as Pvt, Army, 45, released as S/Sgt, 47, after serv. in Adj. Gen. Dept, S.Pac; Philippine Liberation Medal. Mem: Kans. Oil Scouts Asn. (past pres); Kans. Asn. of Petroleum Landmen (past v.pres); Lions; Masonic Blue Lodge Consistory Shrine; Koinonia Fraternity. Rel: Disciples of Christ. 1967 Legal Res: Topeka, Kans. No mailing address available. (1967)

STROUD, JAMES ERNEST R
Mayor, Amarillo, Tex.
b. Weatherford, Okla, 5/8/12; s. Jesse Washington Stroud and Smantha Albright S; m. 5/20/33 to Nell Dale Hume; c. Patricia (Mrs. Tucker), Sherelle (Mrs. Culp), Tim H, Richard R. and James Ernest, Jr. Educ: Southwest. State Col, Okla, 2 years; W. Tex. State Col. exten. course, 54. Polit. & Govt. Pos: Founder and pres, Millions of Americans for Goldwater, 63-64; del, Rep. Nat. Conv, 64; mayor, Amarillo, Tex, 67-; Tex. state dir, Mayors for Nixon, 68; Rep. Presidential elector, 68. Bus. & Prof. Pos: Pres, N.Mex. Welding Supply Co, 33-41; owner, J. Ernest Stroud & Co, 41-; pres, Tex-Air Gas Co, 48-55 and Stroud Develop. Co, 55-; owner, Trades Fair Center, 61-; pres, JesCOm, Inc, 62- Rel: Christian. Legal Res: 3007 S. Ong St, Amarillo, Tex. 79109.

STROUD, JAMES WILLIAM D
Tex. State Rep.
b. Denison, Tex, 6/4/14; s. Lynn Stroud and Rose Hickman S; m. 10/7/60 to Mary Ellon Birdwell; c. James William, Jr, Robert Lynn, George Winton, Douglan Alan and Paul Jeffrey. Polit. & Govt. Pos: Regional ration banking officer, region mgr. dist. center, Off. Price Admin, 42-47; regional dir, U.S. Census Bur, Dallas, 48-64; Tex. State Rep, 64- Bus. & Prof. Pos: Dep. to regional acct, Home Owners Loan Corp, 35-42; pres, Liberty Packing Co, Inc, 40- Mem: Bd. mem, N.Tex. Chap, Multiple Sclerosis Soc. and E.Dallas Dem. Club; Dem. Men of Dallas Co; Phi Sigma. Rel: Christian Church. Mailing Add: 5507 McCommas, Dallas, Tex. 75206.

STROUD, ROBERT EUGENE D
Chmn, Shawnee Co. Dem. Cent. Cmt, Kans.
b. Peabody, Kans, 7/28/23; s. Lakin Monroe Stroud and Lucy Adelaine Underwood S; m. 3/21/51 to Mary Lou Noller; c. Linda Lee and Laurie Ann. Educ: Kans. Univ, A.B, 49; Univ. of Mo, Kans. City, D.D.S, 53; Tau Kappa Epsilon; Xi Psi Phi. Polit. & Govt. Pos: Chmn, Shawnee Co. Dem. Cent. Cmt, Kans, 67-; del, Dem. Nat. Conv, 68; pres, Kans. State Bd. of Dental Exam, 68- Bus. & Prof. Pos: Dentist, Topeka Kans, 53-69. Mil. Serv: Entered as Pvt, Air Force, 43, released as Cpl, 45, after serv. in 409th Inf. 103rd Div, ETO, 44-45; Combat Inf. Badge; Three Battle Stars. Publ: 'The Dentists Challenge,' 63 and 'The Dental Hygienist,' 64, Dent. Hygiene. Mem: Soc. For the Preservation of Oral Health (past pres); Am. Acad. of Dental Practice Admin; Midwest Soc. of Periodontists; Am. Asn. of Endodontists; Am. Asn. of Dental Bd. Exam; Elks; Cosmopolitan Club; Mason; Scottish Rite; Shrine. Rel: Protestant. Legal Res: 4910 West Hills Dr, Topeka, Kans. 66606. Mailing Add: 4301 Huntoon, Topeka, Kans. 66604.

STROUD, WILLIAM HUGH R
S.C. State Rep.
b. Greenville, S.C; s. George Thurmond Stroud and Luna Freeman S; m. 6/14/40 to Dorothy Donald Harris; c. Toni Donne and William Hugh, Jr. Educ: Furman Univ, B.S, 38; Chi Beta Phi. Polit. & Govt. Pos: S.C. State Rep, 67- Bus. & Prof. Pos: Food broker and owner, W.H. Stroud Co; teacher, biol, high sch, 41-43. Mil. Serv: Entered as A/S, Naval Res, 44, released as Lt, 46, after serv. in Pac; Lt.(Ret), Naval Res, 58; Am. Area Ribbon; Asiatic-Pac. Area Ribbon with 2 Stars; Philippine Liberation Ribbon. Mem: Nat. Food Brokers Asn; past pres, Piedmont Food Brokers Asn; Rotary; Elks. Rel: Methodist. Legal Res: R.R. 2, Piedmont, S.C. 29673. Mailing Add: P.O. Box 5985, Station B, Greenville, S.C. 29606.

STROUP, ROBERT LEE R
N.Dak. State Sen.
b. Stanton, N.Dak, 6/17/15; s. Robert Martin Stroup and Margaret Adams S; m. 6/10/39 to Lillian R. Pridt; c. Robyn Jean (Mrs. Edmund Vinje), Robert L, II, M. James, Thomas Allen and Elizabeth Ann. Educ: Concordia Col, Moorhead, Minn, B.A, 37; Pi Kappa Delta. Polit. & Govt. Pos: Park Cmnr, Hazen Park Bd, N.Dak, 52-; N.Dak. State Sen, 66- Bus. & Prof. Pos: secy, Stanton Grain Co, Stanton, N.Dak, 39-; pres, Hazen Lumber Co, Hazen, 47-; secy, Sunrise Homes Inc, 65- Mem: N.Dak. Law Enforcement Coun; Mercer Co. Planning Cmn; Mason; Elks; Soc. of Am. Mil. Engrs; C. of C; past pres, N.Dak. Retail Lumbermen's Asn; pres Northwest Lumbermen Inc. Named Boss of the Year, Hazen Jr. C. of C, 67. Rel: Lutheran. Mailing Add: 317 E. Fourth St, Hazen, N.Dak. 58545.

STROUP, STANLEY G. R
Pa. State Sen.
b. Somerset City, Pa, 9/18/02; s. Samuel D. Stroup and Blanche N. S; m. to La Rue Kathleen Robinson; c. Gordon E. Esquire and Kathleen A. Riggs. Educ: Juniata Col; Pa. State Col; Univ. Pittsburgh; Dickinson Sch. of Law. Polit. & Govt. Pos: Pa. State Rep, 54-60; Pa. State Sen, 60-; alternate del, Rep. Nat. Conv, 68. Bus. & Prof. Pos: Former teacher, athletic coach and prin; pres, Keystone Army and Navy Schs; attorney with Dept. of Justice, 47-54; partner in law firm of Stroup and Stroup. Mil. Serv: War Serv. Dir, Army and Navy Radio Training Stas, 41-46. Mem: Pa. and Am. Bar Asns; Rotary (past mem, 45-50 and past pres, 51); Bedford City Bar Asn. (past pres, 51-61); Am. Judicature Soc; Mason; Univ. Club of Pittsburgh; dir, Bedford City Branch, Pa. Asn. for the Blind; dir, Mem. Hosp. of Bedford City; chmn, Bedford City Chap, Am. Red Cross. Rel: St. John's Reformed Church, Bedford. Mailing Add: 8-10 Court House Square, Bedford, Pa. 15522. (1967)

STROWIG, CALVIN ARTHUR R
Speaker, Kans. House Rep.
b. Paxico, Kans, 12/31/23; s. Homer F. Strowig and Stella Hoffman S; m.

8/1/48 to Betty Lou Isley; c. Pamela and Catherine. Educ: Kans. State Univ, $1\frac{1}{2}$ years. Polit. & Govt. Pos: Kans. State Rep, 57th Dist, 63-64, 54th Dist, 65-66, 92nd Dist, 67-, Majority Floor Leader, Kans. House Rep, 67-68, Speaker of the House, 69- Bus. & Prof. Pos: Owner and mgr, Abilene Theatres, Kans, 47-; v.pres, Anadarko Theatre Corp, Okla, 54-; v.pres, Capitol Drive In Theatre, Iowa, 56- Mil. Serv: Entered as Aviation Cadet, Air Force, 43, released as 1st Lt, 46, after serv. in 1342 BU Mobil Air Transport Squadron, China-Burma-India, 44-45; Distinguished Flying Cross; Air Medal with Oak Leaf Cluster; Asiatic-Pac. Ribbon with Four Campaign Stars; Presidential Unit Citation. Mem: United Motion Picture Asn; C. of C; Am. Legion; VFW; Elks; Mason (Chap. Commandery); Consistory; Shrine; Jesters; Rotary. Rel: Lutheran. Mailing Add: 1112 N. Buckeye, Abilene, Kans. 67410.

STRUCKMEYER, FRED C, JR. D
Chief Justice, Ariz. Supreme Court
b. Phoenix, Ariz, 1/4/12; s. Fred C. Struckmeyer, Sr. and Inez Walker S; m. 4/17/48 to Margaret Mills; c. Chris, Jan Holly, Karl Larson and Kent Mills. Educ: Univ. Ariz. Col. Law, LL.B, 36. Polit. & Govt. Pos: Trial judge, Maricopa Co. Superior Court, Ariz, $4\frac{1}{2}$ years; justice, Ariz. Supreme Court, 55-, chief justice, 60-61 and 66- Mil. Serv: Army Inf, 4 years, released as 1st Lt; Bronze Star; Silver Star; Purple Heart. Distinguished Serv. Award, Greater Phoenix Coun. for Civic Unity, 55; 75th Anniversary Cert. of Award, 60, Medallion of Merit, Univ. Ariz. Rel: Episcopal. Legal Res: 7151 N. Third St, Phoenix, Ariz. 85020. Mailing Add: Rm. 229, Capitol Bldg, Phoenix, Ariz. 85007.

STRUEBING, WILMER HENRY R
b. Brillion, Wis, 4/2/10; s. William F. Struebing and Minnie Schaefer S; m. 2/14/37 to Henrietta Vaupel; c. Mary Lee (Mrs. Hoffman), William F, Jr, George H. and James R. Educ: Brillion Pub. Schs. Polit. & Govt. Pos: Pres. sch. bd, Brillion, Wis, 51-57, town chmn, 57-65; mem, Co. Bd. Supvrs, Calumet Co, 57-65; Wis. State Assemblyman, 63-65; chief clerk, Wis. State Assembly, 65- Bus. & Prof. Pos: Salvage dealer, 39-; farmer, 46- Mem: Lions; hosp. bd, Calumet Mem. Hosp, 57- Rel: Lutheran; mem. church coun. Mailing Add: Route 2, Brillion, Wis. 54110.

STRUNA, MARJORIE CONRAD D
State Cent. Committeewoman, Fourth Cong. Dist, Ohio Dem. Party
b. Lima, Ohio, 4/9/16; d. Herbert O. Conrad and Frieda J. Miller C; m. 7/19/43 to William Frank Struna; c. William Conrad. Educ: Ohio North. Univ, B.S. in Educ; Col. of Law, 2 years; West. Reserve Univ. Polit. & Govt. Pos: Southwest regional v.pres, Federated Women of Ohio, 57-59, 61-63 & 65-67, financial secy, 59-61 and trustee, 63-65; cand. for cong, Fourth Dist, Ohio, 58 & 62; state cent. committeewoman, Fourth Cong. Dist, Ohio Dem. Party, 58-; v.chairwoman, Dem. State Exec. Cmt, 64-66; alternate del, Dem. Nat. Conv, 64 & 68. Mem: Life mem, Nat. Educ. Asn; Northwest and Lima Teachers Asns; Ohio Educ. Asn; Int. Reading Asn; League of Women Voters. Rel: Catholic. Mailing Add: 2816 Lakewood, Lima, Ohio 45805.

STRYKER, HAROLD B. D
b. Rising City, Nebr, 12/28/15; m. 6/15/39 to Talbot Stryker; c. Two. Educ: Midland Col; Univ. Nebr. Col. Agr, 2 years. Polit. & Govt. Pos: Former mem, Sch. Bd; chmn, Co. Dem. Party, Nebr, 8 years; former, Nebr. State Sen, chmn, Legis. Coun, 63-64; acting Gov, Nebr, occasionally, 64. Bus. & Prof. Pos: Farmer and farm mgr. for absentee owners; heavy machine operator for road construction; instr, Vet. Voc. Agr, 18 months; officer work, 3 years; licensed prfnl. engr, Nebr. Mem: Chmn, and committeeman, Farm Security Admin. and Farmers Home Admin; chmn. and mem, Butler Co. Redistricting Cmt; chmn. bd. of dirs, Agr. Prods. Utilization Asn; past mem, bd. dirs, of Butler Co. Farm Loan Asn; Mason; Elks; Air Force Asn. Rel: Methodist Episcopal Church. Mailing Add: Route 2, Rising City, Nebr. 68658.

STUART, DOUGLAS S. R
Mem, Abington Town Rep. Cmt, Mass.
b. Eustis, Maine, 10/23/25; s. E. Allen Stuart and Mary Knapp S; m. 8/19/48 to Elizabeth Fairbanks Hall; c. Douglas S, Jr, Anne Elizabeth, Jonathan Lincoln and Heidi Johanna. Educ: Northeast. Univ. Polit. & Govt. Pos: Mem, Abington Town Rep. Cmt, Mass, currently, former chmn. and v.chmn; former mem. and chmn, Abington Bd. of Park Cmnr, 7 years; coordinator, Plymouth Co. Cong. Elec. and Gov. John A. Volpe Campaign Cmt; co. coordinator, Mass. Buckley for Auditor Cmt. Bus. & Prof. Pos: Mem, Bd. of Dirs, Abington Scholarship Found. Cmt. Mil. Serv: Entered as Pvt, Army, 44, released as Cpl, 44, after serv. in 75th Inf. Div. Mem: Nat. Office Furniture Dealers Asn; former mem, Abington Red Cross Cmt. and Abington Rotary. Rel: First Parish Church; mem, Adv. Cmt. Mailing Add: 151 Myers Ave, Abington, Mass. 02351.

STUART, EDWARD, JR. Conservative
V.Chmn, First Cong. Dist. Cmt. and State Cent. Cmt, Va. Conservative Party
b. Boston, Mass, 6/15/17; s. Edward Stuart and Helen Fox S; c. Edward, III, Diane (Mrs. Perry) and Bruce. Educ: Univ. Maine, B.S. in Forestry, 37; Harvard Univ, civil affairs, 44; Biltmore Forest Sch, forest engr, 45; Univ. Chicago Appraisal Inst, 65; Xi Sigma Pi; Scabbard & Blade; Phi Eta Kappa; M Club; Forestry Club; Pale Blue Key; Maine Outing Club. Polit. & Govt. Pos: Precinct worker and chmn, Northumberland Co. Rep. Party, 48-60; secy-treas, Middlesex Co. Rep. Party, 60-64 and chmn, 64-65; chmn, Middlesex Co. Va. Conservative Party, 65- and v.chmn, First Cong, Dist, 66- Bus. & Prof. Pos: Forester, Oxford Paper Co, 37-38, Penobscot Chem. Fibre, 38 and U.S. Forest Serv, 38-42; forester and lumberman, 46-56; consulting forester and appraiser, East. Forestry, Inc, 56- Mil. Serv: Entered as 2nd Lt, Army, 42, released as Capt, 46, after serv. in Civil Affairs Div, ETO, 44-46; Croix Militaire, Belgium, Commendation, Am. Serv, German Occupation and Victory Medals; European-African-Middle East. Serv. Medal with Four Battle Stars. Publ: 'Affects of Thinning-Black Hills,' J. of Forestry, 44;'Special Factors in Appraising Timberland,' Appraisal & Valuation Manual, 60; 'A Timber Management Contract,' The Consultant, 66. Mem: Soc. Am. Foresters; Nat. Real Estate Bd; Cong. on Surveying & Mapping; Am. Soc. Appraisers; Va. Forests, Inc; Asn. of Consult. Foresters; Va. Real Estate Asn; Va. Forestry Coun; Glou.Mathews-Middlesex Bd. of Realtors; SAR; Am. Legion. Rel: Protestant. Legal Res: Stuart Landing, Wake, Va. 23176. Mailing Add: Box 6, Wake, Va. 23176. (1967)

STUART, EUGENE PAGE R
Ky. State Rep.
b. Louisville, Ky, 10/20/27; s. Eugene Griffin Stuart and Mary Belle Page S; m. 4/30/55 to Mary Dannenhold; c. Eugene Page, Jr. Educ: Univ. Louisville, B.S. in Mkt, 51; Sigma Chi. Polit. & Govt. Pos: Ky. State Rep, 48th Legis. Dist, 64- Mil. Serv: Entered as A/S, Navy, 46, released as Seaman 1/C, 48. Mem: Louisville Bd. of Ins. Agents; Jr. C. of C.(past pres); C. of C; v.pres, Louisville Zool. Cmn. Outstanding Young Man in Louisville and Jefferson Co, 63. Rel: Episcopal. Legal Res: 6403 Coventry Court, Prospect, Ky. 40059. Mailing Add: Starks Bldg, Louisville, Ky. 40202.

STUART, GEORGE B. R
Solicitor, Cumberland Co, Pa.
b. Carlisle, Pa, 7/31/12; s. Walter Stuart, Jr. and Laura Peffer S; single. Educ: Univ. Pa, B.S. in Econ, 34; Dickinson Sch. of Law, LL.B, 38; Theta Chi. Polit. & Govt. Pos: Mem, Pa. State Labor Rels Bd, currently; solicitor, South Middleton Twp, Middlesex Twp, Dickinson Twp. and Cumberland Co, currently; chmn, Cumberland Co. Rep. Party, currently; chmn, Zoning Bd. Adjust, Carlisle, currently; past trial exam, Pub. Utilities Cmn; past solicitor, East Pennsboro Twp, North Middleton Twp, Hampden Twp. and Mt. Holly Springs. Mil. Serv: Entered Army, 42, released 45, after serv. in Off. Strategic Serv, Supreme Hq, AEF, ETO, 42-45; Bronze Star. Mem: VFW; Am. Legion. Rel: Protestant; currently trustee and former treas, First Presby. Church. Legal Res: 201 S. Pitt St, Carlisle, Pa. 17013. Mailing Add: 3 S. Hanover St, Carlisle, Pa. 17013.

STUART, ROBERT D, JR. R
Rep. Nat. Committeeman, Ill.
b. Hubbard Woods, Ill, 4/26/16; s. Robert Douglas Stuart and Harriet McClure S; m. 5/21/38 to Barbara McMath Edwards; c. Robert Douglas, III, James McClure, Marian McClure (Mrs. Donaldson C. Pillsbury) and Alexander Douglas. Educ: Princeton Univ, B.A, 37; Yale Law School, LL.B, 46. Polit. & Govt. Pos: Pres, Lake Co. Rep. Fedn. and precinct committeeman, Ill, 62-64; twp. auditor, Lake Co, Ill, 62-64; Rep. Nat. Committeeman, Ill, currently; del, Rep. Nat. Conv, 68. Bus. & Prof. Pos: With Quaker Oats Co, 47-, pres, 62-; dir, Continental Assurance Co. and Continental Casualty Co, 56-; dir, 1st Nat. Bank of Chicago, 65-; dir, CNA Financial Corp, 67-; dir, United Air Lines, 68- Mil. Serv: Entered as 2nd Lt, Army, 42, released as Maj, 46. Rel: Presbyterian. Legal Res: 1601 W. Conway Rd, Lake Forest, Ill. 60045. Mailing Add: 345 Merchandise Mart, Chicago, Ill. 60654.

STUART, ROBERT STERLING R
Maine State Sen.
b. Rangeley, Maine, 12/7/21; s. Charles Sprague Stuart and Edith Sterling S; m. 11/3/45 to Virginia Stanforth; c. Nancy, Gail and Robert, Jr. Educ: Bowdoin Col, B.A, 44; Columbia Univ. Sch. of Dent. and Oral Surg, D.D.S, 47; Alpha Delta Phi. Polit. & Govt. Pos: Mem, Brunswick Rep. Town Cmt, Maine, 65-, treas, 67-; Maine State Sen, currently, chmn. joint standing cmt. on health and insts, 104th Legis. and mem. joint standing cmt. on educ. Bus. & Prof. Pos: Author, Health study for 20 mem. of Cong, Wash, D.C, 66; staff dentist, Upward Bound and Head Start Prog, 67-; mem. Adv. Cmt. on Dent. Health, Maine State Dept. of Health and Welfare, 67-; mem. Ed. Adv. Bd, Dent. Div, Med. Commun, Inc, 68- Mil. Serv: Entered as Lt, Air Force, 47, released as Capt, 49, after serv. in Korea, Maj, Res, currently. Publ: Bend Over Backwards, 67; 'Preventive Dental Care—a Health Message for Patients,' Dent. Surv, 3/69. Mem: Rotary Int.(pres, Brunswick Club, 68); Brunswick Area United Fund (pres, 68); Brunswick-Topsham Mil. Commun. Coun. Rel: Episcopal. Mailing Add: 15 Meadowbrook Rd, Brunswick, Maine 04011.

STUART, WILLIAM CORWIN R
Justice, Iowa Supreme Court
b. Knoxville, Iowa, 4/28/20; s. George Corwin Stuart and Edith Abram S; m. 10/20/46 to Mary Elgin Cleaver; c. Corwin, Cullen, Melanie and Valerie. Educ: State Univ. Iowa, A.B, 40, J.D, 42; A.F.I, Omicron Delta Kappa; Order of Coif; Phi Kappa Psi; Phi Delta Phi. Polit. & Govt. Pos: City attorney, Chariton, Iowa, 47-49; Iowa State Sen, 53-61; justice, Iowa Supreme Court, 62- Bus. & Prof. Pos: Partner, Stuart and Stuart Law Firm, 46-62. Mil. Serv: Entered as Cadet, Naval Air Corps, 43, released as Lt.(jg), 45. Mem: Iowa State and Am. Bar Asns; Am. Judicature Soc; AF&AM; Shrine; Am. Legion; Lions. Rel: Protestant. Legal Res: 216 S. Grand, Chariton, Iowa 50049. Mailing Add: P.O. Box 130, Chariton, Iowa 50049.

STUBBLEFIELD, FRANK A. D
U.S. Rep, Ky.
b. Murray, Ky, 4/5/07; married; c. Three. Educ: Univ. Ky. Col. of Commerce, B.S. Polit. & Govt. Pos: U.S. Rep, Ky, 58- Bus. & Prof. Pos: Retail drug bus. Mem: Ky. R.R. Cmn, 51- Legal Res: Murray, Ky. 42071. Mailing Add: 4619 Albemarle St, Washington, D.C. 20016.

STUBBS, ARCHIE ROY R
Secy, S.C. Rep. Party
b. Gloucester Co, Va, 11/25/10; s. James Monroe Stubbs, Sr. and Alma Harriett Roy S; m. 8/14/37 to Marion Elizabeth Hoffmann; c. Jon Archer, Kent Parker and Carl Roy. Educ: Col. of William and Mary, class, 31. Polit. & Govt. Pos: Pres. of precinct, Greenville Co. Rep. Party, S.C, 62-64, secy, 62-66; mem, Greenville Co. Exec. Cmt, 64-; secy, S.C. Rep. Party, 65-; Presidential Elector for Nixon, 68. Bus. & Prof. Pos: Home off, Independence Indemnity Co, Phila, 31-33; adjuster, Liberty Mutual Ins. Co, Boston and Providence, 33-36 and Am. Mutual Liability Ins. Co, Chicago, 36 & 37; S.C. mgr, Kemper Ins. Group, 37- Publ: Address as Ins. Indust. Rep. on the Commemoration Day Prog, 30th Anniversary of the S.C. Workmen's Compensation Law, Sept. 3, 65, now appearing in book form pub. by the S.C. Indust. Cmn. Mem: Chmn, Inter-Co. Arbitration Cmt, 57-60; pres, Columbia Claim Mgr. Coun, 61; pres, Exchange Club of Greenville, 67-68; v.pres. and dir, S.C. Rifle and Pistol Asn, 67-; Greenville Little Theatre; Nat. Rifle Asn. Baseball, track, big game hunting. Rel: First Presbyterian. Mailing Add: 405 McDonald Ave, Greenville, S.C. 29609.

STUBENHOFER, JAMES ANTHONY D
Chmn, Chase Co. Dem. Cent. Cmt, Kans.
b. Elmdale, Kans, 1/24/33; s. Karl William Stubenhofer and Bertha Bechel-

mayr S; m. 6/21/58 to Dona Sheridan; c. Scot James. Educ: Elmdale Rural High Sch, Kans, grad. Polit. & Govt. Pos: Mem, Cottonwood Falls City Coun, Kans, currently; chmn, Chase Co. Dem. Cent. Cmt, 68- Mil. Serv: Entered as Pvt, Army, 53, released as Cpl, 55, after serv. in 714 Rwy. Operating Bn, Ft. Eustis, Va. Mem: Am. Legion (Comdr, Post 78, 59, 62, 64 & 68, V.Comdr, 61, 63 & 67, Adj, 60); Boy Scouts (adv. cmt); Brotherhood of Locomotive Fireman & Engineman. Rel: Catholic. Mailing Add: Cottonwood Falls, Kans. 66845.

STUBENVOLL, KURT HUGO R
b. Oakwood, Wis, 10/27/94; s. Dr. Carl E. Stubenvoll and Caroline Rodenbeck S; m. 9/20/17 to Madge de Lacey. Educ: Carrol Col; Northwest. Univ. Polit. & Govt. Pos: Former chmn, Shawano Co. Rep. Party, Wis; chmn, Eau Claire Co. Rep. Party, 32-46. Bus. & Prof. Pos: Product control mgr, U.S. Rubber, Eau Claire, 17-52; tech. dir, U.S. Rubber Tire Div, 52-58. Mem: Mason; Shrine. Rel: Protestant. Mailing Add: 651 Putnam St, Eau Claire, Wis. 54701.

STUCKEY, JAMES HENRY D
b. Kingstree, Ky, 10/20/24; s. Cleon W. Stuckey and Annie Laurie Blakeley S; m. 5/26/46 to Emma Lucille Newton. Educ: Clemson Col, 41-42; Univ. Ga, B.S.F, 48. Polit. & Govt. Pos: Forester of State Cmn. of Forestry, 48-51; S.C. State Rep, 55-56, 63-64 and until 68. Bus. & Prof. Pos: Forestry consult. Mil. Serv: Air Force, World War II, 43-46. Mailing Add: Box 65, Kingstree, S.C. 29566. (1967)

STUCKEY, JAY CLARENCE R
Ariz. State Rep.
b. Geneva, Ind, 9/24/16; s. Clarence Otis Stuckey and Grace Pape S; m. June 39 to Elizabeth M. Lancashire; c. Jay C, Jr, Lawrence L, Grace and Elizabeth. Educ: Univ. of Ariz, B.A, 39. Polit. & Govt. Pos: Ariz. State Rep, 67- Bus. & Prof. Pos: Operates gen. ins. agency. Mem: Mason; Shrine; Rotary; Jr. C. of C. Gulich and Seeton, Camp Fire Girls. Rel: Episcopal. Mailing Add: 2608 N. Dayton, Phoenix, Ariz. 85006.

STUCKEY, JOHN M, JR. R
b. Rodessa, La, 8/9/39; s. John M. Stuckey and Eleanor Harrist S; m. 10/30/65 to Sandra Ridenhour. Educ: La. State Univ, B.A, 61, M.A, 63; George Washington Nat. Law Center, 66; Pi Sigma Alpha; Kappa Sigma Polit. & Govt. Pos: Staff, Rep. Nat. Cmt, 66; consult, Rep. Coord. Cmt, 66-68; legis. asst, U.S. Rep. Brock, Wash, D.C, 66-68. Mil. Serv: Entered as 2/Lt, Army, 61, released as Capt, 69, after serv. in Off. of Asst. Chief for Intel, Pentagon, 63-66. Legal Res: 804 S. Overlook Dr, Alexandria, Va. 22305. Mailing Add: 115 Cannon House Off. Bldg, Washington, D.C. 20515.

STUCKEY, WILLIAMSON S. JR. D
U.S. Rep, Ga.
b. 1935; m. to Ethelynn. Educ: Univ. of Ga, B.B.A, LL.B. Polit. & Govt. Pos: U.S. Rep, Ga, 67- Bus. & Prof. Pos: Pres, Stuckey Timberland, Inc; part owner, candy mfg. co, candy store chain. Mem: Rotary; Elks; Cent. Ga. Coun. of Boy Scouts; Mason; Moose. Rel: Episcopal. Legal Res: Eastman, Ga. 31023. Mailing Add: 515 Cannon House Office Bldg, Washington, D.C. 20515.

STUCKEY, WILLIAMSON SYLVESTER, SR. D
b. Eastman, Ga, 3/26/09; s. William Ira Stuckey and Mary Tripp S; m. to Ethel Mullis; c. Williamson Sylvester, Jr. and Lynda Carol. Educ: Univ. Ga; Lambda Chi Alpha; Sigma Delta Kappa. Polit. & Govt. Pos: Former Ga. State Rep. Bus. & Prof. Pos: Candy mfr. Rel: Methodist. Mailing Add: Eastman, Ga. 31023. (1967)

STUDDS, GERRY EASTMAN D
b. Mineola, N.Y, 5/12/37; s. Eastman Studds and Beatrice Murphy S; single. Educ: Yale Univ, B.A, 59, M.A, 61; St. Anthony Hall. Polit. & Govt. Pos: For. Serv. Officer, U.S. State Dept, 61-63; exec. asst. to Presidential consult, White House, 63-64; legis. asst. to U.S. Sen, 64; coordinator, Sen, Eugene McCarthy's New Hampshire presidential primary campaign, 68; del. and mem. Platform Cmt, Dem. Nat. Conv, 68; mem, N.H. Dem. State Cmt, 68-69. Bus. & Prof. Pos: Teacher, West Haven Public Sch, Conn, 59-60; teacher, St. Paul's Sch, Concord, N.H, 65- Mem: Am. Hist. Asn; Asn. Am. Historians. Legal Res: St. Paul's Sch, Concord, N.H. 03301. Mailing Add: 16 Black Horse Lane, Cohasset, Mass. 02025.

STUECKEMANN, WALTER FREDERICK R
Chmn, Hodgeman Co. Rep. Party, Kans.
b. Great Bend, Kans, 3/3/26; s. Gustav Stueckemann and Augusta Junghärtchen S; m. 3/22/47 to Marjorie Ann Liston; c. William F, Linda Kay, Pamela Sue and Daniel Lee. Educ: Park Col, 45; Univ. Kans, A.B, 48, LL.B, 50; Phi Alpha Delta. Polit. & Govt. Pos: State v.chmn, Young Rep, Kans, 59-61, Fifth Dist. chmn, 61-63; co. attorney, Hodgeman Co, 59-67; chmn, Hodgeman Co. Rep. Party, 64-; city attorney, Jetmore, 65- Mil. Serv: Entered as A/S, Naval Res, 44, released as Ens, 46, after serv. in Am. Theater; Am. Theater and Victory Ribbons; Unit Citation; Lt.(jg) (Ret), Naval Res. Mem: Am, Kans. and S.W. Kans. Bar Asns; Mason; Consistory; Shrine; Clown Unit; Odd Fellows; Lions; VFW; Am. Legion; Exec. Bd, Boy Scouts (Scoutmaster, Troop 160, Jetmore, 56-58 & 67-). Rel: Methodist. Mailing Add: Jetmore, Kans. 67854.

STUELPNAGEL, DAN R
b. Huron, S.Dak, 1/7/10; m. to Elva; c. John and Jean. Educ: Yankton Col. Polit. & Govt. Pos: City cmnr, Yankton, S.Dak, 5 years, mayor, 56-57; S.Dak. State Rep, 62-64; S.Dak. State Sen, 64-66. Bus. & Prof. Pos: Egg processing and banking. Mem: Mason; Shrine; Elks; United Commercial Travelers; Eastern Star; Jesters. Rel: Congregational. Mailing Add: Yankton, S.Dak. 57078.

STULL, JOHN O. R
Calif. State Assemblyman
b. Corwith, Iowa, 8/30/20; s. Dr. Claude Stull and Mabel Frances Stilson S; m. 5/13/44 to Babbie Bogue; c. Sinara. Educ: Univ. Iowa, B.A, 42; Gen. Line Sch, U.S. Navy, Newport, R.I, 47-48; Alpha Phi Omega. Polit. & Govt. Pos: Mem, Calif. Rep. State Cent. Cmt, 64; coordinator, Rep. Assocs, 64; precinct chmn, 80th Assembly Dist, 64; Calif. State Assemblyman, 67- Mil. Serv: Entered V-5 Prog, Navy, 42, as Comdr, 63 (Ret), served as Commanding Officer, U.S. Fleet Gunnery Sch, San Diego, Exec. Officer, U.S.S. Southerland, Off. Naval Intel, Com Trans Div. Staff, Commanding Officer, Landing Ship Medium Rocket and Tank. Publ: Guns are Not Gone Yet, 64 and The Last Pathfinder, 66, U.S. Naval Inst; plus others. Mem: Am. Legion; Farm Bur; Naval Inst; ROA. Rel: Protestant. Legal Res: 460 Parkwood Lane, Leucadia, Calif. 92024. Mailing Add: 714 Second St, Encinitas, Calif. 92024.

STUMPF, EDWARD ADAM, III D
b. Richmond, Va, 1/12/20; s. Edward A. Stumpf, Jr. and Marie Nott S; m. 5/23/41 to Emily Montgomery; c. Katherine (Mrs. Neal Butler), Edward A, IV and Shelley Liane. Educ: Va. Mil. Inst, B.S. in Chem, 41. Polit. & Govt. Pos: Mem, President's Club, Wash. D.C, 64-67; mem, State Dem. Exec. Cmt, Tex, 66-68; alternate del, Dem. Nat. Conv, 68. Bus. & Prof. Pos: Chemist, Burlington Mills, High Point, N.C, 46; mem, fire prev. and eng. bur, Houston, Tex, 46; v.pres, Am. Gen. Ins. Co, Houston, 47-; chmn. of bd, Great South. Bank and mem. of bd, Main Bank of Houston, currently. Mil. Serv: Entered as Aviation Cadet, Air Force, 41, released as Maj, 46. Mem: Chmn, bd. trustees, St. Joseph Hosp; bd. trustees, St. Thomas Univ; mem. bd. Better Bus. Bur; mem, bd, Duchesne Acad; mem. bd, Alley Theatre; mem. bd, Houston Found; mem. bd, State Employees Retirement Syst; mem. bd, Southwest. Diabetic Found; Mem. Dr. Country Club; Warwick Club; Rudi's; Town Club; charter mem. K. of C. Coun; Sirloin & Saddle Club; Ky. Col; Citadel; Headliners. Outstanding Citizen Award, Houston, 67. Rel: Catholic. Mailing Add: 4 Powderhorn Lane, Houston, Tex. 77024.

STURGEON, ALONZO HOLMES D
Treas, Wilkinson Co, Miss.
b. Natchez, Miss, 12/13/31; s. Alonzo Hackett Sturgeon and Mamie Sue Ellis S; m. 12/4/53 to Bettye Jane Moore; c. Alonzo Holmes, Jr. Educ: Univ. South. Miss, B.S. cum laude, 59; Tulane Univ, LL.B, 61; Univ. Miss, J.D, 68; Phi Kappa Phi; Phi Alpha Theta; Pi Gamma Mu; Pi Kappa Pi; Phi Delta Kappa; Phi Delta Phi. Polit. & Govt. Pos: Miss. State Rep, Wilkinson Co, 64-68; Co. auditor, youth court referee, chancery court clerk, co. clerk and co. treas, Wilkinson Co, Miss, 68- Bus. & Prof. Pos: Attorney-at-law, Natchez, Miss, 61-68; prof. polit. sci, Univ. South. Miss, 62-, dean admis, 64-67. Mil. Serv: Entered as Pvt E-1, Army, 51, released as 2nd Lt, 53, after serv. in 31st Inf. Div, Ft. Polk, La, Fourth Army, 52-53. Publ: Sociological Jurisprudence, South. Quart, 65. Mem: Am. and Miss. Bar Asns; Am. Judicature Soc; Mason; RAM. Rel: Church of Christ. Mailing Add: P.O. Box 36, Woodville, Miss. 39669.

STURGEON, VERNON L. R
Mem, Calif. Rep. State Cent. Cmt.
b. San Luis Obispo Co, Calif. 10/1/15; m. 1938 to Esther Matson S; c. Three. Educ: Calif. Pub. Sch. Polit. & Govt. Pos: Mem, city coun, Paso Robles, Calif, 52-60, mayor, currently; Calif. State Sen, 60-66; mem, Calif. Rep. State Cent. Cmt, currently. Bus. & Prof. Pos: Farmer and dairyman; milk distributorship in Paso Robles, 46- Mem: Paso Robles C. of C; Lions; Mason; Scottish Rite Bodies; Elks; Shrine. Rel: Congregational. Mailing Add: 2840 Spring St, Paso Robles, Calif. 93446. (1967)

STURGES, BENJAMIN RUSH R
Mem, Rep. Cmt, North Kingstown, R.I.
b. Providence, R.I, 12/4/08; s. Rush Sturges and Elizabeth Hazards S; m. 9/2/33 to Sandol Stoddard; c. Dorothy, Rush, II and Sandol (Mrs. Harsch). Educ: Yale Univ, A.B, 31, LL.B, 34. Polit. & Govt. Pos: Mem, First Ward Rep. Cmt, Providence, R.I, 37-47; mem, Rep. Cmt, North Kingstown, 54-; councilman, North Kingstown, 62-69; alternate del, Rep. Nat. Conv, 68. Mil. Serv: Entered as Lt, Navy, 42, released as Comdr, 46, after serv. in Pac, 43-45; 2 Bronze Stars; Commendation Ribbon. Rel: Episcopal. Legal Res: R.F.D. 71, Saunderstown, R.I. 02874. Mailing Add: 2110 Industrial Bank Bldg, Providence, R.I. 02903.

STURGILL, BARKLEY JENNINGS D
Co. Attorney, Floyd Co, Ky.
b. Lackey, Ky, 7/4/28; s. Troy Bartram Sturgill and Dorothy Maggard S; m. 7/11/58 to Nancy Lewis; c. Patricia Lee, Dorothy Lewis, Sarah Catherine and Barkley J, Jr. Educ: Univ. Ky, A.B, 49; Wash. & Lee Univ, LL.B, 52; Lamp and Cross; Phi Alpha Delta; Sigma Chi. Polit. & Govt. Pos: Co. attorney, Floyd Co, Ky, 62-; pres, Ky. Young Dem, 64; mem, Ky. State Dem. Cent. Exec. Cmt, 64; del, Dem. Nat. Conv, 64 & 68; mem, Ky. Crime Cmn, 67. Rel: Methodist. Legal Res: 321 Central Ave, Prestonsburg, Ky. 41653. Mailing Add: Box 366, Prestonsburg, Ky. 41653.

STURGIS, DICK R
Mem, Ark. Rep. State Exec. Cmt.
b. Arkadelphia, Ark, 1/13/36; s. J.P. Sturgis and Ruby Selph S; m. 12/30/54 to Kay Golden; c. Paula Kay, Mark and Richard. Educ: Univ. Ark, B.S.B.A, 57; Psi Kappa Alpha. Polit. & Govt. Pos: Chmn, Clark Co. Rep. Cmt, Ark, chmn, Fourth Cong. Dist. Rep. Cmt, mem, Ark. Rep. State Exec. Cmt. and chmn, Clark Co. Elec. Cmn, currently. Bus. & Prof. Pos: Managing partner, Sturgis Land Co, Arkadelphia, 57- Mem: Rotary Int; Farm Bur. Rel: Methodist. Legal Res: 311 N. Sixth, Arkadelphia, Ark. 71923. Mailing Add: Box 87, Arkadelphia, Ark. 71923.

STURR, DOROTHY MERTZ R
Mem, Calif. Rep. State Cent. Cmt.
b. Northumberland, Pa, 10/21/26; d. Blair Hobson Mertz and Catherine Bloskey M; m. 6/5/48 to Dr. Robert Porch Sturr, Jr; c. Judy and Bobby Blair. Educ: Jefferson Medical Sch. of Nursing, Phila, R.N. Polit. & Govt. Pos: Mem, Calif. Rep. State Cent. Cmt, 66-; parliamentarian, Downey Fed. Rep. Women, 67-68. Mem: Pres, Southeast Med. Auxiliary, 68-69; ment. cmt. health, Los Angeles Co. Med. Auxiliary, 69- Rel: Episcopal. Mailing Add: 9041 Charloma Dr, Downey, Calif. 90240.

STUTLER, FRED D
b. Boynton, Mo, 6/13/26; s. William P. Stutler and Wineva Gray S; m. 4/8/47 to Eldrith McLean; c. Larry Wayne and Steven Alan. Educ: Mo. Univ;

Washburn Univ. Polit. & Govt. Pos: Area supvr, Mo. State Tax Cmn; former Mo. State Rep. Mil. Serv: Entered as Cadet V-5, Marine Corps, 43, released as Capt, 52, after serv. in Pac; Lt. Col, Marine Corps, currently; Distinguished Flying Cross with 4 Stars; Air Medal with 5 Stars; Presidential Unit Citation; Korean Presidential Unit Citation; Korean Theater Ribbon with 3 Stars; Victory Medal. Mem: Mason. Rel: Protestant. Mailing Add: Milan, Mo. 63556.

SUBER, MARTIN GAY R
Exec. Dir, S.C. Rep. Party
b. Abbeville, S.C, 8/23/37; s. John Robert Suber and Mildred Cochran S; m. 7/20/60 to Magdalena Emanuel; c. Robert Gay Emanuel and John Carlos Cochran. Educ: Wofford Col, 55-56; Univ. S.C, B.S. in Bus. Admin, 59. Polit. & Govt. Pos: Exec. committeeman, S.C. Rep. Party, 65-68, exec. dir, 69- Bus. & Prof. Pos: Employee, J.R. Suber & Sons, Whitmire, S.C, 61-63; v.pres, Suber Bros, Inc, 63-68. Mil. Serv: Entered as Airman Basic, Air Force Res, 59, released as Airman 1/C, 66; 2nd Lt, Air Force Res. Mem: Shrine; A&FM; Nat. Rifle Asn; Jaycees; dist. chmn, Nat. Fedn. Independent Bus; S.C. Archeol. Soc. Rel: Methodist. Legal Res: 303 Laurel Springs Rd, Columbia, S.C. 29206. Mailing Add: P.O. Box 5247, Columbia, S.C. 29205.

SUBLETT, HARRY F. D
b. Redding, Calif, 5/26/24; s. Floyd D. Sublett and Vera M. Tracy S; m. 4/22/45 to Norma Raedean Pope; c. Kathy Deane. Educ: McGeorge Law Sch, 1 year. Polit. & Govt. Pos: Pres, E. Yolo Dem. Club, Calif, 60-66; chmn, Fourth Cong. Dist. Dem. Coun, 62-66; del. and mem, Calif. Dem. State Cent. Cmt, 62-68; exec. v.pres, Dem. North. Calif, 67-; cmnr, Youth and Health Adv. Cmn, 67-; del, Dem. Nat. Conv, 68; elector, Electoral Col, 69. Bus. & Prof. Pos: Pres, Sublett Enterprises, Sacramento, Calif. Mil. Serv: Entered as A/S, Navy, 42, released as Spec. Q 1/C, 45, after serv. in Naval Intel, Pac. Theatre, 42-45. Rel: Unitarian. Mailing Add: 500 Laurel Lane, West Sacramento, Calif. 95691.

SUCHKO, PAUL D
b. Smithdale, Pa, 12/6/21; s. Michael Suchko and Anna Petrucyak S; m. to Helen M. Kassy; c. three. Polit. & Govt. Pos: Pa. State Rep, 64-67. Bus. & Prof. Pos: Merchant. Mil. Serv: U.S. Army, WW II, 99th Inf. Div, ETO, 42-45. Mem: VFW; Am. Legion; Moose. Mailing Add: 209 Water St, W. Newton, Pa. 17075. (1967)

SUDDARTH, THOMAS HENRY, JR. D
b. Newbern, Tenn, 10/9/23; s. Thomas Henry Suddarth and Oneita Springer S; m. 7/24/48 to Jane Watkins Carrington; c. Betsy Lee and Thomas Sterling. Educ: Univ. N.C, B.S. in Commerce, 48; Univ. N.C. Law Sch, LL.B, 51; Phi Delta Phi. Polit. & Govt. Pos: Law clerk for Chief Judge John J. Parker, U.S. Court of Appeals, Fourth Circuit, N.C, 51-52; v.chmn, Fourth Precinct, Dem. Party, Lexington, 55-62; solicitor, Davidson Co. Court, 58-62; attorney, Davidson Co, 62-66; chmn, Davidson Co. Dem. Exec. Cmt, 62-66; del, Dem. Nat. Conv, 64. Mil. Serv: Entered as Pvt, Army, 43, released as Sgt, 45, after serv. in 95th Inf. Div, 379th Regt, ETO, 44-45; Combat Inf. Badge; Good Conduct Medal; ETO Ribbon with 3 Stars; Bronze Star; Oak Leaf Cluster. Publ: Articles in Univ. N.C. Law Rev, 50-51. Mem: Am, N.C. and Davidson Co. Bar Asns; N.C. State Bar; 22nd Judicial Dist. Bar Asn; Jr. Order; Kiwanis; Dutch Club; Am. Legion. Rel: Baptist. Mailing Add: 408 Country Club Dr, Lexington, N.C. 27292.

SUEPPEL, WILLIAM FRANCIS D
Co-Chmn, Orgn. Cmt, Iowa Dem. Conf.
b. Iowa City, Iowa, 9/23/29; s. Francis William Sueppel and Catherine Striegel S; m. 6/11/55 to Patricia Ann Tierney; c. Kathleen Ann, William John, Thomas Edward, Sara Marie, Kristin Lynn, Steven Francis, Richard James and Robert Patrick. Educ: St. Ambrose Col, B.A, 50; N.Am. Col, Rome, Italy, S.T.D, 53; Univ. Iowa Law Sch, J.D, 58; Order of the Coif; Delta Epsilon Sigma. Polit. & Govt. Pos: Mem, Kennedy for Pres. Cmt, First Cong. Dist, Iowa, 60; chmn, Johnson Co. Dem. Party, 60-63; city attorney, Iowa City, 61-63; cmnr. pub. safety, Iowa, 63-66; chmn, Citizens for Hughes for Gov, Iowa, 66; state chmn, Kennedy for Pres, 68; state chmn, Citizens for Hughes for Senate, 68; del, Dem. Nat. Conv, 68; co-chmn, orgn. cmt, Iowa Dem. Conf, currently. Bus. & Prof. Pos: Assoc, Meardon Law Form, 58-63 & 66-68; partner, Meardon, Sueppel & Downer Law Firm, 69- Mil. Serv: Entered as Pvt, Army, 53, released as Cpl, 55, after serv. in Camp Gordon, Ga. Mem: Am, Iowa and Johnson Co. Bar Asns; Am. Judicature Soc; Am. Asn. Motor Vehicle Adminstr; Iowa Good Roads Asn; Elks; K. of C; Bus. Develop, Inc. Distinguished Serv. Award, Iowa City, Iowa, 63. Rel: Catholic. Legal Res: 1408 Bristol Dr, Iowa City, Iowa 52240. Mailing Add: 100 S. Linn St, Iowa City, Iowa 52240.

SUGG, ANDREW JACKSON R
Chmn, Webster Co. Rep. Party, Miss.
b. Bellefountaine, Miss, 7/26/11; s. John Kirk Sugg and Lucie Emma Haney S; m. 10/26/62 to Annie Lee Blanton. Educ: Wood Jr. Col, Mathiston, Miss, 2 years; Delta State Teachers Col, Cleveland, Miss, 1 year. Polit. & Govt. Pos: Co. chmn, Agr. Stabilization and Conserv. Cmt, 56-58; chmn, Webster Co. Rep. Party, Miss, 68- Bus. & Prof. Pos: Inspector, Miss. Pub. Serv. Cmn, 58-64; pres, Sapa Water Asn, 65-69. Mil. Serv: Inactive Naval Res, 42-43, MM 2/C. Rel: Baptist. Mailing Add: Route 2, Eupora, Miss. 39744.

SUITS, MARGARET ANN R
30th Sen. Dist. Committeewoman, Rep. State Exec. Cmt, Tex.
b. Altus, Okla, 8/2/17; d. Fred Charles Hage and Pearl Weber H; m. 10/28/38 to Tom Ellis Suits. Polit. & Govt. Pos: Co. v.chmn, Hale Co. Rep. Party, Tex, 65-, precinct chmn, 68-; 30th Sen. Dist. committeewoman, Rep. State Exec. Cmt, Tex, 66-; alternate del, Rep. Nat. Conv, 68. Bus. & Prof. Pos: Partner, Kelly-Suits Agency, 49- Mem: Independent Ins. Agents; Am. Angus Asn. Legal Res: 1610 W. First, Petersburg, Tex. 79250. Mailing Add: Box 226, Petersburg, Tex. 79250.

SULCER, KENNETH SAUNDERS D
b. Palestine, Ark, 11/1/25; s. Mack Farlin Sulcer and Nannie Thomas S; m. 11/13/60 to Doris Jean Holloway; c. Kenneth, Jr, Voysey, Kevin, Kathy, Cynthia and Kenda. Educ: Shelby Co. Sch. Aeronaut; Bus. Sch. Mgt; Draftsman's Sch, degree in aerodynamics. Polit. & Govt. Pos: Alderman, Joiner, Ark, 48, treas, 50; Ark. State Rep, 51-66, past speaker pro-tempore, Ark. House of Rep; cand. for Gov, Ark, 66. Bus. & Prof. Pos: Former automobile, lumber and hardware dealer; owner of Planters Furniture Co, Planters Antiques, Independent Ins. Agency, Sulcer Invest. Co. and Real Estate Rentals and partner in Osceola House Rentals, Inc, currently. Mem: Past pres, Joiner Rotary, 12 years; co. fund chmn, Miss. Co. Heart Asn, Ment. Health Asn, Am. Red Cross and Easter Seal Dr; co. fund chmn. and bd. mem, Miss. Co. Tuberc. Asn. and Retarded Children's Asn; past bd. mem, Tuberc. Asn, Heart Asn. and Ark. Asn. for Crippled. Received Outstanding Arkansan Award, 57; spec. recognition from many clubs for sponsoring bill to create Ark. Children's Colony. Rel: Baptist; Sunday School teacher, First Baptist Church. Mailing Add: 100 East Dr, Osceola, Ark. 72370.

SULHOFF, PAUL H. R
b. Wheatland, Wyo, 9/5/24; s. Paul A. Sulhoff and Anne Hertle S; m. 6/16/51 to Jane Doornink; c. Paula Jane, Steven William and James D. Educ: Iowa Univ, B.A. in Econ, 47 and J.D, 50; Phi Gamma Delta; Phi Delta Phi. Polit. & Govt. Pos: Mem, Pottawattamie Co. Zoning Admin, 62-; pres. sch. bd, Council Bluffs Iowa, 63-64; precinct committeeman, Rep. Party, 63-; chmn, Pottawattamie Co. Rep. Cent. Cmt, Iowa, 65-67. Mil. Serv: Entered as A/S, Navy, 43, released as Lt.(jg), 46. Mem: Pottawattamie Co. and Iowa Bar Asns; Mason; Elks; Sertoma Club. Rel: Presbyterian. Mailing Add: 1644 Madison Ave, Council Bluffs, Iowa 51501. (1967)

SULLIVAN, AGNES C. R
b. Des Moines, Iowa, 1905; Educ: Spearfish Normal and Bus. Col. Polit. & Govt. Pos: S.Dak. State Rep, 60-66; Cty. Treas; Dep. Cty. Treas; Register of Deeds and City Treas; chmn, Rep. Cty. Com. Bus. & Prof. Pos: Former Sch. teacher. Mem: Bus. and Prof. Women's Club; Governor's Cmt. Status of Women; State Pub. Aff. Rel: Catholic; Guild; Holy Rosary Club. Mailing Add: Lemmon, S.Dak. 57638. (1967)

SULLIVAN, BERRY JACKSON D
b. Phenix City, Ala, 8/22/31; s. William Berry Sullivan and Thelma Carter S; m. 5/23/53 to Suzanne Gardner; c. Jean Elizabeth and Berry Jackson, Jr. Educ: Univ. Ga, B.S.A, 52; Sigma Nu. Polit. & Govt. Pos: Ga. State Rep, Dist. 95, Post One, until 68. Bus. & Prof. Pos: Pres, Sullivan Oil Co, 54-; partner, Francis Lake Invests, 63-; treas, Florida-Georgia Corp, 64- Mil. Serv: Entered as 2nd Lt, Army, 52, released as 1st Lt, 54. Mem: Elks; Valdosta Country Club; Valdosta Exchange Club. Rel: Episcopal. Mailing Add: 703 Gornto Rd, Valdosta, Ga. 31601.

SULLIVAN, CHARLES LOTEN D
Lt. Gov, Miss.
b. New Orleans, La, 8/20/24; s. Jennie Leona Lewis S; m. to Mary Lester Rayner; c. Charles Lester, David Hewitt, Mary Loten and John Marshall. Educ: Tulane Univ; Univ. Miss, LL.B; Phi Alpha Delta. Polit. & Govt. Pos: Former munic. judge, Clarksdale, Miss. and former dist. attorney, 11th Judicial Dist; Lt. Gov, Miss, 68- Bus. & Prof. Pos: Attorney-at-law, Clarksdale; pres. and chmn. bd, N.Miss. Savings & Loan Asn, 60- Mil. Serv: Entered as Pvt, Army Air Corps, 42, released as 2nd Lt, 45, after serv. as Pilot, Korean Conflict; Lt. Col, Miss. Air Nat. Guard. Mem: Miss. and Am. Bar Asns; Mason; Lions; Am. Legion. Man of the Year, United Press Int, 59; Distinguished Serv. Award, Miss. Jaycees, 60; Distinguished Civilian Serv. Award, Miss, 69. Rel: Baptist. Legal Res: 426 W. Second St, Clarksdale, Miss. 38614. Mailing Add: New Capitol Bldg, Jackson, Miss. 39205.

SULLIVAN, DAVID JOSEPH, JR. R
b. Bridgeport, Conn, 7/12/31; s. David J. Sullivan and Irene Shannahan S; m. 5/21/60 to Mildred G. Gaffney; c. Kathleen Anne, David J, III and Michael Patrick. Educ: Fordham Col, B.S, 53; Georgetown Univ. Law, LL.B, 58. Polit. & Govt. Pos: Former chmn, Rep. Town Cmt, Bridgeport, Conn; del, Constitutional Conv, Conn, 65. Bus. & Prof. Pos: Attorney, Willis and Willis, Bridgeport, Conn. Mil. Serv: Entered as 2nd Lt, Army, 54, released as 1st Lt, 56. Mem: State and Local Bar Asns. Rel: Roman Catholic. Legal Res: 290 Lake Ave, Bridgeport, Conn. 06605. Mailing Add: 955 Main St, Bridgeport, Conn. 06603.

SULLIVAN, DONALD J. D
b. New York, N.Y, 7/18/29; s. Joseph Sullivan and Johnanna Sweeney S; m. 1/28/56 to Theresa M. Carway; c. Daniel B. and Theresa Ann. Educ: Iona Col; Brooklyn Law Sch. Polit. & Govt. Pos: Secy. bldg. dept, N.Y.C, 58-59; N.Y. State Assemblyman, 59-65; Judge, N.Y, 66- Bus. & Prof. Pos: Attorney-at-Law, N.Y. Mem: Bronx Co. Bar Asn. Rel: Catholic. Mailing Add: 1035 Grand Concourse, Bronx, N.Y. 10452.

SULLIVAN, EDWARD JOSEPH D
b. Cambridge, Mass, 2/25/21; s. Michael A. Sullivan and Catherine Hart S; single. Educ: Rindge Tech. High Sch. Polit. & Govt. Pos: Councillor, Cambridge, Mass, 50-58, mayor, 56-57 and clerk of courts, 50-58. Bus. & Prof. Pos: Gen. mgr, M.A. Sullivan Trucking, Inc; partner, Sullivan Twomey Ins. Agency; dir, Univ. Trust Co. Mil. Serv: Entered as Seaman, Navy, 40, released as Boatswain Mate 2/C, 45, after serv. in 2nd Spec. Bn, S.Pac. Mem: Local 379, Int. Brotherhood of Teamsters & Chauffeurs; Am. Legion; VFW; Elks; Hibernians; Irish-Am. Assocs. of Middlesex Co; Clover Club of Lowell; Riverside Boat Club. Rel: Roman Catholic. Mailing Add: 1010 Memorial Dr, Cambridge, Mass. 02138.

SULLIVAN, ELMER LINDSLEY D
b. Phila, Pa, 11/3/30; s. Robert Edmund Sullivan, Sr. and Marion Lindsley S; m. 2/4/67 to Jean Louise Carhart; c. Jonathan Patrick. Educ: Dartmouth Col, A.B, 52; Gen. Theol. Sem, N.Y.C, S.T.B, 55; Phi Beta Kappa. Polit. & Govt. Pos: Del, Dem. Nat. Conv, 68; chmn, New Dem. Coalition of Union Co, N.J, 69- Bus. & Prof. Pos: Rector, St. Luke's Church, Trenton, N.J, 55-67 and St. Augustine's Church, Elizabeth, 67- Rel: Episcopal. Mailing Add: 230 Locust St, Roselle, N.J. 07203.

SULLIVAN, FRANCIS DANIEL D
Mem, Cuyahoga Co. Dem. Exec. Cmt, Ohio
b. Cleveland, Ohio, 10/7/08; s. Daniel Martin Sullivan and Florence Adams

S; m. 1/12/35 to Catherine Burkart; c. Francis D, Jr, Robert James, Patricia Ann (Mrs. John M. Horvath) and William Thomas. Educ: John Carroll Univ, A.B, 34; Le Club St. Charles; Glee Club; Little Theatre Soc. Polit. & Govt. Pos: Right-of-Way exam, Ohio Dept. of Hwy, 35-39; mem, Cuyahoga Co. Dem. Exec. Cmt, Ohio, 48-; Ohio State Rep, 49-63; mem, Cuyahoga Co. Dem. Cent. Cmt, 50-; mem, Ohio State Dem. Cent. Cmt, 57-58; Ohio State Sen, 63-68. Bus. & Prof. Pos: Inspector, Rep. Steel Corp, 40-51, qual. control engr, 51- Mem: Former mem, USW; Cleveland City Club; Citizens League of Cleveland; K. of C. (4°); Cleveland Welfare Fedn. Cmt. for Prevention of Juvenile Delinquency; Citizens Adv. Cmt, Sagamore Hills Children's Psychiatric Hosp; bd. of trustees, Cleveland Guid. Center; exec. bd, Consumers League of Ohio. Rel: Roman Catholic. Mailing Add: 1485 Royalwood Rd, Broadview Heights, Ohio 44147.

SULLIVAN, HERMON HUIT R
Chmn, Tuscoloosa Co. Rep. Party, Ala.
b. Gordo, Ala, 1/14/06; s. Elijah Sullivan and Lou Vente Hannah S; m. 8/23/34; to Brinabee Campbell; c. Harley Eugene and Beverley Mae (Mrs. McGregor). Educ: George Washington Univ, LL.B. Polit. & Govt. Pos: With Fed. Bur. Investigation identification div, 30-39, spec. agent, 39-60; chmn, Tuscaloosa Co. Rep. Party, Ala, 65- Mil. Serv: Cpl, Marine Corps, 24-28. Mem: Mason (32°); Shrine; Former FBI Agents Asn. Mailing Add: 38 Southmont Dr, Tuscaloosa, Ala. 35401.

SULLIVAN, JEAN R
V.Chmn, Ala. Rep. Party
b. Selma, Ala, 5/9/28; d. Arthur Goldsby Sample and Roberta Wood S; m. 7/13/47 to Ira Oliver Sullivan; c. Arthur F, Ira Kent, James A, Connie Jean and Teresa Anne. Educ: Albert G. Parrish High Sch, grad, 46; Ala. Col, 1 year; Nat. Honor Soc; Epsilon Sigma Alpha. Polit. & Govt. Pos: Exec. mem, Dallas Co. Rep. Party, Ala, 62-; del, Ala. State Rep. Conv, 62, 64, 66 & 68; chmn, Glenn Andrews Cong. Campaign, Dallas Co, Ala, 64 & 66; pres, Dallas Co. Rep. Women, 64-67; del, Rep. Nat. Women's Conf, 64-67; mem, Ala. State Rep. Exec. Cmt, 66-; del, Rep. Nat. Conv. and mem. platform cmt, 68; v.chmn, Ala. Rep. Party, Fourth Dist, 69- Bus. & Prof. Pos: Bd. dirs, Ala. Lenders Asn, 66- Mem: Women for Constitutional Govt; Elks Emblem Club; C. of C; Capitol Hill Club; pres, Selma City Coun, PTA, 65-66. Outstanding Den Mother of Boy Scouts, 56-60. Rel: Methodist. Mailing Add: 311 Cresthaven Court, Selma, Ala. 36701.

SULLIVAN, JEROME CECIL, JR. D
b. Duncan, Okla, 5/7/31; s. Jerome Cecil Sullivan and Lucille Lawrence S; m. 8/20/54 to Marilynn Virginia Dannewitz; c. Sheryl Lynn, Sharon Cecile and Shanna Kaye. Educ: Univ. Okla, B.A, 56, LL.B, 56; Phi Alpha Delta; Delta Tau Delta. Polit. & Govt. Pos: Okla. State Rep, 62-66; asst. co. attorney, Stephens Co, Okla, 56-62. Prof. Pos: Pres, Stephen Co. Bar Asn, 57. Mem: Stephens Co. and Okla. Bar Asns; Duncan and Okla. Jr. C. of C; Duncan C. of C; Elks. Rel: First Christian Church. Legal Res: 1316 North 13th, Duncan, Okla. 73533. Mailing Add: B-2 Perkins Bldg, Duncan, Okla. 73533.

SULLIVAN, JOHN FRANCIS D
b. Washington, D.C, 7/27/35; s. Charles J. Sullivan and Rose Fitzmorris S; m. 7/8/60 to Patricia Dailey; c. Timothy J, John F, Jr. and Maureen. Educ: Mt. Saint Mary's Col, Emmitsburg, Md. Polit. & Govt. Pos: Admin. asst. to U.S. Sen. Daniel B. Brewster, Md, 62-68. Mil. Serv: Entered as Pvt, Marine Corps, 57, released as Capt, after serv. in 2nd Marine Div. Rel: Catholic. Mailing Add: 10813 Pleasant Acres Dr, Adelphi, Md. 20783. (1967)

SULLIVAN, JOHN JOSEPH, JR. D
b. Boston, Mass, 8/14/20; s. John Joseph Sullivan and Catherine V.S. Educ: Harvard Col, A.B. Polit. & Govt. Pos: Admin. Asst, Rep. Rodino, N.J. Mil. Serv: Capt, Naval Res, 42-58, Comdr, currently; served in various ships and stations in Pac; all World War II and Korean campaign ribbons except ETO. Mem: UNS world-wide; mgr, cons, Wash, 58-61. 1967 Legal Res: 2121 Virginia Ave. N.W, Washington, D.C. No mailing address available. (1967)

SULLIVAN, JOHN JOSEPH, JR. D
V.Chmn, Quincy City Dem. Cmt, Mass.
b. Boston, Mass, 2/22/41; s. John Joseph Sullivan, Sr. and Mary C. Flynn S; m. 10/29/61 to Eleanor T. Mitchell; c. John J, III and James T. Educ: Quincy Jr. Col, 3 years; Stonehill Col, 2 years. Polit. & Govt. Pos: Dem. nominee for sheriff, Norfolk Co, Mass, 62; mem, Ward 5 Dem. Cmt, Quincy, 63-; cand. for Norfolk Co. cmnr, 64; v.chmn, Quincy City Dem. Cmt, 68-; admin. asst. to Norfolk Co. Cmnr, 68- Mil. Serv: Entered as Seaman Recruit, Coast Guard Res, 58, released as QM3, 66, after serv. in Res. Units in Boston. Mem: K. of C; United Fund; Cardinal Cushing Assembly (4°). Rel: Catholic. Mailing Add: 19 Winthrop Ave, Quincy, Mass. 02170.

SULLIVAN, JOHN M.
Coun. of Hampden City, Mass.
b. Springfield, Mass; m. to Mary L. Desmarais. Educ: St. Michael's Col; Am. Int. Col; Boston Col. Law Sch, LL.B. Polit. & Govt. Pos: Coun. of Hampden City, Mass, currently; coun, Springfield City; attorney adv, Fed. Govt. and Springfield Ord. Dist. at Springfield Armory, 8 years; former exec. dir. and secy, Springfield Redevelopment Authority. Bus. & Prof. Pos: Attorney. Mil. Serv: Navy, Comdr, carrier pilot; Naval Res. Mem: Hampden City Bar Asn; Am. Legion; VFW; Elks; K. of C. Rel: Catholic; Catholic Inter-racial Coun. Mailing Add: 151 Breckwood Blvd, Springfield, Mass. 01109. (1967)

SULLIVAN, JOHN RAYMOND D
Mayor, Richland, Wash.
b. Lowell, Mass, 6/14/29; s. Edward J. Sullivan and Jane Stack S; m. 12/12/53 to Helen Ruth Bartlett; c. Karen, Katherine, Brian and Karla. Educ: Gonzaga Univ, LL.B, 57; Gonzaga Univ. Young Dem. Polit. & Govt. Pos: Precinct committeeman, 57-63; del, Wash. State Conv, 62 & 64 and Nat. Conv, 64; mayor, Richland, Wash, 64- Bus. & Prof. Pos: Munic. judge, Richland, 58-62. Mil. Serv: Entered as Pvt, Army, 51, released as Pfc, 53, after serv. in 6014th Area Serv. Unit, Med. Detachment, Sixth Army. Mem: Wash. Bar Asn; atomic energy cmt, Am. Pub. Power Asn, 66; Wash. State Urban Study Tour of Europe, 66; Local 100 Clerks Union; Am. Legion. Rel: Catholic. Legal Res: 1302 Cottonwood Dr, Richland, Wash. 99352. Mailing Add: 601 Knight St, Richland, Wash. 99352. (1967)

SULLIVAN, JOSEPH A. D
Pa. State Rep.
b. Phila, Pa, 8/9/11; s. John Sullivan and Jennie Daly S; m. to Anna Becht. Educ: Parochial sch, Phila. Polit. & Govt. Pos: Pa. State Rep, 58-; mem, 25th Ward Exec. Cmt; del, Dem. Nat. Conv, 68. Bus. & Prof. Pos: Steel researcher; dist. rep, State Workmen's Ins. Fund. Mem: Hibernians; Men of Malver; K. of C; Richmond Polish Asn. Mailing Add: 2152 E. Ann St, Philadelphia, Pa. 19134. (1967)

SULLIVAN, KEVIN CORNELIUS D
Mass. State Rep.
b. Tewksbury, Mass, 1/9/32; s. John Dennis Sullivan and Mary Sullivan S; m. to Margaret Agnes Mackey; c. Kevin A, Paul, John D, Mary K. and David. Educ: Portia Law Sch, LL.B, 68. Polit. & Govt. Pos: Chmn, Tewksbury Town Dem. Cmt, Mass, 60-67; selectman, Tewksbury, Mass, 65-; Mass. State Rep, 69- Bus. & Prof. Pos: Pres. and treas, Sullivan Homes Inc, Tewksbury. Mil. Serv: Entered as Seaman Recruit, Navy, 52, released as Seaman, 54, after serv. in MCB-1, 1st Marine Air Wing, 52-54; Korean Serv. Ribbon. Mem: Elks. Rel: Catholic. Mailing Add: 200 North St, Tewksbury, Mass. 01876.

SULLIVAN, LEONARD, JR. R
Dep. Dir, Southeast Asia Matters, Defense Research & Eng, Off. Secy. Defense
b. N.Y.C, 12/2/25; s. Leonard Sullivan and Marjorie Dodd S; m. 3/5/60 to Margo Murray Blackley; c. M. Dianne and L. Jason. Educ: Mass. Inst. Tech, B.S, M.S. and A.E; Sigma Xi; Delta Psi, pres, Tau Chap, 48-49. Polit. & Govt. Pos: Dep. asst. dir, Tactical War Plan/Combat Syst, Defense Research & Eng, 64-65, asst. dir, 65-66, dep. dir, Southeast Asia Matters, 66- Bus. & Prof. Pos: Aero eng, Grumman Aircraft Eng. Co, 50-57, asst. chief, preliminary design, Bethpage, N.Y, 57-60, chief, 60-62, mgr, Adv. Syst, 62-64. Mil. Serv: Entered as Pvt, Marine Corps, 44, released as Pfc, 46, after serv. in Combat Intel, CONUS/Occup. of Japan. Publ: 'Special R&D for Vietnam,' Sci. Tech, 10/68; 'Ten Lessons Learned in RVN,' J. of Defense Research, 5/69. Mem: St. Anthony Club of N.Y; Kenwood Golf and Country Club; MIT Club of Wash; chmn, planning bd, Village of Old Field, N.Y, 62-64. Knight of Vietnam, Fifth Class, Awarded by President Thieu, 69. Rel: Presbyterian. Mailing Add: 3637 49th St. N.W, Spring Valley, Washington, D.C. 20016.

SULLIVAN, LEONOR KRETZER D
U.S. Rep, Mo.
b. St. Louis, Mo; d. Frederick William Kretzer and Eleanor Jostrand K; wid. of John Berchmans Sullivan. Educ: Wash. Univ, St. Louis. Polit. & Govt. Pos: U.S. Rep, Third Dist, Mo, 52- Bus. & Prof. Pos: Exec. mgr, Felt and Tarrant Comptometer Co, 27-41. Mem: Am. Legion Auxiliary; League of Women Voters; Nat. Dem. Women's Club. Rel: Roman Catholic. Legal Res: 5966 Columbia Ave, St. Louis, Mo. 63139. Mailing Add: 2221 Rayburn Bldg, Washington, D.C. 20515.

SULLIVAN, MIKE D
Okla. State Rep.
b. Poteau, Okla, 12/2/38; s. B.T. Sullivan and Vada Wise S; m. 3/12/68 to Carolyn Kay McCoy; c. Kimberling Kay, Johnathon Kirk, Richard Mark and Jeffrey Michael. Educ: Poteau Commun. Col, Edmond, Okla, $1\frac{1}{2}$ years; Cent. State Col, Edmond, $2\frac{1}{2}$ years; Okla. City Univ. Sch. of Law; Univ. Tulsa Sch. Law, LL.B, 65; Phi Alpha Delta. Polit. & Govt. Pos: Dir. financial responsibility; asst. attorney, LeFlore Co, Okla, 65-67; Okla. State Rep, Dist. Three, 68- Bus. & Prof. Pos: Secy, Poteau Parking Authority, Okla, 68-69. Mem: LeFlore Co. and Am. Bar Asns; del, Okla. Bar Asn, 65-68; Odd Fellows; Kiwanis; Okla. Farmers Union; bd. dir, Poteau Commun. Chest; bd. dir, Poteau C. of C. Rel: Methodist. Legal Res: 1806 Cruce, Poteau, Okla. 74953. Mailing Add: Box 65, Poteau, Okla. 74953.

SULLIVAN, OLYER U. R
b. Clinton, Miss, 12/27/16; s. Olyer U. Sullivan, Sr. and Jenny L. Lewis S; m. 8/9/41 to Alice Marie Lissard; c. Richard Charles, Jenny Leona, Mary Alice and Katherine. Educ: Tulane Univ; Jone Co. Jr. Col. Polit. & Govt. Pos: Past chmn, Tippecanoe Co. Rep. Cent. Cmt, Ind; chmn, First Precinct, Tippecanoe, 62; campaign mgr, Lafayette Rep. Party, 63; controller, Lafayette, 64-68. Bus. & Prof. Pos: Dist. mgr, Procter & Gamble Co, 47-59; v.pres. in sales and traffic, U.S. Overseas Airline, 59; owner-mgr, M. & J. Schnaible Co, Inc, 59- Mil. Serv: Entered as Pvt, Air Force, 41, released as 1st Lt, 45, after serv. in 13th Air Force, S.Pac. Mem: Kiwanis; Elks; Am. Legion. Rel: Baptist. Mailing Add: 816 S. Ninth St, Lafayette, Ind. 47905.

SULLIVAN, RICHARD JOSEPH D
b. Bronx, N.Y, 5/17/21; s. Joseph William Sullivan and Kathryn McKenna S; m. Nov. 1952; c. Richard Joseph, Regina A, Joseph, Patricia, Teresa, Kimberly and James. Educ: Fordham Col. and Law Sch, B.A, and LL.B. Polit. & Govt. Pos: Chief counsel, Cmt. on Pub. Works, U.S. House of Rep, 57- Mil. Serv: Army, 39th and Ninth Inf. Div, N.Africa, Sicily, ETO; Eight Battle Stars; Combat Inf. Badge. Rel: Catholic. Mailing Add: 5722 N. 28th St, Arlington, Va. 22207.

SULLIVAN, THOMAS F. D
b. Braddock, Pa; s. Michael Sullivan and Bridget Haney S; m. to Florence Mannion. Educ: St. Thomas High Sch. Polit. & Govt. Pos: Pa. State Rep, 60-67. Bus. & Prof. Pos: Elec. worker, Westinghouse Elec. Corp, E. Pittsburgh. Mailing Add: 721 Broadway, East McKeesport, Pa. 19033. (1967)

SULLIVAN, THOMAS J. D
Mem. Exec. Cmt, N.Y. State Dem. Cmt.
b. Elmira, N.Y, 5/22/26; s. William E. Sullivan and Nora O'Neill S; m. 8/28/48 to Mary Marinan; c. John M, Daniel J, Kathleen A. and Thomas J. Educ: Niagara Univ, B.B.A. cum laude, 50; Union Univ, Albany Law Sch, LL.B, 53. Polit. & Govt. Pos: Regional v.chmn, mem. steering cmt. to reorganize

div. and del. to conv, Young Dem. Div. Dem. Party, 55-57; committeeman, Chemung Co. Dem. Cmt, 56-, towns chmn, 57, mem. exec. cmt, 57-, v.chmn, 58 and chmn, 59-60; del, N.Y. State Dem. Conv, 58, 62, 64 & 66 and Dem. Nat. Conv, 60 & 64; corp. counsel, Elmira, 60-61; counsel, Elmira Water Bd. and Elmira Cemetery Cmn, 60-61; mem. exec. cmt, N.Y. State Dem. Cmt, 62-; town attorney, Catlin, Chemung Co, N.Y, 66- Mil. Serv: Entered as Seaman, Navy, 44, released as PO, 46. Mem: Sect. Judicial Admin, Am. Bar Asn; Munic. Law Sect, N.Y. State Bar Asn; Chemung Co. Bar Asn; Nat. Inst. Munic. Law Officers; former mem, N.Y. State Asn. Corp, Counsels; Boy Scouts (cmt. mem, Troop 62); Notre Dame High Sch. Parents Asn. and Athletic Asn; K. of C.(adv, coun, 229); Hibernians; Elks; Am. Legion; Elmira Asn. Commerce; Jr. C. of C.(former mem. and officer). Rel: Catholic. Legal Res: 917 W. Third St, Elmira, N.Y. 19405. Mailing Add: 312 Lake St, Elmira, N.Y. 14902.

SULLIVAN, THOMAS QUINN D
Chmn, Dawson Co. Dem. Cent. Cmt, Mont.
b. Hamilton, Mont, 2/1/33; s. John Thomas Sullivan and Phillis Flanagin S; m. 4/12/53 to Mildred Lee Belgard; c. Alice Jeanette, Laura Lenore, Thomas Michael, Charles Pertis,and Patrick Glen. Educ: Stevensville High Sch, grad, 51. Polit. & Govt. Pos: Precinct committeeman, Dawson Co. Dem. Cent. Cmt, Mont, 64, chmn, 65-; mem, Mont. Dem. Cent. Cmt, 65. Bus. & Prof. Pos: Sr. testboardman, Mt. States Tel. & Tel. Co, Glendive, Mont, 66- Mil. Serv: Entered as Pvt, Air Force, 51, released as Airman 1/C, 55, after serv. in Strategic Air Command, 55, S/Sgt, Air Force Res, 55-62; Korean Serv. Ribbon; UN Ribbon; Good Conduct Medal. Mem: VFW; K. of C; Toasmasters; IBEW. Rel: Catholic. Legal Res: 119 Maple Ave, Hillcrest Addition, Glendive, Mont. 59330. Mailing Add: Box 1373, Glendive, Mont. 59330.

SULLIVAN, ULIE BASCOM D
b. Gordo, Ala, 1899; s. Tobias Sullivan; m. 7/27 to Oliva Ball; c. Eulie Eugene, Joe Owen. Educ: Massey Bus. Col; LaSalle Exten. Univ. Polit. & Govt. Pos: Ala. State Rep, 58-66; Pickens Cty. tax collector, 34-48. Mem: Mason; Civitan. Rel: Baptist. Mailing Add: Reform, Ala. 35481. (1967)

SULLIVAN, VINCENT AUGUSTINE D
Mem, Conn. State Dem. Cent. Cmt.
b. Moosup, Conn, 7/12/17; s. John L. Sullivan and Annette Potvin S; m 11/28/40 to Theresa F. Despathy; c. Maureen B.(Mrs. Deyo), Susan M. and Faye T. Educ: Providence Col, 35-36. Polit. & Govt. Pos: Mem. bd. selectmen, Plainfield, Conn, 51-55, Judge, Munic. Court, 55-60 and chmn, Dem. Town Cmt, 56-; field rep. for U.S. Sen. Thomas J. Dodd, 59; mem, Conn. State Dem. Cent. Cmt, 60-; Probate Judge, Dist. of Plainfield, 62; mem, Dem. State Platform Cmt, 62; del, Dem. Nat. Conv, 64 & 68; del, Conn. State Constitutional Conv, 65; State Senate Advisor, Appropriations Cmt, Conn. Gen. Assembly, 69. Bus. & Prof. Pos: Secy, Plainfield Indust. Found, Inc, Conn, 65- Mil. Serv: Entered as Pvt, Air Force, 42, released as Sgt, 45, after serv. in 9th Air Force, Anti-Submarine Patrol, Caribbean and European Theaters; Air Medal; ETO Ribbon with 5 Stars; Anti-Submarine Patrol Ribbon with 1 Star; Occupation and French Ribbons; M/Sgt, Army Res, 48-60. Mem: 1st World War II Comdr, Godrea-McMahon Post 91, Am. Legion, Moosup, Conn; Elks; K. of C; Lions; clerk, Moosup Fire Dist. Rel: Roman Catholic. Mailing Add: Box 788, Moosup, Conn. 06354.

SULLIVAN, WALTER JOSEPH D
Mayor, Cambridge, Mass.
b. Cambridge, Mass, 3/2/23; s. Michael Andrew Sullivan and Mary C. Hart S; m. 7/27/46 to Marion Ann Colarusso; c. Marion, Mary, Maureen, Michael and Walter. Educ: Cambridge High & Latin Sch, Mass, grad, 41. Polit. & Govt. Pos: Mass. State Rep, 51-52; city coun, Cambridge, 59-, mem. sch. cmt, 68-, mayor, 68-; del, Dem. Nat. Conv, 68. Bus. & Prof. Pos: Asst. clerk, Middlesex Superior Court, Cambridge, 59-; clerk, Charlesbank Trust Co, 66 and v.pres, treas. and mem. bd. dirs, 67-; ins. broker. Mil. Serv: Pvt, Air Force, 42-46; Pac. Theatre Medal; Good Conduct Medal; Pac. Combat Ribbon. Mem: Nat. Sch. Cmt. Asn; Mass. Legis. Asn; U.S. Conf. Mayors; Elks; VFW; K. of C.(4°); Shamrock Soc; Am. Legion (nat. security cmn); Boy Scouts; chmn, Youth Opportunity Cmt; chmn, March of Dimes-Retarded Children-Heart Fund. Hon. Ky. Col. Rel: Catholic. Mailing Add: 28 Putnam Ave, Cambridge, Mass. 02129.

SULLIVAN, WILLIAM LITSEY D
Ky. State Sen.
b. 1921. Educ: Centre Col, B.A; Univ. of Ky, LL.B. Polit. & Govt. Pos: Commonwealth attorney, Henderson, Union and Webster Counties, 59-60; Ky. State Sen, Fourth Dist, 66-, pres. pro tem, 69- Bus. & Prof. Pos: Attorney-at-law. Mil. Serv: Army Air Corps, World War II. Mem: Henderson Co, Ky. and Am. Bar Asns; Past Pres, Rotary; Ky. Cmnr. of Aeronauts, 58-59. Rel: Presbyterian. Mailing Add: Henderson, Ky. 42420.

SUMMER, A. F. D
Attorney Gen, Miss.
Mailing Add: State Capitol, Jackson, Miss. 39205.

SUMMERFIELD, ARTHUR ELLSWORTH R
b. Pinconning, Mich, 3/17/99; s. William Henry Summerfield and Cora Edith Ellsworth S; m. 7/22/18 to Miriam W. Graim; c. Gertrude Miriam (Mrs. MacArthur) and Arthur E. Educ: Hon. D.B.A, Cleary Col, 56; LL.D, Defiance Col, 53, Univ. Mich, 57, Miami Univ, 59 and Thiel Col, 61. Polit. & Govt. Pos: Former regional v.pres, Post War Planning Cmn, chmn, 43-45; finance dir, Rep. State Cent. Cmt, Mich, 43-45; Rep. Nat. Committeeman, Mich, 44-68; regional v.chmn, N.Cent. Div, Rep. Party, Mich, 46; chmn, Rep. Nat. Cmt, 52-53; U.S. Postmaster Gen, 53-61. Bus. & Prof. Pos: Real estate broker, 19-24; distributor, Pure Oil Co, Flint, Mich, 24-37; pres, Summerfield Chevrolet Co, Flint, 29-; dir, Genesee Co. Real Estate Asn; pres, Byrant Properties Corp, 38-; dir, Mich. Auto. Dealers Asn, 42-; pres, Sico Enterprises Corp, Lumbermans' Mutual Casualty Co, Chicago, Am. Motorists Ins. Co, Chicago and Kemper Life Ins. Co, Boston; trustee, Cleary Col. Publ: U.S. Mail, The Story of United States Postal Service, 60. Mem: Mason (33°); K.T; Shrine; Elks; Flint City Club (former pres. and dir); Kiwanis; Detroit Club; Athletic Club; Metrop. Club; Capitol Hill Club, Wash, D.C; U.S. C. of C; Everglades Club. Legal Res: 2952 Parkside Dr, Flint, Mich. 48503. Mailing Add: Genesee Bank Bldg, Flint, Mich. 48502.

SUMMERS, FRANK LESTON D
b. Middletown, Ind, 11/2/01; s. William Lincoln Summers and Cora M. Cummings S; m. 3/28/25 to Oneita May Bushong; c. George Edwin, Sara Lee, Carolyn and John Mark. Polit. & Govt. Pos: Inspector, Agr. Stabilization & Conserv. Cmn, 23-24; letter carrier, Middletown Post Office, Inc, 28-43; mem. council, Henry Co, 58-62; Ind. State Rep, 64-69; field inspector, Ind. Dept. Revenue, 67-69. Bus. & Prof. Pos: V.pres, Cadiz, Ind. Telephone Co, 62-, pres, 65. Mil. Serv: Pvt, Air Force, 22-23. Mem: Nat. Farmers Orgn; chmn, Henry Co. Christian Rural Overseas Prog, 58-66; chmn, Wilbur Wright Birthplace Cmn. Rel: Church of Christ. Mailing Add: R.R. 1, Box 282, Middletown, Ind. 47356.

SUMMERS, FRANK WYNERTH D
Assoc. Justice, Supreme Court, La.
b. Abbeville, La, 9/5/14; s. Clay Ralph Summers and Esther LeBlanc S; m. 6/22/40 to Marie Beverly Miller; c. Frank W, II, Preston M, Susan P, Clay James, William C. and Beverly M. Educ: Univ. Southwest. La, B.A, 38; Tulane Univ, LL.B, 38; Phi Delta Phi; Phi Kappa Sigma. Polit. & Govt. Pos: Dist. Judge, 15th Judicial Dist, La, 52-55; Assoc. Justice, Supreme Court, La, 60- Bus. & Prof. Pos: Attorney-at-law, gen. practice, Abbeville, La, 38-41, 45-52 and 55-60. Mil. Serv: Entered as Ens, Naval Res, 41, released as Lt. Comdr, 45, after serv. in Off. Naval Intel. and Pac. Theater. Publ: 'Some Merits of Civil Jury Trials,' Tulane Law Rev, Dec, 1964. Mem: Pres, Tulane Law Alumni Club, 62-63; hon. mem, St. Thomas More Cath. Lawyers Asn; former mem, La. Dist. Judges Asn, Vermilion Parish, La. State and Am. Bar Asns, La. Dist. Judges Asn. and Am. Judicature Soc; former pres, Abbeville Country Club; former chmn, U.S. Savings Bonds Prog; K. of C. Coun. 2281; past pres, 15th Judicial Dist. Bar Asn; past dist. chmn. and coun. pres, Boy Scouts; past comdr, Am. Legion Vermilion Post 29; VFW; former parish chmn, Am. Red Cross; hon. mem. Order of Coif, Tulane Univ, hon. mem. Blue Key, Loyola Univ. South. Recipient Silver Beaver Award, Boy Scouts, 60. Rel: Catholic. Legal Res: 500 Second St, Abbeville, La. 70510. Mailing Add: Supreme Court Bldg, 301 Loyola Ave, New Orleans, La. 70112.

SUMNER, E. AMOS D
b. Vilas, Fla, 6/2/24; m. to Earline Stoutamire; c. Earnest, Melba, Reginald, Archie and Sally. Educ: Univ. of Ga, B.S, 49; Omicron Delta Kappa; GRIDIRON; Alpha Zeta; AGHON. Polit. & Govt. Pos: Fla State Rep, 64-66. Bus. & Prof. Pos: Forestry. Mil. Serv: Marine Corps, World War II; Guam Campaign; Purple Heart. Mem: Soc. of Am. Farmers; Farm Foresters Asn; C. of C. Liberty Co; Mason; Am. Legion; Farm Bur; Cattlemens Asn; PTA. Rel: Methodist. Mailing Add: P.O. Box 8, Hosford, Fla. 32334.

SUMNERS, CECIL LAMAR D
Miss. State Sen.
b. Belmont, Miss, 9/13/20; married. Polit. & Govt. Pos: Miss. State Sen, currently; former Chancery Clerk. Bus. & Prof. Pos: Lawyer. Mem: Mason (32°); Shrine; WOW; Am. Legion; VFW; Lions; Miss. State Bar Asn; Farm Bur. Rel: Baptist. Mailing Add: 311 S. Fulton St, Iuka, Miss. 38852. (1967)

SUNDBORG, GEORGE D
b. San Francisco, Calif, 3/25/13; s. Charles A. Sundborg and Annie Budgen S; m. 2/26/38 to Mary Frances Baker; c. Pierre Joseph, George Walter, Jr, Rosemary (Mrs. William Bridges Hunter, III), Stephen Vincent and Sarah. Educ: Univ. Wash, A.B. in Journalism, 34; Sigma Delta Chi. Polit. & Govt. Pos: Supvr, Alaska Merit Syst, 40-41; sr. planning technician, Nat. Resources Planning Bd, 41-43; asst. U.S. dir, N.Pac. Planning Proj, Dept. of State, 43-44; indust. analyst, Bonneville Power Admin, 44-46; mem, Thoron Rate Rev. Cmt, Alaska R.R, 46; gen. mgr, Alaska Dvelop. Bd, 46-47 & 51-53; exec. asst. to Gov, Alaska, 47-51; del, Alaska Constitutional Conv, 55-56; admin. asst. to U.S. Sen. Ernest Gruening, Alaska, 59-69; asst. to dir, Bur. Outdoor Recreation, 69- Bus. & Prof. Pos: Reporter and city ed, Grays Harbor Daily Washingtonian, 35-38; reporter and ed. writer, Daily Alaska Empire, 39-41; ed. and publisher, Juneau Independent, 53-57; ed, Fairbanks Daily News-Miner, Alaska, 57-58; former correspondent for various news serv. and periodicals. Publ: Opportunity in Alaska, 45 and Hail Columbia, 54, Macmillan; Statehood for Alaska: The Issues Involved and the Facts About the Issues, Alaska Statehood Asn, 46. Mem: Alaska and Nat. Press Clubs; charter mem. and first pres, Alaska State Soc; v.pres, Senate Press Secy. Asn. Legal Res: Anchorage, Alaska. Mailing Add: 2361 49th St. N.W, Washington, D.C. 20007.

SUNDET, A. O. Conservative
Minn. State Sen.
b. Fillmore Co, 1904; married. Polit. & Govt. Pos: Minn. State Rep, 52, 54 & 56; Minn. State Sen, 58- Bus. & Prof. Pos: Owner, Sundet Mobile Home Sales. Mailing Add: Route 3, Faribault, Minn. 55021. (1967)

SUNDLUN, BRUCE GEORGE D
b. Providence, R.I, 1/19/20; s. Walter I. Sundlun and Jane Z. Colitz S; div; c. Tracy W, Stuart A. and Peter Bruce. Educ: Tabor Acad, Mass, 38; Williams Col, B.A, 42; Harvard Law Sch, LL.B, 49; Delta Upsilon. Polit. & Govt. Pos: Asst. U.S. Attorney, D.C, U.S. Dept. Justice, 49-51 and spec. asst. to Attorney Gen, civil div, 51-54; del, Dem. Nat. Conv, 64 & 68. Bus. & Prof. Pos: Partner, Amram, Hahn & Sundlun, Attorneys, D.C, 54-; dir, v.pres, secy. and gen. counsel, Outlet Co, Providence, R.I, 60-; incorporator and dir, Commun. Satellite Corp, D.C, 62-; dir, secy. and gen. counsel, Exec. Jet Aviation, Inc, Columbus, Ohio, 64- Mil. Serv: Entered as Aviation Cadet, Air Force, 42, released as Capt, 46, after serv. in 384th Bomb Group, Third Ferry Group, ETO and Pac, 43-45; Col, Res, 45-61; Distinguished Flying Cross; Air Medal with Cluster; Purple Heart. Mem: Bar Asn. D.C; R.I, Fed. and Am. Bar Asns; Fed. City Club; Army-Navy Club; City Tavern Asn; Univ. Club R.I; Century Country Club, Williams, N.Y; Williams Club, N.Y; Harvard Club of Boston; Warrenton Hunt, Va; Bristol Yacht Club, R.I. Rel: Jewish. Mailing Add: 700 Colorado Bldg, Washington, D.C. 20005.

SUNDLUN, WALTER IRVING R
b. Providence, R.I, 9/9/90; s. Morris Sundlun and Eva Meisel S; c. Bruce G. and Walter I, Jr. (deceased). Educ: Boston Univ, LL.B, 22. Hon. Sc.D, R.I. Col. of Pharm. and Allied Sci, 50. Polit. Pos: Rep. cand. for U.S. Sen,

R.I, 54; one of floor mgrs. for Wendell Willkie at Rep. Nat. Conv, 40 and later mem. his Personal Adv. Cmt. during campaign for Presidency of the U.S; del, Rep. Nat. Conv, 36 and 32. Bus. & Prof. Pos: Pres. and treas, Cross-Country Invest. Co, Inc, Manning Realty Co, Inc, Dorrance Realty Co, Thayer-Waterman Co, Roger Williams Hotel, Inc. and the Walmac Co, Inc. Publns: Author, Poems, including 'The Soldier's Plea,' pub. by Providence J. Co. and made part of the Harris Collection by Brown Univ; 'Plea for the Human Family' and 'Unknown Soldier,' plus others. Mem: U.S. Supreme Court Bar; Supreme Court of R. I. Bar; R.I. Bar; U.S. Circuit Court of Appeals for the 1st Circuit Bar; U.S. Customs Court Bar and Dist. Court of the U.S. of Am. for the Dist. of R.I. Bar; Barry Merry Lodge 29, F&AM; Jewish Home for Aged of R.I; Jewish Orphanage of R.I; Nat. Coun. Am.Jewish Cmt; Ledgemont Country Club; one of the organizers and founders of the Miriam Hosp. Received Civil Award from Eagles; Hon. Award for being founder of Camp Jori for needy children of R.I; pub. speaker for Catholic Charity Fund on many occasions. Rel: Jewish; pres, Temple Beth-El, Providence, R.I, 37-42 and 51-55. Legal Res: 23 Half Mile Rd, Barrington, R.I. 02806. Mailing Add: 1138 Hospital Trust Bldg, Providence, R.I. 02903. (1967)

SUNDSTROM, FRANK L. R

b. Massena, N.Y, 1/5/01; s. Charles Sundstrom and Nora Lillian Vandevener S; m. 12/26/36 to Jean Ross Johnstone; c. Jean (Mrs. W.G.M. Farrell) and Frank L, Jr. Educ: Cornell Univ, grad, 24; Sigma Delta Chi; Phi Kappa Psi. Polit. & Govt. Pos: Chmn, Rep. City Cmt, East Orange, N.J, 38-48; U.S. Rep, 11th Cong. Dist, N.J, 43-49. Bus. & Prof. Pos: Partner, Burton, Dana & Co, Brokers, 31-; v.pres. & dir, Schenley Distillers, Inc, 55-; v.pres. & dir. of pub. rels, Schenley Indust, Inc, 55-; v.pres, The Tobacco Inst, 69- Mem: Cong. Country Club, Wash, D.C; Capitol Hill Club, Wash, D.C; Montclair Golf Club, N.J; Touchdown Club of N.Y; Cornell Club of Essex Co, N.J. Walter Camp All American Football Tackle, 23. Rel: Episcopal. Legal Res: 21 Hickory Dr, Maplewood, N.J. 07040. Mailing Add: 1776 K St. N.W, Washington, D.C. 20006.

SUPENA, RONALD STEVE D

Mem, Du Page Co. Dem. Cent. Cmt, Ill.

b. Wichita, Kans, 7/9/33; s. Steve A. Supena and Bessie L. Trampota S; m. 9/1/56 to Nancy E. Novy; c. Mary E, Mark S, Wayne G, Paul J. and Ann G. Educ: St. Procopius Col, Lisle, Ill, 51-54; De Paul Univ. Col. Law, LL.B, 58; N.Y. Univ. Sch. Law, LL.M. in Taxation, 63; Delta Theta Phi. Polit. & Govt. Pos: Trial Attorney, Off. of Chief Counsel, Internal Revenue Serv, 62-66; alternate del, Dem. Nat. Conv, 68; precinct committeeman, Precinct 36, Du Page Co. Dem. Party, Ill, 68-; mem, Du Page Co. Dem. Cent. Cmt, 68- Bus. & Prof. Pos: assoc, Pritchard, Chapman, Pennington, Montgomery & Sloan, Chicago, Ill, 66-67; partner, Chapman, Pennington, Montgomery, Holmes & Sloan, 68- Mil. Serv: Entered as 1st Lt, Air Force, 58, released as Capt, 62, after serv. in Judge Advocate Gen. Dept, Strategic Air Command & Air Defense Command; Air Force Res, 62-, Capt. Mem: Fed, Am, Ill. State, Iowa and Chicago Bar Asns; Judge Advocates Asn; Bohemian Lawyers Asn; St. Procopius Col. Alumni Asn.(dir, 67-, v.pres, 67-69, pres, 69-); K. of C. Delta Theta Phi scholarship key, 58. Rel: Catholic. Mailing Add: 862 Cambridge, Elmhurst, Ill. 60126.

SUSKI, EDWARD D

Mich. State Rep.

b. Flint, Mich, 9/9/28; m. 1955 to Elaine Fink; c. Kathy Ann and Edward Daniel. Polit. & Govt. Pos: Mich. State Rep, 64- Bus. & Prof. Pos: Journeyman electrician. Mil. Serv: Army. Mem: Past pres, N.Flint Bus. Asn; past pres, N.Flint Dem. Club; Dom Polski Club. Rel: Catholic. Mailing Add: 3117 Dexter Ave, Flint, Mich. 48506.

SUTHERLAND, JAMES FREDERICK R

b. Martins Ferry, Ohio, 7/16/27; s. Frederick Pelham Sutherland and Anna Obrist S; m. 8/2/51 to Diana Westlake; c. Laurie, Judith Ann and Eve. Educ: Washington & Jefferson Col, B.A, 48; Univ. of Pa, M.D, 52; Phi Delta Theta; Phi Chi. Polit. & Govt. Pos: Rep. cand, U.S. Rep, Ohio, 68. Bus. & Prof. Pos: Pres, Staff Martins Ferry Hosp, 69- Mil. Serv: Entered as A/S, Navy, 45, released as Lt(jg), 46; Navy Res, 57-, Lt. Comdr. Mem: past pres, Belmont Co. Med. Soc; Mason (32°); Am. Legion. Rel: Protestant. Mailing Add: 78 N. Ridge Dr, Martins Ferry, Ohio 43935.

SUTHERLAND, PAUL OSCAR D

b. Flint, Mich, 8/25/24; s. George W. Sutherland and Ann Peterson S; m. 5/30/58 to Josephine R. Meyers; c. Paula Diane. Educ: Univ. Mich; Univ. Wis. Polit. & Govt. Pos: Treas, Ninth Dem. Cong. Dist, Mich, 55-56 and chmn, 62-67; v.chmn, Mason Co. Dem. Cmt, 58-64. Mil. Serv: Entered as Seaman, Navy, 44, released as Seaman 2/C, 45, after serv. in ETO. Mem: V.pres, Cluster 5, Fed. Poverty Act and exec. bd, Mason Co. Commun. Action Group; pres, Region Seven Allied Indust. Workers, AFL-CIO, pres, Mason Co. Coun. and chief steward, Local 132 AIW. Rel: Swedish-Lutheran. Mailing Add: 5563 Rasmussen Rd, Ludington, Mich. 49431. (1967)

SUTPHIN, WILLIAM HALSTEAD D

b. Browntown, N.J, 8/30/87; s. James Taylor Sutphin and Charlotte Brown S; m. 10/19/22 to Catharine Bonner; c. Susan and William T. Educ: High Sch. and Woods Bus. Col. Polit. & Govt. Pos: U.S. Rep, 31-43; mayor, Matawan, N.J, 15-27. Mil. Serv: Pvt, B. Troop, 1st Sq, N.J. Cavalry, released as Sgt; re-entered serv. as Lt, Cavalry, 17, discharged as Capt, Air Serv, 19; Mexican Border and French Serv. Ribbons. Mem: Holland Soc; Sons of Revolution; Mason; Elks; Am. Legion; VFW. Rel: Presbyterian. Mailing Add: 102 West St, Berlin, Md. 21811.

SUTTON, EMMAZETTE COLLIER D

V.Pres, Okla. Fedn. Dem. Women's Clubs

b. Gotebo, Okla, 5/15/15; d. Frank A. Collier and Mittie L. Hawkins C; m. 1/31/42 to LeRoy Sutton; c. Beth Anne (Mrs. Charles Emet Graft) and granddaughter, Leesa Anne Graft. Educ: Southwest. State Col, 1 year; Keen's Bus. Col, Clinton, Okla, 1 year; charter mem. Hon. Soc. Polit. & Govt. Pos: Dem. precinct co-chmn, Clinton, Okla; asst. co. supt. schs, Washita Co, 39-43 and Custer Co, 57-62; v.pres, Okla. Fedn. Dem. Women's Clubs, 67-; alternate del, Dem. Nat. Conv, 68; chmn, Okla. Fedn. Dem. Women's Clubs Conv, 68, spec. adv, 69. Mem: Pres, Lincoln PTA, 53-56, Clinton PTA Coun. and Okla. State Bd, PTA, 55-57. Rel: Methodist. Mailing Add: 1128 Lee Ave, Clinton, Okla. 73601.

SUTTON, GLENN WALLACE D

Chmn, U.S. Tariff Cmn.

b. Milan, Ind, 7/25/04; s. Chester Wallace Sutton and Goldie Tucker S; m. 12/30/30 to Rachel Sibley; c. William Wallace. Educ: Ind. Univ, B.S, 26 and A.M, 27; Ohio State Univ, Ph.D, 38; Beta Gamma Sigma; Alpha Kappa Psi; Phi Kappa Phi; Phi Eta Sigma; Phi Chi Theta; Omicron Delta Kappa. Polit. & Govt. Pos: Dir, Nat. Tabulation Off, Urban Studies of Consumer Purchases and Income, Bur. Labor Statistics, U.S. Dept. Labor, Southeast. States, Atlanta, 36 and Chicago, 37 and dir, Survey of State, Co. and Munic. Employ. & Payrolls, Southeast. States, Atlanta, 39-40 and nat. dir, Phila, 41 and cmnr, U.S. Tariff Cmn, 54-69, chmn, 69- Bus. & Prof. Pos: Acct, Groubs Wholesale Grocery, Seymour, Ind, 22 and Farmers' Coop. Elevator Co, 23; research asst. and ed, Ind. Bus. Rev, Ind. Univ, 25-27; ed, Idaho Econ. Rev. and instr. of econ, Univ. Idaho, 27-29; prof. of finance, chmn. finance div, ed, Ga. Bus. Rev, dir, Bur. Bus. Research and Vet. Affairs Off, dir, Savannah Div. and Grad. Div, Col. Bus. Admin, Univ. Ga, 29-54. Mil. Serv: Entered as Lt, Navy, 42, released as Comdr, 45, after serv. in Fasron 152; Aviation Wing Staff 67; Air Task Group 671; Am. Theater Ribbon; Defense Medal; Capt. (Ret), Naval Res, 64. Mem: Am. Statist. Asn; Am. Econ. Asn; South. Econ. Asn; Am. Finance Asn; Am. Asn. Univ. Prof; Mason; Rotary; Gridiron Club; Am. Legion; Naval Airmen of Am; Naval Res. Asn; U.S. Naval Inst; Navy League; Am. Inst. of Mgt; Cosmos Club. Rel: Methodist. Legal Res: 649 Oglethorpe Ave, Athens, Ga. 30601. Mailing Add: U.S. Tariff Commission, Eighth and E Streets N.W, Washington, D.C. 20436.

SUTTON, HAROLD PUTNAM R

b. Ainsworth, Nebr, 4/29/88; s. Harvey Putnam Sutton and Eliza Burns Munson S; m. 11/10/19 to Gladys Fuller; c. Lois (Mrs. Wayne B. Allen), Harvey and Suzanne (Mrs. Robert G. Boekel). Educ: Univ. Nebr, 08; McCormich Med. Col, O.D; Kappa Sigma. Polit. & Govt. Pos: Chmn, Red Willow Co. Rep. Party, Nebr, over 15 years; chmn, Citizens Party, McCook, Nebr, over 20 years; chmn, Red Cross Disaster Relief Cmt, Red Willow Co, 40 years; del, Rep. Nat. Conv, 68. Bus. & Prof. Pos: Mem, Nebr. Aeronaut. Cmn, 44. Mil. Serv: Entered as Pvt, Army Air Corps, 17, released as 2nd Lt, 18, after serv. in Air Serv, Talliferro Field and Cadet Training and Aerial Gunnery, 18; Res, 18-30, 1st Lt.(Ret). Mem: Nebr. Optometrical Asn; Nat. Aeronaut. Asn; Nebr. Jewelers Asn.(pres, 51); Nebr. Irrigation Asn.(pres, 56); Nebr. Reclamation Asn.(pres, 55); Mason; Shrine; K. of P; Am. Legion (Post and Dist. Comdr). Rel: Protestant. Rel: Protestant. Mailing Add: 803 George W. Norris Ave, McCook, Nebr, 69001.

SUTTON, JOHN EDWIN, JR. 'MATT' D

b. Gettysburg, S.Dak, 6/21/31; s. John Edwin Sutton and Mildred Hanson S; m. 1/1/58 to Helen Ruth Tande; c. Nancy. Educ: S.Dak. State Univ, B.A, 52; Blue Key; Scabbard & Blade; Alpha Zeta. Polit. & Govt. Pos: Mem, Bd. of Supvr, Sully Co. Soil and Water Conserv. Dist, S.Dak; S.Dak. State Rep, Dist, 13, 63-67. Bus. & Prof. Pos: Ranching. Mil. Serv: 2nd Lt, Army, 52-53. Mem: S.Dak. Quarter Horse Asn.(pres, 62 & 63); dir, S.Dak. Hereford Asn, 68-; dir, Beef Improv. Fedn, 68-; Mason; Shrine; Stock Growers; Farmers Union; Farm Bur; Am. Legion; Jaycees; Sully Co. Crop Improv. Asn. Sully Co. Outstanding Young Farmer; Sully Co. Distinguished Serv. Award. Rel: Lutheran. Mailing Add: Agar, S.Dak. 57520.

SUTTON, LEONARD v.B. D

b. Colorado Springs, Colo, 12/21/14; s. Benjamin Edmund Sutton and Anne von Bibra S; m. 3/4/38 to Janette Elsie Gabor. Educ: For. Trade Course, Stuttgart, Germany, 35; Colo. Col, B.A. in polit. sci, 37; Nat. Inst. Pub. Affairs, grad. fel. in govt, 37-38; Univ. Denver Sch. Law, LL.B, 41; Phi Delta Phi; First Voters Club; Int. Rels. Club. Polit. & Govt. Pos: Attorney, El Paso Co. Planning Cmt, 41-42 & 46-50, bd. adjustment, 46-50; chief, legal br, Calif. Qm. Depot, 45-46; town attorney, Manitou Springs, 46-50; mem, Dem. State Cent. Cmt, Colo, 48-56 & 63-66; del. and mem. various cmts, State Dem. Assemblies and Conv, many times; chmn, Colo. State Rules Rev. Cmt, 2 terms; mem, Colo. Dem. State Cent. and Exec. Cmts, 8 years; chmn, El Paso Co. Dem. Cmt, 2 terms and mem. exec. cmt, several times; co. campaign dir, 2 terms and finance chmn, 2 terms; chmn, Co. Assembly and Conv, several times; chmn, Fourth Judicial Dist, 2 terms; precinct committeeman, 3 terms; dist. capt, 2 terms; former mem. and past pres, El Paso Co. Young Dem. Club; del, Dem. Nat. Conv, 52; state chmn, Jefferson-Jackson Day Dinner Cmt, 55; justice, Colo. Supreme Court, 56-68, chief justice, 60 & 66; chmn, U.S. For. Claims Settlement Cmn, 68- Bus. & Prof. Pos: Attorney-at-law, Colo. and dir. various corp, 48-56. Mil. Serv: Entered as Pvt, Army, 42, released as Capt, 46, after serv. in Inf. Ski Troops, 253rd Qm. Pack Co. and Calif. Qm. Depot; Army Commendation Medal; Am. Theater Ribbon; Victory Medal. Publ: 'World Peace Through Foreign Trade,' DePaul Law Rev, autumn 67; 'American Claims Against Yugoslavia,' Vol. 3, 69 and 'American Claims Against Cuba,' Int. Lawyer; plus others. Mem: Trustee, Inst. of Int. Educ, 62-64, hon. trustee, 65-; Inst. of Judicial Admin, N.Y. Univ; Am. Judicature Soc; state chmn, Colo. Jr. Bar Conf, 48; Am. Bar Asn, chmn, Cmt. on Int. Courts, 63-66; Cmt. on World Peace Through UN, 64-66; World Peace Through Law Cmt, Colo. Bar Asn, 63-, former chmn; treas, El Paso Co. Bar Asn, 47-49; World Peace Through Law Fedn, 64-; Fed, Int. and Inter-Am. Bar Asns; Wash. For. Law Soc; El Paso Lodge 13, AF&AM, Al Kaly Shrine, Rocky Mt. Consistory, KCCH (32°); Am. Legion; Cosmos; Rotary; Torch; Garden of Gods Club. Admitted to practice law in Colo. and D.C; collector of paintings, minerals, coins and rare books. Rel: Episcopal. Legal Res: 1604 W. Cheyenne Rd, Colorado Springs, Colo. 80906. Mailing Add: 3919 Watson Place, N.W, Washington, D.C. 20016.

SUTTON, PERCY E. D

m. to Leatrice; c. Pierre Monte, Cheryl Lynn. Educ: Prairie View Col, Hempstead, Tex; Tuskagee Inst, Ala; Hampton Inst, Va; Columbia Univ; Brooklyn Law Sch. Polit. & Govt. Pos: N.Y. State Assemblyman, 64-Jan, 67. Bus. & Prof. Pos: Attorney. Mil. Serv: Grad, Air Univ, Maxwell Field, Ala; Capt, U.S.A.F, WW II; combat stars in Italian and Mediterrean Theatres; Int. Off. in Wash, D.C. and Trial Judge Advocate, U.S.A.F. during Korean War. Mem: Past Chmn, Speakers Bur, V.Pres. & Pres, N.Y. Branch NAACP;

Legal Counsel, N.Y. CORE; consultant, SNCC; Legal Counsel, Baptist Ministers Conf. of Greater NYC; lay adv. bd, Harlem Hosp; Bd, Am. Comm. on Africa; Bd, Harlem Neighborhood Asn; Counsel, Harlem United Block Asn; Counsel, Harlem's Coun. on Jobs and Freedom; Co-Chmn, United Coun. of Harlem Orgns. Mailing Add: 311 W. 118th St, New York, N.Y. 10026. (1967)

SUTTON, TRIBLE DIX D
b. Henrico Co, Va, 5/24/02; s. John Trible Sutton and Florence May Dix S; m. 9/19/22 to Bessie Bertha McAlister; c. Dorothy May and Howard Trible. Educ: Richmond Col, 19-21; T.C. Williams Sch. of Law, LL.B, 46. Polit. & Govt. Pos: Past chmn, Henrico Co. Dem. Cmt, Va; former Va. State Del. Bus. & Prof. Pos: Clerk, acct. dept, C. & O. Rwy, 21-27; lawyer, 28- Mem: Am, Va. and Richmond Bar Asns; Past Master, Glen Allen Lodge 131 AF&AM; Scottish Rite; Mason (32°); past moderator, Dover Baptist Asn. Rel: Baptist; past secy, Virginia Baptist Board of Missions. Legal Res: 8202 Fredonia Rd, Richmond, Va. 23227. Mailing Add: 700 Bldg, Richmond, Va. 23219.

SVAHN, ESTHER MARILU R
b. Spokane, Wash, 3/16/23; d. Nick Caferro and Luisa Maria Domanico C; m. 7/20/41 to Albert Russell Svahn; c. John Alfred, Robert Russell and Richard Gustaf. Educ: San Diego City Col, Cert. in Real Estate. Polit. & Govt. Pos: Co-chmn, Hq. Yes on Proposition 14, 64; chmn, Victory Squad, 66; chmn, Rep. Hq, Point Loma-Ocean Beach, Calif, 66; area chmn, 55 precincts, Ocean Beach, 66-67; pres, Point Loma-Ocean Beach Rep. Women Fedn, 67-68, third v.pres, San Diego Co, 69; mem, Calif. Rep. State Cent. Cmt, 67-69; chmn, youth activities, South. Div, Calif. Fedn. Rep. Women, 68-69, San Diego Co, 69. Bus. & Prof. Pos: Owner, Swan Real Estate, San Diego, Calif, 68. Mem: Nat, San Diego and La Mesa Bd. of Realtors; Calif. Real Estate Asn; Point Loma-Ocean Beach Realty Asn; San Diego bd, Ethics, Credentials and Make Am. Better Cmts; pres, Pearl Harbor Submarine Officers Wives, 59; pres, Eleventh Naval Dist. Officers wives, 61. Rel: Catholic. Mailing Add: 4437 Alhambra, San Diego, Calif. 92107.

SVALINA, NICK D
b. Chicago, Ill, 10/16/10; c. four. Educ: Pearson Real Estate Sch; Ill. Inst. Polit. & Govt. Pos: Mem, Tenth Ward Dem. Club, Ill; dep. sheriff, Cook Co; mem. staff, Superior Court Clerk's Off; chancery clerk; Former Ill. State Rep. Bus. & Prof. Pos: Real estate broker. Mil. Serv: Army, 2 years, one year in Asiatic-Pac. Theatre. Mem: Past comdr, South Chicago VFW Post No. 4104; past vice pres, East Side Lions; South Chicago Am. Legion Post No. 493; Tenth Ward Dem. club rep. in the S. E. Civic Fedn; South Chicago Commun. Coun; Roseland Moose, Legion of the Moose; South Chicago Fraternal Order of Eagles; Polish Nat. Alliance; Croatian Fraternal Union; active in youth progs. Rel: Sacred Heart Church. Mailing Add: 10723 S. Ave. F, Chicago, Ill. 60617. (1967)

SVILAR, DANIEL P. 'MIKE' D
Wyo. State Sen.
b. Hudson, Wyo, 1/12/29; s. Dan W. Svilar and Bessie Sevanovich S; single. Educ: N.Mex. State Univ, B.S. in Mech. Eng, 52; Univ. Wyo, LL.B, 58; Sigma Tau. Polit. & Govt. Pos: Chmn, Fremont Co. Dem. Cent. Cmt, Wyo, 60-64; Wyo. State Rep, 65-66; Wyo. State Sen, 67- Mil. Serv: Entered as 2nd Lt, Air Force, 52, released as 1st Lt, 54; 1st Lt, Air Force Res. Publ: Alimony in Ex Parte Proceedings and Comment on Wyoming Account's Receivable Statute, Wyo. Law Journal, 58. Mem: Wyo. State and Fremont Co. Bar Asns; Am. Soc. Mech. Engr; Am. Legion; Elks. All-Border Conf. Basketball Team, N.Mex. State, 52; All-Air Force Basketball Team, 53. Mailing Add: Hudson, Wyo. 82515.

SWAFFORD, HOWARD GRAHAM R
Tenn. State Rep.
b. Jasper, Tenn, 10/11/19; s. John Aaron Swafford and Ida Graham S; m. 5/8/48 to Claude Galbreath; c. Howard Graham, Jr. and Claudia Mae. Educ: Univ. Tenn, B.S. in Bus. Admin, 41, J.D, 47; Sigma Alpha Epsilon; Phi Alpha Delta. Polit. & Govt. Pos: City Judge and Recorder, South Pittsburg, Tenn, 48-59, Cmnr. of Streets and Pub. Works, 56-58; Rep. committeeman, Third Cong. Dist, 50-54, Rep. Presidential Elector, 64; chmn, Marion Co. Rep. Exec. Cmt, 56-57; Tenn. State Rep, 12th Flotorial Dist, 68- Bus. & Prof. Pos: Lawyer, Partnership of Raulston & Swafford, 47- Mil. Serv: Entered as Aviation Cadet, Navy, 42, released as Lt.(jg), 45, after serv. in U.S.S. S.Dak. in Pac, Southwest Pac. Theatre; Capt, Nat. Guard, South Pittsburg Heavy Mortar Co, 278th Inf, 50-52. Mem: Tenn. and Am. Bar Asns; Tenn. Trial Lawyers Asn; Mason; C. of C; Am. Legion. Rel: Methodist. Legal Res: 704 Contour Ave, South Pittsburg, Tenn. 37380. Mailing Add: Box 355, South Pittsburg, Tenn. 37380.

SWALLOW, GROVER R
Nev. State Assemblyman
b. Meadow, Utah, 10/23/27; s. Thomas Charles Swallow and Vanda Duncan S; m. 9/7/48 to Emily Brookie Condie; c. Condie Thomas, Dana Lee, Brookie Cay, Vanda, Roxanne, Joseph Bruce, Emily Gayle, Dorcas Dawn and Grover Marion. Educ: Idaho State Univ, B.S, 49. Polit. & Govt. Pos: Chmn, Lincoln Area Develop. Cmt, 63-64 & 67-, Nev. Area Develop. Cmt, 65-66; Nev. State Assemblyman, White Pine and Lincoln Counties, 68- Bus. & Prof. Pos: Owner, Caliente Pharm, 57- Mem: Nev. State Pharm. Asn; Rotary. Rel: Latter-day Saint. Legal Res: Box 267, Panaca, Nev. 89042.

SWALLOW, JOSEPH PATRICK R
Mich. State Rep.
b. Alpena, Mich, 12/31/32; m. 2/28/69 to Jane S. Richards. Educ: Grad. Cent. Mich. Univ, B.S; Detroit Col. of Law, J.D. Polit. & Govt. Pos: Mich. State Rep, 64-; former prosecuting attorney of Alpena Co. Bus. & Prof. Pos: Partner, Law Firm, Swallow, Jason and Wenzel, 66- Mil. Serv: Army, Inf, 1st Lt, discharged 58; Capt, Army Res. Mem: Pres, 26th Judicial Bar Asn; pres, Alpena Boy's Club Bd. of Dirs; Mich. State Bar Cmt. on Conserv; Boy's Club Alumni Asn; Optimist Club. Rel: Lutheran. Mailing Add: 504 First St, Alpena, Mich. 49707.

SWALLOW, RICHARD ALDEN R
V.Chmn, Jefferson Co. Rep. Cent. Cmt, Kans.
b. Oskaloosa, Kans, 11/7/05; s. Guy A. Swallow and Caroline Carlotta Clark S; single. Educ: Washburn Col, LL.B, 27 and A.B, 28. Polit. & Govt. Pos: City attorney, Valley Falls, Kans, 34-42 and Perry, Kans, 60-; co. attorney, Jefferson Co, 42-47 and 51-55; v.chmn, Jefferson Co. Rep. Cent. Cmt, 61- Mil. Serv: Entered as Pvt, Army, 42, released as T-5, after serv. in 301 Eng. Bn, 76th Div, Atlantic Seaboard. Mem: Jefferson Co. Bar Asn; Mason; Eastern Star; Am. Legion. Rel: Presbyterian. Mailing Add: Oskaloosa, Kans. 66066.

SWAN, ARTHUR ROBERT R
Mem, Exec. Cmt, Rep. State Cent. Cmt, Minn.
b. Rochester, Minn, 12/5/20; s. William Edward Swan and Rose Aulwes S; m. 1/19/46 to Jacqueline Jean Vincent; c. Kathleen, Barbara, Cynthia and Thomas. Educ: Rochester Jr. Col, A.A, 41; Univ. Minn, B.S.L, 47 and J.D, 49. Polit. & Govt. Pos: Mem, Olmsted Co. Rep. Cent. Cmt, Minn, 52-; alternate del, Rep. Nat. Conv, 52, del, 64; v.chmn, First Rep. Cong. Dist, Minn, 55-59, chmn, 60-65 and del-at-lg, 65-; mem, exec. cmt, Rep. State Cent. Cmt, 60-; mem, Minn. Munic. Cmn, 67- Mil. Serv: Entered as Pvt, Army, 42, released as Maj, 46, after serv. in 63rd Med. Bn, ETO, 44-45; ETO Campaign Ribbon with 3 Stars; Am. Theater Ribbon. Mem: Am. and Minn. State Bars; Elks; Mason; Am. Legion; VFW; C. of C; Kiwanis; mem, adv. bd, Rochester State Jr. Col.(past chmn); past pres, Rochester Coun. of Churches; dir, Rochester Col. Found.(past pres). Rel: Episcopal. Mailing Add: 809 Fifth St. S.W, Rochester, Minn. 55901.

SWAN, JAMES D. R
Wis. State Sen.
b. Neosho Falls, Kans, 2/20/03; s. James D. Swan and Mary Rosina Bishop S; m. 6/27/25 to Edith Brigham; c. Nancy (Mrs. Douglas), Emily (Mrs. deLuca) and Penny (Mrs. Wallen). Educ: Princeton Univ, B.S, 25. Polit. & Govt. Pos: Wis. State Sen, 15th Dist, 67- Bus. & Prof. Pos: Adv. mem, Bd. of Gov, Chicago Mercantile Exchange, Ill, 50-51. Publ: Tech. Publ. Mem: Past pres, Wis. Potato Growers Asn, 50-51; past pres, Vegetable Growers of Am, 54-55; mem, Nat. Pilots Asn; mem, Farm Bur. Rel: Episcopal. Legal Res: Route 2, Elkhorn, Wis. 53121. Mailing Add: State Capitol, Madison, Wis. 53702.

SWAN, MARY FLETCHER. See GAYLORD, MARY FLETCHER

SWAN, ROBERT AUSTIN, JR. D
b. Topeka, Kans, 5/19/42; s. Robert Austin Swan, Sr. and Rosemary Schmidt S; single. Educ: Univ. Kans, B.A, 64, M.A, 69; Univ. Reading, Eng, 64-65; Univ. Buenos Aires, Rotary Fel, 66; Omicron Delta Kappa; Beta Theta Pi. Polit. & Govt. Pos: Dem. cand, U.S. House Rep, Kans, 68; mem, Original Steering Cmt, New Dem. Coalition of Kans, 69. Bus. & Prof. Pos: Dir, Evelyn Wood Reading Dynamics Inst, 68; pres, Univ. Enterprises, Inc, 68-; instr, Univ. Kans, 69; spec. agent, New York Life Ins. Co, 69- Publ: 'University of Kansas and the Peace Corps,' Peace Corps, 62. Mem: Hon. mem, 40 et 8; Am. Legion. A room in Childrens' Rehabilitation Unit at Univ. Kans. Med. Center named in his honor for cerebral palsy charity work. Rel: Presbyterian. Legal Res: 3636 W. 11th, Topeka, Kans. 66604. Mailing Add: 503 E. 22nd St, Terr-Cottage, Lawrence, Kans. 66044.

SWAN, SARA VICTORIA D
b. Banner Elk, N.C, 6/20/22; d. Roby Alan Shomaker and Sara Fina Reece S; m. 11/30/46 to Charles Park Swan. Educ: Newland High Sch, N.C, grad, 39. Polit. & Govt. Pos: Mgr. woman's div. for Gov. Gordon Browning, Anderson Co, Tenn, 48; mgr. for Sen. Estes Kefauver's nomination for Pres, Nashville Co, 52; mem, Knox Co. Dem. Exec. Cmt, 56-69; pres, Dem. Women's Club, 58-59; treas, Young Dem. Club, 58-60; cmt. mem. for John F. Kennedy, 60; mgr. women's div. for Gov. Buford Ellington, Knox Co, 66, for Mayor Leonard Rogers, 68; alternate del, Dem. Nat. Conv, 68. Bus. & Prof. Pos: Cost acct, Carbide and Carbon, 44-50. Mem: Knoxville Woman's Club (past pres); Arthritis Found.(first v.pres); bd. mem, Am. Cancer Soc; Knox Co. Coun. Garden Clubs (second v.pres). Vol. of the year, Am. Cancer Soc; Knoxville's First Lady; Colonial, Gov. Staff. Rel: Baptist. Mailing Add: Beechwood Rd, Knoxville, Tenn. 37920.

SWANNER, JOHN MacDONALD
b. Washington, N.C, 2/11/22; s. John MacDonald Swanner and Mae Spain S; m. 4/29/50 to Mary Elizabeth Blount; c. Susan Lyon and Elizabeth Blount. Educ: Univ. N.C, Chapel Hill, B.S. in Commerce, 48; Phi Beta Kappa; Beta Gamma Sigma; Phi Gamma Delta. Polit. & Govt. Pos: Staff Dir, Cmt. on Standards of Off. Conduct, U.S. House of Rep, 67- Bus. & Prof. Pos: V.pres, Rodar Leasing Corp, Wash, D.C, 57-67. Mil. Serv: Entered as Pvt, Army, 42, released as T/Sgt, 46, after serv. in various units, ETO, 45-46. Mailing Add: 11119 Stephalee Lane, Rockville, Md. 20852.

SWANSON, ARTHUR R. R
Ill. State Sen.
b. Roseland, Ill. Educ: Morgan Park Jr. Col. Polit. & Govt. Pos: Ill. State Sen, 62-66 & 69- Bus. & Prof. Pos: Realtor. Mil. Serv: Combat paratrooper. Mem: Pres, Kiwanis Club of Roseland; Pres, Roseland Real Estate Bd; Dir, South End C. of C; Moose; Chicago Real Estate Bd. Mailing Add: 604 E. 103rd St, Chicago, Ill. 60628. (1967)

SWANSON, CHARLES EDWARD R
b. Galesburg, Ill, 1/3/79; s. Peter Swanson and Hannah Mathilda Johnson S; m. 6/29/10 to Ione Westcott; c. Cynthia (Mrs. Burke) and Stukely. Educ: Knox Col, A.B, 02; Northwest. Univ. Law Sch, LL.B, 07; Phi Alpha Delta. Polit. & Govt. Pos: Attorney, Pottawattamie Co, Iowa, 15-22; chmn, Pottawattamie Co. Rep. Party, 22-28; U.S. Rep, Iowa, 29-33; chmn, Coun. Bluffs Bd. Tax Rev, 48-66. Bus. & Prof. Pos: Pres, Park Bldg, Corp, 38-66. Mem: Pres, Iowa State Co. Attorneys Asn, 19; Am. and Iowa Bar Asns; past Master, AF&AM; past Exalted Ruler, Elks; pres, Pottawattamie Co. Bar Asn, 48; pres, Kiwanis, 24. Rel: Presbyterian. Legal Res: 518 Clark Ave, Council Bluffs, Iowa 51501. Mailing Add: 311 Park Bldg, Council Bluffs, Iowa 51501.

SWANSON, CLARENCE WILLIAM R
b. Orion, Ill, 10/30/05; s. Luther Swanson and Marie Johnson S; m. 11/22/47 to Joanne Krull; c. Linda (Mrs. Baldwin) and Jerry. Educ: Augustana Col, A.B, 28; Univ. Iowa, M.A, 40; Omicron Nu Omicron. Polit. & Govt. Pos: Supt. of schs, Marshall Co, Ill, 43-; Rep. precinct committeeman, Pre-

cinct One, 68- Mem: Nat. Educ. Asn; Ill. Educ. Asn.(pres, Ill. Valley Div, 50); Ill. Asn. of Co. Supt. of Schs; Rotary (pres, Lacon Club, 51); Mason; Commandery; Shrine; Lacon Country Club; Marshall Co. Farm Bur. Rel: Lutheran. Mailing Add: 913 Harmony Lane, Lacon, Ill. 61540.

SWANSON, GERTRUDE GAY CLAIRE R
Mem, Calif. Rep. State Cent. Cmt.
b. Milwaukee, Wis, Sept; d. Carl G. Loeber and Betsy Beyer L; m. 7/1/34 to Ray Oscar Swanson; c. Philip Ray and Linda Gay (Mrs. Alan Charles). Educ: Univ. Calif. Los Angeles, A.B. in Econ. and Polit. Sci. and Jr. High Sch. Teaching Credential; Alpha Chi Delta (pres, 34-37); Pi Sigma Alpha; Nu Delta Omicron; pres, Beta Sigma Omicron, 32-36. Polit. & Govt. Pos: Treas, Pomona Valley Rep. Women's Club, Federated, Calif. 50-60, auditor, 60-, pres, 63-64; mem, Calif. Rep. State Cent. Cmt, 60-; secy, Rep. Coord. Coun. 62, treas, 63-64, pres, 67; received various spec. polit. assignments and cand. campaign appointments including Glenard P. Lipscomb, Cong, 24th Dist, George Murphy, Calif. Sen. Houston Flournoy for State Controller and James Whetmore, Peter Scharbarum and William Campbell, Calif. State Legis; mem, Personnel Bd. Exam, City Pomona, currently. Mem: Calif. State Ment. Health Asn.(spec. citizen's bd); life mem, Univ. Calif, Los Angeles Alumni Asn; Bank of Am. Scholarship Rev. Bd; Lutheran Laymen's League; Lutheran Braille Workers; Lutheran Women's Missionary League; Good Shepherd Lutheran Home Bd. Blunt Hist. Cup, Los Angeles C. of C; For. Trade Award. Rel: Lutheran. Mailing Add: 1891 Fairview Place, Pomona, Calif. 91766.

SWANSON, HARRY BROOKS R
Mem, Washoe Co. Rep. Cent. Cmt, Nev.
b. Reno, Nev, 6/4/28; s. Harry Swanson and Cleo Brooks S; m. 8/6/50 to Irene Fulton; c. Karen, Kathey and Kyle Brooks. Educ: Univ. Nev, B.A, 50; Univ. Calif, Hastings Col. of Law, LL.B, 53; Order of the Coif; Alpha Tau Omega; Phi Alpha Delta. Polit. & Govt. Pos: Asst. city attorney, Reno, Nev, 53-54; Nev. State Assemblyman, 58-64; mem, Washoe Co. Rep. Cent. Cmt, 58-; del, Rep. Nat. Conv, 64. Bus. & Prof. Pos: Partner, Richards & Swanson, 56-62 and Swanson & Swanson, 62- Mil. Serv: Entered as 2nd Lt, Air Force, 54, released as 1st Lt, 56, after serv. in Staff Judge Adv. Off, Malmstrom Air Force Base, Strategic Air Command, Mont. Publ: 'Sherrer v. Sherrer & the Future—A Prophesy,' Am. Bar Asn. Jour, 8/54; ed, Nev. Bar Asn. Jour, 58-63. Mem: Am, Nev. and Washoe Co. Bar Asns; dir, Nev. Wildlife Fedn, Ducks Unlimited, Nev, and Nev. Cancer Soc; Elks; Lions; C. of C. Rel: Methodist. Legal Res: 2001 Sierra Sage Lane, Reno, Nev. 89502. Mailing Add: P.O. Box 2417, Reno, Nev. 89505.

SWANSON, JAMES C. DFL
Minn. State Rep.
b. 1934. Educ: Dunwoody Inst, 52-55, sheet metal degree; Colo. State Univ, 65; Mankato State Col, 66; Univ. Minn, B.S, 69. Polit. & Govt. Pos: Mem, Portland Elem. PTA; Minn. State Rep, currently; mem, Richfield Citizens Tax Cmn, 64-69; elected dir, Richfield Sch. Bd, Dist. 280, 65-68; elected Officials Rev. Cmn, 65-66; app. subchmn, Keith Metro Task Force Cmn, 66. Bus. & Prof. Pos: Journeyman sheet metal worker, 55-63; instr, Dunwoody Indust. Inst. Mem: Minn. and Am. Voc. Asn; Metrop-Suburban Area Sch. Bds. Asn; Richfield DFL Club; Richfield Jaycees; AFL-CIO; COPE. Outstanding Young Man, 69. Mailing Add: 6827 Fifth Ave, Richfield, Minn. 55423.

SWANSON, R. JOHN R
b. Red Oak, Iowa, 11/22/20; s. R.J. Swanson and Ruth Wright S; m. 1/2/46 to Margaret Seibert; c. Ralph, Ben, Mark, David and Bruce. Educ: State Col. Iowa, 38-40; State Univ. Iowa, B.A, 47, Col. Law, J.D, 48; State Univ. Iowa Law Review; Phi Delta Phi; Phi Kappa Psi. Polit. & Govt. Pos: Mem. technical sect, Fed. Bur. Investigation, U.S. Dept. Justice, 42; attorney, Montgomery Co, Iowa, 51-55; mem, Red Oak Sch. Bd, 55-58; chmn, Montgomery Co. Rep. Cent. Cmt, Iowa, 60-66. Bus. & Prof. Pos: Trustee, Murphy Memorial Hosp, Red Oak, Iowa, 49-66. Mil. Serv: Entered as Pvt, Army Air Force, 42, released as S/Sgt, 45, after serv. in ETO, 44-45; 2nd Lt, Army Air Force Res; ETO Ribbon; Good Conduct Medal; Bronze Star. Mem: Am, Iowa, Southwest Iowa and Montgomery Co. Bar Asns; Elks; Lions; Mason; Am. Legion; Farm Bur. Rel: Congregational. Legal Res: 1119 Boundary, Red Oak, Iowa 51566. Mailing Add: 209 Coolbaugh St, Red Oak, Iowa 51566.

SWANSON, WAYNE R
State Treas, Nebr.
b. Omaha, Nebr, 12/31/14; m. 6/22/46 to Ruth McDonald; c. two. Educ: Spec. bus. training. Polit. & Govt. Pos: State Rwy. Cmnr, Nebr, 56-67; State Treas, Nebr, 67- Bus. & Prof. Pos: Former owner excavating bus; plumber. Mil. Serv: Navy, World War II. Mem: Past chmn, State Rwy. Cmnrs; Eagles; Odd Fellows; Mason; hon. life mem, Crestview Lodge, Sarpy Post 9675, VFW. Rel: Baptist. Mailing Add: 1809 S. 53rd St, Lincoln, Nebr. 68506.

SWANSTROM, DWIGHT ALEXANDER Conservative
Minn. State Rep.
b. Duluth, Minn, 4/28/05; s. Adolph Frederick Swanstrom and Catherine Witherspoon Stewart S; m. 10/30/28 to Anna Jean Kearns; c. Mary (Mrs. Patterson), Fred, Lorne, William and Jonathan. Educ: Univ. of Minn, B.A, 67; Sigma Chi; Alpha Kappa Psi. Polit. & Govt. Pos: Mem, Bldg. Appeals Bd, Duluth, Minn, 35-63; Minn. State Rep, 45-55 & 65- Bus. & Prof. Pos: Pres, Dwight Swanstrom Co. Mil. Serv: Cpl, Minn. State Guard, 45-47; Good Conduct, Serv. Medal, State of Minn. Mem: Pres, W. End. Bus. & Civic Club, 40-; dir, Duluth Auto Club, 40-; Minn. Asn. of Independent Ins. Agents; Mason (Past Master); Scottish Rite; Shrine; Moose. Legion of Honor, Grand Council, DeMolay. Rel: Presbyterian; Chmn. bd. of trustees, Presbytery of Duluth. Legal Res: 1325 Lincoln Park Dr, Duluth, Minn. 55806. Mailing Add: 31 N. 21st Ave. W, Duluth, Minn. 55806.

SWANTON, MARY ELLEN CASHIN D
b. Modesto, Calif, 2/3/15; d. Francis Patrick Cashin and Leone Allison C; m. 1/5/43 to Donald Jackson; children by first husband, Lester J. Newell, Sr, m. 32, div, 42; c. Lester J, Jr, Michael G. and Patricial Ellen. Educ: Univ. Hawaii, B.A. cum laude, 67, M.A, 69; Columbia Univ, Grad. work. Polit. & Govt. Pos: Chmn, Gov. Advisory Cmn. on State Insts, Nev, 59; chmn, Gov. Ad Hoc Cmn. on the Status of Women, Hawaii, 64-; pres, 13th Precinct, 17th Dist, Honolulu Dem. Party, 64-; secy, 17th Dist. Dem. Club, 66-; del, Dem. Nat. Conv, 68. Publ: 'Effects of Tourism on American Samoa,' 67; 'Visitor Perception of the Physical and Cultural Environment of American Samoa,' M.A. thesis, 12/68; 'The Geographic Factors in Tourism: Case Study, American Samoa,' Am. Pac. Coast Geogr. Conf, Pac. Area Travel Asn. Libr, San Francisco, 69. Mem: Am. Asn. of Geogr; Asn. of Pac. Coast Geogr; Bishop Museum Asn; Hawaii Fedn. Bus. & Prfnl. Women's Clubs (bd. dirs, 62-69, first v.pres, 69-); Nev. Fedn. Bus. & Prfnl. Women's Clubs (bd. dirs, 52, 59 & 60); Nat. Fedn. of Bus. & Prfnl. Women's Clubs,(pres, Reno, Nev. Club, 53-54); Nat. Orgn. Women; Manoa-Kai Bus. & Prfnl. Women's Club (pres, 66-67); NAACP; Friends of the Library. Sinclair Library Prize for Effects of Tourism on Am. Samoa, 67. Rel: Roman Catholic. Mailing Add: 725 A 15th Ave, Honolulu, Hawaii 96816.

SWANTON, WILLIAM FRANCIS R
b. Casper, Wyo, 4/17/19; s. William Joseph Swanton and Nora Tobin S; m. 3/8/43 to Celia Jane Bon; c. William Lawrence, Bonnie Jane, Nancy Ann and Phillips Randall. Educ: Univ. Wyo, B.S, 43; Denver Univ, LL.B, 45; Phi Delta Phi; Phi Delta Theta. Polit. & Govt. Pos: Wyo. State Rep, 50-66, minority floor leader, Wyo. House of Rep, 65-66 and Wyo. State Sen, 67-68; city attorney, Casper, Wyo, 52-53; Wyo. Rep. Coun. of State Govt, 56-66. Bus. & Prof. Pos: Dir, Pineview Develop. Co, 52-66; pres, Swift Realty Co, 55-66. Mil. Serv: 2nd Lt, Army, 43-44, with serv. in 44th Inf. Div. Mem: Am, Colo, Wyo. and Natrona Co. Bar Asns; Lions; K. of C; Elks; Am. Legion. Rel: Catholic. Mailing Add: 1028 S. Beech, Casper, Wyo. 82601. (1967)

SWARTS, JOSEPH ANDREW R
Chmn, Sixth Cong. Dist. Rep. Party, Mo.
b. Kansas City, Kans, 2/19/17; s. John Lloyd Swarts and Agnes McOwen S; m. 11/26/42 to Thelma Rose Osborn; c. Elizabeth (Mrs. Tom Feeney), Joseph Andrew, Thomas Arthur, Michael Alan and Robert Anthony. Educ: Kansas City Jr. Col, Kans. Polit. & Govt. Pos: Pres, Platte Co. Rep. Club, Mo, 52-55; chmn, Platte Co. Rep. Cent. Cmt, 66-, Sixth Cong. Dist. Rep. Party, 68- Mem: Past Grand Knight, Tri-Co. K. of C, Past Faithful Capt. of Lt. T. Fitzsimmons, K. of C.(4°); Optimist (distinguished pres, South Platte Club, 58-60); Platte Co. Bus. & Prof. Club (mem. chmn, 68). Rel: Catholic. Legal Res: 7511 W. 71 Hwy, Kansas City, Mo. 64151. Mailing Add: 7607 W. 71 Hwy. N.W, Kansas City, Mo. 64151.

SWARTZ, EDWARD STOVER R
b. Hummelstown, Pa, 5/13/10; s. Martin Oliver Swartz and Mary Stover S; m. 8/23/36 to Helen Rose Wagner; c. Edward Oliver. Polit. Pos: Del, Rep. Nat. Conv, 64; Pa. State Rep, 51-52. Bus. Pos: Self employed except for two years, 29-31, with the Marcus Hook Nat. Bank, Pa. Mem: Pres, Pa. Attractions Asn. and Citizens for Constitutional Govt; secy, Pa. Cavemen's Asn. Gubernatorial candidate of Constitutional Party, 66. Rel: Evangelical United Brethren. Legal Res: R.D. 3, Hummelstown, Pa. 17036. Mailing Add: P.O. Box 206, Hummelstown, Pa. 17036.

SWAYZE, FRANCES G. R
b. Council Bluffs, Iowa, 2/11/01; d. William A. Goehring and Lilian Huff G; m. 7/8/23 to Thomas Allen Swayze (deceased); c. Shirley (Mrs. W. Harry Dearth), Gretchen (Mrs. R. William Wilbert), Thomas Allen, Suzanne (Mrs. C.E. Rector) and George. Educ: Univ. Puget Sound, B.A, 22; Pi Beta Phi. Polit. & Govt. Pos: Wash. State Rep, 53-66; training officer, Dept. Motor Vehicles, Wash, 66- Bus. & Prof. Pos: Research asst, Univ. Puget Sound. Mem: PEO; League Women Voters; Am. Asn. Univ. Women; Bus. & Prfnl. Women. Mailing Add: 5716 N. 33rd, Tacoma, Wash. 98407.

SWAYZE, RUTH U. R
m. to Donald Swayze, March, 1946; c. Sandi, Michael. Educ: Bridgewater State Col, 42, B.S. in educ; Rutgers Sch. of Soc. Work, M.S.W, 66. Polit. & Govt. Pos: Cand. U.S. Rep, N.J; Rep. City and Co. Cmts. Bus. & Prof. Pos: Research chemist; soc. worker; Elec. Engr, Dept. MIT and also research metallurgy dept. Mem: League of Women Voters; Urban League of Union Co; NASW; Cath. Human Rels. Coun. of Union Co; State Dept. of Insts. and Agencies, 64 as field rep. in commun. ment. health serv. Mailing Add: 47 Sayre St, Elizabeth, N.J. 07206. (1967)

SWAYZE, THOMAS ALLEN, JR. R
Wash. State Rep.
b. Tacoma, Wash, 12/8/30; s. Thomas Allen Swayze and Frances Goerhing S; m. 7/5/57 to Marliss Marie McCann; c. Sharon Marie, Sandra Lynne, Glenn Thomas and Kristin Kay. Educ: Univ. Puget Sound, A.B, 53; Univ. Wash, LL.B, 54; Kappa Sigma; Phi Alpha Delta. Polit. & Govt. Pos: Chmn, Pierce Co. Rep. Cent. Cmt, 64-65; Wash. State Rep, 26th Dist, 65- Bus. & Prof. Pos: Partner, Muscek, Adams, Swayze & Baker, Tacoma, Wash, 63- Mil. Serv: Entered as Pvt, Army, 54, released as Spec-4, 56, after serv. in Hq. 6023 Personnel Unit. Mem: Am, Wash. State and Tacoma-Pierce Co. Bar Asns; Am. Judicature Soc; Elks; Gyro; Young Men's Bus. Club; C. of C. Rel: Methodist. Mailing Add: 3408 N. 24th St, Tacoma, Wash. 98406.

SWEARENGEN, FRANK BRADFORD R
Chmn, Tallahatchie Co. Rep. Cmt, Miss.
b. Oakland, Miss, 4/14/26; s. Sam A. Swearengen and Eunice Willingham S; m. 3/20/49 to Betty Brock; c. Frank B, Jr, Sherry and Leigh. Educ: Miss. State Univ, 49. Polit. & Govt. Pos: Chmn, Tallahatchie Co. Rep. Cmt, Miss, 60- Bus. & Prof. Pos: Farmer, 52-66. Mil. Serv: Army Air Force, 44-46; entered Res, 50, released as Lt, after serv. in S.Pac. & ETO. Mem: Farm Bur. Rel: Methodist. Mailing Add: Macel Rd, Philipp, Miss. 38950.

SWED, JEANETTE D
Dem. Nat. Committeewoman, Wis.
b. Milwaukee, Wis, 7/2/08; d. Louis Goldberg and Dora Padway G; m. 11/17/29 to Abe Swed; c. Sandra and Jordan Lewis. Educ: Pub. schs, Milwaukee. Polit. & Govt. Pos: Del, Dem. Nat. Conv, 64 & 68; mem. steering cmt, Project Head Start, 64-; Dem. nat. committeewoman, Wis, 64- Bus. & Prof. Pos: Partner, Abe L. Swed Co. Investments, 45-; partner, Lewis Center, 62-; dir, J. Swed Shoe Co. Mem: V.pres, Milwaukee Chap, Haddassah, 28; pres, City of Hope, 34-36; treas. and dir, Protective Serv. for Children, 63; mem. exec. bd, Wis. Sr. Citizens, 63-; Jewish Home for Aged, 63-; Univ.

Wis. Athletic Scholarship Fund; Brandeis Univ. Women's Group; NAACP; Haddassah; B'nai B'rith. Recipient, Nurse of Mercy Award, City of Hope, 60. Legal Res: 9363 N. Sleepy Hollow Lane, Milwaukee, Wis. 53217. Mailing Add: 615 E. Michigan St, Milwaukee, Wis. 53202. (1967)

SWEDA, JOSEPH D
Wis. State Assemblyman
b. Lublin, Wis, 1/3/26. Educ: Lublin and Withee High Schs. Polit. & Govt. Pos: Town chmn, 55; mem. co. bd. and chmn, 58-; chmn, Co. Dem. Unit, 59-61; Wis. State Assemblyman, 62- Bus. & Prof. Pos: Farmer. Mil. Serv: Army Air Force, World War II, 45-46. Mem: Am. Legion (adj, 3 years and post comdr, 8 years); Boy Scouts (chmn, local cmt); Co. Farmers Union (dir, 2 years). Mailing Add: Route 1, Lublin, Wis. 54447. (1967)

SWEDLUND, PAUL J. D
N.Dak. State Rep.
b. Velva, N.Dak, 7/3/34; s. Tony Swedlund and Lois Nopp S; m. 6/8/69 to Ann Kramer. Educ: N.Dak. State Univ, B.S, 67; Soc. Adv. Educ. Polit. & Govt. Pos: N.Dak. State Rep, 69- Bus. & Prof. Pos: Farmer, 60- Mil. Serv: Pvt, Army, 58-59. Mem: Farmers Union; Nat. Farmers Orgn. Rel: Lutheran. Mailing Add: Velva, N.Dak. 58790.

SWEEN, ROBERT HAROLD R
Chmn, Franklin Co. Rep. Cmt, Maine
b. Minneapolis, Minn, 3/24/38; s. Harold Casper Sween and Virginia Graef Hodgkins S; m. 8/24/63 to Constance Jack; c. twins, Sonna Anne and Kristin Remol. Educ: Univ. Maine, B.S, 63; Alpha Tau Omega. Polit. & Govt. Pos: Dist. chmn, Maine Young Rep. Party, 67-68; mem, Maine Rep. Platform Cmt, 68; chmn, Franklin Co. Rep. Cmt, 68- Mem: Farmington, Maine Bus. Men's Asn. (pres, 65-66); AF&AM; Royal Arch; K.T. Rel: Methodist. Mailing Add: North Highlands, Wilton, Maine 04294.

SWEENEY, DAVID F, JR. D
b. Providence, R.I, 4/7/30; m. to Jean Nardone. Educ: Univ. R.I, acct. degree, 52; Boston Univ. Sch. of Law, LL.B, 59. Polit. & Govt. Pos: R.I. State Rep, 61-66. Bus. & Prof. Pos: Attorney and acct. Mil. Serv: Navy, Officer on destroyer, 52-56, active duty in N. Atlantic and Mediterranean; Lt, Naval Res, currently. Mailing Add: 69 Westwood Ave, Cranston, R.I. 02905. (1967)

SWEENEY, EDWARD J. D
b. Princeton, N.J, 6/4/13; m. to Mary Pierre; c. Patricia, Michael and two grandsons. Educ: Rutgers Univ. Polit. & Govt. Pos: N.J. State Assemblyman, 59-68. Bus. & Prof. Pos: Chmn, Grievance Cmn, Local 3355, 44-50; v.pres, Local 3355, 50-52; legis. dir, Cent. Jersey Indust. Coun, CIO, 52; pres, Local 3355, 52-62; mem, State CIO Coun. Legis. Cmn, 54; second v.pres, Mercer Co. Labor Union Coun; union rep; third v.pres, State CIO Coun. Mem: Exec. cmn. and bd. gov, Del. Valley United Fund; chmn, Multiple Sclerosis Dr. for Princeton; campaign mgr, Princeton Dem. Club, 57-59; pres, Princeton Dem. Club, 58, 61 & 64; Mercer Co. Planning Bd; K. of C; Elks; Lions. Mailing Add: 181 N. Harrison St, Princeton, N.J. 08540. (1967)

SWEENEY, JAMES ALOYSIUS, JR. D
N.H. State Rep.
b. Manchester, N.H, 5/4/34; s. James Aloysius Sweeney, Sr. and Clara Allaire S; m. 10/20/62 to Beverly Joan Lester; c. James A, III and Laurie Ann. Educ: Univ. N.H, 52-53 & 55-56; St. Anselms Col, 57-58; Phi Delta Upsilon; Neuman Club. Polit. & Govt. Pos: Selectman, Ward 10, N.H, 66-67 & 68-69; N.H. State Rep, 67-68 & 69- Mil. Serv: Entered as Pvt, Army, 53, released as Pfc, 55; Nat. Defense Serv. Medal; Good Conduct Medal. Rel: Roman Catholic. Mailing Add: 25 Fogg Ave, Manchester, N.H. 03102.

SWEENEY, JAMES MICHAEL, JR. R
Chmn, Lee Co. Rep. Exec. Cmt, Fla.
b. Tappan, N.Y, 4/14/13; s. James M. Sweeney and Alice Janet Fisher S; m. 6/19/38 to Florence Dale George; c. David James and Alice Dale (Mrs. Scott). Educ: Rutgers Univ, 6 months, elec. eng. Polit. & Govt. Pos: Tax assessor, Town of Orangetown, N.Y, 55-58; dep. tax assessor, Lee Co, Fla, 63-; chmn, Lee Co. Rep. Exec. Cmt, 65- Mil. Serv: Entered as A/S, Coast Guard, 42, released as Boatswain, 45, after serv. in Port Security, New York Harbor; N.Am. Ribbon; Victory Ribbon; Good Conduct Medal. Mem: Mason; Shrine; Am. Legion; Lions (past pres); C. of C. (past pres); comnr, Fire Dist. (fire chief). Rel: Presbyterian; supt. of Sunday Sch, Chapel by the Sea. Mailing Add: 226 Connecticut St, Ft. Myers Beach, Fla. 33931.

SWEENEY, PATRICK A. D
Ohio State Rep.
b. Cleveland, Ohio, 1941; single. Educ: Tenn. Col; Washburn Univ; Kans. Univ; Univ. Md. Polit. & Govt. Pos: Ohio State Rep, 67- Bus. & Prof. Pos: Mfr's rep. Mil. Serv: Air Force. Legal Res: 3535 W. 100th St, Cleveland, Ohio 44111. Mailing Add: State Capitol Bldg, Columbus, Ohio 43215. (1967)

SWEENEY, ROBERT EMMETT D
b. Cleveland, Ohio, 11/4/24; s. Martin L. Sweeney (former Congressman from Ohio); m. to Patricia; c. Robert P, Daniel E, William A, Martin L, John B, James M, Thomas F, Mary Brigid, Alice Marie, Edward D, Patricia, Eileen Theresa and Catherine Pearl. Educ: Georgetown Univ; Baldwin-Wallace Col; Cleveland-Marshall Law Sch, LL.B. Polit. & Govt. Pos: Former spec. counsel to the attorney gen, Ohio; Dem. nominee for attorney gen, Ohio, 62 & 66; U.S. Rep, Ohio, 64-66, mem, Ad Hoc Subcmt. on Appalachian Regional Develop, U.S. House of Rep, 65, mem, House Pub. Works Cmt. and Subcmts. on Roads and Rivers and Harbors, 65-66. Bus. & Prof. Pos: Former asst. dir. of law, Cleveland, Ohio; practicing attorney-at-law, Cleveland, 51- Mil. Serv: World War II Vet. Mem: Cleveland, Cuyahoga, and Ohio State Bar Asns; Cleveland Athletic Club. Rel: St. Raphael's Church. Mailing Add: 26821 Bruce Rd, Bay Village, Ohio 44140.

SWEENEY, STEWART GREGORY R
b. Jerseyville, Ill, 8/28/17; s. John Patrick Sweeney and Mary Ellen Lahey S; single. Educ: High Sch. grad. Polit. & Govt. Pos: Sgt-at-Arms, Ill. State Sen, 61-65, doorman, 41-57; former chmn, Co. Rep. Cent. Cmt. Mil. Serv: Entered as Pvt, Army, 41, released as Pfc, 43, after serv. in Antiaircraft Command. Mem: Am. Legion; K. of C; Elks Lodge 954. Rel: Catholic. Mailing Add: 109-A W. Pearl, Jerseyville, Ill. 62052. (1967)

SWEENEY, TOM BELL, JR. R
b. Wheeling, W.Va, 11/18/03; s. Thomas B. Sweeney and Nell Zurmuehlin S; single. Educ: St. Paul's Sch, Concord, N.H, grad, 22; Yale Univ, New Haven, Conn, Ph.B, 26; Alpha Delta Phi. Polit. & Govt. Pos: Pres, Young Rep. Club, W.Va, 34-38; W.Va. State Sen, 38-42; Rep. nominee, U.S. Sen, 40, 46 & 54; del-at-lg, Rep. Nat. Conv, 48, 56, 60 & 64; Rep. nominee, U.S. House Rep, First Dist, 68. Bus. & Prof. Pos: Staff, Time Mag, N.Y, 27-28; staff, Herald Tribune, 28-29; agent, Equitable Life Assurance Soc, W.Va, 33-40; gen. agent, Equitable Life, 40-64; pres, Thomas B. Sweeney Investment Co, 57- Mil. Serv: Entered as Lt, Naval Res, 42, retired as Comdr, 68, after serv. in Naval Air Transport Serv, Atlantic and Pac, 43-46. Publ: Starward Ark, (play) produced by Eddie Dowling, 58; Leaky Roof Circuit, (play) produced by State Theatre of Ky, 63; 'If Verne Could Look at NASA,' Nat. Review, 5/69. Mem: W.Va. Nat. Asn. of Life Underwriters (former pres); Kiwanis; Eagles; Moose; Elks; Yale Clubs of N.Y. & Pittsburgh; Am. Legion; VFW; Amvets; OX5 Club. Rel: Presbyterian. Mailing Add: Hawley Bldg, Wheeling, W.Va. 26003.

SWEENY, JAMES H, JR. D
Fla. State Rep.
b. Port Jervis, N.Y, 9/23/05; s. James H. Sweeny and Elizabeth Horan S; m. 7/31/65 to Christine Pounds Britt; c. James H, III and Thomas F. Educ: Georgetown Univ; Stetson Univ, LL.B; Sigma Nu. Polit. & Govt. Pos: Fla. State Rep, Volusia Co, 48- Mem: Am. and Fla. Bar Asns; Elks; C. of C. Rel: Catholic. Legal Res: 777 Stratford Dr, Country Club Estates, DeLand, Fla. 32720. Mailing Add: P.O. Box 970, DeLand, Fla. 32720.

SWEET, HOWARD C. R
b. Providence, R.I, 8/6/98. Educ: Brown Univ, 20. Polit. & Govt. Pos: Mem, Charlestown Rep. Town Cmt; mem, Charlestown Town Coun, 54-56 and pres, 56-62; R.I. State Rep, 63-68. Bus. & Prof. Pos: Retired; pres, Starkweather and Shepley, N.Y. Mil. Serv: Vet. Mem: V.chmn, S. Co. Dist, BSA; Navy League; Newcomer Soc. of N. Am; Words Unlimited; Shrine. Mailing Add: Old Post Rd, RFD, Westerly, R.I. 02891. (1967)

SWEET, JOHN M. R
Alaska State Rep.
b. Sept. 29; s. John King Sweet; m. June 10 to Mirabel D; c. Mirabel Anne, Patricia Jane, John Hamlin, Robert Matthew, Thomas Andrew, Timmothy Frank and Betty Lou, Howard Lee and Patricia Ann Nunnally. Polit. & Govt. Pos: Alaska State Rep, Dist. Eight, 69- Bus. & Prof. Pos: Dist. explorationist, Atlantic Richfield Co, 50- Mil. Serv: Entered as Pvt, Marines, 43, released as Cpl, 46, after serv. in Pac. Theatre, 44-45. Publ: 'Developments on Alaska,' Bul. Am. Asn. Petroleum Geologists, 64. Mem: charter mem, Am. Inst. Prfnl. Geologists; Am. Asn. Petroleum Geologists; F&AM; Scottish Rite. Rel: Presbyterian. Mailing Add: 3000 Sheldon Jackson, Anchorage, Alaska 99504.

SWEET, LOWELL ELWIN R
Chmn, Walworth Co. Rep. Party, Wis.
b. Flint, Mich, 8/10/31; s. Leslie E. Sweet and Donna Latta S; m. 8/29/53 to Mary Ellen Ebben; c. Lawrence Edward, Diane Marie and Sara Anne. Educ: Wayne Univ, B.A, 53; Univ. Wis, Madison, L.L.D, 55; Alpha Sigma Phi; Phi Alpha Delta; secy, Wayne Univ. Young Rep, 51-52. Polit. & Govt. Pos: Chmn, Walworth Co. Young Rep, Wis, 58-60; chmn, Wis. Young Rep, First Dist, 59; Elkhorn area chmn, Walworth Co. Rep. Party, Wis, 61-65, v.chmn, 65-67, chmn, 67-; mem. platform cmt, Wis. State Rep. Conv, 66, v.chmn. rules cmt, 67, mem. credentials cmt, 68, resolutions cmt, 69. Bus. & Prof. Pos: Attorney-partner, Morrissy, Morrissy, Sweet & Race, Elkhorn, Wis, 57- Mil. Serv: Entered as Pvt, Army, 55, released as Specialist E-4, 57 after serv. in Counter-Intelligence Corps, Fifth Army Area-Continental U.S. as Agent, 56-57. Mem: Am, Wis. and Walworth Co. Bar Asns; Am. and Wis. Trial Lawyers Asns; Am. Judicature Soc; Lions Int; Am. Legion; Moose; Knights of Columbus. Outstanding Young Man-Elkhorn Award; Jr. C. of C; Certificate of Award for Services Rendered, Am. Red Cross. Rel: Roman Catholic. Mailing Add: 242 Winsor St, Elkhorn, Wis. 53121.

SWEET, ROBERT WORKMAN R
Dep. Mayor, N.Y.C.
b. Yonkers, N.Y, 10/15/22; s. James Allen Sweet and Delia Workman S; m. 7/3/48 to Lois Clapp; c. Robert W, Jr, Deborah Adams, Ames Kendall, Eliza Hill and James Allen II (deceased). Educ: Yale Col, B.A, 44, Yale Law Sch, LL.B, 48; Dean's List; Pierson Col. Debating Club; Chi Psi; Yale Dramat; Yale-Raft Scholarship; Intramural Athletics. Polit. & Govt. Pos: Former asst. secy. and mem. bd, N.Y. Young Rep. Club; founder, Youth for Eisenhower, 51; chmn, N.Y.C. Youth for Eisenhower, 52; exec. dir, N.Y. State Citizens for Eisenhower Clubs, 52 & 56; asst. U.S. attorney and asst. chief civil dir, N.Y.C, 53-55; asst. campaign mgr. for Carolyn K. Simon, 57; campaign mgr. former N.Y. State Sen. Whitney N. Seymour, Jr; campaign mgr. John J. Gilhooley Rep. Cand. Controller, N.Y.C; mem. Lawyer's Cmt. Reelect. Congressman John V. Lindsay; mem, Vet. Cmt. Reelec. John V. Lindsay, 64; mem, Rep. Citizens Cmt. U.S. Manhattan Coordinator for John V. Lindsay, 65; exec. asst. to mayor, N.Y.C, 66, dep. mayor, 66-; del, Rep. Nat. Conv, 68. Mil. Serv: Entered as Ens, Naval Res, 43, released as Lt.(jg), after serv. as commun, gunnery and exec. officer, in P.C. type vessels, Pac, 43-46. Mem: Phi Delta Phi; Asn. of the Bar City of N.Y. (mem. President's Spec. Cmt, Civil Rights Under Law); N.Y. State, Am. and Fed. Bar Asn; Am. Judicature Soc; Citizens Union; For. Policy Asn; Nat. Coun. Aging; Am. Legion (past comdr, Willard Straight Post); Century Asn; Navy League Commun. Serv. Soc. (cmt. on aging); Protestant Coun; Planned Parenthood of Manhattan and Bronx; Yorkville Youth Coun; Timber Trails Country Club. Rel: Episcopal; Vestryman, St. Georges Episcopal Church, Manhattan. Legal Res: 433 E. 85th St, New York, N.Y. 10017. Mailing Add: City Hall, New York, N.Y. 10007.

SWEETING, RICHARD W. R
Mem, Rep. Exec. Town Cmt, Sweden, N.Y.
b. Clarkson, N.Y, 10/3/17; s. Walter Sweeting and Alice Barton S; m. 6/7/41

to Helen Wilson. Educ: High Sch. Polit. & Govt. Pos: Councilman, village bd, 48-54; alternate del, Rep. Nat. Conv, 64; mem, Rep. Exec. Town Cmt, Sweden, N.Y, currently. Mil. Serv: Entered as Pvt, Army, 46, released as T-5, 47. Mem: Monroe Lodge 173; Elks. Rel: Protestant. Mailing Add: 34 Hillcrest Pkwy, Brockport, N.Y. 14420. (1967)

SWEETLAND, MONROE MARK D
b. Salem, Ore, 1/20/10; s. Dr. George J. Sweetland and Mildred Mark S; m. 10/15/34 to Lillie Megrath; c. Barbara (Mrs. Smith) and Rebecca. Educ: Wittenberg Univ, A.B, 30; Cornell and Syracuse Univs, grad. work; Pi Kappa Alpha. Polit. & Govt. Pos: Alternate del, Dem. Nat. Conv, 40, del-at-lg, 48-64 and mem, Platform Cmt, 52-64; mem, War Prod. Bd, 41-43; Dem. nat. committeeman, Ore, 48-56; Ore. State Rep, 52-54; Ore. State Sen, 54-63; mem, Ore. Adv. Cmn, U.S. Civil Rights Cmn, 56-61; assoc. dir, Johnson-Humphrey Campaign, 64. Bus. & Prof. Pos: Publisher, Ore. Dem, 48-57 and Ore. weekly newspapers, Milwaukie, Molalla and Newport, 45-64; lectr. journalism, Padjadjaran Univ, Bandung, Indonesia, 63-64; legis. consult, West. States Cmn, Nat. Educ. Asn, 64- Mil. Serv: Entered as Asst. Field Dir, Am. Red Cross, 43, released as Field Supvr, Okinawa, 45, after serv. in Pac. Theater, Marshall Islands and Okinawa Combat Opers. Oregon's First Citizen for Educ, Ore. Educ. Asn, 60; received award from Japanese-Am. Citizens League and West Coast Region Merit Award, NAACP, 61; founded Indonesian-Am. Soc. of U.S, 62. Rel: Methodist. Mailing Add: 1651 Yorktown Rd, San Mateo, Calif. 94402.

SWEEZY, JOHN W. R
b. Indianapolis, Ind, 11/14/32; s. William C. Sweezy and Zuma F. McNew S; m. 7/14/56 to Carole S. Harman; c. John W, Jr. and Bradley E. Educ: Purdue Univ, B.S.M.E, 56; Ind. Univ, Bloomington, M.B.A, 58; Butler Univ; Univ. Ga; Ind. Cent. Col; Sigma Iota Epsilon; Student Senate; Int. Asn; DeMolay; chmn, Region 5, Collegiate Young Rep, 56. Polit. & Govt. Pos: Treas, Marion Co. Young Rep, Ind, 56-58; Rep. precinct committeeman, Marion Co, 58-66, Rep. ward chmn, 66-, twp. chmn, 67-, mem, Bd. of Sanit. Cmnrs, 68, dir. of pub. works, 69-; v.chmn, 11th Dist. Rep. Party, 68; alternate del, Rep. Nat. Conv, 68. Bus. & Prof. Pos: Design engr, Allison Div, Gen. Motors Corp, Indianapolis, Ind, 56-57; asst. to John Mee, Ind. Univ, 58; power sales engr, Indianapolis Power & Light Co, 58-69. Mil. Serv: Entered as Pvt. E-1, Army, 53, released as Cpl. E-4, 55, after serv. in 15th Finance Disbursing Sect, Continental Command; Good Conduct Medal; Nat. Defense Serv. Medal. Mem: Great Lakes Power Club; Am. Soc. Mech. Engrs; Soc. for Adv. Mgt; Teamsters Union. Rel: Methodist. Mailing Add: 166 N. Gibson, Indianapolis, Ind. 46219.

SWENSON, DUAINE VINCENT D
S.Dak. State Rep.
b. Woonsocket, S.Dak, 3/27/19; s. Edward Joseph Swenson and Theresa Privet S; m. 8/25/43 to Rosemary Agnes Basham; c. Carole (Mrs. Rodney D. Shriver), Dale Vincent and Lila Agnes. Educ: Woonsocket High Sch, grad, 37. Polit. & Govt. Pos: Precinct committeeman, Sanburn Co. Dem. Party, S.Dak, 58-69; S.Dak. State Rep, Dist. 32, 66-; del, Coun. of State Govt, 69- and Four-State Cmt. on Water and Related Natural Resources, 69- Bus. & Prof. Pos: Owner and mgr, Farm and Ranch, 43-53 & 59-69, I.H.C. Implement, 53-59. Mem: K. of C; Elks; Woonsocket Commercial Club; Sanborn Co. Farmer Union Coop; PTA. Rel: Catholic. Mailing Add: Route 3, Box 5, Woonsocket, S.Dak. 57385.

SWENSON, GLEN W. Non-Partisan
b. 1910; married; c. Two. Educ: Univ. Minn. Law Sch, 35. Polit. & Govt. Pos: Minn. State Sen, 62-66; Minn. State Rep, 53-62. Bus. & Prof. Pos: Attorney; dir, Buffalo Nat. Bank; Wright Cty. State Bank; Monticello and Rockford State Bank, Rockford. Mil. Serv: WWII. Mem: Am. Legion; VFW. Mailing Add: 109 Division, Buffalo, Minn. 55313. (1967)

SWENSON, JACK HUGHES R
b. Spanish Fork, Utah, 5/19/12; s. Isaac Swenson and Mary Hannah Hughes S; m. 1/24/33 to Phebe LaVern Jex; c. Barbara S. (Mrs. Burke), David H, Jack J, Edward J. and Richard I. Educ: Univ. Utah, 31-32. Polit. & Govt. Pos: Mem. city coun, Spanish Fork, 46-50; Utah State Rep, 51-52; secy, Utah State Rep. Cent. Cmt, 55-60; del, Rep. Nat. Conv, 64. Mem: Cent. Utah Life Underwriter's Asn; Pres, Spanish Fork Jaycees, 40-41 and Utah State Jaycees, 41-42; pres, Spanish Fork Kiwanis, 56 and lt. gov, First Div, Utah-Idaho Dist. Kiwanis, 66; pres, Spanish Fork C. of C. Rel: Latter-day Saint. Mailing Add: 58 W. Second N, Spanish Fork, Utah 84660.

SWENSON, LEON HUGHIE R
Idaho State Sen.
b. Spanish Fork, Utah, 11/6/11; s. Jos. A. Swenson and Cornielia Nielsen S; m. 12/23/38 to Dorothy Nelson; c. Susan (Mrs. Dale Bishop), Sharon Lee (Mrs. Alan Bingham), Carolyn, Lucile, Douglas Leon, Leland Joseph and Eileen. Educ: Utah State Univ, B.S, 35; Sigma Nu; Agr. Club; Livestock Judging Team. Polit. & Govt. Pos: Idaho State Rep, Dist. 12, 65-69; Idaho State Sen, 69- Bus. & Prof. Pos: Agriculturist, Amalgamated Sugar Co, 36-45. Mem: Farm Bur; Countrymens Club. Rel: Latter-day Saint. Mailing Add: R.R. 2, Nampa, Idaho 83651.

SWENSON, ROSS GREELEY D
b. Belleville, Kans, 8/2/93; s. John A. Swenson and Jennie S. Arbuthnot S; m. 8/1/17 to Mabel Walker; c. Jack L, Victor E. and R.G. Educ: Bus. col, 1 year. Polit. & Govt. Pos: Co. chmn, Dem. Party, 38-66; del, Dem. Nat. Conv, 48-56; supvr, U.S. Census, 50; treas, Dem. State Cmt, 52-56; mem. bd. rev, State Alcoholic Beverage Control Cmn, 69- Mem: AF&AM; Kiwanis. Rel: Christian Church. Mailing Add: 1810 O St, Belleville, Kans. 66935.

SWETT, DANA MALCOLM R
Mem, Maine Rep. State Cmt.
b. Ashland, Maine, 6/8/25; s. Charles Frederick Swett and Alice Metcalf S; m. 7/10/64 to Linda Rose McCrum; c. Deanna Jo (Mrs. David Berry). Educ: Ashland Pub. Schs, dipl, 32-44; N.Y.A, Dexter, Maine, Machinist, 44-45. Polit. & Govt. Pos: Treas, Aroostook Co. Rep. Cmt, 58-62, chmn, 64-66; chmn, Ashland Rep. Town Cmt, 60-64; mem, Maine Rep. State Cmt, 66- Bus. & Prof. Pos: Safety dir, Maine Pub. Serv. Co, 61- Mem: Am. Soc. Safety Engrs; New England Electric Coun; Nat. Safety Coun; F&AM; dir, Cent. Am. Chap, Am. Red Cross; clerk, Ashland Indust. Develop. Corp; Rotary (secy, Presque Isle Club); chmn, North Star Dist, Boy Scouts of Am, exec. bd, Katahdin Area Coun; corp. bd, Arthur R. Gould Mem. Hosp. Rel: Episcopal. Mailing Add: 28 Cedar St, Presque Isle, Maine 04769.

SWIATEK, FRANK E. D
Mem, Erie Co. Dem. Exec. Cmt, N.Y.
b. Buffalo, N.Y, 3/5/43; s. Edward T. Swiatek and Clara Kopera S; m. 10/16/65 to Elizabeth Anne Yore; c. Jennifer A. and Jeffrey F. Educ: Canisius Col, B.S. Polit. & Govt. Pos: Alternate del, Dem. Nat. Conv, 68; councilman, Cheektowaga, 68- and chmn, youth bd, 68-; mem, Erie Co. Dem. Exec. Cmt, currently. Bus. & Prof. Pos: Asst. basketball coach, Canisius Col, currently; life ins. agent, State Mutual of Am, Buffalo, currently. Mem: Buffalo Life Underwriters. Rel: Roman Catholic. Mailing Add: 64 W. Cavalier, Cheektowaga, N.Y. 14225.

SWICK, FRANK H. D
b. Linden, Ind, 7/19/84; s. Charley Swick and Minnie Cook S; m. 9/28/09 to Carrie Wilson; c. Geraldyn (Mrs. Griffith). Polit. & Govt. Pos: Game warden, Wash, 23, state fisheries inspector, 33-54; city councilman, Ridgefield, 44-56, mem, Port Cmn, 54-, mayor, 56-60; dep. sheriff, Clark Co, 54-55, tax collector, 55-56; precinct committeeman, North Precinct, Ridgefield, 63- Mem: F&AM; C. of C; Rep. of Civil Defense; Grange; Farm Bur; v.pres, Ft. Vancouver Hist. Soc; Eastern Star; White Shrine of Jerusalem. Man of the Year, Ridgefield, Wash; Plaque for Commun. Leader, 68. Mailing Add: 802 Pioneer Ave, Ridgefield, Wash. 98642.

SWIDLER, JOSEPH C. D
b. Chicago, Ill, 1/28/07; s. Abraham Swidler and Dora Cromer S; m. 5/5/44 to Gertrude Tyrna; c. Ann and Mark L. T. Educ: Univ. Chicago, Ph.B. cum laude, 29, J.D, 30; Order of Coif; Phi Delta Phi; Tau Delta Phi. Polit. & Govt. Pos: Asst. solicitor, Dept. of Interior, 33, attorney, 33-36, asst. gen. counsel, 36-39; solicitor, Tenn. Valley Authority, 39-41; consult, Alien Property Bur, Dept. of Justice, 41-42; spec. consult, War Prod. Bd, 42-43; gen. counsel and secy, Tenn. Valley Authority and chmn, Retirement Syst. Bd, 45-57; chmn, Fed. Power Cmn, 61-65, cmnr, 61 and mem, Water Resources Coun, 64-65. Bus. & Prof. Pos: Private law practice, Chicago, Ill, 30-33 and Knoxville and Nashville, Tenn, 57-61; partner, Swidler & Freeman, 66-67 and Swidler & Belnap, 68- Mil. Serv: Entered as Yeoman, Navy, 43, released as Lt, 45, after serv. in Indust. Readjustment Br, Navy Dept, Wash, D.C. Publ: Contrib, TVA The First Twenty Years, Univ. Ala. and Univ. Tenn. Presses, 56 and numerous articles in utility trade journals. Mem: Fed. and Am. Bar Asns; U.S. Nat. Cmt, World Power Conf, 61-65. Mailing Add: 9504 Michaels Court, Bethesda, Md. 20034.

SWIFT, ALLAN BYRON D
b. Tacoma, Wash, 9/12/35; s. Arnold Byron Swift and M. Orrill Peterson S; m. 8/27/56 to Paula Jean Jackson; c. Margaret Amy and Lauri Ann. Educ: Whitman Col, 54-55; Cent. Wash. State Col, B.A, 57. Polit. & Govt. Pos: Admin. asst. to U.S. Rep. Lloyd Meeds, 65- Bus. & Prof. Pos: Staff announcer, KVOS Radio, 57-58, opers. dir, 58-60 and Int. Good Music, 60-61; pub. affairs dir, KVOS-TV, Inc, 61-65. Publ: 'Rapport and the Cyclopean Eye,' Science Educ, 64. Mem: Nat. Acad. of Radio and TV Arts and Sci; Lions; C. of C. Produced and Directed a TV program entitled, Tide Pool Critters, which was awarded the Am. Legion Gold Mike for America's best local TV Program in the interests of youth. Rel: Unitarian. Legal Res: Bellingham, Wash. Mailing Add: 8820 Trafalgar Court, Springfield, Va. 22151.

SWIFT, EARLE LINWOOD R
b. Attleboro, Mass, 7/18/97; s. Harrison Clifton Swift and Cora Almira Bixby S; m. 5/15/46 to Louise Gleason Colby; c. Dale Harrison and Beverly Almira. Educ: Brown Univ, 15-16; Boston Univ, 17-18; Delta Kappa Epsilon. Polit. & Govt. Pos: Mem, Attleboro Munic. Coun, Mass, 31-38, chmn, Finance, Accounts and Sch. Matters, 34-38; chmn, Sarasota Co. Rep. Exec. Cmt, Fla, 64-69. Bus. & Prof. Pos: Salesman, Remington Rand, Inc, 18-24, dist. mgr. libr. bur, 25-26, bur. mgr, 27-46, br. mgr, Remington Rand Div, Sperry Rand Corp, 46-60; dir, Gulf Gate Nat. Bank and S.Sarasota Co. Mem. Hosp, currently. Mem: Mason (32°); Shrine; v.commodore, Venice Yacht Club, 66; W.Coast Yacht Club Coun. Del, 66; U.S. Power Sq; dir, Happiness House Rehabilitation Center, Inc, Sarasota & Manatee Co. Rel: Protestant. Mailing Add: 425 Bayshore Dr, Venice, Fla. 33595.

SWIFT, HENRY ROBINSON D
b. Burlington, Vt, 2/18/16; s. Elijah Swift and Cynthia Lynch S; m. 3/25/44 to Elizabeth G. Peirce; c. Elizabeth Hawley, James Peirce, Henry Robinson, Jr. and Richard Hamilton. Educ: Univ. Vt, Ph.B, 37; Columbia Univ. Teachers Col, 41; South. Conn. State Col, M.S, 69. Phi Beta Kappa; Delta Psi. Polit. & Govt. Pos: Rep, Westport Town Meeting, 51; mem. bd. educ, Cheshire, 59-66; del, Conn. Constitutional Conv, 65; Conn. State Rep, 83rd Dist, 67-68; mem, New Eng. Bd. Higher Educ, 69-; mem, State Bd. Educ. Arbitration Panel, 69- Bus. & Prof. Pos: Textbook salesman, Allyn & Bacon, publishers, 38-41; salesman, engr. and asst. mgr, S. New England Tel. Co, 46-50, mgr, 50-56 and personnel supvr, 56- Mil. Serv: Entered as Pvt, Army, 41, released as 1st Lt, 46, after serv. in Counter Intel. Corps, Second Serv. Command, N.Y. Publ: Running A Happy Family, 60 and Community Groups & You, 64, both w. Elizabeth P. Swift, John Day Co. Rel: Protestant. Mailing Add: 399 Patton Dr, Cheshire, Conn. 06410.

SWIG, BENJAMIN HARRISON D
b. Taunton, Mass, 11/17/93; s. Simon Swig and Fannie S; m. 12/24/16 to Mae Aronovitz; wid; c. Melvin M, Betty (Mrs. Dinner) and Richard L. Educ: Taunton High Sch. Hon. LL.D, Univ. Santa Clara, 62; Hon. L.H.D, Hebrew Union Col. Jewish Inst. Relig, 64. Polit. & Govt. Pos: Mem, President's Cmt. on Traffic Safety. Bus. & Prof. Pos: Hotel owner and operator, Cali Calif; chmn. bd, Fairmont Hotel Co; pres, Fairmont-Roosevelt Hotel Co; pres. and dir, Mission Inn Co; chmn. bd, West. Dairy Prod, Inc; treas, Diversified Equities Corp; chmn. and pub. interest dir, Fed. Home Loan Bank San Francisco; mem. bd. dirs, Lilli Ann Corp. and Cartier, Inc; founder and chmn. bd. dirs, Careers Unlimited for Women; financial adv, Blackfeet Indians, Browning, Mont; civilian aide to Secy. of Army for North. Calif. Mem:

Am. Friends of Hebrew Univ. and Tel Aviv Univ; legacy develop. cmt, Anti-Defamation League, B'nai B'rith; nat. adv. bd. dirs. and chmn. exec. cmt, San Francisco Chap, Asn. U.S. Army; bd. dirs, Brandies Camp Inst. of West and Brandeis Youth Found, Brandeis Inst; bd. trustees and co-chmn. several cmts, Brandeis Univ; regional v.chmn, Brandeis Univ. Assocs; dir, Calif. Safety Coun; statewide tax cmt. and cmt. on state personnel practices, Calif. State C. of C; Armed Forces Sect, San Francisco C. of C; dir, Calif. Taxpayers' Asn; nat. bd. trustees, Children's Asthma Research Inst. and Hosp; exec. cmt. and chmn. site cmt, Citizens Cmt. for San Francisco World's Fair of 70-71; Soc. Hon. Fels, City of Hope; Commonwealth Club San Francisco; Concordia-Argonaut Club San Francisco; assoc. chmn, nat. adv. cmt, Dropsie Col; nat. cmt, w.coast chmn. and v.chmn, Soc. Founders, Albert Einstein Col. Med; bd. gov, Hebrew Union Col-Jewish Inst. Relig; hon. gov. and hon. fel, Hebrew Univ, Jerusalem; bd. dirs. and bd. gov, Jewish Theol. Seminary Am. and Action Cmt. San Francisco; nat. coun, Joint Defense Appeal; v.chmn. adv. bd, Mary's Help Hosp; bd. dirs, Modern Hebrew Day Sch; San Francisco Adv. Bd, nat. bd, nat. exec. cmt. and nat. spec. gifts cmt, Nat. Conf. Christians and Jews; hon. mem, Presidio Officers' Open Mess, San Francisco; Press Club San Francisco; Eleanor Roosevelt Cancer Found. and Mem. Found; life mem, San Francisco Adv. Bd. and chmn. exec. cmt, State Adv. Bd, Salvation Army; affil, San Francisco Real Estate Bd; chmn, adv. cmt. and co-chmn, finance cmt, San Francisco World Trade Center Authority; bd. dirs. and hon. life mem, bd. trustees, Union of Am. Hebrew Congregations; hon. nat. chmn. and exec. cmt, United Jewish Appeal; bd. regents and pres, Heritage Found, Univ. Santa Clara; bd. gov. and v.chmn, bd. overseers, West Coast Univ. Judaism; hon. v.chmn, W.Coast Div, Yeshiva Univ; mem. cmts, adv. bd, bd. dirs, bd. gov, chmn. or mem, numerous Jewish and commun. cultural, hist, educ, relig, welfare, financial or develop. insts. Awards & Citations: Knight of St. Sylvester, 66; Hon. Ky. Col, 66; Star of Solidarity, Italian Repub, 64; Keystone Award, Boys' Clubs Am, 61, Bronze Keystone, 63; Medal of Valor, State of Israel, 63; Outstanding Civilian Serv. Medal, Dept. of Army, 60; Cert. of Appreciation, Selective Serv. Syst, Dept. of Army, U.S. Army Terminal Command, Pac. and U.S. Air Force, 63, Asn. U.S. Army, 60, San Francisco Bd. Educ, 58, Camp for Living Judaism, Saratoga, 55 and Jewish Theol. Seminary and Salvation Army, 54; Louis Marshall Medal, Jewish Theol. Seminary Am, 62; Michelangelo Award, Boy's Towns Italy, Inc, 62; citations from Hebrew Univ, Jerusalem, 54, Prime Minister, Repub. Korea, 54 and Univ. Judaism, 51; many other awards and honors. Rel: Jewish. Mailing Add: Fairmont Hotel, San Francisco, Calif. 94106.

SWIGER, JAMES EPHRAIM R

b. Yankee Hill, Ohio, 7/4/94; s. William Lewis Swiger and Elsie Myrtle Crabtree S; m. 7/16/30 to Miriam Loraine Brant; c. James Morris and Louis Andre. Polit. & Govt. Pos: Twp. clerk and sch. bd. clerk, Newton Twp, Ohio, 28-32; mem, Pike Co. Bd. of Electors; cent. committeeman and finance committeeman, Rep. Party, Ohio, 62- Bus. & Prof. Pos: Mgr, Pike Co. Farm Bur. and Coop. Asn, 26-51. Mil. Serv: Pvt, Marine Corps, 18-19; Expert Rifleman; Victory Medal. Mem: Farm Bur; Am. Legion; Rep. Club; World War I-Barracks 1860. Rel: Protestant. Mailing Add: 201 S. Mullen, Waverly, Ohio 45690. (1967)

SWIGER, JOE EDWARD R

b. Harrison Co, W.Va, 7/22/40; s. Omar Tilman Swiger and Josephine S; m. 2/19/61 to Constance Jean Norris; c. Michael Tilman, Sandra Jane, Laura Ann and Edward Glen. Educ: Fleet Sonar Sch, U.S. Navy; RCA Inst. Polit. & Govt. Pos: Chmn, Warren Co. Rep. Party, Va, 66-67. Bus. & Prof. Pos: Elec. engr, Potomac Edison Co, 61-66. Mil. Serv: Entered as E-1, Navy, 58, released as SOG-2 P-1, 61; Good Conduct Medal. Mem: Jr. C. of C.(dir); Little League, Inc; chmn, Potomac Edison Emp. Asn; Isaac Walton League of Am. Rel: Protestant. Legal Res: 629 Midland Ave, Front Royal, Va. 22630. Mailing Add: Box 1538, Front Royal, Va. 22630. (1967)

SWINDOLL, GEORGE MITCHELL D

Miss. State Rep.

b. Slate Spring, Miss, 6/11/31; s. Bryant Shaw Swindoll and Hattie Mitchell S; m. 6/16/62 to Nancy McGuire; c. Reuben M. and George B. Educ: Univ. Miss, B.A.E, 55, Law Sch, M.Ed, 58 and LL.B, 63; Tau Kappa Alpha; Alpha Phi Omega; Beta Theta Pi. Polit. & Govt. Pos: Miss. State Rep, 60- Publ: 'To The People Of Calhoun County,' Monitor-Herald & Calhoun Co. J, 60-66. Mem: Toastmasters Int; Am. and Miss. Bar Asns; Am. Farm Bur; exec. dir, Citizens Coun. of Am; bd. trustees, Northwest Jr. Col. Named One of Outstanding Young Men of Am, 65. Rel: Baptist. Mailing Add: Box 158, Calhoun City, Miss. 38916. (1967)

SWINFORD, JOHN McKEE D

Chmn, Harrison Co. Dem. Cmt, Ky.

b. Cynthiana, Ky, 4/19/32; s. Mac Swinford and Benton Peterson S; m. 3/22/63 to Mary Katherine Foster; c. James Lewis and Willaim Kinney. Educ: Princeton Univ; Univ. Mich. Sch. of Law; Univ. Mich. Student Bar Asn. Polit. & Govt. Pos: Mem, Harrison Co. Dem. Cmt, 60-, chmn, 68-; Ky. State Rep, 62-66. Bus. & Prof. Pos: Dir, Cynthiana Businessmen's Club, 60-62 & 65-66 and Cynthiana Harrison Co. C. of C, 64-67. Mil. Serv: Entered as Pvt, Army, 54, released as Specialist 3/C, 56; Good Conduct Medal. Mem: Ky. State and Am. Bar Asns; Am. Legion. Rel: Presbyterian. Legal Res: 106 S. Elmarch Ave, Cynthiana, Ky. 41031. Mailing Add: E. Pike St, Cynthiana, Ky. 41031.

SWISHER, JAY C. R

m. to Mary; c. Five. Educ: Univ. S.Dak. Polit. & Govt. Pos: S.Dak. State Rep, 67. Bus. & Prof. Pos: Farmer and rancher. Mil. Serv: Ninth Armored Div, 3 years. Mem: Brown Co. Livestock and Crop Improv. Asn; Quarter Horse Asn; Kiwanis; past chmn, Wesley Found, North. State Col. Rel: Methodist. Mailing Add: Putney, S.Dak. 57402. (1967)

SWISHER, PAUL W. R

Ind. State Sen.

b. Waverly, Ind, 2/22/18; s. Charles Omer Swisher and Leafy Deborh Minnett S; m. 1/24/37 to Louise Duncan; c. Janet Marie (Mrs. Max MacKenzie), Paula Louise (Mrs. Herbert V. Schelm) and Charles Duncan. Educ: Mooresville High Sch, grad, 36. Polit. & Govt. Pos: Ind. State Sen, 68- Bus. & Prof. Pos: Gen. foreman, Allison Div. of G.M.C, Indianapolis, Ind, 42-48; owner and operator, Mooresville Feed & Supply Co, Ind, 48-61; sales mgr, Vestal Motor Co, Inc, 61-69. Mem: F&AM; Scottish Rite. Rel: Society of Friends. Mailing Add: P.O. Box 85, Mooresville, Ind. 46158.

SWITASKI, ANNA-MAE R

V.Chmn, Conn. State Rep. Cent. Cmt.

b. Philadelphia, Pa, 8/24/09; d. James Francis Havlick and Isabel Mitchell Thompson H; m. 2/12/36 to Bernard John Switaski; wid. Educ: Cent. Conn. State Col, 29. Polit. & Govt. Pos: Organizer, Conn. Young Rep, 34; mem, Conn. State Rep. Cent. Cmt, 39-52, v.chmn, 50-; asst. to Secy. of State, Conn, 43-45 & 47-49; engrossing clerk, Conn. Gen. Assembly, 49; del, Rep. Nat. Conv, 44, 52, 56, 60, 64 & 68 and mem, Nat. Platform Cmt, 56 & 64; pres, Conn. Coun. Rep. Women's Clubs, 50-68; mem. adv. bd, Nat. Fedn. Rep. Women, 50-68 & 70-72; mem, Annual Assay Cmn, U.S. Mint, 59; mem, Conn. Cmn. to Revise Elec. Laws, 61-62; mem, Gov. Cmn. to Study Qualifications of Electors, 67-69. Bus. & Prof. Pos: Teacher, New Britain Jr. High Schs, Conn, 29-40. Legal Res: 273 Main St, Farmington, Conn. 06032. Mailing Add: Republican State Central Committee, 410 Asylum St, Hartford, Conn. 06103.

SWITZER, MARY ELIZABETH

Adminstr, Soc. and Rehabilitation Serv, Dept. of Health Educ. and Welfare

b. Newton, Upper Falls, Mass, 2/16/00; d. Julius Switzer and Margaret Moore S; single. Educ: Radcliffe Col, A.B, 21; hon. mem, Phi Beta Kappa. Founders Day Award, Radcliffe Col, 69; Hon. L.D.H, Tufts Univ, 55, Gallaudet Col, 55, West. Col. for Women, 61, Temple Univ, 66, Manhattanville Col. of Sacred Heart, 66, N.Y. Univ, 67, Russel Sage Col, 69 and Hofstra Univ, 69; J.D, Adelphi Col, 57 and Smith Col, 67; D.H, Boston Univ, 60 and Duke Univ, 62; D.M.S, Woman's Med. Col. of Pa, 60; D.S, Calif. Col. of Med, 63; D.P.S, Springfield Col, 64; D.P.A, Assumption Col, 69. Polit. & Govt. Pos: Various pos, U.S. Treas. Dept, 22-34 and asst. to Asst. Secy. of Treas. in Charge of Pub. Health, 34-39; asst. to Fed. Security Agency Adminstr, 39-50; dir, Off. of Voc. Rehabilitation, Dept. Health, Educ. and Welfare, 50-61, cmnr, Voc. Rehabilitation Admin, 61-67 and adminstr, Soc. and Rehabilitation Serv, 67- Publ: 'Strong Role for Public Welfare,' UN, Econ. and Soc. Coun, Report of the Int. Conf. of Ministers Responsible for Soc. Welfare, 10/68; 'The Social and Rehabilitation Service—Its Philosophy and Function,' Blindness, 68; 'SRS Will Fight Dependency Ills,' U.S. Med, 1/69; plus others. Mem: Adv. cmt, Human Resources Found; adv. coun, Mended Hearts, Inc; health careers cmt, Nat. Health Coun; prfnl. adv. coun, Epilepsy Asn. Am; bd. overseers, Florence Heller Grad. Sch. for Adv. Studies in Soc. Welfare, Brandeis Univ; bd. trustees, Menninger Found; bd, World Rehabilitation Fund, Melvin J. Maas Mem. Rehabilitation Fund and Patrician Arms Nursing Home; bd. visitors, Women's Col. of Duke Univ; bd. dirs, Asn. for the Aid of Crippled Children and Georgetown Univ; first v.pres, Nat. Conf. on Soc. Welfare, 68; hon. mem, Am. Cong. Phys. Med. and Rehabilitation, Am. Psychiat. Asn. and Am. Phys. Therapy Asn; Nat. Asn. Hearing and Speech Agencies; U.S. Cmt, Int. Conf. on Soc. Welfare; World Coun, prfnl. adv. cmt. and U.S. Cmt, Int. Soc. for Rehabilitation of the Disabled; life mem. Nat. Rehabilitation Asn.(past pres); adv. fel, World Fedn. Occup. Therapists; Am. Asn. of Workers for the Blind; Am. Pub. Welfare Asn; fel, Am. Pub. Health Asn; Nat. Conf. Cath. Charities; corporate mem, Nat. Assembly for Soc. Policy and Develop; Nat. Asn. of the Deaf; Nat. Acad. Pub. Admin; Alexandria Asn. for Retarded Children; sch. of nursing cmt. and bd. dirs, Alexandria Hosp; Alexandria Bd. Health; President's Cmt. on Employ. of the Handicapped; contributing mem, Newton-Wellesley Hosp. Aid Asn; Cmt. to Study the Role and Function of Gallaudet Col; Am. Newspaper Women's Club; Radcliffe Club, Wash, D.C; Women's Nat. Dem. Club. Numerous medals, plaques, cert, citations and distinguished serv. awards from various orgn. Rel: Episcopal. Mailing Add: 422 Underhill Place, Alexandria, Va. 22305.

SWOBE, C. COE R

Nev. State Sen.

b. Reno, Nev, 5/23/29; s. John Bradford Swobe and Maxine Elizabeth Bridgman S; m. 12/19/59 to Janet Quilici; c. Caryn Coe and Jaclyn. Educ: Univ. of Nev, B.S, 54; Univ. of Denver, LL.B, 58; Phi Alpha Delta; Sigma Nu. Polit. & Govt. Pos: Pres, Univ. Nev. Alumni Asn. Young Rep, 53-54; legis. bill drafter, Nev, 58-59; U.S. Attorney, Dist. of Nev, 59-61; Nev. State Assemblyman, 63-64, Minority Floor Leader, Nev. State Assembly, 65-66; chmn, Platform Cmt, Rep. State Conv, 66; Nev. State Sen, 66- Bus. & Prof. Pos: Assoc, law firm, Sidney W. Robinson, 62-67; private practice law, 67- Mil. Serv: Entered as Airman 3/C, Air Force, 50, released as Airman 1/C, 52. Mem: Washoe Co, Nev. and Am. Bar Asns; Young Rep. of Washoe Co; Elks; Toastmasters; Univ. of Nev. Alumni Asn; dir, Sigma Nu; Nev. Area Coun, Boy Scouts; Press Club; Prospectors; exec. mem, Salvation Army. Selected Young Man of the Year, Reno Jr. C. of C, 63. Rel: Methodist. Legal Res: 675 Starlight Circle, Reno, Nev. 89502. Mailing Add: P.O. Box 1588, Reno, Nev. 89501.

SWOPE, JOHN W. 'BILLY' R

b. Garrard, Ky, 12/3/94; s. John William Swope and Mary Lilian Gulley S; single. Educ: Univ. of Ky; Georgetown Univ; Universite de Toulouse, France; Delta Chi. Polit. & Govt. Pos: Former Ky. State Sen. and Minority Caucus Chmn. Bus. & Prof. Pos: Attorney at Law. Mil. Serv: Entered as Pvt, Army, 17, released as Sgt, 335th Infantry, AEF, France, 17-18. Mem: Mason; DAV. Mailing Add: Box 668, Lancaster, Ky. 40444.

SYAS, GEORGE D. R

Nebr. State Sen.

b. Omaha, Nebr, 2/11/11; m. 12/7/40 to Pauline Frances Crowder; c. Two. Educ: Omaha N. High Sch, grad. Polit. & Govt. Pos: Chmn, 12th Ward Rep. Cmt, 8 years; Nebr. State Sen, 51- Bus. & Prof. Pos: Machinist, Union Pac. R.R, 33 years. Mem: Former mem, Young Rep, Cent. Park Men's Club, Cent. Park Sch. and McMillan Jr. High Sch. PTA; Omaha N. High Sch. PTA; life mem, Belvidere Sch. PTA; Mason; Eastern Star; RAM; K.T; AAONMS; Men's Club of Florence; Belvidere Club; N. Omaha Commercial Club; IAMAW. Award of Merit, Am. Asn. Conserv. Info, 60; Sch. Bell Award, Omaha Educ. Asn, 64; Nat. Recreation and Park Asn. Award, 66; Nebr. Coun. of Sportsmen's Award, 67. Rel: Congregational; Former mem. bd. of trustees, Cent. Park Congregational Church. Mailing Add: 5312 Fontenelle Blvd, Omaha, Nebr. 68111.

SYBERT, CORNELIUS FERDINAND D

b. Loretto, Pa, 9/16/00; s. Alphonsus Sybert and Anna Haid S; m. 8/31/27 to Elizabeth Johnson; c. Cornelius Ferdinand, Joan Elizabeth, George Joseph and Suzanne Marie. Educ: Loyola Col, A.B, 22; Univ. Md, LL.B, 25. Polit. & Govt. Pos: Secy-treas, Dem. State Cent. Cmt, Md, 30-34; counsel, Howard Co. Cmnrs, 31-34; states attorney, Howard Co, 34-46; Md. State Sen, 50-54, Speaker, Md. House of Del, 46-50; Attorney Gen, Md, 54-61; Assoc. Judge, Md. Court of Appeals, 61-65. Bus. & Prof. Pos: Newspaper reporter, Baltimore News, 22-25; Attorney-at law, 25-; dir, Cent. Bank, Howard Co, 38-61. Mem: Am, Md. and Howard Co. Bar Asns; K. of C. Rel: Roman Catholic. Legal Res: 3910 St. Johns Lane, Ellicott City, Md. 21043. Mailing Add: 3701 Court House, Dr, Ellicott City, Md. 21043.

SYKES, JAMES THURMAN D
Mem. Bd. Supvr, Dane Co, Wis.
b. Cedar Rapids, Iowa, 7/12/35; s. John James Sykes and Edith Waddell S. Larson; m. 6/21/58 to Marguerite Svensson; c. Kathleen Ellen, Sven Steven and Julie Elizabeth. Educ: Univ. Minn, Duluth, B.S, 57; Kent State Univ, M.A, 65; Univ. Wis, 62-; Bulldog Award for Serv, Student Cmn; pres. Bd. of Publ. Polit. & Govt. Pos: Peace Corps Field Rep, 61-63; state treas, Am. for Dem. Action, Wis, 63-; mem, Dane Co. Dem. Party, 67-68; del, Wis. State Dem. Conv, many times; del, Dem. Nat. Conv, 68; mem, Bd. of Supvr, Dane Co, Wis, 68- Bus. & Prof. Pos: Prog. dir, YMCA, Iowa State Univ, 59-60, Univ. Wis, 60-68, dir, Brazil Exchange, 66-68, teacher, Univ. Wis. Center Syst, 67 and dir. pub. serv, Wis. Cheeseman, 68- Publ: 'What is a Christian Association?,' 66 and 'Why the YMCA Speaks,' 67, Asn. Forum. Rel: Quaker. Mailing Add: 2100 Rowley Ave, Madison, Wis. 53705.

SYKES, JAY GILBERT D
b. Phila, Pa, 5/4/22; s. Charles Robert Sykes and Belle Potamkin S; m. 6/14/52 to Katherine Agnes Border; c. Charles Jay. Educ: Rutgers Univ, B.A. 42; Univ. Wash. Law Sch, J.D, 50; Phi Epsilon Pi. Polit. & Govt. Pos: State campaign dir, McCarthy for Pres, Wis. primary, 67-68; del, Dem. Nat. Conv, 68. Bus. & Prof. Pos: Bur. ed, Middletown Times Herald-Record, N.Y, 60-63; ed. writer, Milwaukee Sentinel, Wis, 63-67; lectr, Univ. Wis-Milwaukee, 67- Mil. Serv: Entered 42, released as Sgt, 45, after serv. in Signal Intel. Serv: European and Mediterranean Theaters, 43-45. Publ: Wisconsin Gets a Sales Tax, McGraw, 65; 'The McCarthy Campaign,' Madison Capital-Times, 5-6/69. Mem: Am. and Wash. State Bar Asns; Am. Judicature Soc; Am. Vet Cmt; Wis. Civil Liberties Union (chmn). Award for Distinguished Reporting of Pub. Affairs, Am. Polit. Sci. Asn, 63. Rel: Jewish. Mailing Add: 8327 N. Regent Rd, Fox Point, Wis. 53217.

SYKES, MARY FLANDERS R
Mem, Exec. Cmt, Vt. State Rep. Cmt.
b. Manchester, N.H, 9/14/30; d. Franklin Flanders and Florence Emerson F; m. 7/11/53 to Richard Lee Sykes; c. Rebecca Lee, Katherine Chase and Franklin Thomas. Educ: Duke Univ, A.B. in Hist, 52; co-ed, Duke Chronicle, 51-52. Polit. & Govt. Pos: Secy, Brattleboro Town Rep. Cmt, 57-63 and v.chmn, 63-; del, Vt. State Conv, 60 & 64; corresponding secy, Vt. Fedn. of Rep. Women, 61-63, second v.pres, 63-65, first v.pres, 65-67, pres, 67-69; mem, Windham Co. Rep. Cmt, 61-; alternate del, Rep. Nat. Conv, 64; rep, Brattleboro Town Meeting, 65-; mem. exec. cmt, Vt. State Rep. Cmt, 65- Bus. & Prof. Pos: Asst. ed, Duke Univ. Alumni Register, 52-53. Mem: Am. Asn. Univ. Women; Eastern Star; Brattleboro Mem. Hosp. Auxiliary; Weare Grange, 43-48. Rel: Baptist. Mailing Add: South St, Brattleboro, Vt. 05301.

SYLVESTER, BARBARA THORNTON D
Dem. Nat. Committeewoman, S.C.
b. Florence, S.C, 3/8/29; d. Hugh Bernard Thornton, Sr. and Ola Mae Williamson T; m. 6/30/54 to Dr. Joseph George Sylvester; c. Pamela Mae and Elsa April. Educ: Mars Hill Col, N.C, 1 year; West. Caroline Col, 1 year. Polit. & Govt. Pos: V.chmn, Florence Co. Dem. Party, S.C, 62-64; alternate del, Dem. Nat. Conv, 64, del, 68; coordinator, Lady Bird Spec, S.C, 64; dir. women's activities, S.C. Dem. Party, 64-66; co-dir, S.C. Campaign for Humphrey-Muskie, 68; Dem. Nat. Committeewoman, S.C, 68-; mem. bd. dirs, Florence Co. Off. of Econ. Opportunity and mem, Rules Cmn. of Dem. Party, 69; secy, State Juvenile Correction Bd, 69-; mem. Credentials Cmt, Dem. Nat. Cmt, 69- Bus. & Prof. Pos: S.C. Del, Woman's Auxiliary to the Am. Med. Asn, 56; pres, Pee Dee Med. Auxiliary, 60-61, civil defense chmn, 61-62; pres, McLeod Infirmary Med. Auxiliary, 61-62; commun. serv. chmn, S.C. Med. Auxiliary, 61-62, third v.pres, 62-63. Mem: Adv. to Troop 112, Girl Scouts, 62-67; chmn, Red Cross Vol, Florence Co, 62-67, bd. dirs, 64-67; chmn. women vol, Florence Co. Civil Defense Prog, 68; bd. dirs. and chmn. state conv, S.C. Asn. Retarded Children, 68; v.pres, Florence Co. Asn. Retarded Children, 68, pres, 69. Rel: Episcopal. Mailing Add: 510 Camellia Circle, Florence, S.C. 29501.

SYMINGTON, JAMES W. D
U.S. Rep, Mo.
b. New York, N.Y, 9/28/27; s. Sen. Stuart Symington and Evelyn Wadsworth S; m. 1/24/53 to Sylvia Caroline Schlapp; c. Julia Hay and Jeremy Wadsworth. Educ: Yale Univ, B.A, 50; Columbia Univ, LL.B, 54. Polit. & Govt. Pos: Asst. city counsr, St. Louis, Mo, 54-55; U.S. For. Serv, London, 58-60; dep. dir. Food for Peace, White House, 61-62; admin. asst. to Attorney Gen. of U.S, 62-63; dir, Pres. Cmt. on Juvenile Delinquency, 65-66; consult, Pres. Cmn. Law Enforcement and Admin. of Justice, 65-66; Chief of Protocol, Dept. of State, 66-68; U.S. Rep, Second Dist, Mo, 69- Bus. & Prof. Pos: Assoc. attorney, law firm, 55-58, 60-61 & 63-65. Mil. Serv: Marine Corps, 45-46. Mem: Mo. Bar Asn; Am. Fedn. Musicians. Mailing Add: 1533 Longworth House Office Bldg, Washington, D.C. 20515.

SYMINGTON, JOHN FIFE, JR. R
b. Baltimore, Md, 8/27/10; s. John Fife Symington and Arabella Hambleton S; m. 3/18/39 Martha Frick; c. Helen Clay (Mrs. Minturn V. Chace), Arabella Hambleton (Mrs. Edward N. Dane), Martha Howard Frick (Mrs. Marshall Jenney) and J. Fife, III. Educ: Princeton Univ, B.A, 33. Polit. & Govt. Pos: Former co-chmn, Rep. in Action Cmt, Baltimore Co, Md; cand, U.S. Rep, Second Dist, Md, 58, 60 & 62; chmn. and trustee, Rep. Assocs, Baltimore Co, Inc, 59; mem, Cmt. to Revise Constitution and By-Laws of Rep. Party, Md, 59; chmn, Rep. State Finance Cmt, Md, 63, 64 & 65; former chmn, Second Rep. Cong. Dist, Md; former mem. exec. cmt, Md. State Rep. Cent. Cmt, U.S. Ambassador Extraordinary and Plenipotentiary, Trinidad and Tobago, 69. Bus. & Prof. Pos: Mech. helper, Glenn L. Martin Co, 33-34; traffic rep, Pan Am. Airways, 34-35, traffic and operations rep, 35-36, supvr, Argentine Off, 36-37, mgr, Atlantic, 37-39, sr. rep. in Europe, 39-40, asst. to mgr, Atlantic Div, 41-42, exec. head off, 42-46 and exec. asst. to sr. v.pres. and regional mgr, 46-48; pres, Baltimore Co. Supply Co, 48- Mil. Serv: Entered as Lt.(jg), Naval Res, assigned Pan Am. World Airways Spec. Serv. Mem: Chmn, Baltimore Co. Cancer Crusade, 59 and v.chmn. for Trade and Indust, 62; past dir, Child Welfare League of Am; bd. mgrs, Md. Training Sch. for Boys; past pres. and dir, Md. Children's Aid Soc, Inc; Baltimore Co. Health and Welfare Coun; past hon. dir, Timonium Rotary; chmn. bd. and chief exec. officer, Garrison Forest Sch. Girls. Rel: Episcopal. Mailing Add: Seminary Ave, Lutherville, Md. 21093.

SYMINGTON, LLOYD D
b. New York, N.Y, 9/28/13; s. Charles J. Symington and Elizabeth Lloyd S; m. 9/6/41 to Nancy E. Glover; c. Lloyd, Jr, Donald L, Marion E and Nicholas S. Educ: Princeton Univ, A.B, 36; Univ. Va, LL.B, 39; Phi Beta Kappa. Polit. & Govt. Pos: With Off. of Legal Counsel, War Prod. Bd, Wash, D.C, 42-46; del, Dem. Nat. Conv, 68. Bus. & Prof. Pos: Partner, Fowler & Symington, now, Leva, Hawes, Symington, Martin & Oppenheimer, Wash, D.C, 46- Mem: Am. and Fed. Bar Asns; Barristers; Fed. City Club; Metrop. Club; Wash. Nat. Symphony (pres). Rel: Episcopal. Mailing Add: 3030 Chain Bridge Rd. N.W, Washington, D.C. 20016.

SYMINGTON, STUART D
U.S. Sen, Mo.
b. Amherst, Mass, 6/26/01; s. William Stuart Symington (deceased) and Emily Harrison S.(deceased); m. 3/1/24 to Evelyn Wadsworth; c. Stuart and James; six grandchildren. Educ: Yale Univ, A.B, 23. Polit. & Govt. Pos: Chmn, Surplus Property Bd, 45; Asst. Secy. of War for Air, 46; First Secy, Air Force, 47; chmn, Nat. Sec. Resources Bd, 50; adminstr, Reconstruction Finance Corp, 51; U.S. Sen, Mo, 52-, mem, Cmts. on Aeronaut. and Space Sci, Armed Serv, For. Rels, Appropriations for Armed Serv. and Space, Dem. Policy, Dem. Steering and Joint Econ, U.S. Senate. Bus. & Prof. Pos: Employee, various elec. and iron and steel co, 23-37; pres, Emerson Elec. Mfg. Co, 38-45. Mil. Serv: Army, 17-19. Mem: Am. Legion; Mason (32°); Shrine. Medal for Merit, 47; Distinguished Serv. Medal, 52. Rel: Episcopal. Legal Res: 230 S. Brentwood, St. Louis, Mo. 63105. Mailing Add: Senate Office Bldg, Washington, D.C. 20510.

SYMONS, JOYCE D
Mich. State Rep.
b. Detroit, Mich, 9/10/27; married, 1945; c. Jill, Gary and Mark. Educ: Detroit West. High Sch, grad. Polit. & Govt. Pos: Mich. State Rep, 64- Mem: PTA; Elba Marettes; Women's Auxiliary of Elba Mar Boat Club; Women's Traffic Club; Women of Moose; v.pres, Int. Motor Rate Coun; past v.pres, Mich. Motor Rate Coun. Rel: Presbyterian. Mailing Add: 9648 Buckingham, Allen Park, Mich. 48101. (1967)

SYNHORST, MELVIN D. R
Secy. of State, Iowa
b. Orange City, Iowa, 1/21/14; s. Hugo Synhorst and Ethel Lucas S; m. 5/31/42 to Alice Rossing; c. Robert B. and William J. Educ: Univ. Iowa, B.A. and J.D. Polit. & Govt. Pos: Secy. of State, Iowa, currently. Bus. & Prof. Pos: Attorney-at-law, Des Moines, Iowa. Mil. Serv: Lt.(jg), Naval Res, World War II. Mem: Nat. Asn. Secy. State (past pres); Am. Legion; Mason; Shrine Recipient, Am. Heritage Found. Award for Outstanding Citizenship, 61. Legal Res: 37 Foster Dr, Des Moines, Iowa 50312. Mailing Add: State Capitol, Des Moines, Iowa 50319.

SZABO, DANIEL R
Dep. Asst. Secy. of State for Latin Am. Affairs
b. Budapest, Hungary, 3/23/33; s. Alexander Szabo and Maria Berger S; m. 7/3/55 to Corine Holiber; c. Nancy Beth and Peter Stuart. Educ: City Col. of New York, B.A, 57; Sch. of Adv. Int. Studies, John Hopkins Univ, M.A, 59; Omicron Chi Epsilon; Tau Delta Phi. Polit. & Govt. Pos: Int. economist, U.S. Tariff Cmn, 59-60; desk officer, U.S. Dept. of Commerce, Viet Nam, Cambodia and Laos, 60-63; spec. asst. to Sen. Jacob K. Javits, N.Y, 63-69; Dep. Asst. Secy. of State for Latin Am. Affairs, 69- Mil. Serv: Entered as Pvt, Army, 54, released as Sp-3, 56, after serv. in 101st Airborne Div. Publ: 'The U.S. Point 4 and the UN Technical Assistance Program,' City Col. Bus. and Econ. Rev, fall 56. Mem: Alumni coun, Sch. of Adv. Int. Studies, John Hopkins Univ; Nat. Acad. of Econ. and Polit. Sci; exec. cmt, Far East. Luncheon Group. Mailing Add: 11600 Danville Dr, Rockville, Md. 20852.

T

TABB, BUCK D
b. Miller Co, Ga, 6/10/11; s. Wm. Richard Tabb and Wright McLendon T; m. 2/29/30 to Elizabeth E. Williams; c. Thomas Leroy (deceased), William B. Educ: Miller Co. Schs. Polit. & Govt. Pos: Ga. State Rep, 57-66. Bus. & Prof Pos: City Police Off, Colquitt, 46-; Dep. Sheriff, Miller Co, 25 yrs. Mem: Southeast. Fox Hunters Asn; Farm Bur; Peace Offs. Asn; Livestock and Farm Asn. Rel: Baptist. Mailing Add: Colquitt, Ga. 31737. (1967)

TABER, JOHN (WILLIAM) R
Chmn, Lincoln Co. Rep. Party, Okla.
b. Chandler, Okla, 2/10/32; s. George McKinley Taber and Grace Leake T; m. 12/29/56 to Gloria J. Graber; c. John W, III, Holly J. and Steven L. Educ: Okla. State Univ, B.A, 55, LL.B, 61; Willamette Univ. Law Sch, 58-60; Phi Delta Phi; Sigma Phi Epsilon. Polit. & Govt. Pos: Asst. co. attorney, Lincoln Co, Okla, 61-63; legal mem, Lincoln Co. Sanity Bd, 61-66; city attorney, Chandler, Okla, 63-66; chmn, Lincoln Co. Rep. Party, Okla, currently. Mil. Serv: Entered as 2nd Lt, Army, 55, released as 1st Lt, 58, after serv. as Aviator, Inf, Schofield Barracks, Hawaii, 56-58. Mem: Okla. and Am. Bar Asns; Am. Trial Lawyers Asn; pres, Jaycees, Chandler, Okla, 62, Chandler High Sch. Alumni Asn, 63 and Lincoln Co. Bar Asn, 63-64; chmn, Lincoln Co. Cancer Soc, 62-63; Mason; Lions; C. of C.(dir, Chandler Chap). Rel: Episcopal. Legal Res: 703 E. Third, Chandler, Okla. 74834. Mailing Add: P.O. Box 366, Chandler, Okla. 74834. (1967)

TABOR, JOHN K. R
b. Pittsburgh, Pa; m. to Kate Hill Williams; c. John, Jr. and William. Educ: Yale Univ, 42; Cambridge Univ, Eng. Henry Fel, M.A, 47; Harvard Univ. Sch. Law, LL.B, 50. Polit. & Govt. Pos: Secy. of Commerce, Pa, 63-67, Secy. on Internal Affairs, 67-68, Secy. of Labor and Indust, 68-69; alternate del, Rep. Nat. Conv, 68; Rep. nominee for mayor, Pittsburgh, 69. Bus. & Prof. Pos: Counsel, Nuclear Materials & Equip. Corp; attorney and partner, Kirkpatrick, Pomeroy, Lockhart and Johnson, 53-69; assoc, Kirkpatrick, Lockhart, Johnson & Hutchinson, 69- Mil. Serv: Lt, Navy, World War II, Pac. Theatre. Mem: United Fund; Red Cross; Am. Cancer Soc; Pittsburgh Skin Cancer Soc; Pittsburgh Experiment; Action for For. Policy; For. Policy Admin; Carnegie Inst. Arts Festival; Masaryk Publ. Trust. Rel: Episcopal. Mailing Add: 5440 Aylesboro Ave, Pittsburgh, Pa. 15217.

TABOR, PAULINE EDWARDS D
Okla. State Rep.
b. Henryetta, Tex, 11/26/07; d. John Waite Edwards and Lillie Barrett E; wid. Educ: East Central State Col, Okla, B.A, 32. Polit. & Govt. Pos: Precinct co-chmn, Dem. Party, Durant, Okla, 60-68; Okla. State Rep, 63-; v.pres, State Dem. Women's Club, 64-66, mem, Status of Women, State of Okla, 64-66; mem, President Johnson's Woman Power Bank, 66-68. Mem: Bus. & Prfnl. Women's Club; Delta Kappa Gamma; Lady Elk; Farm Bur; Garden Club; United Daughters Confederacy; Delphian Study Club; Fortnightly Federated Women's Club. Woman of Year, Okla, 64; Distinguished mem, Bus. Women's Club. Rel: Baptist. Mailing Add: 1224 W. Main, Durant, Okla. 74701.

TACHE, ROGER PETER R
Chmn, Fall River Rep. City Cmt, Mass.
b. Fall River, Mass, 6/22/34; s. Robert Tache and Malvina Talon T; m. 8/25/62 to Nancy Ann Shaughnessy; c. R. Peter and Elizabeth Ann. Educ: Southeast. Mass. Tech. Inst. Polit. & Govt. Pos: Pres, Young Rep. Club, Mass, 60-61; chmn, Fall River Rep. City Cmt, 64-; appointments secy. to Gov. John A. Volpe, Mass, 67-69. Bus. & Prof. Pos: Indust. engr, Honeywell Corp, 58-63; sr. indust. engr, The Foxboro Co, 63-; staff assoc, Southeast. Mass. Univ, 69- Mil. Serv: Entered as Pvt, Army Nat. Guard, released as S/Sgt; Outstanding Soldier of Month, Ft. Bliss, Tex. and Soldier of the Month, Ft. Dix, N.J. Mem: Toastmasters Int; Quequeenan Club. Rel: Catholic. Mailing Add: 78 Wingold St, Fall River, Mass. 02720.

TACKE, JOHN BERNARD D
b. Cottonwood, Idaho, 12/4/34; s. Elvin Herman Tacke and Magdelene Catherine Unteriner T; m. 4/18/60 to Pamela Ann Parr. Educ: St. Edwards, A.B, magna cum laude; Georgian Univ, Rome, Italy, Ph.L; George Wash. Univ. Law Sch, LL.B. and LL.M. Polit. & Govt. Pos: Staff asst. to U.S. Sen. Church, Idaho, 60-62; former admin. asst. to U.S. Rep. White. Bus. & Prof. Pos: Lawyer. Mil. Serv: Ens, Coast Guard, 59-60. Mem: Phi Delta Phi; Idaho, Am. and D.C. Bar Asns. Mailing Add: 8914 Mangum Place, Alexandria, Va. 22308.

TACKETT, BOYD ANDERSON D
b. Black Springs, Ark, 5/9/11; s. John Starks Tackett and Myrtle Sandum T; m. 4/26/36 to Norma Virginia Armstrong; c. Boyd Anderson, Jr, Rebecca Lou, Terri Norma and Toni Joe. Educ: Ark. Polytech. Col; Ouachita Col; Univ. Ark. Law Sch. Polit. & Govt. Pos: Ark. State Rep, 37-41; prosecuting attorney, Ninth Judicial Dist, Ark, 41-45; Ark. police cmnr, 45-48; U.S. Rep, Ark, 49-53. Bus. & Prof. Pos: Practicing attorney-at-law, 36- Mil. Serv: Entered as Pvt, Army, 43, released as Cpl, 44, after serv. in Eighth Serv. Command. Mem: Pres, Miller Co. Bar Asn, Ark, 55-56; Mason (32°); Rotary; Kiwanis; Am. Legion. Licensed to practice law before Ark. Supreme Court, U.S. Court of Appeals, Eighth Circuit and U.S. Supreme Court. Rel: Methodist. Legal Res: 2021 Beech St, Texarkana, Ark. 75501. Mailing Add: 517 State National Bank Bldg, Texarkana, Ark. 75501.

TADYCH, ALBERT R. D
b. Milwaukee, Wis, 3/23/32. Educ: Marquette Univ, B.A, 54 and LL.B, 58; Alpha Kappa Psi; Delta Theta Phi. Polit. & Govt. Pos: Wis. State Assemblyman, 60-66; mem, 12th Ward Dem. Unit. Bus. & Prof. Pos: Attorney; former brewery worker; truck driver, U.S. Post Off; assembler. Mem: Milwaukee and Wis. Bar Asns; Brewery Workers Union; Marguette Alumni Asn. Mailing Add: 2006 S. 15th St, Milwaukee, Wis. 53204. (1967)

TAFT, ALEXANDER McKAIG R
b. Greenville, N.H, 6/19/26; married; c. three. Educ: Dartmouth Col. Polit. & Govt. Pos: V.chmn, Mascenic Sch. Dist, N.H; N.H. State Rep, 59-65; coordinator of fed. funds, State of N.H, currently. Bus. & Prof. Pos: Pres. and treas, Greenville Elec. Lighting Co. Mil. Serv: Army, 46-47. Mem: Souhegan Lodge 67, Bektash Temple. Rel: Protestant. Mailing Add: Greenville, N.H. 03048.

TAFT, CHARLES P. R
City Councilman, Cincinnati, Ohio
b. Cincinnati, Ohio, 9/20/97; s. William H. Taft and Helen Herron T; m. 10/6/17 to Eleanor Chase, wid. 1961; c. Eleanor (Mrs. Hall), Sylvia (Mrs. Lotspeich), Seth, Cynthia (Mrs. Morris), Lucia C.(deceased), Rosalyn R, (deceased) and Peter R. Educ: Yale, B.A, 18, LL.B, 21; Phi Delta Phi; Yale Basketball Hall of Fame; Beta Theta Pi. Hon. LL.D, Yale, 52. Polit. & Govt. Pos: Prosecuting attorney, Hamilton Co, Ohio, 27-28; U.S. mediator, Toledo Autolite Strike, 34; chmn, Hamilton Co. Charter Cmn, 34-35; chmn, U.S. Little Steel Mediation Bd, 37; city councilman, Cincinnati, Ohio, 38-42, 48-51 & 55-, mayor, 55-57; dir, Commun. War Serv, Dept. Health, Educ. and Welfare, 41-43; chmn, U.S. Adv. Cmt, Vol. For. Aid, 41-; Dir, Off. Wartime Econ. Affairs, State Dept, 43-45; pres, City Charter Cmt, Ohio, 46-48; Rep. Nominee for Gov, 52. Bus. & Prof. Pos: Dir, Ohio Nat. Life Ins. Co, 37-, Taft Broadcasting Corp, 57-68. Mil. Serv: Entered as Pvt, Army, 17, released as 1st Lt, 19, after serv. in 12th Field Artil, 2nd Div, France, 18; Verdun Medal; European Serv; Capt, Army Res, 19-39. Publ: City Management, Farrar Strauss, 34, You and I and Roosevelt, 36 and Democracy in Politics and Economics, 51. Mem: Cincinnati, Ohio State and Am. Bar Asns; trustee, Cmn. for Econ. Develop; trustee, Carnegie Inst. of Wash; Am. Legion; gen. chmn, Cincinnati Commun. Chest, 34. Received U.S. Medal for Merit, 1946. Rel: Episcopal. Legal Res: 6 Burton Woods Lane, Cincinnati, Ohio 45229. Mailing Add: 1003 First National Bank Bldg. Cincinnati, Ohio 45202.

TAFT, JAMES L, JR. R
R.I. State Sen.
b. Providence, R.I, 10/21/30; s. James L. Taft and Katherine McGrath T; m. 10/1/55 to Sallyanne Fitzpatrick; c. Sarah W, Mary F, Eleanor W. and Jamie Lin. Educ: Col. of the Holy Cross, B.S, 52; Boston Col. Law Sch, LL.B, 55. Polit. & Govt. Pos: Councilman, Cranston, R.I, 58-60; chmn, Cranston Rep. City Cmt, 63-; R.I. State Sen, 63- Bus. & Prof. Pos: Attorney-at-Law. Mem: Am. and R.I. Bar Asns; Jaycees; Rotary; Am. Red Cross. Admitted to practice law before U.S. Supreme Court, R.I. Supreme Court and Fed. Dist. Court. Rel: Catholic. Mailing Add: 53 Fairfield Rd, Cranston, R.I. 02920. (1967)

TAFT, KINGSLEY A. R
Chief Justice, Supreme Court, Ohio
b. Cleveland, Ohio, 7/19/03; s. Frederick L. Taft and Mary Alice Arter T; m. 9/14/27 to Louise Dakin; c. Dr. Charles K, Dr. Kingsley A, Jr, Sheldon A. and Dr. David D. Educ: Amherst Col, A.B. cum laude, 25; Harvard Law Sch, LL.B. cum laude, 28; Phi Beta Kappa; Phi Kappa Psi; Phi Alpha Delta. Hon. LL.D, Amherst Col, 50, Baldwin Wallace Col, 52 and Kenyon Col, 69. Polit. & Govt. Pos: Ohio State Rep, 33-34; mem. bd. educ, Shaker Heights, Ohio, 39-43, pres, 42; U.S. Sen, Ohio, 46-47; Judge, Ohio Supreme Court, 49-63; Chief Justice Supreme Court, Ohio, 63- Bus. & Prof. Pos: Assoc, McKeehan, Merrick, Arter & Stewart, 28-39, partner, 40-48. Mil. Serv: Entered as Capt, Army, 43, released as Maj, 46, after serv. in Ord. Dept; Army Commendation Ribbon with Oak Leaf Cluster. Publ: 'Protecting the Public From Mapp versus Ohio,' Am. Bar J; 9/64. Rel: Methodist. Mailing Add: 231 N. Drexel Ave, Columbus, Ohio 43209.

TAFT, ROBERT, JR. R
U.S. Rep, Ohio
b. Cincinnati, Ohio, 2/26/17; s. Robert A. Taft and Martha Bowers T; m. 6/27/39 to Blanca Noel (deceased); c. Robert A, II, Sarah (Mrs. Winfield P. Jones II), Deborah and Jonathan D. Educ: Yale Univ, B.A, 39; Harvard Law Sch, LL.B, 42; Delta Kappa Epsilon; Phi Alpha Delta. Hon. LL.D, Centre Col. Ky, 65. Polit. & Govt. Pos: Ohio State Rep, 55-62, Majority Floor Leader, Ohio House of Rep, 61-62; del, Rep. Nat. Conv, 56, 60 & 64; U.S. Rep, Ohio, 63-64 & 67-, mem, Banking and Currency, For. Affairs, Educ. and Labor Cmts, pres, 88th Cong. Republican Freshmen Reps; chmn, Rep. Coord. Cmt. Task Force on Functions of Fed, State and Local Govts and chmn, Rep. Conf. Research Cmt, currently. Bus. & Prof. Pos: Partner, Taft Stettinius & Hollister, 51-63 & 65-66; chmn. bd, Cincinnati Terminal Warehouses, Inc, 65- Mil. Serv: Ens, Naval Res, 42, active duty in Atlantic, Mediterranean and Pac. Theaters, 42-46. Publ: 'Republican Committee on Program and Progress,' Decisions for a Better America, 60; 'The Middle Ground of a Midwest Republican,' Saturday Review, 8/22/64; one of Cong. sponsors of compilation, The Conservative Papers, 64. Mem: Am, Ohio and Cincinnati Bar Asns; Nat. Lawyers Club; Bentley Post Chap, Am. Legion; Am. Ordinance Asn. Rel: Episcopal. Mailing Add: 4300 Drake Rd, Cincinnati, Ohio 45243.

TAFT, SETH CHASE R
b. Cincinnati, Ohio, 12/31/22; s. Charles P. Taft and Eleanor Chase T; m. 6/19/43 to Frances Prindle; c. Frederick, Thomas, Cynthia and Tucker. Educ: Yale Col, B.A, 43; Yale Law Sch, LL.B, 48; Phi Beta Kappa; Order of the Coif. Polit. & Govt. Pos: Mem, Cuyahoga Co. Charter Cmn, Ohio, 58-59; c cand. Mayor of Cleveland, 67. Bus. & Prof. Pos: Assoc, Jones, Day, Cockley & Reavis, Attorneys, 48-58, partner, 58- Mil. Serv: Entered as Ens, Naval Res, 43, released as Lt.(jg), 46, after serv. as 1st Lt. on U.S.S. Doran, Atlantic, Mediterranean and Pac. Theatres; Theatre Ribbons. Mem: Cleveland, Cuyahoga Co. and Ohio Bar Asns. Jr. C. of C. Man of Year, 55. Rel: Episcopal. Legal Res: 6 Pepper Ridge Rd, Cleveland, Ohio 44124. Mailing Add: 1750 Union Commerce Bldg, Cleveland, Ohio 44115.

TAFT, WILLIAM W. R
Ohio State Sen.
b. Cleveland, Ohio, 1934; married; c. two sons. Educ: Amherst Col; Harvard Law Sch. Polit. & Govt. Pos: Ohio State Rep, 60-64; Ohio State Sen, 67- Bus. & Prof. Pos: Lawyer; mem. bd. trustees, Cleveland State Univ. Mil. Serv: Army. Mem: Mental Health Asn. Legal Res: 17331 Fernway Rd, Shaker Heights, Ohio 44120. Mailing Add: State Capitol Bldg, Columbus, Ohio 43215. (1967)

TAIRA, NORMAN TAKEO D
Exec. Secy, Hawaii State Dem. Cent. Cmt.
b. Paia, Maui, Hawaii, 4/10/30; s. father (deceased) and Kamado Adaniya T; m. 8/22/53 to Doris Len Tai Ching; c. Nadine Naomi and Norman Takeo, Jr. Educ: Hawaii Sch. of Acct, Honolulu, 48-50. Polit. & Govt. Pos: Exec. secy, Hawaii State Dem. Cent. Cmt, 66-; alternate del, Dem. Nat. Conv, 68; precinct pres, Eighth Dist, Ninth Precinct, Hawaii, 68- Mil. Serv: Entered as Pvt, Army, 51, released as Cpl, 53, after serv. in 425th Transportation Traffic Regulation Group, Korean Commun. Zone, Taegu, Korea, 52-53. Mem: Kaneohe Jr. C. of C.(pres, 59-60); Hawaii State Jr. C. of C.(v.pres, 60-61). Mailing Add: 46-226 Punawai St, Kaneohe, Hawaii 96744.

TAITANO, RICHARD FLORES D
Sen, Guam Legis.
b. Agana, Guam, 5/14/21; s. Juan San Nicolas Taitano and Rosario Sablan Flores T; m. 6/20/59 to Magdalena Ignacio Santos; c. Taling Maria, Richard Flores and John Joseph. Educ: Berea Col, B.A, 49; Univ. Pa, 49-50; Pi Gamma Mu; Int. Club. Polit. & Govt. Pos: Land surveyor, Guam Naval Dept. Pub. Works, 40-46; trainee economist, Guam Dept. Commerce, 50-51; asst. budget officer, Govt. Guam, 51-52, dir. finance, 52-61; del, White House Conf. Aging, 53; del, S.Pac. Conf, 59; dir. off. territories, Dept. Interior, 61-64; spec. presidential ambassador, Samoa Independence, 62; adv, Am. Del. S.Pac. Cmn, 62; mem. White House Mission, Trust Territories of the Pac. Islands, 63, dep. high cmnr, 64-66; asst. gov, Guam, 66; chmn, Dem. Party Guam, 67-; Sen, Guam Legis, 67- Bus. & Prof. Pos: Teacher, pub. schs, Guam, 37-40; Chmn, Educ. Found. Micronesia, 67-69; chmn, Guam Br. Health Educ. Lift

Proj, Inc, 69- Mem: Munic. Finance Officers Asn. U.S. and Can; Am. Welfare Asn; Am. Personnel Asn; Am. Soc. Pub. Admin; Phi Kappa Phi; World Federalist; Am. Civil Liberties Union; Int. Platform Asn; Am. Dem. Action; Mason; Am. Red Cross (pres, Guam chap, 58-59, dir. and treas, 68-69). Rel: General Baptist. Legal Res: Dededo, Guam 96910. Mailing Add: P.O. Box 1328, Agana, Guam 96910.

TAKAHASHI, SAKAE D
Hawaii State Sen.
b. Makaweli, Kauai, Hawaii, 12/8/19; s. Tomonosuke Takahashi and Tori T; m. 7/6/46 to Elizabeth Wulff; c. Karen, Kathryn, Mark and Brian. Educ: Univ. Hawaii, B.S, 41; Rutgers Univ, J.D, 48. Polit. & Govt. Pos: City and co. supvr, Honolulu, Hawaii, 51-52; treas, Territory of Hawaii, 52-53; Hawaii Territorial Sen, 54-59; Hawaii State Sen, 59- Mil. Serv: Entered as 2nd Lt, Army, 41, released as Maj, 46, after serv. in 100th Bn, 442nd Regt, Mediterranean Theatre, 43-45, Army Res, 46-63, Col; Purple Heart, Bronze Star; Legion of Merit. Mem: Hawaii and Am. Bar Asns. Legal Res: 3828 Old Pali Rd, Honolulu, Hawaii 96817. Mailing Add: P.O. Box 2335, Honolulu, Hawaii 96804.

TAKETA, GRAYSON S. D
Mem, Calif. Dem. State Cent. Cmt.
b. San Jose, Calif, 11/8/34; s. Harry Toshinaga Taketa and Miyeko Iseri T; single. Educ: Univ. Calif, Berkeley, B.S.Ch.E, 57; Univ. Santa Clara, J.D, 62; Alpha Sigma Nu. Polit. & Govt. Pos: Secy, Santa Clara Co. Dem. Cmt, Calif, 66-68; nominee, U.S. Rep, Tenth Dist, Calif, 68; mem, Calif. Dem. State Cent. Cmt, 68- Bus. & Prof. Pos: Attorney, Becklund, Siner & Taketa, 64-69. Mil. Serv: Entered as Pvt, Army, 57, released as Pfc, 59, after serv. in Army Chem. Corps; Good Conduct Medal. Mem: Bd. trustees, Santa Clara Co. Bar Asn; Am. and Calif. State Bar Asns. Rel: Buddhist. Legal Res: 3369 Kirkwood Dr, San Jose, Calif. 95117. Mailing Add: P.O. Box 579, San Jose, Calif. 95106.

TAKITANI, HENRY T. D
Hawaii State Rep.
b. Eleele, Kauai, Hawaii, 3/8/24; s. Kanichi Takitani and Mitsu Yamanaka T; m. 9/3/49 to Shirley Shizue Shimizu; c. Sheila Chieko, Cheryl Mitsu and Roxanne Toshie. Educ: Ill. Col, B.A, 51. Polit. & Govt. Pos: Hawaii State Rep, currently. Bus. & Prof. Pos: Secy-treas, K. Takitani Enterprise, 50; owner, H. & S. Garden Center, Maui, 65; pres, House of Colors, 67. Mil. Serv: Entered as Pvt, Army, 44, released as Pfc, 46, after serv. in 442nd Inf, Italy, 45-46. Rel: Congregational. Mailing Add: 262 Ekoa Place, Wailuku, Maui, Hawaii 96793.

TAKUSHI, TOKUICHI D
Mem, Hawaii Dem. Cent. Cmt.
b. Waipahu, Oahu, Hawaii, 1/11/10; s. Ushi Takushi and Kana Nakasone T; m. 8/22/37 to Doris Kimiye Shimabukuro; c. Morris T, Floyd T. and Karen L. (Mrs. Shishido). Educ: Mid-Pac. Inst. Polit. & Govt. Pos: Mem, Hawaii Dem. Co. Cmt, 32-58; del, Hawaii State Dem. Conv, 32-68; mem, C&C Parks and Recreation Cmn, 47-48; mem, C&C Traffic Safety Cmn, 49-50; mem, Hawaii Liquor Cmn, 52; mem, Hawaii Dem. Cent. Cmt, 58-70, asst. secy, 62-66; del. and mem, Credentials Cmt, Dem. Nat. Conv, 60, del. and hon. secy, 64, del, 68; sgt-at-arms, Hawaii State Senate, 62-66; Dem. presidential elector, 68. Mem: Founder and dir, Hui Makaala Orgn, 46-69. Plaque for Outstanding Dem. of the Year, 66. Rel: Protestant. Mailing Add: 31 Coelho Way, Honolulu, Hawaii 96817.

TALBERT, S. WATSON D
S.C. State Rep.
b. Columbia, S.C, 7/15/40; s. C. Laney Talbert and Mary Catherine Power T; m. 8/15/60 to Penny Ann Dixon; c. Earl Rawls and S. Watson, Jr. Educ: Univ. of S.C, four years in polit. sci. Polit. & Govt. Pos: U.S. Senate page, 3 years; S.C. State Rep, 63- Bus. & Prof. Pos: Retail liquor dealer, 69- Mem: WOW; Richland Co. and S.C. Farm Burs; Palmetto Sertoma Club. Rel: Episcopal; Vestry mem, Good Shepherd Episcopal Church. Mailing Add: 4501 Trenholm Rd, Columbia, S.C. 29206.

TALBOT, A. EDWARD R
Mass. State Rep.
Married; c. one son. Educ: Amesbury High Sch, grad. Polit. & Govt. Pos: Selectman, Amesbury, 9 years, chmn. bd, 8 years; Mass. State Rep, 63- Bus. & Prof. Pos: Former foreman, New Eng. Wood Heel Co. Mil. Serv: Army Vet. Mem: Am. Legion; LaFayette Naturalization Club; St. Jean the Baptist Soc. Mailing Add: 190 Main St, Amesbury, Mass. 01913. (1967)

TALBOT, ALAN CHARLES R
Chmn, Yolo Co. Rep. Cent. Cmt, Calif.
b. San Diego, Calif, 11/8/20; s. Ray L. Talbot and Lillian Ione Draper T; m. 6/12/42 to Barbara Lucille Murray; c. Robert A, Daryl K. and Alan C, Jr. Educ: La Salle Exten. Univ, Law course, $1\frac{1}{2}$ years. Polit. & Govt. Pos: Mem, San Diego Police Dept, Calif, 48-59; dep. sheriff and dep. coroner, Tuolumne Co, 61-63; mem, Calif. Dept. of Corrections, 63-; registered legis. advocate, 65; instnl. rep, Golden Empire Coun, Boy Scouts, 65; mem, Yolo Co. Rep. Cent. Cmt, 65, chmn, 69-; pres, United Rep. of Calif, Yolo Co, 65-66; mem. bd. dirs, E. Yolo Cmt. for Self Govt, 67- Bus. & Prof. Pos: Prod. control planner, Solar Aircraft, San Diego, 41-48; self employed, rental bus, 59-60. Mil. Serv: Entered as Pvt, Army Air Force, 43, released as Cpl, 45, after serv. in Second Air Force, Alaska, 44-45; Pac. Theatre Medal. Mem: Calif. Correctional Officers Asn.(pres, CMF chap, 64-). Rel: Protestant. Mailing Add: 1705 Michigan Blvd, West Sacramento, Calif. 95691.

TALBOT, PHILLIPS
b. Pittsburgh, Pa, 6/7/15; s. Kenneth Hammet Talbot and Gertrude Phillips T; m. 8/18/43 to Mildred Aleen Fisher; c. Susan, Nancy and Bruce Kenneth. Educ: Univ. Ill, B.A, B.S.J, 36; London Sch. Oriental Studies, 38-39; Univ. Chicago, Ph.D, 54; Phi Beta Kappa. Hon. LL.D, Mills Col, 63. Polit. & Govt. Pos: Trustee, Coun. Econ. and Cultural Affairs, 53-61, Asia Soc, 57-61 and J.D.R, 3rd Fund; Asst. Secy. of State for Near E. and Asian Affairs Dept. of State, 61-65; U.S. Ambassador to Greece, 65-69. Bus. & Prof. Pos: Reporter. Chicago Daily News, 36-38; assoc, Inst. Current World Affairs, 38-41, part time assoc, 46-51; correspondent in India, Pakistan for Chicago Daily News, 46-48 & 49-50; vis. asst. prof. polit. sci, Univ. Chicago, 48-50; vis. lectr, Columbia Univ, 51; exec. dir. and trustee, Am. Univ. Field Staff, 51-61. Mil. Serv: 2nd Lt, Cavalry, Officers Res. Corps, 36; 1st Lt, Brevet Capt, Ill. Nat. Guard, 37-38; Lt. Comdr, Naval Res, 41-46. Publ: Ed, South Asia in the World Today, 50; author, India and America (with S.L. Poplai), 58. Mem: Coun. on For. Rels; Am. Polit. Sci. Asn; Asn. Asian Studies; Royal Cent. Asian Soc. Rel: Presbyterian. Mailing Add: 3634 Upton St. N.W, Washington, D.C. 20008.

TALCOTT, BURT L. R
U.S. Rep, Calif.
b. Billings, Mont, 2/22/20; s. Burt Breckinridge Talcott and Hester V. Lacklen T; m. 9/6/42 to Lee G. Taylor; c. Ronald T. Educ: Stanford Univ, B.A, 42, LL.B, 48; Phi Delta Phi; Sigma Chi. Polit. & Govt. Pos: Cmnr, Recreation-Parks, Salinas, Calif, 52-54; supvr, Monterey Co, 55-62; U.S. Rep, 12th Dist, 63-; del, Rep. Nat. Conv, 68. Bus. & Prof. Pos: Self-employed attorney, 48-; attorney, Pioda, Leach, Stave, Bryan, Ames & Talcott, 62- Mil. Serv: Entered as Aviation Cadet, Army Air Force, 42, released as 1st Lt, 45, after serv. in 15th Air Force, ETO, 43-45, German Prisoner of War, 14 months; Air Medal with Clusters; Purple Heart with Cluster. Mem: Monterey Co. and Calif. Bar Asns; Am. Legion; C. of C; Commonwealth Club of Calif; Elks; Rotary. Rel: Methodist. Legal Res: Salinas, Calif. 93901. Mailing Add: House of Representatives, Washington, D.C. 20515.

TALIAFERRO, LEWIS D
b. Kenton, Tenn, 10/25/21; s. James Lyndel Taliaferro and Ruby Taylor T; m. 1/9/53 to Bettye Frances Knox; c. Elizabeth Wythe, Margaret Knox and Mary Lyndel. Educ: Memphis State Univ, B.S, 43; Univ. Va, LL.B, 49; Delta Theta Phi; Sigma Phi Epsilon. Polit. & Govt. Pos: Tenn. State Sen, 60-66; chmn, Dem. Party for Shelby Co, 66-68; del, Dem. Nat. Conv, 68. Bus. & Prof. Pos: Partner, Law Firm of Hoffman, Taliaferro, Dwyer, Hughes & McWhorter, Memphis, Tenn, presently. Mil. Serv: Entered as Midn, Navy, 43, released as Lt, 45, after serv. in Amphibious Forces, Pac; Presidential Unit Citation. Mem: Mason, Scottish Rite, Shriner; Am. Legion; 40 et 8; VFW. Named Outstanding Young Man of Memphis, 53. Rel: Church of Christ. Mailing Add: 6360 Heather Dr, Memphis, Tenn. 38117.

TALISMAN, MARK ELLIOT D
b. Cleveland, Ohio, 7/16/41; s. Julius Joel Talisman (deceased) and Rosalyn Seidenberg T; single. Educ: Harvard Col, Cambridge, A.B. cum laude; George Wash. Univ, D.C, grad. studies in pub. affairs, 2 years. Polit. & Govt. Pos: Admin. asst. to U.S. Rep. Charles A. Vanik, 63-; mem. operating exec. adv. bd, Cleveland Coun. for Econ. Opportunity, 64-; mem, Cleveland Health Manpower Coun, 64-; mem, Cleveland Summer Arts Festival, 66-; mem, Ad Hoc Cmt. on Camping, 66-; mem, V.pres. Cmn. on Youth Opportunity, 67-68; mem, Mayor's Cmn. on Youth Opportunity, 68-; mem, Bi-Partisan Intership Cmt, U.S. House of Rep, 69- Bus. & Prof. Pos: Chmn, East. Area Jr. Red Cross, 57-58; co-chmn, Nat. Jr. Red Cross, 58-59; chmn, Admin. Assts. Seminar Group, 64-68; intern, Off. Int. Rels, Am. and Nat. Red Cross; founder and proj. dir, Oper. Govt. Which Produced 40 Half Hours of TV on Three Branches of Fed. Govt, 64-69 Publ: Harvard Student Guide to Vineyards of France, Cambridge, 64; numerous articles on photography, cooking and wine notes to friends, to be publ. soon. Mem: Am. Polit. Sci. Asn; Admin. Assts. Study Group; Harvard Clubs of Cleveland and Wash; Nat. Cmt. for Civic Responsibility; B'nai B'rith. David McCord Prize for Artistic Endeavor, Harvard Univ, 63; Outstanding Photographer Awards; Ten 1-Man Nat. Color Photographic Shows. Rel: Jewish. Legal Res: 3616 Ingleside Rd, Shaker Heights, Ohio 44120. Mailing Add: 408 A St. N.W, Washington, D.C. 20003.

TALKINGTON, ROBERT VAN R
Kans. State Rep.
b. Dallas Co, Tex, 8/23/29; s. William Henry Talkington and Nannie T; m. 3/25/51 to Donna Jill Schmaus; c. Jill, Jacki, James Thomas and Lisa. Educ: Tyler Jr. Col, Tex, A.A, 49; Univ. Kans, B.S, 51; Univ. Kans. Sch. Law, LL.B, 54; Phi Delta Phi; Sigma Alpha Epsilon, recipient Bessemer-Lindsay Award; K-Club. Polit. & Govt. Pos: Attorney, Allen Co, Kans, 57-63; co-chmn, Allen Co. Young Rep. Club, 58-62; Second Dist. chmn, Kans. Day Club, 59; del, Rep. State Conv, 64; chmn, Allen Co. Rep. Cent. Cmt, 64-68; treas, Kans. State Rep. Cmt, 64-; city attorney, LaHarpe, 65-; city attorney, Moran, 68-; Kans. State Rep, 69- Mil. Serv: Army, 54-56, Counter Intel. Corps. Mem: Pres, Allen Co. Bar Asn, 65 & 66, secy, 58-59; prog. cmt, Bar Asn. of Kans, 63-; pres, Iola Kiwanis Club, 63; Am. Bar Asn; Sect. of Real Property, Probate & Trust Law; Elks; Allen Co. Country Club; Am. Legion; Mason; York Rite; Shrine. Rel; Presbyterian. Legal Res: 20 W. Buchanan, Iola, Kans. 66749. Mailing Add: Iola State Bank Bldg, Iola, Kans. 66749.

TALLEY, DON L. D
Wash. State Sen.
b. Tacoma, Wash, 1918; m. to Dolores T; c. four. Educ: High sch, grad. Polit. & Govt. Pos: Wash. State Sen, third term, currently. Bus. & Prof. Pos: Checker for the Port of Longview. Mil. Serv: Navy. Mem: Mason; Elks; Moose; Eagles; Am. Legion; DAV. Mailing Add: 1817 Bloyd, Kelso, Wash. 98626. (1967)

TALLEY, H. ANDREW R
Dir. State Fedn. Young Rep, Del.
b. Wilmington, Del, 3/19/35; s. Lewis H. Talley and Beatrice Andrew T; m. 4/5/58 to Marilyn Mayo; c. Andrew S. and R. Bradford. Educ: Univ. Del, 52-57; Alpha Tau Omega. Polit. & Govt. Pos: Pres, Brandywine Hundred Young Rep, Del, 67-68; admin. asst, Peterson for Gov. Campaign, 68; research dir, Del. Rep. State Cmt, 69; prothonotary, New Castle Co, Del, 69-; pres, New Castle Co. Young Rep, 69-; dir, State Fedn. Young Rep, 69- Bus. & Prof. Pos: Dist. sales mgr, Equitable Life Assurance Soc. of U.S, 60-64 and life ins. salesman, 65-68. Mil. Serv: Entered as Pvt, Army, 57, released as Sgt, 63, after serv. in MP Bn, Berlin Crisis, 61-62. Named Outstanding Area Young Rep. for New Castle Co. Rel: Protestant. Mailing Add: 2505 Dorval Rd, Wilmington, Del. 19803.

TALMADGE, HERMAN EUGENE D
U.S. Sen, Ga.
b. McRae, Ga, 8/9/13; s. Eugene Talmadge and Mattie Thurmond T; m.

12/24/41 to Leila Elizabeth Shingler; c. Herman E, Jr. and Robert S. Educ: Univ. Ga, LL.B, 36; Sigma Nu; Omicron Delta Kappa. Polit. & Govt. Pos: Gov, Ga, 48-55; U.S. Sen, Ga, 57- Mil. Serv: Entered as Ens, Navy, 41, released as Lt. Comdr, 45. Publ: You and Segregation, Vulcan Press, 55. Mem: Mason; Shrine; Am. Legion; 40 et 8; VFW; Ga. Farm Bur; Ga. and Am. Bar Asns. Rel: Baptist. Legal Res: Lovejoy, Ga. 30250. Mailing Add: 347 Senate Office Bldg, Washington, D.C. 20510.

TAMARGO, RAY, JR. D
Chmn, Dem. Exec. Cmt. Hillsborough Co, Fla.
b. Tampa, Fla, 1/29/32; s. Ramiro Tamargo and Violet Alvarez T; div; c. Gina Rae, Lisa Rae and Ted Ray. Educ: Univ. Fla, 48-50; Univ. Tampa, B.S, 58; Stetson Univ. Col. of Law, LL.B, 61; Phi Alpha Delta. Polit. & Govt. Pos: Spec. asst. attorney gen, Fla, 61; precinct committeeman, Dem. Exec. Cmt. Hillsborough Co, Fla, 62-, chmn, 66-; cmnr, Hillsborough Co. Charter Cmn, 65-67; asst. pub. defender, Hillsborough Co, 67-; chmn, Fla. Dem. Co, 69; cmnr, Hillsborough Co. Home Rule Charter Cmn, 69. Mil. Serv: Entered as Pvt, Army, 54, released as Sp-3, 56, after serv. in Corps Engr, Ft. Belvoir, Va. Mem: Tampa-Hillsborough Co, Fla. and Am. Bar Asns; Pub. Defenders' Asn; United Civic Orgn; Jaycees. Legal Res: 2712 Myrtle Ave, Tampa, Fla. 33602. Mailing Add: 311 N. Morgan, Tampa, Fla. 33602.

TAMBOURINE, LORETTA JOYCE R
Mem, Rep. Cent. Cmt, Calif.
b. Chicago, Ill, 2/20/32; d. Harold F. Hanssen and Grace Brookbank H; m. 9/9/50 to Angelo Thomas Tambourine; c. Karen Anne, Steven Thomas, Scott David, Daniel Bruce and David Joseph. Educ: Maine Township High Sch, Des Plaines, Ill, grad, 50. Polit. & Govt. Pos: Ed, Anaheim Rep. Assembly, Calif, 62 & 63 and dir, 64; alternate, Calif. Rep. State Cent. Cmt, 65-67 and mem, 66-68 & 69-; campaign dir, State Sen. John G. Schmitz, 66; v.pres, Del Prado Rep. Women Federated, 67-68; co. primary campaign dir, Rafferty for U.S. Senate, 68; dir-at-lg, Calif. Rep. Assembly, 68-69. Bus. & Prof. Pos: Co-owner, Excel Bus. Serv, Fullerton, Calif, 63- Rel: Roman Catholic. Mailing Add: 504 N. Buttonwood St, Anaheim, Calif. 92805.

TAMMS, ERWIN GEORGE R
Wis. State Assemblyman
b. Milwaukee, Wis, 1/4/31; s. Erwin Cornielius Tamms and Florence Muehl T; m. 10/17/53 to Ruth Hubbell; c. George Alan, Judith Rae and Sandra Lee. Educ: Wash. High Sch, grad, 49; Univ. Wis-Milwaukee, Spec. Interest Courses. Polit. & Govt. Pos: Wis. State Assemblyman, 69- Bus. & Prof. Pos: Pres, Tamms Lithography, 53- Rel: Lutheran. Mailing Add: 3233 N. 92nd St, Milwaukee, Wis. 53222.

TANAKA, FRANCIS TORAO D
V.chmn, State Cent. Cmt, Dem. Party Hawaii
b. Lihue, Hawaii, 8/15/32; s. Jack Torao Tanaka and Aimee Matsumoto T; m. 6/21/58 to Marjorie Hanako Tagawa. Educ: Univ. Hawaii, B.A, 56, M.S, 61. Polit. & Govt. Pos: Chmn, Ninth Dist: 66-68; alternate del, Dem. Nat. Conv, 68; v.chmn, Honolulu Co. Hosp, Adv. Coun, 68-; v.chmn, State Cent. Cmt, Dem. Party of Hawaii, 68- Bus. & Prof. Pos: Chief chemist, Honolulu Gas Co, Ltd, 62-66, tech. supt, 66-; admin. asst. to Rep. Robert C. Oshiro, 65-69. Mil. Serv: Entered as Pvt, Army, 56, released as Pfc, 58, after serv. in Seventh Div, Korea. Mem: Am. Chem. Soc; Am. Soc. of Training and Develop; Jaycees; Toastmasters; Wahiawa Commun. and Businessmen's Asn. Mailing Add: 1803 Laniloa Place, Wahiawa, Hawaii 96786.

TANCK, MARLIN LAVERN D
b. Brokaw, Wis, 10/12/34; s. Norman Walter Tanck and Anna Hoffman T; m. 10/22/55 to M. Dixie Smith; c. Erik Norman. Educ: Univ. Wis, B.A, 56, M.A, 69. Polit. & Govt. Pos: Coordinator, Manitowoc Co. Citizens for Johnson-Humphrey, Wis, 64 & 68; v.chmn, Manitowoc Co. Dem. Party, 65-66, chmn, 67-68; coordinator, Manitowoc Co. Citizens for Lucey, 66, Manitowoc Co. Citizens for Humphrey-Muskie, 68 and Manitowoc Co. Citizens for LaFollette, 68. Bus. & Prof. Pos: Teacher, Lincoln High Sch, Manitowoc, Wis, 59-66; instructional consult, Cooperative Curriculum Develop. Center, 67-69. Mil. Serv: Entered as Pvt, Army Res, 57, released as Sgt. E-6, 63, after serv. in Second Bn, 334th Regt, 84th Div. Publ: 'Teaching Concepts, Generalizations, and Constructs,' 1969 Yearbook of the Nat. Coun. For Soc. Studies. Mem: Nat. and Wis. Coun. for Soc. Studies; Nat, Wis. and Manitowoc Educ. Asns; Wis. State Soc. Studies Cmt. Mailing Add: 3407 S. Tenth St, Route 3, Manitowoc, Wis. 54220.

TANESZIO, THERESA D
Conn. State Rep.
b. New Haven, Conn, 9/10/15; d. Vincenzo Gambardella and Lucy Curcio G; m. 9/24/51 to Anthony Thomas Taneszio; c. Janet Acampora and Paul Manganella. Polit. & Govt. Pos: Town committeewoman, New Haven Dem. Cmt, 60-; bd. mem, State Fedn. Dem. Woman's Clubs, 60-; justice of peace, New Haven, 61-; Conn. State Rep, 107th Dist, 67- Mem: Melebus Club Auxiliary; Int. Ladies Garment Workers Union; pres, Albertus Magnus Col. Circle. Rel: Catholic. Mailing Add: 40 Downing St, New Haven, Conn. 06513. (1967)

TANNER, LYNN D
Ariz. State Rep.
b. Fruitland, N.Mex, 8/14/24; s. Arthur B. Tanner and Elsie Taylor T; m. 9/11/54 to Eva Lou Tangreen; c. David Lynn, Vicki, Toynette, Gregory Lynn and Lyneva. Educ: Cent. High Sch, Kirtland, N.Mex, dipl, 42. Polit. & Govt. Pos: Ariz. State Rep, Dist. 3, 69-, mem. Indian Affairs Adv. Cmt, Ariz. State House of Rep, 69-; mem. Gov. Adv. Cmt. on Alcoholism and Drug Abuse, Ariz. State Health Dept, 69-, mem. Tech. Adv. Cmt, 69- Bus. & Prof. Pos: Pres. and dir, Tan-Tan Industs, Inc, Winslow, Ariz, 63-66, Tanner Investment Corp, Phoenix, currently and Golden Empire Minerals Corp, currently. Mil. Serv: Entered as Pvt, Air Force, 44, released as S/Sgt, 45, after serv. in 20th Air Force, S.Pac. Theater, 44-45; Distinguished Flying Cross; Air Medal with Three Oak Leaf Clusters; Four Battle Stars; Victory Medal; Good Conduct Award. Mem: Nat. Soc. State Legislators; N.Am. Asn. of Alcoholism Progs. Rel: Latter-day Saint. Legal Res: 708 Kinsley Ave, Winslow, Ariz. 86047. Mailing Add: P.O. Box 118, Winslow, Ariz. 86047.

TANNER, MARIETTA JONES D
b. Willow Grove, Pa, 3/7/27; d. George H. Jones and Mary Dickens J; m. 11/16/59 to Cyrus S. Tanner; c. Stephanie Lynne and Cyrus David. Educ: W.Va. State Col, B.A, 49; N.Y. Univ, 51-56; City Col, N.Y, 67-69; Alpha Kappa Mu; Alpha Kappa Alpha. Polit. & Govt. Pos: Mem, Bronx Co. Dem. Cmt, N.Y, 68; del, Dem. Nat. Conv, 68 and Bronx Co. Judicial Conv, 69; secy, Bronx Cmt. for Dem. Voters, 69. Bus. & Prof. Pos: Teacher, N.Y.C, 56-; dir. spec. projs, Haryou Act, Harlem, N.Y, 64-66; dir, Hunts Point Head Start, Bronx, 67-68; coordinator, Para-Prfnl. Training Unit, Bd. of Educ, Dist. 12, N.Y, 68- Publ: 'The Community Conscious,' The Amsterdam News, 67-68. Mem: League of Women Voters; NAACP; Bronx Coun. on the Arts. Commun. Serv. Award, 64. Rel: Protestant. Mailing Add: 1825 Anthony Ave, Bronx, N.Y. 10457.

TANNER, WILLIAM EDGAR R
b. Covington, Ky, 5/3/30; s. Harmon Edgar Tanner and Edna Black T; m. 6/5/54 to Anna Lois Young; c. Cynthia and Amber. Educ: Univ. Ky, Eng. Col, 48, 53-56. Polit. & Govt. Pos: Campaign mgr, Boone Co. Rep. Party, Ky, 62, 63, 64 & 66; precinct capt, Devon, Boone Co, 63-66; secy-treas, Boone Co. Rep. Exec. Cmt, 64-66; admin. asst. to U.S. Rep. M. Gene Snyder, Ky, 67- Bus. & Prof. Pos: Fingerprint clerk, Fed. Bur. of Invest, 49-51; Engr, Western Elec. Co, 56; eng. assoc, Cincinnati and Suburban Bell Telephone Co, 56-67. Mil. Serv: Entered as Pvt, Army, 51, released as Pfc, 53, after serv. in Signal Corp, European Theatre, 52-53. Rel: Baptist. Legal Res: Walton, Ky. Mailing Add: 10803 Norman Ave, Fairfax, Va. 22030.

TANOUS, WAKINE GREGORY R
Maine State Sen.
b. Van Buren, Maine, 11/7/31; s. Thomas Tanous and Alice Shalala T; m. 2/9/55 to Anna Dorothy McKeon; c. Gregory G, Arlene A, Theresa M, Nolan H, Alice Rose, Wakine G. and Peter C. Educ: Boston Col, A.A, 51; Portland Univ. Law Sch, LL.B, 55; Marquette Debating Club. Polit. & Govt. Pos: Mem, East Millinocket Rep. Town Cmt, Maine, 56-59; area chmn. for reelection of Sen. Margaret Chase Smith, 60-66; area chmn. for reelection of Gov. John H. Reed, 62-66; mem, Penobscot Co. Rep. Cmt, 65-69; mem, Penobscot Co. Steering Cmt, 67-69; Maine State Sen, Dist, 27, 69- Bus. & Prof. Pos: Attorney-at-law, 55- Mem: Maine, Penobscot Co. and Am. Bar Asns; Maine Trial Lawyers Asn; Nat. Asn. of Claimants' Counsel of Am; Am. Jurisp. Soc; Elks; K. of C; C. of C; Kiwanis; PTA; St. Peter's Parish Coun; Katahdin Friends of Exceptional Children; Boy Scouts (Katahdin Area Coun. exec. bd). Silver Beaver, Citizenship Award. Rel: Roman Catholic. Legal Res: 29 Main St, East Millinocket, Maine 04430. Mailing Add: 1 Spruce St, East Millinocket, Maine 04430.

TANSLEY, JAMES E. D
Conn. State Sen.
b. 1930. Educ: Univ. of Conn, B.A. and M.A. in teaching. Polit. & Govt. Pos: Conn. State Sen, 62- Bus. & Prof. Pos: Asst. prof. educ. and dir. of Educ. Placement, Univ. Bridgeport, 69- Mailing Add: 86 Shadee Lane, Waterbury, Conn. 06706.

TANZELLA, SEPTEMIO VINCENT D
b. Easton, Pa, 9/30/17; s. Domenic Tanzella and Anna Caporaso T; m. 1/25/48 to Mary Ann Picone; c. Vincent Joseph, Gary Steven and Michele. Educ: Easton High Sch, grad, 35. Polit. & Govt. Pos: Committeeman, Sixth Ward West. Dem. Party, 52-58; alternate del, Dem. Nat. Conv, 64. Bus. & Prof. Pos: Linotype operator, Easton Express, 46-65; mechanical supt, Phillipsburg Free Press, N.J, 65-67; v.pres, Gen. Printing Co, Easton, Pa, 67- Mil. Serv: Entered as Pvt, Army, 42, released as Tech. 5th, 45, after serv. in Sixth Armored Div, 25th Engr, ETO, 44-45; Good Conduct Medal; ETO Ribbon with Five Battle Stars. Mem: Printing House Craftsmen; past pres, Bi-State Indust. Quoit League; Order Sons of Italy in Am; Order of Fleas; Pioneer A.A; VFW; Amvets; Am. Legion; Castel Club; Jacksonian and Seventh Ward Dem. Club; Int. Typographical Union; United Papermakers and Paperworkers. Rel: Roman Catholic. Mailing Add: 902 Lehigh St, Easton, Pa. 18042.

TANZMAN, NORMAN D
N.J. State Sen.
b. N.Y.C, 7/4/18; m. to Marion Schwartz; c. Rona and Jane. Educ: Rutgers Univ; Ind. Univ. Polit. & Govt. Pos: N.J. State Assemblyman, 60-67; N.J. State Sen, 67- Bus. & Prof. Pos: Partner, Jacobson, Goldfarb and Tanzman Co, currently. Mil. Serv: Coast Guard, World War II. Mem: Middlesex Co. Bd. Realtors (past pres); Realtors Multiple Listing Syst. Middlesex Co.(past pres); N.J. and Nat. Asns. Real Estate Bd; Am. Inst. Real Estate Appraisers (former mem, bd. dirs); Inst. Real Estate Mgt; sr. mem, Soc. Residential Appraisers; Woodbridge Twp. Planning Bd, 54-, chmn, 55-60; State Tax Policy Cmn; chmn, bd. trustees, Barron Free Pub. Libr; charter mem, Woodbridge Lions Club; bd. dirs, Am. Red Cross; bd. gov, Perth Amboy Gen. Hosp; dir, Edison Bank, Edison, N.J; bd. dirs, Woodbridge Drama Festival; bd, Anti-defamation League, B'nai B'rith. Received Commun. Serv. Award as Realtor of the Year in Middlesex Co. for Outstanding Civic Serv, 59; Legislator of the Year, N.J. Asn. of Chosen Freeholders, 66. Rel: Jewish; Mem, bd. dirs, Congregation Adath Israel. Mailing Add: 290 Hobart St, Perth Amboy, N.J. 08861.

TAPLIN, BEN F. D
b. Wausau, Wis, 1896; m. to Elizabeth T. Polit. & Gov. Pos: Wash. State Rep, until 66. Bus. & Prof. Pos: Retired. Mil. Serv: WW I. Mem: Elks Lodge No. 896, Lewiston, Idaho; Vet. of WW I; Hells Canyon Barracks No. 224, Clarkston. Mailing Add: 1228 6th St, Clarkston, Wash. 99401. (1967)

TAPPER, GEORGE G. D
b. Brooklyn, N.Y, 10/1/16; m. to Amy Gibson. Polit. & Govt. Pos: Fla. State Rep, 47-52; Fla. State Sen, 25th Dist, 53-56 and Fifth Dist, 64-66. Bus. & Prof. Pos: Pres, Marianna and Blountstown R.R. Co. Mil. Serv: Capt, Air Force, 42-45; 11 Decorations. Mem: Rotary; C. of C.(pres, St. Joe Chap); Am. Legion; Elks; K. of C. Rel: Catholic. Mailing Add: 1600 Constitution Dr, Port St. Joe, Fla. 32456. (1967)

TAPSCOTT, JOHN D
Iowa State Rep.
b. 1930; married; c. six. Educ: Am. Inst. of Bus. Polit. & Govt. Pos: Iowa State Rep, 67- Bus. & Prof. Pos: Asst. to regional dir, Post Off. Dept, St. Louis. Rel: Christ the King Catholic Church. Mailing Add: 1302 Watrous Ave, Des Moines, Iowa 50315. (1967)

TARBURTON, HATTIE WALLS D
V.Pres, Del. Fedn. Dem. Clubs
b. Kenton, Del, 7/4/10; d. William Charles Walls and Ella L. Stutz W; m. 9/18/37 to Franklin N. Tarburton. Educ: Beacom Col, 32. Polit. & Govt. Pos: Supvr. benefits sec, Unemployment Compensation Cmn, 36-42; dep. dir, Motor Vehicle Dept, Del, 52-54 and dir. safety responsibility, 56-; secy, Pub. Serv. Cmn, Del, 54-56; secy, Sixth Dist. Dem. Club, 56-58, v.pres, 62-64 and pres, 65-; chmn. ways and means cmt, Kent Co. Dem. Women's Club, 58-60; v.pres, Kent Co. Dem. Women's Club, 60-62 and pres, 62-64; dir, Del. Fedn. Dem. Clubs, 64-66 and v.pres, 65-; gen. chmn, Del. Fedn. Dem. Conv, 65. Bus. & Prof. Pos: Secy, Prudential Ins. Co, 32-36; dir. and secy, Del. State Hwy. Fed. Credit Union 64-65 and dir. and asst. to treas, 66. Mem: Chmn. region one, Am. Asn. of Motor Vehicle Adminstr, Safety Responsibility, 66- Rel: Baptist. Mailing Add: R.F.D. 1, Wyoming, Del. 19934. (1967)

TARPINIAN, CHARLES SIMON D
b. Lowell, Mass, 6/14/29; s. Charles J. Tarpinian and Laura Marie Poudrier T; m. 11/26/53 to Estelle B. Trudeau; c. Craig, Glenn and Gail. Educ: Univ. Conn, B.A, 51; Univ. Conn. Sch. Law, LL.B, 54. Polit. & Govt. Pos: Mem, Mansfield Dem. Town Cmt, Conn; del, Conn. Constitutional Conv, 65; presidential elector, 64. Mil. Serv: Entered as E-2, Army, 55, released as C.I.C, 57. Mem: Adv. Coun, Am. Bar Asn; Conn. Bar Asn; Past Grand Knight, St. Jude Coun. 4313, K. of C, (4°); Alhambra, Alahor Caravan 87, Norwich, Conn; past pres, Exchange Club of Willimantic, Conn; past mem, Bd. Control, Exchange Clubs of Conn; adminstr, Franco Am. Club of Willimantic; dir, Salvation Army. Rel: Roman Catholic. Legal Res: Mansfield City Rd, Mansfield, Conn. 06250. Mailing Add: R.F.D. 3, Willimantic, Conn. 06226. (1967)

TARR, CURTIS WILLIAM R
Asst. Secy. of the Air Force for Manpower and Reserve Affairs
b. Stockton, Calif, 9/18/24; s. Florence William Tarr and Esther Julia Reed T; m. 2/5/55 to Elizabeth May Myers; c. Pamela E. and Cynthia L. Educ: Stanford Univ, A.B, 48, Ph.D, 52; Harvard Univ, M.B.A, 50; Kappa Alpha. Hon. D.H.L, Ripon Col, 65 and Grinnell Col, 69. Polit. & Govt. Pos: Staff mem, Second Hoover Cmn, 54-55; Rep. cand, U.S. House Rep, Second Dist, Calif, 58; Asst. Secy. of the Air Force for Manpower and Reserve Affairs, 69- Bus. & Prof. Pos: Research asst. and instr, Harvard Grad. Sch. Bus, 50-52; v.pres, Sierra Tractor Co, Calif, 52-58; lectr, Chico State Col, 53-55; asst. dir. summer session, Stanford Univ, 61-62,asst. dean. sch. humanities and sciences, dir. summer session and lectr, 62-63; pres, Lawrence Univ, 63-69. Mil. Serv: Army, 43-46. Mem: Rotary; Univ. Club Chicago; Wis. Acad. Sci, Arts and Letters. Rel: Protestant. Legal Res: Appleton, Wis. 54911. Mailing Add: 1504 Highwood Dr, Arlington, Va. 22207.

TARR, FREDERICK HAMILTON, III R
Auditor, Mass. Young Rep. Asn.
b. Newton, Mass, 9/20/35; s. Frederick Hamilton Tarr, Jr. and Elizabeth Rogers T; single. Educ: Wash. and Lee Univ, B.S. in Biol, 58; Pi Kappa Phi. Polit. & Govt. Pos: Chmn, Rockport Rep. Town Cmt, 63-; del, Mass. Rep. Conv, 64 & 66; subdivision control officer, Rockport Planning Bd, 64-; dir, Essex Club, 64-; mem. exec. cmt, Mass. Young Rep. Asn, 65; auditor, Mass. Young Rep. Asn, 66- Bus. & Prof. Pos: Biologist, Arthur D. Little, Inc, 64-66; scientist, Am. Sci. & Eng, 65-66; prfnl. rep, Merck Sharp & Dohme, 66- Mil. Serv: Entered as Recruit, Army, 58, released as Specialist E-5, 62, after serv. in U.S. Army Security, Japan. Mem: F&AM; Mason; Commandery; Shrine; Boston Mus. of Sci; Jaycees. Rel: Episcopal. Mailing Add: 133 Marmion Way, Rockport, Mass. 01966. (1967)

TARRO, RICHARD EDWARD D
b. Providence, R.I, 12/18/29; m. to Carol Ann Donfrancesco. Educ: New Eng. Inst. of Anat. and Embalming, Boston, Mass. Polit. & Govt. Pos: R.I. State Rep, 65-68. Bus. & Prof. Pos: Funeral dir. Mil. Serv: Army, 51-53. Rel: Holy Ghost Church; Holy Name Soc. Mailing Add: 262 Knight St, Providence, R.I. 02909. (1967)

TART, CHARLES GRAHAM D
N.C. State Rep.
b. Sampson City, N.C, 9/8/18; s. Eura Morton Tart and Mollie McLamb T; single. Educ: Univ. of N.C, B.A, 39. Polit. & Govt. Pos: Clerk of Superior Court, Sampson City, 50-54; N.C. State Rep, 63- Bus. & Prof. Pos: High sch. teacher, Midway High Sch, Sampson City; farming interest in Sampson City; owns and operates tourist bus. Mil. Serv: Navy, 44-46, Specialist A, 2/C PO. Mem: Nat. Educ. Asn; v.pres, Classroom Teachers Asn, Sampson City, 63-65 and pres, 65-; Sampson City Farm Bur. Fedn. Rel: Methodist. Mailing Add: 709 Cutchin St, Clinton, N.C. 28328. (1967)

TARTER, WELDON MURPHY R
Bonus Mem, Colo. Rep. State Cent. Cmt.
b. Edgemont, S.Dak, 9/14/21; s. Thomas Barrett Tarter and Maud Murphy T; m. 6/5/49 to Virginia Lee Richmond; c. Barrett Richmond and Paul Robert. Educ: Colo. Col, B.A, 50; Univ. Denver, LL.B, 52; Kappa Sigma; Phi Delta Phi. Polit. & Govt. Pos: Precinct committeeman, El Paso Co. Rep. Party, Colo, 53-60; secy, El Paso Co. Rep. Cent. Cmt, 56-58, chmn, 58-69; Bonus mem, Colo. Rep. State Cent. Cmt, 58-; mem, Fourth Judicial Cent. Cmt, 58-; mem, Third Cong. Rep. Cent. Cmt, 58-; del, Rep. Nat. Conv, 68. Bus. & Prof. Pos: Partner, Tarter & Tarter, Attorneys, Colorado Springs, 54- Mil. Serv: Entered as A/S, Navy, 41, released as Radioman 1/C, 47, after serv. in U.S.S. Lexington and U.S.S. Saratoga, Pac. Theatre, 41-47; Pac. Theatre Ribbon with Eight Stars; Am. Defense Ribbon with Star. Mem: El Paso Co, Colo. and Am. Bar Asns;Am.Red Cross (bd); Legal Aid Soc.(bd); Pikes Peak Ment. Health Center (bd); secy. bd, Kappa Sigma Alumni; AF&AM; Consistory; Elks; C. of C. Rel: Protestant. Legal Res: 2409 Chelton Rd, Colorado Springs, Colo. 80909. Mailing Add: 203 Mining Exchange Bldg, Colorado Springs, Colo. 80902.

TARTT, ESTELLE HURT R
Committeewoman, Tex. State Rep. Party
b. Galveston, Tex, 5/18/08; d. Boling Grafton Tartt and Emma Price Hurt T; single. Educ: Baylor Col, B.A, 30; Univ. Tex, grad. work in Govt, 30; South. Methodist Univ, grad. work in Govt, 46-47. Polit. & Govt. Pos: Asst. precinct chmn, Galveston Rep. Party, Tex, 65-66; committeewoman, Tex. State Rep. Party, 66-; alternate del, Rep. Nat. Conv, 68. Bus. & Prof. Pos: First grade teacher, Galveston Pub. Schs, Tex, 30-33, hist. and civics teacher, Ball High Sch, 33-35 & 35-46, civics teacher, 55-64. Mem: Delta Kappa Gamma; Galveston and Tex. Classroom Teachers Asns; Wednesday Club. Mailing Add: 1009 Marine, Galveston, Tex. 77550.

TARVER, RAY DARRYL D
b. Natchitoches, La, 12/24/20; s. R. D. Tarver and Lula Elzby T; m. 3/3/56 to Evelyn Marie Youngblood; c. Suzanne Marie. Educ: Northwest. State Col; Loyola Univ. Polit. & Govt. Pos: La. State Rep, 64-68. Mil. Serv: Entered as Pvt, Army, 41, released as 1st Lt, 46, after serv. in ETO; 5 Campaign Stars. Mem: Am. and La. State Dent. Socs; Lions; Elks; Mason; Cattlemen's Asn. Rel: Baptist. Legal Res: 429 Henry Ave, Natchitoches, La. 71457. Mailing Add: 618 Second St, Natchitoches, La. 71457. (1967)

TARWATER, WILLIAM RAYMOND D
Okla. State Rep.
b. Duncan, Okla, 11/24/21; s. Olin P. Tarwater and Ola Carmichael T; m. 4/4/43 to Jean Johnson; c. Judy and William O. Educ: Okla. Univ, 2 years; Delta Upsilon. Polit. & Govt. Pos: Chmn, Stephen Co. Dem. Cent. Cmt, Okla, 59-68; Okla. State Rep, 66- Mil. Serv: Entered as Cadet, Air Force, 42, released as Capt, 46; re-entered 51, released as Maj, 53, after serv. in Research and Develop. Command, Pac, and U.S; Two Air Medals; Seven Unit Citations. Mem: Rotary; Elks; C. of C; Indust. Found; Nat. Asn. Independent Businessmen; Am. Legion. Pres, Okla. Golf Asn. Rel: Methodist. Mailing Add: 1001 N. Ninth, Duncan, Okla. 73533.

TASCA, HENRY J.
U.S. Ambassador to Morocco
b. Providence, R.I, 8/23/12; m. to Lina Federici; c. four. Educ: Temple Univ, B.A. and hon. LL.D, 66; Univ. of Pa, M.A, 34, Ph.D, 37; London Sch. of Econs. Polit. & Govt. Pos: Econ. analyst, Div. of Trade Agreements, State Dept, 37-38; econ. adv, Nat. Defense Cmn, 40-41; U.S. Treas. Dept. rep. Am. Embassy, Rome, 45-48; adv. to U.S. Spec. Rep. Averill Harriman in Europe for Marshall Plan and NATO, 49-52; spec. rep. of President for Korean Econ. Affairs, 53-54; dir, U.S. Opers. Mission in Italy, 54-56; minister, Dir. Off. on Econ. Affairs, Bonn, 56-60; Dept. Asst. Secy. of State for African Affairs, 60-65; U.S. Ambassador to Morocco, 65- Bus. & Prof. Pos: Asst. dir. of Trade Regulation and Commercial Policy Proj, Rockefeller Found, 39-40. Mil. Serv: Navy, Lt. Comdr, 41-45. Publ: Author, Several books on int. trade. Medal of Freedom for work with Mediterranean Allied Force Hq, 46. Mailing Add: U.S. Embassy, Rabat, Morocco.

TATE, EARL HENRY D
b. Spencer, N.C, 9/19/03; s. William Wallace Tate and Emma Lassiter T; m. 4/1/34 to Kathryn Haynes; c. Virginia (Mrs. Raymond Compton), Patricia (Mrs. Charles Weaver) and William Wallace, II. Educ: Univ. of N.C, Pharmacy Sch, Ph.G, 23-25. Polit. & Govt. Pos: Mayor, Lenoir, N.C, 37-61; N.C. State Rep, 63-65 & 67. Bus. & Prof. Pos: Pharmacist; pres, and mgr, Lenoir Drug Co. Mem: N.C. Pharmaceutical Asn.(v.pres, 62, pres, currently); Am. Pharmaceutical Asn; Nat. Asn. of Retail Druggists; Mason; Shrine, Potentate of Oasis Temple, Charlotte, N.C, 61; Moose Lodge; K. of P; Royal Order of Jesters; Lenoir-Morganton Airport Authority, 40-50, chmn, currently; pres, N.C. League of Munic, 48; Caldwell City Bd. of Health, 37-61; pres, Lenoir C. of C, 52-54; dir, Lenoir Merchants' Asn, 61-62; trustee, Caldwell Mem. Hosp, 48-61; bd. of trustees, N.C. Teachers & State Employees' Retirement Bd, 58-54; N.C. Med. Care Com, 58-61. Rel: Methodist; Bd. of Stewards, 50-52. Mailing Add: 229 Norwood St, Lenoir, N.C. 28645.

TATE, JAMES HUGH JOSEPH D
Mayor, Phila, Pa.
b. Phila, Pa, 4/10/10; s. Edward Tate; m. 6/20/42 to Anne M. Daley; c. Francis X. and Anne Marie. Educ: Temple Univ. Evening Law Sch, LL.B, 38; Strayer's Bus. Col; St. Joseph's Col. Indust. and Labor Rels. Sch. Polit. & Govt. Pos: Pa. State Rep, 40-46; mem, City Coun, 51-55 and pres, 55-62; mayor, Phila, 62-; del, Dem. Nat. Conv, 68. Mem: V.pres, Nat. League of Cities; adv. bd, U.S. Conf. of Mayors; chmn, Regional Conf. of Elected Officials; dir. exec. cmts, Food Distribution Center; Old Phila. Develop. Corp; Phila. Industr. Develop. Corp; Hero Scholarship Fund; Phila Zool. Gardens; Conv. and Tourist Bur; Hosp. Survey Cmt; trustee, Univ. Pa; K. of C.(past grand knight); dir, WHYY Broadcasting Sta, Phila. Rel: Roman Catholic. Legal Res: 4029 N. Seventh St, Philadelphia, Pa. 19140. Mailing Add: Room 215, City Hall, Philadelphia, Pa. 19107. (1967)

TATE, RUTH EVELYN D
Mem, Ark. State Dem. Cmt.
b. Laneburg, Ark, 10/6/13; d. Claude McRae Gann and Emily Ward Gann Ingram; m. 8/15/37 to Walter Frank Tate, Wid; c. Walter F. Tate, Jr.(deceased) and Amanda (Mrs. Wunnenberg). Educ: Cora Donnell Sch. Nursing, Prescott, Ark, 32-35; Foster Bus. Col; South. State Col. Polit. & Govt. Pos: Chmn, Ouachita Co. Dollars for Dem. Dr, Ark; coordinator, Vol. Women Works Campaign for Congressman David Pryor, Ark, 66; v.chmn, Ouachita Co. Dem. Cent. Cmt, 67-; mem, Ark. State Dem. Cmt, 13th Judicial Dist, 67-; asst, Sen. William Fulbright Campaign, 68; del, Dem. Nat. Conv, 68; mem. speakers bur, Ark. Young Dem. Club, 69- Mem: Camden Bus. & Prfnl. Club (pres); C. of C; Ark. Women's Dem. Club; Ark. Farm Bur. Fedn; Ark. Wood Prod; Keep Ark. Green; Westside Hardwood Club; Fairview PTA (past pres);Ouachita Co. PTA (past pres); Camden Garden Club (past pres); Camden Coun. Garden Clubs (past pres); hon. mem. Tate Park Garden Club; Ark. Fedn. Garden Clubs (past v.pres. and mem. bd, 25 years); life mem. Nat. Coun. State Garden Clubs; Am. Rose Soc; Am. Daffodil Soc; Camden Teen Town Coun; Girl Scout Leader; Eastern Star; Am. Legion Auxiliary; VFW; Bethesda Asn.(secy-treas. 41-); Ark. Hist. Soc.(v.pres, 61-); Ouachita Co. Hist. Soc.(v.pres); Old State Capitol of Ark.(vol. hostesses). Master Flower Arranger and Flower Show Judge. Rel: United Methodist; Women's Soc. Christian Serv, Couples Class, First United Methodist Church, Camden, Ark. Mailing Add: 902 Tate St. S.W, Camden, Ark. 71701.

TATLEY, HERBERT MELVIN R
b. Minneapolis, Minn, 2/26/37; s. Rev. Melvin Norman Tatley and Gertrude Einsler T; m. 12/28/60 to Esther Berith Edwards; c. Karen Joanna.

Educ: Luther Col, B.A, 59; Delta Men's Club. Polit. & Govt. Pos: Justice of peace, St. Joseph Twp, St. Croix Co, Wis, 62-63; Pre. precinct committeeman, St. Croix Co, Wis, 62-63; chmn, Pepin Co. Rep. Orgn, 65-68. Bus. & Prof. Pos: Pres, Pepin Teachers Asn, Wis, 64-65. Mil. Serv: Army Res, hon. discharge, 63. Mem: Wis. Educ. Asn; Nat. Rifle Asn. Rel: Lutheran. 1967 Legal Res: Pepin, Wis. No mailing address available. (1967)

TATMAN, AUBREY C. R
Mem, Rep. State Cent. Cmt, La.
b. Bayou Chicot, La, 4/20/15; s. Howard W. Tatman and Beulah Courtney T; m. 12/19/37 to Juanita Russell; c. Gwendolyn (Mrs. Harold Burcham) and Aubrey, Jr; Grandchildren; Cary Burcham and Noel Burcham. Educ: High Sch. Polit. & Govt. Pos: Mem, Rep. State Cent. Cmt, La, currently; supvr. of Census; asst. in Bankruptcy Sales. Mem: Bayou Chicot Masonic Lodge 430. Rel: Methodist. Mailing Add: R.R. Three, Ville Platte, La. 70586.

TATUM, WAUGANTHA GRADY 'TUT' D
State Finance Chmn, Dem. Women's Club of Fla.
b. Seminary, Miss, 2/16/20; d. Grover Cleveland Grady and Zilphia Lucretia Herrin G; m. 12/8/44 to John Hervey Tatum; c. Blanche Anne (Mrs. Horn), John Hervey, Jr. and Ross Grady. Educ: Hinds Jr. Col, Miss, 3 years. Polit. & Govt. Pos: Mem, Cemetery Bd, Ft. Walton Beach, Fla, 56-61, mem, Parks and Recreation Bd, 56-64; pres, Miracle Strip Dem. Women's Club, 66-; del, Dem. Nat. Conv, 68; state finance chmn, Dem. Women's Club of Fla, 68- Bus. & Prof. Pos: Secy. and Leasing Agent, John Tatum Mfrs, Inc. 66-; Pres, Tatum Investment Corp, 69- Mem: Exec. cmt, Ft. Walton Beach Hosp, 59-68; bd. dirs, Ft. Walton Beach Tennis Club; Ladie's Golf Asn, Ft. Walton Beach (pres, 65-66); Ladie's Golf Asn, Lake Lorraine Country Club; mem. house cmt, Ft. Walton Yacht Club, 6 years. Hon. Spec. Dept. Sheriff, Okaloosa Co; nominated for Most Outstanding Dem. Woman of Fla. Rel: Baptist. Mailing Add: 305 Brooks, Fort Walton Beach, Fla. 32548.

TAURIELLO, ANTHONY FRANCIS D
b. Buffalo, N.Y, 8/14/99; s. Sebastian Tauriello and Lucia Tita T; single. Educ: Cumberland Univ. Sch. Law, LL.B, 29; Palmer Col. of Chiropractic, 3 years. Polit. & Govt. Pos: Mem. Bd. of Supvr, Erie Co, N.Y, 33-37; mem, Buffalo Common Coun, 38-41, 48 & 54-57; Dep. City Treas, Buffalo, N.Y, 42-45; Exam, Reconstruction Finance Corp, Buffalo Off, 46-47; U.S. Rep, N.Y, 49-50; chmn, Buffalo Munic. Housing Authority, 61-; del, Dem. Nat. Conv, 68. Bus. & Prof. Pos: Owner, Niagara Hudson Liquor Store, Buffalo, N.Y, 41-64. Mem: K. of C; Eagles; Elks. Rel: Catholic. Mailing Add: 618 Seventh St, Buffalo, N.Y, 14213.

TAWES, JOHN MILLARD D
b. Crisfield, Md, 4/8/94; s. James Tawes and Alice Byrd T; m. 12/25/15 to Helen Avalynne Gibson; c. Jimmie Lee (Mrs. William R. Wilson) and Philip W. Polit. & Govt. Pos: Clerk of Court, Somerset Co, Md, 30-38; state comptroller, Md, 38-47 & 50-58, bank cmnr, 47-50, gov, 59-66; del, Dem. Nat. Conv, 68. Bus. & Prof. Pos: Secy-treas, Tawes Shipbuilding Co, 17-19 and Tawes Banking Co, 19-45; dir, Bank of Crisfield, currently. Mem: Past pres, Nat. Asn. State Auditors, Comptrollers and Treas; Hibernian Soc. Baltimore; Md. Soc. Pa; Crisfield Fire Dept; past pres, Chesapeake Bay Fishing Fair Asn; Elks; K. of P; Mason; Shrine; Eastern Star; Rotary; Scimeter; dir, Md-Ready Mem. Hosp. Rel: Methodist. Mailing Add: Hall Hwy, Crisfield, Md. 21817.

TAYLOR, ADA C. R
b. Whitefield, N.H; wid. Educ: Teachers' Col. Polit. & Govt. Pos: N.H. State Rep, 47-68. Bus. & Prof. Pos: Teacher. Mem: Sch. bd. Rel: Baptist. Mailing Add: Whitefield, N.H. 03598. (1967)

TAYLOR, BALCOM SHAW D
b. Danville, Va, 4/8/03; s. Silas Maxwell Taylor and Maria Wilson T; single. Educ: Lincoln Univ; Harvard Univ; Patrick Sch. of Pharm, Mass, A.B. and PH.G; Alpha Phi Alpha; Delta Rho; Varsity Club, Lincoln Univ. Polit. & Govt. Pos: Chmn, Dem. League; chmn, Ward Cmt, 56-65; del-at-lg, Dem. Nat. Conv, 60-64; v.pres. Dem. City Cmt, Boston, Mass. Bus. & Prof. Pos: Pres. and treas, Lincoln Drug, Inc; pres. and treas, Pioneer Club, Inc; pres, Independent Renewel & Develop. Co. Mem: Pres, Lincoln Univ. Alumnae Asn; east. dir, Lincoln Univ. Asn; Mass. Pharmaceut. Asn; Elks; Masons; Neighborhood Improvement Asn; Boston Urban League; Brotherhood Sleeping Car Porters; Boston's Prfnl. & Bus. Men's Club, Inc; Pigskin Club, Inc, Wash, D.C. Rel: Baptist. Mailing Add: 924 Tremont St, Boston, Mass. 02120.

TAYLOR, BELOIT D
b. Corning, Ark, 1/28/97; s. Judge Felix Grundy Taylor and Viola Beloate T; m. 2/23/24 to Harriett Walthall Daniel; c. Virginia Lee (Mrs. Randall). Educ: South. Methodist Univ, 17; Univ. Ark, B.A, 19; George Wash. Univ, LL.B, 23; Beta Gamma Sigma; Kappa Alpha Order, Quo Vadis; Kappa Beta Phi; Blackfriars. Hon. LL.D, Univ. Ark, 60. Polit. Pos: Mem, Ark. State Dem. Cmt, 44-66 and secy, 36-40; secy, Pulaski Co. Dem. Cmt, Ark, 51-66 and mem, 30-51; del, Dem. Nat. Conv, 64 and 40-56; del, Pulaski Co. Dem. Conv, 32-64; secy, Ark. del. to Dem. Nat. Conv, 40; chmn, Ark. State Finance Cmt, 33. Govt. Pos: V.chmn, Adv. Cmt. to Univ. Ark. Med. Sch, 54-; spec. assoc. justice, Supreme Court of Ark, 55; mem, sub-cmt. of Nat. Vol. Mortgage Credit Exten. Cmt. for Region 12, Fed. Housing and Home Finance Agency, 50-54; trustee, Univ. Ark, 37-41; mem, Ark. Centennial Cmn, 36 and War Mem. Cmn, 30; spec. judge, Civil Div, Munic. Court, Little Rock, 27-30; attorney and exam, Fed. Trade Cmn, 23-25; clerk, Passport Div, U.S. Dept. of State, 20-22; enumerator, Bur. of Census, U.S. Dept. of Commerce, 20; dep. co. clerk, Clay Co, Ark, 19-20. Bus. & Prof. Pos: Gen. counsel, officer, dir. for several insts. and orgns. Mil. Serv: Pvt, Army, 18, serv. as Officer's Cand, Field Artil. Cent. Training Sch. Mem: Am, Fed, Ark. and Pulaski Co. Bar Asns; legal sect, Am. Life Conv; Asn. of Life Ins. Counsel; pres, Univ. Ark. Gen. Alumni Asn, 36 and 53 and Endowment and Trust Fund Bd, 54-55; Am. Legion, Post Comdr, M.M. Eberts Post 1, 29-30 and Judge Adv, Dept. of Ark, 30-37; adv. bd, Pulaski Co. Red Cross; Salvation Army; pres, Young Businessmen's Asn. of Gr. Little Rock, 30-31; Little Rock Country Club; Top of the Rock Club. Received Distinguished Alumnus Citation, Univ. Ark, 57. Rel: Protestant. Legal Res: 2211 North Beechwood Rd, Little Rock, Ark. 72207. Mailing Add: 512 Donaghey Bldg, Little Rock, Ark. 72201. (1967)

TAYLOR, CHARLES H. R
N.C. State Rep.
b. Brevard, N.C, 1/23/41; s. Robert Glenn Taylor and Loee English T; single Educ: Wake Forest Univ, B.A. and LL.B; outstanding sr; outstanding third-year law student; v.pres, Student Body; pres, Legis. and Phi Alpha Delta. Polit. & Govt. Pos: Rep. Cong. Campaign, 62; mem, N.C. State Rep. Exec. Cmt. and N.C. State Cent. Cmt; N.C. State Rep, 67-, Minority Leader, 69-; mem. bd. dirs, Nat. Rep. Legislators Conf. Bus. & Prof. Pos: Managing dir, Transylvania Tree Farms and Southeast. Real Estate and Discount Co. Mil. Serv: Air Force Res. Publ: Articles in Wake Forest Univ. Law Rev. and numerous newspaper and mag. articles promoting West. N.C. timber indust. Mem: Nat. adv. bd, Brevard Music Center; state officer, Nat. 4-H Orgn. and coordinator of leadership; 4-H Honor Club; dist. justice, Phi Alpha Delta. Selected One of State's Outstanding 4-H Alumni, 67. Rel: Baptist; Mem, N.C. Baptist Found. Mailing Add: P.O. Box 66, Brevard, N.C. 28712.

TAYLOR, CYNTHIA GOOCH R
Secy, Macoupin Co. Rep. Cent. Cmt, Ill.
b. Carlinville, Ill, 7/5/15; d. John Thomas Gooch and Margaret Gotthardt G; m. 11/2/47 to Edward Parker Taylor, Jr; c. Edward P, III and Thomas G. Educ: Carlinville Commun. High Sch, grad, 33. Polit. & Govt. Pos: Precinct committeeman, Third Precinct, Carlinville, Ill, 66-; pres, Carlinville Rep. Women's Club, 67-69; secy, Macoupin Co. Rep. Cent. Cmt, 68- Mem: Am. Legion Auxiliary; Carlinville Rep. Women's Club. Rel: United Methodist. Mailing Add: 320 S. Plum, Carlinville, Ill. 62626.

TAYLOR, DAVID SURRATT D
S.C. State Rep.
b. Laurens Co, S.C, 7/17/27; s. Benjamin Gideon Taylor and Grace Surratt T; m. 4/30/49 to Dorothy Lee Drummond; c. David S, Jr, F. Drummond, Connie G. and J. Adam. Educ: Clemson Univ, 1 year. Polit. & Govt. Pos: S.C. State Rep, Laurens Co, 63-64 & 67- Bus. & Prof. Pos: Owner, Taylor Real Estate, Laurens, S.C, 63- Mil. Serv: Entered as A/S, Navy, 45, released as Radarman 3/C, 48, after serv. in U.S.S. Chuckawan, ETO, 46-47; Am. Defense, World War II Victory and Europe-Africa-Middle East Campaign Medals. Mem: Rotary; VFW (Comdr, S.C. Orgn, 61-62, chmn, South. Conf, 63-64); Mason; Shrine. Laurens Co. Vet. of the Year, 62. Rel: Methodist. Mailing Add: 104 Barksdale Circle, Laurens, S.C. 29360.

TAYLOR, DENNIS DELTON R
b. Foydada, Tex, 12/2/19; s. John Tilford Taylor and Della Roberts T; m. 12/24/39 to Rachel Mae McClure; c. John Raymond, Joe David and Tom Dennis. Educ: Tex. Tech. Col; Former Students Asn. of Tex. Tech. Col. Polit. & Govt. Pos: Co-chmn, Rep. Party, Tex, 60-61 & 63-66; cand. for Tex. State Rep, 62. Mem: Co. pres, Tex. Farm Bur, 54-59; Crosby Co. Lions, 59-64; mem, Study Migrant Workers, Tex, 61. Rel: Ordained Minister of Primitive Baptist Church. Mailing Add: 1032 Chatterton St, Grinnell, Iowa 50112.

TAYLOR, DON LEE R
Treas, Wis. Ninth Cong. Dist. Rep. Club
b. Milwaukee, Wis, 12/16/32; s. Carl Taylor and Alma Neely T; m. 11/29/58 to Carol Grace Knaebe; c. Wendy Sue, Scott Clay, Jenifer Jo and Ty Rock. Educ: Univ. Wis, B.B.A, 54; Delta Sigma Rho; Sigma Phi Epsilon. Polit. & Govt. Pos: Chmn, Waukesha Co. Young Rep, Wis, 58-59; v.chmn, Second Cong. Dist. Young Rep, 59-60, chmn, 60-61; treas, Wis. Fedn. of Young Rep, 61-63, chmn, 63-65; mem, Wis. Rep. State Cmt, 63-65; del, Rep. Nat. Conv, 64; treas, Wis. Ninth Cong. Dist. Rep. Club, 65- Bus. & Prof. Pos: Employee, Waukesha State Bank, 54-59, asst. cashier, 59-61, asst. v.pres. and dir, 61-66, v.pres. and dir, 66-69, pres. and dir, 69- Mil. Serv: Entered as 2nd Lt, Army Res, 55, released as 1st Lt, 57, after serv. in Army Finance Center, Indianapolis, Ind. Mem: Rotary; Aircraft Owners and Pilots Asn; bd. dirs, YMCA. Private Pilot with instrument rating. Rel: Presbyterian; Elder, First Presbyterian Church, Waukesha. Mailing Add: S 23 W27100 Shananagi Lane, Waukesha, Wis. 53186.

TAYLOR, EDWARD FORT D
Chmn, Granville Co. Dem. Exec. Cmt, N.C.
b. Oxford, N.C, 1/13/06; s. Thomas George Taylor and Mildred Kennon T; m. 10/19/38 to Susan Davis. Educ: Univ. S.C, 25-27; Univ. N.C, LL.B, 30. Polit. & Govt. Pos: Chmn, bd. of elec, Granville Co, N.C, 32-40, co. attorney, 40-46 and solicitor, Recorders Court, 48-56; chmn, Granville Co. Dem. Exec. Cmt, 46-; chmn, bd. of trustees, Granville Co. Libr, 51- Bus. & Prof. Pos: Dir, Oxford Nat. Bank, 65- Mil. Serv: Pvt, Army, 42-43. Mem: Granville Co. and N.C. Bar Asns; N.C. Bar, Inc; Kiwanis; Thorndale Country Club; Am. Legion. Rel: Episcopal. Legal Res: 214 Gilliam St, Oxford, N.C. 27565. Mailing Add: Box 812, Oxford, N.C. 27565. (1967)

TAYLOR, EILEEN GERMAN R
Mem, Calif. Rep. State Cent. Cmt.
b. Los Angeles, Calif, 12/13/16; d. Russell Alger German and Glenna Kays G; m. 2/24/40 to Edwin Melancthon Taylor; c. Joan, John and Victoria (Mrs. Edmondson). Educ: Santa Maria Jr. Col, A.A, 36; Santa Barbara State Col, 36-37; Delta Psi Omega. Polit. & Govt. Pos: Mem, San Luis Obispo Co. Grand Jury, Calif, 65-66; mem, San Luis Obispo Co. Juvenile Justice Cmn, 68-; mem, Calif. Rep. State Cent. Cmt, 68-; mem, San Luis Obispo Co. Juvenile Delinquency Prev, 69-; pres, Santa Lucia Rep. Women's Club, 69- Bus. & Prof. Pos: Partner, Cert. Freight Lines, Calif, 52-; secy, Phelan & Taylor Produce Co. Inc, 54- and Cienega Ranches Inc, 68- Mem: Federated Woman's Club of Arroyo Grande; San Luis Obispo Co. Heart Asn; Commun. Hosp. Vol; San Luis Obispo Antique Car Club; life mem, Arroyo Grande Women's Club (past pres). Tiffany Award, Calif. Federated Women's Club, State Conv. Flower Show; named San Luis Obispo Co. Fair Woman of the Year. Rel: Episcopal. Mailing Add: 1029 Ash St, Arroyo Grande, Calif. 93420.

TAYLOR, ERICH A. O'DRISCOLL D
R.I. State Sen.
b. Newport, R.I, 1/4/02; s. Alexander O'Driscoll Taylor, Jr. and Martha Stanton Cozzens T; single. Educ: Rogers High Sch, R.I, 18. Polit. & Govt. Pos: R.I. State Rep, 41-45; chmn, Newport Rent Control Bd, R.I, 50; city councilman, Newport, 56-57 & 61-62; R.I. State Sen, Dist. 49, currently. Bus.

& Prof. Pos: Reporter, Newport Herald, 20-28; teacher, Portsmouth Priory Sch, 28-32 & 41- Mil. Serv: Seaman 1/C, Navy, 44-45. Publ: Battle of Rhode Island, 1778, 28. Mem: Mediaeval Acad. of Am; Nat. Educ. Asn. Chem. Teachers; Am. Asn. Physics Teachers; past pres, R.I. Biol. Soc; Nat. Sci. Teachers Asn; hon, Sons of Rev; life mem, Am. Legion Post 7, R.I; Col, Newport Artil. Co; hon. nat, Fleet Res. Asn. Received Order of Merit from President, German Fed. Republic, 66. Rel: Episcopal. Mailing Add: 522 Broadway, Newport, R.I. 02840.

TAYLOR, FRANK LILE, JR. D
Gen. Counsel to Speaker, W.Va. House of Del.
b. Charleston, W.Va, 4/13/36; s. Frank Lile Taylor and Anne Carrington Brown T; m. 5/23/64 to Jacquette Ann Maffett; c. Blair Maffett and Paige Anderson. Educ: Univ. of Va, B.A, 57; Col. of Law, W.Va. Univ, LL.B, 60. Polit. & Govt. Pos: Clerk, judiciary cmt, W.Va. House of Del, 61-62; W.Va. State Sen, 17th Sen. Dist, Kanawha Co, 64-66; gen. counsel to Speaker, W.Va. House of Del, presently. Bus. & Prof. Pos: Partner, Kay, Casto & Chaney, Attorneys-at-law, 60-; mem. bd. of dirs, Goodwill Industs. of Kanawha Vall y, Inc, 61- and Boys' Co, Inc, 64-; secy. and mem. bd. of dirs, Goodwill Industs. of Am, Inc, 65-; mem. adv. bd, Buckskin Coun, Inc, Boy Scouts, 65- Mem: Am, W.Va. and Kanawha Co. Bar Asns; W.Va. State Bar; Am. Judicature Soc; AF&AM; Scottish Rite; York Rity; Beni Kedim Temple AAONMS; Royal Order of Jesters; Rotary. Rel: Presbyterian. Mailing Add: 1913 Woodside Circle, Charleston, W.Va. 25314.

TAYLOR, FRED MONROE R
b. Nampa, Idaho, 2/25/01; s. Robert F. Taylor and Pearl Christine T; m. 3/17/29 to Gwen E. McLeod; c. Jacqueline Rae and Marta Kaye. Educ: Univ. of Idaho, LL.B, 26; Phi Alpha Delta; Sigma Nu. Polit. & Govt. Pos: Prosecuting Attorney, Valley Co, Idaho, 27-33 & 35-38; Idaho State Sen, 43-51; City Attorney, Boise, Idaho, 44-45; U.S. Dist. Judge, Idaho, 54- Bus. & Prof. Pos: Pvt. law practice, Boise, 38- Mem: Idaho Bar Asn; Mason. Rel: Episcopal. Legal Res: 3607 Crescent Rim, Boise, Idaho 83704. Mailing Add: Federal Bldg, Boise, Idaho 83702.

TAYLOR, GENE R
Rep. Nat. Committeeman
b. Sarcoxie, Mo, 2/10/28; m. 1947 to Dorothy Wooldridge; c. Linda and Larry. Educ: Southwest Mo. State Col. Polit. & Govt. Pos: Former mayor, Sarcoxie, Mo; mem, Jasper Co. Rep. Cmt, 56, chmn, 58; chmn, Seventh Cong. Dist. Rep. Cmt, Rep. State Cmt, 62-; Rep. Nat. committeeman, currently; del, Rep. Nat. Conv, 68. Bus. & Prof. Pos: Automobile dealer. Mem: Sarcoxie C. of C; Mo. State C. of C; Scottish Rite; Shrine. Rel: Methodist. Mailing Add: P.O. Box 308, Sarcoxie, Mo. 64862.

TAYLOR, GEORGE B. D
Polit. & Govt. Pos: Ind. State Rep, 63-66. Bus. & Prof. Pos: Employee, Emge Packing Co, Ft. Branch, Ind. Mil. Serv: Marine Corps. Mem: V.pres, Gibson Co. Cent. Labor Union; VFW; Am. Legion; Local 172 United Packinghouse Workers of Am. Rel: Baptist. Mailing Add: RFD 3, Princeton, Ind. 47570.

TAYLOR, H. RALPH D
b. Somerville, Mass, 11/2/18; s. Louis Taylor and Freda Pearlson T; m. 11/18/45 to Henrietta Medalia; c. Allan B, Robert S. and David L. Educ: Harvard Univ, A.B, 39, M.P.A, 47; La. State Univ, M.A, 40. Polit. & Govt. Pos: Spec. asst. to dir, Mass. State Housing Bd, 48-51; dir, Somerville Housing Authority, 51-55; dir, New Haven Redevelop. Agency, Conn, 55-59; asst. secy. for model cities, U.S. Dept. Housing and Urban. Develop, 66-69. Bus. & Prof. Pos: Exec. v.pres, Renewal & Develop. Corp, 59-64; pres, Taylor-Hurley Assocs. and H.R. Taylor Mgt. Corp, 64-66; exec. v.pres, M.D-City Developers, Inc, Wash, D.C, currently. Mil. Serv: Entered as Pvt, Army, 41, released as S/Sgt, 45, after serv. in Italy. Mem: Nat. Asn. Housing & Redevelop velop. Off; Nat. Housing Conf. Rel: Jewish. Legal Res: Conn. Mailing Add: 608 Seventh St. S.W, Washington, D.C. 20024.

TAYLOR, HARRY GRANT R
Chmn, Macon Co. Rep. Cent. Cmt, Ill.
b. Flat Rock, Ill, 9/20/08; s. Ulysses Grant Taylor and Lena Gillespie T; m. 2/16/33 to Marion Gambrel; c. Jeffrey and Jack. Educ: James Millikin Univ, A.B, 30; Delta Sigma Phi; Kappa Phi Kappa; Alpha Omega. Polit. & Govt. Pos: Precinct committeeman, Rep. Party, Ill, 34-; chmn, Macon Co. Rep. Cent. Cmt, 48-; pres, Ill. Rep. Co. Chmn. Asn, 59-; del, Rep. Nat. Conv, 68. Bus. & Prof. Pos: Pres, Decatur Warehouse Co, Inc, 30- Mem: Elks. Rel: Presbyterian. Mailing Add: 1340 W. Wood St, Decatur, Ill. 62522.

TAYLOR, HERBERT J. D
N.Mex. State Sen.
b. 1931. Educ: Univ. of N.Mex; plus 132 hours in geol; Kappa Sigma. Polit. & Govt. Pos: N.Mex. State Rep, until 67; N.Mex. State Sen, 67- Bus. & Prof. Pos: Gasoline wholesaler. Mil. Serv: Marine Corps. Mem: C. of C; Red Cross Disaster chmn; Elks. Rel: Episcopal. Mailing Add: 1602 Linda Dr, Gallup, N.Mex. 87301. (1967)

TAYLOR, HERMAN WARD 'POP' D
N.C. State Rep.
b. Magnolia, N.C, 6/6/00; s. Maj. Bayard Taylor and Mary Vance Ward T; m. 8/24/29 to Ruth Vernon Eborn; c. Charlotte Vance (Mrs. John Hardin Best) and Herman Ward, Jr. Educ: N.C. State Univ, B.S. in Agr. Educ, 26 and M.S. in Agronomy, 27; Alpha Zeta; Phi Kappa Phi. Polit. & Govt. Pos: Chmn, N.C. Emergency Econ. Stabilization Task Group, 66-67; N.C. State Rep, Wake Co, N.C, 68- Bus. & Prof. Pos: Substitute for prof. on leave, N.C. Agr. Exp. Sta, Raleigh, N.C, 27; mem. staff, Pa. Salt Mfg. Co, S.W. Ga, 28; with fed-state fruit and vegetable inspection serv, 28; asst. farm agent, Beaufort Co, N.C, 28; farm agent, Edgecombe Co, 29-34; sr. economist, Agr. Adjust. Admin, U.S. Dept. of Agr, 34-35; swine exten. specialist, N.C. State Univ, 35-40 and mkt. specialist, 40-42; dir. of alumni affairs and secy, N.C. State Univ. Alumni Asn, 42-65; Retired 65; lobbyist before N.C. Gen. Assembly, N.C. Fertilizer Mfrs. Asn, 67. Mil. Serv: Pvt, Army, 18, with serv. in Students Army Training Corps; 2nd Lt, Army Res, 26-31. Publ: Ed. and historian, A History of Alfred and Elizabeth Robinson Ward, Their Antecedents and Descendents, 45; co-auth, A Legend in Stone, 65; ed, N.C. State Alumni News, 42-65. Mem: Wake Co. Retired Citizens Asn; Nat. Asn. of Retired Civil Employees; Citizens Law and Order Crusade; Protestants and Other Am. United for Separation of Church and State; Nat. Geog. Soc; Student Aid Asn; life and contributing mem, N.C. State Univ. Alumni Asn; Cary Dog House Club; Royal and Ancient Order of Hopping Fleas; life mem, N.C. Sheriff's Asn; Alderman Hist. Asn. (pres, 67-, past pres. and secy). N.C. Chap. of Alpha Zeta named chap. room, 'Pop' Taylor Room, 52; mem. cmt, Z. Smith Reynolds Found. to Build N.C. State Univ. Faculty Club; Recognition Dinner Honoring H.W. 'Pop' Taylor, N.C. State Col, 65. Rel: Methodist; Served on off. bd. of Magnolia, St. James, Tarboro, Edenton St. and Fairmont, Raleigh Methodist churches; past pres, Edenton St. Men's Bible Class; pres, Fairmont Church Wesley Bible Class. 3 years; mem. off. bd. and finance cmt. and pres, Methodist Men, United Fairmont Methodist Church, currently. Mailing Add: 2820 Bedford Ave, Raleigh, N.C. 27607.

TAYLOR, HERSCHEL KENNETH D
Mem, Exec. Cmt, Rowan Co. Dem. Party, Ky.
b. Barterville, Ky, 6/22/28; s. Spencer Taylor and Edith Sparks T; m. 12/2/49 to Audrey Pearl Rayburn; c. Herschel Kenneth, Jr. and Steven Douglas. Educ: East. Ky. State Univ, 1 year. Polit. & Govt. Pos: Active in every state, local and nat. political campaign, 55-, chmn, finance chmn, 55-; del, Dem. Nat. Conv, 68; mem. exec. cmt, Rowan Co. Dem. Party, Ky, 69- Bus. & Prof. Pos: Pres, Rowan Motor Sales, Inc, 51-; partner, TWS Co, 64-; secy, Cadth, Inc, 68- Mem: Morehead C. of C.(pres, 55 & 66); Mason. Rel: Protestant. Mailing Add: 425 W. Main St, Morehead, Ky. 40351.

TAYLOR, HIRAM BROGDEN D
b. Andalusia, Ala, 4/8/12; s. W. Mallie Taylor and Icy Della Dauphin T; m. to Joyce Hatton; c. Betty Joan (Mrs. Phillip M. Trew), Hiram Brogden, Jr. Educ: Attended sch. in Sanford and Opp. Polit. & Govt. Pos: Ala. State Sen, 63-66; Ala. State Rep, 55-63; mem. City Coun, 48-52. Bus. & Prof. Pos: Ins. and automobile bus. at Georgiana, 39- Mem: Mason; Eastern Star; Butler Cty. Conserv. Club; Kiwanis Club. Rel: Methodist. Mailing Add: Box 278, Georgiana, Ala. 36033. (1967)

TAYLOR, HOBART, JR. D
b. Texarkana, Tex, 12/17/20; s. Hobart Taylor, Sr. and Charlotte Wallace T; m. 1/21/51 to Lynnette Dobbins; c. Albert and Hobart, III. Educ: Prairie View State Col, A.B, 39; Howard Univ, A.M, 41; Univ. Mich, LL.B, 43; Omega Psi Phi. Polit. & Govt. Pos: Research asst, Mich. Supreme Court, 44-45; asst. prosecuting attorney, Wayne Co, Mich, 49-50, corp. counsel, 51-61; spec. counsel, President's Cmt. Equal Employ. Opportunity, 61-62, exec. v.chmn, 62-65; spec. asst. to V.President of U.S., 62-63; assoc. counsel, President of the U.S, 64-65; dir, Export-Import Bank of U.S, 65-68. Bus. & Prof. Pos: Jr. partner, Bledsoe & Taylor, 45-48; sr. mem, Taylor, Patrick, Bailer & Lee, 58-61; pres, Beneficial Life Ins. Soc, 59-61; partner, Dawson, Quinn, Riddell, Taylor & Davis, D.C, 68-; dir, Realty Equities Corp, currently. Mem: Fed, Am, Mich. and Detroit Bar Asns; Econ. Club of Detroit; Nat. Lawyers Club; Detroit Press Club; Int. Club. Rel: Unitarian. Legal Res: Detroit, Mich. Mailing Add: 723 Washington Bldg, Washington, D.C. 20005.

TAYLOR, HOWARD EZRA R
b. Barton, Vt, 11/13/01; m. to Mary Wheeler; c. one daughter. Educ: Albany schs. Polit. & Govt. Pos: Vt. State Rep, 59-66. Bus. & Prof. Pos: Tourist bus. Mem: Elks; pres, Willoughby Lake Trout Club, 5 years. Rel: Catholic. Mailing Add: R.F.D. 2, Box 125, Orleans, Vt. 05860. (1967)

TAYLOR, HOYT PATRICK, JR. D
Lt. Gov. of N.C.
b. Wadesboro, N.C, 4/1/24; s. H.P. Taylor and Inez Wooten T; m. 3/17/51 to Elizabeth Lockhart; c. Elizabeth Ann, Hoyt Patrick III and Adam Lockhart. Educ: Univ. N.C, B.S, 45, Law Sch, LL.B, 48; Phi Gamma Delta; Delta Sigma Pi; Phi Delta Phi. Polit. & Govt. Pos: Mem, Young Dem; N.C. State Rep, 55-66, Speaker, N.C. State House of Rep, 65-66; Lt. Gov. of N.C, 69- Bus. & Prof. Pos: Lawyer. Mil. Serv: Marine Corps, 45-46, 51-52, 1st Lt. Rel: Methodist. Mailing Add: Wadesboro, N.C. 28170.

TAYLOR, JAMES M. R
b. Pleasant Hill, Mo, 11/30/20; m. 7/23/45 to Bettye Jo Carter; c. Bruce J, Mark S. and Candace Jo. Educ: Kans. City, Mo. Pub. Schs. Polit. & Govt. Pos: Mo. State Sen, 62-67. Bus. & Prof. Pos: Sales pos. with Equitable Life Assurance Soc. of the U.S, 45-; pres, East. Jackson Co. Jr. Achievement, 67-68; pres, Raytown C. of C, 68; pres, Raytown Hist. Soc, 69. Mil. Serv: Air Force, Capt, 2 1/2 years; 6 months with 15th Air Force in Italy as navigator. Mem: Shrine and prerequisite bodies of York Rite Masonry; charter mem, Raytown Rotary Club; Independence C. of C. Rel: Christian Church. Mailing Add: 6201 Lane, Raytown, Mo. 64133.

TAYLOR, JEANNE M. D
b. Lincoln, Nebr, 10/6/26; d. John M. Moon (deceased) and Almeda Crawford M. (deceased); m. 12/28/49 to Samuel Clayton Taylor, M.D; c. John S, Daniel M, Sarah L, Martha E. and Andrew C. Educ: Doane Col, Crete, Nebr, 4 years. Polit. & Govt. Pos: Chmn, Canyon Co. Citizens for Kennedy, Idaho, 60; del, Dem. Nat. Conv, 68; precinct committeewoman, Canyon Co, Idaho, 68-; mem, Rules and Credentials Cmt, Dem. Party of Idaho, 69. Mem: Idaho and Southwest Medical Auxiliaries; Nampa Commun. Scholarship Cmt; PTA. Rel: Episcopal. Mailing Add: 1629 Park Ave, Nampa, Idaho 83651.

TAYLOR, JOHN D
b. Salem, Ohio, 5/4/97; s. Ralph Day Taylor and Sarah Brown T; m. 10/19/16 to Lena Catherine Howell; c. John, Jr. Polit. & Govt. Pos: Mem, Columbiana Co. Dem. Exec. Cmt, Ohio, 33-58; Ohio State Sen, 37-38; chmn, Dem. State Conv, 38; mem, Ohio Cmt. for Interstate Coop, 39-41; chmn, Salem, Ohio Dem. Cmt, 40-50; v.chmn, Ohio Little Hoover Cmn, 50-54; Dem. nominee for Lt. Gov. of Ohio, 56; del-at-lg, Dem. Nat. Conv, 60 & 64; mem, Salem, Ohio Charter Cmn, 62-63. Bus. & Prof. Pos: Printer apprentice, Farm & Dairy, Salem News, 12-17; monotype typesetter, Am. Mag, 17-18; rep, Lanston Monotype Co, 19-26; self-employed, Graphic Arts Prod. Develop. & Direct Mail Advert. Consult, 27-65; dir, Printing Indust. of Ohio, 40-

50. Mil. Serv: Serv. as Am. Red Cross Field Dir. attached to Army, Ft. Benning, 43-44. Publ: Manual on Sales Letter Writing, Direct Mail Advert, 64; 'Church Fund Raising,' Church Mgt, 34; 'Direct Mail and Political Campaign,' The Reporter of Direct Mail Advert, 4/66. Mem: Mason. Typographical Achievements: Keepsake book, gift to President of U.S. from State of Fla; Orationes for Cath. Church, Papal Apostolic Blessing. Rel: Episcopal. Legal Res: State Route 558, R.D. 3, Box 26, Salem, Ohio 44460. Mailing Add: Apt. 7B-4848 N.E. 23rd Ave, Ft. Lauderdale, Fla. 33308.

TAYLOR, JOHN EARL D
b. Bland Co, Va, 2/7/18; s. Joseph Taylor and Cora Combs T; m. 3/17/43 to Evelyn; c. Robert, Carol (Mrs. Carl Briggs) and Beverly. Educ: Hollybrook High Sch. Polit. & Govt. Pos: Dem. Precinct Cmt; Chmn, Clinton Co. Dem. Party, 56-69. Bus. & Prof. Pos: Service Station Operator, Standard Oil Co, 59-68. Mil. Serv: Entered as Pvt, Army, 41, released as T/Sgt, 45, after serv. in Ord. Corp, Asiatic Pac, 45 and ETO, 6 months. Mem: Operating Engrs; VFW; Moose; Eagles. Rel: Protestant. Mailing Add: 622 Fourth Ave. S, Clinton, Iowa 52732.

TAYLOR, JULIAN A. D
b. Hertford, N.C, 5/14/02; s. William A. Taylor and Roberta Fortune T; m. 1932 to Margaret P. Morris; c. Mauryne E, Doris R, Jewelle A, Julian A, Jr, Shirlee A. and Patricia R. Educ: Howard Univ; Columbia Univ; Univ. Chicago. Polit. & Govt. Pos: Chmn, Ansonia Munic. Planning Cmn, 56-; hearing examiner, Conn. Civil Rights Cmn, 58-; consult, Sen. Abraham Ribicoff, 64-; del-at-lg, Dem. Nat. Conv, 60 & 64. Bus. & Prof. Pos: Pastor, Macedonia Baptist Church, 38- Mem: Pres, Conn. Baptist Missionary Conv, 55-, Lower Naugatuck NAACP, 42- and N.Eng. Baptist Training Union Conv, 50-; v.pres, Nat. Baptist Conv, U.S.A, Inc, 55-; James F. Wilkens F&AAMPHA and New Haven Consistory F&AAPMPHA; bd. dir, Conn. State Reformatory; exec. bd, Conn. Coun. Churches. Rel: Baptist. Mailing Add: 133 W. Park Ave, New Haven, Conn. 06511.

TAYLOR, LUCAS PARNELL R
b. Huntingdon, Tenn, 4/17/11; s. James Lucas Taylor and Lola Routon T; m. 1943 to Christine Crawley; c. Robert Lucas and James Vincent. Educ: High sch. and bus. educ. Polit. & Govt. Pos: Chmn, Carroll Co. Rep. Party, Tenn, until 67; cmnr, Carroll Co, 53-54; co. mgr. for Rep. Julian Hurst; treas, sch. bd. Bus. & Prof. Pos: Owner, Taylor Pontiac Co, Huntingdon, Tenn, 47- Mil. Serv: Entered Army, 41, released as Cpl. Mem: Elks; Rotary; Mason. Rel: Methodist. Mailing Add: Northwood Dr, Huntingdon, Tenn. 38344. (1967)

TAYLOR, GEN. MAXWELL DAVENPORT, U.S.A. (RET.)
Chmn, President's For. Intel. Adv. Bd.
b. Keytesville, Mo, 8/26/01; s. John Earle Maxwell Taylor and Pearle Davenport T; m. 1/26/25 to Lydia Gardner Happer; c. John Maxwell and Thomas Happer. Educ: U.S. Mil. Acad, B.S, 22; Engr. Sch, 22-23; Field Artil. Sch, 32-33; Command and Gen. Staff Sch, 33-35; Army War Col, 39-40. Hon. D.Eng, N.Y. Univ, 46; LL.D, Bowdoin Col, 48, Univ. Mo, 51, Williams Col, 52, Pa. Mil. Col, Trinity Col. and Yale Univ, 56, The Citadel, 59 and Phillips; other hon. degrees from Lafayette Col, 56, Seoul Univ, 58 and Univ. Pittsburgh, 62. Polit. & Govt. Pos: Instr. French and Spanish, U.S. Mil. Acad, 27-32; studied Japanese lang. in Tokyo, 35-39; asst. mil. attache, Peking, 39; spec. mission to Latin Am. Countries, 40; chief of staff and artil. comdr, 82nd Airborne Div, 42; div. comdr, 101st Airborne Div, Sicilian and Ital. Campaigns, 43-44, West. Front, 44-45; supt, Mil. Acad, 45-49; chief of staff, Am. Forces in Europe, 49; comdr, Am. Mil. Govt, Army Forces, Berlin, 49-51; dep. chief of staff opers. and admin. of Army, 51-53; comdr, Eighth Army, Korea, 53; comdr, Army Forces, Far East, 54; U.S. and UN comdr, Far East, 55; Chief of Staff, Army, 55-59; chmn. bd, chief exec. officer and dir, Mex. Light & Power Co, 59-60; mil. rep. to President of U.S, 61-62; chmn, Joint Chiefs of Staff, 62-64; U.S. Ambassador to South Vietnam, 64-65; spec. consult. to President of U.S, 65-; chmn, President's For. Intel. Adv. Bd, currently. Honors and Decorations: Silver Star with Oak Leaf Cluster; Distinguished Serv. Cross; Distinguished Serv. Medal with Two Oak Leaf Clusters; Legion of Merit; Bronze Star; Purple Heart; Unit Citation; Hon. Knight Comdr, Order Brit. Empire; Hon. Companion, Order of Bath (mil. div) and Distinguished Serv. Order, Eng; Comdr, Legion of Honor and Croix de Guerre with Palm, France; Cross of Grand Officer, Order of Leopold, Order of Crown with Palm and Grand Officer, Croix de Guerre with Palm, Belgium; Order Mil. Merit First Class, Mex; Chief Comdr, Legion of Honor, P.I; Grand Officer, Order of Boyaca, Columbia; Taeguk Distinguished Mil. Serv. Medal, First and Second Awards, Repub. of Korea; Grand Officer, Order of Mil. Merit, Brazel; Comdr, Mil. Order of Ayacucho, Peru; Cloud and Banner Medal with Grand Cordon, China; Comdr, Mil. Order of Italy; Grand Off. Order of Mil. Merit, Italy; Militaire Willems-Orde, Fourth Class, Netherlands; Thai Most Noble Order of the Crown of Thailand, First Class; Cordon of Trinity Medal with Plaque, Ethiopia; Higher Comdr. Cross, Order of George the First, Greece. Publ: Uncertain Trumpet, 60. Mem: Pres, Lincoln Center for Performing Arts, 61; Univ. Club; River Club, N.Y.C; Chevy Chase Club; Army-Navy Club. Rel: Protestant. Legal Res: 3505 Chevy Chase Lake Dr, Chevy Chase, Md. 20015. Mailing Add: The White House Office, Washington, D.C. 20500.

TAYLOR, MYRON CHARLES R
Secy. and Treas, Hancock Rep. Town Cmt, Vt.
b. Whiting, Vt, 10/24/96; single. Educ: State Sch. of Agr, 16. Polit. & Govt. Pos: Justice of the Peace, Overseer of the Poor; town clerk and treas, Hancock, Vt, 47-; secy. and treas, Hancock Rep. Town Cmt, 48-; Vt. State Rep, 53-60 & 62-66. Bus. & Prof. Pos: Retired from the plywood co. in Hancock, 61. Rel: Methodist. Mailing Add: Box 46, Hancock, Vt. 05748.

TAYLOR, NELSON WHITFORD, III D
b. Beaufort, N.C, 8/17/28; s. Bayard Taylor and Jean Thackston T; m. 6/9/51 to Nancy Frazier Derrickson; c. Walter Derrickson, Nelson W, IV, and Bayard Beckwith. Educ: The Citadel, 45-47; Univ. of N.C, A.B, 49, Law Sch, J.D, 55; Delta Theta Phi; Theta Chi. Polit. & Govt. Pos: N.C. State Rep, Third Dist, 67-68. Bus. & Prof. Pos: Attorney and counsr. at law, Beaufort, N.C, currently. Mil. Serv: Entered as Ens, Navy, 51, released Lt.(jg), 54; ETO Ribbon; Good Conduct Medal. Publ: 'Net Worth Method in Tax Fraud Prosecutions, N.C. Law Rev, 54. Mem: Am. and N.C. Bar Asns; Am. Trial Lawyers Asn; N.C. Acad. of Trial Lawyers; Elks; Am. Nat. Red Cross. Rel: Episcopal. Legal Res: 2001 Shepard St, Morehead City, N.C. 28557. Mailing Add: P.O. Box 180, Beaufort, N.C. 28516.

TAYLOR, NORMAN COLLINS R
b. Lowell, Mass, 10/29/23; s. Ralph G. Taylor and Mildred Collins T; m. 7/8/50 to Adele Stemmler; c. Daniel C, Andrew S, Samuel E, and Martha E. Educ: Brown Univ, B.S. in Eng. Polit. & Govt. Pos: Chmn, Woodbury Rep. Town Cmt, Conn, until 68. Mil. Serv: Entered as Ens, Navy, 42, released as Lt, 46, after serv. in Asian Theatre. Rel: Congregational. Mailing Add: School St, Woodbury, Conn. 06798. (1967)

TAYLOR, OWEN BARNEY D
Chmn, Nowata Co. Dem. Party, Okla.
b. Sallisaw, Okla, 11/19/12; s. Sam Taylor and Janie Barnett T; m. 12/23/39 to Velma Griffiths; c. Brenda (Mrs. Mel Martin), Gwen (Mrs. Herman Edwards), Barney Delano and Stratton. Educ: Northeast State Col, B.S, 46; Okla. State Univ, M.S, 57. Polit. & Govt. Pos: Okla. State Rep, Sequoyah Co, 45-51; Supt. of Co. Schs, Sequoyah Co, Okla, 59-62 and Nowata Co, 68-69; del, Dem. Nat. Conv, 68; chmn, Nowata Co. Dem. Party, 68- Mem: Lions; Am. Teachers Asn, Okla. Rel: Baptist. Mailing Add: Box 55, Alluwe, Okla. 74049.

TAYLOR, PAUL REED R
b. Benton, N. Y, 4/26/05; m. to Mary H. Hall Yates; c. Daniel R, Jane E. Reeder. Educ: Hamilton Col, AB; Yale Univ, LL.B. Polit. & Govt. Pos: N.Y. State Assemblyman (from Yates Co) 58-66, (from Monroe Co) 34-35. Bus. & Prof. Pos: Attorney. Mem: Yates Co, N. Y. State and Am. Bar Asns; Asn. of the Bar of the City of N. Y; Grange; Farm Bur. Rel: First Presbyterian Church of Penn Yan. Mailing Add: 342 Main St, Penn Yan, N. Y. 14527. (1967)

TAYLOR, PAUL WORDEN, JR. R
Chmn, Indian River Co. Rep. Exec. Cmt, Fla.
b. Poughkeepsie, N.Y, 2/6/28; s. Paul Worden Taylor and Margaret Vandewater T; m. 11/25/50 to Barbara Jane Nodine; c. Kristen Lee, Paul Worden, III and Donald Nodine. Educ: Amherst Col, B.A, 48; Univ. Rochester Grad. Sch, M.S. in Bact, 51; Univ. Rochester Sch. Med. & Dent, M.D, 53; Phi Beta Kappa; Sphinx-Amherst. Polit. & Govt. Pos: Pres, Young Rep. Club. Indian River Co, Fla, 64, secy, 65; Rep. precinct committeeman, Indian River Co, 65; chmn, Indian River Co. Rep. Exec. Cmt, 66-; trustee, Indian River Co. Hosp. Dist, 69- Bus. & Prof. Pos: Vice chief staff, Indian River Mem. Hosp. Staff, 66, 67, chief of staff, 68. Mil. Serv: Entered as 1st Lt, Air Force, 55, released as Capt, 57, after serv. in 4455th Air Force Hosp, Donaldson Air Force Base, Greenville, S.C. Publ: 4 articles in Medical Literature. Mem: Pres, Beachland Sch. PTA, 61-62; fel, Am. Col. Surgeons; Am. Med. Asn; Fla. Med. Asn; Indian River Co. Med. Soc; Am. Col. Obstetricians-Gynecologists; Fla. Obstet. and Gynec. Soc; South. Med. Asn; Rotary. Rel: Methodist. Mailing Add: 3805 Indian River Dr, Vero Beach, Fla. 32960.

TAYLOR, RANDALL ALFORD D
b. Huntington, W.Va, 10/17/28; s. Thomas H. Taylor and Betty Elizabeth Roby T; m. 10/17/52 to Reba Jane Ellis; c. Sheila Jane. Educ: Marshall Univ; Palmer Col. of Chiropractic. Polit. & Govt. Pos: Councilman, Point Pleasant, W.Va, 61-63; W.Va. State Sen, 64-68. Bus. & Prof. Pos: Chiropractor. Mem: Mason; Odd Fellows; W.Va. Chiropractic Soc, Inc; W.Va. Hist. Soc; Mason Co. C. of C; chap. chmn, Mason Co. Polio Found; pres, W.Va. Chiropractor's Soc, Inc. Named Chiropractor of the year in W.Va, 61. Rel: Methodist. Mailing Add: 715 Main St, Point Pleasant, W.Va. 25550.

TAYLOR, RICHARD 'DICK' D
b. Everett, Wash, 1918; m. to Irene T; c. three. Educ: St. Martin's Col, grad; Stanford Univ. Polit. & Govt. Pos: Wash. State Rep, third term, until 68. Bus. & Prof. Pos: Operator, sporting goods store. Mem: Elks. Mailing Add: 721 Fifth St, Mukileto, Wash. 98275. (1967)

TAYLOR, PHILIP RAYMOND D
Chmn, Bibb Co. Dem. Exec. Cmt, Ga.
b. Dublin, Ga, 11/1/33; s. Evan Augustus Taylor and Eula Bush T; m. 10/21/61 to Elizabeth Lester; c. Emily Elaine and Lester Leigh. Educ: Mercer Univ, A.B, 55, Walter F. George Sch. Law, LL.B, 57; Blue Key; Kappa Alpha Order. Polit. & Govt. Pos: Ga. State Rep, Bibb Co, 61-62; Ga. State Co-chmn, Young Citizens for Johnson Presidential Campaign, 64; alternate del, Dem. Nat. Conv, 64; chmn, Bibb Co. Dem. Exec. Cmt, 67-; mem. subcmt. on reorgn, and cmt. selec. del. to nat. conv, Ga. State Dem. Party, 69-; elec. supt, Bibb Co. Gen. Elec. Bus. & Prof. Pos: Ed. bd, Mercer Law Rev, 55-57; partner, Law Firm, Harris, Russell & Watkins, Macon, 60- Mil. Serv: Army, 57-58, Pvt, Ga. Nat. Guard, 59-66, Capt, Judge Adv. Gen. Corps. Publ: 'Contracts - Communications of Acceptance-when Effective (case note),' 55 and 'Torts-Liability of Contracts,' 57, Mercer Law Rev. Mem: Am. and Ga. Bar Asns; Macon Bar Asn.(pres, 66); C. of C; Elks; Macon C. of C.(cmt. state and local govt); Kappa Alpha Order Alumni Asn.(past pres). Rel: Episcopal. Legal Res: 690 Malvern Hill Dr, Macon, Ga. 31204. Mailing Add: 1200 Georgia Power Bldg, Macon, Ga. 31201.

TAYLOR, ROBERT CAMPBELL D
b. Princeton, Ky, 8/8/30; s. Rumsey Barnes Taylor and Eleanor Hayes C; m. 6/16/56 to Sarah Robinson Sharp; c. Robert Campbell, Jr, Vernon Sharp, Harrison Hayes and Douglas Robinson. Educ: Vanderbilt Univ, A.B, 52, Law Sch, LL.B, 55; Omicron Delta Kappa; Phi Delta Phi; Sigma Alpha Epsilon. Polit. & Govt. Pos: Law clerk, Ky. Court of Appeals, 55-56; Tenn. State Rep, 59-60; Tenn. State Sen, 61-66; co-mgr, Buford Ellington Gubernatorial Campaign, Tenn, 66; mem, Libr. and Arch. Cmn, State of Tenn, 67-; alternate del, Dem. Nat. Conv, 68. Bus. & Prof. Pos: Assoc, Trabue-Sturdivant-Harbison, 56-62; partner, Trabue-Minick-Sturdivant-Harbison, 62-65, Taylor & Schlater, 65- Mem: Nashville, Tenn. and Am. Bar Asns; Am. Trial Lawyers Asn; Tenn. Hosp. Asn. Distinguished Serv. Awards, Jaycees, 58, Tenn. Hosp. Asn. and Tenn. Conserv. League, 65; Nashville Young Man of the Year, 58. Rel: Baptist. Legal Res: 2140 Chickering Lane, Nashville, Tenn. 37219. Mailing Add: Life and Casualty Tower, Nashville, Tenn. 37219.

TAYLOR, ROY A. D
U.S. Rep, N.C.
b. Vader, Wash, 1/31/10; s. Arthur A. Taylor and Lola Morgan T; m. 5/8/32

to Evelyn Reeves; c. Alan and Toni. Educ: Asheville-Biltmore Col, 29; Maryville Col, B.A, 31; Asheville Univ. Law Sch, 36. Polit. & Govt. Pos: N.C. State Rep, 47-53; co. attorney, Buncombe Co, N.C, 49-60; U.S. Rep, N.C, 60- Mil. Serv: Entered as Lt.(jg), Navy, 43, released as Lt, 46, after serv. as Comdr, Landing Ship, Tank, Pac. Theater, 44-45. Mem: Dist. Gov, Lions, 52. Rel: Baptist. Legal Res: 110 Connally St, Black Mountain, N.C. 28711. Mailing Add: 2453 Rayburn House Office Bldg, Washington, D.C. 20515.

TAYLOR, SAM GUTHRIE D
Chmn, Burnet Co. Dem. Party, Tex.
b. Bertram, Tex, 7/3/07; s. Sam Houston Taylor and Willie Guthrie T; m. 11/25/31 to Sarah Elizabeth McFadin; c. Billy Ira. Educ: Southwestern Univ, 25-27; Tex. Univ, B.B.A, 29; Pi Kappa Alpha. Polit. & Govt. Pos: Chmn, Burnet Co. Dem. Party, Tex, 44- Bus. & Prof. Pos: Partner and mgr, S.H. Taylor Hardware and S.H. Taylor Ranch, 36-; v.pres, Pedernales Elec. Coop, 45- Mem: Mason; Lions; Farmers Union. Hon. Lone Star Farmers Degree, Future Farmers of Am. Rel: Baptist. Mailing Add: P.O. Box 237, Bertram, Tex. 78605.

TAYLOR, SELWYN HART D
Chmn, Ward Three Dem. Party, N.H.
b. Rumford, Maine, 10/12/26; s. Nathaniel Taylor and Blanche Hart T; m. 6/6/48 to Lois Edith Baker; c. Leslie Jane and Deborah Lee. Educ: Univ. Mass, B.S, 51. Polit. & Govt. Pos: Alternate del, Dem. Nat. Conv, 68; chmn, Ward 3 Dem. Party, N.H, 68- Bus. & Prof. Pos: Mem. staff, United Airlines, Chicago, Ill, 54-60, programmer, Denver, Colo, 60-65; sr. software engr, Sanders Assocs, Nashua, N.H, 65- Mil. Serv: Entered as A/S, Navy, 44, released as Qm. 2/C, 47, after serv. in Pac. Theatre, 45-46; World War II Victory Medal; Am. Area Campaign Medal; Asiatic-Pac. Campaign Medal with One Star. Mem: Asn. for Computer Machinery. Rel: Unitarian-Universalist. Mailing Add: 20 Lock St, Nashua, N.H. 03060.

TAYLOR, VAN B. D
b. Boles, Ark, 7/22/36; s. Claud E. Taylor and Flo Brazil T; m. 3/7/59 to Judy N. Hood; c. Robert Glenn, Toni Denise and David Riley. Educ: Ark. Tech, Russellville; Ark. Law Sch, Little Rock. Polit. & Govt. Pos: Dep. prosecuting attorney, 63; Ark. State Rep, 65-68. Mem: Jr. C. of C; Farm Bur; Ark. and Am. Bar Asns. Rel: Methodist. Mailing Add: Box 447, Waldron, Ark. 72958. (1967)

TAYLOR, VIRGINIA WILLETT R
Mem, Calif. Rep. State Cent. Cmt.
b. Atascadero, Calif, 1/23/26; d. Oscar Louis Willett and Georgetta Pemberton W; m. 1/6/45 to Wayne Grensted Taylor; c. Sandra Lee (Mrs. Ronald L. Webb), Georgia Ann, Marsha Gail and Anita Jeanne. Educ: Redlands Univ, 43-44; Univ. Calif, Berkeley, 44-45; Mex. City Col, 51-52; San Diego Mesa Col, 69; Alpha Tau Delta; Alpha Epsilon Delta. Polit. & Govt. Pos: Field secy, 36th Cong. Dist, San Diego Co. Rep. Cent. Cmt, Calif, 62 & 63; co-chmn, Elec. Anal. Cmt, Rep. Assocs, 63-65; treas, Oak Park Federated Rep. Women's Club, 64-65; mem, Calif. Rep. State Cent. Cmt, 64-66 & 68-, research analyst, 65; pres, San Diego City and Co. War Against Litter Cmt, Inc, 66-68; chmn, 200th Anniversary Rubbish Roundup, San Diego, 68; chmn, exec. cmt, Tom Hom for 79th Assembly Dist, 68; chmn, 200th Anniversary Hist. Souvenirs and Mementoes, 68-69; pres, North Park Rep. Assembly, 69-; mem, San Diego Co. Rep. Cent. Cmt, 69- Bus. & Prof. Pos: Secy. to dir, Dept. econ, Gen. Petroleum Corp, 48-49; secy. to eng. supvr, Tidewater Assoc. Oil Co, 54-56; steno clerk IV, San Diego Co. Pub. Adminstr. Div, Calif, 56-59, legal secy, 59-63; secy. to Ed. Herb Klein, The San Diego Union, 63-67. Mem: Budget rev. cmts, United Commun. Serv, 61-67; Rainbow Girls Parents Club; Burlingame Club; participant, Keep Am. Beautiful Conf, 67 & 69; initiator, San Diego Co. Environ. Quality Control Coun, 69. Presidential Citation, U.S. and Mex. Border Develop. Cmn, 68. Rel: Protestant. Mailing Add: 2520 San Marcos Ave, San Diego, Calif. 92104.

TAYLOR, WARREN A. D
b. Chehalis, Wash, 1891; married; c. Two; Eight grandchildren. Polit. & Govt. Pos: Alaska Territorial Rep, 33-35, 45-46, 49, 55 & 57; mem, Constitutional Conv. and Statehood Cmt; Alaska State Rep, 59-66. Bus. & Prof. Pos: Attorney-at-law, 27- Mem: Mason; Am. Bar Asn; Am. Judicature Soc; Am. Legion; Am. Trial Lawyers Asn. Mailing Add: P.O. Box 200, Fairbanks, Alaska, 99701.

TAYLOR, WILLIAM H. D
Polit. & Govt. Pos: Ind. State Sen, until 68. Bus. & Prof. Pos: Ins. agent. Mil. Serv: Navy. Mem: K. of C; Lions; Elks; C. of C; Am. Legion. Rel: Roman Catholic. Mailing Add: 2204 Southwest Rd, LaPorte, Ind. 46350. (1967)

TAYLOR, WILLIAM L. D
b. Brooklyn, N.Y, 10/4/31; s. Harry Taylor and Sarah Levine T; m. 6/20/54 to Harriet Rosen; c. Lauren R, Deborah L. and David S. Educ: Brooklyn Col, A.B. cum laude, 52; Yale Univ. Law Sch, LL.B, 54; Yale Law Sch. Grad. Bd. Polit. & Govt. Pos: Secy, President's Sub-Cabinet Cmt. on Civil Rights, 61-64; gen. counsel, asst. staff dir. and spec. asst. to Staff Dir, U.S. Cmn. on Civil Rights, 61-64, staff dir, 65-68; mem, President's Cmn. for the Observance of Int. Human Rights Year, 68. Bus. & Prof. Pos: Law clerk, Corp. Counsel of N.Y.C, 54; attorney, NAACP Legal Defense and Educ. Fund, Inc, 54-58; legis. rep, Americans for Dem. Action, 59-61; mem, Coun. on Community Affairs, Fed. Bar Asn, 68; sr. fel, Yale Law Sch, 68-69; lectr, Yale Col, 69. Mil. Serv: Entered as Pvt, Army, 56, released as Specialist 4/C, 58, after serv. as Adj. Gen, U.S. Publ: 'Are Minority Groups Getting Fair Treatment from Unions and Management?' Marquette Bus. Rev, Winter, 63; 'Civil Disobedience: Some Observations on the Strategies of Protest,' Legal Aspects of the Civil Rights Movement, Wayne State Univ. Press, 6/65; 'Federal Programs and Civil Rights,' The Community and Racial Crises, Practicing Law Inst, 66. Mem: Secy, Nat. Civil Liberties Clearing House, 60-61; nat. bd, Am. for Dem. Action, 63-65; Neighbors, Inc. Legal Res: 1325 Iris St. N.W, Washington, D.C. 20012. Mailing Add: 53 Edgemere Rd, Hamden, Conn. 06517.

TAYLOR, WILLIAM M. R
b. Thomasville, Ga, 5/11/23; s. Thomas H. Taylor and Evelyn Murphy T; m. 2/18/56 to Shirley Ann Warner; c. Erin Warner and William Bradford. Educ: Ariz. State Univ, B.S, 48; Ariz. State Univ. Athletic Scholarship; Delta Chi; Letterman's Club. Polit. & Govt. Pos: Mem, Young Rep. Club, Charlotte, N.C, 52; mem, Mechlenberg Co. Young Rep. Club, N.C; mem, Mechlenberg Co. Rep. Exec. Cmt, mem. finance cmt; precinct orgn. chmn, Rep. C. Raper Jonas, 54; mem. campaign cmt, Jonas for Cong, 56; participant, Eisenhower for Pres. Campaigns, 52 & 56; participant, various local Rep. cand. campaigns; mem, Duval Co. Rep. Exec. Cmt, Fla, mem, Duval Co. Rep. Men's Club; Duval Co. organizer, Floridians for Nixon-Lodge, 60, campaign mgr. and coordinator, Northeast Fla; mem, Duval Co. Young Rep. Club, chmn, 62; participant, Young Rep. Leadership Training Sch, Wash, D.C. 62; mem, Fla. Fed. Young Rep, 63-; del. to all state and nat. Young. Rep. Conv; adv, Young Rep. Trust Fund Cmt; mem. campaign cmt. to elect William F. Murfin chmn. of Rep. State Exec. Cmt. of Fla; co-chmn, Kirk Appreciation Dinner, 66; mem, Tom Slade Adv. Cmt, 66; chmn, Duval Co. Re-Registration Dr, 66; dist. finance chmn, Fla. State Rep. Exec. Cmt, 67; del, Rep. Nat. Conv, 68; host cmt. cand, Fla. House of Rep, dist. 24, 68. Bus. & Prof. Pos: Salesman, Bemis Bros. Bag Co, 48-54; agent, Jefferson Standard Life Ins. Co, 54-57; gen. agent, Manhattan Life Ins. Co, 57-64; supt. of agencies, Peninsular Life Ins. Co, 64-; v.pres, George Washington Life Ins. Co, 67; gen. agent, Provident Life & Accident Ins. Co, 67-; v.pres, W.H. Collings Co, Inc. Mil. Serv: Entered as A/S, Naval Res. with serv. in European and Asiatic Theatres; Commendation Ribbon; Qualified Submarine Badge; Submarine Combat Pin with Four Stars; Good Conduct Medal; Am, European and Asiatic Theatre Ribbons. Mem: Nat. Asn. of Life Underwriters; Northeast Fla. Estate Planning Coun; Sales and Marketing Executives of Jacksonville; Mason; Scottish Rite; Shrine. Rel: Methodist. Legal Res: 7660 Holiday Rd. S, Jacksonville, Fla. 32216. Mailing Add: 6565 Beach Blvd, Jacksonville, Fla. 32216.

TAYLOR, WILLIAM MERLE D
b. Seattle, Wash, 7/16/33; s. William Merle Taylor and Mary Elizabeth Hager T; m. 12/18/65 to Patricia Clair Allen; c. Jessup and Cory. Educ: Univ. South. Calif, B.A, 55, Gen. Secondary, 64; San Francisco Theol. Sem, B.D, 60; Phi Kappa Psi. Polit. & Govt. Pos: North. Calif. chmn, Citizens for Kennedy Campaign, 67-68; Marin Co. co-chmn, Robert Kennedy Primary, 68; del, Dem. Nat. Conv, 68; dir, Inst. for Polit-Cultural Dynamics, 69- Bus. & Prof. Pos: Minister, Presby. Church, 60-63; teacher, Reseda High Sch, 64-66; mgr. broker, Taylor, Tatum and Assocs, Mutual Funds, Life Ins, Calif, 66- Mil. Serv: Entered as 2nd Lt, Marines, 55, released as 1st Lt, 57, after serv. in Inf. and Track Coach, 1st Marine Div, Camp Pendleton, Calif, 56-57; former Capt. Res, 57-60. Publ: Numerous Columns Pacific Sun (newspaper), 68-69. Mem: Rotary, South. Calif. Track Alumni; San Francisco Theol. Sem. Alumni. Mem, 2 Nat'l Championship Track Teams, 54, 55; Capt, Univ. South. Calif. Cross Country Team, 54. Legal Res: 22 Woodside Court, San Anselmo, Calif. 94960. Mailing Add: 412 Red Hill Ave, San Anselmo, Calif. 94960.

TAYLOR, WILLIE MARGARET D
b. Canadian, Tex, 12/2/99; d. George Wesley Little and Hannah Eller L; m. 4/16/18 to Zack Taylor; c. Dick and Ruth. Educ: High Sch. Polit. & Govt. Pos: Chairwoman, Lea Co. Dem. Party, N.Mex, 56-66, mem, Dem. Cent. Cmt, 45-66; mem, N.Mex. State Dem. Cent. Cmt, 50-66; pres, Tatum Women's Club, 24 yrs. Mem: Am. Legion Auxiliary; Eastern Star. Rel: Methodist. Mailing Add: Box 205, Tatum, N.Mex. 88267. (1967)

TAYMOR, BETTY D
Committeewoman, State Dem. Cmt, Mass.
b. Baltimore, Md, 3/22/21; d. William Bernstein and Tillie Blum B; m. 6/7/42 to Melvin Lester Taymor; c. Michael, Laurie (Mrs. William Reed Beer) and Julie. Educ: Goucher Col, A.B, 42; Boston Univ. Grad. Sch, M.A. in Govt, 67. Polit. & Govt. Pos: Committeewoman, State Dem. Cmt, Mass, 56-, v.chmn, 65-68; del-at-lg, Dem. Nat. Conv, 60, 64 & 68 and mem, Platform Cmt, 68; mem, U.S. Nat. Cmn, UNESCO, 61- Bus. & Prof. Pos: Lectr, dept. govt, Simmons Col, 68-69; instr, dept. polit. sci, Northeast. Univ, currently. Awarded Elizabeth King Ellicott fel. from Goucher Col, 59 for develop. of polit. educ. for women in U.S. Rel: Jewish. Mailing Add: 44 Fairfax St, West Newton, Mass. 02165.

TAYOUN, JAMES JOSEPH D
Pa. State Rep.
b. Phila, Pa, 3/27/30; s. Solomon Tayoun and Nora Matter T; m. 1/4/68 to Dolores Michael; c. Yasmine, Nora, James, Jr, David and Paul. Educ: Villanova Univ, 47-48; Temple Univ, B.S. in Journalism, 51; Sigma Delta Chi. Polit. & Govt. Pos: Dem. leader, First Ward, Phila, Pa, 69-; Pa. State Rep, 183rd Legis. Dist, 69- Bus. & Prof. Pos: Owner, Mid. East Restaurant Inc, 59-; owner, Tayoun Bros, Inc, 67- Mil. Serv: Entered as Pvt, Army, 53, released as Sgt, 55, after serv. in Seventh Inf. Div, Korea, 54-55; Good Conduct Medal; Korean Serv. Ribbon; Presidential Unit Citations. Rel: Roman Catholic. Legal Res: 533 Morris St, Philadelphia, Pa. 19148. Mailing Add: 1011 Ellsworth St, Philadelphia, Pa. 19147.

TEAGARDEN, OSCAR LESLIE D
b. W.Va, 2/24/96; s. Jefferson Davis Teagarden and Ida Ash T; m. 7/18/18, wid; 2nd m. 8/21/63 to Mary Kathleen Hook; c. James L. and Rosemar (Mrs. Coleman). Educ: Marietta, Ohio. Polit. & Govt. Pos: Mayor, Oak Harbor, Ohio, 36-46; chmn, Ottawa Co. Dem. Cent. Cmt, 36-46; del, Dem. Nat. Conv, 68. Bus. & Prof. Pos: Pres, J. Weller Co, Oak Harbor, Ohio, 32-, Nat. Bank of Oak Harbor, 34- and Lake Erie Canning Co, Sandusky, 36-; v.chmn, Ohio Turnpike Cmn, 49- Mil. Serv: Entered as Pvt, 18, released as 2nd Lt. Mem: Elks; Boy Scout Coun; 4-H. Rel: Catholic. Mailing Add: 435 Church St, Oak Harbor, Ohio 43449. (1967)

TEAGUE, CHARLES McKEVETT R
U.S. Rep, Calif.
b. Santa Paula, Calif, 9/18/09; s. Charles Collins Teague and Harriet McKevett T; m. 4/27/29 to Marjorie Cowden; c. Norma (Mrs. James B. Potter, Jr), Alan McKevett and Judith (Mrs. Robert H. Kenyon). Educ: Stanford Univ. 31, Law Sch, 34; Beta Theta Pi; Phi Delta Phi. Polit. & Govt. Pos: U.S. Rep, 13th Dist, Calif, 55- Bus. & Prof. Pos: Attorney-at-Law, 34-35. Mil. Serv: Entered as 1st Lt, Army Air Corps, 42, released as Maj, 45; Army Air Corps Commendation. Mem: Rotary Int; Mil. Order of the World Wars; Capitol Hill Club. Rel: Protestant. Legal Res: Country Club Rd, Ojai, Calif. 93023. Mailing Add: 1414 Longworth House Office Bldg, Washington, D.C. 20515.

TEAGUE, CHARLES WOODROW D
b. Thomasville, N.C, 5/27/13; s. Lonnie Edwards Teague and Dora Mae Lassiter T; m. 10/14/39 to Jessie Perry; c. Kathy Randle, Penny Randle and Charles Woodrow, Jr. Educ: Waek Forest Col, Law Sch, LL.B, 34; Gamma Eta Gamma. Polit. & Govt. Pos: Chmn, Wake Co. Bd. of Elec, N.C, 60-64; chmn, Wake Co. Dem. Exec. Cmt, 64-68; del, Dem. Nat. Conv, 64 & 68. Bus. & Prof. Pos: Bd. of Gov, N.C. Bar Asn, 62-65; councilor, N.C. State Bar, 69- Mil. Serv: Entered as Lt.(jg), 42, released as Lt. Comdr, 46, after serv. in Pac; Pac. Theater Ribbon. Mem: Wake Co, N.C. and Am. Bar Asns; Am. Judicature Soc; Int. Asn. of Ins. Attorneys; Kiwanis; Raleigh C. of C; Carolina Country Club. Rel: Presbyterian. Legal Res: 3341 White Oak Rd, Raleigh, N.C. 27609. Mailing Add: 508 First Federal Bldg, Raleigh, N.C. 27602.

TEAGUE, ELMER WILSON D
b. Jasper, Ga, 10/28/23; s. Francis M. Teague and Sara Pettiegrew T; m. 9/19/42 to Willie Grace Blackwell; c. Larry Donald, Glenn Allen. Educ: Canton High Sch. and Dawsonville High Sch. Polit. & Govt. Pos: Ga. State Rep, 61-66. Bus. & Prof. Pos: Automobile dealer. Mil. Serv: U.S. Army, WW II, 43-46; 3 Battle Stars, ETO. Mem: Elks. Rel: Baptist. Mailing Add: Marietta, Ga. 30060. (1967)

TEAGUE, OLIN E. D
U.S. Rep, Tex.
m. to Freddie Dunman; c. James M, John O. and Jill Virginia. Educ: Tex. Agr. and Mech. Col, 28-32. Polit. & Govt. Pos: U.S. Rep, Tex, 46-, chmn, Vet. Affairs Cmt. and Subcmt. Manned Space Flight, U.S. House Rep; mem, Bd. of Visitors, U.S. Mil. Acad, 55- Bus. & Prof. Pos: Employee, Post Office, Animal Husbandry Dept, Tex. Agr. and Mech. Col. and R.R. Mil. Serv: Nat. Guard, 3 years; entered as 2nd Lt, Army, 40, released as Col, 46, after serv. in Inf, commanded First Bn, 314th Inf, 79th Div; decorated 11 times; Silver Star with two clusters; Bronze Star with two clusters; Purple Heart with two clusters; Combat Infantryman's Badge; Army Commendation Ribbon; French Croix de Guerre with Palm. Authored and sponsored the Korean War Vet. Bill that was made Pub. Law 550. Legal Res: College Station, Tex. 77840. Mailing Add: 2311 Rayburn House Office Bldg, Washington, D.C. 20515.

TEAGUE, SAM D
Fla. State Sen.
b. 1922; married; c. Five. Educ: Univ. Fla. Polit. & Govt. Pos: Mayor, Tallahassee, Fla; Fla. State Sen, currently. Bus. & Prof. Pos: Past pres, Fla. Savings and Loan League; chmn, Commonwealth Corp; v.pres, Leon Fed. Savings & Loan Asn. Mil. Serv: Marine Corps, World War II. Mailing Add: 713 Rebecca Dr, Tallahassee, Fla. 32303.

TEALE, STEPHEN P. D
Calif. State Sen.
b. San Francisco, Calif. Educ: L.A. Col. of Osteopathic Physicians and Surgeons, grad. Polit. & Govt. Pos: Mem. bd. supvrs, Calaveras Co, Calif, 5 years; Calif. State Sen, 58-; mem, Calif. Dem. State Cent. Cmt, currently. Bus. & Prof. Pos: Physician and surgeon. Mem: Lions; Calif. Osteopathic Asn. Legal Res: West Point, Calif. 95255. Mailing Add: 5082 State Capitol, Sacramento, Calif. 95814. (1967)

TEASDALE, JOSEPH PATRICK D
Prosecuting Attorney, Jackson Co, Mo.
b. Kansas City, Mo, 3/29/36; s. William B. Teasdale and Adah Downey T; single. Educ: Rockhurst Col, B.S, 57; St. Louis Univ. Sch. of Law, LL.B, 60. Polit. & Govt. Pos: Law clerk to Judge Albert A. Ridge, U.S. Dist. Court, 60-61; asst. U.S. Attorney, Kansas City, Mo, 62-66; prosecuting attorney, Jackson Co, 67-; del, Dem. Nat. Conv, 68. Mil. Serv: Entered as Airman 3/C, Air Force, 61, released as Airman 2/C, 67, after serv. in Carrier Wing. Rel: R Roman Catholic. Legal Res: 6440 Paseo, Apt. 2, Kansas City, Mo. 64131. Mailing Add: 7-M Jackson County Court House, 415 E. 12th St, Kansas City, Mo. 64106.

TEBBS, DANIEL A. R
b. Panguitch, Utah, 5/24/08; s. Fielding Burnes Tebbs and Ruth Asay T; m. 9/21/33 to Nedra Henvie; c. Veda, J. Daniel, Janice, Victor Louis, Joyce and Lucinda. Educ: Univ. Utah, 28-30; Henager Bus. Col, 36-38; Delta Sigma Pi. Polit. Pos: Co. Chmn, Rep. Party, Utah, 60-65. Govt. Pos: Utah State Rep, 63-66; mayor, Panguitch, 57-63, city councilman, 54-57 and 40-44. Bus. & Prof. Pos: Pres, Powell Woolgrowers Asn, 60-65; dir, W. Panguitch Irrigation Co, 58-66; secy-treas, Cattle Asn, 40-50. Mem: Lions; Farm Bureau. Rel: Latter-day Saint. Mailing Add: 10 S. Main, Panguitch, Utah 84759. (1967)

TEBELIUS, JOHN JAMES R
b. Harvey, N.Dak, 9/20/11; s. George Tebelius, Sr. and Charlotta Reiswig T; m. 7/25/46 to Iona Marie Kolbe. Educ: Univ. Minn, LL.B, 37. Polit. & Govt. Pos: State's attorney, Wells Co, N.Dak, 42-53; Rep. precinct committeeman, Second Ward, Harvey, 66-; alternate del, Rep. Nat. Conv, 68; attorney, Farmers Home Admin, Wells Co, N.Dak, 69- Mem: Am. Bar and N.Dak. State Bar Asns; C. of C.(v.pres, 59, pres, 60); Kiwanis; Gr. N.Dak. Asn. Rel: Seventh Day Adventist. Legal Res: 905 Allen Ave, Harvey, N.Dak. 58341. Mailing Add: 805 Lincoln Ave, Harvey, N.Dak. 58341.

TEBO, MARYANNE D
Assoc. Chmn, Franklin Co. Dem. Party, N.Y.
b. Tupper Lake, N.Y, 7/26/32; d. Eugene Gagnier and Catherine Gagnier Tice; m. 9/10/53 to Harvey S. Tebo, Jr; c. John, James and Mary Beth. Educ: Pilgrim State Hosp, R.N, 54; Plattsburgh State Sch, Cert. Polit. & Govt. Pos: Dem. Womens Chmn, Tupper Lake, N.Y, 67-68; assoc. chmn, Franklin Co. Dem. Party, 68- Bus. & Prof. Pos: Sch. Nurse Teacher, Tupper Lake Cent. Sch, N.Y, 54- Rel: Catholic. Legal Res: 13 Lincoln Dr, Tupper Lake, N.Y. 12986. Mailing Add: P.O. Box 1203, Tupper Lake, N.Y. 12986.

TECSON, JOSEPH A. R
Treas, Cook Co. Rep. Party, Ill.
b. Chicago, Ill, 4/4/28; s. Joseph Tecson and Jeanette Lanahan T; m. 1954 to Caroline R. Rees; c. Andrew, Sarah and David. Educ: Ripon Col, B.A, 52; Univ. Wis. Law Sch, LL.B. and J.D, 54. Polit. & Govt. Pos: Committeeman, Riverside Twp. Rep. Party, Ill, 66-; spec. asst. to Ill. Attorney Gen, 69; treas, Cook Co. Rep. Party, 69- Bus. & Prof. Pos: Lawyer and partner with Abel J. De Haan. Mil. Serv: Entered as A/S, Navy, 46, released as PO 3/C, 47, after serv. in Naval Air Branch as Radio-Radar Operator, on U.S.S. Shangrila, Air Group Five, 46-47. Publ: 'Should Impeaching Documents go to the Jury?,' 57 and 'Use of the Plea of Guilty in Civil Action,' 60, Trial Lawyers Guide; 'Let's Combine Law Days with School Days,' Ill. State Bar J, 68. Mem: Am, Ill. and Chicago Bar Asn; Trial Lawyers Club of Chicago; Mason. Rel: Presbyterian. Legal Res: 230 Maplewood Rd, Riverside, Ill. 60546. Mailing Add: One N. LaSalle, Chicago, Ill. 60602.

TEDESCO, SAMUEL JOSEPH D
b. Bridgeport, Conn, 2/22/15; s. Joseph Tedesco and Elizabeth Gelormine T; m. 6/6/42 to Evelyn DeGruttola; c. Joseph. Educ: Univ. of Ky, A.B, 36; Boston Univ, LL.B, 38; Nat. Col. of Trial Judges, Reno, Nev, grad, 68; Phi Sigma Kappa. Polit. & Govt. Pos: Conn. State Rep, 40-48; Conn. State Sen, 50-52; Judge of City Court, Bridgeport, Conn, 55-57, Mayor, 57-65; Lt. Gov, Conn, 62-66; Judge of Superior Court, currently; chmn, Narcotics Control Cmn, 69- Bus. & Prof. Pos: Lawyer, admitted to the Conn. Bar Asn, 38; practiced before Conn. Courts, including the Supreme and Fed. Courts. Mil. Serv: During World War II served in five countries in ETO; awarded a battle star and the Medal of Hon. by City of Versailles. Mem: K. of C; Am. Legion; VFW; Sons of Italy. Mailing Add: 172 High Point Lane, Fairfield, Conn. 06430.

TEDFORD, JOHN ROY, JR. R
Chmn, Sutton Co. Rep. Party, Tex.
b. Dallas, Tex, 3/27/36; s. John Roy Tedford, Sr. and Harriet Clark T; m. 6/5/57 to Dell Davis; c. Gregg Laurence and Valerie. Educ: South. Methodist Univ, Bachelor of Music, 57; Phi Mu Alpha. Polit. & Govt. Pos: Chmn, Sutton Co. Rep. Party, Tex, 62-; alternate del, Rep. State Conv, 64. Bus. & Prof. Pos: Free lance musical dir, theaters in U.S. and Can; musical dir, Dallas Summer Musicals, 68-69; free lance composer and arranger for indust. shows; rancher, Sutton Co, Tex. Mem: Am. Fedn. Musicians; Tex. Sheep and Goat Raisers Asn. Rel: Methodist. Legal Res: 610 Allen Dr, Sonora, Tex. 76950. Mailing Add: P.O. Box 956, Sonora, Tex. 76950.

TEEFEY, DAN D
b. Mt. Sterling, Ill, 11/14/23; s. Edward Teefey and Loretta Geisler T; m. 10/16/48 to Jean Factor T; c. Edward, Jan, Susan, Sharon. Educ: Quincy Col, Univ. of Ill. Polit. & Govt. Pos: Ill. State Rep. -66. Bus. & Prof. Pos: Owns and operates Teefey Grain Co. Mil Serv: USAF, WW II, Pilot. Mem: Past-pres, Ill. Feed Asn; Past-pres, Mt. Sterling Rotary Club; Dir. Brown Cty. Fair Asn; C. of C; K. of C; Elks. Mailing Add: 400 S. W. Cross St, Mt. Sterling, Ill. 61081. (1967)

TEEL, ROBERT JEROME D
b. 1/30/21; s. Henry Addison Teel and Beunnie Lee Rudd T; m. 7/25/41 to Mary George T; c. Robert J, Jr, Frank S, George W. and Carlton L. Educ: Howard Col; Univ. Ala, B.A, 46, LL.B, 48. Polit. & Govt. Pos: Mayor of Rockford, Ala, 60-63; Ala. State Rep, 63-66. Bus. & Prof. Pos: Lawyer, 49- Mil. Serv: Army, 43-46. Mem: Masons. Rel: Baptist. Mailing Add: Teel & Teel, Rockford, Ala. 35136.

TEETER, HOWARD M. R
Mem, Mich. State Rep. Cent. Cmt.
b. Union City, Mich, 2/13/07; s. Herbert M. Teeter and Lillian M. Steidle T; m. 1/4/37 to Marian M. Warner; c. Robert M, Philip W. and John H. Educ: Albion Col, A.B, 29; Univ. Mich. Law Sch, 30. Polit. & Govt. Pos: Alderman, Coldwater, Mich, 39-46, Mayor, 46-47; chmn, Coldwater Rep. Cmt, 40-; mem, Mich. State Rep. Cent. Cmt. and Exec. Cmt. Bus. & Prof. Pos: Rep. and mgr, Equitable Life Assurance Soc. of U.S, 30-67. Mem: Nat. Asn. Life Underwriters; Mich. State Underwriters Asn; Life Leaders of Mich; Million Dollar Round Table; Rotary; Elks. Rel: Presbyterian. Legal Res: 156 Church St, Coldwater, Mich. 49036. Mailing Add: 2 West Chicago St, Coldwater, Mich. 49036.

TEETER, ROBERT E. R
Chmn, Phillips Co. Rep. Party, Ark.
b. Pottsville, Ark, 12/11/29; s. Ray Teeter and Virginia Wade Alexander T; m. 6/3/51 to Helen Lucille Porter; c. Terri Lynn. Educ: State Col. Ark, 2 years; Cybick Sch. of Design, N.Y, 1 year; Sigma Tau Gamma. Polit. & Govt. Pos: Mem, War Mem. Stadium Cmn, Ark, 67-; chmn, Phillips Co. Rep. Party, 68-; mem, Civil Serv. Cmn, West Helena, 68- Mil. Serv: Entered as Seaman, Navy, 47, released as Hospitalman 2/C, 52, after serv. in First Marine Div, Korea as Field Med. Technician, 51-52. Mem: Lions Int. Rel: Baptist. Legal Res: 132 S. Fourth St, West Helena, Ark. 72390. Mailing Add: Box 2463, West Helena, Ark. 72390.

TELLES, RAYMOND
b. El Paso, Tex, 9/5/15; married; c. Two. Educ: Int. Bus. Col, 34; Tex. West. Col. Polit. & Govt. Pos: Acct, Bur. of Prisons, U.S. Dept. of Justice, 34-41 & 47-48; co. clerk, El Paso Co, Tex, 48-56; mayor, El Paso, 57-61; U.S. Ambassador to Costa Rica, 61-67. Mil. Serv: Maj, Army, 41-47; Army Air Force, 51-52, chief of lendlease for Army Air Forces for Latin Am; Col, Air Force Res; Bronze Star. Mailing Add: 1304 N. Saint Vrain, El Paso, Tex. 79901. (1967)

TELLEZ, ROBERT GONZALES D
b. Anthony, N.Mex, 12/28/17; s. Esteban G. Tellez and Maria Gonzales T; m. 9/23/39 to Ofelia Davila; c. Mary Grace (Mrs. Swartz), Abel, Roberta Ofelia, Martha Anne and Esteban, II. Educ: N.Mex. State Univ, 2 years. Polit. & Govt. Pos: Cmnr, Dona Ana Co, N.Mex, 55-58; mem, N.Mex. Dem. State Cent. Cmt, 65-67; chmn, Dona Ana Co. Dem. Party, 67-68; state committeeman, U.S. Dept. of Agr, 68-69. Bus. & Prof. Pos: Farmer, 40-68; off. mgr, Santo Tomas Gin Asn, 41-68; off. mgr. and secy-treas, Santo Tomas Produce Asn, 57-67; co-owner, Consolidated Southwest Produce, Inc, 68. Mem: Secy-treas, Mesilla Valley Ginners Asn, 47-; Elks; K. of C. Citations from N.Mex. State Dem. Party Orgn. Rel: Catholic. Mailing Add: P.O. Box 638, Mesquite, N.Mex. 88048.

TEMMEY, LEO ALBERT R
b. Onida, S.Dak, 11/6/94; s. Lawrence A. Temmey and Annie O'Connor T; m. 11/18/20 to Rose Tracy; c. Larry A. and Robert J. Educ: S.Dak. State

Univ, B.A; Univ. Minn, LL.B; Phi Sigma Kappa. Polit. & Govt. Pos: State's attorney, Beadle Co, S.Dak, 30-35; attorney gen, S.Dak, 39-42; cand. for Gov, 42; del, Rep. Nat. Conv, 48; Rep. State Chmn, S.Dak, 60-65; mem, Rep. Nat. Cmt, 60-65. Mil. Serv: 1st Sgt, Co. I, 355th Inf, World War I; Lt. Col, Staff Under Secy. of War, Bd. of Contract Appeals, World War II. Mem: Pres. State Asn, Elks, 39-40; State Comdr, Am. Legion, 35-36 and Nat. V.Comdr, 36-37; Rotary. Legal Res: 547 Nebraska Ave. S.W, Huron, S.Dak. 57350. Mailing Add: F&M Bank Bldg, Huron, S.Dak. 57350.

TEMPLAR, GEORGE R
b. Cowley Co, Kans, 10/18/04; s. John Templar and Lottie E. Linn T; m. 3/29/24 to Helen Marie Bishop; c. Ted M. and Joan L. (Mrs. Smith). Educ: Washburn Univ, LL.B. cum laude. Polit. & Govt. Pos: Kans. State Rep, 33-41; mem, Kans. Judicial Coun, 39-41, 45-49 & 53; Kans. State Sen, 45-53; U.S. Attorney for Kans, 53-54; U.S. Dist. Judge, 62- Mem: Int. Acad. Trial Lawyers; Nat. Lawyers Club; chmn. bd. trustees, Southwest. Col; Mason; Consistory; Shrine; DeMolay Legion of Honor. Rel: Methodist. Mailing Add: 2864 Knollwood Court, Topeka, Kans. 66611.

TEMPLE, RICHARD DAVIS DFL
Chmn, Douglas Co. Dem-Farmer-Labor Party, Minn.
b. Fargo, N.Dak, 6/23/32; s. Frank Issac Temple and Esther Pohlman T; m. 8/15/59 to Barbara C. Stephenson; c. Kristin Ann, Richard Scott and Allisa Jeanne. Educ: Univ. Wis, Madison, B.S. Econ, 58; N.Dak. State Univ, M.S. Hist, 61; Theta Chi. Polit. & Govt. Pos: Secy, Douglas Co. Dem-Farmer-Labor Party, 64-68 and chmn, 68-; del, Dem. Nat. Conv, 68. Bus. & Prof. Pos; Staff teacher, Sch. Dist. 206, Minn, 61- Mil. Serv: Entered as Seaman, Naval Res, 53, released as ETN 3/C, 55, after serv. in Korea; 7 years Naval Res. Mem: Minn. Coun. Soc. Studies; Minn. and Alexandria Educ. Asns; Am. Legion. Rel: Episcopal. Mailing Add: Mounted Route, Country Club Heights, Alexandria, Minn. 56308.

TEMPLETON, DANIEL SHERIDAN R
Mem, Lancaster City Coun, Pa.
b. Lancaster, Pa, Dec. 1906; s. Harry Templeton and Mable Fox T; m. 3/1/29 to Dorothy M; c. Janet, Daniel, Jr. and Dorothy Jane. Educ: Lancaster Boys High Sch. Polit. & Govt. Pos: Rep. committeeman, 28 years; investr, Pa. State Treas, 50-61; mem, Lancaster City Coun, Pa, 54-58 and 62- Bus. & Prof. Pos: Self-employed, amusement bus, 30 years. Mem: Elks; Moose. Rel: Lutheran. Mailing Add: 812 Fremont St, Lancaster, Pa. 17603. (1967)

TENDICK, TED O. Conservative
married; c. Five daughters. Educ: Rochester Jr. Col; Univ. Minn. Bus. & Prof. Pos: Farmer. Mil. Serv: Korean War, B-29 gunner. Mem: Farm Bur; Minn. Crop Improvement Asn; Lions Club. Rel: Presbyterian. Mailing Add: Hayfield, Minn. 55940. (1967)

TENNEY, JOHN RICHARD R
Justice, N.Y. State Supreme Court
b. North Arlington, N.J, 3/4/30; s. George MacIntosh Tenney and Alice Wiedman T; m. 7/28/56 to Cynthia Ann Roberts; c. John William, Robert Warren, Claudia Lynn and Jane Elizabeth. Educ: Colgate Univ, A.B, 52; Cornell Univ, LL.B, 55; Pi Delta Epsilon; Sigma Nu; Phi Delta Phi; Maroon Key; Konosioni. Polit. & Govt. Pos: Upstate Rep. campaign mgr. for attorney gen, 55 and comptroller, 66; dist. capt, Kings Co. Rep. Cmt, 56-58; asst. attorney gen, N.Y. State, 58-59; alternate del, State Rep. Conv, 58 & 62 and del, 64 & 66; del, Judicial Conv, 59-62 & 64-66; finance chmn, Oneida Co. Rep. Cent. Cmt, N.Y, 60-62 and chmn, 62-68; mem, Oneida Co. Adv. Cmt, 61-66; del, Rep. Nat. Conv, 64 & 68; justice, N.Y. State Supreme Court, Fifth Judicial Dist, 68- Bus. & Prof. Pos: Partner, Ferris Kehoe, Tenney & Murnane, Esquires; pres, Oneida Madison Penny Savers, Inc, 65-66. Mem: N.Y. State, Am. and Oneida Co. Bars; N.Y.C. Bar Asn; N.Y. State Trial Lawyers Asn; Oneida Co. Bar Asn.(dir, 64-65); Kiwanis; YMCA (bd. mem); C. of C; Farm Bur; Utica Zool. Soc; dir, Girl Scout Coun. Rel: Presbyterian; Deacon; Elder, 68-69. Legal Res: 15 Slaytonbush Lane, New Hartford, Utica, N.Y. 13501. Mailing Add: Court House, Utica, N.Y. 13501.

TENNEY, NATHAN BOYD R
Ariz. State Sen.
b. Stanley, Ariz, 6/15/15; s. Nathan Orson Tenney and Myrtle Wear T; m. 4/10/39 to Rachel Teeples; c. John, Diane (Mrs. Paul Timothy), Carl, Jeanine (Mrs. Ronald Neagle), Harold, Dennis, Merle and Ronald. Educ: High sch, grad, 34. Polit. & Govt. Pos: Ariz. State Rep, 62-64; Ariz. State Sen, 64- Bus. & Prof. Pos: Retail feed merchant, 26 years; rancher. Mem: Leader, 4-H, 4 years; cub scouting, 5 years; active in church affairs, 30 years. Rel: Latter-day Saint. Mailing Add: Senator Hwy, Prescott, Ariz. 86301.

TENZER, HERBERT D
b. New York, N.Y, 11/1/05; s. Michael Tenzer and Rose Steier T; m. 6/26/30 to Florence R. Novor; c. Barry and Diane (Mrs. Sidel). Educ: N.Y. Univ, LL.B, 27. Polit. & Govt. Pos: Former U.S. Rep, N.Y. and former mem, Judiciary Cmt. Bus. & Prof. Pos: Sr. partner, Tenzer, Greenblatt, Fallon & Kaplan, Esqs; gen. partner in real estate firms; bd. chmn, Barton's Candy Corp, 40-60; former bd. mem, Metrop. Indust. Bank and Queens Nat. Bank; former dir, Am. Trust Co. Mem: Dir, N.Y. Co. Lawyers Asn. and N.Y. Univ. Law Alumni Asn; counsel, Confectioners Indust. Rels. Bd; pres, Nat. Coun. to Combat Blindness, Inc; chmn, Confectionery Div, N.Y. City Cancer Cmt; bd. Chronic Disease Hosp; founder and gen. dir, United Jewish Appeal of Gr. N.Y; chmn, S. Shore Div, Albert Einstein Col. of Med. and Confectionery and Allied Trades Div, UJA; hon. pres, Yeshiva of Crown Heights and Congregation Beth Sholom; organizer and past chmn, Conf. and Allied Trades Div, Fedn. Jewish Philanthropies; chmn, Rescue Children, Inc; past chancellor, K. of P: Grand St. Boys Asn; Long Island Lodge B'nai B'rith; F&AM; A.A.S.R; Mason (32°); Woodmere Country Club; N.Y. Univ. Club; nat. secy, Synagogue Coun. of Am. Rel: Jewish. Legal Res: 15 Waverly Place, Cedarhurst, N.Y. 11559. Mailing Add: 235 E. 42nd St, New York, N.Y. 10017.

TEPNER, JESS FREDRICK D
Chmn, Knox Co. Dem. Party, Nebr.
b. Plainview, Nebr, 3/14/07; s. Frank Tepner and Jennie Sirek T; m. 6/1/30 to Florence Koppelman; c. Frank L. and Vicky Lynn. Educ: High Sch. Polit. & Govt. Pos: Chmn, Knox Co. Dem. Party, Nebr, 42-; mem, Creighton City coun, 47-52; mem. of the State of Nebr. New Car Dealers License Bd, 58-; Presidential Elector, 68. Mem: Former mem, Commercial Club; Future Farmers of Am; Shrine; Mason; Dem. Century Club. Rel: Congregational. Mailing Add: P.O. Box 47, Creighton, Nebr. 68729.

TERHORST, FRIEDA CATHERINE D
V.Chmn, Vigo Co. Dem. Cent. Cmt, Ind.
b. Columbus, Ohio, 4/2/00; d. Casper Hirschman and Marie Riedl H; wid. Educ: Wabash Commercial Col. Polit. & Govt. Pos: V.Chmn, Vigo Co. Dem. Cent. Cmt, Ind, 42-; bd. mem, Voters Registration Off, 45; committeeman, 50. Mem: Dem. Womens Club. Rel: Catholic. Legal Res: 811 S. Fourth St, Terre Haute, Ind. 47807. Mailing Add: Room 3, Vigo Co. Court House, Terre Haute, Ind. 47801.

TERLAJE, EDWARD SALAS D
V.Speaker, Guam Legis.
b. Agana, Guam, 8/26/34; s. Francisco Flores Terlaje and Maria Salas T; m. 8/16/58 to Shirley Coulter; c. Edward Lawrence, Thomas Francisco, Ricardo Mark, Therese Marie, Maria Kathyrn and John Coulter. Educ: Creighton Univ, B.S, 57, Law Sch, J.D, 60; Delta Theta Phi. Polit. & Govt. Pos: Dep. Island attorney and asst. attorney gen, Govt. Guam, 60-61; Sen, Guam Legis, 61-, mem, Cmt. Educ. and Labor, Cmt. Judiciary and Cmt. on Finance and Taxation, 61-64; pub. improv. chmn, Select Cmt, Juvenile Delinquency, v.speaker, 68-; del, Dem. Nat. Conv, 68 & 68. Bus. & Prof. Pos: Attorney-at-law, 61- Mem: Am. and Nebr. State Bar Asns; Guam Bar Asn. (pres, 68-69); Holy Name Soc. Guam; admitted to practice law by Supreme Court of State of Nebr, Dist. Court Guam, U.S. Court Claims. Rel: Roman Catholic. Mailing Add: P.O. Box 1719, Agana, Guam 96910.

TERRELL, THOMAS F. D
b. Pocatello, Idaho, 7/25/20; s. Robert M. Terrell and Ollie Ruebel T; m. 12/24/40 to Elizabeth Lee Pentz; c. Thomas F, III, Philip R. and Patricia L. Educ: Kemper Mil. Sch, A.A, 39; Univ. Idaho, 40; Mil. Hon. Soc; Band, Drum & Bugle Corps; Best Non-Commissioned Officer Award; Kemper News Staff; Mil. Police. Polit. & Govt. Pos: Idaho State Rep, 54-65, chmn, Ways and Means Cmt, Idaho House of Rep, 59-61, sr. mem, Ins, Banking & Pub. Utilities Cmt, 61-65, Appropriations Cmt, 63-65 and Joint Finance Cmt, 63-65; del, Dem. Nat. Conv, 60; mem, Pre-Legis. Budget Cmt, 60, 62 & 64; chmn. platform cmt, Dem. State Cmt, 62 & 64; exec. dir, Pub. Employee Retirement Syst. of Idaho, 65- Bus. & Prof. Pos: Asst. mgr, Fox Intermountain Theaters, 40-41; v.pres. and mgr, Guaranty Ins. Agency, Inc, 41-60; dir. econ. develop, Pocatello C. of C, 60-63; v.pres. and dir, Guaranty Fed. Savings & Loan Asn, 63-65. Mil. Serv: Pvt, Marine Corps, 43. Mem: Pocatello Asn, Ins. Agents (past pres); Idaho Asn. Ins. Agents (past pres); Nat. Asn. of State Retirement Adminstr; Munic. Finance Officers Asn. of U.S. and Can; Nat. Coun. on Teacher Retirement; Elks (Past Exalted Ruler,); Am. Legion; Voiture; 40 et 8; C. of C; Pocatello Golf & Country Club (past pres); past chmn, Bannock Co. Chap, Am. Red Cross; Kiwanis (past dir, Pocatello Club); bd. mem, Fundsy. Distinguished Citizen Award, Statesman Newspaper, 69. Mailing Add: 3110 Crescent Rim Dr, Apt. 102, Boise, Idaho 83704.

TERRILL, ALBERT LEE D
Majority Leader, Okla. State Senate
b. Walters, Okla, 3/8/37; s. Albert Terrill and Ruth Elliot Gardiner T; m. 3/29/56 to Sandra Kay Cullar; c. Lisa Dianne, Leah Suzanne and Todd Albert. Educ: Abilene Christian Col; Southwest. State Col, B.A; all-conf. fullback; letterman in football, basketball, track. Polit. & Govt. Pos: Okla. State Sen, Dist. 32, 65-, chmn, Educ. Cmt, mem, Cmts. on Bus, Indust. & Labor Rels. and Roads, Hwy. and Pub. Safety, Majority Leader, Okla. State Senate, 69- Bus. & Prof. Pos: Pres, Okla. Preferred Finance & Loan Corp, De'Ninth Bldg. Corp, Royal Enterprises, Inc. and Sheridan Warehouses, Inc; v.pres, Lawton Enterprises, Inc. and Kincannon, Inc; asst. prin, Lawton Pub. Schs, 1 year and teacher and coach, 4 years. Mem: Nat. Asn. Sec. Prin; former Lawton Legis. Rep, Okla. Educ. Asn; v.pres. and state pub. rels. chmn. and bd. dirs, Okla. Consumer Finance Asn; Abilene Christian Col. Nat. Develop. Coun; assoc. mem, bd. trustees, Okla. Christian Col; adv. bd, Relig. Heritage of Am; Jr. C. of C; Cameron Col. and Roads and Transportation Cmts, Lawton C. of C; bd. dirs. and past pres, Breakfast Optimist Club; bd. dirs, past pres. and 1966 Campaign Fund dir, YMCA; bd, Lawton Boys Club; Comanche Co. Cmt. on Children and Youth; Ment. Health Asn; Parliamentarian, Lawton PTA Coun; West. Hills PTA; Lawton Commun. Concert Asn; Lawton Philharmonic Soc; sponsoring mem, Lawton Commun. Theater; Lawton Knife and Fork Club; Comanche Co. Hist. Soc. Rel: Church of Christ; adult Bible class teacher; mem, Educ. and Budget Cmts. Legal Res: 811 N.W. 51st St, Lawton, Okla. 73501. Mailing Add: P.O. Box 1093, Lawton, Okla. 73501.

TERRIS, BRUCE JEROME D
Chmn, Wash, D.C. Dem. Cent. Cmt.
b. Detroit, Mich, 8/3/33; s. Charles Zachary Terris and Ruth Singer T; m. Aug. 1958 to Shirley Duval; c. Elizabeth and Jessica. Educ: Harvard Col, A.B. summa cum laude, 54; Harvard Law Sch, LL.B. magna cum laude, 57, article ed, Harvard Law Rev, 56-57; Georgetown Univ. Grad. Sch, 57-60; Phi Beta Kappa. Polit. & Govt. Pos: Asst. to solicitor gen, Wash, D.C, 58-65; co-chmn, Nat. Conf. on Law and Poverty, 65; asst. dir, Nat. Crime Cmn, 65-67; asst. to the Vice President, 67-68; mem, campaign staff of Sen. Robert Kennedy, 68; chmn, Wash, D.C. Dem. Cent. Cmt, 68- Bus. & Prof. Pos: Consult, Crime, Poverty, Legal Serv. to the Poor, Wash, D.C, 67; vis. prof. law, Cath. Univ. Am, 67-68; exec. dir, Anacostia Assistance Corp, 68-69; consult, Crime, Poverty, Law, Housing, Urban Probs, 69-; sr. attorney, Center on Law and Social Policy, currently. Publ: The Responsibility of City Government: Win the War or Preserve the Peace; New Jersey Municipalities, 68; 'The Role of the Police,' Ann Am. Acad. Polit. Sci, 11/68. Mem: Exec. cmt, Housing Develop. Corp; bd, Capital E. Found; bd. Commun. Action, Inc. Rel: Catholic. Mailing Add: 1855 Shepherd St. N.W, Washington, D.C. 20011.

TERRY, CHARLES LAYMEN, JR. D
b. Camden, Del, 9/17/00; s. Charles Laymen Terry, Sr. and Elizabeth Maxson T; m. 6/30/24 to Jessica Irby; c. Charles L, III. Educ: Swarthmore Col; Univ. Va; Wash. & Lee Univ, LL.B, 23; Phi Sigma Kappa; Phi Delta Phi.

Polit. & Govt. Pos: Secy. of state, Del, 36-37; assoc. judge, Superior Court, 37-57 and presiding judge, 57-62; assoc. justice, Supreme Court, 62-63 and Chief Justice, 63-64; gov, State of Del, 65-69; del, Dem. Nat. Conv, 68. Bus. & Prof. Pos: Mem, Firm of Wolcott & Terry, 23-37. Mem: Wilmington Club. Rel: Episcopal. Mailing Add: 448 N. State St, Dover, Del. 19901. (1967)

TERRY, GEORGE ALVIN R
b. Oneida, Tenn, 12/19/26; s. William Claude Terry and Paralee Cowan T; m. 6/9/50 to Sarah Ellen Winn; c. Stephanie Rhea, Saralee Winn, Sereessaa Louise and Rachel Cowan. Educ: Univ. of Tenn, B.S. in Bus. Admin, 50; Lambda Chi Alpha. Polit. & Govt. Pos: Rep. chmn, Scott Co, Tenn, 52-56; Tenn. State Rep, 57-59; Tenn. State Sen, 61-65. Bus. & Prof. Pos: Mgr, Ben Franklin Store, Oneida, Tenn, currently; v.pres, Terry Motor Co. Inc, currently, First Trust & Savings Bank, 68- Mil. Serv: Entered as Pvt, Army, 44, released as 2nd Lt, 46, after serv. in Armored Forces, ETO, 46. Mem: Am. Legion; Kiwanis; Scott Co. Conserv. League; Nat. Cmt. for Support of Pub. Schs; Nat. Trust for Historic Preservation in U.S. Outstanding Commun. Serv. Award, 68. Rel: Church of Christ. Mailing Add: P.O. Box 432, Oneida, Tenn. 37841.

TERRY, HARRIET ELEANOR D
Chmn, Pratt Co. Dem. Cent. Cmt, Kans.
b. Cullison, Kans, 1/12/12; d. Horace Ramer Walters and Mary Palestine Waggoner W; m. 8/23/29 to Harold Glenn Terry; c. Eleanor Ann (Mrs. Moon) and Roger Allen. Educ: Cullison High Sch, Pratt Co, Kans, 25-29. Polit. & Govt. Pos: V.chmn, Pratt Co. Dem. Cent. Cmt, Kans, 66-68, chmn, 68-; mem, Kans. Dem. State Cmt, 66-; finance chmn. and mem. state exec. cmt, State Federated Dem. Club, 67-69; coordinator of 11 counties, Robinson for Senate Campaign, 68; alternate del, Dem. Nat. Conv, 68; finance chmn, Local Dem. Club, 68- Bus. & Prof. Pos: Avon rep, 55-69. Mem: Pansy Rebecca Lodge; Kans. Genealogical Soc; Royal Neighbors of Am; Ladies Auxiliary to BRT; VFW Auxiliary. Achievement awards; top sales awards; pres. with co-awards; co. bond awards. Rel: Baptist. Mailing Add: 319 Curtis, Pratt, Kans. 67124.

TERRY, JOHN HART R
N.Y. State Assemblyman
b. Syracuse, N.Y, 11/14/24; s. Frank Terry and Saydee Hart T; m. 4/15/50 to Jean Taylor Phelan; c. C. Jean, Jr, Lynn, Susan and Carole. Educ: Univ. Notre Dame, 43; Syracuse Univ. Col. of Law, LL.B, 48; v.pres, Nat. Cath. Col. Students; Louis Marshall Soc. Polit. & Govt. Pos: Supvr, 12th Ward, Onondaga Co, N.Y, 48-58; coordinator, Gubernatorial Campaign, N.Y. State Rep. Cmt, 58; asst. appointments officer to the Gov, 59, asst. secy. to Gov, 59-61; campaign chmn, Onondaga Co. Rep. Cmt, 61; N.Y. State Assemblyman, 63- Bus. & Prof. Pos: Sr. partner, Law Firm of Smith, Sovik, Terry, Kendrick, McAuliffe & Schwarzer, 48- Mil. Serv: Entered as Pvt, Army, 43, released as 1st Lt, 46, after serv. in 94th and 80th Inf. Divs, ETO, 44-46; Bronze Star with Oak Leaf Cluster; Purple Heart; ETO Medal with Four Battle Stars; Combat Inf. Award. Mem: Am, N.Y. State and Onondaga Co. Bar Asns; N.Y. state chmn, United Serv. Orgn; bd. of dirs, Diocese of Syracuse, Cath. Youth Orgn; Citizens Found; Founder, Bishop Foery Found; Am. Legion; 40 et 8; VFW; DAV; Mil. Order of the Purple Heart; Bellevue Country Club; Liederkranz Club; Univ. Club. Rel: Roman Catholic. Legal Res: 99 Wellesley Rd, Syracuse, N.Y. 13207. Mailing Add: 200 Empire Bldg, Syracuse, N.Y. 13202.

TERRY, PEYTON HUBER R
Chmn, Valley Co. Rep. Cent. Cmt, Mont.
b. Wolf Point, Mont, 8/23/23; s. James E. Terry and Maude Stone T; m. 7/2/50 to Constance Agnes Whitmus; c. Cheryl Kay, Paula Rae and Joel Peyton. Educ: Univ. N.Dak. Polit. & Govt. Pos: Treas, Nutter for Gov. Club, Mont, 60; Valley Co. Campaign chmn, Battin for Cong. Club, 61-66; finance chmn, Valley Co. Rep. Cent. Cmt, 62-66; alderman, Glasgow, 63-65; chmn, Valley Co. Rep. Cent. Cmt, 66- Mem: Mont. Stockgrowers; Mont. and Nat. Automobile Dealers Asns; Glasgow Auto Dealers Asn.(pres, 64-); Northeast. Mont. Asn. for Retarded Children (pres, 66-); Kiwanis (pres, Glasgow Club, 60); C. of C. (dir, Glasgow Chap, 63-65); Masonic Bodies; Shrine; Elks. Rel: Methodist. Legal Res: 730 Park, Glasgow, Mont. 59230. Mailing Add: Box 391, Glasgow, Mont. 59230.

TERRY, W. CLAUDE, JR. R
Dist. Chmn, Scott Co. Rep. Party, Tenn.
b. Oneida, Tenn, 2/4/29; s. W. Claude Terry and Paralee Cowan T; m. 6/3/55 to Fayrene Sexton; c. Gail Sue, Patricia Lou, Wilda Jane and William Claude, III. Educ: Univ. Tenn, B.S, 50; Lambda Chi Alpha. Polit. & Govt. Pos: Dist. chmn, Scott Co. Rep. Party, Tenn, currently; mgr, U.S. Senate Co. Rep. Campaign and del, Rep. Nat. Conv, 64; Mem, sch. bd. Tenn. Bus. & Prof. Pos: Pres, Terry Motor Co. Inc, Oneida, Tenn. Mil. Serv: Entered as 2nd Lt, Army, 51, released as 1st Lt, 53. Mem: Am. Legion; Kiwanis. Rel: Church of Christ. Mailing Add: Box 13, Oneida, Tenn. 37841.

TERRY, WALTER E. R
Wis. State Sen.
b. Baraboo, Wis, 2/26/09. Educ: Notre Dame Univ, Ph.B, 32. Polit. & Govt. Pos: Wis. State Assemblyman, 58-66; Wis. State Sen, currently. Bus. & Prof. Pos: Farmer; former field auditor, Wis. Pub. Welfare Dept. Mem: Officer in various state and city dairy coop. Mailing Add: Route 3, Baraboo, Wis. 53913. (1967)

TESCHER, MATH CARL D
b. Independence, Wis, 9/17/93; s. Peter Tescher and Antonitte Gass T; m. 1/16/16; c. Peter, Alvin, Marie (Mrs. Bewmaus), Cecelia (Mrs. Jack Rutelege), Tom, Dona May (Mrs. Jim Lowman), Alice (Mrs. John Megness), Toney, Rosmarie (Mrs. Lloyd Brown), Roslie (Mrs. Al Lang), Joan (Mrs. Roy Kittleson) and Jim. Educ: Pub. Schs. Polit. & Govt. Pos: Mem, Sentinel Bute Sch. Bd, 9 years; mem bd, Co. Cmnrs, 35-37; N.Dak. State Rep, 55-66; del, Dem. Nat. Conv, 68. Bus. & Prof. Pos: Farmer and Rancher. Mem: Grazing Asn; Stockmans Asn.(mem. Brand and Theft Bd, 10 years); K. of C. Rel: Catholic; Trustee, St. Michael Church, 25 years. Mailing Add: Sentinel Butte, N.Dak. 58654.

TESKE, HERB D
b. Miller, S.Dak, 11/16/28; s. Julius T. Teske and Leona Medworth T; m. 12/26/52 to Marilyn Johnson; c. Jody, Kathy and Nancy. Educ: Dakota Wesleyan Univ, B.A, 50; Colo. State Col, M.A, 58. Polit. & Govt. Pos: S.Dak. State Rep, 60-66; exec. secy, S.Dak. Dem. Party, 65-67. Bus. & Prof. Pos: Lake Region Educ. Planning Center, currently. Mil. Serv: Entered as Pvt, E-1, Army Nat. Guard, 46, currently Maj, S.Dak. Nat. Guard. Mem: Nat. and S.Dak. Educ. Asns; Lions Int. Rel: Lutheran. Legal Res: 313 First St. S.W, Watertown, S.Dak. 57201. Mailing Add: 124 First Ave. N.W, Watertown, S.Dak. 57201.

TESMAN, BRUCE ROBERT D
b. Brooklyn, N.Y, 11/7/34; s. Meyer Tesman and Esther Kedersky T; m. 12/17/55 to Sylvia Ada Siegel; c. Alan, Jacqueline, Elyse and Bret. Educ: Thomas Jefferson High Sch, Brooklyn, N.Y, 4 years. Polit. & Govt. Pos: V.pres, Deer Park Dem. Club, N.Y, 64 & 65; v.pres, Suffolk Co. Young Dem, 64-66; committeeman, Babylon Town Dem. Cmt, 64-, treas, 69-; zone leader, Deer Park Dem. Cmt, 65-68; campaign mgr. for Frank O'Conner, Babylon, 66; del, Suffolk Co. Judicial Conv, 66, 67 & 68; alternate del, Dem. Nat. Conv, 68. Mailing Add: 32 Bolling Lane, Deer Park, N.Y. 11729.

TESSENDORF, RAMONA ROBERTA R
V.Chmn, Pottawatomie Co. Rep. Party, Kans.
b. Onaga, Kans, 4/6/30; d. Robert Fredrick Hartwich and Martha Minnie Marten H; m. 1/30/59 to Harold Dean Tessendorf. Educ: Onaga Rural High Sch, Kans, grad, 48; Clark's Secretarial Sch, Topeka, grad, 54. Polit. & Govt. Pos: Committeewoman, Millcreek Twp, Kans, 60-; alternate del, Rep. Nat. Conv, 68; alternate to del-at-lg, Second Dist, Kans, 69; v.chmn, Pottawatomie Co. Rep. Party, 69- Bus. & Prof. Pos: Typist, State of Kans, 53-55, secy, 55-59; Dental Asst. to Dr. Don H. Morrow, 59-61; cashier, United Telephone Co. of Kans, Inc, 62-64. Mem: St. Paul's Lutheran Ladies Aid; Northeast Pottawatomie Co. Rep. Women's Club. Rel: Lutheran, Mo. Synod. Mailing Add: Onaga, Kans. 66521.

TESSIER, EUGENE JOSEPH, JR. R
b. N. Smithfield, R.I, 9/20/29; s. Eugene Joseph Tessier and Elizabeth M. Authelet T; m. to Joan Knowles Lockwood; c. Deborah, Leslie, Nancy, Stephen and Stephanie. Educ: Johnson & Wales Bus. Col, Bus. Admin, 50. Polit. & Govt. Pos: Cand, Warwick City Coun, Ward 5, R.I; chmn, Warwick Rep. City Cmt, 62-65; cand, R.I. State Rep, 64. Bus. & Prof. Pos: Mem, R.I. Rubber Club, 60- Mem: Narraganset Bay Power Squadron; Harmony Lodge 9 F&AM; Scottish Rites; Providence Plantations; Past Exalted Officer, War Auxiliary Police; Sword of Bunker Hill; Warwick Citizens League; Warwick Young Rep. Club. High Sch. Football Capt, 48; Class B. Co-Champ. Football team, 46. Rel: Episcopal. Mailing Add: 59 Hope Ave, Warwick, R.I. 02889.

TESTO, ROBERT JAMES D
b. Bridgeport, Conn, 3/3/20; s. Christopher Testo and Rose Sarlo T; m. 1/17/45 to Elva Grace Kirkland; c. Robert J, Jr, Christopher, Mildred Rose, Mary Beth, Vincent, Rozalie, Laura Ann, Raymond, Ramona, Donna and Diana. Educ: Fordham Univ. and Fordham Law Sch. Polit. & Govt. Pos: City alderman, Bridgeport, Conn, 50-52 and city attorney, 65-; former speaker, Conn. House of Rep; asst. majority leader, 59-61; Conn. State Rep. 60-69; asst. minority leader, 61-66; alternate del, Dem. Nat. Conv, 68. Mil. Serv: Entered as Pfc, Marine Corps, 43, released as Capt, 46, after serv. in Second Marine Air Wing. Mem: Bridgeport Chap, Fairfield Co. Leukemia Soc; Italian Commun. Center; K. of C.(4°); Holy Name Soc, St. Joseph's Church; Savoy Athletic Club; Am. Legion; Mill River Country Club; Algonquin Club. Rel: Catholic. Legal Res: 85 Russo Terr, Bridgeport, Conn. 06606. Mailing Add: 1115 Main St, Bridgeport, Conn. 06603. (1967)

TETENBAUM, SIDNEY JOSEPH D
Mem, Calif. Dem. State Cent. Cmt.
b. Bronx, N.Y, 8/30/22; s. Simon Tetenbaum and Bertha Hantman T; m. 4/12/53 to Carolyn Liever; c. Anne Marie and Alan David. Educ: City Col. N.Y, B.S, 43; N.Y. Univ, M.E.E, 48; Yale Univ, M.S, 49; Ph.D, 52; Phi Beta Kappa; Sigma Xi. Polit. & Govt. Pos: Mem. and officer, Santa Clara Co. Dem. Cent. Cmt, Calif, 54-66, mem, 56-58 & 60-; mem. bd. dirs, Calif. Dem. Coun, 55-57; mem, Calif. Dem. State Cent. Cmt, 58-; co-chmn, Tenth Cong. Dist. Dem. Cmt, 60-66; mem, Calif. Dem. State Exec. Cmt, 60-66 & 68- Bus. & Prof. Pos: Sci. investr, panel on electron tubes, Columbia Univ, 46-48; research asst, physics dept, Yale Univ, 50-52; research engr, Varian Assocs, Palo Alto, Calif, 52-54; sr. engr, adv. develop. engr. and eng. specialist, Gen. Tel. and Electronics, Calif, 54-63; research scientist and staff scientist, Lockheed Research Labs, 63- Mil. Serv: Entered as Pvt, Air Force, 43, released as Sgt, 46, after serv. in Signal Corps, attached to Air Forces. Publ: 'Microwave Spectrum of Br CN at Six Millimeters,' 5/52, and 'Nonlinear Interaction of an Electromagnetic Wave with a Plasma Layer in the Presence of a Magnetic Field,' 7/64, Phys. Rev; 'Observation of an Emission Peak at Plasma Cutoff,' Phys.Rev. Letters, 7/67. Mem: Am. Phys. Soc; Research Soc. Am. Holder of two patents on Microwave Switches. Rel: Hebrew. Mailing Add: 1650 Edmonton Ave, Sunnyvale, Calif. 94087.

TETLOW, HORACE G. D
Treas, Mahoning Co. Dem. Party, Ohio
b. Washingtonville, Ohio, 1/27/10; s. Harold A. Tetlow and Edna R. Vignon T; m. 1/27/40 to Elizabeth J. Bumphrey; c. John J. II and Albert A. Educ: Mt. Union Col, B.A; West. Res. Univ. Law Sch, LL.B; Delta Theta Phi; Alpha Tau Omega; Order of the Coif. Polit. & Govt. Pos: Mem. exec. cmt, Mahoning Co. Dem. Cent. Cmt, Ohio; chief dep, Mahoning Co. Probate Court, 46-63; recorder, Mahoning Co; treas, Mahoning Co. Dem. Party, 63- Bus. & Prof. Pos: Attorney-at-Law, 36-; mem, Mahoning Co. Ment. Health and Retardation Bd, 68-; mem. bd. dir, Mahoning Co. Legal Assistance Asn, 68- Mil. Serv: Entered as Seaman, Navy, 43, released as Lt.(sg), 46, after serv. in Command 12 Staff; Am. Theater Ribbon. Mem: Pres, Mahoning Co. Bar Asn, 52-53; mem. Exec. Cmt. Ohio State Bar Asn, 60-63; Elks; Mason; Am. Legion; C. of C, Youngstown, Ohio. Rel: Methodist. Mailing Add: 4395 Meadowview Dr, Canfield, Ohio 44406.

TEUTSCH, ERIKA D
b. Germany; d. Hans Teutsch and Anna H.T; single. Educ: Swarthmore Col, B.A. with honors, 43; Columbia Univ, 47-48; Mortar Bd. Polit. & Govt. Pos: Research asst, O.S.S, Wash, D.C, 44-45; economist, Mil. Govt, Berlin, 46-47; admin. asst. to U.S. Rep. William F. Ryan, N.Y, 63- Bus. & Prof. Pos: Econ-

omist, Fed. Reserve Bank, N.Y, 48-52; assoc. economist, Off. of Messrs. Rockefeller, 52-62. Legal Res: New York, N.Y. Mailing Add: 303 House Office Bldg, Washington, D.C. 20515.

TEWES, DONALD E. R
b. Merrill, Wis, 8/4/16; s. Herman F. Tewes and Mabel Rickman T; m. 8/17/46 to Myra Torhorst; c. James and Barbara. Educ: Valparaiso Univ, B.A. cum laude, 38; Univ. Wis, LL.B, 40; Hon. Social Sci. and Debate Socs. Polit. & Govt. Pos: Cong. campaign chmn, Wis. Rep. Party, 47-55, chmn, Second Cong. Dist, 53-56, mem. exec. cmt, Wis. Rep. Party, 53-56; chmn, Coun. Econ. Develop, Wis, 53-55. Bus. & Prof. Pos: Attorney-at-law, gen. practice, Merrill, Wis, 40-42; pres, Tewes Plastics Corp, Waukesha, Wis, 47- Mil. Serv: Entered as Pvt, Air Force, 42, released as Maj, 46, after serv. in 14th Air Force Flying Tigers under Gen. Chennault; Air Medal for flying combat; Chinese and other theater medals; various campaign ribbons. Mem: Various legal Asns; Young Rep. Hall of Fame; Kiwanis (past pres); Jaycees (past pres); Am. Legion; VFW; 14th Air Force Asn. Prfnl. pub. speaker; indust. consult; guest instr, col. and univ; Civic Leader Award, C. of C. Rel: Lutheran. Mailing Add: 244 Frederick St, Waukesha, Wis. 53186.

THACIK, ANNE SMITH R
b. Glen Richey, Pa, 12/12/18; d. Pybus Delaun Smith and Mary Hutchinson S; m. to George J. Thacik; c. one, grandchildren, one. Educ: Univ. Buffalo; Pa. State Univ. Polit. & Govt. Pos: Precinct registr, Pa, 48-; area v.chmn, Clearfield Co. Rep. Cmt, 54-60; mem, Clearfield Co. Rep. Exec. Cmt, 54-60; adv, Clearfield Co. Young Rep, 55-57; pres, Clearfield Co. Coun. Rep. Women, 55-61; mem, Clearfield Co. Rep. Publicity Cmt, 58-59; mem, Clearfield Co. Rep. Finance Cmt, 59-60; chmn, Clearfield Co. Rep. Fund Dr. Nixon-Lodge Campaign, 60; regional polit. activities chmn, Pa. Coun. Rep. Women, 62, mem. bd. dirs, 63-, chmn. polit. activities, 63, 64 & 65, mem. conv. cmt, 65, chmn. annual conv, 66, recording secy, 66-67 and pres, 68-; mem. Sch. Commun. Planning, Pub. Serv. Inst, Pa, 63; v.chmn, Clearfield Co. Rep. Cong. Campaign, 64; chmn, Curwensville Borough Planning Cmn, 64-; adv, Clearfield Co. TAR, 65-66; mem. adv. bd, Clearfield Co. Planning Cmn, 65-; mem. adv. bd, Clearfield Co. Develop. Coun, 65-; del-at-lg, Rep. Nat. Conv, 68; mem. bd. dirs, Nat. Fedn. Rep. Women, mem. nominating cmt, 69, Nat. Fedn. Rep. Women del, Am. Acad. Polit. & Soc. Sci, 69. Bus. & Prof. Pos: Operator, Woodhurst Nursery and Antiques, currently. Mem: PTA (pres, Curwensville Schs, 52); Curwensville Woman's Club (secy, 45); Curwensville Area Band Mothers (pres, 53); Curwensville Alumni Asn.(pres, 41 & 66); Six Degree Grange; Govt. Cmt. 100,000 Pennsylvanians; Pa. State Antique Asn. Rel: United Presbyterian; Church Sch. Dept. Supt, United Presby. Church, Curwensville, Pa, Mem. Bd. Christian Educ. Mailing Add: 201 McLaughlin St, Curwensville, Pa. 16833.

THAIN, CARL ERNEST R
Chmn, Pittsburg Co. Rep. Party, Okla.
b. Waukomis, Okla, 11/19/18; s. Charles Thain and Clara Keefer T; m. 5/29/48 to Irene M. Boyle; c. Debra Dianne. Educ: Univ. Okla, B.S, 47. Polit. & Govt. Pos: Chmn, Pittsburg Co. Rep. Party, Okla, 66- Bus. & Prof. Pos: Pres, C.E. Thain Co, Inc, McAlester, Okla, 56- Mil. Serv: Entered as 2nd Lt, Army, 41, released as Maj, 46, after serv. in 456th Parachutist Field Artil. Bn, 82nd Airborne Div, ETO, 42-46, Lt. Col, Res, 46-69; Holland Order of King William; Belgian Fourragere; French Fourragere; Purple Heart; ETO Campaign Medal with Six Battle Stars; Parachute Wings with Star. Mem: Elks; McAlester Country Club; Am. Legion; VFW; ROA. Rel: Episcopal. Mailing Add: 610 E. Indiana, McAlester, Okla. 74501.

THALER, SEYMOUR R. D - Liberal
N.Y. State Sen.
b. N.Y.C, 8/31/19; m. to Mildred G. Intner; c. Frederic and Joan. Educ: Brooklyn Col, Brooklyn Law Sch, LL.B. cum laude and J.S.D. cum laude; Columbia Univ, grad. work. Polit. & Govt. Pos: Dep. asst. attorney gen, 43; asst. counsel, Hotel Case Prep. Sect; law asst, Temporary City Housing Rent Cmn, 48; dep. comnr, N.Y.C. Dept. of Invests, 54-58; asst. to Gov. Harriman's counsel during 30-day bill period, 55-56; N.Y. State Sen, 58 and currently. Bus. & Prof. Pos: Lawyer, Thaler and Kandel. Mailing Add: 63 Groton St, Forest Hills, N.Y. 11375. (1967)

THATCH, WILLIAM R. D
Chmn, Big Horn Co. Dem. Party, Wyo.
b. Lovell, Wyo, 7/27/27; s. Roy Thatch and Alice Wilkerson T; m. 12/5/52 to LaVerne Sessions; c. Susan and Vicky. Educ: Univ. Wyo; Psi Chi. Polit. & Govt. Pos: Staff mem. off. of solicitor, Dept. of Interior, 56-58; city attorney, Lovell, Wyo, 58-62; chmn, Big Horn Co. Dem. Party, Wyo, currently. Bus. & Prof. Pos: Attorney-at-law, Lovell, Wyo, 58- Mil. Serv: PO 3/C, Navy, 45-46; Pac. Theatre Ribbon; Victory Medal. Mem: Mason; Am. Legion: Kiwanis. Rel: Latter-day Saint. Mailing Add: 464 E. Third, Lovell, Wyo. 82431. (1967)

THATCHER, RAYMOND S. D
b. Thompson, Conn, 1/10/03; m. one daughter. Polit. & Govt. Pos: Conn. State Comptroller, -67; former mem. Pub. Utilities Cmn; app. a State Auditor, 56; elected a mem. of the Conn. Constitutional Conv, 65. Mailing Add: East Hampton, Conn. 06424. (1967)

THAXTER, SIDNEY WARREN R
b. Portland, Maine, 4/21/14; s. Sidney St. Felix Thaxter and Phyllis Schuyler T; m. 9/25/42 to Willamain Cranmer McPhee; c. Sandra McPhee, Sidney St. Felix, II, Philip Schuyler and John Cranmer. Educ: Harvard Col, B.S, 37, Harvard Law Sch, LL.B, 40. Polit. & Govt. Pos: Chmn, Cumberland Co. Rep. Cmt, Maine, 50-54; chmn, Maine del. to Rep. Nat. Conv, 52; chmn, Maine Citizens for Eisenhower Cmt, 52 & 56; mem, Maine Rep. State Cmt, 54-58; mem, Portland City Coun, 65-67; mem, Cape Elizabeth Town Coun, 67-; pres, Coun. of Govts. of the Gr. Portland Region, 69- Bus. & Prof. Pos: Partner, Linnell, Perkins, Thompson, Hinckley & Thaxter, 48- Mil. Serv: Entered as Ensign, Navy, 41, released as Lt. Comdr, 45, after serv. in Submarines, Pac. Fleet; Submarine Combat Pin; Unit Commendation, Atlantic, Pac. and ETO Campaign Ribbons and others. Mem: Cumberland Co, Maine State and Am. Bar Asns; Maritime Law Asn. of U.S. Rel: Episcopal. Legal Res: R.D. 1, Ocean House Rd, Cape Elizabeth, Maine 04107.

THAXTON, RICHARD RAY R
b. Las Animas, Colo, 11/12/41; s. Archie Ray Thaxton and Dorothy Lois Inskeep T; m. 2/27/60 to Marlene Desiree Kost; c. Pamela Lynne. Educ: Otero Jr. Col, A.A, 64; Univ. Denver, B.A, 66; Univ. Denver Grad. Sch, 67; Phi Theta Kappa; Phi Alpha Theta; Pi Gamma Nu. Polit. & Govt. Pos: State treas, Colo. Col. Rep, 64-65, state chmn, 65-66; proj. adminstr, Colo. Proj, Rep. Nat. Cmt, 66; research dir, Colo. Rep. Party, 66-68, exec. dir, 68-69. Bus. & Prof. Pos: V.pres, Merrill Research Assocs, Dallas, Tex, 69- Rel: Presbyterian. Mailing Add: 15741 Regal Hill Circle, Dallas, Tex. 75240.

THEIS, FRANK J. DFL
Minn. State Rep.
b. Poland, 1919; m. to Alice; c. two sons and two daughters. Educ: Winona High Sch, Minn. Polit. & Govt. Pos: Minn. State Rep, 64- Bus. & Prof. Pos: Printer-pressman, 29 years. Mem: Dir, Winona Commun. Chest; v.pres, Family Serv-Margaret Simpson Home. Selected Outstanding Labor Man of the Year, Winona, 64. Mailing Add: 517 E. Seventh St, Winona, Minn. 55987. (1967)

THEIS, PAUL ANTHONY R
Pub. Rels. Dir, Nat. Rep. Cong. Cmt.
b. Ft. Wayne, Ind, 2/14/23; s. Albert Peter Theis and Josephine Kinn T; single. Educ: Univ. Notre Dame, B.A. in Journalism, 48; Georgetown Univ, B.S. in For. Serv, 49; Am. Univ, Pub. Rels, 49-52. Polit. & Govt. Pos: Pub. rels. officer, President Eisenhower's Inaugural Cmt, 56; admin. asst. to U.S. Rep, 55-57; radio-TV dir, Nat. Rep. Cong. Cmt, 58-60, pub. rels. dir, 60-; v.chmn. for publicity, President Nixon's 1969 Inaugural Cmt, Nov. 68 to Jan. 69. Bus. & Prof. Pos: Reporter, Army Times, 49 and Wash. Bur, Fairchild Publ, 50-53; Wash. Correspondent, Newsweek Mag, 53-54. Mil. Serv: Entered as Aviation Cadet, Army Air Corps, 43, released as 1st Lt, 46, after serv. as Pilot, 15th Air Force, 97th Heavy Bombardment Group, Italy, 44-45; Maj, Air Force Res, 67; Air Medal with Two Oak Leaf Clusters; ETO Ribbon with Six Battle Stars; Am. Theater Ribbon. Publ: Co-ed, Who's Who in American Politics, R.R. Bowker Co, 67 & 69. Mem: Nat. Press Club; Nat. Aviation Club; Capitol Hill Club; Tantallon Country Club; Notre Dame and Georgetown Univ. Alumni Clubs; Res. Officers Asn. Co-inventor of polit. game, Hat in the Ring. Rel: Catholic. Mailing Add: 38 Ivy St. S.E, Washington, D.C. 20003.

THELIN, HOWARD JAMES D
b. Van Nuys, Calif, 2/7/21; s. John Conrad Thelin and Emma Sophia Boettger T; m. 11/8/58 to Vivien June Odell; c. David Paul, William Howard and Richard John. Educ: Univ. Calif, Los Angeles, B.A; Univ. South. Calif. Law Sch, LL.B. Polit. & Govt. Pos: Calif. State Assemblyman, 56-66; Judge of Munic. Court, Los Angeles, currently. Mil. Serv: Army Inf. Div, overseas 3 years. Mem: Los Angeles, Co. Bar Asn; Lawyers Club; Legion Lex; Elks; Am. Legion; VFW. Rominger Award for best ed. in Am. Legion publ, 53; Freedom Found. Award for essay on Americanism, 55; Serv. to Mankind Award, for leadership in Polit. and commun. betterment, North Los Angeles Dist. of Sertoma, 60. Rel: Catholic. Mailing Add: 632 Robin Glen Dr, Glendale, Calif. 91202.

THEOBALD, GEORGE ANNA R
Rep. Nat. Committeewoman
b. Lincoln, Nebr, 12/16/17; d. Harry Maynard Lehr and Ethel Pearce L; m. 5/2/36 to Clement Walter Theobald; c. Shannon (Mrs. Anthony M. Devoe), Mary Katherine (Mrs. David A. Ness) and Joan (Mrs. Peter J. Peterson). Educ: Univ. of Nebr, 35-36; Univ. of Buffalo, 55; Kappa Delta. Polit. & Govt. Pos: Co-chmn, Citizens for Eisenhower, Del, 52; exec. v.pres, Young Rep, New Castle Co. Rep. Cmt, 58-64; Rep. Nat. Committeewoman from Del, 64-; alternate del, Rep. Nat. Conv, 68; cmnr, Wilmington Housing Authority, 69- Bus. & Prof. Pos: Mem. bd, Greater Wilmington Housing Corp, 69- Mem: League of Women Voters. Legal Res: 213 W. 14th St, Wilmington, Del. 19801. Mailing Add: 810 King St, Wilmington, Del. 19801.

THEOBALD, MAXINE ANDREE R
Mem, Calif. Rep. State Cent. Cmt.
b. Bakersfield, Calif, 10/13/34; d. Andrew Jackson Whitley and Mary Pearl Abercrombie W; m. 6/6/55 to George Edward Theobald, Jr; c. Michelle Suzanne, George Edward, III and Grant Andrew. Educ: Bakersfield Col, Calif, A.A, 55; Lance and Shield. Polit. & Govt. Pos: Chmn, Ways and Means Cmt, Redding Rep. Women, Federated, Calif, 64, pres, 65-66, parliamentarian, 67-68 and v.pres, 69-; mem, United Rep. of Calif, 64-, corresponding secy, 67-68; mem, First Assembly Dist. Rep. Cmt. and Second Cong. Dist. Rep. Cmt, 65-; mem, Shasta Co. Rep. Cent. Cmt, 64-, prog. chmn, 69-; mem, Shasta Co. Reagan Cmt, 66-; chmn, Shasta Co. Women for Nixon, 68; mem. and on state speakers bur, Calif. Rep. State Cent. Cmt, 69- Bus. & Prof. Pos: Real estate sales and property mgt. and part owner, Real Estate Assocs, 63- Publ: Co-ed, Rep. Women's News. Mem: Shasta Co. Bd. of Realtors; Calif. Real Estate Asn; Nat. Asn. of Real Estate Boards; Eastern Star; Mother's Club of Job's Daughters; Toastmistress, Int; Beta Sigma Phi; Delta Theta Tau; Redding Mus. League; Redding Mus. Sponsor's Asn; Commun. Concert Asn; Women of the Elks; bd. dirs, Mem. Hosp. Auxiliary. Hon. sponsor and social adv. to the pres, North. Calif. Coun, Beta Sigma Phi. Rel: Baptist. Mailing Add: 3288 Wilshire Dr, Redding, Calif. 96001.

THEOBALD, ROBERT A. D
Chmn, Summit Co. Dem. Cent. Cmt, Colo.
b. Breckenridge, Colo, 3/24/15; m. to Lois Gessford; c. Robin G. Educ: Univ. Colo, A.B, 35; Univ. Denver, LL.B, 38; Sigma Phi Epsilon. Polit. & Govt. Pos: Co. attorney and dep. dist. attorney, Summit Co, Colo, 46-50; chmn, Summit Co. Dem. Cent. Cmt, 46-; Colo. State Sen, 47-53; Dir. of Revenue, 56-61; Mayor, Blue River, 63-; mem, Summit Co. Sch. Bd, 64- Bus. & Prof. Pos: Counsel, Colo. Press Asn, 60- Mil. Serv: Entered as Pvt, Air Force, 42, released as Flight Officer, 46, after serv. in Air Transport Command. Mem: Colo. Bar Asn; Elks; Denver Athletic Club. Mailing Add: Breckenridge, Colo. 80424.

THEODORE, NICHOLAS GERALD R
Supt, U.S. Mint, Phila, Pa.
b. Media, Pa, 10/23/37; s. George Theodore and Alice Bowden T; m. 9/25/65

to Patricia Ann Kilmon. Educ: Univ. Notre Dame, B.S. in Acct, 59; Villanova Sch. of Law, J.D, 62. Polit. & Govt. Pos: Supt, U.S. Mint, Phila, Pa, 69- Mem: Del. Co. Bar; Del. Co. Bar Asn; Supreme and Superior Court of Pa. and the Fed. Dist. Court for the East. Dist; Jaycees; Media Swimming and Rowing Club; Vesper Club. Rel: Catholic. Legal Res: 7 Lafayette Circle, Media, Pa. 19063. Mailing Add: U.S. Mint, Independence Mall, Philadelphia, Pa. 19106.

THEODORE, NICK ANDREW D
b. Greenville, S.C, 9/16/28; s. Andrew Theodore and Lula Meros T; m. 4/25/55 to Emilie Demosthenes. Educ: Furman Univ, B.A, 52. Polit. & Govt. Pos: S.C. State Rep, 62-66; S.C. State Sen, 66-68; chmn, S.C. Appalachian Cmn. and dir, Gr. Greenville YMCA, currently. Bus. & Prof. Pos: Ins, Cain Co. Mem: Past dir, Co. Red Cross; ex. com, S.C. Jaycees; Pres, S.C. Jr. C. of C, 61-62; March of Dimes Chmn; Pres, Jaycees, 57-58; Master Coun. Greenville Order of DeMolay, 45; State Master Coun. S.C. DeMolay, 47. Rel: Greek Orthodox; Secy, St. George Greek Orthodox Church. Mailing Add: 404 Yorkshire Dr, Greenville, S.C. 29607.

THERIOT, ROY RAOUL D
La. State Comptroller
b. Erath, La, 6/26/14; s. Lastie Theriot and Emerite Barras T; m. 6/7/47 to Helen Roberts; c. Barbara (Mrs. DeBlanc), Roy R, Jr. and Samuel Houston. Educ: Univ. Southwest. La, pre-law, 33-35; Tulane Univ, LL.B, 36-39. Hon. S.M.D, Boswell Inst, 66. Polit. & Govt. Pos: Mayor, Abbeville, La, 54-60; La. State Comptroller, 60- Bus. & Prof. Pos: Lawyer, 39-54. Mil. Serv: Entered as Pvt, Air Force, 42, released as T/Sgt, 46; Am. Theater of Operation Medal; Good Conduct Medal. Mem: Lions Int. (past dist. gov); Am. Legion; Amvets; La. Farm Bur; Boy Scouts Am.(past Vermilion Dist. Chmn); Bayou Girls Scouts Coun.(past pres). Rel: Catholic. Mailing Add: 406 S. Louisiana Ave, Abbeville, La. 70510.

THEURER, GARY LLOYD R
b. Idaho Falls, Idaho, 3/21/29; s. Lloyd Michael Theurer and Gretta Tibbitts T; m. 12/23/53 to Berenice Steele; c. John Michael, Douglas Steele and James Gary. Educ: Utah State Univ, B.S, 51; George Washington Univ. Law Sch, LL.B, 54; Phi Kappa Phi; Phi Delta Phi; Sigma Chi. Polit. & Govt. Pos: Asst. attorney gen, State of Utah, 57-59; chmn, Voting Dist, Salt Lake Co, Utah, 60-62 and Legis. Dist, 62-66; Utah State Rep, 67-68. Bus. & Prof. Pos: Asst. gen. attorney, Union Pac. R.R. Co, 59-64; gen. law practice, Salt Lake City, 64- Mil. Serv: Entered as 2nd Lt, Air Force, 54, released as 1st Lt, 56, after serv. in Judge Adv. Gen. Corps, North. U.S. and Germany. Mem: Am. and Utah Bar Asns; pres, Salt Lake Chap, I.C.C. Practitioners Asn; YMCA; Utah State Univ. Alumni Coun. Rel: Latter-day Saint. Mailing Add: 1430 E. Stratford Ave, Salt Lake City, Utah 84106. (1967)

THIBAUDEAU, JOSEPH P. D
R.I. State Rep.
b. Manchester, N.H, 4/17/26; m. to Jeanine T. Educ: R.I. Radio Sch; Univ. of R.I, exten. courses. Polit. & Govt. Pos: R.I. State Rep, 61- Bus. & Prof. Pos: TV repairs and sales. Mil. Serv: Army, 44-46. Mailing Add: 49 Whitman St, Pawtucket, R.I. 02860. (1967)

THIBEAULT, JOSEPH A. D
R.I. State Rep.
b. Cumberland, R.I, 1/19/19; m. to Dorothy T. Educ: Northeast. Univ. Polit. & Govt. Pos: R.I. State Rep, 61-; first dep. speaker, 65. Bus. & Prof. Pos: Ins. spec. agent; radio announcer, Sta. WEAN, 42-54. Mem: Various fraternal and soc. orgn. Mailing Add: Eight Cushing St, Cumberland, R.I. 02864. (1967)

THIBODEAU, EUGENE E. D
R.I. State Rep.
b. Esmond, R.I, 10/5/16; s. Hubert Thibodeau (deceased) and Amanda Fortin T; m. 6/7/47 to Lillian Juliette Blanchard; c. Lillian Laura and Andre Joseph. Polit. & Govt. Pos: Mem, Smithfield Budget Cmt, 47-48; councilman, Smithfield Town Coun, 48-52; mem, Smithfield Sch. Cmt, 56-64, chmn, 62-64; R.I. State Rep, 64- Bus. & Prof. Pos: Owner, Thibodeau's Poultry and Vegetable Farm, 46- and Thibodeau's Printing Serv, 60- Mil. Serv: Entered as Pvt, Army Air Corps, 42, released as Sgt, 43. Mem: Past comdr, Am. Legion; R.I. Sheep Coop; past pres, Poultry Producers Asn. of R.I; pres, R.I. Agr. Coun. Trustee East. States Exposition, Springfield, Mass. Rel: Catholic. Mailing Add: Sebille Rd, Esmond, R.I. 02917.

THIEM, EZRA GEORGE R
b. Chicago, Ill, 7/8/97; s. Theodore J. Thiem and Sophia Offner T; m. 7/8/26 to Jane P. Weaver; c. Mrs. Jane T. Hill and Theodore George. Educ: Univ. Ill, B.S, 21 cum laude; Medill Sch. of Journalism, Northwest. Univ, 24; John Marshall Law Sch, 27-28; Sigma Delta Chi; Alpha Zeta. Polit. & Govt. Pos: Ill. State Rep, 65-66. Bus. & Prof. Pos: Asst. ed, Prairie Farmer, 23-26; ed. and dir. of info, Ill. Agr. Asn, 26-39; agr. ed, reporter and staff writer, Chicago Daily News, 40-62; free-lance writer, 62- Mil. Serv: ROTC, 16-18. Publ: 'The Keys to Better Rels. Between Mgt. and Labor,' 45; 'The Hodge Scandal,' 63; contrib. to numerous agr. mag. Mem: Farm House; Chicago Newspaper Vets; Headliners; Newspapers Farm Ed. Asn; Mason. Joint Pulitzer Prize Winner, most disintereste and meritorious pub. serv. of any newspaper, 49; Recipient of Freedom Citation, 51; Citation and Award, Ill. Press Asn, 56; Rotary Club of Chicago Award and Citation, 56; Publitzer Pub. Serv. Award, 56. Legal Res: 1856 Sherman Ave, Evanston, Ill. 60433. Mailing Add: Sun Times Plaza, 401 N. Wabash Ave, Chicago, Ill. 60611. (1967)

THIES, LOUIS CARL R
Chmn, Sheridan Co. Rep. Party, Nebr.
b. Wayne Co, Nebr, 11/25/05; s. Fred Theis and Augusta Wolff T; m. 1927 to Ada Peterson; c. Alois (Mrs. Kenneth Herrman) and Randal. Educ: Hay Springs High Sch, Nebr, 21-25. Polit. & Govt. Pos: Mayor, Hay Springs, Nebr, 56-58; chmn, Sheridan Co. Rep. Party, 67- Bus. & Prof. Pos: Pres, Panhandle Wholesale, Inc, Alliance, Nebr, 57-68; v.pres, Randy Mkt, White Clay, Nebr, 15 years and Lou's Shoeland, Rapid City, S.Dak, 10 years; pres, Hay Springs Indust. Co, Inc, 10 years. Mem: Mason; York Rite; Scottish Rite; Shrine; Elks. Rel: Methodist. Mailing Add: Hay Springs, Nebr. 69347.

THIESSEN, CORNIE R. D
Mont. State Sen.
b. Mountain Lake, Minn, 7/7/10; s. David Thiessen, Sr. and Agnetha Holzreichter T; m. 11/25/38 to Ailee E. Buck; c. Anita Sue and James Everett. Educ: Northwest Nazarene Col, B.A, 36; Pasadena Col, M.A, 40; Sigma Lambda Alpha. Polit. & Govt. Pos: Mem. adv. cmt, Rural Elec. Admin, Mont. 54-56; chmn, Mont. Kefauver for President Club, 56; del, Dem. Nat. Conv, 56, 60 & 68; Mont. State Sen, 59-; pres, Mont. Humphrey for President Club. 60. Bus. & Prof. Pos: Secy-treas, Lower Yellowstone Rural Elec, 44-67, pres, 67-; bd. mem, Commun. Mem. Hosp 48-66; pres, Mid Rivers Tel, 52-57; bd. mem, St. Paul Bible Col, 52-66; bd. mem, Nat. Tel. Asn, 54-57; dir. mem, Richland Homes, 58-; secy-treas, Upper Mo. Gen. & Trans, 58-; v.pres. Basin Elec. Power Coop, 61-; mem. bd. mgrs, Christian Missionary Alliance, 61-; v.pres, Mo. Basin Syst. Group, 65-69. Mem: Farmer Union; Int. Toastmasters. Received Good Govt. Award, Jaycees, 66. Rel: Christian & Missionary Alliance. Mailing Add: Box 195, Lambert, Mont. 59243.

THIGPEN, JUDSON ARLEDGE, JR. 'BUD' D
Miss. State Rep.
b. Shaw, Miss, 11/29/26; married. Polit. & Govt. Pos: Miss. State Rep, currently. Bus. & Prof. Pos: Agent, Standard Oil Co; real estate broker. Mem: VFW; Am. Legion; Citizens Coun; Cleveland Vol. Fire Dept. Rel: Baptist. Mailing Add: 601 Deering St, Cleveland, Bolivar City, Miss. 38732. (1967)

THILL, LEWIS D. R
b. Milwaukee, Wis, 10/18/03; s. Dr. Dominic P. Thill and Mary Pierron T; m. 11/29/47 to Carol Jean Werner; c. Mary, John, Lewis, Jr, Dorothy and Carol Louise. Educ: Marquette Univ, A.B; Univ. of Wis, LL.B. Polit. & Govt. Pos: U.S. Rep, Wis, 39-43. Rel: Roman Catholic. Mailing Add: 13360 Marquette Ave, Elm Grove, Wis. 53122.

THIMLAR, J. RILEY D
Polit. & Govt. Pos: Ind. State Rep, -66. Bus. & Prof. Pos: Farmer. Mil. Serv: Navy Air Corps. Mem: Dir, FHA, Miami and Cass Ctys; Masonic Lodge; Shrine; Scottish Rite; Eagles; PTA Asn; Order of Eastern Star. Rel: Methodist. Mailing Add: R.R. 2, Royal Center, Ind. 46978. (1967)

THISS, GEORGE RAYMOND R
Chmn, Minn. Rep. State Cent. Cmt.
b. Minneapolis, Minn, 12/12/27; s. Charles R. Thiss and Alice Newhouse T; m. 2/25/67 to Joyce Zniewski. Educ: Univ. Minn, B.A, 50; N.Y. Univ, M.S, 52; Delta Kappa Epsilon. Polit. & Govt. Pos: Bd. mem, Hennepin Co. Young Rep. League, Minn, 57-61, chmn, 59-61; mem, Hennepin Co. Rep. Cmt, 59-63, v.chmn, 63; del, Nat. Conv, Minn. Young Rep. League, 59, 61 & 63, nat. committeeman, 61-63; mem. exec. cmt, Minn. Rep. State Cent. Cmt, 61-, first v.chmn, 63-65, chmn, 65-; liaison, Col. Fedn, 61-63; officer, Hennepin Co. Finance Cmt, 63; del, Rep. Nat. Conv, 68. Bus. & Prof. Pos: Asst. buyer, Hahne & Co, Newark, N.J, 52-55; store mgr, Thiss Luggage, 55-61. Mem: Jr. C. of C; chmn, UN Week, Minneapolis, 59-60 & 62-63; pres. bd. trustees, mem. and treas, Breck Sch. Alumni Asn; Rotary; Independent Sch. chmn, United Fund, 63 & 64; Teachers Div, Independent Sch. Asn. of Cent. States. Rel: Episcopal. Legal Res: 5025 Normandale Court, Minneapolis, Minn. 55436. Mailing Add: 4940 Viking Dr, Minneapolis, Minn. 55435.

THOMAS, A. J, JR. 'ARCH' D
b. Lake Butler, Fla, 12/23/23; m. to Jean Snodgrass; c. A. J, John M, Elizabeth Ann. Educ: Univ. of Fla, LL.B, 1948. Polit. & Govt. Pos: Fla. State Rep, 60-66; Co. Attorney and Co. Prosecuting Attorney 1959; City Attorney 1953-; Co. Vets. Serv. Officer 48-55. Bus. & Prof. Pos: Lawyer. Mil. Serv: U.S. Air Force, WWII. Mem: Past Dept. Comdr, Am. Legion; Past Pres, Starke Rotary Club; 1st Fed. Savings & Loan Asn. of Starke; Pres, Bradford Co. Fair Asn. Rel: Baptist. Mailing Add: 208 S.E. Sixth St. Ft. Lauderdale, Fla. 33301. (1967)

THOMAS, A. JAN, JR. D
Ark. State Rep.
b. Fayetteville, Ark, 8/27/37; s. Albert Janney Thomas and Evelyn Williams T; m. 12/29/61 to Frederica Rae Russell; c. Jelyn Rae, Albert Janney, III and Heather Hope. Educ: Univ. Ark, B.S.B.A, 59; Univ. Ark. Law Sch, LL.B, 62; Acacia; Delta Theta Phi. Polit. & Govt. Pos: Asst. City Attorney, West Memphis, Ark, 64; Ark. State Rep, Dist 28, Pos. 2, 69- Mem: Am. and Ark. Bar Asns; Crittenden Co. Bar. Asn.(secy-treas, 63, v.pres, 64, pres, 66); Northeast Ark. Bar Asn.(secy-treas, 69); Rotary Int; Jaycees; Farm Bur; C. of C. Distinguished Serv. Award, Jr. C. of C, 68. Rel: United Methodist. Legal Res: P.O. Box 507, Clarkedale, Ark. 72325. Mailing Add: P.O. Box 282, West Memphis, Ark. 72301.

THOMAS, ALFRED VICTOR D
Chmn, Sixth Cong. Dist. Dem. Cmt, Va.
b. Roanoke, Va, 11/9/29; s. Ellis James Thomas and Genevieve Nero T; m. 11/25/46 to Dorothy Marie Lucas; c. Alfred V, Jr, William Eric, Genevieve Cecelia and Thomas Patrick. Educ: Va. South. Col, 58; Univ. Va, 64. Polit. & Govt. Pos: Pres, Roanoke, Va. Young Dem. Club, 65-66; dir, Young Dem. Clubs Va, 66-69; chmn, Roanoke Va. City Dem. Cmt, 67; del, Dem. Nat. Conv, 68; chmn, Sixth Cong. Dist. Dem. Cmt, 68- Bus. & Prof. Pos: Owner, E. J. Thomas Mkt, 49- Mil. Serv: Army, 47, Pvt, serv. in 33rd Combat Team, C.Z. Mem: Elks; Dokkies; K. of P; WOW. Rel: Catholic. Mailing Add: 1301 Orange Ave. N.E, Roanoke, Va. 24012.

THOMAS, CHRISTOPHER YANCEY R
Kans. State Sen.
b. Roanoke, Va, 1/5/00; s. Frank Watkins Thomas and Elizabeth Carson T; m. 6/12/22 to Dorothea Louise Engel; c. Christopher Yancey, Jr, Dorothea Louise (Mrs. Joe Dickey) and Betsy (Mrs. Paul Dring). Educ: Purdue Univ, B.S. in mech. eng, 21 and mech. engr, 26; Tau Beta Pi; Sigma Delta Chi; Beta Theta Pi. Polit. & Govt. Pos: Mem, Bd. of Educ, Pittsburg, Kans, 38-42; councilman, Mission Hills, 55-59 and mayor, 59-63; chmn, Johnson Co. Rep. Cent. Cmt, 62-66; del, Rep. Nat. Conv, 64; mem. and former chmn, Kans. Water Resources Bd; Kans. State Sen, 69- Bus. & Prof. Pos: Chem. engr, Pittsburg & Midway Coal Mining Co, 29-41, chmn, 63-65; v.pres, Spen-

cer Chem. Co, 41-59, v.chmn, 59-60 and chmn, 60-63; dir, Johnson Co. Nat. Bank & Trust Co, Prairie Village, Kans, 53-; v.pres. and dir, Spencer Found, Kansas City, 56- Mil. Serv: Pvt, Army, 18. Mem: Am. Soc. Mech. Engrs; Am. Inst. Mining Engrs; Nat. Soc. Prfnl. Engrs; Kansas City Press Club; Kans. Eng. Soc; Kansas City Engrs. Club; Am. Legion; Elks; Mirza Shrine and other Masonic Bodies; trustee, Farm Found, Chicago; Kans. State C. of C.(v.pres, 63, pres, 64, chmn, 65). Rel: Methodist. Mailing Add: 5519 E. Mission Dr, Shawnee Mission, Kans. 66208.

THOMAS, EDWARD PHILIP R
Chmn, Frederick Co. Rep. Cent. Cmt, Md.
b. Frederick, Md, 8/3/28; s. Edward P. Thomas (deceased) and Louise G. Firmin T; m. 12/2/58 to Lois Anne Viola; c. Stephen, Anne, Sue and Patricia. Educ: Wash. and Lee Univ, B.A, 50; Sigma Delta Chi; Phi Kappa Sigma; Sigma Club, Wash. and Lee Univ. Polit. & Govt. Pos: Chmn, Frederick Co. Rep. Cent. Cmt. Md, 66-; alternate del, Rep. Nat. Conv, 68; mem. exec. cmt, Md. State Rep. Cent. Cmt, 69- Bus. & Prof. Pos: Sports dir. and asst. news dir, WSLS-TV & Radio, Roanoke, Va, 53-60; pres. and gen. mgr, Terrace Lanes Inc, Frederick, Md. and Edgewood Lanes, Inc, Gettysburg, Pa, 60- Mil. Serv: Entered as Pvt, Army, 50, released as Sgt, 52, after serv. in 31st Inf. Div. and European Hq. Command. Mem: Secy-treas, Md. Bowling Proprietors Asn, 7 years; pres, Md. Tenpin Bowling Proprietors Asn; bd. dirs, Bowling Proprietors Asn. Am; Lions; Elks; Touchdown Club; VFW; Am. Legion; Cotillion Club; Catoctin Club; bd. dirs, YMCA. Rel: Episcopal. Mailing Add: 710 Wyngate Dr, Frederick, Md. 21701.

THOMAS, ELWYN D
Justice, Fla. Supreme Court
b. Ankona, Fla, 7/5/94; s. Harry S. Thomas and Julia Eldred T; m. 6/18/24 to Eva Banes; c. Patricia (Mrs. Walter M. Meginniss) and Pamela Elwyn. Educ: John B. Stetson Univ. Acad, B.S, 12, Col. Law, LL.B, 15; Phi Alpha Delta; Alpha Kappa Psi; Phi Beta Kappa; Sigma Nu. Polit. & Govt. Pos: Prosecuting attorney, Fla, 16-18; city attorney, Ft. Pierce, 18-25 and Vero Beach, 19-23; circuit judge, 25-38; justice, Fla. Supreme Court, 38-, chief justice, 47-49 & 59-61. Mil. Serv: Coast Artil, 18. Publ: Articles in Law Reviews, Univ. Fla, Univ. Tenn. and George Wash. Univ. Mem: Bd. Fels, Inst. of Judicial Admin; bd. fels, Am. Bar Found; chmn, Sect. of Judicial Admin, Am. Bar Asn, 56-57; Supreme Justice, Phi Alpha Delta, 56-58; Mason; Am. Legion, 48 yrs; former mem, Tallahassee Rotary Club. Rel: Episcopal. Legal Res: Supreme Court Bldg, Tallahassee, Fla. 32304. Mailing Add: 1480 Sycamore St, Tallahassee, Fla. 32303.

THOMAS, EUSTACE KIRK D
b. E. Charlotte, Vt, 3/25/00; married; c. four sons and six daughters. Educ: St. Michael's High Sch, Winooski, Vt. Polit. & Govt. Pos: Sch. dir, 30-; town overseer of the poor, 36-47; Vt. State Rep, 48-49, 61, 63 & 65. Bus. & Prof. Pos: Farmer. Mem: Grange; Optimist. Rel: Catholic. Mailing Add: Shelburne, Vt. 05482. (1967)

THOMAS, FREDA KATHERINE D
Mem, Dem. Nat. Cmt. for S.Dak.
b. King City, Mo, 6/5/05; d. Charles Spaht and Elizabeth Graham S; m. 8/7/52 to Herbert Thomas; c. Ann Wilinson (Mrs. C. A. Lother). Polit. & Govt. Pos: Mem, Dem. Nat. Cmt. for S.Dak, 60- Bus. & Prof. Pos: Partner, Thomas Realty Co, Pierre, S.Dak, 52-; proprietor, Paul's Greenhouse, Pierre, until 52. Mem: Zonta Int. Club (pres, Pierre-Ft. Pierce Chap). Mailing Add: St. Charles Hotel, Pierre, S.Dak. 57501. (1967)

THOMAS, JAMES KAY D
b. Charleston, W.Va, 2/23/02; s. George E. Thomas and Jean Susan Kay T; m. to Julia Lewis Roseberry; c. Julia Roseberry (Mrs. Payne) and James Kay, Jr. Educ: Wash. and Lee Univ, LL.B, 26. Polit. & Govt. Pos: W.Va. State Del, 32-40, Speaker, W.Va. House of Del, 37-41; Attorney Gen, W.Va, 42-43; first asst. to Attorney Gen, W.Va, 45-48; cmnr. of Motor Vehicles, W.Va, 65-68. Bus. & Prof. Pos: Lawyer; former assoc, Firm of Hill, Thomas, Neff & Morris; gen. counsel and asst. secy, Atlantic Greyhound Corp, 48-59, v.pres. and gen. counsel, 59, v.pres, South. Greyhound Lines Div, 59-65, retired, 65. Mil. Serv: Entered as Capt, Army Air Corps, 42, released as Lt. Col, after serv. in Africa, Italy, Sicily, Corsica, France and Germany; 7 Battle Stars; Am. and European Theatre Serv. Medals; Bronze Star. Mem: Charleston Rotary; Am. and W.Va. State Bar Asns; Mason; Shriner; Elks; Edgewood Country Club; Press Club; mem, Bd. Trustees, Charleston Gen. Hosp, pres, Bd. Trustees, 5 years; bd. dirs, W.Va. C. of C. Rel: Methodist. Mailing Add: 11 Norwood Rd, Charleston, W.Va. 25314. (1967)

THOMAS, JAMES P. D
b. McKinney, Tex; m. to Betty Griffin; c. Jamie and Max. Educ: Baylor Univ, B.A; Ohio State Univ, M.A; N. Tex. Univ; Univ. Wash. Polit. & Govt. Pos: Colo. State Sen, 65-68; chmn, Otero Co. Dem. Cmt. Bus. & Prof. Pos: Partner, produce Firm of Ike, Griffin, Holder & Thomas; v.pres, Frozen Foods, Inc. Mem: Rotary; Quarterback Club; Nat. Onion Asn; Nat. Rifle Asn; Phi Alpha Theta. Rel: Baptist. Mailing Add: Route 2, Box 511, Rocky Ford, Colo. 81067. (1967)

THOMAS, JERRY D
Fla. State Sen.
b. West Palm Beach, Fla, 4/30/29; s. Larry Arthur Thomas (deceased) and Irene Lee T; m. 11/21/51 to Imogene Hair 'Jeannie'; c. Robbie Lee, Larry Arthur, II, Kenneth Cook, Jerry Leroy and Cindy Lynn. Educ: Palm Beach Jr. Col, A.A, 49; Fla. State Univ, B.S, 51 and grad. study; Fla. Atlantic Univ. Grad. Sch, M.E, 67; Grad. Schs. of Bus. in Sr. Bank Mgt, Harvard and Columbia Univs; Omicron Delta Kappa; Gold Key; Pi Alpha Sigma; Sigma Nu. Polit. & Govt. Pos: Dir. and adminstr, Fla. Securities Cmn, 55-57; Fla. State Rep, 60-64; Fla. State Sen, 64- Bus. & Prof. Pos: Chmn. of the bd, First Bank of Jupiter/Tequesta, 63-, First Marine Bank & Trust Co, 64-, First Commercial Bank of Live Oak, 66- and Marine Nat. Bank of Jacksonville, 68-; chmn. and pres, Bancstock Corp. of Am, 64- and First Nat. Bank & Trust Co, 66-; former mem. of two nat. stock exchanges. Mil. Serv: Entered as Seaman, Navy, released as Midn; reentered as Cpl, Marine Corps, released as Capt. Publ: 'Florida's Political Uniqueness,' Smoke Signals, 52; 'Florida Securities Commission Protects Investors,' Capitol Post, 56. Mem: Palm Beach Co. chmn, U.S. Savings Bond Div; Fla. State Univ. Alumni Asn; dir, Children's Home Soc. of Fla; dir, S. Fla. Fair & Exposition; bd. of adv, Fla. State Univ. Found, Inc; former dir, Fla. Heart Asn; past chmn. and pres. of bd, Heart Asn. of Palm Beach and Martin Counties; bd. of gov, Fla. Vision Found; mem. adv. bd, J. Edwin Larson Found. for Ins. Educ; Izaak Walton League of Am; Gr. West Palm Beach and North. Palm Beach C. of C; past pres, Palm Beach Lions Club; Am. Legion; Tiger Bay Club; Islanders; Fla. and Am. Bankers Asns; mem. bd. of gov, Nat. Asn. of Small Bus. Investment Co. Chosen for Allen Morris Awards as Most Outstanding First Term Mem. of Fla. House of Rep, 61, Most Outstanding First Term Mem. of Fla. Senate, 65 and Most Outstanding Second Term Mem. of Fla. Senate, 67; Named One of Five Outstanding Young Men of Fla, 61 and State Good Govt. Award, 67, Fla. Jr. C. of C; Water and Soil Conserv. Award, Nat. and Fla. Wildlife Fedn. Rel: Presbyterian; Elder. Legal Res: Route 1, Box 19960, Jupiter, Fla. 33458. Mailing Add: First Marine Bank & Trust Co, Riviera Beach, Fla. 33404.

THOMAS, JOHN J. R
Ind. State Rep.
b. Rockville, Ind, 11/14/23; s. Joe J. Thomas and Hazel Gross T; m. 12/23/45 to Jessie Sparks; c. Jana, Jamie and Joanna. Educ: Ind. Univ, LL.B, 48; Phi Eta Sigma; Sigma Delta Kappa. Polit. & Govt. Pos: Prosecuting attorney, Clay Co, Ind, 51-58 and co. attorney, 62-; Ind. State Rep. and asst. majority leader, currently. Bus. & Prof. Pos: Attorney, Brazil, Ind, 48- Mil. Serv: Entered as Air Cadet, Air Force, 43, released as Sgt, 46. Mem: Clay Co, Ind. and Am. Bar Asns; Trial Lawyers Asn; Ind. Univ. Alumni Asn; Nat. Coun. Bd. and past pres, Wabash Valley Coun, Boy Scouts; pres, Ind. Prosecutors Asn, 54-55; Elks; Am. Legion; past pres, Brazil Rotary Club; Clay Co. Farm Bur; F&AM, Scottish Rite. Rel: Methodist; Conf. Lay Leader, United Methodist Church. Mailing Add: 823 N. Meridian, Brazil, Ind. 47834.

THOMAS, JOHN PEARCE, JR. R
b. Hopkinsville, Ky, 9/30/20; s. John Pearce Thomas and Agnes Flack T; m. 11/12/55 to Marjorie Bryant; c. Karen (Mrs. Roger McCauley), Marjorie Bryant; Carroll Kennedy and Stephen Brook. Educ: Amherst Col, B.A, 43; Delta Upsilon. Polit. & Govt. Pos: Cmnr. of Waterworks, Tulsa, Okla, 54-56; mem, Tulsa Utility Bd, 56-61 & 66-; dir, Rep. City Campaign, Tulsa, 58, 60, 62 & 64; chmn, Okla. Rep. State Finance Cmt, 60-61; del, Rep. Nat. Conv, 60 & 68, del. and housing chmn. for Okla, 64; mem. exec. cmt, Campaigns of Henry Bellmon for Gov, 62, U.S. Sen, 68, Bud Wilkinson for U.S. Sen, 64 and Dewey Bartlett for Gov, Okla, 66; chmn, Tulsa Co. Rep. Finance Cmt, 63-64; traveling rep, Citizens for Goldwater in States of Pa, Ill. and Ind, 64. Bus. & Prof. Pos: Asst. to chmn. bd, Nat. Tank Co, 56-67; self-employed developer and investor, 67- Mil. Serv: Entered as Pvt, Army, 42, released as Capt, 47, after serv. in 66th Inf, 71st Div, ETO; 5 Battle Stars; Purple Heart; Bronze Star, Am. Theatre and European Theatre; German Occup, Combat Infantryman's Badge. Mem: Effective Citizens Orgn.(past dir, pub. affairs chmn, currently). Rel: Protestant. Mailing Add: 2607 E. 26th Place, Tulsa, Okla. 74114.

THOMAS, JOSEPH N. R
b. Gary, Ind, 2/22/29; s. Ray C. Thomas and Josephine Kelley T; m. 6/17/56 to Bonnie Lee Trapp; c. Jeanine E, Nancy G. and Charna K. Educ: Ind. Univ, B.S. with honors, 51; Harvard Law Sch, LL.B. cum laude, 54; Beta Gamma Sigma; Acacia Blue Key; Chancery Club. Polit. & Govt. Pos: Del, Rep. State Conv, 64, 66 & 68; alternate del, Rep. Nat. Conv, 68; chmn, Ind. Port Cmn, 69-; presidential appointee, St. Lawrence Seaway Adv. Cmn, 69- Bus. & Prof. Pos: Partner, Law Firm of Thomas, Thomas, Burke & Richardson, 57-, managing partner, 62-; bd. dirs, Gary Nat. Bank, 69- Mil. Serv: Entered as 1st Lt, Air Force, 54, released 57, after serv. in 326th Fighter Group, Cent. Air Defense Command. Mem: Gary and Ind. Bar Asns; Ind. Asn. of CPA; Gary Kiwanis Club (bd. dirs, 68-); Gary Jaycees (treas, 59, exec. v.pres, 60, bd. dirs, 60-63). Award for Highest Grade in Ind. CPA Exam, 51. Rel: Presbyterian; Elder. Mailing Add: 504 Broadway, Room 1016, Gary, Ind. 46402.

THOMAS, KATHLEEN PHYLLIS R
Mem, Calif. Rep. State Cent. Cmt.
b. Bakersfield, Calif, 4/8/17; d. Harry Joseph Hendry and Catherine Belshaw H; m. 4/25/43 to George Preston Thomas; c. Patricia Eileen (Mrs. McCoey), George Preston, Jr. and Catherine Jane. Educ: Bakersfield Jr. Col, A.A, 37; Univ. Calif, Berkeley, A.B. and Teaching Credential, 40; San Jose State Col, pupil-personnel credential, Polit. & Govt. Pos: Rep. precinct worker, Morgan Hill, Calif, 52-69; secy, Morgan Hill Rep. Assembly, 60-62, dir, 67-69; mem, Calif. Rep. State Cent. Cmt, 67- Bus. & Prof. Pos: Teacher, Live Oak High Sch, 40-45, head counsr, 53-69. Mem: Am. and Calif. Personnel & Guid. Asns; Eastern Star. Sch. awards. Rel: Episcopal. Legal Res: 17350 Hill Rd, Morgan Hill, Calif. 95037.

THOMAS, NELSON EDISON D
Mem, Roanoke Co. Dem. Cmt, Va.
b. Floyd, Va, 4/10/17; s. Josiah Ananias Thomas and Malinda Arbella Landcaster T; m. 8/3/38 to Edna Ellen Hale; c. Larry W. and Sue Ellen. Polit. & Govt. Pos: Floyd Co. committeeman, Fed. Housing Admin, 60-62; real estate appraiser, Va. Dept. of Taxation, 60-66; Floyd Co. Dem. campaign mgr, 61; mem, Floyd Co. Dem. Cmt, Va, 62-66; del, Dem. Nat. and Va. Conv, 64; mem, Roanoke Co. Dem. Cmt, Va, currently. Bus. & Prof. Pos: Beef cattle producer, 49-65. Mil. Serv: Pvt, Army Air Corps, 43. Mem: Am. Legion; DAV; Va. Asn. of Assessing Officers; Nat. Farmers Union; Ruritans; Aberdeen Angus Asn. Rel: Baptist. Mailing Add: 4887 Brookwood Dr, Roanoke, Va. 24018. (1967)

THOMAS, NORMA GILES D
V.Chmn, Utah State Dem. Party
b. Provo, Utah, 4/18/24; d. Charles Edward Giles and Bertha Bateman G; m. 4/17/45 to Daniel W. Thomas (deceased); c. Daniel G. and Charles Howard. Educ: Brigham Young Univ, 1 year. Polit. & Govt. Pos: V.chmn, Utah Co. Young Dem, 45-46; v.chmn, Utah Co. Dem. Cmt, 47-48; v.chmn, Utah State Dem. Party, 66-; del, Dem. Nat. Conv, 68; cmnr, Utah State Liquor Cmn, 69- Mem: Lions. Rel: Latter-day Saint. Mailing Add: 371 East 300 South, Provo, Utah 84601.

THOMAS, PAT FRANKLIN D
Chmn, Fla. State Dem. Exec. Cmt.
b. Quincy, Fla, 11/21/33; s. Pat Thomas and Verna Peacock T; m. to Mary

Ann Jolley; c. Ann Jolley and John Pat. Educ: Univ. Fla, degree in agr. econ; state v.pres, Future Farmers Am; pres, Alpha Gamma Rho; pres, sr. class; Blue Key. Polit. & Govt. Pos: Mem, State Campaign Staff of Agr. Cmnr, Doyle Conner, Fla; area coordinator, Successful Cong. Campaign; mem, Gadsden Co. Dem. Party; chmn, Gadsden Co. Presidential Campaign Reception, 64; Dem. State Committeeman, Gadsden Co, 66-; chmn, Fla. State Dem. Exec. Cmt, 66-; organizing chmn. state del, Dem. Nat. Conv, 68. Bus. & Prof. Pos: Serv. rep, Fla. Farm Bur, 60-62; owner, Gen. Ins. Agency, 62- Mil. Serv: Army, serv. in Korean War. Mem: Pres, Gadsden Co. Asn. of Ins. Agents, 66, Quincy Jr. C. of C, 66; past pres, Quincy Rotary and Men of the Church; mgr, C. of C, Quincy, 2 years; Fla. Asn. of Ins. Agents; Am. Legion; Am. Cancer Soc; Mason (32°); Shrine; Sawano Country Club, Quincy. Selected, One of Five Outstanding Young Men, Fla. Jaycees, 67. Rel: Presbyterian. Legal Res: Highway 90, P.O. Box 488, Quincy, Fla. 32351. Mailing Add: P.O. Box 488, Quincy, Fla. 32351.

THOMAS, PETER W. R
N.J. State Assemblyman
m. to Barbara Feuchsel; three children. Educ: Rutgers Univ, A.B. and Rutgers Univ. Law Sch, LL.B; Phi Delta Phi; Beta Theta Pi. Polit. & Govt. Pos: Past pres, Morris Co. Young Rep. Club and Chatham Young Rep. Club, N.J, former legis. asst. to Morris Co. Assemblyman; counsel to Rep. Co. Cmt, 61-65; Morris Co. Campaign Chmn, 63; Morris Co. Campaign Chmn. for Sen. Cand. Bernard M. Shanley, 64; asst. Morris Co. counsel and munic. counsel, Borough of Kinnelon; chmn, Morris Co. Rep. Cmt, N.J, 65-; del, N.J. Constitutional Conv, 66; alternate del, Rep. Nat. Conv, 68; N.J. State Assemblyman, 68- Bus. & Prof. Pos: Instr. bus. law, Rutgers Univ, 55-60; partner, Lum, Biunno & Thompkins; counsel to and mem, Chatham Emergency Squad; guest lectr, N.J. Inst. for Continuing Legal Educ; former counsel to Morris-Somerset P.B.A, Local 139. Publ: Contributing writer to N.J. Law Practice series. Mem: N.J. and Morris Co. Bar Asns; Am. Bar Asn.(mem. munic. law & ins. negligence and compensation law sect. and former N.J. chmn. world peace through law cmt); Chatham Anti-Jetport Asn.(secy); Speakers' Bur. and Legal Cmt. of Jersey Jetport Site Asn; charter mem, Chatham Area Jr. C. of C; former fund drive cmt. chmn, Newark United Appeals; former fund drive chmn, YM-YWCA; former mem, Chatham Baseball Cmt; former Little League coach; past pres, Rutgers Alumni Asn. of Morris Co; former mem, Rutgers Law Sch. Alumni Coun; Chatham Hist. Soc; Chatham Commun. Players. Recipient Jaycee Distinguished Serv. Award, Chatham, 64; Outstanding Norris Co. Rep. Award, 66. Mailing Add: 25 Rowan Rd, Chatham, N.J. 07928.

THOMAS, REESE SAMUEL R
b. Dalton, Ga, 6/3/18; s. Sam W. Thomas and Lucy Patterson T; m. 8/31/41 to Margaret Strickland; c. Tim C, Kay, Jan. Educ: Pleasant Grove High Sch, 38. Polit. & Govt. Pos: Judge Court of Appeals; Ga. State Sen, 63-64. Bus. & Prof. Pos: Carpet mill supvr, Cabin Crafts, Inc. Mem: Mason, Past Master Cohutta Lodge No. 64. Rel: Baptist. Mailing Add: Dalton, Ga. 30720. (1967)

THOMAS, RENO HENRY R
Pa. State Rep.
b. Beavertown, Pa, 7/11/22; s. Herbert Franklin Thomas and Ada Hetrick T; m. 4/2/44 to Phyllis Ellen Middleswarth; c. Gayle Ellen and Wendy Lou. Educ: Pa. State Univ, B.S. agr. educ, 43; Alpha Tau Alpha. Polit. & Govt. Pos: Mem, West Snyder Sch. Bd, 47-62; cmnr, Pa. State Farm Show, 63-; Pa. State Rep, 68- Bus. & Prof. Pos: Owner and mgr, Brooks End Farm, 45-69; pres, Pa. Yorkshire Coop. Inc, 54-; pres, Am. Yorkshire Club Inc, 62-64. Mem: Pa. Livestock and Allied Industs. Asn; exec. cmt, Meat Animal Eval. Center for Pa; Moose; Pa. Farmers Asn; Grange; Beavertown Fire Co; State Coun. Farm Orgn; Pa. Agr. Exten. Asn. State Master Farmers Award, 64; Ford Farm Efficiency Award, 67; Commun. Leader of Am, 68. Rel: United Church of Christ. Mailing Add: R.D. 1, Beavertown, Pa. 17813.

THOMAS, RICHARD CLARK R
Secy. of State Vt.
b. Washburn, Maine, 5/3/37; s. Orin A. Thomas, Jr. and Amelia Woodman T; m. 11/28/64 to Clara Betty Wright; c. twins, Lisa Rae and Leslie Lynn. Educ: Middlebury Col, B.S. in Polit. Sci, 59; Georgetown Law Sch, 62-63; Sigma Phi Epsilon. Polit. & Govt. Pos: Prfnl. staff mem, Sen. Cmt. On Commerce, 63; res. and press asst. to U.S. Sen. W.L. Prouty, Vt, 63-65; coordinator, campaign of U.S. Sen. Winston Prouty, Vt, 64; exec. dir, Vt. State Rep. Cmt, 65-67; secy, Legis. Apportionment Bd, 69-; chmn, Pub. Records Adv. Bd, 69-; chmn, Travel Info. Coun, 69-; Cmnr. of For. Corporations, 69-; Secy. of State, Vt, 69- Bus. & Prof. Pos: Reporter, Construction News & Statist. Div, McGraw-Hill Pub. Co, N.Y.C, 60-63. Mil. Serv: Entered as 2nd Lt, Army, 59, served in Hq. and Hq. Co, Third Bn, 304th Training Regt; Capt, Army Artil. Standby Res. Publ: Vermont Almanac and Government Guide, 66. Mem: Vt. Soc. of Asn. Exec. Secretaries; Nat. Asn. of Secretaries of State; Vt. Hist. Soc. (trustee, 69-); Rotary; Am. Legion. Rel: Baptist. Mailing Add: 17 Pinewood Rd, Montpelier, Vt. 05602.

THOMAS, RICHARD JOSEPH D
Mem, Wash. Co. Dem. Exec. Cmt, Ohio
b. Columbus, Ohio, 8/22/26; s. Henry Harlan Thomas and Pauline Rohr T; m. 2/14/53 to Rose Marie Peschan; c. Gregory, Stephanie and Johanna. Educ: Ohio State Univ, A.B, 49 and LL.B, 51; Phi Delta Phi; Tau Kappa Epsilon. Polit. & Govt. Pos: Attorney, Ohio Dept. of Liquor Control, 51-55; Ohio Presidential Elector, 60; chmn, Wash. Co. Dem. Exec. Cmt, 62-67, mem, 62-; del-at-lg, Dem. Nat. Conv, 64; mem, Marietta City Bd. of Health, 66; mem, Wash. Co. Bd. of Elections, 66-; mem, Marietta City Planning Cmn, 67- Bus. & Prof. Pos: Mem, Unemployment and Workmen's Compensation Cmt, Ohio State Bar Asn, 65- Mil. Serv: Navy, 44-46. Mem: Ohio State and Wash. Co. Bar Asns; Am. Trial Lawyers Asn; exec. bd, Wash. Co. Chap, Am. Red Cross; Lions; Marietta Area C. of C. Legal Res: 101 Merryhill Dr, Marietta, Ohio 45750. Mailing Add: 306 First National Bank Bldg, Marietta, Ohio 45750.

THOMAS, ROBERT C. R
Chmn, Juab Co. Rep. Party, Utah
b. Castleford, Idaho, 3/2/15; s. George Foster Thomas and Lucinda Cherrington T; m. 7/4/38 to Winona Calking; c. Chyrle (Mrs. Terry L. Nelson) and R. Bruce. Educ: Albion State Normal, Dipl, 35. Polit. & Govt. Pos: Chmn, Juab Co. Rep. Party, Utah, 65- Bus. & Prof. Pos: Teacher, Castleford Sch. Bd, 38-41; Field Geologist, The Anaconda Co, 42-69, Resident Engr, 69- Mem: Inst. Mining, Metallurgical & Petroleum Engrs; F&AM (Past Master); Elks (Past Exalted Ruler). Mailing Add: P.O. Box 118, Eureka, Utah 84628.

THOMAS, SIM ALLEN JR. D
b. Nixburg, Ala, 9/17/04; s. Sim Allen Thomas; Fannie Smith T; m. 6/15/35 to Kate Carlton; c. Virginia (Mrs. Ralph C. Moseley). Educ: Howard Col; George Washington Univ; Auburn Univ, B.S, in pharm. Polit. & Govt. Pos: Ala. State Rep. for 18 years, -66; mem. Eufaula City Coun. for 8 years. Bus. & Prof. Pos: Druggist, 31- Mem: Bd. of Trustees of Auburn Univ; Bd. of Ala. State Hosp; Mason; Shriner. Rel: Presbyterian. Mailing Add: Eufaula, Ala. 36027. (1967)

THOMAS, STAN, JR. D
Mo. State Rep.
b. Liberty, Mo, 10/17/23; m. 2/6/48 to Margaret Finney; c. Mike, Pat and Brian. Educ: William Jewell Col, B.A; Sigma Nu. Polit. & Govt. Pos: Past. pres, Clay Co. Young Dem, Mo; Mo. State Rep, 88th Dist, 64-, v.chmn, Fees and Salaries Cmt, Mo. House of Rep, mem, Interstate Coop. Cmt. and Bills Perfected and Passed Cmt; del, Dem. Nat. Conv, 68. Bus. & Prof. Pos: Eng. serv. rep, 48-51; owner of disposal serv, 49-; athletic coach and algebra teacher, 51-53. Mil. Serv: Naval Res, World War II (3 years). Mem: AF&AM; Mason; Shrine; past pres, Liberty Jaycees; Beta Xi; v.pres, Liberty Shrine Club. Rel: Methodist. Mailing Add: Room 401, Capitol Bldg, Jefferson City, Mo. 65101.

THOMAS, STANLEY BUDDINGTON, JR. R
Dep. Asst. Secy, Dept. of Health, Educ. and Welfare
b. N.Y.C, 4/28/42; s. Stanley B. Thomas, Sr. and Marion Y. T; m. 6/27/64 to Patricia Strickland; c. Kimberly and Kelly. Educ: Yale Univ, B.A, 64; Delta Kappa Epsilon. Polit. & Govt. Pos: Asst. to Mayor John V. Lindsey, N.Y.C, 66; dep. asst. secy, Dept. of Health, Educ. and Welfare, 69- Bus. & Prof. Pos: Asst. to v.pres. and secy, Time, Inc, 64-66, mgr, Col. Bur, 67-68; mgr, personnel rels, Philip Morris, Inc, 69. Mem: Yale Club of N.Y; former chmn, N.Y.C. Young Rep. Club; Nat. Negro Rep. Assembly. Rel: Episcopal. Legal Res: 501 W. 156th St, New York, N.Y. 10032. Mailing Add: 1435 Fourth St. S.W, Washington, D.C. 20024.

THOMAS, THEODORE FREDERICK R
Mem, Calif. Rep. State Cent. Cmt.
b. Los Angeles, Calif, 5/7/25; both parents deceased; m. 1/31/55 to Evelyn Caccialanza; c. Gary Steven and Bruce Scott. Educ: City Col. of San Francisco, A.A, 48; Los Angeles State Col, B.S, 60. Polit. & Govt. Pos: Pres, Studio City Young Rep, Sherman Oaks, Calif, 63; pres, Studio City UROC, 64-65; mem, Calif. Rep. State Cent. Cmt, 64- and Los Angeles Co. Cent. Cmt, 68- Bus. & Prof. Pos: V.pres, Los Angeles Fastener Asn, 69. Mil. Serv: Entered as Seaman, Navy, 42, released as SH 2/C, 46, after serv. in ETO and Pac. Theatre, 43-46; reentered during Korean War, 50-51; Pac. Area Medal with five stars; European Medal with two stars; Korean Serv. Medal; UN Medal; Am. Theatre Ribbon; China Serv. Medal; World War II Victory Medal; Philippine Govt. Medal. Mem: San Fernando Valley businessmen and prfnl. orgns. Rel: Protestant. Mailing Add: 11940 Weddington St, North Hollywood, Calif. 91607.

THOMAS, THOMAS PAUL D
Councilman, City of Bristol, Conn.
b. North Tarrytown, N.Y, 8/3/12; s. Paul Thomas and Justine Benedict T; m. 9/14/40 to Eleanor Dorothy Northrop; c. Thomas P, Jr, Suzanne H. and George N. Educ: High sch. Polit. & Govt. Pos: Cmnr, Parking Authority, 60-63 and first selectman, 63-65; councilman, City of Bristol, Conn, 63-; mem, Dem. Town Cmt, Bristol, Conn, 64- Bus. & Prof. Pos: Telegraph operator, 35-40 and mgr, West. Union Tel. Co, 40- Mem: K. of C; Elks; Commercial Telegraphers Union, AFL-CIO, Local 146. Rel: Catholic. Legal Res: 19 Driftwood Rd, Bristol, Conn. 06010. Mailing Add: Box 932, Bristol, Conn. 06010. (1967)

THOMAS, VINCENT D
Calif. State Assemblyman
m. 11/5/47 to Mary DiCarlo T; c. Mary Virginia and Vincent, Jr. Educ: Univ. Santa Clara, Ph.B, 32; Law Sch, Univ. Santa Clara, 32-34; Loyola Law Sch, 34-36; minor sports coach, Univ. Santa Clara, 30-34. Polit. & Govt. Pos: Presidential Elector, Calif, 40 & 44; Calif. State Assemblyman, 40- Bus. & Prof. Pos: Phys. Educ. Instr, 33-34; chmn, Joint Legis. Audit Cmt, 63- Mem: Elks; Redmen; Pac. Marine Fisheries Cmn. Mailing Add: 255 W. 5th St, San Pedro, Calif. 90731.

THOMAS, WILLIAM
b. 1925. Educ: High sch, grad. Polit. & Govt. Pos: Minn. State Rep, until 66. Bus. & Prof. Pos: Cargill, Inc, 55-60; George Cook Construction, 60-63; Utility Serv. Co, 63-66; supvr, Shaklee Prod. Mil. Serv: Navy, 3 years. Mem: VFW; Cooties-IWO; Projectionist Union,Local 563. Rel: First Christian Church; First Divine Science. 1967 Legal Res: Minneapolis, Minn. No mailing address available. (1967)

THOMAS, WILLIAM FRANKLIN, JR. D
Chmn, Pulaski Co. Dem. Cmt, Va.
b. Pulaski, Va, 1/2/34; s. William Franklin Thomas and Virginia Mason Saunders T; m. 9/8/62 to Nora Gertrude Davis. Educ: Emory and Henry Col, 50-52; Univ. Richmond, B.S. in B.A, 54; Univ. Va, LL.B, 57; Soc. Adv. Mgt; Phi Gamma Delta. Polit. & Govt. Pos: Del, Dem. State Convs, Va, 56-68 and mem. resolutions cmt, 68; del, Ninth Dist. Dem. Convs, 58-68 and keynote speaker and permanent chmn, 68; del, Dem. Nat. Conv, 60; chmn, Pulaski Co. Dollars for Dem. Campaign, 60; secy-treas, Pulaski Co. Dem. Cmt, 61-67 and chmn, 67-; co. co-campaign mgr, Gov. Mills E. Godwin, Jr, 65; co. co-campaign primary mgr, Harry F. Byrd, Jr. for U.S. Sen, 66. Bus. & Prof. Pos: Partner, Gilmer, Sadler, Ingram, Thomas & Sutherland, Attorneys, 60- Mem: Pulaski Co. Bar Asn.(pres, 64-65); Va. State Bar; Va. State Bar Asn; Elks (treas, 67-68); Pulaski Jaycees (pres, 69-70); AF&AM, Worshipful Master, Masonic Lodge, 63. Rel: United Methodist. Mailing Add: 2211 Pleasant Hill Dr, Pulaski, Va. 24301.

THOMASON, BENJAMIN WALTER D
b. Greenville City, S.C; s. Benjamin Arnold Thomason and Emma Leake T; m. 6/21/22 to Janette Martin; c. Jeanne Meredith, Benjamin Walter Jr. and William Martin. Educ: Furman Univ, B.A, 21; Southern Baptist Theol. Sem, ThM, 25. Polit. & Govt. Pos: N.C. State Rep, 63-66; Mayor of Brevard, N.C; N.C. State Sen. Bus. & Prof. Pos: Pastor, First Baptist Church, Brevard, N.C, 18 years. Mil. Serv: Navy, 18, Chief PO; Lt.(sg), Naval Res, 42-43. Mem: Mason (32°). Mailing Add: P.O. Box 783, Brevard, N.C. 28712. (1967)

THOMASON, LARRY WILSON D
Ga. State Rep.
b. Atlanta, Ga, 2/4/42; s. Robert Wilson Thomason and Carrie Cleveland T; m. 6/9/63 to Ida Olivia Baker; c. Laura. Educ: Fla. State Univ, $3\frac{1}{2}$ years; Emory Univ, B.A; Emory Univ. Sch. Law, LL.B; Delta Tau Delta; Phi Delta Phi; Pershing Rifles. Polit. & Govt. Pos: Asst. City Attorney, Decatur, Ga, 66; Legis. Counsel, DeKalb Del, Ga. Gen. Assembly, 68; Ga. State Rep, 69-, secy, 19-Man DeKalb Legis. Del, Ga. Gen. Assembly, 69. Bus. & Prof. Pos: Self-employed Attorney, Decatur, Ga, 65-; part-time faculty mem, Sch. of Bus. Law, Ga. State Col, Atlanta, Ga, 69- Publ: 'A Democrat Speaks Out', Weekly Opinion Column, Decatur-DeKalb News, 69-70. Mem: Decatur-DeKalb Bar Asn.(treas, 66-68, v.pres, 69-); State Bar of Ga; Am. Bar Asn; Am. Trial Lawyers Asn; Elks; Kiwanis Int; DeKalb C. of C; Fla. State Univ. Alumni Asn.(divisional pres); Emory Univ. Alumni Asn; Druid Hills Civic Asn. Rel: Baptist. Legal Res: 811 Oakdale Rd, Atlanta, Ga. 30307. Mailing Add: 406 Decatur Federal Bldg, Decatur, Ga. 30030.

THOMASON, ROBERT EWING D
b. Shelbyville, Tenn, 5/30/79; s. Dr. Benjamine R. Thomason and Susan Olivia Hoover T; m. 8/18/27 to Abbie Long T; c. William Ewing, Isabelle. Educ: Southwest. Univ, Georgetown, Tex, B.S, 98; Univ. Tex, LL.B, 00. Polit. & Govt. Pos: U.S. Rep, Tex, 31-47; mayor of El Paso, 27-31; mem. Tex. State House of Reps, 17-21 (speaker, 20-21); U.S. Dist. Judge, West. Dist. Tex. Bus. & Prof. Pos: Lawyer, 00-; law practice, El Paso, Tex, 12-; dist. attorney, Gainsville, 02-06. Mem: Kappa Sigma; Phi Delta Phi; Mason (33°). Rel: Presbyterian. Legal Res: 1918 N. Stanton St, El Paso, Tex. 79901. Mailing Add: Federal Building, El Paso, Tex. 79901. (1967)

THOMPSON, ADA McCALL D
Mem, Calif. Dem. State Cent. Cmt.
b. Elmhurst, Ill, 2/11/30; d. Mahlon McCullough McCall and Eva Work M; m. 7/17/54 to Paul Oscar Thompson; c. Eric McCall and Scott William. Educ: Bryn Mawr Col, 48-50; Southwest. Col, 68- Polit. & Govt. Pos: 37th Cong. Dist. dir, Calif. Dem. Coun, 67-69; mem. Chula Vista Ethics Bd, Chula Vista City Cmn, 67-; del, Dem. Nat. Conv, 68; mem, Calif. Dem. State Cent. Cmt, 68- Mem: League of Women Voters (first pres, Chula Vista Club, 62-63); hon. life mem, PTA (v.pres. and pres, 65-69); Am. Civil Liberties Union; Bryn Mawr Col. Club of South. Calif.(student interviewer); UN Asn. Speakers Bur. Rel: Unitarian; Church Coun. Mailing Add: 1060 Las Bancas Court, Chula Vista, Calif. 92011.

THOMPSON, ALAN D
Wash. State Rep.
b. Geneva, Iowa, 1927; m. to Barbara R; c. four sons. Educ: Univ. Nebr; Univ. Calif, B.A; Beta Theta Pi. Polit. & Govt. Pos: Wash. State Rep, currently. Bus. & Prof. Pos: Publisher weekly newspapers, Cowlitz Co. Advocate and Lewis Co. News. Mil. Serv: Navy. Mem: Elks. Mailing Add: 310 Cowlitz View Dr, Castle Rock, Wash. 98611.

THOMPSON, ALBERT C. JR. R
b. Tacoma, Wash, 1919; m. to Nancy T; c. two. Educ: Univ. Wash. Polit. & Govt. Pos: Wash. State Sen, second term, until 66. Bus. & Prof. Pos: Owner and operator, retail drug store. Mailing Add: 2300 108th S.E, Bellevue, Wash. 98004. (1967)

THOMPSON, ALBERT WILLIAM D
Ga. State Rep.
b. Ft. Benning, Ga, 6/29/22; s. Charles Edward Thompson and Mary Elizabeth Houser T; m. 6/6/53 to Dorothy O. Jackson; c. Eloise Marie, Charles E, III and Albert W, Jr. Educ: Savannah State Col, B.S, 42; Howard Univ, LL.B, 50. Polit. & Govt. Pos: Ga. State Rep, Dist. 110, 66- Mil. Serv: Entered as Pvt, Army, 43, released as Sgt, 43, after serv. in 41st Eng. Regt, ETO, 42-44. Mem: State Bar Ga; Columbus Lawyer's Club; Am. Legion; C. of C. Man of the Year, Progressive Club, 65. Rel: Baptist. Mailing Add: 4154 Swann St, Columbus, Ga. 31903. Mailing Add: 210 Ninth St, Columbus, Ga. 31901.

THOMPSON, ALLEN CAVETT D
Mayor, Jackson, Miss.
b. Jackson, Miss, 11/05/06; s. Allen Thompson and Mattie Cavett T; m. 9/4/29 to Evana Shelby; c. Allen Cavett, Evana S. (Mrs. James Mayo McKay) and William I. Educ: Univ. Miss, B.A, 27, LL.B, 29; admitted to Miss. Bar, 31. Polit. & Govt. Pos: Mem, Miss. Legis, 40-44; excise tax cmnr, Miss, 46-48; mayor, Jackson, Miss, 49-; del, U.S. Int. Union Cities, Brighton, Eng, 51. Bus. & Prof. Pos: Instr. of Greek, Univ. Miss, 27-29; prof. of hist. and geog, Blue Mt. Col, 29-31; law practice, Jackson, 31-49; visiting prof. of Greek, Millsaps Col, 34-35. Mil. Serv: Lt.(jg) to Lt. Comdr, Naval Res, World War II. Mem: Am. Munic. Asn.(pres, 54-55); Miss. Munic. Asn.(past pres); U.S. Conf. Mayors; Am. and Miss. Bar Asns; Mason; Shrine. Rel: Methodist. Legal Res: 810 Fairview St, Jackson, Miss. 63755. Mailing Add: City Hall, P.O. Box 17, Jackson, Miss. 63755. (1967)

THOMPSON, ALLEN F. R
b. 1927. Polit. & Govt. Pos: N.Mex. State Rep, 61-67. Bus. & Prof. Pos: Rancher. Mil. Serv: Vet. Mem: Mason; Eastern Star; Farm Bur. Rel: Protestant. Mailing Add: Solano, N.Mex. 87746. (1967)

THOMPSON, ANNE MARIE R
Secy, Otero Co. Rep. Cent. Cmt, Colo.
b. Des Moines, Iowa, 2/7/20; d. George H. Sheely and Esther S. Mayer S; m. 7/31/49 to James Ross Thompson; c. Annette (Mrs. Robert McCracken), James Ross, Jr. and Dana Marie. Educ: Univ. Iowa, B.A, 40; Theta Sigma Phi; Chi Omega. Polit. & Govt. Pos: Colo. State Rep, 56-60; secy, Colo. Rep. Cent. Cmt, 60-61; secy, Colo. Fedn. Rep. Women, 62-65, third cong. dist. dir, 69-; secy, Otero Co. Rep. Cent. Cmt, 62-; pres, Rocky Ford Rep. Women's Club, 64-66. Bus. & Prof. Pos: Co-publisher, Rocky Ford Daily Gazette, 54- Mem: Colo. Authors League; Colo. Press Women; Nat. Fedn. Press Women; PEO; Am. Asn. Univ. Women; Bus. and Prfnl. Women's Club. Colo. Woman of Achievement in Journalism, Colo. Press Women, 68. Rel: Methodist. Legal Res: 1010 Lincoln, Rocky Ford, Colo. 81067. Mailing Add: P.O. Box 430, Rocky Ford, Colo. 81067.

THOMPSON, ARTHUR E. R
b. Wilmot, N.H, 12/28/04; married; c. two. Educ: Wilmot Elem. Sch. and Tilton Sch. Polit. & Govt. Pos: Libr. messenger for the N.H. House of Rep, 25 & 27; former town auditor; forest fire warden; sch. treas. and moderator; town treas; town moderator; N.H. State Rep, 59-68. Bus. & Prof. Pos: Farm work. Mem: Grange; Wilmot Vol. Fire Dept. Rel: Baptist. Mailing Add: Wilmot Flat, N.H. 03287. (1967)

THOMPSON, BARBARA COOPER R
N.H. State Rep.
b. Rochester, N.H, 12/18/16; d. Burt Randall Cooper and Lillian Foss C; div; c. Sandra Grigg, Mark, Boyen and Betsy. Educ: Colby Jr. Col. for Women, A.A, 37; Boston Univ, B.S. in Soc. Sci, 39; Univ. N.H, Grad. Studies, 40, 65 & 68; Delta Delta Delta. Polit. & Govt. Pos: Del, N.H. Constitutional Conv, 64; clerk of health and welfare, N.H. State Insts. Cmt; legis. chmn, Rochester Women's Rep. Club, N.H, 69; N.H. State Rep, 69- Bus. & Prof. Pos: Social Worker, N.H. State Hosp, 40-43, Rochester Schs, 65-68. Mem: Past bd. mem, N.H. Med. Auxiliary; past pres, Strafford Co. Med. Auxiliary; Bd. mem, N.H. Social Welfare Seacoast Coun; Region VI Dist. chmn, Gov. Cmt. on Vocational Rehabilitation; Eastern Star; N.H. Educ. Asn; N.H. Soc. Welfare Coun; v.chmn, N.H. Easter Seal Appeal, 69. Rel: Congregational. Mailing Add: Gronegate Apts, Hill Rd, Rochester, N.H. 03867.

THOMPSON, BRONALD D
b. Fillmore, N. Dak, 5/15/11; married; c. six. Educ: Pub. Schs. Polit. & Govt. Pos: N. Dak. State Sen, 59-61; former alderman; Mayor of Oberon. Bus. & Prof. Pos: Elevator mgr. Mem: Farmers Union; Odd Fellows. Rel: Lutheran. Mailing Add: Oberon, N. Dak. 58357. (1967)

THOMPSON, BURRELL A. D
Ark. State Sen.
b. Paragould, Ark, 11/27/33; s. Alfred C. Thompson and Ruth Wadley T; m. 7/25/52 to Martha Ann Marshall; c. Kevin and Lissa. Polit. & Govt. Pos: Dep. tax collector, Green Co, Ark, 54-58, co. tax collector, 62-68; Ark. State Sen, 23rd Dist, 69- Bus. & Prof. Pos: Co-owner, Thompson Ins. Agency. Mil. Serv: Entered as Pvt, Army, 55, released as SP-3, 57; S/Sgt, Res, 57-63. Mem: Am. Legion; Kiwanis. Rel: Methodist. Mailing Add: Route 4, Paragould, Ark. 72450.

THOMPSON, CARL WILLIAM D
Wis. State Sen.
b. Washington, D.C, 3/15/14; s. Carl William Thompson and Hannah Hegge T; m. 1942 to Marion Foster; c. Anne, Jane, Margaret and Elizabeth. Educ: Lutheran Col, 32-33; Univ. Wis, Ph.B, 36 and LL.B, 39. Polit. & Govt. Pos: Alderman, Stoughton, Wis, city attorney, 42; Dem. Presidential elector, 48; Dem. cand. for Gov, Wis, 48 & 50; Dem. Nat. Committeeman, Wis, 49-56; Wis. State Assemblyman, 53-59; Wis. State Sen, 59-; alternate del, Dem. Nat. Conv, 60. Bus. & Prof. Pos: Attorney-at-law, 39-; real estate broker, 53- Mil. Serv: Entered as Pvt, Army, 42, released as 1st Lt, 46, after serv, in Army Intel. Rel: Lutheran. Legal Res: Route 3, Stoughton, Wis. 53589. Mailing Add: Box 227, Stoughton, Wis. 53589.

THOMPSON, CLARK WALLACE D
b. La Crosse, Wis, 8/6/96; s. Clark Wallace Thompson and Jessie Hyde T; m. 11/16/18 to Libbie Moody; c. Clark W, Jr. and Libbie (Mrs. Stansell, deceased). Educ: Univ. Ore, 15-17; Phi Delta Theta. Polit. & Govt. Pos: U.S. Rep, Tex, 33-34 & 47-67. Bus. & Prof. Pos: Consult, Clark W. Thompson Co, Galveston, Tex, 20-32; consult. dir. pub. rels, Am. Nat. Ins. Co, 36-40; dir, Wash. Operations, Tenneco Inc, currently. Mil. Serv: Entered as Pvt, Marine Corps, 17; released as Col, 46, after serv. in 2nd Div, 2nd and 3rd Brigades, Hq. Marine Corps, Southwest Pac, 40-46; Col, Res, 46; Legion of Merit; Res. Spec. Commendation; Good Conduct Medal; Organized Marine Corps Res. Ribbon. Mem: AF&AM; KCCH (32°); Shrine; Eagles; Red Men; C. of C; VFW; Am. Legion. Rel: Episcopal. Legal Res: 1616 Driftwood Lane, Galveston, Tex. 77550. Mailing Add: 3301 Massachusetts Ave. N.W, Washington, D.C. 20008.

THOMPSON, DENHAM MICHAEL BURGESS 'MIKE' R
b. Miami, Fla, 10/15/39; s. Thomas Denham Thompson and Sybil Valletta Bodden T; m. 11/22/61 to Patricia Elaine Carpenter. Educ: Univ. Miami, B.A, 61; Sigma Delta Chi scholarship; Omicron Delta Kappa; Sigma Delta Chi; Kappa Alpha Mu; Order of Iron Arrow; Lead and Ink. Polit. & Govt. Pos: Special Asst, Gov. War on Crime, Fla, 67; Fed-State Coordinator for Fla, Wash, D.C, 67-68; Conv. Site Coordinator, Nixon for Pres. Cmt, 68; Rep. nominee for U.S. Rep, Fla, 66 & 68; Dade Co. chmn, Bafalis for Gov. Cmt, 69-70. Bus. & Prof. Pos: Asst. news ed, asst. mag. ed. and Sunday ed, The Miami News, 61-66; v.pres, Long Advertising Agency Inc, Miami, Fla, 68- Mil. Serv: Entered as Pvt, Army, 62, released as Sp-5, 68, after serv. in 35th Surg. Hosp, Fla. Nat. Guard and 324th Gen. Hosp, Army Res, Coral Gables, Fla; Expert Rifleman's Medal. Publ: 'Youth in Cuba' Miami News, Assoc. Press Syndication, 2/60. Mem: Fla. Inst. of Pub. Affairs (trustee); South Fla. Young Am. for Freedom (former pres); Dade Co. Young Rep. (former v.pres); Fact Finders Forum; South Dade Rep. Club; honorary mem, Anti-Communist Cuban Col. of Journalists. Ed. of Best Col. Paper in South, Am. Newspaper Guild, Memphis Chap, 60; Hist. Medal, Univ. Miami, Mr. Executive of Tomorrow, Alpha Delta Sigma; Am. Legion Citizenship Medal. Rel: Episcopal. Mailing Add: 2516 Madrid St, Coral Gables, Fla. 33134.

THOMPSON, DONALD L. R
b. McCook, Nebr, 5/23/09; m. 5/4/35 to Marie L. Hesterwerth; c. one. Educ: McCook High Sch, grad. Polit. & Govt. Pos: Nebr. State Sen, 55-66;

speaker of 1961 session; former mem, Local Sch. Bd; past rep. city chmn, and mem, State Bd. of Agr; chmn, Red Willow Co. Rep. Party, currently. Bus. & Prof. Pos: Farmer and stockman. Mem: Adv. bd, Nebr. Resources Cmt. and Nebr. Stockgrowers Asn; past pres, Nebr. Fair Mgrs. Asn; Nebr. Hereford Asn; Jr. C. of C.(past state secy, Nebr. Chap); bd. mem, Red Willow City Fair, 18 years and secy, 14 years; past dir, Frenchman Cambridge Irrigation Dist; adv. cmt, Univ. Nebr. Col. of Agr; pres, Rep. Valley Conserv. Asn. Rel: Protestant. Mailing Add: Route 3, 410 Cherokee Rd, McCook, Nebr. 69001. (1967)

THOMPSON, FRANK, JR. D
U.S. Rep, N.J.
b. Trenton, N.J, 7/26/18; s. Frank Thompson, Sr. and Beatrice Jamieson T; m. 1/10/42 to Evelina Van Metre; c. Anne (Mrs. Henderson) and Evelina. Educ: Wake Forest Law Sch. Hon. LL.D, Princeton Univ, 69. Polit. & Govt. Pos: N.J. State Assemblyman, 49-54; Asst. Minority Leader, N.J. State Assembly, 50 and Minority Leader, 54; U.S. Rep, N.J, 54-, mem, Cmt. Educ. and Labor, House Admin. Cmt, chmn, Spec. Subcmt. on Labor and chmn, Subcmt. on Libr. and Memorials, U.S. House of Rep; chmn, Nat. Voters Registrn. Cmt, Presidential Campaign, 60. Mil. Serv: Entered Navy, 41, released 48, Comdr, U.S.S. LCI, 428 and LCI Rocket Squadrons, 48 and 63; three combat decorations for action at Iwo Jima and Okinawa; Comdr, Naval Res. Bn, active duty on staff of Comdr, East. Sea Frontier, 52-54. Mem: Am. Vet. Cmt, Am. Legion; VFW; Franklin D. Roosevelt Mem. Cmn; trustee, J.F. Kennedy Center. Rel: Catholic. Legal Res: 455 W. State St, Trenton, N.J. 08618. Mailing Add: 383 W. State St, Trenton, N.J. 08618.

THOMPSON, GEORGE R
b. St. Paul, Minn, 7/6/18; s. George Thompson and Hilda Grinde T; m. 5/30/42 to Marion E. Gunderson Taylor; c. Diane Elizabeth, George Gunnar III and David Louis. Educ: Wis. State Col, River Falls, 36-37; St. Olaf Col, B.A, 40; Univ. of Wis, M.A, 41, LL.B, 47; Univ. of Besancon, France, 45. Polit. & Govt. Pos: Mem, LaCrosse Police Cmn, Wis, 52-54; dist. attorney, LaCrosse, 54-60; attorney gen, Wis, 63-65. Mil. Serv: Army, World War II. Mem, Bd. dirs, Wis. Easter Seal Soc; Wis. Lutheran Welfare Soc; Am. Bar Asn; Wis. State Bar; Am. Legion; LaCrosse C. of C; Mason; Optimist; Eagles; Elks. 1967 Legal Res: Madison, Wis. No mailing address available. (1967)

THOMPSON, GEORGE KING R
b. Jamaica, Iowa, 11/24/87; s. William Jenkins Thompson and Ida King T; m. 12/17/21 to Grace Ione Byfield; c. George King, Jr. and William Byfield. Educ: Univ. Iowa, B.A, 11, LL.B, 14. Polit. & Govt. Pos: Justice and Chief Justice, Supreme Court of Iowa, 51-65; Judge, 18th Judicial Dist. of Iowa, 41-50; attorney, Linn Co, Iowa, 33-40. Mem: Mason (32°), KCCH, Shrine; Iowa State and Linn Co. Bar Asns; Rel: Presbyterian. Mailing Add: 2613 Meadowbrook Dr. S.E, Cedar Rapids, Iowa 52403. (1967)

THOMPSON, GERALD FRANKLIN D
Chmn, Jewell Co. Dem. Party, Kans.
b. Mankato, Kans, 4/27/10; s. Charles Thompson and Pearl Eilers T; m. 7/2/33 to Erma May Hunt; c. two stepchildren; 1 granddaughter. Educ: High sch, 2 years. Polit. & Govt. Pos: Wheat cmnr, State Kans. Wheat Cmn, 57-61; chmn, Jewell Co. Dem. Party, Kans, currently. Bus. & Prof. Pos: Jewell Co. bargainer, Nat. Farmers Orgn, 67-69, mem, dist, state and nat. cmts. in recent years. Mem: Nat. Farmers Orgn; Lions (pres, 1 year). Rel: Christian Church of N.Am. Mailing Add: 527 Northwest St, Mankato, Kans. 66956.

THOMPSON, JAMES R
Auditor of Pub. Acct, Ky.
b. Louisville, Ky, 11/13/31; s. Frank Barton Thompson and Ida Webb T; m. 3/29/54 to Alice Dupee; c. Elizabeth, Emery, James, Jr. and Samuel. Educ: Yale Univ, B.S, 54; Univ. Louisville, LL.B, 62. Polit. & Govt. Pos: Auditor Pub. Acct, Ky, 69- Bus. & Prof. Pos: Pres, Old South Life Ins. Co, Louisville, 59- Mil. Serv: Entered as Pvt, Marine Corps, 50, released as Pfc, 51. Rel: Episcopal. Mailing Add: Harrods Creek, Ky. 40027.

THOMPSON, JAMES L. R
Wyo. State Sen.
b. Douglas, Wyo, 12/18/19; m. to Harriett; c. two. Educ: Univ. of Wyo; Curtis Wright Tech. Inst. of Aeronaut, grad. Polit. & Govt. Pos: Wyo. State Rep, currently. Bus. & Prof. Pos: Rancher. Mem: Elks; Wyo. Wool Growers; Wyo. Stock Growers Asn; 4-H leader, Niobrara Country Club, 11 years. Rel: Congregational. Mailing Add: Lance Creek, Wyo. 82222. (1967)

THOMPSON, JIMMY EUGENE D
b. Clarendon, Tex, 3/1/22; s. Curtis Eugene Thompson (deceased) and Margaret Velma Cash T; m. 9/25/48 to Margaret Faye Quebe; c. Fred Eugene, James Alexander and Margaret Ann. Educ: Univ. Tex, Austin, B.A, 42, LL.B, 47; Order of the Coif; Phi Delta Phi; Chancellors; The Tejas Club. Polit. & Govt. Pos: Chmn, Gray Co. Dem. Party, Tex, 54-68; trustee, Pampa Ind. Sch. Dist, Gray and Roberts Co, Tex, 68- Bus. & Prof. Pos: Attorney-at-law. Mil. Serv: Army, 42-46. Mem: Am. and Gray Co. Bar Asns; State Bar of Tex.(dir, 60-63); Pampa Rotary Club (pres, 68-69); dir, Pampa Fine Arts Asn; mem. exec. bd, Adobe Walls Coun. Boy Scouts. Rel: Baptist. Legal Res: 1912 Dogwood, Pampa, Tex. 79065. Mailing Add: P.O. Box 1461, Pampa, Tex. 79065.

THOMPSON, JOHN COLBY R
Chmn, Winnebago Co. Rep. Cent. Cmt, Iowa
b. Forest City, Iowa, 4/9/20; s. Merle M. Thompson (deceased) and Dora Colby T.(deceased); m. to Clara Peterson (deceased); c. Robert P. Educ: Forest City High Sch, grad, 37. Polit. & Govt. Pos: Finance officer, Winnebago Co. Rep. Cent. Cmt, Iowa, 48-66, chmn, 66-; chmn, Forest City Park Bd, 55-68. Bus. & Prof. Pos: Chmn, Forest City Asn. of Independent Ins. Agents, 55-68. Mil. Serv: Entered as Pvt, Air Force, 42, released as S/Sgt, 45, after serv. in Am. and Asiatic Pac. Theatres and Europe-Africa-Middle East, 42-45; 2 Stars. Mem: Iowa Asn. of Independent Ins. Agents; Nat. Soc. of Pub. Acct; Iowa Asn. of Acct; Mason; Eastern Star; Scottish Rite Bodies; Shrine; Am. Legion; VFW; Rotary. Rel: Methodist. Legal Res: 635 N. Seventh St, Forest City, Iowa 50436. Mailing Add: 121 School St, Forest City, Iowa 50436.

THOMPSON, JOHN ELBERT, JR. R
Chmn, Columbus Co. Rep. Party, N.C.
b. Wilmington, N.C, 7/8/37; s. John Elbert Thompson Sr. and Katherin McLean T; single. Educ: The Citadel, B.S, 59. Polit. & Govt. Pos: Town councilman, Whiteville, N.C, 67-; chmn, Columbus Co. Rep. Party, 67-; alternate del, Rep. Nat. Conf, 68. Bus. & Prof. Pos: Partner, Columbus Supply Co, 62- Mil. Serv: Entered as 2nd Lt, Army, 59, released as 1st Lt, 62, after serv. in First Cavalry Div, Eighth Army, 61-62; Capt, N.C. Nat. Guard, 63-; Army Aviator. Mem: Civitan. Rel: Presbyterian. Legal Res: 617 N. Madison St, Whiteville, N.C. 28472. Mailing Add: P.O. Box 425, Whiteville, N.C. 28472.

THOMPSON, JOHN F. R
b. San Jose, Calif, 7/6/96; s. Peter Thompson and Lydia Yager T; m. 2/16/29 to Gladys Lillian Tonkin; c. Bettie Louise (Mrs. J. Hughes) and Jack R. Educ: High Sch. and Bus. Col. Polit. Pos: Mem, Calif. State Rep. Cent. Cmt, 64-66; del. Rep. Nat. Conv, 64; Calif. State Sen, 50-63; Calif. State assemblyman, 42-50; presidential elector, 56 and 52. Govt. Pos: Asst. marketing specialist, Dept. Agr, 40 and 41. Mil. Serv: Entered Merchant Marine, 17, released as Fireman 1/C, 18. Mem: Mason, Shrine, Scottish Rite; Elks; Eagles; Moose; Native Sons of Golden West; Grange. Rel: Protestant. Mailing Add: R.R. 3 Box 408, San Jose, Calif. 95121.

THOMPSON, JOHN ROGER R
Chmn, Wythe Co. Rep. Party, Va.
b. Charlottesville, Va, 6/25/27; s. John Bascom Thompson and Alice Jamison T; m. 6/30/56 to Patricia Sue Shaffer. Educ: Univ. Va; Univ. Va. Law Sch, LL.B, 56. Chmn, Wythe Co. Rep. Party, Va, 66-; Commonwealth attorney, Wythe Co, 68-; chmn, 12th Legis. Dist. Rep. Party, 69. Mil. Serv: Entered as Pvt, Army, 46, released as 2nd Lt, 47, after serv. in ETO. Rel: Methodist. Legal Res: 580 Withers Rd, Wytheville, Va. 24382. Mailing Add: 182 W. Main St, Wytheville, Va. 24382.

THOMPSON, LAWRENCE RUSSELL D
Va. State Del.
b. Rustburg, Va, 10/5/10; m. to Pauline J. Carwile. Educ: Univ. Richmond. Polit. & Govt. Pos: Va. State Del, 55- Bus. & Prof. Pos: Attorney-at-Law. Mil. Serv: Naval Res, Lt. Comdr. Mem: Am. Legion; Mason; Lions; Moose. Mailing Add: Rustburg, Va. 24588.

THOMPSON, LLEWELLYN E, JR.
b. Las Animas, Colo, 8/24/04; m. 10/2/48 to Jane Monroe Gollet; c. Jenny and Sherry. Educ: Univ. Colo, B.A, 28. Polit. & Govt. Pos: V.consul, Colombo, Ceylon, 29; v.consul, Geneva, Switz, 33, consul, 33; second secy, consul, Moscow, 41; U.S. Del, 1st UN Session, London, Eng, 46; dep. dir. for East. European Affairs, 46; dep. dir. for European Affairs, 48; minister-counselor, Am. Embassy, Rome, Italy, 50-52; U.S. High Cmnr, Austria, 52-55, U.S. Ambassador, 55-57; U.S. Ambassador, U.S.S.R, 57-62 & 66-69; State Dept. Ambassador-at-lg, 62-66; acting dep, Under Secy. of State for Polit. Affairs, 64-66. President's Award for Distinguished Fed. Civilian Serv, 52. Mailing Add: 3915 Watson Place N.W, Wash, D.C. 20016.

THOMPSON, LOCKWOOD D
b. Cleveland, Ohio, 7/4/01; s. Amos Burt Thompson and Jeanne Lockwood T; single. Educ: Williams Col, A.B, 23; Harvard Law Sch, LL.B, 26; Phi Beta Kappa; Delta Kappa Epsilon. Polit. & Govt. Pos: Presidential elector, 32 & 36; del, Ohio Repeal Conv, 33; mem, Ohio Bd. Liquor Control, 33-35; pres, Young Dem. Clubs, Ohio, 36-38; del, Dem. Nat. Conv, 36 & 64; mem, Bd. Elec, Cuyahoga Co, 38-40; trustee, Ohio State Univ, 38-43 & 46-51, chmn. bd, 42; mem, Draft Bd. 20, Cuyahoga Co, 40-42; judge, Court of Appeals, Eighth Dist, 51-52; mem. bd. trustees, Cleveland Pub. Libr, 55-, v.pres, 56-59, pres, 64-69; gen. counsel, Ohio Turnpike Cmn, 56-; chmn. bd. ethics, City of Cleveland, 64-69. Bus. & Prof. Pos: Lawyer, Baker, Hostetler & Sidlo, Cleveland, 26-42; fiscal trustee, Phillis Wheatley Asn, 38-; law off. of Lockwood Thompson, Cleveland, 46-; chmn, Ohio Cmt. for Fair Employ. Practices, 49-51; trustee, Golden Age Center, Cleveland, 54-62. Mil. Serv: Entered as Capt, Army Air Force, 42, released as Major, 46, after serv. in Tex. and Europe; on legal staff of Allied Control Cmn, Italy, 44; Forward Echelon of Com. Z, London,44; mem, U.S. Foreign Claims Cmn, Rheims, Brussels, 44-45; 5 Battle Stars; French Reconnaissance Medal. Mem: Cleveland, Cuyahoga and Ohio Bar Asns; adv. coun, Cleveland Mus. of Art; Int. Coun, Mus. Modern Art, N.Y; Int. Sponsor, Space Ltd, London, Eng; Phi Beta Kappa (pres, Cuyahoga Co. Br, 58-59); Union Club of Cleveland; City Club of Cleveland; Athletic Club of Columbus. Was organizer and 1st pres. of Cleveland Soc. for Contemporary Art. Mailing Add: 11901 Carlton Rd, Cleveland, Ohio 44106.

THOMPSON, MARGUERITE PEYTON D
b. Georgetown, Colo; d. Thomas Phillip Peyton and Anna Marie Kearns P; m. to Dr. Lester E. Thompson, wid. Educ: Univ. Colo, M.A, B.A. and B.E; Lamont Sch. Music, Denver; Denver Col. Music; Conservatory, Vienna, Austria; Kappa Delta Pi; Sigma Alpha Iota; Delta Delta Delta. Polit. & Govt. Pos: Dem. Nat. Committeewoman, Colo, 38-60; mem, Dem. Nat. Adv. Coun, 52-58; mem, Nat. Adv. Cancer Coun, 52-56; v.chmn, West. States Dem. Conf; del, Dem. Nat. Conv, 48, mem. planning cmt, 5 times; v.chmn, Colo. State Dem. Party, 34-38. Bus. & Prof. Pos: Music teacher, Boulder Pub. Schs, Colo, 59-60; music supvr, pub. schs, Salida, 43-46 and 38-39, Pueblo, 28-30 and Boulder, 27-28; mem. faculty, Col. Music, Univ. Colo, 26-27. Mem: State music chmn, Colo. Fedn. Women's Clubs; Musician's Soc. Denver; Int. Hon. Mem, Beta Sigma Phi; nat. v.pres, Am. Legion Auxiliary, 30-31, past nat. music chmn, past nat. child welfare chmn, past nat. World War Orphan Educ. Chmn. and past state pres, Colo; pres, Colo. Fedn. Music Clubs, 54-56; state legis. chmn, Am. Asn. Univ. Women, 56. Rel: Catholic. Mailing Add: 2325 13th St, Boulder, Colo. 80302. (1967)

THOMPSON, OLIVER L, JR. R
Minority Leader, R.I. House of Rep.
b. Denver, Colo, 5/26/10; s. Oliver L. Thompson, Sr. and Mary Walsh T; m. 5/29/45 to Ann Elizabeth O'Brien; c. Oliver L, III, W. Brian, John M, Ann Elizabeth, Mary Patricia and James C. Educ: Providence Col; Mass. Inst. Tech; Boston Univ. Law Sch, LL.B, 35; Law Rev, Boston Univ. Polit. & Govt. Pos: Councilman, Barrington Town Coun, R.I, 48-52, pres, 52-56; R.I. State Rep, 56-, Dep. Minority Leader, R.I. House of Rep, 60-61, Minority Leader, 62- Bus.

& Prof. Pos: Mem, Realtors Wash. Cmt, Nat. Asn. of Real Estate Bd, 64-; chmn. East. Shore Adv. Bd, Indust. Nat. Bank of R.I, 69- Publ: Numerous articles, technical and political papers. Mem: Nat. dir, Nat. Asn. of Real Estate Bd, 62-65; pres, R.I. Realtors Asn, 62-63 and bd. dir, 62-65; bd. dir, Providence Bd. of Realtors, 62-65; pres, Bristol Co. Asn. of Ins. Agents, 66-67; VFW; Am. Legion; K. of C. Rel: Roman Catholic. Legal Res: 55 Washington Rd, Barrington, R.I. 02890. Mailing Add: 201 Washington Rd, Barrington, R.I. 02890.

THOMPSON, PAHL E. R
Chmn, Mills Co. Rep. Party, Iowa
b. Cantril, Iowa, 12/24/10; s. James B. Thompson and Olive A. T; m. 3/2/35 to Helen H. Hall; c. Fred R, Roger D. and Ralph H. Educ: Tri City Barber Col, Des Moines, Iowa; Drake Univ. Polit. & Govt. Pos: Chmn, Mills Co. Rep. Party, Iowa, 64- Bus. & Prof. Pos: Barber, 29; mgr, N.W. Bell Tel. Co, 34. Mem: Mason; Rotary. Rel: Methodist. Mailing Add: 5 N. Myrtle St, Glenwood, Iowa 51534.

THOMPSON, R. BURNETT, JR. R
b. Middletown, N.Y, 5/17/26; s. Ralph B. Thompson and Eva Birckhead T; m. 8/19/50 to Ramona Elmer; c. R. Burnett, III, Barbara Ruth and Brenda Faith. Educ: Houghton Col, B.A, 49; George Wash. Univ, 64-66. Polit. & Govt. Pos: Admin. Asst. to U.S. Rep. G. William Whitehurst, Va, 69- Bus. & Prof. Pos: Pastor, Wesleyan Methodist Church, Silver Creek, N.Y, 49-57 and Hamburg, N.Y, 57-59; dist. mgr, Encyclop. Britannica, Wash, D.C. and Va. Beach, Va, 57-68. Mil. Serv: Entered as Pvt, Air Corps, 44, released as Aviation Cadet, 45, after serv. in Pre-Flight. Rel: Methodist. Mailing Add: 4218 Sleepy Hollow Rd, Annandale, Va. 32003.

THOMPSON, RALPH GORDON R
Okla. State Rep.
b. Oklahoma City, Okla, 12/15/34; s. Lee Bennett Thompson and Elaine Bizzell T; m. 9/5/64 to Barbara Irene Hencke; c. Lisa Irene, Elaine and Maria. Educ: Univ. Okla, B.B.A, 56 and LL.B, 61; Phi Alpha Delta; Beta Theta Pi. Polit. & Govt. Pos: Okla. State Rep, 67-; state chmn, Okla. Young Civic Leaders for Nixon-Agnew, 68. Mil. Serv: Entered as 2nd Lt, Air Force, 57, released as 1st Lt, 60, after serv. as Spec. Agent, Off. of Spec. Invests, Nationalist China; Maj, Air Force Res. Mem: Am, Okla. and Oklahoma Co. Bar Asns; pres, Okla. Young Lawyers Conf, 65; pres, Okla. City Lawyers Club, 69; trustee, Okla. Bar Found; ROA; v.chmn. and dir, Okla. Co. Chap, Am. Red Cross. Outstanding Young Man of Oklahoma City, 67; One of Three Outstanding Young Oklahomans, 67-68. Rel: Episcopal. Legal Res: 1109 Huntington, Oklahoma City, Okla. 73116. Mailing Add: 2120 First National Bldg, Oklahoma City, Okla. 73102.

THOMPSON, RICHARD J. R
b. Underwood, N.Dak, 5/13/13; m. 10/20/38 to Dorothy Gross. Educ: Pub. schs. Polit. & Govt. Pos: N.Dak. State Rep, 49-59; N.Dak. Pub. Serv. Cmnr, 60-67. Bus. & Prof. Pos: Farmer. Mem: Elks; former mem. bd. dirs, McLean Co. Elect. Coop. and McLean Co. Independent. Rel: Methodist. Mailing Add: 609 Eighth St, Bismarck, N.Dak. 58501.

THOMPSON, RICHARD KEITH R
b. Columbus, Ind, 7/1/28; s. Albert B. Thompson and Vivian Wooden T; m. 7/24/65 to Jean Ann Slayton; c. Sean Keith and Amy Elizabeth. Educ: Butler Univ, B.S, Journalism, 50; Sigma Delta Chi; Sigma Nu. Polit. & Govt. Pos: Indexer-researcher, Joint Cmt. on Printing, Wash, D.C, 54-63; Researcher, Goldwater for Pres. Cmt, 64; Researcher, House Rep. Conf, 65-66; admin. asst, U.S. Rep. McClure, Idaho, 67- Mil. Serv: Entered as Airman 2/C, Air Force, 51, released as S/Sgt, 53, after serv. in 122nd A C and W Squadron. Rel: Presbyterian. Legal Res: 756 S. State St, North Vernon, Ind. 47265. Mailing Add: 7424 Hopa Court, Alexandria, Va. 22306.

THOMPSON, ROBERT MOODY R
b. Starksboro, Vt, 10/23/20; m. to Arlene Gwendolyn Blair; c. one son and three daughters. Educ: Bristol High Sch. Polit. & Govt. Pos: Town lister, 61-; Vt. State Rep, 63-66. Bus. & Prof. Pos: Lumberman and carpenter. Rel: Methodist. Mailing Add: R.D. 1, Starksboro, Vt. 05487. (1967)

THOMPSON, RONALD L. R
b. Shamokin, Pa, 8/19/99; s. Willis Daniel Thompson and Elizabeth Taylor T; m. 7/9/21 to Elsie Marie Calvert; c. George Harvey. Educ: Univ. Pittsburgh, B.S, 23. Polit. & Govt. Pos: Cmnr, Mt. Lebanon Twp, Pa, 32-40; Pa. State Rep, 41-69. Bus. & Prof. Pos: Partner, Vernon Gold & Silver Co, 22- Mil. Serv: Entered as Pvt, First Pa. Calvalry Nat. Guard, 28th Div, 17, released as Lt. Col, Air Force, 59, after serv. in Air Force Training Command, 41-44; Lt. Col.(Ret), Air Force; World War I Ribbon with Six Battle Stars; World War II Defense Ribbon. Mem: Vet. Groups; Mason; Elks; SAR; City Farmers Club. Rel: Methodist. Mailing Add: 224 Parker Dr, Pittsburgh, Pa. 15216.

THOMPSON, ROSCOE MULLINS D
Ga. State Rep.
b. Columbus, Ga, 7/12/15; s. Clarence A. Thompson and Mary Mullins T; m. 7/5/41 to Mary Barr; c. Carol (Mrs. T. Hodge), Cathy (Mrs. T. McCosh) and Alice F. Educ: Univ. Ga. Polit. & Govt. Pos: Asst. Attorney Gen, Ga, 47-48; chmn, Columbus Dem. Exec. Cmt, Ga, 49-53; City Attorney, Columbus, Ga, 55-59; Ga. State Rep, Muscogee Co, 66- Mil. Serv: Entered as Pvt, Army, 42, released as Capt, 47; Am. Theatre Ribbon. Mem: Columbus lawyers club (pres, 51-52). Rel: Methodist. Legal Res: 1725 Stark Ave, Columbus, Ga. 31906. Mailing Add: P.O. Box 706, Columbus, Ga. 31902.

THOMPSON, S. FLETCHER R
U.S. Rep, Ga.
b. College Park, Ga, 2/5/25; s. R. Standish Thompson and Mary Spencer T; m. 11/23/46 to Kathryn Cochran; c. Charles Lawrence and Deborah Jean. Educ: Emory Univ, A.B, 48; Woodrow Wilson Col. Law, LL.B, 57; Sigma Delta Kappa. Polit. & Govt. Pos: Ga. State Sen, 64-66; U.S. Rep, Ga, 67-; del, Rep. Nat. Conv, 68. Bus. & Prof. Pos: Attorney-at-law; pres, Aero Ins. Co. Mil. Serv: Army Med. Corps, 43; Army Air Corps, 43-46; Air Force, 50-53. Mem: Past nat. v.pres, Nat. Aviation Trades Asn; dir, Int. Lawyer-Pilots Bar Asn; past mem, East Point Rotary Club; past dir. and v.pres, Lakeside Country Club. Rel: Methodist; Trustee, First Methodist Church, East Point. Legal Res: 2631 Hogan Rd, East Point, Ga. 30344. Mailing Add: 514 Cannon House Office Bldg, Washington, D.C. 20515.

THOMPSON, STANLEY EMIL D
b. Hurdland, Mo, 9/19/03; s. Henry Emil Thompson and Lottie L. Merrell T; m. 7/19/51 to Cleone Keller; c. Betty Jean (Mrs. DeLapp) and Janet. Educ: Kirksville State Teachers Col, exten. courses. Polit. & Govt. Pos: Chmn, Mont. Dem. Labor Adv. Cmt, 52-56; del, Dem. Nat. Conv, 52, 56, 60, 64 & 68; secy, Mont. Dem. State Cent. Cmt, 56-61, exec. secy, 60-61; mem, Mont. Air Pollution Cmt. and Apprenticeship Training Coun; mem, Mont. Small Bus. Admin. Admission Coun, currently. Bus. & Prof. Pos: Int. Rep, IBEW, 46-60, int. v.pres, 62- Mem: IBEW; Mason; Consistory, K.T, Commandery, Al BeDoo Shrine Temple; Elks; Order of Ky. Cols. Rel: Methodist. Legal Res: 402 W. 22nd St, Red Lodge, Mont. 59068. Mailing Add: Box 1147, Red Lodge, Mont. 59068.

THOMPSON, THEO ASHTON D
b. Ville Platte, La, 3/31/16; s. Chester Allen Thompson and Rosa Soileau T; m. 4/8/60 to Leatrice Soileau. Educ: La. State Univ, 32-34. Polit. & Govt. Pos: Traveling auditor, La. Hwy. Cmn, 34-40; staff, State Dept. Finance, 40, mem. bd. adv. to educ, Munic. Acct. and Auditing, 51, representative, La. Nat. Assembly States for Develop. Civil Defense Prog. and U.S. Dept. State La; chmn. bd. trustees, State Retirement Syst, 47-53; state budget officer and financial adviser, La. State Legis, 48-52; U.S. Rep, La, 53-66. Mil. Serv: Army Air Force. Mem: Nat. Asn. State Budget Officers (mem, Nat. Cmt. Govt. Acct); Amvets (mem. Nat. Finance Cmt); Am. Legion. Rel: Catholic. Mailing Add: 504 N. Dossman St, Ville Platte, La. 70586.

THOMPSON, TOMMY GEORGE R
Wis. State Assemblyman
b. Elroy, Wis, 11/19/41; s. Allan Thompson and Julia Dutton T; single. Educ: Univ. Wis, B.S, 63 and J.D, 66; Phi Delta Phi. Polit. & Govt. Pos: Legis. messenger, State Capitol, Wis; polit. intern for U.S. Rep, Thompson, 63; v.chmn, Collegians for Goldwater, 63-64; mem, Young Rep. of Wis; Wis. State Assemblyman, 67- Bus. & Prof. Pos: Attorney-at-Law, 66- Mil. Serv: Pvt, Army Res, 66. Mem: Wis. Bar Asn; Jaycees. Rel: Catholic. Mailing Add: 1407 Academy, Elroy, Wis. 53929.

THOMPSON, TYLER D
b. Corona, Calif, 10/18/15; s. Francis Forbes Thompson and Sadie Tyler T; m. 6/19/37 to Phyllis Elizabeth Oechsli; c. Francia (Mrs. Donald E. Hunter), Wendy, Heidi, Becky and Peter. Educ: Calif. Inst. Tech, B.S, 36; Boston Univ. Sch. Theol, S.T.B, 39; Boston Univ. Grad. Sch, Ph.D, 50; Tau Beta Pi. Polit. & Govt. Pos: Second Ward chmn, Evanston Dem. Party, Ill, 56, mem. exec. bd, currently; pres, Evanston Dem. Club, 57-59, mem. exec. bd, currently; Dem. nominee for Congressman, 13th Dist, 60; Dem. twp. committeeman, Evanston and mem, Cook Co. Dem. Cent. Cmt, 66-68. Bus. & Prof. Pos: Pastor, Barre Methodist Church, Mass, 37-39; teacher and pastor, Methodist Mission, Singapore, 39-46; pastor, Weston Methodist Church, Mass, 46-49; asst. prof. relig. and philos, Allegheny Col, 49-51; assoc. prof. philos. of relig, Garrett Theol. Sem, 51-55, prof, 55-, dir. summer sessions, 59- Publ: Religion and Education, Historical Perspective and Current Problems, Ill. State Univ, 67; 'God Deserves Better,' Christian Century, 10/61; 'Left, Right, and Middle-of-the-Road,' Classmate, 3 & 4/64. Mem: Am. Theol. Soc, Midwest Div.(pres, 65-66); Am. Philos. Asn, West. Div; Am. Acad. of Relig; Evanston Human Rels. Coun.(pres, 53-55); Am. Civil Liberties Union (chmn, Ill. Div, 59-64). Am. Asn. of Theol. Schs. faculty fel, 64-65. Rel: Methodist. Mailing Add: 1618 Ashland Ave, Evanston, Ill. 60201.

THOMPSON, VERLA DARLENE R
Secy, Mercer Co. Rep. Cent. Cmt, Ill.
b. Viola, Ill, 12/8/32; d. Earl Clair Thompson and Sylvia Anderson T; single. Educ: Aledo High Sch, grad. Polit. & Govt. Pos: Chief dep. treas, Mercer Co, Ill, 53-; corresponding secy, Mercer Co. Young Rep, 60-63; secy, Mercer Co. Rep. Cent. Cmt, 63- Mem: Nat. Fedn. Rep. Women; Ill. Co. Treas. Asn; Mercer Co. Young Rep. March of Dimes Drive Awards, Nat. Found. Rel: Methodist. Mailing Add: Route 2, Box 182, Aledo, Ill. 61231.

THOMPSON, WAYNE W. R
Secy, Minn. Second Cong. Dist. Rep. Cmt.
b. Tyler, Minn, 11/17/35; s. Wesley Howard Thompson and Wayva Baustian T; m. 8/18/57 to Martha Elizabeth Engebretson; c. Philip Rolf, Rachel Lynn, Nathan David and Lois Marie. Educ: St. Olaf Col, B.A, 57; Lutheran Theol. Sem, B.D, 61. Polit. & Govt. Pos: Chmn, McLeod Co. Rep. Cmt, Minn, 67-69; secy, Minn. Second Cong. Dist. Rep. Cmt, 69- Bus. & Prof. Pos: Pastor, Good Shepherd Lutheran Church, Lake Wilson, Minn, 61-65, Bethel Lutheran Church, Lester Prairie, 65-69 and Faith & Our Saviour's Lutheran Church, Madelia, 69- Mem: U.S. Jaycees. Jaycees Spark Plug & Key Man Awards. Rel: Lutheran. Mailing Add: 222 Abbot Ave. S.W, Madelia, Minn. 56062.

THOMPSON, WILLIAM C. D
b. N.Y.C, 10/26/24; m. to Elaine Allen; c. two. Educ: Brooklyn Col, B.A; Brooklyn Law Sch, LL.B. Polit. & Govt. Pos: N.Y. State Sen, 64-66; co. cmnr. and chmn. of cmn. on rules and regulations, Sixth Assembly Dist. Regular Dem. Orgn; mem, bd. dirs, United Action Dem. Asn; mem, Borough Pres. Commun. Dist. Planning Bd. No. Six. Bus. & Prof. Pos: Attorney. Mil. Serv: Army, Platoon Sgt, Co. A, 370th Inf. Regt, 92nd Div, World War II; Purple Heart; Three Battle Stars; Combat Inf. Badge. Mem: NAACP (exec. bd. and chmn, Legal Redress Cmt, Brooklyn Br; regional dir); Elks; YMCA; Bus. and Prfnl. Men's Luncheon Club; Am. Bar Asn; Bedfore Stuyvesant Lawyers Asn. Rel: St. Philips Episcopal Church. Mailing Add: 768 Putnam Ave, Brooklyn, N.Y. 11221. (1967)

THOMPSON, WILLIAM CARRINGTON D
Va. State Sen.
b. Chatham, Va, 11/6/15; m. to Margaret Sue Colbert. Educ: Hampden-Sydney Col; Univ. Va. Law Sch, LL.B, 39. Polit. & Govt. Pos: Asst. attorney gen. of Va, 46-47; commonwealth attorney of Pittsylvania Co, 48-55; Va.

State Del, 60-68; del, Dem. Nat. Conv, 68; Va. State Sen, currently. Bus. & Prof. Pos: Lawyer. Mil. Serv: Navy. Mem: Elks; Rotary. Rel: Baptist. Legal Res: R.F.D. 2, Box 3, Chatham, Va. 25531. Mailing Add: Box 610, Chatham, Va. 25531. (1967)

THOMPSON, WILLIAM CHARLES R
Mem, Calif. Rep. State Cent. Cmt.
b. Laguay, Mo, 12/21/28; s. James Harry Thompson and Pearl Robertson T; m. 2/22/57 to Juanita Christine Hale; c. Steven Drake and Laurie Rena. Educ: Humboldt State Col, 55-56. Polit. & Govt. Pos: Campaign chmn, State Senate Candidate, Calif, 68; assoc. mem, Humboldt Co. Rep. Cent. Cmt, 69-; mem, Calif. State Rep. Cent. Cmt, 69- Bus. & Prof. Pos: Realtor, Calif Real Estate Assoc, 57- Mil. Serv: Entered as Pvt, Marines, 52, released as Cpl, 54, after serv. in First Marine Air Wing. Mailing Add: 1212 Fern Dr, Eureka, Calif. 95501.

THOMPSON, WILLIAM ISAAC SHELBY D
b. Jackson, Miss, 11/24/36; married. Polit. & Govt. Pos: Miss. State Rep, until 68. Bus. & Prof. Pos: Gen. ins. and realtor. Mem: Mason; Jaycees; Jackson Exchange Club; Jackson Citizens Band Radio Club; Millsaps & Ole Miss; Kappa Sigma; Alumni Asn. of Miss. State. Rel: Methodist. Mailing Add: 715 Brookwood Rd, Jackson, Miss. 39206. (1967)

THOMSON, JAMES CLAUDE, JR. D
Mem. Adv. Bd, Mass. Dem. Coun.
b. Princeton, N.J, 9/14/31; s. James Claude Thomson and Margaret Cook T; m. 12/19/59 to Diana Duffy. Educ: Univ. Nanking, China, 48-49; Yale Univ, B.A, 53; Cambridge Univ, Eng, B.A, 55; Harvard Univ, M.A, 59, Ph.D, 61; Phi Beta Kappa; Zeta Psi; Scroll and Key. Polit. & Govt. Pos: Spec. Asst. to Gov. Chester Bowles, Conn, 56; spec. asst. to U.S. Congressman, 59-61; spec. asst. to Undersecy. of State, 61; spec. asst. to President's Spec. Rep. and Adv. on African, Asian and Latin Am. Affairs, 61-63; spec. asst. to Asst. Secy. of State for Far East. Affairs, 63-64; staff mem, Nat. Security Coun, 64-66; mem. adv. bd, Mass. Dem. Coun, 69- Bus. & Prof. Pos: Teaching fel. and tutor, Harvard Univ, 56-59, asst. prof. hist. and research fel, Kennedy Inst. of Polit, 66- Publ: While China Faced West, Harvard Univ. Press, 69; 'Dragon Under Glass—Time for a New China Policy', 10/67 & 'How could Vietnam Happen?,' 4/68, Atlantic Monthly. Mem: Am. For. Serv. Asn; Asn. Asian Studies; Elizabethan. Overseas Press Club Award for Mag. Writing on For. Affairs, 68. Rel: Presbyterian. Legal Res: 21 Sibley Court, Cambridge, Mass. 02138. Mailing Add: East Asian Research Center, 1737 Cambridge St, Cambridge, Mass. 02138.

THOMSON, JAMES McILHANY D
Va. State Del.
b. New Orleans, La, 8/9/24; s. Paul Jones Thomson and Gretchen Bigelow T; m. 11/15/52 to Sarah Edna Jennings; c. Sarah Jennings and Teresa Lindsay. Educ: Va. Mil. Inst, A.B, 47; Univ. Va, LL.B, 50; Beta Theta Pi. Polit. & Govt. Pos: Clerk to Judge Bennett Champ Clark, U.S. Court of Appeals, D.C, 50-51; mem. prfnl. staff, U.S. Senate Judiciary Cmt, 51-52; Va. State Del, 56-, majority leader, 68- Bus. & Prof. Pos: Partner, Clarke, Richard Moncure & Whitehead, 53-63; dir. and secy, Fidelity Savings and Loan Asn, 62-65; attorney, James M. Thomson, 63-65 & 67-; chmn. bd. and pres, City Bank and Trust Co, 64-; partner, Thomson, Gannon, Thomas & Cacheris, 65-67. Mil. Serv: Entered as Pvt, Marines, 43, released as 2nd Lt, 46; Am. Theater Ribbon; Good Conduct Medal. Mem: Alexandria, Va. and Am. Bar Asns; Va. Code Cmn, 60-67, chmn, 63-67; Va. Adv. Legis. Coun, 68-; Civitan; Am. Legion; 40 et 8; Eagles; Odd Fellows; Alexandria C. of C; Va. C. of C; SAR; Sons of Confederate Vets; Young Dem.(pres, 53-55). Distinguished Serv. Award, Jr. C. of C, 55. Rel: Episcopal. Legal Res: 1325 Kingston Ave, Alexandria, Va. 22302. Mailing Add: P.O. Box 1138, Alexandria, Va. 22313.

THOMSON, LEONARD S. R
Mem, Calif. State Rep. Cent. Cmt.
b. San Diego, Calif, 10/6/12; s. Albert Charles Thomson and Ernestina Louise Fisher T; m. 6/17/39 to Helen Grady; c. Carol Helen. Educ: Calif. Col, China; Phi Chi. Polit. & Govt. Pos: Mem, Calif. State Rep. Cent. Cmt, 48-; mem, Kern Co. Rep. Cent. Cmt. and chmn, 60-64; dir, Kern Co. Water Dist; mem, State Park and Recreation Cmn, 67-69, state chmn, 69- Bus. & Prof. Pos: Employ. with Evans MacCormack & Co, Inc, Stock and Bonds and production mgt, Honolulu Oil Corp. Mil. Serv: Entered as Lt, Army, 42, released as Capt, 47, after serv. as Liason Officer and Field Comdr, Chinese Supreme Command, China, 44-46; 2 Bronze Stars; Purple Heart; Meritorious Serv. Medal; China Theater Ribbon with 3 Battle Stars; China White Cloud Citation. Publ: The White Snake, Greenwich, 60. Mem: Am. Petroleum Inst; Rotary Int; Commonwealth Club of Calif; Farm Bur; Am. Legion; DAV; Sierra Club; United Rep. Calif; chmn, Westside United Rep. Voted Outstanding Citizen of West Side, 58. Rel: Presbyterian. Mailing Add: 111 East Lucard St, Taft, Calif. 93268.

THOMSON, THYRA GODFREY R
Secy. of State, Wyo.
b. Florence, Colo, 7/30/16; d. John Godfrey and Rosalie Altman G; m. 8/6/39 to Edwin Keith Thomson, wid. Dec, 1960; c. William John, II, Bruce Godfrey and Keith Coffey. Educ: Univ. of Wyo, B.A, cum laude, psychol, 39; Alpha Kappa Psi; Psi Chi; Pi Beta Phi; Iron Skull; Spurs. Polit. & Govt. Pos: Mem, Marshall Scholarships Cmt, Pac. Region, 64-68; del, 72nd Int. Wilton Park Conf, Eng, 65; sponsor, Atlantic Coun. of the U.S, 65; chmn, Pub. Lands Cmt, West. Conf. of the Coun. of State Govts, 65-66; mem, 19 state bds. and cmns; Secy. of State, Wyo, currently. Bus. & Prof. Pos: Mem, Invest. Co. Cmt, N.Am. Securities Adminstrs, 65-69. Publ: 'Watching Washington,' column in 14 newspapers, while living in nation's capital, 54-60. Mem: Alpha Chap, Omicron Delta Epsilon; Beta Gamma Sigma; Wyo. Press Women; PEO. Rel: Presbyterian. Selected Woman of Distinction for 69-71, Int. Conv. of Alpha Delta Kappa, hon. soc. of women educators. Mailing Add: 204 E. 22nd St, Cheyenne, Wyo. 82001.

THOMSON, VERNON WALLACE R
U.S. Rep, Wis.
b. Richland Center, Wis, 11/5/05; s. A.A. Thomson and Ella Wallace T; m. 6/6/36 to Helen A. Davis; c. Susan (Mrs. Robert Turner), Patricia M. and Vernon W, Jr. Educ: Carroll Col, Waukesha, Wis, 23-25; Univ. Wis, Madison, B.A, 27; Univ. Wis. Law Sch, Madison, LL.B, 32; Order of Coif; Phi Delta Phi; Chi Phi. Hon. LL.D, Carroll Col, 57. Polit. & Govt. Pos: Wis. State Assemblyman, 35-51; speaker of assembly, 39, 41 & 43 and Rep. Floor Leader, 45, 47 & 49; Attorney Gen, Wis, 51-57, Gov, 57-59; U.S. Rep, Wis, 60-, mem, U.S. House Rep. Cmt. on For. Affairs. Bus. & Prof. Pos: Teacher, Viroqua, Wis, 27-29; attorney-at-law, Richland Center, 32-; C.C.C. Enrolling Officer for Richland Co, 33-35; city attorney, Richland Center, 33-37 & 42-44; pres, Richland Center Libr. Bd, 39-51; mayor, Richland Center, 44-51. Mem: Wis. and Am. Bar Asns; Mason (33°). Rel: Presbyterian. Legal Res: 578 E. Second St, Richland Center, Wis. 53581. Mailing Add: House Office Building, Washington, D.C. 20515.

THOR, JOHN CARL D
Chmn, Stanton Co. Dem. Party, Nebr.
b. Stanton, Nebr, 12/8/18; father deceased; m. 2/12/41 to Joan Drahota; c. David John, Timothy Craig, John Michael and James John. Polit. & Govt. Pos: Mem, Nebr. Dem. State Cent. Cmt, 66 & 68; chmn, Stanton Co. Dem. Party, 66- Bus. & Prof. Pos: Chmn, Stanton Pilger Drainage Dist, 67- Mem: Norfolk Bd. Realtors (chmn, 66); Home Builders; life mem, Cattle Feeders Asn; K. of C; Boy Scouts (chmn, Stanton Co. Troop). Legal Res: R.F.D, Norfolk, Nebr. 68701. Mailing Add: 107 E. Omaha Ave, Norfolk, Nebr. 68701.

THORBURN, ROSE WOODGATE R
Chairwoman, Sixth Cong. Dist. Rep. Party, Minn.
b. Slayton, Minn, 6/18/00; d. George Hardinge Woodgate and Margaret Ronald W; m. 12/7/24 to Lloyd Mungo Thorburn (deceased); c. William Brown. Polit. & Govt. Pos: Chairwoman, Lyon Co. Rep. Cmt, Minn, 53-57; chairwoman, Seventh Cong. Dist. Rep. Party, 57-60; recording secy, Rep. Women's Clubs, 57-58, dist dir, 59-60; mem, Minn. Finance Steering Cmt, 60; del, Rep. Nat. Conv, 60, 64 & 68; pres, Minn. Fedn. of Rep. Women, 61-62; chairwoman, Sixth Cong. Dist. Rep. Party, 64-; mem, City of Marshall Charter Cmn, currently. Bus. & Prof. Pos: Dir, West. State Bank of Marshall, Minn, 58- Rel: Episcopal. Mailing Add: 417 N. Third St, Marshall, Minn. 56258.

THORESEN, WALTER PAUL D
b. Ableman, Wis, 10/9/18; s. Elmer Thoresen and Hildaborg Paulsen T; m. 6/6/41 to Jean Frances Tingle; c. Judith (Mrs. Howe), Kristine and Susan. Educ: Carroll Col, Wis, B.A, 41; Univ. Wis, M.A, 46; Univ. Minn, Ph.D, 63; Phi Delta Kappa; Pi Gamma Mu; Phi Theta Pi; Tau Kappa Epsilon. Polit. & Govt. Pos: Chmn, La Crosse Co. Dem. Party, Wis, 60-61; oper. support chmn, Third Dist. Dem. Party, 61-68 and treas, 63-68; legis. asst. and researcher, U.S. Sen. Gaylord Nelson, 63; state chmn, Reynolds for Gov. Cmt, 64; del, Dem. Nat. Conv, 64; del-at-lg, admin. cmt, Wis. Dem. Party, 64-68. Bus. & Prof. Pos: High sch. teacher, S.Dak. and Wis, 41-43 and Wis, 46-47; prof. and chmn. dept. of social and golf coach, Wis. State Univ, La Cross, 47- Mil. Serv: Entered as Midn, Navy, 43, released as Lt.(sg), 46, after serv. in S.Pac, 43-45. Mem: Am. and Midwest Sociol. Asns; secy-treas, Wis. Sociol. Asn; F&AM; La Crosse Citizens Educ. Cmt; bd. dirs, La Crosse Co. Coop; chmn. bd, La Crosse Sr. Citizens Center. Rel: United Church of Christ. 1967 Legal Res: La Crosse, Wis. No mailing address available. (1967)

THORESON, WILLIAM JOHN R
N.Dak. State Sen.
b. York, N.Dak, 12/17/19; s. Carl John Thoreson and Elizabeth Cochrane T; m. 9/15/42 to Ruth Carlson; c. Carl William, Elizabeth (Mrs. Tufte), Anne Lynn, John Anthony and William John, Jr. Educ: Univ. N.Dak, 1 year; N.Dak. State Univ, 1 year. Polit. & Govt. Pos: Mem, York Sch. Bd. and Leeds Spec. Dist. Sch. Bd, N.Dak, 48-; v.chmn, Benson Co. Rep. Party, 61-63; N.Dak. State Sen, 12th Legis. Dist, 68- Bus. & Prof. Pos: Owner, W.J. Thoreson Farm, 48-; owner and mgr, C.J. Thoreson Elevator, York, 48-; owner, Leeds Elevator Co, 65- Mil. Serv: Entered as Storekeeper 3/C, Coast Guard, 42, released as Storekeeper 2/C, 45, after serv. in U.S.S. Grand Rapids, Atlantic Theatre, 44. Mem: N.Dak. Farmers-Grain Dealers Asn.(past pres); Nat. Feed and Grain Dealers Asn; Mason; Shrine; Elks; Am. Legion (past dist. dep); VFW; 40 et 8; Farm Bur; Farmers Union. Rel: Am. Lutheran. Mailing Add: York, N.Dak. 58386.

THORN, JERI A. D
b. Pampa, Tex, 1/12/37; d. L. R. Archer and Roberta Hedges A; m. 10/18/56 to Jim Thorn, Jr; c. Lisa Maria and Todd Fletcher. Educ: Southwest. Col, Winfield, Kans. Polit. & Govt. Pos: State v.chmn, Collegiate Young Dem, 57; chmn, Citizens for Kennedy-Johnson, 60; secy, Chautauqua Co. Dem. Cent. Cmt, Kans, 60-62 and chmn, 64-68. Mem: Past pres, Beta Sigma Phi; chmn, Cancer Soc; leader, Brownie Girl Scouts. Named One of Nine Outstanding Young Women in the Nation in Dem. Polit. by Dem. Nat. Cmt, 66. Rel: Episcopal. 1967 Legal Res: Sedan, Kans. No mailing address available. (1967)

THORNBERRY, JONATHAN MICHAEL D
b. Conroe, Tex, 1/22/42; s. Owen Thomas Thornberry and Leona Wiggins T; m. 12/22/66 to Nevadia Vick; c. Rachel Elizabeth. Educ: Tex. A&M Univ, B.S, 64. Polit. & Govt. Pos: Co. judge, Montgomery Co, Tex, 67-; del, Conroe, Tex. and Nat. Dem. Conv, 68; mem. exec. cmt, Houston Galveston Area Coun. of Govt, 69. Bus. & Prof. Pos: Pvt. bus. Mem: Farm Bur; Tex. and Nat. Assocs. of Real Estate Bds; hon. mem, Future Farmers Am. Only husband and wife to receive State of Tex. 4-H Alumni Recognition Award. Rel: Baptist. Legal Res: Route 4, Box 484, Conroe, Tex. 77301. Mailing Add: County Judges Office, Courthouse, Conroe, Tex. 77301.

THORNBERRY, WILLIAM HOMER D
b. Austin, Tex, 1/09/09; s. William Moore Thornberry and Mary Lillian Jones T; m. 2/24/45 to Eloise Engle; c. Molly; David and Kate. Educ: Univ. Tex, B.B.A, 32, LL.B, 36; hon. mem, Order of the Coif. Hon. LL.D, Gallaudet Col. Polit. & Govt. Pos: Tex. State Rep, 37-40; Dist. Attorney, Travis Co, Tex, 41-42; mem, City Coun, Austin, 46-48, mayor pro tem, 47-48; U.S. Rep, Tex, 49-63; del-at-lg, Dem. Nat. Conv, 56 & 60; U.S. Dist. Judge, West. Dist, Tex, 63-65; U.S. Judge Court Appeals, 65- Bus. & Prof. Pos: Law practice, Austin, 36- Mil. Serv: Lt. Comdr, Navy, 42-46. Mem: Tex, Am. and Travis

Co. Bar Asns; Am. Legion; Mason (32°); KCCH; Shrine; Kiwanis. Silver Beaver Award, Boy Scouts; Distinguished Alumnus Award, Ex-Students' Asn, Univ. Tex, 65. Rel: Methodist. Legal Res: 1403 Hardouin St, Austin, Tex. 78703. Mailing Add: U.S. Court House, Austin, Tex. 78701.

THORNBURG, LACY HERMAN D
b. Charlotte, N.C, 12/20/29; s. Jesse LaFayette Thornburg and Sarah Ann Zeigler T; m. 9/6/53 to Dorothy Frances Todd; c. Sara Frances, Lacy Eugene and Jesse Todd. Educ: Mars Hill Jr. Col, 50; Univ. N.C, B.A, 52; Law Sch, LL.B, 54; pres, Phi Alpha Delta, Univ. N.C. Law Sch. Chap, 53-54. Polit. & Govt. Pos: V.pres, West. Dist. N.C. Young Dem. Cmt, 59; town attorney, Dillsboro and Webster, 60-62; cong. staff asst. to Hon. Roy A. Taylor, 60-62; city attorney, Jackson City, 60-; N.C. State Rep, 61-66; alternate del, Dem. Nat. Conv, 68. Bus. & Prof. Pos: Lawyer; sr. partner, Law Firm of Hall, Thornburg & Holt. Mil. Serv: Pfc, Army, 47-48. Mem: N.C. and Am. Bar Asns; Lions; Jaycees; Mason. Rel: Presbyterian; Pres, Men of Church, 57; Supt, Sunday Sch, 57-60; Deacon, 58-60. Mailing Add: 28 Main St, Sylva, N.C. 28779. (1967)

THORNBURROW, SAMUEL RAYMOND D
Chmn, Marshall Co. Dem. Party, Kans.
b. St. Joseph, Mo, 7/26/12; s. Samuel Thornburrow and Etta Carney T; m. to Ferne Grubb (deceased). Educ: St. Mary's Col, Kans. Polit. & Govt. Pos: Chmn, Marshall Co. Dem. Party, Kans, 60-; del, Dem. Nat. Conv, 68; adv, Commodity Credit Corp, Wash, D.C, 68-69. Bus. & Prof. Pos: Bank cashier; mgr, Archer-Daniels Feed & Grain Co; loan agent and supvr, Commodity Credit Corp; supvr, Farm Security Corp; owner, farms and feed lots, cattle opers. Mem: Moose; K. of C. Rel: Catholic. Legal Res: 1505 Jenkins, Marysville, Kans. 66508.

THORNBURY, WILLIAM GORDON R
Mem, Calif. Rep. State Cent. Cmt.
b. Haynesville, La, 3/14/04; s. William Yearsley Thornbury and Lorena Kocher T; m. 5/8/31 to Blanche Hinderer; c. Ann (Mrs. Mowatt). Educ: Venice High Sch, grad, 22; Univ. Calif, Los Angeles, 22-24. Polit. & Govt. Pos: Mem, Personnel Bd, Calif, 48-57; councilman, Santa Monica City Coun, 57-62; mem, Calif. Rep. State Cent. Cmt, 69- Mem: Santa Monica Ins. Agents (past pres); Santa Monica Bd. of Realtors; Elks; Shrine; Lions; F&AM; Sciots; Mason. Plaques from various orgn. and city of Santa Monica. Rel: Protestant. Legal Res: 1117 21st St, Apt. 1, Santa Monica, Calif. 90403. Mailing Add: 2953 Lincoln Blvd, Santa Monica, Calif. 90405.

THORNE, WILLIAM H. D
b. London, Ont, Can, 3/4/02; married; c. William H, Daniel, Dorene. Educ: Jr. Col, Collegiate Inst. in London, Ont. Polit. & Govt. Pos: Mich. State Rep, 58-66; former mem. of the sch. bd; justice of the peace; twp. clerk; city clerk. Mem: Masons; Rotary Club; Elks. Rel: Baptist. Mailing Add: 4830 Carolee Lane, Dearborn Heights, Mich. 48125. (1967)

THORNHILL, LUCILLE WOOTEN D
W.Va. State Del.
b. Winston-Salem, N.C, 4/21/17; d. Richard Stephen Wooten and Inez Cordelia Shipp W; m. 12/13/41 to Robert Emmett Thornhill; c. Margaret Alice and Novie Ann. Educ: Capitol City Commercial Col, 1 year; Benjamin Franklin Sch. of Acct, 3 years; Southeast Univ, Wash, D.C, 1½ years. Polit. & Govt. Pos: Mem, Mercer Co. Dem. Exec. Cmt, W.Va, 60-, assoc. chmn, 64-; pres, Mercer Co. Women's Dem. Club, 60-64; dir, Fifth Cong. Dist. W.Va. Fedn. Dem. Women, 62-66; v.pres, W.Va. Fedn. Dem. Women, 66-69; W.Va. State Del, 66 & 69- Bus. & Prof. Pos: Admin. asst. chief claims div, Gen. Acct. Off, Wash, D.C, 35-41; mgr, Easley-Wilson Co. Real Estate, Bluefield, W.Va, 43-45; bookkeeper, Thornhill, Tinning and Plumbing Co, 46- Mem: Mercer Co. Women's Dem. Club; Mercer Co. Dem. Club; W.Va. Fedn. Dem. Women; Mercer Co. Ment. Health Asn; Bluefield Civic League; Fincastle Country Club. Dem. Vol. Worker of the Year, W.Va, 64. Rel: Baptist. Mailing Add: 2410 Cliffmont Ave, Bluefield, W.Va. 24701.

THORNHILL, LYNN R
Okla. State Rep.
b. Sand Creek, Okla, 9/24/04; s. William Andrew Thornhill and Mary Edna Witt T; m. 7/29/25 to Maurine Allie Garrett; c. Beverly Lynn (Mrs. Leonard A. Gibson) and Sharon Adair (Mrs. Jerry Harris). Educ: Wikita Pub. Schs, Okla. Polit. & Govt. Pos: Mem, Wakita Town Bd, Okla, 48-62 and mayor, Wakita, 50-62; Okla. State Rep, 39th Dist, 62-; mem, Okla. World Fair Cmn, 63-64. Bus. & Prof. Pos: Owner, Thornhill Serv, 25 years; partner, Thornhill-Gibson Oil Co, 15 years. Mem: Shrine; Consistory; Mason (past master); Lions (past pres); Quarter-Back club (past pres); Alumni Asn.(past pres). Rel: Baptist. Mailing Add: P.O. Box 25, Wakita, Okla. 73771.

THORNTON, EDMUND BRAXTON R
Mem, Ill. Rep. Finance Coord. Cmt.
b. Chicago, Ill, 3/9/30; s. George A. Thornton and Suzanne Woodward T; m. 12/31/64 to Elizabeth Oakes Moore; c. twins, Jonathan Butler and Thomas Volney and twins, Susan Oakes and Amanda Braxton. Educ: Yale Univ, B.A, 54; Yale Develop. Bd, 67-69; Delta Kappa Epsilon. Polit. & Govt. Pos: Chmn, La Salle Co. Rep. Finance Cmt, 62-68, mem, 69-; dir, United Rep. Fund, Ill, 65-; mem, Ill. Nature Preserves Cmn, 66; del, Rep. Nat. Conv, 68; chmn, All-Ill. Victory Gala Cmt, 69; mem, Gov. Adv. Coun, 69; mem, Ill. Rep. Financing Coord. Cmt, 69. Bus. & Prof. Pos: Pres. and chief exec. officer, Ottawa Silica Co, 62; dir, Ill. Mfrs. Asn, 66; mem. adv. bd, Assoc. Employers of Ill, 69-; pres, Ottawa C. of C, 69- Mil. Serv: Entered as 2nd Lt, Marine Corps Res, 54, released as 1st Lt, 56. Publ: Architectural Tour of Ottawa, Illinois, La Salle Co. Mem: Nat. Indust. Sand Asn; Am. Ceramic Soc; Int. Platform Asn.(gov, 67); La Salle Co. Hist Soc.(pres, 64-70); State of Ill. Hist. Sites Surv.(chmn, 69); Capitol Hill Club; Univ. Club of Chicago; Adventurers Club; Raquett Club; Chicago Club. George Washington Citizen of the Year, 67; Distinguished Serv. Award, Ottawa Jaycees, 69; Boss of the Year, Aishi Chap, Nat. Secretaries Asn, 68. Rel: Congregational. Legal Res: Route 1, Ottawa, Ill. 61350. Mailing Add: P.O. Box 1, Ottawa, Ill. 61350.

THORNTON, JEAN TYROL R
Conn. State Rep.
b. Glastonbury, Conn, 9/28/21; d. Edward Howard Tyrol and Olive Bidwell T; m. 12/2/43 to Delmar O. Thornton; c. Malcolm E, Kirk R. and Barbara J. Educ: Glastonbury High Sch, grad. Polit. & Govt. Pos: Registr. of Voters, Glastonbury, Conn, 56-62; v.chmn, Rep. Town Cmt, Glastonbury, 58-65; Conn. State Rep, 63-; alternate del, Rep. Nat. Conv, 68. Mil. Serv: Entered as Pvt, Women's Army Corps, 42, released as 2nd Lt, 44. Rel: Congregational. Mailing Add: 349 Hubbard St, Glastonbury, Conn. 06033.

THORNTON, LA-VERNE W. R
Chmn, Chatham Co. Rep. Party, N.C.
b. Pittsylvania Co, Va, 2/17/37; s. Perry James Thornton and Ethel Pruitt T; m. 3/23/57 to Alma Lucille Baker; c. La-Visa Jo and Perry James. Educ: Va. Polytech. Inst, B.S, 59. Polit. & Govt. Pos: Chmn, Chatham Co. Rep. Party, N.C, 66-; town councilman, Goldston, N.C, 66-; fourth cong. dist. chmn, Nixon Campaign, N.C, 68. Bus. & Prof. Pos: Plant mgr, Pomona Pipe Prod, Gulf, N.C, 69- Mem: Lions; Jaycees. Rel: Methodist. Legal Res: Windsow and Goldbar, Goldston, N.C. 27252. Mailing Add: P.O. Box 133, Goldston, N.C. 27252.

THORNTON, LEO MAZE R
Ore. State Rep.
b. Dayton, Ore, 4/13/22; s. Ladrue Leslie Thornton and Rada Antrim T; m. 6/27/43 to Patricia Remster; c. Virginia (Mrs. Wildermuth) and Elizabeth. Educ: Cascade Col, A.B, 45; Univ. Ore, 45-46; West. Baptist Sem, Portland, Ore, 48-49; West. Evangel. Sem, Portland, Ore, B.D, 50; hon. Dr. of Letters and Laws. Polit. & Govt. Pos: Rep. precinct committeeman, Clackamas Co, Ore, 63; cand, Ore. State Rep, Clackamas Co, 65; mem, Clackamas Co. Rep. Cent. Cmt, 65-; mem, Ore. State Rep. Cent. Cmt, 67-; Ore. State Rep, Clackamas Co, 67-, mem. Labor and Mgt. Cmt, 67-68, Educ. Cmt. & Pub. Health Cmt. and Chmn. Pub. Welfare Cmt, 67- Bus. & Prof. Pos: Pastor, 50-58; v.pres, West. Evangel. Sem, Portland, Ore, 58- Mil. Serv: Entered as 1st Lt, Army, 55, served in 413th Regt. and 364th Civil Affairs; Maj, Army Res, currently. Mem: Nat. Asn. Evangel; Ore. Hist. Soc; Ore. Retarded Childrens Asn; Isaac Walton League; YMCA; Nat. ROA; Farm Bur. Rel: Evangelical. Mailing Add: 17954 S.E. River Rd, Milwaukie, Ore. 97222.

THORNTON, O. FRANK D
Secy. of State, State of S.C.
b. Mullins, S.C, 7/26/05; s. Oscar Fontaine Thornton (deceased) and Lucendia Cooper T.(deceased); m. 8/19/33 to Rosa Waring; c. Rosa (Mrs. J.M. Cherry, Jr) and Frances (Mrs. Roy H. Shelton). Educ: Univ. S.C, LL.B, 28. Polit. & Govt. Pos: Mem, Dem. Exec. Cmt. and State and Co. Elec. Bd, S.C; S.C. State Rep, 35-36, reading clerk, S.C. House of Rep, 36-50; Secy. of State, State of S.C, 50- Bus. & Prof. Pos: Ed, Clover Herald; attorney-at-law and city attorney, Clover. Mem: Chmn, State Fund Drive, Crippled Children Soc, 60-61; dir, Lions, 61-62 & 66-67; dir, Richland-Lexington United Fund, 66-67; dir, Travelers Aid Soc, 66-67; pres, Nat. Asn. of Secy. of State, 59-60; Elks; Mason; secy. and bus. mgr, Salisbury-Spencer Baseball Club of Piedmont League, 27-29; bd. trustees, S.C. State Libr. Rel: Methodist. Mailing Add: 712 Arbutus Dr, Columbia, S.C. 29205.

THORNTON, ROBERT ERNEST D
b. Archer City, Tex, 8/5/28; s. E.G. Thornton and Ann Renfro T; m. 4/14/49 to Carol Loafman; c. Jamie. Educ: Univ. Wyo, summer 48; Tex. Christian Univ, B.A, 49; Law Sch, Univ. Tex, LL.B, 52; Phi Delta Phi. Polit. & Govt. Pos: Del, local and state conv, 52-68; del, Dem. Nat. Conv, 68. Publ: Auth, various case notes and book rev. and assoc. ed, Tex. Law Rev, 51-52. Mem: Am. Bar Asn; Young Co. Bar Asn. (pres, 56); Rotary; bd. of regents, Midwestern Univ. Mailing Add: Box 8, Olney, Tex. 76374.

THORNTON, ROBERT Y. D
State Attorney Gen, Ore.
b. Portland, Ore. Educ: Stanford Univ, B.A; Univ. of Ore; George Washington Law Sch, J.D. Polit. & Govt. Pos: State Attorney Gen, Ore, 52-; worked as law clerk for Justice of U.S. Court; performed legal servs. for Legis. Ref. Serv. of Cong; asst. attorney, U.S. Dept. of Interior; city attorney of Tillamook,Ore; Ore. State Rep. Bus. & Prof. Pos: Lawyer; law practice Medford and Tillamook. Mil. Serv: Army, 5 years, Lt, Col. Co-auth. of reference book, U.S. Constitution. Mailing Add: Dept. of Justice, State Office Bldg, Salem, Ore. 97310.

THORP, JOHN S, JR. D
N.Y. State Assemblyman
b. Rockville Center, N.Y, 9/29/25; m. to Dolores Hartig; c. John, Richard and Patricia. Educ: Holy Cross Col, 45; Brooklyn Law Sch, 49. Polit. & Govt. Pos: Past pres, Dem. Club; Dem. Co. Committeeman, N.Y, 46-; N.Y. State Assemblyman, 64- Bus. & Prof. Pos: Attorney. Mil. Serv: Navy, World War II. Mem: Nassau Co. Bar Asn; Cath. Lawyer Guild; past pres, Lions Club; C. of C; K. of C; Holy Name Soc. Mailing Add: 92 Voorhis Ave, Rockville Centre, N.Y. 11570.

THORP, MITCHELL LEON D
Mem. Exec. Cmt, Wash. Co. Dem. Orgn, Tenn.
b. Knoxville, Tenn, 7/1/10; s. Benjamin Thorp and Molly Gerber T; m. 3/20/42 to Hilda Rose Rapport; c. Stephanie Mae, Allan Bertram and Marjorie Jean. Educ: Univ. Baltimore, LL.B, 34; Nu Beta Epsilon. Polit. & Govt. Pos: Del, Dem. Nat. Conv, 64 and mem, Permanent Orgn. Cmt, 64; del, Tenn. State Dem. Conv, 64; chmn, Johnson City Area Indust. Cmn, 66; v.mayor, Johnson City, 66; mem. exec. cmt, Wash. Co. Dem. Orgn, currently; mem, Tenn. Indust. Cmn, 68; mem. urban govt. affairs cmt, Nat. Asn. Home Builders, 69. Bus. & Prof. Pos: Pres, Thorp & Co, Inc, E. Tenn. Enterprises and Johnson City Yankees, 66-; v.pres, Tenn. Iron & Paper Inc. and Standard Steel Cabinet, 66- Mem: C. of C; Rotary; Mason; Shrine; Elks; Home Builders Asn; Inst. of Scrap Iron & Steel; Johnson City Country Club; Johnson City Little League. Received Nat. Merit Award, Little League Baseball, 63 and Mr. Baseball, Park & Recreation Award, 65. Rel: Jewish; Pres, B'nai Sholom Congregation. Mailing Add: 1312 Iris Ave, Johnson City, Tenn. 37601.

THORPE, JAMES 'JIM' R
Ohio State Rep.
Married; c. three. Educ: Mt. Union Col; William McKinley Sch. of Law.

Polit. & Govt. Pos: Ohio State Rep, 61-64 & 67-; Ohio State Sen, 65-66. Bus. & Prof. Pos: Attorney. Mil. Serv: Air Force. Mailing Add: State Capitol Bldg, Columbus, Ohio 43215. (1967)

THORSGARD, ENOCH ARNOLD R
N.Dak. State Rep.
b. Northwood, N.Dak, 3/30/17; s. Arne Thorsgard and Clara Markre T; m. 5/31/42 to Madeline Wasness; c. Carol (Mrs. Harold Luuke), Graydon, Betty, John and Ruth. Educ: Northwood High Sch, grad; N.Dak. State Univ, short Agr. Course. Polit. & Govt. Pos: Rep. Precinct Committeeman, Lind Twp, N.Dak, 50-; N.Dak. State Rep, 19th Dist, 69- Bus. & Prof. Pos: Owner and operator, Sunrise Acres, 41-; pres. and treas, Baserier Champlin Inc, 65- Mem: Dir, Fed. Land Bank Asn, Grand Forks; Greater N.Dak. Asn; Lions; Farm Bur; dir, Northwood Hosp. & Home Asn; Farm Mgr. Asn; 4-H Club Leader, 25 years. Outstanding Young Farmer of Grand Forks trade Area, 53. Rel: Lutheran. Mailing Add: Northwood, N.Dak. 58267.

THORSON, HARRY T. R
b. Milan, Minn, 8/17/02; s. Gulmun Thorson and Anne Graves T; m. 6/24/29 to Inga C. Gysland; c. James Donald, Thomas Allen and Mary (Mrs. Gullickson). Educ: Dakota Bus. Col, 18-19. Polit. & Govt. Pos: State committeeman, Weston Co. Rep. Party, Wyo, 54-55; chmn, Wyo. State Rep. Party, 55-60; Rep. nat. committeeman, Wyo, 60-64; chmn, Land and Water Conserv. Cmn, 65-67; chmn, Gov. Cmn. Reorgn. State Govt, 67-69; del, Rep. Nat. Conv, 68; dir, Wyo. Fedn. Rocky Mt. States, 69. Bus. & Prof. Pos: Forman, Ill. Pipe Line Co, Casper, 23-32; supt, Osage Trust, 32-41; independent crude oil producer, 41-; pres, Black Hills Bentanite Co, Mills, 47-; pres, Toco Corp, Newcastle, 66- Mem: Mason; Elks. Rel: Lutheran. Legal Res: 26 S. Senecca, Newcastle, Wyo. 82701. Mailing Add: Box 338, Newcastle, Wyo. 82701.

THOUTSIS, TIMOTHEOS MICHAEL R
Chmn, Paxton Rep. Town Cmt, Mass.
b. Epirus, Greece, 5/27/27; s. Haralambos Michael Thoutsis and Helen Liazos T; m. 7/13/58 to Candy Latham. Educ: Worcester Jr. Col, A.A, 48; Syracuse Univ, B.S, 50. Polit. & Govt. Pos: State exam, Mass. Dept. Ins, 54-; v.pres, Young Men's Rep. Club, 55-56, pres, 56-57; Finance Chmn, Paxton Rep. Town Cmt, 64-65, chmn, 66- Bus. & Prof. Pos: Distributor, Proctor & Gamble, 51-52; asst. buyer, Filene's, 52-53. Mil. Serv: Navy, World War II. Mem: Syracuse Univ. Alumni of Gr. Worcester; Paxton Bd. of Appeals; DAV; Am. Legion. Rel: Greek Orthodox. Mailing Add: 6 William Allen Dr, Paxton, Mass. 01612.

THRANE, RALPH ORVILLE R
b. Kindred, N.Dak, 12/15/32; s. Palmer Thrane and Gunda Simmons T; m. 2/3/55 to Loanne Brager; c. Peter. Educ: Concordia Col, B.A, 54; Stanford Univ, M.B.A, 58. Polit. & Govt. Pos: Chmn, Le Sueur Co. Nixon Vols, Minn, 60; del, Co, Dist. and State Rep. Conv, 60-64, 65 & 68-69; chmn, Second Cong. Dist. Young Rep. League, 61-62, first v.chmn, Second Cong. Dist. Rep. Cmt, 62-63; state dir, Young Rep. League Minn, 63-64; chmn, Co. Rep. Finance Cmt, 65; area chmn, Minn. State Rep. Finance Cmt, 65-66; alternate del-at-lg, Rep. Nat. Conv, 68; state chmn, Nixon-Agnew Speakers Bur, 68; indust. cmnr, Chanhassen Village, Minn, 68. Bus. & Prof. Pos: Research asst, Grad. Sch. Bus, Stanford Univ, 57; mkt. research analyst, Green Giant Co, Le Sueur, Minn, 59-62, profit dir. corn and snap beans, 62-65, asst. to pres, Green Giant Can. Ltd, Windsor, Ont, 65-66; dir, profit planning, 67- Mil. Serv: Entered as E-1, Army, 54, released as E-4, 56, after serv. in Army Band, Ft. Shafter, Honolulu, Hawaii, 55-56. Mem: Am. Mkt. Asn; PTA (co-chmn, sch. dist. concerned citizens cmt, 69); Sunrise Hills Civic Asn.(secy-treas). Outstanding Young Rep. Minn, Young Rep. League Conv, 62. Rel: Lutheran. Mailing Add: R.R. 4, Excelsior, Minn. 55331.

THREET, EWING JACKSON D
Chmn, Coffee Co. Dem. Exec. Cmt, Tenn.
b. Murfreesboro, Tenn, 8/12/26; s. James Herbert Threet and Dera Wood T; m. 8/8/46 to Ann Ray Beachboard; c. Stephen Ewing, Virginia Dianne and James Herbert. Educ: George Peabody Col. for Teachers, Nashville, Tenn, 46-49; Univ. Tenn. Col. Dent, D.D.S, 52, M.S, 53. Polit. & Govt. Pos: Councilman, Manchester, Tenn, 56-58; mem, Indust. Cmn, Tenn, 60-; Tenn. State Sen, 61-63; del, Tenn. Constitutional Conv, 65-; chmn, Coffee Co. Dem. Exec. Cmt, Tenn, 65- Bus. & Prof. Pos: Dir. and secy-treas, Home Fed. Savings & Loan Asn, 64- Mil. Serv: Entered as A/S, Navy, 44, released as Yeoman 2/C, 46, after serv. in Seabees, Pac; 3 Battle Stars; Good Conduct Medal. Mem: Chmn, Coun. on Legis, Tenn. State Dent. Asn, 61- and pres, 4th Dist. Dent. Soc, 61-62; Am. and Tenn. Dent. Asns; Pierre Fanchard Acad, Brit. Royal Soc. of Health; Soc. Dent. for Children; Mason; Lions; Toastmasters; C. of C; Am. Legion; VFW; Nat. Cmt. for Support of Pub. Schs; Tenn. Citizens for Better Schs; Manchester Golf and Country Club. Rel: Church of Christ. Legal Res: 1800 Sycamore Dr, Manchester, Tenn. 37355. Mailing Add: 116 East Fort, Manchester, Tenn. 37355.

THRESHER, IRENE K. R
b. Cologne, Germany, 7/6/00; d. Max A. Kattwinkel and Rosa E. Grossmann K; m. 11/27/23 to Brainerd Alden Thresher; c. Naomi (Mrs. Colyer), Sonia (Mrs. Weaver), Rosemary (Mrs. Edson) and Brainerd Colby. Educ: Vassar Col, B.A, 21. Hon. D.H.L, Emerson Col, 57. Polit. & Govt. Pos: Mem, Newton Rep. City Cmt, Mass, 36-66; mem, Newton Sch. Cmt, 42-51; v.chmn, Fifth Middlesex Mass. State Rep. Cmt, 51-61; del. or alternate del, Rep. Nat. Conv, 52-64; pres, Mass. Fedn. Rep. Women, 55-58; mem, Mass. Rep. State Cmt, 55-68, v.chmn, 55-58; v.chmn, Mass. Rep. Finance Cmt, 59-62; chmn, Newton Housing Authority, 60-65; trustee, Mass. Ment. Health Center, 62-68. Mem: Am. Asn. of Univ. Women; Mass. Asn. for Mental Health; Mass. Legislators Asn; League of Women Voters; Boston Vassar Club; bd, Med. Found; pres, Homemaker Serv; pres, Newton Commun. Chest and Coun; bd, New Eng. Home for Little Wanderers; bd. United Fund of Greater Boston, 57-59. Rel: Protestant. Mailing Add: 2020 N. Atlantic Ave, Cocoa Beach, Fla. 32931.

THROCKMORTON, ADEL FOSTER R
b. Madrid, Iowa, 4/21/93; s. Edward Walter Throckmorton and Lura Woods T; m. 1/3/18 to Florence Miles; c. Jean Lavon (deceased) and Dr. Marion A. Educ: Southwest. Col, Kans, A.B, 20, LL.D, 50; Univ. of Kans, A.M, 29; Baker Univ, L.H.D, 63; Phi Delta Kappa. Polit. & Govt. Pos: Co. Supt. Pub. Instr, Sedgwick Co, Kans, 39-49; State Supt. of Pub. Instr, Kans, 49-66; mem, Kans. Teacher Retirement Bd, 49-66; mem, Kans. State Exec. Coun, 49-66; mem, Kans. Budget Rev. Bd, 65-66. Bus. & Prof. Pos: Newspaper publisher, News, Clearwater, Kans, 32-36. Mil. Serv: Entered as Pvt, Army, 17, released as Sgt, 19, after serv. in Co. C, 110th Field Serv. Bn, 35th Div. in U.S. and ETO; Serv. Bars for St. Mihiel Offensive, Meuse-Argonne Offensive and French Sectors. Publ: 'How Good are Kansas Schools,' Kans. Farmer Stockman, 63; miscellaneous articles in Kans. Teacher, 4-H Jour, Dept. of Educ. Publ. and others, 49-65. Mem: Nat. Educ. Asn; Kans. State Teachers Asn; Am. and Kans. Asns. of Sch. Adminstr; Mason; VFW; YMCA; Am. Legion; Optimist Int; bd. trustees, Baker Univ. Rel: Methodist. Mailing Add: 1225 Van View Court, Wichita, Kans. 67204.

THUET, PAUL ANTHONY D
b. St. Paul, Minn, 11/13/16; s. Paul Anthony Thuet and Annie Chalmers Reid T; m. 10/19/40 to Marian Shellman; c. Stephen Paul and William Frederick. Educ: Univ. Minn, B.S.L, 37, LL.B, 39; Beta Theta Pi; Phi Delta Phi. Polit. & Govt. Pos: City attorney, S.St. Paul, Minn, 47-49, acting Munic. Judge, 49-58; enforcement dir, Minn, U.S. Off. Price Stabilization, 51-53; chmn, Bd. Aeronaut, S.St. Paul, 53-56; mem, Korean Bonus Appeal Bd, Minn, 56-58; Minn. State Sen, 13th Dist, 59-67, former Minority Leader, Minn. State Senate. Bus. & Prof. Pos: Claim mgr, St. Paul Fire & Marine Ins, 40-47; Sr. partner, Beaudoin, Thuet, Todd & Pavlak, 47-60 and Thuet & Todd, 60- Mil. Serv: Entered as Pvt, Army, 44, released as T/Sgt, 46, after serv. in Judge Adv. Staff, Okinawa Base Command, Ryukyus Islands, Pac. Theater, 45-46; Asiatic-Pac. Theater Ribbon; Army of Occup. Medal; Japanese Victory Medal; Good Conduct Medal. Mem: Am. Bar Asn; bd. of gov, Minn. Bar Asn, 56-58; pres, 1st Dist. Bar Asn, 55; Am. Judicature Soc; Am. Acad. of Polit. Sci; bd. of gov, Nat. Soc. of Legis; VFW; Am. Legion; pres, Lions, 52; bd. of dirs. and v.pres, S.St. Paul C. of C, 56-58; St. Paul Athletic Club. Rel: Presbyterian. Mailing Add: 401 Marian Place, South St. Paul, Minn. 55075.

THULL, EUGENE NICHOLAS D
Chmn, Mitchell Co. Dem. Party, Kans.
b. Cawker City, Kans, 2/12/16; s. John George Thull and Florence Smith T; m. 10/23/45 to Frances Kathryn Heinen; c. Barbara, Tracy, Michael, Virginia and Scott. Educ: Salt City Bus. Col. Polit. & Govt. Pos: Chmn, Mitchell Co. Dem. Party, Kans, 58-; councilman, Cawker City, 61-66. Mil. Serv: Entered as Pvt, Air Force, 42, released as T/Sgt, 45, after serv. in Southeast. Tech. Training Command. Mem: K. of C. 1868; Am. Legion; Lions. Rel: Catholic. Mailing Add: Box 106, Cawker City, Kans. 67430.

THUMMEL, GLENN FRANK R
Chmn, Shelby Co. Rep. Cent. Cmt, Iowa
b. Bedford, Iowa, 7/25/14; s. Frank C. Thummel and Alice E. Butts T; m. 7/27/41 to Vera Dorothy; c. Craig, Ann and Kristen. Educ: Northwest Mo. State Col; Univ. Iowa. Polit. & Govt. Pos: Chmn, Shelby Co. Rep. Cent. Cmt, Iowa, currently; treas, Rep. Cent. Cmt. Bus. & Prof. Pos: Internal revenue agent U.S. Govt. Treas. Dept, 48-55; secy-treas, Home Fed. Savings & Loan, 55- Mil. Serv: Entered as Pvt, Air Force, 42, released as Lt, 45. Mem: Am. Legion; Kiwanis Int; Mason; Shrine; K.T; Harland Planning Bd. and Zoning and Appeal Bd; YMCA (secy. bd, West. Iowa Chap); Soc. of Savings and Loans Controllers. Rel: Methodist. Mailing Add: 712 Durant St, Harlan, Iowa 51537. (1967)

THURBER, MARY D. R
Vt. State Rep.
b. Prairie du Chien, Wis, 8/5/12; d. Louis De Vierville Dousman and Sarah Easton D; m. 11/15/33 to Richard Bourne Thurber; c. Mary T.(Mrs. Ralph H. Clark, III), Julia B.(Mrs. J. Dynan Candon) and W.S. Thurber. Educ: Carleton Col, A.B, 33; Phi Beta Kappa. Polit. & Govt. Pos: Chmn, Dist. 30, Vt, 64-66; Vt. State Rep, Dist. 30, currently. Mem: Farm Bur; dir, Chittenden Co. Red Cross, Vt. Coun. on World Affairs and Howard Family Serv. Center. Rel: Episcopal. Mailing Add: West Wind Farm, Charlotte, Vt. 05445.

THURLAND, GENEVIEVE I. D
Dem. Nat. Committeewoman, V.I.
b. Christiansted, V.I, 10/16/14; d. Peter Gregory Thurland Sr. and Ruth Adeline Simmonds T. Educ: Christiansted High Sch, V.I, grad, 30. Polit. & Govt. Pos: Switchboard operator, V.I. Govt, 45-60; treas, V.I. Unity Party, 60-63; Dem. nat. committeewoman, V.I, currently. Bus. & Prof. Pos: Teacher, Christiansted High Sch, 34-36. Mem: Secy, Commun. Chest, 62-64 and St. Croix Concert Asn, 65-66; finance chmn, Bus. and Prfnl. Women's Club, 64-65. Rel: Roman Catholic. Mailing Add: 9 New St, Christiansted, St. Croix, V.I. 00820.

THURM, WILLIAM HENRY D
Mem, Calif. Dem. State Cent. Cmt.
b. Otterville, Ill, 10/26/06; s. Carl Henry Thurm and Mary Welch T; m. 9/23/44 to Lorene Bernice O'Dell; c. Mark William. Educ: Medora High Sch, Ill, grad, 26; Beaumont Night Sch, St. Louis, Mo, Business, 28; Kroger Bus. Admin, 30. Polit. & Govt. Pos: Mem, Kern Co. Dem. Cent. Cmt, Calif, 60-; mem, Calif. Dem. State Cent. Cmt, 60-; area chmn. for Gov. Pat Brown and Lt. Gov. Glenn Anderson Campaigns, Calif, 62-66; pres, Desert Empire Dem. Club, Ridgecrest, 62- Bus. & Prof. Pos: Owner, W.H. Thurm Co. (Sewing Machines), 50- Publ: 'The Sewing Family,' Elna Co, Geneva, Switzerland, (Elna News), 66. Mem: Charter mem, Elks, Ridgecrest; Toastmasters Int. (area gov, 65); AFL Plumbers & Steamfitters Local Union 460, Bakersfield; Amateur Trapshooting Asn, Vandalia, Ohio (nat. shooter, 50-). Winner of trip to Europe, World Contest of Necchi-Elna, 57; 1/4 Century Mem, AFL, 67. Rel: Protestant. Mailing Add: 333 N. Sanders, Ridgecrest, Calif. 93555.

THURMAN, JOHN HOWARD R
Chmn, Peach Co. Rep. Cmt, Ga.
b. Americus, Ga, 7/10/26; s. James Howard Thurman and Bertha Schroeder T; m. 3/2/51 to Mary Anne Thomas; c. John Howard, Jr, C. Michael, Susan Ann, Martha Kay and Thomas D. Educ: Ga. Inst. Tech, B.S.Ch.E, 47; Kappa Alpha. Polit. & Govt. Pos: Chmn, Peach Co. Rep. Cmt, Ga, 66- Bus. & Prof. Pos: Plant engr, Woolfolk Chem. Works, Ft. Valley, Ga, 47-58; plant supt, 58-

Mil. Serv: Entered as A/S, Naval Res, 44, released as Ens, 46. Mem: Kiwanis. Rel: Roman Catholic. Mailing Add: R.F.D. 1, Box 6, Ft. Valley, Ga. 31030.

THURMAN, MARJORIE CLARK D
Dem. Nat. Committeewoman
b. Atlanta, Ga, 6/17/28; d. Henry Clay Clark and Jessie Early Clark Boynton; m. 11/20/48 to Ross H. Thurman; c. Sandra Lynn. Educ: Emory Univ, 45-46; Draughon Sch. Commerce, 46-47; Atlanta Law Sch, LL.B, 49, LL.M, 50. Polit. & Govt. Pos: Young Dem. Committeewoman, 57-63, pres, Fulton Co. Young Dem, Ga, 58-62; gen. counsel, Young Dem. of Am, 59-61; mem, Presidential Inaugural Cmt, 60; del, NATO Exchange of Young Polit. Leaders, 61; mem, Ga. State Dem. Exec. Cmt, 63-; Dem. Nat. Committeewoman, 63-; del, Dem. Nat. Conv, 64 & 68, mem. platform and arrangements cmts, 64, mem. site cmt. and cmt. on permanent orgn, 68. Bus. & Prof. Pos: Practice of law, 49-; mem, Law Firm of Leachman, King & Thurman, 56- Mem: Am, Ga. and Atlanta Bar Asns; Ga. Asn. of Women Lawyers; Old War Horse Lawyers Club; Am. Judicature Soc; Equity Club; Women's C. of C; Atlanta Bus. & Prfnl. Women's Club; League of Women Voters; Gov. Cmn. on Status of Women; Atlanta Asn. UN; Atlanta Cmt. for Int. Visitors. Rel: Methodist. Legal Res: 5450 Glenridge Dr. N.E, Atlanta, Ga. 30305. Mailing Add: 2301 National Bank of Georgia Bldg, Atlanta, Ga. 30303.

THURMOND, DAVID XAVIER D
b. Russellville, Ky, 9/21/49; s. Hal Hart Thurmond and Ida Elizabeth Hite T; single. Educ: Bellarmine Col, 2 years. Polit. & Govt. Pos: Christian Co. Chmn, McCarthy for Pres, Ky, 68; Bellarmine Col. chmn, Katherine Peden for Sen, 68; del, Dem. Nat. Conv, 68. Freshman of the Year, Bellarmine Col, 68, Lennihan Award for Commun. Serv, 69. Rel: Roman Catholic. Mailing Add: 110 S. Sunset Circle, Hopkinsville, Ky. 42240.

THURMOND, EDWIN M. R
Chmn, Calloway Co. Rep. Cmt, Ky.
b. Murray, Ky, 12/31/16; s. Luby F. Thurmond and Ruby Miller T; m. 8/8/42 to Virginia Gephart; c. Ed Michael and Patricia Louise. Educ: Murray State Univ, 34-37. Polit. & Govt. Pos: Secy, Calloway Co. Rep. Orgn, 46-50 & 52-55 and treas, 50-52; chmn, Calloway Co. Rep. Cmt, Ky, 56- Bus. & Prof. Pos: Owner and operator, Thurmond's Coal & Feed Mill of Murray, Ky; partner, Leon Smith, Ky. Country Ham Oper, Hazel, Ky. Mil. Serv: Entered as Pvt, Army, 41, released as Sgt, 45, after serv. in Med. Corps, U.S. Mem: Am. Legion; Moose; Am. Feed Dealers Asn; Nat. C. of C; Nat. Fedn. of Independent Businessmen. Rel: Church of Christ. Legal Res: 203 S. 13th St, Murray, Ky. 42071. Mailing Add: Box 143, Murray, Ky. 42071. (1967)

THURMOND, STROM R
U.S. Sen, S.C.
b. Edgefield, S.C, 12/5/02; s. John William Thurmond and Eleanor Gertrude Strom T; m. 11/7/47 to Jean Crouch, deceased 1/6/60; m. 12/22/68 to Nancy Moore. Educ: Clemson Col, B.S, 23; State of S.C. Law Course, 30. Hon. LL.D, Bob Jones Univ, 48, Presby. Col, 60 and Clemson Col, 61; D.M.S, The Citadel, 61; L.H.D, Trinity Col, 65. Polit. & Govt. Pos: City and co. attorney, several years; co. supt. educ, 29-33; del, Dem. Nat. Conv, 32, 36, 48, 52, 56 & 60, chmn. S.C. del, and nat. committeeman, 48; S.C. State Sen, 33-38; circuit judge, 38-46; Gov. S.C, 47-51; States' Rights Dem. cand, Pres, U.S, 48; chmn, South. Gov. Conf, 50; U.S. Sen, S.C, 55-, mem, Armed Serv, Judiciary, Appropriations (defense) and Rules Cmts, U.S. Senate; del, Rep. Nat. Conv, 68. Bus. & Prof. Pos: Farmer; athletic coach and teacher, 23-29; admitted to S.C. Bar, 30; attorney-at-law, 30-38 & 51-55; admitted to practice in all Fed. Courts including U.S. Supreme Court. Mil. Serv: Army, 42-46, serv. in Hq, First Army, 82nd Airborne Div, Europe and Pac. Theaters and Normandy Invasion; Maj. Gen, Army Res; Five Battle Stars; Legion of Merit; Bronze Star Medal with V; Army Commendation Ribbon; Purple Heart; Presidential Distinguished Unit Citation; Third Army Cert. Achievement; OCAMG Cert. of Achievement; Dept. of Army Cert. Appreciation; French Croix de Guerre; Belgian Order of the Crown. Mem: ROA (past nat. pres); Mil. Govt. Asn. (past nat. pres); Am. Bar Asn. Rel: Baptist. Legal Res: Box 981 Aiken, S.C. 29801. Mailing Add: Senate Office Bldg, Washington, D.C. 20510.

THURSTON, GEORGE O. R
N.H. State Rep.
b. Errol, N.H, 4/19/98; married; c. one. Educ: Errol pub. schs. and Colebrook Acad. Polit. & Govt. Pos: Selectman, Town of Errol, N.H, 24 years; moderator 10 years; N.H. State Rep, currently. Bus. & Prof. Pos: Filling sta. and elec. servicing; mgr, Errol Munic. Elec. Light Dept, 26 years. Mil. Serv: World War II. Mem: Am. Legion. Rel: Congregational. Mailing Add: Errol, N.H. 03579. (1967)

THURSTON, LEWIS BYRON, III R
Res. Dir, N.J. Rep. State Cmt.
b. Hackensack, N.J, 4/19/37; s. Lewis Byron Thurston, Jr. and Dorothea Gras T; m. 2/19/66 to Mary Jane Freriks; c. Linda Jane. Educ: Colgate Univ, A.B. honors in polit. sci, 59; Univ. Va. Law Sch, 59-60; Eagleton Inst. Polit, Rutgers Univ, A.M, 63; Pi Sigma Alpha. Polit. & Govt. Pos: Res. assoc, div. info. & res, N.J. Legis, 63-66; res. asst, N.J. Legis. Reapportionment & Cong. Redistricting Cmn, 64; res. assoc, N.J. Constitutional Conv, 66; secy. to Rep. mem, N.J. Apportionment Cmn, 66-; res. dir, N.J. Rep. State Cmt, 66-; secy. to majority, N.J. State Sen, 68- Bus. & Prof. Pos: Admin. asst. to trust officer, Chase-Manhattan Bank, N.Y.C, 61-62. Mil. Serv: E-1, Army, 60-61, Ft. Dix, N.J, Res, 61-66. Publ: 'The Basis of Legislative Apportionment,' N.J. Constitutional Conv, 66; plus others. Rel: Presbyterian. Mailing Add: 306 Glenn Ave, Trenton, N.J. 08638.

THWEAT, THEODORE OLIVER D
b. Prince George, Va, 8/12/09; s. Edward Thweat and Irene Brower T; m. 7/14/42 to Virginia Patterson. Educ: Va. State Col, B.S; Sigma Chi. Polit. & Govt. Pos: Alternate del, Dem. Nat. Conv, 68. Bus. & Prof. Pos: Sch. teacher, 14 years. Mem: Voters League; Odd Fellows; Elks. Rel: Baptist. Mailing Add: Route 2, Box 113, Disputanta, Va. 23842.

TIBBETS, MARGARET JOY
Dep. Asst Secy, Bur. of European Affairs, Dept. of State
b. Bethel, Maine, 8/26/19; single. Educ: Wheaton Col, A.B, 41; Phi Beta Kappa; Bryn Mawr Col, M.A, 42, Ph.D, 44. Polit. & Govt. Pos: Research analyst, Off. of Strategic Serv, 44-45; career officer, Dept. of State For. Serv, 45-, research asst, 45-49, attache, London, 49-51, 2nd secy, London, 51-54, consul, Leopoldville, Cameroons, French Equatorial Africa, 54-57, officer, polit-mil. affairs, Off. of Europe Regional Affairs, 58-59, spec. asst. to dir, Int. Coop. Admin, 59-61, 1st secy, Brussels, 61-63, Sr. Seminar in For. Policy, 63-64, U.S. Ambassador to Norway, 64-69, dep. asst. secy, Bur. of European Affairs, 69- Mem: Dir, Am. For. Serv. Asn, 57-59. Legal Res: Bethel, Maine 04217. Mailing Add: Dept. of State, Washington, D.C. 20520.

TIBBITTS, WAYNE EVERETT D
Idaho State Rep.
b. Providence, Utah, 5/17/03; s. Lorenzo Edwin Tibbitts and Mary Almeda Marler T; m. 6/30/27 to LaRetta Bessie Jones (deceased); m. 10/30/63 to Lela E. Drake; c. Marjorie J, Barbara G. and Errol Wayne. Educ: High Sch. Polit. & Govt. Pos: Idaho State Sen, Jefferson Co, 63-66; Idaho State Rep, 69- Mem: Rigby Rotary; Jefferson Co. Cattlemen's Asn. Rel: Latter-day Saint. Mailing Add: P.O. Box 125, Lorenzo, Idaho 83432. (1967)

TIBERI, THOMAS J. D
Pa. State Rep.
b. Butler, Pa, 4/10/19; s. John Tiberi and Palm Rose T; m. to Margaret Bovard; c. Five. Educ: Duquesne Univ, B.E. Polit. & Govt. Pos: City chmn, 57-58 and co. chmn, 58-64; Pa. State Rep, 64- Bus. & Prof. Pos: Teacher; auditor. Mil. Serv: Navy, World War II. Mem: Dir, Butler Co. Rec. Bd; hon. mem, AFL-CIO State Employees; Am. Legion. Mailing Add: 109 2nd St, Butler, Pa. 16001.

TICE, WAYNE K. R
b. McPherson, Kans, 9/21/24; s. Galen M. Tice and Ruth O. Kilmer T; m. 6/22/47 to Jean Louise Bell; c. Beverly J, David W. and Robert G. Educ: Univ. of Kans, A.B, 46, M.D, 48; Alpha Omega Alpha; Nu Sigma Nu. Polit. & Govt. Pos: City councilman, Independence, Mo, 62-64; alternate del, Rep. Nat. Conv, 64; pres, Independence-Blue Twp. Rep. Club, Mo, 64-66. Bus. & Prof. Pos: Secy, Nebr. State Radiological Soc, 58; mem, Exec. Coun, Jackson Co. Med. Soc, 64- Mil. Serv: Entered as 1st Lt, Army, 50, released as Capt, 53, after serv. in 35th Sta. Hosp, Kyoto, Japan, Far East. Command, 51-53. Mem: Am. Med. Asn; Mo. State and Jackson Co. Med. Socs; Local and State Radiological Socs; Dipl, Am. Bd. Radiology; Radiological Soc. of N.Am; Am. Col. of Radiology; C. of C. Rel: Presbyterian; Trustee. Mailing Add: 3504 Delaware, Independence, Mo. 64050.

TICEN, THOMAS E. DFL
Minn. State Rep.
b. Rockford, Ill, 12/9/27; s. Merritt Earl Ticen and Theresa J. Whalen T; m. 6/23/56 to Yvonne Pahl; c. Joanne Marie, Mary Theresa and Thomas E, Jr. Educ: St. Thomas Col, B.A, 48; Univ. Minn, J.D, 52. Polit. & Govt. Pos: Minn. State Rep, Dist 27 A, 67- Bus. & Prof. Pos: Attorney, Kempf & Ticen, Bloomington, Minn, 54- Mil. Serv: 1st Lt, Army, 52-54, serv. in Judge Adv. Gen. Corps, Pentagon; Capt, Res, 54-64. Rel: Catholic. Mailing Add: 5400 Southwood Dr, Bloomington, Minn. 55431.

TIDMORE, SAMUEL EDWARD, IV D
b. Decatur, Ill, 10/28/38; s. Samuel Tidmore and Ida Finley T; m. 11/8/59 to Carol Robinson; c. Tamarah and Nichelle. Educ: Ohio State Univ, B.Ed. Polit. & Govt. Pos: Admin. asst. U.S. Rep. Louis Stokes, Ohio. Bus. & Prof. Pos: Player, Cleveland Browns Football Club, 62-63; pub. rels, Carling Brewing, 63; teacher, Cleveland Pub. Schs, 64; stock broker, Hartzmark & Co, 64-69; financial adv, prfnl. man, planning, 67- Mem: Inner City Bus. Club; Pace Asn; Gr. Cleveland Growth Corp. Legal Res: 16407 Nicholas Ave, Cleveland, Ohio 44120. Mailing Add: 1229 Longworth Bldg, Washington, D.C. 20515.

TIDWELL, JACK QUINN D
b. Haskell, Tex, 11/30/30; s. Jack Tidwell and Trudie Isbell T; m. to Carole Ferguson; c. Scott Martelle and Nancy Lyn. Educ: Hardin-Simmons Univ, B.A, 51; Univ. Tex. Sch. Law, LL.B, 54; Alpha Chi; Acacia; Phi Alpha Delta. Polit. & Govt. Pos: Dist. attorney, 70th Judicial Dist, Odessa, Tex, 61-69; alternate del, Dem. Nat. Conv, 68. Bus. & Prof. Pos: Partner, Tidwell & Abbott, Abilene, Tex, 54-55, Cayton & Tidwell, Lamesa, 55-56 and Deaderick, McMahon, Cox, Todd & Tidwell, 69-; assoc, McDonald & Shafer, Odessa, 56-59. Mil. Serv: Entered as Pvt, Tex. Nat. Guard, 48, released as 1st Lt, 57, after serv. in 36th Inf. Div. Mem: Ector Co. Bar Asn.(pres, 59); State Bar of Tex; Tex. Asn. of Defense Counsel; Am. Bar Asn; charter fel, Tex. Bar Found. Rel: Presbyterian. Legal Res: 1700 N. Whitaker, Odessa, Tex. 79760. Mailing Add: P.O. Box 485, Fifth Floor, First State Bank Bldg, Odessa, Tex. 79760.

TIEMANN, NORBERT T. R
Gov, Nebr.
b. Minden, Nebr, 7/18/24; s. The Reverend M.W. Tiemann and Alvina Rathart T; m. 7/19/50 to Lorna Bornholdt; c. Mary Catherine, Norbert, Jr, Lorna and Amy. Educ: Univ. Nebr, 49. Polit. & Govt. Pos: Mayor, Wausa, Nebr, 3 terms; Gov, Nebr, 67-; mem. exec. cmt, Nat. Gov. Conf, Wash, D.C. Bus. & Prof. Pos: Pres, Commercial State Bank, Wausa; asst. mgr, Nebr. Hereford Asn; exec. secy, Nat. Livestock Feeders Asn; dir. indust. rels, Nat. Livestock and Meat Bd, Chicago; mem. exec. coun, Lutheran Church in Am, N.Y.C. Mil. Serv: S/Sgt, Army, 43-46, Pac. Theater; 2nd Lt, Army Res, 52, Germany. Mem: Nebr. C. of C; Am. Legion; VFW; 4-H; Boy Scouts. Rel: Lutheran. Mailing Add: 1425 H St, Lincoln, Nebr. 68508.

TIEDEN, DALE L. R
Iowa State Rep.
b. 10/11/22; s. Lewis Tieden and Grace Fisher T; single. Educ: Elkader Jr. Col; Univ. Iowa. Polit. & Govt. Pos: Iowa State Rep, currently. Bus. & Prof. Pos: Farmer until 59; mgr, Feed and Livestock Yard. Mem: Secy, Co. Farm Bur. and Twp. Agr. Cmts; Mason. Rel: United Church of Christ. Mailing Add: Garnavillo, Iowa 52034. (1967)

TIERNAN, ROBERT OWENS D
U.S. Rep, R.I.
b. Providence, R.I, 4/24/29; s. Joseph J. Tiernan and Mary E. McConnell T;

m. 7/13/53 to Dorothy Ann McNally; c. Michael Moss, Robert O, Jr. and Christopher Paul. Educ: Providence Col, A.B, 53; Cath. Univ. Sch. of Law, LL.B, 56; Spike Shoe Club. Polit. & Govt. Pos: R.I. State Sen, 61-66; U.S. Rep, R.I, 67-, mem, Cmt. Interstate and For. Commerce and Cmt. on Post Office and Civil Serv, U.S. House of Rep; del, Dem. Nat. Conv, 68. Bus. & Prof. Pos: Partner, Gallogly, Beals, Tiernan and Sweeney. Mem: Am. Bar Asn, Banking and Corp. Sect; Elks. Rel: Roman Catholic. Legal Res: 1922 Warwick Ave, Warwick, R.I. 02889. Mailing Add: House Office Bldg, Washington, D.C. 20515.

TIERNEY, JAMES
Mich. State Rep. D
b. Jackson, Mich; married; c. Nancy, Alice, Sue, Timothy and Gail. Educ: Attended tech. schs. and night sch. Polit. & Govt. Pos: Mem, Common Coun, Mich, 44-54; chmn, Bd. of Appeals of Zoning Bd, 47-54; mayor of Garden City, 56-60; mem, Wayne Co. Bd. of Supvr, 56-60; Mich. State Rep, 64- Bus. & Prof. Pos: With Ford Motor Co. Mil. Serv: Army, 3 years. Mem: V.Chmn, Garden City Recreation Cmt, 41-44; Odd Fellows; F&AM; Optimist Club; PTA. Awarded the Ford Motor Co. Citizen of the Year Award. Rel: Baptist. Mailing Add: 5633 Arcola St, Garden City, Mich. 48135.

TIERNEY, LAURENCE E, JR. D
Powhatan, W.Va, 4/29/06; s. Laurence Edward Tierney and Nora Clark T; m. 7/22/30 to Katherine Graham Baker; c. Ann (Mrs. Smith). Educ: Yale Univ, B.S, 29; Sigma Xi; Delta Psi. Polit. & Govt. Pos: Del, Dem. Nat. Conv, 48, 52, 56, 60 & 64; chmn, Nat. Bituminous Coal Adv. Coun, Dept. of Interior, 49-52; mem, ARA Drafting Cmt, W.Va, 60; mem, IDA, W.Va, 61-; U.S. rep, Coal Econ. Coun, Geneva, Switz, 63. Bus. & Prof. Pos: Pres, dir. and treas, Laurence E. Tierney Land Co. and Mohawk Land Co, 30-; dir, Bluefield Supply Co, 30-; pres. and dir, Flat Top Nat. Bank, 30-63, chmn. bd. and dir, 63-; pres. and dir, East. Coal Corp, 33-; dir, W.Va. Armature Co, 40-; pres. and dir, Citizens Underwriters Agency, 41-65, chmn. bd, 65-; pres. and dir, Leatherwood Co, 45-65, chmn. bd. dirs. and treas, 65- Mem: Dir, Nat. Coal Policy Conf; pres, W.Va. Coal Mining Inst, 45; dir, Nat. Coal Asn, v.pres, 47-54; treas-dir, South. Coal Producers Asn; dir, W.Va. Coal Asn, 44-64, pres, 54-64; regional pres, South. W.Va. Coun. Boy Scouts, 36-52; Univ. Club, Bluefield, W.Va. and Wash, D.C; Yale Club; N.Y; Press Club, Charleston, W.Va; Bluefield Country Club; Fincastle Co. Club; C. of C; Bluefield Commun. Concert Asn. Rel: Roman Catholic. Legal Res: 625 Mt. View Ave, Bluefield, W.Va. 24701. Mailing Add: Box 370, Bluefield, W.Va. 24701.

TIETJEN, THEODORE
Chmn, Perkins Co. Rep. Party, Nebr. R
b. Byron, Nebr, 12/6/34; s. Theodore Tietjen Sr. and Lilly Schluefer T; m. 9/25/60 to Louise C. Pollmann; c. Sheryl Kay and Theodore Scott. Educ: Univ. Nebr, B.S, 58; Ag Men. Polit. & Govt. Pos: Precinct chmn, Byron Rep. Party, Thayer Co, Nebr, 60-62; mem, Thayer Co. Rep. Cent. Cmt, 62-65; dist. chmn. for Ralph Beerman, 64; dist. chmn. for Sen. Curtiss, 66; chmn, Perkins Co. Rep. Party, 68- Bus. & Prof. Pos: Byron Chem. Inc, Nebr, 63-66 and pres. and div. mgr, Grant Div, 68-; gen. mgr, Valmont MidContinent Inc, Valley, 66-67. Mil. Serv: Entered as Pvt, Army, 56, released as SP-3, 58, after serv. in Fourth Army, Guided Missile Artillery Units, 56-58. Mem: Nebr. Fertilizer Inst; C. of C; Grant Area Jr. C. of C; bd. dirs, Grant Indust. Develop. Corp; Lions. Outstanding Young Men Award, 69; Outstanding Committeeman, Grant Jaycees, 69. Rel: Lutheran. Mailing Add: 405 Warren Ave, Grant, Nebr. 69140.

TIFFANY, JOHN JEWETT, II
Conn. State Rep. R
b. New London, Conn, 1/6/32; s. Leon Hammond Tiffany and Gwendolyn Willet T; m. 12/3/66 to Susan Bradeen. Educ: Univ. Conn, B.S, 54; Phi Kappa Phi; Gamma Chi Epsilon. Polit. & Govt. Pos: Mem, Lyme Bd. of Selectmen, Conn, 59-61; mem, Lyme Bd. Educ, 63-, chmn, 65-; Conn. State Rep, 63-; mem, Lyme Rep. Town Cmt, 64. Bus. & Prof. Pos: Partner, Tiffany Farms, 56. Mil. Serv: Entered as Pvt, Army, 54, released as SP-3, 56, after serv. in Corps of Eng. Mem: Farm Bur; Grange; Dairy Herd Improv. Asn. Rel: Protestant. Mailing Add: R.F.D, Old Lyme, Conn. 06371.

TIGHE, CHARLES D
b. Fargo, N.Dak, 1/21/27; s. Benjamin C.B. Tighe and Jennie Hebenstreit T; m. 9/3/56 to Dorothy Mushik. Educ: Univ. of N.Dak, Ph.B, 51, LL.B, 51. Polit. & Govt. Pos: Asst. State's Attorney, McKenzie Co, N.Dak, 52-53, Burleigh Co, 53-55; mem, N.Dak. Econ. Develop. Cmn, 61-65; Lt. Gov, N.Dak, 65-69. Bus. & Prof. Pos: Partner, Garaas & Tighe, 52-53, Jensen & Tighe, 53-57; private law practice, Bismarck, 57-; organizer of life ins. co, N.Dak, S.Dak. and Mont. Mil. Serv: Navy, 44-46. Mem: Bd. Regents, Mary Col; Am, N.Dak. and Burleigh Co. Bar Asns; Am. Trial Lawyers Asn. Legal Res: 1108 W. Highland Acres Rd, Bismarck, N.Dak. 58501. Mailing Add: 316 N. Fifth St, Bismarck, N.Dak. 58501. (1967)

TIGHE, CHARLES MOON
Chmn, Essex Rep. Town Cmt, Conn. R
b. Bronxville, N.Y, 9/29/34; s. Charles William Tighe and Jeanette Moon T; m. 6/23/56 to Nancy Watson; c. Alexander W, Leila M. and Jason E. Educ: Harvard Col, A.B, 57; Law Sch, LL.B, 60; Hasty Pudding Club; Delphic Club. Polit. & Govt. Pos: Chmn, Essex Rep. Town Cmt, Conn, 68- Bus. & Prof. Pos: Partner, Copp, Brenneman and Tighe, Attorneys, New London, Conn, 60- Mil. Serv: Entered as Pvt, Army Res, 54, released as SP-6, 61, after serv. in Army Security Agency. Mem: Am. Judicature Soc; Am. Bar Asn.(sect. on taxation); Conn. Bar Asn; Thames Club. Rel: Episcopal. Mailing Add: Donald Rd, Essex, Conn. 06426.

TILLERY, BILLY PROWELL
Mem, Miss. State Rep. Cent. Cmt. R
b. Laurel, Miss, 2/6/31; s. Judge Prowell Tillery and Mildred Lofton T; m. 6/26/57 to Beverly Walker; c. Jan, Lisa, Lynn and Susan. Educ: Jones Jr. Col, Ellisville, Miss; Miss. State Univ; Centenary Col; Tennis Scholarship; E Club; M Club. Polit. & Govt. Pos: Former co. chmn, Jones Co, Miss; mem, Miss. State Rep. Cent. Cmt, currently. Mil. Serv: Entered as Recruit, Navy Res, 48, released as Gunners Mate 2/C. Rel: Church of Christ. Mailing Add: 1024 Woodland Hills, Laurel, Miss. 39440.

TILLMAN, JIM KING
Fla. State Rep. R
b. Adel, Ga, 6/23/35; s. Andrew Lee Tillman and Virginia Maples T; m. 8/30/58 to Mary Wells; c. James McGregor, John Daniel, Teresa Lee and Jimi Lynn. Educ: Fla. State Univ, B.S, 61. Polit. & Govt. Pos: Dep. sheriff, Leon Co, Fla, 56-61; counsr, Sarasota Co. Juvenile Ct, 61-63, chief counsr, 63-65; mem, Sarasota Co. Rep. Exec. Cmt, 66-68; Fla. State Rep, 117th Dist, 67- Mil. Serv: Entered as Airman 3/C, Air Force, 53, released as Airman 1/C, 57, after serv. in security service. Mem: Sarasota Co. and Fla. Cattlemen's Asns; Farm Bur; Fla. Quarter Horse Asn; Sarasota Youth for Christ; Aircraft Owners and Pilots Asn; VFW. Rel: Methodist. Legal Res: Route 2, Box 355, Sarasota, Fla. 33577. Mailing Add: 2046 Main St, Sarasota, Fla. 33577.

TILLOTSON, J. C.
Kans. State Sen. R
b. Lenora, Kans, 2/4/06; s. H. R. Tillotson and Maude Johnston T; m. 6/23/35 to Maxine M. Middleton; c. John C. and Carolyn L. Educ: Washburn Univ, Topeka, Kans; Kappa Sigma. Polit. & Govt. Pos: Co. attorney, Kans, 35-43; Rep. Co. Chmn, Norton, 52-62, mem. sch. bd, 54-62; Kans. State Rep, 60-66, Speaker Pro Tem, Kans. House of Rep, 65-66; pres, Kans. Day Club, 65; Kans. State Sen, 69- Mem: V.pres, Kans. State C. of C, 56; pres, Northwest Kans. Bar Asn, 56 and Kans. Co. Attorneys Asn, 40; Mason; Rotary; Farm Bur. Rel: Methodist. Legal Res: 712 N. First, Norton, Kans. 67654. Mailing Add: 109 S. State, Norton, Kans. 67654.

TILLS, RONALD H.
N.Y. State Assemblyman R
b. Buffalo, N.Y, 5/1/35; s. Roland H. Tills and Doris Ellathorpe T; m. 5/6/60 to Elizabeth Clarkson; c. Susan and Thomas Nash. Educ: Univ. Buffalo, LL.B, 59; Phi Kappa Psi. Polit. & Govt. Pos: Mem. zoning bd. appeals, Hamburg, N.Y, 61-62, asst. town attorney, 62-63, town justice, 63-68; N.Y. State Assemblyman, 147th Assembly Dist, 69- Mil. Serv: Entered as E-1, Army Res, 59, released as Sgt, 65, after serv. in 98th Regt. Mem: N.Y. State Magistrates Asn; Erie Co. Bar Asn; F&AM; Hamburg Lions Club (past pres); Moose; Farm Bur; Hamburg Young Rep; Scope; Hamburg Rep. Club; Hamburg C. of C; Hamburg Vol. Fire Co; Erie Co. and Southwest. Vol. Firemans Asns. Rel: Methodist. Mailing Add: 43 Union St, Hamburg, N.Y. 14075.

TILSON, JOHN QUILLIN R
b. New Haven, Conn, 8/27/11; s. John Quillin Tilson and Marguerite North T; m. 9/14/34 to Catherine Elizabeth Jackson; c. John Q, III, Thomas D. and Rebecca E. Educ: Yale, B.A, 33, Law Sch, LL.B, 36; Beta Theta Pi. Polit. & Govt. Pos: Alderman, New Haven, Conn, 35-37; Conn State Rep, 53-55; alternate del, Rep. Nat. Conv, 56, del, 64; chmn, Hamden Town Rep. Cmt, Conn, 64-68. Bus. & Prof. Pos: Partner, Wiggin and Dana, 36- Mil. Serv: Entered as Lt.(jg), Navy, 43, released as Lt. Comdr, 46; Lt. Comdr, Naval Res, 51-53. Mem: Pres, Conn. Bar Asn, 62; Am. Bar Asn. Rel: Congregational. Mailing Add: 4 Marshall Rd, Hamden, Conn. 06517.

TILTON, JOHN HAVEMEYER
N.H. State Rep. R
b. New York, N.Y, 8/4/25; married; c. Three. Educ: Hampden-Sydney Col; U.S. Naval Acad; Yale Sch. of Fine Arts. Polit. & Govt. Pos: N.H. State Rep, currently. Bus. & Prof. Pos: Commercial artist. Mil. Serv: Navy, 43-46. Rel: Episcopal. Mailing Add: 2 Merrill St, Littleton, N.H. 03561. (1967)

TILTON, JOHN J.
Chmn, Jackson Co. Rep. Cmt, Iowa R
b. Maquoketa, Iowa, 1/31/15; s. Clyde E. Tilton and Dolly Shattuck T; m. 1940, div, 62; c. Ann, Carol, Deborra, John and James. Educ: Univ. Iowa, B.S. and M.D, 40; Intern at St. Mary's Hosp, Duluth, Minn. Polit. & Govt. Pos: Coroner, Jackson Co, Iowa, 41-48, medical examiner, 67-; mem, City Coun, Bellevue, 49-53, mayor, 53-56; chmn, Jackson Co. Rep. Cmt, 64- Mem: Iowa State Med. Soc; Am. Med. Asn; Jackson Co. Med. Soc.(pres, 49, 55, 66); Rotary (pres, 66); Am. Acad. Gen. Practitioners; Mason. Rel: Presbyterian. Legal Res: 137 Riverside Ave, Bellevue, Iowa 52031. Mailing Add: 200 S. Riverview, Bellevue, Iowa 52031.

TIMM, ROBERT DALE
Rep. Nat. Committeeman, Wash. R
b. Harrington, Wash, 10/2/21; s. Otto Timm and Florence Thornbrue T; m. 9/23/44 to Patricia Davies; c. Luanne (Mrs. Caylor) and Terri. Educ: Univ. Wash, B.A. in Econ, 43; Sigma Alpha Epsilon. Polit. & Govt. Pos: Precinct committeeman, Lincoln Co, Rep. Party, Wash, 47-63; mem. bd. educ, Harrington Schs, 48-51; pres, Lincoln Co. Young Rep, 49-50; Wash. State Rep, 51-59, chmn, Rep. Caucus and mem, Legis. Coun, Wash. State House of Rep, 55-59; mem, West. Interstate Cmt. Agr. and Educ, Boulder, Colo, 55-59 and Cmt. Higher Educ, 55-61; mem, Lincoln Co. Bd. Educ, 57-61; mem, Agr. Adv. Cmt. U.S. Dept. Agr, Wash, D.C, 58-60; Rep. nat. committeeman, 58-; treas-v.chmn, Rep. West. Conv, 63-; asst. to Gov. Evans, Olympia, Wash, 65, secy-chmn, Utilities and Transportation Cmn, 65-67, chmn, 67- Bus. & Prof. Pos: Owner-mgr, wheat and investment property, 47-; dir. bd. trustees, Fidelity Mutual Savings Bank, 58-; dir, Great Northwest Life Ins. Co, 59-65; dir-secy-treas, Timmco, Inc, 65-; founder and dir, S.Sound Nat. Bank, 67- Mil. Serv: Pvt, Marine Corps, 42-43. Mem: Nat. Asn. Regulatory Cmnrs.(cmt. gas safety and supply); Elks; Lions; Am. Legion; Spokane Club; Wash. Athletic Club; Olympia Country and Golf Club; Harrington Golf Club; Grange. Rel: Congregational. Mailing Add: Route 6, Box 111, Olympia, Wash. 98501.

TIMMINS, WILLIAM JOSEPH, JR.
Chmn, Trumbull Co. Dem. Exec. and Cent. Cmt, Ohio D
b. Boston, Mass, 7/27/17; s. William J. Timmins, Sr. and Mary Gould T; m. 9/7/46 to Mary Alice Heltzel; c. Mary Lawretta (Mrs. John Bramblett), Margaret Ann, William J, Brion, John, Elizabeth, Ann and Bridget. Educ: Kirksville Col. Osteopathy and Surg, D.O, 41; Kansas City Univ. Physicians and Surgeons, M.D, 43; Cath. Univ. Am, 47-50; Phi Sigma Gamma. Polit. & Govt. Pos: Committeeman, Dem. Party, Ohio, 60-; chmn, Trumbull Co. Dem. Exec. and Cent. Cmt, 60-; mem, Pres. Club, 62-68; chmn, Trumbull Co. Bd. Elec, 62-; mem, Dem. State Adv. Cmt, 63-; del, Dem. Nat. Conv, 64; mem, Ohio Electoral Col, 64; chmn, Ohio Hist. Markers Asn, 64-65; chmn, Ohio

State Dem. Co. Chmn. Rules Cmt, 64-68; trustee, Ohio Elec. Off. Asn, 66- Bus. & Prof. Pos: Chief of staff, Warren Gen. Hosp, 60- Mem: Ohio and Am. Osteopathic Asns; Am. Col. Gen. Practice; life mem, Am. Cmt. Maternal and Child Welfare; Rotary; Elks; K. of C.(4°); Trumbull Country Club. Rel: Roman Catholic. Mailing Add: 3280 E. Market St, Warren, Ohio 44484.

TIMMONS, JON EMIL R
Secy, Stark Co. Rep. Cent. Cmt, Ill.
b. Canton, Ill, 10/27/43; s. Alfred Dale Timmons and Nettie Lucille Hillman T; m. 6/16/63 to Anita Lynn Armstrong; c. Paul David. Educ: Blackhawk E. Col, 1969. Polit. & Govt. Pos: Secy, Stark Co. Rep. Cent. Cmt, Ill, 66-; Rep. precinct committeeman, Toulon Township, Stark Co, 66; pres, Stark Co. Young Rep, 67- Bus. & Prof. Pos: Bookkeeper and teller, Anderson State Bank, 61-; part time assoc, J. C. Penney & Company, 67- Mem: Lake Calhoun Asn.(asst. treas, 68-); Knox County Farm Bur; 1200 Club of Ill. Rel: Lutheran. Mailing Add: 207 North Franklin St, Toulon, Ill. 61483.

TIMMONS, WILLIAM EVAN R
Dep. Asst. to the President
b. Chattanooga, Tenn, 12/27/30; s. Owen Walter Timmons and Doris Eckenrod T; m. 9/28/66 to Mimi Bakshian; c. Karen Leigh, Kimberly Anne and William Evan, Jr. Educ: Georgetown Univ, B.S.F.S. 59; George Washington Univ, 59-61. Polit. & Govt. Pos: Aide to U.S. Sen. Alexander Wiley, Wis, 55-62; exec. dir, Rep. Party of Tenn, 62; campaign mgr, Brock for Cong. Campaign, 62, 64, 66 & 68; mem. faculty, Numerous Nat, Regional, State and Local Rep. Campaign Workshops, 63-; admin. asst. to U.S. Rep. Bill Brock, Tenn, 63-69; conv. coordinator, Nixon for Pres, 68; dir. cong. rels, Nixon-Agnew Campaign, 68; Dep. Asst. to the President, 69- Mil. Serv: Entered as Pvt, Air Force, 51, released as S/Sgt, 54, after serv. in 20th Fighter-Bomber Wing, ETO, 52-55; Korean Conflict Medal; Good Conduct Medal. Mem: A&FM; Scottish Rite; Jaycees; Am. Legion; C. of C. Nat. Outstanding Young Rep. Year, 65. Rel: Episcopal. Legal Res: 230 Federal Bldg, Chattanooga,Tenn. 37402. Mailing Add: 9501 Newbold Place, Bethesda, Md. 20034.

TIMS, MARJORIE HOLLINGSWORTH R
b. New Orleans, La, 8/12/18; d. Dr. Salathiel Lamar Hollingsworth and Fannie Evans H; m. 6/21/41 to Lowry Lamar Tims; c. Lowry Lamar, Jr, Robert Lewis, James Irving and Douglas Austin. Educ: Miss. State Col. Women, B.S. in Home Econ, 39; Gamma Sigma Epsilon. Polit. & Govt. Pos: Pres, Bolivar Co. Rep. Women's Club, Miss, 63-64; v.chmn, Bolivar Co. Rep. Party, 63-65; del. and mem, Permanent Orgn. Cmt, Rep. Nat. Conv, 64; pres, Miss. Fedn. of Rep. Women, 65-67. Mem: DAR; Huguenot Soc; Magna Charta Dames; Cleveland Jr. Auxiliary; pres, MFRW, 69- Rel: Methodist. Mailing Add: 401 First Ave. S, Cleveland, Miss. 38732.

TINGE, ROLF REID D
b. Cleveland, Ohio, 2/25/32; s. Henry Ralph Tinge and Hazel Roney T; m. 12/22/51 to Marjorie E. Richards; c. Susan, Roma, Nancy, Michael and Mary Jo. Educ: Ohio State Univ, 2 years. Polit. & Govt. Pos: Precinct committeeman, Dem. Party, Newbury Twp, Geauga Co, Ohio, 60-; exec. secy, Geauga Co. Dem. Party, 62-66, exec. chmn, 66-68; del, Ohio Dem. State Conv, 68; del, Dem. Nat. Conv, 68. Bus. & Prof. Pos: Owner, Valley Motors, Bainbridge, Ohio, 56-60; Construction Foreman, R. Wantz & Sons, Novelty, 60-68; salesman, fleet mgr, Bedford Ford, Inc, Bedford, 69- Mil. Serv: Entered as Pvt, Army Res, 50, released as M/Sgt, 65, after serv. in 83rd Div, Res; Good Conduct Medal; Sharpshooter Award; Ten-Year Ribbon. Mem: Chagrin Valley Jaycees; West Geauga Jaycees; Eagles; Ohio State Alumnae Asn, Geauga Co. Chap. Rel: Protestant. Mailing Add: 15807 Thomas St, Chagrin Falls, Ohio 44022.

TINGLE, GEORGE W. D
b. Millsboro, Del, 3/28/07; married. Educ: Del. Pub. Schs. Polit. & Govt. Pos: Md. State Del, 63-67; co cmnr, Washington Co, 60-62. Bus. & Prof. Pos: Restaurant owner. Mil. Serv: Coast Guard, 25-27. Mem: Elks; Masons; Shrine; Tall Cedars of Lebanon; Fraternal Order of Police; H.D.H. Hunting and Fishing Club; Nat. Grange; Patrons of Husbandry; Conococheague Sportsmen's Club, Inc; Alsatia Club. Mailing Add: 302 N. Potomac, Hagerstown, Md. 21740. (1967)

TINGLER, ANDREW JACKSON D
Chmn, Covington-Alleghany Co. Dem. Cmt, Va.
b. Craig Co, Va, 5/5/95; s. Emma Fridley Tingler; m. 1922 to Dorothy Womack; c. Virginia (Mrs. John R. Payne, III), Henry Womack and June A. (Mrs. Marion Content Buie). Educ: Daleville Col; Wash. and Lee Univ. Polit. & Govt. Pos: Chmn, Covington-Alleghany Co. Dem. Cmt, Va, currently; chmn, 18th Sen. and Sixth House Dem. Cmts; gen. registr, Covington. Bus. & Prof. Pos: Real estate. Mem: AF&AM; Odd Fellows; Moose; Mason; Blue Lodge; Scottish Rite; Shrine, Kazim Temple. Rel: Presbyterian. Legal Res: 420 W. Riverside Ave, Covington, Va. 24426. Mailing Add: 128 S. Maple Ave, Covington, Va. 24426.

TINKER, CAROL WICKS R
N.Mex. State Rep.
b. Claire City, S.Dak, 12/21/20; d. Leroy S. Wicks and Alta Ness W; m. 10/17/42 to George Edward Tinker, III; c. George Edward IV, Ann (Mrs. Willard Robert Baker, Jr), Tanya Lynn, Randy Catherine and Susan Christine. Educ: Highlands Univ, 3 years; Delta Zeta; drama club; Alpha Psi Omega; cheerleader; choir; SPURS. Polit. & Govt. Pos: Secy. for Rep. gubernatorial cand, N.Mex, 64; chmn, San Miguel Co. Rep. Party, 65-68; San Miguel Co. Campaign Dir. for Congressman Manuel Lujan, Anderson Carter, and primary cand. for gov, Clifford Hawley; N.Mex. State Rep, Dist. One, San Miguel Co, 68- Bus. & Prof. Pos: Secy, Horwath & Horwath, Cert. Pub. Accts, 41-42; secy, U.S. Army, Salzburg, Austria, 49. Mem: Bus. & Prfnl. Women's Club; Rep. Women's Club; Officers Wives Club (past pres, Brooks Field and Ottis Air Force Base Clubs); PTA (past off). Good neighbor award, Stars and Stripes Newspaper, Edinburgh, Scotland. Rel: Lutheran, Missouri Synod. Mailing Add: 902 Third Street, Las Vegas, N.Mex. 87701.

TINKER, RICHARD WILLIAM R
Chmn, Ionia Co. Rep. Cmt, Mich.
b. West Branch, Mich, 5/21/29; s. Frederick Tinker and Flossie M. Strong T; m. 6/25/60 to Carole June Sparkie; c. Douglas F, Todd H, R.V. Carleton and Lisa Cae. Educ: Univ. Mich, B.A, 53; Druids; Delta Tau Delta. Polit. & Govt. Pos: Mem. exec. cmt, Ionia Co. Rep. Cmt, Mich, 61, treas, 62-68, chmn, 68- Mil. Serv: Entered as Pvt, Army, 53, released as Cpl, 55, after serv. in 76th Tank Bn. Mem: Jaycees; Elks. Distinguished Serv. Award, Jaycees. Rel: Methodist. Mailing Add: 410 Pearl, Belding, Mich. 48809.

TINNIN, NELSON B. D
Mo. State Sen.
b. Hornersville, Mo, 10/8/05; m. 1927 to Lora Bolliner; c. Brent Bollinger. Educ: S.E. Mo. State Col; S.W. Mo. State Col; Univ. of Mo, B.S. Polit. & Govt. Pos: Chmn, Dunklin Co. Soil Dist, Mo, 49-; mem, Mo. State Soil Dist. Cmn, 8 years; pres, Mo. Soil Dist. Asn; Mo. State Sen, 60-; app. to Gov. Adv. Cmt. on Water Sheds, 61. Bus. & Prof. Pos: Elem. prin, Mo, 7 years; teacher voc. agr, Hornersville High Sch, 17 years; cotton planter assoc. with Hollywood Gin and Elevator Co, Inc, currently. Mem: Mason (32°), Past Master, Lodge; Scottish Rite; Shrine; Eastern Star; Boy Scout Cmnr, Seminole Dist; Mo. Cotton Producers Asn. Awarded plaque by Hornersville Alumni Asn. for Serv. Rendered and Hon. Achievement, 62; various other awards and plaques. Rel: Methodist; Chmn. of Bd, 4 years. Mailing Add: Hornersville, Mo. 63855. (1967)

TINSTMAN, ROBERT MECHLING
b. Johnstown, Pa, 4/4/28; s. Carl C. Tinstman and Irene Mechling T; m. 6/6/53 to Shirley Mae Overall; c. Robert O, Torre R. and Tracy D. Educ: Pa. State Univ, B.S, 50; Univ. Pa, M.A, 55; Tau Beta Pi; Sigma Tau; Alpha Rho Chi; Scarab. Polit. & Govt. Pos: Asst. city mgr, Kansas City, Mo, 54-59, mgr, Downtown Cmt, 59-60; city mgr, Abilene, Tex, 60-63; city mgr, Oklahoma City, Okla, trustee, Oklahoma City Airport Trust and Oklahoma City Munic. Improv. Authority, 63-67; city mgr, Austin, Tex, 67- Mil. Serv: Army, 51-54. Mem: Bd. dirs, Tex. Munic. League, 62-63; Int. City Mgrs. Asn; Am. Soc. Pub. Admin; Munic. Finance Officers Asn; Am. Pub. Works Asn. Mailing Add: P.O. Box 1088, Austin, Tex, 78767.

TIPPS, PAUL D
Mem. exec. cmt, Montgomery Co. Dem. Party, Ohio
b. Cincinnati, Ohio, 7/27/36; s. Charles P. Tipps and Alma Metz T; m. 4/3/69 to Judith Leiter; c. Deborah, Penny, Tamara, Polly and Anthony. Educ: Univ. Dayton, B.S, 60; Chase Col. Law, 67. Polit. & Govt. Pos: Mem. exec. cmt, Montgomery Co. Dem. Party, Ohio, 66-; Dem. cand, U.S. House of Rep, 68; del, Dem. Nat. Conv, 68. Bus. & Prof. Pos: Pres, Paul Tipps Realtors, 60-; bd. dirs, Dayton Area Bd. Realtors, 65-67. Mil. Serv: Entered as 2nd Lt, Army, 60, released as 2nd Lt, 61, after serv. in Training Co, U.S, 60-61; 1st Lt, Spec. Forces Unit, 61-66; Parachutist Badge, Grad. Spec. Warfare Sch, 65. Publ: 'Advertising & Public Relations for the Realtor,' 9-10/66 and 'Professional Cooperation: The Realtor's Key to Success,' 11-12/66, J. of Property Mgt; 'Charles Whalen: Space Age Politician,' Vanguard, 4/69. Mem: Inst. Real Estate Mgt; Dayton Area Bd. Realtors; Dayton Jaycees; Gem City Dem. Club. One of Ten Outstanding Young Men in Dayton, 67. Rel: Catholic. Mailing Add: 2508 Shroyer Rd, Dayton, Ohio 45419.

TIPSWORD, ROLLAND FORTNER D
Ill. State Rep.
b. Monticello, Ill, 8/19/25; s. Leo Clemit Tipsword and Jossie Fortner T; single. Educ: East. Ill. State Univ, 43; Univ. Idaho, B.A, 49; Northwest. Univ, LL.B, 51; Phi Beta Kappa; Phi Alpha Delta; Delta Tau Delta. Polit. & Govt. Pos: States attorney, Christian Co, Ill, 60-66; Ill. State Rep, 52nd Dist, 67- Bus. & Prof. Pos: Partner, Coale, Taylor, Tipsword and Fraley. Mil. Serv: Entered as A/S, Navy, 43, released as radio Technician 2/C, 46, after serv. in Pac. Area, 44-45; Pac. Combat Area Ribbons. Mem: Christian Co. Bar Asn.(v.pres, 66-69, pres, 69-); Ill. State Bar Asn; AF&AM; Ansar Shrine, Springfield Consistory; VFW; Am. Legion, Elwood Commandery; Elks; Moose; Eagles; Assoc. Grand Patron Easter Star, 69-; White Shrine. Rel: Presbyterian. Mailing Add: 801 Taylorville Blvd, Taylorville, Ill. 62568.

TIPTON, RICHARD McKANE R
V.Chmn, Cherokee Co. Rep. Party, Ga.
b. Gastonia, N.C, 10/14/32; s. John Paul Tipton, Sr. and Annie Margaret McKane T; m. 10/9/59 to Donna Claire Vaughn; c. Richard Vaughn, Ron Barton, Ann Claire and Rhonda Amelia. Educ: Gonzaga Prep, 3 years. Polit. & Govt. Pos: V.chmn, Cherokee Co. Rep. Party, Ga, 68- Bus. & Prof. Pos: Cotton classer, George H. McFadden & Co, Fresno, Calif, 51-58 and Burlington Cotton Co, Greenville, S.C, 58-64; asst. purchasing agent, Fieldcrest Mills, Eden, N.C, 64-65; mgr, fibers dept, Canton Textile Mills, Inc, Canton, Ga, 66- Mem: Fiber Buyers Dir, Ga. Textile Manufacturers Asn; past pres, Greenville Jr. C. of C, S.C. Legal Res: 380 Jarvis St, Canton, Ga. 30114. Mailing Add: c/o Canton Textile Mills, Inc, Canton, Ga. 30114.

TIRRELL, LORING VINSON R
N.H. State Rep.
b. South Weymouth, Mass, 9/28/96; s. Theron Loring Tirrell and Caroline Bertha Costello T; m. 1/8/21 to Mary Jane Holbrook; c. Muriel (Mrs. Bourque), Theron L, Natalie (Mrs. Wolfe) and Jean (Mrs. Brooks). Educ: Mass. Agr. Col, B.S, 20; Univ. Mass, M.S, 40; Univ. N.H, hon. D.Sc, 68; Alpha Zeta; Theta Chi. Polit. & Govt. Pos: Mem, Budget Cmt, Durham, N.H, mem, Zoning Bd. of Adjust, 55-; N.H. State Rep, 69- Bus. & Prof. Pos: Instr. in animal sci, Mass. Agr. Col, 20-21, Univ. N.H, 21-26, prof, 30-66; livestock specialist, Univ. Conn, 26-30. Mil. Serv: Entered as Pvt, Army, 18, released as Lt. Col, 46, after serv. in Inf. and Mil. Police; Hon, Army Res, 56- Mem: Am. Soc. of Animal Sci; Am. Legion; Vet. World War I. Distinguished Teacher Award, Am. Soc. of Animal Sci, 67; Distinguished Equine Award, Agr. Serv. Found, 67; Morgan Horseman of the Year, 67. Rel: Protestant. Mailing Add: R.D. 1, Durham, N.H. 03824.

TISDALE, NELSON G. R
Mich. State Rep.
b. Midland Twp, Mich, 8/30/01; married; c. Lois (Mrs. M. Walrod), Nelson G. and Willard G. Polit. & Govt. Pos: Former Supvr, mem. Sch. Bd. and Fair Bd, Midland, Mich; Mich. State Rep, 60- Bus. & Prof. Pos: Farmer. Mem: C. of C; Rotary; Elks. Rel: Latter-day Saint. Mailing Add: 1135 Poseyville Rd, Midland, Mich. 48640. (1967)

TISDALE, WILLIAM APPLETON D
Miss. State Rep.
b. Sumrall, Miss, 9/1/20; s. William Jennings Tisdale and Margaret Churchill T; m. 12/19/45 to Florence Constance Hoffman; c. William Edward, Paul Appleton, George Jennings, David Lee (deceased), Constance Margaret and Jill Florence. Educ: Tulane Univ. Med. Sch, M.D, 52. Polit. & Govt. Pos: Miss. State Rep, Harrison Co, 68- Bus. & Prof. Pos: Pres. med. staff, Howard Mem. Hosp, Biloxi, Miss, 65- Mil. Serv: Entered as A/S, Navy, 39, released as Chief Pharmacist Mate, 45, after serv. in Amphibious Forces and Seventh Fleet, 12th Fleet and Third Fleet, 43-45; Am. Theatre Ribbon; Pac. Theatre Ribbon; Philippine Liberation Ribbon with Two Stars; Occup, Victory and Am. Defense Medals; Good Conduct Medal with One Star. Mem: Coast Co, Miss. State and Am. Med. Asns; Am. Bd. Gen. Practitioners; Am. Red Cross (dir, Biloxi, Miss, 57-58, Disaster med. officer, 59-67); VFW; Am. Legion; Mason (32°); C. of C. Rel: Episcopal. Mailing Add: 1610 W. Bayview, Biloxi, Miss. 39530.

TITTLE, WILLIAM OSBORNE D
Chmn, Morris Co. Dem. Cmt, Tex.
b. Daingerfield, Tex, 5/15/04; s. Luther Walker Tittle and Cora Phillips T; m. 8/27/24 to Edna Brown; c. Donald A, Sue (Mrs. Harold C. Ehemann) and Billie Ed (deceased). Educ: E. Tex. State; Kalir Club. Polit. & Govt. Pos: Mayor, Daingerfield, Tex, 55-56; tax assessor and collector, Northeast Tex. Munic. Water Dist, 56-57; chmn, Morris Co. Dem. Cmt, Tex, currently. Bus. & Prof. Pos: Bus. mgr, Ivan Frizzell Parts Co. and Ford Motor Co, Mt. Pleasant, Tex, 47-49; off. mgr, Tyler Serv. Parts Co, Tyler, 50-51; mgr, Wadel-Connally Co, Mt. Pleasant, 53; teacher, Daingerfield High Sch, 54; gen. mgr, W.O. Irwin Interests, 57- Mil. Serv: Entered as Storekeeper 2/C, Navy, 44, released as Storekeeper 1/C, 45, after serv. in Mil. Govt, Pac; Philippines and Okinawa Campaign Ribbons. Mem: Mason; Kiwanis; Am. Legion; Retail Merchants. Rel: Methodist. Legal Res: 500 Madison, Daingerfield, Tex. 75638. Mailing Add: P.O. Box 603, Daingerfield, Tex. 75638. (1967)

TITUS, DOUGLAS LEROY R
Chmn, Mansfield Rep. Town Cmt, Mass.
b. Foxboro, Mass, 8/14/34; s. Chester L. Titus and Florence A. Strang T; m. 8/30/58 to Patricia Louise Santucci; c. Kym Ann, Douglas L. II, Donald F. II, Dennis J. and Pauline A. Educ: Boston Univ, 2 years; Mass. State Teachers Col, Bridgewater, 2 years. Polit. & Govt. Pos: Coordinator, John Quinlan for Senate Cmt, 64 & 66, Walter O'Brien for State Rep. Cmt, 64 & 66 and John Volpe for Gov. Cmt, 66 & 68; chmn, Mansfield Rep. Town Cmt, 68-; Notary Pub, 69-; Mem, Fraudulent Claims Bur, Mass, 69- Mil. Serv: Entered as Pvt, Army Paratroopers, 53, released as Cpl, 56, after serv. in Green Beret Tenth Spec. Forces Group, ETO, 54-56; Good Conduct Medal; Paratrooper Wings; Parachute Rigger Wings. Mem: K. of C.(Grand Knight); Good Govt. Cmt; 4-H Club. Star Coun. Award, K. of C. Rel: Catholic. Legal Res: 400 Maple St, Mansfield, Mass. 02048. Mailing Add: 147 S. Main St, Mansfield, Mass. 02048.

TITUS, HERBERT WILLIAM D
b. Baker, Ore, 10/17/37; s. Rulon Lars Titus and Berneice Corbett T; m. 7/22/62 to Marilyn Joyce Guthrie; c. Channa, Troy and Breck. Educ: Univ. Ore, Eugene, B.A, 59; Harvard Law Sch, LL.B, 62; Phi Beta Kappa. Polit. & Govt. Pos: Attorney, U.S. Dept. Justice, Wash, D.C, 62-63; spec. asst. U.S. Attorney, Kansas City, Mo, 63-64; alternate del, Dem. Nat. Conv, 68. Bus. & Prof. Pos: Asst. prof. law, Univ. Okla, 64-66; assoc. prof. law, Univ. Ore, 66- Mem: Am. Civil Liberties Union; Ore. Environ. Coun. Mailing Add: 3238 Edandale Lane, Eugene, Ore. 97405.

TOBIAS, ANSEL WALTER R
Kans. State Rep.
b. Lyons, Kans, 3/6/12; s. Walter James Tobias and Iva Stokes T; m. 7/29/34 to Helen Monroe; c. Ann Rosalle (Mrs. Ron Wingfield). Educ: Kans. State Univ. Polit. & Govt. Pos: Mem, Rice Co. Hosp. Dist. 1, Kans, 58-65; Kans. State Rep, 65- Bus. & Prof. Pos: Pres, Tobias Birchenough Inc, 48- Mem: Kiwanis; Mason; Shrine; Town & Country Club; Kans. Ready-Mix Asn. Rel: First Christian Church; Elder. Mailing Add: R.R. 2, Box 470, Lyons, Kans. 67554. (1967)

TOBIAS, JEAN FRANCES D
b. Mound City, Ill, 6/15/22; d. Francis John Campbell and Eleanor Lucille Tilley C; m. 4/17/43 to Lloyd Delmore Tobias, Jr; c. Lloyd D., III, Gregory John, Jane Diane, James Richard and Celeste Marie. Educ: Mound City Commun. High Sch, Ill, 4 years. Polit. & Govt. Pos: Dem. precinct committeeman, Ohio, 52-; dep. dir, Bd. of Elec, Fairfield Co, 65-; secy-treas, Fairfield Co. Dem. Exec. Cmt, 67-69; secy, Fairfield Co. Dem. Cent. Cmt, 68-69. Mem: Elks Ladies Club; Federated Dem. Women of Ohio; Lancaster-Fairfield Co. Camp Fire Girls; bd. and cmt, Citizens Cmt. for Better Schs; Ohio Elec. Off. Orgn; Tenth Dist. Dem. Action Club; Fairfield Co. Dem. Womens Club; Fairfield Co. Dem. Sr. Club. Rel: Catholic. Mailing Add: 219 Wilson Ave, Lancaster, Ohio 43130.

TOBIASSEN, THOMAS JOHAN R
Fla. State Rep.
b. Omaha, Nebr, 11/21/31; s. Thoralph Johan Tobiassen and Goldie Marie Grimm T; m. 11/27/59 to Audrey Irene Neumann; c. Thomas J, Jr. and Todd J. Educ: Ohio State Univ, B.M.E, 59; Sigma Chi. Polit. & Govt. Pos: Membership Chmn, Young Rep. Club of Pensacola, Fla, 67; Fla. State Rep, 68- Bus. & Prof. Pos: Sr. engr, Monsanto Co, Pensacola, Fla, 61- Mil. Serv: Entered as Pvt, Army, 53, released as Pfc, 55, after serv. in Corps of Engrs, Korea, 54-55; Good Conduct Medal. Mem: Registered Prfnl. Engr. in Fla; Pensacola C. of C. Rel: Lutheran. Mailing Add: 811 Woodbine Dr, Pensacola, Fla. 32503.

TOBIASZ, RAYMOND JOSEPH D
Wis. State Assemblyman
b. Milwaukee, Wis, 5/10/16; s. John Tobiasz and Antoinette Murach T; m. 11/23/40 to Mabel Dorothy McKillip; c. John Edward, Lawrence Alan and Sharon Ann. Educ: High Sch. Polit. & Govt. Pos: Committeeman, Dem. Party of Wis, 56-60; Wis. State Assemblyman, 11th Dist, 61-; alternate del, Dem. Nat. Conv, 68. Bus. & Prof. Pos: Owner, Toby's Gift, Hobby & Smoke Shop, 50-63 and Midwest Scraping & Alignment Co, 53-55. Mil. Serv: Entered as Pvt, Army, 45, released as Pfc, 46, after serv. in 24th Div, Pac; Asiatic-Pac. Ribbon; Army Occup, Japan and Victory Medals. Mem: Amvet; Am. Legion; S. Div. Civic Orgn; K. of C; Polish Nat. Alliance. Coin Collecting. Rel: Roman Catholic. Mailing Add: 3145 S. 50th St, Milwaukee, Wis. 53219. (1967)

TOBIN, DAVID SPENCE D
b. Boston, Mass, 3/16/39; s. James Gerard Tobin and Mary Spencer T; m. to Antonia D. Pompeo. Educ: Suffolk Univ. Law Sch; Boston Col, B.S. Polit. & Govt. Pos: Mass. State Rep, 65-68. Bus. & Prof. Pos: Ins. underwriter, Employers Group of Ins. Co, Inc, 63-65. Mil. Serv: Entered as Pvt, Army, 59, released as A 2/C, 62; 2nd Lt, Air Force Res, 66. Mem: K. of C; Mass. Legis. Asn; Boston Col. Alumni Asn; Boston Col. Downtown Club; VFW; Rel: Roman Catholic. 1967 Legal Res: Boston, Mass. No mailing address available. (1967)

TOBIN, DICK R
Wyo. State Sen.
b. Casper, Wyo, 6/6/18; m. to Marialyce. Educ: Casper Col, A.A; Univ. of Wyo, J.D. Polit. & Govt. Pos: U.S. Dist. Court Cmnr; former city attorney; Dist. Court Cmnr; chmn, Wyo. Statute Rev. Cmn; House Attorney, 57; Sen. Attorney, 59; Wyo. State Rep, 2 years; Wyo. State Sen, 6 years. Bus. & Prof. Pos: Attorney-at-law. Mem: K. of C; Red Cross; Boy Scouts; Natrona Co. Bar Asn.(pres); Wyo. Bar Asn; Am. Bar Asn; Am. Trial Lawyers Asn; C. of C. Recipient of State J.C. Distinguished Serv. Award. Rel: Catholic; pres, Wyo. Catholic Charities. Mailing Add: 413 E. 11th St, Casper, Wyo. 82601.

TOBRINER, MATHEW OSCAR D
Assoc. Justice, Calif. Supreme Court
b. San Francisco, Calif, 4/2/04; s. Oscar Tobriner and Maud Lezinsky T; m. 5/19/39 to Rosabelle Rose; c. Michael Charles and Stephen Oscar. Educ: Stanford Univ, A.B, 24, M.A, 25; Harvard Law Sch, LL.B, 27; Univ. Calif. Sch. Law, S.J.D, 32; Phi Beta Kappa; Order of the Coif; Delta Sigma Rho. Polit. & Govt. Pos: Assoc. Justice, Calif. Court of Appeal, First Appellate 59-62; Dist, Div. One, San Francisco, Assoc. Justice, Calif. Supreme Court, 62- Bus. & Prof. Pos: Assoc, David Livingston and Lawrence Livingston, 28-30, late Judge Milton D. Sapiro, 30-32; Chief Attorney, Solicitor's Off, U.S. Dept. Agr, 32-36; practice of law, Tobriner, Lazarus, Brundage & Neyhart, San Francisco, 36-59. Mil. Serv: Seaman 1/C, San Francisco Volunteer Port Security Force, Coast Guard, 43-45. Publ: Co-author, 'Principles and Practices of Cooperative Marketing (with the late Prof. E. G. Mears, Stanford Univ), Ginn & Co, 26; 'The Individual and the Public Service Enterprise in the New Industrial State' (with Joseph Grodin), Calif. Law Rev, 11/67; 'Individual Rights in an Industrialized Society,' Am. Bar Asn. J, 1/68. Mem: San Francisco Bar Asn.(bd. dirs, 59); Legal Aid Soc. of San Francisco (pres, 61-62); Barrister's Club (one of founders and second pres, 30); Lawyers' Club of San Francisco; Am. Bar Asn.(co-chmn, Cmt. on Nat. Labor Rels. Act, 57-58, mem, Sect. on Labor Rels. Law); Calif. State Bar (Cmt. on Admin. Agencies, 55); chmn, San Francisco Jewish Commun. Rels. Coun, 62-64; quart. chmn, Commonwealth Club, 60. Rel: Jewish. Mailing Add: 3494 Jackson St, San Francisco, Calif. 94118.

TOBRINER, WALTER NATHAN D
b. Washington, D.C, 7/2/02; s. Leon Tobriner and Blanche Barth T; m. 7/20/33 to Marienne E. Smith; c. Constance E. (Mrs. David Povich) and Matthew W. Educ: Princeton, A.B, 23; Harvard, LL.B, 26; Phi Beta Kappa. Polit. & Govt. Pos: Mem. bd. of trustees, Nat. Cultural Center; mem, Wash. Bd. of Educ, 52-61, pres. bd, 57-61; del, Dem. Nat. Conv, 56, 60 & 64; cmnr, D.C. Govt. and pres. bd. of cmnrs, 61-67; U.S. Ambassador, Jamaica, 67-69. Bus. & Prof. Pos: Attorney-at-law, 27-; prof. law, Nat. Univ. Law Sch, 33-50; dir, Blue Cross Plan, 53-61; pres, Garfield Mem. Hosp, 52-55, Lisner Home, 54- and Wash. Hosp. Center, 59-61. Mil. Serv: Lt. Col, Army Air Force, 43-46. Mem: Nat. Press and Cosmos Clubs. Mailing Add: 6100 33rd St. N.W, Washington, D.C. 20015.

TODD, CARL P. D
Secy, Jackson Co. Dem. Cmt, Ill.
b. Grand Tower, Ill, 9/1/13; s. John W. Todd and Sarah Anderson T; m. 9/3/35 to Vera A. Palisch; c. Carleen (Mrs. Ralph Neumann) and Malcolm J. Educ: Grand Tower High Sch, Ill, 12 years. Polit. & Govt. Pos: Conserv. investr, Jackson Co, Ill, 50-52, co. treas, 54-58 and dep. treas, 58-61; supvr, Grand Tower Twp, 50-54; state produce inspector, Agr. Dept, 61-69; secy, Jackson Co. Dem. Cmt, Ill, 64- Bus. & Prof. Pos: Owner, serv. sta, 36-54. Mil. Serv: Entered as Seaman, Navy, 43, released as Radarman 2/C, 45, after serv. in Amphibious Forces, S.Pac, 43-45. Mem: Int. Brotherhood of Operating Engrs; Am. Legion; 40 et 8; VFW; Lions. Rel: Protestant. Mailing Add: Main and Harrison St, Grand Tower, Ill. 62942.

TODD, PAUL HAROLD, JR. D
b. Kalamazoo, Mich, 9/22/21; s. Paul H. Todd and Adeline Allias T; m. 46 to Ruth Newell; c. George, Paul A, Charles and Elizabeth. Educ: Cornell Univ, B.S. in chem, 43; Univ. Chicago, grad. work in econ, 46. Polit. & Govt. Pos: Chief exec. officer, Planned Parenthood-World Population, 67-; U.S. Rep, 3rd Dist, Mich, 65-66. Bus. & Prof. Pos: Chmn. Bd, Kalamazoo Spice Extraction Co, 65 and founder and pres. Mil. Serv: Entered as Pvt, Army, 43, released as 1st Lt, 45, after serv. in China-Burma-India Theater; Bronze Star; Soldiers' Medal. Mem: Am. Chem. Soc; Am. Econ. Asn; Economet. Soc; Inst. of Food Tech. Rel: Protestant. Mailing Add: 3713 W. Main St, Kalamazoo, Mich. 49007. (1967)

TODD, WEBSTER BRAY R
b. Yonkers, N.Y, 8/27/99; s. John R. Todd and Alice Bray T; m. to Eleanor Prentice Schley; c. Kate T.(Mrs. Thompson), John R, II, Webster B, Jr. and Christine T. Educ: Princeton Univ, A.B, 22; Jesus Col, Cambridge, Eng, 22-23; Fordham Univ, LL.B, 27. Polit. & Govt. Pos: Chmn, Willkie for President Clubs, N.J, 40; treas, N.J. State Rep. Cmt, 46-48, chmn, 61-69; chmn, N.J. State Rep. Finance Cmt, 48-53, treas, 58; campaign mgr, Eisenhower Primary, 52; dir, Off. Econ. Affairs, U.S. Mission to NATO and European Regional Orgn, 53-54; mem, U.S. del, UN Econ. and Soc. Coun, 54; chmn, N.J. State Rep. Exec. Cmt, 58-61; chmn, N.J. del, Rep. Nat. Conv, 64, del, 68.

Bus. & Prof. Pos: Pres, Todd & Brown, Inc, 28-45; partner, J.H.Whitney, 46; dir, Bell Aircraft, Am. Wheelabrator, Hawkeye-Security, 47-56; dir. and chmn. exec. cmt, Equity Corp, 47-56; dir, Stevens Inst, Metrop. Life Ins. Co, Princeton Aviation Corp. and Millbrook Sch, currently. Mem: N.Y. State Bar; River Club; Maidstone Club; Union Club; Vet. Asn, 17th Regt, N.Y; trustee, The Training Sch; adv. cmn, Bonnie Brae Farm for Boys. Rel: Presbyterian. Legal Res: Box 146, Oldwick, N.J. 08858. Mailing Add: 250 Park Ave, New York, N.Y. 10017. (1967)

TODD, WEBSTER BRAY, JR. R
N.J. State Assemblyman
b. N.Y.C, 12/1/38; s. Webster Bray Todd, Sr. and Eleanor Schley T; m. 10/24/64 to Sheila Mitchell O'Keefe; c. William Walker and Whitney de Forest. Educ: Univ. Lausanne, Switz. 56-57; Princeton Univ, A.B. in Geol, 61; Stanford Law Sch, 61-62; Ivy Club. Polit. & Govt. Pos: Rep. munic. chmn, Bedminster Twp, N.J, 65-67; N.J. State Assemblyman, Eighth Dist, 68-, chmn, Taxation Cmt, N.J. State Assembly, 68, mem, 69, mem, Appropriations Cmt, 68 & 69, chmn, Study Cmn. Captial Spending, 69 and mem, Tax Exempt Study Cmn, 69. Bus. & Prof. Pos: V.pres, Basking Ridge Aviation, 62-64; pres, Princeton Aviation Corp. and Princeton Air-Research Park, 64-; partner, Gen. Aviation Eng, 66-; chmn. membership cmt, Nat. Air Taxi Conf, 67, Commuter Airline Cmt, 67-69, CANY Scheduling Cmt, 68-69 and mem. Commuter Airline Wash. Nat, currently. Mem: Princeton Nassau Club; N.Y.C. Wings Club; Wash. Nat. Aviation Club; Somerset Hills Country Club; Essex Fox Hounds; Wash. Univ. Club; Rotary Club; mem. voc. scholarship rev. bd, Princeton; Quiet Birdmen. Rel: Episcopal. Legal Res: Blackacre, Rattlesnake Bridge Rd, Far Hills, N.J. 07931. Mailing Add: Box 185, Far Hills, N.J. 07931.

TODD, WILLIAM GIBSON D
b. Mitchell, Ga, 6/11/03; s. J. N. Todd and Mittie Cooper T; m. 1/1/25 to Lena Kitchens; c. Wm. Franklin, Miriam, James Dwight, Aaron Hardy, Bernard Gibson. Educ: Mitchell, Gibson and Wren Schs; Mercer Univ. Polit. & Govt. Pos: Ga. State Rep, 49-66; Glascock Co. Sch. Supt, 41-49. Bus. & Prof. Pos: Teacher; farmer. Mem: Mason. Rel: Baptist. Mailing Add: Gibson, Ga. 30810. (1967)

TOFT, MARJORY MAYO R
Chmn, Childress Co. Rep. Cent. Cmt, Tex.
b. Swearingen, Tex, 5/16/23; d. Boss L. Mayo and Gladys Sears M; m. 6/1/45 to Raymond Leroy Toft; c. Todd Mayo. Educ: Art Courses, Fitz Gallery, 61-66. Polit. & Govt. Pos: Unit supvr, Childress Army Air Base, Tex, secy-bookkeeper, Signal Corps, 43-45; chmn, Childress Co. Rep. Cent. Cmt, 58- Mem: Area Arts Found; Tex. Fine Arts Asn; Univ. Readers Book Club; Tex. Fedn. Women's Dept. Club; Friends of Libr. Sponsor, Rodeo Girls representing Tex. in Madison Sq. Garden, 42; artist, shows Amarillo and N.Y.C, one-man shows in Tex. and Okla. Rel: Methodist. Mailing Add: 409 G. S.E, Childress, Tex. 79201. (1967)

TOKASH, GEORGE DERMER D
b. Weirton, W.Va, 1/1/35; s. Michael Tokash and Margaret Dermer T; m. 12/22/56 to Dolores Ruth Fisher. Educ: W.Va. Univ, B.A. and M.A; Univ. Pittsburgh. Polit. & Govt. Pos: Mem, Young Dem. Club, W.Va; W.Va. State Del, 64-66. Bus. & Prof. Pos: High sch. guid. dir. Mil. Serv: Army, Armored Cavalry; Army Res. Mem: W.Va. Univ. Alumni Asn; Prfnl, Nat. and W.Va. Educ. Asns; Classroom Teachers Asn; Nat. Coun. of Teachers of Eng; Nat. Cong, PTA; Weirton Suburban Boosters; Jaycees. Rel: Baptist; former dir, Men and Boy's Activities, Weirton Christian Center; former supt, Sunday Sch. and mem, Bd. of Deacons. Mailing Add: Weirton, W.Va. 26062. (1967)

TOKITA, TURK T. D
b. Lihue, Hawaii, 5/25/20; s. Tetsushiro Tokita and Tsuta Watanabe T; m. 6/23/57 to Emiko Sueoka; c. Lane T, Mari L. and Ken. M. Educ: Inst. Design, Chicago, A.A, 50. Polit. & Govt. Pos: Pres, Kauai Young Dem. Club, Hawaii, 48-52, dir, 52; secy, Lihue Dem. Precinct Club, 52-65, state conv. del, 56-64 and co. committeeman, 66-68; admin. asst. to Bd. of Supvr, Kauai Co, 57-66; mem, Kauai Charter Cmt, Kauai Co, 63-64; del, Dem. Nat. Conv, 64; exec. secy, Kauai Co. Dem. Party, Hawaii, 64-68; supvr, Registrn. and Ration Books, Econ. Stabilization Div, Kauai Co. Dept. Agr, 66. Bus. & Prof. Pos: Photographer, Turk's Photo, 51-59; dir, Kauai Mortuary, Inc, 64; mem. adv. bd, Investment Equity Life Ins. Co, Hawaii, 64-66, F.A.R, 65-66. Mil. Serv: Entered as Pvt, Army, 42, released as S/Sgt, 45, after serv. in 442nd Inf, R.C.T, Asiatic Pac, 42-43 and ETO, 43-45; Purple Heart; Presidential Unit Citation; Bronze Star; Good Conduct Medal; European, Mediterranean, African, Am. and Asiatic Pac. Campaign Ribbons. Mem: DAV; 442nd Vet. Club; Am. Legion; Hawaii Govt. Employ. Asn. Rel: Protestant. Legal Res: 2794 Pikake St, Lihue, Hawaii 96766. Mailing Add: P.O. Box 1047, Lihue, Hawaii 96766. (1967)

TOLAND, DENNIS PATRICK D
b. S. Boston, Mass, 1920. Educ: Mass. Trade Shops Sch; Boston Sch. of Indust. Rels; Gabriel Richard Inst. in Quincy. Polit. & Govt. Pos: Nominee for city coun. in 65; mem, Ward 5 Dem. Com. Bus. & Prof. Pos: Boston Edison Co. Mem: U.W.U.A. Local 369; United Fund chmn, 65; N. Quincy K. of C. Coun; Montclair Men's Club. Mailing Add: 133 Clay St, Quincy, Mass. 02140. (1967)

TOLEN, GEORGE ROY D
b. Shelbyville, Ind, 2/21/21; s. George Roy Tolen and Hazel Richey T; m. 4/4/42 to Jane Elise Erni; c. Ted Pralle and Jean Elise. Educ: Hanover Col, 38-40; Ind. Univ, LL.B, 48; Phi Delta Theta; Sigma Delta Kappa(pres, 48). Polit. & Govt. Pos: Dem. precinct committeeman, Shelby Co, Ind, 45-48; judge, Shelbyville City Court, 63; chmn, Shelby Co. Dem. Cent. Cmt, 64-66 and 67-69; v.pres, Ind. State Dem. Conv, 66; del, Dem. Nat. Conv, 68. Mil. Serv: Entered as Yeoman 3/C, Navy, 41, released as Chief Yeoman, 45, after serv. on USS Ranger and USS Belleau Wood, European, Atlantic and Pac. Theaters, 42-45; Presidential Unit Citation; European Theater Ribbon with One Star; Am. Theater Ribbon; Pac. Theater Ribbon with Eight Stars; Good Conduct Medal; Victory Medal. Mem: Ind. and Am. Bar Asns; Shelby Co. Bar Asn.(pres, secy. and treas, 48-50, 59); Tenth Dist. Bar Asn.(pres, 59); Ind. Trial Lawyers' Asn; Gov. Adv. Bd. on Alcoholism, 62-67; Am. Legion; VFW; Eagles; Nat. Muzzle Loading Rifle Asn; Nat. Rifle Asn; Bengal Conserv. Club; Lions (pres, Shelbyville Club, 55). Rel: Presbyterian; Deacon; Trustee and pres. Bd. Trustees. Mailing Add: 1708 Culbertson Rd, Shelbyville, Ind. 46176.

TOLER, JAMES L. D
Mayor, Garland, Tex.
b. Plano, Tex, 2/21/35; s. Allen Berryman Toler and Ruth Back T; m. 6/25/55 to Sarah Baker; c. Amy Ruth, James Larkin, Jr, Tobin Daniel and Nancy Jane. Educ: Baylor Univ, B.A, 57; E. Tex. State Univ, M.A, 62; Phi Delta Kappa. Polit. & Govt. Pos: Mayor, Garland, Tex, 63-; del, Dem. Nat. Conv, 68. Bus. & Prof. Pos: Owner, Jim Toler & Co, 62- Mem: Nat. Asn. Real Estate Bd; Tex. Real Estate Asn; Garland Real Estate Bd; Garland Civitan Club; C. of C. Realtor of the Year, 65; Outstanding Young Men of Am, 67. Rel: Baptist. Legal Res: 1330 Phoebe Lane, Garland, Tex. 75040. Mailing Add: 307 Garland Bank Bldg, Garland, Tex. 75040.

TOLES, ELWIN BONDS D
Ga. State Rep.
b. Cherokee Co. Ala, 3/16/16; s. John Glaznor Toles and Jennie Rose Bonds T; m. 4/28/37 to Mildred Louise Williams. Educ: Lyerly High Sch, grad, 33; Tenn. Temple Col, 2 years; pres, Student Body, 51. Polit. & Govt. Pos: State coordinator, Governor's Cmt on Employment of the Handicapped, 69; Ga. State Rep, Ninth Dist, 69- Bus. & Prof. Pos: Owner, Toles Furniture Co, 45-69; salesman, J.L. Todd Auction Co, 65-69. Mem: Kiwanis; pres, Laymen Evangelism of Ga. Lt. Col, aide-de-camp, Gov. Staff, Ga. Rel: Baptist; First V.Pres, Ga. Baptist. Mailing Add: 1114 Park Blvd, Rome, Ga. 30161.

TOLES, J. PENROD D
Chmn, N.Mex. State Dem. Party
b. 1929. Educ: N.Mex. Mil. Inst, B.S; Wash. and Lee Univ, LL.B; Univ. Tex. Sch. of Law, postgrad. law; Phi Alpha Delta; Phi Gamma Delta. Polit. & Govt. Pos: Chmn, Chaves Co. Dem. Party, N.Mex, 58-60; N.Mex. State Sen, 61-67; chmn, N.Mex. State Dem. Party, 68- Bus. & Prof. Pos: Attorney; independent oil operator and investments; mem. bd. dirs, Indust. Develop. Corp. and First Nat. Bank, Roswell, N.Mex. Mil. Serv: Army Res, 5 years; Army of Occup. in Germany, 2 years. Mem: Roswell Pub. Libr; Boy Scouts, Conquistador Coun. Rel: Methodist. Mailing Add: P.O. Drawer 1300, Roswell, N.Mex. 88201.

TOLLEFSON, THOR CARL R
b. Perley, Minn, 5/2/02; s. Christian Toffefson and Bertha Jacobson T; m. 11/24/34 to Eva M. Keuss T; c. Rosemary, Karley, Janie. Educ: Univ. of Wash, LL.B, 30. Polit. & Gov. Pos: U.S. Rep, Wash, 47-65; Pros. Attorney, Pierce Co, Wash, 39-46, 32-34. Bus. & Prof. Pos: Private Law Practice, 66-, 34-38, 30-32; Admitted to the Wash. Bar, 30; Mech. and millworker, 15-22 Mem: Phi Delta Phi; Alpha Sigma Phi; Mason 32nd degree; Shriner; Scottish Rite ; Elks; Moose; Kiwanian. Rel: Lutheran. Mailing Add: 3839 E. G St, Tacoma, Wash. 98404. (1967)

TOLMACH, JANE LOUISE D
Chmn, South Women's Div, Calif. Dem. State Cent. Cmt.
b. Havre, Mont, 11/12/21; d. Robert Francis McCormick and Veronica Tracy M; m. 9/9/46 to Daniel Michael Tolmach; c. James, Richard, Eve, Adam and Jonathan. Educ: Univ. Calif, Los Angeles, A.B, 43; Smith Col, M.S.S, 45; Gamma Phi Beta. Polit. & Govt. Pos: Mem, Ventura Co. Dem. Cent. Cmt, Calif, 53-, chmn, 59-62; alternate del, Dem. Nat. Conv, 56 & 64, del, 60 & 68; mem, Oxnard City Planning Cmn, 57-62, v.chmn, 59-62; mem, Ventura Co. Grand Jury, 58; mem, Calif. Dem. State Cent. Cmt, 58-; chmn, South Women's Div, 66-; mem, bd. trustees, Camarillo State Hosp, 59-68, chmn, 67 & 68; mem, gov. bd, Oxnard Union High Sch. Dist, 65-. Rel: Roman Catholic. Mailing Add: 656 Douglas Ave, Oxnard, Calif. 93030.

TOMAN, ANDREW JOHN D
Coroner, Cook Co, Ill.
b. Chicago, Ill, 2/21/05; s. John Toman and Bertha Sefcik T; m. 6/3/39 to Emily Marianne Serhant; c. John Andrew. Educ: Univ. Chicago and Univ. Ill, Champaign, B.S, 27; Univ. Ill. Col. Med, Chicago, M.D, 29. Polit. & Govt. Pos: Pub. health dir, City of Berwyn Health Dept, Ill, 57-60; coroner, Cook Co, 60-; del, Dem. Nat. Conv, 68. Bus. & Prof. Pos: Intern, Cook Co. Hosp, Chicago, Ill, 29-31; resident, X-ray Dept. and Path. Dept, 31-32; med. supt, House of Correction, 32-52; instr. of surg. and med. nursing, Hosp. St. Anthony de Padua Nursing Sch, 37-39; clin. instr, Dept. of Surg, Stritch Med. Sch, Loyola Univ, Chicago; attending physician and surgeon, Hosp, St. Anthony de Padua, Chicago and Mac Neal Mem, Berwyn; med. dir, Armour & Co, Union Stockyards, Chicago, 53-57. Mil. Serv: Entered as Lt. Comdr, Naval Med. Corps, 43, released as Comdr, 46, after serv. in Naval Res. Med. Corps, Pac. Theatre, 44-45; Am. Theater Medal; Asiatic-Pac. Medal; Victory Medal; World War II Medal. Mem: Am. Med. Asn; Ill. State Med. Soc; Chicago Med. Soc.(Cmt. on Emergency Med. Serv); Cook Co. Traffic Safety Cmn; Chicago Civil Defense Corps; Pub. Safety and Welfare; Joint Maternal and Infant Welfare of Cook Co; Am. Cancer Soc; Spec. Agents Asn; Ill. Police Asn; Nat. Asn. of Coroners; Ill. State Coroners Asn; Am. Acad. of Forensic Sci. Nat. Asn. of Co. Off; Am. Legion; VFW; Am, Mid.W. and Ill. Pub. Health Asns; Cook Co. Hosp. Interns Asn; Royal League; Lions; Elks; Moose; Bohemia Club; Swedish Club; life mem, Art Inst. of Chicago; Phi Beta Pi; adv. bd, Necropsy Serv. to Coroners, Dept. of Pub. Health, State of Ill; Chicago Soc. of Med. Jurisp; Inst. of Med. of Chicago; Pittsburgh Inst. of Legal Med; Cmt. on Trauma, Am. Col. of Surgeons. Rel: Protestant. Legal Res; 287 Southcote Rd, Riverside, Ill. 60546. Mailing Add: Room 408, Civic Center, Chicago, Ill. 60602.

TOMASI, LAWRENCE JAMES D
Vt. State Rep.
b. Barre, Vt, 2/26/06; s. Anthony Tomasi and Rose Massucco T; c. Patricia Duane and Lawrence J, Jr. Educ: Norwich Univ, 28; Holy Cross and Univ. Vt, 29-30 & 31-32; Univ. McGill, D.D.S, 37. Polit. & Govt. Pos: Vt. State Rep, Dist. 18, 67- Rel: Catholic. Legal Res: 46 Court Sq, Windsor, Vt. 05089. Mailing Add: 72 Main St, Windsor, Vt. 05089. (1967)

TOMCZYK, EDWARD J. DFL
Minn. State Rep.
Married; c. Five. Polit. & Govt. Pos: Right of Way Agent, Hennepin Co. Engrs. Off; Minn. State Rep, 47- Mem: K. of C; Eagles; E. Side Men's Club. Rel: Catholic. Mailing Add: 1614 California St. N.E, Minneapolis, Minn. 55413

TOMLIN, EDWIN MERRILL R
b. Augusta, Ga, 3/16/23; s. Ray Silver Tomlin and Dollie Moore T; m. 6/18/46 to Frances Ann Fish; c. Ann, John Marc, Tracy Edward and Michael Timothy. Educ: Cent. Col; Univ. Mo, B.S, 44; Univ. Tenn, M.D, 46; Phi Beta Pi. Polit. & Govt. Pos: Chmn, Cabarrus Co. Rep. Exec. Cmt, N.C, 64-68. Mil. Serv: Entered as Seaman recruit, Naval Res, 43, released as Comdr, Med. Corps, 56; Chinese and Korean Theater Ribbons; Presidential Unit Citation. Mem: Am, N.C. and South. Med. Asns; Am. Urological Asn; Am. Col. of Surgeons; Am. Bd. of Urology; Rotary; Moose. Rel: Presbyterian. Mailing Add: 158 Lecline Dr. N.E, Concord, N.C. 28025. (1967)

TOMLIN, JOHN R. D
N.Mex. State Rep.
b. Albuquerque, N.Mex, 4/20/26; s. Roy A. Tomlin (deceased) and Sallie Mackey T; m. 6/20/50 to Ina L. Carwile; c. John Timothy, Joel Mackey and Jennifer Lee. Educ: N.Mex. State Univ, B.S, 50, M.A, 55; Alpha Tau Alpha; Alpha Delta Theta; Sigma Phi. Polit. & Govt. Pos: V.pres, Las Cruces Co. Dem. Party, N.Mex, 66-69; N.Mex. State Rep, 69- Bus. & Prof. Pos: Pres, Picacho Cotton Gin Coop, 60-69; chmn, research and educ. cmt, Dona Ana Co. Farm Bur, 62-69. Mil. Serv: Entered as Recruit, Army, 44, released as Sgt, 46, after serv. in Inf, ETO, 45-46. Mem: Soil Sci. Soc; N.Mex. Educ. Asn; Rifleman; Mason; Boy Scouts (cmt, troop 70); York Rite; Farm Bur; Shrine; Elks. State Farmer Degree, N.Mex, 44. Rel: Presbyterian; Ruling Elder. Mailing Add: Route 2, Box 267, Las Cruces, N.Mex. 88001.

TOMLINSON, JOHN D. DFL
V.Chmn, Ramsey Co. Dem-Farmer-Labor Party, Minn.
b. Oak Park, Ill, 12/3/29; s. Dewey Tomlinson and Ruth Kincaid T; m. 7/7/51 to Martha Blake; c. Nancy, Diane and David. Educ: Univ. Minn, B.Ch.E, 52; Tau Beta Pi. Polit. & Govt. Pos: Campaign coordinator, U.S. Rep. Joseph Karth, Dist. Four, Minn, 68; del, Dem. Nat. Conv, 68; v.chmn, Ramsey Co. Dem-Farmer-Labor Party, Minn, 68- Bus. & Prof. Pos: Chem. engr, 3M Co, St. Paul, Minn, 55-60, research mgr, 60-68, research analyst, 68- Mil. Serv: Entered as Ens, Navy, 52, released as Lt.(jg), 55, after serv. in U.S.S. Stribling, Atlantic Fleet, 52-55. Rel: Unitarian. Mailing Add: 2232 Conway St, St. Paul, Minn. 55119.

TOMPKINS, WILLIAM FINLEY R
b. Newark, N.J, 2/26/13; s. William Brydon Tompkins and Elizabeth Finley T; m. 12/16/49 to Jane Davis Bryant; c. William F, Jr. Educ: Wesleyan Univ, 35; Rutgers Univ. Sch. Law, 40; Delta Kappa Epsilon. Polit. & Govt. Pos: N.J. State Assemblyman, 51-53; U.S. Attorney, N.J, 53-54; Asst. Attorney Gen, U.S, 54-58; chmn, Cmn. to Study Capital Punishment, 64; del, Rep. Nat. Conv, 64 and N.J. Constitutional Conv, 66. Mil. Serv: Entered as Pvt, World War II, commissioned Inf. Officers Cand. Sch, Ft. Benning, Ga, Commanding Officer, U.S. War Crime Off, Saigon, French Indo-China, U.S. Prosecutor War crime trials in Singapore. Publ: The Traffic in Narcotics, Funk & Wagnall. Mem: V.pres, Fed. Bar Asn, N.Y, N.J. and Conn, 66; special cmt. on minimum standards, Admin. of Criminal Justice, Am. Bar Asn, 64-; pres, bd. trustees, Newark Acad, 64-69, chmn, 69. Received Annual Award by Soc. Former Spec. Agents, F.B.I. for outstanding contributions to the advancement of law enforcement, 59; First Americanism Citation for Meritorious Serv. from S.Mt. Lodge, B'nai B'rith, 55; Honor Roll of Inf. Officer Cand. Hall of Fame, Ft. Benning, Ga. Rel: Methodist. Legal Res: 589 Ridgewood Rd, Maplewood, N.J. 07040. Mailing Add: 550 Broad St, Newark, N.J. 07102.

TOMPOS, WILLIAM D
W.Va. State Sen.
b. Monongahela, Pa, 2/17/14; s. Rudolp Stephen Tompos and Mary Martha Dugan T; m. 5/9/42 to Helen Bambrick; c. Thomas William and Raymond Stephen. Educ: Hancock Co. Pub. Schs. Polit. & Govt. Pos: W.Va. State Del, 56; W.Va. State Sen, 60- Bus. & Prof. Pos: Clerical and serv. work. Mil. Serv: Army, 42-45, attached to 43rd Inf. Div, serv. in Asiatic-Pac. Theatre, 3 years, discharged with rank of Sgt; 5 Battle Stars; 1 Arrowhead Award. Rel: Christian Church. Mailing Add: 3241 West St, Weirton, W.Va. 26062. (1967)

TOMYL, MICHAEL R
Educ: Harvard, S.E.C; Ins. Inst. of Am, Inc. Polit. & Govt. Pos: Chmn, Mass. Coun. of Young Reps; Jr. Nat. Committeeman from Mass; v.chmn, New Eng. Regional Labor Com. of Young Rep. Nat. Fed; del. to Nat. Young Rep. Conv; mem. Rep. Town Com; mem. Billerica Bd. of Appeals; elected Town Meeting mem. Mem: Chmn, Red Cross; Red Cross Bd. of Dir; chmn, Heart Fund Dr, awarded a citation for outstanding serv. by Am. Heart Asn; chmn, Children's Hosp. Med. Center Dr; pres. of Ins. Chap. of Mass. State Employees. Mailing Add: 26 Chelmsford Rd, N. Billerica, Mass. 01826. (1967)

TONE, SUSAN BROWN R
b. Hinsdale, Ill, 1/13/41; d. Harry Whiting Brown (deceased) and Dorothy Lueders Brown Webster; m. 7/27/63 to John Wolfe Tone; c. Tracy Elizabeth and Catherine Hilary. Educ: Drake Univ, 59-62; Delta Gamma. Polit. & Govt. Pos: Block worker and area capt, Hinsdale, Ill, 60-62 and Ottumwa, Iowa, 64-65; precinct committeewoman, Rep. Party, Ottumwa, 65-67 and West Des Moines, 67-69; mobile registr, Ottumwa, 66; del, Rep. Co. Conv, 66 & 68; del, Rep. State Conv, 68; chmn, Ottumwa Rep. Workshops, 64-67; campaign coordinator for local cand, 66; state secy, Iowa Rep. Workshops, 67-68 & 68-69; alternate del, Rep. Nat. Conv, 68; co-chmn, attendance, prom. and Invitations subcmt, Gov. UN Day Cmt, 69; pres, Wapello Co. Women's Rep. Club, 69- Bus. & Prof. Pos: Secy-travel agent, Robinson Travel Serv, Hinsdale, Ill, summer, 59-61; secy-exec, Chicago Title & Trust Co, 62-63. Mem: Des Moines Art Center (jr. art. mus. vol); Compass Duplicate Club; Iowa Fedn. Rep. Women; Polk Co. Young Rep; Iowa Rep. Workshops. Rel: Episcopal. Mailing Add: 180 E. Alta Vista, Ottumwa, Iowa 52501.

TONER, FELIX J. D
Chmn, Southeast Dist. Dem. Party, Alaska
b. Phila, Pa, 4/19/14; s. Felix J. Toner and Elizabeth O'Rourke T; m. 10/17/41 to Mary Vander Leest; c. Kathleen T.(Mrs. Steven K. Boley), Marijo C, Nora Ann and Stacy B. Educ: Univ. Notre Dame, B.S. in Eng, 39. Polit. & Govt. Pos: Precinct chmn, Juneau Dem. Party, Alaska, 52-54, chmn, Southeast Dist. Dem. Party, 54-56 & 68- and state chmn, 56-60; chmn, State Reapportionment Adv. Bd, 65-66; mem. bd. exam, State Alaska Adv. Cmt. Select Cmt. Small Bus, U.S. Sen, 68-69; del, Dem. Nat. Conv, 68. Bus. & Prof. Pos: Mine engr, Alaska Juneau Gold Mining Co, 40-44; assoc. engr, Corps. of Engrs, 44-46; consult. engr, Toner & Nordling, Registered Engrs, 46- Mem: Am. Soc. Civil Engrs; Nat. Soc. Prfnl. Engrs; Elks; C. of C; Alaska Miners Asn. Rel: Roman Catholic. Legal Res: 127 W. Seventh St, Juneau, Alaska 99801. Mailing Add: Box 570, Juneau, Alaska 99801.

TONEY, ADAM D
W.Va. State Del.
b. Dothan, W.Va, 3/3/38; s. C. L. 'Jimbo' Toney and Claris Fisher T; m. 1/24/59 to Mary Jane Massie; c. Lisa Jo and Charlie Adam. Educ: W.Va. Inst. Tech, B.S, 61; Brunswick Bowling Mgt, Chicago, Ill, 62. Polit. & Govt. Pos: Second V.Pres, Fayette Co. Young Dem, W.Va, 69; mem, State Educ. Cmt, 69; W.Va. State Del, 69- Mem: Prfnl. Bowlers Asn; W.Va. Bowling Proprietors Asn; W.Va. Inst. Tech. Alumni Asn; Lions; Moose; C. of C; Oak Hill Athletic Club; Fayette Co. Sportsmen Asn. Rel: Baptist. Mailing Add: 600 Central Ave, Oak Hill, W.Va. 25901.

TONGIER, GLEN LEROY R
b. Coffeyville, Kans, 12/17/24; s. Russell Maynard Tongier and Effie Belle Johnson T; m. 7/28/51 to Sharon Lynn Oakes; c. Cheryl Ann and John David. Educ: Univ. Kans, A.B, 49, LL.B, 51; Alpha Tau Omega; Phi Delta Phi; Big 8 Conf. Tennis Doubles Champion, 48, Univ. Kans. and Tennis Coach, 51. Polit. & Govt. Pos: Mem. State Exec. Cmt. and Third Dist. Chmn, Young Rep, Kans, 53-57; attorney, Montgomery Co, 59-63; Rep. Precinct Committeeman, 60-66; chmn, Montgomery Co. Rep. Cent. Cmt, 64-66; mem. bd. educ, Unified Sch. Dist. 445, 65-; mem. bd. trustees, Coffeyville Jr. Col, 65- Mil. Serv: Entered as A/S, Navy, 43, released as ARM 3/C, 46. Mem: Legis. Cmt, Kans. Asn. Sch. Bds; Montgomery Co, Kans. and Am. Bar Asns; Mason, Blue Lodge, Chapter, Commandery; Rotary; Am. Legion; 40 et 8. Rel: Methodist. Legal Res: 707 Highland, Coffeyville, Kans. Mailing Add: Plaza Bldg, Coffeyville, Kans. 67337.

TOOHER, JOSEPH JOHN, JR. D
b. Stamford, Conn, 6/27/30; s. Joseph J. Tooher and Mary Louise Brennan T; single. Educ: Univ. Conn, B.S, 52, Sch. Law, LL.B, 55. Polit. Pos: Chmn, Stamford City Dem. Cmt, Conn, 64-66. Govt. Pos: Prosecutor, Circuit Court, Conn, 62-63; prosecutor, City Court, Stamford, 60. Bus. & Prof. Pos: Partner in Law Firm, Moore, Epifanio and Tooher, Stamford, Conn. Mil. Serv: Entered as Pvt, 55, Army, released as SP-2, 57. Rel: Roman Catholic. Mailing Add: 48 Hillside Ave, Stamford, Conn. 06902. (1967)

TOOLE, FRAMPTON WYMAN, JR. D
b. Aiken, S.C, 9/18/23; s. Frampton Wyman Toole and Lillian Jones T; m. 10/24/53 to Betty Julia McLure; c. Frampton W, III and Harriet Celeste. Educ: Univ. S.C, A.B. cumlaude, 43; Harvard Univ, LL.B, 49; Blue Key; Kappa Alpha Order; Lincoln's Inn. Polit. & Govt. Pos: S.C. State Rep, Aiken Co, 52-56, 62-66; S.C. State Sen, 67-68. Bus. & Prof. Pos: Law Partner, Toole & Toole, Attorneys, 49- Mil. Serv: Entered as Ens, Naval Res, 43, released as Lt, 46, after serv. in Light Cruiser and Amphibious Forces, Pac; 3 Theater Campaign Ribbons; 2 Battle Stars; Lt. Comdr, Naval Res, Retired, 63. Mem: Am. and S.C. Bar Asns; Aiken Businessmen's Club; Aiken Outing Club; Aiken Cotillion; Highland Park Country Club; Palmetto Club; Am. Legion. Rel: Presbyterian. Legal Res: 1445 Forest Hill Ave, S.W, Aiken, S.C. 29801. Mailing Add: P.O. Box 403, Aiken, S.C. 29801.

TOON, MALCOLM
U.S. Ambassador to Czech.
b. Troy, N.Y, 7/4/16; s. George Toon and Margaret Harcomb Broadfoot T; m. 8/28/43 to Elizabeth Jane Taylor; c. Barbara Jane, Alan Malcolm and Nancy Margaret. Educ: Tufts Univ, A.B, 37; Fletcher Sch. Law and Diplomacy, M.A, 39; Middlebury Col, 50; Harvard Univ, 50-51; Tufts Varsity Club. Polit. & Govt. Pos: Research technician, Nat. Resources Planning Bd, 39-41; career officer, Dept. of State For. Serv, 46-; for. serv. officer, Warsaw, Budapest, Moscow, Rome, Berlin and Wash, D.C, 46-60; mem. U.S. del, Nuclear Test Conf, Geneva, Switz, 58-59, Four Power Working Group, Wash, D.C, London and Paris, 59, For. Ministers Conf, Geneva, 59 and Ten Nation Disarmament Cmt, Geneva, 60; assigned to U.S. Embassy, London, 60-63; counsr. polit. affairs, Moscow, 63-65; assigned Dept. of State, Wash, D.C, 65-69; U.S. Ambassador to Czech, 69- Mil. Serv: Entered as Ens, Navy, 42, released as Lt. Comdr, 46, after serv. in PT Squadron 9, S.Pac. and S.W. Pac, 43-45; Bronze Star Medal. Mem: Am. For. Serv. Asn; Kenwood Golf and Country Club, D.C; Royal Automobile Club, London, Eng. Superior Honor Award, Dept. of State, 65. Legal Res: Northboro, Mass. Mailing Add: U.S. Embassy, Prague, Czechoslovakia.

TOON, THOMAS P. D
Polit. & Govt. Pos: Ind. State Rep, 63-68; Evansville City Clerk, 48-51. Bus. & Prof. Pos: Ins. and Real Estate. Mil. Serv: WW II, U.S. Army Vet. Mem: Eagles; Cent. Turners, Inc. Rel: Catholic. Mailing Add: 1100 S. Grand Ave, Evansville, Ind. 47713. (1967)

TOPE, ROBERT R. R
Exec. Dir, Fla. Rep. State Exec. Cmt.
b. Orlando, Fla, 10/1/39; s. Thomas W. Tope and Marjorie Fender T; m. 2/12/59 to Gretchen Wolsey; c. Anne Elizabeth, Amy Louise and Carrol Marjorie. Educ: Orlando Jr. Col, 2 years; Jones Col, 1 year. Polit. & Govt. Pos: Precinct committeeman, Rep. Party, Seminole Co, Fla, 67, campaign mgr. for State Sen. Ken Plante, 67 and cong. cand, William F. Herlong, 68; co. cmnr, Seminole, 68; exec. dir, Fla. Rep. State Exec. Cmt, 69- Bus. & Prof. Pos: Pres, Tope Bros. Fruit Co. Inc, 59- Mil. Serv: Marine Corps, 56-62; Res. Mem: Intermediate Harvesters and Handlers Asn; Fla. Farm Bur; PTA; Fla. Citrus Mutual; Fla. Peace Officers Asn; Seminole Co. Sportsmen Asn; Ear Club. Named Young Farmer of the Year, South Seminole Jaycees. Rel: Congregational. Mailing Add: 1123 Glen Arden Way, Altamonte Springs, Fla. 32701.

TOPPER, ISADORE R
Mem, Exec. Cmt, Franklin Co. Rep. Orgn, Ohio
b. Toledo, Ohio, 11/14/03; s. Michael Topper and Rebecca Finkelstein T; m.

12/28/28 to Ida Kaplan. Educ: Univ. Toledo, B.A, 25; Ohio State Univ. Col. Law, LL.B, 27; Phi Delta Phi. Polit. & Govt. Pos: Precinct committeeman, Lucas Co. Rep. Orgn, Ohio, 26-32; Asst. Attorney Gen, Ohio, 31-37, Counsel to Attorney Gen, Ohio, 40-45 & 49-; alternate del-at-lg, Rep. Nat. Conv, 56, 60 & 64; mem, Nat. Rep. Club, N.Y.C; mem, exec. cmt, Franklin Co. Rep. Orgn, Ohio, currently. Publ:'The Effect of the Ohio Administrative Procedure Act on Procedure before the Board of Liquor Control,' Ohio State Law J, Vol 13, No. 4, 52. Mem: Chmn, Admin. Law Cmt, and mem, House of Dels, Ohio State Bar Asn; Am. Bar Asn; Am. Judicature Soc; Columbus Bar Asn; charter mem, bd. trustees. and past pres, Ohio Asn. of Attorneys Gen; Elks; Lawyers Club, N.Y.C; B'nai B'rith; regional bd, Anti-Defamation League; trustee, United Jewish Fund and Coun; former trustee, Temple Israel, Columbus, Ohio; bd. trustees and past pres, Winding Hollow Country Club; past pres, Alumni Asn. of Col. Law, Ohio State Univ. and nat. chmn, Financial Aids Fund: President's Club, Ohio State Univ; bd. trustees, Heritage House; Ohio State Univ. Alumni Asn; Univ. Toledo Alumni Asn. First recipient of Distinguished Alumnus Award, Student Bar Asn, Col. Law, Ohio State Univ, 64. Rel: Jewish. Legal Res: 55 South Remington Rd, Bexley, Columbus, Ohio 43209. Mailing Add: 17 South High St, Columbus, Ohio 43215.

TORGERSON, CARROL HOWARD R
N.Dak. State Sen.
b. Bainville, Mont, 9/26/19; s. Herman Torgerson and Margaret Huso T; m. 2/9/46 to Maxine Phyllis Rhodes; c. Michael. Educ: N.Dak. State Univ, 2 terms. Polit. & Govt. Pos: Admin. asst, co. fieldman and off. mgr, Griggs Co. Agr. Stabilization and Conserv. Cmt, 38-42; N.Dak. State Sen, 16th Dist, 63-66 and 23rd Dist, 66-, Asst. Majority Floor Leader, N.Dak. State Senate, 67, v.chmn, Judiciary Cmt, 65 and Finance and Taxation Cmt, currently; mem. tax cmt, Midwest Coun. of State Govt, currently; mem. finance and taxation cmt, Soc. Welfare and Vet. Affairs Cmt, currently. Bus. & Prof. Pos: Mgr, Shepard Farmers Elevator & Grain Co, 46-52; owner and operator, Ford-Mercury Garage, 52-59 and Torgersons Variety Store and Coffee Shop, 60-65; auctioneer and real estate broker, Torgersons Real Estate & Auction Serv, N.Dak, 60- Mil. Serv: Entered as PO 3/C, Navy, 42, released as PO 1/C, 45, after serv. in 75th CB Bn, S.Pac, 42-45. Mem: N.Dak. and Nat. Auctioneers Asns; N.Dak. and Nat. Realtors Asns; VFW; Elks; Cooperstown Commercial Club (past pres); Am. Legion (past state comdr); Farm Bur; Farmers Union; N.Dak. Am. Legion State Exec. Cmt; Nat. Am. Legion Legis. Cmn. Rel: Lutheran; Past Pres, Trinity Lutheran Church. Mailing Add: Cooperstown, N.Dak. 58425.

TORKELSON, LOWELL JEROME R
b. Edmore, N.Dak, 7/15/28; s. John E. Torkelson and Ruth Chellberg T; m. 8/28/48 to Barbara Mae Twaddle; c. Nicki, Kitti and Zachary Thomas. Educ: Dakota Bus. Col, 1 year. Polit. & Govt. Pos: Treas, Cascade Co. Young. Rep. Mont, 62-64, v.chmn, 64-65; v.chmn, Mont. Young Rep, 64-65; del, Nat. Young Rep. Conv, 65-67; asst. finance chmn, Mont. Rep. Party, 66-69; del, Rep. Nat. Conv, 68. Bus. & Prof. Pos: Inspector, Anaconda Wire & Cable Co, 51-54; salesman, Fuller Brush Co, 54-55; sales supvr, retail sales supvr. and merchandiser, Union Oil Co. of Calif, 55-69. Mem: Advert. Club Great Falls. Rel: Christian Church of N.Am. Mailing Add: 800 51 St. S, Great Falls, Mont. 59401.

TORRES, FRANK D
b. New York, N.Y, 1/25/28; s. Felipe N. Torres and Flerida Berrios T; m. 5/6/50 to Yolanda Iola Marquez; c. Andrea Lynn, Ramon Miguel and Analisa Nadine. Educ: City Col. New York; St. John's Univ. Law Sch; Manhattan Sch. Music; Arista; Alpha Phi Omega. Polit. & Govt. Pos: Asst. Dist. Attorney, Bronx, N.Y, 59-63; N.Y. State Assemblyman, 63-64; assoc. govt. appeal agent, Local Bd. 25, 66; mem, N.Y. City Coun. Against Poverty, 66-; Urban Develop. spec, Region One, U.S. Dept. Housing and Urban Develop, currently. Bus. & Prof. Pos: Dir. and founder, Pamela C. Torres Day Care Center, 59-; dir. and counsel, Ponce de Leon Fed. Savings & Loan, 60- Rel: Catholic. Legal Res: 23 Renfrew Rd, Spring Valley, N.Y. 10977. Mailing Add: Dept. of Housing and Urban Development, Washington, D.C. 20410.

TORRES, JESUS U. D
Sen, Guam Legis.
b. Agana, Guam, 6/16/27; s. Joaquin Torres and Maria A. Unpingco T; single. Educ: Columbia Univ, N.Y; Univ. Minn, B.A, 53; William Mitchell Col. Law, St. Paul, Minn, LL.B, 61. Polit. & Govt. Pos: Secy, Guam State Dem. Party, 64-65, chmn, 65-; Sen, Guam Legis, 69- Bus. & Prof. Pos: Attorney at Law, 61- Mil. Serv: Entered as Pvt, Army, 54, released as Specialist 3/C, 56, after serv. in Heavy Motor Co, 25th Div. and 27th Inf. Regt; Good Conduct Medal. Mem: Guam Bar Asn. Rel: Catholic. Legal Res: Santa Rita, Guam 96910. Mailing Add: P.O. Box 1719, Agana, Guam 96910. (1967)

TORRES, MAX E. V. R
Chmn, Las Animas Co. Rep. Cent. Cmt, Colo.
b. Torres, Colo, 2/4/12; s. Emilio Torres and Eufemia Vallejos T; m. 6/14/42 to Della Ann Cordova; c. Felix, Max Anthony and George. Educ: Trinidad High Sch, grad, 31; Trinidad Jr. Col, 31-33; Adams State Col. and Colo. State Col. Polit. & Govt. Pos: V.chmn, Adv. Cmt, U.S. Civil Rights Cmn, 59-69; chmn, Las Animas Co. Rep. Cent. Cmt, Colo, 61-; chmn, Colo. Civil Rights Cmn, 64-69. Bus. & Prof. Pos: Rancher, 31-; bd. mem, Model Land & Irrigation Co, 50-69; secy. and bd. mem, Purgatoire River Water Conservancy Dist, 60-69. Mem: Las Animas Co. Livestock Asn. Rel: Catholic. Mailing Add: 1108 E. Main St, Trinidad, Colo. 81082.

TORRES, STEVE S, JR. R
b. 1938. Educ: Univ. of Wash, B.A; Univ. of N.Mex, grad. work; Delta Tau Delta. Polit. & Govt. Pos: N.Mex. State Rep, until 67. Bus. & Prof. Pos: Corp. Exec, Torridge Corp; pres, restaurant and lounge. Mil. Serv: N.Mex. Nat. Guard, 6 years. Mem: C. of C; Hist. Soc. Mailing Add: 733 N. Calif, Socorro, N.Mex. 87801.

TORRES SANTIAGO, CARLOS LUIS Popular Dem, P.R.
Rep, P.R. House of Rep.
b. Coamo, P.R, 5/24/38; s. Pablo Torres Vazquez and Dolores Santiago De T; m. 10/14/68 to Nilda Zayas Pratts; c. Carlos Jose. Educ: Coamo High Sch, 3 years. Polit. & Govt. Pos: Rep. and mem, Gov. Cmn, P.R. House of Rep, 69-; pres, Coamo Popular Dem. Party, currently. Mem: Pres, Club Soc. Recreativo; Lions Int. Rel: Catholic. Mailing Add: 82 H.W. Santaella, Coamo, P.R. 00640.

TORREY, ELIZABETH N. R
Vice-Chairwoman, Minn. Rep. State Cent. Cmt.
b. Red Wing, Minn, 5/24/25; d. Louis William Nordly and Florence Isabella Brown N; m. 9/25/52 to Marshall George Torrey; c. Robert Marshall and James Marshall. Educ: Carleton Col, Northfield, Minn, B.A, magna cum laude, 47; Phi Beta Kappa. Polit. & Govt. Pos: Rep. precinct chairwoman, Red Wing, Minn, 56-58, Rep. city chairwoman, 58-61; chairwoman, Goodhue Co. Rep. Party, 61-63; vice-chairwoman, First Cong. Dist. Rep. Party, 63-65, chairwoman, 65-69; del, Rep. Nat. Conv, 68; vice-chairwoman, Minn. Rep. State Cent. Cmt, 69- Bus. & Prof. Pos: Claims Supvr, Employers Mutuals of Wausau, 47-52. Rel: Episcopal. Mailing Add: 1617 Poplar Dr, Red Wing, Minn. 55066.

TORVINEN, ROY LEE R
Nev. State Assemblyman
b. Tacoma, Wash, 6/19/27; s. Roy Torvinen and Ora Sparling T; m. 5/30/59 to Helen Lorraine Norris; c. Todd Lee, Karen Lynn, Thomas Craig and James Norris. Educ: Univ. Nev, B.A, 53; Georgetown Univ. Law Sch, LL.B, 53; Lambda Chi Alpha. Polit. & Govt. Pos: Mem, Washoe Co. Rep. Cent. Cmt, Nev, 57-69; asst. city attorney, Reno, 56-59, city attorney, 59-63; Nev. State Assemblyman, Washoe Co, 67- Bus. & Prof. Pos: Private law practice, Reno, Nev, 63-69. Mil. Serv: Entered as Pvt, Army, 46, released as Pfc, 48, after serv. in 24th Div, Japan, 47-48. Mem: Washoe Co, Nev. State and Am. Bar Asns; Admitted to practice law in D.C; Elks; Kiwanis Int. Rel: Protestant. Legal Res: 1465 McKinley Dr, Reno, Nev. 89502. Mailing Add: 1 E. First St, Reno, Nev. 89501.

TOTMAN, RALPH WRIGHT R
b. Greenfield, Mass, 2/27/00; s. Horace Eugene Totman and Nellie E. Wright T; m. 7/18/53 to Mildred Josephine Carton. Educ: Dartmouth Col, B.S, 22; Northeast. Univ, LL.B, 32; Boston Univ, 30 hours towards M.Ed; Lambda Chi Alpha. Polit. & Govt. Pos: Legal Consult, Off. Indust. Personnel Security Rev, N.H, 55-59; del, N.H. State Rep. Conv, 61, 63 & 65; former N.H. State Rep, chmn, Judiciary Cmt, N.H. House of Rep, 61, 63 & 65, mem, Legis. Coun, 63-64; del, N.H. Constitutional Conv, 64. Bus. & Prof. Pos: Headmaster, Walpole High Sch, N.H, 22-27; housemaster, Brookline High Sch, Mass, 27-42. Mil. Serv: Pvt, Army, 18; 1st Lt, Army Air Force, 42-47, Col.(ret), 55. Mem: Mass. and N.H. Bar Asns; Mason; Shrine; Elks; Am. Legion; Soc. of Mayflower Descendants. Rel: Unitarian. Mailing Add: Forest Rd, Alstead, N.H. 03602. (1967)

TOTTEN, DONALD LEE R
b. Brooklyn, N.Y, 2/19/33; s. Edgar L. Totten and Louise Florentine T; m. 6/11/55 to Joyce Anderson; c. Diana, Robert and Kathleen. Educ: Univ. Notre Dame, B.S.M.E, 55. Polit. & Govt. Pos: Committeeman, Schaumburg Rep. Twp. Cmt, Ill, 66- Bus. & Prof. Pos: Indust. engr, Int. Register, Chicago, Ill, 60; plant mgr, Morton Mfg, Libertyville, 60-67, Farr Co, Crystal Lake, 67- Mem: Ill. State C. of C; Am. Mgt. Asn. Rel: Roman Catholic. Mailing Add: 193 Woodlawn St, Hoffman Estates, Ill. 60172.

TOUGH, E. A. R
Chmn, Emmons Co. Rep. Party, N.Dak.
b. Linton, N.Dak, 6/29/13; married; c. Three. Educ: Bus. Col. Polit. & Govt. Pos: Mem. bd, Co. Cmnr, N.Dak, 46-50; mem, Strasburg City Coun, 53-55; N.Dak. State Rep, 55-65; chmn, Emmons Co. Rep. Party, 68-; asst. chief clerk, N.Dak. House Rep, 67-69. Bus. & Prof. Pos: Farmer. Mailing Add: Strasburg, N.Dak. 58573.

TOUHY, JOHN P. D
Ill. State Rep.
b. 4/19/19; m. to Mary; c. Debbie, Nancy and Jackie. Educ: Georgetown Univ; DePaul Law Sch. Polit. & Govt. Pos: Ill. State Rep, currently, Minority Whip, Ill. House of Rep. Mil. Serv: Army, $4\frac{1}{2}$ years, more than 2 years overseas. Mem: VFW; Georgetown Club of Chicago. 1967 Legal Res: Chicago, Ill. No mailing address available. (1967)

TOVREA, RICHARD LELAND D
V.Chmn, Montrose Co. Dem. Party, Colo.
b. Nucla, Colo, 7/29/39; s. Leland Carl Tovrea and Lolo Mae Bishop T; m. 4/17/60 to Lana Faye Mitchel; c. Stephanie Lynn, Vickie Liegh and Michelle Lenae. Educ: West. State Col, Gunnison, 57-60; Univ. Colo, 64; Kappa Delta Mu. Polit. & Govt. Pos: Precinct Chmn, Arapahoe Co. Dem. Party, 60-61; Precinct chmn, Montrose Co. Dem. Party, 64-69, v.chmn, 68- Bus. & Prof. Pos: Foreman, Allied Chem, Denver, Colo, 66-67; partner, Tovrea & Sons, 67- Mem: Moose; C. of C; Nucla and Naturita Jr. C. of C; Rel: United Church of Christ. Mailing Add: Box 459, Nucla, Colo. 81424.

TOWE, THOMAS EDWARD D
b. Cherokee, Iowa, 6/25/37; s. (William) Edward Towe and Florence Tow T; m. 8/21/60 to Alice Ruth James; c. James Thomas. Educ: Earlham Col, Richmond, Ind, B.A, 59; Univ. Paris, L'Institut d'Etude Politique, 56; Univ. Mont. Law Sch, LL.B, 62; Georgetown Univ. Law Sch, LL.M, 65; Univ. Mich. Law Sch, 65-66; Phi Kappa Phi; Phi Delta Phi. Polit. & Govt. Pos: Treas, Univ. Mont. Young Dem. Club, 60; first v.pres, Yellowstone Co. Dem. Club, Mont, 68; cand, Mont. House Rep, 68; del, Mont Dem. State Conv, 68; del, Dem. Nat. Conv, 68. Bus. & Prof. Pos: Attorney-at-law, 67- Mil. Serv: Entered as 1st Lt, Army, 62, released as Capt, 65, after serv. in Judge Adv. Gen. Corps, Pentagon, D.C, 63-65; Capt, Res, 65-; Army Commendation Medal. Publ: 'Personal Jurisdiction Over Non-Residents and Montana's New Rule 4B,' Mont. Law Rev, fall 62; 'Criminal Pretrial Procedure in France,' Tulane Law Rev, 4/64; 'Fundamental Rights in the Soviet Union: A Comparative Approach,' Univ. Pa. Law Rev, 1/67. Mem: Am. and Mont. Bar Asns; Am. Civil Liberties Union; Optimist; Am. Hereford Asn; ROA. Rel: Quaker. Mailing Add: 2640 Burlington Ave, Billings, Mont. 59102.

TOWER, JOHN GOODWIN R
U.S. Sen, Tex.
b. Houston, Tex, 9/29/25; s. Joe Z. Tower and Beryl Goodwin T; m. 3/21/52 to Joza Lou Bullington; c. Penelope, Marian and Jeanne. Educ: Southwest. Univ, B.A, 48; South. Methodist Univ, M.A, 53; London Sch. of Econ. and Polit. Sci, 52-53. Hon. LL.D, Howard Payne Col, Brownwood, Tex, 63; hon. Litt. D, Southwest. Univ, Georgetown, Tex, 64. Polit. & Govt. Pos: U.S. Sen, Tex, 61-, mem, Cmts. on Armed Serv. and Banking and Currency, mem, Joint Cmt. on Defense Prod, chmn, Rep. Nat. Senatorial Cmt, currently; del, Rep. Nat. Conv, 68. Bus. & Prof. Pos: Asst. prof. polit. sci, Midwest. Univ, 51-60. Mil. Serv: Entered Navy, 43, released as Seaman 1/C, 46, after serv. on Naval Gunboat, Asia; mem, Naval Res. Mem: Southwest. Social Sci. Asn; Am. Asn. of Univ. Prof; Am. Polit. Sci. Asn; Int. Polit. Sci. Asn; Am. Legion; U.S. Naval Inst; Tex. Hist. Soc; C. of C; Univ. Kiwanis; Bd. Dir, Wichita Falls Symphony Orchestra; Worthy Grand Procurator, Kappa Sigma; Shrine. Named Kappa Sigma Man of Year, 61; Five trips to Southeast Asian Combat Zone, 65, 66 & 67. Rel: Methodist; mem. bd. stewards, Wichita Falls. Legal Res: 1609 Sparks St, Wichita Falls, Tex. 76302. Mailing Add: Old Senate Office Bldg, Washington, D.C. 20010.

TOWERY, ROLAND KENNETH R
Asst. Dir, U.S. Info. Agency
b. Smithville, Miss, 1/25/23; s. Wiley Azof Towery and Lonie Bell Cowart T; m. 5/4/47 to Louise Cook; c. Roland Kenneth, Jr. and Alice Ann. Polit. & Govt. Pos: Press secy, U.S. Sen. John Tower, Tex, 63-65, admin. asst, 64-69; asst. dir, U.S. Info. Agency, 69- Mil. Serv: Entered as Pvt, Army, 41, released as Cpl, 46, after serv. in Battery C, 60th CAC, Philippines, 41-45; Purple Heart; Presidential Unit Citation with Two Oak Leaf Clusters; Asiatic Pac. Theater Campaign with Two Bronze Stars; Philippine Defense Ribbon with One Bronze Star; Am. Defense Serv. Ribbon with One Bronze Star. Mem: Sigma Delta Chi; Mason. Pulitzer Prize, 55. Legal Res: 1709 Norris Dr, Austin, Tex. 78704. Mailing Add: 6803 Old Chesterbrook Rd, McLean, Va. 22101.

TOWNE, CARROLL EDMUND R
Vt. State Rep.
b. Milton, Vt, 11/2/26; m. to Nina Belle Hazen; c. four sons, four daughters. Educ: Milton High Sch. Polit. & Govt. Pos: Trustee, Sch. Bd, Milton, Vt, 58-60; former mem, Rep. Town Cmt; Vt. State Rep, 63- Bus. & Prof. Pos: Dairy farming. Mem: F&AM; Mason; Past Master's Asn; Eastern Star; Am. Farm Bur. Rel: Congregational. Mailing Add: Route 3, Milton, Vt. 05468.

TOWNES, CLARENCE LEE, JR. R
b. Richmond, Va, 1/21/28; s. Clarence Lee Townes, Sr. and Alice Smith T; m. 6/9/51 to Grace Elizabeth Harris; c. Clarence Lee, III, Michael Steven, June Elizabeth and Lisa Fracine. Educ: Va. Union Univ, B.S. in Commerce, 50; Phi Beta Sigma. Polit. & Govt. Pos: V.chmn, Richmond Rep. Cmt, Va, 63-65; cmnr, Richmond Redevelop. & Housing Authority, 63-; mem, Richmond Biracial Cmt, 64-; v.chmn, Third Dist, Va. Rep. Cmt, 64-; treas, Nat. Negro Rep. Assembly, 64-; asst. to chmn, Rep. Party of Va, 65-; mem. adv. cmt. to chmn, Rep. Nat. Cmt, 66-; alternate del, Rep. Nat. Conv, 68. Bus. & Prof. Pos: Circulation mgr, Norfolk J. & Guide, 44-48; agent, Va. Mutual Benefit Life Ins. Co, 48-50, agency asst, 51-56, agency supvr, 56-64 and dir. of training, 64- Mil. Serv: Entered as Pvt. E-2, Army, 51, released as 2nd Lt, 53, after serv. in Am. Theater. Mem: Master Mason, M.W. Prince Hall Grand Lodge of Va, F&AM, Inc; Int. Frontiers of Am; Astoria Beneficial Club. Rel: Baptist. Mailing Add: 604 W. Lancaster Rd, Richmond, Va. 23222. (1967)

TOWNSEND, CLAIRE STEWART R
Mem, Calif. Rep. State Cent. Cmt.
b. Butte, Mont, 8/23/26; d. Arthur Dayton Stewart and Olga Fylpaa S; m. 2/2/52 to Warren E. Townsend; c. Sharon Elizabeth, Robert Stewart and John Christie. Educ: San Francisco City Col, A.A, 46; Univ. Calif, B.S, 48; Alpha Delta P. Polit. & Govt. Pos: Mem, San Francisco Young Republicans, Calif, 48-52; precinct capt, San Francisco Rep. Party, 52; precinct capt, Fremont Rep. Party, 62 & 68; mem, Calif. Rep. State Cent. Cmt, 68-; secy, Tri-Cities Chap, Calif. Rep. League, 69- Bus. & Prof. Pos: Owner, Dry Cleaning Plants, 62- Mem: Childrens Home Soc; Am. Red Cross (mem. bd, Oakland-S. Alameda Chap). Rel: Episcopal. Mailing Add: 4355 Mattos Dr, Fremont, Calif. 94536.

TOWNSEND, GARY PATTERSON D
b. Ft. Worth, Tex, 5/28/46; s. Donald E. Townsend, Sr. and Mary Blessing T; single. Educ: Calif. State Col. Los Angeles, B.S, 69; Blue Key; Sigma Alpha Epsilon; pres, Assocs. Students, 67-68; exec. coordinator, Calif. State Col. Student Pres. Asn, 67-68; mem. nat. supv. bd, U.S. Nat. Students Asn, 67-68. Polit. & Govt. Pos: Co-chmn, South. Calif. Students for Kennedy, Calif. Presidential Primary, 68; del, Dem. Nat. Conv, 68; mem. nat. steering cmt, Coalition for an Open Conv, 68; co-chmn Calif. Dem. Student Alliance, 68; mem, campaigns for Humphrey-Muskie for President, 68, Cranston for Senate, 68, George E. Brown for Cong, 68 and Bradley for Mayor, 69; founder and past chmn, Calif. Kennedy Action Corps, 68-69; treas. and co-founder, Inst. Soc. Adv, 68-69; exec. coordinator, Student Idea Center for Dem. Action, 69; chmn. state legis. action cmt, Calif. Fedn. Young Dem, 69; Optimist Youth Appreciation Award. Legal Res: 225 Palmetto, Apt. 6, Alhambra, Calif. Mailing Add: 241 S. Olive, Alhambra, Calif. 91801.

TOWNSEND, HOBART LAMAR, JR. D
b. Memphis, Tenn, 8/9/34; s. Hobart Lamar Townsend and Ruth Ellen Jennings T; m. 4/21/62 to Ruth Evelyn Dodson; c. Kyle Lamar. Educ: Univ. Tenn, B.S. in Bus. Admin, 56; Southwest. Grad. Sch. Banking, South. Methodist Univ, dip, 65; Sigma Chi. Polit. & Govt. Pos: Mgr, Decatur Co. Olgiati for Gov, Dem. Primary, Tenn, 62; mem, Decatur Co. Dem. Exec. Cmt, 62-64, chmn, 64-66 & 68; coordinator, Seventh Cong. Dist. Hooker for Gov, Dem. Primary, 66; city councilman, Parsons, 68-; mem, Decatur Co. Planning Cmn, 69; magistrate, Decatur Co, 69- Bus. & Prof. Pos: Officer, Farmers Bank, 57- Mil. Serv: 2nd Lt, Army, 57, serv. in Air Defense Artillery Center, Ft. Bliss, Tex; Capt, Army Res, 66. Mem: Past pres, Jr. Bankers Section, Tenn. Bankers Asn, 66; Elks; Rotary. Rel: Southern Baptist. Mailing Add: 201 W. Fourth St, Parsons, Tenn. 38363.

TOWNSEND, JAMES BAKER D
Okla. State Rep.
b. Haileyville, Okla, 11/23/27; s. John Dunn Townsend and Rose Baker T; m. 8/8/49 to June Marie Childers; c. James Lawrence, Jeffrey Paul and Jay Arthur. Educ: Okla. Mil. Acad, 45. Polit. & Govt. Pos: Okla. State Rep, 64- Mil. Serv: Entered as Pvt, Army, 46, released as Pfc, 47, after serv. in Far East. Mem: Locomotive Firemen and Enginemen; Elks; VFW; Okla. Bow Hunters; Pottawatomie Co. Cattlemen's Asn; Lions; Toastmasters. Rel: Baptist. Mailing Add: Route 4, Box 194, Shawnee, Okla. 74801. (1967)

TOWNSEND, JAMES TERRELL D
b. Brady, Tex, 2/28/35; s. Aubrey Lynn Townsend and Billie Butler T; m. 6/2/57 to Sylvia Nixon; c. Terri Lynn and Craig Nixon. Educ: Univ. Tex, B.B.A, 57, LL.B, 59; Phi Alpha Delta; Lambda Chi Alpha. Polit. & Govt. Pos: Tex. State Rep, 74th Dist, 59-63 and 65th Dist, 63-67. Bus. & Prof. Pos: Exec. dir, Tex. Motor Transportation Asn, currently. Mem: Mason; C. of C; Rotary. Rel: Baptist. Legal Res: 1915 S. Pine St, Brady, Tex. 76825. Mailing Add: Box 1669, Austin, Tex. 78767.

TOWNSEND, KILIAEN VAN RENSSELAER R
Ga. State Rep.
b. Garden City, N.Y, 10/6/18; s. Edward Nichol Townsend and Beatrice Nicholas T; m. 5/9/49 to Mary Campbell Everett; c. Kiliaen Van Rensselaer, Jr. Educ: Williams Col, A.B, 39; Univ. Va. Law Sch, LL.B, 42; Phi Delta Phi; Raven Soc; Chi Psi. Polit. & Govt. Pos: Secy, Fulton Co. Rep. Party, Ga, 48; del, Rep. Nat. Conv, 52; Ga. State Rep, 115th Dist, 65-, Minority Whip, Ga. State House of Rep. Mil. Serv: Entered as Pvt, Army, 42, released as 2nd Lt, 46. Mem: Atlanta Lawyers Club; Ga. Bar Asn; Rotary. Rel: Protestant. Mailing Add: 955 Coronado Dr. N.W, Atlanta, Ga. 30327.

TOWNSEND, MARY E. D
b. Greenville, Ind, 8/17/26; d. Vernon Duvall and Ethel Huffman D; m. 11/8/46 to Clyde Stuart Townsend; c. Clyde Stuart, II and Sherri Lynn. Educ: Ind. State Univ. Polit. & Govt. Pos: Dem. V.Committeeman, Ind, 54-62; Dem. Precinct Committeeman, 62-66; v.chmn, Floyd Co. Dem. Cent. Cmt, 64-66. Mem: Eastern Star; Younger Woman's Federated Club. Rel: Presbyterian. Mailing Add: 205 Spickert Knob Rd, New Albany, Ind. 40920.

TOWNSEND, REBEKAH FAUCETT R
Pres, Del. Fedn. Rep. Women
b. Georgetown, Del, 10/20/02; d. James William Faucett and Nellie Smith Coverdale F; m. 4/17/20 to Eben Alden Townsend, Jr; c. Dorothy Isabel (Mrs. Donald Eugene Robertson); Eben Alden III (deceased). Educ: Georgetown High Sch; Bus. Sch; Art Lessons under Clarence Flatt, 59-61, Univ. Del, Cert. Pub. Speaking, 64; Yale Univ, Campaign Mgt, Seminar, 66. Polit. & Govt. Pos: Chmn. publicity and Americanism chmn, Sussex Co. Rep. Women's Club, Del, 58-62, pres, 60-62, ex officio mem. as guid. counsr, 64-; treas, Del. Fedn. Rep. Women, 62-64, pres, 64-; chmn. prog. and v.pres, Georgetown Rep. Women's Club, 66-; v.chmn, Nixon-Agnew for Sussex Co, 68; coordinator, Women for Nixon, 68; del, Rep. Nat. Conv, 68. Publ: Reports to clubs, state and national bds, for Rep. Women and the Gen. Fedn. Women's Clubs. Mem: Georgetown New Century Club (v.pres, librarian 2 years, pres, chmn. trustees); Sussex Mace and Gavel Club; (v.pres); Georgetown Rep. Women's Club (v.pres); Sussex Co. Rep. Women's Club (pres, ex officio mem. as guid. counsr); Nat. Asn. Parliamentarians (historian, Del. State Asn); Women's Soc. Christian Serv; Nat. Fedn. Rep. Women (nat. bd); Delmarva Rehabilatation Center Crippled Children and Adults (bd. mem). Award, 4-H, 17; Pres. First Award, Del. Fedn. Women's Clubs, 59 and 60; Best All Around Club Women, Georgetown New Century Club, 65; Silver Medallion, Nat. Fed. Rep. Women, 66; Citation, 67; Pin Award, 68. Rel: Methodist Episcopal; Sunday Sch. Teacher, Mem, Official Bd, Circle Leader and Class Officer. Mailing Add: R.D. 1, Box 11, Georgetown, Del. 19947.

TOWNSEND, RICHARD TAYLOR D
b. Laurens, S.C, 9/24/40; s. Thomas Pickney Townsend and Virginia Taylor T; m. 8/31/63 to Donna Doyle Evans; c. Allison. Educ: Clemson Univ, B.S. Indust. Mgt, 62; Univ. S.C, LL.B, 65; Indust. Mgt. Soc; Sigma Alpha Zeta; Phi Delta Phi. Polit. & Govt. Pos: Chmn, Laurens Co. Dem. Party, S.C, 66-68; alternate del, Dem. Nat. Conv, 68. Mem: Am. and S.C. Bar Asns; Laurens Co. Bar Asn.(pres, 67-68); S.C. and Am. Trial Lawyer's Asns; Rotary; Jr. C. of C; pres, Laurens C. of C, 66-67. Peace Fund Award, Clemson Univ. Rel: Episcopal. Legal Res: 208 Owings St, Laurens, S.C. 29360. Mailing Add: P.O. Box 215, Laurens, S.C. 29360.

TOWNSEND, W. WAYNE D
Educ: Grad, Purdue Univ; Alpha Gamma Rho. Polit. & Govt. Pos: Ind. State Rep, 59-66. Bus. & Prof. Pos: Farmer. Mil. Serv: Army Counterintelligence Corps, 54-56. Mem: State Livestock Sanit. Bd; bd. of dir, Marion Gen. Hosp; Grant Cty. Asn. for Ment. Health; state dir, Purdue Ag. Alumni; former dir, Grant Cty. Fair Bd; United Fund; Masons; Scottish Rite; Elks. Rel: Friends Church. Mailing Add: R.R. 1, Upland, Ind. 46989. (1967)

TOWNSEND, WILBURN BRANSON D
Chmn, Decatur Co. Bd. of Educ, Tenn.
b. Parsons, Tenn, 8/17/07; s. Elie Mansfield Townsend and Cordelia Harrison T; m. 11/23/30 to Ema Lou Long; c. Nancy (Mrs. Yarbro), Janell (Mrs. Evans) and Branson. Educ: Union Univ, 29; Univ. Tenn, 31. Polit. & Govt. Pos: Tenn. State Rep, 41 & 61; del, Dem. Nat. Conv, 52, 60 & 64, alternate del, 68; chmn, Decatur Co. Dem. Cmt, Tenn, 58; chmn, Decatur Co. Bd. of Educ, currently. Bus. & Prof. Pos: Gen. ins. consult, 36 years. Mem: Shrine; Lions; Elks. Rel: Baptist. Mailing Add: 403 Virginia Ave, Parsons, Tenn. 38363. (1967)

TOWSE, DANIEL CHARLES R
Mass. State Rep.
b. Somerville, Mass, 12/5/24; s. Charles Frederick Towse and Evangeline Lynch T; m. 8/1/48 to Marian MacDonald; c. Linda Joyce, Janet Elaine and Amy Evangeline. Educ: Stoneham High Sch, 4 years. Polit. & Govt. Pos: Mem, Stoneham Planning Bd, Mass, 59-66; mem, Stoneham Conserv. Cmn, 63-; mem, Rep. Town Cmt, Stoneham, 64-; mem, Stoneham Bd. of Selectmen, 65-69; Mass. State Rep, 21st Middlesex Dist, 69- Bus. & Prof. Pos: Park

and Forestry Supvr, Stoneham, 23 years. Mil. Serv: Entered as Pvt, Army, 43, released as Sgt, 45, after serv. in 76th Inf. Div, Third Army, ETO, 44-45; Unit Citation; Combat Inf. Badge; Three Battle Stars. Mem: Mass. Arborists; Mass. Selectmens Asn; New Eng. Park and Forestry Asn; Mass. Legislators Asn; Am. Legion; VFW; Appalachian Mt. Club; Moose; Kiwanis; Boy Scouts. Rel: Congregational. Mailing Add: 7 Congress St, Stoneham, Mass. 02180.

TOWSON, WILLIAM MALCOLM D
b. Montrose, Ga, 5/3/23; s. William Franklin Towson and Bertha Ashley T; m. 6/4/53 to Dorothy Blanche Perkins; c. Andrew Ashley, James Vernon, Margaret Ann and William Malcolm, Jr. and stepchildren, Allen Kirk and Dorothy Marlene Hazlett. Educ: Univ. Ga, LL.B, 49; Delta Theta Phi; asst. student ed-in-chief, Ga. Bar J, 47-49. Polit. & Govt. Pos: Co. Attorney, Bd. Cmnrs, 65-66; Ga. State Rep, 63-64; City Attorney, Bd. of Alderman, 63-64 and 54-55; Ga. State Sen, 61-62. Bus. & Prof. Pos: Attorney, self-employed. Mil. Serv: Entered as Pvt, Cavalry, 45, released as S/Sgt, 46, after serv. in Pac. Mem: Dublin Circuit Bar Asn; Am. Judicatory Soc; State Disciplinary Bd, Ga. Bar Asn; State Bar Ga; Gov. Cmn. on Judicial Selection; Gov. Staff; Elks; VFW; Am. Legion; Civitan; Laurens Co. Farm Bur; Dublin Country Club; Band Boosters Club; Touchdown Club; Hilcrest Orgn. of Parents and Teachers; Laurens Co. Salvation Army Bd. Rel: Methodist; Chmn, Cmn. on Missions, Bd. Stewards; First Methodist Church, Dublin, Ga. Legal Res: Route 1, Dublin, Ga. 31021. Mailing Add: Box 2069, Court Square Station, Dublin, Ga. 31021. (1967)

TRACY, ROGER WAHLQUIST, JR. R
Ohio State Rep.
b. Columbus, Ohio, 9/26/38; s. Roger Walker Tracy and Elizabeth Wahlquist T; m. 5/21/66 to Elizabeth Ebel. Educ: Miami Univ, B.S. in Bus. Admin, 60; Ohio State Univ, J.D, 63; Beta Theta Pi; Phi Delta Phi. Polit. & Govt. Pos: Spec. messenger for President and the White House Staff, 59; state campaign mgr, Tracy for State Auditor Cmt, 62; res. asst, Ohio Legis. Reference Bur, 63; admin. asst, Off. of Auditor of State, Ohio, 64; asst. dir, Ohio Citizens for Goldwater-Miller, 64; nat. committeeman, Ohio League Young Rep. Clubs, 66; Ohio State Rep, 60th Dist, 67- Bus. & Prof. Pos: Attorney-at-law, 65-; lectr. polit. sci, Ohio State Univ, 68- Mil. Serv: Airman Basic, Air Force Res, 64, served in Judge Adv. Off, 906th Combat Support Squadron, Sgt, Air Force Res, 69. Mem: Columbus and Ohio State Bar Asns; Ohio Hist. Soc; Miami and Ohio State Univ. Alumni Asns. Rel: Episcopal. Mailing Add: 1116 S. High St, Columbus, Ohio 43206.

TRACY, TOM D
b. Butte, Mont, 5/2/28; s. Thomas Tracy and Florence Bubach T; m. 8/24/49 to Margaret M. Killgallon; c. Colleen, Kathleen, Maureen, Geraldine, Tommy Pat and John Fitzgerald Kennedy. Educ: Butte Bus. Col. Polit. & Govt. Pos: Mont. State Rep, 63-67; Mont. State Sen, 67-69. Bus. & Prof. Pos: Bus. rep, IAMAW, 65- Mil. Serv: Entered as A/S, Navy, 45, released as Seaman 1/C, 46. Mem: K. of C; IAMAW. Rel: Catholic. Mailing Add: 2425 Nettie St, Butte, Mont. 59201. (1967)

TRACY, WILLIAM ALLAN D
b. Seattle, Wash, 12/30/40; s. Bernie William Tracy and Mildred Barnard T; single. Educ: Univ. Wash, B.A, 65 & 66; Phi Alpha Theta; Theta Xi; Pi Omicron Sigma. Polit. & Govt. Pos: Dem. committeeman, Precinct 98, Dist. 34, Seattle, Wash, 66-69, Precinct 100, Dist. 34, 69-; dist. campaign chmn, John O'Connell Gov, 34th Dist, 68; alternate del, Dem. Nat. Conv, 68; campaign chmn, A.A. Marinaro Co. Coun, Coun. Dist. Nine, South King Co, 68-69; alternate del. King Co. Young. Dem. Clubs Joint Coun. to Co. Dem. Cent. Cmt. Exec. Bd. Bus. & Prof. Pos: Census trainer and supvr, U.S. Bur. Census, Seattle, Wash, 67; teacher, Highline Sch. Dist, Seattle, 67- Mem: Highline, Wash. and Nat. Educ. Asns; Seattle Young Dem.(pres); Sunset PTA (v.pres). Alumnus of Year Award, Theta Xi, 66. Mailing Add: 3425 S. 176th St, Apt. 160, Seattle, Wash. 98188.

TRAEGER, JOHN ANDREW D
Tex. State Rep.
b. Wichita Falls, Tex, 7/6/21; s. Albert Edward Traeger and Bonnie Lois Forman T; m. 6/21/43 to Margaret Bernice Vivroux; c. Betty Camille, Jeanne Marie, John A, Jr. and James Edward. Educ: Tex. Wesleyan Col, 38-39; Tex. Lutheran Col, 39-41; past pres, Tex. Lutheran Col. Athletic Asn. Polit. & Govt. Pos: City councilman, Seguin, Tex, 58-62, mayor pro tem, 60-61; Tex. State Rep, 41st Dist, 63- Mil. Serv: Entered as Pvt, Army Air Force, 41, released as Capt, 45, after serv. in Continental U.S, grad, Army Air Force, Statist. Sch, U.S. Army Artil Sch. and Nuclear Warfare Sch; Lt. Col, Artil. Bn. Comdr, Tex. Nat. Guard, currently. Mem: Lions (past pres. and zone chmn, Seguin Club); Elks (Past Exalted Ruler and trustee, Seguin Lodge; pres, Seguin C. of C. and Guadalupe Co. Commun. Fund; dist. chmn, Guada-Coma Boy Scout Dist; pres, Quarterback Club and Little League; Am. Legion. Rel: Methodist; Mem, Bd. of Stewards. Mailing Add: 503 S. Austin St, Seguin, Tex. 78155. (1967)

TRAIN, RUSSELL ERROL R
Under Secy, Dept. of the Interior
b. Jamestown, R.I, 6/4/20; s. Rear Admiral Charles Russell Train and Errol Cuthbert Brown T; m. 5/27/54 to Aileen Ligon Bowdoin; c. Nancy (Mrs. St. John Smith), Emily Ligon, Charles Bowdoin and Errol Cuthbert. Educ: Princeton Univ, A.B. 41; Columbia Univ, LL.B. 47. Polit. & Govt. Pos: Staff Attorney, Joint Cmt. Internal Revenue Taxation, U.S. Cong, 47-53; clerk, Cmt. on Ways and Means, U.S. House Rep, 53-54, minority adv, 54-55; head legal adv. staff and asst. to the secy, Treas. Dept, 56-57; judge, U.S. Tax Court, 57-65; Under Secy, Dept. of the Interior, 69- Bus. & Prof. Pos: Pres, Conservation Found, 65-69. Mil. Serv: Entered as 2nd Lt, Army, 41, released as Maj, 46, after serv. in Field Artil, Pac, 45-46; Pac. Campaign Medal with One Battle Star. Rel: Episcopal. Mailing Add: 3101 Woodland Dr. N.W, Washington, D.C. 20008.

TRANSUE, ANDREW JACKSON D
b. Clarksville, Mich, 1/12/03; s. Charles John Transue and Nina Winks T; m. 8/31/35 to Vivian A. Chappel; c. Tamara Louise (Mrs. James Royle) and Andrea Ann (Mrs. Marc Haidle). Educ: Detroit Col. of Law, LL.B, 26, J.D, 68. Polit. & Govt. Pos: Prosecuting attorney, Genesee Co, Mich, 33-37; U.S. Rep, Mich, 37-39; dist. dir, Sixth Dist, Mich, U.S. Census, U.S. Dept. of Commerce, 39-40; assoc. govt. appeal agent, local bd, Selective Serv. Syst, 41-54; mem. appeal bd. panel, 54-66; assoc. govt. appeal agent, 66-; life mem, U.S. Judicial Conf, Sixth Circuit. Mem: U.S. Court of Appeals Third Circuit and Sixth Dist, U.S. Supreme Court, U.S. Dist. Court East. Dist. of Mich. Bars; pres, Genesee Co. Bar Asn, 44-45; Am. Bar Asn; Cmt. on Character and Fitness, Cmt. on Constitutional Law, Cmt. on Condemnation Proceedings, State Bar of Mich; Am. Judicature Soc; Lawyers Club, Univ. Mich; hon. fel, Harry S. Truman Libr. Inst; Mason; F&AM; Elks; Lions. Rel: Methodist. Legal Res: 1647 N. Grand Traverse St, Flint, Mich. 48503. Mailing Add: 813 Mott Foundation Building, Flint, Mich. 48502.

TRAUTMANN, ARTHUR DALLAS D
Chmn, Dist. 31 Dem. Party, N.Dak.
b. Robinson, N.Dak, 10/14/34; s. William A. Trautmann and Martha Wiesser T; m. 8/28/55 to Velma E. Hanson; c. Wesley, LaDonna and Lanna. Educ: Robinson High Sch, grad, 52. Polit. & Govt. Pos: Precinct committeeman, Dem. Party, N.Dak, 64-; chmn, Dist. 31 Dem. Party, 67-; mem, State Resolutions Cmt, 68. Bus. & Prof. Pos: Farmer and rancher, currently. Mem: Eagles; Farmers Union; bd. dir, Kidder Co. Fair; Nat. Farmer's Orgn; Robinson Wildlife Fedn. Rel: Lutheran. Mailing Add: Robinson, N.Dak. 58478.

TRAUTMANN, GEORGE LAMBERT D
b. Staples, Minn, 6/11/24; s. John Julis Trautmann and Elsie Orando T; m. 11/16/64 to Betty Jane Regalia; c. Joan Carol, Brian James, Edward James and Mark Joseph. Educ: Blackduck High Sch, grad; Seattle Photography Sch, grad, 48. Polit. & Govt. Pos: Sewer cmnr, S.W. Suburban, Seattle, Wash, 65-66; Wash. State Rep, 31st Dist, 66; Dem. chmn, 31st Dist, 67-69; alternate del, Dem. Nat. Conv, 68. Mil. Serv: Entered as Recruit, Navy, 43, released as PO 2/C, 46, after serv. in Squadron 16 Navy Air Radio Man, Pac, 45-46; Air Medal. Mem: Pres, White C. of C, 64-65; pres, Northwest Dist. Exchange Club, 69-; Exchange Club of Highline; Elks; Toastmasters; Glen Acres Golf and Country Club. Rel: Roman Catholic. Mailing Add: 11629 19th S.W, Seattle, Wash. 98146.

TRAVERS, ALFRED, JR. D
R.I. State Rep.
b. Providence, R.I, 10/14/24; m. to Concetta. Polit. & Govt. Pos: R.I. State Rep, 61- Bus. & Prof. Pos: Indust. engr. Mailing Add: 53 Armstrong Ave, Providence, R.I. 02903. (1967)

TRAVERS, F. WARREN D
Troy, N.Y, 12/6/27; m. to Joanne P. Pemrick; c. Martin G, Theresa M. Educ: Siena Col. BA, cum laude; Albany Law Sch, LL.B. Polit. & Govt. Pos: N.Y. State Sen, 1964-Jan, 1967; Co. Attorney, U.S. Farm Home Admin; Advocate of Troy Coun. Bus. & Prof. Pos: Lawyer. Mil. Serv: USAF, Philippine Islands area. Mem: Sec, Rensseler Co. Bar Asn; N.Y. & Am. Bar Asn; K. of C. Mailing Add: 393 Eighth Ave, Troy, N.Y. 12182. (1967)

TRAWEEK, FLORENCE IRENE R
V.Chmn, Deaf Smith Co. Rep. Party, Tex.
b. El Paso, Tex, 9/7/12; d. Humboldt Casad and Mattie Maude Garrison C; m. 6/2/39 to Curtis Richard Traweek; c. Sabra. Educ: N.Mex. A&M Col, B.S. and B.A, 34; Zeta Tau Alpha. Polit. & Govt. Pos: Committeewoman, 30th Sen. Dist. Rep. Party, Tex, 52-58 & 61-64; acting postmaster, Hereford, 58-61; alternate del, Rep. Nat. Conv, 64; v.chmn, Deaf Smith Co. Rep. Party, Tex, currently. Bus. & Prof. Pos: Sch. teacher, N.Mex, 34-41. Mem: Bd. dirs, Aggie Alumni Asn, N.Mex. State Univ, 66-67; Farm Bur. Rel: Episcopal. Mailing Add: R.R. 3, Hereford, Tex. 79045. (1967)

TRAWEEK, KENNETH EDWARD R
b. Birmingham, Ala, 5/16/29; s. James Edward Traweek and Elsie Word T; m. 3/20/54 to Carol Jean Biggs; c. Kenneth E, Jr, William Andrew, Jodie Carol and Edith Ami. Educ: Samford Univ, 49; Sigma Nu. Polit. & Govt. Pos: Mem, Jefferson Co. Rep. Exec. Cmt, Ala, 62; mem. nominating cmt, Ala. State Rep. Conv, 62, chmn. credentials cmt, 64 and mem. credentials cmt, 66; admin. v.chmn, Jefferson Co. Rep. Cmt, 64-65, chmn, 65-68; mem, Ala. State Rep. Exec. Cmt, 65-68. Bus. & Prof. Pos: Draftsman, Turner, Smith & Batson, Architects, 48-61; assoc, Albie, Reeves, Smith, Architects, 61- Mil. Serv: Entered as Pvt, Army, 52, released as Cpl, 54, after serv. in 187th Combat Engrs, Iceland. Mem: Lions Int; past pres, Birmingham Chap, Construction Specifications Inst. Rel: Methodist. Mailing Add: 1120 Dogwood Lane, Birmingham, Ala. 35205. (1967)

TRAXLER, J. ROBERT D
Mich. State Rep.
b. Kawkawlin, Mich, 7/21/31; m. 1962 to Louida Repkie; c. Tamara and Brad. Educ: Bay City Jr. Col; Mich. State Univ, B.A. in Polit. Sci, 53; Detroit Col. of Law, LL.B, 59. Polit. & Govt. Pos: Asst. Prosecutor, Bay Co, Mich, 60-62; Mich. State Rep, 62-, Majority Floor Leader, Mich. House of Rep, 65-66, Asst. Minority Floor Leader, 67- Bus. & Prof. Pos: Attorney. Mil. Serv: Army, 53-55. Mem: Am. and Mich. Bar Asns; dir, Bay Co. Ment. Health Soc. Rel: Episcopal. Mailing Add: 2712 N. Van Buren, Bay City, Mich. 48706. (1967)

TRAYLOR, LAWRENCE MILTON R
Mem, Va. State Rep. Cent. Cmt.
b. Oklahoma City, Okla, 3/26/28; s. Edward L. Traylor and Mildred Moore T; wid; c. Lawrence, Jr. and Richard; m. 10/17/68 to Nancy Tingle; c. David (stepson). Educ: American Univ, B.S, 53, LL.B, 56; Delta Theta Phi. Polit. & Govt. Pos: Chmn, Norrhumberland Co. Rep. Cmt, Va, 56-; v.chmn, Eighth Dist. Rep. Cmt, 62; mem, Va. State Rep. Cent. Cmt, 64-; Rep. cand, U.S. Senate, Va, 66. Bus. & Prof. Pos: Attorney-at-Law, 56- Mil. Serv: Entered as Pvt, Army, 46, released as Cpl, 48, after serv. in Gen. Hq, Far East Command, 47. Mem: Am. Trial Lawyers Asn; Va. Bar Asn. Rel: Methodist. Legal Res: Lottsburg, Va. Mailing Add: Heathsville, Va. 22473.

TRAYLOR, LEE CLYDE R
Mem, Ala. State Rep. Exec. Cmt.
b. Ft. Payne, Ala, 8/29/32; s. Hugh Clyde Traylor and Lorine Guest T; m. 11/14/53 to Nancy May Norris; c. Michael Lee, Dennis Hugh and Karen

Lynne. Educ: Emory Univ, A.B, 54; Emory Law Sch, 56-57; Univ. Ala. Law Sch, LL.B, 59; Sigma Chi; case note ed, Ala. Law Rev. Polit. & Govt. Pos: City recorder, Ft. Payne, Ala, 64-; mem. Ala. State and Co. Exec. Cmt, Rep. Party, currently. Bus. & Prof. Pos: Attorney-at-law, 59-; pres, Northeast Ala. Farmers Produce Mkt, 63-65, mem. bd. dirs, 63-; registered wrestling official, Ala. High Sch. Athletic Asn, 67-69; mem. bd. dirs. and secy, Mt. Manor Nursing Home, 67- Mil. Serv: Entered as Pfc, Army, 54, released as Sp-3, 56, after serv. in 575th Ord. Amunition Co. Ft. Hood Tex. Publ: 'Residences Furnished Officers by Corporation,' Digest of Tax Articles, 5/59. Mem: N.Am. Judges Asn; Dekalb Co, Ala. and Am. Bar Asns; Ala. Trial Lawyers Asn; Ala. Claims Asn; Ala. Munic. Judges Asn; Am. Judicature Soc; DeKalb Co. Tourist Asn; DeKalb Co. Red Cross; DeKalb Co. Safety Coun; Boy Scouts; C. of C; secy, Northeast Ala. Hunting Club; secy-treas, Ft. Payne Gun Club; Nat. Rifle Asn; Mason; Eastern Star; Shrine; RAM; Shrine Circus Daddy Club; Phi Delta Phi; secy, Ft. Payne Jaycees. Jaycee Spoke Award. Rel: Baptist. Legal Res: 205 S.W. Eighth St, Ft. Payne, Ala. 35967. Mailing Add: P.O. Box 316, Ft. Payne, Ala. 35967.

TRAYLOR, W. S. D
b. Norfolk, Va, 1926; m. to Shirley T; c. two dtrs. Educ: William and Mary Col. Polit. & Gov. Pos: Wash. State Rep, until 66. Bus. & Prof. Pos: Restaurant owner. Mil. Serv: Coast Guard, 4 yrs, W.W. II; Korean War, 1 yr. Mem: Elks; Am. Legion; VFW; Masons. Mailing Add: Route 2, Box 2400, Port Angeles, Wash. 98362. (1967)

TRAYNOR, STUART J. D
b. Gillespie, Ill, 9/4/19; m. to Alacoque Smith T; c. six. Educ: St. Louis U, LL.B, 50. Polit. & Gov. Pos: Ill. State Rep. Bus. & Prof. Pos: Admitted to practice law, Mo. and Ill; Law Practice, 50-, Taylorville, Ill. Mil. Serv: Motor Torpedo Boat Squadron 13. Mem: Am. Legion; VFW; K. of C; Pres, Christian-Moultrie-Shelby Area Asn. for the Crippled. Rel: Catholic. Mailing Add: 302 E. Market, Taylorville, Ill. 62568. (1967)

TREADWAY, RICHARD FOWLE R
Mem, Mass. Rep. Finance Cmt.
b. Williamstown, Mass, 6/5/13; s. Lauris Goldsmith Treadway and Helen Fowle T; wid; c. Jonathan, James, Lauris Ann and David; m. 6/10/67 to Suzanne Clery Herter. Educ: Dartmouth Col, B.A, 36; Harvard Bus. Sch, Adv. Mgt. Course, 48; Phi Kappa Psi; Casque & Gauntlet Sr. Soc. Polit. & Govt. Pos: Mass. State Sen, 52-54; chmn. exec. cmt, Mass. State Rep. Cmt, 56-60; pres, Mass. Rep. Club, 59-60; mem, Boston Ward Five Rep. Cmt, 60-69; Rep. nat. committeeman, 62-64; chmn, Gov Adv. Cmt. on Tourism, 65-; former mem, Sturbridge Town Rep. Cmt; mem, Cambridge Ward Eight Rep. Cmt. and Mass. Rep. Finance Cmt, currently. Bus. & Prof. Pos: Pres, Treadway Inns Corp, 48-64, chmn, 64-69, dir, 69-; v.pres, Boit, Dalton & Church, Inc. and v.chmn. of bd, Harbor Nat. Bank, 65-67. Mil. Serv: Entered as Pvt, Marine Corps, 43, released as 1st Lt, 45. Rel: Episcopal. Mailing Add: 23 Sparks St, Cambridge, Mass. 02138.

TREADWELL, CLYDE TRAFFORD R
b. Danbury, Conn, 4/5/08; s. David Hendrick Treadwell and Alice Trafford T; m. 12/28/35 to Elinor Howes; c. David H, Clyde T. and Daryl H. (Mrs. Robert D. Bristol, Jr). Educ: Weslyan Univ; Beta Theta Pi. Polit. & Govt. Pos: Conn. State Rep. until 67; chmn, Brookfield Town Rep. Cmt, 63-65, treas, 61-63; chmn, Danbury Town Rep. Cmt, 48. Bus. & Prof. Pos: Personnel Supvr, Danbury Fair, Inc, 66; mortgage officer, Fairfield Co. Trust Co, 65. Mem: Wesleyan Univ. Fairfield Co. Alumni Club; Exchange Club; Union Lodge 40 AF&AM; Soc. of Real Estate Appraisers; Officers Club of Conn; State Police Asn. of Conn; Danbury Bridge Club; Candlewood Bridge Club; Red Cross. Rel: Congregational. Mailing Add: 65 Meadowbrook Rd, Brookfield, Conn. 06804. (1967)

TREADWELL, DONNIE E. 'DON' D
b. Holmes Co, Fla, 2/27/23; m. to Margaret Bradley; c. Gloria, Donna and Dwight. Educ: Univ. Fla, B.A.A, 58, M.A, 68. Polit. & Govt. Pos: Former Fla. State Rep. Bus. & Prof. Pos: Voc. agr. teacher. Mil. Serv: Army Air Corps, World War II; Army, Korean War; Maj, Fla. Nat. Guard, currently. Mem: V.chmn, Holmes Co. Develop. Cmn, 60-; v.chmn, Northwest Fla. Develop. Cmn, 62-63; pres, Holmes Co. Educ. Asn; v.pres, Dist. Fla. Educ. Asn. Gov. Award for Promoting Co. Rel: Baptist. Mailing Add: 28 Dale St, Pensacola, Fla. 32503.

TREAT, WILLIAM WARDWELL R
Mem, Rep. Nat. Cmt. from N.H.
b. Boston, Mass, 5/23/18; s. Joshua Treat, II and Clara Atwood T; m. 2/22/47 to Vivian S. Baker; c. Mary, Esther and Jonathan Buck, II. Educ: Univ. Maine, B.A, 40; Columbia Univ, 40-41; Boston Univ, 43-45; Harvard Univ, M.B.A, 47. Polit. & Govt. Pos: Judge, Seabrook Munic. Court, N.H, 52-; chmn, N.H. Rep. State Cmt, 54-58; mem, Rep. Nat. Cmt. from N.H, 54-58 & 60-, del-at-lg, 60; del, N.H. Constitutional Conv, 55 & 59; judge, Probate Court, Rockingham Co, N.H, 57-; prog. chmn, Rep. Nat. Conv, 64. Bus. & Prof. Pos: Partner, Treat Agency, 38-60; chmn. bd, Hampton Nat. Bank, 58-; mem, Bd. Incorporation, N.H. Savings Bank, 64- Publ: Author, Treat on Probate, 3 vols, 68; 'Introduction to Sales Management,' 48. Mem: Dir, N.H. Children's Aid Soc; N.H. Taxpayers Asn; AAA; Am, Maine, N.H. and Rockingham Co. Bar Asns; Acad. of Polit. Sci; A.L; Kiwanis; Harvard Club; St. Botolph Club; Asn. Munic. Judges. Awarded Claude Dewing Graton Prize, 39. Rel: Episcopal. Legal Res: 47 Park Ave, Hampton, N.H. 03842. Mailing Add: 36 High St, Box 498, Hampton, N.H. 03842.

TREBER, RICHARD E. D
Educ: Ball State Teachers' Col. Polit. & Govt. Pos: Ind. State Rep, 63-66; past pres, Grant Cty. Young Dems. Bus. & Prof. Pos: Pres, Treber Sheet Metal Works, Inc. Mem: Marion Contractors Asn; Aero Club; Optimist Club; FOP; Grant Cty. Plumbing and Heating Asn. Rel: Methodist; official bd. mem, First Methodist Church. Mailing Add: 3654 S. Washington St, Marion, Ind. 46592. (1967)

TREE, MARY ENDICOTT PEABODY D
Mem, U.S. Del. to UN
b. Lawrence, Mass, 4/12/17; d. Malcolm E. Peabody and Mary Parkman P; m. 7/28/47 to Ronald Tree; c. Frances, Penelope. Educ: La Petite Ecole Florentine, Florence, Italy, 34-35; Univ. Pa, 36-39. Hon. D.H.L, Russell Sage Col, 62, Hobart & William Smith Cols, 66 and Franklin Pierce Col, 68; LL.D, Univ. Pa, 64, Drexel Inst. Tech. and Bard Col, 65. Polit. & Govt. Pos: Mem, Hospitality Div, Inter-Am. Affairs, 42-43; mem, N.Y. State Dem. Cmt, 54-59; mem, Fair Housing Practices Panel, N.Y.C, 58, Cmn. Human Rights, 59-61; Dem. Adv. Coun, 59-60; mem, U.S. Del. to UN, 61-, U.S. Rep. to UN Human Rights Cmn, 61-64 and personal rep. of Secy. Gen. to UN Int. Sch, 66-; del-at-lg, N.Y. State Constitutional Conv, 67. Bus. & Prof. Pos: Researcher, Life Mag, 43-45; urbanist and lectr. and mem, Llewelyn-Davies & Assoc, City Planning Firm, currently. Mem: UNA, Asia, African-Am. Inst. Founder, Sydenham Hosp.(interracial). Rel: Episcopal. Mailing Add: 123 E. 79th St, New York, N.Y. 10021.

TREECE, JAMES LYLE R
b. Colorado Springs, Colo, 2/6/25; s. Lee Oren Treece and Ruth Smith T; m. 8/7/49 to Ruth Juljane Rome; c. James Van, Karen Gail, Teryl Amy, Jamilyn Jill and Carol Taryn. Educ: U.S.Naval Acad, 44-46; Mesa Col, A.S, 46; Univ. Colo, J.D, 50; Phi Alpha Delta. Polit. & Govt. Pos: Area chmn, Rep. Assocs, Colo, 56; spec. asst. attorney gen, Colo, 56-57, 62-63 & 65-66; dist. finance chmn, Denver Rep. Cent. Cmt, 58, city finance chmn, 59, dist. capt, 59-64 and city judiciary chmn, 62-68; campaign chmn, Sherman Finesilver, 62 and Cmt. for John Brooks, Jr, 64; mem, Colo. Rep. State Cent. Cmt, 63-65; mem, State Bd. Pub. Welfare, 63-68, chmn, 67-68; alternate del, Rep. Nat. Conv, 64; Denver campaign chmn, Joseph Shoemaker for Lt. Gov. Cmt, Colo, 66; mem, Gov. Cmt. Health and Med. Serv, 66-68; metrop. Chmn, Nixon for Pres. Cmt, 68; Munic. Judge, Greenwood Village, 68-69; U.S. Attorney, Dist. of Colo, 69- Bus. & Prof. Pos: Mem. firm, Yegge, Hall, Treece & Evans and predecessor firms, 51-69. Mil. Serv: Entered as Midn, Navy, 44, released, 46, after serv. in Naval Acad; Victory Medal; Am. Theatre Medal. Mem: Law Club; Fed, Arapahoe and Am. Bar Asns; Denver Bar Asn.(bd. trustees, 59-62, v.pres, 65-66); Colo. Bar Asn.(mem, chmn. and v.chmn, Negligence Trial Sect, 62-63, bd. gov, 68-); Defense Lawyers Asn; Denver Claimmen's Asn; Fed. Exec. Bd; chmn, State Bd. Soc. Serv, 68-69; Health Facilities Planning Coun; Southeast Denver Civic Asn.(chmn, 62-66); Metrop. Law Enforcement Asn; pres, U.S. Naval Acad. Alumni Asn, 69. Named to Trial Lawyers Hall of Fame; Selected Southeast Denver Pacemaker; Commun. Leader Award, 69. Rel: Lutheran. Mailing Add: 12 Cottonwood Lane, Littleton, Colo. 80120.

TREGONING, MARGOT A. D
Idaho State Rep.
b. Utica, Nebr, 5/20/15; d. William F. Schultz (deceased) and Martha DeBoer S. (deceased); m. to Edward Tregoning, wid; c. Diana and Terry. Educ: Kearney State Teachers Col, 1 year; St. Lukes Sch. Nursing, Spokane Wash, R.N. Polit. & Govt. Pos: Mem, Idaho Hosp. construction Adv. Coun, 66-68; Idaho State Rep, 66-; mem, Idaho Comprehensive Health Planning Cmt, Environ. Health Cmt, 68- Mem: Idaho State Nurses Asn.(bd. dirs, 58-62); Soroptimist Club. Honorary Recognition Award, Idaho State Nurses Asn, 69. Rel: Lutheran. Mailing Add: Box 188, Wardner, Idaho 83875.

TREMBLAY, WILFRED JOSEPH, SR. D
N.H. State Rep.
b. Can, 2/16/03; s. Charles Napoleon Tremblay and Mary Bilodeau T; m. 8/1/27 to Jeanne Marie Boisvert; c. Roger J, Roland E, Leon J, Victor A, Annette (Mrs. Langley), Louis J, Wilfred J, Jr, John J. and Louise M. Educ: Lebanon High Sch, 1 year. Polit. & Govt. Pos: Postmaster, Lebanon, N.H, 35-43; Cmnr, Lebanon Housing Authority, 65-; N.H. State Rep, 69- Bus. & Prof. Pos: Merchant, Lebanon, N.H, 43-51. Mem: Dir, Assoc. Grocers of N.H, 48-51; dir, Lebanon C. of C, 48; K. of C; pres, Holy Name Soc. Rel: Catholic. Mailing Add: 15 Eldridge St, Lebanon, N.H. 03766.

TREMPER, WILLIAM DAVID, JR. D
Chmn, Fayette Co. Dem. Cent. Cmt, Ind.
b. Connersville, Ind, 2/25/26; s. William David Tremper, Sr. and Esther Fattig T; m. 2/25/49 to Lois Lucille Voorhees; c. William David, III and Leanne. Educ: Harrisburg High Sch, Connersville, Ind, grad, 44. Polit. & Govt. Pos: Precinct committeeman, Fayette Co. Dem. Cent. Cmt, Ind, 52-64, treas, 59-62 and chmn, 62- Mil. Serv: Entered as A/S, Navy, 44, released as Signalman 2/C, 46, after serv. in Amphibs, Am. Theater and Asiatic-Pac. Korean Occupation. Mem: Am. Legion; F&AM; Shrine; 40 et 8; Scottish Rite; Amvets. Bronze Award, Boy Scouts. Rel: United Methodist. Mailing Add: 420 Fountain, Connersville, Ind. 47331.

TRENBEATH, WILLIAM GRANT R
N.Dak. State Sen.
b. Neche, N.Dak, 8/31/16; married; c. five. Educ: State Sch. of Sci. Polit. & Govt. Pos: N.Dak. State Sen, currently, chmn, Natural Resources Cmt. and Nat. Coun. Govs. Cmts. on Sugarbeet Indust, mem, Gov. Cmt. on Migratory Labor, N.Dak. State Senate. Bus. & Prof. Pos: Farmer. Mem: Officer in many agr. commodity and water develop. asns; Farm Bur; Shrine. Rel: Methodist. Mailing Add: Neche, N.Dak. 58265.

TRENOR, CHARLES ODIE D
b. Houston, Miss, 11/30/99; married. Polit. & Govt. Pos: Miss. State Rep, 56-67. Bus. & Prof. Pos: Acct; livestock; teacher. Mem: Mason; Rotary; Exchange; Lions; Chickasaw City Develop. Found; v.pres, Chickasaw City Fair Asn. Rel: Baptist. Mailing Add: Route 3, Box 70, Houston, Miss. 38851. (1967)

TRENT, DELMUS R
Chmn, Hamblen Co. Rep. Exec. Cmt, Tenn.
b. Treadway, Tenn, 3/10/18; s. Frank Trent and Dollie Greene T; m. 6/25/41 to Lois Kite; c. Patricia Ann, Mary Margaret and James Fred. Educ: Whitesburg High Sch. Grad. Polit. & Govt. Pos: Tenn. State Rep, 56-58 & 60-62; alternate del, Rep. Nat. Conv, 68; chmn, Hamblen Co. Rep. Exec. Cmt, Tenn, currently. Bus. & Prof. Pos: Owner, Trent Land & Auction Co, 44- Mem: Elks; Moose; Lions. Rel: Baptist. Legal Res: 1907 Magnolia Ave, Morristown, Tenn. 37814. Mailing Add: Box 517, Morristown, Tenn. 37814.

TREPANIER, ALBERT EDWARD D
b. Proctor, Vt, 4/8/22; s. Edward Henry Trepanier and Pauline Vigneau T; m. 10/4/42 to Jean Austin; c. Dianne and Debora. Educ: Tulane Univ, 41;

Ethan Allen Club. Polit. & Govt. Pos: Alderman, Burlington, Vt, 64; chmn. ways and means cmt, Vt. State Dem. Party, 64-68; Burlington Traffic Cmnr, 65-66; Burlington Airport Cmnr, 66-68; alternate del, Dem. Nat. Conv, 68; Burlington Police Cmnr, 68- Bus. & Prof. Pos: Pres, Chittenden Auto Dealers Asn, 67-68. Mil. Serv: Entered as Pvt, Army, 41, released as Capt, 46, after serv. in Seventh Inf. Div, Pac, 43-46; Res, 46-47, Ret; Silver Star; Bronze Star; Purple Heart with Four Oak Leaf Clusters; Presidential Citation; Combat Inf. Badge. Mem: DAV; Elks; Am. Legion; VFW; Univ. Vt. Centennial Club (v.pres). Rel: Catholic. Mailing Add: 4 Vine, Burlington, Vt. 05401.

TREPP, GLORIA F. R
V.Chmn, Dickinson Co. Rep. Party, Mich.
b. Chicago, Ill, 11/18/24; m. 5/10/52 to LaVern O. Trepp; c. Devereaux, Laird, Wendell, Erik and Andrea. Educ: Northwest. Univ, 2 years. Polit. & Govt. Pos: Co. del; v.chmn, Dickinson Co. Rep. Party, Mich, currently. Bus. & Prof. Pos: Housewife; mem. off. staff, Pine Mt. Lodge, winter seasons. Mem: Exec. secy, Dickinson Co. Coun. for the Arts; past pres, Iron Mountain Music Club; Matinee Musicale; Iron Mountain-Kingsford Women's Club; Alpha Chap, Phi Gamma Nu; active in Women's Hosp. League. Rel: Lutheran. Mailing Add: 1126 Bay Shore Dr, Iron Mountain, Mich. 49801.

TRETHEWAY, BERNICE RUTH R
V.Pres, Berrien Co. Rep. Cmt, Mich.
b. Baltic, Mich, 12/15/18; d. Bernard Manderfield and Florence M; m. 3/8/41 to Martin J. Tretheway; c. Martin J. and Janet R. Educ: Suomi Col, 2 years. Polit. & Govt. Pos: Clerk, Lincoln Twp, 63-; v.pres, Berrien Co. Rep. Cmt, 69- Bus. & Prof. Pos: Dep. co. treas, Houghton Co, 40-42; secy, Berrien Co. Chapter, Mich. Twp. Asn, 67-68. Mem: League of Women Voters; Lakeshore Lianas; Berrien Co. Rep. Women. Rel: Episcopal. Mailing Add: 5572 Donald St, Stevensville, Mich. 49127.

TRIBBITT, SHERMAN W. D
m. to Jeanne Webb; c. James, Carole and Tip. Educ: Goldey-Beacom Col. Polit. & Govt. Pos: Del. State Rep, 57-64, Speaker, Del. House of Rep, 59-65; Lt. Gov. of Del, 65-69. Bus. & Prof. Pos: Owner and operator, Odessa Supply Co. Mil. Serv: Navy, World War II; Presidential Unit Citation. Mem: Pres, Odessa Bldg. and Loan Asn; dir, Farms Mutual Ins. Co. and Farmer's Bank of Smyrna; Past Master, Union Lodge 5. Rel: Methodist. Mailing Add: Odessa Heights, Del. 19730.

TRIBBLE, JOSEPH JAMES R
b. Forsyth, Ga, 8/30/20; s. James Augustus Tribble and Frances Nixon T; m. 11/25/48 to Laura Jean Boddiford; c. James Nixon, Kathryn Tracy, Craig Rigdon and Carol Lisa. Educ: Ga. Inst. of Tech, B.S. in Mech. Eng, 42; Alpha Tau Omega. Polit. & Govt. Pos: Chmn, Chatham Co. Dem. Exec. Cmt, Ga, 54-57; state chmn, Ga. Draft Goldwater Cmt, 63-64; Ga. State Sen, 63-66; state chmn, Rep. Party of Ga, 64-65; del. and chmn. Ga. del, Rep. Nat. Conv, 64, del, 68; mem, Ga. Rep. State Exec. Cmt, Chatham Co. Rep. Exec. Cmt. and First Cong. Dist. Rep. Exec. Cmt, 64-; chmn, Rep. State Conv, 66; cand, U.S. Rep, Ga, 68. Bus. & Prof. Pos: Asst. plant supt, Union Bag-Camp Paper Corp, 46-65, power plant supt, 65- Mil. Serv: Entered as CPO, Maritime Serv, 43, released as Lt.(sg), 46, after serv. as Asst. Engr, Atlantic, Mediterranean, India and Pac, 43-45; N.Atlantic, Mediterranean, Pac. Theater and Attack Ribbons. Mem: Past v.pres, Savannah Jr. C. of C, Ga; Civitan Club. Rel: Methodist. Mailing Add: 402 Arlington Rd, Savannah, Ga. 31406.

TRICE, J. MARK R
Secy. for U.S. Senate Minority
b. Washington, D.C, 10/22/02; m. to Margaret Ann Linkins; c. Linda Jean Smith. Educ: Georgetown Univ, LL.B, 28. Polit. & Govt. Pos: Page, U.S. Senate, 16-19, secy. to Sgt-at-Arms, 19-29, dep. sgt-at-arms, 32-46, Secy. for Majority, 47-49, Secy. for Minority, 49-53 & 55-, Secy. of U.S. Senate, 53-54. Bus. & Prof. Pos: Attorney, 29-32. Mem: Cong. Country Club. Rel: Methodist. Legal Res: 5017 Worthington Dr, Westmoreland Hills, Md. 20016. Mailing Add: Office of the Secretary for Minority, S337 U.S. Senate, Capitol Bldg, Washington, D.C. 20510.

TRIGO, DENNIS New Progressive, P.R.
b. Rio Piedras, P.R, 5/23/38; s. Dionisio Trigo and Carmen M. Margarida T; m. 4/19/65 to Rosa Mercedes Ferraivoli; c. Mercedes Del Carmen and Maria Cristina. Educ: Georgetown Univ, B.A, 62; Phi Eta Mu. Polit. & Govt. Pos: Del, Dem. Nat. Conv, 68. Bus. & Prof. Pos: Pres, Caribbean Traveler Mag, currently; v.pres. and dir, Caribair Airlines, currently. Mil. Serv: Entered as 2nd Lt, Army, 62, released as 1st Lt, 64, after serv. in Inf. Antilles Command and Army Forces South. Command. Mem: Regional Export Expansion Coun; C. of C. Rel: Roman Catholic. Mailing Add: 552 Trigo St, Santorce, P.R. 00907.

TRIMARCHI, EUGENE JAMES D
Chmn, Indiana Co. Dem. Cmt, Pa.
b. Indiana, Pa, 7/4/22; s. Eugene James Trimarchi and Vera Carnabuci T; m. 5/1/48 to Clara Hosfeld Byers; c. Nell Vera and Julia Elizabeth. Educ: Pa. State Univ, B.A, 43. Polit. & Govt. Pos: Chmn, Indiana Co. Dem. Cmt, Pa, 48-; investr, Dept. of Labor and Indust, 55-58; del, Dem. Nat. Conv, 56; mem, Pa. Turnpike Cmn, 58-61; Secy, Commonwealth of Pa, 61-62. Bus. & Prof. Pos: Secy, Foremost Consumer Discount Corp, 63-, Greensburg Consumer Discount Corp, 65-; exec. v.pres, Conemaugh Valley Bank, 65- Mil. Serv: Entered as Seaman, Navy, 44, released as Lt.(jg), 45, after serv. in Amphibious Div, Pac. Rel: Roman Catholic. Mailing Add: R.R. 2, College Lodge Rd, Indiana, Pa. 15701. (1967)

TRIMBLE, JAMES WILLIAM D
b. Osage, Ark, 2/3/94; s. Matthew Allen Trimble and Anna MacFarlane T; m. 2/14/22 to Ruth Maples; c. James Kerry and Martha Carol (deceased). Educ: Univ. Ark; Skull & Torch. Polit. & Govt. Pos: U.S. Rep, 3rd Dist, Ark, 45-67; clerk and tax collector, Carroll Co, Ark, 4 yrs; dep. prosecuting attorney, 4th Judicial Dist, 2 yrs, prosecuting attorney, 8 yrs. and judge, 6 yrs. Mil. Serv: Army, World War I. Mem: Masonic orgns; Am. Legion; Lions; Odd Fellows; Farm Bur; Farmers Union. Rel: Methodist. Mailing Add: Berryville, Ark. 72616. (1967)

TRIPLETT, WILLIAM KARROL R
Mem, Calif. Rep. State Cent. Cmt.
b. Delano, Calif, 8/8/40; s. Blythe C. Triplett and Laura Stuhr T; m. 1/27/62 to Arlene Ann Jakovich; c. Stephen. Educ: Univ. Calif, Berkeley, A.B, 62; Hastings Col. Law, J.D, 65; Theta Xi. Polit. & Govt. Pos: Mem, Calif. Rep. State Cent. Cmt, 69-; mem, Kern Co. Rep. Cent. Cmt. Bus. & Prof. Pos: Acct, Ernst & Ernst, Oakland, Calif, 65-66; dep. co. counsel, Bakersfield, 66-67; dep. dist. attorney, 67-68; partner, Yinger & Triplett, Attorneys, 68- Mem: Calif. State and Kern Co. Bar Asns; Elks; Jaycees. Rel: Protestant. Legal Res: 2909 Staunton Court, Bakersfield, Calif. 93306. Mailing Add: 812 H St, Bakersfield, Calif. 93304.

TRIPP, JOHN THORNTON R
N.H. State Rep.
b. Farmington, N.H, 7/18/97; s. Charles Henry Tripp and Ella Bickford T; m. 12/11/20 to Blanche V. Ricker; c. Lorna E.(Mrs. Donald Clough). Educ: Rochester High Sch, N.H, grad, 15. Polit. & Govt. Pos: Clerk, U.S. Post Off. Dept, N.H, 20-64, retired 64; N.H. State Rep, 68-; mem, sch. bd, Rochester, N.H, currently. Mem: Grange (Past Master, N.H. State); Mason; Eastern Star (past Patron). Rel: Protestant. Mailing Add: 32 Adams Ave, Rochester, N.H. 03867.

TROJANOWSKI, ANTONI P. R
Chmn, Bridgeport Rep. Town Cmt, Conn.
b. Monroe, Conn, 6/29/23; s. Antoni Trojanowski and Helen Brukiewicz T; m. 9/21/46 to Helen Lemanski; c. Donna L. Educ: Univ. Conn, 2 years. Polit. & Govt. Pos: Bd. Fire Cmnrs, Bridgeport, Conn, 67-; chmn, bridgeport Rep. Town Cmt, currently. Bus. & Prof. Pos: Pres, Trojanowski Ins. Real Estate, 47- Mil. Serv: Entered as Seaman, Navy, 43, released as PO, 46, after serv. in Seabees, Pac. Theatre, 43-45. Mem: Independent Ins. Asn; Gr. Bridgeport Bd. Realtors; Polish Falcons; St. Michael's Holy Name; Football Hall of Fame; K. of C. Rel: Catholic. Legal Res: 70 Amos St, Bridgeport, Conn. 06606. Mailing Add: 1401 E. Main St, Bridgeport, Conn. 06608.

TROLLEY, RICHARD JOSEPH D
Mayor, Taylor, Mich.
b. Detroit, Mich, 11/15/29; s. Vincent Trolley and Adeline Quatro T; m; c. Paula, Pamela and Deborah. Educ: Wayne State Univ, B.A. in Econ; Wayne State Univ. Law Sch, 1 year. Polit. & Govt. Pos: Trustee, Taylor Twp. Sch. Bd, Mich, 56-57, treas, 57-59, secy, 59-61, pres, 61-63; twp. trustee, Taylor, 63, twp. treas, 63-67, twp. supvr, 67-68; del, Dem. Nat. Conv, 68; mayor, Taylor, 68-; mem, 15th Cong. Dist. Dem. Party, currently. Bus. & Prof. Pos: Partner, C & T Underwriters, Allen Park, Mich, 64-; salesman, AAA. Mem: Mich. Asn. of Independent Ins. Agents; Rotary; Great Soc. Dem. Club; Metrop. Club; past pres, Wayne Co. Treas. Asn; former dir, Wayne Co. Asn. of Sch. Bd. Rel: Catholic. Legal Res: 21875 Superior, Taylor, Mich. 48180. Mailing Add: 23555 Goddard Rd, Taylor, Mich. 48180.

TROM, SOPHUS VERNON R
b. Kindred, N.Dak, 6/26/01; s. Olaf K. Trom and Olava Johnson T; m. 9/9/23; c. four. Educ: N.Dak. State Sch. of Sci. Polit. & Govt. Pos: City auditor, Casselton, N.Dak, 58-; N.Dak. State Rep, 59-61. Mem: Commun. Club; Mason. Rel: Lutheran. Mailing Add: Casselton, N.Dak. 58012.

TROMBLEY, MICHAEL JEROME R
b. Bay City, Mich, 12/10/33; s. Clare F. Trombley and Sarha Ingersol T; div; c. Peter D. and Tad F. Educ: Menlo Col, Calif; Stanford Univ; Univ. of Mo; Blue Key; Phi Delta Phi. Polit. & Govt. Pos: Chmn, Boone Co. Rep. Cmt, Mo, 64-66. Bus. & Prof. Pos: Attorney, 59- Mil. Serv: Entered as 2nd Lt, Marine Corps, 55, released as 1st Lt, 57. Mem: Mo. and Am. Bar Asns; Am. Judicature Soc; Mason, Shriner. Rel: Episcopal. Mailing Add: 1103 S. Glenwood, Columbia, Mo. 65201. (1967)

TROTT, BERNARD L. R
Chmn, Fourth Judicial Dist. Rep. Party, Colo.
b. Kearney, Nebr, 10/29/23; s. Lewis Walker Trott and Eleanor Knutson T; m. 4/8/44 to Betty Jane Moore; c. Jeffrey Bernard and Diane Elaine. Educ: Nebr. Wesleyan Univ, B.A, 47; Univ. Mich. Law Sch, J.D, 49; Phi Kappa Phi; Pi Kappa Delta; Crescent. Polit. & Govt. Pos: City councilman, Mission, Kans, 52-54; chmn, Fourth Judicial Dist. Rep. Party, Colo, 61-; mem, El Paso Co. Rep. Cent. Cmt, 61-; del, Rep. Co, State, Cong. and Judicial Dist. Conv, 64-66 & 68; mem, El Paso Co. Rep. Exec. Cmt, Colo, 65-; alternate del, Rep. Nat. Conv, 68. Mil. Serv: Entered as Pvt, Army Air Corps, 43, released as 2nd Lt, 45, after serv. in A-26 Bombardment Group, U.S, Capt, Res, 45-57. Publ: Various articles, Mich. Law Rev, 48-49. Mem: Am. and Colo. Bar Asns; El Paso Co. Bar Asn.(trustee, 64-65); Garden of the Gods Club; Broadmoor Golf Club; Torch Club; Winter Night Club. Rel: Congregational. Mailing Add: 23 Broadmoor Ave, Colorado Springs, Colo. 80906.

TROTTER, DAN R
b. Columbia, S.C, 11/25/29; s. Daniel Jacob Trotter and Lillian Lewis T; m. 10/5/50 to Patricia Williams; c. Dan Lewis, Richard Williams and Christina. Educ: Univ. South Carolina, B.S. in Elec. Eng, 49. Polit. Pos: Alternate del, Rep. Nat. Conv. and pres, Sumter Co. Conv, S.C, 64; treas, S.C. Rep. Party, 63-64; chmn, Sumter Co. Rep. Party, 62-64. Govt. Pos: Mem, Housing Bd. of Adjustment, Sumter, S.C, 64-65. Bus. & Prof. Pos: Pres, Trotter Construct. Co, 54-66. Mem: Kiwanis; Sunset Country Club. Rel: Presbyterian. Legal Res: 42 Buford St, Sumter, S.C. 29150. Mailing Add: P.O. Box 236, Sumter, S.C. 29150. (1967)

TROTTER, WILLIAM PERRY D
Dem. Nat. Committeeman, Ga.
b. Manchester, Ga, 11/2/19; s. McKie M. Trotter and Tudor Perry T; m. 8/5/50 to Julia Thomason; c. Jefferson William and William Perry, Jr. Educ: Vanderbilt Univ, B.A, 41; Univ. Ga, LL.B, 47; Phi Delta Phi; Omicron Delta Kappa; Phi Delta Theta. Polit. & Govt. Pos: Ga. State Sen, 51-52 & 57-58; Ga. State Rep, 59; dir. of Pub. Safety, Ga, 59-61; Dem. Nat. Committeeman, 62- Bus. & Prof. Pos: Troup Co. Attorney, 61- Mil. Serv: Entered as Aviation Cadet, Air Force, 42, released as Maj, 46, after serv. in Troop Carrier Command, Asiatic-Pac. Theater, 44-45; Air Medal; Philippine Liberation Me-

dal; Six Pac. Campaign Ribbons. Mem: Ga. and Am. Bar Asns; VFW; Elks. Prfnl. Baseball, Little Rock, Ark, 41. Rel: Episcopal. Mailing Add: 323 Lane Circle, La Grange, Ga. 30240.

TROUPE, JAMES PAL D
Mo. State Rep.
b. Dudley, Ga, 12/4/09; s. Charley Henry Troupe and Mary Blanche Williams T; m. 2/5/27 to Gertrude Thompson; c. Ernestine (Mrs. Hinton), James, Jr, Delores (Mrs. Warren), Marvin, Donald, Wallace, Vernon and Newton. Educ: N.East. High Sch, Detroit, Mich, grad, 26. Polit. & Govt. Pos: Cmnr, St. Louis Housing Authority, Mo, 51-54; Mo. State Rep, 54-, chmn. Labor Cmt, Mo. State House of Rep, 67-; committeeman, Fifth Ward St. Louis Dem. City Cent. Cmt, 64-68. Bus. & Prof. Pos: Rep, AFL-CIO, USW, 44. Mem: Frontier Internal Club; NAACP; USW Am. Union. Rel: Catholic. Mailing Add: 1538 Hogan St, St. Louis,Mo. 63106.

TROUT, BARBARA ANN R
Mem, Colo. Rep. State Cent. Cmt.
b. Omaha, Nebr, 1/18/27; d. Leroy Glen Lambert and Bernice Wilcox L; m. 6/17/50 to Norman Lee Trout; c. Cheryl, Stanley and Brian. Educ: Univ. S.Dak, B.A, 49; Alpha Phi. Polit. & Govt. Pos: Rep. committeewoman, precinct 606, Jefferson Co, Colo, 61-65 and precinct 412, 65-69; visitor's aid, Colo. State Legis, 63-64 and messenger 69; mem, Colo. Rep. State Cent. Cmt, 65-67 and 69-; chmn. spec. serv. cmt, Jefferson Co, Colo, 66-68; sponsor, Lakewood High Sch. TARS, 66-68. Rel: Episcopal. Mailing Add: 11882 W. 27th Dr, Lakewood, Colo. 80215.

TROUTMAN, FRANK, JR. R
Co. Cmnr, Richmond Co, Ga.
b. Atlanta, Ga, 11/1/34; s. Frank Troutman and Mary Frank Satterfield T; m. 1/22/55 to Joan Castleberry; c. Lee, Mary Stewart, Katherine and Frank, III. Educ: Univ. Ga, A.B, 56, LL.B, 58; Omicron Delta Kappa; Phi Beta Kappa; Phi Delta Phi; Sigma Alpha Epsilon. Polit. & Govt. Pos: V.chmn, Richmond Co. Rep. Party, Ga, 66; first v.chmn. and acting state chmn, Rep. Party of Ga, 66; del, Rep. Nat. Conv, 68; co. cmnr, Richmond Co, 69- Bus. & Prof. Pos: Pres, Castleberry's Food Co, Augusta, 65- Received Young Man of The Year. Richmond Co. Jaycees, 69. Rel: Episcopal. Legal Res: 3030 Bransford Rd, Augusta, Ga. 30904. Mailing Add: P.O. Box 1010, Augusta, Ga. 30903.

TROUTT, TERRY L. D
b. Kennett, Mo, 11/1/19; married; c. Linda Ann, Connie Lee. Polit. & Govt. Pos: Mich. State Rep, 64-66; mem. of the State Bd. of Equalization; supvr, Romulus Twp; chmn, Wayne Co. Bd. of Supvrs. Bus. & Prof. Pos: Mgr, Metro Motel Apts. Mil. Serv: World War II. Mem: Chmn, 16th Dem. Cong. Orgn; VFW; Amvets; Wayne Co. Sportsman's Club. Rel: Baptist. Mailing Add: 16365 Farnum St, Romulus, Mich. 48174. (1967)

TROWBRIDGE, C. ROBERTSON R
N.H. State Rep.
b. Salem, Mass, 3/31/32; s. Cornelius P. Trowbridge and Margaret Murdock Laird T; m. 7/7/55 to Lorna Sagendorph; c. James R, Cornelia T, Beatrix S. and Philip R. Educ: Princeton Univ, A.B, 54; Harvard Univ, LL.B, 57. Polit. & Govt. Pos: N.H. State Rep, currently, chmn, Pub. Works Cmt, mem, Exec. Cmt. Citizens Task Force, and chmn, Cheshire Co. Del, N.H. State House of Rep. Bus. & Prof. Pos: V.Pres, Yankee, Inc; publisher, Yankee Magazine and the Old Farmer's Almanac. Mem: Rotary. Rel: Episcopal. Mailing Add: Box 271, Dublin, N.H. 03444.

TROWBRIDGE, ELTON D
Wyo. State Rep.
b. Holt Co, Nebr, 12/15/05; m. to Irene; c. Two. Educ: Nebr. Wesleyan Univ; Univ. of Nebr. Polit. & Govt. Pos: Wyo. State Rep, currently. Bus. & Prof. Pos: Ranching and ins. Mem: Lions; Farm Bur; Wyo. Stock Growers Asn. Rel: Presbyterian. Mailing Add: P.O. Box 547, Saratoga, Wyo. 82331.

TROXEL, OLIVER LEONARD, JR.
U.S. Ambassador, Zambia
b. Sherburn, Minn, 9/29/19; s. Oliver Leonard Troxel and Rinice Annette Nanninga T; m. 3/10/56 to Holly Eva Hirsch. Educ: George Washington Univ, A.B, 40; Col. of William and Mary, M.A, 41. Polit. & Govt. Pos: Admin. Asst, War Dept, 41-43; For. Serv. Officer, Dept. of State, 46-, Second Secy-Vice Consul, Am. Embassy, Manila, Philippines, 46-48, Tel Aviv, Israel, 48-51, Int. Economist, Dept. of State, 51-57, First Secy-Consul, Am. Embassy, Addis Ababa, Ethiopia, 57-59, Army War Col, Carlisle Barracks, Pa, 59-60, Int. Rels. Officer, Dept. of State, 60-63, Dep. Chief of Mission and Consul Gen, Am. Embassy, Accra, Ghana, 63-66, Dir, Off. Research and Analysis for Africa, Dept. of State, 66-69 and U.S. Ambassador Extraordinary and Plenipotentiary, Zambia, 69- Mil. Serv: Entered as Pvt, Army, 43, released as T/Sgt, 46, after serv. in Inf, Mediterranean Theatre, 44-46; Bronze Star. Mem: Am. Soc. of Int. Law. Dept. of State Honor Award, 56, Superior Honor Award, 66. Legal Res: 2512 14th Ave. Ct, Greeley, Colo. 80631. Mailing Add: c/o Dept. of State, Washington, D.C. 20521.

TROXELL, LEONA MAE R
Mem. Exec. Cmt, Nat. Fedn. Rep. Women
b. Johnstown, N.Y, 4/22/13; d. Rev. Frank Anderson, D.D. and Clara Bergen A; m. 12/15/51 to Col. Nolan Troxell. Educ: Drake Univ, B.A, 34, M.A, 38; Phi Beta Kappa; Phi Sigma Iota; Psi Chi; Alpha Xi Delta; Alpha Lambda Delta. Polit. & Govt. Pos: Serv. club dir, U.S. Army Spec. Servs, 41-43; dir, U.S. Army Spec. Servs. Arts & Crafts, ETO, 48-52; pres, Faulkner Co. Rep. Women's Club, 54-56 and White Co. Rep. Women's Club, 62-63; twp. committeeman, Faulkner and White Co, 54-; v.chairwoman, Faulkner Co, 56-61; second v.pres, Ark. Fedn. Rep. Women, 59-63; secy-treas, Second Cong. Dist, 62-64; Ark. Pub. Dir, 10th and 11th Annual Women's Spring Conf; pres, Ark. Fedn. of Rep. Women, 63-67; mem. bd. dir, Nat. Fedn. Rep. Women, 63-, mem. nominating cmt, 67 and mem. exec. cmt, 67-; mem, Rep. State Exec. Cmt. and Rep. State Cent. Cmt, 63-; alternate del, Rep. Nat. Conv, 64; v.chairwoman, White Co. Rep, 64- Bus. & Prof. Pos: Asst. dean of women and instr, French and Spanish, Drake Univ, 35-40; asst. house supvr, Katharine Gibbs Sch, Boston, Mass, 40-41; hosp. recreation worker, Am. Red Cross, 43-45; dean of women, Drake Univ, 46-48. Mem: Former mem, State and Nat. Asn. of Deans of Women; PEO; Am. Asn. of Univ. Women (state legis. chmn, 69-); Eastern Star; Ark. Div, state bd. dir. and exec. cmt, Am. Cancer Soc; Am. Legion Auxiliary; Home Demonstration Club; Alpha Xi Delta Alumnae Club; Ark. Art Center; Drake Univ. Alumni; VFW Auxiliary; Ark. Asn. of Ment. Health. Chmn, Gov. Cmn. on the Status of Women, 67- Rel: Baptist, Sunday Sch. Teacher. Mailing Add: P.O. Box 61, Rose Bud, Ark. 72137.

TROXELL, RICHARD KIMBALL Constitution Party
Chmn, Tex. State Constitution Party Exec. Cmt.
b. Tulsa, Okla, 9/9/28; s. John Nill Troxell and Janice Meredith Kimball T; m. 12/28/49 to Betty Lynn Riedel; c. Mildred Ann, Laura Lynn, Richard, Jr. and David Riedel. Educ: South. Methodist Univ, B.A, 50; Delta Tau Delta. Polit. & Govt. Pos: Chmn, Tex. State Constitution Party Exec. Cmt, 66- Bus. & Prof. Pos: Owner, Troxell & Assocs, Advert, 50. Mem: Kiwanis; South. Methodist. Univ. Alumni Asn; Asn. of Indust. Advertisers; Raquet Club. Rel: Methodist. Legal Res: 12134 Broken Bough, Houston, Tex. 77024. Mailing Add: P.O. Box 52061, Houston, Tex. 77052.

TROXELL, SAMUEL ARTHUR R
N.C. State Rep.
b. Lorane, Pa, 11/24/92; s. John Eshelman Troxell and Sarah Ann Hertzog T; m. 12/1/20 to Trula May Bost; c. Sarah Catherine (Mrs. Greene). Educ: Catawba Col, A.B, 16; Theol. Sem. United Church of Christ, Pa, B.D, 19. Polit. & Govt. Pos: Mayor, Rockwell, N.C, 57-63; N.C. State Rep, 67- Bus. & Prof. Pos: Minister, United Church of Christ, 19-59; spec. agent, John Hancock Life Ins, 59- Mem: Lt. gov, N.C. Dist, Civitan Club, 58-59; C. of C, Salisbury, Rowan Co. and N.C. Rel: United Church of Christ. Mailing Add: P.O. Box 65, Rockwell, N.C. 28138.

TROY, MATTHEW JOSEPH, JR. D
City Councilman, N.Y.C.
b. Brooklyn, N.Y, 9/23/29; s. Matthew Joseph Troy, Sr. and Maude Gallagher T; m. 9/4/54 to Dolores G. Saville; c. Dolores, Jr, Matthew J, III, Maureen V, Mary P, Therese C, Michael C, Kevin F. and Catherine M. Educ: Georgetown Univ, A.B, 51; Fordham Univ. Sch. of Law, LL.B, 56. Polit. & Govt. Pos: Dem. dist. leader, Queens Co, N.Y, 60-; chmn, Queens Co. Dem. Cmt, 62-63; city councilman, N.Y.C, 64-; del, Dem. Nat. Conv, 68. Bus. & Prof. Pos: Attorney, Troy, Saville & Troy, Law Firm, 63- Mil. Serv: Entered as Pvt, Army, 51, released as Cpl, 53, after serv. in Mil. Police, Asian Theatre, 52-53; 1st Lt, Res, 57- Rel: Roman Catholic. Legal Res: 230-36 88th Ave, Queens Village, N.Y. 11427. Mailing Add: 218-29 Jamaica Ave, Queens Village, N.Y. 11428.

TRUAN, CARLOS FLORES D
Tex. State Rep.
b. Kingsville, Tex, 6/9/35; s. Charles Truan and Santos Flores T; m. 6/21/63 to Elvira Munguia; c. Carlos, Jr, Veronica and Rene. Educ: Tex. A&I Univ, B.B.A, 59; Nat. John Cardinal Newman Hon. Soc; Newman Club; Bus. Club; Student Coun. Adv. Bd. Polit. & Govt. Pos: Tex. State Rep, Dist. 45, Place 2, 69- Bus. & Prof. Pos: Field underwriter, N.Y. Life Ins. Co, Corpus Christi, 60- Publ: Tex. Bilingual Educ. Act, 69. Mem: Nat. Asn. of Life Underwriters; Tex. State Adv. Cmt; U.S. Civil Rights Cmn; Tex. Educ. Agency Adv. Cmt. on Bilingual Educ; LULAC; mem, bd. dirs, Southwest Coun. of La Raza, Inc; Am. G.I. Forum; Sertoma. Outstanding Young Man of 1967, Jaycees; N.Y. Life's Man of the Year, 1967 for S. Tex; LULAC Man of the Year, 1966; Tex. Outstanding LULAC Dist. Dir. of the Year, 1967. Rel: Roman Catholic. Legal Res: 3821 Marion St, Corpus Christi, Tex. 78415. Mailing Add: P.O. Box 2547, Corpus Christi, Tex. 78403.

TRUAX, COMBS CRAIG R
b. Gosport, Ind, 12/28/28; s. Edward Combs Truax and Elva Craig T; m. 2/13/53 to Ellamae J. Whitmire; c. Debra, Edward, Thomas, Mary and David. Educ: Ind. State Univ, 48-50. Polit. & Govt. Pos: Pub. rels. dir, Pa. State Rep. Cmt, 56-59, exec. dir, 59-62; chmn, Pa. State Rep. Party, 63-68. Mil. Serv: Entered as Pvt, Army, 46, released as Sgt, 48, after serv. in 34th Inf. Regiment, 24th Div; recalled as Seaman, Navy, 51, released as Journalist 3/C, 54, after serv. in Naval Training Command, Bainbridge, Md, 51-54. Rel: Protestant. Mailing Add: 2707 N. Second St, Harrisburg, Pa. 17110. (1967)

TRUE, JAMES BENJAMIN 'JIM' D
Miss. State Rep.
b. New Orleans, La, 12/20/05; married. Polit. & Govt. Pos: Mem, Citizens Coun, Miss; Miss. State Rep, currently. Bus. & Prof. Pos: Pres, Jim True & Co, Inc, currently. Mem: F&AM; Consistory; SAR; Gulfport Chap, Gulf Coast Jr. Col. Dist. Alumni Asn; C. of C; John Birch Soc. Mailing Add: 1110 31st Ave, Gulfport, Miss. 39501. (1967)

TRUEBLOOD, AILEEN NASH 'BOBBIE' R
Mem, Calif. Rep. State Cent. Cmt.
b. Exeter, Devonshire, Eng, 10/30/24; d. Ernest Arthur Alfred Montague Nash and Florence Mary Townsend N; m. 7/10/46 to Fred Willette Trueblood, Jr; c. Fred Willette, III, John Christopher, Michael Devon and Kyltie Anne. Educ: Bishop Blackall Sch. for Girls, Exeter, Devonshire, Eng. Polit. & Govt. Pos: Rep. and campaign chmn, Lt. Gov. Ed Reinecke, Santa Clarita Valley, Calif, 64-; mem, Newhall Saugus Rep. Campaign Coun, 65-; mem, Calif. Rep. State Cent. Cmt, 67-; former first v.pres. and corresponding secy, Newhall-Saugus Rep. Women's Club, pub. rels. chmn, currently; first v.pres, United Rep. of Newhall-Saugus; campaign chmn, Councilman James B. Potter, campaign co-chmn, Assemblyman Newt Russell, Santa Clarita Valley, 69. Bus. & Prof. Pos: Soc. ed. and columnist, Newhall Signal, Newhall, Calif, 54-68 and Record Press, Newhall, Calif, 68-69; columnist, View from Valencia, Valencia, Calif, 68- Mil. Serv: Vol. in Royal Observer Corps, World War II, Eng. Mem: Beta Sigma Phi (past chap. pres); bd. mem, Newhall-Saugus-Valencia Asn. of Fine Arts, Inc; bd. mem, William S. Hart High Sch. Dist. Scholarship Found, 65-69. Rel: Episcopal. Mailing Add: 23244 W. Eighth St, Newhall, Calif. 91321.

TRUEX, RUTH OLMSTED R
Conn. State Rep.
b. East Hartford, Conn, 8/10/12; d. Horace Bigelow Olmsted and Julia Williams O; m. 7/6/35 to Edward Hamilton Truex; c. Ann Elizabeth (Mrs. Steele),

Joan Barton, Edward H. and Richard H. Educ: Mt. Holyoke, A.B, 32 and A.M, 34. Polit. & Govt. Pos: Secy, Wethersfield Conn. Bd. Educ, 56-64, chmn, 64-66; Conn. State Rep, 23rd Dist, 67- Bus. & Prof. Pos: Research asst, Mt. Holyoke Col, 32-34, mem. faculty, 34-37; research asst, Inst. of Int. Studies, Yale Univ, 38-41. Rel: Protestant. Mailing Add: 37 Farmingdale Rd, Wethersfield, Conn. 06109.

TRUJILLO, LARRY ENOCH D
b. Fort Garland, Colo, 8/9/40; s. Arthur O. Trujillo and Rose Atencio T; m. 8/10/63 to Ellynn Bailey; c. Renae Ellynn, Sharon Rose and Larry E, Jr. Educ: McCurdy High Sch, grad; Southwest. Inst. of Criminology course for Criminal Invest, completed, 64. Polit. & Govt. Pos: Probation officer, Pueblo, Colo, 64-; del, Third Cong. Dist. Dem. Conv, 66; del, Pueblo Co. Dem. Conv, 66 & 68; dist. capt, Pueblo Dem. Party, 67; del, Colo. State Dem. Conv, 68; alternate del, Dem. Nat. Conv, 68. Mil. Serv: Entered as Airman 3/C, Air Force, 58, released as Airman 1/C, 62, after serv. in Strategic Air Command; Appreciation Award from Comdr. Hq. Squadron 40th Bomb Wing for Outstanding Serv. Mem: Colo. Probation, Parole & Corrections Asn; Colo. Adult Probation Asn; Sunrise Lions; Footprinters; Travelers Protective Asn.(second v.pres. for state); Citizens Serv. Orgn.(past pres, 67); Am. GI Forum. Citizens Serv. Award, Citizens Serv. Orgn, 67; Award of Appreciation, Pueblo Police Dept. Rel: Protestant. Mailing Add: 1105 Catalpa, Pueblo, Colo. 81001.

TRUMAN, HARRY S D
b. Lamar, Mo, 5/8/84; s. John Anderson Truman and Martha Ellen Young T; m. 6/28/19 to Bess Wallace; c. Mary Margaret (Mrs. Clifton Daniel). Educ: Field Artil. Sch, Ft. Sill, Okla, 17-18; Kansas City Sch. of Law, 23-25. Polit. & Govt. Pos: Judge, Jackson Co. Court, Mo, 22-24, presiding judge, 26-34; U.S. Sen, Mo, 34-45; chmn, Spec. Cmt. to Investigate Nat. Defense Prog; Vice President, United States, 45, President, 45-53. Bus. & Prof. Pos: With Kansas City Star, 01; timekeeper for R.R. contractor, 02; with Nat. Bank of Commerce and Union Nat. Bank, Kansas City, 03-05; operated family farm, 06-17. Mil. Serv: Army, World War I, served as 1st Lt, Battery F and Capt, Battery D, 129th Field Artil, 35th Div, AEF, discharged as Maj, 19; Col, Field Artil, Army Res, 27- Publ: Years of Decision, Vol. I, 55; Years of Trial and Hope, Vol. II, 56. Mem: Mason (Past Grand Master, Mo). Rel: Baptist. Mailing Add: 219 N. Delaware St, Independence, Mo. 64055. (1967)

TRUMAN, THEODORE D
b. Biddeford, Maine, 12/11/29; s. Peter Throumoulos; single. Educ: Maine Maritime Acad, B.S, 51. Polit. & Govt. Pos: Trustee, Maine Maritime Acad; mem, Dem. 500 Club, Maine; former Maine State Rep. Bus. & Prof. Pos: Owner, Lighthouse Motor Inn, Truman & Co. Instnl. Foods and Fed. Realty Co. Mil. Serv: Merchant Serv, 51-56, Korean Conflict; reentered as Ens, Naval Res, 56, released as Lt, 58, after serv. in Suez Crises, 56; Lt. Comdr, Naval Res. Mem: Mason; Shrine; Elks; Ahepa; Navy League. Rel: Greek Orthodox. Legal Res: 28 Birch St, Biddeford, Maine 04005. Mailing Add: 67 Alfred St, Biddeford, Maine 04005. (1967)

TSAPIS, CALLIE D
b. Weirton, W.Va, 4/26/23; d. Louis S. Tsapis and Stella Mastromichalis T; single. Educ: W.Va. Univ, B.A, 45; W.Va. Col. Law, LL.B, 48; Phi Beta Kappa; W.Va. Law Quart. Staff. Polit. & Govt. Pos: Asst. Prosecutor, Hancock Co, W.Va, 52-56; mem, W.Va. Dem. State Exec. Cmt, 57-65; W.Va. State Del, Hancock Co, 59-65 & 67-69. Mem: W.Va, Am. and Hancock Co. Bar Asns; W.Va. State Bar; Rebekah; Jefferson Grange; Bus. & Prfnl. Women's Club. Rel: Greek Orthodox. Mailing Add: 103 School St, Weirton, W.Va. 26062. (1967)

TSCHETTER, MENNO D
S.Dak. State Rep.
b. Yale, S.Dak, 10/18/19; s. John M. Tschetter and Mary M. Hofer T; m. 2/7/49 to Betty Jean Johnson; c. Neil Jon, Gary Eugene and Bruce Elden. Educ: Huron Col, B.A, 49; Huron Col. Football Team, 4 yrs. Polit. & Govt. Pos: S.Dak. State Rep, Beadle Co, 64- Bus. & Prof. Pos: Pres, Chicago and North Western Rwy. Fed. Credit Union, 62- Mil. Serv: Entered as Seaman, Navy, 42, released as Yeoman 1/C, 46, after serv. in N.Atlantic, 27 months; Am. Theater Ribbon; Good Conduct Medal. Mem: Pres, Izaak Walton League, 64-65; pres, Huron Lodge 809, Brotherhood of Rwy. Clerks and Local Griever; Cub Scouts; Boy Scouts. Mailing Add: R.R.1, Box 248, Huron, S.Dak. 57350.

TSOMPANAS, PAUL LEE R
b. Grove City, Pa, 1/20/37; s. Nick Tsompanas and Amelia DeSalvo T; m. 8/22/59 to Mary Eva Patron; c. Michelle, John, Stephen and Michael. Educ: Pa. State Univ, B.A, 58; Sigma Delta Chi; Alpha Phi Delta. Polit. & Govt. Pos: Admin. asst. to U.S. Rep. Bob Wilson, Calif, 66- Bus. & Prof. Pos: Reporter and city ed, Clovis News-Journal, Clovis, N.Mex, 60-61; reporter, San Diego Eve. Tribune, Calif, 61-64; cong. correspondent, Copley News Serv, Wash, D.C, 64-66; co-publisher, Wash. Waterline, Wash, D.C, 67- Mil. Serv: Entered as Ens, Navy, 58, released as Lt.(jg), 60, after serv. in U.S.S. Cabildo as Commun. Officer, 58-60. Publ: Articles in various popular trade journals. Mem: Nat. Press Club; Bull Elephants of Capitol Hill; Rutherford Civic Asn. E.H. Shaffer Award, N.Mex. Press Asn; Copley Journalism Award. Rel: Catholic. Legal Res: San Diego, Calif. Mailing Add: 4602 Marley Rd, Fairfax, Va. 22030.

TSUTRAS, FRANK GUS D
b. Williamson, W.Va, 10/18/29; s. Gus Tsutras and Karnitia Savas T; m. 6/20/54 to Helen Athanasios Kouros; c. Constandinos 'Dean'. Educ: W.Va. Univ, B.S. in Bus. Admin, 51, grad. study, 55-57; Sigma Phi Epsilon. Polit. & Govt. Pos: Field coordinator, ARA, 61-65; admin. asst. to U.S. Rep. Kee, W.Va, 66- Bus. & Prof. Pos: Mgr, Merchants Prod. Div, Williamson Supply Co, 57-58; mgr. and dir, Tug Valley C. of C, 58-61. Mil. Serv: 1st Lt, Air Force, 51-53, serv. in 3800 Motor Vehicle Squadron, Sch. of Aviation Med. and Off. Spec. Invests; Capt, Air Force Res, 57-58. Mem: Moose; Elks; Ahepa; Am. Legion. Rel: Greek Orthodox. Legal Res: Williamson, W.Va. 25661. Mailing Add: 3112 N. Rosser St, Alexandria, Va. 22300. (1967)

TUBB, THOMAS JEFFERSON D
Chmn, Clay Co. Dem. Exec. Cmt, Miss.
b. Amory, Miss, 8/14/99; s. Brice Milton Tubb and Iler Rebecca West T; m. 4/13/29 to Sarah Frances Spalding; c. Judith (Mrs. Noel) and Thomas Murray. Educ: Univ. Miss, B.S, 21, LL.B, 22; Phi Delta Phi. Polit. & Govt. Pos: Mem, Clay Co. Dem. Exec. Cmt, 26-, chmn, 32-; mem, Miss. Dem. Exec. Cmt, 32-64, chmn, 44-56; mem, Legal Educ. Adv. Cmt. State Miss, 54-56; mem. bd. trustees, Inst. Higher Learning State Miss, 56-64, pres, 62-64. Bus. & Prof. Pos: Mem. bd. dirs, Clay Co. Fed. Savings and Loan Asn, 35-; mem. bd. dirs, First Nat. Bank, 44- Mil. Serv: Army, 18, Pvt, serv. in Students Army Training Corps, Univ. Miss. Mem: Clay Co. Miss. State and Am. Bar Asns; Miss. Defense Lawyers Asn; Miss. Bar Found; Int. Asn. Ins. Counsel; Defense Res. Inst; F&AM; Odd Fellows; Am. Legion; Rotary; C. of C. Rel: Christian Church N.Am. Legal Res: 521 Grove St, West Point, Miss. 39773. Mailing Add: P.O. Box 324, West Point, Miss. 39773.

TUBBY, ROGER W.
U.S. Rep. to European Off. of UN, Geneva, Switzerland
b. Greenwich, Conn, 12/10/10; m. to Anne Williams; c. Four. Educ: Yale Univ, B.A, 33; Yale Law Sch; London Sch. of Econ. Polit. & Govt. Pos: Info. specialist, Bd. of Econ. Warfare, 42-44; dir. of info, For. Econ. Admin, 44-45; asst. to adminstr, For. Econ. Admin, 45; dir. of info. for Off. of Int. Trade, Dept. of Commerce, 45-46; press officer, exec. asst. for press rels, State Dept, 46-50; asst. press secy, press secy, President Truman, 50-53; asst. to Adlai Stevenson Presidential Campaign, 56; Asst. Secy. of State for Pub. Affairs, 61-62; U.S. Rep. to European Off. of UN, Geneva, 62- Bus. & Prof. Pos: Report, Bennington Banner, Vt, 38-40, managing ed, 40-42; co-publisher, Adirondack Daily Enterprise, Saranac Lake, N.Y, 53-; owner, Lake Placid, N.Y. News, 60- Mem: Pres, Adirondack Park Asn; N.Y. Adv. Cmt. on Natural Resources. Mailing Add: C/O U.S. Mission, 80 Rue de Lausanne, Geneva, Switz.

TUBIAK, JOHN D
b. Meriden, Conn, 12/20/22; s. John Tubiak (deceased) and Mary Swiatek T; m. 2/1/47 to Agnes M. St. Peter; c. Carol Ann and Lisa Marie. Educ: Univ. Hartford, B.A. and M.Ed; grad. study at St. Joseph Col. and Univ. Conn; Gamma Sigma Nu. Polit. & Govt. Pos: Mem, Glastonbury Parking Authority, Conn, 61-65; pres, Glastonbury Young Dem, 62-64; rep, Town Meeting for Tomorrow, Glastonbury, 64; justice of peace, Glastonbury, 64-; chmn, Glastonbury Dem. Town Cmt, 64-; Glastonbury Rep, Capitol Region Planning Agency, 65-; mem. legis. cmt, Gov. Task Force on Educ, 69. Bus. & Prof. Pos: V.pres, Conn. State Fedn. of Teachers, 69- Mil. Serv: Air Force, 42, served with 20th Air Force Ninth Bombardment Group in Southwest Pac, released 46. Mem: Charter mem, East Hartford Fedn. of Teachers and pres, 61-63; v.pres. and legis. chmn, Conn. State Fedn. Teachers. Glastonbury Dem. Man of the Year Award, 69. Rel: Roman Catholic. Mailing Add: 78 Shallowbrook Lane, Glastonbury, Conn. 06033.

TUCHMANN, CAROL J.
b. New York, N.Y, 7/29/44; d. Frederick C. Tuchmann and Hildegard Jung T; single. Educ: Smith Col, A.B, magna cum laude, 65; Phi Beta Kappa. Polit. & Govt. Pos: Summer Intern to U.S. Rep. F. Bradford Morse, Mass, 64; Legis. Aide to U.S. Rep. Ogden R. Reid, N.Y, 65-67, Legis. Asst, 67-69 and Admin. Asst, 69-; Summer Dir, Smith Col, Intern Prog, 66 & 67. Mailing Add: 1831 23rd St. N.W, Washington, D.C. 20008.

TUCHOW, GERALD D
Exec. V.Chmn, 13th Cong. Dist. Dem. Party, Mich.
b. Detroit, Mich, 2/26/30; s. Morris Tuchow and Gertrude Gold T; m. 4/7/57 to Marilyn Alice Spiro; c. Jonathan, Matthew and Lincoln. Educ: Wayne State Univ, B.A, 52; Univ. Mich, LL.B, 57; George Wash. Univ. Polit. & Govt. Pos: V.chmn, First Cong. Dist. Dem. Party, Mich, 62; chmn, State Tenure Cmt, 63; nominee, State Bd. of Educ, 63; del, Dem. Nat. Conv, 64; sch. bd. attorney, Brownstown Sch. Dist, Mich; city attorney, Flat Rock; exec. v.chmn, 13th Cong. Dist. Dem. Party, 64- Bus. & Prof. Pos: Partner, Law Firm of Gazley & Tuchow, currently. Mil. Serv: Entered as Pvt, Army, 52, released as Cpl, 54, after serv. in Wash, D.C. Army Audiology Center. Mem: Mich. and Detroit Bar Asns; Am. Trial Lawyers Asn; Rotary Int.(pres, Local Club); dir, Lafayette Park Commun. Asn; dir, Fact Finders Club of Detroit; pres, Lafayette Park Dem. Club; treas, Chrysler Sch. Parent-Teacher Coun. Legal Res: 1314 Nicolet Place, Detroit, Mich. 48207. Mailing Add: 2200 Commonwealth Bldg, Detroit, Mich. 48226. (1967)

TUCK, ANN LITTON ROWLAND R
Pres, Tenn. Fedn. of Rep. Women
b. Louisville, Ky, 4/1/26; d. Edgar Coleman Rowland and Ida Litton Major R; m. 9/18/48 to James Richard Tuck; c. Ann Litton, James Coleman and Mary Barbour. Educ: Sweet Briar Col, 44-46; Vanderbilt Univ, B.A, 48; Kappa Alpha Theta. Polit. & Govt. Pos: Co. co-chmn, Nixon-Lodge Campaign, Tenn, 60; v.pres. Fifth Cong. Dist, Tenn. Fedn. Rep. Women, 61-66, pres, 66-; off. mgr, Rep. Co. Hq, Nashville, 64; co-chmn, Davidson Co. Young Rep. Club, 65; secy, Davidson Co. Rep. Primary Bd, 67-68; chief engrossing clerk, Tenn. House of Rep, 69- Bus. & Prof. Pos: Asst. lab. technician, Biol. Dept, Vanderbilt Univ, 47-48; asst, Bus. Research Dept, Gen. Shoe Corp, Nashville, Tenn, 48-50. Mem: League of Women Voters; Nashville Symphony Guild; Ladies Hermitage Asn; Fifth Dist. Rep. Women's Club. Rel: Methodist. Mailing Add: 4403 Iroquois Ave, Nashville, Tenn. 37205.

TUCK, EDWIN ALVIS D
Ala. State Rep.
b. Eutaw, Ala, 9/8/10; s. Edwin Acquilla Tuck and Laura Shaw Neal T; m. 10/28/39 to Elizabeth Burton Wedgworth; c. Bettie Neal (Mrs. Hamilton) and Nancy Louise (Mrs. Hitt). Educ: Univ. of Ala, 29-30; Christian Theol. Sem, Butler Univ, 57. Polit. & Govt. Pos: Mem, Green Co. Bd. Educ, Ala, 56-64, pres, 60-64; Ala. State Rep, Greene Co, 64- Bus. & Prof. Pos: Partner, Eutaw Grocery Co, 46- Mil. Serv: Entered as Pvt, Army, 44, released as Cpl, 46, after serv. in S.Pac; New Guinea and Philippine Campaign Ribbons. Mem: V.pres, Ala. Cmt. for Better Schs; pres, C. of C; Mason; Lions; 23 Club; Am. Legion; VFW; Farm Bur. Rel: Disciples of Christ. Legal Res: 1014 Mesopotamia, Eutaw, Ala. 35462. Mailing Add: P.O. Box 554, Eutaw, Ala, 35462.

TUCK, JAMES RICHARD R
Metrop. Councilman, Nashville, Tenn.
b. Weakley Co, Tenn, 10/15/17; m. 9/18/48 to Ann Rowland; c. Ann, James and Mary. Educ: Vanderbilt Univ, A.B, 42, LL.B, 47; Phi Beta Kappa; Omicron Delta Kappa; Delta Kappa Epsilon. Polit. & Govt. Pos: Asst. U.S. Attorney, Middle Dist. of Tenn, 56-58; chmn, Davidson Co. Rep. Party, 62; U.S. Cmnr, Mid. Dist. Tenn, 63; metrop. councilman, Nashville & Davidson Co, 63-; del, Rep. Nat. Conv, 68. Bus. & Prof. Pos: Asst. v.pres. and counsel, Nat. Life and Accident Ins. Co, currently. Mil. Serv: Entered as Pvt, Air Force, 42, released as 1st Lt, 45, after serv. as pilot, CBI Theater, 43-45, Res, Lt. Col.(Ret); Air Medal; Distinguished Flying Cross. Rel: Methodist. Mailing Add: 4403 Iroquois Avenue, Nashville, Tenn. 37205.

TUCK, WELDON WALTER R
Chmn, Halifax Co-South Boston Rep. Cmt, Va.
b. Durham, N.C, 8/11/41; s. Emmett Apple Tuck and Pauline Waller T; m. 8/20/66 to Sarah Wallton Carpenter. Educ: Va. Episcopal Sch, 57-60; Hampden-Sydney Col, B.A, 64; Kappa Sigma. Polit. & Govt. Pos: Organizer, Young Rep. Club, Hampden-Sydney Col, 62; mem, Va. State Rep. Cent. Cmt, 62-; chmn, Halifax Co-S.Boston Rep. Cmt, Va, 63-; del, Rep. Nat. Conv, 64; chmn, Fifth Dist. Rep. Cmt, Va, 65-; cand, Va. State Del, 65; cand, U.S. Rep, Va, 68. Bus. & Prof. Pos: Investment broker, Mason & Lee, Inc, 66- Mem: Jr. C. of C; Halifax Country Golf Club. Rel: Episcopal. Legal Res: 1350 Jeffress, South Boston, Va. 24592. Mailing Add: Security Bldg, South Boston, Va. 24592.

TUCK, WILLIAM MUNFORD D
b. Halifax Co, Va, 9/28/96; s. Robert James Tuck and Virginia Susan Fitts T; m. 2/26/28 to Eva Lovelace Dillard; stepson Lester Layne Dillard. Educ: Wash. and Lee Univ, LL.B, 21; Phi Delta Phi; Omicron Delta Kappa; Sigma Phi Epsilon. Hon. LL.D, Hampden Sydney, Col, 46, Elon Col, N.C, 47, William and Mary Col, 48 and Wash. and Lee Univ, 49. Polit. & Govt. Pos: Va. State Del, 24-32; chmn, Halifax Co. Dem. Cmt, Va, 28-31; Va. State Sen, 32-42; Lt. Gov, Va, 42-46, Gov, 46-50; chmn, Fifth Dist. Dem. Cmt, Va, 51-52; chmn, Va. State Dem. Exec. Cmt, 52; U.S. Rep, Va, 53-69. Mem: Mason (33°); SAR and various other orgn. Rel: Baptist. Mailing Add: South Boston, Va. 24592.

TUCKER, CAROLYN COSTIN R
b. Indianapolis, Ind, 6/17/27; d. James W. Costin and Mildred Chandler C; m. 10/8/49 to John D. Tucker; c. John David, Jr. and Tracy Lee. Educ: DePauw Univ, B.A, 49; Kappa Kappa Gamma. Polit. & Govt. Pos: Census taker, U.S. Govt, 50; dep. assessor, Marion Co, Ind, 50-54; precinct vice committeewoman, Marion Co. Rep. Cmt, 50-60; del, Rep. Nat. Conv, 52, alternate del, 56, 60 & 64; mem, Gov. Cmn. on Handicapped, Ind, 59-; precinct committeewoman and v.chmn, Twp, 60-; chmn. women's div, Greater Indianapolis Rep. Finance Cmt, 68- Bus. & Prof. Pos: Dir. of Pub. Educ, Crossroads Rehabilitation Center, 62- Mem: Pub. Rels. Soc. of Am; Pub. Rels. Coun. of Health and Welfare Orgn; educ. cmt, Pub. Rels. Soc. of Am. Hosp. Asn; Int. Platform Asn; Jr. League of Indianapolis; 500 Festival Asn; Commun. Serv. Coun. Golden Quill Award, Woman's Press Club of Ind, 68. Rel: Methodist. Mailing Add: 6160 Afton Crest, Indianapolis, Ind. 46220.

TUCKER, CHARLOTTE PAIGE D
b. Louisville, Ky, 10/7/00; d. Newton Paige and Charlotte Boyd P; m. 4/13/36 to Thomas Walter Tucker. Educ: Bowling Green High Sch, Ky, grad, 19; Chicago Musical Col, Ill. Teacher's Cert. in Violin, Hist. of Music, Harmony, Ear Training and Pedagogy, 23; Iota Phi Lambda. Polit. & Govt. Pos: Treas, Merrill Twp. Bd, Bitely, Mich, 66-; v.pres, Newaygo Co. Dem. Women's Cmt, 66-67, pres, 67-; del, Dem. Nat. Conv, 68. Bus. & Prof. Pos: Prfnl. photographer and owner, Portrait Studio, Chicago, Ill, 20-37; violin teacher, 20-37. Mem: Budget chmn, Federated Women's Orgn, Chicago, Ill, 32-37 and YWCA, 34-36; pres, Federated Women Prfnl. & Bus. Club, 34-36; Auxiliary, VFW, Idlewild, Mich. Honored Precinct Worker for Ninth Dist, Mich, 69. Rel: Presbyterian. Mailing Add: Route 1, Box 66, Bitely, Mich. 49309.

TUCKER, HENRY HARRIS R
R.I. State Rep.
b. Central Falls, R.I, 7/18/05; m. to Annie Balme. Educ: Alexander Hamilton Inst; Univ. R.I. Polit. & Govt. Pos: Former cmnr, William Blackstone Dist, R.I; served on Lincoln Jr. High Bldg. Cmn. and Lincoln Elem. Sch. Bldg. Cmn; mem, Sch. Cmt, 53-57, Planning Bd, 14 years and Budget Bd, 7 years; R.I. State Rep, 59- Bus. & Prof. Pos: Prod. supvr. Mem: Pres, Charles Edwin Lawton Mem. Masonic Home Asn, Central Falls; F&AM (Past Master, Jenks Lodge 24, Pawtucket); Blackstone Valley Hist. Soc; Limerock Grange P. of H; former mem, Blackstone Valley Exec. Cmt, Boy Scouts. Silver Beaver Award, Boy Scouts. Mailing Add: 569 River Rd, Lincoln, R.I. 02865. (1967)

TUCKER, JACK NORRIS D
Miss. State Sen.
b. Charleston, Miss, 5/15/21; s. Harry Randolph Tucker and Lucy Barnett Rolfe T; m. 9/12/48 to Pattye Sue Williams. Educ: Holmes Jr. Col, Goodman, Miss, 40-42; La. State Normal Col, Natchitoches, 1 semester, 43; Univ. of Ga, pre-flight training, 43; Univ. of Miss, B.A, 48, LL.B, 50 and J.D, 68; Phi Delta Phi; Delta Kappa Epsilon. Polit. & Govt. Pos: Chmn, Elec. Cmn, Tunica Co, Miss, 52-56; Miss. State Sen, 60-, chmn, Cmt. on Educ, Miss. State Senate, 64- Bus. & Prof. Pos: Dir, Rotary, presently; lawyer. Mil Serv: Entered as Aviation Cadet, Naval Res, 42, released as Lt.(jg), 46, after serv. in Am, European and Pac. Theatres; Am. and European Theatre Ribbons. Mem: Rotary; Am. Legion; VFW; Am. and Miss. Heart Asns; Am, Miss. and Clarksdale Bar Asns; Boy Scouts. Meritorious Award, Miss. Heart Asn; Cert. of Appreciation, Am. Heart Asn. Rel: Methodist. Mailing Add: P.O. Box 826, Tunica, Miss. 38676.

TUCKER, JOE B. D
b. Ringgold, Ga, 1/28/33; s. Herman B. Tucker and Carrie North T; m. 12/26/53 to Margaret Anne Goolsby; c. L. Gail, J. Lynn, Clay B. and S. Beth. Educ: Mercer Univ, A.B, 54; Walter F. George Sch. of Law, LL.B, 56; Lambda Chi Alpha; Delta Theta Phi. Polit. & Govt. Pos: Local Bd. Appeal Agent, Ringgold. Ga, 58-64, city attorney, Ringgold and Catoosa Co; Ga. State Rep, 63-66. Bus. & Prof. Pos: Attorney. Mem: Jaycees; pres, Civitan Club, 58; secy, Rotary, 57-58; dir, Coosa Develop. Asn, 58-62. Outstanding Young Man of the Year, 64. Rel: Baptist. Mailing Add: Ringgold, Ga. 30736.

TUCKER, MEMORY KING D
b. Statham, Ga, 9/19/97; s. Memory James Tucker and Udora Lanier T; m. 2/20/16 to Margaret Hill; c. Susie (Mrs. Reuben L. Rockwell), Margaret (Mrs. Carl A. Blount, II), Mary Elizabeth (Mrs. Charles A. Evans, II), grandchildren; Memory Margaret Rockwell, Reuben Luckie Rockwell, Jr, Susan Tucker Rockwell, Carl Ashton Blount III, King Tucker Blount, Leonard Hill Blount, Alva Lanier Blount, Charles Andrew Evans, Jr, William King Evans, Peter Michael Evans, John Kitchens Evans. Educ: Statham High Sch. Polit. & Govt. Pos: Ga. State Rep, 59-66; Housing Authority, chmn; Hosp. Authority, chmn; Burke Co. Bd. of Cmnr, 44-52; mayor, City of Waynesboro, 38-42; city coun, 35-36. Bus. & Prof. Pos: Pres, Bank of Waynesboro. Rel: Presbyterian. Mailing Add: Waynesboro, Ga. 30830. (1967)

TUCKER, RALPH D
b. Hymera, Ind, 9/30/09; s. Jacob H. Tucker and Rosa-Ann Doty T; m. 9/26/36 to Virginia E. Waade; c. Marcia (Mrs. Ray) and Shelia. Educ: Wiley High Sch, Terre Haute, Ind, grad. Polit. & Govt. Pos: City clerk, Terre Haute, Ind, 38-42 and mayor, 48-68; del, Dem. Nat. Conv, 48, 52, 56, 60, 64 & 68; Dem. nominee for Gov, 56. Bus. & Prof. Pos: Gen. mgr, Nat. Lit. Asn, 42-47; pres, Ralph Tucker Agency, Inc, 68- Mem: Mason; Elks; Many citations by nat, state, govt, C. of C. and civic groups. Rel: Protestant. Mailing Add: 341 Barton Ave, Terre Haute, Ind. 47807.

TUCKER, RAY M. D
Ga. State Rep.
b. Cork, Ga, 4/11/27; s. Arthur Washington Tucker and John Torbet T; single. Educ: Walter F. George Sch. of Law, Mercer Univ, LL.B, 52; A.B, 54; Kappa Sigma. Polit. & Govt. Pos: Ga. State Rep, 63- Bus. & Prof. Pos: Attorney-at-law. Mil. Serv: Army, World War II, 45-46, T/5 Army Res, 46-49; Korean War, 52-54, First Lt. Mem: Mason; Elk; Am. Legion; Lions; Treas, McDonough Lions Club, 58-59, v.pres, 59-61, pres, 61-62; Dist. Govt, Dist. 18, Lions Int, 62-63. Rel: Methodist. Mailing Add: McDonough, Ga. 30253.

TUCKER, STERLING D
V.Chmn, D.C. City Coun.
b. Akron, Ohio, 12/21/23; s. John Clifford Tucker and Una Vinson T; m. 8/14/48 to Edna Alloyce Robinson; c. Michele Alloyce and Lauren Alloyce. Educ: Univ. Akron, B.A, 46, M.A, 50; Alpha Phi Alpha; Debate Team; officer, Student Coun. Polit. & Govt. Pos: V.chmn, D.C. City Coun, 69- Bus. & Prof. Pos: Asst. exec. dir, Akron Urban League, Ohio, 49-53; exec. dir, Canton Urban League, 53-56 and Wash. Urban League, D.C, 56-; dir. Field Serv, Nat. Urban League, 68- Publ: Beyond the Burning: Life and Death of the Ghetto, Asn. Press, 68; Why the Ghetto Must Go, Pub. Affairs Pamphlet 423, 68; Black Reflections on White Power, William B. Eerdmans Publ. Co, 69. Mem: Nat. Asn. of Soc. Workers; Acad. of Cert. Soc. Workers; exec. bd, metrop. area, Nat. Asn. of Soc. Workers; v.pres, metrop. area, Urban Coalition; Interreligious Cmt. on Race Rels; bd, Metrop. Wash. Coun. of Churches; Adv. Cmt. on human resources, U.S. Jr. C. of C. Outstanding Young Man of the Year Award, Wash. Jr. C. of C, 64; Citation from Repub. of Liberia, 66. Rel: Episcopal. Mailing Add: 6505 16th St. N.W, Washington, D.C. 20012.

TUCKER, WENDELL O. D
Chmn, Stanton Co. Dem. Cent. Cmt, Kans.
b. Johnson, Kans, 1/22/27; s. Herman Lawrence Tucker and Luella Warren T; m. 4/5/44 to Ethel Lorene Lewis; c. Judith Kay and Wendell Lee. Educ: Johnson High Sch, Kans. Polit. & Govt. Pos: Chmn, Stanton Co. Dem. Cent. Cmt, Kans, 64- Mem: Hon. mem. Legion Club, Post 79; chmn, Stanton Co. Soil Conserv. Dist; past chmn, Stanton Co. Exten. Coun; Stanton Co. Park Bd. of Trustees; past mem, Farm Bur. Bd; Odd Fellows; Elks. Rel: Methodist. Mailing Add: Box 468, Johnson, Kans. 67855. (1967)

TUCKER, WILLIAM EDWARD R
Asst. Attorney Gen, Colo.
b. Idabel, Okla, 9/2/34; s. Owen F. Tucker and Dixie Stiles T; m. 11/25/55 to Nancy Louise Henkins; c. Desiree and Gayle Ann. Educ: S.Dak. Sch. Mines, B.S, 56; Okla. Univ. Sch. Law, LL.B, 62; Phi Alpha Delta; Alpha Delta; Scabbard and Blade; Theta Tau. Polit. & Govt. Pos: Mem, Presidential Campaign Speakers' Center, 64; treas, Denver Young Rep, 64, pres, 65, mem, bd. of dirs, 65-66; mem, State Exec. Bd, Colo. Young Rep, 64-66; Nat. chmn, Young Rep. Speakers' Cmt, 65-66; gen. counsel, Young Rep. League, Colo, 66-; asst. attorney gen, Colo, 66- Mil. Serv: 1st Lt, Army, 55-56. Publ: 'Advertising Prescriptions--End of the Prohibition Era?' Nat. Asn. Bd. of Pharm. Quart, summer 69. Mem: Colo, Okla. and Am. Bar Asns; chmn, Govt. Affairs Cmt, Denver Jaycees, 66; Denver Athletic Club; admitted to practice before Colo, Okla. and U.S. Supreme Courts. Rel: Methodist. Legal Res: 5660 E. Eldorado Place, Denver, Colo. 80222. Mailing Add: Suite 1030, Western Federal Savings Bldg, Denver, Colo. 80202.

TUCKER, WILLIAM HUMPHREY D
b. Boston, Mass, 9/8/23; s. William H. Tucker and Marion Thomas T; m. 6/19/48 to Caroline E. Aitken; c. Sandra J. and Karen D. Educ: Boston Univ. Sch. of Law, LL.B, cum laude, 49; Ed, Boston Univ. Law Rev. Polit. & Govt. Pos: Cmnr, Interstate Commerce Cmn, 61-65, chmn, 66-67; del, Dem. Nat. Conv, 68. Bus. & Prof. Pos: Attorney-at-Law, Athol and Boston, Mass, 49-61; partner, law firm Saxon Maguire & Tucker, 68; v.pres. corporate admin, Penn Cent. Co, 68-69; v.pres, New Eng. Penn Cent. Co, 69- Mil. Serv: Entered as Pvt, Army, 42, released as Sgt, 45, after serv. in 505th Parachute Regt, 82nd Airborne Div, ETO, 43-45; Maj, Army Standby Res; French and Belgian Fourragere; Dutch Order of Wm. Laniard; Sicily, Naples-Foggia, Normandy, Holland, Ardennes and Cent. Europe Campaign Ribbons with Stars; Purple Heart with Cluster; Campaign Infantryman's Badge; Presidential Unit Citation. Publ: 'The Public Interest in Railroad Mergers,' Boston Univ. Law Rev, spring 62; 'The Quiet Crisis in Transportation,' Interstate Commerce Cmn. Practitioners' J, 12/64; 'The Coming of Age in Trucking,' Commercial Car J, 11/65. Mem: Am. Bar Asn; Cong. Country Club; Wash. Athletic Club; Stone Horse Yacht Club; past pres, 82nd Airborne Div. Asn;

chmn. bd, 82nd Airborne C-47 Club, Inc; ICC Practitioners Asn; New Eng. Coun; New Eng. R.R. Club; U.S. Bicentennial World Expo. Distinguished Pub. Serv. Award, Boston Univ; Distinguished Young Gentleman Award, C. of C. Rel: Methodist. Legal Res: 39 Neel Rd, Harwichport, Mass. 02646. Mailing Add: 46 Indian Spring Rd, Milton, Mass. 02186.

TUDAN, VICTOR JOHN D
Conn. State Rep.
b. Winthrop, Mass, 2/17/21; s. John Tudan and Fannie T; m. 2/9/47 to Lillian Palechuck; c. Gerald, Linda, Jon, Mary Ellen, Christine and Patricia Ann. Educ: Weaver High Sch, grad, 39. Polit. & Govt. Pos: Mem, Windsor Dem. Town Cmt, Conn, 50- and treas, 10 years; clerk, Windsor Munic. Court, 54-56; Conn. State Rep, 61-, chmn, Interim Cmt. on Indust. Develop, Conn. State House of Rep, 64-, chmn. cmt, State Develop, and v.chmn, Statewide Airport Study Cmt, 67-; Senate clerk, Cmt. on State Develop, 63- Mil. Serv: Entered as Pvt, Army, 42, released as S/Sgt, 45, after serv. in ETO; 5 Battle Stars; Verdun Medal; Good Conduct Medal; Unit Citation. Mem: VFW; K. of C; Elks; Windsor Hist. Soc. Rel: Roman Catholic. Mailing Add: 63 White Rock Dr, Windsor, Conn. 06095.

TUERK, FRED JAMES R
Ill. State Rep.
b. Peoria, Ill, 7/19/22; s. Fred W. Tuerk and Anna L. Meagher T; m. 3/17/45 to Mary M. Kieffer; c. Mary Anne, Therese Ellen, William F, John A, Barbara M, Ellen E, Margaret M. and Tina L. Educ: St. Ambrose Col, 40-42; Univ. Mo, Columbia, B.A. in Journalism, 46; Beta Theta Pi. Polit. & Govt. Pos: Trustee, Peoria Park Dist, Ill, 63-; Ill. State Rep, 69- Mil. Serv: Entered as A/S, Navy, 42, released as Lt.(jg), 46, after serv. in ETO, 44-45; Am. Theatre Medal; European Theatre Medal with One Star. Mem: Sigma Delta Chi; Int. Coun. of Indust. Ed; Ill. Valley Press Club (secy, 62, pres, 63); K. of C; Peoria Asn. of Commerce; C. of C. Recipient of Freedoms Found. Medal; several co. mag. and newspaper Citations of Excellence. Rel: Catholic. Mailing Add: 3212 N. Avalon Place, Peoria, Ill. 61604.

TUFTS, J. ARTHUR R
N.H. State Sen.
b. Lowell, Mass, 12/28/21; married; c. 4. Educ: Univ. of N.H, B.S, 48; Boston Univ, M.Ed, 61. Polit. & Govt. Pos: N.H. State Rep, 61-, Pres, N.H. State Senate, currently. Bus. & Prof. Pos: Nurseryman; hockey coach and official; square dance teacher; trustee, Univ. N.H. Mil. Serv: World War II Med. Serv. Corps. Mem: Nat. Recreation Asn; N.H. Hort. Soc; Am. Asn. for Health, Phys. Educ. and Recreation; Nat. Ice Hockey Officials Asn; Rockingham Asn. for Retarded Children; 4-H Leader. Rel: Unitarian. Mailing Add: 198 High St, Exeter, N.H. 03833.

TUGGLE, KENNETH HERNDON R
Cmnr, U.S. Interstate Commerce Cmn.
b. Barbourville, Ky, 6/12/04; s. Jesse Davis Tuggle and Sue Gregory Root T; m. 8/20/37 to Vivian Shifley; c. Kenneth Jesse and Sarah Baldwin. Educ: Univ. Ky, A.B, 26; Union Col, LL.D, 46; Delta Theta Phi; Omicron Delta Kappa; Tau Kappa Alpha; Pi Kappa Alpha. Polit. & Govt. Pos: Chmn, Ky. Legis. Coun, 43 & 45; Lt. Gov. of Ky, 43-47, pres, Ky. State Senate, 44-46, mem. bd. mgr, Coun. State Govt, 44 & 47; del-at-lg, Rep. Nat. Conv, 48 & 52; mem, Ky. Cmt. on Resources and Functions of State Govt, 50-52; cmnr, U.S. Interstate Commerce Cmn, 53-, chmn, 59; chmn. U.S. del, Sixth Session, Int. Labor Orgn, Hamburg, Germany, 57. Bus. & Prof. Pos: Pres, Union Nat. Bank, Barbourville, Ky, 34-53. Mem: Founder mem, Am. Soc. of Traffic and Transportation; Am. Judicature Soc; Ky, Am. and Fed. Bar Asns; mem, Jurisp. Cmt, Ky. Bankers Asn, 44-47; Nat. Lawyers Club; Cong. Country Club, Wash, D.C; trustee, Union Col, Barbourville, Ky; trustee, Am. Mus. of Safety. Rel: Methodist. Legal Res: 115 Pine St, Barbourville, Ky. Mailing Add: Interstate Commerce Commission, 12th and Constitution Ave. N.W, Washington, D.C. 20423.

TUIA, MUAGUTUTI'A FA'ATAMALA Am. Samoa Party
Speaker, Am. Samoa House Rep.
b. Sauniatu, West. Samoa, 9/18/20; s. Api Tuia and Salafai Faimalelagi T; m. 4/8/46 to Betty Umeo Logau; c. Mataniu (Mrs. Toelupe), Evelyn (Mrs. Satele), Milton, Minnie, Ralph and Clarie. Polit. & Govt. Pos: Rep, Am. Samoa House Rep, 61-, Speaker of House, 61-62 & 66-; mem. polit. status, Govt. Am. Samoa, 67-69. Bus. & Prof. Pos: V.pres, Samoa Construction Co, Ltd, 61-68, pres, 69-; local practitioner in High Court of Am. Samoa, 61- Rel: Latter-day Saint. Legal Res: Mapusaga, Tutuila, Am. Samoa 96920. Mailing Add: Nu'uuli, Tutuila, P.O. Box 668, Am. Samoa 96920.

TULLER, PAUL RAYMOND R
Chmn, Blandford Rep. Town Cmt, Mass.
b. Westfield, Mass, 12/15/38; s. Edwin Franklin Tuller and Florence Smith T; single. Educ: Westfield State Col, B.S.Ed, 60, M.Ed, 65. Polit. & Govt. Pos: Secy, Ward Five Rep. Cmt, Westfield, Mass, 63-64; secy, Blandford Sch. Study Cmt, 68; temporary rep, Gateway Regional Dist. Sch. Cmt, 68-69, mem, 69-; chmn, Blandford Rep. Town Cmt, 68- Bus. & Prof. Pos: Teacher, Westfield Sch. Syst, Mass, 60-; dir, academically talented prog, Franklin Sch, Westfield, 67-; licensed real estate broker. Mem: Westfield, Mass. and Hampden Co. Teachers Asns; Nat. Educ. Asn; Mass. Asn. Sch. Cmt; Blandford Hist. Soc. (bd. dirs). Rel: Congregational. Mailing Add: Main St, Blandford, Mass. 01008.

TULLEY, JOSEPH P. R
Ohio State Rep.
b. 1922; m. to Mary Rita Keating; c. Deborah, Timothy, Candace, Ellen, Sarah, Patrick and Mary Kate. Educ: John Carroll Univ, B.A; Alpha Sigma Nu; West. Reserve Univ. Law Sch, LL.B. Polit. & Govt. Pos: Ohio State Rep, 67-, chmn, Judicial Admin. Subcmt, 69-70; Willoughby Prosecuting Attorney; Planning and Zoning Cmn. and Charter Cmn, Mentor Village. Mil. Serv: Navy and Naval Res, 17 years, World War II, Korean Conflict; discharged as Lt. Mem: Bd. of dirs, Mentor Commun. Fund; past pres, Lake Co. Bar Asn; Murray Estates Improv. Asn, Holy Name Soc. of St. Mary Parish; past chmn, Mentor United Fund, Cath. Serv. Bur. Adv. Bd; past trustee, C. of C, Rotary; pres, Union of Holy Name Soc; Dep. Grand Knight, K. of C. Legal Counsel, Citizens for Decent Lit. Rel: Roman Catholic. Mailing Add: 7535 Acacia Dr, Mentor, Ohio 44060.

TULLIO, LOUIS JOSEPH D
Mayor, Erie, Pa.
b. Erie, Pa, 5/17/17; s. Anthony Tullio and Ersilia Nardone T; m. 6/21/41 to Mary Cecilia McHale; c. Betty Ann (Mrs. Eisworth), June Cecilia (Mrs. Geisler) and Marilyn Lou; Five grandchildren. Educ: Holy Cross Col, B.S, 39; Boston Univ, M.Ed, 57. Polit. & Govt. Pos: Asst. dir, Health and Physical Educ, Erie City Sch. Dist, Pa, 57-60; secy. and bus. mgr, Erie City Sch. Dist, 60-65; mem. exec. cmt, Erie and Erie Co. Dem. Parties; Mayor, Erie, Pa, 66-; del, Dem. Nat. Conv, 68. Bus. & Prof. Pos: Asst. to the Pres, Gannon Col; high sch. teacher. Mil. Serv: Entered as Ens, Navy, 43, released as Lt, 45. Mem: Dir, Harborcreek Sch. for Boys, Little Gridders of Erie, Inc, Booker T. Washington Center, Erie Chap. United Serv. Orgn. and Soap Box Derby, 64-66; bd. trustees, Erie Pub. Libr. and Mus; Youth Opportunities Exec. Coun; Dollars for Scholars Orgn; Fathers Club of Mercyhurst Prep. Sch; Citizens Adv. Cmt. to Erie City Sch. Dist; Cath.Charities of Erie, Inc. Received Prfnl. Honor Award of Pa. Health, Physical Educ. and Recreation; named Little All Am. Coach of Year. Rel: Catholic. Mailing Add: 660 E. Grandview Blvd, Erie, Pa. 16509.

TUMPACH, JOSEPH JOHN D
Chmn, DuPage Co. Dem. Party, Ill.
b. Baltimore, Md, 12/7/12; s. James Carl Tumpach and Ella Kochanski T; m. 5/18/40 to Cecilia Ann Janik; c. Daniel Joseph. Polit. & Govt. Pos: Twp. chmn, Downers Grove, Ill, 56-58, precinct committeeman, Downers Grove Dem. Party, 56-; field supvr, Dept. Pub. Instr, 58-60; chmn, DuPage Co. Dem. Party, 58-; admin. asst. Fed. Surplus Property, 60-64; Ill. State Rep, 64-69. Bus. & Prof. Pos: Owner grocery store, 45-51 and motel, 45-62; real estate salesman, Ill, 65- Mil. Serv: Entered as A/S, Navy, 43, released as Water Tender 1/C, 45; Purple Heart. Mem: Elks; Moose; UAW; Amvets; Am. Legion. Rel: Catholic. Mailing Add: 4644 Righland Ave, Downers Grove, Ill. 60515. (1967)

TUNNELL, JOE D
b. Grand Saline, Tex, 6/4/18; s. Homer Elisha Tunnell and Bertha Cade T; m. 8/25/50 to Ruth Ann Savage; c. Jo Ann, John Wesley and Thomas Rusk. Educ: North Tex. State Univ, B.S, 39; Southern Methodist Univ, LL.B, 48. Polit. & Govt. Pos: Criminal Dist. Attorney, Van Zandt Co, Tex, 51-58; Asst. U.S. Attorney, East. Dist, Tex, 58-60, U. S. Attorney, 60-61. Bus. & Prof. Pos: Attorney-at-Law, Tyler, Tex, 61- Mil. Serv: Entered as CPO, Navy, 42, released as Lt.(jg), 45, after serv. in North Africa and South Pac. Mem: Mason. Rel: Methodist. Mailing Add: 1030 Amherst St, Tyler, Tex. 75701

TUNNEY, JOHN VARICK D
U.S. Rep, Calif.
b. N.Y.C, 7/26/34; s. Gene Tunney and Mary Lauder T; m. 2/5/59 to Mieke Sprengers; c. Edward Eugene, Mark Andrew and Arianne Sprengers. Educ: Yale Univ, B.A, 52-56; Acad. Int. Law, The Hague, 57; Univ. Va. Law Sch, LL.B, 59; Delta Psi. Polit. & Govt. Pos: U.S. Rep, 38th Dist, Calif, 64- Bus. & Prof. Pos: Attorney, Cahill, Gordon, Reindel & Ohl, 59-69, private practice, 63-64; lectr, Univ. Calif, Riverside, 61-62. Mil. Serv: Entered as 1st Lt, Air Force, 60, released as Capt, 63. Mem: Calif. Bar Asn; Academia Internationalis-Lex et Scientia; Lions; Jr. C. of C; Riverside Aiding Leukemia Stricken Am. Children; Rel: Roman Catholic. Legal Res: 4715 Jackson St, Riverside, Calif. 92503. Mailing Add: 429 Cannon House Office Bldg, Washington, D.C. 20515.

TUNNO, DAVID A. D
b. Studa, Pa, 7/10/23; s. Ben Tunno and Clara Morelli T; m. 5/4/42 to Eva Louise Smith; c. Ben Michael, David Harold and Charlotte Louise. Polit. & Govt. Pos: Admin. asst. to U.S. Rep. Tunney, Calif, currently. Bus. & Prof. Pos: Prom. publicity dir, advert. co. Mil. Serv: Maj, Air Force, 41-62, serv. in Halpro Task Force, 376 Heavy Bombardment, 98th Bomb Group in Mid. East, European and Asiatic Theatres; Asiatic-Pac. Campaign Medal; European Medal with 10 Battle Stars; SCM; Silver Star; Distinguished Flying Cross; Soldier's Medal; Air Medal with 4 Oak Leaf Clusters; Purple Heart; Army Commendation Medal; Air Force Commedation Medal; Presidential Unit Citation with 3 Oak Leaf Clusters; Joint Chiefs of Staff dep. comdr. serv, Air Force; All-Serv. Football Team, 41; Heavyweight Champion, Lowry Air Force Base, 47-48; mgr, Air Force Champion Baseball Team, 48-51. Legal Res: Riverside, Calif. Mailing Add: 530 N St. S.W, S-706, Washington, D.C. 20024. (1967)

TUNOA, TAGOA'I MATAGIESE D
Rep, Am. Samoa House of Rep.
b. Vaitogi, Am. Samoa, 10/14/36; s. Soa Tunoa and Luafalemana Aiavao T; m. 1/14/67 to Tagiilima G. Muasau; c. Wei Lie and Lei Lie. Educ: York Col, 58-60; Abilene Christian Col, B.S, 62; Univ. Hawaii, 62-63; Yale Univ, M.P.H, 65. Polit. & Govt. Pos: Asst. hosp. adminstr, Govt. Am. Samoa, 68-; Rep, Am. Samoa House Rep, 69-, chmn. House Rules Cmt, 69- Mem: Am. Col. of Hosp. Adminstr; Samoa Nei Asn.(past pres); Jaycees. Scholarship Award, High Sch. of Am. Samoa, 55. Rel: Congregational. Legal Res: Vaitogi, Am. Samoa 96920. Mailing Add: L.B.J. Tropical Medical Center, Pago Pago, Am. Samoa 96920.

TUPLING, WILLIAM LLOYD D
b. Saskatoon, Sask, Can, 5/13/15; s. Harry Tupling and Florence Irene White T; m. 6/12/38 to Gladys Irene Battleson; c. Edward William, Timothy Carolyn, Margery Ann and Mary Lee. Educ: Univ. Ore, B.A, 39; Sigma Delta Chi; Alpha Tau Omega; Friars. Polit. & Govt. Pos: Mgr, Al Ullman for Cong. Cmt, 54 and Maurine Neuberger for Sen. Cmt, 60; press secy. to U.S. Sen. Richard L. Neuberger 55-57, admin. asst, 57-60; admin. asst. to U.S. Sen. Maurine Neuberger, 60-66; state coordinator, Ore. Johnson-Humphrey Cmt, 64; Wash. Rep. Sierra Club, 67- Bus. & Prof. Pos: Idaho Mgr, United Press Asns, 40-42, war correspondent, 43-45; publisher, Idaho Pioneer Statewide, 46-53. Mem: Nat. Press Club; Potomac River Power Squadron; bd. of dirs, Chesapeake Found. Rel: Episcopal. Mailing Add: 3619 Tilden, N.W, Washington, D.C. 20008.

TUPPAN, GLENDA RANA R
Mem, Calif. Rep. State Cent. Cmt.
b. Belleville, Ark, Sept. 27; d. P. Rana and E.B. Hudson R; m. 8/8/48 to

George Richard Tuppan; c. Ranalyn and Randy. Educ: Manual Arts High Sch, grad, 44. Polit. & Govt. Pos: Rep. precinct capt, Whittier, Calif, 50, area chmn, 52-59, registrn. chmn, 60-; mem, Calif. Rep. State Cent. Cmt, 66- Mem: Rep. Women (charter pres, Rancho La Habra Women Club, 68); pres, PTA, 60; ed, Heights Life, La Habra Heights Improv. Asn, 63-64, soc. chmn, 65-66. Rel: Lutheran. Mailing Add: 1010 West Rd, Whittier, Calif. 90603.

TUPPER, STANLEY R. R
b. 1/25/21; c. Stanley, Jr. Polit. & Govt. Pos: Mem. and chmn. bd. of Selectmen, Boothbay Harbor, Maine, 48-50; Maine State Rep, 52; cmnr. of Sea and Shore Fisheries for State of Maine, 53-57; U.S. Rep, Maine, 60-66; U.S. Ambassador, Can. World Exhib, 67. Bus. & Prof. Pos: Lawyer. Mil. Serv: Navy. Legal Res: Boothbay Harbor, Maine 04538. Mailing Add: 1819 H St. N.W, Washington, D.C. 20006.

TURCOTT, THOMAS R
V.Chmn, Emmet Co. Rep. Cmt, Mich.
b. Boyne City, Mich, 6/19/23; m. 5/29/47 to Margaret Strehl; c. Riley, Michael, Casey, Patricia, Laura, Kathy, Janie, Mary and Danny. Educ: O.D. Polit. & Govt. Pos: Campaign chmn. for Alger-Cobo-Nixon-Griffin; mem. city coun, Petoskey, Mich; v.chmn, Emmet Co. Rep. Cmt, currently. Bus. & Prof. Pos: Optometrist. Mem: Elks; Am. Legion; bd. dirs, Little League. Legal Res: 722 Mitchell, Petoskey, Mich. 49770. Mailing Add: 312 Mitchell, Petoskey, Mich. 49770.

TURCOTTE, CLIFFORD LAWRENCE D
Mem. Exec. Cmt, Iron Co. Dem. Party, Mich.
b. Pentoga, Mich, 3/27/21; s. Arthur Turcotte and Evelyn Belongie T; m. 11/8/41 to Aurelia Florence Hodkiewicz; c. William Arthur, Robert Allen, Susan Mary and Donna Rae. Educ: Stambaugh High Sch, grad, 38. Polit. & Govt. Pos: City Cmnr, Stambaugh, Mich, 57-58, 60-62 & 63-66, and mayor, 59-60 & 62-63; charter mem, City Co. Planning Cmt, 62-; chmn. pro tem, Iron Co. Bd. Supvr, 63-64 and chmn, 64-67; charter mem, Iron and Dickenson Ment. Health Unit, 64-; chmn, Iron Co. Dem. Party, 67-69 and mem. exec. cmt, 69- Bus. & Prof. Pos: Dir, Hanna Employee's Fed. Credit Union, 62 & 66, v.pres, 63 and pres, 64-65; v.chmn, Iron and Dickenson Co. Commun. Action Agency, 67-70 and chmn, 68-69. Mil. Serv: Entered as Pvt, Army Air Force, 43, released as Sgt, 46, after serv. in 4000 Army Air Force Base, 64-46; Am. Theatre Ribbon; Good Conduct and World War II Victory Medals. Mem: Am. Legion; Elks; Iron Co. Sportsmen Club; USW. Rel: Catholic. Mailing Add: 417 Eighth St, Stambaugh, Mich. 49964.

TURK, EDMUND JOHN D
Councilman, 23rd Ward, Cleveland, Ohio
b. Cleveland, Ohio, 1/7/25; s. Joseph Turk and Rose Skerbec T; single. Educ: John Carroll Univ, B.S.S; John Marshall Law Sch, LL.B; Delta Theta Phi. Polit. & Govt. Pos: Councilman, 23rd Ward, Cleveland, Ohio, 61- Mil. Serv: Entered as Seaman, 43, released as PHM 2/C, 46, after serv. in Atlantic-Pac, Occupation Forces, Japan. Mem: Ohio State, Cuyahoga Co. and Cleveland Bar Asns; Citizens League of Greater Cleveland, Ohio; comdr, Catholic War Vets, Post 1655; 2nd v.pres, Slovenian Mutual Benefit Asn. Rel: Roman Catholic. Legal Res: 1046 E. 69th St, Cleveland, Ohio 44103. Mailing Add: 6411 St. Clair Ave, Cleveland, Ohio 44103.

TURK, JAMES CLINTON R
Va. State Sen.
b. Roanoke, Va, 5/3/23; s. James Alexander Turk and Geneva Alice Richardson T; m. 8/21/54 to Barbara Louise Duncan; c. Ramona Leah Duncan, James Clinton, Jr, Robert Malcolm Duncan, Mary Elizabeth and David Michael. Educ: Roanoke Col, A.B, 49; Wash. & Lee Univ, LL.B, 52; Omicron Delta Kappa; Phi Beta Kappa; Order of the Coif; Pi Kappa Phi; Phi Alpha Delta. Polit. & Govt. Pos: Va. State Sen, 13th Dist, 59-, Minority Leader, Va. State Senate, 66-; mem, Rep. State Cent. Cmt, 64- Bus. & Prof. Pos: Law partner, Dalton, Poff & Turk, 52-; mem. bd. dirs, First & Merchants Nat. Bank, Radford, Va. and mem. bd. trustees, Radford Commun. Hosp. Mil. Serv: Entered as Pvt, Army, 43; released as S/Sgt, 46, after serv. in 2154 Army Serv. Unit, Am. Theater; Capt, Army Res, 49- Mem: Va. State Bar; Radford, Montgomery, Floyd, Va. State and Am. Bar Asns; Va. Trial Lawyers Asn; Asn. of Defense Counsel; Highland Club, Radford; Rotary; Shenandoah Club, Roanoke; Downtown Club, Richmond; Am. Legion; 40 et 8; Shrine. Rel: Baptist. Legal Res: 1002 Walker Dr, Radford, Va. 24141. Mailing Add: P.O. Box 1089, Radford, Va. 24141.

TURLEY, STANLEY F. R
Speaker, Ariz. House of Rep.
b. Snowflake, Ariz, 2/27/21; s. Fred A. Turley and Wilma Fillerup T; m. 10/17/44 to Cleo Fern Olson; c. Tauna Lee, Margo Yvonne, Jana, Fredrick C, Miriam K, Lisa and Leslie. Educ: Brigham Young Univ, 3 years. Polit. & Govt. Pos: Ariz. State Rep, 64-; Speaker, Ariz. House of Rep, 67- Bus. & Prof. Pos: Bd. Dirs, Ariz. Cotton Growers. Mil. Serv: Entered as Pvt, Air Force, 44, released as Pfc, 46. Mem: Farm Bur; Rotary, Chandler, Ariz; Ariz. Cattle Growers Asn. Rel: Latter-day Saint. Mailing Add: 2650 E. Southern Ave, Mesa, Ariz. 85201.

TURLINGTON, RALPH D. D
Fla. State Rep.
b. Gainesville, Fla, 10/5/20; m. to Ann Gellerstedt; c. Donald and Katherine. Educ: Univ. Fla, BSBA; Harvard Univ, MBA, 42. Polit. & Govt. Pos: Fla. State Rep, 50-; del, Dem. Nat. Conv, 68. Bus. & Prof. Pos: Ins. Mil. Serv: Army, World War II and Korea. Mem: Exchange Club; Elks; Am. Legion; VFW. Rel: Baptist. Mailing Add: 117 N.E. 16th Ave, Gainesville, Fla. 32601.

TURNBULL, WILLIAM S. D
Dem. Nat. Committeeman, Fla.
b. Richmond, Va, 3/15/24; s. Nathaniel Turnball and Marguerite Massie T; m. 9/4/48 to Shirley Eileen Wells; c. Laurie Eileen and William S, Jr. Educ: Univ. Fla, 46-48; John B. Stetson Univ, LL.B, 49; Sigma Alpha Epsilon. Polit. & Govt. Pos: Precinct committeeman, Orange Co. Dem. Exec. Cmt, Fla, 54-66, chmn, 63-67; committeeman, Fla. Dem. Exec. Cmt, 66 and chmn, Fifth Dist. Cong. Cmt; del, Dem. Nat. Conv, 68; Dem. Nat. Committeeman, Fla, currently. Mil. Serv: Entered as Aviation Cadet, Navy, 42, released as Ens, 45; Lt. Comdr, Navy Res, 45-66. Publ: 'Alimony and Property Settlement in Florida,' Florida Bar J, 58; 'Zoning Practice,' Florida Real Property Practice Manual, 3rd Volume, 66. Mem: Chmn, Real Property Section, Fla. Bar Asn, 66; Am. and Orange Co. Bar Asns; pres, Downtown Orlando Coun. Rel: Episcopal. Mailing Add: 2602 Middlesex, Orlando, Fla. 32803.

TURNER, ALTON LEE D
Ala. State Sen.
b. Luverne, Ala, 7/12/25; s. Marvin Lee Turner and Lilla Mae Dismuke T; m. 7/21/50 to Sonya Margaretha; c. Janice Mac Stevens; Alison Leigh and Alynn Leslie. Educ: Univ. Ala, LL.B, 50; Omicron Delta Kappa; Ala. Law Rev; Farrah Order of Jurisprudence; pres, Pi Kappa Phi. Polit. & Govt. Pos: Solicitor, Grenshaw Co, Ala, 52-58; Ala. State Sen, 59-63 & 67-; Ala. State Rep, 63-66. Bus. & Prof. Pos: Lawyer, Luverne, Ala, 50- Mil. Serv: Navy, 43-46, Ens; Lt. Col, Judge Adv. Gen. Staff, Ala. Nat. Guard, currently. Mem: Mason. Rel: Baptist. Mailing Add: Box 207, Luverne, Ala. 36049. (1967)

TURNER, CHARLES RUTLEDGE R
b. Baltimore, Md, 10/23/14; s. Anthony Vernon Turner and Anna Heil T; m. 3/11/39 to Elizabeth Jones; c. Donna (Mrs. James) and C. Rutledge, Jr. Educ: High Sch. Polit. & Govt. Pos: Chmn, Md. State Rep. Cent. Cmt, Dorchester, Co, 44-66; cmnr. and secy, State Accident Fund, 55-59; chmn, Dorchester Co. Liquor Control Bd, 67-; mem, First Cong. Cmt. of Md. for Congressman Rogers C.B. Morton. Bus. & Prof. Pos: Clerk, Phillips Packing Co, Inc, 31-36, sales promotion mgr, 36-48; pres, A. Vernon Turner & Sons, Inc, 48-66. Mem: Elks. Gardening, Camping, Hunting and Fishing. Rel: Methodist. Mailing Add: 1203 Hambrooks Blvd, Cambridge, Md. 21613.

TURNER, ELMA JUANITA R
V.Chmn, Washoe Co. Rep. Party, Nev.
b. Milton, Ore, 10/31/19; d. Elmer Shipp and Millie Modrell S; m. 6/21/38 to Fred Frank Turner; c. Patricia Y.(Mrs. George W. Farren, IV) and Fred E. Educ: High sch. Polit. & Govt. Pos: Del, Rep. State Conv, 66 & 68; del, Rep. Co. Conv, 66 & 68; v.chmn, Washoe Co. Rep. Party, Nev, 66-; del, Rep. Nat. Conv, 68. Rel: Protestant. Mailing Add: 485 Stearns Circle, Reno, Nev. 89502.

TURNER, ETHEL WINBORN R
Mem, Bd. Dirs, Okla. Fedn. Rep. Women
b. Houston, Tex, 10/2/25; d. James Ethel Winborn and Lena Franke W; m. 6/10/46 to Samuel Roland Turner; c. LeAnne Davidson, James Winborn and Andrew Roland. Educ: Vanderbilt Univ, B.A. Polit. & Govt. Pos: Co. coordinator, Crawford for U.S. Senate Campaign, Okla, 62; mem, Tulsa Co. Rep. Exec. Cmt, 62-66; first cong. dist. coordinator, Oklahomans for Goldwater, 63-64 and Goldwater Pres. Campaign, 64; dist. dir, Tulsa Co. Rep. Party, 63-66; alternate del-at-lg, Okla. Rep. Party, 64; mem, Okla. State Rep. Exec. Cmt, 65-67; mem, Gov. Cmn. on Status of Women, 67-; state co-chmn, Nixon for Pres. Cmt, 67-68 and Nixon Presidential Campaign, 68; state chmn, Okla. Women for Nixon, 68; mem. bd. of dirs, Okla. Med. Polit. Action Cmt, 68- and Okla. Fedn. of Rep. Women, 69- Mem: Bd. mem. and v.pres, Auxiliary to the Tulsa Co. Med. Asn, 58-67, secy, dist. coun; v.pres. Tulsa Co. Unit, Pro-Am, 63-, state bd. mem, 64-; dist. coun, Auxiliary to Okla. State Med. Asn, 64-65, recording secy, 66-67, state legis. chmn, 68-; v.pres, Jr. Auxiliary Children's Day Nursery, 65-66; Okla. coun, Auxiliary to South. Med. Asn, 68-; Univ. Club of Tulsa; Phi Beta Pi Alumnae Asn; Vanderbilt Univ. Alumnae Asn; Tulsa Philharmonic Asn; Tulsa Opera Guild; Auxiliary, Children's Day Nursery; patron mem, Miss Okla. Pageant; Fedn. of Rep. Women; Med. Auxiliaries. Rel: Disciples of Christ. Mailing Add: 5652 S. Delaware, Tulsa, Okla. 74105.

TURNER, GRANVILLE NICHOLAS D
b. Limestone Co, 8/8/29; s. Cordy Franklin Turner and Bertha Jane Bailey T; m. 10/21/46 to Anne Crouch; c. Stephen Dwight, Sandra Anne, Margaret Kathy, Kimberly Sue. Educ: E. Limestone High Sch. Polit. & Govt. Pos: Ala. State Rep, 59-66. Bus. & Prof. Pos: Cattle breeder, farmer, and bus. man. Mem: Lions Club; Mason; Shriner; Woodmen of the World; Co. Farm Bur. of Limestone Co; Tenn. and Am. Short Horn Breeders Asn; mem. Limestone Co. Hosp. Bd; Trustee, E. Limestone High Sch; secy. and treas, Ala. Short Horn Breeders. Rel: Presbyterian. Mailing Add: Route 2, Box 37, Trinity, Ala. 35673. (1967)

TURNER, HARRY WOODRUFF R
b. Blairsville, Pa, 5/2/39; s. James McKinnie Turner and Dorthy Title T; single. Educ: Univ. Pittsburgh, B.A, 61; Harvard Law Sch, LL.B, 64; Omicron Delta Kappa; Druids; Lincoln's Inn Soc. Polit. & Govt. Pos: Chmn, Pa. Youth for Nixon Lodge, 60; chmn, Action Cmt, Indiana Co, Pa, 62; trustee, Torrance State Hosp, 65-; Rep. nominee, Pa. House Rep, 66; campaign dir, Bob Friend for Controller of Allegheny Co, 67; chmn, New Generation for Nixon, Pa, 68; alternate del, Rep. Nat. Conv, 68; campaign dir, Pomeroy for Pa. Supreme Court, 69. Bus. & Prof. Pos: Attorney, Kirkpatrick, Lockhart, Johnson & Hutchison, Pittsburgh, Pa, 64- Mem: Am. and Pa. Bar Asns; Am. Judicature Soc; Harvard-Yale-Princeton Club of Pittsburgh; Univ. Club of Pittsburgh; Hist. & Landmarks Found. of Pittsburgh. Rel: Presbyterian. Legal Res: 140 S. Spring St, Blairsville, Pa. 15717. Mailing Add: 1100 Oliver Bldg, Pittsburgh, Pa. 15222.

TURNER, IRBY, JR. D
b. Belzoni, Miss, 5/7/32; married. Polit. & Govt. Pos: City attorney, Belzoni, Miss, 59-; Miss. State Rep, 60-69. Bus. & Prof. Pos: Attorney. Mem: Miss. Bar Asn; Rotary; Delta Coun; Farm Bur; Mason; Sons Confederate Vets. Rel: Methodist. Mailing Add: Box 447, Belzoni, Miss. 39038. (1967)

TURNER, JAMES HARVEY D
Miss. State Rep.
b. Conway, Miss, 8/21/30; s. Clarence Evans Turner and Pearl McCrory T; single. Educ: Singleton High School, Carthage, Miss, grad, 48. Polit. & Govt. Pos: Del, Dist. and State Dem. Caucus and Conv, Miss, 68; Miss. State Rep, 28th Dist, 68-, mem. agr, livestock and poultry, co. affairs, roads, ins. and ferries and bridges cmt, Miss. House Rep; dep. dist. cmnr, Leake Co. Soil

Conserv, currently; pres, Choctaw, Attala and Leake Co. Yochanookany River Develop. Dist, currently. Bus. & Prof. Pos: Cattle and row crop farmer, Carthage. Mem: Nat. and Miss. Asns. Life Underwriters; Miss. State Fraternal Cong.(pres, 66-67); Miss. Cattlemen's Asn; Miss. and Leake Co. Farm Bur; WOW (past pres. Camp 648, Carthage, dist. mgr. Ins. Soc, currently); 4-H (pres. Leake Co. Adv. Coun, 65, pres. Adult Leaders Coun, S.W. Dist, Miss, 65-66); Mason (past Master, Pearl River Lodge, secy, currently); Royal Arch (past High Priest, Carthage Chap. 46, secy, currently); Carthage Coun. Royal and Select Masters (past Illustrious Master, Lodge 34, secy, currently); Commandry Knights Templar; Shrine Club (past pres, Leake Club, v.pres, currently); Shrine (membership cmt, Hamasa Temple); Coun. Super Excellent Masters; Order of High Priesthood; Coun. of Thrice Illustrious Masters. Rel: Baptist; Chmn. Bd. Deacons; Choir Dir; Sunday Sch. Teacher; Dept. Dir. Training Union, Center Hill Baptist Church. Mailing Add: Route 6, Box 107, Carthage, Miss. 39051.

TURNER, JOHN RAYMOND D
Ky. State Sen.
b. 1910. Educ: Morehead State Col. Polit. & Govt. Pos: Ky. State Sen, 62-; chmn, Breathitt Co. Dem. Party, currently; former elec. cmnr. Bus. & Prof. Pos: Merchant. Mil. Serv: Army. Rel: Christian. Mailing Add: Jackson, Ky. 41339. (1967)

TURNER, JOSEPH WILLIAM, JR. R
Mem, Dougherty Co. Rep. Exec. Cmt, Ga.
b. Bainbridge, Ga, 11/29/25; s. Joseph William Turner, Sr. and Ouida M. Ingman T; m. 6/9/48 to Mildred Elizabeth Macleod; c. Joseph W, III, Norman Lawrence, David Macleod and Elizabeth Grace. Educ: N. Ga. Col, 43; Clemson Univ, 46-48. Polit. & Govt. Pos: Pres, Dougherty Co. Young Rep. Club, Ga, 61-64; chmn, Draft Goldwater Cmt, Dougherty Co, 64; chmn, Dougherty Co. Rep. Party, 64-66; mem, Dougherty Co. Rep. Exec. Cmt, 66- Bus. & Prof. Pos: Jr. engr. and draftsman, Donald F. Lindstrom Construction Engr, 49-51; mechanical engr, Ga. Cooling & Heating Co, 51-55; mechanical engr, Albany Architects & Engrs, 55-59; consulting engr, self-employed, 59- Mil. Serv: Entered as Pvt, Army Air Force, 43, released as Aviation Cadet, 45; Maj, Air Force Res, currently. Mem: Am. Consulting Engrs. Coun; Ga. Soc. of Prfnl. Engrs; Consulting Engrs. Asn. of Ga; Am. Legion; Kiwanis; Albany Lodge 24, F&AM, Wm. Penn Chap. 15, RAM, St. Pauls Commandery 24; Clemson Alumni Asn; Assoc. Dinner Club; Doubelgate Country Club. Rel: Methodist. Legal Res: 5005 Old Dawson Rd, Albany, Ga. 31702. Mailing Add: P.O. Box 1047, Albany, Ga. 31702.

TURNER, LESTER CECIL D
b. Sycamore, Ga, 6/16/18; s. Marion Newton Turner and Hattie Lou Couch T; m. 7/21/62 to Clairessa Adcock Tracy; c. Mary Elizabeth. Educ: Univ. Ga, B.B.A, 45; Atlanta Law Sch, LL.B; Blue Key; Sigma Nu Phi; Alpha Kappa Psi; Sigma Nu. Polit. & Govt. Pos: Mem, Bd. of Aldermen, Atlanta, Ga, 62-; Ga. State Rep, 67-68. Rel: Baptist. Mailing Add: 1779 Merton Rd, N.E, Atlanta, Ga. 30306. (1967)

TURNER, LLOYD L. Non-partisan
Mayor, Waterloo, Iowa
b. Garrison, Iowa, 5/16/24; s. William Turner and Margaret Nellist T; m. 12/9/42 to Viola Hostetler; c. Teri and Tom. Educ: State Col. of Iowa, 3½ years. Polit. & Govt. Pos: Supt, Riverfront Cmn, Waterloo, Iowa, 54-61; dir, Civil Defense, Black Hawk Co, Iowa, 61-65; mayor, Waterloo, currently. Mil. Serv: Entered as Pvt, Army, 43, released as Pfc, 45, after serv. in Off. War Info, Pac. Theater; Two Bronze Stars; Asiatic and Pac. Theater Ribbon. Mem: Amvets; Am. Legion; Elks; Kiwanis. Rel: Presbyterian. Legal Res: 2546 W. Ninth St, Waterloo, Iowa, 50702. Mailing Add: City Hall, Waterloo, Iowa 50705.

TURNER, MARIE R. D
V.Chmn, Ky. Dem. State Exec. Cmt.
b. Hindman, Ky, 6/9/00; d. John M. Roberts and Louranie Watts R; m. to Ervine Turner (deceased); c. Lois Irene, John Raymond and Treva Louraine T. (Mrs. Howell). Educ: Morehead Univ, A.B. Polit. & Govt. Pos: Supt, Breathitt Co. Schs, Ky, 31-69; v.chmn, Ky. Dem. State Exec. Cmt, 64-; del, Dem. Nat. Conv, 68. Bus. & Prof. Pos: Pres, Citizens Bank of Jackson, 68- Gov. Award for Outstanding Schs; Univ. Award for Outstanding Educ. Progs. Rel: Christian Church of N.Am. Mailing Add: Jackson, Ky. 41339.

TURNER, RALPH FRANKLIN, JR. D
b. Akron, Ohio, 12/30/21; s. Ralph Franklin Turner and Sarah Dunlap T; m. 12/16/44 to Mary Jane Frankenburger; c. David, Carol and James. Educ: Akron Univ; Phi Delta Theta. Polit. & Govt. Pos: Ohio State Rep, Summit Co, 65-66. Bus. & Prof. Pos: Asst. traffic mgr, Polsky's, 47-48; control scheduler and training prog, Goodyear Tire & Rubber Co, 49, supvr. prod, 50. Mil. Serv: Entered as Cadet, Air Force, 42, released as 1st Lt, 45, after serv. in 8th Air Force; ETO Ribbon; Air Medal with 3 Clusters; Distinguished Flying Cross. Mem: AF&AM; Moose; Goodyear Squadron Alumni; Akron Univ. Alumni Asn. Rel: Presbyterian. Mailing Add: 1666 11th St, Cuyahoga Falls, Ohio 44221.

TURNER, RICHARD C. R
Attorney Genera, State of Iowa
b. Avoca, Iowa, 9/30/27; s. Joe W. Turner and Elizabeth Clark T; m. 11/30/56 to Charlotte Forsen; c. Joe W, II, Amy Elizabeth and Mark Howard. Educ: Univ. Iowa, B.A, 50, J.D, 53; Theta Xi; Phi Delta Phi. Polit. & Govt. Pos: Town clerk, Avoca, Iowa, 53-60; asst. co. attorney, Pottawattamie Co, Iowa, 54-56; Iowa State Sen, 61-65; attorney gen, State of Iowa, 67- Bus. & Prof. Pos: Lawyer, Turner & Turner, Attorneys, 53-54; Turner, Williams & Turner, 54-60 and Turner & Walsh, 60-67. Mil. Serv: Entered as Pvt, Air Force, 44, released as Sgt, 47, after serv. in 20th Air Force, Pac, 46-47. Mem: Am, Iowa, S.W. Iowa and Pottawattamie Co. Bar Asns; Am. Trial Lawyers Asn; Iowa Acad. Trial Lawyers; Am. Judicature Soc; Am. Legion; 40 et 8; Elks. Rel: Presbyterian. Legal Res: Council Bluffs, Iowa 51501. Mailing Add: 1054 21st St, West Des Moines, Iowa 50265.

TURNER, ROBERT WILSON
S.C. State Rep.
b. Johnsonville, Florence Co, 10/3/23; s. Robert W. Turner and Elizabeth Cameron T; m. 5/18/47 to Natalie Richardson; c. Robert, Janet, Karen, Sherryl and Nancy. Educ: Birmingham South. Col, 43-44. Polit. & Govt. Pos: S.C. State Rep, 59- Bus. & Prof. Pos: Realtor, owner Robert W. Turner Agency. Mil. Serv: Air Force, 43-46. Mem: Secy, N.Charleston Exchange Club, 54; v.pres, Charleston Soc. of Residential Appraisers, 58; Mason; Dorchester Lodge 369; Am. Legion; pres. Charleston Real Estate Bd, 57; pres. N.Charleston Jr. C. of C, 58; pres. N.Charleston Bus. and Prfnl. Men Asn, 53. Mailing Add: 501 Parkside Dr, North Charleston, S.C. 29406. (1967)

TURNER, ROY R. R
Chmn, York Co. Rep. Party, S.C.
b. Ft. Payne, Ala, 4/26/29; s. Rufus Clinton Turner and Zelda Clayton T; m. 10/22/60 to Elsa Louise Heckendorf; c. John Edward and Joyce Ellen. Educ: Ga. Inst. of Tech, B.E.E, 55; Eta Kappa Nu; Ga. Tech. Philos. Soc. Polit. & Govt. Pos: Committeeman, S.C. Rep. Exec. Cmt, 64-66; chmn, York Co. Rep. Party, 66-; presidential elector, S.C, 68; alternate del, Rep. Nat. Conv, 68. Bus. & Prof. Pos: Elec. engr, Rust Eng. Co, 55-61, Celanese Corp. Am, 61- Mil. Serv: Entered as Pvt, Air Force, 46, released as M/Sgt, 52, after serv. in Alaskan Command, 48-49 and Morocco, 51-52. Mem: Am. Inst. of Elect. & Electronic Engrs; Nat. Speleological Soc; Nat. Soc. Prfnl. Engrs. Rel: Lutheran. Mailing Add: 1008 Magnolia Dr, Rock Hill, S.C. 29730.

TURNER, VIRGINIA PRICE D
b. Wrightsville, Ga, 10/18/17; d. Arthur Bridges Price and Nancy Harrison P; div. Educ: Univ. Ga, B.S.H.E, 39. Polit. & Govt. Pos: Supvr, Farm Security Admin, Dept. of Agr, 39-45; Secy. to U.S. Rep, Ray J. Madden, Ind, 46- Bus. & Prof. Pos: Teacher, Harrison High Sch, Ga, 36-39. Mem: Served in all elected positions, D.C. DAV Auxiliary and was appointed Nat. Exec. Committeewoman, 46-56; Gulls, Potomac River Power Squadron; served in every elective off, Wash, Co. Club, 4-H. Rel: Episcopal. Mailing Add: 14 Third St. N.E, Washington, D.C. 20002.

TURNER, WAYNE 'ANDY' D
Chmn, Clark Co. Dem. Party, Ill.
b. Marshall, Ill, 8/2/21; s. James M. Turner and Fanny Carpenter T; m. 3/17/43 to Edythe Smitley; c. Terry Ann, Susan Lynn, Sally Jo, James Andrew, David Andy and Mary Beth. Educ: Univ. Ill, 40-41. Polit. & Govt. Pos: Mem, City Coun. of Marshall, Ill, 51-55; pres, Clark Co. Young Dem. Club, 52-56; chmn, Clark Co. Dem. Party, 56-; alternate del, Dem. Nat. Conv, 68. Bus. & Prof. Pos: Union officer, Local 7-641, OCAWIU, AFL-CIO, 50-59, int. rep, 59- Mil. Serv: Entered as Seaman, Navy, 42, released as Electrician's Mate 2/C, 45, after serv. in Am. and Asiatic Pac. Theaters; Victory Medal; Asiatic Pac. Ribbon; Good Conduct Medal; Am. Theater Campaign Ribbon; Electrician's Mate 2/C, Naval Res, 48-52. Mem: Am. Legion; VFW; Moose; OCAWIU, AFL-CIO. Mailing Add: Box 68, Marshall, Ill. 62441.

TURNER, WAYNE CALLAWAY R
Chmn, Plumas Co. Rep. Cent. Cmt, Calif.
b. Red Bluff, Calif, 8/5/20; s. Donald A. Turner and Evelyn M. Callaway T; married; c. Dale Wayne and Daryl Jack. Educ: Jr. Col. Polit. & Govt. Pos: Chmn, Plumas Co. Rep. Cent. Cmt, Calif; mem, Calif. Rep. State Cent. Cmt, 69- Mil. Serv: Electrician Mate 2/C, Navy, World War II. Mem: Mason. Rel: Protestant. Mailing Add: Box 87, Caribou, Calif. 95915. (1967)

TURNETTE, NORMAN L. R
V.Chmn, Los Angeles Co. Rep. Cmt, Calif.
b. Los Angeles, Calif, 1/1/30; s. Anthony Turnette and Nila Wion T; m. 2/18/51 to Barbara Jean Niederhaus; c. Mark G. and Renee M. Educ: Mt. San Antonio Col, A.A, 50. Polit. & Govt. Pos: Mem, 58th Assembly Dist. Rep. Cent. Cmt, Calif, 62-, chmn, 64-69; v.chmn, Los Angeles Co. Rep. Cmt, 62-; asst. treas, state bd, Calif. Rep. Assembly, 66; personnel cmn. mem, Charter Oak Unified Sch. Dist, 69-; chief consult, Senate Rep. Caucus, Calif. State Senate, currently. Bus. & Prof. Pos: Chief indust. engr, Marshall Indust, 56-66; partner, Pub. Affairs Assoc, 66-69; gen. mgr. and part owner, Air Col. of Corona, Calif, 69- Mil. Serv: Entered as Cpl, Army, 50, released as 1st Lt, 53; Calif. Nat. Guard, 40th Div, 48-50 & 53-61; Capt, Army Res. Mem: Jaycees; pres, Covina Club, 61-62. Rel: Lutheran. Mailing Add: 5008 Arroway Ave, Covina, Calif. 91722.

TURNHAM, PETE BENTON D
Ala. State Rep.
b. Penton, Ala; s. Joseph Henry Turnham and Fannie May Sessions T; m. 8/30/43 to Nettye Kathryn Rice; c. Diane Dale, Timothy Neil, Ruthmary Kay and Joseph. Educ: Ala. Polytech. Inst, B.S, 44; Auburn Univ, M.S, 48; Univ. Paris; Pa. State Col. Polit. & Govt. Pos: Mem, Lee Co. Sch. Bd, Ala, 55-58; Ala. State Rep, 59- Bus. & Prof. Pos: With A.P.I. Exten. Serv, 48-54; sales rep, Marshall and Bruce Co, Ala, 54-64; conducted several research projects on dairy cattle. Mil. Serv: Army, 43-59, Capt.(Ret); serv. as Comdr, Combat Inf. Units, France, Germany, and Austria; Maj, Army Res, Mil. Intel. Serv, currently. Rel: Baptist. Legal Res: 606 Moore Mill Rd, Auburn, Ala. 36830. Mailing Add: Box 935, Auburn, Ala. 36830. (1967)

TURNQUIST, ARNOLD G. D
Chmn, Foster Dem. Town Cmt, R.I.
b. Glocester, R.I, 4/5/09; m. to Hilda S. Educ: Sch. of Glocester and Providence. Polit. & Govt. Pos: Mem, Adv. Coun. on Forests, R.I, 10 years; R.I. State Sen, 63-66; chmn, Foster Dem. Town Cmt, R.I, currently. Bus. & Prof. Pos: Lumber mfr. and power equip. distributor. Mem: Pres, Foster Lions; Past Master, Ponagansett Grange. Mailing Add: Winsor Rd, Box 155, R.F.D. 1, Foster, R.I. 02825. (1967)

TURSHEN, MAX M. D
b. Brooklyn, N.Y; s. Abraham Turshen and Mary Penziner; m. to Rose Lubin (deceased); c. Ethan Allen, Meredith Belle and Keith Jay. Educ: City Col. New York; N.Y. Univ. Law Sch. Polit. & Govt. Pos: Former chmn, Local Sch. Bd, Brooklyn, N.Y; former Asst. Attorney Gen, N.Y; N.Y. State Assemblyman, 36-62. Bus. & Prof. Pos: Attorney-at-law. Mem: Fed. and Brooklyn Bar Asns; bd. dirs, Lawyers Club; K. of P; Vet. Lodge; Jewish Fed. Charities; Brooklyn Jewish Educ. Asn; Jewish Cong; dir, Yeshiva Rambam; Pub. Off. Cmt, Brooklyn Boy Scouts Lunchoree; bd. dir, Youth

Coun, 63rd Precinct; v.pres, Clarendon Dem. Club First Assembly Dist. Many placks and Man of the Year Awards by charitable and fraternal orgns. Rel: Hebrew. Mailing Add: 1580 E. 13th St, Brooklyn, N.Y. 11230.

TUTEN, JAMES RUSSELL D
b. Appling Co, 7/23/11; m. to Hazel Wicker; c. James, John, Ernest, Mark. Educ: S. Ga. Col, Douglas, Ga; Ga. South. Col, Statesboro, Ga; Gridiron Secret Soc. of Univ. of Ga. Polit. & Govt. Pos: U.S. Rep, Ga, Nov, 62-66; Mayor, Brunswich, 58-62; Brunswich City Cmnr, 56-62; Chmn, Bd. of Trustees, Brewton Parker Col. Bus. & Prof. Pos: Farmer, teacher, bricklayer, businessman, and bldg. contractor. Mem: Mason; York Rite and Scottish Rite; Shriner, past dist. master of 11th Masonic Dist. of Ga, and past grand marshall of Grand Lodge of Ga; Eastern Star; Brunswich Glynn Co. C. of C; Kiwanian. Rel: Baptist deacon, First Baptist Church, Brunswick, Ga, 11 yrs; chmn. of bd. of deacons, 2 yrs. Mailing Add: 214 Noland St, Falls Church, Va. 22046. (1967)

TUTTLE, ELBERT R
s. J. Walton Tuttle; m. to Marian J. Dyan; c. three. Educ: Boston Univ. Col. of Bus. Admin; Boston Univ. Law Sch. Polit. & Govt. Pos: Mem, Framingham Rep. Town Cmt, Mass, 57-62; mem. Bd. Selectmen, Framingham, 62-65; Mass. State Rep, 65-69. Bus. & Prof. Pos: Lawyer. Mil. Serv: Army Inf; serv. as officer, Korean Conflict. Mailing Add: 6 Myrna Rd, Framingham, Mass. 01701. (1967)

TUTTLE, ELSEBETH H. R
Committeewoman, N.Y. State Rep. Cmt.
b. Brewster, N.Y, 5/6/15; d. George W. Heinen and Gertrude Thomas H; m. 12/11/41 to Edward Stannard Tuttle; c. Timothy Clark and Edward Stannard, Jr. Educ: Gaines Bus. Sch, grad, 37. Polit. & Govt. Pos: Secy, Putnam Co. Dept. of Pub. Welfare, N.Y, 37-46; exec. secy. to officers, Fed. Reserve Bank, Jacksonville, Fla, 37-40 & 42-46; pres, Putnam Co. Women's Rep. Club, 66-; v.chmn, Putnam Co. Rep. Cmt, 67-; Putnam Co. rep. for State Sen. Bernard G. Gordon, 67-; clerk, N.Y. State Legis. Cmt. on Ins. Rates and Regulations, 67-; committeewoman, N.Y. State Rep. Cmt, 68- Mem: DAR (v.regent, Enoch Crosby Chap, currently); Southeast Mus; N.Y. State Fedn. of Rep. Women; Nat. Fedn. of Rep. Women; auxiliary mem, Putnam Commun. Hosp; lead singer in women's barbershop quartette, "The Goldusters." Rel: Methodist. Mailing Add: Starr Ridge Rd, Brewster, N.Y. 10509.

TUTTLE, JAMES D
Chmn, Hayes Co. Dem. Exec. Cmt, Tex.
b. Martindale, Tex, 8/30/11; s. Calvin Tuttle and Eleanor Gregg T; m. 9/10/35 to Margaret Cook; c. Margaret. Educ: Southwest. Tex. State Col. Polit. & Govt. Pos: City councilman, San Marcos, Tex, 56-60; chmn, Hayes Co. Dem. Exec. Cmt, currently. Mem: Kiwanis; Mason; Scottish Rite; AF&AM; Shrine; Farm Bur. Rel: Episcopal. Mailing Add: Box 2210, San Marcos, Tex. 78666.

TUTTLE, ROBERT BRADFORD R
b. Warren, Mass, 5/20/32; s. Vernon B. Tuttle and Bernice Roberts T; m. 6/18/55 to Ann Bedell; c. R. Bradford, III, Mark J. and Richard E. Educ: Univ. Mass, B.S; Cornell Univ, grad. study, 2 years. Polit. & Govt. Pos: Mem, Warren Rep. Town Cmt, Mass, 56-69, chmn, 60-65; del, Rep. State Conv, 3 times; chmn, Warren Sch. Cmt. Bus. & Prof. Pos: Mem, Laurel State Fruit Packers, Inc, 58-66; dir. and mem, Mass. Fruit Growers Asn, 58-; dir, Hwy. Area Orgn, 65-66. Mem: AF&AM; v.pres, Rotary Club of the Brookfields. Mailing Add: Southbridge Rd, Warren, Mass. 01083. (1967)

TUTTLE, VIVIAN GILMAN R
b. Ft. Stanton, N.Mex, 10/27/13; m. to Elmer E. Tuttle; c. one. Educ: N.Y. High Sch. Polit. & Govt. Pos: Auditor, West Wardsboro, Vt, 54-, town clerk, 63-; Vt. State Rep, 63-66; former mem. bd. dirs, W.River Develop. Asn. Bus. & Prof. Pos: Housewife. Mem: Eastern Star; CAUSE; West. Wardsboro Ladies Circle. Rel: Methodist. Mailing Add: West Wardsboro, Vt. 05360. (1967)

TWARDUS, JOHN D
N.H. State Rep.
b. Lawrence, Mass, 1/1/98. Educ: St. Mary's High Sch; Newmarket, N.H. Polit. & Govt. Pos: N.H. State Rep, 59-; overseer of poor and selectman of Newmarket. Bus. & Prof. Pos: Retired govt. employee. Mil. Serv: World War I; F.B.I, Navy, World War II, Naval Shipyard, Portsmouth, N.H. Mem: Past Comdr. and life mem, Robert G. Durgin Post 67, Newmarket; state comdr, Vets. of World War I; Hosp. chmn, World War I, N.H; Nat. Hosp. Chmn, World War I, U.S.A. Organized the Vets. Asn. at the Naval Shipyard in 44, and Barracks of World War I, 57 at the Naval Shipyard, Portsmouth; served as Comdr. and Serv. Officer. Rel: Catholic. Mailing Add: 36 Packers Falls Rd, Newmarket, N.H. 03857.

TWETEN, KENNETH R
N.Dak, State Rep.
b. Grand Forks, N.Dak, 8/27/28; married; c. one. Educ: Pub. Schs. Polit. & Govt. Pos: N.Dak. State Rep, 59-, chmn, Transportation Cmt, 63 and Cmt. on Gen. Affairs, 67, v.chmn, Cmt. on Appropriations, 69. Bus. & Prof. Pos: Farmer. Mem: Farm Bur; Steering Cmt, Nat. Potato Coun, 66. Rel: Lutheran. Mailing Add: 2816 Clover Dr, Grand Forks, N.Dak. 58201.

TWIGGS, HOWARD FABING D
N.C. State Rep.
b. Cincinnati, Ohio, 10/27/32; s. Samuel Warren Twiggs and Ruth Fabing T; m. 6/7/58 to Anne Miller; div; c. Elizabeth Anne, Mary Catherine and Jennifer Margaret. Educ: Wake Forest Col, B.S, 54 & LL.B, 57; Omicron Delta Kappa; Kappa Alpha Order; Phi Delta Phi. Polit. & Govt. Pos: N.C. State Rep, 67- Mil. Serv: Entered As Pvt, Army, 58, released as 1st Lt, 64, after serv. in 108th Regt, Raleigh, N.C. Mem: Chmn. Exec. Cmt, Wake Co. Bar Asn, 63; pres, Raleigh Jaycees, 63-64 and Wake Co. Ment. Health Asn, 64-65; dir, Raleigh C. of C, 63-64; bd. dir, N.C. Crippled Children's Asn. and N.C. Ment. Health Asn. Rel: Episcopal. Mailing Add: 3939 Glenwood Ave, Raleigh, N.C. 27609.

TWINAME, JOHN DEAN R
Dep. Adminstr, Soc. and Rehabilitation Serv, Dept. of Health, Educ. and Welfare
b. Mt. Kisco, N.Y, 12/27/31; s. Clarence George Twiname and Constance Ulmer T; m. 8/8/55 to Carolyn Anderson; c. Karen Lynn, Jeanne Copeland and Julia Dean. Educ: Cornell Univ, A.B, 53; Harvard Grad. Sch, George Baker Scholar, 55-57, M.B.A, 57. Polit. & Govt. Pos: Dep. adminstr, Soc. and Rehabilitation Serv, Dept. of Health, Educ. and Welfare, 69- Bus. & Prof. Pos: Sales rep, Am. Hosp. Supply Div, Am. Hosp. Supply Corp, Evanston, Ill, 58-60, prod. research mgr, 61-62, Midwest area sales mgr, 62-63, asst. to pres, 63-64, mkt. mgr, 64-67, v.pres, mkt. serv, 68-69. Mil. Serv: Entered as 2nd Lt, Army, 53, released as 1st Lt, 55, after serv. as Artil-Bn. Intel. Officer. Mem: Pres. bd. mgr, Chicago Bus. Indust. Proj; Econ. Club of Chicago; Chicago Exec. Club; Wilmette Human Rels. Cmt. Rel: Christian; Elder, Winnetka Presby. Church. Mailing Add: 3407 N St. N.W, Washington, D.C. 20007.

TWITTY, FRANK STARLING D
Mem, State Dem. Exec. Cmt, Ga.
b. Camilla, Ga, 8/29/07; s. Thomas B. Twitty and Tennie Wood T; m. 8/5/29 to Margaret Elisabeth Almand; c. Margaret Leah (Mrs. Charles R. Adams, Jr.); Frank S. Jr; Louise Almand (Mrs. Raymond Steele). Educ: Mercer Univ, LL.B, 28; Alpha Tau Omega; Delta Theta Phi. Polit. & Govt. Pos: City attorney, Camilla, Ga, 38-; Ga. State Rep, 45-64, Floor Leader, Ga. State House of Rep, 51-54 & 59-62; mem, State Dem. Exec. Cmt, Ga, 51-54, 59-62 & 67-; gen. counsel, Ga. Sheriffs Asn, 60-; co. attorney, Mitchell Co, 65- Bus. & Prof. Pos: Attorney-at-law. Mem: Mason; Shrine; WOW; dist. gov, Rotary; pres. and dir, C. of C. Rel: Baptist. Mailing Add: Camilla, Ga. 31730.

TWOMBLY, MARGARET ANN 'PEGGY' D
b. Salt Lake City, Utah; d. Daniel Joseph Cavanagh and Pearl Langford C; m. 12/27/45 to Phillip Sidney Twombly; c. Michael Phillip, Kathleen (Mrs. Robert Keith McKellogg), Patricia Ann, Sheila Mary and Daniel Cavanagh. Educ: Maryhurst Col, B.S, 44. Polit. & Govt. Pos: Mem. exec. cmt, Calif. Dem. State Cent. Cmt, 60-69; pres, Fullerton Dem. Women's Club, Calif, 69- Mem: Mem. exec. cmt, Friends of the Col, Calif. State, Fullerton; Assistance League Damas De Caridad (past pres); past pres, Vol. Bur, Jr. Ebell Club, and Jr. Assistance League; charter mem, Nat. Charity League; St. Jude's Hosp. Guild Assistance League; hon. life mem, PTA. Rel: Roman Catholic. Mailing Add: 1106 Richman Knoll, Fullerton, Calif. 92632.

TWOMEY, GEORGE E. R
Mass. State Rep.
b. Newburyport, Mass, 2/3/20; s. Eugene A. Twomey and Anna M. Keller T; m. 9/29/44 to Doris M. Creeden; c. G. Michael, Stephen P. and Kathleen A. Polit. & Govt. Pos: Mass. State Rep, 21 Essex Dist, 64- Bus. & Prof. Pos: Funeral dir. Mil. Serv: Entered as A/S, Coast Guard, 42, released as BM 1/C, 45. Rel: Catholic. Mailing Add: 193 High St, Newburyport, Mass. 01950.

TYDINGS, JOSEPH DAVIES D
U.S. Sen, Md.
b. Asheville, N.C, 5/4/28; s. Millard E. Tydings and Eleanor Davies T; m. 8/20/55 to Virginia Reynolds Campbell; c. Mary Campbell, Millard E, II, Emlen Davies and Eleanor Davies. Educ: Univ. Md, B.A, 51; Univ. Md. Law Sch, LL.B, 53; Phi Eta Sigma; Phi Kappa Phi; Omicron Delta Kappa; Scabbard and Blade; Phi Kappa Sigma; pres, Student Govt. Hon. LL.D, C.W. Post Col, L.I. Univ. and Parsons Col, 67. Polit. & Govt. Pos: Pres, Young Dem. Clubs of Md, 53-55; city attorney, Aberdeen, 54-60; Md. State Del, 55-61; coordinator for the States of Fla. and Del, Kennedy for Pres. and polit. agent and campaign mgr, Md. Presidential Preferential Primary, 60; U.S. Attorney for Md, 61-63; pres, Jr. Bar Asn. of Baltimore City, 62-63; del, Int. Penal Conf, Bellagio, Italy, 63, Interpol Conf, Helsinki, Finland, 63, Mex-U.S. Interparliamentary Conf, Mexico City, 65, Coun. of Intergovt. Cmt. for European Migration, Geneva, Switz, 66 and NATO Assembly, Brussels, Belgium, 68; U.S. Sen, Md, 65- Mil. Serv: Entered as Pvt, Army, 46, released as Cpl, 48, after serv. in Inf, ETO. Publ: 'An Argument for Additional Law Clerks for the Court of Appeals,' Student Lawyer J, 1/67; 'Home Rule for D.C: The Case for Political Justice,' 3/67; 'A Federal Verdict of Not Guilty by Reason of Insanity and a Subsequent Commitment Procedure,' Md. Law Rev, spring 67. Mem: Pres, Jr. Bar Asn. Baltimore City, 62-63; v.pres, Am. Judicature Soc, 68-69; sect. coun, Sect. of Criminal Law and Sect. of Judicial Admin, Md. Bar Asn, 67-69; Metrop. Bd. Dirs, YMCA, 62-63; chmn, Md. Chap, Nat. Multiple Sclerosis Soc, 61. Received Commendation, Md. Legis. Correspondents's Asn, 60 and 61; Outstanding Young Man of Year, Baltimore Jr. C. of C, 63; DAV Award, 66; Prince George's Pub. Rels. Asn. Award for Distinguished Achievement, 67; Menorah Award, B'nai B'rith, 67; Asn. of Fed. Investr. Legis. Award, 67; Am. Trial Lawyers Citation of Distinction in Exceptional Serv. to our Nat. Welfare, 68; Sidney Hollander Award of Distinction, Am. Jewish Cong, 68. Rel: Episcopal. Legal Res: Oakington, Havre de Grace, Md. 21078. Mailing Add: Senate Office Bldg, Washington, D.C. 20510.

TYGART, JAMES CHARLES, SR. R
Chmn, Berrien Co. Rep. Party, Ga.
b. Miami, Fla, 12/8/27; s. Jeff Davis Tygart and Fredia Goetz T; m. 1947 to Marjorie West; c. Lana Joy, Peggy Ann, James Charles, Jr, Timothy Davis and Cynthia Elaine. Educ: Ga. Inst. Tech, 3 years. Polit. & Govt. Pos: Chmn, Berrien Co. Rep. Party, Ga, 64- Bus. & Prof. Pos: Pres, New Ideal Sprayer Co, 50-65; S.E. regional sales mgr, Frick Co, 65-68; pres, Obsolete Chevrolet Parts Co, 69- Mil. Serv: Entered as Pvt, Air Force, 45, released as Pfc, 47, after serv. in Eighth Air Force. Mem: Elks; Moose; Boy Scouts; MMM Club. Rel: Methodist. Mailing Add: Route 3, Box 32, Nashville, Ga. 31639.

TYLER, HERBERT H. D
Md. State Del.
b. Hooper's Island, Md, 9/21/12; married. Educ: Wesley Col, Dover, Del. Polit. & Govt. Pos: Md. State Del, 59-; del, Dem. Nat. Conv, 68. Bus. & Prof. Pos: Businessman. Mem: 15th Dist. Dem. Club; pres, Fourth Councilmanic

Dist. Dem. Club; Manor Dem. Club; Lockridge Merchants Asn; Optimists; Holy Name Soc; Loch Raven Rod and Gun Club. Mailing Add: 1022 Green Acre Rd, Towson, Md. 21204. (1967)

TYLER, WILLIAM ROYALL
b. Paris, France, 10/17/10; s. Royall Tyler and Elisina De Castelvecchio T; m. 7/31/34 to Bettine Mary Fisher-Rowe; c. Royall and Matilda Eve Thompson. Educ: Oxford, Eng, B.A, 33; Harvard, Mass, M.A, 41; Phi Beta Kappa. Hon. D.Litt, Marlboro Col, Vt. Polit. & Govt. Pos: Off. of War Info, N.Africa and France, 42-45; asst. dir, Off. of Int. and Educ. Exchange, 46-48; pub. affairs officer, Paris, 48-52; counselor, Paris, 52-54; dep. dir, Off. of West. European Affairs, 54-57, dir, 57; del, UN 12th Gen. Assembly, 57-58; counselor, Bonn, 58-61; dep. asst. secy. of state for European Affairs, 61-62; asst. secy. of State for European Affairs, 62-65; career officer, U.S. Dept. of State For. Serv, 52-; U.S. Ambassador to the Netherlands, 65-69. Bus. & Prof. Pos: For. banking, 33-38; mgr, Short Wave Radio Sta, 40-42; dir, Dumbarton Oaks Research Libr. and Collection, 69. Mem: Am. Acad. Arts and Sci; hon. mem, Colonial Soc. of Mass; hon. mem, Societe Des Amis Du Musée De Dijon. Medal of Freedom; Knight, Order of the Legion of Honor, France. Rel: Episcopal. Mailing Add: 1735 32nd St, N.W, Washington, D.C. 20007.

TYNDALE, ELMONT SCOTT R
Maine State Rep.
b. N.Y.C, 7/25/00; s. Charles William Tyndale and Jennie Byington T; m. 12/19/37 to Alice Emmons. Educ: Columbia Univ, 22; Alexander Hamilton Bus. Col, 1 year. Polit. & Govt. Pos: Maine State Rep, 61-64 & 69-, asst. majority floor leader and house chmn, pub. utilities cmt, Maine House of Rep, 63-64, chmn, Bills in Third Reading, currently, auth. of over 35 bills now state laws; mem, Rep. Town Cmt, currently. Bus. & Prof. Pos: Nat. rep, Sylvania Elec. Prod, Inc, 39-54; mfr, Emmons Loom Binder Mfg. Co, 54-59, semi-retired. Mem: Lighting Engrs. Soc; Necomen Soc. of N.Am; Mason; K. of P; Odd Fellows; dir, Webber Hosp; dir, Waban Asn. for Retarded Children; Elks; chap. chmn, Red Cross. War Man Power Cmn. Award for outstanding serv. in recruitment of labor for vital war material, Manhattan Proj, World War II. Rel: Protestant; trustee of church. Mailing Add: Emmons Clock Farm, Kennebunkport, Maine 04046.

TYNER, MAYME R
Rep. State Committeewoman, Fla.
b. Laurel Hill, Fla, 3/15/06; d. Mack Tyner and Effie Campbell T; m. 12/23/34 to Richard Eugene Pilcher; div; c. Sara Jane (Mrs. Kay Marvin Eoff). Educ: Fla. State Col. for Women, L.I, 28, A.B. in Educ, 30; Fla. State Univ, M.A. in Educ, 50; Sci. Soc; Col. 4-H Club. Polit. & Govt. Pos: Del, Rep. Nat. Conv, 56, 60 & 68, alternate del, 64; secy, Fla. State Rep. Exec. Cmt, 54-66 and asst. secy, 66-; Rep. state committeewoman, Fla, 54- Bus. & Prof. Pos: Teacher of Eng, Pub. Schs. of Okaloosa, Walton and Calhoun Counties of Fla, 30-34 & 38-57. Mem: Secy, Local Realtor Bd, 60-62 & 66, pres, 63, v.pres, 64; Fla. and Nat. Asns. of Realtors; secy, Fla. Coun. of Eng. Teachers, 48; dir, Co. Chap. Red Cross, 57-63, pilot chmn, 59. Rel: Presbyterian. Legal Res: Route 1, Box 14, Laurel Hill, Fla. 32537. Mailing Add: 317 N. Main St, Crestview, Fla. 32536.

TYRE, RALPH CHARLES D
Fla. State Rep.
b. Lake City, Fla, 9/19/33; m. to Ruth Lord; c. Dottie Ruth. Polit. & Govt. Pos: Fla. State Rep, 64- Bus. & Prof. Pos: Petroleum Jobber. Mil. Serv: Nat. Guard, 52-63, Discharged as Sgt. Mem: First v.pres, Lake City Jaycees; Elks; Moose; WOW; C. of C; QB Club. All-State Football Team 1951; Mr. J. C, 63. Rel: Baptist. Legal Res: 1422 E. Duval, Lake City, Fla. 32055. Mailing Add: P.O. Box 608, Lake City, Fla. 32055. (1967)

TYRELL, JACK RIX R
Mayor Pro-Tem, Temple City, Calif.
b. Alhambra, Calif, 5/6/21; s. John J. Tyrell and Ruth Sands T; m. 7/2/43 to Marion Mallman; c. Sandra Sue, Jon Sands and Randy Rix. Educ: Pasadena Jr. Col, A.A, 41; Univ. South. Calif, A.B, 49; Univ. South. Calif. Sch. Law, J.D, 52. Polit. & Govt. Pos: Councilman, Temple City, Calif, 60-, mayor, 62 & 66, v.mayor, 65 & 69, mayor pro-tem, currently; secy, Calif. Contract Cities Asn, 63-64, second v.pres, 64-65, first v.pres, 65-66, pres, 66-67. Bus. & Prof. Pos: Life guard, Alhambra, Calif, summers 39-51; master router, Vega Aircraft, Burbank, 41-42; welder's helper, grinder, metal worker, inspector, shipping clerk, asst. sales mgr. and sales engr, C.E. Howard & Co, Los Angeles, 45-48; attorney-at-law, 54-56; partner, Davidson, Tyrell & Davidson, Alhambra, 56- Mil. Serv: Entered as Aviation Cadet, Navy, 42, released as Lt, 45, after serv. in Fleet Air Detachment. Mem: Am. and Los Angeles Bar Asns; Nat. and Calif. Trial Lawyers Asns; South. Dist, Fed. Bar of Calif; Legionlex, Univ. South. Calif; State Bar of Calif; Phi Alpha Delta; F&AM; Scottish Rite (32°); Shrine; Alhambra Hi Twelve; Pasadena Tournament of Roses Asn; Am. Legion, Alhambra; Alhambra Exchange Club; Dist. Attorney's Adv. Coun, Los Angeles Co; San Gabriel Valley Boy Scouts (dir); Temple City C. of C. Rel: Episcopal. Mailing Add: 5709 N. Alessandro, Temple City, Calif. 91780.

TYSON, BERTRAND OLIVER D
b. Baton Rouge, La, 10/3/31; s. Straudy Auston Tyson (deceased) and Olivia Byrd T. (deceased); m. 7/1/67 to Maureen Baggal; c. Lisa Camille, Celeste Olivia, Bertrand O, Jr. and Michelle Asante'wa. Educ: Howard Univ, B.S, 50; Meharry Med. Col, M.D, 59; Alpha Phi Alpha. Polit. & Govt. Pos: Del, Dem. Nat. Conv, 68; mem, White House Conf. on Youth and Children, 69- Bus. & Prof. Pos: Gen. practice of med, Plaquemine, La, 60-68; resident, Dept. of Obstetrics and Gynecology, Harvard Med. Sch, Beth Israel Hosp, Brookline, Mass, currently. Mil. Serv: Entered as Pvt, Army, 52, released as Cpl, 54, after serv. in Med. Detachment, U.S. Publ: Several research articles as a medical student. Mem: Nat. Med. Asn; Iberville Parish Med. Soc. Rel: Protestant. Mailing Add: 79 Aspinwall Ave, Brookline, Mass. 02146.

TYSON, CHARLES ELWOOD R
Exec. Dir, Macomb Co. Rep. Cmt, Mich.
b. Berwin, Ill, 4/12/44; s. William Henry Tyson and Margaret Collins T; single. Educ: Univ. Wis, Madison, 62-63; Grand Rapids Jr. Col, A.B.S, 66; West. Mich. Univ, 66-68. Polit. & Govt. Pos: Pres, Grand Rapids Jr. Col. Rep. Club, Mich, 65-66; staff asst, Fifth Dist. Rep. Cmt, 66; treas, Mich. Fedn. of Col. Rep, 66-67; dir, Region Five, Col. Rep. Nat. Cmt, 67-68; adv, Kent Co. TAR, 67-68, dir, Mich. TAR Camp, 68 & 69; exec. dir, Macomb Co. Rep. Cmt, 68-; regional v.pres, Mich. Fedn. of Young Rep, 69. Bus. & Prof. Pos: Acct. clerk, Cornelius Co, Anoka, Minn, 63-64; pres, Novak and Co. Inc, Mt. Clemens, Mich, 68-69. Mem: External v.pres, Gr. Mt. Clemens Jaycees, 69-; Mich. Rep. Exec. Dir. Asn; v.pres, Roe Found. Rel: Episcopal; Vestryman, Grace Episcopal Church. Mailing Add: 108 Lincoln, Mt. Clemens, Mich. 48043.

TYSON, JOHN M. D
b. Jacksonville, Fla, 8/26/25; s. James Jordan Tyson; Mrytice McCaskill T; m. to Grace Harris Durant; c. John M. Jr, William Jordan. Educ: Sigma Alpha Epsilon; Phi Delta Phi. Polit. & Govt. Pos: Ala. State Sen, 63-66; Ala. State Rep, 55-59. Mil. Serv: Naval Air Res. Mem: Am. Legion; Mason. Rel: Presbyterian. Mailing Add: 1804 Hunter Ave, Mobile, Ala. 36606. (1967)

TYUS, E. LEROY D
Chmn, First Cong. Dist. Dem. Party, Mo.
b. Brownsville, Tenn, 2/4/16; s. O. T. Tyus and Odelia Parker T; m. 1945 to Marie Holton; c. Cheryl and Cathy. Educ: Lane Col, Jackson, Tenn, 3 years; Lincoln Law Sch, St. Louis, Mo, 1 year; Alpha Phi Alpha; Vagabond's Inc; Lamb's, Inc. Polit. & Govt. Pos: Mo. State Rep, 50-60; committeeman, 20th Ward, Mo, 60-; Constable, Eighth Magistrate Dist, 62-; del, Dem. Nat. Conv, 68; chmn, First Cong. Dist. Dem. Party, 68- Bus. & Prof. Pos: Operated Army Canteen, St. Louis Mo, 42-45; Tavern and Hotel owner, 45-50; Real Estate Broker, 50-; Operate Security Agency, 66- Received Certificate of Merit in area of Legislative Serv, Lane Col, 52. Rel: Catholic. Mailing Add: 5225 Lexington, St. Louis, Mo. 63115.

U

UBAN, CHARLES J. D
b. Thomson, Iowa, 6/29/21; s. John L. Uban and Mildred U; m. to Emma Jo Schnucker; c. John, Jolynn, Stephen, Mark and Mary Ann. Educ: Iowa State Univ, B.S, 49. Polit. & Govt. Pos: Iowa State Rep, until 66; former Dem. Precinct Committeeman. Bus. & Prof. Pos: Oil Jobber in Waterloo. Mil. Serv: Pilot for the China Nat. Aviation Corp, World War II. Mailing Add: 10 Winter Ridge Rd, Cedar Falls, Iowa 50613. (1967)

UBERTI, E. JAMES R
Chmn, Ansonia Rep. Town Cmt, Conn.
b. Shelton, Conn, 8/29/34; s. Anthony Uberti and Lena Sticco U; m. 6/29/57 to Marilyn Ferla; c. James G. and Teresa M. Educ: Univ. Bridgeport, 1½ years. Polit. & Govt. Pos: Chmn, Ansonia Young Rep, Conn, 66-67; chmn, Ansonia Rep. Town Cmt, 67- Bus. & Prof. Pos: Partner, Derby Glass Co, 56-; gen. distributor, Holiday Magic, Inc, 67- Mil. Serv: Entered as Pvt, Army, 54, released as Pfc, 56, after serv. in Qm. Corps. Mem: Jaycees; Auto Glass Installers of Conn. Rel: Roman Catholic. Mailing Add: 19 Finney St. Extension, Ansonia, Conn. 06401.

UDALL, MORRIS KING D
U.S. Rep, Ariz.
b. St. Johns, Ariz, 6/15/22; s. Levi S. Udall and Louise Lee U; m. 12/1/68 to Ella Royston. Educ: Univ. Ariz, LL.B. with distinction, 49; pres, student body, 48; co-capt, basketball team and all-conf. forward. Polit. & Govt. Pos: Chief dep. co. attorney, Pima Co, Ariz, 51-52 and co. attorney, 53-54; del, Dem. Nat. Conv. and chmn, Ariz. Volunteers for Stevenson, 56; U.S. Rep, Ariz, Second Cong Dist, 61-, mem, Post Off. and Civil Serv. Cmt, Interior and Insular Affairs Cmt, chmn, Fed. Compensation Subcmt, U.S. House of Rep, presently. Bus. & Prof. Pos: Partner, Udall & Udall, 49-61; co-founder and dir, Bank of Tucson and Catalina Savings & Loan Asn. Mil. Serv: Entered as Pvt, Army, 42, released as Capt, Air Force, 46, after serv. in 20th Air Force, Iwo Jima, Saipan, Guam, Pac. Theatre. Publ: Arizona Law of Evidence, West Publishing Co, 60-; The Job of the Congressman (w. Donald G. Tacheron), Bobbs-Merrill Co, 66. Mem: V.pres, Ariz. State Bar Asn. and chmn, Modern Courts Cmt, 60; pres, Tucson YMCA, 60; trustee, Ariz-Sonora Desert Museum. Played prfnl. basketball with Denver Nuggets, Nat. Basketball League, 48-49. Rel: Latter-day Saint. Legal Res: 142 S. Calle Chaparita, Tucson, Ariz. 85716. Mailing Add: 119 House Office Bldg, Washington, D.C. 20515.

UDALL, STEWART LEE D
b. St. Johns, Ariz, 1/31/20; s. Levi S. Udall and Louise Lee U; m. 8/1/46 to Ermalee Webb; c. Thomas, Scott, Lynn, Lori, Denis and James. Educ: Univ. of Ariz, LL.B, 48. Hon. LL.D, Dartmouth Col, Wesleyan Univ, Syracuse Univ, Dickinson Col; L.I. Univ, Wash. Col. and Harvard Univ. Polit. & Govt. Pos: U.S. Rep, Ariz, 55-60; Secy. of Interior, 61-69. Bus. & Prof. Pos: Attorney-at-law, Tucson, Ariz, 48-54; chmn. of bd, The Overview Group, 69- Mil. Serv: Army Air Force, 44. Publ: The Quiet Crisis, Holt, Rinehard & Winston, 63; 1976: Agenda for Tomorrow, Harcourt, Brace & World, 68. Mem: Am. Bar Asn. Rel: Latter-day Saint. Legal Res: Tucson, Ariz. Mailing Add: 1700 Pennsylvania Ave. N.W, Washington, D.C. 20006.

UDINE, FRED FRANCIS D
b. Redlands, Calif, 12/15/05; s. Frank Oscar Udine and Orrie Bell Koehler U. Educ: North. Ariz. Univ. Polit. & Govt. Pos: Ariz. State Sen, 55-67. Mem: Mason, Shriner. Rel: Methodist. Mailing Add: R.R. 1, Box 140, Williams, Ariz. 86046. (1967)

UECKER, WILMONT M. D
S.Dak. State Sen.
b. 5/4/14; m. 6/28/40 to Mavis V. Tipton; c. Jolene and Collene. Educ: Raymond Independent Sch. Polit. & Govt. Pos: Mem. town cmt. and town assessor; mem. sch. bd; co. ASCS committeeman; S.Dak. State Rep, 59; S.Dak. State Sen, 64- Rel: Lutheran. Mailing Add: Raymond, S.Dak. 57258.

UEHLING, ROBERT O. R
Wis. State Assemblyman
b. Wis. Rapids, Wis, 4/23/15. Educ: Wis. Univ, B.A, 39, LL.B, 41. Polit. &

Govt. Pos: Admin. officer, State Selective Serv. Syst, Wis, 52-57; alderman, Madison, Wis, 58-60; Wis. State Assemblyman, 60- Bus. & Prof. Pos: Title and trust officer, 46-52; Attorney, 57- Mil. Serv: Army, 41-45. Mem: Am, State and Co. Bar Asns; Elks; Optimist Club; Nat. Guard Officers Asn. Mailing Add: 4330 Keating Terr, Madison, Wis. 53711. (1967)

UHLENBERG, FRANK L. R
b. Kenosha, Wis, 4/22/07; married; c. two. Educ: Univ. of Wis; Mil. Law, U.S. Navy; Teachers Col, Keene, N.H. Polit. & Govt. Pos: N.H. State Rep, 63-67; Notary Pub; Justice of the Peace; former mem, Gilmanton Budget Cmt. Bus. & Prof. Pos: Machinist; diesel engr; high sch. teacher. Mil. Serv: Navy, 24 years active duty, retired. Mem: V.pres, Belknap Co. Farm Bur; VFW; past pres, Belknap Co. 4-H Fair Asn; Farm Bur. Legis. Adv. Cmt; 4-H Adv. Coun, 4-H leader 20 years; former mem, Belknap Co. Exten. Serv. Finance Cmt. Rel: Chmn, Prudential Cmt, United Church of Gilmanton. Mailing Add: R.F.D. 1, Gilmanton Iron Works, N.H. 03837.

UHLER, LEWIS KNIGHT R
Mem, Calif. Rep. State Cent. Cmt.
b. Alhambra, Calif, 11/22/33; s. James Carvel Uhler and Mavis Fay Warrell U; m. 12/26/55 to Cynthia Louise Ross; c. James Ross, Jonathan Knight and Kirk Lewis. Educ: Yale Univ, B.A, 55; Univ. Calif, Barkeley, J.D, 58; Yale Key; Calliopean Soc. Polit. & Govt. Pos: Admin. asst. to Congressman John H. Rousselot, Calif, 61 & 62; del, Young Rep. Nat. Conv, 63; area dir, Goldwater for President Cmt, 64; asst. to pub. rels. dir, Citizens for Goldwater-Miller, Wash, D.C, 64; partner, Pub. Affairs Assocs, 66-69; alternate mem, Los Angeles Co. Rep. Cent. Cmt, Calif, 67 & 68; mem, Calif. Rep. State Cent. Cmt, 67-; cmnr, Calif. Law Rev. Cmn, 68- Bus. & Prof. Pos: Partner, Garvey Ingram & Baker, Attorneys, Covina, Calif, 63- Mil. Serv: Entered as 2nd Lt, Army, 58, released as 1st Lt, 60, after serv. in Army Intel, Continental U.S. Mem: State Bar of Calif; various local, co, state and nat. Bar Asns; pres, Yale Club of South. Calif; past pres, Edgewood Family Counseling Agency; Covina Rotary Club; Aircraft Owners & Pilots Asn. Rel: Protestant. Mailing Add: 541 N. Segovia, San Gabriel, Calif. 91775.

UHLMAN, WESLEY CARL D
Wash. State Sen.
b. Cashmere, Wash, 3/13/35; s. Warner Uhlman and Dorcas Zimmerman U; m. 12/30/57 to Laila Hammond; c. Wesley Carl, Jr. and Daniel Willard. Educ: Seattle Pac. Col, 52-54; Univ. Wash, B.A, 56, Law Sch, LL.B, 59; Pi Sigma Alpha; Phi Alpha Delta; Model UN; Theta Delta Chi. Polit. & Govt. Pos: Chmn. and pres, 32nd Dist. Dem. Cmt. and Dem. Club, Seattle, Wash, 58-62; chmn, First Cong. Dist. Dem. Caucus, 60; Wash. State Rep, 58-66, chmn, Cmt. on Ways and Means and Cmt. on Higher Educ, 60-62, Wash. State House of Rep; Wash. State Sen, 66- Mil. Serv: 1st Lt, Wash. State Nat. Guard and v.pres, 63-64. Mem: Bd. dirs, Wallingford Boys Club; bd. dirs, N. Cent. C. of C. and chmn, Laws and Regulations Cmt, 64; Kiwanis; Odd Fellows; Mason. Received Outstanding Young Men of America Award, Jaycees, 58. Rel: Methodist; Lay Delegate. Mailing Add: 207 College Club Bldg, Seattle, Wash. 98104. (1967)

UKKELBERG, CLIFFORD Conservative
Minn. State Sen.
b. 3/17/04; married; c. three. Educ: Univ. Minn. Sch. of Agr. Polit. & Govt. Pos: Minn. State Rep, 54-56; Minn. State Sen, 58-; formerly with Fed. Farm Credit Off, 12 years; former mem, local sch. bd. and local PCA. Bus. & Prof. Pos: Owner and operator, farm in partnership with son; instr. agr, adult educ. Mem: 4-H Club Leadership. Mailing Add: Clitherall, Minn. 56524. (1967)

ULLMAN, AL D
U.S. Rep, Ore.
b. Great Falls, Mont, 3/9/14; m. 1941 to Anita Curfman; c. Three. Educ: Whitman Col, B.A, 35; Columbia Univ, M.A. pub. law, 39; Beta Theta Pi. Polit. & Govt. Pos: U.S. Rep, Ore, 56-, mem, Ways and Means Cmt. and Dem. Cmt. on Cmts; del, Dem. Nat. Conv, 68. Bus. & Prof. Pos: Teacher, Port Angeles, Washington High Sch, 2 years. Mil. Serv: Commun. Officer afloat in S. and S.W. Pac. Rel: Presbyterian. Legal Res: Baker, Ore. 97403. Mailing Add: 2410 Rayburn House Office Bldg, Washington, D.C. 20515.

ULMER, ELDON ROBERT R
State Finance Chmn, Rep. Party of Alaska
b. Boise, Idaho, 11/15/18; s. T.C. Ulmer and Winnifred Tarter U; m. 5/1/42 to Lillian Virgin; c. Robert Brent, Jerry Eldon, Scott Alan, Sue Ellen and Reed Christian. Educ: Idaho State Univ, B.S. in Pharm, 43. Polit. & Govt. Pos: Finance chmn, S. Cent. Dist. Rep. Party, Alaska, 67; del, Rep. Nat. Conv, 68; del, Alaska State Rep. Conv, 68; del, S. Cent. Rep. Party Conv, Alaska, 68; state finance chmn, Rep. Party of Alaska, 68- Mil. Serv: Entered as Seaman, Navy, 43, released as Lt.(jg), 46, after serv. in U.S.S. Rhind, Destroyers, S.Pac. Theatre, 44-46; World War II and Pac. Theatre Medals. Mem: Alaska Pharmaceutical Asn.(dir); Alaska State Bd. of Pharm.(v.pres); Am. Cancer Soc.(treas. Alaska div, 68-69); Anchorage Businessmen's Asn. (treas, 60, pres, 63); Downtown Anchorage Merchants Asn.(bd. dirs, 68-69); Boy Scouts (treas, Alaska div). Rel: Protestant. Legal Res: 5204 Strawberry Rd, Anchorage, Alaska 99504. Mailing Add: P.O. Box 1420, Anchorage, Alaska 99501.

ULMER, WALTER JULIUS R
Mont. State Rep.
b. Hebron, N.Dak, 10/12/15; s. Emanual Ulmer and Magdalene Heinle U; m. 3/1/41 to LaVonne Delores Watters; c. Gregory Leland and Judy Jo (Mrs. Burke). Educ: N.Dak. State Col, 34-37; Iowa State Col, B.S, in Civil Eng, 40. Polit. & Govt. Pos: Chmn, Custer Co. Cent. Cmt, Mont, 61-64; Mont. State Rep, 64- Mil. Serv: Entered as 2nd Lt, Army, Corps of Engrs, 41, released as 1st Lt, Hq. S.O.S. ETO, 43. Mem: Lions; Elks; Miles City and Mont. C. of C; Red Cross Bd. of Dirs; dir, Mont. Auto Asn. Rel: Presbyterian; Elder, First Presbyterian Church. Mailing Add: 121 S. Merriam, Miles City, Mont. 59301.

ULRICH, WILFRID J. D
Ind. State Sen.
Educ: Notre Dame, 29. Polit. & Govt. Pos: Mem, Ind. Bd. of Pharm, 50-54; Ind. State Sen, 63- Bus. & Prof. Pos: Registered pharmacist and owner of drugstore; dir, First Nat. Bank, Aurora; pres, Aurora Indust. Develop. Corp. Mem: Pres, Ind. Pharmaceutical Asn, 50; past officer, mem. Hilforest Found; Polio, Tuberc. and Ment. Health Asns; Aurora Farmers Fair Asn; K. of C.(4°); Rotary; Men of Milford, Medievalists; C. of C; past chmn, Dearborn & Ohio Co. Red Cross; Adv. Bd. Sch. of Pharm, Butler Univ. Named Ind. Pharmacist of Year, 65. Rel: Catholic. Mailing Add: 403 Main St, Aurora, Ind. 47001.

UMPHREY, JAMES MORRIS R
Chmn, Huron Co. Rep. Party, Mich.
b. Detroit, Mich, 9/20/23; s. Edwin S. Umphrey and Ione Morris U; m. 8/21/48 to Barbara J. Merrill; c. Mary Patricia and Martha Merrill. Educ: Cent. Mich. Univ, A.B, 49; Wayne State Univ, LL.B, 51; Phi Sigma Epsilon; Sigma Nu Phi. Polit. & Govt. Pos: Rep. dist. chmn, Eighth Cong. Dist, Mich; prosecuting attorney, Huron Co, 53-62; finance chmn, Huron Co. Rep. Party, 62-64, chmn, 65-; mem, Mich. State Rep. Cent. Cmt, 62-65; alternate del, Rep. Nat. Conv, 68. Bus. & Prof. Pos: Mem, Bd. Trustees, Cent. Mich. Univ, 65- Mil. Serv: Entered as Pvt, Air Force, 43, released as S/Sgt, 45, after serv. in 31st Sq, 5th Bomb Group, 13th Air Force, Southwest Pac; Air Medal; Southwest Pac. Campaign Ribbon with 5 Battle Stars; Philippine Campaign Ribbon; Philippine Liberation Medal. Mem: Mich, Huron Co. and 24th Judicial Circuit Bar Asns; Am. Judicature Soc; pres, Mich. Prosecutor's Asn, 60-61; dir, Nat. Dist. Attorney's Asn, 61-62; Rotary; Elks; Verona Hills Country Club. Rel: Episcopal. Legal Res: 123 N. Stanley, Bad Axe, Mich. 48412. Mailing Add: 249 E. Huron Ave, Bad Axe, Mich. 48413.

UNDERHILL, FREDERICK WILLIAM, JR. R
Committeeman, Mass. Rep. State Cmt.
b. Melrose, Mass, 8/31/38; s. Frederick W. Underhill and Vera Bisbee U; m. 11/26/65 to Nancy Ellis; c. Kimberly, Mark Jason and Matthew James. Educ: Boston Univ, B.S, 63; Phi Psi. Polit. & Govt. Pos: Town auditor, Rochester, Mass, 62-65, mem. finance cmt, 64-66 and mem. sch. cmt, 67-; asst. co. treas, Plymouth Co, Mass, 67-; committeeman, Mass. Rep. State Cmt, 68- Bus. & Prof. Pos: Head admin. clerk, Treas. Off, Plymouth Co, 64-67. Mem: Plymouth Co. Treas. Asn; secy, Plymouth Co. Retirement Asn; Elks; Lions; chmn, Rochester Rep. Town Cmt; secy, Plymouth Co. Rep. Club; Rochester Hist. Soc. Rel: Congregational. Mailing Add: High St, West Wareham, Mass. 02576.

UNDERWOOD, CAMILLA KNOTTS R
Secy, Orangeburg Co. Rep. Party, S.C.
b. Orangeburg, S.C, 2/16/41; d. Joseph Evander Knotts and Camilla Brailsford K; m. 8/21/65 to Charles Wilburn Underwood; c. Charlotte Moultrie. Educ: Columbia Col, S.C, A.B. in educ, 64; Kappa Delta Epsilon; Alpha Psi Omega. Polit. & Govt. Pos: Nat. Committeewoman, Young Rep, S.C, 63-65; Region IV co-dir, Nat. Young Rep, 63-65; del, Young Rep. Nat. Conv, 63 & 65; alternate del, Rep. Nat. Conv, 64; adv, Teen-Age Rep, S.C, 65-68; secy, Orangeburg Co. Rep. Party, 68-; treas, Orangeburg Co. GOP Women, 68- Bus. & Prof. Pos: Dir. pub. rels, Youth for Goldwater, Wash, D.C, 64; teacher, Minnie Howell, Atlantic, Ga, 65; teacher, Ellis Avenue, Orangeburg, S.C, 67-68. Rel: Episcopal. Mailing Add: 2537 Jackson Dr, Orangeburg, S.C. 29115.

UNDERWOOD, CECIL HARLAND R
b. Joseph's Mills, W.Va, 11/5/22; s. Silas Henry Underwood and Della Forrester U; m. 7/25/48 to Hovah V. Hall; c. Cecilia Ann, Craig Hall and Sharon Sue. Educ: Salem Col, A.B, 43; W.Va. Univ, A.M, 52; Pi Kappa Delta; Sigma Pi Epsilon. Hon. Doctors Degree, Marietta Col; Bethany Col; W.Va. Univ; West Va. Tech; Concord Col; W.Va. Wesleyan Col; W.Va. State Col; Salem Col; West. New Eng. Col. Polit. & Govt. Pos: W.Va. State Del, 44-56, Minority Leader, W.Va. State House of Delegates, 49-56; pres, Young Rep. League, 46-50; parliamentarian, Young Rep. Nat. Conv, 50; Gov, W.Va, 57-61; mem. cmt. on prog, Rep. Nat. Cmt, 59; mem. exec. cmt, Nat. Gov. Conf, 59-60; temporary chmn, Rep. Nat. Conv, 60, del-at-lg, 60 & 64; nominee for Gov, W.Va, 64; chmn, Work Force on Prog, W.Va. Rep. Revival. Bus. & Prof. Pos: Teacher, St. Mary's High Sch, W.Va, 43-46; mem. staff, Marietta Col, 46-50; v.pres, Salem Col, 50-56 and Island Creek Coal Co, 61-64; v.pres, civic affairs, Monsanto Co, 65-67; pres, Franswood, Inc, 67-; pres, Cecil H. Underwood Assocs, 66-; bd. dir, W.Va. Life Ins. Co, 61-; bd. dir, Huntington Fed. Savings & Loan Asn, 61- Mil. Serv: Pvt, Army Res, 42-43. Publ: State Papers and Public Addresses, 25th Governor West Virginia, State of W.Va, 63; Legislative Process in West Virginia, W.Va. Univ, 52. Mem: Pub. Rels. Soc. of Am; Nat. Munic. League; Int. Platform Asn; Am. Polit. Sci. Asn; Mason; Elks; Moose; v.chmn, Region IV, Boy Scouts; bd. dirs, W.Va. Div-state crusade chmn, 63-64, Am. Cancer Soc. Rel: Methodist. Legal Res: 1930 S. Englewood Rd, Huntington, W.Va. 25701. Mailing Add: P.O. Box 319, Huntington, W.Va. 25708.

UNDERWOOD, JAMES MARTIN R
b. Pittsburgh, Pa, 2/27/09; s. Fred Perry Underwood and Jean Martin U; m. to Ann Saxman; c. Ann (Mrs. Potts), James M, Jr, Thomas S. and Charles P. Educ: Univ. Pittsburgh, B.S, 30; Harvard Univ, Grad. Sch. Bus. Admin, M.B.A, 32; Phi Delta Theta. Polit. & Govt. Pos: Chmn, Young Rep. of Westmoreland Co, Pa, 39-40; councilman, Latrobe, 43-; Rep. nominee for U.S. Rep, 28th Dist, Pa, 40; mem, Pa. State Rep. Cmt, 58-63; del, Rep. Nat. Conv, 60 & 68; mem, exec. cmt, Pa. Rep. Party, 63-65. Bus. & Prof. Pos: Partner, investment coun, Morgan, Underwood, Butler, Pittsburgh, Pa, 32-35; teacher, St. Vincent Col, Latrobe, 32-36; asst. to pres, Vulcan Mold & Iron Co, 35-40, pres, 46-68; pres, Halund Co, 40-44; sales mgr, Latrobe Steel Co, 44-46; chmn. bd. and pres, Vulcan, Inc, 68- Publ: 'The Trustee Game Demands Alert Players,' Mod. Hosp, 12/67; 'How to Serve on a Hospital Board,' Harvard Bus. Rev, 7/69. Mem: Am. Iron & Steel Inst; Am. Foundrymen's Asn; Am. Inst. Mining and Metallurgical Engrs; Rolling Rock Club; Duquesne Club, Pittsburgh; F&AM. Trustee, Univ. Pittsburgh. Rel: Presbyterian. Legal Res: Indian Hill, Depot St. Exten, Latrobe, Pa. 15650. Mailing Add: Box 70, Latrobe, Pa. 15650.

UNDERWOOD, JOE COLUMBUS D
b. Mount Vernon, Ga, 8/8/11; s. Luther C. Underwood and Tink Morrison U; single. Educ: Brewton Parker Jr. Col; Nat. Univ, Wash, D.C, LL.B. Polit. & Govt. Pos: Ga. State Rep, 55-68, Asst. Floor Leader, Ga. State House of Rep, 61-68; former mayor, Mt. Vernon, two terms. Bus. & Prof. Pos: Attor-

ney. Mil. Serv: Naval Res, 42-46. Mem: Mason; Elks; Lions. Rel: Methodist. Mailing Add: Mt. Vernon, Ga. 30445. (1967)

UNDERWOOD, MALCOLM STANLEY, JR. R
Treas, Rep. Party, Va.
b. Shamokin, Pa, 3/24/30; s. Malcolm Stanley Underwood and Ruby Newton U; m. 8/27/59 to Jacqueline T. Atwell; c. Kathryn O, Carl Clifford, Elizabeth A. and Malcolm Stanley, III. Educ: Univ. Va, Charlottesville, B.A, 51, LL.B, 59; Pi Delta Epsilon; Kappa Alpha Order; Sigma Nu Phi; German Club. Polit. & Govt. Pos: Mem, Henrico Co. Rep. Cmt, Va, 60-65; del, each Va. State Rep. Conv. since 60; mem. and treas, Third Dist. Rep. Cmt, 62-; mem, Chesterfield Co. Rep. Cmt, 65-; mem, Va. Rep. State Cent. Cmt, 68-; treas, Rep. Party Va, 68- Bus. & Prof. Pos: Asst. trust officer, United Va. Bank-State Planters, 64-67, trust officer, 67-68 and head trust real estate and mortgage dept, 68- Mil. Serv: Entered as Pvt, Marine Corps, 52, released as 1st Lt, 54, after serv. in Fleet Marine Force, Pac. Theatre, Res, 54-68, Lt. Col. Mem: Va. State Bar Asn; Am. Inst. of Banking; Marine Corps League; Marine Corps Reserve Officers Asn; Mil. Order of the World Wars. Rel: Methodist. Mailing Add: 8400 Bayfield Dr, Richmond, Va. 23235.

UNDERWOOD, MELL G. D
b. Rose Farm, Morgan Co, Ohio, 1/30/92; s. James G. Underwood and Sarah Newlon U; m. June, 1916 to Flora Lewis, wid; c. Mell, Jr, Max L, Linda (Mrs. Wing) and Ned L. Educ: Ohio State Univ; Ohio Univ. Polit. & Govt. Pos: Former prosecuting attorney, Perry Co, Ohio; U.S. Rep, 11th Dist, Ohio, 22-36; Judge, U.S. Dist. Court, Ohio, 36- Mem: Am, Ohio and Columbus Bar Asns; Masons; Aladdin Temple; Elks. Rel: Baptist. Legal Res: New Lexington, Ohio. Mailing Add: New Federal Bldg, 85 Marconi, Columbus, Ohio 43216.

UNDERWOOD, RALPH RUDOLPH D
b. Reynolds, Ga, 4/27/23; s. Udolpho Sikes Underwood and Martha Brown U; m. 11/21/45 to Nora Irene Windham; c. Gloria Lynn, Kathy Irene, Ralph Rudolph, Jr. Educ: Grad. Martha Berry Schs; Georgia Southwestern; attended Univ. of Tenn. Polit. & Govt. Pos: Ga. State Rep, 61-66. Bus. & Prof. Pos: Indust. Loans. Mil. Serv: WWII, Pfc, 43. Mem: Masons; VFW; Am. Legion. Rel: Baptist. Mailing Add: Butler, Ga. 31006. (1967)

UNGER, SHERMAN EDWARD R
Gen. Counsel, Dept. of Housing and Urban Develop.
b. Chicago, Ill, 10/9/27; s. Milton I. Unger and Helen Strong U; m. 12/29/53 to Polly Van Buren Taylor; c. Cathleen Estelle and Peter Van Buren. Educ: Miami Univ, B.A, 50; Univ. Cincinnati Col. Law, J.D, 53; Beta Theta Pi. Polit. & Govt. Pos: Mem. personal staff, Richard Nixon Presidential Campaign, 60, chief of briefing staff, 68; asst. campaign dir, Rep. Cong. Cmt, 62; admin. aide to Richard Nixon, N.Y.C, 64; spec. asst. to nat. chmn, Rep. Nat. Cmt, presidential campaign, 64; cmnr, Ohio State Water and Sewer Cmn, 65-69; gen. counsel, Dept. of Housing and Urban Develop, 69- Bus. & Prof. Pos: Attorney-at-law and partner, Frost & Jacobs, 56-69. Mil. Serv: Entered as Pvt, Army, 46, released as Pfc, 47; entered as 2nd Lt, Air Force, 53, released as 1st Lt, 56, after serv. in Alaskan Air Command, Alaska. Mem: Cincinnati, Ohio and Am. Bar Asns; World Peace Through Law Center; Univ. Club; Queen City Club; Cincinnati, Ohio; Cincinnati Country Club; Metrop. Club, Wash. D.C. Rel: Presbyterian. Legal Res: 3975 Indian Hill Rd, Cincinnati, Ohio 45243. Mailing Add: 451 Seventh St. S.W, Washington, D.C. 20410.

UNGERER, JAMES L. R
Kans. State Rep.
b. Marysville, Kans, 2/12/23; s. Fred M. Ungerer and Carolina Zech U; m. 12/14/47 to Nelda June Bargmann; c. James Lowell, Jeffrey Lynn, Marna Jean and Jon Lindsey. Educ: High Sch. Polit. & Govt. Pos: Chmn, Marshall Co. Rep. Cent. Cmt, Kans, 4 years; mayor, Marysville, 65-; first v.pres, Mayors' Orgn. of League of Kans. Munics, 66; treas, Kans. Rep. State Cmt, 66-; Kans. State Rep, 54th Dist, 69- Mil. Serv: Entered as Pvt, Army Air Corps, 41, released as M/Sgt, 45, after serv. in 20th Air Force, Pac; Army Res, 45-48 and Capt.(Ret), Army Nat. Guard, 48-62. Mem: Pres, Kiwanis Club, 64; chmn. bd. dirs, Commun. Mem. Hosp, 64; comdr, SMNR 163, Am. Legion, 58; comdr, VFW, 55 and 56; bd. dirs, C. of C, 60-61; DAV; Mason; Moose; Eagles. Rel: Protestant. Legal Res: 1010 Ann St, Marysville, Kans. 66508. Mailing Add: Box 327, Marysville, Kans. 66508.

UNGERLEIDER, ROBERT D
b. Phillipsburg, N.J, 7/21/13; s. Morris Ungerleider (deceased) and Mary Feldmesser U.(deceased); m. 8/3/52 to Louise Bressler; c. Lisa, Susan and Pamela. Educ: Lafayette Col, B.A. magna cum laude, 34; Univ. Pa. Law Sch, LL.B, 39; Phi Beta Kappa. Polit. & Govt. Pos: Chief Enforcement counsel, Off. Price Admin, 41-45; first asst. dist. attorney, Northampton Co, Pa, 56-60; del, Dem. Nat. Conv, 64 & 68. Mem: Northampton Co. Bar Asn.(pres, 58); Pa. and Am. Bar Asns; Am. Judicature Soc; Am. Trial Lawyers Asn; solicitor and bd. dirs, Northampton Co. Childrens Bur, 64-65; dir. Bethlehem C. of C; coun-dir, Pa. C. of C; Kiwanis. Rel: Hebrew. Legal Res: 1703 N. New St, Bethlehem, Pa. 18018. Mailing Add: 1509 Easton Ave, Bethlehem, Pa. 18017.

UNGERMAN, MAYNARD IVAN D
b. Topeka, Kans, 12/5/29; s. Irvine E. Ungerman and Hanna Friedburg U; m. 6/25/50 to Elsa Leiter; c. William Charles, Karla Beth and Rebecca Diane. Educ: Stanford Univ, B.A. cum laude, 51 and LL.B, 53; Phi Alpha Delta. Polit. & Govt. Pos: Dem. precinct chmn, Tulsa Co, Okla, 56-67; chmn, credentials cmt, Tulsa Co. Dem. Party, 64 and chmn, First Dist, 66; alternate del, Dem. Nat. Conv, 64, del, 68; coordinator, State Dem. Cent. Cmt, 64; mem. inaugural cmt, President Lyndon Johnson and Vice President, Hubert Humphrey, 65; presidential appointee, Nat. Citizens Cmt. Commun. Rel, 65-; chmn. assoc. housing cmt, Commun. Rel. Cmn, 65-; Gov. appointee, Okla. Acad. State Goals, 66-; chmn, Tulsa Co. Dem. Cent. Cmt, 67-69. Bus. & Prof. Pos: Mem. bd. ed, Stanford Law Rev, 51-53; partner, Ungerman, Grabel, Ungerman & Leiter, Attorneys, 53-; v.chmn, labor law cmt, Okla. State Bar, 67- Mil. Serv: Entered as 1st Lt, Air Force, 53, released 56, after serv. in Judge Adv. Gen. Dept; Air Force Res. Capt.(Ret); Nat. Defense Serv. Award. Mem: Tulsa Co. Bar Asn.(exec. cmt, 62-63, 65-66, chmn, unauthorized practice of law cmt, 65-66); Okla, Am. and Fed. Bar Asns; Commercial Law League Am.(chmn. jr. mem, 61, recording secy, 66-67); Am. Judicature Soc; Univ. Club Tulsa; v.pres, Southwest Region, Anti-Defamation League and chmn, Okla. Sect; Nat. Cmt. Am. Jewish Joint Distribution Cmt; past pres, B'nai Emunah Men's Club; past v.pres, B'nai Emunah Synagogue; past v.pres, Tulsa Family and Children Serv; bd. mem, Oklahomans for Indian Opportunity; bd. med, Neighbor for Neighbor; treas, New Day, Inc. Cert. Merit, Tulsa Co. Bar Asn, 64; Distinguished Serv. Award, Oklahomans for Indian Opportunity, 68. Rel: Jewish. Legal Res: 3732 E. 71st St, Tulsa, Okla. 74135. Mailing Add: Sixth Floor, Wright Bldg, Tulsa, Okla. 74103.

UNRUH, ERNEST ARTHUR R
Kans. State Rep.
b. Newton, Kans, 4/26/20; s. Henry F. Unruh and Susie Hiebert U; m. 11/9/46 to Dorothy Irene Dudte; c. Rodney Irl, Teresa Maureen and LaDonna Marie. Educ: Bethel Col. Polit. & Govt. Pos: Kans. State Rep, 88th Dist, 53- Mil. Serv: Entered as Aviation Cadet, Navy, 41, transferred to Army Air Force, 42, released as 1st Lt, 45, Second Air Force, U.S. Rel: Mennonite. Mailing Add: 2021 N. Main, Newton, Kans. 67114.

UNRUH, GEORGE MacDONALD R
N.Dak. State Sen.
b. Albany, N.Y, 9/10/20; s. George Edward Unruh and Dana M. MacDonald U; m. 12/4/43 to Elaine L. Berg; c. George M, Jr. and Vincent Paul. Educ: Colgate Univ, 37-39; Univ. N.Dak, LL.B, 51; Phi Kappa Tau. Polit. & Govt. Pos: N.Dak. State Rep, 18th Dist, 65-68, chmn, Legis. Research Cmt, 67-69; N.Dak. State Sen, 18th Dist, 68- Bus. & Prof. Pos: Attorney at Law, Homestead, Fla, 51-59, Grand Forks, N.Dak, 59-; pres, Vaberg Co, 66- Mil. Serv: Entered as Aviation Cadet, Navy, 42, released as Lt, 45, after serv. as Naval Aviator, Pensacola, Fla. as flight instr. and Marshall Islands, 43-45. Mem: Fla. and N.Dak. Bar Asns; Lions (past pres, Redland Dist. Club, Homestead, Fla. and Grand Forks Club, N.Dak); Elks; Am. Legion. Rel: Lutheran. Mailing Add: 1513 Cottonwood St, Grand Forks, N.Dak. 58201.

UNRUH, JESSE MARVIN D
Assembly Dem. Leader, Calif. State Legis.
b. Newton, Kans, 9/30/22; s. Isaac P. Unruh and Nettie Laura Kessler U; m. 11/2/43 to Virginia June Lemon; c. Bruce, Bradley, Robert, Randall and Linda Lu. Educ: Wayland Baptist Col, Plainview, Tex, 39-40; Univ. of South. Calif, Los Angeles, A.B, 48; Chubb Fellowship, Yale Univ; Politician in Residence, Rutgers Univ; Artus; Trojan Knights; Blue Key; Skull and Dagger. Polit. & Govt. Pos: Calif. State Assemblyman, 54-, Speaker of the Assembly, 61-69, Assembly Dem. Leader, 69-; chmn, Calif. del, Dem. Nat. Conv, 68. Bus. & Prof. Pos: Lectr, Univs. of Calif, Wash, Wis, Mo, Utah and Stanford Univ, 65-66; mem. staff at Eagleton Inst, Rutgers Univ, 65- Mil. Serv: Entered as Seaman, Navy, 42, released as Aviation Metalsmith 2/C, 45, after serv. in Asian and Pac. Theaters; Good Conduct Medal. Mem: Am. Legion; Inglewood C. of C. Rel: Protestant. Legal Res: 8315 Byrd Ave, Inglewood, Calif. 90305. Mailing Add: Rm. 4112, State Capitol, Sacramento, Calif. 95814.

UNZICKER, DR. WAYNE D
b. Montrose, S.Dak, 5/30/26; married to Idamae Gere Unzicker; c. Jayne. Educ: Creighton Univ, Omaha; Dakota Wesleyan Univ, Mitchell; Chicago Col. of Chiropody and Pedicure Surg. Polit. & Govt. Pos: S.Dak. State Rep, 62-69; del, Dem. Nat. Conv, 68. Mem: Nat. Asn. of Podiatrists; pres, S.Dak. Asn. Podiatrists; v.pres, S.Dak. Jaycees; K. of C; Am. Legion; 40 et 8; Elks; Lions. Rel: Catholic. Mailing Add: 817 W. Ash, Mitchell, S.Dak. 57301. (1967)

UPCHURCH, RUBLE R
Mem, Rep. Exec. Cmt, Tenn.
b. Forbus, Tenn, 6/3/03; s. Raymond Gregg Upchurch and Freely Ann Crabtree U; m. 5/19/35 to Jessie Helen Reagan; 2nd m. 12/11/54 to Janie Rose Dyer; c. Patricia Ann, Ruble, Jr. and Willard Charles; step-children, Linda, Joe and Eddie Booher. Educ: Tenn. Tech. Univ, B.S, 35; Univ. Tenn, M.S, 53; D.A.R. Award for Excellence in Am. Hist, 35. Polit. & Govt. Pos: Mem, Rep. Speaker's Bur, 32, 36 & 40; secy, Fentress Co. Rep. Primary Bd, Tenn, 36-46; pres, Fentress Co. Young Rep. Club, 40-42; mem. and secy, Fentress Co. Equalization Bd, 40-42; chmn, Fentress Co. Rep. Exec. Cmt, 40-42 & 60-, secy, 46-56; mem, Fentress Co. Elec. Cmn, 48-50 & 68-69; mem, Rep. Exec. Cmt, Tenn, 50-; mem, Fentress Co. Jury Cmn, 59-69; co. campaign mgr, Nixon-Lodge Ticket, Mid. Tenn, 60; del, Rep. Nat. Conv, 60; v.pres. and mem, Fentress Co. Libr. Bd, 61-66 and mem. bldg. cmt, 64-66; historian, Fentress Co, 68-69. Bus. & Prof. Pos: Rep, Progress Tailoring Co, 27-30, World Book Encyclop, 48-49 and Compton's Encyclop, 60-62; prin, teacher and supvr, Fentress Co. Schs, 29-66; agent and rep, N.Y. Life Ins. Co, 30-33; student instr. of hist, Tenn. Tech. Univ, 35; pres, Upper Cumberland Supvr, 47-48; secy, Upper Cumberland Prin, 64-65; instr. adult educ, Fentress Co, Tenn, 68-69. Mil. Serv: Pvt, Tenn. State Home Guard, 40-43. Publ: A Supervisory Program for Fentress County Schools, Univ. Tenn, 53. Mem: Life mem, Nat. Educ. Asn; Save Children Fedn; Tenn. Tech. Alumni Asn; Univ. Tenn. Alumni Asn; York Inst. Alumni Asn; Nat. Educ. Asn. 50 Club; Tenn, Fentress Co. and Middle Tenn. Educ. Asns; Rotary; Ruritan Nat; Farm Bur; Wolf River Commun. Club; pres, Epworth League, 31-41; The Coun. of South. Mt; WOW; v.pres, Young Farmers & Home Makers, 50; York-Hull Develop. Asn, 67-69; Lions; pres, Fentress Co. Hist. Soc, 68-69. Name placed by President Eisenhower on Rep. Mem. in Hall of Presidents at Gettysburg, 61; selected as one of the outstanding community leaders for E. Tenn, 62. Rel: Methodist. Legal Res: Forbus, Tenn. 38561. Mailing Add: P.O. Box 457, Jamestown, Tenn. 38556.

UPDIKE, ROBERT ELMER R
Chmn, Crook Co. Rep. Cent. Cmt, Wyo.
b. Newcastle, Wyo, 8/8/32; s. Walter Emerson Updike and Dorothy Rodgers U; m. 3/29/52 to Dorothy Isabelle Gibbs; c. Daniel W, Thomas J, Michael J. and Kenneth H. Educ: Univ. Tulsa, 50-51, Univ. Wyo, 51-52. Polit. & Govt. Pos: V.chmn, Crook Co. Rep. Cent. Cmt, Wyo, 62-64, chmn, 66- Mem: Mason; Scottish Rite; AAONMS; Lions Int. Rel: Methodist. Mailing Add: Box 8, Moorcroft, Wyo. 82721.

UPHAM, CHESTER ROBERT, JR. R
Dist. committeeman, State Rep. Exec. Cmt, Tex.
b. Mineral Wells, Tex, 5/19/25; s. Chester Robert Upham and Ida Irene

Shafer U; m. 12/16/46 to Virginia Frances Lee; c. Barbara Lee (Mrs. Garrett), Mary Kathleen, Chester Robert, III and Richard Lee. Educ: Univ. Tex, Austin, B.S.M.E, 45; Tau Beta Pi; Pi Tau Sigma; Phi Gamma Delta. Polit. & Govt. Pos: Dir, Palo Pinto Co. Munic. Water Dist, Tex, 60-; dist. committeeman, State Rep. Exec. Cmt, 64-; alternate del, Rep. Nat. Conv, 68. Bus. & Prof. Pos: Dir. and v.pres, Brazos River Gas Co, Tex, 47-58; managing owner, Upham Oil & Gas Co, 55-; dir, Loveland Ski Corp, Georgetown, Colo, 56-; dir, Texaramics Inc, Mineral Wells, Tex, 64-; dir, City Nat. Bank, 66- Mil. Serv: Entered as A/S, Navy, 43, released as Ens, 45, after serv. in 16th Fleet. Rel: Protestant. Legal Res: 1301 N.W. Seventh Ave, Mineral Wells, Tex. 76067. Mailing Add: P.O. Box 940, Mineral Wells, Tex. 76067.

UPTON, DAVID FREDERICK R
b. Benton Harbor, Mich, 11/13/21; s. Frederick Stanley Upton and Margaret R. Beckley U; m. 6/19/48 to Harriet Woodworth Skinner; c. Margaret Woodworth, Betsy Ingersol, Benjamin Mather and David Skinner. Educ: Univ. Mich, B.S. in mech. eng. and indust. eng, 48; Michigamua; Alpha Delta Phi. Polit. & Govt. Pos: Treas, Berrien Co. Rep. Party, Mich, 54-58, mem, finance cmt, 56-, chmn, 66-68; del, Rep. State Conv, 56-66; mem, St. Joseph Harbor Authority, 58-; del, Mich. State Constitution Conv, 61-62; Mich. State Rep, 63-64; admin. asst. Mich. State Hwy. Cmn, 65; mem, Mich. Mental Health Adv. Coun, 66-69, chmn, 69-; del, Rep. Nat. Conv, 68. Bus. & Prof. Pos: Mem. exec. dept, Kaiser-Fraizer, 48-50; mem. mgt, Whirlpool Corp, 50-58, dir. purchases, 58-61 and dir. materials control, 60-61; pres, Benton Harbor Abstract & Title Co, 65- Mil. Serv: Entered as A/S, Naval Res, 43, released as Lt.(jg), 46, after serv. in Amphibious Forces, Pac; Atlantic, Pac. Area Ribbons; Iwo Jima, Okinawa and Japan Occupation Ribbons. Mem: Bd. dirs, Mich. United Fund; chmn, Berrien Co. Ment. Health Serv. Bd; bd. of dirs, Mich. Soc. for Mental Health, 65-; regional chmn, Mich. Week Found, 65-66; trustee, Kalamazoo Col, 68-; Twin Cities Rotary; St. Joseph River Yacht Club; Great Lakes Cruising Club; Lake Mich. Yachting Asn; Point O'Woods Golf and Country Club; bd. dirs, Twin Cities C. of C. Rel: Congregational. Mailing Add: 200 Ridgeway, St. Joseph, Mich. 49085.

URBAN, THOMAS NELSON, JR. D
Mayor, Des Moines, Iowa
b. Des Moines, Iowa, 5/26/34; s. Thomas Nelson Urban and Helen U; m. to Mary Bright; c. Vicki, Nina, Tom and Bill. Educ: Harvard Univ, B.A, 56, M.A, 60. Polit. & Govt. Pos: Campaign mgr. for change in city mgr. and ward-coun-mgr. form of govt, Des Moines, Iowa; mayor, Des Moines, Iowa, 68- Mem: Sertoma; C. of C. Rel: Congregational. Legal Res: 4225 Greenwood Dr, Des Moines, Iowa 50312. Mailing Add: City Hall, E. First and Locust St, Des Moines, Iowa 50307.

URBANSKE, LEO, JR. D
b. Wash, D.C, 1/11/23; s. Leo Urbanske and Lois Blosser U; m. 12/10/43 to Theresa Ida Hungerbuhler; c. Amie (Mrs. B.P. Bruggeman), Lois (Mrs. Lewis Hansen), Carol, Leo, III and Mary. Educ: Va. Polytech. Inst. Polit. & Govt. Pos: Mem, Arlington Dem. Cmt, Va, 48-56, 59 & 61, chmn, 54-55; mem, Tenth Dist. Dem. Cmt; secy, A.B.C, 56, chmn, 57-58; mem, Bd. Equalization, Real Estate Assessments, 57-58; mem, Arlington Co. Bd, 59-67, chmn, 61 & 66; mem, Va. State Dem. Cent. Cmt, 64-68; mem, Arlington Co. Legis. Adv. Cmt, 69- Bus. & Pros. Pos: Secy-treas, Local 2336, CWA, AFL-CIO, 48-50, v.pres, 51-52, pres, 52-56; with C. & P. Tel. Co, presently. Mil. Serv: Entered as Pvt, Army-Air Force, 43, released as Cpl, 46, after serv. in Control Tower Opers, China-Burma-India, 45; China-Burma-India Theater Ribbon; Am. Theater Ribbon; Good Conduct Medal; Cpl, Air Force Res, 46-49. Mem: Exec. dir, North Va. Apt. Asn, 68-; v.pres. exec. officers coun, Nat. Apt. Asn, 69-; Yorktown High Sch. PTA; Nellie Custis PTA; Coun. of Govt, D.C. Area; Wash. Metrop. Area Transit Authority, 65-66; Arlington Hist. Soc; N. Va. Transportation Cmt. Va. Polytech. Inst, football. Rel: Methodist. Mailing Add: 4600 37th St. N, Arlington, Va. 22207.

URBIGKIT, WALTER C, JR. D
b. Burris, Wyo, 11/9/27; s. Walter Carl Urbigkit and Bertha Esther Miller U; m. 8/16/53 to Marian Myrna Chilton; c. Marcia Jill, Cynthia Louise, Robert Dale and Brenda Kay. Educ: Univ. Wyo, B.A, 49, LL.B, 51; Phi Beta Kappa; Phi Kappa Phi; Delta Sigma Rho. Polit. & Govt. Pos: Asst. co. attorney, Laramie Co, Wyo, 58-60; v.chmn, Laramie Co. Dem. Cent. Cmt, 59-60 & 64-66; chmn, State Selective Serv. Appeal Bd, 60-; treas, Wyo. State Dem. Cent. Cmt, 61-65, exec. secy, 66-68; mem, Laramie Co. Welfare Bd, Wyo, 66; treas, Bd. of Trustees, Sch. Dist. 1, Cheyenne, Laramie Co, Wyo, 67-; del, Dem. Nat. Conv, 68. Mil. Serv: Pvt, Army, 51-52, serv. in 10th Inf. Mem: Chmn, Civil Rights Cmt, Wyo. State Bar, 65-66; secy-treas, Laramie Co. Bar, 57-58, v.pres, 58-59; Laramie Co. Bar Asn; Am. Bar; Nat. Asn. of Homebuilders; Nat. Judicature Soc; attorney, Citizens Cmt. for Reapportionment; dist. gov. and Cheyenne Club pres, Civitan Int; Am. Legion; Nat. Asn. for Retarded Children. Rel: Congregational. Legal Res: 508 Cornell Lane, Cheyenne, Wyo. 82001. Mailing Add: P.O. Box 247, Cheyenne, Wyo. 82001.

URBINA URBINA, DAVID New Progressive, P.R.
Rep, P.R. House of Rep.
b. Guaynabo, P.R, 4/16/37; s. Salvador Urbina and Natividad U; m. 4/14/61 to Maria F. Calvo; c. David Salvador and Miguel Angel. Educ: Univ. P.R, 56-57; Univ. Salamanca, LL.B, 62. Polit. & Govt. Pos: Rep, P.R. House of Rep, 65-, mem, Finance Cmt, 65-68, chmn, 69-, mem, Planification Cmt, 65-68. Bus. & Prof. Pos: Lawyer, Urbina, Bauza and Bauza, 63. Mem: Colegio de Abogados de P.R; Logia Odfelica; Cooperative de Credito de Guaynabo; Asociación Graduados Universidades Españolas; Exchange Club. Rel: Evangelical. Legal Res: Calle Madrid H-14, Urb. Clementina, Guaynabo, P.R. 00657. Mailing Add: Box 104, Guaynabo, P.R. 00657.

URIE, H. THOMAS R
N.H. State Rep.
b. Orford, N.H, 10/29/96; married; c. Two. Educ: Colby Col, Waterville, Maine. Polit. & Govt. Pos: Former mem, Sch. Bd, N.H; former chmn, New Hampton Rep. Town Cmt, N.H; former Co. Del. Chmn; Co. Conv, 57; N.H. State Rep, 55- Bus. & Prof. Pos: Mfr. Mil. Serv: Navy Res, Ens, World War I. Mem: Mason (32°); K.T; Shrine, Bektash Temple. Nat. Legis. Conservationist of the Year, 67. Rel: Congregational. Mailing Add: New Hampton, N.H. 03256.

USHER, ETTER T. 'E.T.' D
b. Chiefland, Fla, 12/13/26; m. to Helen Hiers; c. Lynetta, Tommy. Polit. & Govt. Pos: Fla. State Sen, 63-66; mem, Levy Co. Sch. Bd. Bus. & Prof. Pos: Timber and cattle. Mil. Serv: Navy. Mem: Mason; Farm Bur; Cattlemen's Asn. Rel: Methodist. Mailing Add: P.O. Box 312, Chiefland, Fla. 32626. (1967)

USHIJIMA, CHARLES T. D
Hawaii State Rep.
b. Hilo, Hawaii, 8/17/32; s. Sakae Ushijima and Satsuki Tanaka U; m. 8/1/59 to Rachel A. Tagomori; c. Shaun S. Educ: Univ. Hawaii, B.S, 55. Polit. & Govt. Pos: Hawaii State Rep, 68- Mil. Serv: Sp-3, Army, 56-58, served in Adj. Gen. Corps, West. Germany. Mem: Hawaii Bankers Asn; Hawaii Jaycees (past state pres); Hawaii C. of C. One of Hawaii's Ten Outstanding Young Men, 58. Mailing Add: 3566 Kumu Place, Honolulu, Hawaii 96822.

USHIJIMA, JOHN T. D
Hawaii State Sen.
b. Hilo, Hawaii, 3/13/24; s. Buhachi Ushijima and Sano Nitahara U; m. 6/6/54 to Margaret S. Kunishige. Educ: Grinnell Col, Iowa, A.B, 50; George Wash. Univ. Law Sch, LL.B, 52; Phi Delta Phi. Polit. & Govt. Pos: Hawaii State Sen, 59- Bus. & Prof. Pos: Dir. and v.pres, Royal State Nat. Ins. Co, 62-; dir, Am. Security Bank, 63- Mil. Serv: Entered as Pvt, Army, 43, released as Sgt, 46; Presidential Unit Citation; 442nd Regt. Combat Team Ribbon; ETO Ribbon; Victory Ribbon. Mem: 442nd Vets. Club. of Hawaii; Y's Mens Club; YMCA. Rel: Protestant. Mailing Add: 114 Melani St, Hilo, Hawaii 96720.

UTHLAUT, RALPH, JR. R
Mo. State Rep.
b. Big Springs, Mo, 12/18/33; m. 12/12/53 to Carol Jean Kattlemann; c. Mark, Michael, Rhonda Sue. Educ: Univ. of Mo, Normandy Br. Polit. & Govt. Pos: Mo. State Rep, 62- Bus. & Prof. Pos: Farmer. Mil. Serv: Army, 54-56, 41st Field Artil. Group, Hqs. Battery, Ft. Sill, Okla. Mem: Mo. Farm Bur; Montgomery City Jr. C. of C. Rel: Methodist. Mailing Add: New Florence, Mo. 63363. (1967)

UTT, JAMES BOYD R
U.S. Rep, Calif.
b. Tustin, Calif, 3/11/99; s. Charles Edward Utt and Mary M. Sheldon U; m. 5/7/21 to Charlene E. Dripps; c. James S. Educ: Santa Ana Jr. Col, A.S, 44; Univ. of South. Calif. Law Sch, LL.B, 46. Polit. & Govt. Pos: Calif. State Assemblyman, 33-37; U.S. Rep, Calif, 53- Mem: Mason, Shrine; K. of P; Native Sons, Calif; Elks; Lions; Izaak Walton. Legal Res: 2233 E. Catalina St, Santa Ana, Calif. 92701. Mailing Add: 2346 Rayburn Bldg, Washington, D.C. 20515.

UTT, MAX EDDY R
Mem, Calif. Rep. State Cent. Cmt.
b. Columbus City, Iowa, 9/23/02; s. John Erwin Utt and Mary Elva Eddy U; m. 3/23/32 to Bonnie Jean Lockwood; c. Virginia (Mrs. Robert F. Stockton) and Roger Lockwood. Educ: Pomona Col, B.A, 24; Harvard Law Sch, LL.B, 27. Polit. & Govt. Pos: Chmn, Citizens Legis. Adv. Cmn. to Calif. Legis, 57-61; mem, Calif. Rep. State Cent. Cmt, 68- Mem: Am. and Calif. Bar Asns; Rel: Presbyterian. Legal Res: 1706 Highland St, Glendale, Calif, 91202. Mailing Add: 634 S. Spring St, Los Angeles, Calif. 90014.

UTTER, MILES WAYNE R
Chmn, Sioux Co. Rep. Party, S.Dak.
b. McIntosh, S.Dak, 4/26/34; s. Ernest S. Utter and Christin Moser U; m. 4/22/57 to Delores R. Ternes; c. Kevin, Kurt, Kim, Kelly, Kary, Karen, Kip, Karmen and Kam. Educ: McIntosh High Sch, S.Dak, grad. Polit. & Govt. Pos: Precinct committeeman, Rep. Party, N.Dak; mem, 35th Legis. Dist. Rep. Exec. Cmt; chmn, Sioux Co. Rep. Party, currently. Bus. & Prof. Pos: Publisher, Selfridge J, 57- Mil. Serv: Entered as Pvt, Army, 53, released as Cpl, 55, after serv. in 511th Airborne, 11th Airborne Div. Mem: Am. Legion; Selfridge Betterment Club. Rel: Catholic. Mailing Add: Selfridge, N.Dak. 58568.

UTTON, ALBERT EDGAR D
b. Aztec, N.Mex, 7/6/31; s. Charles H. Utton and Desda Wood U; m. 6/28/58 to Mary Weighill Lodge; c. Jennifer Lodge and John Weighill. Educ: Univ. N.Mex, B.A. with honors, 53; Oxford Univ, B.A. with honors, 56, M.A. in Juris, 59; Univ. London, 57-58; Yale Univ, 61-62; Phi Kappa Phi; Sigma Chi; Alpha Phi Omega. Polit. & Govt. Pos: Treas, Lawyers for Johnson, N.Mex, 64, state chmn, Lawyers for the President, 64-67; chief platform draftsman, N.Mex. Dem. Party, 66; state pres, N.Mex Dem. Coun, 66-68; chmn, Issues Cmt, N.Mex. Dem. Reorgn. Cmt, 67-68; chmn, Cent. N.Mex. Citizens for Kennedy, 68, state chmn, N.Mex. Citizens for Kennedy, 68; state chmn, N.Mex. Citizens for Humphrey-Muskie, 68; chmn, Educators for Chavez for Gov, N.Mex, 68; alternate del, Dem. Nat. Conv, 68. Bus. & Prof. Pos: Partner, Simms and Garcia, 59-61; law prof, Univ. N.Mex, 62- Mil. Serv: Entered as 2nd Lt, Air Force, 56, released as 1st Lt, 58, after serv. in Judge Adv. Gen. Corp, Hq. Third Air Force; Capt, Air Force Res, 58- Publ: Co-author, Vol. 2, Water Law, Allen Smith, 66; 'Providing Legal Services in a Cross-Cultural Situation,' Kans. Law J, 67; 'Institutional Arrangements for Developing North Sea Oil and Gas,' Va. J. Int. Law, 68. Mem: Asn. Am. Law Schs; Int. Law Asn; secy, Albuquerque Cmt. on For. Rels; Coronado Monument Soc. Rel: Episcopal. Mailing Add: Box 266, N. Star Route, Corrals, N.Mex. 87048.

V

VACCA, PASCHAL PATRICK D
Ala. State Sen.
b. Hillsville, Pa, 9/6/01; s. John Vacca and Philomena Robbio V; m. 8/18/20 to Lelia Frances Bryant. Educ: St. Vincents Col, Pa; Youngstown Bus. Col, Ohio; Sch. of Tech. and Birmingham Sch. of Law, LaSalle Ext. Univ, LL.B. Polit. & Govt. Pos: Former, Munic. judge and city attorney, Tarrant, Ala; former Ala. State Rep; Ala. State Sen, 67- Bus. & Prof. Pos: Law practice,

Birmingham, Ala, 37- Mil. Serv: Served with Am. Red Cross as asst. field dir. attached to armed forces. Mem: Mason; Shrine; Elks; Eagles; past dist. gov. of the Civitan. Rel: Methodist. Mailing Add: 929-930 Frank Nelson Bldg, Birmingham, Ala. 35203.

VACCARO, VINCENT R
b. Bristol, R.I, 1/25/23; m. to Mary Vitullo. Educ: Bryant Col; St. Norberts Col, Green Bay, Wis. Polit. & Govt. Pos: R.I. State Rep, 63-66; former mem, Bristol Rep. Town Cmt. Bus. & Prof. Pos: Planner in prod. controls. Mil. Serv: Army Signal Corps, 43-46, serv. in Pac. Mem: Bristol Coun, K. of C; Am. Legion; assoc. mem. Ever Ready Fire Co. Rel: Catholic; communicant, Our Lady of Mt. Carmel Church. Mailing Add: 96 Peck Ave, Bristol, R.I. 02809. (1967)

VACCO, ANTHONY R
Mayor, Evergreen Park, Ill.
b. Chicago, Ill, 9/24/24; s. Carmen Vacco and Rose Esposito V; m. 8/18/46 to Patricia Ann Nelson; c. Sandra (Mrs. Johnson), Anthony, Jr. and Darlene. Educ: Crane Tech. High Sch, Chicago, Ill, grad, 42. Polit. & Govt. Pos: Chmn, Zoning Bd. Appeals, Evergreen Park, Ill, 61-65, trustee, 65-68, mayor and pres. bd. trustees, 68- Bus. & Prof. Pos: Home delivery dist. mgr, Field Enterprises Newspaper Div, 53-69. Mil. Serv: Entered as Pvt, Army, 43, released as S/Sgt, 45, after serv. in Med. Corps, S.Pac. Theatre; Bronze Star; Good Conduct Medal. Mem: Am. Legion; VFW; Rep. Orgn. Worth Twp.(past pres); Rep. Orgn. Evergreen Park (past pres); United Home Owners Orgn. Evergreen Park; Southeast Improv. Asn; Sons of Italy; St. Bernadette's Holy Name Soc. Bowling and Civic Awards. Rel: Roman Catholic. Legal Res: 9632 S. Mozart Ave, Evergreen Park, Ill. 60642. Mailing Add: 9418 S. Kedzie Ave, Evergreen Park, Ill. 60642.

VAGLEY, ROBERT EVERETT D
Dir, Gen. Subcmt. on Labor, Cmt. on Educ. and Labor, U.S. House of Rep.
b. New Eagle, Pa, 1/31/40; s. William Stuart Vagli and Lillian Tesi V; single. Educ: Pa. State Univ, B.S, 61, M.A, 63; Phi Kappa Theta. Polit. & Govt. Pos: With Cent. Intel. Agency, 63-64; dir, Select Subcmt. on Educ, Cmt. on Educ. and Labor, U.S. House of Rep, 65, dir, Gen. Subcmt. on Labor, 66-; pres, Capitol Hill Young Dem, 68-69. Mem: Univ. Club, Wash, D.C; Woodlawn Country Club, Mt. Vernon, Va; Cong. Secretaries Club; Pa. State Alumni Asn; Westchester Sports Club. Rel: Roman Catholic. Legal Res: 334 Chestnut St, Monessen, Pa. 15062. Mailing Add: 201 I St. S.W, Washington, D.C. 20024.

VAGNOZZI, ALDO D
Chmn, 19th Cong. Dist. Dem. Orgn, Mich.
b. Roseto, Italy, 10/4/25; s. Attilio Vagnozzi and Maria Grazia Sinibaldi V; m. 1/22/49 to Lois Margaret Carl; c. Steven, Paul, Nancy and Barbara. Educ: Wayne State Univ, B.A, 48; Omicron Delta Kappa; Pi Delta Epsilon. Polit. & Govt. Pos: Alternate del, Dem. Nat. Conv, 60, del. and mem, platform cmt, 68; treas, Oakland Co. Dem. Cmt, Mich, 66-68; secy, 68; chmn, 19th Cong. Dist. Dem. Orgn, 67-; sch. bd. mem, Farmington, 69- Mil. Serv: Entered as Pvt, Army, 43, released as Sgt, 46, after serv. as Lang. Interpreter, U.S, 44-46. Mem: Int. Labor Press Asn.(exec. coun); Detroit Press Club; Am. Newspaper Guild (secy, 53-54); Am. Vet. Cmt. Winner, Int. Labor Press Asn. Journalism Contest, several years. Rel: Catholic. Mailing Add: 26193 Kiltartan, Farmington, Mich. 48024.

VAIL, DONALD R
Mem, Westchester Co. Rep. Cmt, N.Y.
b. Yonkers, N.Y, 5/15/21; s. John I.B. Vail and Margaret M. Gray V; m. 7/13/51 to Priscilla A. Luke; c. Melissa G, Mary B, Lucia and Donald Angus. Educ: Princeton Univ, 42; Harvard Law Sch, 48. Polit. & Govt. Pos: Mem, Westchester Co. Rep. Cmt, N.Y, currently; treas, Bedford Town Cmt; chmn, 13th Elec. Dist, Bedford. Bus. & Prof. Pos: Partner, Alexander & Green, Law Firm, N.Y. Mil. Serv: Entered as Seaman 2/C, Navy, 42, released as Capt, Marine Corps Res, 45. Mem: Am. Bar Asn; Bar Asn. of N.Y.C; trustee, North. Westchester Hosp. Rel: Vestryman, St. Matthew's Church, Bedford, N.Y. Mailing Add: Guard Hill Rd, Bedford, N.Y. 10506.

VAIL, JOANE RAND DFL
Chairwoman, Fourth Cong. Dist. Dem-Farmer-Labor Party,
b. Waltham, Mass, 11/16/28; d. Herbert Smythe Rand, Sr. and Pauline Murphy R; m. 11/24/56 to Dr. David Jameson Vail; c. David Rand, Garrett Murphy, Sara Jameson and Michael Walsh. Educ: Boston Univ, 45-46 & 50-51; McLean Hosp. Sch. Nursing, Waverley, Mass, 47-50, R.N, 50; Univ. Md, 52-54; Univ. Minn, Minneapolis, 59- Polit. & Govt. Pos: Legis. dist. chairwoman, Dist. 48N, Minn, 62-65; del, Minn. Dem. State Conv, 64, 65, 66, 67, 68 & 69; chairwoman Ramsey Co. Dem-Farmer-Labor Party, 65 & 68-69; chairwoman, Fourth Cong. Dist. Dem-Farmer-Labor Party, 65-68 & 69-; mem, Minn. Dem-Farmer-Labor Exec. and Cent. Cmt, 65-69; del, Dem. Nat. Conv, 68. Bus. & Prof. Pos: Head Nurse, instr. nursing and dir. nursing educ, State of Md, 52-56. Mem: Nat. League of Nursing; Am. Nurses Asn; League of Woman Voters. Rel: Unitarian. Mailing Add: 127 Sixth St, White Bear Lake, Minn. 55110.

VAILE, VICTOR EDWARD, III R
Chmn, Polk Co. Rep. Exec. Cmt, Fla.
b. Canton, Ohio, 9/16/33; s. Victor Edward Vaile, Jr. and Zana Dietz V; m. 4/23/60 to Marcia Anne Juday; c. Brian Edward. Educ: Ohio State Univ, B.S, 55 and M.D, 59; Nat. Pre-med. Hon. Soc; Phi Chi. Polit. & Govt. Pos: Legis. chmn, Westwood Young Rep. Calif, 60-61 and pres, 61-62; legis. chmn, Los Angeles Co. Young Rep, 61-62 and first v.pres, 62-63; precinct dir, West Los Angeles, 61-63; Shell for Gov. Vol, Santa Monica Hq, 62; mem. 60th Assembly Dist. Rep. Cmt. and mem. 28th Cong. Dist. Rep. Cmt, Rep. State Cent. Cmt, 62-63; region IX v.pres, Calif. State Young Rep, 63; del, Young Rep. Nat. Conv, 63 & 67; mem, Goldwater for Pres. Campaign, Lawton, Okla, 64; chmn, Winter Haven YAF, Fla, 65-67; pres, Heart of Fla. Young Rep, 66-67; membership chmn, Fla. Fedn. Young Rep, 66-67; Rep. committeeman, Precinct 42, Winter Haven, Fla, 66-; chmn, Polk Co. Rep. Exec. Cmt, 67-; chmn, Fla. Friends of Reagan, 68; alternate del, Rep. Nat. Conv, 68. Bus. & Prof. Pos: Speakers bur, Los Angeles Co. Med. Asn, 62-63; v.pres, Santana Toastmasters, Ft. Sill, Okla, 64-65. Mil. Serv: Entered as 1st Lt, Army, 63, released as Capt, 65, after serv. in U.S. Army Hosp, Ft. Sill, Okla, 63-65; Cert. of Achievement. Publ: Ed, Trumpeteer, Heart of Florida Newsletter, 67- and The Statesman, Fla. Young Rep. Newsletter, 69- Mem: Polk Co. Med. Asn. (secy-treas, 68-); Fla. and Am. Med. Asns; Am. Asn. Physicians and Surgeons; Am. and Fla. Dermatology Asn; Kiwanis; bd. dirs, Winter Haven C. of C, 67-; bd. dirs, Heart of Fla. Young Rep. One of Top Ten Young Rep, Fla, 67-68. Rel: Episcopal; former mem. Vestry, St. Pauls Episcopal Church. Mailing Add: 800 Ave. L S.E, Winter Haven, Fla. 33880.

VAILLANCOURT, EUGENE D
b. Cape Madeleine, Can, 1/28/99; m. to Bernadette Bourbeau; c. three. Educ: Cape Madeleine schs. Polit. & Govt. Pos: Vt. State Rep, 64-66; dir. and exec. mem. of United Farmers Coop. of New Eng; lister and selectman, Berkshire. Bus. & Prof. Pos: Farmer. Mailing Add: Enosburg Falls, Vt. 05450. (1967)

VALASI, JOHN SIUFAGA
Rep, Am. Samoa House of Rep.
b. Am. Samoa, 2/5/32; s. Siufaga Valasi and Apaula Vo'a V; m. 1958 to Fau Viagalelei; c. Lilien, Manatua and Finau. Educ: Samoana High Sch, 49-53. Polit. & Govt. Pos: Rep, Am. Samoa House Rep, currently, asst. chmn, P.W.D. Cmt, mem. Judicial Cmt, Educ. Cmt. and Budget Appropriations Cmt, currently; mem, Wage and Labor Bd, Govt. Am. Samoa, currently. Bus. & Prof. Pos: Night mgr. and auditor, Pago Int. Continental Hotel, 55- Publ: Articles in local newspaper, Daily Bul. Rel: London Missionary Soc. Legal Res: Vaitogi Village, American Samoa 96920. Mailing Add: P.O. Box 1131, American Samoa 96920.

VALCOURT, RICHARD ROGER R
Chmn, Kennebec Co. Rep. Cmt, Maine
b. Fall River, Mass, 11/29/41; s. Roger Valcourt and Angeline C. Bernier V; m. 9/11/65 to Cheryl Marjorie Crossley; c. Jordan Roger (deceased), Jean Louise and Shariah Angeline. Educ: Bates Col, 58-60; Cambridge Sch. of Broadcasting, dipl, 61; Elkins Inst. of Electronics, dipl, 61; LaSalle Exten. Univ, LL.B, 66; Kennebec Valley Bates Club. Polit. & Govt. Pos: Campaign dir, Goldwater for Pres, Fall River Area, Mass, 64; asst. sgt-at-arms, Rep. State Conv, 64, mem, Ballot & Tally Cmt, 66, del. and press officer, 68; v.chmn, Mayor's Citizens Adv. Cmt, Fall River, Mass, 64-65, pub. rels. dir. and chmn, fed. affairs subcmt, 64-65; mem, Rep. City Cmt, 64-65; v.pres, Greater Fall River Young Rep, 64-66; del, Mass. Young Rep. Asn, 64-66, cand. for pres, 66; mem, Cambridge Young Rep, 66; mem, Rep. City Cmt, Augusta, Maine, 67-69, v.chmn, 68-69; chmn, Augusta Planning Bd, 68-69; mem, Kennebec Co. Civil Defense Policy Cmt, 68-69; chmn, Kennebec Co. Rep. Cmt, 68-; mem, Gov. Task Force on the Maine Environment, 69. Bus. & Prof. Pos: Announcer, engr. & newsman, Radio Sta. WSAR, Fall River, Mass, 61-63; mem. staff, Valcourt Indust. Supply Co, Inc, 63-64; asst. to dir. and acting dir. of informational research, West. Islands Publ, Boston, 64-66; field consult, Maine Heart Asn, Augusta, Maine, 66-67; news dir, Radio Sta. WFAU, 67-; campaign dir, pub. rels, Commun. Concepts, 68-; pub. rels. consult, Natural Resources Coun. of Maine, 68- Publ: 'Year End Review,' (annual feature with Gov. of Maine on events of preceding year), Radio Stat. WFAU, 12/67 & 12/68; 'The Minority Report' (a feature on racial probs. in Maine with Gov. Kenneth Curtis), CBS Radio Network, 1/69; 'Health and Welfare Report' (series of weekly progs. with off. of Dept. of Health & Welfare on types or extent of serv. offered by state agencies), Radio Sta. WFAU and other Maine stas, 69. Mem: Int. Brotherhood of Elec. Workers, AFL-CIO, 63; mem. of the corp, Cerebral Palsy Center, Fall River, Mass, 65-66; Augusta Area C. of C; v.chmn. for pub. rels, Kennebec Valley Community Chest, 68, chmn. for pub. rels. and mem, exec. cmt, 69; Maine Asn. of Planners; founding v.pres, Friends of Lithgow Pub. Libr, Augusta, Maine, chmn, Libr. Improvement Cmt, 67-69. Outstanding Serv. Award, 68 and Community Serv. Award, 69, Community Chest; One of five cand. for Outstanding Young Man of Year Award, Augusta Jaycees, 68. Rel: Roman Catholic. Mailing Add: 8 Winter St, Augusta, Maine 04330.

VALDEZ, JOE LUIS R
Mem, N.Mex. State Rep. Exec. Cmt.
b. Parkview, N.Mex, 10/9/16; s. Jose Gregorio Valdez and Rebecca Ortiz V; m. 6/1/36 to Rosemary Sanchez; c. Rebecca Carlotta (Mrs. Marlow), Jeanette Marie (Mrs. Gonzalez), Joseph David, Rosemary and Kelly Anne. Educ: Albuquerque High Sch; Cutter Carr Flying Sch, commercial instrs. license. Polit. & Govt. Pos: Mem, N.Mex. State and Bernalillo Co. Rep. Exec. Cmts; dir, Courtesy and Info, N.Mex, 60-62. Mem: Am. Legion Post 13; Elks. Rel: Catholic. Mailing Add: 1507 Cornell N.E, Albuquerque, N.Mex. 87106. (1967)

VALDEZ, JOYCE RUBY R
Mem, Calif. Rep. State Cent. Cmt.
b. Supreme, Ala, 7/17/28; d. Rev. Thomas Lecial Anderson and Ruby Jane Bradley A; m. 12/17/48 to Frank Valdez; c. Dennis Ray, Victoria Lee, Valerie Lynn and Valinda Lou. Educ: Pasadena Jr. Col, 2 years; Scholarship Soc. Polit. & Govt. Pos: Mem, Calif. Rep. State Cent. Cmt, 67-68, 69-, mem. cand. research, 67-68, co-chmn, Festival Latino KMEX, 67; mem, Los Angeles Co. Rep. Cent. Cmt, 67-68, 69-, mem. platform cmt, 68-; mem, 45th Assembly Dist. Rep. Cent. Cmt, 67-68, 69-; mem, United Rep. Calif, Alhambra Rep. Club, Calif. Rep. Assembly, 67-; sustaining mem, Rep. Nat. Cmt, 67-; co-chmn, Gov. Reagans Rally Los Angeles, 68; chmn, Rep. Activities, Nat. Teen-Age Fair, Hollywood, 68; dinner chmn, Gov. Reagans Fund Raisers for State Finances, 69; v.chmn, 29th Cong. Dist. Rep. Cent. Cmt, 69-; secy, 28th Sen. Dist. Rep. Cent. Cmt, 69-; v.chmn, Rep. Cent. Cmt. Youth Cmt. and chmn, Rep. Cent. Cmt. Youth Coord. Coun, 68-; mem, Rep. State Finance Cmt, 69-; cmnr, Calif. Indust. Welfare Cmn, 69- Bus. & Prof. Pos: Model, Catalina, Inc, 43-45; retail clerk-advert-promotionals, Mod. Village Stores, Inc, 43-58; owner and operator, Supermarket chain, Los Angeles and Orange Co, Calif, 58-66. Mem: Food Employers Coun, Retail Clerk Union; South. Calif. Mkt. Chain Local; Spartan Grocers Asn; Fedn. Bus. & Prfnl. Women; Dep. Registra Voters, Los Angeles Co; YWCA; Emotional Health Asn; Muscular Dystrophy; City of Hope; United Crusade; Am. Red Cross; Am. Heart Asn. Highest Achievement Award, Rep. Cent. Cmt. Los Angeles Co, 68. Rel: Protestant. Mailing Add: 1001 S. Valencia St, Alhambra, Calif. 91801.

VALE, R. L. 'BOB' D
Tex. State Rep.
b. Roma, Tex, 12/4/31; s. Joseph J. Vale and Maria Garcia V; m. 10/28/58

to Therea J. Finnegan; c. Kathleen M, Michael G. and Shelagh A. Educ: St. Mary's Univ. Sch. of Law, LL.B. magna cum laude, 54; Delta Theta Phi, scholarship key, Jr. year; St. Thomas Moore, Barristers. Polit. & Govt. Pos: Tex. State Rep, 68th Dist, 64- Mil. Serv: Entered as 2nd Lt, Army, 54, released as 1st Lt, 56, after serv. in Korea. Mem: San Antonio Bar Asn; San Antonio Jr. Bar Asn; Tex. Trial Lawyers Asn; Am. Asn. of Trial Attorneys; Alumni Senate, Delta Theta Phi; Lulacs; G.I. Forum; Eagles; Northeast Dem. Club. Rel: Catholic. Legal Res: 358 Springwood Lane, San Antonio, Tex. 78216. Mailing Add: 801 Tower Life Bldg, San Antonio, Tex. 78205.

VALENCIA, ROSS HAINES D
Mem, Calif. Dem. State Cent. Cmt.
b. Bisbee, Ariz, 6/6/27; s. Gabriel Valencia and Emma Haines V; m. 4/3/48 to Carmen Lopez; c. Ross, Vance, Camille, Rosalie and Gabriel. Educ: Los Angeles City Col, 46-47; Univ. South. Calif. Exten. Sch. Polit. & Govt. Pos: Coordinator, voter registrn, Viva Johnson Campaign, 64; coordinator, voter registrn. and Get-Out-the-Vote, 30th Cong. Dist, 64; mem, Calif. Dem. State Cent. Cmt, 64-; v.chmn, Cmt. on Anti-Poverty in East Los Angeles, 67; adv. mem, City Human Rels, Los Angeles, 67-69; chmn, U.S. Cmn. on Crime and Delinquency for East Los Angeles, 68; campaign dir, Garcia for Assembly, 68; admin. asst. to Calif. State Assemblyman Alex P. Garcia, 69- Bus. & Prof. Pos: Mgr, Foster's Dent. Lab, Inglewood, Calif, 47-49; owner, V.P. Dent. Lab, 49-64; mgr, Nobilium Restorations, Los Angeles, 65-67; bus. rep, Dent. Technicians Union, Local 100, 67-68. Mil. Serv: Entered as Enlisted Man, Navy, 45, released as PO 3/C, 46, after serv. in FPO, San Francisco, Calif. Mem: Calif. Dent. Technicians; Am. Legion; K. of C; Coun. of Mexican-Am. Affairs; PTA; Boy Scouts; Mexican-Am. Labor Coun; Mexican-Am. Polit. Asn. Order of Merit, Boy Scouts; Hon. Life Membership, PTA. Rel: Roman Catholic. Legal Res: 1162 S. Esperanza St, Los Angeles, Calif. 90023. Mailing Add: 257 S. Spring St, Los Angeles, Calif. 90012.

VALENTI, JACK JOSEPH D
b. Houston, Tex, 9/5/21; m. 6/1/62 to Mary Margaret Wiley; c. Courtenay Lynda, John Lyndon and Alexandra Alice. Educ: Univ. of Houston, B.A, 46; Harvard, M.B.A, 48. Polit. & Govt. Pos: Spec. asst. to President Lyndon Johnson, 63-66. Bus. & Prof. Pos: Pres, Motion Picture Asn. of Am, Inc, 66-; dir. and mem. bd. of trustees, John F. Kennedy Cultural Center, 66-; dir. and mem. bd. of trustees, Am. Film Inst; dir, Trans World Airlines, 68- and Corp. for Pub. Broadcasting, 68- Mil. Serv: Entered as Pvt, Army Air Force, 42, released as 1st Lt, 45, after serv. in 57th Bomb Wing, 12th Air Force, 321st Bombardment Group, Italian Theatre, Distinguished Flying Cross; Air Medal with Four Clusters; Distinguished Unit Citation with One Cluster; European Theatre Ribbon with Three Battle Stars. Publ: Ten Heroes and Two Heroines, Premier Publ. Co, 57; The Correctives of Glory, McGraw-Hill, 70. Named Outstanding Young Man of Houston, 55. Rel: Catholic. Legal Res: Houston, Tex. Mailing Add: c/o Motion Picture Association of America, Inc, 1600 Eye St. N.W, Washington, D.C. 20006.

VALENTINE, WILLIAM ANTHONY R
Mayor, Rome, N.Y.
b. Rome, N.Y, 6/14/13; s. Joseph A. Valentine and Elizabeth Uvanni V; m. 5/31/41 to Hazel Beckley; c. Michael J. and Susan. Educ: Niagara Univ, B.S, in Econ, 38. Polit. & Govt. Pos: Alderman, Rome, N.Y, 60-64, city chmn, 62-63, Mayor, 64-; alternate del, Rep. Nat. Conv, 68. Bus. & Prof. Pos: Cent. Planner, Alcoa, 39-64. Mem: Int. Asn. Basketball Off; exec. cmt, N.Y. State Conf. Mayors; chmn. bd. adv, N.Y. State Annsville Youth Camp; Air Force Asn.(mem. bd. dirs); Elks; K. of C; Moose. Rel: Roman Catholic. Mailing Add: 916 W. Thomas St, Rome, N.Y. 13440.

VALEO, FRANCIS R. D
Secy, U.S. Senate
b. Brooklyn, N.Y, 1/30/16; s. James C. Valeo and Lucy Powell V; m. 10/19/58 to Rita MacDonald. Educ: N.Y. Univ. B.A, 36 and M.A, 42; Am. Univ, 46-48. Polit. & Govt. Pos: Consult, Senate For. Rels. Cmt, 52-58; majority secy, U.S. Senate, 63-66; secy, U.S. Senate, presently. Mil. Serv: Entered as Pvt, 42, released as Sgt, 46; Bronze Star. Mem: Am. Acad. Polit. Sci. Legal Res: New York, N.Y. Mailing Add: 3019 Ordway St. N.W, Washington, D.C. 20008.

VALIER, CHARLES E. R
Mo. State Rep.
b. St. Louis, Mo, 6/5/40; s. Charles E. Valier, Jr. and Musa Lewis V; m. 5/4/63 to Michelle Gunter; c. Michelle Lamy. Educ: Yale, B.A, 62; N.Y. Univ. Grad. Sch. of Bus, M.B.A, 65; Univ. of Mo. Law Sch, J.D, 68; Beta Theta Pi. Polit. & Govt. Pos: Mo. State Rep, 67- Bus. & Prof. Pos: With the Bank of New York, N.Y.C, 63-65; assoc, Peper, Martin, Jensen, Maichel & Hetlage, St. Louis, Mo, 68- Mil. Serv: Entered as Pvt, Marine Corps, 62, released as Cpl, 63. Mem: Yale Club; John Marshall Club; Racquet Club. Rel: Presbyterian. Legal Res: 14 N. Kingshighway, St. Louis, Mo. 63108. Mailing Add: House Post Office, Jefferson City, Mo. 65101.

VALLEE, ROLAND S. D
Mayor of Manchester, N.H.
b. Manchester, N.H, 11/13/29; s. Wilfred Vallee and Marie Anne V; m. 7/26/52 to Ida D. Dubois; c. Debra Ann, Steve Roland, Dale Marie, Celeste Ida, Laura Elizabeth and Paul Arthur. Educ: Berklee Sch. Music, Boston, Mass, 54-55; St. Anselm's Col, 57-60; Univ. N.H. 1 year. Polit. & Govt. Pos: Alderman, Ward 14, N.H, 61; cmnr, Manchester Airport Authority, 61; del, Dem. State Conv, 62; nat. committeeman, N.H. Young Dem. Club, 62-65; del, Dem. Nat. Conv, 64; Mayor, Manchester, N.H, 64-; Dem. Nat. Committeeman, N.H. Dem. Party, 67-68. Bus. & Prof. Pos: Carpenter, 48; cabinetmaker, Hermsdorf Store Fixture Mfg. Co, 53-55; owner, pres. and treas, Val Construction, Inc, 55-; pres. and treas, Valco Realty, Inc, 60-; corporator, Manchester Savings Bank, 62. Mil. Serv: Entered Navy, 48, serv. in U.S. Mediterranean, Europe and Korea, released 53; Good Conduct Medal; Korean Ribbon; ETO Ribbon. Mem: Dir, N.H. Homebuilders Asn, 58-59, treas, 60 and v.pres, 61-62; dir, N.H. Cerebral Palsy Asn, 60-61; pres, Manchester Asn. Homebuilders, 62-64; Commun. Chest drives; Retarded Children Fund drives; Heart Fund drives; Cath. Charities; Cath. War Vet. Post 1352; Am. Legion William A. Jutras Post 43; Queen City Mem. Post 8214; Club Mont-Calm; Club Mont-Royal; K. of C.(4°); hon. mem, Kiwanis; Club Jolliet; Aircraft Owners and Pilots Asn; Nat. Realtors Flying Asn; Nat. Asn. Real Estate Bds; Nat. Asn. Homebuilders; Asn. Commerciale Franco-Americaine, Inc; Navy League; dir, Manchester C. of C, 62; Eagles Aerie; N.H. Munic. Asn; Nat. League of Cities; Conf. of Mayors; hon. mem, Optimist Club. Featured in article depicting accomplishments of young man of Franco-Am. descent, Maclean Mag, Canada, 63; selected Outstanding Young Man of Year, Manchester Jaycees, and one of three for N.H, 64; received citation for outstanding youth work, Cath. War Vet, 59. Rel: Catholic. Mailing Add: 94 Bellevue St, Manchester, N.H. 03103.

VALLIERE, LORRAINE SHARON D
Mem: Calif. Dem. State Cent. Cmt.
b. Los Angeles, Calif, 2/23/41; d. John Sosoka and Mary Kovach S; m. 7/26/58 to Edward James Valliere; c. Christina Lorraine, Susan Marie, Andrea Yvette and Victoria Lynn. Educ: Los Angeles City Col, 1 year; Bakersfield Jr. Col, summer. Polit. & Govt. Pos: Mem, Calif. Dem. State Cent. Cmt, 68- Bus. & Prof. Pos: Mem, br. coun, Am. Inst. Banking, Sierra Chap, 69- Mem: League Women Voters. Rel: Protestant. Mailing Add: 579 W. Memory Lane, Porterville, Calif. 93257.

VALSANGIACOMO, ORESTE VICTOR D
Vt. State Rep.
b. Barre, Vt, 10/31/19; s. Giulio Valsangiacomo and Giuseppina Poletti V; m. 1/19/42 to Helen Louise Emslie; c. Oreste, Jr. and Jon C. Polit. & Govt. Pos: Chmn, Barre City Dem. Cmt, Vt, 52-54; Justice of the Peace, Barre City Bd. of Civil Authority, 52-; chmn, Wash. Co. Dem. Cmt, 54-56 & 65-, committeeman, 56-60; Vt. State Rep, Dist. 7-3, Barre City, 67-, mem, Commerce Cmt, Vt. State House of Rep, currently. Bus. & Prof. Pos: Legis. chmn, Vt. Asn. of Ins. Agents, 62- and Vt. Asn. Real Estate Bds, 63-; Secy, Northeast. Vt. Bd. of Realtors, Inc, 63-65, pres, currently; past mem, Vt. Indust. Bldg. Authority. Mil. Serv: Entered as Sgt, Army, 41, released as Capt, 46, after serv. in 335th Inf. Div, ETO, recalled as Maj, 50, released in 52, after serv. in 172nd Inf. 43rd div, NATO; Lt. Col, Inactive Army Res, 62; Am. Defense, Am. Campaign and ETO Ribbons; German Occup. Victory Medals; Combat Inf. and Expert Inf. Badges; Bronze Star with Cluster; Purple Heart. Mem: Rotary; Elks; VFW; DAV; Am. Legion; Barre Fish & Game Asn; 43rd Div. Asn; 84th Div. Asn; Vt. Nat. Guard. Off. Asn; Barre Country Club. Rel: Catholic. Mailing Add: 31 Sheridan St, Barre, Vt. 05641.

VAN ALSTYNE, DAVID, JR. R
Chmn. Finance Cmt, Bergen Co. Rep. Orgn, N.J.
b. Louisville, Ky, 1/3/97; s. David Van Alstyne and Ella Peay V; m. 10/20/23 to Janet Graham; c. Joan (Mrs. Edward F. Johnson), Keats (Mrs. Evans Smith), Ellen (Mrs. Richard C. Starrett) and David III (deceased). Educ: Williams Col, B.A, 18; Delta Kappa Epsilon. Polit. & Govt. Pos: N.J. State Assemblyman, 40-41; N.J. State Sen, 43-53, majority leader, N.J. State Senate, 48, pres, 49; mem, State Tax Cmn, N.J, 44-45; chmn, Joint Legis. Juvenile Deliquency, 46; mem, State Aid Cmt. Educ, 46 & 50; chmn, N.J. Regional Planning Cmt, 46 & 50; mem. defense coun, Englewood, N.J, 46; chmn, Joint Legis. Appropriations Cmt, 47; Acting Gov, 49; chmn, N.J. Metrop. Rapid Transit Cmn, 52-53; cmnr, Port N.Y. Authority, 54-55; v.chmn, N.Y-N.J. Metrop. Rapid Transit Cmn, 54; chmn. finance cmt, Bergen Co. Rep. Orgn, currently. Bus. & Prof. Pos: Sr. partner, Van Alstyne, Noel & Co, 32-; chmn. bd, New Idria Mining & Chem. Co, 40-; dir. and chmn. exec. cmt, United Piece Dye Works, 43-; dir, Whippany Paper Bd. Co, Inc, 61-, Einson-Freeman & Detroy Corp, C.F. Kirk Labs, Inc, Educ. Systs, Inc, Schott Indust. Inc, Canrad Precision Indust. Inc. and Nyvatex Oil Co. Mil. Serv: Vol, French Army, serv. as sect. comdr, Ambulance Corps, transferred, U.S. Army, 17, 1st Lt; Croix de Guerre. Mem: Holland Soc; Ky. Colonels; Am. Field Serv; Am. Legion; VFW; SAR; Invest. Bankers Asn; Bond Club; Bergen Co. United Fund (pres); Constitutional Conv; bd. trustees and finance cmt, Horace Man Sch; Point O'Woods Asn.(dir, mem, finance cmt); Fairleigh Dickinson Univ; trustee, Bergen Commun. Col; bd. mgrs, Commun. Chest Englewood. Key Man, N.J. Rep. Finance Cmt; chmn, Rep. Club Englewood. Rel: Unitarian. Legal Res: 115 Chestnut St, Englewood, N.J. 07631. Mailing Add: 4 Albany St, New York, N.Y. 10006.

VAN ANTWERP, JAMES CALLANAN, JR. R
Chmn, First Cong. Dist. Rep. Exec. Cmt, Ala.
b. Mobile, Ala, 9/24/23; s. James Callanan Van Antwerp and Fanny Imahorn V; m. 8/11/63 to Elizabeth Margret Barrett; c. James Callanan, III, Elizabeth Ann and John David. Educ: U.S. Naval Acad, B.S, 46. Polit. & Govt. Pos: Treas, Mobile Co. Rep. Party, Ala, 62-65; mem, Mobile City Planning Cmn, 62-, chmn, 62-63 & 67-68 and secy, 65-; mem, Rep. State Cmt, 62-; chmn, Mobile Co. Rep. Exec. Cmt, 65-68; del-at-lg, Rep. Nat. Conv, 68; chmn, First Cong. Dist. Rep. Exec. Cmt, Ala, 68- Mil. Serv: Entered as Midn, Navy, 42, released as Lt, 54, after serv. in Japan, Pac. and Atlantic, Mediterranean Sixth Fleet, last five years in submarines. Mem: V.pres, Mobile Asn. of Independent Ins. Agents, 59 and pres, 60; bd. of dirs, Ala. Realtors, 61-62; v.pres, Mobile Bd. Realtors, 61 and pres, 62. Rel: Catholic. Legal Res: 2750 Fontainebleau Dr. N, Mobile, Ala. 36606. Mailing Add: 901 Van Antwerp Bldg, Mobile, Ala. 36602.

VAN BREE, IVAN R
Mem, Vt. Rep. State Cmt.
b. Toronto, Ont, Can, 8/27/97; s. Isaac E. Van Bree and Bella Bene V; m. 8/26/22 to Dorothy Putnam; c. Lt. Peter Putnam (deceased) and Patricia (Mrs. Thornton Hall Hough). Educ: Colgate Univ, A.B. in Econ. and Sociol, 21; Phi Gamma Delta; Scalp and Blade; hon. alumnus, Princeton Univ, 46. Polit. & Govt. Pos: Mem, Corinth Town Rep. Cmt, Vt, 63-, v.chmn, 69-; Grand Juror, Corinth, 64-; mem, Vt. Rep. State Cmt, 67-; del. and mem, Platform Subcmt, Vt. Rep. State Conv, 68; campaign aide for Gov. Deane C. Davis, Vt, 68; mem, Bd. Civil Authority, Orange Co, 68-, Justice of the Peace, 68-; mem, State Parole Bd, 69- Bus. & Prof. Pos: Commercial mgr, N.Y. Tel. Co, Buffalo, 21-24; broker and agent, gen. ins, 24-25; agency mgt. of Life, Accident and Group Dept, Travelers Ins. Co. of Hartford, Conn, 25-38, group ins. mgr, N.Y.C, 38-60; retired, 60; owner and operator, Tree Farm 72, Am. Tree Farm Syst. and Vt. Forest Industs. Cmt, currently. Mil. Serv: Mil. training, 4 years. Mem: Dir, Cent. Conn. Valley Asn; Vt. 251 Club; Vt. Hist. Soc; Mason; Asn. of Paroling Authorities. Rel: Episcopal; Former Sr. Warden. Mailing Add: Fair Acres Farm, Taplin Hill, East Corinth, Vt. 05040.

VANCE, CLIFFORD M. R
b. Henry Co, Iowa, 8/10/02; s. William R. Vance and Nellie Elliott V; m. to Doris Chancler; c. Randall S, Marilyn J. (Mrs. Beemblossom); four grandchildren. Educ: Univ. of Iowa, B.A, 24; J.D, 26. Polit. & Govt. Pos: Co. attorney, Iowa, 29-32; pres, Henry Co. Bar, 42-62; bd. of govs, Iowa State Bar, 44-46; Iowa State Rep, 57th Gen. Assembly; Iowa State Sen, until 67, pres. pro tempore, Iowa State Senate, 60th and 60th Extra Gen. Assembly. Bus. & Prof. Pos: Land owner and operator; gen. law practice, 26- Mem: Co, State and Am. Bar Asns; Past pres, Rotary; Mason (32°); Shrine. Mailing Add: 304 N. Main St, Mt. Pleasant, Iowa 52641.

VANCE, CYRUS ROBERTS D
b. Clarksburg, W.Va, 3/27/17; s. John Carl Vance and Amy Roberts V; m. 2/15/47 to Grace Elsie Sloane; c. Elsie Nicoll, Amy Sloane, Grace Roberts, Camilla and Cyrus Roberts. Educ: Yale Univ, B.A, 39, LL.B, 42. Hon. LL.D, Marshall Univ, 63, Trinity Col, 66, Yale Univ, 68, W.Va. Univ, 69. Polit. & Govt. Pos: Spec. counsel, Preparedness Investigating Sub-Cmt, Senate Armed Serv. Cmt, 57-60; consult. counsel, Spec. Cmt. on Space and Astronaut, U.S. Senate, 58; gen. counsel, Dept. of Defense, 61-62; Secy. of the Army, 62-64; Dep. Secy. of Defense, 64-67; spec. rep. of the President in Cyprus crisis, Nov-Dec, 67 and in Korea, Feb, 68; U.S. Negotiator, Paris Peace Conf. on Vietnam, 68-69. Bus. & Prof. Pos: Asst. to pres, Mead Corp, 46-47; assoc, Simpson, Thacher & Bartlett, N.Y.C, 47-56, partner, 56-61, 67 & 69- Mil. Serv: Entered as Midn, Navy, 42, released as Lt, 46, after serv. in Pac, 42-46; various combat ribbons. Publ: The Administration of Justice in Civil Disorders,' Judicature, 4/68. Mem: Am. and N.Y. State Bar Asns; Bar of the City of New York; fel, Am. Col. Trial Lawyers; v.chmn. and dir, Am. Red Cross, 68-; trustee, Yale Univ, 68-; Century Asn; Links Club, N.Y.C; Metrop. Club, Wash, D.C. Medal of Freedom, 69. Mailing Add: 2 E. 93rd St, New York, N.Y. 10028.

VANCE, ELIZABETH MARY D
b. Mt. Pleasant, Utah, 10/15/06; d. Charles W. Averett and Mary Christensen A; m. 12/31/27 to John M. Vance; c. Mary Lou (Mrs. Gene Seiffert), Jack and Bard. Educ: Ogden High Sch, grad; Henagers Bus. Col. Polit. & Govt. Pos: Dep. Recorder, Weber Co, Utah, 33; v.chmn, Weber Co. Young Dem; v.chmn, Utah State Young Dem, chmn; chmn. and committeewoman, Nat. Dem. Party; worked for Gov. Maw as mgr, State Store, Utah; supvr, U.S. Census, 10 North Counties, Utah, 50; field rep. for Sen. Frank E. Moss, 2 years; secy, City Cmnr; Utah State Rep, 7 times; rep, Anti-Discrimination Div, Utah State Indust. Cmn, currently; alternate del, Dem. Nat. Conv, 68. Mem: Delta Kappa Gamma Int.(hon. mem, Ogden Chapter); Bus. & Prfnl. Women's Club; Alife Iota; Doe, Elks; Eagles Auxiliary; Trainman Auxiliary; VFW; Order Women Legislators. Rel: Latter-day Saint. Mailing Add: 1136 12th St, Ogden, Utah 84404.

VANCE, HELEN RAINEY D
b. Cullman, Ala, 2/7/34; d. Charles R. Rainey and Alberta Hauk R; m. 10/4/53 to Robert S. Vance; c. Robert S, Jr. and Charles R. Educ: Univ. Ala, Tuscaloosa, 51-53; Univ. Ala, Birmingham, 67-69; Alpha Chi Omega. Polit. & Govt. Pos: Secy-treas, Young Dem. of Ala, 52-53; mem. staff of U.S. Sen. Lister Hill, Ala, 53-54; del, Dem. Nat. Conv, 68. Rel: Episcopal. Mailing Add: 2824 Shook Hill Rd, Birmingham, Ala. 35223.

VANCE, HOWARD GRANT R
b. Sedgwick, Ark, 9/24/15; s. B. B. Vance and Elsie Crader V; m. 5/9/39 to Wanda Grace Sellers; c. Ann (Mrs. Bailey), Howard Eugene and David Boston. Educ: Ark. State Col. Polit. & Govt. Pos: Mem, Ark. State Rep. Cmt, 58-64; del, Rep. Nat. Conv, 60, 64 & 68; mem, State Rep. Exec. Cmt, 60-66; committeeman, First Cong. Dist, currently. Bus. & Prof. Pos: Owner, Vance Real Estate, 52-; gen. mgr, B.B. Vance & Sons, Inc, 42-58, pres, 58- Mem: Rotary; past pres, Walnut Ridge High Sch. Alumni Asn. Rel: Methodist. Mailing Add: c/o General Delivery, Sedgwick, Ark. 72465. (1967)

VANCE, ROBERT SMITH D
Chmn, Ala. State Dem. Party
b. Talladega, Ala, 5/10/31; s. Harrell Taylor Vance and Mae Smith V; m. 10/4/53 to Helen Rainey; c. Robert S, Jr. and Charles R. Educ: Univ. Ala, B.S, 50, LL.B, 52; George Wash. Univ, LL.M, 55; Omicron Delta Kappa; Beta Gamma Sigma; Delta Chi. Polit. & Govt. Pos: Chmn, Ala. State Dem. Party, 66- Bus. & Prof. Pos: Partner, Jenkins, Cole, Callaway & Vance, Attorneys at Law, 64- Mil. Serv: Entered as 2nd Lt, Army, 52, released as 1st Lt, 54; Major, Army Res, at present. Mem: Am, Ala. and Birmingham Bar Asns; Civitan Club. Rel: Episcopal. Legal Res: 2824 Shook Hill Rd, Birmingham, Ala. 35223. Mailing Add: 933 Frank Nelson Bldg, Birmingham, Ala. 35203.

VANCE, SHELDON BAIRD
U.S. Ambassador, Repub. of the Congo
b. Crookston, Minn, 1/18/17; s. Erskine Ward Vance and Helen Baird V; m. 12/28/39 to Jean Chambers; c. Robert Clarke and Stephen Baird. Educ: Carleton Col, A.B, 39; Harvard Law Sch, LL.B, 42. Polit. & Govt. Pos: Econ. analyst and third secy, Am. Embassy, Rio de Janiero, Brazil, 42-46; U.S. v.consul, Nice, France and Monaco, 46-49; U.S. Consul, Martinique, W.Indies, 49-51; Belgium-Luxemburg Desk Officer, Dept. of State, Wash, D.C, 51-54; first secy, Am. Embassy, Brussels, 54-58; chief, Personnel Placement Branch for Africa, Middle East and S.Asia, Dept. of State, Wash, D.C, 58-60; student, Sr. Seminar in For. Rels, Dept. of State, 60-61, dir, Office of Cent. African Affairs, 61-62; dep. chief of mission, Am. Embassy, Addis Ababa, 62-66; sr. for. serv. inspector, Dept. of State, 66-67; U.S. Ambassador, Chad, 67-69 and Repub. of the Congo, 69- Bus. & Prof. Pos: Lawyer, Ropes, Gray, Best, Coolidge & Rugg, Boston, Mass, 42. Mem: Mass. Bar; For. Serv. Asn; Lions. Rel: Presbyterian. Legal Res: 8510 Lynwood Place, Chevy Chase, Md. 20015. Mailing Add: Am. Embassy, Kinshasa, Dept. of State, Washington, D.C. 20521.

VAN CLEAVE, THOMAS WINLOCK D
Chmn, Bienville Parish Dem. Exec. Cmt, La.
b. St. Louis, Mo, 1/9/06; s. Thomas Richard Van Cleave and Fanny Winlock V; m. 10/12/28 to Lelia Stark; c. Barbara (Mrs. Joiner). Educ: Rice Univ, 4 years. Polit. & Govt. Pos: Past pres, Bienville Parish Police Jury, La, mem, 44-; mem. and chmn, Bienville Parish Dem. Exec. Cmt, 56-; mem. and pres, Red River Econ. Develop. Coun, Econ. Develop. Admin, 58- Bus. & Prof. Pos: Mgr. then owner, Ice Bus-Mfg. Plant, cotton ginning and cotton buyer, sold feeds and fertilizers, Gibsland, 28-58; semi-retired, now managing timber lands and investments. Mem: Lions. Rel: Baptist. Mailing Add: Gibsland, La. 71028.

VAN CLIEF, DANIEL GOOD D
Va. State Del.
b. Cleveland, Ohio, 2/14/25; s. Ray Alan Van Clief and Margaret Good V; m. 5/22/46 to Margaret L. Robertson; c. Daniel Good, Jr. and Barry Robertson, twins, Jan Courtlandt and Alan Sterling. Educ: Fishburne Mil. Acad, high sch. dipl. Polit, & Govt. Pos: Mem, Albemarle Co. Dem. Cmt, Va, 65-; chmn, Scottsville Dist. Dem. Cmt, 66-; mem, Va. Cmn. of Outdoor Recreation, 66-; mem, Va. State Dem. Finance Cmt, currently; Va. State Del, 68-; mem, Va. Adv. Cmt. on Aviation, 68-; mem, Rural Affairs Study Cmn, 68- Bus. & Prof. Pos: Farmer-financier, Nydrie Farms, Esmont, Va, 45-; past dir, Thomas Jefferson Corp, Charlottesville; officer and dir, Fasig-Tipton Co, N.Y, currently; dir, Md. State Fair, currently; v.pres-dir, Crown Colony Club, Ltd, Chub Cay, Bahamas, currently; dir, Village Green Corp, Charlottesville, Va, currently; dir, Alderman 250 Corp, currently; trustee, Miller Sch. of Albemarle, 68-; former mem. bd. gov, Belfield Sch; dir, Grayson Found, Lexington, Ky, currently; mem. sponsor cmt, Univ. Va. Grad. Sch. of Bus, currently. Mil. Serv: Army, 4th Inf. Div, ETO, World War II; ETO Ribbon with Silver Star and Bronze Arrowhead. Mem: Trustee, Thoroughbred Owners & Breeders Asn. of Am, Jamaica, N.Y; dir, Va. Thoroughbred Asn.(past pres); Jockey Club, N.Y; exec. bd, Stonewall Jackson Coun, Boy Scouts; exec. cmt, Charlottesville YMCA; Vestryman, Christ Church, Glendower, Va.(5 years). Rel: Episcopal. Mailing Add: Old Woodville, Esmont, Va. 22937.

VAN COTT, GEORGE E. R
N.Y. State Assemblyman
b. Mt. Vernon, N.Y; second m. Apr. 1960 to Cassandra Pappas; c. Robert, Jacqueline (Mrs. John Barra), George, Jr, Cassandra Ileana and Peter Pappas. Educ: Wesleyan Univ. Polit. & Govt. Pos: N.Y. State Assemblyman, 88th Assembly Dist, 60-; former supvr, Westchester Bd. of Supvrs; past pres. and mem, Mt. Vernon Common Coun. Bus. & Prof. Pos: Advert. exec, Lennen and Newell, N.Y.C. Mem: Adv. bd, Blind Serv. Agency; dir, PAL; bd. of trustees, Mt. Vernon Hosp; adv. bd, Westchester Lighthouse; former mem. bd. of dirs, Mt. Vernon YMCA; past pres. and campaign chmn, Mt. Vernon Community Chest; dir, Mt. Vernon Police Athletic League; bd. of dirs, Westchester Mentally Ill Children; Am. Hellenic Educ. Progressive Asn. Rel: Bd. of Deacons and Bd. of Trustees, Community Church at Circle. Mailing Add: 4 Laurel Ave, Mt. Vernon, N.Y. 10552.

VanDALSEM, JOSEPHINE FERN R
Chmn, Brown Co. Rep. Party, Kans.
b. Fairview, Kans, 2/11/09; d. Charles Clerance O'Roke and Cicely Monroe O; m. 8/13/30. Polit. & Govt. Pos: Chmn, Brown Co. Rep. Party, Kans, 60- Mem: Kans. Farm Bur; Hiawatha Co. Club; pres, Southwest Brown Co. Women's Rep. Club; precinct committeewoman, Hiawatha Bowling Asn. Rel: Unity. Mailing Add: Box 36, Fairview, Kans. 66425.

VAN DEERLIN, LIONEL D
U.S. Rep, Calif.
b. Los Angeles, Calif, 7/25/14; s. Lionel Van Deerlin, Sr. and Gladys Mary Young V; m. 10/8/40 to Mary Jo Smith; c. Lionel James, Lawson John, Victoria, Elizabeth, Mary Susan and Jeffrey. Educ: Univ. of South. Calif, 37, B.A, Journalism. Polit. & Govt. Pos: U.S. Rep, Calif, 63-, mem, Cmt. on Interstate and For. Commerce and Subcmt. on Commun. and Power, U.S. House of Rep, presently. Bus. & Prof. Pos: Newspaperman; radio and TV news ed. and analyst. Mil. Serv: Army, overseas serv. in Mediterranean Theatre. Rel: Episcopal. Legal Res: San Diego, Calif. Mailing Add: 211 Cannon House Office Bldg, Washington, D.C. 20515.

VANDEN HEUVEL, WILLIAM J. D
b. Rochester, N.Y, 4/14/30; s. Joost Vanden Heuvel and Alberta Demunter V; m. 12/5/58 to Jean Stein; c. Katrina and Wendy. Educ: Deep Springs Jr. Col, 2 years; Cornell Univ, B.A, 50 and Law Sch, LL.B, 52; Order of the Coif. Polit. & Govt. Pos: Spec. asst. to U.S. Ambassador to Thailand, William J. Donovan, 53-54 and to Attorney Gen. Robert Kennedy, 62-64; spec. counsel to Gov. Harriman of N.Y, 58; regional adminstr, Off. of Econ. Opportunity, N.E. U.S, 64-65; v.pres, N.Y. Constitutional Conv, 67; del, Dem. Nat. Conv, 68. Bus. & Prof. Pos: Attorney-at-law, Donovan, Leisure, Newton & Irvine, 52-59, Javits, Moore & Trubin, 59-62 and Stroock, Stroock & Lavan, 65- Mil. Serv: Entered as 1st Lt, Air Force, 52, released as Capt, 54, after serv. in Judge Adv. Gen. Dept; Order of White Elephant. Publ: Triumph and Tragedy of Hungary, 56; Robert F. Kennedy: On His Own, 63-68, Doubleday, 69. Mem: Pres, Int. Rescue Cmt. Rel: Catholic. Mailing Add: 150 E. 72nd St, New York, N.Y. 10021.

VANDERET, ROBERT CHARLES D
Chmn, The Kennedy Cmt. for a Reformed Party
b. Brooklyn, N.Y, 4/12/47; s. James G. Vanderet and Bernadette Cecelia Heaney V; single. Educ: Univ. Calif, Los Angeles, B.A, 69; Regents Scholar, Clarence Dykstra Mem. Scholar. Polit. & Govt. Pos: Del, Dem. Nat. Conv, 68; Chmn, South Calif. Citizens for Kennedy and Los Angeles Citizens for Gun Control, 68; chmn, The Kennedy Cmt. for a Reformed Party, 69- Publ: 'Confrontation and the Campus,' Dem. Bul, 4/69. South. Calif. B'nai B'rith Student of the Year, 65. Rel: Roman Catholic. Legal Res: 7003 Walker Ave, Bell, Calif. 90201. Mailing Add: 613 Gayley Ave, Los Angeles, Calif. 90024.

VANDERHOOF, JOHN D. R
Speaker, Colo. State House of Rep.
b. Rockyford, Colo, 5/27/22; s. Roy Elvin Vanderhoof and Irene Church V; m. 4/3/43 to Lois June Taggart, div; c. Bruce and Linda. Educ: Glendale Col, Calif, A.A. Polit. & Govt. Pos: Colo. State Rep, 55-, Minority Leader, Colo. House of Rep, 55-62 & 65-66, Speaker of the House, 63-64 & 67-; del, Rep. Nat. Conv, 68. Bus. & Prof. Pos: Owner, Van's Sporting Goods, Glenwood Springs, Colo, 46-55; pres, Glenwood Indust. Bank, 55- and Bank of Glenwood, 63- Mil. Serv: Entered as Aviation Cadet, Navy, 42, released as

Lt.(jg), 45, after serv. in Pac; Purple Heart; Distinguished Flying Cross; Two Air Medals. Mem: AF&AM; Kiwanis; Elks; Eagles; Am. Legion; VFW; Shrine. Rel: Methodist. Mailing Add: 338 Park Dr, Glenwood Springs, Colo. 81601.

VANDER JAGT, GUY R
U.S. Rep, Mich.
b. Cadillac, Mich, 8/26/31; s. Harry Vander Jagt and Marie Copier V; m. 4/4/64 to Carol Doorn; c. Virginia Marie. Educ: Hope Col, B.A, 53; Yale Univ. Divinity Sch, B.D, 57; Univ. Mich. Law Sch, LL.B, 60. Polit. & Govt. Pos: Mich. State Sen, 65-67; U.S. Rep, Mich, 67- Bus. & Prof. Pos: News Dir, WWTV, 56; lawyer, Warner, Norcorss & Judd. Publ: 'Evidentiary Problems of Medical Tests,' Practical Lawyer, 61. Mem: Rotary; Mason. Rel: Presbyterian. Legal Res: 1201 Lake Mitchell Dr, Cadillac, Mich. 49601. Mailing Add: U.S. House Office Building, Washington, D.C. 20515.

VANDER KOOI, BENJAMIN DFL
Chmn, Rock Co. Dem-Farmer-Labor Party, Minn.
b. Worthington, Minn, 2/24/19; s. William Vander Kooi and Jessie Roarda V; m. 9/4/42 to Kathryn C. Kooiman; c. Jane (Mrs. Hagedorn), Kathryn, Benjamin, Jr, Ann and Sue. Educ: Calvin Col, 41; Univ. Minn. Law Sch, B.S. and LL.B, 49. Polit. & Govt. Pos: Claims supvr, Minn. Adjusted Compensation Div, 49-50; v.chmn, Rock Co. Dem-Farmer-Labor Party, 50-54, treas, 54-62, chmn, 62-66 & 68-; govt. appeal agent, Selective Serv, 51-; dep. registr. of motor vehicles, Motor Vehicle Dept, 54-64; mem, Dem. State Cent. Cmt, 66-69. Bus. & Prof. Pos: Attorney-at-law, Luverne, Minn, 50- Mil. Serv: Entered as Seaman 2/C, Naval Air Corps, 41, released as Lt. Comdr, 62, after serv. as Naval Aviator; Lt. Comdr, Naval Air Corps Res, until 62. Mem: Minn. Bar Asn; Rotary; Am. Legion; VFW; C. of C. Park Bd; Farmers Union. Winner of Broodman Oratorical Contest, 40. Rel: Christian Reformed Church; mem, bd. trustees; supt, Sunday Sch. Mailing Add: Box 116, RFD 1, Luverne, Minn. 56156.

VANDERLAAN, ROBERT R
Mich. State Sen.
b. Grand Rapids, Mich, 6/4/30; m. 1951 to Mildred Bouma; c. Linda Beth and Robert J. Educ: Calvin Col, A.B, 52; Univ. Mich, M.A, 57. Polit. & Govt. Pos: Mich. State Sen, 62-; former clerk, trustee and supvr. of Paris Twp. Bus. & Prof. Pos: Teacher hist. & govt, South Christian High Sch, 7 years; part-time Calvin Col, 62. Mem: South YMCA bd. of dirs. Rel: Christian Reformed. Mailing Add: 4745 Curwood S.E, Grand Rapids, Mich. 49508. (1967)

VANDERPERREN, CLETUS J. D
Wis. State Assemblyman
b. Pittsfield, Wis, 3/4/12. Educ: Mills Center Sch. Polit. & Govt. Pos: Wis. State Assemblyman, 58-; former town chmn, Green Bay, Wis. and former mem. co. bd, 16 years. Bus. & Prof. Pos: Farm owner and operator. Mem: Farm Bur; Local Dairy Herd Improv. Coop; past pres. and treas, Tri-Co. Fire Dept. Mailing Add: Route 5, Green Bay, Wis. 54303. (1967)

VANDERPLOEG, JAN B. D
b. Holland, Mich, 7/5/00; married; c. Three daughters. Educ: Hope Col, A.B, 22; West. Theol. Sem; Harvard Univ; Mich. State Univ. Polit. & Govt. Pos: Councilman, North Muskegon, Mich, 47-53; secy, Ninth Cong. Dem. Cmt, 54-60; chmn, Muskegon Co. Dem. Cmt, 57-58; bd. of trustees, Mich. State Univ, 57-63; Dem. cand. for U.S. Rep, Mich, 58; mem, Gov. Cmn. on the Employ. of the Older Worker, 58-60; Presidential elector, 60; del, Dem. Nat. Conv, 64; Mich. State Sen, 64-66. Bus. & Prof. Pos: Landscape architect; teacher, Ravenna High Sch. Mil. Serv: World War I. Mem: Planning Bd. of N. Muskegon, 46-47; pres, Mich. Men's Fel. of Congregational Churches, 50-52; lay minister, 52-56; asst. moderator of Mich. Congregational Conf, 53; treas, Geriatrics Coun. of Gr. Muskegon, 56-63; hon. alumnus of Mich. State Univ, 59; Hon. adv, Assoc. of Gov. Bd. of Univs. and Cols. Jonathan Walker Award of the Urban League of Gr. Muskegon. Rel: Unitarian. Mailing Add: 190 N. Whitehall Rd, N.Muskegon, Mich. 49445.

VANDERPOEL, WAYNE GAYLORD R
Wyo. State Sen.
b. Lodi, Wis, 10/16/19; s. Theodore Louis Vanderpoel and Idelia Rutlin V; m. 6/11/69 to Sally Rouse; c. Sally Jo Keeline (stepdaughter), Gay and Philip R. Educ: Oshkosh State Teachers Col, 2 years; Mass. Inst. Tech, 1 year; Univ. Wyo, B.A, 48. Polit. & Govt. Pos: Rep. precinct committeeman, Wyo, 58-64; chmn, Goshen Co. Rep. Party, 64-66; Wyo. State Sen, Goshen Co, 66- Bus. & Prof. Pos: Mem. and chmn, Goshen Co. Welfare Bd, 58-65; mem. and pres, East. Wyo. Col, 59-68. Mil. Serv: Entered as Pvt, Air Force, 41, released as Capt, 46, after serv. in First Army Air Force; Capt, Wyo. Nat. Guard, 51-63, serv. in 115th Field Artil. Group as Air Force Pilot. Mem: Am. Legion, Torrington; Wyo. Farm Bur. Rel: Episcopal. Legal Res: Huntley, Wyo. 82218. Mailing Add: P.O. Drawer V, Torrington, Wyo. 88240.

VANDERPOOL, WILLIAM S, JR. R
Chmn, Poweshiek Co. Rep. Party, Iowa
b. El Paso, Tex, 2/1/22; s. Wm. S. Vanderpool and Nettie Ware V; m. 11/5/48 to Virginia Bliss Fowlkes; c. Carol Marie, Wm. S, III and James David. Educ: Duke Univ, A.B, 43 and LL.B, 48; La. State Univ, M.A, 52 and Ph.D, 53; Phi Alpha Delta; Sigma Nu. Polit. & Govt. Pos: Trial attorney, Anti-Trust Div, Justice Dept, 48-50; v.pres, Young Rep, La. State Univ. and Baton Rouge, 52; chmn, Poweshiek Co. Rep. Party, Iowa, 63-; dir, Prog. in Practical Polit, Grinnell Col, 65-66. Bus. & Prof. Pos: Prof, Grinnell Col, 53- Mil. Serv: Entered as Midn, Navy, 43, released as Lt.(jg), 46, after serv. in Pac. Theater. Publ: Articles on Logic, 56, Propaganda Services, 56 and Parliamentary Procedure, 57, J. Weston Walch. Mem: Arbitrator, Am. Arbit. Asn; Speech Asn. of Am; D.C. Bar Asn; bd. mem, Kiwanis and Commun. Hosp. Rel: Methodist. Mailing Add: 1313 Main, Grinnell, Iowa 50112.

VANDETTE, EDMUND FREDERICK R
Chmn, Houghton Co. Rep. Party, Mich.
b. Houghton, Mich, 8/8/32; s. Bernard Vandette and Elsie Hietala V; m. 10/11/54 to June Helen Randell; c. Edmund Mark and Robert Alan. Educ: North. Mich. Univ, B.S, 58; Univ. Mich, M.A, 59; Ohio State Univ, work on Ph.D; Kappa Delta Pi; Alpha Phi Omega. Polit. & Govt. Pos: Pres, Men's Rep. Club, Houghton Co, Mich, 67-68; chmn, Houghton Co. Rep. Party, 68-; west. regional chmn, Upper Peninsula of Mich, 69; del, Rep. State Conv, 69. Bus. & Prof. Pos: Assoc. prof, Mich. Tech. Univ, 59- Mil. Serv: Entered as A/S, Navy, 51, released as Fireman 1/C, 53, after serv. in U.S.S. Sea Robin, SS407, Submarine Serv, Atlantic Theatre; Am. Nat. Defense Medal; Submarine Dolphins. Mem: Am. Asn. Univ. Profs; Mich. Tech. Univ. Faculty Asn; Copper Country Kiwanis; Elks. Outstanding Teacher of the Year Award, Adult Educ. Asn. Mich. Rel: Catholic. Mailing Add: U.S. 41, Chassell, Mich. 49916.

VAN DOREN, CHARLES NORTON
Dep. Gen. Counsel, Arms Control and Disarmament Agency
b. Orange, N.J, 4/7/24; s. Durand H. Van Doren and Marie Norton V; m. Nov. 1967 to Regina Ridder; c. Catherine Joan Harris (stepdaughter), Harold Charter, Rebecca Elsie, Margaret Alice and Marie Regina. Educ: Harvard Col, 42-43 & 46; Columbia Law Sch, LL.B, 49; ed, Columbia Law Rev, 47-49. Polit. & Govt. Pos: V.pres, South Orange-Maplewood Adult Sch, 59-61; legal adv. to U.S. Disarmament Del, 63; asst. gen. counsel, Arms Control and Disarmament Agency, 63-64, dep. gen. counsel, 64-, acting gen. counsel, 69; U.S. Rep. to Conf. on Non-Nuclear States, 68. Bus. & Prof. Pos: Assoc. lawyer, Simpson Thacher & Bartlett, N.Y.C, 49-60, partner, 61. Mil. Serv: Entered as Pvt, Army, 43, released as T-5, 45, after serv. in First Cavalry Div, Pac. Theater. Mem: Am. Soc. Int. Law; N.Y. Co. Lawyers Asn; Fed. Bar Asn. Harvard Prize Scholarship, 42-43; Harlan Fiske Stone Scholar, Columbia Law Sch, 46-47; Meritorious Honor Award, Arms Control and Disarmament Agency, 67, Outstanding Performance Awards, 67 & 68. Rel: Unitarian. Mailing Add: 1387 Locust Rd. N.W, Washington, D.C. 20012.

VAN DRIE, RUDY ARIE R
Asst. Majority Floor Leader, Iowa House Rep.
b. Ashton, Iowa, 1/5/31; s. Gerritt Van Drie and Sophio Feberwee V; m. 8/1/58 to Gladys Vander Woulde; c. Karen Jo and Karla Ann. Educ: Northwest. Jr. Col, 51; Univ. Iowa, B.A, 55. Polit. & Govt. Pos: Iowa State Rep, 67-, asst. majority floor leader, Iowa House Rep, 69- Bus. & Prof. Pos: Pres, Ideal Develop. Co, Inc; pres, Ames Shopper Guides of Iowa; secy-treas. and pres, Nat. Shopper Asn. Mil. Serv: Cpl, 85th Inf. Mem: Secy, Jaycees; pres, Sertoma; chmn. and mem. bd, Cancer Drive; chaplain and v.comdr, Am. Legion; chmn, Ames, Iowa Safety Cmn. Mailing Add: State Capitol, 10th and Grand Ave, Des Moines, Iowa 50139.

VAN DUSEN, RICHARD CAMPBELL R
Under Secy, Dept. of Housing and Urban Develop.
b. Jackson, Mich, 7/18/25; s. Bruce Buick Van Dusen and Helen Campbell V; m. 6/28/49 to Barbara Congdon; c. Amanda, Lisa and Katherine. Educ: Univ. Minn, B.S, 45; Harvard Law Sch, LL.B, 49. Polit. & Govt. Pos: Mich. State Rep, 54-56; del, Mich. Constitutional Conv, 61-62; legal adv. to Gov, Mich, 63; del, Rep. Nat. Conv, 64, alternate del, 68; Under Secy, U.S. Dept. of Housing and Urban Develop, 69- Bus. & Prof. Pos: Attorney, Dickinson, Wright, McKean & Cudlip, 49-62 & 64-69. Mil. Serv: Entered as A/S, Navy, 43, released as Ens, 46, after serv. in Pac. Mem: Am. and Detroit Bar Asns; State Bar of Mich. Rel: Episcopal. Legal Res: Birmingham, Mich. 48010. Mailing Add: 8300 Burdette Rd, Bethesda, Md. 20034.

VAN DUYNE, FREDERICK WILLIAM R
Chmn, Seventh Dist. Rep. Cmt, Mich.
b. Newark, N.J, 7/15/32; s. Frederick William Van Duyne, Jr. and Florence Goddard V; m. 9/6/56 to Gloria Dawn MacArthur; c. Kimberly, Bethany, Alexander, Jennifer and Abigale. Educ: Cornell Univ, 54, Med. Col, 58; Zeta Psi. Polit. & Govt. Pos: Mem, Genesee Co. Finance Cmt, Mich, 61-64; del, State Rep. Conv, 64 & 68; former chmn, Genesee Co. Rep. Party; mem, Mich. State Bd. of Registrs. in Med, 66-; chmn, Seventh Dist. Rep. Cmt, presently; del, Rep. Nat. Conv, 68. Bus. & Prof. Pos: Chief of gen. practice, Genesee Mem. Hosp, 65-66, vice chief of staff, currently; secy. of gen. staff, McLaren Gen. Hosp, 66. Mem: Am. Med. Asn; Mich. State and Genesee Co. Med. Socs; Acad. of Gen. Practice; Flint Acad. of Med; Rotary. Rel: Episcopal. Mailing Add: 1490 Briarcliffe Dr, Flint, Mich. 48504.

VAN DYK, R. DANIEL D
b. Bellingham, Wash, 11/25/42; s. Ralph A. Van Dyk and Wilamina Johanna Troost V; m. 8/15/64 to Jerilyn Kay Noteboom; c. Jeffrey Daniel. Educ: Wash. State Univ, M.S, 67; Alpha Zeta; Phi Kappa Phi. Polit. & Govt. Pos: Chmn, Dem. Club, Lynden, Wash, 67-69; del. and chmn, Whatcom Co. Dem. Conv, 68; del, Dist, State and Nat. Rep. Conv, 68; precinct committeeman, Whatcom Co. Dem. Party, 68- Bus. & Prof. Pos: Owner and mgr, Vandy Farm, 66- Publ: Nitrate Toxicity Problems-A Research Review, Agr. Exten. Serv. of the Va. Polytechnic Inst, 66, Effects of Various Levels of Monosodium Glutamate in Calf Starter Rations, Washington State Univ, 67, 'Influence of Practical Diets on Fore-stomach Development of the Calf,' J. of Dairy Science, 66. Mem: Am. Dairy Sci. Asn; Kiwanis; Washington State Dairy Fedn; Holstein-Friesian Asn. of Am. Rel: Methodist. Mailing Add: 7585 Noon Rd, Lynden, Wash. 98264.

VAN ENGELEN, W. DEAN R
Chmn, Cassia Co. Rep. Cent. Cmt, Idaho
b. Burley, Idaho, 9/28/29; s. Henry C. Van Engelen and Addie Schmidt V; m. 7/17/49 to Eyvonne Campbell; c. Deana Beth, Debra Lynn and Henry Craig. Educ: Wash. Univ, St. Louis, B.S. in Bus. Admin, 51; Eta Mu Pi. Polit. & Govt. Pos: Precinct committeeman, Cassia Co. Rep. Cent. Cmt, Idaho, 60-64, chmn, 64- Bus. & Prof. Pos: Gen. mgr, Van Engelens, Inc, 54- Mem: Kiwanis; People-to-People; Idaho Employers Coun; C. of C. Rel: Methodist. Legal Res: 85 Van Engelen Dr, Burley, Idaho 83318. Mailing Add: P.O. Box 70, Burley, Idaho 83318. (1967)

VAN ESCHEN, JOHN EDWARD D
b. Ackley, Iowa, 10/12/28; s. John C. Van Eschen and Rose Finger V; m. 5/20/56 to Shirley A. Brandt; c. James Eric and John Brandt. Educ: State Univ. Iowa, B.A, 48; Univ. North. Iowa, 48-50; State Univ. Iowa Law Sch, J.D, 58. Polit. & Govt. Pos: Pres, Greene Commun. Sch. Bd, Iowa, 62-; Dem. nominee for U.S. Rep, 68. Mil. Serv: Entered as Seaman Recruit,

Navy, 52, released as Lt, 56, after serv. aboard Fleet Ships, Atlantic, 3 years. Mem: Local, Co, State and Nat. Bar Asns; Am. Legion; Elks. Rel: Presbyterian. Mailing Add: Greene, Iowa 50636.

VAN EXEM, ELIZABETH HAWLEY GASQUE D
b. Rice Creek Plantation, S.C, 2/26/92; d. John Meade Hawley and Emma Maria Nelson Entzminger H; wid; c. Elizabeth (Mrs. Perry), Doris (Mrs. Beeker), Thomas Nelson and John Allard Gasque. Educ: Furman Univ. Polit. & Govt. Pos: Former mem, Dem. Nat. Speakers' Bur. and former S.C. State Rep. Bus. & Prof. Pos: Tree farmer, 56-66. Publ: Magazine articles. Mem: Patroness, Delta Omicron; mem. and officer, several literary and civic clubs; pres, Study Club and Church Auxiliary; DAR; Colonial Dames; life mem, Cong. Club. Writer dramatic progs; received medal for dramatics. Rel: Episcopal. Mailing Add: Cedar Tree Plantation, Ridgeway, S.C. 29130.

VAN GILST, BASS D
Iowa State Sen.
b. Pella, Iowa, 4/14/11; s. Peter Van Gilst and Nellie Klein V; m. 11/26/37 to Harriet E. DeBrum; c. Ken, Carl, Elaine, Mark, Diane and Joleen. Polit. Pos: Iowa State Sen, 65- Bus. & Prof. Pos: Pres, Marion-Mahaske F.S. Services, at present, past treas, Extention Coun; past pres, Sch. Bd. Mem: Farm Bur; C. of C; Oskaloosa Lions. Rel: Christian Reformed Church. Mailing Add: Route 4, Oskaloosa, Iowa 52577. (1967)

VAN GINKEL, JAMES R
Chmn, Cass Co. Rep. Cent. Cmt, Iowa
b. Prairie City, Iowa, 2/27/23; s. John Christian Van Ginkel and Caroline Van Nimwegen V; m. 6/27/53 to Marvel Crumpacker; c. James Carol, Jane Ann and John Christian. Educ: Univ. of Iowa, B.S.C, 48; Drake Univ, Des Moines, Iowa, J.D, 53; Delta Theta Phi; Omicron Delta Kappa; Am. Law Student Asn. Polit. & Govt. Pos: Attorney, Cass Co, Iowa, 59-64; chmn, Cass Co. Rep. Cent. Cmt, 66- Mil. Serv: Entered as Aviation Cadet, Army Air Force, 42, released as 1st Lt, 45, after serv. in ETO; ETO Ribbon; Air Medal With Four Oak Leaf Clusters. Mem: Am. and Iowa State Bar Asns; Elks; Mason; Lions; Am. Legion; Amvets; VFW. Rel: Methodist. Mailing Add: 1210 East 13th St, Atlantic, Iowa 50022.

VAN HEYDE, ROBERT LEE D
State Cent. Committeeman Ohio Dem. Party
b. Columbus, Ohio, 1/7/30; s. Clyde Leo Van Heyde and Emma Walker V; m. 5/29/55 to Renee Michael; c. Christina, Robert Lee, Jr, Theresa, Eric, Renee and Thomas Jefferson. Educ: Ohio State Univ, B.A, 56, LL.B, 59, J.D, 66. Polit. & Govt. Pos: City councilman, Columbus, Ohio, 58-61; mem, Columbus Metrop. Airport, 65-69, chmn, 66-68; alternate del, Dem. Nat. Conv, 68; State Cent. Committeeman, Ohio Dem. Party, 68- Bus. & Prof. Pos: Attorney-at-law, 59- Mil. Serv: Entered as Seaman, Navy, 48, released as RM 3/C, 52, after serv. in Atlantic, 48-52. Mem: Am, Inter-Am. and Ohio Bar Asns; YMCA; Urban League; Navy League; Elks. Rel: Catholic. Legal Res: 761 Highland Dr, Columbus, Ohio 43214. Mailing Add: 895 S. High St, Columbus, Ohio 43206.

VAN HOLLEN, CHRISTOPHER
Dep. Asst. Secy, Bur. of Near East. & S.Asian Affairs, Dept. of State
Mailing Add: Dept. of State, 2201 C St. N.W, Washington, D.C. 20520.

VAN HOLLEN, JOHN CARTER R
Wis. State Assemblyman
b. Rhinelander, Wis, 6/27/33; s. Byron Floyd Van Hollen and Nila Edith Carter V; m. 12/2/61 to Rosella M. Wipperfurth; c. Susan Janelle, Peggy Marie and John Byron. Educ: Univ. Wis, B.S, 58. Polit. & Govt. Pos: Mem, bd. of dirs, Barron Co. Rep. Party, Wis, 64-, finance chmn, 65-66; v.chmn, Chetek Planning Cmn, 65-66; Wis. State Assemblyman, Barron and Washburn Counties, 67- Bus. & Prof. Pos: V.Pres, Chetek Area Credit Union, 65- Mil. Serv: Entered as Pvt, Army, 54, released as Cpl, 56, after serv. in NATO, Europe, 55-56; Sgt, Army Res, 56-57. Mem: Nat. Asn. of Life Underwriters; Mason, Consistory, Shrine; Odd Fellows; Chetek Rod and Gun Club; C. fo C; Lions; Elks; Indianhead Asn. Rel: Lutheran. Mailing Add: 720 Lakeview Dr, Chetek, Wis. 54728.

VAN HOOMISSEN, GEORGE A. D
Dist. Attorney, Multnomah Co, Ore.
b. Portland, Ore, 3/7/30; s. Frederick J. Van Hoomissen and Helen Flanagan V; m. 6/4/60 to Ruth M. Niedermeyer; c. George Thomas, Ruth Anne and Madeleine. Educ: Univ. of Portland, B.A, 51; Georgetown Univ. Law Sch, J.D, 55; Georgetown Law Center, LL.M, 57; Blue Key; Phi Delta Phi. Polit. & Govt. Pos: Ore. State Rep, 59-62; nat. committeeman, Young Dem. Ore, 60-62; del, Ore. Dem. State Conv, 62 & 66; Dist. Attorney, Multomah Co, 62-; del, Dem. Nat. Conv, 64 & 68. Mil. Serv: Entered as Pvt, Marine Corps Res, 47, released as 1st Lt, 53, after serv. in First Marine Div, FMF, Korea, 52-53; Lt. Col, Marine Corps Res; Distinguished Flying Cross; Air Medal with 5 Gold Stars. Mem: K. of C; Am. Legion; Nat. Dist. Attorney Asn.(v.pres, 66-); Fed. Bar Asn.(pres, Ore. Chap); Ore. UN Asn.(pres). Rel: Catholic. Mailing Add: 2127 S.W. Edgewood Rd, Portland, Ore. 97201.

VAN HOOSE, WENDELL R
Ky. State Sen.
b. 1913. Polit. & Govt. Pos: Ky. State Sen, 52-58, 64-, Rep. Floor Leader, 56, 58 & 64, Ky. State Senate. Bus. & Prof. Pos: Farmer. Mem: Pres. Johnson Co. Farm Bur. Rel: Baptist. Mailing Add: Tutor Key, Ky. 41263. (1967)

VAN HORN, CLARK D
N.Dak. State Sen.
b. Minnewaukan, N.Dak, 6/1/11; married; c. One. Educ: Valley City and Minot Teachers Cols. Polit. & Govt. Pos: N.Dak. State Sen, 59- Bus. & Prof. Pos: Farmer. Mem: Am. Legion; Farmers Union. Mailing Add: Parshall, N.Dak. 58770. (1967)

VAN HORN, DELMAR R
b. Perry, Iowa, 10/8/24; s. Delmar Guy Van Horn and Leone Burk V; m. 2/23/47 to Dorothy Burdine; c. Gary Guy, Kent Michel and Todd Vincent. Educ: Univ. Iowa, 42 and 43; Pershing Rifles. Polit. & Govt. Pos: Precinct chmn, Greene Co. Rep. Party, Iowa, 50-60 and former chmn; mem, Young Rep. State Farm Cmt, 52; del, Rep. Nat. Conv, 68. Bus. & Prof. Pos: Pres, Shriver-Van Horn Construct, 58; v.pres, Am. Athletic Equipment Co, 62 and Beaver Creek Distillery, 66. Mil. Serv: Entered as Pvt, Army, 42, released as Sgt, 47 after serv. in ETO. Mem: Rotary; VFW; Am. Legion; Elks. Outstanding Young Farmer Award, Ideal G.I. Farm Family Award. Rel: Christian Church. Legal Res: Maple Hill Place, Jefferson, Iowa 50129. Mailing Add: Box 111, Jefferson, Iowa 50129. (1967)

VAN HORN, LYLE CECIL R
b. Cerro Gordo, Ill, 4/14/12; s. William C. Van Horn and Bessie Chapman V; m. 5/17/38 to Ruth J. Iliff; c. Thomas D. and Warren M. Educ: Ill. Wesleyan Univ, B.S, 36; Theta Chi. Polit. & Govt. Pos: Alternate del, Rep. Nat. Conv, 64 and del, 68; mem, Gov. Adv. Coun, 69-; mem, Agr. Export Adv. Cmt, Ill. Dept. of Agr, 69- Bus. & Prof. Pos: Pres, Van Horn Hybrids, Inc, 55-69. Mem: Past pres, Ill. Crop Improv. Asn, Ill. Seed Dealers Asn. and Ill. Found. Seeds; Piatt Co. Farm Bur; Mason; Shrine; Bloomington Consistory. Rel: United Methodist. Mailing Add: 121 Arnold Dr, Cerro Gordo, Ill. 61818.

VAN HORN, MICHAEL R
State Chmn, United Rep. of Calif.
b. Prague, Czechoslovakia, 6/15/28; s. Anthony Jednorozec and Libuse Nygrynova J; m. 12/23/60 to Joyce Darlene Walters; c. Connie D, Vickie L. and Michael Anthony. Educ: Charles Univ, Prague, 3 years of Architecture. Polit. & Govt. Pos: V.pres, Young Rep. of Los Angeles Co, Calif, 61; assembly dist. chmn, United Rep. of Calif, 63, gov, Area 11, 64-66, state v.chmn, 67-68, state chmn, 68- Mil. Serv: Mem, Special Forces of Czechoslovakia Army, 48; Mem, Blesk, Partisan Group against German Forces, 44-45. Seven Partisan and Military Awards. Mem: Dir. Los Angeles Jr. C. of C, 58-60; dir, Culver City Jr. C. of C, 60-62, v.pres, 63; United Farmers Agent's Asn.(nat. pres, 68-). Citizenship, Republican and Speaking Awards. Rel: Baptist. Legal Res: 3749 Malibu Vista Dr, Malibu, Calif. 90265. Mailing Add: 11048 W. Washington Blvd, Culver City, Calif. 90230.

VANIK, CHARLES ALBERT D
U.S. Rep, Ohio
b. Cleveland, Ohio, 4/6/13; s. Charles Anton Vanik and Stella Kvasnicka V; m. Feb, 1947 to Betty M; c. Phyllis Jean and John Charles. Educ: Adelbert Col, West Reserve Univ, A.B, 33; West. Reserve Law Sch, LL.B, 36. Polit. & Govt. Pos: Referee, Ohio State Indust. Cmn, 36; attorney-exam, Ohio State Dept. of Hwy, 37; mem, Cleveland City Coun, 38-39; Ohio State Sen, 40-41; mem, Cleveland Bd. of Educ, 41-42; mem, Cleveland Libr. Bd, 46-47; assoc. judge, Cleveland Munic. Court, 47-54; U.S. Rep, 21st Dist, Ohio, 55-; del, Dem. Nat. Conv, 68. Bus. & Prof. Pos: Attorney-at-law, Vanik, Monroe, and McIntyre, 36- Mil. Serv: Entered as Ens, Naval Res, 42, released as Lt.(sg), 46, after serv. in Amphibious Forces, Invasions of N.Africa, Sicily and Okinawa. Mem: Cleveland and Cuyahoga Co. Bar Asns. Rel: Roman Catholic. Legal Res: 24455 Lake Shore Blvd, Euclid, Ohio 44123. Mailing Add: 2463 Rayburn House Office Bldg, Washington, D.C. 20515.

VANLANDINGHAM, A. BASEY D
Mo. State Sen.
b. Boone Co, Mo, 3/30/20; m. 12/31/39 to Lorane Glasock; c. A. Basey II, Forrest Barry, Becky Lynn. Educ: Univ. of Mo. Polit. & Govt. Pos: Mo. State Rep, 56-60, Speaker Pro Tem, Mo. State House of Rep; Mo. State Sen, 60-, mem, Pres. Adv. Bd. Natural Resources, 60-61, Midwest Agr. Cmt, Coun. of State Govt; v.chmn. and chmn, Cmt. on Agr, chmn, Cmt. on Educ, mem, Appropriations, Banks & Banking, Financial Inst, Correctional Inst, Employ. Security and Pub. Health and Welfare Cmts, Mo. State Senate; former pres, Mo-Ark. Basin Flood Control Dist. Six. Bus. & Prof. Pos: Livestock and grain farming, 25 years. Mem: Elks; Past Grand Master, Masonic Grand Lodge of Mo; AF&AM; Past Grand High Priest, Mo. Grand Chap, RAM; Mo. Consistory One, Ararat Shrine Temple, Kansas City, Mo. Received Balanced Farming Award for Boone Co, 56; Received St. Louis Globe-Democrat award for Meritorious Pub. Serv. as the outstanding freshman Rep. in the 69th Gen. Assembly. Rel: Christian. Mailing Add: 12 Glenview Plaza, Columbia, Mo. 65201. (1967)

VAN LARE, FRANK E. R
b. Gates, N.Y; m. to Dorothy R. Harward; c. Donald Frederick. Educ: Gates and Rochester, N.Y. Schs. Polit. & Govt. Pos: N.Y. State Sen, 50-66; former mem, Rochester City Coun; former v.mayor, Rochester; former chmn. Temporary State Cmn. on Water Resources Planning. Bus. & Prof. Pos: Fuel bus, owner of ABC Fuels; former claim investr. for BR & PR. R. Mem: Past pres. 19th Ward Rep. Club; past pres, Retail Fuel Merchants Asn. of Rochester; past chmn, Cmt. of Mgt. of the Arnet and YMCA; Damascus Temple AAONMS of Rochester; K.T; Liederkrantz Club; Holland-Am. Benevolent Soc; Rochester Ad Club; Lalla Rookh Grotto; Moose. Annual Civic Award of Rochester Fraternal Order of Eagles. Mailing Add: 96 Roxborough Rd, Rochester, N.Y. 14619. (1967)

VAN LENGEN, GEORGE HENRY D
b. Syracuse, N.Y, 12/29/14; s. Nicholas Warner Van Lengen and Augusta Merschroth V; m. 2/5/36 to Gertrude Godard; c. Peter, James, Donna and Nicholas. Educ: Wesleyan Univ, 36; Harvard Law Sch, 39; Alpha Delta Phi. Polit. & Govt. Pos: Chmn, Onondaga Co. Dem. Cmt, 62-66; mem. exec. cmt, N.Y. Dem. State Cmt, 63-66; secy, N.Y. State Senate, 65-66; Dem. committeeman, Onondaga, N.Y, 66-69. Bus. & Prof. Pos: Pres, M. P. Amusement Co, Inc, 60-; chmn. bd. dirs, The Prosperity Co, Syracuse, N.Y, 64. Mil. Serv: Pvt, Army, 43, serv. in Ft. Eustis, Va. Mem: N.Y. and Am. Bar Asns; Am. Legion. Rel: Protestant. Mailing Add: 3998 Griffin Rd, Syracuse, N.Y. 13215.

VAN LOAN, ANNA S. R
b. Manchester, 8/20/12; married; c. Four. Educ: Pembroke Col. Polit. & Govt. Pos: N.H. State Rep, 63-66; mem. sch. bd. Rel: Protestant. Mailing Add: 62 Wallace Rd, Bedford, N.H. 03102. (1967)

VAN MARK, JACK R
b. Torrington, Wyo, 7/4/30; m. to Hanna; c. three. Educ: Univ. Wyo, B.S. Polit. & Govt. Pos: Wyo. State Rep, 3 terms. Bus. & Prof. Pos: V.pres,

Wyo. Farmers Grain Food Co. Mem: Farm Bur; Goshen Co. Wheat Growers (past pres); Wyo. Wheat Growers (past pres). Selected as one of the Outstanding Young Men in Am, Jaycees, 64 and Outstanding Young Farmer, Wyo, 66. Mailing Add: 3027 Alta Vista, Torrington, Wyo. 82240.

VAN METER, CRAIG D
b. Charleston, Ill, 8/25/95; s. John Van Meter and Ina Craig V; m. 4/7/21 to Eliza Haynes; c. Alice. Educ: Univ. Ill, LL.B, 17; Order of Coif; Phi Delta Phi; Phi Delta Theta. Polit. & Govt. Pos: Del, Dem. Nat. Conv, 32; Asst. Attorney Gen, Ill. Inheritance Tax Div, 32-33; judge, Fifth Judicial Circuit, Ill, 33-36; appeal agent, Draft Bd, 2, Coles Co, 41-45; Master-in Chancery, Fed. Court, East Dist, Ill, 51-65. Bus. & Prof. Pos: Lawyer, Mattoon, Ill, 19-; partner, Craig & Craig, 23-; mem. legal cmt, Interstate Oil Compact Cmn, 51-52; dir, Cent. Nat. Bank of Mattoon, Mattoon Title & Trust Co. and U.S. Grant Hotel Co. Mil. Serv: 2nd Lt, Army, 17-19. Mem: Am. and Seventh Fed. Circuit Bar Asns; Ill. Bar Asn.(chmn. exec. cmt. mineral law, 55-56); Am. Col. Probate Counsel; Am. Judicature Soc; Soc. Trial Lawyers; Chicago; Mattoon Asn. Commerce (past dir. indust. cmt); Bd. Educ, Mattoon, 25-31; v.pres. bd. dirs, United Fund, 63-64; former pres. bd. dirs, Mem. Methodist Hosp; Univ. Ill. Found; Am. Legion (post comdr, 19). Rel: Episcopal. Legal Res: 300 Wabash Ave, Mattoon, Ill. 61938. Mailing Add: 1807 Broadway, Mattoon, Ill. 61938.

VANN, DAVID J. D
Chmn, Ala. Independent Dem. Party
b. Roanoke, Ala, 8/10/28; s. Clyde Harold Vann and Ruth Johnson V; m. 4/24/65 to Lillian Foscue; c. Lillian Ruth and Cora Elizabeth. Educ: Univ. Ala, B.S. in Commerce, 50 and LL.B, 51; George Wash. Univ, LL.M, 53; Beta Gamma Sigma; Omicron Delta Kappa; Farrah Order of Jurisp; Phi Alpha Delta. Polit. & Govt. Pos: Law clerk, Justice Black, U.S. Supreme Court, 53-54; chmn, Jefferson Co. Dem. Campaign Cmt, Ala, 60-62; chmn, Ala. Independent Dem. Party, 67-; alternate del, Dem. Nat. Conv, 68. Bus. & Prof. Pos: Assoc. attorney, White, Bradley, Arant, All & Rose, 54-63; partner, Vann & Patrick, 63-64 and Berkowitz, Lefkovits, Vann & Patrick, 65- Mil. Serv: Entered as Pvt, Army, 46, released as Sgt, 47, after serv. in 31FA Br, Seventh Div, Korea; 1st Lt, Counter Intel, Res, 51-53. Mem: Birmingham, Ala. and Am. Bar Asns; Am. Judicature Soc; Nat. Munic. League; Secy. Law Sch. Found, Univ. Ala; K. of P; Lions; Young Men's Bus. Club of Birmingham. Rel: Methodist. Legal Res: 4201 Cliff Rd, Birmingham, Ala. 35222. Mailing Add: 1400 City National Bank Bldg, Birmingham, Ala. 35203.

VANN, EARL D
Pa. State Rep.
b. Wilmington, N.C, 10/18/13; s. Joseph Vann and Carrie Eagles V; m. 2/15/36 to Ada Gladden. Educ: S. Phila. High Sch, grad, 31; Univ. Pa, 45-46 & 60-62; Phi Beta Sigma. Polit. & Govt. Pos: State bldg. inspector, Dept. Labor and Indust, Phila, Pa, 55-63; clerk, Bd. of Rev. of Taxes, 63-64; Pa. State Rep, 64-; tax revenue collector, Phila, Pa, 65-66. Bus. & Prof. Pos: Owner, Beer Distributing, 45-55. Mil. Serv: Entered as A/S, Coast Guard, 42, released as 3/C Signalman, 45, after serv. in Seventh Fleet Task Force, Pac. Theatre, 43-45. Mem: Am. Legion; NAACP; Urban League; Fellowship Cmn; YMCA; Los Hermanos; Pa. Athletic Cmn; Phila. Asn. Basketball Referees; Baseball Umpires; Cent. Pa. Athletic Asn; Carmen Chiumento; secy, 36th Ward Dem. Party. Local 1163 State, Co. and Munic. Workers Award; Phi Beta Sigma Man of the Year Award, 67; Los Hermanos Outstanding Achievement Award; Rheingold Beer Commun. Achievement Award. Rel: Episcopal. Mailing Add: 1329 S. 22nd St, Phila, Pa. 19146.

VANN, FRANK COCHRAN D
Ga. State Sen.
b. Camilla, Ga; s. Emory Judson Vann, Jr. and Mary Cochran V; m. 2/23/57 to Alicine Janie Cagle; c. Frank Cochran, Jr, Elizabeth Janie, Mary Georgia and Scott Emory. Educ: Va. Mil. Inst, B.A, 49; Univ. Fla. Col. of Law, 49-50; Univ. Ga. Col. of Law, LL.B, 51; Judge Advocate Gen. Sch, Univ. Va, 52-53; Kappa Alpha; Phi Delta Phi. Polit. & Govt. Pos: Solicitor, Camilla and Pelham City Courts, Ga, 56-64; secy, Mitchell Co. Dem. Exec. Cmt, 66-; Ga. State Sen, Tenth Dist, 69- Bus. & Prof. Pos: Attorney-at-law, 51-; dir, Planters & Citizens Bank, 52-, v.pres, 69- Mil. Serv: 1st Lt, Army, 52-54, with serv. in Korean Base Sect, Korea, 53-54; Bronze Star; Presidential Unit Citation; Korean Serv. Medal with Two Battle Stars; UN Serv. Medal; Korean Presidential Unit Citation; Nat. Defense Serv. Medal. Mem: Mitchell Co. Bar Asn; S. Ga. Judicial Bar Asn.(past pres); State Bar of Ga. (mem. bd. gov, 67-68); Am. Judicature Soc; Lions (past pres, Camilla Club, present ed. Club Bul, dist. gov, Dist. 18-C, Lions Int, 64-65, state chmn, Constitution and Bylaws Cmt. of Multiple Dist. 18); trustee, Ga. Lions Lighthouse Found; C. of C.(charter mem, Camilla chap, pres, 68); VFW; mem. local bd. trustees, Mitchell Co. PTA (past co-pres). Outstanding Zone Chmn. Award Dist. 18-C Lions, 62-63; Outstanding Deputy Dist. Gov, 63-64. Rel: United Methodist; Mem. off. bd, Camilla United Methodist Church. Legal Res: 227 Main St, Camilla, Ga. 31730. Mailing Add: P.O. Box 387, Camilla, Ga. 31730.

VAN NATTA, FREDERICK WILLIAM R
b. Portland, Ore, 12/1/38; s. George G. Van Natta and Irene Breithaupt V; m. 9/6/59 to Marie Dawn Fahlstrom; c. Mary Louise and Michelle Marie. Educ: Willamette Univ, B.A. in Polit. Sci, 60; Univ. Ore, M.A. in Polit. Sci, 63; chmn, Univ. Young Rep. Club, 59-60. Polit. & Govt. Pos: Treas, Columbia Co, Ore. Rep. Cent. Cmt, 60-61; fieldman, Ore. Rep. State Cmt, 62; asst. to chmn, Pa. Rep. State Cmt, 63-64; reg. coordinator, Scranton for Pres. Cmt, 64; asst. to the Speaker, Ore. State House of Rep, 65 & 67; exec. dir, Lane Co. Rep. Cent. Cmt, Ore, 65-67; exec. dir, Rep. State Legislator's Asn, 65-68; pres, Pub. Affairs, Inc, Salem, 67-; west. regional dir, Reagan for Pres. Cmt, 68. Mil. Serv: Entered as Pvt E-1, Ore. Nat. Guard, 56, released as S/Sgt. E-6, 65, after serv. in 41st Div. Mem: Ore. Cattlemen's Asn; West. Livestock Asn; Ore. Pub. Rels. Roundtable; Nat. Sch. Pub. Rels. Asn; Grange; Jr. C. of C; Nat. and Ore. Fedn. of Young Rep. Mailing Add: 347 Ewald St. S.E, Salem, Ore. 97302.

VAN NOSTRAND, MAURICE A. R
Iowa State Rep.
b. Benedict, Nebr, 2/9/25; s. Alton Van Nostrand and Etta Query V; m. 2/20/44 to Carol R. Cummings; c. Gregory, Kevin and James. Educ: Univ. Nebr; Phi Gamma Delta. Polit. & Govt. Pos: Iowa State Rep, 63-64 & 67-; del, Rep. Nat. Conv, 68. Bus. & Prof. Pos: Mgr, Van Nostrand Grain Co, Iowa, 46-64; ed, Council Bluffs Nonpareil and assoc. ed, 64-; pres, Oakland Feeding Corp. and Van Nostrand Grain Co, presently; mem. bd, Avoca Nursing Home and Avoca Mfg. Corp, presently. Mil. Serv: Entered as Pvt, Air Force, 44, released as Aviation Cadet, 46. Mem: V.pres, Council Bluffs C. of C. Rel: Presbyterian. Mailing Add: 1011 N. Cherry St, Avoca, Iowa 51521.

VAN PATTEN, CECIL ROBERT D
Chmn, Malheur Co. Dem. Cent. Cmt, Ore.
b. Malheur City, Ore, 10/10/14; s. Chester Arthur Van Patten and Tina Whitworth V; m. 12/25/40 to Esther Johanna Jeppsen; c. Kay Jean, Janet Lee, George Frederick and Cecil Robert, Jr. Educ: West. States Chiropractic Col, D.C, 46, N.D, 47. Polit. & Govt. Pos: V.chmn, Malheur Co. Dem. Cent. Cmt, Ore, 56-60 & 62-; city councilman, Ontario, Ore, 56-63; mem, Malheur Co. Libr, 64-, chmn, 64-68, v.chmn, 69; mem, Dist. 8C Sch. Bd, 65-69, chmn, 68. Mem: Pres, Ore. Chiropractic Asn, Dist. 7, 56-65; Am. and Ore. Chiropractic Asns; Elks; Ontario C. of C. Rel: Episcopal. Mailing Add: 265 N. Oregon St, Ontario, Ore. 97914.

VAN PELT, WILLIAM K. R
b. Glenbeulah, Wis, 3/10/05; m. 11/14/62 to Anne Trimble; c. Peter, Julie, Ann. Polit. & Govt. Pos: U.S. Rep, Wis, 51-65; Chmn, Fond Du Lac Co. Rep. Cmt, 6 years. Mem: Mason; Elk; Kiwanis. 1967 Legal Res: Glenbeulah, Wis. No mailing address available. (1967)

VAN RENSSELAER, STANLEY L. R
b. Wilton, N.Y, 7/13/11; s. Leslie H. Van Rensselaer and Maud Murphy V; m. 9/6/36 to Dorothy Ericson; c. Anne K, Kristina M. and Jane M. Educ: Syracuse Univ, pre-law, 30-32; Albany Law Sch, LL.B, 35; Delta Kappa Epsilon. Polit. & Govt. Pos: Spec. agent, Fed. Bur. Invest, 41-45; city judge, Sartoga Springs, N.Y, 50-61; N.Y. State Assemblyman, 118th Dist, Saratoga Co, 61-66; chmn, Crime Victims Compensation Bd, 67- Mem: N.Y. State and Saratoga Co. Bar Asns; Lions; Elks; Mason Fraternities; DeMolay, Legion of Honor. Rel: Presbyterian. Mailing Add: 153 Philadelphia St, Saratoga Springs, N.Y. 12866.

VAN ROEKEL, GERRIT R
Iowa State Rep.
b. Leighton, Iowa, 6/11/99; s. Henry Van Roekel and Mina Veenschoten V; m. 8/27/24 to Edna J. De Bruin; c. Ray A. and Ermina Harriet (Mrs. Donald J. Bruggink). Educ: Cent. Col, B.A, 24; Advansonian Lit. Soc. Polit. & Govt. Pos: Iowa State Rep, 67- Bus. & Prof. Pos: Store mgr, Safeway Stores Inc, 25-45; bd. admissions, Cent. Col, 45-48; bus. mgr, 48-64; retired, 64. Mem: Kiwanis Int; C. of C; Golf and Country Club; C Club; Mens Brotherhood. Rel: Reformed Church in Am. Mailing Add: 209 Union St, Pella, Iowa 50219.

VAN SANT, JOHN T. R
Pa. State Sen.
b. Delano, 11/2/15; s. Homer M. Van Sant and Frieda Sharkey V; m. to Alice Jane Zeigler; c. Sandra Ann, Nancy Jane. Educ: Westminster Col, Fulton, Mo; Muhlenberg Col; Beta Theta Pi. Polit. & Govt. Pos: Pa. State Rep, 50-54; Pa. State Sen, 55- Bus. & Prof. Pos: Pub. rels; ins. rep. Mil. Serv: U.S. Navy, World War II. Mem: Greenleaf Lodge; F&AM; Am. Legion; VFW; Alumni Varsity A Club; Italian Club; Sportsmen's and Rep. Orgns; Macungie, Pomona, State, Nat. Granges; DAV. Mailing Add: 102 N. Tenth St, Allentown, Pa. 18102.

VAN SANTVOORD, GEORGE D
Vt. State Rep.
b. Bennington, Vt, 8/5/91; m. to Alice D. Beal; c. 4. Educ: Yale, B.A, 12; Oxford Univ, B.Litt, M.A; hon. degrees from Williams Col, Princeton Univ. & Yale Univ. Polit. & Govt. Pos: Vt. State Sen, 59; Vt. State Rep, 65-; mem. bd, Bennington Mus. & Free Libr. Bus. & Prof. Pos: Retired teacher; owner and operator of dairy farm, currently. Mil. Serv: Entered as Sgt, Army, 16, released as 2nd Lt, 19, after serv. in 39th and 167th Inf; Croix de Guerre; wounded in action. Mem: Farm Bur. Rel: Congregational. Mailing Add: Box 767, Bennington, Vt. 05201.

VAN SICKLE, TOM R. R
Kans. State Sen.
b. Hume, Mo, 6/22/37; s. Vincent Van Sickle and Welcome Hinderliter V; m. 12/19/64 to Suzanne Galvin. Educ: Baker Univ, 55-58; Kans. Univ, B.A. in polit. sci, 59; Washburn Univ. Law Sch, LL.B, 61, J.D, 66; Delta Tau Delta; Phi Alpha Delta. Polit. & Govt. Pos: V.chmn, Young Rep. Club, Baker Univ, 57; Kans. State Rep, 58-60; exec. secy, Young Rep. Nat. Fedn, 59-61, nat. committeeman from Kans, 63-65, chmn, 65-67; chief page, Rep. Nat. Conv, 60; Kans. State Sen, Seventh Dist, 60-, chmn, Ways and Means Cmt, Kans. State Senate; v.chmn, Cmt. on Cmts, mem, Commercial and Financial Insts. Cmt, Judiciary Cmt. and Legis. and Cong. Apportionment Cmt, mem, State Finance Coun; v.chmn, Arn for Senate Cmt, 62; campaign adv, Lukens for Young Rep. Nat. Fedn. Chmn, 63; asst. to nat. dir, Draft Goldwater Cmt, 63; asst. coordinator conv. activities and asst. to dirs. field opers, Goldwater for Pres. Cmt, 64; dir. field opers, Citizens for Goldwater-Miller, 64. Bus. & Prof. Pos: With Coca Cola Bottling Co, 58; advert. rep, Ft. Scott Tribune, Kans, 59; staff asst, Menninger Found, Topeka, 61-63. Mem: Grange; Farm Bur; Jaycees; 4-H Club. Selected 1 of Outstanding Young Men of Am, Jaycees, 65; Man of Year, Ft. Scott Jaycees, 59; State 4-H Leadership Champion, 55. Rel: Methodist. Legal Res: Ft. Scott, Kans. Mailing Add: P.O. Box 630, Ft. Scott, Kans. 66701.

VAN VELZOR, JAMES DANIEL R
Wyo. State Rep.
b. Warren, Mich, 4/11/22; s. Roscoe D. Van Velzor and Marie A. Kelly V; m. 5/27/43 to D. Darleen Boyd; c. M. Sue (Mrs. Mike King) and M. Jo. Educ: Central High Sch, Lansing, Mich, grad, 41. Polit. & Govt. Pos: Wyo. State Rep, 67-68 & 69- Bus. & Prof. Pos: Owner, Van Velzor's House of Music, Cheyenne and Casper, Wyo, 60- Mil. Serv: Entered as Pvt, Army Air Corps, 41, released as Capt, 47, after serv. in Ninth Inf. Div, ETO, 44; Combat Inf.

Badge; Purple Heart. Mem: Lions; Cheyenne Exec. Club; AF&AM; Mason (32°); life mem, DAV; Cheyenne C. of C; Casper C. of C. Hon. Mem, Wyoming VFW. Rel: Baptist. Mailing Add: 1807 Milton Dr, Cheyenne, Wyo. 82001.

VAN VOORHIS, JOHN R
b. Rochester, N.Y, 6/14/97; s. Eugene Van Voorhis and Allis Sherman V; m. 6/2/28 to Linda Gale Lyon; c. Emily (Mrs. Harris), Allis (Mrs. D'Amanda) and Eugene. Educ: A.B, Yale; Phi Beta Kappa. LL.D, Hobart Col, 53, Union Col, 54, Univ. Rochester, 58, N.Y. Law Sch, 65 and Brooklyn Law Sch, 66. Polit. & Govt. Pos: Justice, Supreme Court, Seventh Judicial Dist, 37; assoc. justice, Appellate Div, Supreme Court, First Dept, 47; assoc. judge of Court of Appeals, N.Y, 53-67. Bus. & Prof. Pos: Mem. law firm, John Van Voorhis' Sons, Rochester, N.Y, 22-36; mem. law firm br, Jefferson, Friedman, Van Voorhis & Wise, currently. Rel: Episcopal. Legal Res: 714 Rock Beach Rd, Rochester, N.Y. Mailing Add: 65 Broad St, Rochester, N.Y. 14614.

VANZANDT, EDWARD EARL D
Chmn, Warren Co. Dem. Party, Ky.
b. Henderson, Ky, 6/21/14; s. Wynn Vanzandt and Eva Elliott V; m. 3/30/36 to Edna Ray Cotten; c. Sandra Lee. Educ: High Sch, Louisville, Ky. Polit. & Govt. Pos: Alderman, Bowling Green, Ky, 63-; chmn, Warren Co. Dem. Party, 64-; del, Dem. Nat. Conv, 68. Bus. & Prof. Pos: Owner, Haxby News Co, 54- Mil. Serv: Entered as Pvt, 43, released as Capt, 45, after serv. in Second Div, ETO. Mem: Elks; Optimist; Am. Legion; VFW. Rel: Baptist. Mailing Add: 920 Richland Dr, Bowling Green, Ky. 42101. (1967)

VARALLO, MARY A. D
Councilman-at-lg, Phila, Pa.
b. Philadelphia, Pa; d. Agostino Frascone and Catarina Fortunato F; m. to Alfred Varallo. Educ: Univ. of Pa, cert. in polit. sci. Hon. L.H.D, Cabrini Col, 62; hon. D.Mus, Combs Col. of Music, 63. Polit. & Govt. Pos: Pa. State Rep, 45-60, Majority Whip, Pa. House of Rep, 59-60; del, Dem. Nat. Conv, 56, alternate del, 60, mem. electoral col, 60 & 64; state chmn, Columbus Day Celebrations, Pa, 57-63; councilman-at-lg, Phila, Pa, 60-67; dir. nat. bd. gov, Columbus Day Cmt, 69- Mem: Bd. gov, Ital. Exec. of Am, Inc, 68; bd. dir, Am. Cancer Soc, 68-; bd, Phila. 1976 Bi-Centennial Corp, 68-; Distinguished Daughters of Pa; Bus. & Prfnl. Women's Club; Nat. Order of Women Legislators; adv. bd, Cabrini Col, Am. Cmt. on Italian Migration and Sons of Italy in Am; hon. bd. mem, Phila. Grand Opera Co, pres, Main Line Women's Cmt, 68- Elected to Legion of Hon. of Chapel of Four Chaplains; elected to S. Phila. Hall of Fame, 62; Received State Woman of Year Award, Order Sons of Italy in Am, 61; AMITA Nat. Award to Outstanding Women in Arts, Sci. and Pub. Serv, 63; Pub. Serv. Award, Twenty-one Jewel Square Club, Outstanding Cath. Woman of Year, K. of C, Award of Merit, Italian-Am. Press, Radio, TV and Pub. Rels. Asn, Nat. Award, Am. Cmt. on Italian Migration and Woman of Year Award, Phila. Women's Realty Bd, 65; Star of Solidarity from Pres. of Italy; citations from Fedn. Negro Women in Phila, Zion African Methodist Episcopal Church, Southwest. Businessmen's Asn. and Missionary Sisters of Sacred Heart. Rel: Catholic; Organist and Choir Dir, Church of St. Donato, Phila; wrote hymn to St. Frances Xavier Cabrini, which was used at Canonization exercises. Mailing Add: 1900 John F. Kennedy Blvd, Philadelphia, Pa. 19103.

VARGAS, RICHARD ENRIQUE D
b. Los Angeles, Calif, 1/27/32; s. Arcadio Vargas and Balvina Ruiz V; single. Educ: Calif. State Col. at Los Angeles, B.A, 69; Downtown Alumni Asn. Polit. & Govt. Pos: Del, Dem. Nat. Conv, 68. Bus. & Prof. Pos: Community Organizer, Council of Mexican-Am. Affairs, 69. Mem: United Mexican-Am. Students; Calif. Fedn. of Young Democrats; Kennedy Democrats. Rel: Catholic. Mailing Add: 7921 Bell Ave, Los Angeles, Calif. 90001.

VARGAS, SYBIL ROSE HUNT D
V.Chmn, Dem. Cent. Cmt, Ore.
b. Kelowna, B.C, Can, 5/26/12; d. Jack Kinard Pitcairn and Elsie Kempe P; m. 11/25/34 to Fredwick Anthony Vargas; c. Gilbert Fredwick. Educ: Madonna Col, Letchworth, Eng; Ursuline Convent, Bideford, Eng. Polit. & Govt. Pos: Pres, Jane Jefferson Club, 59-60 and treas, 64; v.chmn, Dem. Cent. Cmt, Ore, 62-64 & 66- and chmn, 64-66. Rel: Episcopal. Mailing Add: 1299 Granite Hill Rd, Grants Pass, Ore. 97526.

VARILEK, ELVERN D
S.Dak. State Rep.
b. 10/18/25; m. to Margaret Durham; c. Donna, Tommy, Michael, Kathy and Lory. Educ: High sch. Polit. & Govt. Pos: Former committeeman, Agr. Stabilization & Conserv. Serv; former mem, Clerk Co. Sch. Bd, Geddes, S.Dak; S.Dak. State Rep, 60-, Minority Leader, 63-65, mem. exec. bd, Legis. Research Coun. and adv. Cmt, S.Dak. State House of Rep. Bus. & Prof. Pos: Ranching. Mem: Pres, S.Dak. State Angus Asn; chmn, S.Dak. Cent. Angus Asn; PTA; 4-H Leader; Mason; Oriental Consistory; El Riad Shrine. Rel: Methodist. Mailing Add: Geddes, S.Dak. 57342. (1967)

VARLEY, ANDREW PRESTON R
Iowa State Rep.
b. Stuart, Iowa, 12/2/34; s. James Preston Varley and Esther Schutz V; m. 8/23/59 to Marilyn Ann Saucke; c. Warren Andrew, Thomas James and John David. Educ: Iowa State Univ, B.S, 57; N.C. State Univ, M.S, 61; Phi Kappa Phi; Alpha Zeta; Alpha Gamma Rho. Polit. & Govt. Pos: Iowa State Rep, 67- Rel: Lutheran. Mailing Add: R.R. 2, Stuart, Iowa 50250.

VARLEY, JOSEPH L. D
R.I. State Sen.
b. Central Falls, R.I, 5/18/09. Educ: Central Falls High Sch. Polit. & Govt. Pos: Former mem, Charter Cmn, Central Falls, R.I. and mem, City Coun, 54-58; R.I. State Rep, 63-66 & 69- Bus. & Prof. Pos: Bank teller. Mil. Serv: Air Force, serv. in Ninth Serv. Command, Finance Sect, 4 years. Mailing Add: 92 Clay St, Central Falls, R.I. 02863. (1967)

VARNEY, CHARLES D
b. Clinton, Iowa, 3/22/03; s. Elmer Varney and Enga V; m. 1/2/26 to Jessie Merle Steffey; c. one. Educ: Bryant Sch, Clinton, Iowa. Polit. & Govt. Pos: Iowa State Rep, until 66; former mem. exec. bd, Clinton, former mem, Solicitation Rev. Bd. and Dem. Cent. Cmt; former Dem. Precinct committeeman; v.pres, Second Dist. COPE. Mil. Serv: Nat. Guard, $4\frac{1}{2}$ years. Mem: Am. Red Cross; Eagles. Rel: Lutheran. Mailing Add: 2128 McKinley St, Clinton, Iowa 52732. (1967)

VARNEY, T. I. D
W.Va. State Del.
b. Barnabus, W.Va, 10/20/18; s. T. B. Varney and Verda Hatfield V; m. 3/6/46 to Neill Smith; c. David B, Eva Lynn. Educ: Bowling Green Bus. Univ. Polit. & Govt. Pos: W.Va. State Del, 64-; former employee, Pub. Serv. Cmn. Bus. & Prof. Pos: Probation Officer. Mil. Serv: Air Force. Mem: Moose; Fraternal Order of Police; VFW; former pres, Rotary Club. Rel: Protestant. Mailing Add: Box 127, Matewan, W.Va. 25678. (1967)

VARNON, CLIFF WALTER D
Chmn, Bowie Co. Dem. Exec. Cmt, Tex.
b. Buckholts, Tex, 11/4/17; s. Willie D. Varnon and Bessie Mae McDuff V; m. 3/24/43 to Jennie May Larsen; c. Cliff, Jr. Educ: Univ. Tex, 3 yrs. Polit. & Govt. Pos: Chmn, Bowie Co. Dem. Exec. Cmt, Tex, 60-; Presidential elector from First Sen. Dist, 68. Mem: Texarkana Bd. of Realtors (pres, 64-66); Four States Life Underwriters (pres, 52); Civitan (pres, 50). Rel: Episcopal. Legal Res: 902 Texas Ave, Texarkana, Tex. 75501. Mailing Add: P.O. Box 1242, Texarkana, Tex. 75501.

VARNUM, CHARLES HENRY R
Mich. State Rep.
b. Jonesville, Mich, 7/9/33; s. Henry Varnum and Mae V; c. Barbara and Mitchell. Educ: Ferris Inst, Big Rapids, Mich, 51-54; Hillsdale Col, grad, 59. Polit. & Govt. Pos: Mich. State Rep, 107th Dist, at present; councilman and mayor pro-tem, Manistique City Coun, 64-; mem, Schoolcraft Co. Bd. Supvrs, 11th Cong. Dist. Exec. Cmt. and Mich. State Athletic Bd. of Control. Prof. Pos: Teacher, Manistique Pub. Schs, 59- Mil. Serv: Sgt, Marine Corps, 51-54. Mem: VFW; Rotary Int; Elks; former pres, Manistique Teachers Asn. Named Young Man of Year, Manistique Jaycees, 65. Mailing Add: 531 Oak St, Manistique, Mich. 49854.

VASCONCELLOS, JOHN BERNARD D
Calif. State Assemblyman
b. San Jose, Calif, 5/11/32; s. John Bernard Vasconcellos and Teresa Jacobs V; single. Educ: Univ. Santa Clara, B.S. in hist. magna cum laude, 54 and LL.B. cum laude, 59; Alpha Sigma Nu. Polit. & Govt. Pos: Travel secy, Gov. of Calif, 60-61; chmn, Speaker's Bur, Gov. Campaign, Calif, 62; co. chmn, Young Citizens for Johnson, 64; Calif. State Assemblyman, 24th Dist, 67-; del, Dem. Nat. Conv, 68; Santa Clara Co. co-chmn, Sen. Robert Kennedy for Pres. Campaign, 68. Bus. & Prof. Pos: Partner, Ruffo & Oneto, 65-67. Mil. Serv: Entered as 2nd Lt, Army, 54, released as 1st Lt, 56. Mem: State Bar Cmt. on Legis; chmn, State Bar Local Admin. Cmt. No. 4; former dir, San Jose Jr. C. of C; bd. dirs, Cath. Soc. Serv; found. mem, St. Thomas More Soc; chmn, Fund Drive for John F. Kennedy Trade Inst, 65-66; adv. bd, San Jose Concert Series; bd. dirs, San Jose Chap. Am. Red Cross; former mem, bd. drs, San Jose United Serv. Orgn; chmn, exec. cmt, San Jose Citizens Bond Cmt, 66. Rel: Roman Catholic. Mailing Add: 100 W. Rincon Ave, Suite 207, Campbell, Calif. 95008.

VASHON, DORIS LOUISE D
Mem, Calif. Dem. State Cent. Cmt.
b. Waterville, Maine, 2/14/27; d. Aldelbert Louis Couture and Lena Carey C; m. 12/9/44 to Richard Robert Vashon; c. Suzanne Marie, Patricia (deceased), Daniel (deceased), Judith (deceased), Stephen (deceased), Ann (deceased) and Betty Jean (deceased). Educ: Waterville High Sch, 40-43. Polit. & Govt. Pos: Secy, Mary O'Keefe Dem. Club, Calif, 61-63; pres, Riverside Dem. Forum, 64-67; co. chmn, Milton Gordon for Secy. of State, 66; orgn. chmn, Fedn. of Dem. Clubs, 67-69; pres, Riverside Dem. Action League, 67-69; mem. and pub. chmn, Co. Dem. Cent. Cmt, 68-; mem, Calif. Dem. State Cent. Cmt, 68- Mem: V.pres, Northside Improv. Asn; Park and Recreation Cmnr; Inland Area Urban League; Urban Coalition; PTA pres, Fremont Elem. Sch, 64-65 and Cent. Jr. High Sch, 68-69; Am. Legion Auxiliary; Eagles Auxiliary. Outstanding Serv. Award, Coun. on Polit. Educ, AFL-CIO. Rel: Catholic. Mailing Add: 1635 Fairmount Blvd, Riverside, Calif. 92501.

VASSELL, ROBERT M. R
b. Omaha, Nebr, 1/20/37; s. Fred Walter Vassell and Freda Cordes V; single. Educ: Univ. Miami, A.B, 59; Univ. Nebr, Lincoln, 60-61, 63 & 65; Univ. Nebr, Omaha, 66-68. Polit. & Govt. Pos: Alternate del, Rep. Nat. Conv, 68; moderator, Young Rep. Club, Col. St. Mary, Omaha, Nebr, 68- Bus. & Prof. Pos: Teacher Eng, West Point High Sch, Nebr, 59-60 and David City High Sch, 63-66; instr. Eng, Huron Col, 68 and Col. St. Mary, Omaha, 68-69. Publ: Poetry published in lit. mag. Mem: Renaissance Soc. of Am; Douglas Co. Young Rep. Club. Nat. teaching fel; reading assistantship. Rel: Congregational. Mailing Add: 520 N. 86th St, Omaha, Nebr. 68114.

VAUGHAN, DAVID N, JR. D
b. Fairmount, Ga, 2/2/35; s. David N. Vaughan and Agnes Richardson V; m. 9/29/68 to Mary Colquitt; c. Stephen David, Lynn and Darrell. Educ: N.Ga. Col; Univ. Ga; Phi Alpha Delta; Delta Tau Delta. Polit. & Govt. Pos: Asst. Solicitor Gen, Cherokee Judicial Circuit, Ga, 62; Ga. State Rep, 14th Dist, 65-68; Dist. Attorney, Cherokee Judicial Circuit, 69- Mem: Dist. Attorneys Asn; Ga. Forest Asn; Exchange Club; Shrine; Elks; Farm Bur; C. of C. Rel: Methodist. Legal Res: 134 Leake St, Cartersville, Ga. 30120. Mailing Add: P.O. Box 534, Cartersville, Ga. 30120.

VAUGHAN, GRANVIL B. R
Mo. State Rep.
b. Leota, Mo, 5/17/21; m. 2/17/43 to Idell Vest; c. Karyn Sue and Reta Kay. Educ: Howell Co, Mo. Pub. Schs. Polit. & Govt. Pos: Mo. State Rep, 62- Bus. & Prof. Pos: Farmer; owned serv. sta, 14 years. Mil. Serv: Army, World War II, $3\frac{1}{2}$ years, Pac. Theatre. Mem: VFW; Am. Legion. Rel: Protestant. Mailing Add: R.F.D. 1, West Plains, Mo. 63775. (1967)

VAUGHAN, HUGH SLAVENS D
Mem, Mo. State Dem. Cmt.
b. Urbana, Mo, 9/2/16 to William D. Vaughan and Josephine Slavens V; m.

1/16/43 to Monte Jean Johnson; c. Barbara Sue (Mrs. Wilson), Patricia (Mrs. Ames), Judith K, Hugh Allen and Robert James. Educ: Univ. Mo, 34-38; Phi Kappa Psi. Polit. & Govt. Pos: Chmn, Dallas Co. Dem. Cmt, Mo, 56-; mem, Mo. State Dem. Cmt, 66- Bus. & Prof. Pos: Pres, Bank of Urbana, 5 years. Mil. Serv: Entered as Pvt, Army, 43, released as Capt, 45, after serv. in Ninth Armored Div, ETO, 44-45; Bronze Star. Mem: Lions; AF&AM; Scottish Rite; Shrine. Rel: Methodist. Mailing Add: Urbana, Mo. 65767.

VAUGHAN, ROBERT LEE, SR. D
Miss. State Rep.
b. Kansas City, Mo, 6/12/27; m. to Martha St. John. Polit. & Govt. Pos: Miss. State Rep, 65- Bus. & Prof. Pos: Owner, Vaughan Milling Co, Inc. Mem: Mason; F&AM; Eastern Star; Am. Legion; Farm Bur; Miss. Cattlemen's Asn; Lions; Claiborne Co. C. of C; Aircraft Owners & Pilots Asn. Rel: Presbyterian. Mailing Add: Box 467, Port Gibson, Miss. 39150. (1967)

VAUGHN, CHARLES R. R
b. Olney, Ill, 2/17/22; s. Charles Vaughn and Elsie Ray V; m. 12/4/43 to Elizabeth Gassmann; c. Ann, Carol, Charles B, Kathleen, John R, Allen Z, Mary G, Ray W. and Frank E. Educ: James Millikin Univ, B.S, 43; Univ. Ill, LL.B, 48; Sigma Alpha Epsilon. Polit. & Govt. Pos: Asst. States Attorney, Richland Co, Ill, 48-52, States Attorney, 52-64 & 68-; alternate del, Rep. Nat. Conv, 64; Chmn, Percy for Gov, 64 and Percy for Sen, 23rd Cong. Dist, 66. Bus. & Prof. Pos: Dir, First Nat. Bank, Olney, Ill, 62-66. Mil. Serv: Entered as Pfc, Marine Corps, 42, released as 1st Lt, 46, after serv. in 5th Amphibious Corps, Pac; Navy Unit Commendation; Am, Pac. and Occup. Japan Theater Ribbons. Mem: Richland Co. and Ill. Bar Asns; Am. Legion; VFW; Elks. Rel: Catholic. Mailing Add: 507 N. Boone St, Olney, Ill. 62450.

VAUGHN, CLARENCE ROLAND, JR. D
Ga. State Rep.
b. Conyers, Ga, 1/22/21; s. Clarence Roland Vaughn and Mary Guinn V; m. 6/14/42 to Doris Elizabeth Henson; c. Alvin Henson and Clarence Roland III. Educ: N.Ga. Col, 39; Univ. of Ga, LL.B, 46. Polit. & Govt. Pos: Ga. State Sen, 59-60; Ga. State Rep, 61- Bus. & Prof. Pos: Attorney. Mil. Serv: U.S. Army, 42-46, Capt; Bronze Star. Mem: Mason; Lions; Am. Legion; VFW; Elks. Rel: Methodist. Mailing Add: Conyers, Ga. 30207.

VAUGHN, EARL W. D
Speaker, N.C. House of Rep.
b. Reidsville, N.C, 6/17/28; s. John H. Vaughn and Lelia F.V; m. 12/20/52 to Eloise Freeland Maddry; c. Mark Foster, John Maddry, Stuart E. and Mary Rose. Educ: Pfeiffer Jr. Col; Univ. N.C, A.B, 50, Law Sch, LL.B, 52; Phi Delta Phi. Polit. & Govt. Pos: Attorney for town of Draper, N.C, 55-; pres, Tri-City Rescue Squad, 57; secy-treas, Rockingham Co. Dem. Exec. Cmt; pres, Rockingham Co. Young Dem. Club; solicitor, Leaksville Recorder's Court, 59-60; N.C. State Rep, 61-, past Majority Leader, N.C. House of Rep, Speaker, 67-; attorney, City of Eden, 67- Bus. & Prof. Pos: Lawyer. Mil. Serv: Army, 54-57. Mem: N.C. State and Rockingham Co. Bar Asns; Rotary (pres, Draper Club, 55). Rel: Methodist; chmn. off. bd, 57, mem. bd. of trustees, 55- Mailing Add: Fieldcrest Rd, Eden, N.C. 27288.

VAUGHN, JACK HOOD
U.S. Ambassador to Colombia
b. Columbus, Mont, 8/18/20; s. Lige Hood Vaughn and Lona Blair Cox McCaslin V; m. 2/9/46 to Joanne Cordes Smith; c. Kathryn and Carol. Educ: Univ. Mich, B.A, 43, M.A, 47. Polit. & Govt. Pos: Dir, Bi-Nat. Center, La Paz, Bolivia, U.S. Info. Serv, 49-52; dir. program off, Panama, Int. Coop. Admin, 52-56, La Paz, Bolivia, 56-58 and Europe and Africa, 58-60; dir, U.S. Overseas Mission, Dakar, Senegal, 60-61; dir, Latin Am. Region, Peace Corps, 61-64; U.S. Ambassador to Panama, 64-65; dir, Peace Corps, 66-69; U.S. Ambassador to Colombia, 69- Bus. & Prof. Pos: Prof, Univ. Mich, 46-47, Univ. Pa, 48-49 and Johns Hopkins Sch. of Int. Studies, 58. Mil. Serv: Entered as 2nd Lt, Marine Corps, 43, released as 1st Lt, 46, after serv. in 22nd Marine Regt, Pac; Capt, Marine Corps Res, 50; Navy Commendation Ribbon. Publ: Practical English, (2 vols), Pub. in Bolivia and Costa Rica. Legal Res: 502 Wolfe St, Alexandria, Va. 22314. Mailing Add: American Embassy, Bogota, Columbia.

VAUGHN, RAYMOND C. R
Kans. State Rep.
Polit. & Govt. Pos: Kans. State Rep, 65- Bus. & Prof. Pos: Owner, Coffey Co. Livestock Mkt; partner, Eureka Auction Sale. Mil. Serv: Navy. Mem: Mason; Am. Legion; VFW; Sch. Bd; Kans. High Sch. Activities Assoc; Coffey Co. Fair Bd. Rel: Methodist; Conf. Finance Bd, Methodist Church. Mailing Add: 428 Yuba, Box 252, Burlington, Kans. 66839. (1967)

VAUGHN, RAYMOND LUKE R
Chmn, Douglas Co. Rep. Party, Ga.
b. Atlanta, Ga, 5/26/23; s. Robert Livingston Vaughn and Iley Conner V; m. 12/28/46 to Helen Chapman; c. Rodney Bryan and Vickie Darline. Educ: Douglas Co. High Sch. Polit. & Govt. Pos: Chmn, Douglas Co. Rep. Party, Ga, 64-; cand, Ga. State Rep, 66. Mil. Serv: Entered Navy, 42, released, Navy Air Force, 47. Rel: Southern Baptist; Deacon. Legal Res: R.F.D. 1, Douglasville, Ga. 30134. Mailing Add: P.O. Box 567, Douglasville, Ga. 30134. (1967)

VAUGHNS, WILLIAM ELMORE R
Mem, Alameda Co. Rep. Cent. Cmt, Calif.
b. San Francisco, Calif, 4/10/02; s. Wilson Vaughns and Milinda Anderson V; m. 3/20/35 to Mildred Lucille Anderson; c. Sharon Renee (Mrs. Wilson) and grandson, Scott Wilson. Educ: Golden Gate Col. Schs. of Real Estate Ins, 52-53; Oakland City Col, A.A, 62. Polit. & Govt. Pos: Chmn, 17th Assembly Dist. Coord. Coun, Calif, 66-; mem, Alameda Co. Rep. Cent. Cmt, 68- Bus. & Prof. Pos: From messenger, mail and distribution dept. to various pos, Pac. Fire Rating Bur, 18-64, supt, dept, 64-66; retired. Mem: First Worshipful Master, W.J. Anderson Lodge 59, F&AM; Grove St. Neighborhood Coun; Alameda Co. Rep. League; past pres, Oakland-Albany-Berkeley Speakers Club; Rep. Fund Raising Cmt. Rel: Protestant. Mailing Add: 1421 Sacramento St, Berkeley, Calif. 94702.

VAYO, GERARD A. R
Chmn, Chelmsford Rep. Town Cmt, Mass.
b. Lowell, Mass, 12/14/20; s. Myles E. Vayo and Winifred Clohsey V; single. Educ: Bentley Col, Acct. Cert, 50; Lowell Commercial Col, dipl, 40. Polit. & Govt. Pos: Treas, Chelmsford Rep. Town Cmt, Mass, 54-56, chmn, 56-; personnel bd. mem. and secy, Chelmsford, 56-60, bd. mem, Commun. Action Cmt, 66, chmn, 68-; del, Mass. Rep. State Conv, 56-64; v.pres, Chelmsford Rep. Club, Mass, 64- Bus. & Prof. Pos: Cost acct, Corps of Engrs, U.S. Army, 40-42 & 46-48, chief, Mil. Pay Dept, Finance Dept, Ft. Devens, Mass, 48-51; prin, Gerard A. Vayo, Pub. Acct, 51- Mil. Serv: Entered as Aviation Cadet, Army Air Force, 42, released as T/Sgt, 45, after serv. in 445th Bomb Group, 702nd Squadron, Second Bombardment Div, Eighth Air Force, ETO; Distinguished Flying Cross; Air Medal with Three Oak Leaf Clusters; World War II Victory Medal; Europe-Africa-Middle East Campaign Ribbon with Five Battle Stars; Good Conduct Medal; Am. Theater Ribbon; Distinguished Unit Citation. Mem: Nat. Soc. Pub. Acct; Elks; Am. Legion; Lowell Hist. Soc; DAV; Air Force Asn; exec. bd, Boy Scouts, Lowell, Mass. Coun. Rel: Roman Catholic. Mailing Add: 249 Chelmsford St, Chelmsford, Mass. 01824.

VEAL, JOSEPH HOLLIDAY R
Rep. State Committeeman, Fla.
b. Daniel Boone, Ky, 2/23/23; s. Marvin Speed Veal and Ida Perry V; m. 4/10/48 to Mary Riley; c. James Warren. Educ: Duke Univ, B.A, 43; C.L.U, Am. Col. Life Underwriters, 66; Alpha Tau Omega; BOS. Polit. & Govt. Pos: Del, Rep. Nat. Conv, 64; co. sch. trustee, 64-66; precinct committeeman, Rep. Party, Fla; Rep. State Committeeman, Fla, 66- Mil. Serv: Entered as A/S, Naval Res, 44, released as Lt.(jg), 46, after serv. in Pac, Marshall Islands, 46. Mem: Nat. Asn. Life Underwriters (mem. bd, 64); Oratorio Soc; ACA; United Serv. Orgn; Rotary; Pensacola Country Club. Rel: Episcopal. Mailing Add: 900 Fairway Dr, Pensacola, Fla. 32507.

VEALE, ROADS R
Mem, Sonoma Co. Rep. Cent. Cmt, Calif.
b. Spokane, Wash, 4/13/40; s. Henry Veale and Mariana Gray V; m. 11/23/63 to Gayle Miller; c. Jennifer and Jodi. Educ: Santa Rosa Jr. Col, 1 year; Golden Gate Col, San Francisco, 3 years. Polit. & Govt. Pos: Mem, Sonoma Co. Rep. Cent. Cmt, Calif, 69- Mil. Serv: Entered as Pvt, Army, 58, released as Sp-4, 61, after serv. in 24th Med. Unit. Mem: Rotary; bd. dir, YMCA; bd. dirs, Santa Rosa C. of C. Rel: Protestant. Mailing Add: 4343 Wallace Rd, Santa Rosa, Calif. 95404.

VEGHTE, HENRY, JR. R
Vt. State Rep.
b. Johnston, N.Y, 2/21/04; m. to Anne Berry; c. 5. Educ: Gloversville Bus. Sch; N.Y. Univ, Bachelor of Commercial Sci. Polit. & Govt. Pos: Mem, Vt. Develop. Cmn; town auditor, 9 years; Justice of the Peace, 60-; selectman, 63-; Vt. State Rep, 65-; mem, Joint Sch. Bd. Bus. & Prof. Pos: Glove mfr. Mem: Elks; A.I.V. Rel: Presbyterian. Mailing Add: Stage Pico Pines, Rutland, Vt. 05701.

VEITCH, AGNES BELL R
Third V.Pres, Nat. Fedn. of Rep. Women
b. Shenandoah Junction, W.Va, 8/4/99; d. Wesley Porter Bell and Mercy Lee Boyer B; m. 7/3/22 to Samuel L. Veitch; c. Donald Guilford and Boyer Lewis. Educ: Shephard Col, Shepherdstown, W.Va, grad; Temple Univ; Univ. Pittsburgh. Polit. & Govt. Pos: Third V.pres, Nat. Fedn. of Rep. Women, 65-; pres, Pa. Coun. Rep. Women, 61-66; committeewoman, Penn Wynne Dist, 22 yrs; v.chmn, Lower Marion Twp. Rep. Cmt, 2 terms; mem. bd. dirs, Pa. Coun. Rep. Women and state chmn. membership and prog; past pres, Lower Marion-Narberth Coun. Rep. Women. Bus. & Prof. Pos: Supvr, pub. sch. music; assoc. ed. of nat. magazine, 6 yrs; dir, soc. serv, Pennhurst State Sch. Mem: Past pres, Penn Wynne Library Asn; past pres, Maine Line Bus. & Prfnl. Women's Club and former state officer; past pres, Philadelphia Chap. Women's Auxiliary, Lafayette Col. and past nat. pres; N.S. Daughters of Am. Revolution; United Daughters of Confederacy; past pres, Women's League of Penn Wynne; bd. Main Line Fed. Churches; corresponding secy. and dir, Hathaway Shakespeare Club; dir, Philadelphia Soroptimist Club; chmn. membership cmt, Matinee Musical Club; bd. mgrs, Main Line YMCA; dir, Women's Div, United Fund Drive; Women's Cmt. of Philadelphia Orchestra; Emergency Aid. Rel: Presbyterian; Mem, Exec. Cmt. and Women's Asn; charter mem, Chris-West Hope Presbyterian Church, organist and choir dir, 5 yrs, supt, Beginners Dept, mem, Bd. Deacons; Bryn Mawr Presbyterian Church. Mailing Add: 1238 Page Terrace, Villanova, Pa. 19085. (1967)

VELASQUEZ, WALDO R
Mem, Rep. State Cent. Cmt, Calif.
b. Ignacio, Colo, 11/1/19; s. Miguel Velasquez and Josephine Montoya V; m. to June Patricia Cowherd; c. Priscilla. Educ: Chama High Sch, N.Mex, grad; El Rito Normal Sch, 1 year. Polit. & Govt. Pos: Mem. Rep. State Cent. Cmt, Calif. and Co. Cent. Cmt, 64-; Rep. Cand, U.S. House Rep, 68. Mem: Pres, San Francisco Tip Club, 59; pres, Optimist Club, 64; pres, Spanish Speaking Citizens, 66. Commended by Calif. State Legis. Rel: Catholic. Mailing Add: 130 Milton St, San Francisco, Calif. 94112.

VELÁZQUEZ, LUIS MAGÍN Popular Dem, P.R.
b. Carolina, P.R, 9/30/20; s. Pablo Velázquez and Manuela Walker V; m. 3/17/47 to Mary Morales; c. Luis Magín, Luis Raúl and Pablo Ramón. Educ: Univ. P.R, Rio Piedras, P.R. Polit. & Govt. Pos: P.R. State Rep, 61-69, chmn, Commerce & Indust. Cmt, P.R. State House of Rep, 66-69; chmn, Popular Dem. Party, Carolina, P.R. Bus. & Prof. Pos: V.pres, Bd. of Dirs, Metrop. Savings & Loan Asn, Carolina, P.R. Mil. Serv: Entered as Pvt, Army, 42, released as Sgt, 46, after serv. in 65th Inf. Regt, Caribbean; Am. Theater Serv. Medal; Good Conduct Medal; Victory Medal; Overseas Serv. Ribbons. Mem: Planning Bd. Cmt; Civil Air Patrol; Am. Legion. Rel: Catholic. Legal Res: Bo. Martín Gonzáles, Carolina, P.R. 00630- Mailing Add: Box 545, Carolina, P.R. 00630. (1967)

VELEZ ITHIER, MANUEL Popular Dem, P.R.
Rep, P.R. House of Rep.
b. Cabo Rojo, P.R, 2/20/14; s. Gregorio Velez Irizarry (deceased) and Maria D. Ithier V; m. 1/25/45 to Gregoria Ortiz Nazario; c. Manuel, Maria Magda-

lena and Anais. Educ: Agr. & Mech. Col, Mayaguez, P.R, B.S.A, 39; Univ. P.R, Dipl. in Sch. Supv. and Admin, 61. Polit. & Govt. Pos: Chmn, local cmt, Algarrobo Co. Popular Dem. Cmt, P.R, 60-64; mem, Vega Baja Popular Dem. Munic. Cmt, 64-; Rep, P.R. House of Rep, 69- Bus. & Prof. Pos: Local dir. civil defense, Vega Baja, P.R, 51-60. Mem: P.R. Teachers Asn.(pres, Vega Baja Chap, 48-57); Mason (Worshipful Master, Brisas Del Caribe Number 86, 60-61); pres, SSS Vega Baja Local Bd. Number 73, 60-68; P.R. Agronomist Col.(pres, Manati Chap, 67-68); F&AM; Odd Fellows. Year Agronomist, 67. Rel: Presbyterian. Legal Res: Algarrobo Ward Route 155 Km. 66 Hm. 3, Vega Baja, P.R. 00763. Mailing Add: P.O. Box 865, Vega Baja, P.R. 00763.

VENABLE, ABRAHAM SYLVESTER
Dep. Dir, Off. of Minority Bus. Enterprise, Dept. of Commerce
b. Washington, D.C, 4/10/30; s. Abraham Venable and Mattie Foy V; m. 1/11/53 to Anna Graham; c. Karen, Douglas and Stephen. Educ: Howard Univ, B.A, 51 and M.A, 53. Polit. & Govt. Pos: Economist, Bus. and Defense Serv. Admin, Dept. of Commerce, 63-64, conciliation specialist, Commun. Rels. Serv, 64-66, dir, Affirmative Actions, 66-68 and dep. dir, Off. of Minority Bus. Enterprises, 69- Bus. & Prof. Pos: Regional mkt. rep, Anheuser-Busch, Inc, Budweiser Beer, 57-60; pres, Venable Assocs, Inc, 60-61 and New World Labs, Inc, 61-62; v.pres. mkt, Fearonce Beauty Prod. Co, 62-63. Publ: 'Mobilizing Dormant Resources: Negro Entrepreneurs,' MBA, 5/67. Mem: Nat. Asn. of Mkt. Developers; Nat. Bus. League. Awarded one year govt. fel. at the Woodrow Wilson Sch. of Pub. and Int. Affairs, Princeton Univ. Rel: Presbyterian. Mailing Add: 1415 Whittier Place N.W, Washington, D.C. 20012.

VENABLE, JACK BENTON D
b. Wetumpka, Ala, 2/25/39; s. Benton Knowles Venable and Maydell Smith V; m. 6/7/64 to Josephine Mann; c. Cameron Julia. Educ: Auburn Univ, B.S, 61. Polit. & Govt. Pos: Admin. asst. to U.S. Rep. Bill Nichols, Ala, 67- Bus. & Prof. Pos: Producer-dir, Auburn Univ. Educ. TV, 60-61; news dir, WCCB-TV, Montgomery, Ala, 62-63; dir. news and pub. affairs, WSFA-TV, 63-67. Mil. Serv: Entered as Pvt, Army Res, 56, released 1st Lt, 68, after serv. in various res. units and 31st Dixie Div, Ala. Nat. Guard. Mem: Delta Sigma Chi; Jaycees. Rel: Presbyterian. Legal Res: P.O. Box 320, Wetumpka, Ala. 36092. Mailing Add: 2007 Kenley Court, Alexandria, Va. 22308.

VENEMAN, JOHN G, JR. R
Under Secy, Dept. of Health, Educ. and Welfare
b. Corcoran, Calif, 10/31/25; s. John G. Veneman and Bertha Van Konynenburg V; m. 7/22/47 to Nita D. Bomberger; c. Ann Margaret, John Gerrit and Jane Elizabeth. Educ: Ariz. State Col, 44; Univ. Tex, 44-45. Polit. & Govt. Pos: Trustee, Empire Union Sch, Calif, 57-59; mem, grand jury, Stanislaus Co, 57-59, chmn. bd. supvr, 59-62; Calif. State Assemblyman, 30th Dist, 62-69; legis. mem, State Social Welfare Bd, 64-69; state chmn, Robert Finch Campaign for Lt. Gov, 66; Under Secy, Dept. of Health, Educ. and Welfare, 69- Mil. Serv: A/S, Navy, 44. Mem: Dir, Stanislaus Co. Farm Bur, 62-65; pres, Growers Harvesting Cmt, 60 and Empire Lions, 57; master, Empire Grange, 52; Elks; Gr. Modesto C. of C; Calif. State C. of C; Am. Legion; Commonwealth Club of San Francisco. Young Man of Year, Modesto Jr. C. of C, 60; Selected to attend Legis. Seminar, Eagleton Inst. of Politics, 66. Rel: Presbyterian. Legal Res: Modesto, Calif. Mailing Add: 1431 Woodacre Dr, McLean, Va. 22101.

VENNEBERG, BINA CLARICE D
b. Meyers Falls, Wash, 7/1/12; d. George Harvey Hammer and Bina Josephine Bartlett H; m. 8/19/31 to William Henry Venneberg; c. Leonard H, Shirley M.((Mrs. Meier), Christina C. (Mrs. Sampson), Marlene J. (Mrs. Badgley) and Rachel Susan (Mrs. Kevin Imper). Educ: High Sch; Girls League. Polit. & Govt. Pos: Precinct Committeewoman, Chelan Co, 60-; state committeewoman, Chelan Co. Cent. Cmt, 63; del, Nat. Dem. Conv, 64. Bus. & Prof. Pos: Real Estate Salesman, Scofield Realtors, 66- Mem: PTA; Camp Fire; Wash. State Federated Women's Clubs; Manson Garden Club; Belle Reeves Dem. Women's Club; Chelan Co. Dem. Cmt; Grange. Rel: Protestant. Legal Res: Boetzkes Ave, Manson, Wash. 98831. Mailing Add: P.O. Box 196, Manson, Wash. 98831.

VENTERS, CARL VERNON D
b. Richlands, N.C, 1/18/06; s. Wayne Brinson Venters and Julia G. Stevens V; m. 4/30/30 to Margaret Dean Burnette; c. Carl V, Jr, Wayne Burnette and Margaret Gayle. Educ: Univ. of N.C, A.B, 26 and LL.B, 29; Phi Gamma Delta; Phi Delta Phi. Polit. & Govt. Pos: Co. solicitor, N.C, 47-48; N.C. State Rep, 49-61 & 63-65; mem, N.C. Adv. Budget Cmn, 55-58, chmn, 57-58; N.C. State Sen, 65-66. Publ: American Law Reports-Annotations, Edward Thompson Co, Northport, N.Y, 30-35. Mem: Onslow Co. Bar Asn.(pres, 62); Fourth Judicial Bar Asn.(pres, 62); N.C. Bar Asn; Am. Judicature Soc; Kiwanis; Farm Bur; Moose. Rel: Episcopal. Legal Res: 6 E. Bayshore Blvd, Jacksonville, N.C. 28540. Mailing Add: Box 160, Jacksonville, N.C. 28540.

VENTERS, W. ODELL D
b. Johnsonville, 3/29/17; s. Willie Venters and Lizzie Abrams V; m. 6/6/36 to Nina Barfield. Educ: Pub. Sch, Johnsonville, S.C. Polit. & Govt. Pos: Mem, Town Coun, Johnsonville, S.C, 50-55, mayor, 55-60; S.C. State Rep, 61-69. Bus. & Prof. Pos: Merchant, owner, Venters Dept. Store. Mem: S.C. Jr. C. of C. Distinguished Serv. Award as one of the outstanding young men of State of S.C, 50. Mailing Add: Johnsonville, S.C. 29555. (1967)

VERHOEFF, HOWARD L. R
b. Flagler, Colo, 6/21/10; married; c. three. Polit. & Govt. Pos: Colo. State Rep, 66-67; former Rep. committeeman, Flagler and Denver, Colo, 8 years. Bus. & Prof. Pos: Pres, Local 675 Brick and Clay Workers Union, chief negotiator, 10 years. Mailing Add: 538 S. Osceola St, Denver, Colo. 80219. (1967)

VERKLER, JERRY THOMAS D
b. Black Rock, Ark; s. Jewel T. Verkler and Sylvia Thomas V; m. to Mary Frances Keadle; c. Gail, Alison, Kimberly and Jerry, Jr. Educ: Univ. N.Mex, B.A, 54; George Wash. Univ. Law Sch, LL.B, 60; Pi Kappa Alpha; Young Dem; Phi Alpha Delta. Polit. & Govt. Pos: Legis. asst. to U.S. Sen. Clinton P. Anderson, N.Mex, 56-60; staff dir, U.S. Sen. Cmt. on Interior and Insular Affairs, 61-; del, Va. Dem. Conv, 68. Mil. Serv: 2nd Lt, Marines, 54, serv. in 2nd Marine Div; Maj, Marine Corps Res. Mailing Add: 7922 Greeley Blvd, Springfield, Va. 22152.

VERLOT, FRANK O. R
Mem, Calif. Rep. State Cent. Cmt.
b. Ghent, Belgium, 10/18/41; s. Maximillian G. Verlot and Eva Danilevitz V; m. 6/24/67 to Marian Elizabeth Berkner. Educ: Mass. Inst. Tech, B.S, 63; Stanford Univ, M.S, 64, Post Master's Study, 64-67; Burcon. Polit. & Govt. Pos: Pres, Mass. Inst. Tech. Young Rep, 61-63; chmn, San Mateo Co. Youth for Reagan, Calif, 66; pres, Stanford Univ. Young Rep, 66-67; assoc. mem, Calif. Rep. State Cent. Cmt, 67-68, mem, 69-; campaign chmn, Dorwin for Assembly, 24th Dist, Calif, 68; alternate mem, Santa Clara Co. Rep. Cent. Cmt, 68, mem, 69-; San Francisco Bay Area v.pres, Calif. Young Rep, 68-; Rep. precinct chmn, Santa Clara Co, 69- Bus. & Prof. Pos: Thermodynamics engr, Grumman Aircraft Eng. Corp, Bethpage, N.Y, 63-65, Lockheed Space & Missiles Co, Sunnyvale, Calif, 66-68; proj. engr, prog. mgt, United Tech. Center, 68- Mem: Am. Soc. Mech. Engrs; Am. Inst. Aeronaut. & Astronaut; Commonwealth Club of Calif; Sierra Club. Rel: Roman Catholic. Mailing Add: 1540 Klamath Dr, Sunnyvale, Calif. 94087.

VERNON, MANFRED CLAUDE D
Chmn, Whatcom Co. Dem. Cent. Cmt, Wash.
b. Duesseldorf, Germany, 5/23/07; s. Otto Vernon and Johanna Scheuer V; m. 12/17/46 to Hally Weis; c. Bonnie Joan, Abbie Ruth, Stephen Michael and Wendy Margaret. Educ: Univ. Cologne, LL.B, 29; Univ. Berlin, J.D, 33; Stanford Univ, Ph.D, 48; Pi Sigma Alpha. Polit. & Govt. Pos: Br. chief in research, U.S. Dept. of State, 51-53; chmn, Whatcom Co. Dem. Cent. Cmt, Wash, 67- Bus. & Prof. Pos: Instr. polit. sci, Univ. Mich, 47-51; from assoc. prof. to prof, Univ. Ala, 53-64; Fulbright prof, Univ. Ankara, 60-61; prof, West. Wash. State Col, 64-, chmn, dept, 64-68. Mil. Serv: Entered as Pvt, Army, 41, released as S/Sgt, 45, after serv. in Inf. and Signal Corps, Southwest Pac. Theatre, 44-45; Good Conduct Medal and several others. Publ: Devlet Sistemleri (Government Systems), Univ. Ankara, 61; New Sourcebook in Major European Governments, World Publ, Co, 66; contrib. ed, Handbook of Historical Concepts, Philos. Libr, 66. Mem: Am, South, West. and Pac. Northwest Polit. Sci. Asns; Am. Asn. Univ. Prof; Int. Studies Asn. Univ. Mich. and Univ. Ala. research grants; Fulbright lect. grant to Turkey, 60-61. Mailing Add: 528 Fieldstone Rd, Bellingham, Wash. 98225.

VEROSKE, FREDERICK ANTHONY R
Wash. State Rep.
b. Chelan, Wash, 11/29/28; s. John Veroske and Pearl Anthony V; m. 9/21/49 to Joyce Hinton; c. Melissa Jean, Kim Ellen and Rebecca Ann. Educ: Calif. Col. of Mortuary Sci, Los Angeles, Calif, 50. Polit. & Govt. Pos: City councilman, Lynden, Wash, 60-; Wash. State Rep, 65- Mem: State and Nat. Funeral Dirs. Asn; West. Farmers Asn; Cattlemans Asn; Grange; Mason; Elks; Kiwains; C. of C; Planning Cmn; Yacht Club; Golf and Country Club. Rel: Methodist. Mailing Add: 723 17th St, Bellingham, Wash. 98225.

VER PLANK, JOEL P. R
Chmn, Ottawa Co. Rep. Party, Mich.
b. Zeeland, Mich, 2/18/37; s. Joseph Ver Plank and Jessemine Cross V; m. 1/31/59 to Susan Yates; c. Elizabeth. Educ: Albion Col, B.A, 59; Delta Tau Delta. Polit. & Govt. Pos: Del, Rep. Party, Livonia, Mich, 64-66 and Holland, Mich, 66-; state secy, United Rep. of Mich, 68-69; chmn, Ottawa Co. Rep. Party, 69- Bus. & Prof. Pos: Teacher, Almont Community Sch, 59-62 and Livonia Pub. Schs, 62-65; supvr, Royal Casket Co, Zeeland, Mich, 65-69, asst. secy-treas, 69- Mem: Holland Jaycees; v.pres, Zeeland C. of C. Rel: Protestant. Mailing Add: 559 Elmdale Court, Holland, Mich. 49423.

VERRIKER, WILLIAM J. D
Conn. State Sen.
b. Waterbury, Conn, 7/13/02; s. Edward Verriker and Bridget Lehan V; m. 6/12/48 to Ferande Genier; c. Margaret, William and John. Polit. & Govt. Pos: Chmn, Waterbury Bd. Police Cmnrs, Conn, 40-44, 56-57 & 60; treas, Waterbury Dem. Town Cmt, 52-60, chmn, 60-64; mem, Waterbury Bd. Fire Cmnrs, 59; Conn. State Sen, 59- Bus. & Prof. Pos: Pres, Verriker Paint & Wallpaper Co, 26- Mem: Elks; Exchange Club; Nat. Asn. of State Legislators; Conn. Paint Salesmen Club; Waterbury C. of C; Waterbury Country Club. Rel: Roman Catholic. Mailing Add: 77 W. Ridge Dr, Waterbury, Conn. 06078. (1967)

VESICH, ANTHONY JOSEPH, JR. D
La. State Rep.
b. New Orleans, La, 12/25/25; s. Anthony J. Vesich, Sr. and Lucy Ellen McCormack V; m. 12/27/47 to Rita Mae Curtis; c. Lucy Ellen and Anthony J, III. Educ: Loyola Univ, LL.D, 51; Delta Theta Phi. Polit. & Govt. Pos: La. State Rep, 56- Mil. Serv: Entered as A/S, Navy, 43, released as Torpedoman 2/C, 46, after serv. in Pac. Theatre, 44-46. Rel: Catholic. Mailing Add: 20 Killdeer St, New Orleans, La. 70124.

VESSELLA, PETER ANTHONY D
V.Pres, Young Dem. Clubs of Am.
b. West Pittsburg, Pa, 6/7/34; s. James Joseph Vessella and Helen Pavkovich V; m. 7/6/57 to Rosemary Huzinec; c. Mark, Suzanne, Lorrin and Maret. Educ: Duquesne Univ, B.S. in B.A, 56; Alpha Phi Delta. Polit. & Govt. Pos: Pres, Lawrence Co. Young Dem. Club, Pa, 62-64; dir. of orgn, Young Dem. Clubs of Pa, 65-66, pres, 66-68, v.pres, 68-, nat. committeeman, 69-; mem. policy cmt, Pa. Dem. State Cmt, 66-68, mem. speakers bur, 66-, mem. rules change cmt, 69; mem. exec. bd, Lawrence Co. Dem. Cmt, 66-; pres, Ellport Coun, Ellwood City, 66-; alternate del, Dem. Nat. Conv, 68. Bus. & Prof. Pos: Pres, Motel/Hotel Enterprises, 61-; owner and pres, X-V Fund, 68-; pres, 7-L Corp, 69. Mil. Serv: Entered as Ens, Navy, 57, released as Lt.(jg), 61, after serv. in U.S.S. Iowa, 57, U.S.S. Leyte, 58-59 and U.S.S. Cinclantflt, 60-61; Lt, Naval Res, 61- Mem: Lions; Moose; Lawrence Co. Borough Officials Asn. Young Man of the Year, 67; named one of the Outstanding Young Men of Am, 68 and one of the Community Leaders of Am, 69. Rel: Roman Catholic. Mailing Add: 317 Golf Ave, Ellport, Ellwood City, Pa. 16117.

VEST, ALTON HARRY R
Chmn, Mercer Co. Rep. Exec. Cmt, W.Va.
b. Floyd, Va, 4/3/91; s. Abraham Lincoln Vest and Emma Evangeline Thur-

man V; m. 6/15/21 to Ella Mastin Bailey; c. Harry Lincoln (deceased), Glen Mastin (deceased), Robert Alton and Eugene Thurman. Educ: Floyd Co. Free Schs, Va, 98-07; Pizzaro Grammar Sch, 07-08. Polit. & Govt. Pos: Census enumerator, Floyd Co, Va; mayor, Bluefield, W.Va, 45-49; Rep. capt, Precinct 30, Bluefield, 48, 49 & 52; campaign mgr, Mercer Co, 64; chmn, Mercer Co. Rep. Exec. Cmt, 65-; gen. chmn, Don Clark for Cong. Cmt, W.Va, 68; presidential elector, Fifth Cong. Dist, 68. Mil. Serv: Entered as Pvt, Army, 17, released as M/Sgt, 19, after serv. in Hosp. Med. Corps, France, 17-19; Good Conduct Medal. Mem: Bluefield Life Underwriters Asn.(pres, 52); W.Va. Life Underwriters Asn.(secy-treas, 54); South. W.Va. Ins. Asn.(pres, 55); Nat. Asn. Life Underwriters; Am. Legion (post comdr, Riley Vest Post No. 9, 39-, sixth dist. comdr, 42-44, state historian, 41); Kiwanis; AF&AM; Shrine; C. of C; Mercer Co. Rep. Club; Elks; Moose; Beni-Kedem Temple. 25 Years Perfect Attendance, Bluefield Kiwanis Club; 50 Year Pin, AF&AM, 66; Distinguished Citizenship Award, Am. Legion, 62; Man of the Year, Jr. C. of C, 46. Rel: Presbyterian; Elder, Westminster Presby. Church; Pres, Presby. Men, W.Va. Presby. Church, 63; Cmnr, Gen. Assembly, 64. Mailing Add: 2100 Wythe Ave, Bluefield, W.Va. 24701.

VETTER, KENNETH EUGENE R
City Councilman, Bakersfield, Calif.
b. Lindsay, Calif, 9/7/28; s. Fred L. Vetter and Alyce M. Chapman V; m. 5/14/54 to Betty L. Ellis; c. Kay Leslie, Frederick Joseph, Stephen Kenneth and Jeffrey Matthew. Educ: Lindsay High Sch, grad; Stanford Univ, 2 years. Polit. & Govt. Pos: City councilman, Bakersfield, Calif, 67- Bus. & Prof. Pos: Owner, Ken Vetter Ins, 55- Mil. Serv: Entered as Seaman, Navy, 46, released E-T 2/C, 48, after serv. in U.S.S. Lyman K. Swenson DD, 47-48. Mem: Elks; Lions Int. Rel: Catholic. Legal Res: 129 Cypress, Bakersfield, Calif. 93304. Mailing Add: P.O. Box 2424, Bakersfield, Calif. 92809.

VEYSEY, VICTOR VINCENT R
Calif. State Assemblyman
b. Eagle Rock, Calif, 4/14/15; s. Charles Francis Veysey and Nettie Shelley V; m. 7/20/40 to Janet Donaldson; c. Ann (Mrs. Al Kosky), John Charles, Thomas Frank and Mark Edward. Educ: Calif. Inst. Tech, B.S. in Eng; Harvard Univ, M.A. in Bus. Admin. Polit. & Govt. Pos: Mem. and past clerk and pres, Brawley Sch. Bd, Calif; mem. adv. cmt, Southwest Irrigation Field Sta, U.S. Dept. Agr; mem. and past chmn, Adv. Cmt. for Exten. Serv. and Meloland Field Sta, Univ. Calif; Calif. State Assemblyman, 75th Dist, 63-, chmn, Cmt. on Educ. and mem, Ways and Means Cmt, Calif. State Assembly, currently; past chmn, Co. Cmt. on Sch. Dist. Orgn. Bus. & Prof. Pos: Farmer, Imp. Valley, Calif, 49-; indust. rels. mgr, plant mgr. and then works mgr, Calif. Inst. Tech. and Rocket Div, Gen. Tire and Rubber Co. of Calif; instr. and asst. prof, econ, indust. rels. and indust. mgt, Calif. Inst. Tech, 7 yrs. Mem: Bd. mem, Imperial Valley Col, 3 yrs; Imperial Co. Sugar Beet Growers Asn.(pres, Dist. 9, 4 yrs, also secy. and v.pres); dir. state bd, Calif. Beet Growers; coun. cmnr, Boy Scouts; pres, Brawley Coun, Camp Fire Girls; commun. leader, Brawley 4-H Club; dir, United Fund; Rotary Int; Elks. Man of Year in Educ. Award, Phi Delta Kappa, 61. Rel: Presbyterian; Elder. Legal Res: 5203 Highway 111, Brawley, Calif. 92227. Mailing Add: 141 South Sixth St, Brawley, Calif. 92227.

VICINO, ROBERT JAMES D
Conn. State Rep.
b. Ft. Lee, N.J, 9/7/30; s. Rocco Vicino and Blanche Wovers V.(deceased); m. 7/30/54 to Arlene Levesque; c. Robert John, Carol Ann, Cynthia Ann and Stephen James. Educ: Bristol High Sch, grad, 48; Univ. Hartford, 1 year. Polit. & Govt. Pos: Pres, Young Dem. Club, Bristol, Conn, 60-61; selectman, Bristol, 62-64; chmn, First Dist. Dem. Party, 62-65; Conn. State Rep, 34th Dist, 67- Mil. Serv: Entered as Pvt, Air Force, 49, released as S/SGT, 53, after serv. in Far E. Air Force. Publ: 'Insurance,' Rough Notes Inc, 6/62. Mem: Dir, Conn. Bd. Realtors; past pres. and v.pres, Bristol Bd. Realtors. Rel: Catholic. Legal Res: 282 Fall Mountain Rd, Bristol, Conn. 06010. Mailing Add: 36 High St, Bristol, Conn. 06010.

VICK, GABE T. D
Chmn, Parker Co. Dem. Party, Tex.
b. Weatherford, Tex, 5/24/31; s. Joseph J. Vick and Era Greenfield V; m. 5/8/54 to Luanne Johnson; c. Gabe T, Jr, Randol J. and Michael F. Educ: Weatherford Col, 48-49; Univ. Tex, Austin, B.B.A, 52, LL.B, 56; Phi Kappa Tau; Phi Alpha Delta. Polit. & Govt. Pos: Judge, Parker Co, Tex, 62-66; chmn, Parker Co. Dem. Party, 67- Mil. Serv: Entered as 2nd Lt, Army, 52, released as 1st Lt, 54, after serv. in 593rd Transportation Traffic Regt. Detachment, Seoul, Korea, 53-54; Maj, Judge Adv. Gen. Corps, Res, 54-; Commendation Ribbon; Korean Serv, Am. Nat. Defense and UN Medals. Mem: Tex. Bar Asn; Parker Co. Bar Asn.(pres, 67); Optimist; K. of P; VFW. Rel: Episcopal. Legal Res: 1303 Bois d'Arc, Weatherford, Tex. 76086. Mailing Add: P.O. Box 51, Weatherford, Tex. 76086.

VICKERS, EARL M. D
b. Montgomery, W.Va, 4/30/23; s. Charles Milton Vickers and Helen Montgomery V; m. 6/28/47 to Betty Beach; c. Henry Beach, Montgomery, Frank Wysor, Helen, Ann. Educ: W.Va. Inst. of Tech; Univ. of Richmond and Wash. and Lee Univ, LL.B. Polit. & Govt. Pos: Mem, 11th Sen. Dist. Dem. Exec. Cmt, W.Va, 54-60; former pres, Fayette Co. Commun. Action Coun; former spec. agent, Fed. Bur. Invest; former chmn, Montgomery Dem. Exec. Cmt, W.Va; former mem, Bd. of Park Cmnrs; former mem, Montgomery Urban Renewal Authority; W.Va. State Del, 60-66, former Majority Leader, W.Va. State House of Del. Bus. & Prof. Pos: Mem. bd. dirs, New River Gorge Develop. Corp; pres, Fayette Co. Develop. Corp. Mil. Serv: Navy, Lt.(jg), World War II. Mem: Past pres, Fayette Co. Bar Asn; W.Va. State Bar and Am. Bar Asns; exec. bd, Buckskin Coun. Boy Scouts; AF&AM; Lions. Rel: Presbyterian. Mailing Add: Montgomery, W.Va. 25136. (1967)

VICKERS, JEAN M. R
b. Lake City, Colo, 8/1/14; d. John Nerr McCloughan and Linnie Pearl Hunt M; m. 8/21/34 to John Henry Vickers; c. Sally Ann (Mrs. Harold David), Lester Howard, Jon Theodore and Joseph Duncan. Educ: Lake City High Sch. and Rubicam Bus. Sch, St. Louis, Mo, 32 & 33. Polit. & Govt. Pos: Dep. co. treas, Hinsdale Co, Colo, 32-50, clerk to Ration Bd. during World War II, dep. co. clerk, 53-55, co. clerk and recorder, 55-; town treas, Lake City, 60- Bus. & Prof. Pos: Mem. staff, Frank Dial Tire Co, Pampa, Tex, 50-52. Mem: Pres, Colo. State Asn. of Co. Clerks and Recorders, currently; Rebekah. Rel: Episcopal. Legal Res: 7 Gunnison Ave, Lake City, Colo. 81235. Mailing Add: Box 218, Lake City, Colo. 81235.

VICKERS, MARIE D
Postmaster, Pratt, Kans.
b. Syracuse, Kans, d. John Francis Cleary and Margaret Nelson C; m. 5/30/46 to E. C. Vickers, Jr; wid. Educ: Betts Sch. of Bus, Arkansas City, Kans. Polit. & Govt. Pos: Precinct committeewoman, Kans, 52-; v.chmn, Breeding for Cong. Cmt, 56-59; v.chmn, Fifth Dist. Dem. Cmt, 59-60; v.chmn, State Dem. Cmt, 60-63; del, Dem. Nat. Conv, 60 & 64; mem. adv. coun, Small Bus. Admin, 62-; Dem. Nat. Committeewoman, Kans, 63-66; coord, Women's Activities, Johnson-Humphrey Campaign, 64; postmaster, Pratt, Kans, 66- Bus. & Prof. Pos: Mem, Pres. Coun, St. Marys of Plains Col, 65- Mem: Park Hill Country Club; Bus. & Prfnl. Womens Clubs; C. of C; Int. Platform Asn. Selected Community Leader of Am; Selected as One of 2000 Distinguished Women of Achievement of the World. Rel: Catholic. Mailing Add: 117 Champa, Pratt, Kans. 67124.

VICKERY, HAROLD JAY R
N.H. State Rep.
b. Rochester, N.H, 5/12/93; s. William Vickery and Ida G. Bickford V; wid; c. William D. Educ: Rochester High Sch, N.H, grad. Polit. & Govt. Pos: Selectman, Rochester, N.H; N.H. State Rep, 67- Mem: Farm Bur; Rochester Grange. Rel: Quaker. Mailing Add: R.F.D. 2, Rochester, N.H. 03867.

VIDAL, DAGMAR LUND D
Dem. Committeewoman, Third Dist, Iowa
b. Hampton, Iowa, 12/10/17; d. Peter Lauritzen Lund and Mette Miller L; m. 6/22/44 to Lewis Leonard Vidal; c. Katherine, Robert, Peter and Leonard. Educ: Grand View Col, 35-36; Iowa State Teachers Col, 38-39; Univ. Minn, summer Sch; Colo. State Univ. Polit. & Govt. Pos: Dem. precinct committeewoman, pres, Dem. Women's Club and secy, Franklin Co. Dem. Cent. Cmt, 60-66; Dem. committeewoman, Third Dist, Party, Iowa, 64-; mem. adv. bd, Iowa Center for Educ. in Polit, 65-; mem, Dem. State Cent. Cmt, Iowa Voters Cmt, 66-; del, Dem. Nat. Conv, 68. Mem: Pres, Hospital Auxiliary, 58-62; secy, N.Iowa Area Develop. Cmn. Tax Study, 65-66. Rel: Lutheran. Mailing Add: 218 Central Ave. E, Hampton, Iowa 50441. (1967)

VIEHMEYER, GLENN
b. Gandy, Nebr, 12/3/00; s. George Julius Viehmeyer and Clara Belle Parker V; m. 12/1/24 to Catherine Kelly Smith; c. Joyce Lucille (deceased) and Glenn Robert. Educ: High Sch. Polit. & Govt. Pos: Asst. forester, U.S. Forest Serv, 35-40; supt, Niobrara State Park, Nebr. Game Cmn, 40-43; former Nebr. State Sen, 45th Dist. Bus. & Prof. Pos: Farmer and rancher, Logan Co, Nebr, 20-35; prof. hort, Univ. Nebr, 43-; lectr, U.S. and Can. Publ: 'Reversal of Evolution in the Genus Penstemon,' Am. Naturalist, 58; 'Chrysanthemum Improvement,' Bul. Univ. Nebr; 'Penstemon In Your Garden.' Mem: Am. Rose Soc; Am. Genetic Asn; Can. Soc. for Hort. Sci; Am. Penstemon Soc; Soc. for Study of Evolution; Nebr. Ornithologists Union; Nebr. Roadside Coun; State, Co. and Local Commun. Beautification Cmts; Nebr. Fedn. of Garden Clubs; Nat. Fedn. of State Garden Clubs. Botanist and plant explorer; internationally recognized plant breeder. Mailing Add: Route 4, North Platte, Nebr. 69101.

VIENS, NOEL DAVID D
b. E. Ga, Vt, 12/23/22; m. to Edna Rubyor; c. 11. Educ: UVM. Polit. & Govt. Pos: Vt. State Sen, 61-66; Interstate Cmn. on Lake Champlain Basin; Champlain Waterway Cmn; Interstate Coop. Cmn. Bus. & Prof. Pos: Restaurant and cabin owner. Mil. Serv: ROTC at UVM. Mem: Lions Club; Moose; 3° K. of C. Rel: Catholic. Mailing Add: S. Hero, Vt. 05486. (1967)

VIERA-MARTINEZ, ANGEL New Progressive, P.R.
Speaker, P.R. House of Rep.
b. Gurabo, P.R, 11/18/15; s. Nieves Viera and Alejandrina Martínez V; m. 12/22/52 to Gladys Villeneuve; c. Angel and Harry. Educ: Univ. P.R, B.A. and LL.B. Polit. & Govt. Pos: Asst. dist. attorney, San Juan, P.R, 46-49, dist. attorney, 49-55; Rep. Precinct Two and Speaker, P.R. House of Rep, 69- Mem: P.R. and Am. Bar Asns; Am. Judicature Soc. Rel: Catholic. Legal Res: 1213 Luccheti St, Santurce, P.R. 00907. Mailing Add: House of Representatives, P.O. Box 2268, San Juan, P.R. 00903.

VIGEANT, AGNES MARTIN R
Pres, R.I. Fedn. of Rep. Women
b. Paisley, Scotland, 11/6/01; d. John Millar Martin and Margaret Campbell Renwick M; wid. Educ: Abercorn High Sch, Paisley, Scotland, grad, 19; R.I. Sch. of Design, dress design, 44. Polit. & Govt. Pos: Mem, Rep. Ward Cmt, Providence, R.I, 34-44; mem, Barrington Rep. Town Cmt, 64-69; mem, R.I. Rep. State Cmt, 65-69; pres, R.I. Fedn. of Rep. Women, 67-; del, Rep. Nat. Conv, 68; mem, Joint Legis. Coun. of R.I. Bus. & Prof. Pos: Mem. textile staff, Atlantic Yarn, Providence, R.I, 28-67; retired. Mem: Am. Legion; pres, Providence Chap. I, Widows of World War I, Inc; R.I. State Coun. of Sr. Citizens. Rel: Presbyterian. Mailing Add: 89 Spring Ave, Barrington, R.I. 02890.

VIGIL, CHARLES S. D
b. Trinidad, Colo, 6/9/13; s. Jose Urbano Vigil and Andieita Maes Martinez V. Educ: Univ. Colo; Lambda Chi Alpha. Polit. & Govt. Pos: Dist. attorney's off, Third Dist. Colo, 37-40 & 48-49; U.S. Attorney, Colo, 49-52; Electoral Col, Dem, 60; del, Dem. Nat. Conv, 64. Mil. Serv: Entered as Ens, Coast Guard, 42, released as Lt.(sg), after serv. in Cuban Flotilla. Publ: Psychology and the Law. Mem: Comdr, 984, VFW, 49; Lions; Elks; Am. Legion; Am. Bar; Am. Judicaute; Int. Bar; Int. Law. Legal Res: Trinidad, Colo. 81082. Mailing Add: 1804 Security Life Bldg, Denver, Colo. 80202.

VIGNEAU, ROBERT A. D
Mass. State Rep.
b. Dorchester, Mass, 11/4/20; s. Albert G. Vigneau and Helen R. Mehlinger V; m. 6/28/47 to Alice V. McHugh; c. Mary A, Therese M, Robert A, Jr, Peter J, Paul F. and Patrice A. Educ: Mass. Univ. Exten; Benedictis George

Sch. Art; Northeast. Univ. Polit. & Govt. Pos: Selectman, Burlington, Mass, 46-47 & 64-; mem, Dem. Town Cmt, 65-; Mass. State Rep, 69- Bus. & Prof. Pos: Pub. Acct, currently. Mil. Serv: Entered as Pvt, Army, 42, released as Lt, 45, after serv. in First Armored Div, N.Africa and Italy, ETO, 43-45; Silver Star; Purple Heart. Mem: Am. Legion; DAV; VFW; K. of C; Amputated Vet. Asn. Rel: Catholic. Mailing Add: 5 Elm Ave, Burlington, Mass. 01803.

VIGORITO, JOSEPH PHILLIP D
U.S. Rep, Pa.
b. Niles, Ohio, 11/10/18; m. to Florence Hoppe; c. Tina, Barbara and Linda. Educ: Wharton Sch. of Finance, Univ. of Pa, B.S. econ, 47; Univ. of Denver, M.B.A, 49. Polit. & Govt. Pos: U.S. Rep, Pa, 64- Bus. & Prof. Pos: CPA; asst. prof, Pa. State Univ. Mil. Serv: Army, 1st Lt, 42-45; Purple Heart. Legal Res: Erie, Pa. Mailing Add: 328 Cannon House Office Bldg, Washington, D.C. 20515. (1967)

VILARINO, JOSEPH R
Del, Calif. Rep. State Cent.
b. Inglewood, Calif, 3/14/26; s. John Vilarino and Josephine Cippresso V; m. 2/29/48 to Marian Stach; c. Steven, Jeffrey and Ronald. Educ: High Sch, 4 years. Polit. & Govt. Pos: Commun. chmn. and finance chmn, Nixon Campaign, 46th Assembly Dist, Calif, 68; del, Calif. Rep. State Cent. Cmt, 68- Bus. & Prof. Pos: Faculty, El Camino Col, 64-65; mem, Electronic Adv. Cmt, Calif, 66; pres, Riviera Village Asn, 69. Mil. Serv: A/S, Navy, 44, released as Quartermaster, 3/C, 46, after serv. in U.S. Amphibious Forces, South West Pac, 44-46. Mem: Riviera Village Businessmens Asn; Redondo Beach C. of C; Riveria Village Rotary (v.pres, 69); Riveria Village Merchants Asn. Rel: Protestant. Mailing Add: 721 31st St, Manhattan Beach, Calif. 90266.

VILLAR, EMERY L. D
La. State Rep.
b. Bnignac, La, 10/2/20; s. John Daniel Villar, Sr. and Josephine Blackwell V; m. 9/6/41 to Winnie Marie Gautreau; c. Dianne V.(Mrs. Herin), Dolores V. (Mrs. Smith) and Ronald P. Educ: Gonzales High Sch, grad. Polit. & Govt. Pos: Sch. bd. mem, Seventh Ward, Ascension Parish, La, 51-60; La. State Rep, Ascension Parish, 60- Bus. & Prof. Pos: Supvr, Humble Oil and Refining Co, 50- Mem: F&AM. Rel: Baptist. Legal Res: 701 Bayou Narcissee, Gonzales, La. 70737. Mailing Add: P.O. Box 787, Gonzales, La. 70737.

VILLARREAL, CARLOS C. R
Adminstr, Urban Mass Transportation Admin, Dept. of Transportation
b. Brownsville, Tex, 11/9/24; s. Jesus Jose Villarreal and Elisa L. Castaneda V; m. 8/25/25 to Doris Ann Akers; c. Timothy John and David Leroux. Educ: U.S. Naval Acad, B.S, 48; U.S. Navy Postgrad, M.S, 50. Polit. & Govt. Pos: Adminstr, Urban Mass Transportation Admin, Dept. of Transportation, 69- Bus. & Prof. Pos: Mgr, marine and indust. oper, Gen. Elec. Co, Cincinnati, Ohio, 56-66; v.pres. mkt. and admin, The Marquardt Corp, Van Nuys, Calif, 66-69. Mil. Serv: Entered as Ens, Navy, 48, released as Lt, 56, after serv. in Destroyers and minesweepers, Atlantic and Pac. Fleets. Mem: Am. Inst. Aeronaut. and Astronaut; Soc. Naval Architects and Marine Engrs; Navy League of U.S; Asn. of U.S. Army; chmn. holding cmt, Boy Scouts, Indian Hill, Ohio; Univ. Clubs, Wash, D.C. and Cincinnati, Ohio; Army-Navy Club, Wash, D.C. Rel: Catholic. Mailing Add: 11802 Old Gate Rd, Rockville, Md. 20852.

VILLELA, RUY SANTOS R
Chmn, New Bedford Rep. City Cmt, Mass.
b. New Bedford, Mass, 11/16/39; s. Vasco Antunes Villela and Caroline Santos V; m. 7/16/66 to Margaret Rose Conley; c. Caroline Marie. Educ: Boston Col, A.B, 61; Portia Law Sch, LL.B, 66; Southeast. Mass. Club. Polit. & Govt. Pos: Legal asst, Dept. Attorney Gen, Commonwealth of Mass, 67-69; chmn, New Bedford Rep. City Cmt, Mass, 68- Bus. & Prof. Pos: Incorporator, Southeast. Bank and Trust Co, New Bedford, Mass, 68-; clerk of corp, 69- Mil. Serv: Entered as Seaman Recruit, Coast Guard, 62, released as Seaman, 68, after serv. in ORTUPS, Mass; Inactive Res, 68- Mem: Mass. and New Bedford Bar Asns. Rel: Roman Catholic. Mailing Add: 1353 Rockdale Ave, New Bedford, Mass. 02740.

VINCENT, ARTHUR J. D
b. Somersworth, 7/15/91; married; c. 2. Educ: Somersworth Schs. Polit. & Govt. Pos: N.H. State Rep, 59-67; former mem. City Coun; Sch. Bd; City treas. Bus. & Prof. Pos: Retired shoe factory exec. Mem: Eagles; K. of C. Rel: Catholic. Mailing Add: 121 Green St, Somersworth, N.H. 03878. (1967)

VINCENT, CURTIS RALPH R
Secy. and Treas, Paulding Co. Rep. Exec. and Cent. Cmt, Ohio
b. Paulding, Ohio, 1/27/16; s. Forrest Vincent and Maudy Grieger V; m. 11/4/39 to Alice Zielke; c. Frederick Curtis. Educ: Am. Sch. Drafting & Eng, 2 years. Polit. & Govt. Pos: Maintenance supt, Div. 1, State of Ohio, 57-60; secy, treas. & campaign mgr. for Congressman Delbert L. Latta, Fifth Dist, Ohio, 62-; secy. & treas, Paulding Co. Rep. Exec. & Cent. Cmt, 68- Bus. & Prof. Pos: Freelance draftsman, 60-; diversified farming, Paulding Co, Ohio, 27 years. Rel: Lutheran. Mailing Add: R.R. 2, Paulding, Ohio 45879.

VINCENT, DWIGHT HAROLD R
Chmn, 15th Cong. Dist. Rep. Party, Mich.
b. Akron, Ohio, 4/29/30; s. Harold S. Vincent and Frances H. Hill V; m. 12/27/52 to Cynthia S. Stein; c. George H, Patricia L. and Emily H. Educ: Univ. Mich, A.B. in Law, 53, J.D, 57; Alpha Tau Omega; Delta Theta Phi. Polit. & Govt. Pos: Chmn, Dearborn Heights Rep. Party, Mich, 61-63; mem, Mich. State Rep. Cent. Cmt, 63-64; chmn, 15th Cong. Dist. Rep. Party, Mich, 64-; del, Rep. Nat. Conv, 68. Mil. Serv: Entered as Ens, Navy, 52, released as Lt(jg), 55, after serv. in U.S.S. Rogers, Korean Theatre; Comdr, Naval Res, 66; Three Battle Stars, Korean War; China Theater Extended Medal; United Nations Medal; Korean Ribbon. Mem: Am, Mich. and Detroit Bar Asns.(mem, Labor Rel. Sect, 57-). Rel: Lutheran. Mailing Add: 837 S. Beech Daly, Dearborn Heights, Mich. 48125.

VINCENT, L. L. D
W.Va. Dept. of Welfare Cmnr.
b. Marion Co, 10/24/07; s. Charles and Anne Vincent; m. to Mary Virginia Bowman. Educ: Fairmont State Col, A.B; W.Va. Univ. Sch. of Soc. Work, grad. work. Polit. & Govt. Pos: Former co. dir, field rep, dist. adminstr, asst. dir. med. serv. and asst. cmnr, Marion Co. Dep. of Pub. Assistance, W.Va, dir. dept, 36; W.Va. Dept. of Welfare Cmnr, 65- Mil. Serv: Lt. Comdr, Naval Res, 3 years. Mailing Add: Room 732, State Office Bldg. 1, Charleston, W.Va. 25305. (1967)

VINCENT, ROBERT CARR R
Chmn, Cimarron Co. Rep. Party, Okla.
b. Pampa, Tex, 12/1/30; s. Clifton Eli Vincent and Edna Carr V; m. 11/1/61 to Margaret Ann Weatherly; c. Dawn, Carr, John and Clifton. Educ: Tex. Tech. Col, B.B.A, 53. Polit. & Govt. Pos: Chmn, Cimarron Co. Rep. Party, Okla, 67- Bus. & Prof. Pos: Rancher. Mil. Serv: Entered as Pvt, Army, 53, released as E-3, 55, after serv. in 42nd Field Artillery Bn, Germany, 54-55; Nat. Defense Serv, Army Occup. and Good Conduct Medals. Mem: Am. Nat. Cattlemen's Asn; Panhandle Livestock Asn; Farm Bur; Panhandle Plains Hist. Soc. Rel: Episcopal. Mailing Add: Route 1, Box 64, Boise City, Okla. 73933.

VINING, CHARLES LEROY, JR. D
La. State Rep.
b. Darnell, La, 9/28/35; s. Charles Leroy Vining, Sr. and Bobbie Jean White V; m. 5/28/56 to Jessie Stevie Stuart; c. Vicki Vonn, Charles L, III and Richard Albert. Educ: Northeast La. State Col, B.S.P.E. Polit. & Govt. Pos: La. State Rep, 32nd Dist, E. and W.Carroll Parishes, 68-, mem, Cmts. on Agr, Game, Fish and Oysters, Labor and Indust, Pub. Health and Welfare and Transportation and Hwy, La. House of Rep, currently. Bus. & Prof. Pos: Teacher and coach, Transylvania Jr. High Sch, 60-65; farmer, E.Carroll Parish, 60-69; contractor, Vining Brothers and Beck Inc, 65-; rural mail carrier, U.S. Post Office Dept, 66-68. Mil. Serv: Entered as Pvt, Army, 53, released as Sp-4, 56, after serv. in 79th Engr. Bn. Overseas, Japan, Camp Eta Jima and Camp Okubo, 54-56; Army Res, 56-61; Nat. Defense Serv. Medal; Korean Serv. Medal; UN Serv. Medal. Mem: Future Farmers of Am; 4-H Club; Allied Youth; pres, E.Carroll Parish Teachers Asn, 65; Mason; Farm Bur. Rel: Baptist; Sunday School Superintendent, Sondheimer Baptist Church. Mailing Add: Route 1, Box 185, Sondheimer, La. 71276.

VINJE, MARTIN E. R
b. Vottineau, N.Dak, 7/10/99; married. Educ: State Sch. of Forestry. Polit. & Govt. Pos: N.Dak. State Rep, 53-66. Bus. & Prof. Pos: Merchant. Mem: Am. Legion; Masonic Orders; Bottineau C. of C. Rel: Lutheran. Mailing Add: Bottineau, N.Dak. 58318. (1967)

VINOVICH, RALPH R
b. Peoria, Ill, 6/23/28; s. Ralph Vinovich (deceased) and Martha Mrvos V. (deceased); m. 11/24/62 to Mary Catherine Reynolds; c. Sam Matthew and Paul David. Educ: Am. Univ, B.S, 67. Polit. & Govt. Pos: Spec. asst, U.S. Sen. Everett M. Dirksen, Ill, 55-67; admin. asst, U.S. Rep. Robert H. Michel, Ill, 67- Bus. & Prof. Pos: Grain buyer, J. Younge Grain Co, Peoria, Ill, 46-51 and W.W. Dewey & Sons, 53-55. Mil. Serv: Entered as Seaman Recruit, Navy, 51, released as PO 3/C, 53, after serv. in U.S. Naval Sta, Atlantic Fleet, Bermuda. Rel: Protestant. Legal Res: 2600 W. Starr St, Peoria, Ill. 61605. Mailing Add: 2701 Parkway Place, Cheverly, Md. 20785.

VINSON, CARL D
b. Baldwin Co, Ga, 11/18/83; s. Edward S. Vinson and Anne Morris V; wid. Educ: Ga. Mil. Col, Milledgeville; Mercer Univ, LL.B, 02. Polit. & Govt. Pos: Co. Court Solicitor, Ga, 06-10; Ga. State Rep, 09-12; Judge, Baldwin Co. Court, 12-16; Former chmn, Naval Affairs Cmn; U.S. Rep, Ga, 13-32, 33-52 & 55-64. Bus. & Prof. Pos: Mem, law firm Hines & Vinson. Rel: Methodist. Mailing Add: Milledgeville, Ga. 01061. (1967)

VINSON, ROY FURMAN D
Chmn, Motley Co. Dem. Party, Tex.
b. Matador, Tex, 4/15/21; s. Oscar Vinson and Maud Hudson V; m. 11/27/43 to Beverly Gray; c. Roger Furman and Linda (Mrs. Perryman). Educ: Tex. Tech. Univ, 37-41. Polit. & Govt. Pos: Chmn, Motley Co. Dem. Party, Tex, 60- Mil. Serv: Entered as Pvt, Army, 42, released 1st Lt, 46, after serv. in Co. E, 307th Inf, 77th Div, Pac. Theatre, 44-45; Purple Heart; Bronze Star with Oak Leaf Cluster; Presidential Unit Citation. Mem: Farm Bur; Mason; Shrine. Rel: Methodist. Mailing Add: Star Route, Flomot, Tex. 79234.

VIOLETTE, ELMER H. D
Maine State Sen.
b. Van Buren, Maine, 2/2/21; s. Vital E. Violette and Estell Bosse V; m. 9/2/46 to Marcella Belanger; c. Dennis, Louise, Mark, Thomas and Paul. Educ: Ricker Jr. Col; Boston Univ. Law Sch, 50. Polit. & Govt. Pos: Former mem, Maine Cmt. on Children and Youth; Maine State Rep, 42 & 46-48; chmn, Van Buren Dem. Cmt, 54- and Aroostook Co. Dem. Cmt, 58-; judge, Van Buren Munic. Court, 57-61; Maine State Sen, 64-; del, Dem. Nat. Conv, 68. Bus. & Prof. Pos: Trustee, Ricker Col; chmn. bd. trustees, Van Buren Light and Power Dist; dir, Northeast Pub. Power Asn; former chmn, Van Buren Housing Authority; trustee, Van Buren Commun. Hosp; chmn, Maine Citizens for Dickey-Lincoln Sch. Hydroelectric Proj. Mil. Serv: Entered as Pvt, Army Air Force, 42, released as M/Sgt, 46. Mem: Rotary; Am. Legion; K. of C; PTA; Aroostook and Maine Bar Asns; Christian Family Movement. Rel: Roman Catholic. Legal Res: 42 Violette St, Van Buren, Maine 04785. Mailing Add: Box 56, Van Buren, Maine 04785. (1967)

VIOLETTE, WOODROW THOMAS D
Conn. State Rep.
b. Lewiston, Maine, 7/22/24; s. Thomas Ulysses Violette and Amelia Pelletier V; m. 4/5/47 to Helen B. Sobota; c. Barbara Ann and Lori Jean. Educ: Bristol Tech. High Sch, 2 years. Polit. & Govt. Pos: Mem, Citizens Action Cmt, Bristol, Conn, 61-63, city treas, 63-69; Conn. State Rep, 69- Bus. & Prof. Pos: Machine operator, New Departure Hyatt Div, Gen. Motors Corp, 42-; coordinator, UAW Retired Workers, Bristol, 57-69. Mil. Serv: Entered as Pvt, Army, 43, released as T-5, 46, after serv. in Army Transportation Corps, China, Burma and India; Army Res, 46-49; Good Conduct Medal; Asiatic Pac. Theatre Campaign Ribbon; Victory Medal. Mem: Labor leader, UAW; Polish Legion of Am. Vet; Franco Am; dir, United Fund and Boys Club; Nat. Coun. of Sr. Citizens, New Eng; coordinator, Bristol Hosp; Nat. Coun. Adv. Staff. Rel: Catholic. Mailing Add: 26 Putnam St, Bristol, Conn. 06010.

VIRELLA, JOSE HORACIO CORA R
b. Arroyo, P.R, 6/26/03; s. Fidel Cora and Ezequiela Virella C; m. April, 1928 to Julia Maisonet Sanchez; c. Emma Josefina, Julio Fidel and Josefa Dolores. Educ: LL.B. degree. Polit. & Govt. Pos: P.R. State Rep, 28-40 & 64-66; ins. specialist, Off. of the Supt. of Ins, 35-59 and former ins. specialist, Off. of the Cmnr. of Ins; former chief of claims & complaints, Indust. Cmn, P.R. Bus. & Prof. Pos: Elem. teacher, Govt. of P.R, 23-28; gen. ins. agent, Reliable Serv. Ins. Agency, Inc, San Juan; mgr, Providence Ins. Agency and Caribbean Ins. Co, San Juan, 59-62. Mem: Asn. Pro Bienestar De La Familia, dir; Cruz Azul De P.R, Regente; Henry George Sch. of Social Sci; Mason; Odd Fellows. Rel: Methodist. Mailing Add: 1656 Nueva St, Stop 24, Santurce, P.R. 00901. (1967)

VIRTS, CHARLES CLIFTON D
Md. State Del.
b. Leesburg, Va, 3/3/10; s. Charles Clifton Virts and Maude Smith V; m. 5/30/42 to Stella Anne Overman; c. Cynthia (Mrs. Wickless) and Charles Clifton, III. Educ: Univ. Va, 31-34; Univ. Md, LL.B, 40. Polit. & Govt. Pos: Md. State Del, 47- Mem: Pres, Frederick Co. Bar Asn, 59-60; chmn, Ft. Detrick Boy Scouts, 65-66; presiding justice, Elks, 684, 56-66 and Exalted Ruler, 51; Moose, 371; Yellow Springs Lions; Nat. Grange. Rel: Episcopal. Legal Res: 423 Lee Place, Frederick, Md. 21701. Mailing Add: 5 W. Church St, Frederick, Md. 21701. (1967)

VITANZA, THOMAS ANTHONY D
Chmn, Chenango Co. Dem. Cmt, N.Y.
b. Buffalo, N.Y, 11/6/32; s. Thomas Vitanza and Jennie Bauda V; m. 4/11/55 to Joan Cavanagh; c. Thomas, Karen, Michael, Deborah and Mary. Educ: LeMoyne Col, B.A, 55; Syracuse Law Sch, LL.B, 58; Alpha Sigma Nu. Polit. & Govt. Pos: City committeeman, Second Ward, Norwich, N.Y, 65-; chmn, Chenango Co. Dem. Cmt, 68- Mem: N.Y. State and Chenango Co. Bar Asns; N.Y. State Trial Lawyers Asn; Elks; K. of C; Kiwanis. Rel: Roman Catholic. Legal Res: 39 Canasawacta St, Norwich, N.Y, 13815. Mailing Add: Box 695, Norwich, N.Y. 13815.

VITEK, JOHN M. D
b. 1907; c. one son, three grandchildren. Educ: Tilden Tech. High Sch; spec. training in real estate and ins. Polit. & Govt. Pos: Former Ill. State Rep; former mem, 11th Ward Dem. Orgn. Bus. & Prof. Pos: Former reporter for Narod Bohemian Newspaper, 5 years; real estate and title expert, Cook Co, 15 years; former jr. engr, Hwy. and Road Construction, 4 years; real estate and ins. broker, currently. Mem: Holy Name Soc; K. of C.(4°); 11th Ward Property Owner's Asn. Citation as chmn, Bridgeport Civilian Defense for outstanding work in the servicemen's center, World War II. Mailing Add: 2953 S. Union Ave, Chicago, Ill. 60616. (1967)

VIVIAN, WESTON E. D
b. Newf, Can, 10/25/24; m. to Anne Biggs, wid. 4/23/69; c. Byron, Alice, Leslie and Sarah. Educ: Union Col, B.S, 45; Mass. Inst. Tech, M.S, 49; Univ. Mich, Ph.D. in Elec. Eng, 59. Polit. & Govt. Pos: Cand. for City Coun, Ann Arbor, Mich, 58 & 59; chmn, Ann Arbor City Dem. Cmt, 59-60; U.S. Rep, Second Cong. Dist, Mich, 65-66, mem, Sci. and Astronaut. Cmt, U.S. House of Rep; Dem. nominee for Cong, Second. Dist, 66 & 68; mem. pub. eval. cmt. for state tech. serv. prog, U.S. Dept. of Commerce, 67-68; chmn. cmt. on admin. of training progs, Dept. of Health, Educ. & Welfare, 67-68; mem, Nat. Cmt. on U.S-China Rels, 68-69; organizer, Robert Kennedy for President Campaign, Mich, 68. Bus. & Prof. Pos: Summer staff mem, Lincoln Labs, Mass. Inst. Tech; consult, Nat. Coun. on Marine Resources and Ocean Eng, Wash, D.C, 67, Bendix Aviation Corp. and Corps. of Engrs; research engr. and lectr. elec. eng, Univ. Mich, 51-60; founder, v.pres. and mem. bd. dirs, Conductron Corp, Ann Arbor, 60-65; founder and v.pres, KMS Industs, Ann Arbor, Mich, 67-68; consult, Great Lakes Basin Cmn, Ann Arbor, 68; mgr. astrotype div, Info. Control Systs, Inc, 68-; nat. lectr, Asn. for Comput. Machinery, 69; chmn, Spuntech Housing, Inc, 69- Mem: Sigma Xi; Am. Phys. Soc; NAACP; Former bd. mem, Ann Arbor and Mich. United Funds. Rel: Unitarian. Mailing Add: 2717 Kenilworth Dr, Ann Arbor, Mich. 48104.

VLAHOS, ROBERT PETER D
Committeeman, Ill. Dem. Cent. Cmt.
b. Paris, Ill, 1/13/30; s. George Peter Vlahos and Velva Clark V; m. 1/29/50 to Myrtle Rose Shaver; c. Barbara Joan, Jennifer Jill, Robert Peter, Cynthia Denise and David Clark. Educ: Paris High Sch, 44-47. Polit. & Govt. Pos: Committeeman, Ill. Dem. Cent. Cmt, 66- Bus. & Prof. Pos: Equipment Operator, State of Ill, 61- Mil. Serv: Entered as Pvt, Air Force, 48, released as S/Sgt, 53, after serv. in Dent. Corps. Mem: Elks; Am. Legion. Rel: Baptist. Mailing Add: R.R. 2, Paris, Ill. 61944.

VOELKER, ROY E. R
Chmn, Mahaska Co. Rep. Cmt, Iowa
b. Winona, Minn, 4/5/23; s. Edward A. Voelker and Bernice Edwards V; m. 4/29/56 to Shirley Sigman. Educ: Gregg Col, Chicago, Ill, 46. Polit. & Govt. Pos: Off. shorthand reporter, Iowa Eighth Judicial Dist, 46-47 and Iowa Sixth Judicial Dist, 47-69; precinct committeeman, Rep. Party, 60-68; chmn, Mahaska Co. Rep. Cmt, Iowa, 66- Bus. & Prof. Pos: Ed, Nat. Shorthand Reporter, Nat. Shorthand Reporters Asn, 53-66. Mil. Serv: Entered as Pvt, Army Air Corps, 42, released as S/Sgt, 46, after serv. in U.S. Strategic Air Forces, ETO, 43-46; Am. and ETO Ribbons. Mem: Bd. mem, Nat. Shorthand Reporters Asn, 69-; Iowa Shorthand Reporters Asn.(pres, 63-64); bd. mem, Iowans for Right to Work, 68-; Iowa Voting Machine Cmn, 69-; AF&AM; Am. Legion. Cert. Shorthand Reporter, Iowa; Cert. of Proficiency, Nat. Shorthand Reporters Asn. and Distinguished Serv. Award for outstanding serv. to shorthand reporting profession, 68; Gregg Diamond Medal (shorthand award); Expert Rifleman, Nat. Rifle Asn. Mailing Add: 1510 S. First St, Oskaloosa, Iowa 52577.

VOGEL, CHARLES JOSEPH D
b. Otter Tail Co, Star Lake Twp, Minn, 9/20/98; s. Philip Francis Vogel and Anna Marie Jenson V; m. 8/22/25 to Fern Nesbitt; c. Janet Dunsmoor (Mrs. Elver T. Pearson) and Jon Nesbitt. Educ: Huron Col, 17-18; Univ. Minn, LL.B, 23; Order of the Coif; Phi Kappa Delta; Phi Alpha Delta. Polit. & Govt. Pos: Chmn, N.Dak. State Dem. Party, 37-39; Dem. Nat. committeeman, N.Dak, 38-40; nominee for U.S. Sen, N.Dak, 40; U.S. Dist. Judge, N.Dak, 41-54; U.S. Circuit Judge, 54-; Chief Judge, U.S. Court of Appeals, Eighth Circuit, 65- Bus. & Prof. Pos: Practicing attorney, 23-41. Mil. Serv: Entered as Pvt, Army, 18, released as Sgt, 19, after serv. in Signal Corps and Tank Corps. Mem: Am. Bar Asn; Am. Judicature Soc; bd. of gov, Neuropsychiatric Inst; Am. Legion. Rel: Episcopal. Legal Res: 1701 10th St. S, Fargo, N.Dak. 58102. Mailing Add: P.O. Box 1350, Fargo, N.Dak. 58102. (1967)

VOGEL, JOHN HENRY R
Kans. State Rep.
b. Stuttgart, Kans, 5/14/16; s. John Henry Vogel and Margaret Veeh V; m. to Irene Dorothy Schaake; c. Nancy Sue and Gerald Max. Educ: Univ. Kans, B.S. in Bus, 39; Alpha Kappa Psi. Polit. & Govt. Pos: Kans. State Rep, currently. Bus. & Prof. Pos: Dir, Douglas Co. State Bank; Farmer, Stockman and Businessman; mem, Bd. of Gov, Lawrence Higher Educ. Loan Prog. Mem: C. of C.(dir, Lawrence Chap); life mem, Univ. of Kans. Alumni Asn. One of ten Kans. Farm Bur. Leaders of The Year, 63. Rel: Lutheran. Mailing Add: Route 4, Lawrence, Kans. 66044.

VOGEL, RAYMOND HENRY R
Chmn, Tenth Cong. Dist. Rep. Cmt, Mo.
b. Pocahontas, Mo, 10/6/15; s. John Arthur Vogel and Emma Mirly V; m. 9/6/42 to Rosalind Justus; c. John Justus, Raymond Henry, Jr. and Martha Ann. Educ: Southeast Mo. State Col, B.S, 37; Col. Law, Univ. Iowa, J.D, 40; Pi Kappa Delta; Delta Theta Phi. Polit. & Govt. Pos: Spec. Agent, Fed. Bur. Invest, 40-46; prosecuting attorney, Cape Girardeau Co, Mo, 49-54; Mo. State Rep, 57-58; City Attorney, Cape Girardeau, 59-64; mem, Mo. State Bd. of Training Schs, 65-69; spec. asst. attorney gen, currently; chmn, Cape Girardeau Co. Rep. Cent. Cmt, currently; chmn, Tenth Cong. Dist. Rep. Cmt, currently. Bus. & Prof. Pos: Practicing Attorney, 46- Mem: Cape Girardeau Co. Bar Asn.(Pres, 60); Mo. Bar; Am. Bar Asn; Am. Trial Lawyers Asn; Rotary; Mason; Cape Girardeau Co. Club. Rel: Methodist. Legal Res: Six S. Fountain St, Cape Girardeau, Mo. 63701. Mailing Add: P.O. Box 307, Cape Girardeau, Mo. 63701.

VOGLER, JAMES B. D
N.C. State Rep.
b. Charlotte, N.C, 4/13/95; s. James A. Vogler and Susan Caroline Alexander; m. 6/12/16 to Lillian Raymells Ketchie; c. Col. James B, Jr, John T, Mrs. Louis H. Layne. Educ: Baird's Mil. Inst. Polit. & Govt. Pos: Assisted in establishment, U.S.A. Food Stamp Prog, N.C, 29; N.C. State Rep, 36-41, 45-47, 51, 55-57 & 61-; secy, N.C. Food and Grocery Distributors Code Authority during N.R.A. organizing N.C. under the N.R.A. for food and grocery indust; mem, Fair Trade Coun, Charlotte and Macklenburg Co. Mem: Pres, Nat. Asn. Food Trade Execs; Asparagus Club Int; Southeast. Food Trades Exec. Asn; past pres, Am. War Dads, Charlotte; Charlotte Optimist Club; Travelers Protective Asn; United Commercial Travelers; Mason (32°); Masonic Fel. Club; Excelsior Lodge 261, Charlotte; RAM; Scottish Rite· Azusa Grotta; Shrine Oasis Temple. Rel: Methodist. Mailing Add: 2011 Randolph Rd, Charlotte, N.C. 28801. (1967)

VOHDIN, WALTER J. D
N.J. State Assemblyman
b. Newark, N.J, 11/9/09. Polit. & Govt. Pos: N.J. State Assemblyman, 61-; mem, Adv. Coun. on Disability Benefits, Div. Employ. Security; mem, Newark Parking Authority and Essex Co. Welfare Bd. Bus. & Prof. Pos: Bus. mgr. Bricklayers, Mason, Plasterers Union Local 16, AFL-CIO. Mem: Elks. Mailing Add: 62 19th Ave, Newark, N.J. 07103. (1967)

VOIGT, CARL EMIL R
b. James, S.Dak, 5/6/95; s. Carl Voigt and Minnie Affeldt V; m. 7/3/20 to Eula Manwaring; c. Carl E, Jr. and Robert S. Educ: Huron Col, B.S, 18, hon. LL.D, 68. Polit. & Govt. Pos: Former chmn, Minnehaha Co. Rep. Cent. Cmt, S.Dak; del, Rep. Nat. Conv, 64. Bus. & Prof. Pos: Mgr, Huron Br, Northwest. Nat. Bank, until 43; pres, until 60, chmn. bd, 60-61; v.pres, Northwest Bancorporation, Minneapolis, Minn, 51; bus. consult, 60- Mil. Serv: Entered as Pvt, Army, 18, released as Cpl, 19, after serv. in Co. C, 314th Engrs, 89th Div, France and Germany. Mem: Mason (Past Grand Master); chmn, Grand Masters Conf, D.C, 64-65; Rotary (past gov, Dist. 561); Elks; Am. Legion; Greater S.Dak. Asn; past pres, Sioux Falls and Huron C. of C; Boy Scouts; YMCA; trustee, Huron Col. Received honors in football, basketball and track; Cosmopolitan's Citizen of Year, 64. Rel: Presbyterian. Mailing Add: 1603 S. Fourth Ave, Sioux Falls, S.Dak. 57105.

VOINOVICH, GEORGE V. R
b. 1936. Educ: Ohio Univ, B.A; Ohio State Univ, LL.B. Polit. & Govt. Pos: Asst. Attorney Gen, Ohio, 63; Ohio State Rep, 67-69. Bus. & Prof. Pos: Attorney. Legal Res: 17717 Crestland Rd, Cleveland, Ohio 44119. Mailing Add: 793 E. 152nd St, Cleveland, Ohio 44110.

VOLCKER, PAUL A. D
Under Secy. of the Treas. for Monetary Affairs
b. Cape May, N.J, 9/5/27; s. Paul A. Volcker and Alma Klippel V; m. to Barbara Marie Bahnson; c. Janice and James. Educ: Princeton Univ, B.A. summa cum laude, 49; Harvard Grad. Sch. of Pub. Admin, M.A. in Polit. Econ. and Govt, 51; Rotary Found. fel, London Sch. Econ, 51-52; Phi Beta Kappa. Polit. & Govt. Pos: Research asst, Fed. Reserve Bank of New York, summers 50 & 51, with Domestic Research Div, 53-55, spec. asst, Securities Dept, 55-57; jr. mgt. asst, Treas. Dept, 51, dir, Off. of Financial Anal, 62-63, Dep. Under Secy. for Monetary Affairs, 63-65, Under Secy. for Monetary Affairs, 69-; chmn, Tech. Adv. Group, Balance of Payments Adv. Cmt, Dept. of Commerce, 66 & 67. Bus. & Prof. Pos: Mem. faculty, N.Y. Inst. of Finance, 53-57; financial economist, Chase Manhattan Bank, 57-62 & 65-69. Mem: Am. Econ. Asn; Am. Finance Asn; Metrop. Econ. Asn; Nat. Asn. of Bus. Economists. Recipient, Arthur S. Flemming Award, One of Ten Outstanding Young Men in Fed. Serv; Exceptional Serv. Award, Treas. Dept, 65. Legal Res: Montclair, N.J. Mailing Add: Treasury Dept, 15th and Pennsylvania Ave, Washington, D.C. 20220.

VOLET, WILLIAM B. D
b. Brooklyn, N.Y, 3/14/03; s. Jacob Volet and Kate Yagastow V; m. 1/1/33 to Lottie Hecht; c. Andrew Martin. Educ: N.Y. Univ. Polit. & Govt. Pos:

Secy. to Judge Franklin Taylor, N.Y.C, 26-49; admin. asst. chmn, N.Y.C. Transit Authority, 49-53; exec. asst. to comptroller, State of N.Y, 55- Mem: Nat. Dem. Club; Unity Club, Brooklyn; exec. mem, Parkway Dem. Club; Lenox Hill Dem. Club; Elks; Moose. Mailing Add: 245 E. 63rd St, New York City, N.Y. 10021. (1967)

VOLK, AUSTIN NICHOLAS R
N.J. State Assemblyman
b. N.Y.C, 12/28/18; s. Nicholas Volk and Helen Diehl V; single. Educ: Brown Univ, A.B, 41; Delta Kappa Epsilon. Polit. & Govt. Pos: Councilman, Englewood, N.J, 55-56, councilman-at-lg. and pres, City Coun, 57-59, mayor, 60-63 & 66-67; N.J. State Assemblyman, 68- Bus. & Prof. Pos: V.pres, Nicholas Volk & Co, Inc, 46-69. Mil. Serv: Entered as A/S, Navy, 40, released as Lt, 46, after serv. in Amphibious Forces, S.Pac. Theatre, 42-44, reentered, 50, released as Lt. Comdr, 54, after serv. as Commanding Officer, U.S.S. Landing Ship, Tank 525 and Comdr, Oper. Develop. Force, Korea; Capt, Naval Res, 62; Atlantic Pac. Theatre Medal with three Stars; Nat. Defense Medal; Letter of Commendation; Naval Res. Medal; World War II Victory Medal. Mem: Am. Polit. Sci. Asn; Naval Order; Soc. of Am. Wars; Coun. of State Govt; Navy League; Am. Legion; VFW. Rel: Catholic. Mailing Add: 378 Walnut St, Englewood, N.J. 07631.

VOLKEMA, HAROLD JAMES R
b. Holland, Mich, 5/29/30; s. Claus Volkema and Susan DeVries V; m. 8/30/51 to Shirley Ann Bolt; c. Thomas Bolt, Barbara Jo, Jane Kay, Mary Lynn and James Lewis. Educ: Calvin Col, A.B, 53; grad. work at Mich. State Univ, West. Mich Univ. and Univ. Mich. Polit. & Govt. Pos: City councilman, Holland, Mich, 60-64; Mich. State Sen, 64-66. Bus. & Prof. Pos: Teacher, Schs. for Christian Educ, 53-62; sports dir, WHTC, 53-63; owner-mgr, Volkema's Book Stores, 62-64. Mil. Serv: Entered as Pvt, Army Nat. Guard, 48, released as Sgt, 61. Rel: Faith Christian Reformed Church. Mailing Add: 197 W. 22nd St, Holland, Mich. 49423. (1967)

VOLKEMA, RUSSELL H. D
b. Moline, Mich, 5/23/20; s. Andrew Volkema and Hazel Reminga V; m. 6/30/50 to Lois Jean; c. Colette, Daniel, Michael and Kimberly. Educ: Calvin Col, A.B, 51; Univ. Miami Sch. Law, J.D, 53; exec. ed, Miami Law Quart. Polit. & Govt. Pos: Dem. nominee for U.S. Rep, Ohio, 68. Mil. Serv: Entered as Seaman 2/C, Navy, 42, released as Lt, 46, after serv. in Naval Air Corps, Pac. Theatre, 43-45; Presidential Unit Citation; Pac. Theatre Medal with 6 Battle Stars. Publ: 'Volkema's Ohio Forms for Pleading a Negligence Case'. Mem: Phi Delta Phi; pres, Bryan Inc; Am. Bar Asn; Am. Trial Lawyers Asn.(committeeman, 67-69); Franklin Co. Trial Lawyers (pres, 62-63); Ohio Academy Trial Lawyers Asn.(pres, 64-66); Am. Legion. Rel: Christian Reformed Church. Mailing Add: 88 E. Broad St, Columbus, Ohio 43215.

VOLKER, JULIUS R
b. Lancaster, N.Y, 6/18/03; s. William J. Volker and Ermelinda Schwartz V; m. 10/15/31 to Loretta A. O'Neill; c. Joel V. and Dale M. Educ: Canisius Col, B.A, 24; Buffalo Law Sch, LL.B, 27. Polit. & Govt. Pos: Councilman, Lancaster, N.Y, 34-35, Justice of the Peace, 36-39, town attorney, 40-41, 52-53 & 55-56; N.Y. State Assemblyman, 45-66; counsel Civil Defense Cmn, 48; counsel, Constitutional Conv, 67. Mem: Erie Co. and N.Y. State Bar Asns; Elks (Past Exalted Ruler); Moose; Knights of St. John (4°); K. of C. (4°); Rotary (past pres). Rel: Roman Catholic. Mailing Add: 44 Bloomfield Ave, Depew, N.Y. 14043.

VOLLACK, ANTHONY F. D
Colo. State Sen.
b. Cheyenne, Wyo, 8/7/29; s. Luke Vollack and Opal Johnston V; m. 8/2/58 to Imojean Shelton; c. Leah A. Educ: Colo. State Univ, B.S. in econs, 51; Univ. Denver, LL.B, 56; Phi Delta Phi; Sigma Nu. Polit. & Govt. Pos: Treas, Colo. Young Dem, 59-60, pres, 60-61; pres, Jefferson Co. Young Dem, 60-61; dep. dist. attorney, First Judicial Dist, 60-61; committeeman, Jefferson Co. Dem. Party, 61-65; mem, Colo. State Dem. Cent. Cmt, 62-63; dist. capt, Jefferson Co. Dem. Cent. Cmt, 62-65; Colo. State Sen, 65- Mil. Serv: Entered as 2nd Lt, Air Force, 51, released as 1st Lt, 53. Mem: Colo. and First Judicial Dist. Bar Asns; Arvada Jr. C. of C; Elks; Friends of the Libr. League, Jefferson Co. and Arvada; dir, Jefferson Co. Chap, Nat. Found, March of Dimes; Jefferson Co. Govt. Asn; Industs. for Jefferson Co. Rel: Protestant. Mailing Add: 6360 Reed St, Arvada, Colo. 80002. (1967)

VOLPE, JOHN ANTHONY R
Secy. of Transportation
b. Wakefield, Mass, 12/8/08; s. Vito Volpe (deceased) and Philomena Benedetto V. (deceased); m. 6/18/34 to Jennie Benedetto; c. John A, Jr. and Jean (Mrs. Roger Rotondi). Educ: Westworth Inst, grad. Hon. Dr. Eng, D.P.A, L.H.D. and LL.D. Polit. & Govt. Pos: Dep. chmn, Mass. Rep. State Cmt, 50-53; Cmnr. Pub. Works, Mass, 53-56; First Fed. Hwy. Adminstr, Fed. Interstate Hwy. Prog, 56-57; Gov, Mass, 60-62 & 64-69; del, Rep. Nat. Conv, 60, 64 and 68; Secy. of Transportation, 69- Bus. & Prof. Pos: Founder, Construction Co, Malden, Mass, 33-69. Mil. Serv: Entered as Lt.(jg), Navy, 43, released as Lt. Comdr, 46, after serv. in Civil Engr. Corps. Mem: Past pres, Asn. Gen. Contractors of Am, Soc. Am. Mil. Engrs, Assoc. Gen. Contractors Mass. and Gr. Boston C. of C; state chmn, Mass. Cancer Crusade; Capitol Hill Club; Bon Secours Hosp. Guild, Methuen, De Cordova Museum; hon. mem, Columbian Squires, K. of C. Lodge 269; hon. mem, Local Union 877, Am. Fedn. of State, Co. and Munic. Employees, AFL-CIO; Italian-Am. War Vet. Rel: Catholic. Legal Res: Mass. Mailing Add: Dept. of Transportation, Washington, D.C. 20590.

VOLSTAD, EDWARD J. (EDDIE) DFL
b. Minneapolis, Minn, 1/2/96. Educ: Pub. Schs; spec. studies in elevator construction. Polit. & Govt. Pos: Minn. State Rep, 43-66. Bus. & Prof. Pos: Clothing buyer. Mem: Past Fifth Dist. Comdr, VFW; Clerks Union; Am. Legion; Chief warden, 12th Zone Air Raid Corps. 1967 Legal Res: 3327 25th Ave. S, Minneapolis, Minn. No mailing address available. (1967)

VONALT, FRED L. D
b. Angola, Ind, 2/2/42; s. Paul Christian Vonalt and Eula Faye Garrell V; m. 9/22/62 to Margaret Ellen Palumbo; c. Christina and Faye. Educ: Bowling Green State Univ, B.S.Ed, 64; Mich. State Univ, 68-69. Polit. & Govt. Pos: Mem, Sandusky Co. Dem. Exec. Cmt, Ohio, 65-68; city councilman, Fremont, Ohio, 66-67; alternate del, Dem. Nat. Conv, 68. Bus. & Prof. Pos: Teacher, Ross High Sch, Fremont, Ohio, 64-67, Bettsville High Sch, Ohio, 67-68 and Marysville schs, Marysville, Mich, 68- Mem: Marysville, Mich. and Nat. Educ. Asns. Mailing Add: 1320 Colorado Ave, Marysville, Mich. 48040.

VonBLASKEWICZ, BETTY JANE R
V.Chmn, Delta Co. Rep. Party, Mich.
b. Detroit, Mich, 10/8/22; d. Earle Moore Porter and Vera Donovan P; m. 9/1/50 to Henry Robert VonBlaskewicz; c. Christine and William. Educ: Cass Tech. High Sch, 4 years. Polit. & Govt. Pos: V.chmn, Delta Co. Rep. Party, 69- Bus. & Prof. Pos: Charge clerk, J.L. Hudson Co, Detroit, Mich, 41-42; receptionist, Smith & Wilks, 42-46; off. clerk, Gen. Motors Bldg, 46-50. Mem: Child's Welfare Club of Gladstone, Mich. Rel: Protestant. Mailing Add: 1611 Minneapolis Ave, Gladstone, Mich. 49837.

von CHRISTIERSON, KARL R
Mem, Calif. Rep. State Cent. Exec. Cmt.
b. Madera, Calif, 1/20/16; s. Sune von Christierson and Katheryn Gilbert C; m. 1/11/40 to Elise Shryock; c. Sigurd and Eric. Educ: Temple Univ, 2 years; Univ. Calif, Davis, summer courses. Polit. & Govt. Pos: Mayor, Soledad, Calif, 44-52; trustee, Soledad Elem. Sch, 48-52 and Monterey Co. Salinas Elem. Sch. Dist, 54-58; mem, Monterey Co. Rep. Cent. Cmt, 58-, chmn, 61-68; mem, Rep. State Cent. Finance Cmt, 60-; mem, Calif. Rep. Assembly, 60-; chmn, Rep. Co. Chmn. Asn, 62-66; mem, Calif. Rep. State Cent. Exec. Cmt, 62-; secy, Rep. State Cent. Cmt, 64-68; mem, Calif. Rep. League, 64- Mem: Growers-Shipper Vegetable Asn.(chmn, research cmt, 66-67); Farm Bur; founding dir, Calif. Tomato Growers Asn.(chmn, grower-shipper legis. cmt, 67-); Hort. Crops Adv. Cmt, Wash, D.C; Commonwealth Club; Corral de Tierra Country Club; Press & Union League; Capitol Hill Club. Silver Beaver Award. Rel: Episcopal. Legal Res: 1370 Byron Dr, Apt. 32, Salinas, Calif. 93901. Mailing Add: P.O. Box 719, Salinas, Calif. 93901.

VON HOLTUM, JOHN E. DFL
Chmn, Nobles Co. Dem-Farmer-Labor Party, Minn.
b. Tyler, Minn, 11/27/26; s. Edmund Von Holtum and Ellen Maher V; m. 8/26/49 to Patricia M. Hefferan; c. Edmund Dennis, Michael John, Katherine, Ellen, Elizabeth, William, John and Patrick. Educ: Univ. Minn, B.S, 49 and LL.B, 50. Polit. & Govt. Pos: Former dep. registr. of motor vehicles, Minn; chmn, Nobles Co. Dem-Farmer-Labor Party, presently and secy, 60-65. Mil. Serv: Entered as Pvt, Army, 44, released as Cpl, 47, after serv. in 8th Photo Tech. Squadron, ETO, 46; Good Conduct Medal; ETO Ribbon. Mem: Am. and Minn. State Bar Asns; Am. Trial Lawyer's Asn; Elks; VFW; Am. Legion; C. of C. Rel: Roman Catholic. Mailing Add: 803 West Lake Ave, Worthington, Minn. 56187.

VOORHEES, DONALD EDWIN R
Iowa State Rep.
b. Winfield, Kans, 9/8/30; s. Martin J. Voorhees and Margaret Kanitz V; m. 9/8/48 to Laurene Ann Chambers; c. Nancy (Mrs. Richard Richter), Donald Edwin, Jr, Susan Laurene and Ross Lee. Educ: Bus. Course, Am. Sch, Chicago. Polit. & Govt. Pos: Iowa State Rep, 67- Mem: Hon. mem, VFW; Elks; all local off, Hutchinson Jaycees; state v.pres, Kans. Jaycees, 55-56; nat. dir, Iowa Jaycees, 65-66. Rel: Lutheran, Mo. Synod. Mailing Add: 2201 W. Fourth, Waterloo, Iowa 50701.

VOORHIS, HORACE JERRY D
b. Ottawa, Kans, 4/6/01; s. Charles Brown Voorhis and Ella Ward Smith V; m. 11/27/24 to Alice Louise Livingston; c. Alice Nell, Charles Brown and Jerry Livingston. Educ: Yale, A.B, 23; Claremont Col, M.A, 28; St. Francis Xavier Univ, LL.D, 53. Polit. & Govt. Pos: U.S. Rep, Calif, 37-47. Bus. & Prof. Pos: Traveling rep, YMCA in Germany, 23-24; worker, Ford Assembly Plant, Charlotte, N.C, 24-25; teacher, Allendale Farm Sch, Lake Villo, Ill, 25-26; dir, Dray Cottage, Home for Boys, Laramie, Wyo, 26-27; head master and trustee, Voorhis Sch. for Boys, 28-37; spec. lectr, Pomona Col, 30-35; secy, Group Health Asn. Am, 47-; exec. dir, Coop. League of U.S, 47-67, consult, 67- Mem: Am. Pub. Health Asn; Nat. Cath. Rural Life Conf; Am. Country Life Asn; Phi Delta Kappa; Phi Beta Kappa; United World Fedns. Publ: Out of Debt, Out of Danger, Confessions of a Congressman, The Christian in Politics; Am. Coops. Rel: Episcopal. Legal Res: 736 Oak St, Winnetka, Ill. 60093. Mailing Add: 53 W. Jackson Blvd, Chicago, Ill. 60604.

VOSS, JOHN HARM R
Kans. State Sen.
b. Downs, Kans, 6/18/89; s. George Voss and Elizabeth Buikstra V; wid; c. Lorraine and Althea. Polit. & Govt. Pos: Chmn, Osborne Co. Rep. Party; Rep. precinct committeeman; treas, State Rep. Cmt; del, Rep. Nat. Conv, 60; Kans. State Sen, 24th Dist, 63-64 & 67- Bus. & Prof. Pos: Owner, Voss Implement & Supply. Co, Voss Grain & Seed Co, Inc. and Voss. Mfg. & Distributing, 12- Mem: Kans. Livestock Asn; Kans. Grain Dealers Asn.(dir); State Grain Adv. Cmt; C. of C; Elks; AF&AM; Royal Order of Jesters; Farm Bur; Rotary; Shrine; exec. cmt, Coronado Coun. Boy Scouts; Beloit Country Club. Rel: Methodist. Mailing Add: 511 Division, Downs, Kans. 67437.

VOSS, WILLARD NEW D
Chmn, Ripley Co. Dem. Cent. Cmt, Ind.
b. Milan, Ind; s. Henry Voss and Mary Luhing V; single. Educ: Milan High Sch, Ind, grad, 17. Polit. & Govt. Pos: Treas, Ripley Co. Dem. Cent. Cmt, Ind, 29-32, chmn, 64-; clerk, Ripley Co. Circuit Court, 34-41; mgr, Milan License Br, 65-69. Rel: Protestant. Mailing Add: Route 2, Milan, Ind. 47031.

VOSTI, LAURENCE R
Mem, Calif. Rep. State Cent. Cmt.
b. Salinas, Calif, 5/21/40; s. John A. Vosti and Dorothy Graham V; married. Educ: Univ. Calif, Berkeley, A.B, 64. Polit. & Govt. Pos: Coordinator, Bay Area Cols. and mem, Alameda Co. Coord. Cmt, Rockefeller for Pres, 64; v.pres, South Co. Young Rep, Calif, 65; v.pres, Alameda Co. Young Rep, 66, chmn, 67-68; treas. Alameda Co, Robert Finch for Lt. Gov, 66; mem, Alameda Co. Coord.

Cmt, Flournoy for Controller, 66; mem. coord. cmt, Lewis Sherman for State Sen, 66; mem. bd. dirs, East Bay Rep. Alliance, Calif, 66-69, treas, 68-69; mem. bd. dirs, Calif. Young Rep, 67-68; mem, Calif. Rep. State Cent. Cmt, 67-; mem. speakers bur, Nixon for Pres, 68; pub. rels. chmn, Ray Moser for State Assemblyman, 68; trustee, Bay Area Rep. Alliance, 68-69; mem. adv. cmt, State Sen. Lewis Sherman, 68-69. Bus. & Prof. Pos: Mgr. commercial div, Adams & Adams Realtors, Castro Valley, 64-68; pres, Cultural Condominium Inc, San Francisco, 66-69; in real estate sales and develop, Grubb & Ellis Co, Oakland, 68- Mil. Serv: Entered as Pvt, Army, 61, released as SP-5, 67, after serv. in 458th Mil. Intel. Unit. Rel: Epsicopal. Mailing Add: 65 L Red Hill Circle, Tiburon, Calif. 94920.

VOXLAND, ROY L. Conservative
Minn. State Rep.
b. Goodhue Co, 1899; married; c. Five. Educ: Sch. of Agr, Univ. of Minn. Polit. & Govt. Pos: Former supvr, S. Goodhue Soil Conserv. Dist; former twp. supvr; Minn. State Rep, 45-, chmn, Minn. Legis. Bldg. Cmn. Bus. & Prof. Pos: Farmer. Mem: Active in farm and Community orgns. Mailing Add: R.F.D, Kenyon, Minn. 55946.

VRDOLYAK, EDWARD ROBERT D
Committeeman, Ill. Dem. Cent. Cmt.
b. Chicago, Ill, 12/28/37; s. Peter J. Vrdolyak and Matilda Vrdolyak V; m. 9/8/62 to Denise M. Danaher; c. Peter T. and John K. Educ: St. Joseph Col, Ind, A.B, 59; Univ. Chicago, J.D, 63. Polit. & Govt. Pos: Committeeman, Ill. Dem. Cent. Cmt, 68- Bus. & Prof. Pos: Attorney-at-law, 63- Mem: Chicago Bar Asn; Am. Judicature Soc; Tenth Ward Dem. Club; former state legal adv, all League of United Latin Am. Citizens Coun. in Ill; chmn, Boy Scouts Fund Dr; K. of C.(4°); Lions; C. of C; El Dallo Club; Eagles. Rel: Catholic. Legal Res: 1630 E. 92nd St, Chicago, Ill. 60617. Mailing Add: 1925 E. 95th St, Chicago, Ill. 60617.

VREELAND, GEORGE WASHINGTON, JR. R
Mem, Calif. Rep. State Cent. Cmt.
b. Stevbenville, Ohio, 1/2/19; s. George W. Vreeland and Maritta York Sisson V; m. 1/24/48 to Virginia Aileen Sisson; c. Maritta Sisson and Harriet Ann. Educ: Cornell Univ, B.S. in A.E; Phi Delta Theta. Polit. & Govt. Pos: Div. chmn, Rep. Precinct Orgn. 47th Assembly Dist, Calif, 56, area chmn, 60-69; mem, Calif. Rep. State Cent. Cmt, 64-; unit and assembly dist. chmn, United Rep. of Calif, 66- Bus. & Prof. Pos: Various eng. capacities, U.S. Steel Corp, 48-69. Mil. Serv: Entered as 2nd Lt, Army Ord. Dept, 41, released as Capt, 46, after serv. in 350th Ord. Bn, S. Pac, 43-46; Res, Maj.(Ret). Mem: Am. Soc. Metals; Am. Soc. Iron and Steel Engrs; Am. Soc. Non-Destructive Testing. Rel: Episcopal. Mailing Add: 3425 Huntington Dr, Pasadena, Calif. 91107.

VUKASIN, JOHN PETER, JR. R
Mem, Calif.Rep. State Cent. Cmt.
b. Oakland, Calif, 5/25/28; s. John Peter Vukasin and Natalie Lubibratich V; m. 7/1/56 to Carol Sue Davis; c. John Peter, III, Kirk Edwin, Alexander George, Kim Joan and Karen Lynn. Educ: Univ. Calif, A.B, 50, Sch. Law, J.D, 56; Phi Kappa Phi; Phi Delta Phi; Sigma Phi. Polit. & Govt. Pos: Alameda Co. chmn, Nixon-Lodge Campaign Cmt, 60; mem, Calif. Rep. State Cent. Cmt, 62-; chmn, Bay Area Rep. Alliance, 63; v.chmn, Goldwater for President Campaign Cmt, Calif, 64; del, Rep. Nat. Conv, 64. Bus. & Prof. Pos: Attorney-at-law, 56; secy, Feran, Inc, 62-; arbitrator, Am. Arbit. Asn, 63-; vis. prof. of bus. law, Calif. State Col, currently. Mil. Serv: Army, 51-53. Publ: Digest of California Cases on Eminent Domain, Calif. Dept. of Pub. Works, 57; 'The Anti-Merger Law of the United States: Yesterday, Today, Tomorrow,' Antitrust Bul, 5-6/58; 'The Grand Jury, Useful or Useless,' J. of the State Bar of Calif, 7-8/59. Mem: Am. and Alameda Co. Bar Asns; Am. Bar Asn. Sect. on Corp. Banking and Bus. Law; State Bar of Calif; Am. Arbitration Asn; Calif. State Automobile Accident Study Cmn. and chmn, Accident Prev. Cmt; Alameda Co. Retirement Bd; dir, East Bay Activity Center for Emotionally Disturbed Children; life mem, Univ. Calif. Alumni Asn; dir, Univ. Club of Alameda Co; Athenian-Nile Club; Yerba Buena Lodge 403, F&AM, Oakland Consistory, Scottish Rite; Rotary. Rel: Serbian Eastern Orthodox. Legal Res: 250 Sheridan Ave, Piedmont, Calif. 94611. Mailing Add: Suite 1515, Financial Center Bldg, Oakland, Calif. 94612. (1967)

VUKELICH, THOMAS D. DFL
b. Virginia, Minn, 7/9/09; married; c. Six. Educ: Virginia Jr. Col; Winona Teachers Col. Polit. & Govt. Pos: City assessor, Gilbert, Minn, 35-38; Minn. State Rep, 39-45; Minn. State Sen, 45-66. Bus. & Prof. Pos: Supvr, St. Louis Co. Bd. of Educ, presently. Mem: Gilbert C. of C; K. of C. Mailing Add: 312 Nebraska Ave, Gilbert, Minn. 55741.

VUKOVICH, GEORGE D
b. Youngstown, Ohio, 9/8/26; s. John Vukovich and Mary Vukovich V; m. 6/24/50 to Helen Bogovich; c. Carol and Sonia. Educ: Youngstown Univ, 1 year; Lincoln Mgt. Inst. Polit. & Govt. Pos: Dem. councilman, Seventh Ward, Youngstown, Ohio, 60-64; clerk of the munic. courts, Youngstown, Ohio, 64-; alternate del, Dem. Nat. Conv, 68. Mil. Serv: Entered as Pvt, Army, 51, released as Cpl, 53, after serv. in Inf, ETO, 51-52; Army Leadership Sch. Award; Good Conduct Medal. Mem: Ohio Asn. Munic. Courtclerks; Croatian Fraternal Union; Slovak Catholic Sokols; Elks; Lions; Dem. Club; Am. Croatian Citizens; Ursuline Sisters Century Club; Soc. for the Blind and Disabled; Urban League; CWV; USW; Resolution of Serv, City of Youngstown, 64. Councilman Serv. Award, Seventh Ward; Man of the Year 1967, L.O.B.S. 1 Lodge. Rel: Catholic. Mailing Add: 2640 Cooper St, Youngstown, Ohio 44502.

W

WACKETT, BYRON F. R
Wis. State Assemblyman
b. Randolph, Wis, 3/21/12. Educ: Randolph pub. schs. Polit. & Govt. Pos: Mayor, Watertown, Wis, 46-49; Wis. State Assemblyman, 52- Bus. & Prof. Pos: Serv. station operator; former salesman. Mem: Past pres, Wis. Asn. of Petroleum Retailers; chmn, Watertown Chap. Red Cross, 50-52. Mailing Add: 100 Oak Hill Court, Watertown, Wis. 53094. (1967)

WADDELL, JAMES MADISON, JR. D
S.C. State Sen.
b. Boydell, Ark, 11/1/22; s. James Madison Waddell, Sr. and Mabel Gibson W; m. 1/2/46 to Natalie Lavis; c. James M, V, Michael Gibson and John Spencer. Educ: The Citadel, B.S. in Civil Eng, 47. Polit. & Govt. Pos: S.C. State Rep, 55-60; S.C. State Sen, 60- Bus. & Prof. Pos: Gen. agent, Pilot Life Ins. Co, 49-; pres, Citizens Ins. Agency, 55- and Riveracres Develop. Corp, Beaufort, S.C, 63- Mil. Serv: Entered Orgn. Res. Corps, 42, active duty, Inf, 43-46, Capt, serv. in 335th Inf. Regt, 84th Inf. Div, Germany; Purple Heart; Europe-Africa-Mid. East. Ribbon with Two Battle Stars; Am. Theatre Medal; Victory Medal; Combat Inf. Badge. Mem: Past pres, C. of C; mem. bd. regents, Beaufort Mem. Hosp; Mason; Beaufort Yacht Club; Asn. Citadel Men; Navy League; DAV; Moose; Retired Officers' Asn; Sertoma; Nat. Sojourners; VFW. Rel: Presbyterian; Elder, First Presbyterian Church, Beaufort, S.C. Mailing Add: Battery Creek, P.O. Box 547, Beaufort, S.C. 29902.

WADDINGHAM, A. THORPE D
b. Milford, Utah, 8/19/23; s. Lindsay Bailey Waddingham and Lois Bohn W; m. 5/29/46 to Norma Michaelsen; c. Brent Michael Dana Lee, Lois Ann, Linda LaRue and Richard Thorpe. Educ: Snow Col, 47-48; George Washington Univ, LL.B, 51; Phi Delta Phi. Polit. & Govt. Pos: City attorney, Delta, Utah, 58-63; Utah State Sen, 59-67, chmn, Standing Cmt. on Educ. and Welfare, Utah State Senate, 59-61, mem, Utah Legis. Coun, 59-63, v.chmn, 61-62, chmn, Legis. Auditing Cmt, 61-63; pres. of the Senate, 61-62, Majority Leader, 65-67; chmn, Utah Del, West. States Water Coun, 65-; mem. adv. cmt, State Tech. Serv. Act, Utah, 66- Mil. Serv: Entered as Cadet Pvt, Air Force, 42, released as 1st Lt, 46, after serv. in 15th Air Force, ETO, 44-46; ETO Ribbon; Purple Heart; Air Medal. Mem: Utah State Bar Asn.(pres, 63); Utah State Bar Cmn, 58-63; South. Utah Bar Asn; VFW; Am. Legion; Kiwanis. Distinguished Serv. Award, Utah Jr. C. of C, 57. Rel: Latter-day Saint. Mailing Add: Box 177, Delta, Utah 84624.

WADDINGTON, JOHN A.
b. Salem, N.J, 5/10/11; s. John R. Waddington and Irene W; m. 1933 to Kathryn Mulhern; c. John T. and Preston L. Educ: Univ. Del, A.B. in Bus. Admin; Rutgers Univ, grad. study. Polit. & Govt. Pos: N.J. State Assemblyman, 54-55; N.J. State Sen, 56-69, Minority Leader, 58, Majority Leader, 66 & 67; mem, N.J. Adv. Cmt. to Nat. Civil Rights Cmt. and chmn, 58-60; chmn, Salem Co. Human Rels. Cmt; asst. dir, Salem Co. Bd. of Freeholders, 69, freeholder, 69- Bus. & Prof. Pos: Coach and teacher, Salem High Sch, N.J, 32-34; personnel supvr, E.I. Dupont Co, 35-; instr, evening sch, Rutgers Univ, 42-45; relief and rehabilitation worker in Italy, Am. Friends Serv. Cmt, 45-46. Rel: Society of Friends. Mailing Add: Light House Rd, Route 3, Salem, N.J. 08079.

WADE, EDWIN WINSLOW
Mayor, Long Beach, Calif.
b. Jamestown, N.Dak, 10/15/03; s. Harry M. Wade and Marian A. Eaton W; m. 11/18/25 to Mary Bruce Garrick; c. Betty Jo. Educ: Student in Eng, Correspondence Sch. Polit. & Govt. Pos: Mayor, Long Beach, Calif, currently. Bus. & Prof. Pos: Sales engr, South. Eng. Co, Wilmington, Calif, 33-35; partner and gen. mgr, Marine Specialty Co, 35-41, pres. and gen. mgr, Marine Specialty Co, Inc, 41- Mem: Chmn, Armed Serv. Cmn, Long Beach, Calif; Independent Bus. Mens Asn. of Gr. Long Beach; past patron, Eastern Star; Mason (past pres, Long Beach Chap). Legal Res: 4155 Greenbrier Rd, Long Beach, Calif. 90808. Mailing Add: Gaylord and Hayes, Long Beach, Calif. 90813.

WADE, GEORGE N. R
Pa. State Sen.
b. Emlenton, Pa, 8/13/98; m. to Anna Ruth Platt. Polit. & Govt. Pos: Mem, Camp Hill Sch; mem, Camp Hill Borough Coun; Pa. State Rep, 30-34; Pa. State Sen, 40- Bus. & Prof. Pos: Former East. Mgr, Ohio Nat. Life Ins. Co; chmn. bd, Cumberland Co. Nat. Bank & Trust Co. Mil. Serv: A.E.F, World War I, France. Mem: Past Comdr, Am. Legion; past pres, Ohio Nat. Builders' Club; pres, Harrisburg Commun. Chest; chmn, Harrisburg Area Commun. Chest War Fund, 44. Mailing Add: 312 N. 26th St, Camp Hill, Pa. 17011.

WADE, HUGH JOSEPH D
b. Dougherty, Iowa, 6/29/01; s. John Francis Wade and Mary Dougherty W; m. 6/29/33 to Madge Clara Case; c. Hugh Gerald, Suzanne (Mrs. McKeown) and Michael Howard. Educ: Univ. of Iowa, LL.B, 24; Phi Kappa. Polit. & Govt. Pos: Agent, Fed. Bur. Invest, 25-28; Alaska dir, Nat. Recovery Admin, 33-34; attorney, Social Security Bd, 35-36; territorial dir, Fed. Security Agency, 37-50; area dir, Alaska Off. Bur. Indian Affairs, Alaska Native Serv, 50-53; treas, Territory of Alaska, 54-59; former Secy. of State Alaska. Bus. & Prof. Pos: Attorney, private practice, 24-25; attorney, Nelson Bros. Bond & Mortgage, 28-30 and Eskimo Pie Corp, 30-31; asst. to pres, West. TV Corp, 31-33. Mem: Am. and Alaska Bar Asns; Rotary; Pioneers of Alaska. Rel: Catholic. Mailing Add: 628 Basin Rd, Juneau, Alaska 99801. (1967)

WADE, RICHARD CLEMENT D
b. Des Moines, Iowa, 7/14/22; s. Clement F. Wade and Mabel McNichols W; m. 8/21/48 to Louise Carroll. Educ: Univ. Rochester, B.A. & M.A; Harvard Univ, M.A. & Ph.D. Polit. & Govt. Pos: N.Y. State v.chmn, Stevenson-Kefauver Cmt, 56; N.Y. State v.chmn, Kennedy-Johnson Cmt, 60; chmn, Ill. Citizens for Kennedy, 68; chmn, Ill. Citizens for McGovern, 68; del, Dem. Nat. Conv, 68; cmnr, Chicago Housing Authority, 69- Bus. & Prof. Pos: Prof. Am. hist, Univ. Chicago, 62- Publ: The Urban Frontier, Harvard Univ, 59; Slavery in the Cities, Oxford Univ, 64; Chicago, Growth of a Metropolis, Univ. Chicago, 69. Mailing Add: 5422 S. Blackstone Ave, Chicago, Ill. 60615.

WADESON, HARRY R
b. Alice, N.Dak, 7/20/96; married; c. one. Educ: Pub. schs, Alice, N.Dak. Polit. & Govt. Pos: N.Dak. State Rep, 47-51; N.Dak. State Sen, 53-61. Bus. & Prof. Pos: Farmer; pres, Fingal State Bank. Mil. Serv: World War II. Mailing Add: Alice, N.Dak. 58003. (1967)

WADSWORTH, CHARLIE DOSTER Independent
b. Autauga, Ala, 2/10/80; s. Malcolm Smith Wadsworth and Petonia Alexander W; m. 6/25/02 to Mary Ethel Smyly, wid; c. Sadie Sophronia, Charles

Danile, Clara Nell, Alma Ruth and William Wood. Educ: Univ. Ala, 3 years. Polit. & Govt. Pos: Chmn. and Secy, Dem. Exec. Cmt, Autauga Co, Ala, 40 years; state and co. tax collector, 11 years; mem, Dem. Exec. Cmt, Prattville, Ala, 2 years; justice of peace; appraiser, Fed. Land Bank; chmn. bd. trustees, Prattville Sch; mem. and chmn, Ration Bd, World War II. Bus. & Prof. Pos: Agent-distributor, Standard Oil Co, Ky, 21-53. Mem: 25 Year Club, Standard Oil Co; Univ. Ala. Alumni Asn; Lions; Farm Bur. Rel: Methodist; chmn, Wesley Bible Class. Mailing Add: 439 N. Chestnut St, Prattville, Ala. 36067.

WADSWORTH, HERBERT ROBINSON, JR. D

b. Live Oak, Fla, 6/15/31; s. Herbert Wadsworth and Susie Kinnard W. Educ: Univ. Fla, B.S, 53; Fla. Blue Key; Sigma Delta Chi; bus. mgr, Fla. Alligator; Sigma Alpha Epsilon. Polit. & Govt. Pos: Admin. asst, Rep. Fuqua (Fla.), 62- Bus. & Prof. Pos: Ed, Suwannee Dem. Newspaper, 53-61. Mem: Fla. Press Asn, bd. dir; Jaycees, pres, v.pres, nat. dir; Kiwanis, pres; C. of C, v.pres; Mason, worshipful master, dist. dep. grandmaster; Shriner; Childrens Com. of Morocco Temple. Numerous awards, including Ed.Oscar; Outstanding Young Man, Suwannee Co, 54. Rel: Presbyterian. Legal Add: Live Oak, Fla. 32060. Mailing Add: 458 New Jersey Ave. S.E, Washington, D.C. 20003. (1967)

WADSWORTH, JAMES J. R

Mem, Fed. Communications Cmn.

b. Groveland, N.Y, 6/12/05; s. James Wolcott Wadsworth, Jr. and Alice Hay W; m. 6/16/27 to Harty Griggs Tilton (deceased 12/31/65); c. Alice Tilton (Mrs. Trowbridge Strong); m. 5/22/67 to Mary A. Donaldson. Educ: Yale, A.B, 27; Alfred Univ, LL.D, 37; Bowdoin Col, LL.D, 64. Polit. & Govt. Pos: N.Y. State Assemblyman, 31-41; dir. pub. serv. div, War Assets Admin, 45-46; spec. asst. to adminstr, Econ. Coop. Admin, 48-50; acting dir, Civil Defense Off, 50; dep. adminstr, Fed. Civil Defense Admin, 51; Dep. U.S. Rep. to UN, 53-60, permanent U.S. Rep. to UN, 60-61; mem, Fed. Communications Cmn, 65- Bus. & Prof. Pos: Asst. mgr, Indust. Rels, Curtiss Wright Corp, Buffalo, 41-45; dir, Govt. Affairs Dept, Air Transport Asn. of Am, 46-48; chmn. bd. of trustees, Freedom House, 61; pres, Peace Research Inst, 61-62. Publ: Auth, The Price of Peace; The Glass House. Mem: Trustee, People to People, U.S. Cmt. Dag Hammarskjold Found; bd. dir, U.S. Cmt. for UN; Meridian Found; UN Asn, USA, V.Pres, 64-; Coun. For. Rels; Chevy Chase Club Int, Pres, 63- (Wash); Yale Club (N.Y). Rel: Episcopal. Mailing Add: 6717 Tulip Hill Terr, Washington, D.C. 20016.

WADSWORTH, JAMES LEO D

Dist. Attorney, Lincoln Co, Nev.

b. Alamo, Nev, 5/21/22; s. James Allen Wadsworth and Lois Stewart W; m. 9/26/51 to Kathleen Vickers; c. James Vickers and Felicia Kathleen. Educ: Brigham Young Univ, A.B, 48; George Wash. Univ, J.D, 52. Polit. & Govt. Pos: Nev. State Assemblyman, Lincoln Co, 49-50; admin. asst. to Dir, Off. Airports, Civil Aeronaut. Admin, 50-52; dist. attorney, Esmeralda Co, Nev, 60-62; asst. city attorney, North Las Vegas, 63-64, assoc. city judge, 64-66; dist. attorney, Lincoln Co, 66- Mailing Add: Box 446, Pioche, Nev. 89043.

WADSWORTH, WILLIAM L. D

b. Hawthorne, Fla, 5/6/14; m. to Frances E. Faulkner; c. Susan Lotta, Penelope Gail and Whilhelmenia L. Educ: Univ. Fla; The Citadel, A.B, 38; Stetson Univ, LL.B, 49. Polit. & Govt. Pos: Fla. State Rep, 56-66; Circuit Judge, Fla, 67- Bus. & Prof. Pos: Attorney. Mil. Serv: Army, World War II. Rel: Presbyterian. Mailing Add: P.O. Box 896, Bunnell, Fla. 32010. (1967)

WAGENSELLER, SHERMAN FREDERICK R

Chmn, Los Angeles Co. Rep. Cent. Cmt, Calif.

b. Los Angeles, Calif, 6/22/27; s. Hudson Henry Wagenseller and Florence Dimity W; m. 7/21/63 to Janet Triplett; c. Hudson Whitney, Sharman Kathleen, Trent Bradford, Ward Frederick and Laine Triplett. Educ: Univ. of South. Calif, 46-48. Polit. & Govt. Pos: Mem, Calif. Rep. State Cent. Cmt, 64-; mem, Los Angeles Co. Rep. Cent. Cmt, 60th Dist, 64-; chmn, currently; mem, Dist. Attorney Adv. Cmt, Los Angeles Co, 66-69; v.pres, Young Rep. Los Angeles Co; membership and orgn. chmn, Calif. Young Rep. Bus. & Prof. Pos: Pres, Swag Oil Co, 59-; v.pres, Merchants Exchange Bldg, Inc, 66-, Cooper Bldg. Co, Inc, 66- and Wagenseller & Durst Security Corp, 67- Mil. Serv: Entered as Seaman 2/C, Navy, 45, released as AMM 3/C, 46, after serv. in Naval Air Force; Victory Medal. Mem: Rotary Int; Trojan Club. Rel: Presbyterian. Mailing Add: 1767 Old Ranch Rd, Los Angeles, Calif. 90049.

WAGER, ELI D

N.Y. State Assemblyman

b. N.Y.C, 2/2/26; s. Nathan Wager and Rose Kligman W; m. 1/22/49 to Lila G. Kupferberg; c. Daryl Lynne and Ruth Ellen. Educ: City Col, N.Y, B.B.A; N.Y. Law Sch, LL.B. Polit. & Govt. Pos: N.Y. State Assemblyman, 20th Assembly Dist, 65-66, 15th Assembly Dist, 66-67 & 68- Bus. & Prof. Pos: Partner, Wager & Shane, 62-66, Wager, Shane & Ehrlich, 66-69 and Wager & Ehrlich, 69- Mil. Serv: Entered as Pvt, Army, 44, released as S/Sgt, 46, after serv. in Third and 70th Inf. Div, ETO, 45-46; Two Battle Stars. Publ: Author of five studies on town govt. Mem: King and Nassau Co. Criminal Bar Asns; Am, Brooklyn and Nassau Co. Bar Asns; N.Y. State Bar; VFW; Jewish War Vet; Am. Legion; Kiwanis; Mason. Rel: Jewish. Legal Res: 615 Woodmere Blvd, Woodmere, N.Y. 11598. Mailing Add: 158 Third St, Mineola, N.Y. 11501.

WAGER, ROBERT D

b. Rockford, Ill, 3/3/34; s. Maurice P. Wager and Ruth Kanter W; m. 7/3/66 to Deborah Miller. Educ: Pomona Col, B.A, 56; Stanford Law Sch, LL.B, 59; Harvard Law Sch, LL.M, 60. Polit. & Govt. Pos: Attorney, Anti-trust Div, Dept. of Justice, 60-61; legal asst. to Gerald H. Brown, Nat. Labor Rels. Bd, 61-63; legis. asst. to U.S. Rep. James C. Corman, 63-64; asst. to dep. chmn, Dem. Nat. Cmt. and asst. counsel, Spec. Equal Rights Cmt, 65-66; counsel, Senate Subcmt. on Exec. Reorgn, Senate Cmt. on Govt. Opers, 66- Publ: Democratic Registration and Get-Out-The-Vote Manual, 66. Mailing Add: 103 G St. S.W, Washington, D.C. 20024. (1967)

WAGGONER, JAMES THOMAS, JR. D

Ala. State Rep.

b. Birmingham, Ala, 1/8/37; s. James Thomas Waggoner and Nell Harris W; m. 3/14/58 to Marilyn Louise Mitchell; c. Mark Thomas, Scott Mitchell and Marilyn Ann. Educ: Auburn Univ, $2\frac{1}{2}$ years; Birmingham South. Col, A.B; Birmingham Sch. Law, LL.B. and J.D; Alpha Kappa Psi; Eta Sigma Phi; Sigma Delta Kappa; Kappa Alpha Order. Polit. & Govt. Pos: Ala. State Rep, Jefferson Co, 66- Mem: Indust. Developers Asn, Ala; Civitan; Mason; Shrine; Eagles; YMCA; PTA; chmn, Jefferson Co. Cystic Fibrosis Fund Drive, 68. Rel: Church of Christ. Legal Res: 1829 Mission Rd, Birmingham, Ala. 35216. Mailing Add: P.O. Box 2641, Birmingham, Ala. 35202.

WAGGONER, ROBERT ERNEST R

b. Elgin, Ill, 10/4/18; s. Ernest C. Waggoner and Madeline Sadler W; m. 12/20/42 to Beverly Jean Giedd; c. Jeffrey R, Melissa and Priscilla. Educ: Northwest. Univ, B.S.S, 41; Univ. S.Dak, M.A, 47. Polit. & Govt. Pos: Asst. bill clerk, U.S. House Rep, Wash, D.C, 53; exec. dir, Iowa Rep. State Cent. Cmt, 54, admin. asst, U.S. Sen. Thomas E. Martin, Iowa, 55-57; Rep. cand, U.S. House Rep, Sixth Dist, 58; spec. asst, Exec. Off. President, 59; regional dir, Off. Civil & Defense Mobilization, Denver, Colo, 60-61; admin. asst, U.S. Rep. Donald G. Brotzman, Second Dist, Colo, 63-64; exec. secy, Gov. John A. Love, Denver, Colo, 65- Bus. & Prof. Pos: Instr. polit. sci. and speech, Ft. Dodge Jr. Col, Iowa, 47-53; west. regional mgr, Wonder Steel Corp, Denver, Colo, 62. Mil. Serv: Army, 42-46. Rel: Congregational. Mailing Add: 10581 W. 22nd Place, Lakewood, Colo. 80215.

WAGGONER, SAM W. D

State Hwy. Cmnr, Miss.

b. Leake Co, Miss, 10/22/22; s. Sam Wilder Waggoner, Jr. and Ruth Ayres W; m. 4/3/46 to Mary Elizabeth Smith; c. Joe Ayres and Mary Jane. Educ: Univ. Miss, B.S. in Civil Eng, 43; Am. Soc. of Civil Eng; Sigma Theta Psi; Phi Kappa Psi. Polit. & Govt. Pos: State hwy. cmnr, Miss, 68- Bus. & Prof. Pos: Co. engr, Newton Co, Miss, 63-67; city engr, Brandon and Newton, 63-67. Mil. Serv: Entered as A/S, Navy, 42, released as Lt.(jg), 47, after serv. in U.S.S. Nutmeg, ETO, 44-46; Naval Res.(Ret). Mem: Miss. Soc. of Prfnl. Engrs; Am. Legion (past state comdr, Miss); VFW; 40 et 8; Mason; Moose; past pres, Newton Jr. C. of C; state chmn, Pub. Educ. Cmt; bd. dir, Am. Cancer Soc, Miss; Gov. Cmt. to Keep Miss. Beautiful; Farm Bur. Rel: Baptist. Legal Res: 109 Bingham St, Newton, Miss. 39345. Mailing Add: P.O. Box 214, Newton, Miss. 39345.

WAGGONNER, JOE D, JR. D

U.S. Rep, La.

b. Plain Dealing, La, 9/7/18; s. Joe D. Waggonner, Sr. and Elizzibeth Johnston W; m. 12/14/42 to Mary Ruth Carter; c. David and Carol Jean. Educ: La. Polytech. Inst, B.A. Polit. & Govt. Pos: Mem, Bossier Parish Sch. Bd, 54 & 60, pres, 56; mem, La. State Bd. Educ, 60; pres, United Schs. Cmt, La, 61; U.S. Rep, La, 61- Bus. & Prof. Pos: Operator, wholesale petrol. prod. distribution agency, N.Bossier Parish, La, currently. Mil. Serv: Lt. Comdr, Navy, World War II and Korea, 51-52. Mem: Mason; Shrine; Elks; Am. Legion; 40 et 8; Lions; Kappa Sigma; pres, La. Sch. Bds. Asn, 61. Rel: Methodist. Legal Res: Plain Dealing, La. 71064. Mailing Add: House Office Bldg, Washington, D.C. 20515.

WAGNER, AUBREY J. Independent

Dir. and Chmn. Bd, Tenn. Valley Authority

b. Hillsboro, Wis, 1/12/12; s. Joseph M. Wagner and Wilhelmina Filter W; m. 9/9/33 to Dorothea J. Huber; c. Audrey Grace, Joseph Michael, James Richard and Karl Edward. Educ: Univ. Wis, B.C.E. magna cum laude, 33; Tau Beti Pi; Chi Epsilon; Phi Kappa Phi; Phi Eta Sigma; Lambda Chi Alpha; Scabbard and Blade. Hon. LL.B, Newberry Col, 66. Polit. & Govt. Pos: Jr. hydraulic engr. to chief river transportation div, Tenn. Valley Authority, 34-51, asst. gen. mgr, 51-54, gen. mgr, 54-61 and dir. and chmn. bd, 62-; mem, Pres. Appalachian Adv. Coun, 63-65, Recreation Adv. Coun, 65-69 and Cost Reduction Coun, 68- Bus. & Prof. Pos: Lectr, Agr. and Nat. Resources Session, Seminar in Am. Studies, Salzburg, Austria, 68. Mem: Tenn. Archael. Soc; Ft. Loudoun Asn. Rel: Lutheran; mem. Exec. Coun, Lutheran Church of Am, 62- Legal Res: 1600 Cedar Lane, Knoxville, Tenn. 37918. Mailing Add: 403 New Sprankle Bldg, Knoxville, Tenn. 37902.

WAGNER, BETTY JOY R

b. Chicago, Ill, 3/3/26; d. Percy Evan Wagner and Elizabeth McGeeney W; single. Educ: Vassar Col, B.A, 47. Polit. & Govt. Pos: Alternate del, Rep. Nat. Conv, 68; mem, Gov. Adv. Coun, 69; various offices, 43rd Ward Regular Rep. Orgn, Chicago, Ill. Bus. & Prof. Pos: Mem, real estate div, Marshall Field & Co, Chicago. Mem: Vassar Col. Alumnae Asn; Katherine Gibbs Alumnae Asn; Gold Coast Clippers Investment Club. Rel: Protestant. Mailing Add: 1360 N. Lake Shore Dr, Chicago, Ill. 60610.

WAGNER, COLMAN H, SR. D

m. 7/9/19 to Thekla Kimmel; c. Colman L. Jr, Richard A, Corinnee. Educ: S.Dak. State Univ, B.S, 17. Polit. & Govt. Pos: S.Dak. State Rep, 64-66. Bus. & Prof. Pos: Retired farmer; Co. Exten. Agent, 22 years. Mem: Masons; A. F. & A.M; Epsilon Sigma Phi; Squanto; hon. mem, Clark F.F.A; past pres, secy, Clark Rotary; retired Co. Exten. Agents Emeritus. Mailing Add: Clark, S.Dak. 57225. (1967)

WAGNER, DALE EARL D

Nat. Chmn, Col. Young Dem. Clubs of Am.

b. Des Moines, Iowa, 11/28/41; s. Earl Raymond Wagner and Bernice Elizabeth Taylor W; m. 5/29/69 to Stephany Louise Joy. Educ: Am. Inst. of Bus, 57-59; Drake Univ, B.A. in polit. sci, 64; George Wash. Univ; Hastings Col. Law, Univ. Calif; Am. Univ, M.A, 67; Univ. Md, Ph.D, 69; Omicron Delta Kappa; Air Force ROTC Band and Drake Univ. Band. Polit. & Govt. Pos: V.pres, Jasper Co. Young Dem, Iowa, 58; pres, Drake Univ. Young Dem, 60-61; asst. to Cmnr. of Ins, State Dept. of Ins, Iowa, 60-64; Fifth Cong. Dist. Committeeman, Young Dem. Clubs of Iowa, 61-62; regional chmn, Nat. Fedn. Col. Young Dem, 61-63; state pres, Young Dem. Clubs of Iowa, 62-64; del, Dem. Nat. Conv, 64; chmn, Presidential Inaugural License Tag Cmt, 64-65; nat. chmn, Col. Young Dem. Clubs of Am, 64- and chmn, Col. Young Dem. Del. to U.S. Youth Coun, World Assembly of Youth, N.Y.C; cong. patronage,

U.S. Rep. Winfield K. Denton, Ind, 66; research asst, Rep. Richard Fulton, Tenn, 66-67; asst, Rep. Don Edwards, Calif, 67. Bus. & Prof. Pos: Research asst, Bur. of Governmental Research, Univ. Md, 67-69; asst. prof. polit. sci, Univ. Akron, Ohio, 69- Mem: Am. and Midwest Polit. Sci. Asns; Am. Acad. Polit. and Soc. Sci; Am. Polit. Items Collector; Am. Soc. for Pub. Admin; Am. Civil Liberties Union; Md. Soc. for Pub. Admin; Md. Civil Liberties Union. Awarded Week in Wash. Internship, Iowa Citizenship Clearing House, 61. Mailing Add: Department of Political Science, University of Akron, Akron, Ohio 44304.

WAGNER, FLOYD E. R
b. Cass Co, Mich, 6/13/98; m. 1917 to Esther Z. English; c. 3 daughters, 1 son. Educ: S.Bend Col. of Commerce. Polit. & Govt. Pos: Mich. State Rep, 58-66; former chmn, War Price Rationing Bd; Cass co. clerk, 18 years; postmaster, 5 years; on various sch, village and twp. bds. Mem: Life mem, Masonic Lodge 290, Vandalia; Elks Lodge 889; Clerk's Asn. Rel: United Church. Mailing Add: 205 N. Broadway, Cassopolis, Mich. 49031.

WAGNER, GEORGE D, JR. D
b. St. John, Wash, 10/28/24; s. George D. Wagner and Lura J. Lee W; m. 12/20/46 to Trudy A. Vowell Weldon; c. David M, Steven J. and Robert J. Educ: Wash. State Univ, B.S, 46-51; Sigma Xi, Phi Lambda Upsilon; Alpha Chi Sigma; Pi Kappa Alpha. Polit. & Govt. Pos: Mem. city coun, Albion, Wash, 54-56 and police judge, 56-57; chmn, Ventura Co. Dem. Coun, Calif, 62-64; chmn, Conejo Valley Dem. Club, Calif, 61-62 & 63-64; alternate del, Dem. Nat. Conv, 64; co. campaign chmn. for U.S. Sen, 64; mem, Ventura Co. Dem. Cent. Cmt, Calif, 64-65; chmn, Ventura Co. Dem. Vol, 64-65; admin. asst. for Wash. State Rep, 65-69; campaign chmn. for Wash. State Sen, 66; chmn, Wash. State Citizens for Kennedy, April, 67; precinct committeeman, Buenna Precinct, King Co, 68- Bus. & Prof. Pos: Molecular spectroscopist, Wash. State Univ, 53-57, instr. math, 55-57; Research engr, The Boeing Co, 57-60, mgt, 65-; profj. engr, Packard-Bell, 60-62; supvr, Westinghouse, 62-63; br. chief, Northrop Space Labs, 63-65. Mil. Serv: Entered as Pvt, Marine Corps, 42, released as Cpl, 45, after serv. in First Marine Div, S.Pac, 43-45; Purple Heart. Publ: 'Synthesis of beta-alkyl-alpha-Bromoacrylic Ethyl Esters,' J. Chem. Soc. 74, 909, 52; 'Vibrational Spectra and Structure of Monomeric Cyanamide and Dutero-cyanamide,' J. Phys. Chem, 64, 1480, 60; 'Visible and Infrared Spectral and Radiometric Measurements of Solid-Propellant Rocket Plumes,' IRIS 5, 1, 281, 60. Mem: Am. Chem. Soc; Soc. for Applied Spectros; Coblentz Soc; Am. Asn. for the Adv. Sci; Infrared Info. Symposium; Lions. Mailing Add: 10600 S.E. 256th, Apt. 212A, Kent, Wash. 98031.

WAGNER, JEANNETTE SECHRIST R
b. Wadsworth, Ohio, 2/3/15; d. Sterling G. Sechrist and Phoebe Trew S; m. 3/27/38 to Paul G. Wagner; c. Christine (Mrs. Hacker) and Sterling G; Educ: Ind. Univ, 33-34; Akron Univ, A.B, 37; Delta Gamma. Polit. & Govt. Pos: Rep. precinct committeeman, Ohio, 54-; mem, 23rd Cong. Dist, Ohio State Sch. Bd, 58-; alternate del, Rep. Nat. Conv, 64. Bus. & Prof. Pos: Treas, Wagner-Green Co, 45- Mem: Womans City Club, Cleveland; West. Reserve Woman's Rep. Club. Rel: Protestant. Mailing Add: 37855 Jackson Rd, Chagrin Falls, Ohio 44022.

WAGNER, JERRY D
b. New Haven, Conn, 8/2/26; s. Nathan Wagner and Clara Themper W; m. 5/30/50 to Salley Jeanne Hurvitz; c. Jonathan, Paula and Michael. Educ: Yale Univ, B.S, 46; Harvard Univ, LL.B, 49. Polit. & Govt. Pos: Mem, Bloomfield Dem. Town Cmt, Conn, 55-69; Conn. State Rep, 59-60; mem, State Cmn. on Intergovt. Coop, 59-61; town attorney, Bloomfield, 60-61; mem, Bloomfield Redevlop. Cmn, 63-68; del, Dem. Nat. Conv, 64; Dem. nominee for Conn. State Sen, 66; counsel to Conn. State Senate Majority, 67-68; spec. asst, Citizens for Humphrey-Muskie, 68. Bus. & Prof. Pos: Attorney-at-law, currently. Mil. Serv: Entered as Pre-Aviation Cadet, Army Air Force, 44, released as Pvt, 45. Mem: Conn. Bar Asn; exec. cmt. and ethics cmt, Hartford Co. Bar Asn; Am. Bar Asn; Hartford Yale Club; chmn, Hartford Jewish Commun. Rel. Cmt, 63-69; past pres, Conn. Jewish Commun. Rels. Coun, 61-63; pres, Conn. Div, Am. Jewish Cong, 61-69; v.chmn, Nat. Commun. Rels. Adv. Coun, 69; chmn, Conn. Youth and Govt. Cmt, YMCA, 69; mem, Regional Adv. Cmt, Gr. Hartford Town Meeting; Mason; Scottish Rite; Civitan; Am. Legion; Jewish War Vet; Urban League. Received Outstanding Young Man of Year Award, Jaycees, 62. Rel: Jewish. Mailing Add: 4 Craigemore Rd, Bloomfield, Conn. 06002.

WAGNER, JOHN EDWIN D
b. Pollock, La, 8/6/91; s. Thomas Jefferson Wagner and Minerva Maxwell W; m. 5/14/13 to Carolyn LaCroix; c. James Edwin. Polit. & Govt. Pos: Alderman, Dermott, Ark, 18 years; chmn, Chicot Co. Dem. Cmt, 25 years. Bus. & Prof. Pos: Mem. staff, La. Sawmill Co, Glenmora, La, 15-18, White Construction Co, Dermott, Ark, 18-20 and Walker Transfer Co, 20-23; salesman, Texaco Dist, 23-36; jobber, Lion Oil Co, 36-59. Mem: Mason; C. of C; Rotary. 25 Year Serv. Award, Lion Oil Co; 50 Year Membership Award, Mason. Rel: Methodist; Chmn. Bd. Trustees. Mailing Add: 200 S. Norwood, Dermott, Ark. 71638.

WAGNER, JOSEPH NICHOLAS D
Idaho State Rep.
b. Annamoose, N.Dak, 11/1/05; s. William Wagner and Helen Meisch W; m. 3/30/32 to Fern Margaret Lewis; c. Virginia Ann (Mrs. Hogard), William J, Margaret Helen (Mrs. Inghram), Janet Lenore (Mrs. Sonnichsen) and Robert J. Educ: High sch. educ. Polit. & Govt. Pos: Mayor, Grangeville, Idaho; Idaho State Rep, Dist. Six, currently. Mem: Pres, Lions, Grangeville, Idaho; secy, Grangeville C. of C. Rel: Catholic. Mailing Add: 2828 Sunset Dr, Lewiston, Idaho 83501.

WAGNER, KENNETH DAVID R
Mem, Calif. Rep. State Cent. Cmt.
b. Selinsgrove, Pa, 5/18/26; s. Charles E. Wagner and Nora E. Hetick W; m. 3/13/48 to Inez M. Spaid; c. Sherrie I. and Lorraine L. Educ: Bloomsburg State Col, Pa, B.S. in Educ, 54; grad. studies, Bucknell Univ, Stanford Univ, Duke Univ, Univ. South. Calif. and Calif. State Cols. at Long Beach and Los Angeles; Phi Sigma; Nu Epsilon Pi. Polit. & Govt. Pos: 19th Cong. Dist. pres. and mem. exec. bd, Los Angeles Co. Rep. Assembly, Calif, 67-69; v.pres, Greater Whittier Rep. Assembly, 67-69; alternate mem, Los Angeles Co. Rep. Cent. Cmt, 51st Assembly Dist. Cent. Cmt, 67-69, mem, 69-; assoc. mem, Calif. Rep. State Cent. Cmt, 67-69, mem, 69-; mem. gov. bd. trustees, Whittier City Sch. Dist, 69- Bus. & Prof. Pos: Teaching assignments in all areas of Biol. Sci, 56-; prof. expert-teacher workshop leader, Plastic Tech. for Teachers, 59, Atomic Info. for Civilian Use, 60; student cafeteria coord. and supvr, Manual Arts High Sch, Los Angeles, 62-67, counseling and guid. adv, 67, audio visual serv. coord, 67-68, health serv. coord. and dept. chmn, 68- Mil. Serv: Entered as Aviation Cadet, Army Air Force, 44, released as S/Sgt, 46, after serv. in 9222 Transport Serv. Unit, ETO, 45-46; Good Conduct Medal; Meritorious Serv. Award; ETO, ATO, and World War II Victory Medals; Crew Mem. Wings. Mem: Calif. Teachers Asn; Assoc. Classroom Teachers of Los Angeles; Nat. Sci. Teachers Asn; Fellow Am. Asn. for the Adv. of Sci; Whittier Area and Los Angeles Co. Sch. Trustees Asns; Calif. and Nat. Sch. Bd. Asns; F&AM; Nat. Rifle Asn. Freedom Found. Medal; U.S. Nat. Cancer Inst. STAR Award Medal; One of Calif. Outstanding Young Men of 62; Distinguished Serv. Award, City of Whittier, 62; Commendatory Resolutions from Calif. Senate and Assembly, Los Angeles Co, City of Los Angeles, City of Whittier, House of Rep. and Commonwealth of Pa; Calif; Conserv. Coun. Merit Award; Calif. finalist, Am. Ten Outstanding Young Mem, 63. Rel: Lutheran. Mailing Add: 13621 E. Philadelphia St, Whittier, Calif. 90601.

WAGNER, ROBERT F. D
b. N.Y.C, 4/20/10; s. Robert F. Wagner; m. 1942 to Susan Edwards (deceased), m. July 1965 to Barbara Joan Cavanagh; c. two sons. Educ: Yale Univ, A.B, 33, LL.B, 37; Harvard Univ. Sch. Bus. Admin, 34. Polit. & Govt. Pos: N.Y. State Assemblyman, 38-41; city tax cmnr, N.Y.C, 46; cmnr, Housing and Bldgs, 47; chmn, City Planning Cmn, 48; del, Dem. Nat. Conv, 48, 52, 56, 60, 64 & 68 and chmn, N.Y. Del, 60 & 64; pres, Borough of Manhattan, Gr. N.Y.C, 49-53; mayor, N.Y.C, 54-66; First V.pres, N.Y. State Constitutional Conv, 67-; U.S. Ambassador to Spain, 68-69. Mil. Serv: Eighth Air Force, 42-45, Lt. Col. Mailing Add: Wagner, Quillinan & Tennant, 350 Fifth Ave, New York, N.Y. 10001.

WAGNER, THEODORE FRANKLIN R
Chmn, Roane Co. Rep. Exec. Cmt, Tenn.
b. Madison, S.Dak, 4/7/21; s. Charles Carroll Wagner and Eldred Brown Lawrence W; m. 4/20/50 to Pauline Lucienne Audette; c. Karen Elizabeth, Theodore Franklin, Jr. and Annette Evelyn. Educ: U.S. Mil. Acad, B.S, 45; Univ. Tenn, Knoxville, M.S, 55. Polit. & Govt. Pos: Chmn, Roane Co. Rep. Exec. Cmt, Tenn, 66-; mem. city coun, Kingston, Tenn, 67- Bus. & Prof. Pos: Mgt. trainee, Curtiss Candy Co, Chicago, Ill, 49-51; admin. asst, nuclear div, Union Carbide Corp, 51-67, univ. rels. rep, 67-; mem. bd. dirs, First Nat. Bank and Trust Co, Rockwood and chmn. adv. bd. dirs, Kingston Off. Mil. Serv: Entered as Pvt, Army, 39, released as 1st Lt, 49, after serv. in various Bn, ETO, 45-47 and 204 TC Car Co. and hq. command, Mediterranean Theatre, 47; Res, 49-67, Lt. Col; ETO and World War II Victory Medals. Mem: Rotary. Rel: Christian Science. Mailing Add: 707 Sunset Dr, Kingston, Tenn. 37763.

WAGNER, VERNON E. R
N.Dak. State Rep.
b. Golden Valley, N.Dak, 6/13/26; s. Alex R. Wagner and Katie Miller W; m. 5/29/65 to Mary Dean Andrus. Educ: N.Dak. State Univ, B.S. in Pharm, 48; Phi Kappa Phi; Rho Chi; Sigma Alpha Epsilon. Polit. & Govt. Pos: Precinct committeeman, Burleigh Co. Rep. Party, N.Dak, 54-60; secy, N.Dak. Rep. Cent. Cmt, 60-63; N.Dak. State Rep, 63- Bus. & Prof. Pos: Pharmacist, Serv. Drug, 48-54; partner-mgr, Clin. Pharm, Bismarck, 54-67; asst. exec. secy, N.Dak. Med. Asn, 67- Mem: Am. and N.Dak. Pharmaceut. Asns; Nat. Asn. Retail Druggists; N.Dak. Heart Asn; dir, Bismarck C. of C; dir, Am. Heart Asn; past pres, N.Dak. Jaycees. Rel: Lutheran. Mailing Add: 809 Ave. A West, Bismarck, N.Dak. 58501.

WAGNER, WILLIAM FREMONT, JR. R
b. San Angelo, Tex, 10/24/33; s. Dr. William Fremont Wagner and Margret Colina Pratt W; m. 4/12/58 to Artemisa Suárez; c. William, III, Alexander and Michael. Educ: Mexico City Col, B.A. in Philosophy, 59 and M.A. in Spanish, 61. Polit. & Govt. Pos: Advisor, Louisburg Col. Young Rep, N.C, 62-; mem. bd. elec. Franklin Co. Rep. Party; chmn, Franklin Co. Rep. Party, 64-69. Bus. & Prof. Pos: Prof, Spanish, Louisburg, Col, 61- Mil. Serv: Entered as Seaman, Navy, 52, released as Qm. 3/C, 57, after serv. in Submarines, Underwater Demolition Team 12, Korea. Publ: 'A Sabbath Tale,' translation from Spanish, Short Story Int, 1965. Mem: Am. Asn. of Teachers of Spanish and Portuguese; Rotary. Rel: Catholic. Legal Res: Box 175A, Route 1, Louisburg, N.C. 27549. Mailing Add: Louisburg College, Louisburg, N.C. 27549. (1967)

WAILES, THOMAS WILLIAM D
b. Hereford, Tex, 4/4/15; s. Samuel Wailes and Anna Lory W; m. 4/13/40 to Dorothy Beatrice Wood; c. Jan Lee (Mrs. Piland), Mary Frances and Donald Arthur. Educ: Colo. State Univ, 34-35. Polit. & Govt. Pos: Mem. bd. educ, Sch. Dist. 22, Bennett, Colo, 45-59; pres. bd. dirs, Bennett Fire Protective Dist, 63-; Colo. State Rep, 65-67. Mem: AF&AM; Eastern Star; Bennett Consistory 1, Denver; Farmers Union. Rel: Presbyterian; Elder, Bennett Presbyterian Church. Mailing Add: R.F.D. 1, Bennett, Colo. 80102.

WAINWRIGHT, STUYVESANT R
b. New York, N.Y, 3/16/21; s. Carroll L. Wainwright and Edith Kathrine Gould W; m. 4/23/61 to Mary Grace Harris; c. Stuyvesant, Jonathan Mayhew, Janet Snowden, Laura Livingston. Educ: Yale, LL.B, 47. Polit. & Govt. Pos: U.S. Rep, N.Y, 53-61, spec. cong. mission to Far East, 53. Bus. & Prof. Pos: With Satterlee, Warfield and Stephens, N.Y.C, 47-49; mem. firm Evarts, Baltzell, Wainwright & Baker, 49-52; partner, Wainwright & Matthews, Huntington, N.Y, 53-64; lawyer, Walker & Beale, N.Y.C, 65- Mil. Serv: Office of Strategic Servs, Army, 42-45. Mem: St. Nicholas Soc; The Loyal Legion; VFW; Phi Delta Phi; Chi Psi; Mason; Union, Univ, N.Y.C; Maidenstone Club, L.I; Royal Bermuda Yacht Club; chmn, Maidenstone Invitation Int. Tennis Tournaments, 50-52. Legal Res: East Hampton, L.I, N.Y. 11401. Mailing Add: 444 Madison Ave, New York, N.Y. 10022. (1967)

WAKATSUKI, JAMES HIROJI D
Hawaii State Rep.
b. Honolulu, Hawaii, 8/17/29; s. Shichizaemon Wakatsuki and Sachi Kobayashi W; m. 2/9/57 to Irene Natsuko Yoshimura; c. Janie Toshie, Stuart Kazuo and Cora Akemi. Polit. & Govt. Pos: Hawaii State Rep, currently, chmn, Finance Cmt, 69-70. Mil. Serv: Entered as Recruit, Army, 48, released as Pfc, 49, after serv. in Pac; Army Res, 49-55. Legal Res: 1462 Ala Mahamoe St, Honolulu, Hawaii 96819. Mailing Add: Suite 311, 1022 Bethel St, Honolulu, Hawaii 96813.

WAKEMAN, WILLIAM THOMSON R
Mem, Rep. Nat. Finance Cmt, Fla.
b. Stamford, Conn, 5/25/23; s. Francis Salmon Wakeman and Louise Thomson W; m. 11/26/60 to Nancy Deere Wiman; c. Catherine Theresa and Rufus II. Educ: Kenyon Col; Delta Kappa Epsilon. Polit. & Govt. Pos: Mem, Rep. Nat. Finance Cmt, Fla, currently; chmn, Fla. Rep. Finance Cmt, 63-65; del-at-lg, Rep. Nat. Conv, 64; dep. sheriff, Palm Beach Co, Fla. Mil. Serv: Entered as Aviation Cadet, Navy, 42, released as Qm. 3/C, 46, after serv. in S.Pac; Guam, Okinawa and Iwo Jima Theater Ribbons. Mem: Bd. of Dirs, Palm Beach Co. Chap, Am. Red Cross; Palm Beach Civic Asn; Eng. Speaking Union; Soc. Colonial Wars; Everglades Club; Palm Beach; Coral Beach Club; John Birch Soc; Screen Actors Guild; Am. Fedn. of TV & Radio Artists. Rel: Christian. Mailing Add: El Brillo Way, Palm Beach, Fla. 33480. (1967)

WALBRIDGE, JOHN TUTHILL, JR. R
Mem, 11th Cong. Dist. Rep. Exec. Cmt, Mich.
b. Lakeland, Fla, 12/10/25; s. John T. Walbridge and Mabel Thornton W; m. 6/14/47 to Mary Lou Sailor; c. John T, III and Mary Lewis. Educ: Yale, B.S; Hale Found. Polit. & Govt. Pos: Co. chmn, Rep. Party, Mich, 62-65; former mem, Gov. Cmt. Party Principles; del, Rep. Nat. Conv, 64; mem, 11th Cong. Dist. Rep. Exec. Cmt, 64- Bus. & Prof. Pos: Exec. v.pres, Early Am. Fence Co, 56-59, pres, 59-; pres, North Land & Lumber Co, 60- and Am. Timber Homes, Inc, 61- Mil. Serv: Seaman 2/C, Navy, 44-46 in U.S.S. Marlboro, Atlantic. Mem: Chmn, Mich. White Cedar Asn; C. of C; Escanaba Country Club. Rel: Episcopal. Mailing Add: 215 S. Sixth St, Escanaba, Mich. 49829.

WALCH, JOHN MacARTHUR DUNSMORE R
Committeeman, Essex Co. Rep. Party, N.J.
b. St. Joseph, Mo, 2/8/26; s. Donald Elbra Walch and Ruth Dunsmore W; m. 6/27/50 to Zelda Sofman; c. Donald Elbra, Jonathan, Grace Ann and Elizabeth. Educ: Mass. Inst. Tech, B.S.E.E; Delta Tau Delta, Deer Lake Club. Polit. & Pos: Committeeman, Rep. Party, Ridgefield, N.J, 54-59, mem, Bd. Health, 59; committeeman, Essex Co. Rep. Party, 60-; pres, Nutley Rep. Club, 66-67; campaign mgr, Nutley, 68, mem, Nutley Cmn. Elec, 68; alternate del, Rep. Nat. Conv, 68; pres. bd. dirs, Nutley Family Serv. Br, 68-69. Bus. & Prof. Pos: Educ. counsr, Mass. Inst. Tech, 54-; prfnl. engr, N.J, 54-; sr. engr, Pub. Serv. Elec. & Gas Co, 69- Mil. Serv: Entered as Pvt, Army, 43, released as Sgt, 46, after serv. in Combat Engr, South Pac, 44-46. Mem: Sr. mem, Inst. Elec. and Electronics Engrs; Elks; Capitol Hill Club; Nutley Rep. Club. United Commun. Fund and Coun. of Essex and West Hudson Vol. Award, 68. Rel: Episcopal. Mailing Add: 166 Highfield Lane, Nutley, N.J. 07110.

WALDIE, JEROME RUSSELL D
U.S. Rep, Calif.
b. Antioch, Calif, 2/15/25; s. George Daniel Waldie and Alice Crosiar W; m. 6/20/48 to Dorothy Joanne Gregg; c. Jill, Jonathon and Jefferey. Educ: Univ. Calif. at Berkeley, A.B, 50; Univ. Calif. Boalt Law Sch, LL.B, 53. Polit. & Govt. Pos: Calif. State Assemblyman, 58-66 and Majority Leader; U.S. Rep, Calif, 66- Mil. Serv: Entered as Pvt, Army, 43, released as T/5, Army and Signal Corps, 46. Mem: Odd Fellows; Elks; Am. Legion; Moose. Rel: Congregational. Legal Res: 500 Lynn, Antioch, Calif. 94509. Mailing Add: Room 408, Cannon Office Bldg, Washington, D.C. 20515.

WALDO, WILLARD H. R
Nebr. State Sen.
b. DeWitt, Nebr, 4/2/12; m. 6/2/33 to Beulah Plucknett; c. Arley, Max and Willa (Mrs. George Cammack). Educ: Univ. Nebr, grad, 34; Alpha Gamma Rho; Gamma Sigma Delta; Alpha Zeta; Phi Delta Kappa. Polit. & Govt. Pos: Nebr. State Sen, 57-61 and 68- Bus. & Prof. Pos: Voc. instr. and coach, Stapleton, Nebr, 34-36; co. agent, Franklin Co, 36-40 and Cass Co, 40-46; pres, Nebr. Livestock Breeders & Feeders Asn; dir, United Duroc Record Asn, Nebr. Sheep Breeders, Nebr. Swine Coun. and Nebr. Swine Accrediting Agency; chmn, State Brucellosis Cmt, 53-57 and Nebr. Farmers Home Admin, 55-56; dir, Nebr. Crop Improv. Asn, 56-62; chmn. and nat. dir, Nat. Farm Policy Coun, 60; chmn, Nebr. Hog Cholera Control Cmt, 62; v.chmn, Nebr. Cmt. on Pub. Rels. for Agr, 62; past v.pres, Nat. Swine Disease Research Found; del, Nebr. Stockmen's People to People Goodwill Tour, S.Am, 63 and People to People Govt. Off. Del. throughout Europe and Soviet Union; farmer, currently. Mil. Serv: Prisoner of War, 44-46. Mem: Pres, Gage Co. Fair, 54-55; DeWitt Civic Club (past pres); Univ. Nebr. Alumni Asn.(past dir); Nebr. Duroc Breeders (past secy); Nebr. Milking Shorthorn Breeders Asn. (past secy); Boy Scouts (former leader); 4-H (former leader); hon. mem, Nebr. Future Farmers and Nebr. Vet. Med. Asn; Nebr. Coun. for Better Educ; Nebr. Stock Growers; Tax Farmers of Am. Asn; Nebr. State Hist. Soc; Knights of Ak-Sar-Ben. Honor Farm Family, 52; Award and past v.pres, Nebr. Hall of Agr. Achievement; Skelly Superior Achievement in Agr; Gage Co. Outstanding Farmer Citizen Award, 57; One of four Nat. Swine Prod. awarded trip to Europe, 59; Agr. Achievement Award for leadership in every phase of agr, Ak-Sar-Ben, 62; Outstanding Alumnus Award, Alpha Gamma Rho, 62; Nebr. Co. Agent Award, 62; Livestock Award, Block and Bridle Club, 67; Homestead King, 67; Award of Merit, Gamma Sigma Delta, 68. Rel: Methodist; Mem. of the Bd. Mailing Add: DeWitt, Nebr. 68341.

WALDOR, MILTON A. R
N.J. State Sen.
b. Newark, N.J, 9/28/24; s. Jack M. Waldor and Rose Lowe W; m. 11/6/50 to Mona McClosky; c. Cathy Lynn and Mitchell Ross. Educ: Rutgers Univ. Sch. of Law, J.D; Sigma Alpha Mu. Polit. & Govt. Pos: N.J. State Sen, 11th Dist, Essex Co, 68- Bus. & Prof. Pos: Lawyer, Waldor & Hochberg, currently. Mil. Serv: Entered as Aviation Cadet, Air Force, released as 1st Lt, 45, after serv. in 7th Bomb Group, China-Burma-India Theatre, 44-45; Distinguished Flying Cross; Air Medal with Oak Leaf Cluster. Publ: Peddlers of Fear, Lynn Ross Publ. Co, 66. Mem: Essex Co. Bar Asn; Am. Trial Lawyers Asn; Past nat. comdr, Jewish War Vet. of U.S; dir, Anti Defamation League of B'nai B'rith, N.J; mem, President's Cmn. to Employ the Physically Handicapped. John F. Kennedy Outstanding Citizens Award, Jewish War Vet; Honorary Citizen of Calif, Ga, Md, Fla. and Minn. Rel: Hebrew. Legal Res: 37 Waddington Ave, West Orange, N.J. 07052. Mailing Add: 1180 Raymond Blvd, Newark, N.J. 07102.

WALDRIP, HELEN C. R
Committeewoman, Independence Co. Rep. Cmt, Ark.
b. Kearney, Nebr, 1/13/13; d. George Nama and Mary Deeb N; m. 5/28/50 to William J. Waldrip, Jr; c. William J, III and stepson, Jack W. Educ: Clarkson Mem. Hosp, Omaha, Nebr, R.N; LaSalle Col, 1 year; Wayne Univ, 1 year. Polit. & Govt. Pos: Committeewoman, Independence Co. Rep. Cmt, Ark, 56-; alternate del, Rep. Nat. Conv, 68. Mil. Serv: Entered as 2nd Lt, Army Nurse Corps, 42, released as 1st Lt, 45, after serv. in 252nd Sta. Hosp. and 16th Evacuation Hosp, ETO, Fifth Army, 43-45; Special Commendation from Gen. Mark Clark for Meritorious Serv. Performed while on detached serv. with 93rd Evacuation Hosp. on the Anzio Beachhead. Mem: Am. Legion. Rel: Episcopal. Legal Res: Hwy. 167, Batesville, Ark. 72501. Mailing Add: Box 610, Batesville, Ark. 72501.

WALDRON, DAVID REEDER D
b. Tremonton, Utah, 1/12/10; s. Thomas Orsen Waldron and Agnes Bowen W; m. 12/17/35 to Carmen Halverson; c. James H, Nancy Ann and Susan W. (Mrs. Sweet). Educ: Utah State Univ, B.S, 33; Alpha Kappa Psi; Scabbard and Blade; Sigma Phi Epsilon; Alpha Delta Epsilon. Polit. & Govt. Pos: Various Dem. state cmt. assignments, Utah, 50-60; mem, Utah Pub. Sch. Survey Cmn, 52-54; Utah State Sen, Box Elder Co, 65-67. Mil. Serv: 2nd Lt, Army, 33. Mem: Pres, Box Elder Co. Fair Bd; Golden Spike Rodeo Corp; Garland Beet Growers Asn. and North Box Elder Farm Bur; dir, Asn. of Gen. Contractors; Elks; Lions; Ambassador Athletic Club. Rel: Latter-day Saint. Mailing Add: 402 N. First E, Tremonton, Utah 84337. (1967)

WALDRON, JOHNIE JAMES R
Nebr. State Sen.
b. Callaway, Nebr, 12/17/36; s. Johnie Abither Waldron and Addie Bonde W; single. Educ: Univ. Nebr, B.S, 61, M.A, 68, J.D, 70. Polit. & Govt. Pos: Nebr. State Sen, 67-; alternate del, Rep. Nat. Conv, 68. Mil. Serv: Entered as 2nd Lt, Army, 61, released as 1st Lt, 63, after serv. in Chem. Support Units, Third Army Area; Capt, Army Res, 63- Rel: Protestant. Mailing Add: Callaway, Nebr. 68825.

WALDRON, ROBERT EDWIN R
Mich. State Rep.
b. Brookline, Mass, 1/25/20; s. Robert George Waldron and Adelaide Merrimon W; m. to Helen Miller; c. Margaret, William and Mary Leslie. Educ: Dartmouth Col, A.B, 46; Univ. Mich. Law Sch, LL.B, 49; Phi Sigma Alpha. Polit. & Govt. Pos: Mich. State Rep, 55-, Majority Leader, Mich. State House of Rep, 63-64, Minority Leader, 65-66 & 69- and Speaker House, 67-68; chmn, Wayne Co. Rep. Party, 64-66. Bus. & Prof. Pos: Attorney-at-law, 49- Mil. Serv: Entered as Pvt, Air Force, 42, released as Capt, 46, after serv. in Ninth Air Force Strike Signal Corps, European Theater Ribbon. Mem: Am, Mich. and Detroit Bar Asns; Am. Legion. Rel: Episcopal. Legal Res: 532 University Place, Grosse Point, Mich. 48230. Mailing Add: 17350 W. Ten Mile Rd, Southfield, Mich. 48075.

WALDROP, RALPH LOY R
Chmn, Transylvania Co. Rep. Exec. Cmt, N.C.
b. Cherryfield, N.C, 1/16/13; s. John Lewis Waldrop and Addie Ross W; m. 9/4/42 to Kathryn Grace Stall; c. Ralph Loy, Jr, Larry R, Jean Ann and Nancy Sue. Educ: Mars Hill Col, 30-31; Furman Univ, B.S, 33. Polit. & Govt. Pos: Mem, Catheys Creek Rep. Precinct Cmt, N.C, 48-50; mem, Transylvania Co. Rep. Exec. Cmt, 52-55, chmn, 58- Bus. & Prof. Pos: Shift control supvr, Paper Div, Olin Mathieson Chem. Corp, Pisgah Forest, N.C, 39- Mil. Serv: Entered as 1st Lt, Chem. Warfare Serv, Army, 41, released as Capt, Chem. Corps, 46, after serv. in 256th Chem. Lab. Co, Asiatic-Pac. Area, 45; Army Res, 36-41 & 46-64, Lt. Col.(Ret); Am. Defense Medal; Asiatic-Pac, Am. Theater and Philippines Liberation Ribbons; Victory Medal; Armed Forces Res. Campaign and Serv. Medal. Mem: Mason. Rel: Baptist. Mailing Add: R.R. 2, Box 669, Brevard, N.C. 28712.

WALGREN, GORDON LEE D
Wash. State Sen.
b. Bremerton, Wash, 3/7/33; s. Jess Nelson Walgren and Grace Barber W; m. 6/5/63 to Sue Kathlyen Proctor; c. Kathy and Tracey. Educ: Univ. Wash, B.A, 55, LL.B. and J.D, 57; Delta Upsilon; Phi Delta Phi. Polit. & Govt. Pos: Prosecuting attorney, Kitsap Co, Wash, 58-62; Wash. State Rep, 66-68; city attorney, Bremerton, 66-; Wash. State Sen, 68- Publ: 'Due Process and Contempt,' Wash. Law Rev, 56. Mem: Nat. Trial Lawyers Asn; Am. and Wash. State Bar Asns; pres, Kitsap Co. Bar Asn, 68-69; Nat. Dist. Attorneys Asn; F&AM; Shrine; Elks; Eagles; Kiwanis. Freedoms Found. Award, Valley Forge. Rel: Protestant. Mailing Add: 5533 Erland Point Rd, Bremerton, Wash. 98310.

WALK, ETHEL EDNA D
State Committeewoman, Wash. Dem. Party
b. Kittitas, Wash, 11/4/15; d. Tom Martin II and Anna Laura Nightingale M; m. 12/30/41 to Ernest Paul Walk; c. Anna Laura (Mrs. John M. Folline), Larry C, Ernest Paul Karl and Mary Louisa (Mrs. Dale E. Pelham). Educ: High sch. grad. Polit. & Govt. Pos: State committeewoman, Wash. Dem. Party, Pac. Co, 53-60 & 69-; organized, Women's Dem. Club, 54; precinct committeewoman, Pac. Co. Dem. Party, 56-58; del, Wash. State Fedn. Dem. Women's Clubs Convs, 56-68, state educ. chmn, 63-66 and state treas, 66-; del, Dem. Co. and State Convs, 56-68; first pres, Valley Dem. Women's Club, 59; chmn, 25th Dist. Kennedy Campaign, 60; v.chmn, Pierce Co. Dem. Cent. Cmt, 60-68; Dem. committeewoman, Tide Haven Precinct, 60-; co-chmn, 4 for 64 Campaign, 64; instr, Precinct Training Classes, 64; del, Dem. Nat. Conv, 68; chmn, Women for Humphrey, 68; chmn, Precinct Training Course, 69; chmn. and

active in several Dem. campaign including that of Gov. Rosellini, Land Cmnr, Bert Cole, Secy. of State Vic Myers and co. cands. Publ: Handbook for Washington State Federation of Democratic Women, 66. Mem: Eastern Star; 27th Dist. Dem. Club; Valley Women's Dem. Club; Bus. Women's Dem. Club; pres, Pierce Co. Dem. Women's League, 68. Rel: Protestant. Mailing Add: 5701 Fourth St. E, Tacoma, Wash. 98404.

WALKER, ALAN LEE D
Chmn, Lawrence Co. Dem. Cent. Cmt, Ind.
b. South Bend, Ind, 7/21/34; s. Chester Eugene Walker and Lura True W; m. 8/28/54 to Donnera Phillips; c. Gloria Jean and Elizabeth Anne. Educ: Evansville Col, 52-55; Univ. Cincinnati, 55-56; Acacia. Polit. & Govt. Pos: Mem, Lawrence Co. Dem. Elec. Bd, Ind, 63-66; chmn, Lawrence Co. Dem. Cent. Cmt, 66- Bus. & Prof. Pos: Advert. salesman and sportscaster, Radio Sta. WBIW, Bedford, Ind, 61- Mil. Serv: Entered as Pvt, Marine Corps Res, 52, released as M/Sgt, 66, after serv. in Marine, Army and Air Corps Res. Mem: F&AM; U.S. Power Squadron; Bedford Little Theater; Rotary. Rel: Presbyterian. Mailing Add: 1412 Fifth St, Bedford, Ind. 47421.

WALKER, ANNA MAE D
V.Chmn, Owen Co. Dem. Cent. Cmt, Ind.
b. Spencer, Ind, 12/4/22; d. James Edward Taylor and Gladys McAuley T; m. 5/9/38 to Charles Harold Walker; c. Charles Mc, Patricia Darlene, Janet Suzann and James Roy. Educ: Freedom High Sch. Polit. & Govt. Pos: V.chmn, Owen Co. Dem. Cent. Cmt, Ind, currently; precinct committeeman, Owen Co. Dem. Cmt, 52- Mem: Eastern Star 425; Spencer Past Matrons Club; Am. Auxiliary. Rel: Methodist. Mailing Add: Route 1, Spencer, Ind. 47460. (1967)

WALKER, CHARLES RAY R
Chmn, Jefferson Co Rep. Exec. Cmt, Tex.
b. Beaumont, Tex, 9/24/27; s. Clyde Howell Haywood Walker and Mary Estelle Ray W; m. 6/30/62 to Patricia Joann Brandow; c. Earl Howell and Caroline Ray. Educ: Lamar Jr. Col, A.A, 45; Baylor Univ, B.S, cum laude, 47; Univ. Tex. Sch. Med, M.D, 51; Beta Beta Beta; Alpha Epsilon Delta; Phi Chi, Zeta Chap. Polit. & Govt. Pos: Pres, N.Jefferson Co. Rep. Club and precinct chmn, Precinct Four, Jefferson Co, 62-64; chmn, Jefferson Co. Rep. Exec. Cmt, Tex, 64-; del, Rep. Nat. Conv, 68. Bus. & Prof. Pos: Instr. radiology, Univ. Tex. Sch. of Med, 55-56; asst. prof, 58-59; radiologist, Lake Charles Mem. Hosp, La, 56; dep-chief-of-radiology, U.S. Marine Hosp, San Francisco, 56-57; chief-of radiology, U.S. Marine Hosp, Baltimore, 57-58; radiologist, Beaumont, Tex, 60- Mil. Serv: Entered as Sr. Asst. Surgeon, Capt, U.S. Pub. Health Serv, 56, released as Sr. Surgeon, Lt. Col, 58, after serv. in Hosp. Div, Baltimore and San Francisco, 56-58. Mem: Pres, La-Tex. Gulf Coast Radiol. Soc, 65-66; Am. Col. of Radiol; Tex. Med. Asn; Jefferson Co. Med. Soc; dir, Tex. Physicians' Guild, 68-; Beaumont Club; treas, Tex. Gulf Hist. Soc, 68-; pres, Paul Revere Chap, SAR, 67-69; Surgeon, Tex. Div, Sons of Confederate Vet, 67-68, Third Lt. Comdr, 68-; Adjutant, Dick Dowling Camp, Sons of Confederate Vet, 68- Rel: Methodist. Legal Res: 5770 Fleetwood Lane, Beaumont, Tex. 77706. Mailing Add: 3155 Stagg Dr, Beaumont, Tex. 77701.

WALKER, CHARLS EDWARD R
Under Secy. of the Treas.
b. Graham, Tex, 12/24/23; s. Pinkney Clay Walker and Sammye McCombs W; m. to Harmolyn Hart; c. Carolyn and Charls Edward, Jr. Educ: Univ. Tex, B.B.A, 47 and M.B.A, 48; Wharton Sch. of Finance, Univ. Pa, Ph.D. in Econ, 55. Polit. & Govt. Pos: Assoc. economist, Fed. Reserve Bank of Phila, 53-54 and Dallas, 54-61, v.pres, 58-61; asst. to Secy. of the Treas. Robert B. Anderson, 59-61; Under Secy. of the Treas, 69- Bus. & Prof. Pos: Instr. finance, Univ. Tex, 47-48, assoc. prof, 50-54; instr, Wharton Sch. of Finance, Univ. Pa, 48-50; economist and spec. asst. to pres, Repub. Nat. Bank of Dallas, Tex, 55-56; exec. v.pres, Am. Bankers Asn, 61-69. Mil. Serv: Pilot, Army Air Force, World War II. Publ: Co-ed, The Banker's Handbook; plus articles for econ. and other jour. Mem: Trustee, Joint Coun. on Econ. Educ: former mem. bd. ed, J. of Finance. Legal Res: Riverside, Conn. 06878. Mailing Add: Treasury Dept, 15th and Pennsylvania Ave, Washington, D.C. 20220.

WALKER, CLAUDE A. R
b. Chicago, Ill, 8/24/05; married; c. three sons and three grandchildren. Educ: Lewis Inst; Loyola Univ. Law Sch, LL.B. Polit. & Govt. Pos: Ill. State Rep, until 64; chmn, Ration Bd, 4 years; chmn, Cook Co. Civil Serv. Cmn, 6 years. Bus. & Prof. Pos: Exec. Secy, Chicago Accredited Newspapers; past pres, Ill. Press Asn; ed, publisher, newspapers, Lemont, Argo, Forest Park, and Oak Park, Ill. Mem: Chicago Headline Club; Secy, Cook Co. Suburban Publishers Asn; charter mem, Chicago Press Club; past pres, Kiwanis; past pres, Forest Park C. of C; past chmn, Community Chest Fund; Forest Pub, Inc. Mailing Add: 422 Circle Ave, Forest Park, Ill. 60130. (1967)

WALKER, E. S. JOHNNY D
b. Fulton, Ky, 6/18/11; s. John Karr Walker and Annie Stephens W; m. 1/17/39 to Pauline Marie Wernicke; c. Janet and Stephen Michael. Educ: Univ. of N.Mex, 31-35; Nat. Univ, 36. Polit. & Govt. Pos: Organizer and first dir, N.Mex. Oil and Gas Acct. Cmn; N.Mex. State Rep, 49-53, majority whip; cmnr, N.Mex. Land Off, 53-56 & 60-64; cmnr, Bur. of Revenue of N.Mex, 59; mem, N.Mex. Investment Coun; mem, N.Mex. Forestry Cmn; mem, N.Mex. Oil Conserv. Cmn; U.S. Rep, N.Mex, 65-69. Bus. & Prof. Pos: Part owner, Free Fraser Pharm, Adobe Motel, Santa Fe, N.Mex. Mil. Serv: Army, Vet, World War II, N.Africa and Europe. Mem: VFW; Am. Legion; Elks. Mailing Add: 2207 Cerrillos Rd, Santa Fe, N.Mex. 87501. (1967)

WALKER, EARL SIDNEY R
b. Wilmerding, Pa, 9/6/15; s. Sidney Walker and Laura Mensdorf W; m. to Mary Loughead; c. two. Educ: Duquesne Univ, A.B; Lutheran Theol. Sem, B.D. Polit. & Govt. Pos: Pa. State Rep, 62-69; committeeman, chmn, East Pittsburgh Rep. Party. Bus. & Prof. Pos: Lutheran Clergyman; St. John's Lutheran Church, Ford City, 48-52; Hebron Luth. Church, East Pittsburgh, 52-; CIO mem. while employed by Westinghouse Air Brake Co. Mil. Serv: Air Force, World War II, 44 months; aerial navigator, 2 years, Pac, 1st Lt. Mem: Pres, East Pittsburgh Rotary. Mailing Add: 416 Franklin St, East Pittsburgh, Pa. 15112. (1967)

WALKER, FRED H. D
b. Valdosta, Ga, 9/30/20; s. John A. Walker and Bessie Thompson W; m. 12/02/47 to Waunee Wheeler; c. Linda Aleen, John A. II, Fred Harding, Jr. and Wanda Gail. Educ: Univ. Ga. Law Sch, LL.B, 42. Polit. & Govt. Pos: Ga. State Rep, 57-66. Bus. & Prof. Pos: Attorney-at-Law. Mil. Serv: Air Force Res, World War II, Maj, Judge Adv. Gen's Dept, Res. Mem: Shrine, Elks. Rel: Elder, 1st Christian Church. Mailing Add: P.O. Box 1507, Valdosta, Ga. 31601.

WALKER, HARRY BURTON, JR. R
b. Millville, N.J, 6/12/22; s. Harry Burton Walker and Ada Harris W; m. 11/20/53 to Priscilla Hoffman; c. Peggy Ada, Harry Burton, III and Ernest T. Educ: Earlham Col, 39-41; Bowdoin Col, B.S, 43; Temple Univ. Med. Sch, M.D, 48; Chi Psi; Phi Chi. Polit. & Govt. Pos: Alternate del, Rep. Nat. Conv, 68. Bus. & Prof. Pos: Anesthesiologist. Mil. Serv: Entered as 1st Lt, Air Force, 53, released as Capt, 55, after serv. in 3415 Hosp. Unit, Denver. Mem: Am. Med. Asn; Rotary; Am. and Colo. Socs. Anesthesiologists; Arapahoe Co. Politalkers (pres, 65). Rel: Protestant. Mailing Add: 3445 S. Columbine Circle, Englewood, Colo. 80110.

WALKER, HENRY C. D
b. Senaca, S.C, 7/19/06; s. H.C. Walker and Mary Alice Buchanan W; m. 6/1/32 to Bess Suber. Educ: Univ. of S.C, A.B, 29, LL.B, 47. Polit. & Govt. Pos: S.C. State Sen, 49-52, 61-69. Bus. & Prof. Pos: Lawyer; prin. and coach, Ridgeland High Sch, 29-36; supt, Hardeeville Sch, 36-37; supt. of educ, Jasper Co. 37-43; S.C. Indust. Cmt, 51-60. Mil. Serv: Navy, Gunnery Officer, 43-45, Atlantic and Mediterranean. Mem: Blue Key; Mason; Am. Legion. Rel: Baptist. Mailing Add: Box 818, Ridgeland, S.C. 29936. (1967)

WALKER, JACK E. R
Majority Leader, Ill. State House of Rep.
b. Dahinda, Ill, 7/15/10; s. Stephen Eugene Walker and Ida McIntyre W; m. 6/13/47 to Pearl Huizenga; c. Karen (Mrs. Hobgood), Kathy Kay and Jack, Jr. Educ: Univ. Ill. and Knox Col, 29-32; John Marshall Law Sch, LL.B, 40; Lambda Chi Alpha. Polit. & Govt. Pos: Former village attorney, Dixmoor, Thornton Twp. and Lan-Oak Park Dist; former sch. bd. attorney, Cook Co. Sch. Dist. 171; village attorney, Lansing, Calumet Park and Thornton, currently; sch. bd. attorney, Cook Co. Sch. Dist. 158, currently; pres, Thornton Twp. Reg. Rep. Orgn, 51; Ill. State Rep, 57-, Majority Whip, Ill. State House of Rep, 67-68 and Majority Leader, 69- Mem: Am, Ill. and Chicago Bar Asns; past pres, Harvey-Calumet Bar Asn, Lansing Lions Club, S.Suburban Shrine, Calumet Shrine Club and Lansing Commun. Chest; AF&AM; AAONMS; Elks; Odd Fellows; Aircraft Pilot's Asn. Rel: Methodist. Mailing Add: 18018 Arcadia, Lansing, Ill. 60438.

WALKER, JAMES LORENZO D
Fla. State Rep.
b. Marco, Fla, 11/1/20; s. Forrest Walker and Adnie Prine W; m. 1/3/42 to Marguerite Louise Lanier; c. Barbara Ann and Carolyn Sue. Educ: Naples High Sch, grad; Hemp Hill Diesel Sch, Grad. Diesel Engr. Polit. & Govt. Pos: Mem, Collier Co. Cmn, Fla, 50-56; Fla. State Rep, 56-, speaker pro tempore, Fla. House of Rep, 67- Bus. & Prof. Pos: Real Estate Broker; dir, First Nat. Bank Naples and Naples Commun. Hosp. Mil. Serv: Entered as Pvt, Army Air Corps, 43, released as S/Sgt, Cent. Instruction Sch. for Flexible Gunnery, Am. Theater, 46. Mem: Former post comdr, Am. Legion; past pres, Lions and Collier City Tuberc. & Health Asn. Rel: Church of God. Legal Res: 1537 Gordon Dr, Naples, Fla. 33940. Mailing Add: P.O. Box 475, Naples, Fla. 33940.

WALKER, JOHN A. R
b. Hamilton Co, Iowa, 6/5/12; m. to Violet Michaels; c. John A, II, Nancy Louise and Steven. Educ: Ellsworth Jr. Col, Iowa Falls, Iowa; Am. Inst. of Bus, Des Moines; Grinnell Col. Polit. & Govt. Pos: Iowa State Sen, until 66; Iowa State Rep, 4 terms. Bus. & Prof. Pos: Farming; banking; with J.C. Penney Co, Inc, several states. Mem: Eastern Star; Mason; Odd Fellows; numerous other orgns. Rel: Lutheran. Mailing Add: Williams, Iowa 50217. (1967)

WALKER, LILLIAN W. D
La. State Rep.
b. Meridian, Miss, 5/8/24; d. Rudolph Blanche Walker and Maggie Elizabeth George W; m. 5/25/42 to Edward Everett Walker; c. Edward T. and Betti H. Educ: Meridian Jr. Bus. Col, grad. Polit. & Govt. Pos: La. State Rep, East Baton Rouge Parish, currently and chmn, Contingent Expense Cmt. and Joint Legis. Cmt. on Exceptional Children and mem, Appropriations and Pub. Health, Welfare and Charitable Insts. Cmts, La. State House of Rep; mem, Coun. on Ment. Retardation Planning; hon. v.chmn, La. Cmn. on Status Women; mem, Gov. Cmt. on Employ. Handicapped and Gov. Hwy. Safety Cmt; del, Dem. Nat. Conv, 60; former mem, 100 Mem. Cmt. on Educ. Curriculum Study for State Dept. Educ. and State Adv. Coun. on Ment. Health. Bus. & Prof. Pos: Owner, Baton Rouge Agency, La, 56- Mem: Nat. Asn. for Retarded Children; bd. mem. and past pres, La. and Baton Rouge Asns. for Retarded Children; bd. mem, Baton Rouge Arthritis Asn; bd. mem, Audubon Coun. and former troop leader, Girl Scouts; Baton Rouge Ins. Exchange; past pres, Baton Rouge Bus. & Prfnl. Women's Club; bd. mem, Baton Rouge Zonta; La. Coun. Soc. Welfare; Nat. Order Women Legislators; Nat. Asn. State Legislators; Nicholson Post, Am. Legion Auxiliary; former mem, Govt. Affairs Cmt, Baton Rouge C. of C; past pres, Broadmoor Elem. Sch. PTA; former chmn, Women's Div, United Givers Fund; past capt, YMCA Bldg. Fund Drive; former soc. coordinator, Nat. Dairy Princess Contest; former judge, Jr. Achievement Fair; former mem, Baton Rouge Sheltered Workshop Bd. and La. Orgn. for State Legis. Achievements: Civitan Int. Award, 60; Nat. Dairy Asn. Award, 60; Cert. of Merit, New Orleans Asn. for Retarded Children, 62; Cert. of Appreciation, Baton Rouge Asn. for Retarded Children, 64; Louisianian of Year Award, La. Asn. Broadcasters, 64; Outstanding Mem. Award, Zonta Int, 65; Appreciation Award, Audubon Girl Scout Coun, 65; Pres. Cup Award, La. Asn. for Retarded Children, 66; Cert. of Appreciation, Baton Rouge Ins. Exchange, 66; Niki Award, La. Fedn. of Bus. & Prfnl. Womens Clubs, 68; Man of the Quarter Award, La. Asn. of Ment. Health, 69. Rel: Presbyterian. Legal Res: 655 Cora Dr, Baton Rouge, La. 70815. Mailing Add: P.O. Box 66451, Baton Rouge, La. 70806.

WALKER, LLOYD EDWARD R
Chmn, Montcalm Co. Rep. Cmt, Mich.
b. Greenville, Mich, 6/17/29; s. Ralph Walker and Dora Van Oss W; m. 12/28/57 to Marcia L. Richmond; c. Theresa Theodora, Mary Karen, John Lloyd, Paul Frederick and Wendy Lea. Educ: Greenville High Sch. Polit. & Govt. Pos: City councilman, Greenville, Mich, 64-; chmn, Greenville Bd. of Health, 66-; mem, bd. of supvr, Montcalm Co, 67 & 68; mem, Mid-Mich. Bd. of Health, 68; mem, Areawide Comprehensive Health Planning Unit, 68-; chmn, Montcalm Co. Rep. Cmt, Mich, 69- Bus. & Prof. Pos: Right-of-way Buyer, currently. Mil. Serv: Entered as Pvt, Army, 51, released as Cpl, 52, after serv. in 197th Regt. Combat Team, Alaska. Mem: Regional coordinator, Mich. Cath. Conf. Educaid Effort; Rotary; Am. Legion; K. of C; Sigma Theta. Rel: Catholic. Mailing Add: 610 S. Franklin St, Greenville, Mich. 48838.

WALKER, LLOYD JULIUS D
b. Hailey, Idaho, 9/30/28; s. Lloyd William Walker and Agatha Diebenow W; m. 4/25/52 to Mary Eileen Fallon; c. Lloyd W, II, Francis Patrick and Mary Nora. Educ: Harvard Univ, A.B, 50, LL.B, 55. Polit. & Govt. Pos: Del, Dem. Nat. Conv, 60 & 64; chmn, Twin Falls Co. Dem. Cent. Cmt, Idaho, 58-60 and Idaho State Dem. Cent. Cmt, 62-65; cand. for Dem. Nomination for Gov, Idaho, 66; Dem. precinct committeeman, Third Precinct, Idaho. Bus. & Prof. Pos: Partner, Kramer, Walker, Pope & Plankey, Idaho, 57-66. Mil. Serv: Entered as Pvt, Army, 51, released as Cpl, 53, after serv. in Hq. & Hq. Battery, 12th Anti-aircraft Artil. Group, Seventh Army, ETO, 51-53. Mem: Elks; Am. Legion; C. of C. Rel: Roman Catholic. Mailing Add: 311 Eighth Ave, North, Twin Falls, Idaho 83301. (1967)

WALKER, MERLE ROYSE, II R
Chmn, Henderson Co. Rep. Party, Tex.
b. Laurel, Miss, 8/27/22; s. Ray Mattox Walker and Marian Tippy W; m. 3/26/48 to Betty Ross Moseley; c. Wynne Worth, Merle Royse, III and Ross Moseley. Educ: De Pauw Univ, B.A; Tex. Univ. Grad. Sch. Polit. & Govt. Pos: Acting postmaster, Athens, Tex, 59-62; del, Tex. State Rep. Conv. and Nominating Conv, 64 & 66; chmn, Henderson Co. Rep. Party, Tex, currently. Bus. & Prof. Pos: Realtor, CMB, Merle Walker Real Estate, 63-66; life ins. agent, Ohio Nat. Life, 64-65, Standard Life Ins. Co, 65 and West. Rep. Life, 66; teacher math, Henderson Co. Jr. Col, 66. Mil. Serv: Entered as A/S, Naval Res, 43, released as Lt.(jg), 46; Southwest Pac. Area Ribbon; Philippines Ribbon. Mem: Athens Little Theater; Rotary; Mensa; Jr. Col. Teachers Asn; Tex. Real Estate Asn; Nat. Asn. Real Estate Bd. Mailing Add: 508 Robbins Rd, Athens, Tex. 75751.

WALKER, PRENTISS LAFAYETTE R
b. Smith Co, Miss, 8/17/17; s. W.L. Walker and Melissa Mayfield W; m. 5/4/37 to Dimple Howell; c. Jan (Mrs. Magee) and Treta. Educ: Miss. Col, 36. Polit. & Govt. Pos: Mem, Miss. State Fish & Game Cmn, 60; campaign mgr, Unpledged Electors Movement, Fourth Dist, Miss, 60; U.S. Rep, Fourth Dist, Miss, 65-68; del, Rep. Nat. Conv, 68. Bus. & Prof. Pos: Owner, Walker's Supermarket, 37-63; pres, Walker Egg Farms, Inc, 55- Mil. Serv: Entered as Pvt, Army, 44, released as Pvt. 1/C, after serv. in Pac. Theater. Mem: Mason; Am. Legion; Lions; Mize Improv. Club; past pres, Miss. Fox Hunter's Asn; South. Miss. Fox Hunter's Asn. Rel: Baptist; Deacon, Baptist Church. Mailing Add: P.O. Box 38, Mize, Miss. 39116. (1967)

WALKER, STANLEY CLAY D
Va. State Del.
b. Norfolk, Va, 7/2/23; m. to Sibyl Bruce Moore. Educ: Fork Union Mil. Acad; Norfolk Bus. Col. Polit. & Govt. Pos: Va. State Del, 64-; mem, Norfolk Citizens Adv. Cmt, Norfolk City Recreation Cmn and Norfolk City Sch. Bd. Bus. & Prof. Pos: Partner and officer, structural steel fabrication, erection, and eng. firm. Mil. Serv: World War II, Army, Europe. Mem: Past v.pres, Norfolk Cosmopolitan Club; past pres, Kempsville Puritan Club; Norfolk Executives Club; Corinthian Lodge 266, AF&AM; past pres, Tidewater Toastmasters Club. Rel: Methodist; official bd. mem. Mailing Add: 1298 Kempsville Rd, Norfolk, Va. 23502. (1967)

WALKER, WILLIAM H, III R
Tenn. State Rep.
b. Memphis, Tenn, 10/28/33; s. William H. Walker, Jr. and Evelyn Brandon W; m. 6/26/59 to June Elisabeth Derryberry; c. Alison and Brandon. Educ: Union Univ, 51-53; Univ. Tenn, B.S, 58, M.S, 61; Alpha Tau Omega. Polit. & Govt. Pos: Tenn. State Rep, Crockett and Haywood Co, 68- Bus. & Prof. Pos: Supvr, Haywood Co. Soil Conserv. Dist. Bd, 64-; dir, Haywood Co. Farmers Coop, 66-; dir, Haywood Co. Farm Bur, Brownsville, 66- Mil. Serv: Entered as Pvt, Army, 55, released as Sgt, 56, after serv. in 613th Artil. Bn, Ft. Bragg, N.C, 55-56. Mem: Tenn. and Nat. Soybean Asn; Tenn. and Nat. Holstein-Friesian Asns; Farm Bur. Rel: Baptist. Mailing Add: Route 3, Box 195, Brownsville, Tenn. 38012.

WALKER, WILLIAM HENRY D
Secy, Lake Co. Dem. Cent. Orgn, Ind.
b. El Dorado, Ark, 8/9/14; s. Sidney Walker and Lila Jackson W; m. 10/19/59 to Dorothy Hicks; c. William Henry, Jr, Sidney Vincent and Sybil Roberta. Educ: Prairie View Col, 32-34; Wilberforce Univ, 35-37; De Paul Law Sch, LL.B, 47; Kappa Alpha Psi. Polit. & Govt. Pos: Juvenile probation officer, Lake Co, Ind, 48; dep. prosecuting attorney, East Chicago, 47 and asst. city attorney, 51; del, Dem. Nat. Conv, 60 & 64; state civil rights coordinator, Pres. Campaign, Ind, 60; secy, Lake Co. Dem. Cent. Orgn, 62-; attorney, East Chicago Water Dept, 64-69; spec. consult. to State Dem. Cent. Cmt, 66-67; mem. Campaign staff, H.H. Humphrey, 68. Bus. & Prof. Pos: Bd. mem, Ind. Vocational Tech. Col. Bd, 65-; chmn, Northwest Regional Inst. Mem: Am, Nat, Ind. and East Chicago Bar Asns; Am. Judicature Soc; Am. Trial Lawyers Asn; North Ind. Polit. Action Alliance; Mason (32°); life mem. NAACP; Crippled Children's Soc. of Lake Co; United Commun. Serv. Orgn. of East Chicago; East Chicago Boys Club; treas, Lake Co. Arthritis & Rheumatism Fund; Twin City Recreation League. Rel: Methodist. Legal Res: 2307 Purdue Dr, East Chicago, Ind, 46312. Mailing Add: 2208 Broadway, East Chicago, Ind. 46312.

WALKER, WILLIAM O. R
Dir, Dept. of Indust. Rels, Ohio
b. Selma, Ala, 9/19/96; s. Alex Walker and Annie Jones W; m. 6/12/54 to Naomi E. Russell. Educ: Wilberforce Univ, 16; Omega Psi Phi. Polit. & Govt. Pos: City councilman, Cleveland, Ohio, 40-46; dir, Dept. of Indust. Rels, Ohio, 63-; mem, Rep. State Cent. Cmt; ward leader, Rep. Party; alternate del, Rep. Nat. Conv, 68. Mem: Pres, Cleveland Chapter Urban League, NAACP, Nat. Newspaper Pub. Asn, Cleveland Bus. League. Rel: St. James African Methodist Episcopal Church. Legal Res: 3198 Ashwood Rd, Cleveland, Ohio 44120. Mailing Add: 1949 E. 105th St, Cleveland, Ohio 44106.

WALKLEY, FRANK R
N.Y. State Assemblyman
b. Oneida, N.Y, 10/17/21; m. to Margaret Curtis; c. Sarah, Lincoln, Jennifer, Donna and Margaret. Educ: Cornell Univ, B.S. in agr. econ. Polit. & Govt. Pos: Former town supvr. and justice of the peace; N.Y. State Assemblyman, 64- Bus. & Prof. Pos: Farm Operator. Mil. Serv: Navy, Lt.(jg). Mem: Farm Bur; Am. Legion; Oakland Lodge 379, F&AM; past pres, Castile Commun. Club; chmn. adv. bd, Empire Livestock Mkt. Coop; past co. pres, Dairyman's League Coop; pres. bd. mgrs, Wyo. Co. Commun. Hosp; Erie-Niagara Regional Water Resources Bd; Regional Fish and Wildlife Mgt. Bd. Rel: Dir, trustee, chmn. of off. bd, United Community Church. Mailing Add: Castile, N.Y. 14427.

WALL, ARTHUR J. R
b. Hawley, Pa, 1/20/98; s. Theodore F. Wall and Mary Bryant W. Educ: Wyoming Sem. Polit. & Govt. Pos: Pa. State Rep, 32-38 & 52-67; co. cmnr, Wayne Co, 12 years. Bus. & Prof. Pos: Feed bus, 22-46; retired, 46. Mil. Serv: Aviation Corps, Army, World War I. Mailing Add: 301 Eighth St, Honesdale, Pa. 18431. (1967)

WALL, FRANK TRACY D
b. Gillsburg, Miss, 3/5/08; married. Polit. & Govt. Pos: Miss. State Rep, 52-60. Bus. & Prof. Pos: Dairy Farmer. Rel: Baptist. Mailing Add: Route 2, Liberty, Miss. 39645. (1967)

WALL, H. EWING D
Chmn, Prince William Co. Dem. Cmt, Va.
b. Richmond, Va, 4/9/99; s. Charles Clements Wall and Loveline Cutler Ewing W; m. 11/20/26 to Laura Lillard Fray (deceased) and 9/8/39 to Anne Stribling Moncure; c. H. Ewing, Jr. and Marion Moncure. Educ: Hampden Sydney Col, 18-19; Kappa Sigma. Polit. & Govt. Pos: Councilman, town clerk and treas, Quantico, Va, 20's-32; chmn, Prince William Co. Dem. Cmt, currently. Bus. & Prof. Pos: Secy-treas, Group III, Va. Bankers Asn, 50-58, treas, 59-, pres, Va. Bankers Asn, 62. Mil. Serv: Pvt, Students Army Training Corps, 18. Rel: Presbyterian. Legal Res: Fuller Rd, Quantico, Va. 22134. Mailing Add: 301 Potomac Ave, Quantico, Va. 22134.

WALL, HARRY D
Dem. Nat. Committeeman, Idaho
b. Bowerston, Ohio, 9/1/03; s. William Wall and Lulu Seifried W; wid. Polit. & Govt. Pos: Idaho State Sen, 45-50; Dem. Nat. Committeeman, Idaho. Mem: Elks. Rel: Episcopal. Legal Res: Box 436, Lewiston, Idaho. 83501. Mailing Add: 611 Main, Lewiston, Idaho. 83501.

WALL, JAMES L. D
Chmn, Randolph Co. Dem. Cent. Cmt, Ind.
b. Pleasant Hill, Ohio, 12/21/05; s. Fred L. Wall and Daisy J. Jellison W; m. to Mary I. Heaston; c. Susan L.(Mrs. William Patton), Judith A.(Mrs. John Hevel) and Nancy K.(Mrs. John Mitchell). Educ: Ball State Univ, 23-27. Polit. & Govt. Pos: Dem. precinct committeeman, Ind, 28-32; mem, Bd. of Educ, Winchester, 50-54, pres, 58-62; mem, City Park Bd, 52-56; chmn, Randolph Co. Dem. Cent. Cmt, 64- Bus. & Prof. Pos: Sch. teacher, 24-28; mgr, Miller-Jones Shoe Co, Rushville, Ind, 28-33; agent, Metrop. Life Ins. Co, New Castle, 33-37; mgr. and owner, Wall's Brownbilt Shoe Store, Winchester, 37-57; supt. dist, Ind. State Hwy. Cmn, Indianapolis, 64-69; retired. Mem: Elks. Rel: Presbyterian. Mailing Add: 700 West South, Winchester, Ind. 47394.

WALL, JOE D
Chmn, Houston Co. Dem. Exec. Cmt, Ga.
b. Winder, Ga, 12/24/29; s. Albert Glenn Wall and Ettie Whitehead W; m. 3/9/53 to Sara Helen Jones; c. Joseph Gregory, Steven Douglas and Gary Albert. Educ: High sch. Polit. & Govt. Pos: Mem, adv. cmt, City of Warner Robins, Ga, 65-; chmn, Houston Co. Dem. Exec. Cmt, 66- Bus. & Prof. Pos: V.pres, Wall Tire Serv, Inc, Warner Robins, Ga, 53-; v.pres, Klein & Wall Tire Serv, Inc, Perry, currently; v.pres, Wall Tire Distributors, Inc, currently; pres, Tamie Land Develop. Co. Inc, 65- Mil. Serv: Entered as Seaman, Navy, 47, released as SKSN, 50; after serv. in U.S.S. Tolovana. Mem: Air Force Asn; Rotary Int; Elks; Mason; Scottish Rite; Shrine; Warner Robins C. of C. Rel: Methodist. Legal Res: 618 Arrowhead Trail, Warner Robins, Ga. 31093. Mailing Add: P.O. Box 668, Warner Robins, Ga. 31093.

WALL, JOHN F. R
Ill. State Rep.
b. Chicago, Ill, 8/10/13; married; c. 2 sons. Educ: St. Barbara Roman Cath. Parochial Sch; Tilden Tech. High Sch; Englewood Eve. Sch. Polit. & Govt. Pos: Alderman, 11th Ward, 47-51; Rep. Ward Committeeman, 52-; supt. of private employ. agencies, Ill. Dept. of Labor, 55-61; Ill. State Rep, 62-64 & currently; mem, Ill. Rep. State Cent. Cmt, 68- Bus. & Prof. Pos: Dir, Wash. Savings & Loan Asn; operated Wholesale Grocery and Meat Bus. and Cleaning and Laundry; operates Archer Loomis Recreation Bowling Lanes. Mem: Archbishop Quigley Coun, K. of C; St. Barbara's Holy Name Soc. Rel: Roman Catholic. Legal Res: 2874 S. Hillock Ave, Chicago, Ill. 60608. Mailing Add: 2903 Archer Ave, Chicago, Ill. 60608. (1967)

WALL, JOHN M. R
Chmn, Chautauqua Co. Rep. Cmt, Kans.
b. Sedan, Kans, 10/1/06; s. Nathan B. Wall and Flora J. Inglefield W; m. 5/7/39 to Beth K. Keller; c. Nancy. Educ: Univ. Kans, B.S, 28, LL.B, 31; Pi Kappa Alpha. Polit. & Govt. Pos: State attorney, Kans, 33-36, co. attorney, Chautauqua Co, 37-42 & 46-50; chmn, Chautauqua Co. Rep. Cmt, 50-; del-at-lg, Rep. Nat. Conv, 56. Bus. & Prof. Pos: Attorney-at-law, 31-33 & 37- Mil. Serv: Entered as Pvt, Army, 42, released as Capt, 46, after serv. in 98th and 25th Inf. Divs, Pacific Theater. Mem: Kans. Bar Asn; past pres, Sedan C. of C; Am. Legion. Rel: Episcopal. Legal Res: 405 N. Montgomery, Sedan, Kans. 67361. Mailing Add: P.O. Box 96, Sedan, Kans. 67361.

WALLACE, CARL S. R
Spec. Asst. to the Secy. and Dep. Secy. of Defense
b. Ontario, Wis, 9/27/18; s. David Wallace and Mae McQueen W; m. 2/22/41 to Marian E. Jones; c. Carl S, Jr. and Mary Ann. Educ: Univ. Wis, Ph.B, 43. Polit. & Govt. Pos: Admin. asst. to U.S. Rep. Melvin Laird, Wis, 65-69; Spec. Asst. to the Secy. and Dep. Secy. of Defense, 69- Bus. & Prof. Pos: Mgr. Wausau Off, Wis. State Employ. Serv, 51-53; mgr. Stevens Point Area C. of C, 53-65. Mil. Serv: S/Sgt, Army, 42-45, with serv. in Co. M, 417th Inf, 76th Div, ETO; Two Bronze Stars. Mem: Elks; Kiwanis; Am. Legion. Rel: Methodist. Legal Res: Stevens Point, Wis. 54481. Mailing Add: 8312 Ashwood Dr, Alexandria, Va. 22308.

WALLACE, E. HOWARD D
Chmn, Medina Co. Dem. Exec. Cmt, Tex.
b. Pearsall, Tex, 7/7/24; s. John G. Wallace and Josie Jerkins W; m. 8/29/42 to Doris Schott; c. William Howard, Danny J. and Vicki A. Educ: Am. Inst. of Banking; South. Methodist Univ. Polit. & Govt. Pos: Alderman and mayor pro tem, Devine, Tex, 64-; chmn, Medina Co. Dem. Exec. Cmt, 67- Bus. & Prof. Pos: Warehouse supt, Sweeney & Co, San Antonio, Tex; v. pres. and cashier, Median Valley State Bank, Devine, 52- Mil. Serv: Army, 43. Mem: Pres, Winter Garden Bankers Asn; C. of C; bd. dir, Devine Golf Asn; St. Joseph Soc. Rel: Catholic. Mailing Add: 203 Cardinal Dr, Devine, Tex. 78016.

WALLACE, FRED, JR. R
b. 1914. Polit. & Govt. Pos: Ky. State Rep, 64-69; former chmn, Muhlenburg Co. Rep. Exec. Cmt. Bus. & Prof. Pos: Retail hardware. Mem: Central City C. of C. Rel: Methodist; former mem, Bd. of Stewards, First Methodist Church. Mailing Add: Central City, Ky. 42330. (1967)

WALLACE, GEORGE CORLEY Am. Independent Party
b. Clio, Ala, 8/25/19; s. George Corley Wallace and Mozelle Smith W; m. 5/22/43 to Lurleen Burns (deceased); c. Bobbie Jo, Peggy Sue, George C. III and Lee. Educ: Univ. of Ala, LL.B. Polit. & Govt. Pos: Ala. State Rep, 51-55; judge, Third Judicial Circuit, 55-63; Gov, Ala, 63-66; cand. for Pres, U.S, 68. Bus. & Prof. Pos: Lawyer. Mil. Serv: Army, Sgt, 42-45, 58th Combat Wing, China, Burma, India, Marianna Islands; 20th Air Force, B-29 Flight Engr, Air offensive over Japan. Mem: VFW; Am. Legion; Mason. Rel: Methodist. Mailing Add: P.O. Box 1968, Montgomery, Ala. 36103.

WALLACE, GERALDINE ELIZABETH D
V.Chmn, Second Dist. Dem. Party, Ind.
b. Freeland Park, Ind, 6/13/06; d. William Anderson Bowman and Lottie Jane Miller B; m. 6/26/28 to Alvin Eldo Wallace; c. June (Mrs. Thomas Timothy), Mary (Mrs. Dennis Plantenga) and Wanda (Mrs. Arnold Wilson). Educ: Ind. State Univ, Terre Haute, 4 years; Butler Univ, 1 year. Polit. & Govt. Pos: Vice precinct committeeman, Benton Co. Richland Twp. Dem. Party, Ind, 50-69; vice chmn, Benton Co. Dem. Party, 60-69; v.chmn, Second Dist. Dem. Party, 68-; del, Dem. Nat. Conv, 68. Bus. & Prof. Pos: Kindergarten teacher, Benton Cent. Pub. Schs, 53-68. Mem: Am. Legion Auxiliary; DAR. Jenny Award, Dem. Women of Ind. Rel: Presbyterian; Choir dir, 20 years. Mailing Add: Earl Park, Ind. 47942.

WALLACE, GLENN CHARLES 'GUS' R
Chmn, Cedar Co. Rep. Cent. Cmt, Iowa
b. Rhodes, Iowa, 6/24/25; s. James E. Wallace and Florence Lemkuhl W; m. 6/30/50 to Kathryn Ann Crist; c. Jane and Jennifer. Educ: Marshalltown Jr. Col, 1 year; Iowa State Univ, 1 1/4 years; Mo. Univ, Columbia, 1 1/4 years. Polit. & Govt. Pos: Precinct committeeman, Rep. Party, Iowa, 58-; finance chmn, Cedar Co. Rep. Cent. Cmt, 59-63, chmn, 66- Bus. & Prof. Pos: Farmer, 51- Mil. Serv: Entered as Pvt, Air Force, 43, released as Lt, 45. Mem: Am. Legion; Farm Bur. Fedn. Rel: Methodist. Legal Res: R.R. 1, Clarence, Iowa 52216.

WALLACE, JOSEPH CLARK D
b. Indianapolis, Ind; s. Ross H. Wallace and Mary-Joe Clark W; single. Educ: Franklin and Marshall Col, B.S, 29; Ind. Univ, LL.B, 34 and J.D, 36; Sigma Delta Kappa. Polit. & Govt. Pos: Ind. State Rep, 39-40; Indianapolis City Councilman, 48-68. Mil. Serv: Entered as Pvt, Army, 42, released as 2nd Lt, 45 after serv. in 3rd Army ETO. Mem: Indianapolis, Ind. and Am. Bar Asns; Am. Legion; Mason, Scottish Rite. Rel: Methodist. Legal Res: 1840 N. Pennsylvania St, Indianapolis, Ind. 46202. Mailing Add: 130 E. Washington St, Indianapolis, Ind. 46204.

WALLACE, LISLE L. R
b. Sheridan, Ind, 3/30/02; s. Lee O. Wallace and Angeline Spencer W; m. 9/8/21 to Margaret Anne Geyler; c. Mary (Mrs. Smith), Phil Wallace and Anne (Mrs. Nichols). Educ: Ind. Univ, LL.B; Sigma Delta Kappa. Polit. & Govt. Pos: Admin. asst. to Sen. Wm. E. Jenner, 44; chmn, Ind. Dept. Conserv, 45-48; co-chmn, Chicago Off, Rep. Party Nomination Cmt, 48; Ind. campaign mgr, Robert Taft, 52; chmn, Sixth Dist. Rep. Party, Ind, 58-62. Mem: Columbia Club, Indianapolis, Ind. Mailing Add: 403 E. Fifth St, Sheridan, Ind. 46069.

WALLACE, MATTHEW BREVARD, JR. R
b. Huntersville, N.C, 9/18/13; s. M.B. Wallace and Alma Oehler W; m. 7/25/38 to Ruth Davis; c. Sandra and M. Brevard, III. Educ: Davidson Col, B.S. in chem, 34. Polit. & Govt. Pos: Chmn, Florence Co. Rep. Party, 64-66, finance chmn, 68-69; precinct committeeman, Rep. Party, 66- Bus. & Prof. Pos: Indust. supvr, Dupont Co. Plant, Florence, S.C, 41-60, employee rels. supt, Dupont Co. Plant, Florence, S.C, 60-66; mem, Florence Co. Dist. 1 Sch. Bd, 67- Mem: Am. Soc. Personnel Adminstr; past pres. and past zone chmn, Lions; Pee Dee Tech. Soc; pres, Florence Co. United Fund, 69-70. Rel: Presbyterian. Mailing Add: 1336 Clarendon Ave, Florence, S.C. 29501.

WALLACE, ROBERT ASH D
b. Cordell, Okla, 5/26/21; s. John Marshall Wallace (deceased) and Allie Stewart W; m. 12/9/43 to Luna Agnes Campbell; c. Robert C, Wendy A. and Douglas S. Educ: Okla. State Univ, 38-42; Univ. Wash, B.A, 45; Univ. Chicago, Ph.D, 56; Sigma Tau; Blue Key; Pi Sigma Alpha; Sigma Alpha Epsilon. Polit. & Govt. Pos: Legis. asst. to U.S. Sen. Paul H. Douglas, 49-54; staff dir, U.S. Senate Cmt. on Banking and Currency, 55-59; consultant to U.S. Sen. John F. Kennedy, 59-61; Asst. Secy. of Treas, U.S. Treas. Dept, 61-69. Bus. & Prof. Pos: Eng, Boeing Airplane Co, Seattle, Wash, 42-45; instr, Ill. Inst. of Tech, Chicago, Ill, 48-49; v.chmn. bd, Exchange Nat. Bank of Chicago, 69- Publ: Federal Expenditures, A Detailed Analysis, Am. Assembly, Columbia Univ, 52; Factors Affecting the Stock Market (with others), U.S. Govt. Printing Off, 55; Congressional Control of Federal Spending, Wayne State Univ. Press, 60. Mem: Am. Acad. of Polit. & Soc. Sci; Am. Polit. Sci. Asn. U.S. Treas. Exceptional Serv. Award, 65; U.S. Treas. Alexander Hamilton Award, 68. Rel: First Christian Church. Legal Res: 237 E. Delaware Place, Chicago, Ill. 60611. Mailing Add: 130 S. La Salle, Chicago, Ill. 60603.

WALLACE, ROBERT BUFORD D
b. Charleston, S.C, 4/9/35; s. Oliver T. Wallace and Thelma Fogle W; m. 8/30/58 to Joy Holcombe; c. Kimberly, Robyn, O. Theodore, Lisa and Krystie. Educ: Univ. S.C, LL.B, 59; Kappa Sigma Kappa; Omicron Delta Kappa; Sigma Phi Epsilon; Alpha Tau Omega; Wig & Robe. Polit. & Govt. Pos: Chmn, Charleston Co. Dem. Party, S.C, 66-68; solicitor, Ninth Judicial Circuit, 69- Mil. Serv: Entered as A/S, Navy, released as Fireman, 61, after serv. in Naval Res. Mem: Exec. cmt, Charleston Co. Bar Asn; S.C. Bar Asn; S.C. Trial Lawyers Asn; dist. Dep. Grand Master, First Masonic Dist, Masons; Exchange Club Charleston. Rel: Episcopal. Legal Res: 536 Pelzer, Mt. Pleasant, S.C. 29464. Mailing Add: P.O. Box 388, Charleston, S.C. 29402.

WALLACE, ROBERT LEWIS R
Chmn, Iowa Co. Rep. Cent. Cmt, Iowa
b. Williamsburg, Iowa, 5/8/22; s. John R. Wallace and Lois Howes W; m. 10/4/64 to Margaret Jeanne Davis Norton; c. Stephen K. Norton, Kathleen G. Norton, Claudia J. Norton and Robin Jeanne Wallace. Educ: Williamsburg High Sch, grad. Polit. & Govt. Pos: Chmn, Iowa Co. Young Rep, Iowa, 52-56; policy chmn, Iowa Young Rep, 54-56; Rep. precinct committeeman, 54-61; chmn, First Dist. Young Rep, 56-59; chmn, Iowa Co. Rep. Cent. Cmt, currently. Bus. & Prof. Pos: Farmer, 46-61; ins. rep. Indust. Casualty Ins. Co, Chicago, Ill, 61- Mil. Serv: Entered as Pvt, Army, 43, released as S/Sgt, 46; Good Conduct Medal; Am. Theater Ribbon. Mem: Mason; Eastern Star; Am. Legion; Farm Bur. Rel: Methodist. Mailing Add: 802 W. Welsh, Williamsburg, Iowa 52361. (1967)

WALLACE, WILLIAM LEWIS D
S.C. State Sen.
b. York, S.C, 5/2/11; s. John Robert Alexander Wallace and Nettie Lou Gardner W; m. 11/25/39 to Elyn Colgin; c. Mary Elyn Carroll, JoAnn Kathrine and Peatsa Christina. Educ: LaSalle Exten. Univ. Polit. & Govt. Pos: S.C. State Rep, 40-48; S.C. State Sen, 48-56 & 69-; chmn. planning bd. and platform and resolution cmt, State Dem. Exec. Cmt, 46-; del-at-lg, Dem. Nat. Conv, 52, 56 & 64; mem. adv. coun, Nat. Dem. Party. Bus. & Prof. Pos: Realtor, merchant and cattle rancher. Mem: Elks; WOW; C. of C. Rel: Presbyterian. Mailing Add: 16 Roosevelt, York, S.C. 29745. (1967)

WALLACH, LOUIS D
b. New York City, N.Y, 5/7/24; s. Arthur Wallach and Lena Rosiner W; m. 9/15/46 to Mildred N. Aufrichtig; c. Michael J. and Tom H. Educ: St. John's Univ. Law Sch, LL.B, 46. Polit. & Govt. Pos: N.Y. State Assemblyman, 55-64; judge, The Civil Court, N.Y, 65- Bus. & Prof. Pos: Attorney-at-Law, 47-64. Mil. Serv: Army, Pvt, 43. Mem: Elks; Philonomic Coun; N.Y. State and Queen's Co. Bar Asns. Rel: Jewish. Legal Res: 110-11 Queen's Blvd, Forest Hills, N.Y. 11375. Mailing Add: 126-06 Queen's Blvd, Kew Gardens, N.Y. 11415.

WALLANDER, JEROME BRANDVOLD R
b. Williston, N.Dak, 4/7/25; s. Selmer Brandvold Wallander and Elna Scott W; m. 6/29/58 to Marjorie Jean Ertmann; c. Karen and Daniel. Educ: Univ. Mont, B.A. and LL.B; Sigma Alpha Epsilon. Polit. & Govt. Pos: Former Mont. State Rep, Fourth Dist. Bus. & Prof. Pos: V.pres. and counsel, First State Bank of Froid, Mont, currently. Mil. Serv: Entered as A/S, Navy, 43, released as Disbursing Clerk 2nd, 46, after serv. in USS Paul Hamilton, Am. and Pac. Theaters; re-entered as Disbursing Clerk 2nd, Navy, 51, released as 52, after serv. in Mil. Air Transport Squadron 8, Hawaii; Asiatic-Pac. Medal; Am. Campaign Medal; Victory Medal; Philippine Liberation Medal. Rel: Protestant. Mailing Add: Froid, Mont. 59226. (1967)

WALLER, MARGIE WEST R
Mem, Ala. State Rep. Exec. Cmt.
b. New Orleans, La, 6/4/25; d. William A. West, Jr. and Estelle Flaspoller W; m. 4/23/49 to Luther Hill Waller, Jr; c. Susan Murray, Janet Maultsby and Marguerite Estelle. Educ: Newcomb Col, Tulane Univ, B.A; Kappa Kappa Gamma. Polit. & Govt. Pos: Past treas. and v.pres, Ala. Fedn. Rep. Women; v.chmn, Montgomery Co. Rep. Exec. Cmt, 60-; del, State Rep. Conv, 62, 64, 66 & 68; alternate del, Rep. Nat. Conv, 64 & 68; mem, Ala. State Rep. Exec. Cmt, 66- Mem: Jr. League. Rel: Presbyterian. Mailing Add: 2307 Allendale Place, Montgomery, Ala. 36111.

WALLER, SAMUEL CARPENTER D
Mem, Richmond Co. Dem. Exec. Cmt, Ga.
b. Augusta, Ga, 5/3/18; s. Harcourt E. Waller and Josephine C. Carpenter W; m. 4/18/52 to Anna B. Maxwell; c. Anna M, Laura C. and Amelia C. Educ: Princeton Univ, A.B, 40; Harvard Law Sch, LL.B, 48. Polit. & Govt. Pos: Mem. city coun, Augusta, Ga, 50-56, city attorney, 64-; former chmn, Richmond Co. Dem. Exec. Cmt, Ga, mem, 66- Bus. & Prof. Pos: Former pres, Augusta Library; mem. bd. dir, First of Ga. Ins. Co, 56-68; cmnr, Nat. Conf. of Cmnrs. on Uniform State Laws, 65- Mil. Serv: Entered as 2nd Lt, Army, 41, released as Capt, 45, after serv. in 63rd Inf. Div, ETO; Bronze Star. Mem: Kiwanis; mem. bd. gov, State Bar of Ga, 67- Rel: Episcopal; Registrar, Diocese of Ga; dep. to gen. conv, Episcopal Church, 58- Legal Res: 600 Gary St, Augusta, Ga. 30904. Mailing Add: 1500 Georgia Railroad Bank Building, Augusta, Ga. 30902.

WALLHAUSER, GEORGE MARVIN R
b. Newark, N.J, 2/10/00; s. Dr. Henry Joseph Frederick and Rachel Apolonia Vogt W; m. 5/26/26 to Isabel Towne; c. George Marvin, Henry

Towne. Educ: Univ. Pa, B.A, 22; Columbia Univ, 42; Phi Sigma Kappa. Polit. & Govt. Pos: Former pres. and mem. bd, Bur. Family Serv, Orange and Maplewood, N.J; chmn. planning bd, Maplewood, 46-54; mem, Twp. Cmt, 54-57; U.S. Rep, N.J, 59-65. Bus. & Prof. Pos: Mem. staff, U.S. Realty & Investment Co, 28-, treas, 47-, v.pres, 56-, dir, 40; dir, Maplewood Bank & Trust Co. and Yorkwood Savings & Loan Asn. Mil. Serv: Naval Res, World War I. Mem: Am. Legion; Mason; Elks. Rel: Methodist. Legal Res: 31 Kensington Terr, Maplewood, N.J. 07060. Mailing Add: 972 Broad St, Newark, N.J. 07060.

WALLIN, JEAN ROGERS D
N.H. State Rep.
b. Hibbing, Minn, 1/13/34; d. William John Rogers and Rhea Madison R; m. 6/12/54 to Donald Frank Wallin; c. Rikka Louise and Amy Suzanne. Educ: Va. Junior Col, Minn, 1 year; Univ. Minn, Minneapolis, 2 years. Polit. & Govt. Pos: N.H. State Rep, 67-; del. and mem. rules cmt, Dem. Nat. Conv, 68; Dem. Nat. Committeewoman, N.H, 68-; mem, Nashua Sch. Bd, 68- Mem: N.H. Civil Liberties Union; League of Women Voters; Order of Women Legislators. Rel: Unitarian, Universalist. Mailing Add: 3 Durham St, Nashua, N.H. 03060.

WALLIN, MYRON JOSEPH R
Chmn, N.Dak. Dist. Two Rep. Party
b. Minot, N.Dak, 3/13/23; s. John Adolph Wallin and Hattie Spooner W; m. 5/2/43 to Fern Grindeland; c. Gary Wayne, Jerry Lee and Craig Myron. Educ: Noonan High Sch, 4 years. Polit. & Govt. Pos: Justice of the Peace, Harmonious Twp, Burke Co, N.Dak, 48-50; state committeeman and conv. del, Rep. Orgn. Cmt, 52; postmaster, U.S. Post Off, Crosby, 57-61; del, Rep. State Conv, 64 & 68; chmn, N.Dak. Dist. Two Rep. Party, 68- Mem: N.Dak. Soc. Farm Mgt. and Rural Appraisal; Mason (past master); Concordia Lutheran Church Mens' Club (past chmn); charter mem, Crosby Jaycee's; Moose (bd. dirs); Kiwanis (bd. dirs). Rel: Lutheran. Mailing Add: 601 First St. S.E, Crosby, N.Dak. 58730.

WALLING, BARBARA ECKHOFF R
b. New Sharon, Iowa, 4/6/27; d. Tom Eckhoff and Alice Howell E; m. 12/22/47 to Charles Lee Walling; c. Arthur Knight, Thomas Henry and Anne. Educ: Christian Col, Columbia, Mo. Polit. & Govt. Pos: Pres, Mahaska Co. Club of Rep. Women, Iowa, currently; pub. rels. chmn, Fourth Dist. Rep. Women, currently; alternate del, Rep. Nat. Conv, 68. Bus. & Prof. Pos: Staff writer, Oskaloosa Daily Herald, currently. Publ: Numerous articles for Oskaloosa Daily Herald. Rel: Episcopal. Mailing Add: 1103 Woodland Rd, Oskaloosa, Iowa 52577.

WALLING, ROBERT D
Ga. State Sen.
b. Fernaldina, Fla, 9/13/27; s. Robert Walling and Mary-Lee Smith W; m. 10/4/52 to Mildred Bruce Fraser; c. Carol Leigh, Lynne Elizabeth, Robert Fraser and Gregory Bruce. Educ: Ga. Tech, B.S, 50; Emory Univ, LL.B, 56; Yale Univ, LL.M, 60. Polit. & Govt. Pos: Asst. Attorney Gen, Ga, 58-59; Ga. State Rep, 66-69; Ga. State Sen, 69- Bus. & Prof. Pos: Asst. prof. of Law, Emory Univ. Law Sch, 60-63; partner, Haas & Holland, 63- Mil. Serv: Lt, Naval Res. Rel: Presbyterian. Mailing Add: 1001 Oxford Rd, Atlanta, Ga. 30306.

WALLING, WILLIS R. R
Chmn, Morris Co. Rep. Cmt, N.J.
b. Newark, N.J, 8/6/21; s. Willis H. Walling and Gladys Smith W; m. 11/4/43 to Margaret P. Stager; c. Susan M. (Mrs. Hauser), Jeanne Lynn and Diane Carol. Educ: I.C.S, Scranton, Pa. 8 years. Polit. & Govt. Pos: Co. cmt, Hanover Twp, N.J, 60- and munic. chmn, 64-65; dist. chmn, indust. finance chmn. and mem. exec. cmt, Morris Co. Rep. Cmt, 67-68 and co. chmn, 68- Bus. & Prof. Pos: Sales mgr, Swann Eng. Corp, N.J, 49-54; sales mgr, Damascus, Tube, Pa, 54-58 and exec. v.pres, 58-59; pres-treas, Swan Mfg. Corp, N.J, 60- and chmn. bd, 66- Mil. Serv: Entered as Pvt, Army, 42, released as Capt, 45, after serv. as pilot, 371st Fighter Group, ETO, 44-45, Capt, Res, 45-50; Air Medal with Five Clusters; Presidential Citation. Publ: 'Metal Specifications for Pools,' Swimming Pool Age, 67; 'Purchasing of Metals for Pool Use,' Calif. Pool, 67; 'Foreign Sales Development,' N.J. Int. Commerce. Mem: Nat. Swimming Pool Inst; Nat. Recreation & Parks Asn. Rel: Protestant. Mailing Add: 21 Hilltop Circle, Whippany, N.J. 07981.

WALLINGFORD, SAMUEL P, MRS. R
m. 3/26/66 to Samuel P. Wallingford. Polit. & Govt. Pos: Former v.chmn, Sedgwick Co. Young Rep. Club, Kans; exec. secy, Abraham Lincoln Rep. Club, 36-48; mem. state bd. Kans. Young Rep, 39; former v.chmn. adv. bd, Sedgwick Co. Rep. Women's Club; former mem. adv. bd, Sedgwick Co. Rep. Cent. Cmt; alternate del, Rep. Nat. Conv, 56 & 60; Rep. precinct committeewoman, 58-66. Mailing Add: 300 N. Terr. Dr, Wichita, Kans. 67208. (1967)

WALLIS, CHARLES L. R
Chmn, Yates Co. Rep. Cmt, N.Y.
b. Hamilton, N.Y, 5/1/21; s. The Rev. Robert S. Wallis and Caroline L. W; m. to Betty Barbe Watson. Educ: Univ. Redlands, A.B; Univ. Rochester, M.A; Colgate Rochester Divinity Sch, B.D; Delta Alpha. Polit. & Govt. Pos: Del, Rep. N.Y. State Conv, 62 & 66; del, Rep. Nat. Conv, 68; chmn, Yates Co. Rep. Cmt, N.Y, currently. Bus. & Prof. Pos: Minister, 1st Baptist Church, Canandaigua, 43-46, Keuka Col. Church, 46-65 and Keuka Park Church, 65-; chaplain, Vet. Admin. Hosp, 44-46; mem. Eng. Staff, Keuka Col, 45-, lectr. philos. and relig, 54-61 and prof. Eng. and chmn. dept, 59-; ed, Pulpit Preaching, 48-; ed. staff, Interpreter's Bible, 53-57; consult. ed, Harper & Row, Publishers, 54-; contrib, World Book Encyclop; ed, N.Y. Folklore Quart, 55-62; ed. assoc, Ministers Manual, 55-; ed. fel, Ministers Research Found, Inc, 56-59; bd. mgrs, Am. Baptist Hist. Soc, 61-; adv. ed, Chapel Books, 64- Publ: Co-author, Christmas in Our Hearts, Revell; ed, Treasury of Sermon Illustrations, Abingdon; ed, The Funeral Encyclop, Harper, plus many others. Mem: Chap. adv, Sigma Tau Delta and Pi Delta Epsilon; Poetry Soc. Am; Am. Asn. Univ. Prof; N.Y. Folklore Soc; Soc. Biblical Lit; Am. Acad. Relig; past master, Mason; past patron, Eastern Star; past pres, Rotary; Nat. Coun Teachers of Eng; Col. Eng. Asn; N.Y. Educ. Coun. Rel: Baptist. Mailing Add: Keuka College, Keuka Park, N.Y. 14478.

WALLIS, J. B. D
b. Patton, Mo, 10/6/29; s. Chas. J. Wallis and Ida O. Yount W; single. Educ: Southeast Mo. State Col, B.A, 54. Polit. & Govt. Pos: Del, Dem. Nat. Conv, 64. Bus. & Prof. Pos: Chevrolet dealer, 60- Rel: Methodist. Mailing Add: Marble Hill, Mo. 63764. (1967)

WALLNER, MARY D
Dem. Nat. Committeewoman, S.Dak.
m. to Frank Wallner. Polit. & Govt. Pos: Mgr, Dem. Hq. Polit. Campaigns, S.Dak, 58 & 60; State Dem. Cent. Committeewoman; Dem. Nat. Committeewoman, S.Dak, 65- Bus. & Prof. Pos: Art teacher. Mem: McKennan Hosp. Auxiliary; Crippled Childrens Hosp-Sch. Auxiliary; St. Mary's Altar Soc; bd. dir, Sioux Falls Civic Fine Art Center. Mailing Add: 2605 Poplar Dr, Sioux Falls, S.Dak. 57105.

WALLOP, MALCOLM R
Wyo. State Rep.
b. New York, N.Y, 2/27/33; s. Oliver Malcolm Wallop and Jean Moore W; m. 3/27/67 to Judith Warren; c. Malcolm Moncreiffe, Paul Stebbins, Oliver Matthew and Amy Vail. Educ: Yale, B.A, 54; St. Anthony Club. Polit. & Govt. Pos: Rep. precinct committeeman, Big Horn, Wyo, 64-69; Wyo. State Rep, Sheridan Co, 69- Bus. & Prof. Pos: Owner, Polo Ranch, Wyo, 58-; pres, Fairway Acres Inc, 59-68; pres, Mt. Flying Serv, Sheridan, Wyo, 60-64. Mil. Serv: Entered as 2nd Lt, Army, 55, released as 1st Lt, 57, after serving in 269th Field Artillery and 40th Field Artillery Group, Fifth Army, 55-57. Mem: Aircraft Owners & Pilot's Asn; Wyo. Farm Bur; Wyo. Stock Growers; Am. Nat. Cattleman's Asn; Elks. Rel: Episcopal. Mailing Add: Polo Ranch, Big Horn, Wyo. 82833.

WALSH, BASIL BARRY R
b. E. Rupert, Vt, 1/9/98; m. to C. Mae Thorpe; c. two daughters; eight grandchildren. Educ: Middlebury Col, B.S, 23; grad. work, Univ. of Vt. Polit. & Govt. Pos: Justice of the peace, Vt, 48; old age forwarding officer, 48-49; selectman, 48-57 & 60-; mem, Gov. Adv. Cmt. on Pub. Law 566; Vt. State Rep, 49-57 & 63-66. Bus. & Prof. Pos: Pvt. real estate investment; dir. and treas, Vt. Thorpe Camp for Crippled Children, Inc, 33- Mem: Past pres, Brandon Rotary Club; St. Paul's Lodge 25, F&AM; Farmers Chap. 9, RAM; Farmers Coun, 9, RSM; Mt. Calvary Commandery, 1; K.T. Cairo Temple, Shrine; bd, Neshobe River Flood Control Proj; treas, Otter Valley Watershed Asn; trustee, U.V.M, 55-61. Rel: Congregational. Mailing Add: Brandon, Vt. 05733. (1967)

WALSH, DANIEL CLIFFORD D
b. Hand Co, S.Dak, 7/13/01; s. Daniel Walsh and Alzina Burke W; m. 7/6/33 to Verniece Eva Davey; c. Margaret Ann. Educ: Marquette Univ, LL.B, 29. Polit. & Govt. Pos: States attorney, Hand Co, S.Dak, 30-35; asst. attorney gen, S.Dak, 35-39. Bus. & Prof. Pos: Practicing attorney, 29- Mem: S.Dak. Bar Asn. Rel: Roman Catholic. Legal Res: 223 W. Second Ave, Miller, S.Dak. 57362. Mailing Add: 112 W. Second St, Miller, S.Dak. 57362.

WALSH, DANIEL MICHAEL, JR. D
Treas, Hampden Co, Mass.
b. Springfield, Mass, 1/27/09; s. Daniel Michael Walsh and Anna Q. Rodgers W; m. 11/10/37 to Mary M. Hallahan; 2nd m. 7/1/65 to Patricia F. Mangan McMahon; c. Marita A, Daniel M, III and Timothy J. Walsh; stepchildren, Maribeth C, P. Faith, George F, Gregory M, Margaret T. and Kevin C. McMahon. Educ: Holy Cross Col, A.B, 29; Harvard Law Sch, 30; Northeast. Univ, LL.B, 35. Polit. & Govt. Pos: Del, Mass. State Dem. Conv, 36-38 & 60-62; mem, Mass. Gov. Coun, 41-42; treas, Hampden Co, Mass, 49-; alternate del, Dem. Nat. Conv, 64. Bus. & Prof. Pos: Corporator, Springfield Inst. for Savings. Mil Serv: Entered as Lt.(jg), Naval Res, 43, released as Lt.(sg), 46, after serv. as Fighter Dir, 45; Lt.(sg).(Ret), Naval Res; Asiatic-Pac. Theater Ribbon; Presidential Unit Citation. Mem: Pres, Springfield Asn. Ins. Agents, 52-54, Mass. Asn. Ins. Agents, 54-56, Serra Club Springfield, 65-66 and Mass. Asn. Contributory Retirement Bds, 69-; former dir, Automobile Club Springfield, v.pres, currently; Mass. and Nat. Asns. Co. Treas; K. of C.(4°); Elks; Am. Legion; ROA; Navy League. Rel: Roman Catholic. Legal Res: 46 Oxford Rd, Longmeadow, Mass. 01106. Mailing Add: 52 State St, Springfield, Mass. 01103.

WALSH, EUGENE PETER D
Mem, State Dem. Cmt, Mo.
b. St. Louis, Mo, 9/18/27; s. John Patrick Walsh and Edna Downey W; m. 6/30/51 to Mary Loretta Finazzo; c. Suzanne and Patrick. Educ: St. Louis Univ. Sch. Law, LL.B, 50; Delta Theta Phi. Polit. & Govt. Pos: Mo. State Rep, 53-56; legal asst. to Gov. Mo, 65-66; del, Dem. Nat. Conv, 68; mem, State Dem. Cmt, 68- Bus. & Prof. Pos: Attorney-partner, Law Firm, Aubuchon & Walsh, 53- Mil. Serv: Entered as A/S, Navy, 45, released as Seaman 1/C, 46, after serv. in Amphibious Forces, U.S, Third Fleet. Mem: St. Louis and Am. Bar Asns; Mo. Bar Asn. (former mem. bd. gov.); Lawyers Asn. St. Louis (past pres). Rel: Catholic. Mailing Add: 8 Kirken Knoll, St. Louis, Mo. 63131.

WALSH, FRANCIS P. D
Married; c. two. Polit. & Govt. Pos: Cand, Mass. State Rep. Bus. & Prof. Pos: Retired Police Sgt, Lynn Police Dept. Mem: Past Pres, Mass. Police Asn; Secy-Treas, Lynn Br, Mass. Police Asn, 30 years . Misc: Father of the 40 hour work week Bill; commendation for rescuing two children from drowning in Holyoke St. clay pits and for apprehending slayer of Patrolman Francis Quinn 2/15/53. Rel: Roman Catholic. Mailing Add: 54 Locust St, Lynn, Mass. 01904. (1967)

WALSH, JACK R
b. New York, N.Y, 2/17/34; s. Patrick Walsh and Mary Waters W; m. 8/25/56 to Kathleen Pekin; c. Brian, Kevin, John, Jr, James, Brendan, Terrie and Sheila. Educ: Georgetown Univ, A.B, 56. Polit. & Govt. Pos: Supvr, First Dist, San Diego Co, Calif, 69- Mailing Add: County Administration Bldg, 1600 Pacific Hwy, San Diego, Calif. 92101.

WALSH, JOHN BERNARD, JR. D
City Councilman, Norwalk, Conn.
b. Torrington, Conn, 12/6/32; s. John B. Walsh and Lenore O'Connor W; m.

10/10/59 to Gail Mary D'Abato; c. John B, III, Carol A, Barbara J. and Laurie J. Educ: Univ. Conn, B.A, 54; Boston Col. Law Sch, LL.B, 59. Polit. & Govt. Pos: City councilman, Ward A, Norwalk, Conn, 63-, pres, 67-68. Bus. & Prof. Pos: Law clerk, Keogh and Candee, 59-61; claimsman, Travelers Ins. Co, 65- Mil. Serv: Entered as Pvt, Army, 54, released as Pfc, 56, after serv. in Germany. Mem: Metrop. Regional Planning Agency; Hibernians; St. Philip's Holy Name Soc. Rel: Catholic. Mailing Add: 11 Delaware Ave, Norwalk, Conn. 06851.

WALSH, JOHN J. D
N.Y. State Assemblyman
b. Manhattan, N.Y; m. to Mary Smith; c. Thomas, Clare, Maureen, James, Margaret. Educ: Fordham Col. & Law Sch. Polit. & Govt. Pos: N.Y. State Assemblyman, 58- Bus. & Prof. Pos: Attorney. Mil. Serv: World War II. Mem: Fred H. Meyer Post, VFW; youth bd, Inwood Commun. Coun; Holy Name Soc; Wash. Heights, Boys, Inc; Shamrock Post, CWV; Nat. Conf. of Christians & Jews; Ancient Order of Hibernians; Elks Lodge No. 1. Mailing Add: 91 Park Terr. W, New York, N.Y. 10034. (1967)

WALSH, JOHN RICHARD D
b. Martinsville, Ind, 5/22/13; s. John N. Walsh and Edna Rude W; m. 6/25/41 to Helen Louise Stewart; c. John R, II, Stephen R, Timothy R. and Helen Kathleen. Educ: Ind. Univ. Law Sch, LL.B, 34 and J.D, 38. Polit. & Govt. Pos: Dep. Attorney Gen, Ind, 41; U.S. Rep, Ind, 49-51; Secy. of State, Ind, 58-60; del, Dem. Nat. Conv, 60; attorney, Madison Co, Ind, 65-66. Mil. Serv: Entered as Pvt, Army, 42, released as T/Sgt, 43. Mem: Pres, Madison Co. Bar Asn, 65-66. Rel: Methodist. Legal Res: 2016 Melody Lane, Anderson, Ind. 46012. Mailing Add: 464 Citizens Bank Bldg, Anderson, Ind. 46011.

WALSH, JOHN T. D
Pa. State Rep.
b. Pittsburgh, Pa, 12/21/98; s. John W. Walsh and Ellen Daley W; m. to Henrietta A. Clay; c. five; 11 grandchildren. Educ: Univ. of Pittsburgh. Polit. & Govt. Pos: Pa. State Rep, 52- Bus. & Prof. Pos: Chief clerk, master mech. off, Nat. Tube Co, 3 years; clerk to yardmaster, B&O R.R, 1 year; retired contractor. Mil. Serv: World War I; chmn, Draft bd; World War II and Korea. Mem: Past comdr, VFW, quartermaster, Post 514, 30 years; Am. Legion; Elks; K. of C; A.O.H; Moose; Eagles; CWV; World War I Vet; Lions; YMCA; Youghiogheny Country Club; dir, McKeesport Boys Club. Rel: Catholic. Mailing Add: 1415 Fremont St, McKeesport, Pa. 15132. (1967)

WALSH, JOSEPH WILLIAM D
R.I. State Rep.
b. Providence, R.I, 8/28/41; s. William A. Walsh and Ethel M. Horowitz W; m. 7/5/68 to Joyce Ioanes. Educ: Providence Col, A.B, 63; Georgetown Law Sch, J.D, 66. Polit. & Govt. Pos: Clerk, Mil. Court of Appeals, 64; mem. of the staff of Congressman John Fogarty, Providence, R.I, 66-67; asst. city solicitor, Warwick, 67-68; R.I. State Rep, 69- Bus. & Prof. Pos: Attorney-at-Law, Providence, 67- Mem: Am. and R.I. Bar Asns. Legal Res: 210 Partition St, Warwick, R.I. 02888. Mailing Add: 931 Industrial Bank Bldg, Providence, R.I. 02903.

WALSH, LAWRENCE E. D
Calif. State Sen.
b. Huntington Park, Calif, 9/8/26; s. George A. Walsh and Bertha Inez W; m. to Joan A. Walsh; c. Donovan P. and Lawrence H. Educ: Huntington Park High Sch; Los Angeles Traffic Inst. Polit. & Govt. Pos: Planning and Zoning Cmnr, Huntington Park, Calif. 58-62; bd. dir, Co. Sanit. Dist. One; Huntington Park City Councilman, 62-64; mayor, Huntington Park, 65-67; Calif. State Sen, 67- Bus. & Prof. Pos: Owner, Walsh Equip. Co, 52- Mil. Serv: Naval Air Corps, World War II. Mem: Elks; K. of C; Native Sons of Golden West; Jr. C. of C; Am. G.I. Forum. Sole Recipient, Presidential Award for Leadership and Outstanding Civic Serv, Jr. C. of C. Mailing Add: 6055 E. Washington Blvd, Suite 629, Commerce, Calif. 90022.

WALSH, RICHARD A. R
Ill. State Rep.
b. Chicago, Ill, 11/25/30; m. 1959 to Patricia; c. Richard, Jr, Mark, Patrick, Brian. Educ: Loyola Univ, Ill, B.S. in Commerce, J.D. Polit. & Govt. Pos: Ill. State Rep, 62- Bus. & Prof. Pos: Passed bar exam, Ill. and Wis; lawyer. Mil. Serv: Naval Res, 54-57; Lt.(jg), legal off. aboard Battleship Iowa. Mem: W. Suburban, Ill. and Chicago Bar Asns. Legal Add: 1003 N. Elmwood Ave, Oak Park, Ill. 60302. Mailing Add: 134 N. LaSalle St, Chicago, Ill. 60602.

WALSH, ROBERT V. D
b. Grayville, Ill; div; c. Patrick Robin. Educ: Univ. of Ill, 49, Col. of Law, 3 years. Polit. & Govt. Pos: Ill. State Rep, 62-66. Bus. and Prof. Pos: Farming opers; real estate; oil prod, 50- Mil. Serv: Army, World War II, 2 years. Mem: Phi Alpha Delta legal fraternity; Am. Legion; Elks; Moose; Wabash Valley Asn; Farm Bur; Shrine. Mailing Add: 221 W. North St, Grayville, Ill. 62844. (1967)

WALSH, STARIA DFL
b. 1916. Educ: Col. of St. Scholastica, B.A, 38. Polit. & Govt. Pos: Secy, Dem-Farmer-Labor Fifth Ward Club, Minn, 54-58; mem, Brooklyn Park Planning Cmn, 63-; secy, 29th Ward Dem-Farmer-Labor Club, currently. Bus. & Prof. Pos: Former br. off. mgr, Nat. Mkt. Research Agency; formerly dir, psychol. testing, RCA, Bloomington, Ind, 42-45; partner, off. mgr. and advert. mgr, sales agency. Mailing Add: 7025 Kentucky Ave. N, Brooklyn Park, Minn. 55428.

WALSH, THOMAS A. D
Mo. State Rep.
b. St. Louis, Mo. Polit. & Govt. Pos: Mo. State Rep, 47-; del, Dem. Nat. Conv, 68. Mailing Add: 1820 Warren St, St. Louis, Mo. 63106. (1967)

WALSH, THOMAS JOSEPH D
b. Parnell, Iowa, 9/5/29; s. Bart Thomas Walsh and Mary Alice Gallagher W; m. 2/6/54 to Marie Katherine Sprengelmeyer; c. Kevin Thomas, Brian Duggan, Michael Kieran, Kathleen Marie and Terra Ann. Educ: St. Edwards Univ, 47-49; Univ. Dayton, B.S. in bus. admin, 51; DePaul Law Sch, Chicago, Ill, 54. Polit. & Govt. Pos: Chmn, DeKalb Co. Young Dem, Ill, 59; cand, clerk circuit court, DeKalb Co, 60; chmn, 15th Cong. Dist. Ill. Young Dem, 61; chmn, 14th Cong. Dist. Ill. Young Dem, 62; cand, Nat. Committeeman, Ill. Young Dem, 63; alternate del, Dem. Nat. Conv, 64; div. leader, York Twp. Dem. Orgn, 64-66, trustee, 64-; Dem. precinct committeeman, York Twp, 64-; chmn. regional bd. dirs, Young Dem. Ill, 65; cand, asst. supvr, York Twp, 65; mem. exec. bd, DuPage Co. Dem. Cent. Cmt, 65; pres, DuPage Co. Young Dem, 65, chmn. exec. bd, 66-; cand, State Dem. Cent. Cmt, 14th Cong Dist, 66; committeeman, DuPage Co, 66- Bus. & Prof. Pos: Real estate salesman, Lombard, Ill, 65-66; v.pres, Mastech, Inc, Chicago, 65-66; ins. broker, DuPage Co, 66. Mem: Soc. for Adv. of Mgt; Elks; K. of C; Civil Air Patrol; Ill. Sheriffs Asn; Toastmasters, Int; Little League; Police Auxiliary; Box Scouts. Rel: Catholic. Mailing Add: 1703 S. Fairfield, Lombard, Ill. 60148.

WALSH, WILLIAM D. R
Ill. State Rep.
b. Chicago, Ill, 2/5/24; m. to Barbara Kennedy; c. William, Jr, Cynthia, Julie, Peter, Elizabeth, Thomas, David and Terrence. Educ: Northwest. Univ; Loyola Univ, B.S.C. Polit. & Govt. Pos: Pres, Proviso Twp. Young Rep, Ill; mem, Park Dist. Bd. Cmnrs; Ill. State Rep, currently. Bus. & Prof. Pos: Real estate and ins. bus. with father and brother, John, P.M. Walsh & Co. Mil. Serv: Navy, World War II. Mem: Kiwanis; St. Francis Xavier Holy Name Soc. Rel: Catholic. Mailing Add: 801 N. Kensington Ave, La Grange Park, Ill. 60525. (1967)

WALSH, WM. EDWIN R
b. Oswego, N.Y, 1/29/03; s. William Edwin Walsh and Mary Schneider W; m. 8/6/32 to Marian Kardell; c. William Edwin, III. Educ: Willamette Univ. and Law Sch. Polit. & Govt. Pos: Dist. Attorney, Coos Co, Ore, 30-32; Ore. State Sen, 41-52; mem, Statute Rev. Coun, State of Ore, 49-51; pres, Ore. State Senate and Acting Gov, 49-51; del, Rep. Nat. Conv, 52; mem, State Bd. Higher Educ, Ore, 53-64, pres, 61-64; state chmn, Rockefeller for President Cmt, 64; mem. bd. dir, Southwest. Ore. Commun. Col, 66- Bus. & Prof. Pos: Dir. and v.pres, Ore. State Motor Asn, 52-; mem. bd. trustees, Willamette Univ, 53- Mem: Bd. gov, Ore. State Bar, 51-54; pres, Coos Co. Bar Asn, 35; Am. Bar Asn; Eastern Star; Elks; Mason; Shrine. Legal Res: 888 Telegraph Dr, Coos Bay, Ore. 97420. Mailing Add: P.O. Box 359, Coos Bay, Ore. 97420.

WALSH, WILLIAM FRANCIS R
Mayor, Syracuse, N.Y.
b. Syracuse, N.Y, 7/11/12; s. Michael J. Walsh and Mary Egan W; m. 5/15/43 to Mary Dorsey; c. William, James, Joseph, Mary, Martha, Patricia and Michael. Educ: St. Bonaventure Col, A.B. in sociol, 34; Catholic Univ; Univ. Buffalo, M.A. in sociol, 49; Syracuse Univ, Ph.D. course work completed in sociol. Polit. & Govt. Pos: Mayor, Syracuse, N.Y, 62-; cmnr. Asst. area supvr, N.Y. State Dep. of Social Welfare, 46-47; area dir, N.Y. State Cmn. Against Discrimination, 47-56; dir. of research, Onondaga Co, 57-59, cmnr. of welfare, 60-61; mayor, Syracuse, N.Y, 62- Mil. Serv: Entered as Pvt, Army, 41, released as Capt, 45, after serv. in Sixth Air Serv. Area Command, Mid-Pac, 45; Pac. Theater of Operations Ribbon; Good Conduct Medal. Mem: Exec. cmt, N.Y. State Conf. of Mayors; N.Y. State Munic. Police Training Coun; Gov. Adv. Cmn. for Law Enforcement; President's Adv. Cmn. on Intergovernmental Rels; U.S. Conf. of Mayors; trustee, Syracuse Univ. and Maria Regina Col; Commun. Facilities and League Study Cmt, Nat. League of Cities; Tip Hill Post, Am. Legion; VFW; Hibernians; Bellevue Country Club; Calvary Club; Otisco Lake Rod and Gun Club. Rel: Roman Catholic. Legal Res: 522 Schuyler St, Syracuse, N.Y. 13204. Mailing Add: 201 City Hall, Syracuse, N.Y. 13202.

WALSH, WILLIAM L. D
R.I. State Rep.
b. Providence, R.I, 6/11/97; m. to Lillian M. Educ: Providence schs. Polit. & Govt. Pos: R.I. State Rep, 59- Bus. & Prof. Pos: Salesman. Mil. Serv: Sgt. Maj, Army. Mem: Past mem, A.G.V.A; K. of C; Elks. Mailing Add: 158 Chandler Ave, Cranston, R.I. 02911. (1967)

WALSTROM, LOIS JEAN D
Mem, Dem. State Cent. Cmt, Nebr.
b. West Bend, Iowa, 2/3/25; d. Grover Cleveland Carter and Antoinette Mikes C; m. 5/20/44 to Dr. Veryl Walstrom; c. Verlyn Cleve and Julie Carter. Educ: North. Iowa Univ, 43; Kans. State Univ, B.S, 46; Phi Beta Kappa. Polit. & Govt. Pos: Mem, Dem. State Cent. Cmt, Nebr, 64-; alternate del, Dem. Nat. Conv, 68. Publ: Several articles and pictures in Nat. Art Magazines. Rel: Methodist. Mailing Add: Verdigre, Nebr. 68783.

WALSTROM, VERYL ARMOUR D
Mem, Nebr. State Dem. Cent. Cmt.
b. Spencer, Iowa, 6/1/21; s. Oscar Benhart Walstrom and Esther Emma Kruse W; m. 5/20/44 to Lois Jean Carter; c. Verlyn Cleve and Julie Carter. Educ: Iowa State Col, B.S. in agron, 42; Kans. State Col, D.V.M, 46; Agron. Club; Jr. Am. Vet. Med. Asn. Polit. & Govt. Pos: Alternate del, Dem. Nat. Conv, 64; mem, Nebr. Judicial Nominating Cmn, 64 and Nebr. Bd. of Educ. Servs, 66-; v.chmn, Knox Co. Dem. Cmt; mem, Nebr. State Dem. Cent. Cmt, currently. Mil. Serv: Entered as Pvt, Army Chem. Warfare Serv, 42, released as Cadet, 44. Mem: Editorial Exec. Cmt, Nebr. Vet. Med. Asn, 66; Exec. Cmt, Nebr. Livestock Sales Inspectors, 64; Am. Vet. Med. Asn; Am. Legion; Masonic Lodge, Oriental Consistory of S.Dak; Royal Soc. of Health. Does experimental work in use of tranquilizer guns. Rel: Methodist. Mailing Add: Verdigre, Nebr. 68783.

WALTER, MABEL VICTORIA D
V.Chmn, Stevens Co. Dem. Party, Kans.
b. Forgan, Okla, 6/14/27; d. John Raymond Groves and Bonnie Izora Hodges G; m. 10/26/47 to Selman Eugene Walter; c. Michael Thomas. Educ: Beaver High Sch, grad. Polit. & Govt. Pos: V.chmn, Stevens Co. Dem. Party, 66-; secy-treas, Dist. 122 Dem. Party, 68-69. Bus. & Prof. Pos: Secy, Rep. Nat. Gas Co, Hugoton, 57-62, Southwest. Savings & Loan, 62-66 and See-More Cable, 67- Rel: Christian. Legal Res: 119 N. Jackson, Hugoton, Kans. 67951. Mailing Add: Box 1101, Hugoton, Kans. 67951.

WALTER, MERWYN H. D
Chmn, Miner Co. Dem. Party, S.Dak.
b. 10/5/11; m. 12/6/37 to Audrey Iwerks; c. Robert. Educ: Sch. of Agr, S.Dak. State Univ, 1 year. Polit. & Govt. Pos: Mem, draft bd. and bd. of educ, Miner Co, S.Dak; chmn, local sch. bd; supvr, Miner Co. Soil and Water Conserv. Dist; S.Dak. State Sen. until 66; chmn, Miner Co. Dem. Party, currently. Bus. & Prof. Pos: Farmer; dir, Miner Co. Crop & Livestock Asn. Mem: Miner Co. F.H.A, bd. mem; Mason; Eastern Star. Rel: Presbyterian; Trustee and Elder. Mailing Add: Roswell, S.Dak. 57312. (1967)

WALTER, PAUL WILLIAM, JR. R
b. Cleveland, Ohio, 9/5/46; s. Paul William Walter and Susan E. Hamilton W; single. Educ: Lake Forest Col; Case-Res. Univ, currently. Polit. & Govt. Pos: Del, Rep. Nat. Conv, 68. Bus. & Prof. Pos: Assoc, Law Off. of Walter, Haverfield, Buescher & Chockley, Cleveland, Ohio, currently. Rel: Protestant. Mailing Add: 23976 Lyman Blvd, Shaker Heights, Ohio 44122.

WALTER, VIVIAN D
b. Oakland, Calif, Aug. 6; d. Abe S. Cohn and Ella Jacobson C; m. 5/22/53 to Stephen Walter; c. Daphne Bransten, Jennifer Snarskis and Edwin J, 2nd Educ: Univ. Calif, Berkeley, 3 years; Pasadena Commun. Playhouse Sch. Theatre, 3 years. Polit. & Govt. Pos: Mem. pub. rels, Adlai Stevenson, 56, John F. Kennedy 60 and Gov. Edmund G. Brown, 66; mem, Gov. Adv. Cmt. on Aid to Totally Disabled, Calif, 59-65; mem, State of Calif. Ment. Retardation Prog. and Standards Bd, 65-; del, Dem. Nat. Conv, 68; First for Robert F. Kennedy Club, 68; chmn. adv. cmt, Calif. Dem. State Cent. Cmt; founding mem and bd. mem, Dem. Women of Bay Area. Bus. & Prof. Pos: Advert. copy writer, I Magnin & Co, San Francisco and The Emporium; pub. rels, Red Cross, Palace Hotel and Vivian Seay Walter. Legal Res: California.

WALTERS, CHARLES TIMOTHY D
b. Cumberland, Ky, 5/3/38; s. Gifford Jerome Walters and May Farmer W; m. 7/30/61 to Leah Patricia Studebaker; c. Camille and Robert Benton. Educ: Georgetown Col, B.A, 60; Univ. Ky. Law Sch, LL.B, 64; Lambda Chi Alpha. Polit. & Govt. Pos: Ky. State Rep, 73rd Legis. Dist, 67-69; commonwealth attorney, 25th Judicial Dist, 70- Mem: Ky. and Clark Co. Bar Asns; Kiwanis; Clark Co. Hist. Soc. Rel: Baptist. Mailing Add: 224 W. Hickman St, Winchester, Ky. 40391.

WALTERS, ELMER ELMO D
Md. State Del.
b. Baltimore, Md, 9/29/10; s. Raymond William Walters and Charlotte E. Stichel W; single. Educ: Baltimore Polytech. Inst. Polit. & Govt. Pos: Md. State Del, 54- Mil. Serv: Entered as Yeoman 2/C, Navy, 42, released as Printer 1/C, 45. Mem: Eagle. Track, baseball, softball, soccer, basketball and volley ball. Rel: Lutheran. Mailing Add: 17 N. Curley St, Baltimore, Md. 21224. (1967)

WALTERS, HERBERT STANFORD D
Dem. Nat. Committeeman, Tenn.
b. Leadvale, Tenn, 11/17/91; m. 7/23/28 to Sarah Ruckman Lockridge. Educ: Carson-Newman Col; Castle Heights Col; Univ. Tenn. Polit. & Govt. Pos: Mem, State Dem. Exec. Cmt, 44-; Dem. Nat. Committeeman, Tenn, 45-; U.S. Sen, Tenn, 63-64; former mem, Tenn. Gov. Adv. Staff, Former chmn, Bd. of Licensing Gen. Contractors and former chmn, Morristown Power and Water Cmn; trustee, Univ. Tenn; del, Dem. Nat. Conv, 68. Bus. & Prof. Pos: Dir, Hamilton Nat. Assocs, 45-; chmn. bd. and exec. officer, Hamilton Nat. Bank, Morristown, Tenn, dir, 47-; dir, Nashville Gas Co, 50- and Tenn. Gas Co, 56-; v.pres. and dir, Concrete Materials, Inc, currently. Mem: Mason; Elks; Kiwanis; C. of C; Rotary. Rel: Presbyterian. Mailing Add: 620 W. Second North St, Morristown, Tenn. 37813.

WALTERS, JOHN BAILY R
Chmn, Linn Co. Resp. Cent. Cmt, Iowa
b. Rockford, Ill, 1/8/21; s. Reuben Ransom Walters and Mae Louise Baily W; m. 2/14/43 to Ann Louise Engberg; c. James S, Martha A, Thomas J. and Mary L. Educ: Coe Col, B.A. in Econ, 46; Am. Col. Life Underwriters, C.L.U, 51; Tau Kappa Epsilon. Polit. & Govt. Pos: Bd. mem, City Plan Cmn, Cedar Rapids, Iowa, 66-; chmn, Linn Co. Rep. Cent. Cmt, 67- Bus. & Prof. Pos: Agent, Nat. Life Ins. Co. of Vt, 46-60, gen. agent, 60-68, agent, 68- Mil. Serv: Entered as Air Cadet, Army Air Corps, 43, released as 1st Lt, 45, after serv. in Ninth Air Force, ETO, 44-45; Air Medal with Five Oak Leaf Clusters; ETO Ribbon with Two Battle Stars. Mem: Life Underwriters Asn; Am. Soc. of Chartered Life Underwriters; Cedar Rapids Estate Planning Coun; Iowa Leaders Round Table; C. of C; Elks; Optimist. C. of C. Civic Serv. Award. Rel: Presbyterian. Legal Res: 2325 Hillcrest Dr. S.E, Cedar Rapids, Iowa 52403. Mailing Add: 709 Dows Bldg, Cedar Rapids, Iowa 52401

WALTERS, JOHNNIE McKEIVER R
Asst. Attorney Gen, Tax Div, Dept. of Justice
b. Hartsville, S.C, 12/20/19; s. Tommie Ellis Walters and Lizzie Lee Grantham W; m. 9/1/47 to Donna Lucile Hall; c. Donna Diane, Lizbeth Kathern, Hilton Horace and John Roy. Educ: Furman Univ, A.B, 42; Univ. Mich. Law Sch, LL.B, 48; Quaternion Club. Polit. & Govt. Pos: Attorney, chief counsel's off, Internal Rev. Serv, Wash, D.C, 49-53; Asst. Attorney Gen, Tax Div, Dept. of Justice, 69- Bus. & Prof. Pos: Attorney, tax dept, Texaco, Inc, N.Y.C, 53-61; attorney and partner, Geer, Walters & Demo, Greenville, S.C, 61-69. Mil. Serv: Entered as Pvt, Air Force, 42, released as 1st Lt, 45, after serv. in 450th Bomb Group (H), Italy, 44-45, Capt, Res, 45-55; Air Medal with Clusters; Purple Heart; Distinguished Flying Cross. Mem: S.C, Greenville Co. and Am. Bar Asns; Rotary (pres, Greenville Club, 68-69); C. of C; Cmt. for Total Develop. of Greenville; bd. dirs, United Fund, Greenville; Greenville Little Theatre; Greenville Symphony Asn. Rel: Baptist; Pres, Ives Bible Class, First Baptist Church of Greenville, 66. Legal Res: 1327 Oberon Way, McLean, Va. 22101. Mailing Add: Room 4143, Dept. of Justice, Washington, D.C. 20530.

WALTON, CHARLES A. D
Polit. & Govt. Pos: Former dep. prosecutor, Marion Co, Ind; former bailiff, Superior Court, Ind; former Ind. State Rep; c. attorney, Marion Co, 67- Mem: Phi Alpha Delta; Kappa Alpha Psi; Pi Sigma Alpha; NAACP; Elks. Rel: Baptist. Mailing Add: 156 E. Market St, Indianapolis, Ind. 46204.

WALTON, FRANK EDWARD D
b. Kinney Co, Tex, 11/6/94; s. Mark Crodus Walton and Kathryn Weave W; m. 10/31/20 to Jaynette Cope; c. Frank Edward, Jr. Educ: West Point grad. Polit. & Govt. Pos: Chmn, Johnson Club and John Connally Club, Val Verde Co, Tex; former chmn, Val Verde Co. Dem. Cmt. Bus. & Prof. Pos: Partner, Waltons Bros, 11- Mil. Serv: Pvt, Army, 18. Mem: Charter mem, Am. Legion; Sch. Trustee; Lions. Baseball. Rel: Methodist. 1967 Legal Res: Del Rio, Tex. No mailing address available. (1967)

WALTON, GEORGE D. R
Chmn, Cent. Dist. Rep. Party, Alaska
b. Springfield, Mo, 6/3/32; s. William H. Walton (deceased) and Verda W.(deceased); m. 5/19/67 to Maxine L. Ryman; c. Donald R. and Deborah A. Polit. & Govt. Pos: v.chmn, Cent. Dist. Rep. Party, Alaska, 67-68 and chmn, 68- Mil. Serv: Entered as Airman, Air Force, 52, released as Airman 1/C, 56, after serv. in Alaskan Air Command, 54-55. Mem: Alaska State Life Underwriters (pres, 67-68); Fairbanks Asn. Life Underwriters (pres, 61-62); pres, Fairbanks Jaycees, 62-63; dir, Golden Heart Lions; Lions. Rel: Methodist. Legal Res: 2675 Valkeetna, Fairbanks, Alaska 99701. Mailing Add: P.O. Box 318, Fairbanks, Alaska 99701.

WALTON, JAMES NEUMAN, JR. R
Chmn, McCulloch Co. Rep. Party, Tex.
b. Marlin, Tex, 9/14/24; s. James Neuman Walton, Sr. and Elizabeth Parsons W; m. 8/15/47 to Agnes Elizabeth Rose Robinson; c. Betsy and Jim. Educ: Tex. A&M Col, 42. Polit. & Govt. Pos: Chmn, McCulloch Co. Rep. Party, Tex, 66- Bus. & Prof. Pos: Partner, Walton Pontiac Co, Marlin, Tex, 46-48; owner, Brady Auto Supply, 48-66, Ozona Auto Supply, 59-66 and J & B Trailer Sales, 69- Mil. Serv: Entered as Pvt, Army Air Force, 42, released as 1st Lt, 46, after serv. in 309th Bombardment Group and Sixth Ferry Group, China-Burma-India, 44 and as Air Transport Command Hump Pilot, Asia, 44-45; 1st Lt, Air Force Res, 69; Air Medal; Distinguished Flying Cross; Presidential Unit Citation; three major battle stars. Mem: Past dir, Automotive Wholesalers of Tex; Am. Legion; Hump Pilots Asn; Air Force Hist. Asn; Lions. Rel: Presbyterian. Mailing Add: 1007 W. 12th, Brady, Tex. 76825.

WALTON, JOSEPH MAURICE D
b. Cleveland, Ohio, 7/11/26; s. Joseph Francis Walton and Dorothy Evelyn Daley W; m. 10/25/47 to Marguerite Josephine Monroe; c. Joseph P, Mary Elizabeth, Marguerite, Gerald R, Robert G, Nancy, D. Michael and Suzanne. Educ: John Carroll Univ, 46-47. Polit. & Govt. Pos: Councilman, Jamestown, Pa, 54-58; mem. exec. cmt, Mercer Co. Dem. Ctm, 56-66, chmn, 64-66; charter mem, Mercer Co. Planning Cmn, 57-59; chmn, Joyce for Cong. Campaign, 24th Cong. Dist, 62; mem, Pa. Adv. Coun, Small Bus. Admin, 63-, mem, Nat. Adv. Coun, 65-, chmn, West. Pa. Adv. Coun, 66-; del, Dem. Nat. Conv, 64; cand. for Pa. State Sen, 50th Dist, 66; mem, Pa. Dem. Policy Cmt, 66. Bus. & Prof. Pos: Pres, Jamestown Paint Co, 52-, chmn, 54-; trustee, Greenville Hosp, 59-; dir, First Nat. Bank of Mercer Co, 61- Mil. Serv: Entered as A/S, Navy, 44, released as Yeoman 3/C, 46, after serv. in Mine Warfare Div, Atlantic Theater; Atlantic Theater and Victory Ribbons. Mem: Fedn. Soc. Paint Tech; Elks; Nat. Farmer's Union; K. of C.(4°); exec. bd, Mercer Co. Boy Scouts; Greenville Country Club; Iroquois Club. Rel: Roman Catholic. Mailing Add: 15808 Oakhill Rd, East Cleveland, Ohio 44112.

WALTON, LEONARD S. D
Mich. State Rep.
b. Detroit, Mich, 2/28/29; married; c. Karen and Daniel. Educ: Officers Res. Corps. Sch, San Pedro, Calif, grad. Polit. & Govt. Pos: Mich. State Rep, 62- Mil. Serv: Korean Conflict, 51-53. Mem: K. of C; Am. Legion; Irish Am. Club; 17th Dist. Dem. Club; Mic-Mac Athletic Club; Barney McCosky Booster Club. Civilian Citation for outstanding serv. and coop. rendered to the Detroit Police Dept, 62. Rel: Roman Catholic. Mailing Add: 9244 Burt, Detroit, Mich. 48228.

WALTON, PEGGY SHOLAR D
b. Wilmington, N.C, 7/1/21; d. Ralph L. Sholar and Annie Clyde Benton S; m. 12/25/47 to Linwood Graham Walton, Sr; c. Cheryl Ann and Linwood. Educ: Univ. N.C. at Greensboro, 38-41. Polit. & Govt. Pos: Mem, price div, Off. Price Admin, 44-45; co-chmn, Seventh Cong. Dist. Dem. Campaign Cmt, N.C, 62, mem. planning cmt, rally, 64; mem, N.C. State Dem. Campaign Cmt, 62; pres, Dem. Women of Columbus Co, 62-64, coordinator, 64-66; mem, Columbus Co. Dem. Exec. Cmt, 62-; advisor, Columbus Co. Teen Dem, 63-66; alternate del, Dem. Nat. Conv, 64; coordinator, Dem. Women of Seventh Cong. Dist, 64-65; v.chmn, First Precinct Dem. Exec. Cmt, 64-; mem, N.C. Atomic Energy Adv. Cmt, 64- Bus. & Prof. Pos: Secy, Triangle Construction Co, 42-44 and Avant & Sholar, Inc, 45-47; v.pres, Walton-Sholar Hardware, Inc, 59-61; commun. serv. consult, Columbus Co. Commun. Action, Inc, 64-65; secy, Ballard, McKim & Sawyer, Architects, 66- Mem: Whiteville Country Club; Whiteville Woman's Club; bd. dirs, Columbus Co. Cancer Soc, Columbus Co. Mental Health Asn. and Whiteville Commun. Rels. Coun. Rel: Methodist. Legal Res: 404 North Thompson St, Whiteville, N.C. 28472. Mailing Add: P.O. Box 726, Whiteville, N.C. 28472. (1967)

WALTZ, RALPH H. R
Educ: Ohio State Univ, B.S, M.A. Polit. & Govt. Pos: Former Ind. State Rep; Majority Caucus chmn, 61. Bus. & Prof. Pos: Farmer; businessman; past pres, Nat. Asn. of Swine Records; former secy. and ed, Nat. Swine Record Asn; former instr. of speech and Romance lang, Ohio State Univ. and Univ. of Iowa. Mem: Blue Lodge; Scottish Rite; Shrine; Indianapolis Press Club. Rel: W. River Friends Church. Mailing Add: Hagerstown, Ind. 47346. (1967)

WALZ, NORMAN JOSEPH D
b. Detroit Lakes, Minn, 7/18/15; s. Mark E. Walz and Margaret Ketten W; m. 6/21/37 to Kathryn Ann Fasching; c. Margaret Ann, Mary Kay, Frank Joseph, Thomas Fredrick, Louis Marie, Pauline Lucille and William Patrick. Educ: Detroit Lakes High Sch. Polit. & Govt. Pos: Minn. State Sen. until 67; mem, City Coun, Detroit Lakes, 53 and 54. Bus. & Prof. Pos: Oil Refinery Representative. Mil. Serv: Fireman, Navy, 33-35. Mem: Eagles; Elks: K. of C. Rel: Catholic. Mailing Add: 1140 West Ave, Detroit Lakes, Minn. 56501. (1967)

WAMBLE, BURTON MAX D
Ga. State Rep.
b. Taft, Fla, 7/8/28; s. Reddin Grover Wamble and Nellie Mae Townsend W; m. 5/16/48 to Peggy Joyce Shiver; c. Dorothy Nell and Patricia Joyce. Educ: Fla. South. Col, 1 year. Polit. & Govt. Pos: Committeeman, Grady Co. Dem. Exec. Cmt, Ga, 61-65, chmn, 65-67; Ga. State Rep, Dist. 69, 67- Bus. & Prof. Pos: Credit mgr, Faulk Chevrolet Co, Cairo, Ga, 52-54; cashier, H.V. Kell Wholesale Grocery Co, 55-58; owner-operator, Wamble Bookkeeping Serv, 58-; owner-operator, Burton M. Wamble - Marketer, Sinclair Oil Distributorship, 63-68; sales rep, Investors Diversified Serv, Inc, Minneapolis, Minn, 68- Mil. Serv: Entered as A/S, Navy, 46, released as Storekeeper 1/C, 52, after serv. in Atlantic Fleet, on U.S.S. Sicily CVE-118, 33 months and on U.S.S. Mellette APA 156, 22 months. Mem: Am. Legion; Rotary; Farm Bur; Grady Co. Livestock Asn; Ga. Livestock Asn; Cairo Co. Club; Am. Horseshow Asn; Tenn. Walking Horse Breeders and Exhibition Asn; Whigham Commun. Club; Cairo-Grady Co. C. of C.(dir, 67-). Rel: Baptist. Mailing Add: Route 1, Box 119, Cairo, Ga. 31728.

WAMEL, RUFUS HENRY, JR. D
Chmn, Hildago Co. Dem. Party, N.Mex.
b. 1923. Educ: Univ. S.C, B.S. in Mech. Eng. Polit. & Govt. Pos: N.Mex. State Sen, 57-67; chmn, Hildago Co. Dem. Party, currently. Bus. & Prof. Pos: Rancher-farmer. Mem: Elks. Rel: Protestant. Mailing Add: Animas, N.Mex. 88020. (1967)

WAMPLER, WILLIAM CREED 'BILL' R
U.S. Rep, Va.
b. Pennington Gap, Va, 4/21/26; s. John Sevier Wampler (deceased) and Lillian Wolfe W. (deceased); m. 8/29/53 to Mary Elizabeth Baker; c. Barbara Irene and William Creed, Jr. Educ: Va. Polytech. Inst, B.S, 48; Univ. Va. Law Sch, 49-50; Sigma Nu Phi. Polit. & Govt. Pos: U.S. Rep, 9th Dist, Va, Special asst. to Gen. Mgr, Atomic Energy Cmn; pres, Young Rep. Fedn. of Va, 50; U.S. Rep, Ninth Dist, Va, 52-54, 67-; chmn, Ninth Dist. Rep. Party, 65-66. Bus. & Prof. Pos: Former owner and operator, furniture and carpet bus, Bristol, Va; newsman, Bristol Herald Courier, Virginia-Tennessean and Big Stone Gap Post. Publ: 'Shall We Let Them Vote?' Woman's Day, 12/53; 'Brief Thoughts on Election Reform,' Va. Record Mag, 10/68. Mem: Bd. Visitors, Emory and Henry Col; Am. Legion; 40 et 8; mem-at-lg, Sequoyah Coun, Boy Scouts. Freedoms Found. Award for Woman's Day Article; Watchdog of Treasury Award for 100% Voting Record for Econ. in 90th Cong, Nat. Assoc. Businessmen, Inc, 68; Appreciation Plaque, Va. State Letter Carriers, 68; Outstanding Citizen of the Year, Bristol, Va-Tenn, VFW, 68. Rel: Presbyterian. Legal Res: 812 Long Crescent Dr, Bristol, Va. 24201. Mailing Add: 323 Cannon House Office Building, Wash, D.C. 20515.

WANAMAKER, FLOYD ALLISON 'PAT' R
Wash. State Rep.
b. Port Townsend, Wash, 8/3/10; s. Clarence Ira Wanamaker and Blanche Brown W; m. 9/26/38 to Irene Eliza DeVries; c. Jacqueline Lou, John Edward, Patrick Allison and Robert Edward. Educ: Univ. Wash, 30-34. Polit. Govt. Pos: Wash. State Rep, Tenth Dist, 67- Rel: Methodist. Mailing Add: Route 1, Box 193-A, Coupeville, Wash. 98239. (1967)

WANER, JOHN LOUIS R
b. Chicago, Ill, 8/3/14; s. Ludwig Wojnarowski and Anna Kwiatkowski W; m. 9/28/35 to Anna Kusek; c. Joan (Mrs. Alfred E. Roman), James L, Arthur G. and Linda. Educ: Gordon Tech. High Sch, 4 years; Englewood Bus. Col, 2 years. Polit. & Govt. Pos: Dir, Fed. Housing Authority, North. Ill, 60-61; Chicago campaign mgr, Charles H. Percy for Sen, 66; del, Rep. Nat. Conv, 68. Bus. & Prof. Pos: Chmn. bd, Waner Heating & Air Conditioning Corp, pres, Waner & Waner Enterprises, Ltd, dir, Time Savings & Loan Asn. and dir, Garfield Ridge Trust & Savings Bank, currently. Mem: Home Builders Asn. of Chicago; Am. Inst. Eng. Tech; K. of C; Elks; Polish Roman Cath. Union; Polish Nat. Alliance; Kiwanis; C. of C; hon. mem, Kennedy High Sch. Key Club; Chicago Journeymen Plumbers Union; Sheet Metal Workers. Man of the Year Award, Polish Daily News, 60; Bishop Tien Award. Rel: Roman Catholic. Mailing Add: 5414 Archer Ave, Chicago, Ill. 60638.

WANER, MAY FILLMORE R
Mem, Calif. Rep. State Cent. Cmt.
b. Palmer, Mass, 5/26/93; d. Willard F. Fillmore and Ada E. Clark F; m. 9/16/23 to Thomas Redman Waner, wid; c. Janice (Mrs. Max C. Wilson) and Howard Gerald. Educ: Boston Univ, 16-18. Polit. & Govt. Pos: Dep. co. assessor, Bus. Div, Los Angeles Co, Calif, 42-63; precinct chmn, Rep. Assembly Dist, Los Angeles, 58-60; victory squad chmn, 63rd Rep. Assembly Dist, 68, Hq. chmn, 69; mem, Calif. Rep. State Cent. Cmt, 69- Bus. & Prof. Pos: Teacher bus. courses, high schs. on East Coast, 12-16; teacher bus. training, col. with Teacher Training, 16-20; bookkeeper, various bus. off, West Coast, 20-23. Mem: Am. Legion Auxiliary; Nat. Asn. Parliamentarians; Int. Toastmistress Clubs. Honors and Awards from Los Angeles Co. Rep. Cent. Cmt. for 40 years of Precinct Work. Rel: Protestant. Mailing Add: 3662 W. 62nd St, Los Angeles, Calif. 90043.

WANGEN, MARVIN EUGENE DFL
V.Chmn, First Dist. Dem-Farmer-Labor Cmt, Minn.
b. Albert Lea, Minn, 4/21/31; s. Arnold Marvin Wangen and Frieda Drommerhausen W; m. 7/12/53, wid; m. 1/18/63 to Harriet Ann Landaas; c. Claudia Ann, Diane Lynette, Janis Marie and Aaron Albert. Educ: Dunwoody Indust. Inst; Minneapolis Art Inst. Polit. & Govt. Pos: V.chmn, Freeborn Co. Dem-Farmer-Labor Cmt, Minn, 61-63, chmn, 63-66; mem, State Dem-Farmer-Labor Cent. Cmt, 61-; del, State Dem-Farmer-Labor Conv, 62-68, mem, Credentials Cmt, 62; del, Dem. Nat. Conv, 64; mem, First Dist. Dem-Farmer-Labor Exec. Cmt, 65- Bus. & Prof. Pos: Self-employed silk-screen printing, 55-56; art dir. and prod. mgr, Ad-Art Co, 56-59; art dir. and copywriter, Nat. Coops, Inc, 59-65, Church Offset Printing, Inc, 65- Mil. Serv: Entered as Pvt, Army Signal Corps, 52, released as Cpl, 55, after serv. in Joint Commun. Center as Cryptographer, Field Command, Armed Forces Spec. Weapons Proj, 52-55; Nat. Defense Ribbon. Received Dept. of Defense Award for Cartoon-of-the-Month, 4/54. Rel: Lutheran. Mailing Add: 2013 Tower Rd, Albert Lea, Minn. 56007.

WANNAMAKER, WILLIAM WHETSTONE, JR. R
b. Orangeburg, S.C, 5/18/00; s. William Whetstone Wannamaker and Lyall Matheson W; m. 9/3/25 to Evelyn Townsend; c. William Whetstone, III, Mary Lyall (Mrs. George M. Morris) and Evelyn Townsend (Mrs. J.T. Richards). Educ: The Citadel, B.S, 19; Cornell Univ, C.E, 21; Sigma Alpha Epsilon. Hon. Dr. Eng, The Citadel, 66. Polit. & Govt. Pos: Del, S.C. State Rep. Conv, 54-68, pres, 58-60; mem, S.C. State Rep. Cmt, 54-66; mem, Rep. Nat. Cmt, 56-66; del, Rep. Nat. Conv, 56, 60 & 64; presidential elector, S.C, 68. Bus. & Prof. Pos: Draftsman-designer-chief party resident engr, S.C. State Hwy. Dept, 21-27; pres, Wannamaker & Wells, Inc, 27-58, chmn. bd, 59-69; mem. bd. visitors, The Citadel, 46-66. Mil. Serv: Entered as Lt. Comdr, Naval Res, 40, released as Capt, 45, after serv. in Civil Eng. Corps, Continental U.S. and Pac; Capt.(Ret), Naval Res. Mem: Am. Soc. Civil Engrs; S.C. Soc. Engrs; Am. Legion; Soc. Colonial Wars; SAR; Son. Confederate Vet; Army and Navy Club, Wash, D.C; Carolina Yacht Club, Charleston; Palmetto Club, Columbia. Legal Res: 1225 Broughton N.W, Orangeburg, S.C. 29115. Mailing Add: P.O. Box 542, Orangeburg, S.C. 29115.

WANNAMAKER, WILLIAM WHETSTONE, III R
Chmn, Fifth Cong. Dist. Rep. Party, S.C.
b. Orangeburg, S.C, 11/1/26; s. William Whetstone Wannamaker, Jr. and Evelyn Townsend W; m. 9/13/47 to Betty Ray Davis; c. Ray, Harriet (Mrs. Willis Sheorn), William W, IV, Preston Davis, Amelia Townsend and Sarah Boyd. Educ: The Citadel, B.S, 49; Cornell Univ, B.Ch.E, 52; Univ. S.C; Alpha Chi Sigma. Polit. & Govt. Pos: Former chmn, Kershaw Co. Young Rep. Club; former pres. and del, Young Rep. State Conv; former poll watcher and pres, Rep. Precinct Club; former pres. and del, Rep. City Conv, Camden; former, Rep. City Exec. Cmt, Camden; former pres. and del, Kershaw Co. Rep. Conv; former del, Rep. State Conv. and second v.pres, State Conv, 66; alternate del, Rep. Nat. Conv, 60 & 68 and del. and pres. elector, 64; chmn. and former secy, Kershaw Co. Exec. Cmt; chmn, Fifth Cong. Dist. Rep. Party, currently; exec. dir, S.C. Nixon for Pres. Cmt, 68. Bus. & Prof. Pos: Spec. proj. supvr, Wannamaker Chem. Co, Inc, 42-49; tech. engr, E.I. du Pont de Nemours & Co, 52-59; former newspaper writer; pres. and chief chemist, Wateree Chem. Co, Inc, 56-; high sch. teacher, Thomas Sumter Acad, 65-, headmaster, 66-68; first v.pres, Hynes Chem. Res. Corp, currently. Mil. Serv: Entered as A/S, Navy, 44, released as Coxswain, 46, after serv. aboard U.S.S. Union AKA 106, Pac; Lt, Naval Res.(Ret); Naval Res. Medal; Am. Theatre, Asiatic-Pac. and Japan Occupation and China Serv. Ribbons; Armed Forces Res. and World War II Victory Medals. Mem: Am. Chem. Soc; S.C. Soc. Engr; Nat. Soc. Prfnl. Engrs; prfnl. engr, S.C. and Del, prfnl. chemist; fel, Am. Inst. of Chemists; bd, Joseph Kerslaw Acad; Am. Ord. Asn; Navy League; life mem, Asn. Citadel Men; Camden C. of C; past pres, Camden Rotary Club. Awarded Army-Navy E, High Explosives Worker, World War II. Rel: Episcopal. Legal Res: 314 Chestnut St, Camden, S.C. 29020. Mailing Add: P.O. Box 7, Lugoff, S.C. 29078.

WANSACZ, JOHN D
Pa. State Rep.
b. Old Forge, Pa, 10/7/36; s. William Wansacz and Anna Blaschak W; m. 7/26/69 to Maryann Presty. Educ: Old Forge High Sch, grad, 55. Polit. & Govt. Pos: Pres. and organizer, Old Forge Young Dem, Pa, 62; mem, Lackawanna Co. Dem. Steering Cmt, 65; Pa. State Rep, currently. Mem: Lackawanna Co. Dem. Clubs; LWIU; Keystone Consistory. Rel: Russian Orthodox Greek Catholic. Legal Res: 620 Hickory St, Old Forge, Pa. 18518. Mailing Add: House of Representatives, Harrisburg, Pa. 17105.

WANSTREET, CLARENCE PAUL D
W.Va. State Del.
b. Clarksburg, W.Va, 3/16/21; s. George Lee Wanstreet and Margurite Greiver W; m. 6/23/52 to Mary Hurley; c. Brent Lee and Brenda Kay. Educ: Polit. & Govt. Pos: W.Va. State Del, 69- Bus. & Prof. Pos: Dist. mgr, B.F. Goodrich, Hartford, Conn, 51-60; mgr, Discount Tire Serv, Inc, Clarksburg, 60-69. Mil. Serv: Entered as Seaman, Navy, 47, released as CPO, 51, after serv. in C.Z, East. Command, Naval Res, 51-55. Mem: Nat. Tire Dealers & Retreaders Asn; Elks; VFW; Am. Legion; Moose; Eagles. Rel: Protestant. Mailing Add: 207 Sycamore St, Clarksburg, W.Va. 26301.

WANVICK, ARNE C. DFL
Minn. State Sen.
Polit. & Govt. Pos: Mem, Duluth-Superior High Bridge Cmn, Minn; secy, Interim Cmn, Seaway Port Authority; Minn. State Rep, 33-39 & 43-64; Minn. State Sen, 64- Bus. & Prof. Pos: Mercantile bus, formerly; painting contractor. Mem: Moose. Mailing Add: 215 W. Third St, Duluth, Minn. 55806. (1967)

WARBURTON, HERBERT B. R
b. Wilmington, Del, 9/21/16; s. William Herbert Warburton and Lela Wingate W; m. 12/11/41 to Elizabeth Grimm. Educ: Univ. Del, A.B, 38; Dickinson Sch. Law, Carlisle, Pa, LL.B, 41; Phi Kappa Phi; Alpha Psi Omega; Sigma Phi Epsilon; Corpus Juris. Polit. & Govt. Pos: Spec. Minority Counsel, First Asst. City Solicitor, Wilmington, Del, 47-51; Dep. Attorney Gen, Del, 47-51; chmn, Del. State Young Rep, 47-51; chmn, Young Rep. Nat. Fedn, 51-53; U.S. Rep, Del, 53-55; cand, U.S. Senate, 54; spec. asst. to Secy. of Labor, U.S. Dept. of Labor, 55-57; gen. counsel, Post Off. Dept, 57-61; minority counsel, Govt. Cmt, U.S. House of Rep, 62-64. Bus. & Prof. Pos: Attorney-at-Law, Wilmington, Del, 46-55; v.pres, Balogh & Co. Investments, D.C, 61-62; exec. dir, Am. Orthotic and Prosthetic Asn, Am. Bd. for Cert. in Orthotic and Prosthetic, 66- Mil. Serv: Entered as 1st Lt, Army, 41, released as Maj, 45, after serv. in Counter-Intel. Corps, Am. Defense. Rel: Protestant. Mailing Add: 8500 Beech Tree Rd, Bethesda, Md. 20034.

WARD, ALINE FRANCES R
Vt. State Rep.
b. Camden, N.J, 6/17/98; d. John P. Hollopeter and Margaret Smith H; m. 6/29/21 to Merlin Burton Ward; c. Richard Smith, Lois Evans (Mrs Tierney) and Holly Merlin. Educ: Syracuse Univ, B.A, 20; Univ. Vt, summer 49; Delta Kappa Gamma; Delta Gamma; Eta Pi Upsilon. Polit. & Govt. Pos: Mem, Moretown Sch. Bd, Vt, 39-; Vt. State Rep, 47 & 53, Dist. 69, 69-; pres, Vt. State PTA, 53-56; del, Rep. Nat. Conv, 56, alternate del, 68; mem, Gov. Cmt. of Children and Youth, 60-; Vt. State Sen, Wash. Co, 61 & 63; pres, Vt. State

Sch. Dir, 61-63; mem, Vt. Rep. State Cmt, 64-; pres, Vt. Fedn. Rep. Women, 69- Bus. & Prof. Pos: Eng. teacher, Camden High Sch, N.J, 20. Mem: Am. Asn. of Univ. Women (legis. chmn); Vt. Farm Bur; Vt. Women's Club; trustee, Vt. Col. Rel: Methodist. Mailing Add: Box 535, Moretown, Vt. 05660.

WARD, ARTHUR ODELL D
Mem, Hendry Co. Dem. Exec. Cmt, Fla.
b. Live Oak, Fla, 3/29/92; s. La Fayette Ward and Catherine Clark W; m. Janie Wilson, wid, 42; m. Carolyn Fleming, wid, 66; c. Edwin O, Mildred W. (Mrs. Francis) and Grace W. (Mrs. Faulkner). Educ: Suwannee High and Southern Bus. Col. Polit. & Govt. Pos: Mem, Hendry Co. Sch. Bd, Fla, 28-30 & 41-43; co. tax collector, Hendry Co, 49-64; mem, Hendry Co. Dem. Exec. Cmt, 54-, resigned as chmn, 66. Bus. & Prof. Pos: Cashier and store mgr, Standard Lumber Co, 17-29; mgr. commissaries, U.S. Sugar Corp, 29-47; drug store, self employed, 48. Mem: Hon. mem, Clewiston Kiwanis Club; Fla. Tax Collectors Asn; Elks; F&AM; Eastern Star; Hendry Co. Farm Bur. Rel: Methodist. Legal Res: 404 W. Osceola, Clewiston, Fla. 33440. Mailing Add: P.O. Box 1206, Clewiston, Fla. 33440.

WARD, CHARLES LELAND D
b. Celina, Tex, 7/6/18; s. Charles Lee Ward (deceased) and Annie L. Allen W; m. 11/1/42 to Mary Lois Barrett. Educ: Univ. Okla, B.A, 50; Sigma Delta Chi; Phi Beta Kappa; Tau Kappa Epsilon. Polit. & Govt. Pos: Admin. asst. to House Majority Leader, Rep. Albert, Okla, currently. Bus. & Prof. Pos: Ed, Heber Springs Times, Ark, 36-39; off. mgr, State N.Y.A. off, 41; bur, chief, Daily Oklahoman, 47-48; asst. mgr, Okla. Press Asn, 48-49; news ed, Poteau News, 50-55; managing ed. and gen. mgr, Durant Democrat, Okla, 55-59. Mil. Serv: Army Air Force, 42-46. Mem: Rotary, past pres; v.pres, Durant Camp Fire Coun; Durant C. of C; v.chmn, Nat. Found. for Infantile Paralysis, 57-59; pub. chmn, United Fund, Durant, Okla. Rel: Methodist. Legal Res: Durant, Okla. Mailing Add: 1600 S. Eads, Apt. 1121 S, Arlington, Va. 22202.

WARD, CLEVELAND RAY D
b. Sparta, Tenn, 7/22/07; s. Wayman Franklin Ward (deceased) and Emma Mayes W.(deceased); m. 10/17/28 to Sarah Catherine Sparkman; c. James, Tom, Mary (Mrs. Dorsie Poole) and Sue (Mrs. Jerry Bancroft). Polit. & Govt. Pos: Mem, White Co. Sch. Bd, Tenn, 38; Tenn. State Rep, 51; first mayor, Doyle, 63; chmn, White Co. Dem. Primary Cmt, 63. Bus. & Prof. Pos: Organizer, C. Ray Ward & Co, 28 and partner, 53; pres, Tenn-Valley Oxygen Co. Inc, 59, Growers Tobacco Warehouse, 59-65 and Farmers Burley Warehouse, 60-63. Mem: Tenn. Insurors Asn.(pres, 53); Burley Auction Warehouse Asn; C. of C.(pres, White Co. Chap, 48); Rotary; Elks; Mason; K.T; Shrine. Insuror of the Year, State of Tenn, 53. Rel: Methodist. Legal Res: Sparta Rd, Doyle, Tenn. 38559. Mailing Add: Box 38, Doyle, Tenn. 38559.

WARD, DAVID ELMER D
b. Fort Myers, Fla, 9/26/09; s. David Thomas Ward and Molly Ethel Johnson-Cox W; m. 6/3/37 to Martha Katherine Carlton; c. David Elmer, Jr, Mary Nell and Robert Doyle Carlton. Educ: Univ. Fla, Gainesville; Cumberland Univ. Law Sch, LL.B; U.S. Naval War Col, Newport, R.I. Polit. & Govt. Pos: Spec. asst. James B. Forrestal, Secy. of Navy and first Secy. of Defense; Judge, Lee Co. Court, Fla, 33-39; Fla. State Sen, Lee, Collier, Hendry and Monroe Co, 39-41; del, Dem. Nat. Conv, 68. Bus. & Prof. Pos: Bookkeeper, Gen. Mercentile; confidential clerk, First Nat. Bank, Ft. Myers, Fla, 26-28; organizer and attorney, Fla. Fish Prod. Asn; organizer and attorney, Fla. Shrimp Prod. Asn; sr. mem, Carlton, Fields, Ward and others, Lawyers, Tampa and Orlando, Fla. Mil. Serv: Entered Navy, 42, released as Lt. Comdr, 45, after serv. in Atlantic, Caribbean and Pac. Theaters; Navy Commendations and various other commendations. Publ: Florida Parole and Probation Act and Constitutional Amendment Act; Florida Drivers and Highway Patrol Act; Florida Governmental Study and Recommendation. Mem: Fla. Bar Asn. (v.pres); Tampa Co, Hillsborough Co. and Am. Bar Asns; Calooshachee Cattleman's Asn; Am. Judicature; trustee, Fla. Baptist Children's Home Soc; trustee, Fla. Children's Home Soc. Rel: Baptist. Legal Res: 4417 Bayshore Blvd, Tampa, Fla. 33611. Mailing Add: 20th Floor, Exchange National Bank Bldg, Tampa, Fla. 33601.

WARD, GORDON A. D
b. Edgeley, N.Dak, 5/22/26; s. Charles William Ward and Eleanor Grace Whitman W. (deceased); m. 8/27/58 to Betty Lou Butler; c. Cheryl Denise (deceased). Educ: Northern State Teachers Col, B.S, 50; Univ. Wyo, Coe fel. and M.A, 58; Stanford Univ, Stanford-Gen. Elec. fel, postgrad. work. Polit. Pos: Wyo. State Rep, 65-66; precinct worker, Dem. Party, prior to 65. Bus. & Prof. Pos: Sr. v.prin, Natrona Co. High Sch, Wyo, 64-66. Mil. Serv: Entered as Seaman, Navy, 44, released as PhoM 3/C, 46, after serv. in Photo Interpretation Squadron, Pac, 45-46; Three Unit Commendations; Asiatic-Pac. Ribbon; Am. Theater Ribbon; Philippine Theater Ribbon; Three Battle Stars. Publns: 'Teachers and Politics,' Wyo. Educ. Asn. Mag, 4/66; numerous articles for professional papers and mags. Mem: Hon. mem, Police and Protective Asn. Wyo; Nat. Asn. of Secondary Sch. Principals; pres, Classroom Teacher's Asn, 60-61; del, Nat. Educ. Asn. and Wyo. Educ. Asn, 61-62; chmn, bus. and prfnl. affairs, Kiwanis; Am. Legion; VFW; C. of C; Oil City Diners Club. Rel: Presbyterian. Mailing Add: 3211 S. Coffman, Casper, Wyo. 82601. (1967)

WARD, HAROLD R, JR. R
b. Minneapolis, Minn, 10/24/15; s. Harold R. Ward and Harriet Loring W; m. 6/29/39 to Rosamond de Laittre; c. Harriet L.(Mrs. Price), Harold R, III, Eleanor Del (Mrs. Westcott) and Karl Del. Educ: Amherst Col, B.A, 39; Alpha Delta Phi. Polit. & Govt. Pos: Mem, bd, Montecito Sanitary Dist, Calif, 59-60 and Embarcadero Improv. Dist, 61-62; chmn, Reagan for Gov. Cmt, 66; alternate del, Rep. Nat. Conv, 68. Bus. & Prof. Pos: V.pres, Bateman Eichler, Hill Richards, Santa Barbara, Calif, 62-; v.pres, F.H. Peavey & Co, Minneapolis, Minn, 57-60. Mil. Serv: Entered as Ens, Navy, 42, released as Lt. Comdr, 46, after serv. in Univ. Ill. NROTC and ETO, 43-45; ETO-Normandy Invasion, N.African Invasion and S.Am. Ribbons. Mem: Rotary. Rel: Episcopal. Legal Res: 246 Toro Canyon Rd, Carpinteria, Calif. 93013. Mailing Add: 1030 State St, Santa Barbara, Calif. 93101.

WARD, HORACE TALIAFERRO D
Ga. State Sen.
b. LaGrange, Ga, 7/29/27; m. Educ: Morehouse Col, A.B. with honors, 49; Atlanta Univ, A.M, 50; Northwest. Univ, J.D, 59; Alpha Phi Alpha. Polit. & Govt. Pos: Chmn, Seventh Ward, Fulton Co. Dem. Party, Ga, 64; Ga. State Sen, 39th Dist, 64-; mem, Fulton Co. Dem. Exec. Cmt, 66-; mem, Ga. Dem. State Exec. Cmt, 67-; chmn. exec. cmt, Fulton Co. Dem. Club, 67-; dep. city attorney, Atlanta, Ga, 69- Mil. Serv: Entered as Pvt, Army, 53, released as Sp-4, 55, after serv. in Korea, 54-55; Good Conduct Medal. Mem: Atlanta Bar Asn; Gate City Bar Asn.(treas, 69-); Ga. State Bar Asn. Mailing Add: 172 Milton St. S.W, Atlanta, Ga. 30314.

WARD, LAURA IDA D
Committeewoman, N.J. Dem. State Cmt.
b. Walpack, N.J, 1/22/16; d. Irvin Robbins and Elizabeth Bogart R; m. 11/9/40 to Charles Baxter Ward; c. Mary Alice (Mrs. Silverstein) and Charles Baxter, Jr. Polit. & Govt. Pos: Committeewoman, Sussex Co. Dem. Cmt, N.J, 49-66, mem, exec. cmt, 53-; past pres, Sussex Co. Women's Dem. Club, 63-64; alternate del, Dem. Nat. Conv, 64; past pres, Lake Region Dem. Club, 65; committeewoman, N.J. Dem. State Cmt, 53- Bus. & Prof. Pos: Partner, Newton Sport Shop, 57- Mem: Past matron, Melchoir Chap. 131, Eastern Star. Rel: Presbyterian. Legal Res: Paulinskill Lake Rd, Fredon Twp, N.J. 07860. Mailing Add: P.O. Box 295, Newton, N.J. 07860. (1967)

WARD, LEW O. R
Chmn, Garfield Co. Rep. Party, Okla.
b. Oklahoma City, Okla, 7/24/30; s. Llewellyn Orcutt Ward, II and Addie Reisdorph W; m. 10/29/55 to Myra Beth Gungoll; c. Casidy Ann and William Carlton. Educ: Okla. Mil. Acad, 3½ years; Okla. Univ, B.S, 53; Alpha Tau Omega. Polit. & Govt. Pos: Co. coordinator, Dewey Bartlett for Gov, 66; chmn, Garfield Co. Rep. Party, Okla, 66-; co. chmn, Henry Bellmon for Senate, 68. Bus. & Prof. Pos: Petroleum engr, Delhi Taylor Oil Corp, 55-57; partner and petroleum engr, Ward-Gungoll Oil Investments, 57-69; oil producer and oper, L.O. Ward Oil Opers, 65-69. Mil. Serv: Entered as 2nd Lt, Army, 53, released as 1st Lt, 55, after serv. in Corps of Engrs, Far East, 54-55. Mem: Am. Inst. Mining & Metallurgical Engrs; Soc. of Petroleum Engrs; Okla. Independent Petroleum Asn; Mason; Scottish Rite; Shrine; Am. Bus. Club; Rotary. Legal Res: 1621 Indian Dr, Enid, Okla. 73701. Mailing Add: Box 1187, Enid, Okla. 73701.

WARD, ROBERT MIDDLETON D
Chmn, Champaign Co. Dem. Cmt, Ohio
b. Urbana, Ohio, 2/2/13; s. Dow Ward, Sr. and Blanke Middleton W; m. 1/27/35 to Sara Louise; c. Robert M, Jr, Barbara Louise (Mrs. Prince) and Harriet Jill (Mrs. Discher). Educ: Westville Pub. Schs, Ohio, 12 years. Polit. & Govt. Pos: Chmn, Champaign Co. Dem. Cmt, Ohio, 67- Bus. & Prof. Pos: Mem. and pres, Ohio State Bd. Agr, 6 years; mem, Ohio Expos. Cmn, 6 years, secy, currently; pres, Ohio Swine Breeders & Feeders Asn; pres, Westville Grain Co. Mem: Mason; Shrine; K. of P. Rel: Methodist. Mailing Add: Route 2, Urbana, Ohio 43078.

WARD, ROBERT W. R
Secy. State, Alaska
b. Northeast. Wash, 11/26/29; m. to Peggie Garske; c. Kenneth, Robert, Jr. and Karen. Polit. & Govt. Pos: Mem. city coun, Ketchikan, Alaska, 61-64, borough chmn, 63-66; cmnr. admin, Alaska, 66-67; acting Secy. State, Alaska, 67-69, Secy. State, 69- Bus. & Prof. Pos: With, Ketchikan Pulp Co, Alaska. Mem: Jaycees; C. of C; Rotary; Elks; Toasmasters; Little League; Babe Ruth League. Rel: Methodist. Mailing Add: Pouch AA, Juneau, Alaska 99801.

WARD, SARA ELIZABETH LITTLE D
b. Dresden, Tenn, Apr. 7; d. Dr. Richard M. Little and Ina Allen Bobbitt L; m. to Charles Wesley Ward, wid; c. Dr. John Wesley Ward. Educ: McFerrin Private Sch; Wash. Sem, Atlanta, Ga; Watkins Inst, Nashville, Tenn. Polit. & Govt. Pos: Personal secy. to U.S. Sen. Kenneth McKellar, Tenn, 40-53; secy. and admin. asst. to U.S. Rep. Tom Murray, 53-67; mem, House Post Off. and Civil Serv. Cmt. Staff, 67- Mem: Pilot Club of Wash, D.C; Cong. Secy. Club; U.S. Senate Asn. of Admin. Assts. and Secys; Eastern Star; Tenn. State Soc; Tenn. Hist. Soc. Rel: Methodist. Legal Res: Greenfield, Tenn. 38230. Mailing Add: 2745 29th St. N.W, Washington, D.C. 20008.

WARD, THOMAS HENRY D
b. Baltimore, Md, 2/28/27; s. Thomas Joseph Ward and Louise Dietz W; m. 7/25/58 to Joyce McCartney; c. Kathleen, Patrick, Tracey and Megan. Educ: Georgetown Univ. Sch. For. Serv, B.S, 50; Univ. Md. Sch. Law, LL.B, 53; Johns Hopkins Univ. Grad. Sch. in Hist, 54-58; Gamma Eta Gamma. Polit. & Govt. Pos: Sgt-at-Arms, Dem. Nat. Conv, 60, alternate del, 68; councilman, Baltimore City Coun, Md, 63-67; dist. campaign mgr. on behalf of numerous candidates in various elections; mem, Mayor's Cmt. to Determine Econ. Feasibility of Acquiring Baltimore Transit Co, 65, mem, Mayor's Cmt. on Redistricting, 66; mem, Archit. and Hist. Cmn, Baltimore City, 67; mem. subcmt, chmn, Ways and Means Cmt. and Pub. Transportation Cmt, Legis. Coun. of Md, 67. Bus. & Prof. Pos: Practicing attorney, 53-; secy. and mem. bd. dirs, Colonial Savings & Loan Asn. Mil. Serv: Entered as Pvt, Army Parachute Inf, 45, released as 2nd Lt, 47, after serv. in Pac. Theatre, 46-47; Army Res, 47-52. Publ: Ed, Mt. Royal Dem. Club and Baltimore Heritage, Inc, newsletters. Mem: Baltimore City and Md. Plaintiff's Bar Asns; former exec. secy, Property Owner's Asn; pres, Baltimore Heritage, Inc; past pres, Linden Ave. Improv. Asn; Soc. for Preservation of Fed. Hill, Montgomery St. and Fells Point (bd. mem); Civil War Round Table (former secy); Md. Hist. Soc;.Nat. Parks Asn; Mt. Royal Dem. Club (past pres. and founder); Am. Legion (second V.Comdr, Post 4, Judge Advocate Gen, Baltimore Dist). Rel: Presbyterian. Mailing Add: 1325 Bolton St, Baltimore, Md. 21217.

WARD, THOMAS MORGAN D
b. Shreveport, La, 1/19/35; s. Edward Morgan Ward and Bradys Louise Alexander W; m. 6/10/61 to Louise Taylor Harrison. c. Thomas Morgan, Jr, Louise Harrison and Margaret Harrison. Educ: La. State Univ, B.A, 57, M.A, 65; South. Baptist Theol. Sem, Ky, B.D, 61; Phi Alpha Theta; Kappa Sigma. Polit. & Govt. Pos: Chmn. bd. dirs, Bluegrass Area Econ. Opportunity Coun,

Ky, 66-68; Mem, Woodford Co. Dem. Exec. Cmt; alternate del, Dem. Nat Conv, 68; Cand, Ky. House Rep, 52nd Legis. Dist, 68; mem, Whitehouse Conf. Children and Youth, 70- Bus. & Prof. Pos: Minister, Pisgah Presby. Church, Woodford Co, Ky, 65-; instr. relig, Midway Jr. Col, Ky, 68- Crusade for Freedom Award, 57. Rel: Presbyterian. Legal Res: Route 1, Sugar Hill, Versailles, Ky. 40383. Mailing Add: P.O. Drawer 569, Versailles, Ky. 40383.

WARD, VIVIENNE T. R
Third V.Pres, Mich. State Fedn. of Rep. Women
b. Matteson, Mich, 10/15/99; m. 5/28/19 to Howard Ward; c. Dorothy (Mrs. Linville), Dr. Donald and Duane Gardner. Polit. & Govt. Pos: Mem, Branch Co. Rep. Cmt, Mich, 61-, v.chmn, currently; third v.pres, Mich. State Fedn. of Rep. Women; coordinator for Women's Rep. Activities in Fourth Dist; alternate del, Rep. Nat. Conv, 68; organizer of many Rep. Youth Groups and Rep. Women's Clubs. Mem: Bronson Woman's Club; Ladies Advance, Mothers of World War II; former chmn, local Red Cross; past pres, PTA, Bronson Women's Club, Branch Co. Fedn. of Women's Clubs and Southwest Dist. of Mich. Fedn. of Women's Clubs; dir, Branch Co. Cancer Bd. Rel: Congregational; past pres, Women's Div, Bronson Congregational Church. Mailing Add: 240 W. Chicago St, Bronson, Mich. 49028.

WARD, WAYMAN 'TOM' D
Justice of Peace, White Co, Tenn.
b. Doyle, Tenn, 5/12/34; s. C. Ray Ward and Sarah Catherine Sparkman W; m. 9/18/57 to Pattye Jo Kirby; c. James Thomas, Lorie Ann, Sara Jane, Nancy Lynn and John Cleveland. Educ: Tenn. Tech. Univ, B.S, 59. Polit. & Govt. Pos: Mem, Young Dem, Tenn, 61-; justice of peace, White Co, 66- Mil. Serv: Entered as Pvt, Army Security Agency, 53, released as Cpl, 56, after serv. in 8609 Reconnaissance Unit, Far East, 54-56. Mem: Tenn. Insurors Asn; Jaycees (State v.pres, 68, exec. v.pres. for external affairs, 69). Named Jaycee of Year, 66 and Outstanding Young Man of White Co, 69. Rel: Church of Christ. Legal Res: Belle Meade Subdivision, Sparta, Tenn. 38583. Mailing Add: Box 217, Sparta, Tenn. 38583.

WARD, WYMAN BURTON R
Chmn, Granby Rep. Town Cmt, Conn.
b. Burlington, Vt, 1/7/34; s. Kenneth Hiram Ward and Florence Miles W; m. 8/13/55 to Dorothy Francis Peck; c. Cynthia Kim and Donna Kay. Educ: Bryant Col, B.S.B.A, 53; Beta Iota Beta; Bus. Admin. Soc; Student Senate. Polit. & Govt. Pos: Dist. coordinator, Granby Rep. Town Cmt, Conn, 61-64, chmn, 64-; secy, Indust. Develop. Cmn, 62-64; Justice of the Peace, 62- Bus. & Prof. Pos: Personnel asst, Pratt & Whitney, Inc, 58-62, employ. supvr, 62-66; employ. supvr, Chandler Evans, Inc, 66-; advisor, Ward Tech. Inst, 69- Mil. Serv: Entered as Pvt, Army, 56, released as Sp-5, 58, after serv. in 290th Armored Field Artil, Fifth Army; Good Conduct Medal. Mem: Chandler Evans Mgt. Club and Mens Club; East. Seaboard Apprenticeship Coun; Hartford Indust. Mgr. Club; Metal Workings Trades Apprenticeship Coun. Rel: Episcopal. Mailing Add: 6 Zimmer Rd, Granby, Conn. 06035.

WARDEN, ROBERT P. R
b. Joplin, Mo, 1/9/31; m. 6/25/55 to Kathryn Meyer; c. Donald, Janet, John and Cris. Educ: Univ. Mo, A.B, LL.B. Polit. & Govt. Pos: Mo. State Rep, 60-66. Bus. & Prof. Pos: Attorney. Mil. Serv: Lt, Air Force, Judge Advocate Gen. Dept. Mem: Beta Theta Pi. Rel: Methodist. Mailing Add: 415 N. Moffet, Joplin, Mo. 64801. (1967)

WARDER, FREDERICK L. 'RED' R
N.Y. State Assemblyman
b. Geneva, N.Y, 9/17/12; m. to Justine Crandall; c. Susan (Mrs. Peebles), Karen (Mrs. Adkinson) and Frederick W. Educ: Univ. Rochester. Polit. & Govt. Pos: Past chmn. of finance, Geneva, N.Y; past pres, Geneva Common Coun; mayor, Geneva, 58-59; N.Y. State Assemblyman, 62-, chmn, Labor Cmt. Bus. & Prof. Pos: Mfr. of Tents. Mem: Finger Lakes Coun. of Mayors; v.pres, Soc. of the Genesee and the Lakes; Genesee Agr. Soc; Ontario Co. Agr. Soc; Ontario Co. Vol. Firemans Asn. and Hydrant Hose Co; YMCA; Univ. Club; Rotary; Rod and Gun Club; Theta Delta Chi; chmn, Citizens for Eisenhower, 52-56. Rel: Episcopal. Mailing Add: 100 Lewis St, Geneva, N.Y. 14456.

WARDER, JOHN MORGAN DFL
b. Ellsworth, Kans, 1/7/27; s. Warner First Warder (deceased) and Buelah Dillard W; m. 11/27/52 to Margie Lucille Harrison; c. Linda, Kent and David. Educ: Univ. Kans, B.A, 52; Alpha Phi Alpha. Polit. & Govt. Pos: Del, Dem-Farmer-Labor City and Co. Conv, Minneapolis, Minn, 63, 65, 67 & 69; dir. and clerk, Minneapolis Bd. of Educ, 64-69; mem, Ward Caucus Screening Cmts, 66 & 68; del, Dem. Nat. Conv. and secy, Minn. Del, 68. Bus. & Prof. Pos: Purchasing agent, Litho Supply Depot, Inc, Minneapolis, 52-60, v.pres, 60-68; asst. to pres, First Bank Syst, 68-69; trustee, Macalester Col, 69; pres, First Plymouth Nat. Bank, 69- Mil. Serv: Entered as Pvt, Army, 46, released Cpl, 48, after serv. in Air Force. Mem: Minneapolis Urban League; bd. mem, Children's Hosp. of Minneapolis, Inc, Twin City Inst. for Talent Youth, Minneapolis Urban Coalition, United Fund and Small Bus. Admin. Minnesota-Wisconsin Adv. Coun; Minneapolis Club. Rel: Baptist. Mailing Add: 5133 Garfield Ave. S, Minneapolis, Minn. 55419.

WARDLOW, FLOYD H, JR. D
Chmn, Turner Co. Dem. Exec. Cmt, Ga.
b. Ashburn, Ga, 4/29/21; s. Floyd H. Wardlow, Sr. and Nora Pickel W; m. 7/10/42 to Linnie Powell; c. Floyd Hill, III and Jimmy. Educ: Ga. South. Col, 38-40; Univ. Ga. Law Sch, LL.B, 58; Phi Delta Phi. Polit. & Govt. Pos: Ga. State Rep, Turner Co, 52-53; chmn, Turner Co. Dem. Exec. Cmt, 66- Mil. Serv: Entered as Cadet, Navy, 40, released as Lt, 45, after serv. as combat flight instr; Air Medal with Five Gold Stars; Letters of Commendation. Mem: Mason; Shrine; Am. Legion; 40 et 8. Rel: Baptist. Legal Res: Ashburn, Ga. 31714. Mailing Add: P.O. Box 647, Ashburn, Ga. 31714.

WARE, FREDA CATHERINE R
Mem, Calif. Rep. State Cent. Cmt.
b. Golden, Colo, 9/9/16; d. Edward Cowperthwaite and Freda Jeuck C; m. 3/7/41 to Arnold Grassel Ware; c. Stephen, Randolph and Mary Ann. Educ: Univ. Colo, B.A, 38; Alpha Chi Omega. Polit. & Govt. Pos: Pres, S. Pasadena Rep. Women's Club, Federated, Calif, 64; mem, Calif. Rep. State Cent. Cmt, 68- Rel: Congregational. Mailing Add: 630 Camino Cerrado, S. Pasadena, Calif. 91030.

WARE, GEORGE CHURCH R
b. Brookline, Vt, 4/11/80; m. to Esther Andrews; c. 1 son. Polit. & Govt. Pos: Town lister, Vt; rd. cmnr; mem, Soil Conserv. Cmn; selectman, 50-; Vt. State Rep, 61-66. Bus. & Prof. Pos: Resort owner; farmer; retired. Mem: Newbrook Fire Dept. Rel: Baptist. Mailing Add: Newfane, Vt. 05345. (1967)

WARE, JACK R
b. Jermyn, Tex, 9/23/18; s. Harry Eugene Ware and Agnes Sampley W; m. 12/26/42 to Helen Franzes Ryan; c. Michael O, Melinda K. and K. Patrick. Educ: Baylor Univ, 37-38; Tex. Christian Univ, 43. Polit. & Govt. Pos: Chmn, Denver Co. Young Rep. League, Colo, 53; precinct committeeman and area supvr, Denver Co. Rep. Party, 54-58; admin. asst. to U.S. Sen. Gordon Allott, Colo, 62- Bus. & Prof. Pos: Mgr, Wade-Tex Theaters, Gainesville, Tex, 40-41; asst. sales mgr, Panther Oil & Grease Mfg. Co, Ft. Worth, 42-51; v.pres, MotoRoyal Oil Co, Denver, Colo, 51-55; self-employed sales mgt. and prom. consult, 55-62. Rel: Protestant. Mailing Add: 14221 Chesterfield Rd, Rockville, Md. 20853.

WARE, JAMES CRAWFORD D
Ga. State Rep.
b. Colon, C.Z, 2/2/15; s. Rigdon Mims Ware and Emily Virginia Shackleford W; m. 6/16/44 to Gwynneth Mary Woodhouse; c. Suzanna Emily (Mrs. O'Donnell), John Rigdon, Peter Woodhouse and David Anthony Mims. Educ: Univ. Ore. Polit. & Govt. Pos: Mem, Hogansville City Bd. Educ, 41; Ga. State Rep, 61- Bus. & Prof. Pos: Owner, J. Crawford Ware Ins. & Real Estate, 47-69; pres, Ware Bros, Inc, 56-60; pres, Hogansville Warehouse Co, 64- Mil. Serv: Entered as Pvt, Army, 42, released as Tech. Sgt, 45, after serv. in ETO; European-African-Mid. East. Theater Ribbon with Three Bronze Stars. Mem: Kiwanis; Am. Legion; VFW; Farm Bur; C. of C; State and Nat. Independent Ins. Agents Asns; State and Nat. Asns. of Real Estate Bds; Tri-County and Troup Co. Sportsmans' Clubs. Rel: Baptist. Legal Res: 17 Taliaferro Dr, Hogansville, Ga. 30230. Mailing Add: P.O. Box 305, Hogansville, Ga. 30230.

WARE, JOHN H, III R
Pa. State Sen.
b. 8/29/08; s. John H. Ware, Jr. and Clara Edwards W; m. to Marian R. Snyder; c. four. Educ: Univ. of Pa, B.S. Polit. & Govt. Pos: Burgess, Oxford, Pa; mem, State Bd. of Welfare, 61; mem, Pa. Hist. and Museum Cmn, 62; chmn, Chester Co. Develop. Coun; former pres, Young Rep. of South. Chester Co; Rep. dist. chmn; former Rep. co. committeeman; mem, Co. Exec. Cmt; Pa. State Sen, 60-, chmn, Rep. Caucus. Bus. & Prof. Pos: Bus. exec; newspaper publisher; chmn, Am. Water Works Co; pres, Pa. Fuel Gas, Inc. Mem: Beta Theta Pi; past dist. gov, Rotary Int; pres, Coatesville YMCA; pres, Chester Co. Co, Boy Scouts; trustee, Lincoln Univ, W. Nottingham Acad, Univ. of Pa, and Pa. Col. Optom; dir, State YMCA, Chester Co. Tuberc. Soc; gov, East. Pa. Arthritis-Rheumatism Found. Rel: Presbyterian; Treas. and Trustee, Presbytery of Donegal, Synod of Pa. Mailing Add: 55 S. Third St, Oxford, Pa. 19363.

WARE, JOHN THOMAS R
Fla. State Rep.
b. Chattanooga, Tenn, 11/14/31; s. Col. James E. Ware and Marguerite McQue Ware; m. Doris Gregory; c. G. Scott, Stacey, Sheryl, Sheila and Steven Edwin. Educ: Univ. Fla, 49-50; Fla. State Univ, B.S. pub. admin, 57; Stetson Col. of Law, J.D, 61; pres, Lambda Chi Alpha and Inter Fraternity Coun, 56-57. Polit. & Govt. Pos: Fla. State Rep, 64-66 & 68-; city attorney, St. Petersburg Beach, 67. Bus. & Prof. Pos: Attorney-at-Law. Mil. Serv: Navy, Korean War, 50-54. Mem: St. Petersburg Bar Asn; Fla. Acad. of Trial Lawyers; Fla. and Am. Bar Asns; St. Petersburg Trial Lawyers Asn. Mailing Add: 2540 Fairway Ave. S, St. Petersburg, Fla. 33712.

WARE, LEONARD R
Mem, Calif. Rep. State Cent. Cmt.
b. Everett, Wash, 1/19/28; s. Dwight Ware and Ruth Hulbert W; m. 2/27/60 to Jeanne Bailard; c. Laura Ruth, Lincoln, Jennifer and Pamela. Educ: Univ. Wash, 47-50; Syracuse Col. Law, LL.B, 53; Delta Kappa Epsilon; Phi Delta Phi. Polit. & Govt. Pos: Asst. U.S. Attorney, Dept. Justice, 53-55; City Planning Cmnr, Palo Alto, Calif, 65-67; mem, Lawyers Cmt. for Civil Rights Under Law, 65-; dir, Calif. Rep. League, 65-69, pres, 68-69; alternate del, Rep. Nat. Conv, 68; mem, Calif. Rep. State Cent. Cmt, 69- Mailing Add: 2600 El Camino Real, Palo Alto, Calif. 94306.

WARE, RICHARD ANDERSON R
Prin. Dep. Asst. Secy. of Defense for Int. Security Affairs, Dept. of Defense
b. Staten Island, N.Y, 11/7/19; s. John Sayers Ware and Mabelle Anderson W; m. 3/20/42 to Lucille Henney; c. Alexander W, Janet M, Bradley J. and Patricia E. Educ: Lehigh Univ, B.A, 41; Wayne State Univ, M.P.A, 43; Phi Beta Kappa; Phi Alpha Theta. Polit. & Govt. Pos: Asst. dir, Mich. Joint Legis. Cmt. on State Reorgn, 50-52; secy, Gov. Cmn. to Study Prisons, 52-53; polit. analyst, Rep. Nat. Cmt, 64; Prin. Dep. Asst. Secy. of Defense for Int. Security Affairs, Dept. of Defense, 69- Bus. & Prof. Pos: Research asst, Detroit Bur. of Govt. Research, 41-42; personnel technician, Lend-Lease Admin, 42-43; research assoc, Citizens Research Coun. of Mich, 46-49, asst. dir, 49-56; secy, Relm Found. and Earhart Found, 56- Mil. Serv: Entered as Pvt, Army Air Corps, 43, released as T/Sgt, 46. Publ: 'A Proposal for a Legislative Auditor General,' essay, 51; 'The Case for Reorganization,' monograph, 52; 'Governmental Research: Challenge & Response,' monograph, 66. Rel: Presbyterian. Legal Res: 2815 Washtenaw Rd, Ann Arbor, Mich. 48104. Mailing Add: Room 4E813, The Pentagon, Washington, D.C. 20301.

WARE, WAYMON WALTER Freedom Socialist Party
b. Clarksville, Tex, 12/5/14; s. Gene Ware and Daisy Estelle Choice W; m. 11/7/42 to Florestine Roberts; c. Dorthy Pearl and Billie Don. Educ: San Antonio Jr. Col, 36-37; Univ. Wash, 47-52. Polit. & Govt. Pos: Cand, U.S. Rep, Wash, formerly and chmn, Freedom Socialist Party until 68. Bus. & Prof. Pos: Building contractor, self-employed, 52-; lectr, Cent. States Col, 67-

Mil. Serv: Entered as Pvt, Army, 42, released as Sgt, 45, after serv. in 260th Mil. Police Co, S.Pac. Theatre; 43-45; Campaign Ribbons; Good Conduct and Marksman Medal. Mem: Former off, Seattle Improv. Asn. Mailing Add: 1622 35th Ave, Seattle, Wash. 98122.

WAREHAM, LEVADA E. R
Secy, Trumbull Co. Rep. Exec. & Cent. Cmts, Ohio.
b. Warren, Ohio, 8/6/21; d. Charles Allen Wright and Sarah Seybert W; m. 10/19/40 to Roscoe H. Wareham; c. Sally (Mrs. Welke), Deborah and Patricia. Educ: Warren G. Harding High Sch, Warren, Ohio, 3 years. Polit. & Govt. Pos: Secy. & v.pres, Howland Rep. Club, Ohio, 63, pres, 64, legis. chmn, 69; Rep. precinct committeeman, Howland Precinct M, Trumbull Co, 63-69; secy, Trumbull Co. Rep. Exec. & Cent. Cmt, 64-; polit. dir, Warren City Women's Club, 69. Rel: Protestant. Mailing Add: 4300 Stonybrook Dr, Warren, Ohio 44484.

WARF, J. H.
Cmnr. of Educ, Tenn.
b. Maury Co, Tenn, 9/13/04; m. 1932 to Martha Josephine Kistler. Educ: Mid. Tenn. State Col, B.S; George Peabody Col, M.A. Polit. & Govt. Pos: Mem, Tenn. State Bd. of Educ, 55-62; cmnr. of educ, Tenn, 63- Bus. & Prof. Pos: Elem. and sec. sch. teacher, asst. prin. and prin, Lewis Co, 21-29; Lewis Co. supt, 29-62. Mem: Tenn. Educ. Asn; Tenn. Pub. Sch. Officers' Asn; Am. Asn. of Sch. Adminstrs; Tenn. Sch. Bd. Asn; Dept. of Rural Educ, Nat. Educ. Asn; Sigma Club; Middle Tenn. State Col; Coord. Cmt. for Higher Educ. in Tenn; Develop. Coun, Univ. Tenn. Rel: Methodist. Mailing Add: Cordell Hull Bldg, Nashville, Tenn. 37219. (1967)

WARFIELD, EDWIN, III D
Md. State Del.
b. Baltimore, Md, 6/3/24; married. Educ: Cornell Univ; Johns Hopkins Univ; Univ. of Md, B.S, 50. Polit. & Govt. Pos: Md. State Del, 63- Bus. & Prof. Pos: Newspaper publisher and farmer. Mil. Serv: Air Force; Chief of Staff, Md. Air Nat. Guard. Mem: Chmn, Gov. Cmn. on the Expansion of the Univ. of Md. Mailing Add: 15 E. Saratoga St, Baltimore, Md. 21202. (1967)

WARFIELD, WILLIAM S, IV R
Mont. State Rep.
b. Chicago, Ill, 12/25/19; s. William S. Warfield, III and Hildegarde Ware W; m. 6/30/48 to Norma Patrick; c. William S, V, Christine, James Patrick and Katharine. Educ: Princeton Univ, A.B, 42; Princeton Elm Club. Polit. & Govt. Pos: Mem, city-co. airport bd, Livingston, Mont, 51-68; mem, bd. of trustees, Sch. Dist. 10, Park Co, 55-; Mont. State Rep, 67- Mil. Serv: Entered as A/S, Navy, 42, released Lt, 46, after serv. in U.S.S. Pac. 1133rd, S.W. Pac, 43-45; Bronze Star; Unit Commendation. Mem: Am. Legion; Farm Bur. Rel: Episcopal. Mailing Add: Hoffman Rd, Livingston, Mont. 59047.

WARGO, JOSEPH G. D
Pa. State Rep.
b. Olyphant, Pa, 8/4/22; s. Andrew P. Wargo and Anna Wasilisin W. Educ: Olyphant Sr. High Sch. Polit. & Govt. Pos: Mem, Lackawanna Co. Dem. Clubs, Pa; Pa. State Rep, 48- Mil. Serv: 109th Inf, Nat. Guard, peacetime; World War II, Sgt, 168th Inf, 34th Div, N.Africa, Italy; lost left leg, Battle of Casino. Mem: DAV; Am. Legion; life mem, Throop Blvd. Mem. Post 7251, VFW; Lions; K. of C. Coun. 1005; Centennial Club, Olyphant. Mailing Add: 408 Cleveland St, Olyphant, Pa. 18447. (1967)

WARLICK, GEORGE HUNTER R
N.C. State Rep.
b. Kings Mountain, N.C, 8/1/31; s. Charles Ervin Warlick, Sr. and Madge Patterson W; m. 3/24/62 to Anna Grace Dell; c. Cherrie Dell. Educ: Davidson Col, A.B, 57; Duke Univ. Law Sch, LL.B, 60; Order of the Coif; Sigma Phi Epsilon; Delta Theta Phi. Polit. & Govt. Pos: N.C. State Rep, 68-; mem. Local Govt. Study Cmn, 69- Bus. & Prof. Pos: Attorney, Dockery, Ruff, Perry, Bond & Cobb, Charlotte, N.C, 60-63; attorney, Hovey & Warlick, Hickory, 63-69; attorney, private practice, 69- Mil. Serv: Entered as Seaman Recruit, Navy, 51, released as 2/C PO, 54, after serv. in Seventh Fleet Flag Allowance, Korea, 51-52 and Mobile Construction Bn. Nine, Philippines and Aleutians, 52-54; UN Serv, Korean Serv. and Good Conduct Medals. Publ: 'North Carolina Section-Encyclopedia of Banking & Commercial Law,' Banking Law J. Mem: Am. and N.C. Bar Asns; Kiwanis. Rel: Methodist. Legal Res: 227 31st Ave. N.W, Hickory, N.C. 28601. Mailing Add: P.O. Box 182, Hickory, N.C. 28601.

WARMAN, EDWARD ALLEN D
Ill. State Rep.
b. Oak Park, Ill, 6/23/26; s. Jacob Warman and Ethel Colt W; m. 9/5/49 to Doris Mae Miller; c. Robin Sheryl, Robert Evan and Jeffrey Glenn. Educ: Chicago-Kent Col. Law, LL.B, 50; Nu Beta Epsilon. Polit. & Govt. Pos: Pres, 49th Ward Young Dem, 55-56; precinct capt, 49th Ward, Chicago, 55-58; precinct committeeman, 59-66; asst. attorney gen, Ill, 61-64; mem. steering cmt, Niles Twp. Dem. Orgn, Ill, 63-66; Ill. State Rep, 65- Bus. & Prof. Pos: Participant, Rutgers Univ. Eagleton Sch. of Politics Seminar, 67. Mil. Serv: Entered as Pvt, Army, 44, released as Tech. Sgt, 46, after serv. in 91st Mil. Govt. Hq. and Hq. Co, Japan, 45-46. Mem: Legis. cmt, Chicago Bar Asn, 65-68, local govt. cmt, 64-68; bd. mgrs, Niles Twp. Bar Asn, 63-64 & 65-66; legis. cmt, Decalogue Soc. of Lawyers, 64-68; past post comdr, Jewish War Vets; PTA; B'nai B'rith; dir, South Fairview Property Owners; Rotary Int; Am. Acad. of Polit. and Soc. Sci; Acad. of Polit. Sci. Rel: Hebrew. Legal Res: 6419 Lockwood Ave, Skokie, Ill. 60076. Mailing Add: 4400 Oakton St, Skokie, Ill. 60076.

WARNER, BERTHA DIGGS R
Third V.Chmn, Kings Co. Rep. Cmt, N.Y.
b. Richland, Ga, 5/2/12; d. James Jones and Elizabeth Thornton J.(deceased); m. 1934 to Jacob A. Diggs, div; m. 10/24/54 to Louis Johnson Warner; c. Betty Jean Diggs (Mrs. Luther L. Dix, Jr). Educ: Cent. Sch. of Bus, 36-38; Columbia Univ, cert, 53; Pohs Inst, licensed real estate broker, 67. Polit. & Govt. Pos: Mem, Rep. Speakers Bur, city, state and nat, 34-56; fifth ward secy, Erie Co. Rep. Cmt, N.Y, 34-44; mem, N.Y. State Legis. Cmn. to Investigate Condition of the Urban Negro Population, 38; orgn. and exec. dir, Crispus Attucks Rep. League, 38-55; asst. campaign mgr, Rep. State Cmt, 42; mem, Nat. Rep. Planning Cmt, Erie Co, N.Y, 42; alternate del, Rep. Nat. Conv, 44 & 68; mem, Eisenhower for Pres. Cmt, 52; pub. mem, Housing Adv. Cmt, N.Y. State Div. Housing, 61-69; third v.chmn, Kings Co. Rep. Cmt, N.Y, 68- Bus. & Prof. Pos: Secretarial asst, Erie Co. Clerk's Off, Buffalo, N.Y, 40-44; Secy. of Labor, State of New York, 44-55; mgr, Warner & Warner Realty Co, 55-69; legis. chmn, Empire State Sunday Sch. Cong, 65-69. Publ: Home and Family Seminar, Nat. Baptist, 56; 'A Proposal for a State Commission for Community Development,' newsletter proj, 65; 'The Responsibilities of Citizenship,' The Baptist, 66. Mem: Pres. adv. coun, Pace Col; Am. Acad. Polit. and Soc. Sci; adv, Edward Corsi Labor Mgt. Inst; Vis. Nurse Asn. Brooklyn; Karen Lectr. Serv. Pub. Serv. Award, N.Y. State Civil Serv. Citation In-Serv. Training, 50; The N.Y. Bible Soc. Award, 61; Silver Cup, Nat. Rep. Negro Coun; Meritorious Serv, Am. Legion, State Employees' Post. Rel: Baptist; Deaconess, Mt. Olivet Baptist Church. Mailing Add: 1245 Union St, Brooklyn, N.Y. 11225.

WARNER, CLARENCE E. R
Chmn, Okla. Rep. State Party
b. Booker, Tex, 10/31/38; s. Virgil O. Warner and Mabel Arnett W; m. 6/5/60 to Ona C. Oldfield; c. Catharine Lynette. Educ: Kans. State Teachers Col, B.A, 60; Okla. State Univ, M.S, 66; Lambda Delta Lambda; Kappa Mu Epsilon; Phi Lambda Upsilon; Alpha Kappa Lambda. Polit. & Govt. Pos: Chmn, Garfield Co. Young Rep. Club, Okla, 65 & 66; Rep. precinct chmn, Garfield Co, 65-68; Sixth Dist. chmn, Okla. Young Rep. Fedn, 67-68; Rep. state committeeman, Garfield Co, Okla, 67-68; chmn, Okla. Educ, Coun, 67-68; chmn, Okla. Rep. State Party, 69-; admin. asst. to U.S. Rep. John N. Happy Camp, Okla, 69- Bus. & Prof. Pos: Instr, Sterling Col, Kans, 63; asst. prof. chem, Phillips Univ, Enid, Okla, 63-68. Mil. Serv: Capt, Army Nat. Guard, Okla, 57-; Res. Forces Medal. Mem: Am. Chem. Soc; Am. Asn. Univ. Prof. Rel: Methodist. Mailing Add: 11201 Dover Court, Surrey Hills, Yukon, Okla. 73099.

WARNER, DALE IRVING R
Mich. State Rep.
b. Williamston, Mich, 2/3/41; s. Russell Lewis Warner and Kathryn Crippen W; single. Educ: Mich. State Univ, B.A, 62; Univ. Mich, LL.B, 65; Phi Eta Sigma; Phi Kappa Phi; Delta Chi; Green Helmet; Blue Key; Excalibur; speaker and v.pres, All-Univ. Student Govt. and mem, Student Cong. Polit. & Govt. Pos: Precinct del, Eaton Co. Rep. Conv, Mich, 62-64; alternate del, Rep. Nat. Conv, 64; state chmn, Mich. Fedn. Col. Rep, 64-65; dir, Fifth Region Col. Rep. Nat. Cmt, 65-66; spec. asst. to State Chmn. for Youth Activities, Rep. State Cent. Cmt, 65-66; mem. and finance chmn, Eaton Co. Rep. Exec. Cmt, 65-66; Mich. State Rep, 65- Bus. & Prof. Pos: Attorney-at-law. Mem: Mich. State Bar Asn; Eaton Co. Farm Bur. Received Ford Found. Legis. Fel, 65-66. Rel: Baptist. Legal Res: 9188 Cockroft Rd, Eaton Rapids, Mich. 48827. Mailing Add: P.O. Box 937, Lansing, Mich. 48904.

WARNER, DOROTHY MARIE R
Treas. South. Div, Calif. Fedn. of Rep. Women
b. Albion, Ill, 9/3/22; d. Ross Lewis Davis and Ruth Easton D; m. 12/30/42 to Kenneth J. Warner; c. Kathleen Jo. Educ: Ind. Univ, Bloomington, 2 years. Polit. & Govt. Pos: Pres, Thousand Oaks Rep. Women's Club, Federated, Calif, 61-62; co-chmn, Nixon for Gov. Cmt, Conejo Valley, 62; v.pres, Ventura Co. Fedn. of Rep. Women, 63-64, precinct chmn, 65-66; chmn, Goldwater for Pres. Cmt, Conejo Valley, 64; Americanism chmn, South. Div, Calif. Fedn. of Rep. Women, 64-65, precinct chmn, 66-67, treas, 68-; precinct chmn. and v.chmn, Ventura Co. Rep. Cent. Cmt, Calif, 65-; mem. precinct steering cmt, Calif. Rep. State Cent. Cmt, 65-68. Publ: 'Guide for Republican Women,' South. Div, Calif. Fedn. of Rep. Women, 68. Mem: Conejo Commun. Coun. (past youth chmn, secy, currently); Conejo Beautiful, Inc.(past chmn); Conejo Valley Garden Club; Audubon Soc; Delphian Soc. One of Fifty in State of Calif. to Receive Gov. Reagan's Award of Precinct Excellence, 68. Rel: Lutheran. Mailing Add: 2066 Penrose Court, Thousand Oaks, Calif. 91360.

WARNER, IVAN D
b. New York, N.Y, 2/18/19; m. to Helen E. Nichols. Educ: City Col. New York; Am. Univ; N.Y. Law Sch, LL.B. Polit. & Govt. Pos: Secy. to U.S. Rep. Isidore Dollinger; N.Y. State Assemblyman, 58-60; N.Y. State Sen, 60-68; del, Dem. Nat. Conv, 68. Bus. & Prof. Pos: Attorney. Mem: V.chmn, Nat. Conf. of Christians and Jews; Bronx chmn, Bronx Co. Dem. Cmt; NAACP; Urban League of Gr. N.Y; bd. of dir, Bronx Co. Bar Asn; New York Co. Lawyers Asn; Harlem Lawyers Asn; bd. of mgr, Bronx Div, Protestant Coun; chap. 37, St. George Asn. of Bus. and Prof. Men; Forest Neighborhood House; E. Tremont Neighborhood Asn; Lawyer's Div, United Jewish Appeal; co-chmn, 42nd precinct PAL; E. Bronx Commun. Coun; dist. cmt, March of Dimes; Boy Scouts; Prospect-Longwood Civic Asn; Lions Club of Bronx; exec, Jackson Dem. Club, 78th Assembly Dist, Bronx. Rel: Episcopal; Hon. Vestryman, Trinity Episcopal Church. Mailing Add: 748 E. 175th St, Bronx, N.Y. 10457. (1967)

WARNER, JEROME R
Nebr. State Sen.
b. Waverly, Nebr, 11/23/27; s. Charles J. Warner and Esther Anderson W; single. Educ: Univ. Nebr, B.Sc, 52; Alpha Zeta, Gamma Sigma Delta, Block and Bridle; Farm House. Polit. & Govt. Pos: Nebr. State Sen, 25th Dist, 66-, Speaker Nebr. State Senate, 69- Rel: Covenant. Mailing Add: Waverly, Nebr. 68462.

WARNER, JOAN FLEENOR D
Exec. Secy, Summit Co. Dem. Party, Ohio
b. Weston, W.Va, 5/11/09; d. David D. Rich and Anna Elizabeth Skidmore R; m. 11/28/66 to Guy O. Warner. Educ: Actual Bus. Col, Akron, Ohio, Secy. Cert, 29; Akron Univ, 32; Case Col. Eng, Cleveland, Ohio, 45-46. Polit. & Govt. Pos: Sr. Inspector govt. material, Army Ord. Dept, 46-49, Army Eng. Corp, 47-49; state dep. registrar motor vehicles, Ohio, 50-54; chmn, Fifth Ward Dem. Precinct Committee People, pres, Fifth Ward Dem. Club and exec. secy, Summit Co. Dem. Party, Ohio, 50-; state sales tax agent, Ohio, 61-63; mem, State and Nat. Fedn. Dem. Womens Club. Bus. & Prof. Pos: Secy, Firestone Tire & Rubber Co, Akron, Ohio, 32-45; owner and mgr, J & H Restaurant, 46- Mem: Exec. off, Firestone Auxiliary 7 and AFL-CIO Auxiliary Coun; Women's Bus. Asn; state dep, Daughters of Am; Women's Benefit Asn;

German Am. Club; Am. Legion Auxiliary. Testimonial dinner for registering more Dem. than anyone in Summit Co, Akron, Ohio. Rel: Protestant. Mailing Add: 1032 Neptune Ave, Akron, Ohio 44301.

WARNER, JOHN WILLIAM R
Under Secy. of the Navy, Wash, D.C.
b. Washington, D.C, 2/18/27; s. Dr. John William Warner, Sr. and Martha Stuart Budd W; m. 8/7/57 to Catherine Conover Mellon; c. Mary Conover, Virginia Stuart and John William, IV. Educ: Wash. and Lee Univ, B.S, 49; Univ. Va, LL.B, 53; Beta Theta Pi; Phi Alpha Delta. Polit. & Govt. Pos: Law clerk, Judge E. Barrett Prettyman, Circuit Judge, U.S. Court of Appeals, 53-54; spec. asst. to U.S. Attorney, 56-57; asst. U.S. Attorney, Justice Dept, 57-60; advanceman, Nixon Campaign Staff, 60; nat. dir, United Citizens for Nixon/Agnew, 68; mem. staff, Off. President-elect, 68-69; Under Secy. of the Navy, Wash, D.C, 69- Bus. & Prof. Pos: Lawyer; partner, Hogan & Hartson, 60-68. Mil. Serv: Entered as Seaman, Navy, 44, released as ETM 3/C, 46, recalled as Pvt, Marine Corps, 49, released as Capt, 61, after serv. in First Marine Air Wing, Korea, 51-52. Mem: Am. Bar Asn; Wash. Inst. For. Affairs; Metrop. Club; Burning Tree Club and Chevy Chase Club, Wash, D.C; trustee, Protestant Episcopal Cathedral Found; World Peace Through Law Center; Va. Mus. Fine Arts; trustee, Wash. and Lee Univ. Rel: Episcopal. Legal Res: Milldale Farms, Box 24, White Post, Va. 22663. Mailing Add: 3240 S St. N.W, Washington, D.C. 20007.

WARNER, ROBERT EDSON D
b. Gallipolis, Ohio, 4/11/31; s. Robert Warner and Ada Roush W; m. 6/26/54 to Mary Lou Clark; c. Ruth Christina, Margaret Elizabeth, Deborah Marie and Elizabeth Rebecca. Educ: Antioch Col, B.S, 54; Univ. Rochester, Ph.D, 59; Union Carbide and Carbon fel, 56-57; Nat. Sci. Found. fel, 57-59. Polit. & Govt. Pos: Chmn, 13th Cong. Dist. Citizens for McCarthy Cmt, Ohio, 68; alternate del, Dem. Nat. Conv, 68. Bus. & Prof. Pos: From instr. to asst. prof, Univ. Rochester, 59-61; asst. prof, Antioch Col, 61-63; from asst. to assoc. prof, Univ. Manitoba, 63-65; assoc. prof, Oberlin Col, 65- Publ: Polarization in 217 Mev p-n and p-p Scattering (with J.H. Tinlot), Phys. Rev, 61; Bremsstrahlung Production in 48 Mev p-p Collisions, Can. J. Phys, 66; Deuteron Breakup by 42 Mev α-particles (with R.W. Bercaw), Nuclear Physics, 68; plus 11 others. Mem: Am. Asn. Univ. Prof; Am. Phys. Soc; Am. Asn. Physics Teachers; Am. Asn. Adv. Sci; Am. Civil Liberties Union. Rel: Congregational. Mailing Add: 236 Forest St, Oberlin, Ohio 44074.

WARNER, SETH WILLMARTH R
b. Addison, Vt, 10/2/07; married; c. 1 daughter. Educ: Vt. State Sch. of Agr. Polit. & Govt. Pos: Town lister and auditor, 9 years; Vt. State Rep, 61-66. Bus. & Prof. Pos: Farming; house restoration; pres. and dir, Middlebury Nat. Farm Loan Asn; rep. on Stockholders Cmt, Fed. Land Bank for Vt. and N.H, 2 years; dir, Prod. Credit Asn, Burlington, 3 years. Mem: Master, Grange, 2 years. Rel: Episcopal. Mailing Add: R.D. 1, Vergennes, Vt. 05491. (1967)

WARNICK, ROBERT WILLIAM R
Utah State Rep.
b. Bell, Los Angeles, Calif, 6/27/37; s. Frederick Wise Warnick and Mary Ellen Daly W; m. 11/18/60 to Carol Julian; c. Gina Michelle, Troy Julian and Daren Robert. Educ: Brigham Young Univ, 57-58 & 60-61; Univ. Utah, B.S. in Polit. Sci, 63. Polit. & Govt. Pos: Del, Utah State Rep. Conv, 64 & 68; Utah State Rep, 69- Bus. & Prof. Pos: Field rep, Utah State Med. Asn, 63-67; agent, Mass. Mutual Life, 67; sales rep, Pfizer Labs, 67- Mil. Serv: Entered as Pvt, Army, 55, released as SP-3, 57 after serv. in Sixth Armored Cavalry and 11th Armored Cavalry, European Command, Germany, 56-57. Mem: Exec. cmt, Utah Chap, Arthritis Found; home safety cmt, Utah Safety Coun; Legis. Intern to Utah State Senate from Hinckley Inst. Practical Polit, 66. Rel: Latter-day Saint; Bishop. Mailing Add: 2731 Glen Heather Ave, Salt Lake City, Utah 84121.

WARNKE, CURTIS B. Non-Partisan
b. Wood Lake, Minn, 1932. Educ: Univ. Minn. Polit. & Govt. Pos: Minn. State Rep, 58-66; del, Dem. Nat. Conv, 68. Rel: Methodist. Mailing Add: Wood Lake, Minn. 56297. (1967)

WARNKE, FRANK J. D
b. Havre, Mont, 1933. Educ: Cent. Wash. Col. of Educ; $1\frac{1}{2}$ years, Univ. Wash, polit. sci. maj. Polit. & Govt. Pos: Wash. State Rep, until 66. Bus. & Prof. Pos: Pub. Affairs consult; legis. dir, Pub. Sch. Employees. Mil. Serv: Coast Guard, 3 years. Mem: Kiwanis; Jr. C. of C. Mailing Add: 29457 51st St. S, Auburn, Wash. 98002. (1967)

WARREN, CHARLES D
Calif. State Assemblyman
b. Kansas City, Mo, 1927; m. 1963 to Audrey Paul Warren. Educ: Yale Univ; Univ. Calif, B.A, 49; Hastings Col. of Law, LL.B, 52. Polit. & Govt. Pos: Chmn, Dem. State Cent. Cmt; Calif. Coun. of Dem. Clubs; Calif. State Assemblyman, 63-; del, Dem. Nat. Conv, 68. Mil. Serv: Sgt, Army, 44-46. Mem: Urban League; Nat. Panel of Arbitrators, Am. Arbit. Asn; Wilshire and Calif. State Bar Asns. Mailing Add: 1411 W. Olympic Blvd, Los Angeles, Calif. 90015.

WARREN, CLIFFORD ERNEST D
Chmn, Small Bus. Cmt, West. State Dem. Conf.
b. Seattle, Wash, 1/25/19; s. John L. Warren and Esther Smith W; m. 5/20/38 to June Lorraine Crate. Polit. & Govt. Pos: Chmn, Small Bus. Cmt, West States Dem. Conf, 62-; precinct chmn, Dem. Party, 64-65; del, Dem. Nat. Conv, 68. Bus. & Prof. Pos: Pres, Warren Painting Co, Inc, 50- Mil. Serv: Painter 1/C, Navy, 42-45, serv. in 40th Naval Construction Bn, Pac; Asiatic-Pac. Campaign Ribbon with Three Stars; Army, Distinguished Unit Citation; Good Conduct Medal. Mem: Elks; Mason; Scottish Rite; Shrine; Arctic Club; Wash. Athletic Club. Rel: Protestant. Legal Res: 2650 Marston Dr, Anchorage, Alaska 99503. Mailing Add: P.O. Box 1124, Anchorage, Alaska 99501. (1967)

WARREN, DELBERT CLAYTON R
Chmn, Montgomery Co. Rep. Party, Ky.
b. Bath Co, Ky, 5/3/30; s. Clark Warren and Ina Vertna Karrick Bogie W; m. July 1960 to Wanda Bryant; c. Ronald, Nancy, Melanie, Kimberly and Brent. Polit. & Govt. Pos: Chmn, Montgomery Co. Rep. Party, Ky, 68- Bus. & Prof. Pos: Pres, Warren Builders, Inc; Pres, Warren Lumber Co. Inc; V.Pres, Gate City Bowling Lanes. Rel: Protestant. Legal Res: 107 Ronameki Dr, Mt. Sterling, Ky. 40353. Mailing Add: P.O. Box 486, Mt. Sterling, Ky. 40353.

WARREN, DOUGLAS STEWART R
b. West Hollywood, Calif, 9/28/34; s. Charles Brown Warren and Louise Evangeline Watt W; m. 12/4/66 to Betty June Handley; c. Cynthia Dawn and Douglas Scott. Educ: Utah State Univ, B.S. in Polit. Sci, 59; Univ. Colo, grad. work in Law, 59-62; Rep. Col. League (officer, Utah State Univ. Club, 57-59, chmn, Univ. Colo. Club, 61-62). Polit. & Govt. Pos: Capt, Rep. Dist, Riverside, Calif, 55-57; co-chmn, Bill Kreg for U.S. Rep, Calif, 56; state coordinator, Hill High Sch. Rep. Party, Colo, 59-60; capt, Rep. Dist, Denver, 63-65; chmn, Colo. State Goldwater for Pres. Speakers Bur, 64; chmn, Ore. State Young Rep. First Voter Prog, 67-68; exec. secy, Ore. State Young Rep. Fedn, 68; Rep. nominee for U.S. Rep, Third Dist, Ore, 68-69. Mil. Serv: Entered as Airman, Air Force, 51, released as Airman 3/C, 53, after serv. in 69th Fighter Bomber Squadron, Korea, 52-53; Presidential Citation; 2 Battle Stars; Sigman Rhee Citation. Publ: Position Papers for 1968 Congressional Compaign. Mem: Jr. C. of C; C. of C. Rel: Latter-day Saint. Mailing Add: 3109 S.E. Claybourne, Portland, Ore. 97202.

WARREN, EARL R
b. Los Angeles, Calif, 3/19/91; s. Methias H. Warren and Chrystal Hernlund W; m. 10/14/25 to Nina P. Meyers; c. James C, Virginia (Mrs. John Daly), Earl, Dorothy (Mrs. Carmine Clemente), Nina Elizabeth (Mrs. Stuart Brien) and Robert. Educ: Univ. Calif, B.L, 12 and J.D, 14; Phi Delta Phi; Sigma Phi. Recipient numerous hon. degrees. Polit. & Govt. Pos: Clerk, assembly judiciary cmt, Calif. Legis, 19; dep. city attorney, Oakland, Calif, 19-20; dep. dist. attorney, Alameda Co, Calif, 20-23, chief dep, 23-25, dist. attorney, 25-39; alternate del, Rep. Nat. Conv, 28, del, 32 and mem. nat. exec. cmt, temporary chmn. and keynote speaker, 44; chmn, Calif. Rep. State Cent. Cmt, 34-36; Rep. Nat. Committeeman, Calif, 36-38; attorney gen, Calif, 39-43, Gov, 43-53; cand, V.Pres. of U.S, 48; spec. ambassador of U.S. to Coronation of Queen Elizabeth II, 53; chmn. bd. trustees, Nat. Gallery of Art, 53-; chancellor bd. regents, Smithsonian Inst, 53-; Chief Justice of U.S, 53-69; chmn, Int. Bd. of Overseers, Harry Truman Int. Center for the Adv. of Peace in Jerusalem, 69- Bus. & Prof. Pos: Research assoc, Bur. Pub. Admin, Univ. Calif, 32-40. Mil. Serv: 1st Lt, Army Inf, 17-18; Capt, Army Res, until 36. Mem: State Bar of Calif; Alameda and Sacramento Co. Bar Asns; Am. Acad. Arts and Sci; trustee, Nat. Geog. Soc; Am. Philos. Soc; pres, Nat. Asn. Attorneys Gen, 40-41; Mason (32°, grand master, Calif, 35-36); Olympic, Commonwealth, Bohemian, Athens Athletic, Claremont Country, Jonathan, Calif, Sutter and Del Paso Country Clubs. Mailing Add: Sheraton Park Hotel, Washington, D.C. 20008.

WARREN, EARL W. D
Wis. State Assemblyman
b. Hurley, Wis, 2/25/02. Educ: Ironwood, Mich. Bus. Col. Polit. & Govt. Pos: Mem, Racine Co. Bd, Wis, 48-55; Wis. State Assemblyman, 54- Bus. & Prof. Pos: Assembler in radiator factory, 36; formerly operated own bus. Mem: Elks; AFL-CIO; Eagles; United Commercial Travelers. Mailing Add: 2809 Virginia St, Racine, Wis. 53405. (1967)

WARREN, EDWARD J. DFL
Chmn, Olmsted Co. Dem-Farmer-Labor Cent. Cmt, Minn.
b. Orrville, Ohio, 2/25/25; s. Henry B. Warren and Beulah Hofer W; m. 9/12/45 to Eunice Kathleen Golberg; c. Barry, Kathleen, Mark, Wendy and Robert. Polit. & Govt. Pos: Mem, Olmsted Co. Dem-Farmer-Labor Cent. Cmt, Minn, 58- and chmn, 64-; mem, Olmsted Co. Dem-Farmer Labor Exec. Cmt, 60- and chmn, 64-; mem, Minn. Dem-Farmer-Labor Cent. Cmt, 64- Bus. & Prof. Pos: Lab. technician, Mayo Clinic, 52. Mil. Serv: Entered as A/S, Navy, 42, released as Chief Pharmacist's Mate, 47, after serv. in Asiatic-Pac. Theater, 3 years; Inactive Naval Res, 48-53. Mem: K. of C. Rel: Roman Catholic. Mailing Add: 715 Tenth Ave. S.W, Rochester, Minn. 55901. (1967)

WARREN, GEORGE MARVIN, JR. D
Va. State Sen.
b. Bristol, Va, 8/19/22; m. to Merle Musser Watkins W. Educ: Emory and Henry Col, B.A; Univ. of Va, LL.B. Polit. & Govt. Pos: Former cmnr, West. Dist. of Va; Va. State Sen, 64- Bus. & Prof. Pos: Lawyer. Mil. Serv: Navy, 3 years, S.W. Pac. Mem: Elks; Mason; Commonwealth Club. Rel: Presbyterian. Legal Res: 100 Wallace Pike, Bristol, Va. 24201. Mailing Add: 600 Reynolds Arcade Bldg, Bristol, Va. 24201. (1967)

WARREN, HARLAND D. R
b. Serena Twp, Ill, 8/18/16; m. to Helen Bowers; c. three. Educ: Univ. Ill. Polit. & Govt. Pos: State attorney, LaSalle Co, Ill, 52-60; Ill. State Rep, 62-64. Bus. & Prof. Pos: Lawyer. Mil. Serv: Navy, 42-46, serv. in Amphibious Forces, S.Pac. Mem: Ill. Bar and U.S. Supreme Court; Am. Legion; VFW; Shrine. Legal Res: 722 Green St, Ottawa, Ill. 61350. Mailing Add: 118 W. Madison St, Ottawa, Ill. 61350. (1967)

WARREN, HUGH J. D
b. Collins, Mo, 6/7/16; s. Henry Jacob Warren and Emma Hare W; m. 2/15/35 to Joycie Davis; c. Charles H. Polit. & Govt. Pos: Mem, Stone Co. Dem. Cmt, Mo, 56-57, chmn, 64-66. Bus. & Prof. Pos: Partner-mgr, Warren Lumber Co, 36-66; owner-mgr, Crane Lumber Co, 65. Mil. Serv: Entered as A/S, Navy, 43, released as CPO, 45; 6 Pac. Theater Ribbons with 7 Battle Stars. Mem: Am. Tech, Chicago; Mason; Past Master, Shrine, Commandery. Rel: Protestant. Legal Res: Galena, Mo. 65656. Mailing Add: Crane, Mo. 65633.

WARREN, JACK A, JR. D
Miss. State Rep.
b. D'Lo, Miss, 11/29/07; married. Polit. & Govt. Pos: Mem, Mendenhall Sch. Bd; Miss. State Rep, 68- Bus. & Prof. Pos: Cattleman and farmer; pub. rels; dir, Farm Bur, Miss. Land & Timber Corp. Mem: Mason; Shrine; Eastern Star; pres, Simpson Co. Soil Conserv. Dist. Cmn; first v.pres, SE Livestock Asn; C. of C; Lions. Rel: Methodist. Mailing Add: D'Lo, Miss. 39062.

WARREN, JAMES E. D
b. Ludowici, Ga, 12/31/21; s. Leroy B. Warren, Sr. and Laura Fisher W; m. 9/21/45 to Mary Ila McElveen; c. James E. Jr, Joseph Barnwell, Jill Ann, Jamie Ila and John Shepard. Educ: Ludowici High Sch, 40. Polit. & Govt. Pos: Ga. State Rep, 63-64. Bus. & Prof. Pos: Sales rep, Giant Portland Cement Co, Carolina Giant Div, 57- Mil. Serv: 1st Sgt, 41-45; Korean Conflict, 1st Lt, 50-52; Philippine Liberation Ribbon with Bronze Star; Am. Defense Serv. Ribbon; Distinguished Unit Badge; Asiatic Pac. Theatre Ribbon with 4 Bronze Stars; Good Conduct Medal. Mem: Mason; Shrine; cmnr, Am. Legion, 55; VFW. Rel: Baptist. Mailing Add: Jesup, Ga. 31545. (1967)

WARREN, JOE E. D
Kans. State Sen.
b. Silverdale, Kans, 9/17/12; s. James Edmond Warren and Phoebe Harkelroad W; m. 9/4/32 to Pauline Goff; c. James E. and Helen Jane (Mrs. Fair). Polit. & Govt. Pos: Dir. sch. bd, King Sch. Dist. 58, Kans, 38-59; treas, Spring Creek Twp, 50-54; committeeman, Cowley Co. Agr. Stabilization and Conserv. Cmt, 50-54; Kans. State Sen, 57-, chmn, Dem. Caucus, Kans. State Senate, 64-, mem, Kans. Legis. Coun, currently, chmn, Livestock Subcmt. and v.chmn, Agr. Subcmt, currently; chmn, Cowley Co. Soil Conserv. Dist, 60-; mem, Adv. Coun. Unemploy. Security, Secy. Labor, 64-68; alternate del, Dem. Nat. Conv, 68. Mem: Grange; G.F. Forum; Rotary; Elks. Rel: Presbyterian. Mailing Add: R.R. 1, Maple City, Kans. 67102.

WARREN, JOHN E. 'JACK' R
Chmn, Black Hawk Co. Rep. Cent. Cmt, Iowa
b. Rockford, Ill, 12/28/12; s. Ezra H. Warren and Mary Elizabeth Diamond W; m. 9/25/33 to Audrey E. Showalter; c. Audrey E.(Mrs. Harold C. Andrews), Jacqueline (Mrs. Richard Roberts), Adelor J. and Sari Ann. Educ: Rockford High Sch, Ill, grad; Chicago Sch. of Traffic; La Salle Correspondence Sch. of Bus. Polit. & Govt. Pos: Finance chmn, Black Hawk Co. Rep. Party, Iowa, 61 and Third Dist. Rep. Party, 66; chmn, Black Hawk Co. Rep. Cent. Cmt, 63-; state chmn, Rep. Party of Iowa, 67; mem, Rep. Nat. Cmt, currently. Bus. & Prof. Pos: Secy-treas, Warren Transport, Inc, Waterloo, Iowa; pres, Warren Real Estate, Inc; v.pres, Warren Bros, Inc; v.pres. and treas, A & F Finance; and Tripoli Grain and Feed. Mem: V.pres, Iowa Motor Truck Asn, 66; exec. bd, Common Carrier Conf, Irregular Route, chmn, Specified Commodities Div. and Pub Rels. Legis. Cmt; bd. of dir, Waterloo Indust. Develop. Asn; chmn. legis. cmt. and bd. of dirs, Waterloo C. of C; past pres. and mem. bd. of dirs, Machinery Haulers Asn; trustee, Judson Col, Elgin, Ill; Mason, K.T, Shrine; Elks; Moose; former cub master, Boy Scouts;Sunnyside Country Club; Goodfellows; Knife and Fork Club. Rel: Baptist. Legal Res: 2112 W. Fourth St, Waterloo, Iowa 50701. Mailing Add: P.O. Box 420, Waterloo, Iowa 50704.

WARREN, JOHN FISKEN 'JACK' R
Chmn, Smith Co. Rep. Party, Tex.
b. Dallas, Tex, 7/31/29; s. John Edwin Warren and Majorie Fisken W; m. 7/14/51 to Patricia Payne; c. William Edwin, Nancy Bentley and Donald Payne. Educ: N.Mex. Mil. Inst, 2 years; Univ. Tex, 3 years; Phi Kappa Psi. Polit. & Govt. Pos: Rep. Precinct chmn, Smith Co, Tex, 60 & 62; del, Tex. State Rep. Conv, 60, 62, 64, 66 & 68; co.chmn, George Bush Sen. Campaign, 64; co. chmn, John Tower Sen. Campaign, 66; chmn, Smith Co. Rep. Party, 66-; mem, State Rep. Task Force on Revenue and Taxation, 67; alternate del, Rep. Nat. Conv, 68; mem, State Cmt. on Fed. Employ, 69. Bus. & Prof. Pos: Oil scout, Gulf Oil Co, summers; landman, Humble Oil and Ref. Co, Tyler, Tex, 56-63; independent oil operator, 63- Mil. Serv: Entered as 2nd Lt, Army, 54, released as 1st Lt, 66, after serv. in Tenth Inf. Div. and First Inf. Div; discharged from Res. with rank of Capt, 63. Mem: Independent Petroleum Asn. Am.(dir); Am. Asn. Petroleum Landmen; Community Concert Asn. of Tyler(dir); Tyler Independence Day Celebration Cmt.(dir. and chmn); Kiwanis. Rel: Episcopal; Past Vestryman and Past Sr. Warden, Christ Episcopal Church. Legal Res: 1932 Montrose, Tyler, Tex. 75701. Mailing Add: 803 Citizens Bank Bldg, Tyler, Tex. 75701.

WARREN, LINDSAY C, JR. D
N.C. State Sen.
b. Washington, N.C, 10/8/24; s. Lindsay C. Warren and Emily D. Harris W; m. 9/4/48 to Grace J. Bowen; c. Adrienne B, Emily H. and Grace J. Educ: Univ. N.C, B.S, 48 and J.D, 51; Phi Delta Phi. Polit. & Govt. Pos: N.C. State Sen, 63- Bus. & Prof. Pos: Lawyer. Mil. Serv: Lt.(jg), Coast Guard Res, 43-46. Mem: Am. and N.C. Bars; bd. trustees, Wayne Co. Mem. Hosp; Goldsboro Bd. of Educ, 59-62. Rel: Presbyterian. Mailing Add: 208 Ridgewood Dr, Goldsboro, N.C. 27530. (1967)

WARREN, ROBERT WILLIS R
Attorney Gen, Wis.
b. Raton, N.Mex, 8/30/25; s. The Reverend George R. Warren and Clara Joliffee W; m. 8/23/47 to Laverne D. Voagen; c. Cheryl Lynn, Iver Eric, Gregg Alan, Treiva Mae and Lyle David. Educ: Univ. Pa, Army basic eng. course, 44; Macalester Col, B.A. magna cum laude in econ, 50; Univ. Minn, M.A. in pub. admin, 51; For. Serv. Inst, 51-52; Univ. Wis. Law Sch, LL.B, 56; pres, Student Body, 49-50; Nat. Soc. Sci. Hon. Soc; Eta Gamma. Polit. & Govt. Pos: For. Affairs Off, U.S. Dept. of State, 51-53; secy, Brown Co. Vol. Rep. Cmt, 58; asst. dist. attorney, Brown Co, 59-60, dist. attorney, 61-64; Wis. State Sen, Second Dist, 65-69; Attorney Gen, Wis, 69- Bus. & Prof. Pos: Shipfitter's helper, Sturgeon Bay Shipbuilding and Drydock Co, 43; G.I. Loan Agent and Counsr, Bank of Sturgeon Bay, 46; mem, Godfrey, Godfrey and Warren, Elkhorn, Wis, 56-57; partner, Warren and Boltz, Attorneys, Green Bay, Wis, 57-59, Smith, Will & Warren, 65-69. Mil. Serv: Entered as Pvt, Army Res, 43, released as T/4, 46, after serv. in 377th Inf. Regt, 95th Div, 613th Ord. Basic Armor Maintenance and 889th Heavy Automotive Maintenance Co, ETO, 44-46; Combat Infantryman's Badge; Purple Heart; ETO Ribbon. Mem: Wis. Dist. Attorneys Asn; Wis. and Brown Co. Bar Asns; YMCA; Elks; Monday Optimists; Boy Scout Dist. Cmt; Mil. Order of Purple Heart; VFW; DAV; Family Serv. Asn. Rel: Methodist. Legal Res: 209 Glacier Dr, Madison, Wis. 53705. Mailing Add: State Capitol, Madison, Wis. 53702.

WARREN, STEWART B. D
N.C. State Sen.
b. Newton Grove, N.C, 3/10/16; s. John C. Warren and Flora Grantham W; m. 6/28/47 to Lottie Fay West; c. Betsy Faye and George Stewart. Educ: Campbell Col, 33-34; Univ. N.C, A.B, 37; Univ. N.C. Law Sch, LL.B, 39. Polit. & Govt. Pos: Chmn, Sampson Co. Dem. Exec. Cmt, N.C, 46-60; Sampson Co. Attorney, 52-60; city attorney, Clinton, 61-; N.C. State Sen, 61- Mil. Serv: S/Sgt, Army, Counter Intel. Corps, 42-46. Mem: Am. and N.C. Bar Asns; Young Dem. Club; Am. Legion; Lions Int. Rel: Methodist. Mailing Add: Box 745, Clinton, N.C. 28328. (1967)

WARRINER, D. DORTCH R
Mem, Va. State Rep. Cent. Cmt.
b. Brunswick Co, Va, 2/25/29; s. Thomas Emmett Warriner, Sr. and Maria Clarke Dortch W; m. 1/31/59 to Barbara Ann Jenkins; c. Susan Wells, David Thomas Dortch and Julia Cotman. Educ: Univ. Va, LL.B, 57; Univ. N.C, B.A, 51; Order of the Holy Grail; Kappa Alpha Order; Sigma Nu Phi. Polit. & Govt. Pos: Chmn, Greensville Co. Rep. Cmt, Va, 63-; del, Rep. State Conv, 64, 65, 68 & 69; alternate del, Rep. Nat. Conv, 64, del, 68; mem, Va. State Rep. Cent. Cmt, 64- and exec. cmt, 68-; nominee for Attorney Gen. of Va, 65; co-chmn, Va. Nixon for Pres. Cmt, 68; chmn, Fourth Cong. Dist. Rep. Party, 68- Mil. Serv: Entered as Ens, Navy, 51, released as Lt.(jg), 54, after serv. with Atlantic Fleet; Lt, Naval Res, 57- Mem: Va. and Am. Bar Asns; Greenville Bar Asn.(secy, 60-); Va. Trial Lawyers Asn; dist. gov, Lions, 65-66; Va. Farm Bur. Fedn. Rel: Protestant. Legal Res: 100 State St, Emporia, Va. 23847. Mailing Add: 332 S. Main St, Emporia, Va. 23847.

WARSCHAW, CARMEN H. D
Dem. Nat. Committeewoman, Calif.
b. Los Angeles, Calif, 9/4/17; d. Leo M. Harvey and Lena Brody H; m. 7/31/38 to Louis Warschaw; c. Hope and Sue (Mrs. Robertson). Educ: Univ. South. Calif, A.B. cum laude, 39; Alpha Kappa Delta. Polit. & Govt. Pos: Mem. exec. cmt, Dem. State Cent. Cmt, Calif, co-chmn; pres, Dem. Club; mem, Los Angeles Co. Dem. Cent. Cmt; mem. exec. cmt, Calif. Fedn. Young Dem; del, Dem. Nat. Conv, 56, 60, 64 & 68, mem. permanent orgn. cmt, 60; pres, Dem. Women's Forum, 56-57 & 58-59; chmn. women's div, Dem. State Cent. Cmt, 58-64; mem, State Bd. Soc. Welfare, 59; mem, Fair Employment Practices Cmn, 59-64, chmn, 64; chmn, Dem. State Cent. Cmt. of South. Calif, 64-66; Dem. nat. committeewoman, 68-; mem, Nat. Citizens Adv. Cmt. for Commun. Serv. Mem: Bd. dir, Pac. W. Coast Anti-Defamation League, B'nai B'rith; Commun. Rels. Coun, J.F.C. Commun. Serv. Award in Human Rels, Pac. Southwest Region Bd, Anti-Defamation League, B'nai B'rith, 64; Mem, Am. Revolution Bicentennial Cmn. of Calif; Woman of the Year, Los Angeles Times, 68. Mailing Add: 2324 N. Vermont, Los Angeles, Calif. 90027.

WARSHAFSKY, TED M. D
Court Cmnr, Milwaukee Co, Wis.
b. St. Louis, Mo, 12/6/26; s. Israel Warshafsky and Ida Wacks W; m. 7/10/50 to Dolores Anne Weiss; c. Beth, Michael and Lynn. Educ: Univ. Ill, 44; Univ. Wis, B.B.A, 49; Univ. Wis. Law Sch, J.D, 52. Polit. & Govt. Pos: Chmn, Milwaukee Civil Liberties Union, Wis, 62-66; del, Wis. Dem. State Conv, 63, 66, 67, 68 & 69; parliamentarian, Milwaukee Co. Dem. Party, 66-67; court cmnr, Milwaukee Co, 66-; co-chmn, Concerned Dem, 67; co-chmn, McCarthy for Pres, 67-68; v.chmn, Wis. Dem. Del. and del, Dem. Nat. Conv, 68; bd. mem, Wis. Civil Liberties Union, 68-69; chmn, Milwaukee Dem. Coalition, 69. Bus. & Prof. Pos: Sr. partner, Warshafsky, Rotter & Tarnoff, 64- Mil. Serv: Entered as Pvt, Marines, 44, released as Pfc, 46, after serv. in Fleet Marine Force, Pac. Theatre, 45-46. Publ: Collateral Cross Examination, Bankcroft Whitney, 67. Mem: Chmn. ins. and negligence sect, Wis. Bar Asn; Am. Bar Asn; pres, Wis. Acad. Trial Lawyers; Am. Judicature Soc; nat. secy, educ. dir. and current nat. exec. bd. mem, Am. Trial Lawyers Asn. Numerous prfnl. and bar asn. honors and awards. Rel: Jewish. Mailing Add: 2228 E. Newberry Blvd, Milwaukee, Wis. 53211.

WARTINBEE, D. RUSSELL R
b. La Crosse, Wis, 11/11/03. Educ: Wis. Univ, law training, 25-26, B.Mus, 34; Minn. Univ, M.A, 48. Polit. & Govt. Pos: Wis. State Assemblyman, 60-66. Bus. & Prof. Pos: Teacher, music, 27-42 and hist. and soc. studies, 42- Mem: La Crosse Musicians' Asn.(past pres); dir, La Crosse Concert Band, 39. Mailing Add: 1444 Wood St, La Crosse, Wis. 54601. (1967)

WARTNER, ALOYS, JR. R
b. Harvey, N. Dak, 10/6/06; married. Educ: Univ. of N. Dak; Phi Delta Theta. Polit. & Govt. Pos: N. Dak. State Sen, 57-61. Bus. & Prof. Pos: Attorney-at-Law. Mem: Elks; Mason; Shrine; Eagles; Am. Bar Asn; Judge Advocates Asn. Mailing Add: Harvey, N. Dak. 58341.

WARWICK, ROBERT FRANKLIN R
Asst. Secy, N.C. Rep. Party
b. Wilmington, N.C, 5/26/36; s. James Franklin Warwick and Virginia Cayce W; m. 9/11/55 to Catherine Herring; c. Carol Diane and Steven James. Educ: Wilmington Col, 55; Univ. N.C, B.S. in Bus. Admin, 58; Chi Phi. Polit. & Govt. Pos: Treas. and finance chmn, New Hanover Rep. Exec. Cmt, N.C, 62-; treas, New Hanover Co. Rep. Party, 62-; del, Rep. Nat. Conv, 64, alternate del, 68; precinct chmn, S. Wilmington Precinct, 64-65; mem, finance cmt, N.C. Rep. Party, 66-; chmn, Gardner for Gov. Campaign Seventh Dist, 68; finance chmn, Seventh Cong. Dist, N.C, 68-; mem, N.C. State Rep. Cent. Cmt, 68-; asst. secy, N.C. Rep. Party, 68- Bus. & Prof. Pos: Clerk auditor of Freight Receipts Off, Atlantic Coast Line R.R. Co, 54-55; partner, Staff Cert. Pub. Acct, 58-62 and C.S. Lowrimore & Co, Cert. Pub. Acct, 62-; instr, spec. acct. courses, Wilmington Col, 62-63. Publ: 'Multiple Corporations,' Series of Articles for N.C. Newspapers, 67. Mem: Nat. Accounting Asn; Am. Inst. of Cert. Pub. Accts; N.C. Asn. of Cert. Pub. Accts; pres, Cape Fear Area Soc. Cert. Pub. Accts, 66; Kiwanis; Pine Valley Country Club; Admiral, N.C. Navy. Rel: Baptist. Mailing Add: 23 Pickett Dr, Wilmington, N.C. 28401.

WARYAS, VICTOR C. D
b. Poughkeepsie, N.Y, 2/28/15; m. to Elynore Kuklin; c. Joanne (Mrs. Daniele) and Victor C, Jr. Educ: Poughkeepsie Schs. Polit. & Govt. Pos: City chamberlain, Poughkeepsie, N.Y, 50-52; mayor, Poughkeepsie, 59-65; N.Y. State Assemblyman, 64-69; mem, State Bd. of Canvassers Rep. the Speaker of N.Y. State Assembly, Moses Weinstein, 68; mem, Spec. Cmn. tc Consider Legis. Pertaining to Human Organism Transplants; Spec. Legis. Coordinator to Minority Leader N.Y. State Assembly, Stanley Steingut, 69. Bus. & Prof. Pos: Ins. agent. Mil. Serv: Navy. Mem: Past pres, Polish-Am.

Citizen Club; past pres, Exchange Club; Moose; Am. Legion; Poughkeepsie C. of C.(mem. bd. dir); bd. dir, Dutchess Co. Chap, Red Cross. Selected by U.S. State Dept. as one of four U.S. Mayors to Visit Poland as a Rep. of U.S. in People to People Prog, Oct, 63. Rel: Catholic. Mailing Add: P.O. Box 132, Poughkeepsie, N.Y. 12602.

WASDEN, WILEY ANDERSON, JR. R
Chmn, Ga. State Rep. Party
b. Millen, Ga, 1/23/37; s. Wiley Anderson Wasden and Katherine Carr W; m. 8/30/58 to Mary Bell Harrison; c. Wiley A, III and Robert Hancock. Educ: Univ. Ga. Polit. & Govt. Pos: Former chmn, First Cong. Dist. Rep. Party, Ga; former mem, Ga. Rep. State Exec. Cmt. and Chatham Co. Tax Broadening Cmt; mem, Co. and Dist. Rep. Exec. Cmts; an organizer, first Rep. Primary, Savannah; chmn, Ga. State Rep. Party, 69- Bus. & Prof. Pos: Former asst. trust officer, The Citizens & South. Nat. Bank, Savannah; mem. bd. dirs, Darvoe Advert. Agency; treas. and dir, Abercorn Investors, Inc; v.pres. and dir, Savannah Oxygen & Supply Co; gen. partner, Adams & Wasden Enterprises; pres, Wiley A. Wasden Co. Mil. Serv: Entered as Pvt, Army, 56, released as Sgt, 63, after serv. in Inf. Unit. Mem: Former dist. v.pres, Ga. Alumni Soc; former dir, YMCA; chmn. bd. trustees, Savannah Country Day Sch; bd. dirs, C. of C, Savannah; treas. and trustee, Telfair Acad. of Arts & Sci; treas, Girl Scout Coun, Inc; co.chmn, Joint Ga-Ga. Tech. Found; Mayor's Youth Opportunity Coun; steering cmt. and former v.pres, Bulldog Club of Savannah; grad, Commun. Leadership Seminar; Little Theatre; Savannah Art Asn. Rel: Episcopal. Legal Res: 80 Dolan Dr, Grimball Point, Savannah, Ga. 31406. Mailing Add: 206 Factors Walk, Savannah, Ga. 31401.

WASHBURN, C. LANGHORNE R
Dir, U.S. Travel Serv, Dept. of Commerce
b. Livermore Falls, Maine, 7/14/18; s. Stanley Washburn and Alice Langhorne W; m. 12/17/66 to Judith Davies; c. Cary Langhorne, J. Tayloe, Alice, Alexandra and Pamela. Educ: Univ. Va; Delta Upsilon; Univ. Va. Flying Club. Polit. & Govt. Pos: Co-founder, Young Indust. for Eisenhower, 52; dir. spec. events, Nat. Citizens for Eisenhower, 52, v.chmn. cong. cmt, 54; chmn, Eisenhower Bandwagon Opers, 52 & 56, dir. campaign activities, 56; dir. finance cmt, Rep. Nat. Cong. Cmn. and dir, Rockefeller for Pres. Cmt, 64; exec. dir, Rep. Cong. Boosters Club, 64-69; dir. finance, Rep. Nat. Finance Cmt, 65-69; mem, Nixon Presidential Campaign, 69; dir, U.S. Travel Serv, Dept. of Commerce, 69- Bus. & Prof. Pos: Asst. to the pres, Hiller Aircraft, Hiller Helicopter Corp, 47-54; exec. v.pres, Bernard Relin & Assocs, 56-59; consult. assoc, Towne-Oller Assocs, 59-60; pres, Automated Preference Testing Corp, 60-61; v.pres, A.C. Nielsen Co, 61-64. Mil. Serv: Entered as Ens, Navy, 41, released as Lt.(sg), 45, after serv. in Pac. Theater, 42-45; Pac. Theater Ribbon with Five Campaign Stars; Navy Air Medal with Gold Star. Publ: 'Snowbound Aloft,' Flying, 4/57. Mem: Olympic Club; N.Y.C. Union Club; Wash, D.C. Fed. City Club and Capitol Hill Club; Nantucket Yacht Club. Rel: Episcopal. Legal Res: 3333 Prospect N.W, Washington, D.C. 20007. Mailing Add: U.S. Travel Service, Department of Commerce, Washington, D.C. 20230.

WASHBURN, ELWOOD CONRAD R
Chmn, Greenwich Rep. Town Cmt, Conn.
b. Stamford, Conn, 3/18/14; s. Chester C. Washburn and Elsie A. Stahl W; m. 2/1/47 to Pauline Kolok. Educ: Univ. Ala, 33-35; N.Y. Univ, B.S, 49, M.A, 52; Univ. Ala. Baseball Team, 35. Polit. & Govt. Pos: Mem, Greenwich Rep. Town Cmt, Conn, 49-, dist. leader and mem. exec. cmt, 58-63, chmn, 58-; mem. exec. cmt, Fairfield Co. Rep. Orgn, 63- Bus. & Prof. Pos: Dir. of athletics and varsity coach, football, baseball and basketball, Edgewood Sch, 46-49; head coach, varsity basketball, Greenwich High Sch, 53-56; chmn, Greenwich Elem. Sch. Phys. Educ. Staff, 62-64. Mil. Serv: Pvt, Army, 41-45, serv. in Coast Artil, Balloon Barrage, Engrs, 780th Engr. Petrol. Distribution Co, N.Africa, China-Burma-India, 43-45; Mediterranean and China-Burma-India Campaign Ribbons. Mem: Greenwich and Conn. Educ. Asns; Conn. Phys. Educ. and Health Asn; Old Timers' Athletic Asn, Greenwich, Conn. and Port Chester, N.Y. and Stamford, Conn; Ninth Dist. Vets. Asn, Glenville, Conn. Honors, Port Chester, N.Y. Old Timers Athletic Asn, 64 and Greenwich Old Timers Athletic Asn, 67. Rel: Lutheran. Mailing Add: 73 Pemberwick Rd, Byram, Conn. 10573.

WASHER, HARRIET HUNT R
Committeewoman, Wash. Co. Rep. Party, N.Y.
b. Kingsbury, N.Y, 6/23/15; d. Orville P. Hunt and Loretta Wilson H; m. 6/24/33 to Edgar Tuttle Washer; c. Robert Edgar. Educ: Adirondack Bus. Col, Glens Falls, N.Y, grad, 33. Polit. & Govt. Pos: Dep. town clerk and bookkeeper to supvr, Kingsbury, N.Y, 46-52, town clerk, 52-; committeewoman, Wash. Co. Rep. Party, 47-; secy, Kingsbury Rep. Town Cmt, 48-65, secy-treas, 63-65; v.chmn, Wash. Co. Rep. Cmt, 53-68. Bus. & Prof. Pos: Stenographer, Glens Falls Hosp, N.Y, 38; typist, Wash. Co. Clerk's Off, Hudson Falls, 46. Publ: 'What My Faith Means to Me—A Citizen', The Church Woman, 3/55. Mem: Hudson Falls Bus. and Prfnl. Women's Club; Cmt. to Organize Town Clerk's Training Schs, N.Y. State Asn. of Towns; Hudson Falls Women's Civic League; Tri-Co. Br, Nat. Farm and Garden Asn; Eastern Star; Wash. Co. Coun. of United Church Women; Wash. Co. Rep. Women's Club; Wash. Co. Hist. Soc; Wash. Co. Home Bur. and Exten. Serv; Lake George Opera Festival Asn; Operetta Club; Local Concert Asn; Wash. Union Coun. of Baptist Women; N.Y. State Baptist Women. Selected as Woman of the Year by local bus. and prfnl. women's club, 68; recognized and presented with a place for serv. rendered in Wash. Co. Rep. Women's Club. Rel: Baptist. Mailing Add: 33 Pearl St, Hudson Falls, N.Y. 12839.

WASHINGTON, HAROLD D
Ill. State Rep.
b. Chicago, Ill, 4/15/22; s. Roy L. Washington and Bertha Jones W; single. Educ: Roosevelt Univ, Chicago, Ill, B.A, 49; Northwest. Univ. Law Sch, J.D, 52; Nu Beta Epsilon. Polit. & Govt. Pos: Precinct capt, mem. adv. bd. and asst. dir. of elec, Third Ward Regular Dem. Orgn, Chicago, Ill, 52-; asst. city prosecutor, Corp. Counsel's Off, Chicago, Ill, 54-58; pres, Third Ward Young Dem, 58-61; arbitrator, Ill. State Indust. Cmn, 60-64; Ill. State Rep, currently. Mil. Serv: Entered as Pvt, Army, 42, released as 1st Sgt, 46, after serv. in 1887th Eng. Aviation Bn, Pac, 43-46; Mariannas Campaign Ribbon. Mem: Cook Co, Ill. and Nat. Bar Asns; Am. Vet. Asn. Rel: Catholic. Legal Res: 4950 S. South Parkway Ave, Chicago, Ill. 60615. Mailing Add: 4950 Martin L. King Dr, Chicago, Ill. 60607. (1967)

WASHINGTON, JAMES A, JR. D
Gen. Counsel, U.S. Dept. of Transportation
b. Asheville, N.C, 2/17/15; s. James A. Washington, Sr. and Vivian B. Alston W; m. 1/4/35 to Ada Collins; c. Grace C.(Mrs. Alexander), Eleanor J.(Mrs. Jackson), Vivian A.(Mrs. Johnson), James A, III, Stephen C, Michael G, Diana V. and Carlton C. Educ: Howard Univ, A.B, 36; Howard Univ. Sch. Law, LL.B, 39; Harvard Law Sch, LL.M. magna cum laude, 41; Omega Psi Phi; Sigma Delta Tau. Polit. & Govt. Pos: Attorney, U.S. Dept. of Justice, 42-46; bd. mem, Nat. Capital Housing Authority of D.C, 61-66; chmn, D.C. Pub. Serv. Cmn, 61-66; gen. counsel, U.S. Dept. of Transportation, 69- Bus. & Prof. Pos: Prof. law, Howard Univ. Sch. Law, 46-61, Langston prof, 66-69, dean, 69; vis. prof, Wash. Col. Law, Am. Univ, summers, 60-61, Georgetown Law Center, summer 61. Publ: 'Right of Privacy in the United States,' Harvard Law Sch, 41; 'The Program of the Civil Rights Section of the Department of Justice,' J. on Negro Educ, summer 51; 'One or Three, Which Should It Be? Conjectures of Three-Judge Court Procedure,' (with George M. Johnson), Howard Law J, 55. Mem: Nat. and Wash. Bar Asns; Phi Alpha Delta; chmn, Police Commun. Rels. Inst, Nat. Conf. Christians and Jews, Inc, 67; chmn, model cities cmt, D.C. Health and Welfare Coun, 67-68; chmn, Reconstruction and Develop. Corp, 69-; bd, Nat. Capital Area Coun, Boy Scouts; bd, Travelers Aid Soc; bd, Health and Welfare Coun. Rel: Episcopal. Mailing Add: 4302 13th St. N.W, Washington, D.C. 20017.

WASHINGTON, LENA GENEVA R
Mem, Calif. Rep. State Cent. Cmt.
b. Florence, Ala, 11/16/14; d. Benjamin B. Fields and Effie Hewitt F; m. 11/27/35 to Clarence Wilson Washington; c. Melva (Mrs. Ellis Veil). Educ: Los Angeles City Col, 2 years; Univ. West, 1 year; Beta Pi Sigma; Westsiders of the 30's. Polit. & Govt. Pos: Mem, Calif. Rep. State Cent. Cmt, currently, exec. dir. and membership secy, 48-69, secy, speaker's bur, 69-; secy, Californians for Sen. George Murphy Orgn, 69- Bus. & Prof. Pos: Mem, Women's Polit. Study, 36-, secy. to founder; mem, Westside Fedn, 61-; mem. and co-organizer, Rep. Assocs. Bus. Women, 62- Mem: PTA; Urban League. Progress Award and Serv. Award, Beta Pi Sigma; Citations from Compton Rep. Club and Santa Monica Commun. Club; 'Salute to Lena,' Cosmopolitan Rep. Voters League Study Club; 20 years serv. to Rep. State Cent. Cmt; awards from Women's Polit. State Cmt; Westside Rep. Women; Los Angeles Co. Cent. Cmt. Rel: Methodist. Mailing Add: 1726 W. 22nd St, Los Angeles, Calif. 90007.

WASHINGTON, NAT WILLIS D
Wash. State Sen.
b. Coulee City, Wash, 5/2/14; s. Nat Willis Washington and Gladys Fuller W; m. 4/24/45 to Wanda Florence Wells; c. Nat W, Jr. and Thomas F. Educ: Univ. Wash, B.A, 36, LL.B, 38; Phi Delta Phi; Beta Theta Pi; Fir Tree; Oval Club. Polit. & Govt. Pos: Wash. State Rep, 49-51; pres, State Young Dem, 50; Wash. State Sen, 51-; chmn, West. Interstate Hwy. Cmt. and Nat. Legis. Hwy. Cmt; chmn, Senate Hwys. Cmt, 60-; mem. gov. bd, Coun. State Govt; v.chmn. exec. cmt, Nat. Cmt. Uniform Traffic Laws and Ordinances. Bus. & Prof. Pos: Attorney, Bonneville Power Admin, Dept. of Interior, 39-42. Mil. Serv: Entered as 1st Lt, Army Air Corps, 42, released as Lt. Col, 47, after serv. in Second Air Force, 12th Tactical Air Command, Germany; Lt. Col, Judge Adv. Gen. Dept, Air Force Res. Mem: Wash. State Bar Asn; Mason; Grange. Rel: Episcopal. Mailing Add: 42 C St. N.W, Ephrata, Wash. 98823.

WASHINGTON, WALTER E. D
Mayor-Cmnr, D.C.
b. Dawson, Ga, 4/15/15; s. William Washington and Willie Mae Thornton W; m. 12/26/41 to Bennetta Bullock; c. Bennetta (Mrs. Jules Rosette). Educ: Howard Univ, A.B, 38, LL.B, 48; Am. Univ. grad. course pub. admin, 39-43. Hon. LL.D, Fisk Univ, Georgetown Univ. and Cath. Univ. Am, 68. Polit. & Govt. Pos: Jr. housing asst, Alley Dwelling Authority, 41, housing mgr, Nat. Capital Housing Authority, 45-51, various exec. pos, 51-61, exec. dir, 61-66; chmn, N.Y.C. Housing Authority, 66-67; mayor-cmnr, D.C, 67- Mem: Past pres. and mem. bd. dirs, Southwest Settlement House; mem. bd. dirs, Nat. Capital Area United Serv. Orgn; mem, United Commun. Serv. Cmt. Juvenile Delinquency and United Commun. Serv. Corrections Sect; mem. model cities and metrop. develop. adv. cmt, Dept. Housing and Urban Develop, 67; mem. ins. panel, Nat. Adv. Cmn. Civil Disorders, 67; LeDroit Park Civic Asn.(past pres); Big Bros.(bd. dirs); Wash. Urban League (bd. dirs. and chmn. nominating cmt); Wash. Action Youth (bd. dirs); United Planning Orgn.(bd. dirs); Nat. Capital Area Coun. Boy Scouts (bd. dirs); Coun. Churches Gr. Wash.(bd. dirs); Vis. Nurses Asn.(bd. dirs); Health and Welfare Coun, Nat. Capital Area (v.pres); secy. bd. dirs, United Givers Fund. Howard Univ. Alumni Award for Distinguished Achievement in Pub. Serv, 63; Commun. Serv. Award, Meritorious Commun. Serv, Health and Welfare Coun, Nat. Capital Area, 63; Nat. Civil Serv. League Medal, 64. Rel: Baptist. Legal Res: 408 T St. N.W, Washington, D.C. 20001. Mailing Add: 520 District Bldg, 14th and E St. N.W, Washington, D.C. 20004.

WASIELEWSKI, THADDEUS FRANCIS D
b. Milwaukee, Wis, 12/2/04; s. Francis Stanley Wasielewski, M.D. and Felicia H. Baranowski W; m. 10/28/39 to Stephanie Mary Gorak; c. Francis Thomas, Stephanie Felicia (Mrs. James S. Fay), Janina Maria, Mary Constance and John Thaddeus. Educ: Univ. Mich, B.A, 27; Marquette Univ. Law Sch, J.D, 31; Delta Theta Phi; Eschweiler Senate. Polit. & Govt. Pos: U.S. Rep, Wis, 41-47; mem, Wis. State Dem. Cent. Cmt, 47-48; del, Dem. Nat. Conv, 48. Mem: Elks; bd. dir, Milwaukee Repertory Theater; Am, Wis. State and Milwaukee Co. Bar Asns; bd. dir, United Fund, 52-57. Rel: Roman Catholic. Legal Res: 2530 N. Summit Ave, Milwaukee, Wis. 53211. Mailing Add: 637 W. Mitchell St, Milwaukee, Wis. 53204.

WASKOW, ARTHUR I. New Party
Mem, Nat. Cmt, New Party
b. Baltimore, Md, 10/12/33; s. Henry B. Waskow and Hannah Osnowitz W; m. 8/26/56 to Irene Elkin; c. David Franklin and Susanna. Educ: Johns Hopkins

Univ, B.A, 54; Univ. Wis, M.A, 56 and Ph.D, 63; Phi Beta Kappa; Alpha Epsilon Pi (master, Psi Chap). Polit. & Govt. Pos: Precinct chmn, Dem. Party, Madison, Wis, 58-59; legis. asst, U.S. House of Rep, 59-61; mem. exec. cmt, Nat. Conf. for New Polit, 65-67; mem. steering cmt, Coalition for an Open Conv, 68; alternate del, Dem. Nat. Conv, 68; mem. nat. cmt, New Party, 68- Bus. & Prof. Pos: Sr. staff, Peace Research Inst, 62-63; resident fel, Inst. of Policy Studies, 63- Publ: The Limits of Defense, 62 and From Race Riot to Sit-in, 66, Doubleday; The Freedom Seder: A new Haggadah for Passover, Micah Press, 69. Mem: Am. Hist. Asn; Students for a Dem. Soc, 63-68; secy, Adams-Morgan Commun. Coun, 67-68; chmn, Center for Emergency Support, 67-69; Jews for Urban Justice (mem, steering cmt); Jewish Commun. Coun. (mem, urban probs. cmt); Conf. on Peace Research in Hist; Resist; New Univ. Conf; South. Student Organizing Cmt. Rel: Jewish. Mailing Add: 1808 Wyoming Ave. N.W, Washington, D.C. 20009.

WASSENBERG, SHIRLEY MAE D
b. Oketo, Kans, 11/5/27; d. Elijah Orville Keck and Cora Oehm K; m. 1/6/49 to Henry G. Wassenberg; c. Henry Arnold, Ellen Kaye, Daniel Orville, Amy Carlene, Janis Christine and Thomas Andrew. Educ: Marysville High Sch. grad. Polit. & Govt. Pos: V.chmn, Marshall Co. Dem. Party, Kans, 58-69; secy, Second Dist. Dem. Party, 60-62, v.chmn, 64-69; alternate del, Dem. Nat. Conv, 68. Mem: Beta Sigma Phi; Am. Legion Auxiliary; Kans. Dem. Century Club; Kans. Fedn. of Womens Dem. Clubs. Rel: Catholic. Mailing Add: 209 N. 11th St, Marysville, Kans. 66508.

WASSER, JOSEPH D
V.Chmn, Sullivan Co. Dem. Cmt, N.Y.
b. New York, N.Y, 12/9/20; s. Sam Wasser and Esther Weingarten W; m. 12/24/44 to Ethel Apter; c. Ellen Sue and Martin Barry. Educ: St. John's Univ, B.A, 43. Polit. & Govt. Pos: Chief, consumer goods div, Off. Price Stabilization, N.Y.C, 50-53; magistrate, Thompson, N.Y, 54-; del, Dem. State Conv, 64 & 66; v.chmn, Sullivan Co. Dem. Cmt, 67-; alternate del, Dem. Nat. Conv, 68. Bus. & Prof. Pos: Dir, Co. Trust Co, Monticello, 58-; v.pres, Monticello Hosp, 60-67; cmnr, Sullivan Co. Condemnation Bd, 67-; mem, Mid-Hudson Pattern for Progress Cmn, State Univ, N.Y, New Paltz, 68- Mil. Serv: Entered as Pvt, Army, 43, released as 1st Lt, 46, after serv. in Adj. Gen. Dept; Res, 46-50. Mem: Pres, Kiwanis, 65; justice subordinate forum, Elks, 65-67; Mason; Jewish War Vet; Am. Legion; Izaak Walton League; pres, Sullivan Co. Magistrates Asn, 60-63; Magistrates Asn; Monticello Vol. Fire Dept. Rel: Hebrew. Legal Res: 7 Roosa Ave, Monticello, N.Y. 12701. Mailing Add: P.O. Box 192, Monticello, N.Y. 12701.

WASTVEDT, GILMAN R
b. Hatton, N.Dak, 5/24/08; married; c. two. Educ: Union Commercial Col. Polit. & Govt. Pos: N.Dak. State Rep, 61-66; former mem, Bd. of Co. Cmnrs. Bus. & Prof. Pos: Farmer. Mem: Eagles; Mason; Scottish Rite; Shrine. Rel: Lutheran. Mailing Add: Hatton, N.Dak. 58240.

WATAHA, PAUL JOHN D
Mayor, Rock Springs, Wyo.
b. Rock Springs, Wyo, 12/1/24; s. John Joseph Wataha and Susan Steffan W; m. 12/17/47 to Dorothy Jo Manley; c. John Charles, Paul Jay and Joseph Frank. Educ: Univ. Wyo; Sigma Alpha Epsilon. Polit. & Govt. Pos: Finance dir, Sweetwater Co. Dem. Cmt, 56-65; mem, Stream Pollution Coun, Wyo, 58-59; Mayor, Rock Springs, Wyo, 58-; mem. adv. coun, Small Bus. Admin, 64-65. Bus. & Prof. Pos: Owner, Paul J. Wataha, Pub. Acct, 50-; pres, Wyo. Asn. Pub. Accts, 57-59; state dir, Nat. Soc. Pub. Accts, 58-64. Mem: C. of C; Elks; Eagles; Lions; Nat. Soc. Pub. Accts; Wyo. Asn. Pub. Accts; Int. Soc. Tax Consults; Nat. Platform Asn; Univ. Wyo. Alumni Asn; Nat. Asn. Fed. Enrolled Tax Accts. Outstanding Young Man of Rock Springs, Jr. C. of C, 51; Outstanding Young Man of Wyo, Jr. C. of C, 58. Rel: Catholic. Legal Res: 1946 Opal St, Rock Springs, Wyo. 82901. Mailing Add: 725 North Front St, Rock Springs, Wyo. 82901.

WATERFIELD, HARRY LEE D
b. Calloway Co, Ky, 1/19/11; s. Burnett Waterfield and Lois Burton W; m. 6/1/33 to Laura Ferguson; c. Rose Gayle (Mrs. Hardy), Nancy (Mrs. Dudgeon) and Harry Lee, II. Educ: Murray State Col, B.S, 32. Polit. & Govt. Pos: Ky. State Rep, 38-50, Speaker, Ky. State House of Rep, 44-46; secy, Ky. State Dem. Party, 44-47 & 56-59; Lt. Gov, Commonwealth of Ky, 55-59 & 63-67; chmn, Ky. Legis. Res. Cmn. and Ky. Disabled Ex-Servicemen's Bd, 55-59 and Ky. Indust. Develop. Finance Authority, 58-59; del, Dem. Nat. Conv, 68. Bus. & Prof. Pos: Publisher, Hickman Co. Gazette, 34-; pres, Ky. Press Asn, 42; pres. and chmn. bd, Investors Heritage Life Ins. Co, 60-; pres, Ky. Investors, Inc, 63- and chmn. bd, currently. Mem: Mason; Shrine; Rotary; Farm Bur; C. of C; chmn, Nat. Asn. Lt. Gov, 66-67. Rel: Christian Church. Legal Res: R.R. 3, Clinton, Ky. 42031. Mailing Add: 200 Capital Ave, Frankfort, Ky. 40601.

WATERHOUSE, THOMAS, JR. R
b. Lowell, Mass, 10/9/06; married; c. Two sons. Educ: Pub. schs. Polit. & Govt. Pos: Chmn, Bd. of Selectmen, Windham, N.H, 15 years; N.H. State Rep, 51-61; N.H. State Sen, 61-68. Bus. & Prof. Pos: Merchant. Mem: St. Marks' Lodge Number 44. Rel: Protestant. Mailing Add: Mammoth Rd, Windham, N.H. 03087. (1967)

WATERMAN, EDWIN PAYN Conservative, N.Y.
Regional V.Chmn, Capital Dist. Conservative, N.Y.
b. Little Falls, N.Y, 4/14/02; s. George Dean Waterman and Crescida Gott W; m. 11/11/44 to Margaret Anna Melroy. Educ: Union Col, B.S, 24; Delta Upsilon. Polit & Govt. Pos: Budget research asst, N.Y, 39-41; mem. E.Nassau Cent. Sch. Bd, 60-64; treas, New Yorkers for Goldwater-Miller, Rensselaer Co, N.Y, 64; legis. rep, Conservative, N.Y, 64 and regional v.chmn, Capitol Dist, 65-; Conservative Cand, N.Y. State Assemblyman, 65. Bus. & Prof. Pos: Sales rep, Gen. Elec. Co, 24-29 and Edward B. Smith, Inc, Investments, 29-31; swimming instr, 31-39; purchasing agent, RCA, Harrison, N.J, 41-47; self-employed, personal investments, 47-66. Mil. Serv: Entered as Pvt, N.Y. Nat. Guard, 37, released, 40, after serv. in 101st Calvary. Publ: How to Live Happily, Warwick Press, 46. Rel: Methodist. Mailing Add: Tsatsawassa Lake Rd, East Nassau, N.Y. 12062. (1967)

WATERMAN, JEREMIAH COLWELL R
V.Chmn, D.C. Rep. Cmt,
b. Westfield, N.J, 1/18/04; s. Marcus B. Waterman and Grace Hampson W; m. 9/1/26 to Mary Fager; c. Suzanna (Mrs. Howard K. Gray) and Judith (Mrs. Owen P. Jacobsen). Educ: Princeton Univ, A.B, 26; Columbia Univ, J.D, 31; Phi Delta Phi; Princeton Terrace Club. Polit. & Govt. Pos: Mem, Zoning Bd. of Appeals, Mamaroneck, N.Y, mem, town coun, 51-59; mem, D.C. Rep. Cmt, 64-, v.chmn, 68- Bus. & Prof. Pos: Gen. attorney, South. Pac. Co, N.Y.C, 52-59, Wash, D.C, 59-66; counsel, Steptoe & Johnson, 66- Mil. Serv: Army, 26-39, released as 1st Lt, 39; serv. in 442nd Field Artil. Res. Publ: 'Special Report on War Delay Cases,' War Delay Law Cmt, Asn. of Am. Railroads, 45. Mem: Am. and D.C. Bar Asns; Am. Judicature Soc; N.Y. Co. Lawyers Asn; Asn. of Interstate Commerce Practitioners; Nat. Press Club, Wash, D.C; Metrop. Club; Capitol Hill Club; Cong. Country Club. Rel: Episcopal. Legal Res: 2807 O St, N.W, Washington, D.C. 20007. Mailing Add: 1250 Connecticut Ave, Washington, D.C. 20036.

WATERS, ALONZO L. R
b. Oak Orchard-on-the-Ridge, N.Y, 9/6/93; m. to Mary Hazard, 54; c. Robert E. Educ: Miami Univ, Oxford, Ohio. Polit. & Govt. Pos: Postmaster Medina, N.Y, 27-36; mem. and former pres, Medina Bd. of Educ, 38-49; N.Y. State Assemblyman, 48-66. Bus. & Prof. Pos: Publisher, Medina Daily J. Register. Mil. Serv: 308th Field Artil, World War I. Mem: Past Master, past dist. dep, Medina Lodge 336, F&AM; past high priest, Medina Chap. RAM; past illustrious master, Alpha-Omega Coun. of RAM; Genesee Commandery K.T; Ismailia Temple AAONMS; past exalted ruler, Medina Lodge Elks; past pres, N.Y. State Elks Asn, 33-34; past pres, Medina Rotary Club; past comdr, James P. Clark Post; past co. comdr, Am. Legion; Lincoln Post, VFW of Medina; past pres, Medina Adver. Club; past pres, Orleans Motor Club; Officer, Lewistown Trail Coun, Boy Scouts; Medina Lodge of Moose; Sigma Chi; Lemuel Cook Chap, SAR; N.Y. State Publishers Asn; Assoc. Dailies; Orleans Co. War Coun; World War II; Pres, Orleans Co. Welfare Coun, 38-40. Rel: Episcopal; Diocesean Trustee. Mailing Add: 410 W. Center St, Medina, N.Y. 14103.

WATERS, ERROL T. D
Chmn, Idaho Dem. Party
b. Merced, Calif; m. to Grace Hughes. Educ: Weiser High Sch, Idaho, grad. Polit. & Govt. Pos: Chmn, Washington Co. Dem. Party, Idaho, seven terms; committeeman, Ada Co. Dem. Party, 58-65 and Idaho Dem. Cmt, 63-65; chmn, Idaho Dem. Party, 65- Bus. & Prof. Pos: Former dir, Payette Div, Idaho Power Co; automobile bus, 21-51. Mem: Elks; Boise Valley Hi-De-Ho Travel Trailer Club. Legal Res: 7124 McMullen St, Boise, Idaho 83701. Mailing Add: P.O. Box 445, Boise, Idaho 83701.

WATERS, JEAN R
b. Wadsworth, Ohio, 3/11/29; d. Leon C. Waters and Ada Becker; single. Educ: Sharon High Sch, grad, 47. Polit. & Govt. Pos: Chief dep. clerk, Common Pleas Court, Medina Co, Ohio, 50-68, clerk, 68-; committeeman, Precinct B Rep. Cent. Cmt, 66-68; committeeman, Sharon Twp. Rep. Cent. Cmt, 68-; secy, Medina Co. Rep. Cent. Cmt, 69; second v.pres, Medina Co. Rep. Women's Club, 69; dist. chmn, Seventh Dist. Ohio Clerk of Courts Asn, 69. Bus. & Prof. Pos: With Ohio Eng. Co, Medina, Ohio, 47-50. Mem: YWCA; hon. mem, Young Rep. Club. Rel: Lutheran. Mailing Add: R.D. 2, 5723 Boneta Rd, Medina, Ohio 44256.

WATERS, JERRY B. R
b. St. Francis, Kans, 1/6/33; s. Roy Waters and Bertha Zimbleman W; m. 9/12/53 to Janice LaVern Miller; c. Ricki, Jeffrey and Brent. Educ: Kans. State Univ, B.S, 54; Mich. State Univ, M.S, 58, Ph.D, 65. Polit. & Govt. Pos: Research analyst and asst. pub. dir, Mich. Rep. State Cent. Cmt, 60-61; legis. and research asst. to U.S. Sen. James B. Pearson, Kans, 66-67, admin. asst, 67- Bus. & Prof. Pos: Instr, Dept. Econ. and Sociol, Kans. State Univ, 61-64, asst. prof, Dept. Polit. Sci, 64-66. Mil. Serv: Entered as 2nd Lt, Air Force, 54, released as 1st Lt, 57, after serv. in 91st Fighter Bomber Squadron, Third Air Force, Eng, 55-57; Capt, Air Force Res, 57-62. Publ: Co-author, 'Values, Expectations and Political Predispositions of Italian Youth,' Midwest Jour. Polit. Sci, 2/61; 'Reapportionment: The Legislative Struggle,' In: Representation and Misrepresentation, ed. Robt. Goldwin, Rand McNally & Co, 68. Mem: Am. Polit. Sci. Asn; Midwest Conf. Polit. Scientists; Asn. Admin. Assts. Rel: Protestant. Legal Res: 2449 Hobbs Dr, Manhattan, Kans. 66502. Mailing Add: 3411 Raymond St, Chevy Chase, Maryland. 20015.

WATERS, JOHN B, JR. R
b. Sevierville, Tenn, 7/15/29; s. J.B. Waters, Sr. and Myrtle Paine W; m. 4/8/53 to Patsy Temple; c. John B, III and Cynthia Beth. Educ: Univ. Tenn, B.S, 52 and J.D, 61; Scarrbean Sr. Soc; Phi Sigma Kappa; Phi Alpha Delta. Polit. & Govt. Pos: Mem, Tenn. Rep. State Exec. Cmt, 62-69 and v.chmn, 64-66; del, Rep. Nat. Conv, 68; fed. co-chmn, Appalachian Regional Cmn, 69- Bus. & Prof. Pos: Assoc, Hailey, Waters & Jarvis, Attorneys; mem, Sevierville Housing Authority, 58-69; chmn, Sevier Co. Indust. Develop. Bd, 64-69. Mil. Serv: Entered as Ens, Naval Res, 52, released as Lt, 56, after serv. in U.S.S. Conway, Atlantic and Sixth Fleet. Mem: Am. Judicature Soc; Am. and Fed. Bar Asns; Mason; Am. Legion; Lions; Elks. Rel: Baptist. Legal Res: Route 1, Waters Edge, Sevierville, Tenn. 37862. Mailing Add: 1666 Connecticut Ave, Washington, D.C. 20019.

WATERS, TROY L. R
Chmn, Izard Co. Rep. Party, Ark.
b. Yorktown, Ark, 1/16/29; s. Timothy Bell Waters and Corma Lee Smith W; m. to Billie Vivian Weaver; c. Carol Lynn and Robert Troy. Educ: Ark. Col, Batesville, B.S.E. Polit. & Govt. Pos: Chmn, Izard Co. Rep. Party, Ark, 65-; field rep, Second Cong. Dist. Rep. Party, 67-68; dir, Ark. State Dept. of Pub. Welfare Commodity Distribution Div, 69- Bus. & Prof. Pos: Sch. teacher, 53-67. Mem: Mason. Lillian McGillicuddy Award. Rel: Protestant. Legal Res: Guion, Ark. 72540. Mailing Add: P.O. Box 5254, North Little Rock, Ark. 72115.

WATERS, VIRGINIA MOZINGO D
b. Dodge Center, Minn, 9/10/19; d. Marion Edgar Mozingo and Joy Williams M; m. 1/16/44 to Franklin Eugene Waters; c. Joel, Daniel and Camilla. Educ:

Long Beach Jr. Col, 37-39; Occidental Col, A.B, 41; Univ. Calif, Los Angeles, Calif. State at Long Beach and Columbia, grad. work; Alpha Phi. Polit. & Govt. Pos: Cand, city coun, Long Beach, Calif, 66; Dem. cand, Calif. State Assembly, 39th Dist, 68. Bus. & Prof. Pos: Pub. rels. dir, Barcus-Berry, Inc, Long Beach, Calif, 67; with Pavlina Waters, Ltd, Int. Promotions and Pub Rels, currently. Publ: Autopariahnism, Sociological Essay; co-ed, Pavlina Messman—Dear John and Tom, Pòemes Choisis, Pavlina Messman—Systematic Cycle, Pavlina Messman—Transfer to Another Death Cell and Pavlina Messman—Pornography Unveiled, 59. Mem: Belmont Shore Bus. & Prfnl. Women's Club; Jr. League of Long Beach (past pres.); pres. and founder, Family Serv. Guild of Long Beach; C. of C. Rel: Episcopal. Mailing Add: 1485 La Perla, Long Beach, Calif. 90815.

WATERS, WILLIAM BAXTER D
Mo. State Sen.
b. Lathrop, Mo, 4/26/15; m. 5/15/43 to Ellen B. Nesbitt. Educ: William Jewell Col, A.B; Univ. of Mo. at Kansas City, LL.B. Polit. & Govt. Pos: Probate Judge, Clay Co, Mo, 47-55; mem, Dem. State Cmt, 51-56; Mo. State Sen, 56- Bus. & Prof. Pos: Attorney, Lawson & Hale, now Hale, Coleberd, Kincaid & Waters, 41- Mil. Serv: Army. Mem: Lions; Am. Legion; VFW. Rel: Christian. Mailing Add: First Office Bldg, Liberty, Mo. 64068.

WATKINS, ARTHUR VIVIAN R
b. Midway, Utah, 12/18/86; s. Arthur Watkins and Emily A. Gerber W; m. 6/18/13 to Andrea Rich; c. Nedra Reese, Arthur Rich, Don Rich, Venna Swalberg, Jeanene Scott, and Nina Palmer. Educ: Brigham Young Univ, 03-06; N.Y. Univ, 09-10; Columbia Univ, LL.B, 12; Univ. Utah, LL.D, 59. Polit. & Govt. Pos: Asst. co. attorney, Salt Lake City, Utah, 14-17; dist. judge, 28-33; counsel, Provo River Water Users Asn, 35-46; cmnr, Utah State Bar; mem, Platform Cmt, Rep. Nat. Conv, 44 & 56; U.S. Sen, Utah, 47-58, co-sponsor, Colo. River Storage Proj. and numerous other reclamation proj, chmn, Select Cmt. to Consider Censure Charges Against Sen. Joseph McCarthy, Wis, 54; assoc. mem, Indian Claims Cmn, Wash, D.C, 59-60, chief cmnr, 60-69. Bus. & Prof. Pos: Publisher, Orem-Geneva Times and Utah Valley News, 42-46; rancher and fruit farmer. Publ: Enough Rope (McCarthy Censure Proceedings), Prentice-Hall and Univ. Utah Press; Reclamation in the Upper Colorado River Basin State, (in prep) Univ. Utah Press. Mem: Life mem, Kiwanis. Rel: Latter-day Saint. Mailing Add: 777 East South Temple, Salt Lake City, Utah 84102.

WATKINS, BRUCE RILEY D
b. Parkville, Mo, 3/20/24; s. Bruce Watkins and Olivia Hughes W; m. 12/3/60 to Rhae Tate; c. Bruce R, Jr. and Robert G. Educ: Bordentown High Sch, N.J, grad; Air Force Col. Training, Rockhurst Col, Kansas City, Mo; Worsham Col, Chicago, Ill. Polit. & Govt. Pos: City councilman, Kansas City, Mo, 63-66; circuit clerk, Jackson Co, 67-; del, Dem. Nat. Conv, 68. Bus. & Prof. Pos: V.pres, Watkins Brothers Mem. Chapels, Kansas City, Mo, 45- Mil. Serv: Entered as Pvt, Army, 43, released as 2nd Lt, 45, after serv. as Bombardier-Pilot, Tuskegee, Ala, 44-45. Mem: Mason; Shrine; Elks; NAACP; YMCA; Boys Clubs; chmn, Freedom Inc. Rel: Baptist. Mailing Add: 4616 E. 51st, Kansas City, Mo. 64130.

WATKINS, CHARLES HENRY D
b. St. Paul, Kans, 12/3/05; s. Charles Henry Franklin Watkins and Effie Janette Harrah W; m. 7/7/29 to Minnie Esther Farris; c. Ralph Franklin and Ruth Elizabeth. Polit. & Govt. Pos: Kans. State Rep, 63-68. Mem: Partners of the Alliance (del, Third Interam. Conf, Lima, Peru, 68 and Fourth Interam. Conf, Salt Lake City, Utah, 69); state chmn, Kans. UNESCO, 59-60; AF&AM. Rel: Christian. Mailing Add: Route 3, Erie, Kans. 66733.

WATKINS, G. ROBERT R
U.S. Rep, Pa.
b. Hampton, Va, 5/21/02; m. to Hilda J. Smerbeck; c. Robert G. and Dwain Joseph. Polit. & Govt. Pos: Cmnr, Delaware Co, Pa, 4 years, sheriff, 4 years; Pa. State Sen, 12 years; U.S. Rep, Pa, 64- Bus. & Prof. Pos: Owner, Chester Stevedoring Co, 20-31; owner, Blue Line Transfer Co, 32-; breeder, thoroughbred horses, 37- Legal Res: West Chester, Pa. 19380. Mailing Add: 1015 Longworth House Office Bldg, Washington, D.C. 20515. (1967)

WATKINS, JAMES PAUL R
b. Loudon, Tenn, 12/16/12; s. Edward Elihu Watkins and Rachel A. Hooker W; m. 12/31/35 to Blanche A. Johnson; c. Linda R.(Mrs. Winstead), Sarah K. and Rebecca C.(Mrs. Brewster). Educ: Univ. Tenn, A.B, 35, LL.B. and J.D, 36. Polit. & Govt. Pos: Chmn, Loudon Co. Primary Bd, Tenn, 36-58; Asst. Attorney Gen, Fourth Judicial Circuit, 50-58, Dist. Attorney Gen, 58-; alternate del, Rep. Nat. Conv, 68. Mil. Serv: Pvt, Army, 44, 16th Med. Bn, U.S. Mem: Loudon Co. Bar Asn; pres, Tenn. Dist. Attorney Asn; bd. dirs, Am. Dist. Attorney Asn; Am. Legion; Appeal Agent, Local Draft Bd, 17 years. Rel: Methodist. Legal Res: Route 1, Loudon, Tenn. 37774. Mailing Add: P.O. Box 384, Loudon, Tenn. 37774.

WATKINS, JOE A. D
b. Granville Co, N.C, 5/25/08; s. John S. Watkins and Belle Norwood W; m. 10/1/38 to Doris Poole; c. Jo Anna and Doris Poole. Educ: Wake Forest Col, A.B, 31. Polit. & Govt. Pos: Cmnr, Oxford, N.C, 45-54, mayor-pro-tem, 53-54; N.C. State Rep, 55-66. Bus. & Prof. Pos: Automobile dealer; dir, Oxford Nat. Bank and Oxford Credit Union. Mem: N.C. Auto Dealers Asn, pres, 58-59; Nat. Auto Dealers Asn; Kiwanis; former pres, v.pres. and dir, Granville Co. C. of C. Mailing Add: 105 Pine Cone Dr, Oxford, N.C. 27565. (1967)

WATKINS, JOSEPH WESLEY, III D
Secy, Miss. Dem. Exec. Cmt.
b. Greenville, Miss, 9/17/35; s. Joseph Wesley Watkins, Jr. and Mary Alice Catlette W; m. 12/20/57 to Jane Magruder; c. Gordon Estes and Marjorie Laurin. Educ: U.S. Naval Acad, 53-54; Univ. Miss, B.A, 57, LL.B, 62; Phi Alpha Delta; Sigma Alpha Epsilon. Polit. & Govt. Pos: Trial attorney, Tax Div, U.S. Dept. Justice, Wash, D.C, 62-67; pres, Wash. Co. Young Dem, Miss, 67-; attorney, Miss. Loyal Dem. Challenge, Dem. Nat. Conv, 68, del, 68; mem, Wash. Co. Dem. Exec. Cmt, 68-; secy, Miss. Dem. Exec. Cmt, 68- Mil. Serv: Entered as Ens, Navy, 57, released as Lt.(jg), 59, after serv. in U.S.S. Edmonds, Pac. Fleet, 57-59. Mem: Miss. and Wash. Co. Bar Asns; Kiwanis Int; Greenville Symphony Asn; Twin Cities Theatre Guild; Miss. Coun. Human Rel; Greenville Art Asn; Miss. Soc.(v.pres); Univ. Miss. Alumni Asn.(pres, 66). Rel: Episcopal. Mailing Add: 1211 Kirk Circle, Greenville, Miss. 38701.

WATKINS, PARHAM MC ATEE (P. M.) D
b. Port Gibson, Miss, 1/17/17; married. Polit. & Govt. Pos: Miss. State Sen, 52-56 & 60-68; Miss. State Rep, 56-60. Bus. & Prof. Pos: Lawyer. Mem: Blue Key; Am. Legion; Citizens Coun; C. of C; State Bar Asn. Rel: Presbyterian. Mailing Add: Port Gibson, Miss. 39150. (1967)

WATKINS, RALPH A, JR. D
b. Phoenix, Ariz, 7/29/26; s. Ralph A. Watkins and Ruby Lena Formby W; m. 10/23/51 to Patricia Mae Reilly; c. Cynthia E. and Ralph A, III. Educ: N.Mex. Mil. Inst, 44; Ariz. State Univ, B.A, 51. Polit. & Govt. Pos: Former Dem. Precinct Committeeman and former chmn, Dem. Dist. 37, Ariz; exec. secy, Ariz. State Fair Cmn, 57-59; cand, U.S. Rep, Ariz, 66; Dem. Nominee, Third Cong. Dist, 68; del, Dem. Nat. Conv, 68. Bus. & Prof. Pos: Salesman, Bankers Life Nebr. Ins, 61; part owner, Watkins Chevrolet, Watkins Manor Apt. and two ranches; mem, Bd. Continental Security Guard, currently. Mil. Serv: Capt, Marine Corps, World War II and Korean War; retired from Marine Corps Res, 63. Mem: Nat. Exec. Cmt. and former comdr, Am. Legion; Ariz. State Univ. Alumni Asn.(pres, 65-66); state chmn, Cancer Soc, 67; Buckeye C. of C; pres, Buckeye Develop. Corp; pres, Univ. Club, Phoenix; past mem, Estrella Park Bd; Small Bus. Adv. Bd; El Zaribah Shrine; Royal Order Jesters. Has private pilot's license. Rel: Community Church; former bd. mem. and Financial chmn. Mailing Add: 801 E. Edison, Buckeye, Ariz. 85326.

WATKINS, RALPH AUSTIN D
b. Hertha, Kans, 7/26/02; s. Henry Franklin Watkins and Effie Jeanette Harrah W; m. 10/2/26 to Genevra Lavon Nance; c. Russell Austin. Polit. & Govt. Pos: Okla. State Rep, Canadian Co, 43 & 58-68 and chmn. and v.chmn, Okla. House Cmt. on Labor Rels. Bus. & Prof. Pos: Signal maintainer, Chicago, Rock Island & Pac. R.R, 27-53 and signal testman, 53-; legis. rep, Brotherhood of R.R. Signalmen, 49-59 and gen. chmn. and secy, 52. Mem: El Reno Flyers Inc; First Okla. gov, Soaring Soc. Am; Aircraft Owners and Pilots Asn; Mason (32°); Amaranth, past patron; Toastmasters Int; bd. mgr, Rock Island Employees Hosp. Asn; dir, El Reno United Fund; C. of C; Kiwanis. Commercial pilot with instr. rating, former private pilot exam; Silver C 82, Soaring Soc. Am; Sportsman Award, Soaring Contest, Wichita Falls, Tex, 49; Lamp Lighter Award, Canadian Co. Teacher's Asn, 65. Rel: Baptist. Mailing Add: 1414 W. Shuttee, El Reno, Okla. 73036.

WATKINS, RICHARD WRIGHT, JR. D
Chmn, Butts Co. Dem. Exec. Cmt, Ga.
b. Indian Springs, Ga, 2/14/20; s. R. Wright Watkins and Dovie Bryans W; m. 10/22/50 to Martha Elizabeth Hood; c. Margaret Ann, Rachael and Hazel Virginia. Educ: Maryville Col, A.B. in econ, 42; Univ. Ga, J.D, 47; Phi Delta Phi. Polit. & Govt. Pos: Ordinary, Butts Co, Ga, 57-64; chmn, State Bd. of Corrections, 64-; treas, Sixth Cong. Dist. Dem. Exec. Cmt, 66-; chmn, Butts Co. Dem. Exec. Cmt, 66- Bus. & Prof. Pos: Dir. and attorney, Citizens & South. Bank of Jackson, Ga, currently. Mil. Serv: Entered as Pvt, Army Air Force, 42, released as Sgt, 45, after serv. in Fifth Air-Sea Rescue Squadron, ETO, re-entered Judge Adv. Gen. Corps, 51, released as 1st Lt, 52; Lt. Col, Judge Adv. Gen. Corps, Army Res; ETO Ribbon with 5 Battle Stars. Publ: 'Criminal Jurisdiction of Ordinary Courts in Georgia' In: Handbook for Ordinaries of Georgia, Univ. Ga, 65. Mem: Past pres, Flint Judicial Circuit Bar Asn; Elks; Mason; Shrine; Kiwanis; Am. Legion; VFW; Farm Bur. Rel: Presbyterian. Legal Res: 169 Dempsey Ave, Jackson, Ga. 30233. Mailing Add: P.O. Box 105, Jackson, Ga. 30233.

WATKINS, SAM HOUSTON D
b. 1914. Polit. & Govt. Pos: Ky. State Rep, 62-68. Bus. & Prof. Pos: Finance co. pres; oil producer; farmer. Mil. Serv: Naval Merchant Marine, World War II. Mem: Mason; Pendennis Club; Ky. Hist. Soc; Farm Bur. Mailing Add: Elizabethtown, Ky. 42701. (1967)

WATKINS, WILLIAM FORBES, JR. D
Chmn, Prince Edward Co. Dem. Cmt, Va.
b. Millen, Ga, 4/10/26; s. William F. Watkins and Susie Bone W; m. 8/20/49 to Norma Louise Soyars; c. Sally Anne, William Norman and Richard Forbes. Educ: Va. Mil. Inst; Hampden Sydney Col; Univ. Va. Law Sch; Omicron Delta Kappa. Polit. & Govt. Pos: Mayor, Farmville, Va, 58-63; chmn, Prince Edward Co. Dem. Cmt, Va, currently. Mil. Serv: Seaman 2/C, Navy, 44-46. Mem: Va. State Bar Asn; Nat. Dist. Attorney's Asn; Va. Trial Attorney's Asn; v.pres, Judicial Bar Asn; Va. Commonwealth's Attorneys Asn; Mason; Lions. Rel: Presbyterian. Legal Res: R.F.D. 6, Farmville, Va. 23901. Mailing Add: P.O. Box 81, Farmville, Va. 23901.

WATSON, ALBERT W. R
U.S. Rep, S.C.
b. Sumter, S.C, 8/30/22; s. Claude A. Watson (deceased) and Eva Clark W; m. 5/24/48 to Lillian Williams; three children. Educ: Univ. S.C, LL.B, 50; Pi Kappa Delta. Polit. & Govt. Pos: S.C. State Rep, 55-58, 60-62; U.S. Rep, S.C, 63- Bus. & Prof. Pos: Attorney. Mil. Serv: Air Force, 42-46. Mem: Am. Legion; VFW: Farm Bur; Mason; Lions; Nat. Chmn, Voice of Democracy Prog, sponsored by U.S. Jr. C. of C. Rel: Baptist. Mailing Add: House Office Bldg, Washington, D.C. 20515.

WATSON, ARTHUR CHOPIN D
Chmn, Dem. State Cent. Cmt, La.
b. Natchitoches, La, 12/15/09; s. Arthur William Watson and Eugenie Chopin W; m. 4/27/35 to Marion Eugenia Hickman, 'Gene'; c. Marion (Mrs. O. J. Bienvenu), Saidee (Mrs. Guy R. Newell) and Eugenie Chopin. Educ: Spring Hill Col, B.A; Tulane Univ, LL.B. & J.S.D; Order of the Coif; Kappa Sigma; Phi Delta Phi; Tulane Law Sch. Club. Polit. & Govt. Pos: Chmn, La. State Dem. Cmt, 40-; mem, Natchitoches Parish Dem. Cmt, 44-; del, Dem. Nat. Conv, 68; chmn, Dem. State Cent. Cmt, 68- Bus. & Prof. Pos: Partner, Watson, Brittain & Murchison, Attorneys, 33-; pres, Progressive Mutual Bldg. & Loan Asn, 64-; chmn. bd, Exchange Bank & Trust Co, 66- Publ:

'Alluvion and Dereliction' Tulane Law Review, 33. Mem: Am. Bar Asn; Elks (Past Exalted Ruler); Lions; La. Bar Asn.(bd. gov, 56-58, House Del, 59-67); Jr. Bar La.(pres, 42-43). Man of the Year, Natchitoches C. of C, 66. Rel: Catholic. Legal Res: 501 Parkway Dr, Natchitoches, La. 71457. Mailing Add: P.O. Box 226, Natchitoches, La. 71457.

WATSON, BILLY JAMES R
Chmn, Greenup Co. Rep. Exec. Cmt, Ky.
b. Salyersville, Ky. 7/18/38; s. Hager Watson and Tressie Jackson W; m. 6/4/60 to Janice Maggard; c. JuJuana Dawn. Educ: Morehead State Univ, A.B, 58, M.A, 64; Crescendo Club. Polit. & Govt. Pos: Educ. dir, Gov. Louie B. Nunn Campaign, Greenup Co, Ky, 67; mem. finance cmt, Greenup Co. Rep. Campaigns, 67-; del, Greenup Co. Young Rep. Club, 68; chmn, Greenup Co. Rep. Exec. Cmt, 68- Bus. & Prof. Pos: Independent contracting musician, Ky, Ohio and W.Va, 58-; band dir, Wurtland High Sch, Ky, 58-66; band dir, Portsmouth High Sch, Ohio, 66-; chmn, instrumental music dept, Portsmouth City Schs, 66- Mem: Ohio Educ. Asn; Portsmouth City Teachers Asn; Ohio Music Educators Asn; Music Educators Nat. Conf; Am. Fedn. Musicians; WOW. Outstanding Grad. Senior, Ky. Colonel. Rel: Baptist. Mailing Add: Adena St, Wurtland, Ky. 41144.

WATSON, CALEB POWERS D
b. Center, Ala, 6/10/95; s. Benjamin Franklin Watson and Martha Boyd W; m. 6/25/31 to Evelyn Sangster Smith; c. C. P. Jr, Earl Ford, Martha Jeanne, David Michael, Susan Frances. Educ: Hearn Acad; Mercer Exten. Sch; Howard Col. Polit. & Govt. Pos: Ga. State Sen, 59-60; Ga. State Rep, 63-64; mem, Molena City Coun, 64-67. Mil. Serv: State Guard under direction of Internal Security; full time Chaplain (Maj). Mem: Mason. Rel: Baptist minister; missionary. Mailing Add: Molena, Ga. 30258.

WATSON, ED RAYMOND D
b. Wallisville, Tex, 7/20/20; s. Raymond Fieldon Watson and Ella Gertrude Syer W; m. 5/7/48 to Susan Geraldine Eaves; c. Dan Aubrey, Deborah Ellaine (Mrs. Moake), Faith Marie and Donald Wayne. Educ: Univ. Houston, 45; San Jacinto Jr. Col, 67-68. Polit. & Govt. Pos: Del, Dem. Precinct, Co. and State Conv, Tex, 48-; del, Dem. Nat. Conv, 68. Mil. Serv: Entered as A/S, Navy, 42, released as Boatswain Mate 2/C, 45, after serv. in Naval Armed Guard, European, Atlantic, Mediterranean, Asiatic, Pac. and Caribbean Theatres, Korean War, 50-51 , serv. in Japan, China, Philippines and Malay; European Theater Medal with Two Stars; Atlantic Theatre Medal with Two Stars; Asiatic Theater Medal with Two Stars; Korean Medal; Good Conduct Medal. Mem: Nat. Dem; Harris Co. Dem; Tex. Dem; OCAWIU (Steward, Local 4-367, 48-, pres, 52-56, v.pres, 64-, Legis. Rep, Dist. 4, 68-); exec. bd, Harris Co. AFL-CIO, 64-; adv. bd, Tex. Safety Cmt, 68-; Am. Legion; Eagles; labor participation cmt, United Fund, 66- Rel: Baptist. Mailing Add: 802 Harvard St, Deer Park, Tex. 77536.

WATSON, FRANK RUNDELL R
b. Livingston, Wis, 12/1/99; s. John William Watson and Lydia Rundell W; m. 2/13/25 to Agnes Louella Peterson; c. Jean (Mrs. Laird). Educ: Univ. of Wis, Platteville, B.A. and B.E, 29. Polit. & Govt. Pos: Wyo. Cmnr, West. Interstate Cmn. for Higher Educ, 7 years; sch. supt, Worland, Wyo, 26-57, mayor and mem. city coun, 50-56; Wyo. State Rep, Washakie Co, 61-63; Wyo. State Sen, Washakie Co, 63-67; del, Rep. Nat. Conv, 64; rep, Wyo. State Senate, Wyo. Youth Coun, 65-66. Mil. Serv: Pvt, Army, 18-19. Mem: Life mem, Nat. Educ. Asn; pres, Wyo. Educ. Asn, 44-45; pres, Northwest Educ. Asn, 36-37; Elks; Mason; Shrine; Shrine Club; Lions; Am. Legion; C. of C. Baseball player and coach; Coached five Am. Legion Jr. baseball teams to State Championship. Rel: Episcopal. Mailing Add: 1301 Coburn Ave, Worland, Wyo. 82401.

WATSON, JACK W. R
b. Council Bluffs, Iowa, 7/21/16; s. De Vere Watson and Freole Placek W; m. 1/21/48 to Ann Tipler; c. Michele. Educ: Univ. Iowa, B.A, 38; George Wash. Univ, LL.B, 55. Polit. & Govt. Pos: Secy. to U.S. Rep. Ben Jensen, Iowa, 39-42 & 59-65, asst. clerk, House Admin. Cmt, 47-59, minority clerk, House Appropriations Cmt, 64-65; exec. dir, Midwest Resources Asn, 66; admin. asst. to U.S. Rep. Wiley Mayne, Iowa, 67- Mil. Serv: Entered as Ens, Navy, 42, released as Lt. Comdr, 47, after serv. in various stas, Mediterranean & European Theatres, 42-46; Three European Theatre Stars; Secy. of Navy Letter of Commendation. Mem: Am. Legion; Int. Club of Wash. Rel: Methodist. Legal Res: Council Bluffs, Iowa. Mailing Add: 2707 N. Nelson St, Arlington, Va. 22207.

WATSON, JAMES EDWIN, III D
Majority Whip, W.Va. House of Delegates
b. Fairmont, W.Va, 11/8/17; s. James E. Watson, Jr. and Eleanor Blackford W; m. 5/5/42 to Henrietta Altidel Weager; c. Eleanor W.(Mrs. Laughlin), Claire W.(Mrs. Wolverton, Jr) and Sue Adele. Educ: Colgate Univ, B.A, 41; W.Va. Univ. Law Sch, LL.B, 49; Phi Gamma Delta. Polit. & Govt. Pos: W.Va. State Del, 53-57 & 59-, majority whip, 59-, chmn. redistricting cmt, 63-64 and chmn. judiciary cmt, 65-; asst. prosecuting attorney, Marion Co, 63; alternate del, Dem. Nat. Conv, 68. Bus. & Prof. Pos: Pres, Mid-City Recreation, Inc, 52-; sr. partner, Watson & Snyder, 62-; pres, Marion Pallet Co, Fairmont, W.Va, 66- Mil. Serv: Entered as Pvt, Army, 41, released as Maj, 46, after serv. in 42nd Inf. Div, SHAEF Mission, Norway, European Theater, 44-45; Lt. Col.(Ret), Army Res, 55-66; Bronze Star; Norwegian Medal of Freedom; Purple Heart; Army Commendation Ribbon; Am. and European Theater Ribbons. Mem: Am, W.Va. and Marion Co. Bar Asns; W.Va. State Bar; Res. Officers Asn; Bowling Proprietors' Asn. of Am; pres, W.Va. Bowling Proprietors' Asn, 63-68; Rotary; Elks; Moose; Am. Legion; VFW; Fraternal Order of Police; Sons of Revolution; Fairmont Field Club; Izaac Walton League. Rel: Episcopal. Legal Res: 111 Circle Dr, Fairmont, W.Va. 26554. Mailing Add: Room 510, First National Bank Building, Fairmont, W.Va. 26554.

WATSON, JOHN CRAWFORD D
b. Iola, Ill, 10/30/16; s. Percy Mayfield Watson and Hallie Grace Moore W; m. 6/30/46 to Dorothy Eloise Walton; c. Theresa Joan (Mrs. Russell Kraft Nuzum III), Timothy John, John Lynn and Holly Grace. Educ: McKendree Col, 38-39; Ill. Col, 39-41 & 46-48; Sigma Beta Rho; Phi Alpha. Polit. & Govt. Pos: Dem. Cand, U.S. House Rep, 19th Dist, Ill, 58 & 60; asst. dir, Dept. Registration and Educ, State of Ill, 61-64 and dir, 64-69; del, Dem. Nat. Conv, 68; Dem. committeeman, Precinct 15, Jacksonville, 68-; mgr. admin. serv. Ill. State Libr, Off. Secy. of State, 69- Bus. & Prof. Pos: Minister, Methodist Parish, Sailor Springs, Ill, 38-39, Naples and Oxville, 39-41, Golden, 41-42 and Detroit, Ill, 46-49, Disciples of Christ, Maroa, 49-51, and Abingdon, 51-61. Mil. Serv: Merchant Marine, 42-46. Mem: Mason; Odd Fellows. Rel: Disciples of Christ. Mailing Add: 101 Chestnut St, Jacksonville, Ill. 62650.

WATSON, JOHN L. R
b. Danbury, Conn, 6/13/24; s. Edmund B. Watson and Helen Hughes W; m. 8/2/45 to Eda Cereda; c. John Michael and Anthony Lewis. Educ: Univ. Cincinnati, Col. Bus. Admin, 46-48; Univ. Cincinnati, Col. Law, LL.B, 50; Alpha Kappa Psi; Beta Gamma Sigma; Phi Alpha Delta. Polit. & Govt. Pos: Dir, Clermont Co. Bd. Elec, Ohio, 57-; del, Rep. Nat. Conv, 68. Mil. Serv: Entered as Pvt, Army, 43, released as 2nd Lt, 46, after serv. in 2nd Constabulary, ETO, 45-46. Mem: Am. Judicature Soc; Ohio State Bar Asn; Clermont Co. Bar Asn.(pres, 58); Am. Legion; VFW; Royal Oak Country Club. Rel: Protestant. Mailing Add: 359 S. Fifth St, Williamsburg, Ohio 45176.

WATSON, MELVILLE E. D
Educ: Ind. Univ. Polit. & Govt. Pos: Hancock Co. prosecuting attorney, 47-58; Ind. State Sen, 59-66. Bus. & Prof. Pos: Attorney, Farm Security Admin, 40-41. Mil. Serv: Army. Mem: Co, State and Am. Bar Asns; Kiwanis; Elks; Am. Legion; Scottish Rite. Rel: Methodist. Mailing Add: Thayer Bldg, Greenfield, Ind. 46140. (1967)

WATSON, MURRAY, JR. D
Tex. State Sen.
b. Mart, Tex, 5/14/32; s. Murray Watson and Ethel Bryson W; m. 8/15/59 to Greta Candace Warren; c. Milicent 'Missy.' Educ: Baylor Univ, B.B.A, 52; Baylor Univ. Sch. of Law, LL.B, 54; grad. study in econ; Delta Sigma Pi; Acct. Club; Tyron Coteria; Order of Artus; Arnold Air Soc-Baylor; Air Force ROTC Most Outstanding Third Cadet; Phi Alpha Delta (pres); pres, Baylor Law Sch. Student Body, 59-60; faculty supvr, TARUS Soc. Polit. & Govt. Pos: Tex. State Rep, 55-62, mem, State Affairs, Judicial Munic. and Pvt. Corp, Game and Fish and Sch. Dist. House Cmts, Tex. House of Rep, 55th Session, mem, State Affairs, Judicial Munic. and Pvt. Corp, Sch. Dist. and Representation before the Legis. House Cmts, 56th Session, chmn, Ins. Cmt. and Interim Study Cmt. Studying Tex. Utilities, temporary chmn, Appropriations Cmt, mem, State Affairs, Munic. and Pvt. Corp, Revenue and Tax, Rules, Tex. Legis. Coun. and Interim Study Cmts. for classroom facilities in insts. of higher learning, loan shark regulation, ment. health work in pub. schs. and regulation of hosp. ins. house cmts, 57th Session; Tex. State Sen, 63-, v.chmn. Rules Cmt, mem, State Affairs, Banking, Ins, Jurisp, Oil and Gas, Pub. Health, Transportation and Livestock and Agr. Senate Cmts, 58th Session, chmn. State Dept. and Insts. and Arterial Streets Study Cmts, v.chmn, Transportation and Deaf Study, mem, Rules, Banking, Ins, Oil and Gas, Game and Fish, Jurisp, State Affairs, Constitutional Amendments, Mil. and Vet. Affairs and Tex. Legis. Coun. Senate Cmts, 59th Session, chmn. Ins, v.chmn, Agr, Livestock, Interim Health Ins. Investigation Study and Interim Voc. Tech. Educ. Study, mem, Banking, Constitutional Amendments, Labor and Mgt, Rels, Finance, Transportation, Tex. Legis. Coun, Game and Fish and Jurisp. Senate Cmts, 60th Session, Pres. Pro-Tem, Tex. Senate, 69- Bus. & Prof. Pos: Assoc, feed bus. and livestock oper, Mart, Tex, 49-54; bill clerk, Tex. House of Rep, 54-55; attorney-at-law, Mart, 55-59; faculty supvr, Tarus Sch, 59-60; prof. bus. law, Baylor Univ, 59-60; partner, Watson and Rogers, Attorneys, Waco, 59-61; attorney-at-law, Mart, 61-62; assoc, Jones, Boyd, Westbrook and Lovelace, Attorneys, 62-67; vis. instr, McLennan Commun. Col, 67-68; partner, Watson and Weed, Attorneys, 67-; vis. prof. state admin. law, Baylor Univ. Sch. Law, 69- Publ: 'What Baylor Meant to Me,' Baylor Line, Sept. Ed, 57; 'Promoting Sound Leadership,' Tex-O-Key, Feb. Ed, Vol. II, No. 6; 'Trends in Rehabilitation Concepts,' J. Asn. for Phys. and Ment. Rehabilitation, July-Aug. Ed, 64, Vol. 18, No. 4. Mem: Dir, pres. and v.pres, Cent. Tex. Mus; pres. and dir, Cent. Tex. Indust. Develop. Coun; Lions; C. of C.(bd. dir, Waco Chap, 68-); Farm Bur; Cattle Raisers Asn; Kiwanis; Toastmaster's; Waco Jr. Bar Asn; Farm and Ranch Club; Jr. C. of C.(dir, Waco Chap, 59-60); Waco-McLennan Co. Bar Asn; State Bar of Tex; Mason; Scottish Rite (master, Waco, 65-67); dir, McLennan Co. and Cent. Tex. Tuberc. Asns; Lighthouse for the Blind; Shrine; Am. Bar Asn, 55-59. Distinguished Serv. Citation, Tex. State Asn. Fire Fighters, 63; Distinguished Serv. Award, Waco Jaycees, 64; Distinguished Serv. Award, Voc. Agr. Teachers Asn, 64; Distinguished Serv. Award, Tex. Ment. Health Asn, 64; Outstanding Citizen Award, Mart C. of C, 64; Citation of Appreciation, Asn. for Phys. and Ment. Rehabilitation, 64; Outstanding Layman's Award, San Gabriel Baptist Church, 65; Awards from McLennan Co. Tuberc. Asn. and Christmas Seal Chmn, 66; Hon. Lifetime Mem, Sojourners, 66; Citation of Appreciation, Tex. Asn. for Ment. Health, 66; Gold Farmer Award, Tex. Future Farmers of Am, 67; Outstanding Pub. Serv, Waco Jr. C. of C, 67; Hon. Future Farmers Award, Rosebud Chap, Future Farmers of Am, 67; Distinguished Serv. Award, Mart Future Farmers of Am, 67; Outstanding Serv. Award for Good Govt, Mem. State Chiropractors Asn, 67; Outstanding Serv. Award, Tex. Asn. of the Deaf and Tex. Soc. of Interpreters for the Deaf, 67; Murray Watson Day, Waco City Coun, 67; Hon. Chmn. of Mother's March, Waco March of Dimes, 67; Blazers, Waco C. of C, 67; Lifetime and Hon. Fireman, Killeen, 67; President's Cmt. Citation for outstanding work with handicapped people, 69; Distinguished Serv. Award, Killeen Boy Scout Troop, 69. Rel: Methodist. Legal Res: 308 Texas Ave, Mart, Tex. 76664. Mailing Add: Room 337, State Capitol Bldg, Austin, Tex. 78711.

WATSON, TERRY DURWARD D
b. Concordia, Kans, 12/6/42; s. Durward Albert Watson and Marvel Bliss W; single. Educ: St. Benedict's Col, A.B. summa cum laude, 64; Univ. Kans, 64-65; Washburn Univ, J.D, 68; Phi Alpha Delta. Polit. & Govt. Pos: Research asst, Bd. Co. Cmnrs, Kans, 65-66; nat. committeeman, Young Dem. Clubs Kans, 65-67 and pres, 67-68; treas, Shawnee Co. Dem. Action Cmt, 66-67; staff asst, Kans. Dem. State Cmt, 66-67; admin. asst, Gov. Robert Docking, 67-68; del, Dem. Nat. Conv, 68; pres, U.S. Youth Coun, 68-69; mem. exec. cmt, World Assembly of Youth, currently. Bus. & Prof. Pos: Ed-in-chief, The Rambler, St. Benedict's Col; trustee, Nat. Assembly for Soc. Policy & Develop, currently. Mem: Am. Judicature Soc; Acad. Polit. Sci; Adv.

Coun, Int. Movement Atlantic Union; Elks; K. of C. Valedictorian, St. Benedict's Col. Rel: Roman Catholic. Legal Res: 631 W. Main St, Osborne, Kans. 76473. Mailing Add: 315 E. 53rd, New York, N.Y. 10022.

WATSON, THOMAS ARNIE D
Miss. State Sen.
b. Carrollton, Miss, 6/25/09; s. William Edward Watson and Mittie Steele W; m. 6/24/56 to Bervil Elder. Educ: Holmes Jr. Col, diploma, 33; Delta State Teachers Col, 46; Miss. State Univ, B.A. pending, 35, 50 and 65. Polit. & Govt. Pos: Carroll Co. Tax Assessor, Miss, 48-56; Miss. State Sen, 56-60, 64-66 & 68-, chmn, Pub. Welfare, v.chmn. Forestry, Agr. Appropriations, Co. Affairs, Educ, Game and Fish and Penitentiaries Cmts; mem, Miss. Legis. Coun; crew chief, U.S. Census Bur, 60. Bus. & Prof. Pos: Teacher, soc. sci, Carroll Co. Schs, Miss, 45-47. Mil. Serv: Entered as Pvt, Miss. Nat. Guard, 40, released as Sgt, Army, 45, after serv. in Hq. Battery, 114th Field Artil, 18th Airborne Corps, ETO, 44-45; Good Conduct Medal; ETO Ribbon; Three Bronze Stars. Mem: VFW; Am. Legion; Farm Bur; Miss. Cattlemen's Asn; Lions; C. of C. Rel: Church of Christ. Legal Res: P.O. Box 1, North Carrollton, Miss. 38947. Mailing Add: Mississippi State Senate, Jackson, Miss. 39205.

WATSON, WILLIAM ABNER, JR. D
V.Chmn, Prince Edward Co. Dem. Party, Va.
b. Darlington Heights, Va, 2/15/99; s. William Abner Watson, Sr. and Adlaide Ford W; m. 2/14/24 to Louise Newton Brightwell; c. William Abner, III and James Maxey. Educ: Univ. Richmond; Smithdeal Massey Bus. Col, Richmond, Va. Polit. & Govt. Pos: Del, Dem. State Conv, 12 years; del, Nat. Dem. Conv, 64 & 68; v.chmn, Prince Edward Co. Dem. Party, Va, currently. Bus. & Prof. Pos: Pres, W.A. Watson & Sons Ins. Agency, Farmville, Va, 24-; pres, Am. Health Ins. Agency, 42-; pres, Odd Fellows Home of Va, Inc, Lynchburg, 20 years. Mil. Serv: Army, 18, Pvt. Mem: Odd Fellows; AF&AM; Farmville C. of C. (past pres); Farmville Area Develop. Corp. (past pres). Rel: Baptist. Legal Res: 700 First Ave, Farmville, Va. 23901. Mailing Add: Box 567, Farmville, Va. 23901.

WATSON, WILLIAM EDWARD D
Chmn, Brooke Co. Dem. Party, W.Va.
b. Jane Lew, W.Va, 7/31/36; s. Jefferson Bassell Watson and Mary Bush W; m. 9/3/58 to Mara Louise Linaberger; c. Lynn Ellen. Educ: W.Va. Wesleyan Col, A.B, 58; George Wash. Univ, J.D, 61. Polit. & Govt. Pos: Solicitor, Wellsburg, W.Va, 65-; chmn, Brooke Co. Dem. Party, 65-; mem, W.Va. Dem. State Exec. Cmt, 67- Bus. & Prof. Pos: Attorney-at-law, Pinsky, Mahan, Barnes & Watson, 61- Mil. Serv: Entered as Pvt, Army Res, 62, released as Sgt, 68, after serv. in Fourth Med. Tank Bn; Army Res, currently. Mem: Nat. Asn. of Defense Lawyers in Criminal Cases; Am. and W.Va. State Bar Asns; Kiwanis. Rel: Methodist. Mailing Add: 2000 Main, Wellsburg, W.Va. 26070.

WATSON, WILLIAM MARVIN D
b. Oakhurst, Tex, 6/6/24; s. William Marvin Watson, Sr. and Lillie Mae Anderson W; m. to Marion Baugh; c. Winston Lee, Kimberly Baugh and William Marvin, III. Educ: Baylor Univ, B.B.A, 49, M.A, 50; Ouachita Univ, L.H.D, 68. Polit. & Govt. Pos: Mem, State Dem. Exec. Cmt, Tex, 58-64, chmn, 64-65; spec. asst. to President Lyndon B. Johnson, 65-68; Postmaster Gen, 68-69. Bus. & Prof. Pos: Exec. asst. to the pres, Lone Star Steel, Dallas, Tex, 56-65; state v.pres, Red River Valley Asn, Shreveport, La; from secy. to pres, Northeast Tex. Munic. Water Dist; pres, Occidental Int. Corp, 69- Mil. Serv: Entered as Pvt, Marines, released as Sgt. Mem: Mason; Shrine. Rel: Baptist. Legal Res: 100 Hughes Circle, Daingerfield, Tex, 75638. Mailing Add: 1717 Pennsylvania Ave. N.W, Suite 1201, Washington, D.C. 20006.

WATT, JAMES GAIUS R
Dep. Asst. Secy. for Water and Power Develop, Dept. of the Interior
b. Lusk, Wyo, 1/31/38; s. William G. Watt and Lois M. Williams W; m. 11/2/57 to Leilani Bomgardner; c. Erin Gaia and Eric Gaius. Educ: Univ. Wyo. Col. Bus. and Indust, B.S. with honors, 60, Law Sch, J.D, 62; Omicron Delta Kappa; Phi Kappa Phi; Alpha Tau Omega; Iron Skull; pres, Phi Epsilon Phi; ed, Wyo. Law J, 2 years; Teaching fel, 60-62. Polit. & Govt. Pos: Personal asst, Milward L. Simpson, 62; legis. asst. and counsel to former U.S. Sen. Milward L. Simpson, 62-66; consult. to Secy. Walter Hickel, Dept. of Interior, 69, Dep. Asst. Secy. for Water and Power Develop, 69- Publ: 'Federal Tax Liens: Divesture,' Wyo. Law J, fall 61; 'Conservation Not Conversation, Cong. Record, 3/67; 'Economic Implications of Pollution Control,' Indust. Water Eng, 1/68. Mem: Am. Bar Asn; Wyo. State Bar; Bar of the Supreme Court of U.S; Full Gospel Businessmen's Fel. Int; sr. assoc, U.S. C. of C; Wyo. State Soc; Alpha Tau Omega Alumni Group. Thomas Arkle Clarke Award, Alpha Tau Omega. Rel: Southern Baptist. Legal Res: Wheatland, Wyo. 82201. Mailing Add: 5407 Keppler Rd, Camp Springs, Md. 20031.

WATT, ROBERT DELANSON D
Mont. State Rep.
b. Marion Co, Ind, 8/27/99; s. Charles Columbus Watt and Minne Ellen Royster W; m. 3/12/65 to Mabel Hardy Benson; stepson Gordon Benson. Educ: Univ. Mo, Columbia, B.A, 24; Ind. Univ, Bloomington, M.A, 28; various courses at Butler Univ, Ind. Univ, Indianapolis and Univ. Mont; Phi Delta Kappa; Lambda Chi Alpha. Polit. & Govt. Pos: Mont. State Rep, Dist. 26, Missoula Co, 63-, mem, Interim Cmt. for Rev. of Sch. Laws, Mont. House of Rep, 65 & 66, mem, Mont. Constitutional Rev. Cmn. and Legis. Coun. to Study and Recommend Changes in Tax Struct, currently. Bus. & Prof. Pos: Teacher of govt, Ind. High Schs, 25-28, Mont. High Schs, 32-58; supt, Missoula Co. Schs, Mont, 58-63. Mil. Serv: Entered as Technician Pvt, Army Ordnance, 42, released as Sgt, 45, after serv. in 603rd Ordnance Bn, N. African and Ital. Theatres, 43-45; Campaign Ribbon with Three Battle Stars. Publ: Matters dealing with legis. or local or state problems in local publ. Mem: Life mem, Nat. and Mont. Educ. Asns; Elks; Moose; VFW; Am. Legion; Missoula Rose Soc; Nat. Asn. of Retired Persons and Retired Teachers Asn; Local Non-profit Corp. for Develop. of Low-income Housing; Lions; founder and pres, Mont. Fairer Taxes Asn. Rel: Christian Church. Mailing Add: 451 Kensington Ave, Missoula, Mont. 59801.

WATTS, JESSE CLAYBORNE D
b. Durham, N.C, 9/9/02; s. Ewell L. Watts and Martha Ann Pleasants W; m. 11/13/24 to Marquerite Couch; c. William C. Educ: Trinity Col, Duke Univ, 20-22. Polit. & Govt. Pos: Co. supt. of schs, Talbot Co, Ga, 37-45; Ga. State Rep, 63-64; aid to Speaker of House of Rep, Ga, 65-66; part-time pres. of senate, Ga, 68-69; part-time aide to Lt. Gov, Ga, 69- Bus. & Prof. Pos: Owner, dept. store, 41-69; teacher, Morehead City, N.C. and Geneva, Ga; supt. of Talbot Co. Schs; businessman. Mem: Lions, 26 years. Rel: Methodist. Mailing Add: Talbotton, Ga. 31827.

WATTS, JOHN CLARENCE D
U.S. Rep, Ky.
b. Nicholasville, Ky, 7/9/02; m. to Nora Wilburn; c. Lillian Frances. Educ: Univ. of Ky, A.B, 25, LL.B, 27; Phi Delta Phi. Polit. & Govt. Pos: Police judge, Nicholasville, Ky, 29-33; co. attorney, Jessamine Co, 33-45; chmn, Jessamine Co. Dem. Party, 28 years; Ky. State Rep. and Majority Leader, Ky. House of Rep, 47-48; Cmnr. of Motor Transportation, Ky, 48-51; U.S. Rep, Ky, 51- Bus. & Prof. Pos: Lawyer, farmer, banker. Mem: K. of P; Lions. Legal Res: Nicholasville, Ky. Mailing Add: 2411 Rayburn House Office Bldg, Washington, D.C. 20515. (1967)

WATTS, LAWRENCE D
b. Pinetop, Ky, 11/9/02; s. Simeon Watts and Aggie Jane Hall W; m. 11/8/33 to Velma Honeycutt; c. Sue Carol, Jakie, Imogene, Simeon Kit, Alonzo Laird, Sharon Dale, Barry Lawrence and Melissa Lynn. Polit. & Govt. Pos: Postmaster, Pinetop, Ky, 33-41; Ky. State Rep, 48-50 & 64-66; supvr, Soil Conserv. Serv, Agr. Stabilization & Conserv. Serv, 9 years. Bus. & Prof. Pos: Merchant, 31-41; coal operator, 60-66. Mil. Serv: Entered as Pvt, Army Res, 24, released as Pfc. Rel: Baptist. Mailing Add: Pinetop, Ky. 41843. (1967)

WATTS, LEE R. R
Chmn, Adams Co. Rep. Cent. Cmt, Iowa
b. Hedrick, Iowa, 2/27/98; s. George W. Watts and Estella White W; m. 2/19/19 to Fern Hedges; c. Evelyn (Mrs. Gamrath), Kathryn (Mrs. Harrison), Marilyn (Mrs. Reinhold), Beverly (Mrs. Glasgow), Ruth (Mrs. Tranbarger) and Donna (Mrs. Peckham). Educ: Drake Univ, LL.B, 25. Polit. & Govt. Pos: Mayor, Corning, Iowa, 45-46; chmn, Iowa State Hwy. Cmn, 47; attorney, Adams Co, 52-62; chmn, Adams Co. Rep. Cent. Cmt, 66- Mil. Serv: Entered as Radio Apprentice, Navy, 17, released as Radioman 3/C, 21. Mem: Iowa State Bar Asn; past pres, Third Judical Dist. Bar Asn, Adams Co. Fair Asn, Corning C. of C. and Iowa Asn. of Sailors and Marines; past dist. comdr, Am. Legion; dir, Corning Housing Cmn; Mason; Shrine; Eastern Star; Farm Bur. Rel: Presbyterian. Legal Res: 703 Grove Ave, Corning, Iowa 50841. Mailing Add: 407 Seventh St, Corning, Iowa 50841.

WATTS, SAMUEL HARVEY D
Secy, Crawford Co. Dem. Cent. Cmt, Ill.
b. Brazil, Ind, 2/25/09; s. Daniel Voorheis Watts and Mary Elizabeth W; m. 12/29/32 to Florence Rose Houston; c. Shelia Rose (Mrs. William L. Snyder) and Samuel H; grandchildren, Tawny Yvonne Watts, Jill Lynette Snyder and William Bradley Snyder. Educ: Stauton High Sch, Ind, 4 years. Polit. & Govt. Pos: State oil well inspector, Crawford Co, Ill, 61-; secy, Crawford Co. Dem. Cent. Cmt, 61-; mem. sch. bd, Palestine Elem. Sch. and Palestine Commun. Dist Two; mem. Village bd, Palestine. Mem: Moose (Moose Legion Fel. Degree); Elks; Eagles; Wardads; Lions; pres, 25th Anniversary, C. of C. Man of the Year Award, Eagles. Rel: Christian Church. Mailing Add: 307 W. Market, Palestine, Ill. 62451.

WAUGH, WILLIAM THOMAS D
b. Pleasant Hill, Ill, 6/15/09; s. William T. Waugh and Dot Thomas W; m. 12/27/33 to Dora Lee Wood; c. Karin Wells. Polit. & Govt. Pos: Mem, Ill. Dem. Cent. Cmt, until 69. Mem: Moose; Elks; Farmers Union. Rel: Methodist. Mailing Add: Pleasant Hill, Ill. 62366.

WAUGMAN, WILLIAM I. R
married; c. Five. Polit. & Govt. Pos: Alaska State Sen, 67-68. Bus. & Prof. Pos: Owner, Wood River Guides and Outfitters. Mem: V.pres, Alaska State C. of C; bd. of dir, Fairbanks C. of C; First Nat. Bank; Alaska Gold Panners; Tanana Valley Sportsmen's Asn; Nat. Rifle Asn. Mailing Add: 114 Slater Dr, Fairbanks, Alaska 99706. (1967)

WAX, JOHN CALLAWAY R
Mem, Miss. State Rep. Exec. Cmt.
b. Amory, Miss, 12/21/20; s. John Cayce Wax and Rozelle Callaway W; m. 5/1/43 to Billie Louise Clifton; c. Michael Terry and David Callaway. Educ: Univ. Miss, B.A, 42. Polit. & Govt. Pos: Mem, Miss. State Rep. Exec. Cmt. and chmn, Monroe Co. Rep. Party, 64-; chmn, Fed. Housing Cmn, Amory, Miss. and Bd. of Trustees, Amory Munic. Libr. 65- Bus. & Prof. Pos: Partner, The Wax Co, Amory, 52- Mil. Serv: Entered as Midshipman, Navy, 42, released as Lt, 45. Mem: Ala. and South. Seedsmen's Asns; Am. Seed Research Found; bd. of trustees, Gilmore Mem. Hosp; past pres, Miss. Seedsmen's Asn. and Amory Kiwanis Club; Am. Legion. Rel: Methodist; Chmn. Official Bd, First Methodist Church, Amory, 65. Mailing Add: 906 Tenth Ave. N, Amory, Miss. 38821.

WAXMAN, HENRY ARNOLD D
Calif. State Assemblyman
b. Los Angeles, Calif, 9/12/39; s. R. Louis Waxman and Esther Silverman W; single. Educ: Univ. Calif, Los Angeles, B.A. in Polit. Sci, 61; Univ. Calif, Los Angeles Sch. Law, J.D, 64; Pi Sigma Alpha. Polit. & Govt. Pos: State pres, Calif. Fedn. Young Dem, 65-67; Calif. State Assemblyman, 61st Dist, 69- Bus. & Prof. Pos: Attorney at law, Los Angeles, Calif. Mem: Calif, Los Angeles & Beverly Hills Bar Asns; Am. Jewish Cong; Am. Civil Liberties Union; NAACP; Ephebian Soc; Sierra Club; Guardians for the Jewish Home for the Aged. Rel: Jewish. Mailing Add: 5208 W. Pico Blvd, Los Angeles, Calif. 90019.

WAXMAN, RICHARD STANLEY D
Maine State Rep.
b. Portland, Maine, 11/3/44; s. Gerald Robert Waxman and Beatrice Helfont W; single. Educ: Bates Col, B.A, 69. Polit. & Govt Pos: Pres, Bates Col. Young Dem. Club, 67-68; Maine State Rep, 69- Mem: B'nai B'rith. Rel: Jewish. Mailing Add: 84 Machigonne St, Portland, Maine 04102.

WAY, HOWARD R
Calif. State Sen.
Educ: Univ. Calif. Polit. & Govt. Pos: Former mem, Calif. State Govt. Orgn. and Econ. Cmn; former mem, Fair Bd, 8 years; former Exeter High Sch. trustee, 8 years; Calif. State Sen, 62-, Pres. Pro Tempore, Calif. State Senate, 69-, chmn, Senate Rules Cmt, currently; mem, Calif. Rep. State Cent. Cmt, currently; del, Rep. Nat. Conv, 68. Bus. & Prof. Pos: Farmer and fruit grower. Mem: Kiwanis (past Lt. Gov); former dir, Co. March of Dimes and Cancer Crusade Campaigns; state dir, Self-Help Enterprises, Inc. Mailing Add: 708 E. Cedar, Exeter, Calif. 93221.

WAYNE, RALPH E. D
Tex. State Rep.
b. Wellington, Tex, 12/14/32; s. L.J. Wayne; m. to Laurel Sue Collins; c. Melanie Sue, Ralph E, Jr. and Carla Diane. Educ: W.Tex. State Univ, B.A, 53; Alpha Chi; Sigma Nu. Polit. & Govt. Pos: Tex. State Rep, 64-, mem, Rules, Conservation and Reclamation, State Schs. and Hosp, Aeronaut. and Penitentiaries Cmts. and Legis. Coun, Hwy. Beautification, Deaf and Hard of Hearing, Dependent and Neglected Children and Capitol Brochure Interim Cmts, Tex. House of Rep, 60th Session, chmn, House Admin. Cmt, mem, Rules, State Affairs, Banks and Banking and Labor Cmts. and Legis. Coun, 61st Session, chmn, Fed. Rels. Cmt, mem, Urban Affairs, Labor, Common Carriers and Pub. Health Cmts, 61st Session; former del, South. Regional Educ. Conf. on Qual. in Higher Educ; former mem, Econ. Develop. Conf, Coun. of South. States Govt; former del, Nat. Legis. Conf; statewide campaign mgr. for Lt. Gov. Ben Barnes, 68. Mil. Serv: Army, 54. Mem: Past bd. mem, Plainview YMCA, United Fund and Red Cross; chmn. legis. cmt, C. of C; past v.chmn, Civic Develop. Cmt; past chmn, Aviation Cmt; bd, Tex. Partners of Alliance; Mason (32°); York Rite; Shrine; regional membership chmn, Dallas Scottish Rite Consistory. Legal Res: 2306 W. Fifth St, Plainview, Tex. 79072. Mailing Add: House of Representatives, Capitol Sta, Austin, Tex. 78711.

WAYRYNEN, RAY J. D
Speaker, Mont. House Rep.
b. Hancock, Mich, 9/24/22; s. Martin Wayrynen and Annie Heikkila W; m. 7/26/42 to Nielsine Caroline Lowney; c. Linda Rae. Educ: Worsham Col, Chicago, Ill, 48. Polit. & Govt. Pos: Mont. State Rep, 57, minority leader, Mont. State House, 63- and speaker, 65-; alternate del, Dem. Nat. Conv, 68. Bus. & Prof. Pos: Pres. and chmn. bd, Wayrynen Funeral Home, 57- Mil. Serv: Entered as SF 3/C, Navy Seebees, 43, released as SF 2/C, 45, after serv. in Southwest and West. Pac. Mem: Mason; Scottish Rite; Shrine; Order of Jesters; Am. Legion; VFW; Kiwanis; United Commercial Travelers; Odd Fellows. Rel: Lutheran. Legal Res: 1800 Florence Ave, Butte, Mont. 59701. Mailing Add: 133 E. Broadway, Butte, Mont. 59701. (1967)

WEANER, KARL HULL R
Mem, Ohio State Rep. Cent. Cmt.
b. Defiance, Ohio, 5/2/07; s. Karl A. Weaner and Zora E. Hull W; m. 2/1/32 to Dorothy Houck; c. Zora J. (Mrs. Matson) and John W. Educ: Defiance Col, 26-28; Ohio State Univ. Law Sch, LL.B, 31; Pi Kappa Alpha; The Stollers. Polit. & Govt. Pos: City solicitor, Defiance, Ohio, 32-34; prosecuting attorney, Defiance Co, 35-41; judge, Court of Common Pleas, 47; mem. and pres, Defiance City Bd. of Educ, 49-58; cmnr, app. by Supreme Court of Ohio, Bd. on Grievances and Discipline, 63-; chmn, Defiance Co. Rep. Cent. Cmt, and Finance Cmts; mem, Ohio State Rep. Cent. Cmt, Fifth Dist, currently. Mil. Serv: Entered as Lt.(jg), Navy, 42, released as Lt.(sg), 46, after serv. in Naval Air Force, Caribbean and Mil. Govt, Okinawa, 46; Am-European-Asiatic Theater Ribbon. Mem: Exec. Committeeman, Ohio State Bar Asn, 62-64; pres, Defiance Co. Bar Asn, 51-52; pres, Northwest. Ohio Bar Asn, 35; Am. Col. Probate Counsel; Int. Asn. of Ins. Counsel; Nat. Asn. of R.R. Trial Counsel; Am. Judicature Soc; Am. Bar Asn; Mason; Elks; Eagles; Am. Legion; Grange; Rotary. Rel: Evangelical United Brethren. Legal Res: 722 East High St, Defiance, Ohio 43512. Mailing Add: State Bank & Trust Bldg, Defiance, Ohio 43512.

WEANT, EDWARD O, JR. D
b. Westminster, Md, 4/9/18; married. Educ: West. Md. Col, A.B, 41; Harvard Grad. Sch. of Bus. Admin; Univ. of Md, LL.B, 49. Polit. & Govt. Pos: Md. State Sen, 59-65; Assoc. Judge, Fifth Judicial Circuit, Md, 65- Mil. Serv: Army, 42-46. Mem: Past chmn, Carroll Co. Bar Asn; past pres, Westminster C. of C; past comdr, Carroll Post 31, Am. Legion; VFW; pres, Mem. Soc. of Senates Past; chmn. bd, Friends of Psychiatric Research, Inc. Mailing Add: Box 190, Westminster, Md. 21157.

WEARIN, OTHA DONNER D
b. Hastings, Iowa, 1/10/03; s. Joseph Andrew Wearin and Mary Jane Donner W; m. 1/2/31 to Lola Irene Brazelton; c. Martha Jane (Mrs. R.L. Rasmusen) and Rebecca Joe (Mrs. Allen F. Pulk). Educ: Tabor Col, 16-21; Grinnell Col, B.A, 24; Int. Inst. of Agr, grad. work, 27; Grinnell Col, Honor G Club and Commun. Serv. Award, 59. Polit. & Govt. Pos: Dem. Precinct Committeeman, Hastings, Iowa, 24-32; Iowa State Rep, 28-32; U.S. Rep, 32-38; mem, U.S. Alien Enemy Hearing Bd, South. Dist. Iowa, Mills Co. Bd. of Educ, 48-58 and Iowa State Aging Cmn, 65-; Iowa State Dem. Cent. Committeeman, 43-53. Bus. & Prof. Pos: Farm mgr, Brazelton & Wearin Farms, 37-; pres, bd. dir, Clarinda Prod. Credit Asn, 46- Publ: I Remember Hastings, 65, Political Americana, 67 and Clarence Ellsworth, 67, World Publ. Co, Shenandoah, Iowa; plus two others. Mem: Ak-Sar-Ben; Friends of the Land; Los Angeles, Denver, Omaha and Wash, D.C. Corrals of the Westerners. Collector of Western Americana. Rel: Congregational. Mailing Add: Nishna Vale Farm, Hastings, Iowa 51540.

WEARY, LAWRENCE CLIFTON D
Committeeman, Calif. Dem. State Cent. Cmt.
b. Columbia, Miss, 10/22/28; s. Ollie James Weary and Lora Smith W; m. 6/11/54 to Olevia Beatrice Riser; c. Mable Beatrice. Educ: South. Univ, grad, 57; Univ. Calif, Los Angeles, 68; Pepperdine Col, 68-69. Polit. & Govt. Pos: Mem, Carson Dem. Club, Calif, 68-; field rep. to Calif. State Assemblyman Larry Townsend, 68-; committeeman, Calif. Dem. State Cent. Cmt, 68- Bus. & Prof Pos: Pres, Commun. Action for Better Schs, 68; pres, Compton Christian Sch. Bd; teacher indust. arts; real estate broker. Mil. Serv: Entered as Pvt, Army. 51, released as Cpl, 53, after serv. in 933rd Antiaircraft Artil, Korea, 51-52. Mem: Calif. Teachers Asn; Calif. Indust. Educ. Asn; v.pres, Compton Civic League, 67; NAACP; South. Univ. Alumni Asn; Sr. Achievement Club. Thompson Award, Campfire Girls. Rel: Christian Church of N.Am. Mailing Add: 2633 W. Bennett St, Compton, Calif. 90220.

WEATHERFORD, JOHN WILLIAM D
b. Decatur, Ill, 1/5/24; s. Earl Oliver Weatherford and Mae Fields W; m. 4/17/48 to Louise Hardin Fristoe; c. Laura, Alice and John. Educ: Millikin Univ, B.A, 47; Univ. N.Mex, M.A, 48; Univ. Mich, M.A.L.S, 54. Polit. & Govt. Pos: Secy, Butler Co. Dem. Cent. Cmt, Ohio, 66-68. Bus. & Prof. Pos: Assoc. dir, univ. librn. and assoc. prof. libr. sci, Miami Univ, 57- Mil. Serv: Entered as Pvt, Army, 43, released as S/Sgt, 46, after serv. in Engrs, Europe and Korea, 45-46. Publ: 'Vicomte de Vaux,' Ont. Hist. Quart, 55; 'Short Life of Manhattan, Ohio,' 56 and 'Warren K. Moorehead,' 56, Ohio Hist. Quart. Mailing Add: 122 Beechpoint, Oxford, Ohio 45056.

WEATHERFORD, WADE STACKHOUSE, JR.
b. Manning, S.C, 5/10/20; s. Wade S. Weatherford Sr. and Susie Richbourg W; m. 10/28/44 to Eleanor Redyke; c. Chip, Rick and Lynn. Educ: Univ. of N.C, A.B, cum laude, 43; Univ. of S.C, LL.B, 48; Phi Beta Kappa. Polit. & Govt. Pos: S.C. State Rep, 61-66; S.C. State Sen, 67-68. Bus. & Prof. Pos: Lawyer. Mil. Serv: Comdr, Naval Res; World War II. Mailing Add: 308 Union St, Gaffney, S.C. 29340. (1967)

WEATHERLY, ROY JAMES R
b. Hurdsfield, N.Dak, 11/5/20; s. Newton E. Weatherly and Delilah Bacus W; m. 11/10/50 to Patricia Ann Boynton-Smith; c. Laurence Ross, Steven Roy, Arthur Alan and Suzan Louisa. Educ: Bismarck Jr. Col, grad, 41; Univ. Puget Sound, B.A, 48. Polit. & Govt. Pos: Auditor, Wash. State Tax Cmn, 50-53; councilman, White Salmon City Coun, 54-58; precinct committeeman, Rep. Party, Wash, 62-63; chmn, Klickitat Co. Rep. Cmt, 63-66; campaign chmn, Klickitat Co. for A. Ludlo Krame for Secy. of State, 68. Mil. Serv: Entered as Seaman 2/C, Navy, 42, released as Lt.(jg), 45, after serv. in Naval Air Corps, Atlantic. Mem: White Salmon Bus. & Prfnl. Asn.(secy-treas, 66-68, pres, 68-); AAONMS; Eagles; Elks; VFW; White Salmon Vol. Fire Dept; Lions (pres, 69-); Boys Scouts (troop coun, Troop 384 and cmt. chmn, Explorer Post 384). Rel: Methodist. Legal Res: 890 N.E. Stauch St, White Salmon, Wash. 98672. Mailing Add: P.O. Box 1088, White Salmon, Wash. 98672.

WEATHERSBY, WILLIAM HENRY
b. Clinton, Miss, 11/30/14; m. to Ruth Mowers; c. William Jeffrey, Anne Delano and Amanda Maali. Educ: Miss. South. Col, B.S, 34; Univ. Mo, B.J, 35. Polit. & Govt. Pos: Pub. affairs Officer, Cairo, 51-56; Nat. War Col, 57-58; dep. asst. dir. for Near East, S.Asia and Africa, U.S. Info. Agency, 58-60, dir. of personnel, 60-61, dep. dir. for policy, 69-; counselor for Pub. Affairs, New Delhi, 61-65, minister-counselor, U.S. Embassy, 68-69; U.S. Ambassador to Sudan, 65-67. Bus. & Prof. Pos: Newspaper reporter, 35-37 & 37-40; ed, news serv, 40-41 & 45-51. Mil. Serv: Navy, Lt, 41-45. Legal Res: San Francisco, Calif. Mailing Add: United States Information Agency, Washington, D.C. 20547.

WEAVER, CHARLES R. R
Minn. State Rep.
b. Anoka, Minn; married; c. Five. Educ: Univ. Minn; William Mitchell Col. of Law. Polit. & Govt. Pos: Mem, Anoka City Charter Cmn, Minn; treas, Anoka Off. Econ. Opportunity; mem, Anoka Co. Rep. Party; Minn. State Rep, 67- Bus. & Prof. Pos: Attorney, Weaver, Talle & Herrick. Mil. Serv: Army. Mem: Pres, Anoka Co. Bar Asn; exec. bd, young lawyers sect, Minn. Bar Asn; C. of C.(mem. educ. cmt, Anoka Chap); Kiwanis; Anoka Chap. for Mentally Retarded (past chmn); Minn. Asn. for Ment. Health (past co. chmn); chmn, Anoka Boy Scouts Fund Dr, 61. Mailing Add: 830 River Lane, Anoka, Minn. 55303. (1967)

WEAVER, EDWARD MYERS, JR. R
Chmn, Lancaster Co. Rep. Cent. Cmt, Nebr.
b. Columbus, Nebr, 6/9/27; s. Edward Myers Weaver, Sr. and Phyllis Ruth McAnn W; m. to Lois Jean Kaminska; c. Matthew L. Educ: Univ. Nebr, 45-46. Polit. & Govt. Pos: Chmn, Lancaster Co. Rep. Cent. Cmt, Nebr, 66-; chmn, First Cong. Dist, Nebr, 69; mem. exec. cmt, Rep. Party, Nebr, currently; mem, Nebr. Aeronautics Cmn, currently. Bus. & Prof. Pos: Past pres, Weaver Potato Chip Co; dir, Lincoln Bank South, at present. Mil. Serv: Entered as Pvt, Army, 52, released as Sgt, 54. Mem: Dir. and past pres, Potato Chip Inst, Int. and chmn, Prod. & Tech. Steering Cmt; Exec. Cmt, Nebr. Potato Coun; dir, Lincoln C. of C. and Nebr. Asn. of Commerce and Indust; Kiwanis; Am. Legion. Rel: Presbyterian. Mailing Add: 2645 S. 70th St, Lincoln, Nebr. 68506.

WEAVER, GEORGE DUNCAN, JR. D
Chmn, Newport Dem. City Cmt, R.I.
b. Newport, R.I, 6/27/18; s. George Duncan Weaver and Kathryn Sampson W; m. 3/19/42 to Eleanor Sperling; c. Steven Dennis and Matthew Duncan. Polit. & Govt. Pos: Mem, Personnel Appeals Bd, Newport, R.I, 58; mem, Newport Dem. City Cmt, 64-, chmn, 67-; mem, Hist. Dist. Cmn, Newport, 66. Mailing Add: 9 Chestnut St, Newport, R.I. 02840.

WEAVER, GEORGE LEON PAUL D
b. Pittsburgh, Pa, 5/18/12; s. George J. Weaver and Josephine Snell W; m. 9/7/41 to Mary F. Sullivan. Educ: YMCA Sch, Chicago, Ill, 40-42; Howard Univ. Law Sch, 42-43. Hon. LL.D, Howard Univ, 62. Polit. & Govt. Pos: Mem, War Relief Cmt, 41-42; dir, Civil Rights Cmn, 55-58; spec. asst. to Secy. of Labor, 61; Asst. Secy. of Labor for Int. Affairs, 61-69; spec. asst. to dir. gen, Int. Labor Orgn, currently. Bus. & Prof. Pos: Asst. to secy-treas, CIO, 42-45; asst. to pres, IUE, 58-60; del. or rep. U.S, numerous int. labor orgn. meetings. Eleanor Roosevelt Key for Outstanding Serv. to the World Commun, Roosevelt Univ, 61, Tan Sri Hon. Award, Govt. Malaya, 63; Kim Khanh Medal Second Class, Labor Medal First Class, Repub. S.Vietnam, 68; La Grande Officier, Repub. Federale du Cameron, by President El Hadj Ahmadou Ahidjo, 69. Mailing Add: 3819 26th St. N.E, Washington, D.C. 20018.

WEAVER, JAMES D. R
b. Erie, Pa, 9/27/20; m. to Harriet Zesinger; c. Eight. Educ: Syracuse Univ, B.S, 41; Univ. Pa. Med. Sch, 44; Erie Conservatory of Music. Polit. &

Govt. Pos: With Pa. Bur. of Voc. Rehabilitation, 60-62; del. to White House Conf. on Aging, 61; U.S. Rep, Pa, 62-64. Bus. & Prof. Pos: Physician; rehabilitation consult. Mil. Serv: Army, Med. Corps, Capt, 46; commanding officer and chief of surgery, 382nd Sta. Hosp, Ascom, Korea, 47-48; Lt. Col, Air Force Res; aerospace consult. to Air Force. Mem: Am. Legion; VFW; Am. Musicians; Kiwanis; Erie Co. Motor Club; Pa. Heart Asn; Pa. Health Coun; Pa. Acad. of Gen. Practice; past pres, Erie C. of C; past pres, Erie Co. Med. Soc; hon. chmn, Inter-Faith Chapel, Warren State Hosp; Nat. Acad. of Sci. consult. at Biennial Sci. Conf; chmn, Christmas Seal campaign, Erie and Crawford Co. Erie Man of the Year Award, 50. Mailing Add: 1605 Washington Plaza N, Reston, Va. 22070. (1967)

WEAVER, JAMES HOWARD D
b. Brookings, S.Dak, 8/8/27; s. Leo C. Weaver and Alice J. Flittie W; m. 6/11/55 to Sally Cummins; c. Regan, Allison and Sarah. Educ: Univ. Ore, B.Sc, 52; Sigma Nu. Polit. & Govt. Pos: Exec. secy, Ore. Legis. Interim Cmt. on Agr, 59-60; del, Dem. Nat. Conv, 60 & 64. Bus. & Prof. Pos: Real Estate Invest, 61- Mil. Serv: Entered as A/S, Navy, 45, released as Storekeeper 3/C, 46. Mem: Metrop. Civic Club. Mailing Add: 2301 Spring Blvd, Eugene, Ore. 97403. (1967)

WEAVER, JOHN WILLIAM R
Mayor, Elkhart, Ind.
b. Elkhart, Ind, 10/10/27; s. Harmon Jacob Weaver and Lillian Beatrice Rapp W; m. 4/27/52 to Norma Ann Richardson; c. John William, II, Cynthia Ann, Steven Harmon and Robert Frederick. Educ: Purdue Univ, B.S.C.E; Bucknell Univ; Tau Beta Pi. Polit. & Govt. Pos: City Engr, Elkhart, Ind, 53-56 and Nappanee, 53-58; mayor, Elkhart, 64- Mil. Serv: Navy, V-5 Prog; 49-64 Seabees, Lt(jg). Mem: Elcona Country Club; Exchange Club; Hon. Rotarian; Mason (32°). Rel: First Evangelical United Brethren. Mailing Add: 719 Prospect St, Elkhart, Ind. 46514.

WEAVER, LONNIE LEROY DFL
Chmn, Lake of the Woods Co. Dem-Farmer-Labor Party, Minn.
b. Lake Park, Iowa, 11/2/07; s. William Howe Weaver and Annie Jones W; m. 11/15/27 to Clarene Ruby Evans; c. Merle Leroy, Robert Dean, Karen (Mrs. Fred Sherk) and Janell Gay (Mrs. Ben Saunders). Educ: Silver Lake Twp. High Sch, Lake Park, Iowa, grad, 28. Polit. & Govt. Pos: Dickinson Co. chmn. for Gov. Herschel Loveless, Iowa; Dem. precinct chmn, Silver Lake Twp; chmn, Dickinson Co. Dem. Party; chief inspector, Tax Cmn, State of Iowa, 55-60; Acting Postmaster, Lake Park, 60-63; chmn, Lake of the Woods Co. Dem-Farmer-Labor Party, Minn, 65- Bus. & Prof. Pos: Gen. contractor, 40-55; owner and proprietor, Bayview Lodge, currently. Mem: AF&AM; Shrine. Rel: Methodist. Mailing Add: R.R, Baudette, Minn. 56623.

WEAVER, PHILLIP HART R
b. Falls City, Nebr, 4/9/19; s. Arthur J. Weaver and Evelyn Maude Hart W; m. 4/6/46 to Betty Jane Burner; c. Phillip Arthur, Frederick William, Edwin Burner, Douglas Charles and Daniel Hart. Educ: St. Benedicts Col, 38-39; Univ. Nebr, A.B, 42; Alpha Tau Omega. Polit. & Govt. Pos: Civilian admin. asst. to Asst. Chief of Staff, Fifth Army, Chicago, 49-50; U.S. Rep, Nebr, 55-62, mem, Cmts. on Vet. Affairs, Interior and Insular Affairs and Appropriations, Cong. del, NATO Parliamentary Conf, Europe, 60 and Interparliamentary Union Conf, Brasilia, 62 and former pres, 84th Rep. Club, U.S. House of Rep; spec. consult. to U.S. Secy. of Agr. and dep. dir, FOD, Rural Commun. Develop. Serv, 63-69, acting admin, Rural Commun. Develop. Serv, 69- Bus. & Prof. Pos: Staff announcer, radio stas, KGNF, KFAB, KFOR, KVAK, 38-40; agent gen. ins. and finance bus, 46-49; owner, Weaver Motor Sales, 50-55; partner, Smith-Weaver Motors, 55-56; trustee, Trinity Co. Timber Interests. Mil. Serv: Entered as 2nd Lt, Army, 42, released as Capt, 46, after serv. in Airborne Troops, ETO; Combat Infantryman's Badge; Bronze Star with Oak Leaf Cluster; Lt. Col, (Ret), Army Res. Mem: Bd. gov, Nebr. State Soc; former dir, Nebr. New Car Dealers Asn; Mason (32°), Shrine; Past Exalted Ruler, Elks; past comdr, VFW; Am. Legion; C. of C. Rel: Presbyterian. Legal Res: 1906 Fulton St, Falls City, Nebr. 68355. Mailing Add: 13207 Overbrook Lane, Bowie, Md. 20715. (1967)

WEAVER, ROBERT CLIFTON R
b. Wash, D.C, 12/29/07; s. Mortimer Grover Weaver and Florence Freeman W; m. 7/18/35 to Ella Haith; c. Robert (deceased). Educ: Harvard Col, B.S. cum laude, 29, Harvard Univ, M.A, 31, Ph.D, 34; Omega Psi Phi; Lambda Alpha. Polit. & Govt. Pos: Dep. cmnr, N.Y. State Div. of Housing, 55; adminstr, N.Y. State Rent Cmn, 55-58; v.chmn, Housing and Redevelop. Bd, N.Y.C, 60-61; adminstr, Housing and Home Finance Agency, Wash, D.C, 61-66; secy, U.S. Dept. of Housing and Urban Develop, 66-68. Bus. & Prof. Pos: Lectr, Northwest. Univ; visiting prof, Teachers Col, Columbia Univ. and N.Y. Univ. Sch. Educ, 48-50; dir, Opportunity Fels, John Hay Whitney Found, 50-55; consult, Ford Found, N.Y.C, 59-60; pres, Baruch Col, City Univ. of N.Y.C, 68- Publ: Negro Labor, 46 and The Negro Ghetto, 48, Harcourt, Brace; The Urban Complex, Doubleday, 64; Dilemmas of Urban America, Harvard, 65; over 100 articles on housing, urban develop, labor and race rels. probs. Mem: Fel, Am. Acad. of Arts and Sci; bd. mem, Am. Heritage Found, Col. of V.I, Planning Found. of Am, visiting cmt, Joint Center for Urban Studies, Mass. Inst. Tech. and Harvard Univ; Cmt. on Econ. Develop; Freedom House; For. Policy Asn. Lectr, Columbia, Mass. Inst. Tech, Cornell, Rutgers, Wesleyan, Mt. Holyoke, Smith, Haverford, Wash. Univ. and others. Mailing Add: 215 E. 68th St, New York, N.Y. 10021.

WEAVER, WOOD W. R
b. Rolfe, Iowa, 4/27/18; s. Merle O. Weaver and Bess Wood W; m. 12/28/46 to Elaine Bunte; c. Susan, James and Merle. Educ: Iowa Falls High Sch; Ellsworth Jr. Col. Polit. & Govt. Pos: Alternate del, Rep. Nat. Conv, 68. Mil. Serv: Entered as 3/C PO, Navy, 42, released CPO, 45, after serv. in 100 CB-Navy, Pac. Theatre, 43-45; Citation, Pac. Theatre. Mem: Assoc. Gen. Contractors (Iowa pres, 62); Iowa Limestone Asn.(pres, 56); Nat. Crushed Stone (exec. bd.); Shrine; Mason; Elks; VFW; Am. Legion; Farm Bur. Rel: Protestant. Mailing Add: 116 Glen Dr, Iowa Falls, Iowa 50126.

WEBB, DERICK V. R
m. to Elizabeth C; c. Four sons and two daughters. Educ: Yale Univ. and Cornell Agr. Col. Polit. & Govt. Pos: Chmn, Rep. State Cmt, Vt, formerly. Bus. & Prof. Pos: Owner and mgr, Shelburne Farms. Mil. Serv: Army, 97th Inf, 42-46. Mailing Add: Shelburne Farms, Shelburne, Vt. 05482.

WEBB, DOUGLAS J. R
Nev. State Assemblyman
b. Washington, D.C, 12/15/29; m. 8/13/50 to Leslie Eraut; c. Suzanne M, Kimron D, Marie K. and Laureen L. Educ: Willamette Univ, 48-50; Univ. Portland, 50-52; Sigma Chi. Polit. & Govt. Pos; Nev. State Assemblyman, 66- Mailing Add: 5733 Wedekind Rd, Sparks, Nev. 89431.

WEBB, JAMES EDWIN D
b. Granville Co, N.C, 10/7/06; s. John Frederick Webb and Sarah Gorham W; m. 1938 to Patsy Aiken Douglas; c. Sarah Gorham and James Edwin, Jr. Educ: Univ. N.C, A.B. in Educ, 28; George Wash. Univ. Law Sch, 32-35; Phi Beta Kappa; Phi Delta Phi; Acacia. Hon. LL.D, Univ. N.C, 49, Syracuse Univ, 50, Colo. Col, 57, George Wash. Univ, 61, Univ. Fla, 63, Univ. Del, 63, Univ. Vt, 64, Duke Univ, 66 and N.Mex. State Univ, 66; Sc.D, Univ. Notre Dame, 61, Wash. Univ, 62, Univ. Kansas City, 62, Boston Col, 63, Mo. Valley Col, 64, Univ. Ala, 64, Univ. Miami, 65, Brandeis Univ, 65, Ripon Col, 66, N.Y. Univ, 67; Univ. Toledo, 67 and W.Va. Univ, 68; D.P.A, Northwest. Univ, 62; D.H.L, Oklahoma City Univ, 62, Nebr. Wesleyan Univ, 65, Rose Polytech. Inst, 65 and Wake Forest Univ, 69; D.C.L, Univ. Pittsburgh, 63; L.H.D, Wayne State Univ, 65; D.Eng, Rensselaer Polytech. Inst, 66; Dr. Sci. and Commerce, Drexel Inst. Tech, 67. Polit. & Govt. Pos: Secy. to U.S. Rep. Edward W. Pou, N.C, 32-34; exec. asst. to Under Secy. of the Treas, Wash, D.C, 46; dir, U.S. Bur. of the Budget, Exec. Off. of President, 46-49; mem, President's Adv. Cmt. on Mgt, 49-52; alternate gov, Int. Bank for Reconstruction and Develop. and Int. Monetary Fund, 49-52; Under Secy. of State, 49-52; mem, Adv. Coun. on Study of Civil Serv, Cmt. on Post Off. and Civil Serv, U.S. Senate, 55-57; mem. exec. cmt, U.S. Cmt. for the UN, N.Y.C, 55-60; mem. nat. adv. cancer coun, U.S. Pub. Health Serv, 56-60; mem. Spec. Stockpile Adv. Cmt. to Dir. of Defense Mobilization, 57-58; mem, Panel of Consult. on Med. Research and Educ. to Secy. Marion B. Folsom, Dept. of Health, Educ. and Welfare, 57-58; mem, President's Cmt. to Study the U.S. Mil. Assistance Prog, 58-59; mem, Career Exec. Bd, 58-59; mem. adv. cmt, Presidential Transition Proj, The Brookings Inst, 60-61; mem, President's Cmt. on Equal Employ. Opportunity, 61-65; mem, Fed. Coun. for Sci. and Tech, 61-68; mem. and adminstr, Nat. Aeronaut. and Space Coun, 61-68; mem, President's Cmt. on Manpower and President's Adv. Cmt. on Supersonic Transport, 64-68. Bus. & Prof. Pos: Secy. to pres, R.G. Lassiter Co, Raleigh, N.C, 24-25; secy. to Bur. of Educ. Research, Univ. N.C, Chapel Hill, 28-29; law clerk, Parham & Lassiter, Attorney's, Oxford, N.C, 29-30; law student and asst. in the off. of O. Max Gardner, Attorney, Wash, D.C, 34-36; personnel dir. and asst. to pres, then secy-treas. and later v.pres, Sperry Gyroscope Co, Brooklyn, N.Y, 36-43; attorney-at-law, Gardner, Morrison & Rogers, Wash, D.C, 45-46; trustee, George Wash. Univ, 51-63; mem. research inst, Univ. Okla, 54-61, chmn. gen. adv. cmt, 57-58; mem. indust. adv. bd, Okla. State Univ, 54-61; regional v.pres, Nat. Munic. League, N.Y.C, 55-58; trustee, Nat. Center for Educ. in Polit, N.Y, 60-63; mem. adv. coun, Sch. of Indust. Mgt, Mass. Inst. Tech, 60-63; chmn, Distinguished Civilian Serv. Awards Bd, 61-63; dir. of numerous companies and organizations; attorney-at-law, Wash, D.C, currently. Mil. Serv: Pfc, Marine Corp Res, 30-31; 2nd Lt, Fleet Marine Corps Res, Naval Aviator, 31-32; 2nd Lt, 1st Lt, then Capt, Marine Corps Res, 32-44, Maj, Ninth Marine Aircraft Wing and Command Officer, First Marine Air Warning Group, 44-45, Lt. Col, 50-66 and (Ret), 66. Publ: Governmental Manpower for Tomorrow's Cities, (with John J. Corson), McGraw-Hill, 62; 'From Runnymede to Ganymede,' in Speaking of Space and Aeronautics, 7/67; 'Space Age Management,' The McKinsey Lecture Series, Columbia Univ, 68, McGraw-Hill. Mem: Trustee and chmn. bd. trustees, Meridian House Found, Wash, D.C.(pres, 60-62); trustee, chmn. bd. trustees and pres, Urban Studies, Inc, Wash, D.C; coun, Am. Soc. for Pub. Admin.(pres, 66-67); trustee, Cmt. for Econ. Develop; Nat. Acad. of Pub. Admin.(treas, 68-); trustee Nat. Geographic Soc; pres. adv. bd, Nat. Kidney Found; Am. Bar Asn; D.C. Bar Asn; Marine Corps Reserve Officers Asn; Am. Legion; Air Force Asn; Am. Polit. Sci. Asn; Am. Acad. Polit. and Soc. Sci; Acad. Polit. Sci; Nat. Civil Serv. League; Fed. City Coun; Univ. Film Asn. (trustee, 58-61); Am. Astronaut. Soc; Am. Asn. for the Adv. of Sci; Inst. of Aerospace Sci; Aerospace Med. Asn; Nat. Space Club (bd. gov, 68-); Frontiers of Sci. Found. of Okla.(pres, 56-57); Aero Club of Wash; Hon. Order of Ky. Cols; Am. Judicature Soc; AF&AM; Alfalfa Club; Army and Navy Country Club; Chevy Chase Club; Nat. Capitol Dem. Club; Metrop. Club; Univ. Clubs, Wash, D.C. and N.Y.C; Brook Club of N.Y.C. Mgt. Achievement Award, Soc. for the Adv. of Mgt, 64; Crowell Award, Am. Ord. Asn, 66; Collier Trophy, 66; Elec. to Okla. Hall of Fame, 67; Award for Achievement, Nat. Aviation Club, 67; Univ. Mich. Sesquicentennial Award, 67; Mount St. Mary's Col. Dubois Medal, 67; Silver Buffalo Award, Boy Scouts, 68; NASA Distinguished Serv. Medal, 68; Presidential Medal of Freedom, 68. Rel: Presbyterian. Legal Res: 134 Robert S. Kerr Ave, Oklahoma City, Okla. 73102. Mailing Add: 2800 36th St. N.W, Washington, D.C. 20007.

WEBB, JAY LEON R
Idaho State Rep.
b. Idaho Falls, Idaho, 10/29/34; s. A.J. Webb and Anna M. McDermott W; m. 12/2/61 to Mary Jane Milbrath; c. Anna M. Educ: Univ. Idaho, B.A, 56 and LL.B, 59; Phi Alpha Delta; Phi Gamma Delta. Polit. & Govt. Pos: Attorney, Boise Co, Idaho, 65-66; Idaho State Rep, 67- Mil. Serv: Air Force, Idaho Nat. Guard, 59; Capt, Army Res, currently. Mem: Third Judicial Dist. Bar Asn. Rel: Protestant. Legal Res: 1421 Garfield, Boise, Idaho 83706. Mailing Add: Box 292, Boise, Idaho 83701. (1967)

WEBB, JOHN W. R
Mo. State Rep.
b. Picher, Okla, 3/11/32; s. Jesse Lee Webb and Daphne Iona Huddleston W; m. 9/3/55 to Mona Genile Woodmansee; c. Laura Lee, William Wesley and Lisa Lynne. Educ: Joplin Jr. Col, Mo, 53-54; Kans. State Col, Pittsburg, B.S, 56; Univ. Mo. Sch. of Law, Columbia, LL.B, 59; Phi Theta Kappa; Phi Alpha Delta. Polit. & Govt. Pos: City attorney, Webb City, Mo, 61-66; mem, Bd. of Educ, Webb City, 61-67; Mo. State Rep, 134th Dist, 67- Mil. Serv: Entered as Pvt, Air Force, 50, released as S/Sgt, 53. Mem: Secy-treas, Jasper Co. Bar Asn; Mo. Bar Integrated, Jefferson City; Am. Legion; Rotary (v.pres, Webb City Club); v.pres, Webb City C. of C. Rel: Presbyterian. Mailing Add: 602 W. Broadway, Webb City, Mo. 64670.

WEBB, JULIAN D
Ga. State Sen.
b. Byronville, Ga, 10/02/11; s. Vester Ottis Webb and Flossie Woodruff W; m. 9/25/35 to Jo Smith; c. Joanna (Mrs. Henry Clayton Custer), Julianna (Mrs. Robert Edward Cheshire, III); Grandchildren: Julianna Webb and Henry Clayton Custer, Jr. and Joanna Merritt and Robert Edward Cheshire, IV. Educ: Mercer Univ, A.B. and LL.B, 32; Sigma Pi; Phi Alpha Delta. Polit. & Govt. Pos: City attorney, Donalsonville, Ga, 45-; mem, Constitution Revision Cmn, 63-64 & 69; mem, State Dem. Exec. Cmt, 63-; Ga. State Sen, 11th Dist, 63-, asst. floor leader, Ga. State Senate, 63-64 and floor leader, 64-66, pres. pro tem, 66-68. Bus. & Prof. Pos: Admitted to Ga. Bar, 32; legal practice, Augusta, 33; mem. legal dept, Farm Credit Admin, 33-42; attorney-at-law, currently. Mem: Pataula Circuit Bar Asn.(pres, 44-46 & 62); Am. Bar Asn; Am. Judicature Soc; Ga. Bar Asn.(mem. bd. gov, 46-48 & 68-); State Bar Disciplinary Bd, 64-67; del, World Conf. on Peace Through Law, Geneva, 67; Lions (pres, Donalsonville chap, 45); Mason; Shrine;(potentate, Hasan Temple, 58); pres, S. Ga. Home for Aging Am, 63-68; C. of C.(dir, Donalsonville Chap). Rel: Methodist; Del, World Conf. Methodist, London, 66. Mailing Add: Box 277, Donalsonville, Ga. 31745.

WEBB, KATHLEEN CECELIA D
Secy, Santa Cruz Co. Dem. Cent. Cmt, Calif.
b. Cresco, Iowa, 9/21/16; d. Francis Patrick Farrell and Nell Pollitt F; m. 1/30/43 to William Marion Webb; c. William Farrell and Pamela Joan. Educ: Watsonville High Sch, 4 years. Polit. & Govt. Pos: Secy, Santa Cruz Co. Dem. Cent. Cmt, Calif, 64-; mem, Calif. Dem. State Cent. Cmt, 68- Mem: Armed Forces Wives Club; Hui Nao Wahine, Hawaii; Am. Red Cross; Am. Cancer Soc; Watsonville Women's Club. Rel: Catholic. Mailing Add: 29 Shady Oaks Dr, Watsonville, Calif. 94076.

WEBB, MAURICE EVERETT D
b. Bloom, Kans, 12/8/13; s. Loris Everett Webb and Clara Crotinger W; m. 4/3/33 to Hattye Mae Allen; c. Peggy (Mrs. Schoen), Everett Eugene, Mark Allen and Michael Ray. Educ: High schs, Sterling and Dodge City, Kans, 4 years. Polit. & Govt. Pos: Dem. precinct committeeman, Hodgeman Co, Kans, 40-69; Kans. State Rep, 55-56; chmn, Hodgeman Co. Dem. Party, 56-69; mem, Kans. State Bd. of Health, 68- Bus. & Prof. Pos: Adminstr, Hodgeman Co. Hosp, Jetmore, Kans, 56-69. Mem: Am. and Kans. Hosp. Asns; Lutheran Hosp. Asn. of Kans; Am. Col. of Med. Adminstr; Lions; Nat. Farmers Union. Rel: Lutheran. Legal Res: 107 N. Clay, Jetmore, Kans. 67854. Mailing Add: P.O. Box 322, Jetmore, Kans. 67854.

WEBB, ROBERT MAURICE, JR. D
Miss. State Rep.
b. Greensburg, La, 4/20/32; s. Robert Maurice Webb, Sr. and Bertha Rayborn W; m. 6/17/56 to Sandra Wesson; c. Robert M, III, John Julius and William Pascal. Educ: Copiah-Lincoln Jr. Col, 52-53; La. State Univ, 54-55. Polit. & Govt. Pos: Mem, Bd. of Alderman, Saltillo, Miss, 67; Miss. State Rep, Lee and Itawamba Counties, 68- Bus. & Prof. Pos: Adjuster, Am. For Loyalty Group, Baton Rouge, La, 57-60; self-employed, farmer and ginner, 60- Mil. Serv: Entered as Pvt, Army, 52, released Cpl, 54, after serv. in First Armored Div. Mem: Mason; Shrine; Eastern Star; Lee Co. Farm Club; Civitian; Am. Legion; VFW. Lee Co. Farmer of Year, 64. Rel: Presbyterian; Elder. Mailing Add: Box 190, Saltillo, Miss. 38866.

WEBB, WILLIAM EDWIN, JR. D
b. Statesville, N.C, 12/6/15; s. William Edwin Webb and Bertha Fleming W; m. 5/4/47 to Martha Plott; c. William E, III and James B. Educ: Mitchell Col, 33-34; Univ. N.C, A.B, 37; Kappa Sigma. Polit. & Govt. Pos: Mem, Dem. Nat. Cmt, 64-68; del, Dem. Nat. Conv, 68. Bus. & Prof. Pos: Chmn, bd, Mitchell Col, 57-64. Mil. Serv: Entered as A/S, Naval Res, 41, released as Lt. Comdr, 45, after serv. in Atlantic Escort and Amphibious Off, ETO, 42-45; Two Commendation Medals; Pre-Pearl Harbor Medal; Atlantic and ETO Serv. Ribbons. Mem: Pres, Carolinas Chap, Soc. Chartered Property & Casualty Underwriters; pres, N.C. Asn. Ins. Agents; pres, Nat. Asn. Ins. Agents, 65-66; Rotary; Elks; Am. Legion; VFW. Rel: Presbyterian. Legal Res: 202 Ridgeway, Statesville, N.C. 28677. Mailing Add: Box 827, Statesville, N.C. 28677.

WEBBER, ALBERT RAYMOND D
Conn. State Rep.
b. New Haven, Conn, 9/28/13; s. Louis Webber and Fannie Ostrow W; m. 5/20/43 to Sally Goodmark; c. Michelle, Lawrence, Priscilla and Jordon. Polit. & Govt. Pos: Conn. State Rep, 58-; mem, New Haven Bd. of Aldermen, and Zoning Appeals. Bus. & Prof. Pos: Pres, A.R. Webber Co. Mil. Serv: Pvt, Army, 42. Mem: Woodbridge C. of C; Probus Club; mem. bd, New Haven Rehabil. Center and Commun. Center, Home for the Aged; chmn, adv. bd, New Haven Regional Center for the Ment. Retarded. Rel: Jewish. Mailing Add: 109 Stevenson Rd, New Haven, Conn. 06515.

WEBBER, FREDERICK LEROY R
b. Portland, Maine, 1/4/38; s. Leon True Webber and Patricia Conti W; m. 12/30/65 to Ann Chamberlain Bouker; c. John Frederick and Jennifer True. Educ: Yale Univ, B.A. in Hist, 61; Yale Key; Phi Gamma Delta. Polit. & Govt. Pos: Admin. asst. to U.S. Rep. John Dellenback, Ore, 68- Bus. & Prof. Pos: Legis. liaison, Nat. Forest Products Asn, Wash, D.C, 66-68. Mil. Serv: Entered as 2nd Lt, Marine Corps, 61, released as Capt, 66, after serv. in Third and Second Div, West. Pac. and E. Coast, Major, Marine Corps Res, 66-; Letter of Commendation for Combat Duties in Dominican Repub. Mem: Yale Club, Wash, D.C; Jaycees (Capitol Hill Chap); Marine Corps Res. Fourth Civil Affairs Group. Rel: Congregational. Mailing Add: 7819 Penley Place, Springfield, Va. 22151.

WEBBER, HENRY EARL III D
Chmn, Sumner Co. Dem. Party, Tenn.
b. Nashville, Tenn, 9/11/39; s. Henry Earl Webber Jr. and Margrete Hodsen W; m. 8/27/62 to Sonja Loerita Perry; c. Margrete, Lacy and Helen. Educ: Univ. Tenn, 1 year; George Peabody Col, 2 years; Epsilon Alpha Sigma. Polit. & Govt. Pos: Chmn, Sumner Co. Young Dem, Tenn, 64-68; alternate del, Dem. Nat. Conv, 68; chmn, Sumner Co. Dem. Party, 68- Bus. & Prof. Pos: V.pres, Gallatin Block Co, Tenn, 61- Mil. Serv: Specialist 5/C, Army Res, 61-67. Mem: Chmn, Tenn. Jr. C. of C. Three Legion of Merit Awards. Rel: Methodist. Mailing Add: 915 Harris Dr, Gallatin, Tenn. 37066.

WEBER, ARNOLD ROBERT
Asst. Secy. for Manpower, Dept. of Labor
b. N.Y.C, 9/20/29; s. Jack Weber and Lee Smith W; m. 2/8/54 to Edna Files; c. David B, Paul L. and Robert C. Educ: Univ. Ill, B.A, 50, M.A, 52; Mass. Inst. Tech, Ph.D, 58; Phi Beta Kappa; Phi Eta Sigma. Polit. & Govt. Pos: Asst. Secy. for Manpower, Dept. of Labor, 69- Bus. & Prof. Pos: Asst. prof. indust. rels, Mass. Inst. Tech, 57-58; asst. prof, Grad. Sch. Bus, Univ. Chicago, 58-60, assoc. prof, 60-64, prof, 64-69, dir. faculty research, 66-69; vis. prof. indust. rels, Stanford Univ, 66. Mil. Serv: Entered as A/S, Coast Guard, 52, released as Lt.(jg), 54, after serv. in U.S.C.G.C. Wauchusetts, Pac. and Korean Areas, 52-54; Am. Defense, UN and Korean Theatre Medals. Publ: Union Decision-making and Collective Bargaining, Univ. Ill, 53; ed, The Structure of Collective Bargaining: Problems and Perspectives, Free Press, 61; co-auth, Strategies for the Displaced Worker, Harper & Row, 66. Mem: Am. Asn. Univ. Prof; Indust. Rels. Research Asn; Nat. Acad. Arbitrators. Rel: Jewish. Legal Res: Chicago, Ill. Mailing Add: Dept. of Labor, Washington, D.C. 20210.

WEBER, ELMER OTTO R
Chmn, Wayne Co. Second Rep. Dist. Orgn, Mich.
b. Saginaw, Mich, 10/29/23; s. Otto Weber and Emma Bluemlein W; m. 6/10/50 to Pearl Margaret Kluck; c. Karlton Richard and Carol Ann. Educ: Gen. Motors Inst, 42-43; Univ. Mich, B.B.A, 48, M.B.A, 49; Sigma Nu; treas, Student Legis. Polit. & Govt. Pos: Trustee, Northville Bd. Educ, Mich, 64-66; exec. secy, Wayne Co. Second Rep. Dist. Orgn, 65-67, chmn, 67-; alternate del, Rep. Nat. Conv, 68. Bus. & Prof. Pos: Indust. rels. mgr, Fostoria Plant, Ford Motor Co, 61-63, mgr. salaried personnel, Gen. Parts Div, 63-67, supvr. pos. eval, Ford Motor Co, 67- Mil. Serv: Entered as Cadet, Air Force, 43, released as 1st Lt, 45, after serv. in First Troop Carrier, China-Burma-India, 44-45; Capt. Res, 45-53; Air Medal with Three Clusters; Distinguished Flying Cross with Two Oak Leaf Clusters. Mem: PTA; Teen Center Bd. Outstanding Young Man, Jaycee 1956, Boss of the Year, 63; Ford Citizen of the Year, Ford Co, 66. Rel: Lutheran. Mailing Add: 20360 Woodhill Rd, Northville, Mich. 48167.

WEBER, GARRY ALLEN D
City Councilman, Dallas, Tex.
b. Oelwein, Iowa, 2/25/36; s. Arthur Albert Weber and Eleanore Lincoln W; m. 1/6/68 to Barbara Jane Post. Educ: South. Methodist Univ, B.B.A, 58; Phi Alpha Delta; Kappa Alpha. Polit. & Govt. Pos: Co-chmn, Young Men for Cabell, Earle Cabell Congressman's Club, Dallas, Tex, 66-68; campaign chmn. for Earle Cabell, 68; del, Dem. Nat. Conv, 68; mem, Cmn. to Study Mortgage Interest Rates, Wash, D.C, 68-69; city councilman, Dallas, 69- Bus. & Prof. Pos: Chmn. bd, Weber, Hall, Cobb & Caudle, Inc, Dallas, Tex, 64- Mem: Bd. dirs, March of Dimes; dir, Goodwill Industs, Dallas; bd. dirs, Dallas Co. Hosp. Dist; Salesmanship Club of Dallas; mem. cmt, Goals for Dallas; United Fund Cmt; dir, N.Dallas C. of C. Rel: Methodist. Legal Res: 3131 Maple Ave, Dallas, Tex. 75201. Mailing Add: 1800 LTV Tower, Dallas, Tex. 75201.

WEBER, GEORGE D. D
b. Eureka, Mo, 3/2/25; m. 8/2/47 to F. Roberta Harrison; c. Carole Ann, George David, Samuel Christopher, Thomas Stuart, Robert Clay, Diana Lynn. Educ: Col. of Eng, Univ. of Mo. Polit. & Govt. Pos: Mo. State Rep, 64-66. Bus. & Prof. Pos: Farmer; real estate broker; pres, Investors Real Estate Investment Trust. Mil. Serv: Marine Corps, 44-46. Mem: K. of C; Lions; Am. Legion; VFW. Rel: Catholic. Mailing Add: Eureka, Mo. 63025.

WEBER, MARY E. D
Dem. Nat. Committeewoman, Wash.
b. Ironton, Ohio, 6/24/11; d. Charles John Willis and Sue Ella Gholson Sloat W; m. 10/28/44 to Earl Weber; c. Dawn and Karen. Educ: Marshall Univ, A.B, 33; Ohio State Univ, 34-36; Univ. Chicago, 40; Cleveland Inst. Fine Arts; Univ. Wash, 53; Delta Kappa Gamma; Glee Clubs; Debate; French Club; German Club; Drama. Polit. & Govt. Pos: Dem. Precinct committeewoman, 11 years; organizer, Dem. Woman's Clubs; mem, Off. Price Admin. Rental Adv. Bd, Seattle, King and Snohomish Co, Wash, 46-53; pres. rep, Dem. Nat. Conv, 50, del, 64 & 68; del, Wash. State Dem. Conv, 56-66; pres, Grant Co. Dem. Women's Club, 61-64; chmn, Grant Co. Dem. Platform Cmt, mem, State Dem. Platform Cmt. and del, White House Conf. Dem. Women, 66, del, West. States Dem. Conf, Los Angeles, 67; former committeewoman, Wash. State Dem. Cent. Cmt; state co-chmn, Cmt. to Reform Elec. Process and Humphrey for Pres. Cmt; Dem. Nat. Committeewoman, Wash, 68- Bus. & Prof. Pos: Music, Eng, Latin and debate teacher, 32-42; co-owner and mgr, Auto and Farm Implement Co, 48-54; co-owner farm, Columbia Basin Irrigation Proj, 53-; photographer, Pac. Northwest Gardens, 56; co-ed, Smoke Signals, Wash. State Fedn. of Garden Clubs, 58-61. Mil. Serv: Army, 42-44, civilian employee, Army Corps Engrs; President's Blue Serv. Ribbons. Mem: Exec. secy, Columbia Basin Landowners' Asn, 59-63; state finance chmn, 50 and state prog. chmn, Wash. League Women Voters, 51; rep. pres, Delta Kappa Gamma to nat. polit. conv. to seek more representation for women, 40; Daughters of Nile; El Karnak Temple (Spokane Shrine Affiliate); Eastern Star; White Shrine of Jerusalem; v.pres, Quincy PTA; Am. Legion Auxiliary; conserv. chmn, Wash. Fedn. of Garden Clubs, 67-69. Bronze Medal for Hort. from Am. Iris Soc, 59; Blue Ribbon Winner, Seattle World's Fair Flower Show for Design Depicting Century 21 Sci. Center, 61; Sweepstakes Winner, Rocky Reach Dam Driftwood Show, Wenatchee, 64; Outstanding Commun. Leader, 68. Rel: Presbyterian. Mailing Add: Route 1, Box 173, Quincy, Wash. 98848.

WEBER, O. J. D
b. Bay City, Tex, 7/12/25; s. Otto James Weber and Margaret Holland W; m. 5/28/43 to Ann Hooton; c. Carol Ann (Mrs. Paddock) and James Lee. Educ: Southwest Tex. State, 1 year; Univ. Tex, Austin, B.A, 41; Yale Univ, LL.B, 49; Phi Beta Kappa. Polit. & Govt. Pos: Secy. to Congressman Lyndon B. Johnson, Wash, D.C, 41-42; sen. dist. campaign mgr. for Gov. John Connally, Tex, 62-68; del, State Dem. Conv, 64, 66 & 68; del, Dem. Nat. Conv, 68. Bus. & Prof. Pos: Attorney, Baker, Botts, Shepherd & Coates, Houston,

49-55; partner, Mehaffy, Weber, Keith & Gonsoulin, Beaumont, 55- Mil. Serv: Entered as Pvt, Air Force, 42, released as Capt, 46, after serv. as a Radar Staff Officer, Air Force Training Command, 43-46; Commendation Medal. Mem: Am. and Tex. State Bar Asns; Jefferson Co. Bar Asn.(past pres. and dir); Fedn. of Ins. Counsel; Tex. Asn. of Defense Counsel (v.pres. and past dir); Beaumont Club; Beaumont Country Club; Lions (past pres, Downtown Club); Friends of the Abilene Christian Col. Libr.(past pres); Knife & Fork Club (past pres); hon. mem, Am. Fedn. of Musicians; fel, Tex. Bar Found. Rel: Church of Christ. Legal Res: 1980 Thomas Rd, Beaumont, Tex. 77706. Mailing Add: 1400 San Jacinto Bldg, Beaumont, Tex. 77701.

WEBER, ROBERT H. D
b. Bridgeton, N.J, 12/14/19; s. Howard A. Weber and Luta Wolfe W; m. 9/7/46 to Janice Frazier; c. Thomas Wolfe, Linda J, Robert H, Jr, Jeffrey W, Peter Adrian and Stephen Shaw. Polit. & Govt. Pos: N.J. State Assemblyman, 57-58; N.J. State Sen, 59-65, Minority Leader, N.J. State Senate, 65; mem, N.J. State Bd. of Control, Dept. Insts. and Agencies; alternate del, Dem. Nat. Conv, 68. Mil. Serv: Radio Officer, Merchant Marines. Rel: Methodist. Legal Res: Main St, Greenwich, N.J. 08323. Mailing Add: 134 N. Pearl St, Bridgeton, N.J. 08302.

WEBER, THOMAS D
b. Phila, Pa, 4/26/16; s. Carl A. Weber (deceased) and Gertrude Stier W (deceased); m. 4/1/45 to Mary Louise Cole; c. Thomas C. and Marilyn B. Educ: Princeton Univ, A.B, 38; Columbia Univ, A.M, 40, Ph.D, 51; Dial Lodge. Polit. & Govt. Pos: Councilman, Borough of Metuchen, N.J, 59-64 and mayor, 66-67; alternate del, Dem. Nat. Conv, 68. Bus. & Prof. Pos: Instr. hist, Rutgers Univ, 45-49, asst. prof, 49-55 and assoc. prof, 55- Mil. Serv: Entered as Pvt, Army, 41, released as T/Sgt, 45, after serv. in Mil. Police, Qm. C. and Eighth Div, Eng, N.Africa, Italy, 42-45. Publ: Northern Railroads and the Civil War, 1861-5, Kings Crown, 52; Heritage of First Presbyterian Church of Metuchen, N.J, Georgian Press, 67. Mem: Am. Hist. Asn; Orgn. Am. Historians; Am. Asn. Univ. Prof; Metuchen Dem. Club. Rel: Presbyterian. Mailing Add: 99 Beacon Hill Dr, Metuchen, N.J. 08840.

WEBER, WILLIAM V. R
Mich. State Rep.
b. Viroqua, Wis, 11/9/01; m. 6/3/28 to Esther E. Wahlstien; c. John L. and William Paul. Educ: Univ. Iowa, B.A, 28, M.A, 29 and Ph.D, 32; Alpha Phi Sigma. Polit. & Govt. Pos: Mem, Kalamazoo Co. Cmt, Mich, 50-; chmn. zoning bd. of appeals, Kalamazoo, 54-67; Kalamazoo City Rep, Kalamazoo Co. Bd. Supvrs, 63-67; chmn. educ. and research cmt, Rep. State Cent. Cmt, 63-; mem, Rep. Third Cong. Dist. Cmt. and Kalamazoo Exec. Rep. Cmt, 64-; Mich. State Rep, 67- Mil. Serv: Entered as Lt, Navy, 43, released as Comdr, 46. Mem: Am. and Mid-West Polit. Sci. Asns; Mich. Pub. Admin. Asn; Mason; Elks; Am. Legion. Rel: Congregational. Mailing Add: 1612 Evanston, Kalamazoo, Mich. 49001.

WEBER, WINNIE PAULA D
b. Ellington, Mo, 7/4/36; d. Paul Faulkenberry and Lillian Williams F; m. 2/23/63 to H. Glenn Weber. Educ: Southwest Mo. State Col, B.S. in Educ, 63; Univ. Mo, M.S. in Educ, 67, scholarship, Guid. and Counseling Inst, 1 year; Independent Orgn. Students. Polit. & Govt. Pos: Pres, Jefferson Co. Women's Dem. Clubs, Mo, 63-65; Dem. committeewoman, Meramec Twp, Jefferson Co, 64-69; del, Dem. Nat. Conv, 68; pres, Eighth Cong. Dist, Women's Dem. Clubs, Mo, 68- Bus. & Prof. Pos: Teacher, Mo. Pub. Sch. Syst, 53-66; counsr, Pkwy Sch. Dist, St. Louis Co, Mo, 66-69. Mem: Mo. State Teacher's Asn; Nat. Educ. Asn; Mo. Guid. Asn; Eastern Star. Appeared on prog. at Am. Personnel and Guid. Asn, Dallas, Tex, 67. Rel: Methodist. Mailing Add: House Springs, Mo. 63051.

WEBSTER, DEAN KINGMAN R
Rep. State Committeeman, Mass.
b. Andover, Mass, 5/16/29; s. D. Kingman Webster, Jr. and Mina Muirhead W; m. 6/15/68 to Eliza Tabb Mason. Educ: Phillips Acad; Williams Col, B.A. Polit. & Govt. Pos: Mem, Andover Rep. Town Cmt, Mass, 60-64; del, Rep. State Conv, 60-66; cand, Mass. State Senate, 62; pres, Gr. Lawrence Young Rep, 62-63; alternate del, Rep. Nat. Conv, 64; Rep. State Committeeman, Mass, Fourth Essex Dist, currently. Bus. & Prof. Pos: Pres, H.K. Webster Co; corporator, Lawrence Savings Bank; dir, Bay State Merchants Nat. Bank. Mil. Serv: Entered as 2nd Lt, Marine Corps, 51, released as 1st Lt, 53, after serv. in First Marine Div, Korea; UN and Korean Serv. Medals. Mem: Delta Phi; VFW; Gr. Lawrence Jaycees; v.pres, Lawrence YMCA; past pres, Mass. Soc. for Prev. of Cruelty to Children, Merrimack Valley Dist; past pres, Lawrence Y's Men's Club; dir, New Eng. Grain and Feed Council; dir, Am. Feed Mfg. Asn; gen. chmn, United Fund of Gr. Lawrence 1970 Campaign. Rel: Episcopal. Mailing Add: 11 Longwood Dr, Andover, Mass. 01810.

WEBSTER, DeWITT TALMADGE D
b. Shuqualak, Miss, 9/16/00; s. Dr. Milton Alexander Webster and Alice Parks W; m. 6/26/23 to Carmen Elise Labat; c. Muriel A.(Mrs. Cooper) and D.T, Jr. Educ: Straight's Col, 2 years; Cincinnati Col. of Embalming, 2 years. Polit. & Govt. Pos: Del, Dem. Nat. Conv, 68; mem, Lauderdale Co. Dem. Exec. Cmt, Miss, 69. Bus. & Prof. Pos: Owner and mgr, Metrop. Funeral Home, Philadelphia and Meridian, Miss, 24-; pres, Metrop. Burial Ins, 60-; realtor, 61- Mem: Toastmaster Club; NAACP. Rel: Catholic. Legal Res: 1414 28th Ave, Meridian, Miss. 39301. Mailing Add: P.O. Box 5802, Meridian, Miss. 39301.

WEBSTER, DONALD ALBERT R
Asst. to Secy. of Treas.
b. Rochester, N.Y, 12/9/30; s. Albert C. Webster and Madeline Vandenbush W; m. 3/30/59 to Helen Long. Educ: Hamilton Col, B.A, 53; Sch. Adv. Int. Studies, Johns Hopkins Univ, M.A, 55; Pi Delta Epsilon; Delta Sigma Rho; Tau Kappa Epsilon. Polit. & Govt. Pos: Research asst. to Sen. Frederick G. Payne, Wash, D.C, 55-56; asst. to asst. Admin, Gen. Serv. Admin, 59-61; minority economist, Joint Econ. Cmt. of Cong, 62-68; staff mem, Nixon Campaign Staff and Presidential Transition Cmt, 68-69; Asst. to Secy. of Treas, 69- Bus. & Prof. Pos: Writer, Cong. Quart, Wash, D.C, 61-62. Mil. Serv: Entered as A/S, Navy, 56, released as Lt.(jg), 59, after serv. in Heavy Photographic Squadron 62, 56-58. Mem: Am. Econ. Asn; Am. Polit. Sci. Asn; Nat. Economists Club; Capitol Hill Club, Wash, D.C; Phi Beta Kappa. Rel: Protestant. Legal Res: 1624 Creek St, Rochester, N.Y. 14625. Mailing Add: 4615 Sedgwick St. N.W, Washington, D.C. 20016.

WEBSTER, FRANKLIN D
Ky. State Rep.
b. 1889. Educ: East. Ky. State Col, A.B; Univ. Ky, M.A. Polit. & Govt. Pos: Ky. State Rep, 62- Bus. & Prof. Pos: Retired teacher. Mil. Serv: Army, World War I. Rel: Baptist. Mailing Add: 9 Summit Ave, Williamstown, Ky. 41097. (1967)

WEBSTER, RICHARD M. R
Mo. State Sen.
b. Carthage, Mo, 4/29/22; m. 1948 to Janet Poston Whitehead; c. Richard M, Jr. and William Lawrence. Educ: Univ. Mo; Columbia Univ, LL.B, 48. Polit. & Govt. Pos: Mo. State Rep, 50-56; Mo. State Sen, 62- Bus. & Prof. Pos: Attorney and stockman. Mil. Serv: Coast Guard, 41-45; Naval Res, 45- Mem: Mason; K. of P. Rel: Presbyterian. Mailing Add: 1725 S. Garrison, Carthage, Mo. 64836. (1967)

WEBSTER, ROBERT L. R
Chmn, Fayette Co. Rep. Party, Pa.
b. Brownsville, Pa, 9/7/24; s. Thomas J. Webster and Janet Thompson W; m. 8/21/48 to Wilma O'Brien; c. Robert L, Jr, Danny L. and Thomas W. Educ: St. Vincent's Col, 44; Univ. Pittsburgh, LL.B, 51. Polit. & Govt. Pos: Chmn, Fayette Co. Young Rep, Pa, 52-56; dir, State Fedn. Young Rep, 55-57; chmn, Fayette Co. Rep. Party, 66-; del, Rep. Nat. Conv, 68. Bus. & Prof. Pos: Attorney-at-Law, 51- Mil. Serv: Entered as Flight Engr, Air Force, 43, released as Flight Engr, 46, after serv. in Fourth Air Force. Mem: Fayette Co, Pa. and Am. Bar Asns. Rel: Protestant. Mailing Add: 421 High St, Brownsville, Pa. 15417.

WEBSTER, ROLAND H. D
b. Washington, Vt, 9/14/23; single. Educ: Spaulding High Sch. Polit. & Govt. Pos: Vt. State Rep, 65-66. Bus. & Prof. Pos: Stonecutter; instr, S.C.S. Mil. Serv: Army, Philippines, 43-46. Mem: 4-H leader; Civil Defense. Rel: Universalist. Mailing Add: Box 76, Washington, Vt. 05675. (1967)

WEBSTER, RONALD ARTHUR R
Attorney Gen, Knox Co, Tenn.
b. Morgan Co, Tenn, 12/21/38; s. Paris Guthrie Webster and Myrtle Hill W; m. 9/9/67 to Dianne Elizabeth Sharp. Educ: Univ. Tenn, B.S, 60, Col. Law, J.D, 62; pres, Phi Delta Phi, 61-62; Tau Kappa Alpha; Sigma Chi. Polit. & Govt. Pos: Pres, Univ. Tenn. Youth for Nixon-Lodge, 60; Tenn. State Rep, Knox Co, 64-68; mem, Knox Co. Rep. Exec. Cmt, Tenn, 64-; mem, Tenn. Rep. State Exec. Cmt, currently; treas, Knox Co. Young Rep. Club, 65-66; trial attorney, Knoxville, 65-67; attorney gen, Knox Co, 68- Mem: Am, Tenn. and Knoxville Bar Asns; Am. Trial Lawyers Asn; Mason; YMCA; Sen. Country Club; Deane Hill Country Club. Rel: Baptist. Legal Res: 1631 Laurel Ave. S.W, Knoxville, Tenn. 37916. Mailing Add: Criminal Court Bldg, Knoxville, Tenn. 37902.

WEBSTER, WALTER E, JR. R
Mem, Maine State Rep. Cmt.
b. Kingston, N.H, 7/14/16; s. Walter E. Webster, Sr. and Bertha Kruger W; m. 4/6/45 to Mary Ellen Romaine; c. Walter, III, Susan Ann, Mary Elizabeth, John Norman, David Henry, Martha Louise and Jane Catherine. Educ: Univ. N.H. Polit. & Govt. Pos: Town Rep. Chmn, Maine, 60-62; mem, Co. Rep. Cmt, 62-; Co. Rep. Chmn, 64-65; mem, Maine State Rep. Cmt, currently. Bus. & Prof. Pos: Salesman, Laird de Vou, Inc, 56-, mem. bd. dir, 62- and treas, 69- Mem: Mason; Am. Legion; Am. Soc. Tool & Mech. Engrs; Farm Bur. Rel: Methodist. Mailing Add: Pond Rd, South Berwick, Maine 03908.

WEBSTER, WARREN RAYMOND R
Chmn, Knox Co. Rep. Exec. Cmt, Tenn.
b. Morgan Co, Tenn, 12/25/21; s. Paris Guthrie Webster and Myrtle Hill W; div; c. Richard Alan, Martha Carol, Sara Joyce and Thomas Raymond. Educ: Univ. Tenn, B.A; Univ. Tenn. Col. of Law, LL.B; Sigma Nu; Phi Alpha Delta. Polit. & Govt. Pos: Chmn, Rep. Primary Cmn, Tenn, 56-57; chmn, Knox Co. Rep. Exec. Cmt, 57-60 & 64-; field secy. for U.S. Rep. Howard H. Baker, Sr, 59-61; mem, Second Cong. Dist. Exec. Cmt, Tenn, 64-; del, Rep. Nat. Conv, 68. Bus. & Prof. Pos: Attorney-at-Law, 53- Mil. Serv: Entered as Aviation Cadet, Navy, 43, commissioned 2nd Lt, Marine Corps, 44, released, 46, after serv. in Pacific Theater; recalled to serv. with VMR 152, Korean War, 50, released as Major, 62; Pac. Campaign Ribbon with Two Combat Stars. Mem: Mason (32°); Shrine; Elks; Knoxville, Tenn. and Am. Bar Asns. Rel: Baptist. Legal Res: 2822 E. Fifth Ave, Knoxville, Tenn. 37914. Mailing Add: Suite 1100 Hamilton Bank Bldg, Knoxville, Tenn. 37902.

WEDWORTH, JAMES Q. D
Calif. State Sen.
b. Ill, 1919; m. to Muriel Berube; c. Ronald, Diane, Susan and Albert. Educ: Ill. and La. Pub. Schs. Polit. & Govt. Pos: Mem, Hawthorne City Coun, Calif, 53-66, mayor, 58-66; Hawthorne rep, S.Bay Mayor's Coun, West Basin Water Dist, Los Angeles Co. Sanit Dist, Rapid Transit Selection Bd, League of Independent Cities, Am. Munic. League and Nat. Mayors' Coun; Calif. State Sen, 66-, v.chmn, Cmt. on Educ, Calif. State Senate, mem, Govt. Efficiency, Local Govt, Joint Cmt. on Legis. Orgn, Legis. Bldg. Space Needs and Senate's Rep. on the Gov. Automatic Data Processing Policy Cmts, mem, Constitution Revision, State Educ, Marine and Coastal Resources Cmns, former mem, Fish and Game, Water Resources, Agr. and Natural Resources Cmts. Bus. & Prof. Pos: Mgr, U.S. Navy Exchange, 45-49; employee, Northrop Corp, 49-53; operator, Schwinn Bicycle Agency and Fuller Paint Store, 53- Mil. Serv: Navy, 41-45. Mem: Bd. dirs. and chmn. youth cmt, Hawthorne Rotary Club; Winners Club; Boy Scouts; PTA; Elks; Little League; Pop Warner Football; Am. Field Serv; Am. Bicycle Asn; chmn, Local Heart Fund and Cerebral Palsy Dr. Rotarian of the Year, Hawthorne Rotary, 57. Rel: Lutheran. Mailing Add: 5303 W. 141st St, Hawthorne, Calif. 90250.

WEED, MARION R
b. Wheelock, Vt, 1/23/97; wid; c. three sons and two daughters. Educ: Lyndon Inst. Polit. & Govt. Pos: Vt. State Rep, 61-66; chmn, Caledonia Co.

Rep. Cmt. Bus. & Prof. Pos: Farmer and musician; Sutton Sch. Dir. Mem: West Burke Grange; Caledonia Co. Farm Bur; Am. Legion Auxiliary; Caledonia Exten. Serv; Lyndon Inst. Bd. of Trustees and Corporators; Commun. Sch. for Retarded Children. Rel: Methodist. Mailing Add: Box 399, Lyndonville, Vt. 05851.

WEEKS, ARTHUR DeWITTE D
b. White Plains, N.Y, 11/15/27; s. George Albert Weeks and Sara Sloman W; m. 10/7/50 to Johanna Grieb; c. Rebecca and Geoffrey DeWitt. Educ: Dickinson Col, A.B, 53; Dickinson Law Sch, LL.B, 56; Sigma Alpha Epsilon. Polit. & Govt. Pos: Sch. dir, York Suburban Sch. Dist, Pa, 58-65; registration chmn, York Co. Dem. Orgn, 62, area leader, 62-64, mem. nominating cmt, 63 and mem. exec. cmt, 64-66; alternate del, Dem. Nat. Conv, 64; asst. solicitor, York Co, Pa, 69- Bus. & Prof. Pos: Instr. Bus. law, York Jr. Col, 58-60; instr. real estate law, Pa. State Univ, York Campus, 64-69. Mem: Pa. and York Co. Bar Asns; Am. Judicature Soc; Am. Trial Lawyers Asn; Sertoma Club; Boy Scouts; Arthritis and Rheumatism Found. ASCAP Award, 56. Rel: Protestant. Mailing Add: 760 Erlen Dr, York, Pa. 17402.

WEEKS, CAMERON S. D
b. Tarboro, N.C, 11/19/10; s. George Earle Weeks and Lena Rivers Pittman W; m. 12/18/35 to Glennes Dodge; c. Ronald Dodge. Educ: Univ. N.C. Law Sch, LL.B, 36. Polit. & Govt. Pos: N.C. State Rep, Edgecombe Co, 41; mem, State Dem. Exec. Cmt, 52-54; N.C. State Sen, 53, 55, 56, 65 & 66. Bus. & Prof. Pos: Attorney-at-Law; bd. dir, Atlantic and N.C. R.R, 54; bd. trustees, Consolidated U.N.C, 57- Mem: N.C. and Am. Bar. Asns; N.C. Bar Inc. Rel: Presbyterian. Mailing Add: 505 St. Andrew St, Tarboro, N.C. 27886.

WEEKS, EDNA BATCHELDER R
N.H. State Rep.
b. Laconia, N.H, 4/28/06; d. Edward C. Batchelder and Nellie Parkman B; m. 10/22/32 to George Newton Weeks; c. Cynthia W. (Mrs. Smith) and Carolyn G. Educ: Univ. N.H, B.S, 28; Phi Kappa Phi; Delta Kappa; Delta Chi; Phi Lambda Phi; Phi Eta Phi. Polit. & Govt. Pos: Mem, Greenland Sch. Bd, N.H, 34-43; secy, Greenland Selectmen, 57-; N.H. State Rep, Dist. 23, 59-; clerk, Co. Del, 61- Bus. & Prof. Pos: Teacher math. and head dept, Sanborn Sem, 28-32; private tutor, 50-65. Mem: Order of Women Legis; N.H. Farm Bur; Greenland Grange; trustee, N.H. 4-H Found; Eastern Star. Rel: Protestant. Legal Res: 160 Newington Rd, Greenland, N.H. 03840. Mailing Add: Box 93, Greenland, N.H. 03840.

WEEKS, JOHANNA GRIEB D
Mem, York Co. Dem. Exec. Cmt, Pa.
b. Uniontown, Pa, 5/5/27; d. Nevin Henry Grieb and Elizabeth Egleston G; m. 10/7/50 to Arthur DeWitte Weeks; c. Rebecca and Geoffrey DeWitt. Educ: Mont. State Univ, 45-47; Millersville State Col, B.S, 62; Towson State Col, M.Ed, 67. Polit. & Govt. Pos: Mem, York Co. Dem. Exec. Cmt, Pa, 67-; alternate del, Dem. Nat. Conv, 68. Bus. & Prof. Pos: Teacher, York City Sch. Syst, 67- Mem: York City Educ. Asn. Rel: Protestant. Mailing Add: 760 Erlen Dr, York, Pa. 17402.

WEEKS, RAYMOND D
Ala. State Rep.
b. Columbus, Ga, 8/18/08; s. Henry L. Weeks and Minnie Kate Tillery W; m. 9/11/32 to Jennie Dee Robinson; c. Brenda and Barbara; seven grandchildren. Educ: Birmingham-South. Col, 3 years; Kappa Pi; Theta Chi. Polit. & Govt. Pos: Mem: State Dem. Exec. Cmt, Ala, 46, 50, 54 & 60; del, Dem. Nat. Conv, 52, 56 & 60; Ala. State Rep, 14th Dist, 66- Bus. & Prof. Pos: Advert. mgr, Jefferson Theater, 31-33; sales mgr, Ala. Outdoor Advert. Co, 33-69. Mil. Serv: Entered as A/S, Navy, 42, released as PO 1/C, after serv. in Air Wing, Am. Theater; Am. Theater Ribbon; Commendation and Victory Medals. Mem: Ala. State Ment. Health Asn.(former dir. and officer); Multiple Sclerosis Soc. (former dir); life mem, Soc. Hygiene Asn. U.S.(former dir); Red Cross (former dir); Commun. Chest (former dir); Polio Found.(former dir); organizer and first chmn, March of Dimes, 34; Jr. C. of C.(pres, Birmingham Chap, 40); C. of C.(former dir, Birmingham Chap); hon. mem, U.S. Jr. C. of C; State Comdr, Am. Legion, 62-63, Mason; Shrine; life mem, Elks; Eagles; Aero Club; Nat. Aeronaut. Asn; Civitan; Monday Morning Quarterback Club; Touchdown Club Wash; Young Men's Bus. Club; Sales Exec. Club; Traffic and Transportation Club: Asn. U.S. Army; Navy League; Air Force Asn. U.S; VFW: Sons of Confederate Vet; life mem, K.T. Credited with founding Am. Vet. Day, Nov. 11; Nat. Citation for Distinguished Achievement of our Am. Way of Life, Freedoms Found; Nat. Commun. Serv. Award, VFW; Commendation Award, Am. Legion; Pres, Citation, Asn. U.S. Army; Outstanding Civilian Serv. Medal, U.S. Army, 66; Commendations, all br. mil. serv; only civilian to receive Golden Acorn Award for distinguished serv. to commun, state and nation, 87th Maneuver Area Command, 68. Rel: Methodist. Legal Res: 101 N. 26th St, Birmingham, Ala. 35203. Mailing Add: 3420 Altamont Rd, Birmingham, Ala. 35205.

WEEKS, SINCLAIR R
b. West Newton, Mass, 6/15/93; s. John Wingate Weeks and Martha A. Sinclair W; m. 1/3/48 to Jane Tompkins Rankin; c. Frances Lee, John W, Jr, Martha S, Sinclair, Beatrice and William D. Educ: Harvard Univ, A.B, 14. Polit. & Govt. Pos: Treas, Rep. Nat. Cmt, 41-44; U.S. Sen, Mass, 44; chmn, Rep. Finance Cmt, 49-52; Secy. of Commerce, 53-58. Bus. & Prof. Pos: Clerk to asst. cashier, First Nat. Bank, Boston, 14-23; dir, N.H. Ins. Co. and Lancaster Nat. Bank; chmn, Reed and Barton Corp; hon. dir, United-Carr, Inc. and First Nat. Bank, Boston; limited partner, Hornblower & Weeks; chmn. bd. trustees, Wentworth Inst; trustee, Univ. N.H, Fessenden Sch, Newton, Mass, and Amos Tuck Sch. Bus. Admin, Dartmouth. Mil. Serv: Capt, F.A, Army, 17-19, AEF in France. Rel: Unitarian. Legal Res: Lancaster, N.H. 03584. Mailing Add: 4600 Prudential Center, Boston, Mass. 02199. (1967)

WEEKS, WILLIAM DOWSE R
Mass. State Sen.
b. West Newton, Mass, 5/9/26; s. Sinclair Weeks and Beatrice Dowse W; m. 6/19/53 to Frances Ravenel Prioleau Menefee; c. Frances P, Margaret D, William D, Jr. and Charles S. Educ: Milton Acad, Milton, Mass; Harvard Col, A.B, 49; Univ. Va. Law Sch, LL.B, 55. Polit. & Govt. Pos: Mass. State Sen, Norfolk and Plymouth Dist, 65- Bus. & Prof. Pos: Attorney, partner, Boyd, MacCrellish & Weeks, Boston, Mass, currently. Mil. Serv: Entered as Pvt, Army Air Force, 44, released as Pfc, 45. Mem: Am, Mass. and Boston Bar Asns; Mason; Overseer, Boys Clubs of Boston; dir, Mass. Soc. for Prevention of Cruelty to Children; World Affairs Coun. of Boston and N. Conway Inst; trustee, Arthritis and Rheumatism Found; New Eng. Deaconess Hosp. Corp. Rel: Unitarian. Mailing Add: 134 Border St, Cohasset, Mass. 02025.

WEEMS, MACK DAWSON D
b. Scott Co, Miss, 12/21/03; married. Polit. & Govt. Pos: Miss. State Rep, 62-68. Bus. & Prof. Pos: Farmer; former supt. of educ; teacher. Mem: Lions; Miss Educ. Asn; Miss. Cattlemen's Asn; Farm Bur; Mason. Rel: Methodist. Mailing Add: 291 Second Ave, Forest, Miss. 39074. (1967)

WEFALD, JON MICHAEL DFL
b. Minneapolis, Minn, 11/24/37; s. Olav Wefald and Walma Ovrom W; m. 6/8/63 to Ruth Ann Joynt. Educ: Pac. Lutheran Univ, B.A, 59; Wash. State Univ, M.A, 61; Univ. Mich, Ph.D, 65; fel, Univ. Mich; Phi Kappa Phi. Polit. & Govt. Pos: Dem-Farmer-Labor nominee for U.S. Rep, 68. Bus. & Prof. Pos: Teaching asst, Wash. State Univ, 59-61; teaching fel, Univ. Mich, 61-63; assoc. prof. hist, Gustavus Adolphus Col, 65- Mem: Am. Hist. Asn; Orgn. of Am. Historians; Phi Alpha Theta; Jaycees. Rel: Lutheran. Mailing Add: 619 W. Chestnut, St. Peter, Minn. 56082.

WEGEMER, CHARLES W. D
Chmn, Elk Co. Dem. Cmt, Pa.
b. St. Marys, Pa, 4/22/19; s. John F. Wegemer and Rose Keller W; m. 5/8/43 to Ruth W. Micheau; c. Bernadette, Barbara, Christine, Charlotte and Kimberly. Polit. & Govt. Pos: Chmn, Benzinger Twp. Dem. Cmt, Pa, 53-59; assessor, Elk Co, Pa, 53-59; secy-treas, Elk Co. Dem. Cmt, 60-64, chmn, 66-; field auditor, Pa. Dept. Auditor Gen, 62- Bus. & Prof. Pos: Ins. agent, C.W. Wegemer Ins. Agency, 47- Mil. Serv: Entered as Pvt, Army, 42, released as Pfc, 45. Mem: Past Grand Knight, St. Marys Coun, K. of C. 567; past pres, St. Marys Lions Club, and St. Marys Commun. Develop. Coun. Rel: Roman Catholic. Mailing Add: 334 Brussells St, St. Marys, Pa. 15857. (1967)

WEGNER, GLEN EUGENE R
Dep. Asst. Secy. for Health Legislation, Dept. of Health, Educ. and Welfare
b. Kendrick, Idaho, 1/25/39; s. Glen August Wegner and Jean Fry W; single. Educ: Col. Idaho, B.S. in Zool. and B.S. in Psychol, 60; Univ. Wash. Sch. Med, M.D, 64; Boston City Hosp, Mass, intern, 64-65; Johns Hopkins Univ, residency and fel, 65-67; Am. Univ, Wash, D.C, law, 67-69; Abbotts; Intercollegiate Knights. Polit. & Govt. Pos: Clin. research assoc, Nat. Inst. of Child Health and Human Develop, Nat. Insts. of Health, Dept. of Health, Educ. and Welfare, 67-68, spec. asst. to the Surgeon Gen. and to the Asst. Secy. for Health and Sci. Affairs, 68-69, Dep. Asst. Secy. for Health Legis, 69- Bus. & Prof. Pos: Clinical research assoc, Nat. Insts. of Health, Bethesda, Md, 67-68. Mil. Serv: Lt. Comdr, Pub. Health Serv, 67-69, with serv. as surgeon, Nat. Insts. of Health and the Off. of the Surgeon Gen. Mem: Am. Med. Asn; Md. Med. and Chirurgical Soc; Diplomat, Nat. Bd. of Med. Exam; Student Am. Bar Asn. White House Fel; Col. Man of the Year. Rel: Protestant. Legal Res: Kendrick, Idaho 83537. Mailing Add: 3417 Dent Place N.W, Washington, D.C. 20007.

WEGNER, ROBERT J. D
b. Paterson, N.J, 2/14/13; m. to Grace A. McBride; c. Kathleen (Mrs. Edward G. Tidabach) and Robert J. Jr. Educ: Holy Cross Col, Worcester, Mass. Polit. & Govt. Pos: Mem, N.J. Tenement House Cmn, 41-49; police and fire cmnr, Paterson, 49-56; pres, Paterson Plant Mgt. Cmn, 56-; exec. dir, Paterson Parking Authority; former N.J. State Assemblyman. Mem: Hon. life mem. State Patrolman's Benevolent Asn; hon. life mem. Fireman's Mutual Benevolent Asn; Past Exalted Ruler and hon. life mem, Paterson Elks Lodge. Mailing Add: 445 E. 39th St, Paterson, N.J. 07504. (1967)

WEHMEYER, CLARKE HAID R
Chmn, Callaway Co. Rep. Cmt, Mo.
b. Cedar City, Mo, 1/10/11; s. John Herman Wehmeyer and Anna Haid W; m. 6/29/63 to Catherine Baker. Educ: Jefferson City High Sch, grad. Polit. & Govt. Pos: Securities clerk, Mo. Ins. Dept, 41-46; chmn, Callaway Co. Rep. Cmt, Mo, 66- Mem: AF&AM; Prince of Peace Commandry; RAM; RSM; Eastern Star; Shrine. Rel: United Church of Christ. Mailing Add: Holts Summit, Mo. 65043.

WEHMEYER, VICTOR WILLIAM R
Chmn, Warren Co. Rep. Cmt, Mo.
b. Warrenton, Mo, 3/16/04; s. Herman Henry Wehmeyer and Henrietta Koelling W; m. 5/8/32 to Louisa Caroline Fredericka Schnarre; c. Roxana Louise (Mrs. Schroeder). Educ: Grad. Chillicothe Bus. Col, Mo. Polit. & Govt. Pos: Pres, Mo. Co. Assessors Asn, 28-30 & 52-53; constable, Pinckney Twp, Warren Co; co. assessor, Warren Co, 42-62 and co. collector, 62-; chmn, Warren Co. Rep. Cmt, currently; v.pres, Mo. State Co. Collectors Asn, 63-64. Mem: Daggett Lodge 492 AF&AM, 39 years. Rel: Methodist. Mailing Add: Route 1, Box 99, Marthasville, Mo. 63357.

WEICHMAN, DAVID EDWARD R
Iowa State Rep.
b. Newhall, Iowa, 9/22/21; s. Harry Edward Weichman and Elizabeth Meyer W; single. Educ: State Univ. Iowa, B.A, 47, J.D, 48; Delta Theta Phi. Polit. & Govt. Pos: Field rep, Iowa Dept. Pub. Safety, 48; law clerk, 53rd Iowa Gen. Assembly, 49; town treas, Newhall, Iowa, 53-; justice of the peace, Benton Co, Iowa, 56-60; Iowa State Rep, 61-62 & 69- Bus. & Prof. Pos: Attorney-at-Law, 50- Mil. Serv: Entered as Pvt, Air Force, 42, released as 1st Lt, 45, after serv. in 15th Air Force, 44-45; Lt. Col, Res, 45-; Air Medal with three Oak Leaf Clusters; Distinguished Flying Cross. Mem: Benton Co, Iowa State and Am. Bar Asns; Am. Legion; VFW; Farm Bur; Izaak Walton League, Newhall Commercial Club; Boy Scouts. Rel: Lutheran. Mailing Add: 313 Third St. E, Newhall, Iowa 52315.

WEICKER, LOWELL PALMER, JR. R
U.S. Rep, Conn.
b. Paris, France, 5/16/31; s. Lowell P. Weicker and Mary Bickford W; m.

6/13/53 to Marie Louise Godfrey; c. Scot Bickford and Gray Godfrey. Educ: Yale Univ, B.A, 53; Univ. Va, LL.B, 58; Phi Gamma Delta; Phi Alpha Delta. Polit. & Govt. Pos: Conn. State Rep, 62-68; First Selectman, Greenwich, 63-67; U.S. Rep, Fourth Cong. Dist, Conn, 69- Bus. & Prof. Pos: Partner, Nickerson, Weicker, Talcott & Cohen, Greenwich, Conn. Mem: Greenwich, Conn. and Am. Bar Asns; Exchange Club; Greenwich Coun. Boy Scouts. Rel: Episcopal. Legal Res: Round Hill Rd, Greenwich, Conn. 06830. Mailing Add: Room 1007, Longworth House Office Bldg, Washington, D.C. 20515.

WEIDEMEYER, C. MAURICE D
b. Hebbville, Md, 10/22/06; married. Educ: John Hopkins Univ; Columbus Univ. Sch. of Law, LL.B, M.P.L, LL.M, 36. Polit. & Govt. Pos: Cmnr. land off, Annapolis, Md, 51; trial magistrate, 51-52; Md. State Del, 63-67; del, Md. Constitutional Conv, 67-68. Bus. & Prof. Pos: Beach operator and corp. pres. Mil. Serv: Army. Mem: Am, Md. and Anne Arundel Co. Bar Asns; Elks; Moose; Shrine; Tall Cedars of Lebanon; Am. Legion; Annapolis Yacht Club. Mailing Add: 236 Main St, Annapolis, Md. 21401.

WEIDENBAUM, MURRAY LEW R
Asst. Secy. of the Treas. for Econ. Policy
b. Bronx, N.Y, 2/10/27; s. David Weidenbaum and Rose Warshaw W; m. 6/13/54 to Phyllis Green; c. Susan, James and Laurie. Educ: City Col. N.Y, B.B.A, 48; Columbia Univ, M.A, 49; Princeton Univ, Banbury fel, 52-54, Ph.D, 58; Omicron Delta Epsilon. Polit. & Govt. Pos: Jr. economist, N.Y. State Dept. of Labor, 48-49; fiscal economist, U.S. Bur. of the Budget, Wash. D.C, 49-57; mem, Bus. Research Adv. Coun, U.S. Bur. of Labor Statist, 59-63; mem, Research Adv. Coun, Wash. State Dept. of Commerce and Econ. Develop, 60-63; mem, panel of econ. consult, U.S. Arms Control and Disarmament Agency, Wash, D.C, 61-62; mem, Task Force on Inventory Fluctuations and Econ. Stabilization, Joint Econ. Cmt, 62; mem, President's Cmt. on the U.S. Dept. of Labor Fiftieth Anniversary Year, 62; exec. secy, President's Cmt. on the Econ. Impact of Defense and Disarmament, 64; mem, Independent Study Bd. and chmn, Tech. Adv. Cmt, U.S. Dept. of Commerce, 67; Asst. Secy. of the Treas. for Econ. Policy, 69- Bus. & Prof. Pos: Sr. opers. analyst, Gen. Dynamics Corp, Ft. Worth, Tex, 57-58; corporate economist, Boeing Co, Seattle, Wash, 58-63; sr. economist, Stanford Research Inst, Menlo Park, Calif, 63-64. Publ: The Modern Public Sector, Basic Books, Inc, 69; 'The Timing of the Economic Impact of Government Spending,' Nat. Tax J, 3/59; 'Arms and the American Economy,' Am. Econ. Rev, 5/68. Mem: Charter mem, Nat. Asn. Bus. Economists; Am. Econ. Asn; Am. Statist. Asn; Nat. Tax Asn; Regional Sci. Asn; Conf. of Bus. Economists; Nat. Economists' Club (bd. dirs). Rel: Jewish. Legal Res: 568 Bedford Ave, University City, Mo. 63130. Mailing Add: 124 Grafton St, Chevy Chase, Md. 20015.

WEIDNER, CHARLES RICHARD D
Mem, Exec. Cmt, Calif. State Dem. Cent. Cmt.
b. Minneapolis, Minn, 10/11/18; s. Peter C. Weidner and Lillian Halbe W; m. 8/16/40 to Diane Glantz; c. Susan, Janet and Linda. Educ: Univ. Minn, B.A, 40. Polit. & Govt. Pos: Mem, Exec. Cmt, Calif. State Dem. Cent. Cmt, 64-, Health Rev. and Prog. Coun, State of Calif, 66-; chmn, Contra Costa Co. Dem. Cent. Cmt, 64- Bus. & Prof. Pos: Pres, Charles R. Weidner Co, Calif, 56- Mem: Exec. Bd, Health Facilities Planning Asn, Contra Costra Co, 63-; Nat. Found. Health, Welfare and Pension Plans; West. Pension Conf; Lions. Rel: Unitarian. Mailing Add: 41 Viking Drive, Pleasant Hill, Calif. 94523. (1967)

WEIDNER, MARVIN DETWEILER R
Pa. State Rep.
b. Telford, Pa, 8/29/11; s. William R. Weidner and Alverda H. Detweiler W; m. 8/31/35 to Mary Elyonta Breece; c. Kurt S. Educ: Pa. State Univ. Exten, real estate, 64-65 and appraising, 65-66. Polit. & Govt. Pos: Tax collector, Borough of Telford, Pa, 46-63; mem, Bucks Co. Rep. Exec. Cmt, 61-; treas, Bucks Co, 64-66; Pa. State Rep, 67- Bus. & Prof. Pos: Chief clerk, Norfolk & West. Rwy. Co, 43-53; gen. agent, Winston-Salem Southbound Rwy. Co, 53-63. Mem: MacCalla Lodge 596, F&AM; Telford Volunteer Fire Co; Lions; C. of C. Rel: Indian Creek United Church of Christ. Mailing Add: 21 South Hamilton St, Telford, Pa. 18969.

WEIKEL, EVELYN JANE R
b. Cheyenne, Wyo, 8/30/14; d. Dr. Carlton Byford, Frank and Carrie Trout Anderson F; m. 1/5/36 to Karl Frederick Weikel; c. William Carlton. Educ: Comnock Col, 32-34; Southwest. Univ, 35; Phi Beta Epsilon. Polit. & Govt. Pos: Mem, Clark Co. Rep. Cent. Cmt, Nev, 54-; orgn. chmn, Nev. Fedn. of Rep. Women, 60-65 and second v.pres, 62-65; pres, Nel-Ser Rep. Women's Club, 62-67; life mem, Young Rep; mem, Nev. State Rep. Platform and Finance Cmts, 64-66 and Nev. State Rep. Cent. Exec. Cmt, 64-68; Rep. Nat. Committeewoman, Nev, 64-68; mem. resolutions cmt, Rep. West. Conf, 65. Bus. & Prof. Pos: Spec. dep, Clark Co. Sheriff's Off, Nev, 52-; chmn, Clark Co. Beef Promotion, 58-; secy-treas, Searchlight Property Corp, 60-64 and secy, 64- Mem: Bd. dirs, Clark Co. Polio Found, 58-64; pres, Clark Co. Civil Defense Women's Orgn, 58-; life mem, Nat. Rifle Asn; Nev. Cowbelles; Am. Nat. Cowbelles; Nat. Sheriff's Asn; Clark Co. Sheriff Asn; Job's Daughters; Pac. Coast Club; Capital Hill Club. Rel: Episcopal. Mailing Add: YKL Ranch, Searchlight, Nev. 89046. (1967)

WEIKER, BRYCE LAMAR D
Mem, Ohio State Dem. Exec. Cmt.
b. Republic, Ohio, 1/17/21; s. Ai Levi Weiker and Nona Cook W; m. 5/3/43 to Fern Eileen Vogt; c. Judith (Mrs. Watson) and Terry. Educ: Ohio State Univ, 2 years; Alpha Gamma Rho. Polit. & Govt. Pos: Mem. bd. of educ, Republic, Ohio, 50-62; mem, Seneca Co. Dem. Exec. Cmt, 58-, chmn, 66-; mem, State Bd. of Educ, Ohio, 62-; mem, Ohio State Dem. Exec. Cmt, 69- Bus. & Prof. Pos: Self-employed farmer, 45-47; artificial breeding serviceman, Noba Inc, Tiffin, Ohio, 46-51, Holstein sire selector, 51-61, supvr. servicemen, 61-65 and gen. sales mgr, 65- Mil. Serv: Entered as Pvt, Army, 42, released as T/Sgt, 45, after serv. in Hq, Asian Theatre, 44-45; Theatre Decorations. Publ: Numerous articles for trade papers, 56- Mem: Dairy Shrine Club; Ohio Dairyman's Asn; Lions; Am. Legion; Grange; Farm Bur; Holstein-Friesian Asn. Hon. State Farmer Degree, Ohio Future Farmers of Am. Rel: Protestant. Mailing Add: R.R. 2, Republic, Ohio 44867.

WEIL, SIDNEY, JR. D
Co-Chmn, Hamilton Co. Dem. Party, Ohio
b. Cincinnati, Ohio, 9/12/26; s. Sidney Weil and Ida Ackerman W; m. 9/9/50 to Dorothy Louise Coomer; c. Rex and Bruce. Educ: Univ. Cincinnati, 46-48; LL.B, 50; Order of the Coif; Phi Delta Phi. Polit. & Govt. Pos: Chmn, Hamilton Co. Dem. Exec. Cmt, 64-68; mem, Hamilton Co. Bd. Elec, 66-; del, Dem. Nat. Conv, 68; co-chmn, Hamilton Co. Dem. Party, 68- Bus. & Prof. Pos: Lectr, law, Univ. Cincinnati Col. Law, 51-67; partner, Nichols, Wood, Marx & Ginter, Attorneys, 60-67; partner, Beckman, Lavercombe, Fox & Weil, Attorneys, 67- Mil. Serv: Entered as Pvt, Army, 44, released as S/Sgt, 46, after serv. in 106th Inf. Div, ETO, 45-46. Mem: Judicial Selection Cmt, Cincinnati Bar Asn; trustee, Commun. Chest; Hamilton Co. Welfare Adv. Bd; dir, Planned Parenthood Asn. Legal Res: 8 Belsaw Place, Cincinnati, Ohio 45220. Mailing Add: 1714 First National Bank Bldg, Cincinnati, Ohio 45202.

WEILE, ERIC IGNATZ D
Md. State Del.
b. Germany, 9/29/07; s. Louis Weile and Hedwig Michaelis W; m. 9/28/48 to Helen Alice Grevinsky; c. Spencer Girard and Lisa Gail. Educ: Handelshochschule, Berlin, Germany, 20. Polit. & Govt. Pos: Md. State Del, 66- Publ: Weile's Gazette, 15000 Ed, semi-annually, 40- Mem: Pres, Optimist Int, Langley Park, Md, 58; Pres, Langley Park, C. of C, 60; B'nai B'rith (pres, 68-69); Restaurant Asn. Greater Wash; Argo Lodge (pres); Grange; Dem. Clubs. Man of the Year, B'nai B'rith. Rel: Jewish. Mailing Add: 921 Ray Rd, Hyattsville, Md. 20783.

WEINBERGER, CASPAR WILLARD R
State Dir. of Finance, Calif.
b. San Francisco, Calif, 8/18/17; s. Herman Weinberger and Cerise Carpenter Hampson W; m. 8/16/42 to Jane Dalton; c. Arlin Cerise (Mrs. Richard Paterak) and Caspar Willard, Jr. Educ: Harvard Col, A.B, 38; Harvard Law Sch, LL.B, 41; Phi Beta Kappa. Polit. & Govt. Pos: Mem. of Assembly, Calif. State Legis, 21st Assembly Dist, 52-58; v.chmn, Calif. Rep. State Cent. Cmt, 60-62, chmn, 62-64; chmn, Cmn. on Calif. State Govt. Orgn. and Econ, 67-68; state dir. of finance, Calif, 68- Bus. & Prof. Pos: Former staff book reviewer, San Francisco Chronicle and San Francisco Mag, Calif; law clerk, U.S. Circuit Judge William E. Orr, Ninth Circuit Court of Appeals, San Francisco, 45-47; attorney-at-law, Heller, Ehrman, White & McAuliffe, 47-, partner, 59- Mil. Serv: Entered as Pvt, Army, 41, released as Capt, 45, after serv. in 41st Inf. Div, Pac. Theatre and on Intel. Staff of Gen. Douglas MacArthur; Bronze Star. Publ: Semi-weekly column on Calif. state govt. in numerous Calif. newspapers, 59-68; moderator, 'Profile: Bay Area,' weekly local pub. affairs prog, KQED TV, San Francisco, Calif. Mem: Am. Bar Asn; State Bar of Calif; bd. trustees, Bay Area Educ. TV Asn; Boy Scouts (exec. bd, San Francisco Coun); League of Women Voters of Calif, Inc. (adv. cmt); bd. trustees, Mech. Inst; Nat. Citizens Cmt. for Pub. TV, N.Y; San Francisco Health Facilities Planning Cmt; bd. gov, San Francisco Heart Asn; YMCA (gov. mem, San Francisco). Rel: Episcopal; Vestryman, St. Luke's Episcopal Church, San Francisco, Calif. Mailing Add: State Capitol, Sacramento, Calif. 95814.

WEINER, CHARLES R. D
b. Philadelphia, Pa, 6/27/23; s. Max Weiner and Bessie Chairney W; m. 8/24/44 to Edna G. Gerber; c. William, Carole and Harvey. Educ: Univ. Pa, A.B, 47; Temple Univ, LL.B, 47. Polit. & Govt. Pos: Asst. Dist. Attorney, Phila. Co, Pa, 52; Pa. State Sen, Seventh Dist, 52-67, Minority Leader, 59-60 & 63-64 and Majority Leader, 61-62, Pa. State House of Rep; mem, Pres. Adv. Cmn. on Intergovt. Rels, chmn, Pa. Cmn. on Interstate Coop. and v.chmn, Joint State Govt. Cmn; mem, Pa. State Bd. Pub. Welfare. Bus. & Prof. Pos: Attorney-at-Law, Weiner, Basch, Lehrer & Cheskin; dir, Phila. Psychiat. Center and Wharton Center. Mil. Serv: Entered as Seaman, Navy, 42, released as Lt, 46. Mem: Am, Pa. and Phila. Bar Asns; Co. Bd. Law Exam; v.chmn, Cmt. for Elimination Co. Restriction; bd. trustees and exec. cmts, Fedn. Jewish Charities and Allied Jewish Appeal Phila; Phila. Tribune Charities; YMCA; Commun. Chest; Big Brothers Asn; Crime Prevention Asn; Coun, Jewish Fedn. Welfare Funds, Inc. Phila. Fel. Award; various awards from civic and commun. agencies and orgn. Legal Res: 3214 Ridge Ave, Philadelphia, Pa. 19132. Mailing Add: 1420 Walnut St, 11th Floor, Philadelphia, Pa. 19102. (1967)

WEINER, MAURICE D
b. Brooklyn, N.Y, 8/18/30; s. Charles Weiner and Esther Brand W; single. Educ: City Col. N.Y, B.B.A, 51; New Sch. Social Research, grad courses, 53-55; pres, Econ. Club; ed, Bus. and Econ. Rev. Polit. & Govt. Pos: 56th Assembly Dist. chmn, Roybal for Cong, Los Angeles, Calif, 62; precinct orgn. chmn, Bradley for Coun, 63; statewide officer, Calif. Dem. Coun, 64-67; exec. bd. mem, Jones for Los Angeles Bd. Educ, 65; exec. dir, Calif. for Liberal Representation, 65-69; dep. to city councilman, City Council, Los Angeles, 65-; campaign mgr, Nova for Los Angeles Bd. Educ, 67; alternate del, Dem. Nat. Conv, 68; mem. exec. cmt. Peace & Equality Slate, Calif. Dem. Party, 68; campaign mgr, Bradley for Mayor, Los Angeles, 69. Bus. & Prof. Pos: Asst. housing mgr, N.Y.C. Housing Authority, 50's; methods and planning analyst, Citizens Nat. Bank, Los Angeles, Calif, 60-62; admin. asst, Los Angeles City Schs, 62-65, admin. analyst, 65. Mem: Oxford Theater (bd. dirs); NAACP; Am. Civil Liberties Union. Rel: Jewish. Mailing Add: 1129 W. 27th St, Los Angeles, Calif. 90007.

WEINER, PHYLLIS D
Committeewoman, 23rd Rep. Dist. Dem. Party, Del.
b. Bronx, N.Y, 7/1/29; d. William Futterman and Anna Resnick F; m. 7/10/48 to Samuel Weiner; c. Eric and Jeffrey. Educ: L.I. Univ, 52; Ind. Univ, 60-61. Polit. & Govt. Pos: Dist. capt, Dem. Club, N.Y, 50-59; committeewoman, 23rd Rep. Dist. Dem. Party, Del, 64-, chairwoman, 68; secy, 14th Rep. Dist. Dem. Party, 67-68; del, Dem. Nat. Conv, 68. Mem: Girl Scout Leader; Nat. Coun. Jewish Women; Hadassah. Green Cord Award for five years good serv. in scouting. Rel: Jewish. Mailing Add: 2210 Gheen Rd, Wilmington, Del. 19808.

WEINER, STEPHEN S. D
b. Morristown, N.J, 6/11/39; s. Elizabeth Berger, father deceased; m. 8/23/64 to Patricia Shields. Educ: Univ. Calif, Los Angeles, B.S, 61, M.S. in eng, 63; Tau Beta Pi; life mem, Eng. Soc. of Univ. Calif, Los Angeles. Polit.

& Govt. Pos: Admin. Asst. to U.S. Rep. James C. Corman, 64-68. Bus. & Prof. Pos: Intern in Pub. Affairs, Coro Found, 63-64. Mem: Am. Inst. of Planners; Am. Civil Liberties Union. Rel: Jewish. 1967 Legal Res: Canoga Park, Calif. No mailing address available. (1967)

WEINGAND, ALVIN CARL D
b. North Platte, Nebr, 6/11/04; s. Claude O. Weingand and Augusta Tanger W; div; c. Christopher. Educ: Univ. of Calif, Berkeley, A.B, 26; Artus; Alpha Sigma Phi. Polit. & Govt. Pos: Mem, Co. Planning Cmn, Calif, 38-42; mem, Montecito Sanit. Dist. and Co. Dem. Cent. Cmt; chmn, Montecito Fire Cmn; Calif. State Sen, until 67. Bus. & Prof. Pos: Owner, San Usidro Ranch, Calif, 35-65. Mil. Serv: Entered as Lt, Navy, 42, released as Lt. Comdr, 45, after serv. in Supply Corps, S.Pac, 43-45. Mem: Dir, 19th Dist. Agr. Asn; Valley Club; Coral Casino; Montecito Country Club. Rel: Lutheran. Mailing Add: 900 San Usidro Lane, Santa Barbara, Calif. 93103.

WEINREB, ILENE SPACK D
City Councilman, Hayward, Calif.
b. Kansas City, Mo, 11/9/31; d. Henry Mitchell Spack and Mary Botwinik S; m. 8/21/51 to Marvin Seymour Weinreb, M.D; c. Rachel, Deborah and Judith. Educ: Univ. Chicago, M.A, 53; Univ. Calif, Berkeley. Polit. & Govt. Pos: Asst. dir. housing, Off. of Econ. Opportunity, Eden Twp, Calif, 66-67; committeewoman, Calif. State Dem. Party, 67 & 68; city councilman, Hayward, Calif, 68- Mem: League of Women Voters; Am. Asn. of Univ. Women; Alameda-Contra Costa Auxiliary, Medical Society; B'nai B'rith. Rel: Jewish. Mailing Add: 30504 Prestwick Ave, Hayward, Calif. 94544.

WEINSTEIN, JACK M. R
b. New York, N.Y, 6/29/36; s. Martin Weinstein and Helen Lax W; m. 7/26/64 to Doran Polikoff; c. Loren Gay and Justin David. Educ: N.Y. Univ, B.S, 56, N.Y. Univ. Grad. Sch. Bus. Admin, M.B.A, 58 and J.D, 60; Phi Alpha Kappa; Pi Lambda Phi. Polit. & Govt. Pos: Rep. nominee, U.S. House Rep, 68; law secy, Supreme Court, Queens Co, N.Y, 69- Bus. & Prof. Pos: Partner, Black, Brownstein and Weinstein, Attorneys, 61-; counsel, Queensboro Soc. Prev. Cruelty to Children, 67-; counsel, Am. Mensa Cmt, 67- Mem: Asn. Bar City New York; N.Y. State and Queens Co. Bar Asns; Am. and N.Y. State Trial Lawyers Asns; bd. dirs, United Cerebral Palsy of Queens; Mensa. Rel: Jewish. Legal Res: 140-09 69th Rd, Flushing, N.Y. 11367. Mailing Add: 90-50 Parsons Blvd, Jamaica, N.Y. 11432.

WEINSTEIN, MOSES M. D
N.Y. State Assemblyman
b. New York, N.Y; m. to Muriel M. Marshall; c. Jonathan, Peter and Jeremy. Educ: Brooklyn Col; Brooklyn Law Sch, LL.B. Polit. & Govt. Pos: N.Y. State Assemblyman, 58-, majority leader, 65-, speaker of the assembly, 68-69; exec, John F. Kennedy Regular Dem. Club; chmn, exec. cmt, Queens Co. Dem. Orgn, 62; nominee, N.Y. Supreme Court. Bus. & Prof. Pos: Attorney-at-Law. Mil. Serv: Army, ETO. Mem: Coun, United Serv. for New Ams; League for Retarded Children; Pride of Judea Children's Home; Kew Garden Hills Little League; treas, Queens Co. Multiple Sclerosis Soc; Queens Childrens Rehabilitation Serv; Mid-Queens Child Guild Center. Mailing Add: 138-33 78th Dr, Kew Gardens Hills, Flushing, N.Y. 11367.

WEINTRAUB, CLAIRE D
b. Miami, Fla, 6/1/05; d. Isidor Cohen and Ida Hirsh C; m. 10/16/28 to Sydney Louis Weintraub; c. Albert Laurence. Educ: Fla. State Univ, 2 years; Univ. Miami, B.A, 28, hon. L.H.D; Delta Phi Epsilon. Polit. & Govt. Pos: Del, Dem. Nat. Conv, 56, 64 & 68. Mem: Pres, Dade Co. Citizens Safety Coun; chmn, Practical Nurse Bd. Voc. Sch; past pres. and trustee, Museum of Sci. Outstanding Citizen's Award. Rel: Jewish. Mailing Add: 3030 Brickell Ave, Miami, Fla. 33129.

WEIR, DAVID LEROY R
Co. Engr, Ashtabula Co, Ohio
b. Ashtabula, Ohio, 1/23/37; s. Kenneth J. Weir and Zada Gray W; m. 7/31/60 to Judith Ellen Reed; c. Jack Kenneth and Wesley Reed. Educ: Ohio North. Univ, B.S.C.E, 59; Kappa Kappa Psi; Phi Mu Delta. Polit. & Govt. Pos: Asst. co. sanit. engr, Ashtabula Co, Ohio, 62-65, co. engr, 65-, co. sanit. engr, 65-66 & 69-; alternate del, Rep. Nat. Conv, 68; pres, Young Rep, Ashtabula Co, Ohio, 68-69. Bus. & Prof. Pos: Partner, Weir & Weir Eng. & Surv, 59-62. Mil. Serv: Entered as Pvt, Army, 59, released as Sgt. E-5, 65, after serv. in Co. E, 308th Engr. Bn, 83rd Inf. Mem: Rotary; C. of C; Boy Scouts; United Appeal; United Commun. Serv; Ashtabula Co. Twp. Trustees and Clerks Asn; Northeast. Ohio Co. Sanit. Engrs. Asn; bd. dirs, Co. Engrs. Asn. of Ohio; DeMolay (Chevalier). Rel: Episcopal. Mailing Add: 106 N. Market St, Jefferson, Ohio 44047.

WEIR, JULIAN PAUL R
Chmn, House Dist. Six Rep. Party, Alaska
b. Ballinger, Tex, 8/15/23; s. Joseph Elmer Weir and Lola Agnes Ross W; m 3/10/52 to Sumike Inoue; c. Joseph Paul. Educ: N.Mex. Col. Agr. & Mech. Arts, 2 years. Polit. & Govt. Pos: Alternate-del, Rep. Nat. Conv, 68; Rep. precinct committeeman, Glennallen, Alaska, 68-; chmn, House Dist. Six Rep. Party, 68- Bus. & Prof. Pos: Mechanic, Pan Am. World Airways, San Francisco, Calif, 53-60; Lineman, Alaska Commun. System, U.S. Air Force, Glennallen, Alaska, 63-67; owner and operator, Glennallen Texaco Serv. Sta, 67- Mil. Serv: Entered as A/S, Naval Res, 41, released as Aircraft Mechanic 1/C, 45; T/Sgt, Marine Corps Res, 47-53, serv. in VMR 152, Japan, Korea, Hawaii and Calif; Distinguished Flying Cross. Mem: White House Conf. on Children and Youth; Am. Legion (Past Comdr, Glennallen Post 27, active in Legion affairs, currently); Nat. Rifleman Asn. Rel: Christian. Mailing Add: Mile 182 Glenn Highway, Box 275, Glennallen, Alaska 99588.

WEIS, JOHN HARVEY R
Ohio State Rep.
Married; c. Two. Educ: Ohio Univ, B.A. Polit. & Govt. Pos: Mayor, Lancaster, Ohio, 5 terms; Ohio State Rep, 63- Bus. & Prof. Pos: Pres, Lancaster Beauty Supply, Inc. Mailing Add: 130 Briarwood Ct, Lancaster, Ohio 43130.

WEISENBERG, WEBB R
Chmn, Lawrence Co. Rep. Party, S.Dak.
b. Lead, S.Dak, 11/9/23; s. Webb Weisenberg and Lottie Lewis W; m. 6/7/47 to Maxine Lorraine Smith; c. Terry. Educ: Lead High Sch. Polit. & Govt. Pos: Chmn, Lawrence Co. Rep. Party, S.Dak, 64- Bus. & Prof. Pos: Asst. recreation dir, Homestake Mining Co, currently. Mil. Serv: Entered as Pvt, Army, released as 1st Sgt, Inf, Italy, 45; Bronze Star; Italian Campaign Ribbons. Mem: Am. Legion; VFW. Rel: Methodist. Legal Res: 204 Anderson, Lead, S.Dak. 57754. Mailing Add: Homestake Club, Lead, S.Dak. 57754. (1967)

WEISENBORN, CLARA ELIZABETH R
Ohio State Sen.
b. Dayton, Ohio, 2/9/07; d. William J. Nies and Edna Clara Hartung N; m. 8/23/23 to Herbert Edison Weisenborn; c. Donald Harold and Howard Ellwood. Educ: Bus. Col; Delta Kappa Gamma. Polit. & Govt. Pos: Ohio State Rep, Montgomery Co, 53-66; Ohio State Sen, 67- Bus. & Prof. Pos: Daily columnist, Dayton J. Herald, 42-, garden ed, 43-; v.pres, Imperial Bank, Vandalia, currently. Mem: Bus. & Prfnl. Women; extension chmn, Altruse Int; pres, Dayton Altruse Club; Eastern Star; Ladies of 89; Am. Legion; Ohio Soc. for Blindness: pres, Ohio State Univ. Club. Women of the Year Award, Bus. & Prfnl. Women, 62; Rep. Women of the Year, 65. Rel: Lutheran. Mailing Add: 4940 Chambersburg Rd, Dayton, Ohio 45424.

WEISENSEL, RUSSEL R. R
Wis. State Assemblyman
b. Columbus, Wis, 12/23/31; s. August J. Weisensel and Julia Schmidt W; m. 4/24/54 to Mary E. Devine; c. David R, Daniel J, Kathleen A, Maureen A. and Brian L. Polit. & Govt. Pos: Wis. State Assemblyman, currently. Bus. & Prof. Pos: Farmer. Mem: Nat. 4-H Club Congress, 51; K. of C; Madison Area Retardation Coun; Help Educ. the Emotionally Disturbed; chmn, Dane Co. Day Care Bd. Wis. Handicapped Person of the Year, 68. Rel: Catholic. Mailing Add: Rt. 2, Twin Lane, Sun Prairie, Wis. 53590.

WEISENSTINE, ERNEST MOORE D
Mem, Guernsey Co. Dem. Cent. Cmt, Ohio
b. Cambridge, Ohio, 11/30/91; s. McClelland Weisenstine and Mary S. Burris W; m. 9/3/13 to Celia Margaret Stewart; c. Savonna (Mrs. Cox) and Ernest, Jr. Educ: Cambridge Bus. Col, 1 year. Polit. & Govt. Pos: Mem, Guernsey Co. Dem. Cent. Cmt, Ohio, 40-; clerk, Cambridge Twp, Ohio, 60-; chmn, Ohio Dem. State Cent. Cmt, 66-67. Bus. & Prof. Pos: Grocer, 13-21 & 46-57; salesman, 21-46. Mem: Odd Fellows. Grand Decoration of Chivalry. Rel: Protestant. Mailing Add: 1932 Wheeling Ave, Cambridge, Ohio 43725.

WEISGERBER, WILLIAM DENNY R
Councilman, Milpitas, Calif.
b. Bend, Ore, 5/5/30; s. Sherman Nash Weisgerber and Olive Edith Denny W; m. 2/12/49 to Marianne Tillery; c. Pamela Kay and William Denny, Jr. Educ: Boise Jr. Col, 48-49 & 53-54; San Jose State Col, 54-55; Univ. Calif, Los Angeles, 64; Life Underwriters Training Course Grad. Courses I, II & III, 68-69. Polit. & Govt. Pos: Councilman, Milpitas, Calif, 61 & 66-; inter-city coun. rep, Santa Clara Co, Calif, 61-; rep, Asn. Bay Area Govt, 61-; chmn, Mayors Cmt, Santa Clara Co, 62-63; mem, Milpitas Co. Water Bd, 62-64; mayor, Milpitas, Calif, 62-66; mem, Santa Clara Transportation Cmt, 63-, and chmn, 68-; mem, Local Agency Formation Cmn, 64- and chmn, 68-; assoc. mem, Calif. Rep. State Cent. Cmt, 66-68, mem, 68-; v.chmn, Santa Clara Planning Policy Cmt, 68 and chmn, 69-; mem, League of Calif. Cities Annexation Cmt, 69-; chmn, Santa Clara Co. Sports Arena Conv. Cmt, 69- Bus. & Prof. Pos: Cert. Prosthodontist and orthodontist, Am. Bd. for Certification, 61-; ins. agent, State Farm Ins. Co, 65- Mil. Serv: Entered as Pvt, Marine Corps, 49, released as S/Sgt, 53, after serv. as Platoon Sgt, Seventh Marines, First Marine Div, Korean Theatre, 53; Navy Cross; Purple Heart; Presidential Unit, Navy Unit and Korean Presidential Unit Citations; Korean, Nat. Defense and UN Serv. Medals. Mem: Elks; life mem, DAV; VFW; Marine Corps League; Rotary (past pres); Toastmasters Club (past pres); C. of C; Businessman's Asn, Milpitas, Calif. Named Area and Dist. Speech Winner, 68. Rel: Presbyterian. Mailing Add: 195 Casper St, Milpitas, Calif. 95035.

WEISL, EDWIN L, JR. D
b. New York, N.Y, 10/17/29; s. Edwin Louis Weisl, Sr. and Alice Todriff W; m. to Reyna Lander; c. Angela. Educ: Yale Univ, 47-51; Columbia Law Sch, 53-56. Polit. & Govt. Pos: Asst. spec. counsel, Senate Preparedness Investigation Subcmt, 57-59; del, Dem. Nat. Conv, 60, 64 & 68; mem, N.Y. Co. Dem. Cmt, 60-; campaign dir, N.Y. State Dem. Cmt, 64; asst. attorney gen, Dept. of Justice, 65-69. Bus. & Prof. Pos: Attorney, Simpson, Thacher & Bartlett, 56-65, partner, 64-65 & 69- Mil. Serv: Entered as Ensign, Navy, 51, released as Lt.(jg), 53, after serv. in Korea and as Asst. Spec. Cong. Liaison Officer, Navy Dept, Wash, 53; Korean, UN and Am. Defense Serv. Ribbons; South Korean Presidential Unit Citation. Mem: Am, Fed, N.Y. State and D.C. Bar Asns; Asn. of the Bar of the City of New York. Rel: Jewish. Legal Res: 2411 California St. N.W, Washington, D.C. 20008. Mailing Add: Suite 613, 1735 Eye St. N.W, Washington, D.C. 20006.

WEISS, PETER D
b. Vienna, Austria, 12/8/25; s. Emil Weiss and Paula Hahn W; m. 6/17/56 to Cora Rubin; c. Judith, Tamara and Daniel. Educ: St. John's Col, B.A, 49; Yale Law Sch, LL.B, 52. Polit. & Govt. Pos: Chmn, Manhattan Adv. Coun, N.Y. State Div. of Human Rights, 65-68, chmn, Bronx Adv. Coun, 68-; chmn, For. Policy Coun. of N.Y. Dem, 66-68; mem, Gov. Cmt. to Rev. Laws and Procedures in the Area of Human Rights, 67-68; del, Dem. Nat. Conv, 68; chmn, Bronx Coalition for a Dem. Alternative, 68; mem. exec. cmt, New Dem. Coalition of N.Y, currently. Bus. & Prof. Pos: Exec. dir, Int. Develop. Placement Asn, N.Y, 52-54; assoc, Langner, Parry, Card & Langner, 54-64; partner, 64-69; partner, Weiss, David, Fross & Lehrman, 69- Mil. Serv: Entered as Pvt, Army, 44, released as Sgt, 46, after serv. in Mil. Intel. Serv, U.S, 45-46. Publ: 'The Permanent Sabotage,' Nation, 53; 'Private Investment in French-Speaking Africa,' Rutgers Law Rev, 63; 'Negroes and Jews,' Cong. Bi-Weekly, 67. Mem: N.Y. State Bar; Asn. of the Bar of the City of N.Y.(past chmn, Cmt. on African Law); Am. Bar Asn; Am. and N.Y. Patent Law Asns; past v.chmn, Cmn. on Indust. Property, Int. C. of C; pres, Am. Cmt. on Africa; trustee, Inst. for Policy Studies; gov. coun, Am. Jewish Cong, 66-68, N.Y. Met coun, 66-; pres, Fund for Tomorrow, Inc; dir, Givat Hariva Educ. Found; dir, Nat. Cmt. on Discrimination in Housing; exec. cmt, Nat. Emergency Civil Liberties Cmt. Convicted of Disorderly Conduct in Munic. Court, Chicago for upholding First Amendment rights during Dem. Nat. Conv, 68. Rel: Jewish. Mailing Add: 5022 Waldo Ave, Bronx, N.Y. 10471.

WEISS, SAMUEL ARTHUR D
b. Krotowica, Warsaw, Poland, 4/15/02; s. Israel Weiss and Sadie Golden W; m. 6/29/30 to Jeannette Estelle Hoffman; c. Joy Arlene (Mrs. S.R. Cohen) and James Edgar. Educ: Univ. Pittsburg, 20-21; Duquesne Univ, B.S.B.E, 25; Duquesne Univ. Law Sch, LL.B, 27, J.D, 60; Sigma Alpha Mu. Polit. & Govt. Pos: Pa. State Rep, 35-39; U.S. Rep, Pa, 40-47; Judge, Common Pleas Court, Allegheny Co, Pittsburgh, Pa, 46-67. Bus. & Prof. Pos: Former dep. cmnr, Nat. Prfnl. Football League and referee, 42-54; private law practice. Mem: Lions; Odd Fellows; Eagles; Elks; Allegheny Co. Civic Club; Mason; East. Intercol. Group (official). Outstanding Alumnus Award, Duquesne Univ, 49; Boys Club Outstanding Citizens Award, 50; B'nai B'rith Humanitarian Award, 60; First Hall of Fame, Duquesne Univ, 63; Man of the Year Award, Allegheny Co. Sportsmans Asn. Rel: Jewish. Legal Res: 4601 Fifth Ave, Pittsburgh, Pa. 15213. Mailing Add: 908 City-County Bldg, Pittsburgh, Pa. 15219.

WEISSENBORN, LEE D
Fla. State Sen.
b. St. Louis, Mo, 3/19/29; s. Julius S. Weissenborn and Pauline L. W; m. to Esther Byrd; c. James, Carol and Stephen. Educ: Univ. Fla, B.S, 51, LL.B, 56; Phi Alpha Delta. Polit. & Govt. Pos: Pres, Young Dem. Dade Co, Fla, 57-59; pres, Young Dem, Fla, 59-61; mem, Nat. Cmt. Young Dem. Am, 59-61; del, Dem. Nat. Conv, 60; host chmn, Young Dem. Nat. Conv, 61; Fla. State Rep, 63-66; Fla. State Sen, currently. Bus. & Prof. Pos: Attorney-at-law. Mil. Serv: Marine Corps Res, 51-53, Capt. Mem: Miami-Dade Co. C. of C; Fla, Am. and Dade Co. Bar Asns; Past Comdr, Coral Gables Am. Legion; dir, Hialean-Miami Springs C. of C. Rel: Episcopal. Legal Res: 1850 N.E. 186th St, North Miami Beach, Fla. 33162. Mailing Add: Suite 1112, Ainsley Bldg, 14 N.E. First Ave, Miami, Fla. 33132.

WELCH, BETTY JOAN R
b. Grubbs, Ark, 3/3/36; d. O.R. Roden and Mercedes Ragsdale R; m. 7/25/54 to Billy Van Welch; c. Billy Van, Jr. and Joel Roden. Educ: Ark. State Col, 57. Polit. & Govt. Pos: Del, Nat. Fedn. Rep. Women Biennial Conv, 67; adult adv, Newport TAR, Ark, 67-68; pres, Jackson Co. Rep. and Independent Women's Club, 67-68; White River regional dir, Ark. Fedn. Rep. Women, 68 and mem. bd. dirs, 69-; del. and mem. resolutions cmt, Rep. State Conv, 68; secy. and treas, Jackson Co. Rep. Cmt, 68; alternate del, Rep. Nat. Conv, 68; mem, Gov. Cmn. Status Women, 68-69. Mem: Jackson Co. Saddle Club; Jackson Co. Farm Bur. Rel: Church of Christ. Mailing Add: P.O. Box 27, Auvergne, Ark. 72008.

WELCH, CHARLES, JR. R
Utah State Sen.
b. Leicester, Eng, 5/9/09; s. Charles Welch and Gertrude Parker; m. 8/26/38 to Jane Seare; c. Linda (Mrs. Farrell Bennett), Jacquelyn (Mrs. Grant Davis), Janet (Mrs. Keith Kirkham) and Susan. Educ: Univ. Utah, B.A, 31, Law Sch, J.D, 35. Polit. & Govt. Pos: Utah State Rep, 55-64, speaker, Utah State House Rep, 63-64; Utah State Sen, 65-; pres, West. Conf. Coun. State Govt, 64-65; chmn. Bd. Coun. State Govt, 66-67. Mil. Serv: Utah Nat. Guard. Mem: Am. Bar Asn; Utah State Bar (pres, 64-65); Salt Lake Co. Bar Asn.(pres, 58-59); Sugarhouse Lions Club. Rel: Latter-day Saint. Mailing Add: 1940 Michigan Ave, Salt Lake City, Utah 84108.

WELCH, GORDON DANIEL R
City Councilman, Brown City, Mich.
b. Gladwin, Mich, 2/15/21; s. John Elson Welch and Mary Webb W; m. 5/17/41 to Edna Loraine Jickling; c. Sharon Kay (Mrs. Ronald Cook), Linda D.(Mrs. Ronald Campbell) and George S. Educ: Brown City High Sch, grad, 38. Polit. & Govt. Pos: City councilman, Brown City, Mich, 66-; co-chmn, Harvey for Congress Cmt, 68; finance chmn, Sanilac Co. Rep. Cmt, 67-69, chmn, 69. Bus. & Prof. Pos: Sales mgr, Fruehauf Trailer Co, Saginaw, Mich, 55-58; real-estate broker and land developer. Rel: Methodist. Mailing Add: 7208 Lincoln St, Brown City, Mich. 48416.

WELCH, HAYWARD OLIVER D
b. Preston, Ga, 11/8/35; s. Thomas Russell Welch and Sarah Ann Mainor W; wid. Educ: Ga. State Col, B.B.A. in Acct, M.B.A. in Mgt. and cand. for D.B.A; pres, Beta Alpha Psi and Grad. Club. Polit. & Govt. Pos: Chmn, Young Georgians for Sanders, Fifth Dist; treas, Young Dem. Club Fulton Co; mem, Gov. Carl Sanders' Escort Cmt; off. del, Ga. Dem. Conv, 62; co-chmn, Jefferson-Jackson Day Dinner, 63; alternate del, Dem. Nat. Conv, 64; pres. and treas, Young Dem. Clubs Ga; mem, Gov. Staff; mem. exec. cmt, Ga. Dem. Party; secy, Local Govt. and Revenue Study Cmt. and chmn, subcmt. of three to write cmt. report; asst. state supt. schs; comptroller, DeKalb Co. Dem. Party, Ga; State Planning Officer and Liaison Officer for Land and Water Conserv. Prog, currently; Ga. Rep. on Appalachian Region Cmn, Pub. Land Law Rev. Cmn. and Resources Adv. Bd, currently; Gov. Alternate to Coastal Plains Regional Cmn, currently; Fed. State Rels. Coordinator for Ga, currently. Bus. & Prof. Pos: CPA; consult. to several large firms, 6 years; indust. acct, 2 years; fed. acct, 2 years; consult. in financial mgt. and budgeting in educ, State of Ga, 3 years; asst. prof, Ga. State Col; pres, Empire State Enterprise, Inc, Govt. Research Corp. Am. and Leisure Time Corp. Am; treas, Gr. Atlanta Develop. Corp. Mil. Serv: Entered as Pvt, Army, 55, released as SP-4, 47, after serv. in Finance Corps; Cert. of Achievement for Work in Installing Acct. Control Mgr. Syst. at Ft. McPherson, Ga. Publ: Several articles, manuals and important reports, including Ga. Jaycee Govt. Affairs Manual, U.S. Jaycee Govt. Inspection Manual, First State Orgn. Manual for Young Dem. Clubs Ga. and book for Gov. Conf. on Educ, Georgia's Biggest Investment: Education. Mem: V.pres. and secy-treas, Am. Soc. for Pub. Admin; Am. Inst. CPA; Am. Inst. Execs, Inc; Am. Econ. Asn; Soc. for Adv. Mgt; Am. Asn. Univ. Prof; Systs. and Procedures Asn; Am. Acct. Asn; Pub. Personnel Asn; v.chmn. govt. acct. cmt, Ga. Soc. Cert. Acct; Am. Acad. Polit. and Soc. Sci; Am. Inst. Mgt; Asn. Sch. Bus. Off; Asn. for Educ. Data Syst; nat. dir. and asst. chmn. govt. affairs, U.S. Jaycees; prog. dir, Jr. Chamber Int. and U.S. Del, World Cong; chmn. govt. affairs and dir. programming, Ga. Jaycees; exec. v.pres, Southeast Atlanta Jaycees; dir, Atlanta Jr. C. of C; co-organizer, Students for Free Enterprise, Inc; treas, Ga. State Booster Club; financial adv, Fayetteville Flat Shoals Civic Asn; drive capt, Ga. Soc. for Crippled Children, Inc. U.S. Merchant Marine Acad. Scholarship; Emory Univ. Grad. Sch. Fel; Ga. State Col. Doctoral Prog. Fel; Ga. Winner, Govt. Affairs Award, U.S. Jr. C. of C; Selected One of Outstanding Young Men of Am. Rel: Baptist. Mailing Add: 215 Piedmont Ave. N.E, Atlanta, Ga. 30312.

WELCH, JOHN L. D
N.H. State Rep.
b. 6/11/16; married; c. two. Educ: Manchester Schs. Polit. & Govt. Pos: N.H. State Rep, currently. Bus. & Prof. Pos: Stephen Spinning Co. Mil. Serv: Army, 3 years. Rel: Catholic. Mailing Add: 39 Ashland St, Manchester, N.H. 03104. (1967)

WELCH, LOUIE D
Mayor, Houston, Tex.
b. Lockney, Tex, 12/9/18; s. Gilford E. Welch and Nora Shackelford W; m. 12/17/40 to Ida Faye Cure; c. Guy Lynn, Gary Dale, Louis Gilford, Shannon Austin and Tina Joy. Educ: Abilene Christian Col, B.A, magna cum laude, 40. Polit. & Govt. Pos: Councilman-at-Lg, Houston City Coun, Tex, 50-52, 56-62, pres, 58-59; mem, Houston Legis. Cmt, 56-; v.pres, League Tex. Munic, 57-58; mayor, Houston, Tex, 63-; del, Dem. Nat. Conv, 68. Bus. & Prof. Pos: Mem. bd. of dirs, Houston Christian Schs. and Abilene Christian Col; pres, Welch Indust, Inc, Houston, 55-; exec. v.pres, Tex. Gulf Indust, 56-57; pres, Louie Welch & Co, Inc, 62-63. Mem: Tex. Mayors & Councilmens Asns; Tex. Construction Coun.(past mem. exec. bd); Auto Wholesalers of Tex. Mailing Add: Mayor's Office, City Hall, Houston, Tex. 77002. (1967)

WELCH, RODNEY RAY R
Mem, Calif. Rep. State Cent. Cmt.
b. Phillipston, Mass, 1/9/98; s. Albert Franklin Welch and Mary Bosworth W; m. Ruth Zan Crandall; c. June (Mrs. Arnold Doimer), Doris, Gilbert, Rodney Ray, Jr, Dale and Alan. Educ: Phillipston Pub. Sch. number 6, 4 years; Riverbend Pub. Sch, 4 years. Polit. & Govt. Pos: Mem, Calif. Rep. State Cent. Cmt, 68- Bus. & Prof. Pos: Apprentice, Union Twist Drill Co, Athol, Mass, 13-17; toolmaker, Remington Arms, Bridgeport, Conn, 17-18; Goodard & Goodard, Detroit, Mich, 19-20; Gorham Tool Co, 21-25; supt, Morse Counterbox and Tool Co, 25-27; founder, Welch Industs, 27 and pres, currently. Army 'E' Flag for outstanding performance. Rel: Protestant. Mailing Add: P.O. Box 35, Idyllwild, Calif. 92349.

WELCH, RONALD E. D
m. to Serena Lupico; c. two. Educ: Suffolk Univ, A.B. in Polit. Sci. and Suffolk Law Sch, LL.B. Polit. & Govt. Pos: Spec. asst. to city solicitor Haverhill, Mass. Bus. & Prof. Pos: Attorney. Mil. Serv: Army, 2 years. Mem: Former dir, Greater Haverhill Jaycees; radio publicity chmn, Am. Cancer Soc. Crusade, 66. Mailing Add: 88 Carmel Rd, Andover, Mass. 01810.

WELCOME, VERDA FREEMAN D
Md. State Sen.
b. Lake Lure, N.C; d. John Nuborn Freeman and Docia Proctor Freeman; m. 12/21/35 to Henry Cecil Welcome; c. Mary Sue. Educ: Morgan State Col, B.S, 39; N.Y. Univ, M.A, 43. Hon. LL.D, Howard Univ, 68. Polit. & Govt. Pos: Md. State Del, 59-62; Md. State Sen, 63- Mem: Delta Sigma Theta; Baltimore Mus. of Art; Baltimore Urban League; League of Women Voters; Md. Hist. Soc; Md. League of Women Voters; Nat. Order of Women Legislators; NAACP; Nat. Coun. of Negro Women; Women's Coop. League; Am. for Dem. Action; Int. League for Peace and Freedom; Baltimore Chap, Univ. Women; Baltimore Grand Jurors Adv. Group, Inc; Citizens Planning and Housing Cmn; Md. Chap, UN; Baltimore Chap, Multiple Sclerosis Soc. Woman of the Year Award, Women's Auxiliary to the Nat. Med. Asn, 62; Distinguished First Award, Am. Negro Emancipation Centennial Cmn. of Ill, 63; Citation for Outstanding Achievement in Legis. Govt, Delta Sigma Theta, 63; Citation for Significant Contribution in the Field of Polit, Nat. Coun. of Negro Women, 63; Citation for Contributions in the Field of Polit. and Govt, Col. Alumnae Club of the Nat. Asn. of Col. Women, 64; World's Fair Citizenship Day Award for Achievements in Govt. and Polit, League of Women Voters Day, New York's World's Fair, Sept. 17, 64; Citation in Recognition of Outstanding Achievement in the Field of Commun. Serv, Pi Omega Chap, Omegi Psi Phi, 64; Outstanding Achievement Award, The Women of Morgan State Col, 63; The 1965 Medgar Evers Human Rights Award, 23rd Annual Award of the Capital Press, 66; Cert. of Appointment of Hon. Mayor of Braxton Village, Braxton Village Men's Club, 66; 40 Hour Cert. for Vol. Citizens, Cmt. for Voter Registrn, 64; Award for Re-elec. to High Off. on Founder's Day of Lambda Kappa Mu, 67; Plaque, Alumna of the Year, Morgan State Col, Alumni Asn, 67; Commun. Serv. Award, Baltimore Chap, Bus. and Prfnl. Women's Clubs; Cert. of Merit, Baltimore Chap, Howard Univ. Alumni Asn; Distinguished Alumni Citation, Coppin State Teachers Col, Baltimore; Citation to an Outstanding Soror, Baltimore Alumnae Chap, Delta Sigma Theta; Cert. of Merit, Kappa Chap, Iota Phi Lambda; Afro-Am. Newspaper Award, Baltimore; Eighth Annual Emma V. Kelly Achievement Award, Daughters of the Int. Order of World Elks; Plaque, Baltimore Chap, Jack and Jill of Am; Plaque, Achievement Award, Beta Sigma Tau Alumni Chap; Trophy, Fourth Annual Md. Debutante Ball. Rel: Presbyterian. Mailing Add: 2101 Liberty Heights Ave, Baltimore, Md. 21217.

WELDEN, JACQUES ROGER R
Chmn, Contra Costra Co. Rep. Cent. Cmt, Calif.
b. Evanston, Ill, 9/6/27; s. George Claypool Welden and Eleanor Brown W; m. 8/20/50 to Jacquelen Rae Thompson; c. Kathryn Jean, David Roger, Bruce Arthur and Barbara Denise. Educ: Univ. Utah; Univ. Calif, Berkeley; San Francisco Law Sch; Pi Kappa Alpha; Phi Alpha Delta. Polit. & Govt. Pos: Mem, Contra Costra Co. Rep. Cent. Cmt, Calif, 60-, chmn, 64-; mem, Rep. Cong. Adv. Cmt, 64-66; chmn, Legis. Co. Cmnr. Asn. of Calif, 65-66; chmn, Bay Area Co. Chmn, 66. Bus. & Prof. Pos: Sr. Partner, Corbett & Welden, Attorneys, 67- Mil. Serv: Entered as Pvt, Army, 44, released as Cpl, 46; Good Conduct Medal; Am. Theater Ribbon. Mem: Lawyer's Club of San Francisco (bd. dir, 65-, pres, 69); bd. dir, Bar Asn. of San Francisco, 62; pres, Barristers Club, 62; chmn, Sports Youth Coun, Jr. C. of C, 60-61; Am. Bar Asn; Calif. State Bar; Elks Lodge 3, San Francisco; Lions; San Francisco Jr. C. of C; Rep. League; mem. Troop 99 Cmt, Boy Scouts; pres. and chmn. bd. trustees, Arlington Commun. Club, 66-67. Played lead in a number of plays and wrote skits for little theater groups. Rel: United Church of Christ; Mem. endowment cmt, 69. Mailing Add: 38 Avon Rd, Kensington, Calif. 94707.

WELDEN, WILLIAM BIDWELL R
b. New York, N.Y, 1/9/02; s. Reuben William Welden and Alice Louise Bidwell W; m. 4/26/30 to Lillian Walsh. Educ: Yale Col, 23; Univ. Conn; Univ. Hartford; Phi Beta Kappa; Sigma Xi; Yale Water Polo Team. Polit. &

Govt. Pos: Mem, Simsbury Sch. Bd, Conn, 24-29 and Finance Bd, 55-60; Conn. State Rep, 65-67. Bus. & Prof. Pos: Owner, Welden Hardware, 26-58, Welden Farm Equip, 41-56 and Welden Realty, 60-66. Mem: Conn. Hardware Asn. (pres, 50); New Eng. Farm Equip. Dealers Asn.(pres, 52); Choral Club of Hartford; Avon Country Club; AF&AM; Rotary. Yale, Water Polo Team. Rel: Methodist. Legal Res: 100 Farms Village Rd, Simsbury, Conn. 06070. Mailing Add: P.O. Box 553, Simsbury, Conn. 06070.

WELDISHOFER, JAMES R. R
b. Toledo, Ohio, 4/24/29; s. William M. Weldishofer and Adelaide Wieman W; m. 6/28/52 to Ann Cherry; c. Luanna Sue, Jenny Lynn, Sandra Jo and John J. Educ: Toledo Univ, 47-48; Ohio State Univ, B.Sc. in bus. admin, 51; Beta Alpha Psi; Lambda Chi Alpha. Polit. & Govt. Pos: Rep. Precinct Committeeman, Ohio, 61; asst. twp. chmn, Sylvania Twp, Ohio, 63- and trustee, 65-; Ohio State Rep, 67-68. Bus. & Prof. Pos: Indust. acct, Gen. Motors, 51-60; dist. mgr, H&R Block, Inc, 60- Rel: Methodist. Mailing Add: 5635 Mitchaw Rd, Sylvania, Ohio 43560. (1967)

WELDON, JIMMIE DALE D
Tex. State Rep.
b. Port Arthur, Tex, 11/9/28; s. Don E. Weldon, Sr. and Edna Stutes W; m. 2/17/49 to Betty Jane Duplantis; c. Jan Darlene and Julie Danette. Educ: Thomas Jefferson High, Port Arthur, Tex, grad, 47; Int. Correspondence Sch, indust. elec. eng, home study, 52. Polit. & Govt. Pos: City councilman, Port Arthur, Tex, 57-59 and mayor-pro-tem, 58-59; Tex. State Rep, 63- Bus. & Prof. Pos: Pres, Int. Brotherhood of Elec. Workers, Unit 457, Port Arthur, 55-56. Mil. Serv: Entered as Recruit, Tex. Nat. Guard, 48, released as SFC, 53, after serv. in Co. B, 111th Eng, 36th Div. Rel: Protestant. Mailing Add: 3412 Eighth St, Port Arthur, Tex. 77640. (1967)

WELDON, JOHN PHILIP D
Mem, Calif. Dem. State Cent. Cmt.
b. Clare, Mich, 4/19/21; s. William Bruce Weldon and Mary Cedargreen W; m. 2/14/44 to Florence Marie DeClaire; c. Kathleen Marie and Bonnie Jean. Educ: Cabrillo Jr. Col, 65- Polit. & Govt. Pos: Rep. to Cmt. on Polit. Educ, Santa Cruz Cent. Labor Coun, Calif, 63-; mem, Santa Cruz Co. Dem. Cent. Cmt, 64-68; mem, Calif. Dem. State Cent. Cmt, 68- Bus. & Prof. Pos: Apprentice plumber, Santa Cruz and Santa Clara, Calif, 46-51; journeyman plumber, Santa Cruz, 51- Mil. Serv: Entered as A/S, Navy, 40, released as GM 2/C, 46, after serv. in Asiatic-Pac. and Aleutians. Mem: United Asn. of Plumbers and Pipe Fitters of the U.S. and Can; del, Santa Cruz Co. Cent. Labor Coun; Toastmasters Club (treas, 1 year); Moose (past prelate, jr. gov. and gov); Independent Order of Foresters (orator, 1 year); Live Oak Improv. Asn.(pres, $5\frac{1}{2}$ years); VFW. Rel: Protestant. Mailing Add: 217 16th Ave, Santa Cruz, Calif. 95060.

WELDON, WILLIAM KIMBERLY R
Tenn. State Rep.
b. Tulsa, Okla, 6/10/21; s. Henry Cole Weldon and Alice Cecilia Cummings W; m. 6/17/44 to Ann Rudd James; c. Karen Ann, William Kimberly, Jr. and Elizabeth James. Educ: Univ. Okla, 41-42; South. Law Univ, LL.B, 48; Theta Kappa Phi; Ruf Neks; Delta Chi Delta. Polit. & Govt. Pos: Pres, East Memphis Rep. Club, Tenn, 62; mem. steering cmt, Shelby Co. Rep. Party, 62-68, mem. exec. cmt, 62-; Tenn. State Rep, 67-; mem, Legis. Coun, Tenn, 69- Bus. & Prof. Pos: Partner, Adams, James & Weldon, Attorneys, Memphis, Tenn, 54- Mil. Serv: Entered as Aviation Cadet, Navy, 42, served as fighter pilot, Air-Group 4, Pac. Theater, World War II, and as air intel. officer, Korea; Lt. Comdr, Naval Res; Air Medal, twice; Navy Unit Citation; Presidential Unit Citation, 4 times; Korean Presidential Unit Citation. Mem: Memphis and Shelby Co. and Tenn. Bar Asns; K. of C; Naval Res. Asn; Mil. Order of World Wars; Elks; VFW; Serra, Int. Rel: Catholic. Mailing Add: 90 S. Mendenhall, Memphis, Tenn. 38117.

WELIN, BOYD PRESCOTT R
b. Fullerton, Calif, 3/7/04; s. John Emil Welin and Maude Eva Tower W; m. 5/5/34 to Elsie Irene Davis. Educ: Univ. South. Calif, Ph.G, 23, B.S, 27; Blue Key; Phi Delta Chi; Sigma Sigma; Skull and Dagger. Polit. & Govt. Pos: Mem. bd. dirs, Pasadena, Calif, 61-68, chmn. and mayor, 66-68. Bus. & Prof. Pos: Pres, Welin Sater Co, 37-; v.pres. and treas, Brown & Welin, Prescription Pharmacists, 46-67, pres, 67- Mil. Serv: Entered as 1st Lt, Army, 42, released as Maj, 46, after serv. in Med. Admin. Corps, Exec. Off. Port Med. Supply Off, San Francisco Port Embarkation; Asiatic Pac. Theatre Ribbon; Army Commendation Citation. Publ: Excerpts published in Am. Finance Officers J, 66 and Proc. of Nat. Air Pollution Meeting, Wash, D.C, 1967. Mem: Am. Pharmaceutical Asn; Univ. Club; Am. Legion; pres, Gen. Alumni Asn, Univ. South. Calif, 66-67. First Hon. Alumnus Award, Sch. of Pharm, Univ. South. Calif; Hon. Life Membership, C. of C, Pasadena, Calif; resolution for substantial contribution to local govt, particularly Pasadena, Calif. State Senate. Rel: Protestant. Legal Res: 939 Arden Rd, Pasadena, Calif. 91106. Mailing Add: 64 S. Lake Ave, Pasadena, Calif. 91101.

WELLER, CHESTER E. 'BUCK' R
Mem, Canadian Co. Rep. Exec. Cmt, Okla.
b. Gotebo, Okla, 1/17/07; s. James Thomas Weller and Nova Midkiff W; m. 7/30/35 to Elizabeth Summers; c. John Thomas, Richard Summers and Janice Elizabeth. Educ: Bethany Nazarene Col, 27-29. Polit. & Govt. Pos: Precinct chmn, Rep. Party, Okla, 37 & 64-68; mem, Precinct Elec. Bd; mem, Canadian Co. Farm Security Bd. and Tenant Purchase Bd, 41-46; clerk, Sch. Bd, Frisco Rural Dist. 30, 42-45; del, Rep. State Conv, 65, 67 & 69; chmn, Canadian Co. Rep. Party, 67-69; mem, Canadian Co. Rep. Exec. Cmt, 69- Mem: Okla. Hwy. Users Conf.(v.pres. and chmn. legis. cmt, 55-69); Okla. Farm Bur.(dir, 48-61, v.pres, 54-61). Mailing Add: 721 Kingston Dr, Yukon, Okla. 73099.

WELLFORD, HARRY WALKER R
Mem, Tenn. State Rep. Exec. Cmt.
b. Memphis, Tenn, 8/6/24; s. Harry Alexander Wellford and Roberta Prothro W; m. 12/7/51 to Katherine Potts; c. Harry W, Jr, James B, Buckner P, Katherine T. and Allison R. Educ: Wash. & Lee Univ, B.A, 47; Univ. Mich; Vanderbilt Univ, LL.B, 50; Phi Beta Kappa; Phi Alpha Delta; Delta Tau Delta. Polit. & Govt. Pos: Del, Rep. Nat. Conv, 64; campaign mgr. for H. Baker for Sen, 64 & 66; mem. bd. dir, Memphis and Shelby Co. Rep. Asn. and treas, 64-65; Shelby Co. Rep. Chmn, 68-; mem, Tenn. State Rep. Exec. Cmt, Ninth Cong. Dist, currently. Bus. & Prof. Pos: Partner, McCloy, Wellford & Clark, Attorneys, Tenn, 57- Mil. Serv: Entered as A/S, Naval Res, 43, released as Ens, 46, after serv. in Pac, 45; Battle Stars, Okinawa and Pac. Campaigns. Publ: Local Bar Practice Manual, Memphis & Shelby Co. Jr. Bar Asn, 52. Mem: V.pres, Memphis & Shelby Co. Jr. Bar Asn, 55; bd. dirs, Memphis & Shelby Co. Bar Asn, 60-63; Memphis Better Bus. Bur; C. of C. Sam A. Myar Memorial Award for Serv. to Bar and Commun, 64; Memphis Doubles Tennis Championship; Miss. Valley Doubles Tennis Championship. Rel: Presbyterian; Clerk of Session, Idlewild Presbyterian Church. Mailing Add: 91 N. Perkins, Memphis, Tenn. 38117.

WELLMAN, DOUGLAS C. R
Chmn, Moffat Co. Rep. Party, Colo.
b. Denver, Colo, 11/16/30; s. H.W. Wellman, Jr. and Pauline C. Cornish W; m. 11/24/58 to Lucille J. Amen; c. Harrison William and John Douglas. Educ: Colo. A&M Univ, B.S, 53; Sigma Phi Epsilon; Livestock Club; Col. Young Rep. Polit. & Govt. Pos: Publicity chmn, Moffat Co. Rep. Party, Colo, 64-67, chmn, 67- Mil. Serv: Entered as 2nd Lt, Air Force, 54, released as 1st Lt, 56, after serv. in Okinawa. Mem: Moffat Co. Nat. Farmers Orgn; Routt-Moffat Woolgrowers (bd. dirs, 67-69, secy-treas, 69-); Toastmasters (Breeze Hour). Rel: Episcopal. Mailing Add: 624 School St, Craig, Colo. 81625.

WELLMAN, NOVA ELIZABETH WILLIAMS R
b. Blaine, Ky, 1/12/03; d. Noah Cambridge Williams and Norah Leona Boggs W; m. 3/8/22 to Ernest Franklin Wellman (deceased); c. Ernestine (Mrs. Kennedy). Educ: Ky. Normal Col, B.A. in bus. admin, 21. Polit. & Govt. Pos: Former register clerk, Louisa Post Off, Ky, former city clerk and city assessor and former office dep, Co. Court Clerk; mem, Lawrence Co. Bd. Educ, 35-37; mem, Louisa City Coun, 38-40; circuit court clerk, Lawrence Co, Ky, 58-; alternate del, Rep. Nat. Conv, 64. Bus. & Prof. Pos: Off. mgr. and acct, Davis Motors, Louisa, Ky; bookkeeper, Sandy Valley Grocery Co. Mem: Charter mem, Louisa Women's Club. Holder 25 year pin, Eastern Star. Rel: Christian Church; v.chmn, Church Bd. Mailing Add: 310 Sullivan St, Louisa, Ky. 41230. (1967)

WELLS, BILL G. D
Ark. State Rep.
b. Hermitage, Ark, 4/24/30; s. Leslie Washington Wells and L. Elroy Barnett W; m. 11/10/50 to N. Sue Leggett; c. Bill, Jr, Edward C, Alan L. F. and Wm. Kieth. Educ: Ark. A&M. Col. Polit. & Govt. Pos: Mayor, Hermitage, Ark, 56-60; Ark. State Rep, 42nd Dist, 60-; dem. nominee for Lt. Gov. Ark, 68 & 70. Bus. & Prof. Pos: Owner, Bill Wells Ins. Agency, 58- and City Cafe, 62- Mil. Serv: Pvt, Army Airborne, 47-50. Mem: Mason; Lions; VFW; Am. Legion. Rel: Baptist. Mailing Add: Box 188, Hermitage, Ark. 71647.

WELLS, CYRUS CURTIS R
Finance Chmn, Colo. State Rep. Party
b. Detroit, Mich, 10/16/14; s. Pearson Wells and Helen Pillsbury W; m. 7/3/36 to Barbara Holt; c. Peter Curt, Wendy W. (Mrs. Oakes) and Christopher Bruce. Educ: Harvard Univ, B.A, 36; Harvard Bus. Sch, M.B.A, 38; Colo. Univ, M.A. in Polit. Sci, 62. Polit. & Govt. Pos: Asst. to State Chmn, Colo. State Rep. Cent. Cmt, 60-61, field dir, 61-62, exec. secy, 62-64 and secy, 64-69; trustee, Town Coun, 60-62; finance chmn, Colo. State Rep. Party, 69- Publ: Biography of U.S. Senator Eugene Milikin, Colorado. Mem: Past v.pres, Kiwanis. Rel: Lutheran. Mailing Add: 5280 Ridge Trail, Littleton, Colo. 80120.

WELLS, D. WARNER D
b. Jacksonville, Ga, 10/29/03; s. Jasper Brooks Wells and Cora Williams W; m. 12/23/34 to Virlyn Gasset. Educ: Grad. w/honors, Ga-Ala. Bus. Col, 25; Bar Rev. Course at John Marshall Law Sch. Polit. & Govt. Pos: Mayor, Ft. Valley, Ga, 8 months, 53; bd. registrs, Peach Co, 10 years; city coun, Ft. Valley, 8 years; chmn, Dem. Exec. Cmt, Peach Co, 10 years; Ga. State Rep, 57-64; Peach Co. Attorney, 67- Bus. & Prof. Pos: Attorney; admitted bar 45 and practice, Ft. Valley, 45- Mem: Mason. Rel: Baptist. Mailing Add: Ft. Valley, Ga. 31030.

WELLS, DAVID EMERSON R
b. West Grove, Pa, 6/10/29; s. Winfield Scott Wells and Cleo Kennedy W; m. 6/20/53 to Earline Elizabeth Collier; c. Linda Karen, Nancy Ellen and Catherine Elizabeth. Educ: Mars Hill Jr. Col, 49-50; Univ. Va, LL.B, 56; Sigma Chi. Polit. & Govt. Pos: Chmn, Duval Co. Young Rep. Club, Fla, 61; v.chmn, Duval Co. Rep. Cmt, 62-66; nat. committeeman, Fla. Young Rep, 63-65; chmn, Nat. Fed. Young Rep. Nat. Conv. Arrangements, 65; chmn, Fla. Fedn. Young Rep. Clubs, 65-66; legal counsel Fla. Rep. del, Rep. Nat. Conv, 68; Rep. presidential elector, 68; dir. polit. orgn, Nixon-Agnew Cmt. of Fla, 68; exec. dir, Citizens for Nixon of Fla, 68; chief counsel, Fed. Hwy. Admin, 69- Bus. & Prof. Pos: Commerce counsel, A.C.L. R.R. Co, Jacksonville, 56-66; corporate secy. and asst. gen. counsel, Redwing Carriers, Inc, Tampa, 66-69. Mil. Serv: Entered as Pvt, Army, 46, released as Pfc, 49, after serv. in 88th Mech. Cav. Recon. Troop, Trieste, Italy, 46-49, recalled into 151st Combat Eng. Bn, Korea, 50-51; 2nd Lt, Air Force ROTC, Univ. Va, ETO Ribbon; Korean Theater Ribbon; Two Battle Stars; Good Conduct Medal; Army of Occup. Medal. Mem: Am, Va. and Fla. Bar Asns; Asn. Interstate Commerce Cmn. Practitioners; Kiwanis; Mason. Rel: Baptist. Legal Res: 5514 Primrose Lane, Jacksonville, Fla. 32211. Mailing Add: 3807 Great Neck Court, Alexandria, Va. 22309.

WELLS, GORDON W. D
b. Savannah, Ga, 12/6/17; m. to Virginia Cloys; c. Virginia J. and Anna M. Educ: Univ. Fla, 35; Bowling Green Col. of Commerce, 41; Univ. Miami, LL.B, 52. Polit. & Govt. Pos: Asst. co. solicitor, Escambia Co, Fla, 60; Fla. State Rep, 62-68. Bus. & Prof. Pos: Attorney, currently; asst. prof. acct, Univ. Miami. Mil. Serv: Army, 42-46; grad, Officers Cand. Sch; Capt. Finance Dept; Army Commendation Medal. Mem: Fla. and Am. Bar Asns; Jr. Achievement; Gr. Pensacola C. of C; past dir, Pensacola Rotary. Rel: Presbyterian; former deacon, First Presbyterian Church, Pensacola. Mailing Add: P.O. Box 12066, Pensacola, Fla. 32502.

WELLS, GUY JACKSON R
Mem, Exec. Cmt, R.I. State Rep. Cent. Cmt.
b. Providence, R.I, 7/3/30; s. Guy William Wells and Ruth Emory W; m. 11/29/58 to Beverly Jansen; c. Guy William, III, Tracy Elizabeth, Thomas Jansen and Jennifer Jackson. Educ: Princeton Univ, A.B, 52; Boston Univ. Law Sch, LL.B, 57; Court Club. Polit. & Govt. Pos: Mem. at large, R.I. State Rep. Cent. Cmt, 60-, mem.exec. cmt, 66-; chmn, R.I. Nixon Campaign, 68; alternate del, Rep. Nat. Conv, 68. Bus. & Prof. Pos: Partner, Hinckly, Allen Salisbury & Parsons, 58- Mil. Serv: Entered as 2nd Lt, Army, 52, released as 1st Lt, 54, after serv. in Artil, Korea; Maj, Army Res; Army Commendation Ribbon; UN Medal; Korean Serv. Medal; Nat. Defense Ribbon; Army Res. Medal. Mem: R.I. and Am. Bar Asns. R.I. Bar Asn. Award of Merit, 67- Rel: Protestant. Mailing Add: 243 Promenade Ave, Warwick, R.I. 02886.

WELLS, GWENDOLYN MARIE D
b. Kansas City, Kans, 9/23/28; d. William DeWitt Dunlap and Forrest Wilson D; div; c. John H, Jr. Educ: Howard Univ, B.A, 49; Tex. South. Univ. Law Sch, LL.B, 59; Delta Sigma Theta. Polit. & Govt. Pos: Asst. prosecuting attorney, Jackson Co, Mo, 62-63 & 65-66; mem. bd. trustees, Metrop. Jr. Col, Kansas City, 64-68; area dir, Equal Employ. Opportunity Cmn, 68- Rel: Episcopal. Legal Res: 4011 Linwood Blvd, Kansas City, Mo. 64128. Mailing Add: 9727 Mount Pisgah Rd, Silver Spring, Md. 20903.

WELLS, HUBERT HOMER D
b. Homer, Ga, 4/16/11; s. Alfred Moss Wells and Lavada Redd W; m. 8/9/30 to Elizabeth McRee; c. Martha (Mrs. Thomas) and Mell H. Educ: Oconee Co. High Sch, 30. Polit. & Govt. Pos: Mem. bd. trustees, Oconee Co. Schs, Ga, 4 years; city councilman, 7 years and mayor-pro-tem, 4 years; Ga. State Rep, 59-68. Bus. & Prof. Pos: Merchant; automobile-appliance dealer; farmer; dir, Oconee State Bank; bd. dirs, Oconee Farm Bur, 56- Mem: Mason; Shrine; Civitan (pres, Watkinsville, Chap, 57-58). Rel: Christian; Chmn, Bd. of Deacons. Mailing Add: Watkinsville, Ga. 30677. (1967)

WELLS, J. C. D
Chmn, Warren Co. Dem. Cmt, Mo.
b. Wellsville, Mo, 5/2/09; s. John Hayden Wells and Rebbeca Rainey W; m. 6/6/53 to Agnes Marie Herbel; c. Sue (Mrs. Erwin), George, Bruce, Sherri and Nancy. Polit. & Govt. Pos: Chmn, Warren Co. Dem. Cmt, Mo, currently. Bus. & Prof. Pos: Bus driver, T.N.T. Plant, 42-45. Mem: Warren Co. Dem. Club (past pres); Local 600 Union. Rel: Methodist. Mailing Add: 401 McKinley, Warrenton, Mo. 63383.

WELLS, JAMES DALE D
Iowa State Rep.
b. Marathon, Iowa 8/7/28; s. Willard Wallace Wells and Florence Peterson W; m. 6/11/50 to Shirley Ann Clare; c. Linda Sue, Cheryl Kay and Nancy Ann. Educ: Marathon Consolidated Sch, Iowa, grad. Polit. & Govt. Pos: Chmn, Cmt. on Polit. Educ, 66-69; Iowa State Rep, 69- Mil. Serv: Entered as Sgt. 1/C, Army Res, served in 328th Combat Engrs, 6½ years. Mem: Men's Club; recording secy, Retail Wholesale Dept. Store Union, 9 years. Rel: United Methodist. Legal Res: 1229 20th St. S.W, Cedar Rapids, Iowa 52404. Mailing Add: State Capitol, Des Moines, Iowa 50139.

WELLS, JOHN MARVIN R
Councilman-at-Lg, Charleston, W.Va.
b. Charleston, W.Va, 4/19/18; s. John Calvin Wells and Florence Friedman W; m. 11/13/36 to Nancy Elizabeth Kyle; c. Nancy (Mrs. Daniel F. Johnson), John M, Jr, Sally Michael and Robert Michael. Educ: Charleston High Sch, W.Va, dipl, 37. Polit. & Govt. Pos: Ward councilman, Charleston, W.Va, 59-, chmn. finance cmt, City Coun, 63-67, majority leader, 67-68; councilman-at-lg, 67-; v.chmn. Charleston Dist, Rep. Gubernatorial Primary, spring 68; v.chmn, Rep. State Exec. Cmt, summer 68 and currently. Bus. & Prof. Pos: Pres, R.H. Kyle Furniture Co, Charleston, 61- Mil. Serv: Entered as Pvt, Army, 45, released as Cpl, 46, after serv. in Engr. Corps. Mem: Nat. Wholesale Furniture Asn.(past dir, v.pres, pres. and chmn. bd, 62 & 63); Elks; Mason; Shrine; Capital Park Authority; Charleston Civic Center Bd. Man of the Year Award, Nat. Wholesale Furniture Asn. Rel: Presbyterian. Legal Res: 888 Chester Rd, Charleston, W.Va. 25302. Mailing Add: 1352 Hansford St, Charleston, W.Va. 25301.

WELLS, LYNN B. D
b. 1913. Educ: Chillicothe Bus. Col, bus. degree. Polit. & Govt. Pos: Ky. State Rep, 64-68. Bus. & Prof. Pos: Ins. Rel: Baptist. Mailing Add: Sandy Hook, Ky. 41171. (1967)

WELLS, RICHARD DALE R
Supt. Pub. Instr, Ind.
b. Hobart, Ind, 4/24/28; s. Simeon Lester Wells and Pearl Leotta Wasson W; m. 7/2/51 to Jeanette Blake; c. Douglas Wade, Yvonne Lea, Scott Simeon and Brian Richard. Educ: Ind. Univ, B.S, 56, M.S, 66. Polit. & Govt. Pos: del, Ind. State Rep. Conv, 60 & 62; Rep. Precinct Committeeman, Porter Co, Ind, 64-66; v.chmn, Portage Twp. Rep. Orgn, 65; Supt. Pub. Instr, Ind, 67-; Bd. of Trustees, Ball State Univ, Ind. State Univ. and Ind. Voc. Tech. Col, 67-; Bd. of Visitors, Ind. Univ, 67-; mem, steering cmt, Educ. Cmn. of the States, currently. Bus. & Prof. Pos: Classroom teacher, Portage Twp, Porter Co, Ind, 56-57, Gary, 57-67. Mil. Serv: Entered as 2nd Lt, Army, 53, released as 1st Lt, 55, after serv. in Quarter Master Corps, Korean Theatre, 54-55; Korean Serv. Medal; Asian Theatre. Mem: Nat. Educ. Asn; Am. Asn. of Sch. Admin; Sch. Bd. Asn. Rel: Methodist. Legal Res: R.R. 9, Valparaiso, Ind. 46383. Mailing Add: Room 229 State House, Indianapolis, Ind. 46204.

WELSH, EDWARD CRISTY D
b. Long Valley, N.J, 3/20/09; s. Edward Cristy Welsh and Florence E. Delp W; m. 6/15/35 to Carolyn B. White. Educ: Lafayette Col, A.B, magna cum laude, 30; Tufts Col, M.A, 32; Ohio State Univ, Ph.D, 40; Lafayette Col, Litt.D, 63; Clark Univ, LL.D, 65; Phi Beta Kappa; Beta Gamma Sigma; Pi Delta Epsilon. Polit. & Govt. Pos: Mem, Econ. Nat. Resources Cmt, 37; mem, Temporary Nat. Econ Cmt, 40; dir, regional price exec, Ohio, W.Va, Ky. and Ind, 42-44 and price oper. all regions U.S, 44-46 and dep. adminstr, Off. Price Admin, 46; asst. comdr. OTC, Chief Anti-Trust and Cartels Div, Dept. Army, GHQ, Japan, 47-50; mem, For. Investment Bd, Japan, 49-50; asst. to adminstr, econ. adv, Reconstruction Finance Corp, 51-53; legal asst. to Sen. Symington, 53-61; exec. secy, Nat. Aeronaut. and Space Coun, 61-69. Bus. & Prof. Pos: Teacher, econ. dept, various univ, 30-42. Mem: Am. Astronaut. Soc; Am. Inst. of Aeronaut. and Astronaut; Air Force Asn; Am. Ord. Asn; Aerospace Med. Asn; Int. Acad. of Astronaut; bd. gov, Nat. Space Club; bd. dirs, Spaceward Corp. Honored by Army for Major Contribution to Develop. of Private Enterprise in Japan; Recipient Arnold Air Soc. Annual Award, 62 & 68; Nat. Space Club Press Award, 68; Man of the Year in Arts and Letters, Air Force Asn, 68. Mailing Add: 1500 Arlington Blvd, Arlington, Va. 22209.

WELSH, EVELYN MARGARET D
Mem. Bd, Federated Dem. Women of Ohio
b. Youngstown, Ohio, 2/14/03; d. William Albert German and Anna Vaughan G; m. 6/12/22 to William J. Welsh (deceased 1/5/69); c. Evelyn (Mrs. Mahoney) and Eleanore (Mrs. Hill). Educ: High Sch. and Bus. Col. Polit. & Govt. Pos: Cmn. mem, Youngstown Civil Serv; precinct committeewoman, Mahoning Co. Dem. Exec. Cmt; pres, Jackson-Roosevelt Dem. Women's Club, 52-56; pres, Federated Dem. Women of Ohio, 64-65, mem. bd, currently. Bus. & Prof. Pos: Secy, Idora Park, 52-65; ed, Forum Features Mag. of Garden Forum, currently. Mem: Beta Sigma Sorority, Int; VFW Auxiliary; DAV Auxiliary; Parliamentary Study Club; bd, Youngstown Fedn. Women's Clubs; bd, Garden Forum of Gr. Youngstown; Mill Creek Garden Club; 16 Club; Bridge Club; Advisory Bd. mem. and Parliamentarian, PNA Div. 3 of Ohio; Educ. Garden Club of Poland. Rel: Episcopal. Mailing Add: 3453 Bent Willow Lane, Youngstown, Ohio 44511.

WELSH, GEORGE A. R
b. Bay View, Cecil Co, Md, 8/9/78; s. George Welsh and Sarah Pickering W; m. 10/31/21 to Helen Reed Kirk; c. Margaret, Patrick, Deborah. Educ: Temple Univ, 92-94, LL.B, 06, LL.D, 39. Polit. & Govt. Pos: Secy. to mayor, Phila, Pa, 04-06; asst. city solicitor, Phila, 06-07; Asst. Dist. Attorney, Phila, 07-22; U.S. Rep, Pa, 23-33; U.S. Dist. Judge, East. Dist. Pa, 32-; mem. bd. educ, Phila. Co, 11 years. Bus. & Prof. Pos: Lawyer; v.pres, Temple Univ, 39-, exec. bd. and bd. trustees, dir. and secy. for many years. Mem: Mason; K.T; Mid-Day Club. Legal Res: Middletown and Barren Rds, Lima, Pa. 19060. Mailing Add: U.S. Court House, Philadelphia, Pa. 19106. (1967)

WELSH, JOHN T. D
b. Abington, Pa, 7/11/14; s. Richard A. Welsh and Mary E. Mahoney W; m. 6/28/41 to Ruth A. Carlen; c. John T, Jr, Daniel R, Michael B, James D, Richard J. and Dennis R. Educ: Peirce Jr. Bus. Col, acct. course, grad, 32-35. Polit. & Govt. Pos: Committeeman, Bucks Co. Dem. Cmt, Pa, 35-44, secy, 38-44, chmn, 44-52, treas, 58-60 and chmn, 62-68; mem, Bucks Co. Bd. of Cmnrs, 52-56, chmn, 56-60; chmn, Pa. Workmen's Compensation Bd, 60-63; del, Dem. Nat. Conv, 68. Bus. & Prof. Pos: Mem. bd. dir, Bucks Co. Bd. Realtors, 54-60, pres, 61; mem. bd. dirs, Bucks Co. Indust. Develop. Corp, 61. Mem: Pres, Bucks Co. Asn. of Blind, Inc, 65 and 66; past pres. and charter mem, Doylestown Lions Club, 21 yrs. perfect attendance, 45-66; past pres, St. Joseph's Soc, Our Lady of Mt. Carmel Catholic Church, Doylestown. Chosen Realtor of the Year, 65 and Outstanding Catholic Layman, 65. Rel: Catholic. Legal Res: 216 East Ashland St, Doylestown, Pa. 18901. Mailing Add: 62 East Court St, Doylestown, Pa. 18901.

WELSH, MATTHEW EMPSON D
b. Detroit, Mich, 9/15/12; s. Matthew William Welsh and Inez Empson W; m. 9/25/37 to Mary Virginia Homann; c. Janet and Kathryn. Educ: Univ. Pa, B.S. in econ, 34; Ind. Univ. Law Sch, 35 & 36; Univ. Chicago, J.D, 37; Phi Delta Phi; Delta Kappa Epsilon; managing ed, Daily Pennsylvanian. Hon. LL.D, Ind. Univ, St. Joseph's Col, Franklin Col, Ind. State Univ, Vincennes Univ. and Tri-State Col. Polit. & Govt. Pos: Ind. State Rep, 41-44; Ind. State Sen, 55-60, floor leader, 57 & 59; U.S. Attorney, South. Dist. Ind, 50-52; gov, Ind, 61-65; mem. exec. cmt, Nat. Gov. Conf, 63; chmn, Interstate Oil Compact Cmn, 63; Dem. Nat. Committeeman, Ind, 64 & 65; chmn, U.S. Sect, Int. Joint Cmn, U.S. and Can, 66- Bus. & Prof. Pos: Attorney-at-law, Vincennes, Ind, 37-61; partner, Bingham, Summers, Welsh & Spilman, 65-; chmn. bd. trustees, Vincennes Univ; chmn. bd. trustees, Christian Theol. Sem, Indianapolis; mem. bd. mgrs, Lincoln Nat. Variable Annuity Fund A and B; mem. bd. dir, Lincoln Nat. Balanced Fund and Lincoln Nat. Capital Fund of Lincoln Nat. Corp, Ft. Wayne; mem. bd. dir, Security Bank & Trust Co, Vincennes, Farmers State Bank, Eminence and Universal Scientific Co, Vincennes. Mil. Serv: Entered as Lt.(jg), Navy, 43, released as Lt, 46, after serv. in Supply Corps. Mem: Knox Co, Marion Co, Ind. and Am. Bar Asns; Fel. Am. Bar Found; Kiwanis, Elks, Indianapolis Athletic Club; Columbia Club, Nat. Lawyers Club. Rel: Disciples of Christ. Legal Res: 4546 N. Park Ave, Indianapolis, Ind. 46205. Mailing Add: 600 Circle Tower Building, Indianapolis, Ind. 46204.

WELSH, WILLIAM BROWNLEE D
b. Munfordville, Ky, 9/18/24; s. Benjamin T. Welsh and Mary Cocks W; m. 1/25/48 to Jean Justice; c. Charles B; Mary J. and Wm. E. Educ: Berea Col; Univ. of Ky; Maxwell Sch; Syracuse Univ. Polit. & Govt. Pos: Legis. asst. to U.S. Sen. Herbert H. Lehman, N.Y, 52-56; res. dir, Dem. Nat. Cmt, 57-58; mem, Fairfax Co. Dem. Cmt, Va, 59-; admin. asst. to U.S. Sen. Philip A. Hart, Mich, 59-66; admin. asst. to the V.pres, U.S, 66-69; exec. asst. to Chmn, Dem. Nat. Cmt, 69- Mil. Serv: Entered as Pvt, Army, released as Sgt, 46, after serv. in ETO. Mem: Am. Polit. Sci. Asn. Rel: Presbyterian. Mailing Add: 6917 Cherry Lane, Annandale, Va. 22003.

WELTNER, CHARLES LONGSTREET D
b. Atlanta, Ga, 12/17/27; s. Philip Weltner and Sally Cobb Hull W; m. 9/16/50 to Betty Jean Center; c. Elizabeth Shirley, Philip II, Susan Martin and Charles Longstreet. Educ: Oglethorpe Univ, A.B, 48; Columbia Univ, LL.B, 50; Tufts Univ, LL.D, 67; Omicron Delta Kappa. Polit. & Govt. Pos: U.S. Rep, Ga, Fifth Dist, 62-66. Bus. & Prof. Pos: Attorney-at-law. Mil. Serv: Capt, Army. Publ: Southerner, J.B. Lippincott, 66. Rel: Presbyterian. Mailing Add: 33 Walker Terrace N.E, Atlanta, Ga. 30309.

WELTY, ROBERT D
State Treas, Dem. Party, Ore.
b. Portland, Ore, 1/13/15; s. Jacob Welty and Louise E. Lerch W; m. 9/24/39

to Gertrude M. Johnson; c. Robert Wm. and Michael D. Educ: Ore. State Univ, B.S. in elec. eng, 38; Eta Kappa Nu; Sigma Tau. Polit. & Govt. Pos: Field engr, Rural Elec. Admin, Ore, 38-42 & 44-45; treas, Wasco Co. Dem. Cent. Cmt, 56-60, chmn, 60-; state treas, Dem. Party Ore, 63-; del, Dem. Nat. Conv, 64. Bus. & Prof. Pos: Consult. engr, owner, Robert Welty Engrs, The Dalles, Ore, 45- Mil. Serv: Tech. Adv. on Construct, Signal Corps, 42-44. Mem: Pres, Consult. Engrs Asn. of Ore, 62; Consult. Engrs. Coun; Prfnl. Engrs. of Ore; Nat. Soc. of Prfnl. Engrs; mem. Nat. Bd, Asn. of Commun. Engrs; C. of C; Cherry Park Grange; Mid Columbia Develop. Corp; The Dalles Yacht Club. Rel: Lutheran; mem. of coun. Mailing Add: 1607 E. 11th, The Dalles, Ore. 97058.

WEMPLE, CLARK CULLINGS R
N.Y. State Assemblyman
b. Schenectady, N.Y, 7/19/27; s. John Herbert Wemple and Luella Clark W; m. 6/6/53 to Marilyn Greve; c. Mark Vanderpool, Kirk Jameson and Erik Cullings. Educ: Yale Univ, B.A, 50; Albany Law Sch, J.D, 53. Polit. & Govt. Pos: Justice of the Peace, Niskayuna, N.Y, 57-63, town councilman, 63-65; N.Y. State Assemblyman, 66- Bus. & Prof. Pos: Self-employed attorney-at-law, 53-69. Mil. Serv: Entered as Seaman 1/C, Navy, 45, released as SKD 3/C, 46, after serv. in ETO. Mem: N.Y. State, Schenectady Co. and Am. Bar Asns; Am. Arbit. Asn. Rel: Protestant. Mailing Add: 1760 Van Antwerp Rd, Schenectady, N.Y. 12309.

WENGERT, JAMES JOHN D
b. Sioux City, Iowa, 3/23/34; s. Donald Wilbur Wengert and Margaret Pendergast W; m. 12/15/51 to Joanne Wehde; c. Kathryn Ann, Patricia Kay, James John, Jr, Mary Jo, Susan Lynn, Kim Marie and Jean Anne. Polit. Pos: Iowa State Rep, Woodbury Co, 65-66; precinct committeemen, Dem. Cmt, 64, 62 and 60; pres, Young Dem. for Woodbury Co, 59-60. Govt. Pos: Bd. Mem, Econ. Opportunity Mobilization Cmt, 65-; mem, Mayor's Cmt. for International Visitors, 63-64. Mem: K. of C; v.pres, Iowa Fedn. of Labor, AFL-CIO; v.pres, Local 71, United Packinghouse Food and Allied Workers, AFL-CIO, trustee, Woodbury Co. Labor Coun, AFL-CIO. Rel: Catholic. 1967 Legal Res: 1512 W. Second St, Sioux City, Iowa 51103. No mailing address available. (1967)

WENINGER, HOWARD L. D
Chmn, Starke Co. Dem. Cent. Cmt, Ind.
b. North Judson, Ind, 12/13/04; s. Charles W. Weninger and Elizabeth Collier W; m. 6/26/27 to Esther Claire Grimm; c. Kay (Mrs. Croyle) and Howard L. Jr. Educ: Univ. of Mich, 24-26. Polit. & Govt. Pos: Clerk-treas, North Judson, Ind, 36-42, pres, Recreation Bd, 38-42, secy, Sch. Bd, 48-52 and Libr, 51-54; trustee, Wayne Twp, 47-54; chmn, Starke Co. Dem. Cent. Cmt, 52-; chmn, Second Dist. Dem. Cent. Cmt, 61-66; del, Dem. Nat. Conv, 60, 64 & 68. Bus. & Prof. Pos: Dir, Am. State Bank, North Judson, Ind, 53-; pres, Judson Pub. Inc, 64- Mem: Nat. Asn. Independent Ins. Agents; pres, North Judson C. of C, 32 & 44; Mason; Scottish Rite; Shrine; Eagles; Moose; Conserv. Club. Rel: Methodist. Mailing Add: 508 Keller Ave, North Judson, Ind. 46366.

WENKE, PAUL E. R
b. Pender, Nebr, 8/10/17; s. William F. Wenke and Anna Rosacker W; c. Mary Alice and Susan Jane. Educ: Univ. Nebr, A.B. & J.D, 40; Phi Delta Phi; Sigma Phi Epsilon. Polit. & Govt. Pos: Precinct committeeman, Colo, 47; chmn, Larimer Co. Rep. Cent. Cmt, 48-50; probate and juvenile judge, Larimer Co, Colo, 50-51; Majority Leader, Colo. State Senate, 59-67. Bus. & Prof. Pos: Spec. agent, Fed. Bur. Invest, 40-46. Mem: Am, Colo, Nebr. and Wyo. Bar Asns. Cmts. on Legis, 63-; pres, Larimer Co. Bar Asn, 54-55, Ft. Collins C. of C, 58, Larimer Co. Chap. Am. Red Cross, 49-50, Ft. Collins Commun. Chest, 49-50 and Ft. Collins Jr. C. of C, 47-48; Elks Lodge 804. Mailing Add: 504 Rocky Mountain Bldg, Ft. Collins, Colo. 80522.

WENSTROM, FRANK AUGUSTUS R
N.Dak. State Sen.
b. Dover, N.Dak, 7/27/03; s. James August Wenstrom and Anna P. Kringstad W; m. 6/10/38 to Mary Esther Pickett. Educ: Pub. Schs, N.Dak. Polit. & Govt. Pos: N.Dak. State Sen, 57-59 & 67-, mem, Legis. Res. Coun, 59-60 & 69, chmn, Cmt. Audits and Fiscal Rev, 63-64; Lt. Gov, N.Dak, 63-64. Bus. & Prof. Pos: Exec. v.pres, Northwest. Fed. Savings and Loan Asn; farmer, 44-; pub. rels. off, 1st Nat. Bank, Williston, N.Dak, 50-61; asst. to pres, Am. State Bank of Williston, 68- Mem: Secy-Mgr, Williston C. of C, 45-51; Secy-Treas, Upper Mo. Purebred Cattle Breeders Asn, 47-62; Pres, Wms. Co. Wildlife Fedn, 45; Pres, N.Dak. Wildlife Fedn, 47-48; Pres, N.Dak. Reclamation Asn, 57; Mem, Yellowstone-Mo-Ft. Union Cmn, 59-; Roosevelt Nat. Park Com, 54-; Williston Commun. Chest; N.Dak. Soc. for Crippled Children & Adults; N.Dak. & Williston C. of C; Elks; Mason; N.Dak. Easter Seals Chmn, 65. Mailing Add: 516 Third Ave. W, Williston, N.Dak. 58801.

WENTNER, NITA R
Mem. Exec. Cmt, Calif Rep. State Cent. Cmt.
b. Amarillo, Tex, 6/25/21; d. Atha Pike, foster mother; m. to Wayne W. Wentner, wid; c. Martha (Mrs. Philip Koch) and Joy (Mrs. James Pratt). Educ: Loretta Heights Col, 37-38. Polit. & Govt. Pos: Mem, Co. Rep. Cent. Cmt, Calif, 65-; mem. exec. cmt, Calif. Rep. State Cent. Cmt, 66-; asst. appointment secy, Gov. Reagan, 67; mem, Calif. State Personnel Bd, 67-; del. and mem. platform cmt, Rep. Nat. Conv, 68. Bus. & Prof. Pos: Real estate salesman, Calif, 56-; life ins. broker, State of Calif, 64- Mem: Calif. Real Estate Asn; Nat. Underwriters Asn. Rel: Protestant. Mailing Add: 80 Via Robles, Walnut Creek, Calif. 94529.

WENTZIEN, IRWIN H. R
b. Gladbrook, Iowa, 2/25/02; s. H.H. Wentzien, Jr. and Pauline Nissen W; m. 2/15/34 to Vivian Alice Walter; c. Irwin Heinrich, Paul Warren and Michael Brent. Educ: Univ. South. Calif, 21-22; Univ. Iowa, B.S.C, 24. Polit. & Govt. Pos: Del, Iowa Rep. State Conv, 29-64; coun. mem, Gladbrook Sch. Bd, 46-54; chmn, Tama Co. Rep. Party, 59-64, orgn. chmn, 64-69; del, Rep. Nat. Conv, 64. Bus. & Prof. Pos: Hardware merchant, 24- Mem: Hardware Asn; Mason; Boy Scouts; Salvation Army; Commercial Club; Odd Fellows. Rel: Church of Christ. Mailing Add: Gladbrook, Iowa 50635.

WENZEL, FERDINAND EDWARD 'TED' R
V.Chmn, Tuolumne Co. Rep. Cent. Cmt, Calif.
b. Sonora, Calif, 10/5/17; s. Edward George Wenzel and Cora E. Leonard W; m. 11/12/37 to Eloise Vivian Mitchell; c. Sharon P. (Mrs. Stockton) and Gerald E. Educ: Modesto Jr. Col, 35-36; Col. of Commerce, Stockton, Calif, B.A, Bus, 38. Polit. & Govt. Pos: Finance chmn, Tuolumne Co. Rep. Cent. Cmt, Calif, 62-, v.chmn, currently; mem, Calif. Rep. State Cent. Cmt, currently. Bus. & Prof. Pos: Owner, Wenzels Men & Women's Wear, 41- Mem: Sonora Area Bus. Asn; Elks; Lions; N.Calif. Golf Asn; Phoenix Lake Golf & Country Club; E. Clampus Vitus Amatuca Chap; C. of C; Twain Harte Golf Club. Gov. Award for Outstanding Performance as Finance Chmn. Rep. Cent. Cmt, 68. Rel: Protestant. Mailing Add: 316 E. Summit Ave, Sonora, Calif. 95370.

WENZLAFF, THEODORE CHARLES R
Nebr. State Sen.
b. Yankton, S.Dak. 1/8/03; s. John Christian Wenzlaff, Jr. and Johanna Ochsner W; m. 9/30/27 to Frieda Griess; c. Marianne Elizabeth (Mrs. Harold Lewis Zinnecker, Jr), William Frederic and Kathleen Marie (Mrs. James Reid Brockhaus). Educ: Univ. Nebr, 21-22; U.S. Mil. Acad, B.S, 26; Hastings Col, B.A, 56. Polit. & Govt. Pos: City councilman, Sutton, Nebr, 59-61; Nebr. State Sen, 32nd Dist, 68- Bus. & Prof. Pos: Teacher, Eng, Sutton High Sch, 56-57. Mil. Serv: Entered as 2nd Lt, Army, 26, retired as Col, 55, after serv. in ETO, 42-46 and Korea, 53-54, Legion of Merit. Publ: The Life of Johann Christian Wenzlaff (1827-1894), Privately Publ, 63; History of the Hope Reformed Church, Sutton, Nebraska, Hope Reformed Church, 68; 'The Russian Germans Come to the United States,' Nebr. Hist, Vol. 49, No. 4. Mem: Am. Legion; Meadowbrook Golf Club, Hastings, Nebr; v.pres, Am. Hist. Soc. Germans Russia. Rel: Reformed Protestant. Legal Res: Sutton, Nebr. 68979. Mailing Add: P.O. Box 26, Sutton, Nebr. 68979.

WERBE, SUSAN DIANE D
b. Detroit, Mich, 8/17/46; d. Bernard Alvin Werbe and Sally Grossman W; single. Educ: Univ. Calif, Berkeley, B.A, 68; Theta Sigma. Polit. & Govt. Pos: Co-chmn, Berkeley Students for Kennedy, Calif, 68; del, Dem. Nat. Conv, 68. Bus. & Prof. Pos: Asst. research dir, Dem. Study Group, Wash, D.C, 68-69. Rel: Jewish. Legal Res: Sobrante, Calif. Mailing Add: 25611 Greenfield Rd, Southfield, Mich. 48075.

WERNKE, WILLIAM D. R
b. Fairfax, S.Dak, 6/19/33; s. Eugene Wernke and Daisy Loper W; m. 9/22/56 to Catherine Thoene; c. Mark Noah, Kari Lynn and Jay William. Educ: Univ. S.Dak, B.S. in Bus. Admin. with honors, 61; Univ. S.Dak. Law Sch, LL.B, 63; Phi Eta Sigma; Beta Gamma Sigma; Delta Sigma Pi; Delta Theta Phi. Polit. & Govt. Pos: Chmn, Gregory Co. Rep. Party, S.Dak, 65-68; states attorney, Gregory Co, 65-; mem, S.Dak. State Bd. of Educ, 68- Bus. & Prof. Pos: Attorney-at-law, Herman & Wernke, Gregory, S.Dak, 64- Mil. Serv: Entered as Pvt, Army, 53, released as 1st Lt, Artil, 56, after serv. in 82nd Airborne Div, Ft. Bragg, N.C, 54-56; Jump Wings. Mem: S.Dak. States Attorneys Asn; S.Dak. Trial Lawyers Asn; S.Dak. State and Am. Bar Asns; Nat. Asn. of State Bd. of Educ; AF&AM; Elks. Rel: Episcopal. Legal Res: R.R. 2, Gregory, S.Dak. 57533. Mailing Add: Herman & Wernke, Attorneys-at-law, Gregory, S.Dak. 57533.

WERTZ, WILLIAM JENNINGS R
b. Bedford, Pa, 10/28/96; s. Samuel Nye Wertz and Emma Ellen Shaffer W; m. 2/11/20 to Pauline Elouise Pingrey; c. Mary Carolyn (Mrs. McDonald), Renetta Frances (Mrs. Curry) and William Pingrey. Educ: Ottawa Univ, Kans, 15-16; Univ. Kans, LL.B, 19; Delta Theta Phi. Hon. LL.D, St. Benedict Col, 62. Polit. & Govt. Pos: Attorney, Sedgwick Co, Wichita, Kans, 27-31; Kans. State Sen, 41-43; Judge, 18th Dist. Court, Kans, 47-50; Justice, Supreme Court Kans, 50-65. Bus. & Prof. Pos: Mem. bd. dirs, Bethany Col, 58- Mil. Serv: Seaman 2/C, Naval Res, 18, Res, 18-21; re-entered as Capt, Army, 42, released as Lt. Col, 46, after serv. in Off. Judge Adv. Gen. Corps; Col.(Ret), 56. Mem: Wichita, Kans. and Am. Bar Asns; Mason (33°); Wichita Consistory; Shrine; Am. Legion; Mil. Order World Wars; Ret. Officers Asn; Wichita Club. Rel: Lutheran. Mailing Add: 4402 E. English, Wichita, Kans. 67218.

WERVE, MARVIN R. D
b. Kenosha, Wis, 7/21/13; s. Edward Werve and Clair Russell W; m. 8/18/39 to Leonila Dieter; c. Nick, Martha, Mary, Theresa, Patricia and Colleen. Educ: Creighton Univ. Law Sch; pres, Sr. Law Class; col. varsity football. Polit. & Govt. Pos: Former mem, Nebr. Dem. Nat. Cmt; del, Dem. Nat. Conv, 68. Bus. & Prof. Pos: Chmn, Nebr. Multiple Sclerosis Soc, United Commun. Serv. Dr, 65; dir. and treas, Dr. and St. Catherine's Hosps. Dr, currently. Mem: Am. Banking Asn.(installment credit cmt), C. of C; instr, Am. Inst. of Banking; Nebr. Resources Cmt, Nebr. Bar Asn. Rel: Catholic. Legal Res: 473 S. 90th St, Omaha, Nebr. 68102. Mailing Add: The Omaha National Bank, 1620 Farnam St, Omaha, Nebr. 68102. (1967)

WESBERRY, JAMES PICKETT, JR. D
b. Columbia, S.C, 9/22/34; s. James Pickett Wesberry and Ruby Lee Perry W; m. 6/16/51 to Nydia Arminda Lastre; c. Elisa Marie, James Pickett, III and Lillian Sue. Educ: Lamar Sch. Law, Emory Univ; Ga. State Col, B.B.A. in acct. Polit. & Govt. Pos: Page, U.S. House of Rep, 49-51; Lt. Col, Gov. Staff, 55-66; mem, Fulton Co. Dem. Exec. Cmt, Ga, 62-66; Ga. State Sen, dist. 37, 63-68, chmn, Cmt. on Insts. and Ment. Health and mem, Cmt. on Appropriations, Banking and Finance, Health and Welfare, Ga. State Senate, 67-68; chmn, Fulton Co. Senate Del, 65-66; mem, Fulton Co. Young Dem. Bus. & Prof. Pos: CPA and mgt. consult, specializing in govt. and non-profit orgn. acct. syst. and procedures, 56- Publ: Originator and first ed, GO Mag, U.S. Jaycees; Articles in Nat. Civic Rev, Optimist Int. Mag, Cong. Record and Future Mag. Mem: Bd. dirs, Warren Mem. Boys Club; Active Voters and Morningside-Lenox Asn; v.pres, Nat. Soc. State Legislators, 65-66; N.Fulton Fine Arts Found; F&AM; RAM; RSM (hon. life mem, Union Coun); K.T.(hon. life mem, Columbia Commandery); AAONMS; Royal Order of Scotland; Mason; Ga. State Col. Alumni Asn; Am. Inst. CPA; Ga. Soc. CPA; Nat. Asn. Acct; Munic. Finance Officers Asn. of U.S. and Can; C. of C; dir, Atlanta Jaycees, 59-61; treas, Fifth Dist. and state govt. affairs chmn, Ga. Jaycees, 60-61; treas, nat. conv, U.S. Jaycees, 61, nat. govt. affairs chmn, 61-63, asst. nat. treas, 63-64, dir. and mem. exec. cmt, 63-66, nat. treas, 64-65 and nat. v.pres, 65-66; originator, Nat. Govt. Affairs Seminar; former trustee, Nat. Jaycees Ment. Health and Ment. Retardation Fund, Jaycees War Mem. Fund and Jaycees Relig. Activities Fund; Goodwill Indust.(former secy. and dir, Atlanta); dir, Ga. Asn. for Ment. Health; Joint Cmn. on Corrections, Man-

power and Training; adv. coun, Int. Movement for Atlantic Union. Named one of five Outstanding Young Men of Ga, 63; Outstanding State Chmn. Award, Ga. Jaycees; Outstanding Nat. Chmn. Award, U.S. Jaycees. Rel: Baptist. Legal Res: 1876 Windemere Drive, N.E, Atlanta, Ga. 30324. Mailing Add: P.O. Box 8087, Atlanta, Ga. 30306. (1967)

WESLEY, JOHN QUENTIN R
Ky. State Rep.
b. Sturgis, Union Co, Ky, 10/22/29; s. Charles R. Wesley, Sr. and Roberta Wynn W; m. 8/15/55 to Hildegarde Taylor; c. Jeffery Taylor, Katherine Virginia, John Quentin, Jr. and Sara Lincoln. Educ: Bob Jones Univ; West. Ky. State Col; Univ. Ky, LL.B, 54; Phi Delta Phi. Polit. & Govt. Pos: Ky. State Rep, Seventh Dist, 68- Bus. & Prof. Pos: Attorney at law, Wathen & Wesley, 59- Mil. Serv: Entered as 2nd Lt, Air Force, 54, released as 1st Lt, 57, after serving in Procurement & Prod, Air Material Command; Air Force Res, 57-65, Capt. Publ: 'Probate of Wills of Kentucky', Ky. Law J, 54. Mem: Ky. and Am. Bar Asns; Am. Trial Lawyers Asn; Kiwanis; Farm Bur. Rel: Baptist. Legal Res: Wynn Addition, Sturgis, Ky. 42459. Mailing Add: Route 1, Sturgis, Ky. 42459.

WESNER, EDWIN R. R
Chmn, Marion Co. Rep. Cent. Cmt, Ill.
b. Centralia, Ill, 2/12/19; s. Raymond James Wesner and Minnie Rhinholz W; m. 2/8/45 to Jeanne Look; c. Susan (Mrs. Prince), Barbara and Robert. Educ: Centralia High Sch. Polit. & Govt. Pos: Justice of peace, Centralia, Twp, Ill, 55-59 and supvr, 59-; chmn, Marion Co. Rep. Cent. Cmt, 62-; mem, Ill. Rep. Cent. Cmt, currently. Bus. & Prof. Pos: Partner, Wesner Insect Control, 46-61 and Best Exterminating Co, 61- Mil. Serv: Entered as Shipfitter 3/C, Navy, 42, released as Shipfitter 2/C, 45, after serv. in S.Pac. and Mediterranean. Mem: Rotary; Elks; VFW; Am. Legion; Moose. Rel: Christian. Mailing Add: 723 E. Broadway, Centralia, Ill. 62801. (1967)

WEST, CHARLES I. D
b. Washington, D.C, 9/27/08; s. Dr. Charles West (deceased) and Rebekah Baldwin W; m. 6/12/52 to Dorothy Seamon; c. John P. and Rocci S. Educ: Dartmouth Col, 26-29; Howard Univ. Sch. of Med, 29-33; Omega Psi Phi. Polit. & Govt. Pos: Del, Dem. Nat. Conv, 68; mem, U.S. Cmn. for UNESCO, currently. Bus. & Prof. Pos: Private practice, med, 36-; owner and publisher, Las Vegas Voice, 63- Mil. Serv: Entered as 1st Lt, Army Med. Corps, 42, released as Maj, 46, after serv. in Med. Detachment Comdr. and Exec. Officer, ETO and African Theatre, 43-46; Purple Heart; European-African Campaign Medals; Bronze Star. Publ: 'Africa in Today's World,' weekly series, 63-65 and 'Hidden History,' weekly series, 65-67, Las Vegas Voice. Mem: Nat. Med. Soc; Nat. Asn. of Newspaper Publishers; Am. Acad. of Gen. Practice; Int. Elks (past asst. grand med. dir). Legal Res: 1301 Ralston Dr, Las Vegas, Nev. 89106. Mailing Add: P.O. Box 4038, Las Vegas, Nev. 89106.

WEST, FOWLER CLAUD D
b. Bosqueville, Tex, 7/6/40; s. Fowler Clarke West and Bertha Dotson W; single. Educ: N.Tex. State Univ, 58-59; Baylor Univ, B.A, 63; Pi Sigma Alpha; Phi Eta Sigma. Polit. & Govt. Pos: Asst. staff consult, House Agr. Cmt, 65-69; admin. asst. to U.S. Rep. W.R. Poage, Tex, 69- Mil. Serv: Sgt. E-5, Army Nat. Guard, 63-69. Mem: Mason; bd. dirs, Cong. Secretaries Club. Rel: Methodist. Legal Res: 2324 Bosque Blvd, Waco, Tex. 76707. Mailing Add: 215 C St. S.E, Washington, D.C. 20003.

WEST, HAROLD NORMAN D
S.C. State Rep.
b. Rocky Mount, N.C, 8/15/20; s. W. Edgar West, Sr. and Imel Joyce W; m. 7/20/46 to Marjorie Ann Hodges. Educ: Univ. S.C, A.B, 44 and LL.B, 45; Omicron Delta Kappa. Polit. & Govt. Pos: Master in Equity for Berkley Co, 54-60; S.C. State Rep, 61- Bus. & Prof. Pos: Lawyer. Mem: Mason; Rotary; secy-treas, Moncks Corner C. of C. Rel: Baptist; Bd. of Deacons. Mailing Add: Box 716, Moncks Corner, S.C. 29461.

WEST, JAMES CLIFFORD R
Chmn, Marshall Co. Rep. Cent. Cmt, Iowa
b. Des Moines, Iowa, 7/30/32; s. Clifford Leroy West and Marian Brimhall W; m. 2/26/55 to Mary Carol Nelson; c. Guy James and Dean Alden. Educ: Iowa State Univ, B.S, 60; Denver Univ, M.B.A, 61. Polit. & Govt. Pos: Rep. precinct committeeman, State Center Twp, Iowa, 65-68; chmn, Marshall Co. Rep. Cent. Cmt, 68- Bus. & Prof. Pos: Mgr, Brimhall-West Co, 62- Mil. Serv: Entered as Pvt, Air Force, 52, released as S/Sgt, 56, after serv. in 13th Bomb Squadron, Far E. Command, 52-53; Air Medal; UN Serv. Medal; Korean Serv. Medal; Good Conduct Medal. Publ: 'Masonry is for Masons,' 2/66 and 'Charity,' 3-4/68, The Philalethes. Mem: Am. Legion; Mason; Boy Scouts; RAM; K.T; RSM; The Philalethes Soc. Rel: Presbyterian. Mailing Add: 202 Second St. N. W, State Center, Iowa 50247.

WEST, JAMES PASCHAL R
Chmn, Dooly Co. Rep. Party, Ga.
b. 6/17/26; s. Edgar Charles West and Betty Davis W; m. 9/30/44 to Zula Jean Arflin; c. Jeanine, James P, Jr. and David H. Educ: Pinehurst High Sch, grad. Polit. & Govt. Pos: Chmn, Dooly Co. Rep. Party, Ga, 64- Bus. & Prof. Pos: Farmer, currently. Mil. Serv: Entered as Pvt, Army, 45, released as Cpl, 46, after serv. in 925th Anti-Aircraft Artil. Automatic Weapons Bn, Asiatic- Pacific Theatre; Victory Ribbon. Mem: Mason; VFW; Nat. Farm Orgn; Farm Bur. Rel: Baptist. Mailing Add: Route 1, Pinehurst, Ga. 31070.

WEST, JOHN CARL D
Lt. Gov, S.C.
b. Camden, S.C, 8/27/22; s. Shelton J. West and Mattie Ratterree W; m. 8/29/42 to Lois Rhame; c. John Carl, Jr, Douglas Allen and Shelton Anne. Educ: Univ. S.C, LL.B. magna cum laude, 48; Phi Beta Kappa. Polit. & Govt. Pos: Mem, Hwy. Cmn, 48-52, v.chmn, 52; S.C. State Sen, 54-62; Lt. Gov, S.C, 67-, regional v.pres, Nat. Conf. of Lt. Gov, 67-68; del, Dem. Nat. Conv, 68. Bus. & Prof. Pos: Attorney, West, Holland and Fruman, Camden, S.C. Mil. Serv: Army, 42-46; Army Commendation Medal. Mem: Kiwanis; Am. Legion; C. of C; bd. of trustees, Coker Col, Hartsville, S.C; chmn, United Cerebral Palsy Dr. of S.C, 64. Rel: Presbyterian; Deacon, Ruling Elder, Bethesda Presbyterian Church. Mailing Add: P.O. Drawer 100, Camden, S.C. 29020.

WEST, ROBERT EDWARD R
Vt. State Sen.
b. Londonderry, Vt, 8/9/36; s. Lewis Alfred West and Cora Mae Norse W; m. to Judith Kay Seaver. Educ: Amherst Col, B.A, 58; Yale Univ. Law Sch, LL.B, 61; Theta Delta Chi. Polit. & Govt. Pos: Trustee of pub. funds, Manchester, Vt, 62-64, cemetery cmnr, 63-64; Vt. state attorney, Rutland Co, 65-69; grand juror, Rutland, Vt, 65-69; mem, Vt. Digest Cmt, 66-68, chmn, 66-67; del, Vt. Rep. State Conv, 68; del, Vt. Rep. State Platform Conv, 68; Rutland Co. chmn, Vt. Almanac, 68; Rutland city chmn, Vt. Rep. Annual Dinner, 68; justice of the peace, Rutland, 69-; Vt. State Sen, Rutland Co, 69-; mem, Joint Criminal Code Study Cmt, Vt, 69-; mem, Regional Planning Cmt. on Crime Control and Prev, 69; mem, Rutland Co. Rep. Cmt; v.chmn, City of Rutland Rep. Cmt. Mem: Rutland Co, Bennington Co, Vt. and Am. Bar Asns; Nat. Dist. Attorneys Asn; Vt. State Attorneys Asn.(pres, 67-69); C. of C; Traffic Safety Coun; Elks; Grange; Ethan Allen Coun, Boy Scouts; Burr and Burton Sem. Alumni Asn.(pres, 62-66); Green Mountain Club; Crown Point Rd. Asn. Rel: Protestant. Legal Res: 143 Grove St, Rutland, Vt. 05701. Mailing Add: 98 Merchants Row, Rutland, Vt. 05701.

WEST, TED GRADON D
b. Lenoir, N.C, 2/18/29; s. John Wilson West and Elvira Foster W; m. 12/26/50 to Claudine Goble; c. Amanda Anne. Educ: Concord Col, A.B, 54; Univ. N.C. Sch. Law, J.D, 57; National Blue Key; Phi Alpha Delta; assoc. ed, N.C. Law Rev. Polit. & Govt. Pos: Attorney, Tenn. Valley Authority, 57-60; pres, Caldwell Co. Young Dem. Club, N.C, 61-62; v.pres, N.C. Young Dem. Club, 62-63; del, Dem. Nat. Conv, 64. Bus. & Prof. Pos: Attorney, Lenoir, N.C, 60-; pres, Goble and Munday Redi-Mix, Inc, 63-; gen. counsel, Blue Ridge Elec.Corp, 65- Mil. Serv: Entered as Midn, Navy, 48, released as Lt.(jg), 52, after serv. as Naval Aviator, ComAirLant, Sixth Fleet; Nat. Defense, European Occup. and Naval Res. Medals; Lt, Navy Res, 55- Publ: 'Case Notes and Comments,' N.C. Law Rev, 56. Mem: Am. and N.C. Bar Asns; Rotary; Moose; Am. Legion. Rel: Baptist. Legal Res: 9 Beverly Circle, Lenoir, N.C. 28645. Mailing Add: P.O. Box 282, Lenoir, N.C. 28645.

WEST, TOM JAMES R
Kans. State Sen.
b. Topeka, Kans, 6/10/25; s. George William West and Victoria Maria Taffoya W; m. 12/20/46 to Delores Jane Hunt; c. Suzanne Jane (Mrs. Rodney L. Nelson), Janet Marie, Nancy Gail and Tom James, II. Educ: Washburn Univ, A.B, 50; Univ. Kans, M.E, 54; Alpha Beta Kappa; Phi Delta Kappa. Polit. & Govt. Pos: Kans. State Rep, 67-69; Kans. State Sen, 69- Bus. & Prof. Pos: Sch. prin, Highland Park Jr. High, Topeka, Kans, 54-61, Curtis Jr. High, 61-62, Eisenhower Jr. High, 62-63 and Highland Park High Sch, 63- Mil. Serv: A/S, Coast Guard, 43, released Chief Qm, 46, after serv. in USS Eugene, destroyer, Pac. and Atlantic Theatres; Pac. Theatre Medal with three stars; Atlantic Medal with one battle star. Mem: Nat. Educ. Asn; Nat. Asn. of Sec. Sch. and Prin. Rel: Catholic. Mailing Add: 2801 Maryland St, Topeka, Kans. 66605.

WEST, WAYNE GRADE R
b. Andrews, N.C, 6/15/06; s. John Bryant West and Media Wright W; m. 6/8/30 to Mildred Barnard; c. Ronald W, Ramona and Wanda. Educ: Pub. Schs, N.C. Polit. & Govt. Pos: N.C. State Rep, 61-64; cand, N.C. State Rep, 66. Bus. & Prof. Pos: Farmer and cattleman. Mil. Serv: Entered as Pvt, Army, 29, released as Col, 58, after serv. in Transportation Group, Ft. Eustis, Va; ETO and Am. Theater Ribbons; Res, Am. Defense and Victory Medals; Occupation Medal. Mem: Shrine; VFW; AF&AM; Farm Bur. Rel: Baptist. Mailing Add: R.F.D. 1, Warne, N.C. 28909.

WEST, WILSON HENRY R
b. Odin, Ill, 9/13/13; s. Willian John West and Clara Sebastian W; m. 4/1/38 to Sarah Mildred Ingram; c. John Wilson. Educ: South. Ill. Univ, 31-33; St. Louis Univ, M.D, 37. Polit. & Govt. Pos: Del, Rep. Nat. Conv, 68; chmn, St. Clair Co, United Rep. Fund, currently; mem. bd. gov, Ill. United Rep. Fund, currently; mem, Belleville Rep. Club, Ill, currently. Bus. & Prof. Pos: Instr. urology, Wash. Univ, 39-52; pres, Christian Welfare Hosp. Staff, East St. Louis, 61-62; mem. bd. of dirs, Union Nat. Bank, East St. Louis, currently; mem. exec. bd, Christian Welfare Hosp, St. Clair Co, currently. Publ: 'Treatment of Tetanus, Am. Med. Asn, 37. Mem: St. Clair Co. Med. Soc, pres. elec, 69; mem, St. Clair Hosp. Asn; Am. Med. Asn; Ill. State Med. Soc; St. Clair Med. Soc; Mason; Shrine; Consistory; K.T; C. of C. Rel: Methodist. Mailing Add: 14 Oakwood Dr, Belleville, Ill. 62223.

WESTBERRY, HARRY D
Fla. State Rep.
b. Jessup, Ga, 4/30/07; m. to Elizabeth Lenoir. Educ: Univ. of Fla. Exten. and ICS, grad, Steam E.E. Polit. & Govt. Pos: Fla. State Rep, 52- Bus. & Prof. Pos: Mgr. of indust. rels, South. Mills and Woodlands, Owen-Ill. Glass Co. Mil. Serv: Army and Navy, World War II. Mem: Elks; N. Jacksonville Businessman's Club; Mason; Scottish Rite; Shrine; Duval Co. Playground Asn; Am. Legion; VFW; Gator Bowl Asn. Rel: Baptist. Legal Res: 152 Tallulah Ave, Jacksonville, Fla. 32208. Mailing Add: P.O. Box 1620, Jacksonville, Fla. 32201.

WESTBROOK, WILLIAM VERDO, JR. R
b. Jackson, Miss, 12/2/29; s. William Verdo Westbrook and Ruby Thomas W; m. 11/10/50 to Barbara Anne Thomson; c. William V, III, Holley Anne and Mark Thomas. Educ: Univ. Miss, B.B.A, 50; Kappa Sigma. Polit. & Govt. Pos: Pres, Jackson Rep. Party, Miss, 58; del, Rep. Nat. Conv, 60; chmn, Hinds Co. Rep. Exec. cmt, 60-68. Bus. & Prof. Pos: V.pres. and secy, Westbrook Mfg. Co. 55- Mil. Serv: Entered as 2nd Lt, Air Force, 51, released as 1st Lt, 55, after serv. in 468th Strategic Fighter Squadron, 508th Strategic Fighter Wing, Far East Japan, 53. Mem: Kiwanis; River Hills Club of Jackson. Rel: Presbyterian. Mailing Add: 4010 Pinewood Drive, Jackson, Miss. 39211.

WESTERBERG, VICTOR JOHN R
Pa. State Rep.
b. Kane, Pa, 2/6/12; s. Victor J. Westerberg and Anna E. Seaton W; m. 9/25/41 to June Elizabeth Anderson; c. Ann M. (Mrs. Fergusen) and Jean S. (Mrs. Morrow). Polit. & Govt. Pos: Auditor, Wetmore Twp. Road Dist, Pa, 35-37 and secy, 37-42; mem. borough coun, Kane, Pa, 52-56; acting

postmaster, U.S. Post Off, Kane, 59-61; Pa. State Rep, 67th dist, 64- Bus. & Prof. Pos: Partner, Gausman's Garage, 46-61; owner, Kane Truck Sales, Pa, 62- Mil. Serv: Entered as 1st Lt, Army, 42, released as Capt, 46, after serv. in 613 Ordnance Bn, ETO, 44-45. Mem: C. of C.(past pres, Kane Chap); Rotary (past pres, Kane Chap); dir, McKean Co. Crippled Childrens Soc; Am. Legion; VFW; Kane Area United Fund. Rel: First Methodist. Mailing Add: 630 Greeves St, Kane, Pa. 16735. (1967)

WESTERFIELD, SAMUEL ZAZA, JR.
U.S. Ambassador to Liberia
b. Chicago, Ill, 11/15/19; s. Samuel Zaza Westerfield and Rachael Waddleton W; m. 9/5/45 to Helene Bryant; c. Samuel Zaza and Sheila Helene. Educ: Howard Univ, A.B. magna cum laude, 39; Harvard Univ, M.A, 49, Ph.D, 50. Polit. & Govt. Pos: Treas, All-Citizens Registration Cmt, Atlanta, Ga, 57-58; U.S. Rep. to numerous int. conf; assoc. dir. debt analysis staff, Treas. Dept, 61, sr. adv. to dir, Off. Int. Affairs, 61-63; dep. asst. secy, Bur. Econ. Affairs, Dept. of State, 63-64, dep. asst. secy. econ. and planning, Bur. African Affairs, 64-69; U.S. Ambassador to Liberia, 69- Bus. & Prof. Pos: Instr. econ. and statistics, Howard Univ, summers, 40, 41 & 45; asst. prof. econ, W.Va. State Col, 45-46; asst. prof. econ. and chmn. dept. econ. and bus. admin, Lincoln Univ, 47-50; assoc. prof. econ, Atlanta Univ, 50-52, prof. econ. and dean, sch. bus. admin, 52-61; vis. prof, Harvard Grad. Sch. Bus, 59-60; guest lectr, Univ. Col, Ibadan, Nigeria, 60 and Univ. Col, Addis Ababa, Ethiopia, 60. Mem: Urban League (bd. dirs, Atlanta Chap, 56-59); Am. Econ. Asn; Kappa Mu; Int. Club. Anson Phelps Stokes Scholar, 40-42; Rosenwald Found. Fel, 40-42; Soc. Sci. Research Coun. grant, 44-45; Am. Univs. Prog-Merrill Trust Fund Grant, 60. Legal Res: 4801 Colorado Ave. N.W, Washington, D.C. 20011. Mailing Add: U.S. Embassy, Monrovia, Liberia.

WESTERHOLM, LEO LYDER R
Chmn, Calhoun Co. Rep. Party, Tex.
b. Danevang, Tex, 2/7/22; s. Peter H. Westerholm and Astrid Hojrup W; m. 10/5/56 to Dorothy June Edwards; c. Sheila Ruth and Hans Kurt. Educ: Texas Arts & Indust. Col, Kingsville, Tex, B.S, 48. Polit. & Govt. Pos: Chmn, Calhoun Co. Rep. Party, Tex, 62- Bus. & Prof. Pos: Personal Producer, Southland Life Ins. Co, 53- Mil. Serv: Entered as Pvt, Army, 42, released as Pfc, 45, after serv. in 101st Airborne Div, ETO, 44; Presidential Citation; ETO Ribbon with one star; Captured during Normandy Invasion, Prisoner of War. Mem: Gulf Coast Asn. Life Underwriters; Lions (past pres.); Red Cross. Recipient, Lion of the Year Award, 60; 15 year pin, Red Cross. Rel: Methodist. Legal Res: 202 Sunnydale, Port Lavaca, Tex. 77979. Mailing Add: Box 44, Port Lavaca, Tex. 77979.

WESTFALL, RAYMOND E. 'JOHNNY' R
Mo. State Rep.
b. Halfway, Mo, 2/28/11; s. Linley B. Westfall and Mertie Vincent W; m. 11/21/37 to Ethel Faye Neill; c. Morris G. Educ: Drury Col, Adult classes, 57; Dale Carnegie Course. Polit. & Govt. Pos: Mo. State Rep, 140th Dist, 69- Bus. & Prof. Pos: Owner and operator, Grocery Store & Gen. Store, 37-45; salesman, Springfield Grocery Co, 44-66; owner and operator, Bolivar Candy & Tobacco Co, 48-; co-owner, Mo. Student Supply Co, 57-; former co-owner and now owner, Sho-Me Toy Co, 64- Mem: Lions (past pres, Halfway Club); Springfield Booster's Club (past pres); hon. mem, Future Farmers of Am. Rel: Baptist; Sunday sch. teacher, 25 years. Legal Res: Halfway, Mo. 65663. Mailing Add: Capital Bldg, Jefferson City, Mo. 65101.

WESTIN, LESLIE E. Conservative
b. St. Paul, Minn, 1917; m. to Harriet Holmberg; c. John, Robert and Edward. Educ: Univ. Minn. Polit. & Govt. Pos: Minn. State Sen, 54-66; dir, commun. serv, Minn. Cmt. Higher Educ, currently. Publ: 'Higher Education in the Solution of Community Problems,' State of Minn, 6/68; 'Action Education,' In: Planning 1968, Am. Soc. Planning Officials, 9/68. Mem: Nat. Univ. Extension Asn; Am. Soc. Planning Officials; Urban Am, Inc. Minn. Outstanding Young Man of the Year, Jr. C. of C, 52. Legal Res: 2160 Edgerton, St. Paul, Minn. 55117. Mailing Add: Minnesota Committee Higher Education, 550 Cedar Capitol Square, St. Paul, Minn. 55111.

WESTLAKE, JAMES ROGER R
Ga. State Rep.
b. Kansas City, Mo, 2/11/28; s. Roger A. Westlake and Helen Treadway W; m. 5/14/46 to Joyce Rosemary Covey; c. Joyce Ann, Beverly Jeanne, James R, Jr. and Richard Christopher. Educ: Univ. Mo, 44-45; Ga. State Col, B.B.A, 58 and M.B.A, 60; Beta Gamma Sigma; Delta Sigma Pi; Sigma Chi. Polit. & Govt. Pos: Ga. State Rep, 119th Dist, 65-68, 75th Dist, 68-, Minority Caucus Chmn, 69-; Fourth Cong. Dist, Rep. Party,Chmn, 66-68; del, Rep. Nat. Conv, 68; del. from Ga. Legis. to Inauguration, 69. Bus. & Prof. Pos: Columnist, Right Side of the Aisle, Decatur-DeKalb News; pres, South. Agencies, Inc, 49- Mil. Serv: Entered as A/S, Navy, released as Seaman 1/C, 46, after serv. in S.Pac, 45-46; Am. and Asiatic Theater Ribbons; World War II Victory Medal. Publ: Life Insurance Salesman, 63; 'Agent's Point of View,' Chartered Property & Casualty Underwriters News, 4/66. Mem: Soc. of Chartered Property & Casualty Underwriters; Soc. of Chartered Life underwriters; Optimist Club; Nat. Asn. Independent Ins. Agents. Rel: Presbyterian; Ordained Ruling Elder. Legal Res: 3930 West Side Place, Ellenwood, Ga. 30049. Mailing Add: 3375 Glenwood Rd, Decatur, Ga. 30032.

WESTLAND, JACK R
b. Everett, Wash, 12/14/04; s. Alfred John Westland and Hortense Horan W; m. 8/59 to Helen M. Geis; c. John T. Educ: Univ. of Wash, LL.B, 26; Phi Delta Phi; Psi Upsilon. Polit. & Govt. Pos: U.S. Rep, Wash, 53-64. Mil. Serv: Comdr, USN Res, WW II. Mem: Mason (Shriner); Rotary Int. Misc: Nat. Amateur Golf Champion, 52- Mailing Add: P.O. Box 326, Pebble Beach, Calif. 93953. (1967)

WESTPHAL, ALBERT H. R
Treas, 16th Cong. Dist. Rep. Cmt, Mich.
b. Neche, N.Dak, 11/3/97; s. Herman Henry Westphal and Amelia Walters W; m. 8/27/27 to Elsie A. Timian; c. George Albert and Sandra L. (Mrs. Milton C. Lewis, III); grandchildren, Debbie and Kevin Lewis. Educ: Univ. South. Minn, grad, 18; Mankato Commercial Col, Minn, grad; Dakota Bus. Col, Fargo, N.Dak, B.B.A; LaSalle Exten. Univ, Chicago, grad. law; Wayne State Univ, 1 year; Gamma Delta. Polit. & Govt. Pos: Precinct del, Rep. Party of Mich. 38-; mem, Citizens Adv. Cmt, Wyandotte, 63-; charter mem, Wyandotte Rep. Club; mem, 16th Cong. Dist. Rep. Cmt, 65-, treas, 69-; alternate del, Rep. Nat. Conv, 68. Bus. & Prof. Pos: Acct. clerk, Detroit Copper Brass Rolling Mills, 25-30, chief clerk, Anaconda Am. Brass Co, 33-42, chief timekeeper, 42-60, retired; instr, Twin City Commercial Col, Hancock, real estate salesman, Judd Realty Co, 63- Mem: Nat. Bus. Educ. Asn; Lutheran's Laymens League; Goodfellows; Hon. Order of Ky. Col. Rel: Lutheran. Mailing Add: 2433 17th St, Wyandotte, Mich. 48192.

WESTWOOD, JACK RICHARD R
b. Sioux City, Iowa, 7/5/26; s. Arthur Gerald Westwood and Hilda Losenstein W; m. 4/10/52 to Barbara Clemons; c. Victoria Lee, Elizabeth Ann, Jack Richard, II and Cameron Glenn. Educ: Colo. State Univ, B.S. in agr; Phi Delta Theta. Polit. & Govt. Pos: Chmn, Big Horn Co. Rep. Cent. Cmt, Mont, 64-69. Bus. & Prof. Pos: Owner, Westwood Ins. Agency, 63-; secy-treas. and mgr, Westwood Cattle Co, 63- Mil. Serv: Entered as Pvt, Army, 45, released as Pfc, 47, after serv. in Army Med. Corps; Good Conduct Medal; Am. Theater Ribbons. Mem: Mont. Independent Ins. Agents; Mason (32°); Shrine; Black Horse Patrol; Farm Bur; Farmers Union; Elks; Lions; Colo. State Alumni Asn; Am. Legion; dir, Big Horn Co. Soil and Water Conserv. Cmt; Nat. Farm Orgn. Del. to Russia, Soil Conserv. Serv. Rel: Baptist; Deacon, Little Brown Baptist Church. Mailing Add: Box 183, Lodge Grass, Mont. 59050.

WESTWOOD, JEAN MILES D
Dem. Nat. Committeewoman, Utah
b. Price, Utah, 11/22/23; d. Frances Marion Miles and Nettie Potter M; m. 9/6/41 to Richard Elwyn Westwood; c. Richard Elwyn, Jr. and Beth (Mrs. Vernon Davies). Educ: Carbon Jr. Col, 40 & 46-47; Univ. Utah, Utah State Univ, Univ. Colo. and San Diego State Col, selected classes of interest. Polit. & Govt. Pos: Mem, various campaign cmts, 54-; committeeman or dist. v.chmn, Dist. 453, Salt Lake Co, Utah, 54-; mem, Jordan Dist. Study Staff, Utah Merit Study Cmn, 58-60; mem, various Dem. Party Functions and Cmts, 58-; del, Utah Woman's Legis. Coun, 60-61 & 67-69; co-chmn, Salt Lake Co. Dem. Get Out The Vote and Canvass, 62; nat. state and co. del, Dem. Party, 64; women's campaign mgr. for U.S. Rep. David S. King, 64; mem, Utah Young Dem, Sagebrush Club, Jane Jefferson Club and Salt Lake Women's Dem. Club; field rep, Staff of U.S. Rep, David S. King, 65-66; mem. exec. bd, Utah 100 Club, 65-66; mem, Utah State Dem. Cent. Cmt, 65-; chaplain, Salt Lake Co. Women's Dem. Club, 66; del, Dem. Nat, State and Co. Conv, 67-69, mem. platform cmt, Dem. Nat. Conv, 68; coordinator, Humphrey Campaign Utah, State Elec. Hqs, 68; Dem. Nat. Committeeman, 68-; mem. exec. cmt, Dem. Nat. Cmt, 69. Bus. & Prof. Pos: Partner-secy, Westwood Mink Farm, Utah, 44-66; secy, Utah Mink Show, 51-54; secy, Westwood Enterprises, 66-; v.pres, West. Pools Inc, 68- Publ: 'Great Lakes News,' Am. Fur Breeder, 57-62; ed, Nat. Annual, Fur Broadcaster, 51-52. Mem: Am. Acad. of Polit. and Soc. Sci; hon. mem, Eugene Field Soc, Nat. Asn. of Authors and Journalists; Emba Mink Breeders Asn; Great Lakes Asn; Alpine Country Club; Beta Sigma Phi; Am. Legion Auxiliary; nat. Conv, del, PTA, 61; leader, 4-H Clubs, 7 years; Ballet West Asn; Utah Consumer's League; Am. Civil Liberties Union; v.pres, Salt Lake Co. Dem. Women's Club, 67-68. Short Story and Poetry Writing, First Place in Writer's Digest Annual Short Story Contest; Book Rev. and Lectrs, Women's Clubs. Rel: Latter-day Saint. Mailing Add: 1624 West 8600 South, West Jordon, Utah 84084.

WETHERBY, LAWRENCE WINCHESTER D
Ky. State Sen.
b. Middletown, Ky, 1/2/08; s. Dr. Samuel D. Wetherby and Fanny Yenowine W; m. 4/24/30 to Helen Dwyer; c. Lawrence, Jr, Suzanne and Barbara. Educ: Univ. Louisville, LL.B, 29; Omicron Delta Kappa; Delta Upsilon. Polit. & Govt. Pos: Judge, Jefferson Co. Juvenile Court, Ky, 43-47; chmn, 34th Legis. Dist. Dem. Cmt, 43-56; Lt. Gov, Ky, 47-50, Gov, 50-55 and chmn, South. Gov. Conf, 54-55; secy, Ky. State Dem. Cent. Cmt, 47-52, secy, 60-65 and mem. finance cmt, 65-; del, Dem. Nat. Conv, 48-68; mem, State Constitution Assembly, 64-66; Ky. State Sen. and Pres. Pro-Tem, Ky. State Senate, 66- Bus. & Prof. Pos: Attorney-at-law, 29-; dir, Lincoln Income Life Ins. Co, 40-; v.pres. and dir, Brighton Engr. Co, 56- Mil. Serv: Ky. Nat. Guard, 25-29. Mem: Franklin Co. and Ky. State Bar Asns; C. of C; Frankfort Country Club. Named Ky. Man of the Year, 52, Ky. Sportsman of Year, 54 and Mr. Recreation, Ky, 56. Rel: Methodist. Mailing Add: Weehawken Lane, Frankfort, Ky. 40601.

WETHERELL, HOWARD HENDERSON D
Committeeman, Fla. State Dem. Exec. Cmt.
b. Daytona Beach, Fla, 7/13/29; s. Carl Frederick Wetherell and Bertha Lee Henderson W; m. 12/19/57 to Diana Lee Daniel; c. Margaret L, Elizabeth J. and David H. Educ: Marion Inst, Ala, A.S, 49; Univ. Ala, 49-50; Univ. Berlin, 51-52; Fla. State Univ, B.S, 54 and postgrad; Sigma Chi; founder, Epsilon Zeta Chap, Sigma Chi, Fla. State Univ. Polit. & Govt. Pos: Pres, Volusia Co. Young Dem, Fla, 57-58; treas, Volusia Co. Dem. Exec. Cmt, 58-65; dist. v.pres, Fla. State Young Dem, 59; chmn, North Peninsula Zoning Dist. Bd. of Adjust, 59-60; pres. and dir, Northeast Dem. Club Volusia Co, 61-62; U.S. Rep. campaign mgr, Fifth Cong. Dist, Fla, 62; dist. chmn, Oper. Cleansweep, Dem. Get-Out-the-Vote, 62; mem, Ormond Beach Financial Adv. Cmt, currently; mem, Ormond Beach Police Pension Fund Trustee, currently; committeeman, Fla. State Dem. Exec. Cmt, 67-; alternate del, Dem. Nat. Conv, 68. Bus. & Prof. Pos: Research analyst, Fla. State Dept. of Educ, Tallahassee, 53-54; asst. exec. secy, Sigma Chi Int. Fraternity Hq, Evanston, Ill, 54-55; pub. sch. teacher, Volusia Co. Schs, Fla, 55-56; admin. asst. to pres, Ellinor Corp, 56-57; dir. commun. rels, First Fed. Savings & Loan of Daytona Beach, 58-64, asst. v.pres, 64-66 and v.pres, currently. Mil. Serv: Entered as Inductee, Army, 51, released as Sgt, 53, after serv. in Army Combat Engrs, Army Occup. Forces, Europe; Army Occup. Serv. Medal; NATO and Good Conduct Medals. Mem: Savings Insts. Mkt. Soc; Am. Savings & Loan Inst.(past pres, Daytona Beach Chap); Fla. State Savings & Loan League; life mem, Sigma Chi Int. Fraternity; Kiwanis Int; Daytona Beach and Ormond Beach C. of C; Am. Legion; VFW; Vet. Businessmen Club; Daytona Beach Area Execs. Club (former v.pres); Oceanside Country Club; Ponte Vedra Club; Fla. State Soc. for Crippled Children (bd. dirs); Volusia Co. Easter Seal Soc. for Crippled Children. Jr. C. of C, Outstanding Young Men of Am. Publ, 65;

Merit Awards for Outstanding Serv, Jr. C. of C, Daytona Beach C. of C; Northeast Dem. Club Volusia Co. and Volusia Co. Crippled Children Soc; Sigma Chi Presidential Citation for Outstanding Alumni Serv; Fla. Newspaper Advert. Execs. Cert. of Merit for Outstanding Advert. Financial Classification. Rel: Presbyterian. Mailing Add: 76 S. Halifax Dr, Ormond Beach, Fla. 32074.

WETHERELL, ROSE CLAIRE D
V.Chmn, Idaho State Dem. Cent. Cmt.
b. Flandreau, S.Dak, 2/18/19; d. Thomas James Hart and Margaret Louise Hefferon H; m. 8/28/43 to Robert Miles Wetherell, wid; c. Michael Edward, Dennis Hart, Ellen Ann and Robert Thomas; Educ: Univ. Calif, Berkeley, 2 years; Mercy Hosp. Sch. Nursing Council Bluffs, Iowa, R.N. Polit. & Govt. Pos: State Committeewoman, Elmore Co, Idaho, 50-; secy, Elmore Hosp. Bd, Elmore Co. Mem. Hosp, 56-59; v.chmn, Idaho State Dem. Cent. Cmt, 62-del, Dem. Nat. Conv, 68. Bus. & Prof. Pos: Asst. dir, USO Mountain Home, 52-54; indust. nurse, Hughes Aircraft, 61-63; owner-mgr, Guaranty Title & Abstract Co, Mountain Home, 66- Mil. Serv: Entered as Ens, Navy, 42-43, serv. in Bremerton, Wash. Mem: Am. Legion, Legion Auxiliary; Elkettes; Idaho Nurses Asn; C. of C.(bd. dir, 69-70), Am. Contract Bridge League; Catholic Altar Soc; pres, Am. Field Serv. Rel: Roman Catholic. Legal Res: 440 N. Eighth East, Mountain Home, Idaho 83647. Mailing Add: 150 S. Third, East, Mountain Home, Idaho 83647.

WETLAUFER, BRUCE ALVAH R
Chmn, Green Lake Co. Rep. Party, Wis.
b. Montello, Wis, 10/13/21; s. Alvah Henry Wetlaufer and Edith Parrott W; m. 10/13/60 to Patricia Brady; c. Kathy Ann. Educ: Univ. Wis, Madison, B.S, 48; Lambda Chi Alpha. Polit. & Govt. Pos: Treas, Green Lake Co. Rep. Party, Wis, 63-64, chmn, 64-; Green Lake Co. chmn, Citizens for Goldwater, 64 and Citizens for Nixon, 68. Mem: Pres, Med. Rep. Club, Madison, Wis, 56-57; dir, Dane Co. Pharmaceutical Asn, 57-58, pres, 60-61; pres, Green Lake C. of C, 63-64; Am. and Wis. Pharmaceutical Asns; Nat. Asn. Retail Druggists; Lions; Univ. Wis. Alumni Club. Rel: Catholic. Mailing Add: 387 Princeton Rd, Green Lake, Wis. 54941.

WETZEL, DARREL ERNEST D
Treas, Darke Co. Dem. Exec. Cmt, Ohio
b. Greenville, Ohio, 1/6/12; s. Fred Wetzel and Racheal Ernest W; m. 3/4/36 to Berniece Roosa; c. Roberta, Betty Lou, Carolyn, Margaret, Wayne, and Dennis. Polit. & Govt. Pos: Mem, Gettysburg Sch. Bd, Ohio 42-54 and Darke Co. Sch. Bd, 54-68; trustee, Van Buren Twp, 12 years; treas, Darke Co. Dem. Exec. Cmt, 61-; alternate del, Dem. Nat. Conv, 64. Mem: Co. and State Trustees Asns; Darke Co. Farm Bur; Scottish Rite; Shrine; Mason (32°); assoc. supvr, Soil Conserv. of Darke Co; dir, Miami Valley Tobacco Growers Coop. Asn. Rel: Evangelical United Brethren. Mailing Add: R.F.D. 2, Greenville, Ohio 45331.

WEV, OSCAR C. B. R
Chmn, Hanover Co. Rep. Party, Va.
b. Richmond, Va, 5/8/07; s. Oscar Neill Wev and Nellie Baughan Bosquet W; m. 7/16/36 to Lillian Dixon; c. Lynda (Mrs. Frank C. Cowatch), Penelope (Mrs. A. Jonathan Frere), Peter and Pamela (Mrs. James A. Hart). Educ: Univ. Va, 2 years; U.S. Coast Guard Acad, B.S. Polit. & Govt. Pos: Chmn, Hanover Co. Rep. Party, Va, 66- Bus. & Prof. Pos: Retired farmer since 65. Mil. Serv: Entered as Pvt, Army, 27, graduated from U.S. Coast Guard Acad. as Ens, 31, released as Capt, 64; Commendation Ribbon; Am. Defense Ribbon with Star; Am. Theater Ribbon; European Theater with Star; Pac. Theater Ribbon with 5 Stars; Philippine Liberation Ribbon with 2 Stars; Greek Naval Medal 1st Class. Helped design, and commanded for 3 years, U.S. Coast Guard Cutter Courier, a vessel operated Voice of America, 51-54. Mem: Mason; Mil. Order of World Wars; Hanover Country Club. Rel: Presbyterian. Mailing Add: R.R. 1, Box 476, Ashland, Va. 23005.

WEWEL, LARRY LOU D
b. Newport, Nebr, 8/29/40; s. Lou F. Wewel and Reda Schriener W; single. Educ: Wayne State Col, B.F.A. in Educ, 67; Pi Kappa Delta; pres, Young Dem. Club; pres, Pre-Law Club; pres, Int. Rels. Club. Polit. & Govt. Pos: Pres, Nebr. Young Dem. Clubs, 66-68; mem. exec. bd, Nat. Young Dem. Clubs U.S, 66-68; mem. exec. bd, Nebr. Dem. Party, 66-68; alternate del, Dem. Nat. Conv, 68. Bus. & Prof. Pos: Rancher, Newport, Nebr, 58-; research dir, Int. Chem. Workers Union, Akron, Ohio, 67- Mem: Sandhills Cattle Asn; K. of C; Rel: Catholic. Legal Res: Box L Ranch, Newport, Nebr. 68759. Mailing Add: 733 W. Market St, Apt. 708, Akron, Ohio 44303.

WEYRENS, JERRY PHILIP Conservative
b. St. Cloud, Minn, 12/6/32; s. Hugo A. Weyrens and Alma Storkamp W; m. 4/24/65 to Mary Ellen Byrne; c. Molly Irene. Educ: Univ. Minn. Sch. Agr, Cert, 52. Polit. & Govt. Pos: Chmn, Sch. Bd. Dist, Minn, 52 & 55-64; chmn, St. Cloud Metrop. Planning Cmn, 66-67. Bus. & Prof. Pos: Owner, Angushire Golf Course (pres, 66-); owner, Angus Acres, Housing Develop; mem. bd. trustees, St. Cloud Hosp. Mil. Serv: Entered as Pvt, Army, 54, released as Sp-2, 56, after serv. in ETO, 54-56. Mem: Bd. mem, Univ. Minn. Alumni Asn, St. Cloud Chap, 64-67; bd. mem, St. Cloud Hosp. Extended Care Facility, 66; Past Exalted Ruler, Elks Lodge 516, 62-63; Rotary Int; K. of C.(4°); Minn. Angus Asn; Minn. Crop Improv. Asn; v.pres, St. Cloud Libr. Bd. and St. Cloud Rotary Club. Rel: Catholic. Mailing Add: Angus Acres, St. Cloud, Minn. 56301.

WHALEN, CHARLES WILLIAM, JR. R
U.S. Rep, Ohio
b. Dayton, Ohio, 7/31/20; s. Charles William Whalen and Coletee E. Kelleher W; m. 12/27/58 to Mary Barbara Gleason; c. Charles E, Daniel D, Edward J, Joseph M. and Anne E. Educ: Univ. Dayton, B.B.A, 42; Harvard Univ. Grad. Sch. Bus. Admin, M.B.A, 46; Eta Mu Pi. Polit. & Govt. Pos: Ohio State Rep, 55-60; Ohio State Sen, 61-66. Bus. & Prof. Pos: V.pres, Dayton Dress Co, 46-52; from asst. prof. to prof. retailing, Univ. Dayton, 52-63, prof. econ. and chmn. dept, 63-; v.pres, Whalen Invest Co, 54- Mil. Serv: Entered as Pvt, Army, 43, released as 1st Lt, 46, after serv. in 628th Qm. Refrigeration Co, 44-45 and Base Sect. Spec. Serv. Officer, India-Burma Theater, 45-46. Publ: Co-auth, How To End The Draft: The Case For An All-Volunteer Army, Nat. Press, Inc. Mem: Am. Legion; Eagles; Sertoma Club; VFW; K. of C. Rel: Roman Catholic. Mailing Add: 204 Lookout Dr, Dayton, Ohio 45419.

WHALEN, GEORGE EDWIN D
State Committeeman, N.Y. State Dem. Cmt.
b. Dover Plains, N.Y, 11/27/19; s. Thomas P. Whalen and Lillian Flagler W; m. 6/24/51 to Mildred E. Roberto; c. George Patrick and Thomas James. Educ: Fordham Univ, A.B, 41; Albany Law Sch, LL.B, 43. Polit. & Govt. Pos: Mem, Dutchess Co. Dem. Cmt, N.Y, 46-; town clerk, Dover, N.Y, 46-47, supvr, 48-53 & 56-59; mem, N.Y. State Dem. Cmt, 53-; counsel to comptroller of N.Y. State, 59-61; co. attorney, Dutchess Co, 64-65; chmn, Dutchess Co. Dem. Cmt, N.Y, 65-69; state committeeman, 97th assembly dist, N.Y. State Dem. Cmt, 68-; del, Dem. Nat. Conv, 68. Bus. & Prof. Pos: Attorney, 43- Mem: Am, N.Y. State and Dutchess Co. Bar Asns; K. of C; Grange; Elks. Rel: Catholic. Legal Res: Dover Plains, N.Y. 12522. Mailing Add: Route 22, Dover Plains, N.Y. 12522.

WHALEN, HORACE KING R
Md. State Del.
b. Bethesda, Md, 2/8/09; s. Benjamin Peyton Whalen and Edith Gittings W; m. 8/6/32 to Elizabeth Seeds; c. Donald P. and Barbara (Mrs. Cantor). Educ: U.S. Mil. Acad, B.S, 32. Polit. & Govt. Pos: Precinct chmn, Montgomery Co. Rep. Party, Md, 64-; Md. State Del, 66-, co-chmn, Montgomery Co. Del, Md. Gen. Assembly, 67-; del, Rep. Nat. Conv, 68. Bus. & Prof. Pos: Spec. partner, Sade & Co,(mem, N.Y. Stock Exchange), 58-62 & 65-; gen. partner, 62-65. Mil. Serv: Entered as 2nd Lt, Army, 32, retired as Col, 62, after serv. in various units including 12th Army Group, ETO, 43-45; Legion of Merit; Bronze Star; Commendation Medal; Various For. Awards from France, Belgium, Luxembourg and Japan. Mem: 12th Army Group Asn; Army and Navy Town Club, Wash, D.C; Asn. of U.S. Army. Rel: Protestant. Mailing Add: 7400 Arrowwood Rd, Bethesda, Md. 20034.

WHALEN, PETER J. D
b. Chicago, Ill, 9/20/98; married; c. 2 daughters. Educ: Bus. Col, acct. 2 yrs. Polit. & Govt. Pos: Ill. State Rep, 62-64; 17th Ward Regular Dem. Orgn, Chicago. Bus. & Prof. Pos: Gen. supvr, Cook Co. Hwy. Dept. Mem: AFL. Rel: Catholic. 1967 Legal Res: 8029 S. Vincennes Ave, Chicago, Ill. No mailing address available. (1967)

WHALEY, BEVERLY ANNE R
Secy, Rep. Co. Cent. Cmt. of San Francisco
b. Sidney, Mont, 7/14/27; d. Franklin Richard Whaley and Mathilda Block W; single. Educ: Univ. Wash, B.A, 49; Kappa Kappa Gamma. Polit. & Govt. Pos: V.chmn, San Francisco Young Rep, 58-59; chmn, 24th Assembly Dist, Rep. Co. Cent. Cmt. San Francisco, 59, mem, 65-, registrn. chmn, 66-68, secy, 66-; secy. to Congressman William S. Mailliard, 59-60; mem, Calif. Rep. State Cent. Cmt, 62- Bus. & Prof. Pos: Secy, E.S. Merriman & Sons, San Francisco, 61- Rel: Episcopal. Mailing Add: 940 Baker St, San Francisco, Calif. 94115.

WHALLEY, JOHN IRVING R
U.S. Rep, Pa.
b. Barnesboro, Pa; s. James H. Whalley and Ann Ashurst W; m. to Ruth Anderson; c. John and Ruth. Educ: Cambria Rowe Bus. Col, Johnstown, Pa. Polit. & Govt. Pos: Pa. State Assemblyman, 50-55; Pa. State Sen, 55-60; U.S. Rep, Pa, 60- Bus. & Prof. Pos: Automobile, Banking, Coal, Ins. and Real Estate. Rel: Presbyterian. Legal Res: 1309 Park Ave, Windber, Pa. 15963. Mailing Add: 1235 Longworth House Office Bldg, Washington, D.C. 20515.

WHAM, JAMES BUNDY R
b. Centralia, Ill, 10/10/18; s. Charles Wham and Sarah Pauline Bundy W; m. 6/24/41 to Phyllis Jane Wright; c. Sarah Jane (Mrs. Cary) and Jennifer Jean. Educ: Univ. Ill, B.S, 44, Col. of Law, J.D, 46; Order of the Coif; Sigma Chi. Polit. & Govt. Pos: Del, Rep. Nat. Conv, 52, 60, 64 & 68; Rep. precinct committeeman, Centralia Twp, Ill, 50-; Judge, Ill. Court of Claims, 53-61. Bus. & Prof. Pos: Partner, Wham & Wham Attorneys, Centralia, Ill, 47- Mil. Serv: Entered as Pvt, Army Air Corps, 41, released as Maj, 45 after serv. in 62nd Troop Carrier Group, 12th Air Force, ETO, 42-45; Bronze Star; Campaign Medals for serv. in Eng, N.Africa, Sicily and Italy. Mem: Ill, Fed. and Marion Co. Bar Asns; fel. Am. Col. of Trial Lawyers; Int. Soc. of Barristers; Ill. Soc. of Trial Lawyers; Am. Legion; VFW; 40 et 8; Rotary; Elks. Rel: Methodist. Legal Res: 407 S. Pine, Centralia, Ill. 62801. Mailing Add: 212 E. Broadway, Centralia, Ill. 62801.

WHARTON, CLYDE WILSON D
Committeeman, Noble Co. Dem. Cent. Cmt, Ohio
b. Marion Twp, Noble Co, Ohio, 8/10/13; s. Danford K. Wharton and Bessie McElfresh W; m. 8/15/36 to Margaret Fetkovich; c. Joyce (Mrs. Robert Sholtis), Judith Ann (Mrs. Gilbert Wheeler), David C. and James A. Educ: High sch, grad, 31. Polit. & Govt. Pos: Co. recorder, Noble Co, Ohio, 41-47; committeeman, Noble Co. Dem. Cent. Cmt, 56-; mem, Exec. Cmt, 60-, chmn, 60-; presidential elector, 64; mem, Ohio State Dem. Exec. Cmt, 69- Bus. & Prof. Pos: Accounting dept, Cent. Ohio Coal Co, Cumberland, Ohio, 46- Mem: Dem. Action Club; Noble Co. Dem. Club. Rel: Protestant. Mailing Add: R.R. 4, Caldwell, Ohio 43724.

WHARTON, J(AMES) ERNEST R
b. Binghamton, N.Y, 10/4/99; s. James H. Wharton and Mae Dibble W; m. to Marion K. Turner. Educ: Union Col, B.A; Albany Law Sch, LL.B, 19. Polit. & Govt. Pos: Surrogate Co. Judge, also judge, Children's Court of Schoharie Co, 41 & 47; U.S. Rep, N.Y, 51-65. Bus. & Prof. Pos: Lawyer, claim and legal dept, Travelers Ins. Co, 20-29; attorney-at-law, Richmond, N.Y, 29-32. Mil. Serv: Army, Pvt, World War I. Mailing Add: Richmondville, N.Y. 12149.

WHATLEY, ROBERT EUGENE 'BOB' R
b. Amarillo, Tex, 11/4/31; s. T. W. Whatley and Jewell Lucille White W; m. 8/3/62 to Dominica Romero; c. Thomas Wayne, Brenda Ann and Terry William. Educ: East. N.Mex. Univ, 1 year; Univ. N.Mex, 1 year. Polit. & Govt. Pos: Precinct chmn, Clovis Rep. Party, N.Mex, 66; mem, Curry Co.

Rep. Cent. Cmt, 66; del, N.Mex. Rep. Conv, 66; mem. exec. cmt, Curry Co. Young Rep, 66; Rep. cand, N.Mex. State Sen, Curry and Roosevelt Co, 66; del, Nat. Young Rep. Conv, 67; mem, N.Mex. Rep. State Cent. Cmt, 67; mem, N.Mex. Penitentiary Bd. Cmnr, 67; alternate del, Rep. Nat. Conv, 68; Rep. cand, N.Mex. State Treas, 68. Bus. & Prof. Pos: Conductor, AT-SF R.R, 51-63; owner, West. Oil Co, 63-; owner, Mr. Frisky Drive-Inns, 63- Mil. Serv: Entered as Pvt, Army, 49, released as Pfc, 56; entered as Pvt, 56, N.Mex. Nat. Guard, released as Sgt, 58; Soldier of the Month, Ft. Chaffee, Ark. Mem: Petroleum Marketing Inst; Am. Legion; Farm Bur; Optimist Club; Jaycees; Clovis Game Protective Asn; Kiwanis; Order R.R. Conductors (first secy); BRT. Received Eagle Scout. Rel: Baptist. Legal Res: 2200 Duckworth, Clovis, N.Mex. 88101. Mailing Add: P.O. Box 1041, Clovis, N.Mex. 88101.

WHATLEY, WILLIS D
b. 1928; married; c. two. Educ: Univ. Tex. Polit. & Govt. Pos: Tex. State Rep, 63-68. Bus. & Prof. Pos: Attorney. Mil. Serv: Korean War. Mailing Add: 2002 Brooktree, Houston, Tex. 77008. (1967)

WHEAT, VIVIAN R
Chmn, Delaware Co. Rep. Party, Okla.
b. Muldrow, Okla, 3/20/00; d. Chester Walker Bethell and Fannie Watts B; wid; c. Charles Bethell. Educ: Univ. Okla, B.A; Columbia Univ, M.A; Univ. Pa; Univ. Calif; Tulane Univ; Col. William and Mary; Pi Gamma Mu; Alpha Phi. Polit. & Govt. Pos: Chmn, Delaware Co. Rep. Party, Okla, 48-52, 67-69 & 69- and co. secy; secy, Okla. State Rep. Cmt. and Okla. State Rep. Exec. Cmt. Bus. & Prof. Pos: Teacher, Cent. State Col, 22-30; teacher, New Orleans Syst, 56-65. Mem: Am. Asn. Univ. Women; Legion Auxiliary; VFW. Rel: Methodist. Mailing Add: Trigo Farm, Star Route, Kansas, Okla. 74344.

WHEATCRAFT, MARTHA CLARK R
Mem, Ohio Rep. State Cent. and Exec. Cmt.
b. Morrow Co, Ohio; d. Col. John R. Clark and Mary Elizabeth Dawson C; m. to Willard W. Wheatcraft, wid; c. Joan (Mrs. Howard E. Samuel). Educ: Columbus Off. Training Sch, Bus. Admin. and Pub. Rels, 18-20. Polit. & Govt. Pos: Chairwoman, Crawford Co. Rep. Cent. Cmt, Ohio, 48- and secy, Crawford Co. Rep. Exec. Cmt, currently; state committeewoman, Ohio Rep. Party, 50-; presidential elector, eighth cong. dist, 56; mem, Galion City Traffic Cmn, 56-60 and Galion Civil Serv. Cmn, 66-68; mem, Crawford Co. Bd. of Elec, 56-; dist. chmn, Neighbor to Neighbor, 62-; chmn, Eighth Dist. Nixon-Agnew Cmt, 68; mem. bd. of mgt, Ohio Fedn. of Rep. Women; mem, Ohio Rep. State Cent. and Exec. Cmt, currently, and mem. policy cmt, 68- Bus. & Prof. Pos: Notary pub, Crawford Co, 50-; dir. pub. rels, Perfection-Cobey Co, Galion, Ohio, 54- and govt. contract adminstr, 56-; v.pres. and dir, Allied Indust. Sales, Inc, 61- Publ: History of Eighth Ohio Dist,(in prep). Mem: Ohio Mfrs. Asn; Defense Supply Agency; Perfection Mgt. Club; Harding Mem. Libr. Asn; Eastern Star (past matron, Burgoyne Chap); White Shrine (past worthy high priestess, Marion Chap); C. of C.(former mem. bd. dirs, Galion Chap); Galion Country Club; Capitol Hill Club; founder and chmn, Ohio's Eighth Cong. Dist. Hist. Found. Organized and sponsored the first Navy-Indust. Day held in U.S, Galion, Ohio, 5/59; Awarded Cert. of Merit and Appreciation, U.S. Army Procurement Dist, Cleveland, Ohio, 5/64. Rel: United Methodist. Legal Res: 705 Cherry St, Galion, Ohio 44833. Mailing Add: P.O. Box 685, Galion, Ohio 44833.

WHEATLEY, CHARLES H. D
b. Baltimore, Md, 8/11/32; married. Educ: West. Md. Col, A.B. 54; Drew Univ; Univ. of Md. Law Sch, LL.B, 59. Polit. & Govt. Pos: Law clerk, Md. Court of Appeals, 59-60; Md. State Del, 63-67. Bus. & Prof. Pos: Lawyer. Mem: Jr. Bar Asn. of Baltimore City; Real Estate Bd. of Gr. Baltimore; Eagles; Moose; Delta Theta Phi; ROA; pres, South. High Sch. Alumni Asn. Mailing Add: 1218 Pine Heights Ave, Baltimore, Md. 21209. (1967)

WHEATLEY, ELECTRA CATSONIS R
b. Washington, D.C, 8/6/33; d. Achilles Catsonis and Anastasia Carzis C; m. 5/12/63 to James E. Wheatley. Educ: Pa. State Univ, B.A. with honors, 55; George Wash. Univ, Nat. Law Center, J.D. with honors, 69; Phi Beta Kappa; Kappa Beta Pi; Pi Gamma Mu; Phi Sigma Iota; Phi Kappa Phi; Alpha Lambda Delta. Polit. & Govt. Pos: Legis. asst. to U.S. Rep. Donald D. Clancy, Ohio, 62-67; admin. asst. to U.S. Rep. John M. Ashbrook, Ohio, 68- Bus. & Prof. Pos: Asst. ed, AERO DIGEST, Washington, D.C, 55-56; ed. asst. and admin. secy, Fairchild Engine & Airplane Corp, 56-57; pub. rel. and exec. suite secy, Kaiser Indust. Corp, 57-60; secy, to pres, George Wash. Univ, 60-62. Mem: Top-Side Aviation Club. Phi Delta Delta Schaeffer Award; Outstanding Second-Year Law Student. Rel: Greek Orthodox. Mailing Add: 7613 Maryknoll Ave, Bethesda, Md. 20034.

WHEATLEY, SEAGAL V. R
b. Houston, Tex, 5/24/35; s. Seagal V. Wheatley and Hilda Claire Guess W; m. 10/28/61 to Beverly Annette Klaver; c. Jill and Julie. Educ: N.Tex. State Univ, B.A, 57; South. Methodist Univ, Dallas, 58; Univ. Tex, LL.B, 60; Delta Theta Phi; Sigma Nu. Polit. & Govt. Pos: Asst. Sgt-at-Arms, Tex. State House of Rep, 58-59; del, Rep. State Conv, 64 & 66; secy, Rep. Lawyer's Coun, 64-66; asst. city attorney Terrell Hills, 65, Corp. Court Judge, 66; chmn, Bexar Co. Rep. Cmt, 65-67; mem, Elec. Law Study Cmt. and State Rep. Finance Cmt, 66; alternate del, Rep. Nat. Conv, 68; U.S. attorney, West. Dist. of Tex, 69- Bus. & Prof. Pos: Partner, Beckmann, Stanard, Wood & Kenne, 60- Mem: Tex. and Am. Bar Asns; San Antonio Bar Asn.(secy, 65, dir, 66); Kiwanis; C. of C. Rel: Presbyterian. Legal Res: 626 Terrell Rd, San Antonio, Tex. 78209. Mailing Add: P.O. Box 1701, San Antonio, Tex. 78206.

WHEATLEY, W. C. D
Polit. & Govt. Pos: Former mem, N.Mex. Bd. of Mgrs. and Coun. of State Govt; N.Mex. State Rep, 49-51; N.Mex. State Sen, 53-67. Bus. & Prof. Pos: Car dealer. Mil. Serv: Civil Air Patrol. Mem: Past pres, C. of C; Nat. Legis. Leaders Conf; Rotary. Rel: Methodist. Mailing Add: 405 Walnut St, Clayton, N.Mex. 88415. (1967)

WHEATLEY, WALTER HENRY R
b. Brookfield, Vt, 8/4/96; m. to Grace Trask; c. two sons and two daughters. Educ: Vt. State Sch. of Agr, 18. Polit. & Govt. Pos: Mem, Agr. Conserv. Prog. Cmn, 38-53; mem, Orange Co. Cmn, Vt, 53-61; mem, Brookfield Rep. Cmt, 56-60; Vt. State Rep, 57-60; chmn, Orange Co. Rep. Cmt. and mem, Vt. State Rep. Cmt, 58-62; pres, Vt. Town Clerks & Treas, 60-62; Vt. State Sen, 63-68. Bus. & Prof. Pos: Farming; Brookfield Town Treas, 42- Mil. Serv: Univ. Vt, S.A.T.C, Pvt, 18. Mem: Mason (past master); Grange; Eastern Star (past patron); Farm Bur.(dir, Orange Co. Bur, 17 years and pres, 2 years); dir, Middle Br. Credit Union, 54- Rel: Congregational; Deacon. Mailing Add: R.F.D, 2, Randolph Center, Vt. 05061. (1967)

WHEELER, ALTON GROVER R
b. Waterbury, Vt, 3/28/91; s. Stedman C. Wheeler and Mabel J. Grover W; m. 5/20/15 to Edythe M. Boyce; c. Evelyn (Mrs. Stagg) and Gordon B. Educ: Norwich Univ, B.S, 14; Sigma Alpha Epsilon. Polit. & Govt. Pos: Auditor, Waterbury, Vt, 18-26, sch. dir, 24-36; trustee, Village of Waterbury, 38-39, pres, 40; mem. budget cmt, Town of Waterbury, 48-68, Village of Waterbury, 60-68; mem, State Selective Serv. Bd, 51-67; mem, Dist. Rep. Cmt, 65-67; mem, Waterbury Town Rep. Cmt; Vt. State Rep, 65-68. Bus. & Prof. Pos: Assoc. with father in lumber bus, 14-24; secy, Pilgrim Plywood Corp, Vt, 24-42, pres. and treas, 42-62. Mil. Serv: Vt. State Guard, Capt, 42-47. Mem: Mason (33°), York and Scottish Rite, Shrine, Grand Master Masons, Vt, 56-57, G.H.P. Grand Chap. of RAM, 44, Appointive Officer Gen. GR. Chap. of U.S, 53-54; Rotary; pres, Waterbury Pub. Libr. Asn. and trustee, 24-69; Waterbury Hist. Soc. Rel: Congregational. Mailing Add: 29 Randall, Waterbury, Vt. 05676.

WHEELER, CHARLES D. R
Ky. State Rep.
Educ: Ashland Jr. Col. Polit. & Govt. Pos: City cmnr, Ashland, Ky, 58-60; farmer exec. v.chmn, Young Rep. Clubs of Ky; former pres, Boyd Co. Young Rep. Club; Ky. State Rep, 64- Bus. & Prof. Pos: Pres, Wheeler & Williams Hardware Co, Inc. Mem: Kiwanis; Toastmaster's Club. Rel: Baptist. Mailing Add: 4330 Grandview Dr, Ashland, Ky. 41101. (1967)

WHEELER, GALE ELDON D
Chmn, Warren Co. Dem. Cent. Cmt, Iowa
b. Argentine, Kans, 7/22/30; s. Ira Arden Wheeler and Ruby Reamy W; m. 9/5/54 to Donna Faye Scull; c. Craig Allen, Zoe Ann, Stephen Kent, David and Thomas. Educ: State Univ. Iowa, B.A, 56. Polit. & Govt. Pos: Dem. precinct committeeman, Norwalk, Iowa, 62-66; chmn, Warren Co. Dem. Cent. Cmt, 66- Bus. & Prof. Pos: Statistician, Blue Cross, Des Moines, Iowa, 56- Mil. Serv: Entered as Pvt, Marine Corps, 48, released as Staff Sgt, 52, after serv. in Marine Corps Recruit Depot, San Diego, Calif, 48-52. Mem: Norwalk Planning & Zoning Cmn; Norwalk rep. and cmn. v.chmn, Cent. Iowa Regional Planning Cmn. Rel: Unitarian. Mailing Add: 610 Lane Ave, Norwalk, Iowa 50211.

WHEELER, HARVEY, JR.
b. Waco, Tex, 10/17/18; m. 1941 to Mimi Arnold; c. Two. Educ: Wabash Col; Univ. Ind, B.A, 46 and M.A, 47; Harvard Univ, Ph.D, 50; Pi Sigma Alpha. Polit. & Govt. Pos: Consult, Md. State Reorgn. Cmn, 53; chmn, Nat. Conf. for New Polit. Bus. & Prof. Pos: Asst. prof, Johns Hopkins Univ, 50-54; assoc. prof. polit. sci, Wash. & Lee Univ, 54-56, prof, 56-62; consult, Fund for the Repub, 58-, sr. fel, Center for the Study of Dem. Insts, 60-, vis. scholar, 61-63, prog. dir, 69- Mil. Serv: Army, 41-46; Mil. Govt, Europe, 44-46. Publ: The Conservative Crisis, 58; Democracy in a Revolutionary Era, 68; contrib, Am. Hist. Rev, West. Polit. Quart, Ethics, Notre Dame Lawyer, Jour. Conflict Resolution and Natural Law Forum; plus others. Mem: Am. Polit. Sci. Asn. Rel: Catholic. Mailing Add: Center for the Study of Democratic Institutions, Santa Barbara, Calif. 93103.

WHEELER, JACK ADRAIN D
Ga. State Rep.
b. Columbus, Ohio, 6/13/21; s. Harold Ellwood Wheeler and Mildred Kiger W; m. 2/23/43 to Josephine Askew; c. Mary Jo (Mrs. Donald R. Dye), Bob Ellwood and Jack Adrain, Jr. Educ: South. Col. Optom, Memphis, Tenn, Dr. of Optom, 48; Omega Delta. Polit. & Govt. Pos: Mayor, Elberton, Ga, 65-66 & 67-68; Ga. State Rep, Dist. 18, 69- Mil. Serv: Entered as Pvt, Army, 42, released as Sgt, 45, after serv. in 513 Ord, H.M. Co, ETO, 43-45; ETO Ribbon; Four Bronze Stars. Mem: Am. Optom. Asn; South. Coun. Optom; Ga. Optom. Asn. (secy-treas, 52, pres, 54, legal-legis. chmn, 56-66); Elks; Am. Legion; VFW; Rotary; C. of C. Ga. Optom. Commun. Serv. Award, 54, 62 & 63; Distinguished Serv. Award, Elbert Co. Jr. C. of C, 62; Distinguished Serv. Award, Elbert Co. C. of C, 63-64. Rel: Baptist. Legal Res: 196 Tusten St, Elberton, Ga. 30635. Mailing Add: P.O. Box 807, Elberton, Ga. 30635.

WHEELER, JAMES WALTER D
Chmn, Cherokee Co. Dem. Exec. Cmt, Ga.
b. Canton, Ga, 10/31/17; s. William Henry Wheeler and Lola Cochran W; m. 5/17/46 to Vern Bassett; c. Rebecca, Carole Ann and James W, Jr. Educ: Clemson Univ, 47. Polit. & Govt. Pos: Mem, Cherokee Co. Dem. Exec. Cmt, Ga, 50-55, secy-treas, 55-66, chmn, 66- Bus. & Prof. Pos: Dir. qual. control, Canton Textile Mills, Ga, 46-61, merchandising coordinator, 61-65, admin. asst, 65-68, mgr. prod. scheduling and control, 68- Mil. Serv: Entered as Pvt, Army, 42, released as Sgt, 45, after serving in 27th Evacuation Hosp, ETO, 44-45; Bronze Arrowhead; 5 Campaign Stars. Mem: Textile & Needle Trades Div, Am. Soc. Qual. Control(charter mem. and officer, 50-); past chmn, Cherokee Co. Red Cross Chap, 8 years; past pres, Canton Lions Club; past chmn. trustees, Canton Elem. Sch. Distinguished Serv. Award, Am. Soc. Quality Control, 62. Rel: Baptist; Past chmn, Bd. Deacons, First Baptist Church. Legal Res: Waleska Hwy, Canton, Ga. 30114. Mailing Add: Box 491, Canton, Ga. 30114.

WHEELER, JOHN HERVEY D
Asst. Treas, N.C. Dem. Cmt.
b. Kittrell, N.C, 1/1/08; s. John Leonidas Wheeler and Margaret Hervey W; m. 12/25/35 to Selena Lucille Warren; c. Julia W.(Mrs. Taylor) and Warren H. Educ: Morehouse Col, A.B, 29; N.C. Col, Durham, LL.B, 47; Omega Psi Phi. Polit. & Govt. Pos: Mem, Sixth Dist. Dem. Legis. Cmt, N.C, 54; mem, Pres. Cmt. on Equal Employ. Opportunity, 61-65; mem, Redevelop. Cmn, Durham, N.C, 61-; del, Dem. Nat. Conv, 64 & 68; v.chmn, Nat. Cmt. for Commun. Rels, Commun. Rels. Serv, 64-; mem, U.S. Adv. Cmn. on Food & Fibers, 65-; mem, Subcmt. on Study Racial Desegregation Pub. Schs, U.S. Cmn. on Civil

Rights, 66-; mem. and asst. treas, N.C. Dem. Cmt, currently. Bus. & Prof. Pos: Mem. bd. dirs, Mutual Savings and Loan Asn, 35-; pres, Mechanics and Farmers Bank, Durham, N.C, 52-; trustee, Cmt. for Econ. Develop, 64-; mem. bd. dirs, Mutual Real Estate Investment Trust, N.Y.C, currently; incorporator and mem. bd, Nat. Corp. for Housing Partnerships, currently; dir. and pres, N.C. Low-Income Housing Corp, currently. Publ: 'Apartheid Implemented by Education in South Africa,' J. Negro Educ, 61; 'Impact of Race Relations on Industrial Relations in the South,' Labor Law J, 7/64; 'Impact of Civil Rights Groups on the Poverty Program,' Duke Univ. Law Rev, 66. Mem: U.S. Supreme Court Bar; N.C. Bar Asn; personnel and urban affairs cmts, Am. Bankers Asn; chmn. ins. and protective cmt, N.C. Bankers Asn; F&AM; Shrine; bd. dirs. and past pres, 4-H Club Found, N.C; Bus. and Finance Cmt, Nat. Coun. of Churches. Rel: African Methodist Episcopal Church; gen. bd. mem. Mailing Add: 302 Formosa Ave, Durham, N.C. 27707.

WHEELER, JOHN R. P. D
b. Greeley, Colo, 12/23/16; s. Charles F. Wheeler and K. Blanche Robinson W; m. 9/13/42 to Laura Jane Coonradt; c. Thomas A, Lorie J. and John D. Educ: Univ. Colo; Hon. Bus. Sch. Fraternity. Polit. & Govt. Pos: Chmn, Colo. Real Estate Cmn, 50-65; Colo. State Rep, 65-67. Bus. & Prof. Pos: Am. Inst. Real Estate Appraisers. Rel: Methodist. Mailing Add: 1900-26 Ave.Court, Greeley, Colo. 80631. (1967)

WHEELER, LOUISE C. D
b. Otterbein, Ind, 7/21/11; d. Thomas B. Carroll and Margaret L. Quigg C; m. 6/29/44 to George W. Wheeler; c. Sue Dianne (Mrs. Schuessler). Educ: High Sch. and Lafayette Bus. Col. Polit. & Govt. Pos: Mem, Kennedy for President Club, Tippecanoe Co, Ind; secy, Branigin for Gov. Cmt, 56, mem. and secy, 66; Dem. V.Committeeman, Fairfield 8, Tippecanoe Co, 56-; v.chmn, Tippecanoe Co, and secy, 2nd Dist, Ind, 58-66; mem, Lafayette City Coun, 59-63, pres, 61-63; Dem. Mem. Bd. Registrn, Tippecanoe Co, 61-66. Bus. & Prof. Pos: Legal secy, Stuart Law Firm, 37-45 and Weigle Law Firm, Lafayette, Ind, Ball & Eggleston, 57-59; mem. Gift Shop Bd, St. Elizabeth Hosp, 51-; elected mem, St. Boniface Parish Coun. and mem, Ecumenical II Coun. in Parish, 68-; mem, Diocesan Coun. of Cath. Women and Chmn. Commun. Activities, 69; app. mem, City Libr. Bd, Lafayette, Ind, 69- Mem: Sigma Phi Gamma Int; Guild of St. Boniface Church; Lafayette Home Demonstration Club; St. Elizabeth Hosp. Auxiliary (pres, 69; elected mem. hosp. lay bd, 69); Cancer Soc; Guild of Cent. Catholic High Sch. Rel: Catholic. Mailing Add: 1201 Digby Dr, Lafayette, Ind. 47905.

WHEELER, ROBERT R. R
Chmn, Ninth Dist. Rep. Party, Mich.
b. Shelby, Mich, 3/10/27; m. July 1948 to Ann Jean Brondyke; c. Norman R. and Gerald A. Polit. & Govt. Pos: Chmn, Oceana Co. Rep. Party and Ninth Dist. Rep. Party, Mich, currently; dist. supvr, Oceana Co; alternate del, Rep. Nat. Conv, 68. Bus. & Prof. Pos: Ins. agent. Mem: Past Master, Mason; past pres, Shelby C. of C. and Shelby Optimist Club; Past Dist. Lt. Gov, Optimist Int; Co. Vet. Trust Fund Cmt, representing Am. Legion; chief, Shelby Vol. Fire Dept. Rel: Congregational; Treas, First Congregational Church. Legal Res: R.D. 2, Shelby, Mich. 49455. Mailing Add: P.O. Box 36, Shelby, Mich. 49455.

WHEELOCK, JOHN NEAL D
Exec. Dir, Fed. Trade Cmn.
b. Spring City, Tenn, 10/20/04; s. William E. Wheelock and Amanda Brown Neal W. Educ: Vanderbilt Univ, B.A, 27, LL.B, 29; Columbia Univ, M.A, 31; Kappa Sigma; Phi Delta Phi. Polit. & Govt. Pos: Attorney for Pub. Works Admin. in D.C, Miss. and Fla, 33-37; exec. dir, Fed. Trade Cmn, 61- Bus. & Prof. Pos: Attorney-at-Law, 31-33. Mil. Serv: Navy Res, Comdr, 42-46. Mem: Fed. Bar Asn; Nat. Press and Lawyers Clubs; Army and Navy Country Clubs. Mailing Add: 3133 Connecticut Ave. N.W, Washington, D.C. 20008.

WHEELOCK, ROBERT WEBB R
Mem, Calif. Rep. State Cent. Cmt.
b. Delta, Colo, 5/10/07; s. Dr. Jay Edson Wheelock and Daisy Britton Webb W; div. Educ: Univ. of Denver, D.D.S, 28; Univ. of Calif. Col. of Dentistry, Oral Surg. and Oro-Facial Prosthesis, 46; Delta Sigma Delta. Polit. & Govt. Pos: Assoc. mem, Calif. Rep. State Cent. Cmt, 62-64, mem, 64- Bus. & Prof. Pos: Private practice, gen. dentistry, Bay City, Tex, 28-31. Mil. Serv: Entered as Lt.(jg), Dental Corps, Navy, 31, Capt.(Ret), 59, after serv. in Staff Positions, Ships, Stas. and Hosp, Staff Dental Officer, Commandant Naval Operating Base, Leyte, Philippines, 44-45 and Staff Dental Officer, Philippine Sea Frontier, 45-46; Letter of Commendation from Commander Naval Operating Base, Leyte Gulf, Philippine Islands, 45; China Serv. Medal; Am. Defense Medal, Two Am. Campaign Medals; World War II Medal. Publ: 'Open Reduction of Fractured Mandible,' J. of Oral Surg, 7/50. Mem: Am. Dental Asn; Royal Soc. of Health, Egn; DeMolay; charter mem, Ocean Beach Town Coun, San Diego, Calif. and Lions Club, Bay City, Tex; Naval Order of the U.S; Mil. Order of World Wars. Cong. Cert. of Appreciation, Congressman Bob Wilson, 60; Cert. of Appreciation in Grateful Recognition of Serv. to Independent Higher Educ. and to Univ. of Denver, 63; Invited to Presidential Inauguration, 69. Rel: Baptist. Mailing Add: 4275 Coronado Ave, San Diego, Calif. 92107.

WHEETLEY, BERNARD RALPH R
b. Pratt, Mo, 8/8/19; s. Arthur A. Wheetley and Flaucie Augusta Deaton W; m. 6/3/39 to Mary Alice Short; c. Sandra Kay (Mrs. Freedman), Sharon Gayle and Susan Lea. Educ: High Sch. grad. Polit. & Govt. Pos: Treas, Poplar Bluff Rep. Cmt, Mo, 62-; del, Rep. State and Nat. Conv, 64; chmn, Butler Co. Rep. Cent. Cmt, Mo, 64-68. Bus. & Prof. Pos: Mem. of staff, Poplar Bluff Printing Co, 31 and part owner and secy-treas, 45- Mil. Serv: Army, 44, wounded, 44, Med. Discharge, 45, after serv. in 329th Inf, 44th Div, ETO; Purple Heart; Combat Infantryman Badge; ETO Campaign Ribbon; Good Conduct Ribbon. Mem: C. of C.(past pres);Kiwanis. Rel: Baptist. Legal Res: 1402 Lurlyn Rd, Poplar Bluff, Mo. 63901. Mailing Add: P.O. Box 4, Poplar Bluff, Mo. 63901.

WHELAN, JOHN JOSEPH D
Mem, Calif. Dem. State Cent. Cmt.
b. San Francisco, Calif, 11/20/17; s. Michael James Whelan and Josephine Welch W; m. 4/22/50 to Marjorie Celise Power; c. Mary Jo and Jeannette Marie. Educ: Univ. San Francisco, A.B. cum laude, 38; Univ. San Francisco Law Sch, J.D, 41. Polit. & Govt. Pos: Co-chmn, Campaign of Munic. Court Judge Clayton Horn for Superior Court, Calif, 64, Campaigns of Kevin O'Shea for San Francisco Bd. Supvr, 65 & 67 and Campaign for Calif. State Assemblyman John F. Foran, 68; mem, Calif. Dem. State Cent. Cmt, 68- Bus. & Prof. Pos: Assoc. with firm of Derby, Sharp, Quinby & Tweedt, San Francisco, Calif, 42-48; partner, Michelson, Whelan & Michelson, 48-64; self-employed attorney, 64- Mem: State Bar Calif; Am. Judicature Soc; Lawyers Club San Francisco; Int. Optimist (Lt. Gov, Zone 1, Pac. Cent. Dist. Club); Hibernian-Newman Club, San Francisco; San Francisco Olympic Club; Native Sons of Golden West, South Parlor; Police Athletic League, San Francisco; Godfather's Club; Druids Soc. Rel: Catholic. Legal Res: 140 Castenada, San Francisco, Calif. 94116. Mailing Add: 235 Montgomery St, San Francisco, Calif. 94104.

WHELAN, ROBERT EDWARD D
Committeeman, N.Y. Dem. State Cmt.
b. Brooklyn, N.Y, 4/8/17; s. Richard Chester Whelan and Agnes Kendall W; m. 8/31/41 to Juliana Catherine Hofstadt; c. Robert Kendall and David Charles. Educ: Grover Cleveland High Sch; Heffley Bus. Sch; Pohs Ins. & Real Estate Sch. Polit. & Govt. Pos: N.Y. State Assemblyman, Third Dist, Queens Co, 63-67; committeeman, N.Y. Dem. State Cmt, 34th Dist, 66- Bus. & Prof. Pos: Owner, Real Estate & Ins. Bur, 56- Mil. Serv: Entered as Pvt, Army, 40; released as Sgt, 45, after serv. in Hq. 1st Army, European Theater. Mem: Past pres, Grover Cleveland High Sch. Alumni Asn; past master, Lexington Lodge 310 F&AM, past most wise master, Chap. of Rose Croix, Consistory, Valley of New York; past comdr, Ridgewood Post 123, VFW; Am. Legion; Property Owners Asn. Rel: Lutheran. Legal Res: 63-67 77th Place, Middle Village, Queens, N.Y. 11379. Mailing Add: 66-27 Fresh Pond Rd, Ridgewood, N.Y. 11227. (1967)

WHELAN, VINCENT EDWARD D
b. San Diego, Calif, 6/12/34; s. Vincent A. Whelan and Adele Prentice W; m. 9/12/58 to Barbara Lee Higgs; c. William Vincent dePaul; Hugh Thomas More and Alexandra Marcella Maria Theresa. Educ: Univ. Notre Dame, 52-53; Univ. Georgetown Sch. For. Serv, B.S. in For. Serv, 56; Univ. Madrid, Spain, 54-55; Stanford Univ, LL.B, 59. Polit. & Govt. Pos: Chmn, Attorneys for Robert F. Kennedy, San Diego Co, Calif, 68; del, Dem. Nat. Conv, 68; pres, Dem. Prfnl. Club San Diego, Calif, 69- Bus. & Prof. Pos: Dir, San Diego Co. Bar Asn, 68- Mem: Am. Bar Asn; Am. Judicature Soc; bd. dirs, St. John's Episcopal Sch. Rel: Roman Catholic. Legal Res: Chula Vista, Calif. 92010. Mailing Add: P.O. Box 568, San Diego, Calif. 92112.

WHETMORE, JAMES EDWARD R
Calif. State Sen.
b. Columbus, Ohio, 3/9/13; s. Edward Claude Whetmore and Anna Garnett Willis W; m. 8/28/48 to Ann R. Hamaker; c. Edward J, Patricia A. and Karen R. Educ: LaSalle Exten. Univ, LL.B, 61. Polit. & Govt. Pos: Calif. State Assemblyman, 63-66; Calif. State Sen, currently. Bus. & Prof. Pos: Owner and operator, Whetmore Orchestra Agency, 35-; attorney, private practice, Calif, 61- Mem: Calif. and Orange Co. Bar Asns; Elks; Optimists; C. of C. Rel: Lutheran. Mailing Add: 1801 North Hills Dr, La Habra, Calif. 90631.

WHETZEL, JONATHAN R
Wash. State Rep.
b. Pittsburgh, Pa, 1927; single. Educ: Princeton, A.B. cum laude, 49; Harvard Law Sch, LL.B. Polit. & Govt. Pos: Wash. State Rep, 64- Bus. & Prof. Pos: Lawyer; gen. mgr, real estate and investment firm. Mil. Serv: Navy. Mailing Add: 1411 Fourth Ave, Seattle, Wash. 98101. (1967)

WHIPPLE, BLAINE D
Dem. Nat. Committeeman, Ore.
b. Martin, S.Dak, 2/22/30; s. Blaine Whipple and Pearl Scott W; m. 8/6/66 to Ines Mae Peterson; c. Judith Lynn Steele (stepdaughter), Robert Bruce Steele (stepson) and Blaine Scott. Educ: Mankato State Teachers Col, 49; Univ. Miss, 50; Univ. Minn, Minneapolis, B.A, 56; Univ. Ore, M.S, 59. Polit. & Govt. Pos: Fourth dist. campaign dir, Re-elect Charles O. Porter to Cong. Cmt, Ore, 58; exec. dir, Ore. Dem. Party, 60-62; Dem. nominee for Cong, First Dist, 62 & 64; alternate chmn, Wash. Co. Dem. Cent. Cmt, 62-66; chmn, Howard Morgan for U.S. Senate Cmt, 66; Dem. nominee, Ore. State Senate, Wash. & Yamhill Co, 66; v.chmn, Wash. Co. Intermediate Educ. Dist, 66-; chmn, Oregonians for McCarthy, 68; del-at-lg, Dem. Nat. Conv, 68; Dem. nat. committeeman, Ore, 68- Bus. & Prof. Pos: Dir, Ore. Small Bus. Admin, 67-68; v.pres, Randall Construction Co. Inc, currently. Mil. Serv: Entered as A/S, Navy, 50, released as Journalist 2/C, 54, after serv. in Mil. Sea Transportation Serv. and Barbers Point Naval Air Sta, Hawaii, 52-54; Good Conduct Medal. Mem: Sigma Delta Chi; Nat. Inst. of Real Estate Bd; legis. cmt, Wash. Co. Bd. of Realtors, 66-68; co-chmn, apt. house cmt, Portland Home Builders Asn; West. Realty Investment Coun; pres, West Tualatin View Elem. Sch; Wash. Co. Pub. Affairs Forum; chmn, Wash. Co. March of Dimes, 4 years; legis. cmt, Laurel Scholls Farmers Union, 61-63. Rel: Protestant. Mailing Add: 8455 S.W. Brookridge, Portland, Ore. 97225.

WHIPPLE, GLADYS LOUISE R
Treas, Grafton Co. Rep. Cmt, N.H.
b. Lebanon, N.H, 11/1/98; d. Frank Leroy Whipple and Annie Brown W; single. Educ: Univ. N.H; courses at Sorbonne, McGill and Middlebury; Alpha Chi Omega. Polit. & Govt. Pos: N.H. State Rep, 57-69; treas, Grafton Co. Rep. Cmt, N.H, currently. Bus. & Prof. Pos: Teacher. Mem: Past pres, dir. Lebanon's Woman's Club; town cmts; Church Orgns; Hosp. Auxiliary; C. of C. Rel: Unitarian. Mailing Add: 17 Shaw St, Lebanon, N.H. 03766.

WHISLER, ROSS S. D
b. Udell, Iowa, 12/3/91; m. 4/15/17 to Lucile Ziegler; c. Denny R. Educ: Udell Pub. Schs. Polit. & Govt. Pos: Former twp. trustee and assessor, Centreville, Iowa, 10 years; secy, Udell Consol. Sch. Bd, 10 years; mem, Udell City Coun, 2 years; Iowa State Rep, 64-66, mem, Claims, Conserv. and Recreation and Steering Cmts, Iowa State House of Rep. Bus. & Prof. Pos: Ins. Rel: Church of the Brethren; Supt. Sunday Schs. Mailing Add: 406 S. 15th St, Centreville, Iowa 52544. (1967)

WHITACRE, JAMES MARION R
Secy, Lake Co. Rep. Exec. Cmt, Ohio
b. Dayton, Pa, 9/30/07; s. Alton Marion Whitacre and Agnes Jane Schrecengost W; m. 10/15/27 to Lilly Victoria Schultz; c. Dorothy Jane (Mrs. Ronald Galloway), David Alton and William James. Educ: John Huntington Tech. Inst, Cleveland, Ohio, 34-35; Chicago Eng. Sch, correspondence course, 41-45. Polit. & Govt. Pos: Rep. precinct committeeman, Precinct B, Ohio, 58-; secy, Lake Co. Rep. Exec. Cmt, 63- Bus. & Prof. Pos: Machinist, Foote-Burti Co, Cleveland, Ohio, 25-39, serv. engr, 39-42; machinist, Ajax Mfg. Co, Euclid, 42-45, asst. supt, 45-56, supt, 56- Mem: F&AM; Scottish Rite (32°); Shrine; Eastern Star. Rel: Presbyterian; Elder, Presby. Church, Willoughby, Ohio. Mailing Add: 5321 Robinhood Dr, Willoughby, Ohio 44094.

WHITAKER, CHARLES JAMES, SR. D
V.Chmn. Richland Co. Dem. Party, S.C.
b. Blythewood, S.C, 9/16/24; s. Richard Mann Whitaker and Priscilla Harrison W; m. 7/20/47 to Ernestine Peay; c. Charles James, Jr, Jacquelyn LaMoris, Willie Roscoe, Venice Lynntine, Donna Druetta and Mamie Laverne. Educ: Benedict Col, B.Th, 61. Polit. & Govt. Pos: V.pres, Greenview Precinct Dem. Party, S.C, 67-; del, Dem. Co. Conv, Dem. State Conv. and Dem. Nat. Conv, 68; v.chmn, Richland Co. Dem. Party, S.C, 68- Bus. & Prof. Pos: Minister, Pine Grove Baptist Church, Great Falls, S.C, 56- and Ridge Branch Baptist Church, Batesburg, 63. Mem: Columbia Ministerial Alliance Club; moderator, Fairfield Co. Baptist Asn, 60-; F&AM; Consistory (32°); Noble, Mystic Shrine, Cairo Temple 125; S.C. Coun. on Human Rels; Columbia Commun. Rels. Coun; Richland Co. Voters' Registrn Coun; chmn, pres, North Columbia Civic Club; Eastern Star (Grand Worthy Patron); trustee, Statewide Home Found; chaplain, S.C. PTA. Outstanding Work Awards, Boys Club of Am, North Columbia Civic Club, Fairwold Elem. Sch, Fairwold Jr. High Sch. and S.C. PTA. Rel: Baptist. Mailing Add: 6308 Benedict St, Columbia, S.C. 29203.

WHITAKER, HAROLD W. R
Vt. State Rep.
b. Newfane, Vt, 5/31/00; m. to Dorothy Douglas; c. Three sons and one daughter. Educ: Leland & Gray Sem, Townshend, Vt; State Sch. of Agr, 23. Polit. & Govt. Pos: Town auditor, Newfane, Vt, 28-38, lister, 30 and selectman, 48-; Vt. State Rep, 61- Bus. & Prof. Pos: Farmer; carpenter. Mem: Newbrook Vol. Fire Co. Rel: Protestant. Mailing Add: Newfane, Vt. 05345. (1967)

WHITAKER, JOHN CARROLL R
Secy. to the Cabinet
b. Victoria, B.C, Can, 12/29/26; s. Clifford Edmund Whitaker and Stella Neville W; m. 9/20/58 to Mary Elizabeth Bradley; c. John Clifford, Robert Carroll, Stephen Bradley, William Burns and James Ford. Educ: Georgetown Univ, B.S.S, 49; John Hopkins Univ, Ph.D. in Geol. Polit. & Govt. Pos: Asst. campaign mgr. for Schedules and Tour for President Richard M. Nixon and Vice President Agnew, 68; Secy. to the Cabinet, 69- Bus. & Prof. Pos: Geologist, Standard Oil of Calif, 53-55; mgr, geophys. sales, Lundberg Explor. Ltd, Toronto, Can, 55-57 and Hycon Aerial Survey, Inc, Pasadena, Calif, 57-59; v.pres, Int. Aero Serv. Co. Div, Litton Industs, Phila, Pa, 59-66 and John C. Whitaker & Co, Wash, D.C, 66-68. Mil. Serv: Entered as A/S, Navy, 44, released as Aerographers Mate 3/C, 46. Publ: 'Geology of Catoctin Mountain: Maryland and Virginia,' 55 and 'Cambrian Clastics in Maryland,' 55, Bul. of Geol. Soc. Am; 'The Proton Nuclear Precession Magnetometer for Airborne Geophysical Exploration,' Oil & Gas J, 57. Mem: Am. Asn. Petroleum Geologists; Geol. Soc. Am; Soc. Explor. Geophysicists; Am. Geophys. Union; Am. Cong. Surveying and Mapping. Rel: Roman Catholic. Mailing Add: 8013 Greentree Rd, Bethesda, Md. 20034.

WHITAKER, TOM, JR. D
b. Tampa, Fla, 8/22/28; m. to Nancy Anne Thompson; c. Thomas Powell, III, Anne Hope, Richard Ellis and Robert Pleasant. Educ: Wash. and Lee Univ. of Tenn, B.S, 52; Univ. Fla, LL.B, 57. Polit. & Govt. Pos: Investr, Fla. Legis. Invest. Cmt, 57; Fla. State Rep, 58-62; Fla. State Sen, 62-66. Bus. & Prof. Pos: Attorney. Mil. Serv: Marine Corps, 52-54. Mem: Setoma Club of Tampa; Am. Legion; Marine Corps League; Jaycees; Elks. Rel: Methodist. 1967 Legal Res: Tampa, Fla. No mailing address available. (1967)

WHITAKER, URBAN G, JR. D
Mem. Calif. Dem. State Cent. Cmt.
b. Colony, Kans, 5/19/24; s. Urban G. Whitaker and Gladys Fackler W; m. 3/18/50 to Jean Knox; c. Susan, Bruce Knox and Keith George. Educ: Occidental Col, B.A, 47; Col. Chinese Studies, Peking, cert, 48; Univ. Wash, Ph.D, 54. Polit. & Govt. Pos: Trustee, San Bruno, Calif. Elem. Schs, 58-60; Dem. nominee, U.S. Rep, 11th Dist, Calif, 68; mem, Calif. Dem. State Cent. Cmt, 68- Bus. & Prof. Pos: Prof. int. rels, San Francisco State Col, 54-, dean undergrad. studies, 69- Mil. Serv: Entered as A/S, Navy Res, 42, released as Lt, 52, after serv. on a destroyer, Pac. Theater, 45-46, 50-52; Letter of Commendation; Presidential Unit Citations. Publ: Nationalism and Internationalism, Chandler, 61; Politics and Power, Harper-Row, 64; The World and Ridgeway, S.C, Univ. S.C, 68. Mem: Nat. Bd. Dirs, UN Asn. U.S, Cmn. to Study Orgn. of Peace; past pres, West. Div, Int. Studies Asn; Am. Fedn. Teachers. Rel: Unitarian. Mailing Add: 1590 Greenwood Way, San Bruno, Calif. 94066.

WHITBECK, WALTER SAMUEL R
b. Lime Rock, Conn, 6/24/91; s. William Henry Whitbeck and Elizabeth Johnstone W; m. 12/4/24 to Carrie E. Marston; m. 4/28/53 to Lois Martin Marston, 2nd ; c. Walter Samuel, Anna Elizabeth and Nelson E. Educ: High Sch. Polit. & Govt. Pos: Conn. State Rep, 61-67. Bus. & Prof. Pos: Operated Salisbury Pharmacy; 25-, pres, Salisbury Pharmacy Inc. Mil. Serv: Entered as Pvt, Army, 18, released as Pfc, and Dispensary Asst, U.S. Gen. Hosp, 18. Mem: Am. Legion; Rotary; Grange; Am. Legion. Rel: Episcopal. Mailing Add: Orchard, Lakeville, Conn. 06068. (1967)

WHITCOMB, EDGAR DOUD R
Gov, Ind.
b. Hayden, Ind, 11/6/17; s. John William Whitcomb and Louise Doud W; m. 5/20/51 to Patricia Louise Dolfuss; c. Patricia Louise, Alice Elaine, Linda Ann, John Doud and Shelley Jean. Educ: Ind. Univ, 36-39; Ind. Univ. Sch. Law, LL.B, 50; Phi Delta Phi. Polit. & Govt. Pos: Ind. State Sen, 51-54; asst. U.S. Attorney, Justice Dept. South. Dist. Ind, 55-56; chmn, Great Lakes Cmn, 65-66; secy. of state, Ind, 66-69, gov, 69- Bus. & Prof. Pos: Lawyer, Whitcomb & Brown, Seymour, Ind, 56- Mil. Serv: Entered as Flying Cadet, Army Air Corps, 40, released as Maj, 46, after serv. in 19th Bombardment Group, Air Transport Command, Fifth Air Force Hq, Asiatic Theater; Col, Air Force Res, 65; Air Medal with Oak Leaf Cluster; Presidential Unit Citation with Six Oak Leaf Clusters. Publ: Escape From Corregidor, Henry Regnery Publ. Co, 58. Mem: Ind. and Am. Bar Asns; Am. Legion; VFW. Rel: Methodist. Mailing Add: 636 N. Poplar, Seymour, Ind. 47274.

WHITE, ALBERT CHARLES, JR. R
b. Boston, Mass, 7/1/31; s. Albert Charles White and Evangeline May Drew W; single. Educ: Northeast. Univ, B.S, 66. Polit. & Govt. Pos: Mem, Rep. Town Cmt, Lynnfield, Mass, 52-68, secy, 56-64 and chmn, 66-68; clerk, Bd. of Selectmen, Lynnfield, 56-57; del, Mass. State Rep. Conv, 58, 62, 64 & 66; mem, Bd. of Registr, Lynnfield, Mass, 60-68, chmn, 68. Bus. & Prof. Pos: Supvr, Joseph T. Ryerson & Son, Inc, Allston, Mass, 54- Mem: Nat. Asn. of Purchasing Mgt; AF&AM, Lynnfield. Rel: Episcopal. Mailing Add: 190 Mt. Auburn St, Watertown, Mass. 02172.

WHITE, BERTA LEE D
Miss. State Sen.
b. Obadiah, Miss, 6/27/14; m. to Gordon White. Polit. & Govt. Pos: Former Miss. State Rep; Miss. State Sen, 68- Bus. & Prof. Pos: Secy. to dir, Hughes Tel. Co. Mem: Leader, 4-H Club; Obadiah Home Demonstration; Center Hill Commun. Develop; Lauderdale Co. Cancer & Ment. Health Bd; Meridian Bus. & Prfnl. Women; Miss. Women's Cabinet; state dir, Farm Bur; trustee, Meridian Pub. Libr. Cmn, Am. Libr. Trustee; Asn. Country Women of the World (del. to Australia, 62). Rel: Presbyterian. Mailing Add: Route 1, R.F.D. 1, Bailey, Lauderdale Co, Miss. 39320. (1967)

WHITE, BEVERLY JEAN D
Vice Chairlady, Tooele Co. Dem. Party, Utah
b. Salt Lake City, Utah, 9/28/28; d. Gustave R. Larson and Helene Sterzer L; m. 4/8/47 to Marion Floyd White; c. Susan Helene (Mrs. John Morris), Douglas Floyd, Robyn Ann, David Scott and Wendy Jo. Educ: Int. Bus. Machines Sch, grad, 48. Polit. & Govt. Pos: Del, Co. and State Convs, Utah, 20 years; dist. vice chairlady, Dem. Party, Tooele, Utah, 58, 59; pres, Lady Dem, 58-59; vice chairlady, Tooele Co. Dem. Party, 61-; appointed, Utah State Bd. Corrections, 66-; mem, State Patronage Cmt, 67-; del, Dem. Nat. Conv, 68. Mem: Officer, PTA; Tooele Co. Lady Dem; Tooele Vol. Firemens Auxiliary. Rel: Latter-day Saint; youth activities, 17 years. Mailing Add: 122 Russell Ave, Tooele, Utah 84074.

WHITE, BYRON R
Assoc. Justice, U.S. Supreme Court
b. Ft. Collins, Colo, 6/8/17; m. to Marion Stearns; c. Charles and Nancy. Educ: Univ. Colo, B.A, 38; Rhodes Scholar, Oxford Univ, 39; Yale Law Sch, LL.B, 46; Phi Beta Kappa; Phi Gamma Delta; Order of the Coif. Polit. & Govt. Pos: Law clerk to Chief Justice of the U.S. Supreme Court, 46-47; Dep. Attorney Gen, U.S, 61-62; Assoc. Justice, U.S. Supreme Court, 62- Bus. & Prof. Pos: Attorney, Lewis, Grant & Davis, Denver, Colo, 47-60. Mil. Serv: Naval Res, World War II. Mailing Add: c/o U.S. Supreme Court, Washington, D.C. 20543. (1967)

WHITE, CARL A. R
N.Dak. State Rep.
b. Tracy, Minn, 10/25/17; s. George A. White and Alethea Louis W; m. 9/11/41 to Jean Y; c. Jason B, Jacquelyn C. and Webb A. Educ: N.Dak. State Univ, 36-38; Univ. Minn, B.B.A, 41; Alpha Tau Omega. Polit. & Govt. Pos: Mem, Exec. Cmt, 21st Dist. Rep. Party, 66-68; N.Dak. State Rep, 69- Bus. & Prof. Pos: Pres, Dairy Queen of West. Can, Ltd, 53-69; secy, Waverly Enterprises, Can, 58-69; dir, Vancouver A & W Drive Inn, Ltd, Can, 60-69; chmn. bd, Moorhead State Bank, 64-69; v.pres, Dairy Queen of Alaska, 64-69. Mil. Serv: Entered as Yeoman 3/C, Navy, 42, released as Lt.(jg), 45, after serv. in Pac. Theatre, 43-45. Mem: Mason; Shrine; Kiwanis. Rel: Protestant. Mailing Add: 41 Woodland Dr, Fargo, N.Dak. 58102.

WHITE, CATHERINE KILMURRAY D
b. Pikesville, Md, 4/19/30; d. Martin Francis Kilmurray and Catherine McGrath K; m. 6/18/55 to Charles Evans White; c. Catherine Elizabeth. Educ: Univ. Md, B.A, 54; Columbia Univ. Sch. Law, J.D, 69; Int. Club. Polit. & Govt. Pos: Mem, Human Rels. Cmn, City of Plainfield, N.J, 66-68; alternate del, Dem. Nat. Conv, 68. Bus. & Prof. Pos: Teacher, Prince George Co, Md, 54-55 & 56-59. Mem: Former chmn, W.Va. Citizen-Consumers League; former pres, Kanawha Valley Human Rels. Coun; former pres, W.Virginians for Improved Health Care; Am. Asn. Univ. Women; Vol. for McCarthy; Plainfield Dem. Club. Mailing Add: 1145 Woodland Ave, Plainfield, N.J. 07060.

WHITE, CHARLES CODY D
Mem, Third Dist. Dem. Exec. Cmt, Ga.
b. Atlanta, Ga, 5/30/06; s. Frank Gilman White and Anna Collier W; m. 6/21/34 to Jane Allison Butler; c. Charles Cody, Jr, Jane Allison (Mrs. James C. Adams) and Robert Christopher (deceased 6/1/68). Polit. & Govt. Pos: Mem, Muscogee Co. Dem. Exec. Cmt, 45-68, v.chmn, 49-56 and chmn, 56-65; mem. bd. educ, Muscogee Co. Sch. Dist, 58-68; mem, Third Dist. Dem. Exec. Cmt, 65-; Cand. for Tax Cmnr, Muscogee Co. Mem: Nat, Ga. and Columbus Asns. Independent Ins. Agents; assoc. mem, Soc. Real Estate Appraisers; div. dir, Ga. Sch. Bds. Asn, 64-67; pres, Columbus High Sch. PTA, 57; pres, Columbus Asn. Ins. Agents, 43; secy, Columbus Lions, 48-51; Columbus Exec. Club. Rel: Baptist. Legal Res: 1623 Carter Ave, Columbus, Ga. 31906. Mailing Add: P.O. Box 135, Columbus, Ga. 31902.

WHITE, CHARLES E. 'PETE' R
b. Oelrichs, S.Dak, 1916; m. to Marjorie Cavanaugh; c. Bill, Jim, Tom. Educ: Oelrich High Sch; Course in agr, Univ. Wyo. Polit. & Govt. Pos: S.Dak. State Rep, 62-66. Bus. & Prof. Pos: Cattle rancher. Mem: Past mem, Fall River Co. Fair Bd; past pres, Co. Farm Bur; past dir, S.Dak. Stockgrowers Asn; 6 years, State Brand Bd, 2 years as pres; Elks. Rel: Methodist. Mailing Add: Oelrichs, S.Dak. 57763. (1967)

WHITE, CLARENCE OTHO D
b. Seadrift, Tex, 12/19/13; s. Joseph Bushrod White and Eulah Williams W; m. 3/29/40 to Margaret Virginia Dunaway; c. Henry Charles and Gloria Jean (Mrs. Fawcett). Educ: Univ. Tex; Randolph Col; Univ. Houston; Hogg Debating Club; Knights of the Round Table. Polit. & Govt. Pos: Mem, Harris Co. Dem. Orgn; del, Dem. Nat. Conv. and Tex. Dem. Conv, 64. Bus. Pos: Partner, Dawson & White Realty Co, 60- Mil. Serv: Pvt, Tex. Nat. Guard, 32-33. Mem: Elks; Odd Fellows; Eagles; Moose; pres. and life mem, Jaycees; Exchange Club; C. of C. Rel: Disciples of Christ. Mailing Add: Dawson & White Realty Co, 7812 Fulton, Houston, Tex. 77022. (1967)

WHITE, CLYDE MILTON D
Secy, 57th Rep. Dist. Dem. Cmt, Ill.
b. Johnston City, Ill, 9/12/07; s. Edgar M. White and Leona E. Newton W; m. 7/27/48; Mildred C. Crompton; c. Gerold F. and David J. Marlow. Educ: High School, 4 years. Polit. & Govt. Pos: Mem. draft bd, Williamson Co, Ill, 62-; investr, Secy. of State, Ill, 64-; secy, 57th Rep. Dist. Dem. Cmt, 66- Bus. & Prof. Pos: Co-owner of coal mine, White & Son Coal Co, Marion, Ill, 30-41. Mil. Serv: Entered as Pvt. Air Force, 42, released as S/Sgt, 45, after serv. in Transport Command ETO, 43-45; reserve, 45-62. Rel: Protestant. Mailing Add: 1116 N. Washington Ave, Johnston City, Ill. 62951.

WHITE, COMPTON I. D
b. 1922. Educ: George Washington Univ. Sch. Engr; Univ. Idaho Sch. Mines. Polit. & Govt. Pos: U.S. Rep, Idaho, 63-67; former mayor, Clark Fork, Idaho; former mem. adv. cmt, Kaniksu Nat. Forest; nominee, U.S. Rep, Idaho, 68. Bus. & Prof. Pos: Farmer; lumber bus; mining; stock raiser. Mailing Add: Box 8, Clark Fork, Idaho 83811. (1967)

WHITE, DAN FREDRICK D
Ark. State Sen.
b. Fort Smith, Ark, 12/3/15; s. William Clarence White, Sr. and Elsie Mae Kell W; m. 8/9/50 to Dorothy Crofton Flocks; c. stepson, Carl Flocks, III. Educ: Cumberland Univ, LL.B, 41; Univ. Ark; Blue Key. Polit. & Govt. Pos: Ark. State Rep, Sebastian Co, 51-57; Ark. State Sen, Dist. four, 57- Bus. & Prof. Pos: Partner, White & Martin, Attorneys, 50- Mil. Serv: Entered as Pvt, Army, 41, released as 1st Lt, 46, after serv. in S.Pac; Two Campaign Ribbons. Mem: Ark, Sebastian Co. Bar Asns; Am. and Ark. Trial Lawyers Asns; Mason; Am. Legion; VFW; Amvets; Univ. Ark. Alumni Asn. Rel: Baptist. Legal Res: 4510 N. M. St, Ft. Smith, Ark. 72901. Mailing Add: 707 First National Bank Bldg, Fort Smith, Ark. 72901.

WHITE, DANIEL H. D
b. Athens, Ga, 11/06/25; s. Daniel Harrison White and Evelyn Woodward W; m. 7/12/59 to Ruby Lee Amerson; c. Ruby Amerson and Evelyn Woodward. Educ: Univ. Ga, LL.B, 50; Delta Theta Phi. Polit. & Govt. Pos: Darien City Attorney; McIntosh Co. Attorney; Ga. State Rep, 57-66. Bus. & Prof. Pos: Attorney; admitted bar 50; began practice 53, Darien, Ga. Mil. Serv: Army Air Force, Pvt, Aviation Cadet, Continental U.S, 43-45. Mem: Mason. Rel: Episcopal. Mailing Add: Darien, Ga. 31305.

WHITE, DONALD BLAISDELL R
Chmn, Lexington Rep. Town Cmt, Mass.
b. Woburn, Mass, 10/1/29; s. Malcolm Stuart White and Edna M. Neville W; m. 1/16/54 to Ellen Parker Holmes; c. Nina Stuart, Melissa Parker, Maria Standish, Lisabeth Mason, Donald Blaisdell, Jr, Charles Parker and Andrea. Educ: Tufts Univ; Theta Delta Chi. Polit. & Govt. Pos: Pres. and secy, Woburn Young Rep. Club, Mass, 57-60; precinct chmn, Lexington Rep. Town Cmt, 64, chmn, 65-; mem, Lexington Rep. Finance Cmt, 68- Bus. & Prof. Pos: Product mgr, Boston Woven Hose, 60-; v.pres. and gen. mgr, Black & Webster Sales, 63- Mil. Serv: Entered as Pvt, Mass. Nat. Guard, 48, released as Sgt, 1/C, 56, after serv. in 182nd Regt. Marksmanship Medals. Mem: Hancock Men's Club; Tufts Alumni Inter Fraternity Coun; Hist. Dist. Cmn. Rel: Protestant. Mailing Add: 73 Hancock St, Lexington, Mass. 02173.

WHITE, DONALD STANLEY D
Mem, Calif. Dem. State Cent. Cmt.
b. N.Y.C, N.Y, 5/2/35; s. Martin White and Florence Meiman W; m. 1/31/60 to Sylvia Phyllis Schostak; c. Stephen and Andrew. Educ: Univ. Calif, Los Angeles, B.A; Univ. Calif. Sch. of Law, Berkeley, LL.B. Polit. & Govt. Pos: Dep. Pub. Defender, Los Angeles, Calif, 61-62, Los Angeles Co, 65-67; mem, Los Angeles Co. Dem. Cent. Cmt, 66-68; cand. for U.S. Rep, 20th Cong. Dist, Calif, 68; mem. and chmn. 20th Cong. Dist. Del, Calif. Dem. State Cent. Cmt, 68- Assoc. dir, Peace Corps, Ghana and Tanzania, 62-65; attorney, Private Law Firm of Morgan, Wenzel, Lynberg, Stearns & Morris, 67- Publ: 'Seagoing Men and Automation,' Marine Cooks & Stewards Union, 61. Mem: Am, Calif. and Criminal Courts Bar Asns; Lawyers Club of Los Angeles. Mailing Add: 1937 Myra Ave, Los Angeles, Calif. 90027.

WHITE, DORIS MAUDE R
b. Watertown, S.Dak, 2/3/11; d. Joseph Henderson Croft (deceased) and Ruby Louise Burk C; m. 9/17/40 to Donald Eugene White; c. Maureen (Mrs. Robert Marlyst) and Jeffrey Dallas. Educ: Watertown High Sch, 24-28. Polit. & Govt. Pos: Precinct committeewoman, Pennington Co. Rep. Cent. Cmt, S.Dak, 54, v.chairwoman 56-60; secy-treas, Karl Mundt for Senate Club, 60; state chairwoman, Women for Nixon-Agnew, 68; alternate del, Rep. Nat. Conv, 68; pub. rels. chmn, S.Dak. Fedn. of Rep. Women; prog. chmn, Local Fedn. of Rep. Women. Bus. & Prof. Pos: Secy, YM-YWCA Bd, 56-60; mem, bd. dir, United Commun. Coun, 67- Mem: PEO. Rel: Episcopal. Legal Res: 2008 Central Blvd, Rapid City, S.Dak. 57701. Mailing Add: P.O. Box 1170, Rapid City, S.Dak. 57701.

WHITE, EDWARD HOMER, JR. D
Speaker Pro Tempore, Md. House of Del.
b. Salisbury, Md, 4/5/11; married. Educ: William and Mary Col. Polit. & Govt. Pos: Md. State Del, 47-, permanent chmn, Dem. Caucus, Md. House of Del, 55-, Speaker Pro Tempore, 63-; chmn, State Water Study Cmn. and State Planning Cmn, 59-; Dem. cand, U.S. Rep, Md, 68; del, Dem. Nat. Conv, 68. Bus. & Prof. Pos: Merchant. Mil. Serv: 1st Sgt, 722nd M.P. Bn. in European Theatre. Mailing Add: 724 Camden St, Salisbury, Md. 21801. (1967)

WHITE, F. CLIFTON R
b. Leonardsville, N.Y, 6/13/18; s. Frederick H. White and Mary Hicks W; m. 6/22/40 to Gladys Bunnell; c. F. Clifton, Jr. and A. Carole. Educ: Colgate, A.B, 40; Cornell Univ. grad. work in govt, 45-47; Delta Sigma Rho; Freeman H. Allan Soc. Polit. & Govt. Pos: Mem. exec. cmt, Youth for Dewey, Rep. Nat. Conv, 48, alternate del-at-lg, 52, del, 68, alternate dist. del, 56, mem, Nixon Staff, 60, mgr, Goldwater Del. Forces, 64; del. and chmn, conv. cmts, Nat. Young Rep. Conv, 49, 51, 53 & 55, chmn, 51; mem, State Sen. Dist. Rep. Cmt, and 36th Cong. Dist. Rep. Cmt; mem, Nat. Young Rep. Exec. Cmt, 49-55; del, N.Y. State Eisenhower Campaign Train and dir, Nixon Campaign Train, 52; judicial dist. chmn, co. gov. and local pres. and treas, N.Y.C. Young Rep; dir, Region 11, Nat. Fedn. Young Rep. and chmn, Nat. Speakers Bur; pres, N.Y. State Young Rep, also chmn, col. div. and club and dist. orgn; assoc. dir. and lectr, State-wide Sch. Polit, Hamilton Col; faculty adv, Ithaca Col. and Cornell Univ. Young Rep. Clubs; co. chmn, city chmn. and committeeman; acting secy. and youth dir, N.Y. State Rep. Cent. Cmt; spec. asst. to N.Y. State Chmn; chmn, N.Y. State Eisenhower Campaign Train and dir, Nixon Campaign Train, 52; del, President's Hwy. Safety Coun, 53; exec. dep. cmnr, 52-55, acting cmnr, N.Y. State Bur. of Motor Vehicles, 55; dir. orgn, Nat. Nixon-Lodge Vols, 60; mgr. and adv. in campaigns for pub. off, local to nat. level; dir, Nat. Draft Goldwater Cmt, 63; nat. dir, Goldwater for President Cmt, 64; nat. dir, Citizens for Goldwater-Miller, 64. Bus. & Prof. Pos: Chmn, soc. sci. dept, Ravena Pub. Schs; instr, dept. of soc. sci, Cornell Univ, 45-50; lectr, dept. of polit. sci, Ithaca Col, 49-51; pres, Pub. Affairs Counsellors, Inc, 57-60; pres, F. Clifton White & Assocs, Inc, N.Y, currently. Mil. Serv: Entered as Pvt, Air Force, 42, released as Capt, 45, after serv. in 390th Bomb Group, Eighth Air Force, ETO, 42-44; Air Medal with Three Oak Leaf Cluster; Distinguished Flying Cross; Distinguished Unit Citation with Cluster. Publ: You Should Be a Politician, Pub. Affairs Counsellors, Inc, 59; Suite 3505, Arlington House, 67. Mem: Am. Polit. Sci. Asn; Am. Acad. Polit. & Soc. Sci; Inst. Fiscal and Polit. Educ.(pres); Acad. Polit. Sci; Am. Asn. Polit. Consult.(v.pres); Int. Asn. Polit. Campaign Consult.(dir); dir, Nat. Rep. Club; Mason (32°); Sons of Revolution. Rel: Presbyterian; Elder, Rye Presbyterian Church, N.Y. Legal Res: 2 Fraydun Place, Rye, N.Y. 10580. Mailing Add: 122 E. 42nd St, New York, N.Y. 10017.

WHITE, FRANK LOUIS D
Tenn. State Sen.
b. Memphis, Tenn, 3/1/24; s. Frank Louis White and Margaret Tyler W; m. 7/29/43 to Geraldine Marguerite Goodwin; c. Frank L, III, Dennis W. and Wanda Mae. Educ: St. Joseph Sem, 41-42; South Law Univ. LL.B, 46-49. Polit. & Govt. Pos: Tenn. State Rep, 61-62; Tenn. State Sen, 63-67. Mil. Serv: Entered as Pvt, Army Air Force, 43, released as Tech. Sgt, 45, after serv. in 30th Bomb Group, Pac. Theater, 44-45; Air Medal with Oak Leaf Cluster; Pac. Theater Ribbons. Mem: Am, Memphis and Shelby Co. Bar Asns; Am. Legion; VFW; Elks. Rel: Catholic. Mailing Add: 4806 Kaye Rd, Memphis, Tenn. 38117. (1967)

WHITE, GEORGE W, SR. R
N.H. State Rep.
b. Newburyport, Mass, 1/9/00; married; c. Ten. Educ: Medford High Sch. Polit. & Govt. Pos: Selectman 12 years; N.H. State Rep, 57- Bus. & Prof. Pos: Retired. Mil. Serv: World War I and World War II. Mem: Grange; Shrine; Consistory; F&AM; Scottish Rite Bodies; Am. Legion; VFW. Rel: Protestant. Mailing Add: Main St, Atkinson, N.H. 03811.

WHITE, H. LABAN D
W.Va. State Del.
b. Spencer, W.Va, 5/1/16; s. H. Laban White, Sr. and Nannie Leigh Cox W; m. 12/23/43 to Gwendolyn Beall; c. Patricia Linda, Nanora Diane and Carol Ann. Educ: Glenville State Col, B.A; W.Va. Univ, LL.B. Polit. & Govt. Pos: City attorney, Clarksburg, W.Va, 49-55; asst. prosecuting attorney, Harrison Co, 56; W.Va. State Del, 56-, Speaker, W.Va. State House of Del, 65-69. Bus. & Prof. Pos: Former teacher and surveyor; lawyer, currently. Mil. Serv: Entered as Pvt, Army, 42, released as Capt, 46, Lt. Col, Army Res. Mem: Am. and W.Va. Bar Asns; W.Va. State Bar; Harrison Co. Bar Asn.(past pres, 63); Elks; Moose; Past pres, Lions Club; Nat. Cong. PTA; United Fund; Harrison Co. Heart Asn; W.Va. Univ, Glenville State and W.Va. Univ. Law Sch. Alumni Asns; Am. Legion; ROA; Asn. U.S. Army; W.Va. dept comdr, Amvets, 50. Rel: Baptist. Mailing Add: Empire Bank Bldg, Clarksburg, W.Va. 26301.

WHITE, HENRY EUGENE R
Mem, Vance Co. Rep. Exec. Cmt, N.C.
b. Vance Co, N.C, 10/27/97; s. Adolphus Eugene White and Maggie Delilah Bobbitt W; m. 9/10/38 to Ann Bruce Clark. Educ: Elon Col, A.B, 22; Wake Forest Col, LL.B, 32; Sigma Phi Beta; Gamma Eta Gamma. Polit. & Govt. Pos: Chmn, Vance Co. Rep. Party, N.C, 36-40, 54-62; alternate del, Rep. Nat. Conv, 68; mem, Vance Co. Bd. Elec, 68-; mem, Vance Co. Rep. Exec. Cmt, 68- Bus. & Prof. Pos: School teacher and prin, Tyro High Sch, Davidson Co, N.C, 22-23, Pilot High Sch, 23-26, Midway High Sch, 26-28 and Hasty High Sch, 28-30; lawyer, Henderson, N.C, 32-40. Mil. Serv: Entered as M/Sgt, Army, 40, released as Lt. Col, 54, after serv. in Judge Adv. Gen. Dept, Ft. Holabird, Md; Philippines, Ryukus and Far East Command; Japan, 47-49 & 50-52; Army Commendation Ribbon; Am. Campaign Medal; World War II Victory Medal; Army of Occup. Medal, Japan; Korean Serv. Medal; UN Serv. Medal; Bronze Star; Nat. Defense Serv. Medal; Korean Presidential Unit Citation. Mem: Co. and state bar asns; Am. Legion; 40 et 8; Ruritan; Elks; N.C. Soc. of Co. and Local Historians; N.C. Soc. for the Preservation of Antiquity. Rel: Methodist. Mailing Add: Route 3, Box 162, Henderson, N.C. 27536.

WHITE, JACK HUTCHINS D
N.C. State Sen.
b. Winston-Salem, N.C, 7/2/25; s. Emmett White and Hannah Elizabeth Hutchins W; m. 6/10/50 to Dorcas Louise Cline; c. Jack H, Jr, Nancy Love and Alyson Elizabeth. Educ: Wake Forest Col, B.S, 51; Wake Forest Sch. of Law, LL.B, 51; Phi Delta Phi. Polit. & Govt. Pos: Solicitor, Kings Mountain Recorder's Court, N.C, 51-53 and Judge, 53-64; N.C. State Sen, 63- Bus. & Prof. Pos: Lawyer. Mil. Serv: Sgt, U.S. Army, 44-46. Mem: N.C. and Am. Bar Asns; pres, Cleveland Co. Bar Asn, 62; Alpha Sigma Phi; Alpha Psi

Omega. Rel: Baptist; Trustee, 57-59; Teacher, Adult Bible Class, 57-; Deacon, 59-61. Mailing Add: 218 Edgemont Dr, Kings Mountain, N.C. 28086. (1967)

WHITE, JAMES E. R
Tenn. State Rep.
b. Nashville, Tenn, 2/18/35; s. James B. White and Helen Irene W; m. 11/26/58 to Sara Jo Wallen; c. Suzanne and James E, Jr. Educ: Mid. Tenn. State Univ, B.S, 60. Polit. & Govt. Pos: Precinct chmn, Tenn. Rep. Party, 64-65; chmn, Co. Precinct Orgn, 65-66; chmn, Young Rep. Club, 68; Tenn. State Rep, Sixth Dist, 69- Bus. & Prof. Pos: Pres, Town & Country Realty Co, 66- Mil. Serv: Entered as Pvt, Marines, 52, released as Sgt, 56, after serv. in Korea, 53-54. Mem: Nashville Bd. Realtors; Tenn. Real Estate Bd; Nat. Asn. Real Estate Bd; dir, Police Assistance League; Jr. C. of C; C. of C; Boy Scout committeeman. Rel: Church of Christ; Deacon. Legal Res: 707 Summerly Dr, Nashville, Tenn. 37209. Mailing Add: 733 Stahlman Bldg, Nashville, Tenn. 37201.

WHITE, JAMES R. R
b. Paterson, N.J, 8/7/30; s. Albert White and Mary Betar W; m. 6/27/54 to Lois Elaine Costa; c. James A, Jeanne M, Mary E, Kathleen A. and David R. Educ: Villanova Univ, B.S. in Econ, 53; N.Y. Univ, M.S, 55. Polit. & Govt. Pos: Councilman, Totowa, N.J, 63-69; alternate del, Rep. Nat. Conv, 68; mem, exec. bd, Passaic Co. Rep. Orgn, currently. Bus. & Prof. Pos: Officer trainee, Citizens Trust, Paterson, N.J, 54; asst. secy, Totowa Savings, 55-61; exec. v.pres, Mahwah Savings & Loan, 62-69. Mem: Bergen Co, N.J. and U.S. Savings and Loan Leagues; Elks; K. of C; pres, C. of C; trustee, Police Athletic League; trustee, Rescue Squad. Rel: Roman Catholic. Mailing Add: 131 Washington Pl, Totowa, N.J. 07512.

WHITE, JAMES WILSON D
Committeeman, Pa. Dem. State Cmt.
b. Pittsburgh, Pa, 12/31/26; s. David White and Elizabeth Wilson W; m. 6/19/48 to Lois E. Wyman; c. Patricia Lee, Nancy Evelyn, Kathleen Elizabeth and Mary Josephine. Educ: Pa. State Univ, B.S, 50. Polit. & Govt. Pos: Supt, Pa. Dept. Hwy, 57-63; pres, Pa. Young Dem. Clubs, 60-62; spec. asst. to pres, Young Dem. Clubs of Am, 63-65; chmn, Pa. Agr. Stabilization and Conserv. Serv, U.S. Dept. of Agr, 64-69; alternate del, Dem. Nat. Conv, 68; nat. chmn, Nat. Cmt. for Improv. of Rural Am, 69; committeeman, Pa. Dem. State Cmt, 69- Bus. & Prof. Pos: Co-owner, Homestead Farms, Kittanning, Pa, 50-; pres, White Enterprises, 60-; secy-treas, Manor Minerals Inc, 63-; mem. exec. bd, Pa. Rural Area Develop. Cmt, 65-69; first v.pres, Mid. Armstrong Co. Develop. Orgn, 69. Mil. Serv: Entered as A/S, Navy, 44, released as Seaman 1/C, 46, after serv. in S.Pac, Philippines, 45-46; Philippine and Pac. Theatre Ribbons. Mem: Pa. Stone Producers Asn; Nat. Farmers Union; Elks; Rotary; VFW; Am. Legion; C. of C. Appointed U.S. Del. of Young Polit. Leaders to NATO, 65. Rel: Presbyterian. Legal Res: 354 N. Jefferson St, Kittanning, Pa. 16201. Mailing Add: 265 S. Jefferson St, Kittanning, Pa. 16201.

WHITE, JEAN CHRISTENSEN R
Mem, Calif. Rep. State Cent. Cmt.
b. Franksville, Wis, 8/19/34; d. Norman W. Christensen and Esther Hansen C; m. 6/16/56 to Robert Cecil White; c. Douglas Hunter and Carol Andersen. Educ: Northwest. Univ, B.S. in Journalism, 56; Theta Sigma Phi; Alpha Omicron Pi. Polit. & Govt. Pos: Rep. precinct sect. chmn. in North San Diego, San Diego Co. Rep. Cent. Cmt, 61-64, exec. secy, 64-66, mem, currently, ed, San Diego Rep, 69-; campaign coordinator, Assemblyman Pete Wilson, 76th Dist, 66, dist. secy, 66-68; mem, Calif. Rep. State Cent. Cmt, 69- Mem: Clairemont Rep. Women's Club; Rep. Assocs; Speech and Hearing Center Auxiliary to Children's Hosp; Alpha Omicron Pi Alumnae Chap. Rel: Presbyterian. Mailing Add: 3151 Fryden Court, San Diego, Calif. 92117.

WHITE, JOHN COYLE D
Cmnr, Tex. Dept. of Agr.
b. Newport, Tex, 11/26/24; s. Edward H. White and Carrie L. Campbell W; c. John Richard, Edward Prince and Jake Rayburn. Educ: Tex. Tech. Col, B.S, 42-46; Tex. A&M Univ, grad. work; Kappa Sigma. Polit. & Govt. Pos: Cmnr, Tex. Dept. of Agr, 51- Bus. & Prof. Pos: Dir, Sch. of Agr, Midwest. Univ, 48-50; area dir, Vet. Vocational Agr. Schs, 46-48. Mem: Past pres. South. Asn. of Cmnrs. and Secys. of Agr; Nat. Asn. of State Depts. of Agr; Optimist. Chosen as one of Life Magazine's Ten Most Outstanding Young Men of the Year, 52; Fed. Land Bank Award for Outstanding Serv. to Am. Agr, 68; French Ordre du Merite, Top French Govt. Agr. Award, 69. Mailing Add: Drawer BB, Austin, Tex. 78711.

WHITE, JOHN E. R
Ky. State Rep.
b. Manchester, Ky. 2/6/20; s. Charles H. White and Nora Sizemore W; m. 4/25/42 to Wintress Hacker; c. John Thomas and Charles Douglas. Polit. & Govt. Pos: Ky. State Rep, 60-; mem, Constitution Revision Assembly, Ky. Bus. & Prof. Pos: Theater owner and mgr, 52- Mem: Kiwanis; Clay Co. Develop. Asn. Merit Award in Conserv. of Natural Resources. Rel: Baptist. Mailing Add: 116 Wayne St, Manchester, Ky. 40962. (1967)

WHITE, JOHN L. R
N.J. State Sen.
b. Camden, N.J, 4/1/30; married; c. Four. Educ: Franklin and Marshall Col, Lancaster, Pa; Temple Univ. Sch. of Law, 55. Polit. & Govt. Pos: Past chmn, Woodbury Zoning Bd. of Adust; Asst. Co. Solicitor for Gloucester Co. Bd. of Chosen Freeholders; N.J. State Assemblyman, 64-68; N.J. State Sen, 68- Bus. & Prof. Pos: Attorney-at-law; mem. bd. dir, Mantua Bldg. and Loan Asn; dir, Nat. Bank of Mantua. Mem: Woodbury Kiwanis; Florence Lodge 87, F&AM; Excelsior Consistory, AASR; Crescent Temple, AAONMS, Trenton, N.J; bd. dir, Woodbury Savings & Loan Asn; bd. trustees, Underwood-Mem. Hosp, Woodbury. Rel: Presbyterian. Mailing Add: 193 Briar Hill Lane, Woodbury, N.J. 08096.

WHITE, JOSHUA WARREN, JR. D
Va. State Del.
b. Norfolk, Va, 8/27/16; m. to Dorothy Lee Winstead. Educ: Wash. and Lee Univ. Polit. & Govt. Pos: Mem, Second Dist. Dem. Cmt; Va. State Del, 62- Bus. & Prof. Pos: Pres. and treas, Old Dominion Paper Co; Va. Nat. Bank, Norfolk Bd. Mil. Serv: Navy, discharged, 45, Lt. Comdr. Mem: Bd. Dir, Norfolk Gen. Hosp; United Commun. Fund; Edgewater Home for Boys and Girls; Va. Coun. of the Small Bus. Admin; trustee, Tidewater Develop. Coun; Hampton Rds. Coun. of Navy League, USA (mem. bd); Norfolk German Club; Princess Anne Country Club. Rel: Presbyterian; Deacon, First Presbyterian Church. Mailing Add: C/O Old Dominion Paper Co, 44th & Colley Ave, Norfolk, Va. 23508.

WHITE, JULIA HUMPHREYS R
N.H. State Rep.
b. Portsmouth, N.H, 12/13/95; wid; c. Two. Educ: Portsmouth schs. Polit. & Govt. Pos: Co. chmn, Rep. Ward Cmt, N.H, mem. exec. dept. and adminstr, 3 terms; former selectman; ballot inspector, Portsmouth City Coun; N.H. State Rep, 59- Mem: Pres, Fed. Rep. Women's Club of Portsmouth; Graffort Club; Womans City Club; Fleet Res. Auxiliary (nat. defense chmn, past pres, past secy-treas); PTA; St. John's Guild; Ranger Chap, DAR; Rep. City Club. Rel: Episcopal. Mailing Add: 35 Salter St, Portsmouth, N.H. 03801. (1967)

WHITE, KATHARINE ELKUS D
b. New York, N.Y, 11/25/06; d. Abram I. Elkus and Gertrude Hess E; m. 10/3/29 to Arthur Joske White; c. Lawrence E. and Frances (Mrs. John Cohen). Educ: Vassar Col, A.B, 28. Hon. LL.D, Douglass Col, Rutgers Univ, 67. Polit. & Govt. Pos: Mayor, Red Bank, N.J, 50-56; chmn, N.J. Hwy. Authority, 54-64; v.chmn, N.J. Dem. State Cmt; N.J. State Committeewoman, Monmouth Co; acting treas, N.J, 61; pres, Cmt. for Traffic Safety, 61-63; chmn, adv. coun, 63-64; Annual Assay Coin Cmn; U.S. Ambassador to Denmark, 64-68. Mem: Pres. bd. mgrs, N.J. State Hosp; trustee, Red Bank YMCA; trustee, Monmouth Co. Orgn. for Soc. Servs; trustee, Rutgers Univ, 69-; Am. Asn. Univ. Women; Int. Fedn. Univ. Women; Dem. Nat. Club; N.J. State Dem. Orgn. Grand Cross of Order of the Dannebrog. Legal Res: Elkridge-Harding Rd, Red Bank, N.J. 07701. Mailing Add: P.O. Box 261, Red Bank, N.J. 07701.

WHITE, KEVIN HAGAN D
Mayor, Boston, Mass.
b. Boston, Mass, 9/25/29; s. Joseph C. White and Patricia Hagan W; m. 6/7/56 to Kathryn Galvin; c. Mark, Caitlin, Elizabeth and Christopher. Educ: Williams Col, A.B, 52; Boston Col. Law Sch, LL.B, 55; Harvard Grad. Sch. Pub. Admin. Polit. & Govt. Pos: Legal aide to Dist. Attorney, Boston, Mass, 56-58 and asst. dist. attorney, Boston, 58-60; secy, Commonwealth of Mass, 61-68; mayor, Boston, 68- Bus. & Prof. Pos: Corp. counsel, Standard Oil of Calif, 55; partner, Cameron & White, 56- Mem: Boston, Am. and Mass. Bar Asns; Mass. Trial Lawyers Asn; Nat. Asn. of Secretaries of State. Rel: Catholic. Legal Res: 158 Mt. Vernon St, Boston, Mass. Mailing Add: Office of the Mayor, City Hall, City Hall Square, Boston, Mass. 02201.

WHITE, LAWRENCE CLERMONT R
b. Wood Co, W.Va, 7/17/84; s. Michael White and Mary Ann Holleron W; m. 6/17/21 to Ora Myrtle Hupp; c. Grace (Mrs. Robert L. Dimmick), Joyce (Mrs. Robert H. Ford), Lawrence Clermont, Jr, Joseph Byron C, Frank Ellsworth and Robert Bruce. Educ: Fairmont Normal, standard normal cert, 17; W.Va. Univ; Marietta Col; Ohio Univ; George Peabody Col. for Teachers, B.S, 26 and M.A, 28; Psi Chap, Phi Delta Kappa; World Affairs Club; Peabody Masonic Club; YMCA. Polit. & Govt. Pos: Supt, Wood Co. Schs, W.Va, 19-23; former mem, Wood Co. Planning Cmn; clerk, Wood Co, 47-; del, Rep. Nat. Conv, 60 & 64; Rep. precinct organizer and supvr. of precinct capt. Publ: Ed, Directory of Wood County, W.Va. Schs, 19; ed, Wood Co. Sch. J, 19-23; Resume of Local Government with added features, 56. Mem: V.pres, Co. and Circuit Clerks Asn; dir, W.Va. Co. Officials Asn; mem. bd. dirs, NARC; pres, Wood Co. Teachers Asn; secy, W.Va. Co. and Dist. Supts. Asn; secy, S.Parkersburg Improv. Asn; mem. and del, Nat. and State Educ. Asns; Wood Co. Farm Bur; secy, Rural Tel. Co; Odd Fellows; Mason, Scottish Rite (32°), Shrine; leader and organizer, Boy Scout Award Exam. Rel: Methodist; Pres, Christian Endeavor; pres, Methodist Men; church trustee, Sunday sch. supt, Bible class teacher and cert. Lay Minister. Mailing Add: 1704 20th St, Parkersburg, W.Va. 26101. (1967)

WHITE, LEE C. D
b. Omaha, Nebr, 9/1/23; s. Herman Henry White and Ann Ruth Ackerman W; m. 12/31/44 to Dorothy Bernice Cohn; c. Bruce D, Roslyn A, Murray L, Sheldon R. and Laura H. Educ: Univ. Nebr, B.S, 48, LA.B, 50. Polit. & Govt. Pos: Attorney, Legal Div, TVA, 50-54; mem, Hoover Cmn, 54-55; asst. to Joseph P. Kennedy; legis. asst. to Sen. John F. Kennedy, 54-57; counsel, U.S. Sen. Small Bus. Cmt, 57-58; admin. asst. to Sen John S. Cooper, 58-61; asst. spec. counsel to President John F. Kennedy, 61-63; assoc. counsel to President Johnson, 63-65; spec. counsel to President Lyndon B. Johnson, 65-66; chmn, Fed. Power Cmn, 66-69. Bus. & Prof. Pos: Partner, Semer, White & Jacobsen, currently. Mil. Serv: Army, 43-46. Mailing Add: 3216 W. Coquelin Terrace, Chevy Chase, Md. 20015.

WHITE, LUKE D
b. Washington, Ind, 3/13/13; s. William Nelson White and Mary E. Campbell W; m. 6/24/37 to Margaret Zechiel; c. Barbara Ann, Mary Patricia and Kipling Nels. Educ: Wabash Col, A.B, 34; Ind. Univ, J.D, 36; Phi Beta Kappa; Order of the Coif; Tau Kappa Alpha; Pi Delta Epsilon; Phi Delta Phi; Beta Theta Pi. Polit. & Govt. Pos: Del, Ind. Dem. State Conv, 46-58; mem, Covington Sch. Bd, 54-61; del, Dem. Nat. Conv, 56, 60, 64 & 68; mem, Ind. State Bd. Educ, 61-69. Bus. & Prof. Pos: Partner law firm, White & White, 36-; pres, The Fountain Trust Co; officer and dir, various corps. Mil. Serv: Army Air Force, 43-45. Rel: Methodist. Mailing Add: 702 Sixth St, Covington, Ind. 47932.

WHITE, MARVIN L. D
Nev. State Sen.
b. 1934. Polit. & Govt. Pos: Nev. State Assemblyman, 67-69; Nev. State Sen, 69- Bus. & Prof. Pos: Mgr, Ins. Agency; pres, 2 Investment Corp. Mem: Pres, Nev. Life Underwriters Asn; v.chmn, Sunrise Dist. Boy Scouts. Rel: Latter-day Saint. Mailing Add: 1729 Arrowhead Ave, North Las Vegas, Nev. 89030. (1967)

WHITE, PRESSLEY BYRNE D
b. Norfolk, Va, 9/4/05; m. to Veronica Garis W. Educ: Maury High Sch; Grant's Law Sch, Norfolk. Polit. & Govt. Pos: Former asst. judge, Princess Anne Co. Court; former chmn, Electoral Bd. Princess Anne Co; Va. State Del, 60-68; judge munic court, Virginia Beach, 68- Bus. & Prof. Pos: Attorney-at-Law. Mem: State Bar; Norfolk-Portsmouth and Va. State Bar Asn; Rotary; Ruth Lodge No. 89; John Walters Chap; Grice Commandery, Khedive Temple (trustee) Shrine; Hardy Bible Class, past Pres; Va. Beach-Princess Anne Shrine Club, past Pres; Princess Anne Country Club. Rel: Presbyterian. Mailing Add: 106 66th St, Virginia Beach, Va. 23451.

WHITE, RAY D. R
Tenn. State Rep.
b. Chattanooga, Tenn, 5/10/38; s. Raymond E. White and Lorraine Piper W; m. 4/21/62 to Bonnie Lou George; c. Laurie and David. Educ: Univ. Chattanooga, 4 years; Lambda Chi Alpha. Polit. & Govt. Pos: Tenn. State Rep, Hamilton Co, Seventh Dist, 68- Bus. & Prof. Pos: Licensed gen. contractor, Ray White Construction Co, currently. Mil. Serv: Entered as Pvt, Army, 62, released as SP-5, 64, after serv. in Army Security Agency, Okinawa, 63-64; Good Conduct Medal; Expert Medal for M-14 Rifle. Mem: Home Builders Asns. of Chattanooga and Tenn; Nat. Asn. Home Builders; Jaycees; Lambda Chi Alpha Alumni Asn. Rel: Protestant. Mailing Add: 5814 Northwoods View, Hixson, Tenn. 37343.

WHITE, RAY M. D
b. Millersburg, Ohio, 10/3/01; s. Charles R. White and Bertha V. Mast W; m. 6/15/23 to Cecile C. Calhoun; c. Mary Barbara (Mrs. Ned Scheetz). Polit. & Govt. Pos: Ohio State Rep, 45-52; dir. info. and educ. sect, Ohio Dept. of Natural Resources, 52-54; admin. asst, Gov. Lausche, Ohio, 54-57 and Sen. Lausche, 57-68. Bus. & Prof. Pos: News ed. and publisher, Millersburg, Ohio, 24-53. Publ: Ohio Strip Mine Reclamation Act, Ohio Dept. of Natural Resources Unification Law. Mem: Sigma Delta Chi; Buckeye Press Asn; Outdoor Writers Asn, Ohio; past treas, Ohio News Asn; Outdoor Writers Asn. of Am; Ohio Forestry Asn; Ohio Acad. Sci; Friends of the Land; past pres, Blue Pencil Club, Rotary and Millersburg C. of C. Rel: Methodist. Legal Res: Millersburg, Ohio 44654. Mailing Add: 4501 Arlington Blvd, Arlington, Va. 22203. (1967)

WHITE, RICHARD D
Exec. Asst, Nebr. Dem. Party
b. Valentine, Nebr, 1/2/42; s. Francis White and Emma Peters W; single. Educ: Nebr. Wesleyan Univ, B.A, 64; Blue Key; Pi Kappa Delta. Polit. & Govt. Pos: Del, Dem. Nat. Conv, 68; exec. asst, Nebr. Dem. Party, 69- Rel: Methodist. Legal Res: 231 Edna St, Valentine, Nebr. 69201. Mailing Add: 5403 Huntington, Lincoln, Nebr. 68504.

WHITE, RICHARD CRAWFORD D
U.S. Rep, Tex.
b. El Paso, Tex, 4/29/23; m. to Katherine Huffman W; c. Rodrick James, Richard Whitman, Raymond Edward. Educ: El Paso High Sch; Civilian Mil. Training Camp, San Antonio; Tex. West. Col; Univ. Tex, B.A, 46; Univ. Tex. Law Sch, LL.D, 49; Phi Alpha Delta; Sigma Alpha Epsilon. Polit. & Govt. Pos: Tex. State Rep, 55-58; U.S. Rep, Tex, 64-, mem, Armed Serv, Post Off. and Civil Serv. Cmts, U.S. House of Rep. Bus. & Prof. Pos: Lawyer licensed to practice before the U.S. Supreme Court. Mil. Serv: Marines, Pac. Theatre; Japanese interpreter-rifleman Bougainville, Guam, Iwo Jima; Purple Heart. Mem: El Paso C. of C; Tex. Univ. Ex-Students Asn; El Paso Co. Bar Asn; State Bar of Tex, Am. Bar Asn; El Paso Hist. Soc; Kiwanis. Rel: Episcopal. Legal Res: El Paso, Tex. Mailing Add: 4217 Leland St, Chevy Chase, Md. 20015.

WHITE, RICHARD H. Conservative
Minn. State Rep.
b. Minneapolis, Minn, 1914; married; c. three. Educ: Univ. Minn, B.S.L, LL.B. Polit. & Govt. Pos: F.B.I. Agent, 42-46; Minn. State Rep, 62- Bus. & Prof. Pos: Partner, Cloutier, Gallagher, White & James Attorneys, Minneapolis, Minn, currently. Legal Res: 1777 Knox Ave. S, Minneapolis, Minn. 55403. Mailing Add: 610 Midwest Plaza, Minneapolis, Minn. 55402.

WHITE, ROBERT SIEMENS R
Mont. State Rep.
b. Roy, Mont, 11/30/21; s. Claude H. White and Anna Siemens W; m. 12/26/43 to Lorraine B. Woolley; c. Lauriann Mary, Cheryl Donalouise and Bobbe Joleyne. Polit. & Govt. Pos: Mont. State Rep, State Constitution Rev. Interim Cmn, currently. Mil. Serv: Entered as Pvt, Army, 42, released as Tech. 3/C, 45; Good Conduct Medal; Presidential Unit Citation; ETO Ribbon with Four Battle Stars. Mem: Exalted Ruler, Elks, 66-67; pres, Lions Club, 61-62; Mason; Shrine; Al Bedoo; Farm Bur; Stock Growers Asn; VFW; Am. Legion. Rel: United Presbyterian; elder. Mailing Add: R.R. 2, Lewistown, Mont. 59457.

WHITE, ROSE MARIE D
Mem, Dem. Nat. Cmt.
b. Lincoln, Calif, 9/15/08; d. Joseph Oscar Amadio and Evelyn Ann Brusco A; m. 4/29/29 to William Walter White; c. James Edward. Educ: Lincoln Union High Sch, Lincoln, Calif, 24-28. Polit. & Govt. Pos: Mem, Calif. Dem. State Cent. Cmt, currently; exec. bd. mem, Union Labor Party, San Francisco, currently; mem. disaster corps, San Francisco City and Co, 69-; mem, Dem. Nat. Cmt, currently. Bus. & Prof. Pos: Bus. rep, Local 2565, Indust. Carpenters, 41- Mem: Del, Bay Dist. Coun. of Carpenters; pres, New Mission Terrace Improv. Asn, 10 years; del, exec. bd, Alemany Dist. Coun, San Francisco; Druids; Golden Gate Circle; San Francisco Sons of Italy. Rel: Catholic. Mailing Add: 306 Delano Ave, San Francisco, Calif. 94112.

WHITE, RUTH FORBES D
b. Wanchese, N.C, 9/8/98; d. Clemond Z. Forbes and Elvina Etheridge F; m. 2/12/19 to William E. White (deceased); c. Caroline (Mrs. Garland E. Bell). Educ: Univ. N.C, 2 years; Cornelian Lit. Soc. Polit. & Govt. Pos: Postmaster, Colerain, N.C, 27-57; del, State Dem. Conv, 39-; del, Co. Dem. Conv, 58-68; pres, Bertie Co. Dem. Women, 60-63; bd. mem, Bertie Co. Welfare Dept, 61-65, chmn. bd, 65-68; del, Nat. Dem. Conv, 64; v.chmn, Colerain Precinct, 65-69. Bus. & Prof. Pos: Sch. teacher, Colerain Pub. Sch, 24-27. Publ: 'History of Colerain,' N.C. Hist. Soc. Mag, 40; 'History of Plantations on Chowan River,' Bertie Co. Chronicle, N.C. Mag. and Dept. Archives and Hist. Mem: Pres, Colerain Womans Club; Bertie Co. Historic Soc; Hist. Hope Found; Bertie Co. Hosp. Auxiliary. Rel: Baptist; Deacon, Baptist Church. Mailing Add: River St, Colerain, N.C. 27924.

WHITE, SOMERS HAYES R
Ariz. State Sen.
b. Sterling, Kans, 3/1/31; s. Paul A. White and Bertrude Brown W; m. 12/10/55 to Nancy Butler; c. Trudy, Polly and Tucker. Educ: Amherst Col, B.A, 53; Harvard Bus. Sch, M.B.A, 59; Rep. Campaign Mgt. Sch, grad, 67; Chi Phi. Polit. & Govt. Pos: Ariz. State Sen, 69- Bus. & Prof. Pos: Bus. asst. to trust officer, Chase Manhattan Bank, N.Y, 53, exec. training prog, 55-57; head off, Valley Nat. Bank, Phoenix, 59-60; asst. v.pres, Guaranty Bank, Phoenix, 60-61; pres, N.W. Bank, Seattle, Wash, 61-65; exec. v.pres, Pioneer Bank, Ariz, 65-; pres, Somers H. White Co, Mgt. Consults, 66- Mil. Serv: Entered Army, 54, released as Sgt, 55, after serv. in 17th Inf. Regt, Korea, 18 months; seventh Div. Cert. of Achievement; Korean Serv, Nat. Defense, UN Serv. and Good Conduct Medals. Mem: Dir, Phoenix Advert. Club; dir, Sales and Mkt. Execs. Asn; dir, Phoenix Soc. Financial Analysts; mem, Pub. Rels. Soc. Am; Int. Platform Asn; past pres, Harvard Bus. Club of Phoenix. Youngest Bank President in Am. Rel: Catholic. Legal Res: 2208 E. Missouri, Phoenix, Ariz. 85016. Mailing Add: P.O. Box 1617, Phoenix, Ariz. 85001.

WHITE, THOMAS JACKSON D
N.C. State Sen.
b. Concord, N.C, 3/6/03; s. Thomas Jackson, Sr. and Mary Isabelle Culp W; m. 12/29/37 to Virginia Edwards Turley; c. Isabelle White (former marriage), Mrs. Sarah Ellen White Archie, Thomas Jackson III, Mrs. Virginia Turley Moseley (Step-daughter). Educ: Charlotte Univ. Sch, 17; Bailey Mil. Inst, 18-19; Concord High Sch, 19-20; N.C. State Col, 20-22; Univ. of N.C. State Law Sch, 24-27. Polit. & Govt. Pos: Co. attorney, Lenoir Co. N.C, 38-64; N.C. State Rep, 53-59; mem, N.C. Adv. Budget Cmn, 61-, chmn, 63-68; N.C. State Sen, 61-69, chmn, Senate Finance Cmt, 61 and chmn, Senate Appropriations Cmt, 63-67; chmn, N.C. Art Mus. Bldg. Cmn, 67-; trustee, Univ. N.C, 65-, mem. exec. cmt, 67-; legis. counsel to Gov. N.C, 69. Bus. & Prof. Pos: Delegate to Legis. Work Conf, South. Regional Ed. Bd, Sept, 56. Mil. Serv: Co. E, 120th Inf, N.C. Nat. Guard, 21-24. Mem: Lenoir Co. Bar Asn, (pres, 52); Sixth Dist. Bar Asn.(pres, 54); N.C. State Bar Asn, Inc; N.C. Bar Asn; Am. Bar Asn; Am. Judicature Soc; Phi Gamma Delta (Epsilon Chap, Univ. N.C); Phi Alpha Delta (law); Fel, Am. Col. Trial Lawyers; Richard Caswell Masonic Lodge No. 705; AF&AM; Sphinx Club; Moose; Elks, Kinston Lodge No. 740. Rel: Episcopal. Mailing Add: P.O. Box 187, Kinston, N.C. 28501.

WHITE, THOMAS W. D
b. Detroit, Mich, 10/31/37. Educ: Univ. Mich; Wayne State Univ, B.A. in Hist, grad. work in Sociol. Polit. & Govt. Pos: Field investr, Prog. in Civil Rights and Intergroup Rels, Detroit Commun. Rels. Cmn, Mich; tech. aide, Detroit Civil Serv. Cmn, 1 year; soc. worker, Wayne Co. Bur. of Soc. Aid, 2 years; Mich. State Rep, 64-67. Mem: NAACP; Trade Union Leadership Coun; Am. Civil Liberties Union; Cong. on Racial Equality. Mailing Add: 79 Massachusetts, Highland Park, Mich. 48203. (1967)

WHITE, WILLIAM JOHNSON D
b. Columbia, N.C, 1/7/98; s. William White and Victoria Kemp W; m. 11/26/25 to Veva Merle Collins W; c. William Johnson, Jr. Educ: Univ. N.C. Polit. & Govt. Pos: Register of Deeds, Tyrell Co, N.C, 22-26; mayor, Columbia, 27-31; chmn, Tyrell Co. Bd. Educ, 36-38; former chmn, Tyrell Co. Dem. Exec. Cmt; supt, Tyrell Co. Schs, 43-53; N.C. State Rep, 63-66. Bus. & Prof. Pos: Retail merchant. Mem: Mason; Eastern Star (past Worthy Patron, Columbus Chap. 281); N.C. Merchants Asn; past pres, Columbia Rotary Club; pres, South. Albemarle Asn. Rel: Methodist; steward, teacher, men's Bible class. Mailing Add: Columbia, N.C. 27925.

WHITE, WILLIAM L. R
b. Almena, Kans, 4/21/08; s. Bertram Calvin White and Gertrude Hays W; m. 4/22/34 to Lucile E. West; c. Myrna Lea (Mrs. Temple) and Bonnie Mae (Mrs. Maul). Educ: Arapahoe High Sch, 22-26. Polit. & Govt. Pos: Chmn, 18th Sen. Rep. Cent. Cmt, Colo, 62-66; chmn, Cheyenne Co. Rep. Cent. Cmt, 62-; chmn, 57th Representative Rep. Cent. Cmt, 66-68; cmnr, Colo. State Bd. Stock Inspection, 67- Bus. & Prof. Pos: Mem, Cheyenne Co. Hosp. Bd, 46-50; mem, Sch. Bd, Arapahoe Sch. Dist, 48-56; chmn, Cheyenne Agr. Stabilization & Conserv. Serv. Coun, 48-56; owner and operator, State Line Ranch, currently. Mem: Odd Fellows (past Grand Chmn); Colo. and Cheyenne Co. Farm Bur; Colo. Cattleman Asn; Cheyenne Co. Livestock Asn. Rel: Protestant. Mailing Add: Arapahoe, Colo. 80802.

WHITEAKER, PEARL WALLACE D
b. Pine Bluff, Ark, 7/8/35; s. Joseph W. Whiteaker and Laura Muse W; m. 2/16/58 to Mary Ada Latta; c. Gregory Wallace, Mary Denise and Scott Murray. Educ: Ark. A&M, 2 summers; Southwest. at Memphis, A.B, 58; Univ. Miss, M.B.S, 61; Sigma Nu. Polit. & Govt. Pos: Asst, U.S. Rep. Oren Harris, Ark, 65; admin. asst, U.S. Sen. John L. McClellan, Ark, 66- Bus. & Prof. Pos: Mgr, Merritt-LeMay Realty Co, 60-61; asst. to pres, Ark. Col, 62-64; math. teacher, Pine Bluff Pub. Schs, 58-59. Mem: Ark. Real Estate Asn; Kiwanis. Rel: Presbyterian. Legal Res: 720 Kentucky, Pine Bluff, Ark. 71601. Mailing Add: 8415 Thames, Springfield, Va. 22151.

WHITEHEAD, DONALD WHARTON R
V.Pres, Norfolk Co. Rep. Club, Mass.
b. Auburn, N.Y, 6/23/29; s. Louis H. Whitehead and Dorothy Hawthorne W; m. 2/28/50 to Margaret S. Sharpe; c. John L, Donna L, Karen A, Robert S. and Donald W, Jr. Educ: Williams Col, A.B, cum laude; Northeast. Univ. Sch. Law, LL.B, cum laude, Harvard Law Sch; Tufts Univ, Pub. Affairs Fel. Polit. & Govt. Pos: V.pres, Norfolk Co. Rep. Club, Mass, 57-; chmn, Rep. Town Cmt, Stoughton, 57-; admin. asst. to U.S. Rep. Hastings Keith, 62; campaign mgr, Curtis for U.S. Sen. Cmt, 62, Ames for State Sen. Cmt, 62 & 64, Hahn for State Treas. Cmt, 64 and Retain Sales Tax Cmt, 66; asst. at-

torney gen, Commonwealth of Mass, 63-64; field coordinator, Rep. Nat. Cmt, 68; regional dir, Mid-Atlantic States Nixon-for-President Cmt, 68. Mem: State and Local Bar Asns; Rising Star Lodge, AOFAM. Rel: Protestant. Legal Res: 453 Morton St, Stoughton, Mass, 02072. Mailing Add: c/o Hahn & Whitehead, 44 Bromfield St, Boston, Mass. 02108.

WHITEHEAD, EDWIN H. 'ED' D
Wyo. State Rep.
Educ: Univ. Wyo. Polit. & Govt. Pos: Past pres, Wyo. Young Dem; del, Dem. Nat. Conv, 60; chmn. platform cmt, Dem. State Conv, Wyo, 66; Wyo. State Rep, 67- Bus. & Prof. Pos: Businessman. Mailing Add: 2974 Kelley Dr, Cheyenne, Wyo. 82001. (1967)

WHITEHEAD, EMREY LEE R
S.Dak. State Rep.
b. Fort Worth, Tex, 4/9/99; s. Thomas J. Whitehead and Imogene Mallinson W; m. 9/11/32 to Audrey M. Golloday. Educ: Cent. High Sch, St. Joseph, Mo, 4 years. Polit. & Govt. Pos: Co. Cmnr, Pennington Co, S.Dak, 40-58; pres, Black Hills Commun. Asn, 49-50; pres, S.Dak. State Asn. Co. Cmt, 52-53; mem, S.Dak. State Racing Cmn, 52-53; S.Dak. State Rep, Pennington Co, 67- Bus. & Prof. Pos: Owner, Whitehead Ins. Agency & Real Estate, 36-67. Mem: Mason; Elks; Lions. Legal Res: 614½ St. Joseph St, Rapid City, S.Dak. 57701. Mailing Add: Box 745, Rapid City, S.Dak. 57701.

WHITEHEAD, ROBERT S. D
b. Elwood, Ind, 8/29/15; s. V. W. Whitehead and Dorothy Smith W; m. 5/10/44 to Betty J. McDowell; c. Susan and Betsy. Educ: Univ. Notre Dame, 34-35; Ind. Univ, A.B, 41, LL.B, 48; Phi Delta Phi; Phi Kappa Psi. Polit. & Govt. Pos: Dep. prosecuting attorney, Howard Co, Ind, 48-52; del, Dem. Nat. Conv, 52; city attorney, Kokomo, Ind, 52-60; attorney, Kokomo-Center Twp. Consolidated Sch. Corp, 54-; attorney, Howard Co, Ind, 61-; chmn, Ind. State Hwy. Cmn, 65-69. Mil. Serv: Entered as Pvt, Army, 41, released as Capt, 45, after serv. in Coast Artil, Aleutian and Alaskan Theaters, 42-45. Mem: Am, Ind. State and Howard Co. Bar Asns; Elks; Kokomo Country Club; VFW. Rel: Presbyterian. Mailing Add: 100 S. Buckeye, Kokomo, Ind. 46901.

WHITEHEAD, TRUMAN JACK R
Secy, Fulton Co. Rep. Cent. Cmt, Ill.
b. Canton, Ill, 7/26/28; s. Howard J. Whitehead and Kathryn Jump W; m. 11/23/51 to Ina Mae Berkley; c. Linda Diann, Truman Jay, Dennis Allen, Ellen Sue, Teresa Rena and Caryl Beth. Educ: West. Ill. Univ, B.S. in Educ, 51. Polit. & Govt. Pos: Co. chmn, Gov. Ogillvie, Fulton Co, Ill, 68; Rep. committeeman, Precinct Four, Lewiston, Ill, chmn, Lewistown Rep. Twp. Cmt. and representative committeeman, 46th Rep. Dist, currently; mem. patronage cmt. and exec. cmt, Fulton Co. Rep. Cent. Cmt, currently and secy, 68- Bus. & Prof. Pos: Secy, Lewistown Grade Sch. Dist. 141, 64-67. Mem: AF&AM (secy, Lewistown Lodge No. 104 and past master); Boy Scouts (chmn, Lewistown Pack No. 132 and past chmn, Cub Scout Pack No. 132); 1200 Club of Ill. Rel: Methodist. Mailing Add: 1124 S. Illinois St, Lewistown, Ill. 61542.

WHITEHEAD, WILLIAM SCHOLL R
Mem, Renegotiation Bd.
b. Denver, Colo, 5/27/07; s. Morgan Thomas Whitehead (deceased) and Mayme Elsie Scholl W.(deceased); m. 2/2/34 to Dorothy Childs; c. William Scholl, Jr. Educ: Wharton Sch. Finance, Univ, Pa, 3½ years; Beta Theta Pi. Polit. & Govt. Pos: Mem. staff, Securities and Exchange Cmn, Wash, D.C, 35-40; mem. staff, Off. Price Admin, 40-42; mem. staff, War Assets Admin, 46-47; mem, Renegotiation Bd, 69- Bus. & Prof. Pos: Mgt. consult, Ives, Whitehead & Co, Inc, 48-69. Mil. Serv: Col.(Ret), Army Res, 67; Legion of Merit; Army Commendation Medal with Oak Leaf Cluster. Mem: Army-Navy Country Club; Beta Theta Pi Alumni Asn. of Wash. Rel: Episcopal. Mailing Add: 2600 S. 16th St, Arlington, Va. 22204.

WHITEHILL, GRACE ELFREDA R
Vt. State Rep.
b. Coventry, Vt, 8/12/00; m. to Lucian; c. two sons; four daughters. Educ: Derby Acad. Polit. & Govt. Pos: Former clerk and chmn, currently clerk; mem. sch. bd, 46-; Vt. State Rep, 65- Bus. & Prof. Pos: Housewife. Mem: Seymour Home Dem Club; Morgan United Church Coun. Rel: Methodist. Mailing Add: Island Pond, Vt. 05846.

WHITEHURST, GEORGE WILLIAM R
U.S. Rep, Va.
b. Norfolk, Va, 3/12/25; s. Calvert Stanhope Whitehurst and Laura Tomlinson W; m. 8/24/46 to Jennette Franks; c. Calvert Stanhope and Frances Seymour. Educ: Washington and Lee Univ, B.A, 50; Univ. Va, M.A, Hist, 51; W.Va. Univ, Ph.D. Am. Diplomatic Hist, 62; Delta Upsilon. Polit. & Govt. Pos: Mem, Mayor's Cmn. on Crime and Delinquency, Norfolk, Va, 66-68; U.S. Rep, House Rep, Second Dist, 69- Bus. & Prof. Pos: Mem, Dept. Hist, Old Dominion Col, 50-68 and dean student affairs, 63-68; news analyst, WTAR-TV, Norfolk, 62-68. Mil. Serv: Entered as A/S, Navy, 43, released as ARM 2/C, 46, after serv. in Torpedo Squadron 88, U.S.S. Yorktown, Pac, 45; Air Medal with Star. Mem: Am. Hist. Asn; Va. Student Personnel Asn; Am. Legion; Lions; Norfolk Coun. Alcoholism; Norfolk Forum; Norfolk Roundtable; Tidewater Coun. Health and Welfare; past pres, Tidewater Chap, Am. Cancer Crusade; Tidewater Chap, Am. Asn. UN. Rel: Methodist; former chmn. official bd, Ghent Methodist Church. Legal Res: 7320 Glenroie Ave, Norfolk, Va. 23505. Mailing Add: 1227 Longworth House Office Bldg, Washington, D.C. 20515.

WHITEHURST, SAM LATHAM D
b. New Bern, N.C, 7/30/22; s. Fred Hancock and Sallie Tingle W; m. 2/1/69 to Carolyn Purser; c. Sam Latham, Jr, Frances Whitehurst (Mrs. Gurley) and Fred Hancock, II. Educ: Fishburne Mil. Sch, N.C. State of the Univ. of N.C, Raleigh. Polit. & Govt. Pos: N.C. State Rep, 53-63, mem, Legis. Coun, 63-64; N.C. State Sen, 64-69; former chmn, Ins. Cmn. and Driver Educ. Cmn. Bus. & Prof. Pos: Farmer; pres, Dairy Farmer Inc; dir, N.C. Dairy Found; dir, Atlantic E. Carolina Rwy; exec. dir, N.C. Soft Drink Assoc, Raleigh, 68- Mil. Serv: Cpl, Army, 43-45. Mem: Pres, Craven Co. Chap, N.C. State Alumni Asn; past pres, Craven Co. Farm Bur; AF&AM; Rotary; VFW; Am. Legion; Scottish Rite. Rel: Methodist. Legal Res: Bayboro Rd, New Bern, N.C. 28560. Mailing Add: P.O. Box 2302, Raleigh, N.C. 27602.

WHITENER, BASIL LEE D
b. York Co, S.C, 5/14/15; s. Levi L. Whitener and Laura Barrett W; m. 9/26/42 to Harriet Priscilla Morgan; c. John Morgan, Laura Lee, Basil L, Jr. and Barrett S. Educ: Rutherford Col, 31-33; Univ. S.C, 33-35; Duke Univ, LL.B, 37; Phi Delta Phi; Omicron Delta Kappa. Hon. LL.D, Belmont Abbey Col, 60 and Pfeiffer Col, 65. Polit. & Govt. Pos: N.C. State Rep, 41; solicitor, 14th Dist, N.C, 46-56; del, Dem. Nat. Conv, 48 & 60; U.S. Rep, N.C, 57-69. Bus. & Prof. Pos: Instr. bus. law, Belmont Abbey Col, 38-40; attorney-at-law, 37- Mil. Serv: Entered as Ens, Navy, 42, released as Lt, Naval Res, 45; Maj, Air Force Res; Secy. of Navy Commendation Ribbon; Am. Area, European-African-Middle East. Area Campaign Ribbons with Two Combat Stars. Mem: Pres, Gaston Co. Bar Asn, 50, Gen. Statutes Cmn, 46 and Cmn. to Study Improvement of Admin. of Justice, 47-49; bd. adv, Belmont Abbey Col; N.C. and Am. Bar Asns; Am. Trial Lawyers Asn; hon. life mem, Gastonia Jr. C. of C; Kiwanis; Elks; Am. Legion; 40 et 8; VFW; Mason (32°), York and Scottish Rite Bodies, Shrine. Recipient POSA Merit Medallion Award, 66; Watchdog of the Treasury Award from Nat. Associated Businessmen, Inc, 66. Rel: Methodist; Mem, Official Bd. Legal Res: 1854 Montclaire, Gastonia, N.C. 28052. Mailing Add: Box 1, Gastonia, N.C. 28052.

WHITFIELD, J. CHARLES, JR. D
b. Beaumont, Tex, 12/16/21; s. Joseph Charles Whitfield, Sr. and Grace Belle See W; m. 10/17/44 to Mary Florence Ingalls; c. James Charles and Charlotte Marie. Educ: Univ. Tex, B.B.A, 43; Univ. Houston Col. of Law, 54-55; South Tex. Col. of Law, LL.B, 57; Delta Sigma Pi. Polit. & Govt. Pos: Tex. State Rep, Dist. 22, Position 8, 59-67. Bus. & Prof. Pos: Attorney-at-Law, 58- Mil. Serv: Entered as Seaman, Naval Res, 42, released as Lt. Comdr, 66, after serv. in World War II and Korean War, 6 years active duty in Pac; Lt. Comdr.(Ret), Naval Res, until 66; Naval Res. Medal; Atlantic Serv. Ribbon; UN Serv. Medal; Victory Medal; S.W. Pac. Ribbon. Mem: Harris Co. Bar Asn; cmt. on state legis, Am. Bar Asn; Am. Asn. of Defense Lawyers in Criminal Cases; Odd Fellows. Rel: Baptist. Legal Res: 5808 Charlotte St, Houston, Tex. 77005. Mailing Add: 1006 Houston Bar Center Building, 723 Main at Rusk, Houston, Tex. 77002.

WHITING, HAROLD JOHNSON R
Utah State Rep.
b. Springville, Utah, 2/25/08; s. James William Whiting and Harriet Anna Johnson W; m. 6/10/31 to Marie Jensen; c. Harriet (Mrs. Ronald J. Clark), James William, Lynn Jensen and Phyllis (Mrs. Robert L. Haymond). Educ: Brigham Young Univ, B.A, 30; N.Y. Univ, grad. sch. Polit. & Govt. Pos: City councilman, Springville, Utah, 50-60; Utah State Rep, 67- Bus. & Prof. Pos: Order clerk, Great Atlantic Tea Co, Garden City, L. I, N.Y, 30-34; pres, Whiting Haymond Construction Co, Springville, Utah, 35- Mem: Assoc. Gen. Contractors of Am.(v.pres, Utah Chap, 52-53, pres, 53-54); Jr. C. of C; Lions; C. of C. Rel: Latter-day Saint. Mailing Add: 165 East Fourth North, Springville, Utah 84663.

WHITING, THELMA P. Independent
b. Springfield, Mass, 6/12/25; d. George O. Packard and Edith Elsie Snyder P; m. 12/1/55 to Carroll William Whiting; c. Laurie Anne. Educ: Famous Writers Sch, Westport, Conn, 1½ years. Polit. & Govt. Pos: Chmn, Cummington Citizens for Eisenhower, Mass, 52; secy. bd. selectmen, Cummington, 52-57, Town Finance Cmt, 58-63, Bd. Health, 62-65, secy, Regional Sch. Dist, Planning Cmt, 63-; chmn, Rep. Town Cmt, Cummington, 52-60, secy, 60-62; coordinator for U.S. Sen. Cand. Edward Brooke, Cummington, 66; secy, Cummington Hist. Cmn, 67- Bus. & Prof. Pos: Bookkeeper, Cummington Mfg. Co, Mass, 56-68; govt. reporter, Daily Hampshire Gazette, Northampton, 68- Publ: Newspaper features. Mem: Cummington Village Ladies Soc; Hillside Agr. Soc; Cummington Mother's Club; Cummington Hist. Cmt; Community Leaders of Am, 68; The Two Thousand Women of Achievement, 69. Rel: United Church of Christ. Legal Res: Thayer Corner Rd, Cummington, Mass. 01026. Mailing Add: Box 114, Cummington, Mass. 01026.

WHITLEY, CLYDE H. R
N.C. State Rep.
b. Stanley County, N.C, 10/3/18; s. M.D. Whitley and Ida Rose Herrin W; m. 12/16/39 to Opal J. Almond; c. Tony, June, Gail and Judson. Educ: Ridgecrest High Sch; ICS Bus. Sch, 40. Polit. & Govt. Pos: Co. Cmnr, Purchasing Agent, N.C, 56-58; N.C. State Rep, 61- Bus. & Prof. Pos: Plumbing & Heating Contractor. Mem: Stanly Baptist Exec. Cmt; Teacher, Sunday Sch. Group Leader, Stanly Baptist Asn; Mission Baptist Church. Rel: Baptist. Mailing Add: Box 2310 Charlotte Rd, Albemarle, N.C. 28001.

WHITLEY, DANIEL P, JR. D
b. Albemarle, N.C, 12/2/18; s. Daniel P. Whitley and Ruth Irene Snotherly W; m. 12/21/41 to Sally Edgerton; c. Daniel P, IV and Ann. Educ: High Point Col; Univ. N.C, A.B, 38, LL.B, 41. Polit. & Govt. Pos: N.C. State Rep, 63-68. Bus. & Prof. Pos: Attorney-at-law. Mil. Serv: Lt. Comdr, Navy, World War II, 41-45; Korean Conflict, 51-53. Mem: High Point Bar Asn.(pres, 60); N.C. Bar Asn; Phi Delta Phi; High Point Friends Meeting; past pres, Men of the Meeting, 58-59. Mailing Add: 1101 Clyde Place, High Point, N.C. 27262.

WHITLOCK, DOUGLAS R
b. Terre Haute, Ind, 10/3/04; s. Charles Chester Whitlock and Birdella E. Smith W; m. 6/18/29 to Mary Ellen Jenkins; c. Douglas, II, Marilyn (Mrs. Robert Long) and Sandra (Mrs. Theodore Driscoll, Jr). Educ: Ind. Univ, B.S, 26, J.D, 28; Alpha Tau Omega; Gamma Eta Gamma. Polit. & Govt. Pos: Chmn, Young Rep, Ind, 28-30; pres, Young Rep. Nat. Fedn, 30-32; exec. dir, Eisenhower Campaign Tour Cmt, 52 and Goldwater Campaign Tour Cmt, 64. Bus. & Prof. Pos: Sr. partner, Whitlock & Tait. Mem: Devereux Found; chmn. bd, Structural Clay Prod. Inst; U.S. C. of C; pres, Producers Coun, 43-45; chmn, Bldg. Prod. Inst; Am. and D.C. Bar Asns; Ind. Soc. Wash. Decorated Knight Comdr. of Liberia; Order of Merit, Haiti. Rel: Episcopal. Mailing Add: 2550 Massachusetts Ave. N.W, Washington, D.C. 20008.

WHITLOCK, JAMES E. D
b. 1934. Educ: Bellarmine Col; Univ. Ky. Polit. & Govt. Pos: Ky. State Rep, 62-68. Bus. & Prof. Pos: Real estate broker; v.pres, Old Ky. Home Realty Bd; ins. agent; exec. v.pres. and dir, Taylor Co. Fed. Savings & Loan Asn. Mil. Serv: Marine Corps. Mem: Jaycees; K. of C; Am. Legion. Rel: Catholic. Mailing Add: 407 Lebanon Ave, Campbellsville, Ky. 42718.

WHITLOW, WYATT RODNEY D
b. Oakland, Ky, 7/24/82; s. Alphaus Whitlow and Betty Cole W; m. 6/6/40 to Melba Newbill; c. Melba (Mrs. Smith) and Wm. Rodney (deceased). Educ: Potter's Col, 3 years. Polit. & Govt. Pos: Ky. State Rep, Warren Co, 06, Todd Co, 46; with State Dept. of Agr, 56; chmn, Todd Co. Dem. Party, 66. Bus. & Prof. Pos: Farmer. Mem: Lions Club (charter mem); Farm Bur; Dark Fired Tobacco Growers' Asn; Responsible for soil conserv. in Todd Co. Rel: Christian Church of N.Am. Mailing Add: Box 214, Spring St, Guthrie, Ky. 42234.

WHITMAN, REGINALD NORMAN R
Fed. R.R. Adminstr, Dept. of Transportation
b. Jasmin, Sask, Can, 10/15/09; s. Norman L. Whitman and Irene Haverlock W; m. 1/31/32 to Opal Vales; c. James, Richard and Donna (Mrs. Ronald Throener). Educ: St. Joseph Col, Sask, grad; Harvard Bus. Sch, admin. mgt. Polit. & Govt. Pos: Gen. mgr, Alaska R.R, Dept. of Interior, Anchorage, 55-56; mem, Alaska's North Cmn, 67; fed. R.R. adminstr, Dept. of Transportation, 69- Bus. & Prof. Pos: From telegrapher to dispatcher, trainmaster, rules examiner and terminal trainmaster, Great North. Rwy, 29-53, supt, Cascade Div, 53-57, gen. mgr, Lines E, 57-69, former pres, Lake Superior Terminal and Transfer R.R. and former v.pres, Portal Pipe Line Co. Mil. Serv: Served as 1st Lt, 732nd R.R. Oper. Bn, 43-44. Mem: Nat. Defense Transportation Asn; Am. Legion. Rel: Catholic. Mailing Add: 6308 Stoneham Lane, McLean, Va. 22101.

WHITNEY, CHARLES THOMAS J. D
Pres, Young Dem. Clubs of Iowa
b. Des Moines, Iowa, 8/6/44; s. Charles H. Whitney and Ethyl Terry Jackson W; m. 10/26/62 to Ellen Kae Shiffer; c. JoEllen. Educ: Drake Univ. Polit. & Govt. Pos: NEC Col. Young Dem. Clubs of Am; state chmn, Am. Christmas Trains and Trucks for Viet Nam, 65; Young Dem. rep, Operation Support, 65-66; pres, Young Dem. Club of Drake Univ, 65-66; exec. secy, Young Dem. Clubs of Iowa, 65-66 and pres, currently; mem, Polk Co. Dem. Cent. Cmt, 66. Legal Res: 1607 Pioneer Rd, Des Moines, Iowa 50320. Mailing Add: 500 Shops Bldg, Des Moines, Iowa 50309. (1967)

WHITNEY, CLOY E. R
Mo. State Rep.
b. Fort Morgan, Colo, 11/15/10; m. 1934 to Anne M. Wood; c. Larry and Carol Anne. Educ: Mo. State Col, Kirksville, B.S. Polit. & Govt. Pos: Kirksville City Coun, Mo, 8 years; Kirksville Bd. of Educ; Mo. State Rep, 62-, Educ, Ins, Mil. and Vets. Affairs and Accounts Cmts. Bus. & Prof. Pos: Ins. Mil. Serv: Navy, World War II, Lt, Commun. Off, Adm. Nimitz' Staff. Mem: Mason; Am. Legion; 40 et 8; VFW; Rotary; Shrine. Rel: Baptist. Mailing Add: 8 Center Rd, Kirksville, Mo. 63501.

WHITNEY, IRA DEXTER R
b. Stamford, Vt, 4/6/02; m. to Anna Mae Foucard; c. One son and one daughter. Educ: Drury High Sch; Bliss Bus. Col, N. Adams, Mass. Polit. & Govt. Pos: Selectman, Mass, 26-29; 2nd constable, 32-37; chmn. planning and bldg. cmt, Stamford Elem. Sch, 58-60; lister, Stamford, 58-60; lister, Glastenbury, 59-62; Vt. State Rep, 65-68. Bus. & Prof. Pos: Former dairyman. Mem: Trustee, Stamford Vol. Fire Dept; past pres, Bennington Co. Farm Bur. Rel: Baptist. Mailing Add: R.F.D. 1, North Adams, Mass. 01247. (1967)

WHITNEY, JOHN ADAIR R
Md. State Del.
b. Cincinnati, Ohio, 1/25/32; s. Nathanial Ruggles Whitney and Helen Loos W; m. 12/22/56 to Linda Hollis Leary; c. William Nathaniel, Jane Hollis and Anne Dickson. Educ: Williams Col, B.A, 53; Harvard Law Sch, LL.B, 56; Phi Beta Kappa; Chi Psi. Polit. & Govt. Pos: Md. State Del, 67- Bus. & Prof. Pos: Attorney, Pope, Ballard & Loos, 59- Mil. Serv: Entered as Officer Cand, Navy, 56, released as Lt, 59, after serv. in Off. Judge Adv. Gen, Navy Dept, 57-59; Lt. Comdr, Naval Res. Mem: Am. and Md. State Bar Asns; Bar Asn. of D.C. Rel: Presbyterian. Legal Res: 8007 Aberdeen Rd, Bethesda, Md. 20014. Mailing Add: 700 Brawner Bldg, 888 17th St, N.W, Washington, D.C. 20006.

WHITNEY, RAMEY CHARLES R
Nebr. State Sen.
b. Elba, Nebr, 11/16/08; s. Zachariah Faulkner Whitney and Lillian Dell R; m. 2/7/31 to Doris Ella Bemis; c. Charles Bemis and Charlene Rae (Mrs. Tirro). Educ: Univ. Nebr, B.S, 31, M.A, 36; Univ. Minn, Ph.D.(econ), 46; Alpha Zeta; Gamma Sigma Delta; Delta Sigma Pi; Pi Gamma Mu; Kappa Sigma Pi. Polit. & Govt. Pos: Mayor, Chappell, Nebr, 58-62; Nebr. State Sen, 64- Bus. & Prof. Pos: Asst. prof. agr. econ, Colo. State Univ, 37-41; res. economist, Bur. Agr. Econ, U.S. Dept. Agr, 41-43; assoc. prof. agr. econ, Univ. Mo, 43-46; Univ. Nebr, 46-55. Publ: Prospective Income from Average Size Farms on Grade Two Missouri Land, Univ. Mo, 46; Artificial Grain Drying in Nebraska, 52 and The Valuation of Rental Housing, Omaha and Lincoln, 54, Univ. Nebr. Mem: West. Farm Econ. Asn; Nebr. Wheat Growers Asn; Farm Bur; Rotary Int; C. of C. Rel: Methodist. Mailing Add: 1482 Fifth St, Chappell, Nebr. 69129.

WHITNEY, ROBERT E. D
Committeeman, Ill. Dem. Cent. Cmt.
b. Carrier Mills, Ill, 7/22/21; s. George Whitney and Blanche Lewis; m. 10/14/44 to Julia Maller; c. Gloria Stout, Julene Clift, Robbie Dewar and stepson Fred Williams. Polit. & Govt. Pos: Dem. committeeman, Precinct one, Carrier Mills, Ill, 46-54; v.pres, Young Dem. Ill, 48; state auto investr, Ill, 49-53; committeeman, Ill. Dem. Cent. Cmt, 62-; mem. Ill. Real Estate Exam. Cmt, Dept. Registrn. and Educ, 64- Bus. & Prof. Pos: Mem. and dir, Egyptian Real Estate Bd. Mil. Serv: Entered as CPO, Navy, 42, released 45, after serv. in U.S.S. LST 384, ETO, 30 months; Five Battle Stars; Good Conduct Medal. Mem: Am. Legion (past comdr, 2 terms); VFW. Rel: Methodist. Mailing Add: 18 W. Walnut, Harrisburg, Ill. 62946.

WHITNEY, SHIRLEY R
b. Cincinnati, Ohio, 5/20/14; d. Samuel Freedman and Mary Jacobs F; m. 11/24/49 to James C. Whitney; c. Sally (Mrs. Louis Nothwang) and John S. Post; 4 grandchildren. Educ: Comnock Girls Sch, Los Angeles, Calif, 4 years; Chouinart Art Sch, 3 years. Polit. & Govt. Pos: Secy, Reseda West Valley Dem. Club, 64 & 65, pres, 65 & 66; secy, 64th Assembly Dist. Dem. Coun, 64 & 65 and 22nd Cong. Dist. Dem. Coun, 64 & 65; off. mgr, State Assembly Dem. Cand, 64, off. mgr. and asst. campaign mgr, 66 and off. mgr, 68; mem, Calif. Dem. State Cent. Cmt, 66-69; mem, Los Angeles Co. Dem. Cent. Cmt, 67. Mem: Life mem. Calif. Rifle and Pistol Asn; life mem. Nat. Rifle Asn.(cmt. firearms safety, 69 and pub. rels. vol). Mailing Add: 19540 Victory Blvd, Reseda, Calif. 91335.

WHITSITT, VIRGIL H. R
Chmn, Phillips Co. Rep. Party, Kans.
b. Phillipsburg, Kans, 7/6/21; s. Carl C. Whitsitt (deceased) and Grace White W.(deceased); m. 6/6/53 to Jeanette Pittman; c. Peggy and Lois. Educ: Univ. Kans, A.B, 48; Alpha Kappa Lambda. Polit. & Govt. Pos: Chmn, Phillips Co. Rep. Party, Kans, 68- Bus. & Prof. Pos: Owner, V.H. Whitsitt Real Estate & Ins. Agency, Phillipsburg, Kans, 48- Mil. Serv: Entered as Pvt, Army Air Corps, 42, released as 1st Lt, 46, after serv. in Base Air Depot 2, Eighth Air Force, ETO, 43-46; Maj, Kans. Nat. Guard. Mem: Lions; VFW; C. of C. Rel: United Methodist. Legal Res: Phillipsburg Twp, Phillipsburg, Kans. 67661. Mailing Add: Box 222, Phillipsburg, Kans. 67661.

WHITSON, EDMUND RAYBURN 'RAY' D
Chmn, Fifth Cong. Dist. Dem. Cmt, Okla.
b. Oklahoma City, Okla, 5/21/30; s. Perry C. Whitson and Rebecca R. Hays W; m. 3/4/50 to Carolyn J. Hammon; c. Rebecca, Esta and Eddie. Educ: Univ. Okla, B.A, 52, M.A, 56; Pi Gamma Mu. Polit. & Govt. Pos: Chmn, Citizen's Adv. Cmt, Edmond, Okla, 66-68; chmn, Fifth Cong. Dist. Dem. Cmt, 67-; del, Dem. Nat. Conv, 68. Mil. Serv: Entered as 2nd Lt, Air Force, 52, released as 1st Lt, 54, after serv. in Air Force Security Serv. Mem: Am. Asn. Univ. Prof.(pres, Cent. State Col. Chap, 59-61 & 69-); Okla. Educ. Asn; Southwest. Soc. Sci. Asn. Rel: Methodist. Mailing Add: 911 N. Washington, Edmond, Okla. 73034.

WHITTAKER, EARL HORTON R
Chmn, Piute Co. Bd. Cmnrs, Utah
b. Circleville, Utah, 4/6/06; s. James Christopher Whittaker and Hannah Horton W; m. 9/13/31 to Beryl Brinkerhoff; c. Amaralyn Treece (Mrs. Lancaster) and Earl Horton, Jr. Educ: Univ. Utah, 28-30; Delta Sigma Pi; Sigma Nu. Polit. & Govt. Pos: Utah State Rep, 49-50 & 65-66; chmn, Piute Co. Bd. of Cmnrs, 69- Bus. & Prof. Pos: Livestock grower, farmer and theater owner and operator. Rel: Latter-day Saint. Mailing Add: Circleville, Utah 84723.

WHITTAKER, FREDERICK WILLIAM R
b. New Haven, Conn, 1/26/13; s. Frederick William Whittaker (deceased) and Annie May Penney W; m. 9/14/40 to Shirley Louise Johns; c. Barbara Anne (Mrs. Donald P. Bakker) and Frederick Mark. Educ: Bowdoin Col, A.B, 44; Bangor Theol. Sem, B.D, 44; Yale Univ, Ph.D, 50; Phi Beta Kappa. Hon. D.D, Bowdoin Col. and Ricker Col. Polit. & Govt. Pos: Chmn, City Coun, Maine, 59-62 and Bangor City Coun, 62; Maine State Sen, 63-64; del, Rep. Nat. Conv, 64; mem, Bangor City Rep. Cmt, Penobscot Co. Rep. Cmt. and Dist. Rep. Cong. Cmt; chmn, Maine Educ. Conf. Bd, 64-67. Bus. & Prof. Pos: Secy, Freight Traffic Dept, New Haven R.R. Co, 29-39; minister, First Parish Church, Yarmouth, Maine, 43-44 and Huntington Congregational Church, Shelton Conn, 44-48; prof. of hist, Bangor Theol. Sem, 48-; pres, 52- Mem: Am. Soc. of Church Hist; Mason. Rel: United Church of Christ; Ordained Minister. Legal Res: 15 Fifth St, Bangor, Maine 04401. Mailing Add: 300 Union St, Bangor, Maine 04401.

WHITTAKER, PHILIP N. R
Asst. Secy. of the Air Force
b. Chestnut Hill, Pa, 11/7/18; m. 11/6/48 to Elizabeth Stevenson; c. Elizabeth T, Stephen A, Philip N, Jr. and Nancy C. Educ: Univ. Pa, B.A. in Eng. and Bus, 40. Polit. & Govt. Pos: Asst. Adminstr. for Indust. Affairs, NASA, 68-69; Asst. Secy. of the Air Force, 69- Bus. & Prof. Pos: Student salesman, Int. Bus. Machines Corp, Phila, Pa, 46, sr. salesman, Portland, Maine, 46-48, br. off. mgr, Montpelier, Vt, 48-49, admin. asst, N.Y.C, 49-54, mgr. contract rels, 54-59, mgr. contracts, Fed. Systs. Div, Rockville, Md, 59-63, dir. contracts, 63-65, dir. of mkt. and contracts, 65, v.pres, Fed. Systs. Div, Gaithersburg, Md, 65-68. Mil. Serv: Entered as Ens, Navy, 41, released as Lt. Comdr, 46, after serv. in N.Z. Mem: Nat. Security Indust. Asn; Aerospace Indust. Asn. of Am, Inc; Electronics Indust. Asn; Coun. of Defense and Space Indust. Asn.(former mem, Policy Cmt); Indust. Adv. Coun, Dept. of Defense; bd. adv, Nat. Contract Mgt. Asn. Legal Res: 11009 Spring House Court, Potomac, Md. 20854. Mailing Add: Dept. of the Air Force, Pentagon, Washington, D.C. 20330.

WHITTEN, CHARLES ALVIN R
b. Eatonton, Ga, 7/5/93; s. Charles Alvin Whitten, Sr. and Clyde Hearn W; m. 10/31/40 to Octavia Pollard; c. Charles A, Jr, Varue, Richard D. and Francois H. Educ: Univ. Ga, LL.B, 17; Delta Tau Delta. Polit. & Govt. Pos: Cashier of Customs, Dist 19, U.S. Customs Serv, Mobile, Ala, 19-27; spec. agent, Fed. Bur. of Invest, 27-48; chmn, Putnam Co. Rep. Cmt, Ga, 67-68. Bus. & Prof. Pos: Owner, lumber and timber bus, 50-60. Mil. Serv: Entered as Seaman 2/C, Navy, 17, released as PhM 2/C, 19; Good Conduct and World War I Serv. Ribbons. Mem: Athelstan Club, Mobile, Ala; East. Shore Yacht Club, Mobile; Bachelors Club; Am. Legion, Mobile; Elks Club, New Orleans, La; Blue Lodge Mason (32°), Scottish Rite, Shrine, Mobile, Ala. Rel: Methodist. Mailing Add: 407 Jefferson Ave. N, Eatonton, Ga. 31024.

WHITTEN, JAMIE LLOYD D
U.S. Rep, Miss.
b. Cascilla, Miss, 4/18/10; s. Alymer Guy Whitten and Nettie Viola Early W; m. 6/20/40 to Rebecca Thompson; c. James Lloyd and Beverly Rebecca (Mrs. Walter Merritt, III). Educ: Univ. Miss. Literary and Law Depts, 27-32; Phi Alpha Delta; Beta Theta Pi. Polit. & Govt. Pos: Miss. State Rep, 32-33; Dist. Attorney, 17th Dist, 33-41; U.S. Rep, Miss, 41- Publ: That We May Live, D. Van Nostrand Co, 66. Mem: Lions; Mason; Rotary. Rel: Presbyterian. Legal Res: Charleston, Miss. 38921. Mailing Add: 2413 Rayburn House Office Building, Washington, D.C. 20515.

WHITTEN, JOHN WALLACE, JR. D
Chmn, Tallahatchie Co. Dem. Exec. Cmt, Miss.
b. Cascilla, Miss, 2/26/19; s. John Wallace Whitten and Janie Allbritton W;

m. 9/16/43 to Marianne Thaxton; c. John Wallace, III and Gordon Thaxton. Educ: Univ. Miss, LL.B. and J.D, 40; Beta Theta Pi. Polit. & Govt. Pos: Investr, U.S. Dept. Labor, Birmingham, Ala, 40-41; chmn, Tallahatchie Co. Dem. Exec. Cmt, Miss, 50- Mil. Serv: Entered as Pvt, Army, 41, released as Capt, 46, after serv. in 97th Inf. Div, Europe and Japan, 41-46; Bronze Star Medal. Mem: Miss. State Bar; Am. Legion. Rel: Protestant. Legal Res: Jennings St, Sumner, Miss. 38957. Mailing Add: Courthouse Square, Sumner, Miss. 38957.

WHITTON, REX MARION D
b. Jackson Co, Mo, 8/7/98; s. Shelley Whitton and Susan Catharine Rucker W; m. 4/22/25 to Callie Maud Lowe; c. Rex Marion, Jr. Educ: Univ. Mo, B.S, 20 and D.Sc, 61. Polit. & Govt. Pos: Various positions, Mo, 20-51, chief engr, Mo. State Hwy. Dept, 51-61; Fed. Hwy. Adminstr, Wash, D.C, 61-67. Mem: Exec. cmt, past chmn, Hwy. Research Bd; mem. bd. trustees, William Jewell Col; Am. Asn. State Hwy. Officials, past pres; Nat. Acad. Sci; Am. Road Builders Asn; Am. Soc. Civil Engrs; Mo. Soc, Prfnl. Engrs; Mason (K.T, Shrine, Jester). Recipient Thomas H. McDonald Award, 60; George S. Bartlett Award, 58. Rel: Methodist. Mailing Add: 4320 Montclair, Independence, Mo. 64055.

WHITTOW, WAYNE F. D
Wis. State Sen.
b. Milwaukee, Wis, 8/16/33. Educ: Univ. of Wis, Milwaukee, B.B.A, 63, M.B.A, 66. Polit. & Govt. Pos: Wis. State Assemblyman, 60-66; mem, 16th Ward Dem. Unit; Wis. State Sen, currently. Bus. & Prof. Pos: Mgt. consult, formerly in traffic admin. Mil. Serv: Army, 55-57. Mem: Eagles; St. Joseph Children's Home Athletic Asn; Bluemound Rd, State St. and Vliet St. Adv. Asns. Mailing Add: 4921 W. Washington Blvd, Milwaukee, Wis. 53208.

WHORTON, BILL G. R
b. London, Ark, 7/28/26; s. Joseph A. Whorton and Lottie Love W; m. 12/6/46 to Geraldine Barnes; c. David Lynn, Denise Lee and Dana Lee. Educ: Northeast. State Col, grad. in bus. admin, 49. Polit. & Govt. Pos: Exec. dir, Sedgwick Co. Rep. Cent. Cmt, Kans, 59-60; campaign mgr, Andrew F. Schoeppel for U.S. Sen, 60, spec. asst. to U.S. Sen. Andrew F. Schoeppel, 61-62; state chmn, Goldwater for Pres. Cmt, Kans, 63-64 and Citizens for Goldwater-Miller, 64; Rep. precinct committeeman, Kans. Bus. & Prof. Pos: Gen. mgr, Wash. World, 62-63; v.pres, Farm and Ranch Life Ins, 64-65; pres, Key Securities, Inc, Wichita, Kans, 65- and Agr. and Indust. Develop. Inc, 66- Mil. Serv: Entered as Pvt, Air Force, 44, released as Sgt, 46, after serv. in Fifth Air Force, Pac. and Japan, 46. Mem: VFW; Am. Legion; Mason; C. of C. Rel: Baptist. Mailing Add: 7416 Tanglewood Lane, Wichita, Kans. 67206. (1967)

WHORTON, J. D. R
Okla. State Rep.
b. Locust Grove, Okla, 12/18/27; s. Dorsey Homer Whorton, Sr. and Ona Yingst W; m. 4/18/52 to Patricia Lee Burchett; c. Saundra Olean (Mrs. Gary Gotfredson), J.D, Jr, Dwight Lee, Ernest Dwayne and Tina Deann. Educ: Locust Grove Okla. High Sch, 42-46. Polit. & Govt. Pos: Rep. State Committeeman, Mayes Co, 63-68; Okla. State Rep, Dist. 8, 68- Mem: Odd Fellows; Elks; C. of C; Rotary; Okla. Cattlemen's Asn. Rel: Methodist. Mailing Add: Star Route, Pryor, Okla. 74361.

WICK, CARL B. R
b. Detroit, Mich, 12/24/25; s. Gabriel Wick and Jenny Hanson W; m. 4/7/67 to Joyce Y. Carlson; c. Danny and Jacqueline. Educ: Univ. South. Calif, A.B, 50. Polit. & Govt. Pos: Pres, Calif. Young Rep, 59; treas, CRA, 60; pres, Calif. for Goldwater, 63 & 64. Bus. & Prof. Pos: Owner, Northridge-Reseda Ins. Asn, 56-66. Mil. Serv: Entered as Pvt, Army Air Force, 43, released as Pfc, 45. Mem: Am. Legion; Rotary. Rel: Protestant. Legal Res: 8365 Chimineas, Northridge, Calif. 91324. Mailing Add: Box 312, Reseda, Calif. 91135.

WICKER, J. SHELTON D
b. Sanford, N.C, 12/10/17; s. S.A. Wicker and Sally Jane Stone W; m. 8/3/42 to Clarice M. Burns; c. Bobby, Sharon, Michael, Dennis, John and James. Educ: N.C. State Col, B.S. in Agr, 41. Polit. & Govt. Pos: Mem, Lee Co. Bd. of Cmnrs, N.C; N.C. State Rep, 53-66. Bus. & Prof. Pos: Wholesale gas and oil jobber, Shell Oil Co, Lee and Harnett Counties, N.C. Mil. Serv: Entered Army, 42, released as 1st Lt, 46, after serv. in 290th Inf, 75th Div. Mem: Lions; Elks; 40 et 8; VFW; Am. Legion; Lee Co. Wildlife Club; trustee, Gr. Univ. of N.C, Exec. Cmt. Rel: Methodist. Mailing Add: Burns Hill Dr, Sanford, N.C. 27330.

WICKERSHAM, VICTOR EUGENE D
b. Lone Rick, Ark, 2/9/06; s. Frank M. Wickersham and Lillie Mae Sword W; c. LaMelba Sue (Mrs. Everett Renberger), Galen, Nelda (Mrs. Samuel L. Holston, Jr) and Victor II; eleven grandchildren. Educ: Mangum Jr. Col; Bus. Col, LaSalle Exten. Univ. Polit. & Govt. Pos: Co. off, Okla, 24-35; state off, 35 & 36; U.S. Rep, Okla, 41-46, 49-56 & 61-64. Bus. & Prof. Pos: Chief clerk, State Bd. Pub. Affairs, Oklahoma City, Okla, 35-36; bldg. contractor, 37; agent, John Hancock Mutual Life Ins. Co, 38; life ins. agent, 38-41; agent, broker and realtor, Wash, D.C, 45 & 46; leading agent, Repub. Nat. Life Ins. Co. of Dallas, 65-; consult, 65-69. Mem: Pres, PTA, Wash, D.C, 49-50; pres, Okla. State Soc, D.C, 55-56; mem, State Coun. Christian Churches, 58-59; former pres, State Court Clerk's Asn, 29-30; former Scoutmaster, Mangum, Okla, 32-33; AF&AM; Mason (32°); Shrine; Elks; Odd Fellows; WOW. Former Top-4-H Club Winner, State Fair, 24; Spec. Cong. Cmt. during Harry S Truman Admin. and on a Spec. Cong. Cmt. during Dwight Eisenhower Admin. Rel: Christian Church; pres, S.W. Dist, Christian Endeavor, Christian Churches, 20-21; secy. church bd, pres, Cent. Christian Church Bd. and Sunday Sch. Teacher, 33-34; Elder Emer, Nat. City Christian Church, Wash, D.C; Elder, Cent. Christian Church, Mangum, Okla. Mailing Add: 1901 N. Oklahoma Ave, Mangum, Okla. 73554.

WIDEMAN, EDMUND CHARLES, JR. D
Dem. Luzerne Co. Cmnr.
b. Wilkes Barre, Pa, 6/17/17; s. Edmund Charles Wideman and Adele Braun W; m. 9/28/66 to Ann Azat Hayes; c. Edmund Charles, III and Janice. Educ: St. Bonaventure Univ, B.S. in bus. admin. Polit. & Govt. Pos: Chmn, Luzerne Co. Bd. of Assessors, Pa, 60-63; Dem. Luzerne Co. Cmnr, 64- Bus. & Prof. Pos: Pres, Gr. Wilkes Barre Real Estate Bd, 58-60 and Property Owners of Luzerne Co, 59-60. Mil. Serv: Entered as Ens, Navy, 42, released as Lt, 45, after serv. in Pac. Area; Atlantic, Pac, Philippine and Okinawa Theater Ribbons; Presidential Unit Citation. Mem: Am. Legion; Greater Wilkes Barre Real Estate Bd; Westmoreland Club; Elks. Rel: Roman Catholic. Legal Res: 33 S. Dawes Ave, Kingston, Pa. 18704. Mailing Add: 31 W. Market St, Wilkes Barre, Pa. 18701.

WIDNALL, WILLIAM BECK R
U.S. Rep, N.J.
b. Hackensack, N.J, 3/17/06; m. to Marjorie Soule; c. Barbara and William S. Educ: Brown Univ, Ph.B, 26; N.J. Law Sch, LL.B, 31. Polit. & Govt. Pos: N.J. State Assemblyman, 46-50; U.S. Rep, N.J, 50-; del, Rep. Nat. Conv, 68. Bus. & Prof. Pos: Lawyer. Mem: Bergen Co. Bar Asn. Rel: Episcopal. Legal Res: Saddle River, N.J. 07458. Mailing Add: 2309 Rayburn House Office Bldg, Washington, D.C. 20515. (1967)

WIEDEMANN, ANNA BELLE D
Okla. State Rep.
b. Piedmont, Okla, 7/22/31; d. John William Palmer and Ruby Heckes P; m. 9/11/49 to Carl Henry Wiedemann, Jr; c. Brenda Kay. Educ: Okarche Pub. High Sch, grad, 49; Automobile and Casualty Ins. License, 52; Life Ins. License, 67. Polit. & Govt. Pos: Pres, Dem. Women's Orgn. of Canadian Co, Okla, 67-68; co-chmn, Canadian Co. Dem. Cent. Cmt, 67-68; Okla. State Rep, Dist. 43, Canadian Co, 69- Bus. & Prof. Pos: Practical nurse, 5 years. Mem: C. of C; Dem. Women's Orgn; Exten. Homemakers Club; Jefferson Bryan State Club; Bus. & Prfnl. Women's Club; Ohoyohoma State Club; Okla. Cattlemens Asn; Okla. and Nat. CowBelles Asns. Rel: Lutheran. Mailing Add: R.R. 1, Piedmont, Okla. 73078.

WIEDENMAN, WALTER V. D
b. Milford, Minn, 4/27/99; m. 6/23/28 to Ada P. Quincey; c. Charles D, Jack A. and Richard V. Educ: Univ. Minn, 2 years. Polit. & Govt. Pos: S.Dak. State Rep, 65-66. Mil. Serv: Pvt, Army, 18. Mem: Mason, Shrine; Am. Legion; Elks: Odd Fellows; Kiwanis; U.S. C. of C. Rel: Protestant. Mailing Add: 620 N. Lee Ave, Madison, S.Dak. 57042.

WIENGES, OTHNIEL HENRY, JR. D
S.C. State Rep.
b. St. Mathews, S.C, 12/27/24; s. Henry and Celeste George Wienges; m. to Carolyn Phillips. Educ: Univ. S.C, A.B, 47. Polit. & Govt. Pos: Former mem. bd. trustees, Calhoun Co. Sch. Dist. 1, S.C; chmn, S.C. Rural Area Develop. Cmt; S.C. State Rep, 63- Bus. & Prof. Pos: Farmer. Mil. Serv: Naval Res, Lt.(jg), 43-46, Seventh Amphibious Force. Mem: Bd. dir, S.C. Farm Bur. Mkt. Asn; Mason; 40 et 8; Univ. S.C. Educ. Found; pres, S.C. Crop Improv. Asn; pres, S.C. Found. Seed Asn. Rel: Presbyterian; Deacon, First Presbyterian Church, St. Mathews. Mailing Add: St. Mathews, S.C. 29135. (1967)

WIERZBICKI, FRANK V. D
Mich. State Rep.
b. Detroit, Mich, 3/10/25; s. Joseph Wierzbicki and Margaret Oleksy W; single. Educ: Univ. Detroit, B.B.A, 53; Kappa Sigma Kappa. Polit. & Govt. Pos: Supvr, Wayne Co. Bd. of Supvrs, 64-66; Mich. State Rep, 25th Dist, 67- Bus. & Prof. Pos: Frank V. Wierzbicki and Co, CPA's. Mil. Serv: Entered as Seaman 2/C, Navy, 43, released as Gunners Mate 3/C, 46. Mem: Am. Inst. CPA's; Mich. Asn. of CPA's; Polish Roman Catholic Union; Moose, Dearborn Lodge 1620; Usher's Club, St. Hedwig Parish, Detroit, Mich; Polish Nat. Alliance. Rel: Catholic. Mailing Add: 3185 Gilbert Ave, Detroit, Mich. 48210. (1967)

WIESNER, SUSAN ANN D
b. Manitowoc, Wis, 4/16/47; d. Harold W. Wiesner and Agnus Brault W; single. Educ: Univ. Wis, Madison, B.S. in Sec. Educ, 69; Eta Kappa Lambda. Polit. & Govt. Pos: Chmn, Manitowoc Co. Young Dem, Wis, 62-63; non-col. chmn, Wis. Young Dem, 63-65, admin. rep, 65-68; del, Wis. Dem. Conv, 66 & 68; mem. state steering cmt, Wis. Concerned Dem, 68; mem. nat. staff, Sen. Eugene McCarthy, Ind, 68; alternate del-at-lg, Dem. Nat. Conv, 68. Rel: Roman Catholic. Legal Res: 2613 Wollmer St, Manitowoc, Wis. 54220. Mailing Add: 430 Gorham St, Madison, Wis. 53706.

WIETING, LEROY JAMES D
Tex. State Rep.
b. Runge, Tex, 2/28/27; s. Herman William Wieting and Rose Marie Kubala W; m. 9/9/45 to Dorris Willene Atlkins; c. Leroy James, Jr. and Beckie Lynette. Educ: Tex. A&I; Univ. Corpus Christi. Polit. & Govt. Pos: City secy, Portland, Tex, 58-60, tax assessor collector, 58-62 and city mgr, 60-62; Tex. State Rep, currently. Bus. & Prof. Pos: Personnel rep, personnel dept, Reynolds Metal Co, currently. Mem: Kiwanis; Tex. City Mgrs. Asn; Tax Assessor-Collector Asn. Rel: Baptist. Mailing Add: 114 Janin Circle N, Portland, Tex. 78374.

WIGDERSON, MAURICE BRAYTON R
b. Antigo, Wis, 5/17/18; s. David L. Wigderson and Myrth Smith W; m. 7/18/42 to Miriam Margaret Martin; c. William David, Patricia K. (Mrs. Wandra) and Michael Brayton. Educ: Univ. Wis, Ph.B, 42, LL.B, 50, J.D, 66; Gamma Eta Gamma. Polit. & Govt. Pos: Chmn, Dane Co. Rep. Cmt, Wis, 49-51 and Ozaukee Co. Rep. Cmt, 64-65; arbitrator, Nat. Mediation Bd, 64- Bus. & Prof. Pos: Labor consult-attorney, Wigderson, Lindholm, Brigger and Vanesca, 50-57; chief counsel-dir, Air Line Pilot's Asn, 57-64; dir, Air Line Employee's Asn, 65-, v.pres, 69- Mil. Serv: Entered as Pvt, Army Air Force, 42, released as Capt, 45, after serv. in Combat Cargo Wing, China-Burma-India Theater; Air Medal. Mem: Am. and Wis. Bar Asns; VFW; Air Line Employee's Asn; pres, Great Dane Club of Milwaukee. Rel: Catholic. Mailing Add: 224 W. Birchwood Lane 139 N, Mequon, Wis. 53092.

WIGEN, JORIS ODIN R
Cmnr. of Ins, N.Dak.
b. Hettinger, N.Dak, 5/5/17; s. J.O. Wigen and Gea Sether W; m. 7/4/43 to

Phyll G. Vevle; c. Richard, Joan and Ann. Educ: St. Olaf Col, B.A, 39. Polit. & Govt. Pos: Finance chmn, Burleigh Co. Rep. Cmt, N.Dak, 62-64; treas, N.Dak. State Rep. Cent. Cmt, 64-69; cmnr. of Ins, N.Dak, 69- Bus. & Prof. Pos: Mgr, West. Adjust. and Inspection Co, 50-57; owner-mgr, Noble Adjust. Co, Bismarck, 57- and Kwiki Carwash, 65- Mil. Serv: Entered as Pvt, Army, 41, released as Capt, 46, after serv. as Air Force Pilot, 440th Troop Carrier GP, ETO, 44-45; Air Medal with Two Oak Leaf Clusters; Presidential Unit Citation; Am. Defense Ribbon; ETO Ribbon with seven Battle Stars; Am. Theater Ribbon; Victory Medal. Mem: Bd. dirs. and exec. cmt, Bismarck C. of C; past secy. and exec. cmt, Mo. Slope Lutheran Homes; past pres, Bismarck Kiwanis Club. Rel: Trinity Lutheran. Mailing Add: 1255 W. Highland Acres Rd, Bismarck, N.Dak. 58501.

WIGFIELD, RALPH D
b. Sampsel, Mo, 4/9/15; m. 6/29/40 to Grace Louise Goben; c. Mrs. Jim Cole, Eoyce Elaine and Kenneth Wayne. Educ: Pub. schs, Livingston and Daviess Co, Mo. Polit. & Govt. Pos: Mo. State Rep, 54-66, chmn, Banks and Banking cmt, mem. Appropriations and Eleemosynary Insts. and Local Govt. Cmt, Mo. State House of Rep. Bus. & Prof. Pos: Farmer. Mem: Past Noble Grand, Odd Fellows. Rel: Baptist. Mailing Add: R.F.D. 4, Chillicothe, Mo. 64601. (1967)

WIGGIN, CHESTER M, JR. R
b. Conway, N.H, 6/4/17; s. Chester M. Wiggin and Frances Starkey W; m. 10/20/62 to Joyce A. Guyer. Educ: Dartmouth Col, A.B, 39; Boston Univ, LL.B, 42; Kappa Kappa Kappa. Polit. & Govt. Pos: Former legal aide to Secy. of the Navy; former mem, Pub. Utilities Cmn; exec. secy, Bd. of Corrections Naval Records, 47-53; admin. asst. to U.S. Sen. Bridges, N.H, 53-61 and to U.S. Sen. Cotton, N.H, 62- Mil. Serv: Entered as Pvt, Marine Corps, 43, released as Capt, 47, after serv. in Inf, Pac, 43-45 and Second Marine Div, 45-47; Lt. Col, Marine Corps Res.(Ret); Bronze Star. Mem: Supreme Court, N.H. and D.C. Bar Asns. Mailing Add: 4201 Massachusetts Ave. N.W, Washington, D.C. 20016. (1967)

WIGGIN, FRANK L. R
Polit. & Govt. Pos: Former pres. Peabody City Coun; former coun. at large; Rep. City Cmt, former cand. for mayor. Bus. & Prof. Pos: Boston Registry of Motor Vehicles. Mil. Serv: WWII. Mem: Coach and umpire Essex Co. High Sch, Am. Legion baseball leagues. Mailing Add: 5 Park St, Peabody, Mass. 01906. (1967)

WIGGIN, RALPH M, SR. R
b. Bedford, N.H, 7/16/90; married; c. Five. Educ: McGaw Inst; Univ. N.H. Polit. & Govt. Pos: Road agent, N.H; town and sch. moderator, Bedford; town clerk; former selectman; N.H. State Sen, 49; former N.H. State Rep. Bus. & Prof. Pos: Retired farmer. Mem: Mason; Grange; Farm Bur; Unity Club; Bedford Sportsman's Club. Rel: Presbyterian. Mailing Add: 109 Meetinghouse Rd, Bedford, N.H. 03102. (1967)

WIGGINS, CHARLES DELMAR R
Rep. State Committeeman, Okla.
b. Lancaster, Mo, 2/2/05; s. George Henry Wiggins and Mary Elizabeth Coons W; m. 1/10/48 to Mary Katheryn Donaldson; c. Larry Don. Educ: Panhandle A&M Col, Goodwell, Okla. Polit. & Govt. Pos: Rep. Precinct Committeeman, Texas Co, Okla, 26-62; Bur. of Census, 60; Rep. Chmn, Texas Co, 62-67; Rep. State Committeeman, Texas Co, Okla, 67-; Nixon for President Co. Chmn, 68; Camp for Cong. Co. Chmn, 68. Bus. & Prof. Pos: Pub. sch. teacher, 23-39; farmer, 35-69. Mem: Farm Bur; Band Parents; Coin Club; Nat. Rifle Asn. Rel: Methodist. Mailing Add: Route 3, Guymon, Okla. 73942.

WIGGINS, CHARLES E. R
U.S. Rep, Calif.
b. El Monte, Calif, 12/3/27; m. 1946 to Yvonne L. Boots; c. Steven L. and Scott D. Educ: Pasadena City Col, Pasadena, Calif, A.A, 49; Univ. South. Calif, Los Angeles, Calif, B.S, 53; Univ. South. Calif. Sch. of Law, Los Angeles, Calif, LL.B, 56. Polit. & Govt. Pos: Pres, El Monte Coord. Coun; pres, El Monte Young Rep, 49; del, Nat. Young Rep. Conv, 49; alternate, L.A. Co. Rep. Cent. Cmt, 50; mem, Rep. Cong. Section Cmt, 50; mem, Lieberg for Cong. Campaign Cmt, 58; chmn, El Monte Planning Cmt, 58-60; mem, Rousselot for Cong. Campaign Cmt, 60 & 62; mem, El Monte City Coun, 60-64; finance chmn, Miller for Assembly Campaign, 62; town chmn, Nixon for Gov. Campaign, 62; mem, Los Angeles Co. Cent. Cmt, 62-66; mem, Rep. State Cent. Cmt, 62-66; Calif. State Assemblyman; mem, Walton for Cong. Campaign Cmt, 64; finance chmn, Lancaster for Assemblyman Campaign, 64; town chmn, Younger for Dist. Attorney Campaign, 64; mayor, El Monte, 64-66; U.S. Rep, Calif, 66- Bus. & Prof. Pos: Research attorney, Judge Frank Swain, 56-57; attorney-at-law, 57-58; partner, Wood & Wiggins, Attorneys, 58-66. Mil. Serv: Army, 45-48, 50-52, discharged 1st Lt, Inf; Combat Inf. Badge. Mem: Am, Calif. and Pomona Valley Bar Asns; Univ. South. Calif. Law Alumni; Univ. South. Calif. Legion Lex; pres, Friendly El Monte Cmt; Lions; pres, Jr. C. of C. Distinguished Serv. Award; ed, Univ. South. Calif. Law Rev, 55-56. Rel: Methodist. Mailing Add: 11001 Valley Mall, El Monte, Calif. 91731.

WIGGINS, MATTHEW EDWIN
b. Danville, Ala, 4/30/98; s. Charles Tucker Wiggins and Sidney Breedlove W; m. 10/9/29 to Lelia Katherine Harper; c. Lorna Anice and Katherine Diane (Mrs. R. Ledbetter). Educ: Albany Bus. Col. Polit. & Govt. Pos: Pres. Birmingham City Coun, Ala, 63- Bus. & Prof. Pos: Various supvry. pos, Ala. Power Co, 18-46, asst. treas, 46-52 and treas, 52-63. Mem: Mason (32°); Shrine; Boy Scouts; treas, Kiwanis. Rel: Methodist; Mem, Southeast. Jurisdictional Coun, 64-68. Silver Beaver Award, Boy Scouts, 53; Birmingham 1965 Civic Salesman of the Year, Award from the Sales and Marketing Executives of Birmingham. Legal Res: 1416 44th St, W, Birmingham, Ala. 35208. Mailing Add: Room 315, City Hall, Birmingham, Ala. 35203.

WIGGINS, TED R
b. Dozier, Covington Co, Ala; m. to Glenda; c. Scott, Beverly. Educ: Univ. Ala. Law Sch, 49. Polit. & Govt. Pos: Butler Co. Rep. Exec. Comm. Bus. & Prof. Pos: Farm equip. dealer, 14 years. Mil. Serv: Army, Inf. Mailing Add: Greenville, Ala. 36037. (1967)

WIGGINS, WARREN WILLIAM D
Dep. Dir, Peace Corps
b. Phoenix, Ariz, 9/1/22; s. Chester N. Wiggins and Barbara Reed W; m. 6/9/44 to Edna Abell; c. William, Karen, Lisa, John, David and Mark. Educ: Univ. Colo, B.A, 46; Harvard Univ. M.P.A, 49. Polit. & Govt. Pos: Sr. U.S. econ. adv, Philippines Govt, 54; dep. dir. and acting dir, U.S. For. Assistance Mission, LaPaz, Bolivia, 57; asst. dep. dir. for progs, Int. Coop. Admin, 59 and dep. dir. Far East Oper, 60; assoc. dir. prog. develop. and oper, Peace Corps, 61-65, dep. dir, 65- Mil. Serv: Entered as Pvt, Air Force, 43, released as 1st Lt, 45, after serv. in China-Burma-India; Air Medal with Cluster; Distinguished Flying Cross. Recipient Arthur S. Flemming Award as one of Ten Outstanding Young Men in Fed. Govt, 62. Rel: Unitarian. Mailing Add: 7106 Rebecca Dr, Alexandria, Va. 22307. (1967)

WIGGINS, WILLIAM J. D
b. Carrollton, Ga, 3/18/24; s. Camp Wiggins and Percy Fleming W; m. 8/30/64 to Mary Brinkley. Educ: W. Ga. Col; Univ. Ga, LL.B, 48; Sigma Nu. Polit. & Govt. Pos: Solicitor, City Court of Carrollton, Ga, 53-61; Ga. State Rep, 63-68. Bus. & Prof. Pos: Attorney-at-law, Carrollton, Ga. Mil. Serv: Lt, Naval Air Force, World War II. Mem: F&AM. Rel: Baptist. Mailing Add: Carrollton, Ga. 30117. (1967)

WIGODA, PAUL THEODOR D
Alderman, Chicago, Ill.
b. Peoria, Ill, 6/18/22; s. Hugh M. Wigoda and Rebecca B. W; m. 6/17/45 to Rose Woloshin; c. William S, Gary I. and Robert M. Educ: Univ. Ill, 40-42; Roosevelt Univ, B.A, 48; DePaul Univ, J.D, 50. Polit. & Govt. Pos: Alderman, 49th Ward, Chicago, Ill, 59-; del, Dem. Nat. Conv, 68. Bus. & Prof. Pos: Attorney, 50-; lectr. polit. sci, Mundelein Col, 65-67 and Loyola Univ, Ill, 69- Mil. Serv: Entered as A/S, Navy, 42, released as PhM 1/C, 45, after serv. in Fleet Marines, S.Pac, 43-45. Mem: Chicago Bar Asn; Decologue Soc. Lawyers; Am. Legion; Jewish War Vet; B'nai B'rith; Chicago Plan Cmn. Rel: Jewish. Legal Res: 1535 W. North Shore Ave, Chicago, Ill. 60626. Mailing Add: 111 W. Washington, Chicago, Ill. 60602.

WIKTORSKI, CHESTER ROMAN D
b. Chicago, Ill, 5/14/34; s. Chester R. Wiktorski and Helen Placek W; single. Educ: North Ill. Teachers Col, B.A, 55. Polit. & Govt. Pos: Ill. State Rep, 57-67, mem, Gov. Task Force on Educ, 65-66, Compact on Educ. Cmt, 66 and chmn, Ill. Sch. Problems Cmn, 66, Ill. State House of Rep. Bus. & Prof. Pos: Teacher, Chicago Pub. Schs, Ill, 55-65; asst. v.pres, Parkway Bank, 65- Mem: Chicago Soc, Intercollegiate Coun; Chicago Teachers Union; K. of C; Holy Name Soc; City Club; PTA. Rel: Catholic. Mailing Add: 5300 W. Drummond Place, Chicago, Ill. 60639. (1967)

WILBER, ROLAND C. R
Chmn, Idaho Rep. Party
b. 4/5/04; m. to Marie. Polit. & Govt. Pos: Former chmn, Idaho Rep. State Finance Cmt. and Nez Perce Co. Rep. Party; del, Rep. Nat. Conv, 68; chmn, Idaho Rep. Party, 68- Bus. & Prof. Pos: With pub. rels. dept, Potlach Industs. Legal Res: 1322 Eighth St, Lewiston, Idaho 83501. Mailing Add: P.O. Box 628, Lewiston, Idaho 83501.

WILBUR, GEORGE CRAIG D
b. Flint, Mich, 1/23/46; s. Maurice D. Wilbur (deceased) and Helen V. Jentz W. Educ: Wis. State Univ, River Falls, 64-67; Univ. Wis, Madison, 67-68. Polit. & Govt. Pos: Numerous positions in Wis. Young Dem; mem. staff, David Carley for Gov. Campaign; nat. committeeman, Wis. Young Dem, 67-68; aide to Patrick J. Lucey, McCarthy for Pres. Nat. Staff, 68; state chmn, Wis. Students for McCarthy, 67-68; mem. nat. ad hoc steering cmt, Students for McCarthy, 68-69. Bus. & Prof. Pos: Bus. mgr. for student govt, Wis. State Univ, River Falls, 66-67. Mem: Am. Civil Liberties Union; Wis. New Dem. Coalition; Tarrant City Grape Boycott Cmt, Tex. Rel: Methodist. Mailing Add: 1933 Sheridan St, Madison, Wis. 53704.

WILBURN, CORDELL HULL D
Chmn, Trousdale Co. Dem. Exec. Cmt, Tenn.
b. Dixon Springs, Tenn, 3/12/08; s. Booker Wilburn and Cynthia Johnson W; m. 12/25/34 to Evelyn Wiles; c. Betty Louise (Mrs. Thomas D. McAnulty) and Frank Wiles. Educ: Univ. Tenn, B.S.A, 32; Midd. Tenn. State Univ, A.B, 54; Phi Delta Kappa. Polit. & Govt. Pos: Supt, Trousdale Co. Schs, Tenn, 48-60; chmn, Trousdale Co. Dem. Exec. Cmt, 55-; supt, Hartsville Area Voc. Tech. Sch, 64- Mil. Serv: Entered as 2nd Lt, Tenn. State Guard, 39, released as 1st Lt, 44, after serv. in Hartsville. Mem: Trousdale Co. Farm Bur; Hartsville Kiwanis Club (pres, 48); Ky-Tenn. Dist. Kiwanis (lt. gov. dist. 17, 65). Rel: Baptist. Mailing Add: Melrose Dr, Hartsville, Tenn. 37074.

WILBURN, JERRY D
Miss. State Rep.
b. Mantachie, Miss, 9/18/40; s. E.C. Wilburn and Lula Wren W; m. 8/8/65 to Margaret Ann Silas; c. Bronson Gane. Educ: Itawamba Jr. Col, Fulton, Miss; Miss. State Univ, Starkville, Miss. Polit. & Govt. Pos: Miss. State Rep, 64- Bus. & Prof. Pos: Pub. rels. and job promoter, Cook, Coggins, Kelly & Cook, Engrs. Mil. Serv: Lt, Army, 62-69. Mem: Mason; Scottish Rite. Outstanding Young Men of Am, 65. Rel: Methodist. Mailing Add: P.O. Box 36, Mantachie, Miss. 38855.

WILBURN, WESLEY MILTON D
Pres, Young Dem. of Wash.
b. Walnut Ridge, Ark, 6/17/41; s. Raymond Cleo Wilburn and Elizabeth Blanche Herron W; m. 11/26/65 to Irene Diane Palmer. Educ: Everett Community Col, Wash, Assoc. Arts & Sci, 68; Phi Beta Kappa; Pi Ro Phi. Polit. & Govt. Pos: Pres, Wash. Asn. Community Cols, 67-68; pres, Everett Community Col. Young Dem, 67-68; pres, Young Dem. of Wash, 68-; del-at-lg, Dem. Nat. Conv, 68; campaign mgr, Wash. State Rep. Richard King, 68; legis. clerk, Dem. caucus, Wash. State House Rep, 69- Bus. & Prof. Pos: Buyer, purchasing dept, Lockheed Shipbuilding & Construction Co, Seattle, Wash, 64-66. Mil. Serv: Entered as Pvt, Army, 58, released as Sgt, 64, after serv. in 183rd Airborne Inf. Brigade, Pac. Theatre, Okinawa, 60-64; Command Soldier of the Month, 12/62; Second Place, U.S. Army Pac. Theatre Rifle Matches. Man of the Year, Everett Community Col, 68. Rel: Baptist. Mailing Add: 6702-200 S.W, Lynnwood, Wash. 98036.

WILCOCK, FRED R
b. Burnley, Eng, 7/23/92; m. to Ruth Barber; c. One son. Educ: Manchester Univ, M.Sc; Drew Univ. Theol. Sch, 22. Polit. & Govt. Pos: Mem, Rep. Co. Cmt, Vt; chmn, Sheffield Rep. Town Cmt; town moderator; Justice of Peace; Vt. State Rep, 61-66. Bus. & Prof. Pos: Former minister. Mem: Mason; hon. mem, Rotary and Kiwanis. Rel: Methodist. Mailing Add: Sheffield, Vt. 05866. (1967)

WILCOX, JON PAUL R
Wis. State Assemblyman
b. Berlin, Wis, 9/5/36; s. Everett Emerson Wilcox and Irma Elsie Weinkauf W; m. 6/8/63 to Jane Ann Heller; c. Jeffrey Jon and Jennifer Jane. Educ: Ripon Col, A.B, 58; Univ. Wis. Law Sch, J.D, 65; Phi Alpha Delta; Sigma Nu. Polit. & Govt. Pos: Wis. State Assemblyman, 69- Bus. & Prof. Pos: Assoc, Steele, Smyth, Klos & Flynn, Law firm, LaCrosse, Wis, 65-66; partner, Hacker & Wilcox, Law firm, Wautoma, 66-; partner, J & G Farms, 66- Mil. Serv: Entered as 2nd Lt, Army, 59, released as 1st Lt, 61, after serv. in Mil. Police Corp. Mem: Wis. and Am. Bar Asns; Wis. Law Alumni Bd. of Visitors; Am. Trial Lawyers Asn; Am. Judicature Soc; Jr. C. of C; Rotary; Mason; Ripon Col. Alumni Asn. Rel: Am. Lutheran. Mailing Add: Box 157, Wautoma, Wis. 54982.

WILCOX, OMA ELLISON R
b. Layton, Utah, 4/20/09; d. Laurence Ephraim Ellison and Catherine Adams E; m. 4/12/36 to George Benjamin Wilcox; c. Catherine Ellison. Educ: Utah State Univ; Univ. of Utah; Weber State Col; Brigham Young Univ. Polit. & Govt. Pos: V.chmn, Davis Co. Rep. Cent. Cmt, Utah, 56-58; voting dist. v.chmn, Layton Voting Dist. 11, 56-60; alternate del, Rep. Nat. Conv, 60, del. and mem. resolutions cmt, 64; v.chmn, Utah State Rep. Cent. Cmt, 62-65; city councilman, Layton, Utah, 61-; parliamentarian, Salt Lake Womens' Rep. Club; mem. state adv. cmt, Designing Educ. for the Future, 67-; mem. state bd, Div. of Welfare, 67-; mem. state bd, Utah Fedn. Women's Rep. Club, 68- Bus. & Prof. Pos: Secy, First Nat. Bank of Layton, 62-; dir, Farmers Union, 65- Mem: Bd. Trustees, Weber State Col, 61-65; pres, Women's State Legis. Coun. of Utah, 61-63, parliamentarian, 65-67. Rel: Latter-day Saint. Mailing Add: 1877 E. Gentile St, Layton, Utah 84041.

WILCOX, ROBERT CLAYTON R
Ariz. State Sen.
b. Burlington, Vt, 7/31/21; s. Frederick Clayton Wilcox and Irene Marion Pecue W; m. 6/29/47 to Frances McLean; c. Judith Ann and Rebecca Susan. Polit. & Govt. Pos: Ariz. State Rep, 61-66; Ariz. State Sen, 67- Bus. & Prof. Pos: Dir, Prfnl. Photographers of Am, 62- Mem: Mason, Shrine; Kiwanis. Rel: Methodist. Mailing Add: 601 E. Orangewood, Phoenix, Ariz. 85020.

WILDE, ALMA LEE R
Secy, Anderson Co. Rep. Exec. Cmt, Tenn.
b. Greenville, S.C, 12/16/21; d. Fred Ervin O'Dell and Daisy Bishop O; m. 5/12/40 to Andrew Gene Wilde; c. Gerald Gene, Diane Louise, Stephen Lee and Robin Kay. Polit. & Govt. Pos: Secy, Anderson Co. Rep. Exec. Cmt, Tenn, 63-; v.pres, Rep. Voters Serv. Club, 64; alternate del, Rep. Nat. Conv, 64; del, State Rep. Conv, Tenn, 64. Bus. & Prof. Pos: Secy. and off. mgr, Refrigeration Serv. Co, 65-66. Rel: Baptist. Mailing Add: 780 W. Outer Dr, Oak Ridge, Tenn. 37830. (1967)

WILDE, ORVIN GERAL D
b. Fairview, Utah, 8/11/33; s. Orvin Eskel Wilde and Verl Miner W; m. 8/21/53 to Rosalie Hall; c. Orvin Jeffery, Ruth Ann, Denise, Allison and Gregory James. Educ: Brigham Young Univ, B.S, 56, M.S, 63; Theta Alpha Phi; Polit. & Govt. Pos: Voting dist. chmn, Provo, Utah, 64-65; ward chmn, Dem. Party, Provo, 65-68, precinct chmn, 68-; mem. bd. trustees, Utah Coun. Improv. Educ, 66-69, pres, 68-69; del, Dem. Nat. Conv, 68. Bus. & Prof. Pos: Chmn, Wasatch Front Educ, Coun, 63-64; pres, Asn. Local Pres, 65-66. Mem: Life mem, Nat. Educ. Asn; Utah Educ. Asn.(trustee, 66-69); Speech Arts Asn. Utah; Alpine Educ. Asn.(pres, 64-65); Nat. Forensic League. Rel: Latter-day Saint. Mailing Add: 815 North 300 West, Provo, Utah 84601.

WILDER, ALICE F. R
Rep. Nat. Committeewoman, S.C.
b. Richmond, Va, 1/1/04; m. 7/16/38 to M.A. Wilder; c. Marion Archer, Jr. and Mary Alice (Mrs. Hastings Wyman, Jr). Educ: Univ. S.C, A.B, 23. Polit. & Govt. Pos: Helped establish first GOP orgn. in Precinct One, Aiken, S.C, 61; mem, Aiken Co. Rep. Exec. Cmt, 61-; mem, Precinct One Rep. Exec. Cmt, Aiken, 62-68; charter mem. and first v.pres, Aiken Co. Rep. Women's Club, pres, 65-; mgr, Watson for Cong. Hq, Aiken, 65 and Aiken Co. Campaign Hq, fall 66; chmn, Agenda Cmt, Aiken Co. Rep. Conv, 66 & 68; secy, Aiken Co. Rep. Party and Aiken City Rep. Party, currently; Rep. Nat. Committeewoman, S.C, 69- Bus. & Prof. Pos: Teacher, Pub. Schs, 23-39; headmistress, Aiken Day Sch, 39-55; organizer and teacher, Mead Hall, Parish Day Sch, Episcopal Church, 55-65. Rel: Episcopal; Sunday Sch. teacher and former head, Women of the Church, St. Thaddeus' Church. Mailing Add: P.O. Box 443, Aiken, S.C. 29801.

WILDER, GEORGE WARREN R
Mem, State Rep. Cmt, N.H.
b. Portsmouth, N.H, 3/8/37; s. Stowe Wilder and Mary Chapen W; m. 6/16/64 to Caroline Mary Burton; c. Maria Laina and George Warren, III. Educ: Univ. N.H, B.A, 60; Lambda Chi Alpha. Polit. & Govt. Pos: Del, Rep. State Conv, N.H, 64; mem, N.H. State Rep. Cmt, 66-; cmnr, Housing Authority, Portsmouth, 66-; chmn, Portsmouth Rep. City Conf, 66-; chmn, Portsmouth Rep. Party, currently. Bus. & Prof. Pos: Partner, John Sise & Co, 64; dir, Portsmouth Ment. Health Clinic, N.H, 64- Mil. Serv: Entered as 2nd Lt. Army, 60, released as 1st Lt, 63; Parachute Badge; Capt, Army Res, 66. Mem: N.H. Independent Ins. Asn; v.pres, Portsmouth Jr. C. of C, 64-65; chmn, Red Cross Fund Drive, 65; coach, Portsmouth High Hockey Team, 65-66; pres, N.H. Asn. of Ment. Health Clinics, 66; Rotary; Elks. Rel: Episcopal. Legal Res: Regina Rd, Portsmouth, N.H. 03801. Mailing Add: 345 State St, Portsmouth, N.H. 03802. (1967)

WILDER, HARVEY A. DFL
b. 2/17/07; m. to Bernice; c. Four. Educ: Central High Sch, Crookston; Northwest. Agr. Col, Crookston. Polit. & Govt. Pos: Minn. State Rep, 57-66; Crookston City Coun, 7 years. Bus. & Prof. Pos: Grain farmer. Mil. Serv: Nat. Guard, 5 years in State Guard, WWII; 1 1/2 years, Nat. Guard Korean Conflict. Mem: Masonic Orders; trustee, Covenant Mission Church; Salvation Army Bd; Elks; Eagles; Cloverleaf Local Minn. Farmers Union, 25 years; Vets. Co. I, Minn. Nat. Guard; Pearl Harbor Day Minute Men. Rel: Protestant. Mailing Add: 202 S. Hubbard St, Crookston, Minn. 56716. (1967)

WILDER, JOSEPH M. 'JOE' D
b. Bronson, Fla, 1/8/18; m. to Carnet S. Clark; c. Shirley Beckham, Bobby Joe, Jannie Lee and Kay Helene. Polit. & Govt. Pos: Mem, City Coun, Cedar Key, Fla; mem, Sch. Adv. Bd; Fla. State Rep, 64-66. Bus. & Prof. Pos: Motel mgr, Marine Boat Ways. Mem: C. of C. Rel: Church of Christ. Mailing Add: Box 356, Cedar Key, Fla. 32625. (1967)

WILDER, RAYMOND EDWARD R
Mem. Exec. Cmt, El Paso Co. Rep. Cent. Cmt, Colo.
b. Muskegon, Mich. 10/7/31; s. Raymond F. Wilder and Alma E. Wenger W; m. 9/10/55 to Patricia A. Erickson; c. Ann, John, Nancy, Janet, Sandra and James. Educ: Mich. State Univ, B.A, 57; Univ. Colo. Sch. of Law, LL.B, 60; Phi Eta Sigma; Phi Kappa Phi; Phi Gamma Mu; Phi Alpha Theta. Polit. & Govt. Pos: Dep. dist. attorney, El Paso Co, Colo, 61-63; Rep. precinct committeeman, El Paso Co, 62-64; Colo. State Rep, 67-69; mem. exec. cmt, El Paso Co. Rep. Cent. Cmt, 69-; chmn, Rep. Mens Club of El Paso Co, 69- Bus. & Prof. Pos: Sr. partner, Quigley, Wilder, Helwig & Palermo, 63- Mil. Serv: Entered as Pvt, Marines, 50, released as Sgt, 53, after serv. in First Marine Div, Korea, 52-53, Maj, Res, 54-69. Mem: Am, Colo. and El Paso Co. Bar Asns; Pikes Peak Kiwanis. Rel: Protestant. Mailing Add: 16 Lake Ave, Colorado Springs, Colo. 80906.

WILDEY, GEORGE S. R
b. Peekskill, N.Y, 12/11/94; married; c. one daughter. Educ: Ill. Inst. Tech. Polit. & Govt. Pos: N.H. State Rep, 61-67; former chmn, local sch. bd. Bus. & Prof. Pos: Retired fire prev. engr. Mil. Serv: Marine Corps, in charge of Intel. and Internal Security; Air Force, WWII. Mem: F&AM; Westmoreland Men's Club, past dep. N.H. State Grange. 1967 Legal Res: Westmoreland, N.H. 03467. No mailing address available. (1967)

WILENTZ, DAVID T. D
Dem. Nat. Committeeman, N.J.
Mailing Add: 252 Madison Ave, Perth Amboy, N.J. 08862.

WILENTZ, ROBERT N. D
N.J. State Assemblyman
b. Perth Amboy, N.J, 2/17/27; m. to Jacqueline Malino. Educ: Princeton Univ; Harvard Col, A.B, 49; Columbia Law Sch, LL.B, 52. Polit. & Govt. Pos: Legis. asst. to late Sen. Bernard M. Vogel; app. by N.J. Supreme Court to Cmt. on Rev. of the Law of Evidence and to Ethics Cmt. of Middlesex Co; N.J. State Assemblyman, currently app, N.J. Adv. Coun, 69- Bus. & Prof. Pos: Lawyer; partner, Wilentz, Goldman & Spitzer. Mil. Serv: Navy, World War II. Mem: Past pres, Perth Amboy C. of C; chmn, United Fund and Red Cross Blood Prog; prfnl. div, United Jewish Appeal Campaign, High Sch. Scholarship Fund; v.pres, Perth Amboy Jewish Commun. Coun; YMHA; exec. cmt, Perth Amboy Gen. Hosp; past counsel, E. Brunswick Bd. of Educ; counsel, Middlesex Co. Col. and Middlesex Co. Chap. of CORE; N.J. State Bar Asn. Mailing Add: 252 Madison Ave, Perth Amboy, N.J. 08861.

WILENTZ, WARREN W. D
Educ: Univ. Va; Rutgers Univ. Law Sch. Polit. & Govt. Pos: Cand. U.S. Sen, N.J, 66; Co. Counsel, 60-66; Prosecutor, Middlesex Co, 56-60. Bus. & Prof. Pos: Attorney; incorporator of Co. Econ. Opportunity Prog; Dir, Co. Legal Aid Prog. to aid poor. Mil. Serv: Combat Vet, World War II. Mem: United Fund; Sister Kenny Fund; City of Hope; Red Cross; UNICEF; United Jewish Appeal. Misc: Established 1st co. police training sch. & consumers frauds div. Rel: Jewish. Mailing Add: 252 Madison Ave, Perth Amboy, N.J. 08861. (1967)

WILETS, LAWRENCE D
b. Oconomowoc, Wis, 1/4/27; s. Edward Wilets and Sophia Finger W; m. 12/21/47 to Dulcy Elaine Margoles; c. Ileen S, Edward E. and James D. Educ: Univ. Wis, Madison, B.S. with high honors, 48; Princeton Univ, M.A, 50, Ph.D, 52; Phi Eta Sigma; Phi Beta Kappa. Polit. & Govt. Pos: Finance chmn, Los Alamos Co. Stevenson for Pres, N.Mex, 56; exec. secy, Wash. State Scientists and Engrs. for Johnson-Humphrey, 64; bd. mem, N.End Dem. Club, Seattle, 64-65; bd. mem, Metrop. Dem. Club, 66-68; chmn, King Co. McCarthy for Pres, 67-68; v.chmn, 46th Legis. Dist. Dem. Orgn, 67-68; del, Dem. Nat. Conv, 68. Bus. & Prof. Pos: Research assoc, Calif. Radiation Lab, 53; Nat. Sci. Found. Fel, Inst. Theoret. Physics, Copenhagen, 53-55; staff mem, Los Alamos Sci. Lab, N.Mex, 55-58; mem, Inst. Adv. Study, Princeton, N.J, 57-58; prof. physics, Univ. Wash, 58- Mil. Serv: Entered as Seaman 1/C, Navy, 45, released as ETM 2/C, 46, after serv. on U.S.S. Philippine Sea, Atlantic, 46. Publ: Theories of Nuclear Fission, Oxford Press, 64; 'Isotope Shifts in Atomic Spectra,' In: Encyclopedia of Physics, Springer, 57; more than 50 articles in physics journals. Mem: Fel, Am. Phys. Soc; Am. Asn. Univ. Prof; Fedn. Am. Scientists; Sigma Xi; Am. Asn. Adv. Sci; B'nai B'rith. Physics Dept. Honors, Univ. Wis, 48. Rel: Jewish. Mailing Add: 8534 53rd Court N.E, Seattle, Wash. 98115.

WILEY, CHARLES VICTOR D
Chmn, Plymouth Co. Dem. Party, Iowa
b. Carthage, S.Dak, 3/28/15; s. Charles Arthur Wiley and Vera Means W; m. 11/22/41 to Helen Theresa Brauch; c. Monica (Mrs. Jack Collins) and Kristine. Educ: High sch, grad, 33. Polit. & Govt. Pos: Chmn, Plymouth Co. Dem. Party, Iowa, 66- Mailing Add: 45 Third Ave. S.E, LeMars, Iowa 51031.

WILEY, JUNIOR LEE R
Chmn, Clay Co. Rep. Party, Ark.
b. Piggott, Ark, 6/26/26; s. Claude Elbert Wiley and Gladies W; m. 5/19/51 to Martha Gaye Winstead; c. Rhonda Faye, Gary Neal and Bruce Wayne. Educ: Greenway High Sch, 40-44. Polit. & Govt. Pos: Chmn, Clay Co. Rep. Party, Ark, 69- Bus. & Prof. Pos: Builder and contractor; farmer; cattle bus; nurs-

ing homes corp. Mil. Serv: Entered as Pvt, Army, 45, released as Cpl, 46, after serv. in U.S. Mem: Bd. mem, Ark. Polled Hereford Asn. Rel: Baptist. Mailing Add: S. 12th St, Piggott, Ark. 72422.

WILKERSON, WALTER D, JR. R
State Committeeman, Tex. Rep. Party
b. Marlin, Tex, 6/7/30; s. Walter Dumas Wilkerson and Frances Burnitt W; m. 12/19/54 to Neddie Jane Bullock; c. Nancy Ellen and Mark Howard. Educ: Tex. A&M Univ, B.S, 51; Univ. Tex. Southwest. Med. Sch, M.D, 55; Phi Eta Sigma; Phi Kappa Phi. Polit. & Govt. Pos: Chmn, Montgomery Co. Rep. Party, Tex, 64-; state committeeman, Tex. Rep. Party, 65-; del, Rep. Nat. Conv, 68. Mil. Serv: Lt. MC, Navy, 56-58. Mem: Am. Acad. Gen. Practice; Am. and Tex. Med. Asns. Rel: Methodist. Mailing Add: 1516 N. San Jacinto St, Conroe, Tex. 77301.

WILKERSON, WILLIAM AVERY 'BILL' D
Miss. State Rep.
b. Benndale, Miss, 3/9/38; married. Polit. & Govt. Pos: Miss. State Rep, currently. Bus. & Prof. Pos: Teacher; timber farmer. Mem: Mason; Jaycees; George Co. Sportsmanship & Boating Club; Farm Bur. Rel: Methodist. Mailing Add: Box 255, Lucedale, Miss. 39452. (1967)

WILKES, WILSON BRYANT D
Ga. State Budget Dir.
b. Adel, Ga, 3/24/17; s. William Bryant Wilkes and Georgia Giddens W; m. 3/22/47 to Ruby Ellison; c. step-daughter Mary Dee (Mrs. James Boatman). Educ: Univ. Ga, 37, Commerce Degree; Pi Kappa Alpha. Polit. & Govt. Pos: Ga. State Rep, 49-52 & 59-64; Ga. State Sen, 53-54; Ga. State Budget Dir, 64- Bus. & Prof. Pos: Gen. agent, Fire, Life & Casualty Ins; Farmer. Mil. Serv: Entered as Pvt, Army, 41, released as Maj, 45, after serv. in Air Force, 15th Air Force, Europe, 44-45; Lt. Col, Air Force Res; Seven Oak Leaf Clusters; Presidential Citation with One Oak Leaf Cluster. Rel: Baptist. Mailing Add: 1939 Gotham Way, N.E, Atlanta, Ga. 30334.

WILKIE, CARROLL WELDON R
N.C. State Sen.
b. Fletcher, N.C, 4/27/27; s. Grover C. Wilkie and Jennie Dockings W; m. 3/31/53 to Elizabeth Anne Wright; c. Rebecca Marie and Stephen Carroll. Educ: West. Carolina Univ, B.S, 50. Polit. & Govt. Pos: N.C. State Sen, 32nd Dist, 69- Mil. Serv: Army, 45-46, serv. in first Inf, First Serv. Command; Good Conduct Medal. Mem: N.C. Motor Carriers; Fletcher Mens Club; Hoopers Creek Commun. Club (founder and organizer, 68); Boy Scouts (cub scout master, 64-68); Henderson Co. PTA (coun. pres, 66-67) Rel: Baptist. Mailing Add: Route 1, Fletcher, N.C. 28732.

WILKIE, GERHART D
N.Dak. State Rep.
b. Rolette Co, N.Dak, 2/15/07; married; c. Four. Educ: Pub. Schs. Polit. & Govt. Pos: N.Dak. State Rep, 61- Bus. & Prof. Pos: Farmer. Mem: Sportsmen's Club; Crop Improv. Asn; Farmers Union. Rel: Lutheran. Mailing Add: Rolla, N.Dak. 58367. (1967)

WILKINS, EDNESS KIMBALL D
Wyo. State Sen.
b. Casper, Wyo; d. Wilson S. Kimball and Edness Jane Merrick K; m. to Capt. Roland Wilkins, wid; c. Dr. Charles. Educ: Univ. Ky; Univ. Nebr. Polit. & Govt. Pos: Chief clerk, State Auditor's Off, Cheyenne, Wyo, 24-28; secy. and asst. to Dir. Mint, Wash, D.C, 33-47; personnel officer, Bur. of Reclamation, Casper, Wyo, 47-50; mgr, Casper Water and Sanitation Dept, 50-54; Wyo. State Rep, 55-66, minority leader, 63, speaker pro-tem, 65, speaker, 66; Wyo. State Sen, 67- Bus. & Prof. Pos: Owner, Kimball Ranch, Casper, Wyo, 52-; pres, Hjorth Oil Royalty Co, Casper, 58- Publ: Many articles on history of Wyo. Mem: Past pres, Wyo. State Hist. Soc. and Wyo. State Pioneer Asn; Salvation Army Bd; Red Cross Bd; Cmn. on Status of Women; Old Fort Caspar Cmn; Wyo. 75th Anniversary Cmn; C. of C; Bus. & Prfnl. Women's Club; Wyo. Stockgrowers' Asn; League of Women Voters; Am. Asn. Univ. Women; Zonta; Eastern Star; Farm Bur; Izaak Walton League. Rel: Episcopal. Mailing Add: 433 Milton Ave, Casper, Wyo. 82601.

WILKINS, GEORGE T. D
b. Anna, Ill, 1/16/05; s. B. Frank Wilkins and Nellie Mae Hileman W; m. 7/4/26 to Mary A. Treece; c. George T, M.D. Educ: South. Ill. Univ, B.Ed, 37; Univ. Ill, M.A, 40; McKendree Col, LL.D, 58; Phi Delta Kappa; Kappa Phi Kappa; track letterman, South. Ill. Univ. Polit. & Govt. Pos: Co. Supt. of Schs, Madison Co, Ill, 47-59; Supt of Pub. Instr, Ill, 59-63; mem, Sch. Problems Cmn, Ill, 59-66; pres, Mid-West Coun. of Chief Sch. Officers, 62-63; v.chmn, Urban Problems Cmn, State of Ill, 68-69. Bus. & Prof. Pos: Assoc. dir, Pub. Rels, Commun. Media, Info. Serv, South. Ill. Univ, Edwardsville Campus; prof, grad. sch, educ. div, South. Ill. Univ. and Monticello Col, Shurtleff Col. and McKendree Col; chmn. bd, Nathan Hale Fire & Casualty Co. and Nathan Life Ins. Co; Supt. of Schs, Wolf Lake, Thebes and Madison, Ill, 19 years; mem. bd. dir, Nathan Hale Investment Corp. and Vernon Investment Corp. Publ: 'Strengthening Science Teaching in Elementary Schools,' Ill. Educ. J, 60; School Building Construction, Stipes Pub. Co, 68; The School Law, Am. of Edwardsville, Inc, 68. Mem: Ill. and Am. Asn. Sch. Adminstrs; Ill. Asn. for Higher Educ; Nat. Educ. Asn.(life); past dist. gov, Rotary; Mason (32°); Shrine; Moose; Eastern Star. Officiated 2006 High Sch. and Col. Football and Basketball Games; Elected Hall of Fame-Hon. Coach, Ill. Teams Won More than 400 Games; Cert. of Appreciation and Recognition for Pioneering in the Develop. of Instructional TV and Radio in the Schs. of Ill. Rel: Presbyterian. Mailing Add: 2611 Cleveland Blvd, Granite City, Ill. 62040.

WILKINS, HAROLD EDWARD R
b. Presque Isle, Maine, 7/24/23; s. Clyde Lamkin Wilkins and Inez Wills W; m. 11/20/49 to Eileen Laura Northway; c. Belinda, Geoffrey Northway, Martha and Derek Wills. Educ: Randolph-Macon Col, B.S, 43; Med. Col. of Va, M.D, 47; Phi Beta Kappa; Omicron Delta Kappa; Phi Delta Theta; Phi Chi. Polit. & Govt. Pos: Dir, Calif. Rep. Assembly, 63-64, v.pres, 65-66 & 69; assoc. mem, Calif. Rep. State Cent. Cmt, 64-69; alternate del, Rep. Nat. Conv, 68; mem, Bd. of Med. Exam, Calif, 69- Bus. & Prof. Pos: Private practice of internal med, 54- Mil. Serv: Entered as Pfc, Army, 43, released as Maj, 54, after serv. in 5001st Med. Group, Alaskan Air Command, 51-53. Mem: Am, Calif. and Los Angeles Co. Med. Asns; Am. Soc. of Internal Med; SAR; Am. Legion. Rel: Methodist. Mailing Add: 9850 Hasty Ave, Downey, Calif. 90240.

WILKINS, ROY
b. St. Louis, Mo, 8/30/01; s. William D. Wilkins and Mayfield Edmondson W; m. 9/15/29 to Aminda Badeau. Educ: Univ. Minn, A.B, 23. Bus. & Prof. Pos: Ed, Crisis Mag; managing ed, Kans. City Call, 23-31; asst. secy, NAACP, 31-49, secy, 49-50, adminstr, 50-55, exec. secy, 55-64 and dir, 65- Springarn Medal, NAACP. Legal Res: 147-15 Village Rd, Jamaica, N.Y. 11435. Mailing Add: 1790 Broadway, N.Y. 10019.

WILKINS, WILLIAM THOMAS, JR. R
Exec. dir, Miss. Rep. Party
b. Cotton Plant, Ark, 1/17/40; s. William Thomas Wilkins, M.D. and Sue Ellen Brown W; m. 8/18/61 to Martha Ann Huddleston; c. Martha Ellen and William Thomas. Educ: Millsaps Col, 58-60; Univ. Miss, B.P.A, 62, M.A, 66; Delta Sigma Phi; Pi Sigma Alpha; v.pres, Kappa Sigma; publisher, Campus Conservative, 60-62. Polit. & Govt. Pos: Exec. dir, Miss. Rep. Party, 62-; orgn. dir, Gubernatorial Campaign, Miss, 63, campaign mgr, 67; research dir, Presidential Campaign, 64, campaign coordinator, 68, Munic. Campaigns, 65, Senate and House Campaigns, 66; campaign mgr, Spec. Cong. Campaign, 68; exec. dir, South. Asn. of Rep. State Chmn, 69- Publ: 'Mississippi's 1963 General Election: An Analysis,' 64 and 'How to Hold a Primary: A Statutory Digest,' 65, 66 & 69, Miss. Rep. Party; 'The Role of Political Interest Groups in the Mississippi Legislature,' Univ. Miss, 66. Mem: Am. Polit. Sci. Asn; Miss. Hist. Soc. Rel: Presbyterian. Legal Res: 1677 Wilhurst St, Jackson, Miss. 39211. Mailing Add: P.O. Box 1178, Jackson, Miss. 39205.

WILKINSON, CHARLES BURNHAM 'BUD' R
Spec. Consult. to the President
b. Minneapolis, Minn, 4/23/16; s. Charles P. Wilkinson and Edith Lindbloom W; stepmother Ethel Grace W; m. 8/27/38 to Mary Shifflett; c. James G. 'Jay' and Charles P. 'Pat'. Educ: Univ. Minn, Minneapolis, B.A. Eng, 37; Syracuse Univ, M.A, Eng. Educ, 40; Psi Upsilon. Polit. & Govt. Pos: Consult. to President Kennedy on Physical Fitness, President's Coun. Physical Fitness, Wash, D.C, 61-64; Rep. Nat. Committeeman, Okla, 68-; Spec. Consult. to the President, 69- Bus. & Prof. Pos: Asst. football coach, Syracuse Univ, 37-42; asst. football coach, Univ. Minn, Minneapolis, 42-43; football coach and athletic dir, Univ. Okla, 46-61; pres, Lifetime Sports Found, 65-69; pregame analyst and color commentator, col. football telecasts, NCAA Game of the Week, 65- Mil. Serv: Entered as Ens, Navy, 43, released as Lt. Comdr, 45, after serv. in V-5 Prog, Pac, 44-45. Publ: Oklahoma Split-T Football, 52 and Modern Defensive Football, 57, Prentice Hall; Modern Physical Fitness, Viking Press, 67. Mem: Am. Football Coaches Asn.(pres, 58); Am. Legion. Big Ten Medal-Outstanding Scholar-Athlete, 37; B'nai B'rith Award; One of Nation's Ten Outstanding Young Men, U.S. Jr. C. of C, 50; Nat. Brotherhood Citation, Nat. Conf. Christians and Jews, 59; Univ. Okla. Distinguished Serv. Citation; Sports Illustrated Silver Anniversary All-Am. Award, 62; Nat. Football Found. Hall of Fame, 69. Rel: Episcopal. Legal Res: 2543 W. Main, Norman Okla. 73069. Mailing Add: 2801 New Mexico Ave. N.W, Washington, D.C. 20007.

WILKINSON, ERNEST LeROY R
b. Ogden, Utah, 5/4/99; s. Robert Brown Wilkinson and Annie Cecilia Anderson W; m. 8/15/23 to Alice Valera Ludlow; c. Ernest Ludlow, Marian, Alice Ann, David Lawrence and Douglas Dwight. Educ: Weber Col, 17-18; Brigham Young Univ, A.B, 21; George Wash. Univ, J.D, 26; Harvard, S.J.D, 27; Delta Theta Phi, Hon. LL.D, Brigham Young Univ, 57. Polit. & Govt. Pos: Supt, Camp Good Will, Wash, 25; dep. supt. of ins, N.Y. State, 31; mem, Nat. Cmt. of Army and Navy Chaplains, 47-50; mem, Gov. Cmt. Representing Utah, White House Conf. on Educ, 55; del, Rep. Nat. Conv, 56, 60 & 68; mem, Nat. Cmt. to Evaluate United Serv. Orgn, 62; Rep. Cand, U.S. Senate, 64. Bus. & Prof. Pos: Mem. of faculty, Weber Col, Ogden, Utah, 21-23 and Bus. High Sch, Wash, D.C, 23-26; prof. law, N.J. Law Sch, 27-33; assoc, Law Firm, Hughes, Schurman & Dwight, N.Y.C, 28-35; partner, Law Firm, Moyle & Wilkinson, Wash, D.C, 35-40 and Law Firm, Wilkinson, Cragun & Barker, 51-; head, Law Firm of Ernest L. Wilkinson, 40-51; pres, Brigham Young Univ, 50-64 & 65-; chancellor, Unified Church Sch. Syst, Church of Jesus Christ of Latter-day Saints; mem. bd. dirs, Deseret News Pub. Co, Salt Lake City, Utah, 54-, Beneficial Life Ins, Co, 57- and KSL, Inc. and Radio Serv. Corp. of Utah, 60-, mem. bd. trustees, Utah Found, Salt Lake City and Found. for Econ. Educ, Irvington-On-Hudson, N.Y, 60-; mem. bd. dirs, Rolling Hills Orchard, 61- and Ellison Ranching Co, Tuscarora, Nev, 62- Mil. Serv: Pvt, Army, 18. Publ: Decline & Possible Fall of the American Republic, Bookcraft, 65. Mem: Fel. Am. Bar Found; Wash, D.C, Utah State and N.Y. State Bars; Accreditation Cmn. for Bus. Schs, 61-64; mem. bd. visitors, Valley Forge Freedoms Found, 64-; mem. bd. dirs, Nat. Right to Work Cmt, Inc, 64-; Am. Legion; Order of the Coif; hon. mem, Rotary; C. of C; Alta Club. Awarded George Washington Medal by Freedoms Found. for Speech on Free Enterprise, 61, for Independence Day Ed, 67 and for 'Whither America' Address, 68. Rel: Latter-day Saint. Mailing Add: Brigham Young University, Provo, Utah 84601.

WILKINSON, JOHN ARCHBELL R
Mem, N.C. Rep. Cent. Cmt.
b. Pantego, 10/22/09; s. Samuel Walter Wilkinson and Pattie Archbell W; m. 8/25/39 to Beulah Marie Gaither; c. Pattie Archbell and Margaret Gaither. Educ: Univ. of N.C. grad, 32; Tau Kappa Alpha. Polit. & Govt. Pos: Pres, N.C. Young Rep, 41-42; campaign dir, Nat. Young Rep, 42, v.chmn, 46; mem, Nat. Platform Cmt, San Francisco, 64; mem, N.C. Rep. Cent. Cmt, 66- Mil. Serv: Entered as Pvt, Army, 42, released as M/Sgt, 45, after serv. Harbor Defense Key West, Fla. Publ: First prize Scribner's Commentator National Essay Contest on American Foreign Policy, 41. Mem: Pres, N.C. 2nd Dist. Bar Asn, 60 and N.C. 1st Dist. Bar Asn, 56; Am. Judicature Soc; Am. Legion; Mason; Am. Farm Bur; past pres, Washington Yacht & Country Club. Rel: Protestant. Legal Res: Country Club Rd, Washington, N.C. 27889. Mailing Add: P.O. Box 732, Washington, N.C. 27889.

WILKINSON, MARY ANN R
V.Chmn, Gogebic Co. Rep. Party, Mich.
b. Manistique, Mich, 6/16/41; d. John William Kelly and Monica McConnell K;

m. 8/8/64 to Thomas John Wilkinson; c. Patricia Claire. Educ: Mich. State Univ, 59-62; North. Mich. Univ, B.S, 64; Univ. Mich, 67-68; Phi Kappa Delta. Polit. & Govt. Pos: Precinct del, Flint, Mich, 67-68; v.chmn, Gogebic Co. Rep. Party, 68- Bus. & Prof. Pos: Teacher high sch. Eng, Trenary, Mich, 64-65; teacher speech, Eng. and coached debate, Flint North. High Sch, 65-68; teacher Eng, Wakefield Pub. Schs, 69, Ironwood High Sch, 69- Mem: Mich. and Nat. Educ. Asns; Mich. Teachers of Speech; Jaycettes; Theatre North; Urban League; Rotary Auxiliary; Ironwood Women's Club; Ironwood Coun. of the Arts. Rel: Roman Catholic. Mailing Add: 1116 E. Margaret St, Ironwood, Mich. 49938.

WILKINSON, ROBERT DAWSON, JR. R
Chmn, Dallas Co. Rep. Party, Ala.
b. Macon, Ga, 12/31/18; s. Robert Dawson Wilkinson Sr. and Frankie Jones W; m. 12/20/41 to Dorothy Jarvis; c. Linda Kaye. Educ: Ala. Polytech. Inst B.S. in Mech. Eng, 40; Stanford Univ, grad. study, 46-47; Sigma Phi. Polit. & Govt. Pos: Chmn, Dallas Co. Rep. Party, Ala, 62- Bus. & Prof. Pos: Owner, Splendid Cafe, 48-64; owner, Sky Hill Farm, 52-; concessionaire, Downtown Dinner Club, 64-; pres, Dallas Co. Pvt. Sch. Found, 65-66, mem. bd. dir, 67-; owner, Downtown Restaurant and Graystone Restaurant. Mil. Serv: Entered as Lt, Army, 40, released as Capt, 48, after serv. in Air Force, Pac. Area and Okinawa. Mem: Ala. Cattlemen's Asn; pres, Dallas Co. Private Sch. Found, Inc; Ala. Farm Bur; Masonic Blue Lodge 305, Commandery 5. Rel: Presbyterian. Mailing Add: R.R. 2, Box 233B, Selma, Ala. 36701.

WILKINSON, ROBERT MELVIN R
City Councilman, Los Angeles, Calif.
b. Nebr, 4/11/21; s. Ray David Wilkinson and Katherine Lambert W; m. 5/13/44 to Marjorie Philp; c. Barbara (Mrs. Michael Lima), Noreen and Robert, Jr. Educ: Univ. South. Calif, B.E, 47; Sigma Phi Epsilon. Polit. & Govt. Pos: City councilman, 12th Dist, Los Angeles, Calif, 53-57 & 67-; exec. secy, Los Angeles Harbor Cmn, 57-65. Mil. Serv: Qm, 1/C, Navy, 42-45, Caribbean Theatre. Mem: Am. Legion; Reseda; bd. dirs, Japan-Am. Soc; Winnetka C. of C.(v.pres); West Valley Asn. C. of C.(pres); life mem, PTA; commun. adv. planning cmt, San Fernando Valley State Col; bd. trustees, Vet. For. Affairs; Los Angeles-Nagoya, Japan Sister City Cmt. Rel: Protestant. Mailing Add: 17319 Rayen St, Northridge, Calif. 91324.

WILKINSON, RONALD JOE R
Chmn, Sedgwick Co. Rep. Party, Kans.
b. Wichita, Kans, 4/9/34; s. Virgil Milton Wilkinson and Edythe Catherine Wiske W; m. 10/18/69 to Sidney Beattie; c. Stuart Alan and Shelley Anne. Educ: Univ. Wichita, A.B, 56; George Wash. Univ. Law Sch, 56; Washburn Univ. Law Sch, LL.B, 58; pres, Student Bar Asn, 57-58; Delta Theta Phi. Polit. & Govt. Pos: Mem, City-Co. Health Bd, Kans, 63-64; chmn, Sedgwick Co. Young Rep, 64-65; munic. judge, Wichita, 65-67; chmn, Kans. Young Rep, 65-67; chmn, Sedgwick Co. Rep. Party, Kans, 67-; mem, Metrop. Area Planning Cmn, 69- Bus. & Prof. Pos: Chmn, Law Day Cmt, 64. Mil. Serv: Entered as Airman, Air Nat. Guard, 58, released as Capt, 64; Del, Nat. War Col. Strategy Seminar, 60. Mem: Wichita and Kans. Bar Asns; Masonic Orgn. Outstanding Young Man of Wichita, 67. Rel: Protestant. Mailing Add: 2422 Wilson, Wichita, Kans. 67202.

WILKS, MAX D
b. Milton, Fla, 2/9/36; m. to Patricia Mohr; c. Terry Max, John Frederick, Cathy Patricia. Educ: Auburn Univ, BEE, 1958. Polit. & Govt. Pos: Fla. State Rep, 64-66. Bus. & Prof. Pos: Elec. Eng. and Construction. Mem: Milton Jr. C. of C; Milton Quarterback Club; Fla. Adult Ed. Asn. Rel: Baptist. 1967 Legal Res: 1101 Berryhill Rd, Milton, Fla. No mailing address available. (1967)

WILL, CALVIN EVERT R
b. Detroit, Mich, 4/2/36; s. Frederick Edward Will, Jr. and Irene Hoffman W; m. 10/24/65 to Lila Mae Siegert. Educ: Univ. Mich, B.B.A, 58. Polit. & Govt. Pos: Trustee, Caledonia Twp, Mich. and Alcona Co. Libr. Bd, 60-; secy, Alcona Co. Rep. Cmt, 64-65 and chmn, 65-68. Bus. & Prof. Pos: Partner, Will's Gun Shop, 59, owner, 64- Mem: Secy-treas, Lost Lake Woods Club, 65-66; P.K. Fletcher Gun Club; life mem, Nat. Rifle Asn; Alpena City Rifle League; Hubbard Lake Sportsmen's & Imp. Asn. Rel: Lutheran. Mailing Add: Spruce, Mich. 48762.

WILLARD, JAMES E. R
Pa. State Sen.
b. Vandergrift, Pa, 11/20/03; s. James Willard and Edith Barher W; m. to Cornelia E. Anderson; c. Two daughters. Educ: Homestead Pub. schs, Farrell High Sch, Farrell, Pa. Polit. & Govt. Pos: Rep. committeeman, Shenango Twp, Pa, 50-51; Pa. State Rep, 56-67; Pa. State Sen, 67- Bus. & Prof. Pos: Mfr, burial vaults and graveside equip. Mem: Charter mem, past pres, W. Middlesex Kiwanis Club, Lt. Gov, Div. 2, Kiwanis Int, 55; Keydron Masonic Lodge 389; Sharon Elks 103; Odd Fellows; Ancient Accepted Scottish Rite Valley of New Castle; Zem Zem Temple. Rel: Presbyterian. Mailing Add: R.F.D. 2, Pulaski, Pa. 16143. (1967)

WILLARD, KENNETH ROLLAH R
b. Nunda, N.Y, 11/13/02; s. Oscar J. Willard and Frank Rollah W; m. 3/16/28 to Helen Gillette; c. Dale Gillette, Jacquelyn L. (Mrs. Klein) and Stephen R. Educ: Manlius Sch; Rochester Bus. Inst; Eastman Sch. of Music; Columbia Col. Polit. & Govt. Pos: Trustee, Nunda, N.Y, 27-33, mayor, 33-57; N.Y. State Assemblyman, Livingston Co, 57-65; N.Y. State Sen, 53rd and 59th Dists, 65-67; del, N.Y. State Constitutional Conv, 67. Bus. & Prof. Pos: Secy-treas, Nunda Casket Co, Inc, 24- Mem: Rotary; Genesee State Col. Coun; Livingston Co. Libr. Syst; Genessee Coun, Boy Scouts; Mason; Farm Bur. Rel: Presbyterian. Mailing Add: Nunda, N.Y. 14517.

WILLEFORD, GEORGE R
Chmn, Cameron Co. Rep. Cmt, Tex.
b. Dallas, Tex, 10/23/21; s. George Willeford and Joy Brenner W; m. 3/27/48 to Ann Jennings; c. George, III, Allison Ann and Joy Hale. Educ: Tex. A&M Univ, B.S, 43; Univ. Tex. Med. Br, M.D, 46; Phi Pho Sigma. Polit. & Govt. Pos: Chmn, Cameron Co. Rep. Cmt, Tex, 60-62 & 66-; exec. committeeman, Rep. Exec. Cmt, 62-66. Mil. Serv: Entered as 1st Lt, Air Force Med. Corps, 46, released as Capt, Flight Surgeon, 48, after serv. in Komaki Airdrome, Fifth Air Force Hq, Far East, 46-49. Publ: Medical Word Finder, Parker Pub. Co, 66. Mem: Tex. and Am. Med. Asns; Tex. Pediatric Asn; Am. Acad. of Pediatrics; Am. Bd. of Pediatrics; Rotary; Cameron Co. Farm Bur. Rel: Episcopal. Mailing Add: 1019 E. Parkwood, Harlingen, Tex. 78550.

WILLEFORD, MILTON ELMO D
Mem, Calif. Dem. State Cent. Cmt.
b. Livingston, Tenn, 1/6/11; s. Sidney Lee Willeford and Retta Burroughs W; m. 8/13/61 to Helen Elaine Fast; c. Rhetta Ann (Mrs. Hinton), Sidney L. and Susan M. Educ: Tenn. Polytech. Inst, S.S, 32. Polit. & Govt. Pos: Mem, Tulare Co. Dem. Cent. Cmt, Calif, 44-47; inheritance tax appraiser, Calif, 61-; pres, Fresno Dem. Businessmen's Asn, 63-64; mem, Calif. Dem. State Cent. Cmt, currently. Bus. & Prof. Pos: Partner, Willeford, Levey & Co, 55- Mem: Am. Inst. of CPA; Calif. Soc. of CPA; State of Calif. Treasurers' Asn; Calif. State Inheritance Tax Appraisers' Asn; Mason (32°); Shrine; Elks. Rel: Protestant. Mailing Add: 151 W. Keats Ave, Fresno, Calif. 93704. (1967)

WILLENS, HOWARD PENNEY D
Mem, Wash, D.C. Dem. Cent. Cmt.
b. Oak Park, Ill, 5/27/31; s. Joseph Robert Willens and Helen Green W; m. 6/13/54 to Susan Popkin; c. Jonathan, Margaret, Sarah and Patricia. Educ: Stanford Univ, 1 year; Univ. Mich, B.A, 53; Yale Law Sch, LL.B, 56; Phi Beta Kappa; Pi Sigma Alpha; Zeta Beta Tau. Polit. & Govt. Pos: Second asst, Criminal Div, U.S. Dept. of Justice, 61-63, first asst, 64-65; asst. counsel, President's Cmn. on the Assassination of President Kennedy, 63-64; exec. dir, President's Cmn. on Crime in D.C, 65-66; mem, Wash, D.C. Dem. Cent. Cmt, 68-; del, Dem. Nat. Conv, 68. Bus. & Prof. Pos: Assoc, Kirkland, Ellis, Hodson, Chaffetz & Masters, Wash, D.C, 59-61; partner, Wilmer, Cutler & Pickering, 67- Mil. Serv: Entered as Pvt, Army, 57, released as Cpl, 58, after serv. in Fourth Inf. Div, Ft. Louis, Wash, Mem: Am. and Fed. Bar Asns; Bar Asn. of Wash, D.C. Rel: Jewish. Legal Res: 3307 Newark St. N.W, Washington, D.C. 20008. Mailing Add: 900 17th St. N.W, Washington, D.C. 20006.

WILLETT, CHARLES K. R
b. Rock Falls, Ill, 1/4/05; c. two sons. Educ: U. of Ill, B.S, Civil Eng. Polit. & Gov. Pos: Ill. House of Rep, 66th-73rd Gen. Assemblies. Bus. & Prof. Pos: Consult. Engr. Mem: Am. Soc. Civil Engrs; Ill. and Nat. Soc. Prfnl. Engrs; Elks; Mason. Rel: Presbyterian. Mailing Add: Dixon, Ill. 61021. (1967)

WILLETT, DOUGLAS WARREN D
b. Haynes, N.Dak, 5/25/37; s. Warren H. Willett and Alma C. Christman W; m. 9/17/59 to Grace Marie Bartholomew; c. Sean D, Michelle R, Lon A, Renata D. and Bryce W. Educ: S.Dak. Sch. Mines and Tech, B.Sc, 59; Calif. Inst. Tech, Ph.D, 63. Polit. & Govt. Pos: Alternate del, Dem. Nat. Conv, 68. Bus. & Prof. Pos: Assoc. prof, Univ. Alta, 62-66; assoc. prof, Univ. Utah, 66- Publ: 'On a Nonlinear Boundary Value Problem . . . ,' Arch. Rational Mech. & Anal, 66; 'Boundedness of Solutions of Equation $\ddot{x} + f(x, \dot{x}) + g(x) = o$,' SIAM J, 66; 'On the Oscillatory Behavior of the Solutions of Second Order Linear Differential Equations,' Annales Polonici Math, 68. Mem: Am. Math. Soc; Math. Asn. Am; Can. Math. Cong; Unione Matematica Italiano; New Dem. Coalition, Utah. Mailing Add: 3730 E. Millstream Dr, Salt Lake City, Utah 84109.

WILLEY, EDWARD EUGENE D
Va. State Sen.
b. Frederick Co, Va, 4/7/10; m. to Twyla Sutton Layton. Educ: Med. Col. of Va, Sch. of Pharm. Polit. & Govt. Pos: Former city councilman, Richmond, Va; Va. State Sen, 52- Bus. & Prof. Pos: Owner, Willey Drug Co. Mem: Mason; Shrine; various fraternal, prfnl. and civic orgns. Rel: Methodist. Mailing Add: 4510 Newport Dr, Richmond, Va. 23227. (1967)

WILLEY, RICHARD CROSMAN R
b. Bar Harbor, Maine, 9/14/06; s. Clifford Morton Willey and Bertha Conners W; m. 12/25/32 to Winifred Lois Rollins; c. Alice, Karen, Joan and Richard, Jr. Educ: Univ. Maine; Sigma Alpha Epsilon. Polit. & Govt. Pos: Mem, Ellsworth City Coun, Maine, 48-50; Maine State Rep, 52-54 & 54-56; Maine State Sen, 56-58, 58-60 & 65-67; Maine State Liquor Cmnr, 60-63; v.chmn, Gov. Exec. Coun, currently. Bus. & Prof. Pos: Asst. mgr, Willey's Inc, 26-60, pres-treas-mgr, 60-64; Liquor Vendor's Rep, J.A. Dougherty's Sons, Inc, 64- Mem: All Masonic Bodies, including Shrine; Grange; Lions. Rel: Congregational. Mailing Add: 24 Birch Ave, Ellsworth, Maine 04605.

WILLIAMS, ALAN D, JR. R
b. Phila, Pa, 2/16/27; s. Alan D. Williams and Vivian Folwell W; m. to Mary Jane Wilbur; c. four. Educ: Wharton Sch, Univ. of Pa, B.S; Univ. of Oslo, Norway; Univ. Pa. Law Sch, LL.B; pres, William Draper Lewis Law Club; treas, Law Class, Univ. Pa, 53. Polit. & Govt. Pos: Asst. Dist. Attorney, Bucks Co, Pa, 58; Pa. State Rep, 58-67. Bus. & Prof. Pos: Instructor, Delaware Valley Col. of Sci. & Agr, Doylestown. Mil. Serv: Army, 45-47. Mem: Bucks Co, Pa. Supreme and Superior Courts; Am. Bar Asn; Cent. Bucks. Jr. C. of C; Am. Legion. Mailing Add: 353 E. State St, Doylestown, Pa. 18901. (1967)

WILLIAMS, ALBERT D
Tenn. Cmnr.
b. Davidson Co, Tenn, 5/30/88; m. to Irma Neblett W; c. Dr. Charlotte Williams (Mrs. Allen). Educ: Vanderbilt Univ; Cumberland Univ, LL.B. Polit. & Govt. Pos: Judge, Fifth Judicial Circuit, Tenn, 23-; Tenn. Cmnr, 63-; has sat on Tenn. Supreme Court as Spec. Judge on numerous occasions. Mem: Tenn. Bar Asn; past pres, Nashville Bar Asn. Counsel and Chmn, Evidence Cmt. of Int. Tribunal in Tokyo, Japanese War Crimes Trials. Mailing Add: State Office Bldg, Nashville, Tenn. 37219. (1967)

WILLIAMS, ALBERT CLARK R
Ariz. State Rep.
b. Encino, N.Mex, 11/20/25; s. Albert H. Williams and Hallie A. Walker W; m. 11/20/45 to Viola B. Cary; c. Gary A. and Diane C. Educ: East. N.Mex. Univ, B.S, 53; Univ. Ariz, M.B.A, 55. Polit. & Govt. Pos: Ariz. State Rep, Pima Co, 67- Bus. & Prof. Pos: Auditor, Hughes Aircraft Co, 57- Mil.

Serv: Entered as Seaman, Navy, 43, released as Aviation Radioman 3/C, 46, after serv. in S.Pac, 44-45. Mem: Nat. Mgt. Asn; Nat. Acct. Asn; Elks; Masonic Lodge Aaron, Tucson, Tucson Consistory (32°), K.T, York Rite, Sabbar Shrine Temple; Royal Orders of Jesters. Rel: Methodist. Mailing Add: 4342 E. 16th St, Tucson, Ariz. 85711.

WILLIAMS, ALEXANDER SAMUEL, III D
Coroner, Lake Co, Ind.
b. Huntsville, Ala, 3/26/22; s. Alexander Samuel Williams, II and Ola Grace Hicks W; m. 2/25/45 to Annie Ruth Malone; c. Annette Yvonne, Alexander Samuel, IV, Charles Darryl and David Ronald. Educ: Gary Col, 39-41; Univ. Chicago, 41-43; Meharry Med. Col, M.D, 46; Kappa Pi; Alpha Phi Alpha. Polit. & Govt. Pos: Coroner, Lake Co, Ind, 45-; mem, Gary Redevelop. Cmn, 60-, Ind. Criminal Justice Cmn, 64-69 and Lake Co. Law Enforcement Coun, 65-; del, Dem. Nat. Conv, 68. Bus. & Prof. Pos: Dir, Stewart Settlement House, 57-; mem. adv. bd, Bank of Ind, 58-68; chmn. bd. dirs, Bank of Century, 68- Mil. Serv: Pfc, Army, 43-46, serv. in ASTP, U.S. Publ: 'Traffic Deaths in Lake County,' J. of Ind. State Med. Asn, 12/66; 'Traffic Deaths in Lake County Indiana,' (a 2 year study), Med. Times, 10/68. Mem: Lake Co. and Ind. State Med. Socs; Am. Med. Asn; Nat. Coroner's Asn; Vet. in Polit; v.pres, Northwest Ind. United Fund, 69-; Kiwanis Int; C. of C; Fraternal Order of Police. Frontier's Citizenship Award; safety awards, USW, 68; Commun. Serv. Award, Radio Sta. WMPP; safety awards, Ind. Blue Cross-Blue Shield; Letter of Commendation from Nat. Safety Coun, 68. Rel: Methodist; Trustee, Deloney Methodist Church. Legal Res: 1925 Taft St, Gary, Ind. 46404. Mailing Add: 751 Washington St, Gary, Ind. 46402.

WILLIAMS, ARTHUR R
b. Lawrence, Mass, 12/14/15; s. Michael Joseph Williams and Elizabeth Rodger W; m. 11/16/40 to Elizabeth Lauder Wilkinson; c. Arthur Kenneth and Keith Andrew. Educ: Northeast. Univ. Col. Liberal Arts, Sch. Law and Grad. Sch. Law. Polit. & Govt. Pos: Mass. State Rep, 57-68; moderator, Town of Andover, 65-; legis. secy. to Gov. Volpe, 68- Bus. & Prof. Pos: Attorney-at-Law; spec. Justice, First Dist. Court of North. Middlesex, currently. Mil. Serv: Entered as Pvt, Army, 41, released as 1st Lt; Lt. Col, Army Res, currently; Presidential Unit Citation; S.Pac. Campaign Medal; Three Battle Stars. Mem: Lawrence and Essex Co. Bar Asns; pres, Essex Co. Legislators Asn; Mason; ROA; Elks; Lions; VFW; Am. Legion. Rel: Congregational. Mailing Add: 149 Haverhill St, Andover, Mass. 01810.

WILLIAMS, ARTHUR FOSTER R
b. Bath, Maine, 7/3/26; s. John Winslow and Kaiulani Sewall W; m. 6/30/56 to Hanne Vrede Nielsen; c. Astrid, Nathaniel and John. Educ: Bowdoin Col, B.A; Wesleyn Col, 1 year; Univ. Vt, 2 years; Alpha Delta Phi. Polit. & Govt. Pos: Vt. State Rep, 62-66; dir, Vt. Coun. on the Arts, 65-67, asst. dir, 68; chmn, State Bd. Historic Sites, 65- Mil. Serv: Vol, Am. Field Serv, 44-45, ETO and World War II Victory Medals. Mailing Add: Waitsfield, Vt. 05673.

WILLIAMS, AUDREY PATTERSON 'DICK' D
b. Allendale, S.C, 11/28/04; s. Angus Patterson Williams and Catherine Rebecca Bennett W; m. 10/15/33 to Lucille Tuten. Educ: Pub. schs. Polit. & Govt. Pos: S.C. State Rep, 49-50; S.C. State Sen, 63-66. Bus. & Prof. Pos: Automotive parts jobber; merchant; owner, Dick's Motor Serv. Mailing Add: Allendale, S.C. 29810. (1967)

WILLIAMS, AVON NYANZA, JR. D
Tenn. State Sen.
b. Knoxville, Tenn, 12/22/21; s. Avon Nyanza Williams, Sr. and Carrie Belle Cole W; m. 7/22/56 to Joan Marie Bontemps; c. Avon Nyanza, III and Wendy Janette. Educ: Johnson C. Smith Univ, A.B, 40; Boston Univ. Law Sch, LL.B, 47, LL.M, 48; Omega Psi Phi. Polit. & Govt. Pos: State chmn, Tenn. Voters Coun, 68-; Tenn. State Sen, 19th Dist, 69- Bus. & Prof. Pos: Attorney at law, Knoxville, Tenn, 49-53, Nashville, 53-; cooperating attorney, NAACP Legal Defense Educ. Fund, Inc, N.Y.C, 49-; bank attorney, Commun. Fed. Savings & Loan Asn, Nashville, 62-; lectr. dent. jurisprudence, Meharry Med. Col, 66- Mil. Serv: Entered as Pvt, Army Air Force, 43, released as 1st Lt, 46, after serv. in S.Pac, 44-46; Res, 46-69, Lt. Col; S.Pac. Campaign Ribbon; World War II Ribbon. Publ: 'Race Relations—A Community Problem,' New South & Negro Digest, 63. Mem: Am. and Fed. Bar Asns; Am. Judicature Soc; Davidson Co. Trial Lawyers Asn; NAACP (exec. bd. Nashville Br); South. Regional Coun.(bd. dirs); Tenn. Voters Coun.(gen. chmn); Tenn. Coun. Human Rels; Sigma Pi Phi. Citizen of the Year, Omega Psi Phi; Serv. Award, East Nashville Civic Club; Cert. Merit, Johnson C. Smith Univ, Agora Assembly and NAACP Youth Coun; Distinguished Serv. Award, Nashville Br. NAACP. Rel: Presbyterian; Elder, St. Andrews Presbyterian Church. Legal Res: 1818 Morena St, Nashville, Tenn. 37208. Mailing Add: 1414 Parkway Towers, Nashville, Tenn. 37219.

WILLIAMS, BEATRICE JACQUART R
b. Larned, Kans, 10/28/11; d. Henry Joseph Jacquart (deceased) and Ann Robinson J; m. 12/26/68 to James Alfred Williams. Educ: Washburn Univ, 30-32; Ft. Hays State Col, A.B, 35; Phi Gamma Delta; Kappa Alpha Theta. Polit. & Govt. Pos: Kans. State Rep, 57-67; dist. rep. for U.S. Sen. Bob Dole, 67- Bus. & Prof. Pos: Ed, Johnson, Plains, Ulysses and Sublette, Kans, 30. Mil. Serv: Entered as Pvt, W.A.C, released as Capt, 46. Mem: Kans. Citizens Safety Coun; Mineral Resources Coun; Kans. Asn. of Ment. Health Bd; Ft. Hays Endowment; Federated Women's Club; Bus. & Prfnl. Women's Club; Kans. Newspaper Women; State Bd. Kans. Presswomen; Republican Women; Kans. Heart Asn; Salvation Army; Girl Scouts; Eastern Star (past matron); Am. Legion Auxiliary (past pres); mem. bd, Kans. Adv. Cmn. Inst. Mgt. and Commun. Health and Valley Hope Treatment Center. Distinguished Alumni Award, Ft. Hays State Col, 65. Rel: Christian Church. Mailing Add: 708 Central, Dodge City, Kans. 67801.

WILLIAMS, BEN C. D
b. Port St. Joe, Fla, 5/5/14; m. to Alyce Todd; c. J.A. and William R. 'Bo'. Polit. & Govt. Pos: Fla. State Rep, 62-68. Bus. & Prof. Pos: Electrician. Mem: Mason; charter mem. and founding high priest, St. Joseph's Chap. Number 56, RAM; founding pres, St. Joe Shrine Club; past mem, PTA. Rel: Baptist. Mailing Add: P.O. Box N, Port St. Joe, Fla. 32456. (1967)

WILLIAMS, BETTIE McLEAN ZACHER R
b. Hartford, Conn, 1/16/16; c. Louis Edmund Zacher and Marie Theresa Z; m. 1953 to Edward I. Williams, Jr; c. Sheridan Zacher, Nicholas McLean, Preston J. and Gardiner T. Educ: Wellesley Col. Polit. & Govt. Pos: Former mem, Women's Nat. Rep. Club, D.C. League of Rep. Women and Rep. Orgn, V.I; chief photographer, Citizens for Eisenhower, 52; mem, Rep. Nat. Cmt, V.I, 51-64; asst. to State Finance Chmn, 51-; postal adv, V.I, 57-61. Bus. & Prof. Pos: Photographer, Second Fahnestock South Sea Expedition; with Am. Mus. Nat. Hist, 40; on staff, radio sta. WIIC, Hartford, 42-43; free-lance photographer, 48-58. Mem: Soc. Woman Geographers; Photog. Soc. Am; St. Croix C. of C; Wellesley Club; Sulgrave Club; Tennis Club; Country Club. Mailing Add: Christiansted, St. Croix, V.I. 00820. (1967)

WILLIAMS, BROWARD D
Fla. State Treas.
b. Graceville, Fla, 8/25/11; s. James T. Williams and Emma Louetta Register W; m. 5/13/42 to Monetha Duggar; c. Shirley Ann (Mrs. W. Dunbar). Educ: Univ. Fla, 31-35; Fla. Blue Key; Alpha Kappa Psi; Phi Kappa Tau. Polit. & Govt. Pos: Chief clerk to State Treas, Fla, 38-42, admin. asst, 50-63; mem, Fla. Installment Land Sales Bd, 63-65; coordinator, Fla. Gov. Cabinet and Congressman in Johnson-Humphrey Campaign, 64; mem. bd. dir, Fla. Citizens Safety Coun, 65-68; Fla. State Treas, Ins. Cmnr. and State Fire Marshall, 65-; dir, Gov. Highway Safety Cmn, 68; del-at-lg, Dem. Nat. Conv, 68; mem. policy cmt, Fla. Nat. Forum on Fed. Rels. of Local Govt, 69. Bus. & Prof. Pos: Ins. agent, Fla. Asn. of Ins. Co, 48-50, exec. dir, 63-65. Mil. Serv: Ens, Navy Res, 42-45; Asiatic Pac. Theater Medal; Am. Theater Medal; Victory Medal; Purple Heart. Mem: Nat. Asn. Ins. Cmnrs; Nat. Asn. State Auditors, Comptrollers and Treas; Nat. Fire Protection Asn; Int. Asn. of Fire Chiefs; Fla. Peace Officers Asn; Fla. Firemans Asn; Cmt. on Ins. Terminology, Am. Risk & Ins. Asn, 69-; Fla. Health Planning Adv. Coun; Fed. Flood Ins. Adv. Cmt; adv. cmt, Fla. Jaycees Ment. Health and Retardation Cmt; bd. dir, Hope Sch. of Miami; bd. trustees, Fla. Sheriffs Boys Ranch; Blue Goose; past area comdr. and mem, nat. security coun, Am. Legion; 40 et 8; VFW; Kiwanis; Elks; Mason (32°); Shrine. Rel: Methodist. Legal Res: 1503 Marion Ave, Tallahassee, Fla. 32303. Mailing Add: State Treasurer's Office, State Capitol, Tallahassee, Fla. 32304.

WILLIAMS, C. HERSCHEL D
b. Marissa, Ill, 1/8/27; s. Cale Joshua Williams and Stella R. Young W; m. to Opal Marie Blackwell; c. Joan Carol. Educ: South. Ill. Univ, 48-49; St. Louis Univ, 49-50; Wash. Univ, 53-54; Nu Epsilon Alpha. Polit. & Govt. Pos: Treas, Randolph Co, Chester, Ill, 62-66; alternate del, Dem. Nat. Conv, 64; mem, Little Egypt Regional Port Dist, 65- Bus. & Prof. Pos: Exec. v.pres, Evansville Building and Loan, 68-; pres, Sparta Rotary Club, 69-70. Mil. Serv: Entered as Pvt, Army, 51, released as Cpl, 53, after serv. in Hq. Med. Div, Heidelberg, Germany, 52-53. Mem: Hope Lodge 162, AF&AM; VFW Post, Chester, Ill; Eastern Star; White Shrine. Rel: Protestant. Mailing Add: 213 N. Vine, Sparta, Ill. 62286.

WILLIAMS, CARL MICHAEL R
Colo. State Sen.
b. Douglas, Wyo, 11/9/28; s. John Walter Williams and Eleanor Powers W; m. 12/29/57 to Ginny Lee Downer; c. Eleanor Lee Payne and Michael Carl. Educ: Univ. N.C, B.A, 50; Univ. Wyo, J.D, 56; Kappa Sigma. Polit. & Govt. Pos: Colo. State Sen, 68- Bus. & Prof. Pos: Pres, Televents, 57- Mil. Serv: Entered as Pvt, Air Force, 50, released as Capt, 58, after serv. in Wyo. Air Nat. Guard, 53-58. Publ: Contrib, Law J. Mem: C. of C; Am. Legion. Rel: Episcopal. Legal Res: 160 Cherry St, Denver, Colo. 80220. Mailing Add: 280 Columbine, Denver, Colo. 80206.

WILLIAMS, CARRINGTON D
Va. State Del.
b. Brookneal, Va, 6/21/19; m. to Carla Elaine Shriner. Educ: Johns Hopkins Univ, A.B, 40; Univ. Va, LL.B, 42; mem. staff, Va. Law Rev, 42. Polit. & Govt. Pos: Va. State Del, 66- Bus. & Prof. Pos: Lawyer. Mil. Serv: Entered Army Air Force, 42, released as Capt, 46, after serv. in Pac. Theatre. Mem: Johns Hopkins Club; Delta Phi; Omicron Delta Kappa; Va. State Bar Asn; Va. State Bar. Rel: Episcopal. Mailing Add: 3543 Half Moon Circle, Falls Church, Va. 22040.

WILLIAMS, CHARLES SHELDON D
b. Winsted, Conn, 3/12/35; s. Othneil Glanville Williams and Janet Barbara Sheldon W; m. 6/20/64 to Katherine Brown Johnston; c. Sarah McNaughton and Rachel Penfield. Educ: Hamilton Col, A.B, 57; Yale Univ. Divinity Sch, B.D, 64; Chi Psi. Polit. & Govt. Pos: Mem, Mayor's Ad-Hoc Cmt. Summer Planning for Youth, Wash, D.C, 66-67, Ad-Hoc Cmt. on Rebuilding H St, 68-69; mem. and strategist, Capitol Hill Concerned Citizens for Peace, 67-; alternate del, Dem. Nat. Conv, 68; mem. city planning cmt, D.C. Dem. Cent. Cmt, 68-; assoc. commun. educator and dir. of conf. and insts, Commun. Educ. Div, Fed. City Col, Wash, 68- Bus. & Prof. Pos: Ordained clergyman, Potomac Asn, United Church of Christ, 64-, bd. dirs, 66-69; mem, Race Inst, 69- Mil. Serv: Entered as A/S, Naval Res, 57, released as Lt.(jg), 61, after serv. in J-2, Intel. Directorate, Fleet Intel. Center, 57-59 and joint staff, Joint Chiefs of Staff, 59-61; Dept. of Defense Medal. Mem: Nat. Univ. Exten. Asn. Rel: United Church of Christ. Mailing Add: 530 Cedar St, Washington, D.C. 20012.

WILLIAMS, DAISY LEE D
Secy, S.Dak. Dem. State Cmt.
b. Ava, Mo, 11/19/30; d. Oscar Bryan Denney and Pansy Henson D; m. 11/16/52 to Joe Williams. Polit. & Govt. Pos: Precinct committeewoman and secy, Dewey Co. Dem. Cmt, 58-62; del. and mem. orgn. cmt, Dem. Nat. Conv, 60; secy, S.Dak. Dem. State Cmt, 62-; mem. nat. cmt, Citizens for Johnson and Humphrey, 64; mem. reception cmt. and traveling host, Mrs. Hubert Humphrey, 64; orgn. and recording secy, Dem. State Conv, 64, del, 66. Rel: Methodist. Mailing Add: 706 South Potter, Gettysburg, S.Dak. 57442. (1967)

WILLIAMS, DAVID CARY R
b. Santa Monica, Calif, 6/22/35; s. Donald Cary Williams and Katherine Adams W; m. 9/8/62 to Cynthia Cora Irwin. Educ: Harvard Col, nat. scholarships, 53-57, A.B, 57; Mass. Inst. Tech, Nat. Sci. Found. fel, 57-61, Ph.D,

62; Phi Beta Kappa; Phi Lambda Upsilon; Sigma Xi. Polit. & Govt. Pos: Mem, Los Alamos Citizens for Goldwater, N.Mex, 64; mem. exec. bd, Los Alamos Young Rep, 65-66; alternate del, Rep. Nat. Conv, 68; precinct div. chmn, Bernalillo Co. Rep. Party, N.Mex, 69- Bus. & Prof. Pos: Postdoctoral fellow, Princeton Univ, 62-64, Los Alamos Sci. Lab, 64-66; research staff mem, Sandia Laboratories, 66- Publ: 'Angular Momentum Effects in Nuclear Evaporation Processes: Charged Particle Emission,' (with T. D. Thomas), 67 and 'The Analysis of Nuclear Evaporation Spectra: Charged Particle Emission,' (with T.D. Thomas), 68, Nuclear Physics; 'Levels of ^{42}Ca and ^{46}Ca as Observed in the ^{40}Ca(t,p) and ^{44}Ca(t,p) Reactions,' (with J.D. Knight and W.T. Leland), Phys. Rev, 67. Mem: Am. Phys. Soc; Am. Chem. Soc; Am. Asn. Adv. Sci; N.Y. Acad. Sci. Mailing Add: 1300 Espanola N.E, Albuquerque, N.Mex. 87110.

WILLIAMS, DAVID JOHN R
b. Shaft, Md, 5/29/08; s. David John Williams and Mary Ann Yates W; m. 12/17/32 to Margaret Louise Coleman; c. Ruth (Mrs. Warnick), Ethel (Mrs. Spalding), Margaret (Mrs. Jones), Mabel (Mrs. Smith), Betty (Mrs. Schlerth) and David John, Jr. Polit. & Govt. Pos: Chief Judge of Elec, Midland, Md, 44-54; mem, Md. State Rep. Cent. Cmt, 54-58; trial magistrate, Allegany Co, 56-58; Md. State Del, 58-60 & 62-66; clerk, Midland, 60-62. Bus. & Prof. Pos: Former coal miner; process worker, Celanese Corp, 37-48; mine operator, 48-54; blueprint clerk, 54-59; traffic clerk, Cumberland Cement and Supply Co, 59. Mem: Mason; Shrine; Eastern Star; K. of P; Fire Co. Rel: Methodist; mem, Official Bd. Trustee and Assoc. Dist. Lay Leader. Legal Res: Cemetery Rd, Midland, Md. 21542. Mailing Add: Box 54, Midland, Md. 21542. (1967)

WILLIAMS, DONALD W. D
b. Berlin, N.H, 1/26/29; married; c. Four. Educ: Berlin High Sch. Polit. & Govt. Pos: Former N.H. State Rep. Mil. Serv: Army Air Force, 18 months. Rel: Catholic. Mailing Add: 41 Verdun St, Berlin, N.H. 03570. (1967)

WILLIAMS, EDWARD MORGAN R
b. Ottawa, Kans, 11/26/39; s. Albert Joseph Williams and Lucille Williams W; m. 12/20/59 to Lynda Beth Angell; c. Jon Douglas, Denise Adele and Daren Randall. Educ: Ottawa Univ.(Kans), B.A, 61; Univ. Kans, M.A, 62; Woodrow Wilson Fel; Phi Beta Kappa. Polit. & Govt. Pos: Chmn, Ottawa Univ. Collegiate Young Rep, 60-61 and faculty adv, 66-69; precinct committeeman, Plains Twp. Rep. Party, Kans, 62-66; chmn, Meade Co. Rep. Cent. Cmt, 62-66; mem. exec. cmt, mem. bd. dirs. and chmn, Rep. Assocs. of Southwest Kans, 65-66; mem. Kans. del, Young Rep. Nat. Leadership Training Sch, 65; chmn, Franklin Co. Rep. Cent. Cmt, 67-69; co-chmn, Third Dist, Kans. Rep. State Finance Cmt, 69- Bus. & Prof. Pos: Gen. mgr, Plains Equity Exchange, 62-66; asst. prof, Ottawa Univ.(Kans), 66-69; state dir, Farmers Home Admin, 69- Mem: Am. Econ. Asn; Orgn. Am. Historians; Am. Agr. Econ. Asn; Agr. Hist. Soc; Econ. Hist. Asn; Nebr. State Hist. Soc; Kans. State Hist. Soc; Lions; Ottawa Country Club; Kans. Rep. State Cmt-Fivescore Club; Franklin Co. Day Care, Inc; Kaw Coun. Boy Scouts; Ottawa Little Symphony Asn; Native Sons and Daughters of Kans; Ottawa Univ. O Club; Mid.West Area Faith at Work Team. Eagle Scout; Wall Street J. Award; Distinguished Serv. Award, Plains Jaycees, 65 and Ottawa Jaycees, 69; Distinguished Jayhawker, 64. Rel: Baptist. Mailing Add: 3340 W. 34th St. Court, Topeka, Kans. 66614.

WILLIAMS, EDWARD VERNON D
Idaho State Rep.
b. Lewiston, Idaho, 1/17/28; s. Gilbert Murrey Williams and Viva White W; m. 8/25/55 to Barbara Lee Gill; c. Susan Nolt, Ronald and Richard. Educ: North. Idaho Col. Educ, 48-51; Univ. Idaho, B.S. in Educ, 55. Polit. & Govt. Pos: Idaho State Rep, Nez Perce Co, 63-; Asst. Minority Leader, Idaho House of Rep, Dist. 7, 67-69, Minority Leader, 69- Mil. Serv: Entered as Pvt, Army, 46, released as Sgt, 48, after serv. in Korea Co. B, Sixth Eng. Combat Bn, Asiatic-Pac. Theatre; re-entered as Sgt, 51, released as M/Sgt, 52, after Serv. in C Battery, 148th Field Artil. Bn, Ft. Carson, Colo; Capt.(Ret), Army Res. and Idaho Nat. Guard, 68. Mem: Idaho and Nat. Educ. Asns; VFW; Am. Legion; Elks. Rel: Protestant. Mailing Add: 3418 12th St, Lewiston, Idaho 83501.

WILLIAMS, ERLE RUPERT R
Mem, First Territorial Rep. Cmt, V.I.
b. St. Thomas, V.I, 7/4/98; s. Joseph A. Williams and Helen A. Wells W; m. 9/12/23 to Florence A. Stephens; c. Ruth (Mrs. Klint) and Norma Celine (Mrs. Wm. McCarey). Educ: Northwest. Univ, A.B, 50. Polit. & Govt. Pos: Secy-treas, V.I. Rep. Orgn, 61; mem, First Territorial Rep. Cmt, 63- Bus. & Prof. Pos: Asst. ed, West End News, 58 and St. Croix Avis, V.I, 60. Mil. Serv: Entered as Pvt, Army, 42, released as S/Sgt, 45, after serv. in 100th Qm. Railhead Co, Seventh Army, N.Africa and ETO, 43; Good Conduct Medal; Rome Arno & European-African-Middle East. Serv. Ribbons; Am. Defense Serv. Medal; Victory Ribbon. Mem: Comdr, Alexander Hamilton Post 85, Am. Legion; membership and past cmt, Nat. Hq. Rel: Anglican. Legal Res: 10 A2B King St, St. Croix, V.I. 00820. Mailing Add: Christiansted, St. Croix, V.I. 00820.

WILLIAMS, ESTHER ROBBINS D
b. Harrison, Mich, 7/24/20; d. Stephen Leonard Robbins and Cora Belle McFadden R; m. 12/1/40 to Frank Williams; c. Jeffrey and Timothy. Educ: Harrison High Sch, Mich, grad, 38. Polit. & Govt. Pos: Dem. precinct del, 14th Cong. Dist, Detroit, Mich, 64-69; first v.chmn, 14th Dist. Dem. Orgn, Mich, 66, womens cmt. chmn, 66, commun. rels. chmn, 67, dist. chmn, 68, exec. bd. mem, 69, precinct del, 69; del, Dem. Nat. Conv, and treas, Mich. Del, 68. Bus. & Prof. Pos: Supvr, Stouffers, Inc, Detroit, Mich, 60; instr, Leadership Training Inst, 64-66; rep. in Wayne Co. Probate Court, The Legal Advertiser, Highland Park, 66- Mem: Past mem. exec. bd, PTA, Edwin Denby High Sch. Mothers' Club, United Found and March of Dimes; chmn, Citizens for Schs, 58-62. Cert. of Honor, for Serv. to Detroit Schs, Detroit Bd. Educ. Rel: Lutheran. Mailing Add: 15881 Collingham Dr, Detroit, Mich. 48205.

WILLIAMS, EVAN S. R
b. Mainsburg, Pa, 2/15/22; s. Evan C. Williams and Nellie Squires W; m. to Louise Eadie; c. Four. Educ: Cornell Univ, A.B, LL.B. Polit. & Govt. Pos: Pa. State Rep, 58-68. Bus. & Prof. Pos: Attorney-at-law. Mil. Serv: B-17 Pilot, WSAF, 447th Bomber Group, Eng, 43-45. Mailing Add: Troy, Pa. 16947. (1967)

WILLIAMS, F. JAMES, JR. D
b. Brooklyn, N.Y, 6/6/13; s. Frank J. Williams and Zetta Fickeisen W; m. 9/19/59 to Elizabeth Wagner; c. Peter James and Pamela (Mrs. Donald Cady). Educ: Duke Univ. Polit. & Govt. Pos: Asst. to cmnr, N.Y. State Dept. of Agr, 56-58; del-at-lg, N.Y. State Dem. Conv, 58; dir, N.Y. State Indian Affairs, 58-59; cmnr, Hudson River-Black River Regulating Dist, 59-; alternate del-at-lg, Dem. Nat. Conv, 64. Bus. & Prof. Pos: V.pres, Johnson Bros. Lumber, 38-56, pres, 56-59; pres, Sugar Hill Farms, 53-60, Classic Cue of Saratoga, 63-66 and Allen Wine & Liquor Store, Albany, 65- Mem: Pleasant Valley Grange; F&AM (32°); Shrine; Univ. Club of Albany; Albany Country Club; Lake Placid Club. Rel: Episcopal. Mailing Add: 17 Loudon Hts. N, Loudonville, N.Y. 12211. (1967)

WILLIAMS, FLOYD BERT R
Chmn, Brisco Co. Rep, Tex.
b. Kirkland, Tex, 5/13/15; s. Bert Thomas Williams and Ethel Rae Coats W; m. 3/11/43 to Diamond Dorthy Howard; c. Martina Jane (Mrs. Ray A. Mattheus) and Annette. Educ: Tex. Tech. Col, 39-41. Polit. & Govt. Pos: Chmn, Brisco Co. Rep, Tex, 61- Bus. & Prof. Pos: Farmer, 46- Mil. Serv: Entered as Pvt, Air Force, 42, released as Sgt, 45, after serv. in Ground Crew. Mem: Farm Bur; Nat. Farmers Orgn. Rel: Baptist. Legal Res: 201 Loretta St, Silverton, Tex. 79257. Mailing Add: P.O. Box 741, Silverton, Tex. 79257.

WILLIAMS, FRANCIS XETON D
Committeeman, Ill. Dem. Cent. Cmt.
b. Springfield, Ill, 8/1/15; s. Hobert T Williams and Elizabeth Spring W; m. 6/4/36 to Hedy Mrosko; c. Sharon and Paul VanDaele, James O, Thomas J. and Robert F. Educ: Cathedral Boys High Sch, 4 years. Polit. & Govt. Pos: Dem. precinct committeeman, Ill, 62-; chmn, Moline City Dem. Cmt, 64-; inspector of agr, Ill, 65-68; bd. rev, Rock Island Co, 68-; committeeman, Ill. Dem. Cent. Cmt, 44th Dist, 68- Mem: Eagles; Ill. Registered Sanitarian; hon. mem, Policemens Benovolent & Protective Asn. of Ill, 69. Rel: Catholic. Mailing Add: 1426 27th St, Moline, Ill. 61265.

WILLIAMS, FRANKLIN H. D
b. Flushing, N.Y, 10/22/17; s. Arthur Lee Williams and Alinda Lowry W; m. 5/27/44 to Shirley Broyard; c. Franklin, Jr. and Paul Anatole. Educ: Lincoln Univ, A.B, 41; Fordham Law Sch, LL.B, 45; Phi Kappa Epsilon; Alpha Phi Alpha. Hon. LL.D, Lincoln Univ. and Elizabethtown Col; hon. D.H.L, Windham Col. Polit. & Govt. Pos: Asst. Attorney Gen, Calif, 59-61; spec. asst. to dir, U.S. Peace Corps, 61-62. dir, Div. of Univ, Pvt. and Int. Cooperation, 62-63, dir, African Regional Off, 63; U.S. Rep. to UN Econ. and Soc. Coun, 64-65; U.S. Ambassador to Ghana, 65-68; alternate rep, 19th Session of UN Gen. Assembly, 64-65; dir, Urban Center, Columbia Univ, 68- Mil. Serv: Army, 42-43. Mem: Am. Arbitration Asn; Coun. on For. Rels; For Policy Asn. Rel: Methodist. Mailing Add: 52 W. 89th St, New York, N.Y. 10024.

WILLIAMS, FRANKLIN TAYLOR, JR. R
Chmn, Md. Rep. State Cent. Cmt.
b. Cecil Co, Md, 4/1/21; s. Franklin Taylor Williams, Sr. and Ella Simmers W; m. 8/14/43 to Florence Elizabeth Helbig; c. Allaire Diane, Franklin Taylor, III and Andrea Danielle. Educ: Goldey Sch. Bus, 2 years, grad, 39. Polit. & Govt. Pos: Secy, Md. Rep. State Cent. Cmt, 58-62 and chmn, 62-; del, Rep. State Conv, Md, 58-64 and Rep. Nat. Conv, 64. Bus. & Prof. Pos: Mgr, Elkton Auto Sales Corp, 40-48; owner, Williams Motor Co, 48- Mil. Serv: Entered as Yeoman 3/C, Coast Guard, 42, released as Lt, 46, after serv. in Wash, D.C, Hq. and Camp Lejeune, N.C, European and Asiatic Pac. Theaters, 25 months; Am. Theater Ribbon with One Star; Asiatic Theater Ribbon with One Star; ETO Ribbon with Two Stars; Presidential Unit Citation. Mem: Nat. Automobile Dealers Asn; Mason, Shrine; Am. Legion; VFW; Rotary Int. Rel: Presbyterian. Mailing Add: 120 Walnut Lane, Elkton, Md. 21921. (1967)

WILLIAMS, FRED D
Mo. State Rep.
b. Columbus, Miss, 7/6/35; m. Oct. 1956 to Etta Prather; c. Anthony, Archell, Candace, Ursula and DeEldra. Educ: Hubbard Bus. Col; Univ. Mo. Polit. & Govt. Pos: Block chmn, Dem. Party, St. Louis, Mo, 4 terms; mem. and employ. chmn, West-End Neighborhood Adv. Cmt; mem, West-End Commun. Conf. and 26th Ward Beautification Cmn; area chmn. for poverty prog; precinct capt, 28th Ward Dem. Orgn, former secy. and head precinct capt; mem, 25th and 26th Wards Dem. Orgn; Mo. State Rep, 68-, mem. atomic energy and indust. develop, fed-state rels. and labor cmts, Mo. House Rep. Bus. & Prof. Pos: Prod. planner, McConnell Douglas Corp, 12 years. Mil. Serv: Marine Corps, 52, Korea. Mem: Mason (Master, former jr. warden). Rel: Methodist. Mailing Add: 5621 Chamberlain Ave, St. Louis, Mo. 63112.

WILLIAMS, G. MENNEN D
b. Detroit, Mich, 2/23/11; s. Henry Phillips Williams and Elma Mennen W; m. 6/26/37 to Nancy Lace Quirk; c. G. Mennen, Jr; Nancy Quirk (Mrs. Theodore Ketterer, Jr) and Wendy; grandchildren, G. Mennen Williams, III, Lee Ann Monroe Williams, and Julia Quirk Ketterer. Educ: Princeton Univ, A.B, 33; Univ. Mich. Law Sch, J.D, 36; Phi Beta Kappa; Order of the Coif; Phi Delta Phi; Quadrangle Club; Liberal Club; Phi Gamma Delta. Hon. degrees, Wilberforce Univ, Lawrence Inst. Tech, Mich. State Univ, Univ. Liberia, Univ. Mich, Aquinas Col, St. Augustine's Col, Ferris Inst, West. Mich. Univ. and Lincoln Univ. Polit. & Govt. Pos: Mem. social security bd, Social Security Admin, 36-37; asst. attorney gen, Mich, 37-38; exec. asst. to U.S. Attorney Gen, 39-40; mem. criminal div, U.S. Dept. Justice, 40-41; exec. asst. to Gen. Counsel, Off. Price Admin, 41, dep. dir. for Mich, 46-47; mem, Mich. Liquor Control Cmn, 47-48; Gov, Mich, 49-61; chmn. nationalities div, Dem. Nat. Cmt, 54-61, v.chmn, 55-61 and mem. adv. coun, 57-61; Secy. of State for African Affairs, U.S. Dept. of State, 61-66, U.S. Ambassador, Republic of the Philippines, 68-69. Bus. & Prof. Pos: Mem, Griffiths, Williams & Griffiths, Law Firm, Mich, 48. Mil. Serv:

Entered Navy, 42, released as Lt. Comdr, 46, after serv. in Fast Carrier Task Forces and Strategic Bombing Survey, Japan; 10 Battle Stars; Legion of Merit with Combat V; 3 Presidential Unit Citations; Pac, Philippine and Am. Campaign Ribbons. Publ: A Governor's Notes, Univ. Mich, 61. Mem: Fed, Mich. and Detroit Bar Asns; Mason; Eagles; Elks; Moose; Nat. Grange; Amvets; Am. Legion; VFW; Am. Vets Cmt; Navy Club; Res. Officers Asn; SAR; Ahepa; Steuben Soc; Edelweiss; Univ. Club of Detroit; Detroit Country Club; various sportsmen's and conserv. orgns. Grand Officer, Order of Orange Nassau, Netherlands; Grand Comdr, Royal Order of Phoenix, Greece; Humane Band of African Redemption, Liberia; Polonia Restituta, Polish Govt. in Exile. Rel: Episcopal. Mailing Add: 25 Tonnancour Place, Grosse Pointe Farms, Mich. 48236.

WILLIAMS, GALE R
Ill. State Rep.
b. Ava, Ill, 8/3/22; m. 12/9/47 to Helen Falkenheim W. Educ: Trico High Sch. Polit. & Govt. Pos: Ill. State Rep. currently; coroner, Jackson Co, 56; former dist. gov, 25th Dist. Young Rep. Bus. & Prof. Pos: Owner, trailer sales bus. Mil. Serv: Marine Corps. Mem: Elks; Mason; Mississippi Valley Consistory; Ainad Temple; Eastern Star; Moose; Am. Legion. Rel: Baptist. Mailing Add: 1313 N. 16th Murphysboro, Ill. 62966.

WILLIAMS, GEORGE JOEL D
b. Axson, Ga, 12/16/02 (then McDonald); s. George W. Williams and Matilda Vickers W; m. 11/24/30 to Mary H. Ritchie; c. Rosemary, George Joel Jr. Educ: Ga. Normal Bus. Col, 26, 29. Polit. & Govt. Pos: Ga. State Rep, 59-66. Bus. & Prof. Pos: Farmer; former sch. teacher; pres, bd. of dir. of Farmers Mutual Exch. Corp, 10 years. Mem: Trustee and chmn. Satilla High Sch. Rel: Missionary Baptist; chmn. bd. deacons. Mailing Add: Axson, Ga. 31624. (1967)

WILLIAMS, GEORGE 'WHITEY' R
Chmn, Shelby Co. Rep. Orgn, Ill.
b. Shelbyville, Ill, 1/6/93; s. Asa Wilse Williams and Margaret Dannenbarger W; m. 1/27/20 to Nellie Frances Stewardson; c. Frances Evelyn, Dorothy Jane and Kathryn Ann. Educ: Sparks Bus. Col, 11-13. Polit. & Govt. Pos: Mem. staff, Attorney Gen. Off, Ill, 30-32, with Dept. of Pub. Safety, 41, investr, Mines and Minerals, 41-42; supt, Parks and Memorials, 42-49 and supvr, Liquor Control Cmn, 53-61; chmn, Shelby Co. Rep. Orgn, 34- and precinct committeeman, 44-; mem, Shelbyville City Coun, 14 years; pres, Shelby Co. Airport Authority, 54-; mem, Ill. Rep. State Cent. Cmt, currently. Bus. & Prof. Pos: Salesman, Moore Decorating Co, St. Louis, Mo, 13-18 and Seck DeVault Paint Co, Springfield, Ill, 50-52; owner, painting and decorating co, Shelbyville, Ill, 20-41. Mil. Serv: Pvt, Army, 18-19; serv. in Co. B-335th Inf, 84th Div, tranferred to Co. H-363rd Inf, 91st Div. in the Argonne Forest then to Belgium Drive; 2nd Lt, Army Res, 19-23. Mem: Mason; Moose; Past Comdr. and charter mem, Am. Legion; Past Comdr, VFW and 40 Hommes Et. 8 Chevaux. Rel: Presbyterian. Mailing Add: 610 West North Third St, Shelbyville, Ill. 62565. (1967)

WILLIAMS, GLEN MORGAN R
Mem, Va. State Rep. Cent. Cmt.
b. Jonesville, Va, 2/17/20; s. Hughy May Williams and Hattie Hines W; m. 11/17/62 to Jane Slemp; c. Janet Susan, Judith Ann, Rebecca Lynn and Melinda Jane. Educ: Milligan Col, A.B; Univ. Va, LL.B; The Raven Soc; Order of the Coif; Delta Theta Phi; Va. Law Rev. Polit. & Govt. Pos: State v.chmn, Young Rep. of Va, 48; commonwealth attorney, Lee Co, Va, 48-52; dist. chmn, Ninth Dist, Rep. Party, 50; Va. State Sen, 54; del, Rep. Nat. Conv, 60 & 68; U.S. Cmnr, Cumberland Gap Nat. Hist. Park, 63; cong. cand, Ninth Dist, Va, 64; chmn, Lee Co. Rep. Cent. Cmt, 64-; mem, Va. State Rep. Cent. Cmt, 68- Bus. & Prof. Pos: Pres, Lee Farmer's Warehouse, Inc, 52-65. Mil. Serv: Entered as A/S, Navy, 42, released as Lt.(sg), 46, after serv. as Commanding Officer, USS Seer, Pac; Atlantic Theater Ribbon; Mediterranean Theater Ribbon with Two Stars; Pac. Theater Ribbon with One Star; Citation from Comdr. Minecraft, Pac. Fleet. Mem: Pres, Lee Co. Bar Asn, 65; Am. Legion; 40 et 8; Powell Valley Shrine Club, Cyrene Commandery 21, RAM; Lions; Lee Players; PTA. Rel: Disciples of Christ. Mailing Add: P.O. Box 6, Jonesville, Va. 24263.

WILLIAMS, GORDON OLIVER R
b. Sunderland, Mass, 10/30/25; s. Walter Roberts Williams and Ruth Louise Clark W; m. 8/15/59 to Mary Lou Belden; c. Darryl Ladd, David Clark, Brian Oliver and Mary Ruth. Educ: Calif. State Polytech. Col, B.S, 63. Polit. & Govt. Pos: State appointed mem, Hatfield Housing Authority, Mass, 67-; chmn, Hatfield Rep. Town Cmt, 68-69. Mem: Farm Bur; New Eng. Milk Producers Asn. Rel: Protestant. Legal Res: 9 Depot Rd, Hatfield, Mass. 01066. Mailing Add: Box 5, North Hatfield, Mass. 01066.

WILLIAMS, GRANVILLE OLIVER R
Okla. State Sen.
b. Mutual, Okla, 2/2/07; s. Edward Paul Williams and Elizabeth Scheirman W; m. 3/12/31 to Lois A. Greene; c. Joe E, Karen (Mrs. Laubhan) and J. Douglas. Educ: Okla. State Univ, 23-24. Polit. & Govt. Pos: Okla. State Sen, Dist. 28, 64-, Woodward-Woods Co, 62-64; del, Rep. Nat. Conv, 68. Bus. & Prof. Pos: Owner, G.O. Williams Auto Co. and G.O. Williams Oil Co, 39- Mem: Woodward C. of C; Farm Bur. and others. Golf. Rel: Methodist. Mailing Add: 1718 Cedar, Woodward, Okla. 73801.

WILLIAMS, HARRISON ARLINGTON, JR. D
U.S. Sen, N.J.
b. Plainfield, N.J, 12/10/19; m. 1948 to Nancy S. McGlone; c. Nancy, Peter, Wendy, Jonathan and Nina. Educ: Oberlin Col, A.B, 41; Columbia Law Sch, LL.B, 48; Georgetown Univ. Sch. of For. Serv. Hon. LL.D, Rutgers Univ, 60. Polit. & Govt. Pos: U.S. Rep, N.J, 53-56; U.S. Sen, N.J, 58-; del, Dem. Nat. Conv, 68. Bus. & Prof. Pos: Attorney-at-law, N.J. Mil. Serv: Naval Res, pilot, 4 years. Mem: N.J. Tercentenary Celebration Cmn, Woodrow Wilson Mem. Cmt; Adv. Cmn. Unitarian Layman's League; N.J. Bar Asn; exec. cmt, Dem. Nat. Cmt. Nationalities Div; Elks. First Recipient Father Raymond A. McGowan Award, Nat. Coun. for the Spanish Speaking, 63. Rel: Presbyterian. Legal Res: 231 Elizabeth Ave, Westfield, N.J. 07090. Mailing Add: U.S. Senate Bldg, Washington, D.C. 20510.

WILLIAMS, HENRY LEE R
b. Richmond, Va, 4/29/35; s. Lunsford A. Williams and Ruth Puckett W; m. 6/29/56 to Beverly Fleer; c. Debbie Jean and Lynder Lee. Polit. & Govt. Pos: Chmn, Chesterfield Co. Rep. Cmt, Va, 66-68. Bus. & Prof. Pos: Pres, Shelter-All of Va. Inc, 64. Mem: Lions; past pres, Chester Jaycees; pres, Chester Civic Asn; pres, Curtis PTA. Rel: Lutheran. Mailing Add: 10 Oakland St, Chester, Va. 23831. (1967)

WILLIAMS, HOWARD DALE R
Okla. State Rep.
b. Baxter Springs, Kans, 6/30/32; s. Onie Monroe Williams (deceased) and Dora Ison W; m. 12/17/55 to Betty Jean Marks; c. Howard Dale, II and Linda LuJean. Educ: Northeast. Okla. A&M Jr. Col, 50-51; Baylor Univ, 52-54; Am. Canoe Asn. Polit. & Govt. Pos: Okla. State Rep, Dist. 78, 64- Bus. & Prof. Pos: Pres, Cord Automobile Int. and dir, South. Equitable Life Ins. Co, currently. Rel: Southern Baptist. Mailing Add: 1924 S. Lakewood Ave, Tulsa, Okla. 74112. (1967)

WILLIAMS, JAMES B, JR. R
Chmn, Carroll Co. Rep. Cmt, Miss.
b. Memphis, Tenn, 2/16/30; s. James Barney Williams and Volney Williamson W; m. 12/28/57 to Katharine George Saunders; c. James Barney, III and Katharine Elizabeth. Educ: Univ. Miss, B.A, 52, M.A, 59; Beta Theta Pi. Polit. & Govt. Pos: Chmn, Carroll Co. Rep. Cmt, Miss, 64- Mil. Serv: Entered as 2nd Lt, Army, 52, released as 1st Lt, 54, after serv. in Eighth Army, Korea, 53-54; Capt, Army Res; Commendation Ribbon; Korea Presidential Unit Citation. Mem: Miss. Educ. Asn; Rotary; Am. Legion. Rel: Episcopal. Legal Res: Cotesworth, North Carrollton, Miss. 38947. Mailing Add: P.O. Box 165, North Carrollton, Miss. 38947.

WILLIAMS, JAMES BAIRD D
Mem, Calif. Dem. State Cent. Cmt.
b. Vandervoort, Ark, 7/27/13; s. John Williams and Martha Ann Harbison W; m. 3/19/33 to Arlene Blankenship; c. Lynda Gay (Mrs. Jack M. Tipton) and Judith Ann (Mrs. David J. Spence). Educ: San Antonio Col, 31-33; Sul Ross State Col, 34. Polit. & Govt. Pos: Dem. cand. for Calif. State Assemblyman, 33rd Assembly Dist, 68; mem, Fresno Co. Dem. Cent. Cmt, Calif, 68-; mem, Calif. Dem. State Cent. Cmt, 68-; econ. develop. officer, Model Cities Prog, Fresno, 69- Bus. & Prof. Pos: V.pres, Balfour, Guthrie & Co. Ltd, San Francisco, 55-66; exec. secy, Calif. Egg Coun, 66-67. Mem: F&AM. Rel: Methodist. Legal Res: 5440 Columbia Dr, S, Fresno, Calif. 93727. Mailing Add: City Hall, Fresno, Calif. 93721.

WILLIAMS, JAMES W. D
Mo. State Rep.
b. St. Joseph, Mo, 11/10/20; m. Dec. 48 to Anita F. Hurst; c. Sandra Kay and Barbara Jo. Educ: Platt Bus. Col. Polit. & Govt. Pos: Charter mem, Buchanan Co. Young Dem. Club, Mo; Mo. State Rep, 58-, chmn, Cmn. Motor Vehicle and Traffic Regulations, mem. Appropriations Cmt. and Legis. Research Cmt, Mo. State House of Rep. Bus. & Prof. Pos: Route salesman, Pearl Brewing Co, St. Joseph, Mo. Mil. Serv: Army Air Corps, 3 years. Mem: AF&AM; Scottish Rite; Shrine; Eastern Star; Eagles; Am. Legion. Rel: Methodist. Mailing Add: 2010 N. Fourth St, St. Joseph, Mo. 64505.

WILLIAMS, JEANETTE K. D
Exec. Bd. Mem, Wash. State Dem. Cent. Cmt.
b. Seattle, Wash, 6/11/17; d. Dr. Louis Herman Klemptner and Olga Krelova K; m. 8/8/42 to David Houston Williams; c. Patricia Ellen and George Frederick. Educ: Univ. Wash, B.A, 37; Am. Conservatory of Music, B.M, Violin, 38, M.M, Violin, 39, M.M, Composition, 40; Sigma Alpha Iota; Phi Mu. Polit. & Govt. Pos: Exec. bd. del, King Co. Dem. Cent. Cmt, Wash, 60, v.chmn, 61-62 and chmn, 63-64, 65-66 & 67-68; exec. bd. mem, Wash. State Dem. Cent. Cmt, 67-68 & 69-; del. and mem. Platform Cmt, Dem. Nat. Conv, 64 & 68; pub. rels. chmn, Wash. State Fedn. Dem. Women's Clubs, 69. Bus. & Prof. Pos: Performing musician, dir. and arranger from Chicago to Los Angeles, 38-42. Mem: Musicians Union; Urban League; League of Women Voters; 46th Dist. Dem. Precinct Orgn; City Wide Dem. Womens' Club; Young Women's Dem. Club; Bus. and Prfnl. Women. Rel: Protestant. Mailing Add: 7132 58th N.E, Seattle, Wash. 98115.

WILLIAMS, JENNIE WINONA R
b. Sheridan Co, Wyo, 5/13/94; d. Allen Williams and Nina Condit W; single. Educ: Grinnell Col, 16-17; Univ. Colo, A.B, 23; Univ. Calif, Berkeley, summer, 24; Univ. Denver, M.A, 32. Polit. & Govt. Pos: State high sch. inspector, Wyo. State Dept. of Educ, 25-29; precinct committeewoman, Ucross, 42-55, Sheridan, 57-60; v.chmn, Sheridan Co. Rep, Cent. Cmt, 60-68; mem, Gov. Cmt. on Educ, 62-63; del, Rep. Nat. Conv, 64. Bus. & Prof. Pos: Chmn. Eng. Dept, Sheridan Col, 58-67; mem, State Libr, Archives and Hist. Bd, 67- Mem: Farm Bur; DAR; Am. Asn. Univ. Women; Wyo. State Hist. Soc; Am. Legion Auxiliary; Nat. pres, Home Demonstration Coun, Nat. Exten. Homemakers' Coun, 52-54. Rel: Presbyterian. Mailing Add: 410 S. Main St, Sheridan, Wyo. 82801.

WILLIAMS, JOE D
b. Seymour, Mo, 10/26/14; s. Asbury Williams and Ida Daughtery W; m. 11/16/52 to Daisy Lee Denney. Polit. Pos: Del, Dem. Nat. Conv, 64. Bus. & Prof. Pos: Owner, Williams Grain & Mfg. Co, at present. Mem: Mason. Rel: Methodist. Mailing Add: 706 S. Potter, Gettysburg, S.Dak. 57442. (1967)

WILLIAMS, JOHN BELL D
Gov, Miss.
b. Raymond, Miss, 12/4/18; s. Gnaves Kelly Williams and Maude E. Bedwell W; m. 10/12/44 to Elizabeth Ann Wells; c. Marcia Elizabeth, John Bell and Kelly Wells. Educ: Hinds Jr. Col, 36-38; Univ. of Miss; Jackson Sch. of Law, LL.B, 40. Polit. & Govt. Pos: Prosecuting attorney, Hinds Co, Miss, 44-46; U.S. Rep, Miss, 47-67; Gov, Miss, 68- Bus. & Prof. Pos: Attorney-at-law. Mil. Serv: Army Air Corps, 41-44. Mem: Miss. State Bar Asn; Am. Legion; VFW; Air Forces Asn; Lions. Rel: Baptist. Legal Res: Raymond, Miss. 39154. Mailing Add: State Capital Bldg, Jackson, Miss. 39205. (1967)

WILLIAMS, JOHN CORNELIUS, JR. D
S.C. State Rep.
b. Spartanburg, S.C, 11/9/38; s. John Cornelius Williams, Sr. and Clare

Dowling Williams Marr; m. 8/22/64 to Lucia Counsell Moir; c. Mary Stewart and Meredith Dowling. Educ: Wofford Col, A.B, 60; Univ. S.C. Law Sch, LL.B, 64; Sigma Alpha Epsilon. Polit. & Govt. Pos: S.C. State Rep, 69- Mil. Serv: Entered as Pvt, Marine Corps Res, 60, released as Cpl, 65; Sharpshooter with rifle. Mem: S.C. and Spartanburg Co. Bar Asns; S.C. Trial Lawyers Asn; AFM; Mason (32°); Shrine; Lions; Phi Delta Phi; Spartanburg Co. Young Dem. Rel: Episcopal. Mailing Add: 400 Lake Forest Dr, Spartanburg, S.C. 29302.

WILLIAMS, JOHN JAMES R
U.S. Sen, Del.
b. Frankford, Del, 5/17/04; s. Albert Frank Williams and Anna Hudson W; m. 5/4/24 to Elsie E. Steele; c. Blanche (Mrs. Baker) and grandchildren, Janet Rae McCarty, Lora W. Baker and Holly A.Baker. Educ: Frankford High Sch. Polit. & Govt. Pos: U.S. Sen, Del, 47- Bus. & Prof. Pos: Grain bus. Mem: Mason; Shrine; Rotary. Rel: Methodist. Legal Res: Millsboro, Del. 19966. Mailing Add: 2213 New Senate Office Bldg, Washington, D.C. 20510.

WILLIAMS, JOHN RICHARD 'JACK' R
Gov, Ariz.
b. Los Angeles, Calif, 10/29/09; s. James Maurice Williams and Laura LaCossitt W; m. 6/5/42 to Vera May; c. Rick, Michael Maurice and Nikki. Educ: Phoenix Jr. Col. Polit. & Govt. Pos: Pres, Phoenix Housing Authority, Ariz, 44-47; councilman, Phoenix, 53-54, mayor, 56-60; Gov, Ariz, 67-; del, Rep. Nat. Conv, 68. Bus. & Prof. Pos: Dir, Radio Sta. KOY, 29-; secy-treas, Key Investment Co, KOY, Inc; former dir, Radio Sta. KTUC, Tucson; former newspaper columnist, Phoenix Gazette. Mem: Phoenix Jr. C. of C.(pres, 46); Lions; Kiva Club; Cloud Club; Ariz. Club; Phoenix Press Club; Exec. Club; White Mt. Country Club. Phoenix Man of the Year Award, 53. Rel: Episcopal. Mailing Add: 2323 N. Central, Phoenix, Ariz. 85004.

WILLIAMS, JOHN TAYLOR R
b. Bemis, Tenn, 8/13/11; s. Oliver M. Williams (deceased) and Annie Williamson W; m. 12/25/33 to Thelma Lucille Argo; c. John T, Jr. and Richard H. Educ: Lambuth Col, 31-32; Univ. Tenn. Exten. Course, Cert. Indust. Eng, 43; SA, Lambuth Col. Polit. & Govt. Pos: Mayor, Trezevant, Tenn, 45-47; U.S. Marshal, West. Dist. Tenn, Memphis, 55-60; Rep. nominee, U.S. House Rep, 68. Bus. & Prof. Pos: Ins. broker, 45-55 & 61-; sales mgr, Diversified Securities, Memphis, Tenn, 60-61; v.pres, First U.S. Corp, 61. Mil. Serv: Nat. Guard. Mem: Tenn. Bankers Asn; Lions; Young Bus. Men's Club (past pres); C. of C.(past pres); Outstanding Sales Award; Salesman of the Year; and Salesman of the Month Award; President Awards for Outstanding Sales. Rel: Methodist. Mailing Add: 955 Reddoch Cove, Memphis, Tenn. 38117.

WILLIAMS, JOSEPH P. D
Mayor, Metropolis, Ill.
b. Brownfield, Ill, 1/10/12; s. Frank D. Williams and Millie McCool W; m. 3/14/31 to Ola Evelyn Travelstead; c. Betty Jo (Mrs. Joe Bowman), Billy Eugene, Kenneth P, Roma (Mrs. Weatherford) and Shelia Ann (Mrs. Steve Woodward). Educ: Metropolis Commun. High Sch, 1 year. Polit. & Govt. Pos: Mayor, Metropolis, Ill, 57- Mil. Serv: Entered as Pvt, Army, 44, released as Pfc, 45, after serv. in Med. Corps, Ninth Serv. Command; Sharpshooter Medal. Mem: Am. Legion, Lions; United Brotherhood of Carpenters. Rel: Protestant. Mailing Add: 106 W. Fifth St, Metropolis, Ill. 62960.

WILLIAMS, JOSEPH RULON D
State Auditor, Idaho
b. Samaria, Idaho, 4/14/04; s. Lewis Williams and Sara Morse W; m. 8/18/30 to Eva Lauraine Gyllenskog; c. Joseph Roger, Bruce, Linda Lou (Mrs. Root), Susan Jolaine (Mrs. Winkler), Neal Morse, Milton Lee and Kristin May. Educ: Univ. Idaho, 25-29; Int. Corresponding Sch, 32; Sigma Chi. Polit. & Govt. Pos: Chmn, Ada Co. Dem. Party, Idaho, 32-48; state pres, Young Dem. Idaho, 46, nat. committeeman, Young Dem, 47; dep. state auditor, Idaho, 41-47, state auditor, 59-; postmaster, Boise, 48-52. Bus. & Prof. Pos: Real estate broker, Boise, 47- Mem: Kiwanis; Boy Scouts; Nat. Asn. State Auditors, Comptrollers and Treas.(v.pres); Nat. Conf. of State Soc. Security Adminstr. (nat. secy). Rel: Latter-day Saint. Mailing Add: 801 N. 20th, Boise, Idaho 83702.

WILLIAMS, KENNETH OGDEN D
Miss. State Rep.
b. Clarksdale, Miss, 1/18/24; s. Peter Fairley Williams and Robbie Mae Casey W; m. 6/14/69 to Frances Lott; c. Frances. Educ: Vanderbilt Univ, Nashville, Tenn, B.A, 49; Phi Delta Theta. Polit. & Govt. Pos: Miss. State Rep, 60-; del, Dem. Nat. Conv, 56-60. Mil. Serv: Entered as Pvt, Army, 43, released as Sgt, 46, after serv. in Hq. Bty, 91st Observation Bn, Field Artil, ETO, 16th Corp, Ninth Army, 44-46; Bronze Star; Three Battle Stars. Mem: VFW; Am. Legion; Delta Coun; Planters Club. Rel: Baptist. Legal Res: 620 Oakhurst Ave, Clarksdale, Miss. 38614. Mailing Add: P.O. Box 729, Clarksdale, Miss. 38614.

WILLIAMS, LaVERGNE HOBART R
b. Wells Co, Ind, 8/22/96; s. Thomas E. Williams and Elizabeth Hines W; m. 11/26/46 to Mary Tylanda; c. LaVergne E. Educ: High Sch. Polit. & Govt. Pos: Conn. State Rep, 49-67. Bus. & Prof. Pos: Research, Gunver Mfg, 57-66; sales mgr, The National Cash Register Co, 23-46. Mem: Mason; Grange; City Club of Hartford; Avon Country Club; Columbia Lions. Rel: Methodist. Mailing Add: Collins Rd, Columbia, Conn. 06327. (1967)

WILLIAMS, LAWRENCE G. R
U.S. Rep, Pa.
b. Pittsburgh, Pa, 9/15/13; m. to Margery; c. Kathy and James. Educ: Drexel Inst. of Tech. Polit. & Govt. Pos: U.S. Rep, Pa, 66-; Springfield Twp. Cmnr, 52-66; pres, Bd. of Cmnrs; Del. Co. rep. to Pa-Jersey Transportation Study, Southeast Pa. Transportation Authority and Del. Valley Regional Planning Cmn. Bus. & Prof. Pos: Asst. to v.pres. of mfg, Curtis Pub. Co. Mil. Serv: Army Air Corps. Mem: Past pres, Pa. State Asn. of Twp. Cmnrs; Am. Legion. Mailing Add: 56 S. Brookside Rd, Springfield, Pa. 19064.

WILLIAMS, LEE D
b. Denver, Colo, 7/7/25; s. Floyd Lee Williams and Effie Lingo W; m. 10/14/45 to Vickie Strohmaier; c. Floyd Lee, III. Educ: Univ. Ark, LL.B, 53; Omicron Delta Kappa; Gamma Delta; Delta Theta Phi. Polit. & Govt. Pos: Admin. asst. to U.S. Sen. J.W. Fulbright, Ark, currently. Bus. & Prof. Pos: Attorney-at-Law, Fayetteville, Ark, 53-55. Mil. Serv: Entered as Pvt, Army, 44, released as S/Sgt, 47, after serv. in ETO; ETO Ribbon with Bronze Battle Star; Europe-African-Middle East. Ribbon; Am. Theater Ribbon; Victory Medal; Army of Occupation Medal. Mem: Ark. Bar Asn; Nat. Press Club; U.S. Senate Asn. of Admin. Assts. Rel: Lutheran. Legal Res: Fayetteville, Ark. 72701. Mailing Add: 7215 Burtonwood Dr, Alexandria, Va. 22307.

WILLIAMS, LEROY, JR. D
Chmn, Ohio Co. Dem. Cent. Cmt, Ind.
b. Rising Sun, Ind, 9/24/21; s. Clifford Leroy Williams and Leola Fry W; m. 1/25/47 to Clara Beatrice Browning; c. Kenneth Lee, Connie Lou, Sandra, Karen Sue and Sharon Ann. Educ: Rising Sun Schools, 12 years. Polit. & Govt. Pos: Precinct committeeman, Rising Sun Dem. Party, Ind, 12 years; councilman, Rising Sun, 10 years; co. cmnr, Ohio Co, 7 years; chmn, Ohio Co. Dem. Cent. Cmt, 66- Mem: Mason; Am. Legion; Nat. Farmers Orgn. Rel: Church of Christ. Mailing Add: R.R. 2, Dillsboro, Ind. 47018.

WILLIAMS, LUKE GLADSTONE, JR. R
b. Spokane, Wash, 10/4/23; s. Luke Campbell Williams and Grace Murray W; m. 10/19/47 to Beuletta Nordby; c. Brenda Louise and Mark Edward. Polit. & Govt. Pos: City councilman, Spokane, Wash, 62-; state chmn, Citizens for Goldwater, 64; former v.chmn, Wash. State Rep. Finance Cmt. Bus. & Prof. Pos: Pres, Williams Bros. Mfg. Co, 48-, Am. Sign & Indicator Corp, 58- and Electronic Mfg. Co, 61- Mil. Serv: Entered as A/S, Navy, 42, released as Torpedoman 2/C; 46, after serv. in S.Pac. Mem: Asn. Wash. Industs. (pres); Bd. Nat. Asn. Mfgs; Mason (32°); Shrine. Rel: Presbyterian. Mailing Add: 931 Comstock Court, Spokane, Wash. 99203.

WILLIAMS, LYNN ALFRED D
b. Chicago, Ill, 1/6/09; s. Lynn Alfred Williams and Helen Harvey W; m. 9/12/32 to Dora du Pont; c. Eve (Mrs. Noonan), Ann (Mrs. Jennett), Lynn A, III, Dora (Mrs. Keller) and Susan (Mrs. Lenfestey). Educ: Yale Univ, A.B, 29; Harvard Univ, LL.B, 32; Mass. Inst. Tech, spec. student, 32-33. Polit. & Govt. Pos: Dem. cand. for U.S. Rep, 64; committeeman, New Trier Dem. Orgn, Ill, 66- Bus. & Prof. Pos: Secy, Stewart-Warner Corp, 38-42, v.pres, 42-47; pres, Great Books Found, 47-48, chmn, 48-; v.pres, Univ. Chicago, 48-51; pres, Anocut Eng. Co, 54- Mailing Add: 1175 Whitebridge Hill, Winnetka, Ill. 60093.

WILLIAMS, MARSHALL BURNS D
S.C. State Sen.
b. Norway, S.C, 1/17/12; s. C.H. Williams and Maude Metts W; m. to Margaret Shecutt; c. Burns, Ann, Mary Ashley and Charles. Educ: Univ. S.C, B.S, 33; LL.B, 36. Polit. & Govt. Pos: S.C. State Rep, 47-52; S.C. State Sen, 53- Bus. & Prof. Pos: Lawyer and farmer. Mil. Serv: Lt. Comdr, Navy Air Corps, 42-46. Mem: Pres, S.C. Young Dem. Clubs, 39-40. Mailing Add: Box 316, Orangeburg, S.C. 29115. (1967)

WILLIAMS, MATT R
b. Magdalena, N.Mex, 5/15/41; s. Frank Williams and Eleanor Lockwood McClintock W; single. Educ: N.Mex. Mil. Inst, 60. Polit. & Govt. Pos: Chmn, Catron Co. Rep. Cent. Cmt, N.Mex, 65-68. Bus. & Prof. Pos: Rancher, 60- Mil. Serv: Pvt, Army, 62; Sgt, N.Mex. Nat. Guard, 66- Mem: N.Mex. Farm and Livestock Bur. Rel: Protestant. Mailing Add: P.O. Box 192, Quemado, N.Mex. 87829. (1967)

WILLIAMS, MELBA RUTH D
b. Cullman, Ala; d. William Claiborne Jones and Rebecca McGill J; m. 10/21/44 to Harry Bixler Williams, Jr; c. Harry Bixler, III and Randolph Claiborne. Educ: Ala. Col, B.S, 42; Univ. N.C, grad. study in pub. admin, 46-47; Mortar Bd; Kappa Delta Pi; Sigma Alpha Sigma; Publ. Bd. Res; Pi Tau Chi; Alpha Lambda Delta; Lambda Sigma Pi; LeCercle Francias. Polit. & Govt. Pos: Mem, Montgomery Co. Personnel Bd, Md, 58-59; precinct v.chmn, Montgomery Co. Dem. Party, 58-59; chmn, DeKalb Dem. Club, 61-62; v.chmn. and secy, DeKalb Co. Dem. Exec. Cmt, 62-68; mem, Ga. Dem. Exec. Cmt, 62-; del. and mem. credentials cmt, Dem. Nat. Conv, 64, del, 68; mem, Ga. Cmn. on Status of Women, 64-; v.chmn. and mem, Ga. State Elec. Bd, 64- Bus. & Prof. Pos: Personnel officer and res. assoc, Tenn. Valley Authority, 44-46; teacher, DeKalb Co, Ga, 49-50; asst. dir. pub. rels, Presbyterian Church, 50-52; research, Atlanta Area Metrop. Planning Cmn, 61-62 and Bell and Stanton, Pub. Rels, 65-66; consultant to Secy. of State, Ga, 67-68; conf. coordinator, Inst. of Govt. and Continuing Educ. Center, Univ. Ga, 68-69. Publ: 'Handbook for Georgia Voter Registrars,' 'Handbook for Georgia Election Officials' and 'Handbook for Georgia Municipal Election Officials,' Secy. of State and Inst. of Govt, Univ. Ga, 68. Mem: Pub. Admin. Asn; PTA; Ga. Fedn. of Women's Clubs; Sorosis of Athens. Rel: Methodist. Mailing Add: 620 Forest Rd, Athens, Ga. 30601.

WILLIAMS, MURRELL DWAYNE R
Chmn, Eighth Rep. Cong. Dist, Mo.
b. Grovespring, Mo, 9/24/23; s. William McKinley Williams and Ethel Lee Perryman W; m. 4/7/46 to Marilyn May Glass; c. Deanna May, Karen Jane, Brenda Merle and Zelma Lee. Educ: Morgan High Sch, Mo. Polit. & Govt. Pos: Treas, Laclede Co, Mo, 47-51; chmn, Laclede Co. Rep. Cent. Cmt, 60-; chmn, Eighth Rep. Cong. Dist, 64- Mil. Serv: Entered as Pvt, Army, 44, released as Sgt, 46, after serv. in Armoured Inf. Training Unit, Ft. Knox, Ky. Mem: Am. Legion; Odd Fellows; Kiwanis; Laclede Co. Rep. Club. Rel: Baptist. Mailing Add: 451 Harwood Ave, Lebanon, Mo. 65536. (1967)

WILLIAMS, NAT McDONALD, JR. D
Chmn, Thomas Co. Dem. Exec. Cmt, Ga.
b. Thomasville, Ga, 4/14/27; s. Nat McDonald Williams and Vivian Bowers W; m. 12/2/50 to Peggy Lucas; c. Ann, Mac, Joan and Jim. Educ: Marion Inst, 43-45; U.S. Naval Acad, 45-47; Univ. N.C, B.S. in Chem, 49; Phi Beta Kappa; Kappa Alpha Order. Polit. & Govt. Pos: Chmn, Thomas Co. Dem.

Exec. Cmt, Ga, 64-; mem, Thomasville Sch. Bd, 65-, chmn, 69- Bus. & Prof. Pos: Pres, Scat Oil Co, 58-, Interstate Enterprises, 59- Mil. Serv: Entered as Midn. 4/C, Navy, 45, released as Midn. 3/C, 47 after serv. in U.S. Rel: Methodist. Legal Res: Pine Tree Blvd, S.W, Thomasville, Ga. 31792. Mailing Add: P.O. Drawer 649, Thomasville, Ga. 31792.

WILLIAMS, NEIL A. R
Chmn, Osage Co. Rep. Party, Kans.
b. Lyndon, Kans, 7/14/32; s. Clifford H. Williams and Grace M. Lindsay W; m. 11/26/50 to Lo-Ree N. White; c. Gary N, Bruce A, Kent B. and Kimberley R. Educ: Lyndon Pub. Schs, 12 years. Polit. & Govt. Pos: Chmn, Osage Co. Rep. Party, Kans, 68- Bus. & Prof. Pos: Owner and mgr, Williams Motor Co, Lyndon, Kans, 50- Mem: C. of C; Lyndon Housing Proj. Rel: Methodist. Legal Res: 304 W. Eighth, Lyndon, Kans. 66451. Mailing Add: P.O. Box 252, Lyndon, Kans. 66451.

WILLIAMS, NORMA OTTEY D
b. Washington, D.C, 2/26/14; d. Reginald Charles Ottey and Lillie House O; m. 1/27/40 to Henry G. Williams. Educ: Miner Teachers Col, 31-33; Bus. Sch. Polit. & Govt. Pos: Admin. asst, Civilian Aide to Secy. of War, 41-44; secy, admin. asst. to Secy. Commerce, 47-50; admin. aide, Nat. Selective Serv. Syst, 51-54; admin. asst. to U.S. Rep. William L. Dawson, 54- Rel: Lutheran. Mailing Add: 1632 South St. N.W, Washington, D.C. 20009.

WILLIAMS, ODD R
b. Kansas City, Mo, 9/2/26; s. Russell Dick Williams and Mary Elizabeth Gossard W; m. 6/10/53 to Jonell Ashcraft; c. Lynn, Kimberly, Dick Clifton, Evan and Russell Ashcraft. Educ: Univ. Kans, B.S. in Bus, 49, J.D, 52; Sigma Chi; Phi Delta Phi. Polit. & Govt. Pos: Kans. State Rep, 57-64, speaker pro tem, Kans. House of Rep, 63-64, mem, Kans. Legis. Coun, 63-64; alternate del, Rep. Nat. Conv, 60; mem. exec. cmt, Gov. Econ. Develop. Cmt, 63-64; mem, Kans. Constitutional Rev. Cmn, 63-64; finance chmn, Douglas Co. Rep. Cent. Cmt, 64-; legis. liason for Gov. of Kans, 65-66; del. and mem. rules cmt, Rep. Nat. Conv, 68. Bus. & Prof. Pos: Co-chmn, John Outland Scholarship Fund, Univ. Kans, 49-, nat. chmn, Greater Univ. Fund, 65-66, dir, Univ. of Kans. Athletic Bd, 66- and mem. and chmn, Coun. for Progress, Univ. Kans, 67-69; dir, Douglas Co. State Bank, 52-, H.D. Lee Co, Shawnee Mission, 66-, Lawrence, Kans. Indust. Develop. Corp, 66- and Center for Research and Indust, Inc, Lawrence, Kans, 68- Mil. Serv: Entered as 2nd Lt, Air Force, 52, released as 1st Lt, 54, after serv. at Maxwell Air Force Base, Montgomery, Ala. and Manzando Air Force Base, Albuquerque, N.Mex, 52-54. Mem: Kans. Bar Asn; Kansas City Club; Topeka Country Club; Lawrence, Kans. Country Club; Rotary; Elks; Am. Legion. Man of the Year, Jr. C. of C, Lawrence, Kans, 62; pres, Kans. Day, 65-66. Rel: Protestant. Legal Res: 700 California St, Lawrence, Kans. 66044. Mailing Add: Box 530, Lawrence, Kans. 66044.

WILLIAMS, PAT D
Mont. State Rep.
b. Helena, Mont, 10/30/37; s. Shelton Williams and Elizabeth Keough W; m. 6/10/65 to Carol Ann Griffith; c. John Griffith. Educ: Univ. Mont, 56-58; William Jewell Col, 58-59; Univ. Denver, B.S, 61; West. Mont. Col, grad. work, 62. Polit. & Govt. Pos: Pres, Silver Bow Co. Young Dem, Mont, 62-64; del, Dem. State Conv, 64; regional v.pres, Young Dem, 64-65 and mem. state exec. cmt, 65-66; mem, state speakers bur, Mont. Dem. Orgn, 64-; Mont. State Rep, 66- Bus. & Prof. Pos: Elementary teacher, Butte, Mont, 63- Mil. Serv: Entered as Pvt. E-1, Nat. Guard, 61; released as Sgt, E-5, 67. Rel: Roman Catholic. Mailing Add: 1728 Thornton, Butte, Mont. 59701. (1967)

WILLIAMS, PATRICK NEHEMIAH D
Chmn, Dem. Party, V.I.
b. Christiansted, St. Croix, V.I, 9/28/28; s. Norman Williams and Ingerborg Cassimeer W; m. 12/21/51 to Inex Maria Byron; c. Glenice Ingerborg, Sharon Maria, Lindel Alphonso, Wayne, Patrice-Ann, Patrick Maurice and Raymond Jerome. Educ: High Sch, Grad, 59. Polit. & Govt. Pos: V.I. State Sen, 63-65; consult, V.I. Legis, 65-; chmn, Dem. Party, V.I, 66-; mem, Traffic & Safety Cmn, 66-; chmn, Voc. & Tech. Educ, 67-; v.chmn, Cmn. Aging, 67-; v.chmn, Comprehensive Health Planning, 67-; del, Dem. Nat. Conv, 68; chmn, Bd. Pub. Educ. TV, 69; Bus. & Prof. Pos: Mgr, Alexander Hamilton Supply and Hardware, 59-60; mgr, Abramson's Enterprises, 60; asst. store mgr, Merwin Hardware Inc, 60-62. Mil. Serv: Entered as Pvt, Marine Corp, 51, released as Cpl, 53, after serv. in second Med. Bn; Second Marine Div. Mem: Boy Scouts (exec. cmt); Navy League U.S. (first v.pres, St. Croix Chap); Am. Voc. Asn. Rel: Catholic. Legal Res: Estate Grove Place, St. Croix, V.I. 00850. Mailing Add: P.O. Box 22, Kingshill, St. Croix, V.I. 00850.

WILLIAMS, PAUL E. D
b. Pike Co, Mo, 9/1/23; m. 8/22/48 to Harriet Marie Rollins; c. Nita Sue, Mary Lou, Paul Rollins, Karen Lynn. Educ: Univ. Mo, Columbia, A.B, 52, LL.B, 53. Polit. & Govt. Pos: Judiciary prosecuting attorney, Pike Co, Mo, 55-62; Mo. State Rep, 62-66, v.chmn, Cmt. Higher Educ, mem, Cmt. on Agr, and Cmt. on Fees and Salaries, Mo. State House of Rep. Bus. & Prof. Pos: Practicing attorney; admitted Mo. Bar, 53. Mil. Serv: Air Force, 43-45, Mid-west Pac. Theater. Mem: Elks; Lions; Am. Legion. Rel: Presbyterian. Mailing Add: Bowling Green, Mo. 63334. (1967)

WILLIAMS, ROBERT D
b. Graceville, Fla, 3/30/19; m. to Josephine Josey; c. Robert, Kay and Linda. Educ: Univ. Fla, B.S.E, 40. Polit. & Govt. Pos: Fla. State Rep, 60-62; Fla. State Sen, 62-66. Bus. & Prof. Pos: Research Analyst for Fla. Legis. Ref. Bur. Mil. Serv: Army, 43-46; Spec. Training Unit OSC, Served Overseas in AFWESPAC. Mem: Past zone chmn, pres, dir. and secy, Lions; Jackson Co. C. of C; bd. dir, Sch. Adv. Bd; PTA; Gramer Develop. Corp; secy, Jackson Co. Develop. Coun; past bd. dir, Jackson Co. Develop. Coun. Rel: Methodist; Past Chmn, Bd. of Stewards; Teacher, Men's Bible Class. Mailing Add: 1210 Walton Dr, Tallahassee, Fla. 32303. (1967)

WILLIAMS, ROBERT D. D
b. Armona, Calif; m. to Evelyn Whitman; c. Robert Jr, Jack and Mike. Educ: Fresno State Col, A.B, 39. Polit. & Govt. Pos: Calif. State Sen, 60-66; chmn, Kings Co. Bd. of Supvr. Bus. & Prof. Pos: Businessman. Mil. Serv: Vet. Mem: Elks; Kiwanis; Am. Legion; past mem, Nat. Ment. Health Adv. Coun; Salvation Army Adv. Coun; former chmn, Kings Co. March of Dimes; past pres, San Joaquin Valley Supvr. Asn. 1967 Legal Res: Hanford, Calif. No mailing address available. (1967)

WILLIAMS, ROBERT KELSEY D
Chmn, Wabash Co. Dem. Cent. Cmt, Ill.
b. West Salem, Ill, 1/19/19; s. Forrest Lake Williams and Rozella Kelsey W; m. 9/18/53 to Virginia Josephine Nagy; c. Verlin Eugene and Jeannine Rochelle. Educ: Bone Gap High Sch, Ill, grad. Polit. & Govt. Pos: Dem. committeeman, Precinct Six, Mt. Carmel, Ill, 66-; chmn, Wabash Co. Dem. Cent. Cmt, 68-; investr, Ill. Commerce Cmn, 68- Mil. Serv: Entered as Pvt, Army Air Force, 43, released as Cpl, 46, after serv. in Second Air Force, Am. Theatre, 32 months. Mem: Am. Legion (Past Comdr, Post 423, Mt. Carmel); VFW; Civitan Int.(Lt. Gov, Midwest Dist. and pres, Mt. Carmel Club). Rel: Protestant. Legal Res: 903 Pear St, Mt. Carmel, Ill. 62863. Mailing Add: Box 135, Mt. Carmel, Ill. 62863.

WILLIAMS, ROD D
b. Louisville, Ky, 10/8/37; s. James Dudley Williams and Gladys Marie Hopkins W; m. 9/10/66 to Marlene Marie Martin; c. James Michael. Educ: Bakersfield Jr. Col, A.A, 61; San Francisco State Col, B.A. in Polit. Sci, 63; Hastings Col. Law, LL.B. and J.D, 66; Alpha Gamma Sigma; Phi Sigma Alpha; Phi Alpha Delta. Polit. & Govt. Pos: Del, Dem. Nat. Conv, 68. Bus. & Prof. Pos: Partner, Young, Wooldridge, Paulden, Self & Williams, 66- Mem: Kern Co, Am. and Calif. Bar Asns; Am. Trial Lawyers; Jr. C. of C; March of Dimes; Kern Co. Ment. Health Asn; Elks. Rel: Protestant. Mailing Add: 2429 Bay St, Bakersfield, Calif. 93301.

WILLIAMS, SMALLWOOD EDMOND D
V.Chmn, Dem. Cent. Cmt, D.C.
b. Lynchburg, Va, 10/17/07; s. Mary Broadus; m. 5/16/28 to Verna Lucille Rapley; c. Smallwood, Jr. (deceased), Pearl, Wallace and Yvonne. Educ: Terrell Law Sch; Howard Univ. Sch. Relig; Am. Bible Col, B.D, 48. Hon. D.D, 49 & 50. Polit. & Govt. Pos: Mem, Dem. Cent. Cmt, D.C, 54-64, v.chmn, 64-; mem, President's Cmt. on Relig. Resources in Ment. Retardation; del, Dem. Nat. Conv, 64. Bus. & Prof. Pos: Presiding Bishop, Bible Way Church of Our Lord Jesus Christ World Wide, 57; chmn, Apostolic Interorganizational Fel, 63-; co-chmn, Cmt. on Race Rel. Interrelig; chmn, Golden Rule Apts, Inc, 66. Mem: NAACP; chmn, D.C. Chap, South. Christian Leadership Conf, 62-65; Wash. Urban League; Wash. Home Rule Cmt. Selected for Afro-Am. Newspaper Roll of Honor, Wash, D.C, 47; Washington's Most Prominent Radio Minister, 44; won trip around world as most popular radio minister, Afro-Am. Newspaper Poll, 43. Rel: Bible Way Church of Our Lord Jesus Christ World Wide. Legal Res: 4720 16th St, N.W, Washington, D.C. 20011. Mailing Add: 1130 New Jersey Ave, N.W, Washington, D.C. 20001.

WILLIAMS, SQUIRE NEEDHAM D
b. Frenchburg, Ky, 11/8/17; s. Squire Needham Williams and Mary Lee Spencer W; m. 8/24/46 to Doris Macauley; c. Janice Lee, Squire N, III, Laura Macauley and Kathryn Doris. Educ: Univ. Ky, A.B, 39, LL.B, 42; Pi Sigma Alpha; Sigma Chi. Polit. & Govt. Pos: Asst. Attorney Gen, Ky, 48-54; judge pro-tem, Franklin Co, 56-57; spec. circuit judge, 57-59; judge, Court of Appeals of Ky, 59-69. Mil. Serv: Entered as Midshipman, Navy, 42, released as Ens, 45, after serv. in Naval Aviation, S. Pac. Mem: Am. and Ky. Bar Asns; VFW. Rel: Presbyterian. Mailing Add: 120 West Todd St, Frankfort, Ky. 40601.

WILLIAMS, THAYNE S. R
b. Mt. Vernon, Ind, 9/7/96; married; c. two daughters. Educ: Purdue Univ. Polit. & Govt. Pos: N.H. State Rep, until 67. Bus. & Prof. Pos: West. Elec. Co.(retired). Mil. Serv: World War I, 18-19. Mem: Tel. Pioneers; Mason. Rel: Protestant. Mailing Add: Eaton Center, N.H. 03832. (1967)

WILLIAMS, THOMAS HENDRIX D
b. Autryville, N.C, 3/18/16; s. Nathan Thomas Williams and Penny Jackson W; m. 1/29/44 to Shirley Leidich; c. Holly Gayle (Mrs. David Owen) and Terry Hendrix. Educ: Campbell Col, 36; Elon Col, AB Business, 38; Wake Forest Univ, LL.B, 41; Univ. of Ariz, 44. Polit. & Govt. Pos: Spec. agent, Fed. Bur. Invest, 41-43 & 46-50; clerk, Superior Court and judge, Juvenile Court, Cumberland Co, N.C, 56-62; chmn, Cumberland Co. Dem. Party, 64-68; alternate del, Dem. Nat. Conv, 68. Bus. & Prof. Pos: Attorney, Fayetteville, N.C, 50-56 & 63- Mem: Exchange Club Fayetteville. Mailing Add: 1033 Bragg Blvd, Fayetteville, N.C. 28301.

WILLIAMS, THOMAS MARVIN, SR. D
b. Mena, Ark, 2/15/90; married. Polit. & Govt. Pos: Co. agent, State Exten. Serv, Miss; agr. develop. agent; Miss. State Sen, 52-68. Bus. & Prof. Pos: Merchant; employee, Mo. Pac. R.R. Mem: Past pres, State Exten. Workers Asn; Mason; Rotary. Rel: Methodist. Mailing Add: Box 210, Lexington, Miss. 39095. (1967)

WILLIAMS, W. WALTER R
b. Monroe Co, Iowa, 12/30/94; s. Alfred Williams and Ada Johnson W; m. 7/7/58 to Ruth Garrison; c. Walter B, Marjorie (Mrs. Myers) and Judy (Mrs. Zimmerman). Educ: Univ. Wash, B.S, 16; Parsons Col, Hon. Doctorate, 56, Pac. Univ, 66; Phi Beta Kappa; Tau Beta Pi; Phi Lambda Upsilon; Phi Delta Kappa; Sigma Chi. Polit. & Govt. Pos: Chmn, Wash. State Defense Coun, 41-45; chmn, Wash. State Rep. Party, 51; nat. chmn, Citizens for Eisenhower-Nixon, 52; Under Secy. of Commerce, U.S. Govt, 53-58; finance chmn, Wash. State Rep. Cmt, 59-60; chmn, Gov. Adv. Cmt, Dept. of Commerce and Econ. Develop, 64-67; v.chmn, Nat. Rep. Finance Cmt, 66-68; alternate del, Rep. Nat. Conv, 68. Bus. & Prof. Pos: Pres. and chmn. bd, Continental Inc, Seattle, Wash, 27- Mil. Serv: Pfc, Army, 17, released in 18, after serv. in Aviation Sect, Signal Corps, Chem. Warfare Serv. and Air Ground Sch, Univ. Calif. Squadron 55. Mem: Rainier Club; Harbor Club; Wash. Athletic Club. Seattle First Citizen Award and others. Rel: Congregational. Legal Res: 2035 Parkside Dr. E, Seattle, Wash. 98102. Mailing Add: Continental, Inc, 701 Second Ave, Seattle, Wash. 98104.

WILLIAMS, WALTER BAKER R
Wash. State Sen.
b. Seattle, Wash, 5/12/21; s. W. Walter Williams and Anna W; m. 7/6/45 to Marie Davis Wilson; c. Kathryn, Marcia, Bruce and Wendy. Educ: Univ. Wash, B.A, 43, Harvard Law Sch, LL.B, 48; Phi Beta Kappa; Alpha Delta Phi. Polit. & Govt. Pos: Chmn, 43rd Dist. Rep. Orgn, Wash, 58-60; Wash. State Rep, 61-63; Wash. State Sen, 63- Bus. & Prof. Pos: Partner, Bogle, Bogle & Gates, 60-63; pres, Continental, Inc, 63- Mil. Serv: Entered as Yeoman 2/C, Naval Res, 42. released as 1st Lt, Marine Corps Res, 46; Pac. Theater Ribbon; Presidential Unit Citation. Mem: Seattle, Wash. State and Am. Bar Asns; Mortgage Bankers Asn. of Am; Seattle Rotary Club; Seattle-King Co. Munic. League; World Affairs Coun. Rel: Congregational. Mailing Add: 3871 45th Ave. N.E, Seattle, Wash. 98105.

WILLIAMS, WALTER J. D
Chmn, McLennan Co. Dem. Party, Tex.
b. Christoval, Tex, 11/27/00; s. Thomas Z. Williams and Clara Tuttle W; m. 12/12/25 to Lucy Sue Abney; c. Lucille (Mrs. Brigham). Educ: Baylor Univ, B.A; M.A; Univ. Mich, Ph.D; Sigma Xi. Polit. & Govt. Pos: Chmn, McLennan Co. Dem. Party, Tex, 62- Bus. & Prof. Pos: Prof. math. and chmn. dept, Baylor Univ, 37- Mem: Am. Asn. for Adv. Sci; Am. Math. Soc; Am. Astronomical Soc. Rel: Baptist. Legal Res: 902 Speight Ave, Waco, Tex. 76706. Mailing Add: Mathematics Dept, Baylor University, Waco, Tex. 76703.

WILLIAMS, WILLIAM EDWARD R
b. Washington C.H, Ohio, 5/30/25; s. Edward L. Williams and Marie Bushong W; m. 10/11/47 to Jane Mark; c. Gregory, Wendi and Mark. Educ: Univ. Cincinnati, B.S. in archit, 52; Scarab. Polit. & Govt. Pos: Alternate del, Rep. Nat. Conv, 64; v.pres, Rep. Club of Fayette Co, Ohio, 66- Bus. & Prof. Pos: Dir, Wash. Develop. Corp, 60- and Commun. Improv. Corp, 63-64. Mil. Serv: Entered as A/S, Naval Res, 43, released as Aerographer's Mate 3/C, 46, after serv. on U.S.S. Chaffee and U.S.S. Midway, Atlantic, 44-46; 2nd Lt, Air Force Res, 52; Atlantic Theater and Am. Theater Serv. Ribbons; Good Conduct Medal. Mem: Assoc. Gen. Contractors of Am; v.pres, Ohio Jr. C. of C, 59-60; pres, Wash. Court House Jaycees, 56-67; pres. and dir, Wash. Court House C. of C, 62-64; U.S. C. of C; Ohio Info. Cmt; Am. Legion; life mem. and sen. 2334, Jr. Chamber Int; Rotary Int; League of Ohio Sportsmen; Buckeye State Sheriffs Asn; Nat. Rifle Asn. Rel: Methodist; trustee and bd. mem. Mailing Add: R.R. 2, Washington C.H, Ohio 43160.

WILLIAMS, WILLIAM FREDERICK R
Mem, N.C. State Rep. Exec. Cmt.
b. Rutherfordton, N.C, 12/17/21; s. John Hampton Williams and Maude Hardin W; m. 12/23/51 to Eva Mae Beam; c. Pamela Kay and Tina Gail. Educ: Bowling Green Col. of Commerce, B.A, 49. Polit. & Govt. Pos: V.chmn, Rutherford Co. Rep. Exec. Cmt, N.C, 46-48, chmn, 66-; mem, N.C. State Rep. Exec. Cmt, 56-60 & 66-; mem, Rutherfordton Planning Cmn, 60-; del, Rep. Nat. Conv, 64. Bus. & Prof. Pos: Gen. off. mgr, Excelsion Mills, Inc, Union, S.C, 53-62; controller, Doncaster Collar & Shirt Co, Rutherfordton, 59-62; secy. and controller, Deering Milliken Serv. Corp, Spartanburg, S.C. 62-65; from admin. asst. to v.pres. and gen. mgr, Magnolia Finishing Plant, Pacolet Indust, Inc, Blacksburg, S.C. 66- Mil. Serv: Entered as Pvt, Army, 42, released as S/Sgt, 46, Mem: Former chap. dir, Nat. Asn. of Accts; Am. Legion; Kiwanis; Rutherfordton Golf Club. Rel: Presbyterian. Mailing Add: 310 Tanner St, Rutherfordton, N.C. 28139.

WILLIAMS, WILLIAM G. R
Mont. State Rep.
b. Missoula, Mont, 6/12/27; s. John F. Williams and Alice W. Preston W. (deceased); m. 4/27/51 to LaRee Leatham; c. Cathy June, David L, Dennis W, Robin Kaye and Michelle Marie. Educ: High sch. Polit. & Govt. Pos: Mont. State Rep, 65- Bus. & Prof. Pos: Ranch mgr, 54-59. Mil. Serv: Entered as A/S, Navy, 44, released as Fireman 2/C, 45. Mem: Mont. Farm Bureau; Am. Legion; Townsend Rodeo Asn. Rel: Latter-day Saint. Mailing Add: Toston, Mont. 59643. (1967)

WILLIAMS, WILLIAM MARCUS D
Ga. State Rep.
b. Hazelhurst, Ga, 1/16/10; m. 1/09/32 to Jessie Deane Glaze; c. William Roger, Beverly Patricia, Carol Deane and Virginia Diane; grandchildren, Richard Michael, Mary Kathleen and William Marcus. Educ: Hazelhurst High Sch, 27. Polit. & Govt. Pos: Secy, Hall Co. Dem. Exec. Cmt, Ga, 48-54; Ga. State Rep, 55-56 & 59- Bus. & Prof. Pos: Secy-treas, Bell Petroleum Co; Shell Jobbers. Mem: Mason. Rel: Baptist. Mailing Add: 1628 Thomson Bridge Rd, Gainesville, Ga. 30501. (1967)

WILLIAMS, WILLIAM VAN R
Co. Chmn, Rep. Party, Ala.
b. Greenville, Ala, 12/8/25; s. John Robbins Williams and Myra L. Ware W; m. to Nell Langford; c. Sara Catherine and James Brittain. Educ: Auburn Univ; Birmingham South. Col. Polit. & Govt. Pos: Co. chmn, Rep. Party, Ala. Mil. Serv: Entered as Pvt, Marines, 44, released as Lt, 45, after serv. in Okinawa and Korea. Mem: Lions; Am. Legion; Farm Bur; Police Res. Rel: Baptist. Mailing Add: P.O. Box 368, Greenville, Ala. 36037.

WILLIAMS, WILTON ALBERT D
b. Monroe, N.C, 5/30/10; s. Wilton Alexis Williams and Lillian Marsh W; m. 4/28/33 to Edith Belk; c. Sarah W.(Mrs. Harrelson), Sybil W.(Mrs. Gore), Dr. Larry A. and Samuel. Educ: Wingate Jr. Col, N.C; Wake Forest Col; Appalachian State Col. Polit. & Govt. Pos: Mayor, Tabor City, 46-52; judge, Columbus Co, N.C, 58- Mem: Rotary; Mason; Shrine, Sudan Temple. Rel: Baptist. Mailing Add: 107 E. Fifth St, Tabor City, N.C. 28463. (1967)

WILLIAMS, YORK W, JR. R
b. Gourd, Ark, 10/24/29; s. Rev. York W. Williams, Sr.(deceased) and Lillie Rucker W; m. 8/20/53 to Cloteal Emerson; c. Carl Keith and Thalya Beata. Educ: Morris-Booker Mem. Sch, Dermott, Ark, Dipl, 46; Ark. A.M. and N. Col, A.B. in Econ, 56; Univ. Colo, M.A. in Econ, 61; Southwest. Baptist Theol. Sem, 64; Alpha Kappa Mu; Sigma Rho Sigma. Polit. & Govt. Pos: Mem, exec. cmt, Ark. State Rep. Party, 68-69; mem. adv. coun, Ark. Coun. on Commun. Serv. and Continuing Educ, 68-69; Rep. cand. Ark. House Rep, 69. Bus. & Prof. Pos: Mem. exec. bd, Ark. Coun. Human Rels; bd. dirs, Chicot Mem. Hosp. Bd; pres. and founder, Dermott Commun. Planning Orgn; pres, Morris Booker Baptist Col, 11 years; teacher, Lincoln Co. Schs, 3 years; pastor, Rose Hill Baptist Church, 5 years; bd. trustees, Ark. A.M. and N. Col, 1 year. Publ: Articles in Ark. Teachers Asn. Bul, Nat. Baptist Sunday Sch. Informer, Nat. Baptist Voice and Quart. Rev. Higher Educ. Among Negroes. Mem: Chicot Co. Teacher Asn; Dist. One Teachers Asn.(pres, 4 years); Ark. and Am. Teachers Asns; Nat. Educ. Asn; Nat. Asn. Sec. Sch. Prin; Dist. One Adminstr. Asn.(v.pres); Ark. Educ. Asn.(exec. cmt, 1 year). Rel: Baptist, Trustee, St. Paul Baptist Church; mem, Ark. and Nat. Baptist Conv. Mailing Add: 200 N. Drew, Dermott, Ark. 71638.

WILLIAMSON, ALLEN D
Okla. State Rep.
b. Ripley, Okla, 12/20/09; s. Armstead R. Williamson and Ida D. W; m. to Margaret Adele McKinley; c. Charles F. Foster (stepson). Educ: Okla. State Univ; Cent. State Teachers Col; Sigma Phi Epsilon. Polit. & Govt. Pos: Okla. State Rep, Dist. 33, 66-, chmn. Subcmt. Revenue and Taxation. Bus. & Prof. Pos: Teacher, Rural Sch, Cushing, Okla, 32-42; landman, Thomas N. Berry & Co, 54-57. Mil. Serv: Entered Seabees, 42, released as Gunners Mate 1/C, 45, after serv. in 572nd Unit, S.Pac. Mem: Landman's Asn; Independent Oil Producers Asn; Am. Petrol. Inst; C. of C; Rotary; Okla. Consistory; Shrine. Rel: Methodist. Mailing Add: 940 E. Cherry St, Cushing, Okla. 74023.

WILLIAMSON, ARTHUR W. D
N.C. State Rep.
b. Cerro Gordo, N.C, 11/6/12; s. Marshall Edcar Williamson and Annie Bell W; m. 1/20/62 to Catherine Price Rothrock; c. Five. Educ: Wake Forest Col, 29. Polit. & Govt. Pos: Chmn, Columbus Co. Bd. of Cmnrs, N.C, 40-50 and Columbus Co. Bd. of Educ, 53-54; mem, Columbus Co. Bd. of Health, 44-47 and Columbus Co. Bd. of Welfare, 45-50; dist. supvr, U.S. Census, Seventh Cong. Dist, 50; N.C. State Sen, 55 & 59; N.C. State Rep, 61- Bus. & Prof. Pos: Farmer; fertilizer dealer. Rel: Baptist. Mailing Add: Chadbourn, N.C. 28431. (1967)

WILLIAMSON, BLAKE ARTHUR R
Kans. State Rep.
b. Edwardsville, Kans, 7/24/01; s. Roy Chadwick Williamson and Minnie Kuhu W; m. 8/39/27 to Ruth Imogene Belknap; c. Edith Rae (Mrs. Brocku) and Betsy Gail (Mrs. Dwight Chattaway). Educ: Kans. Univ, J.D, 23; Phi Alpha Delta. Polit. & Govt. Pos: City attorney, Edwardsville, Kans, 28-42; asst. co. counsr, Wyandotte Co, Kans, 29-31 and co. counsr, 31-33; mem, Legis. Coun, 31-45; attorney, State Bd. of Med. Registrn. and Exam, 32-42 and State Civil Serv. Bd, 47-; Kans. State Rep, 36th Dist, 35-41 and 45-; v.chmn, State Bd. of Welfare, 49-54. Bus. & Prof. Pos: V.pres, Kans. Valley R.R, 54-60; pres, Midwest Investors, 60-; secy-treas, Wyandotte Investors, Inc, 61-; chmn. bd. dirs, Fidelity State Bank, 65- Mil. Serv: Entered as Capt, Army, 42, released as Lt. Col, 46, after serv. in Judge Adv. Gen. Dept, Am. Theatre and ETO; Legion of Merit. Publ: Various articles, Kans. Bar J, 47-60. Mem: Wyandotte Co. Bar Asn.(pres, 39-40); pres, Wyandotte Co. Heart Asn, 41-42; Kans. and Am. Bar Asns; Am. Judicature Soc; fel, Am. Col. Trial Lawyers; Mason; Shrine (past potentate); Am. Legion; 40 et 8; C. of C. Citation, Kans. Welfare and Ment. Health Asn; Citation, Kans. Asn. of Blind; Commun. Leader of Am, 68. Rel: Protestant. Mailing Add: 1865 Edwardsville Dr, Edwardsville, Kans. 66022.

WILLIAMSON, ERNEST WILFERT D
Mem. Exec. Cmt, Shelby Co. Dem. Party, Tenn.
b. New Albany, Miss, 7/18/21; s. George Williamson and Della Story W; m. 9/10/41 to Ruby Ann Tuggle; c. Gwendolyn Alfredia, Ernest Wilfert, Jr. and George Keith. Educ: Am. Theol. Sem, B.Th, 49; Le Moyne Col, Tenn, A.B, 52; Fisk Univ, M.A, 61. Polit. & Govt. Pos: Del, Dem. Nat. Conv, 68; counsr, State Div. of Juvenile Probation, Tenn, 68-69; mem, State Employ. Security Coun, 68-; mem. exec. cmt, Shelby Co. Dem. Party, 69- Bus. & Prof. Pos: Pres, Minister's Mutual Fel, 66- Mil. Serv: Entered as Pvt, Army, 43, released as T/Sgt, 45, after serv. in 656th Ord. Ammunition Co, ETO. Mem: Pres, 26th Ward Civic Club, 60-61; Mason; F&AM; Elks; NAACP; South. Christian Leadership Conf. Col, Gov. Staff, Tenn, 68. Rel: Baptist; Pastor. Mailing Add: 1392 Melrose Cove, Memphis, Tenn. 38106.

WILLIAMSON, EUGENE THOMAS DFL
b. Minneapolis, Minn, 11/29/31; s. Ingvald Williamson and Ethel Bement W; m. 9/27/58 to Virginia McCoy; c. Thomas, Terri, David and Diane. Educ: N.Dak. State Univ, B.S, 53; Univ. Minn. Law Sch, LL.B, 58; Phi Delta Phi; Scabbard and Blade; Univ. Minn. Dem-Farmer-Labor, Int. Rels. Club; Independent Students Asn. Polit. & Govt. Pos: Mem, N.Dak. Young Dem, 52-53; mem, Minn. Young Dem-Labor-Farmer Party, 55-58; mem, Second Ward, Dem-Labor Farmer-Labor Club, Minneapolis, 55-59; spec. Munic. Judge, Int. Falls, 60-63; precinct chmn, Koochiching Co. Dem-Farmer-Labor Party, 60-66 and chmn, 65-68; del, Eighth Cong. Dist. and Minn. State Dem-Farmer-Labor Conv, 60-68; co. attorney, Koochiching Co, 63-; mem, City Planning Bd. and Libr. Bd. Bus. & Prof. Pos: Assoc, Robins, Davis & Lyons, St. Paul, Minn, 58-59; attorney-at-law, 59- Mil. Serv: Entered as 2nd Lt, Army, 53, released as 1st Lt, 55, after serv. in Eighth Inf. Div, Fifth Army Area, U.S. Army Res, 3 years. Mem: Am, Minn, 15th Dist. and Koochiching Co. Bar Asns; Am. Legion; Mason; Falls Citizens Scholarship Found. Rel: Protestant. Legal Res: 923 Riverside Dr, International Falls, Minn. 56649. Mailing Add: Box 171, International Falls, Minn. 56649.

WILLIAMSON, JO C. D
b. Urbana, Ill, 3/27/09; s. Francis E. Williamson and Etta Mae Creamer W; m. 3/17/34 to Meryl Sanders; c. Jo Ann (Mrs. Higgs) and Donald F. Educ: Univ. Ill, A.B, 31 and LL.B, 33; Theta Chi; letter winner, Tribe of the Illini. Polit. & Govt. Pos: Secy, to U.S. Rep, 37-38; dir, attorney, Off. Price Admin. Rent Control, 43-45; del, Dem. Nat. Conv, 64 & 68; former asst. attorney gen, Ill. Mem: Ill. State and Am. Bar Asns; dir, Champaign Co. Bar Asn, 64; pres, Urbana Rotary Club, 57; chmn, Champaign Co. Cancer Soc, 54 and Boy Scout Coun, 41; Torch; C. of C. Rel: Presbyterian. Mailing Add: 2022 Zuppke Circle, Urbana, Ill. 61801.

WILLIAMSON, JOHN C. D
b. Oskaloosa, Kans, 12/15/12; m. 3/17/45 to Laurel Jean Stewart W; c. Sally, John, Richard and Robert. Educ: Univ. Calif. Polit. & Govt. Pos:

Mem. bd. trustees, Fruitvale Elem. Sch. Dist, 49-59; chmn, Kern Co. Dem. Cent. Cmt, 54-58; Calif. State Assemblyman, until 66; asst. to pres, Sacramento State Col, 67; exec. dir, Joint Cmt. on Open Space Lands, 67- Bus. & Prof. Pos: Serv. sta. owner and operator. Mil. Serv: Infantry, 1st Lt. Mem: V.pres, Nat. Cong. of Petroleum Retailers, 55-56; pres, Calif. Gasoline Retailers, 52-53; Am. Legion; VFW; Lions; Security Lodge 581, F&AM. Rel: Congregational. Mailing Add: 328 Balboa Ave, Davis, Calif. 95616.

WILLIAMSON, ODELL D

b. Ash, N.C, 11/19/19; s. John Bun Williamson and Love W; m. 11/24/40 to Virginia Alma. Educ: Waccamaw High Sch. Polit. & Govt. Pos: N.C. State Rep, 47, 49, 53, 63-69. Bus. & Prof. Pos: Real estate developer; farmer; merchant. Mil. Serv: Capt, Field Artillery, Army, 42-45. Rel: Methodist. Mailing Add: Shallotte, N.C. 28459.

WILLIAMSON, RAYMOND DANIEL, JR. R

Mem, Calif. Rep. State Cent. Cmt.

b. San Francisco, Calif, 6/4/38; s. Raymond D. Williamson and Pauline Luby W; m. 11/9/63 to Carol Ann Munstermann; c. Raymond Daniel, Deborah Ann and Kevin Michael. Educ: Univ. San Francisco, B.S, 59; Kendrick Hall Sch. Law, Univ. San Francisco, J.D, 63; Phi Alpha Delta. Polit. & Govt. Pos: Pres, San Francisco Young Rep, Calif, 66; assoc. mem, San Francisco Co. Rep. Cent. Cmt, 66, 68 & 69; dep. city attorney, San Francisco, 66-; mem, Calif. Rep. State Cent. Cmt, 68- Bus. & Prof. Pos: Asst. trust officer, Wells Fargo Bank, San Francisco, Calif, 63-66. Mil. Serv: Entered as 2nd Lt, Army, 60, released as Capt, 67, after serv. in 91st Div, Army Res. Mem: State Bar of Calif; Bar Asn. of San Francisco; Barristers Club of San Francisco; bd. dir, San Francisco Civic League of Improv. Clubs; Vet. Polit. Coun. of San Francisco; Gleeson Libr. Assocs. Rel: Catholic. Mailing Add: 286 28th Ave, San Francisco, Calif. 94121.

WILLIAMSON, STANLEY H. R

N.H. State Rep.

b. East Providence, R.I, 6/29/19; married; c. Three. Educ: Boston Univ, A.B, 40, A.M, 41. Polit. & Govt. Pos: Trustee, Horizon's Edge Sch, N.H; former pres. bd. trustees, Hampshire Country Sch; former dir, Dartmouth-Lake Sunapee Region; mem, Goshen-Lempster Coop. Sch. Bd, Newport Area Sch. Study Cmt. and Goshen Budget Cmt; del, Rep. State Constitution Conv. and mem, Platform Cmt, 64; alternate del, Rep. Nat. Conv, 64; N.H. State Rep, 61- Bus. & Prof. Pos: Life underwriter. Mem: Former pres, Twin State Valley Underwriters Asn; former dir, N.H. Asn. of Life Underwriters; Sunapee and Goshen-Lempster Parents Club; troop committeeman, Goshen Boy Scouts; Civilian Pub. Serv, 41-45. Rel: Quaker. Mailing Add: Box 1, Wendell, N.H. 03783.

WILLIAMSON, WALTER EDWARD D

b. Magnolia, Ark, 11/10/07; s. Walter Otis Williamson and Willie Lee Merritt W; m. 6/8/41 to Sue Lee Harris; c. Walter Edward, Jr, Susanne (Mrs. Steven Barr), Sara Beth and James Thomas. Educ: Henderson State Col, A.B, 30; Garland Lit. Soc. Polit. & Govt. Pos: Circuit and chancery clerk, Columbia Co, Ark, 35-41; mayor, Magnolia, 55-57; chief clerk on Interstate and For. Commerce Cmt, U.S. House of Rep, 57- Bus. & Prof. Pos: Mgr, C. of C, Magnolia, Ark, 46-50; pres. and owner, Ford Chair Factory, 50-58. Mil. Serv: Entered as Pvt, Army, 42, released as Capt, 46, after serv. in Inf. Sch, Ft. Benning, Ga. and IRTC, Camp Fannin, Tex. Mem: Mason; Lions Int. (former Dist. Gov); Am. Legion. Rel: Methodist. Legal Res: Magnolia, Ark. Mailing Add: 2125 Rayburn Bldg, Washington, D.C. 20515.

WILLIS, DOYLE D

Tex. State Rep.

b. Kaufman Co, Tex, 8/18/08; s. Alvin Willis and Eliza Phillips W; m. 2/14/42 to Evelyn McDavid; c. Doyle Willis, Jr, Dan, Dina and Dale. Educ: Univ. Tex, Austin, B.A. and B.S, 34; Georgetown Univ. Law Sch, 4 years, LL.B; Theta Xi; Gamma Eta Gamma. Polit. & Govt. Pos: Tex. State Rep, Tarrant Co, 47-52 & 69-; Tex. State Sen, 52-62; City councilman, Ft. Worth, Tex, 63-64. Bus. & Prof. Pos: Attorney-at-law, Ft. Worth, Tex, currently. Mil. Serv: Enlisted in Mil. Intel. Engrs, 41, released as Maj, 46, after serv. in Asiatic-Pac. Theatre, 44-45; Bronze Star and 4 Battle Stars. Mem: Tarrant Co. and Tex. Bar Asns; VFW (Dept. of Tex. Comdr, 58-59); Am. Legion (Comdr. Bothwell Kane Post, 67-68); pres, ROA; Tarrant Co, Tex, 48-49. First v.pres, Tex. Jr. Bar Asn, 42-43. Rel: Methodist. Mailing Add: 3316 Browning Court, Fort Worth, Tex. 76111.

WILLIS, EDWIN EDWARD D

b. Arnaudville, La, 10/2/04; s. Olanda Willis and Julia Hardy W; m. 12/9/29 to Estelle Bulliard; c. Bob; foster child, Joseph A. Educ: Loyola Univ, New Orleans, La, LL.B, 26. Polit. & Govt. Pos: La. State Sen, 47-48; U.S. Rep, La, Third Cong. Dist, 48-69. Bus. & Prof. Pos: Attorney-at-Law, St. Martinville, La, 26-46. Mem: La. Bar Asn; Am. Judicature Soc; K. of C; Rotary (former pres, St. Martinville Rotary). Highest Award-Medallion of Patriotic Order Sons of Am. Rel: Roman Catholic. Legal Res: 420 N. Pinaud St, St. Martinville, La. 70582. Mailing Add: 422 S. Main St, St. Martinville, La. 70582.

WILLIS, GEORGE LEWIS D

b. Ashland, Ky, 9/17/23; s. Otis Willis and Sarah M. W; m. 6/29/51 to Carolyn Schnaitter; c. Kelley, Julia and Georgia. Educ: Ind. Univ, A.B, 48; Univ. N.C, M.A, 50; Ind. Univ, Ph.D, 53. Polit. & Govt. Pos: Exec. dir, Hamilton Co. Dem. Party, Ohio, 58-64; mem, Hamilton Co. Bd. of Elecs, 58-66; del, Dem. Nat. Conv, 60, alternate del, 64; chmn, 12th Ward Dem. Orgn, Cincinnati, 66-; precinct committeeman, Ward 12, Cincinnati; del, Wis. Dem. State Conv, 67-68 & 69. Bus. & Prof. Pos: Asst. prof. of polit. sci, Univ. Cincinnati, 54-58; vis. lectr. in pub. admin, Univ. Ky, 64-66; assoc. prof. of polit. sci, Wis. State Univ, Oshkosh, 66-68, chmn. dept, 68-69; prof. polit. sci, Univ. Toledo, Toledo, Ohio, 69- Mil. Serv: Entered as Pvt, Air Force, 43, released as 1st Lt, 46, after serv. in 322nd Bomb Sq, ETO, 44-45; Capt, Air Force Res; ETO Campaign Ribbon. Publ: 'Politics of 22nd Amendment,' West. Polit. Quart, 52; 'Electronic Vote Counting in a Metropolitan Area,' Pub. Admin. Rev, 3/66. Mem: Am. Soc. for Pub. Admin; Am. Polit. Sci. Asn. Rel: Methodist. Mailing Add: Department of Political Science, University of Toledo, Toledo, Ohio 43606.

WILLIS, J. THERON D

b. Columbia, La, 9/13/17; s. L. David Willis and Leola Meredith W; m. 6/19/43 to Olivia Coffie; c. Roger David, Mary Stephanie and John Geoffrey. Educ: La. Polytech. Inst; La. State Univ. Sch. Med, M.D, 42; Mayo Clinic, resident in surgery, 43-44 and 46-48. Polit. & Govt. Pos: Chmn, La. State Hosp. Bd, 64-; v.chmn, Gov. Cmn. on Medicare, 66; mem, Regional Cmt. on Heart, Cancer and Stroke. Bus. & Prof. Pos: Pres. staff, Baptist Hosp, 50-, St. Francis Cabrini Hosp, Alexandria, La, 56-; consult. in surg, Huey P. Long Mem. Hosp. Mil. Serv: Entered as 1st Lt, Army, 44, released as Capt, 46, after serv. as Chief Gen. Surg. and Asst. Chief Surg, Gen. Hosp. Center, Camp Edwards, Mass, 45-46. Publ: 'Fat Replacement in Lymph Nodes,' thesis for M.S. in surg, Univ. Minn. and Mayo Clin, 48. Mem: Am. Med. Asn; 2nd v.pres, La. State Med. Soc, 59-60, 1st v.pres, 62-63 and 64-66, mem, cmts. on legis. and pub. policy, 64-66, pres. elect, 66-67, pres, 67-68; Rapides Parish Med. Soc; La. Orgn. for State Legislators, 58-66. Rel: Episcopal. Legal Res: 1924 Marye, Alexandria, La. 71301. Mailing Add: 2417 Texas, Alexandria, La. 71301. (1967)

WILLIS, JAMES H. D

b. Wilburton, Kans, 6/9/25; s. George Willis and Clara Mae Watson W; m. to Nancy Leigh Hadley; c. Michelle Lynn, Nancy Marie, Lianna Jean (Mrs. Ken Crandell) and Jimmy Lee. Educ: Joplin Sr. High Sch, 4 years; Am. Sch, Chicago, Ill. Polit. & Govt. Pos: Pres, Young Dem. Club, Joplin, Mo, 48; treas, Jasper Co. Dem. Club, 49-50; Dem. committeeman, Tenth Precinct, Joplin, 50-60 & 62-68; chmn, West. Dist. 135 Dem. Party, 66-68; acting postmaster, Joplin Mo, 68-69. Bus. & Prof. Pos: Buyer, Christman's Dept. Store, Joplin, Mo, 48-56; sales mgr, Macy's Dept. Store, 56-69. Mil. Serv: Entered as Pvt, Army, 43, released as T/Sgt, 45, after serv. in 37th Inf. Div, Asia Pac, Philippines; Purple Heart; Bronze Star; Combat Inf. Badge with Three Battle Stars. Publ: 'Give Me Back Georgia,' Stars & Stripe, 44. Mem: Elks; Boy Scouts; Am. Legion (Past Post Comdr); VFW (Past Post Cmdr, Dist Comdr, State Inspector, State Chief Staff, State Judge Advocate, V.Chmn, Nat. Credentials); United Serv. Orgn; Joplin Soft Ball Cmn; United Fund; pres, March of Dimes Jasper Co. Rel: Protestant. Mailing Add: 706 N. Wall, Joplin, Mo. 64801.

WILLIS, KATHERINE R

Chmn, Van Buren Co. Rep. Cmt, Mich.

b. Chicago, Ill, 11/26/16; m. 6/6/36 to Frank Willis, Jr; c. Penny (Mrs. Padden), Bruce and Tara Kathleen. Educ: Ind. Univ, 1 year. Polit. & Govt. Pos: Mem, Fourth Dist. Rep. Cmt, 59-; v.chmn, Van Buren Co. Rep. Cmt, Mich, 62-68, chmn, 68-; pres, Rep. Women, 65-, state chmn, Rep. Women's Conf, Chicago, Ill, 67. Bus. & Prof. Pos: Homemaker. Mem: Bus. & Prfnl. Women's Asn; Eastern Star; v.chmn, PTA; secy, Zoning Bd; Paw Paw Hosp. Bd. Mailing Add: Route 1, Shaw Rd, Lawton, Mich. 49065.

WILLIS, RICHARD ROBINSON R

Secy-Treas, Fayette Co. Rep. Exec. and Cent. Cmts, Ohio

b. Ashville, N.C, 5/20/29; s. Richard Rochester Willis and Mary Haglen W; m. 2/19/49 to Gaynelle June Heath; c. David R, Dale H, Dawn M. and Douglas C. Educ: Denison Univ, 2 years; Beta Theta Pi. Polit. & Govt. Pos: Rep. presidential elector, 56; mem, Rep. Bd. of Elec, 57-63; officer, Young Rep. Club, 49-64; mem. finance cmt, Ohio Young Rep. Club, formerly, and Fayette Co. Rep. Exec. Cmt, 50; committeeman, Fayette Co. Rep. Cent. Cmt, 52-, v.chmn. and chmn; secy-treas, Fayette Co. Rep. Exec. and Cent. Cmts, currently. Bus. & Prof. Pos: Pres, Willis Ins. Inc, Washington Court House, Ohio, 49-69. Mem: Ohio Asn. of Ins. Agents Inc; bd. dirs, Midwest. Indemnity Ins. Co; Lions (past pres); Symposcarchs Buckeye Boosters, Inc; Elks; Eagles; Shrine; Mason. Rel: Baptist. Legal Res: 450 Rawlings, Washington Court House, Ohio 43160. Mailing Add: Box E, Washington Court House, Ohio 43160.

WILLIS, WILLIAM PASCAL D

Okla. State Rep.

b. Anadarko, Okla, 10/17/10; s. Robert Garnett Willis and Lulu Wyatt W; m. 9/19/36 to Zelma Bynum; c. Diane, Joyce, Billie Jean, Herbert, Zelma Marie, William, Jr. and Doak. Educ: E.Cent. State Col, B.A, 36; Tulsa Univ, M.A, 48; Pres, Int. Rels. Club, E.Cent. State Col, 35-36. Polit. & Govt. Pos: Mayor, Locust Grove, Okla, 38-44; Okla. State Rep, Fourth Dist, 58- Mil. Serv: Entered as Pvt, Army, 44, released as S/Sgt, 44, after serv. in 627th Field Artil. Mem: Mason; Shrine; Am. Legion; C. of C; Tahlequah Kiwanis; Cherokee Nat. Hist. Soc. Rel: Baptist. Mailing Add: 1 Valley, Tahlequah, Okla. 74464.

WILLITS, JOHN BIRDCELL D

Mem. Staff, Nat. Mediation Bd.

b. Huron, S.Dak, 8/30/21; s. John Birdcell Willits and Sarah Dunn W; m. 6/14/46 to Helen Louise Sperla; c. John, Elaine, Laura, Charles, Thomas, Julie, Vickie and Jane. Educ: Worsham Col, 45; Delta Pi Epsilon. Polit. & Govt. Pos: Del, Dem. Nat. Conv, 64; Mont. State Rep, 65 & 67; chmn, Cascade Co. Dem. Coord. Cmt, 66-; mem. staff, Nat. Mediation Bd, 62- Bus. & Prof. Pos: Cmnr, Boy Scouts, 62; state chmn, Trainmen's Polit. Educ. League, 66. Mil. Serv: Entered as Seaman, Coast Guard, 42, released as Seaman 1/C, 43, after serv. in Life Saving Serv. Mem: Cascade Co. Wildlife Asn; Brotherhood of R.R. Trainmen; Am. Legion; Eagles. Rel: Catholic. Legal Res: 1620 Fifth Ave. N, Great Falls, Mont. 59401. Mailing Add: 2823 Mosby St, Alexandria, Va. 22305.

WILLMARTH, DAVID GERARD D

Chmn, Wood Co. Dem. Cent. Cmt, Ohio

b. Toledo, Ohio 6/19/35; s. Gerard Ellsworth Willmarth and Helen Evelyn Munger W; m. 6/23/56 to Mary Lou Mallendick; c. Teri Lyn, Mark Stephen, Lori Ann, Michael David and Lisa Michele. Polit. & Govt. Pos: Pres, Wood Co. Dem. Club, Ohio, 62-66; pres, Wood Co. Young Dem, 63; secy, Wood Co. Dem. Exec. Cmt, 68-; chmn, Wood Co. Dem. Cent. Cmt, 68- Bus. & Prof. Pos: Asst. advert. dir, Sentinel-Tribune, Bowling Green, Ohio, 57-64; sales mgr, WAWR-FM Radio, 64-65; prod. supvr, Photo-Jour. Press, 65-68, West Toledo Herald, Toledo, 68- Mem: Northwest. Ohio Newspaper Asn; Soc. for Preservation and Encouragement of Barbershop Quartet Singing in Am, Inc; Toastmaster's Club. Rel: Reorganized Latter-day Saint; Ordained Minister. Mailing Add: 525 N. Prospect St, Bowling Green, Ohio 43402.

WILLNER, DON S. D
Ore. State Sen.
b. New York, N.Y, 5/22/26; s. Morris R. Willner and Beatrice Bergman W; m. 8/1/52 to Patience Durand; c. Jennifer Russell, Sarah Newlin, Anna Herrick and Rebecca Bennett. Educ: Harvard Col, A.B. magna cum laude, 48; Harvard Law Sch, LL.B, 51; Phi Beta Kappa. Polit. & Govt. Pos: Ore. State Rep, Multnomah Co, 57-59; Ore. State Sen, 63- Bus. & Prof. Pos: Practicing attorney, Wash, D.C, 51-52; partner in law firm, Willner, Bennett & Leonard, 52- Mil. Serv: Entered as Pvt, Army, 45, released as Cpl, 46, after serv. in various branches, Maritime Serv, 44-45, A/S. Publ: 'Government Regulation of Local Union Democracy,' Labor Law J, 52. Mem: Am. and Multnomah Co. Bar Asns; Ore. State Bar; dir, Portland C. of C, 66-; v.pres, Pac. Northwest Regional Coun. of Boys Clubs of Am; Mason; Am. Legion; Grange; Ore-Wash. Farmers' Union; Portland City Club. Legal Res: 930 S.W. Englewood Dr, Lake Oswego, Ore. 97034. Mailing Add: 900 Corbett Bldg, Portland, Ore. 97204.

WILLOX, JAMES A. R
Wyo. State Rep.
b. 1936; s. James Willox; m. to Sue. Educ: Univ. Wyo. Polit. & Govt. Pos: Wyo. State Rep, 67- Bus. & Prof. Pos: Rancher. Mil. Serv: Armed Forces Vet. Mem: Legis. chmn, Converse Co. Farm Bus; Wyo. Stock Growers; Moose; Am. Legion; Jaycees. Rel: Episcopal. Mailing Add: Route 6, Box 23, Douglas, Wyo. 82633. (1967)

WILLS, MARSHALL THEODORE 'TED' R
N.C. State Rep.
b. Indianapolis, Ind, 12/31/20; s. Rev. Alvin Lamar Wills and Helen Holton W; m. 11/7/42 to Betty Jean Broughton; c. Marshall Ward, Graylan Broughton, Barry Lamar, Mary Jeanette and Helen Lydell. Educ: Officers Cand. Sch, Ft. Monmouth, N.J, 43; Northwest. Univ, B.S, 47; Kappa Sigma; Univ. Theatre; Waa-Mu. Polit. & Govt. Pos: Indust. engr, State Govt, Raleigh, N.C, 58-60; N.C. State Rep, Forsyth Co, 69- Bus. & Prof. Pos: Sales Rep, WPTF Radio-WNAD, Raleigh, N.C, 47-52, Lamburt-Hudnut Div, 53-59; indust. hunter, Winston-Salem C. of C, 59-62; with area develop, Potomac Edison, Hagerstown, Md, 62-63; state Westinghouse distributor, Winston-Salem, N.C, 63- Mil. Serv: Entered as Pvt, Army Signal Corps, 42, released as 1st Lt, 46, after serv. in 3139 Motor Messenger, ETO, 44-46; 5 Battle Stars; various company citations. Publ: 'Speculative Industrial Buildings in the Eastern United States,' Am. Indust. Develop. Coun. J, 1/66. Mem: South Indust. Develop. Coun; Am. Indust. Develop. Coun; Winston-Salem C. of C; Forsyth Rep. Party. Rel: Chirstian Science. Mailing Add: 4144 Robinhood Rd, Winston-Salem, N.C. 27106.

WILMARTH, W. ELERY R
Committeeman, Colo. State Rep. Cent. Cmt.
b. Santa Maria, Calif, 5/18/34; s. Wilson E. Wilmarth and Emily White W; m. 11/5/57 to Nancy Pulver; c. Douglas E, Jennifer K. and Perry M. Educ: Wesleyan Univ, B.A, 56; Colo. Univ, LL.B, 63; Sigma Nu; Phi Delta Phi. Polit. & Govt. Pos: Rep. precinct committeeman, Boulder, Colo, 61-62, Ft. Collins, 64-; committeeman, Colo. State Rep. Cent. Cmt, 69- Mil. Serv: Entered as Ens, Navy, 57, released as Lt, 61, after serv. in Patrol Squadron 50 and Fleet Air Intel. Training Center, Pac. Mem: Larimer Co, Colo. and Am. Bar Asns; Elks; Lions; North. Colo. Yacht Club; Ft. Collins Munic. Golf Asn; South Col. Commun. Asn. Mailing Add: 1411 Hillside Dr, Ft. Collins, Colo. 80521.

WILMER, HENRY BOND R
Chmn. Exec. Cmt, Mecklenburg Co. Rep. Party, N.C.
b. Phila, Pa, 4/9/20; s. Harry Bond Wilmer and Helen Lewis Parker W; m. 3/20/43 to Mary Van Der Voort; c. Henry Bond, Jr, Emily, Helen P. and Molly. Educ: Princeton Univ, 39-42. Polit. & Govt. Pos: Co. cmnr, Mecklenburg Co, N.C, 62-64; mem, Planning & Zoning Cmn, 67-; chmn. Exec. Cmt, Mecklenburg Co. Rep. Party, 68- Bus. & Prof. Pos: Agent, Prudential Ins. Co. Am, 54- Mil. Serv: Entered as Aviation Cadet, Marines, 41, released as Capt, 45, after serv. in Third Marine Airwing, Pac. Theatre, 44-45; Res, Maj.(Ret); Unit Commendation. Citizenship Award, Charlotte, N.C; Citizenship Award, Prudential Ins. Co; Cert. of Appreciation, Charlotte-Mecklenburg Sch. Bd. Rel: Episcopal. Mailing Add: 2136 Malvern Rd, Charlotte, N.C. 28207.

WILLSON, GEORGE AUSTILL D
b. New Orleans, La; s. George Massey Willson and Josephine Tompkins W; m. 10/27/34 to Anna Marie Flynn; c. Joan Marie, M.D.(Mrs. Charles King). Educ: Univ. South. Calif; Pac. Coast Sch. Law, LL.B, 44. Polit. & Govt. Pos: Calif. State Assemblyman, 52nd Assembly Dist, 58-66; councilman and mayor, Huntington Park, 48-58. Bus. & Prof. Pos: Attorney at Law, 44- Mem: Univ. South. Calif. Alumna Asn; Elks; Moose; Eagles; past pres, Sertoma; C. of C; Red Cross; adv. bd, Salvation Army; sponsor, YMCA. Rel: Episcopal. Legal Res: 4035 Santa Ana St, Huntington Park, Calif. 90255. Mailing Add: 3400 Florence Ave, Huntington Park, Calif. 90255.

WILSCAM, RODERICK ALBERT R
b. Galesburg, Ill, 8/25/27; s. Frederick Vital Wilscam and Lily Ekstrom W; m. 8/4/51 to Mollie Lou Kennedy; c. Janet Marie, Karen Jane and Linda Gay. Educ: Knox Col, B.A, 53. Polit. & Govt. Pos: Mem, bd. finance, Rocky Hill, Conn, 63-64, clerk, 64-; mem, Rocky Hill Rep. Town Cmt, 64-66, chmn, 66-69; mem, Libr. Bldg. Cmt, 64-; del, Rep. State Conv, 66. Bus. & Prof. Pos: Underwriter, Travelers Ins. Co, 53- Mil. Serv: Entered as Pvt, Army, 44, released as Technician, 4/C, 46, after serv. in 179th Finance Disbursing Unit, Japan; 2nd Lt, Army Res, 62. Rel: Methodist. Mailing Add: 24 Valley Brook Rd, Rocky Hill, Conn. 06067. (1967)

WILSON, A. K. R
Chmn, Perry Co. Rep. Party, Ohio
b. Corning, Ohio, 8/20/09; s. Clifford Wilson and Eura Koher W; m. 3/25/33 to Verna Hammer; c. Clifford Dale, Beverly Lama and Pamela. Educ: Moxahala High Sch, Ohio, 24 & 25; New Lexington High Sch, Ohio, 26-27. Polit. & Govt. Pos: Councilman, Somerset, Ohio, 46-54; cmnr, Perry Co, 55-64 & 67-; Ohio State Rep, 65-66; chmn, Perry Co. Rep. Party, 68- Bus. & Prof. Pos: Laborer, Pa. R.R, Newark, 27-29; clerk, Kroger, New Lexington, Ohio, 29-33; miner, Buckingham Coal Co, Congo, 33-37; salesman, Monumental Life Ins, Zanesville, 37-39; grocery owner and operator, Somerset, 39-48; farm equip. owner and operator, Somerset, 48- Mem: Lions; Mason; Eagles; Grange; Farm Bur; Civic Asn. Rel: Protestant. Legal Res: North Dr, Somerset, Ohio 43783. Mailing Add: Box 6043, Somerset, Ohio 43783.

WILSON, ALICE MARIAN EDMONDSON D
b. Robersonville, N.C, 2/26/30; d. Roy Sutton Edmondson, Sr. and Louise Matthews E; m. 6/27/54 to James Floyd Wilson, Jr. 'Sam'. Educ: Oak City High Sch, grad, 48. Polit. & Govt. Pos: Off. mgr, Edgecombe Co. Dem. Party, N.C, 60; woman's co. chmn, Edgecombe Co. Dem. for Moore, 63; secy, Edgecombe Co. Young Dem, 63-65; off. mgr, Edgecombe Co. Dem. Party for Scott, 68; alternate del, Dem. Nat. Conv, 68; hon. mem. Cmt. to Notify Vice-President, 68; dir, Gov. Morehead Sch. for the Blind, Raleigh, N.C, 65-69. Bus. & Prof. Pos: Secy, Bateman Ins. Agency, Tarboro, 48-49; receptionist, Edgecombe-Martin Co. Elec. Membership Corp, 49-59; exec. secy, Tarboro United Fund, 59-68. Publ: Monthly article, Elec. Corp. Mag, 57-59; Easter Story, Daily Southerner, 58; Prayer for Peace, Am. Legion Auxiliary Mag. Mem: Edgecombe Co. Hist. Soc; Women's Cmt, Edgecombe Martin Co. Elec. membership Corp; Coastal Plain Heart Asn; Am. Legion Auxiliary. United Fund Award for Outstanding Serv; hon. mention, State Am. Legion Conv; page to pres, State Am. Legion Auxiliary at State Conv. Rel: Baptist. Legal Res: Route 1, Bethel, N.C. 27812. Mailing Add: P.O. Box 154, Tarboro, N.C. 27886.

WILSON, ANNE CHAPMAN R
V.Chmn, Dade Co. Rep. Exec. Cmt, Fla.
b. St. Louis, Mo. 8/24/29; d. Thomas Howard Chapman and Gean La Mont C; div; c. Anne Rebecca, Francis Gavin, Jr. and Dwight Collins. Educ: Univ. Miami, 1 year. Polit. & Govt. Pos: First v.pres, Dade Co. Young Rep, 64-65; del, Young Rep. Nat. Conv, 65; state TAR chmn, Fla. Fedn. Young Rep, 65-67; co. committeewoman, Dade Co. Rep. Exec. Cmt, 66- and v.chmn, 66-; del, Rep. Nat. Conv, 68. Bus. & Prof. Pos: Circulation mgr, Investment Sales Monthly, Miami, 65-68; admin. asst. to dir, Miami Art Center, 68. Publ: Book Reviews, Presby. J, 65-67. Excellence Award, Am. Security Coun. Bus. Citizenship Competition, 67. Rel: Presbyterian. Mailing Add: 3710 Battersea Rd, Miami, Fla. 33133.

WILSON, BENJAMIN H. R
Pa. State Rep.
b. Mt. Carmel, Pa, 1/25/25; s. Benj. H. Wilson and Esther B. Marshall W; m. 7/15/50 to Jean Terry; c. Sheryl and Denise. Educ: Pa. State Univ, B.A, 49. Polit. & Govt. Pos: Rep. Committeeman, Warminster, Pa, 54-58; mem, Bucks Co. Rep. Cmt, 56-59; tax collector, Warminster Twp, 58-; Pa. State Rep, 67- Bus. & Prof. Pos: Salesman, Minn. Mining & Mfg. Co, 49-53; Manufacturer's Rep, 53-64. Mil. Serv: Entered as Pvt, Army Air Force, 43, released as 2nd Lt, 46, after serv. in S.Pac. Mem: Am. Legion; VFW; F&AM; AAONMS; Caldwell Consistory; C. of C. Rel: Presbyterian. Mailing Add: 1215 W. County Line Rd, Warminster, Pa. 18974.

WILSON, CARROLL DEAN D
Conservator, Knox Co, Ill.
b. Nauvoo, Ill, 9/22/30; s. Robert Wilson and Edna Mae Grotts W; m. 6/28/50 to Barbara Jean Jones; c. Kathleen Joan and Carolyn Jean. Educ: West. Ill. Univ, B.S, 57, top 10% of class, M.S. in Educ, 60; U.S. Hist. Club; Young Dem. Club. Polit. & Govt. Pos: Mem, Citizens Adv. Cmt, Ill. Off. Econ. Opportunity, 65; pres, Knox Co. Young Dem, Ill, 65; Dem. Cand. for Knox Co. Supt. Schs, 66; pub. adminstr and conservator, Knox Co, 67-; Dem. precinct committeeman, Sixth Precinct, Galesburg, 68; alternate del, Dem. Nat. Conv, 68. Bus. & Prof. Pos: Elem. prin. and teacher, Henderson Co, Ill, 57-58; teacher, counsr. and dean of boys, Sch. Dist. 205, Galesburg, 59- Mil. Serv: Entered as A/S, Navy, 52, released as PO 3/C, 54, after serv. in U.S.S. Philippine Sea CVA-47, Pac. Area; Korean Serv. Medal. Publ: 'Using Test Results and Teacher Evaluation in Identifying Gifted Pupils,' Am. Personnel and Guid. J, 4/63. Mem: Nat. and Ill. Educ. Asns; Am, Ill. and Galesburg Fedn. Teachers; Ill. Personnel & Guid. Asn; Elks. Am. Legion. Rel: Protestant. Mailing Add: 1051 N. Broad St, Galesburg, Ill. 61401.

WILSON, CHARLES H. D
U.S. Rep, Calif.
b. Magna, Utah, 2/15/17; s. Charles H. Wilson and Janet C. Hunter W; m. 3/23/47 to Dorothy Elizabeth Gibbel; c. Stephen Charles, Donald Herbert, Kenneth Alan and William John. Polit. & Govt. Pos: Cmnr, Los Angeles Pub. Housing Authority, 52-54; Calif. State Assemblyman, 55-63; U.S. Rep, 31st Dist, Calif, 63- Mil. Serv: Entered as Pvt, Army, 42, released as S/Sgt, 45, after serv. in 218th Replacement Co, ETO; Good Conduct, Victory, Am. Campaign and European-African-Middle East. Campaign Medals. Mem: Angeles Mesa Masonic Lodge, Los Angeles; Al Malaikah Shrine; Inglewood Am. Legion Post; 3rd Div. Post, VFW; Inglewood Shrine Club; Sowela Shrine Club; Inglewood Elks Lodge; Crenshaw C. of C; Inglewood C. of C. Rel: United Church of Christ. Legal Res: 5934 Madden Ave, Los Angeles, Calif. 90043. Mailing Add: 4801 Randolph Dr, Annandale, Va. 22003.

WILSON, DOLA N, JR. D
Co. Attorney, Chouteau Co, Mont.
b. Miles City, Mont, 8/15/20; s. Dola N. Wilson, Sr. and Blanche Sarff W; m. 8/26/52 to Myrl Morris; c. Darla (Mrs. Robert Andruik), William C, John J, Mary C. and Elizabeth J. Educ: Univ. Mont, B.A, 49, B.A. in Bus. Admin. and LL.B, 50. Polit. & Govt. Pos: Chief legal adv, Mont. House of Rep, 51; attorney, Mont. State Fish & Game Dept, 51-52; supvr, Corp. License Tax Div, Mont. Bd. of Equality, 53-54; co. attorney, Chouteau Co, Mont, 57-58, 61-62 & 66- Mil. Serv: Entered as Pvt, Army Air Force, 42, released as T/Sgt, 45, after serv. in Ninth Air Force, ETO, 44-45; Good Conduct Medal; Air Medal with 8 Clusters; Distinguished Flying Cross; Purple Heart; Am. Theatre Medal; ETO with 5 Battle Stars; Presidential Citation; Letter of Commendation. Mem: Am. and Mont. Bar Asns; AF&AM; Scottish Rite Consistory (32°); VFW (post comdr, Ft. Benton, Mont, 60, dist. comdr, Dist. 2, Mont, 63, dept. inspector, Mont, 67 and dept. chief of staff, Mont, 68); DAV; Farmers Union. Rel: Protestant. Mailing Add: 1309 Franklin St, Ft. Benton, Mont. 59442.

WILSON, DONALD JAMES 'DON' R
Ore. State Rep.
b. Hebron, N.Dak, 10/8/21; s. Virgil Irvin Wilson and Ella Underdahl W; m. 7/8/61 to Ruth Elinor Goodwin; c. Carrie Evans and Michael Montgomery.

Educ: Stanford Univ, B.A, 43; Willamette Univ, LL.B, 55; Phi Delta Phi; Delta Upsilon. Polit. & Govt. Pos: Ore. State Rep, Benton-Lane Co, 65-, chmn, Judiciary Cmt. and mem, public welfare, interstate cooperation cmt. and judicial coun. Mil. Serv: Entered as Yeoman 2/C, Navy, 42, released as Lt.(jg), 46, after serv. in S.Pac; Lt, Naval Res, 46-66; Seven Campaign Ribbons. Mem: Ore. State and Lane Co. Bar Asns; Mason; Elks. Rel: Protestant. Mailing Add: 2425 Charnelton St, Eugene, Ore. 97405.

WILSON, EARL R
Ind. State Sen.
b. Huron, Ind, 4/18/06; s. James E. Wilson and Annie Hill W; m. 6/15/31 to Elsie Bex; c. Linda Sue and Phillip E. Educ: Ind. Univ, B.A. and M.S. Polit. & Govt. Pos: U.S. Rep, Ind, 41-58 & 60-64; Ind. State Sen, 68- Mem: Mason; Shrine. Rel: Baptist. Mailing Add: 2003 O, Bedford, Ind. 47421.

WILSON, EARL D. R
Chmn, Allen Co. Rep. Party, Ky.
b. Holland, Ky, 10/18/14; s. Enoch George Wilson and Fairnie Holland W; m. 7/16/32 to Willie Ruth Lones; c. Earl Dennis and Merle Jean (Mrs. Conder). Educ: Schs, Holland, Ky, 12 years. Polit. & Govt. Pos: Chmn, Allen Co. Rep. Party, Ky, 68- Mailing Add: Holland, Ky. 42153.

WILSON, ELAINE M. D
b. Grand Rapids, Mich, 1/18/24; d. Lawrence Edward Popma and Gladys Bolder P; m. 11/22/46 to Peter Wilson; c. James L, David L. and Bruce E. Educ: Cath. Cent. High Sch, grad, 42. Polit. & Govt. Pos: Chmn, VIP Prog. and Dollars for Dem, 62; mem. exec. bd, Kent Co. Dem. Cmt, Mich, 64, v.chmn, 65-67; mem, Dem. Women's Club; chmn, Jefferson-Jackson Dinner in Kent Co. and coordinator, Williams for Sen. Campaign, Kent Co, 66; out state chmn, Oper. Support, Dem. Party of Mich, mem, Off. of Econ. Opportunity Planning Cmt, area v.chmn, United Fund Campaign and mem, Cmt. of 100, Model Cities Cmt, 68; mem, VCS Leadership Cmt, 68-69. Mem: Corresponding secy, Grand Rapids PTA Coun, 66-; treas, Creston High PTA, 65-66; mother v.pres, Crestview Sch. PTA, 65-66 and exec. bd. mem, 64-66; Riverside Jr. High PTA; NAACP. Rel: Catholic. Mailing Add: 2421 Plainfield N.E, Grand Rapids, Mich. 49505.

WILSON, ELTON DAKOTA D
Linn Co. Dem. Chmn, Kans.
b. Mound City, Kans, 9/27/96; s. Dakota Jay Wilson and Daisy McAuley W; m. 9/23/20 to Jennie Alexander; c. William E. and Jenneta W.(Mrs. Headrick). Polit. & Govt. Pos: Campaign mgr, Robert Docking, Delano Bass and J. Floyd Breeding; del, Dem. Nat. Conv, 64; chmn, Linn Co. Dem. Party, Kans; Dem. Committeeman, Mound City Twp, 69; Linn Co. Dem. Chmn, 69- Mil. Serv: Navy, 17-18, serv. in France. Mem: Mason; life mem, Am. Legion (Post Serv. Officer, Hewitt-New Post 240, 60-69). State Legion Officer; Child Welfare Chmn. Rel: Protestant. Mailing Add: 713 Fletcher, Mound City, Kans. 66056.

WILSON, FRANK G. R
Vt. State Rep.
b. Warehouse Point, Conn, 8/2/19; s. Cassius I. Wilson and Naomi Darden W; m. 12/3/39 to Constance Roby; c. James H, Steven J. and Gregory D. Educ: Brattleboro High Sch, grad, 37. Polit. & Govt. Pos: Vt. State Rep, Dist. 13-2, 68- Bus. & Prof. Pos: Pres, Basketville, Putney, Vt, 41- Mil. Serv: Entered as Seaman 3/C, Navy, 44, released as Seaman 2/C, 45. Mem: Elks. Rel: Episcopal. Mailing Add: Kimball Hill, Putney, Vt. 05346.

WILSON, FRANK WILEY D
b. Knoxville, Tenn, 6/21/17; s. Frank Caldwell Wilson and Mary Wiley W; m. 4/6/42 to Helen Elizabeth Warwick; c. Frank Carl and William Randall. Educ: Univ. Tenn, A.B, 39, LL.B, 41; Phi Kappa Phi; Order of the Coif. Polit. & Govt. Pos: Co. attorney, Anderson Co, Tenn, 48-50; mem, Bd. Educ, Oak Ridge, 56-61; U.S Dist. Judge, East. Dist, Tenn, 61- Bus. & Prof. Pos: V.pres, Bank of Oak Ridge, Tenn, 52-61. Mil. Serv: Entered as Pvt, Army Air Force, 42, released as S/Sgt, 46; Italian Theater Ribbon. Publ: 'Federal Habeas Corpus,' Vanderbilt Law Review, June, 66; 'A Fair Trial and A Free Press,' Neiman Reports, Dec, 65; 'Era of Gideon vs. Wainwright,' Tenn. Bar J, May, 65. Mem: Am. Judicature Soc; Am. and Tenn. Bar Asns; Rotary Int. Rel: Methodist. Legal Res: 103 Stratford Way, Signal Mountain, Tenn. 37377. Mailing Add: U.S. District Court, Chattanooga, Tenn. 37402.

WILSON, GEORGE E, JR. R
Rep. Nat. Committeeman, Tenn.
b. Rockwood, Tenn, 7/26/21; m. 4/12/47 to Chalmers; c. George E, III, Emmie N. and Madge T. Educ: Vanderbilt Univ, grad, 43. Polit. & Govt. Pos: Chmn, Roane Co. Rep. Party, Tenn, 52-56, Second Cong. Dist. Rep. Party, 58-63 and Tenn. State Rep. Party, 63-64; chmn, Tenn. Del, Rep. Nat. Conv, 64; Rep. Nat. Committeeman, Tenn, 68- Bus. & Prof. Pos: Hosiery mfr, with Burlington Mills, Inc, 4 years and Roane Hosiery, Inc, 19 years. Mem: V.pres, Tenn. Mfrs. Asn, 68-; bd, Nat. Asn. of Hosiery Mfrs; Rotary; Hosp. Bd; Commun. Chest; Cancer Soc; Am. Legion; VFW. Rel: Presbyterian. Legal Res: 702 Cumberland St, Harriman, Tenn. 37748. Mailing Add: P.O. Box 431, Harriman, Tenn. 37748.

WILSON, GEORGE HOWARD D
b. Mattoon, Ill, 8/21/05; s. George Duncan Wilson and Helen Maude Bresee W; m. 6/26/29 to Myrna Kathryn Reams; c. Jane Kathryn, Sandra Kay, Myrna Lee and George Howard, II. Educ: Phillips Univ, A.B, 26; Univ. Mich. Law Sch, 26-27; Univ. Okla, LL.B, 29; Order of the Coif; Phi Delta Phi; Delta Sigma Rho; Acacia. Polit. & Govt. Pos: Spec. agent, Fed. Bur. Invest, 34-38; city attorney, Enid, Okla, 39-42; U.S. Rep, Okla, 49-50; dir Okla. State Crime Bur, 51-52; superior court judge, Enid, Garfield Co, Okla, 52-68; Chief Judge Dist. Court, Div. One, Fourth Judicial Dist, Okla, 69- Mil. Serv: Entered as Capt, Army, released as Col, 45, after serv. in Judge Adv. Gen. Corps; Col, Army Res; Commendation Medal. Publ: 'The Role of a Trial Judge in the Trial of a Negligence Action,' Vol. 7, Defense Law J, 1960. Mem: Garfield Co, Okla. State and Am. Bar Asns; Legionnaire of Hon, DeMolay, 51; Commodore by Okla. Gov, 52; Soc. Former Spec. Agents of Fed. Bur. Invest; Mason; K.T, Scottish Rite; former bd. mem. Enid Post. Am. Legion; past pres. and past lt. gov, Kiwanis; mem. exec. bd, Enid YMCA; past pres. and campaign chmn, Enid Commun. Chest; former chmn. adv. bd, St. Marys' Hosp, Enid; coun. v.pres, Boys Scouts, Cherokee Strip Coun. Admitted to practice before: Okla. Supreme Court, U.S. Supreme Court, U.S. Dist. Court, West. Dist, Okla, Nebr. Supreme Court, U.S. Dist. Court and North. Ill. Rel: Presbyterian; Elder, 31- Mailing Add: 1724 W. Cherokee, Enid, Okla. 73701.

WILSON, HARLAN YATES, JR. R
W.Va. State Del.
b. Charleston, W.Va, 5/2/30; s. Harlan Yates Wilson, Sr. and Glenna Poling W; m. 6/25/60 to Betty Phillips; c. Nicole Lyn. Educ: Morris Harvey Col, 1 year. Polit. & Govt. Pos: W.Va. State Del, 69- Bus. & Prof. Pos: V.pres, Wilson Funeral Home, Inc, 50- Mil. Serv: Pvt, Army Nat. Guard, 48, Capt, Res, 48-69. Mem: Kiwanis; Edgewood Country Club; Army-Navy Club of Charleston; West Side Bus. Asn; Nat. Guard Asn. of U.S. and W.Va. Rel: Methodist. Mailing Add: 1010 Summit Dr, Charleston, W.Va, 25302.

WILSON, HAROLD STALETS R
Fla. State Sen.
b. Chicago, Ill, 9/28/21; s. Harold Bennett Wilson and Luella Stalets W; m. 1/19/63 to Mary Ellen Rusin; c. Jennie Ellen and Janice Mary. Educ: Univ. Chicago, B.A, 42; Harvard Law Sch, LL.B, 53; Delta Sigma Pi. Polit. & Govt. Pos: Asst. pub. defender, Pinellas Co, Fla, 63; city attorney, Safety Harbor, Fla, 62-65; Assoc. Munic. Judge, Indian Rocks Beach, 66; Fla. State Sen, 20th Dist, 66- Mil. Serv: S/Sgt, Army Signal Corps, 43-46; Am. Campaign Medal; Asiatic-Pac. Campaign Ribbon; Southern Philippines Liberation Medal. Mem: Fla, Clearwater and Largo Bar Asns; Pinellas Co. Trial Lawyers' Asn. Rel: Catholic. Mailing Add: 1406 Maple Forest Rd, Clearwater, Fla. 33516.

WILSON, HARRY S. D
V.Chmn, Second Dist. Dem. Party, Del.
b. Philadelphia, Pa, 7/22/16; s. Sol Wilson and Lena Abelson W; m. 8/7/41 to Helen Berg; c. Suzanne and Lawrence Alan. Educ: Univ. Del. Polit. & Govt. Pos: V.chmn, Second Dist, Dem. Party, Del, v.pres, Ninth Ward Dem. Club and committeeman, Second Elec. Dist, currently. Del, State Rep, Second Dist. and chmn, House Ins. and Banking Cmt, until 67. Bus. & Prof. Pos: Indust. life ins. salesman, Equitable Life Ins. Co, Washington, D.C, 40-50; ins. broker, self-employed, Del, 50-66. Mil. Serv: Entered as Pvt, Army, 43, released as Sgt, 45, after serv. in ETO. Mem: Am. Legion; VFW; B'nai B'rith. Rel: Jewish. Mailing Add: 2004 N. Broom St, Wilmington, Del. 19802.

WILSON, HENRY HALL, JR. D
b. Monroe, N.C, 12/6/21; s. Henry Hall Wilson and Annie Sanders W; m. 1/11/44 to Mary C. Walters; c. Jean, Nancy and Henry H, III. Educ: Duke Univ, B.A, 42, LL.B, 48. Polit. & Govt. Pos: N.C. State Rep, 53-59; pres, N.C. Young Dem. Club, 55-57; del, Dem. Nat. Conv, 56 & 60; Dem. nat. committeeman, N.C, 61; admin. asst. to President of U.S, 61-67. Bus. & Prof. Pos: Attorney-at-Law, Monroe, N.C, 48-61; pres, Chicago Bd. of Trade, 67- Mil. Serv: Entered as Pvt, Army, 43, released as 1st Lt, 46. Rel: Baptist. Legal Res: Winnetka, Ill. Mailing Add: Chicago Board of Trade, 141 W. Jackson Blvd, Chicago, Ill. 60604.

WILSON, HOKE SMITH D
b. Nahunta, Ga, 2/07/17; s. Joseph S. Wilson and Minnie Hendrix W; m. 4/5/37 to Mary Bryan; c. Jo Ann, Hubert and Charles. Educ: Nahunta Schs. Polit. & Govt. Pos: Ga. State Rep, 63-66. Bus. & Prof. Pos: Sinclair Gas & Oil Distributor. Mil. Serv: Navy. Rel: Methodist. Mailing Add: Nahunta, Ga. 31553.

WILSON, HUGH MAL R
Mem, Caldwell Co. Rep. Exec. Cmt, N.C.
b. Rutherfordton, N.C, 5/3/30; s. H. Mal Wilson and Ruth Scruggs W; m. 8/18/56 to Martha Whitehead; c. Karen, Lynne and Robert. Educ: Mars Hill Col, A.A, 49; Wake Forest Col, B.B.A, 51, Law Sch, LL.B, 56; Alpha Kappa Psi; Phi Delta Phi. Polit. & Govt. Pos: Mem, Caldwell Co. Rep. Exec. Cmt, N.C, 58-; mem. bd. elecs, Caldwell Co, 62-, tax attorney, 65-; del, Rep. Nat. Conv, 64. Bus. & Prof. Pos: Attorney-at-Law, 56-62; attorney, Seila, Wilson & Palmer, 62-; Caldwell Co. Attorney, 66- Mil. Serv: Entered as Pvt, Air Force, 51, released as Airman 2/C, 53, after serv. in Hq. ROTC. Mem: N.C. Acad. Trial Lawyers; Am. Trial Lawyers Asn; N.C. State Bar; N.C, 25th Dist. and Caldwell Co. Bar Asns; Jaycees; Am. Legion; pres, Lenoir-Caldwell Co. C. of C; 69- Outstanding Young Man Award, 64. Rel: Baptist. Legal Res: 125 Circle Dr, Lenoir, N.C. 28645. Mailing Add: Box 638, Lenoir, N.C. 28645.

WILSON, IRL DONAKER D
Chmn, Montgomery Co. Dem. Cmt, Va.
b. Calhoun Co, Iowa, 5/21/88; s. John Francis Wilson and Hariett Donaker W; m. 11/26/14 to Belle Seely; m. 6/20/53 to Eleanor Atkins; c. Irl Donaker, Jr. Educ: Iowa State Col, D.V.M, 14, Ph.D, 30; Pa. State Col, M.S, 18; Alpha Zeta; Phi Kappa Phi; Gamma Sigma Delta; Sigma Xi; Phi Sigma Kappa. Polit. & Govt. Pos: Mem, Va. State Bd. Vet. Med. Exam, 32-46; collab, U.S. Bur. Animal Indust, 36-41; mem, U.S. Govt. Alaska Reindeer Surv. and Appraisal Cmt, 38-39; mem, Va. Cmn. on Animal Indust. and Vet. Col, 46; Rockefeller Found. appointee to cmt. to survey Nat. Univ. of Latin Am. Countries, 49; U.S. Agency for Int. Develop. educ. adv, India, 58-60; U.S. State Dept. lectr, Kabul Univ, 61; chmn, Montgomery Co. Dem. Cmt, Va, 67-; chmn, 13th Dist. Dem. Cmt, 67- Bus. & Prof. Pos: Vet, Blue Earth, Minn, 14-16; prof, Pa. State Col, 16-23; prof. and head dept. biol, Va. Polytech. Inst, 23-58. Mil. Serv: 2nd Lt, Iowa State Cadet Corps. Publ: 'Bovine Coccidiosis,' Va. Agr. Exp. Sta. Bul, 30; 'Veterinary Education in Developing Countries,' Am. Inst. Biol. Sci. Bul, 12/63; 'Those Interesting Afghans,' Sci. Educ, 10/67; 'What the People of Other Nations Really Think of Us,' Sci. Educ, 11/69. Mem: Va. Acad. Sci; Va. and Am. Vet. Med. Asns; Am. Inst. Biol. Sci; Theta Kappa Psi; Sigma Delta Psi; Torch; Mason; Shrine; Univ. Club; Shenandoah Club. Paper presented on animal husbandry and vet. educ. at the First Pan Am. Vet. Cong, Lima, Peru, 51; A.M. Mills Award, 64; Va. Vet. of the Year, 68. Rel: Episcopal. Mailing Add: 1303 Oak Dr, Blacksburg, Va. 24060.

WILSON, J. FRANKLIN R
Mem, D.C. Rep. Cmt.
b. Talladega, Ala, 6/28/86; s. Stewart Henry Wilson and Leah Catherine

Cameron W; m. 6/25/48 to Nellie B. Taylor. Educ: Howard Univ, A.B, 14; Law Sch, LL.B, 17. Polit. & Govt. Pos: Mem, D.C. Rep. Conv, 24-; former sr. v.chmn, D.C. Rep. Cmt, mem, currently; alternate del, Rep. Nat. Conv, 36, del, 40, 52, 60 & 64. Mil. Serv: Entered as Pvt, Army, 18, released as Sgt, 19, after serv. in 317th Trench Mortar Battery, Metz Sector. Mem: D.C. Bar; Am. Legion (former dept. judge advocate, D.C. Dept). Numerous awards for serv, Wash, D.C. Draft Bd. and Am. Legion. Rel: Congregational. Legal Res: 6445 Luzon Ave. N.W, Apt. 316, Washington, D.C. 20012. Mailing Add: 1020 U St. N.W, Washington, D.C. 20001.

WILSON, JAMES R
Committeeman, Chelan Co. Rep. Cent. Cmt, Wash.
b. Peshastin, Wash, 4/3/21; s. L. E. Wilson and Juna B. Smith W; m. 9/28/45 to Alvis June Richardson; c. Linda and David. Educ: Wenatchee Valley Col, 40-42; Wash. State Univ, B.S, 47; Tau Beta Pi; Sigma Tau; Phi Kappa Phi. Polit. & Govt. Pos: Precinct committeeman, Chelan Co. Rep. Cent. Cmt, Wash, 50-69, dist. cmnr, 54-56, committeeman, 56-58 & 68-, chmn, 66-68. Mem: Trustee, Chelan Co. Hist. Soc, 56-64, pres, 60-62. Mailing Add: Box 812, Cashmere, Wash. 98815.

WILSON, JEROME L. D
b. Wash, D.C, 7/16/31; m. to Frances Elizabeth Roberts; c. Four. Educ: Colgate Univ, B.A, 53; War Memorial Scholar. Polit. & Govt. Pos: N.Y. State Sen, 62-66; former asst. to Manhattan Borough Pres, Edward R. Dudley. Bus. & Prof. Pos: Pres. and founder, Coun. for Parks and Playgrounds; former mem. of exec. staff, Nat. Urban League; Publicity and Pub. Rels. Work. Mil. Serv: 1st Lt, Air Force; serv. in Germany; Air Force Commendation Ribbon. Mem: Episcopal Soc. for Racial and Cultural Unity; Mayors Cmt. against Exploitation of Workers; NAACP; E. Harlem Cmt. Planning Bd; Yorkville Civic Coun; Group Work and Recreation Cmt. of Commun. Coun. of N.Y.C; Dem. and Liberal Party Clubs. Received John F. Kennedy Memorial Award from Recreational Employees, AFL-CIO, 64. Rel: Protestant. Mailing Add: 517 E. 82nd St, New York, N.Y. 10028. (1967)

WILSON, JOE MACK D
Ga. State Rep.
b. Marietta, Ga, 12/11/19; m. 6/1/45 to Mary Elizabeth Fullen Holloway; c. Joe Michael, Stephen Holloway and David McKelvey. Educ: Ga. Tech, 39-44. Polit. & Govt. Pos: Mem, Cobb Co. Dem. Exec. Cmt, Ga; Ga. State Rep, 61-Bus. & Prof. Pos: Retail merchant. Mem: Elks; bd. of dir, Aidmore Hosp; Atlanta Area Metrop. Planning Cmn. Rel: Methodist. Mailing Add: 306 Northcutt S.W, Marietta, Ga. 30060. (1967)

WILSON, JOHN BENJAMIN, JR. D
b. Frederick, Okla, 1/27/12; s. John Benjamin Wilson and Anna Harris W; m. 8/12/61 to Renate; c. John Jeffrey. Educ: Okla. Univ, B.A, 35, LL.B, 37; Kappa Alpha South. Polit. & Govt. Pos: Asst. co. attorney, Tillman Co, Okla, 39-40; city attorney, Frederick, formerly; chmn, Tillman Co. Dem. Party, formerly. Bus. & Prof. Pos: Attorney-at-law, Wilson & Wilson, 46-55, Wilson & Massad, 55- Mil. Serv: Entered as 1st Lt, Army, 41, released as Maj, 46, after serv. in 208th Field Artil. Group, ETO, 43-46; Lt. Col.(Ret), Judge Adv. Gen. Corps, Army Res, 65; Bronze Star; ETO Medal with three Stars. Mem: Okla. and Am. Bar Asns; VFW; Am. Legion; Lions Int; Mason. Rel: Baptist. Legal Res: 403 E. Floral Ave, Frederick, Okla. 73542. Mailing Add: Box 606, Frederick, Okla. 73542.

WILSON, JOSEPHINE EVADNA R
b. Ensign, Kans; d. Henry Reuben and Mary E. Scott Smith R; m. 11/22/45 to Woodrow Bankhead Wilson. Educ: Kans. Univ; George Washington Univ. Polit. & Govt. Pos: Legis. liaison secy, Selective Serv, 40-45; secy. to cmnr, Hoover Cmn, 48-49; secy. to U.S. Reps, 55-66; minority legis. clerk, off. of minority leader, U.S. House of Rep, 56- Bus. & Prof. Pos: Legal secy, 35-40. Mem: Woman's Soc. of Christian Serv; Capitol Hill Club. Rel: Methodist. Legal Res: Paola, Kans. 66071. Mailing Add: 3816 Van Ness St. N.W, Washington, D.C. 20016.

WILSON, KENNETH E. D
b. Tacoma, Wash; m. to Orestes T; c. Kay Michele. Educ: Univ. Chicago Law Sch, J.D; Alpha Phi Alpha. Polit. & Govt. Pos: Asst. Attorney Gen, Ill, 49-52; Asst. State Attorney, Cook Co, 52; former Ill. State Rep. Bus. & Prof. Pos: Lectr. law, N.W. Univ. Law School's Sch. for State Attorneys, 54-55. Mil. Serv: Corps of Engrs, World War II. Mem: Mason; Shrine; VFW; bd. dir, Jane Dent Home for Aged People; former judge advocate, Am. Legion, George L. Giles Post; Ill, Cook Co. and Chicago Bar Asns. Rel: Congregational; bd. of Deacons and chmn. bd. trustees, Church of the Good Shepherd. Mailing Add: 4524 S. Parkway Blvd, Chicago, Ill. 60653. (1967)

WILSON, KENNETH L. R
b. 3/27/08; m. to Anna M. Kuhlewind; c. Kenneth, Jr, Jean Anne and Jane Lewis. Educ: Newark Acad. and Kingston High Sch. Polit. & Govt. Pos: Supvr, Woodstock, N.Y, 44-53; majority leader, Ulster Co. Bd. of Supvrs, 49-53; former chmn, Ulster Co. Rep. Cmt. and N.Y. Rep. State Cmt; N.Y. State Assemblyman, 53-69. Bus. & Prof. Pos: Real estate mgt, trustee, Saugerties Savings Bank; adv. bd, Nat. Bank of Orange and Ulster Counties. Mem: Past pres, Federated Sportmen's Club of Ulster Co. Mailing Add: Woodstock, N.Y. 12498. (1967)

WILSON, L. EARLE D
b. Craftsbury, Vt, 7/14/04; m. to Mary M. Tatro; c. Two. Educ: Univ. Vt. Polit. & Govt. Pos: Sch. dir, Craftsbury, Vt, 20 years; town moderator, 32-; Vt. State Rep, 57, 59 & 65-67. Bus. & Prof. Pos: Ins. agent and broker; retired farmer. Mem: Former pres, Northeast. Vt. Develop. Asn, 53-54; Mason; Eastern Star; Farm Bur. Rel: Congregational. Mailing Add: Craftsbury, Vt. 05826. (1967)

WILSON, LAVERNE BLAIR D
b. Pitcairn, Pa, 6/26/09; d. Gilbert Albert Blair and Margaret Wilson B; m. 5/31/38 to Dr. Ray Carleton Wilson; c. Dr. Wm. E, Richard C. and Dr. Gilbert McLaughlin. Polit. & Govt. Pos: Employee, Fed. Govt, until 38; mem. bd. dirs, Clearfield Co. Dept. Pub. Assistance; mem, Pres. Cmt. on Employ. Handicapped; mem, Gov. Cmts. on Handicapped and Aging; mem, DuBois Area Sch. Bd, Pa; local coordinator for Milton J. Shapp, cand. for Gov; co. coordinator for Genevieve Blatt; cand. for U.S. Sen; mem, Dem. Women's Club, DuBois Area; treas, DuBois Area Dem. Club; del, Dem. Nat. Conv, 60 & 64; precinct chairlady, Dem. Party, Pa, 63-; co. chmn, White House Conf. on Aging, currently. Bus. & Prof. Pos: Co-founder, Goodwill Industries, DuBois, Pa. Mem: Bd. dir, DuBois Area United Fund; Pa. Citizens Coun; Maple Ave. and DuBois Hosp. Auxiliaries; Nat. Rehabilitation Asn; C. of C; bd. dir, home nursing chmn, first aid instr, Bloodmobile Aid, Civil Defense Aid, mem, disaster preparedness cmt. and supvr. training, home nurses and teachers, Am. Red Cross; adv. bd, Jefferson Co. Asn. for Retarded Children; organizer and pres. bd, Sheltered Workshop Cmt; bd, Ridgway Psychiat. Clin. Recipient of Much Coveted Benjamin Rush Award, Jefferson Clearfield Co. Med. Soc. Photography; home nursing; first aid. Rel: Presbyterian. Mailing Add: 119 E. Washington Ave, DuBois, Pa. 15801.

WILSON, MALCOLM R
N.Y. Lt. Gov.
b. N.Y.C, 2/26/14; s. Charles H. Wilson; m. to Katharine McCloskey; c. Kathy and Anne. Educ: Fordham Col, B.A, 33; Fordham Law Sch. Hon. Degrees from Alfred Univ, Brooklyn Law Sch, Canisius Col, Fordham Univ, Pace Col, St. Bonaventure Univ, Siena Col, Le Moyne Col, St. John Fisher Col. and Manhattan Col. Polit. & Govt. Pos: N.Y. State Assemblyman, 38-58; N.Y. Lt. Gov, 58- Bus. & Prof. Pos: Partner, Kent, Hazzard, Wilson, Freeman & Greer, Attorneys, currently. Mil. Serv: Navy, World War II; Comdr. Navy Gun Crew on Ammunition Ship in Mediterranean and European Theaters; Normandy Invasion, 6/44. Mem: V.pres, Yonkers Gen. Hosp; dir, CYO of Archdiocese of N.Y; N.Y. State, Am. and Westchester Co. Bar Asns; K. of C; Hiberians; Friendly Sons of St. Patrick; adv. bd, Mt. Mercy Col; coun. of regents, St. Francis Col; bd. regents, St. John Fisher Col; Grand St. Boys Asn; N.Y. State Farm Bur; bd. trustees, Nat. Conf. Christians and Jews; chmn, Capital City Cmn; bd. trustees, Fordham Univ. Rel: Catholic. Mailing Add: 24 Windsor Rd, Yonkers,(Scarsdale P.O), N.Y. 10583.

WILSON, PATTY HELEN R
Chairwoman, Eighth Dist. Rep. Cmt, Minn.
b. Minneapolis, Minn; d. Roy Stewart Nelson (deceased) and Angela Marie Gehrke N; m. 9/8/51 to Leonard Alfred Wilson; c. Patricia Marie and Gary David. Educ: Univ. Minn, Minneapolis, B.A, 48 and 1 year grad. study; Minn. Col. Rep. Fedn. Polit. & Govt. Pos: Mem, Minn. State Bd. Young Rep, 52-57; v.chairwoman, Minn. Young Rep. League, 53-54 and chairwoman, 54-57; del, Nat. Young Rep. Conv, 54, 56 & 58; co-chmn, Midwest Coun. Young Rep, 55-57; del, Minn. Rep. State Cent. Cmt, 55-; alternate del, Rep. Nat. Conv, 56, del, 68; secy, Minn. Legis. Session, 57; chairwoman, Carlton Co. Women's Rep. Club, 63; v.chairwoman, Minn. Eighth Dist. Rep. Cmt, 63-66 and chairwoman, 66-; chairwoman, several cand. cmts, 65-68. Bus. & Prof. Pos: Mem, research staff, Indust. Rels. Sect, Calif. Inst. Tech, Pasadena, Calif, 45-46; research sci, Indust. Rels. Cent, Univ. Minn, Minneapolis, 47-54. Publ: Author, many articles of a tech. nature in the field of personnel and indust. rels. Mem: Am. Asn. Univ. Women; Lawyers' Wives Minn; Univ. Minn. Alumni Asn; Nat. Fedn. Rep. Women; Duluth Woman's Club; Cloquet Country Club; Univ. Minn. Alumni Club; Cloquet Commun. Players. Rel: Lutheran. Mailing Add: 540 Webbeking Dr, Carlton, Minn. 55718.

WILSON, PETE R
Calif. State Assemblyman
b. Lake Forest, Ill, 8/23/33; s. James Boone Wilson and Margaret Callahan W; m. 7/14/68 to Betty Weedn Robertson. Educ: Yale Univ, B.A, 55; Univ. Calif. Sch. Law, LL.B, 62; Phi Delta Phi; Zeta Psi. Polit. & Govt. Pos: Campaign Aide to V.Pres, Richard M. Nixon in gubernatorial race, 62; asst. exec. dir, Rep. Assocs. of San Diego Co, 63-64; exec. dir, San Diego Co. Rep. Cent. Cmt, 64-65; legal serv. officer, precinct cmt, Calif. State Rep. Cent. Cmt, 65-; Calif. State Assemblyman, 76th Dist, 67-, Minority Whip, 67 & 68, chmn. Cmt. on Urban Affairs and Housing, chmn. Cmt. on Drug Abuse Cmn. of the Californias and chmn. Legis. Subcmt. Gov. Interagency Coun. on Drug Abuse, 69; chmn. of cmt. to name Presidential Electors, Rep. Calif. State Conv, 68. Bus. & Prof. Pos: Partner, Davies & Burch, Attorney's, Calif. Mil. Serv: Entered as 2nd Lt, Marine Corps, 55, released as 1st Lt, 58, after serv. in Fourth Marines, Hawaii, 56-58. Publ: 'Drug Abuse as a Legislative Problem,' Calif. Sch. Health Asn. J, 5/68. Mem: San Diego Co, Calif. State and Fla. State Bar Asns; Int. Cmn. of the Californias; state adv. cmn, Marine and Coastal Resources; Kiwanis; YMCA; Calif. Commonwealth Club; San Diego C. of C; Navy League. Selected to Rep. Calif. at 1968 Eagleton Inst. of Politics, Rutgers Univ. Annual Seminar for Outstanding State Legislators; Outstanding Young Man of San Diego, Jr. C. of C, 69. Rel: Episcopal. Mailing Add: 4146 Genesee Ave, San Diego, Calif. 92117. Mailing Add: 233 A St, San Diego, Calif. 92101.

WILSON, ROBERT CARLTON 'BOB' R
U.S. Rep, Calif.
b. Calexico, Calif, 4/5/16; s. George Wellington Wilson and Olive Blanche Richardson W; m. 10/24/36 to Laura Jean Bryant; c. Frances (Mrs. James Wilson), Mary Ann (Mrs. Michael Chapple) and Bryant. Educ: San Diego State Col; Otis Art Inst. Polit. & Govt. Pos: U.S. Rep, Calif, 36th Dist, 53-, mem, Armed Serv. Cmt; Campaign Coordinator for Richard M. Nixon, 56; chmn, Nat. Rep. Cong. Cmt, 61- Bus. & Prof. Pos: V.pres, The Tolle Co, San Diego. Mil. Serv: Pvt, Army, 44-45; Lt. Col, Marine Corps Res, currently. Publ: John J. Montgomery the Forgotten Man of Aviation. Mem: Adv cmt, Who's Who in Am. Polit, 67 & 69; San Diego Adv. Coun, Boys' Club; Chula Vista Rotary; Am. Legion, Chula Vista Post 434; Elks Lodge 168; Aztec Alumni Asn, San Diego State Col; San Diego Advert. and Sales Club; founder, Rep. Assoc; Harbor Lions; SAR; Navy League Retired Officers Asn; hon. mem, Kiwanis and Optimists; Hon. life mem, Fleet Res. Asn; Jr. C. of C. Int. Recipient Floats Award, Pasadena Tournament of Roses; Named Chef of West, Sunset Mag; Received Award as One of Ten Congressmen Who Had Done Most for Young People of Am, Redbook Mag; Award for Work on Doctor Draft Legis, Med-Dent. Vet. Orgns; Award for Outstanding Work in Behalf of Minority Groups, Filipino-Am. Vet. Orgn. Legal Res: San Diego, Calif. Mailing Add: 2235 Rayburn Building, Washington, D.C. 20515.

WILSON, ROBERT EDWARD R
b. Greensboro, Vt, 7/31/09; m. to Harriette Riddell W; c. Three sons, one daughter. Educ: Univ. Vt, B.S. Polit. & Govt. Pos: Sch. dir, Greensboro,

Vt, 50-55 & 66; village trustee, 58-67; Vt. State Rep, 57-60 & 63-67. Bus. & Prof. Pos: Radio-TV repair. Mem: Grange; Vt. State Firefighters Asn. Rel: Presbyterian. Mailing Add: Greensboro, Vt. 05841. (1967)

WILSON, ROBERT IZOD D
Chmn, Kerr Co. Dem. Party, Tex.
b. Junction, Tex, 2/17/94; s. Horace Ernest Wilson and Jane Graham W; m. 1938 to Jessie Mae McCalmont; c. Linda Mary and Kathleen Izod (Mrs. Jenkins). Educ: Univ. Tex, 4 years. Polit. & Govt. Pos: Chmn, Kerr Co. Dem. Party, Tex, currently. Bus. & Prof. Pos: Attorney-at-law, 19- Mil. Serv: 2nd Lt, Army, World War I, Maj, World War II, serv. in U.S. Mem: Various Bar Asns; Vet. Orgn; Elks. Rel: Protestant. Mailing Add: 249 Travis St, Kerrville, Tex. 78028.

WILSON, ROBERT MASON D
b. Edgewood, R.I, 5/24/23; s. Thomas Ford Wilson and Florence Turner W; m. 5/25/46 to Marilyn Mundy; c. Philip, Mundy and Peter. Educ: Mass. Inst. Tech, 43-44; Brown Univ, B.S, 48. Polit. & Govt. Pos: Sch. dir, chmn, clerk and v.chmn, Bennington Rural Schs, Inc, Vt, 58-62; chmn, Joint Steering Cmt. of Bennington-Bennington Southwest Sch. Study, 60-61; dir. and v.chmn, Mt. Anthony Union High Sch. Dist, 61-63; mem, Gov. Task Force on Educ, Vt, 63; Vt. State Sen, Bennington Co, 65-66; mem, Vt. State Hwy. Bd, Dept. of Hwy, 66-68; cmnr, Vt. Develop. Dept, 68- Bus. & Prof. Pos: Engr-mgt. trainee, Ford Motor Co, Dearborn, Mich, 48-50, zone sales mgr, Natick, Mass, 50-53; gen. mgr, South. Maine Motors, Kennebunk, Maine, 53-55; pres. and gen. mgr, Wilson Ford, Inc, Bennington, Vt, 55-68; v.pres. and dir, Bennington Weavers, Inc, 66-68. Mil. Serv: Entered as Pvt, Army Res, 41, released as S/Sgt, 46, after serv. in 309th Inf. Regiment, ETO, 43-46; Bronze Star; 2 Battle Stars. Mem: Bennington Rotary Club; Gr. Bennington Asn. Rel: Unitarian. Mailing Add: P.O. Box 13, Waitsfield, Vt. 05673.

WILSON, ROBERT TERRY D
b. Dora, Ala, 4/23/22; s. William Myrick Wilson; Katie Bell Dobbs W; m. to Ruth Eleanor McDaniel; c. Sandra Sue, Robert Terry, Jr, Sally Ruth, Alice Kaye. Educ: Stetson Law Sch, Deland, Fla; Univ. of Ala, 50. Polit. & Govt. Pos: Ala. State Sen, 63-67. Bus. & Prof. Pos: Lawyer. Mil. Serv: Air Force, T/Sgt, 65 Combat Missions. Mem: Mason; Shriner. Rel: Methodist. Mailing Add: Box 1090, Jasper, Ala. 35501. (1967)

WILSON, ROGER WESLEY R
b. Macon, Ga, 3/8/28; s. John Wesley Wilson and Hattie Lou Griffith W; m. 4/25/53 to Ruth Merkel Dunwody; c. Howard Wesley, John Fletcher, Steven Lee and James Michael. Educ: Univ. S.C, B.B.A, 50; Sigma Chi; Blue Key; Lettermens Club. Polit. & Govt. Pos: Ga. State Rep, 66-68; chmn, Sixth Dist. Rep. Party, 68-69; mem, Macon-Bibb Co. Hosp. Authority, 68- Bus. & Prof. Pos: Pres, Wilson Elec. Supply Co, 50- and Southeast. Chap Elec. Apparatus Serv. Asn, 62. Mil. Serv: Entered as Lt, Air Force Res, released as 1st Lt, Air Nat. Guard. Mem: Eagles; Elks; Masons; Macon Civic Club. Rel: Episcopal. Mailing Add: 2975 King Alfred Dr, Macon, Ga. 31204.

WILSON, SALLY JO R
Mem, Calif. Rep. State Cent. Cmt.
b. Grand Island, Nebr, 12/5/42; d. Claude Laverne Wilson and Geraldine Scott W; single. Educ: Mark Keppel High Sch, Alhambra, Calif, grad, 64. Polit. & Govt. Pos: Precinct Capt, Alhambra Precinct Orgn, Calif, 64-65, Monterey Park Precinct Orgn, 67-68; mem, Calif. Rep. State Cent. Cmt, 69- Bus. & Prof. Pos: Interchange Bur. Asst, Credit Mgr. Asn, Los Angeles, 62-64; supvr-Forms Control, Transamerica Financial Corp, 64- Mem: Bus. Forms Mgt Asn; Monterey Park Rep. Women's Federated. Rel: Protestant. Mailing Add: 2013 South Stoneman Ave, Alhambra, Calif. 91801.

WILSON, W. R. 'SQUIBB' D
b. Fairview, W.Va, 10/6/13; s. R. J. Wilson and Jettie Pearl Tennant W; m. 7/22/40 to Mary Eleanor Talbott; c. Mikell Ann and Julia Kay. Educ: Fairmont State Col, A.B, 35; Columbia Univ, M.A, 39; W.Va. Univ, grad. work, 46 and Univ. Pittsburg, 47. Polit. & Govt. Pos: W.Va. State Del, 56-68. Bus. & Prof. Pos: Athletic dir, Fairmont State Col, 39-66; inventor and pres, Z Bar, Inc, 58-65; dir, Elsco, Educators Invest. Serv. Co, 66. Mil. Serv: Entered as Ens, Navy, 42, released as Lt.(jg), 45, ETO; Asian-Mid East. and Invasion of France Ribbons. Publ: Isometric Exercises, Privately Published, 58; 'Little League Try Out System,' Little Leaguer, 52. Mem: Nat. Educ. Asn; Am. Asn. Higher Educ; Am. Asn. of Coaches; Am. Asn. Health, Phys. Educ. & Recreation; ABCA; MCEA; Rotary; Elks; Am. Legion; 40 et 8; Fairmont Develop. Asn. Organizer, first little leaguers and pony leagues, Va. and W.Va; Selected as Man Who Had Done Most for Sports in W.Va, Sportwriters and Sportcasters, 52. Rel: Methodist. Mailing Add: 1 Camden Rd, Fairmont, W.Va. 26554. (1967)

WILSON, WILL R. R
Asst. Attorney Gen, Criminal Div, Dept. of Justice
Mailing Add: Dept. of Justice, Constitution Ave. & Tenth St. N.W, Washington, D.C. 20530.

WILSON, WILLIAM E. D
b. Scottsburg, Ind, 3/1/96; s. W. L. Wilson and Edith Tipps W; m. 8/30/34 to Myrtle Z. Huffman. Educ: Hanover Col, A.B, 18, LL.D, 61; Ind. State Teachers Col, A.M, 31; LL.D, Ball State Univ, 47. Polit. & Govt. Pos: State Supt. of Pub. Instr, Pa, 59-67. Bus. & Prof. Pos: Former sch. supt, teacher and prin, Pa; instr, Ind. State Univ, Southeast. Campus, currently. Mil. Serv: World War I. Legal Res: 203 Maple Wood St, Jeffersonville, Ind. 47130. Mailing Add: Indiana State University, Southeastern Campus, Warder Park, Jeffersonville, Ind. 47130. (1967)

WILSON, WILLIAM LANEY D
Chmn, State Dem. Cent. Cmt, Md.
b. Cumberland, Md, 5/9/14; s. William Laney Wilson, Sr. and Rhea Myers W; m. 5/16/42 to Elizabeth Lee Gracie; c. Amanda L. Educ: Wash. & Lee Univ, A.B, 36, Law Sch, LL.B, 38; Omicron Delta Kappa; Phi Delta Phi; Kappa Alpha. Polit. & Govt. Pos: Chmn, Md. State Dem. Cent. Cmt, 48-54 & 61-, state treas, 68-; chmn, Housing Authority, Cumberland, 50-52 and Civil Serv. Cmn, Allegany Co, 57-60; v.pres, Md. State Bd. Educ, 60-67; del, Dem. Nat. Conv, 68. Bus. & Prof. Pos: Dir, First Nat. Bank & Trust Co, Md, 55-; pres, Queen City Brewing Co, 57-; dir, Cumberland Brewing Co, 58- and U.S. Brewers Asn, 67- Mil. Serv: Entered as Ens, Naval Res, 41, released as Lt. Comdr, 46. Mem: V.pres, Md. State Bar Asn, 55; pres, Allegany Co. Bar Asn, 64; pres. bd. trustees, State Cols. of Md, 63-; dir, Sacred Heart Hosp; pres, Cumberland C. of C, 62; Am. Legion; VFW; Mason; Elks; Eagles. Rel: Episcopal; Sr. Warden. Legal Res: 527 Washington St, Cumberalnd, Md. 21502. Mailing Add: Liberty Trust Bldg, Cumberland, Md. 21502.

WILSON, WILLIAM ORVAL D
Chmn, Greene Co. Dem. Cent. Cmt, Ill.
b. Coal City, Ill, 1/14/11; s. William Wilson and Agnes Hunter W; m. 6/7/33 to Marguerite Zboyovski; c. Marguerite and William Joseph. Educ: High Sch, grad. Polit. & Govt. Pos: Chmn, Greene Co. Dem. Cent. Cmt, Ill, currently. Bus. & Prof. Pos: Asst. mine mgr, Superior Coal Co, 42-52; grocer, Southside Market, 46-69; owner, Wilson's Tavern, 52-64; farmer, Calhoun and Greene Co, Ill, 59-69. Mem: Carrollton and Eldred Sportsman Club; Farm Bur; Ill. Valley Econ. Develop. Corp. Rel: Christian. Mailing Add: 314 Church St, Carrollton, Ill. 62016.

WILSON, WILLIAM P. D
b. Independence, Mo, 12/31/37; s. Harry Wilson and Charline W; single. Educ: Iowa State Univ; Am. Univ, B.A; Sigma Nu; Pi Sigma Alpha. Polit. & Govt. Pos: Iowa State Rep, until 66; Nat. Committeeman Young Dem. Clubs of Iowa; former mem. staff of U.S. Rep. Merwin Coad. Bus. & Prof. Pos: V.pres, Aaron Gold & Assoc. Mem: Jaycees; NAACP; Iowa State Cyclone Club. Rel: Methodist. Mailing Add: 6211 N. Winthrop, Chicago, Ill. 60626.

WILSON, WOODROW R
Nev. State Assemblyman
b. 1916. Polit. & Govt. Pos: Mem. adv. cmt, U.S. Civil Rights Cmn; Nev. State Assemblyman, 67-; del, Rep. Nat. Conv, 68. Bus. & Prof. Pos: Mem. staff, Am. Potash and Chem. Co, Henderson, Nev; treas. and mgr, Westside Fed. Credit Union. Mem: NAACP; Nev. Voters League. Mailing Add: 625 Frederick Ave, Las Vegas, Nev. 89106. (1967)

WILT, RAYMOND E. R
Pa. State Rep.
b. Ross Twp, Pa, 12/5/07; s. Jacob Wilt and Caroline Wieland W; m. to Marcella Newman; c. five. Educ: Pittsburgh Schs. Polit. & Govt. Pos: Pa. State Rep, 50-; chmn, Ross Twp. Rep. Cmt. Bus. & Prof. Pos: Hauling contractor. Mem: Moose; Elks; Kiwanis; Mason; Commandery K. T, Syria Mosque Shrine; Allegheny Co. and State Fireman's Asns; N.Park Sportsman Club; AFL; F&AM; RAM. Mailing Add: 131 Enger Ave, Pittsburgh, Pa. 15214.

WILT, THORNTON W. D
Chmn, Jefferson Co. Dem. Party, W.Va.
b. Jefferson Co, W.Va, 10/25/16; s. Thomas W. Wilt and Cecilia Staubs W; m. 8/2/41 to Katherine Hodges; c. Anne Hodges, Thornton W, Jr, Katherine, G. Thomas and Sarah Beth. Educ: Shepherd Col. Polit. & Govt. Pos: W.Va. State Rep, 62-68; chmn, Jefferson Co. Dem. Party, currently. Bus. & Prof. Pos: Sales mgr. Mem: C. of C; Theta Sigma Chi. Rel: Lutheran. Mailing Add: Bolivar Heights, W.Va. 25426. (1967)

WILT, WILLIAM W. R
Pa. State Rep.
b. Altoona, Pa, 4/15/18; s. Harry E. Wilt and Estella Williams W; m. to Marjorie Jane Benton; c. Two sons. Educ: Hollidaysburg High Schs. Polit. & Govt. Pos: Pa. State Rep, 62- Bus. & Prof. Pos: Tel. repairman. Mil. Serv: Army, 43-45, ETO. Mem: Fedn. of Tel. Workers of Pa; Am. Legion; VFW; former master, Juniata Lodge, F&AM; former pres, Hollidaysburg Sportsmen's Club; Blair Co. Fedn. of Sportsmen's Club. Mailing Add: 1211 Maple Ave, Hollidaysburg, Pa. 16648. (1967)

WIMBERLY, HELEN DAMERON D
b. Iowa City, Iowa, 10/30/97; d. James Lewis Dameron and Mattie Winston D; m. 7/19/52 to Joseph Waddell Wimberly; c. William Hutchason Beshears, Jr. Educ: Whitney Carr Scholarship, Univ. Iowa, 16-20, B.A, 20; Univ. Chicago Sch. of Soc. Serv, summers 36, 38 & 40; Drake Univ-Univ. Iowa Summer Sch; Delta Sigma Theta; Cosmopolitan Club. Polit. & Govt. Pos: secy, Polk Co. Dem. Cent. Cmt, Iowa; del, Dem. State Conv, 64 & 66; del, Dem. Statutory Conv, 68; alternate del, Dem. Nat. Conv, 68; precinct committeewoman and mem. exec. bd, Polk Co. Dem. Womans Activities Club, Iowa, currently. Bus. & Prof. Pos: Probation officer, Polk Co. Juvenile Court, Iowa, 33-43; exec. dir, Germantown Br, YWCA, Phila, Plainfield, N.J, 45-46; social worker, N.Y. State Dept. of Welfare, 46-48, Iowa State Bd. of Control, 48-52 and Chicago Dept. of Welfare, 52-55; probation officer, Polk Co. Juvenile Court, 57-63; retired. Mem: Cmt. on Crime and Delinquency, Iowa Welfare Assn; past pres, Iowa Asn. of Colored Womens Clubs; Social Action Cmt, Iowa Coun. of Churches. Rel: African Methodist Episcopal; Pres. Laymens Orgn, St. Paul African Methodist Episcopal Church. Mailing Add: 2720 Amick Ave, Des Moines, Iowa 50310.

WIMMER, JAMES WILLIAM, JR. D
Chmn, State Dem. Party, Wis.
b. Portage, Wis, 10/20/35; s. James William Wimmer and Alice Bauer W; m. 8/6/67 to Mary Alice Cullen; c. Leslie Ann. Educ: Univ. Wis, Madison, B.A, 59; Beta Theta Pi; MACE. Polit. & Govt. Pos: Admin. asst. to Gov, Wis, 59-62 and Speaker of Wis. State Assembly, 65-66; del, Dem. Nat. Conv, 68; chmn, State Dem. Party, Wis, 69- Bus. & Prof. Pos: Pres, Intergovt. Research Assoc, Madison, Wis, 67- Mil. Serv: Entered as 2nd Lt, Army, 62, released as 1st Lt, 64, after serv. in U.S. forces overseas, NATO; Capt, Inactive Reserves, currently; Army Commendation Award. Rel: Presbyterian. Legal Res: 411 Wisconsin Ave, Wisconsin Dells, Wis. 53965. Mailing Add: 222 E. Main St, Madison, Wis. 53703.

WINCHESTER, LUCY ALEXANDER R
Soc. Secy, The White House
b. Lexington, Ky, 1/11/37; d. James Holloway Alexander and Lucy Moulthrop

A; div; c. Lucy. Educ: Finch Jr. Col, dipl, 57; Univ. Ky, B.A, 60. Polit. & Govt. Pos: Mem. staff, protocol off, U.S. Mission to U.N, 60; guide, U.N, 60-62; hostess, VIP room, Nixon Hq, Rep. Nat. Conv, 68; soc. secy, The White House, 69- Bus. & Prof. Pos: Owner and mgr, Alexander Farms, Lexington, Ky, 62-69. Legal Res: Lexington, Ky. 40504. Mailing Add: 1600 Pennsylvania Ave, Washington, D.C. 20006.

WIND, HERBERT HAMILTON, JR. D
Secy. and Treas, Grade Co. Dem. Party, Ga.
b. Cairo, Ga, 6/7/15; s. Herbert Hamilton Wind, Sr. and Isola Vanlandingham W; m. 5/22/37 to Catherine Stephens; c. Robert Hamilton and Herbert Wesley. Educ: Middle Ga. Col, 33-34. Polit. & Govt. Pos: Chmn, Grade Co. Dem. Party, Ga, secy. and treas, 46- Bus. & Prof. Pos: Ed, The Cairo Messenger, 46-68, publ, 68-, pres, Messenger Publ. Co, Inc, Cairo, Ga, 56- Mem: Rotary; Ga. Press Asn; Am. Newspaper Asn; Grady Co. Farm Bur. Rel: Methodist. Legal Res: R.F.D. 2, Cairo, Ga. 31728. Mailing Add: P.O. Box 30, Cairo, Ga. 31728.

WINDINGSTAD, HAROLD OLIVER, JR. DFL
b. Dawson, Minn, 8/26/29; s. Harold Oliver Windingstad, Sr. and Alvina Simonson W; m. 6/20/53 to Dolores Lucille Hoyles. Educ: Dawson High Sch, grad, 47. Polit. & Govt. Pos: V.chmn, Lac qui Parle Co. Dem-Farmer-Labor Party, Minn, 58-59, chmn, 60-69; v.chmn, Sixth Dist. Dem-Farmer-Labor Party, 65-69; del, Dem. Nat. Conv, 68. Bus. & Prof. Pos: Farmer, currently. Mem: Farmers Union; chmn, West. Tri-Co. Commun. Action Coun; chmn, Sch. Bd. Dist. 61. Rel: Lutheran. Mailing Add: Dawson, Minn. 56232.

WINDON, BERNARD MILROY R
b. Winfield, W.Va, 5/19/40; s. Chester Windon and Arminta Gill W; single. Educ: Moody Bible Inst, Ill, 61; Westmont Col, Calif, 64. Polit. & Govt. Pos: Exec. dir, Sixth Dist. Rep. Party, La, 64-65; exec. dir, Young Rep. Nat. Fedn, 65-67. Mem: Jaycees. Rel: Baptist. 1967 Legal Res: Washington, D.C. No mailing address available. (1967)

WINDSHEIMER, WALTER W. R
Mem, Benton Co. Rep. Finance Cmt, Wash.
b. Oakdale, Pa, 8/8/13; s. John Windsheimer and Anne Louise Bernhart W; single. Educ: Waynesburg Col, B.Sc, 38; Activities Hon. Soc; pres, Scholastic Hon. Soc. Polit. & Govt. Pos: Chmn, nuclear energy subcmt, Benton Co. Rep. Platform Cmt, Wash, 58; finance chmn, Benton Co. Rep. Party, 61 & 62, co. chmn, 67 & 68; mem, electronic data processing cmt, Wash. Rep. State Cent. Cmt, 67-68; alternate del, Rep. Nat. Conv, 68; del, Rep. State Conv, 68. Bus. & Prof. Pos: Field supvr, Agr. Exten. Agency, 39-40, chemist, Universal Cyclops Steel Co, 40-41; supvr, E.I. DuPont Co, 41-45; prod. and eng. mgr, Gen. Elec. Co, 46-65; admin. specialist and prin. engr, Douglas United Nuclear, Inc, 65- Mem: Am. Nuclear Soc; Am. Soc. Chem. Engrs; Elks; Grange. Rel: Lutheran. Mailing Add: 58 Park St, Richland, Wash. 99352.

WINDSOR, JULIUS GAYLE, JR. D
Ark. State Rep.
b. Tulsa, Okla, 6/4/20; s. Julius Gayle Windsor and Bertha Lewis W; m. 12/16/44 to Betty Kraft; c. Margaret (Mrs. Clark), Mary Elizabeth and John Gayle. Educ: Univ. Calif, Los Angeles, B.A, 46; Ark. Law Sch, LL.B, 52; Theta Chi. Polit. & Govt. Pos: Ark. State Rep, Pulaski Co, 57-63 & 67- Bus. & Prof. Pos: Self-employed lawyer and public acct, 49- Mil. Serv: Entered as Aviation Cadet, Army Air Corps, 41, released as Capt, 46, after serv. in 2nd and 3rd Air Force, Continental U.S, 42-46. Mem: Ark. and Am. Bar Asns; Lions Int; Am. Legion. Rel: Baptist. Legal Res: 1019 N. Arthur, Little Rock, Ark. 72207. Mailing Add: 1040 Tower Bldg, Little Rock, Ark. 72201.

WINEBRENNER, TOMMY LEE R
Minority Postmaster, U.S. House of Rep.
b. Wolf Lake, Ind, 1/14/36; s. Heber Winebrenner and Francis Marker W; m. 6/11/60 to Barbara Berry; c. Pamela Lee and Mark Lewis. Educ: Am. Univ, B.S, 60; George Wash. Univ. Law Sch; Alpha Tau Omega. Polit. & Govt. Pos: Page boy, U.S. House of Rep, 53-54, asst, mgr. minority tel, 55-63 and Minority Postmaster, 62- Mem: Fed. Lodge, F&AM; Capitol Hill Club. Rel: Methodist. Legal Res: La Porte, Ind. 46350. Mailing Add: 8418 Crown Place, Alexandria, Va. 22308.

WINELAND, FRED L. D
Md. State Sen.
b. Wash, D.C, 8/16/26; married. Educ: Am. Univ; Southeast. Univ. Polit. & Govt. Pos: Young Dem. Club of Prince George's Co; Oxon Hill Dem. Club; past pres, Ft. Wash. Dem. Club; Co. Coun. of Dem. Clubs; campaign chmn, Prince George's Co. Primary Elec, 62; campaign v.chmn, Prince George's Co. Gen. Elec, 62; Md. State Rep, 63-65; campaign chmn, Prince George's Co. Gen. Elec, 64; Md. State Sen, 65- Bus. & Prof. Pos: Motion picture theatre and closed circuit TV owner. Mil. Serv: Navy. Mem: Md. Farm Bur; South. Md. Bd. of Trade; Aircraft Owners and Pilots; Nat. Rivers and Harbors Cong; C. of C; Southeast Hosp. Action Cmt; Variety Club; area chmn, UGF; Mason; Shrine; Oxon Hill Lions Club; VFW; Allentown Rd. Vol. Fire Dept. Rel: Methodist; Pres, Bd. of Trustees, Ft. Washington Methodist Church. Mailing Add: 1100 W. Riverview Rd, Silesia, Md. 20022.

WINFIELD, MARY JONES D
Dem. Nat. Committeewoman, N.C.
b. Valdosta, Ga, 1/16/16; d. Henry Davis Jones and Ethel Mae Hightower J; m. 6/28/35 to John Augustus Winfield; c. Frances Ann (Mrs. Bowers), Mary Virginia (Mrs. Dowdy), Gloria Jean and John Scott. Educ: Ga. State Woman's Col, 34-35; E.Carolina Univ, 36. Polit. & Govt. Pos: Dem. chmn, Yeatesville Precinct, N.C, 58-68; alternate del, Dem. Nat. Conv, 68; v.chmn, Beaufort Co. Dem. Party, 68-; Dem. Nat. Committeewoman, N.C, 68- Mem: State pres, Home Demonstration Clubs, 64; local sch. bd, 6 years, dist. three sch. bd, 2 years, chmn, Better Schs. Beaufort Co, 9 years; Gov. Sanford appointee, Spec. Cmn. Libr. Resources; bd. dirs, Mt. Olive Col; Tuberc. Asn; Cancer Bd; South. Albemarle Asn. Outstanding Club Woman, 64; Atlantic and Pac. Leadership Award, 65; Outstanding Church Woman Albemarle Dist, 66; Rural Elec. Asn. Rural Award, 68; featured as outstanding Women Farm Mgrs. South. Region, Farm and Ranch Mag; Tar Heel of the Week, New and Observer. Rel: Freewill Baptist; Sunday Sch. Teacher, 15 years; numerous speeches in Albemarle Dist. Mailing Add: Route 1, Pinetown, N.C. 27865.

WING, ADA SCHICK R
b. Bartlett, Ill, 10/14/96; d. August Schick and Augusta Meyer S; div; c. Wilbur Schick Wing (deceased). Educ: Elgin Acad. Jr. Col, 1 year. Polit. & Govt. Pos: Pres, Santa Barbara Co. Rep. Women, Calif, 56-60; mem, Santa Barbara Co. Rep. Cent. Cmt, 62-66; mem, Calif. Rep. State Cent. Cmt, 64-69; mem, Gov. Reagan's Adv. Cmt. on Ment. Illness, 68-; Rep. precinct chmn, Santa Barbara Co, currently. Bus. & Prof. Pos: Teacher, Ill, 18; off. mgr, Chicago, Ill, 20-25; asst. to dir. of defunct banks, Terra Bella and Woodlake, Calif, 32-34; ins. agent, Aetna Life, 40-43; mgr, orange grove, Terra Bella, Calif, 49-65. Mem: Rep. Women's Club; Carpenteria Women's Club; Ment. Health Asn.(pres. women's bd, Santa Barbara Asn). Rated first of ten best precinct chmn. in Calif. Rel: Protestant. Mailing Add: 3675 La Entrada Rd, Santa Barbara, Calif. 93105.

WING, FRANCIS WILLIAM R
Chmn, Freetown Rep. Town Cmt, Mass.
b. Fall River, Mass, 1/19/41; s. Hilda S. Neal; m. 7/1/67 to Lois Ann Bennett. Educ: Wentworth Inst, A.E. in Prod. Eng, 62; Northeast. Univ, B.S. in Indust. Tech, 66. Polit. & Govt. Pos: Mem, Bd. of Pub. Welfare, Freetown, Mass, 63-68, mem, Bd. of Selectmen and Bd. of Health and police cmnr, 63-69; mem, Freetown Rep. Town Cmt, 63-, chmn, 68-; pres, Bristol Co. Selectmen's Asn, 65-66; mem. exec. bd, Mass. Selectmen's Asn, 65-66; mem, Pub. State Welfare Cmt, 68- Bus. & Prof. Pos: Indust. engr, Aerovox Corp, New Bedford, Mass, 63-64, Raytheon Co, 69-; head of qual. control, J.I. Paulding, 64-65; syst. engr, Cornell Dubilier, 65-69. Mem: Am. Soc. of Qual. Control; AF&AM; bd. trustees, Bristol Commun. Col, 67-; Lions. Youngest elected selectman in Mass. history. Rel: First Christian. Mailing Add: 238 Elm St, Assonet, Mass. 02702.

WING, LEONARD ARCHIE R
Finance Chmn, Rep. Cent. Cmt, Mont.
b. Comfrey, Minn, 6/20/06; s. Arthur Carl Wing and Sophie Olivia Swanson W; m. 2/23/33 to Eula Cora Thompson; c. David Arthur. Educ: Mont. State Univ; Phi Kappa Phi; Alpha Zeta; Scabbard & Blade. Polit. & Govt. Pos: Chmn, Gallatin Co. Rep Cent. Cmt, Mont, 63-64 & 65; committeeman, First Dist. Mont. Rep. Cent. Cmt, 64-; finance chmn, Rep. Cent. Cmt, currently; del, Rep. Nat. Conv, 68. Bus. & Prof. Pos: Finance inst. employee, 32-40; cattle rancher, 32- Mil. Serv: Entered as Pvt, Army, 23, released as Lt. Col, 46, after serv. in 41st Div, Pac; Silver Star; Bronze Star; Air Medal; Combat Inf. Medal. Mem: Mason; C. of C; Shrine; Farm Bur; Mont. Stock Growers Asn. Rel: Lutheran. Mailing Add: Route 3, Box 72, Bozeman, Mont. 59715.

WINGARD, GEORGE FRANK R
Ore. State Rep.
b. Amboy, Wash, 11/6/35; s. Sylvester Caroll Wingard and Edna English W; m. to Rhea Mae Henault; c. Carol Lynne and Gail Ann. Educ: Univ. Ore, 2 years; Ore. State Univ, 2 years; Sigma Chi. Polit. & Govt. Pos: Councilman, Eugene City Coun, Ore, 66-; Ore. State Rep, 69- Bus. & Prof. Pos: Owner, EDCO, currently; owner and pres, Wingard Construction, Inc, currently; co-owner, J & W, Inc, currently. Mem: Urban Land Inst; Metro Civic Club; Elks; C. of C. Jr. First Citizen of Eugene, 68; One of Ore. Five Outstanding Young Men, 68. Rel: Presbyterian. Mailing Add: 2323 Fairmount, Eugene, Ore. 97403.

WINGARD, JOHN P. Conservative
Minn. State Rep.
b. Brooklyn Center, Minn, 1927; married; c. Four. Educ: Univ. Minn, B.A. Polit. & Govt. Pos: Justice of Peace, Brooklyn Center, Minn, 54-62; Minn. State Rep, 62- Bus. & Prof. Pos: Farmer. Distinguished Serv. Award and Outstanding Farmer's Award, Jr. C. of C. Mailing Add: Route 1, Champlin, Minn. 55316. (1967)

WINGATE, CLAUDE E. D
b. Hilliard, Fla, 3/15/23; m. to Elizabeth Ament 'Betty Jo'; c. LeeNora Jo, Janet, Claudia, Wayne and Monta. Polit. & Govt. Pos: Fla. State Rep, 62-66. Bus. & Prof. Pos: Millwright; pub. rels. Mil. Serv: Navy, 42-45, Navy Carrier Div, Oper. Training Units. Mem: Past pres, Kraft Athletic Club; membership cmt, Am. Legion Post 54; v.pres. state coun. and exec. bd. of dirs, Dist. 112 Int. Asn. of Machinists; bd. of dirs, Fernandina Beach Boat Club; F&AM; Temple Lodge 23; charter mem, Nassau Co. Young Dem. Rel: Baptist. Mailing Add: 631 N. Fletcher Ave, Fernandina Beach, Fla. 32034. (1967)

WINGATE, RICHARD ANTHONY R
Chmn, Voluntown Rep. Town Cmt, Conn.
b. Brooklyn, N.Y, 5/27/37; s. Elsdon Anthony Wingate and Florence Maybeck W; m. 8/16/58 to Dorothy Ann Daycock; c. Mark Anthony, Belinda Jo, Elizabeth Claire and Matthew Jon. Educ: State Univ. N.Y, Oswego, B.S, 58; Ind. Univ, M.S, 60; Epsilon Pi Tau; Delta Kappa Kappa. Polit. & Govt. Pos: Justice of the Peace, Voluntown, Conn, 68-; chmn, Voluntown Rep. Town Cmt, 68- Bus. & Prof. Pos: Indust. Arts Teacher, Stonington High Sch, 61- Mil. Serv: Entered as Seaman Recruit, Naval Res, 54, released as Seaman, 62. Mem: Nat. and Conn. Educ. Asns; East. Conn. Indust. Arts Asn; Voluntown Vol. Fire Dept; Mason; Eastern Star. Rel: Congregational. Legal Res: Pendelton Hill, Voluntown, Conn. 06384. Mailing Add: R.F.D. 1, North Stonington, Conn. 06359.

WINGE, HERBERT CLAYTON R
Chmn, Third Region Seventh Cong. Dist. Rep. Party, Minn.
b. Van Hook Twp, N.Dak, 9/15/23; s. Albert Nicoli Winge and Mabel Gregerson W. (deceased); m. 5/28/50 to Alice Cape; c. Vernon, Carol, Joyce and Marlys. Educ: Univ. N.Dak, B.A, 49, B.S, 50; Northwest. Univ. & Med. Sch, M.D, 52; Wesley Mem. Hosp, Chicago, Internship, 52-53; Sacred Heart Hosp, Yankton, S.Dak, G.P. Residency, 53-54; Phi Beta Pi. Polit. & Govt. Pos: Chmn, Traverse Co. Rep. Party, Minn, 63-69; finance chmn, Third Region Seventh Cong. Dist. Rep. Party, 65-69, chmn, 69-; health officer, Wheaton, 67- Bus. & Prof. Pos: Private medical practice, 54-; chief of staff, Wheaton Commun. Hosp, 67- Mil. Serv: Entered as Pvt, Army Med. Dept, Ft. Snelling, Minn, 43, released as T/4, 46, after serv. in 20th Armored Div, ETO; Good Conduct Medal; Bronze Star Medal; European Theater Ribbon. Mem: W.Cent. Minn. Med. Soc; Am. Med. Asn; Minn. State Med. Asn;(mem. policy and liaison cmt); Am.Acad. Gen. Practice; Minn. Acad. Gen. Practice (mem. cmt.

on med. econ); Mason; chmn, Traverse Co. Cancer Soc. Rel: Presbyterian. Legal Res: 702 Fifth Ave. N, Wheaton, Minn. 56296. Mailing Add: 11 Tenth St. N, Wheaton, Minn. 56296.

WINGE, RALPH M. D
b. Van Hook, N.Dak, 8/25/25; s. Albert N. Winge and Mabel C. Gregerson W; single. Educ: N.Dak. State Univ, B.S, 53. Polit. & Govt. Pos: N.Dak. State Rep, 59-69, mem, Legis. Research Cmt, 61-65 & 67-69. Bus. & Prof. Pos: Farmer, Van Hook, N.Dak, 43-53; farmer, Litchville, N.Dak, 53- Mem: Farmers Union; Sons of Norway. Rel: Lutheran. Mailing Add: Route 2, Box 81, Litchville, N.Dak. 58461.

WINGETT, ERNEST A. D
b. Pratts Fork, Ohio, 4/2/04; s. Wm. E. Wingett and Minnie Whetstone W; m. 6/13/31 to Maxine Spencer. Educ: Ohio Univ, B.S, 30; Columbia Univ. Polit. & Govt. Pos: Mayor, Racine, Ohio, 46-56 & 58-64; del, Dem. Nat. Conv, 64; chmn, Meigs Co. Dem. Exec. Cmt, Ohio, 65-66. Bus. & Prof. Pos: Teacher, 25 & 37; bus. mgr, newspaper, Pomeroy, Ohio, 44-53; teacher, Ravenswood High Sch, 63-66. Mem: Ohio Educ. Asn; Nat. Educ. Asn; Mason, F&AM, Commandery. Rel: Methodist. Mailing Add: Elm St, Racine, Ohio 45771. (1967)

WINGFIELD, LOTUS MAE D
Secy, Yuma Co. Dem. Party, Colo.
b. Mildred, Colo, 10/5/11; d. C. C. Duff and Estie A. Eastin D; m. 10/5/35 Educ: Yuma Co. High Sch, 2 years; Am. Sch. Correspondence course, 2 years. Polit. & Govt. Pos: Committeewoman, Precinct 19, Yuma Co. Dem. Party, Colo, 37-69; clerk, U.S. Post Off, 40-50, U.S. Postmistress, 50-54; v.pres, secy. and treas, Yuma Co. Jane Jefferson Clubs, 55-60, pres, 62-63; secy, Yuma Co. Dem. Party, 69- Mem: Eastern Star (all degrees and Worthy Matron); hon. mem, Extension Homemakers Club (state treas, 56-59); youth leader, Farmers Union, 40-44; leader, 4-H, 41-54. Rel: Methodist. Mailing Add: Eckley, Colo. 80727.

WINGO, CECIL D
Chmn, Brazoria Co. Dem. Party, Tex.
b. Poteau, Okla, 3/11/29; s. Cecil Wingo, Sr. and Mabel Todd W; m. 11/4/50 to Dorothy Sue Matthews; c. Stewart Matthew. Educ: U.S. Dept. Justice, Border Patrol Acad, 56; Univ. Tex, 60; Univ. Houston, 64. Polit. & Govt. Pos: Constable, precinct one, Brazoria Co, Tex, 60-64; chmn. co. del, State Dem. Conv, 66 & 68; chmn, Brazoria Co. Dem. Party, 67-; alternate del, Dem. Nat. Conv, 68. Bus. & Prof. Pos: Proj. engr, Wallace Indust. Construction, Houston, 64; proj. engr, Sam P. Wallace Co, 64 and proj. mgr, 68; sales engr, Knost Eng. and Construction, currently. Mil. Serv: Enlisted, Navy, 45, released 49, after serv. in destroyers, N.Atlantic and Caribbean; Maj, Tex. Mil. Forces, 61-; Victory Medal; Am. Theatre Medal. Mem: Am. Legion; State Guard Asn; dir, Brazoria Co. Fair Asn; Eagles. Rel: Presbyterian. Mailing Add: 9 Kaysie, Angleton, Tex. 77515.

WINKEL, MORTON ARNOLD D
b. New York, N.Y, 3/8/30; s. Walter L. Winkel and Leah Neidenberg W; m. 6/27/59 to Geneva June Swearingen; c. Phyllis, Berganini, Douglas and Dina. Educ: N.Y. Univ, B.A, 51; Columbia Law Sch, LL.B, 54. Polit. & Govt. Pos: Treas, Multnomah Co. Dem. Cent. Cmt, Ore, 63-65, chmn, 65-68. Bus. & Prof. Pos: Law clerk, Justice George Rossman, Ore. Supreme Court, 56-57; assoc, Reinhardt, Coblens and Stoll, 59-61; partner, Reinhardt, Coblens, Stoll and Winkel, 62-68; attorney and dist. judge pro tem, Multnomah Co, 69- Mil. Serv: Entered as Pvt, Army, 54, released as Pfc, 56, after serv. in Antilles. Mem: Am. Bar Asn; Ore. State Bar; Multnomah Bar; Portland City Club; Am. Civil Liberties Union; Jewish Commun. Center; bd. dir, Ore. Consumer League, 67-; Portland UN Asn, 69- Rel: Jewish. Legal Res: 3619 S.W. 38th Ave, Portland, Ore. 97221. Mailing Add: 500 Corbett Bldg, Portland, Ore. 97204.

WINKELMAN, ROBERT BERNARD, JR. D
b. Philadelphia, Pa, 5/12/23; s. Robert Bernard Winkelman and Nora Devitt W; m. 10/28/50 to Pauline Petraits; c. Eileen, Nora and Robert, III. Educ: La Salle Col, B.S. in acct, 44; Mt. St. Mary's Col, Emmitsburg, Md; Temple Univ. Polit. & Govt. Pos: Chmn, 58th Ward Dem. Exec. Cmt, Pa, 61-64; city councilman, Tenth Dist, Phila, 62-63; alternate del, Dem. Nat. Conv, 64; dep. cmnr, Dept. of Pub. Property, Phila, 64- Mil. Serv: Entered as A/S, Navy, 43, released as Lt, 46, after serv. in Signal Corps, Naval Construction Bns, Pac. Area, 44-46. Mem: Nat. Asn. of Life Underwriters; K. of C. Rel: Roman Catholic. Mailing Add: 850 Bartlett St, Philadelphia, Pa. 19115.

WINKELMAN, WILLIAM PRATT R
Iowa State Rep.
b. Lohrville, Iowa, 1/14/33; s. Ewart Cain Winkelman and Marjorie Pratt W; single. Educ: Iowa State Univ, B.S, 54; Alpha Gamma Rho. Polit. & Govt. Pos: Councilman, Lohrville, Iowa, 60-61; organizing chmn, Calhoun Co. Young Rep, 62; Iowa State Rep, Calhoun Co, 62-, mem, Higher Educ. Facilities Cmn, Iowa State House of Rep, 67- and chmn, Iowa Develop. Cmt, 69-; alternate del, Rep. Nat. Conv, 64. Bus. & Prof. Pos: Pres, Lohrville Commercial Club, 59; proprietor, Winkelman Farms, 58-; dir, Am. Shetland Pony Club, 62-65; committeeman, Am. Horse Shows Asn, 62-67, dir. and v.pres, 67-; dir, Welsh Pony Soc. Am, 64; dir, Iowa Soc. Preservation Historic Landmarks, 67- Mil. Serv: Entered as 2nd Lt, Air Force, 55, released as 1st Lt, 57; Capt, Air Force Res, 62- Mem: Pres, Lohrville High Sch. Alumni Asn, 60-65; cmnr, N.W. Iowa to United Presbyterian Gen. Assembly, U.S.A, 60; pres, Chap. 17, Nat. Sojourners, 57; mem. of commandery, Consistory, Shrine. Univ. Merit of Leadership Award, Iowa State Univ, 53 and 54. Rel: Presbyterian. Mailing Add: R.R. 2, Lohrville, Iowa 51453.

WINKELMANN, HERMAN PAUL D
Mo. State Rep.
b. St. Louis, Mo, 6/22/12; s. Ernest A. Winkelmann and Clara I. Paule W; m. 10/10/34 to Julianna Marie Fleis; c. Julianna Christi 'Judy'(Mrs. Eugene Louis LaBarge). Educ: St. Louis Col. of Pharm. and Allied Sci, Ph.G, 33; Omega Phi. Polit. & Govt. Pos: Chmn, Decent Lit. Cmn. for St. Louis, Mo, 54-65; mem, Mo. Bd. Pharm, 56; nominee, Mo. State Rep, Dist. 48, 66; pres, Bd. Aldermen Lakeshire, St. Louis Co, 66-68; mem, Gov. Coun. on Commun. Affairs, 68-; Mo. State Rep, Dist. 48, 69- Bus. & Prof. Pos: Exec. mgr, St. Louis Pharmacists Asn, 44-62; bus. mgr, Nat. Asn. of Retail Druggists Conv. in St. Louis, 52 & 59. Mem: Nat. Asn. of Retail Druggists; Am. and Mo. Pharmaceutical Asns; Cinchona Club; Vet. Druggist; Citizens for Decent Lit; Metrop. Pharmaceutical Secretaries Asn.(pres, mem, and secy, 44-62); Alumni Asn. St. Louis Col. of Pharm. and Allied Sci.(pres, 52-54); St. Louis Diabetes Asn.(pres, 61-65); Arthritis and Rheumatism Found, East. Mo. Chap. (treas); Hampton Lions (first v.pres, 68-69); mem. lay adv. bd, Incarnate Word Hosp; St. Louis Chap, Nat. Cath. Pharmacists Guild (pres); Elks. Man of the Year Award, Sch. Pharm, Univ. Mo. at Kansas City Alumni Asn, 52; Pharmacist of the Year, St. Louis Col. Pharm. Alumni Asn, 60. Rel: Catholic; Pres, Catholic Laymen's Retreat League, 59-60. Mailing Add: 10111 Stonell Dr, Lakeshire, St. Louis Co, Mo. 63123.

WINKLES, FRED LARRY R
Ga. State Rep.
b. Carrollton, Ga; s. Riley Steven Winkles and Annie Gertrude Potts W; m. 12/22/51 to Harriett Ann Spruell; c. Fred Larry, Jr, Gwendolyn Nell, Michael Anthony and Stephan Allen. Educ: Ga. State Col, B.B.A, 57; Alpha Kappa Psi. Polit. & Govt. Pos: Ga. State Rep, 67- Mil. Serv: Entered as Pvt, Army, 51, released as Cpl, 53. Mem: Am. Col.Life Underwriters. Rel: Presbyterian. Mailing Add: 878 Falcon Dr, Atlanta, Ga. 30311.

WINN, CECELIA LOUISE D
Mem, Dem. State Cmt, N.H.
b. Nashua, N.H, 4/24/07; d. John Winn and Cecelia Degnan W; single. Educ: Keene State Teachers' Col, grad; Harvard Univ; Boston Univ; Univ. N.H, M.E; Nashua, N.H. Col. Club. Polit. & Govt. Pos: Nashua Women's Dem. Chmn, 62-66, pres, 63-65; mem, Status of Women, N.H, 63; N.H. Women's Chmn. for President Johnson, 64; del. and mem. credentials cmt, Dem. Nat. Conv, 64; del, N.H. Dem. Conv, 64 & 66; mem, Hundred Dollar State Dem. Club; mem, N.H. Dem. Cmt, 66-; mem, Dem. State Cmt, N.H, 66-; Co. Dem. V.Chmn, 68-; Women's City Chmn, 68- Bus. & Prof. Pos: Guidance counselor, Nashua Sch. Dept, 28- Publ: Polit. articles in defense of Dem. Party. Mem: N.H. Personnel and Guidance Asn; New England and Nat. Guidance Asns; Bay State Beagle Club; Gr. Lowell Beagle-Brunswick Foxhound Club; pres, Nashua Teachers' Coun and Nashua Cath. Women's Guild; Cath. Daughters of Am; AFL-CIO Nashua Teachers Union; Emblem Club. Proposed and raised funds for monument in mem. of John F. Kennedy, erected in front of Nashua City Hall; breeder and trainer of show beagles, winner many nat. and int. championships. Rel: Roman Catholic. Mailing Add: 12 Middle St, Nashua, N.H. 03060.

WINN, JOHN RALPH D
b. San Jose, Calif, 7/1/32; s. Ralph G. Winn and Aurelie La Prairie W; m. 1/1/58 to Anne Fryer Threlkeld; c. Donald John and Patricia Anne. Educ: Golden Gate Col. Polit. & Govt. Pos: Former mem, Calif. Dem. State Cent. Cmt; mem, San Benito Co. Dem. Cent. Cmt. and chmn, 61-66. Bus. & Prof. Pos: V.pres and gen. mgr, Winn Ins. Agency, 55- Mil. Serv: Entered as Seaman, Coast Guard, 52, released as Boatswain's Mate, 54, after serv. in Far East; Korean War Medal. Mem: Elks; VFW; Am. Legion; San Francisco Ins. Forum; Nat. and Calif. Ins. Brokers Asn. Legal Res: 1341 Sunnyslope Rd, Hollister, Calif. 95023. Mailing Add: P.O. Box 220, Hollister, Calif. 95023. (1967)

WINN, LARRY, JR. R
U.S. Rep, Kans.
b. Kansas City, Mo, 8/22/19; s. Edward Lawrence Winn and Gertrude Shepherd W; m. 5/5/42 to Joan Ruth Elliott; c. Edward Lawrence, III, Robert Elliott, Douglas Shepherd, Janet Gay and Cynthia Joan. Educ: Univ. Kans, B.A, 41; pres, Sigma Delta Chi and Phi Kappa Psi; dir, Mem. Union Bldg. Polit. & Govt. Pos: Past chmn, Third Cong. Dist. Rep. Party, Kans; past mem, Kans. State Rep. Exec. Cmt; U.S. Rep, Third Dist, Kans, 67- Bus. & Prof. Pos: Employee, WHB Radio Sta, 2 years; employee, N.Am. Aviation, 2 years; pub. rels. dir, Am. Red Cross, Kansas City, 2 years; private builder, 2 years; v.pres, Winn-Rau Corp, Overland Park, 50-; mem. bd. dirs, Southgate State Bank, Prairie Village; mem, Kans. Univ. Develop. Cmt. Mem: Nat. dir, Nat. Asn. Home Builders; dir. and past pres, Home Builders Asn. Gr. Kansas City; v.pres, Home Builders Asn. Kans; former v.pres, Kans. Coun. Boys Scouts and nat. coun. rep; former mem. bd. dirs, Johnson Co. United Funds Coun. and Commun. Chest Gr. Kansas City; adv. bd, Gr. Kansas City Jr. Achievement, Inc. and Shawnee Mission Hosp; People to People; Farm Bur; Rotary. Silver Beaver Award, Boy Scouts. Rel: Christian Church. Legal Res: Overland Park, Kans. Mailing Add: 510 Cannon House Office Bldg, Washington, D.C. 20515.

WINSLOW, EUGENE CLINTON D
Mem, Vt. State Dem. Cmt.
b. West Rutland, Vt, 7/5/19; s. Howard C. Winslow and Lydia Ratti W; m. to Katharine Holloway, separated; c. Holly Joan (Mrs. Stephenson), Heidi Gene, Peter Howard, Paul Rupert and Katharine Jill. Educ: Middlebury Col, A.B, 40; Univ. R.I, M.S, 42; Cornell Univ, Ph.D, 44; Sigma Xi; Kappa Psi; Kappa Delta Rho. Polit. & Govt. Pos: Pres, South Kingstown Town Coun, R.I, 55-61; secy, Munic. Chief Exec. Asn. of R.I, 57-61; mem, Vt. Student Assistance Corp, 65-69; mem, Vt. Constitutional Revision Cmn, 67-; mem, Vt. State Dem. Cmt, 67-; del, Dem. Nat. Conv, 68. Bus. & Prof. Pos: Instr, asst. prof, assoc. prof. and prof, Univ. R.I, 46-64; pres, Windham Col, 64- Mil. Serv: Entered as Ens, Navy, 44, released as Ens, 46, after serv. in Naval Res, Pac. Theatre, 45; Capt, Naval Res, 45-68. Publ: Basic Principles of Chemistry, D. Van Nostrand, 58; Laboratory Exercises and Problems in Basic Chemistry, W.C. Brown, 59. Mem: Am. Chem. Soc; N.E. Asn. of Chem. Teachers; Am. Civil Liberties Union. Rel: Congregational. Mailing Add: Windham College, Putney, Vt. 05346.

WINSLOW, JULIAN EMMETT D
b. Winfall, N.C, 2/14/97; s. Charles Cook Winslow; Martha Leigh W; married; c: Julian Emmett, Jr. and Mrs. Paul Baumgartner. Educ: Univ. of Tex. Polit. & Govt. Pos: Sheriff, Perquimans Co, N.C, 32-46; mem, Cong. Cmt, 37-49; N.C. State Sen, 49, 51, 59, 61-66; mem, Dem. Exec. Cmt, 49-; del, Dem. Nat. Conv, 52 & 56; cmnr, State Hwy. and Pub. Works Cmn, 53-57.

Bus. & Prof. Pos: Farmer, fertilizer manufacturer, oil jobber. Mil. Serv: Air Corps, 2nd Lt, Dec, 17 - Oct, 19; Res. Army Air Corps, 2nd Lt, Oct, 19 - Oct, 24. Mem: Order of Daedalians; N.C. Oil Jobbers Asn; N.C. Hardware Dealer's Asn; N.C. Merchants Asn; (32°) Mason; Shrine, Sudan Temple. Rel: Episcopal; mem. of Vestry. Mailing Add: Hertford, N.C. 27944.

WINSTEAD, WILLIAM ARTHUR D
b. Union, Miss, 1/6/04; s. Thomas Emerson Winstead and Ida Collins W; m. 4/26/33 to Etna B. Johnson; c. William Arthur. Educ: Clark Mem. Col, Newton, Miss, 27-29; Miss. South. Col, Hattiesburg, B.S, 31; Univ. Ala, 33. Polit. & Govt. Pos: Supt. of educ, Neshoba Co, Miss, 36-43; U.S. Rep, Miss, 43-64. Mem: Miss. Educ. Asn; Miss. Elem. Accrediting Cmn; State Orgn. for Co. Supts, chmn; v.pres, Neshoba Co. Fair; Mason. Mailing Add: Philadelphia, Miss. 39350. (1967)

WINSTEIN, STEWART R. D
Finance Officer, 19th Cong. Dist. Dem. Cmt, Ill.
b. Viola, Ill, 5/18/14; s. A. Winstein and Esther Meyer W; m. 11/30/60 to Dorothy Shock Adams; c. Arthur. Educ: Augustana Col, A.B, 35; Univ. Chicago, J.D, 38. Polit. & Govt. Pos: Pub. adminstr, Rock Island Co, Ill, 60-; finance officer, 19th Cong. Dist. Dem. Cmt, Ill, 63-; del, Dem. Nat. Conv, 68. Mem: Am, Ill. State and Rock Island Co. Bar Asns; Elks. Rel: Jewish. Legal Res: 3535 24th St, Rock Island, Ill. 61202. Mailing Add: P.O Box 428, Rock Island, Ill, 61201.

WINTER, JOHN BURTON R
Minn. State Rep.
b. St. Paul, Minn, 1/22/30; s. John B. Winter and Irene Drake W; m. 11/20/51 to Beverly Nelson; c. John David, James Robert and Lynn Marie. Educ: Macalester Col, 47-50. Polit. & Govt. Pos: Mayor, North St. Paul, Minn, 62-66, mem, Metrop. Planning Cmt, 66; Minn. State Rep, 67- Bus. & Prof. Pos: Mgr, order dept, Microtone Hearing Aids, 52-54; agent, Mutual Serv. Ins. Co, 54-56; owner, John Winter Agency, 56-62 and pres, John Winter Agency, Inc, 62-; dist. mgr, Am. Mutual Life Ins. Co, 65- Mil. Serv: Entered as Cpl, Marine Corps, 50, released as S/Sgt, 52, after serv. in MGCIS-1, Korea, 50-51; T/Sgt, Res, 47-62; Presidential Unit Citation; Distinguished Unit Citation; Organized Res. Ribbon; Korean Serv. Ribbon with Three Stars; Marine Res. Ribbon; UN Medal. Mem: Minn. Life Underwriters Asn; Minn. Civil Air Patrol; Am. Legion; AF&AM. Rel: Presbyterian. Mailing Add: 2611 E. First Ave, North St. Paul, Minn. 55109.

WINTER, MADELINE FIELD R
Chmn, Richmond Rep. Town Cmt, Mass.
b. Lanesboro, Mass, 5/25/22; d. George Allen Field (deceased) and Edith Young F; m. 4/19/47 to James Emory Winter, Jr; c. Douglas Paul. Educ: Bishop Mem. Training Sch. for Nurses, Pittsfield Gen. Hosp, 1 year; Berkshire Bus. Col; Dale Carnegie Course, grad. Polit. & Govt. Pos: Secy, Richmond Rep. Town Cmt, Mass, 55-68, chmn, 68-; del, Mass. Rep. State Conv, 66; del, Berkshire Co. Rep. Asn, 67- Bus. & Prof. Pos: Librn. and garden ed, Berkshire Eagle, Pittsfield, Mass, 67- Mem: Pittsfield Gen. Hosp. Auxiliary; Women's Club Pittsfield. Rel: Congregational. Mailing Add: Dublin Rd, Richmond, Mass. 01254.

WINTER, NADINE P. D
b. N.C; d. Samuel Poole and Elnora Kenion P; div; c. Alan and Reginald, Jr. Educ: Hampton Inst; Fed. City Col, D.C, currently. Polit. & Govt. Pos: Del, Dem. Nat. Conv, 68. Bus. & Prof. Pos: Exec. dir, Hospitality House, 62-69. Mem: Nat. Bus. & Prfnl. League. Over 44 Awards and Trophies for Commun. Work. Rel: Episcopal. Mailing Add: 513 Eighth St, N.E, Washington, D.C. 20008.

WINTER, R. EULALIE D
Chmn, Petroleum Co. Dem. Cent. Cmt, Mont.
b. Churches Ferry, N.Dak, 1/1/98; d. William Spence Sterrett and Mary McGovern S; wid; stepdaugther, Mary Hazel (Mrs. James R. Gibson). Educ: St. Mary's High Sch, Calgary, Alberta, grad, 17; Alberta Normal, Teaching Credits, 18; Dillon Normal, Mont, Teaching Credits, 20 & 22. Polit. & Govt. Pos: Precinct committeewoman, Petroleum Co. Dem. Cent. Cmt, Mont, 30-58, chmn, 66- Mem: Am. Legion Auxiliary; Ladies Auxiliary, VFW; Royal Neighbors of Am; Petroleum Co. Cowbelles; Nat. Retired Teachers Asn. Rel: Catholic. Mailing Add: Box 24, Winnett, Mont. 59087.

WINTER, WILLIAM FORREST D
b. Grenada, Miss, 2/21/23; s. William Aylmer Winter and Inez Parker W; m. 10/10/50 to Elise Varner; c. Anne, Elise and Eleanor. Educ: Univ. Miss, B.A, 43, LL.B, 49; Omicron Delta Kappa; Phi Delta Phi; Phi Kappa Phi; Phi Delta Theta. Polit. & Govt. Pos: Miss. State Rep, 48-56; Miss. State Tax Collector, 56-64, State Treas, 64-68. Bus. & Prof. Pos: Attorney, Watkins, Pyle, Edwards, Ludlam, Winter and Stennis, Jackson, Miss, 68- Mil. Serv: Entered as Pvt, Army, 43, released as Maj, 46, after serv. in 86th Inf. Div, Pac. Mem: Am. and Miss. Bar Asns; v.pres, Nat. Asn. for Ment. Health, 65-66. Rel: Presbyterian. Legal Res: 1415 E. Northside Dr, Jackson, Miss. 39211. Mailing Add: Box 427, Jackson, Miss. 39205.

WINTERBERG, EDWARD JOSEPH D
b. Covington, Ky, 5/21/46; s. Nicholas Edward Winterberg and Mary Louise Clayton W; single. Educ: Univ. Ky. North. Commun. Col, A.S; Univ. Ky, B.A. Econ, Col. Law, currently; Phi Alpha Delta. Polit. & Govt. Pos: Asst. state coordinator, Ky. Citizens for McCarthy, summer 68; del, Ky. State Dem. Conv, 68; del, Dem. Nat. Conv, 68; state chmn, Ky. Youth Coalition for Humphrey-Muskie, 68; pres, Univ. Ky. New Dem. Coalition, currently; Ky. Rep, Nat. Cmt. New Dem. Coalition, currently. Bus. & Prof. Pos: V.pres, Claywin Develop. Corp, Erlanger, 67- Rel: Roman Catholic. Legal Res: 531 Rosary Dr, Erlanger, Ky. 41018. Mailing Add: P.O. Box 113, Erlanger, Ky. 41018.

WINTERS, JOHN WESLEY D
V.Chmn, Wake Co. Dem. Exec. Cmt, N.C.
b. Raleigh, N.C, 1/21/20; s. Charlie Winters and Lillie Summerville W; m. 2/3/41 to Marie Montague; c. Frances (Mrs. Carter), John W, Jr, Michael C, Donna F, Naomi R, Rebecca J, Roland E. and Seanne M. Educ: L.I. Univ; Va. State Col; Shaw Univ, hon. LL.D; Omega Psi Phi. Polit. & Govt. Pos: Mem, Raleigh City Coun, N.C, 61-67; v.chmn, Wake Co. Dem. Exec. Cmt, 65-; alternate del, Dem. Nat. Conv, 68. Bus. & Prof. Pos: Pres, John W. Winters & Co, 57; pres, Madonna Acres, Inc, 59; regional v.pres, Nat. Bus. League; mem. bd. mgr, Mechanics & Farmers Bank. Mem: Nat. Asn. Home Builders (bd. dirs); Raleigh Bus. & Prfnl. League. Citizen of the Year, Omega Psi Phi, 61; Alpha Kappa Alpha Award, 66. Rel: Catholic. Mailing Add: 507 E. Martin St, Raleigh, N.C. 27601.

WINTERS, LEO D
State Treas, Okla.
b. Hooker, Okla, 11/7/22; s. David Winters and Gertrude Strochin W; m. to Patti Hill. Educ: Panhandle A. & M. Col, A.B, 50; Univ. Okla, LL.B, 57. Polit. & Govt. Pos: Secy, State Elec. Bd, Okla, 55-62; Lt. Gov, Okla, 63-67, State Treas, 67- Bus. & Prof. Pos: Pres, Alaskan Livestock Co, Kodiak, Alaska, 56-; Law Firm, Grove, Winters & Cloud, 60-67. Mil. Serv: Air Force, pilot. Mem: Am. Quarter Horse Asn; Mason (32°). Mailing Add: Box 53411, Oklahoma City, Okla. 73105.

WINTERS, LESLIE ROLAND R
Chmn, Cottonwood Co. Rep. Party, Minn.
b. Roland, Man, 12/26/21; s. Jacob Winters and Helen Kienits W; m. 11/12/46 to Ruby Verna Reimer; c. Dean Wayne, Brian Jay, Dale Alan and Patricia. Educ: Bingham Lake High Sch. Polit. & Govt. Pos: Mem. bd, Co. Agr. Stabilization & Conserv. Serv, Minn, 65-67; chmn, Cottonwood Co. Rep. Party, 67-; mem, Co. Zoning & Planning Bd, 68-69. Bus. & Prof. Pos: Bd. dirs, Five Star Dairyland Coop, 57-68, secy-treas, 68-; Adult 4-H Leader, 58-64. Mem: Cottonwood Co. Dairy Herd Improv. Asn.(pres); Cottonwood Co. Farm Bur.(past v.pres). Rel: Mennonite. Mailing Add: R.R. 1, Bingham Lake, Minn. 56118.

WINTERS, MARY LOU D
b. Monroe, La, 2/22/35; s. Tola Oren Trawick and Mary Hamilton T; m. 6/3/57 to Harry Hall Winters, III, M.D; c. Harry Hall, IV, Martha Roan, Mary Catherine, Hamilton Stephens and twins, Caroline and Amanda. Educ: La. State Univ, B.S, 56 and M.E, 57; Phi Alpha Theta; Chi Omega. Polit. & Govt. Pos: Mem, Gov, John McKeithen's Inaugural Cmt, La, 64 & 68; del, Dem. Nat. Conv, 64 & 68; chmn, La. Juvenile Probation and Parole Coun, 65-; mem, La. State Welfare Bd, 66-71. Mem: DAR; PTA; Am. Cancer Soc; Caldwell Resource Develop. Asn; state pre-sch. chmn, bd. mgrs, La. State PTA; chmn, Bishop's Drive for Centenary Col, 64; dir, Caldwell Resource Develop. Asn, 64-; co-chmn, La. Art and Folk Festival, 64-; chmn. for La, Nat. Freedom from Hunger, 64; pres, Caldwell Parish Cancer Soc. Unit, 63-; dir, Coffee Co, Tenn, Red Cross Home Serv, 58-60; Chi Omega Alumnae; Bayou Desiard Country Club; Caldwell Farm Bur. Rel: Methodist. Mailing Add: P.O. Box 645, Columbia, La. 71418.

WINTON, GORDON HARVEY, JR. D
b. Merced, Calif, 8/21/13; s. Gordon H. Winton and Mildred Stoddard W; m. 2/12/38 to Agnes Mattson; c. Douglas Kent and Salli Sue. Educ: Univ. Calif, Berkeley, A.B, 35; San Francisco Law Sch, LL, B, 46. Polit. & Govt. Pos: Mem, Merced Co. Dem. Cent. Cmt, Calif, 36-38; city attorney, Livingston, 48-60; mem. bd. educ, Merced City, 51-55; pres. bd. freeholders, Merced Co, 52; Calif. State Assemblyman, 31st Assembly Dist, 57-67; chmn, North. Calif. Dem. Cent. Cmt, 60-62; legis. rep, Sch. Adminstr, Asns. of Calif, 67-69. Mil. Serv: Entered as Ens, Naval Res, 41, released as Comdr, 45, after serv. in Am. & Mediterranean Theaters; Comdr, Naval Res,(Ret); Am. Defense Medal; Am. Theater Ribbon; African-Mid. East. Theater Ribbon; Naval Res. and Victory Medals. Mem: Calif. Bar Asn; pres, Merced Co. Bar Asn, 50; Elks; Masons; Rotary; state commander, VFW, 53-54; Am. Legion; Odd Fellows; Farm Bur; Grange; Japanese Am. Citizen League. Rel: Methodist. Mailing Add: 143 W. 20th St, Merced, Calif. 95340.

WIQUEST, WALTER WILLIAM D
b. Lyon Mountain, N.Y, 1/31/97; m. to Myrle Grafton W; c. One daughter. Educ: Graniteville Sch, Vt. Polit. & Govt. Pos: Justice of Peace, 20 years; selectman; Vt. State Rep, 59-67. Bus. & Prof. Pos: Cabinet work, 4 years; stationary engr, 12 years; life ins. agent, 27 years; former automobile salesman. Mem: Barre Fish and Game Club; Williamstown Credit Union; Eastern Star; Odd Fellows; F&AM; Fraternity Rebekah Lodge 50. Rel: Methodist. Mailing Add: Williamstown, Vt. 05679. (1967)

WIRKKALA, MATT LEANDER DFL
Chmn, Wadena Co. Dem-Farmer-Labor Party, Minn.
b. Sebeka, Minn, 2/21/96; s. Matt Wirkkala and Ida Susanna Hihnala W; m. 12/24/26 to Lempie Wilhelmiina Hendrickson. Polit. & Govt. Pos: Chmn, Wadena Co. Dem-Farmer-Labor Party, Minn, 55-; del, Dem. Nat. Conv, 60. Bus. & Prof. Pos: Farmer; dist. mgr, Ins. Co, 45-50, spec. agent, 50-55. Mem: Minn. Hist. Soc; Sebeka Conserv. Club; Suomi Seura. Rel: Lutheran. Mailing Add: Sebeka, Minn. 56477. (1967)

WIRTH, HELEN IRMIGER D
Recording Secy, 14th Cong. Dist. Dem. Off. Orgn, Mich.
b. Detroit, Mich, 5/17/17; d. Alphonse L. Irmiger and Mary Elizabeth Niederer I; m. 11/14/34 to Joseph V. Wirth, Jr; c. Joseph C, Robert A. and Thomas C. Educ: Wayne State Univ, 1 year. Polit. & Govt. Pos: Mem, Exec. Bd, 14th Cong. Dist. Dem. Off. Orgn, Mich, 48-, recording secy, currently; mem, Mich. State Dem. Cent. Cmt, 56-62; del, Dem. Nat. Conv, 56 & 64; chmn, Grosse Pointe Woods Bd. of Canvassers, 65- Bus. & Prof. Pos: Chmn, credit cmt, C.J. Fed. Credit Union, 47-; bookkeeper and secy, Local 7, UAW, currently, recording secy, COPE, 62-67. Mem: Legis. chmn, Detroit Nor Re Bus, Bus. and Prfnl. Women, Mich, 63-67, pres, 69-, nat. del. to Golden Conv, 69; Detroit Garden Center; Int. Inst. of Detroit; Detroit Round Table, Nat. Conf. Christians & Jews; Office and Prfnl. Employees Indust. Union 42; Founders Soc, Detroit Inst. of Arts; Nat. Asn. of Accts; Dodge Local 3, UAW; Women's Dem. Club 14th Dist; League of Women Voters; Nat. Air Force Asn. Amity Scholarship in human rels, Univ. Mich, from Nat. Conf. Christians and Jews, 55. Rel: Catholic. Mailing Add: 1237 Hampton Rd, Grosse Pointe, Mich. 48236.

WIRTHLIN, MADELINE BITNER R
b. Holliday, Utah, 4/15/93; d. Brenaman Barr Bitner and Martina Marjory Halseth B; m. 9/14/16 to Joseph Leopold Wirthlin (deceased); c. Joseph B, Judith W.(Mrs. Parker), Gwendolyn W.(Mrs. Cannon), Richard B. and David B.

Educ: Univ. Utah, grad, 14. Polit. & Govt. Pos: Pres, Salt Lake Women's Rep. Club, 45-46; pres, Utah Fedn. Women's Rep. Clubs, 51-53, prog. chmn, 67-69; del, State and Nat. Conv, 51-56, mem, State and Nat. Platform Cmts, 52; mem, State Bd. of Educ, 52-59; Rep. Nat. Committeewoman, Utah, 64-68. Bus. & Prof. Pos: Teacher, Granite and Salt Lake Schs, Utah, 14-16; dir, Wirthlin's Inc, 50- and J.L.W. Co, 55- Mem: Authors Club; Forum; Guide Dogs for the Blind; Contemporary Readers; Womens State Legis. Coun; Utah State Textbook and Curriculum Cmn; exec. cmt, Utah Div. Voc. Rehabilitation; Murray City Libr. Bd. Hon. Golden Gleaner Award, Church of Jesus Christ of Latter-day Saints, 55. Rel: Latter-day Saint. Mailing Add: 654 W. 5300 S, Murray, Utah 84107.

WIRTZ, W. WILLARD

b. DeKalb, Ill, 3/14/12; s. William Wilbur Wirtz and Alpha Belle White W; m. 1936 to Mary Jane Quinsenberry; c. Richard and Philip. Educ: North. Ill. State Teachers Col, 28-30; Univ. Calif, Berkeley, 30-31; Beloit Col, A.B, 33; Harvard Law Sch, LL.B, 37. Hon. LL.D, Univ. Mich, Univ. of R.I, Amherst Col. and Monmouth Col. Polit. & Govt. Pos: Asst. gen. counsel, Bd. of Econ. Warfare, 42-43; gen. counsel and pub. mem, War Labor Bd, 43-45; chmn, Nat. Wage Stabilization Bd, 46; mem, Trust Fund and Fed. Disability Ins. Fund; Under Secy. of Labor, 61-62, Secy. of Labor, 62-69, chmn, President's Cmt. on Manpower, President's Adv. Cmt. on Labor-Mgt. Policy, Missile Sites Labor Cmn, Interdepartmental Cmt. on Status of Women and President's Cmt. on Corp. Pension Funds and Other Private Retirement and Welfare Prog, co-chmn, Fed. Interagency Cmt. of Nat. Cmn. on Automation, Tech. and Econ. Progress, mem, Cabinet Cmt. on Econ. Growth, Fed. Develop. Planning Cmt. for Appalachia, Fed. Interagency Cmt. on Educ, President's Coun. on Aging and on Phys. Fitness and Adv. Coun. of President's Cmt. on Employ. of Handicapped, Bd. Trustees of Fed. Old Age and Survivors Ins. Bus. & Prof. Pos: Teacher Eng, Kewanee High Sch, Ill, 33-34; Instr. law, Univ. Iowa, 37-39; assoc. prof. law, Northwest. Univ, 39-42, prof. law, 46-61; partner, Stevenson, Rifkind & Wirtz, 55-61. Publ: Labor and the Public Interest, Harper and Row, 64. Mem: Fel, Am. Acad. of Arts and Sci. Mailing Add: 5009 39th St. N.W, Washington, D.C. 20016.

WISE, CARL FRANCIS R

Chmn, Stark Co. Rep. Party, Ohio

b. Niles, Ohio, 10/23/00; s. Sherman G. Wise and Hannah Meredith W; m. 8/28/24 to Ruth B. Hammen; c. Carl F, Jr. and Dale E. Educ: E. Ohio Bus. Col, 20. Polit. & Govt. Pos: Councilman, Canton, Ohio, 36-37, mayor, 52-58; mem, City Civil Serv. Cmn, 38-45; chmn, Stark Co. Rep. Party, 60-; del, Rep. Nat. Conv, 64. Bus. & Prof. Pos: Pres, Canton Real Estate Bd, 31, 42 & 43; dir, Peoples Fed. Savings & Loan Asn, 37-66. Mem: C. of C; Canton Bd. of Realtors; YMCA; pres, Al Koran Shrine, 48; Elks; Mason; Rotary; Brookside Country Club; Ohio League of Sportsmen. Rel: Christian Church. Legal Res: 1308 Buena Vista Blvd. N.E, Canton, Ohio 44714. Mailing Add: 327 Second St. S.W, Canton, Ohio 44702.

WISE, CHARLES DAVIDSON R

Ind. State Sen.

b. Huntington, W.Va, 6/13/26; s. Fred Eugene Wise and Maggie Harshbarger W; m. 3/22/47 to Juanita Irene Meadows; c. Sandra Lyn. Educ: Marshall Univ, 46-48 & 50-51; W.Va. Univ, A.B. and M.S, 50; Univ. N.Mex, Ph.D, 62; Chi Beta Phi; Phi Sigma. Polit. & Govt. Pos: Ind. State Rep, 67-68; Ind. State Sen, 69- Bus. & Prof. Pos: Boy Scout nature counsr, Camp Arrowhead, Ona, W.Va, summers, 50 & 51; teacher, St. Albans High Sch, W.Va, 51-53; instr, Amarillo Col, 55-57; research scientist, Univ. Tex, 58-60; prof, Ball State Univ, 61- Mil. Serv: Entered as Pvt, Army, 44, released as Pfc, 46, after serv. in Americal Div, Asiatic-Pac. Theatre, 45-46; Asiatic-Pac. Theatre, Japan Occup. and Philippine Liberation Ribbons; World War II Victory Bar; Good Conduct Medal. Publ: 15 articles on sci. and sci. educ. in numerous mag. Mem: Am. Soc. Limnology and Oceanography; Am. Microscopical Soc; Biol. Soc. Wash, D.C; Lions Int; Am. Legion; VFW; Amvets; Travelers Protective Asn. Rel: Presbyterian. Mailing Add: 711 University Ave, Muncie, Ind. 47303.

WISE, HENRY SEILER D

b. Mt. Carmel, Ill, 7/16/09; s. Henry Wise and Ida Seiler W; m. 12/10/38 to G. Louise Hawkins; c. H. Michael, Marilyn, Patricia, David and Susanne. Educ: Wash. Univ, St. Louis, Mo, A.B, 33, LL.B, 33; Phi Delta Phi; Sigma Alpha Epsilon. Polit. & Govt. Pos: Precinct committeeman, 36-66; chmn, Vermilion Co. Dem. Orgn, Ill, 48-54, mem. exec. cmt, 60-66; cmnr, Court of Claims, State of Ill, 49-53; alternate del, Dem. Nat. Conv, 52, del, 56, 60 & 64; mem, Ill. Parole and Pardon Bd, 60-66; pres, Vermilion Co. Young Dem. Orgn; U.S. Dist. Judge, 66- Mem: Am. and Illinois Bar Asns; pres, Vermilion Co. Bar Asn, 50; Am. Judicature Soc; v.pres, Danville C. of C, 58-60; Nat. Farmers Union; Elks; K. of C; Danville Country Club. Rel: Roman Catholic. Mailing Add: 507 Chester Ave, Danville, Ill. 61832.

WISE, JAMES ALAN D

b. Tulsa, Okla, 7/28/24; s. Edward Marvin Wise and Mary Frazer W; m. 8/17/46 to Ann Winifred Rodgers; c. Theresa Ann, Mary Andrea and Julia Alana. Educ: Univ. Md, overseas. Polit. & Govt. Pos: Admin. asst. to U.S. Rep. William R. Anderson, Sixth Dist, Tenn, 65- Bus. & Prof. Pos: Admin. asst, Guided Missiles Br, Vitro Corp. of Am, 63-64. Mil. Serv: Entered as A/S, Navy, 41, released as Cmn. Warrant Officer, W-3, 63, after serv. in various commands throughout the world; Commendation Ribbon; Good Conduct Medal; Am. Defense Medal with Star; Am. Theater Ribbon; Asiatic-Pac. Theater Ribbon with 3 Stars; European-African-Middle East Theater Ribbon with 2 Stars; Victory, Philippine Liberation, Navy Occupation and China Serv. Medals. Mem: Am. Legion; VFW; Elks; Mason (3°); Nat. Sojourners; Heroes of '76; Daedalians; Cong. Secy. Club; Burro Club; Nat. Capital Dem. Club. Rel: Methodist. Legal Res: Waverly, Tenn. 37185. Mailing Add: 900 Caroline St, Woodbridge, Va. 22191.

WISE, JAMES H. D

b. Abbeville, Fla, 7/15/12; m. to Clarissa Johnson; c. James William, Peggy Claire and Laura Jo. Educ: Pub. Schs. of Ala. and Fla. Polit. & Govt. Pos: Fla. State Rep, 48-50 & 56-66; former pres, City Coun, Crestview. Bus. & Prof. Pos: Mail Contractor and rental properties. Mem: Shrine; Mason; WOW. Rel: Church of Christ. Mailing Add: 302 East Cedar Ave, Crestview, Fla. 32536. (1967)

WISE, JOHN NORMAN D

V.Chmn, Highland Co. Dem. Exec. Cmt, Ohio

b. Lynchburg, Ohio, 4/16/00; s. Andrew D. Wise and Flora Trautwine W; m. 6/23/27 to Helen Gladys Barnhizer; c. Norman. Educ: Lynchburg High Sch, grad. Polit. & Govt. Pos: Chmn, Dem. Cent. Cmt, Ohio, 65; mem, Dem. Exec. Cmt, Ohio, 66-68; secy, Dem. Cent. Cmt, Ohio, 67; v.chmn. exec. cmt, Dem. Party, Ohio, 67-; chmn, Highland Co. Bd. Elec. Bus. & Prof. Pos: Salesman, West. & South. Life Ins. Co, Hillsboro, Ohio, 39-44, branch mgr, Hillsboro and Maysville, Ky, 44-64; retired. Mem: Mason; Scottish Rite; Shrine; Elks; Hist. Soc. Rel: Methodist. Legal Res: 70 Willettsville Rd, Hillsboro, Ohio 45133. Mailing Add: Box 472, Hillsboro, Ohio 45133.

WISE, ROBERT C. D

Pa. State Rep.

b. Williamsport, Pa, 5/21/25; s. Victor C. Wise and Alice Shaw Mahaffey W; m. to Margaret L. Browne; c. Three. Educ: Calif. Inst. of Tech, B.S; Dickinson Sch. of Law, J.D. Polit. & Govt. Pos: Asst. dist. attorney, Lycoming Co, Pa, 56-60; Pa. State Rep, 64- Bus. & Prof. Pos: Lawyer. Mil. Serv: Lt, Navy, World War II, Korea. Mem: Kiwanis; Mason; Am. Legion; dir, N.Cent. Automobile Club; Williamsport Redevelop. Authority. Rel: Episcopal. Mailing Add: 820 Louisa St, Williamsport, Pa. 17701.

WISE, SEELIG BARTELL D

b. Jonestown, Miss, 8/7/13; married. Polit. & Govt. Pos: Former Miss. State Sen. Bus. & Prof. Pos: Farmer. Mem: Kappa Sigma; Am. Legion; Soc. of Former Spec. Agents of Fed. Bur. of Investigation; trustee, Coahoma Co. Hosp; exec. secy, Miss. Asn. Hosp. Gov. Bds. Rel: Baptist. Mailing Add: Box 7067, Jonestown, Miss. 38639. (1967)

WISEMAN, EARL LEROY R

b. Fulton Co, Ohio, 1/8/10; s. Ben Wiseman and Orpha Laverna Morr W; m. 12/25/35 to Pauline Byronna Zimmerman; c. David Earl, Nancy Lee (Mrs. Stoddard) and Thomas LeRoy. Educ: East. Mich. Univ; Bowling Green State Univ. Polit. & Govt. Pos: Councilman-at-lg, Port Clinton, Ohio, 56-60; Ohio State Rep, Ottawa Co, 62-67. Bus. & Prof. Pos: Pres, Wiseman Agency, Inc, currently. Mem: Mason; pres, Commercial Teachers' Club. Rel: Lutheran. Legal Res: 308 E. Tenth St, Port Clinton, Ohio 43452. Mailing Add: P.O. Box 67, Port Clinton, Ohio 43452.

WISER, C. LAWRENCE D

Md. State Del.

b. Berwyn Heights, Md, 8/3/30; s. Floyd J. Wiser and Alice E. W; m. 6/28/52 to Mary E. Hodge; c. Robert, Glenn, Caroline and Susan. Educ: Univ. Md, B.S. in econs, 52; George Wash. Univ, LL.B, 58, LL.M, 60; Omicron Delta Kappa; Delta Theta Phi. Polit. & Govt. Pos: Md. State Del, currently. Bus. & Prof. Pos: Sr. attorney, Marriott Corp. Mil. Serv: Entered as 2nd Lt, Air Force, 52, released as 1st Lt, 54. Mem: Del, Montgomery Co. Coun. PTA; del, Allied Civic Group; bd. dirs, Bethesda-Chevy Chase C. of C; pres, Stoneybrook Civic Asn Rel: Baptist. Mailing Add: 12702 Littleton St, Silver Spring, Md. 20906.

WISHEK, MAX ALBERT R

b. Ashley, N.Dak, 8/29/01; s. John Henry Wishek and Nina Farley W; m. 4/8/25 to Viola Hezel; c. Max A, Jr. and Sally Lovell. Educ: Univ. N.Dak, 2 years; Univ. Mich, LL.B, 24; Sigma Delta Kappa. Polit. & Govt. Pos: States attorney, McIntosh Co, N.Dak, 31-38 & 39-40; govt. appeal agent, World War II, 39-40; del, Rep. Nat. Conv, 48-64; Rep. precinct committeeman, 62-; Rep. presidential elector, 68. Bus. & Prof. Pos: Lawyer; banker; dir, N.Dak. Taxpayers Asn, 60-66. Mem: N.Dak. and Am. Bar Asns; Indust. Cmt, Greater N.Dak. Asn; Odd Fellows; Lions. Rel: Lutheran. Mailing Add: Ashley, N.Dak. 58413.

WISTI, ANDREW HENRY D

b. Chassell, Mich, 3/16/32; s. William Andrew Wisti and Hilda Lantto W; m. 9/25/52 to Ruth Wayrynen; c. Mark, Daniel and Eric. Educ: Mich. State Univ, 49-51; Detroit Col. Law, LL.B, 56. Polit. & Govt. Pos: Mich. State Rep, 59-60; former mem, Mich. State Dem. Cent. Cmt; chmn, Houghton Co. Dem. Cmt, 62-69; del, Dem. Nat. Conv, 64 & 68. Mil. Serv: Entered as Pvt, Army, 52, released as S/Sgt, 54. Mem: Am. Trial Lawyers Asn; VFW; Am. Legion. Rel: Lutheran. Mailing Add: Hancock, Mich. 49930.

WITCHER, ROGER KENNETH R

Tenn. State Rep.

b. Red Boiling Springs, Tenn, 5/8/20; s. Ponie Oscar Witcher and Lena Russell W; m. 5/7/44 to Maitred Yates Neel; c. Sue Lynne, Deborah Neel, Russell Yates, Sandra Lucile and Roger Kenneth, Jr. Educ: Memphis State Univ, B.S, 48; Chi Beta Phi. Polit. & Govt. Pos: Mem, Macon Co. Bd. Educ, Tenn, 50-; del, Rep. Nat. Conv, 60 & 68, alternate del, 64; chmn, Macon Co. Rep. Party, 60-; Tenn. State Rep, 65- Bus. & Prof. Pos: Owner, Kenneth Witcher Lumber Co. Mil. Serv: Entered as Hosp. Corpsman, 2/C, Navy, 42, released as Ph.M. 2/C, 45. Mem: Am. Legion; Farm Bur; Lions. Rel: Baptist. Mailing Add: Red Boiling Springs, Tenn. 37150.

WITHERBEE, C. G. D

b. Frazer, Mont, 1922; m. to Mary; c. Six. Educ: High sch. Polit. & Govt. Pos: Wash. State Rep, until 66. Bus. & Prof. Pos: Exec. v.pres, Seahurst Investment Co. Mem: Mason; Elks; PTA; Machinists Union; YMCA. Mailing Add: 13647 24th Ave. S, Seattle, Wash. 98168. (1967)

WITHERS, CHARLES DUDLEY

b. Greenville, S.C, 4/15/16; s. James Dudley Withers and Ella Dorroh W; m. 12/16/44 to Jane Dunham. Educ: Furman Univ, 33-35; Wash. and Lee Univ, B.S, 37. Polit. & Govt. Pos: Career officer, U.S. Dept. of State For. Serv, 40-; For. Serv. Auxiliary, 43; assigned to Leopoldville, Belgian Congo, 43-45; v.consul, Bombay, India, 46-48; officer and secy. in Diplomatic Serv, 47; detailed to Dept. of Commerce, 48-49; consul, Dacca, 49-51; first secy. to consul, Karachi, Pakistan, 51-54; Imp. Defense Col, London, 61; Sr. For. Serv. Inspector, 62-63; U.S. Ambassador to Repub. of Rwanda, 63-66; sr. exam, Bd. Exam, For. Serv, 67- Mem: Kappa Alpha. Rel: Episcopal. Mailing Add: U.S. Dept. of State Foreign Service, Washington, D.C. 20521. (1967)

WITHERSPOON, DOROTHY KARPEL D
Mem, Colo. Dem. State Cent. Cmt.
b. Joliet, Ill, 2/19/36; d. John Karpel and Margaret Kuban K; m. 6/9/56 to Leon Clifford Witherspoon; c. Jay Robert, Leanne M, Paul Jon and Todd M. Educ: Joliet Twp. High Sch, Ill, 4 years. Polit. & Govt. Pos: Dist. v.capt, Jefferson Co. Dem. Party, Colo, currently; Jefferson Co. co-chmn, Robert F. Kennedy Presidential Campaign, 68; mem, Colo. Dem. State Cent. Cmt, 69- Mem: Colo. Young Dem; Denver Metro Fair Housing. Rel: Catholic. Mailing Add: 12281 W. Kentucky Dr, Denver, Colo. 80228.

WITHERWAX, CHARLES H. Conservative, N.Y.
Chmn, Bronx Co. Conservative Party Cmt, N.Y.
b. Schroon Lake, N.Y, 7/24/34; s. Halsey J. Witherwax and Elizabeth Bingham W; m. 7/11/59 to Rita Gormley; c. Daria Mary and Clare Maura. Educ: N.Y. State Maritime Col, B.S, 56; Union Univ. Albany Law Sch, LL.B, 59; Pres, Student Coun. and commodore, N.Y. State Maritime Col. Yacht Club, 54-55; comdr, Cadet Battalion, 55. Polit. & Govt. Pos: Organizer and chmn, Douglas MacArthur Conservative Club, N.Y, 62-65; chmn, Bronx Co. Conservative Party Cmt, 62-; cand. for Dist. Attorney of Bronx Co, 63; state committeeman, N.Y. Conservative Party, 63-, state exec. committeeman, 66- Bus. & Prof. Pos: Attorney-at-Law, 62- Mil. Serv: Entered as Lt.(jg), Navy, 59, released as Lt, 61, after serv. in 2nd and 6th Fleets, East Coast U.S.A. and Mediterranean 59-61; Lt. Comdr, Naval Res. Mem: Bronx Co. Bar Asn; Independent Bar Asn; Coun. of Am. Master Mariners; U.S. Naval Inst; North East Bronx Commun. Coun; Bronx Taxpayers Coun. Rel: Roman Catholic. Mailing Add: 88 Marine St, City Island, N.Y. 10464.

WITHROW, MRS. W.W. 'JACKIE' D
W.Va. State Del.
b. Mabscott, W.Va; d. Charles Frank Neubert and Willie Lee Flanagan N; m. 4/20/43 to William W. Withrow. Educ: Beckley pub. schs. Polit. & Govt. Pos: W.Va. State Del, 60-; mem, Gov. Cmn. on the Handicapped, Gov. Adv. Cmn. on Ment. Health and Gov. Cmn. on the Status of Women; past pres, Raleigh Co. Young Dem. Club. Bus. & Prof. Pos: Real estate saleswoman. Mem: Eastern Star; Raleigh Co. Park Bd; Bus. and Prfnl. Woman's Club of Beckley; Beckley Child Care Auxiliary; Raleigh Co. Dem. Woman's Club; Am. Legion Auxiliary; charter pres, Gulf Woman's Club; bd. of dir, Mental Health Asn. of Raleigh Co; Sophia High Sch. Scholarship Fund; Jr. Hist. Soc. of Woodrow Wilson High Sch. and Rhododendron Girls State. Rel: Baptist; Sunday Sch. teacher, Friendship Baptist Church; sponsor BYF. Mailing Add: Sophia, W.Va. 25921.

WITKOWSKI, LEO VICTOR D
Chmn, Deaf Smith Co. Dem. Party, Tex.
b. David City, Nebr, 8/23/13; s. Frank James Witkowski and Anna Zeleny W; m. 8/7/40 to Louise Christine Weil; c. Rita Sue (Mrs. Huckert), Lou Ann, Gerald and Jane Latrice. Educ: Tex. A&M Univ, B.S. Polit. & Govt. Pos: Chmn, Deaf Smith Co. Dem. Party, Tex, 62- Bus. & Prof. Pos: Mem. adv. bd, Producers Grain Corp, 56-60 & 61-67; mem, 17 Man Agr. Steering Cmt, Tex. A&M Univ, 67. Mem: Tex. Asn. of Wheat Growers (pres, 63-69); Tex. Farmers Union (bd. dirs, 66-69); bd. dirs, Nat. Asn. of Wheat Growers, 64-69; bd. dirs, Dimmitt Wheat Growers, 54-60 & 61-67; pres, Amarillo Diocesan Coun. of Cath. Men, 60-62; C. of C; K. of C. Rel: Catholic. Mailing Add: 215 N. Texas Ave, Hereford, Tex. 79045.

WITMAN, WILLIAM, II
b. Harrisburg, Pa, 1/31/14; s. Horace Montgomery Witman and Clara Wallower W; m. 9/24/47 to Melpomene Maria Fafalios. Educ: Yale Univ, B.A, 35. Polit. & Govt. Pos: Asst. trade cmnr, Caracas, 35-39; v.consul and third secy, Beirut, 39-44; acting commercial attache and third secy, Ankara, 44-45; asst. commercial attache, second secy. and consul, Am. Embassy, Athens, 45-48; consul, Bombay, 48-49; officer-in-charge, India-Nepal-Ceylon Affairs, Dept. of State, 49-52; counsr. of legation and consul gen, Am. Legation, Tangier, 52-55; dep. dir. Off. of S.Asian Affairs, 55-56; dep. dir, Off. of N.African Affairs, 57; first secy, Am. Embassy, Paris, 57-60; dir, Off. of N.African Affairs, Dept. of State, 60-62; For. Serv. Officer, Class One, 63; Sr. Seminar in For. Policy, 63-64; U.S. Ambassador to Repub. of Togo, 64-67; mem, Policy Planning Coun, 67-69; dir, Inter-African Affairs, 69-; mem, U.S. Del, UN Gen. Assembly, 62, 65 & 66 and spec. emergency session, 67, SEATO Ministerial Meeting, Karachi, 57, Second Law of the Sea Conf, Geneva, 60 and UN Econ. Coop. Admin. Conf, Addis Ababa, 61; chief, U.S. Del, Tripartite Consultations on Horn of Africa, Rome, 62; personal rep. of President with rank of Spec. Ambassador to Algerian Independence Ceremonies, 62. Mem: For. Serv. Asn; Yale Club, D.C. Recipient, Superior Serv. Award, Dept. of State, 63. Rel: Presbyterian. Legal Res: Harrisburg, Pa. Mailing Add: 2500 25th St. N, Arlington, Va. 22207.

WITT, BOSTON E. D
b. Carlsbad, N.Mex, 11/22/31; s. Charles Gilreath Witt and Alene Q. Price W; m. 12/30/59 to Kathleen Avery; c. Boston Randell and Roger Gilreath. Educ: Univ. N.Mex, B.B.A, 58; LL.B, 59; Sigma Alpha Epsilon. Polit. & Govt. Pos: Asst. Attorney Gen, N.Mex, 59-61, Dep. Attorney Gen, 61-64, Attorney Gen, 65-69, mem, Space & Atomic Energy Cmt. Bus. & Prof. Pos: Partner, Law Firm of Stanley, Witt and Quinn, currently. Mil. Serv: Entered as Pvt, Army, 50, released as 1st Lt, 53, after serv. in Seventh Inf. Div, Korea, 52-53. Mem: Ad. bd, Am. Automobile Asn; Nat. Asn. of Attorneys Gen; Elks; Am. Legion. Rel: Methodist. Mailing Add: Old Santa Fe Trail, Santa Fe, N.Mex. 87501.

WITT, CARTER H. D
Tenn. State Rep.
b. Pulaski, Tenn, 10/10/37; s. Carter H. Witt and Mary Abernathy W; m. to Judith Lanier; c. Carter H, V and George Lanier. Educ: Vanderbilt Univ, B.A, 60; Mid. Tenn. State Univ, 65- Polit. & Govt. Pos: Mem, Giles Co. Dem. Cmt, Tenn, 66-; Tenn. State Rep, 69- Mil. Serv: 2nd Lt, Army Field Artil, 61, served in 38th Artil; Res, 61-, Capt. Mem: Pres, Giles Co. Educ. Asn; Tenn. Educ. Asn; dir, U.G.F. Giles Co; dir. Giles Co. Ment. Health Center; Civitan. Rel: Methodist. Mailing Add: Route 1, Lynnville, Tenn. 38472.

WITTE, MICHAEL BENNETT D
Mem, Calif. Dem. State Cent. Cmt.
b. Chicago, Ill, 11/18/35; s. Henry Oscar Witte and Ella Bella Rubenstein W; m. 8/12/62 to Roberta Elaine Shafton; c. Jill Suzanne and Jennifer Lynn. Educ: San Diego State Col, B.S, 60; Univ. San Diego, J.D, 64; Zeta Beta Tau. Polit. & Govt. Pos: Mem, Calif. Collection Agency Adv. Bd, 64-65; mem, Calif. Dem. State Cent. Cmt, 68- Bus. & Prof. Pos: Law partner, Hinchy, Katz, Witte, Wood & Anderson, Calif, 65- Mil. Serv: Entered as Airman, Air Force, 54, released as Airman 2/C, 58, after serv. in Base Command, Ramey Air Force Base, P.R, 56-58. Mem: Am, Calif. State and San Diego Co. Bar Asns; F&AM; dir, San Diego Hebrew Home for the Aged; dir, Guardians of San Diego. Rel: Jewish. Legal Res: 6931 Everglades, San Diego, Calif. 92119. Mailing Add: 3232 Fourth Ave, San Diego, Calif. 92103.

WITTEMAN, ORVILLE P. D
b. Hitchcock, S.Dak, 1892; married; c. Three. Educ: N.Dak. State Univ. Agr. and Appl. Sci. Polit. & Govt. Pos: N.Dak. State Rep, 57-59; N.Dak. State Sen, 61-66. Bus. & Prof. Pos: Farmer. Mem: Am. Legion; Mason. Rel: Lutheran. Mailing Add: Mohall, N.Dak. 58761. (1967)

WITTENMEYER, CHARLES E. R
Mem, Rep. Nat. Cmt, Iowa
b. Centerville, Iowa, 9/3/03; s. Thomas William Wittenmeyer and Maggie E. Lantz W; m. 3/4/31 to Dorothy P. Proctor; c. Sheila (Mrs. F. D. Goar). Educ: Drake Univ, J.D, 28; Phi Alpha Delta Delta; Phi Gamma Lambda; Theta Nu Epsilon; Helmet & Spurs. Polit. & Govt. Pos: Chmn, Scott Co. Young Rep, Iowa, 34-36, Second Dist. Young Rep, 36-38 and Scott Co. Rep. Cent. Cmt, 38-56; city attorney, Davenport, 44-54; chmn, Rep. City Cent. Cmt, 44-57; del, Rep. Nat. Conv, 44, 56, 60, 64 & 68 and chmn, Cmt. on Credentials, 64 and Rules and Order of Bus. Cmt, 68; First Dist. chmn, Iowa Rep. Cent. Cmt, 52-56; mem, Rep. Nat. Cmt, Iowa, 56-, mem, Exec. Cmt, 60-64 and Task Force on Functions of Fed, State and Local Govt. Bus. & Prof. Pos: Dir, First Nat. Bank of Davenport; trustee, Fejervary Home, Davenport, Iowa. Mem: Scott Co. and Am. Bar Asns; life mem. Iowa Bar Asn; Acad. of Polit. Sci; Izaak Walton League of Am; Iowa Farm Bur. Asn; Mason (32°), Shrine, Legion of Honor; pres, Jr. C. of C, Davenport, Iowa, 36; Davenport C. of C; Davenport Club; Des Moines Club; Lincoln Club of Iowa; life mem. Iowa Hist. Soc; pres, Drake Law Sch. Alumni Asn, 50. Rel: Methodist. Legal Res: 301 Forest Rd, Davenport, Iowa 52803. Mailing Add: 826 Davenport Bank Bldg, Davenport, Iowa 52801.

WITWER, SAMUEL WEILER R
V.Pres, United Rep. Fund of Ill.
b. Pueblo, Colo, 7/1/08; s. Samuel Weiler Witwer and Lulu Richmond W; m. 8/14/37 to Ethyl L. Wilkins; c. Samuel Weiler III, Michael Wilkins, Carole Ann (Mrs. Peter C. Dalton) and David R. Educ: Dickinson Col, Ph.B, 30; Harvard Univ, LL.B, 33; Simpson Col, LL.D, 55; Omicron Delta Kappa; Sigma Chi. Polit. & Govt. Pos: Mem, Ill. Cmt. Constitutional Rev, 50-55; state chmn, Ill. Citizens for Eisenhower-Nixon, 56; Ill. Chmn. of USO, 58-63; Rep. Cand. for U.S. Sen, Ill, 60; mem, Rep. Nat. Finance Cmt, v.pres, United Rep. Fund of Ill, currently. Bus. & Prof. Pos: Lawyer, Witwer, Moran & Burlage, 33-; gen. counsel, Ill. Cmt. for Constitutional Conv, Inc, currently. Publ: Auth, Laymen's Day Message. Mem: Am, Ill, Chicago Bar Asns; dir, Chicago Coun. For. Rels. and Chicago Urban League; Legal Club; Union League Club; Commercial Club; Law Club; Am. Law Inst; pres. bd. trustees, Dickinson Col; secy. bd. trustees, Chicago Wesley Mem. Hosp; trustee, Garret Theol. Sem. Recipient Chicagoans of the Year Citation, 54; Chicagoan of the Year in Law Award, Jr. C. of C, 68. Rel: Methodist; dir, Methodist Corp, 60-64; mem, Judicial Coun, currently. Mailing Add: 111 Abingdon Rd, Kenilworth, Ill. 60043.

WIXSON, DOUGLAS CHARLES R
Okla. State Rep.
b. W. Clarksville, N.Y, 10/17/99; s. Lewellyn G. Wixson and Ellen M. Butts W; m. 9/9/49 to Helen Porterfield Gilger; c. James David and Douglas C, Jr. Educ: High sch. and bus. sch. Polit. & Govt. Pos: Okla. State Rep, 62- Bus. & Prof. Pos: V.pres, Marketing, Sunray D X Oil Co. and Predecessors, 19-64. Mem: Mason; Tulsa Petroleum Club; Tulsa Country Club. Rel: Presbyterian. Mailing Add: 3420 E. 56th Place, Tulsa, Okla. 74135.

WOFFORD, JAMES MASON
b. Cross Anchor, S.C, 6/24/21; s. James L. Wofford and Sallie Aiken W; m. 2/14/42 to Dorothy McIntyre. Educ: Cross Anchor High Sch. Polit. & Govt. Pos: Mem. Co. Bd. of Educ, S.C, 49-64; former secy, Co. Bd. of Educ; S.C. State Rep, until 66. Bus. & Prof. Pos: Merchant. Mem: Pres, Lions Club, 61; Master Masonic Lodge, 52-53; Woodruff C. of C; co-chmn, Commun. Chest, 60-61. Rel: Baptist; music dir, Cross Anchor Baptist Church. Mailing Add: 224 S. Main St, Woodruff, S.C. 29388. (1967)

WOGAN, JOHN BEUGNOT, JR. R
Chmn, Denver Co. Rep. Cent. Cmt, Colo.
b. Boston, Mass, 6/29/26; s. John Beugnot Wogan and Grace McLain W; m. 12/30/49 to Katrina Himes, wid. 3/31/66; c. Michael B, John M, Eilleen C, Hilary W, Christopher H, Katrina Whitney and Lisa M. Educ: U.S. Mil. Acad, West Point, N.Y, B.S, 49 Polit. & Govt. Pos: Secy, Denver Co. Rep. Cent. Cmt, Colo, 63-66, chmn, 66-; mem, Citizens Capital Improv. Budget Cmt, Denver, 64-; del, Rep. Nat. Conv, 68. Bus. & Prof. Pos: Pres, 245 Columbine Corp, 60-; pres, Wakonda West, Inc. and the Canterbury Corp. Mil. Serv: Entered as 2nd Lt, Air Force, 49, released as Maj, 60, after serv. in 61st Troop Carrier Sq, Hq. Far East Command; Maj, Air Force Res, 60-; Bronze Star Medal; Air Medal with Two Oak Leaf Clusters; Presidential Unit Citation, U.S and Korea; Korean Serv. Ribbons with Two Arrowheads; Six Battle Stars; World War II Am. Theater Ribbon. Mem: Denver Athletic Club; Univ. Club; Denver City Club; Air Force Asn. Rel: Catholic. Legal Res: 100 Gaylord St, Denver, Colo. 80206. Mailing Add: 245 Columbine St, Denver, Colo. 80206.

WOJTKOWSKI, THOMAS CASMERE D
Mass. State Rep.
b. Pittsfield, Mass, 9/18/26; s. Frank Wojtkowski and Anna Yuhaski W; m. 7/21/62 to Anne Everest; c. Thomas C, Jr. and Marcella. Educ: Champlain Col, A.A, 49; George Wash. Univ, B.S, 52; Portia Law Sch, LL.B; Nat. Journalism Fraternity. Polit. & Govt. Pos: Mem, Berkshire Dist, Mass. State Dem. Cmt; Mass. State Rep, 57-, chmn, Cmt. on Educ, Mass. House of Rep, 57-59, Cmt. on Agr, 57-60 and Cmt. on Judiciary, 60-64 and mem, Cmt. on Ways and Means, 65-66; chmn, Berkshire Co. Dem. Party, currently. Mil. Serv: En-

tered as A/S, Navy, 44, released as Pharmacist's Mate 3/C, 46, after serv. in Asiatic Pac, Am. and Japanese Occupations; Asiatic Pac. Campaign Ribbon. Mem: Mass. and Berkshire Bar Asns; Polish Nat. Alliance; Am. Legion; VFW; bd. dirs, Hillcrest Hosp. Rel: Roman Catholic. Mailing Add: 85 Ridge Ave, Pittsfield, Mass. 02101. (1967)

WOLBACH, ROBERT ALBERT D
b. N.Y.C, 9/3/30; s. Robert Paul Wolbach and Alberta Falck W; m. 12/24/66 to Judith Romney; c. Sarah Aulene. Educ: Cornell Univ, B.A, 51, Ph.D, 54; U.S. Pub. Health Serv. fel, N.Y. Univ, 60-61, M.D, 61. Polit. & Govt. Pos: Voting dist. chmn, Dem. Party, Salt Lake Co, Utah, 65-66 and legis. dist. secy, 65-66; del, Dem. Co. Conv, 65-66 & 68-69; del, Dem State Conv, 65-66 & 68-69; alternate del, Dem. Nat. Conv, 68. Bus. & Prof. Pos: Instr. physiol, N.Y. Univ, 56-61; asst. prof. physiol, Univ. Utah, 62-68 and assoc. prof. physiol, 69- Mil. Serv: Entered as Pvt, Army, 54, released as Sp-2, 56, after serv. in Med. Serv. Corps, ROTC, Harvard Med. Sch, 55-56; Good Conduct Medal. Publ: 'Sulfhydryl Groups and Structure of Hemoglobin,' J. Gen. Physiol, 55; 'Arteriographic Changes in Experimental Frostbite,' 56 and 'Effects of Glucose, Phlorizin and Parathyroid Extract on Renal Tubular Transport of Phosphate in Chicken,' 67, Am. J. Physiol. Mem: Sigma Xi; Harvey Soc. of N.Y; Mt. Desert Island Biol. Lab. Corp; Am. Physiol. Soc; Am. Heart Asn; Am. Soc. of Nephrology; Am. Civil Liberties Union; NAACP; Nat. Cmt. for a Sane Nuclear Policy; chmn, Coalition for Dem. Action. Legal Res: 1111 S. 13th East, Salt Lake City, Utah 84105. Mailing Add: Dept. of Physiology, University of Utah Medical Center, Salt Lake City, Utah 84112.

WOLBANK, EDWARD W. D
Ill. State Rep.
b. N.Y.C, 4/14/13. Educ: YMCA Col, Chicago. Polit. & Govt. Pos: Ill. State Rep, 62- Bus. & Prof. Pos: Antique dealer. Mil. Serv: Marine Corps, Pac. Area. Mem: Am. Legion; Moose. Rel: Catholic. Mailing Add: 619 N. State St, Chicago, Ill. 60610. (1967)

WOLCOTT, OLGA DORAN D
b. Colesburg, Iowa, 8/12/04; d. James Doran and Frances Brown D; m. 1929 to Milton Harold Wolcott; c. Sister Mary Fatima O.P. and Rose Marie. Educ: Mason City Jr. Col. Polit. & Govt. Pos: Iowa State Rep, until 66. Bus. & Prof. Pos: Teacher. Mem: Deanery pres. Mason City Coun. of Cath. Women; 1st v.pres. Dubuque Archdiocesan Coun; co. chmn, Cerro Gordo Federated Women's Clubs; Farm Bur; League of Women Voters; Bus. & Prfnl. Women; Wigwam and Wagon Campers; Rake and Hoe Co. Garden Club; Mason City Friends Libr. Bd. Rel: Catholic. Mailing Add: Rockwell, Iowa 50469. (1967)

WOLCOTT, RAYMOND OLIVER R
Minn. State Rep.
b. Winnebago, Nebr, 5/25/12; s. Raymond Franklin Wolcott and Blanche Baldridge W; m. 4/6/40 to Anna Margaret Swenson; c. Raymond Oliver, Jr. and John Baldridge. Educ: Univ. Minn, B. A, 34, J.D, 37; Lambda Chi Alpha. Polit. & Govt. Pos: Attorney, Tax Dept, Minn, 37-39; chief, interpretation and rules section, corp. finance div, U.S. Securities and Exchange Cmn, 39-45; Minn. State Rep, 67- Bus. & Prof. Pos: Sr. assoc, Cravath, Swaine & Moore, Attorneys, N.Y.C, 45-50; chief counsel, Honeywell, Inc, Aero Div, Minneapolis, Minn, 50-59; asst. v.pres. and chief counsel, Ling, Temco, Vought, Inc, Dallas, Tex, 59-62; assoc. counsel, Investors Diversified Serv, Inc, Minneapolis, Minn, 62- Mil. Serv: ROTC. Mem: Am, Minn, Hennepin Co, N.Y. and Tex. Bar Asns; Am. Judicature Asn; co-founder and secy, Edina Little League Baseball, 52-57; co-founder and secy, AAU Swim Club of Edina, 57-59; chmn, Boy Scout Harriet Dist. Coun, 56; Citizens League of Minneapolis. Rel: Methodist. Mailing Add: 4110 Coffman Lane, Minneapolis, Minn. 55406.

WOLD, JOHN S. R
U.S. Rep, Wyo.
b. East Orange, N.J, 8/31/16; s. Dr. Peter Irving Wold and Mary Helff W; m. 9/28/46 to Jane Adele Pearson; c. Peter Irving, II, Priscilla Adele and John Pearson. Educ: St. Andrews Univ, Scotland; Union Col, A.B, 38; Cornell Univ, M.S, 39; Sigma Xi; Alpha Delta Phi. Polit. & Govt. Pos: Wyo. House of Rep, Wyo. State Rep, 57-59; chmn, Wyo. Rep. State Cmt, 60-64; chmn, West. States Rep. State Chmn. Asn; mem, Rep. Nat. Cmt, 60-64, mem. exec. cmt, 62-64; Rep. nominee, U.S. Senate, Wyo, 64; U.S. House Rep, 91st Cong, 68-; U.S. Rep, Wyo, 69- Bus. & Prof. Pos: Consulting Physicist, Bur. Ord, Dept. of the Navy, 41-42; dir, Fedn. Rocky Mt. States; v.pres, Rocky Mt. Oil and Gas Asn. Mil. Serv: Entered as Ens, Navy, 42, released as Lt.(sg), 46, after serv. in Bur. of Ord, Com. Serv. Pac. III, gunnery & exec. officer, destroyer escort duty, Atlantic & Pac. Publ: Various articles on oil, gas, coal, geology in nat. publ. Mem: v.pres, 91st Club; Am. Legion; VFW. Rel: Episcopal. Legal Res: 1231 W. 30th St, Casper, Wyo. 82601. Mailing Add: 1323 Longworth House Office Bldg, Washington, D.C. 20515.

WOLD, PETER BERTRAM, JR. R
Mem, N.Dak. Rep. State Exec. Cmt.
b. Hillsboro, N.Dak, 11/19/26; s. Peter Bertram Wold and Marie Gadberry W; m. 9/16/56 to Anne Markham; c. Mary Kate, Peter Benson, Jeffrey, Nancy and Leif. Educ: State Sch. Forestry, Bottineau, N.Dak, A.S, 48; N.Dak. State Univ, B.S, 50; Univ. N.Dak, M.S, 56. Polit. & Govt. Pos: Finance chmn, Sixth Dist. Rep. Party, N.Dak, 56-64, dist. chmn, 64-; mem, N.Dak. Rep. State Exec. Cmt, 64-; chmn, N.Dak. Rep. Platform Cmt, 68; del, chmn. N.Dak. del. and mem. platform cmt, Rep. Nat. Conv, 68; chmn, N.Dak. Rep. State Research Cmt, 68- Mil. Serv: Entered as Seaman, Navy, 43, released as Motor Machinist's Mate 3/C, 46, after serv. in Naval Amphibious Units, S.Pac. Theatre, 44-46; 1st Lt, Army Res, 54- Mem: Nat. Soc. Prfnl. Engrs; Consulting Engrs. Coun. of the U.S; Am. Legion; Elks; Mason; Shrine; Nat. C. of C; Lions Int. Rel: Methodist. Mailing Add: 509 Nichol St, Bottineau, N.Dak. 58318.

WOLD, SIGURD R
b. Duluth, Minn, 4/24/96; s. Peter A. Wold and Anna Marie W; div; c. Robin Louise. Educ: Univ. Alaska, Fairbanks, Alaska. Polit. & Govt. Pos: Former Alaska State Rep, former mem. cmts, Health, Welfare and Educ. and Local Govt, Alaska State House of Rep. Bus. & Prof. Pos: Pres, Miners Lumber Co, 38-43, Sig. Wold Storage & Transfer, 41-62 and Denali Transportation Corp, 55-66. Mil. Serv: Entered as Pvt, Army, 17, released as Sgt, 19, after serv. in 803rd Aero Squadron. Mem: Mason; Elks; Pioneers of Alaska; Rotary; Am. Legion; Nat. Defense Transportation Asn. Rel: Lutheran. Legal Res: 504 Monroe St, Fairbanks, Alaska 99701. Mailing Add: Box 791, Fairbanks, Alaska 99701.

WOLD, THOMAS CLIFFORD R
Chmn, 21st Dist. Rep. Party, N.Dak.
b. Rugby, N.Dak, 6/24/37; s. Omar Clifford Wold and Gladys Antony W; m. 10/17/59 to Patricia Rae Levasseur; c. Tracey Jean, Jennifer Jo and Kelly Ann. Educ: Univ. N.Dak, Ph.B, 60, LL.B, 62; Blue Key; Sigma Chi. Polit. & Govt. Pos: Chmn, Cass Co. Young Rep, N.Dak, 63-65, mem. exec. cmt, 63-; v.chmn, N.Dak. Young Rep, 66, state chmn, 67; campaign chmn, 21st Dist. Rep. Party, 66, finance chmn, 67-68, chmn, 68-; mem. exec. cmt, N.Dak. State Rep. Party, 68-; mem, Fargo City Airport Authority, 69. Bus. & Prof. Pos: Partner Law Firm, Pancratz, Wold & Johnson, 64- Mem: Am, N.Dak. and Cass Co. Bar Asns; Elks; Kiwanis; Jr. Achievement; Fargo-Moorhead Area Found. N.Dak. Jaycees Govt. Affairs Award, 65. Rel: Catholic. Mailing Add: 806 18th Ave. S, Fargo, N.Dak. 58102.

WOLF, BEN J. R
Mem, Pub. Serv. Cmn, N.Dak.
b. McIntosh Co, N.Dak, 6/4/07; married; c. Seven. Educ: Pub. Schs. Polit. & Govt. Pos: Mayor, Zeeland, N.Dak, 4 terms; N.Dak. State Rep, 11 terms, Speaker of House, N.Dak. House Rep, 57, Majority Floor Leader, 59-61; mem. Pub. Serv. Cmn, currently. Bus. & Prof. Pos: Bulk oil plant operator. Legal Res: Zeeland, N.Dak. 58581. Mailing Add: State Capitol, Bismarck, N.Dak. 58501. (1967)

WOLF, CHARLES WILLIAM R
b. Hamilton Twp, Adams Co, Pa, 3/6/12; s. James Guy Wolf and Nora M. Baugher W; m. 12/4/52 to Mary Elizabeth Eckert; c. James C. and Jeffrey W. Educ: Gettysburg Col, A.B, 34; Harvard Law Sch, LL.B, 39; Phi Sigma Iota; Phi Beta Kappa; Gettysburg Col. Hon. Soc. Polit. & Govt. Pos: Legal adv. to Commanding Gen, U.S. Air Force in Europe, Wiesbaden, Germany, 47-49; co. solicitor, Adams Co, Pa, 54-61; chmn, Adams Co. Rep. Finance Cmt, 55-60; attorney, Commonwealth of Pa, 60-62; del, Rep. Nat. Conv, 68. Bus. & Prof. Pos: Practicing attorney, 50- Mil. Serv: Entered as Pvt, Army, 42, released as 1st Lt, 47, after serv. in Hq, U.S. Air Force in Europe, ETO, 44-47; Cert. of Commendation, Hq. U.S. Air Forces in Europe; One Battle Star. Mem: Adams Co, Pa. and Am. Bar Asns; Am. Judicature Soc; Mason; Shrine; Lions; Am. Legion; VFW; Elks. Charter Alumnus, Eisenhower Col; Bd. of Fels, Gettysburg Col. Rel: Lutheran. Legal Res: 225 Lincolnway E, New Oxford, Pa. 17350. Mailing Add: 112 Baltimore St, Gettysburg, Pa. 17325.

WOLF, CHARLES WILLIAM D
Chmn, White Co. Dem. Party, Ind.
b. Chalmers, Ind, 2/1/24; s. Adlai Wolf, Sr. and Mary Woods W; m. 12/2/45 to Kathleen Munsterman; c. Mark and Marcia. Educ: Reynolds High Sch, 30-42. Polit. & Govt. Pos: City councilman, Reynolds, Ind, 46-50, twp. trustee, Reynolds, Ind, 50-58, precinct committeeman, Dem. Party, Reynolds, Ind, 56-; chmn, White Co. Dem. Party, Ind, 64- Bus. & Prof. Pos: Salesman, Hicksgas, Monticello, Ind, 54-57; sales mgr, Pearson's LP Gas, Delphi, 57- Mem: Moose. Rel: Lutheran. Mailing Add: Box 121, Reynolds, Ind. 47980.

WOLF, ED R
b. Gaylord, Kans, 9/27/02; s. August Wolf and Anna Maria Imke W; m. 5/25/32 to Esther Ann Akens. Educ: Gaylord Pub. Sch. Polit. & Govt. Pos: Chmn, Smith Co. Young Rep, Kans, 36; v.chmn, Smith Co. Rep. Cent. Cmt, 60-64, chmn, 64-67; presidential elector, First Dist, Kans, 64. Mem: Farm Bur. Rel: German Baptist. Mailing Add: R.D. 1, Gaylord, Kans. 67638.

WOLF, FRANK C. R
Ill. State Rep.
b. Chicago, Ill; m. Amelia W. Educ: Northwest. Univ; YMCA Bus. Col. Polit. & Govt. Pos: Precinct capt. and orgn. secy, 23rd Ward Regular Dem. Orgn, 20 years; former chief bailiff, Munic. Court of Chicago; former admin. secy, City of Chicago Treas, Bd. Inspectors, City of Chicago and House of Correction Supts, 33-49; alternate del, Dem. Nat. Conv, 68; Ill. State Rep, currently; mem, Ill. Dem. State Cent. Cmt, currently. Bus. & Prof. Pos: Admin. asst, Cook Co. Recorder of Deeds, Ill. Mailing Add: 4046 W. 26th St, Chicago, Ill. 60623. (1967)

WOLF, HAROLD E. 'HAL' R
Wash. State Rep.
b. Yelm, Wash, 1926; m. to Peggy W; c. Three. Educ: Univ. Puget Sound, B.A. Polit. & Govt. Pos: Wash. State Rep, 64-; Majority Whip, Wash. House of Rep, currently, mem. Legis. Coun, 67- Bus. & Prof. Pos: Grocer. Mil. Serv: Navy. Mem: Lions; Elks; Moose; Mason. Mailing Add: Clark Rd, Yelm, Wash. 98597.

WOLF, HERBERT CHRISTIAN D
Chmn, Clark Co. Dem. Exec. and Cent. Cmt, Ohio
b. Baltimore, Md, 4/6/23; s. Carl George Wolf and Margaret Umhau W; m. 6/18/47 to Margaret Schroder; c. Gretchen, Gary, Martin, Allen and Miriam. Educ: Johns Hopkins Univ, A.B, 43; Lutheran Theol. Sem, B.D, 47; Univ. Chicago, M.A, 59; Harvard Univ, Th.D, 68; Omicron Delta Kappa; Danforth Found. Study Grant, 61-62 & 64-65; Martin Luther fel, 61-62 & 64-65; Alpha Tau Omega. Polit. & Govt. Pos: Chmn, Clark Co. Dem. Cent. and Exec. Cmt, Ohio, 66-; del, Dem. Nat. Conv, 68; mem, Clark Co. Bd. Elec, 68- Bus. & Prof. Pos: Instr. relig, Mich. State Univ. and campus pastor, Univ. Lutheran Church, 48-57; from asst. prof. to assoc. prof, Wittenberg Univ, 57- Publ: Kierkegaard and Bultmann: The Quest of the Historical Jesus, Augsburg, 65; 'An Introduction to the Idea of God as Person,' J. of Bible and Relig, 1/64. Mem: Am. Asn. Univ. Prof; Am. Acad. Relig; Am. Theol. Soc; Ministerium, Lutheran Church in Am; Ohio Dem. Chmn. Asn.(secy, 66-). Rel: Lutheran. Mailing Add: 1126 N. Fountain Ave, Springfield, Ohio 45504.

WOLF, KATIE LOUISE D
Dem. Nat. Committeewoman, Ind.
b. Wolcott, Ind, 7/9/25; d. John H. Munsterman and Helen Brtulag M; m.

12/2/45 to Charles W. Wolf; c. Mark and Marcia. Educ: Ind. Bus. Col, 43-44. Polit. & Govt. Pos: V.chmn, White Co. Dem. Party, Ind, 60-64; v.chmn, Second Cong, Dist. Dem. Party, 64-68; clerk, White Co, 68-; Dem. Nat. Committeewoman, Ind, 68- Bus. & Prof. Pos: Co. registrn. officer, White Co, Ind, 60; mgr, White Co. License Br, 60-68. Mem: Bus. & Prfnl. Women's Club; Ind. State Ment. Health Asn; White Co. Ment. Health Asn.(legis. chmn); Ind. Asn. for Retarded Children (mem. chmn); Kappa Kappa Sigma. Rel: Lutheran. Mailing Add: Box 121, Reynolds, Ind. 47980.

WOLF, KENNETH MOHR R
Mont. State Rep.
b. Grinnell, Iowa, 7/28/36; s. Gilbert Wolf and Maxine Mohr W; m. 11/12/66 to Michel Bernice Hall; c. Kenneth Allen, Cory Lyndell, Jody Kay and Jay Allen. Educ: Montezuma High Sch, Iowa, 12 years. Polit. & Govt. Pos: Mont. State Rep, 67- Bus. & Prof. Pos: Owner-mgr, Ken's Standard Serv, Ken's U-Haul, Ken's Intermountain Transportation Depot and Ken's Wrecker Serv, 61- Mem: Jaycees (pres, Shelby Chap, 63-64, state v.pres, Mont, 64-65, state pres. cand, 66, pres, 69-70, nat. dir, 65-66); pres, Toastmasters, 63-64; AF&AM; Optimist. Distinguished Serv. Award, 65; Named One of Five Outstanding Young Men of Montana, 67. Rel: Methodist. Mailing Add: 1126 Second St. S, Shelby, Mont. 59474.

WOLF, LAURENCE GRAMBOW D
b. N.Y.C, 9/4/21; s. Edward Andrew Wolf and Anna Charlotte Grambow W; m. 9/6/52 to Norma Roberts Rienhardt; c. Steven Rienhardt, Allen Jonathan and Eric Laurence Harold. Educ: City Col, N.Y, B.S, 43; Columbia Univ, M.A, 47; Syracuse Univ, Ph.D, 66. Polit. & Govt. Pos: Alternate del, Dem. Nat. Conv, 68. Bus. & Prof. Pos: Assoc. prof, Dept. Geog, Univ. Cincinnati, 52- Mil. Serv: Entered as Pvt, Army, 43, released as Sgt, 46. Publ: 'The Metropolitan Tidal Wave in Ohio, 1900-2000, Econ. Geog, 4/69. Mem: Asn. Am. Geog; Am. Geog. Soc; Ohio Acad. Sci; Am. Asn. Univ. Prof. Rel: Unitarian. Mailing Add: 3402 Whitfield St, Cincinnati, Ohio 45220.

WOLF, LEONARD GEORGE D
b. Mazomanie, Wis, 1925; s. Frank C. Wolf and Gertrude Linley W; m. 7/2/49 to Marilyn Margaret Adams; c. Steven Michael, Ann Marilyn and Jennifer Elizabeth. Polit. & Govt. Pos: U.S. Rep, Iowa, 59-60; Food for Peace dir, Brazil, 61-65. Bus. & Prof. Pos: Travel lectures on Europe, Iron Curtain countries youth activities, urban and rural; proprietor, retail feed bus, 53-59; prog. dir, Operation Ninos for Latin Am, 65-68; exec. dir, Am. Freedom from Hunger Found, 68- Mil. Serv: Navy, World War II. Mailing Add: 8205 Ft. Foote Rd. N.W, Washington, D.C. 20022.

WOLF, LOIS RUTH D
Mem. Calif. Dem. State Cent. Cmt.
b. Glen Flora, Wharton, Tex, 9/4/97; d. Louie L. Benthall and Mattie M. Zernial B; m. 9/12/15 to Leon Aaron Wolf, wid; c. Maxine Lois (Mrs. Sam Brownstein). Educ: Texas City, Texas High Sch, 13-15. Polit. & Govt. Pos: Chmn. ways and means cmt, San Joaquin Co. Dem. Women's Club, 58-69; mem, 30th Assembly Dist. Get Out the Vote Campaign, 15th Cong. Dist. Cand, 58-69; mem, Sixth Sen. Dist. and 12th Assembly Dist. Dem. Party, 60-69; chmn, Dem. Party Fair Booth, 60-69; mem. finance cmt, San Joaquin Co. Dem. State Cent. Cmt. 65-; mem. women's div, Calif. Dem. State Cent. Cmt, 67-69, mem, 68-; Dem. precinct chmn, French Camp and Lathrop, Calif, 69. Mem: Am. Bus. Womens Asn; life mem, Hadassah (Ways and Means Cmt, Stockton Chap, 40-69); Dem. Womens Club. Recipient of Woman of the Year Serv. Award, Hadassah, 64; in recognition of dedication and loyalty to Dem. Party, Dem. Womens Club Declared Feb. 15th, 68 to be Lois Wolf Day. Rel: Protestant. Mailing Add: 2144 W. Raymond Ave, Stockton, Calif. 95203.

WOLF, PAUL ARNOLD D
Chmn, Stevens Co. Dem. Cent. Cmt, Kans.
b. Geneseo, Kans, 1/8/21; s. Frank Wolf and Lillie Arnold W; m. 7/22/51 to Marion Greenlee; c. Franklin, Carol and Douglas. Educ: Univ. Kans, B.S. in Bus, 47, LL.B, 52; Phi Alpha Delta. Polit. & Govt. Pos: Kans. State Rep, 55-61; chmn, Stevens Co. Dem. Cent. Cmt, 62-; co. attorney, 63-; del, Dem. Nat. Conv, 68. Bus. & Prof. Pos: Pres. and dir, Southwestern Savings & Loan Asn, 62- Mil. Serv: Entered as Pvt, Army, 42, released as Capt, 46. Mem: Lions; Knife & Fork. Rel: Methodist. Mailing Add: 115 N. Jackson, Hugoton, Kans. 67951.

WOLF, THERESA CATHERINE D
Secy, Lee Co. Dem. Cent. Cmt, Ill.
b. Dixon, Ill, 1/2/38; d. Ralph George Wolf and State Brimblecom W; m. 5/26/56 to Harold Joseph Wolf; c. Cynthia, Ralph, Christine, Suzette and Doreen. Educ: Student, Sauk Valley Jr. Col, currently. Polit. & Govt. Pos: Secy, Lee Co. Young Dem, Ill, 64 & 65, pres, 66 & 67; clerk, South Dixon Twp, 65-69, Dem. precinct committeeman, 68-; chmn, Ladies for Brinkmeier, 68; chairwoman, Lee Co. Dem. Party, 68-; secy, Lee Co. Dem. Cent. Cmt, 68- Mem: Secy, Lee Co. Heart Asn; first v.chmn, South Dixon Unit, Lee Co. Home Exten. Rel: Catholic. Mailing Add: R.R. 2, Box 79, Dixon, Ill. 61021.

WOLF, WILLIAM HENRY D
Chmn, Hancock Co. Dem. Cmt, Ind.
b. Indianapolis, Ind, 8/5/20; s. Paul Henry Wolf and Ora Sarah Jones W; m. 4/20/50 to Mary Jane Vermillion; c. Sarah, Martha, Pamela and Paula. Educ: Earlham Col, A.B, 42; Harvard Bus. Sch, 43; Ind. Univ. Sch. of Law, J.D, 50. Polit. & Govt. Pos: Chmn, Hancock Co. Dem. Cmt, Ind. and Dem. Sixth Dist, currently; del, Dem. Nat. Conv, 68. Mil. Serv: Entered as Ens, Navy, 46, released as Lt.(sg), after serv. in Am. Embassy, Havana, Cuba. Mem: Am. and Ind. State Bar Asns; Am. Trial Lawyers Asn; Am. Legion; Elks; 40 et 8. Rel: Quaker. Legal Res: 207 W. McKenzie Rd, Greenfield, Ind. 46140. Mailing Add: P.O. Box 452, Greenfield, Ind. 46140.

WOLFE, BERNARD B. D
Ill. State Rep.
b. Chicago, Ill, 7/1/14; s. Ira W. Wolfe and Kate Davis W; m. 11/17/35 to Harriett Poncher; c. Michele (Mrs. Polovin) and Richard. Educ: Crane Jr. Col, A.A, 33; Chicago-Kent Col. Law, LL.B, 37; mem. exec. cmt, Round Table; chancellor, Nu Beta Epsilon; pres, sr. class. Polit. & Govt. Pos: Rent enforcement attorney, Chicago Defense Rental Area, 42-43; regional chief enforcement attorney, Off. Price Admin. and war surplus goods enforcement coordinator, 46; mem. Tri-Park Commun. Coun, N.River Cmn. and exec. bd, 40th Ward Regular Dem. Orgn; dir, Peterson Park Improv. Asn, 49-, pres, 57-59, chmn. bd, 60-62; Ill. State Rep, 15th Dist, 64-, mem. Cmts. on Judiciary, Personnel and Pension and Liquor Regulation, Ill. House Rep. Bus. & Prof. Pos: Partner, Lochtan and Wolfe. Mil. Serv: Entered as Ens, Navy, 43, released as Lt.(jg), 45, after serv. as Commanding Officer, Armed Guard Gun Crew; Commendation, Armed Guard; Lt.(Ret), Naval Res. Publ: 'Magic of Membership,' Workshop Conf, Dept. Urban Renewal, Chicago, 8/64. Mem: Fed, Ill. and Chicago Bar Asns; Decalogue Soc. of Lawyers; Am. Judicature Soc; City Club; chmn, Tri-Park Commun. and Am. Red Cross Commun. Fund Drives; chmn, Tri-Park Commun, Am. Cancer Soc, 64-66; dir, past pres. and bd. chmn, Henry Davis 400, Heart Surg.Research Orgn; B'nai B'rith; Moose; Am. Legion; Jewish War Vet; Men's Club AG Beth Israel. Recipient Am. Legion Citation, 65; President's Award for Outstanding Commun. Serv, Peterson Park Improv. Asn, 65; Achievement Award, Mount Sinai Hosp; Legis. Excellence Award, Peterson Park Improv. Asn, 66. Rel: Jewish. Legal Res: 6052 N. Lawndale Ave, Chicago, Ill. 60645. Mailing Add: 77 W. Washington St, Chicago, Ill. 60602. (1967)

WOLFE, CARLTON FLOYD D
b. Perinton, N.Y, 7/29/16; s. Charles J. Wolfe and Sophia Fishback W; m. 7/2/40 to Harriett Hickey; c. Jeanne Marie. Educ: Hobart Col, B.A, 50; State Univ. N.Y. at Geneseo, M.S, 55. Polit. & Govt. Pos: Dem. committeeman, N.Y, 60-; del, Dem. Nat. Conv, 68. Mil. Serv: Entered as Pvt, Marine Corps, 42, released as Cpl, 45, after serv. in Ninth Defense Bn, Pac. Theatre, 43-45. Mem: Pres, Letchworth Cent. Teachers Asn, 59; Mason; Am. Legion; Silver Lake Golf Club (bd. dirs, 67-, pres). Rel: Protestant; Mem. Bd. Trustees, Warsaw United Church. Mailing Add: 61 W. Court St, Warsaw, N.Y. 14569.

WOLFE, DALLAS R
W.Va. State Sen.
b. Colebank, W.Va, 9/1/95; s. Oliver Wolfe and Beuna Lindsey W; m. 10/2/28 to Virginia Jones; c. William P, Dallas Jr, Mrs. R.N. Smith, Mrs. Dan Orescanin. Educ: Alderson-Broaddus Col. Polit. & Govt. Pos: W.Va. State Del, 34; W.Va. State Sen, 60- Bus. & Prof. Pos: Millwright, former teacher, farmer, mfr. of hardwood lumber, serv. sta, motel and restaurant bus. Mil. Serv: Navy, World War I. Mem: Mason (32°); Shrine; AF&AM (past master); RAM (past high priest); Am. Legion; VFW; Taylor Co. Sportsman Asn; Preston Co. Rifle Club; Kasson Ruritan Club; Rowlesburg Lions Club; K.T.(past comdr); local union No. 1775 U.B. of C. and A. Rel: Baptist. Mailing Add: Rowlesburg, W.Va. 26425. (1967)

WOLFE, LOUIS E. DL
b. Plattsburgh, N.Y, 7/14/33; m. to Zena Shane. Educ: Cornell Univ, A.B, LL.B. Polit. & Govt. Pos: N.Y. State Assemblyman, 64-68; Bus. & Prof. Pos: Lawyer with O'Connell and Wolfe. Mem: Shrine; Elks; N.Y. State and Clinton Co. Bar Asns. Mailing Add: 6 Mason Dr, Plattsburgh, N.Y. 12901. (1967)

WOLFE, RICHARD B. R
Mem, Mt. Vernon Rep. Precinct Cmt, Iowa
b. Mt. Vernon, Iowa, 7/14/06; s. Dr. Thomas L. Wolfe and Ora Bair W; m. 7/3/35 to Caroline L. Weseman; c. Dorothy Louise and Douglas Daniel. Educ: Cornell Col, Iowa, B.A, 27; Univ. Iowa, J.D, 30; Delta Theta Phi. Polit. & Govt. Pos: Mem, Mt. Vernon Rep. Precinct Cmt, Iowa, 50-; alternate del-at-lg, Rep. Nat. Conv, 64. Mem: Linn Co. and Iowa State Bar Asns; v.pres, Mt. Vernon C. of C, 45-46 and pres, 46-; pres, Lions, 50-51; pres, Hillcrest Country Club, 61. Rel: Methodist. Legal Res: 214 W. Third St, S, Mt. Vernon, Iowa 52314. Mailing Add: Box 174, Mt. Vernon, Iowa 52314.

WOLFE, STEPHEN CHARLES R
Okla. State Rep.
b. Saginaw, Mich, 11/19/40; s. Frank Burleigh Wolfe and Helen M. Galehr W; m. 6/8/68 to Joey Darleen Harbour; c. Lea Marie. Educ: Wash. and Lee Univ; Westminster Col, Fulton, Mo, B.A. in Polit. Sci, 62; Okla. Univ. Sch. Law, J.D, 65; Alpha Phi Omega; Phi Gamma Delta; Phi Alpha Delta; YMCA; Westminster Men of Song Glee Club. Polit. & Govt. Pos: Mem, Tulsa Co. Young Rep; officer, Westminster Young Rep. Club, 62; Okla. State Rep, 76th Dist, currently. Bus. & Prof. Pos: Attorney-at-law, 65-; licensed real estate broker, 68- Mil. Serv: 2nd Lt, Army, Mil. Police Corps, Mem: Am, Okla. and Tulsa Co. Bar Asns; Am. Trial Lawyers Asn. Rel: First Presbyterian. Legal Res: 1533 S. Indianapolis, Tulsa, Okla. 74112. Mailing Add: 407 Mayo Bldg, Tulsa, Okla. 74102.

WOLFF, LESTER LIONEL D
U.S. Rep, N.Y.
b. New York, N.Y, 1/4/19; m. to Blanche Silver; c. Bruce, Diane. Educ: N.Y. Univ, 39. Polit. & Govt. Pos: Chmn. adv. cmt, Subcmt. on Consumers Study, U.S. House of Rep, 57; mem, U.S. Trade Mission, Philippines, 62, Malaysia and Hong Kong, 63; U.S. Rep, N.Y, 64- Bus. & Prof. Pos: Lectr. mkt, 39-41; head mkt. dept, Collegiate Inst, 45-49; TV moderator and producer, 'Between the Lines,' 48-60; TV producer, 'Showcase' and 'Wendy Barrie Show,' 55-58; former mem. bd, Noramco Dugan's and Madison Life Ins. Co; former chmn. bd, Coordinated Mkt. Agency. Mil. Serv: Maj, pub. rels. officer, squad comdr, Civil Air Patrol Auxiliary. Mem: Trustee, Nat. Jewish Hosp. Denver and Deborah Hosp. Legal Res: Great Neck, N.Y. Mailing Add: House Office Bldg, Washington, D.C. 20515.

WOLFREY, BERNICE R
b. Waterbury, Conn, 1/3/28; d. Herbert C. Wolfrey and Minnie Cooper W; div. Educ: Va. State Col; N.Y. Sch. of Interior Design; Pratt Inst; Honor Soc, Va. State Col. and ed, Va. Statesman, 48 & 49; Alpha Kappa Alpha. Polit. & Govt. Pos: Secy-treas, Rep. Party of St. Croix, V.I, 62-63; secy, Rep. Party of St. Croix, V.I, 63-; former nat. committeewoman, V.I. Rep. Party. Rel: Baptist. Legal Res: 265 Richmond, Christiansted, St. Croix, V.I. 00820. Mailing Add: P.O. Box 1444, Christiansted, St. Croix, V.I. 00820. (1967)

WOLFSON, LOUIS, II D
Fla. State Rep.
b. Miami, Fla, 9/19/27; s. Mitchell Wolfson and Frances Cohn W; m. 11/21/51 to Lynn Rabin; c. Lynda Louise, Louis, III and Frances Jo. Educ:

Grinnell Col; Univ. Miami, B.A, 52; Alpha Epsilon Pi. Polit. & Govt. Pos: Fla. State Rep, Dade and Monroe Co, 63- Bus. & Prof. Pos: Dir. and v.pres, WFGA-TV, Jacksonville, Fla, 59-; owner, KVOS-TV, Bellingham, Wash, 60-61; sr. v.pres, Wometco Enterprises, Inc, 61-69. Mil. Serv: Entered as Seaman 3/C, Navy, 44, released as Seaman 1/C, 46. Mem: Miami Beach C. of C; Nat. Legis. Conf. Fed-State Rels. Cmt; Fla. Asn. of Broadcasters; TV Pioneers; Tiger Bay Political Club; Suwanee River Citizens Asn; Miami Kiwanis; Footlighters Club; Vancouver Univ. Club; Miami Beach Civic League; Miami Club; Eagles; Elks; Tallahassee Caucus Club; Dade Co. Ment. Health Asn; Miami Beach Taxpayers' Asn; Fla. Sheriff Asn. Nat. Award of Merit; Fla. State Univ. Interfraternity Coun. Cert; Nat. Soc. of State Legislator's Award; Commun. Leaders of Am. Award; Fla. Sheriffs' Boys Ranch Award. Rel: Jewish. Legal Res: 4595 N. Meridian Ave, Miami Beach, Fla. 33140. Mailing Add: 306 N. Miami Ave, Miami, Fla. 33128.

WOLLENHAUPT, RALPH EUGENE R
Chmn, Adair Co. Rep. Cent. Cmt, Iowa
b. Massena, Iowa, 5/9/18; s. Frederick George Wollenhaupt and Ida Sophia Gaulke W; m. 7/10/55 to Janet Kari Johnson; c. Kurt Fred. Educ: Drake Univ, B.A, 52, M.A, 68; Grad. Sch. Banking, Univ. Wis, grad, 61; Agr. Credit Sch, Iowa State Univ, grad, 64; Phi Beta Kappa. Polit. & Govt. Pos: Secy. to U.S. Naval Attache, U.S. Embassy, Ottawa, Ont, Can, 45-48; Rep. precinct committee, Summerset Twp, Iowa, 62-66; chmn, Adair Co. Rep. Cent. Cmt, 65- Bus. & Prof. Pos: V.pres, State Savings Bank, Fontanelle, Iowa, 62-64, exec. v.pres. and cashier, 64- Mil. Serv: Entered as PO 1/C, Navy, 41, released as Chief PO 45, after serv. in Intel. Serv, East. Can. Mem: AF&AM; Scottish Rite (32°); Shrine; Eastern Star; Am. Legion (dept. finance officer, Iowa Dept, 66-); Farm Bur. Rel: Methodist. Mailing Add: 110 Benton St, Fontanelle, Iowa 50846.

WOLLSTADT, PAUL R
Dep. Asst. Secy. Manpower Research and Utilization, Dept. Defense
b. Rockford, Ill, 7/28/10; s. John P. Wollstadt and Hilda Ekstrom W; m. 6/19/34 to Elzada Elizabeth Rogers; c. Roger Davis, David Carl and Loyd James. Educ: Univ. Ill, A.B, 32; Phi Eta Sigma. Polit. & Govt. Pos: Dep. Asst. Secy. Manpower Research and Utilization, Dept. Defense, 69- Bus. & Prof. Pos: Writer and ed, Rockford Newspapers, Inc, Ill, 32-45; ed, Nat. Petroleum News, Cleveland, Ohio, 45-51; asst. mgr. pub. rels, Mobil Oil Corp, N.Y.C, 51-58, asst. to chmn, 58-59, v.pres, 59-63, sr. v.pres, 63-69. Mem: Nat. Press Club; Maplewood Country Club; Cloud Club. Rel: Presbyterian. Legal Res: 77 Slope Dr, Short Hills, N.J. 07078. Mailing Add: 2111 Jefferson Davis Hwy, Apt. 1111-S, Arlington, Va. 22202.

WOLTERMANN, GERHARD HENRY D
City Alderman, Columbus, Mont.
b. Columbus, Mont, 12/25/16; s. Gerhard Fred Woltermann and Helena Anna Mehrens W; m. 11/3/38 to Agnes Cecila Matovich; c. Gary, Mary Lou (Mrs. Jim Hoover), Ronald and Paula. Polit. & Govt. Pos: City alderman, Columbus, Mont, 59- Bus. & Prof. Pos: Owner, Git's Mobile Sta. & Big Sky Motel, 46- Mem: Kiwanis. Rel: Catholic. Mailing Add: Pike and Allen St, Columbus, Mont. 59019.

WOMACK, GERALDINE S. R
b. Summertown, Ga, 10/28/30; d. John Thomas Sherrod and Sara Mae Kirkland S; m. 11/25/49 to Robbie E. Womack; c. Gerry Elaine and Linda Gail. Educ: Summertown High Sch, grad, 47; Ryan's Bus. Col, Savannah, Ga, 48; high sch. athletic, commercial and scholarship medals. Polit. & Govt. Pos: Secy, Jenkins Co. Rep. Party, Ga, 56-60, chmn, 60-65; dist. dir, Rep. Women's Club, 60-65. Bus. & Prof. Pos: Payroll clerk, South. Paperboard Corp, Port Wentworth, Ga, 48-49; secy, Harrison Ins. Agency, Millen, Ga, 57-58. Mem: VFW Auxiliary; Home Demonstration Club, v.pres, Rural Letter Carriers Auxiliary, PTA; Women's Soc. for Christian Serv. Rel: Methodist; Communion Steward and Spiritual Life Secy. Mailing Add: R.F.D. 2, Millen, Ga. 30442. (1967)

WONG, CHUNG-MING R
Dir, Off. of Saline Water, Dept. of the Interior
b. 4/22/20; U.S. citizen; s. Tong Wong and Oy-Kwan Wong W; m. 5/19/46 to Irene Kia-Yu Hoh; c. Wai-so and Conrad Wai-pac. Educ: Tsing Hua Univ, China, B.S.M.E. summa cum laude, 42; Purdue Univ, M.S.M.E, 47; Columbia Univ, Ph.D, 58; Sigma Xi; Tau Beta Pi; past pres, Pui-Ching Alumni Asn; past pres, Chinese Engrs. and Scientists Asn, Calif. Polit. & Govt. Pos: Former mem, Aeronaut. and Space Cmt, Mayor's Off, Los Angeles, Calif; chmn, Prfnl. Cmt. for Nixon-Agnew, South. Calif, 68; dir, Off. of Saline Water, Dept. of the Interior, 69- Bus. & Prof. Pos: Instr, Sun Yat-sen Univ, China, 42-46; prof, Univ. Bridgeport, N.Y. Univ. and Brooklyn Polytech. Inst, 48-54; sr. scientist and mgr. thermodynamics, research and adv. develop, AVCO Mfg. Co, 54-56; asst. chief design engr, Repub. Aviation Corp, L.I, N.Y, 56-58; asst. mgr, Propulsion and Material Div, Missile and Space Co, Lockheed Aircraft Corp, Sunnyvale, Calif, 58-59; chief scientist and tech. asst. to the pres, United Tech. Corp, United Aircraft, 59-61; directorate asst, TRW Syst, Redondo Beach, 61-63; chief engr, Structures and Auxiliary Syst, Northrop Corp, Hawthorne, 63-66; sr. exec. adv, McDonnell Douglas Corp, Los Angeles, 66-69. Mil. Serv: Entered Nationalist Chinese Air Force, 46, released as 1st Lt, 47, after serv. in Chinese Theatre. Publ: Space Electronics Science and Technology, 65 and Advance Propulsion Systems for Space Application, 67, West. Periodical Publ; Advance Aerospace Structures, 66; VTOL Aircrafts, 67; Marine Sciences, Am. Inst. of Aeronaut. and Astronaut. Monogr. Series, 67; plus six books and over twenty tech. papers. Mem: Chmn, Int. Symp. on Space Tech. and Sci, Tokyo, 63 & 67; Propellant and Combustion Cmt, Am. Inst. of Aeronaut. and Astronaut, 63-67, secy, 67-68; chmn, Lect. Series Cmt, Symp. Cmt. and Field Trip Cmt; nat. tech. dir. and v.chmn, Am. Astronaut. Soc, 65-68; Sigma Xi; Am. Asn. Adv. Sci; Am. Physical Soc; Am. Asn. Col. Prof; Am. Soc. Mech. Engrs; PTA; Cub Scouts; Tennis Club. Scholarship Awards, Case Inst. Tech, 47; elected Best Prof. by student body, Univ. Bridgeport, 49-52; Scholarship Awards, DuPont de Nemours & Co, 50-68; Aerospace Sci. Award, Am. Inst. of Aeronaut. and Astronaut, 63; adv, Space and Aeronaut. Task Force, U.S. Cong, 63-65; Ministry of Exam. Highest Achievement Award, China. Rel: Presbyterian. Legal Res: 1501 Bel Air Rd, Los Angeles, Calif. 90024. Mailing Add: Office of Saline Water, Dept. of the Interior, Washington, D.C. 20240.

WONG, FRANCIS ALVIN D
Hawaii State Rep.
b. Honolulu, Hawaii, 7/18/36; s. Francis Y. Wong and Elizabeth Chong W; m. 6/14/58 to Shirley Anne Chun; c. Catherine Anne, Francis, Jr, Timothy Gerard and Mary Anne. Educ: Georgetown Col, B.S, 58; Georgetown Univ. Law Center, J.D, 60. Polit. & Govt. Pos: Staff mem, Off. of U.S. Sen. John F. Kennedy, 58-59; research asst, Off. of U.S. Sen. Oren E. Long, 59-62; pres, Dem. Precinct, Pearl City, Hawaii, 64-66; Hawaii State Rep, 67- Bus. & Prof. Pos: Real Estate Broker, Francis A. Wong & Assocs, 62-; Attorney-at-Law, 62- Mem: Bar Asn. of Hawaii; Am. Trial Lawyers Asn; Am. Bar Asn; Pacific Palisades Commun. Asn; Pearl City Commun. Asn; Waianae Businessmen's Asn; Hale Mohalu Hosp. Auxiliary; Leeward YMCA; Palisades PTA; Our Lady of Good Counsel PTG. Recipient Distinguished Serv. Award, U.S. Jr. C. of C, 65; One of Three Outstanding Young Men in Hawaii, Hawaii Jaycees, 68. Rel: Catholic. Mailing Add: 2023 Aamanu St, Pearl City, Hawaii 96782.

WON PAT, ANTONIO BORJA D
Wash. Rep, Territory of Guam
b. Sumay, Guam, 12/10/08; s. Ignacio Won Pat and Maria Suriano Borja W; m. 3/22/32 to Ana Salas Perez; c. Aveline (Mrs. Ploke), Marilyn A, Jacqueline (Mrs. Coats), Ellen (Mrs. Chargualaf), Anthony B, Jr, Rosalind (Mrs. Wise), Judith T, Mark V. and Denise J. Educ: Guam Normal Schs, 28-40. Polit. & Govt. Pos: Assemblyman, Guam Assembly, 36-41; Sen, Guam Legis, 50-64, speaker, 50-64; Wash. Rep, Territory of Guam, 65-; del, Dem. Nat. Conv, 68. Bus. & Prof. Pos: Sch. teacher, Guam, 28-33; elem. sch. prin, 34-40; high sch. teacher, 40-41; private bus. in imports, wholesale and retail, 45-54, real estate broker and ins. agent, 54; pres. and chmn. bd, Guam Commercial Corp, Inc, 46-54. Mem: Am. Acad. Polit. & Soc. Sci; Am. Soc. Pub. Admin; hon. mem. Rotary; Jr. C. of C.(pres. Guam Chap, 46-48); Guam Lions Club (pres, 48-50); D.C. Coun. Navy League, Nat. Capital Dem. Club; Capitol Hill Club. Commun. Leader Am. Award, 69. Rel: Catholic. Legal Res: Sinajana, Guam 96910. Mailing Add: 200 Maryland Ave. N.E, Suite 301, Washington, D.C. 20242.

WOO, GEORGE K. W. D
b. Kwangtung, China, 11/6/10; s. Matthew J. Woo and Loo Shee W; m. 6/25/36 to Rosalie Yee Quil; c. Lisa Jane and Matthew James. Educ: Va. Mil. Inst, B.S, 34; Univ. Pittsburgh, grad. work, 39; W.Va. Univ, grad. work, 45- Polit. & Govt. Pos: Mem, South Charleston Dem. Exec. Cmt, 54; mem, Kanawha Co. Dem. Exec. Cmt, 60; mem, South Charleston Recreation Cmn, 66; W.Va. State Del, 67-68. Bus. & Prof. Pos: Chief chemist, Evans Lead Div, Nat. Lead Co, 39- Mem: Kanawha Valley Indust. Emergency Planning Coun; Aquarium Soc. Charleston; Mason (past master); York Rite (past comdr); Shrine; Scottish Rite. Rel: Presbyterian; Deacon, First Presby. Church of South Charleston. Mailing Add: 5141 Ohio St. S.W, South Charleston, W.Va. 25309.

WOOD, BERNARD PENDLETON R
Chmn, Adams Co. Rep. Exec. Cmt, Miss.
b. Natchez, Miss, 2/7/38; s. Bernard Pendleton Wood and Helen Mae Miles W, both deceased; m. 12/29/60 to Lucianne A; c. Lucianne Campbell and Helen Elizabeth. Educ: La. State Univ, B.S, 60; Delta Kappa Epsilon. Polit. & Govt. Pos: Chmn, Adams Co. Rep. Exec. Cmt, Miss. Bus. & Prof. Pos: Pres, Wood's Automotive, Inc, 58-; treas, Natchez Elec. & Supply, Inc, 64- Mil. Serv: Naval Res, 55-63. Mem: Master Mason, Andrew Jackson Lodge; Rotary. Rel: Episcopal. Mailing Add: 407 S. Union St, Natchez, Miss. 39120.

WOOD, CHARLES ROSS R
Chmn, Clay Co. Rep. Cent. Cmt, Iowa
b. Spencer, Iowa, 1/13/41; s. Charles Edward Wood and Louise Carstensen W; m. 6/16/62 to Carol Ann Rosien; c. Courtney Anne and Matthew Charles. Educ: State Univ. Iowa, 59-60; Iowa State Univ, B.S. in Animal Sci, 63, George Gund Scholar, 63-64; Block and Bridle; Phi Kappa Psi. Polit. & Govt. Pos: Chmn, Clay Co. Young Rep, Iowa, 65-66 and Clay Co. Rep. Cent. Cmt, 66- Bus. & Prof. Pos: Dir. and exec. v.pres, Welco Feed Mfg. Co, Inc, 63- Mem: 4-H Club Leader; Am. Soc. Animal Sci; Spencer C. of C.(dir, 65-68); Master Mason. Produced Int. Grand Champion Steer, 58. Rel: Congregational; Dir, Bd. of Educ, 66-69. Mailing Add: 1010 Fourth Ave. W, Spencer, Iowa 51301.

WOOD, CLYDE NORRIS R
Chmn, Young Co. Rep. Party, Tex.
b. Salado, Tex, 8/16/17; s. Fred Bruce Wood and Lanora Birdwell W; m. 8/27/40 to Teny Blanche Merrill; c. Joanna (Mrs. Bill Watson) and Danny Bruce. Educ: McMurry Col, Abilene, Tex, B.S, 40; Tex. Tech. Col, B.S. in Agr, 50, M.S, 52; I.H.R. Polit. & Govt. Pos: Chmn, Young Co. Rep. Party, Tex, 67- Bus. & Prof. Pos: Teacher, Truscott Independent Sch. Dist, Tex, 40-, Rotan Independent Sch. Dist, 41-42, Throckmorton Independent Sch. Dist, 42-44 & 46-48 and Graham Independent Sch. Dist, 50-58. Mil. Serv: Entered as Pvt, Army, 44, released as Pfc, 46, after serv. in 138th Engr. Combat Bn, ETO, 44-46; ETO Victory Medal; Good Conduct Medal; Rhineland and Cent. Europe Battle Stars. Mem: Voc. Agr. Teachers Asn; Tex. State Teachers Asn. Scholarship, N.Tex. State Teachers Col. Rel: Methodist. Mailing Add: Royal Lane, The Oaks Apt. 11 A, Graham, Tex. 76046.

WOOD, CONSTANCE RICE D
Mem. Exec. Bd, N.H. Dem. State Cmt.
b. Marlboro, Mass, 2/1/22; d. John E. Rice and Helen Ellis R; m. 3/19/44 to Robert Kenneth Wood; c. Robert K, Jr, Jeffrey Bullard and Durinda Rice. Educ: Syracuse Univ, A.B, 43; Colby Jr. Col, 1 year. Polit. & Govt. Pos: Treas, Cheshire Co, McCarthy for Pres. Cmt, N.H, 68; alternate del, Dem. Nat. Conv, 68; Keene City chmn, Hoeh for Cong. Campaign, 68; mem, exec. bd, N.H. Dem. State Cmt, 69- Mem: UN Asn; League of Women Voters; Elliot Commun. Hosp. Ladies Aid; Center for Human Concerns; Cheshire Homes Inc; Dem. City Club; Keene Country Club. Rel: Unitarian-Universalist; pres. bd. trustees, Keene, N.H. Unitarian-Universalist Church. Mailing Add: 63 Arch St, Keene, N.H. 03431.

WOOD, DOROTHY MERTIS R
V.Chmn, Brown Co. Rep. Party, S.Dak.
b. Aberdeen, S.Dak, 4/23/28; d. John Carl Lowitz and Bertha Papke L; m.

6/15/47 to Royal J. Wood; c. James Royal, Bonnie Anita, Peggy Annette and Amy Louise. Educ: Warner High Sch, grad, 46. Polit. & Govt. Pos: Exec. secy, Brown Co. Rep. Serv. Off, S.Dak, 66-; v.chmn, Brown Co. Planning Cmn, 67-69; Brown Co. del, S.Dak. State Rep. Conv, 68; v.chmn, Brown Co. Rep. Party, S.Dak, 68-; S.Dak. del, Nat. Women's Fedn. of Rep. Women, Wash, D.C, 69. Mem: Pres, Rieck-Morgan Legion Auxiliary, Warner, 47-48; held various off, Merry Workers Exten. Club, 47-69; pres, Warner PTA, 63-64; Dist. 8 pres, S.Dak. PTA, 64-66; pres, Northeast. S.Dak. Cerebral Palsy Asn, 66-69; chmn, Brown Co. Mother's March of Dimes, 66-69; chmn, Voters Serv. and mem. bd, Aberdeen League of Women Voters, 66-68; chmn, Equal Rights for Women Cmt. Rel: Lutheran; Sunday Sch. Supt, St. John Lutheran Church, Warner, 50-51, Sunday Sch. Teacher, 52-65, Choir mem, currently. Mailing Add: Warner, S.Dak. 47579.

WOOD, FREDA B. D

b. Salt Lake City, Utah, 10/27/11; d. Gustave Fred Bushman and Freda Hertel B; m. 11/28/29 to Joseph Herbert Wood; c. Jack Bushman, Patricia (Mrs. Petersen) and William Joseph. Educ: Salt Lake Bus. Col, acct. & secretarial courses, 26-27; Univ. Utah, exten. courses in polit. sci, 58-59, cert, 59. Polit. & Govt. Pos: Del, Dem. Co. and Dist. Conv, Utah, 40-; bd. mem. planning cmn, N.Salt Lake City, 50-56, city recorder, 50-60, councilwoman finance dept, 50-62; del, Dem. State Conv, 52-; charter pres. and organizer, South Davis Jane Jefferson Club, 56, past pres. and auditor, 65-66; trustee and charter bd. mem, S.Davis Co. Sewer Improv. Dist, 59, clerk-treas, 59-; bd. mem, Utah State Retirement Bd, 66, mem. investment cmt, 67- Bus. & Prof. Pos: Del. to Int. Union of Local Authorities for Utah Munic. League, Wash, D.C, 61, Brussels, Belgium, 63. Mem: Int. Union Local Authorities; Am. Soc. for Pub. Admin; Garden Bouquet Club; bd. mem, Utah Munic. League, 58-59; del, Women's Legis. Coun, Utah, 58-; charter mem. and former v.pres, Soc. Multiple Handicapped Children, 56-59; secy, Utah Chap, Nat. Munic. Clerks Asn, 57; bd. mem, South Davis Youth Center, 55-57; PTA; United Fund and others. Rel: Latter-day Saint. Mailing Add: 56 South Main, North Salt Lake, Utah 84054.

WOOD, GEORGE ARTHUR R

Chmn, East Lyme Rep. Town Cmt, Conn.

b. Anderson, S.C, 6/30/21; s. Edward Murray Wood and Beulah Francis LeCroy W; m. 10/24/42 to Carolyn Marie Puckett; c. Larry Renner, Stephen Murray, Joan Marie and Charles Arthur. Educ: Greenville Col, 41; Mitchel Col, 57-58. Polit. & Govt. Pos: Chmn, East Lyme Rep. Town Cmt, Conn, 68- Bus. & Prof. Pos: Research psychologist, Gen. Dynamics Elec. Boat Div, Groton, Conn, 62- Mil. Serv: Entered as A/S, Navy, 42, released as Chief Engineman, 61, after serv. in Submarine Serv, Pac, Theatre, 42-45; Navy Unit Citation; Good Conduct Medal with 4 Stars; Am. Campaign, Asiatic Campaign, and Victory Medals; Submarine Combat Insignia with 7 Stars. Publ: Submarine Advanced Casualty Control, Gen. Dynamics Elec. Boat Div, 2/69. Mem: Am. Legion; East Lyme Arts Coun. Rel: Protestant. Mailing Add: 7 Penncove Rd, Niantic, Conn. 06357.

WOOD, GEORGE MATTHEW D

N.C. State Sen.

b. Camden, N.C, 4/30/26; s. Freshwater Pool Wood and Elsie Griffin W.(deceased); m. 8/12/50 to Winifred Jones; c. Gail Griffen, George M, Jr, David Lloyd, Joanne Jones and Robert Graham. Educ: N.C. State Univ, B.S. in Agronomy, 50; Gamma Sigma Delta; Sigma Chi. Polit. & Govt. Pos: N.C. State Rep, 63-66; N.C. State Sen, 67- Bus. & Prof. Pos: V.pres, F.P. Wood & Son, Inc, 52 and v.pres, F.P. Wood & Son of Elizabeth City, Inc, 60; pres, Carolina Transit, Inc, 62; bd. dir, South. Loan & Ins. Co, 64-; mem, State Capital Planning Cmn, 65. Mil. Serv: Entered as Seaman, Maritime Serv, 43, released as Ens, 46; Atlantic and Pac. War Theater Ribbons. Mem: Past pres, N.C. State Alumni Asn. and Camden Lions Club; adv. bd, Chowan Col; adv. coun, Sch. of Agr, N.C. State Univ. and bldg. cmt, N.C. State Univ; bd. trustees, Univ. N.C; dir, Nat. Grain & Feed Dealers Asn; Wolfpack Club; Va-Carolina Grain & Feed Dealers Asn; Nat. Potato Chip Asn; Farm Bur; Mason; Shrine; Elizabeth City Golf Club. Bus. Character Award, Red Book; Outstanding Young Farmer Award, Jaycees, 61; Meritorious Serv. Award, N.C. State Univ. Alumni Asn, 67. Pub. Speaker. Rel: Presbyterian, Deacon, 55-56, Elder, 66. Mailing Add: Camden, N.C. 27921.

WOOD, GORDON THOMPSON R

Chmn, Douglas Co. Rep. Cent. Cmt, Ore.

b. Seattle, Wash, 4/24/30; s. Harold Sidney Wood and Muriel Sellers W; m. 6/19/54 to Phyllis Julia Warneke; c. Scott Denison, Peter Gordon and Kelsey Lyle. Educ: Univ. Wash, 47-50 & 52-54; Acacia. Polit. & Govt. Pos: Chmn, Douglas Co. Rep. Cent. Cmt, Ore, 68-; mem. electoral col, 68; mem. exec. bd, Law Enforcement Planning Cmn, 69-; mem, Roseburg-Douglas Co. Airport Adv. Cmn, 69- Mil. Serv: Entered as Pvt, Air Force, 50, released as Airman 1/C, 52, after serv. in 28th Air Div, West. Air Defense Force, 50-52. Mem: Cert. Ins. Agent; Ore. Asn. Independent Ins. Agents; Douglas Co. Ins. Agents Asn; pres, Roseburg Area C. of C, 67; pres, Douglas Co. Chap, Ore. Pilots Asn, 66; chmn, Douglas Co. Nat. Found. March of Dimes, 62-65; pres, Roseburg Kiwanis Club, 69; Trustee, Elks, 68-; Moose; Aircraft Owners and Pilots Asn; Roseburg Country Club. Rel: Lutheran. Legal Res: 933 S.E. Glen, Roseburg, Ore. 97470. Mailing Add: P.O. Box 1326, Roseburg, Ore. 97470.

WOOD, HARLINGTON, JR. R

Dir. Exec. Off. for U.S. Attorneys, Dept. of Justice

b. Springfield, Ill, 4/17/20; s. Harlington Wood and Marie Green W; m. 7/27/45 to Rosemary Miller; c. Alexa. Educ: Univ. Ill, A.B, 42, J.D, 48; Delta Kappa Epsilon. Polit. & Govt. Pos: Legal adv. to Lt. Gov. of Ill, 52; spec. asst. attorney gen, Ill, 54-58; U.S. attorney, S. Dist. of Ill, 58-61; mem. bd. dir, Ill. Bur. of Race Track Police, 63-65; mem, Ill. Crime and Investigating Cmn, 63-68; ballot security officer, Rep. Nat. Cmt, 64, participant in seminars and consult. on legal aspects of elec, 64-68; dir, Exec. Off. for U.S. Attorneys, Dept. of Justice, 69- Bus. & Prof. Pos: Attorney-at-law, Wood & Wood, Springfield, Ill, 48-58 & 61-69. Mil. Serv: Entered as 2nd Lt, Army, 42, released as Maj, 46, after serv. in Air Force and Transportation Corps, ETO and Asian Theatre, 43-45; Commendation Medal. Mem: Ill, Am. and Fed. Bar Asns; Am. Trial Lawyers Asn; Nat. Dist. Attorneys Asn; Urban League; Abraham Lincoln Asn. Rel: Protestant. Legal Res: R.R. 6, Old Jacksonville Rd, Springfield, Ill. 62707. Mailing Add: P.O. Box 985, Washington, D.C. 20044.

WOOD, JANE R

V.Pres, Calif. State Rep. Cent. Cmt.

b. Merced, Calif, 8/25/24; d. Charles Kenneth Safford and Isabel Burton S; m. 11/11/45 to James Ritchie Wood; c. Kenneth James and Dorothy Jane. Educ: Merced Jr. Col; Col. Pac, Stockton, Calif; San Joaquin Co. Hosp, R.N. Polit. & Govt. Pos: Chmn, Merced Co. Rep. Cent. Cmt, Calif, 60; v.pres, Calif. Rep. State Cent. Cmt, 65- Mil. Serv: Cadet Nurse, Navy, 45. Mem: Atwater High Sch. PTA; Fruitland Womens Improv. Club; Atwater Womens' Club; Merced Hosp. Assistance League. Rel: Episcopal. Mailing Add: P.O. Box 207, Atwater, Calif. 95301. (1967)

WOOD, JOE T. D

Ga. State Rep.

b. Gainesville, Ga, 10/23/22; s. Ernest W. Wood and Martha Ann Reynolds W; m. 4/4/42 to Helen Thrasher; c. Joe T, Jr. Educ: Univ. Ga, 2 years; Gridiron Soc. Polit. & Govt. Pos: Ga. State Rep, 11th Dist, 65- Mil. Serv: Entered as Pvt, Army, 42, released as 1st Sgt, 46. Mem: Elks; Am. Legion; VFW; Gainesville Farm Bur; Chattahoochee Country Club. Rel: Baptist. Legal Res: 1435 Cumberland Dr. N.E, Gainesville, Ga. 30501. Mailing Add: P.O. Box 736, Gainesville, Ga. 30501.

WOOD, JOHN DUDLEY R

b. New York, N.Y, 12/5/30; s. Horace Eugene Wood and Anna Lucretia Bennett W; m. 12/29/56 to Roberta Harrison; c. Eric Dudley, Ethan Keller and Claudia Elaine. Educ: Ohio Wesleyan Univ, 48-51; Case Inst. Tech, B.S, 53; Lehigh Univ, M.S, 59, Ph.D, 62; Sigma Xi; Pi Mu Epsilon; Delta Tau Delta. Polit. & Govt. Pos: Del, Rep. Nat. Conv, 68. Bus. & Prof. Pos: Student engr, Am. Tel. & Tel. Co, N.Y, 53-54; prod. metallurgist, Kaiser Aluminum & Chem. Corp, Haethorpe, Md, 56-58; instr, Lehigh Univ, 58-61 and prof, 62-; research metallurgist, Aluminum Co. Am, New Kensington, Pa, 61-62. Mil. Serv: Entered as 2nd Lt, Air Force Res, 54, released as 1st Lt, 56, after serv. in Wright Air Develop. Center, Wright Patterson AFB, Ohio, 54-56; Korean Conflict Medal. Publ: Many technical articles. Mem: Am. Soc. Metals; Inst. Metals; Am. Inst. Mining, Metallurgical and Petroleum Engrs; Am. Soc. Testing and Materials; Lehigh Pocono Cmt. of Concern; Northampton Cmt. for Responsive Govt. Rel: Unitarian. Mailing Add: 25 E. Goepp St, Bethlehem, Pa. 18018.

WOOD, JOHN EMMET D

b. Millry, Ala, 9/9/09; s. John Wesley Wood and Ada Wilkins W; m. 6/13/36 to Georgine Onderdonk; c. Roberta Clara. Educ: Univ. Ala; Int. Criminology Sch, Seattle, Wash, 34. Polit. & Govt. Pos: Ala. State Rep, 47-59 & 63-66. Bus. & Prof. Pos: Criminologist; co. coroner. Mil. Serv: Marine Corps, World War II. Mem: Woodman; Elks; Mason. Rel: Methodist. Mailing Add: Millry, Ala. 36558. (1967)

WOOD, KATHERINE M. R

V.Chmn, Otsego Co. Rep. Cmt, N.Y.

b. Burdette, N.Y, 8/16/05; d. Ralph E. Winton and Nellie Frautz W; m. 6/26/26 to Adelbert E. Wood, wid; c. Robert W. and Karlyn E. Educ: Richfield Springs Training Sch. Polit. & Govt. Pos: Rep. committeewoman, Springfield Center, N.Y, 26-; committeewoman, N.Y. State Rep. Party, 54-58; v.chmn, Otsego Co. Rep. Cmt, N.Y, 58- Bus. & Prof. Pos: Dir. admissions, M.I.B. Hosp, Cooperstown, N.Y, 57-69; adminstr, Order of Eastern Star Home, Oriskany, 69- Mem: Adminstr. Long Term Care Facilities of N.Y; Criterion Prfnl. Women's Club; bd. visitors, Binghamton State Hosp; Eastern Star (Grand Matron, 53); DAR. Rel: Episcopal. Legal Res: P.O. Box 125, Springfield Center, N.Y. 13468. Mailing Add: Order of Eastern Star Home, Oriskany, N.Y. 13424.

WOOD, LEONA BERYL R

Secy, Nev. Rep. State Cent. Cmt.

b. Pig Pine, Calif, 10/16/22; d. James Steven Crocker and Muriel Osborn C; m. 3/21/42 to George Leslie Wood; c. Lana (Mrs. McAllister), John and Jim. Educ: Bishop Union High Sch, dipl, 40. Polit. & Govt. Pos: Secy, Nev. Rep. State Cent. Cmt, 66-; corresponding secy, Nev. Fedn. Rep. Women, 67- Mem: Am. Bus. Women's Asn.(prog. cmt, 69); secy, Youth Baseball Asn. of Carson City, Nev, 5 years; counsr, Walther League, Bethlehem Lutheran Church, 7 years; pres, Mother's Baseball Asn. of Carson City, 1 year. Am. Legion Award, Grammar Sch, Bishop, Calif, 36. Rel: Lutheran. Legal Res: 412 W. Fifth St, Carson City, Nev. 89701. Mailing Add: Box 829, Carson City, Nev. 89701.

WOOD, LEONARD VICTOR R

Fla. State Rep.

b. Chicago, Ill, 3/3/37; s. Benton Willis Wood and Emma Grady W; m. 12/15/61 to Barbara Alice Parker; c. Benton Nelson, Balen Brent and Annastasia. Educ: Rollins Col, B.A, 59; Duke Univ. Law Sch, LL.B, 62; Omicron Delta Kappa; X-Club; pres, Fla. Intercol. Stud. Govt. Asn. and Rollins Col. Stud. Govt. Asn, 58-59. Polit. & Govt. Pos: Spec. asst. pub. defender, Ninth Judicial Circuit, Fla, 65; Fla. State Rep, 38th Dist, 68- Bus. & Prof. Pos: Partner, Whittaker, Pyle & Wood, Orlando, Fla, 64- Mil. Serv: Marine Corps, 56-62. Mem: Am, Fla. and Orange Co. Bar Asns; Am. Judicature Soc; Am. Acad. Defense Counsel; Fla. Acad. Trial Attorneys. Algernon Sidney Sullivan Leadership Award, 57. Rel: Methodist. Mailing Add: 312 Park Place, Altamonte Springs, Fla. 32701.

WOOD, RANDOLPH CLAY D

b. Warren Co, Tenn, 3/30/17; s. C.I. Wood and Irene Wimberly; m. 12/21/41 to Lois Henry; c. Linda Carol, Larry Clay and John Randolph. Educ: Middle Tenn. State Col, B.S, 41. Polit. & Govt. Pos: Alternate del, Dem. Nat. Conv, 64. Bus. & Prof. Pos: Recording indust. exec; founder, pres, Dot Records, Inc, 50-; founder, pres, chmn. bd, Randy's Record Shop; v.pres, Paramount Pictures Corp, Vin-Sun Music Corp, SunVine Music Corp; pres, Gallatin Music Corp, Dot Records Distributing Corp, Randy-Smith Corp; dir, radio sta. WHIN, Gallatin, Tenn; chmn. bd. Wood Found, Nashville. Mil.

Serv: Army Air Force, 1st Lt, 42-45. Mem: Founder, Hollywood Mus; Peabody Develop. Coun, George Peabody Col. for Teachers; pres. bd, Pepperdine Col; bd. dir, South. Calif. Sch. Theology, Hollywood YMCA, Agr. Tech. Assistance Found; dir, past v.pres, hon. col. Tenn. Mem. Rec. Indust. Am. Asn; Am. Legion; C. of C; Elk; Mason; Shrine; Wilshire Country Club; past pres, Gallatin Lions Club. Rel: Methodist; Trustee. Mailing Add: 301 S. Beverly Glen, Los Angeles, Calif. 90024. (1967)

WOOD, RICHARD GLEE R
Chmn, Hockey Co. Rep. Cent. Cmt, Tex.
b. Mt. Vernon, Ill, 2/21/31; s. K. Glee Wood (deceased) and Stella Edmison W; m. 12/18/54 to Marylea Henderson; c. Brenda, Donald, Margaret and Kay. Educ: Baylor Univ, B.A; Tex. Tech. Col, M.B.A. Polit. & Govt. Pos: Electoral col. nominee, Tex, 60; secy, Lubbock Co. Rep. Party, 60-62; chmn, Hockey Co. Rep. Cent. Cmt, 66- Bus. & Prof. Pos: Owner, Bus. Consult. Serv; chmn. bus. dept, S.Plains Col, Levelland, Tex, 65-67; chmn. dept. bus. & econ, Campbellsville Col, Campbellsville, Ky, 67-69; asst. prof, Sul Ross State Univ, Alpine, Tex, 69- Mem: Nat. Bus. Educ. Asn; Tex. State Jr. Col. Asn; West Econ. Asn. Rel: Southern Baptist. Mailing Add: Sul Ross State Univ, Alpine, Tex. 79830.

WOOD, ROYAL JAMES 'BUD' R
S.Dak. State Rep.
b. Warner, S.Dak, 3/28/22; s. James Lawson Wood and Esther Rehfeld W; m. 6/15/47 to Dorothy Mertis Lowitz; c. James Royal, Bonnie Anita, Peggy Annette, and Amy Louise. Educ: North. State Col, 40-42. Polit. & Govt. Pos: Chmn, Co. Young Rep. Orgn, S.Dak, 43; S.Dak. State Rep, 67- Bus. & Prof. Pos: Past dir, Warner Co-op Sta, 6 years; pres, Warner Co-op Elevator, 9 years; auctioneer, 45- Mem: Past pres, Farm Bur; Mason; past pres, 4-H Asn; PTA; Brown Co. Crop Improvement Asn; Brown Co. Livestock Improvement Asn; Lutheran Brotherhood. Meritorious Award for Serv. to 4-H. Rel: Lutheran; Pres, Church Coun. Mailing Add: Warner, S.Dak. 57479.

WOOD, WARREN KIRCHNER R
Iowa State Rep.
b. Davenport, Iowa, 3/7/32; s. Jasper E.Wood and Helen D. Kirchner W; m. 12/11/60 to Sue Ann Hohenadel; c. Douglas M. and William K. Educ: Univ. Iowa, B.A, 53, J.D, 55; Phi Delta Phi; Acacia. Polit. & Govt. Pos: Staff mem, First U.S. Cong. Dist, Iowa, 59-62; ward alderman, Davenport City Coun, 60 & 61; Iowa State Rep, 67- Mil. Serv: Entered as 2nd Lt, Air Force, 55, released as 1st Lt, 58; Capt, Air Force Res, 58- Mem: Scott Co, State of Iowa and Am. Bar Asns; Mason (32°), Shrine; Gyro Club; IBEW. Rel: Episcopal. Mailing Add: 2706 Fairhaven Rd, Davenport, Iowa 52803.

WOOD, WILLIAM ZENO D
N.C. State Sen.
b. Hamptonville, N.C, 2/15/24; s. Walden Livingston Wood and Mattie Martin W; m. 4/14/46 to Whilma J. Wood; c. William Zeno, Jr, John Walden and Martha Susan. Educ: Wake Forest Col. and Law Sch, LL.B; Beta Club; Phi Alpha Delta. Polit. & Govt. Pos: Chmn, Forsyth Co. Bd. Elec, 53-60 & 66; pres, Wilsonian Dem. Club, 55-56; nat. committeeman, Young Dem. Clubs, N.C, 56-57; regional dir, Young Dem. Clubs of Am, 57-58; mem, N.C. State Dem. Exec. Cmt, 60; N.C. State Rep, 61-63; N.C. State Sen, 65-, mem, N.C. Vet. Cmn, N.C. R.R. Cmn. and N.C. Elec. Laws Rev. Cmn; mem, Platform Cmt, N.C. Dem. Conv, 67. Mil. Serv: Entered as Pvt, Air Force, 44, released as T-5, 46, after serv. in India-Burma; 3 Battle Stars. Mem: Pres, Forsyth Co. Jr. Bar Asn, 63; Mason 32°); Shrine; Moose; Am. Legion; 40 et 8; Optimist; dir, March of Dimes, 66-67; N.C. Bar Asn; Forsyth Co. Jr. Bar Asn.(pres. elect). Rel: Presbyterian. Mailing Add: 4915 Stonington Rd, Winston-Salem, N.C. 27101.

WOODAHL, ROBERT LEE R
Attorney Gen, Mont.
b. Great Falls, Mont, 6/28/31; s. Arvid Bye Woodahl and Margaret R. Fogerty W; m. 10/20/63 to Arlene Rae Depner; c. Brian Arvid, Scott Robert and Kirsten Patrice. Educ: Mont. State Univ, 49-51; South. Methodist Univ, 56; Univ. Mont, B.S, 56, LL.B, 59; Sigma Alpha Epsilon; Phi Delta Phi. Polit. & Govt. Pos: Co. attorney, Teton Co, Mont, 61-68; pres, State Elec. Bd, Helena, Mont, 65-67; attorney gen, Mont, 69- Mil. Serv: Entered as Sgt, Air Force, 51, released as S/Sgt, 52, after serv. in 186th Fighter Squadron, Strategic and Tactical Air Command, 51-52; Good Conduct Medal. Mem: Nat. Asn. of Attorneys Gen; Mont. Bar Asn; Mason; Shrine; Eastern Star; Eagles; Lions; Am. Legion. Rel: Methodist. Legal Res: 1402 Jerome Place, Helena, Mont. 59601. Mailing Add: Office of the Attorney General, State Capitol, Helena, Mont. 59601.

WOODALL, PERRY B. R
Wash. State Sen.
b. Buena, Wash, 11/26/12; s. Perry M. Woodall and Nona Crayne W; m. 10/1/43 to Joye Johnson; c. Patricia Joye. Educ: Yakima Valley Col, 30-32; Univ. Wash, LL.B, 36. Polit. & Govt. Pos: Wash. State Rep, 39-43 & 47-51; v.chmn, Yakima Co. Cent. Cmt, 46; permanent chmn, Wash. State Rep. Conv, 48 & 60; Wash. State Sen, 57-; del, Rep. Nat. Conv, 64. Bus. & Prof. Pos: V.pres, Co. Bar Asn, 39; pres, Cent. Wash. Fair, 39-61; judge adv. Dept. of Wash. Am. Legion, 55; mem. legis. cmt, State Bar Asn, 64-65. Mil. Serv: Entered as Lt.(jg), Navy, 43, released as Lt, 46. Mem: Elks; Eagles; Grange; Farm Bur; Am. Legion. Rel: Baptist. Legal Res: R.R. 1, Toppenish, Wash. 98948. Mailing Add: P.O. Box 507, Toppenish, Wash. 98948.

WOODARD, CARL JUBAL R
b. Cullman, Ala, 8/1/24; s. Milas Homer Woodard and Olivia Faye Summerford W; m. 10/11/44 to Martha Louise Van Meter; c. Carl Gary and Sheila Archer. Educ: Auburn Univ, 1 year. Polit. & Govt. Pos: Chmn, Cullman Co. Rep. Exec. Cmt, Ala. and v.chmn, 63; ed, Cullman Rep. Newsletter, 63- Bus. & Prof. Pos: Mgr, M.H. Woodard Dept. Store, 55-65, owner, Carl's Dept. Store, 65- Mil. Serv: Entered as Pvt, Army Air Force, 43, released as S/Sgt, 44, after serv. in Eighth Air Force, Eng; Air Medal with 5 Oak Leaf Clusters; Distinguished Flying Cross. Mem: VFW; Am. Legion; Ala. Farm Bur; Rotary. Rel: Lutheran; Mo. Synod. Legal Res: 1603 Elizabeth St, Cullman, Ala. 35055. Mailing Add: 305 First Ave. W, Cullman, Ala. 35055.

WOODARD, JOHN RAYNOR D
b. Pendleton, N.C, 7/11/06; s. Donald M. Woodard and Maggie Maddry W; m. 6/4/33 to Bernice Norris; c. John Raynor, Jr. and James Anderson. Educ: Wake Forest Col, B.S, 30. Polit. & Govt. Pos: Treas, Conway, N.C, 41-48; mem, Northampton Co. Bd. Educ, 42-43; mem, Northampton Co. Bd. Cmnrs, 43-48; mem. bd. trustees, Chowan Col, 48-52, chmn. bd, 52; N.C. State Rep, 49-66. Bus. & Prof. Pos: Merchant and farmer. Mem: Conway C. of C.(pres, 56); Conway Ruritan Club (pres, 46-47); Northampton Co. Farm Bur.(pres, 51-52); Mason (master); Shrine; Beechwood Country Club; Chowan Yacht Club; Scottish Rite; York Rite. Rel: Baptist; Deacon, 39-62, Sunday Sch. Supt, 40-46; Sunday Sch. Teacher, 31-40 & 47-64; church clerk, 57-64; chmn. bd. trustees, 53-64. Mailing Add: Conway, N.C. 27820. (1967)

WOODARD, WILLIAM EARL R
Kans. State Rep.
b. Montezuma, Kans, 1/1/23; s. William Earl Woodard and Faye Dodge W; m. 3/9/49 to Peggy Dorene McComas; c. Mark John, Barbara Kay and JoAnn. Educ: Friends Univ, 40-41; Wichita Univ, A.B, 47; Washburn Univ. Law Sch, LL.B, 50; Delta Theta Phi. Polit. & Govt. Pos: Dep. co. attorney, Sedgwick Co, Wichita, Kans, 51-53; co-chmn, Young Rep, Wichita, 55-56; Rep. jr. nat. committeeman, State of Kans, 57-58; police judge, Wichita, 61-63; Kans. State Sen, Sedgwick Co, 65- Mil. Serv: Entered as Cadet, Navy, 42, released as Lt.(jg), 46, after serv. in Naval Air Corp Training Command. Mem: Wichita and Kans. Bar Asns; Am. Legion; Optimist. Rel: Presbyterian. Legal Res: 3822 E. Skinner, Wichita, Kans. 67218. Mailing Add: 815 Union National Bldg, Wichita, Kans. 67202.

WOODARD, WILLIAM PHILIP R
Chmn, East Brookfield Rep. Town Cmt, Mass.
b. Worcester, Mass, 10/23/32; s. George R. Woodard and Carrie E. Herbert W; m. 8/25/60 to Judith Ann Tucker; c. William Thomas, Kathie Anne and Barry Jon. Educ: Worcester Jr. Col; Am. Int. Col, B.A. in Hist, 59; Worcester State Col, M.Ed, 61; Univ. Conn. Polit. & Govt. Pos: Chmn, East Brookfield Rep. Town Cmt, Mass, 63-; mem, East Brookfield Finance Cmt, 63-66. Bus. & Prof. Pos: Teacher soc. sci, Charlton High Sch, 60-66. Mil. Serv: Entered as Pvt, Army, 53, released as SP-3, after serv. in Germany 302 BN, Seventh Corps, 56; Soldier of Month, 302 BN, 55 and 502 Corps, 55. Mem: Chmn, East Brookfield Hist. Soc; Nat. Geographic Soc. Rel: Protestant. Mailing Add: Lake Quaboag, East Brookfield, Mass. 01515. (1967)

WOODCOCK, GEORGE WASHINGTON R
Chmn, Wabash Co. Rep. Party, Ill.
b. Brownsville, Ky, 4/13/30; s. George W. Woodcock, Sr. and Mellittia Van-Meter W; m. 12/20/52 to Margaret Delsey Peet; c. Margaret Nell, Marilyn and George W, III. Educ: West. Ky. Univ, A.B, 54; Univ. Ky. Law Sch, LL.B, 57; Alpha Tau Omega. Polit. & Govt. Pos: U.S. Cmnr, East. Dist, Ill, 61-65; city attorney, Mt. Carmel, 63-66; bd. mem, Selective Serv. Bd. 205, Mt. Carmel, 67-69, Selective Serv. Syst. adv. to Registrants, Wabash Co, currently; State's Attorney, Wabash Co, 68-; chmn, Wabash Co. Rep. Party, 68- Bus. & Prof. Pos: Partner, Law Firm of White & Woodcock, Morgantown, Ky, 57, law firm of McGaughey, McGaughey, Henry & Woodcock, Mt. Carmel, Ill, 58-62; attorney at law, 62- Mil. Serv: Entered as Pvt, Army, 47-48 & 52-53, released as Lt, 53, after serv. in 45th Div, Korea; Combat Infantryman's Badge. Mem: Wabash Co, Ill. State, Am. and Ky. State Bar Asns; Am. Trial Lawyers Asn; Interstate Oil Compact Cmn; v.pres, Bank of Edmonson Co, Brownsville, Ky; Union League Club of Chicago; Shrine; Mason; VFW; Am. Legion; Elks; Moose; Eagles; C. of C. Rel: Episcopal. Legal Res: 139 St. Joseph Ave, Mt. Carmel, Ill. 62863. Mailing Add: P.O. Drawer 433, Mt. Carmel, Ill. 62863.

WOODCOCK, JOSEPH C, JR. R
N.J. State Sen.
b. Cliffside Park, N.J, 11/20/25. Educ: Rutgers Univ, A.B, 50; Univ. of Pa. Law Sch, LL.B, 53. Polit. & Govt. Pos: Bergen Co. Young Rep. Club, N.J; Cliffside Park Rep. Club; campaign mgr, Cliffside Park Rep. Cands, 57; Borough Attorney, Northvale; former Borough Attorney, Cliffside Park; N.J. State Assemblyman, 62-67; N.J. State Sen, 68- Mem: Lions, Cliffside Park; Mem. Post 126, Am. Legion; Whitehead Lodge No. 184, F&AM; past mem, Co. Comm; past mem, Cliffside Park Coun. Mailing Add: 690 Anderson Ave, Cliffside Park, N.J. 07010.

WOODCOCK, LEONARD D
b. Providence, R.I, 2/15/11; s. Ernest Woodcock and Margaret Freel W; m. 5/28/41 to Loula Martin; c. Mrs. Leslie Bluestone, Janet and John. Educ: Wayne State Univ, 28-30; Walsh Inst. Accountancy, 28-30. Polit. & Govt. Pos: Gov, Wayne State Univ, 59-; del, Dem. Nat. Conv, 68. Bus. & Prof. Pos: Staff rep, UAW, 40-47; regional dir, Int. UAW, 47-55, v.pres, 55- Mem: UAW. Legal Res: 1300 Lafayette E, Detroit, Mich. 48207. Mailing Add: 8000 E. Jefferson, Detroit, Mich. 48214.

WOODCOCK, RAYMOND PAUL D
R.I. State Rep.
b. Providence, R.I, 11/1/29; s. William Woodcock, Sr.(deceased) and Valentine Boucher W; m. 6/12/47 to Eileen M. Donahue; c. Raymond, Jr, Stephen F. and William, III. Educ: N.Y. Mergenthaler Linotype Sch, 1 year. Polit. & Govt. Pos: Mem, 34th Representative Dist. Cmt, Dem. Party, R.I, 66-67; R.I. State Rep, Dist. 34, 67- Bus. & Prof. Pos: Apprentice printer, William R. Brown Co, Providence, R.I, 48-53; printer, Providence Journal-Bulletin, 53-55; Lockup-man, Typecraft, Inc, Calif, 55-56; foreman, Shamory Typesetting Serv, 56-60; treas. and gen. mgr, William R. Brown Printing Co, Providence, R.I, 60- Mem: Elks (Leading Knight, Pawtucket Lodge); Warwick Coun, K. of C; Sons of Irish Kings; Friendly Sons of St. Patrick; Shamrock Soc. North Providence; St. Benedict's Holy Name Soc. Rel: Roman Catholic. Mailing Add: 60 La Chance Ave, Warwick, R.I. 02889.

WOODHAMS, DORRIS C. R
V.Chmn, Sedgwick Co. Rep. Cent. Cmt, Colo.
b. Ovid, Colo, 5/24/18; d. Michael Troudtman Cloud and Leona Belle Bowers C; m. 2/2/42 to Charles F. Woodhams; c. Leanna Rae (Mrs. Appleby) and Sharon H.(Mrs. Skrdlant). Educ: Sedgwick Co. High Sch, Julesburg, Colo, grad. Polit. & Govt. Pos: Precinct work, Sedgwick Co. Rep. Party, Colo, 50-55; asst. secy, Sedgwick Co. Rep. Cent. Cmt, 55-57, secy, 57-61 and v.chmn, 61- Bus. & Prof. Pos: Off. clerk, Great West. Sugar Co, Ovid, Colo, 42-51; secy-bookkeeper, Farmers Elevator Co, 51-53; secy-treas, West. Mgt. Corp, Julesburg, Colo, 53- Mem: organizer and charter mem, Ovid Wesleyan Serv.

Guild; Ovid Fedn. Women's Club; Rep. Women's Club. Local Good Neighbor Award, Fedn. Women's Club State Recognition Award for organization and work in Teen Age Traffic Safety Club; numerous cert. in recognition of work in various depts. of Christian Church. Rel: Christian Church of N.Am. Legal Res: 304 Sixth St, Ovid, Colo. 80744. Mailing Add: Box 102, Ovid, Colo. 80744.

WOODHOUSE, MRS. CHASE GOING D
Mem, Sprague Dem. Town Cmt, Conn.
b. Victoria, B.C, Can; d. Seymour Going and Harriet Jackson G; wid; c. Margaret (Mrs. Becker). Educ: McGill Univ, B.A. & M.A; Univ. Berlin and Univ. Chicago, grad. study. Hon. LL.D, Alfred Univ, Allegheny Col. and Univ. Hartford. Polit. & Govt. Pos: Economist chief div. econ, Bur. Home Econ, U.S. Dept. Agr, 26-29; del, Dem. Nat. Conv, 40; Secy. of State, Conn, 40-42; del, Conn. State Dem. Conv, 40-68; Conn. State Rep, Second Dist, 44-46 & 48-50; organizer women's div, Off. of Mil. Govt. of U.S. in Germany, 47; asst. to dir, Off. Price Stabilization; mem, Southeast. Conn. Regional Planning Agency; mem, Sprague Dem. Town Cmt, Conn; mem, New Eng. Gov. Research Cmt, Gov. Cmt. on Libr, 65 and mem, Gov. Cmt. on Br. Univ. in Southeast Conn, 65; mem, Conn. Unemploy. Cmn, 66; mem, Conn. Ment. Health Planning Proj; del, Constitutional Conv. and co-chmn, Cmt. on Resolutions, 66; chmn, Cmn. on Status Women; mem, Gov. Clean Water Task Force; chmn, Sprague Zoning and Planning Cmn, Conn; mem. cmn. on regional, local planning and commun. health orgn, Adv. Coun. to Dept. of Commun. Affairs, 68-; mem. bd. Sponsors, Int. Student Serv, 69- Bus. & Prof. Pos: Assoc. prof. of econ, Smith Col, 18-26; personnel dir, Women's Col, Univ. N.C, 29-34; prof. of econ, Conn. Col, 34-46; dir. serv. bur. for women's orgn, Beatrice Fox Auerbach Found, 54- Publ: Series of books on occupations for women and articles in prfnl. jour. Mem: Past mem. bd. dir, Conn. Fedn. Planning and Zoning Agencies; hon. mem, Delta Kappa Gamma and Omicron Nu. New Eng. Tri-Agents Friend of Exten. Award, 69; Americanization Award, Conn. Valley B'nai B'rith, 69. Rel: Episcopal. Mailing Add: Falcon Farm, Rd. 1, Baltic, Conn. 06330.

WOODHOUSE, EDWIN WILBUR D
b. Mt. Airy, N.C, 2/1/36; s. Wilbur Bradley Woodhouse and Eunice Whaley W; m. 2/4/58 to Betty Smith; c. Edwin Wilbur, Jr, Barry Andrew and Anna Jane. Educ: Louisburg Col, A.A, 56; Pfeiffer Col, B.S, 58; Mem, N.C. Jr. Col. All-Star Basketball Team, 56; basketball scholarship, Pfeiffer Col, 57-58; pres, Men's Student Govt, Louisburg Col, 56 and Pfeiffer Col, 58; v.pres, Monogram Club; mem, Student Coun, Recreation and Physical Educ. Club. Polit. & Govt. Pos: Pres, Louisburg Col. Young Dem. Club, 58; treas, Wake Co. Young Dem. Club, N.C, 62 and treas, 63; staff mem, Judge Dan K. Moore for Gov. Cmt, 64; asst. exec. dir, State Dem. Exec. Cmt, 64, exec. dir, 65-69. Bus. & Prof. Pos: Pres, News Publ. Co, Inc, 67- Mem: Wake Co. Chap, Louisburg Col. Alumni Asn; Cary PTA; Wake Co. Chap, Pfeiffer Col. Alumni Asn; exec. secy, N.C. Poultry Fedn, 69- Received Distinguished Alumni Award, Pfeiffer Col. and Outstanding Young Men of Am. Award, 66. Rel: Church of Christ. Mailing Add: Route 1, Cary, N.C. 27511.

WOODLEE, RICHARD JAMES R
Mayor, Barnesville, Ga.
b. Beersheba Springs, Tenn, 11/16/11; s. Henry Woodlee, Sr.(deceased) and Lena Schwoon W.(deceased); m. 10/9/36 to Sarah Virginia Sims; c. Eleanor V. Polit. & Govt. Pos: Chmn, Lamar Co. Rep. Exec. Cmt, Ga, 52-68; mayor, Barnesville, Ga, 65- Mailing Add: 301 Spencer St, Barnesville, Ga. 30204. (1967)

WOODLEY, EDMUND ETCHISON R
Mem, Rep. State Cent. Cmt, La.
s. John Woodley and Willie Emma Etchison; m. 6/26/54 to Clarice Robinson; c. Scott Etchison. Educ: Centenary Col, Shreveport, La, 42-43 & 46; La. State Univ. Law Sch, Baton Rouge, J.D, 49; Kappa Alpha Order. Polit. & Govt. Pos: Asst. U.S. Attorney, West. Dist, La, 54-59; mem, Rep. State Cent. Cmt, La, 64- Bus. & Prof. Pos: Partner, Law Firm, Cavanaugh, Brame, Holt & Woodley, Lake Charles, La, 59-66; partner, law firm, Holt & Woodley, 67- Mil. Serv: Entered as Pvt, Army, 44, released as Pvt. 1/C, 46, after serv. in 14th Armored Div, 45th Inf. Div, ETO, 44-45; Purple Heart; Combat Inf. Badge; ETO Ribbon with Three Battle Stars. Mem: La. and Am. Bar Asns; Defense Research Inst; Am. Judicature Soc; Maritime Law Asn. of the U.S; Rotary; Am. Legion. Rel: Episcopal. Legal Res: 917 Fair Oak Lane, Lake Charles, La. 70601. Mailing Add: P.O. Box EE, Lake Charles, La. 70601.

WOODMAN, BLAIR G. R
b. Owosso, Mich, 3/15/03; married; c. 1 daughter. Educ: Mich. State Univ, B.S, 25; Epsilon Sigma Phi. Polit. & Govt. Pos: Mich. State Rep, 64-68. Bus. & Prof. Pos: Secy, Shiawassee Co. Agr. Soc, 14 years; mem, Mich. State Univ. Coop. Exten. Serv, 34 years, during which time served as 4-H Club agent and co. agr. agent in Hillsdale Co. and co. exten. dir. in Shiawassee Co. Mem: Kiwanis Club; bd. dirs, Shiawassee Co. United Fund; chmn. mems. and funds cmt, Shiawassee Chap, Red Cross; Shiawassee Co. Agr. Soc.(bd. dirs); assoc. mem. Farm Bur; Grange. Rel: Methodist. Mailing Add: 1473 S. M-47, Owosso, Mich. 48867. (1967)

WOODMAN, DOROTHY E. R
V.Chmn, Boulder Co. Rep. Party, Colo.
b. Denver, Colo, 9/13/14; d. Arnold J. Widmer and Elizabeth A. Decker W; m. 2/20/46 to Howard W. Woodman; c. Michael D, Beth Rose and James M. Educ: Denver high sch, grad, 32; various courses pertaining to interests or work. Polit. & Govt. Pos: Capt, Boulder Co. Rep. Party, Colo, 63-66, v.chmn, 66- Bus. & Prof. Pos: Bookkeeper, Longmont Radio & TV, 53-63; homemaker, 63- Rel: Presbyterian. Mailing Add: 1533 Emery St, Longmont, Colo. 80501.

WOODMANSEE, DONAVIN N. D
Chmn, Clinton Co. Dem. Cent. Cmt, Ohio
b. Sabina, Ohio, 5/29/16; s. John O. Woodmansee and Laura Luttrell W; m. 9/3/39 to Lois Jackson; c. Linda (Mrs. Hartley E. Jackson) and Lelan Keith. Educ: Wayne Twp. High Sch, Lees Creek, Ohio, grad. Polit. & Govt. Pos: Mem, Clinton Co. Dem. Exec. Cmt, Ohio, 60-; chmn, Clinton Co. Dem. Cent. Cmt, 66-; alternate del, Dem. Nat. Conv, 68. Bus. & Prof. Pos: Owner and operator, Woodmansee's Elevators, Melvin and Highland, Ohio, 44- Mem: Mason, Sabina; Valley of Cincinnati Scottish Rite. Rel: United Methodist. Mailing Add: Box 22, Reesville, Ohio 45166.

WOODMANSEE, GERALD LOUIS D
Utah State Rep.
b. Salt Lake City, Utah, 6/27/30; s. Benjamin Louis Woodmansee and Annie Bertha Eugster W; m. 9/28/62 to Joyce Littlewood; c. Pamela Sue, Cynthia Lee, Shelly Kay and Wade Alan. Educ: Univ. Utah, B.S, 56; Lambda Delta Sigma. Polit. & Govt. Pos: Dist. chmn, Dem. Party, Utah, 65-69, legis. chmn, currently; Utah State Rep, 69- Mem: Am. Speech & Hearing Asn; Salt Lake Teachers; Utah and Nat. Educ. Asns. State Handball Championships in Singles and Doubles. Rel: Latter-day Saint. Mailing Add: 877 Catherine St, Salt Lake City, Utah 84116.

WOODRING, RALPH D
b. 2/14/10. Educ: 9th grade. Polit. & Govt. Pos: Granis Sch. Bd, Mont, 18 years; Mont. State Rep, 59; S.Dak. State Rep, 64-66. Mem: K. of C; Lower Shields River Canal Bd, Mont. Rel: Catholic. Mailing Add: 305 E. Lewis, Livingston, Mont. 59047.

WOODRUFF, BYRON EDWIN D
Alternate chmn, Douglas Co. Dem. Party, Ore.
b. Wilroads, Kans, 1/17/18; s. Curtis D. Woodruff and Beulah Gearhart W; m. 9/26/43 to Lillian Coleman Rigby; c. Jeanne (Mrs. Moore); Scott Edwin. Educ: Pac. Univ, B.S, 48, Sch. Optometry, O.D, 49; Omega Delta; Alpha Zeta. Polit. & Govt. Pos: Mem, Douglas Co. Welfare Cmn, 60-68; mem. and first chmn. adv. bd, State Bd. Health, 62-68; del, Dem. Nat. Conv, 68. Bus. & Prof. Pos: Optometric adv, vision surv. of the aged, State Bd. Health, 65-68. Mil. Serv: Entered as Pvt, Army, 40, released as 1st Lt, 44, after serv. in Inf. Replacement Training Center, Ret. Army Res. Mem: Ore. Optometric Asn.(v.pres, 58, pres, 59-61); Am. Optometric Asn; Better Vision Inst; Lions; Elks; Mason; Shrine; Am. Legion; Roseburg Country Club. Rel: Methodist. Legal Res: Box 662 900 Page Rd, Winchester, Ore. 97495. Mailing Add: Box 1168, Roseburg, Ore. 94770.

WOODRUM, DONALD LEE D
Chmn, Irwin Co. Dem. Exec. Cmt, Ga.
b. Irwin Co, Ga, 12/9/00; s. William Milton Woodrum and Laura Turner W; m. 12/20/33 to Lillie Tucker; c. Sara Nelle (Mrs. Rowe), Dianne Lee (Mrs. Atkinson), Lillian Alice (Mrs. Rhodes) and Billy Donald. Educ: Irwin Co. High Sch. Polit. & Govt. Pos: Chmn, Irwin Co. Dem. Exec. Cmt, Ga, 35- Bus. & Prof. Pos: Agriculture. Mem: Mason; chmn, Forestry Cmn. Irwin Co; Farm Bur; Nat. Farm Orgn. Rel: Baptist; Deacon, Bethlehem Baptist Church. Mailing Add: Route 1 Box 222, Ocilla, Ga. 31774.

WOODS, FRANK MONTGOMERY R
b. Chattanooga, Tenn, 3/31/33; s. Frank Montgomery Woods and Josephine Roberts W; m. 2/24/62 to Eunice Kathryn Harrigan; c. Dorine Ross, Frank Montgomery and Kathryn Alexandria. Educ: Cornell Univ, B.S, 54; Phi Kappa Phi; Sphinx Head; Red Key; Ye Hosts; Sigma Phi; Cornell United Relig. Work. Polit. & Govt. Pos: Goldwater precinct chmn, San Francisco Co, Calif. Presidential Primary, 63-64; Goldwater/Miller advanceman, Rep. Nat. Cmt, 64; asst. to North. Calif. campaign chmn, Ronald Reagan Gubernatorial Race, 65-66; spec. asst, Gov. Ronald Reagan's Staff, 67-68; alternate del, Rep. Nat. Conv, 68; mem, Calif. Harbors and Watercraft Cmn, 68- Bus. & Prof. Pos: Various advert. and sales pos, Procter & Gamble, Cincinnati, 54-60; mkt. mgr, Fenco Corp, San Francisco, 60-62; v.pres, Fyrtech Corp, 62-64; v.pres, West. Eleven Mkt. Corp, 64-67; pres, Mkt. Continental, Inc, 67- Mil. Serv: Entered as 2nd Lt, Army, 55, released as 1st Lt, 57, after serv. in Ascom City in Qm. Corp, Seventh Army Command, Far East Theatre, 55-57. Mem: Commonwealth Club San Francisco; Guardsmen of San Francisco; Univ. Club; St. Francis Yacht Club; Cornell Alumni Coun. Rel: Protestant. Legal Res: 2414 Gough St, San Francisco, Calif. 94123. Mailing Add: 1485 Bayshore Blvd, San Francisco, Calif. 94124.

WOODS, JAMES CHRISTOPHER D
Murrysville, Pa, 8/22/39; s. Dorothy W, father (deceased); m. 6/2/62 to Nancy Elizabeth Ryan; c. Jennifer Anne and Craig Andrew. Educ: Univ. Rochester, A.B, 60; Episcopal Theol. Sch, S.T.B, 64. Polit. & Govt. Pos: Committeeman, Ontario Co. Dem. Party, N.Y, 66-67; mem, Allegany Co. Reformed Dem, 67-; del, Dem. Nat. Conv, 68; del, State Conv, Concerned Dem. of N.Y, 69. Bus. & Prof. Pos: Vicar, St. John's Episcopal Church, Phelps, N.Y, 64-67; Episcopal Chaplain, Univ. Rochester, 65-67, Alfred Univ, 67-; asst. minister, Christ Church, Hornell, 67- Mem: Rochester Cmt. Foreign Affairs, Orgn. Coun. on Foreign Affairs, N.Y.C; Nat. Episcopal Study Conf. in Higher Educ. Rel: Episcopal. Mailing Add: 43 Sayles St, Alfred, N.Y. 14802.

WOODS, LUCIUS EARL D
Mem, Colo. Dem. State Cent. Cmt.
b. Yonkers, N.Y, 10/14/21; s. Henry Earl Woods and Esther Potter W; m. 5/27/50 to Ruth Claybourne; c. Henry Earl, Samuel Claybourne and Beverly Nell. Educ: Columbia Univ, B.S, 43, LL.B, 48; Phi Gamma Delta. Polit. & Govt. Pos: Precinct committeeman, Denver, Dem. Party, Colo, 53-60; mem, Denver Dem. Exec. Cmt, 63-; chmn, Colo. Civil Law Subcmt, Presidential Task Force on Ment. Retardation, 64-65; mem, Colo. Dem. State Cent. Cmt, 65-; del, Dem. Nat. Conv, 68. Bus. & Prof. Pos: Lawyer, Denver, 52- Mil. Serv: Entered as A/S, Navy, 42, released as Lt.(jg), 46, after serv. in Atlantic and Pac. Theatres, 43-46. Publ: 'Rebuttal—A Brief on Rosenberg's Judgment,' Ramparts, 12/65. Mem: Denver, Colo. and Am. Bar Asns; Fel, Am. Col. Probate Counsel; Nat. Farmers Union; Am. Civil Liberties Union; South. Christian Leadership Conf; Am. for Dem. Action. Rel: Unitarian. Mailing Add: 855 S. Josephine St, Denver, Colo. 80209.

WOODS, NETTIE JOE D
Mem, Calif. Dem. State Cent. Cmt.
b. Calhoun, Ga, 6/18/26; d. Arthur Reel and Violine Hunt R; m. 5/3/56 to Milford Harrison Woods; c. Reginia Edwards and Kenneth Edwards. Educ: San Diego City Col, 2 years. Polit. & Govt. Pos: Dem. precinct worker, 79th Dist-Area 1056, Calif, 63-68; mem, Calif. Dem. State Cent. Cmt, currently. Bus. & Prof. Pos: Hosp. attendant II, Co. Hosp, San Diego, Calif, 58; off. nurse, Dr. Harold E. Burt, 58-62; private duty nursing, 62-67; nursing asst, U.S. Naval Hosp, San Diego, 67; art coordinator, Mayor's Coun. on Youth Opportunity, 68; classified personnel, San Diego Unified Sch. Dist, 68-69. Mem: Assoc. mem, San Diego Art Inst; San Diego Coun. of Visual Arts (pres). Rel: Protestant. Mailing Add: 5684 Santa Margarita St, San Diego, Calif. 92114.

WOODS, PATRICIA HUCK R
V.Chmn, Midland Co. Rep. Party, Mich.
b. Bethlehem, Pa, 2/26/32; d. George Mark Huck and Helen McBeath H; m. 7/22/52 to Joseph Wilton Woods; c. Michael, Mark and Scott. Educ: Univ. Colo, 49-50; Col. San Mateo, 50-51. Polit. & Govt. Pos: Chmn, Women for Nixon, 68; v.chmn, Midland Co. Rep. Party, Mich, 69- Mem: Bd. dir, Family Serv. Agency of Midland. Rel: Episcopal. Mailing Add: 705 Linwood Dr, Midland, Mich. 48640.

WOODS, THELL MICHAEL R
b. Pontiac, Mich, 7/3/27; s. Dr. Robert V. Woods and Ruth Landguth W; m. 6/20/65 to Roberta Robinson; c. Thell Micah. Educ: Alma Col, B.A, 62; Am. Univ, M.A, 68; Mich. State Univ; Univ. Mich, work toward Ph.D; Psi Chi; Omicron Beta Kappa. Polit. & Govt. Pos: Region sch, Midwest Fedn. of Col. Young Rep, 59-60; pres. and founder, Alma Col. Young Rep. Club, 59-61; dep. clerk, Arcada Twp, Mich, 60-69; mem, Gratiot Co. Rep. Cmt, 60-69, chmn, 65-66; mem, Gov. Romney's Rep. Task Force for Party Evaluation, 65. Bus. & Prof. Pos: Pres. and owner, TMW Enterprises, real estate, land develop, bldg. and contracting, 54-69; pres, Behavorial Inquiry and Design, small firm for production of electronic models for scientific study in psychol, 66; pres, Gratiot-Isabella Bd. Realtors, 69. Publ: Financial Crises in the UN, M.A. Thesis, on file in UN Off, Wash, D.C, 63; column, 'Republican Stand,' Gratiot Co. Herald, 65-66. Mem: Am. Psychol. Asn; Farm Bur; Rep. Men's Club; past chaplain, Alma Jaycees; C. of C; Kiwanis. Travel in 50 Countries and research on UN Functions. Rel: Presbyterian. Legal Res: 4239 Riverview, Alma, Mich. 48801. Mailing Add: 230 N. State, Alma, Mich. 48801.

WOODS, WILLIAM H. R
V.Chmn, Cape May Co. Rep. Exec. Cmt, N.J.
b. Windber, Pa, 8/31/35; s. Dr. William S. Woods and Catherine E. Long W; m. 8/13/60 to Mary E. Bluett; c. Elizabeth and Alice. Educ: Washington and Jefferson Col, A.B, Rutgers Univ, 1 year; Pi Delta Epsilon; Phi Delta Theta. Polit. & Govt. Pos: Tax assessor, Ocean City, N.J, 65-67, co. Rep. committeeman, 65- and exec. v.chmn, Men's Rep. Club, 66-67; v.chmn, Cape May Co. Young Rep, 66-67; v.chmn, Cape May Co. Rep. Exec. Cmt, 66-; co-campaign chmn, Cape May Co, 68. Bus. & Prof. Pos: Spec. agent, Aetna Casualty and Surety Co, 59-63; real estate and ins. broker, Bill Woods Agency, Ocean City, 63- Mil. Serv: Entered as 2nd Lt, Army, 59, released as Capt, 69, after serv. in 990 Eng. Co. Mem: Secy, Ocean City Bd. Realtors; v.chmn, Cape May Co. Ins. Agents Asn; state dir, Exchange Clubs; F&AM; Mason; Ocean City Exchange Club; Ocean City C. of C; Ocean City Men's Rep. Club; Gardens Civic Asn. Rel: Methodist. Legal Res: 356 E. Surf Rd, Ocean City, N.J. 08226. Mailing Add: 218 West Ave, Ocean City, N.J. 08226.

WOODSIDE, HOWARD BUSH R
b. Pittsburgh, Pa, 8/14/21; s. Hugh Nevin Woodside and Kathryn Smith W; m. 1/1/44 to Emmaline Gray Smith; c. Lucille S. and Paisley Anne. Educ: Univ. Wis, B.A, 43, J.D, 48; Phi Eta Sigma; Phi Kappa Phi; Order of the Coif; Beta Theta Pi. Polit. & Govt. Pos: Asst. city attorney, Marshfield, Wis, 48-51; mem. sch. bd, 49-51; v.chmn, Wood Co. Rep. Party, 49-51; chmn, Seventh Dist. Rep. Party, Wis, 61-69; del, Rep. Nat. Conv, 64 & 68, admin. asst. on platform cmt, 64; mem. zoning bd, Plover-Stevens Point, Wis, 65- Bus. & Prof. Pos: Dir, Bank of Plover; attorney-at-law, Emery & Woodside, Marshfield, Wis, 48-51 & 54-56; attorney, Sentry Ins, Stevens Point, 56-62, asst. gen. coun. and asst. secy, 62-; instr. adv. mil. law, U.S. Fifth Army Reserve Officers Judge Advocate Gen. Corps Sch, 58- Mil. Serv: Entered as Cpl, Army, 43, released as Capt, 46, after serv. in Third Inf. Regt, ETO, 44-46; recalled, Capt, 51-54, serv. in 45th Inf. Div, Korea, 51-52; Commendation Ribbon with Medal; ETO Ribbon with Battle Star; Am. Theatre Ribbon; Army of Occup. Ribbon, ETO and Japan; Res. Ribbon; Korean Ribbon with Two Battle Stars; UN Serv. Ribbon; Lt. Col, Judge Adv. Gen. Corps, Army Res, 63. Mem: Am. and Portage Co. Bar Asns; Mil. Law Cmt, Wis. Bar Asn; advert. cmt. and Wis. Legis. Cmt, Health Ins. Asn. of Am; info. at source cmt, Life Ins. Asn. and Am. Life Conv; Mason; Elks; charter pres, Marshfield Kiwanis; dir, Wis. Curling Asn; new club cmt, U.S. Men's Curling Asn; ROA. One of leading Wis. Curlers; Holds Golf Championships in 3 continents. Rel: Presbyterian; Elder. Mailing Add: Route 1, Plover, Wis. 54467.

WOODSON, LAWRENCE EDWARD D
Alderman, St. Louis 20th Ward, Mo.
b. St. Louis, Mo, 12/8/13; s. Edward Woodson and Snodie Bell Casey W; m. 6/10/56 to Jacqueline Barbara Glenn; c. Jesse L. and Christy L. Educ: St. Louis Col. Mortuary Sci, Dipl, 42; Epsilon Nu Delta. Polit. & Govt. Pos: Alderman, St. Louis 20th Ward, 59-, v.pres, Bd. of Alderman; chmn, 20th Ward Dem. Orgn, Mo, 59- Mil. Serv: Entered as Seaman 1/C, Naval Res, 42, released as Specialist T 2/C, 45. Mem: St. Louis Undertakers Asn.(pres, 66-). Rel: Methodist. Legal Res: 4939 Northland Place, St. Louis, Mo. 63112. Mailing Add: 1167 Hamilton Ave, St. Louis, Mo. 63112.

WOODSON, S. HOWARD, JR. D
N.J. State Assemblyman
b. Philadelphia, Pa, 5/8/16; s. Samuel H. Woodson Sr. and Lulu E. Howard W; m. 9/2/39 to Audrey M. Manley; c. Jean and Howard. Educ: Cheyney State Col; Sch. Religion, Morehouse Col, Ga; Atlanta Univ; Kappa Alpha Psi. Polit. & Govt. Pos: V.chmn, Trenton Planning Cmn, N.J, 52-62; councilman-at-lg, Trenton City Coun, 62-65; N.J. State Assemblyman, 66-, chmn, Co. and Munic. Govt. Cmt. and Cmn. to Study Money in Lieu of Taxes for State Owned Lands, N.J. State Legis. and Minority Leader, 68-; del, Dem. Nat. Conv, 68. Bus. & Prof. Pos: Participant, Legis. Seminar, Fla, 69. Mem: Mason; Nat. Soc. State Legislators; League of Munic; Ministerial Conf. Phila; Interdenominational Ministerial Conf, Trenton, N.J. Twice received Citizen of Year Award, N.J; Legislator of the Year, Chosen Bd. Freeholders Asn, 68; Christian and Jews Brotherhood Award, 68; Outstanding Legis. Serv. Award, Civil Serv. Rel: Baptist; Pastor, Shiloh Baptist Church. Legal Res: 838 Edgewood Ave, Trenton, N.J. Mailing Add: 340 Calhoun St, Trenton, N.J. 08618.

WOODWARD, BAILEY D
b. Jenkinsburg, Ga, 3/06/19; s. David O. Woodward and Emily Moore W; m. 12/8/44 to Mary J. Jones; c. David Bailey Jr. and Robert Jones. Educ: Ga. Tech. Polit. & Govt. Pos: Ga. State Sen, 22nd Dist, 57-58; Ga. State Rep, 61-66. Bus. & Prof. Pos: Trucking Bus, farmer and timber. Mil. Serv: Navy, 42. Mem: Mason; Shrine. Rel: Methodist. Mailing Add: Jackson, Ga. 30233. (1967)

WOODWARD, JOE D. D
b. Magnolia, Ark, 3/26/30; s. W.A.G. Woodward, Sr. and Mary Davis W; m. 10/18/52 to Deane Reid; c. Reid and Davis. Educ: South. State Col, A.A, 49; William and Mary Col, 49; Univ. Va, LL.B, 52; Delta Theta Phi; Kappa Sigma. Polit. & Govt. Pos: City attorney, Magnolia, Ark, 56-62, Taylor, Ark, 56-64 and Waldo, Ark, 56-67; del, Dem. State Conv, 56-68; prosecuting attorney, 13th Dist. Ark, 62-66; del, Dem. Nat. Conv, 68. Bus. & Prof. Pos: Dir, Farmers Bank & Trust Co, Magnolia, Ark. Mil. Serv: Army, 52-55, 1st Lt, serv. in Judge Adv. Corps. Mem: Columbia Co. Bar Asn.(pres, 69-); Ark. Bar Asn.(chmn. ethics and grievance cmt); Am. Bar Asn; Am. Trial Lawyers Asn; Boy Scouts (chmn. Columbia Dist); Rotary; Am. Legion. Rel: United Methodist; Chmn Off. Bd, First United Methodist Church Magnolia, 67-68. Legal Res: 707 Sue St, Magnolia, Ark. 71753. Mailing Add: P.O. Box 727, Magnolia, Ark. 71753.

WOODWARD, MARY DAVIS D
Mem, Ark. State Dem. Cent. Cmt.
b. Magnolia, Ark, 7/14/03; d. Joe L. Davis and Ella Arnold D; m. 6/15/25 to Walter Ashton Galloway Woodward, wid; c. Walter Ashton Galloway, Jr, Mary Ann (Mrs. McLaughlin), Joe D. and Mac B. Educ: Galloway Woman's Col, Searcy, Ark, A.B, 24; Hendrix Col, A.B, 36; pres, Laniers, Galloway Woman's Col. Polit. & Govt. Pos: Alderwoman, Magnolia City Coun, Ark, 44-46; mem, State Girl's Training Sch. Bd, 53-56; Fourth Cong. rep, Ark. State Dem. Cmt, 65-69; mem, Ark. State Dem. Cent. Cmt, 65-, Sen. del, 67-68; v.chmn, Columbia Co. Dem. Cent. Cmt, Ark, 66-68. Bus. & Prof. Pos: Partner, Woodward and Kinard, Attorneys at Law, Magnolia, Ark, currently; operator real estate and oil bus. Mem: Life mem, Ark. Hist. Asn.(v.pres, 60-61, pres, 61-62, co-chmn. for annual meeting, 68); organizer and first pres, Columbia Co. Hist. Coun, 50; charter mem, Lafayette Co. Hist. Asn; helped organize, Southwest Ark. Geneological Asn, 64; organizer, Jackson Co. and Jefferson Co. Hist. Asns, 67; UDC (recorder of Mil. Crosses, Ark. Div, 65, pres, Columbia Co. Mem. Chap, 67-68). Ark. Mother of the Year, 54. Rel: Methodist; Pres, Women's Soc. Christian Serv, First Methodist Church, 51. Mailing Add: 813 Partee Dr, Magnolia, Ark. 71753.

WOODWARD, ROY SMITH R
b. Enosburg, Vt, 11/7/92; m. to Lula Mae Shattuck; c. Three sons, Three daughters. Educ: Enosburg High Sch. Polit. & Govt. Pos: Vt. State Rep, 37, 53 & 65-68; dep. sheriff; tax collector; town constable; overseer of the poor; commun. committeeman for A.C.P; high bailiff. Bus. & Prof. Pos: Farmer. Rel: Methodist. Mailing Add: Waterville, Vt. 05452. (1967)

WOODWORTH, LAURENCE NEAL Independent
b. Loudenville, Ohio, 3/22/18; s. Alfred Ray Woodworth and Nora Sheldon W; m. 9/1/40 to Margaret Forest Bretz; c. Laurence Sheldon, Joseph Ray, Esther Margaret and Melissa Mary. Educ: Ohio North. Univ, A.B, 40; Univ. Denver, M.S. in Govt. Mgt, 42; New York Univ, Ph.D, 60; Alpha Phi Gamma; Sigma Phi Epsilon. Hon. J.D, Juniata Col; Hon. D.P.A, Ohio North. Univ. Polit. & Govt. Pos: Economist, Joint Cong. Cmt. on Internal Revenue Taxation, 44-64 and chief of staff, 64-; councilman, Cheverly, Md, 48-59 and mayor, 59-64; pres, Md. Munic. League, 63-64. Rel: United Methodist. Mailing Add: 2810 Crest Ave, Cheverly, Md. 20785.

WOOL, RICHARD IRWIN D
b. New York, N.Y, 3/6/44; s. Edward Wool and Adele Ribler W; single. Educ: Pa. State Univ, B.A, 65; Univ. Md, M.A, 68; N.Y. Univ, 68-; Phi Alpha Theta. Polit. & Govt. Pos: Aide to Hon. Eugene J. Koegh, Wash, D.C, 66; research and writing, Paul O'Dwyer Sen. Campaign, 68; alternate del, Dem. Nat. Conv, 68; coordinator, L.I. Youth for McCarthy, 68. Bus. & Prof. Pos: Teaching asst, Univ. Md, 66-67; research asst, N.Y. Pub. Libr, 68; teaching asst, N.Y. Univ, 68- Legal Res: 54 Avalon Rd, Garden City, N.Y. 11530. Mailing Add: Apt. 6L, 96 Fifth Ave, New York, N.Y. 10011.

WOOLBERT, MAYBELLE SIEGELE D
b. Weehawken, N.J; d. Curt Guenther Siegele and Mabel Schnackenberg S; m. to Robert Gale Woolbert (deceased); c. Susan Gale (deceased) and Richard Curt. Educ: N.Y. Univ, 1 year; Ballard Secretarial Sch, N.Y.C, 1 year. Polit. & Govt. Pos: Precinct committeewoman, precinct capt. and v.chmn, Arapahoe Co. Dem. Party, Colo, 52-58; cand. Arapahoe Co. Clerk, Colo, 58; exec. secy, U.S. Rep. Byron L. Johnson, Colo, 58-60; aide to Congressman Otis G. Pike, N.Y, 61- Bus. & Prof. Pos: Research asst, Coun. For. Rels, N.Y.C, 37-41. Publ: Look at Africa (with Robert Gale Woolbert), For. Policy Asn, 44. Mem: Colo. and Md. League Women Voters. Fel, Wilton Park Conv, Sussex, Eng, 67. Rel: Episcopal. Legal Res: 121 Summit, Englewood, Colo. 80110. Mailing Add: 6628 Rannoch Rd, Bethesda, Md. 20034.

WOOLDRIDGE, HARRY LINN D
Chmn, Freestone Co. Dem. Exec. Cmt, Tex.
b. Bloominggrove, Tex, 9/24/99; s. Henry Harrison Wooldridge and Dessie Tanner W; m. 12/4/21 to Fannie Mae McIlveen; c. Tom Linn and Mary (Mrs. Coleman). Educ: Fairfield High Sch, dipl, 16. Polit. & Govt. Pos: Dep, Internal Revenue Serv, 42-47; chmn, Freestone Co. Dem. Exec. Cmt, Tex, 64- Bus. & Prof. Pos: Bank clerk, Fairfield State Bank, 21-28; salesman and bookkeeper, Parmer Chevrolet Co, 28-42; mgr, Kay Way Builders Supply Co, 47-65; self employed, acct. and tax work, 65- Mem: C. of C; Lions. Rel: Baptist. Mailing Add: Fairfield, Tex. 75840.

WOOLEY, ROBERT PAUL R
Ky. State Rep.
b. Evansville, Ind, 6/15/31; s. Thomas Riley Wooley, Sr. and Lettie Buttrum W; m. 9/6/53 to Carolyn Murray; c. Robert Matthew, Daniel Paul and Jane Murray. Educ: Evansville Univ, A.B, 54; Sigma Alpha Epsilon. Polit. & Govt. Pos: Ky. State Rep, 68- Bus. & Prof. Pos: Salesman, N.Y. Life Ins. Co, Evansville, Ind, 57-59; mgr, N.Y. Life Ins. Co, Louisville-Lexington, Ky, 59-61; self-employed bldg. contractor, Lexington, 62- Mil. Serv: Entered as Officer Cand, Coast Guard, 54, released as Lt.(jg), 57, after serv. in San Juan,

P.R, Gr. Antilles Command. Mem: Nat. Home Builders Asn. Rel: Presbyterian. Mailing Add: 1166 Athenia Dr, Lexington, Ky. 40504.

WOOLFENDEN, MILTON, JR. R
b. New Bedford, Mass, 12/3/25; s. Milton Woolfenden and Emma C. Campbell W; m. 3/22/47 to Marylou Horne; c. Nancy Jeanne, Lynn, Robin Keith, Leslie and Leigh Scott. Educ: Dean Prep Sch, Franklin, Mass, 46-47; Bentley Sch. of Accounting and Finance, Boston, Mass, 48-51. Polit. & Govt. Pos: Elected mem. town coun, Newton, N.J, 56-58, mayor, 58-59; N.J. State Sen, 64-68, asst. minority leader, 67-68. Bus. & Prof. Pos: Chief accountant, Limestone Products Corp. of Am, 51-59, admin. asst, 59-61, first v.pres. and treas, 61-65, pres. and treas, 65-; dir, Hardyston Nat. Bank, Hamburg, N.J, 68- Mil. Serv: Navy, 43-46, serv. in USS Wasp, Seaman 1/C. Mem: Bd. dir. and chmn. of charitable gifts cmt, Newton Mem. Hosp; mem. Frankford Twp. Bd. Educ, N.J; VFW; chmn, Girl Scout Financial Dr; past chmn, March of Dimes Campaign; past pres, Branchville Businessmen's Club; Elks (past Exalted Ruler Lodge 1512); F&AM. Rel: Presbyterian. Mailing Add: R.D. 3, Box 90, Newton, N.J. 07860.

WOOLLEN, CHARLES WESLEY R
Chmn, Ralls Co. Rep. Cmt, Mo.
b. New London, Mo, 3/3/13; s. Charles Wesley Woollen and Grace Jameson W; m. 6/17/40 to Anna Dean Lewis; c. Geraldine (Mrs. Fuqua), Bobbe Grace (Mrs. Winders), Mary J.(Mrs. Keithly), Elizabeth S.(Mrs. Jacobs) and Chas. Wesley. Polit. & Govt. Pos: Off. mgr, Agr. Stabilization and Conserv. Serv, Ralls Co, Mo, 56-61; chmn, Ralls Co. Rep. Cmt, 62- Bus. & Prof. Pos: Farmer. Mil. Serv: Am 3/C, Navy, 31-35. Mem: Am. Farm Bur. Asn. Rel: Christian Church. Mailing Add: Route 1, New London, Mo. 63459.

WOOLLEY, J. RUSSELL R
Chmn, Monmouth Co. Rep. Cmt, N.J.
b. Long Branch, N.J, 10/15/95; s. John W. Woolley and Florence Bennett W; m. 12/25/17 to Wilhelmina R. Krug; c. J. Russell, Jr. and Virginia C.(Mrs. Reilly). Educ: Long Branch Pub. Schs; Hon. degree, Monmouth Col, 65. Polit. & Govt. Pos: Freeholder, Monmouth Co, N.J, 36-39, co. clerk, 39-, chmn, Monmouth Co. Rep. Cmt, 40-; del, Rep. Nat. Conv, 68. Mil. Serv: Entered as Pvt, Army, 17, released as Sgt. Maj, 19. Mem: Am. Legion;VFW; Mason; Elks; Eagles. Rel: Methodist. Legal Res: 580 Cedar Ave, West Long Branch, N.J. 07764. Mailing Add: Box 7, West Long Branch, N.J. 07764. (1967)

WOOLLEY, JOHN ROBERT 'JACK' R
Asst. Secy. for Cong. Rels, Dept. of Housing and Urban Develop.
b. Salina, Kans, 3/15/24; s. Henry Arthur Woolley and Ridotta Parmenter W; m. 10/9/49 to Junette Kathryn Carter; c. Karen Patricia. Educ: U.S. Merchant Marine Acad, B.S, 44; Univ. South. Calif, M.B.A, 49; Alpha Delta Sigma; Delta Chi. Polit. & Govt. Pos: Spec. Asst. to Secy. of Navy, Wash, D.C, 56-58, spec. asst. to Secy. of Defense, 58-59; asst. campaign planning dir, Nixon-Lodge for Pres, 60-61; exec. secy, Orange Co. Rep. Cent. Cmt, Calif, 61-64; asst. to nat. chmn, Rep. Nat. Conv, 64, asst. prog. chmn, 68; exec. dir, Calif. Rep. State Cent. Cmt, 64-66; Asst. Secy. for Cong. Rels, Dept. of Housing and Urban Develop, 69- Bus. & Prof. Pos: Dir. govt. rels, TRW Systs, Redondo Beach, Calif, 66-69. Mil. Serv: Entered as Midn, Navy, 41, released as Lt. (jg), 46, after serv. in U.S.S. Logan, Atlantic, Mediterranean and Pac. Theatres; Capt, Naval Res, 66; Purple Heart; Two Navy Unit Commendations; Secy. of Navy Commendations. Publ: Mechanics of Radio and TV Advertising, Univ. South Calif. Press, 49. Mem: Calif. state pres, Navy League of U.S, 55-56; Bel-Air Country Club, Los Angeles; Cong. Country Club, Wash, D.C; Capitol Hill Club, Wash. D.C. Rel: Episcopal. Legal Res: 584 Dryad Rd, Santa Monica, Calif. 90402. Mailing Add: 344 N St. S.W, Washington, D.C. 20024.

WOOLLEY, NAOMI REBECCA D
b. Salt Lake City, Utah, 8/28/93; d. Benjamin John Beer and Elizabeth Taylor B; m. 4/28/15 to Heber Rumel Woolley; c. Glen B, Richard B. and Nancy Jane (Mrs. Myers). Educ: Univ. Utah, 13-15. Polit. & Govt. Pos: Voting dist. chmn, Dem. State Cent. Cmt, Utah, 50-62; mem, 59-69 and legis. dist. chmn, 62-63; mem, Utah. Dem. Women's Club, 60-68; v.chmn, Salt Lake Co. Dem. Cmt, 63-67; v.chmn, Humphrey for Pres, Utah, 67-68; del. and mem, rules and order of bus. cmt, Dem. Nat. Conv, 68. Bus. & Prof. Pos: Supt, nursery schs, Univ. Utah, 39-46; supvr, Granite Bd. Educ. Nursery Schs, Salt Lake Co, 46-48. Mem: Asn. Childhood Educ.(pres, 40-45); Utah Asn. UN (pres, 60-62); Utah State Hist. Soc.(mem. bd. dirs, 66-69). Award, Utah UN, 60; Award, Asn. Childhood Educ, 62. Rel: Non-sectarian. Mailing Add: 5560 Holladay Blvd, Salt Lake City, Utah 84117.

WOOLNER, SIDNEY HENRY D
b. Centralia, Ill, 1/8/11; s. Sidney Woolner and Olive Krieckhaus W; m. 11/25/36 to Doris Weiss; c. Sally and Tom. Educ: Univ. of Mich, B.A, 32; Phi Beta Kappa; Phi Kappa Phi. Polit. & Govt. Pos: Dep. cmnr, Mich. Corp. and Securities Cmn, 49-51; campaign dir, Mich. Dem. Party, 50-58; dep. dir, Mich. OPS, 51-52, dir, 52-53; dep. Secy. of State, 55-57; chief dep. hwy cmnr, 57-58; exec. secy, Gov. Williams, Mich, 59-60, Gov. Swainson, Mich, 61; Presidential Elector, 60; cmnr, Commun. Facilities Admin, 61-64; Regional Adminstr, O.E.O, 64-66; admin. asst. to U.S. Sen. Philip A. Hart, 66- Bus. & Prof. Pos: Sales prom, ed. employee mag, Detroit Edison Co, Mich, 33-42; sales, prod exec, Jam Handy Orgn, Detroit, 42-49; leasing agent, Realty Mortgage and Investment Corp, Detroit, 53-54. Mailing Add: 3552 Quebec St, N.W. Washington, D.C. 20016.

WOOLSEY, THOMAS G. R
b. Warrensburg, Mo, 4/13/17; m. 2/9/44 to Helen Crowder; c. Thomas G. Jr, Debra Lee. Educ: Westminster Col; Sch. of Law, Univ. Mo, LL.B. Polit. & Govt. Pos: Mo. State Sen, 60-68; prosecuting attorney, Morgan Co, 3 terms. Bus. & Prof. Pos: Lawyer. Mil. Serv: Air Force, World War II. Rel: Protestant. Mailing Add: Mason Bldg, Versailles, Mo. 65084. (1967)

WOOTEN, FRED G. D
W.Va. State Del.
b. Hensley, W.Va, 4/26/06; s. Charles Lee Wooten and Lila N. Rice W; m. 9/7/31 to Alafaire Puckett; c. Judy Gail (Mrs. Ralph Carroll): Mrs. James Broeckel, James Ray. Educ: McDowell Co. Pub. Schs. Polit. & Govt. Pos: W.Va. State Del, 60- Bus. & Prof. Pos: Coal miner, 43 years. Mem: Mason; Shrine; UMW, secy. local union No. 6026, 18 years. Rel: Methodist. Mailing Add: Coalwood, W.Va. 24824. (1967)

WORCESTER, BETTY JEWEL D
V.Chmn, Lyon Co. Dem. Party, Kans.
b. Emporia, Kansas, 12/1/21; d. Golden J. Hollar and Priscilla I. Grimmett H; m. 9/14/40 to Robert Worcester; c. Connie (Mrs. Ned O'Hara), Linda (Mrs. Duwayne Birk) and Jo Ann. Polit. & Govt. Pos: V.chmn, Lyon Co. Dem. Party, Kans, 60- Bus. & Prof. Pos: Legal secy, Wade A. Myers, 57; real estate salesman, Austenfeld-Stevenson, 67. Rel: Christian. Mailing Add: 1004 Prairie, Emporia, Kans. 66801.

WORD, JAMES POWELL D
Tex. State Sen.
b. Meridian, Tex, 6/24/29; s. Charles K. Word and Rosemary Dorman W; m. 4/11/53 to Bobbye Louise Warren; c. Charles B, J.P, Jr. and Amy Alice. Educ: Tarleton State Col, 48-49; Baylor Univ. Law Sch, LL.B, 58; Delta Theta Phi. Polit. & Govt. Pos: Judge, Bosque Co, Tex, 59-62; Tex. State Sen, Dist. 12, 63- Bus. & Prof. Pos: Partner, Word & Word Law Off, 56-68; br. mgr, Waco Savings & Loan, Clifton and Meridian, 63; partner, Word & Vance Law Off, 68- Mil. Serv: Entered as Pvt, Army, 49, released as S/Sgt, 53, after serv. in Intel, Korea, 17 months. Mem: Tex. and Am. Bar Asns; Lions; Meridian Vol. Fire Dept; VFW; first v.pres, Cent. Tex. Indust. Develop. Coun; Am. Legion; C. of C; Gov. Cmt. of 500. Rel: Methodist. Legal Res: 120 S. Erath, Meridian, Tex. 76665.

WORDEN, HENRY O. 'BILL' R
Mont. State Rep.
b. Missoula, Mont, 8/21/12; s. Henry Owen Worden and Mary Jordan W; m. 9/23/60 to Tomme Lu Middleton; c. Margaret Middleton, Henry O, III and William Austin. Educ: Prep Sch, Wash, D.C, 30; Univ. Mont, B.A. in Math, 35; Pi Mu Epsilon; Sigma Chi. Polit. & Govt. Pos: Mont. State Rep, Dist. 26, Missoula Co, 67- Bus. & Prof. Pos: Mem. banking staff, West. Mont. Nat. Bank, Missoula, Mont, 38-66, v.pres. bank, 66- Mil. Serv: Entered as Radio Tech. 2/C, Navy, 42, released as Lt. (jg), 46, after serv. in Naval Air Transport, 45-46. Mem: Elks; Lions; C. of C; past chmn, Missoula-Mineral Co. Red Cross Chap; dir, Missoula Salvation Army. Rel: Episcopal. Mailing Add: 208 Pattee Canyon Dr, Missoula, Mont. 59801.

WORKMAN, DALE H. R
Utah State Rep.
b. Delta, Utah, 6/19/35; s. Meltier Hatch Workman and Edna Horne W; m. 6/3/55 to Darleen May; c. Lynne, Jo Anne, Michael, Dalene, Diane and Pamela. Educ: Col. South. Utah, 1 year; Utah State Univ, B.S, 57; Alpha Kappa Psi. Polit. & Govt. Pos: Voting dist. chmn, Smithfield, Utah, 63-68; Utah State Rep, Dist. 51, Cache Co, 69- Bus. & Prof. Pos: Auditor, U.S. Army Audit Agency, Salt Lake City, Utah, 57-59; cost analyst, Thiokol Chem. Corp, Brigham City, 59-61, supvr. acct, Logan, 61-63, div. controller, 64-69. Mem: Nat. Asn. Acct. Wall Street J. Achievement Award. Rel: Latter-day Saint. Mailing Add: 250 E. First N, Smithfield, Utah 84335.

WORLEY, FRANCIS R
Pa. State Rep.
b. Latimore Twp, Pa, 12/23/13; s. Chester B. Worley and Hermie Masemer W; m. 7/26/35 to Ruth T. Gardner; c. Francis, Jr. and Daniel T. Educ: Pa. State Univ, B.A, 38; Dickinson Sch. Law, LL.B, 41, J.D, 68; George Wash. Univ. Law Sch, LL.M, 52; Univ. Pa. Grad. Sch, M.A. in Int. Affairs, 59. Polit. & Govt. Pos: Justice of the Peace, Latimore Twp, Pa, 39-41; Pa. State Rep, Adams Co, 42-50, 52-62 & 64- Rel: Quaker. Legal Res: Latimore Township, Adams Co, Pa. Mailing Add: House Post Office Box 200, House of Representatives, Harrisburg, Pa. 17120.

WORLOCK, PAUL ANTHONY D
Committeeman, Fifth Ward Dem. Party, Rome, N.Y.
b. Rome, N.Y, 9/21/31; s. Lyle Francis Worlock (deceased) and Angeline McMullin W; m. 5/18/63 to Ines Traversa; c. Jane Ann, Donna Ellen and Paula Aileen. Educ: LeMoyne Col, B.B.A, 52; Fordham Univ. Sch. Law, LL.B, 55. Polit. & Govt. Pos: Councilman, Rome City Coun, N.Y, 59-62; staff asst, Rome Civil Defense Coun, 58-60; pres, Rome Dem. Club, 59-62; N.Y. State Assemblyman, 61-65, Majority Whip, N.Y. State Assembly, 65; research asst, Speaker's Staff, N.Y. State Assembly, 66-; committeeman, Fifth Ward Dem. Party, Rome, currently. Mil. Serv: Entered as Pvt, Army, 55, released as Spec. Agent, Army Res, after serv. in Counter Intel. Corps, 1st Army; Good Conduct Medal; Letter of Recommendation from Maj. Gen. Bean. Mem: Am, N.Y. State, Oneida Co. and Rome Bar Asns; bd. dirs, Rome C. of C, 69-; Adv, Coun. 391, K. of C; bd. dirs, Oneida Co. Unit, Am. Cancer Soc; bd. dirs, Catholic Charities; Ft. Stanwix Coun, Boy Scouts; Sr. Citizens Coun. Rel: Roman Catholic. Legal Res: 909 Turin St, Rome, N.Y. 13440. Mailing Add: 125 N. Washington St, Rome, N.Y. 13440.

WORRILOW, THOMAS HENRY, SR. R
Pa. State Rep.
b. Chester, Pa, 8/15/18; s. Benjamin Scott Worrilow and Sadie McNulty W; m. 11/8/47 to Amelia Mae Owens; c. Thomas Henry, Jr, Diane Marie and Lawrence Richard. Educ: Chester High Sch, grad, 36. Polit. & Govt. Pos: Pa. State Rep, 69- Mil. Serv: Entered as Pvt, Army, 42, released as Sgt, 45, after serv. in 373rd Gen. Serv. Engnrs. Regt, ETO, 43-45; Five Battle Stars. Mem: F&AM; AAONMS; Am. Legion; VFW; ITU; Moyamensing Hook & Ladder Co; Young Men's Rep. Club. Rel: Protestant. Mailing Add: 933 Potter St, Chester, Pa. 19013.

WORSHAM, GEORGE FREDERICK R
b. Clarendon Co, S.C, 7/30/09; s. George Talbert Worsham and Jessie Phillips W; m. 1/17/40 to Sara L. Deer. Educ: Col. of Charleston. Polit. & Govt. Pos: S.C. State Rep, 62-68. Bus. & Prof. Pos: V.pres. and dir. pub. rels, Coburg Dairy, Inc. Mem: Charleston C. of C.(dir); Lions Int.(former dir); Charleston Lions Club (secy-treas); Jr. C. of C.(former pres); Sales and Mkt. Execs. Club (former pres); Charleston Country Club; Sq. and Level Club; Bd. of Coastal Carolina Boy Scouts; YMCA Bd; Scottish Rite; A.F.M.(former Master); Shrine. Rel: Presbyterian; Ruling Elder, Second Presby. Church. Mailing Add: 4 Tarleton Dr. S, Windemere, Charleston, S.C. 29404. (1967)

WORTHINGTON, LORNE R. D
Cmnr. of Ins, Iowa
b. Penticton, B.C, Can, 6/14/38; s. Paul A. Worthington and Alice Marsland W; m. 5/30/59 to Veneta Faye Snethen; c. Penelope Lynn, Deborah Ann, Suzanne Marie and Michael Robert. Educ: State Univ. Iowa, 60 and 56-58; Graceland Col, B.A. cum laude, 64; Lambda Delta Sigma. Polit. & Govt. Pos: Iowa State Rep, 62-64; mem, Gov. Cmt. on Pub. Health, 63-69; former mem, Cmt. on Intergovt. Rels; auditor, Iowa, 65-66; cmnr. of Ins, Iowa, currently. Bus. & Prof. Pos: Off. mgr, Lamoni Sales Corp, 59-64; secy, Lamoni Farms, Inc, 63-64; mem, Exec. Cmt, Nat. Asn. Ins. Cmnrs, chmn, Spec. Auto Insurance Cmt. and mem, Adv. Cmt. Fed. Dept. Transportation, 68-69. Mem: Pres, Lamoni C. of C, 64; v.pres, Graceland Col. Alumni Asn. Outstanding Freshman Legis. Award, 63; Nat. Jaycee Outstanding Young Man Award, 65. Rel: Reorganized Latter-day Saint. Legal Res: Lamoni, Iowa 50140. Mailing Add: State Insurance Dept, Lucas State Office Bldg, Des Moines, Iowa 50319.

WORTHINGTON, ROBERT FLETCHER, JR. D
b. Clinton, 7/17/31; s. Robert Fletcher Worthington, Sr. and Rachael W; m. to Julia McCrary; c. Julia Elizabeth and Katherine Louisa. Educ: Univ. Tenn, J.D, 57; Phi Delta Phi; Sigma Alpha Epsilon. Polit. & Govt. Pos: Ward chmn, Tenn. Dem. Party, 60; mem, Knox Co. State Primary Cmn, 64-66; pres, Knox Co. Young Dem. Club, 66; exec. cmt, Tenn. Young Dem, 66; alternate del, Dem. Nat. Conv, 68. Bus. & Prof. Pos: Partner, Baker, Worthington, Barnett & Crossley, Attorneys, 64- Mil. Serv: Entered as 2nd Lt, Army, released as 1st Lt, 56, after serv. in Third Inf. Div. Mem: Knoxville, Tenn. and Am. Bar Asns. Rel: Presbyterian. Legal Res: 807 Woodland Court, S.W, Knoxville, Tenn. 37919. Mailing Add: Valley Fidelity Bank Bldg, Knoxville, Tenn. 37902.

WORTHY, K(ENNETH) MARTIN Independent
Chief Counsel, Internal Revenue Serv. and Asst. Gen. Counsel, Treas. Dept.
b. Dawson, Ga, 9/24/20; s. Kenneth Spencer Worthy and Jeffrie Martin W; m. 2/15/47 to Eleanor Vreeland Blewett; c. Jeffrie Martin and William Blewett. Educ: The Citadel, 37-39; Emory Univ, B.Ph, 41, J.D, 47; Harvard Univ, M.B.A, cum laude, 43; Omicron Delta Kappa; Phi Delta Theta; Phi Delta Phi. Polit. & Govt. Pos: Chief counsel, Internal Revenue Serv. and asst. gen. counsel, Treas. Dept, 69- Bus. & Prof. Pos: Assoc, Hamel, Morgan, Park & Saunders, Wash, D.C, 48-51, partner, 52-69; lectured before Tax Insts. of Univ. Chicago, Am. Univ, George Wash. Univ, Univ. Tex, N.Y. Univ. and Tulane Univ. and Va, Ky. and South. Fed. Tax Insts. Mil. Serv: Entered as Cpl, Army, 43, released as Capt, 46, after serv. in Transportation Corps, reentered 51, released as Capt, 52, after serv. in Judge Adv. Corps; Army Commendation Ribbon, 46. Publ: Co-auth, Basic Estate Planning, Bobbs-Merrill, 57; 'Carryovers of Deductions, Credits and Other Tax Attributes in Corporate Adjustments and Reorganizations,' Taxes Mag, 12/66; 'Problems of Jointly-Owned Property,' The Tax Lawyer, 69. Mem: Am. Bar Asn.(chmn, Cmt. on Corporate Stockholder Relationships, 62-64, mem. coun, 65-68 and v.chmn, 68-69, Taxation Sect); Bar Asn. of D.C; Ga. State and Fed. Bar Asns; Nat. Tax Asn; tax adv. group, Am. Law Inst, 63-68; del, Montgomery Co. Civic Fedn, 52-61; pres, Bannockburn Citizens Asn, 58-59; Health and Welfare Coun, D.C. Area, 61-62; chmn, Finance Dept, Episcopal Diocese of Wash, 69- Rel: Episcopal. Legal Res: 5305 Portsmouth Rd, Bethesda, Md. 20016. Mailing Add: Room 3024, 1111 Constitution Ave. N.W, Washington, D.C. 20224.

WOUTAT, HELEN LOUISE R
b. Grafton, N.Dak, 5/29/15; d. John A. McIntosh and Evelyn Roberta Smith M; m. 11/1/35 to Philip H. Woutat; c. Paul G, Robert P. and Donald B. Educ: Mayville State Teachers Col, 32-34. Polit. & Govt Pos: Rep. precinct chmn, Grand Forks Co. N.Dak, 56-66; ward chmn, Rep. Nat. Conv, 52, co-chmn, 60 and alternate del, 64; alternate del, N.Dak. State Rep. Conv, 60, del, 62, 64 & 68; pres, N.Dak. Fedn. Rep. Women, 65-67; secy. libr. bd, Grand Forks Pub. Libr, currently. Mem: Patroness, Kappa Alpha Theta, Univ. of N.Dak; PEO; N.Dak. Med. Auxiliary; Deaconess and St. Michael's Hosp. Auxiliaries; Red Cross; N.Dak. and Nat. Fedn. of Rep. Women. Golf Champion, Grand Forks Country Club, 64 and 65. Rel: Presbyterian. Mailing Add: 1205 Lincoln Dr, Grand Forks, N.Dak. 58201.

WOZNIAK, DANIEL DONALD DFL
b. Silver Lake, Minn, 8/26/22; s. George Adalbert Wozniak and Anna Biros W; m. 8/30/47 to Angela Louise Walsh; c. Angela, Victoria, Daniel and George. Educ: Col. St. Thomas, B.A, 43; Univ. Minn, J.D, 48; pres, Nat. Student Coun. Polit. & Govt. Pos: Minn. State Rep, 50-66, Majority Leader, Minn. House of Rep, 8 years; Minority Leader, 6 years; for. serv. reserve officer, State Dept. Mil. Serv: Entered as Cadet, Navy, released as Lt.(jg), after serv. as Naval Aviator. Publ: 'Sales Taxes-Are Regressive,' Local Econ. Rev, 62; 'Billboard Regulation or Blight,' AAA Motorist, 65; 'The Role of a Legislator,' Nat. Coop, 64. Rel: Catholic. Mailing Add: 303 Woodlawn Ave, St. Paul, Minn. 55105.

WRAY, JERRY CLARK R
Chmn, Wash. Co. Rep. Cmt, Idaho
b. Raggelsville, Ind, 6/10/04; s. Clarence Wray and Maargaret Clark W; wid; c. Jon Lee and Jaque. Educ: High sch, Griffith, Ind, 4 years. Polit. & Govt. Pos: Chmn, Wash. Co. Rep. Cmt, Idaho, 51-52 & 68- Bus. & Prof. Pos: Partner, Horner-West Co, 50-67. Rel: Protestant. Mailing Add: 475 E. Main St, Weiser, Idaho 83672.

WRENN, JOHN JOSEPH D
b. Providence, R.I, 8/27/06; s. John J. Wrenn (deceased) and Mary Ann Ginnerty (deceased), m. 7/10/43 to Eleanor Peyton Quarles; c. John Peyton and David Sinclair. Educ: Brown Univ, Extension Div, 37-43. Polit. & Govt. Pos: Former v.pres, Young Dem, R.I; R.I. State Rep, 33-38 & 41-69, former chmn, Finance Cmt, R.I. State House of Rep, chmn, Spec. Unemploy. Ins. Fund Cmn, 35-36, Cmn. on State Fiscal Operations, 57, Cmn. to Study Treatment and Care of Inebriates, 61, Cmn. to Study the Orgn. of State and Local Govt, Dep. Majority Leader, 53-56, Speaker, R.I. House of Rep, 65-69 and former chmn, Cmt. on labor; asst. dist. supvr, Providence Co. Fed. Census, 40; mem, Northwest. State Fire Protection Cmn, 66; del, Dem. Nat. Conv, 68; mem, R.I. Pub. Utilities Cmn, 69- Bus. & Prof. Pos: Ins. broker; mem. bd. dirs, West End Fed. Neighborhood Credit Union, currently. Mem: Urban League of R.I; NAACP. Rel: Catholic. Mailing Add: 177 Bellevue Ave, Providence, R.I. 02907.

WRIGHT, CARL JOHN R
Chmn, Bay Co. Rep. Party, Mich.
b. Buffalo, N.Y. 3/12/11; s. Earl Wright and Nellie Pinney W; m. 11/11/39 to Barbara L. Norton; c. Beverly, Karen and Judith. Educ: Northeast. Univ, B.B.A. Polit. & Govt. Pos: Chmn, Bay Co. Rep. Party, Mich, 65-; alternate del, Rep. Nat. Conv, 68. Bus. & Prof. Pos: Manufacturer agent. Mem: Elks; Consistory, Shrine; Bay City Country Club; Toastmasters. Rel: Congregational. Mailing Add: 411 N. Johnson, Bay City, Mich. 48706.

WRIGHT, CARROLL D
b. Littleton, Ill, 5/2/12; m. to Lurline Lewis; c. Jacqueline Kohl, Michael. Educ: West. Ill, State Teachers Col. Polit. & Govt. Pos: Iowa State Rep, 66-67; Judicial Nominating Cmt; Mayor's Youth Cmt. of Scott Co. Iowa; V.P. of Quad City Fedn. of Labor. Bus. & Prof. Pos: Bus. Rep. of Dist. 102, Int. Asn. of Machinist; with Herman Nelson, Moline, Ill. until 51. 1967 Legal Res: 2619 W. 71st Street, Davenport, Iowa. No mailing address available. (1967)

WRIGHT, CHARLES WESLEY R
b. Topeka, Kans, 8/17/19; s. Charles Wesley Wright and Mary Florence Kanode W; m. 9/2/44 to Alice Clare Brownfield; c. Charles Wesley, III, Douglas Scott and Catherine Clare. Educ: Univ. Kans, B.F.A, 41; Delta Chi. Polit. & Govt. Pos: Cmnr. of Streets, Topeka, Kans, 61-65, mayor, 65-69; exec. dir, Citizens Asn, Kansas City, Mo, 69- Bus. & Prof. Pos: Partner, Patterson-Wright Advert. Agency, Topeka, Kans, 54-61; mem. staff, Advert. & Pub. Rels, Standard Oil Co, 46-54. Mil. Serv: Entered as A/S, Naval Res, 42, released as Capt, 46, after serv. in Fleet Marine Force, Pac. Theatre; Maj.(Ret), Marine Corps Res; S.Pac. and Am. Expeditionary Theatre Ribbons; World War II Victory Bar. Mem: Am. Pub. Works Asn.(first pres, Kans. Chap); AF&AM; Scottish Rite; Shrine; VFW; Am. Legion; Kiwanis; Kansas City Advert. & Sales Exec. Club; trustee, Am. Humanics Found, Kansas City, Mo; Washburn Univ.(former regent); Boy Scouts (Eagle Scout). Scouter's Award and Key; Silver Beaver. Rel: Congregational. Mailing Add: 2036 W. 30th, Topeka, Kans. 66611.

WRIGHT, DEXTER S. R
Ky. State Rep.
b. Linton, Ind, 8/11/21; m. 8/19/44 to Margaret E. Brown; c. Ronnie Sue (Mrs. Robert Steiner) and Dawn Sheree. Educ: Univ. of Louisville, 2 years. Polit. & Govt. Pos: Ky. State Rep, 64-, Minority Whip, Ky. State House of Rep, 68- Mil. Serv: Entered as Pvt, Army, 44, released as Sgt, 46, after serv. in Inf, ETO. Mem: Mason; Scottish Rite; Shrine. Rel: Methodist. Mailing Add: 337 Kenwood Hill Rd, Louisville, Ky. 40214.

WRIGHT, DONALD ORR Conservative
Minn. State Sen.
b. Hennepin Co, Minn; m. to Virna Wood; c. Donald O, Jr. and Charles W. Polit. & Govt. Pos: Minn. State Rep, 27-33, chmn, House Cmt. on Workmen's Compensation; Minn. State Sen, 35-, mem, Liquor Control, Pub. Hwys, Civil Admin, Pub. Welfare, Taxes and Tax Laws Senate Cmts, chmn, Taxes and Tax Law Cmt, 51-69 and chmn, Cmt. on Cmts, 55-61, pres. pro tempore, 53; del, Rep. Nat. Conv, 40; Lt. Gov, 54. Bus. & Prof. Pos: Attorney-at-Law. Mailing Add: 1164 Cedar View Dr, Minneapolis, Minn. 55405.

WRIGHT, DONN HOWARD D
b. Easton, Minn, 7/9/21; s. George Albert Wright and Beatrice Swam W; m. 2/9/44 to Margaret Louise Falk; c. Jan Donn, Robert Carter and Lyn Edward. Educ: Dak. Wesleyan Univ, Mitchell, S.Dak. Polit. & Govt. Pos: S.Dak. State Rep, 62-66; dir. inspections, S.Dak. State Dept. Agr; Lake Twp. Clerk and Mem. Sch. Bd; del, S.Dak. State Dem. Conv, 68. Bus. & Prof. Pos: Farmer; ins. agent, Farmers Union Ins. Co; mail carrier, White Lake, S.Dak; sales rep, News Printing Co, Aberdeen S.Dak; owner, Donn's Dept. Store, Kimball, S.Dak. Mil. Serv: Entered as Pvt, Army, 41, released as Cpl, 45, after serv. in FA, CAC, Postal Serv, Aleutions, Cent. Pac, Palaus, Philippine Islands, 41-45. Mem: Mason; VFW; Am. Legion; Eastern Star; PTA; Farmers Union. 1966 Dem. Cand. for U.S. Senate. Rel: Presbyterian. Legal Res: White Lake, S.Dak. 57383. Mailing Add: Kimball, S.Dak. 57355.

WRIGHT, DONNA GALE R
Mem, Calif. Rep. State Cent. Cmt.
b. Los Angeles, Calif, 2/9/23; d. Glenn Edwin Myers, M.D. and Dorothy Murphy M; m. 7/10/57 to Elwood Wellman Wright, Jr; c. Donna, Glenn, Diana, Susan and Christopher. Educ: Stanford Univ, 40-41. Polit. & Govt. Pos: Area chmn, 21st Assembly Dist. Rep. Party, San Francisco, Calif, 60-64; assoc. mem, San Francisco Co. Rep. Cent. Cmt, 60-, women's v.chmn, 65-66; demonstration chmn, Margaret Chase Smith Presidential Campaign, 64; mem, Calif. Rep. State Cent. Cmt, 64-; campaign coordinator, Mailliard for Cong, 68. Mem: Treas, San Francisco Beautiful, 65-; pres, Vol. for Instl. Aid, 68-69; bd. mem, San Francisco Stanford Womens Club, 62-66. Rel: Protestant. Mailing Add: 70 Commonwealth Ave, San Francisco, Calif. 94118.

WRIGHT, ELBRIDGE JUETTE D
S.C. State Rep.
b. Anderson Co, S.C; s. Benjamin Yancey Wright and Juletta Jane Hanks W; m. 1959 to Christine C. Gregory. Educ: Pub. Schs. of Anderson Co. Polit. & Govt. Pos: S.C. State Rep, 57-58 & 63-; sch. trustee, Anderson Co. Bus. & Prof. Pos: Farmer. Mil. Serv: 18-19. Mailing Add: R.D. 1, Belton, S.C. 29627. (1967)

WRIGHT, ELMA POGGE R
b. Salt Lake City, Utah, 9/11/93; d. Ulrich Christain Pogge and Mary Lovina Williams P; m. 1/19/16 to Earl Stanger Wright; c. Boyd Pogge. Educ: High Sch, grad. Polit. & Govt. Pos: V.chmn, Rep. Cent. Cmt, Idaho, 47-49; del, Rep. Nat. Conv, 48, 52 & 68; pres, Idaho Fedn. Rep. Woman, 56-58. Mem: DAR; Colonial Dames; pres, Nat. Woolgrowers Woman's Auxiliary, 56-57. Rel: Latter-day Saint. Mailing Add: 1144 Sahara Ave, Idaho Falls, Idaho 83401.

WRIGHT, F(RED) GORDON R
Minn. State Rep.
b. Brockville, Ont, Can, 3/27/97; s. Wm. James Wright and Mary Gibson Zealand W; m. 9/14/23 to Clare Laurentine Christiansen; c. John Gordon. Educ: Bexhill Can. Officers Training Sch, Bexhill, Eng, Lt, 17; Northwest.

Col. Law, Minneapolis, LL.B, 23; Univ. Club Minneapolis. Polit. & Govt. Pos: Clerk, Minn. State House of Rep. Judiciary Cmt, 35-39 & 41-43, chief counsel, 51-54; Minn. State Rep, 36th Dist, 55- Bus. & Prof. Pos: Sr. partner, Wright, Wanglie & Zimmerman, Attorneys-at-law, 63- Mil. Serv: Entered as Pvt, Can. Inf, 14, released as Capt, 19, after serv. in 11th Bn. and 43rd Bn. Cameron Highlanders Can, France, Belgium and Germany, 15-19; Mons Star; Serv. and Victory Medals. Publ: 'Articles on Legislation,' Bench & Bar, M.S.B.A, 50' Mem: Chmn. cmt. legis, Minn. State Bar Asn, 44-51; past master, Cataract Lodge 2, AF&AM; Shrine; Univ. Club Minneapolis; v.pres, Minn. Soc. Prevention of Blindness, 66-; chmn. legis. coun, U.S. Nat. Coun, Royal Can. Legion. Silver Beaver Award and Order of the Arrow, Boy Scouts Am. Rel: Christian Science. Mailing Add: 2912 Chowen Ave. S, Minneapolis, Minn. 55416.

WRIGHT, FRED THORNTON R
State Chmn, Utah Rep. Party
b. American Fork, Utah, 2/24/24; s. Frederick Earl Wright and Mary Ann Thornton W; m. 6/5/43 to Doris Tanner Lewis; c. Cathryn W.(Mrs. Cochran), Constance, F. Lewis, Wayne H, Elizabeth, Margaret and Ruth Anne. Educ: Brigham Young Univ, 2 years; Univ. Washington, 1 year; Univ. Calif, Los Angeles, 1 year. Polit. & Govt. Pos: Voting dist. officer, American Fork Rep. Party, Utah, 59-61, chmn, 61-65; chmn, Utah Co. Rep. Party, 65-67 & 68-69, mem. Reapportionment Cmt, 66; mem, Judicial Selection Cmn, Fourth Dist, 67-; State Chmn, Utah Rep. Party, 69- Bus. & Prof. Pos: Aircraft dispatcher, Am. Overseas Airlines, N.Y, 46-47; chief dispatcher, K.L.M. Royal Dutch Airlines, 47-51; raw materials analyst, U.S. Steel Corp, Geneva, Utah, 51- Mil. Serv: Entered as Pvt, Army Air Corps, 43, released as 1st Lt, 46, after serv. in Air Transport Command, ETO, 44-46. Mem: American Fork Hosp. bd. of trustees; Lions (past pres, Am. Fork Club). Rel: Latter-day Saint. Mailing Add: 825 N. First E. St, American Fork, Utah 84003.

WRIGHT, FREDERICK CHRISTIAN, III D
Md. State Del.
b. Hagerstown, Md, 9/4/38; s. Frederick Christian Wright, Jr. and Laura Katherine Roulette W; m. 6/11/66 to Caroline Ann Routzann. Educ: Univ. Va, B.S. in commerce, 60 and LL.B, 63; Omicron Delta Kappa; Phi Alpha Delta; Phi Kappa Sigma; Raven Soc; IMP Soc; Eli Banana Club. Polit. & Govt. Pos: Md. State Del, 66-; mem, Young Dem. Club of Wash. Co. Bus. & Prof. Pos: Assoc, McCauley, Cooey & Berkson, 63; partner, McCauley, Cooey, Berkson & Wright, 67- Mil. Serv: Pfc, Army, 63; Sgt, Army Res, Co. B, 378th Quartermaster Bn. Mem: Md, Wash. Co. and Am. Bar Asns; bd. dirs, Jaycees, 2 terms; Fountain Head Country Club. Rel: Episcopal. Mailing Add: 152 W. Washington St, Hagerstown, Md. 21740.

WRIGHT, GEORGE F. D
Polit. & Govt. Pos: Former del, Conn. State Constitutional Conv; chmn, Stratford Housing Authority, 58; former mem, Stratford Town Coun, 6 years; Conn. State Rep, 59-69, Dem. Whip, Conn. State House of Rep. Mil. Serv: Navy, World War II, Naval Res, 8 years. Mem: Former pres, Stonybrook Sch. Father's Club. Mailing Add: 7 Baird Court, Stratford, Conn. 06497. (1967)

WRIGHT, HILDRED MARGARET D
b. Jet, Okla, 9/10/06; d. Gilbert Marshall Nelson and Lillie Pereau N; m. 10/25/33 to Herbert William Wright; c. Jimmy, Billy, Donna, Jack and Jill. Educ: Enid Bus. Col, grad, 26; Univ. Minn, poetry course, 45-46; Northwest. State Col, refresher courses & income tax acct, 59-63. Polit. & Govt. Pos: Secy-treas, Alfalfa Co. Dem. Cent. Cmt, Okla, 34-36, & 56-64; del, Okla. State Dem. Conv, 36; del, Dem. Nat. Conv, 36 & 64; co-chmn. or secy-treas, First Precinct Third Ward Dem. Party, Cherokee, Okla, over 30 years. Bus. & Prof. Pos: Employee, B.F. Sadil Abstract Co, Wichita, Kans, 30-32 and Cherokee Nat. Bank, 32-33; owner and operator, Wright Abstract Co, 35-50; income tax acct, Attorney H.W. Wright, Cherokee, Okla, 50-66. Publ: Poems, 'Prairie Child' and 'Diurnal Farewell,' Okla. Silver Jubilee, Anthology Poetry Soc. of Okla, 59; 'Poetic Urge' and 'Suffering Father' in Songs of the Free, Crown Publishing Co, N.Y.C, 47; 'You Answered Not,' Capper's Weekly, Topeka, Kans, 52; plus others. Mem: Okla. State Poet Laureate, charter mem. and past pres, Colonial Dames XVII Cent; Past Matron, Eastern Star; bd. dirs, state orgn. and regional dir, Poetry Soc. Okla; past pres, Cherokee Poetry Club; Ohyahoma Club; charter mem, Cherokee Bus. & Prfnl. Women's Club; Cub Scout Den Mother; PTA. Rel: Methodist; Sunday Sch. Teacher, First Methodist Church of Cherokee. Mailing Add: 1117 S. Grand Ave, Cherokee, Okla. 73728. (1967)

WRIGHT, IRA LLOYD D
b. Blacksville, W.Va, 9/7/95; s. Lewis Leasure Wright and Armeda Bell Phillips W; m. 8/21/17 to Effie Glen Howard; c. Howard Lloyd. Educ: Waynesburg Col; W. Chester State Teachers Col; Wash. Col. of Law, LL.B. Polit. & Govt. Pos: Asst. comptroller and asst. finance dir, Panama Canal and Panama R.R. Co, 18-54; chief dep. sheriff, Preston Co, W.Va, 61-64; W.Va. State Del, 64-66; former Preston Co. Rep. State Coun. on Educ. Bus. & Prof. Pos: Lawyer; Teacher, 13-17; retired Fed. Official. Mil. Serv: Officers Res. Corps, Army, 29-39. Mem: D.C. and Canal Zone Bar Asns; Mason; Lions; Modern Woodmen; K. of P; Odd Fellows; Rebekahs; exec. bd, Mountaineer Area Coun, Boy Scouts; Salvation Army adv. bd; Arthurdale Commun. Asn; Preston Co. Hist. Soc; Nat. Asn. of Retired Civil Employees; Nat. Cong. of PTA. Rel: Methodist. Mailing Add: Arthurdale, W.Va. 26520. (1967)

WRIGHT, J. STEWART R
Chmn, McCone Co. Rep. Cent. Cmt, Mont.
b. Glasgow, Mont, 1/17/20; s. Frank C. Wright and Anna Stanley W; m. 8/31/52 to Lois Sylvia Samuelson; c. Jay S, Bruce A, Jan Sylvia and Frank C. Educ: North. Mont. Col, 38-39; Mont State Col, B.S, 42; Alpha Zeta; Phi Kappa Phi. Polit. & Govt. Pos: Bd. mem, McCone Co. Dist. Six Sch. Bd, 49-59; bd. mem, McCone Dist. High Sch. Bd, 53-59; Mont. State Rep, 59-64; chmn, McCone Co. Rep. Cent. Cmt, 66- Bus. & Prof. Pos: Owner, McCone Co. Ranch, 49-69. Mem: Mont. Stockgrowers Asn.(exec. cmt, 65-69); McCone Co. Farm Bur; AF&AM. Rel: Lutheran. Mailing Add: Route C32, Wolf Point, Mont. 59201.

WRIGHT, JAMES C. D
U.S. Rep, Tex.
b. Fort Worth, Tex, 12/22/22; s. James C. Wright and Mary Lyster W; m. to Mary Ethelyn Lemons; c. Jimmy, Virginia Sue, Patricia Kay and Alicia Marie. Educ: Weatherford Col; Univ. Tex. Polit. & Govt. Pos: Tex. State Rep, 47-48; mayor, Weatherford, Tex, 49-54; pres, Tex. League of Munic, 52; U.S. Rep, Tex, 55-, mem, Pub. Works Cmt, Govt. Opers. Cmt. and Mil. Affairs Subcmt, chmn, Watershed Develop. Subcmt, ranking Dem. Mem. and floor leader, spec. subcmt. for Appalachia Develop. Bill, U.S. del. to Interparliamentary Conf, three years, official observer for Gemini Orbital Mission, House Del. to confer with Brit. Legislators and attend Sir Winston Churchill's Funeral, 65; alternate del, Dem. Nat. Conv, 68. Bus. & Prof. Pos: Partner, trade exten. and advert. firm. Mil. Serv: Entered as Pvt, Army Air Force, 41, released as Officer, 46, after serv. as B-24 Pilot, S.Pac; Distinguished Flying Cross. Publ: You and Your Congressman, Coward-McCann, 65; The Coming Water Famine, Coward-McCann, 66; article on Interstate Hwy. Prog, Saturday Evening Pos, 62; plus others. Rel: Presbyterian; Lay worker. Legal Res: Fort Worth, Tex. Mailing Add: Rayburn House Office Bldg, Washington, D.C. 20515.

WRIGHT, JAMES D. D
b. Keokuk, Iowa, 11/2/30; married; c. Three. Educ: Regis Col; Univ. Colo; Univ. Denver. Polit. & Govt. Pos: V.pres, Denver Young Dem, Colo, 57; former Dem. precinct committeeman, Denver and Arapahoe Co; former Colo. State Rep. Bus. & Prof. Pos: Former teacher, Adams City High Sch; part-owner, Mercury Signs Co; guest lectr. hist, Regis Col. Mailing Add: 13406 E. Fifth Place, Aurora, Colo. 80010. (1967)

WRIGHT, JAMES L, JR. R
Pa. State Rep.
b. New York, N.Y, 3/10/25; s. James L. Wright and Rose Fitzsimmons W; m. 1951 to Elaine Norris; c. Duane, Anne, James and Matthew. Educ: Univ. Mich, B.S.E, 51; Registered Prfnl. Engr. Polit. & Govt. Pos: Chmn, bd. supvrs, Middletown Twp, Bucks Co, Pa, 62-65; asst. co. chmn, Bucks Co. Rep. Party, 63-64; Pa. State Rep, 142nd Dist, Bucks Co, currently. Bus. & Prof. Pos: Sr. indust. engr, U.S. Steel, Trenton, N.J, 55- Mil. Serv: Entered as Pvt, Army, 43, released as Capt, 57, after serv. in Eighth Air Force, ETO, 43; Air Medal; Victory Medal; Theater Ribbons. Rel: Catholic. Mailing Add: 116 Hollow Rd, Levittown, Pa. 19056.

WRIGHT, JAMES LASHUA D
Ill. State Rep.
b. Hinsdale, Ill, 8/1/34; s. Charles Aspinall Wright and Vera Lashua W; m. 11/28/65 to Paulette Blanche Hecker; c. James Lashua, Jr. Educ: Hinsdale Twp. High Sch, Ill, 4 years. Polit. & Govt. Pos: Dem. precinct committeeman, 33rd Precinct, Ill, 56-; secy, Dupage Co. Dem. Cent. Cmt, 60-; del, Dem. Nat. Conv, 64; village trustee, Westmont, Ill, 67-; Ill. State Rep, 69- Mem: YMCA Bus. Mens Club. Rel: Protestant. Mailing Add: 219 N. Adams, Westmont, Ill. 60559.

WRIGHT, JAMES LEE D
Chmn, Henderson Co. Dem. Exec. Cmt, Tenn.
b. Sardis, Tenn, 7/4/12; s. James Walter Wright and Fanny Lee Wells W; m. 10/17/36 to Maxine Pierce. Educ: High Sch. Polit. & Govt. Pos: Chmn, Henderson Co. Dem. Exec. Cmt, Tenn, currently; chmn, Henderson Co. Dem. Primary Bd, 52-66. Bus. & Prof. Pos: Partner, Retail Grocery Store, 32-66; owner, Retail Furniture & Appliance Store, 41-66. Mem: Past Master, Constantine Lodge 64; Rotary. Rel: Methodist. Mailing Add: R.F.D. 1, Lexington, Tenn. 38351. (1967)

WRIGHT, J(AMES) SKELLY D
b. New Orleans, La, 1/14/11; s. James Edward Wright and Margaret Skelly W; m. 2/1/45 to Helen Mitchell Patton; c. James Skelly, Jr. Educ: Loyola Univ, Ph.B, 31; Loyola Univ. Sch. Law, J.D, 34; Alpha Delta Gamma; Blue Key; Phi Delta Phi. Hon. LL.D, Yale Univ, 61, Univ. Notre Dame, 62, Howard Univ, 64. Polit. & Govt. Pos: Asst. U.S. Attorney, East. Dist. La, 37-46, U.S. Attorney, 48-49; U.S. Dist. Judge, 49-62; U.S. Circuit Judge, D.C. Circuit, 62- Bus. & Prof. Pos: Teacher, Fortier High Sch, New Orleans, La, 31-35; lectr. Eng. hist, Loyola Univ, 36-37; mem. faculty, Loyola Univ. Sch. Law, 50-62; James Madison Lectr, N.Y. Univ. Sch. Law, 65; Robert H. Jackson Lectr, Nat. Col. State Trial Judge, Univ. Colo, 66; lectr, Univ. Tex. Sch. Law, Austin, 67; Frank Irvine Lectr, Cornell Law Sch, Ithaca, N.Y, 68 Mil. Serv: Entered as Lt.(jg), Coast Guard, 42, released as Lt. Comdr, 45, after serv. in ETO. Publ: 'Public School Desegregation: Legal Remedies for De Facto Segregation,' N.Y. Univ. Law Rev, 4/65; 'Federal Courts and the Nature and Quality of State Law,' Wayne Law Rev, winter 67; 'Role of the Supreme Court in a Democratic Society—Judicial Activism or Restraint?' Cornell Law Rev, 11/68; plus others. Mem: Am. Law Inst; Nat. Adv. Coun, Practicing Law Inst; Judicial Conf. U.S.(standing cmt, Rules of Practice and Procedure, Cmt. on Court Admin. and chmn, Subcmt. Fed. Jurisdiction). Citation in Law, Who's Who in Am, 68. Rel: Roman Catholic. Mailing Add: 5317 Blackistone Rd, Westmoreland Hills, Washington, D.C. 20016.

WRIGHT, JERAULD
b. Amherst, Mass, 6/4/98; s. Gen. William Mason Wright and Marjorie R. Jerauld W; m. 7/23/38 to Phyllis Blagden Thompson; c. Marion Jerauld and William Mason, III. Educ: U.S. Naval Acad, B.S, 17. Hon. Sc.D, Rose Polytech. Inst; LL.D, Col. of William and Mary and Univ. Mass. Polit. & Govt. Pos: Assigned to Presidential Yacht U.S.S. Mayflower, 24-26; White House Aide under President Hoover and President Coolidge, 24-26 & 31-33; mem. bd. nat. intel. estimates, CIA, 61-63; U.S. Ambassador to Repub. of China, 63-66. Mil. Serv: Entered as Ens, Navy, 17, released as Adm, 60, after serv. in Atlantic, Pac, Asiatic, European and Mid. East; Command Ens, U.S. Navy, 17 with serv. in U.S.S. Castine, 17-18, U.S.S. John D. Ford, 22-24 and U.S.S. Md, 26-29; attached Bur. Ord, 29-31; 1st Lt. and Gunnery, U.S.S. Salt Lake City, 31-34; exec. staff U.S. Naval Acad, 34-35, 39-41; aide asst. secy. Navy, 35-36; attached Bur. Ord, 36-37; Comdr, destroyer U.S.S. Blue, 37-39; exec. officer, U.S.S. Miss, 41-42; commanded H.M.S. Seraph in Evacuation French Gen. Giraud from Vichy, France, 42; U.S.N. Mem. of Murphy Clark Group in Secret Submarine Landing, N.Africa, 42; commanded U.S.S. Santa Fe, Pac. Opers, 43-44; assigned to Hq, Comdr-in-Chief, U.S. Fleet & Staff of Comdr. Naval Forces in Europe, also staff of comdr, AEF; amphibious group five, 44-45; comdr, cruiser div. six, 45; head oper. readiness sect, Off. Chief of Naval Opers, 45-49; comdr. amphibious force, Atlantic Fleet,

49-51; U.S. mem. NATO standing group, Wash, 51-52; Comdr-in-Chief, U.S. Naval Forces in East. Atlantic, Mediterranean and Mid. East, 52-54; Supreme Allied Comdr, Atlantic, NATO, 54-60; Comdr-in-Chief, Atlantic and U.S. Atlantic Fleet, 54-60; Awarded D.S.M; Legion of Merit with Gold Star; Bronze Star; Silver Star; Chevalier Legion of Honor, France; For. Decorations, France, Belgium, Netherlands, Portugal, Peru, Brazel, Italy and Colombia. Mem: Pres, U.S. Naval Inst, 57-58; Wash, D.C. Metrop. Club; Alibi Club; Chevy Chase Club. Rel: Episcopal. Mailing Add: 2706 36th St. N.W, Washington, D.C. 20007.

WRIGHT, JOHN COOK D
Mem. Exec. Cmt, New Dem. Coalition of Kans.
b. Los Angeles, Calif, 7/27/33; s. Charles MacPhee Wright and Helen Cook W; m. 6/25/55 to Jo Anne Steinheimer; c. Elizabeth, Jennifer, Melanie and Kennedy Weston. Educ: Harvard Col, A.B. magna cum laude, 54; Stanford Univ, Ph.D, 60. Polit. & Govt. Pos: Precinct chmn, Dem-Farmer-Labor Party, Fridley, Minn, 62-64 and city chmn, 62-63; city councilman, 64-66; del, Anoka Co. Dem-Farmer-Labor Conv, 62-64, 66 & 68; alternate del, Minn. State Dem-Farmer-Labor Conv, 66; v.chmn, Minn. Conf. of Concerned Dem, 67-68; del, Dem. Nat. Conv, 68; chmn, Lawrence, Kans. Chap. of New Dem. Coalition of Kans, 69-; co-founder and mem. exec. cmt, New Dem. Coalition of Kans, 69- Bus. & Prof. Pos: Acting instr. dept. of psychol, Stanford Univ, 59-60; asst. prof. inst. of child develop, Univ. Minn, 60-63 and assoc. prof, 63-68; assoc. prof, dept. of human develop, Univ. Kans, 68- Mil. Serv: Entered as Pvt, Army, 54, released as SP-4, 56, after serv. in Combat Develop. Dept, Signal Corps, Army Electronic Proving Ground, Ft. Huachuca, Ariz, 55-56; Good Conduct Medal. Publ: 'Basic Cognitive Processes in Children,' Monographs of the Soc. for Research in Child Develop, 63; 'Child Psychology,' In: Experimental Methods and Instrumentation in Psychology, (J. Sidowski, ed), Wiley, 65; 'Cognitive Develop,' In: Human Development, (F. Falkner, ed), W.B. Saunders, 67. Mem: Sigma Xi; Am. and Midwest. Psychol. Asns; Am. Asn. Univ. Prof; Psychonomic Soc; Soc. for Research in Child Develop; Am. Asn. for the Adv. of Sci; Am. Civil Liberties Union; NAACP. Nat. Sci. Found. fel, summer 59. Rel: Episcopal. Mailing Add: 3515 W. Fifth Terr, Lawrence, Kans. 66044.

WRIGHT, JOHN G. D
b. Philomath, Ga, 7/08/08; s. Cory William Wright and Georgia Bryan W; m. 7/05/41 to Mary Hinton Dillard. Educ: Univ. Ga, B.A, 25-27; Lumpkin Law Sch, LL.B, 30; Phi Kappa Phi. Polit. & Govt. Pos: Legis. asst. to U.S. Rep. Paul Brown, 24-37 and to U.S. Rep. Charles H. Brand, 32-33; Ga. State Rep, 64-66; Judge, Recorders Court, Washington, Ga, 66-; on Gov. Staff, Ga, 67- Bus. & Prof. Pos: Attorney-at-law, Washington, Ga, 64- Mem: Life mem. Ga. Probation & Parole Asn; Elks. Rel: Presbyterian. Mailing Add: Washington, Ga. 30673.

WRIGHT, JOHN ROBERT D
Tex. State Rep.
b. Dallas, Tex, 12/20/28; s. John Robert Wright and Anne Taylor W; m. 6/16/56 to Topsy Roberson; c. Martha Claire and John Robert, III. Educ: N.Tex. Univ, B.S. in govt, 51; Univ. Tex, LL.B, 54; Delta Theta Phi. Polit & Govt. Pos: Tex. State Rep, Dallas Co, 64- Mem: State Bar of Tex; Dallas Bar Asn; Southwest. Legal Found; Dallas Co. Criminal Bar Asn; Mason; Scottish Rite; Shrine; Rotary. Rel: Baptist. Mailing Add: 801 British, Grand Prairie, Tex. 75050.

WRIGHT, JOHN W. R
Mem, Mass. State Rep. Cmt.
b. 1926; m. to Emily McGarrahan; c. six. Educ: Boston Univ. Sch. Law; Sci. Found. Am, Legal Med. Cert. Polit. & Govt. Pos: Former mem, Town Meeting, Milton, Mass; 8 years; former asst. attorney gen, Chief of Contracts Div, 6 years; former chmn, Rep. Town Cmt; del, Rep. State Conv, 62, 64 & 66; mem, Mass. State Rep. Cmt, currently; alternate del, Rep. Nat. Conv, 68. Bus. & Prof. Pos: Attorney-at-law. Mem: Quincy Bar Asn. (former pres); Pub. Rels. Cmt, Mass. Bar Asn; Norfold Co. Bar Asn; Jaycees; chmn, Cmn, Keep Milton Residential. Mailing Add: 12 Spafford Rd, Milton, Mass. 02186.

WRIGHT, JULES R
b. Nenana, Alaska, 1933; married; c. three. Polit. & Govt. Pos: Alaska State Rep, 67-69. Bus. & Prof. Pos: Contractor. Mem: Pres. Fairbanks Native Asn. Mailing Add: P.O. Box 221, Fairbanks, Alaska 99701. (1967)

WRIGHT, LOUIS CHARLES D
Ala. State Rep.
b. Gadsden, Ala, 5/14/22; s. Louis Clifford Wright and Elizabeth McBrayer W; m. 3/22/44 to Maxine McClendon; c. Adele (Mrs. Joseph E. Miller, Jr), Louis Charles, Jr. and Dennis McClendon. Educ: Auburn Univ, B.S, 43; Univ. Ala, LL.B, 48; Phi Alpha Delta. Polit. & Govt. Pos: Dist. attorney, 16th Judicial Circuit of Ala, 55-63; U.S. Cmnr, North. Dist. of Ala, 63-65; Ala. State Rep, 11th Dist, 67- Bus. & Prof. Pos: Attorney, Ala, 48-; pres, Etowah Co. Bar Asn, 54; partner, Dortch, Wright & Wright, Gadsden, 65-69. Mil. Serv: Entered as A/S, Navy, 43, released as Lt.(jg), 46, after serv. in Am-Pac. Theatre, 43-46; Naval Res, 43-67, Comdr; Am, Pac. Theatre, Philippine Liberation and Naval Res. Ribbons. Mem: Ala. and Am. Bar Asns; Nat. Defense Attorneys Asn; Trial Lawyers Asn; Am. Judicature Soc; Nat. Res. Officers Asn; Mason; Lions; Am. Legion; VFW. Rel: Baptist. Legal Res: 311 Claremont Dr, Gadsden, Ala. 35902. Mailing Add: P.O. Box 405, Gadsden, Ala. 35902.

WRIGHT, LUTHER CLARK, JR. D
S.C. State Rep.
b. Ft. Mill, S.C, 9/7/18; s. Luther C. Wright, Sr. and Margaret E. Starnes W; m. 9/17/39 to Virginia Lee Brown; c. Luther C. III, Elliott Watson. Educ: Chester High Sch, 36. Polit. & Govt. Pos: S.C. State Rep, 57- Bus. & Prof. Pos: Funeral dir. Mil. Serv: 44-45. Mem: Chester Lodge 18, AF&M; Hejaz Temple AAONMS; Am. Legion; Eastern Star; WOW; K. of P; Chester Exchange Club; Chester Co. Develop. Bd; Chester Moose Club. Rel: Trustee, Bethel Methodist Church. Mailing Add: Chester, S.C. 29706. (1967)

WRIGHT, OREN ALVIN R
b. Greenwood, Ind, 8/27/11; s. Harry Wright and Clara Hautsky W; m. 11/10/36 to Ida Ray; c. Newton. Educ: Purdue Univ, 2 years. Polit. & Govt. Pos: Chmn, Johnson Co. Rep. Cent. Cmt, Ind, 57-69. Bus. & Prof. Pos: Farmer and bank dir. Mem: Dir, Ind. State Fair Bd; v.pres, Dorset Sheep Asn. of Am; Odd Fellows; Mason; Shrine; Lions; Farmers Union; Farm Bur. Hall of Fame, Purdue Univ. Rel: Christian. Mailing Add: Route 6, Greenwood, Ind. 46142.

WRIGHT, SYLVESTER MARILYN D
Dir, United Polit. Orgn. of Tex.
b. Dallas, Tex, 2/7/27; s. Calvin Wesley Wright and Mary Mickle W; m. 8/31/47 to Anna Vivian Henderson. Educ: Butler Col, A.A, 45; Bishop Col, B.A, 49, M.A, 54; Minister's Lyceum. Polit. & Govt. Pos: V.chmn, Johnson-Humphrey Campaign for Minority Group, Dallas, Tex, 64; dir, United Polit. Orgn. of Tex, 64-; elec. judge, Precinct 338, Dallas, 64-; chmn, Citizens' Cmt. for Better Law Enforcement, 65; area coordinator, Dem. for Responsible Govt, 66-68; dir, Trinity River Authority of Tex, 66-68; alternate del, Dem. Nat. Conv, 68; moderator, Goals for Dallas, Area Seven, 68; mem, Pres. White House Conf. Civil Rights. Bus. & Prof. Pos: Pastor, Peoples Baptist Church, 57- Mil. Serv: Entered as Pvt, Air Force, 45, released as Pfc, 47, after serv. in First Air Force; Good Conduct Medal. Mem: Interdenominal Minister's Alliance of Dallas (pres, 65-); chmn. steering cmt. of jr. col. prog, Missionary Baptist Gen. Conv. of Tex, 67-; Dallas Coun. Churches (mem. bd); NAACP (bd. mem, S.Dallas Branch); YMCA (mem. bd, Dallas Chap); Urban League of Dallas (mem. bd); United Serv. Orgn.(mem. bd, Dallas Chap); life mem, AF&AM. Bishop Col. Alumnus Award, 67. Rel: Baptist. Mailing Add: 2104 Dugald Place, Dallas, Tex. 75216.

WRIGHT, WILLIAM L. D
Vt. State Sen.
b. 1924. Polit. & Govt. Pos: Vt. State Sen, 67-; chmn, Burlington Parking Cmn, Burlington Police Dept, Vt. Rehabilitation Center; mem, Chittenden and Burlington Planning Cmns; del, Dem. Nat. Conv, 68. Bus. & Prof. Pos: V.pres, Abernethy's; pres, DeGoesbriand Hosp. Assocs. Mem: Pres, Burlington-Lake Champlain C. of C, Burlington Commun. Chest; v.pres, Nat. Retail Merchants Asn. Mailing Add: 57 Brookes Ave, Burlington, Vt. 05401. (1967)

WRIGHT, WILLIAM STEWART, JR. R
b. Indio, Calif, 2/21/24; s. William S. Wright, Sr. and Lidabell Coard W; m. 8/15/43 to Patricia Marie Murch; c. Patricia Jean. Educ: Maricopa High Sch, 4 years. Polit. & Govt. Pos: Co. cmnr, Esmeralda Co, Nev, 67-69. Bus. & Prof. Pos: V.pres, Wright Drilling, Inc, 49-67, pres, 67-; secy, White Mt. Power Coop, 57-61 and First Lake Valley TV Dist, 59-63; v.pres, Monte Cristo Oil Corp, 67-; owner, Union Oil Bulk Plant, Tonopah, Nev, currently; cattle rancher, Dyer, Nev, currently. Mem: Farm Bur. Rel: Protestant. Legal Res: Dyer, Nev. 89010. Mailing Add: Box 951, Tonopah, Nev. 89049.

WUGER, LAVINA MARDEAN R
V.Chmn, Faulk Co. Rep. Party, S.Dak.
b. Faulkton, S.Dak, 1/2/31; d. John William Vogeler and Erma Lillian Border V; m. 1/8/49 to Charles John Wuger; c. Guy Arnold and Nancy Elaine. Polit. & Govt. Pos: V.chmn, Faulk Co. Rep. Party, S.Dak, 68- Bus. & Prof. Pos: Clerk, Northwest. Pub. Serv, Co, 58. Mem: Sunflower Club; 4-H (leader, 14 years); Exten. Club; Faulkton Commun. Club; treas, Faulk Co. March of Dimes. Rel: Methodist; treas, Faulkton Methodist Church, 67- Mailing Add: Box 52, Faulkton, S.Dak. 57438.

WUNSCH, PAUL ROBERT R
Chmn, Kingman Co. Rep. Orgn, Kans.
b. Freeport, Kans, 7/14/01; s. Robert Wunsch and Mathilda Shultz W; m. 11/3/28 to Bula Mae Staley; c. Delores Elaine (Mrs. Stevens) and Robert Staley. Educ: Univ. Kans, A.B, 24 and LL.B, 25; Delta Sigma Rho; Phi Alpha Delta; Sour Owl Soc. Polit. & Govt. Pos: Co. attorney, Kingman Co, Kans, 26-33; Kans. State Rep, 37-45, Majority Floor Leader, Kans. State House of Rep, 39-41 and Speaker of the House, 43-45; Kans. State Sen, 45-65, Pres-Pro-Tem, Kans. State Senate, 49-65; mem, Kans. Legis. Coun, 49- and chmn, 2 years; chmn, Kingman Co. Rep. Orgn, 64-; cand, Gov, Kans, 64. Mem: Fel. Am. Col. Trial Lawyers; Kans. State, Kingman Co, 24th Judicial Dist. and Southwest Bar Asns; Lions; C. of C; AF&AM; K.T. Rel: Presbyterian. Mailing Add: 809 N. Main St, Kingman, Kans. 67068.

WURZ, LOUIS O. R
Mem, Calif. Rep. State Cent. Cmt.
b. Los Gatos, Calif, 9/20/18; s. Louis Otto Wurz and Anna I. Gray W; m. 11/5/66 to Barbara Jane Ellis; c. Margaret (Mrs. Michael Bonifield), Jeannette (Mrs. Fred Pace), Melanie, Robert and Carol Jane. Educ: San Jose State Col, 1 semester. Polit. & Govt. Pos: City councilman, Napa, Calif, 54 & 55; chmn, Agr. Stabilization and Conserv. Serv. Cmt, Napa Co, 64 & 65; mem, Rep. State Cent. Cmt. of Calif, 69- Bus. & Prof. Pos: Self employed, rancher, currently. Mem: Calif. Prune Adv. Bd; Prune Admin. Cmt; 20-30 Club (past pres); Elks; First Cong. Club; Yountville Vol. Firemen's Asn; Napa Co. Farm Bur.(past pres). Rel: Protestant. Legal Res: 7905 Money Rd, Napa, Calif. 94558. Mailing Add: 5135 St. Helena Highway, Napa, Calif. 94558.

WURZEL, RAYMOND C. R
b. St. Clair Co, Mich, 4/1/02; m. 1926 to Ada Quail; five grandchildren. Educ: Mich. State Univ. Polit. & Govt. Pos: Mich. State Rep, 56-66. Bus. & Prof. Pos: Farmer and dairyman. Mem: Mason; Elks; Kiwanis; Commun. Chest. Rel: Methodist. Mailing Add: North St. Post Office, St. Clair, Mich. 48079. (1967)

WYANT, CLINTON W. DFL
Chmn, Eighth Dist. Dem-Farmer-Labor Party, Minn.
b. O'Neill, Nebr, 12/25/31; s. Charles E. Wyant and Mary Cuddy W; m. 9/8/58 to Sophia Stalzer; c. Maria S, Charles R. and Amy Marie. Educ: St. John's Univ, Minn, B.A; William Mitchell Col. Law, B.S.L; St. Paul Col. Law, LL.B; St. Paul Dominic Club; Assoc. Confraternity Club. Polit. & Govt. Pos: Alternate del, Dem. Nat. Conv, 64 and del, 68; del, Minn. State and Dist. Dem-Farmer-Labor Conv. and Aitkin Co. Dem-Farmer-Labor Conv, Waukenabo Precinct, 66; former finance dir, Eighth Dist. Dem-Farmer-Labor Party and chmn, 69-; chmn, Aitkin Co. Dem-Farmer-Labor Party; asst. pub. defender, Minn, 67- Mem: Treas, 15th Judicial Bar Asn, Minn. Bar Asn. and chmn, Water Pollution Control Sub-Cmt; exec. secy, Aitkin Co. Area Resort Asn; state chmn, Jr. C. of C. Commun. Develop. of Minn, 60-

61. Recipient State Gold Medal and Nat. Award, Jr. C. of C. Rel: Roman Catholic. Legal Res: Route 2, Palisade, Minn. 56469. Mailing Add: 8 Second St. N.E, Aitkin, Minn. 56431.

WYATT, ANNE DUNCAN D
b. Louisville, Ky, 4/28/06; d. Dr. Ellis Duncan and Annie Kinnaird D; m. 6/14/30 to Wilson Watkins Wyatt; c. Mary Anne Duncan, Nancy Kinnaird and Wilson Watkins, Jr. Educ: Randolph-Macon Woman's Col, A.B; Phi Mu; pres, Lambda Chap, Quill Driver's. Polit. & Govt. Pos: Mem-at-lg, Dem. Women's Club, Ky, 42-46, parliamentarian, 58-60, prog. chmn, 60-64 and pres, 64-65; mem. speakers' bur, Dem. Nat. Cmt, Wash, D.C, 46; mem, Ky. State Dem. Cent. Exec. Cmt, 64-65. Mem: Dir, Ky. Arthritis Found, 65-; bd. mem, Louisville Free Pub. Libr, 51-60; bd. mem, Urban League, Wash, D.C, 46; mem. budget cmt, Louisville Commun. Chest, 38; bd. mem, War Fund of Louisville, 42 and League of Women Voters, 35-40; pres, Jr. League of Louisville, 36 and Younger Woman's Club, 34 and 35; Woman's Club of Louisville; Federated Woman's Club of Ky; Ky. Lawyers Asn; Ky. Craft Guild; Woman's Nat. Dem. Club; Forest Farmers Asn; Louisville Art Center; Filson Club. Rel: Presbyterian; v.pres, Women of the Second Presbyterian Church, 57. Mailing Add: 1001 Alta Vista Rd, Louisville, Ky. 40205.

WYATT, DONALD WALTER R
Mem, R.I. State Rep. Cmt.
b. Providence, R.I, 4/15/29; s. Andrew Walter Wyatt and Margaret Kenson W; m. 7/1/50 to Marguerite Elizabeth Lyons; c. Colleen, Mark, Donna, Susan and Michael. Polit. & Govt. Pos: Pres, Warwick Young Rep, R.I, 59-61; chmn, Warwick Charter Cmn, 59-61; mem, Third Ward Rep. Cmt, 62-; mem, R.I. State Rep. Cmt, 62-; exec. secy, Governor's Off, 63-69; chmn, Warwick Rep. City Cmt, 65-67; research asst, R.I. State Rep. Cent. Cmt, 69- Bus. & Prof. Pos: Exec. secy, Catholic Youth Orgn, 48-63; pub. rels. mgr, George Cardono and Assocs, 69- Mem: Cath. Broadcasters Asn; Prog. Workers of R.I; Cath. Press Asn; Providence C. of C. Rel: Roman Catholic. Mailing Add: 121 Homeland Ave, Warwick, R.I. 02886.

WYATT, JOSEPH LUCIAN, JR. D
b. Chicago, Ill, 2/21/24; s. Joseph Lucian Wyatt and Cecile Gertrude Zadico W; m. to Marjorie Kathryn Simmons; c. Daniel Winship, Linn Kathryn and Jonathan Burton. Educ: Northwest. Univ, A.B, 47; Harvard Law Sch; Phi Beta Kappa; Phi Eta Sigma; Sigma Alpha Epsilon. Polit. & Govt. Pos: Chmn, Calif. Fedn. Young Dem, South. Div, 52-53; secy, Calif. Dem. Coun, 53-57, pres, 57-61, dir, 61-65; del, Dem. Nat. Conv, 56, 60, 64 & 68; mem, Calif. State Personnel Bd, 61-, pres, 65-67; mem. bd. admin, Calif. Pub. Employees Retirement Syst, 63- Bus. & Prof. Pos: Lecturer, Fiduciary Law, Pac. Coast Banking Sch, 63-; Calif. ed, Trusts and Estates, 63- Mil. Serv: Entered as Pvt, Army Air Force, 42, released as 1st Sgt, 45, after serv. in 442nd Troop Carrier Group, ETO, 44-45. Publ: Trust Administration and Taxation, Revised Second Edition, Matthew Bender, currently. Mem: Am. Bar Asn; Am. Judicature Soc. Rel: Christian Science. Legal Res: 1119 Armada Dr, Pasadena, Calif. 91103. Mailing Add: Suite 704, 3345 Wilshire Blvd, Los Angeles, Calif. 90005.

WYATT, LANDON RUSSELL D
b. Callands, Va, 1/1/91; m. to Mary Beulah Hundley. Educ: Danville Commercial Col. Polit. & Govt. Pos: Va. State Rep, 44-52; Va. State Sen, 54-69; chmn, Finance Cmt. City Coun, 8 years; pres. Bd. of Trustees, Averett Col; trustee Hargrave Mil. Acad. Bus. & Prof. Pos: Automobile dealer; dir, Dan River Mills, Inc; pres. Piedmont Hardware Co; pres. Danville Parts & Body Mfg. Co; pres. Dickerson Buick Corp; dir, Norfolk, Franklin & Danville Rwy. Co; partner, Wyatt Buick Sales Co; pres, First Fed. Bldg. & Loan Asn; dir, Piedmont Broadcasting Corp; v.pres. Danville Livestock Auction Mkt; chmn, Bd. of Dir, Danville Knitting Mills, Inc. Mem: Former pres, Kiwanis; former pres, C. of C; former pres, YMCA; Retail Merchants Asn; dir. Danville Tuberc. Bd; pres, Danville Fair Asn. Elected Danville First Citizen, 39. Rel: Baptist. Mailing Add: Danville, Va. 24541. (1967)

WYATT, WENDELL WILLIAM R
U.S. Rep, Ore.
b. Eugene, Ore, 6/15/17; s. Henry H. Wyatt and Jane Pearl Smith W; m. 10/13/62 to Faye L. Reinecker; c. Ann, Jane and William Wyatt; Sandi and Larry Hill. Educ: Univ. Ore, LL.B, 41; Phi Delta Phi; Beta Theta Pi. Polit. & Govt. Pos: Chmn, Ore. State Rep. Cent. Cmt, 55-57; mem, President Eisenhower's Percy Cmt, 58; chmn, Ore. for Nixon Cmt, 60; U.S. Rep, Ore, First Dist, 64- Bus. & Prof. Pos: Mem, Ore. State Bar Bd. of Gov, 53-55 and House of Del, Am. Bar Asn, 60-66. Mil. Serv: Entered as Aviation Cadet, Navy, 42, released as Capt, Marine Corps, 46, after serv. in FMB 413, S.Pac, 44; Asiatic Theater Ribbon. Mem: Am. Col. of Trial Lawyers; Elks; Mason; Am. Legion; VFW. Rel: Episcopal. Legal Res: Gearhart, Ore. 97138. Mailing Add: 1209 Huntly Place, Alexandria, Va. 22307.

WYATT, WILSON WATKINS D
b. Louisville, Ky, 11/21/05; s. Richard H. Wyatt and Mary Watkins W; m. 6/14/30 to Anne Kinnaird Duncan; c. Mary Anne, Nancy Kinnaird and Wilson Watkins, Jr. Educ: Univ. Louisville, 22-23; LL.B, 27; Knox Col, LL.D, 45. Hon. LL.D, Univ. Louisville, 48. Polit. & Govt. Pos: Trial Attorney, Louisville, Ky, 34; Sinking Fund Cmnrs. Bd, 36; chmn, Louisville Cmt. on For. Rels, 40-41; mayor, Louisville, 41-45; chmn, Louisville Metrop. Area Defense Coun, Twice Awarded Citation of Merit, 42-45; mem. adv. bd, U.S. Conf. Mayors, 42-45; Spec. Rep. Bd. Econ. Warfare, N.Africa, 43; pres, Am. Soc. Planning Offs, 43-44; pres, Ky. Munic. League, 44; del-at-lg, Dem. Nat. Conv, since 44; pres, Louisville Area Develop. Asn, 44-45; pres, Am. Munic. Asn, 45; Housing Expediter and Adminstr. Nat. Housing Agency, 46; Personal Campaign Mgr, Stevenson, 52; co-ordinator Campaign Divs, 56; Ky. Chmn, Treas. Adv. Cmt, U.S. Savings Bonds Prog; chmn, Ky. Econ. Develop. Cmn, 60-63; Dem. Nat. Committeeman, Ky, 60-64; del, Dem. Nat. Conv, 68. Bus. & Prof. Pos: Mem. firm, Garnett & Van Winkle, 27-32; prof, Jefferson Sch. of Law, 29-35; attorney-at-law, 27-35; mem. firm, Peter, Heyburn, Marshall & Wyatt, 35-41; dir, Levy Bros, Inc, Standard Gravure Co, WHAS, Inc, Courier J. and Louisville Times Co, bd. of Roper Pub. Opinion Research Center, I.O.S, Ltd, Fonditalia Mgt. Co, S.A, Regent Fund Ltd. and Fund of Funds Ltd; sr. partner, Wyatt, Grafton & Sloss, 47-; mem. bd. trustees, Univ. Louisville, 50-58, chmn, 51-55. Mem: Dir, Am. Arbitration Asn; Am. and Louisville Bar Asns; Ky. Bar Asn.(secy, 30-34); Fed. Commun. Bar Asn; Am. Law Inst; Nat. Chmn, Jefferson-Jackson Day Dinners, 48-49; Pendennis, Louisville Country; Forest Farmers Asn; Rotary; Harmony Landing Country Club; Nat. Capital Dem; N.Y. Century Club. Recipient, U.S. Treasury Distinguished Serv. Award. Rel: Presbyterian. Mailing Add: Marion E. Taylor Building, Louisville, Ky. 40202.

WYCKOFF, DAVID COLE R
V.Chmn, Somerset Co. Rep. Party, N.J.
b. Somerville, N.J, 6/14/40; s. Frederick Raymond Wykoff and Ruth Cole W; m. 6/5/60 to Kerry Gay Shaffer; c. David Cole, Tracy Carroll, Whitney Ceone, Brent Preston and foster daughter, Susan Courtleigh. Educ: Hope Col; Kappa Eta Nu. Polit. & Govt. Pos: Dist. committeeman, Hillsborough Twp, N.J, 65, chmn. Rep. club, 66 and munic. chmn, 67; v.chmn, Somerset Co. Rep. Party, 68-; chmn, Somerset Co. Ment. Health Bd, 69- Bus. & Prof. Pos: Secy-treas, F.R. Wyckoff Agency, Somerville, N.J, 64-68 and pres, 68- Mem: Secy, Somerset Co. Ins. Agents Asn, 68-; dist. committeeman and mem-at-lg, Boy Scouts; past pres, Temple Christian Day Sch. PTA; Wyckoff Asn. in Am; Green Knoll Golf Course; YMCA, Adventure Tribe. Rel: Protestant; Elder, Neshanic Reformed Church. Mailing Add: Long Hill Rd, Box 90, Neshanic, N.J. 08853.

WYDLER, JOHN W. R
U.S. Rep, N.Y.
b. Brooklyn, N.Y, 6/9/24; m. Oct, 1959 to Brenda O'Sullivan; c. Christopher John, Kathleen Ellen and Elizabeth Ann. Educ: Harvard Law Sch, 50. Polit. & Govt. Pos: With U.S. Attorney's Off, 53-59; mem, N.Y. State Invest. Cmn. on Sch. Construction Irregularities, 59; U.S. Rep, N.Y, 63-; del, Rep. Nat. Conv, 68. Bus. & Prof. Pos: Lawyer; assoc. of A.A. Foreman, 59-61; mem, Wydler, Margolin, Balin, Pares & Soloway, 67- Mil. Serv: World War II, discharged as Sgt, 45; Lt, Air Force Res, Judge Adv. Off. Mem: Am. Legion; VFW; Lions; Ahepa; Sigma Chi; Dist. Attorney's Asn; Fed. and Nassau Co. Bar Asns; Protestant Lawyers' Asn; Mason; Elks; mem. at large, Boy Scouts of Am. Rel: Cathedral of the Incarnation; Mem, Bishop's Men and Men's Asns. Legal Res: 63 First St, Garden City, N.Y. 11530. Mailing Add: 225 Cannon House Office Bldg, Washington, D.C. 20515.

WYLIE, CHALMERS PANGBURN R
U.S. Rep, Ohio
b. Norwich, Ohio, 11/23/20; s. Chalmer C. Wylie and Margaret Pangburn W; m. 9/19/64 to Marjorie Ann Murnane; c. Jacquelyn and Bradley. Educ: Otterbein Col, 39-41; Ohio State Univ, 41-43; Harvard Law Sch, LL.B, 48. Polit. & Govt. Pos: Asst. Attorney Gen, Ohio, 48 & 51-54; asst. city attorney, Columbus, 49-50, city attorney, 54-57; supvr, Indust. Cmn, Ohio, 51-53; pres, Buckeye Rep. Club, 53; pres, Ohio Munci. League, 57; adminstr, Ohio Bur. Workmen's Comp, 57; mem, War Vet. Rep. Club and Capitol City Young Rep. Club; Ohio State Rep, 61-66 and chmn, Govt. Operations Cmt, Ohio State House of Rep; U.S. Rep, Ohio, 66- Bus. & Prof. Pos: Partner, Law Firm Gingher & Christensen, 59-; mem. bd. trustees, Blue Cross of Cent. Ohio, Inc, currently. Mil. Serv: Entered as Pvt, Army, 43, released as 1st Lt, 45, after serv. in 30th Inf. Div, five European Campaigns, World War II; Silver Star; Bronze Star; Croix de Guerre Unit Citation; Belgian Fouragier Unit Citation; Presidential Unit Citation with 2 Oak Leaf Clusters; Purple Heart; Lt. Col. Army Res. Mem: Columbus and Ohio Bar Asns; Ohio Munic. Attorneys Asn.(pres, 55-56); Kiwanis; former mem. bd. trustees, N.Broadway Methodist Church. Named one of Ten Men of Year, Columbus Citizen J. and One of Five Outstanding Young Men in Ohio, 55; received Distinguished Serv. Award, Outstanding Young Man of Year in Columbus, 55. Rel: Methodist. Mailing Add: 1019 Spring Grove Lane, Columbus, Ohio 43085.

WYLIE, WILLIAM M. R
Nebr. State Sen.
b. Antelope Co, Nebr; m. 8/18/24 to Haggard Wylie; c. Maxine, William and Mary. Educ: Pub, normal and bus. schs. Polit. & Govt. Pos: Nebr. State Sen, 61-; treas, Elgin Twp; mem, Co. Bd; mem. and chmn, Co. Welfare Bd; secy-treas, v.pres. of N.E. Nebr. Co. Offs. Asn. Bus. & Prof. Pos: Farmer and livestock breeder. Mem: Antelope Co. Fair Bd; W.Cedar Valley Cemetery Bd; Loan Cmt. of Elgin Coop Bank. Mailing Add: Elgin, Nebr. 68636. (1967)

WYLY, SAM R
Mem, Nat. Rep. Finance Cmt.
b. Lake Providence, La, 10/4/34; s. Charles Joseph Wyly, Sr. and Flora Evans W; m. 5/20/60 to Rosemary Acton; c. Evan Acton, Laurie Louise and Lisa Ann. Educ: La. Polytech. Inst, B.A, 56, Hon. Ph.D, 69; Univ. Mich, M.B.A, 57; W.A. Paton Scholarship; Phi Kappa Phi; Pi Kappa Alpha; Pi Kappa Delta; Beta Sigma Omicron; Omicron Delta Kappa. Polit. & Govt. Pos: Mem, Dallas Co. Rep. Finance Cmt, Tex, 66-68; Tex. finance chmn, 1968 Nixon for Pres. Campaign; del, Rep. Nat. Conv, 68; mem, Nat. Rep. Finance Cmt, 69-; mem, President's Cmt. on White House Fels. and chmn. adv. coun, Off. of Minority Bus. Enterprise, currently. Bus. & Prof. Pos: Sales rep, Serv. Bur. Corp, Dallas, Tex, 58-61; area sales mgr, Honeywell, Inc, 61-63; pres. and founder, Univ. Computing Co, 63-, chmn. bd. dirs, 69- Mil. Serv: Entered as A-3/C, Air Force Res, 57, released as A-2/C, 63, after serv. in Nat. Guard. Mem: Am. Mgt. Asn; Pres. Asn; Young Pres. Orgn; Dallas Citizens Coun; League for Educ. Adv. in Dallas; C. of C; Pres. Club of Univ. Mich; Dallas Petroleum Club; City Club of Dallas. Named One of Five Outstanding Young Men by Tex. Jaycees, 67; Named One of Ten Outstanding Young Men of Am. by U.S. Jaycees, 68; Distinguished Toastmaster for 1969, Big D Chap, Int. Toastmasters. Rel: Christian Scientist. Legal Res: 3905 Beverly, Dallas, Tex. 75205. Mailing Add: 1300 Frito-Lay Tower, Dallas, Tex. 75235.

WYMAN, EUGENE LESTER D
b. Los Angeles, Calif, 7/21/24; s. Abraham Wyman and Betty Koplowitz W; m. 8/29/54 to Rosalind Naomi Wiener; c. Betty Lyn, Robert Alan and Brad Hibbs. Educ: Northwest. Univ, B.S, 47; Harvard Law Sch, LL.B, 49; Delta Sigma Rho; Hardy Scholar, Harvard Legal Aid. Polit. & Govt. Pos: Chmn, South. Calif. Cent. Cmt, 61-62; chmn, Calif. State Dem. Cent. Cmt, 62-64; Dem. Nat. Committeeman, Calif, 64-68; treas, West. States Dem. Conf, 65-, v.chmn, 67; finance chmn, West. States Humphrey for President Campaign, 68; del, Dem. Nat. Conv, 68. Bus. & Prof. Pos: Attorney, Wyman, Bautzer,

Finell, Rothman and Kuchel, Beverly Hills, Calif, currently. Mem: Beverly Hills, Am, Los Angeles and Calif. Bar Asns; Calif. Bar; U.S. Dist. Court, South Dist, Calif; U.S. Supreme Court; Bd. Gov, Cedars-Sinai Med. Center, 64; bd. trustees, Temple Beth Am, 65; Westgate Masonic Lodge; Harvard Club; Big 10 Club; Friars Club; Los Angeles Athletic Club; Beverly Hills Club. Received Reiss-Davis Clinic Citation for work done on behalf of mentally retarded children, 64 and with Mrs. Wyman received Mr. and Mrs. American Citizen Award, Los Angeles B'nai B'rith Lodge 487, 64. Legal Res: 10430 Bellagio Rd, Los Angeles, Calif. 90024. Mailing Add: 9601 Wilshire Blvd, Beverly Hills, Calif. 90210.

WYMAN, IRIS JUANITA D
Committeewoman, State Dem. Exec. Cmt, Tex.
b. Wills Point, Tex, 1/6/15; d. Charles McClendon and La Rita Seago M; m. 6/30/35; to William Claton Wyman; c. William Claton, Jr. and Sally Ann. Educ: High sch. grad. Polit. & Govt. Pos: Committeewoman, State Dem. Exec. Cmt, Tex, 67-; alternate del, Dem. Nat. Conv, 68. Mem: Oak Cliff Country Club; Top-O'Cliff Club. Rel: Methodist. Legal Res: Sorcey Rd, Cedar Hill, Tex. 75104. Mailing Add: Route 1, Box 863, Cedar Hill, Tex. 75104.

WYMAN, LOUIS C. R
U.S. Rep, N.H.
b. Manchester, N.H, 3/16/17; s. Louis E. Wyman and Alice Crosby W; m. 1938 to Virginia E. Markley; c. Jo Ann and Louis E, II. Educ: Univ. N.H, B.S. with hon, 38; Harvard Law Sch, LL.B. cum laude, 41; Phi Kappa Phi; Theta Chi; Kappa Delta Pi; pres, Harvard Legal Aid Bur, 40-41; permanent secy. of class of 41, Harvard Law Sch. Polit. & Govt. Pos: Bd. dir, N.H. Coun. on World Affairs; Citizens Adv. Cmt. to Nat. Cmn. on Govt. Security; gen. counsel to U.S. Senate Cmt. on Campaign Expenditures, 46; secy. to Hon. Styles Bridges, 47; counsel, Joint Cong. Cmt. on For. Econ. Coop, 48-49; attorney gen, N.H, 53-61; chmn, N.H. Cmn. on Interstate Coop, 53-61; mem, N.H. Ballot Law Cmn. and N.H. Judicial Coun, 53-61; cmnr, Uniform State Laws for N.H, 53-61; del-at-lg, Rep. Nat. Conv, 56 & 60; legis. counsel to Gov, N.H, 61; U.S. Rep, N.H, 62-64 & 67- Bus. & Prof. Pos: Partner, Wyman, Bean & Tefft, Law Firm, Manchester, N.H. Mil. Serv: Naval Res, 42-46, Lt. Mem: Am. Bar Asn; chmn, Cmt. on Jurisp. & Law Reform, 61-63; Cmt. on Communist Tactics, Strategy & Objectives, 55-61; pres, Nat. Asn. Attorneys Gen, 56-57; fel. Am. Col. Trial Lawyers; D.C, Fla, Mass. and N.H. Bar Asns; Mason, Shrine, Bektash Temple; VFW; Am. Legion; Elks; SAR. Mailing Add: 121 Shaw St, Manchester, N.H. 03104.

WYND, ELIZABETH S. R
b. 2/16/14; d. Robert S. Steele and Florence Freeman S; m. to James Wynd, Jr.(deceased); c. One daughter. Educ: Dean Sch. of Bus. Polit. & Govt. Pos: Pa. State Rep, 61-67; former dep. co. treas; chmn, Legis. Cmt. of Wyoming Co. Rep. Bus. & Prof. Pos: Housewife; former law secy, Co. reporter. Mailing Add: R.D. 3, Tunkhannock, Pa. 18657. (1967)

WYNN, SPROESSER R
b. Dallas, Tex, 12/18/13; s. William Clement Wynn and Amy Hirschfeld W; m. 4/11/36 to Mildred Patton; c. Carol (Mrs. C. Harold Brown) and Betty (Mrs. Paul J. McDonald). Educ: Tex. Christian Univ, A.B, 33; Univ. Tex, LL.B, 35; Kappa Sigma. Polit. & Govt. Pos: State chmn, Tex. for Tower, 66; chmn, State Rep. Task Force Educ, 67; chmn, Tower Senate Club, 67-; del, Dem. Nat. Conv, 68; chmn, State Rep. Cmt. Del, 68; Rep. nominee, Attorney Gen. Tex, 69. Bus. & Prof. Pos: Dir, First Nat. Bank Ft. Worth, 65-; chmn, Family Law Sect, State Bar, 67-68; dir, First Worth Corp, 67- Mem: Fel. Tex. Bar Found; Consistory; KCCH (32°); Shrine (past potentate). Rel: Disciples of Christ. Legal Res: Apt. 105, 4320 Bellaire Dr. S, Ft. Worth, Tex. 76109. Mailing Add: Continental Bank Bldg, Ft. Worth, Tex. 76102.

WYRICK, DONALD NORWOOD D
b. Idabel, Okla, 1/10/40; s. Thomas Jefferson Wyrick and Hazel Norwood W; m. 6/20/62 to Helen Juan Sullivan; c. Regina Lynn and Jeffrey Lance. Educ: Southeast. State Col, 58-60; South. Methodist Univ, 67; Sigma Tau Gamma. Polit. & Govt. Pos: Chmn, Titus Co. Dem. Cent. Cmt, Tex, 64-68. Bus. & Prof. Pos: V.pres, First State Bank, Idabel, Okla, 67-; pres, McCurtain Co. Prod. Corp, Idabel, 67- Mil. Serv: Entered as Pvt, Army, 60, released as Sgt, 65, after serv. in 49th Armored Div. Mem: C. of C; Nat. Asn. of Bank Auditors and Controllers (pres, 66); pres, Am. Cancer Soc, 64; Idabel Lions; Jaycees (treas, 63 and v.pres, 65); pres, United Fund, 66 & 68; mem, Idabel Bd. Educ; secy, McCurtain Co. Commun. Trust, 69; dir, Bankers Admin. Inst, 63, 66 & 69; dir, Idabel Libr. Bd, 68 & 69. Rel: Baptist. Mailing Add: 510 S.E. Madison, Idabel, Okla. 74745.

WYSE, JACOB FREDERICK R
Chmn, Edgefield Co. Rep. Party, S.C.
b. Lexington Co, S.C, 8/14/15; s. James Kelley Wyse and Martha Adella Fulmer W; m. 6/24/39 to Annie Ruth Bickley. Educ: Clemson Univ. Polit. & Govt. Pos: Chmn, Edgefield Co. Rep. Party, S.C, currently. Mil. Serv: Entered Navy, 45, released as Seaman 1/C, after serv. in Pac. Mem: Am. Legion; 40 et 8; Grange; pres, S.C. Voc. Agr. Asn, 48. Rel: Lutheran. Mailing Add: 509 Roland Ave, Johnston, S.C. 29832. (1967)

WYSINGER, VOSSA EDWARD, JR. R
Dir-at-Lg, Calif. State Rep. Assembly.
b. Fresno, Calif, 8/23/22; s. Vossa Edward Wysinger, Sr. and Kathlyn Boatman W; m. 10/14/43 to Winona Ardez Jones; c. Vernon Edward, Marta Lewis, Myra Lynn and Jeannette (Mrs. Atkins). Educ: Pasadena City Col, Bus. Admin, Dale Carnegie Course, 40-42. Polit. & Govt. Pos: Campaign worker, Gov. Earl Warren and U.S. Sen. William Knowland for Gov. Calif, 50's; sector chmn, Richard Nixon for Pres, 50 precincts, S.W. Berkeley, 60; precinct and sector chmn, Richard Nixon for Gov. Calif, 62; mem. bd. dirs, N.Berkeley Rep. Assembly, 65, v.pres, 66 & 67; mem. bd. dirs, Alameda Co. Coord.Rep. Assembly, 66, area v.pres, 67 & 68, treas, 69-; north. Calif. co-chmn, Stevenson for State Bd. Equalization Campaign Cmt, 66; mem, Alameda Co. Rep. Develop. Cmt, 67; mem. state and nat. affairs cmt, Calif. State Rep. Assembly, 67 & 68, dir-at-lg, 67-; mem. labor cmt, Calif. Rep. State Cent. Cmt, 67 & 68; Rep. cand, U.S. Cong, Seventh Cong. Dist, 68; exec. dir, Rep. Minority Adv. Cmt, 68; adv. and field dir. in minority areas, Robert Hannon, Calif. State Sen. Campaign, 11th Dist, 68; hq. chmn. and asst. to Thomas J. Miles for field opers. in minority areas, Nixon-Agnew Presidential Campaign, 68; mem. Calif. state adv. cmt. and chmn. Berkeley cmt, Max Rafferty U.S. Sen. Campaign, 68. Bus. & Prof. Pos: Real estate developer, Apt. bldgs. and motels, 52-64; property mgr, 64-; author and book publisher, polit. sci. subjects, 64- Mil. Serv: Entered as Seaman, Coast Guard, 43, released as PO 1/C, 45, after serv. in U.S.S. Sterope, S.Pac. Theater, 44-45. Publ: The Celestial Democracy, Celestial Democracy Co, 66; 'Minority Report,' Bayview Mag, 68. Mem: Bd. dirs, Orviss Mem; VFW; Concerned Berkeley Citizens; AFL-CIO (Metal Trades Coun). Rel: Religious Science. Legal Res: 3228 Idaho St, Berkeley, Calif. 94702. Mailing Add: P.O. Box 158, Berkeley, Calif. 94704.

Y

YAGER, JOHN J. R
b. Deer Trail, Colo, 9/6/21; s. Reggie Yager and Elizabeth Jolly Y; m. 12/31/44 to Helen Laverne Shouse; c. Linda Rae, Jeri Lynne and John Corey. Educ: Deer Trail High Sch. Polit. & Govt. Pos: Chmn, Morgan Co. Rep. Party, Colo, 61-69. Bus. & Prof. Pos: Owner, operator and mgr, ranch and farm. Mem: Morgan Co. Farm Bur; Toastmasters Int. Rel: Presbyterian. Mailing Add: 315 Grant, Fort Morgan, Colo. 80701. (1967)

YAHNER, PAUL J. D
Pa. State Rep.
b. Patton, Pa, 11/8/08; s. Ambrose Yahner and Mary Sharbaugh Y; m. to Rosemarie Farabaugh; c. 13. Educ: Pa. State Univ. Polit. & Govt. Pos: Mem, People to People agr. del. touring Communist countries, 63; Pa. State Rep, 64- Bus. & Prof. Pos: Farmer; owner, operator 1,110 acre livestock and poultry farm; dir, First Nat. Bank and Cambria Co. Mutual Fire Ins. Co. Mem: C. of C; Cambria Co. Agr. Exten. Asn; K. of C; Knight of St. George; Pa. Farm Bur. Fedn; Patton Grange. Pa. Master Farmer, 61. Rel: Catholic. Mailing Add: R.D. 1, Box 165, Patton, Pa. 16668. (1967)

YAMAMOTO, TOSHIKO TOSHI R
Mem. Exec. Cmt, Calif. Rep. State Cent. Cmt.
b. Seattle, Wash, 12/1/15; d. Mokuji Yasutake and Tome Watanabe Y; m. 8/19/44 to George Masashi Yamamoto. Educ: Univ. Wash, 39-40; Am. Barber Col, Los Angeles, Calif, grad, 52. Polit. & Govt. Pos: Recording secy, Monterey Park Rep. Women's Federated, Calif, 57-58; second v.pres, Japanese Am. Rep. of South Calif, 66-67, pres, 67-69, Am. of Japanese Ancestry Rep. Club, 69-; corresponding secy, Monterey Park Rep. Club, United Rep. of Calif, 67-68; mem, Calif. Rep. State Cent. Cmt, 67-, secy. nationalities cmt, 67-69, mem. exec. cmt, 69-; alternate del, Rep. Nat. Conv, 68; mem, Calif. adv. coun, Nat. Women for Nixon Cmt, 68; elector, Calif. Rep. Party, 68; mem, Calif. State Bd. Barber Exam, 68- Mem: Japanese Barber Asn. Los Angeles (dir. pub. rels, 56-64); Los Angeles Bonsai Soc.(recording secy, 56-57); Nat. Fedn. Bus. & Prfnl. Women's Club (chmn. appointive cmt, E. Los Angeles Chap, 69-70); Japan Am. Soc; Montebello Rep. Women's Federated; South. Calif. Nisei Women's Golf Asn. Rel: Episcopal. Mailing Add: 253 S. Gerhart Ave, East Los Angeles, Calif. 90022.

YAMASAKI, MAMORU D
Hawaii State Sen.
b. Paia, Maui, Hawaii, 9/6/16; s. Isuke Yamasaki and Sode Kawaoka Y; single. Polit. & Govt. Pos: Mem, Dem. Cent. Cmt, Territory of Hawaii, 54-59; clerk, Senate Ways and Means Cmt, 30th Territorial Legis, 59; Hawaii State Rep, 59-67; mem, Hawaii State Dem. Cent. Cmt, 60-66; Hawaii State Sen, 68- Mem: Former mem. bd. of dirs, KRR Fed. Credit Union; adv. bd, Maui Salvation Army; bd. of dirs, Maui Commun. Chest, Maui Econ. Opportunity and Lahaina Restoration Found. Rel: Buddhist. Legal Res: 238 West Lanai St, Kahului, Maui, Hawaii 96732. Mailing Add: P.O. Box 1516, Kahului, Maui, Hawaii 96732.

YANCEY, ALMA NADINE D
b. Holts Summit, Mo, 5/20/18; d. Frederick William Koelling and Grace Roedel K; m. 11/14/40 to Hudson Brown Yancey; c. Gracia Lynn. Educ: Jefferson City Sr. High, dipl, 36. Polit. & Govt. Pos: Secy, Women's Dem. Club, Callaway Co, Mo, 1 year, treas, 1 year; mem, Callaway Co. Dem. Cent. Cmt, 12 years, secy, 2 years; clerk and key punch operator, Dept. Revenue, 48-49; machine operator, Treas. Dept, 49-50; clerk-typist, Pub. Serv. Cmn, Mo, 55-56; alternate del, Dem. Nat. Conv, 68; del, Dem. State Conv, 68; committeewoman, Cedar Twp. Dem. Party, currently. Mem: Eastern Star; Karim Khan Grotto Auxiliary; Women's Dem. Club, Callaway Co; Dem. State-Club, Mo; Meadow Lake Acres Country Club. Attended two inaugural balls for Gov. Warren E. Hearnes, 65 & 69. Rel: United Church of Christ. Mailing Add: New Bloomfield, Mo. 65063.

YANCEY, KYLE D
b. Tampa, Fla, 1/17/26; s. John Dewey Yancey and Eva Odom Y; m. 6/08/57 to Janet Nicholson; c. Kathryn Ann, Phillip Kyle and Stephen Charles. Educ: Ga. State Col, Atlanta Div, 46-47; Emory Univ, 47-48; Univ. Ga, LL.B, 51. Polit. & Govt. Pos: Ga. State Sen, 33rd Dist, 63-66. Bus. & Prof. Pos: Attorney, admitted to bar 51; admitted to practice in all Appellate Courts, Ga, U.S. Court of Appeals, Fed. Dist. Court and U.S. Supreme Court. Mil. Serv: Air Force; Occup. Medal. Mem: Cobb Co, Ga, and Am. Bar Asns; Lions (pres, 54-55); Mason. Rel: Baptist. Mailing Add: Austell, Ga. 30001.

YANO, VINCENT H. D
Hawaii State Sen.
m. to Eloise Y; c. Six sons and four daughters. Educ: Univ. Dayton, Ohio; Harvard Law Sch. Polit. & Govt. Pos: Hawaii State Sen, 62-, chmn, Pub. Cmt, Hawaii State Senate. Bus. & Prof. Pos: Lawyer; pres, First Financial Savings and Loan Asn, Rubber Stamp House. Mem: Bd. of St. Francis Hosp; bd. of Chaminade Col; bd. of Hawaii Asn. for Retarded Children; former pres, Star of the Sea, St. Louis High Sch. Parent-Teacher Guilds. Appointed Knight of the St. Sylvester by Pope Paul VI. Legal Res: 1466 Pule Place, Chaminade Terrace, Honolulu, Hawaii 96816. Mailing Add: Suite 800, 333 Queen St, Honolulu, Hawaii 96813. (1967)

YARBER, CLEOPHUS KENNETH D
Chmn, Ark. Christian Dem.
b. Ashdown, Ark, 9/23/28; s. Gus Yarber and Clara Jackson Y; m. 5/30/48 to Inez Witherspoon; c. Gussie Ann, Diane, Clara M, Catherine Shuntina, Cleophus, Annothy, Gregory, Darrell, Garland and Marcus. Educ: Tyler Barber Col, 1 year; United Baptist Theol. Sem, 4 years. Polit. & Govt. Pos: Chmn, Ark. Christian Dem, 59-; bd. mem, Coordinating Cmt, 66, 68 & 69 and State Dem. Cmt, 67-68; mem. trustee bd, Ark. Baptist Col, 66 & 68; cmnr, Rural Develop. Authority, 67-; chmn, Ark. Voter Registrn. Cmt, 68; mem, Southwest Develop. Bd. of Dirs, 68; del, Dem. Nat. Conv, 68; jury cmnr; second v.moderator, Southwest. Dist; cand, Bd. Dirs. Labor in Ark. Bus. & Prof. Pos: Owner and mgr, Yarber Barber Shop, 50-; pastor, Lonoke Baptist Church, 57- Mem: Twin City Bus. Civic League; Willo Grove Lodge; Am. Automobile Asn; Humble Travel Club. Rel: Baptist. Mailing Add: 405 Park Ave, Texarkana, Ark. 75501.

YARBOROUGH, FOSTER HALL D
S.C. State Rep.
b. Jenkinsville, S.C, 9/18/21; s. David Glenn Yarborough and Helen Whatley Y; m. 3/22/43 to Elizabeth Wolfe. Educ: Univ. of S.C, B.S, 41. Polit. & Govt. Pos: S.C. State Rep, 57-; Probation Counselor Domestic Rels. Court; supvr, Orangeburg Soil Conserv. Dist. Bus. & Prof. Pos: Attorney-at-law; farmer; prin, Wagener Centralized Schs, 41-42; Cameron Schs, 50-55. Mil. Serv: Air Force, aerial navigator, 42-45; former Capt, Air Force Res. Mailing Add: Box 606, Orangeburg, S.C. 29115.

YARBOROUGH, JESS D
b. Chester, S.C, 12/30/06; s. James Henry Yarborough and Lilly Hardin Y; m. 5/28/33 to Mildred Louise Blanding; c. Mrs. Frank U. Greer, Jesse H, Jr. and James A. Educ: Clemson Univ, grad. and post grad. work; Furman Univ; George Peabody Col. and Univ. of Fla; pres, Jr. Class and Honor Coun. Polit. & Govt. Pos: Cmnr, Dade Co. Cmn, Fla, 49-56; mem, Dade Co. Sch. Bd, 58-60; Fla. State Rep, Dade Co, 63-69; Fla. Pub. Serv. Cmnr, 69- Bus. & Prof. Pos: Pres, State Asn. of Co. Cmnr, Fla, 56 and Fla. Adv. Coun, Coordinates Co. Legis, 56. Mil. Serv: Entered as 1st Lt, Air Force, 42, released as Maj, 46. Mem: Am. Soc. of Appraisers; Nat. Asn. of Realty Bd; Miami Realty Bd; Fla. Turnpike Cmt, 56; past. pres, Miami Kiwanis and Orange Bowl Cmt; Shrine. Honored for outstanding serv. to athletics by Fla. High Sch. Coaching Asn, 42 & 61. Rel: Baptist. Legal Res: 2601 S.W. Fourth St, Miami, Fla. 33135. Mailing Add: 700 S. Adams St, Tallahassee, Fla. 32304.

YARBOROUGH, RALPH WEBSTER D
U.S. Sen, Tex.
b. Chandler, Tex, 6/8/03; s. Charles Richard Yarborough and Nannie Jane Spear Y; m. to Opal Warren; c. Richard Warren. Educ: Sam Houston State Teachers Col; U.S. Mil. Acad, 1 year; Univ. of Tex. Law Sch, LL.B, 27. Hon. D:H.L, Lincoln Col. Polit. & Govt. Pos: Asst. attorney gen, Tex, 31-34; mem, bd. of dirs, Lower Colo. River Authority, 35-36; dist judge, 53rd Judicial Dist, 36-41; presiding judge, Third Admin. Judicial Dist; mem, Tex. Bd. of Law Exam, 47-51; U.S. Sen, Tex, 57-; del, Interparliamentary Union, Brazil, 62, Dublin, Ireland, 65, Canberra, Australia, 66, Tehran, Iran, 66, Palma, Mallorca, Spain, 67, Lima, Peru, 68 and Vienna, Austria, 69; del, Dem. Nat. Conv, 64. Bus. & Prof. Pos: Former teacher; lawyer. Mil. Serv: Inf, Army, discharged Lt. Col, 46. Publ: Frank Dobie: Man and Friend, Potomac Corral of the Westerners, 67; 'Sam Houston—Giant on a Postage Stamp,' Texas Avenue at Main Street, 64; 'Lincoln as a Liberal Statesman,' 112, Lincoln for the Ages, Doubleday, 64. Mem: Travis Co, El Paso and Am. Bar Asns; former dir, State Bar of Tex; Am. Law Inst; Am. Judicature Soc; Nat. Legal Aid Asn. Am. Polit. Sci. Asn; Am. Legion; VFW; Phi Delta Phi; Acacia; Order of the Coif; Mason; Shrine; Moose; hon. mem, Tex. Libr. Asn. Hon. Fel, Postgrad. Center for Ment. Health, N.Y.C; Distinguished Serv. Award, Los Angeles Co, Calif. Rel: Baptist. Legal Res: Austin, Tex. Mailing Add: 110 Maryland Ave. N.E, Washington, D.C. 20002.

YARBROUGH, JOE CONE D
b. Smith Co, Tex, 8/21/20; s. W.E. Yarbrough and Gertie Land Y; m. 12/24/42 to Helen Louise Warmouth; c. Linda Jo (Mrs. William F. Brown, Jr), Diane Louise, Shirley Ann and Evelyn Claudette. Educ: Winnsboro High Sch, grad, 37. Polit. & Govt. Pos: Del, Dem. Nat. Conv, 64 & 68; dist. committeeman, Dem. Party, Tex, 68- Bus. & Prof. Pos: Mem. bd. dirs, Bassett Nat. Bank, El Paso Jr. Col, Fortune Life Ins. Co. and Pub. Serv. Bd, currently; mem. adv. cmt, Univ. Tex, El Paso, currently; mem. bd. mgrs, R.E. Thomason Gen. Hosp, currently. Mem: Bd. dirs, El Paso C. of C, El Paso Boys Club, El Paso United Fund and El Paso YMCA; past pres, El Paso Home Builders Asn; charter pres, El Paso Lower Valley Rotary Club; Mason (32°); Elks; Odd Fellows. Rel: Methodist. Mailing Add: 9540 Desert Ridge, El Paso, Tex. 79926.

YARBROUGH, GEORGE MALONE D
b. Red Banks, Miss, 8/15/16; married. Polit. & Govt. Pos: Miss. State Rep, 52-56; Miss. State Sen, 56-69 and Pres-Pro-Tem, Miss. State Senate, 60-69; acting Lt. Gov, Miss, 67-69. Bus. & Prof. Pos: Farmer; cattle dealer; ins; newspaper. Mem: Mason; Am. Legion; K. of P; 40 et 8; Farm Bur; Lions; Citizens Coun. Rel: Methodist. Mailing Add: Box 17, Red Banks, Miss. 38661. (1967)

YARBROUGH, WALTER HERMAN R
Idaho State Sen.
b. Maywood, Mo. 8/15/12; s. Edward Francis Yarbrough and Amelia M. Herman Y; m. 7/17/41 to Lucy Mae Rocks; c. George Edward, Richard Alan, Stephen Anthony and Walter Carl. Educ: Northeast Mo. State Teachers Col, 3 years. Polit. & Govt. Pos: Chmn, Co. Fair Bd, Idaho, 55-61; Idaho State Sen, 64- Bus. & Prof. Pos: Pres, Boise Valley Angus Asn, Idaho, 56-60; Idaho State Angus Asn, 62-66; v.pres, West. States Angus Asn, 64-; nat. dir, Am. Angus Asn, 67- Mil. Serv: Entered as Pvt, Army Corp Engrs, 41, released as Maj. Construction Engr, 46, after serv. in 1778 Engr. Coast Bn, Pac, 45-46; Lt. Col. Res, 46-63; Presidential Unit Citation. Mem: Mason; Shrine; past comdr, Am. Legion Post 132. Rel: Protestant. Mailing Add: Question Mark Ranch, Grand View, Idaho 83624.

YARDLEY, DAN D
Mont. State Rep.
b. Big Timber, Mont, 10/15/28; s. Ray Yardley (mother deceased); m. 12/25/59 to Jo Anne Frizzelle; c. Thomas Edward and Mary Elizabeth. Educ: Univ. Mont, LL.B, 52 and B.A, 55; N.Y. Univ, LL.M, 56. Polit. & Govt. Pos: Mont. State Rep, Dist. 14, 69- Mil. Serv: Army, 2 years. Mem: Mont. Bar Asn. Legal Res: 802 S. Eighth St, Livingston, Mont. 59047. Mailing Add: P.O. Box 482, Livingston, Mont. 59047.

YARDLEY, JAMES FREDRICK R
Chmn, Garfield Co. Cmn, Utah
b. Hatch, Utah, 11/19/21; s. John Alfred Yardley and Lareta Stoney Y; m. 1/17/45 to Alta Hatch; c. James V. and John Wallace. Educ: Utah State Univ, B.S, 47; Lambda Chi Alpha. Polit. & Govt. Pos: Rep. precinct chmn, Utah, 64-65; chmn, Garfield Co. Rep. Party, 65-69; mem. exec. cmt, Utah Asn. of Co, 68-69; chmn, Five Co. Orgn, 69; chmn, Garfield Co. Cmn, 67- Mil. Serv: Entered as Aviation Cadet, Navy, 42, released as Cadet, 44, after serv. in V 5 Naval Aviation Prog. Mem: Independent Ins. Agents; Lions; Am. Legion; Comdr. Dept. Utah Am. Legion, 63-64; C. of C; Jr. C. of C. Rel: Latter-day Saint. Mailing Add: Panguitch, Utah 84759.

YARDLEY, WILLIAM LAWRENCE R
b. Keene, N.H, 2/20/28; married; c. Five. Educ: Marlboro Schs. Polit. & Govt. Pos: N.H. State Rep, 57-69; former selectman, Marlboro, N.H. Bus. & Prof. Pos: Farmer; operator retail milk bus. Mem: Cheshire Co. Del, road agent; past pres. of Lions Club; Odd Fellows; Grange. Rel: Protestant; dir of Federated Church of Marlboro. Mailing Add: Horse Hill Farm, Marlboro, N.H. 03455. (1967)

YARMOLINSKY, ADAM D
b. N.Y.C, 11/17/22; s. Avrahm Yarmolinsky and Babette Deutsch Y; m. 3/24/45 to Harriet Rypins; c. Sarah, Tobias, Benjamin and Matthew. Educ: Harvard Col, A.B, 43, Yale Law Sch, LL.B, 48. Polit. & Govt. Pos: Law clerk, Judge Charles E. Clark, U.S. Second Circuit Court of Appeals, 48-49; law clerk, Justice Reed, U.S. Supreme Court, 50-51; spec. asst. to Secy. of Defense, 61-64, prin. dep. asst. secy. of defense for int. security affairs, 65-66; dep. dir, President's Task Force on the War Against Poverty, 64; chief, U.S. Emergency Relief Mission, Dominican Repub, 65. Bus. & Prof. Pos: Assoc. firm, Root, Ballantine, Harlan, Bushby & Palmer, N.Y.C, 49-50; Cleary Gottlieb, Friendly & Ball, Wash, D.C, 51-55; lectr, Am. Univ. Law Sch, 51-56; secy, Fund for the Repub, 55-57; pub. affairs ed, Doubleday & Co, 57-59; lectr, Yale Law Sch, 58-59; consult, philanthropic foundations, 59-61; prof. law, Harvard Law Sch, 66-; mem. inst. polit, John Fitzgerald Kennedy Sch. Govt, Harvard, 66. Mil. Serv: Entered as Pvt, Army Air Corps, 43, released as Sgt, 46. Publ: Ed, Case Studies in Personnel Security, Bur. Nat. Affairs, 55; Recognition of Excellence, Edgar Stern Family Found, Free Press Glencoe, 60; articles in magazines and newspapers. Mem: N.Y. and D.C. Bars; Asn. Bar City of N.Y; Am. Bar Asn; Am. Law Inst; Coun. For Rels; Inst. Strategic Studies; Hudson Inst; bd. med, Nat. Acad. Sci; Citizens Housing & Planning Asn.(exec. bd); sponsoring mem, Civil Defense Forum; Inst. Research Poverty (nat. adv. cmt); trustee, Robert F. Kennedy Mem; trustee, Vera Inst. Justice; fel. Am. Acad. Arts & Sci; fel. Ezra Stiles Col; Asn. Harvard Alumni (dir, 65-68). Dept. of Defense Distinguished Pub. Serv. Medal, 66. Legal Res: 6 Longfellow Park, Cambridge, Mass. 02138. Mailing Add: Harvard Law School, Cambridge, Mass. 02138.

YATES, ALBERT R
Chmn, Spencer Co. Rep. Cmt, Ky.
b. Washington Co, Ky, 10/24/98; s. Charles S. Yates and Elma D. Graham Y; m. 2/9/21 to Frances E. Downs; c. Robert D, Frances (Mrs. Florence) and Nancy (Mrs. Heady). Educ: High Sch. Polit. & Govt. Pos: Chmn, Spencer Co. Rep. Cmt, Ky, 58- Bus. & Prof. Pos: Chmn, Spencer Co. Agr. Stabilization and Conserv. Cmt, 40-60; v.pres, West. Dist. Warehousing Corp, 47-66; v.pres, Salt River R.E.C.C, Burdstown, Ky, 50-66; v.pres, West. Dist. Redrying and Storage Corp. Mem: Mason; Spencer Co. Farm Bur. Rel: Baptist. Mailing Add: Fisherville, Ky. 40023.

YATES, GLENN, JR. D
Va. State Del.
b. Walnut Ridge, Ark, 9/7/27; m. to Christina Galatis. Educ: Univ. Pa; Pratt Inst; Univ. Va. Polit. & Govt. Pos: Va. State Del, 66- Bus. & Prof. Pos: Elec. and struct. engr. architect. Mem: C. of C; YMCA; Kiwanis; Torch Club; Am. Cancer Soc; Elizabeth Manor Golf & Country Club. First Honor Award for excellence in design, Portsmouth Pub. Libr, 64. Rel: Greek Orthodox Church. Mailing Add: 405 Sycamore Rd, Portsmouth, Va. 23707.

YATES, ORAL LOVE, SR. D
b. Waynesville, N.C, 7/20/02; s. Dock P. Yates and Emma Queen Y; m. to Pearl Justice; c. Francis Emma (Mrs. Stout) and Oral Love, Jr. Educ: West. Carolina Teachers Col, 21; Cecil's Bus. Col, 22. Polit. & Govt. Pos: Chmn, Crabtree-Iron Duff Sch. Bd, N.C, 36-42; pres, Haywood Co. Farm Bur, 49-50, dir, 58-62; field rep, N.C. Farm Bur, 51-58, dir, Dist. 7, 62-; N.C. State Rep, 51 & 59; N.C. State Sen, 63-66. Bus. & Prof. Pos: Farmer. Mem: Dir, Haywood Co. Ment. Health Asn, 62; asst. dir, Haywood Co. Civil Defense, 60-62; bd. of dirs, Canton Kiwanis Club (pres, 60; Lt. Gov, Div. One, Carolinas Dist, Int. Kiwanis, 68); Brotherhood of Rwy. and Steamship Clerks; dir, Waynesville Chap, Am. Red Cross, 49-58; chmn, Waynesville area, Red Cross, 50; pres, PTA, 47-51; asst. scout master, Troop 8, 45-46; chmn, Scout Cmt. 11, 46-50; Bd. of Temperance, West. Carolina Conf, 42-50; bd. of dirs, Brevard Music Center, 65-; chmn, Bldg. and Finance Cmt, N.C. Farm Bur. Fedn, 67- Rel: Methodist; Lay speaker; supt, Davis Chapel Sunday Sch, 51-57, 64; dist. steward, 42-48; bd. of stewards, 50. Mailing Add: Hill 'n' Dale Farm, Waynesville, N.C. 28786.

YATES, SIDNEY R. D
U.S. Rep, Ill.
b. Chicago, Ill, 8/27/09; m. 1935 to Adeline J. Holleb. Educ: Univ. Chicago, Ph.B, 31 and J.D, 33. Polit. & Govt. Pos: Asst. attorney for Ill. State Bank Receiver, 35-37; asst. attorney gen. to Ill. Commerce Cmn, 37-40; U.S. Rep, Ill, 48-62 & 65-; U.S. Rep. with rank of Ambassador, to Trusteeship Coun.

of UN, 63-64. Bus. & Prof. Pos: Lawyer. Mil. Serv: Lt, Navy. Mem: Am, Chicago and Ill. State Bar Asns; Am. Vet. Cmt; Chicago Coun. on For. Rels: City Club of Chicago; Decalogue Soc. of Lawyers (ed, Bul, 47). Legal Res: 3500 Lake Shore Dr, Chicago, Ill. Mailing Add: 2234 Rayburn House Office Bldg, Washington, D.C. 20515.

YATRON, GUS D
U.S. Rep, Pa.
b. Reading, Pa, 10/16/27; s. George H. Yatron and Theano Lazos Y; m. to Mildred Menzies; c. George and Theana. Educ: Kutztown State Teachers Col; active in scholastic sports. Polit. & Govt. Pos: Mem, Reading Sch. Bd, Pa, 55-61; former Pa. State Rep; U.S. Rep, Sixth Dist, Pa, 68- Bus. & Prof. Pos: Owner, Yatron's Ice Cream, currently. Mem: Dir, Reading Pub. Mus. and Art Gallery; Reading Hosp. Bd. of Mgr; Reading Recreation Bd; Berks Co. Athletic Asn. Rel: Greek Orthodox. Legal Res: 1908 Hessian Rd, Reading, Pa. 19602. Mailing Add: 1510 Longworth House Office Bldg, Washington, D.C. 20515.

YEAGER, WELDON OSBORNE R
Mich. State Rep.
b. Ohio, 7/26/22; s. Carl O. Yeager and Stella F. McCall Y; m. to Page Wise; c. Richard, Mark, Carey and Scott. Educ: Wayne State Univ, B.S. in bus. admin, 56. Polit. & Govt. Pos: Mem, 17th Cong. Dist. Rep. Orgn, Mich, 49-, chmn, 62-64 & 66-68; del, Mich. Constitutional Conv, 61-62; del, Rep. Nat. Conv, 64 & 68; dir, Workmen's Compensation Dept, Mich, 64-67; Mich. State Rep, 69- Bus. & Prof. Pos: Pres, Yeager and Co, Inc, currently. Mil. Serv: Entered as Pvt, Air Force, 40, released as Capt, 46. Mem: Mil. Order of World Wars; Am. Legion; Detroit Press Club; Mich. Cancer Found. Rel: Congregational. Legal Res: Detroit, Mich. Mailing Add: P.O. Box 119, Lansing, Mich. 48901.

YEAGLEY, DONALD RAE D
b. La Paz, Ind, 5/6/20; s. Earl Edgar Yeagley and Ethel Mangun Y; m. 5/10/41 to Evelyn Mae Roush; c. Elizabeth June, Thomas Roy and James Allan. Educ: Bendix Sch. of Tech, Tool & Die Maker, 42. Polit. & Govt. Pos: Ind. State Rep, 59-62; del, White House Conf. on Youth, 60; Ind. State Sen, 62-67; mem, Ind. Conserv. Cmt, 65-66. Bus. & Prof. Pos: Citizenship dir, United Auto Workers, 65-66. Mem: Moose; Local 9, UAW, South Bend, Ind. Rel: Presbyterian. Mailing Add: 4482 N. Priscilla Ave, Indianapolis, Ind. 46226. (1967)

YEATES, CHARLES H. R
Chmn, Allegan Co. Rep. Cmt, Mich.
b. Chichester, Eng, 7/8/16; s. Charles Yeates and Amy H. Yates Y; m. 1/16/48 to Winifred M. Gerry; c. Penelope A. and Alan H. Educ: Univ. London, 34-38. Polit. & Govt. Pos: Chmn, Benzie Co. Rep. Cmt, Mich, 58-64; councilman and mayor-pro-tem, Frankfort City Coun, 62-64; finance chmn, Allegan Co. Rep. Cmt, 65, chmn, 66-; mem, Crippled Children's Cmn, Mich, 67-; del, Rep. Nat. Conv, 68. Bus. & Prof. Pos: Admin. asst, Local Govt. Serv, Eng, 38-39; adminstr, Devizes Hosp, Wilts, Eng, 48-51; acct, Allis Chalmers Mfg. Co, 51-55; adminstr, Paul Oliver Mem. Hosp, Frankfort, Mich, 55-63; adminstr, Allegan Health Center, 63- Mil. Serv: Entered as Pvt, British Army, 39, released as Capt, 48, after serv. in Med. Corps, France, 39-40, Middle East, 40-44 and India, 45-47. Mem: Am. Col. Hosp. Adminstr; past pres, Rotary; Past Master, Mason; Shrine. Rel: Episcopal; Lay reader. Legal Res: 528 Marshall, Allegan, Mich. 49010. Mailing Add: Allegan Health Center, Allegan, Mich. 49010.

YEAW, EARL FRANK R
b. Dover, Vt, 10/25/95; m. to Edna Hager. Educ: Dover schs. Polit. & Govt. Pos: Vt. State Rep, 45-51 & 65-66; former constable, selectman, sch. dir. and justice of the peace, East Dover, Vt. Bus. & Prof. Pos: Contractor and builder (retired). Mem: Mason; Odd Fellows. Rel: Baptist. Mailing Add: East Dover, Vt. 05341. (1967)

YEE, PHOEBE G. D
Mem, Calif. Dem. State Cent. Cmt.
b. Sacramento, Calif, 11/1/23; d. Gee Hing and Wong Yuk Lin H; m. 11/15/46 to Louie F. On, wid; m. 11/27/68 to David Yee; c. Gloria Jeanne, Barbara Ann and Gordon Victor. Educ: Los Angeles City Col, 41. Polit. & Govt. Pos: Worker, Glenn Anderson Campaign and George Brown Congressman and Assemblyman Edward Elliott Campaign; co-chmn, Women's Div, No on Prop. 14; mem, Calif. Dem. State Cent. Cmt, currently. Bus. & Prof. Pos: Owner, Louie F. On & Co. Agency, 46- Mem: Life Underwriters Asn. Los Angeles; Mutual Ins. Agents of Los Angeles; Life Underwriters Asn.(secy, women's div); licensed life and health casualty agent and broker; mutual fund rep. and chartered life underwriter; Chinese Am. Citizens Alliance (women's div); Soo Yuen Fraternal Asn.(womens div); Coun. Oriental Orgn.(v.pres); Los Angeles Chinatown Dem. Club (secy); Lucky Invest. Club (secy. and founder); Oriental Serv. Center Los Angeles (bd. mem). Rel: Congregational; Bd. Trustees, Chinese Congregational Church. Legal Res: 1961 College View Dr, Monterey Park, Calif. 91754. Mailing Add: 5265 E. Beverly Blvd, Los Angeles, Calif. 90022.

YEILDING, NEWMAN MANLY D
Ala. State Rep.
b. Birmingham, Ala, 3/8/00; s. Frank Bee Yeilding and Morgana Bland Y; m. 8/26/29 to Annie Lou Fletcher; c. Newman Manly, Jr, Ann (Mrs. Upton) and Fletcher. Educ: Birmingham-South. Col, A.B, 22, hon. LL.D, 69; Omicron Delta Kappa; Beta Theta Pi. Polit. & Govt. Pos: Ala. State Rep, 67- Bus. & Prof. Pos: Bursar, Birmingham-South. Col, 26-38, treas, 38-50, financial v.pres, 50-65. Mil. Serv: Pvt, Army, 18, served in Student Army Training Corp. Mem: South. Asn. Col. & Univ. Bus. Officers; Nat. Asn. Col. & Univ. Purchasing Agents; Nat. Asn. Purchasing Agents; Mason; The Club; Kiwanis. Rel: Methodist. Mailing Add: 3340 Hermitage Rd, Birmingham, Ala. 35223.

YELENICK, JOHN ANDREW D
Councilman, Denver, Colo.
b. Denver, Colo, 2/4/23; s. John Joseph Yelenick and Amelia Rose Boytz Y; m. 8/4/53 to Maesel Joyce Reed; c. John Joseph, Ann Marie, Mary Therese, Joseph Thomas and James Andrew. Educ: Regis Col, A.B; Univ. Denver. Polit. & Govt. Pos: Mem, Mayors Budget Cmt, Denver, Colo, 50-54; marriage counselor, Domestic Court of Human Rels, Denver, 54; precinct committeeman, 65; city councilman, Denver, currently; cmnr, Urban Renewal Authority, 68-69; mem, Bd. of Water Cmnrs, 69- Bus. & Prof. Pos: Pres, A.M.D.G, Inc, 54- and Your Valet, Inc, 60-; secy-treas, C.V.Y. Corp, 64-69, pres, 69-; dir, Educators Assurance Co, 64- Mil. Serv: Entered as Navy, Ens, 43, released as Lt, 47, after serv. in APA Pac; Am, Atlantic, Pac, Japan Area Ribbons; South. France, Okinawa Invasion Ribbons. Mem: K. of C.(4°); Am. Legion; President's Round Table; Denver C. of C; Int. Platform Asn; Nat. Coun. of Cath. Men; Denver Athletic Club; nat. bd, Confraternity of Christian Doctrine; pres, Archdiocesan; dir, Cystic Fibrosis Asn; Nat. Conf. Christians and Jews. Winner Pius X Medal and Cath. Youth Orgn. Medal, 54; Keynote speaker, Fourth Inter Am. Catechetical Cong, Dallas, 61. Rel: Catholic. Legal Res: 2 S. Dahlia St, Denver, Colo. 80222. Mailing Add: 1330 Leyden St, Denver, Colo. 80220.

YERGIN, ALAN EUGENE D
b. 11/15/29; s. Eugene Horace Yergin and Beatrice Roof Y; m. 8/29/65 to Nora Lee Bow. Educ: Wabash Col, B.A, 51; Ind. Univ, J.D, 58; Phi Delta Theta; Delta Theta Phi. Polit. & Govt. Pos: Dep. prosecuting attorney, Henry Co, Ind, 59; judge, New Castle City Court, 60- Bus. & Prof. Pos: Practicing attorney, New Castle, Ind, 58. Mil. Serv: Entered as Seaman, Navy, 52, released as Lt.(jg), 56, after serv. in Destroyer Div. 322, Korean Theater, 53-54; Lt, Naval Res, 56; Asian Theater and Korean Ribbons. Mem: Am. and Ind. Bar Asns; Elks; Moose; Eagles; VFW; Am. Legion; Westwood Country Culb. Rel: Protestant. Legal Res: 1522 Valley Dr, New Castle, Ind. 47362. Mailing Add: 1258½ Broad St, New Castle, Ind. 47362.

YESKO, JEROME L. D
b. Paterson, N.J, 8/13/18; m. to Salley Elaine Nestrel; c. Jill and Orrin. Educ: N.Y. Univ, B.A, 39; Univ. Pa. Law Sch; Rutgers Univ. Sch. Law, LL.B, 43. Polit. & Govt. Pos: Former N.J. State Assemblyman; acting magistrate, Paterson, 52-59. Bus. & Prof. Pos: Attorney. Publ: Assoc. ed, Torts, Am. Trial Lawyers Asn. J. Mem: N.J, N.Y, Am. and Fed. Bar Asns; v.pres, N.J. Asn. of Plaintiffs' Trial Lawyers; Hillsdale Dem. Club; v.pres, Jewish Welfare Bd. of Bergen Co; B'nai B'rith; Passaic Valley Chap; Moose; trustee, Passaic Co. Bar Asn; Bergen Co. Chap, N.Y. Univ. Alumni Asn. Rel: Jewish. Mailing Add: 218 Paul Court, Hillsdale, N.J. 07642. (1967)

YETKA, LAWRENCE ROBERT D
V.Chmn, Dem. Party, Minn.
b. Cloquet, Minn, 10/1/24; s. Frank Yetka and Martha Norkowski Y; m. 11/11/50 to Ellen Marie Fuller; c. Frank Barry, Lawrence George and Christopher Hubert. Educ: Univ. Minn, B.B.L, 47 and LL.B, 48; Nat. Honor Soc. Polit. & Govt. Pos: Chmn, Students for Humphrey Re-election Cmt. for Mayor, Minneapolis, Minn, 47; mem, Minn. State Dem. Exec. Cmt; Chmn, Young Dem. Clubs, Carlton Co, 48-50; v.chmn, Carlton Co, 50-68; staff attorney, Off. Price Stabilization, Dept. of Commerce, 51-52; Minn. State Rep, 51-61, chmn, Judiciary Cmt, Minn. State House of Rep, 55-61; mem, Great Lakes Cmn, 57-59; attorney, Duluth Port Authority, 57-60; chmn, Citizens for Kennedy, 60; chmn, Eighth Cong. Dist. Dem. Party, Minn, 62-66; munic attorney for numerous sch. dist. and other munic; city attorney, Cloquet, 64-; mem, Minn. State Judicial Coun, 65-; v.chmn, Dem. Party, Minn, currently; del, Dem. Nat. Conv, 68. Bus. & Prof. Pos: Sr. partner, Yetka & Newby Law Firm, Cloquet, Minn, 49-; mem. bd. of dirs, Carlton Co. Fed. Savings and Loan Asn, 58- Mem: Pres, Carlton Co. Bar Asn; 11th Judicial Dist. and Am. Bar Asns; Am. Judicature Soc; Eagles; C. of C; incorporator and mem, Cloquet Commun. Hosp. Asn, 54-65 and Cloquet Commun. Chest; past pres, Cloquet Civic Affairs Coun. Coach, Little League Baseball, Cloquet Champions, 3 years. Rel: Lutheran. Legal Res: 1707 Selmser Ave, Cloquet, Minn. 55720. Mailing Add: 124½ Avenue C, Cloquet, Minn. 55720.

YETTER, VAN D. JR. D
b. Smithfield Twp, Pa, 10/10/13; s. Van D. Yetter and Elsie Schall Y; m. to Katherine Froelich; c. four. Educ: E. Stroudsburg High Sch. Polit. & Govt Pos: Pa. State Rep, 54-67; Supvr, secy-treas, Smithfield Twp. Bus. & Prof. Pos: Farmer; Mobile Home Bus. Mem: Mason; Eagles; Elks; Pocono Mountains Motor Club; Stroudsburg Rotary Club; former pres, Lehigh Valley Farm Equip. Dealers Asn; Pocono Mountains C. of C; Pocono Mountains Sportsmen's Asn. Rel: Mem, Pres. Coun, Lutheran Church. Mailing Add: RFD 2, E. Stroudsburg, Pa. 18360. (1967)

YINGLING, JACOB MATTHIAS R
Md. State Del.
b. Aspers, Pa, 9/30/30; s. Jacob Charles Yingling and Emma Grimes Y; m. 4/5/51 to Genevieve Jean Koontz; c. Stephen Jacob and Randall Mathtew. Educ: Stroudsburg State Col, 48-49; Gettysburg Col, B.A, 52; Alpha Tau Omega; Kappa Phi Kappa. Polit. & Govt. Pos: Md. State Del, 63-; v.chmn, Md. Citizen's Cmt. for Fair Cong. Redistricting, 63-64; pres, Carroll Co. Rep. Club, 64-65; mem. and chmn, Speaker's Bur, Md. World's Fair Cmn, 64-65. Bus. & Prof. Pos: Former v.pres. and dir, J.Y.S.G. Corp; mem, adv. bd, Equitable Trust Co, Baltimore, Md; dir, Westminster Trust Co. and Independent Liberty Life Ins. Co. Mem: Past pres, Md, Del. and D.C. Educ. Salesmen's Asn, Westminster Interdenominational Group and Westminster Babe Ruth League; past, chmn, Carroll Co. Cancer Crusade; past Grand Knight, K. of C; mem, adv. bd, St. Joseph's Hosp, Baltimore; Prfnl. Bookmen of Am; Gov. Club; bd, Baltimore Regional Planning Coun. and Nat. Serv. to Regional Coun. Rel: Roman Catholic. Mailing Add: 178 William Ave, Westminster, Md. 21157.

YLITALO, JOHN RAYMOND
U.S. Ambassador to Paraguay
b. Floodwood, Minn, 12/25/16; s. John Ylitalo and Saima Marie Swen Y; m. 9/19/42 to Jean Sarchet; c. John Raymond, Georgianne, Mary Katherine and Sara Lisa. Educ: Suomi Col, 33-35; St. Olaf Col, B.A, 37; Northwest. Univ, M.B.A, 38; Nat. War Col, grad, 54. Polit. & Govt. Pos: Spec. agent, Fed. Bur. Invest, 41-46; attache, polit. officer, Am. Legation, Helsinki, 46-50; assigned to Dept. of State, Wash, D.C, 50-53; dep. prin. officer, Am. Consulate Gen, Munich Germany, 54-58; consul gen, counsellor of embassy, Am. Embassy, Manila, 59-62; assigned to Dept. of State, Wash, D.C, 62-69; dir, VISA Off, 65-67; prin. off, Am. Consulate Gen, Tijuana, Mex, 67-68; U.S. Ambassador

to Paraguay, 69- Bus. & Prof. Pos: Instr. econ, Univ. Ala, 38-41. Legal Res: 521 First Ave. W, Mobridge, S.Dak. 57601. Mailing Add: U.S. Embassy, Asuncion, Paraguay.

YNGVE, JOHN ANTON R
b. Thief River Falls, Minn, 10/3/24; s. Anton Yngve and Esther Johnson Y; m. to Deborah Ronning; c. Rolf, Aron, Hans, Hal and John P. Educ: Univ. Minn, B.S.L, 49, LL.B, 49; Reed Col, 43; Delta Theta Phi. Polit. & Govt. Pos: Dep. registr, Motor Vehicles, Minn, 46-55; mem, Planning Cmn, Plymouth, 60-61; mem, Third Dist. and Hennepin Co. Rep. Cmt, 60-63; trustee, Plymouth Coun, 61-62; Minn. State Rep, 63-68; chmn, Hennepin Co. Gen. Hosp. Bd. and mem, Hennepin Co. Ment. Health Bd, 65-; mem, Minn. State Rep. Cent. Cmt, 66; chmn, Plymouth Charter Cmt, 69-; regent, Univ. of Minn, 69- Bus. & Prof. Pos: Lawyer-partner, Yngve & Yngve, 50-67; pres, Nortronics Co, Inc, 67- Mil. Serv: Entered as Pvt, Air Force, 43, released as Cpl, 46, after serv. in Okinawa and Japan. Mem: Bd. of dirs, Hennepin Co. Bar Asn, 63; Am. and Minn. Bar Asns; Am. Judicature Soc; C. of C; Rotary; Am. Legion; Mason; Shrine; Golden Valley Golf Club; Hennepin Co. League of Munic. Rel: Protestant. Mailing Add: R.R. 2, Box 480, Wayzata, Minn. 55391.

YOAK, DON D
b. Grantsville, W.Va, 9/19/21; s. Ira Yoak and Fannie Morris Y; m. 9/20/42 to Lucretia M. Smith; c. Mrs. Larry E. Perkins and Denzil E. Educ: Calhoun Pub. Schs. Polit. & Govt. Pos: W.Va. State Del, 52; W.Va. Sgt-at-Arms, State House of Del, 55-65; pres, Roane Co. Young Dem, 59, 60, 61. Mem: Mason; Shrine; Scottish Rite; Eastern Star; Roane Co. Vol. Fire Dept. Rel: Methodist. Mailing Add: Spencer, W.Va. 25276. (1967)

YOCUM, NORMA LENORE R
City Councilman, Alhambra, Calif.
b. Redkey, Ind, 1/10/11; d. Fern Leigh Young and Mattie Rathburn Y; m. 10/2/32 to Sam A. Yocum; c. Virginia Ruth (Mrs. Clyde Fraser), Martha Louise (Mrs. Edward White), Robert Charles and Phyllis Mary. Educ: Cent. Jr. Col, 28-30; Woodbury Bus. Col, 30-31. Polit. & Govt. Pos: City Councilman, Alhambra, Calif, 55-, mayor, 64-66; secy, Calif. State Rep. Assembly, 66 & 68; Rep. nominee for Calif. State Assemblyman, 45th Assembly Dist, 66 & 68; mem, Los Angeles Co. Rep. Cent. Cmt, 66-; mem, Calif. Rep. State Cent. Cmt, 66-; mem, Gov. Adv. Coun. on Atomic Energy Develop. and Radiation Protection, 68. Bus. & Prof. Pos: V.pres, Sam Yocum, Inc, San Gabriel, Calif, currently. Mem: Founder-pres, San Gabriel Valley Coun. of Church Women, 38-45; pres, Alhambra Coord. Coun, 43-45; chmn, Los Angeles Co. Recreation Adv. Cmt, 46-49; pres, Los Angeles Co. Fedn. of Coord. Coun, 50; adv, Los Angeles Co. Fedn. of Youth Coun, 51-53; charter pres, Alhambra Hist. Soc, 66; Bus. & Prfnl. Womens Club of Alhambra; Soroptimist Club of Alhambra-San Gabriel. Woman of the Year, Quota Club, 55; Citizenship Award, Civitan Club, 60; Man of the Year, B'nai B'rith, Woman of the Year in Govt, Calif. Fedn. of Bus. & Prfnl. Women's Clubs and Hon. Citizenship, Granada, Spain, 65; Jaycee of the Year, Jr. C. of C, Mother of the Year, C. of C. and Los Angeles Downtown Bus. Men's Asn, 66. Rel: Protestant. Mailing Add: 1815 S. Fourth St, Alhambra, Calif. 91803.

YODER, EARL M. R
b. Okla, 10/11/27; married; c. three. Polit. & Govt. Pos: Iowa State Rep, 67-69. Bus. & Prof. Pos: Pres, Earl Yoder Const. Co. and Kalona Builder's Supply; dir, Iowa City Housing, Inc, Bus. Ventures, Inc, and Arsenal Life Ins. Co. Mem: Past pres, Optimists Club and Home Builders Asn. of Iowa and of Iowa City; dir, C. of C, Good Will Industs, and Commun. Givers. Rel: Mennonite. Mailing Add: 519 S. Summit, Iowa City, Iowa 52240. (1967)

YOHN, WILLIAM H, JR. R
Pa. State Rep.
b. Pottstown, Pa. 11/20/35; s. William H. Yohn, Sr. and Dorothy Cornelius Y; m. 3/16/63 to Jean Kochel; c. William H, III and Bradley G. Educ: Princeton Univ, A.B, 57; Yale Law Sch, LL.B, 60; Phi Beta Kappa; Cannon Club. Polit. & Govt. Pos: Research intern for U.S. Sen. John Sherman Cooper, Ky, summer 59; secy, Pottstown Police Civil Serv. Cmn, Pa, 61-62; asst. dist. attorney, Montgomery Co, 62-65; chmn, Pottstown Area Young Rep. Asn, 63-65; chmn, Montgomery Co. Rep. Primary Campaign Cmt, 65; chmn, Montgomery Co. Young Rep. Fedn, 66-67; Pa. State Rep, 68-, research coun. to majority leader, Pa. House of Rep, 67-68. Bus. & Prof. Pos: Attorney, Wells, Campbell, Yohn & Wells, Pottstown, Pa, 61- Mil. Serv: Entered as Pvt, Marine Corps Res, 60, released as Cpl, 66. Mem: Montgomery Bar Asn.(dir, 67-); Pa, Am. and D.C. Bar Asns; Jaycees; C. of C; Elks; Pottstown Hist. Soc. Outstanding Young Man of 1968 Award, Pottstown Jaycees. Rel: United Church of Christ. Mailing Add: 1040 Logan St, Pottstown, Pa. 19464.

YONCE, HENRY GRADY D
S.C. State Rep.
b. Johnson, S.C, 11/18/28; s. Luther Silas Yonce and Mertie Yonce Y; m. to Dell Harrison; c. Henry Grady, Jr. and Jeffrey Bryan. Educ: Univ. S.C, B.S. in acct, 48. Polit. & Govt. Pos: S.C. State Rep, 62- Bus. & Prof. Pos: Pres, Yonce Ins. Agency, Inc, 54- Mil. Serv: Entered as Seaman Recruit, Coast Guard, 52, released as Lt.(jg), 54; Lt. Comdr, Coast Guard Res, 62- Mem: Property Cmt; S.C. Ins. Agents Asn. Rel: Baptist. Legal Res: 6617 Arcadia Woods Rd, Columbia, S.C. 29206. Mailing Add: Palmetto State Life Bldg, Columbia, S.C. 29201. (1967)

YONEY, JOHN F. D
b. Smithdale, Pa, 3/27/08; s. Joseph Yoney and Mary Y; m. 6/8/35 to Sophia Podrasky. Educ: Monessen High Sch, grad, 25; Eckel's Sch. of Embalming, Pa. Polit. & Govt. Pos: Mem, Canonsburg Bd. Educ, Pa, 18 years; del, Dem. Nat. Conv, 68. Mem: Nat. Funeral Dirs. Asn. Rel: Catholic. Mailing Add: 216 E. Pike St, Canonsburg, Pa. 15317.

YONKEE, LAWRENCE A. R
Wyo. State Rep.
b. Sheridan, Wyo, 1/13/35; s. Fredrick T. Yonkee and Lillian A. Ponath Y; m. 8/10/57 to Mary Jo Budd; c. Kimberley Anne. Educ: Univ. Wyo, B.S, 59, J.D. with honors, 61; Phi Delta Theta; Potter Law Club; Omicron Delta Kappa Polit. & Govt. Pos: Chmn. Sheridan Police Cmn. and Sheridan Planning Cmn. and mem, Sheridan Co. Libr. Bd; Wyo. State Rep, 63-, chmn, Judiciary Cmt, Wyo. House of Rep, currently; mem, Wyo. Statute Rev. Cmn, 63-68 and Wyo. Legis-Exec. Reorgn. Cmn, 69- Bus. & Prof. Pos: Partner, Redle, Yonkee & Redle, Attorneys-at-law, Sheridan, Wyo, 63-; partner, FTY Ranch Co, Otten, Mont, 69. Mil. Serv: Entered as Pvt, Marines, 53, released as Sgt, 56, after serv. in Fleet Marine Force, Pac, Hawaii, 55-56. Mem: Wyo. State and Am. Bar Asns; Am. Trial Lawyers Asn; Am. Judicature Soc; Rotary; Elks; v.pres. bd. dirs, Univ. Wyo. Alumni Asn. Rel: Roman Catholic. Legal Res: 702 S. Jefferson St, Sheridan, Wyo. 82801. Mailing Add: P.O. Box 765, Sheridan, Wyo. 82801.

YORK, FRED BRANTLEY D
b. Alexander Co, N.C, 10/14/00; s. Keener Wood York and Stella Blaine Beckham Y; m. 1/22/31 to Hixie McLeod; c. Martha. Educ: Rutherford Col, 18-19; Kings Bus. Col, 19-20. Polit. & Govt. Pos: Register of deeds and co. acct, Alexander Co, N.C, 26-34; dep. U.S. marshall, West. Dist. N.C, 34-38; N.C. State Rep, 63-66. Bus. & Prof. Pos: Poultryman. Mem: Mason. Rel: Presbyterian; teacher, men's Bible class, 48-; ruling elder, 50- Mailing Add: Taylorsville, N.C. 28681. (1967)

YORK, JOSEPH FERRELL D
b. Alco, Ark, 2/7/07; s. Andrew Orphus York and Bertha Richardson Y; m. 12/3/31 to Mary Belle Prather. Educ: Univ. Tex, B.A, 27, Med. Branch, M.D, 31; Alpha Omega Alpha; Nu Sigma Nu. Polit. & Govt. Pos: Examiner, Local Draft Bd, Madill, Okla, 40-; chmn, Marshall Co. Dem. Party, 50-69. Mem: V.pres, Okla. Chap. Am. Acad. Gen. Practice; Nat. Membership Cmt, Am. Asn. Physicians and Surgeons; Am. Med. Asn; Okla. State Med. Asn; AF&AM. Rel: Methodist. Mailing Add: 507 Lillie Blvd, Madill, Okla. 73446. (1967)

YORK, STANLEY R
Wis. State Assemblyman
b. Milwaukee, Wis, 8/29/31; s. Wilford Douglas York and Margaret Richardson Y; m. 6/20/53 to Emily Ann Loucks; c. Cynthia Lee, Douglas Charles and Elizabeth. Educ: Beloit Col, B.A, 53; Andover Newton Theol. Sch, B.D, 57; Phi Kappa Psi. Polit. & Govt. Pos: Wis. State Assemblyman, 67- Bus. & Prof. Pos: Pastor, Congregational Church, Red Granite, Wis, 57-59, Union Congregational Church, Berlin, 57-62 and First Congregation Church, River Falls, 62- Rel: United Church of Christ. Mailing Add: 118 N. Third St, River Falls, Wis. 54022.

YORTY, SAM D
Mayor, Los Angeles, Calif.
b. Lincoln, Nebr, 10/1/09; s. Frank Patrick Yorty and Johanna Egan Y; m. 12/1/38 to Betty Hensel; c. William Egan. Educ: Southwestern Univ; Univ. South. Calif. Polit. & Govt. Pos: Calif. State Assemblyman, 36-40 & 49-50; U.S. Rep, Calif, 50-54; mayor, Los Angeles, 61- Bus. & Prof. Pos: Attorney at law, private practice, 40-42, 45-50 & 54-61. Mil. Serv: Entered Army Air Corps, 42, released as Capt, 45, after serv. in 5th Air Force and 6th Army, New Guinea and Philippines. Mailing Add: 12979 Blairwood Dr, Studio City, Calif. 91604.

YOST, JERRY L. D
Co. Cmnr, Adams Co, Colo.
b. Columbus, Ohio, 3/21/32; s. Carl L. Yost and Mary E. Rife Y; m. 1/3/58 to Wanda Watson; c. Zane Murray, Kimberlee Dawn and Tracee Lynn. Educ: Ohio State Univ; Univ. N.Mex; Finance Sch, Ft. Harrison, Ind, 51; pres, Thomas Jefferson Club. Polit. & Govt. Pos: Chief juvenile probation officer and referee, Adams Co, Colo, 61-66; Colo. State Rep, 65-67; co. cmnr, Adams Co, currently. Mil. Serv: Entered as Cpl, Army, 51, released 53, after serv. in Japan; UN Serv. Ribbon; Good Conduct Ribbon. Mem: Elks; VFW; bd. dir, Adams Co. Ment. Hygiene Clinic; adv. bd, Adams Co. War on Poverty. Rel: Unitarian. Mailing Add: 1260 Oak Place, Thornton, Colo. 80229. (1967)

YOSWEIN, LEONARD E. D
b. N.Y.C. Educ: Brooklyn Col, 42; N.Y. Univ. Law Sch, 48. Polit. & Govt. Pos: Former N.Y. State Assemblyman; judge, Civil Court City N.Y, currently. Mil. Serv: Air Force, Capt, 42-46; served in European, China, Burma and India Theatres; awarded Air Medal and Three Campaign Stars. Mem: Linden Lodge; K. of C; B'nai B'rith; past judge advocate, Jewish War Vet, Post 321; N.Y. Co. Lawyers Asn; Fedn. of Jewish Philanthropies, E. N.Y. Div; NAACP; Rel: B'nai Israel Congregation. Mailing Add: 1037 Hendrix St, Brooklyn, N.Y. 11207.

YOU, RICHARD WONSANG D
b. Honolulu, Hawaii, 12/23/16; s. Dong Men You and Mary Choy Y; m. 4/19/43 to Eleanor Chun; c. Pamela and Aleta. Educ: Univ. Hawaii, B.S, 39; Creighton Med. Sch, M.D, 43; intern, Queen's Hosp, Honolulu, 43-44; gen. rotating residency, St. Francis Hosp, Honolulu, 46-47; Gamma Pi Sigma. Polit. & Govt. Pos: Chmn, Gov. Youth Fitness Cmt, Hawaii, 60-62; Hawaii's liaison to President's Coun. on Youth Fitness, 60-63; hon. guest, Inauguration of President John F. Kennedy, 61; v.chmn, Univ. Hawaii Bd. Regents, 61-63; mem, Mayor's Urban Renewal Adv. Cmt, Honolulu, 65-; mem, Humphrey Nat. Cmt, 68; alternate del, Dem. Nat. Conv, 68; mem, Nat. Dem. Flying Donkey Club, 68. Bus. & Prof. Pos: Physician, U.S. Olympic Team, Helsinki, Finland, 52; physician and trainer, U.S. Pan Am. Team, Mexico City, 55; mgr. and trainer-coach of athletes and physician and surgeon, currently. Publ: 'The Progressive XDR System of Athletic Training,' 65; 'The Key to Permanet World Peace,' 67. Mil. Serv: Entered as Pvt, Hawaii Nat. Guard, 32, released as Sgt, 39; re-entered as 1st Lt, Med. Corps, Army, 44, released as Capt, 46, after serv. as Post and Compound Surgeon, Prisoner of War Camp, Hawaii, 45-46; Capt, Med. Corps, Hawaii Nat. Guard, 47-50. Mem: U.S. Del, Int. Symposium of Med. and Physiol. of Sports, Helsinki, Finland, 52; Nat. Bd. Med. Exam, 53-; U.S. Olympic Cmt, 56-; life mem, Univ. Hawaii East West Center, 60-; secy, U.S. Olympic Weightlifting Cmt, 61-; Ancient Order of the Chammori of Guam, 63-; v.pres, Olympian Int, 64-; app. by U.S. Dept. of Commerce to Honolulu Export Expansion Coun, 65-; U.S. Olympic Weightlifting Cmt. for Olympic Games, Munich, Germany, 69- Voted life mem, Helms Athletic Found. and elected to the Int. Helms Hall of Fame for Weightlifting, 68. Mailing Add: 1270 Queen Emma St, Room 106, Honolulu, Hawaii 96813.

YOULE, JOHN CLINTON R
b. Chicago, Ill, 4/4/16; s. John Wilbur Youle and Sadie Muench Y; m. 5/17/41 to Cherie Jeanne Eadie; c. Jessica, Susan and John Clinton. Educ: Wheaton Col, A.B. Polit. & Govt. Pos: Ill. State Rep, 65-67. Bus. & Prof. Pos: Inventor and mfr. of automatic stock gates; commentator and writer, Nat. Broadcasting Co, 46-59; newspaper publisher, five Ill. newspapers, 52-62; invest. banker, Lehman Brothers, 59-66; dir. and v.pres, Donald R. Booz & Assoc, Inc, 66- Mil. Serv: Entered as Pvt, Air Force, 42, released as Maj, 46. Mem: Pres, Youle Christian Found; trustee, Shimer Col; Am. Meteorol Soc; Univ. Club; Exec. Club; Dunham Woods Riding Club; Chicago Club. Rel: Congregational. Legal Res: Whitethorn Rd, Wayne, Ill. 60184. Mailing Add: 20 N. Wacker Dr, Chicago, Ill. 60606. (1967)

YOUNG, ALLAN CHANDLER R
Mem, N.Dak. State Rep. Exec. Cmt.
b. Devils Lake, N.Dak, 6/26/37; s. Ray Duane Young and Jane Mann Y; m. 9/28/57 to Glenda Marie Overbo; c. Carrie Lynn and Stuart Chandler. Educ: Univ. N.Dak, 55-57; Univ. Vienna, Austria, fall 56; Phi Delta Theta. Polit. & Govt. Pos: Sgt-at-Arms, Rep. Nat. Conv, 60; mem, campaign staff, N.Dak. Rep. Party, 60, chmn, Tri-Co. Rally Banquet, 60; Young Rep. Co. chmn, 60-61; del, N.Dak. Rep. Conv, 60, 62, 63, 64, 66 & 68; regional dir, N.Dak. Young Rep, 61-62; campaign chmn. and organizational dir, Ramsey Co. Rep. Party, 62; precinct committeeman, 62 & 66; Three-Co. campaign fieldman, 63; chmn, N.Dak. Del, Nat. Young Rep. Fedn. Conv, 63 & 65; chmn, N.Dak. Young Rep, 63-67; mem, N.Dak. State Rep. Exec. Cmt, 63-67 & 69-; organizational and campaign dir, Ramsey Co, 64; Five-Co. Campaign fieldman, 64; del, Rep. Nat. Conv, 64; grad, Young Rep. Leadership Training Sch, Wash, D.C, 65 & 67; chmn, Lincoln Day Dinner, Dist. 15, 66; mem, Dist. 15, Ramsey Co. Exec. Cmt, 66; mem, N.Dak. Young Rep. State Exec. Cmt, 67-68; v.chmn, Dist. 15, 67-68, organizational chmn, 68, chmn, 68-; mem, N.Dak. Rep. Campaign Cmt, 68; mem, N.Dak. State Rep. Budget and Quota Cmt, 69-; v.chmn, N.Dak. Rep. Publicity Cmt, 69- Bus. & Prof. Pos: Secy-treas, Mann's Dept. Store, 61- Mem: Eagles; Elks; Mason (Past Master); York Rite; Shrine (secy, Lake Region Club, 68); DeMolay (Legion of Honor, 67; N.Dak. State Adv, 67-69); SAR; chmn, City Heart Fund, 61; publicity chmn, United Fund, 60; dir, Jaycee Frolics, 62; dir. and corp. secy, Devils Lake Commun. Develop. Corp, 67-69; Ramsey Co. dir, Gr. N.Dak. Asn, 68; Jaycees; C. of C.(instr, courses); founding mem. and dir, N.Dak. Retail Asn. Named One of the Ten Outstanding State Chmn. by Buzz Lukens, chmn, Young Rep. Nat. Fedn, 65; Distinguished Serv. Award, Devils Lake Jaycees, 68. Rel: Episcopal; Vestryman; Men's Club; Choir. Mailing Add: 1111 Sixth St, Devils Lake, N.Dak. 58301.

YOUNG, BYRON PORTER R
b. Gouldsboro, Maine, 8/18/11; s. Nathan Cole Young and Clara Bunker Y; m. 9/7/40 to Faith Whittier Holden; c. Dennis Julian and Byron Bunker. Educ: Winter Harbor High Sch. Polit. & Govt. Pos: Selectman, Gouldsboro, Maine, 50-66; Maine State Rep, 59-66; Maine State Sen, 67-68; cmnr, Hancock Co, 69- Bus. & Prof. Pos: Pres, Maine Lobstermen's Asn, Inc, 65-66. Mem: Frenchman's Bay Conservation Club. Rel: Protestant. Mailing Add: Ashville, Maine 04607.

YOUNG, C. W. BILL R
Fla. State Sen.
b. Harmarville, Pa, 12/16/30; s. Raymond Edward Young and Wilma Hulings Y; m. 8/20/49 to Marian Ford; c. Pamela Kay, Terry Lee and Kimber. Polit. & Govt. Pos: Former state chmn. and nat. committeeman, Fla. Fedn. of Young Rep; asst. Sgt-at-Arms, Rep. Nat. Conv, 56 & 60; dist. asst. to U.S. Rep. Cramer, 57-60; mem, Pinellas Co. Rep. Exec. Cmt; Fla. State Sen, 19th Dist, 60-, Minority Leader, Fla. State Senate, currently, chmn, Gen. Legis. Cmt, v.chmn, Labor and Indust. Cmt, mem, Finance, Ins, Salt Water Conserv. and Legis. Adv. Cmts; mem, Legis. Coun. and Fla. Constitution Rev. Cmn; treas. of Host Cmt, del. and Nixon Floor Mgr. for Fla, Rep. Nat. Conv, 68; presidential elector, 68. Bus. & Prof. Pos: Owner, C. W. Bill Young Ins, 57-60; pres, Prudential Property and Casualty Ins. Agency, Inc, 60-64; partner, Young & Kyle Ins, 64-; mem, bd. of dirs, St. Petersburg Bank & Trust. Mil. Serv: Entered as Pvt, Fla. Nat. Guard, 48, released as M/Sgt, 57. Mem: Independent Insurors Asn; Million Dollar Club; Founder Life Assurance Co; Independent Ins. Agents Asn. of Fla. and St. Petersburg; Fla. Asn. of Ins. Agencies; v.pres, Pinellas Park Rotary; chmn, Munic. Affairs Cmt. of Pinellas Park Commun. Develop. Asn; YMCA Health Club; Camp Cmt, St. Petersburg YMCA; Moose; Jr. C. of C; Aircraft Owners & Pilots Asn; Ridge Wood Groves Civic Asn. Cmn. of Ky. Col, 63; Am. Legion Award for Meritorious Serv, 63; One of the Outstanding Young Men of Am, U.S. Jr. C. of C, 64; Allen Morris Awards, Second Most Effective in Debate and Second Most Valuable in Fla. State Senate, 67 and Most Valuable Sen. in Fla. State Senate, 69; nominated for St. Petersburg Times Most Valuable Member of Fla. State Senate Award, 67; Distinguished Serv. Award, Nat. Am. Vet. of World War II; Award of Merit, President's Cmn. on Employ. of the Handicapped; Allstate Ins. Nat. Safety Crusade Cert; Good Govt. Award, Pinellas Park Jaycees. Rel: Methodist. Mailing Add: 7880 Ridge Rd, Seminole, Fla. 33540.

YOUNG, CHARLES L. D
Dist. Chmn, Fourth Cong. Dist. Dem. Party, Miss.
b. Meridian, Miss, 8/27/31; s. E.F. Young, Jr. and Velma Beal Y; m. Aug. 1960 to Doretha Corner; c. Deidra, Charles L, Jr, Arthur and Veldora F. Educ: Tenn. State A & I Univ, B.S. in Bus, 51; Tuskegee Inst; Univ. Denver, 58; Kappa Alpha Psi. Polit. & Govt. Pos: Chmn, Lauderdale Co. Dem. Club, Miss, 66 & 69; del, Dem. Nat. Conv, 68; dist. chmn, Fourth Cong. Dist. Dem. Party, 68- Bus. & Prof. Pos: Pres, E.F. Young, Jr. Mfg. Co; pres, Young's Construction Inc; chmn. bd. dirs, Lauderdale Econ. Assistance Prog. Mil. Serv: Entered as Pvt, Army, 52, released as Sgt. 1/C, 54, after serv. in Korea, Second Div; Bronze Star; Good Conduct Medal; Korean Serv. Medal. Mem: Mason; Elks; C. of C.(housing cmt, 68); Meridian Bus. League (pres, 60). Rel: Christian Methodist Episcopal. Legal Res: 3911 12th St, Meridian, Miss. 39301. Mailing Add: 500 25th Ave, Meridian, Miss. 39301.

YOUNG, COLEMAN A. D
Mich. State Sen.
b. Tuscaloosa, Ala, 5/24/18. Educ: Detroit East. High Sch, grad. Polit. & Govt. Pos: Mich. State Sen, 64-; former del, Mich. State Constitutional Conv; del, Dem. Nat. Conv. 68; mem, Dem. Nat. Cmt, currently. Mil. Serv: Army Air Force, 2nd Lt. Mem: NAACP; Booker T. Washington Bus. Men's Asn; Trade Union Leadership Coun; Asn. for the Study of Negro Life and Hist; bd. dirs, Ferndale Coop. Credit Union; spec. rep. AFL-CIO Coun. Rel: Baptist. Mailing Add: 278 E. Forrest, Apt. 7, Detroit, Mich. 48201. (1967)

YOUNG, DALE L. R
State Treas, Rep. Party of Nebr.
b. Palmyra, Nebr, 3/13/28; s. Mike P. Young and Grace Clutter Y; m. 6/18/50 to Norma Shalla; c. Shalla Ann and Philip Mike. Educ: Univ. Nebr, Lincoln, B.S, 50; Theta Xi. Polit. & Govt. Pos: Del, Lancaster Co. Rep. Conv, Nebr, 66 & 68; del, Nebr. State Rep. Conv, 66 & 68; state treas, Rep. Party of Nebr, 66- Bus. & Prof. Pos: V.pres. and cashier, First Nat. Bank & Trust Co, Lincoln, Nebr, 50- Mil. Serv: Entered as Pvt, Army, 44, released as S/Sgt, 46, recalled in 50, released as M/Sgt, 51, after serv. in Am. Theatre. Mem: Am. Inst. Banking; Omaha-Lincoln Soc. Financial Anal; Lincoln Country Club; Govt. Research Inst. Rel: Presbyterian. Legal Res: 2627 Park Ave, Lincoln, Nebr. 68502. Mailing Add: First National Bank & Trust Co, Lincoln, Nebr. 68508.

YOUNG, DAMON MICHAEL D
Ark. State Rep.
b. Nashville, Ark, 12/1/40; s. Howard Cecil Young and Modena McCaskill Y; m. 8/26/61 to Doris Ann Anderson; c. Jerri Ann and Damon Michael, Jr. Educ: Univ. Ark, LL.B, 65. Polit. & Govt. Pos: Co. chmn, Young Dem, 64; chmn, Credentials Cmt, State Young Dem, Ark, 65; city attorney, Texarkana, Ark, 65-67; Ark. State Rep, 67- Bus. & Prof. Pos: Partner, Shaver, Tackett, Young & Patton, Attorneys, 64- Rel: Methodist. Legal Res: 2 Broadmoor Circle, Texarkana, Ark. 75501. Mailing Add: 517-521 State First National Bank, Texarkana, Ark. 75501.

YOUNG, DAVID LEON R
Chmn, Hillsborough Co. Rep. Exec. Cmt, Fla.
b. Miami, Fla, 9/18/28; s. Charles Albert Young and Ercell M. Daniel Y; m. 12/6/57 to Patricia Ann Poggel; c. Richard Scott and Mark David. Educ: Fla. State Univ, B.S, 58; Alpha Kappa Psi. Polit. & Govt. Pos: Chmn, Hillsborough Co. Rep. Exec. Cmt, Fla, 66- Bus. & Prof. Pos: Owner, David Young Ins, 66-; pres, Aviation Travel Asn, 66- Mil. Serv: Entered as Pfc, Air Force, 50, released as Staff Sgt, 54, after serv. in 305th Bomb Wing, Okinawa and England, 52-53. Mem: Treas, Hillsborough Co. Rep. Club. Private Pilot. Rel: Evangelical United Brethren. Mailing Add: 2129 Rambla St, Tampa, Fla. 33612. (1967)

YOUNG, DON D
S.Dak. State Rep.
b. Dow City, Iowa, 3/23/96; m. to Lena Werth; c. Donna and Margaret. Educ: Common Sch. Polit. & Govt. Pos: S.Dak. State Rep, 60-; mem, Twp. Bd, Warner, S.Dak, 13 years and chmn, Sch. Bd, 22 years. Bus. & Prof. Pos: Farmer; dir, R.E.A. Mem: Mason; Scottish Rite; Shrine; Eastern Star; Elks; Am. Legion; chmn, Regional Libr. Bd. Rel: Evangelical United Brethren Church. Mailing Add: Warner, S.Dak. 57479. (1967)

YOUNG, DONALD E. R
Alaska State Rep.
b. Meridian, Calif, 1933; married; c. Two. Polit. & Govt. Pos: Alaska State Rep, 67-; pres, Ft. Yukon City Coun. Bus. & Prof. Pos: Teacher. Mem: Elks; Mason; Dog Mushers Asn; del, Alaska Educ. Asn. Mailing Add: P.O. Box 119, Ft. Yukon, Alaska 99740. (1967)

YOUNG, DOREEN DUNWOODY R
Chairwoman, Madison Co. Rep. Cent. Cmt, Ill.
b. Paris, France, 3/29/22; d. Col. Halsey Dunwoody and Doris Sleator D; m. 6/6/42 to Lafayette T. Young, M.D; c. Ellen (Mrs. Joseph L. Moceri), Patricia (Mrs. Karl Messmer), Mary A, Doris D. and Bizette M. Educ: Wash. Univ, 2 years; Kappa Alpha Theta. Polit. & Govt. Pos: Chairwoman and mem. exec. cmt, Madison Co. Rep. Cent. Cmt, Ill, 64-; mem, Representative Cmt. 55th House Dist, 66 & 68; Cand. for del, Constitutional Conv, 53 Sen. Dist, State Cent. committeewoman, 23rd Cong. Dist, 69- Mem: Former pres, Jr. Serv. League, Alton; former pres, Women's Auxiliary, St. Paul's Episcopal Church; St. Joseph's Hosp. Auxiliary; Madison Co. Med. Auxiliary; Madison Co. Fedn. Rep. Women; Alton Dist. Rep. Club; Ill. Fedn. Rep. Women. Rel: Episcopal. Mailing Add: 3003 Brown St, Alton, Ill. 62002.

YOUNG, ERNEST D. D
b. Baltimore, Md, 5/17/28; married. Educ: Loyola Col, B.S, 55; Univ. of Md. Law Sch, LL.B, 57. Polit. & Gov. Pos: Md. State Del, 63-67. Mem: N.W. Baltimore Dem. Club; Trenton Dem. Club. Mailing Add: 1825 N. Pulaski St, Baltimore, Md. 21217. (1967)

YOUNG, FRANK WESLEY R
Nev. State Assemblyman
b. Waterville, Ohio, 6/18/23; s. William Edward Young, Sr. and Ruth Farnsworth Y; m. 10/8/49 to Jean Elizabeth Smith; c. John Robert and Richard William. Educ: Ohio State Univ, 41-43; Yale, B.E.E, 44, 46-47; Phi Eta Sigma; Eta Kappa Nu; Stadium Club, Ohio State Univ; Wesley Found. Polit. & Govt. Pos: Nev. State Assemblyman, 67-; Nev. rep, West. Insterstate Nuclear Bd, 68- Bus. & Prof. Pos: Teacher, Garden Country Day Sch, Jackson Heights, L.I, N.Y, 48-50; controls engr, M.W. Kellogg Co, Jersey City, N.J, 50-52; instrument engr, AMF Atomics, Greenwich, Conn, 52-58; sr. sci. exec, E G & G, Las Vegas, Nev, 58- Mil. Serv: Entered as Seaman, Naval Res, 43, released as Lt.(jg), after serv. in Field Serv. Group, Naval Research Lab. Mem: Am. Nuclear Soc; Inst. Elec. & Electronic Engrs; Am. Mgt. Asn; Am. Soc. Pub. Admin; Kiwanis; adv. bd, Las Vegas Corps of Salvation Army; exec. bd, Boulder Dam Area Counc. Boy Scouts. Rel: Methodist. Mailing Add: 2113 Barry Way, Las Vegas, Nev. 89106.

YOUNG, FREDERICK NEVIN R
Ohio State Rep.
b. Dayton, Ohio, 1/1/32; s. Robert Frederick Young and Katherine Patterson Y; m. 8/27/51 to Joyce Canney; c. Margaret R, Shirley Kay, Nancy E. and Mary R. Educ: Wesleyan Univ, B.A, 54; Harvard Law Sch, LL.B, 57; Phi Beta Kappa; Beta Theta Pi. Polit. & Govt. Pos: Precinct and Ward Commit-

teeman, Rep. Party, Montgomery Co, Ohio, 57-66; pres, Montgomery Co. Young Rep. Club, 60; state chmn, Ohio League Young Rep. Clubs, 64; mem, Ohio State Rep. Cent. Cmt, 66; Ohio State Rep, 84th Dist, 68- Bus. & Prof. Pos: Partner, Law Firm, Young & Alexander, Dayton, 61- Publ: 'Corporate Separations; Some Recent Revenue Rulings,' Harvard Law Rev, 58. Mem: Harvard Law Sch. Asn. Ohio (past pres); Dayton, Ohio and Am. Bar Asns; Kettering-Oakwood Exchange Club. Rel: Protestant. Mailing Add: 5512 Laureldale Rd, Dayton, Ohio 45429.

YOUNG, GeDELLE BRABHAM D
b. Columbia, S.C, 10/31/13; d. Vernon Brabham and Margaret Cope B; m. 7/18/38 to Martin Dunaway Young; c. Martin Brabham and Margaret Cope (Mrs. J.P. Anderson, Jr). Educ: Ga. State Woman's Col, A.B, 34; Emory Univ, A.B. in Libr. Sci, 35. Polit. & Govt. Pos: Mem, City Bd. of Health and Housing Bd, Columbia, S.C; mem, C.Z. Dem. Party, currently; del, Dem. Nat. Conv, 68. Bus. & Prof. Pos: Librn, Richland Co. Pub. Libr, Columbia, S.C, 36-40; various other libr. pos. in the area. Mem: South. Regional Coun; S.C. Coun. on Human Rights; League of Women Voters. Rel: Humanist. Mailing Add: Box 2016, Balboa Heights, C.Z.

YOUNG, GEORGE C. R
Mass. State Rep.
Educ: Dartmouth Col, A.B; Boston Univ, M.Ed. and Cert. of Adv. Grad. Specialization. Polit. & Govt. Pos: Chmn, Rep. Town Cmt, 10 years; mem. sch. bd, Scituate, Mass, 9 years, chmn, 2 years; Mass. State Rep, currently. Bus. & Prof. Pos: Sch. adminstr, 30 years; acting supt. of schs, twice; prin, Cent. Jr. High Sch, Quincy. Mil. Serv: Entered as Pvt, Army, released as Capt, after serv. in World War II 4 years; Lt. Col, Army Res, 24 years. Mailing Add: 20 Lawson Rd, Scituate, Mass. 02066. (1967)

YOUNG, GUS WILSON D
Ala. State Rep.
b. Heflin, Ala, 2/18/18; s. Ross Brown Young and Nancy Savannah Wade Y; m. 8/20/39 to Murrah Lee Butler; c. Joseph Lloyd and Laura Marylin (Mrs. Harry Truman Morrison). Educ: Ala. Polytech. Inst, B.S, 42; New Orleans Baptist Sem. Polit. & Govt. Pos: Ala. State Rep, 62- Bus. & Prof. Pos: Baptist Minister and farmer. Mem: Mason. Rel: Baptist. Mailing Add: R.R. 1, Graham, Ala. 36263.

YOUNG, HORTENSE HOUSTON D
b. Huntsville, Tex; d. Joshua Houston and Georgia Orviss H; m. 6/22/27 to Dr. Coleman Milton Young, Jr; c. Yvonne (Mrs. William F. Clark) and Coleman Milton, III. Educ: Fisk Univ, A.B; Univ. Ill, Urbana, B.L.S; Univ. Louisville Law Sch, 3 years; Delta Sigma Theta. Polit. & Govt. Pos: Precinct committeewoman, Dem. Party, Louisville, Ky, 40-; cmnr, Ky. Cmn. on Pub. Educ, 60-68; del, Nat. Dem. Conv, 68; committeewoman, Ky. Conv. Del. Cmt, 69- Bus. & Prof. Pos: Mem, Mayors' Legis. Cmt. of Louisville, Ky, 38-60, secy, Mayors' Race Rels. Cmn, 41-44, cmnr, Louisville Munic. Housing Cmn, 57-63; pres, Louisville Asn. of Real Estate Brokers, 64-67. Publ: 'Tense Topics,' (weekly features) Louisville Defender Newspaper, 40-47; 'Women in Politics,' Delta J, 63. Mem: Am. and Ky. Libr. Asns; Nat. Asn. of Real Estate Brokers; League of Women Voters; YMCA; Church Women United; Urban League; NAACP; Nat. Cmt. for Support of Pub. Schs; Jefferson Co. Med. Soc. Auxiliary; Links, Inc; Commun. Action Cmn; bd. Family & Children's Agency; bd. dirs, Kentuckiana Girl Scouts; Third Dist. Womens Dem. Club. Lincoln Key, 47. Rel: United Church of Christ. Legal Res: 818 S. Sixth St, Louisville, Ky. 40203. Mailing Add: P.O. Box 2153, Louisville, Ky. 40201.

YOUNG, JAMES E. D
Asst. State Treas, Ga.
b. Doublas, Ga, 12/03/36; s. Jack Young and Olis Hinson Y; m. 11/06/60 to Jacqueline E. Sikes; c. James Edward, Jr. and Shelley Elaine. Educ: S.Ga. Col, 57. Polit. & Govt. Pos: Asst. cashier, State Treas. Dept, Ga, 58-63; Asst. State Treas, Ga, 63- Mil. Serv: Nat. Guard. Rel: Baptist. Mailing Add: 3355 Casa Linda Dr, Decatur, Ga. 30032.

YOUNG, JAMES MILTON, III Conservative
b. Pittsburgh, Pa, 9/23/28; s. James M. Young, Jr. and Helen Pfiel Y; m. 4/2/55 to Regina Coyne. Educ: Carnegie Inst. of Tech, B.S, 49, M.S, 54. Polit. & Govt. Pos: Chmn, Erie Co. Conservative Party, N.Y, 63-66 and Western Regional chmn. Bus. & Prof. Pos: Research assoc, Mellon Inst, 52-54; tech. serv. rep, Hooker Chem. Co, 55-60, mkt. research analyst, 60-; dist. sales mgr, Haveg Industs, 66- Mil. Serv: 2nd Lt, Army, 50-52; serv. in 378th Engr. Combat Battalion, U.S. and Far East, 52; UN Serv. Ribbon; Korean Combat Ribbon with Three Battle Stars. Mem: Am. Inst. of Chem. Engrs; Atlantic Athletic Club; Univ. Club. Rel: Catholic. Mailing Add: 5225 W. Kingston Court, Atlanta, Ga. 30305.

YOUNG, JOHN D
U.S. Rep, Tex.
b. 11/10/16; s. Phillip M. Young and Catherine Gaffney Y; m. to Jane Gallier; c. Catherine Gaffney, Nancy Rae, John, Jr, Robert Harold and Mary Patricia. Educ: St. Edwards Univ, B.A, 37; Univ. Tex, law student, 37-40. Hon. LL.D, St. Edwards Univ, 61. Polit. & Govt. Pos: Asst. co. attorney, Nueces Co, Tex, 46, asst. dist. attorney, 47-50, co. attorney, 51-52, co. judge, 53-56; U.S. Rep, Tex, 57- Bus. & Prof. Pos: Lawyer. Mil. Serv: Navy. Mem: State Bar of Tex. Legal Res: Corpus Christi, Tex. Mailing Add: 2419 Rayburn House Office Bldg, Washington, D.C. 20515.

YOUNG, JOHN T. R
N.H. State Rep.
b. Merrimac, Mass, 1892; wid; c. Two. Educ: Merrimac High Sch. Polit. & Govt. Pos: N.H. State Rep, currently. Bus. & Prof. Pos: Retired master plumber. Mil. Serv: Pfc, World War I. Mem: Odd Fellows; Vets. World War I, Major Waldron's Sports Club; Am. Legion; N.H. Hist. Soc. Rel: Protestant. Mailing Add: 49 Littleworth Rd, Dover, N.H. 03820. (1967)

YOUNG, JOHN WALLACE D
Okla. State Sen.
b. Sapulpa, Okla, 11/25/23; s. Glenn Olen Young and Thora Kate Shiflet Y; m. 9/6/49 to Claudeen Humes: c. John Mark, David Lee and Bradford Humes. Educ: Tulane Univ, B.Bus. and Acct, M.Bus. and Acct; Okla. Univ, LL.B, 50; Phi Delta Phi; Beta Gamma Sigma; Kappa Sigma. Polit. & Govt. Pos: Fifth Dist. chmn, League of Young Dem, formerly; pres, Student Sen, Okla. Univ, 49; Okla. State Sen, 64- Mil. Serv: Entered as A/S, Navy, released as Lt.(jg); Lt, Naval Res. Mem: C. of C; Lions; Hist. Soc, Sapulpa; Round-Up Club. Rel: Baptist. Legal Res: 1401 E. Lincoln, Sapulpa, Okla. 74066. Mailing Add: P.O. Box 1392, Sapulpa, Okla. 74066.

YOUNG, JOHN WILLIAM R
b. Louisville, Ky, 5/29/16; s. Birch Higgins Young and Bertha May Lindeman Y; m. 8/29/41 to Dorothy Mary Mialback; c. John W, Jr. Educ: Univ. Louisville; Univ. Heidelberg, Germany. Polit. & Govt. Pos: Rep. precinct capt, Louisville, Ky, 50-62, ward chmn, 55-66 and v.pres, Young Rep. Club, 54; mem, Louisville Bd. of Aldermen, 62, pres, 65- Bus. & Prof. Pos: Pub. Rels. man, Oertel Brewing Co, 66. Mil. Serv: Entered as Pvt, Army, 41, released as Cpl, 45, after serv. in First Armored Signal Bn, ETO; ETO Ribbon with Five Battle Stars; Good Conduct Medal. Mem: VFW; Am. Legion; Lincoln Club of Ky; Greater Louisville Labor Coun; COPE; Rep, Brewery Workers Local 20. Capt. High Sch. Basketball team; Du Pont Manual Training 1934. Rel: Protestant. Mailing Add: 3121 McMahan Blvd, Louisville, Ky. 40220. (1967)

YOUNG, MARION WEBSTER R
Chmn, Bee Co. Rep. Party, Tex.
b. Gratis, Ohio, 6/13/05; s. Joel Edwin Young and Grace Hetzler Y; m. 3/1/28 to Beatrice Menier Kimbrough; c. Gwendolyn Menier (Mrs. Richard T. Burke) and Edwin Lanier. Polit. & Govt. Pos: Chmn, Bee Co. Rep. Party, Tex, 62- Bus. & Prof. Pos: Construction engr, Houston Oil Co, Tex, 26-28, construction supt, 28-31, oil scout, 31-36 and dist landman, 36-46; independent oil operator, 46- Mem: Am. Asn. Petroleum Landmen; Corpus Christi Asn. Petroleum Landmen; Mason; Tex. Farm Bur. Silver Beaver, Boy Scouts. Rel: Presbyterian. Mailing Add: P.O. Box 1118, Beeville, Tex. 78102.

YOUNG, MARTIN D
Ga. State Sen.
b. Ben Hill Co, Ga, 9/05/01; s. Samuel S. Young and Dona Player Y; m. 9/30/23 to Lois Hobgood. Educ: Ben Hill and Turner Co. elem. and high sch, 07-20. Polit. & Govt. Pos: Co. cmnr, Ben Hill Co, Ga, 51-56; Ga. State Sen, 45th Dist, 57-58 and 13th Dist, 63- Bus. & Prof. Pos: Farmer and merchant. Mem: Mason; Shrine. Rel: Methodist. Mailing Add: R.R. 2, Rebecca, Ga. 31783. (1967)

YOUNG, MAXCINE D
b. Laurens, S.C, 6/1/07; married; c. John Luther. Educ: S.C. State Col; Gamma Phi Delta. Polit. & Govt. Pos: Mich. State Rep, 60-66; precinct del. for 14 years, bd. mem. of 13th Dem. Cong. Dist. Bus. & Prof. Pos: Real estate saleswoman; exec. secy, Progressive Civic League. Mem: Nat. Coun. of Negro Women; League of Women Voters; NAACP; bus. mgr, Hand of Mercy Club; daughter ruler of Beulah Land Temple of Elks. Rel: Peoples Community Church. Mailing Add: 2038 Delaware St, Detroit, Mich. 48206. (1967)

YOUNG, MELVIN RICHARD R
b. Norfolk, Va, 10/20/10; s. Melvin R. Young and Nola Winingder Y; m. July, 1956 to Mary Ellen Chrisman; c. Sandra, Mary Ellen, Ann and Christopher. Educ: Va. Polytech. Inst, B.S. in indust. eng. Polit. & Govt. Pos: Mayor, Ft. Lauderdale, Fla, 63-65; state chmn, Kirk for Gov. Campaign. Bus. & Prof. Pos: Owner, Ocean Manor Resort Hotel, Ft. Lauderdale, Fla. and pres, Worden-Young Import-Export, currently; dir, Am. Nat. Bank; mem. bd. trustees, Pine Crest Sch. and mem. bd, Nova Univ. Adv. Tech. Mil. Serv: Entered as Lt.(jg), Naval Res, 42, released as Lt. Comdr, after serv. as Naval Aviator. Rel: Presbyterian; Mem. bd. trustees. Mailing Add: Ocean Manor Hotel, P.O. Box 8484, Ft. Lauderdale, Fla. 33310.

YOUNG, MILTON R. R
U.S. Sen, N.Dak.
b. Berlin, N.Dak, 12/6/97; m. 7/7/19 to Malinda V. Benson; c. Wendell M, Duane C. and John M. Educ: N.Dak. State Agr. Col; Graceland Col, Lamoni, Iowa. Polit. & Govt. Pos: Mem. of sch, twp. and col. AAA bd; N.Dak. State Rep, 32-34; N.Dak. State Sen, 34-45, pres. pro tem, 41, Majority Floor Leader, 43; U.S. Sen, N.Dak, 45-, secy, Senate Rep. Conf. Cmt, 48-, ranking Rep, Senate Appropriations Cmt, second ranking Rep, Agr. and Forestry Cmt. Bus. & Prof. Pos: Farmer. Legal Res: LaMoure, N.Dak. 58458. Mailing Add: 2800 Quebec St. N.W, Washington, D.C. 20008.

YOUNG, PAUL E, SR. D
b. 1904. Educ: Cumberland Univ, Tenn, Sigma Alpha Epsilon. Polit. & Govt. Pos: Ky. State Rep, 54-66; former justice of the peace, 18 years. Bus. & Prof. Pos: Farmer; tobacco warehouseman. Rel: Methodist. Mailing Add: Olmstead, Ky. 42265. (1967)

YOUNG, RICHARD A. D
Mich. State Rep.
b. 1/16/27; married; c. Sharon, Michael. Educ: Grad, Univ. of Detroit, B.S. pub. admin; Wayne State Univ, LL.B; now attending Univ. of Mich; Alpha Kappa Psi; Delta Theta Pi. Polit. & Govt. Pos: Mich. State Rep, 64-; former treas. of Dearborn Twp. and Dearborn Heights. Bus. & Prof. Pos: Asst. Prof. at the Univ. of Detroit; attorney at law; formerly employed by the auditor gen. of Detroit; Internal Revenue Serv; Ernst and Ernst, CPA firm. Mil. Serv: Army Air Force. Mem: Treas, Dearborn Heights Goodfellows; Dearborn, Detroit, Mich. and Am. Bar Asns; Dearborn Heights Dem. Club. Rel: Catholic. Mailing Add: 24442 W. Warren Rd, Dearborn Heights, Mich. 48127. (1967)

YOUNG, RICHARD FREEMAN D
Chmn, Garfield Co. Dem. Party, Okla.
b. Swan, Iowa, 4/19/29; s. Ross Theodore Young and Ethlene Freeman Y; m. 4/20/57 to Sharon Lee Lynch; c. Jeffrey Mark, Jennifer Ann and Brenda Lee. Educ: Drake Univ, $1\frac{1}{2}$ years; Iowa State Col, 2 years. Polit. & Govt. Pos: Precinct chmn, Dem. Party, Des Moines, Iowa, 58-60 and Enid, Okla, 62-67; campaign mgr. for gubernatorial cand. Preston Moore, Enid, 66; chmn, Garfield Co. Dem. Party, 67-; del. and hon. v.pres, Dem. Nat. Conv, 68; acting dist.

chmn, Dem. Party, Enid and chmn, Credentials Cmt, Okla. Dem. State Conv, 68. Mil. Serv: Entered as Pvt, Army, 50, released as Sgt. 1/C, 52, after serv. in Army Engrs, Korean War, 50-52; grad, Mil. Law and Army Justice Course; Good Conduct Medal. Mem: Okla. and Enid Claimsmen Asns; C. of C.(v.chmn, govt. affairs cmt, 66); YMCA (dir, youth and govt. prog, 62-65); Mason (32°); Shrine; Odd Fellows; Am. Legion. Rel: Christian; bd. dirs, Cent. Christian Church, 62-66. Legal Res: 908 N. Oakwood Rd, Enid, Okla. 73701. Mailing Add: Box 1863, Enid, Okla. 73701.

YOUNG, ROBERT A. D
Mo. State Sen.
b. St. Louis, Mo, 11/27/23; m. 11/27/47 to Irene Slawson; c. Ann Grace, Robert Anton, Jr. and Margaret Mary. Educ: St. Louis Parochial Schs, McBride High Sch, Normandy High Sch, St. Louis, Mo. Polit. & Govt. Pos: Former chmn, Permanent Cmt. on Correctional Insts. and Probs; chmn, Atomic Energy Cmn; Dem. committeeman, Airport Twp. St. Louis Co, Mo, 52, 54, 56, 58, 60, 64 & 68; Mo. State Rep, 56-62; del, Dem. Nat. Conv, 60, 64 & 68; Mo. State Sen, 62- Mil. Serv: Army, 43-45; 346th Inf, 87th Div, ETO. Mem: Am. Legion; Lions; K. of C; past comdr, St. Ann Mem. Post; VFW; life mem, Amvets; Pipefitters Union. Rel: Catholic. Mailing Add: 3500 Adie Rd, St. Ann, Mo. 63074.

YOUNG, ROBERT ELLIS R
Mo. State Rep.
b. Logansport, Ind, 11/12/19; m. 1/5/52 to Priscilla Mariea; c. John Cobb, Robert Ellis, Jr. and Donald James Mariea. Educ: Wabash Col, Crawfordsville, Ind, B.A; Phi Beta Kappa. Polit. & Govt. Pos: Pub. rels. dir, Citizens' Cmt. for Reports from Kem, 51; field rep, Mo. for Eisenhower, 52; Mo. State Rep, 54-; serv. as asst. minority floor leader in the Seventy-fourth Gen. Assembly and mem. appropriations and agr. cmts. in the Seventy-fifth Gen. Assembly; also serv. on Legis. Research and State Fiscal Affairs Joint Cmts. Bus. & Prof. Pos: Former radio news and newspaper ed; secy, Carthage Indust. Develop. Corp; exec. secy, Carthage, C. of C, 56-68. Mil. Serv: Army, Signal Corps, 41-46. Mem: Am. Legion; Jasper Co. Hist. Soc; C. of C. Execs. of Mo; State Hist. Soc. of Mo; East. Jasper Co. Ment. Health Asn; secy, East. Jasper Co. Hist. Sites Asn; Jasper Co. Develop. Asn; dir, Jasper Co. Unit of Am. Cancer Soc.(pres, 58-59); George Washington Carver Dist. Birthplace Asn.(pres, 60-61, chmn, 60-61 & 67-69, dir, 62, 64 & 66); Civil War Centennial Cmn. of Mo, 58-65; v.chmn, Mo. Tourism Cmn, 67-69; chmn, U.S. Hwy. 71 Asn, 68-69. Received St. Louis Globe-Dem. Newspaper's Meritorious Pub. Serv. Award as the House Mem. most effective in debate for 65-66; 1968 Conservationist of the Year Award from the Conserv. Fedn. of Mo, Sears-Roebuck Found. and Nat. Wildlife Fedn. Rel: Protestant-Episcopal. Mailing Add: 208 W. Macon St, Carthage, Mo. 64836.

YOUNG, ROBERT ELMO R
b. Harrisburg, Pa, 8/28/33; s. Benjamin Franklin Young, Jr. and Reba Koontz Y; single. Educ: Dickinson Col, A.B, magna cum laude with spec. honors in Polit. Sci, 59, Sch. Law, 58-59; Grad. Sch. Pa. State Univ, 59-60; Phi Beta Kappa; Nat. Soc. Sci. Honor Soc; Pi Gamma Mu; Sigma Chi. Polit. & Govt. Pos: Mem, Pa. Rep. Research and Planning Corp, 65-; mem, Young Rep. State Cmt, Pa, 66-67; chmn, Dauphin Co. Young Rep, 66-67; pres, Citizens for a Modern Constitution, 67-; mem, Pa. Gov. Youth Adv. Coun, 67-; mem, Harrisburg Mayor's Citizens Adv. Cmt, 68-; exec. asst. to chmn, appropriations cmt, Pa. State Senate, 68- Bus. & Prof. Pos: Supvr. div. practices, Pa. Power & Light Co, Harrisburg, 60-67. Mil. Serv: Entered as Pvt, Army, 53, released as Specialist 2/C, 56, after serv. in Security Agency, First Army, 53-56; Good Conduct and Nat. Defense Serv. Medals. Mem: Elks; Dickinson Col. Alumni Coun; Harrisburg Commun. Theatre; Muscular Dystrophy Asns. Am; William Penn Mem. Mus. Assocs. Best Alumni Chap. Officer Award, Sigma Chi; Outstanding Young Man of Am, U.S. Jr. C. of C. Rel: Roman Catholic; Lay Lector. Mailing Add: 3401 Rutherford St, Harrisburg, Pa. 17111.

YOUNG, ROBERT WESLEY R
Chmn, Woodstock Rep. Town Cmt, Conn.
b. N.Y.C, 3/31/22; s. Clarence Wesley Young and Dorothy Bruce Y.(deceased); m. 12/27/48 to Charlotte Albiston; c. Douglas Bruce. Educ: State Univ. N.Y; Col. Ceramics, Alfred Univ. B.Sc. in glass tech, 48; N.Mex. Highlands Univ, M.S. in inorganic chem, 51; Alpha Phi Omega. Polit. & Govt. Pos: Mem, Woodstock Rep. Town Cmt, Conn, 58-64, chmn, 64-; justice of the peace, Woodstock, 62-64 & 67- Bus. & Prof. Pos: Sr. glass technician, Research Div, Am. Optical Co, 53-59 & 60-66, head glass develop. labs, 60- and chief research engr, 66-; lectr, chem, Annhurst Col, Conn. Mil. Serv: Entered as Ens, Naval Res, 44, released as Lt.(jg), 46, after serv. in Amphibious Forces, Fifth Fleet, Iwo Jima Theater, 45; Lt. Comdr, Commanding Officer, Naval Res. Research Co, 55; Naval Res. Medal; Armed Forces Medal; Atlantic and Pac. Theater Ribbons; World War II Victory Medal. Publ: Articles on chem. and glass tech, 52-66. Mem: Am. Chem. Soc; Am. Ceramic Soc; Nat. Inst. of Ceramic Engrs; Eagle Scout, Scouts' Key, Silver Beaver, scout cmnr, East. Conn. Coun, Boy Scouts. 4 U.S. patents and 12 patent applications filed in U.S, U.K, France, W. Germany, Can. and Japan. Rel: Congregational. Legal Res: Childs Hill Rd, Woodstock, Conn. 06281. Mailing Add: P.O. Box 104, Woodstock, Conn. 06281. (1967)

YOUNG, SAMUEL H. R
b. Casey, Ill, 12/26/22; m. to Bonnie Ilten; c. Elisabeth, Samuel and Ellen. Educ: Univ. Ill. Champaign-Urbana, LL.B, 47, Law Sch, J.D, 48. Polit. & Govt. Pos: Mem, Evanston Young Rep, 48-55; precinct capt, Evanston Regular Rep. Orgn, 50-55; pres, Ill. Young Rep. Orgn, 51-53; chmn, Ill. Youth for Taft, 52; chief draftsman, Ill. Securities Law, 53; Securities Cmnr, Ill, 53-56; mem. bd. gov, United Rep. Fund, 53-50, chmn. Cook Co. membership dr, 59; chmn, speakers bur, Ill. Rep. State Cent. Cmt, 56; asst. campaign chmn. to Sen. Arthur Bidwill in reelection campaign of Charles F. Carpentier for Secy. of State, 56; Asst. Secy. of State, Ill, 56-58; chief draftsman, Ill. Motor Vehicle Code, 57; cand. Nat. chmn, Nat. Fedn. Young Rep, 59; campaign chmn, Samuel Witwer for U.S. Sen, 60; Rep. committeeman, Northfield Twp, 62 & 66; chmn, Rep. Judicial Slating Cmt. Cook Co, 68; cand, U.S. House Rep, 13th Dist, 68. Bus. & Prof. Pos: Instr. econ. and corp. finance, Univ. Ill, 47-49; instr. bus. finance, Northwest. Univ, 49-50; attorney, U.S. Securities and Exchange Cmn, Chicago, 48-49; assoc, Hinsaw & Culbertson, 49-53; partner, Hinshaw, Culbertson, Moelmann & Hoban, 58-59; partner, Hough, Young & Coale, 59-65; financial v.pres. and secy-treas, Am. Hosp. Supply Corp, 65-66; head law firm, Samuel H. Young Law Off, 66- Mil. Serv: Entered as Pvt, 44, released as Capt, 46, after serv. in paratroops, 13th and 82nd Airborne Div, ETO, 45-46. Publ: Ed. historical and practice note on Ill. Securities Law and Ill. Motor Vehicle Code, Smith-Hurd Annotated Statutes of Ill; various legal articles on securities, corp. and motor vehicle laws. Mem: Am. Soc. Corp. Secretaries; Am. Finance Asn; Econ. Club Chicago; Exec. Club Chicago; Chicago Coun. For. Rels; bd. gov, Home for Destitute and Crippled Children; Cmt. of 76 (past pres); past chmn, Fund Dr. for Citizens of Gr. Chicago; Ill. State Bar Asn.(bd. gov, 58, secy, 59-60, mem. and chmn. various cmts); Chicago Bar Asn.(mem. and chmn. various cmts); Attic Club; Delta Tau Delta. Rel: Community Church. Legal Res: 735 Raleigh Rd, Glenview, Ill. 60025. Mailing Add: 135 S. La Salle St, Chicago, Ill. 60025.

YOUNG, STEPHEN M. D
U.S. Sen, Ohio
b. 5/4/89; s. Stephen M. Young and Belle Wagner Y; m. 1911 to Ruby L. Dawley, wid, 52; c. Stephen and Richard D.(both deceased) and Marjorie L. Educ: West. Res. Univ, LL.B, 11. Hon. Degrees, West. Res. Univ, Kenyon Col. and Cent. State Col. and Chubb Fel, Yale Univ. Polit. & Govt. Pos: Ohio State Rep, 13-17; mem, Ohio Cmn. on Unemploy. Ins, 31-32; U.S. Rep-at-lg, Ohio, 32-34; Allied Mil. Gov, Province Reggio Emilia, Italy, 45; U.S. Sen, Ohio, 58-, former chmn, Subcmt. on Pub. Bldg. and Grounds, U.S. Senate, chmn, Flood Control and Rivers and Harbors Subcmt, mem, Pub. Works Cmt, Armed Serv. and Aeronaut. and Space Sci. Cmts, mem, Spec. Cmt. on Aging. Mil. Serv: Army, Field Artil, 17-18 and Field Serv, N.Africa and Combat Serv, 5th Army, Italy, 42-45; Lt. Col, Army Res; Bronze Star; 4 Battle Stars; Order of Crown Italy and Commendation of Gen. Mark W. Clark. Mem: Past pres, War Vet. Bar Asn. of Cleveland and Cuyahoga Co. Bar Asn. Legal Res: Cleveland, Ohio. Mailing Add: U.S. Senate Bldg, Washington, D.C. 20510.

YOUNG, THOMAS FRANKLIN R
Ore. State Rep.
b. Baker, Ore, 10/7/28; s. Lonnie Franklin Young and Marjorie Snook Y; m. 12/26/53 to Patricia Jeanne Doherty; c. Jeffery Thomas, Holley Ann, Kelley Jean and Christopher David. Educ: Univ. of Ore, B.S, 50; Northwest. Col. of Law, LL.B, 57; Phi Kappa Sigma. Polit. & Govt. Pos: Ore. State Rep, 69- Bus. & Prof. Pos: Attorney, Banta, Silven & Young Law Firm, Baker Ore, 57- Mil. Serv: Entered as Pvt, Army, 51, released as Pfc, 53, after serv. in Chemical Corp. Mem: Rotary; Mason; Scottish Rite; Shrine. Rel: Presbyterian. Mailing Add: 3015 N. Second St, Baker, Ore. 97814.

YOUNG, THOMAS HAROLD R
b. Dunlo, Pa, 9/1/32; s. Harold Edward Young and Mary Thomas Y; m. 1/11/54 to Sara K. Martin; c. Thomas H, Jr, Theodore A, Timothy A, Cathy S, Cynthia A, Carol J, Sara K. and Sylvia A. Educ: Youngwood High Sch, grad, 50. Polit. & Govt. Pos: Committeeman, Westmoreland Co. Rep. Party, Pa, 60-67; chmn, Youngwood Rep. Cmt, 61-66; pres, Hempfield Area Sch. Bd, 65-; mem, Youngwood Planning Cmt, Youngwood Town Coun, 67-69; cong. cand, U.S. House Rep, 21st Cong. Dist, 68. Mil. Serv: Entered as Pvt, Army, 53, released as Sgt, 55, after serv. in Army Security Agency, ETO, 53-55. Mem: Pa. Food Merchants Asn; Cent. Westmoreland C. of C.(chmn, 66, dir, 66); Youngwood Area Prfnl. Asn.(dir, 66-68); Elks; Am. Legion; Youngwood Area Jaycees. One of Top Ten Jaycees in Pa, Spoke Award, 62. Rel: Protestant. Mailing Add: 606 S. Sixth St, Youngwood, Pa. 15697.

YOUNG, WENDELL WILLIAM D
b. Phila, Pa, 7/7/38; s. Wendell W. Young, Jr. and Gladys Brenner Y; m. 10/15/60 to Marilyn Louise Fluehr; c. Wendell W, IV, Brian Joseph and Scott Andrew. Educ: St. Joseph's Col, B.S, 60; Temple Univ, postgrad. work, 60-61; Univ. Pa; Pa. State Univ; Ed. newspaper, Nat. Fedn. Cath. Col. Students, officer of state-wide orgn, 2 years; class rep, 4 years; class officer, 2 years; Dramatics, 3 years; Glee Club, 4 years. Polit. & Govt. Pos: Ward leader, Dem. Party, Phila. Co, Pa, 63-68; mem, Phila. Co. Dem. Exec. Party, 63-68; chmn. various campaigns for Congressmen and Senators, 63-; alternate del, Dem. Nat. Conv, 64 and del, 68; chmn, United Labor Alliance for reelec. of Mayor Tate, 66; bd. dirs, Cmt. on Polit. Educ, 66- Bus. & Prof. Pos: Pres. and chief exec. officer, Retail Clerks Local 1357, 62-; v.pres, Phila. AFL-CIO, 63-; v.pres. and exec. bd. mem, Maritime Port Coun, 64-; chmn, active Ballot Club, Retail Clerks Int. Asn, 67-; secy-treas. and exec. bd. mem, Delaware Valley Food Coun, 68-; prof. ethics-labor mgt, St. Joseph's Col, 68- Mem: Am. Fedn. Teachers; Cath. Philopatrian; Torresdale Frankford Country Club; Northwood Civic Asn; United Fund Exec. Cmt. Youngest Labor Leader, Pa; Formerly Youngest Ward Leader, Phila. Co. Rel: Roman Catholic. Legal Res: 5004 Castor Ave, Philadelphia, Pa. 19124. Mailing Add: 5933 N. Broad St, Philadelphia, Pa. 19141.

YOUNG, WHITNEY MOORE, JR.
b. Lincoln Ridge, Ky, 7/31/21; s. Whitney Moore Young and Laura Ray Y; m. 1/2/44 to Margaret Buchner; c. Marcia Elaine and Lauren Lee. Educ: Ky. State Col, B.S, 41; Mass. Inst. Tech, 42-43; Univ. Minn, M.A, 47; Harvard Univ, 60-61; Alpha Phi Alpha. Hon. LL.D, N.C. Agr. & Tech. Col, 61. Polit. & Govt. Pos: Indust. rels. and voc. guid. dir, St. Paul Urban League, 47-50; exec. secy, Omaha Urban League, 50-58; exec. dir, Nat. Urban League, 61-; mem, President's Cmt. Youth Employ. and adv. cmt, Secy. of Health, Educ. and Welfare; consult, U.S. Pub. Health Dept. Bus. & Prof. Pos: Instr, Sch. Soc. Work, Univ. Nebr, 50-58; dean, Sch. Soc. Work, Atlanta Univ, 54-60; nat. adv. coun, AFL-CIO Commun. Serv. Cmt; adv. bd, N.Y. Sch. Soc. Work, Columbia. Mil. Serv: Army, World War II. Publ: To Be Equal, 64; Intergroup Relations as a Challenge to Social Work Practice, 60; Integration—Role of Labor Education, 59; plus others. Mem: V.pres, Nat. Asn. Soc. Workers. Recipient Outstanding Alumni Award, Univ, Minn, 60; Florina Lasker Award, 60. Mailing Add: 29 Mohegan Place, New Rochelle, N.Y. 10804. (1967)

YOUNG, WILLIAM C. D
b. Paducah, Ky, 4/16/19; s. Thomas R. Young and Virginia A. Prince Y; m. 6/9/41 to Nannie M. Holloway; c. William C, Jr, Thomas, Janice, David and Stanly. Educ: West. Ky. Voc. Sch; Univ. Ky. Polit. & Govt. Pos: Former admin. aid to Gov. of Ky; del, Ky. and Nat. Dem. Conv; precinct capt, Dem. Party. Bus. & Prof. Pos: B.A. Railway Clerks; field dir, Cmt. on Polit.

Educ, AFL-CIO, currently. Mil. Serv: Entered as Pvt, Army, 42, released as Sgt, 46, after serv. in Asia and S.Pac. Mem: VFW. Rel: Baptist. Legal Res: 1038 Washington St, Paducah, Ky. 42001. Mailing Add: P.O. Box 275, Paducah, Ky. 42001.

YOUNG, WILLIAM JOSEPH R
b. Fulton, N.Y, 7/27/28; s. William Henry Young and Ethel Sommers Y; m. 6/21/58 to Jacqueline Ann Newton; c. Lisa Ann, Shonna Louise and Marica Ann. Educ: Becker Jr. Col, A.A. Polit. & Govt. Pos: Treas, Worcester Young Rep. Club, 62-63, pres, 64-65; mem. exec. cmt, Worcester Co. Rep. Club, 64-; chmn, Ward One, Worcester Rep. City Cmt, 67-69. Bus. & Prof. Pos: Asst. treas, Marine Plastics Inc, 60- Mil. Serv: Entered as A/S, Navy, 46, released as EM 3, 49, after serv. in U.S.S. Shannon. Rel: Catholic. Mailing Add: 17 Darnell Rd, Worcester, Mass. 01606.

YOUNG, WOOD HALL R
Mem, N.C. Rep. State Exec. Cmt.
b. Minneapolis, N.C, 12/31/14; s. Pink Lucius Young and Nell Burleson Y; m. 10/26/46 to Frances Elizabeth Buchanan; c. Victoria Nell, Vivian Leigh and Wood Hall, Jr. Educ: Appalachian State Univ, B.S. Polit. & Govt. Pos: Rep. precinct chmn, Minneapolis, N.C, 46-56; chmn, Avery Co. Rep. Party, 58-68; mem, N.C. Rep. State Exec. Cmt, 62-; Rep. cand, U.S. Rep, N.C. Tenth Cong. Dist, 68; alternate del, Rep. Nat. Conv, 68. Mil. Serv: Entered as Pvt, Air Force, 42, released as Pfc, 43. Mem: Mason; York Rite; Shrine; Minneapolis and Avery Co. PTA; Mt. Glynn Country Club; C. of C. Rel: Christian Church of N.Am. Mailing Add: Box 14, Minneapolis, N.C. 28652.

YOUNGBLOOD, CHARLES N, JR. D
Mich. State Sen.
b. Detroit, Mich, 4/24/32; s. Charles N. Youngblood and Lucille Stoll Y; m. 7/11/52 to Delores M. Buttigieg; c. Victoria Ann, Michael Charles, Donna Marie, Cynthia Ann and Cathleen Delores. Educ: Univ. Hawaii, 51-55; Wayne State Univ, 57-59. Polit. & Govt. Pos: Dep. sheriff, Wayne Co, Mich, 55-61; precinct del, Wayne Co, 61; mem, Constitutional Conv, Mich, 61-62; chief investr, Wayne Co. Road Cmn, 62; Mich. State Sen, 63-, mem, Cmts. on Tourist Industs. and Vet. Affairs, Mich. State Senate. Bus. & Prof. Pos: Pres, Pequaming Sales Corp, 65- Mil. Serv: Entered as Seaman Recruit, Navy, 49, released as BMSN 1, 55, after serv. in Korean Conflict; UN Serv, Nat. Defense and Korean Ribbons; Good Conduct Medal. Mem: K. of C; Amvets; Dads' Club; Detroit Police Sgts. and Lts; Mich. Serv. Asn; life mem, DAV. Rel: Catholic. Mailing Add: 17202 Teppert, Detroit, Mich. 48234. (1967)

YOUNGBLOOD, HAROLD FRANCIS R
b. Detroit, Mich, 8/7/07; s. Daniel Youngblood and Loretta Elizabeth Gausley Y; m. to Jennie J. Highstreet; c. Anita (Mrs. Leist), Joan (Mrs. Kostech), Nancy and Kathleen (Mrs. Elleray). Educ: St. Josephs Commercial Col, 27. Polit. & Govt. Pos: Clerk to Secy. of State, Mich, 27-28; clerk Wayne Co. Bd. Auditors, 28-34; U.S. Rep, Mich, 47-48; asst. to H. Stassen, For. Opers. Admin, U.S. State Dept, Berlin, 54-55; Rep. precinct committeeman. Bus. & Prof. Pos: Pres, Youngblood Plumbing & Heating Co. Mil. Serv: Entered Army, 25, released as Sgt, 28, after serv. in C-Co, 125th Inf, U.S.A. Mem: Elks; Lions. Rel: Roman Catholic. Mailing Add: 7333 Calle Arturo, Tucson, Ariz. 85710.

YOUNGDAHL, LUTHER W. D
b. Minneapolis, Minn, 5/29/96; s. John Carl Youngdahl and Elizabeth Johnson Y; m. 6/23/23 to Irene Annet Engdahl; c. Margaret Louise, Luther William Andrew and Paul David. Educ: Univ. Minn, 15-16; Gustavus Adolphus Col, A.B, 19; Minn. Col. of Law, LL.B, 21. Hon. L.H.D. and LL.D. degrees from 15 univs. and cols. Polit. & Govt. Pos: Sr. judge, city attorney, Minneapolis, Minn, 21-23, judge, munic. court, 30-36 and dist. court, Hennepin Co, 36-42; Assoc. Justice, Minn. Supreme Court, 42-47; Gov, Minn, 47-51; judge, U.S. Dist. Court, Wash, D.C, 51-66, sr. judge, 66-; off. del. from State Dept. to Third UN Conf. on Crime and Delinquency; mem, President's Cmt. on Law Enforcement and Admin. of Justice; mem. coun. judges, Nat. Coun. Crime and Delinquency. Mil. Serv: World War I. Awarded Grand Gross of the Royal Order of the North Star by King Gustaf V of Sweden. Legal Res: 4101 Cathedral Ave. N.W, Washington, D.C. 20016. Mailing Add: U.S. Courthouse, Washington, D.C. 20001.

YOUNGDALE, JAMES MARTIN DFL
b. Harcourt, Iowa, 2/8/19; s. Martin E. Youngdale and Eva Anderson Y; m. Dec. 1957 to Margaret Simmons; c. Eric and Mark. Educ: Carleton Col, B.A, 40; Am. Univ, 41; Nat. Inst. Pub. Affairs, 41; Univ. Minn, M.A, Ph.D. cand, 67-70. Polit. & Govt. Pos: Chmn, Swift Co. Democrat-Farm-Labor Party, Minn, 46-48; alternate del, Dem. Nat. Conv, 68; Democrat-Farm-Labor cand. for Cong. six times. Bus. & Prof. Pos: Farmer, Minn, 47-66. Mil. Serv: Entered as Ens, Navy, 42, released as Lt, 45. Publ: Third Party Footprints, Ross and Haines, 67. Mem: Farmer Union; Nat. Farmers Orgn. Grand Order of the Purge, Awarded by Hubert Humphrey, 52. Rel: Protestant. Mailing Add: 157 Williams, S.E, Minneapolis, Minn. 55414.

YOUNGDOFF, THEODORE EUGENE R
Mem, Calif. Rep. State Cent. Cmt.
b. Topeka, Kans, 6/22/17; s. Charles Nelson Youngdoff and Anna Erickson Y; m. 6/10/45 to Naomi Mae Johnson; c. Brenda Jo and Candice C. Educ: San Jose State, 1 year; Heald Col, 1 year. Polit. & Govt. Pos: Secy, Young Rep, San Mateo, Calif, 51; mem, San Mateo Co. Rep. Cent. Cmt, 64-; mem, Calif. Rep. State Cent. Cmt, 64- Mil. Serv: Entered as Pvt, Army, 39, released as Pfc, 40. Mem: Mason. Rel: Methodist. Mailing Add: 500 Occidental Ave, San Mateo, Calif. 94402.

YOUNGER, MILTON M. D
b. Bakersfield, Calif, 7/8/31; s. Louis J. Younger and Celia S. Birnbaum Y; m. 7/19/57 to Betty Lee Hoenshell; c. Lisa Lee, Cynthia Lee and Lynda Lee. Educ: Stanford Univ, A.B. & M.A, 53, LL.B, 56; Theta Chi; Phi Delta Phi. Polit. & Govt. Pos: Del, Dem. Nat. Conv, 68; pres, Kern Co. Dem. Coun, Calif, 68-69. Bus. & Prof. Pos: Partner, Chain & Younger, Bakersfield, 56- Mil. Serv: Entered as E-1, Army, 56, released as Capt, 58. Mem: Am, Calif. and Kern Co. Bar Asns; Am. Trial Lawyers Asn; pres. and bd. mem, Child Guid. Clin, 8 years. Rel: Jewish. Legal Res: 1833 Chevy Chase Dr, Bakersfield, Calif. 93306. Mailing Add: Suite 231 Sill Bldg, 1508 18th, Bakersfield, Calif. 93301.

YOUNGLUND, WALTER ARTHUR R
Colo. State Rep.
b. Weld Co, Colo, 12/20/23; s. Elmer Younglund and Jessie McCarthy Y; m. 4/10/46 to Meryl Gilbert; c. Louetta, Ladonna, Marleen, Marshia, Monty, Fairy, Frankie and Marshal. Educ: Elem. sch, 8 years. Polit. & Govt. Pos: Colo. State Rep, 68- Mil. Serv: With armed serv; Asiatic Ribbon with One Star. Mem: VFW; Am. Legion; Lions. Mailing Add: New Raymer, Colo. 80742.

YOUNKIN, JOSEPHINE COLLINS D
Kans. State Rep.
b. Junction City, Kans, 7/27/03; d. Joseph L. Collins and Agnes Webster C; m. 11/24/23 to Francis Earl Younkin; c. Norma Jean (Mrs. Gayle Milligan) and David Joseph. Educ: Junction City High Sch, Kans, grad, 22. Polit. & Govt. Pos: Treas, Geary Co, Kans, 64-68, dep. co. treas, 68-69; Kans. State Rep, 56th Dist, 69- Mem: Nat. Bus. and Prfnl. Women; Pilot Int; Kans. State Farm Bur. Gray Lady Award, Army Hosp, Ft. Riley, Kans. Rel: Presbyterian. Mailing Add: 128 W. Pine St, Junction City, Kans. 66441.

YOUSO, SEVERYN DONALD D
b. Willmar, Minn, 12/10/10; s. Fred Youso (deceased) and Martha Albright (deceased); m. 2/3/36 to Irene Ellen Henry; c. Betty Jayne, LuVerne, Severin, Jr, Ronald, Gary, Joan M. and Cathy Ann. Educ: St. Cloud Bus. Col. Polit. & Govt. Pos: Chmn, Benton Co. Dem. Party, Minn, 34-69. Mem: Minn. Newspaper Asn; Nat. Press Asn; Foley Bus. Bur; St. Cloud Eagles; K. of C; Foley Sportsman Club. Rel: Catholic. Mailing Add: 411 Third Ave. N, Foley, Minn. 56329.

YOUTZ, HEWITT G. R
Chmn, Fremont Co. Rep. Party, Wyo.
b. San Diego, Calif, 10/7/22; s. H. Fletcher Youtz and Lizzie Gleave Y; m. 4/6/44 to Mildred Josephine Brown; c. Charles, Jo Anne (Mrs. McFarland) and Thomas. Educ: Univ. Wyo, B.S, 47; Alpha Zeta. Polit. & Govt. Pos: State committeeman, Park Co. Rep. Party, Wyo, 61-62; chmn, Fremont Co. Rep. Party, 66-; alternate del, Rep. Nat. Conv, 68. Mailing Add: 929 Sahara Dr, Riverton, Wyo. 82501.

YTURRI, ANTHONY R
Ore. State Sen.
b. Jordan Valley, Ore, 10/19/14; s. Domingo Yturri and Justa Bilbao Y; m. 2/14/42 to Reme Jayo. Educ: Univ. Ore, B.A. and J.D; Phi Beta Kappa; Order of the Coif; Phi Delta Phi. Polit. & Govt. Pos: Ore. State Sen, Malheur, Baker, Harney and Grant Cos, 58-; pres, West. Conf, Coun. of State Govts, 63-64; regional mgr, Coun. of States Govts, 64-66. Mil. Serv: Entered as Pvt, Army, 42, released as Capt, 46, after serv. in Judge Adv. Gen. Dept, Philippines. Mem: Am, Ore. State and Malheur Co. Bar Asns; Judge Advocate's Asn; Am. Judicature Soc; Am. Legion; Elks; Kiwanis. Rel: Catholic. Legal Res: 1010 Eighth Ave. S.W, Ontario, Ore. 97914. Mailing Add: 89 S.W. Third Ave, Ontario, Ore. 97914.

YUNGHANS, ROBERT O. D
b. Kansas City, Kans, 11/29/19; s. Emil F. Yunghans and Edith L. Zane Y; m. 12/31/49 to Kathryn M. O'Toole; c. Joseph, Mary and James. Educ: Kans. State Univ, B.S, 45. Polit. & Govt. Pos: Mem, Seneca City Coun, Kans, 54-60; Kans. State Rep, 60-66; former pres, Kans. Dem. Club. Bus. & Prof. Pos: Ins. Agent, 53- Mil. Serv: Pvt, Army Air Force, 43; Lt. Col, Air Force Res, currently, Dep. Comdr. of Material, 935th Mil. Airlift Group, Richards-Gebaur, Mo. Mem: Kans. Asn. Independent Ins. Agents (former chmn, Rural Agents Cmn); K. of C.(4°); VFW; Am. Legion; C. of C; former chmn, Manepoja Dist, Jayhawk Area Coun, Boy Scouts. Rel: Catholic. Mailing Add: 401 N. Third St, Seneca, Kans. 66538.

YUSE, FRANK T. D
b. Spokane, Wash, 11/15/27; s. Frank Yuse and Mary Tarantina Y; m. 11/30/57 to Adonna H. Nuxoll; c. Mary, Janet, Paul, Rita and John. Educ: Gonzaga Univ, Wash, B.A. and M.A; East. Wash. State Col, B.E. and grad. work; Univ. of Wash, grad. work; John Hays fel. in humanities; Phi Delta Kappa. Polit. & Govt. Pos: Leader, Fifth Legis. Dist, Wash, 63-66; alternate del, Dem. Nat. Conv, 64. Bus. & Prof. Pos: Teacher and coach, Trent Sch. Dist, 56-58 and De Sales High Sch, 59-60; teacher and head dept, Shadle Park High Sch, 60-66. Mem: Elks. Rel: Catholic. Mailing Add: N. 7037 G St, Spokane, Wash. 99208.

Z

ZAAGMAN, MILTON R
Mich. State Sen.
b. Grand Rapids, Mich, 3/28/26; m. 1948 to Martha Haverkamp; c. Milton John, Carol Ruth, James Richard and Cynthia Lynn. Educ: Calvin Col; Wayne State Univ, degree in mortuary sci, 50. Polit. & Govt. Pos: Mich. State Sen, 62-; Co. Bd. of Supvrs, three terms. Bus. & Prof. Pos: Mortician. Mil. Serv: Navy. Mem: Am. Legion; Nat. Asn. of Co. Officials; Mich. Funeral Dirs. Asn. Rel: Christian Reformed. Mailing Add: 2251 Plymouth S.E, Grand Rapids, Mich. 49506.

ZABLOCKI, CLEMENT JOHN D
U.S. Rep, Wis.
b. Milwaukee, Wis, 11/18/12; s. Matt J. Zablocki and Mary Jankowski Z; m. 5/26/37 to Blanche M. Janic; c. Joseph Paul and Jane Frances. Educ: Marquette Univ, Ph.B. and grad. study in educ. Hon. LL.D, Marquette Univ, 66 and Alverno Col, 69. Polit. & Govt. Pos: Wis. State Sen, 42-48; U.S. Rep, Fourth Dist, Wis, 48-; del, Dem. Nat. Conv, 68. Bus. & Prof. Pos: Teacher, choir dir. and organist, Milwaukee. Mil. Serv: Lt. Col, Air Force Res. Publ: Sino Soviet Rivalry, Praeger, 66; 'The United States and Recent Events in Vietnam,' Vital Speeches of Our Day, 12/63; 'We Must Make Our Stand in

Vietnam,' Vietnam, A Report on a Wingspring Briefing, The Johnson Found, 64; 'A Third Pollution,' Nat. Eagle Mag, 6/65. Mem: Atlantic Coun. of U.S; Adv. Bd, Center for Strategic Studies, Georgetown Univ; adv. coun, Korean Cultural and Freedom Found, Inc; Am. Coun. of Polish Cultural Clubs; K. of C.(4°); ROA; Polish Asn. of Am; Polish Nat. Alliance; W. Milwaukee C. of C; Greenfield C. of C; S. Div. Civic Asn; Milwaukee Musicians Asn. Rel: Roman Catholic. Legal Res: 3245 W. Drury Lane, Milwaukee, Wis. 53215. Mailing Add: 2184 Rayburn Bldg, Washington, D.C. 20515.

ZABORSKI, RICHARD J. D
b. Milwaukee, Wis, 1/7/27. Educ: Marquette Univ, B.S, 53; Wis. Univ. Law Sch, postgrad. work. Polit. & Govt. Pos: Wis. State Sen, 54-66, Minority Leader, Wis. State Senate, 63 & 65; former chmn, Milwaukee Co. Dem. Full Employ. Conf. Bus. & Prof. Pos: Commun. rels. Mil. Serv: Army Inf, World War II and Korea; Purple Heart; Nuremberg Trials. Mem: Am. Legion; Holy Name Soc. Mailing Add: 18600 Midland Place, Brookfield, Wis. 53005.

ZABRISKIE, CHARLES VARD R
b. Eureka, Utah, 1/22/23; s. Albert Vard Zabriskie and Kathrynn Thomas Z; m. 3/14/43 to Shirley Thornton; c. Andrew, Richard and Thomas. Educ: Univ. Utah, M.D; Univ. Minn, M.S.(surgery). Polit. & Govt. Pos: Mem, Utah State Rep. Cent. Cmt, 62-69; legis. dist. chmn, Weber Co, Utah, 62; alternate del, Rep. Nat. Conv, 64; secy, Exec. Cmt, Utah Med. Polit. Action Cmt. Mil. Serv: Entered as Pvt, Army, 43, released as Lt. Comdr, Med. Corps, Naval Res. Mem: Am. Med. Asn; Am. Urological Asn; Exchange Club. Legal Res: 1888 27th St, Ogden, Utah 84403. Mailing Add: 950 25th St, Ogden, Utah 84401.

ZACCHINI, RENE A. D
b. Paris, France, 3/28/30; m. to Joan Shipley; c. Norman. Educ: Univ. Fla, B.A, 51; LL.B, 54. Polit. & Govt. Pos: Judge of Munic. Court, Tampa, Fla, 59; Fla. State Rep, 62-66; asst. city attorney, Tampa, 68- Bus. & Prof. Pos: Attorney. Mil. Serv: Army. Mem: Tampa and Hillsborough Co. Bar Asns; Fla. and Am. Bar Asns; Gr. Tampa C. of C; Gr. Tampa Showman's Asn. Mailing Add: 4811 Beachway Dr, Tampa, Fla. 33609.

ZACHARY, WALTER L, SR. R
Chmn, Yadkin Co. Rep. Party, N.C.
b. Yadkinville, N.C, 11/12/11; s. Willis Dobson Zachary and Sallie Inscore Z; m. 6/14/39 to Mary Jo Curry; c. Walter Lee, Jr, and Frank Curry. Educ: Wake Forest Law Sch, 2 years. Polit. & Govt. Pos: Chmn, Yadkin Co. Rep. Party, N.C, 40-; co. attorney, Yadkin Co, 46-56; solicitor, Yadkin Co. Criminal Court, 56- Mil. Serv: Entered as Pvt, Army, 44, released S/Sgt, 46, after serv. in U.S; Army Commendation Ribbon. Mem: N.C. Bar Asn; N.C. State Bar. Rel: Methodist. Mailing Add: Box 608, Yadkinville, N.C. 27055.

ZACHER, HARRY RAYMOND R
b. Elgin, N.Dak, 10/7/25; s. Edward Zacher and Mathlida Zeller Z; m. 10/13/46 to Esther E. Wegner; c. Clayton S. and Jolette S. Educ: Elgin High Sch, grad. Polit. & Govt. Pos: Chmn, Grant Co. Rep. Party, N.Dak, 64-66; Rep. precinct committeeman, Elgin, N.Dak, 66-; co. chmn, Kleppe for U.S. Rep, N.Dak, 68, mem, Kleppe for U.S. Rep. Cmt, 68- Bus. & Prof. Pos: Farmer, 46-50; owner, bar, 50-, trailer court, 58-; real estate broker, 69- Mem: Lions; Commercial Club; Vol. Fireman; Elks; Farm Bur. Rel: Lutheran. Mailing Add: 216 N. Main, Elgin, N.Dak. 58533.

ZACHOS, KIMON STEPHEN R
N.H. State Rep.
b. Concord, N.H, 11/20/30; s. Stephen Zachos and Sophia Bacogianis Z; m. 7/5/57 to Anne Colby; c. Ellen, Elizabeth and Sarah. Educ: Wesleyan Univ, B.A, 52; N.Y. Univ. Sch. of Law, LL.B, 55; Boston Univ. Law Sch, LL.M, 69; Delta Sigma Rho; Sigma Chi; Phi Delta Phi. Polit. & Govt. Pos: Del, N.H. Constitutional Conv, 64; N.H. State Rep. and chmn, Judiciary Cmt, N.H. House of Rep, 69- Bus. & Prof. Pos: Lawyer-partner, Sheehan, Phinney, Bass & Green, Manchester, N.H, 57-69. Mil. Serv: Entered as Pvt, Army, 55, released as Specialist 3/C, 57, after serv. in Third Armored Div, Germany, 56-57. Mem: Am. Bar Asn; Am. Judicature Soc; Ahepa. Citizen of the Year, Manchester YMCA, 65; Brotherhood Award, N.H. Chapter, Conference of Christians and Jews, 66. Rel: Greek Orthodox. Mailing Add: 52 N. Adams St, Manchester, N.H. 03104.

ZACHOS, VICTORIA R
Asst. Chmn, Rep. State Cmt, N.H.
b. Bennington, N.H, 7/6/29; d. Stephen Zachos (deceased) and Sophia Bacogiannis Z.(deceased); single. Educ: Concord Commercial Col, N.H, 48. Polit. & Govt. Pos: New Eng. Secy, New Eng. Coun. Young Rep, N.H, 52-54; chmn, N.H. Coun. Young Rep, 54-60, Nat. committeewoman, 60-64; chmn, Concord Rep. City Cmt, 64-68; asst. chmn. and head, womens div, Rep. State Cmt, N.H, 68- Bus. & Prof. Pos: Legal secy, Off. of Robert D. Branch, 48- Rel: Greek Orthodox. Mailing Add: 82 Warren St, Concord, N.H. 03301.

ZADROZNY, MITCHELL GEORGE R
b. Chicago, Ill, 12/23/23; s. John Zadrozny and Jeanette Ulick Z; single. Educ: Ill. State Univ, B.S, 47; Univ. Chicago, S.M, 49, Ph.D, 56. Polit. & Govt. Pos: Alternate del, Rep. Nat. Conv, 68; secy, 45th Ward Rep. Orgn, 68- Bus. & Prof. Pos: Civilian geogr. analyst, U.S. Dept. of Army, Tokyo, Japan, 50-52; lectr. geog. of Southeast Asia, Univ. Chicago Downtown Col, 53-55; dir. of research, Cambodia-Laos Proj, Univ. Chicago, 54-55; teacher, Wright City Col, 55-63, asst. prof, 63-66, assoc. prof, 66-69, prof, 69- Mil. Serv: Entered as Pvt, Army, 42, released as 2nd Lt, 45, after serv. as Bombardier, Third Army Air Force. Publ: Cambodia Handbook, Human Rels. Area Files Press, 55; Water Utilization in the Middle Mississippi Valley, Univ. Chicago Press, 56; World Regional Geography TV Guide with map supplement, Chicago Bd. of Educ, 62. Mem: Asn. of Am. Geogr; Ill. Geog. Asn; bd. dirs, Chicago Uptown Cmn; Cook Co. Col. Teachers Union; exec. dir, Rep. Orgn. Vol. of Ill. Rel: Catholic. Mailing Add: 4158 N. McVicker Ave, Chicago, Ill. 60634.

ZAFFKE, KERMIT JOHN R
b. Backus, Minn, 7/1/29; s. Aaron Zaffke Sr. and Blanche Bloom Z; m. 12/7/47 to Betty Kathryn Nystrom; c. K. John, Karna, Kendall, Karla, Kelvin and Kent. Educ: Backus High Sch. Polit. & Govt. Pos: Former chmn, Cass Co. Rep. Party, Minn. Rel: Baptist. Mailing Add: Backus, Minn. 56435. (1967)

ZAGONE, NICHOLAS D
b. Chicago, Ill, 2/8/31; m. to Darlene Johnson Z; c. Mary Beth, Theresa Lynn. Educ: DePaul U. Acad; Wright City Col; John Marshall Law Sch; Lawyers Inst. Polit. & Gov. Pos: Ill. State Rep, 62-66. Bus. & Prof. Pos: Lawyer. Mil. Serv: Opers. and Intel. Sect. of Army. Mem: Chicago Bar Asn; Justinian Soc. of Lawyers. Mailing Add: 11 S. LaSalle St, Chicago, Ill. 60603. (1967)

ZAGORIA, SAM R
b. Somerville, N.J, 4/9/19; s. Nathan Zagoria and Rebecca Shapiro Z; m. 12/21/41 to Sylvia Bomse; c. Paul, Marjorie, Ronald. Educ: Rutgers Univ, B.L. in Journalism, 41; Nieman Fellow Harvard, 54. Polit. & Govt. Pos: N.J. Defense Coun, Trenton, 41-42; Fed. Off. Govt. Reports, Newark, 42; admin. asst. to Sen. Clifford P. Case, N.J, 55-65; with Nat. Labor Rels. Bd, Wash, D.C, 65- Bus. & Prof. Pos: Reporter, Daily Home News, New Brunswick, N.J, 40-41 and Wash. Post, 46-55. Mil. Serv: Army Air Force, 42-45. Mem: Nat. Press Club, Wash; Soc. Nieman Fellows; Rutgers Univ. Alumni Asn. Rel: Jewish. Mailing Add: National Labor Relations Board, Washington, D.C. 20570.

ZAGULA, EDWARD ANDREW D
b. Weirton, W.Va, 1/24/25; s. Andrew S. Zagula and Stella Zellers Z; m. 2/11/56 to Beatrice Ciarrocchi; c. Deborah Ann, David Edward and Pamela Marie. Educ: Ga. Tech; Univ. S.C; W.Va. Univ. Polit. & Govt. Pos: Former chmn, Hancock Co. Dem. Exec. Cmt, W.Va; councilman, City of Weirton, W.Va, 56-60. Bus. & Prof. Pos: Pres, Chestnut Bowl Inc, 50-58; attorney at law, 63- Mil. Serv: Entered as A/S, Navy, 43, released as Lt.(jg), 47, after serv. in Pac. Area. Mem: Am. Trial Lawyers Asn; W.Va. Trial Lawyers Asn; Am. and W.Va. Bar Asns; Elks; K. of C; Int. Moose. Rel: Roman Catholic. Legal Res: 200 Donell St, Weirton, W.Va. Mailing Add: 3445 Main St, Weirton, W.Va. 26062. (1967)

ZAHN, DONALD M. R
b. Carey, Ohio, 8/20/23; s. Leo Norman Zahn and Margueritte Simonis Z; m. 10/6/43 to Mary Elizabeth Miller; c. Marilyn, Bruce and Diane. Educ: Bowling Green State Univ, B.S. in educ, 46; Colo. Univ, M.A. in hist, 48; Ohio State Univ, 48-50; Phi Alpha Theta; Alpha Tau Omega. Polit. & Govt. Pos: Archivist, Nat. Archives, 50-57; admin. asst. to U.S. Rep. Jackson E. Betts, Md, 57- Mil. Serv: Pvt, Army, 42-44. Hobbies: Sports and Music. Rel: Catholic. Legal Res: Carey, Ohio 43316. Mailing Add: 6014 85th Place, New Carrollton, Md. 20784.

ZAHNER, KENYON BENEDICT, JR. R
Chmn, Catawba Co. Rep. Exec. Cmt, N.C.
b. Atlanta, Ga. 1/17/30; s. Kenyon Benedict Zahner, Sr. and Harriet Evalina Loyer Lawton Z; m. 12/26/51 to Jane Linn Henley; c. Kenyon B, III, Courtney Linn, Linn Henley, Catherine Cleveland and Cleveland Benedict. Educ: Univ. N.C, Chapel Hill, 49-51; N.C. State Univ, B.S, 55; Phi Delta Theta. Polit. & Govt. Pos: Chmn, Catawba Co. Rep. Finance Cmt, N.C, 63-65; mem, N.C. Rep. State Exec. Cmt, 64-; mem, Tenth Cong. Dist. Rep. Exec. Cmt, 66-; chmn, Catawba Co. Rep. Exec. Cmt, 66- Bus. & Prof. Pos: Poultry specialist, Lindsay-Robinson, Inc, 55-56; mgr, Bumgarner Poultry, Iron Sta, N.C, 56-58; farmer, Catawba Co, 58-61; agent, New Eng. Mutual Life Ins. Co, Boston, Mass, 61- Mil. Serv: Entered as Recruit, Army, 51, released as Specialist 1/C, 53, after serv. in 529th FAOBN and Seventh Army Intel, West. Zone, Germany, 52. Mem: Am. Col. Life Underwriters; Nat. Asn. Life Underwriters; Farm Bur. Rel: Episcopal. Legal Res: Old St. Paul Church Rd, Newton, N.C. 28658. Mailing Add: P.O. Box 1630, Hickory, N.C. 28601.

ZAHOREC, JOSEPH JOHN D
Spec. Events Chmn, Lorain Co. Dem. Exec. Cmt, Ohio
b. Lorain, Ohio, 7/2/20; s. John Steve Zahorec and Mary Marincin Z; m. to Helen M. Jalowiec; c. John J, Jolynne Jaykel, Mary Ellen and Susan. Educ: Lorain High Sch, grad, 38. Polit. & Govt. Pos: Zoning inspector, Black River Twp, Ohio; precinct committeeman, Lorain City Dem. Cent. Cmt; spec. events chmn, Lorain Co. Dem. Exec. Cmt, 66-; alternate del, Dem. Nat. Conv, 68; del, Dem. State Conv, 68. Bus. & Prof. Pos: Music instr; realtor and owner, Zahorec Realty; notary pub. Mem: Lorain Real Estate Bd; Ohio Real Estate Bd.(past pres); Nat. Real Estate Bd.(former dir); Lorain City Club (pres); Lions; Elks; C. of C; Niarol Civic Club; Slovak Club; United Polish Club; Ambassadors Club (past pres); Cent. Bus. Men's Asn.(dir); Lorain City Sustaining Club; Polish Legion of Am. Vet; Polish Am. Citizens Club; Ohio Billion Dollar Club. Realtor of the Year, 65; cand, Man of the Year, 68. Rel: Catholic. Mailing Add: 238 Jefferson St, Lorain, Ohio 44052.

ZAKAIB, PAUL, JR. R
W.Va. State Del.
b. Los Angeles, Calif, 10/20/32; s. Paul Zakaib, Sr. and Hazel Rahal Z; m. to Maria L. De Rito; c. Paul, III. Educ: Morris Harvey Col, A.B. in Polit. Sci, 55; W.Va. Univ, LL.B; Phi Delta Phi; Phi Sigma Phi; pres, W.Va. Univ. Young Rep. Club. Polit. & Govt. Pos: Mem. adv. cmt, W.Va. Young Rep. League, 55-58; chmn, Membership Cmt, Kanawha Co. Young Rep. Club, 58, secy, 59; attorney, W.Va. Dept. Employ. Security, 58-59; clerk, U.S. Dept. Justice, D.C, 58; Attorney, W.Va. State Tax Cmn, 58, W.Va. Dept. Employ. Security, 58-59 and W.Va. Econ. Develop. Agency, 59-60; exec. asst, W.Va. Dept. Commerce, 60-62; W.Va. State Del, 67- Bus. & Prof. Pos: Attorney, Preiser, Greene & Hunt, Charleston, W.Va, currently. Mil. Serv: Entered as Pvt, Army, 52, released as Pfc, 54, after serv. in 34th Regt. Combat Team, Korean Conflict; Cpl, Army Res; Good Conduct Ribbon; UN Command Ribbon; Far East Command Ribbon; Korean Campaign Ribbon with three Stars. Mem: Am. Bar Asn; W.Va. State Bar; Am. Trial Laweyrs Asn; Elks; VFW. Rel: Eastern Orthodox. Mailing Add: 1558 Lee St, Apt. D, Charleston, W.Va. 25311.

ZALLA, ALVIN BERNARD D
b. Cleveland, Ohio, 1/22/31; s. Morris A. Zalla and Celia Sanderson Z; m. 8/16/53 to Shirley Beck; c. David. Educ: Univ. Fla, A.B, 53, LL.B, 56; Fla.

Blue Key; Tau Kappa Alpha; Phi Alpha Delta; Pi Lambda Phi. Polit. & Govt. Pos: Pres, Young Dem. Club, Palm Beach Co, Fla, 60; dep. cmnr, Fla. Indust. Cmt, Workmans Compensation Div, 60-61; city attorney, Palm Springs, 60-; precinct committeeman, Palm Beach Co. Dem. Exec. Cmt, 60-, chmn, 62-65; dist. dir, Young Dem. Fla, 61; nat. committeeman, Young Dem. Clubs Am, Fla, 62-69. Bus. & Prof. Pos: Lawyer, private practice, 56- Mem: Acad. of Fla. Trial Lawyers; Fla. Asn. of Compensation Attorneys; Am. Trial Lawyers Asn; Kiwanis; B'nai B'rith. Rel: Jewish. Legal Res: 325 Mid Pines, Palm Springs, Fla. 33460. Mailing Add: P.O. Box 947, West Palm Beach, Fla. 33402.

ZAMPANO, ROBERT CARMINE D
b. New Haven, Conn, 3/18/29; s. Anthony N. Zampano and Marie Fusco Z; m. 11/23/50 to Dorothea Mae Gilbridge; c. Deborah Lee and Robert Anthony. Educ: Gunnery Sch, Conn, 47; Yale, B.A, 51, LL.B, 54. Polit. & Govt. Pos: Law clerk to U.S. Dist. Judge, Conn, 54-55; chmn, E.Haven Dem. Party, 56-61; Judge, E.Haven, 59-60; counsel, E.Haven, 56-61; exec. secy. rev. div, Superior Court, Conn, 56-61; U.S. Dist. Attorney, Conn, 61-64; U.S. Dist. Judge, Conn, 64- Bus. & Prof. Pos: With Thompson, Weir & Mac Donald, New Haven, Conn, 55-57 and law firm, Zampano & Mager, E.Haven, 59-61. Mem: Pres, E.Haven 175th Anniv. Cmt, 60; co-chmn, New Haven United Fund Drive, 56-57; cmnr, Quinnipiac Boy Scouts, 53; bd. dirs, A.R.C, E.Haven; New Haven, Am. Bar Asns; New Haven Jr. Bar, pres, 57-58; New Haven Jr. C. of C; K. of C; Melebus Club; Yale Club, dir, 60-63; Amity Club, Secy, 61. Mailing Add: 141 Church St, New Haven, Conn. 06510. (1967)

ZAMPIERI, JOHN JAMES D
Vt. State Rep.
b. Ryegate, Vt, 1/19/41; s. Giovianni G. Zampieri and Breatice Demeritt Z; m. to Joyce E. Andreoletti. Educ: Champlain Bus. Col. Polit. & Govt. Pos: Chmn, Ryegate Dem. Town Cmt, Vt, 65-; secy, Caledonia Co. Dem. Cmt, 65-; Vt. State Rep, 65-; trustee, Village South Ryegate, 66-69; del, Dem. Nat. Conv, 68. Bus. & Prof. Pos: Salesman, Nationwide Ins. Co, 63- Mil. Serv: Airman, Vt. Air Nat. Guard, 63- Mem: Woodsville Lions Club; Mi. Sinai Shrine; Montpelier, Vt; Pulaski Lodge 58, F&AM, Well Rivers, Vt; dir, Northeast. Vt. Develop. Asn. Rel: United Presbyterian. Mailing Add: Box 164, South Ryegate, Vt. 05069.

ZANGER, JOSEPH ANTHONY R
Chmn, San Benito Co. Rep. Cent. Cmt, Calif.
b. San Jose, Calif, 12/28/27; s. Dr. Henry George Zanger and Clara A. Cribari Z; m. 6/6/53 to Kathleen Kelsch; c. Wendy, Allene, Joseph C. and Gretchen. Educ: Univ. Santa Clara, 3 years. Polit. & Govt. Pos: San Benito Co. campaign mgr. for State Sen. Donald Grunsky, President Richard Nixon and Farmers for Gov. Reagan, Calif; finance chmn, San Benito Co. Rep. Cent. Cmt, Calif, 65-67, v.chmn, 67-69, chmn, 69-; mem, Calif. Rep. State Cent. Cmt, currently. Bus. & Prof. Pos: Chmn, San Benito Co. Fair Entertainment, 66-69; dir. and pres, San Benito Co. Farm Bur, 69; dir, State Farm Bur. Prune Research Cmt, 69; mem, Fed. Prune Admin. Cmt, 69; mem, Calif. State Prune Adv. Bd, 69; dir. and a founder Calif. Prune Bargaining Asn, 69; owner, Casa de Fruta Complex; owner, Zanger-Casa de Fruta Orchards. Mem: Elks; Santa Clara Co. Horseman Asn.(dir); San Benito Co. Saddle Horse Asn; San Benito Co. C. of C; Health Planning Coun, San Benito Co.(dir). Rel: Catholic. Mailing Add: 6680 Pacheco Pass Hwy, Hollister, Calif. 95023.

ZAPP, JOHN SHEA R
Treas, Rep. State Cent. Cmt, Ore.
b. Nampa; Idaho, 9/28/69; s. George M. Zapp, Sr. and Gertrude Shea Z; m. Joyce C. Boozer; c. Regina M, John, Jr, Megan, Michael and Mark. Educ: Boise Col, A.B, 57; Creighton Sch. of Dent, D.D.S, 61; Boise Col. Pres, 55; Pres, Delta Sigma Delta, 60-61; secy, Inter-Fraternity Coun, 59-60. Polit. & Govt. Pos: Finance chmn, Wasco Co. Rep. Cent. Cmt, 62-63, chmn, 65-67; chmn, Wasco Co. Young Rep, 64-65; state dir, Young Rep. Fedn. Ore, 64-65; chmn, Second Cong. Dist. Rep. Cent. Cmt, 65-67; mem, Rep. State Coord. Cmt, 66-; treas, Rep. State Cent. Cmt, Ore, 67-; chmn. budget cmt, Rep. State Cmt, 67-; treas, Rep. State Exec. Cmt. Ore, 67-; chmn, Biennial Rep. Platform Conv. Ore, 68; alternate del, Rep. Nat. Conv, 68. Bus. & Prof. Pos: Chmn, Mid-Columbia Commun. Col. Cmt, 63-67; v.chmn, State Commun. Col. Governance Cmt, 67-68; dir, Ore. Med. Polit. Action Cmt, 68-; chmn, Dentists of Ore. Polit. Action Cmt, 69- Mil. Serv: Entered as Pvt, Marines, 51, released as Sgt, 54, after serv. in First and Third Marines, Korea, 53-54; Purple Heart. Mem: Multnomah Co. Dent. Soc.(chmn. speakers bur, 68, legis. cmt, 68-); Ore. and Am. Dent. Asns; Am. Soc. of Dent. for Children; Am. Acad. of Gen. Dent; West. Soc. of Periodontology; Lions Int; C. of C; Navy League; Wash. Co. Pub. Affairs Forum. One of Oregon's Ten Outstanding Young Men, 64; Young Man of the Year, 65; Distinguished Serv. Award. Rel: Catholic. Mailing Add: 15485 N.W. Norwich Circle, Beaverton, Ore. 97005.

ZARETZKI, JOSEPH D
N.Y. State Sen.
Married; c. One. Educ: Columbia Col, A.B, 22; Columbia Law Sch, LL.B, 24. Polit. & Govt. Pos: N.Y. State Sen, 48-, Minority Leader, 57- and temporary pres, 65, N.Y. State Senate. Bus. & Prof. Pos: Lawyer. Mil. Serv: World War I. Mem: N.Y. State Bar Asn; Am. Legion; Mason; life mem. NAACP. Mailing Add: 160 Cabrini Blvd, New York, N.Y. 10033.

ZARNOWSKI, ALEXANDER F. R
Mayor, West Haven, Conn.
b. New Haven, Conn, 4/4/15; m. to Helen Mary Gorecki; c. David and Joseph. Polit. & Govt. Pos: Mayor, West Haven, Conn, 66-; mem, Rep. Town Meeting; councilman-at-lg, West Haven City Coun; alternate del, Rep. Nat. Conv, 68. Bus. & Prof. Pos: Treas, Campbell Court Develop. Corp. Mil. Serv: Merchant Marine Serv. Mem: Elks; K. of C; Polish Am. Club; Redmen; Polish Falcons of Am. Koscuiszko Soc. Mailing Add: 429 Blohm St, West Haven, Conn. 06516.

ZAROD, STANLEY JOHN D
Mass. State Sen.
b. Indian Orchard, Mass, 4/11/24; s. Johns Zarod and Sophie Borsa Z; m. 11/28/59 to Isabelle S. Guzik. Educ: Dartmouth Col, A.B, 44; Phi Gamma Delta. Polit. & Govt. Pos: City councilman, Springfield, Mass, 49-57, pres, city coun, 56, acting mayor, Springfield, 57-; Mass. State Sen, 57-67, 69-; dir. interstate coop. cmn, Mass, 67-68. Bus. & Prof. Pos: Self-employed in real estate, 50- Mil. Serv: Entered as Pvt, Marines, 42, released as Cpl, 46, after serv. in Sixth Marine Div, S.Pac, 43-46; Presidential Unit Citation. Mem: Am. Legion; Polish Am. Vet; Elks; K. of C. Rel: Catholic. Mailing Add: 537 Main St, Indian Orchard, Mass. 01051.

ZATEZALO, RUDOLPH EDWARD D
b. Belmont Park, Ohio, 4/7/21; s. Harry Zatezalo and Sarah Popcig Z; m. 1/20/46 to Juanita June Adami; c. Sara Page (Mrs. McCorkle) and Jani Anne. Educ: Wash. Univ, 1 year; Mo. Chiropractic Col, 3 years; Delta Sigma Chi. Polit. & Govt. Pos: Police judge, Clinton, Mo, 54-58; state finance chmn, Gov. Warren Hearnes, 64; exec. asst. to Dem. State chmn, 64-65; exec. dir, Mo. H.H. Humphrey Campaign, 68; del, Dem. Nat. Conv, 68. Bus. & Prof. Pos: Dr. Chiropractic, Clinton, Mo, 49-64; sr. v.pres, Civic Plaza Nat. Bank, Kansas City, Mo, currently. Mil. Serv: Army, 42-46, T-5, serv. in 66th Signal Bn, ETO and Pac. Theatre, 44-46; European Campaign, Philippine Liberation and Good Conduct Medals; Am. Theatre Serv. Medal; Mid. East. Serv. Medal; Asiatic Serv. Medal. Mem: VFW; Am. Legion; Elks (past Exalted Ruler); Mason; Rotary. Rel: Methodist. Legal Res: 10901 Tracy, Kansas City, Mo. 64131. Mailing Add: Civic Plaza National Bank, 13th and Oak, Kansas City, Mo. 64106.

ZAZAS, SYLVIA D
V.Chmn, Marion Co. Dem. Party, Ind.
b. Baltimore, Md, 7/1/21; d. Nathan Levinson and Nettie Gross L; m. 5/16/63 to George J. Zazas; c. Eric, James and Robert. Educ: Goucher Col, B.A, 45; Columbia Univ, summers 42, 43 & 44; Phi Beta Kappa. Polit. & Govt. Pos: Precinct v.committeeman, Dem. Party, Bethesda, Md, 53-56; precinct v.chmn, Marion Co, Ind, 57-69, ward v.chmn, 60-62; del, Dem. Nat. Conv, 68; v.chmn, Marion Co. Dem. Party, 68- Bus. & Prof. Pos: Economist, Fed. Reserve Bd, Wash, D.C, 46-53. Mem: Ind. Art Asn; League of Women Voters; Coun. on World Affairs; state and local Dem. clubs. Mailing Add: 6105 Shawnee Trail, Indianapolis, Ind. 46220.

Z'BERG, EDWIN L. D
Calif. State Assemblyman
b. Sacramento, Calif; m. to Edna Merle Coz; c. Vicki, John and Cynthia Susan. Educ: Univ. Calif, Los Angeles, B.A; Univ. San Francisco of Law, LL.B. summa cum laude, 51. Polit. & Govt. Pos: Calif. State Assemblyman, 58-; former Dep. Attorney Gen; mem, Calif. Dem. State Cent. Cmt. Bus. & Prof. Pos: Lawyer. Mil. Serv: Ens, Naval Res, 44-47; Lt.(jg), Res, currently. Mem: Sacramento Swiss Lodge; Sacramento Jr. C. of C; Foresters; NSGW; VFW. Received Gostic Award, Stanford Jr. High Sch, highest scholastic record in class; Valedictorian, Sacramento Sr. High Sch; received Pres. Scholarship, Univ. San Francisco. Legal Res: 1157 Lancaster Way, Sacramento, Calif. 95822. Mailing Add: 1501 W. Capitol Ave, West Sacramento, Calif. 95691. (1967)

ZEARFOSS, HERBERT KEYSER R
Pa. State Rep.
b. W. Chillisquaque Twp, Pa, 10/13/29; s. Dean Wilson Zearfoss and Susan Keyser Z; m. 12/19/53 to Thelma Mary McCarthy; c. Timothy David, Jonathan Andrew and Sarah Creighton. Educ: Bucknell Univ, A.B, 51; Yale Law Sch, 51-53; Wash. Col. Law, Am. Univ, J.D, 58; Omicron Delta Kappa; Phi Alpha Theta; Tau Kappa Alpha; Pi Sigma Alpha; Theta Chi; Alpha Phi Omega. Polit. & Govt. Pos: Mem, Radnor Twp. Park and Recreation Bd, Pa, 64-66; Justice of the Peace, Radnor Twp, Del. Co, 66-67; Pa. State Rep, 68- Bus. & Prof. Pos: Partner, Fetter & Zearfoss, Lewisburg, Pa, 59-60; asst. counsel, Fidelity Mutual Life Ins. Co, Phila, 60-66; secy-mgr, Ins. Fedn. of Pa, Phila, 66-68; lawyer, Wayne, Pa, 69- Mil. Serv: Entered as S/A, Naval Res, 54, released as Lt, 58, after serv. in Naval Security Sta, Wash, D.C, 54-58; Lt. Comdr, Navy Res, 63; Nat. Defense Serv. Medal; Naval Res. Medal. Publ: 'Gifts of Life Insurance, 4/61 and 'Health Insurance and Federal Tax Collector,' 4/64, Fidelity Field Man. Mem: Phi Alpha Delta; Life, Accident and Health Claims Asn. of Phila; Asn. Life Ins. Counsel; Am, Pa. and Phila. Bar Asns; Yale Club of Phila; Down Town Club of Phila; Waynesborough Country Club. Rel: Episcopal. Mailing Add: 615 Brookside Ave, St. Davids, Pa. 19087.

ZEBROSKI, LEON BERNARD R
b. Stamford, Conn, 11/15/39; s. Stanley A. Zebroski and Joan L. Lenczycki Z; m. to Eileen Mayers; c. David Alexander. Educ: Univ. Dayton, A.E, 62; Univ. Cincinnati, B.S, 62, M.Ed, 64; Iota Lambda Sigma; Hon. Soc. of Prfnl. Trade & Indust. Educators. Polit. & Govt. Pos: Mem, Bd. of Rep, City of Stamford, Conn, 65-66; third v.pres, Pulaski Rep. Orgn, 65-69. Bus. & Prof. Pos: Mgt. consult, Alexander Proudfoot Co, 64- Rel: Roman Catholic. Mailing Add: 39 Glenbrook Rd, Stamford, Conn. 06902.

ZEIGLER, EUGENE NOEL, JR. D
S.C. State Sen.
b. Florence, S.C; s. Eugene Noel Zeigler and Helen Townsend Z; m. 1953 to Anne Marian Lide; c. Belton T, Helen Townsend and Nina McClenaghan. Educ: Univ. of the South, Sewanee, Tenn, B.A, 42; Harvard Univ. Law Sch, LL.B, 49; Omicron Delta Kappa; Blue Key; Phi Beta Kappa. Polit. & Govt. Pos: S.C. State Rep, 61-62; spec. judge, 64-65; chmn, Gov. Interagency Coun. Arts and Humanities, 66; S.C. State Sen, 11th Dist, 67-68 and 16th Dist, 69- Bus. & Prof. Pos: Sr. partner, Zeigler & Townsend, Attorneys, 64- Mil. Serv: Vet, World War II, 4 years serv. on aircraft carriers, Capt. in Naval Res; selected as one of six Naval Res. Officers of 6th Naval Res. Dist. to attend Nat. War Col. in Wash, D.C. for a Defense Strategy Seminar. Rel: Episcopal; Vestryman, St. John's Episcopal Church. Legal Res: 823 Greenway Dr, Florence, S.C. 29501. Mailing Add: P.O. Box 266, Florence, S.C. 29501.

ZEILMANN, STEPHEN HUBERT R
b. Linn, Mo, 5/22/05; s. Louis Zeilmann and Mary Reinkemeyer Z; m. 11/28/28 to Gertrude A. Hastings; c. Jerome L, Richard J. and Nancy Ann (Mrs. Jaegers). Educ: St. Georges Parochial Sch, 14-20. Polit. & Govt. Pos: Mayor, Linn, Mo, 52-56; Mo. State Rep, 58-66; pub. adminstr, Osage Co, 69- Bus. & Prof. Pos: Owner, Zeilmann Bros, 30-68; mem. bd. educ, Linn High Sch, 47-49; fire chief, Linn Vol. Fire Dept, 55-58. Mem: Linn C. of C.(pres,

38-41); Linn Lions Club (pres, 65-66); West. Cath. Union (dep. v.pres, 68-); K. of C.(4°) and Grand Knight, 68- Rel: Catholic. Mailing Add: Linn, Mo. 65051.

ZEISER, BRUCE HUNTER R
Mass. State Rep.
b. Orange, N.J, 6/15/24; s. Bruce Rexford Zeiser and Louise Hunter Z; wid; m. 8/7/64 to Judith Wade Howes; c. Bambie (Mrs. Douglas K. Chard), Bruce Rexford, II, Linda Hunter, Walker Russell, Laurie Cameron and Anne Risley. Educ: Harvard Col, A.B. cum laude, 44; LL.B, 48; Speakers Club; Harvard Lampoon; Hasty Pudding Inst. 1770. Polit. & Govt. Pos: Chmn, R.I. Young Rep, 48-51; asst. counsel, Armed Serv. Petroleum Purchasing Agency, Wash, D.C, 51-52; nat. col. dir, Youth for Eisenhower, N.Y, 52; campaign mgr, Bayard Ewing for U.S. Sen, R.I, 52; spec. attorney, Dept. Justice, D.C, 53-54; asst. to gen. counsel, Fed. Housing Admin, D.C, 54-55; town moderator, Barrington, R.I, 56-59; v.chmn, Essex Co. Rep. Cmt, N.J, 60-62; chmn, Wellesley Rep. Town Cmt, Mass, 64-68; Mass. State Rep, Ninth Dist, 69- Bus. & Prof. Pos: Attorney, Letts and Quinn, Providence, R.I, 49-51; asst. secy, Title Guarantee Co. R.I, 56-59; field rep, Lawyers Title Ins. Corp, N.Y.C, 59-62; mgr, Lawyers Title Ins. Corp, Boston, Mass, 62- Mil. Serv: Entered as A/S, Navy, 43, released as Lt.(jg), 46, after serv. in Combat Commun. Unit,43, Pac, 44-46; Lt, Naval Res. Retired; Navy Unit Commendation Medal. Mem: R.I. Bar; Fed. Bar; U.S. Supreme Court; R.I. and Am. Bar Asns; Wellesley Town Meeting, 63- Rel: Episcopal. Mailing Add: 18 Kenilworth Rd, Wellesley, Mass. 02181.

ZELASKO, ANTONE RICHARD 'TONY' R
b. Tamaroa, Ill, 3/1/23; s. Leo Zelasko and Anna Kreft Z; m. 5/11/46 to Dorothy Mourek; c. Anthony, Jr, Robert and Carolyn. Educ: High Sch. Polit. & Govt. Pos: Precinct committeeman, Perry Co. Rep. Party, Ill, 58-; chmn, Perry Co. Rep. Cent. Cmt, Ill, 62-66. Bus. & Prof. Pos: Line foreman, Ill. State Tel. Co, 65- Mil. Serv: Entered as Pvt, Army, 43, released as Cpl. T-5, 46, after serv. in 371st Engr. Bn, Am. Theater. Mem: K. of C; PTA; IBEW. Rel: Catholic. Mailing Add: Route 1, Box 120, Tamaroa, Ill. 62888. (1967)

ZELENKO, HERBERT D
b. N.Y.C, 3/16/06; s. Barnett Zelenko and Lena Z; m. 12/25/29 to Rhoda Goldberg; c. Audrey (Mrs. Edwin Weiss). Educ: Columbia Col, 26; Columbia Law Sch, 28. Polit. & Govt. Pos: Asst. U.S. Attorney, 33-34; U.S. Rep, N.Y, 54-62. Legal Res: 200 E. 74th St, New York, N.Y. 10021. Mailing Add: 60 E. 42nd St, New York, N.Y. 10017.

ZEMAN, ROBERT THOMAS D
Secy, Peoria Co. Dem. Cent. Cmt, Ill.
b. Peoria, Ill, 5/14/14; s. John C. Zeman and Threasa Halligan Z; m. 6/2/36 to Margaret M. Powers; c. Mary Margaret (Mrs. Hipple), Francis Jean (Mrs. Siegriest) and Carroll Ann (Mrs. Gorman). Educ: Manual Training High Sch, 29-30. Polit. & Govt. Pos: Mem, City Zoning Bd. of Appeals, Peoria, Ill, 60-; secy, Peoria Co. Dem. Cent. Cmt, 69- Bus. & Prof. Pos: Dir, St. Patrick's Parish Credit Union, Peoria, Ill, 26. Mem: Brotherhood Railway, Airline & Steamship Clerks, Freight Handlers, Express & Station Employees; K. of C; Transportation Club of Peoria (treas). Rel: Catholic. Mailing Add: 1304 W. Kettelle St, Peoria, Ill. 61605.

ZEMMOL, ALLEN D
Chmn, 18th Cong. Dist. Dem. Cmt, Mich.
b. Detroit, Mich, 7/30/30; s. Julius Zemmol and Anna Eisenberg Z; m. 1/30/55 to Lita Belle Schechter; c. Miriam Beth, Deborah Ruth and Jonathan Israel. Educ: Univ. Mich, A.B, 52, J.D, 54; Phi Alpha Delta. Polit. & Govt. Pos: Precinct del, Oak Park Dem. Party, Mich, 62-67, mem. bd. canvassers, 64-68; pres, Oak Park Dem. Club, 65-67; Dem. nominee for cong, 18th Cong. Dist, 68; del, Dem. Nat. Conv, 68; precinct del, Southfield Twp. Dem. Party, 68-; chmn. 18th Cong. Dist. Dem. Cmt, 69- Bus. & Prof. Pos: Partner, Dingell, Hylton & Zemmol, Attorneys, 63- Mem: Detroit and Mich. Bar Asns; Am. Judicature Soc; Am. Trial Lawyers Asn; Am. Legion; Jewish War Vet; B'nai B'rith; NAACP; Mich. Asn. Emotionally Disturbed Children. Man of the Year, Oak Park Jr. C. of C, 65. Rel: Jewish. Mailing Add: 21501 W. 13 Mile Rd, Birmingham, Mich. 48010.

ZEMPRELLI, EDWARD P. D
Pa. State Sen.
b. Clairton, Pa, 5/11/25; s. John Zemprelli and Mary Mercurio Z; m. 4/23/49 to Margaret Antoinette; c. Carla. Educ: Pa. State Col, B.A, 45; Univ. Pittsburgh Law Sch, LL.B, 49; Sigma Chi; Skull and Bones; Nat. Forensic Soc; Phi Alpha Delta. Polit. & Govt. Pos: Solicitor, Clairton, Pa, 52-60; former chmn, Clairton Dem. Party; Pa. State Rep, 64-69; Pa. State Sen, 69- Bus. & Prof. Pos: Pres, Copperhead Enterprises Financial Insts. Mem: Am. and Allegheny Co. Bar Asns; Acad. of Trial Lawyers; pres, Clairton Rotary Club, 63-67; mem, bd. of dirs, Clairton Pub. Libr, 66; pres, C. of C, 51; K. of C.(4°); Sons of Columbus; Ital-Am. Instructive Club; Clairton Sportsmen's Club; Croation Fraternal Union; Am. Citizens Club; VFW; Ital. Sons & Daughters of Am. Rel: Roman Catholic. Mailing Add: 1244 Bickerton Dr, Clairton, Pa. 15025.

ZENGE, J. ANDY, JR. R
b. Canton, Mo, 9/10/12; s. J. Andy Zenge and Alice Parmalee Z; m. 11/19/38 to Dorothy Jennings; c. Thomas L. and Linda K. Educ: Culver-Stockton Col, A.B, 34; Univ. Mo. Sch. of Law, LL.B, 36. Polit. & Govt. Pos: Chmn, Lewis Co. Cent. Rep. Cmt, Mo, 62-68; Rep. cand, circuit judge, Mo, 68. Mil. Serv: Entered as Pvt, Marine Corp Res, 43, released as 1st Lt, 46. Mem: Mason; Shrine; Kiwanis; former mem, Rotary Club; Am. Legion. Rel: Christian Church. Legal Res: 907 White St, Canton, Mo. 63435. Mailing Add: 329 Lewis St, Canton, Mo. 63435.

ZENI, FERDINAND J, JR. R
b. Du Quoin, Ill, 10/2/24; s. Ferdinand J. Zeni, Sr. and Lea E. Walzer Z; single. Educ: Northwest. Univ, B.S, 47, Law Sch, J.D, 50; Delta Sigma Chi; Wranglers; Kappa Alpha. Hardy Scholarship, Northwest. Univ. Law Sch, 47-50. Polit. & Govt. Pos: Chmn, Cook Co. Young Rep. Orgn, Chicago, Ill, 54-55; mem. exec. bd, Young Rep. Orgn. Ill, 55-59; pres, 43rd Ward Regular Rep. Orgn, 59-64 and committeeman, 64-; Ill. cmnr, Nat. Conf. Cmnr. on Uniform State Laws, 69- Bus. & Prof. Pos: Attorney-at-Law, Russ & O'Keefe, Chicago, Ill, 50-58; gen. attorney, Montgomery Ward & Co, Inc, 58- Publ: 'Concerted Activities Under National Labor Relations Act,' Ill. Law Rev, 48; 'Wire Tapping,' J. of Criminal Law and Criminology, 50. Mem: Chicago and Am. Bar Asns; Lincoln Park Conserv. Asn. Rel: Roman Catholic. Mailing Add: 1400 Lake Shore Dr, Chicago, Ill. 60610.

ZENOVICH, GEORGE N. D
Calif. State Assmblyman
b. Fresno, Calif, 4/29/22; s. Nicholas F. Zenovich and Eva Sugich Z; m. 8/26/55 to Vera Sarenac; c. Ninon and Marina. Educ: Fresno State Col, B.A, 48; Southwest. Col. of Law, Los Angeles, LL.B, 52; Blue Key. Polit. & Govt. Pos: Mem, Fresno Co. Dem. Cent. Cmt, 56-62; Calif. State Assemblyman, 32nd Dist, 63-, Majority Floor Leader, Calif. State Assembly, 66, 67 & 68 and Dem. Caucus Chmn, 69-; del, Dem. Nat. Conv, 68. Bus. & Prof. Pos: Attorney-at-law, Fresno, Calif, 53- Mil. Serv: Entered as Pvt, 43, released as Cpl, 46, after serv. in 13th Air Force, Pac. Theater; Pac. Theater Ribbon. Mem: Am, Calif. and Fresno Co. Bars; life mem, Musicians Local 210, Fresno and mem. Local 47, Los Angeles; Int. Acad. of Law, Hague, Holland; NAACP; Fresno State Col. Alumni Asn. Rel: Serbian Orthodox. Legal Res: 3238 N. Arthur, Fresno, Calif. 93705. Mailing Add: 1060 Fulton Mall, Fresno, Calif. 93721.

ZEPEDA, BARBARA JOYCE D
Chmn, 43rd Legis. Dist. Dem. Orgn, Wash.
b. Spokane, Wash, 3/21/35; d. Kurt Gaebel and Elsie Katzenberger G; m. Aug. 1958 to Julian Zepeda; c. Lydia Ann. Educ: Univ. Wash, 2 years; Cosmos Club; Young Dem. Polit. & Govt. Pos: Mem, Wash. State Dem. Platform Cmt, 60; Dem. precinct committeewoman, Precinct 43-63, Wash, 60-69; alternate del, Dem. Nat. Conv, 68; chmn, 43rd Legis. Dist. Dem. Orgn, Wash, 69- Bus. & Prof. Pos: Co-owner, Zepeda Instruments, Seattle, currently. Mem: Montlake Commun. Club; PTA; League Women Voters; Am. for Dem. Action; Wash. Dem. Coun. Rel: Baptist. Mailing Add: 1937 25th E, Seattle, Wash. 98102.

ZETTERBERG, STEPHEN INGERSOLL D
Mem, Calif. Dem. State Cent. Cmt.
b. Galesburg, Ill, 8/2/16; s. Arvid P. Zetterberg and Winifred Ingersoll Z; m. 12/26/40 to Connie Lyon; c. Charles, Alan, Pierre and Del. Educ: Pomona Col, A.B, 38; Nat. Inst. Pub. Affairs, D.C, 38-39; Yale Law Sch, LL.B, 42. Polit. & Govt. Pos: Legis. asst, U.S. Sen. Scott Lucas, Calif, 39 & 46; jr. mediation officer, Nat. War Labor Bd, 42; Dem. Cand, U.S. House Rep, 48; Dem. nominee, U.S. House Rep, 50; mem. at various times, Dem. State and Co. Cmts, 48-; mem, Gov. Cmt. on Health Needs of Calif, 59; mem, Gov. Cmt. Health, 59-60; mem, Calif. State Bd. Health, 60-68; mem, Calif. Dem. State Cent. Cmt, 68-; mem, Los Angeles Co. Dem. Cent. Cmt, 68- Mil. Serv: Entered as A/S, Coast Guard Res, 42, released as Lt, 45, after serv. in Section Base, Hawaii and as officer, U.S.C.G. Cutter Tiger, Pac. Ocean Area, 43-46. Publ: Articles in newspapers on polit. and govt. subjects, 63- Mem: Am. Bar Asn; Am. Civil Liberties Union. Mailing Add: 350 Radcliffe Dr, Claremont, Calif. 91711.

ZICKGRAF, WALTER GRANT D
b. Hendersonville, N.C, 11/1/35; s. Grant L. Zickgraf and Thelma Elizabeth Camp Z; m. 1/30/57 to Geraldine Robinson; c. Beth, David. Educ: Univ. N.C, B.S, 58; Phi Delta Theta. Polit. & Govt. Pos: N.C. State Rep, 63-66. Bus. & Prof. Pos: Mgr, Nantahala Lumber Co, Franklin, N.C. Mem: Carolina Lumber and Bldg. Supply Asn, Charlotte, N.C. All Am. Swimmer, Univ. N.C. Rel: Baptist. Mailing Add: Hurst Circle Dr, Franklin, N.C. 28734. (1967)

ZIEBARTH, WAYNE W. D
Nebr. State Sen.
b. Wilcox, Nebr, 8/2/21; s. Herman J. Ziebarth and Martha Habben Z; m. 12/28/47 to Renee England; c. Jennifer, Jane and James. Educ: Midland Col, B.S; Columbia Univ, M.A; Creighton Law Sch; Delta Theta Phi; Kal Beta. Polit. & Govt. Pos: Nebr. State Sen, Dist. 37, 69-; Nebr. cmnr, Educ. Cmn. of the States, 69- Bus. & Prof. Pos: Teacher, Minden Pub. Schs, Nebr; prin. and coach, Wilcox Pub. Schs; dir, Farmers and Merchants Bank, Axtell, currently; farmer, currently. Mil. Serv: Lt, Marines, World War II, Capt, Korean Conflict; Presidential Citation, Okinawa. Mem: Pres, Wilcox Bd. of Educ; secy, Bd. of Educ. Serv. Unit 11; Lions (dist. gov, 66-67, pres, Wilcox Club, currently); bd. dirs, Midland Col; v.pres, Wilcox C. of C; Americanism cmt, Am. Legion; VFW; Elks; PTA; past pres, Dist. VI State Sch. Bd. Asn, past chmn, Hwy. Four Asn; past bd. mem, Bethpage Mission and Trinity Lutheran Church, Axtell. Farm Family of the Month, Hastings C. of C, 59; chosen One of Five Thousand Outstanding Civic Leaders in Am, 67. Rel: Lutheran; Sunday Sch. teacher, Trinity Lutheran Church, Axtell. Mailing Add: Wilcox, Nebr. 68982.

ZIEGLER, HAL WALTER R
Mich. State Rep.
b. Jackson, Mich, 8/23/32; s. Harry Garrett Ziegler and Frances West Z; m. 1/11/58 to Mary Sue Williams; c. Harry Martin, Terence Mace and Hallie Patricia. Educ: Kenyon Col; Jackson Commun. Col; Hillsdale Col, A.B; Wayne State Univ. Law Sch, LL.B; Alpha Delta Phi. Polit. & Govt. Pos: Chmn, Rep. Co. Conv, Mich, 62; mem, President Lincoln Club, 63; del, Rep. State Conv, 56-66; asst. co. prosecutor, Jackson Co. Mich, 62-64, circuit court cmnr, 65-67; Mich. State Rep, 67- Mil. Serv: Entered as Pvt, Army, 64, released as Specialist 3/C, 65, after serv. in 594th T.T.R.G, Command Z, Paris, France, 64-65; Good Conduct Medal; Overseas Ribbon; Nat. Defense. Mem: Jackson Co. Bar Asn. (treas, 63-64); Mich. Co. Bar Asn; Jackson Country Club; Lions; C. of C. Rel: Episcopal. Mailing Add: 2011 Cascades Dr, Jackson, Mich. 49203.

ZIEGLER, PAUL A. D
b. Carmi, Ill, 10/20/11; m. Jan. 1937 to Jessie Shook. Educ: Evansville Col, Ind. Polit. & Govt. Pos: Co. treas, White Co, Ill, 33; former chmn, White Co. Dem. Party and former committeeman; Ill. State Rep, 3 terms; Ill. State Sen, 58-66. Mil. Serv: Army, serv. in N.African and Mediterranean Theatre of Opers. Rel: Evangelical United Brethren Church. Mailing Add: 700 N. Second St, Carmi, Ill. 62821. (1967)

ZIEGLER, ROBERT HOLTON, SR. D
Alaska State Sen.
b. Baltimore, Md, 3/27/21; s. Adolph Holton Ziegler and Lilian Windfohr Z; m. 1/14/50 to Betsy R. Rogers; c. Robert Holton, Jr. and Ann Holton. Educ: Univ. Va, Charlottesville, LL.B, 48; Sigma Nu; Phi Delta Theta; Glee Club. Polit. & Govt. Pos: Alaska State Rep, 57-59, Alaska State Sen, 64- Bus. & Prof. Pos: Pvt. practice law, 48-; mem. firm, Ziegler, Ziegler & Cloudy, currently. Mil. Serv: Entered as Pvt, Army, 42, released as Lt, 46, after serv. in Med. Admin. Corps. Mem: Elks (Past Exalted Ruler); Rotary (past pres); Moose; Am. Legion. Rel: Episcopal. Legal Res: 324 Cedar, Ketchikan, Alaska 99901. Mailing Add: Box 979, Ketchikan, Alaska 99901.

ZIEGLER, RONALD LEWIS R
Press Secy. to the President
b. Covington, Ky, 5/12/39; s. Louis Daniel Ziegler and Ruby Parsons Z; m. 7/30/60 to Nancy Lee Plessinger; c. Cynthia Lee and Laurie Michelle. Educ: Xavier Univ, 57-58; Univ. South. Calif, B.S, 61; Sigma Chi. Polit. & Govt. Pos: Press dir, Rep. State Cent. Cmt. of Calif, 61-62; press aide, Richard Nixon Gubernatorial Campaign Staff, 62; press aide, Staff of Richard Nixon, 68-69; press secy. to the President, 69- Bus. & Prof. Pos: Salesman, Proctor & Gamble Distributing Co, 61; acct. rep, J. Walter Thompson Co, 62-68. Rel: Presbyterian. Mailing Add: 2008 Fort Dr, Alexandria, Va. 22307.

ZIEN, BURT D
b. Milwaukee, Wis, 11/2/12; s. Herman Zien and Florence Holperin Z; m. 3/10/46 to Betty Segal; c. Jimmy. Educ: U. Wis, Madison, B.S. in Mech. Engr, 35, Alpha Tau Sigma. Polit. & Govt. Pos: Clerk, Tenn. Valley Authority, Knoxville, Tenn, 35-37; investr, Dept. of Labor, Tenn, 38-40, field dir, Wage and Hour Div, 40-42 & 47-47; field dir, Nat. Labor Rels. Bd, 47-50; alternate del, Dem. Nat. Conv, 68. Bus. & Prof. Pos: Gen. mgr. and chmn. of bd, Zien Plumbing & Heating, 50- Mil. Serv: Entered as Cadet, Air Force, 42, released as Capt, 46, after serv. in Fifth and 13th Air Force, Pacific, 42-46; Philippine Liberation Ribbon; Asiatic-Pac. Theater Ribbon with Three Bronze Stars. Mem: Heating Contractors Indust. Fund; Sheet Metal Contractors Asn; Plumbing Contractors Indust. Fund; hon. mem, Wis. Chief Police Asn; trustee, Mt. Sinai Hosp; Milwaukee Vol. Equal Employ Opportunity Coun.(exec. bd); Opportunities Indust. Center (adv. bd); Urban League (exec. bd, Home for Aged Jews); Jewish Voc. Serv. Handicapped Workers (contract and prog. cmt); River Oaks Country Club; Univ. Wis. Alumni Asn. and Fund; Dartmouth Col. Parents Fund (Milwaukee chmn). Rel: Jewish; Trustee, Congregation Emanuel B'ne Jeshurun. Mailing Add: 501 E. Lake Terr, Whitefish Bay, Wis. 53217.

ZIFFREN, PAUL D
b. Davenport, Iowa, 7/18/13; s. Jacob Ziffren and Belle Rothenberg Z; m. 5/20/48 to Muriel Averett; c. Kenneth, Abbie and John. Educ: Northwest. Univ, B.S. in speech, 35, Sch. Law, LL.B, 38; Order of Coif; Sigma Delta Chi. Polit. & Govt. Pos: Spec. asst. to Chief Counsel, Bur. Internal Revenue, Treas. Dept, Chicago, 39-40; asst. U.S. attorney in charge of Tax Div, Chicago, 41-42; Dem. Nat. Committeeman, Calif, 53-60; mem, exec. cmt, Dem. Nat. Cmt, 56-60, mem, adv. cmt, 57-60; chmn, Calif. Conv. Cmt, Dem. Nat. Conv, 60; del, Dem. Nat. Conv, 68. Bus. & Prof. Pos: Mem, bd. gov, Cedars-Sinai Hosps, 63-; mem, bd. gov, Film Indust. Workshops, Inc, Los Angeles, 65-; mem, bd. dirs. and secy, Center Theatre Group of Los Angeles, 66-; mem, bd. trustees, Citizens Research Found, Princeton, N.J, 68- Mem: Am, State, Los Angeles Co. and Beverly Hills Bar Asns; Town Hall; World Affairs Coun; v.pres, Northwest. Univ. Law Alumni Asn; exec. cabinet, Music Center Asn, 61-63; Los Angeles Club; Hillcrest Country Club. Rel: Jewish. Legal Res: 23920 Malibu Rd, Malibu, Calif. 90265. Mailing Add: 10889 Wilshire Blvd, Suite 1260, Los Angeles, Calif. 90024.

ZIMMER, JOHN HERMAN R
b. Sioux Falls, S.Dak, 12/30/22; s. John Francis Zimmer and Veronica Berke Z; m. 12/26/46 to Phyllis June Graber; c. June Marie, Mary Joan, Robert Joseph and Judith Maureen. Educ: Augustana Col, 41-42; Mont. State Col, 43; Univ. S.Dak, LL.B, 48; Phi Delta Phi; Delta Theta Phi; A Club. Polit. & Govt. Pos: Chmn, Turner Co. Rep. Cmt, S.Dak, 55-56; states attorney, Turner Co, 55-58 & 62-64; mem, S.Dak. Rep. State Adv. Cmt, 59-60; asst. doorman, Rep. Nat. Conv, 60; minority counsel, strategic and critical materials invest, U.S. Senate Armed Serv. Cmt, 62-63; alternate del, Rep. Nat. Conv, 68. Bus. & Prof. Pos: Mem, S.Dak. Unauthorized Practice of Law Cmt, 58-64, chmn, 58-62. Mil. Serv: Entered as Pvt, Army, 43, released as T-5, 46, after serv. in Signal Serv. Group, Pac; Philippine Liberation Ribbon; Two Bronze Stars; S.Pac. Campaign Ribbon. Mem: S.Dak. State Bar Asn.(bar cmnr, 54-57); Fed, Am. and Minnehaha Co. Bar Asns; Am. Trial Lawyers Asn.(state committeeman, 68-69); S.Dak. Trial Lawyers Asn.(pres, 67-68); VFW; Am. Legion; Marion Commun. Club; S.Dak. Jr. Bar Asn.(pres, 53). Rel: Roman Catholic. Legal Res: 375 S. Broadway, Marion, S.Dak. 57043. Mailing Add: Law Bldg, Parker, S.Dak. 57053.

ZIMMER, WILLIAM HAROLD D
Mont. State Rep.
b. Yankton, S.Dak, 8/31/99; s. Gustavus Adolphus Zimmer and Carry Belle Suter Z; m. 7/20/57 to Alice Luille Sheldon; c. William Frederick and Audrey Lea (Mrs. James E. Madole). Educ: Ninth Grade. Polit. & Govt. Pos: Chmn, sch. bd, Oswego Pub. Sch, Mont, 37-38; chmn, sch. bd, Olney Pub. Sch, 44-47; chmn, Fire Dist, Olney, 61-; Mont. State Rep, 63-66 & 69-; mem. Legis. Coun. Subcmt, currently; pres, Flathead Co. Asn. of Fire Dist, 68-69. Bus. & Prof. Pos: Signal maintainer, Great North. R.R. Mem: Mason (Past Master); Shrine; Moose (Past Gov. and Past State Pres; Past Supreme Lodge Officer of Moose for Mont, Idaho and Alta); Eagles; Great North. Vet. Asn. Rel: Protestant. Mailing Add: Box 68, Olney, Mont. 59927.

ZIMMERMAN, DONALD WAYNE R
b. Olathe, Kans, 4/6/31; s. Roy S. Zimmerman and Dorothy Robinson Z; m. 7/4/54 to Dorothy L. Nevius; c. Steven W, Beverly A. and Richard A. Educ: Kans. State Univ, B.S. in agr, 53; C.L.U, Am. Col. Life Underwriters, 67; Farmhouse Fraternity. Polit. & Govt. Pos: Precinct committeeman, Rep. Party, Kans, 63; Kans. State Rep, 14th Dist, 65-66 and 16th Dist, 67-68. Bus. & Prof. Pos: Flight test asst, Flight Test Sect, Aviation Gas Turine Div, Westinghouse Elec. Co, 56-57; owner, Zimmerman Ins, 57- Mil. Serv: Entered as 2nd Lt, Air Force, 53, released as 1st Lt, 56, after serv. as a jet fighter pilot and aircraft controller with 738th Radar Squadron Air Defense Command; Capt, Air Force Res, 56-59. Mem: Life Underwriters Asn; Am. Soc. Chartered Life Underwriters; Jaycees; C. of C; Optimist Club. Rel: Methodist. Legal Res: 804 Brentwood, Olathe, Kans. 66061. Mailing Add: Box 682, Olathe, Kans. 66061.

ZIMMERMAN, HAROLD SAMUEL R
Wash. State Rep.
b. Valley City, N.Dak, 6/1/23; s. Dr. S. A. Zimmerman and Lulu Wylie Z; m. 9/12/46 to Julianne Williams Z; c. Karen Marie, Steven Walter and Judi Jean. Educ: Valley City, N.Dak. State Teachers' Col; Tex. A&M Univ; Univ. Wash, B.A, 47; Sigma Chi; Sigma Delta Chi. Polit. & Govt. Pos: Former chmn, Cowlitz Co. Rep. Party, Wash; Wash. State Rep, currently. Bus. & Prof. Pos: Circulation agency mgr, Minn. Star-Journal-Tribune Valley City, 40-41; U.S. Forest Serv, Bear Head Mt, 42; reporter, N.Seattle News, 46-47; news ed, Courier Times, Sedro-Woolley, Wash, 47-50; ed-publisher, Cowlitz Co. Advocate, Castle Rock, Wash, 50-57; Post-Record, Camas, Wash, 57- Mil. Serv: Air Force, 42-46. Mem: Former secy-treas. and v.pres, WNPA; pres, WNPA Serv, 62; past state chmn, Nat. Educ. Asn; past pres, C. of C, Castle Rock; dir, Camas-Washougal Jr. Achievement; past bd. mem, Cowlitz Gen. Hosp; bd. mem, Wash. Chap, AAUN; bd. of dir, Clark Co. Am. Red Cross; Young Life Coun. Columbia River Dist; past pres, Kiwanis, Camas, Lions, Castle Rock; Castle Rock FFA, hon. mem. Received first place, essay contest, Univ. Wash, 42; hon. mention, Nat. Educ. Asn, ed. contest, 55. Rel: Methodist; Lay Leader. Mailing Add: 1432 N.E. Sixth Ave, Camas, Wash. 98607.

ZIMMERMAN, JACOB W. D
Del. State Rep.
Educ: Villanova Univ. Polit. & Govt. Pos: Chmn, Del. Agr. Stabilization and Conserv. State Cmt, 61-64; Del. State Rep, 65-, Minority Leader, Del. State House of Rep, 67- Bus. & Prof. Pos: Farmer; dir, Del. Produce Growers, Inc; dir, Nat. Potato Coun; dir, Geriatric Serv. of Del, Inc; trustee, Del. Arts Soc. Mem: Toastmasters. Mailing Add: R.D. 3, Box 117, Dover, Del. 19901.

ZIMMERMAN, LESTER H. R
b. Fermanagh Twp, Pa, 9/10/16; s. Banks A. Zimmerman and Catherine M. Calhoun Z; m. to Violet Lebkicher; c. Lester H, Jr, Jeffry M, Randall E. and Douglas C. Educ: Mifflintown High Sch. Polit. & Govt. Pos: Pa. State Rep, 56-67. Bus. & Prof. Pos: Farmer; food serv. indust. Mil. Serv: U.S, China-Burma-India, 41-45. Mem: Scouter; vet. orgn; Vol. Fire Co; Juniata Co. Sportsman Asn; Union Lodge 324; Zembo Shrine; chmn, March of Dimes Campaign; past pres, Juniata Valley Asn. of the Blind; chmn, Juniata Co. Chap. Nat. Found; Cross Keys Conserv. Club. Rel: Protestant. Mailing Add: 316 Orange St, Mifflintown, Pa. 17059.

ZIMMERMAN, ROBERT C. R
Secy. of State, Wis.
b. Lake, Wis, 1/5/10. Educ: High Sch, grad. Polit. & Govt. Pos: Asst. Secy. of State, Wis, 39-56, Secy. of State, 56-; former cmnr, Pub. Lands and former mem, State Bd. Canvassers. Mil. Serv: Army, World War II. Mem: Madison Press Club; Nat. Asn. Secy. of State. Mailing Add: State Capitol, Madison, Wis. 53702. (1967)

ZIMMERMAN, WILLIAM T. R
b. Alton, Ill, 12/19/01; m. 9/3/28 to Merle Krutzman. Educ: Cent. Wesleyan Col, Warrenton, Mo, B.A, 28. Polit. & Govt. Pos: Mo. State Rep, 56-66. Bus. & Prof. Pos: Owner, Hawthorn and South Haven Terrace Subdivisions, Warrenton, Mo. Mem: Elks; Mo. C. of C; past pres, Warrenton C. of C; Charter Mem. and First V.pres, Warrenton Rotary Club; Charter Mem, Warrenton Lions Club. Rel: College Methodist Church. Mailing Add: 216 S. East St, Warrenton, Mo. 63383. (1967)

ZION, ROGER H. R
U.S. Rep, Ind.
b. Escanaba, Mich, 9/17/21; s. H. G. Zion and Helen Hutchinson Z; m. 2/20/45 to Marjorie Knauss; c. Gayle, Scott and Randal. Educ: Univ. Wis, B.A, 43; Harvard Bus. Sch, 45; pres, Wis. chap, Alpha Delta Phi, 41-43. Polit. & Govt. Pos: U.S. Rep, Eighth Dist, Ind, 67-, mem, Pub. Works Cmt, U.S. House of Rep, currently, mem, Flood Control, Roads and Watershed Develop. Subcmts, Spec. Subcmt. on Fed-Aid Hwy. Prog. and Ad Hoc Subcmt. on Appalachia, currently. Bus. & Prof. Pos: Dir, sales training, Mead Johnson & Co, 54-64, dir, training and prfnl. rels, 64-65; pres, Roger Zion & Assoc, Mkt. Personnel Consult, 66. Mil. Serv: Entered as Aviation Cadet, Navy, 43, released as Lt.(jg), 46, after serv. in Asiatic Pac. Theater. Publ: Keys to Human Relations in Selling, Prentice-Hall, 63; Influencing Human Behavior (record), Businessmen's Record Club, Dvi. of Int. Commun. Inst, 68. Mem: Sales and Mkt. Execs. Int; pres, Evansville chap, Nat. Sales and Mkt. Execs, 62; Am. Legion; VFW; bd. dirs, Rotary, 64; chap. chmn, Am. Red Cross, 60-62; v.pres, Buffalo Trace Coun, Boy Scouts, 60; Wabash Valley Asn. Internationally-known speaker. Rel: Congregational. Legal Res: R.R. 3 Erskine Lane, Evansville, Ind. 47711. Mailing Add: 1226 Longworth Bldg, Washington, D.C. 20515.

ZIPPERER, EDWARD HELMEY D
Ga. State Sen.
b. Savannah, Ga, 8/8/31; s. James Forrester Zipperer and Hattie Mae Helmey Z; m. 7/4/56 to Nina Dorris Arnold; c. Laura Love and Daniel McRae. Educ: Univ. Ga, B.S. in Agr. Eng, 54; Pi Kappa Alpha. Polit. & Govt. Pos: Ga. State Sen, Third Dist, 69- Mil. Serv: Entered as Trainee, Army, 56, released as SP-4, 58 after serv. in Combat Eng; Res, 58-62. Mem: Civitan; Sertoma; Ga. Soybean Asn; Chatham Co. Farm Bur; Effingham Co. Farm Bur; Univ. Ga. Alumni Asn. Rel: Lutheran. Mailing Add: Little Neck Farm, Box 475, Route 4, Savannah, Ga. 31405.

ZIRKELBACH, BARBARA MARILYN FOLEY D
Mem, Colo. Dem. State Cent. Cmt.
b. Denver, Colo, 8/23/27; d. William J. Foley and Grace Litmer F.(deceased); m. 4/28/51 to Harry William Hernon Zirkelbach; c. Paul J, Thomas J, David J, Grace M, Josephine, Amy M, Julie M, Albert J. and Treesa M. Educ: Colo. Univ, 1 year; Denver Univ, 2 years; Univ. Fribourg, Switz, summer; Alpha

Chi Omega; Forensic; Yearbook. Polit. & Govt. Pos: Dist. capt, Dem. Party, Denver Co, Colo, 65-; mem. exec. cmt, R.F. Kennedy for Pres, Denver and Colo, 68; mem, Colo. Dem. State Cent. Cmt, 69- Mem: E.Cent. Human Rels. Coun.(chmn); rep, Metro. Center; capt, United Way; area chmn, Cancer Soc; Muscular Dystrophy; PTA. Rel: Roman Catholic. Mailing Add: 745 Steele, Denver, Colo. 80206.

ZLATNIK, MICHAEL F. R
b. Chicago, Ill, 4/12/13. Educ: Crane Jr. Col; DePaul U. Col. of Law; Chicago Col. of Law. Polit. & Govt. Pos: Ill. State Rep, 4 terms; Spec. Cmnr. to Superior and Circuit Courts of Cook Co. Bus. & Prof. Pos: Lawyer. Mem: Bd. of Govs, City Club of Chicago; Chicago, Ill. and Am. Bar Asn; Decalogue Soc. of Lawyers; Am. Judicature Soc; Elks; B'nai B'rith; Moose; Kiwanis; Chicago Asn. of Comm. and Indust; Rogers Park C. of C; Howard Dist. C. of C; Rogers Park Citizens Traffic Safety Cmt; Gerontological Soc; Vice Pres, Bd. of Commun. Center of Rogers Park; Vice Pres, Bd. of Dir, Rogers Park Zionist Orgn; Bd. of Mgr. of McCormick Chicago Boys Club; Bd. of Lower N. Centers; Am. Acad. of Matrimonial Lawyers; Ill. Rep. Vets. League; Bd. of Dir, Hebrew Theol. Col; Gov. Coun. Am. Jewish Cong. Mailing Add: 6300 N. Sheridan Rd, Chicago, Ill. 60626. (1967)

ZNIDARSICH, KAY R
Secy, Las Animas Co. Cent. Cmt, Colo.
b. Trinidad, Colo, 11/30/36; d. Tony M. Franza and Lucy Guadagnoli F; m. 11/9/57 to William H. Znidarsich. Educ: Trinidad State Jr. Col, Bus. Cert, 58. Polit. & Govt. Pos: Secy, Las Animas Co. Rep. Cent. Cmt, Colo, 61-; secy, Rep. Women's Club, 61-, historian, 69- Mem: Rep. Womens Club; 1200 Club; Cath. Daughter Am. Rel: Catholic. Mailing Add: Route 2, Box 14, Trinidad, Colo. 81082.

ZOLLAR, CHARLES O. R
Mich. State Sen.
b. Chicago, Ill, 1/6/15; married; c. Robin and Michelle. Educ: Mich. State Univ. through continuing educ. courses. Polit. & Govt. Pos: Mich. State Sen, 64-; pres, Pearl Sch. Bd. Bus. & Prof. Pos: Owner Zollar Farms (fruit growers); pres, Aircraft Components, Inc.(aircraft parts); Riverside Enterprises, Inc.(real estate); Zollar Nurseries, Inc.(fruit trees and plant propagation). Mil. Serv: Aviation instr, World War II. Mem: Chmn, Benton Harbor Mkt. Bd, Benton Twp. Housing Cmn, Mich. Cmn. of Agr; pres, Southwest Mich. Strawberry Growers Asn; Elks; Rotary; Am. Legion; Moose; Fraternal Order of Police; Farm Bur; Aircraft Owners and Pilots Asn. Rel: Lutheran. Mailing Add: Box 298, Benton Harbor, Mich. 49022. (1967)

ZOLLICOFFER, ALGERNON AUGUSTUS, JR. D
b. Henderson, N.C, 3/6/24; s. Algernon Augustus Zollicoffer and Fannie Spotswood Cooper Z; m. 4/11/53 to Jane Crichton Lewis; c. Jane Crichton, Allison Caulaincourt, Fannie Cooper and Ellen Lewis. Educ: Univ. N.C, B.S, 47 and Law Sch, J.D, 50; Delta Kappa Epsilon; Phi Delta Phi. Polit. & Govt. Pos: Prosecuting attorney, Vance Co. Recorder's Court, N.C, 55-56; N.C. State Rep, 57-66. Bus. & Prof. Pos: Lawyer. Mil. Serv: Lt.(jg), Naval Res, 43-46. Rel: Episcopal; Vestryman, Holy Innocents Church. Mailing Add: Meadow Lane, Henderson, N.C. 27536.

ZORD, JOSEPH V, JR. R
Pa. State Rep.
b. Baldwin Twp, Pa, 5/2/10; s. Joseph V. Zord and Bertha L. Sexauer Z; m. to Lois Lyden; c. Two. Educ: Curry Bus. Col. Polit. & Govt. Pos: Founder, Whitehall Borough, Pa, councilman, 48-52, Rep. chmn; registrn. chmn. and committeeman, Allegheny Co; Justice of the Peace, 52-60; Pa. State Rep, 64- Bus. & Prof. Pos: Realtor. Mem: Nat. Bd. of Realtors; Pa. Bd. of Realtors; Pittsburgh Bd. of Realtors; Nat. Inst. of Real Estate Brokers; Int. Traders Club; founder, Whitehall Fire Co; Ins. Cmn. of the Borough of Whitehall; charter mem, Whitehall Lions Club; South Hills YMCA. Award of Merit, Allegheny Co. Rep. Ctm, 64; Hon. Cmn. Ky. Col. Mailing Add: 611 Glowood Dr, Pittsburgh, Pa. 15227.

ZORN, WILLIAM AUSTIN D
b. Dothan, Ala, 1/16/27; s. George Harvey Zorn and Myrtle Bush Z; m. 1/01/51 to Claire Council; c. Karen Lee, William Austin, Jr, James Harvey, and Robert Steven. Educ: Univ. Ga, LL.B, 51; Delta Tau Delta. Polit. & Govt. Pos: City attorney, Jesup, Ga, 52-; Ga. State Sen, Sixth Dist, 63-64. Bus. & Prof. Pos: Attorney. Mil. Serv: Army Air Force, 44-46. Mem: Jesup Bar Asn.(pres, 62); Elks; Lions, pres, 54. Rel: Methodist. Mailing Add: Jesup, Ga. 31545.

ZUCKERT, EUGENE M. D
b. N.Y.C, 11/9/11; s. Harry M. Zuckert and Eugenie Adrienne Pincoffs Z; m. 6/24/38 to Kathleen Barnes (deceased); m. 5/5/45 to Barbara E. Jackman; c. Adrienne (Mrs. Chandler R. Cowles), Robert Barnes and Gene (Mrs. Edward F. Downs, Jr). Educ: Yale, B.A, 33, LL.B, 37; Harvard Bus. Sch; Beta Theta Pi. Hon. degrees, George Wash. Univ, 62 and Clarkson Col, 64. Polit. & Govt. Pos: Attorney, U.S. Securities and Exchange Cmn, Wash, D.C. and N.Y.C, 37-40; spec. consult. to Commanding Gen, Army Air Force in Develop. Statist. Control, 43-44; exec. asst. to admin, Surplus Property Admin, Wash, D.C, 45-46; spec. asst. to Secy. of War for Air, 46-47; asst. secy. of Air Force, 47-52; mem, Atomic Energy Cmn, 52-54; Secy. of Air Force, 61-65. Bus. & Prof. Pos: Instr. and subsequently asst. prof. and asst. dean, Harvard Grad. Sch. of Bus. Admin, 40-44; attorney-at-law, Wash, D.C, 54-61; counsel, Lear, Scoutt & Rasenberger, 65-68; partner, Zuckert, Scoutt & Rasenberger, 68- Mil. Serv: Lt.(jg), Naval Res, Off. of Chief of Naval Opers, Wash, D.C. Publ: Atomic Energy for Your Business, 56; 'The Service Secretary; Has He a Useful Role?' For. Affairs, 4/66. Mem: Chmn. of bd, Proj. HOPE. Rel: Episcopal. Legal Res: 141 Hesketh St, Chevy Chase, Md. 20015. Mailing Add: 888 17th St. N.W, Suite 1105, Washington, D.C. 20006.

ZULLO, FRANK NICHOLAS D
Mayor, Norwalk, Conn.
b. Norwalk, Conn, 6/3/32; s. Frank Zullo and Regina Z; m. 4/26/58 to Berenice M. Fischler; c. Lesley Anne. Educ: Fairfield Prep. Sch, 50; Fordham Col, B.S.S, 54, Law Sch, LL.B, 57. Polit. & Govt. Pos: Prosecutor, Norwalk City Court, Conn, 59; mem, Dem. State Cent. Cmt, 60-; Minority Leader, Norwalk Common Coun, 63-65; mayor, Norwalk, 65-; secy, Conn. Conf. of Mayors, 66-67, pres, 68-69; del, Dem. Nat. Conv, 68; mem. adv. bd, U.S. Conv. of Mayors, 68-, mem. bd. of trustees, 69- Bus. & Prof. Pos: Attorney, Santaniello & Culhane, 57-59; partner, Tierney & Zullo, 59- Mil. Serv: Entered as Pvt, Army, 57, released as 1st Lt, Nat. Guard Res. Mem: Conn, Am. and Norwalk-Wilton Bar Asns; past pres, campaign chmn. and mem. bd. dirs, United Fund; bd. dirs, YMCA; chmn, Norwalk-Wilton Chap, Red Cross Water Safety Prog. Selected Young Man of the Year, Jr. C. of C, Norwalk, 58-63. Rel: Roman Catholic. Legal Res: 24 Sawmill Rd, Norwalk, Conn. 06850. Mailing Add: City Hall, South Norwalk, Conn. 06856.

ZumBRUNNEN, LESLIE LEE R
Wyo. State Rep.
b. Kirtley, Wyo, 4/22/08; s. Roy L. ZumBrunnen and Bama Teakel Z; m. 2/2/38 to Olive A. Hanson; c. Katherine C.(Mrs. Larry E. McDaniel) and Melvin L. Educ: Kearney State Teachers Col, Nebr, B.S. in educ, 31; Univ. Wyo, grad. work. Polit. & Govt. Pos: Wyo. State Rep, 67- Bus. & Prof. Pos: Teacher, 33-37; rancher, 37- Mem: Farm Bur; coun. leader, Wyo. State 4-H and Local 4-H Leader. Rel: Methodist. Mailing Add: Lusk, Wyo. 82225.

ZUPAN, ROSE ANN D
b. Pueblo, Colo, 12/15/29; d. Paul Zupan and Mildred Butkovich Z; div; c. Becky Diane. Educ: High Sch, grad, 46. Polit. & Govt. Pos: Second v.pres, Pueblo Co. Young Dem, Colo, 62-63; dep. clerk, Pueblo Co. Court, 62-66; treas, Jane Jefferson Dem. Club, 63; state treas, Colo. Young Dem, 63-64; del, Dem. Nat. Conv. and secy. Colo. Del, 64; mem, State Dem. Cent. Cmt, 65-66; v.chmn, Pueblo Co. Dem. Cent. Cmt, 65-69. Bus. & Prof. Pos: Partner, Zupan Enterprises, Inc, 59-66. Mem: Women's Italian Fidelity Lodge; NAACP; USW, Women's Auxiliary; reporter for Cmt. on Polit. Educ; Bus. and Prfnl. Women. Rel: Catholic. Mailing Add: 501 W. Orman, Pueblo, Colo. 81005. (1967)

ZUPKO, JOHN MICHAEL D
b. Tuxedo Park, N.Y, 1/8/13; s. George Zupko and Mary Ellko Z; m. 11/7/36 to Leora Galloway; c. Michael John. Polit. & Govt. Pos: Precinct chmn, Dem. Party, Utah. 45-54, co. chmn, 58-67; Utah State Rep, Duchesne Co, 65-67; Utah State dir, Farmers Union Green Thumb Prog, 68- Mem: Kiwanis; C. of C; exec. secy, Utah-Idaho Farmers Union Orgn. Rel: Latter-day Saint. Mailing Add: R.R. 1, Roosevelt, Utah 84066.

ZURICK, WILLIAM PHILIP D
Chmn, Northumberland Co. Dem. Finance Cmt, Pa.
b. Shamokin, Pa, 4/28/25; s. Joseph E. Zurick and Gertrude Meyer Z; m. 11/11/46 to Anne Teresa Lascoskie; c. Cecilia, William, Jr, Lorraine Joseph, Mary Carol and James. Polit. & Govt. Pos: Pres, Selinsgrove State Sch. Bd, Pa, 54-62; chmn, Northumberland Co. Dem. Finance Cmt, 56-; del, Dem. Nat. Conv, 60 & 68, alternate del, 64; dir, State Ment. Health Asn, 60-61. Bus. & Prof. Pos: Owner, Zurick & Zurick Lumber Co, 19 years; dir, West Ward S & L Asn, 57-66 and Security of Am. Life Ins. Co, 63-66. Mem: Moose; Elks; Eagles; K. of C; NAACP; Optimists. Rel: Catholic. Mailing Add: R.D. 1, Shamokin, Pa. 17872.

ZWACH, JOHN M. R
U.S. Rep, Minn.
b. Gales Twp, Redwood Co, Minn, 2/8/07; s. Joseph Zwach and Barbara Hammerschmidt Z; m. 6/3/40 to Agnes Schueller; c. Barbara (Mrs. Sykora), Marie, John, Jr, Dennis and Anne. Educ: Mankato State Col; Univ. Minn, B.S. Polit. & Govt. Pos: Minn. State Rep, 34-46; Minn. State Sen, 46-66, Majority Leader, Minn. State Senate, 59-66; U.S. Rep, Minn, 67-; del, Rep. Nat. Conv, 68. Bus. & Prof. Pos: Teacher, prin, supt, 14 years; farmer. Mem: Farm Bur; Nat. Farmers Orgn; Farmers Union; Grange; K. of C. Rel: Roman Catholic. Legal Res: Walnut Grove, Minn. 56180. Mailing Add: 1208 Longworth House Office Bldg, Washington, D.C. 20515.

ZWIER, STANLEY D
b. Passaic, N.J, 11/4/10; s. Paul Zwier and Sophia Polisczcuk Z. m. 7/17/43 to Anna Kapalka; c. Michael Stanley, Norman and Stanley Michael. Polit. & Govt. Pos: Councilman, Clifton, N.J, 54-58 & 62-66, mayor, 58-62. Bus. & Prof. Pos: Pres, M&S Cleaners, Inc, 46-66; secy, JAC Real Co, Inc, 64-66. Mem: Moose; Elks; Optimist; bd. dirs, Boys Club and Girls Club of Clifton; Stanley Zwier League, Ukrainian Cent, Russian-Am. Club; Clifton Dem. Club; Main Dem. Club; Ukranian Nat. Home. Rel: Orthodox. Mailing Add: 114 Marconi St, Clifton, N.J. 07013.

Addenda

Biographies and changes received too late for inclusion in the regular text of the Directory

ARBUCKLE, ROBERT M. R
Utah State Rep.
b. Woods Cross, Utah, 3/30/25; s. James S. Arbuckle and Chloe Mann A; m. 6/12/47 to Joyce Webb; c. Cheryl Gove, Robert W, Debra W, Alan W, Gayle and Lynda. Educ: Utah Univ, 2 years; Wash. State Univ. Polit. & Govt. Pos: Utah State Rep, 65- Bus. & Prof. Pos: Pres, Freeway Heating & Air Conditioning, 56-69. Mil. Serv: Cpl, Air Force, 43-46, with serv. in U.S. Mem: Jaycees; C. of C; Sertoma Club. Rel: Latter-day Saint. Mailing Add: 555 E. Tenth St, Centerville, Utah 84014.

BALL, GEORGE WILDMAN
(additional information to sketch on p. 53)
Polit. & Govt. Pos: U.S. Permanent Rep. to the UN, 68. Bus. & Prof. Pos: Partner, Cleary, Gottlieb, Steen & Hamilton, 46-61, counsel, 66-68 & 69-; chmn, Lehman Bros. Int, 66-68; sr. partner investment banking, Lehman Bros, 69- Publ: The Discipline of Power, Atlantic-Little Brown, 68. Grand Cross, Order of the Crown, Belgium. Legal Res: 860 UN Plaza, New York, N.Y. 10017. Mailing Add: c/o Lehman Brothers, 1 William St, New York, N.Y. 10004.

BAREFIELD, STONE DEAVOURS D
Miss. State Rep.
b. Laurel, Miss, 7/28/27; s. Samuel S. Barefield, Sr. and Dinah Deavours B; m. 12/2/51 to Bonnie Merle Taylor; c. Stone D, Jr, Allen Taylor, Julia Ann and Michael Clayton. Educ: Univ. South. Miss, B.S, 52; Univ. Miss. Sch. Law, LL.B, 54; Kappa Alpha. Polit. & Govt. Pos: Miss. State Rep, 60- Mil. Serv: Merchant Marines, 45-46, Atlantic and Mediterranean Area; entered as Pvt, Marines, 46, released as Pfc, 48, after serv. in Marine Air Wing, Cherrypoint, N.C; re-entered 50, released as Cpl, 51, after serv. in Third Bn, Sixth Marines, Camp LeJune, N.C. Mem: Forrest Co. and Miss. State Bar Asns; F&AM; Lions; Am. Legion; Citizens Coun. Rel: Methodist. Legal Res: Route 4, Hattiesburg, Miss. 39401. Mailing Add: 121 W. Front St, Hattiesburg, Miss. 39401.

BONICELLI, DERITO D
Mayor, Walsenburg, Colo.
b. Ideal, Colo, 12/21/18; s. Morandi Bonicelli and Cotilda B; m. 9/23/40 to Caryl Kathrine Ralya; c. Harold E, Caryl Ann, Debra, Derito James, Celine and Janine. Educ: St. Marys Sch, grad, 37. Polit. & Govt. Pos: Councilman, Walsenburg, Colo, 57-63; chmn, Walsenburg Dem. Party, 63-68; chmn, Huerfano Co. Dem. Party, 68-; mayor, Walsenburg, 69- Bus. & Prof. Pos: Owner, Firestone Store, 45, Misty Haven Resort Cabins, Cuchara, Colo, 65 and B-K Drive-In, 69. Mil. Serv: Entered as Buck Pvt, Army, 41, released as Sgt. Maj, 45, after serv. in 214th Antiaircraft Artil. Gun Bn, ETO, 42-45; Good Conduct and Bronze Star Medals. Mem: Elks; Lions; VFW; Am. Legion. Rel: Catholic. Mailing Add: 323 E. Seventh St, Walsenburg, Colo. 81089.

BRENNAN, THOMAS EMMETT
Chief Justice, Supreme Court of Mich.
b. Detroit, Mich, 5/27/29; s. Joseph Terrance Brennan and Jeannette Sullivan B; m. 4/28/51 to Pauline Mary Weinberger; c. Thomas Emmett, Jr, John Seamus, Margaret Ann, William Joseph, Mary Beth and Ellen Mary. Educ: Univ. Detroit Law Sch, LL.B, 52; Delta Theta Phi; Upsilon Delta Sigma. Polit. & Govt. Pos: Judge, Common Pleas Court, Detroit, Mich, 61-63; judge, Circuit Court, Wayne Co, 63-67; assoc. judge, Supreme Court of Mich, 67-69, chief justice, 69- Bus. & Prof. Pos: Attorney-at-law, Detroit, Mich, 53-61; partner, Waldron, Brennan & Maher, 57-61; adj. prof. polit. sci, Univ. Detroit, 69- Mem: Detroit and Am. Bar Asns; State Bar of Mich; Mich. Cmn. on Law Enforcement and Criminal Justice; Nat. Conf. of Chief Justices; Nat. Col. of Appellate Judges; bd. trustees, Marygrove Col. Rel: Roman Catholic. Legal Res: 19347 Berkeley Rd, Detroit, Mich. 48221. Mailing Add: Supreme Court of Michigan, Lansing, Mich. 48933.

BROWN, AARON S. Deceased 1969.

BROWNE, RUTH T(ERESA)
(additional information to sketch on p. 148)
Educ: Loretto Heights Col, B.A. Sociol, 51. Polit. & Govt. Pos: Dem. precinct committeewoman, 55-; chmn, Clay Co. Dem. Party, 63-68; v.pres, Kans. Cultural Arts Cmn, 66-; secy. Kans. del, Dem. Nat. Conv, 68. Mem: Am. Asn. Univ. Women; Am. Asn. Soc. Scientists; Am. Fedn. Arts; v.pres. & mem. bd, Clay Center Pub. Libr; legis. chmn, Clay Center C. of C, 68-; bd. mem, North. Flint Hills Health Coun; Kans. Club; Kans. Libr. Asn; Cath. Daughters Am; Clay Center Libr. Club; Nat. Educ. Asn. Study Club (past pres).

BURNS, ARTHUR FRANK
Chmn, Fed. Reserve Bd, 70- (see sketch p. 163)

BURNSIDE, MAURICE GWINN
(corrections to sketch on p. 165)
Mem: A founder, Int. Rels. Club of Am. Mailing Add: 2009 Hermitage Rd, Wilson, N.C. 27893.

BUTLER, CHARLES FREDERICK
(correction to sketch on p. 168)
Mailing Add: 1323 Redpath Crescent, Montreal, Que, Can.

CANGELOSI, THEODORE FRANCIS
(corrections to sketch on p. 181)
Legal Res: 2644 E. Lakeshore Dr, Baton Rouge, La. 70808. Mailing Add: P.O. Box 3036, Baton Rouge, La. 70821.

CAPALBY, JOSEPH RICHARD D
V.Chmn, Ariz. Dem. Party
b. Chicago, Ill, 3/11/20; s. Fredrick Capalby and Josephine De Paulo C; m. 7/30/39 to Mary Ellen McDow; c. Patty Jo, Audrey, Joseph Richard, II, Wilma Jeanne (Mrs. Salisbury) and Fred Michael, II. Educ: John L. Marsh Sch. Polit. & Govt. Pos: Chmn, Mohave Co. Dem. Cent. Cmt, Ariz, 66-; del, Dem. Nat. Conv, 68; v.chmn, Ariz. Dem. Party, currently. Rel: Catholic. Mailing Add: 1010 Parkview, Kingman, Ariz. 86401.

CHESROW, FRANK WILLIAM
(additional information to sketch on p. 207)
Polit. & Govt. Pos: Trustee, Bd. Trustees, Metrop. Sanit. Dist, Gr. Chicago, Ill, 48-66, pres, 58-66. Mem: Pres, Soc. Am. Mil. Engrs; Ill. Athletic, Lake Shore and Irish Fel. Clubs; Furniture Club of Chicago. Honors: Knight, Grand Off. Order Repub. of Italy; Vatican, Knight Com. Order of the Holy Sepulchre of Jerusalem; Gentleman in Waiting to Pope Paul VI; Personal Chamberlain Sword & Cape to Pope John XXIII. Legal Res: 400 E. Randolph St, Chicago, Ill. 60601. Mailing Add: 134 S. LaSalle St, Chicago, Ill. 60603.

CROCKETT, KENNEDY McCAMPBELL
U.S. Ambassador to Nicaragua
b. Kingsville, Tex, Jan. 1920; s. Frank H. Crockett and Alice Kennedy C; m. 9/8/43 to Mary Campbell; c. John Kennedy, Laura (Mrs. Wendell Loftis), Judy (Mrs. Federico Faerron), Mary Melinda and Teresa Alice. Educ: N.Tex. Agr. Col, 37-39; Univ. Tex, Austin, 39-42. Polit. & Govt. Pos: With For. Serv, 43-; with Consulate, Nuevo Laredo, Mex, 43-44, v.consul, 44-47; prin. officer, Consulate, La Ceiba, Honduras, 47-48; v.consul, Embassy, Mexico City, Mex, 48-51; prin. officer, Tampico, 51-55; staff asst. and spec. asst. on consular affairs, Dept. of State, 55-56, officer in charge of Mexican Affairs, 56-57, dep. dir, Off. of Caribbean Affairs, 62-65; first secy, Embassy, Guatemala, 57-60; consul, Tijuana, Mex, 60-62; counselor, Embassy, San José, Costa Rica, 65-67; U.S. Ambassador to Nicaragua, 67- Superior Honor Award, Dept. of State, 66. Legal Res. 1602 Washington St, Laredo, Tex. 78040. Mailing Add: P.O. Box 278, Laredo, Tex. 78040.

DAVIS, CHARLES J. Deceased 1969.

DERGE, DAVID RICHARD
(additional information to sketch on p. 293)
Polit. & Govt. Pos: Mem, U.S. Adv. Cmn. on Int. Educ. & Cultural Affairs.

DRISCOLL, KATHLEEN VIRGINIA
(correction to sketch on p. 317)
Bus. & Prof. Pos: Secy, Iowa Co. Agr. Adjust. Admin, 42-46.

GRONOUSKI, JOHN AUSTIN
(additional information to sketch on p. 457)
Bus. & Prof. Pos: Dean, Lyndon B. Johnson Sch. Pub. Affairs, Univ. Tex, Austin, 69-

KELLAM, RONALD LLOYD D
Maine State Sen.
b. Portland, Maine, 10/21/28; s. Robert Murray Kellam and Freda Edith Nelson K; m. 5/24/52 to Hazel Shannon; c. Linda Sue, Steven Paul and Janice Lynn. Educ: Portland Jr. Col, 48-50; Boston Univ. Sch. Law, LL.B, 54, LL.M, 64. Polit. & Govt. Pos: Maine State Rep, 59-60 & 61-62; asst. attorney gen, Maine, 65-66; Maine State Sen, 69- Bus. & Prof. Pos: Attorney-at-Law, Portland, Maine, 54-59. Mil. Serv: Pvt, Army, 46-48. Rel: Protestant. Mailing Add: 63 Caleb St, Portland, Maine 04102.

LeBRETON, EDWARD FRANCIS, JR. D
La. State Rep.
b. New Orleans, La, 8/16/13; s. Edward Francis Le Breton, Sr. and Carmen

Suarez L; m. 1/18/47 to Gladys Lodoiska Gay; c. Edward Francis, III, Gladys Fenner Gay and Robert Aime. Educ: Tulane Univ, 33. Polit. & Govt. Pos: Mem, President of U.S. Automobile Safety Cmt, 52-64; La. State Rep, 52-; treas, Audubon Park Cmn, 54-61; mem, New Orleans Mosquito Control Cmt, 63; del, Dem. Nat. Conv, 64; mem, Gov. Joint Legis. Cmt. on Econ, 64; mem, President of U.S. Adv. Cmt. on Studies of Natural Disaster, Dept. of Housing and Urban Develop, 65; mem, Am. Assembly of Columbia Univ. in coord. with the South. Assembly, 67; mem. by proxy of Speaker of House, La. Stadium and Expos. Dist, 67; pres, Nat. Soc. of State Legislators, 68-; mem, Gov. Joint Legis. Cmt. on Hurrican and Ins. and Joint Interim Legis. Cmt. on State Air Transportation Needs, 69. Bus. & Prof. Pos: Partner, Martin-LeBreton Ins. Agency, New Orleans, La, 38-; mem. bd. dirs, New Orleans Opera House Asn, 60; mem. bd. dirs. and exec. cmt, Nat. Asn. of Casualty and Surety Agents, 64; mem. bd. dirs, Black Gold Marine, Inc, 66, Jackson Homestead Asn, 67 and Int. House, 68. Mil. Serv: Entered as Coxswain, Navy, 42, released as Chief Boatswain Mate, 45, after serv. in N. and S. Atlantic and Gulf of Mex. Publ: Feasibility Study-Conversion of Civil Courts Building for State Opera House-Music Center, New Orleans, La, 64; Legislative Committee on Economy Report on Fire and Extended Coverage Insurance of State of Louisiana, 66 and Employee Group Insurance Coverage for State of Louisiana, 67. Mem: La. and New Orleans Ins. Asns; C. of C.(bd. dirs, New Orleans area, 65); Metairie and New Orleans Country Clubs; Paul Morphy Chess Club; Press Club; New Orleans Lawn Tennis Club; Stratford Club; Plimsoll Club; K. of C; VFW; Franc-Amerique La, Inc; City Club of Baton Rouge; Press Club of Baton Rouge; Camelot; Kappa Alpha Alumni Asn. Rel: Roman Catholic. Legal Res: 1420 First St, New Orleans, La. 70130. Mailing Add: 219 Carondelet St, New Orleans, La. 70130.

LIST, ROBERT FRANK R
Dist. Attorney, Carson City, Nev.
b. Visalia, Calif, 9/1/36; s. Frank W. List and Alice Dove L; m. 7/1/62 to Kathryn Geary; c. Suzanne Kathryn and Franklin Mark. Educ: Utah State Univ, B.S, 59; Univ. Calif. Hastings Col. Law, J.D, 62; Sigma Alpha Epsilon. Polit. & Govt. Pos: Chmn, Young Rep. Club, Carson City, Nev, 63-64; del, Young Rep. Nat. Conv, 63, 65, 67 & 69, chmn. platform cmt, 69; chmn, Young Nevadans for Laxalt Sen. Campaign, 64, Gubernatorial Campaign, 66; del, Rep. co. and state conv, 64, 66 & 68, keynote speaker, Rep. State Conv, 68; del, Young Rep. State Conv, 64-69; chmn, Nev. Young Rep, 65-66; v.chmn, Young Rep. Nat. Fedn, 67; Young Rep. del, Conf. in Vietnam, 67; dist. attorney, Carson City, 67-; del, Rep. Nat. Conv, 68; Young Rep. del, NATO Conf, Brussels, Belgium, 68. Bus. & Prof. Pos: Attorney-at-law, 62-66. Mem: Nev. and Am. Bar Asns; Nev. and Nat. Dist. Attorneys Asns; Rotary; Elks; Reno Exec. Club. Rel: Protestant. Legal Res: 2 Crest Dr, Carson City, Nev. 89701. Mailing Add: P.O. Box 1057, Carson City, Nev. 98701.

MANAFORT, PAUL JOHN R
Mayor, New Britain, Conn.
b. New Britain, Conn, 6/10/23; s. James Vincenzo Manafort and Lena Miglizze M; m. 6/26/49 to Antoinette Cifalu; c. Paul John, Robert Vincent and Dennis Salvatore. Educ: New Britain Sr. High Sch, Conn. Polit. & Govt. Pos: Del, Young Rep. State and Nat. Conv; former mem, New Britain Rep. Town Cmt; alderman, New Britain, 59-60, fire cmn, 60-62, mayor, 65-; co-chmn, Citizens Water Cmt; chmn, Bd. Pub. Works Cmn, 62-64, cmnr, 64-65; v.pres, Conn. Conf. of Mayors, 68, pres, 69. Bus. & Prof. Pos: Former secy-treas, Manafort Bros, Inc, New Britain, Conn; secy-treas, Family Realty, Inc; pres, Schultz Salvage, Inc. Mil. Serv: Entered as Pvt, Army, released as Cpl, after serv. in Combat Engrs, ETO. Mem: Founder and first pres, New Britain Young Rep. Club; Jaycees; dir, Police Athletic League; Generale Ameglio Soc; trustee and charter mem, Sons of Italy; former state adj, Ital. Am. World War Vet, sr. v.comdr, chaplin and judge adv, Bernardino-Badolato Post; Lions; Ealges; Elks; Moose; Order of Alhambra; Good Shepherd Guild; K. of C; Am. Legion; Armenian-Am. Vet. of Conn. Inc; NAACP; Ital. Fraternal Soc. Recipient of Outstanding Boss Award, New Britain C. of C, 55; Distinguished Serv. Award and Hon. Pres, Generale Ameglio Soc, New Britain, Conn. Rel: Catholic. Mailing Add: 45 Overhill Ave, New Britain, Conn. 06053.

MERRITT, GILBERT ROY 'GIL' R
b. Atchison, Kans, 2/28/41; s. Thomas William Merritt, Sr. and Virginia Skelley M; single. Educ: Baker Univ, B.A, 63; Pi Kappa Delta; Alpha Psi Omega; Zeta Chi. Polit. & Govt. Pos: Chmn, Atchison Co. Young Rep, 64-66; Rep. precinct committeeman, Atchison, 65-66; v.chmn, Kans. Fedn. Young Rep, 69; press secy, U.S. Rep. Larry Winn, Jr, Kans, 69-; pres, House Rep. Commun. Asn, 69- Mem: Toastmasters Int.(pres, Haworth Toastmasters 193, 68); Elks. Toastmaster of the Year, Haworth, 67. Rel: Protestant. Legal Res: 1001 N. 13th, Atchison, Kans. 66002. Mailing Add: 510 Cannon Office Bldg, Washington, D.C. 20515.

MORGAN, LEWIS V, JR.
(additional information to sketch on p. 812)
Educ: DePauw Univ, B.A, 51. Polit. & Govt. Pos: Co-chmn, Ill. Cmn. on Atomic Energy, 66-; chmn, House Elec. Cmt, Ill. House of Rep, 67-68, Majority Leader, 69- Bus. & Prof. Pos: Lawyer, Redmond, Morgan, Mraz & Bennorth, currently. Mem: Dir, Bank of Winfield and Wheaton Pub. Libr; bd. gov, Am. Acad. Matrimonial Lawyers. Legal Res: 1213 E. Prairie Ave, Wheaton, Ill. 60187. Mailing Add: 107 N. Hale St, Wheaton, Ill. 60187.

MORSE, FRANK BRADFORD
(additional information to sketch on p. 816)
Polit. & Govt. Pos: Cong. advisor, 18-Nation Disarmament Conf, Geneva; U.S. rep, Coun. of Europe; U.S. del, Interparliamentary Union; U.S. observer, Latin Am. Parliament; chmn, Mem. of Cong. for Peace through Law. Mem: Sponsor, Atlantic Coun; chmn, Anglo-Am. Study Group on African Affairs; dir, Brazilian-Am. Cultural Inst; bd. dirs, Inst. Polit. and Planning, Pan-Am. Develop. Found. and World Affairs Coun. of Boston; founder, Famine Fighters.

MOYNIHAN, DANIEL PATRICK
Domestic Affairs Counsel to the President, 70- (see sketch p. 820)

SALLEY, GUSS C.
(additional information to sketch on p. 1005)
Polit. & Govt. Pos: Mem, Cmts. Pub. Health and Safety and State Parks and Recreation, Mo. House. of Rep, chmn. Mo. Legis. Permanent Joint Cmt. of House and Senate for Penal Insts, Schs. of Correction, State Insts. and Properties.

SANDERS, FRANK
(correction to sketch on p. 1008)
Legal Res: Potomac, Md. 20854.

SCHAAP, GEORGE ALDARUS R
Chmn, Colusa Co. Rep. Cent. Cmt, Calif.
b. Sacramento, Calif, 8/11/19; s. George Aldarus Schaap, Sr. and Maybelle Nirod Niestrath S; m. 4/29/42 to Phoebe Ann Lewis; c. Pamela Ann (Mrs. MacKean) and Craig Aldarus. Educ: Santa Rosa Jr. Col, A.A, 40; Univ. Calif, Los Angeles, 41-42; Calif. Col. Med, M.D, 46; Univ. Vienna, 56-57. Polit. & Govt. Pos: Rep. campaign dir, Fifth Sen. Dist, Calif, 61; chmn, Colusa Co. Rep. Cent. Cmt, 62-; area chmn, N.Cent. Co. Rep. Party, 69. Bus. & Prof. Pos: Sr. resident in med, Los Angeles Co. Hosp, 47-48; pvt. practice of med, Colusa Co, Calif, 48-; resident in surgery, Gen. Hosp, Linz, Austria, 57-58; pres, Valley West Convalescent Hosp, Williams, Calif, 65- Mem: Am. and Calif. Med. Asns; Tri Co. Med. Soc; Mason; Farm Bur; C. of C. County Fair Share quota 100%, 64-68. Rel: Protestant. Mailing Add: 426 Webster, Colusa, Calif. 95932.

SENNETT, WILLIAM CLIFFORD R
Attorney Gen, Pa.
b. Erie, Pa, 6/1/30; s. B. Walter Sennett and Roseanne Cooney S; m. 8/7/54 to Pauline Wuenschel; c. William, Timothy, Patrick, Mark and Kathleen. Educ: Holy Cross Col, B.A, 52; Georgetown Univ. Law Sch, LL.B, 55. Polit. & Govt. Pos: Solicitor, Erie Co. Controller, Pa, 61-63; spec. asst. attorney gen, Commonwealth of Pa, 63-66; admin. asst. to Lt. Gov, Pa, 66-67; Attorney Gen, Commonwealth of Pa, 67-, chmn, Pa. Crime Cmn. and Gov. Liquor Code Adv. Cmn, currently. Bus. & Prof. Pos: Law clerk to John Danaher, U.S. Court of Appeals, D.C, 55-56; assoc, Shreve, Sennett, Couglin & McCarthy, Erie, Pa, 56-65; partner, Knox, Pearson & McLaughlin, 65-66. Mem: Adv. bd, Mercyhurst Col; trustee, St. Vincent Hosp; bd. corporators, Hamot Hosp; Erie Co, Pa. and Am. Bar Asns; Phi Delta Phi; Automotive Asn. Erie (secy-treas, 57-66). Erie Co. Jaycee Man of the Year, 61. Rel: Catholic. Legal Res: 6336 Red Pine Lane, Erie, Pa. 16509. Mailing Add: 3834 Carriage House Dr, Camp Hill, Pa. 17011.

TAYLOR, CHARLES H.
(additiona. information to sketch on p. 1134)
Mem: Bd. dirs, Brevard C. of C. 4-H Outstanding Serv. Award, 69.

State Delegations in the 91st Congress

Number which precedes name of representative designates congressional district.

ALABAMA

Senators
John J. Sparkman (D)
James B. Allen (D)

Representatives (D-5, R-3)
1. Jack Edwards (R)
2. William L. Dickinson (R)
3. George William Andrews (D)
4. William Flynt Nichols (D)
5. Walter Winkler Flowers, Jr. (D)
6. John Hall Buchanan, Jr. (R)
7. Tom Bevill (D)
8. Robert Emmett Jones, II (D)

ALASKA

Senators
Theodore F. Stevens (R)
Mike R. Gravel (D)

Representatives (R-1)
At Large-Howard W. Pollock (R)

ARIZONA

Senators
Paul J. Fannin (R)
Barry M. Goldwater (R)

Representatives (D-1, R-2)
1. John J. Rhodes (R)
2. Morris King Udall (D)
3. Sam Steiger (R)

ARKANSAS

Senators
John L. McClellan (D)
James W. Fulbright (D)

Representatives (D-3, R-1)
1. William V. Alexander, Jr. (D)
2. Wilbur D. Mills (D)
3. John Paul Hammerschmidt (R)
4. David Hampton Pryor (D)

CALIFORNIA

Senators
George L. Murphy (R)
Alan M. Cranston (D)

Representatives (D-21, R-17)
1. Don H. Clausen (R)
2. Harold T. Johnson (D)
3. John Emerson Moss, Jr. (D)
4. Robert Louis Leggett (D)
5. Phillip Burton (D)
6. William Somers Mailliard (R)
7. Jeffery Cohelan (D)
8. George Paul Miller (D)
9. Don Edwards (D)
10. Charles S. Gubser (R)
11. Paul Norton McCloskey, Jr. (R)
12. Burt L. Talcott (R)
13. Charles McKevett Teague (R)
14. Jerome Russell Waldie (D)
15. John J. McFall (D)
16. B. F. Sisk (D)
17. Glenn M. Anderson (D)
18. Robert Bruce Mathias (R)
19. Chet Holifield (D)
20. H. Allen Smith (R)
21. Augustus F. Hawkins (D)
22. James C. Corman (D)
23. Delwin Morgan Clawson (R)
24. Glenard P. Lipscomb (R)
25. Charles E. Wiggins (R)
26. Thomas M. Rees (D)
27. Barry Goldwater, Jr. (R)
28. Alphonzo E. Bell, Jr. (R)
29. George Edward Brown, Jr. (D)
30. Edward R. Roybal (D)
31. Charles H. Wilson (D)
32. Craig Hosmer (R)
33. Jerry Lyle Pettis (R)
34. Richard T. Hanna (D)
35. James Boyd Utt (R)
36. Robert Carlton Wilson (R)
37. Lionel Van Deerlin (D)
38. John Varick Tunney (D)

COLORADO

Senators
Gordon L. Allott (R)
Peter H. Dominick (R)

Representatives (D-3, R-1)
1. Byron Giles Rogers (D)
2. Donald G. Brotzman (R)
3. Frank Edward Evans (D)
4. Wayne Norviel Aspinall (D)

CONNECTICUT

Senators
Thomas J. Dodd (D)
Abraham A. Ribicoff (D)

Representatives (D-4, R-2)
1. Emilio Quincy Daddario (D)
2. William Leon St. Onge (D)
3. Robert N. Giaimo (D)
4. Lowell Palmer Weicker, Jr. (R)
5. John Stephen Monagan (D)
6. Thomas J. Meskill, Jr. (R)

DELAWARE

Senators
John J. Williams (R)
J. Caleb Boggs (R)

Representatives (R-1)
At Large-William Victor Roth, Jr. (R)

FLORIDA

Senators
Spessard L. Holland (D)
Edward J. Gurney (R)

Representatives (D-9, R-3)
1. Robert L. F. Sikes (D)
2. Don Fuqua (D)
3. Charles E. Bennett (D)
4. William Venroe Chappell, Jr. (D)
5. Louis Frey, Jr. (R)
6. Sam M. Gibbons (D)
7. James Andrew Haley (D)
8. William C. Cramer (R)
9. Paul Grant Rogers (D)
10. J. Herbert Burke (R)
11. Claude Pepper (D)
12. Dante B. Fascell (D)

GEORGIA

Senators
Richard B. Russell (D)
Herman E. Talmadge (D)

Representatives (D-8, R-2)
1. George Elliott Hagan (D)
2. Maston Emmett O'Neal, Jr. (D)
3. Jack Thomas Brinkley (D)
4. Ben B. Blackburn, III (R)
5. Fletcher Thompson (R)
6. John James Flynt, Jr. (D)
7. John W. Davis (D)
8. Williamson S. Stuckey, Jr. (D)
9. Phillip Mitchell Landrum (D)
10. Robert Grier Stephens, Jr. (D)

HAWAII

Senators
Hiram Leong Fong (R)
Daniel Ken Inouye (D)

Representatives (D-2)
At Large-Spark Masayuki Matsunaga (D)
At Large-Patsy Takemoto Mink (D)

IDAHO

Senators
Frank Church (D)
Leonard B. Jordan (R)

Representatives (R-2)
1. James A. McClure (R)
2. Orval Howard Hansen (R)

ILLINOIS

Senators
Charles H. Percy (R)
Ralph T. Smith (R)

Representatives (D-11, R-11)
1. William L. Dawson (D)
2. Abner J. Mikva (D)
3. William T. Murphy (D)
4. Edward J. Derwinski (R)
5. John Carl Kluczynski (D)
6. Vacancy
7. Frank Annunzio (D)
8. Dan Rostenkowski (D)
9. Sidney R. Yates (D)
10. Harold R. Collier (R)
11. Roman C. Pucinski (D)
12. Robert McClory (R)
13. Vacancy
14. John Neal Erlenborn (R)
15. Charlotte T. Reid (R)
16. John B. Anderson (R)
17. Leslie C. Arends (R)
18. Robert Henry Michel (R)
19. Thomas F. Railsback (R)
20. Paul Findley (R)
21. Kenneth J. Gray (D)
22. William Lee Springer (R)
23. George Edward Shipley (D)
24. Melvin Price (D)

INDIANA

Senators
Vance Hartke (D)
Birch Bayh (D)

Representatives (D-4, R-7)
1. Ray J. Madden (D)
2. Earl Frederick Landgrebe (R)
3. John Brademas (D)
4. E. Ross Adair (R)
5. Richard L. Róudebush (R)
6. William Gilmer Bray (R)
7. John T. Myers (R)
8. Roger H. Zion (R)
9. Lee Herbert Hamilton (D)
10. David Worth Dennis (R)
11. Andrew Jacobs, Jr. (D)

IOWA

Senators
Jack R. Miller (R)
Harold E. Hughes (D)

Representatives (D 2, R-5)
1. Fred Schwengel (R)
2. John Chester Culver (D)
3. H. R. Gross (R)
4. John H. Kyl (R)
5. Neal Smith (D)
6. Wiley Mayne (R)
7. William J. Scherle (R)

KANSAS

Senators
James B. Pearson (R)
Robert J. Dole (R)

Representatives (R-5)
1. Keith George Sebelius (R)
2. Chester L. Mize (R)
3. Larry Winn, Jr. (R)
4. Garner E. Shriver (R)
5. Joe Skubitz (R)

KENTUCKY

Senators
John S. Cooper (R)
Marlow W. Cook (R)

Representatives (D-4, R-3)
1. Frank A. Stubblefield (D)
2. William H. Natcher (D)
3. William Owen Cowger (R)

4. Marion Gene Snyder (R)
5. Tim Lee Carter (R)
6. John Clarence Watts (D)
7. Carl D. Perkins (D)

LOUISIANA

Senators
Allen J. Ellender (D)
Russell B. Long (D)

Representatives (D-8)
1. F. Edward Hebert (D)
2. Hale Boggs (D)
3. Patrick Thomson Caffery (D)
4. Joe D. Waggonner, Jr. (D)
5. Otto Ernest Passman (D)
6. John Richard Rarick (D)
7. Edwin W. Edwards (D)
8. Speedy O. Long (D)

MAINE

Senators
Margaret C. Smith (R)
Edmund S. Muskie (D)

Representatives (D-2)
1. Peter Nicholas Kyros (D)
2. William Dodd Hathaway (D)

MARYLAND

Senators
Joseph D. Tydings (D)
Charles McC. Mathias, Jr. (R)

Representatives (D-4, R-4)
1. Rogers Clark Ballard Morton (R)
2. Clarence Dickinson Long, Jr. (D)
3. Edward A. Garmatz (D)
4. George H. Fallon (D)
5. Lawrence Joseph Hogan (R)
6. J. Glenn Beall, Jr. (R)
7. Samuel Nathaniel Friedel (D)
8. Gilbert Gude (R)

MASSACHUSETTS

Senators
Edward M. Kennedy (D)
Edward W. Brooke (R)

Representatives (D-8, R-4)
1. Silvio O. Conte (R)
2. Edward P. Boland (D)
3. Philip Joseph Philbin (D)
4. Harold D. Donohue (D)
5. Frank Bradford Morse (R)
6. Michael Joseph Harrington (D)
7. Torbert H. MacDonald (D)
8. Thomas P. O'Neill, Jr. (D)
9. John W. McCormack (D)
10. Margaret M. Heckler (R)
11. James Anthony Burke (D)
12. Hastings Keith (R)

MICHIGAN

Senators
Philip A. Hart (D)
Robert P. Griffin (R)

Representatives (D-8, R-11)
1. John Conyers, Jr. (D)
2. Marvin L. Esch (R)
3. Garry Eldrige Brown (R)
4. Edward Hutchinson (R)
5. Gerald R. Ford (R)
6. Charles E. Chamberlain (R)
7. Donald W. Riegle, Jr. (R)
8. James Harvey (R)
9. Guy Vander Jagt (R)
10. Elford A. Cederberg (R)
11. Philip E. Ruppe (D)
12. James Grant O'Hara (D)
13. Charles Coles Diggs, Jr. (D)
14. Lucien Norbert Nedzi (D)
15. William David Ford (D)
16. John D. Dingell (D)
17. Martha W. Griffiths (D)
18. William S. Broomfield (R)
19. Jack H. McDonald (R)

MINNESOTA

Senators
Eugene J. McCarthy (DFL)
Walter F. Mondale (DFL)

Representatives (D-3, R-5)
1. Albert Harold Quie (R)
2. Ancher Nelsen (R)
3. Clark MacGregor (R)
4. Joseph E. Karth (DFL)
5. Donald MacKay Fraser (DFL)
6. John M. Zwach (R)
7. Odin Langen (R)
8. John A. Blatnik (DFL)

MISSISSIPPI

Senators
James O. Eastland (D)
John C. Stennis (D)

Representatives (D-5)
1. Thomas Gerstle Abernethy (D)
2. Jamie Lloyd Whitten (D)
3. Charles Hudson Griffin (D)
4. Gillespie V. Montgomery (D)
5. William Meyers Colmer (D)

MISSOURI

Senators
Stuart Symington (D)
Thomas F. Eagleton (D)

Representatives (D-9, R-1)
1. William Lacy Clay (D)
2. James W. Symington (D)
3. Leonor Kretzer Sullivan (D)
4. William J. Randall (D)
5. Richard Walker Bolling (D)
6. W. R. Hull, Jr. (D)
7. Durward Gorham Hall (R)
8. Richard H. Ichord (D)
9. William Leonard Hungate (D)
10. Bill D. Burlison (D)

MONTANA

Senators
Michael J. Mansfield (D)
Lee Metcalf (D)

Representatives (D-2)
1. Arnold Olsen (D)
2. John Melcher (D)

NEBRASKA

Senators
Roman L. Hruska (R)
Carl T. Curtis (R)

Representatives (R-3)
1. Robert V. Denney (R)
2. Glenn C. Cunningham (R)
3. David Thomas Martin (R)

NEVADA

Senators
Alan Bible (D)
Howard W. Cannon (D)

Representatives (D-1)
1. Walter S. Baring (D)

NEW HAMPSHIRE

Senators
Norris Cotton (R)
Thomas J. McIntyre (D)

Representatives (R-2)
1. Louis C. Wyman (R)
2. James C. Cleveland (R)

NEW JERSEY

Senators
Clifford P. Case (R)
Harrison A. Williams, Jr. (D)

Representatives (D-8, R-6)
1. John E. Hunt (R)
2. Charles W. Sandman, Jr. (R)
3. James J. Howard (D)
4. Frank Thompson, Jr. (D)
5. Peter H. B. Frelinghuysen (R)
6. William T. Cahill (R)
7. William Beck Widnall (R)
8. Vacant
9. Henry Helstoski (D)
10. Peter Wallace Rodino, Jr. (D)
11. Joseph George Minish (D)
12. Florence P. Dwyer (R)
13. Cornelis E. Gallagher (D)
14. Dominick V. Daniels (D)
15. Edward James Patten (D)

NEW MEXICO

Senators
Clinton P. Anderson (D)
Joseph M. Montoya (D)

Representatives (R-2)
1. Manuel Lujan, Jr. (R)
2. Ed Foreman (R)

NEW YORK

Senators
Jacob Koppel Javits (R)
Charles E. Goodell (R)

Representatives (D-26, R-15)
1. Otis Grey Pike (D)
2. James R. Grover, Jr. (R)
3. Lester Lionel Wolff (D)
4. John W. Wydler (R)
5. Allard K. Lowenstein (D)
6. Seymour Halpern (R)
7. Joseph Patrick Addabbo (D)
8. Benjamin Stanley Rosenthal (D)
9. James J. Delaney (D)
10. Emanuel Celler (D)
11. Frank J. Brasco (D)
12. Shirley Anita Chisholm (D)
13. Bertram L. Podell (D)
14. John J. Rooney (D)
15. Hugh L. Carey (D)
16. John Michael Murphy (D)
17. Edward Irving Koch (D)
18. Adam Clayton Powell, Jr. (D)
19. Leonard Farbstein (D)
20. William Fitts Ryan (D)
21. James H. Scheuer (D)
22. Jacob H. Gilbert (D)
23. Jonathan B. Bingham (D)
24. Mario Biaggi (D)
25. Richard Lawrence Ottinger (D)
26. Ogden Rogers Reid (R)
27. Martin B. McKneally (R)
28. Hamilton Fish, Jr. (R)
29. Daniel E. Button (R)
30. Carleton James King (R)
31. Robert Cameron McEwen (R)
32. Alexander Pirnie (R)
33. Howard Winfield Robison (R)
34. James Michael Hanley (D)
35. Samuel Studdiford Stratton (D)
36. Frank Horton (R)
37. Barber Benjamin Conable, Jr. (R)
38. James Fred Hastings (R)
39. Richard Dean McCarthy (D)
40. Henry P. Smith, III (R)
41. Thaddeus J. Dulski (D-L)

NORTH CAROLINA

Senators
Sam J. Ervin, Jr. (D)
B. Everett Jordan (D)

Representatives (D-7, R-4)
1. Walter Beaman Jones (D)
2. L. H. Fountain (D)
3. David Newton Henderson (D)
4. Nick Galifianakis (D)
5. Wilmer David Mizell (R)
6. Lunsford Richardson Preyer (D)
7. Alton Asa Lennon (D)
8. Earl Baker Ruth (R)
9. Charles Raper Jonas (R)
10. James Thomas Broyhill (R)
11. Roy A. Taylor (D)

NORTH DAKOTA

Senators
Milton R. Young (R)
Quentin N. Burdick (D)

Representatives (R-2)
1. Mark Andrews (R)
2. Thomas S. Kleppe (R)

OHIO

Senators
Stephen M. Young (D)
William B. Saxbe (R)

Representatives (D-6, R-18)
1. Robert Taft, Jr. (R)
2. Donald D. Clancy (R)
3. Charles William Whalen, Jr. (R)
4. William M. McCulloch (R)
5. Delbert L. Latta (R)
6. William H. Harsha (R)
7. Clarence J. Brown, Jr. (R)
8. Jackson Edward Betts (R)
9. Thomas Ludlow Ashley (D)
10. Clarence E. Miller (R)
11. John William Stanton (R)
12. Samuel L. Devine (R)
13. Charles Adams Mosher (R)
14. William Hanes Ayres (R)
15. Chalmers Pangburn Wylie (R)
16. Frank T. Bow (R)
17. John Milan Ashbrook (R)
18. Wayne L. Hays (D)
19. Michael Joseph Kirwan (D)
20. Michael A. Feighan (D)
21. Louis Stokes (D)
22. Charles Albert Vanik (D)
23. William E. Minshall (R)
24. Donald E. Lukens (R)

OKLAHOMA

Senators
Fred R. Harris (D)
Henry L. Bellmon (R)

Representatives (D-4, R-2)
1. Page Belcher (R)
2. Ed Edmondson (D)
3. Carl Bert Albert (D)
4. Tom Steed (D)
5. John Jarman (D)
6. John Newbold Camp (R)

OREGON

Senators
Mark O. Hatfield (R)
Robert William Packwood (R)

Representatives (D-2, R-2)
1. Wendell William Wyatt (R)
2. Al Ullman (D)
3. Edith S. Green (D)
4. John R. Dellenback (R)

PENNSYLVANIA

Senators
Hugh Scott (R)
Richard S. Schweiker (R)

Representatives (D-14, R-13)
1. William A. Barrett (D)
2. Robert N. C. Nix (D)
3. James Aloysius Byrne (D)
4. Joshua Eilberg (D)
5. William Joseph Green (D)
6. Gus Yatron (D)
7. Lawrence G. Williams (R)
8. Edward G. Biester, Jr. (R)
9. G. Robert Watkins (R)
10. Joseph Michael McDade (R)
11. Daniel J. Flood (D)
12. John Irving Whalley (R)
13. Robert Lawrence Coughlin, Jr. (R)
14. William Singer Moorhead, Jr. (D)
15. Fred B. Rooney (D)
16. Edwin D. Eshleman (R)
17. Herman Theodore Schneebeli (R)
18. Robert J. Corbett (R)
19. George A. Goodling (R)
20. Joseph Matthew Gaydos (D)
21. John H. Dent (D)
22. John Phillips Saylor (R)
23. Albert W. Johnson (R)
24. Joseph Phillip Vigorito (D)
25. Frank M. Clark (D)
26. Thomas Ellsworth Morgan (D)
27. James G. Fulton (R)

RHODE ISLAND

Senators
John O. Pastore (D)
Clairborne Pell (D)

Representatives (D-2)
1. Fernand Joseph St. Germain (D)
2. Robert Owens Tiernan (D)

SOUTH CAROLINA

Senators
James Strom Thurmond (R)
Ernest F. Hollings (D)

Representatives (D-5, R-1)
1. L. Mendel Rivers (D)
2. Albert W. Watson (R)
3. William Jennings Bryan Dorn (D)
4. James Robert Mann (D)
5. Thomas Smithwick Gettys (D)
6. John L. McMillan (D)

SOUTH DAKOTA

Senators
Karl E. Mundt (R)
George McGovern (D)

Representatives (R-2)
1. Benjamin Reifel (R)
2. E. Y. Berry (R)

TENNESSEE

Senators
Albert A. Gore (D)
Howard Baker, Jr. (R)

Representatives (D-5, R-4)
1. James Henry Quillen (R)
2. John James Duncan (R)
3. William Emerson Brock, III (R)
4. Joe Landon Evins (D)
5. Richard Harmon Fulton (D)
6. William Robert Anderson (D)
7. L. Ray Blanton (D)
8. Edward Jones (D)
9. Dan Heflin Kuykendall (R)

TEXAS

Senators
Ralph W. Yarborough (D)
John G. Tower (R)

Representatives (D-20, R-3)
1. Wright Patman (D)
2. John Dowdy (D)
3. James Mitchell Collins (R)
4. Ray Roberts (D)

5. Earle Cabell (D)
6. Olin Teague (D)
7. George Bush (R)
8. Robert Christian Eckhardt (D)
9. Jack Brooks (D)
10. J. J. Pickle (D)
11. William Robert Poage (D)
12. James C. Wright (D)
13. Graham Purcell (D)
14. John Young (D)
15. Eligio de la Garza (D)
16. Richard Crawford White (D)
17. Omar Burleson (D)
18. Robert Dale Price (R)
19. George Herman Mahon (D)
20. Henry Barbosa Gonzalez (D)
21. O. Clark Fisher (D)
22. Robert Randolph Casey (D)
23. Abraham Kazen (D)

UTAH

Senators
Wallace F. Bennett (R)
Frank E. Moss (D)

Representatives (R-2)
1. Laurence Junior Burton (R)
2. Sherman Parkinson Lloyd (R)

VERMONT

Senators
George D. Aiken (R)
Winston L. Prouty (R)

Representatives (R-1)
At Large-Robert T. Stafford (R)

VIRGINIA

Senators
Harry F. Byrd, Jr. (D)
William B. Spong, Jr. (D)

Representatives (D-5, R-5)
1. Thomas N. Downing (D)
2. George William Whitehurst (R)
3. David E. Satterfield, III (D)
4. Watkins Moorman Abbitt (D)
5. W. C. Daniel (D)
6. Richard H. Poff (R)
7. John O. Marsh (D)
8. William Scott (R)
9. William Creed Wampler (R)
10. Joel T. Broyhill (R)

WASHINGTON

Senators
Warren G. Magnuson (D)
Henry M. Jackson (D)

Representatives (D-5, R-2)
1. Thomas Minor Pelly (R)
2. Lloyd Meeds (D)
3. Julia Butler Hansen (D)
4. Catherine Barnes May (R)
5. Thomas Stephen Foley (D)
6. Floyd V. Hicks (D)
7. Brockman Adams (D)

WEST VIRGINIA

Senators
Jennings Randolph (D)
Robert C. Byrd (D)

Representatives (D-5)
1. Robert H. Mollohan (D)
2. Harley Orrin Staggers (D)
3. John M. Slack, Jr. (D)
4. Ken Hechler (D)
5. James Kee (D)

WISCONSIN

Senators
William Proxmire (D)
Gaylord Anton Nelson (D)

Representatives (D-4, R-6)
1. Henry Carl Schadeberg (R)
2. Robert William Kastenmeier (D)
3. Vernon Wallace Thomson (R)
4. Clement John Zablocki (D)
5. Henry S. Reuss (D)
6. William Albert Steiger (R)
7. David R. Obey (D)
8. John William Byrnes (R)
9. Glenn Robert Davis (R)
10. Alvin E. O'Konski (R)

WYOMING

Senators
Gale William McGee (D)
Clifford P. Hansen (R)

Representatives (R-1)
At Large-John S. Wold (R)

PUERTO RICO

Resident Commissioner
Jorge Luis Cordova

CLASSIFICATION

Senate		House	
Democrat	57	Democrat	245
Republican	43	Republican	187
Total	100	Total	432

Governors of the States

STATE	GOVERNOR	LT. GOVERNOR
ALABAMA	Albert Preston Brewer (D)	Vacant
ALASKA	Keith Harvey Miller (R)	*
ARIZONA	John Richard Williams (R)	*
ARKANSAS	Winthrop Rockefeller (R)	Maurice L. Britt (R)
CALIFORNIA	Ronald Wilson Reagan (R)	Ed Reinecke (R)
COLORADO	John Arthur Love (R)	Mark Anthony Hogan (D)
CONNECTICUT	John N. Dempsey (D)	Attilio R. Frassinelli (D)
DELAWARE	Russell Wilbur Peterson (R)	Eugene Donald Bookhammer (R)
FLORIDA	Claude Roy Kirk, Jr. (R)	Ray C. Osborne (R)
GEORGIA	Lester G. Maddox (D)	George Thornewell Smith (D)
HAWAII	John A. Burns (D)	Thomas P. Gill (D)
IDAHO	Donald W. Samuelson (R)	Jack M. Murphy (R)
ILLINOIS	Richard Buell Ogilvie (R)	Paul Simon (D)
INDIANA	Edgar Doud Whitcomb (R)	Richard E. Folz (R)
IOWA	Robert D. Ray (R)	Roger W. Jepsen (R)
KANSAS	Robert Blackwell Docking (D)	James H. DeCoursey, Jr. (D)
KENTUCKY	Louie B. Nunn (R)	Wendell H. Ford (D)
LOUISIANA	John Julian McKeithen (D)	Clarence C. Aycock (D)
MAINE	Kenneth M. Curtis (D)	*
MARYLAND	Marvin Mandel (D)	*
MASSACHUSETTS	Francis W. Sargent (R)	Vacant
MICHIGAN	William Grawn Milliken (R)	Vacant
MINNESOTA	Harold LeVander (R)	James B. Goetz (R)
MISSISSIPPI	John Bell Williams (D)	Charles L. Sullivan (D)
MISSOURI	Warren Eastman Hearnes (D)	William Shelton Morris (D)
MONTANA	Forrest H. Anderson (D)	Thomas Lee Judge (D)
NEBRASKA	Norbert T. Tiemann (R)	John Everroad (R)
NEVADA	Paul Laxalt (R)	Ed Fike (R)

* Office of Lt. Governor nonexistent.

STATE	GOVERNOR	LT. GOVERNOR
NEW HAMPSHIRE	Walter Rutherford Peterson (R)	*
NEW JERSEY	Richard J. Hughes (D)	*
NEW MEXICO	David Francis Cargo (R)	E. Lee Francis (R)
NEW YORK	Nelson Aldrich Rockefeller (R)	Malcolm Wilson (R)
NORTH CAROLINA	Robert Walter Scott (D)	Hoyt Patrick Taylor, Jr. (D)
NORTH DAKOTA	William L. Guy (D)	Richard F. Larsen (R)
OHIO	James Allen Rhodes (R)	John William Brown (R)
OKLAHOMA	Dewey Follett Bartlett (R)	George Patterson Nigh (D)
OREGON	Tom Lawson McCall (R)	*
PENNSYLVANIA	Raymond Philip Shafer (R)	Raymond Joseph Broderick (R)
RHODE ISLAND	Frank Licht (D)	J. Joseph Garrahy (D)
SOUTH CAROLINA	Robert Evander McNair (D)	John Carl West (D)
SOUTH DAKOTA	Frank L. Farrar (R)	James Abdnor (R)
TENNESSEE	Earl Buford Ellington (D)	Frank Gorrell (D)
TEXAS	Preston Earnest Smith (D)	Ben F. Barnes (D)
UTAH	Calvin Lewellyn Rampton (D)	*
VERMONT	Deane Chandler Davis (R)	Thomas Lawlor Hayes (R)
VIRGINIA	Mills Edwin Godwin, Jr. (D)	Fred G. Pollard (D)
WASHINGTON	Daniel Jackson Evans (R)	John Andrew Cherberg (D)
WEST VIRGINIA	Arch A. Moore, Jr. (R)	*
WISCONSIN	Warren P. Knowles (R)	Jack R. Olson (R)
WYOMING	Stanley K. Hathaway (R)	*

AMERICAN SAMOA	John M. Haydon	*
GUAM	Carlos Garcia Camacho (R)	*
PUERTO RICO	Luis A. Ferre (R)	*
VIRGIN ISLANDS	Melvin H. Evans (R)	*

* Office of Lt. Governor nonexistent.

Geographical Index

ALABAMA

Abernethy, Louise (R)
Adams, Charles Harris (D)
Adams, James Lowell, Sr. (D)
Albea, Woodrow (D)
Alexander, Dan C, Jr (D)
Allen, Harlan Goline Sr (D)
Allen, James Browning (D)
Allgood, Clarence William (D)
Alonzo, Frank Oliver (D)
Ames, Bobbie (R)
Amos, Mabel S. (D)
Andrews, Arthur Glenn (R)
Andrews, George William (D)
Avery, Richard Moore (D)
Baggett, Agnes Beahn (D)
Bailes, George Lewis, Jr. (D)
Baker, James Willie (D)
Baker, Raymond Excell (D)
Bandouveris, Harry (R)
Barnett, George M. (D)
Barnett, Roy Alexander (D)
Barnett, William Curless (R)
Bassett, Lee Gardner (D)
Beck, William Morris (D)
Bennett, J. Richardson, Jr. (R)
Bentley, Luther Daniel Jr. (D)
Berryman, William Anderson (D)
Bethea, Barron (D)
Bethea, Malcolm (R)
Bevill, Tom (D)
Blanton, John H (D)
Bloodworth, James Nelson (D)
Blount, Winton M. (R)
Blue, John Edward (D)
Bolton, Lyndol (D)
Boston, Hugh Chester (D)
Boutwell, Albert Burton (D)
Bowers, Quinton R. (D)
Boyd, Eloise Agusta Metzger (R)
Boykin, Elizabeth Joseph (R)
Brannan, Louie Wesley (D)
Branyon, James Alexander II (D)
Brassell, Bowen Hill (D)
Brewer, Albert Preston (D)
Brown, Norman Knight (D)
Brown, Ralph D. (D)
Buchanan, John Hall, Jr. (R)
Burgess, Gerald Ray (D)
Burnham, Horace Rupert (D)
Burns, Gary Franklin (D)
Bynum, F. G. (R)
Caldwell, John Jay, Jr. (R)
Callahan, Artemas Killian (D)
Cameron, James Wesley (D)
Camp, Ashley Leonidas, Jr. (D)
Campbell, William Dewey, Jr. (D)
Campbell, William Loy (D)
Cantrell, Berry Dabney Lynchmore (D)
Capps, R. Walter (D)
Carr, Aubrey J. (D)
Carter, Clayton (D)
Casey, John Sears (D)
Castile, George Edward (D)
Cates, John Lewis (D)
Chapman, Charles Hickerson, Jr. (R)
Cherner, Bennett Lee (D)
Childers, Erasmus Roy (R)
Clark, Harry Patrick (D)
Clark, James Sterling (D)
Coleman, Irwin Weldon, Jr. (R)
Coleman, James Samuel, Jr.
Collier, Ernest Sims (D)
Collins, Clara Stone (D)
Collins, Donald L. (R)
Collins, William Montgomery (D)
Compton, Richard Wesley (R)
Connor, Eugene (D)
Cook, James Drexel (D)
Cook, John W. (D)
Cooper, Andrew James, II (D)
Cooper, Roland (D)
Cornett, Homer Wilson, Jr. (D)
Crane, Verbon E. (D)
Crawford, James Francis (D)
Cronin, Donald J. (D)
Crow, James Harris, Jr. (D)
Culpepper, Rufus Horace (D)
Culver, John Lee (D)
Dailey, Steve (D)
Daniel, Van Buren (D)
Davis, Frederick Howard (D)
Davis, Julian Mason, Jr. (D)
Dickinson, William Louis (R)
Dill, Richard F. (D)
Dobbs, Oscar Clarence (D)
Doggett, Roswell Christopher (D)
Dominick, Richard Fahey (D)
Dowling, Young Daniel (R)
Downing, Maurice Albert (D)
Drake, Tom (D)
Drennen, Alan Travis, Jr. (D)
Dumas, William Lawrence, Jr. (D)
Eddins, Edward Oswell (D)
Edington, Patricia Gentry (D)
Edington, Robert Sherard (D)
Edwards, Jack (R)
Edwards, Walter Malcolm (D)
Edwards, William Deara
Elliott, Carl (D)
Ellis, John Hagood (R)
Ellis, Robert Lawson, Jr. (D)
Engel, Mylan Robert (D)
Etheredge, Robert Foster (D)
Evans, Albert Henry, Jr. (D)
Faulk, Roland R. (D)
Fetner, Auey Emory (R)
Fite, Rankin (D)
Flowers, Richmond McDavid (D)
Flowers, Walter Winkler, Jr. (D)
Franks, Vaudry Lee (D)
Frazier, Elva Brindley (D)
French, Robert Bryant, Jr. (R)
Frink, Bettye Jean (D)
Fuller, Charles Eugene, Jr. (D)
Funderburk, Kenneth LeRoy (R)
Gallion, MacDonald (D)
Garner, Mary Texas (D)
Garrett, Walter Eugene (D)
Gay, James Hoyt (R)
Getchell, Earle Duncan (R)
Gilbert, Thomas Martin (D)
Gilchrist, James Robert (D)
Giles, Jack (D)
Gilmore, Eddie Hubert (D)
Givhan, Walter Coats (D)
Glass, Folsom LaMont (D)
Goldthwaite, Alfred Witherspoon (D)
Goodwyn, O. J. (D)
Graham, Anna (R)
Graham, William Hardin (R)
Grant, George McInvale (D)
Graves, John (Independent)
Grenier, John Edward (R)
Grouby, Edward Arthur, Sr. (D)
Hain, B. V. (D)
Hall, David McGiffert (R)
Hall, Earl Wells (R)
Hall, Lilbourne Preston (R)
Hambric, Alton Marshall (D)
Hancock, Oscar Walker (D)
Hand, William Brevard (R)
Hannay, Esther E. (D)
Harman, James Harvey (R)
Hartwig, Asa Charls (R)
Hawkins, Donald Andrew (D)
Hawkins, Donna Kay (D)
Hawkins, John H, Jr. (D)
Headley, Lewis W. (D)
Heflin, Henry Grady (D)
Henderson, William Bruce (R)
Hester, J. Walston (D)
Hill, (Joseph) Lister (D)
Hill, Robert McClellan, Jr. (D)
Hogan, Elwood Leon (D)
Holladay, Hugh Edwin (D)
Hollins, Wilbur Hugo (D)
Holmes, Alvin Adolf (D)
Hooper, Perry O. (R)
Horne, John Elmer (D)
Hornsby, Ernest Clayton (D)
Horton, James Edwin, Jr. (D)
Ingram, Kenneth Frank (D)
Jackson, Jesse Ernest (D)
Jackson, Walter Frank (D)
James, Earl Daniel
James, Henry Parker (D)
Jones, Helen B. (D)
Jones, J. Fletcher (D)
Jones, Ralph Lee (D)
Jones, Robert Emmett, II (D)
Jones, Thomas Applewhite, Jr. (D)
Jorgensen, Natalie Smith (R)
Joseph, William Francis, Jr. (R)
Kahalley, Jameal A. (D)
Kelly, Frances Floyd (R)
Kerr, Robert Mabry (R)
King, Tom Cobb, Jr. (R)
Kolb, James (D)
Langan, Joseph Nicholas (D)
Lawless, Kirby Gordon, Jr. (R)
Lemley, Bill L. (D)
Lindsey, Wallace Henry, III (D)
Little, Dorothy Lynn (D)
Little, Tandy Duncan, Jr. (R)
Livingston, James Edwin (D)
Locke, Hugh Allen Jr. (D)
Locklin, Robert Rives (D)
Lolley, Wilmer Ray (D)
Lowe, Herbert Julian (D)
McAlister, Thomas Buell (R)
McCain, William Clarence (D)
McCarley, William George (D)
McCorquodale, Joseph Charles, Jr. (D)
McDermott, William Henry (D)
McDonald, Sid L. (D)
McDow, James Thomas (D)
McGhee, Flora Devaughan (D)
McKay, Charles Watson, Jr. (D)
McLain, Eugene Milton (D)
McLemore, Carl Ray (R)
McSwean, Robert Horace (D)
Malone, Dan Richard (D)
Manley, Richard Shannon (D)
Marr, Thomas Marshall (D)
Martin, James Douglas (R)
Martin, William Roy (D)
Mashburn, Telfair James (D)
Massey, James Clements (D)
Mathews, Charles T. (D)
Maxwell, Robert Hamilton (R)
Mayhall, Roy (D)
Mays, James McCoy (D)
Meade, Ralph Allison (D)
Meadows, Austin Ruel (D)
Medders, Marion Wardner (R)
Meeks, Julius Paul, Jr. (D)
Merrill, Hugh Davis (D)
Merrill, Pelham Jones (D)
Metcalf, Neil (D)
Millican, Manyon Meadows (R)
Mims, Lambert Carter
Mitchell, Wendell Wilkie (D)
Montgomery, Charles Albert (D)
Moore, Edsel Ford (D)
Mordecai, Frank Selmer (R)
Morrow, Hugh III (D)
Nabors, Ollie Wilson (D)
Nesmith, Carl Dalton (D)
Neville, William Vinkley, Jr. (D)
Nichols, William Flynt (D)
Norris, Palmer Whitten (R)
O'Connor, Carolyn Old (D)
O'Connor, James David (D)
Oden, William Emmett (D)
Owen, Clyde Craddock (D)
Owen, L. Dick, Jr. (D)
Owens, James King, Jr. (R)
Owens, Ruth Johnson (D)
Owens, William Edward, Jr. (D)
Parker, Donald Conant (R)
Patterson, John Malcolm (D)
Patterson, LaFayette (D)
Pearson, Leon P. (D)
Pennington, Harry Lucas (D)
Perloff, Mayer William (D)
Perry, Walter Emmett, Jr. (D)
Peters, James Elbert (R)
Peters, Maxwell (R)
Pierce, Junius Julius (D)
Pitts, Jon Will (R)
Pointer, Sam Clyde, Jr. (R)
Posey, John A. Jr. (R)
Powell, Freddie Delano (D)
Price, Reginald Staunton (D)
Pruitt, David Carl, III (R)
Pruitt, Ira Drayton (D)
Purvis, Mary O. Carnley (D)
Putman, Kathleen Mavourneen (R)
Radney, Tom (D)
Rains, Albert M. (D)
Rains, Hobdy G. (D)
Rast, Holt (D)
Reid, James E. (D)
Reynolds, Edward Harris (D)
Reynolds, Newton Luther
Richerson, Francis Buckner (R)
Riseling, Bob Henderson (R)
Roberts, Kenneth Allison (D)
Roberts, Roscoe O. Jr. (D)
Robertson, Edward D. (D)
Robertson, John Anderson (R)
Roberson, Pat Howell (D)
Robinson, Errol Wayne (R)
Robison, Blanchard Gaillard, Jr. (D)
Robison, Vaughan Hill (D)
Rodgers, Louise V. (D)
Rogers, Charles McPherson Aduston, III (Independent)
Saliba, Alfred J. (R)
Salter, Wiley (D)
Schuler, John Hamilton (R)
Scurlock, Louie M. (D)
Selden, Armistead I, Jr. (D)
Sessions, Paul Trammell (D)
Shackleford, Robert Mitchell, Jr. (R)
Shelton, Allen Clifton (D)
Sherrer, Wayman G. (R)
Sherrod, Henry Floyd (D)
Shores, Arthur Davis (D)
Simpson, Robert Tennent (D)
Sizemore, James Middleton, Jr. (R)

Slate, Ralph E. (D)
Smith, Charles O, Jr. (R)
Smith, Coy (D)
Smith, Joseph W. (D)
Smith, Philip Hardy (D)
Smith, Wilburn (R)
Snell, Charles Sherman (D)
Sparkman, John J. (D)
Spencer, Edward L, Jr. (R)
Stallworth, John Robert, III (D)
Starnes, John Wallace (D)
Steagall, Henry II (D)
Stembridge, Bob Jones (D)
Stewart, Ellis Cameron (D)
Stone, Ernest (D)
Sullivan, Hermon Huit (R)
Sullivan, Jean (R)
Sullivan, Ulie Bascom (D)
Taylor, Hiram Brodgen (D)
Teel, Robert Jerome (D)
Thomas, Sim Allen Jr. (D)
Traweek, Kenneth Edward (R)
Traylor, Lee Clyde (R)
Tuck, Edwin Alvis (D)
Turner, Alton Lee (D)
Turner, Granville Nicholas (D)
Turnham, Pete Benton (D)
Tyson, John M. (D)
Vacca, Paschal Patrick (D)
Van Antwerp, James Callanan, Jr. (R)
Vance, Helen Rainey (D)
Vance, Robert Smith (D)
Vann, David J. (D)
Venable, Jack Benton (D)
Wadsworth, Charlie Doster (Independent)
Waggoner, James Thomas, Jr. (D)
Wallace, George Corley (Independent)
Waller, Margie West (R)
Weeks, Raymond (D)
Wiggins, Matthew Edwin
Wiggins, Ted (R)
Wilkinson, Robert Dawson, Jr. (R)
Williams, William Van (R)
Wilson, Robert Terry (D)
Wood, John Emmet (D)
Woodard, Carl Jubal (R)
Wright, Louis Charles (D)
Yeilding, Newman Manly (D)
Young, Gus Wilson (D)

ALASKA

Barnes, Doris Marian (R)
Boney, George Frank (R)
Bradner, Michael Drake (D)
Brady, Carl Franklin (R)
Briones, Joseph Magdaleno (D)
Brown, Russel Leroy (D)
Browning, Levi Martin (D)
Burgess, Lloyd Albert (R)
Butrovich, John (R)
Cannon, Patricia Elaine (D)
Chance, Genie (D)
Christiansen, Raymond C. (D)
Conwell, Evelyn Lona (R)
Colver, Warren C. (D)
Cornelius, Stanley Preston (R)
Croft, Leland Chancy (D)
Davenny, Robert Alton (R)
Durant, Phil S. (R)
Edwards, G. Kent (R)
Egan, William Allen (D)
Engstrom, Elton E. (R)
Fischer, Victor (D)
Fisher, Lee Elliott (R)
Fitzpatrick, Marjorie Grace (R)
Gain, Kenneth Jay (D)
Gottstein, Barnard J. (D)
Gravel, Mike Robert (D)
Gruening, Ernest (D)
Guess, Eugene (D)
Haggland, P. B. (R)
Hammond, Jay Sterner (R)
Harrigan, Alice Anna (D)
Harris, Frank W. (R)
Hemenway, Robert Bruce (R)
Hensley, William L. (D)
Hickel, Walter, J. (R)
Hohman, George H, Jr. (D)
Holloway, Eager Louis (D)
Holm, Edith Muriel (R)
Homay, Alan (D)
Hoopes, Robert (D)
Jackson, Barry Wendell (D)
Kilcher, Yule F. (D)
Koslosky, Janis Marvin (R)
Le Fevre, Walter (D)
Lomen, Mary Elizabeth (R)
MacCarty, Collin Stewart, Jr.
McCombe, Bob (D)
McKinley, Ira Blakely (R)
McNealy, Robert J. (D)
McVeigh, Richard Lawrence (D)
Martin, Waneta (R)
Meacham, Charles Harding (R)
Miller, Alex (D)
Miller, Keith Harvey (R)
Miller, Terry (R)
Millsap, Claude, Jr. (R)
Moses, Carl Eugene
O'Connell, John W. (D)
Orbeck, Edmund N. (D)
Parsons, James Cecil (R)
Peirce, Walter H. (R)
Phillips, E. Bradford (R)
Poland, Bill Merle (D)
Pollock, Howard W. (R)
Plotnick, Maurice Daniel (D)
Rabinowitz, Jay Andrew (D)
Rader, John L. (D)
Rasmuson, Elmer Edwin (R)
Ray, Bill (D)
Rhodes, Wilma Melissa (R)
Rivers, Ralph Julian (D)
Rothstein, Joseph Marvin (D)
Savage, Emily Gierasch (R)
Schleppegrell, John Daniel (R)
Schwamm, John A. (D)
Scott, Norma Kathleen (D)
Scott, Robert F. (D)
Sheldon, Robert Edwards (D)
Simpson, Jack Raymond (R)
Smith, Donald L. (R)
Smith, V. Maurice (R)
Stephens, Merle Leon (R)
Stepovich, Michael A. (R)
Stevens, Theodore Fulton (R)
Stevenson, Robert D. (D)
Sundborg, George (D)
Sweet, John M. (R)
Taylor, Warren A. (D)
Toner, Felix J. (D)
Ulmer, Eldon Robert (R)
Wade, Hugh Joseph (D)
Walton, George D. (R)
Ward, Robert W. (R)
Warren, Clifford Ernest (D)
Waugman, William I. (R)
Weir, Julian Paul (R)
Wold, Sigurd (R)
Wright, Jules (R)
Young, Donald E. (R)
Ziegler, Robert Holton, Sr. (D)

ARIZONA

Abrams, Stanley Paul (D)
Ackerman, Leopold (D)
Ahee, Joe (D)
Allen, Jesse Willard (R)
Alkire, Alma Asenath (R)
Alspach, Thomas Alan (R)
Arnold, Ben (D)
Baker, George Tone (D)
Baker, William D. (R)
Baldwin, Howard Stanley (R)
Beaman, James Addison (R)
Bean, Robert Ray (D)
Beaty, Orren, Jr. (D)
Bleikamp, Barbara Leota (R)
Bolin, Wesley H. (D)
Bosch, Lovinna (D)
Braden, Margaret Mize (R)
Brown, Jack Albert (D)
Brown, Keith Spalding (R)
Brown, M. J. (D)
Buehl, William Anthony (R)
Burch, Dean (R)
Burgess, Isabel Andrews (R)
Cajero, Bernardo Moreno (D)
Campbell, Cloves Colbert (D)
Capalby, Joseph R. (D) See Addenda
Carney, John (D)
Castillo, Joseph A. (D)
Castro, Raul Hector (D)
Cohen, Marvin S. (D)
Cole, Tom C. (D)
Conlan, John B, Jr. (R)
Conlee, Patricia Ann (R)
Cooper, James LeRoy (R)
Corbett, James Neilson, Jr. (D)
Davids, Craig E. (D)
Davis, Lewis Walter (R)
DeConcini, Dennis (D)
DeWitt, Laron Waldo (R)
Douglas, Lewis W. (D)
Duffield, John Richard (D)
Elliott, James Alton (D)
Elson, Roy Lane (D)
Ely, Herbert Leonard (D)
Everett, Raymond Leo (R)
Face, Albert R. (R)
Fannin, Paul Jones (R)
Farley, Rex Jay (R)
Farmer, Merle L. (D)
Fenn, Henry Forster (D)
Foss, Joseph Jacob (R)
Frandsen, Vigo Bishop (R)
Frank, John Paul (D)
Frantz, Albert Edward, Jr. (D)
Getzwiller, Polly (D)
Gilbert, Andrew Jackson (D)
Giss, Harold C. (D)
Goddard, Samuel Pearson, Jr. (D)
Goetze, Ray A. (R)
Goldwater, Barry Morris (R)
Graham, Milton Henry (R)
Gutierrez, Rosendo (D)
Haines, Don Hugh (D)
Halacy, Daniel Stephen, Jr. (R)
Hamilton, Mary Ellen (R)
Harless, Richard Fielding (D)
Harrison, Mark I. (D)
Hathaway, Robert Richard (D)
Haugh, John H. (R)
Hayden, Carl Trumbull (D)
Hays, Jack D. H. (R)
Hays, Priscilla Harvey (R)
Hazelett, John Martin (R)
Herbert, Richard John (D)
Hesser, Woodrow Cleveland (D)
Hill, Izora R. (D)
Hodge, William Sneed (D)
Holsclaw, Douglas Stanley (R)
House, Lloyd Lynn (D)
Huerta, Joseph Lopez (D)
Husky, Milton J. (D)
Jacquin, William C. (R)
Jenks, Davidson (R)
Jennings, Renz Dixon (D)
Johnson, Christopher T. (R)
Johnson, Raleigh West (R)
Jones, D. Lee (R)
Jones, Herschel Albert (R)
Joyner, Conrad Francis (R)
Kay, Peter (R)
Kelley, Frank (R)
Kitchel, Denison (R)
Kleindienst, Richard Gordon (R)
Kluender, Al (R)
Knoles, Thomas M, Jr. (D)
Koory, Edward Fredrick, Jr. (R)
Kret, David B. (R)
Larson, Mildred (D)
Lasher, Michael Albert, Jr. (R)
Lena, Sam (D)
Lewis, Charles William (R)
Lewis, Orme, Jr. (R)
Liverance, Irma Milde (R)
Lockwood, Lorna E. (D)
McFarland, Ernest William (D)
McLay, James B. (D)
Mahoney, William Patrick, Jr. (D)
Mason, Bruce Bonner (D)
Miller, Robert Evans (D)
Minarik, Frank Stuyvesant (D)
Monplaisir, Maria Ellen (R)
Morrow, Robert Emery (D)
Murray, Michael Webster (D)
Musgrave, Harold Miller (R)
Nelson, Gary Kent (R)
Olson, Richard Carl (D)
Oshrin, Albert Sidney (D)
Pardridge, Marilyn Jones (R)
Peck, Barbara May (R)
Peck, George W. (D)
Pena, Manuel, Jr. (D)
Peterson, Arthur La Verne (R)
Pickrell, Robert W. (R)
Pine, Charles Warren (D)
Platt, Harvey J. (R)
Pritzlaff, John Charles Jr. (R)
Rehnquist, William Hubbs (R)
Reveles, Robert Apodaca (D)
Rhodes, John J. (R)
Riggs, L. Alton (D)
Riley, James Joseph (D)
Ronan, Barbara Hunt (D)
Rosenbaum, Polly (D)
Rosenzweig, Harry (R)
Ross, Edna Genevieve (R)
Ruman, Helen Anne (D)
Scanlan, Robert Joseph (R)
Senner, George Frederick, Jr. (D)
Shaughnessy, Joseph, Jr. (R)
Shelley, James Ernest (R)
Shumway, Boyd Albert (D)
Shumway, Drew (R)
Smith, Darrell Fenwick (R)
Smith, Kent Nephi (D)
Smitherman, William C. (R)
Sossaman, James J. (R)
Staggs, Ralph Eugene (R)
Steiger, Sam (R)
Stewart, Donovan (R)
Stillman, Guy (D)
Stinson, Bess B. (R)
Stone, David Bonesteel (R)
Strong, Robert Campbell
Struckmeyer, Fred C, Jr. (D)
Tanner, Lynn (D)
Tenney, Nathan Boyd (R)
Turley, Stanley F. (R)
Udall, Morris King (D)
Udall, Stewart Lee (D)
Udine, Fred Francis (D)
Watkins, Ralph A, Jr. (D)
White, Somers Hayes (R)
Wilcox, Robert Clayton (R)
Williams, Albert Clark (R)
Williams, John Richard (R)
Youngblood, Harold Francis (R)

ARKANSAS

Adcox, Jimmy Dean (D)
Alexander, William V, Jr. (D)
Alstadt, William Robert (D)
Andrews, George Aristedes (R)
Arnold, William Joshua (D)
Babbitt, Wayne Hubert (R)
Beaumont, William Eustace, Jr. (D)
Becker, Jerome Bill (D)
Beeson, Travis N. (R)
Bell, Clarence E. (D)
Bell, Sara Jo (R)
Bernard, Betty Hill (R)
Bernard, Charles Taylor (R)
Binder, James Shirley (R)
Blair, James B. (D)
Blaylock, Len Everette (R)
Boyce, Charles Wayne (D)
Brandon, James William (D)
Brandon, Phyllis Dillaha (D)
Britt, Henry Middleton (R)
Britt, Maurice L. (R)
Brown, Rolland D. (R)
Brown, Roscoe Delano (D)
Bryant, Garland Lee (D)
Bryant, Kelly (D)
Burleson, David J. (D)
Burns, William Vernon (D)
Burton, Ben Franklin (D)
Burton, Marion B. (R)
Bush, Baker Hoskins (D)
Butler, Richard C, Jr. (R)
Bynum, Preston C. (R)
Capps, John Paul (D)
Carnes, Mrs. Jack (D)
Carney, Cy, Jr. (R)
Catlett, Leon Bidez (D)
Chambers, Melvin Thayer (D)
Clark, Hubert Woody (D)
Clements, Ruth Welch (D)
Cockrill, Sterling Robertson, Jr. (D)
Colay, Harry Bradford (D)
Courtney, Wayne Neely (D)
Crank, Marion Harlan (D)
Cypert, James Dean (D)
Dalton, Herman Udell (R)
De Busk, David Louis (R)
Dishongh, Howard Allan (D)
Durrett, Chadd Lanier, Sr. (D)
Earnhart, Milt (D)
Faubus, Orval Eugene (D)
Faulkner, Robert Wesley (R)
Feild, Kay Carol (R)
Felton, Daniel Henry, Jr. (D)
Fendler, Oscar (D)
Fletcher, Virgil T. (D)
Fogleman, John Albert (D)
Ford, Joe T. (D)
Freed, Melvyn Norris (D)
Fulbright, James William (D)
Galyean, Roy Horton (D)
Garrison, Frank Sheridan (R)
Gathings, Ezekiel Candler (D)
Gooch, James Thomas (D)
Gordon, Edward (D)
Griffee, John Franklin (R)
Griffin, Richard Earl (D)
Grubbs, Lawton Edison (D)
Hall, Nancy Johnson (D)
Ham, Everett Adams, Jr. (R)
Hamilton, Joseph T. (D)
Hammerschmidt, John Paul (R)
Hammons, Otis Parnell (D)
Hardy, Sarah Frances (D)
Harper, Thomas (D)

Harrell, James H. (D)
Harris, Frank Carleton (D)
Harris, Oren (D)
Hartrick, Gordon Dean (R)
Hawkins, Jeffrey Laden (D)
Hawkins, Marlin C. (D)
Hayes, Jesse C. (D)
Heiskell, John N. (D)
Hendricks, Malvin Leon, Sr. (R)
Henley, Leland (R)
Henson, James Harvey (R)
Hinkle, Doris McCastlain (D)
Holleman, Harlan Harmon (R)
Horn, Amos (D)
Hough, Cass Sheffield (R)
House, Mary Corbin (D)
Howell, Max (D)
Hurst, Ella Blanche (D)
Hurst, Quincy Byrum (D)
Johnson, James Douglas (D)
Johnson, Jewelle Richardson (D)
Johnson, Lewis James, Sr. (D)
Johnson, Neal Sox (R)
Jones, Guy Hamilton, Sr. (D)
Jones, James Fred (D)
Jones, James Samuel (D)
Jones, Jimmie (D)
Jones, Mark Perrin, III (D)
Kane, David Ronald (D)
Keel, John Peyton (D)
Kelley, Glen E. (D)
Kelly, William Thomas
Kenkel, Gerhard H. (R)
Keown, Woodrow N. (D)
Kinney, Clarke (D)
Kizer, Bernice L. (D)
Kolb, James Monroe, Sr. (D)
Larey, Bethel Bryan (R)
Ledbetter, Calvin Reville, Jr. (D)
Ledbetter, Joel Yowell (D)
Leonard, Joe Eldon (R)
Lieblong, Warren George (R)
Linder, A. James (D)
Lively, Robbie J. (D)
Lookadoo, J. Hugh (D)
Lowe, Aylmer Lynn (R)
Lowe, Jere B. (R)
McAdams, Herbert Hall (D)
McClellan, John L. (D)
McClerkin, Hayes Candor (D)
McCuiston, Lloyd Carlisle, Jr. (D)
McDonald, Rommie Gean (D)
McGillicuddy, Lillian Grace (R)
McMath, Sidney S. (D)
McQuilkin, Margaret (R)
Malin, Marjorie Claire (D)
Manatt, Frank Bentley (D)
Marks, Dorris Doty (R)
Matthews, Charles Dawson (D)
Matthews, James Madison, Jr. (D)
May, Ronald Alan (R)
Miller, John E. (D)
Mills, Wilbur D. (D)
Nelson, George Neil (D)
Newman, Bobby Gene (D)
Nowotny, George Edward, Jr. (R)
Oglesby, Gladys Martin (D)
Partain, David Owen (D)
Patrick, Danny L. (R)
Peel, David Walker (D)
Pendergrass, Orville Dexter (R)
Penix, Bill (D)
Penn, Thomas Azor (D)
Peterson, Merle Francis (D)
Phillips, Reece W. (R)
Poe, McDonald, Sr. (D)
Pollard, Odell (R)
Poynter, Bill Charles (R)
Prewitt, Taylor Archie (D)
Pryor, David Hampton (D)
Purcell, Joe (D)
Purtle, John Ingram (D)
Ragsdale, Albert George (D)
Rainwater, Wallace Eugene (D)
Raney, James W. (R)
Reeves, Helen Grayson (R)
Rhodes, Joe Edd (D)
Rice, Dale Harvey (R)
Rich, Jack W. (D)
Riley, Bob Cowley (D)
Ritter, Mabel Louise (R)
Rockefeller, Winthrop (R)
Rogers, Judith (D)
Rose, Ivan W. (D)
Routon, Bonnie Anthony (R)
Rule, Herbert Charles, III (D)
Rush, Carolyn Sue (R)
Rush, William Van Jr. (R)
Ryburn, Bennie, Jr. (D)
Shaver, James L, Jr. (D)
Sheeks, Brooks (D)
Sheets, James Lee (R)
Sisco, Friedman (R)
Sisk, Arthur C, Sr. (R)
Smith, Bernard Chester (R)
Smith, Donald Houston (D)
Smith, George Rose (D)
Smith, George William (R)
Smith, Odis Odell (D)
Snyder, Evelyn Boyce (D)
Sparks, Thomas Everett (D)
Spencer, George Lloyd (D)
Stewart, Brice Horace (R)
Stewart, Charles Wesley, Jr. (D)
Still, Eugene Fontaine (D)
Streett, Julian DuVall (D)
Stuckey, Jay Clarence (R)
Sturgis, Dick (R)
Sulcer, Kenneth Saunders (D)
Tackett, Boyd Anderson (D)
Tate, Ruth Evelyn (D)
Taylor, Beloit (D)
Taylor, Van B. (D)
Teeter, Robert E. (R)
Thomas, A. Jan, Jr. (D)
Thompson, Burrell A. (D)
Trimble, James William (D)
Troxell, Leona Mae (R)
Vance, Howard Grant (R)
Wagner, John Edwin (D)
Waldrip, Helen C. (R)
Waters, Troy L. (R)
Welch, Betty Joan (R)
Wells, Bill G. (D)
White, Dan Fredrick (D)
Whiteaker, Pearl Wallace (D)
Wiley, Junior Lee (R)
Williams, Lee (D)
Williams, York W, Jr. (R)
Williamson, Walter Edward (D)
Windsor, Julius Gayle, Jr. (D)
Woodward, Joe D. (D)
Woodward, Mary Davis (D)
Yarber, Cleophus Kenneth (D)
Young, Damon Michael (D)

CALIFORNIA

Ablin, George (D)
Adair, Sidney Arthur (R)
Adams, Earl Clinton (R)
Adams, Frank Pollard (R)
Agostini, Wanda E. (R)
Aitken, Wylie Arthur (D)
Alanson, Ann (D)
Alarcon, Angelita (D)
Alcaraz, Gertrude Elizabeth (D)
Alex, John Maynard (R)
Alexander, Opal Mansur (D)
Alioto, Joseph Lawrence (D)
Allen, Bruce Franklin (R)
Allen, Don A, Sr. (D)
Allen, Joyce Rosetta (D)
Allen, Peter John (D)
Alperson, Joseph Lionel (D)
Amante, Paul Sam (D)
Amerine, Mervin Wells (R)
Anderson, Alvin Bert (R)
Anderson, Clifford R, Jr. (R)
Anderson, Don (R)
Anderson, Glenn M. (D)
Anderson, Jack Z. (R)
Anderson, John Milton (D)
Anderson, Mary Dunn (R)
Andre, Peter Richard (R)
Andrew, Lester M. (R)
Anthony, Philip LaVern (D)
Archer, Roy Robert (D)
Arciga, Carmen (D)
Ardaiz, Aran Alton (R)
Arklin, Arax (R)
Arklin, Henry (R)
Arnebergh, Roger (R)
Arnett, Dixon (R)
Arnold, Alva Lee (R)
Arnold, Stanley (D)
Arvizu, Arthur A. (D)
Ashen, Pete (R)
Astredo, Jane Ann (R)
Axelrod, Daniel Louis (D)
Badger, LeMoyne Smith (R)
Badham, Robert Edward (R)
Bagley, William Thompson (R)
Bailin, Harold A. (D)
Ballard, Reece (D)
Bamberg, Daniel Francis (D)
Baptista, Mary Elsie (D)
Barnard, Aurora Caro (R)
Barnard, Keith W. (R)
Barnes, Dwight H. (D)
Barnum, C. Robert (R)
Barnyak, Mary A. (R)
Barry, Robert R. (R)
Bartel, John W, Jr. (R)
Bartley, William Maurice (D)
Barton, Terry Allen (R)
Basile, James Charles (D)
Baskin, Gordon (D)
Batt, George Kenneth
Baum, Sherry Liss (D)
Beagley, Ronald Francis (D)
Beahrs, John Victor (R)
Beauchamp, Jean M. (R)
Beaver, Jack Aldred (R)
Beaver, Robert F. (R)
Bee, Carlos (D)
Begovich, John C. (D)
Beilenson, Anthony C. (D)
Bell, Alphonzo (R)
Bell, Elvin Charles (D)
Bell, Paul Maxwell (R)
Belotti, Frank P. (R)
Bennett, Lora Marie (R)
Berg, Larry Lee (D)
Berliner, Henry Paul (D)
Berman, Howard Lawrence (D)
Berry, Charles Frederick (R)
Berry, LeRoy (D)
Betts, Bert A. (D)
Beverly, Robert Graham (R)
Biddle, W. Craig (R)
Bigelow, Charles DeForrest (R)
Bilheimer, Stephen Charles (R)
Billings, Guy Earl (D)
Bispo, Naomi Marie (R)
Bispo, William Lawrence (R)
Black, Beulah (D)
Black, Shirley Temple (R)
Black, Thomas Andrew (R)
Blackmer, Margaret Couture (D)
Blair, Robert Earl (R)
Blasier, John Wilber (R)
Boas, Roger (D)
Bondshu, Robert Eugene (R)
Bonicelli, Derito (D)
Booth, Charles Rockwell (R)
Borelli, Frank Peter, Jr. (R)
Bort, Joseph Parker (R)
Boston, Eugene Alfred (R)
Bowe, John Edward (R)
Bowersox, Robert Joseph (D)
Bowler, Ann (R)
Boyce, Merle Hunter (R)
Boynton, Marjorie Chase (R)
Bradford, Marion Tillson (R)
Bradley, Clark Lynn (R)
Bradley, Thomas (D)
Bradley, William Randolph (R)
Brandon, Robert Franklin (R)
Brathwaite, Yvonne Watson (D)
Braun, Virginia Mary (R)
Brekke, Lola M. (R)
Breshears, Carol Ann (D)
Briggs, John Vern (R)
Britschgi, Carl A. (R)
Broad, Eli (D)
Brock, Margaret Martin (R)
Bromfield, Betsy Byron (R)
Bronson, Leisa Graeme (R)
Brooks, John (D)
Brown, Charles Harrison (D)
Brown, Donald Kent (D)
Brown, Edmund Gerald (D)
Brown, Edmund Gerald, Jr. (D)
Brown, Eleanor Mae (R)
Brown, George A. (R)
Brown, George Edward, Jr. (D)
Brown, Gloria Ruth (R)
Brown, James Harvey (D)
Brown, Josephine M. (R)
Brown, Lewis Frank (D)
Brown, Lillian Cunningham (D)
Brown, Lola W. (D)
Brown, Ralph M. (D)
Brown, Richard Ross (R)
Brown, Willie L, Jr. (D)
Browning, James Arthur, Jr. (D)
Buchbinder, Lucie Hahn (D)
Bugatto, B. John (R)
Bunzel, John Harvey (D)
Burgener, Clair W. (R)
Burgess, Barbara Ann (D)
Burke, Robert H. (R)
Burns, Hugh M. (D)
Burton, Phillip (D)
Busterud, John A. (R)
Butcher, William Arthur (D)
Butchko, John Thaddeus (D)
Butler, Bayford Duncan (R)
Butterfield, Alexander Porter (R)
Byers, Robert Keith (R)
Byers, William H. (R)
Byrne, Wm. Matthew (D)
Cade, Lionel Bruce (D)
Calden, Gertrude Beckwith (R)
Calvin, Richard Woodland, Jr. (R)
Camaroda, Pat Joseph (D)
Cameron, Ronald Brooks (D)
Cameron, Ward Francis (D)
Campbell, Alberta W. (R)
Campbell, Anona Jeanne (R)
Campbell, Charles Arthur (R)
Campbell, Jacqueline F. (R)
Campbell, Leslie Kenneth (R)
Canson, Virna M. (D)
Capen, Richard Goodwin, Jr. (R)
Carbone, Eugene R. (D)
Cardona, Lois Eileen (D)
Carey, Jacquelyn Ann (R)
Carlson, Jack Lewis (R)
Carpenter, Dennis E. (R)
Carr, Gladys B. (R)
Carr, James K. (D)
Carrell, Thomas C. (D)
Carreno, Delores Mae (D)
Carrow, Robert Duane (D)
Carsten, Arlene Desmet (D)
Carter, Paul Thomas (R)
Carter, Phillip Leroy (D)
Carter, Robert Thomas (D)
Carvey, Tom B, Jr. (D)
Casattas, Paul Steven (R)
Case, Stewart Stanton (R)
Casey, Jack Tull (D)
Cashion, David Carl (R)
Casillas, Joe David (R)
Castile, Robert O. (D)
Castle, Robert Marvin (D)
Castro, Ramon (D)
Cavnar, Sam (R)
Cenotto, Lawrence Arthur, IV (R)
Cervantes, Alfred F. (D)
Champlain, Robert Alfred (R)
Champlin, Malcolm McGregor (R)
Chandler, Roger Carl (R)
Chapel, Charles Edward (R)
Chapman, Alice Hackett (R)
Chappie, Eugene A. (R)
Chickering, Sherman (R)
Cho, Maria Chungsook (R)
Chrisman, P. Michael (R)
Christensen, Carl L. (D)
Christoffersen, Paul John (D)
Christopher, Warren Minor (D)
Chu, Betty Tom (D)
Clark, Richard Owen (D)
Clarke, Russell Leland (R)
Clausen, Don H. (R)
Clawson, Delwin Morgan (R)
Cleland, Jack Cyril (D)
Cline, Robert Corde (R)
Cobey, James Alexander (D)
Coblentz, William Kraemer (D)
Cochran, Alice Liddle (R)
Cohee, Darwin Dick (R)
Cohelan, Jeffery (D)
Cohn, Nathan (D)
Coil, Henry Wilson, Jr. (R)
Cole, Louis V. (R)
Collier, Charles Russell (R)
Collier, John L. E. (R)
Collier, Randolph (D)
Cologne, Gordon (R)
Comfort, Sylvia Hague (R)
Commons, Dorman Leland (D)
Comstock, Kirke White (D)
Conatser, Ray (D)
Conelly, Carl Robert (R)
Conrad, Charles J. (R)
Cook, James Clifford (D)
Cook, Orrin S. (R)
Cooke, Charles Maynard, Jr. (R)
Coolidge, Glenn E. (R)
Coombs, William Elmer (R)
Cooper, Fred Ferris (D)
Cooper, Gloria Claire (D)
Cooper, Jane Ellen (R)
Cooper, Leon M. (D)
Corbin, Leland Wayne (R)
Corman, James C. (D)
Corrigan, Ione Elaine (D)
Cory, James Kenneth (D)
Costantini, Edmond (D)
Cox, Hazel Irene (D)
Cox, John Edward, Jr. (R)
Crandall, Earle P. (R)
Cranston, Alan MacGregor (D)
Crawford, Carol Forsyth (R)
Crawford, Richard Royce (D)
Cristina, Vernon Joseph (R)
Croft, John Kendrick (D)
Crosby, Jane A. (R)
Crosby, Joseph Marshall (R)

Crose, Jack Curry (D)
Cross, (William) Travis (R)
Crown, Robert W. (D)
Cullen, Mike (D)
Cullen, Rita Beane (D)
Cunningham, Rex M. (D)
Curran, Frank E.
Currigan, Thomas G. (D)
Cusanovich, Lou (R)
Custer, Dorothy Pauline (R)
Cutting, Wendell Riley (R)
Daley, Anne Belisle (D)
Daley, Katherine Fay (R)
Dana, Deane, Jr. (R)
Dance, James Harold, Jr. (R)
Danielson, George Elmore (D)
Dannemeyer, William Edwin (D)
Darby, Helen Almeda (R)
Davey, Mary Curtis (R)
Davis, Lou Ann (R)
Davis, Nada (R)
Davis, Pauline L. (D)
Davis, Wallace Robert (D)
Dawkins, Maurice Anderson (D)
Day, Joan Thomson (R)
Debolt, Edward S. (R)
Deddeh, Wadie Peter (D)
DeDomenico, Paul Domenic (D)
Degnan, June Oppen (D)
Delahanty, George Emmett (R)
Del Junco, Tirso (R)
De Lotto, Bert (D)
Dembosz, Joseph John (D)
Dent, James Wesley (R)
De Paoli, Esther Elayne (R)
Dermody, John Daniel (D)
Dermody, Mary Louise (D)
Despol, John Anton (R)
Deukmejian, George (R)
Dewees, Elaine MacDonald (R)
Dias, Frances Jean (R)
Dickinson, William Streit, Jr. (D)
Dills, Clayton A. (D)
Dills, Ralph C. (D)
Doe, Russell Malloch (R)
Dolwig, Richard J. (R)
Donnelly, Hugh P. (D)
Donovan, Richard J.
Doolin, Don (D)
Dorsey, May Florence (R)
Double, Barbara Turner (D)
Doyle, John Augustine (D)
Drane, Davis Clark (R)
Draper, William Henry, III (R)
Driver, Robert Farr (D)
Dubin, Leonard R. (D)
Ducommun, Charles Emil (R)
Duffy, Gordon W. (R)
Dugan, Paul Fleming (D)
Duguid, Robert Lee (R)
Dunlap, Carter Wesley (R)
Dunlap, John Foster (D)
Dunn, James Randall (R)
Dunn, Lucy M. (D)
Duran, June Clark (R)
Dyal, Ken W. (D)
Dyer, Louise Seeburger (R)
Dymally, Mervyn M. (D)
Eberle, Harold Frederick, Jr. (R)
Edelman, Edmund Douglas (D)
Edwards, Don (D)
Egeberg, Roger O. (D)
Egerman, Howard Douglas (D)
Eller, Armena Morse (R)
Elliott, Alfred James (D)
Elliott, Edward Emerson (D)
Emery, Michael C. (D)
Emett, Robert Lynn (R)
English, Richard Matthew (D)
Erreca, Robert Cronwell (D)
Ertola, John Andrew (D)
Evans, David R. (R)
Evans, James Larkin (D)
Fadem, Jerrold Alan (D)
Fadem, Joyce A. (D)
Fadem, Robert Stanley (R)
Fagan, Michael Robert (D)
Fargher, Lawrence LeRoy (R)
Faries, McIntyre (R)
Farkas, Daniel John (D)
Farr, Fred S. (D)
Fenster, Leo (D)
Ferguson, Dorothy Maude (R)
Ferguson, Rodger O. (R)
Ferrell, F. Douglas (D)
Field, Donald William (R)
Finch, Robert Hutchison (R)
Finkel, Robert S. (D)
Fisher, Audrey Horn (R)
Fisher, Hugo Mark (D)
Fisher, Joel Marshall (R)
Fisher, Priscilla Mary Evelynn (R)
Fitzpatrick, Rosalyn M. (R)
Flagg, Morgan (D)
Fleetwood, Thirvin Dow (D)
Fletcher, Charles Kimball (R)
Flint, Philip Sheridan (R)
Flournoy, Houston Irvine (R)
Foley, John Field (R)
Fong, March K. (D)
Foran, John Francis (D)
Forrest, Erin George (D)
Fowle, Eleanor Cranston (D)
Fowles, Olive Grace (R)
Francis, Louis Patrick (R)
Francois, Terry Arthur (D)
Franzi, Emil Anthony (R)
Freas, Howard George
Freeman, Fulton
Freeman, Kenneth Donald (D)
Freitas, Edward Warren (D)
Frew, Myron H. (D)
Friedman, Frances (R)
Friend, Hazel Irene (R)
Fritz, Abner Marvin (D)
Frizzelle, Nolan (R)
Furra, Leon (D)
Gaffney, Edward McGlynn (D)
Gagan, Michael Stephen (D)
Gage, John Burdette (D)
Gangle, Ruth Alice (D)
Gant, Charles Green (D)
Garabedian, Adria W. (D)
Garabedian, John Michel (R)
Garcia, Joseph Albert (R)
Garrigues, George Louis (R)
Garrigus, Charles B. (D)
Gasdiae, Frank Robert (R)
Gater, David Winfield (R)
Geddes, John Arrington (R)
Geernaert, Gerald L. (R)
Gehres, Leslie Edward (R)
Geier, Robert Albert (R)
Geis, Ellen Florence (R)
Geisler, Margaret S. (D)
Gelber, Louise Carp (D)
Germino, Donald Owen (R)
Gherini, Pier A. (R)
Gibney, Robert Emmet (R)
Gibson, John S. (D)
Gibson, Tyree Jim (D)
Gilbert, William Lewis (D)
Giles, Leon Mansfield (R)
Gill, James Maxwell (D)
Gillenwaters, Edgar Martin (R)
Gillmor, Gary George (D)
Gladson, Charles L. (R)
Gladstein, Nancy Robin (D)
Goady, Charles William (R)
Goldwater, Barry, Jr. (R)
Gomperts, Robert Elliot (D)
Gonsalves, Joe A. (D)
Gonzales, Robert Eugene (D)
Gonzales, Victor Jr. (D)
Gordon, Jean Ella (R)
Gordon, Margaret Shaughnessy (D)
Gordon, Milton G. (D)
Gould, George Benjamin (D)
Gourlay, Islay Mae (R)
Graf, Al N. (R)
Grant, William S. (R)
Green, Mary Louise Katherine (R)
Green, Maxine Wise (R)
Greenawald, Dolores Rose (R)
Greenaway, Roy Francis (D)
Greene, Bill (D)
Greer, Michael Ira (D)
Gregg, James Erwin (D)
Gregory, Norris Paige, Jr. (D)
Griffin, Saundra Lee (D)
Griffith, Richard Alden (R)
Groenen, Jan Henry (R)
Gromala, John Anthony (R)
Gronnebeck, Treva D. (D)
Groom, James Haynes (R)
Grossman, Leon Wolfe (D)
Groves, G. Mark (R)
Grunsky, Donald Lucius (R)
Gruver, William Rand II (D)
Gubser, Charles S. (R)
Guerra, Mark (R)
Guzman, Ralph (D)
Haerle, Paul Raymond (R)
Hagen, Harlan Francis (D)
Hall, Charles Edward (D)
Halley, James Winston (R)
Hand, Lloyd Nelson (D)
Handy, Wendell Taylor (R)
Hanna, Richard T. (D)
Hannaford, Mark Warren (D)
Hannaford, Peter Dor (R)
Hansen, Grant Lewis (R)
Harabedian, Michael Thomas (D)
Harcourt, Richard Lloyd (R)
Harker, Jacqueline Nugent (R)
Harmer, John L. (R)
Harper, Virginia Maughan (D)
Harriman, John H. (R)
Harris, Dave T. (R)
Hart, Peter D. (D)
Harutunian, Albert Theodore, Jr. (R)
Hass, Ewing (R)
Hassenplug, Richard Doss (R)
Hatch, Stanley Craig (D)
Hausey, Willie Robert (D)
Hawkins, Alice Tenneson (R)
Haverkamp, Warren Franklin
Hawkins, Augustus F. (D)
Hayes, James A. (R)
Hearn, Irene Finnerty (R)
Heavey, Patricia W. Durbin (D)
Hecht, W. Arthur (R)
Hedrick, Coleena Wade (R)
Henderson, Mary Warner (R)
Henley, Robert L. (R)
Henry, Harold Eugene (D)
Henson, Burt Martin (D)
Herrema, Lavonne June (D)
Hickerson, Marcus R. (D)
Hiestand, Edgar Willard (R)
Higgins, Sammie L. (R)
High, Thomas William (R)
Higham, William Rolston (D)
Hill, Albert Alan (R)
Hillings, Patrick J. (R)
Hinkle, Paul David (D)
Hirschi, Frank William (R)
Hitt, Patricia Reilly (R)
Hitt, Robert James (R)
Hix, John Denham (R)
Hobdy, Clarence Chester (R)
Hodge, Kenneth Kennedy (R)
Hodgson, James Day (D)
Hoeppel, John Henry (D)
Holdstock, Richard S. (D)
Holifield, Chet (D)
Hollingsworth, William Right (R)
Holmdahl, John W. (D)
Holmes, David William (R)
Holmes, Gordon Conant (R)
Holmes, James Loren (R)
Holsinger, Galen Wright (D)
Hone, Susan Meadows (D)
Horwitz, Larry (D)
Hosking, Mary Katherine (R)
Hosking, Richard (R)
Hosmer, Craig (R)
Hosmer, Lucile Callan (R)
Houghteling, Joseph Cannon (D)
House, Leverette D. (D)
House, Vincent F. (R)
Houston, Henry Ervin (R)
Houston, Norman Oliver (D)
Houston, William Kyle (R)
Howsden, Arley Levern (D)
Huber, Robert Daniel (R)
Huberty, Dorothea Hill Witter (R)
Hulett, Stanley William (R)
Hume, Jaquelin Holliday (R)
Humphreys, George Douglass (D)
Hunter, Jean Lorraine Major (R)
Huntley, William Leonard (D)
Hutton, Louise Phillips (R)
Hyde, Floyd H.
Irwin, Betty J. (R)
Jachens, Norman H. W. (R)
Jackson, Donald Lester (R)
Jackson, Rosella Mildred (R)
Jackson, Thomas Edwin (D)
Jacobs, Harry Michael (D)
James, Louis Earl (R)
James, Ronald R. (R)
Jeffers, Mary L. (D)
Jenkins, Thomas M. (D)
Jensen, Anna Gertrude Bates (R)
Jernegan, John Durnford
Johnson, Beverly Adele (R)
Johnson, Cyrus (R)
Johnson, Gardiner (R)
Johnson, Harold (R)
Johnson, Harold T. (D)
Johnson, Harvey Myers (D)
Johnson, James Edward (R)
Johnson, Ray Eugene (R)
Johnson, Thurman Cleophus (D)
Johnson, U. Alexis
Johnston, Ronald Vernon (D)
Jonas, Allan K. (D)
Jones, Bill (R)
Jones, Napoleon (D)
Jordan, Donald Weller, Jr. (D)
Jordan, Frank Morrill (R)
Jorgensen, Frank E. (R)
Jumani, Beth Virginia (R)
Karabian, Walter John (D)
Kaufman, Vernon (D)
Keas, Jacquelin B. (R)
Keating, Edward Michael
Keatinge, Richard Harte (D)
Keaton, Harry Joseph (R)
Kehoe, John Thomas (D)
Keilbar, Mona Mary (R)
Keller, Emma Knauss (R)
Kelly, Joseph I. (D)
Kenchelian, Karney K. (R)
Kennedy, Goldie L. (D)
Kenney, Edward William (D)
Kennick, Joseph M. (D)
Kenoyer, Kenneth Dale (D)
Kent, Roger (D)
Kenyon, Cecil Clark (R)
Kerr, Bailey Furman (R)
Ketchum, William Matthew (R)
Keyston, David Hill (R)
King, Cecil R. (D)
King, William Theodore (R)
Kirby, Peter (R)
Klein, Herbert George (R)
Klein, Margaree Selma (D)
Knauft, Milford Roy, Jr. (R)
Knight, A. J. (D)
Knight, Evelyn Deloris (D)
Knight, Goodwin S. (R)
Knight, V. Lane (R)
Knott, Walter (R)
Knowland, William Fife (R)
Knox, John Theryll (D)
Knuppel, Shirley LaVaune (R)
Kofman, Abraham (D)
Kopeikin, Leonard I.
Koreski, Donald Eugene (D)
Kraemer, James S. (R)
Krieger, Harvey S. (D)
Kronick, Russell (D)
Krotz, Virla Roper (R)
Krueger, Robert William (R)
Kuchel, Thomas H. (R)
Kutz, Robert Boyne (R)
Kyle, Charles Clayton (R)
Ladd, Kenneth Richard (R)
Lagomarsino, Robert John (R)
Lake, James Howard (R)
Lathen, Bernice A. (D)
Lambros, Theresa (R)
Lamport, Paul H. (R)
Lanterman, Frank D. (R)
Lavery, Vincent Joseph (D)
Lawrence, M. Larry (D)
Leake, Paul Raymond (D)
Leatherman, Jefferson Franklin (R)
Leckman, Henry T. (D)
Le Conte, Dorothy Teagar (D)
Lee, Robert Reid (R)
Leet, Louis (R)
Leggett, Robert Louis (D)
Lehman, Edith Alban (R)
Leinberry, Wilbur Stanley (R)
Leitcher, Elizabeth S. (R)
Lemucchi, Timothy Jon (D)
Lenhart, Thomas B. (D)
Leonoudakis, Stephan Constantine (D)
Leopold, Arthur Fredric (D)
Leslie, Jacques Robert (D)
Levee, Michael Charles, Jr. (D)
Lillie, Arline Whipple (R)
Lindgren, Donald Arthur (D)
Lindholm, Frances Marion (R)
Lindsey, Jack B. (R)
Lippincott, C. Lydon (R)
Lipscomb, Glenard P. (R)
Livanos, Peter E, Jr. (R)
Livermore, Putnam (R)
Lloyd, Jacqueline Vaughan (D)
Lloyd, James Fredrick (D)
Logue, Daniels Charles (R)
Lombardi, Angela Funai (R)
Longaker, Daniel Norman, Jr. (D)
Lonsdale, Howard C. (R)
Lookinland, Paul Russell (R)
Love, Clyde B. (D)
Lowance, Franklin E. (R)
Lowe, David William (D)
Luce, Gordon C. (R)
Lucking, William Alfred, Jr. (R)
Ludwig, Joseph Lafe (R)
Luftig, Rita Sheila (D)
Lundberg, Lois Ann (R)
Lundy, Rayfield (R)
Lynch, John William (D)
Lynch, Thomas Connor (D)
Lyng, Richard (R)
MacBride, Thomas Jamison (D)
McCall, Isodene Marie (R)

McCall, James Kennedy (R)
McCarty, Frank John (R)
McClintock, Darwin Graham (D)
McCloskey, Maxine Elaine (D)
McCloskey, Paul Norton, Jr. (R)
McColl, John Angus (R)
McColley, Pearcy L. (D)
McComb, Marshall Francis (R)
McDaniel, Donald Conley (R)
MacDonald, J. Kenyon (D)
McDonough, Gordon Leo (R)
McElwain, Calvin Lewis (D)
McFall, John J. (D)
McFarland, Mary Ann (R)
McGee, Patrick D'Arcy (R)
McGhee, Milton Lorenzo (D)
MacGillivray, W. Donald (R)
McInnes, Theresa (R)
McKee, Douglas Arthur (R)
Mackey, Malcolm H. (D)
McKillen, Jean Barbara (R)
McKinney, James Grover (R)
McKinnon, Clinton D. (D)
McMillan, Lester A. (D)
MacNair, Robert Wynn (R)
McNeil, Jean McIntyre (R)
McPherson, William Hauhuth (R)
McVaney, Beatrice (D)
McVey, Caroline Marie (D)
Mailliard, William Somers (R)
Maizlish, Leonard Murray (D)
Malek, Frederic Vincent (R)
Malloy, Boyd Edward (D)
Manatt, Charles Taylor (D)
Manibog, G. Monty (D)
Manis, James Edward (R)
Manriquez, Carol Huante (D)
Maple, Barbara D. (R)
Mardian, Robert Charles (R)
Mark, Norman Leroy (R)
Markel, J. Ogden (D)
Marks, Milton (R)
Marler, Fred William, Jr. (R)
Marootian, Simon (D)
Marra, August James (D)
Marriott, Richard Harold (D)
Martell, Kay Patricia (D)
Martin, Clarence Daniel, Jr. (D)
Massey, Horace S. T. (D)
Masterson, William Anthony (D)
Mathews, Elbert G.
Mathias, Robert Bruce (R)
Mattox, Verna D. (R)
Maughmer, Karrol June (R)
May, Bernice Hubbard (D)
May, James Woodrow (D)
Maynard, Robert Tilson (D)
Mazzie, E. C. (R)
Mazzie, Lorraine Gardiner (R)
Meggs, Margarette Brown (R)
Meis, Martha F. (R)
Mellen, Melba J. (R)
Mello, Henry John (D)
Mendelsohn, Robert H. (D)
Mespelt, Roy W. (D)
Meyer, Norman J. (D)
Meyer, William Benedict (D)
Meyers, Charles Walter, Sr. (D)
Michals, Charles (R)
Michaud, Denis Joseph (D)
Milam, Mobley Meadows (D)
Miles, Mary Jo (D)
Miles, Thomas James (R)
Milias, George Wallace (R)
Miller, George Paul (D)
Miller, Howard Benjamin (D)
Miller, John Jose (D)
Miller, Robert Gordon (R)
Miller, Robert John (R)
Miller, Ross Matthew, Jr. (D)
Mills, Billy Gene (D)
Mills, James R. (D)
Milnar, Carol Virginia (R)
Mingo, Jack (R)
Misuraca, Malcolm Anthony (D)
Mitchell, Bruce Tyson (R)
Mitchell, Robert E. (R)
Mize, Dwight Workman (D)
Mobley, Ernest Nelson (R)
Moeller, Beverley Bowen (R)
Moffatt, Norbert Basil (D)
Monagan, Robert Timothy, Jr. (R)
Monce, Raymond Eugene (D)
Monson, Arch, Jr. (R)
Montalvo, Ray Garcia (D)
Moore, Dudley Shields (R)
Moore, J. Max (R)
Moorhead, Carlos J. (R)
Moose, Margaret Ruth (R)
More, David Lewis (R)
Moretti, Robert (D)

Morris, Chester (R)
Morris, Coalson C. (R)
Morrow, Floyd Lee (D)
Moser, Raymond (R)
Moses, William Preston (R)
Mosk, Edna Mitchell (D)
Mosk, Richard Mitchell (D)
Mosk, Stanley (D)
Moss, John Emerson (D)
Moulds, Elizabeth Fry (D)
Mulford, David Donald (R)
Muller, Ella Elizabeth (R)
Munnell, William Arthur (D)
Munroe, Kenneth George (D)
Murphy, Frank, Jr. (R)
Murphy, George Lloyd (R)
Murphy, Robert Joseph, III (R)
Murray, John Joseph, Jr. (R)
Murrell, Cecil Boyd (R)
Musgrove, William L. (D)
Muskey, Nicholas Chris (R)
Myers, Bob J. (D)
Myers, William Blackwell (D)
Nakashima, S. Stephen (R)
Narvid, Ethel Gallay (D)
Naujock, Evelyn Katsis (R)
Neal, Fred Warner (D)
Negri, David (D)
Neibel, Clemett Lee (R)
Nelson, Maynard Dale (R)
Neuman, Jerold Joe (R)
Neumann, Robert G. (R)
Nevins, Richard (D)
Newman, Jeffrey Paul (D)
Newsom, David D.
Nielsen, Vigo Gilbert, Jr. (R)
Ninburg, Daniel Harvey (D)
Nisbet, Eugene G. (D)
Nissen, Ralph Albert (R)
Nixon, Richard M(ilhous) (R)
Noel, Joseph Walter (R)
Nolan, Mae Ella (R)
Norris, William Albert (D)
Norris, William E. (R)
O'Brien, Charles A. (D)
O'Donnell, Gladys (R)
Offutt, David Allen (R)
Ogle, Alice Nichols (R)
O'Keefe, John Cornelius (D)
Olrich, Frank Edwin (D)
O'Neill, Oren George (D)
Orme, Lila Morton (D)
Orozco, Joseph William (R)
Orr, Juanita Elois (D)
Orrick, William Horsley, Jr. (D)
Osgood, Thomas Andrew (D)
Osos, Toby (D)
O'Sullivan, Virgil (D)
Oswald, Robert Leon (R)
Otterson, Margaret LaVerne (R)
Outland, George E. (D)
Pace, Joseph L. (D)
Packard, David (R)
Paddock, Darven Leveree (R)
Page, Donald Kenneth (D)
Paine, Thomas Otten (D)
Palevsky, Max (D)
Palmer, Kenneth A. (D)
Palmer, Thomas Gerald, Jr. (D)
Pardue, Erwin (R)
Park, William Henry (R)
Parker, Ann L. (R)
Parkinson, Gaylord Benton, Jr. (R)
Parkinson, Harvey Vincent (R)
Parshalle, Eve (R)
Partello, Charles Hamilton (D)
Pauley, Edwin Wendell (D)
Pearson, Enid Irene (R)
Pedersen, Esther Irene (R)
Peeke, Harman V.S. (D)
Pelosi, Ronald (D)
Penn, William Frank (R)
Pereira, Stephen Edward (D)
Peters, Alice Boye (R)
Peters, Raymond Elmer (D)
Petersen, Donald Harry (R)
Peterson, Beverly Jane (R)
Peterson, Harriett Monroe (R)
Peterson, Paul Ames (D)
Petris, Nicholas C. (D)
Pettis, Jerry Lyle (R)
Pettitt, James Vanoni (R)
Phillips, Gifford (D)
Pienta, Lillian Louise (D)
Pierce, Nathaniel Peter (D)
Pierre, George (D)
Pike, Emily Goodloe (R)
Pike, Thomas Potter (R)
Pitchess, Peter J. (R)
Poché, Marc B. (D)
Politzer, S. Robert (D)

Pope, Alexander H. (D)
Porter, Carley V. (D)
Pottage, Thomas Michael (R)
Potter, James B, Jr. (R)
Potter, Norma Teague (R)
Posner, Paul M. (D)
Post, Manning J. (D)
Poust, Clara Esther (R)
Powers, Gordon F. (R)
Powers, Lawton Raymond (R)
Pratt, John McKee (D)
Prescott, Robert W. (D)
Prestage, Ethel Marian (R)
Priest, Ivy Baker (R)
Prioleau, Diane Thys (R)
Priolo, Paul V. (R)
Puffer, Thomas Ray (R)
Quevedo, Henry Anthony (R)
Quick, Aaron W. (D)
Rader, Bobby Jewett (R)
Rae, Matthew Sanderson, Jr. (R)
Rafferty, Max (R)
Ralph, Leon Douglas (D)
Ramirez, E. Alice (D)
Ramser, Harold Charles (R)
Raner, Guy Havard, Jr. (D)
Ransom, Edward Duane (R)
Raven, Juanita G. (R)
Ravizza, Eugene Albert (R)
Raynes, Burt Franklin (R)
Raznikov, Richard Alan (D)
Reading, John Harden (R)
Reagan, Bruce Vincent (R)
Reagan, Maureen Elizabeth (R)
Reagan, Ronald Wilson (R)
Reardon, Harold E. (R)
Reddick, Richard Daly (R)
Reed, Dana Whitman (R)
Reed, Thomas Care (R)
Rees, Thomas M. (D)
Reeves, Albert L, Jr. (R)
Regalia, Gwendolyn Whiteford (D)
Regan, Edwin J. (D)
Regan, Walter Edward (R)
Reidy, James Basil, Jr. (D)
Reilly, Jane Bernadette (R)
Reimche, Ruben R. (R)
Reinecke, Ed (R)
Reinhardt, George Frederick
Reinhardt, Stephen (D)
Rendon, Ralph Albert (R)
Reynolds, Jerry Lee (R)
Reynolds, Martha M. (R)
Rhodes, Nina (D)
Richards, William Sidney (R)
Richardson, H. L. (R)
Richardson, Redmond Rodgers (D)
Richardson, Robert Lloyd (R)
Rickman, Geraldine (R)
Ridder, Daniel Hickey (R)
Rider, Joseph Alfred (R)
Rifkin, Julie Kaye (R)
Riley, Emily Odell (D)
Riley, Timothy Crocker (R)
Ring, Eleanor Reynolds (R)
Riordan, (Justine) Kim (D)
Rishwain, Robert James (D)
Ritter, Lucy Elizabeth (D)
Robbins, Paul (D)
Roberti, David A. (D)
Roberts, Anthony Alongi (R)
Roberts, Trevor Carol (R)
Robinson, Arthur Alexander, Jr. (D)
Robinson, Willard James (R)
Rodda, Albert S. (D)
Rodriguez, David (D)
Rodriguez, Jay (D)
Rogan, Richard Robert (D)
Rogers, Stanley (D)
Roosevelt, James (D)
Rosa, Victor Joseph (D)
Ross, John Raymond (R)
Rotelli, Delbert Leroy (R)
Rothman, David Michael (D)
Rotondo, John Louis (D)
Rouse, Allan Preston (R)
Rousselot, John Harbin (R)
Rowen, Elizabeth Gore (R)
Roybal, Edward R. (D)
Ruderian, Harvey Lee (D)
Rumford, William Byron (D)
Rus, William P. (R)
Rusmisel, Jack Raymond (R)
Russ, Joseph, IV (R)
Russell, Fred J. (R)
Russell, Newton R. (R)
Ruston, Bernice Loris (R)
Rutherford, Clara Beryl (R)
Ryan, Leo Joseph (D)
Ryskind, Mary House (R)
Sajor, Edmund Casimer (R)

Salinger, Pierre Emil George (D)
Sanborn, Blake Paul (R)
Sanderson, Gladys Louise (R)
Sandoval, Alice Catherine (D)
Sandstrom, Elsa (R)
Sasine, Robert Gale (R)
Sawicki, John Gerald (R)
Sawyer, Donald Raymond (R)
Sawyer, Wayne Robert (R)
Scalia, Robert Charles (R)
Schaap, George Aldarus (R)
Schabarum, Peter F. (R)
Schachter, Marvin (D)
Schaefer, Mike (R)
Scheidle, Harry F. (R)
Schiller, Charlotte (D)
Schlei, Norbert Anthony (D)
Schlenker, Gerald (D)
Schlesinger, James Rodney (R)
Schma, Donald William (R)
Schmidt, Robin (R)
Schmitz, John G. (R)
Schrade, Jack (R)
Schrette, Roland Donald (R)
Schriefer, Roger Bernard (D)
Schultz, Mike (R)
Schwartz, Howard Leland (R)
Scott, Jeremiah Ronald, Jr. (R)
Scott, Joseph Harold (R)
Sebens, Raymond Willard (D)
Sedgwick, Harold Thomas (R)
Selby, Mary N. (D)
Seligman, Howard L. (R)
Shapiro, Marvin S. (D)
Sharatz, Marguerite Theresa (R)
Shea, John Francis (D)
Shear, William Merrill (R)
Sheinbaum, Stanley K. (D)
Shell, Joseph C. (R)
Shelley, John Francis (D)
Shepherd, Margaret Brown (D)
Sheppard, Harry Richard (D)
Sherman, Lewis Frank (R)
Shernoff, William M. (D)
Shine, Henry Martin, Jr. (R)
Shirpser, Clara (D)
Shoemaker, Winfield Allen (D)
Short, Alan (D)
Shuey, John Arthur (R)
Shumway, James McBride (R)
Siciliano, Rocco C. (R)
Sieroty, Alan Gerald (D)
Silliman, Nevelle I. (R)
Silva, Alexander A, Jr. (D)
Silver, Ethel Marie (R)
Simas, Jean Lenore (R)
Simon, Raymond Clark (R)
Simmons, Raymond Hedilius (R)
Simpson, Robert Lewis (R)
Sinclair, James Moncrieff (D)
Singer, James Milford (D)
Siple, Randolph Edward (R)
Sisk, B. F. (D)
Sloan, Dean (R)
Smalley, K. Maxine (R)
Smith, Bette Belle (R)
Smith, Betty Denny (R)
Smith, Earl Victor, Sr. (D)
Smith, H. Allen (R)
Smith, Janice Mary (R)
Smith, John Kerwin (D)
Smith, Lyman Robert (D)
Smith, Paul Bruce (R)
Smith, Siegmund Wilson (R)
Smith, Steven Earl (D)
Smith, William French (R)
Snyder, Arthur Kress (R)
Snyder, Norman Gene (R)
Soderstrom, Charles Wallace (R)
Song, Alfred H. (D)
Speers, Frederic Warden (R)
Spencer, Ann L. (R)
Sperrazzo, V. James (D)
Sprague, Irvine H. (D)
Sprinkel, Warren Reed (R)
Stancil, Joan M. (R)
Stanley, Mary T. (R)
Steele, Robert Howe (R)
Stefani, J. Robert (D)
Steinberg, Lionel Sanford (D)
Sterbenk, William D. (R)
Sterling, Barry H. (D)
Stern, Howard Morris (R)
Stevens, Robert S. (R)
Stidger, Ruby Jane (D)
Stidham, Jeanne (R)
Stiern, Walter W. (D)
Stiles, Barbara Jean (R)
Stitt, Nancy Catherine (R)
Stivers, Oliver Charles (R)
Stoessel, Walter John, Jr.

Stone, Charles L. (D)
Stonum, Elizabeth Ann (R)
Storke, Thomas More (D)
Story, Patricia Jordan (R)
Stout, Helen Larson (D)
Straight, John Leslie (R)
Strehlow, Arthur Frank (R)
Stringer, Clarence Maine (R)
Stull, John O. (R)
Sturgeon, Vernon L. (R)
Sturr, Dorothy Mertz (R)
Sublett, Harry F. (D)
Svahn, Esther Marilu (R)
Swanson, Gertrude Gay Claire (R)
Sweetland, Monroe Mark (D)
Swig, Benjamin Harrison (D)
Taketa, Grayson S. (D)
Talbot, Alan Charles (R)
Talcott, Burt L. (R)
Tambourine, Loretta Joyce (R)
Taylor, Eileen German (R)
Taylor, Virginia Willett (R)
Taylor, William Merle (D)
Teague, Charles McKevett (R)
Teal, Stephen P. (D)
Tetenbaum, Sidney Joseph (D)
Thelin, Howard James (D)
Theobald, Maxine Andree (R)
Thomas, Kathleen Phyllis (R)
Thomas, Vincent (D)
Thomas, Theodore Frederick (R)
Thompson, Ada McCall (D)
Thompson, John F. (R)
Thompson, William Charles (R)
Thomson, Leonard S. (R)
Thornbury, William Gordon (R)
Thurm, William Henry (D)
Tobriner, Mathew Oscar (D)
Tolmach, Jane Louise (D)
Townsend, Claire Stewart (R)
Townsend, Gary Patterson (D)
Triplett, William Karrol (R)
Trueblood, Aileen Nash (R)
Tunney, John Varick (D)
Tunno, David A. (D)
Tuppan, Glenda Rana (R)
Turner, Wayne Callaway (R)
Turnette, Norman L. (R)
Tsompanas, Paul Lee (R)
Twombly, Margaret Ann (D)
Tyrell, Jack Rix (R)
Uhler, Lewis Knight (R)
Unruh, Jesse Marvin (D)
Utt, James Boyd (R)
Utt, Max Eddy (R)
Valdez, Joyce Ruby (R)
Valencia, Ross Haines (D)
Valliere, Lorraine Sharon (D)
Van Deerlin, Lionel (D)
Vanderet, Robert Charles (D)
Van Horn, Michael (R)
Varga, Richard Enrique (D)
Vasconcellos, John Bernard (D)
Vashon, Doris Louise (D)
Vaughns, William Elmore (R)
Veale, Roads (R)
Velasquez, Waldo (R)
Veneman, John G, Jr. (R)
Verlot, Frank O. (R)
Vetter, Kenneth Eugene (R)
Veysey, Victor Vincent (R)
Vilarino, Joseph (R)
Villarreal, Carlos C. (R)
von Christierson, Karl (R)
Vosti, Laurence R. (R)
Vreeland, George Washington, Jr. (R)
Vukasin, John Peter, Jr. (R)
Wade, Edwin Winslow
Wagenseller, Sherman Frederick (R)
Wagner, Kenneth David (R)
Waldie, Jerome Russell (D)
Walsh, Jack (R)
Walsh, Lawrence E. (D)
Walter, Vivian (D)
Waner, May Fillmore (R)
Ward, Harold R, Jr. (R)
Ware, Freda Catherine (R)
Ware, Leonard (R)
Warner, Dorothy Marie (R)
Warren, Charles (D)
Warren, Earl (R)
Warschaw, Carmen H. (D)
Washington, Lena Geneva (R)
Waters, Virginia Mozingo (D)
Waxman, Henry Arnold (D)
Way, Howard (R)
Weary, Lawrence Clifton (D)
Weathersby, William Henry
Webb, Kathleen Cecelia (D)
Wedworth, James Q. (D)
Weidner, Charles Richard (D)
Weinberger, Caspar Willard (R)
Weiner, Maurice (D)
Weiner, Stephen S. (D)
Weingand, Alvin Carl (D)
Weinreb, Ilene Spack (D)
Weisgerber, William Denny (R)
Welch, Rodney Ray (R)
Welden, Jacques Roger (R)
Weldon, John Philip (D)
Welin, Boyd Prescott (R)
Wentner, Nita (R)
Wenzel, Ferdinand Edward (R)
Werbe, Susan Diane (D)
Westland, Jack (R)
Whaley, Beverly Anne (R)
Wheeler, Harvey, Jr.
Wheelock, Robert Webb (R)
Whelan, John Joseph (D)
Whelan, Vincent Edward (D)
Whetmore, James Edward (R)
Whitaker, Urban G, Jr. (D)
White, Donald Stanley (D)
White, Jean Christensen (R)
White, Rose Marie (D)
Whitney, Shirley (R)
Wick, Carl B. (R)
Wiggins, Charles E. (R)
Wilkins, Harold Edward (R)
Wilkinson, Robert Melvin (R)
Willeford, Milton Elmo (D)
Williams, James Baird (D)
Williams, Robert D. (D)
Williams, Rod (D)
Williamson, John C. (D)
Williamson, Raymond Daniel, Jr. (R)
Willson, George Austill (D)
Wilson, Charles H. (D)
Wilson, Pete (R)
Wilson, Robert Carlton (R)
Wilson, Sally Jo (R)
Wing, Ada Schick (R)
Winn, John Ralph (D)
Winton, Gordon Harvey, Jr. (D)
Witte, Michael Bennett (D)
Wolf, Lois Ruth (D)
Wong, Chung-Ming (R)
Wood, Jane (R)
Wood, Randolph Clay (D)
Woods, Nettie Joe (D)
Woods, Frank Montgomery (R)
Woolley, John Robert (R)
Wright, Donna Gale (R)
Wurz, Louis O. (R)
Wyatt, Joseph Lucian, Jr. (D)
Wyman, Eugene Lester (D)
Wysinger, Vossa Edward, Jr. (R)
Yamamoto, Toshiko Toshi (R)
Yee, Phoebe G. (D)
Yocum, Norma Lenore (R)
Yorty, Sam (D)
Youngdoff, Theodore Eugene (R)
Younger, Milton M. (D)
Zanger, Joseph Anthony (R)
Z'Berg, Edwin L. (D)
Zenovich, George N. (D)
Zetterberg, Stephen Ingersoll (D)
Ziegler, Ronald Lewis (R)
Ziffren, Paul (D)

COLORADO

Abbott, James Charles, Jr. (R)
Abrahamson, Eunice F. (R)
Adams, Ruth May (D)
Akins, Guy Brookins, Jr. (D)
Alberstein, Pearl (D)
Albi, Joe (R)
Allard, Amos Wilson (D)
Allison, Betty Virginia (R)
Allott, Gordon Llewellyn (R)
Alperstein, Arnold (D)
Altamore, Mary (D)
Anderson, Byron (R)
Anderson, Harry Dale (D)
Aspinall, Owen Stewart (D)
Aspinall, Wayne Norviel (D)
Atchison, Jeannine Cowell (D)
Bader, Gerald Louis (R)
Baer, T. John, Jr. (D)
Bain, Jean Knight (R)
Bales, Jane Alexander (R)
Ball, Lois Helen (R)
Banks, Doris Nininger (D)
Banner, Dorothy Bertha (R)
Bastien, Thomas (D)
Baxter, J. Sterling (R)
Beckstead, Lucy (R)
Bender, Stanley B. (D)
Berger, Gertrude Maribelle (R)
Bermingham, John Rutledge (R)
Betz, Fred McLean (D)
Bickley, Charles Henry (D)
Blake, Milton J. (R)
Bledsoe, William E. (R)
Blue, Virginia Neal (R)
Booth, Mary Benson (R)
Boscia, Ida B. (D)
Bradley, Marguerite Lorraine (R)
Bradley, Paul (R)
Brandt, Lorraine Helen (R)
Brannan, Charles F. (D)
Branscomb, Anne Wells (D)
Briggs, Robert Alvin, Jr. (R)
Briscoe, James Price (D)
Brocker, Naida Louise (R)
Brooks, George Henry (D)
Brotzman, Donald G. (R)
Bryant, Ted (R)
Buglewicz, John Valentine (R)
Burch, Palmer Lyle (R)
Burford, Robert F. (R)
Burnett, Gail Tiner (R)
Burney, William E. (D)
Burns, Hugh Allan (D)
Busch, Virginia Marie (D)
Byrne, Charles David (R)
Calabrese, Joseph V. (D)
Carey, David James (D)
Carleno, Harry Eugene (D)
Carleton, Marilyn Jean (R)
Carper, Frances I. (D)
Carroll, John Spencer (D)
Carter, Marian Elizabeth (R)
Caywood, Mary Eudora (R)
Cefkin, J. Leo (D)
Chenoweth, J. Edgar (R)
Chronic, Betty M. (R)
Clement, Robert Frederick (R)
Clifton, O. K. (R)
Cole, Ralph A. (R)
Colgrove, Larry W. (R)
Coloroso, Dominic A. (D)
Conklin, Charles Ross (D)
Conner, Warren John (R)
Conrad, Priscilla Paulette (D)
Cooke, Lucille Ellen (R)
Cottrell, Corinne Louise (R)
Cox, Guy Jackson (R)
Cresswell, Mildred (R)
Crouse, Ruby Rose (R)
Davidson, Evelyn Taylor (D)
Davis, Milford Neil (D)
Deatherage, Alice Eunice (R)
DeBerard, Fay F. (R)
DeMoulin, Charles Joseph (D)
Dillon, Warren Adelbert (D)
Dines, Allen (D)
Di Paolo, Carl Michael (D)
Dire, Michael D. (R)
Donlon, John Joseph (D)
Dominick, Peter Hoyt (R)
Dougherty, Mary B. (R)
Dunbar, Duke (R)
Dunn, Mabel Elaine (D)
Edmonds, Charles Myers (D)
Egan, Rena Adele (R)
Englert, Kenneth Edward (R)
Englert, Lorene Baker (R)
Evans, Frank Edward (D)
Farley, Thomas T. (D)
Fassler, Joseph Leo (D)
Fellers, Vera Lesley (R)
Fenton, Lawrence Lyman (R)
Fentress, George H. (R)
Fix, George Arthur (D)
Flanigan, Robert M. (R)
Foster, William Edward (R)
Fowler, Hugh Charles (R)
Fowler, Leslie R. (R)
Frank, Barbara (D)
Franklin, Cecil DeWayne (D)
Frantz, Albert Thibaut (D)
Freed, Elaine Eilers (D)
Friedman, Don (R)
Fuhr, John D. (R)
Fury, Robert Floyd (R)
Gallatin, Albert Harold (R)
Garnsey, William Smith (R)
Gaylord, Mary Fletcher (R)
Gebhardt, Richard G. (D)
Geddes, Kenneth Whitehill (R)
Gervasini, William Victor (R)
Gilbert, Lela S. (R)
Gillaspey, Clarence James (D)
Gollob, Joseph (D)
Graen, Fred A. (D)
Graham, Jean Charters (D)
Grant, William (D)
Gray, Betty June (D)
Gray, Jo Anne Hastings (R)
Greene, Wilma Ann (D)
Gresham, Mildred Miriam (R)
Grimshaw, Thomas T. (R)
Gustafson, Carl H. (R)
Haas, Al H. (D)
Hall, Fern L. (R)
Hamil, David Alexander (R)
Hamilton, A. C. (R)
Hamilton, Dwight Alan (R)
Hamilton, Paul L. (D)
Hanson, Dean P. (R)
Hanson, Donald Paul (R)
Haring, Nick J. (D)
Hart, Harrie E. (R)
Haskell, Floyd K. (R)
Haver, Mildred Allison (R)
Hibberd, Lucy Reed (D)
High, Mary Ellen (R)
Hill, Jesse Edwin (R)
Hine, Robert Walter (R)
Hines, Paulena Lininger (R)
Hinman, Wallace Porter (R)
Hite, F. Richard (R)
Hoagland, Donald W.
Hochman, William Russell (D)
Hodges, Lloyd James (R)
Hoegh, Leo Arthur (R)
Hogan, Mark Anthony (D)
Horst, Donald J. (D)
Howe, Charles Bryan (D)
Howe, Marilyn Ann (D)
Hubbard, Kenneth Dean (D)
Huffsmith, Judith Ann (R)
Hulshizer, R. Dale (D)
Ibbotson, Gordon Mackenzie (D)
Inouye, Roy Y. (R)
Jackson, George (R)
Jackson, Harley Taylor (R)
Jeanmard, Fuchsia Leonteen (R)
Jensen, Robert N. (D)
Johnson, Byron Lindberg (D)
Johnson, Edwin Carl (D)
Johnson, Gregory Hamilton (R)
Johnson, Orie Carter (D)
Johnstone, Louise Moffit (R)
Jones, Glenn Robert (R)
Jones, Lee Richardson (R)
Kaess, Helen Marie (R)
Keese, William Brewer (R)
Kelley, Donald E. (R)
Kelloff, George (D)
Kemp, Frank Alexander, Jr. (R)
Kendrick, Charles Richard (R)
Keohane, Paul J. (D)
Kester, Bettye Jean (D)
Killam, Anne Loretta (D)
Kinney, William B. (R)
Kinnie, Kenneth Ivan (R)
Klein, Ben (D)
Knous, Robert Lee (D)
Knox, Wayne N. (D)
Koether, Herbert Franklin (R)
Kogovsek, John J. (D)
Kogovsek, Ray P. (D)
Kopel, Gerald L. (D)
Korrell, Rita May (R)
Koster, Harold R. (R)
Kranzler, Richard Martin (D)
Kushnir, Mary Constance (D)
Lahaye, James S. (D)
Lamb, Cecil Port (R)
Lamm, Richard D. (D)
La Mora, Judy Lynne (R)
Lamson, Elizabeth Josephine (R)
Lanaghen, Carol Love (R)
Lancaster, Glen (R)
Leavel, Willard Hayden (D)
Lemkuil, Linda Lee (R)
Lindbloom, Harold Seth (D)
Linke, Edwin Henry (R)
Lisco, Archie L. (D)
Loesch, Harrison (R)
Love, John Arthur (R)
Lowery, Philip E. (D)
Lucas, Andy Delerrian (D)
Lynch, Daniel Francis (D)
McCleave, Mildred Atwood (R)
McComb, Thomas M. (R)
McCormick, Harold L. (R)
McCue, Warren Richard (D)
McCulloch, Robert Winslow (D)
MacDonald, Donald Paul (R)
McElwain, S. Marion (D)
MacFarlane, John Dee (D)
McIntyre, N. J. (R)
MacKendrick, Donald Anthony (D)
McKenna, Ellanore Louise (D)
Mackie, John Golden (R)
McLean, Richard Cameron (D)
McNeil, Hiram A.

McNichols, Stephen L. R. (D)
McRae, Dorothy A. (R)
McVicker, Roy Harrison (D)
Manzanares, Alfonso B. (R)
Mapelli, Roland Lawrence (D)
Martin, Carol Jean (D)
Martinez, Levi (D)
Masco, Dorothy Beryl (R)
Massari, Phillip (D)
Massari, Vincent (D)
Mathews, Roy Palmer (R)
May, Timothy James (D)
Mayhew, Eldon Jay (R)
Mendenhall, Betty Lee (D)
Michael, Patricia M. (R)
Michael, Robert Kern (R)
Miller, Betty Jane (D)
Milliken, John Gordon (D)
Mondragon, Charles Steven, Jr. (D)
Moore, Isaac E, Jr. (D)
Morgan, Wright J. Jr. (R)
Morrison, Beatrice Bethel (D)
Muftic, Felicia Boillot (D)
Muhm, James R. (R)
Mularz, Ruth Louise (D)
Myers, Roderick Douglas (R)
Nally, John Joseph (R)
Neal, Thomas V. (D)
Nelson, John Clifford (R)
Nichols, John William (R)
Norgren, Leigh Hyatt (R)
O'Connor, Gene Anthony (D)
O'Donnell, James T. (D)
Okane, Bernard Patrick (D)
Oliver, Floyd (D)
Oliver, Stella Grace (R)
Osborn, Michael Kindig (D)
Otterstein, Adolph William (D)
Palermo, Constance Joan (R)
Parcell, Lew W. (D)
Parker, Maurice R. (D)
Pascoe, D. Monte (D)
Peterson, Andrienne Tosso (D)
Peterson, Betty Ann (D)
Pierson, Ileta Faye (D)
Poole, James Ford (D)
Porter, Ralph E. (R)
Powers, William Shotwell (R)
Propst, Howard B. (R)
Ragsdale, Howard Arthur (D)
Rehm, Irma Spurgeon (R)
Rehnberg, Rex Delbert (D)
Rider, Lila Catherine (D)
Rivera, Amos (D)
Roberts, Phyllis Arene (D)
Robinson, Brandon Terry (D)
Robinson, Charles K. (R)
Rockwell, Wilson Miller (R)
Rodriguez, Lydia T. (D)
Rogers, Byron Giles (D)
Rogers, Chloe (D)
Rogers, Rowena Emery (R)
Romer, Roy R. (D)
Rosales, John A. (D)
Rosenheim, Robert Chatwell (R)
Rothstein, Robert N. (D)
Rose, Jerome C. (D)
Roushar, Victor Thomas (R)
Roy, Catherine H. (R)
Ruffe, Doris Irene (D)
Russell, Jean Albach (R)
Ruyle, Lydia M. (D)
Sack, Floyd M. (R)
Safran, Hubert Mayer (D)
Sanchez, Paco (D)
Saunders, Allegra (D)
Schafer, John Robert (R)
Scheierman, Mabel M. (R)
Schieffelin, Joseph B. (R)
Schmidt, Eric William (R)
Schoenberger, Charlotte Sally (R)
Schubert, Theodore R. (R)
Scott, Edward Smith (R)
Scott, Tasso Harold (D)
Sears, Betty Jean (R)
Shelton, James Huston (D)
Shook, Robert H. (R)
Showalter, Carl Edward (R)
Showalter, Myrtle May (R)
Singer, M. Keith (R)
Skelton, Darrell J. (D)
Smith, John B. (D)
Snell, Edward Louis (R)
Soash, Richard Morton (D)
Sokol, William (D)
Sonnenberg, Lowell Ernest (R)
Stapp, Robert R. (D)
Sterling, Ernst Hiram (D)
Stieghorst, Lewis Earl (R)
Stienmier, Harold (R)
Stimmel, Don Perry (D)
Stockton, Ruth S. (R)
Strait, Donald E. (D)
Straub, Pearl Ann (D)
Strickland, Ted L. (R)
Sutton, Leonard v.B. (D)
Tarter, Weldon Murphy (R)
Theobald, Robert A. (D)
Thomas, James P. (D)
Thompson, Anne Marie (R)
Thompson, Marguerite Peyton (D)
Torres, Max E. V. (R)
Tovrea, Richard Leland (D)
Treece, James Lyle (R)
Trott, Bernard L. (R)
Trout, Barbara Ann (R)
Troxel, Oliver Leonard, Jr.
Trujillo, Larry Enoch (D)
Tucker, William Edward (R)
Vanderhoof, John D. (R)
Verhoeff, Howard L. (R)
Vickers, Jean M. (R)
Vigil, Charles S. (D)
Vollack, Anthony F. (D)
Waggoner, Robert Ernest (R)
Wailes, Thomas William (D)
Walker, Harry Burton, Jr. (R)
Wellman, Douglas C. (R)
Wells, Cyrus Curtis (R)
Wenke, Paul E. (R)
Wheeler, John R. P. (D)
White, Byron R.
White, William L. (R)
Wilder, Raymond Edward (R)
Williams, Carl Michael (R)
Wilmarth, W. Elery (R)
Wingfield, Lotus Mae (D)
Witherspoon, Dorothy Karpel (D)
Wogan, John Beugnot, Jr. (R)
Woodhams, Dorris C. (R)
Woodman, Dorothy E. (R)
Woods, Lucius Earl (D)
Woolbert, Maybelle Siegele (D)
Wright, James D. (D)
Yager, John J. (R)
Yelenick, John Andrew (D)
Yost, Jerry L. (D)
Younglund, Walter Arthur (R)
Zirkelbach, Barbara Marilyn Foley (D)
Znidarsich, Kay (R)
Zupan, Rose Ann (D)

CONNECTICUT

Adam, Joseph Raymond (D)
Ahearn, Frank Edward (D)
Ajello, Carl Richard (D)
Alaimo, Charles B. (R)
Alcorn, Hugh Meade, Jr. (R)
Alfano, Charles Thomas (D)
Allen, Donald George (R)
Alsop, John De Koven (R)
Altobello, Henry D. (D)
Amenta, Paul S. (D)
Anderson, Gerald Edward (D)
Argazzi, Robert Angelo (R)
Asbell, Bernard (D)
Aspinwall, James Hamilton, III (D)
August, Robert Burton (R)
Avcollie, Bernard Lincoln (D)
Bailey, John Moran (D)
Baker, John Edward (R)
Baldrige, Malcolm (R)
Barbato, Pasquale Angelo (D)
Bard, E. Ronald (R)
Barlow, Boce William (D)
Barnes, John Brearton (D)
Barnes, Wallace (R)
Barringer, Benjamin Lang (R)
Barry, David Michael (D)
Barry, John Joseph (D)
Bartels, Millard (R)
Beck, Audrey Phillips (D)
Becker, Henry Timothy (D)
Beckwith, Robert James (D)
Begg, William Vincent (D)
Bennet, Douglas Joseph, Jr. (D)
Bent, James Edward (R)
Benton, William (D)
Berberick, Frederick Charles, Jr. (R)
Bergeron, Raynald Edward (D)
Bernstein, Myron Ronald (R)
Berry, Louise Spaulding (R)
Bidwell, Arline M. (D)
Bishop, Mary Gertrude (R)
Bliss, Robert Landers (R)
Boatwright, Mary Howard (R)
Boggini, N. Charles (D)
Bolton, Ann D. (R)
Bowles, Chester (D)
Bromley, James Robert (R)
Brown, George R. (D)
Brown, Hoyte G, Jr. (R)
Brown, Ida Baldwin (R)
Brown, Otha Nathaniel, Jr. (D)
Brown, Ralph J. (R)
Buchanan, William Edward (R)
Buckley, Joseph B. (D)
Burns, Bernard John (R)
Bush, Prescott Sheldon (R)
Butterworth, Miriam Brooks (D)
Byington, Homer Morrison, Jr.
Cairns, Robert Thompson (R)
Caldwell, J. Edward (D)
Calhoun, Frank Ellinwood (R)
Caplan, Milton Irving (D)
Carroll, Donald Francis (D)
Carruthers, Thomas G. (R)
Casale, Louis Joseph, Jr. (R)
Casey, Joseph Edward (R)
Ceruzzi, Michael Joseph (D)
Charkoudian, Arppie (R)
Chase, William Roger (R)
Church, James Oliver (R)
Ciarlone, Anthony Michael (D)
Clarke, Hilda Rose (R)
Clynes, James Joseph (D)
Coe, Margaret Wyman (R)
Collins, Constance Sullivan (R)
Collins, Francis James (R)
Compton, Ranulf (R)
Conklin, George William (D)
Cooke, Frank Jerome (R)
Cooper, Francis Loren (R)
Cosgrove, Daniel Patrick (D)
Cotter, William R. (D)
Craig, James Donald (R)
Crampton, Richard Snow (R)
Crockett, Albert Stevens II (R)
Cunningham, Mary Van Zile (R)
Curtin, Margaret Mary (D)
Curtis, Elizabeth Kennedy (D)
Curtis, Sarah Frances (R)
Cutillo, Louis Sabino (D)
Daddario, Emilio Quincy (D)
Danaher, John Anthony (R)
Daniels, John Clifford (D)
Dawson, James Francis (D)
DeBaise, Pasquale John (D)
DeFrances, Guy Robert (R)
Delaney, Blanche Johnson (R)
Della Vecchia, Arthur (D)
Delmonte, Paul A. (D)
Dempsey, John N. (D)
Deno, John Wesley (D)
DeNoia, Richard Joseph (D)
DeRosa, Pasquale Joseph (R)
Devoe, George W. (R)
Dion, Alfred Charles, Sr. (D)
Di Rienzo, John Luke (D)
Dodd, Thomas J. (D)
Donahue, Joseph Patrick (D)
Donovan, Theodore Martin (R)
Doocy, Fred J. (D)
Dowd, Thomas Francis, Jr. (R)
Duda, Richard Joseph (D)
Duffey, Joseph D. (D)
Duffy, Francis Patrick (R)
Dunn, Barbara Baxter (R)
Dupont, Thomas E. (D)
Dzialo, Raymond John (D)
Earle, Ralph Louis, Sr. (R)
Eddy, Frank Vincent (R)
Ely, William Marvin (R)
Erb, Lillian Edgar (R)
Evarts, Katharine Avery (R)
Fabrizio, John Arthur (R)
Fagan, Lawrence James (R)
Falcigno, Paul Anthony (D)
Feeley, Francis B. (D)
Fellows, Douglas Merritt (R)
Fennell, Melvin (R)
Finney, Florence D. (R)
Fischer, William Raymond (D)
Fishbone, William M. (R)
Flaherty, Leo Bernard, Jr. (D)
Flanagan, Ruth Wallace (D)
Fleming, John Grant (D)
Foote, Ellsworth Bishop (R)
Fox, Abijah Upson (R)
Francis, Robert Ellsworth (R)
Frassinelli, Attilio (D)
Frost, Norma W. (R)
Fuller, Franklin Apollos (R)
Gaffney, J. Brian (R)
Genovesi, Donald S. (R)
Genovesi, Vincent Arthur (R)
Gentile, James (D)
Giaimo, Robert N. (D)
Gladstone, Louis I. (D)
Golden, John Matthew (D)
Goldfarb, Alexander A. (D)
Grabowski, Bernard F. (D)
Granquist, Wayne G. (D)
Grasso, Ella Tambussi (D)
Gregory, Edwin Paul (D)
Gregorzek, Joseph (D)
Grey, Robert Thaddeus, Jr. (D)
Griswold, Mary Brooks (D)
Grosby, Eleanor (R)
Gunther, George Lackman (R)
Guzzi, Ralph Joseph (D)
Haflich, Edwin Lurie (D)
Hall, Evelyn Elizabeth (R)
Hammer, Lucy T. (R)
Hamzy, Joseph Amin (R)
Hannon, George William, Jr. (D)
Harlamon, George Peter (R)
Harlan, John Marshall
Harrower, Leontine Lyle (R)
Hartnett, James Joseph (D)
Hausman, Howard E. (R)
Healey, James Thomas (D)
Hebert, Roland Arthur, Jr. (R)
Heck, Wilfred Henry (D)
Hennessy, Francis Xavier (D)
Hickey, William, Jr. (D)
Hicks, Vance Dodsworth (R)
Hill, Mary Bertha (D)
Hogan, Morris Bernard (R)
Holdsworth, Earl Thomas (R)
Houley, Robert D. (D)
Housman, Kenneth Alfred (R)
Houston, Howard Edwin (R)
Huber, Arthur P. (R)
Hughes, John William (R)
Hunt, Robert Richard, Sr. (R)
Huntington, John Willard (D)
Hutchins, Elizabeth Dennis (R)
Hyman, Albert H. (D)
Innes, Allan C. (R)
Irwin, Donald Jay (D)
Ives, Alden Allen (R)
Jackson, Jay Wayne (D)
Janovic, John Peter (D)
Jepson, Alan Herbert (D)
Johnson, Lowell Berthen (D)
Jones, William (D)
Jordan, Robert Lansing (R)
Jordan, William Osborne (R)
Kalenak, Nicholas Paul (D)
Karrel, Oscar (D)
Keena, Thomas Eugene Joseph (D)
Kellis, James George (D)
Kelly, Arthur John (D)
Keyes, Thomas J, Jr. (D)
Killian, Robert Kenneth (D)
King, Edgar A. (R)
Kinsella, George Brendan (D)
Klebanoff, Howard Michael (D)
Kline, Morgan Marshall (R)
Klonoski, Frank J. (D)
Koletsky, Joseph Quint (R)
Kopp, W. Brewster (R)
Kowalski, Frank (D)
Krechevsky, Robert Leon (D)
Lamb, Gerald A. (D)
Later, Chester J. (R)
Lavery, William James (D)
Leary, William Cornelius (D)
Lee, Linda K. (R)
Lee, Richard Charles (D)
Leech, Robinson (R)
Lenzi, Stephen E. (R)
Lester, Helen MacDonald (R)
Liebman, Lawrence Maurice (D)
Lincoln, Emma Ethel (R)
Links, Karl Henry (R)
Lodge, John Davis (R)
Lowden, Elmer Willis (D)
Lowell, James Belden, Jr. (R)
Ludlam, Lillian J. (R)
Lupton, John Mather (R)
Lyons, William Joseph, Jr. (R)
McCaffery, Dorothy Kane (D)
McCarthy, Francis J. (R)
McCarthy, James Joseph, Jr. (D)
McCarthy, John Francis (D)
McColough, Charles Peter (D)
McCue, Agnes Louise (D)
McGovern, Terry Patrick (D)
McGuire, John Andrew (D)
Mackenzie, Hugh Maxwell (R)
McKinney, Stewart Brett (R)
McLoughlin, James Patrick (D)
Macy, John Williams, Jr. (D)
Mahaney, John Daniel (D)
Mahoney, Francis James (D)
Manafort, Paul John (R)
Manna, Mario Joseph (R)
Mansfield, Edward Wilson (D)

Marcus, Edward Leonard (D)
Mariani, Peter P. (R)
Mascolo, Frederic Edward (D)
Massicotte, Joseph J. (D)
May, Edwin Hyland, Jr. (R)
May, Stephanie Middleton (D)
Mayer, William Snyder (R)
Mayers, Thomas Crawford (R)
Maynard, Robert Raymond (D)
Meskill, Thomas J. (R)
Mettler, Rollin Woodruff, Jr. (D)
Middendorf, John William, II (R)
Miller, Albert Edward (R)
Miller, Arthur (Independent)
Miller, Dorothy Risley (R)
Milmore, Thomas Aloysius (D)
Miner, S. Norton (R)
Minetto, John A. (R)
Monagan, John Stephen (D)
Mondani, Thomas P. (D)
Montano, George John (R)
Moore, William Graham (R)
Morano, Albert Paul (D)
Morelli, Carmen (D)
Morris, Arline Winifred (D)
Morris, Bruce Leo (D)
Mullen, John H. (R)
Mulreed, James Nelson (D)
Mulvey, Harold M. (D)
Nickerson, Grant Norwood (R)
Noce, Robert Nicholas (R)
Noyes, Richard Cunningham (R)
O'Connell, Richard T. (R)
O'Connor, J. Raymond (R)
O'Keefe, Arthur B, Jr. (D)
Oliver, Robert G. (D)
O'Neill, Norris Lawrence (D)
Orr, Richard Arthur (R)
O'Sullivan, Patrick Brett (D)
Padula, Louis J. (R)
Page, Stanley Haynes (R)
Palladino, Vincent Oliver (R)
Palmieri, James John (D)
Papandrea, Edward James (D)
Papandrea, John Francis (D)
Parmelee, Alice Emmons (R)
Patterson, J. Tyler, Jr. (R)
Pavetti, Francis James (D)
Perrin, Carl Ellis (D)
Petroni, Romeo Geno (R)
Pickett, John F. (D)
Pinney, A. Searle (R)
Pinney, Harry Ward (D)
Piscopo, Patsy J. (R)
Powers, Arthur B. (D)
Prete, John Donald (D)
Price, Henry John (R)
Pugliese, Joseph Michael (R)
Purtell, William Arthur (R)
Pyne, Lee Edward (R)
Quinn, Timothy Allan (D)
Ransohoff, Babette Strauss (R)
Reed, Gordon Wies (R)
Rees, William H. H. (D)
Reid, Aaron Q. (D)
Repko, Andrew (R)
Reynolds, Merle C, Jr. (D)
Ribicoff, Abraham A. (D)
Rice, Edward W. (D)
Ritter, George Joseph (D)
Rock, Isabel K. (R)
Rogers, Randolph (R)
Rogers, Robert Delwyn (R)
Rosa, Paul James, Jr. (R)
Rose, Rufus Chappell (R)
Rosenthal, Beatrice Holt (D)
Rowley, Evelyn Fish (R)
Rudolf, Jacob Paul (R)
Russell, Edward Wesley (R)
Russell, George Edward (R)
Russo, Gaetano Arthur, Jr. (R)
Rutledge, Catherine Anne (D)
Ryan, Theodore S. (R)
Sabota, Francis Robert (D)
Sadlak, Antoni Nicholas (R)
St. Onge, William Leon (D)
Salamone, Thomas Carmen (D)
Sanger, Richard Calvin (R)
Sarasin, Ronald A. (R)
Satter, Robert (D)
Schaller, Barry Raymond (R)
Schwartz, Ronald M. (R)
Schwend, Renato Timothy (R)
Scully, William James, Jr. (D)
Shakespeare, Frank (R)
Shea, William T. (D)
Sibal, Abner Woodruff (R)
Smith, Margaret Keane (D)
Smith, Richard Parker (R)
Sonnichsen, John William (R)
Stecker, Russell Lee (R)
Stevens, Gerald Fairlie (R)
Stevenson, Russell E, Jr. (R)
Stolberg, Irving Jules (D)
Stroffolino, Louis Joseph (R)
Sullivan, David Joseph, Jr. (R)
Sullivan, Vincent Augustine (D)
Swift, Henry Robinson (D)
Switaski, Anna-Mae (R)
Taneszio, Theresa (D)
Tansley, James E. (D)
Tarpinian, Charles Simon (D)
Taylor, H. Ralph (D)
Taylor, Julian A. (D)
Taylor, Norman Collins (R)
Tedesco, Samuel Joseph (D)
Testo, Robert James (D)
Thatcher, Raymond S. (D)
Thomas, Thomas Paul (D)
Thornton, Jean Tyrol (R)
Tiffany, John Jewett, II (R)
Tighe, Charles Moon (R)
Tilson, John Quillin (R)
Tooher, Joseph John, Jr. (D)
Treadwell, Clyde Trafford (R)
Trojanowski, Antoni P. (R)
Truex, Ruth Olmsted (R)
Tubiak, John (D)
Tudan, Victor John (D)
Uberti, E. James (R)
Verriker, William J. (D)
Vicino, Robert James (D)
Violette, Woodrow Thomas (D)
Wagner, Jerry (D)
Walker, Charls Edward (R)
Walsh, John Bernard, Jr. (D)
Ward, Wyman Burton (R)
Washburn, Elwood Conrad (R)
Webber, Albert Raymond (D)
Weicker, Lowell Palmer, Jr. (R)
Welden, William Bidwell (R)
Whitbeck, Walter Samuel (R)
Williams, LaVergne Hobart (R)
Wilscam, Roderick Albert (R)
Wingate, Richard Anthony (R)
Wood, George Arthur (R)
Woodhouse, Mrs. Chase Going (D)
Wright, George F. (D)
Young, Robert Wesley (R)
Zampano, Robert Carmine (D)
Zarnowski, Alexander F. (R)
Zebroski, Leon Bernard (R)
Zullo, Frank Nicholas (D)

DELAWARE

Babiarz, John Edward (D)
Bartleson, Thomas Lees (R)
Bayard, Alexis Irenee duPont (D)
Benson, David S. (R)
Blendt, Carlton, Jr. (D)
Boggs, J. Caleb (R)
Bookhammer, Eugene Donald (R)
Brown, Fred (R)
Buckson, David Penrose (R)
Bunting, Eugene D. (R)
Burt, Warren Brooker (R)
Burton, Louis Wyatt (R)
Calloway, James Richard (D)
Carney, Robert I. (D)
Carvel, Elbert Nostrand (D)
Cashman, Joseph T. (R)
Castle, Michael Newbold (R)
Conner, Louise Thompson (R)
Cook, Allen Jones (D)
Copeland, Lammot duPont, Jr. (R)
Cripps, George Washington (R)
Davidson, Robert C(arey) (D)
Delker, Audrey P. (R)
Derrickson, Vernon Blades (D)
Dodge, Robert Mapes (R)
Dukes, Elisha (D)
Elston, Dorothy Andrews (R)
Evans, Raymond T. (R)
Everett, Annabelle Smith (D)
Foltz, Andy (R)
Frear, Joseph Allen, Jr. (D)
Frederick, William L. (R)
Gooding, Mary Etta (D)
Gordy, William J. (D)
Gray, George Edward (R)
Greenwood, Evelyn Hanke (R)
Grier, Frank R. (R)
Hale, Everette (R)
Hammond, Reese Leroy (D)
Harkins, Michael Eugene (R)
Harrison, Clayton S, Jr. (R)
Hart, William F. (R)
Haskell, Harry Garner, Jr. (R)
Hearn, Clifford Burton, Jr. (D)
Heckert, Clarice Upson (R)
Hering, George C, III (R)
Hickman, Thomas Edwin, Jr. (R)
Holloway, Herman Monwell (D)
Isaacs, John Donald (R)
Isaacs, M. Martin (D)
Jackson, Isabel Hope (R)
Keil, Charles K. (D)
Kirk, John Francis, Jr. (R)
Kirtley, Donald Ray (R)
Lesher, Herbert A. (R)
Lickle, William Cauffiel (R)
Little, Thomas Lawrence (R)
McCullough, Calvin R. (D)
McDowell, Harris B, Jr. (D)
McMahon, John J, Sr. (D)
Manning, Margaret R. (R)
Martin, Larry K. (R)
Mayhew, Harry Ennis (D)
Moerschel, W. Neal (R)
Moyed, Ralph S. (R)
Murphy, Joseph Richard (R)
Murphy, William Malcolm, Jr. (D)
Pagano, Mario A. (R)
Peirson, Mary Wood (R)
Perry, Christopher Lawrence (R)
Peters, Ralph R. (R)
Peterson, Russell Wilbur (R)
Phillips, William Harrison (D)
Pierce, Grace Wagner (R)
Potter, William Samuel (D)
Quillen, George Robert (R)
Redfearn, B. Wilson (R)
Reed, Eugene Thompson, Sr. (D)
Riddagh, Robert W. (R)
Richeson, Samuel Randolph, Jr. (D)
Rispoli, Marcello (D)
Ross, Daniel J. (R)
Roth, William Victor, Jr. (R)
Sandstrom, Theodore Frederick, Jr. (D)
Scannell, Joseph John (D)
Sebrell, Lorin B. (R)
Seibel, Marion Irma (R)
Shockley, Paul E. (D)
Smith, Albert F. (R)
Stabler, W. Laird, Jr. (R)
Steele, Dean C. (R)
Steen, Curtis W. (D)
Talley, H. Andrew (R)
Tarburton, Hattie Walls (D)
Terry, Charles Laymen, Jr. (D)
Theobald, George Anna (R)
Townsend, Rebekah Faucett (R)
Tribbitt, Sherman W. (D)
Weiner, Phyllis (D)
Williams, John James (R)
Wilson, Harry S. (D)
Zimmerman, Jacob W. (D)

DISTRICT OF COLUMBIA

Abell, Tyler (D)
Acheson, Dean Gooderham (D)
Adams, Eva Bertrand (D)
Akers, Robert Wood
Alexander, Clifford L. (D)
Alexander, Myrl Early (D)
Amory, Robert, Jr. (R)
Andrade, Carolyn Marie (D)
Anton, James (R)
Auchincloss, James Coats (R)
Bacher, Edward Leonard (R)
Bane, David Morgan
Barbee, Juanita E. (D)
Barber, Jesse B, Jr. (D)
Barthelmes, Wes (D)
Batt, William Loren, Jr (D)
Battle, Lucius D.
Baumgart, Merle David (D)
Bazelon, David L. (D)
Beal, Thaddeus R. (R)
Beale, Wilson Thomas Moore
Beasley, Delmar Otis
Beauchamp, Carole Ann (R)
Bechtel, William Russell (D)
Becker, Eugene M. (R)
Bell, David Elliott
Bell, James D.
Bennett, W. Tapley, Jr.
Berliner, Henry A, Jr. (R)
Bindeman, Jacob Edward (R)
Black, John Woodland
Bohlen, Charles E.
Brennan, William J, Jr.
Breuninger, Lewis Talmage (R)
Brimmer, Andrew Felton
Brown, Olga Jamison (D)
Brown, William H.
Brown, Winthrop Gilman
Brownstein, Philip Nathan (D)
Bruce, David K. E.
Bundy, William P. (D)
Burdick, Margaret Carothers (R)
Burling, Edward, Jr. (R)
Burress, Richard Thomas (R)
Burton, Melvin Matthew, Jr. (R)
Bush, Dorothy Vredenburgh (D)
Butler, Robert Neil (D)
Byron, Katharine Edgar (D)
Calhoun, John A.
Califano, Joseph A, Jr. (D)
Campbell, Joseph (R)
Caplin, Mortimer M. (D)
Carle, Jackson T. (D)
Carothers, Neil, III (R)
Carter, Chester Charles
Cater, Douglass (D)
Chambers, Ray Benjamin (R)
Chapin, John Carsten (R)
Chapman, Oscar Littleton (D)
Chase, Seymour M. (D)
Chatelain, Leon, Jr. (R)
Chin-Lee, William (R)
Cipriani, Harriet Emily (D)
Clarke, Biehl Patrick (R)
Cooper, William Hurlbert (R)
Cottam, Howard R.
Coultrap, Susan Ann (R)
Council, Mary Lee (D)
Craft, Kathryn T. (D)
Davis, Richard Hallock
Dean, John (D)
Dickson, Ernest C. (R)
Dixon, Fred L. (R)
Dixon, Paul Rand (D)
Donnelley, Dixon (D)
Douglas, Emily Taft (D)
Dudley, Tilford Eli (D)
Dumont, Donald Albert
Duncan, John Bonner (D)
Dunn, Charles Wythe (R)
Dutton, Frederick G. (D)
Edwards, Leverett
Eichhorn, Janice E. (D)
Elbrick, C. Burke
Ewing, Samuel Evans (R)
Fahy, Charles (D)
Farmer, Thomas Laurence (D)
Feggans, Edward Leland (R)
Feldman, George Joseph
Feldman, Myer (D)
Ferguson, C. Vaughn, Jr.
Ferguson, Clarence Clyde, Jr. (R)
Ferguson, Homer (R)
Fertig, Ralph David (D)
Fielding, Elizabeth May (R)
Fisher, John Brookins (R)
Flax, Alexander Henry
Fletcher, Thomas William (D)
Fletcher, Virginia Carol (D)
Folger, John Clifford (R)
Fortas, Abe (D)
Foster, William Chapman
Frohnmayer, David Braden (R)
Funkhouser, Richard
Gage, William McCutcheon (R)
Garrett, Clyde Davis (R)
Gaud, William S
Gibbons, Boyd H, III (R)
Gibson, James Oliver (D)
Gill, John Worden (R)
Good, Josephine Louise (R)
Good, Robert Crocker (D)
Green, Marshall
Guiles, Samuel Everette (R)
Hadsel, Fred Latimer
Hahn, Gilbert, Jr. (R)
Handley, William J.
Harllee, John (D)
Harris, Patricia Roberts (D)
Harris, Robert Oberndoerfer (D)
Harrison, James Lerlie
Hartel, Arthur Paul, Jr. (R)
Hastings, Wilmot Reed (R)
Hayes, John S.
Henderson, Douglas
Henning, John Francis
Henry, Emil William (D)
Hess, Stephen (R)
Holtzoff, Alexander
Holum, Kenneth
Hoover, John Edgar
Hoyland, Frances Burns (D)
Hyman, Lester Samuel (D)
Imhoff, Lawrence Edward
Izac, Edouard Victor Michel (D)
Jackson, E(dward) Franklin (D)
Jarvis, Norman O. (R)
Jenkins, Alice Elaine Brown (R)

Jones, Roy J. (D)
Kaplowitz, Paul (D)
Kashiwa, Shiro (R)
Kauper, Thomas E. (R)
Kearns, Henry (R)
Kelley, Roger T. (R)
Kertz, Harold Allan (R)
Keyserling, Mary Dublin (D)
Kintner, Robert Edmonds
Knox, Katherine McCook (R)
Koren, Henry Lloyd Thornell
Korth, Fred (D)
Laise, Carol
Lee, H. Rex (D)
Lee, Robert Emmet (R)
Leonhart, William
Lewis, Geoffrey W.
Lilley, Tom (R)
Linder, Harold Francis
Loevinger, Lee (D)
Loftus, Joseph Anthony (R)
Looram, Matthew
MacArthur, Douglas, II
McConaughy, Walter Patrick
McDermott, Edward Aloysious (D)
McEvoy, John Thomas (D)
McFadden, Robert Holland (R)
McGinnis, Edward Francis (R)
McGuire, E. Perkins (R)
McIlvaine, Robinson
MacKinnon, George Edward (R)
McLaughlin, Charles F. (D)
McNemar, Georgia Arlone (R)
McRae, Ray A. (R)
McSweeney, John Morgan
Marks, Leonard Harold (D)
Marriott, Alice Sheets (R)
Martin, William McChesney, Jr.
Mason, Willie C. (R)
Meeker, Leonard Carpenter
Meloy, Francis Edward, Jr.
Menasco, Horace (R)
Miner, Robert Graham
Monroney, A. S. Mike (D)
Moore, Jerry Alexander, Jr. (R)
Morgan, George Allen
Morrison, Dorothy Dunn (D)
Newman, Theodore Roosevelt, Jr. (R)
Nicholson, Ralph William (D)
Oliphant, S. Parker (R)
Oshiki, Kaz (D)
Owen, Henry D.
Owens, Hugh Franklin (D)
Palmer, Joseph, II
Parry, David Thomas (D)
Peckham, Rufus W, Jr. (R)
Péladeau, Marius B.
Pendleton, Edmund E, Jr. (R)
Peterson, Esther Eggertsen (D)
Peterson, John K. L. (R)
Phillips, Channing Emery (D)
Phillips, Kevin Price (R)
Phillips, Richard I.
Pickett, Thomas Augustus (D)
Pine, David Andrew (D)
Pinkett, Flaxie Madison (D)
Popper, David Henry
Porter, Dwight J.
Pott, George P. (R)
Pyrros, James G. (D)
Rauh, Joseph L, Jr. (D)
Read, Benjamin H. (D)
Reardon, Timothy James, Jr. (D)
Reed, J. Duff, III (R)
Reedy, George Edward, Jr. (D)
Resor, Stanley R. (R)
Revercomb, George H. (R)
Reynolds, James Joseph (D)
Rivkin, William R. (D)
Roach, William Neale (D)
Robinson, Spottswood William, III
Rogovin, Mitchell (D)
Rosenthal, Jacob (D)
Ross, Betty B. (D)
Ross, Claude G.
Rowan, Carl Thomas (Independent)
Rowe, Mrs. James Henry, Jr. (D)
Rusk, Dean (D)
Ryan, Robert Joseph
Safran, Daniel (D)
Sauer, Walter Charles
Schaetzel, J. Robert
Schaller, Jerome Donald (D)
Schedler, Spencer Jaime (R)
Schmidt, Richard Marten, Jr. (D)
Schreiber, Ann F. (D)
Schultze, Charles Louis (D)
Scott, Catherine Dorothy (R)
Scott, Donald Lee (R)
Seaborg, Glenn T. (D)
Seamans, Robert Channing, Jr. (R)
Selin, Ivan
Shackleton, Polly (D)
Sheldon, Georgiana H. (R)
Sherman, Norman (D)
Shipley, Carl L. (R)
Shouse, Jouett (D)
Shull, Leon
Siegrist, Robert Ryan (R)
Siena, James Vincent (D)
Simons, William Henry (D)
Simpson, William Walton (D)
Sisco, Joseph John
Smith, Gerard Coad (R)
Spingarn, Natalie Davis (D)
Spingarn, Stephen J. (D)
Staats, Elmer Boyd
Stanley, Eliot Hungerford (D)
Stans, Maurice H. (R)
Steeves, John M.
Stevens, Roger L. (D)
Stewart, Carlyle Veeder, Jr. (R)
Stewart, John George
Stinnett, Ronald F. (D)
Stokley, Robert W.
Streeter, Joyce Katherine (R)
Sullivan, John Joseph, Jr. (D)
Sullivan, Leonard, Jr. (R)
Sundlun, Bruce George (D)
Symington, Lloyd (D)
Talbot, Phillips
Tasca, Henry J.
Taylor, William L. (D)
Terris, Bruce Jerome (D)
Theis, Paul Anthony (R)
Thompson, Llewellyn E, Jr.
Tobriner, Walter Nathan (D)
Train, Russell Errol (R)
Tuchmann, Carol J.
Tucker, Sterling (D)
Tupling, William Lloyd (D)
Turner, Virginia Price (D)
Twiname, John Dean (R)
Tyler, William Royall
Van Doren, Charles Norton
Van Hollen, Christopher
Venable, Abraham Sylvester
Volpe, John Anthony (R)
Wadsworth, James J. (R)
Wager, Robert (D)
Washburn, C. Langhorne (R)
Washington, James A. Jr. (D)
Washington, Walter E. (D)
Waskow, Arthur I. (New Party)
Waterman, Jeremiah Colwell (R)
Weaver, George Leon Paul (D)
Weisl, Edwin L, Jr. (D)
Westerfield, Samuel Zaza, Jr.
Wheelock, John Neal (D)
Whitlock, Douglas (R)
Wilson, J. Franklin (R)
Willens, Howard Penney (D)
Williams, Charles Sheldon (D)
Williams, Norma Ottey (D)
Williams, Smallwood Edmond (D)
Wilson, Will (R)
Windon, Bernard Milroy (R)
Winter, Nadine P. (D)
Wirtz, W. Willard
Withers, Charles Dudley
Wolf, Leonard George (D)
Woolner, Sidney Henry (D)
Worthy, K(enneth) Martin (Independent)
Wright, J(ames) Skelly (D)
Wright, Jerauld
Youngdahl, Luther W. (D)

FLORIDA

Ackel, Fred John (R)
Adair, Charles Wallace, Jr.
Adams, J. M, Jr. (D)
Adams, Tom (D)
Adkins, James Calhoun, Jr. (D)
Alcalde, Hector (D)
Alford, Robert Bruce (R)
Alger, Bruce Reynolds (R)
Alligood, Bob (D)
Allsworth, Emerson (D)
Alvarez, Ted, Jr. (D)
Ambler, William Emerson (R)
Anderson, William McOwan, III (R)
Andrews, William Claud (D)
Arnold, Lynwood (D)
Ashler, Philip Frederic (D)
Askew, Reubin O'D. (D)
Ayers, John Law (D)
Bafalis, Louis A. (R)
Baker, Maxine Eldridge (D)
Balestrieri, Edward Anthony (D)
Barber, Merrill P. (D)
Barron, Dempsey James (D)
Barrow, William Dean (D)
Basford, Bill (D)
Beattie, Jack Robert (R)
Beck, James N. (D)
Bell, John William (R)
Bembry, Payton, Jr. (D)
Bennett, Charles E. (D)
Bennett, Ralph Julian (D)
Bird, Richard Alan (R)
Blackburn, Robert Ed, Jr. (D)
Bledsoe, Lamar (D)
Bloodworth, Burnett Saunders (D)
Bockelman, James F. (D)
Boeke, Richard Frederick (D)
Bolton, Roxcy O'Neal (D)
Boyd, Joseph Arthur, Jr. (D)
Boyd, Wilbur Harrison (D)
Boylston, Emily Mason (R)
Bradley, (Agnes) Alberta (R)
Brake, Robert Merle (D)
Brannen, Robert F. (D)
Breeze, Evelyn Louise Cox (R)
Brilliant, Mollie Wexler (D)
Brown, Richard L. (D)
Brown, Tom Fairfield (R)
Bryant, Cecil Farris (D)
Buckley, John Reed (D)
Burke, J. Herbert (R)
Burns, Findley, Jr.
Butterworth, Jayne Burbridge (R)
Cabanas, Henry Anthony, Sr. (R)
Cable, John Levi (R)
Caldwell, Millard Fillmore, Jr. (D)
Callahan, Carolyn Bossert (D)
Cameron, Sally Freeman (R)
Campbell, Courtney Warren (D)
Campbell, Lehman Shelby (R)
Carlton, Doyle E, Jr. (D)
Carlton, Vassar B. (D)
Carraway, Wilson (D)
Carter, Ralph C. (D)
Chaffee, Florence Esther (R)
Chandler, Ralph C. (R)
Chapman, Joseph F. (D)
Chappell, William Venroe, Jr. (D)
Chiles, Lawton (D)
Clark, John R. (D)
Clark, Richard Wayne (D)
Clark, Stephen Patrick (D)
Cleveland, Mack N, Jr. (D)
Cobbe, Margaret Hammet (D)
Coble, J. Kermit (D)
Collins, Leroy (D)
Condon, Richard Paul (R)
Conner, Doyle E. (D)
Connor, James E. (D)
Conway, William Rayford (D)
Cordiner, Ralph Jarron (R)
Costin, Cecil Guerry, Jr. (D)
Covington, D. D, Jr. (D)
Crabtree, Granville H, Jr. (R)
Crabtree, Paulette (R)
Cramer, Ann Marie Joan (D)
Cramer, William C. (R)
Crecelius, Robert Allen (R)
Crews, John J, Jr. (D)
Crider, John (D)
Crittenden, Earl M. (R)
Cross, J. Emory (D)
Culbreath, John Richard (D)
Curtis, Robert McNown (D)
D'Alemberte, Talbot (D)
Damsey, Joan Roberta (D)
Daniel, C. Welborn (D)
Daves, Joel T. (F)
Davis, Charles E, Jr. (R)
Davis, Hayward H. (D)
Davis, Ira P. (D)
Davis, S. Joseph Jr. (D)
Deeb, Richard J. (R)
de la Parte, Louis Anthony (D)
Devlin, Philip, Jr. (R)
De Young, Robert Cornelius (R)
Dickinson, Fred Otis, Jr. (D)
Dixon, R. Earl (R)
Dougherty, Jean Marie Cordiner (R)
Dressler, James R. (D)
Drew, Edwin Harris (D)
Drummond, Addison Peairs (D)
Drummond, Greg Neal (R)
Dubbin, Murray H. (D)
Ducker, John Lackner (R)
Earle, Lewis Samuel (R)
Eddy, James Rollins (R)
Edwards, Lawrence Kirkland, Jr. (D)
Ell, Leon J. (R)
Ellison, O. Ernest, Jr.
Elrod, Robert Harding (R)
Englander, Sophia (D)
Evans, Hazel Atkinson (D)
Evans, Nancy Whittemore (D)
Ewing, M. Jean (R)
Faircloth, Earl (D)
Fascell, Dante B. (D)
Featherstone, Harold G. (D)
Fee, Frank H. (D)
Feller, Mildred Manley (D)
Fincher, Dick (D)
Firestone, George (D)
Fischer, Thelma Thomas (R)
Fisher, John J. (R)
Fleece, William Harold (R)
Forand, Aimé J. (D)
Fouse, Clara Mae (R)
Fraser, Edwin G. (D)
Frey, Louis, Jr. (R)
Friday, Elmer Otto, Jr. (D)
Frye, William, III (D)
Fulford, William Edmond (D)
Fuller, Joseph C. (D)
Fuqua, Don (D)
Gallen, Thomas M. (D)
Gautier, Ernest William (D)
Gautier, Redmond Bunn, Jr. (D)
Gibbons, Sam M. (D)
Gibson, L. P. (D)
Gibson, William L. (R)
Gillespie, William Miller (D)
Godwin, Ruth Tichi (D)
Gong, Edmond Joseph (D)
Grantham, Jasper Edward (R)
Greene, Harold A. (D)
Greene, Thomas H. (D)
Gregory, James (R)
Griffin, Ben Hill, Jr. (D)
Griffin, J. J, Jr. (D)
Grizzle, Mary R. (R)
Guilford, Frank E. (D)
Gunter, William D, Jr. (D)
Gurney, Edward John (R)
Gustafson, Joel Karl (R)
Haber, Richard Michael (R)
Hagaman, Lloyd Cates, Jr. (R)
Haley, James Andrew (D)
Hall, Muriel Fisher (D)
Harris, Marshall S. (D)
Hartnett, Robert C. (D)
Harvey, Ellery Hale (R)
Haverfield, Robert Metcalfe (D)
Hawkins, Paula F. (R)
Heath, Donald E. (R)
Hector, Robert C. (D)
Hembree, Gerry P. (R)
Hembree, William Lasater (R)
Henderson, Warren S. (R)
Hendricks, Joseph Edward (D)
Herlong, Albert Sydney, Jr. (D)
Herlong, William Frederick, Jr. (R)
Hern, Lester Monroe (R)
High, Robert King (D)
Hodes, Richard S. (D)
Hollahan, George Lovett, Jr. (D)
Holland, Evelyn Faucette (D)
Holland, Spessard Lindsey (D)
Holloway, Vernon Carlyle (D)
Homer, Porter Wyman
Hook, Robert Franklin (R)
Hopping, Wade Lee (R)
Hostettler, Dorie McFetridge (R)
Humphrey, Joseph W. H. (R)
Huntley, Louis L. (D)
Inman, W. M. (D)
James, Bobbie McFee (R)
Johns, Charley Eugene (D)
Johnson, Beth (R)
Johnson, Beth McCollough (D)
Johnson, Dewey M. (D)
Johnson, Elizabeth Jean (R)
Jordan, John W. (R)
Jordan, Russell Clinger, Jr. (D)
Jova, Joseph John
Juarez, Oscar F. (R)
Karst, Arthur E. (D)
Kearns, Tom (D)
Keegan, John Francis (D)
Keeth, Geraldine Audrey (R)
Keller, Leonard (R)
Kershaw, Joseph Lang (D)
Kiefer, Edgar L. (R)
King, Charles James (R)
Kirk, Claude Roy, Jr. (R)
Klein, Henry (R)
Knight, Harry Frank (D)
Knopke, Ray C. (D)
Kohler, Foy David (Independent)
Kruse, Edward H, Jr.
Kurke, Eleanor Bergan (R)
Kyle, Marcus Aurelius (R)
Kynes, James W. (D)
Lancaster, Howell (D)
Land, Henry William (D)
Lane, David Campbell (R)

Lantaff, William C. (D)
Latson, William Roy (R)
Lewis, Gerald (D)
Lieb, Helen Bowman (R)
Liles, Woodie A. (D)
Locke, Nina Spencer (R)
Loeser, Annette Baker (D)
Lytal, Lake Henry (D)
McCarty, John Moore (D)
McClain, Joseph Adolphus, Jr. (R)
McConkey, George M, Jr. (R)
McCort, William (R)
McDonald, John Angus (D)
McDonald, Leon N, Sr. (D)
McElmurray, Jeanne Frances (D)
McIntosh, Anne Magwood (R)
MacKenzie, Mary Ann (D)
McLaughlin, Maurice (D)
McMullen, Daniel G. Jr. (D)
McNulty, Clifford Allen (R)
McPherson, Thomas Allen (D)
McRae, William Allan, Jr. (D)
Malloy, Leah Block (R)
Mancini, Joseph A. (R)
Mann, Robert T. (R)
Manthey, Charles Edwin (R)
Mapoles, Clayton W. (D)
Markham, W. Allen (D)
Martin, William Cabiness (D)
Martinez, Elvin L. (D)
Mathews, John E, Jr. (D)
Matthews, Carey (D)
Matthews, Donald Ray (D)
Mattox, Ray (D)
Mayo, William Taylor (D)
Melton, G. T. (D)
Melvin, Jarrett Green (D)
Messmer, Jack Gustaphe (R)
Meyer, Anne Heineman (D)
Mickle, Charles Abraham (R)
Middlemas, John Robert (D)
Miers, Miley L, II (D)
Milligan, Ida Victoria Collins (R)
Miner, Barbara Paula (D)
Mitchell, Coy J. (D)
Mitchell, Richard O. (D)
Mondres, Marvin D. (R)
Moore, James Francis (R)
Morris, Benjamin Gordon (D)
Morris, Helene M. (R)
Mueller, Frederick Henry (R)
Murfin, William Floyd (R)
Murray, Edward Thomas (D)
Myers, Kenneth Morton (D)
Myers, Paul J. (R)
Myers, William George (R)
Ninos, Anthony (D)
Nock, John Dix, Jr. (R)
Ogden, Carl (D)
Ogle, Ellen Knight (R)
Oka, Kenneth (D)
O'Neill, Alyse Stern (R)
O'Neill, Paul Joseph (R)
O'Neill, William G. (D)
Osborne, Ray C. (R)
Ott, T. Truett (D)
Owens, William E. (D)
Owles, Fae Bidgood (D)
Papy, Bernie, Jr. (D)
Parsons, Willard Ernest (R)
Pawley, William Douglas
Peeples, Joe H. (D)
Pepper, Claude (D)
Perlin, Morton J. (D)
Peterson, James Hardin (D)
Pettigrew, Richard Allen (D)
Phillips, Joel Patrick, Jr. (R)
Pickle, Louise Elizabeth (D)
Pierce, Charlton Louian (D)
Poorbaugh, Jack Morgan (R)
Pope, Verle A. (D)
Poston, Ralph R. (D)
Pratt, Jerome (D)
Price, Ed H. Jr. (D)
Prominski, Henry John (R)
Pruitt, James H. (D)
Pruitt, Prentice (D)
Rainey, Charles E. (R)
Randall, M. T. (D)
Redman, James L. (D)
Reed, Donald H, Jr. (R)
Reed, Nathaniel Pryor (R)
Reedy, W. H. (D)
Reeves, James Jerauld (D)
Regan, Ouida Baggett (D)
Register, William Morell, Jr. (D)
Reilly, Carl Nelson (R)
Renick, Richard Randolph (D)
Reuter, Clifford Silva, III (R)
Roberts, C. A. (D)
Roberts, Emmett S. (D)
Roberts, Houston W. (D)
Robinson, James Carson (D)
Robsion, John Marshall, Jr. (R)
Roddenberry, Ernest (D)
Rogers, Paul Grant (D)
Roosevelt, Elliott (D)
Roundtree, William H. (D)
Rountree, William M.
Rowell, E. C. (D)
Rudd, John Allison (D)
Rude, Arthur Herman (R)
Rupert, Emerson (R)
Rushing, John Slaton (R)
Russell, C. E. (D)
Rust, Robert Warren (R)
Ryan, A. J, Jr. (D)
Sackett, Walter W. Jr. (D)
Saunders, Robert L, Jr. (D)
Savage, John J. (R)
Sayler, Henry B, Jr. (R)
Scarborough, Dan Irving (D)
Schultz, Frederick Henry (D)
Sessums, Thomas Terrell (D)
Sewell, J. Richard (D)
Shank, Clare Brown Williams (R)
Shepard, Julius Jack (D)
Shevin, Robert Lewis (D)
Shields, William Henry (R)
Sikes, Robert L. F. (D)
Simpson, Bryan (D)
Simpson, Clyde Wagner (D)
Slade, Thomas Howell (R)
Smathers, George Armistead (D)
Smith, Donald Eugene (R)
Smith, Harold Kenneth (D)
Smith, Ken (D)
Smith, Raymond Felix (D)
Smith, Richard Waddell (R)
Smith, Robert Lee (D)
Smith, S. C. (D)
Smoak, D. Frank (D)
Southerland, James F. (D)
Spencer, W. Thomas (D)
Spicer, Don L. (R)
Spicola, Guy William (D)
Spottswood, John Maloney (D)
Spring, Lewis N. (R)
Stack, Edward J. (R)
Stafford, Don H. (R)
Stallings, George B, Jr. (D)
Stanley, Leroy R. (R)
Stevens, Tom (D)
Stone, Richard Bernard (D)
Storey, Wallace L. (D)
Stratton, Harry O, Sr. (D)
Strauss, Ronald I. (R)
Strickland, Allison R. (D)
Sumner, E. Amos (D)
Sweeney, James Michael, Jr. (R)
Sweeny, James H, Jr. (D)
Swift, Earle Linwood (R)
Tamargo, Ray, Jr. (D)
Tapper, George G. (D)
Tatum, Waugantha Grady (D)
Taylor, Paul Worden, Jr. (R)
Taylor, William M. (R)
Teague, Sam (D)
Thomas, A. J. Jr. (D)
Thomas, Elwyn (D)
Thomas, Jerry (D)
Thomas, Pat Franklin (D)
Thompson, Denham Michael Burgess (R)
Thresher, Irene K. (R)
Tillman, Jim King (R)
Tobiassen, Thomas Johan (R)
Tope, Robert R. (R)
Treadwell, Donnie E. (D)
Turlington, Ralph D. (D)
Turnbull, William S. (D)
Tyner, Mayme (R)
Tyre, Ralph Charles (D)
Usher, Etter T. (D)
Vaile, Victor Edward, III (R)
Veal, Joseph Holliday (R)
Wadsworth, Herbert Robinson, Jr. (D)
Wadsworth, William L. (D)
Wakeman, William Thomson (R)
Walker, James Lorenzo (D)
Ward, Arthur Odell (D)
Ward, David Elmer (D)
Ware, John Thomas (R)
Weintraub, Claire (D)
Weissenborn, Lee (D)
Wells, David Emerson (R)
Wells, Gordon W. (D)
Westberry, Harry (D)
Wetherell, Howard Henderson (D)
Whitaker, Tom, Jr. (D)
Wilder, Joseph M. (D)
Wilks, Max (D)
Williams, Ben C. (D)
Williams, Broward (D)
Williams, Robert (D)
Wilson, Anne Chapman (R)
Wilson, Harold Stalets (R)
Wingate, Claude E. (D)
Wise, James H. (D)
Wolfson, Louis, II (D)
Wood, Leonard Victor (R)
Yarborough, Jess (D)
Young, C. W. Bill (R)
Young, David Leon (R)
Young, Melvin Richard (R)
Zacchini, Rene A. (D)
Zalla, Alvin Bernard (D)

GEORGIA

Abney, Billy Shaw (D)
Acree, John William (D)
Adams, George Drayton, Jr. (D)
Adams, Ronald Fletcher (D)
Aiken, Isaac Means (I)
Alaimo, Anthony Alfred (R)
Alexander, William Henry (D)
Allen, Henry Banks (D)
Allen, Ivan, Jr. (D)
Allen, James Robert (R)
Allen, Nora Alice (R)
Almand, Bond (D)
Alsobrook, Henry Herman (R)
Altman, James Eston (R)
Amos, William George (R)
Anderson, Charles William (R)
Anderson, John Henry, Jr. (D)
Andrews, Foy Rhyne (D)
Andrews, James Allen (D)
Andrews, Robert (D)
Arnall, Ellis Gibbs (D)
Arnsdorff, B. Frank (D)
Atherton, L. Howard, Jr. (D)
Austin, Ivy Frank (D)
Bagby, George Talmadge (D)
Balkcom, James C, Jr. (D)
Ballard, William Donaldson (D)
Ballew, Robert King (D)
Banister, Bette (R)
Barber, Jack McWhorter (D)
Barnard, Druie Douglas, Jr. (D)
Bateman, Oliver Cromwell (R)
Baugh, James Emory (D)
Baughman, Leon Hodges (D)
Beard, Fred J. (R)
Beck, James Edward (D)
Beckham, Robert Culp (R)
Bedgood, William Randall, Jr. (D)
Bell, Halcyon Alsup (R)
Bell, Robert Hudson (R)
Bennett, Jim T, Jr. (D)
Bentley, George Edward (D)
Bentley, James Lynwood (D)
Berry, Charles Edward (D)
Bertsche, Faith Brown (R)
Black, James Lucius (D)
Blackburn, Ben B, III (R)
Blackburn, James B. (D)
Blackshear, Marmaduke Hardeman (D)
Blair, William Evans (R)
Blalock, Daniel Braxton (D)
Blalock, Edgar (D)
Bolton, Arthur Key (D)
Bond, (Horace) Julian (D)
Bowen, A'Delbert (R)
Bowen, Ralph W. (D)
Bowen, Rooney L. (D)
Bowen, Ross P. (D)
Boyd, Elizabeth Cobb (D)
Brackin, J. O. (D)
Branch, W. Frank (D)
Brantley, Haskew Hawthorne (R)
Brantley, Hines L. (D)
Brewer, Oby T. (D)
Brinkley, Jack Thomas (D)
Brooks, Carolyn Elizabeth (R)
Brooks, George B. (D)
Brooks, Wilson (D)
Broome, Dean Carl (D)
Broun, Paul C. (D)
Brown, Benjamin D. (D)
Brown, Jesse Frances (D)
Brown, Martin Parks (D)
Brown, T. Clayton, Jr. (D)
Buck, Thomas Bryant, III (D)
Buffington, Herbert L, Jr. (D)
Burt, Addison Moore (R)
Burton, Joe Nelson (D)
Burton, Thomas Lawson (R)
Busbee, George D. (D)
Bynum, Knox (D)
Byrd, Garland Turk (D)
Byrd, John Thomas (D)
Caldwell, Johnnie L. (D)
Calhoun, Anne Carter (R)
Callaway, Howard Hollis (R)
Campbell, Charles Edward
Campbell, James Philander, Jr. (R)
Candler, Thomas Slaughter (D)
Cargile, Richard Franklin (R)
Carlton, Milton Augustus, Sr. (D)
Carr, Thomas Caswell (D)
Carter, James Earl, Jr. (D)
Cary, Ashton Hall, Jr. (R)
Cauble, Florence Horkan (R)
Cauble, John A. (R)
Causby, Troy (D)
Chambers, William Clyde (R)
Chambless, Clarence G. (R)
Chandler, Philip M. (D)
Chapman, Cyrus Miller (D)
Cheeks, Donald Edward (D)
Clardy, George L. (R)
Clark, Joe Taylor (D)
Clarke, Harold Gravely (D)
Clements, Charles McCall, III (R)
Clyde, William A. (D)
Coggin, Frank Edward (D)
Coker, Grady N. (D)
Coker, Roy N. (D)
Cole, James William (D)
Collins, John Felton (D)
Collins, Stanley Newcomb, Jr. (R)
Conger, J. Willis (D)
Conner, James L. (D)
Conway, Earl Cranston (D)
Cook, Rodney Mims (R)
Cordell, Joseph Edward (R)
Covington, Dean (D)
Cox, Jay Carroll (D)
Crawford, Abbott Linton (D)
Cullens, J. R. (D)
Daniel, Alice Lee (R)
Davidson, William John (R)
Davis, Earl Thomas (R)
Davis, James Curran (D)
Davis, John W. (D)
Davis, Thelma Faulkner (D)
Davis, Truitt (D)
Davis, Walter Lamar (R)
Dean, James Edward (D)
Dean, Nathan D. (D)
Dean, Roscoe Emory, Jr. (D)
Deen, Hugh Dorsey (D)
Delong, R. Luke (R)
Dennard, Joe L. (D)
DeVane, Marvin Eugene (D)
Dickinson, John Ingram (R)
Dickinson, Richard Kent (D)
Dicus, Harry (D)
Dillard, Benjamin Hall, Jr. (R)
Dixon, Harry Donival (D)
Dodson, Carr Glover (R)
Dorminy, Arthur B. C, Jr. (D)
Downing, Frank O. (D)
Drew, Lionel Edward, Jr. (D)
Duckworth, William Henry (D)
Duncan, Andrew Claude (D)
Duncan, Joseph Elvin (D)
Dykes, Wingate (D)
Echols, Talmage B. (D)
Edenfield, Berry Avant (D)
Edwards, Julian Ward (D)
Egan, Michael Joseph (R)
Elder, David Mayne (D)
Elliott, James Sewell (R)
Elliott, Tyron Clifford (R)
Ellis, Morriss Wren (D)
Ellis, S. Thomas (D)
Etheridge, Jack Paul (D)
Ezzard, Clarence Gray (D)
Farmer, Leon, Jr. (D)
Felton, Jule Wimberly, Jr. (D)
Ferst, Jeanne Rolfe (R)
Fincher, Jack Chambers, Sr. (D)
Fitzpatrick, Duross (R)
Fitzpatrick, Mark William (R)
Fleming, William M, Jr. (D)
Flournoy, Robert Edward, Jr. (D)
Floyd, James H. (D)
Flynt, John J, Jr. (D)
Flynt, Wales Thornton (D)
Fortson, Ben W, Jr. (D)
Foster, Roy Guylus, Jr. (R)
Fowler, James Darwin (R)
Freedman, Claire Friedman (R)
Fulford, Ed (D)
Fuller, Vincent Cefalu (R)
Funk, Arthur Joseph (D)
Fuqua, J. B. (D)
Futch, Sidney (R)
Gardner, Jay D. (R)
Gary, Archie Thomas (D)
Gayner, John M, III (R)

Geer, Peter Zack, Jr. (D)
German, Charles Grady (D)
Gilbert, Robert Bacon, Jr. (D)
Gillis, Carl L, Jr. (R)
Gillis, Hugh Marion (D)
Ginn, Ronald B. (D)
Goode, James Waltom (R)
Gordy, A. Perry, II (R)
Grahl, Daniel Kendall, Sr. (D)
Graves, Charles Edward (D)
Gray, James H. (D)
Greene, William Bernard (D)
Grice, Benning Moore (D)
Grier, J. D, Jr. (D)
Griffin, Robert Alwyn (D)
Griffin, Samuel Marvin (D)
Groover, Denmark, Jr. (D)
Gunter, William B. (D)
Hadaway, John Henry (D)
Hagan, G. Elliott (D)
Haight, David Henry (D)
Hale, Maddox Jerome (D)
Hall, Henry Goodwin (D)
Hall, James Battle (D)
Hall, Robert, Jr. (R)
Harden, Ross Ullman (D)
Hardin, William Henderson (D)
Hardy, Joel Cecil (D)
Harrell, Aubrey Hewlette (D)
Harrington, John Floyd (D)
Harris, James Robin (D)
Harris, Reid Walker (D)
Harrison, Harold (D)
Harrison, Ivan (R)
Harrison, James Edward, III (R)
Harrison, Robert Ward, Jr. (D)
Hawes, Peyton Samuel, Jr. (D)
Hawkins, Herb Clay, Jr. (D)
Heard, Roland Shaefer (D)
Hearn, George J.
Heath, Tim Ray (R)
Henderson, J. H, Jr. (D)
Henderson, Waldo (D)
Herndon, Curtis C. (D)
Herring, Robert F. (D)
Hester, William H. (R)
Hill, Bobby L. (D)
Hill, James Render (D)
Hodges, J. Alex (R)
Holloway, Albert Weston (D)
Holmes, John Paul, Jr. (R)
Hooks, Vendie H, Jr. (D)
Hooper, Thomas Bertron (D)
Hornsby, David Hugo (R)
Horton, Nevils Dudley, Jr. (D)
Horton, Seab Sanford, Jr. (R)
House, Mitchel Patrie, Jr. (D)
Housley, Grady Eugene (D)
Houston, Francis (D)
Howard, John Mell (D)
Howell, William Mobley (D)
Hudgins, Floyd (D)
Hudson, Eugene Talmadge (D)
Huiet, Ben Tillman (D)
Hull, James M, Jr. (D)
Hulsey, Randi Torgesen (R)
Hunt, William J. (D)
Hurst, Joseph J. (D)
Hutchinson, Richard Shirley (D)
Isenberg, Joe (D)
Jackson, Harry Cook (D)
Jernigan, Wallace Lawson (D)
Johnson, Albert Sidney, Sr. (D)
Johnson, Ben(jamin) F(ranklin) (D)
Johnson, Bobby Ware (D)
Johnson, Elston Lowe (D)
Johnson, George Thomas (R)
Johnson, Leroy Reginald (D)
Johnson, Newman Newton (R)
Jones, Charles Maury (D)
Jones, David Campbell (D)
Jones, Frederick Carl, Jr. (D)
Jones, G. Paul, Jr. (R)
Jones, Milton (D)
Jordan, Ben Carlton (R)
Jordan, George (D)
Jordan, James E. (D)
Jordan, William Harvey (D)
Kaler, Irving K (D)
Keadle, Haygood (D)
Keenan, Paul A, Jr. (D)
Keeter, Albert McKinley (R)
Kelly, Roy R. (D)
Kendrick, Edward Storey (D)
Kennedy, Joseph Everett (D)
Killian, William Russell (D)
Kilpatrick, Kenneth (D)
Kimmons, James Royce (R)
Kirkland, Hogan Emil (D)
Knapp, G. Ed(ward) (R)
Knight, Durell Warthen, Jr. (D)
Knight, John Steverson (D)
Knight, William D. (D)
Kopp, John Glenwright (R)
Kreeger, George H. (D)
Krumme, James Leon (R)
Laite, William E, Jr. (D)
Lambert, Ezekiel Roy (D)
Lambros, Nick George (D)
Landrum, Phillip Mitchell (D)
Lane, W. Jones (D)
LeCraw, Julian (R)
Lee, Grover B. (D)
Lee, Robert E, Jr. (D)
Lee, William J. (D)
Lee, William Spencer (D)
Leonard, Gerald H. (D)
Lester, James Luther (D)
Levitas, Elliott Harris (D)
Lewis, E. Brooks (D)
Lewis, Preston Brooks (D)
Lewis, William Hugh (R)
Logan, Benjamin Cicero, Sr. (R)
Loggins, Joseph E. (D)
Lokey, Hamilton (D)
Lokey, Leonard N. (D)
London, Maylon Kermit (D)
Low, Norman C, Jr. (D)
Lowrey, Robert Sidney, Sr. (D)
Lucas, Mary Louisa (D)
McAfee, Lilian Foote (R)
McClatchey, Devereaux Fore (D)
McClelland, Ralph, Jr. (D)
McCorkle, Zack Reshess (D)
McCracken, James Roy (D)
McCutchen, Pleasant Theodore (D)
McCutcheon, Chester M. (R)
McDonald, Thomas James, Jr. (D)
McDonald, Walter Raleigh (D)
McGill, Sam P. (D)
McIntire, Pope Barrow (D)
Mackay, James Armstrong (D)
McKemie, Henry Grady (D)
McKibben, Jadie Clifford (D)
McKinnon, Talmadge (D)
Maclean, Malcolm Roderick (D)
McVey, Lauder Tully (R)
McVey, Walter Lewis, Jr. (R)
McWhorter, William Hugh (D)
Maddox, Lester G. (D)
Mahan, Dauswell Rogers, Jr. (R)
Malone, Judson Perry (R)
Matthews, Dorsey Rudolph (D)
Matthews, Robert Chappelle (D)
Mattingly, Mack Francis (R)
Mays, Troy A. (R)
Meeks, William Thomas, Jr. (D)
Melton, Quimby, Jr. (D)
Merritt, Janet Burton Scarborough (D)
Milford, Charles Patrick (D)
Milford, William Doyle (D)
Milhollin, Henry Roberts (D)
Miller, Mitch (D)
Miller, Zell Bryan (D)
Minge, Jerry Lee (D)
Mitchell, Harlan Erwin (D)
Mitchell, Thomas Marvin (D)
Mixon, Billy Pearson (R)
Mixon, Harry (D)
Moate, Marvin E. (D)
Mobley, Carlton
Moore, Don Cager (D)
Moore, John Harvey (D)
Moore, Thomas Jefferson (R)
Morgan, Handsel Grady (D)
Morgan, Jack H. (D)
Morris, J. Harold (D)
Morrison, Raymond M, Sr. (D)
Morrison, Robert Elliott (D)
Moshier, Terry Allen (R)
Moss, Truett W. (R)
Moye, Charles A, Jr. (R)
Munford, Dillard (R)
Murphy, Thomas Bailey (D)
Murrah, William Nolan, Jr. (R)
Myers, James Frank (D)
Nash, Norris Jewell (D)
Neal, Henry G. (D)
Nessmith, Paul E, Sr. (D)
New, James Grant (R)
New, William Madison (R)
Newton, David Lanier (D)
Noble, Roy V. (D)
Norman, Robert Claude (D)
Odom, Colquitt Hurst (D)
Oglesby, Jamie White (R)
O'Keeffe, Whitney Carter (R)
O'Kelley, William Clark (R)
Oliver, Clinton (D)
O'Neal, John Barnwell (D)
O'Neal, Maston Emmett, Jr. (D)
Overby, Howard Thomas (D)
Owens, Erwin (D)
Padgett, William David (D)
Pafford, Robert C. (D)
Pagel, John Theodore (R)
Palmer, Dwight Wendell (R)
Palmer, Tom Carroll, Jr. (D)
Paris, James W. (D)
Parker, Henry Walstein (D)
Parsons, Joanna Gable (D)
Partridge, Henry F. (D)
Patton, Elbert Earl, Jr. (R)
Payton, Henry N. (D)
Peavy, James Edwin (R)
Pelham, Glenn (D)
Pennington, Brooks Maddox, Jr. (D)
Perry, Eldridge Wells (D)
Peters, William Cooper (D)
Peterson, David C. (D)
Phelps, Jo Minor (R)
Phillips, Glenn Stephens (D)
Phillips, J. Taylor (D)
Phillips, Lewis Milton (D)
Phillips, Ralph Boyd (D)
Phillips, Watson Randolph (D)
Pickard, A. Mac (D)
Pilcher, James Brownie (D)
Pinkston, Frank Chapman (D)
Pittman, Richard Edward (R)
Plunkett, Lamar R. (D)
Ponsell, William King (D)
Poole, Will (D)
Pope, Marion Thomas, Jr. (D)
Posey, Grover Harold (D)
Poss, Edwin Carroll (D)
Powell, Herbert B. (Independent)
Prichard, W. M. (R)
Prince, Jack Alexander (R)
Prince, Jerry Richard (R)
Proctor, Ernest Earl (R)
Quinn, Augustine Statham (R)
Ragland, Joe F. (D)
Rainey, Howard (D)
Raulerson, Louis Thomas (D)
Ray, Jack Bowdoin (D)
Reaves, Henry L. (D)
Rees, Willard Andrew (R)
Reese, James Edwin (R)
Reynolds, Steve (D)
Rhodes, J(ames) R(obert), Jr. (D)
Richardson, Willis Jenkins, Jr.
Roberts, Corbin C. (D)
Rodgers, Henry Benjamin (D)
Rogers, Jimmie Fort (D)
Rogers, John Richard (D)
Rooks, James Orville (R)
Roper, Allen Page (D)
Rowan, Robert A. (D)
Rowland, Emory L. (D)
Rush, Dewey Davent (D)
Russell, Henry Phillip, Jr. (D)
Russell, Richard Brevard (D)
Salome, J. M. (D)
Sancken, George A, Jr. (Independent)
Sanders, Carl Edward (D)
Sanders, H. E. (R)
Sangster, Thomas I. (D)
Satterfield, Frances Gibson (D)
Savage, Carl Preston, Sr. (D)
Scarborough, Homer M, Jr. (D)
Scarborough, John C, Jr. (D)
Schaefer, Orville Tyler (D)
Scheer, George M. (D)
Schloth, William John (R)
Scott, Milford A. (D)
Searcey, William A. (D)
Self, Earl Burdell (D)
Sewell, John William (D)
Sharpe, T. Malone (D)
Shaw, Joseph Tyron, Sr. (D)
Shaw, Robert Jennings (R)
Shea, Bart E. (D)
Sherman, John Hayes, Jr. (R)
Shields, I. Lawrence (D)
Shinall, Robert Phillip, Jr. (R)
Shuman, Jack W. (D)
Simkins, Leroy Hampton, Jr. (R)
Simmons, John Grover (D)
Simpson, Mackie (D)
Sinclair, John Paul (D)
Singer, Sam S. (D)
Smalley, Robert Harris, Jr. (D)
Smith, Arthur C. (D)
Smith, Charles Courtland (D)
Smith, Charles Franklin, Sr. (R)
Smith, Edgar B, Jr. (D)
Smith, George Leon, II (D)
Smith, George Thornewell (D)
Smith, Marilu Crafton (R)
Smith, Priscilla B. (R)
Smith, Richard Russell (D)
Smith, Samuel Lamont (D)
Smith, Stanley Eugene, Jr. (D)
Smith, Virgil T. (D)
Smith, William Armstrong (R)
Snellings, William Ross (D)
Snider, Freddie Rembert (R)
Snow, Wayne, Jr. (D)
Sorrells, Marvin Williams (D)
Spikes, Harry Russell (D)
Spinks, Ford Belmont (D)
Spiva, Ulric Winston (R)
Stalnaker, Paul (D)
Starnes, Richard L, Jr. (D)
Steis, William Burton (D)
Stephens, Jack LeRol (D)
Stephens, Robert Grier, Jr. (D)
Stewart, George Daniel (D)
Stewart, Travis Burns (D)
Story, Earl P. (D)
Strickland, Ernest Willie (D)
Stuckey, Williamson S, Jr. (D)
Stuckey, Williamson Sylvester, Sr. (D)
Sullivan, Berry Jackson (D)
Sutton, Glenn Wallace (D)
Tabb, Buck (D)
Talmadge, Herman Eugene (D)
Taylor, Philip Raymond (D)
Teague, Elmer Wilson (D)
Thomas, Reese Samuel (R)
Thomason, Larry Wilson (D)
Thompson, Albert William (D)
Thompson, Roscoe Mullins (D)
Thompson, S. Fletcher (R)
Thurman, John Howard (R)
Thurman, Marjorie Clark (D)
Tipton, Richard McKane (R)
Todd, William Gibson (D)
Toles, Elwin Bonds (D)
Townsend, Kiliaen Van Rensselaer (R)
Towson, William Malcolm (D)
Tribble, Joseph James (R)
Trotter, William Perry (D)
Troutman, Frank, Jr. (R)
Tucker, Joe B. (D)
Tucker, Memory King (D)
Tucker, Ray M. (D)
Turner, Joseph William, Jr. (R)
Turner, Lester Cecil (D)
Twitty, Frank Starling (D)
Tygart, James Charles, Sr. (R)
Underwood, Joe Columbus (D)
Underwood, Ralph Rudolph (D)
Vaughan, David N, Jr. (D)
Vaughn, Clarence Roland, Jr. (D)
Vann, Frank Cochran (D)
Vaughn, Raymond Luke (R)
Vinson, Carl (D)
Walker, Fred H. (D)
Wall, Joe (D)
Waller, Samuel Carpenter (D)
Walling, Robert (D)
Wamble, Burton Max (D)
Ward, Horace Taliaferro (D)
Wardlow, Floyd H, Jr. (D)
Ware, James Crawford (D)
Warren, James E. (D)
Wasden, Wiley Anderson, Jr. (R)
Watkins, Richard Wright, Jr. (D)
Watson, Caleb Powers (D)
Watts, Jesse Clayborne (D)
Webb, Julian (D)
Welch, Hayward Oliver (D)
Wells, D. Warner (D)
Wells, Hubert Homer (D)
Weltner, Charles Longstreet (D)
Wesberry, James Pickett, Jr. (D)
West, James Paschal (R)
Westlake, James Roger (R)
Wheeler, Jack Adrain (D)
Wheeler, James Walter (D)
White, Charles Cody (D)
White, Daniel H. (D)
Whitten, Charles Alvin (R)
Wiggins, William J. (D)
Wilkes, Wilson Bryant (D)
Williams, George Joel (D)
Williams, Melba Ruth (D)
Williams, Nat McDonald, Jr. (D)
Williams, William Marcus (D)
Wilson, Hoke Smith (D)
Wilson, Joe Mack (D)
Wilson, Roger Wesley (R)
Wind, Herbert Hamilton, Jr. (D)
Winkles, Fred Larry (R)
Womack, Geraldine S. (R)
Wood, Joe T. (D)
Woodlee, Richard James (R)
Woodrum, Donald Lee (D)
Woodward, Bailey (D)
Wright, John G. (D)

Yancey, Kyle (D)
Young, James E. (D)
Young, James Milton, III (Conservative)
Young, Martin (D)
Zipperer, Edward Helmey (D)
Zorn, William Austin (D)

HAWAII

Abe, Kazuhisa (D)
Aduja, Peter A. (R)
Ajifu, Ralph K. (R)
Akizaki, Clarence Yasuo (D)
Alcon, Emilio S. (D)
Ansai, Toshio (R)
Anthony, Joseph Garner
Ariyoshi, George Ryoichi (D)
Au, Bernard E. (R)
Beppu, Tadao (D)
Blaisdell, Neal Shaw (R)
Burns, Barbara Lou (R)
Burns, John A. (D)
Butler, John (R)
Carson, Robert Trebor (R)
Chikasuye, Clesson Y. (D)
Ching, Donald D. H. (D)
Chu, Samuel En Fon (R)
Cingcade, Lester Earl (D)
Cleveland, Harlan (D)
Constantino, Patrick Ronald (D)
Coray, Carla Winn (R)
Costa, Mrs. Mary Meade (R)
Cravalho, Elmer F. (D)
Crossley, Randolph Allin (R)
Devereux, Dorothy Louise (R)
Dillingham, Benjamin Franklin, II (R)
Doi, Nelson K. (D)
Duarte, John Gomes (D)
Edwards, Richard Guy (R)
Farrington, Elizabeth Pruett (R)
Fasi, Frank Francis (D)
Fong, Hiram Leong (R)
Forbes, Eureka Bernice (R)
Fukushima, Yasutaka (R)
Gilkey, Robert C. (D)
Gill, Thomas P. (D)
Goemans, John W. (D)
Gratz, H(omer) Tucker (D)
Hara, Stanley Ikuo (D)
Heen, Walter Meheula (D)
Hirai, Seichi (D)
Ho, Stuart T. K. (D)
Hogan, Robert George (D)
Hudson, Glen Gary (R)
Hulten, John James (D)
Inaba, Minoru (D)
Inouye, Daniel Ken (D)
Johnston, Edward Elliott (R)
Judd, Frank Case (R)
Kaapu, Kekoa David (D)
Kamaka, Hiram K. (D)
Kanbara, Bertram (D)
Kato, James H. (D)
Kellerman, Elizabeth Rountree (R)
Kennedy, Eugene Frederick (R)
Kido, Mitsuyuki (D)
Kim, John En Suk (R)
Kimura, Robert Yutaka (D)
Kobayashi, Bert Takaaki (D)
Koga, George M. (D)
Kondo, Ronald Yoneo (D)
Krueger, Cliff W. (R)
Lanham, John Calhoun (D)
Lee, Kenneth K. L. (D)
Lemke, Herman G. P. (D)
Loo, Frank W. C. (D)
Loo, George Wing Tat (D)
Low, Daniel Tien Kee (R)
Luce, Clare Boothe (R)
Lum, Tennyson Kum Wing (R)
McClung, David Charles (D)
Matsunaga, Spark Masayuki (D)
Miho, Katsugo (R)
Mink, Patsy Takemoto (D)
Minn, Momi Pearl (D)
Minn, Philip P. (D)
Mirikitani, Percy Kiyoshi (R)
Miwa, Ralph M. (D)
Miyake, Howard Y. (D)
Miyake, Noboru (R)
Morioka, Ted T. (D)
Mui, Thomas Lawrence (D)
Nakamura, Yoshiro (D)
Noguchi, George Koji (D)
Norrell, Catherine Dorris (D)
Oda, Howard Kazumi (R)
Okada, Hideo (D)
Oshiro, Robert Chosei (D)
Osorio, Elroy Thomas Leialoha (R)
Overstreet, Frederick Heiskell (R)
Pacarro, Rudolph (D)
Park, Corey Y. S. (D)
Payne, John Howard (R)
Poepoe, Andrew Keliikuniaupuni (R)
Rice, V(irgil) Thomas (R)
Rodby, Leo Bernard, Jr. (D)
Roehrig, Stanley Herbert (D)
Rohlfing, Frederick W. (R)
Saiki, Patricia (R)
Shafer, Esther Virginia (R)
Shelly, Alice E. (R)
Smith, Emma E. (R)
Soares, Wilfred (R)
Souza, James Stanley (R)
Spalding, Philip Edmunds, Jr. (R)
Swanton, Mary Ellen Cashin (D)
Taira, Norman Takeo (D)
Takahashi, Sakae (D)
Takitani, Henry T. (D)
Takushi, Tokuichi (D)
Tanaka, Francis Torao (D)
Tokita, Turk T. (D)
Ushijima, Charles T. (D)
Ushijima, John T. (D)
Wakatsuki, James Hiroji (D)
Wong, Francis Alvin (D)
Yamasaki, Mamoru (D)
Yano, Vincent H. (D)
You, Richard Wonsang (D)

IDAHO

Allen, John Joseph, Jr. (R)
Amyx, Jay S. (R)
Andrus, Cecil D. (D)
Antone, Steve (R)
Aslett, Leona (D)
Ausich, Joseph L. (D)
Barlow, Hubert Rampton (R)
Barnett, Gwen Hughes (R)
Barron, Charles Lee (R)
Bauer, Richard L. (R)
Beal, Joseph Burns (R)
Bean, Woodrow W. (D)
Bilyeu, Charles Edward (D)
Bilyeu, Diane F. (D)
Blanc, Donald Richard (D)
Blick, George Leonard (R)
Bowler, Orson Lloyd (R)
Bozzuto, Victor J. (D)
Branson, Dale R. (D)
Brauner, William Jess (D)
Brocke, George Frank (D)
Brooks, Mary Elizabeth (R)
Brown, Grundy Mortimore (R)
Brunt, A. W. (D)
Budge, Hamer Harold (R)
Bush, Eugene Lorin (R)
Cammack, Wilbert (D)
Carey, Jack Wesley (R)
Cartan, Gloria Harrison (D)
Carver, John A, Jr. (D)
Cenarrusa, Peter Thomas (R)
Chamberlin, Gaylord Bartlett (R)
Chase, Cyril Charles (D)
Christensen, Gerald Othello (R)
Christensen, J. Lloyd (D)
Church, Frank (D)
Claiborn, Jack Dewey (R)
Cobbs, Lyle Richard (R)
Collett, Harold Edwin (D)
Condie, Angus R. (R)
Cowan, Rosa K. (D)
Crapo, Terry LaVelle (R)
Crow, Dolores Jean (R)
Crupper, Gordon (R)
Curtis, Dennis Rex (D)
Daniels, Russel O. (D)
Defenbach, Will S. (R)
Detweiler, Gertrude Homan (R)
Donaldson, Charles Russell (Non-Partisan)
Edwards, John Albert (R)
Egbert, Richard Alexander (D)
Ellsworth, W. Fisher (R)
English, Eleanor Jean (D)
Eriksen, Lu Dean (D)
Fogg, Lorin Russell (R)
Fuller, Wayne P. (D)
Garner, Dale B. (R)
George, John Hendrix (R)
Glenn, Fred Andrew (D)
Goff, Abe McGregor (R)
Gregoire, Edward Paul (R)
Haakenson, Robert Melvin (D)
Hamilton, Clarence James (D)
Hammond, F. Melvin (D)
Hansen, George V. (R)
Hansen, Orval Howard (R)
Hansen, Othello Tanner (R)
Hansen, Rodney Alton (R)
Harding, Ralph Ray (D)
Hart, Mark Fielding (D)
Hartvigsen, Lester A. (D)
Hatch, Mike W. (D)
Healy, Ellen (D)
Hedges, Edward Eugene (R)
Hubbard, Robert Williams (R)
Ingalls, James W. (D)
Jenkins, Edward Gerrard (R)
Johnson, Byron Jerald (D)
Johnston, Ronald Dale (R)
Jones, Stanley Oscar (R)
Jordan, Leonard Beck (R)
Judge, Jim Ervin (R)
Kaufman, Samuel (R)
Kidwell, Wayne Le Roy (R)
Kingsford, Leonard O. (R)
Klein, Edith Miller (R)
Koch, Henry Ferd (R)
Koontz, Robert J. (R)
Lanting, William John (R)
Larson, Dorothy M. (D)
LeGresley, Roscoe Edward (D)
Leonardson, Elmer Charles (R)
Lincoln, Ray William (R)
Lineberger, Lawrence M. (D)
Ling, Roger D. (R)
Little, David (R)
Little, Duane Ewing (D)
Lowe, Jay R. (D)
Lunte, Charles David (R)
McCarter, Joe T. (D)
McClary, James Daly (R)
McClary, Mary Jane (R)
McClure, James A. (R)
McCollum, Joe D. (R)
McKinney, Helen Mathews (R)
McLaughlin, Robert Francis (D)
McMurray, John Odell (R)
McReynolds, Elizabeth Sanford (R)
Manley, Art (D)
Marineau, William Thomas (R)
Markham, Harley Bruce, Sr. (R)
Martin, John E. (R)
Miller, Dean E. (D)
Miller, Neil J. (D)
Mills, William Larry (R)
Mitchell, Thomas (R)
Mix, John Parson (D)
Moon, Marjorie Ruth (D)
Murphy, Arthur Powell (D)
Murphy, Jack M. (R)
Nelson, Alice Mary (R)
Nicholson, Joe David (D)
Niswander, Calvin Elroy (R)
Park, William Anthony (D)
Parsley, Merle David (D)
Patterson, Wilma Randolph (D)
Payton, Willis Osborne (D)
Peavey, John Thomas (R)
Pell, Katherine D. (D)
Pino, John Hardy (D)
Rammell, Arthur Leon (D)
Ravenscroft, Vernon Frank (D)
Reagan, William Angus (D)
Rigby, Ray Wendell (D)
Robbins, Ray (R)
Robson, Robert Morgan (R)
Rowett, Robert Mellen (R)
Russell, J. A. (R)
Ryan, Harold L. (R)
Samuelson, Don W. (R)
Sandberg, John Cecil (D)
Scoresby, Clifford Norman (R)
Shadduck, Louise (R)
Sharp, Joseph Lessil (R)
Shelton, Clara Kathryn (D)
Shepard, Allan G. (R)
Short, E. Russell (R)
Shultz, Margaret Hampton (D)
Sinclair, Orriette Coiner (R)
Smazal, Vincent August (D)
Smeed, Ralph E. (R)
Smith, Richard R. (R)
Smylie, Robert E. (R)
Snow, Harold (R)
Solberg, Nels Leroy (D)
Spradling, Grady R. (D)
Stewart, Joseph Alexander (R)
Stewart, William F. (R)
Swenson, Leon Hughie (R)
Tacke, John Bernard (D)
Taylor, Fred Monroe (R)
Taylor, Jeanne M. (D)
Terrell, Thomas F. (D)
Tibbitts, Wayne Everett (D)
Tregoning, Margot A. (D)
Van Engelen, W. Dean (R)
Wagner, Joseph Nicholas (D)
Walker, Lloyd Julius (D)
Wall, Harry (D)
Waters, Errol T. (D)
Webb, Jay Leon (R)
Wegner, Glen Eugene (R)
Wetherell, Rose Claire (D)
White, Compton I. (D)
Wilber, Roland C. (R)
Williams, Edward Vernon (D)
Williams, Joseph Rulon (D)
Wray, Jerry Clark (R)
Wright, Elma Pogge (R)
Yarbrough, Walter Herman (R)

ILLINOIS

Abercrombie, John Reid (R)
Acton, Charles Edward (R)
Adams, Don W. (R)
Akin, Edward B. (D)
Albrecht, Harold Joseph (R)
Alfeld, Jack A. (D)
Alinsky, Saul David (D)
Alschuler, Benjamin Philip (D)
Alsup, John W. (D)
Altorfer, John Henry (R)
Anagnost, Catherine Cook (R)
Anderson, John B. (R)
Anderson, Raymond E. (R)
Anderson, Robert Lowell (R)
Anderson, Walter (D)
Annunzio, Frank (D)
Arends, Leslie C. (R)
Arrington, William Russell (R)
Arvey, Jacob M. (D)
Austin, Robert (R)
Awerkamp, Thomas James (D)
Babcock, Milton (D)
Babcock, Richard Felt (D)
Bafford, Hallie B. (D)
Bagge, Carl Elmer (R)
Baird, Russell Miller
Baker, Bert (D)
Baker, J. Frederick (R)
Ball, Judson Charles (D)
Baltz, Meade (R)
Barbour, Walworth
Barlow, John Leland (R)
Barron, Francis R. (D)
Barry, Tobias (D)
Barto, Raymond N. (R)
Basso, Romeo James (R)
Beaupre, Jack Raymond (D)
Beck, Leslie Vernon (D)
Benefiel, Philip Baker (D)
Bennett, Lowell E. (R)
Berman, Arthur Leonard (D)
Bernbaum, Maurice Marshall
Bidwill, Arthur John (R)
Bidwill, Neal M. (R)
Bierbaum, May Pearl (R)
Bingle, James Douglas (R)
Bishop, Cecil W. (R)
Black, Creed Carter (R)
Black, Kenneth Wallace (R)
Blackorby, Lila Rose (R)
Blades, Ben C. (R)
Blair, W. Robert (R)
Blanek, Frank Joseph, Jr. (D)
Blase, Nicholas B. (D)
Blaser, William Lawrence (R)
Blickhan, Edith M. (D)
Blouin, Robert Richard (R)
Blume, Joyce Campbell (D)
Blythe, Coy Daniel, Sr. (R)
Bolger, William J. (D)
Borah, Dan V. (R)
Borchers, Albert Webber (R)
Boswell, Paul P. (R)
Bowers, Jack E. (R)
Bowsher, Charles Arthur (D)
Bradford, Robert Edward (R)
Bradley, Gerald Allen (D)
Branson, Fred (R)
Bringham, William Talbert (R)
Brookhart, Samuel Henry (R)
Brouillet, Hector A. (R)
Broverman, Robert Lee (D)
Brown, David Emerson (R)
Brown, Fred James (D)
Broyles, Paul W. (R)
Brydia, George S. (R)
Burditt, George Miller (R)
Burgoon, Garrel (R)
Burhans, Donald Lucas (R)
Burhans, Robert L. (R)
Burke, Donald Francis (D)
Burr, James M. (R)
Byrne, Emmet Francis (R)

Cadigan, Patrick J. (D)
Cairnes, William E. (R)
Caldwell, Lewis A. H. (D)
Callahan, Joe (D)
Calvo, Horace Lawrence (D)
Campbell, Charles M. (R)
Canfield, Robert Roe (R)
Cannon, Joe Wesley (R)
Capuzi, Louis F. (R)
Carpentier, Donald Dee (R)
Carrigan, James D. (D)
Carroll, John W. (R)
Carter, James Y. (D)
Cassidy, John E, Jr. (D)
Ceaser, Paul G. (D)
Chamberlain, William H. (D)
Chancey, C. Ray (D)
Chapman, Eugenia Sheldon (D)
Chapman, James Frederick (D)
Cherry, Robert E. (D)
Chesney, Chester Anton (D)
Chesnutt, John Henry (R)
Chesrow, Frank William (D)
Chew, Charles, Jr. (D)
Childs, John Lawrence (Liberal)
Choate, Clyde L. (D)
Church, Marguerite Stitt (R)
Clabaugh, Charles Wesley (R)
Clark, William George (D)
Clarke, Terrel E. (R)
Cleary, Patrick James (R)
Coleman, Marion Wilford (D)
Collier, Harold R. (R)
Collins, Dennis J. (R)
Combs, James Clinton (R)
Coney, Jack Arthur (R)
Conolly, John Hamilton (R)
Cook, Mercer
Coombes, Dorothy Margaret (R)
Copeland, Edward Jerome (R)
Corbett, Jerry G. (D)
Corbett, Joan Dufner (D)
Costello, Daniel E. (D)
Costello, Joan D. (R)
Coulson, Robert (R)
Course, Kenneth W. (D)
Coutrakon, George P. (R)
Craig, Robert (D)
Creighton, Robert Emmett (D)
Cromwell, James H. (R)
Cronin, A. L. (D)
Cronson, Robert Granville (R)
Cryer, Clifford Eugene (R)
Cunningham, William Johnston, III (R)
Dahlberg, Virginia Isis (R)
Dale, Edwin E. (R)
Daley, Richard J(oseph) (D)
Damron, William Orville (R)
Daniels, Cary (D)
Davidson, W. K. (R)
Davis, Corneal A. (D)
Davis, David (R)
Dawson, Frances Ledlie (R)
Dawson, William L. (D)
Day, Robert George (R)
Degenhardt, Darlene Lucille (D)
DeLaCour, Joseph L. (D)
DeMichaels, LaSalle J. (D)
Derwinski, Edward J. (R)
De Tolve, Anthony Joseph (D)
Deuster, Donald Eugene (R)
Devitt, Eugene Thomas (R)
DiPrima, Lawrence (D)
Dixon, Alan John (D)
Doerr, Ray E. (R)
Dolezal, George E. (R)
Donnewald, James H. (D)
Donovan, Margaret Walsh (D)
Dougherty, Daniel D. (D)
Douglas, Paul H. (D)
Dowling, John Robert (R)
Downes, John P. (D)
Downing, T. Mac (R)
Dowse, Duane Arlo (D)
Drach, George E. (R)
Dristle, Ronald Lee, Sr. (D)
Drummet, J. Dudley (D)
Dubin, Martin David (D)
Duda, Walter (R)
Duffy, Stephen Francis (D)
Dupree, James A. (D)
Dwyer, Robert A. (R)
Dyer, Mrs. Robert C.
Eagleton, Richard Ernest (D)
Eatherly, James Edward (R)
Eberspacher, Edward Christian (D)
Elliott, John D. (R)
Elrod, Richard Jay (D)
Elward, Paul Francis (D)
Erkert, Roger William (R)
Erlenborn, John Neal (R)
Euzzino, Andrew A. (D)
Everett, Reynolds Melville (R)
Ewell, Raymond Whitney (D)
Falls, Arthur Joseph (R)
Fawell, Harris W. (R)
Feehan, Thomas (R)
Fetridge, William Harrison (R)
Findley, Paul (R)
Finley, Morgan M. (D)
Finnegan, Edward R. (D)
Flinn, Monroe Lawrence (D)
Flynn, John James (D)
Fonner, Paul E. (R)
Forker, Paul C. (D)
Forsyth, Don (D)
Foster, Clifton N(eal) (R)
Fraley, Vance Levoy (R)
Fulle, Floyd Theodore (R)
Gamble, Walker Rubin (D)
Gardner, J. Horace (R)
Gaylord, Clayton Russell (R)
Gholson, Jerome Busler (D)
Gibson, Robert Glenn (D)
Gilbert, John G. (R)
Gillies, Frederick Montague (R)
Giorgi, E. J. (D)
Gleason, Clyde K. (R)
Gleason, Martin John (D)
Goddard, Alpheus John, Jr. (R)
Good, James W, Jr. (R)
Gordus, Michael (R)
Gottschalk, Arthur R. (R)
Grady, Homer E. (R)
Graham, Elwood (R)
Graham, John A. (R)
Granata, Peter C. (R)
Graves, G. Eugene (R)
Graves, Parker (R)
Gray, Kenneth J. (D)
Green, Howard E, Jr. (R)
Green, Madge Miller (R)
Greenaway, Robert Francis (R)
Gregory, Dick (Peace)
Grindle, William L. (D)
Groen, Egbert B. (R)
Grow, Dorah Lucile (D)
Gwin, John P. (R)
Habermeyer, Howard William
Hachmeister, Albert William (R)
Haddick, Dean Z. (R)
Hale, Joseph Robert (R)
Hall, Harber Homer (R)
Hall, John Emory (R)
Hammack, Dean Rae (D)
Hancock, William P. (D)
Hansen, Carl R. (R)
Harpstrite, Ben C. (R)
Harrelson, Joseph Edward (D)
Harrington, Margaret Elizabeth (D)
Harris, Thomas Murray (R)
Harris, William Cullen (R)
Harshbarger, Helen Margaret (R)
Hart, Fred J. (R)
Hart, Parker Thompson
Hart, Richard Odum (D)
Haste, James Francis (R)
Hatcher, James Gerald (D)
Haukap, Edward Ralph (D)
Hawkinson, John W. (R)
Hayes, Roger W. (R)
Heady, Marion Benjamin (R)
Heil, Wallace Lee (D)
Heiple, James Dee (R)
Heisler, Donald Eugene (D)
Henneberger, Robert Lawrence (R)
Henson, John R. (D)
Henss, Donald Allen (R)
Hill, John Jerome (D)
Hocking, Bert Whitman (R)
Hoellen, John James (R)
Hoffelder, Walter P. (R)
Hoffman, Benjamin Franklin (D)
Hoffman, Gene Louis (R)
Hoffman, Ronald Kenneth (R)
Holderman, Samuel James (R)
Hollister, Charles Ammon (D)
Holloway, James D. (D)
Holm, Jeanne Antoinette (D)
Holman, Claude W. B. (D)
Holmes, Harold Hubert (D)
Homeier, Christian Henry (R)
Horsley, George William, Sr. (R)
Horstman, Alice Lou (R)
Horstman, Ronald Ralph (R)
Horwitz, Erwin R. (D)
House, Byron O. (R)
Houser, Thomas James (R)
Howarth, Nelson Oliver (R)
Howlett, Michael J. (D)
Hughes, Charles Lendall (R)
Humphrey, William Howard (D)
Hunsicker, Carl T. (R)
Hupe, Lawrence Louis (R)
Hurst, Ronald Alan (R)
Hutar, Patricia (R)
Hutchcraft, James Edwin (R)
Hyde, Henry John (R)
Igo, Irma L. (D)
Ihnen, H. B. (R)
Imle, Albert Robert (D)
Ingram, Robert L. (D)
Ireland, Thomas Robert (R)
Irving, Don (D)
Ives, Timothy Read (D)
Jackson, James William (R)
Janczak, Louis (R)
Jenison, Edward Halsey (R)
Jennings, Janet Roberts (R)
Jensen, Elmer (R)
Jesk, James Wilbert (D)
Jessen, Gudmund Bendix, Jr. (D)
Jevitz, John Louis (R)
Johns, George Peter (R)
Johnson, Larry Alan (D)
Johnson, Rex Duane (R)
Johnson, William Potter (R)
Johnston, Alan R. (R)
Jones, Fannie Gwendolyn (D)
Jones, John David (R)
Jones, John Morton (R)
Jones, Paul F. (R)
Jones, Teddy Albert (R)
Jones, Theodore A. (D)
Jones, William Layman (R)
Joseph, Maurice Franklin (D)
Joslin, Roger (R)
Juckett, Robert S. (R)
Juergens, William G. (R)
Kahoun, Raymond J. (R)
Kane, William B. (R)
Kanter, Samuel A. (R)
Kaplan, Nathan Joseph (D)
Kaplinski, Henry Stanislaus (R)
Karber, James Winfield (D)
Karson, Marc (D)
Katz, Harold A. (D)
Keasler, William Henry (R)
Keegan, Betty Ann Southwick (D)
Keller, Charles F. (D)
Kelly, Charles Henry (D)
Kennedy, David Matthew (R)
Kennedy, Leland J. (D)
Kenney, Virginia Banning (R)
Kerner, Otto (D)
Kerr, Gordon E. (R)
Kezon, Peter Paul (D)
Killey, Ralph Allen (R)
Kilver, Wayne M. (D)
Kinally, Nathan J. (D)
King, Woodrow Wilson (D)
Kipley, Edward Lorenz, Sr. (R)
Kipping, Gregory August (D)
Klaus, Arthur Carl (R)
Klein, Carl Louis (R)
Klingbiel, Ray I. (R)
Kluczynski, John Carl (D)
Knuepfer, Jack Tarrant (R)
Koch, Edward Herman (D)
Koch, Lester Donald (R)
Koeppel, Willard Maurice (R)
Kolski, Edwin Thomas (R)
Koruna, Steven (D)
Krabbe, Louis August (D)
Kraus, Elmer J. (R)
Krier, Raymond Valentine (D)
Kuhle, Donald Lewis (D)
Kunze, Emma Louise (R)
Kusibab, Thad I. (D)
Lahey, Daniel Francis (D)
Landolt, Allan Francis (R)
Lanigan, John J. (R)
Larson, Richard Rosen (R)
Latherow, Clifford Brandon (R)
Laughlin, Everett E. (R)
Laurino, Anthony C. (D)
Lauterbach, Wilbur H. (R)
Law, Robert Dale (R)
Lechowicz, Thaddeus Stanley (D)
Lee, Clyde (D)
Lee, Noble W. (R)
Lehman, Ed (R)
Lehman, Jesse E, Jr. (R)
Lehnhausen, Robert Joseph (R)
Leischner, Ellis Edward (D)
Lenard, Henry M. (D)
Lennon, Arthur Thomas (R)
Lento, Thomas Joseph (R)
Leon, John F. (D)
Leonard, Mack (R)
Lerner, Louis A. (D)
Lesseg, Walter August (R)
Lewellen, Homer William (D)
Lewis, John W, Jr. (R)
Libonati, Roland Victor (D)
Lindberg, George W. (R)
Lindenmeyer, Paul Andrew (R)
Lodestro, Richard L. (R)
Londrigan, James T. (D)
Loughran, Francis J. (D)
Loukas, James Peter (D)
Lovell, Paul Dean (D)
Lovitt, Craig Edward (D)
Lucas, Allen Thurman (D)
Lucas, Scott Wike (D)
Lundquist, Clarence Theodore (D)
Lyman, Frank (D)
Lynch, Francis J. (D)
Lyons, Thomas G. (D)
Lyons, William (D)
McAfee, Garland E. (R)
McAvoy, Walter (R)
McBroom, Edward (R)
McCabe, James L. (D)
McCarthy, Robert W. (D)
McClain, Elmo Francis (D)
McClory, Robert (R)
McConnel, A. B.
McCormick, C. L. (R)
McCormick, Hope (R)
McCormick, William E. (D)
McCulloch, Frank W. (D)
McCully, Dean (R)
McDermott, Michael (D)
McDevitt, Bernard (R)
McFetridge, William Lane (D)
McGah, Joseph Patrick (D)
McGaw, Robert Walter (D)
McGloon, Thomas Arthur (D)
McGowan, Edwin A. (R)
McGrew, Finley (R)
McHenry, Donald Franchot
McIver, Edgar Wilson (R)
Mack, Peter Francis, Jr. (D)
McKenney, Harold Charles (D)
McLaren, Richard Wellington (R)
McLaughlin, James Robert (D)
McLendon, James Andrew (D)
McLoskey, Robert T. (R)
McMahon, Joseph Patrick (D)
McPartlin, Robert F. (D)
Madison, Edward P. (R)
Mahoney, Francis Xavier (D)
Majewski, Chester P. (D)
Mann, Robert E. (D)
Maragos, Samuel C. (D)
Marek, Frank A. (R)
Markert, Louis A. (D)
Marks, Robert (D)
Martenson, David Louis (R)
Marti, Douglas (R)
Martin, Louis Emanuel (D)
Martin, Samuel L. (R)
Mattran, Gerald Charles (R)
Mayhall, James Elwin (R)
Maynard, Richard Edwards (D)
Mayo, Robert Porter (R)
Mays, Robert Alan (R)
Mazewski, Aloysius Alex (R)
Mazor, Leon Louis (D)
Meehan, Leo John (D)
Melas, Nicholas J. (D)
Merlo, John (D)
Merritt, Tom (R)
Metcalfe, Ralph Harold (D)
Meyer, Armin Henry
Meyer, J. Theodore (R)
Meyer, John P. (R)
Meyer, John Richard (R)
Michaels, Ernest Edwin (R)
Michel, Robert Henry (R)
Mikva, Abner J. (D)
Miller, Charles Robert (R)
Miller, Kenneth Walton (R)
Miller, Peter J. (R)
Mills, Ellsworth Luther, II (R)
Mills, Miles E. (D)
Minow, Newton Norman (D)
Mitchell, George Trice (R)
Mitchler, Robert W. (R)
Moberley, Kenneth E. (R)
Moculeski, Chester Francis (D)
Moll, Otto Rudolph (R)
Moore, Don A. (R)
Morgan, Lewis V, Jr. (R)
Morris, John K. (D)
Mudge, Dick H, Jr. (D)
Murphy, William J. (R)
Murphy, William T. (D)
Musch, Warren Roy (R)
Nagel, Harold Derrer (R)
Napolitano, Richard A. (D)
Narusis, Bernard V. (R)

Neff, Clarence Everett (R)
Neistein, Bernard S. (D)
Nelson, Herman G. (R)
Nevills, Willie L. (R)
Newberger, Shel (D)
Nichols, Charles E.
Nimrod, John Joseph (R)
Noecker, Mary Lou (D)
Nowlan, James Dunlap (R)
O'Block, Patrick Michael (D)
O'Brien, Donald J. (D)
O'Brien, Dorothy Gertrude (D)
O'Brien, John Fitzgerald (D)
Ogilvie, Richard Buell (R)
O'Keefe, James L. (D)
Olson, Weslie W. (R)
Oshel, Val (R)
Ostendorf, Alvin Fred (R)
Owens, Thomas Jerome (D)
Ozinga, Frank M. (R)
Page, Ray (R)
Paine, Harry Allen (D)
Palmer, Glen Daniel (R)
Pape, Carl E. (R)
Pappas, Pete (R)
Parkhurst, John C. (R)
Parsons, Albert Roy (R)
Partee, Cecil A. (D)
Peak, Audrey R. (R)
Pearre, Jerome (R)
Pearson, Lloyd Edward (R)
Peden, Preston E. (D)
Percy, Charles Harting (R)
Perkins, William H, Jr. (D)
Peskin, Bernard M. (D)
Peters, Everett R. (R)
Peterson, James E. (R)
Pezman, Alfred Leonard (D)
Pfeffer, Leo (D)
Philip, James Peyton, Jr. (R)
Philippi, Craig M. (D)
Phillips, David Julius (D)
Phillips, Paul S. (R)
Pierce, Daniel Marshall (D)
Pierce, William (D)
Piotrowski, Lillian (D)
Podesta, Robert A. (R)
Polhill, Maxine Laughlin (R)
Pollack, William E. (R)
Powell, Paul (D)
Powers, Frank James (D)
Price, Melvin (D)
Pucinski, Roman C. (D)
Pulliam, Donald Woodrow (D)
Pusateri, Lawrence Xavier (R)
Raffl, Kenneth Albert (R)
Railsback, Thomas F. (R)
Rainville, Harold E. (R)
Randolph, Paul J. (R)
Ratcliffe, C. R. (D)
Rauschenberger, John Kenneth (R)
Rayson, Leland Homer (D)
Redmond, William A. (D)
Reese, Daniel Gunder (R)
Regner, David Joseph (R)
Reid, Charlotte T. (R)
Rentschler, William Henry (R)
Reynolds, Warren G. (R)
Rhodes, Ben S. (R)
Rice, Vilas C. (R)
Ridgeway, William Gilbert (R)
Riechmann, Howard Christ (R)
Rini, Dominic William (D)
Roberts, Virgil H. (R)
Robertson, Hayes (R)
Robinson, Donald Louis (D)
Robinson, Sara Katharine Moore (D)
Robinson, William H. (R)
Rodd, Pat (R)
Romano, Sam (D)
Ronan, James A. (D)
Ropa, Matt (D)
Rose, Thomas Chapin (R)
Rosewell, Edward Joseph (D)
Ross, Leonard Walter (D)
Rossi, Italo Amrerico (R)
Rostenkowski, Dan (D)
Rowe, Harris (R)
Ruddy, Clarence John (D)
Ruddy, Machael A. (R)
Rumsfeld, Donald (R)
Russell, Joe W. (D)
Rybacki, Ray J. (D)
Saal, George L. (D)
Sabonjian, Robert V. (R)
Sanders, James Willis (R)
Sandquist, Elroy C. (R)
Saperstein, Esther (D)
Satterthwaite, Cameron B. (D)
Savickas, Frank David (D)
Sawyer, Eugene, Jr. (D)
Scannell, William Francis (R)
Scariano, Anthony (D)
Schackmann, George Severine (D)
Schaw, Walter A. (R)
Schertzer, Silas Dean (R)
Schilke, Donald Lee (R)
Schilson, Donald Lee (D)
Schirger, William Edward (D)
Schisler, D. Gale (D)
Schlafly, Phyllis (R)
Schleicher, Ben T. (R)
Schlickman, Eugene F. (R)
Schmalzl, Kurt Charles (R)
Schneider, Edward (R)
Schoeberlein, Allen L. (R)
Schraeder, Fred Joseph (D)
Schumacher, Leo William (D)
Schwarz, Adolph C. (R)
Scott, J. W. (D)
Scott, William J. (R)
Seaman, Roger George (D)
Sebo, Walter J. (R)
Self, John Spencer (D)
Sexner, Sidney Jay (D)
Shafer, Earl T. (R)
Shapiro, David Charles (R)
Shapiro, Samuel H. (D)
Shaw, Edward J. (D)
Shea, Gerald W. (D)
Sheehan, Timothy P. (R)
Sherer, Albert William, Jr.
Shipley, George Edward (D)
Shippee, Wiley Wright (D)
Shriver, Robert Sargent, Jr. (D)
Shuman, Charles B. (D)
Simmons, Arthur E. (R)
Simon, Paul (D)
Simon, Raymond F. (D)
Simon, Seymour Frank (D)
Sisler, George Frederick (R)
Slade, Arthur Roy, Sr. (D)
Sloan, Paul Crosier (R)
Small, Roy Curtis (D)
Smith, Frank J. (D)
Smith, Fred J. (D)
Smith, Ralph Tyler (R)
Smith, Robert Louis (D)
Smith, Victor L. (R)
Smrcka, Thomas Carol (R)
Sochowski, Clary S. (D)
Soderstrom, Carl W. (R)
Songer, Jack Douglas (R)
Sours, Hudson Ralph (R)
Speckman, Leon George (R)
Sperling, Jack Irving (R)
Sperry, Kenneth C. (R)
Sprague, Arthur W. (R)
Springer, William Lee (R)
Stahl, David Edward (D)
Stastny, George F. (R)
Stearns, Raymond Milton (R)
Stedelin, Harold David (D)
Stern, Harry L. (R)
Stern, Herbert Lyman, Jr. (D)
Stevenson, Adlai Ewing, III (D)
Stewart, William O. (R)
Stiehl, William D. (R)
Stites, Albert Karl (D)
Stolle, Hellmut W. (R)
Stone, Paul (D)
Stone, William Clement (R)
Story, Harry G. (D)
Stowell, Edward Allen (D)
Stratton, William Grant (R)
Strayhorn, Earl Edward (D)
Stremlau, Joseph P. (D)
Stroger, John Herman, Jr. (D)
Stuart, Robert D, Jr. (R)
Supena, Ronald Steve (D)
Svalina, Nick (D)
Swanson, Arthur R. (R)
Swanson, Clarence William (R)
Sweeney, Stewart Gregory (R)
Taylor, Cynthia Gooch (R)
Taylor, Harry Grant (R)
Tecson, Joseph A. (R)
Teefey, Dan (D)
Thiem, Ezra George (R)
Thompson, Tyler (D)
Thompson, Verla Darlene (R)
Thornton, Edmund Braxton (R)
Timmons, Jon Emil (R)
Tipsword, Rolland Fortner (D)
Todd, Carl P. (D)
Toman, Andrew John (D)
Totten, Donald Lee (R)
Touhy, John P. (D)
Traynor, Stuart J. (D)
Tuerk, Fred James (R)
Tumpach, Joseph John (D)
Turner, Wayne (D)
Vacco, Anthony (R)
Van Horn, Lyle Cecil (R)
Van Meter, Craig (D)
Vaughn, Charles R. (R)
Vinovich, Ralph (R)
Vitek, John M. (D)
Vlahos, Robert Peter (D)
Voorhis, Horace Jerry (D)
Vrdolyak, Edward Robert (D)
Wade, Richard Clement (D)
Wagner, Betty Joy (R)
Walker, Claude A. (R)
Walker, Jack E. (R)
Wall, John F. (R)
Wallace, Robert Ash (D)
Walsh, Richard A. (R)
Walsh, Robert V. (D)
Walsh, Thomas Joseph (D)
Walsh, William D. (R)
Waner, John Louis (R)
Warman, Edward Allen (D)
Warren, Harland D. (R)
Washington, Harold (D)
Watson, John Crawford (D)
Watts, Samuel Harvey (D)
Waugh, William Thomas (D)
Weber, Arnold Robert
Wesner, Edwin R. (R)
West, Wilson Henry (R)
Whalen, Peter J. (D)
Wham, James Bundy (R)
White, Clyde Milton (D)
Whitehead, Truman Jack (R)
Whitney, Robert E. (D)
Wigoda, Paul Theodor (D)
Wiktorski, Chester Roman (D)
Wilkins, George T. (D)
Willett, Charles K. (R)
Williams, C. Herschel (D)
Williams, Francis Xeton (D)
Williams, Gale (R)
Williams, George (R)
Williams, Joseph P. (D)
Williams, Lynn Alfred (D)
Williams, Robert Kelsey (D)
Williamson, Jo C. (D)
Wilson, Carroll Dean (D)
Wilson, Henry Hall, Jr. (D)
Wilson, Kenneth E. (D)
Wilson, William Orval (D)
Wilson, William P. (D)
Winstein, Stewart R. (D)
Wise, Henry Seiler (D)
Wittmond, Carl H. (D)
Witwer, Samuel Weiler (R)
Wolbank, Edward W. (D)
Wolf, Frank C. (R)
Wolf, Theresa Catherine (D)
Wolfe, Bernard B. (D)
Wood, Harlington, Jr. (R)
Woodcock, George Washington (R)
Wright, James Lashua (D)
Yates, Sidney R. (D)
Youle, John Clinton (R)
Young, Doreen Dunwoody (R)
Young, Samuel H. (R)
Zadrozny, Mitchell George (R)
Zagone, Nicholas (D)
Zelasko, Antone Richard (R)
Zeman, Robert Thomas (D)
Zeni, Ferdinand J, Jr. (R)
Ziegler, Paul A. (D)
Zlatnik, Michael F. (R)

INDIANA

Abshier, Charles K. (D)
Achor, Helen E. (R)
Adair, E. Ross (R)
Allen, Lloyd M (R)
Allen, Nola Arlene (R)
Allison, David Lord (R)
Anderson, C. Joseph (D)
Anderson, Edwin Dewey, Sr. (R)
Andrew, Jess Charles, Jr. (R)
Angel, Nick (D)
Annakin, V. Dewey (D)
Applegate, A. Earl (D)
Applegate, K. Edwin (D)
Arnold, Margaret E. (D)
Arredondo, Joe (D)
Arterburn, Norman F.
Augsburger, John Frederick (R)
Babincsak, William E. (D)
Bailey, J. J. (D)
Bailey, John W, Jr. (R)
Bainbridge, Eugene Henry (D)
Bales, Robert H. (R)
Bannon, Edmond Joseph (D)
Barbour, Walter Harris (R)
Barker, Austin E. (D)
Barnhart, Hugh Arthur (D)
Barnhorst, Howard Joseph (R)
Barning, Elsie Christene (D)
Barton, John Joseph (D)
Batchelet, Willis K. (R)
Bauer, Burnett Calix (D)
Bauer, Frederick T. (D)
Bayh, Birch (D)
Bays, Kenneth Bruce (R)
Beamer, George N. (D)
Beardsley, Walter Raper (R)
Beasley, Kern Grant (R)
Beatty, James Ward (D)
Beaver, James Raymond (R)
Beers, Orvas E. (R)
Bell, Richard D. (D)
Beneville, Walter John (D)
Benjamin, Adam, Jr. (D)
Berning, William A. (R)
Biddinger, Frank James (R)
Bierly, George Remy (D)
Bixel, C. Ernest (D)
Blachly, Quentin A. (R)
Bloom, Allen (R)
Bodine, Richard Clay (D)
Boehning, Richard Allen (R)
Boisson, Augusta Nellie (D)
Bole, Ruth Marie (D)
Bond, L. Jean (R)
Borst, Lawrence Marion (R)
Bosma, Charles Edward (R)
Bottorff, John David (D)
Bowen, Otis R. (R)
Bowers, F. Wesley (D)
Bracken, Frank Alexander (R)
Brademas, John (D)
Brand, W. Calvert (R)
Branigin, Roger Douglas (D)
Brassie, Ralph A. (R)
Bray, William Gilmer (R)
Bridgewater, William Kenneth (D)
Bridwell, Robert Vern (D)
Brighton, William J. (D)
Briner, Eugene Murray (D)
Broide, Mace Irwin (D)
Brown, H. Ross (D)
Brown, Juanita Maggie Deich (D)
Brown, Robert Henry (D)
Bruggenschmidt, Joseph G. (D)
Bubb, George William (R)
Budge, Reed William (R)
Bulen, Lawrence Keith (R)
Burdick, Mildred Marya (D)
Burrous, Kermit O. (R)
Burton, Danny L. (R)
Burton, Julia Ann (D)
Bushemi, Marion J. (D)
Byram, Stanley Harold (R)
Byron, Philip E. (D)
Cabell, John Allen (D)
Caesar, Victoria (D)
Callaway, Leland (D)
Carithers, William Richmond (R)
Carmichael, Jack Kemper (R)
Carmichael, Oliver Cromwell, Jr. (R)
Chapleau, Louis Carey (D)
Chaney, Buena (R)
Chase, John William (R)
Chavis, Patrick E, Jr. (D)
Christy, William (D)
Clarkson, C. Jack. (R)
Claudon, Roger Keith (R)
Clemens, Arthur J. (D)
Clingan, Lee (D)
Close, Pat M. (D)
Coblentz, Arthur Paul (R)
Cogan, Gene (D)
Colclesser, Galen A. (R)
Coleman, Floyd Butler (R)
Combs, Gertrude Brown (D)
Conn, Harriette Bailey (R)
Coppes, John F. (R)
Creedon, Richard O. (D)
Crook, Thurman Charles (D)
Crowe, Eugene Burgess (D)
Crumpacker, Shepard J. (R)
Daugherty, David Leroy (R)
Davis, Mildred Christina (D)
Dawson, Carlin F. (D)
Dean, Russell J. (D)
Denbo, Seth Thomas (R)
Dennis, David Worth (R)
Denton, Winfield Kirkpatrick (D)
Derge, David Richard (R)
DeWitt, Clifford M. (D)
Dickerson, Thelma Louise (D)
Dickey, Donald Floyd (R)
Dickinson, Valjean L. (D)

Dillon, John J. (D)
Donaldson, John Weber (R)
Dorbecker, Doris L. (R)
Dowling, Edward C. (D)
Downing, William S. (D)
Drake, Ronald L. (D)
Dutton, Judson Dunlap (R)
Duvall, Leslie (R)
Dye, George W. (R)
Edwards, Choice (R)
Eichhorn, Von Arden (D)
Eilert, David DeWitt (D)
Elder, William J. (D)
Ellis, G. Richard (R)
Ellsasser, Edward Charles, Jr. (D)
Elmore, Dorothy (D)
Emshwiller, Thomas C. (D)
Erwin, William Walter (R)
Essex, Thomas L. (D)
Etherton, Trudy Slaby (R)
Fentress, Leo Freedom (D)
Ferguson, Stephen Luther (R)
Fisher, Ethel Virginia (R)
Fisher, George L. (R)
Flora, Helen Elizabeth (D)
Folz, Richard E. (R)
Ford, Robert C. (D)
France, Mark L. (D)
Fraser, Keith (R)
Frazier, William Gould (R)
Frick, John J. (D)
Friedersdorf, Max Lee (R)
Fruits, Katherine (D)
Gallahan, Russell Wayne (D)
Gardiner, Sherry Biggers (R)
Gardner, George Dexter (D)
Garton, Robert Dean (R)
Gates, Robert E. (R)
Gaylord, E. Frances (R)
Gee, Bill F. (R)
Gentry, Herschel A, Sr. (R)
Gerhart, John Donald (D)
Gigerich, William Edward (D)
Gildea, Austin Cornelius (D)
Givan, Richard Martin (R)
Glaescher, Kennith Parker (D)
Gordon, Robert W. (D)
Grandys, Frances T. (D)
Graves, Marguerite Everett (D)
Green, Clinton (D)
Green, Victor (D)
Greeno, Mabel Emerson (D)
Grills, Nelson Grover (D)
Gubbins, Joan Margaret (R)
Guthridge, Esther Blanch (R)
Gutman, Phillip Edward (R)
Haggerty, Judson Francis (D)
Halleck, Charles Abraham (R)
Hamilton, Ernest Roll (D)
Hamilton, Lee Herbert (D)
Harden, Cecil Murray (R)
Harrison, Joseph William (R)
Hart, John C. (R)
Hartig, Judith Martin (R)
Hartke, Vance (D)
Harvey, Ralph (R)
Hasbrook, Thomas Charles (R)
Hatcher, Richard G. (D)
Hathaway, Lois Eileen (D)
Haworth, Roger Lee (R)
Hayes, Arthur C. (R)
Hebble, Harry Harold (D)
Heckard, William Norman (R)
Heeke, Dennis H. (D)
Heine, Ralph Robert (R)
Hendren, William Foster (D)
Hendricks, Charles O. (R)
Henrichs, Ulric H. (R)
Henry, Hermann Russell (D)
Hensler, Charles Morris (R)
Herring, William H. (D)
Hershey, Lewis Blaine
Hertz, Joseph Harold (D)
Hesler, Harry Ray (R)
Heyde, James Wallace (R)
Hibner, Roy Henry (R)
Hill, Jack Howard (D)
Hill, W. W, Jr. (R)
Hillis, Elwood H. (R)
Hobson, Leathel James (R)
Hodson, Gerald K. (R)
Hoehn, Elmer L. (D)
Hoffer, Giles G. (R)
Holder, Elmo (D)
Holstine, Loretta Marguerite (D)
Hosea, Norma Katherine (D)
Howard, Charles Billy (R)
Howat, Carol L. (D)
Huber, August C. (D)
Huett, Orvil E. (D)
Hughes, Wayne (R)

Hummer, Fannie May (D)
Hunnings, R. H. (R)
Hunter, Donald H. (R)
Hunter, James S. (D)
Jackson, Amos Wade (D)
Jackson, Matthew Ernest (D)
Jackson, Nyle Meringo (R)
Jacobs, Andrew, Jr. (D)
James, Edward (D)
Jessup, Roger L. (R)
Johnson, E. Orville (R)
Johnson, Houston K. (D)
Johnston, Harold Ralph (D)
Jones, Gary L. (D)
Jones, Robert W. (D)
Katz, A. Martin (D)
Keaton, Claris Edmond (D)
Keefe, Robert Joseph (D)
Kellam, James Robert (R)
Kelly, Edward Florian (D)
Kennedy, Nelson D. (D)
Kesler, John A. (D)
Kimmell, Curtis Vollmer (D)
Kirtley, James Marion (D)
Kizer, Marshall Force (D)
Kleinkort, Charles B. (R)
Klepper, Carl J. (R)
Klineman, Alan I. (D)
Konrady, Bernard Wendell (D)
Konrady, Emery L. (D)
Koons, James L. (D)
Kramer, Sidney S. (R)
Krampe, Bernard J. (D)
Kruger, John W. (R)
Krupa, John George (D)
Kruse, Dean Verl (R)
Kuykendall, Rufus Calvin (R)
Lake, Martin (R)
Lamb, Jerry Allen (R)
LaMere, Albert J. (D)
Lamkin, Eugene Henry, Jr. (R)
Landgrebe, Earl Frederick (R)
Lange, Walter Henry (D)
Lankford, Thomas J. (R)
Lapar, William Edward (R)
Lash, Carl D. (R)
Latz, William S. (R)
Lauck, Marie Theresa (D)
Lebamoff, Ivan A. (D)
Lemon, Thos. L. (D)
Leopold, William Wolf (R)
Lesniak, Ben, Jr. (D)
Lesniak, Richard John (D)
Lewis, John M. (R)
Lindley, John William (R)
Lipp, John L. (D)
Lloyd, Daisy Riley (D)
Logan, Cecilia M. (D)
Loughlin, John Joseph (D)
Louie, Willard (D)
Lugar, Richard Green (R)
Lundquist, Eldon F. (R)
McCauley, Philip W. (R)
McComb, Thomas V. (R)
McCord, Eugene Warren (D)
McCormick, Keith C. (R)
McDaniel, Marlin K. (R)
McDermott, Russell William (R)
MacDonald, Elmer (R)
McFall, David Merrill (D)
McGinley, Paul Martin (D)
McGowan, Joseph E. (D)
McKinney, Frank Edward (D)
McKinney, Robert Hurley (D)
Madden, Ray J. (D)
Maddox, Charles M. (R)
Mahowald, Robert E. (D)
Maloney, Anna (D)
Mason, Maurice (D)
Mauzy, Thames L. (R)
Meadors, Albert Murril (R)
Merrill, D. Bailey (R)
Mertz, J. Harold (R)
Mettler, Joe H. (D)
Metzger, David F. (D)
Meyer, William (D)
Miers, Morgan L. (D)
Miles, Hugh E. (D)
Miller, Frances Miron (D)
Miller, John William (R)
Million, Clarence H. (D)
Mills, Morris Hadley (R)
Mishler, Everett Monroe (D)
Moriarty, Daniel Patrick (D)
Morin, Thomas Lee (R)
Moynahan, Thomas Alvin (D)
Mullendore, Herbert Jack (R)
Murakowski, Arthur R. (D)
Murphy, Thomas J. (D)
Mutz, John M. (R)
Myers, John T. (R)

Myers, Rufus H, Jr. (D)
Myers, Walter, Jr. (D)
Neaderhiser, Jack I. (D)
Neff, John F. (D)
New, Jack L. (D)
Newlin, Wilbur E. (R)
Nicholson, Carl Joseph (R)
Noble, Freda Golden (D)
Northrup, Arthur Harry (R)
Norton, William J. (D)
O'Bannon, Robert P. (D)
Onion, Cecil R. (D)
Opperman, Leonard (D)
Orr, Robert Dunkerson (R)
Paarlberg, Don (R)
Palmer, Willard Vincent (D)
Pearson, Jimmy Ray (D)
Pedigo, Kenneth Ray (D)
Pers, John F. (D)
Peterson, Robert E. (D)
Phillips, Orville (D)
Pickett, Robert McQuillious (R)
Piper, Rodney E. (D)
Plaskett, James M. (D)
Plimpton, Theodore Ferry (R)
Poor, Robert Lawrence (R)
Price, John Richard (R)
Prickett, Richard C. (R)
Provost, Perley Herbert, Jr. (R)
Pruitt, Leslie O. (D)
Pryor, W. Irvin (R)
Rahe, Arme Na (D)
Rainbolt, Audie W. (D)
Ramsey, Harvey Kenneth (R)
Raskosky, Edward J. (D)
Rea, Samuel A. (R)
Redmon, Helen Carver (D)
Regnier, Richard Olin (R)
Rice, Charles E.
Rickard, Robert Lee, Jr. (R)
Rickets, J. Ben (D)
Ricketts, Marvel (D)
Riggin, Richard E. (R)
Robbins, Jesse (R)
Rock, Robert Lee (D)
Rogers, David (D)
Rogers, Michael K. (R)
Roland, Paul Gerald (D)
Roorda, Walter John (R)
Roudebush, Richard L. (R)
Roush, J. Edward (D)
Rubin, George Allen (R)
Ruby, John Allen (D)
Ruckelshaus, William Doyle (R)
Ryan, John M. (R)
Rybolt, Gerald W. (R)
Sabatini, Frederick Anthony (R)
St. Angelo, Gordon (D)
Salin, William N. (R)
Scheidt, Virgil D. (R)
Schenk, Charles H. (D)
Schmutzler, Emil Hermann, Jr. (R)
Sebree, William T. (D)
Sendak, Theodore Lorraine (R)
Seybert, Myron Silver (R)
Shank, Richard Eugene (R)
Shea, John A. (D)
Shuee, Charles Edward (D)
Sidle, Charles Lloyd (D)
Simcox, Edwin Jesse (R)
Sines, Thelma L. (D)
Sinks, John R. (R)
Sleet, Thomas Preston (D)
Slenker, Glenn R. (R)
Smith, Dale Augustus (R)
Smith, Robert Leonard (D)
Smith, Roger Hollingshead (R)
Smitherman, Jack N. (R)
Snowden, Gene E. (R)
Snyder, William V. (D)
Sorensen, Philip Chaikin (D)
Spanagel, Harry Borman (D)
Speckner, Robert F. (D)
Stanish, Paul Joseph (D)
Staton, Robert Howard (D)
Steed, Carl (D)
Steers, Edwin Kemp
Stephenson, George Edward (D)
Stewart, Flossie Kledith (D)
Stewart, Harold W. (D)
Stewart, Robert Wendell (D)
Stinson, Dean King (R)
Stoner, Richard Burkett (D)
Striker, Mabel D. (D)
Strong, Jeanette B. (D)
Sullivan, Olyer U. (R)
Summers, Frank Leston (D)
Sweezy, John W. (R)
Swisher, Paul W. (R)
Taylor, George B. (D)
Taylor, William H. (D)

Terhorst, Frieda Catherine (D)
Thimlar, J. Riley (D)
Thomas, John J. (R)
Thomas,Joseph N. (R)
Thompson, Richard Keith (R)
Tolen, George Roy (D)
Toon, Thomas P. (D)
Townsend, Mary E. (D)
Townsend, W. Wayne (D)
Treber, Richard E. (D)
Tremper, William David, Jr. (D)
Tucker, Carolyn Costin (R)
Tucker, Ralph (D)
Ulrich, Wilfrid J. (D)
Voss, Willard New (D)
Walker, Alan Lee (D)
Walker, Anna Mae (D)
Walker, William Henry (D)
Wall, James L. (D)
Wallace, Geraldine Elizabeth (D)
Wallace, Joseph Clark (D)
Wallace, Lisle L. (R)
Walsh, John Richard (D)
Walton, Charles A. (D)
Waltz, Ralph H. (R)
Watson, Melville E. (D)
Weaver, John William (R)
Wells, Richard Dale (R)
Welsh, Matthew Empson (D)
Weninger, Howard L. (D)
Wheeler, Louise C. (D)
Whitcomb, Edgar Doud (R)
White, Luke (D)
Whitehead, Robert S. (D)
Williams, Alexander Samuel, III (D)
Williams, Leroy, Jr. (D)
Wilson, Earl (R)
Wilson, William E. (D)
Winebrenner, Tommy Lee (R)
Wise, Charles Davidson (R)
Wolf, Charles William (D)
Wolf, Katie Louise (D)
Wolf, William Henry (D)
Wright, Oren Alvin (R)
Yeagley, Donald Rae (D)
Yergin, Alan Eugene (D)
Zazas, Sylvia (D)
Zion, Roger H. (R)

IOWA

Allen, Sewell Ellyson (D)
Andersen, Leonard Christian (R)
Anderson, Quentin V. (D)
Anderson, Ralph Wilbur (R)
Arbuckle, Richard Dean (R)
Bailey, Ray V. (D)
Baker, Donald E. (D)
Balloun, Charles F. (R)
Bandstra, Bert Andrew (D)
Baringer, Maurice E. (R)
Barry, Martin Joseph (D)
Battles, Lynn F, Sr. (R)
Beardsley, Harry Winfred (D)
Bedell, George Noble (D)
Beecher, Robert J. (D)
Beeson, Anna Mae (D)
Benda, Kenneth John (R)
Beneke, Donald G. (R)
Bennett, Vernon Nile (D)
Benoit, John Koll, Sr. (D)
Bergman, Irvin Lester (R)
Biermann, Fred (D)
Birkenholz, Carroll Merle (R)
Bleakly, John L. (D)
Blouin, Michael Thomas (D)
Bogenrief, Mattie B. (D)
Boot, Armour (D)
Bosch, Robert D. (R)
Bowin, Donald Albert (R)
Breitbach, Alfred P, Sr. (D)
Bremmer, Edward (D)
Briles, James E. (R)
Brinck, Adrian (D)
Brock, R. Buckman (R)
Bromwell, James Edward (R)
Brown, Joe Raymond (D)
Browne, Stanley Robert Rieve (R)
Buren, John Leonard (D)
Burke, James W. (D)
Burke, Vincent S. (D)
Burns, Robert John (D)
Burrows, John (R)
Busch, Henry W. (R)
Busing, Edward E. (D)
Butler, Elliott Arthur (R)
Caffrey, James Terence (D)
Cameron, Gary L. (D)
Campbell, Herbert Lawrence (R)

Carlson, Elmer Gustav (D)
Carnahan, Cleve L. (D)
Carr, E. Michael (D)
Case, Robert Elroy (R)
Cassidy, Joseph W. (D)
Cavanaugh, James H. (R)
Charlton, Wm. Stuart (R)
Christensen, Perry Lee (R)
Christenson, Ronald Sidney (D)
Christianson, Gale Edward (D)
Clampitt, Bruce Willard (R)
Clapsaddle, R. J. (D)
Clark, Richard Clarence (D)
Clarke, Hugh Hauser (R)
Clinton, Ellaree Avant (D)
Cochran, Dale M. (D)
Coffman, William J. (R)
Cohen, Gertrude S. (D)
Coleman, C. Joseph (D)
Coles, Frank Van de Ven (R)
Condon, Gene F. (D)
Conklin, Willa Charlene (R)
Conmey, Larry J. (D)
Conway, Walter I. (D)
Cooley, Lewis Wallace (R)
Coons, Marion M. (R)
Corey, Dean Orville (R)
Cox, Dean F. (D)
Craig, Paul E. (D)
Crosier, Dale Theron (D)
Crotty, J. Desmond (D)
Culver, John Chester (D)
Cunningham, Ray Crews (R)
Curran, Leigh Raymond (R)
Dawson, Tom Henry (D)
Day, Jacqueline (R)
Debbins, William (R)
DeHart, Pearle Porter (R)
De Koster, Lucas James (R)
Den Herder, Elmer Hans (R)
Denman, William F. (D)
Detje, Albert H. (D)
Dickinson, Clyde Earl (D)
Dircks, Durwood William (R)
Distelhorst, Milton (D)
Doderer, Minnette Frerichs (D)
Dodds, Robert R. (D)
Dolliver, James I. (R)
Donielson, Allen Lee (R)
Dorrington, George Jordan (D)
Dougherty, Tom (D)
Doyle, Donald Vincent (D)
Drake, Richard Francis (R)
Drew, Raymond Patrick (D)
Driscoll, Kathleen Virginia (D)
Duffy, John L. (D)
Dunton, Keith H. (D)
Edgington, Floyd P, Sr. (R)
Edwards, Lee Mark (R)
Elliott, Jack Mark (R)
Ellis, Verna Jeanne (R)
Ellsworth, Barbara Lange (R)
Elvers, Adolph Walter (D)
Ely, John M. (D)
Emerson, Rollo E. (R)
Engebretson, Gary Duane (R)
Erbe, Norman Arthur (R)
Evans, Howard David (D)
Faber, Herman E. (R)
Fair, Fay E. (D)
Felger, Foster F. (D)
Fischer, Harold O. (R)
Fisher, C. Raymond (R)
Flatt, Joseph B. (R)
Fleming, Richard Leo (D)
Floy, Delbert William (D)
Fosness, Irene (D)
Foster, LaMar, Sr. (D)
Franzenburg, Paul (D)
Freeman, Dennis L. (R)
Frey, Tom J. (R)
Frommelt, Andrew G. (D)
Fullerton, Bert (R)
Fullmer, Wayne J. (D)
Fulton, Robert D. (D)
Galetich, Louis Robert (D)
Gallagher, James V. (D)
Gannon, William J. (D)
Garfield, John Clement (D)
Garfield, Theodore Greenlief (R)
Garrett, Loyal Clayton (D)
Gaudineer, Lee H. (D)
Gaul, Dewie J. (D)
Getscher, Edwin Clarke (R)
Gibson, Ben J, Jr. (R)
Gilchrist, Lawrence Barnt (R)
Gillette, Guy Mark (D)
Gillette, Roy Robert (D)
Gillette, W. R. (D)
Gittins, Harry Raymond (R)
Glanton, Willie Stevenson (D)
Gleason, Theodore Michael (D)
Glenn, Gene W. (D)
Gluba, William Evan (D)
Goeken, Robert Lee (D)
Goodwin, Robert Kingman (R)
Graham, J. Wesley (R)
Grassley, Charles E. (R)
Green, Dorothea Marie (D)
Greene, Roy Louis (D)
Greenleaf, Hale Carr, Jr. (R)
Gregerson, Mary Pat (D)
Greigg, Stanley L. (D)
Griffin, Charles F. (R)
Gross, H. R. (R)
Gunderson, Deane Charles (R)
Gwynne, John Williams (R)
Hagedorn, Merle W. (D)
Hamilton, Howard A. (R)
Hammer, Walter Benjamin (R)
Hansen, John Robert (D)
Hanson, Fred Byron (R)
Hanson, Harley Sven (D)
Hanson, Joseph Lyle (R)
Harbor, William H. (R)
Harrison, Dwight Allen (R)
Hayes, Ernest A. (R)
Heaberlin, Stanley M. (D)
Healey, Marie (D)
Hedberg, Arthur Carl, Jr. (D)
Hendricks, Lewis S. (R)
Heying, Hilarius L. (D)
Hickenlooper, Bourke Blakemore (R)
Hicklin, Edwin Anderson (R)
Hill, Eugene Marshall (D)
Hill, William (R)
Hoeven, Charles Bernard (R)
Hogben, Anne (D)
Holden, Edgar H. (R)
Holmes, David H. (R)
Holmes, John A. (D)
Hougen, Chester Orlan (R)
Houston, Harold J. (D)
Hudson, James Weissinger (R)
Huff, William Henry, III (R)
Hughes, Harold Everett (D)
Hughes, Phyllis Josephine (D)
Hullinger, Arlo (D)
Humpleby, Twyla Jean (R)
Hutchins, Charles Eugene (D)
Hutchison, Ervin A. (R)
Hutte, Robert Emmett (D)
Irey, Don F. (D)
Jackson, James H. (D)
Jackson, Lloyd G. (D)
Jackson, Stephen Bernard (D)
Jayne, Edward James (R)
Jebens, John Herman (R)
Jensen, Ben Franklin (R)
Jensen, Donald Hugo (D)
Jepson, Roger W. (R)
Jesse, Norman Gale (D)
Johnson, Harvey William (R)
Johnson, Robert M. L. (R)
Johnson, Thatcher (R)
Johnston, Dan L. (D)
Johnston, Elton Andrew (R)
Jones, Joseph Hillis (R)
Jordan, Clifford Homer (R)
Kampen, Paul D. (D)
Kastrup, Harry Frederick (D)
Keele, Harold O. (D)
Kehe, Luvern William (R)
Keister, Roberta Elaine (D)
Keith, Wayne (R)
Keleher, Leo D. (D)
Kelly, Alberta Metcalf (D)
Kempter, Paul E. (D)
Kennedy, Gene V. (D)
Kennedy, Keith K. (D)
Kennedy, Michael Kelly (D)
Kenyon, Arnold Oakley (R)
Kibbie, John P. (D)
Kibbie, Richard Patrick (D)
Kiilsholm, Karl Erik (R)
Kitner, Arthur J. (R)
Klefstad, Gilbert E. (D)
Klein, James Tackett (R)
Klink, Leslie C. (R)
Kluever, Lester Luverne (R)
Knight, Harold LaVerne (R)
Koch, Edgar Jurgen (R)
Korn, Charles A. (D)
Kosek, Ernest (R)
Kreamer, Robert McDonald (R)
Kruck, Warren J. (D)
Kyhl, Vernon H. (R)
Kyl, John H. (R)
Lamborn, Clifton C. (R)
Lange, Elmer F. (R)
Langland, Walter V. (R)
Laverty, Irene C. (R)
Lawlor, Daniel F. (D)
Lawson, Murray Carter (R)
LeCompte, Karl Miles (R)
Lee, Richard Ernest (R)
Levy, Gerald (D)
Lias, Thomas Lee (R)
Lippold, Donald L. (R)
Lipsky, Joan (R)
Lisle, Vern (R)
Lodwick, Seeley G. (R)
Logemann, Kenneth Lavern (R)
Lomas, Anna Cochrane (R)
Loveless, Herschel Cellel (D)
Lowe, Ralph George (D)
Lucken, John Henry (R)
Lynch, James L. (D)
McCartney, Ralph F. (R)
McCauley, Michael Sylvester (D)
McCluhan, Neil R. (D)
McCormick, Harold Charles (D)
McCreedy, Harry Duane (R)
McCullough, Robert Earl (D)
McDonald, John Cecil (R)
McGill, Donald S. (D)
McIntyre, Scott, Jr. (R)
McManus, Edward Joseph (D)
McNally, James M. (D)
McNamara, Walter Lynn (D)
Madden, Harry C. (D)
Mahan, Bruce E. (D)
Mahon, Donald Duphorne (R)
Main, Franklin Smith (D)
Maley, Walter F. (D)
Maloney, James E. (D)
Markman, Sherwin J. (D)
Martinek, Viola E. (D)
Mathis, Ralph C.
Maule, Elroy (D)
Mayberry, D. Vincent (D)
Mayne, Wiley (R)
Meacham, Al (D)
Meeker, Frederick Edward (D)
Melrose, A. Rae (D)
Mendenhall, John Cecil (R)
Menefee, Maynard Turner (R)
Mensing, A. L. (R)
Messerly, Francis L. (R)
Mezvinsky, Edward M. (D)
Middleswart, James Ira (D)
Millen, Floyd H. (R)
Miller, Charles P. (D)
Miller, Elizabeth Ruby (R)
Miller, Jack Richard (R)
Miller, John S. (D)
Miller, Leroy S. (R)
Miller, Roy A. (R)
Mills, Max Milo (R)
Mincks, Jacob Benjamin (D)
Minglin, Harry J. (R)
Mitchell, Donald J. (D)
Mitchell, Loren H. (D)
Moffitt, Delmont Theodore (R)
Mogged, Charles George (R)
Mohling, Carl Louis (D)
Mohrfeld, Fred (R)
Monaghan, John Bernard (D)
Mondt, Loren Edward (D)
Moore, Fred H. (D)
Moore, Kenneth Merrill (D)
Moore, Lester Leland (D)
Mooty, William Lewis (R)
Morgan, Eldon M. (D)
Mowry, John L. (R)
Moyer, Ruth Eloise (D)
Mueller, Harold F. (D)
Mulgrew, Thomas James (D)
Murray, Donald William (D)
Murray, John J. (D)
Naden, Robert William (R)
Nagle, Daniel Lee (D)
Neely, Marion Robert (R)
Neu, Arthur Alan (R)
Newsom, George Edward (R)
Newton, Robert Edward (D)
Nicholson, Edward Eaton (R)
Nielsen, Alfred (R)
Nielsen, Niels J. (D)
Nims, Daryl Hallett (D)
Noah, Keith S. (R)
Nolting, Fred Wayne (D)
Norris, Paul Gifford, Jr. (R)
Nurse, H. Kenneth (D)
Obermiller, Edward (D)
O'Brien, Donald Eugene (D)
O'Brien, Miles S. (D)
O'Brien, Myrtle A. (D)
Oehlsen, Robert W. (D)
O'Hearn, Trave E. (R)
O'Malley, Bernard John (D)
O'Malley, George E. (D)
Ossian, Conrad (R)
Owen, Kenneth E. (D)
Oxley, Myron B. (D)
Palmer, William Darrell (D)
Pardun, Patricia Jane (R)
Parsons, John Welsey (R)
Patton, James E. (R)
Patton, John W. (D)
Pavich, Emil Sam (D)
Pease, Roger De Vere (R)
Pelton, Charles Howard (R)
Pelzer, Max O. (R)
Perkins, Larry Lee (R)
Peters, Jacob John (D)
Pillers, George Wylie, Jr. (R)
Pinegar, Richard Lee (D)
Platt, Joe-Ann Elizabeth (R)
Potgeter, James Alvin (R)
Potter, Ralph Wilson (R)
Prichard, James McMurtry (R)
Prichard, Robert Daniel (R)
Quinn, James L. (D)
Quirk, Charles Evans (D)
Radl, Richard Martin (D)
Rasmussen, Clark R. (D)
Rathje, Victor Dean (R)
Rauch, Joseph Ralph (D)
Rawlings, Maurice Edward (D)
Ray, Robert D. (R)
Redeker, Stanley Frederick (R)
Redfern, Carroll Irwin (D)
Redman, Richard Elson (R)
Reed, Cecil Arvell (R)
Reed, Glenn T. (D)
Reed, Lois Swallow (R)
Rehder, Merlyn Albert (R)
Reichardt, William J. (D)
Renda, Thomas Anthony (D)
Reno, Max E. (D)
Reppert, Howard C, Jr.
Resnick, James D. (D)
Rex, Clyde (R)
Richards, Elizabeth Miller (D)
Rickert, Dale H. (D)
Rider, Robert E, Sr. (D)
Riehm, Curtis Godfrey (R)
Rigler, Robert Raymond (R)
Riley, Tom Joseph (R)
Roach, Richard Howard (R)
Robinson, Enid (R)
Robinson, Kenneth (D)
Roe, Thomas S. (D)
Roorda, Norman Paul (R)
Runkle, Jerry Chloyd (R)
Ruther, William Richard (R)
Scalise, Lawrence F. (D)
Scherle, William J. (R)
Schimmel, Allan D. (R)
Schmarje, Clarence F. (R)
Schmidhauser, John Richard (D)
Schnepp, Pauline Helen (R)
Schroeder, Jack (R)
Schroeder, Laverne W. (R)
Schuler, Louis Eugene (R)
Schwengel, Fred (R)
Schwieger, Yvonne Ocea (R)
Scott, Burl E. (D)
Shaff, David O. (R)
Shannahan, John (D)
Shaw, Elizabeth Orr (R)
Shirley, Edwin Alan (D)
Shirley, Marvin Scott (D)
Shoeman, John D. (R)
Simpson, Stanley R. (R)
Sloan, Chester Wesley (R)
Sloan, Donald Richard (R)
Smart, William Howard (R)
Smith, Marvin W. (R)
Smith, Mary Louise (R)
Smith, Neal (D)
Smith, Robert Harold (D)
Smith, William R. (D)
Sorg, Nathan F. (R)
Stanley, David (R)
Steffen, Vincent B. (D)
Stegemann, John Dietrich (D)
Steiff, Irma S. (D)
Steiff, Paul Walter (D)
Stephens, Richard L. (R)
Stevenson, M. Ross (D)
Stewart, David Wallace (R)
Stieneke, Donald Junior (D)
Stokes, A. Gordon (R)
Story, Melvin Emmett (R)
Story, Steve Bixler (D)
Strand, Clair (R)
Straub, Joseph J. (D)
Stroburg, Eldon Leonard (D)
Stromer, Delwyn Dean (R)
Strothman, Charles F. (R)
Stuart, William Corwin (R)

Sueppel, William Francis (D)
Sulhoff, Paul H. (R)
Swanson, Charles Edward (R)
Swanson, R. John (R)
Synhorst, Melvin D. (R)
Tapscott, John (D)
Taylor, Dennis Delton (R)
Taylor, John Earl (D)
Thompson, George King (R)
Thompson, John Colby (R)
Thompson, Pahl E. (R)
Thummel, Glenn Frank (R)
Tieden, Dale L. (R)
Tilton, John J. (R)
Tone, Susan Brown (R)
Turner, Lloyd L. (Non-Partisan)
Turner, Richard C. (R)
Uban, Charles J. (D)
Urban, Thomas Nelson, Jr. (D)
Vance, Clifford M. (R)
Vanderpool, William S, Jr. (R)
Van Drie, Rudy Arie (R)
Van Eschen, John Edward (D)
Van Gilst, Bass (D)
Van Ginkel, James (R)
Van Horn, Delmar (R)
Van Nostrand, Maurice A. (R)
Van Roekel, Gerrit (R)
Varley, Andrew Preston (R)
Varney, Charles (D)
Vidal, Dagmar Lund (D)
Voelker, Roy E. (R)
Voorhees, Donald Edwin (R)
Walker, John A. (R)
Wallace, Glenn Charles (R)
Wallace, Robert Lewis (R)
Walling, Barbara Eckhoff (R)
Walters, John Baily (R)
Warren, John E. (R)
Watts, Lee R. (R)
Watson, Jack W. (R)
Wearin, Otha Donner (D)
Weaver, Wood W. (R)
Weichman, David Edward (R)
Wells, James Dale (D)
Wengert, James John (D)
Wentzien, Irwin H. (R)
West, James Clifford (R)
Wheeler, Gale Eldon (D)
Whisler, Ross S. (D)
Whitney, Charles Thomas J. (D)
Wiley, Charles Victor (D)
Wimberly, Helen Dameron (D)
Winkelman, William Pratt (R)
Wittenmeyer, Charles E. (R)
Wolcott, Olga Doran (D)
Wolfe, Richard B. (R)
Wollenhaupt, Ralph Eugene (R)
Wood, Charles Ross (R)
Wood, Warren Kirchner (R)
Worthington, Lorne R. (D)
Wright, Carroll (D)
Yoder, Earl M. (R)

KANSAS

Abbey, Clifford Elza (D)
Adams, Clyde Benton (D)
Addington, Donna Lorene (R)
Allen, Mary Elizabeth (D)
Amis, George Clayton (D)
Anderson, John, Jr. (R)
Anderson, Kenneth Theodore (D)
Anderson, Myrta Jane (D)
Andrews, Mary Eloise Okeson (D)
Andrews, Robert Leon (D)
Angell, Wayne D. (R)
Arnold, Robert Almerine (D)
Arthur, Charles Shirk, Jr. (R)
Arvin, Lester Cave (R)
Avery, William Henry (R)
Aylward, Paul L. (D)
Bachman, G. Craig (R)
Baden, Jo Ann (D)
Bales, Polly Roth (R)
Ball, Steadman (R)
Barnes, Betty Lou (D)
Barnhill, Earl Stanton (D)
Barr, H. J, II (R)
Basgall, Wendelin E. (D)
Bell, Donald Alfred (R)
Bell, L. Claude (R)
Bennett, Mark Lyle, Sr. (R)
Bennett, Robert Frederick (R)
Beougher, Ethel M. (D)
Beymer, James Elton (R)
Blancett, Thomas Joseph (R)
Blangers, Nell Elizabeth (D)
Bogart, Mary Constance (D)
Bogart, Vincent L. (D)
Bower, John David (R)
Boyd, McDill (R)
Breeding, J. Floyd (D)
Breyfogle, John William, Jr. (R)
Bridges, Duane N. (R)
Brock, Robert Lee (D)
Brown, Clarence Ebbert (D)
Brown, Harlow Billings (D)
Browne, James Harold (R)
Browne, Ruth T. (D)
Brueck, Karl Arthur (D)
Brungardt, Kenneth Florian (D)
Bryan, Grover L. (D)
Bubb, Henry Agnew (R)
Buchele, James Paul, Jr. (D)
Bunten, William Wallace (R)
Bunyan, William Price, III (R)
Burke, M. M. (R)
Burkhart, Jean M. (D)
Burkman, Carol Lynn (R)
Carlson, Frank (R)
Carlson, Raymond Franklin (R)
Carpenter, M. John (D)
Carroll, Jane Irene (D)
Chartier, Glenn Dell (D)
Chase, DeWayne Arthur Newton (R)
Chase, Harold H. (R)
Christy, Donald (R)
Coldsnow, Robert A. (R)
Cole, Orville John (R)
Concannon, Donald O. (R)
Cordel, Lawrence A. (D)
Cooper, Clint Marvin (D)
Cox, Gladys (R)
Crabb, Delbert Elmo (R)
Cram, Ole Robert (R)
Creighton, Robert A. (R)
Crist, Harold Howard (R)
Crutcher, John William (R)
Dade, Gladys Mae (R)
Daily, Frank Edward, Jr. (R)
Darby, Harry (R)
Davis, James Parker (D)
Davis, William Ackelson (D)
De Coursey, James H, Jr. (D)
Docking, George Richard (D)
Docking, Marshall (R)
Docking, Robert Blackwell (D)
Docking, Virginia (D)
Doerschlag, Walter A, Jr. (D)
Dole, Robert J. (R)
Dotson, William Francis (D)
Dowell, Richard A. (D)
Dreiling, Norbert R. (D)
Driscoll, Richard Michael (D)
Dunlap, Fred Everett (R)
Dunn, Harry H. (R)
Durfee, Charles Herman (R)
Dwyer, Ronald F. (D)
Edwards, Ellsworth James (R)
Elliott, Wilfred Marion (D)
Ellsworth, Robert F. (R)
Enoch, Donald K. (R)
Euler, Jack Richard (R)
Everett, Donn James (R)
Fatzer, Harold R. (R)
Fletcher, Kathleen (R)
Foster, Ben (R)
Fowler, Raymond William (D)
Francisco, James Lee (D)
French, Jim (R)
Frieden, Erma Rose (D)
Fritz, George H. (R)
Frizzell, Kent (R)
Frost, Jack Wesley (R)
Gaar, Norman Edward (R)
Gabriel, Arthur Wilfred (R)
Gastl, Eugene Francis (D)
George, Newell A. (D)
Golden, John Hollister (R)
Graber, Ben J. (D)
Graber, Walter W. (D)
Graham, Betty June (D)
Grant, Ervin Eugene (R)
Graves, James Thomas (R)
Gray, Oren Lee (R)
Gregg, Marie Ellen (R)
Greiner, Keith Allen (R)
Griffith, Jerry L. (D)
Groesbeck, Arthur Jerome, III (R)
Hall, William Keeny (R)
Hannen, Margaret E. (D)
Hanson, Warren Eugene (R)
Harder, Joseph C. (R)
Harder, Robert Clarence (D)
Harman, Rick (R)
Harrison, Lillian Luella (R)
Hawes, Aaron Edward (D)
Hawes, Bryan (D)
Hayes, John Francis (R)
Healy, H. E. Pat (R)
Hedrick, Clay E. (R)
Heft, Doyle J. (D)
Heide, Walter John (R)
Heimke, Karl Frederic (R)
Heinemann, David John (R)
Hellman, Otis (D)
Henderson, Opal Mae (D)
Henry, Ailee M. (R)
Herrman, Gregory Joseph (D)
Hill, Clyde (R)
Hodge, Frank S. (R)
Hoffman, Judith Linda (D)
Holmes, Laurence Street (D)
Hope, Clifford Ragsdale (R)
Hope, Clifford Ragsdale, Jr. (R)
Hornbaker, Lee Vaughn (D)
Hougland, Gerald Lee (R)
Howard, Kenith Raymond, Jr. (R)
Hoy, Rex Bruce (R)
Hughes, Eva Frances (R)
Hughes, Oliver H. (R)
Humphreys, Frederick M. (R)
Jackson, Samuel Charles (R)
Jacobs, Francis (R)
Jambor, Louise Irma (R)
Janssen, Jack Wesley (D)
Jelinek, George Joseph (D)
Jennison, Harold Stewart (R)
Josserand, Robert Warren (R)
Joyce, Robert H. (D)
Keenan, Robert P. (D)
Kellner, Dorothy Dell (D)
Kessinger, Edward L. (R)
Kidwell, Thomas McKinley (D)
King, Clarence Leroy, Jr. (D)
King, J. D. (R)
Kirk, Polly (R)
Kisner, Ignatius (D)
Klein, Dorothea Elizabeth (D)
Kroeger, Nadine Clara (D)
Krouse, Morris J. (D)
Krueger, Yvonne (R)
Landon, Alfred M. (R)
Lang, John Ernest (D)
Light, William Jasper (D)
Linde, Frederick Adolphus (R)
Littler, Richard L. (R)
Londerholm, Robert Carl (R)
Long, William C, Jr. (R)
Loux, Richard Charles (D)
Love, Clarence Chester (D)
Lueck, Henry Longley (D)
Luke, Clarence D. (D)
Lutz, Harry Francis (R)
Maag, James S. (R)
McClinton, Curtis Realious (D)
McCray, Billy Quincy (D)
McDowell, Joseph Hampton (D)
McGill, Duane S. (R)
McMillin, M. June (D)
Madden, Robert Bruce (D)
Matlack, Don (D)
Meckel, Vivian Miller (R)
Meek, Fred (R)
Meeker, George Wilber (D)
Meeks, Cordell David (D)
Merritt, Gilbert Roy (R). See Addenda
Metz, Daniel Dodds (R)
Miller, Dorothy Jenilee (D)
Mills, Govan (D)
Mize, Chester L. (R)
Moore, Warner (D)
Murray, John Hiram (R)
Myers, Jan (D)
Myers, Wade Alexander (D)
Nettels, George E, Jr. (R)
Newton, Betty Mae (R)
Niles, Irving Russell (D)
Nitsch, John Christian (R)
Noah, Donald Witherell (R)
Noel, James Ellsworth (R)
Nothern, Austin (R)
Nunn, Myrta Mae (D)
Ochs, Tillman Paul (R)
O'Connor, Earl E. (R)
Olander, Gene M. (R)
Otstott, Jesse Lee (D)
Owen, David Carroll (R)
Parker, Letha Mary (R)
Parrish, Robert Ambrose (R)
Patton, James William (R)
Pearson, James Blackwood (R)
Peery, Walter H. (R)
Pfalzgraf, Harold Archer (R)
Pivonka, Charles August (D)
Poizner, Joseph Jacob (D)
Pomeroy, Elwaine Franklin (R)
Porter, Louise M. (R)
Price, Neil Lawson (R)
Prochazka, Joe W. (D)
Ratner, Payne H, Jr. (R)
Reed, Ottwa Luther (D)
Reilly, Edward Francis, Jr. (R)
Rice, Carl Venton (D)
Roberts, Fay Edwin (D)
Roberts, Leona Grace (D)
Roberts, William Logan (D)
Robinson, Jack W. (R)
Robinson, William Ingraham (D)
Rogers, Gerald (R)
Rohmiller, Harold C. (D)
Roniger, Pascal Allen (R)
Rose, Jo Ann (D)
Rosen, Lester L. (R)
Rosenau, Fred W. (D)
Rosenbaum, Walter Elijah (D)
Roulier, Leon (D)
Rudicel, Chandler Clifton (D)
Saia, David Joseph 'Joe' (D)
Saffels, Winona R. (D)
Sanders, Robert R. (R)
Sargent, Stan (R)
Scanlon, Terence J. (D)
Scherff, Judith Sue (R)
Schnittker, John Alvin (D)
Schraeder, Vernon Virgil (D)
Schroeder, Alfred Gustav (R)
Schurter, Marion Eveline (R)
Schwab, Merle Edwin (R)
Schwinn, Tom Lomax (R)
Scott, Beatrice Normadine (R)
Sears, Fred N. (D)
Sebelius, Keith George (R)
Semple, Florence Emma (R)
Shanahan, Elwill M. (R)
Shank, Mary Ellen (D)
Shankel, Buford L. (D)
Shrewder, Roy Valentine (R)
Shriver, Garner E. (R)
Shunn, Maxine Faye (D)
Skubitz, Joe (R)
Sloan, James Wendell (D)
Slocombe, Lawrence Davis (R)
Smith, Eugene Linn (R)
Smith, Glee Sidney, Jr. (R)
Sparks, Billy Schley (D)
Spears, LaVerne H. (R)
Spotts, Oscar Donald (R)
Stadler, Robert Fry (R)
Steineger, John Francis, Jr. (D)
Stockebrand, Maynard Leon (R)
Stone, Gordon Earl (R)
Storey, Bob Wilson (R)
Strahan, Ernest Wesley (R)
Stremel, Nick A. (D)
Stroud, Garner Ramsey (R)
Stroud, Robert Eugene (D)
Strowig, Calvin Arthur (R)
Stubenhofer, James Anthony (D)
Stueckemann, Walter Frederick (R)
Swallow, Richard Alden (R)
Swan, Robert Austin, Jr. (D)
Swenson, Ross Greeley (D)
Talkington, Robert Van (R)
Templar, George (R)
Terry, Harriet Eleanor (D)
Tessendorf, Ramona Roberta (R)
Thomas, Christopher Yancey (R)
Thompson, Gerald Franklin (D)
Thorn, Jeri A. (D)
Thornburrow, Samuel Raymond (D)
Throckmorton, Adel Foster (R)
Thull, Eugene Nicholas (D)
Tillotson, J. C. (R)
Tobias, Ansel Walter (R)
Tongier, Glen Leroy (R)
Tucker, Wendell O. (D)
Ungerer, James L. (R)
Unruh, Ernest Arthur (R)
VanDalsem, Josephine Fern (R)
Van Sickle, Tom R. (R)
Vaughn, Raymond C. (R)
Vickers, Marie (D)
Vogel, John Henry (R)
Voss, John Harm (R)
Wall, John M. (R)
Wallingford, Samuel P, Mrs. (R)
Walter, Mabel Victoria (D)
Warren, Joe E. (D)
Wassenberg, Shirley Mae (D)
Waters, Jerry B. (R)
Watkins, Charles Henry (D)
Watson, Terry Durward (D)
Webb, Maurice Everett (D)
Wertz, William Jennings (R)
West, Tom James (R)
Whitsitt, Virgil H. (R)
Whorton, Bill G. (R)
Wilkinson, Ronald Joe (R)
Williams, Beatrice Jacquart (R)
Williams, Edward Morgan (R)
Williams, Neil A. (R)
Williams, Odd (R)
Williamson, Blake Arthur (R)
Wilson, Elton Dakota (D)

Wilson, Josephine Evadna (R)
Winn, Larry, Jr. (R)
Wolf, Ed (R)
Wolf, Paul Arnold (D)
Woodard, William Earl (R)
Worcester, Betty Jewel (D)
Wright, Charles Wesley (R)
Wright, John Cook (D)
Wunsch, Paul Robert (R)
Younkin, Josephine Collins (D)
Yunghans, Robert O. (D)
Zimmerman, Donald Wayne (R)

KENTUCKY

Adams, William R. (R)
Allen, Paul (D)
Anderson, Carlton Eugene (D)
Anderson, Cecil A. (D)
Antrobus, Randall Leon (R)
Arnett, Sherman Rolen (D)
Arnold, Edgar Frank, Jr. (D)
Ashby, Milton (D)
Back, A. G, Jr. (D)
Ball, Donald Ray (R)
Ballard, Leonard Harrison (R)
Ballenger, Louis E. (R)
Bamberger, Carl A. (R)
Bane, Cora (D)
Barbar, Raymond (D)
Barker, Robert (R)
Barton, Harold Bryan (R)
Barton, Nelda Ann Lambert (R)
Beauchamp, Isaac Emerson (D)
Begley, Elmer (R)
Beliles, Richard Vincent (D)
Bell, Nancy Ballantine (D)
Billings, Bernard E. (D)
Billington, Owen (D)
Bishop, Clay Massey (R)
Black, Harry Gordon (R)
Blandford, Donald Joseph (D)
Blau, Edward John (D)
Blume, Norbert (D)
Blythe, E. Bruce, Jr. (R)
Bogardus, O. A. (R)
Bondurant, James E. (D)
Bonn, Bernard J, Sr. (D)
Booth, John Thomas (D)
Bottom, Curtis Hobbs (R)
Bowman, Wilson Shelby (D)
Brand, George G. (D)
Bratcher, Rhodes (R)
Breathitt, Edward Thompson, Jr. (D)
Breckinridge, John Bayne (D)
Brizendine, Thomas M. (D)
Brooking, John R. S. (R)
Brown, Archie (R)
Brown, Edward G. (D)
Brown, Ernest Eugene (R)
Brown, John Young (D)
Bruce, James Edmond (D)
Buckman, James David (D)
Buky, Fallis Vernon (R)
Burke, Frank Welsh (D)
Burkhart, Stephen (R)
Butler, Paul Clinton (R)
Butler, Wendell P. (D)
Byck, Mary Helen (D)
Caldwell, James M. (R)
Carroll, Julian Morton (D)
Carroll, Thomas Charles (D)
Carter, Abe Parker (R)
Carter, J. C. (R)
Carter, Tim Lee (R)
Caskey, Wilburn (D)
Chandler, Albert Benjamin (D)
Chapman, Thomas E. (D)
Chaudoin, Otis R. (D)
Chelf, Frank, Sr. (D)
Chin, Richard (R)
Clark, Buford Thomas (R)
Clark, Joe P. (D)
Combs, Bert Thomas (D)
Combs, Vera Salyer (D)
Cook, Everett E. (D)
Cook, Marlow Webster (R)
Cooper, John Sherman (R)
Corcoran, Thomas Joseph (D)
Cowan, Boyd Lynn (R)
Cowger, William Owen (R)
Cowherd, Colby F. (D)
Cox, John Henry (D)
Criscillis, William Lee, Jr. (D)
Curlin, William P, Jr. (D)
Davie, John Turney (D)
Davis, Curtis Loran (D)
Davis, Georgia M. (D)
Davis, James Adair (R)
DeMarcus, William Harold (R)
Denham, Mitchel Bertram (D)
Denton, Ashton Lyle (R)
Dickson, Edith Bratschi (R)
Disponett, William David (R)
Dotson, William Shakespeare (D)
Duffy, Martin J, Jr. (D)
Duncan, Oliver O. (R)
Duncan, William Graham, IV (R)
Edmonds, Edwin Benton (R)
Eicher, Bob Henry (R)
Elliott, F. Dunlap (D)
Elliott, Frank, Jr. (R)
Elliott, Humphrey Taylor (R)
Engle, William (D)
Evans, Earl Wesley (R)
Fallin, James Holder (D)
Fannin, Homer Windell (R)
Farnsley, Charles Rowland Peaslee (D)
Farris, Norman Edwin (R)
Ferguson, Bruce Stuart (D)
Flynn, Robert Douglas (R)
Ford, Wendell H. (D)
Forester, William Davis (R)
Frazer, Robert Nunn (R)
Freeman, Edwin (D)
Freeman, Wayne W. (D)
Friend, Kelsey E. (D)
Frymire, Richard L. (D)
Fugazzi, Fred E. (D)
Garrett, Tom (D)
Gay, Clay (R)
Goff, Kenneth Harold (R)
Golden, James Stephen (R)
Gregory, Noble Jones (D)
Hadden, Carl Thompson (D)
Hammons, Owen Cecil (D)
Hampton, Hayes Allen (D)
Hardwick, Ted H. (R)
Hardy, Raymond H. (R)
Hare, Cleve Thomas (R)
Harper, Kenneth Franklin (R)
Harvey, Daryl Preston (R)
Harvey, William Edward (R)
Hatfield, Marshal Joe (R)
Hehl, Lambert Lawrence, Jr. (D)
Helm, Joseph Burge (D)
Helton, James Carter (R)
Henry, William Keith (D)
Hickey, James Clyde (D)
Hill, Edward Polk, III (D)
Hill, Thomas Jefferson, III (D)
Hinkle, Allen Brooks (D)
Hislope, Leonard Russell (R)
Hoe, Harry Morgan (R)
Hoffman, John Stanley (D)
Holbert, Salin (R)
Hopkins, Richard (D)
Hopper, Hubert Carson (R)
House, Luther Porter, Sr. (D)
House, Raymond Durward (D)
House, Val A, Jr. (D)
Howard, Durham W. (R)
Howerton, James William (R)
Hubbard, Carroll, Jr, (D)
Huddleston, Walter (D)
Huff, Gene (R)
Hunt, Howard P, Jr. (D)
Hunt, James E. (R)
Hurst, John Raymond (R)
Hyden, Jesse L. (R)
Irick, Gether (D)
Isler, John J. (D)
Ison, Donald (R)
Jarboe, Joseph Benjamin, Jr. (D)
Johnson, Arthur Lloyd, Jr. (D)
Johnson, Donald L. (R)
Johnson, Fairis (D)
Johnson, Graddy Williams (R)
Johnson, Oz (R)
Johnson, Vernon Lee, Jr. (R)
Jones, Charles J. (R)
Jones, Pleas E. (R)
Jones, William Beaty (R)
Jordan, William R, Jr. (D)
Keene, Bernard (D)
Keller, John L. (D)
Kelly, Ed J. (D)
Kelly, Mary Prudence (D)
Kelly, Stuart Stacy (D)
Kerr, John H, Jr. (R)
Kibbey, Jack Robinson (R)
Kidwell, Alvin (D)
King, Philip E. (D)
Kinkead, Shelby C. (D)
Kipping, Robert Kirtley (R)
Kirtley, Louise Gasser (D)
Knicely, Carroll Franklin (D)
Knott, James W. (R)
Landolt, Gene (D)
Lane, Caswell P. (D)
Lassiter, Charlie (D)
Latta, Clifford B. (D)
Lawrence, H. Bemis (R)
Layne, William Henry (R)
Layson, Jefferson Vimont, Jr. (R)
Lewis, James E. (D)
Locklin, Jack G. (D)
Long, George James (R)
Lovett, Wells Thomas (D)
Lucas, Opal M. (R)
McBrayer, W. Terry (D)
McCallum, Shelby (D)
McCann, Charles William Aloysius (D)
McCowen, Dexter (R)
McGinty, Vernon Charles (R)
McHenry, Gail Pitts (D)
McIntyre, Alex, Jr. (R)
McKinney, Lloyd (R)
McNamara, Nell Guy (D)
Maddox, Henry (D)
Maggard, Jack Samuel (D)
Majors, Damon (D)
Mann, Marcus (D)
Mann, Dr. William C. (R)
Marks, Howard R. (R)
Martin, Ersel (R)
Matthews, Robert (D)
Mazzoli, Romano Louis (D)
Mershon, John Carl (D)
Middleton, Clyde William (R)
Middleton, Edwin G. (R)
Miller, B. Read (R)
Miller, Clarence R. (D)
Miller, James R. (D)
Miller, John D. (D)
Miller, John Robert (R)
Miller, Robert Louis (R)
Miller, Scott, Jr. (R)
Miller, Thomas Rowland (D)
Mills, Don (D)
Mills, Frances Jones (D)
Mitchell, Ralph Wilson (D)
Mobley, Pleaz Wm. (R)
Moorman, Richard Elliott (D)
Morgan, Fred H. (D)
Morris, H. H. (D)
Morton, Thruston B. (R)
Moseley, Douglas Dewayne (R)
Murphy, James E. (D)
Natcher, William H. (D)
Newberry, James H. (D)
Nichols, Henry Lyons (R)
Nickell, James D. (R)
Norris, Raymond (R)
Nunn, Louie B. (R)
Ockerman, Foster (D)
O'Hara, Mary Evelyne (R)
Osborne, Earl Thomas (D)
Overman, Henry (D)
Palmer, Wilson (D)
Palmore, John Stanley, Jr. (D)
Parish, David Andrew (D)
Parsley, Frances Elaine (R)
Parsons, Harold Paul (D)
Patrick, James Fairchild (R)
Payne, S. Tilford, Jr. (R)
Peace, Will K. (R)
Peden, Katherine Graham (D)
Peniston, Louis T. (D)
Perkins, Carl D. (D)
Perkins, Cecil Ray (D)
Pettit, H. Foster (D)
Pickett, Lawrence Edwin (R)
Pile, C. H. (D)
Poston, James Richard (D)
Ragland, Kenneth Neil (D)
Rand, John William (D)
Rankin, Otwell C. (D)
Rattliff, Herman W. (R)
Reeves, John Estill (D)
Reichert, Walter Stewart (R)
Reynolds, Louise Elliott (R)
Reynolds, Robert Jackson (D)
Reynolds, Russell C. (D)
Reynolds, W. J, Jr. (D)
Rickert, Jon Edward (D)
Riddle, M. T. (R)
Riley, Lake (R)
Roberts, Dan J. (D)
Roberts, Price Park (R)
Roberts, Thomas Jefferson (D)
Robinson, William Hobert (R)
Russell, Allen E. (R)
Sanders, Cecil Carlton (D)
Sanders, Roy (D)
Sartin, Frank Comer (R)
Sawyer, E. P. (R)
Schmidt, Arthur Louis (R)
Schweder, Warren Dickens (R)
Sharp, Joshua P. (R)
Sheehan, Gus, Jr. (D)
Shepherd, Rinehart S. (D)
Short, Paul (R)
Siemens, George R. (D)
Siler, Eugene (R)
Sims, John Thaxter (D)
Skaggs, Joel Henry (R)
Smith, Clifford Edwin, Jr. (D)
Smith, W. R. (D)
Smothers, John Madison (D)
Snyder, Marion Gene (R)
Sower, Frank William (D)
Spalding, Lester Helm (D)
Sparks, Harry Magee (D)
Spence, Foster Hoyt (R)
Spragens, Thomas Arthur (D)
Steinfeld, Samuel S. (R)
Stewart, Dan, Jr. (D)
Stovall, Thelma Loyace (D)
Straney, Martin Louis (Independent)
Stuart, Eugene Page (R)
Stubblefield, Frank A. (D)
Sturgill, Barkley Jennings (D)
Sullivan, William Litsey (D)
Swinford, John McKee (D)
Swope, John W. (R)
Tanner, William Edgar (R)
Taylor, Herschel Kenneth (D)
Thompson, James (R)
Thurmond, David Xavier (D)
Thurmond, Edwin M. (R)
Tuggle, Kenneth Herndon (R)
Turner, John Raymond (D)
Turner, Marie R. (D)
Van Hoose, Wendell (R)
Vanzandt, Edward Earl (D)
Wallace, Fred, Jr. (R)
Walters, Charles Timothy (D)
Ward, Thomas Morgan (D)
Warren, Delbert Clayton (R)
Waterfield, Harry Lee (D)
Watkins, Sam Houston (D)
Watson, Billy James (R)
Watts, John Clarence (D)
Watts, Lawrence (D)
Webster, Franklin (D)
Wellman, Nova Elizabeth Williams (R)
Wells, Lynn B. (D)
Wesley, John Quentin (R)
Wetherby, Lawrence Winchester (D)
Wheeler, Charles D. (R)
White, John E. (R)
Whitlock, James E. (D)
Whitlow, Wyatt Rodney (D)
Williams, Murrell Dwayne (R)
Williams, Squire Needham (D)
Wilson, Earl D. (R)
Winchester, Lucy Alexander (R)
Winterberg, Edward Joseph (D)
Wooley, Robert Paul (R)
Wright, Dexter S. (R)
Wyatt, Anne Duncan (D)
Wyatt, Wilson Watkins (D)
Young, John William (R)
Young, Hortense Houston (D)
Young, Paul E, Sr. (D)
Young, William C. (D)
Yates, Albert (R)

LOUISIANA

Allphin, John, Jr. (D)
Anderson, Gertie Feazel (D)
Angers, Robert John (R)
Ardoin, James Madison (D)
Aycock, Clarence C. (D)
Bagwell, Harrison Garey (R)
Barham, Charles Clem (D)
Barham, Erle Edwards (R)
Becnel, Benoit Paul (D)
Belchic, Harriet Cameron (R)
Belton, Acie Julious (D)
Bergeron, Belvin Francis (D)
Bickford, Francis Edward (D)
Bigby, Walter Oliver (D)
Blackwell, Morton Clyde (R)
Blue, George Riebel (D)
Boese, Elsie Jean (R)
Boese, H. Lamar (R)
Boggs, (Thomas) Hale (D)
Bolton, Edgar Simpson (Constitution)
Bonin, Garland L. (D)
Booker, Edward Hamilton (D)
Bourg, Emile Joseph (D)
Bowdon, William George (D)
Boyer, James Gambrell (D)
Brady, Thomas Floyd (D)

Branton, Parey Pershing (D)
Breaux, John Richard (D)
Brinkhaus, Armand Joseph (D)
Brittain, Jack Oliver (D)
Broussard, J. B. (D)
Broussard, Marcus Anson, Jr. (D)
Brown, J. Marshall (D)
Brown, William Kirkland (D)
Burton, George Aubrey, Jr. (R)
Bussie, Victor (D)
Caffery, Patrick Thomson (D)
Calhoun, Nathan Meredith (D)
Calogero, Pascal Frank, Jr. (D)
Casey, Joseph S. (D)
Castellini, William McGregor (R)
Cawthorn, Merle Sloan (D)
Chaisson, Joel Thomas (D)
Ching, Wiletta Parker (R)
Clark, Clabie (D)
Clark, James Erle (D)
Clarke, Jack Wells (D)
Clemons, Ance C, Jr. (D)
Cole, Luther Francis (D)
Colten, A. Thomas (R)
Cotton, W. Davis (D)
Crawford, Floyd O. (R)
Curtis, Henry Baldwin (D)
Darsey, Elton A. (D)
Davis, Jackson Beauregard (D)
DeBlieux, Joseph Davis (D)
deGravelles, Charles Camille (R)
deGravelles, Mrs. Charles Camille (R)
DeJean, Howard Benjamin, Jr. (D)
de la Houssaye, Harry Louis (D)
Delaroderie, Laurence Aldrich (D)
de la Vergne, Hugues Jules, II (R)
Dennis, James Leon (D)
Despot, George Joseph (R)
Diamond, Lloyd Webb (R)
Dixon, Margaret Richardson (D)
Dodd, William Joseph (D)
Downs, Crawford Hugh (D)
Dumas, Woodrow Wilson (D)
Dunbar, Charles Edward, III (R)
Duplantier, Adrian Guy (D)
Duval, Claude Berwick (D)
Easley, Morris Ewell, Sr. (D)
Edwards, E. Neel, Jr. (D)
Edwards, Edwin W. (D)
Eleser, Golda Easley (R)
Ellender, Allen Joseph (D)
Ellis, Frank Burton (D)
Farrar, Reginald Warren, Jr. (R)
Feldman, Martin L. C. (R)
Fernandez, Joachim Octave (D)
Flournoy, Carolyn Clay (R)
Fortier, Donald Louis (D)
Fredlund, Ray (R)
Friedman, Jimmy Elizabeth (D)
Friedman, Sylvan N. (D)
Fruge, Jack C. (D)
Gangelosi, Theodore Francis
Gaudin, Edward Clark (R)
Gauthier, Richard Hugh (D)
Gay, Lizzie Reed (R)
Gibbs, Henry Lawrence, Jr. (D)
Gilbert, J. C. (D)
Gill, William Alexander, Jr. (D)
Glasgow, Leslie L. (R)
Gomer, Pierre Jackson (R)
Graham, Ralph Warren (D)
Granger, Lester Blackwell (R)
Gravel, Camille F, Jr. (D)
Gray, Jack Kenneth (D)
Gremillion, Allen Castle (D)
Gremillion, Jack Paul Faustin (D)
Guglielmo, Dudley A. (D)
Guilliot, Ogden Clarence (D)
Guste, William Joseph (D)
Hainkel, John Joseph, Jr. (D)
Hall, Crayton Green (R)
Hayes, Fredric Granison (D)
Haynes, William G, Jr. (R)
Heath, Joseph Bryan, Jr. (D)
Hebert, F. Edward (D)
Hebert, Percy Daniel (D)
Hecht, Henry Del Banco, Jr. (R)
Heitman, Betty Green (R)
Hendricks, Leonard Monroe, Jr. (R)
Henry, Edgerton L. (D)
Hobbs, Henry Grady (D)
Holstead, George B. (D)
Hood, Elizabeth Hanna (R)
Hudson, Morley Alvin (R)
Hunter, Robert Edward (D)
Hurston, Charles Andrew (D)
Hymel, Gary Gerard (D)
Jones, Robert G. (D)
Jordan, Ingersoll (D)
Karst, Charles Edward
King, Frederick Jenks (R)
King, James Savery (R)
King, Joan Merrin (R)
King, R. Edwin (D)
King, Semmes Walmsley (R)
Kinler, Gladys Veronica (R)
Knight, William Noel (R)
Kouns, Sinclair Bert (D)
Laborde, Paulin Joseph, Jr. (D)
Labouisse, Carolyn Gay (D)
Landreneau, J. Vernon (D)
Leblanc, Charles John (R)
LeBlanc, J. Luke (D)
LeBlanc, John Dennis (D)
LeBreton, Edward Francis, Jr. (D)
See Addenda
Lee, D. R. (D)
Leithman, John Kenneth (D)
Leonard, Herbert Lee (R)
Leonard, Will Ernest, Jr. (D)
Lindh, Patricia Sullivan (R)
Lofaso, Gerald Francis (D)
Long, Blanche R. (D)
Long, Gillis William (D)
Long, Jimmy Dale (D)
Long, Russell B. (D)
Long, Speedy O. (D)
Lowe, Herman Joseph (D)
Lyons, Charlton Havard, Sr. (R)
McCain, Wilbur Teal (D)
McIntosh, James David (D)
McKeithen, John Julian (D)
McSween, Harold Barnett (D)
Manning, Ethel Leonard (D)
Marcantel, Bernard Norman (D)
Marcel, Cleveland Joseph, Sr. (D)
Marionneaux, John Esper, Jr. (D)
Martin, Wade Omer, Jr. (D)
Mauberret, Claude, Jr. (D)
Miller, Frank L. (D)
Miller, Ralph Ross (D)
Miller, Roderick Luke (R)
Mills, Newt V. (D)
Mollere, Jules Gustave (D)
Montgomery, A. Harold (D)
Montgomery, John Willard (D)
Moore, Ellen Bryan (D)
Morial, Ernest Nathan (D)
Morrison, James Hobson (D)
Mouser, Cotys Milner (D)
Needham, Daisy Eudora (R)
Noe, James Albert (D)
Ogilvie, Oscar Phillips (D)
O'Keefe, Michael Hanley (D)
Oubre, George Thurman (D)
Parker, Mary Evelyn (D)
Passman, Otto Ernest (D)
Patten, David Ivy (D)
Paxton, Ralph Eugene (R)
Peltier, Harvey A, Jr. (D)
Polack, Robert (R)
Putnam, Richard Johnson (D)
Rappelet, Albert Otto (D)
Rarick, John Richard (D)
Rathe, Barbara A. (D)
Read, William Brooks (D)
Reggie, Edmund M. (D)
Roberts, Donald Duane (R)
Rush, Samuel Lee (R)
Sadler, James Kenneth, Jr. (R)
Sanders, Joe William (D)
Schiro, Victor Hugo (D)
Segura, Perry (D)
Sheldon, Joe S, Jr. (R)
Shirah, Ross Patrick (R)
Simon, Warren Joseph (D)
Singleton, Ernest (D)
Smith, Ernest Henry (D)
Smith, James P. (D)
Smither, Charles Gabriel (D)
Stagg, Tom (R)
Stear, David Spring (R)
Stinson, Ford Edwards (D)
Stoutz, Edwin A, Jr. (D)
Summers, Frank Wynerth (D)
Tarver, Ray Darryl (D)
Tatman, Aubrey C. (R)
Theriot, Roy Raoul (D)
Thompson, Theo Ashton (D)
Van Cleave, Thomas Winlock (D)
Vesich, Anthony Joseph, Jr. (D)
Villar, Emery L. (D)
Vining, Charles Leroy, Jr. (D)
Waggonner, Joe D, Jr. (D)
Walker, Lillian W. (D)
Watson, Arthur Chopin (D)
Willis, Edwin Edward (D)
Willis, J. Theron (D)
Winters, Mary Lou (D)
Woodley, Edmund Etchison (R)

MAINE

Aiken, Ruth Merle Jones (R)
Allen, Ralph Watson (R)
Baker, Ethel Bowden (R)
Ballou, John Waldo (R)
Barnes, Ralph Anthony (D)
Bartram, Philip Hoyt (R)
Belanger, Joseph A. (D)
Beliveau, Severin M. (D)
Benson, David B. (R)
Benson, Robert Arthur (D)
Berman, Malcolm Irving (R)
Bernard, Donald Joseph (D)
Bernard, Peter (D)
Berry, Richard Nathaniel (R)
Birt, Walter Arthur (R)
Bishop, James Alden (D)
Boisvert, Romeo T. (D)
Bonney, Edward Mayson (D)
Bourgoin, Emile J. (D)
Bowie, Frank Morey (R)
Broderick, Fay Leone (D)
Broderick, Richard Howard (D)
Brown, Dwight A. (R)
Brown, Marion Fuller (R)
Campbell, Joseph Bradburn (R)
Carey, Richard James (D)
Carr, James Drew (R)
Carrier, J. Robert (D)
Carroll, George Arthur (D)
Carswell, Catherine Idella (D)
Carter, Donald Victor (D)
Chisholm, Mary E. (D)
Clark, Carroll Herbert (R)
Coffey, Barbara Jean (D)
Cohen, Nathan (D)
Cook, Sanger Mills (R)
Corson, Neal Craig (R)
Cottrell, John Boardman, Jr. (D)
Cox, David M. (D)
Crane, Henrietta Page (R)
Crommett, Leon James (D)
Cummings, Minnette Hunsiker (R)
Curran, Raymond Joseph (D)
Curtis, Kenneth M. (D)
Dame, Walter B. (R)
Danton, Nicholas William (D)
Deschambeault, Frederic (D)
Dietz, Lew (D)
Dougherty, Esther Hawley (R)
Drigotas, Frank Martin (D)
Dubord, Richard Joseph (D)
Dunbar, Frank Hayden (D)
Dunfey, Robert John (D)
Dutremble, Richard Donald (D)
Dyar, Roswell E. (R)
Edgar, Joseph T. (R)
Edwards, W. Russell, Jr. (D)
Emery, Eugene Marshall (D)
Erwin, James Shrewsbury (R)
Evans, Lee Earl (R)
Farnham, Roderick Ewen (R)
Fortier, Malcolm John (D)
Garland, Peter A. (R)
Gaudreau, Lorenzo J. (D)
Gilbert, Sylvio Joseph (R)
Giordano, Dominic Thomas (D)
Good, Vinal G. (R)
Goodwin, Kathleen Watson (D)
Graham, David Livingstone (D)
Hale, Robert (R)
Hall, Stanley Vernon (R)
Hancock, Frank Ellis (R)
Hanson, Bernice Zilpha (R)
Hanson, Herbert L. (R)
Harding, Edward Perry (R)
Harding, Floyd L. (D)
Haugen, Roy S. (D)
Hathaway, William Dodd (D)
Hewes, Richard David (R)
Hichens, Walter Wilson (R)
Hildreth, Horace A, Jr. (R)
Hoffses, Albert Winston (R)
Hutchins, Christopher (R)
Jalbert, Louis (D)
Jameson, John Henry (R)
Jephson, Evelyn S. (D)
Jewell, Flave M. (R)
Joly, Cyril Matthew, Jr. (R)
Jutras, Philip L. (D)
Katz, Bennett David (R)
Keegan, William Toomey (D)
Kellam, Ronald Lloyd (D)
Kennedy, David J. (R)
King, Spencer M.
Klickstein, David (D)
Kuhn, Brenda (D)
Kyes, Ernest G. (R)
Kyros, Peter Nicholas (D)
Laberge, Romeo Louis (D)
Levesque, Emilien A. (D)
Lewis, Edward Barker (R)
McIntire, Clifford Guy (R)
MacLeod, Kenneth Parker (R)
Marcotte, Roland Louis (D)
Marden, Robert Allen (R)
Marquis, Norman J. F. (D)
Marstaller, Louis John (R)
Martin, John L. (D)
Martin, Marion E. (R)
Micoleau, Charles Judd (D)
Millett, H. Sawin, Jr. (R)
Mills, Kenneth Armour (D)
Mitchell, George John (D)
Monks, Robert A. G. (R)
Morong, Leroy Libby (D)
Muskie, Edmund Sixtus (D)
Nichols, David A. (R)
Nicoll, Donald Eugene (D)
O'Brien, Jadine R. (D)
Osgood, H. Davison, Jr. (R)
Palmer, George Arnold (D)
Payne, Frederick George (R)
Pendergast, M. Abbott (R)
Pennell, Russell Adams (D)
Pert, Edwin Harry (D)
Pike, Sumner Tucker (R)
Pineo, Fred Benjamin, Jr. (D)
Porteous, Louis Robert, Jr. (R)
Poulin, Gaston Gerard (D)
Pratt, John Alden (R)
Prince, Sanford Jack, Jr. (R)
Reed, Carlton Day, Jr. (D)
Reed, John Hathaway (R)
Richardson, Harrison Lambert (R)
Rolde, Neil Richard (D)
Russell, Theodore Henry (D)
Sahagian, Herman D. (R)
Schoenberger, Maralyn Morton (D)
Schoenberger, Walter Smith (D)
Scolnik, Louis (D)
Scott, George William (R)
Scribner, Fred Clark, Jr. (R)
Scribner, Rodney Latham (D)
Shaw, Stanley F. (R)
Shiro, Burton Grant (D)
Shute, Elden H, Jr. (R)
Smith, Frederick Orville, II (R)
Smith, Margaret Chase (R)
Snow, Paris John (R)
Snowe, Peter Trafton (R)
Speers, Jerrold Bond (R)
Starbird, Seaward Glenn, Jr. (D)
Steele, Philip Reed (D)
Stern, Edward (D)
Stillings, Richard Wallace (R)
Stuart, Robert Sterling (R)
Sween, Robert Harold (R)
Swett, Dana Malcolm (R)
Tanous, Wakine Gregory (R)
Thaxter, Sidney Warren (R)
Tibbets, Margaret Joy
Truman, Theodore (D)
Tupper, Stanley R. (R)
Tyndale, Elmont Scott (R)
Valcourt, Richard Roger (R)
Violette, Elmer H. (D)
Waxman, Richard Stanley (D)
Webster, Walter E, Jr. (R)
Whittaker, Frederick William (R)
Willey, Richard Crosman (R)
Young, Byron Porter (R)

MARYLAND

Abrahams, Albert Edward (R)
Abrams, Rosalie Silber (D)
Abramson, Joseph (D)
Abramson, Murray (D)
Adams, Victorine Quille (D)
Adkins, Bertha Sheppard (R)
Agnew, Spiro Theodore (R)
Ahlers, John Clarke (R)
Aiken, Benjamin Otis (D)
Aitken, John Winfield (R)
Alcorn, Janice Carol (R)
Allen, Aris Tee (R)
Allett, Robert G. (R)
Alpert, Maxwell (D)
Alpert, Paul Edwin (D)
Alton, Joseph W, Jr. (R)
Anderson, N. Dale (D)
Anderson, Thomas M, Jr. (R)
Andolsek, Ludwig John (D)
Antonelli, Camillo N. (D)
Aragona, Xavier Angelo (D)
Arnick, John Stephen (D)
Athey, Tyras S. (D)
Baer, John Miller (D)
Bailey, William Disharoon (D)
Baker, Alva Sayrs, Jr. (D)

Baker, James Howard (R)
Baker, Joe M, Jr. (R)
Ball, Robert Myers (D)
Barber, Arthur Whiting (D)
Barbour, Robert Taylor (R)
Barkan, Alexander Elias
Barr, Bruce Reid (R)
Bauman, Robert Edmund (R)
Baumann, Albert F. (D)
Bayley, Ned Duane (R)
Beall, George (R)
Beall, J. Glenn, Jr. (R)
Bean, Joseph Edward (D)
Beattie, Charles Kenneth (R)
Becker, Martin Stanley (D)
Beggs, James Montgomery (R)
Beggs, Mary Harrison (R)
Benner, Robert Willis (R)
Bennett, Earl (D)
Bennett, Homer Lampson (R)
Bennett, Marion T. (R)
Berdes, George Raymond (D)
Berg, William, Jr. (D)
Bertier, Theodore, Jr. (D)
Bertorelli, Joseph A. (D)
Biemiller, Andrew J. (D)
Bishop, John J, Jr. (R)
Black, Walter Evan, Jr. (R)
Blades, Orland Beverly (D)
Blair, Charles Stanley (R)
Blondes, Leonard Saul (D)
Bollard, Robert D. (D)
Boone, Alexander Gordon, Jr. (D)
Bossle, Francis X. (D)
Boyer, Elroy G. (D)
Bray, Elza (R)
Bresler, Charles S. (R)
Brewster, Daniel Baugh (D)
Brightman, Samuel Charles (D)
Briscoe, John Hanson (D)
Brooke, Albert Bushong, Jr. (R)
Browne, Glenn Gordon
Browning, George Mortimer (D)
Buffington, J. Raymond (D)
Bullock, Joseph E. (D)
Burch, Francis B(oucher) (D)
Burgess, Hugh (D)
Burgess, Warren Randolph (R)
Burkhead, William Joseph (D)
Burkheimer, Nancy Brown (D)
Burns, Andrew Joseph, Jr. (D)
Busby, Horace (D)
Buswell, David Hastings (R)
Butler, Earl Dennett (D)
Byron, Goodloe Edgar (D)
Caldwell, James H. (D)
Calvert, William Bailey (D)
Cardin, Benjamin Louis (D)
Cardin, Carl William (R)
Cardin, Jerome S. (D)
Cardin, Maurice (D)
Carpenter, Margaret Wodtke (D)
Cass, Millard (D)
Cassady, Helen B. (D)
Chandler, O. Sheldon (D)
Chester, Joseph Arnathen, Sr. (D)
Christie, John M. (R)
Clark, James F, Jr. (D)
Clark, Lyn Henderson (D)
Clark, Theodore Nichols (R)
Clifford, Clark McAdams (D)
Cohen, Manuel Frederick (D)
Collier, Harry P. (R)
Collins, Charles Edward (D)
Connell, William James (D)
Connellee, Douglas W. (D)
Conroy, Edward Thomas (D)
Cook, Edna Pepper (D)
Cook, Noel Speir (R)
Coolahan, John Carroll (D)
Coopersmith, Esther Lipsen (D)
Cornish, Charles Edward (R)
Corrigan, William P. (D)
Cowen, Eugene S. (R)
Cox, Ernest Y. (D)
Cox, Robert Emmett (R)
Crawford, Jack Frederick (R)
Crawford, Victor Lawrence (D)
Crivella, Barbara Ann (R)
Crowe, Philip K.
Crum, William Bruce (R)
Cummings, Frank (R)
Curran, Gerald Joseph (D)
Curran, J. Joseph (D)
Curran, J. Joseph, Jr. (D)
D'Alesandro, Thomas, Jr. (D)
D'Alesandro, Thomas J, III (D)
Daly, Mavis Glander (R)
Davis, Mary Wright (D)
Davis, W. Lester (D)
Day, J. Edward (D)
Dean, John Wesley, III (R)
Dean, Robert Payne (D)
Della, Charles A. (D)
Della, George Washington (D)
Delphey, Chester Franklin (D)
Dembling, Paul Gerald
Dembowski, James S. (D)
Dentz, Robert Joseph (D)
DePalma, Samuel
Derr, John A. (R)
Deschler, Lewis
Dillon, R(ezon) Samuel, Jr. (D)
Dixon, Isaiah, Jr. (D)
Dixon, Walter Thomas, Sr. (D)
Dize, Carlton Yank (R)
Docter, Charles Alfred (D)
Dorf, Paul Aaron (D)
Dorman, Arthur (D)
Douglas, John Woolman (D)
Douglass, Calvin Albert (D)
Douglass, Robert Lee (D)
Dowell, Bennie C. (D)
Downs, Arthur Walter (R)
Dukert, Joseph Michael (R)
Dulany, William Bevard (D)
Duvall, C. Hayes (D)
Dyer, Margaret Louise (R)
Eisenhower, Milton Stover (R)
Ellis, Clyde T. (D)
Elman, Philip
Emanuel, Meyer M, Jr. (D)
Emerson, N. William (R)
Englund, Merrill Wayne (D)
Epstein, Harvey A. (D)
Evans, Edward T, Jr. (R)
Evans, William Thomas (D)
Fallon, George H. (D)
Fallon, John J. (D)
Fenn, Dan Huntington, Jr. (D)
Finan, Thomas B. (D)
Finger, Harold Ben
Finney, Jervis Spencer (R)
Fornos, Werner H. (D)
Fowler, Henry J. (D)
Frank, Murray (D)
Friedel, Samuel Nathaniel (D)
Friedler, Carl Lobe (D)
Friedman, Edward David (D)
Friedman, Irving (D)
Friedman, Sol J. (D)
Froehlke, Robert Frederick (R)
Frosch, Robert Alan
Gallagher, Francis Xavier (D)
Garbett, Richard Walker (R)
Gardner, John William (R)
Garmatz, Edward A. (D)
Gartland, James Wesley Francis (D)
Gibson, Andrew E. (R)
Gilpin, R. Wayne (R)
Glackin, Paul Louis (D)
Glotfelty, Martha Imogene (R)
Goldstein, Herbert (D)
Goldstein, Louis L. (D)
Goodman, William J. (D)
Gordon, Lincoln
Gore, Louise (R)
Grady, Joseph Harold (D)
Graham, Spencer W. (R)
Gray, Kenneth Elwood (D)
Green, Walter LeRoy (D)
Greer, William Calvin (D)
Groves, Elwood S. (R)
Grumbacher, Richard (D)
Gude, Gilbert (R)
Hahn, Ruby Virginia (D)
Hale, Preston L. (D)
Hall, Edward Thomas (R)
Hampton, Robert Edward (R)
Hanchett, James Granger (R)
Hanna, William Sawyer (D)
Hanson, Royce (D)
Hardwicke, John W. (R)
Harris, Elmer O. (R)
Harris, Frank H. (D)
Harris, John Mathew Wade (R)
Hart, Royal (D)
Hathaway, Michael David (R)
Hellmann, Claude Bernard
Helms, William J, Jr. (D)
Henderson, Frances (R)
Hendrickson, Constance Cooper (D)
Henkin, Daniel Z. (D)
Hepbron, Percy M. (D)
Hergenroeder, Henry Robert, Jr. (D)
Hermann, Albert Bartholomew (R)
Hermann, Sylvia (R)
Hess, Arthur Emil
Hess, W. Dale (D)
Hickey-Evans, Terri R. (R)
Hickman, Carter Malcolm (D)
Hickman, Russell Orlando (D)
Hodges, William L. (D)
Hoffman, Irwin F. (D)
Hoffmann, Frank Nordy (D)
Hogan, Lawrence Joseph (R)
Holt, Marjorie Sewell (R)
Holub, Carl James (D)
Hopkins, Charles A. Porter (R)
Houck, William M. (D)
Hoyer, Steny Hamilton (D)
Hughes, George Raymond, Jr. (R)
Hughes, Harry Roe (D)
Hughes, Thomas Raymond (D)
Hull, Ann Remington (D)
Hunton, Benjamin Lacy (R)
Hurd, Eliot Provoost (R)
Hutchinson, Donald Paul (D)
Huyett, Mildred C. (D)
Hyde, DeWitt Stephen (R)
Hyde, Henry Van Zile, Jr. (R)
James, William S. (D)
Jensen, William Owen, Jr. (D)
Johnson, G. Griffith, Jr. (R)
Johnston, Imogene Bane (R)
Joiner, W. Paul (D)
Jones, James Locke (D)
Jones, Marshall P.
Jones, Marshall William, Jr. (R)
Karey, Joseph Norman (R)
Kaylor, Omer Thomas, Jr. (R)
Kendall, Don Robert (R)
Kenney, Edward Beckham (R)
King, David S. (D)
Kircher, Martin A. (D)
Kirkpatrick, Evron Maurice (D)
Kirkpatrick, William Huntington (R)
Kline, Paul Arthur (R)
Kolnacki, Catherine Fahey
Koonce, Sarah Ada (D)
Kosakowski, Chester G. (D)
Krogseng, David Neil (R)
Krug, Andrew Joseph (D)
Lady, Elaine (R)
Lankford, Richard Estep (D)
Lankler, Alexander MacDonald (R)
Lapides, Julian Lee (D)
Larrimore, W. Garrett (D)
Larson, Clarence Edward (R)
Latham, James C. (D)
Lee, Blair, III (D)
Lee, Lena King (D)
Lee, Ronald Barry (D)
Leonard, Rodney Edwin (D)
Lewis, Stacy Lee (D)
Linton, Samuel Clifton, Jr. (D)
Lipin, Alfred Jerome (D)
Liss, Solomon (D)
Locke, Barry M. (R)
Lockwood, Jane Biggers (R)
Long, Clarence Dickinson, Jr. (D)
Long, Joseph J, Sr. (D)
Long, Robert Charles Biggy (D)
Lowe, Hermus W. (D)
Lowe, Thomas Hunter (D)
Luetkemeyer, John Alexander (D)
Lynch, James H. (D)
Macaulay, Joseph Hugh (R)
McAuliffe, James S, Jr. (D)
McCarty, Maclyn, Jr. (D)
McCourt, Frank J. (D)
McCurdy, M. Jacqueline (D)
MacDaniel, Harold Kemp (D)
McDonough, Raymond J. (D)
McGuirk, Harry J. (D)
Mach, Joseph V. (D)
Machen, Hervey Gilbert, Jr. (D)
McInerney, John S. (R)
McKeldin, Theodore R. (R)
McKinney, Joseph Evans (D)
McMillan, Gaines (D)
McNulty, John F. (D)
McPherson, Harry Cummings, Jr. (D)
McQuade, Frank Joseph, Jr. (D)
McWilliams, William James (D)
Magin, Wilbur Wright (D)
Maguire, John N. (D)
Maguire, Richard (D)
Mahoney, George P. (D)
Malkus, Frederick C. (D)
Malone, J. Edward (D)
Mandel, Marvin (D)
Maneri, Dorothy B. (R)
Mann, Maurice
Marbury, Charles Clagett (D)
Marion, J. Hardin (D)
Markey, David John, III (R)
Marlatt, Ralph Hiers (R)
Marshall, Dennis H. (D)
Mason, Norman Christy (D)
Massenburg, Katherine Black (R)
Mathias, Charles McC, Jr. (R)
Matthews, Richard Carroll (R)
Matthews, Richard Moore (D)
Medairy, Bernard John, Jr. (D)
Meloy, Frances Eanes (D)
Menes, Pauline H. (D)
Merryweather, Thomas L. (D)
Miller, Edward Tylor (R)
Miller, James Rogers, Jr. (R)
Miltich, Paul Andrew (R)
Mitchell, Clarence M, III (D)
Monzel, L. Vincent (R)
Mooney, Thomas Joseph, III (D)
Moore, George Mansfield (R)
Moore, John P. (D)
Morreale, Joseph Francis (R)
Morton, Rogers Clark Ballard (R)
Mrozinski, Benjamin Alexander (D)
Murphy, Charles Springs (D)
Murphy, Margaret Anna (D)
Murphy, Richard James (D)
Nathan, Richard Perle (R)
Needham, James Joseph (R)
Neff, Edwin DeFrees (R)
Nelson, David Aldrich (R)
Nice, Harry Whinna, III (R)
Nimmerrichter, Loretta (R)
Nitze, Paul Henry (D)
Nock, Mary L. (D)
Nolan, John Stephan (R)
Nonnenmacher, Nicholas Thaddeus (R)
North, John-Clarence (D)
Nye, Gerald Prentice (R)
O'Brien, John F. X. (D)
O'Connell, Maurice J. (D)
O'Farrell, Thomas Richard (D)
Olsen, Van Roger (R)
Ordman, Arnold (D)
Orlebeke, Charles J. (R)
Orlinsky, Walter Sidney (D)
Otenasek, Mildred (D)
Palmisano, Angelo Frank (D)
Parker, Peter (R)
Parran, John Thomas, Jr. (D)
Patricelli, Robert E. (R)
Payne, Joseph Bevley (R)
Pedersen, Richard F.
Perrin, Frank G. (R)
Peters, William H, Jr. (D)
Pfrommer, Christopher F, III (D)
Phoebus, Harry T. Jr. (R)
Pilchard, Mark O. (D)
Pine, James Alexander (D)
Polk, Norman E. (D)
Poole, Jerry Wallace (R)
Potter, Charles Edward (R)
Powell, Austin Clifford (D)
Powers, Thompson (D)
Prendergast, William Broderick (R)
Price, George A. (R)
Quigley, James Michael (D)
Quinn, Egbert Lyle (D)
Raley, J. Frank, Jr. (D)
Ramspeck, Robert (D)
Ravnholt, Eiler Christian (D)
Ray, Chester J. (D)
Raymond, Joseph Robert (D)
Rea, James Magruder (D)
Rechtin, Eberhardt (R)
Reed, Lester B. (R)
Reid, Patricia Ann (D)
Reilly, John Richard (D)
Remsberg, E. Earl (R)
Resnick, Alan Marvin (D)
Rinehart, D. Eldred (R)
Risley, Charles E. (D)
Roberson, Donald W. (D)
Rogers, William Pierce (R)
Rolapp, R. Richards (R)
Roney, James Albert, Jr. (D)
Rook, Doris Mae (R)
Rosfeld, Arthur Edward (D)
Rourke, Russell Arthur (R)
Rubenstein, Leon A. (D)
Rummage, Frederick Charles (D)
Rush, William (D)
Rynd, Richard (D)
Sanders, Frank (D)
Sanford, John L, Jr. (D)
Sarbacher, George William, Jr. (R)
Sarbanes, Paul Spyros (D)
Sauerbrey, Ellen Richmond (R)
Saunders, Charles Baskerville, Jr. (R)
Saxon, James J. (D)
Scammon, Richard Montgomery
Scarff, Ross Wilson (R)

Schifter, Richard (D)
Schneider, Nelson Myron (D)
Schroeder, Florence Parks (R)
Scott, David Alan (R)
See, Charles Melberth (R)
Shillito, Barry James (D)
Sickles, Carlton R. (D)
Siegel, Gerald (D)
Silberman, Laurence Hirsch (R)
Silk, James J. (D)
Silver, Edgar P. (D)
Simpkins, Lloyd L. (D)
Smelser, Charles Harold (D)
Smith, Elbert Benjamin, Jr. (D)
Snyder, George Elmer (D)
Snyder, John Wesley
Sparks, E. Clyde (D)
Sparks, John Dudley, Jr. (R)
Spector, Allen Bernard (D)
Spence, Robert Noel (R)
Spencer, Alvie Glenn, Jr. (R)
Spicer, Thomas T. (D)
Stark, Alexander (D)
Staten, Roy Neville (D)
Steers, Newton Ivan, Jr. (R)
Steffey, John W. (R)
Steinberg, Melvin Allen (D)
Steingaszner, Elfrida Helen (R)
Sullivan, John Francis (D)
Sutphin, William Halstead (D)
Swanner, John MacDonald
Swidler, Joseph C. (D)
Sybert, Cornelius Ferdinand (D)
Symington, John Fife, Jr. (R)
Szabo, Daniel (R)
Tawes, John Millard (D)
Taylor, Maxwell Davenport
Thomas, Edward Philip (R)
Tingle, George W. (D)
Trice, J. Mark (R)
Turner, Charles Rutledge (R)
Tydings, Joseph Davies (D)
Tyler, Herbert H. (D)
Vance, Sheldon Baird
Virts, Charles Clifton (D)
Walters, Elmer Elmo (D)
Warburton, Herbert B. (R)
Ward, Thomas Henry (D)
Ware, Jack (R)
Warfield, Edwin, III (D)
Weant, Edward O, Jr. (D)
Weidemeyer, C. Maurice (D)
Weile, Eric Ignatz (D)
Welcome, Verda Freeman (D)
Whalen, Horace King (R)
Wheatley, Charles H. (D)
Wheatley, Electra Catsonis (R)
Whitaker, John Carroll (R)
White, Edward Homer, Jr. (D)
White, Lee C. (D)
Whitney, John Adair (R)
Whittaker, Philip N. (R)
Williams, David John (R)
Williams, Franklin Taylor, Jr. (R)
Wilson, William Laney (D)
Wineland, Fred L. (D)
Wiser, C. Lawrence (D)
Woodworth, Laurence Neal (Independent)
Wright, Frederick Christian, III (D)
Yingling, Jacob Matthias (R)
Young, Ernest D. (D)
Zuckert, Eugene M. (D)

MASSACHUSETTS

Abbott, William Saunders (R)
Abram, Morris Berthold (D)
Abrams, Robert Marshall (D)
Adams, Thomas B. (D)
Aguiar, Antone Souza, Jr. (D)
Akakelian, Hampton (D)
Aleixo, Theodore J, Jr. (D)
Ambrose, Delphin D. (R)
Amesbury, Elizabeth Elwell (R)
Archibald, Ralph Strong (R)
Armstrong, John Alexander (R)
Arnold, Roger W. (R)
Aronson, Robert Samuel (R)
Axelrod, Harry (R)
Babb, Roger Sumner (R)
Backman, Jack H. (D)
Baker, Charles Duane (R)
Baker, Robert William (D)
Baker, William Howard (D)
Barry, Thomas J. (R)
Bartley, David Michael (D)
Basbas, Monte George (R)
Batchelder, Merton K. (R)
Batchelor, Norman Frederick (R)
Batson, Ruth Marion (D)
Beane, Arthur E, Jr. (R)
Beebe, Allison Stanley (R)
Bellotti, Francis Xavier (D)
Belmonte, Robert A. (R)
Bennett, Rosalie B. (R)
Bens, Ralph Joseph, Jr. (R)
Bertonazzi, Louis Peter (D)
Bevilacqua, Francis J. (D)
Bilowz, Walter Gregory (R)
Black, Charles Edwin (R)
Blackham, Ann Rosemary (R)
Bliss, Bruce James (R)
Blizard, Margaret Murray (D)
Blomen, Henning Albert (Socialist Labor Party)
Bly, Belden G, Jr. (R)
Bocko, Stanley J. (D)
Bogdan, Albert Alexander (D)
Boland, Edward P. (D)
Borek, Jo Anne (R)
Bosco, Joseph Angelo (Independent)
Bowler, James J. (D)
Boyle, James Philip (D)
Bradford, Robert Fiske (R)
Bradley, Joseph Gerard (D)
Brandt, Neill Matteson (R)
Brennan, James Francis (D)
Brenton, Marianne Webber (R)
Brett, Joseph E. (D)
Brooke, Edward William (R)
Brown, Jane Phillips (R)
Brown, Matthew (R)
Brown, Richard Gilbert (R)
Browne, Secor Delahay (R)
Brumley, Calvin Edgar (R)
Buckley, John J. (R)
Buczko, Thaddeus Joseph (D)
Buglione, Nicholas Joseph (D)
Burke, George Gerald (D)
Burke, J. Edward (D)
Burke, James A. (D)
Burke, John Patrick Shanahan (D)
Burke, Raymond F. (D)
Burns, James MacGregor (D)
Burtt, Theodore C. (R)
Caldwell, Irene Catherine (R)
Caldwell, Pamela Butler (R)
Campbell, Levin Hicks (R)
Card, Andrew Hill (R)
Carney, Philip N. (D)
Carothers, Charles C, III (R)
Carstensen, Helene Simson (R)
Casdin, Joseph Charles (D)
Casey, John Peter (D)
Cataldo, Paul Amadeo (R)
Cauchon, Robert V. (D)
Cavanaugh, Paul Joseph (D)
Cawley, Robert Lucian (D)
Cherington, Paul W. (R)
Clarke, Clifton Winthrop (R)
Clifford, Jane Elizabeth (R)
Codinha, Paul Phillip (R)
Cogan, John Francis, Jr. (D)
Collatos, Charles Nicholas (D)
Collins, John Frederick (D)
Connolly, Selden Wolcott (R)
Conte, Silvio O. (R)
Conway, James Stephen (D)
Cook, John Lewis (R)
Corriveau, Paul J. (R)
Corso, Philip Louis (R)
Coulter, William Alfred (R)
Courtney, Richard Travers, Jr. (D)
Cox, Archibald (D)
Cox, Gilbert W, Jr. (R)
Craig, Russell H. (R)
Crane, Bruce (R)
Crane, Robert Q. (D)
Craven, James J, Jr. (D)
Craven, Katherine Patricia (D)
Creedon, Robert Stanton, Jr. (D)
Crispin, Marjorie Lawrena (R)
Cronin, George Francis (D)
Cronin, Paul William (R)
Cunningham, Joseph M, Jr. (R)
Curtis, Laurence (R)
Cutler, David (R)
Dabrowski, Edward K.
Dahl, Curtis (R)
Daly, Michael John (D)
Daly, Richard Walker (R)
Davoren, John Francis Xavier (D)
Debar, Frank Richard (R)
DeGuglielmo, Joseph Arcangel (D)
Demers, Richard H. (D)
deRham, Casimir, Jr. (R)
Dever, Edward James (D)
Dibble, Daniel Francis (D)
DiCarlo, Joseph Carmine (D)
DiFruscia, Anthony R. (D)
DiVirgilio, Albert Vincent (D)
Dolan, John F. (R)
Donahue, Richard King (D)
Donoghue, Marion P. (D)
Donoghue, Patrick Joseph (D)
Donohue, Harold D. (D)
Donovan, Eileen Roberta
Donovan, John Francis, Jr. (D)
Dowd, Phoebe Mary (D)
Dowds, James Alexander (R)
Driscoll, John Thomas (D)
Dubino, Helen Mary (R)
Dugan, Robert Joseph (R)
Dullea, Edward J, Jr. (D)
Dwight, Maria Burgee (R)
Dwyer, Claire Buckley (D)
Dyer, Donald J. (R)
Eckstein, Otto (D)
Eisenstadt, Thomas Stephen (D)
Elam, Clarence Richard (R)
Emerson, Galo Putnam, Jr. (R)
Epstein, Rubin (D)
Epstein, Seymour Francis (D)
Evansen, Robert Edward (R)
Fantasia, Mary (D)
Feeney, Joseph Francis (D)
Felloni, Julio (D)
Fitzgerald, John J. (D)
Fitzgerald, John James (D)
Fitzgerald, Patrick F. (D)
Fitzgerald, Pauline McNamara (D)
Flaherty, Charles Francis, Jr. (D)
Flaherty, Michael Francis (D)
Fleming, Richard Thorpe (R)
Flynn, David L. (D)
Fontana, Raymond Joseph (R)
Foster, Eleanor Corinne (R)
Fox, J. Ronald
Frazier, Robert E. (D)
Freedberg, John Michael (R)
Freedman, Frank Harlan (R)
Freeman, Bruce N. (R)
Frenette, Henry N, Jr. (R)
Friedman, Benjamin A. (D)
Fuller, Robert Turner (R)
Furcolo, Foster (D)
Galbraith, J. Kenneth (D)
Galotti, Edward Francis (D)
Gammal, Albert Abraham, Jr. (R)
Gannett, Ann Cole (R)
Garbose, Doris Rhoda (R)
Gaucher, Clifford O. (D)
Gaudette, Donald Roger (D)
Gayron, T. Harold (D)
Geanakos, George J. (R)
Geller, Michael (D)
Giadone, William Biagio (R)
Gilligan, Julie (D)
Glovsky, C. Henry (R)
Gonzals, John Peter (R)
Goodwin, Richard N. (D)
Gordon, Robert H. (R)
Gormalley, Joan Patricia (R)
Gould, Harold D, Jr. (D)
Grant, William Patrick (D)
Graves, Hazel Caroline (R)
Greenberg, Joel Selig (D)
Greene, William C. (R)
Griffin, Walter Joseph (R)
Hall, Godfrey Worth (R)
Hamilton, Daniel (R)
Hammond, George Donald (R)
Hanify, Joseph Edward, Jr. (D)
Hannon, Barry Thomas (D)
Hanson, P. Emery (R)
Harrington, Edward Dennis, Jr. (R)
Harrington, Edward F. (D)
Harrington, Michael Joseph (D)
Harrington, Patrick H. (D)
Harris, J. Edmond (R)
Harrison, David Eldridge (D)
Hatch, Francis Whiting, Jr. (R)
Hawke, Robert Douglas (R)
Hayes, Albert J. (D)
Hays, David Witherow (R)
Hayward, Channing Wayne (R)
Healy, Winston (R)
Heckler, Margaret M. (R)
Henderson, James H. (R)
Hermann, Robert Lambert (R)
Hersey, Ralph Bertram, Jr. (R)
Hines, Arthur Snow (R)
Hines, Peter Francis (D)
Hogan, Charles V. (D)
Holgate, Franklin Wesley (D)
Hollis, Herbert Brown (R)
Holmer, John Kenneth (R)
Holmstrom, Andrew Birger (R)
Horne, Alice M. (R)
Houthakker, Hendrik Samuel (R)
Howard, Edwin Morey, Jr. (R)
Howe, Eunice P. (R)
Howe, Marie Elizabeth (D)
Hughes, H(enry) Stuart (D)
Ivascyn, John Peter (D)
Jackson, Ellen M. (D)
Jazowski, J. Peter, Jr. (R)
Johnson, George Alfred (R)
Johnson, Raymond Allan (R)
Jones, Aubrey Elroy (R)
Jones, Harold Kinsman (R)
Jones, Leona Bromwell (R)
Joyce, Daniel L, Jr. (D)
Kairit, Eleanor Jessie (R)
Kane, Irving Edward (D)
Kane, Katharine D. (D)
Keady, George Cregan, Jr. (R)
Keane, Francis Michael (D)
Kearney, Joseph Matthew (D)
Keith, Hastings (R)
Kelleher, Frank Henry (D)
Keller, Donald Monroe (R)
Kelliher, Walter James (D)
Kelly, James Anthony, Jr. (D)
Kelly, James H. (D)
Kenneally, George Vincent, Jr. (D)
Kennedy, Edward Moore (D)
Kenney, Burton (R)
Kenney, Daniel Joseph (R)
Kenny, Frederick Leo (D)
Khachadoorian, Gregory Benjamin (R)
Kiley, Daniel Patrick, Jr. (D)
Kimball, Edward W. (R)
Kirby, Edward Paul (R)
Kissinger, Henry Alfred
Kitchener, Ruth Mae (R)
Kittredge, Enid Suzanne (R)
Klassen, E. T. (R)
Kossoi, Milton (R)
Kottis, John Gregory (R)
Krock, Edward (D)
Ladeau, George Arthur, Jr. (R)
Lamson, Fred I. (R)
Lane, David Judson (R)
Lane, Thomas J. (D)
Lapointe, Francis Charles (D)
LaRaia, Joseph J. (D)
Laughlin, Lawrence Roy (D)
Leblanc, J. Louis (D)
Lenhoff, Bernard (R)
Liederman, David Samuel (D)
Lilley, John Robert, II (R)
Linsky, Martin A. (R)
Lippman, George Jennings (R)
Locke, David Henry (R)
Lodge, George Cabot (R)
Lodge, Henry Cabot (R)
Lolas, Alexander (D)
Lombard, James Manuel (R)
Long, John Joseph (D)
Longstreet, Victor Mendell (D)
Losch, John Charles (R)
Lurvey, Mildred Edwina (R)
Lyons, Ida Rita (D)
McBride, Anthony P. (D)
McCann, Francis X. (D)
McCarthy, William Augustus (R)
McColgan, Edward Anthony (D)
McCormack, Edward Joseph, Jr. (D)
McCormack, John W. (D)
MacDonald, Robert William (D)
MacDonald, Torbert H. (D)
McGee, Thomas W. (D)
McGlennon, John Austin Shaw (R)
McGuire, Henry M. (D)
McGuire, Joseph Edward (D)
McKenna, Arthur James (D)
McKenna, Patrick E. (R)
MacKenzie, Ronald Conrad (R)
MacLean, William Q, Jr. (D)
McMahon, James Robert, Jr. (D)
Maguire, Robert Charles (D)
Maguire, William James (D)
MaHood, Cecil Heber (R)
Mann, Charles W. (R)
Mann, Theodore D. (R)
Manning, Donald J. (D)
Manning, M. Joseph (D)
Manzi, Albert Paul (R)
Marino, Anthony V. (R)
Marshall, Clifford Holmes (D)
Martin, Baron Hay II (D)
Martin, Joseph F. (R)
Martin, Spencer Ferrin, Jr. (R)
Masterman, Harold (R)
Mastrangelo, Richard Edward (R)
Mendall, Ralph Bertrand, Jr. (R)
Menton, Paul C. (D)
Merrick, Samuel Vaughan (D)

Metayer, Elizabeth Nener (D)
Miller, Howard A, Jr. (R)
Miller, S. Lee (R)
Mitchell, Nicholas Wilfred (D)
Moakley, John Joseph (D)
Monahan, John Leo (D)
Monahan, Maurice Brice (R)
Mooney, Michael L. (D)
Moore, Jonathan (R)
Moore, Roger Allan (R)
Moran, Robert Daniel (R)
Morse, Frank Bradford (R)
Morton, Hugh (R)
Moynihan, Daniel Patrick (D)
Mullen, James G. (D)
Murphy, John Francis (D)
Murray, James Joseph, III (D)
Mushnick, Samuel Winiker (R)
Naurison, Morton Stanley (R)
Nee, Patrick William (D)
Nefussy, Eli Maurice (R)
Neunherz, Lise Jungshoved (R)
Newman, Mary B. (R)
Newth, Thomas M. (R)
Nickerson, Reginald Lee (R)
Nilson, Herbert Tomlin (R)
Nolen, James Richard (D)
Nordberg, Nils Lovering (R)
Norton, Francis Carleton (R)
Norton, Philip Jeffrey (R)
Nuciforo, Andrea Francesco (D)
O'Brien, Chester J. (R)
O'Brien, Lawrence Francis (D)
O'Donnell, Kenneth P. (D)
O'Donnell, Philip Conroy (D)
Ohanian, Charles (D)
Olver, John Walter (D)
O'Meara, George F, Jr. (D)
O'Neill, James Joseph (D)
O'Neill, Thomas P, Jr. (D)
Palmer, Walter Henderson (R)
Parenteau, Carolyn Blanche (R)
Park, Douglas Campbell (R)
Paulin, Camille A. (R)
Paull, Richard Cary (R)
Peabody, Endicott (D)
Peabody, Malcolm, Jr. (R)
Pearson, Eric Gustav (R)
Pease, Lucille Currie (R)
Peck, Raymond Stuart (D)
Pellegrini, Philibert L. (D)
Peoples, Charles Frederick (R)
Perenick, Charles Henry (R)
Peterson, Gunnar Aron Julius (R)
Peterson, Hjalmar Reginald (R)
Philbin, Philip Joseph (D)
Pinanski, Viola R. (R)
Piro, Vincent Joseph (D)
Powers, John E. (D)
Proctor, Helen June (R)
Quinlan, John M. (R)
Quinn, Philip Andrew (D)
Quinn, Robert H. (D)
Randall, Donald H. (R)
Randall, William I. (R)
Ratte, George Joseph (R)
Read, Harry Augustus Sherman (R)
Reinstein, William George (D)
Reis, John C, Jr. (R)
Renahan, Thomas Michael, Jr. (R)
Rescia, George Frank (R)
Reynolds, Richard L. (D)
Reynolds, Robert Charles (R)
Richardson, Elliot Lee (R)
Richmany, James M. (D)
Robert, Ernest (R)
Roberts, Donald Keith (D)
Robinson, Winthrop Lincoln (R)
Rockett, J. Hilary (R)
Rogers, George (D)
Romanos, George Marcus, Jr. (R)
Roodkowsky, Alice May (R)
Rosen, Harold Ellis (R)
Rosner, Henry George (R)
Ryan, Donald Neil (D)
Ryan, William Herbert (R)
Sacchetti, Dominic Vincent (R)
Sacco, George Lawrence, Jr. (D)
St. Cyr, John F. (R)
Sala, Roger Andrew (D)
Salerno, Robert (D)
Salmonsen, Lyman Stanley (R)
Saltonstall, Leverett (R)
Saltonstall, Sally Brooks (R)
Saltonstall, William Lawrence (R)
Sandberg, Chester C. (R)
Sargent, Francis W. (R)
Saulnier, Joseph Douglas (R)
Schoonmaker, Neill Weiss, Jr. (R)
Schwartz, Edna Barbara (D)
Scott, Alphonse A. (R)
Scott, Leonard A. (R)
Sears, John Winthrop (R)
Sears, Philip Mason (R)
Sears, Ruth Parker (R)
Semensi, Joseph John (D)
Serlin, I. Edward (D)
Shattuck, George William (R)
Shea, H. James, Jr. (D)
Sheehan, John Francis (D)
Sheehy, Edward Driscoll (D)
Shinberg, Aaron M. I. (D)
Shinberg, Rose Ruth (D)
Sidd, Allan (D)
Sigourney, Andre R. (D)
Simkin, William E. (D)
Simpson, Russell G. (R)
Sisitsky, Alan David (D)
Skerry, Patrick Joseph (D)
Smith, A. Ledyard, Jr. (R)
Smith, Dennis A. (D)
Smith, James Harold (D)
Smith, James McCormick (R)
Solomon, Bernard (D)
Spaulding, Josiah A. (R)
Spence, William James (D)
Spencer, Anne H. (D)
Stevens, Chandler Harrison, Jr. (Independent)
Stiles, Annie Lovina (R)
Stuart, Douglas S. (R)
Sullivan, Edward Joseph (D)
Sullivan, John Joseph, Jr. (D)
Sullivan, John M.
Sullivan, Kevin Cornelius (D)
Sullivan, Walter Joseph (D)
Tache, Roger Peter (R)
Talbot, A. Edward (R)
Tarr, Frederick Hamilton, III (R)
Taylor, Balcom Shaw (D)
Taymor, Betty (D)
Thomson, James Claude, Jr. (D)
Thoutsis, Timotheos Michael (R)
Titus, Douglas Leroy (R)
Tobin, David Spence (D)
Toland, Dennis Patrick (D)
Tomyl, Michael (R)
Toon, Malcolm
Towse, Daniel Charles (R)
Treadway, Richard Fowle (R)
Tucker, William Humphrey (D)
Tuller, Paul Raymond (R)
Tuttle, Elbert (R)
Tuttle, Robert Bradford (R)
Twomey, George E. (R)
Tyson, Bertrand Oliver (D)
Underhill, Frederick William, Jr. (R)
Vayo, Gerard A. (R)
Vigneau, Robert A. (D)
Villela, Ruy Santos (R)
Walsh, Daniel Michael, Jr. (D)
Walsh, Francis P. (D)
Webster, Dean Kingman (R)
Weeks, William Dowse (R)
Welch, Ronald E. (D)
White, Albert Charles, Jr. (R)
White, Donald Blaisdell (R)
White, Kevin Hagan (D)
Whitehead, Donald Wharton (R)
Whiting, Thelma P. (Independent)
Whitman, Reginald Norman (R)
Whitney, Ira Dexter (R)
Wiggin, Frank L. (R)
Williams, Arthur (R)
Williams, Gordon Oliver (R)
Wing, Francis William (R)
Winter, Madeline Field (R)
Wojtkowski, Thomas Casmere (D)
Woodard, Willliam Philip (R)
Wright, John W. (R)
Yarmolinsky, Adam (D)
Young, George C. (R)
Young, William Joseph (R)
Zarod, Stanley John (D)
Zeiser, Bruce Hunter (R)

MICHIGAN

Abercrombie, Howard Randolph (D)
Ackley, (Hugh) Gardner (D)
Adair, Nira Moore (R)
Adams, Paul Lincoln (D)
Addison, Robert A. (R)
Adrounie, Dorothy (R)
Ahart, Thomas Insell (R)
Allen, Lester J. (R)
Allen, Richard John (R)
Anderson, Harold Earl (R)
Anderson, Thomas J(efferson) (D)
Appelget, Ervin Roy (D)
Archer, Harold Lawrence (D)
Arnett, Homer (R)
Backus, Jean Rae (R)
Baker, Raymond L. (R)
Baldwin, David Rawson (D)
Ballenger, William S, III (R)
Barber, Richard J.
Barber, Robert J. (R)
Barcus, G. Douglas, Jr. (R)
Beadle, Frank D. (R)
Beckwith, Florence Hess (R)
Beedon, Francis W. (D)
Belen, Frederick C(hristopher) (D)
Bengry, Ellsworth Ray (D)
Bennett, John (D)
Bentley, Alvin M, Jr. (R)
Berla, Michael J. (D)
Berlo, David Kenneth (R)
Berry, Michael (D)
Bertz, Ralph Harrison (R)
Bessey, Carol (D)
Bieber, Owen F. (D)
Bielawski, Anthony F. (D)
Bishop, Donald E. (R)
Blue, William Roy (D)
Boos, Wm. A, Jr. (D)
Boucher, George Victor (R)
Bowman, John T. (D)
Boykin, Ulysses W. (R)
Braathen, Clayton Arnold (R)
Bradley, James (D)
Bradley, Russell Wallen (D)
Brennan, Bert C. (R)
Brennan, Thomas Emmett See Addenda
Brickley, James H.
Brighton, Howard (D)
Broomfield, William S. (R)
Brouillette, Francis Delore (D)
Brown, Basil W. (D)
Brown, Daniel R. (D)
Brown, Garry Eldridge (R)
Brown, George Hay (R)
Brown, Jean Isabelle (R)
Brown, Prentiss Marsh (D)
Brown, Thomas Henry (D)
Brown, Thomas L. (R)
Bruff, John Bowman (D)
Buhl, Lloyd Frank (R)
Burdick, Irwin H. (R)
Burk, Rachel Irene (D)
Burns, William Lloyd (R)
Bursley, Gilbert E. (R)
Buth, Martin D. (R)
Butt, Bettie Lou (R)
Calabrese, Sylvia M. (D)
Callahan, James N. (D)
Campbell, Wyman D. (D)
Canfield, John Lemual (R)
Cappaert, LeRoy A. (D)
Carey, Edward Anthony (D)
Carey, Patricia Jean I. (R)
Carter, Michael Laverne (R)
Cartwright, Arthur (D)
Cater, Eugene R. (D)
Cavanagh, Jerome Patrick (D)
Cederberg, Elford A. (R)
Chamberlain, Charles E. (R)
Chambers, Lillian Boyle (R)
Charlton, Fred Russell (R)
Charron, Sanford E. (D)
Chase, Nancy Bastien (R)
Chatterson, Bertha Marie (R)
Clark, Harold B. (D)
Clark, Lee Hinchman (R)
Clements, John V. (R)
Clevenger, Raymond Francis (D)
Closz, Harold F, Jr. (R)
Clunis, Wager Frederick (D)
Cobb, Andrew Whitney (R)
Cohen, Wilbur Joseph (D)
Cohn, Morton Ray (D)
Collins, John Joseph (D)
Conlin, Rollo G. (R)
Connelly, Brian Robert (R)
Conrad, Charles Oscar (D)
Constantini, James K. (D)
Conyers, John, Jr. (D)
Cook, Henry Holden (D)
Cook, Richard Martin (D)
Cooper, Daniel S. (D)
Copeland, William R. (D)
Cowden, Thomas K. (R)
Craig, Roger E. (D)
Cramton, Louis Kav (R)
Crim, Bobby L. (D)
Crowley, Francis A. (D)
Czarnecki, Walter (R)
Darrow, Peter P. (D)
Dartland, Walter T. (D)
Daugherty, John Balcom (R)
Davis, Charles J. (R)
Davis, Stanley J. (D)
De Bruyn, William Edward (R)
De Caussin, Edmund John, Jr. (D)
DeGrow, Alvin James (R)
Del Rio, James (D)
DeMaso, Harry A. (R)
Dessert, Gerald L. (D)
DeStigter, Melvin (R)
Dethmers, John R. (R)
Dexter, Louis Miles (R)
Diggs, Charles Coles, Jr. (D)
Dimmers, David Albert (R)
Dingell, John D. (D)
Dingwell, Robert E. (D)
Dittlinger, Micheal Adam, Sr. (D)
Dively, Michael Augustus (R)
Dobie, Gertrude Agnes (R)
Doherty, Walter Gerard (R)
Doll, Bernard Thomas (R)
Domitrovich, Frank Anthony (D)
Donahue, R. Patrick (D)
Doughty, Warren Browe (D)
Downing, Neil Frederick (D)
Driver, Marjorie M. (R)
Dubbelde, Herman Henry (R)
Dunn, Gerald Raymond (D)
Dunnell, Mildred Hazel (R)
Dwyer, Robert Eugene (D)
Dwyer, Theodore John (R)
Dyell, Mary Laverne (R)
Dzendzel, Raymond D. (D)
Edwards, George (D)
Edwards, George H. (D)
Edwards, Nelson Jack (D)
Eggle, Doris E. (R)
Elliott, Daisy (D)
Elsesser, Betty (R)
Engstrom, Arnell (R)
Ensign, W. Scott (D)
Erlandsen, Einar E. (D)
Esch, Marvin L. (R)
Evans, Hubert Carol (D)
Fairchild, Alfred Charles (D)
Farnsworth, James S. (R)
Farnum, Billie Sunday (D)
Farr, William S, Jr. (R)
Faust, William Paul (D)
Faxon, Jack (D)
Feinstein, Otto (D)
Fenner, Bertine Lorraine (D)
Ferency, Zolton A. (D)
Ferguson, Joel Irving (D)
Ferguson, Rosetta (D)
Fill, Leon (D)
Fina, Eunyce Aloys (R)
Firley, Carl Franklin (R)
Fishman, Alvin (D)
Fitzgerald, George S. (D)
Fitzgerald, William B. (D)
Fitzpatrick, John J. (D)
Flavin, Ray M. (D)
Fleming, James G. (R)
Fletcher, Peter B. (R)
Folks, James N. (R)
Ford, Gerald R. (R)
Ford, Thomas G, Sr. (R)
Ford, William David (D)
Fowler, R. Lynn (R)
Frazier, Lincoln B. (R)
Freeh, Edwin James, Jr. (D)
Frink, Gary R. (D)
Fuller, Ralph C. (R)
Furlong, Frank J. (D)
Galinet, Peter C. (D)
Garrett, James Neal, Jr. (D)
Gast, Roy Andrew (R)
Gaugh, James H. (D)
Gaultier, Gerald Douglas (R)
Geerlings, Edgar Allen (R)
Gettel, Gerhard F. (R)
Gibbons, Delmar Dale (Prohibition Party)
Gibbs, John Allen (R)
Gibson, Catharine (R)
Gillman, Michael J. (R)
Gilman, Gordon St. John (R)
Gilmore, James Stanley, Jr. (R)
Gladstone, William (D)
Glusac, Michael M. (Non-partisan)
Goemaere, Warren N. (D)
Googasian, George Ara (D)
Gould, Lora Ione (D)
Grant, Robert Williams, Jr. (R)
Gray, Charles F. (D)
Gray, Marcus J. (D)
Green, Allison (R)

Green, Joseph Thomas (R)
Griffen, Daniel (D)
Griffin, Robert Paul (R)
Griffiths, Martha W. (D)
Grimes, Thomas Parnell (R)
Griner, Adeline Caltha (D)
Guastello, Thomas (D)
Hafstad, Katharine Clarke (R)
Hall, Richard Harold (D)
Hampton, William Peck (R)
Hare, James McNeil (D)
Harris, Max Brooks (R)
Harrison, James A. (D)
Hart, Adelaide Julia (D)
Hart, Jerome Thomas (D)
Hart, Philip A. (D)
Hartley, Minnie Matilda (R)
Harvey, James (R)
Hastings, Joseph Henry (R)
Hayward, William (R)
Hayworth, Don (D)
Headlee, Richard Harold (R)
Heinz, Lyle Kenneth (D)
Heinze, James Henry (R)
Hellman, Russell (D)
Henderson, Robert G. (R)
Herman, Donald Louis (D)
Hertzberg, Stuart E. (D)
Hicks, David L. (R)
Hill, Rowland Lester (D)
Hipkins, Stella A. (D)
Hobbs, Ruth Josephine (R)
Hobbs, Wendell Wilson (R)
Hoffman, Quincy (R)
Holbel, Diane Erickson (R)
Holbrook, Donald E, Jr. (R)
Holden, Creighton Davidson (R)
Holley, Hubert Lee (D)
Holmes, David S, Jr. (D)
Hood, Raymond W. (D)
Hook, Frank Eugene (D)
Horn, Carl Lewis (R)
Horrigan, Albert R. (D)
Howard, Laurence Edward (D)
Hubbard, Orville L. (R)
Huber, Robert J. (R)
Huey, Arthur Ticknor (R)
Huffman, Bill S. (D)
Huhtala, Ralph E. (R)
Humphrey, W. Hugh (R)
Hunsinger, Josephine D. (D)
Huston, Mary Thelma (D)
Hutchinson, Edward (R)
Huvaere, Valere (D)
Jackson, Murray Earl (D)
Jacobetti, Dominic J. (D)
Jamieson, Norman Leslie (R)
Jeffrey, Mildred (D)
Johns, Roy William (R)
Johnson, Dorr A. (R)
Johnson, Fridolf (D)
Jones, Francis A, III (R)
Kadish, Paul Yale (D)
Kaess, Fred W. (R)
Karoub, James H. (D)
Kavanagh, Thomas Matthew (D)
Kay, Thomas
Keenan, Thomas Le Roy (D)
Kehres, Raymond C. (D)
Keier, Richard Frederick (R)
Kelley, Frank J. (D)
Kelley, Joan Gund (D)
Kelsey, John T. (D)
Kendall, James Allen (R)
Kennedy, Earl (R)
Kildee, Dale E. (D)
Kime, F. Willard (R)
King, Raymond Lamprey (R)
Kinney, Roxie W. (R)
Kirsch, Charles Edward (R)
Klaus, Walter Kloepping (R)
Klei, Louis William (R)
Kleiner, A. Robert (D)
Klempnow, Paul L. J. (D)
Kneen, Richard A. (R)
Knox, Patti (D)
Knox, Victor A. (R)
Koeze, Ella Demmink (R)
Koivisto, Clifford Daniel (R)
Kok, Peter (R)
Kolb, Eugene J. (D)
Kory, Delores Nevada (R)
Koss, Esther Elizabeth (D)
Kramer, Albert A. (D)
Kriekard, Harold Edward (R)
Krnacik, John, Jr. (D)
Krohn, Helen Josephine (D)
Kubert, Carolynne Frances (D)
Kuthy, Eugene Wendel (D)
Lane, Garland (D)
LaPorte, Alfred O. (R)
Laskey, Norma Jean (R)
Lauricella, Sal A. (R)
Law, Arthur J. (D)
Lebenbom, David (D)
Ledman, Eldon Dale (R)
Lee, Albert
Lee, Catherine Patricia (R)
Legg, Louis E, Jr. (R)
Lesinski, T. John
Levey, Nita B. (R)
Levin, Sander M. (D)
Light, Catherine (D)
Light, Eleanor M. (D)
Lincoln, George A. (R)
Lindroos, LaVanne M. (R)
Lipscomb, Willie G, Jr. (R)
Little, Carl O. (R)
Lockwood, Emil (R)
Logan, Irene Elizabeth (R)
Loupee, Eva Celestia (R)
McCauley, John E. (D)
McClure, Harold Milton (R)
McCollough, Lucille Hanna (D)
McCracken, Paul Winston (R)
McDonald, Jack H. (R)
McFern, Genevieve P. (R)
McGoff, John Peter (R)
Machrowicz, Thaddeus Michael (D)
McIntire, John Elmer (D)
Mackie, John C. (D)
McLaughlin, William Francis (R)
McNeely, James Michael (D)
McNeely, Matthew (D)
Magee, Robert (R)
Mahalak, Edward E. (D)
Mahoney, Robert D. (D)
Malmberg, Steven Robert (D)
Mantey, Carl F. (R)
Marek, Richard John (D)
Marlin, Don Lee Roy (D)
Marshall, Frederic J. (R)
Martin, John Butlin (R)
Mastin, Philip Olin, Jr. (D)
Mathes, Donald Taylor (R)
Mattheeussen, Floyd J. (D)
May, Alfred A. (R)
May, Wallace G. (R)
Maynard, Olivia Benedict (D)
Meachum, Robert Lewis (D)
Meader, George (R)
Meekhof, George (R)
Merrelli, George (D)
Merrill, William Hale (D)
Meyer, Frank (R)
Michalski, Edward K. (D)
Miller, Norman Lee (D)
Millhouse, Clifford John (R)
Milliken, William Grawn (R)
Mitchell, Leland Dewight (D)
Mitchell, Robert S. (D)
Moffat, John Weir (R)
Monks, Bruce L. (D)
Monte, Raymond Louis (D)
Montgomery, George F. (D)
Morrison, Clayton T. (R)
Morse, Elizabeth Ann (D)
Mossner, Eugene Donald (D)
Murninghan, Max Ernest (R)
Murphy, Norbert Clinton (D)
Nagel, Gladys S. (R)
Nagelvoort, Bernard Charles (R)
Nedzi, Lucien Norbert (D)
Nelson, LeRoy James (D)
Newhouse, Gerald Francis (R)
Nichols, Haskell L. (R)
Nichols, William Preston (R)
North, Sally Anne (R)
Norvell, John Hugh (R)
Novak, Ethel V. (R)
Novak, Stanley (D)
O'Brien, Bernard F, Jr. (D)
O'Brien, Carl W. (D)
O'Brien, E. D. (D)
O'Hara, James Grant (D)
Olsson, Eleanor (R)
O'Rourke, Peter Edward (R)
O'Toole, Thomas J. (D)
Ott, Alexander Reginald (D)
Paluch, Leo Leon (D)
Parish, Tat (D)
Parris, George Nick (D)
Payne, Howard E. (R)
Pearl, Dorothy Waite (R)
Pears, Don R. (R)
Pember, Robert Wayne (D)
Perlos, Alexander Charles (D)
Peterson, Elly M. (R)
Petitpren, Vincent J. (D)
Phelan, Ellen Skae (R)
Pilch, Alex (D)
Pilot, Larry R.
Pinnick, Siria F. (R)
Pintar, Anton James (D)
Pittenger, Philip Osborn (R)
Pixley, Theodore R, Sr. (D)
Platt, Faun (R)
Plewa, Casmere Joseph (R)
Pobuda, Robert E. (R)
Polley, Ira
Potter, S. Don (R)
Pouzar, Thomas Frank (D)
Powell, Stanley M. (R)
Power, Philip Harwick (D)
Pridgeon, Dean M. (R)
Puffer, K(enneth) Hart (R)
Pulido, Alberto (D)
Putnam, Peggy Joan (R)
Quarker, Dorothy Elaine (D)
Quinn, Donald Lee (R)
Raap, F. Charles (D)
Radant, Kenneth Raymond (R)
Rambo, Agnes McKinnell Wilson (R)
Rathbun, Frank Hugo (D)
Reader, Barbara Jean (R)
Reissing, Theodore Charles, Sr. (R)
Richards, Harold Leland (D)
Richardson, Robert (R)
Riecker, Margaret Ann (R)
Riegle, Donald W, Jr. (R)
Riolo, Michael A. (D)
Roberts, Farrell E. (R)
Robertson, Ruth Elizabeth (R)
Robinson, Edward J. (D)
Robinson, Henrietta (D)
Robinson, Kenneth William (D)
Robinson, Richard Earl (R)
Rockwell, Gordon (R)
Roe, Jerry D. (R)
Rohlfs, Harry E. (R)
Romney, George Wilcken (R)
Root, Cyril H. (R)
Root, Edson V, Jr. (R)
Roth, Stephen J. (D)
Rouse, Eliene Wilhelmina (R)
Rouse, Frederick Oakes (R)
Rozycki, Stanley F. (D)
Ruppe, Philip E. (R)
Ruwe, L. Nicholas (R)
Ryan, Harold Martin (D)
Ryan, William A. (D)
Sackett, Wayne B. (R)
St. Louis, George (D)
Sallade, George Wahr (D)
Sanford, Bernard H. (R)
Sarapo, Donato Frank (R)
Schmidt, Louis Edward (R)
Scholle, August (D)
Schroeder, Arthur E. (D)
Schweigert, Thomas F. (R)
Schwesinger, Chester Robert (R)
Selin, Virginia Mae (D)
Serotkin, David M. (R)
Sharkey, George Edward (D)
Sharpe, Thomas G. (R)
Sheffield, Horace Lindsey (D)
Sheridan, Alfred A. (D)
Sietsema, George (D)
Silver, Paul (D)
Silverstein, Lawrence G. (D)
Simmons, Samuel J. (D)
Sinclair, John Richley (R)
Sladek, Henry Robert (R)
Slingerlend, Robert J. (D)
Smart, Clifford H. (R)
Smit, Raymond J. (R)
Smith, Charlotte Westbrook (R)
Smith, James F. (R)
Smith, Lawrence Peter (D)
Smith, Sheldon B. (R)
Snell, Hilary Fred (R)
Snyder, Joseph M. (D)
Sonneveldt, Chris H.
Sparling, James M, Jr. (R)
Sparrow, David John (D)
Spencer, Roy L. (R)
Sperry, Ralph Russell (D)
Stack, Jack Michael (R)
Staebler, Neil (D)
Stahlin, John Henry (R)
Stamm, Anthony (R)
Steeh, Victor R. (D)
Stein, Ivan C. (R)
Stempien, Marvin R. (D)
Stempien, Ronald Robert (D)
Stepp, Marc (D)
Stevens, J. Harold (R)
Stewart, Melvin James (D)
Stites, Robert Clare (R)
Stockmeyer, Norman Otto (R)
Stolz, Mabel Smith (D)
Stopczynski, Stephen (D)
Summerfield, Arthur Ellsworth (R)
Suski, Edward (D)
Sutherland, Paul Oscar (D)
Swallow, Joseph Patrick (R)
Symons, Joyce (D)
Taylor, Hobart, Jr. (D)
Teeter, Howard M. (R)
Thorne, William H. (D)
Tierney, James (D)
Tinker, Richard William (R)
Tisdale, Nelson G. (R)
Todd, Paul Harold, Jr. (D)
Transue, Andrew Jackson (D)
Traxler, J. Robert (D)
Trepp, Gloria F. (R)
Tretheway, Bernice Ruth (R)
Trolley, Richard Joseph (D)
Troutt, Terry L. (D)
Tuchow, Gerald (D)
Tucker, Charlotte Paige (D)
Turcott, Thomas (R)
Turcotte, Clifford Lawrence (D)
Tyson, Charles Elwood (R)
Umphrey, James Morris (R)
Upton, David Frederick (R)
Vagnozzi, Aldo (D)
Vander Jagt, Guy (R)
Vanderlaan, Robert (R)
Vanderploeg, Jan B. (D)
Vandette, Edmund Frederick (R)
Van Dusen, Richard Campbell (R)
Van Duyne, Frederick William (R)
Varnum, Charles Henry (R)
Ver Plank, Joel P. (R)
Vincent, Dwight Harold (R)
Vivian, Weston E. (D)
Volkema, Harold James (R)
Vonalt, Fred L. (D)
VonBlaskewicz, Betty Jane (R)
Wagner, Floyd E. (R)
Walbridge, John Tuthill, Jr. (R)
Waldron, Robert Edwin (R)
Walker, Lloyd Edward (R)
Walton, Leonard S. (D)
Ward, Vivienne T. (R)
Ware, Richard Anderson (R)
Warner, Dale Irving (R)
Weber, Elmer Otto (R)
Weber, William V. (R)
Welch, Gordon Daniel (R)
Westphal, Albert H. (R)
Wheeler, Robert R. (R)
White, Thomas W. (D)
Wierzbicki, Frank V. (D)
Wilkinson, Mary Ann (R)
Will, Calvin Evert (R)
Williams, Esther Robbins (D)
Williams, G. Mennen (D)
Willis, Katherine (R)
Wilson, Elaine M. (D)
Wirth, Helen Irmiger (D)
Wisti, Andrew Henry (D)
Woodcock, Leonard (D)
Woodman, Blair G. (R)
Woods, Patricia Huck (R)
Woods, Thell Michael (R)
Wright, Carl John (R)
Wurzel, Raymond C. (R)
Yeager, Weldon Osborne (R)
Yeates, Charles H. (R)
Young, Coleman A. (D)
Young, Maxcine (D)
Young, Richard A. (D)
Youngblood, Charles N, Jr. (D)
Zaagman, Milton (R)
Zemmol, Allen (D)
Ziegler, Hal Walter (R)
Zollar, Charles O. (R)

MINNESOTA

Adams, Frank Emil (D)
Adams, James L. (DFL)
Adams, Salisbury (Conservative)
Albertson, Howard Randolph (R)
Alexander, John Grant (Independent Republican)
Allen, Claude H.
Alsop, Donald Douglas (R)
Andeen, Birger Baldwin (D)
Andersen, Elmer Lee (R)
Anderson, Amon Ra (DFL)
Anderson, Carl William (DFL)
Anderson, Dagmar Irene (R)
Anderson, Ernest J. (R)

Anderson, Eugenie Moore (D)
Anderson, Harold J. (R)
Anderson, Irvin Neal (DFL)
Anderson, John Tracy (Non-Partisan)
Anderson, Norval August (R)
Anderson, Thor (Conservative)
Anderson, Wendell Richard (D)
Arne, Richard O. (R)
Ashbach, Arlene Delores (R)
Ashbach, Robert O. (R)
Banen, Abraham Theodore (DFL)
Bang, Otto T, Jr. (Conservative)
Barrette, Emery George (R)
Barry, Hilary D. (D)
Bastovich, John (DFL)
Battles, Everett (DFL)
Beach, Stephen Leeds, III (D)
Becker, Robert William (DFL)
Becklin, Robert C. (Conservative)
Beedle, Ernest Arnold (D)
Benson, C. J. (DFL)
Bergemann, Lawrence Alfred (DFL)
Bergerud, Alf L.
Berghuis, Henry Edwin (R)
Bergland, Bob Selmer (DFL)
Berke, Fred H. (DFL)
Bernat, Leo Allen (DFL)
Bigwood, Robert Maurice (R)
Bischoff, Barney (DFL)
Bjornson, Val (R)
Blackmun, Harry Andrew
Blatnik, John A. (DFL)
Blatz, Jerome V. (Conservative)
Blomquist, Glenn A. (DFL)
Blumer, Arlo R. (R)
Bodger, Richard Alan (R)
Borden, Winston Wendell (D)
Brandl, John Edward (D)
Brandt, Edward R. (R)
Brataas, Nancy Osborn (R)
Brink, Lyman Arnold (R)
Brinkman, Bernard J. (DFL)
Brister, Milton E. (D)
Brown, David Millard (R)
Brown, Robert John (R)
Bundlie, Ordner T, Jr. (DFL)
Burton, Daniel F(rederick) (DFL)
Buss, William (Conservative)
Byrne, Thomas Robert (DFL)
Carlson, Bernard O. (DFL)
Chalupsky, Harry Richard (R)
Chapman, Jerome F. (DFL)
Charles, Erland W. (R)
Chelseth, Archie Donald (R)
Chenoweth, John Craig (D)
Christensen, Robert F. (Conservative)
Christenson, Gerald William (D)
Christgau, Victor
Christianson, Marvin E. (DFL)
Cina, Fred A. (DFL)
Coleman, Nicholas D. (DFL)
Connolly, John Stevens (D)
Conzemius, George Robert (DFL)
Cook, Robert Eugene (R)
Crain, V. Richard (DFL)
Curtis, John F. (DFL)
Dahl, Arden (D)
Dahlin, Melba R. (D)
Daly, Michael James (D)
Davies, John Thomas (DFL)
Dean, William Denard (DFL)
Delaney, Frances I. (DFL)
Dickey, Brad Wilfer (R)
Dickinson, Leonard Ralph (R)
Dillon, Gerald Richard (DFL)
Dirlam, Aubrey William (R)
Dodge, M. Eugene (DFL)
Doering, Lee Everett (R)
Doffing, Godfrey Raymond (D)
Donovan, Joseph L. (DFL)
Dosland, William Buehler (R)
Drexler, John M. (R)
Du Bois, B. F. (DFL)
Dunlap, Robert R. (Non-Partisan)
Dunn, Robert G. (Conservative)
Dunton, Harold Hartley (R)
Duxbury, Lloyd L, Jr. (Conservative)
Dworkin, Martin (DFL)
Eatros, Alexander Michael (D)
Ehlers, Thomas Martin (R)
Eisenman, Jane Morley (R)
Ellingson, Herman E. (R)
Ellison, Charles E, Jr. (DFL)
Enebo, Stanley A.
Engelbrecht, Arthur (DFL)
Erdahl, Arlen Ingolf (R)
Erickson, Carl Wendell (R)
Erickson, Wendell O. (Conservative)
Erlander, Rose (DFL)
Esau, Gilbert D. (Conservative)
Etzell, George Ferdinand (R)
Eustis, Warren Penhall (DFL)
Evenson, Marvin Arnold (DFL)
Everson, Ronald Albin (R)
Farmer, Lyle T. (DFL)
Farr, George A. (D)
Fena, Jack (DFL)
Ferguson, Lawrence W. (D)
Fischer, W. Casper (Conservative)
Fisher, Leo Frank (DFL)
Fitzsimons, Richard W. (Conservative)
Flakne, Gary W. (R)
Flemming, Arthur Sherwood (R)
Foley, Eugene Patrick (D)
Forseth, Donald E. (Conservative)
Forsythe, Robert Ames (R)
France, Alfred E. (Conservative)
Franz, W. J. (Conservative)
Fraser, Donald MacKay (DFL)
Frederick, Melvin Lyle (R)
Fredriksen, Arnold Louis (DFL)
Freeman, Orville Lothrop (D)
French, George A.
Frentz, Roy (R)
Frenzel, William Eldridge (R)
Frerichs, Donald L. (R)
Frick, Arthur, H, Sr. (Conservative)
Fudro, Stanley J. (DFL)
Fugina, Peter X. (DFL)
Gage, Fred Kelton (R)
Gainey, Daniel Charles (R)
Gearty, Edward Joseph (DFL)
Geib, G. Harriet (R)
Geittmann, Ida Mae (D)
Gerling, Gordon Douglas (D)
Gillen, Arthur F. (R)
Glewwe, Rollin Bert (R)
Goetz, James B. (R)
Gorlin, Marilyn Alpern (DFL)
Gorman, George E. (D)
Graven, David Lauren (DFL)
Graw, Joseph P.
Grittner, Karl Frederick (DFL)
Gruhn, Karl (DFL)
Grussendorf, Wm. T. (Conservative)
Grussing, George P. (Conservative)
Gruys, Arnold (DFL)
Gunderson, Maxine Delores (DFL)
Gustafson, Earl B. (DFL)
Gustafson, Wallace F. (Non-Partisan)
Halsted, Charles L. (D)
Halvorson, George Charles, Sr. (R)
Hansen, Melvin E. (R)
Hanson, Henry Elias (D)
Hanson, Richard H. (Conservative)
Hanson, Roger Leon (R)
Hanson, Rudolph (Non-Partisan)
Harper, Warren Wayne, Sr. (D)
Hart, Nathaniel Irwin (DFL)
Hart, Richard T, Jr. (R)
Hartle, Dean Pickett (R)
Haugerud, Neil Sherman (D)
Head, Douglas M. (R)
Heegaard, Peter Anker (R)
Heid, James K. (R)
Heller, Walter Wolfgang (D)
Hennen, James Allen (R)
Henning, H. J. (Conservative)
Henry, John J. (D)
Hetland, James L, Jr. (R)
Heuer, William C. F. (D)
Higgins, Raymond J. (Conservative)
Hilleren, Richard H. (DFL)
Hinman, Keith (DFL)
Hoium, Vernon Stanley (D)
Holand, P. J.
Holman, Kingsley David (DFL)
Holmberg, R(oy) Hopkins (DFL)
Holmquist, Stanley W. (Conservative)
Hoppe, Vernon T. (Conservative)
Horbal, Koryne Emily (DFL)
House, William H. (DFL)
Howatt, Lester A. (Conservative)
Hughes, Jerome Michael (D)
Hughes, Keith F. (Conservative)
Hulstrand, George Eugene (DFL)
Humphrey, George F. (Conservative)
Humphrey, Hubert Horatio (D)
Hunt, John Joseph, Jr. (D)
Imm, Val (DFL)
Jaakola, Raymond Theodore (R)
Jacobsen, Ernie R.
Jacobson, Howard O. (D)
Jensen, Carl Arthur (R)
Jensen, Gloria Natalie (R)
Jensen, Vernon K. (DFL)
Joerg, David Allen (R)
Johnson, C. A. (Conservative)
Johnson, Carl Clifford (R)
Johnson, Carl Marcus (DFL)
Johnson, Charles Clayton (R)
Johnson, Dorothea Alice (R)
Johnson, Harold N. (Non-Partisan)
Johnson, James Buford (DFL)
Johnson, John Warren (R)
Johnson, Norval Stanley (DFL)
Johnson, Robert George
Johnson, Robert Warren (Conservative)
Johnson, Victor L. (DFL)
Johnson, Warren O. (R)
Jones, Marjorie Cornelia (R)
Jopp, Ralph P. (Conservative)
Jorgensen, Jack J. (DFL)
Josefson, J. A. (R)
Joseph, Geraldine M. (D)
Jude, Victor N. (Non-Partisan)
Jungclaus, Walter C. (Conservative)
Kalina, Harold (DFL)
Karth, Joseph E. (DFL)
Keefe, John B. (R)
Keith, A. M. (DFL)
Kendrick, Frank Jenness (DFL)
Ketcham, Douglas Theodore, Sr. (R)
Kildahl, Erling Oliver (R)
King, Kenneth I. (R)
King, Stafford (R)
Kirchner, William G. (Non-Partisan)
Kirkpatrick, Bruce Wilbur (R)
Kivimaki, Elmer Norman (DFL)
Kleinbaum, Jack (Liberal)
Knudsen, Eugene Peter (DFL)
Knutson, Howard Arthur (R)
Knutson, Terrence Andrew (DFL)
Kosloske, John T. (R)
Kramer, Edward G. (Independent)
Krenik, George B. (Conservative)
Krenik, Lauris D. (R)
Krieger, Harold G. (R)
Kroehler, Franklin P. (Non-Partisan)
Kucera, Robert C. (R)
Kvam, Adolph
LaBrosse, Francis (DFL)
Langen, Odin (R)
Larson, Calvin Ruben (R)
Larson, Levern Orville (DFL)
Larson, Lew W. (Conservative)
Larson, Norman J.
Latz, Robert (DFL)
Laufenburger, Roger Allyn (D)
Laughlin, Gloria B. (R)
Lease, M. Harry, Jr. (D)
Lee, L. J. (DFL)
Leiseth, Robert Vernon (R)
Lemme, John Hewett
LeVander, Harold (R)
Liljegren, Dorothy Jean (R)
Lindahl, Bruce (DFL)
Lindstrom, Ernest A. (R)
Long, Verne Everett (R)
Lund, Rhoda S. (R)
Luukinen, (Roberta) Jeanne (R)
McCarthy, Eugene Joseph (DFL)
McCarty, Glenn D. (Conservative)
McGowan, Martin James, Jr. (DFL)
MacGregor, Clark (R)
McGuire, Michael E. (DFL)
MacIver, Dale (DFL)
McKee, John Henry (R)
MacKenzie, Malcolm Kerr (R)
McKnight, Henry T.
McLeod, L. Donald (Conservative)
McMillan, Helen E. (DFL)
Magnuson, Paul A. (R)
Magnusson, Cyrus E. (Independent)
Mahowald, Robert A. (Conservative)
Mammenga, Gene (DFL)
Mann, George (D)
Maruska, Harveydale
Mattson, Robert W. (DFL)
Maxwell, Clinton William (R)
Maxwell, Stephen Lloyd (R)
Metcalf. John Albert (R)
Miller, Charles H. (DFL)
Miller, Darrel R. (DFL)
Miller, Hans R. (Non-Partisan)
Mitchell, C. C. (Conservative)
Mitchell, Don (Conservative)
Moen, Carl Donovan (DFL)
Mondale, Walter Frederick (DFL)
Morlock, Henry Jacob (Conservative)
Mosier, Leo DeWitt (DFL)
Mueller, August B. (Conservative)
Muller, Marilyn Joan (DFL)
Mullin, William Edward, Jr. (DFL)
Munger, Harry Leonard (D)
Munger, Willard M. (DFL)
Murphy, Mary Catherine (DFL)
Murphy, Robert Edward (D)
Murphy, Thomas John (DFL)
Murphy, Louis A. (D)
Naftalin, Arthur (D)
Nee, Kay Evangeline (DFL)
Nelsen, Ancher (R)
Nelson, Alan Dale (R)
Nelson, Harold S.
Nelson, Howard I. (Conservative)
Nelson, Leslie H. (Non-Partisan)
Nelson, Martin A. (R)
Nelson, Rolf Timothy (R)
Nelson, W. C. (DFL)
Newcome, Thomas W. (Non-Partisan)
Nickoloff, Robert Stokely (DFL)
Nielsen, Helga Ragnhild Sorensen (DFL)
Nierengarten, Roger Joseph (DFL)
Noblitt, Harding Coolidge (D)
Nordin, John Herman (DFL)
Norheim, Gordon L. (DFL)
Norton, Fred Carl (DFL)
Novak, Edward G. (DFL)
Nurminen, Birger (DFL)
Nyquist, Dean Allen (R)
O'Brien, William J. (R)
O'Connor, William Thomas (DFL)
O'Dea, Richard W. (DFL)
Ogdahl, Harmon T. (Conservative)
Olson, Alec Gehard (D)
Olson, Jerome Arnold (R)
Olson, John L.
Olson, Robert Charles (R)
Olson, Vern Frank (R)
Olson, Wayne H. (DFL)
O'Neill, Joseph Thomas (R)
Otis, James Cornish, Jr.
Otterson, Laura Gunderson (R)
Pagel, Gary James (DFL)
Parenteau, Marc Duane (R)
Parish, Richard Justus (DFL)
Parks, Clifton (Conservative)
Parsons, Roger Alan (R)
Patterson, Benjamin
Patton, William B. (R)
Pavlak, Raymond (DFL)
Pavlak, Robert Leo (Independent)
Perpich, A. J. (DFL)
Perpich, Rudolph G. (DFL)
Peterson, Charles Thomas (R)
Peterson, Harry William (DFL)
Peterson, John H. (Conservative)
Peterson, Kay G. (D)
Peterson, Paul Kenneth (R)
Peterson, Robert Earl (R)
Pfaender, Thomas Paine (R)
Pfeilsticker, Marion August (DFL)
Pillsbury, Sally Whitney (R)
Pintar, Michael Anthony (DFL)
Plaisance, Vernon Raymond (R)
Podgorski, Anthony (DFL)
Pomeroy, Benjamin Sherwood (R)
Popham, Wayne Gordon (R)
Prifrel, Joseph (D)
Provo, Jack Marlowe (R)
Quie, Albert Harold (R)
Quirin, E. William (DFL)
Rappana, Duane (Conservative)
Rasmussen, Paul A. (DFL)
Reding, Leo John (DFL)
Reichert, Thomas George (R)
Renneke, Earl Wallace (R)
Renner, Robert G. (Conservative)
Richardson, Maryclaire S. (R)
Richie, Richard W. (DFL)
Richter, Anne Thorbeck (D)
Rickert, Robert Taylor (DFL)
Ring, Carolyn Louise (R)
Robbie, Joseph, Jr. (D)
Rolvaag, Karl Fritjof (DFL)
Rosenmeier, Gordon (Conservative)

Rutter, Loren Stanley (DFL)
Ryan, Thomas (Liberal)
Sabo, Martin Olav (DFL)
Salchert, John Joseph (DFL)
Saliterman, Joel A. (DFL)
Salmore, Raphael F. (DFL)
Samardich, George R. (DFL)
Sampson, Curtis Allen (R)
Samuelson, Donald B. (DFL)
Sanford, Loren William (R)
Sathre, Harvey B. (Conservative)
Savelkoul, Donald Charles (D)
Savelkoul, Henry Jerome (R)
Schafer, Ernest Elmer (R)
Scherer, Roger H. (R)
Schmitz, Robert Joseph (DFL)
Schoon, Warren Eugene (R)
Schrom, Edward Joseph (D)
Schumann, Alfred Oscar (R)
Schumann, Marvin C. (Conservative)
Schwarzkopf, Lyall Arthur (R)
Scribner, Duane C. (DFL)
Searle, Rodney N. (Conservative)
Seely, Robert D. (R)
Sether, Virginia Hill (R)
Sharp, John Malcolm (R)
Short, Robert E. (D)
Sillers, Douglas Hugh (R)
Simonson, Harold James (DFL)
Sinclair, Donald (Conservative)
Skaar, Andrew Ordeen
Skeate, John P. (DFL)
Skjervold, Paul Arnold (DFL)
Smaby, Alpha Sunde (DFL)
Smith, Edward J. H. (DFL)
Smith, John Malcolm (DFL)
Smith, Richard Racine (R)
Smith, William Warren, III (DFL)
Sommer, Clifford Carl (R)
Sommerdorf, Vernon L. (DFL)
Spielman, Gordon L. (DFL)
Springer, Erchal John (DFL)
Standafer, Daryl Lloyd (R)
Stangeland, Arlan Inghart (R)
Stassen, Richard J. (R)
Stenvig, Charles (Independent)
Stickney, Charles William (DFL)
Stocker, Luella Heine (R)
Stone, Ivan (Conservative)
Stopka, John P. (D)
Sundet, A. O. (Conservative)
Swan, Arthur Robert (R)
Swanson, James C. (DFL)
Swanstrom, Dwight Alexander (Conservative)
Swenson, Glen W. (Non-Partisan)
Temple, Richard Davis (DFL)
Tendick, Ted O. (Conservative)
Theis, Frank J. (DFL)
Thiss, George Raymond (R)
Thomas, William
Thompson, Wayne W. (R)
Thorburn, Rose Woodgate (R)
Thrane, Ralph Orville (R)
Thuet, Paul Anthony (D)
Ticen, Thomas E. (DFL)
Tomczyk, Edward J. (DFL)
Tomlinson, John D. (DFL)
Torrey, Elizabeth N. (R)
Ukkelberg, Clifford (Conservative)
Vail, Joane Rand (DFL)
Vander Kooi, Benjamin (DFL)
Volstad, Edward J. (DFL)
Von Holtum, John E. (DFL)
Voxland, Roy L. (Conservative)
Vukelich, Thomas D. (DFL)
Walsh, Staria (DFL)
Walz, Norman Joseph (D)
Wangen, Marvin Eugene (DFL)
Wanvick, Arne C. (DFL)
Warder, John Morgan (DFL)
Warnke, Curtis B. (Non-Partisan)
Warren, Edward J. (DFL)
Weaver, Charles R. (R)
Weaver, Lonnie Leroy (DFL)
Wefald, Jon Michael (DFL)
Westin, Leslie E. (Conservative)
Weyrens, Jerry Philip (Conservative)
White, Richard H. (Conservative)
Wilder, Harvey A. (DFL)
Williamson, Eugene Thomas (DFL)
Wilson, Patty Helen (R)
Windingstad, Harold Oliver, Jr. (DFL)
Wingard, John P.(Conservative)
Winge, Herbert Clayton (R)
Winter, John Burton (R)
Winters, Leslie Roland (R)
Wirkkala, Matt Leander (DFL)
Wolcott, Raymond Oliver (R)
Wozniak, Daniel Donald (DFL)
Wright, Donald Orr (Conservative)
Wright, F(red) Gordon (R)
Wyant, Clinton W. (DFL)
Yetka, Lawrence Robert (D)
Yngve, John Anton (R)
Youngdale, James Martin (DFL)
Youso, Severyn Donald (D)
Zaffke, Kermit John (R)
Zwach, John M. (R)

MISSISSIPPI

Abernethy, Thomas Gerstle (D)
Abraham, George Douglas (D)
Adams, Luther Wiley (D)
Ainsworth, Wilburn Eugene, Jr. (D)
Alexander, Wm. B. (D)
Allen, Charles Brenham, Jr. (D)
Anderson, Robert Darrow (D)
Anderson, Robert Edward (D)
Applewhite, Mary Elizabeth (R)
Arnold, John Robert (R)
Ayers, Jake Bertram (D)
Bailey, Howard Taft (D)
Bailey, Joseph Nathaniel, Jr. (D)
Barefield, Stone Deavours (D) See Addenda
Barnes, Thelma Palmer (D)
Barnett, James Arden (R)
Barnett, Ross Robert (D)
Barrett, Esther Scott (R)
Bennett, Otis Bee (D)
Black, Roy Herbert (D)
Blackwell, Charles Gray (D)
Bodron, Ellis Barkett (D)
Bonds, Robert Alexander, Jr. (D)
Boteler, Edgar Lee, Jr. (D)
Boyd, Robert Dunleigh (D)
Brady, Thomas Pickens (D)
Brady, Tullius (D)
Branch, Elwood L. (D)
Breed, William Jack (R)
Brent, Edwin Lea (R)
Brock, H. Burt (D)
Brooks, Gary Harold (D)
Brown, J. Walter (D)
Bryant, Curtis Conway (D)
Bryant, Phillip Davis (D)
Buchanan, Robert Henry (R)
Bullock, Charles Louie (D)
Burgin, William Garmer, Jr. (D)
Burns, Clyde L. (D)
Callicott, William Edward (D)
Cammack, Benjamin Franklin, Jr. (D)
Campbell, Bland Hayden (D)
Cannon, Farrar Huffman (D)
Caraway, William Julius (D)
Carlisle, Jack B. (D)
Carlton, Frank Anderson, Jr. (D)
Carmichael, Gilbert Ellzey (R)
Carr, Andrew Rembert (D)
Carr, Oscar Clark, Jr. (D)
Carruth, George Simmons (D)
Case, George Milton (D)
Chambliss, Donald R. (D)
Clarke, Robert George (Independent)
Collier, Clint C. (D)
Collier, Wilma Bernice Blendt (R)
Collins, Elson K. (D)
Colmer, William Meyers (D)
Cope, William DeLoach (D)
Corr, William Ervin, Jr. (D)
Cossar, George Payne (D)
Craig, Carl H. (D)
Crook, Robert Lacey (D)
Cross, Billy Joe (D)
Cross, Donald Melvin (D)
Cupit, Danny Earl (D)
Dallas, DeVan (D)
Damon, Henry Eugene (R)
Davis, James Preston (D)
Davis, Russell C. (D)
Dean, James Porter (D)
Dean, Kenneth Leon (D)
Deaton, Charles M. (D)
DeCell, Herman Brister (D)
Derian, Patricia Murphy (D)
Donald, Robert Hicks, II (D)
Dorwin, Jack Crosby (R)
Douglas, C. Thomas (D)
Du Bois, Radford Eugene, Jr. (D)
Eastland, James Oliver (D)
Emmons, Rome Augustus, Jr. (R)
Ethridge, William Nathaniel, Jr. (D)
Evans, Jeff W. (D)
Everett, Nathan Clark, Sr. (D)
Evers, Charles (D)
Fagan, Thomas John (R)
Ferguson, George Robert, Jr. (D)
Finnie, Hubert Noel (D)
Forsythe, John Edward (R)
Fortinberry, Toxey Thomas (R)
Foster, Albert James (D)
Fox, Russell Lambert (D)
Franklin, Melvin Madison (D)
Frazier, Bert Lee (R)
Gandy, Edythe Evelyn (D)
Garner, John Bromley (D)
Geoghegan, James Francis (D)
Gillespie, Robert Gill
Gilliam, Godfrey Cline (D)
Gipson, Thomas Zachariah (D)
Gollott, Tommy Arlin (D)
Gordon, Willard Fremont (D)
Gore, Ney McKinley, Jr. (D)
Gore, Teay Norley (D)
Graham, Mack (D)
Graham, Thomas Estus (D)
Greene, Edwin Eugene (R)
Griffin, Charles Hudson (D)
Guyot, Lawrence T, Jr. (D)
Halbrook, David McCall (D)
Harned, Horace Hammerton, Jr. (D)
Harvey, James Ferguson, Jr. (R)
Haynes, Glenn Johnson (R)
Headrick, William Moore (R)
Hennington, Burnette Yarbrough (D)
Henry, Aaron Edd (D)
Henry, Edwards C. (D)
Herrin, Ralph Herman (D)
Hicks, Hervey Owings (D)
Hilbun, Benjamin Franklin, Jr. (D)
Hollinger, John Fielding (D)
Holloman, John Holliday, III (D)
Holyfield, Robert Lee (D)
Hooker, Edwin Wilburn, Sr. (D)
Hooper, James Fullerton, III (R)
Hooper, Virginia Fite (R)
Hough, John Howard (D)
Hughes, Peaster Leo (D)
Hutchinson, Flavous Leo (D)
Johnson, Allen Levi (D)
Johnson, Norman Aaron, Jr. (D)
Johnson, Paul Burney (D)
Johnson, Seymour Bennett (R)
Jones, Henry Lee (D)
Jones, J(esse) Fred (D)
Jones, Rex Kenton (D)
Jones, Walton Morris (D)
Jones, William Valentine, Jr. (D)
Junkin, John Richard (D)
Kennedy, Carroll Henry (D)
Kennedy, John Lloyd (D)
King, William Hampton (D)
Klaus, William J. (R)
Kochtitzky, Robert Boone (D)
Ladner, Heber Austin (D)
Ladner, Hiram Griffin (D)
Laird, H. V. (R)
Lambert, Aaron Colus (D)
LaRue, Fred (R)
Lassiter, Robert L. (D)
Lee, Adrian Gordon (D)
Lee, Albert Ray, Jr. (R)
Lee, Billy Joe (D)
Lee, Paul (D)
Lennon, Robert Lawrence (D)
Lester, Horace Baxter (D)
Lipscomb, James Walton, III (D)
Littlejohn, Talmadge D. (D)
Lomax, William Alexander (D)
Long, Betty Jane (D)
Lott, Chester Trent
Lotterhos, Frederick Jacob, Jr. (D)
Love, James Percy (D)
Love, John Clark (D)
Love, Samuel David (D)
Mabry, Malcolm H, Jr. (R)
McAllister, Lewis Leslie, Jr. (R)
McAlpin, Ehrman T. (D)
McCay, Thomas Scott (R)
McClamrock, Margaret Elizabeth (R)
McClellan, Thompson (D)
McClendon, Burwell Beeman, Jr. (R)
McCormick, Tabot Green (D)
McCoy, Howard Wayne (R)
McCullough, William Todd (D)
McDaniel, Estes Cruden (D)
McDonald, Robert Faucette (R)
McDonnell, Howard Andre (D)
McGaughey, Noel Douglas (D)
McKay, Kelsey B. (R)
McKay, Martha Wagner (R)
Mackey, Oscar Powell (D)
McKinley, William Edward (D)
McLoone, Philip Joseph (D)
McNair, Clarissa Walton (R)
Magee, Douglas McArthur (R)
Majure, Irby Wilmot (D)
Marks, Gordon Sutton (D)
Massey, Alton (D)
Mathis, James Wesley (D)
Meek, Walter Buchanan (D)
Merideth, Horace Lavelle, Jr. (D)
Miller, Albert Virgil (D)
Miller, Joseph Abraham, Jr. (D)
Miller, William M. (D)
Millette, Theodore Joseph (D)
Mitchell, Charles B. (R)
Mitchell, Henry Redman (D)
Mitchell, William Henry (D)
Mitlin, Laurance Robert (D)
Mohamed, Ollie (D)
Montgomery, Gillespie V. (D)
Moore, Dana Clifton, Jr. (D)
Moore, Walter Vernon, Jr. (D)
Morrow, James Anthony (D)
Moss, Joseph Gibson (D)
Mounger, William Donald (R)
Moye, James M. (R)
Mulholland, Joe Henry (D)
Muths, Sherman Lewis, Jr. (D)
Neal, James Huston (D)
Newman, Clarence Benton (D)
Nix, James Elmer (R)
Nixon, Thomas Glenn (D)
Norman, Dovie S. (R)
Ogden, Edwin Bennett, Jr. (R)
Oswald, Robert Holmes (D)
Owen, Ben (D)
Owen, Sank Edward (R)
Page, Matthew John (D)
Palmer, Merle Franklin (D)
Parish, Jerry Edward (R)
Patridge, Corbet Lee (D)
Peebles, Robert Carley (D)
Penton, Marby Robert (D)
Perkins, John Burton (D)
Perry, Bobby Gerald (D)
Perry, Doyle (D)
Peteet, Porter Weaver (R)
Phillips, Alice Snider (D)
Phillips, Rubel Lex (R)
Phillips, Walter E. (D)
Pickering, Charles Willis (R)
Pierce, Clarence Albert, Jr. (D)
Pittman, Edwin Lloyd (D)
Pitts, Hudie (D)
Posey, John Phillip (D)
Powe, William Alison (R)
Powell, John William (D)
Pringle, Charles Kistner (D)
Puckett, Thomas W. (D)
Purvis, Perrin Hays (D)
Rankin, Harry Longino, Jr. (R)
Reed, Clarke Thomas (R)
Reeves, R. B. (D)
Reiff, Lee Herbert (D)
Rester, James Ausbon (D)
Rhodes, Alfred Henry, Jr. (D)
Robertson, Edward Peyton, Jr. (R)
Robertson, James Arthur, Jr. (D)
Robertson, Stokes Vernon (Independent)
Rodgers, Henry L. (D)
Ross, Jim Buck (D)
Ruffin, Susie Bolden (D)
Russum, Julius Franklin (D)
Sanderson, Gaines Milfred (D)
Sanford, I. S. (D)
Scruggs, Cleston (D)
Seabrook, Sterling Withers (D)
Shanahan, Frank Edward, Jr. (D)
Sheely, Katherine Baskervill (R)
Shields, Charlie D. (D)
Sides, Julian Earl, Jr. (R)
Simmons, Ralph Terrell (R)
Simpson, James Charles (D)
Singley, Vasco Monett (D)
Slayden, Gladys (D)
Smith, John Neil (D)
Smith, Wade Orchin (D)
Smith, William Marion (D)
Smith, Willie Conly (D)
Snyder, D. W. (D)
Sowell, J. Ralph, Jr. (D)
Steadman, Hoyt Gay (D)
Stennis, John Cornelius (D)
Stephens, Edgar J, Jr. (D)
Stevens, William Arnald (D)
Stone, Thomas Mitchell (D)
Strickland, Roy Bedford (D)
Strider, Henry Clarence, Sr. (D)

Sturgeon, Alonzo Holmes (D)
Sugg, Andrew Jackson (R)
Sullivan, Charles L. (D)
Summer, A. F. (D)
Sumners, Cecil Lamar (D)
Swearengen, Frank Bradford (R)
Swindoll, George Mitchell (D)
Thigpen, Judson Arledge, Jr. (D)
Thompson, Allen Cavett (D)
Thompson, William Isaac Shelby (D)
Tillery, Billy Prowell (R)
Tims, Marjorie Hollingsworth (R)
Tisdale, William Appleton (D)
Trenor, Charles Odie (D)
True, James Benjamin (D)
Tubb, Thomas Jefferson (D)
Tucker, Jack Norris (D)
Turner, Irby, Jr. (D)
Turner, James Harvey (D)
Vaughan, Robert Lee, Sr. (D)
Waggoner, Sam W. (D)
Walker, Prentiss Lafayette (R)
Wall, Frank Tracy (D)
Warren, Jack A, Jr. (D)
Watkins, Joseph Wesley, III (D)
Watkins, Parham Mc Atee (D)
Watson, Thomas Arnie (D)
Wax, John Callaway (R)
Webb, Robert Maurice, Jr. (D)
Webster, DeWitt Talmadge (D)
Weems, Mack Dawson (D)
Westbrook, William Verdo, Jr. (R)
White, Berta Lee (D)
Whitten, Jamie Lloyd (D)
Whitten, John Wallace, Jr. (D)
Wilburn, Jerry (D)
Wilkerson, William Avery (D)
Wilkins, William Thomas, Jr. (R)
Williams, James B, Jr. (R)
Williams, John Bell (D)
Williams, Kenneth Ogden (D)
Williams, Thomas Marvin, Sr. (D)
Winstead, William Arthur (D)
Winter, William Forrest (D)
Wise, Seelig Bartell (D)
Wood, Bernard Pendleton (R)
Yarbrough, George Malone (D)
Young, Charles L. (D)

MISSOURI

Akers, Herbert S. (R)
Allen, J. S. (D)
Allmon, Ray N. (D)
Anderson, Norman H. (D)
Antoine, William Robert (D)
Armstrong, Orland Kay (R)
Arndt, Elizabeth Moore (R)
Arnold, Jim (D)
Arnold, John Burleigh (D)
Arnold, Luther (R)
Ascoli, Gloria Jean (R)
Auchly, William Joseph (R)
Avery, Omer H. (D)
Aylward, James Patrick, Jr. (D)
Bacon, Mary Elizabeth (D)
Baker, Lloyd J. (D)
Baker, Tom F, III (D)
Bakewell, Claude I. (R)
Banta, Parke M. (R)
Barks, Marion Emmett (R)
Barrett, John P. (D)
Barrow, Letha Jewell (D)
Barrows, Raymond Edwin (R)
Bassman, C. M. (R)
Bauer, M. C. (R)
Bayer, Gary Gray (R)
Beavers, Ruth Jones (D)
Beckerle, Joseph W. (D)
Beery, John Thomas (D)
Belt, Ronald Madison (R)
Berger, Henry Weinberg (D)
Berkley, Richard L. (R)
Berra, Paul M. (D)
Berry, Leland L. (D)
Bess, Joda Lee (R)
Betz, Vernon Elwood (R)
Beydler, Raymond (R)
Bild, Frank (R)
Birk, Raymond Jule (R)
Black, David C. (D)
Blackwell, Earl R. (D)
Blades, Ray (R)
Bockhorst, Estelle Wilferth (R)
Bolling, Richard Walker (D)
Bollinger, Earl A. (D)
Bond, Christopher S. (R)
Bondurant, Keith P. (R)
Bonitt, Edward John (D)
Bowlby, Harold V. (R)
Bowman, Vera Anderson (R)
Brady, Edwin Francis (R)
Brancato, Jasper M. (D)
Brand, James Henry (R)
Brandwein, Carl O. (D)
Branom, Robert H. (D)
Brenton, Fonnie L. (R)
Briggs, Frank P. (D)
Brill, Newton Clyde (R)
Briscoe, Joseph R, Jr. (R)
Bromwich, Elroy William (R)
Broomfield, Charles S. (D)
Brown, Mona Katherine (R)
Burch, Clyde Monroe (D)
Burch, William Alva (R)
Burford, Dorothy Wright (R)
Burlison, Bill D. (D)
Burns, Mary Frances (D)
Bush, Hilary Ashby (D)
Butler, Luna E. (D)
Butters, Shirley Sue (D)
Butzer, Harold Godfrey (R)
Callow, John A. (R)
Calloway, DeVerne Lee (D)
Campbell, Ethan Hubbard (R)
Campbell, J. Teeter (D)
Canaday, Paul D. (R)
Cannon, Edward M. (D)
Cantrell, E. J. (D)
Carnahan, Ernest Bryan, Jr. (D)
Carnahan, Melvin Eugene (D)
Carter, Frank (R)
Carter, Tom M, Sr. (R)
Case, Mervin Roy (R)
Casey, William F. (D)
Cash, Tom (R)
Cason, William J. (D)
Caywood, Delmar Eugene (R)
Cervantes, Alfonso J. (D)
Charles Robert Horne
Childers, Wilson R. (D)
Childress, Harold Noel (R)
Christy, John Grier
Clay, William Lacy (D)
Cleek, Lyman McGarvey (D)
Clements, Homer M. (D)
Comstock, Rolland L. (D)
Conley, John, Jr. (D)
Connors, William R. (D)
Conway, James Francis (D)
Cook, George M. (D)
Copeland, Fred E. (D)
Cothern, Henry D. (D)
Cox, Emil G. (R)
Cox, Hardin Charles (D)
Cox, William Noel (R)
Crandall, Vernie Raymond (D)
Crigler, Bill J. (D)
Crockett, Glen M. (D)
Croley, Boyd T, Sr. (D)
Curtis, Jack (R)
Curtis, Thomas B. (R)
Dale, Clarence Taylor (R)
Dalton, John Montgomery (D)
Dames, Omer J. (D)
Danforth, John Claggett (R)
Darst, Stephen (D)
Davidson, Curtis Vernon (D)
Davis, Donald D. (D)
Davis, Gorus Laurel (R)
Davis, Ilus Winifield (D)
Davis, William T. (R)
De Coster, Richard J. (D)
Degenhardt, Martin P. (R)
Delezene, Larry Keith (R)
Denny, James T. (D)
Devoy, Robert (D)
DeWitt, John Allen (D)
Dickerson, Frank Arthur (R)
Dickey, Charles Hardin, Jr. (D)
Dickson, Harold (R)
Dill, J. Anthony (R)
Dinger, Marvin L. (D)
Donegan, George J. (R)
Donnell, Forrest C. (R)
Dorsey, Robert Schult (D)
Downs, Edward Larson (D)
Downs, John E. (D)
Drebenstedt, Frances Sams (D)
Duensing, George, Jr. (R)
Duncan, Richard Meloan (D)
Dunmire, George Q. (R)
Dwyer, Winifred Brennan (R)
Eads, Edna C. (R)
Eagan, James Joseph
Eagleton, Thomas F. (D)
Eckelmann, Louis Charles, Jr. (R)
Eliot, Thomas Hopkinson (D)
Ellis, Frank C. (D)
Esely, William Joseph (R)
Esser, Harold Joseph (R)
Farley, James Wallace (D)
Feldman, Henry Lee (D)
Fickle, William (D)
Fields, Robert Crump (D)
Fike, Stanley Redfield (D)
Fink, Eric Frank (R)
Fischer, Glennon John (R)
Foley, Charles W. (D)
Franken, John H. (D)
Frappier, J. H. (R)
Freeman, Frankie Muse
Frost, Robert Hockaday (D)
Gann, Donald L. (R)
Garner, Harl A. (D)
Garrett, Howard M. (D)
Garten, Meredith (R)
Gault, Sue Nelle (R)
Giebler, Richard Owen (R)
Gilgour, John Henry (R)
Ginn, Rosemary Lucas (R)
Glover, Kermit P. (D)
Goddard, Ralph E. (D)
Godfrey, James E. (D)
Goode, P. Wayne (D)
Gosser, Marvel G. (R)
Goward, Russell (D)
Graham, Thomas D. (D)
Graham, Willard Woodrow (D)
Gralike, Donald J. (D)
Grant, David Marshall (D)
Gray, John Nicholas (R)
Grellner, John A. (D)
Griffith, Margaret Ruth (R)
Growney, Kenneth L. (D)
Gunter, Robert Sharp (D)
Hailey, Sallie (D)
Hall, Durward Gorham (R)
Hall, James Merwin (R)
Hancock, Don (D)
Hankins, Dewey L. (R)
Hardy, Helen Coleman (D)
Harlow, W. M. (R)
Harper, Roy W. (D)
Harpham, Elmer Dee (D)
Harris, Morran Denver (D)
Hearnes, Warren Eastman (D)
Heckemeyer, Anthony Joseph (D)
Herbst, Ann C. (D)
Hibler, William D, Jr. (D)
Hickey, Patrick Joseph (D)
Hill, J. Morris (R)
Hill, Joseph Wayne (R)
Hillelson, Jeffrey P. (R)
Hocker, Irah Eaves (D)
Holland, Horton Faye (R)
Holliday, Harold L. (D)
Holloran, Mark Richard (D)
Holman, Haskell (D)
Hopfinger, Raymond B. (D)
Houtchens, Delton Louis (D)
Howard, Raymond (D)
Huber, LeRoy James (D)
Huff, Ira Lu (R)
Hughes, Shelby Bond (D)
Hull, W. R, Jr. (D)
Hungate, William Leonard (D)
Hutcheson, John Williams (R)
Ichord, Richard H. (D)
Inglish, John William (D)
James, Vernon M. (R)
Jasper, Norbert J. (D)
Johnson, John J. (D)
Jones, A. Clifford (R)
Jones, Jack C. (D)
Jones, Jean Boswell (R)
Jones, Lem T. (R)
Jones, Paul C. (D)
Jordan, Leon M. (D)
Joynt, John William (D)
Karsten, Frank M. (D)
Kaufmann, Aloys P. (R)
Kay, Buddy (D)
Keane, Jack (D)
Keating, Edgar J. (D)
Kelly, James P. (R)
Kelmel, Dorothy Ellen (R)
Kennedy, Carolyn Burton (R)
Kennedy, Don William (D)
Kennedy, Jewel (R)
Kinchen, Lonnie Lee (D)
King, Bryon Roy (D)
King, Ethyl Bell (R)
King, R. J, Jr. (R)
King, Selby (R)
King, Zola M. (D)
Kirkpatrick, James C. (D)
Kostron, Frank E. (D)
Landgraf, Vernon H. (R)
Landreth, Joseph Franklin (R)
Lane, Perry M. (D)
Lee, Jack Orban (R)
Lee, Lawrence J. (D)
Lewis, John Henry (D)
Lindsey, Jordan (D)
Lisle, Henry L. (D)
Long, Edward V. (D)
Lowther, Gerald Halbert (D)
Lozier, Mary Jones (D)
McCubbin, Carrol J. (R)
McFadin, Richard E. (D)
McGraw, Ann R. (R)
Mackey, Earl Seay (D)
Mackie, William O. (D)
McMullin, John Boyd (D)
McNeal, Theodore D. (D)
McPherson, Michael Claude (D)
Madeson, Marvin Louis (D)
Mann, Elva Don (R)
Manrose, Dorothy Jean (D)
Marriott, B. Gladys (D)
Marriott, Vonceile Janis (D)
Marschalk, John Douglas (R)
Marshall, Richard Milton (R)
Martin, Robert Hugh (D)
Martin, Theodore S. (D)
Marvel, Billy Bryan (D)
Masters, Harold William (R)
Maughmer, Fred H, Jr. (R)
Mayberry, Clifton E. (R)
Mazzuca, Eugene F. (D)
Melton, Emory L. (R)
Melton, Ralph H. (R)
Meyer, Arlie H. (R)
Meyer, Walter L. (D)
Mickelson, Frank Leslie (D)
Middleton, Blanche Jones (D)
Miles, Daniel Black (D)
Miller, Claude J. (R)
Misbauer, Benedict (D)
Moll, Charles Phillip (D)
Moore, James Louis (D)
Moore, William F. (R)
Morris, Mount Etna (D)
Morris, William Shelton (D)
Mosher, Sol (R)
Murray, George E. (R)
Myers, Fern Holt (D)
Nangle, John Francis (R)
Nichols, Fred Harold (R)
Niewoehner, Carl H. (D)
Noland, James Alfred, Jr. (R)
O'Connell, Willoughby L. (D)
O'Connor, Patrick J. (D)
O'Gara, Frank L. (D)
Oliver, Ray (D)
Olson, Leslie O. (R)
O'Reilly, John P. (D)
Orr, Lon Greer (D)
Osbourn, D. R. (D)
Ottinger, Edward E. (R)
Owen, G. Stafford (D)
Owens, Don (R)
Pace, Fred V. (D)
Pace, George H. (D)
Palmer, Hazel (R)
Parker, George Warren (R)
Patterson, Bob Lee (R)
Patterson, J. F. (D)
Patterson, Margot Truman (D)
Pentland, Robert (D)
Perkins, Talford O. (R)
Perry, Ralph Kenneth (R)
Petersmeyer, Vallea Cornelia (R)
Peterson, Irene M. (D)
Petrovic, Alex M. (D)
Phelps, William C. (R)
Pierce, A. Robert, Jr. (R)
Ploeser, Walter Christian (R)
Portell, Clyde F. (D)
Powell, John Duane (R)
Powell, Kathryn (D)
Prange, Robert Louis (R)
Proffer, Marvin E. (D)
Rabbitt, Richard J. (D)
Raiffie, Harry C. (D)
Rains, Joe F. (D)
Randall, Donald Millard (D)
Randall, Wm. J. (D)
Reed, Nell Quinlan (R)
Reed, Ronald Swain, Jr. (D)
Reinhard, James Richard (D)
Reisch, Harold Franklin (R)
Rigby, Vincent Herbert (R)
Riney, James E. (D)
Riney, Patricia Ann (D)
Roach, Criss Warren (D)
Robbins, William Raymond (R)
Roberts, Raymond Rohrer (D)
Roberts, Wilber Eastes (D)
Robinson, Clyde Rayford (D)
Robinson, Frank E. (D)
Robinson, James Luther (D)

Rogers, Ben A. (R)
Rolwing, Francis David (D)
Roos, Lawrence K. (R)
Ross, Henry (D)
Rothman, Kenneth J. (D)
Royster, William Reid (D)
Ruffin, James Edward (D)
Runge, Gilbert Andy (R)
Russell, James (D)
Russell, John Thomas (R)
Russell, Patricia Brown (R)
Ryan, John C. (R)
Ryan, Thomas F. (D)
Saffarrans, Maurice (D)
St. Peter, George T. (R)
Salley, Guss C. (R)
Salomon, Sidney, Jr. (D)
Salveter, Ted C. (D)
Scaglia, Phillip P. (D)
Schapeler, Ruben (D)
Schechter, Maurice (D)
Schneider, John Durbin (D)
Schorgl, James Joseph (D)
Schrader, Leo W. (D)
Schramm, Jack Joseph (D)
Schwabe, Max (R)
Scroghem, Alpheus M. (D)
Seay, William E. (D)
Seiner, James Calvin (D)
Sevits, Willis Lee (R)
Shaffrey, Ina Theresa (D)
Shaver, Gerald Dean (D)
Sheehan, Charles A. (D)
Shenker, Morris A. (D)
Short, Samuel James (R)
Shovell, William Lee, III (D)
Shuey, Don E. (D)
Simcoe, Bernard (D)
Sims, Roydon E. (D)
Skaggs, James Cordell (D)
Skaggs, Raymond Leo (R)
Skelton, Arch Mason (D)
Skelton, Ike N, Jr. (D)
Skelton, John Boone (D)
Slay, Francis R. (D)
Smallwood, Richard Burton (D)
Smith, Elmer Eugene (R)
Smith, Gracchus Lattimore (D)
Smith, Homer Albert (D)
Smith, Robert Charles (D)
Snider, D. Dwain (D)
Snowden, Philip Hugh (D)
Snyder, Robert O. (R)
Somerville, Ronald L. (R)
South, Stephen E. (D)
Southern, Richard Earl (D)
Spain, James Earl (D)
Spainhower, James I. (D)
Speckman, George Raymond (D)
Speer, Alfred Alten (R)
Sponsler, Earl L. (D)
Spradling, Albert M, Jr. (D)
Stark, Lloyd Crow (D)
Steelman, Dorman Lloyd (R)
Stocksdale, Russell Horner (D)
Stoll, Richard Philip (D)
Stone, J. W. (R)
Stotts, Keith Horace (R)
Stutler, Fred (D)
Sullivan, Leonor Kretzer (D)
Swarts, Joseph Andrew (R)
Symington, James W. (D)
Symington, Stuart (D)
Taylor, Gene (R)
Taylor, James M. (R)
Teasdale, Joseph Patrick (D)
Thomas, Stan, Jr. (D)
Tice, Wayne K. (R)
Tinnin, Nelson B. (D)
Trombley, Michael Jerome (R)
Troupe, James Pal (D)
Truman, Harry S (D)
Tyus, E. Leroy (D)
Uthlaut, Ralph, Jr. (R)
Valier, Charles E. (R)
Vanlandingham, A. Basey (D)
Vaughan, Granvil B. (R)
Vaughan, Hugh Slavens (D)
Vogel, Raymond Henry (R)
Wallis, J. B. (D)
Walsh, Eugene Peter (D)
Walsh, Thomas A. (D)
Warden, Robert P. (R)
Warren, Hugh J. (D)
Waters, William Baxter (D)
Watkins, Bruce Riley (D)
Webb, John W. (R)
Weber, George D. (D)
Weber, Winnie Paula (D)
Webster, Richard M. (R)
Wehmeyer, Clarke Haid (R)
Wehmeyer, Victor William (R)
Weidenbaum, Murray Lew (R)
Wells, Gwendolyn Marie (D)
Wells, J. C. (D)
Westfall, Raymond E. (R)
Wheetley, Bernard Ralph (R)
Whitney, Cloy E. (R)
Whitton, Rex Marion (D)
Wigfield, Ralph (D)
Williams, Fred (D)
Williams, James W. (D)
Williams, Paul E. (D)
Willis, James H. II (D)
Winkelmann, Herman Paul (D)
Woodson, Lawrence Edward (D)
Woollen, Charles Wesley (R)
Woolsey, Thomas G. (R)
Yancey, Alma Nadine (D)
Young, Robert A. (D)
Young, Robert Ellis (R)
Zatezalo, Rudolph Edward (D)
Zeilmann, Stephen Hubert (R)
Zenge, J. Andy, Jr. (R)
Zimmerman, William T. (R)

MONTANA

Aasheim, Magnus S. (D)
Amsberry, Jeanne Louquat (R)
Anderson, Forrest H. (D)
Anderson, Helen Fuhs (R)
Anderson, Henry H. (D)
Anderson, LeRoy Hagen (D)
Anderson, Morine R. (R)
Aronow, Cedor Boris (D)
Asbjornson, Julian O. (R)
Aubert, Edward John (D)
Babcock, Tim (R)
Bailey, Elvin Louis (D)
Bailey, Manson Harvey, Jr. (D)
Bardanouve, Francis (R)
Barrett, Fred E. (D)
Bartlett, John Wesley (D)
Beaty, Jeanne Kellar (D)
Beck, Carla Wetzsteon (D)
Beck, Ralph James (R)
Beebe, Margaret Scherf (D)
Bennett, W. F. (R)
Berner, Alice Viola (D)
Blaylock, Chester Merle (D)
Boedecker, Louis Gimmell (D)
Bollinger, Gordon Edward (D)
Borchers, Louis F. (R)
Brenner, John Skoning (R)
Brewer, Clyde Barklow (R)
Brewer, David S. (D)
Burnett, James H. (R)
Campbell, William Richardson (R)
Cannon, Ross W. (D)
Carney, Glenn Edward (D)
Casey, Loran William (R)
Cashmore, William Francis (R)
Castles, Ruth Blake (R)
Castles, Wesley (Non-Partisan)
Cate, Jerome Joseph (D)
Christiansen, Edward William, Jr. (D)
Colburg, Dolores (D)
Conklin, Russel (D)
Cotton, Robert Sanford (D)
Cromer, Ella Mae (R)
Cross, John Melvin (D)
Cumming, Hugh Clifford (D)
Daniels, Marvin Kermit (D)
Darrow, George (R)
Delano, John Lee (R)
Derr, Grace West (D)
Donald, Ann Carberry (R)
Doty, Russell Leigh, Jr. (D)
Dougherty, Eleanor Mary (D)
Doyle, Stanley Morton (Non-Partisan)
Drum, David George (R)
Dybwad, Jean I. (R)
Dye, Robert Floyd (R)
Dzivi, Richard (D)
East, Vic (R)
Erdmann, Marian Sands (R)
Erickson, Leif (D)
Etchart, Mark S. (R)
Fagg, Harrison Grover (R)
Feda, Gerald C. (R)
Fladager, Milton Wallace (R)
Fladmo, Einer Martin (D)
Flynn, G. Elmer (D)
Fraser, Marie Florence (D)
Fraser, Willard E. (Independent)
Gehrett, Virginia Dalton (R)
Gerke, Harold Edward (D)
Giesick, Gary Ronald (R)
Gilfeather, Patrick James (D)
Goodheart, Bernard J. (D)
Graham, Carroll Adrian (D)
Grant, Raymond Armand (D)
Graybill, Leo Carlisle (D)
Groff, William Albert (D)
Gunderson, Jack Edward (D)
Hageman, Alvin William (D)
Hall, John Cleveland (D)
Ham, Donald Jamieson (R)
Harlow, Paul Kidder (D)
Harrison, James Thomas
Harrison, James Thomas, Jr. (R)
Harrison, John Conway (D)
Haswell, Frank I.
Haughey, James McCrea (R)
Hayne, Jack McVicar (R)
Healy, John Edward (D)
Hibbard, Henry Sieben (R)
Hilling, Henry Boyce, Sr. (R)
Himsl, Mathias A. (R)
Hinman, Edna Jane (R)
Hoff, Arthur (R)
Holling, Bing (R)
Holtz, Charlotte Rodger (D)
Holtz, Ronald Walter (D)
Hooks, Patrick F. (D)
Hoven, Gorden Elsworth (D)
Hunt, William Edward (D)
Jacobsen, Glenn Eugene (D)
James, David Farnham (D)
James, Isabel Brenner (R)
Jarussi, John Matthew (D)
Jensen, Millo (R)
Johnson, Edward A. (D)
Johnson, Helen Chaffin (R)
Johnson, Robert Lloyd (R)
Judge, Thomas Lee (D)
Jurcich, Frank John (D)
Kafka, Lada James (D)
Keil, Norma Fern (D)
Kelleher, Robert Lee (D)
Keller, Millett Frederick (R)
Kendall, Orin Parker (D)
Kimmitt, Joseph Stanley (D)
Klindt, Herbert James (R)
Knudsen, D. L. (D)
Koebbe, Lawrence Edwin (D)
Kolstad, Allen C. (R)
Kondelik, Evelyn M. (D)
Kvaalen, Oscar Seigel (R)
Lehrkind, Carl, Jr. (R)
Leininger, William H, Jr. (R)
Leuthold, Louise Pospisil (R)
Lincoln, Jack D. (R)
Lindblom, Rita (D)
Loble, Lester Henry, II (D)
Logan, Frances D. (D)
Lucas, James P. (R)
Lundgren, Conrad F. (R)
Lunstad, Ernest S. (D)
Lynch, Neil Joseph (D)
McAlear, Allen Lee (D)
McCaffery, Joseph James, Jr. (D)
McCallum, George (R)
McDonald, John Kenneth (D)
McDunn, Henry J. (D)
Mackay, William Raynor (R)
McKeon, John Luke (D)
McLaughlin, John James (D)
McNamara, John R. (D)
Mahan, John William (D)
Mahoney, Eugene Henry (D)
Mann, Virginia H. (R)
Manning, Dave Martin (D)
Mansfield, Michael J. (D)
Marbut, Gary Raymond (R)
Marks, Robert L. (R)
Marshall, Walter Henry (D)
Mather, William S. (R)
Melcher, John (D)
Mengel, Eldon R. (R)
Metcalf, Lee (D)
Michels, Lloyd John (D)
Miller, Harriet Evelyn (D)
Moberly, Isabel Carol (R)
Montgomery, Wayne Warren (R)
Murphy, James E. (R)
Murray, Frank (D)
Murray, Roger Stephen (D)
Murray, Thomas F. (D)
Nefzger, Donald Deane (D)
Nelson, Richard Curtis (R)
Nelstead, Keith Torval (R)
Newman, Dan L. (D)
Northey, Harry Thomas (R)
Nugent, James Patrick (D)
O'Hair, Allyn W. (D)
Olsen, Arnold (D)
Omholt, Elmer V. (R)
Pasma, James Jay (D)
Payne, Robert Forrest, Jr. (R)
Pierce, John H. (R)
Powell, Donald Deloss (D)
Rankin, Jeannette (R)
Rankin, Richard J. (R)
Reber, Joseph Bryant, Sr. (D)
Robert, Paris W. (R)
Roe, Teddy W. (D)
Romney, Miles (D)
Rosell, Antoinette Fraser (R)
Rostad, Carl (R)
Rugg, Glen Thomas (R)
Rygg, Maynard Sterling (R)
Sample, Alex K, Jr. (R)
Schoonover, Leland Howard (D)
Scott, Jeffrey J. (R)
Selstad, Tom Aaron (R)
Sheffels, Patricia O. (R)
Sheldon, Clarence E. (D)
Siderius, George E. (D)
Smiley, Richard Durham (R)
Smith, Duane E. (R)
Smith, Edward Bruce (R)
Smith, Paul Thompson (D)
Snoddy, Carol Nadine (R)
Spahr, William Edward (D)
Speare, William James (D)
Stephens, Stanley Graham (R)
Stevens, Edwin Walter (R)
Stranahan, Clinton Goodwin (D)
Stratton, Scott B. (R)
Sullivan, Thomas Quinn (D)
Terry, Peyton Huber (R)
Thiessen, Cornie R. (D)
Thompson, Stanley Emil (D)
Torkelson, Lowell Jerome (R)
Towe, Thomas Edward (D)
Tracy, Tom (D)
Ulmer, Walter Julius (R)
Wallander, Jerome Brandvold (R)
Warfield, William S, IV (R)
Watt, Robert Delanson (D)
Wayrynen, Ray J. (D)
Westwood, Jack Richard (R)
White, Robert Siemens (R)
Williams, Pat (D)
Williams, William G. (R)
Willits, John Birdcell (D)
Wilson, Dola N, Jr. (D)
Wing, Leonard Archie (R)
Winter, R. Eulalie (D)
Wolf, Kenneth Mohr (R)
Woltermann, Gerhard Henry (D)
Woodahl, Robert Lee (R)
Woodring, Ralph (D)
Worden, Henry O. (R)
Wright, J. Stewart (R)
Yardley, Dan (D)
Zimmer, William Harold (D)

NEBRASKA

Adamson, Elvin A. (R)
Allen, Jack Lee (R)
Altig, Delbert Roy (D)
Andersen, Stephen Dale (R)
Apking, William Tappan (R)
Bahensky, Leroy (R)
Baker, Ralph A. (R)
Bancroft, Hobart David (D)
Batchelder, Anne Stuart (R)
Bauer, Hal William (D)
Baum, Glen Frederick (R)
Beckius, John Lawrence (D)
Beermann, Allen Jay (R)
Beermann, Ralph Frederick (R)
Belker, Loren B. (D)
Berger, Bill L. (R)
Berryman, William Robert (D)
Bieber, Donn K. (R)
Biegert, Maurine (D)
Blankenau, Francis Joseph (R)
Blostein, Harold Leon (D)
Boehler, Conrad Joseph (D)
Bohlke, Lloyd Elmer (R)
Bottorff, Lewis Madison (D)
Bowen, Kenneth L. (R)
Bowman, Dale Merdith (D)
Bowring, Eva
Brandt, William B. (R)
Braun, Walter W. (R)
Bridenbaugh, Hal (R)
Brodersen, Robert James (D)
Burbach, Julius W.
Burney, Dwight Willard (R)
Bycroft, Ronald Eugene (R)
Bystrom, Irene Neville (D)
Cada, Frank Joseph (D)
Callan, Clair Armstrong (D)
Carpenter, Terry M. (R)

Cherry, Frank Elliott (R)
Childs, Nancy Jane (D)
Clark, Cloyd Ellsworth (R)
Clarke, Helen Hopkins (R)
Claussen, Peter H. (R)
Cook, William W. (R)
Cooper, Samuel V. (D)
Craft, Cecil I. (R)
Cramer, J. Alan (R)
Crandall, Horace Charles (R)
Cullan, David James (D)
Cunningham, Glenn C. (R)
Cunningham, Mary Rosalie (D)
Cunningham, Sarah Jane McQuaide (R)
Curtis, Carl T. (R)
Damrow, Thomas Herman (D)
Danner, Edward Ray (R)
Davey, Patrick James (D)
David, Thomas O. (D)
Dean, John Bingham (D)
Dean, Thomas Richard (D)
Denney, Robert V. (R)
Dosek, Edwin Francis (D)
Duis, Herbert J. (R)
Duncan, Vernon Fred (R)
Dusatko, Alan A. (D)
Dworak, James Joseph
Edwards, Joseph Robert (R)
Elrod, A. Don (D)
Elrod, Irma Petsch (D)
Erlewine, Dale (Independent)
Everroad, John (R)
Exon, J. James (D)
Felton, Katherine Lofgren (D)
Fleming, George H. (R)
Foote, Kathleen Ackerson (R)
Forrester, M. M. (R)
Fowler, Leonard (D)
Fowler, Marilyn Lee (D)
Fraser, Thomas Jefferson (D)
Fraser, William Charles (R)
Frost, Frank Leslie (R)
Frye, Keith Duane (E)
Galbraith, William Eugene (R)
Gerdes, George C. (R)
Gerhart, H. L. (R)
Gierau, Paul William, III (D)
Gorton, Donald Grant (R)
Gotch, Clifford Roy (R)
Graham, Dolores Jean (R)
Hamilton, John Orville (D)
Hanson, Doyle Robert (D)
Hardin, Clifford Morris (R)
Harding, Frank Emil (R)
Harman, Charles William (D)
Harrison, Robert Dinsmore (R)
Harroun, Harold Franklin (R)
Harsh, Lester (R)
Hasselbalch, Hal Burke (R)
Havens, Florence L. (R)
Healey, Janice Farrell (D)
Herbener, Lloyd Wayne (R)
Hines, Leon C. (D)
Holmquist, Claire Walfred (R)
Hruska, Roman Lee (R)
Hughes, Calista Cooper (R)
Hummel, Lowell Harold (R)
Hunker, Joseph Frederick (D)
Huston, Tedd Clark (R)
Jensen, Hans Otto (D)
Johnson, Elmore Thome (R)
Johnson, Joseph Earl (D)
Johnson, Lance Franklin (R)
Johnson, Ray C. (R)
Juelfs, Stanley R. (R)
Keyes, Orval Andrew (R)
Kirby, Vincent John (D)
Kissack, John Walter (D)
Kjar, Albert A. (D)
Klaver, Sam (R)
Knight, John Ellsworth (R)
Kremer, Maurice A. (R)
Kromberg, Jerome I. (D)
Krueger, Vernon H. (R)
Kruger, Alice L. (R)
Krugler, Arnold Frank (R)
Lambourn, Robert C. (R)
Lange, Ernest J. (D)
Larson, Leonard Robert (R)
Lederman, Jack Sherer (D)
Luedtke, Roland Alfred (R)
Luke, Virginia Pavelka (D)
Luther, Ernest M. (D)
Lynch, Daniel Cornelous (D)
McGinley, Donald F. (D)
Macken, James Lee (R)
Mahoney, Eugene T. (R)
Marcy, Orrin Jay (D)
Marsh, Frank (R)
Martin, David Thomas (R)
Marvel, Richard Douglas (R)
Meier, William Henry (D)
Meyer, Clarence Ardell Henry (R)
Meyer, Fred Charles (D)
Milder, Myron Harry (R)
Mitchell, John C. (D)
Monson, N. Paul (R)
Morrell, Emily A. (D)
Morris, Charles Edward (R)
Morrison, Frank B. (D)
Morrison, Maxine E. (D)
Morrissey, Thomas Lawrence (D)
Moss, Paul Simeon, Jr. (D)
Moulton, William S. (D)
Moylan, Harold Thomas (D)
Moylan, James Harold (D)
Neal, Harvey Ivan (R)
Nelson, Frank (R)
Nelson, Harold Robert (R)
Noble, Joe Clark (R)
Nore, Herbert E. (R)
Norton, William Hayden (D)
Odgaard, John Edmund (R)
Oestmann, Arthur Fred (D)
Orme, Fern Hubbard (R)
Orr, Lorraine (R)
Otto, Arnold Eugene (D)
Palmberg, Maurice Edwin (R)
Payne, Dale L. (R)
Pedersen, Henry Frederick, Jr. (R)
Peterson, Bernice Letitia (R)
Peterson, Val (R)
Pohlenz, Dean (R)
Powers, Leonard H. (D)
Proud, Richard French (R)
Putnam, L. D. (D)
Rasmussen, Eric C. (R)
Rasmussen, Kurt Duevang (D)
Rasmussen, Ross Hans (D)
Reeves, Theodore C. (R)
Riggs, William Robert (D)
Roberts, James Allen (R)
Robinson, Leslie (R)
Romans, Ronald Charles (R)
Ross, Donald Roe (R)
Rothwell, Robert L. (D)
Ruby, Ellis Scott (R)
Ruhnke, Arnold J. (R)
Rule, Charles H. (D)
Russillo, Michael P.
Schaffer, Larry D. (R)
Schimek, Herbert H. (D)
Schmit, Loran (R)
Schreurs, Wayne LeRoy (R)
Schuetz, Jack (R)
Schwab, C. B. (R)
Searcy, Nelson Donald (D)
Seaton, Frederick Andrew (R)
Shaffer, Butler DeLane (R)
Simmons, Ray Clifford (R)
Simpson, Harold Dwaine (R)
Skarda, William R, Jr. (R)
Smith, James Roswell (R)
Solomon, Vicki M. (D)
Spencer, Harry A. (R)
Stalder, Lloyd W. (R)
Steen, Donald Mariner (R)
Stewart, Mary Ruth (R)
Stewart, William A, Jr. (R)
Stromer, Marvin E. (R)
Stryker, Harold B. (D)
Sutton, Harold Putnam (R)
Swanson, Wayne (R)
Syas, George D. (R)
Tepner, Jess Fredrick (D)
Thies, Louis Carl (R)
Thompson, Donald L. (R)
Thor, John Call (D)
Tiemann, Norbert T. (R)
Tietjen, Theodore (R)
Vassell, Robert M. (R)
Viehmeyer, Glenn
Waldo, Willard H. (R)
Waldron, Johnie James (R)
Walstrom, Lois Jean (D)
Walstrom, Veryl Armour (D)
Warner, Jerome (R)
Weaver, Edward Myers, Jr. (R)
Weaver, Phillip Hart (R)
Wenzlaff, Theodore Charles (R)
Werve, Marvin R. (D)
Wewel, Larry Lou (D)
White, Richard (D)
Whitney, Ramey Charles (R)
Wylie, William M. (R)
Young, Dale L. (R)
Ziebarth, Wayne W. (D)

NEVADA

Aalbu, Roy M. (D)
Abbott, George William (R)
Allen, Creighton Hale (R)
Ashworth, Keith (D)
Baring, Walter S. (D)
Batjer, Cameron McVicar (R)
Beyer, Betty (D)
Bible, Alan (D)
Blakemore, Richard Eugene (D)
Brookman, Eileen B. (D)
Brown, B. Mahlon (D)
Bryan, Richard H. (D)
Bunker, Vernon E. (D)
Cannon, Howard Walter (D)
Capurro, Randall Victor (R)
Catt, Virginia Ann (D)
Collins, Jon Richard (D)
Covington, Herbert Louis (D)
Denser, John W. (R)
Dickerson, Harvey (D)
Dini, Joseph Edward, Jr. (D)
Domonoske, Merton Elzwick (R)
Driggs, Don Wallace (D)
Evans, Charles Bordoe, Jr. (R)
Fike, Ed (R)
Foote, Margie Ellen (D)
Frazzini, Mary (R)
Fry, Leslie McGee (R)
Gardella, Hazel Lucille (R)
Getto, Virgil M. (R)
Giannotti, Virginia Lytle (D)
Gibson, James Isaac (D)
Giomi, John Frank (D)
Glaser, Norman Dale (D)
Gottschalk, Gertrude Riordan (D)
Guinan, James J. (D)
Harris, Len (R)
Hecht, Chic (R)
Herr, Helen E. (D)
Hilbrecht, Norman Ty (D)
Hoyt, Merlyn Harold (D)
Hug, Procter Ralph, Sr. (D)
Hulse, James Warren (D)
Humphrey, Lucie King (R)
Hunter, Jack J. (D)
Johnson, Kay (R)
Kellar, Charles L. (D)
Koontz, John (D)
Kruse, Mildred Thomas (D)
Lamb, Harold Edward (R)
Landsman, Albert Michael (D)
Lanning, Charles D. (R)
Laub, William Murray (R)
Laxalt, Paul (R)
Levy, Harry Charles (D)
Lingenfelter, Cornelius Wilson (R)
List, Robert Frank (R)
Lowman, Zelvin Don (R)
Lundberg, Melvin Edward (R)
McDonald, Joseph Francis, Jr. (D)
Macdonald, William (D)
McKissick, Howard Frank, Jr. (R)
Meadows, David Breacy (D)
Mello, Donald Ray (D)
Miller, Thomas Woodnutt (R)
Mirabelli, Michael Anthony (D)
Monroe, Warren Ludwig (D)
Moody, Wilma (D)
Morrison, Robert Lee (D)
Mowbray, John Code (D)
Nash, Victoria C. (D)
Pappas, Leah Aglaia (D)
Parsons, Jewel Etta (D)
Petersen, Marci (D)
Poli, Nancy Carol (D)
Reid, Harry M. (D)
Richards, Paul Augustine (D)
Rose, Robert Edgar (D)
Russell, Charles Hinton (R)
Sawyer, F. Grant (D)
Schouweiler, Bart McClain (R)
Seward, George Horton (D)
Sheerin, Gary Asher (D)
Smith, Boyd Keith (D)
Smith, Janet Margaret (D)
Smith, John Gregory (R)
Smith, Robert Hallock (R)
Springer, Charles Edward (D)
Stone, Clarence F. (D)
Swallow, Grover (R)
Swanson, Harry Brooks (R)
Swobe, C. Coe (R)
Torvinen, Roy Lee (R)
Turner, Elma Juanita (R)
Viani, Giuseppe Joe (D)
Wadsworth, James Leo (D)
Webb, Douglas J. (R)
Weikel, Evelyn Jane (R)
West, Charles I. (D)
White, Marvin L. (D)
Wilson, Woodrow (R)
Wood, Leona Beryl (R)
Wright, William Stewart, Jr. (R)
Young, Frank Wesley (R)

NEW HAMPSHIRE

Adams, Alice E. (R)
Adams, Arthur F. (R)
Adams, Sherman (R)
Ainley, Greta M. (R)
Allan, Stuart B. (R)
Allen, James F. (R)
Andersen, Chris Kenneth (R)
Anderson, Fayne E. (R)
Andrews, William Taylor (R)
Angus, George W. (R)
Avery, Fred (R)
Bailey, Elsie C. (D)
Ballam, Louis S. (R)
Balomenos, Sandra Jean (R)
Barker, Helen A. (R)
Barnard, Roland A. (D)
Barry, James J. (R)
Barry, William H, Jr. (D)
Bartlett, Clarence Edward (R)
Bass, Perkins (R)
Bass, Robert P, Jr. (R)
Bean, Arthur E, Jr. (R)
Beaudoin, Leo E. (D)
Beauvais, John Paul (D)
Bednar, John M. (D)
Belcourt, Agenor (D)
Bergeron, Lucien E. (D)
Bernard, Mary Elizabeth (D)
Bernasconi, Fidele Joseph (R)
Berringer, St. Clair A. (R)
Berry, Dorothy B. (R)
Bigelow, L. Waldo, Jr. (R)
Bingham, James C. (R)
Bissonnette, Oscar (D)
Blaisdell, Clesson J. (D)
Blanchette, Alice Frances (D)
Boggis, Donald Earl (D)
Boire, Henry (D)
Boisvert, Ralph W. (D)
Bolden, Melvin Reed (D)
Borchers, Donald Earl (R)
Bouchard, Arthur A. (D)
Bouchard, Bertrand J. (D)
Boucher, Raymond L. (R)
Bouley, Arthur (D)
Bowlen, Wayne Thomas (D)
Bownes, Hugh Henry (D)
Bownes, Irja Catherine (D)
Bradshaw, John Rogers (R)
Bragdon, Orson H. (R)
Bridges, Webster E, Jr. (R)
Brock, David Allen (R)
Brocklebank, Daniel (R)
Brown, Paul Edward (R)
Brown, Robert C. (R)
Brumer, George (D)
Brungot, Hilda C. F. (R)
Bruton, George A. (D)
Buchanan, Creeley S. (R)
Burleigh, Joseph (R)
Burnham, Roland B. (R)
Bushey, Walter O. (D)
Bussiere, Andrew Joseph (R)
Bussiere, Emile R. (D)
Call, Robert Traip (D)
Campbell, Allan P. (R)
Cann, William Francis (R)
Canney, Ralph W. (R)
Capistran, Armand (D)
Carrier, Maria L. (D)
Carter, Malcolm M. (R)
Casassa, Herbert Alfred (R)
Cavis, Morton Hastings (R)
Chamberlain, Kenneth Wellington (R)
Chamberlain, Leslie M. (R)
Champagne, Edward (D)
Chase, Robert Leon (R)
Chase, Russell Cushing (R)
Chasse, Peter N. (D)
Christie, Roland E, Jr. (R)
Claflin, Russell G. (R)
Clark, Ernest D. (R)
Clark, Shirley M. (R)
Cleveland, James C. (R)
Clough, Barry Lenwood (R)
Clymer, W. B. Shubrick (D)
Cobleigh, Marshall W. (R)
Coburn, Roscoe Newton (R)
Coffin, Fred J. (D)
Coggeshall, Robert Alan (R)
Colburn, Majorie D. (R)
Cole, Stacey Ward (R)
Collishaw, Lyman E. (R)
Cone, John Coit (R)
Cook, George A. (D)
Coolidge, Clyde Rocheleau (R)
Copadis, Nicholas George (R)
Corey, William Walter (D)
Corriveau, Anthony J. (R)

Cote, Joseph Leo (D)
Côté, Margaret Sullivan (D)
Cotton, Norris (R)
Countermarsh, Ernest R. (D)
Cournoyer, Wilfred W. (D)
Coussoule, Hector (D)
Cox, Herschel W. (D)
Craig, William H. (D)
Crouch, Leon Meader (R)
Cullity, William J. (D)
Dale, Thomas James, Sr. (R)
Daniell, Eugene S, Jr. (D)
Davis, Donald C. (R)
Dearborn, Henry (Independent)
DeBlois, Romeo R. (R)
De Lude, Margaret Bowles (R)
Demers, Mary E. (D)
Desgrosseilliers, Emile Joseph (D)
Desjardins, Helen (D)
Desmarais, Raymond J. (D)
Dickinson, R. Dorothea (R)
Drabinowicz, Alice Rose Theresa (D)
Drake, Arthur Miles (R)
Donnelly, Helene Rosalyn (R)
Downing, Maurice J. (D)
Drew, Harold Franklin (R)
Drew, Robert B. (R)
Ducharme, Raymond R. (D)
Dunfey, William Leo (D)
Dwinell, Lane (R)
Earley, Robert Emmett (D)
Eastman, Edwin Winter (R)
Eaton, Joseph March (R)
Edwards, Ellerton H. (R)
Emerson, William O. (R)
Eneguess, Daniel Francis (R)
Engel, David Chapin (R)
English, Robert (R)
Fairbanks, Clyde Gerrish (D)
Faulkner, Ellen (R)
Ferguson, Charles Wright, Jr. (R)
Ferron, Albert J. (R)
Fogg, Edna D. (R)
Foley, Eileen (D)
Forbes, Roxie A. (R)
Fortier, Guy Joseph
Fortin, John O. (D)
Foster, Claude W. (R)
Fox, Arthur H. (R)
Frizzell, Martha McDanolds (R)
Gaffney, William L. (D)
Gage, A. Stuart (R)
Gage, Edward Augustus (R)
Gagnon, Rebecca A. (D)
Gamache, Willibert (D)
Gardner, Van H. (R)
Gay, Charles Henry (R)
Gelt, Jeanette (R)
Gile, Robert Hall (R)
Gilman, George (R)
Gilman, Wiggin S. (D)
Glavin, William Francis (R)
Goedecke, Herbert G. (R)
Goff, John Bryson (D)
Gore, Marion Adams (R)
Gorham, Austen C. (R)
Gorman, Redmon Henry (Non-Partisan)
Gove, William P. (R)
Greeley, Stephen Alonzo (R)
Green, Dorothy (R)
Greene, Elizabeth A. (R)
Gregg, Hugh (R)
Griffin, Margaret A. (R)
Grinnell, Harold C. (R)
Guild, Lawrence W, Sr. (R)
Guilmette, Alfred J. (D)
Gutterson, Mildred E. (R)
Hall, Fred William, Jr. (R)
Halvorson, Alf Halvor (R)
Hamel, Stanley A. (R)
Hanson, Arnold Philip (R)
Hanson, Richard D. (R)
Hartigan, Winifred E. (D)
Hayes, John Donald (R)
Herbert, Edward N. (R)
Hill, Robert Charles (R)
Hilliard, Robert Lee (D)
Hoeh, David Charles (D)
Hoeh, Sandra U. (D)
Holland, John (D)
Hood, Vernon A. (R)
Horan, Richard Henry (R)
Howard, Nelson E. (R)
Huggins, Harry F. (R)
Hunt, Roger L. (D)
Huot, J. Oliva (D)
Hurd, Esther Thompson (R)
Hussey, Daniel James (R)
Jacobson, Alf Edgar (R)
Johnson, Edward Alfred (R)
Johnson, Harry S. (R)
Johnson, William R. (R)
Joncas, Grace Lucille (D)
Junkins, F. LeRoy (R)
Karnis, Theodore Henry (R)
Karsten, Herbert H. (R)
Keane, Michael J. (D)
Keefe, James Thomas (D)
Keefe, William F. (D)
Keenan, Francis Joyce (R)
Keeney, Phyllis Mottram (R)
Kelsey, James R. (R)
Kimball, Hayford T. (R)
King, John W. (D)
Knight, Alice D. Tirrell (R)
Kopperl, George D. (R)
Kurth, Richard Augustin (R)
LaFond, Alphonse A. (D)
Lamontagne, Laurier (D)
LaPlante, Roland Henry (D)
Laroche, Leo (D)
Latour, John H. (D)
Leavitt, James F. (R)
Leclerc, Charles J. (D)
Lemire, George (D)
Leonard, Richard Wilson (D)
Lerandeau, Wilfred P. (D)
Lesage, Romeo R. (D)
LeVasseur, Edward J. (D)
Levesque, Freffle George (D)
Lewis, Robert M. (R)
Lockhart, Richard Spence (R)
Loizeaux, M. Suzanne (R)
Low, Fletcher (R)
Lynbourgh, William B. (D)
Lyon, Cecil Burton
McCarthy, John Francis (D)
McEachern, Paul (D)
McEachern, Raymond Joseph (D)
McGoldrick, Paul J. (R)
McIntyre, Thomas James (D)
Mack, Walter R. (R)
McMahon, Charles T. (D)
McMeekin, Norman A. (R)
Makris, Harry Peter (D)
Maloomian, Sarkis (D)
Manchester, John C. (R)
Manning, Alfred George (D)
Marcotte, Ronald J. (D)
Marrow, George Meredith (D)
Martel, Louis Israel (D)
Martin, Eda C. (R)
Martin, Willard Gordon (R)
Marx, Elanor F. (Independent)
Matheson, L. Keith (R)
Maxham, Paul B. (R)
Maxwell, Diamond Ai (R)
Maynard, William (R)
Meloney, John Mitchell
Merrifield, George R. (R)
Merrill, Shirley Kimball (R)
Michels, John Rudolf (R)
Mitchell, Lester Elbridge, Sr. (R)
Morrill, Arthur H. (R)
Morrison, Bessie Matilda (R)
Morse, Macy Elkins (D)
Morse, Richard A. (R)
Morse, Walter C. (D)
Moulton, Idanelle T. (R)
Murphy, Dennis Edward, Jr. (D)
Murphy, Peter John (D)
Nahil, Sam J. (R)
Nalette, Joseph C. (D)
Neale, Genevieve Shackelford (D)
Nelson, Albert L. (D)
Newell, Henry Chase (R)
Nikitas, Christus M. (D)
Nixon, David Lee (R)
Normandin, Margaret Eulalie (D)
Noyes, Chester Drew (R)
Nyberg, Harry E. (R)
O'Hara, Richard E. (D)
Oleson, Otto H. (D)
Olivier, Charles J. (R)
O'Neil, C. Michael (D)
O'Neil, James E. (R)
O'Rourke, Thomas F. (D)
Osborn, Clayton E. (R)
O'Shan, David (R)
Palazzi, John (R)
Palmer, Mildred L. (R)
Pappagianis, George S. (D)
Parnagian, Aram (R)
Park, Hazel I. (R)
Peabody, Arthur H. (D)
Peever, Leonard B. (R)
Pennington, Luther B, Jr. (R)
Perkins, Mildred Kelley (R)
Peterson, Walter Rutherford (R)
Phelps, Victor E. (D)
Philbrick, Robert D. (D)
Pinkham, Ernest L. (R)
Poliquin, Arthur (D)
Pollock, Stephen W, Sr. (R)
Powell, Wesley (R)
Pratt, Frederick (D)
Preston, Russell Edward (D)
Purdhomme, Leroy H. (D)
Putnam, Rose S. (D)
Quinn, J. Herbert (D)
Quirk, Jeremiah (R)
Radway, Laurence Ingram (D)
Raiche, Robert Edward (D)
Randall, Earle F. (R)
Rayball, Joseph Charles (D)
Read, Maurice W. (R)
Reddy, Samuel, Jr. (R)
Resnick, George J. (R)
Richardson, Mabel Lowe (R)
Riley, Richard D. (D)
Rinden, Paul (R)
Roberts, Milburn F. (R)
Robertson, Douglas Duncan (R)
Roby, Arthur E, Sr. (R)
Rolfe, Ernest L. (R)
Rossley, Eileen G. (D)
Roy, Edgar J. (D)
Rubins, Glenna H. (D)
Rufo, Pasquale V. (R)
Russell, Margaret A. (D)
Sabluski, Frank Charles (D)
Saggiotes, Soterios Arthur (D)
Sanders, Horace W: (R)
Sanders, Wilfred Leroy, Jr. (D)
Sawyer, Frank N. (R)
Savage, Stella Ramsay (R)
Scamman, W. Douglas (R)
Scamman, Walter Douglas, Jr. (R)
Schwaner, Annie Mae (R)
Scott, John L. (R)
Scott-Craig, Mary M. (D)
Senter, Kenneth Lee (R)
Sewall, F. Albert (D)
Shea, John Dana (D)
Shea, Roberta Tolman (R)
Sheehan, John Joseph (D)
Sherman, Kenneth Leland (R)
Sherman, Lloyd G. (R)
Shute, Ralph D. (R)
Sirois, Leo O. (R)
Smith, Manson Bowles (R)
Smith, Roger A. (R)
Smith, Stephen Wells (R)
Soden, Irving Henry (R)
Soucy, Emile J. (R)
Spalding, Kenneth Woodman, Jr. (R)
Spanos, Charles Vaios (D)
Spanos, Harry V. (D)
Spaulding, Roma Alma (R)
Splaine, James Raymond (D)
Spollett, Doris M. (R)
Squires, James Duane (R)
Stafford, George Walter (R)
Stark, Robert L. (R)
Stearns, Clifford Dwight (R)
Stevens, Henry L. (R)
Stratton, Robert J. (R)
Straw, Ezekiel A. (R)
Streeter, Bernard A, Jr. (R)
Studds, Gerry Eastman (D)
Sweeney, James Aloysius, Jr. (D)
Taft, Alexander McKaig (R)
Taylor, Ada C. (R)
Taylor, Selwyn Hart (D)
Thompson, Arthur E. (R)
Thompson, Barbara Cooper (R)
Thurston, George O. (R)
Tilton, John Havemeyer (R)
Tirrell, Loring Vinson (R)
Totman, Ralph Wright (R)
Treat, William Wardwell (R)
Tremblay, Wilfred Joseph, Sr. (D)
Tripp, John Thornton (R)
Trowbridge, C. Robertson (R)
Tufts, J. Arthur (R)
Twardus, John (D)
Uhlenberg, Frank L. (R)
Urie, H. Thomas (R)
Vallee, Roland S. (D)
Van Loan, Anna S. (R)
Vickery, Harold Jay (R)
Vincent, Arthur J. (D)
Wallin, Jean Rogers (D)
Waterhouse, Thomas, Jr. (R)
Weeks, Edna Batchelder (R)
Weeks, Sinclair (R)
Welch, John L. (D)
Whipple, Gladys Louise (R)
White, George W, Sr. (R)
White, Julia Humphreys (R)
Wiggin, Chester M, Jr. (R)
Wiggin, Ralph M, Sr. (R)
Wilder, George Warren (R)
Wildey, George S. (R)
Williams, Donald W. (D)
Williams, Thayne S. (R)
Williamson, Stanley H. (R)
Winn, Cecelia Louise (D)
Wood, Constance Rice (D)
Wyman, Louis C. (R)
Yardley, William Lawrence (R)
Young, John T. (R)
Zachos, Kimon Stephen (R)
Zachos, Victoria (R)

NEW JERSEY

Abbott, Barbara S. (R)
Abbott, Joseph A. (D)
Adams, Homer Mat (D)
Addonizio, Hugh J. (D)
Addonizio, Victor F. (D)
Agnoli, Bruno (D)
Albanese, Vito A. (D)
Allen, Robert F. (D)
Andora, Anthony D. (D)
Armellino, John Ralph (D)
Armenti, Carmen John (D)
Azzolina, Joseph (R)
Bain, Laurence Dixon, Jr. (D)
Barone, Ralph Peter (D)
Bateman, Raymond Henry (R)
Beadleston, Alfred N. (R)
Beam, Jacob Dyneley
Belli, Frank (D)
Betz, Frank Herbert, III (R)
Biancardi, Joseph G. (D)
Biber, Samuel L. (D)
Bigley, A. Donald (D)
Black, David Statler (D)
Bontempo, Salvatore (D)
Bouton, Charlotte Eldredge (D)
Boyd, Robert Stewart (R)
Brady, Maurice V. (D)
Brigiani, Guido J. (D)
Brown, Arnold E. (D)
Brown, John F. (R)
Browne, Robert Span (D)
Browne, William V. (D)
Burke, Jerome U. (R)
Burkhardt, Robert James (D)
Butler, Warren Harold (R)
Butterworth, W. Walton
Cafiero, James S. (R)
Cahill, William T. (R)
Caldwell, Hugh (D)
Campi, P. Paul (D)
Canfield, Gordon (R)
Carino, Anthony Jacob (D)
Carlton, Lee Mark (D)
Carty, Melville A. (D)
Case, Clifford Philip (R)
Citrino, Robert Joseph, Jr. (R)
Clemente, Celestino (R)
Cobb, William Allen (R)
Coleman, James M, Jr. (R)
Collins, Loree (R)
Connor, John Thomas (D)
Cooper, Aldrage B, Jr. (D)
Costa, Catherine Aurora (D)
Costa, Thomas J. (R)
Crabiel, David B. (D)
Crabiel, J. Edward (D)
Cryan, John F. (D)
Curcio, Samuel A. (R)
Curry, Harold J. (D)
Daniels, Dominick V. (D)
Davis, Edwin Letts (D)
Davis, John W. (D)
Davis, Nathaniel
Dealaman, Doris W. (R)
Deitz, William Thomas (D)
Del Tufo, Gerardo L. (R)
DeMarco, Richard M. (R)
Dennis, John Newman (R)
DeVoursney, Martin Thomas (D)
Diamond, Alice Mae (D)
Dichter, David (D)
Dickey, William K, Jr. (R)
Dickinson, Fairleigh Stanton, Jr. (R)
Dillon, C(larence) Douglas (R)
Dimon, John Edward (R)
Dodd, Frank J. (D)
Dono, Bobbie T. (D)
Doren, Joseph C. (D)
Doyle, Norman, Jr. (D)
Driver, Richard John (D)
Duff, John Bernard (D)
Dumont, Wayne, Jr. (R)
Dungan, Ralph Anthony
Dunton, George Albert (D)
Dwyer, Florence P. (R)

Edwards, Margaret Mary (D)
Errico, Chester L. (D)
Esposito, Michael P. (D)
Falcey, Robert M. (D)
Farley, Frank S. (R)
Farrington, Charles Edward (D)
Fay, John J, Jr. (D)
Fekety, John J. (D)
Feldman, Gerald Saunders (D)
Feldman, Matthew (D)
Fernald, Julia Gregg (R)
Fernicola, Nicholas (D)
Fisher, Germaine Edward (D)
Fleming, George Gains (R)
Flynn, Ann Dolores (R)
Flynn, James Jay, Jr. (D)
Forsythe, Edwin B. (R)
Frelinghuysen, Peter H. B. (R)
Friedland, David J. (D)
Gabrielson, Guy George (R)
Gaby, Daniel M. (D)
Gallagher, Cornelius E. (D)
Garibaldi, Peter Paul (R)
Gasser, Robert Alan (D)
Gavan, Henry F. (D)
Gavin, James Aloysius (D)
Gerard, Sumner, Jr. (R)
Gibbons, Harry J. (D)
Giblin, John Joseph (D)
Gladden, Robert E.
Goldman, Maclyn S. (D)
Gorman, Francis John (D)
Graves, Francis Xavier (D)
Grays, Lewis James (R)
Grecco, Joseph (D)
Gregg, Charles Stone (D)
Gross, Nelson G. (R)
Grossi, Anthony J. (D)
Guarini, Frank J, Jr. (D)
Guido, Robert Norman (R)
Hagedorn, Garrett William (R)
Halpin, Robert J. (D)
Hamer, Robert E. (D)
Haskell, Reuben L. (R)
Hauser, Frederick Howard (D)
Hausmann, C. Stewart (R)
Hawes, Judith Mays (D)
Hawk, Elizabeth B. (D)
Heatly, Constance A. (R)
Helstoski, Henry (D)
Henderson, Robert Emmet (D)
Hiering, William Thomas (R)
Higgins, Joseph J. (D)
Higgins, Marion West (R)
Higgins, Thomas S. (D)
Higham, Justus Charles (D)
Hillery, Thomas J. (R)
Holland, Arthur John (D)
Hollander, Sanford Lloyd (D)
Hollenbeck, Harold Capistran (R)
Horn, John J. (D)
Howard, James J. (D)
Howell, Charles Robert (D)
Hughes, Edward Joseph, Jr. (D)
Hughes, Mildred Barry (D)
Hughes, Richard J. (D)
Hume, Edmund Terrence (R)
Hunt, John E. (R)
Hurley, James Richardson (R)
Hyland, Richard Stephen (D)
Hyland, William Francis (D)
Inge, Hutchins F. (D)
Joelson, Charles S. (D)
Kahn, Albert B. (D)
Kaltenbacher, Philip David (R)
Kaser, Leonard H. (R)
Keegan, Joseph M. (D)
Kelly, William F, Jr. (D)
Kendall, William T. (R)
Kennan, George Frost
Kennedy, Walter P. (R)
Kenny, Eugene Patrick (R)
Kervick, John A. (D)
Kiefer, Alfred W. (D)
Kinneally, James Joseph (D)
Kirsch, Nathan S. (D)
Klein, Herbert Charles (D)
Knowlton, Willard Burr (R)
Kopycinski, Stephen Joseph (D)
Kordja, Betty McNamara (D)
Krasnow, Mildred (D)
Krebs, Paul J. (D)
La Corte, Nicholas St. John (R)
Lapidus, I. Richard (D)
Laskin, Lee B. (R)
Lazzio, Thomas (R)
Leiner, Henry Robert (R)
Lembo, Armand E. (D)
Lewis, Lorraine (D)
Ludwig, Donald Joseph (R)
Lynch, John A. (D)

McDermott, Frank X. (R)
McDonough, Peter J. (R)
McGann, Patrick J, Jr. (D)
McGrath, Thomas Charles, Jr. (D)
McGuire, David Kelty (D)
McKim, Adele W. (R)
McLaughlin, John A. (D)
MacLaury, Bruce K. (R)
McLeon, Addison M. (D)
McMillan, Brockway (R)
Mandelbaum, David M. (D)
Maraziti, Joseph J. (R)
Margetts, Josephine Sharon (R)
Margetts, Walter T, Jr. (R)
Merlino, Joseph Piedmont (D)
Meyer, Alice C. (D)
Meyner, Robert Baumle (D)
Miller, John J. (D)
Miller, John L. (R)
Minish, Joseph George (D)
Moore, John Denis Joseph (R)
Moraites, Peter (R)
Musto, William V. (D)
Neuberger, Katherine (R)
Nissley, Eleanore Steffens (R)
O'Connor, Jeremiah F. (D)
Osmers, Frank C, Jr. (R)
Owens, Ronald (D)
Ozzard, William E. (R)
Paini, Arthur William (D)
Parker, Barry T. (R)
Parsekian, Ned J. (D)
Patten, Edward James (D)
Perskie, Marvin D. (D)
Petersen, Arnold (Socialist Labor Party)
Pfaltz, Hugo Menzel, Jr. (R)
Phelps, Phelps (D)
Pierce, Alfred R. (D)
Plechner, Richard Frederick (R)
Policastro, Paul (D)
Politano, Frank James (D)
Ponzio, Arthur W. (D)
Pozen, Walter (D)
Quadara, Dominick Rocko (D)
Randall, Harry, Jr. (R)
Redfield, Reuben Robert (D)
Rhoades, Anna Rosa (R)
Ridolfi, Sido L. (D)
Rimm, Benjamin A. (R)
Rinaldi, Herbert M. (R)
Rinaldo, Matthew John (R)
Ringen, Walter Edwin, Jr. (D)
Robertson, Neil Frederick (D)
Rodino, Peter Wallace, Jr. (D)
Rogers, James Tracy (D)
Rubin, A. Michael (R)
Running, John Mark (D)
Rutherfurd, Douglas (R)
Saltzman, Edward Harold (D)
Samuel, Richard Irving (D)
Sandman, Charles W, Jr. (R)
Schluter, William Everett (R)
Schoel, Richard George (R)
Scholz, Frederick James (R)
Sciro, Frank Joseph (R)
Scott, Frank, Jr. (R)
Sears, Harry L. (R)
Sellars, Richard B. (R)
Serafin, Mary Walus (D)
Shanley, Bernard Michael (R)
Sharp, Thelma P. (D)
Sheehan, Patricia Queenan (D)
Sills, Arthur Jack (D)
Sisco, Edward (R)
Skevin, John M. (D)
Slade, Robert Henry (D)
Smith, Albert S. (R)
Smith, Irene M. (D)
Smith, Walter L, Jr. (R)
Smyth, Henry Dewolf
Snyder, John Parr (D)
Soltesz, Andrew, Jr. (D)
Sorensen, Emil S. (R)
Souter, Sydney Scull (R)
Spencer, Arthur Conover (R)
Stamler, Nelson F. (R)
Stark, Carroll Joseph (D)
Stemmer, Jay A. (R)
Stern, Jere Bart (D)
Sterner, E. Donald (R)
Stetin, Sol (D)
Stevenson, Harry (D)
Stiles, Beatrice May (R)
Stout, Richard Ralston (R)
Straut, Charles H, Jr. (D)
Stretch, D. Allen, Jr. (D)
Sullivan, Elmer Lindsley (D)
Sundstrom, Frank L. (R)
Swayze, Ruth U. (R)
Sweeney, Edward J. (D)

Tanzman, Norman (D)
Thomas, Peter W. (R)
Thompson, Frank, Jr. (D)
Thurston, Lewis Byron, III (R)
Todd, Webster Bray (R)
Todd, Webster Bray, Jr. (R)
Tompkins, William Finley (R)
Van Alstyne, David, Jr. (R)
Vohdin, Walter J. (D)
Volcker, Paul A. (D)
Volk, Austin Nicholas (R)
Waddington, John A.
Walch, John MacArthur Dunsmore (R)
Waldor, Milton A. (R)
Wallhauser, George Marvin (R)
Walling, Willis R. (R)
Ward, Laura Ida (D)
Weber, Robert H. (D)
Weber, Thomas (D)
Wegner, Robert J. (D)
White, Catherine Kilmurray (D)
White, James R. (R)
White, John L. (R)
White, Katharine Elkus
Widnall, William Beck (R)
Wilentz, David T. (D)
Wilentz, Robert N. (D)
Wilentz, Warren W. (D)
Williams, Harrison Arlington, Jr. (D)
Wollstadt, Paul (R)
Woodcock, Joseph C, Jr. (R)
Woods, William H. (R)
Woodson, S. Howard, Jr. (D)
Woolfenden, Milton, Jr. (R)
Woolley, J. Russell (R)
Wyckoff, David Cole (R)
Yesko, Jerome L. (D)
Zagoria, Sam (R)
Zwier, Stanley (D)

NEW MEXICO

Abbott, Ray Gene (R)
Alarid, Michael (D)
Amaya, George D. (D)
Anderson, Clinton Presba (D)
Anderson, Robert Orville (R)
Apodaca, Jerry (D)
Aragon, Manuel Leroy (D)
Armijo, Alex J. (D)
Armijo, Jose Enrique (R)
Armstrong, Gordian Lee (D)
Atchison, Raymond Lee (R)
Baca, Clovis (D)
Bannister, Tillman Arthur (D)
Bartlett, Martin Handley (R)
Begay, Wilbert C. (R)
Bellino, Charlotte Lee (D)
Bigbee, John Franklin, Jr. (R)
Black, Kenneth M. (R)
Black, Sterling F. (D)
Blakeley, James Gary (D)
Blocker, George (D)
Boucher, Mayo Terry (D)
Bowman, Fletcher C, Jr. (D)
Branch, Turner Williamson (R)
Brockman, Eugene Earl (R)
Brooks, Austin (D)
Brown, Frank (D)
Brown, Thomas E. (D)
Brown, Thomas Elzie, Jr. (D)
Bryan, Walker (D)
Budd, Harrell (R)
Burke, Nancy Aelishia (R)
Burkstaller, Sarah Ruth (D)
Burns, Dorothae Vivian (D)
Burroughs, John (D)
Cadwallader, James Kerrick (R)
Campbell, Jack M. (D)
Cargo, David Francis (R)
Carr, Marion P. (D)
Carter, Anderson (R)
Carter, Vincent (R)
Chacon, Matias L. (D)
Chavez, David, Jr. (D)
Chavez, Jose Benito (D)
Chavez, Tibo J. (D)
Coll, Max (R)
Cook, Cecil W. (D)
Cowan, Jim Magee (D)
Daniels, Jack (D)
Davenport, Raymond Wilson, Jr. (D)
Davis, George E. (R)
De Herrera, Joe Henry (R)
Demos, Paul T. (D)
Derizotis, Paris C. (D)
DeVargas, Horace (D)

Donnell, John Dickson (R)
Dow, Arthur L. (D)
Duckworth, William Henry (R)
Dunn, Aubrey L. (D)
Dunn, Marty Hoyle (R)
Dunne, Martha Lucille (R)
Durrett, James Melton, Sr. (D)
Eager, Henry L. (D)
Easley, Mack (D)
Eastham, John P. (R)
Eaves, John M. (D)
English, John C. (R)
Engwall, Carl A, Jr. (R)
Evans, Arthur Hayden (R)
Evans, Ernestine Duran (D)
Evans, Foster (D)
Feil, Paul Arnold (R)
Ferguson, Robert Earl (D)
Ferran, Gilbert Hipolito (R)
Fettinger, George Edgar (D)
Foreman, Ed (R)
Foster, Frank (D)
Foster, Fred W. (D)
Francis, E. Lee (R)
Gallagher, William C. (D)
Gant, Joseph Erwin, Jr. (D)
Garley, Gilbert Manuel, Jr. (D)
Gonzales, Arcenie A. (D)
Gonzales, Fidel C. (D)
Good, Thomas J, Jr. (D)
Goodwin, Martin Brune (R)
Greaser, Willie O. (D)
Greer, Albert R. (D)
Gross, Fred Alfred, Jr. (R)
Grothus, Edward Bernard (D)
Hart, Emmett C. (D)
Hartman, Ralph D. (D)
Hays, Guyton B. (D)
Heidel, Finis Leroy (D)
Helbing, Stephen Couch (R)
Hill, Harold Eugene (D)
Hilton, Ivan Jay (D)
Hoover, Thomas Warren (R)
Howe, Dennis (R)
Johns, Willam Campbell (R)
Johnson, Dewey E. (D)
Johnson, Lawrence H. (R)
Johnston, Kenneth R. (D)
Jordan, Robert Dean (R)
Jymm, Monroe M. (D)
Keil, A(rmin) T(heodore) (R)
Kelly, John Martin (D)
King, Bruce (D)
Kipp, Rex, Jr. (D)
Koch, James H. (D)
Kornegay, Jesse Dexter (D)
Lee, Frances Marron (R)
Lee, Robert M. (R)
Lee, Tom (R)
Lopez, Edward Joseph (D)
Lopez, Junio (R)
Lujan, Jim (D)
Lujan, Manuel, Jr. (R)
Lusk, Georgia Lee (D)
McCarty, Doris Maxine (D)
McCarty, Glen A. (D)
McComas, Elizabeth Mae Veitch (R)
McKim, George William (R)
McKinney, Robert (D)
Maestas, Cirilio Daniel (D)
Mahe, Henry Edward, Jr. (R)
Maloney, James A. (D)
Martin, Robert C. (D)
Martinez, Alex G. (D)
Mather, Richard F. (R)
Mattingly, Rex Max (R)
Mattson, John B, Jr. (R)
Mayer, Katharine (R)
Mayfield, Bobby M. (D)
Mead, Ed V. (D)
Mechem, Edwin Leard (R)
Melbourne, Maxine Joyce (R)
Melbourne, Ralph (R)
Melton, John Calvin (R)
Merino, S. Q. (D)
Mershon, John J. (D)
Miera, Ernest (D)
Miera, Ruben (D)
Miller, Alberta Meryl (D)
Mills, James C. (R)
Mitchell, Albert Knell (R)
Mitchell, Stephen A. (D)
Mondragon, Robert A. (D)
Montoya, Alfonso T. (D)
Montoya, Joseph M. (D)
Moran, Robert Martin (R)
Morgan, Robert C. (D)
Morris, James Paxton (R)
Morris, Thomas Gayle (D)
Murray, Frank A, Jr. (D)

Murray, Robert S. (R)
Neal, Caswell Fincher (D)
Neff, Francine Irving (R)
Noble, Merrill E. (D)
Norvell, David L. (D)
Ortiz, Rudy A. (D)
Ortiz, Willie V. (R)
Pacheco, Fermin (D)
Papen, Frank O'Brien (D)
Parker, Alva J. (D)
Parker, Earl, Sr. (D)
Pattison, Orville Hoyt (R)
Patton, James R. (D)
Peirce, Eugene Willard, Jr. (R)
Pendleton, Raymond A. (R)
Pino, Jose Ortiz, III (D)
Pool, Penta Price (R)
Pope, Georgia Helen (R)
Prince, Bradford H. (R)
Pruit, Ralph Eugene (R)
Quinn, Wesley Marion (R)
Reese, Norman Randolph (D)
Roberts, Austin E. (D)
Robinson, Carlos R. (R)
Rogers, Hamilton (R)
Rogers, Verdon Lee (D)
Rolstad, Bruce Howard (D)
Romero, Moises (R)
Rose, Joe (R)
Rudolph, Joseph H. Milnor (R)
Runnels, Harold Lowell (D)
Ryan, William Murray (R)
Sanborn, Burt D. (R)
Sanchez, Cordelia C. (D)
Sanchez, J. Chris (D)
Sanchez, Maurice (D)
Sandel, Jerry Wayne (D)
Sawyer, Fern (D)
Sawyer, Mrs. U. D. (D)
Sedillo, Filo M. (D)
Shrecengost, William G. (R)
Skeen, Joseph Richard (R)
Skinner, Elmer L. (D)
Smalley, I. M. (D)
Stahl, Jack L. (R)
Standley, Fred M. (D)
Taylor, Herbert J. (D)
Taylor, Willie Margaret (D)
Tellez, Robert Gonzales (D)
Thompson, Allen F. (R)
Tinker, Carol Wicks (R)
Toles, J. Penrod (D)
Tomlin, John R. (D)
Torres, Steve S, Jr. (R)
Utton, Albert Edgar (D)
Valdez, Joe Luis (R)
Walker, E. S. Johnny (D)
Wamel, Rufus Henry, Jr. (D)
Whatley, Robert Eugene (R)
Wheatley, W. C. (D)
Williams, David Cary (R)
Williams, Matt (R)
Witt, Boston E. (D)

NEW YORK

Abrams, Robert (D)
Acevedo, Nicolas C. (D)
Adams, Wilhelmina F. (D)
Adams, William E. (R)
Addabbo, Joseph Patrick (D)
Albano, Vincent Francis, Jr. (R)
Aldrich, Alexander (R)
Allen, James E, Jr. (R)
Amadei, James Robert (R)
Amann, Edward J, Jr. (R)
Ambrose, John Anthony (D)
Anastasio, Frank (D)
Anderson, Robert Bernard (R)
Anderson, Warren Mattice (R)
Aponte, Humberto (D)
Aron, Carl Robert (D)
Aurelio, Richard R. (R)
Aust, Mildred Grace (D)
Badillo, Herman (D)
Bahou, Victor Samuel (D)
Baker, Bertram L. (D)
Balch, Richard H. (D)
Balen, Mark Louis (D)
Ball, George Wildman (D)
Balletta, Vincent R, Jr. (R)
Baranello, Dominic Joseph (D)
Barclay, H. Douglas (R)
Barden, Bryce (R)
Baritz, Loren (D)
Barry, James J. (D)
Barry, John D. (R)
Bartlett, Kenneth G. (R)
Bartlett, Richard James (R)
Basmajian, Walter (D)
Battista, Vito Piranesi (R)
Bazell, Michael Philip (D)
Beame, Abraham David (D)
Becker, Daniel (R)
Becker, Frank J. (R)
Beckman, John Wells (R)
Beeman, Josiah Horton (D)
Begley, Owen M. (D)
Belcher, Taylor Garrison
Bell, H. Clark (R)
Bellanca, Alfonso V. (R)
Bennet, Augustus Witschief (R)
Berger, Harold D. (D)
Berking, Max (D)
Berle, Adolf Augustus (D)
Berle, Peter Adolf Augustus (D)
Berman, Frederic Sanford (D)
Bernstein, Abraham (D)
Bernstein, George Kaskel (R)
Bersani, Leonard F. (R)
Biaggi, Mario (D)
Bikel, Theodore (D)
Bingham, Jonathan B. (D)
Blanchfield, Nina Marie (D)
Block, Ethel Lasher (R)
Bloom, Jeremiah B. (D)
Blumberg, Thelma Nagler (D)
Blumenthal, Albert Howard (D)
Bobroff, Harold (D)
Boehm, David O. (R)
Bolton, Richard Hall (R)
Bookson, Paul P. E. (D)
Bosch, Albert H. (R)
Boulous, Lila Nebhan (D)
Boutelle, Paul Benjamin (Socialist Workers Party)
Boyle, Earl E. (D)
Bradshaw, Lester Joseph, Jr. (R)
Brasco, Frank J. (D)
Breitel, Charles David (R)
Bromberg, Michael D. (D)
Bronstein, Herbert (D)
Bronston, Jack E. (D-L)
Brooks, Doris L. (R)
Brooks, Olive (D)
Brown, Arnold Irwin (D)
Brown, David W. (D)
Brown, Richard A. (R)
Brown, Richard Arthur (D)
Browne, Kenneth N. (D)
Brownell, Herbert (R)
Brownstein, Irwin (D)
Bruno, Jerry (D)
Bryant, Frederick Boyce (R)
Brydges, Earl William (R)
Buchenholz, Jane Jacobs (D)
Buck, Ellsworth Brewer (R)
Buckley, John Timothy (R)
Buckley, William Frank, Jr. (Conservative)
Bunche, Ralph Johnson (D)
Bundy, McGeorge
Burns, Arthur Frank (R)
Burns, John J. (D)
Burns, John M. (R)
Bush, Elmer Ogden (R)
Buttenwieser, Benjamin Joseph (D)
Button, Daniel E. (R)
Byrnes, Lawrence C. (R)
Cabot, Lawrence A. (D)
Caemmerer, John D. (R)
Calkins, John Thiers (R)
Callanan, John P. (R)
Calli, William S. (R)
Campbell, Donald A. (R)
Campbell, Dorothy Mildred (R)
Capanegro, Michael J. (D)
Capozzoli, Louis J. (D)
Cappola, Pasquale (R)
Carey, Hugh L. (D)
Carey, May E. (D)
Cariello, Mario J. (D)
Carmichael, James A, Jr. (D)
Carroll, George Francis (D)
Carroll, James Francis (R)
Casey, Joseph Francis (R)
Caso, Ralph George (R)
Catterson, James M, Jr. (R)
Cavanagh, Edward Francis, Jr. (D)
Celler, Emanuel (D)
Cerosky, Richard A. (R)
Cerulli, Louis Anthony (D)
Chananau, Alexander (D)
Chase, Philip R. (R)
Childs, Theodore F. (D)
Chisholm, Shirley Anita (D)
Chubb, Elizabeth Louise (R)
Cincotta, George A. (D)
Clancy, Jean Theresa (D)
Clark, Ramsey (D)
Clay, Lucius DuBignon (R)
Clements, Mahlon Thompson (R)
Cochrane, John Campbell (R)
Cohen, Joseph (D)
Cohen, Leonard N. (D)
Cohen, Monroe (D)
Cohn, Harold W. (D)
Cole, Donald Dennis (R)
Cole, Thomas David (Conservative)
Cole, Thomas E. (R)
Collum, Thad L. (R)
Conable, Barber Benjamin, Jr. (R)
Conklin, William T. (R)
Connolly, Eugene Paul (D)
Connor, Robert T. (R)
Connorton, John Vincent (D)
Conway, John O'Connor (D)
Cook, Constance E. (R)
Cook, Don W. (R)
Cooke, Walter E. (D)
Cooperman, Arthur J. (D)
Corbett, Lawrence E, Jr. (R)
Corcoran, James Patrick (D)
Corning, Erastus II (D)
Corso, Joseph R. (D)
Cosgrove, John B. (D)
Costanza, Margaret (D)
Costanzo, Nicholas (R)
Costanzo, Robert Frank (D)
Costello, Timothy William (Liberal)
Costikyan, Edward N. (D)
Coudert, Frederic Rene (R)
Cox, Frank P. (D)
Crangle, Joseph F. (D)
Crawford, Edward F. (R)
Crego, Doris Imogen (R)
Crews, John Robert (R)
Crews, Julia L. (D)
Cronin, Robert Joseph (D)
Cunningham, Patrick Joseph (D)
Curley, Lucy A. Alford (D)
Curran, Henry M. (R)
Curran, Paul J. (R)
Cusimano, Fred J. (D)
Daly, Edna M. (R)
Davidoff, Gilbert (D)
Davidoff, Paul (D)
Davidson, Irwin Delmore (D)
Davidson, Muriel SaRells (R)
Davis, Kenneth Newton, Jr. (R)
Davis, Shelby Cullom (R)
Day, Theodore D. (R)
Deardourff, John D. (R)
De Blasi, Pasquale, Sr. (R)
DeJohn, Mary Frances (D)
Delaney, James J. (D)
DeLaney, William Richard (D)
Del Giudice, Michael J. (D)
Derounian, Steven B. (R)
DeSalvio, Louis F. (D)
De Santis, Carl Robert (R)
DeThomasis, Louis (D)
Deutsch, Bernard (D)
Deutsch, Peter (R)
Dewey, Thomas Edmund (R)
DeWind, Adrian W(illiam) (D)
DiCarlo, Dominick L. (R)
Dickens, Lloyd Evertt (D)
Dickinson, Daniel S, Jr. (R)
Di Falco, Anthony G. (D)
Dimond, Francis George (D)
DiPronio, Lena (D)
Doerr, John H. (D)
Dominick, D. Clinton, III (R)
Donno, Aldo David (R)
Donovan, James Hubert (R)
Dooley, Edwin Benedict (R)
Dorn, Francis Edwin (R)
Dow, John Goodchild (D)
Dowd, Joseph (D)
Drajem, Irene Theresa (D)
Droms, Fred William, Jr. (R)
Drumm, Willard C. (R)
Dryfoos, George Ellis (D)
Dubinsky, David (Liberal)
Dudley, Edward Richard D. (D)
Duffy, Thomas A. (D)
Duke, Angier Biddle (D)
Dulski, Thaddeus J. (D-L)
Dunn, Frederick H. (D)
Duryéa, Perry Belmont, Jr. (R)
Dwyer, William Francis (R)
Dyson, John Stuart (D)
Echtman, Irwin M. (D)
Eddy, Vera Louise (R)
Edwards, Deighton Octavius, Jr. (R)
Eggert, Fred W. (D)
Ehrlich, Eleanor Ewing (D)
Emery, James Louis (R)
Engel, Irving M. (D)
English, John Francis (D)
Ernst, Morris Leopold (D)
Erway, Julian B. (D)
Eve, Arthur O. (D)
Fabrizi, John (D)
Farber, Earl Clarence (R)
Farbstein, Leonard (D)
Farenga, Felix Anthony (D)
Farley, James A. (D)
Farmer, James (Liberal, N.Y.)
Farrell, George Joseph, Jr. (R)
Fehrenbach, Edwin Joseph (R)
Fein, Arnold L. (D)
Feldman, Justin N. (D)
Fenton, Isabelle B. (R)
Ferguson, Glenn W.
Ferman, Allan S. (D)
Ferrall, William J. (D)
Ferrari, Dante Louis (D)
Fertig, Harold (D)
Feuer, Mortimer (D)
Field, Frederick Gorham, Jr. (R)
Field, Ruth (D)
Finger, Seymour Maxwell
Fink, Thomas A. (D)
Finkelstein, Jerry (D)
Finley, Joseph Caldwell (R)
Fino, Paul A. (R)
Fischer, Edward Mickael (D)
Fish, Hamilton, Jr. (R)
Fisher, Arnold R. (R)
Flynn, John E. (R)
Folmer, Louis H. (R)
Folsom, Marion Bayard (R)
Fox, J. Lewis (D)
Frankel, Charles (D)
Freda, Carmine (R)
French, Eleanor Clark (D)
Friedman, Beth Holland (D)
Furness, Betty (D)
Galiber, Joseph Lionel (D)
Gallagher, John T. (R)
Gamser, Howard Graham (D)
Garbarino, John Alfred (R)
Garcia, Robert (D)
Garnham, Harold P. (D)
Garnsey, James F. (D)
Gilbert, Jacob H. (D)
Gilhooley, John Joseph (R)
Gill, Kathleen O'Connor (D)
Gillette, Henry E. (D)
Gilman, Benjamin A. (R)
Ginsberg, Martin (R)
Gioffre, Anthony B. (R)
Glavin, James Henry, III (D)
Gliedman, Howard Benjamin (R)
Glinski, Frank J. (D)
Godley, G. McMurtrie
Goldberg, Arthur Joseph (D)
Goldin, Harrison J. (D)
Goldstein, Lewis Howard (D)
Goldstein, Nathaniel Lawrence (D)
Goldstein, Noah (D)
Golombek, Eugene W. (D)
Goodell, Charles Ellsworth (R)
Goodman, Arthur (D)
Goodman, Roy M. (R)
Gordon, Bernard G. (R)
Gottlieb, Stephen Stewart (D)
Greco, Michael John (D)
Greco, Stephen R. (D)
Green, S. William (R)
Greenberg, Samuel L. (D)
Greene, Leonard Robert (R)
Greene, Scott E. (R)
Grieco, Salvatore J. (D)
Griffin, Francis J. (D)
Griffin, James D. (D)
Griffin, Raymond P. (D)
Griffith, William F, Jr. (Conservative, N.Y.)
Griffiths, Arthur H. (D)
Grimm, Peter (R)
Grimsey, J. Herbert (R)
Grossman, Howard M. (D)
Grover, James R, Jr. (R)
Grunfeld, Roselyn E. (D)
Guardino, Alphonse Peter (R)
Gunning, Rosemary Rita (Conservative, N.Y.)
Gutowski, Stanley L. (R)
Hagerty, James C. (R)
Halaby, Najeeb E.
Halbert, Herschel Ogden (D)
Haley, K. Daniel (D)
Hall, Leonard Wood (R)
Halpern, Seymour (R)
Halpin, Stella (D)

Halstead, Fred Wolf (Socialist Workers Party)
Hampton, Mason Lillard, Jr. (Conservative, N.Y.)
Hanley, James Michael (D)
Harcourt, J. Palmer (R)
Hardwick, Arthur, Jr. (D)
Harriman, W. Averell
Harrington, Donald Szantho (Liberal Party, N.Y.)
Harris, Glenn H. (R)
Harris, James Monroe (R)
Harrison, Irving (D)
Harwood, Stanley (D)
Hastings, James Fred (R)
Hausbeck, Albert J. (D)
Hausman, Samuel (R)
Hayduk, Albert T. (R)
Healey, James Christopher (D)
Hearn, George Henry (D)
Hecht, Burton (D)
Hein, Sidney S. (R)
Held, Gerald S. (R)
Hellmuth, James Grant (R)
Hemenway, Russell Douglas (D)
Henderson, Charles D. (R)
Hesterberg, Alexander George (D)
Higgins, Martin Joseph (D)
Hildebrand, George H.
Hinman, George L. (R)
Hirsch, Hilda (R)
Hoak, Bertrand H. (D)
Hoeh, George Charles (D)
Hoffman, Harry S. (Conservative, N.Y.)
Hogan, Frank Smithwick (D)
Hogan, Rosemarie (D)
Hooker, Roger Wolcott (R)
Hope, Leighton A. (R)
Hopf, Peter S. (D)
Hornig, Donald Frederick (D)
Horton, Frank (R)
Howard, Henry Seymour (R)
Howe, Gordon A. (R)
Hudson, Douglas (R)
Hughes, Douglas William (R)
Hughes, John Henry (R)
Huntington, Lawrence Smith (R)
Huntington, Prescott Butler (R)
Ingalls, George Lewis (R)
Ingram, Verner Merritt (R)
Ippolito, Andrew Vincent (D)
Isacson, Leo (D)
Javits, Jacob Koppel (R)
Johnson, Nina Sidler (D)
Jonas, Milton (R)
Jones, Clarence Benjamin (D)
Jones, John J. J. (D)
Jones, Mary Gardiner (R)
Kalish, Louis (D)
Kane, Angeline Betty (D)
Kane, F. James, Jr. (D)
Kapenstein, Ira (D)
Katzenbach, Nicholas de Belleville (D)
Kaye, Allen E. (R)
Keating, Kenneth B. (R)
Keeler, Virginia Lee (D)
Keenan, Edward John (R)
Keenan, William Q. (D)
Kelleher, Neil William (R)
Kelly, Daniel M. (D)
Kelly, Edna F(lannery) (D)
Kelly, Phyllis Matheis (R)
Kelly, Robert F. (R)
Keogh, Eugene James (D)
Kesselring, Leo John (Conservative Party, N.Y.)
Kickbush, Robert James (R)
Kilburn, Clarence Evans (R)
King, Carleton James (R)
Kingman, William Salem (R)
Kingston, John Earl (R)
Kinsolving, Charles McIlvaine, Jr. (D)
Kirsch, Morris (R)
Kirvin, John F. (D)
Kirwin, Arthur Robert (D)
Klein, Aaron Edward (D)
Kleiner, Robert I. (D)
Kline, David Louis (D)
Kline, Helen M. (D)
Knight, Ridgway Brewster
Knorr, Martin J. (R)
Koch, Edward Irving (D)
Kopple, Robert (D)
Kottler, Joseph (D)
Kraf, Harry (D)
Kretchmer, Jerome (D)
Krim, Arthur B. (D)
Krohn, Franklin Bernard (D)
Krupsak, Mary Anne (D)
Kuhnen, Richard F. (R)
Kupferman, Theodore R. (R)
Kurmel, Edward A. (D)
LaFauci, Thomas V. (D)
Lagonegro, Edward Thomas (D)
Lama, Alfred A. (D)
Lamb, Frank T. (D)
Landis, Frederick (R)
Lane, Clarence D. (R)
Langley, Walter B. (R)
Lanigan, Charles Thomas (R)
LaPan, James Edward (D)
Larson, A. William (D)
Laverne, Thomas (R)
LaVigne, Francis C. (D)
Leasure, Kenneth Say (R)
Lee, Charles Marks (R)
LeFever, Rose Isabel (R)
Lefkowitz, Louis J. (R)
Leichter, Franz S. (D)
Lent, Norman F. (R)
Lentol, Edward S. (D)
Leppert, George (D)
Letsen, Royden A. (D)
Levine, Barry S. (D)
Levine, Joseph Samuel (D)
Levine, Philip Michael (R)
Levine, Solomon (D)
Levitt, Arthur (D)
Levy, Eugene (R)
Lewinter, Murray (D)
Lichtman, Sidney Alfred (D)
Liebowitz, Simon J. (D)
Lifset, Harvey Mervin (D-Liberal)
Lill, Raymond Joseph (D)
Lindsay, John Vliet (R)
Lindsay, Robert Goodall (D)
Linowitz, Sol Myron (D)
Lis, John B. (D)
Loeb, John Langeloth, Jr. (R)
Lohrey, Maryann (R)
Lombard, James A. (D)
Lombardi, Tarky James, Jr. (R)
Lomenzo, John P. (R)
Lounsberry, Richard C. (R)
Lounsbury, Robert Hastings (D)
Lovenheim, David A. (R)
Lovett, Robert Abercrombie (D)
Low, Robert A. (Dem-Liberal)
Lowell, Harriette Mary (R)
Lowell, Stanley H. (D)
Lowenstein, Allard K. (D)
Lowery, Thomas John, Jr. (D)
Lowry, Benjamin James (R)
Luddy, William F. (D)
Lyman, Curtis Lee (R)
Lynch, Ida W. (R)
MacCallum, Douglas C. (R)
McCarthy, John G. (R)
McCarthy, Richard Dean (D)
Macomber, William Butts, Jr. (R)
McCormick, Charles F. (D)
McCurn, Neal Peters (D)
McDevitt, Charles F. (R)
McDonough, George Gibson (D)
MacDougal, Harry Martin (R)
McDougal, Jerome R, Jr. (D)
McEwen, Robert Cameron (R)
McFarland, James Thomas (R)
McHugh, Dorothy Barbree (R)
McInerney, Thomas J. (D)
Mackell, Thomas James (D)
McKneally, Martin B. (R)
McManus, Donald Francis (D)
McSpedon, Thomas G. (D)
Magnani, Mauro (Conservative, N.Y.)
Mahoney, J. Daniel (Conservative, N.Y.)
Mahoney, John F, Jr. (D)
Mailer, Norman Kingsley (D)
Mangano, Guy James (D)
Mangano, James V. (D)
Mankiewicz, Don Martin (D)
Manley, Bruce (R)
Marcham, John (D)
Marchi, John Joseph (R)
Maresca, Orest V. (D)
Margiotta, Joseph Michael (R)
Marine, Joseph E. (D)
Marino, Ralph John (R)
Markham, Charles Buchanan (R)
Marks, Jerome Walter (D)
Marra, Mary Ann (R)
Marsha, Howard Clarence (R)
Marshall, Richard L. (R)
Martano, Frank Louis (R)
Marthen, Elsa W. (R)
Marvin, Guy L. (R)
Marwell, Edward Marvin (D)
Mason, Edwyn E. (R)
Mastandrea, Frank J. (R)
Mattar, Edward Paul, III (R)
Mead, John J. S. (R)
Melvin, Kathleen O'Hara (R)
Mercorella, Anthony J. (D)
Metcalf, George R. (R)
Meyer, Frank Straus (Conservative, N.Y.)
Meyerson, A. Frederick (D)
Michaels, George M. (D)
Middendorf, Henry Stump, Jr. (Conservative Party, N.Y.)
Miller, Ethel Allen (R)
Miller, Franklin (D)
Miller, Marilyn Ruth (D)
Miller, William Edward (R)
Mills, Kenneth Adolfo (D)
Milone, Salvatore Anthony (R)
Mintz, Hyman E. (R)
Mitchell, Charlene (Communist Party)
Mitchell, Donald J. (R)
Mitchell, John Newton (R)
Molyneaux, Silas Robarre (D)
Monacelli, William Anthony (D)
Mondello, Ferdinand J. (D)
Montano, Armando (D)
Morganthau, Henry, Jr.
Moriarty, Jeremiah J. (R)
Morrison, Edward Allen (Liberal)
Mosbacher, Emil, Jr. (R)
Mosberg, Irving (D)
Moses, Robert (R)
Motley, Constance Baker (D)
Moyers, Bill D. (D)
Mulhern, John Francis (D)
Multer, Abraham J. (D)
Murphy, John Michael (D)
Murphy, Lawrence P. (D)
Nakasian, Samuel (R)
Nankey, Ralph Wallace (Conservative, N.Y.)
Neuhaus, Richard John (D)
Nezezon, Marie Ann (D)
Nichols, Benjamin (D)
Nickerson, Eugene Hoffman (D)
Niles, Dalwin J. (R)
Norris, Russell Earl, Jr. (Conservative, N.Y.)
Novak, James B. (Conservative, N.Y.)
Novak, Larry F. (D)
Nowicki, Joseph F. X. (R)
Oberwager, Frances Robertson (R)
O'Brien, Leo William (D)
O'Connor, Eugene Paul (D)
O'Connor, Frank Daniel (D)
O'Doherty, Kieran (Conservative, N.Y.)
O'Hara, Donald J.
Ohrenstein, Manfred (D)
Olds, Glenn A.
O'Rourke, James F. X. (R)
Osborn, George W. (R)
Oster, John Edward (R)
Ostertag, Harold Charles (R)
Ottinger, Richard Lawrence (D)
Palmer, George Vincent (D)
Palmer, Vincent A, Jr. (R)
Pandick, Margaret L. (D)
Paradise, Elsie M. (R)
Parillo, Joseph, Jr. (R)
Parsons, J. Graham
Passannante, William F. (D)
Paternoster, Francis Richard (D)
Paterson, Basil A. (D)
Pcionek, Pauline Anna (D)
Pearsall, C. Bruce (R)
Pemberton, John De J, Jr. (R)
Periconi, Joseph F. (R)
Peters, Robert (Conservative, N.Y.)
Petito, Michael N. (D)
Petrie, Donald A. (D)
Petty, John R.
Pfeiffer, Lolita Dawson (D)
Pfeiffer, William Louis (R)
Pheiffer, William Townsend (R)
Pierce, George Adams (D)
Pike, Otis Grey (D)
Pillion, John R. (R)
Pirnie, Alexander (R)
Pisani, Joseph R. (R)
Planer, Richard Andrew (D)
Platt, Thomas C. (R)
Plumadore, Hayward Henry (R)
Podell, Bertram L. (D)
Polansky, Daniel J. (R)
Pomeroy, Robert Watson (R)
Pope, Gregory J. (D)
Portela, Thomas Joseph (D)
Posess, Stanley (D)
Posillipo, Anthony Joseph (D)
Posner, Seymour (D)
Potter, Orlando B. (D)
Powell, Adam Clayton, Jr. (D)
Powers, James Edward (D)
Proller, Nathan (R)
Proudfit, John Graham (R)
Psaty, Martin Melville (D)
Purcell, Francis T. (R)
Quackenbush, Margaret Thompson (R)
Quigley, Robert Joseph (D)
Quinn, John E. (D)
Quinn, Thomas Rodney (D)
Ramos-Lopez, Jose (D)
Rand, William (R)
Rangel, Charles B. (D)
Ray, John Henry (R)
Reid, Ogden Rogers (R)
Reilly, Joseph Matthew (R)
Repicci, Francis C. (D)
Reuss, Frederick M, Jr. (R)
Rice, Michael G. (D)
Rickenbacker, William Frost (Conservative, N.Y.)
Rickman, Herbert Paul (D)
Riegelman, Rosalind (D)
Riesner, Daniel J. (R)
Rios, Carlos M. (D)
Roberson, John (R)
Robison, Howard Winfield (R)
Rockefeller, Nelson Aldrich (R)
Rodell, Martin (D)
Rodino, Robert Joseph (D)
Rodriguez, Eugene (D)
Rogalin, Wilma Clare (R)
Roncallo, Angelo D. (R)
Rooney, John J. (D)
Roosevelt, Franklin Delano, Jr. (D)
Rose, Alex (Liberal)
Rose, Dorothy H. (D)
Rosen, Mildred Pafundi (R)
Rosenbaum, Richard Merrill (R)
Rosenberg, Alex Jacob (D)
Rosenberg, Marvin (D)
Rosenberg, William S. (R)
Rosenblatt, Joseph B. (D)
Rosenblatt, William (D)
Rosencrans, Arthur (D)
Rosenthal, Benjamin Stanley (D)
Rosow, Jerome Morris (Independent)
Rossetti, Frank G. (D)
Rossides, Eugene Telemachus (R)
Roth, Fred M, Jr. (R)
Royall, Kenneth Claiborne (D)
Rubin, Israel (D)
Ruchala, Joseph F. (R)
Rush, Kenneth
Russell, Lloyd A. (R)
Russo, Lucio F. (R)
Ryan, Aileen Barlow (D)
Ryan, Andrew W, Jr. (R)
Ryan, William Fitts (D)
Sabbatino, Jules G. (D)
Sachs, Alice (D)
Sachs, Herbert (D)
Sacks, Alexander (R)
Saddlemire, Carl Lewis (R)
Sadowsky, Edward L. (D)
Safian, A. Chester (D)
St. George, Katharine (R)
St. Lawrence, Joseph Thomas (D)
Salomone, Michael John (D)
Samuel, Howard David (D)
Samuels, Howard Joseph (D)
Samuels, Nathaniel (R)
Satriale, John T. (D)
Schatz, Harold H. (R)
Scheuer, James H. (D)
Schick, John Joseph, Jr. (D)
Schlesinger, Arthur Meier, Jr. (D)
Schlosser, Jack A. (D)
Schmidt, Frederick D. (D)
Schneider, Morris H. (D)
Schoellkopf, Paul A, Jr. (R)
Schoeneck, Charles A. (R)
Schosberg, Paul Alan (D)
Schriever, William W.
Schutzer, Jerome (D)
Schwartz, Murray M. (D)
Schwartzman, Sarah (D)
Schwenk, Edwin Miller (R)
Screvane, Paul R. (D)
Sears, William R. (R)

Sedita, Frank A. (D)
Seergy, Edmund George (R)
Seldin, Abe (R)
Selkirk, Russell (R)
Shaffer, Robert Edwin (D)
Shannon, Janet Loretta (D)
Shapiro, Stanley Lester (R)
Sharpe, John George (R)
Shaw, Edward Walter (Socialist Workers Party)
Sibley, Harper, Jr. (D)
Siciliano, Marion Elizabeth (R)
Siegel, Norma Kaiden (D)
Silk, Robert H. (D)
Silverman, Leonard (D)
Simpson, Robert Foster (Conservative, N.Y.)
Skinner, Elliott Percival (D)
Smith, Bernard C. (R)
Smith, Henry P, III (R)
Smith, Raymond K. (D)
Smith, Robert Franklin (D)
Smith, William T, II (R)
Smythe, Hugh Heyne
Snitow, Virginia L. (D)
Solarz, Stephen J. (D)
Soldini, John Louis (D)
Sorensen, Theodore Chaikin (D)
Southall, Mark T. (D)
Sovik, Laurence (D)
Spadanuta, Barbara Belvek (D)
Spatt, Moses (R)
Speno, Edward J. (R)
Stabile, Joseph Anthony (D)
Stachowski, Stanley Joseph (D)
Stark, Abe (D)
Stein, Andrew Jay (D)
Stein, Robert (D)
Steingut, Stanley (D)
Stella, Anthony Joseph (D)
Stephens, Willis H. (R)
Stevenson, Edward A. (D)
Stewart, Waldaba Hamilton, Jr. (D)
Stillman, John Sterling (D)
Stockmeister, Charles F. (D)
Stone, Norma Walsh (R)
Stopyra, Agnes Theresa (D)
Strasser, George Louis, Jr. (D)
Stratton, Samuel Studdiford (D)
Straub, Chester John (D)
Straus, R. Peter (D)
Strelzin, Harvey Lloyd (D)
Sullivan, Donald J. (D)
Sullivan, Thomas J. (D)
Sutton, Percy E. (D)
Sweet, Robert Workman (R)
Sweeting, Richard W. (R)
Swiatek, Frank E. (D)
Tanner, Marietta Jones (D)
Tauriello, Anthony Francis (D)
Taylor, Paul Reed (R)
Tebo, Maryanne (D)
Tenney, John Richard (R)
Tenzer, Herbert (D)
Terry, John Hart (R)
Tesman, Bruce Robert (D)
Teutsch, Erika (D)
Thaler, Seymour R. (D-Liberal)
Thomas, Stanley Buddington, Jr. (R)
Thompson, William C. (D)
Thorp, John S, Jr. (D)
Tills, Ronald H. (R)
Torres, Frank (D)
Travers, F. Warren (D)
Tree, Mary Endicott Peabody (D)
Troy, Matthew Joseph, Jr. (D)
Tubby, Roger W.
Turshen, Max M. (D)
Tuttle, Elsebeth H. (R)
Vail, Donald (R)
Valentine, William Anthony (R)
Valeo, Francis R. (D)
Vance, Cyrus Roberts (D)
Van Cott, George E. (R)
Vanden Heuvel, William J. (D)
Van Lare, Frank E. (R)
Van Lengen, George Henry (D)
Van Rensselaer, Stanley L. (R)
Van Voorhis, John (R)
Vitanza, Thomas Anthony (D)
Volet, William B. (D)
Volker, Julius (R)
Wager, Eli (D)
Wagner, Robert F. (D)
Wainwright, Stuyvesant (R)
Walkley, Frank (R)
Wallach, Louis (D)
Wallis, Charles L. (R)
Walsh, John J. (D)
Walsh, William Francis (R)
Warder, Frederick L. (R)
Warner, Bertha Diggs (R)
Warner, Ivan (D)
Waryas, Victor C. (D)
Washer, Harriet Hunt (R)
Wasser, Joseph (D)
Waterman, Edwin Payn (Conservative, N.Y.)
Waters, Alonzo L. (R)
Weaver, Robert Clifton (R)
Webster, Donald Albert (R)
Weinstein, Jack M. (R)
Weinstein, Moses M. (D)
Weiss, Peter (D)
Wemple, Clark Cullings (R)
Whalen, George Edwin (D)
Wharton, J(ames) Ernest (R)
Whelan, Robert Edward (D)
White, F. Clifton (R)
Wilkins, Roy
Willard, Kenneth Rollah (R)
Williams, F. James, Jr. (D)
Williams, Franklin H. (D)
Wilson, Jerome L. (D)
Wilson, Kenneth L. (R)
Wilson, Malcolm (R)
Witherwax, Charles H. (Conservative, N.Y.)
Wolfe, Carlton Floyd (D)
Wolfe, Louis E. (DL)
Wolff, Lester Lionel (D)
Wood, Katherine M. (R)
Woods, James Christopher (D)
Wool, Richard Irwin (D)
Worlock, Paul Anthony (D)
Wydler, John W. (R)
Yoswein, Leonard E. (D)
Young, Whitney Moore, Jr.
Zaretzki, Joseph (D)
Zelenko, Herbert (D)

NORTH CAROLINA

Adams, Hoover (D)
Adcox, John (R)
Ainsley, William Franklin (D)
Aldridge, George Irvin (D)
Alexander, Hugh Quincy (D)
Alford, Dallas L, Jr. (D)
Allen, Charles Gice, Jr. (R)
Allen, Gordon Phillip (D)
Alley, Zebulon Doyle (D)
Allsbrook, Julian Russell (D)
Andrews, Ike Franklin (D)
Arledge, James Thurston (D)
Auman, Toffie Clyde (D)
Bagnal, Harry Stroman (R)
Bahnson, Fred F, Jr. (D)
Bailey, Carl Leroy, Jr. (D)
Bailey, James Ruffin (D)
Bailey, Wesley (D)
Baker, Charles Alden (D)
Ballenger, Thomas Cass (R)
Ballentine, Bessie Bangert (D)
Barbee, Allen Cromwell (D)
Barker, Christopher Sylvanus, Jr. (D)
Barnwell, Richard Brantley (R)
Barr, Basil Duke (D)
Barringer, Russell Newton (R)
Bason, Samuel Murphey (D)
Bass, Herbert Edward (R)
Batuyios, James Harry (D)
Baugh, Philip J. (D)
Beall, Albert Creasy (R)
Beard, Robert Quincy (R)
Beatty, Jim (D)
Behr, Lawrence Van der Poel (R)
Belk, Irwin (D)
Bell, Edwin Graham (D)
Bennett, Mark Wilson (D)
Bennett, Thomas S. (R)
Benton, Morris Carey, Jr. (D)
Billings, Claude Elledge, Jr. (R)
Bingham, Donald William (R)
Blue, Julian Hubert, Jr. (R)
Bobbitt, William Haywood
Boger, Gilbert Lee (R)
Bogle, Robert Stover (R)
Bolin, Grover Cleveland, Jr. (R)
Bostian, Teral Thomas (R)
Bowles, Hargrove, Jr. (D)
Bowles, Lawrence Leonard (R)
Brewer, Joe Oliver (R)
Bridges, Henry Lee (D)
Briggs, Bruce Burry (R)
Brinson, Leland Virgil (D)
Britt, David Maxwell (D)
Britt, William Ross (D)
Brookshire, Stanford Raymond (D)
Brown, Clark Samuel (D)
Brown, Glenn William (D)
Broyhill, James Edgar (R)
Broyhill, James Thomas (R)
Brumby, Mary Faye (D)
Bruton, Thomas Wade (D)
Bryan, Joseph McKinley (D)
Bryson, Thaddeus Dillard (D)
Buchanan, Harry E. (D)
Buck, Mildred Reel (D)
Bumgardner, David Webster, Jr. (D)
Bunn, Thomas Davis (D)
Burden, Emmett Wynn (D)
Burney, John J, Jr. (D)
Burnside, Maurice Gwinn (D)
Butler, Algernon Lee (R)
Byrd, Joe K. (D)
Byrd, Robert Bond, Sr. (D)
Calvert, Richard B. (R)
Campbell, A. Hartwell (D)
Campbell, Fred Young (D)
Campbell, Hugh Brown, Jr. (D)
Cannon, Hugh (D)
Carr, Gerald (D)
Carson, James H, Jr. (R)
Carter, Ernest Rawls (R)
Cashion, Roy Wilson (D)
Chandler, Gerald Reid (R)
Chase, Nancy Winbon (D)
Choate, A. Vance (D)
Clark, David (D)
Clark, George Thomas, Jr. (R)
Clark, John Conrad (D)
Clark, Johnny R. (D)
Clark, Richard Schuyler (D)
Coble, John Howard (R)
Cochrane, William McWhorter (D)
Cochrane, William P.
Coggins, Jyles Jackson (D)
Collier, Robert Alvis, Jr. (D)
Conger, Stephen Halsey (Am. Party)
Cook, Dennis Shelton (D)
Cooke, William Leon (D)
Cooley, Harold Dunbar (D)
Cooper, William Vance (D)
Craig, Hubert Maxton, Jr. (R)
Crawford, Charles Raymond (D)
Crawford, Irvin Cooper (D)
Cresimore, James Leonard (R)
Crew, William Lunsford (D)
Croft, Sydney Fraser (D)
Crowell, Lester Avant, Jr. (R)
Currie, Claude (D)
Dagenhart, Ewell Martin (R)
Dalton, Reginald Waldo (R)
Daniels, Jonathan Worth (D)
Daniels, Moncie Lee, Jr. (D)
Dansey, William Ellsworth, Jr. (R)
Davenport, John Edwin (D)
Davis, Clarence Leonard (D)
Davis, John Williams (R)
Dent, Raymond Theodore (R)
Dolley, Stephan Bland, Jr. (D)
Dowdy, Lewis Carnegie (D)
Drake, Wilton Rodwell (D)
Drexel, David Anthony (R)
Dugger, James Allison (D)
Dunlap, Wesley Taylor (R)
Dupree, Franklin Taylor, Jr. (R)
Eagles, Joseph Elliott (D)
Early, Jack Jones (R)
Earnhardt, Wiley J. P, Jr. (D)
East, John Porter (R)
Edwards, Elton (D)
Efird, Hoyle Timothy (D)
Elliott, Guy (D)
Elliott, Marie Spivey (D)
Ellis, Albert Joseph (D)
Ervin, Sam J, Jr. (D)
Euliss, Jack Manning (D)
Eure, Thad (D)
Evans, Martha Wright (D)
Everhart, Elmer Reece (R)
Falls, Robert Zemri (D)
Few, Mary Reamey Thomas (R)
Fields, Frank Paddison (R)
Flaherty, David Thomas (R)
Folger, Fred, Jr. (D)
Folger, Thomas Lewellyn (D)
Forbes, William Alfred (D)
Forsyth, William Frank (D)
Foster, Doris Vesa (R)
Fountain, L. H. (D)
Frank, Jay Frederick (R)
Froelich, Jacob Henry, Jr. (D)
Frye, Henry E. (D)
Fulton, William McKinney (R)
Furr, Dorothy Presser (R)
Futrell, Ashley Brown (D)
Galifianakis, Nick (D)
Gallagher, Christine Shirley (D)
Gallagher, John K. (D)
Gardner, James Carson (R)
Gardner, Reece B. (R)
Garinger, Elmer Henry (D)
Garner, Cyrus Roby, Sr. (R)
Garren, Don Harvey (R)
Gentry, James Worth (D)
Gill, Edwin Maurice (D)
Gilmore, Thomas Odell (D)
Gilmore, Voit (D)
Glenn, Dorothy Norman (D)
Godwin, Philip Pittman (D)
Godwin, Ruffin C. (D)
Godwin, Samuel E. (R)
Goodman, Arthur, Jr. (D)
Graham, William Edgar, Jr. (D)
Graham, William Thomas (R)
Green, James Collins (D)
Green, Walter Guerry (American Party)
Greene, Claude L, Jr. (R)
Greenwood, Gordon Hicks
Gregory, Carson (D)
Gregory, Thorne (D)
Griffin, C. Frank (D)
Griffin, Edward Foster (D)
Grubb, Robert Lay (D)
Gunn, John O. (D)
Gwyn, Allen Hatchett, Jr. (D)
Hackett, Roger C. (D)
Hamrick, Claude Meredith (D)
Hann, John Robert (R)
Hardin, Russell (R)
Harding, Franklin Daniel Boone (R)
Harmon, George McKinley (R)
Harper, George Edward (R)
Harrington, James Elmer, Jr. (R)
Hawfield, Samuel Glenn (D)
Hawkins, Reginald Armistice (D)
Haynes, Jeter L. (R)
Hege, Joe H, Jr. (R)
Henderson, David Newton (D)
Henley, John Tannery (D)
Hester, Robert James, Jr. (D)
Hickman, Anne Kent (R)
Hickman, Marcus Tobias (R)
Hicks, Ernest Lee (D)
Hill, James Henry, Jr. (D)
Hill, William Lanier, II (D)
Hodges, Harold Young (R)
Hodges, Luther Hartwell (D)
Hofler, William Hance (D)
Hollowell, Linwood Branton (D)
Holshouser, James Eubert, Jr. (R)
Hope, Clarence Caldwell, Jr. (D)
Horton, Isaac Joseph (D)
Howell, Herbert Hugh (R)
Hunt, James Baxter, Jr. (D)
Hunter, George Patrick, Jr. (D)
Huskins, Joseph Patterson (D)
Hutchens, James Albert (R)
Hutchens, John Grover (R)
Hyde, Herbert Lee (D)
Ingle, John R. (D)
Isenhour, George Myron, Jr. (R)
Issac, Mack Stewart (R)
Jackson, George Winfield (R)
Jackson, J. Elvin (D)
Jacob, J. Laird, Jr. (D)
Jemison, Howard Allan (R)
Jensen, John Calvin (R)
Jernigan, Roberts Harrell, Jr. (D)
Johnson, Earl (D)
Johnson, Hugh Stewart, Jr. (D)
Johnson, James Calvin, Jr. (R)
Johnson, James Vernor (D)
Johnson, Samuel Henry (D)
Johnston, Thomas Shull (D)
Jonas, Charles Raper (R)
Jones, Arthur H. (D)
Jones, Robert Alden (D)
Jones, Seby Brown (D)
Jones, Walter Beaman (D)
Jordan, B. Everett (D)
Jordan, David Davoe (R)
Kaplan, Stanley Norris (D)
Keith, Frederick R. (R)
Keith, Thomas Joseph (R)
Kincaid, Donald R. (R)
King, Jennings Graham (D)
King, Raymond E, Jr. (D)
Kirby, James Russell (D)
Kirk, Phillip James, Jr. (R)
Kiser, Roger Clinton (D)
Kitchin, Alvin Paul (D)
Koontz, Elizabeth Duncan (D)
Kornegay, Horace Robinson (D)
Lackey, J. M. (D)
Lambert, Joel William (D)
Lambeth, Thomas Willis (D)

Land, W. R, Jr. (D)
Lane, Archie Travers, Sr. (D)
Laney, James Arch (D)
Lang, Wilton Earl, Jr. (D)
Larkins, Charles Haymore, Jr. (D)
Larkins, John Davis, Jr. (D)
Leary, Hilary Ashburn (D)
Leatherman, Clarence Edwin (D)
Lennon, Alton Asa (D)
Lilley, Daniel T. (D)
Lind, Alden E. (D)
Little, Erick Paul (R)
Lockamy, John Nathan (D)
Long, John Fletcher (D)
Love, Jimmy Lewis (D)
Lowney, Jerry, Jr. (D)
Lucas, Walter Clyde (D)
Lupton, Walter Jones (D)
McBryde, Charles Marion (R)
McConnell, David Moffatt (D)
McDaniel, C. Dempsey (R)
McDaniel, Joe Ann (D)
McFadyen, Neill Lauchlin (D)
McGeachy, Neill Hector, Jr. (D)
McGlamery, Wiley A. (D)
McGowen, Faison Wells (D)
McKay, Martha Clampitt (D)
McKissick, Floyd Bixler
McKnight, Ed M. (R)
McLean, Dickson, Jr. (D)
MacLean, Hector (D)
McLendon, Lennox Polk, Jr. (D)
McMillan, Archibald Alexander (D)
McMillan, Roscoe Drake, Jr. (D)
Markham, Allan Whitlock (D)
Marshall, Robert Dixon, Jr. (R)
Martin, Graham A.
Martin, James Grubbs (R)
Matheson, Donald Stuart (D)
Mayo, William Patrick (D)
Meares, Carl Whitten (D)
Merritt, Hugh L. (D)
Messer, Ernest Bryan (D)
Midgett, Lorimer Willard (D)
Mills, Fred Moore, Jr. (D)
Mills, Robert Gray (R)
Mills, William Donald (D)
Mizell, Wilmer David (R)
Mohn, James Franklin (D)
Monroe, Willie Parker (D)
Montgomery, Wayne Swope (R)
Moody, Jack Arthur (D)
Moore, Daniel Killian (D)
Moore, Herman Aubrey (D)
Morgan, Joe Lee (R)
Morgan, Robert Burren (D)
Morris, Sam Cameron (D)
Murphy, Ashley Monroe (D)
Murrow, Calvin Coolidge (R)
Muse, Raymond O'Neal (D)
Newton, David Timothy (R)
Nielson, Eldon Denzel (R)
Nielson, Geraldine R. (R)
Norton, Clyde Monroe (D)
O'Hanlon, Isaac Hawley (D)
Owens, Hollis M, Jr. (D)
Parker, John Rainey, Jr. (R)
Parker, Leon Douglas (R)
Paschall, Joshua Ernest (D)
Pemberton, Clarence Lilly (D)
Pendleton, Don Milton (R)
Penn, Frank Reid (D)
Penny, James F, Jr. (D)
Perry, Leon Wheless (R)
Phillips, Andrew Craig (D)
Phillips, Charles Wiley (D)
Phipps, Luther James (D)
Pickard, Morris Glenn (D)
Pittman, Frank Shields, Jr. (D)
Pittman, Kenneth Alexandria (D)
Pittman, Walter James, Jr. (D)
Pitts, Noah Odas, Jr. (R)
Poovey, Julius Reid (R)
Prestwood, Colon Edward (D)
Preyer, Lunsford Richardson (D)
Pyatt, Wade Henry (R)
Quinn, Dwight Wilson (D)
Ragsdale, Hugh Appleton (D)
Ramsey, Frances Crafton (R)
Ramsey, James Edward (D)
Ratcliff, Frances Jean (R)
Rauch, Marshall Arthur (D)
Raynor, Joseph Bryant, Jr. (D)
Reavis, Charles G. (R)
Reed, Norris Cummins, Jr. (D)
Reid, David Edward, Jr. (D)
Reid, Theodore Edwin (D)
Reid, Thomas Beauregard, Jr. (R)
Riddle, Harry L, Jr. (D)
Ridings, Clarence Osborne (D)
Riggs, Warren Elwood (R)
Ritch, Marvin Lee (D)
Rivers, Robert Campbell, Jr. (D)
Robbins, Mrs. Floyd T. (R)
Roberson, Paul Dawson (D)
Robinson, Mrs. John D. (D)
Robinson, Robert J. (D)
Robinson, Sankey Wright (D)
Rodenbough, Grace Taylor (D)
Rogers, Bobby Wayne (D)
Rogers, Thelma Tharp (R)
Ross, Neill McKay (D)
Rountree, Herbert Horton (D)
Rowe, Marie Rich (R)
Rowe, Roy (D)
Royall, Kenneth Claiborne, Jr. (D)
Royster, Fred S. (D)
Ruffin, William Haywood (Independent)
Ruth, Earl Baker (R)
Saltz, Thomas Leon (R)
Sanford, Terry (D)
Sawyer, Milburn Ercell (D)
Schenck, Joseph Samuel (R)
Scott, Ralph H. (D)
Scott, Ralph James (D)
Scott, Robert Walter (D)
Seagroves, Jessie Ruth (D)
Seay, Thomas Waller, Jr. (D)
Sellers, John Dewey (R)
Semans, Mary Duke Biddle Trent (D)
Sermons, Wayland James (D)
Shaw, Luther Wallace (D)
Short, W. Marcus (D)
Shriver, Donald Woods, Jr. (D)
Shuford, Adrian Lafayette, Jr. (D)
Sink, Joseph Stanford (D)
Slear, John Klump (D)
Smith, Edward Henry (R)
Smith, Frank Lester, Sr. (R)
Smith, Lee Creecy (D)
Snead, Edward Cleo (D)
Snyder, James Eugene (R)
Soles, Robert Charles, Jr. (D)
Somers, Robert Vance (R)
Sowers, Roy Gerodd, Jr. (D)
Spain, Jack (D)
Speed, James Davis (D)
Speros, Gus (D)
Stack, Amos Morehead (R)
Stanford, Donald McIver (D)
Staton, William Wayne (D)
Steele, G. Fred, Jr. (R)
Story, Paul Jackson (D)
Street, J. D. (R)
Strickland, Thomas Edward (D)
Suddarth, Thomas Henry, Jr. (D)
Tart, Charles Graham (D)
Tate, Earl Henry (D)
Taylor, Charles H. (R)
Taylor, Edward Fort (D)
Taylor, Herman Ward (D)
Taylor, Hoyt Patrick, Jr. (D)
Taylor, Nelson Whitford, III (D)
Taylor, Roy A. (D)
Teague, Charles Woodrow (D)
Thomason, Benjamin Walter (D)
Thompson, John Elbert, Jr. (R)
Thornburg, Lacy Herman (D)
Thornton, La-Verne W. (R)
Tomlin, Edwin Merrill (R)
Troxell, Samuel Arthur (R)
Twiggs, Howard Fabing (D)
Vaughn, Earl W. (D)
Venters, Carl Vernon (D)
Vogler, James B. (D)
Wagner, William Fremont, Jr. (R)
Waldrop, Ralph Loy (R)
Walton, Peggy Sholar (D)
Warlick, George Hunter (R)
Warren, Lindsay C, Jr. (D)
Warren, Stewart B. (D)
Warwick, Robert Franklin (R)
Watkins, Joe A. (D)
Webb, William Edwin, Jr. (D)
Weeks, Cameron S. (D)
West, Ted Gradon (D)
West, Wayne Grade (R)
Wheeler, John Hervey (D)
White, Henry Eugene (R)
White, Jack Hutchins (D)
White, Ruth Forbes (D)
White, Thomas Jackson (D)
White, William Johnson (D)
Whitehurst, Sam Latham (D)
Whitener, Basil Lee (D)
Whitley, Clyde H. (R)
Whitley, Daniel P, Jr. (D)
Wicker, J. Shelton (D)
Wilkie, Carroll Weldon (R)
Wilkinson, John Archbell (R)
Williams, Thomas Hendrix (D)
Williams, William Frederick (R)
Williams, Wilton Albert (D)
Williamson, Arthur W. (D)
Williamson, Odell (D)
Wills, Marshall Theodore (R)
Wilmer, Henry Bond (R)
Wilson, Alice Marian Edmondson (D)
Wilson, Hugh Mal (R)
Winfield, Mary Jones (D)
Winslow, Julian Emmett (D)
Winters, John Wesley (D)
Wood, George Matthew (D)
Wood, William Zeno (D)
Woodard, John Raynor (D)
Woodhouse, Edwin Wilbur (D)
Yates, Oral Love, Sr. (D)
York, Fred Brantley (D)
Young, Wood Hall (R)
Zachary, Walter L, Sr. (R)
Zahner, Kenyon Benedict, Jr. (R)
Zickgraf, Walter Grant (D)
Zollicoffer, Algernon Augustus, Jr. (D)

NORTH DAKOTA

Aamoth, Gordon S. (R)
Aas, Lynn W. (R)
Allen, Warren George (R)
Anderson, Scott Gale (D)
Andre, Pearl Isabelle (D)
Andrews, Mark (R)
Annear, Gary (D)
Asbridge, Bernice Muriel (R)
Asheim, John Vernon (R)
Atkinson, Myron Hilton, Jr. (R)
Austin, Ellen Jane (D)
Backes, Richard J. (D)
Baker, Carroll William (R)
Bakken, Albert C. (D)
Balerud, Bert A. (R)
Barden, Joel Ray (D)
Barth, Francis Phillip (D)
Becker, Edwin Charles (R)
Belquist, Russell L. (D)
Belter, Wesley Paul (R)
Berg, Harris Odell (R)
Bernabucci, John Roger, Jr. (R)
Bertsch, Marian N. (R)
Berube, Philip (D)
Bier, Howard F. (R)
Bjorlie, Liv Bergliot (D)
Bloom, Sam O. (D)
Bopp, Leonard A. (D)
Bowman, George McKinley (R)
Bowman, Lawrence G. (R)
Brakke, Thomas Jerome (D)
Bratcher, I. E. (R)
Breum, Ole (D)
Brown, R. Fay (R)
Brunsdale, Clarence Norman (R)
Buechler, Edmund (R)
Bullis, Harold Owen (R)
Bunker, A. G. (R)
Burdick, Quentin N. (D)
Burgum, Katherine K. (R)
Burgum, Leslie R. (R)
Burk, Walter O. (D)
Butler, Francis Jesse (R)
Bye, Howard O. (R)
Carey, Peter John (R)
Carvell, Kevin (Independent)
Cayley, Hubert S. (D)
Christensen, Walter (D)
Christiansen, Lee D. (D)
Christopher, Albert Joseph (R)
Clayburgh, Bennie James (R)
Cockerill, Leon Herbert, Jr. (R)
Collette, Wilfred (D)
Coughlin, John Dennis (R)
Coughlin, Virginia Maurine (R)
Currie, Jack M. (R)
Dahl, Arne (R)
Dahl, Eugene Ralph (R)
Dahl, Math (R)
Davis, Ed N. (R)
Davis, John Edward (R)
Davis, Leonard John (R)
Dawson, Barbara Ann (R)
Devine, Terence D. (R)
Dick, Lawrence (R)
Dickey, Cale (R)
Diehl, Ralph E. (R)
Doherty, Edward William (R)
Dorgan, Byron Leslie (D)
Duncan, Russell (R)
Dvorak, Charles Vincent (D)
Eagles, Aloha Taylor (R)
Eaton, Jonathan Chase, Jr. (D)
Eckes, J. Kenneth (D)
Einarson, F. M. (R)
Elkin, Richard (R)
Engel, Austin George, Jr. (D)
Erickson, Larry Duane (D)
Erickson, Leroy (R)
Erickson, Nellie (D)
Erickson, Orbin A. (R)
Erickson, William A. (D)
Erickstad, Ralph John (R)
Fiedler, Walter R (D)
Fleming, Neil Wayne (D)
Forkner, Richard E. (R)
Forsgren, F. Leslie (R)
Fossum, Chester (R)
Frederickson, Lyle L. (R)
Gackle, William Frederick (R)
Garaas, John O. (D)
Gaukler, George (D)
Gengler, John F. (D)
Gefreh, Adam (R)
George, Harry W. (R)
Gershman, Louis (D)
Gibson, Theodore Morton (R)
Gietzen, William Nicholas (D)
Giffey, Donald Francis (D)
Glaspey, M. E. (D)
Goebel, Eldon E. (R)
Goldberg, Richard W. (R)
Gottlieb, Frank (R)
Grant, Robert Elmer (D)
Gronhovd, Kenneth (D)
Gronvold, A. F. (R)
Gudajtes, Edward Raymond (D)
Gumeringer, Bert (D)
Guy, William L. (D)
Hagen, E. Bruce (D)
Hagen, Orville West (Independent)
Hanson, Helen Wheiland (D)
Harris, Genevieve Irene (R)
Harrison, Reuel Emmett (D)
Hathaway, Donald H. (R)
Hauf, Otto (D)
Haugen, Donnell Wilfred (D)
Haugland, Brynhild (R)
Haverluk, Steve (D)
Hensrud, Ingmen O. (R)
Hernett, Gail H. (R)
Hertz, Gothold (D)
Hickle, Ralph (R)
Hilleboe, Peter Stuart (R)
Hocking, Sydney Burdette (D)
Hoefs, Rudolph Herman (R)
Hoffner, S. F. (D)
Hofstrand, Harold R. (R)
Holand, Donald C. (R)
Hougen, James Richard (R)
Husfloen, Abraham (D)
Idso, Russell (R)
Jacobson, Irven Julian (D)
Jensen, A. J. (R)
Johanneson, Helgi (R)
Johnson, Ernest N. (R)
Johnson, Mary Catherine (D)
Jones, Lloyd Raymond (D)
Jungroth, James Ralph (D)
Kadlec, Ludger (D)
Kee, C. G. (R)
Kelly, Henry William (D)
Kelly, Milton Gudmundur (R)
Kelsch, William Charles (R)
Keogh, Brooks James (R)
Kisse, Dan (R)
Kleppe, Thomas S. (R)
Kline, Allen J. (D)
Knudsen, Milo (R)
Knudson, Harvey Bornemann (R)
Knudson, Kenneth (R)
Kretschmar, Bruce E. (R)
Kruger, Sylvia Morgan (D)
Kuehn, Duane Arthur (R)
Larsen, Richard F. (R)
Larson, Eldon C. (D)
Larson, Guy Frederick (R)
Larson, Harvey Casper (R)
Larson, LeRoy Melvin (R)
Larson, Lester George (D)
Larson, Margaret Brunsdale (R)
Lautenschlager, Lester N. (D)
LaVerdure, Betty (D)
Lazareck, Isadore Luke (D)
Legrid, Gloria Jean (R)
Leibhan, Joe B. (R)
Lillehaugen, C. Arnold (R)
Lindberg, Clifford L. (R)
Linderman, Dale (D)
Link, Arthur A. (D)
Lips, Evan Edwin (R)
Litten, Charles Warner (R)

Longmire, George (R)
Lowe, Kenneth C.
Luick, A. W. (R)
Lynch, Richard H. (R)
McCarney, Robert Patterson (R)
McDonald, Tom Joseph (R)
Magnusson, Kingdon B. (R)
Marion, John Leonard (D)
Matheny, Gordon (R)
Meeker, James George (D)
Meidinger, Roland E. (R)
Meier, Ben (R)
Melland, Robert Bruce (R)
Menz, Joseph (R)
Metzger, Edward (R)
Meyer, Carl A. (D)
Miedema, Ernest John (R)
Miller, Adin R. (R)
Montplaiser, David Henry (D)
Moore, Donald Bruce (R)
Morgan, Ken L. (R)
Mueller, L. C. (R)
Mutch, Duane (R)
Neikircher, John (R)
Nesvig, Jerome (D)
Nicolson, Don (D)
Nord, Oscar (R)
Nygaard, K. O. (D)
Ohlsen, Ferdinand Albert (R)
Olson, Curtis (R)
Olson, Dagny V. (R)
Olson, Florence May (D)
Olson, Gillman C. (D)
Paulson, Clayton Clarence (D)
Paulson, William Lee
Peterson, Barbara Preston (R)
Peterson, Gilman F. (D)
Peterson, M. F.
Peterson, Robert L. (D)
Poling, Clarence C. (D)
Porter, Robert Lawrence (D)
Powers, Anna Bertha Josepine (D)
Prindiville, John D. (D)
Pullin, Roland Buckner (R)
Purdy, Mark F. (D)
Rait, George (D)
Redlin, Rolland (D)
Reeves, Edward Irvin (R)
Reimers, Robert F. (R)
Renfrow, Harry G. (R)
Rickford, Fred E. (R)
Rimestad, Idar
Ringsak, Elton W. (R)
Robinson, Dave M. (R)
Roen, Leland H. (R)
Rolfsrud, Halver (D)
Rowe, John L. (D)
Rundle, Earl Clifford (R)
Samuelson, Jean Margaret (D)
Sands, Ernest Monroe (R)
Sanstead, Wayne Godfrey (D)
Saugstad, Stanley (R)
Saumur, George (R)
Scheresky, Laurence Theodore (R)
Schlosser, James Douglas (R)
Schmit, Nicholas Matthew (D)
Schrock, Clyde W. (D)
Schuler, T. E. (R)
Scott, Ralph (R)
Secrest, T. L. (R)
Seibel, Albert Edgar (R)
Sellie, John Martin (R)
Severson, Stanley Raymond (R)
Shablow, Frank S. (D)
Short, Don L. (R)
Simons, Herbert Edwin (D)
Sinner, George Albert (D)
Skaar, Harold George (D)
Smith, Gordon Bennis (D)
Smykowski, James George (R)
Solberg, Iver (D)
Solberg, Oscar (D)
Sorlie, Oscar J. (R)
Stallman, Thomas R. (D)
Stockman, Jacque (R)
Strinden, Earl Stanford (R)
Stroup, Robert Lee (R)
Swedlund, Paul J. (D)
Tebelius, John James (R)
Tescher, Math Carl (D)
Thompson, Bronald (D)
Thompson, Richard J. (R)
Thoreson, William John (R)
Thorsgard, Enoch Arnold (R)
Tighe, Charles (D)
Torgerson, Carrol Howard (R)
Tough, E. A. (R)
Trautmann, Arthur Dallas (D)
Trenbeath, William Grant (R)
Trom, Sophus Vernon (R)
Tweten, Kenneth (R)
Unruh, George MacDonald (R)
Utter, Miles Wayne (R)
Van Horn, Clark (D)
Vinje, Martin E. (R)
Vogel, Charles Joseph (D)
Wadeson, Harry (R)
Wagner, Vernon E. (R)
Wallin, Myron Joseph (R)
Wartner, Aloys, Jr. (R)
Wastvedt, Gilman (R)
Wenstrom, Frank Augustus (R)
White, Carl A. (R)
Wigen, Joris Odin (R)
Wilkie, Gerhart (D)
Winge, Ralph M. (D)
Wishek, Max Albert (R)
Witteman, Orville P. (D)
Wold, Peter Bertram, Jr. (R)
Wold, Thomas Clifford (R)
Wolf, Ben J. (R)
Woutat, Helen Louise (R)
Young, Allan Chandler (R)
Young, Milton R. (R)
Zacher, Harry Raymond (R)

OHIO

Abel, Glenn Frederick (R)
Abele, Homer E. (R)
Adams, Phillip Wayne (D)
Andrews, John Striker (R)
Applegate, Douglas (D)
Armstrong, Harry Leon (R)
Aronoff, Stanley J. (R)
Ashbrook, John Milan (R)
Ashley, Thomas Ludlow (D)
Atkinson, Beverly Moon (R)
Ayres, William Hanes (R)
Bachman, Ilse (D)
Bachrach, Walton H. (R)
Baker, Herman Merlin (R)
Ballard, John Stuart (R)
Banks, David Owen (D)
Barnes, Earl Thomas (R)
Barnhouse, Thomas Dye (D)
Barrell, Charles Alden (D)
Barrett, Ralph Roland (D)
Bartunek, Allen John (R)
Bartunek, Joseph W. (D)
Batchelder, William George (R)
Battisti, Frank Joseph (D)
Bays, Sondra Kay (D)
Beach, Wilbur Lewis (R)
Bechtold, John A. (R)
Beckman, Vincent H. (D)
Bell, Robert Morse (R)
Belt, William Scott (R)
Bennett, Frank B. (D)
Benson, Daniel Leroy (D)
Berry, Loren Murphy (R)
Betleski, Adrian Francis (D)
Betts, Jackson Edward (R)
Black, Ernest F. (R)
Black, Lila (R)
Bliss, Ray Charles (R)
Blosser, Clarence (R)
Bohn, Ernest John (R)
Bolender, Laura Lou (D)
Bolton, Frances P. (R)
Bolton, Oliver P. (R)
Bond, Robert H. (D)
Borchers, Roger F. (D)
Bow, Frank T. (R)
Bowen, William F. (D)
Bowers, Arthur Robert (D)
Bowyer, Edna L. (R)
Brandow, George William (R)
Breen, Edward (D)
Brennan, Frank Michael (D)
Brents, Alvin Lee (D)
Bricker, Dale Eugene (R)
Bricker, John William (R)
Briley, John Marshall (R)
Bristley, Calvin Wesley, Jr. (R)
Britz, Harland Marshall (D)
Brooks, William Henry (D)
Broughton, Berlin Arthur (R)
Brown, Clarence J, Jr. (R)
Brown, John W(illiam) (R)
Brown, Katharine Kennedy (R)
Brown, Paul Wesley (R)
Brown, Ted W(illiam) (R)
Browne, Roy Edward (R)
Brubaker, Robert Lee (R)
Buchanan, Donald William (R)
Bunstine, Edward Royal (D)
Burke, Thomas A. (D)
Burton, William Smith (R)
Bush, John William (D)
Cadwallader, William Rayburn (R)
Calabrese, Anthony O. (D)
Calabrese, Anthony O, Jr. (D)
Camera, Joseph Leonard (D)
Carmichael, Donald (D)
Carney, John Joseph (D)
Cecile, Robert Earl (D)
Celebrezze, Anthony J. (D)
Celebrezze, James P. (D)
Cermak, Albina Rose (R)
Chaney, Isabelle Caroline (R)
Churchill, Walter Augustus (R)
Clancy, Donald D. (R)
Clark, Curtis Luthur (R)
Close, Albert Stephen (R)
Cloud, Roger (R)
Cmich, Stanley A. (R)
Cole, Charles Morton (R)
Cole, Ralph D, Jr. (R)
Cole, William Jennings Bryan (R)
Coleman, Doris Catherine (R)
Coleman, William L. (D)
Collier, James Bruce (R)
Collins, Oakley C. (R)
Collins, Phil C. (D)
Conley, Harry V. (D)
Contris, Charles Melanchthon (D)
Cook, Howard C. (R)
Costine, Robert Edwin (R)
Coyle, Martin Adolphus (R)
Coyne, John Martin (D)
Creasy, Kenneth Burton (R)
Crewson, Harry Bernarr, Jr. (D)
Crisp, Jack W. (D)
Croskey, Ermine Mary (D)
Cruze, Chester T. (R)
Cunningham, Ronald Leroy (R)
Davidson, Carlton E. (R)
Davis, Emil L. (D)
Davis, Jacob Erastus (D)
Day, James Walter (D)
Dean, Hershel Edwin (D)
DeChant, Edward William (D)
DeLaine, Phillip Morgan (D)
Delon, Richard Marshall (R)
Dennis, Max Hale (R)
Dennison, David Short, Jr. (R)
Dennison, Margaret (R)
Derighter, John Thomas (D)
Devine, Samuel L. (R)
DiPaolo, Roger Fulvio (D)
Dippold, Norbert Clem (D)
Ditmer, Ward Nelson (R)
Dix, Timothy Voorhees (R)
Donahey, Gertrude Walton (D)
Donnellon, Edward James (D)
Driehaus, Donald (D)
Duerk, James Allen (R)
Dumm, Lucille (R)
Dutt, George Frederick (R)
Eardley, James Garfield (R)
Eaton, Anne Kinder (D)
Eckhart, Henry Worley (D)
Eisenberg, Ronald Aaron (R)
Emanuel, Joseph (D)
Ensign, William James (D)
Evans, John F. (R)
Feighan, Michael A. (D)
Feighan, William Mathews (D)
Fell, George Henry (R)
Ferguson, Thomas Edward (D)
Ferguson, Verle Marion (D)
Fichter, Joseph William (D)
Fiocca, Claude Michael (D)
Fisher, Ralph E. (R)
Flannery, James Joseph (D)
Flath, Don Edgar (R)
Floyd, Maynard (D)
Flury, Joseph Edward (D)
Fontana, John Columbus (D)
Ford, John Oberton (D)
Ford, Seabury H. (R)
Fordham, Delbert Arthur (D)
Francis, Wilmer J. (D)
Fraser, Donald Ross (R)
Freeman, Brian A. (R)
Frost, James L. (R)
Frost, Russell Hastings (D)
Fuller, Don Edgar (R)
Gaffney, Betty Jane (D)
Gaines, Clarence Llewellyn (D)
Galbraith, John Allen (R)
Gallagher, Mary Ceceila (D)
Gamble, Michael P. (D)
Garrigan, Edgar L, Jr. (R)
Garvin, William Henry (D)
Gehres, Helen L. (D)
Gehres, Walter Arnold (D)
Gerber, Samuel Robert (D)
Gerken, John Raymond, Jr. (R)
Gillespie, Chester Karl (R)
Gilligan, John Joyce (D)
Gilliland, Roy J. (R)
Gillmor, Paul Eugene (R)
Glenn, John Herschel, Jr. (D)
Goddard, Don Reuben (R)
Gorman, Frank McGown (D)
Gorman, Robert Herancourt (D)
Gradison, Willis David, Jr. (R)
Gray, Theodore Milton (R)
Green, Ben Charles (D)
Greiner, William Merlin (R)
Grose, James H. (R)
Guggenheim, Richard E. (D)
Guyer, Tennyson (R)
Hackett, Hanley Anton (D)
Hackett, Leona Amelia (D)
Hadley, Fred B. (R)
Haines, Joan Renshaw (D)
Hale, Phale Dophis (D)
Hall, F. Riley (R)
Hall, Paul Davis (R)
Hall, Tony P. (D)
Hallett, Lewis Francis (D)
Hammond, Evert Newton (R)
Hanes, Thomas C. (D)
Hapner, Jon Clark (R)
Harbison, Maureen M. (D)
Harding, Dorothy Mae (R)
Harmody, Richard M. (D)
Harnetty, Charles Samuel (D)
Harp, Joseph Robert (D)
Harrod, M. Merle (R)
Harsha, William H. (R)
Harvey, Edward (D)
Hawkins, Clyde E. (R)
Hays, Wayne L. (D)
Heft, Francis J. (R)
Heintzelman, Ross Garfield (R)
Heiser, Karl Florien (D)
Henderson, John Earl (R)
Henderson, Robert Earl (R)
Henderson, Stuart (D)
Herbert, Dorothy Fess (R)
Herbert, John David (R)
Hermanies, John Hans (R)
Hershman, Richard Joseph (R)
Hess, William E. (R)
Hicks, Arch R, Jr. (R)
Hickson, Robert C. (R)
Hiestand, Joseph Franklin (R)
Higgins, Ned Preston (R)
Hill, Thomas E. (D)
Hillyer, William Hudson (R)
Hinig, William E. (D)
Hobstetter, Elizabeth Alice (R)
Hofstetter, Edwin Thomas (R)
Hoiles, William McHenry (R)
Hole, Richard Eugene, II (R)
Hollington, Richard R, Jr. (R)
Hollister, John Baker (R)
Holmes, Robert Edward (R)
Horstman, Robert Anthony (D)
Howard, Walter Boivin (D)
Huffer, Roy Henry, Jr. (D)
Huffman, Frank Howard (D)
Huffman, James Wylie (D)
Hughes, Lawrence Edward (R)
Humphrey, Nelson Hine (D)
Hunt, James Irving (R)
Hutson, Frank Loring, Jr. (D)
Inzetta, James William (D)
Jackson, Amos (D)
Jackson, Cleveland (D)
Jackson, Leo Albert (D)
Jackson, M. Morris (D)
James, Troy Lee (D)
Jeffers, Woodrow Wilson (D)
Jeffrey, Harry Palmer (R)
Jenkins, Jacqueline Ann (D)
Johns, John S. (D)
Johnson, Anice Wismer (R)
Johnson, Danny D. (D)
Johnson, E G. (R)
Johnson, John Edward (D)
Johnson, Karl C. (D)
Johnson, Theodore August (R)
Jolovitz, Herbert Allen (D)
Jones, Casey C. (D)
Jones, Doris Joan (R)
Jones, Elmer Fillmore (R)
Jones, Evelyn Rose (D)
Jones, Fred E. (R)
Jones, Pha L. (R)
Jones, Thelma D. (D)
Jones, Theodore Tanner (R)
Jones, Wilfred Denton (R)
Jump, Harry V. (R)
Kaduk, Frank J. (D)
Kagle, John Henry (D)
Kainrad, Joseph Robert (D)
Kalbfleisch, Girard Edward (R)

Karpinski, Helen Bernice (D)
Keating, Richard Michael (D)
Keefe, Ruth Eleanor (D)
Kelly, John Barnes (R)
Kelly, William James (D)
Kester, John Barton (R)
Keys, John Grant (D)
Kilpatrick, Bishop Robbins (D)
Kirkendall, Mary Margaret (R)
Kirwan, Michael Joseph (D)
Kloeb, Frank LeBlond (D)
Knorek, Lee J. (D)
Knowlton, Daniel David (R)
Koehler, Richard Norman (D)
Kohnen, Ralph Bernard, Jr. (R)
Kornick, Michael (D)
Krabach, Richard Lowell (R)
Kurfess, Charles Frederick (R)
Lamb, Edward (D)
Lampson, Elbert Wellington (R)
Lancione, A. G. (D)
Lancione, Nelson (D)
Lane, Janet Isabel (R)
Lange, Michael Baker (D)
Laser, William Charles (D)
Latta, Delbert L. (R)
Lausche, Frank J. (D)
Laws, Donald Boyd (D)
Lawther, Robert M. (R)
Leahy, Elizabeth Clare (D)
LeBoutillier, Philip, Jr. (R)
Leedy, James K. (R)
Leininger, Theodore E. (R)
Leshy, John (D)
Levering, Robert W. (D)
Levey, Barry (R)
Levitt, Robert Elwood (R)
Lewis, David John (R)
Lindhorst, Ambrose H. (R)
Lindseth, Jon A. (R)
Link, Joseph, Jr. (D)
Linkous, T. Cecil (D)
Little, Sue Lohmiller (R)
Lloyd, Thomas Reese (R)
Locher, Ralph Sidney (D)
Locker, Dale Le Roy (D)
Lohrey, Carl N. (R)
Long, Carol D. (R)
Longley, Iris Hull (R)
Longsworth, John Robert (R)
Love, Rodney Marvin (D)
Lowe, Allen James (R)
Lucas, Ethel Violet (D)
Luckhart, Elton Wagner (R)
Luffman, Don Ramon (D)
Lukens, Donald E. (R)
Lusk, Raymond Francis (R)
McAlister, Robert Beaton (D)
McCarthy, John V. (D)
McCown, David Henry (D)
McCreary, Gerald Fredric (R)
McCulloch, William M. (R)
McDonald, John Cooper (D)
McElroy, Neil H. (R)
McGough, Kent B. (R)
McGovern, Frances (D)
McGowan, Mary Elizabeth (D)
McGrew, Leslie Frank (R)
MacKenzie, Bernice K. (D)
McKenzie, Earl Eugene (R)
McLin, Clarence Josef, Jr. (D)
McNamara, Keith (R)
McQuilkin, Ford Lincoln (R)
Macrae, Clara Delle (R)
McRitchie, Thomas Parke (D)
McSweeney, John (D)
Maddux, Don Stewart (D)
Magers, William L. (R)
Mahoney, Margaret Annette (D)
Maile, Francis A. (D)
Maloney, Michael Joseph (R)
Maloon, James Harold (D)
Maloon, Wayne Allen (D)
Mantle, C. Lee (R)
Marsh, Benjamin Franklin (R)
Martin, Edwin M.
Martin, Roy (R)
Marx, Emil Francis (D)
Mastics, George E. (R)
Mastrangelo, Evelino William (D)
Mathna, Woodrow Wilson (R)
Mauro, Guy J. (D)
Mayfield, Frank Henderson, Jr. (R)
Meekison, David (D)
Meeks, John Neal (D)
Meredith, Harry R. (D)
Messerly, Roberta G. (D)
Metzenbaum, Howard Morton (D)
Mihlbaugh, Robert Holleran (D)
Miller, Clarence E. (R)
Miller, Joseph Kerr (R)
Miller, Ward MacLaughlin (R)
Milleson, Ronald Kinsey (D)
Minshall, William E. (R)
Mitchell, Maxine K. (R)
Moeller, Walter H. (D)
Mohler, Robert Emerson (D)
Mooney, Charles A. (D)
Moore, Margaret W. (D)
Moore, Martha Christine (R)
Moorehead, Tom V. (R)
Morgan, William Nelson (R)
Morris, Christian Purtscher (R)
Morse, Robert Warren (D)
Moser, John Richard (R)
Mosher, Charles Adams (R)
Motley, Raymond Charles (D)
Mottl, Ronald M. (D)
Mounts, Swanson H. (D)
Moyer, Don F. (D)
Musser, Virgil Lee (D)
Mussey, William Howard (R)
Neeper, Alice E. (D)
Netzley, Robert E. (R)
Nichols, Hugh Llewellyn, II (D)
Niehoff, H. Richard Petersen (R)
Nolan, Monica (D)
Nord, Larry Richard (R)
Norris, Alan E. (R)
Novak, Anthony F. (D)
Nowack, Donald Robert (D)
Nye, William B. (D)
Ocasek, Oliver Robert (D)
O'Donnell, Alfred P. Joseph, Jr. (R)
O'Grady, Eugene P. (D)
Okey, Eugene P. (D)
Oldham, Chauncey Marling (R)
Olenick, Stephen R. (D)
Oliver, Jack Laronso (D)
Oliver, Jack Phillip (R)
O'Neill, C. William (R)
O'Neill, Henry Martin, Jr. (R)
Osborne, Edward Beryl (D)
Otterman, Robert James (D)
Ours, Ralph Warden (R)
Page, Fugate Foster (R)
Patterson, James F. (R)
Paulo, Walter H. (R)
Pease, Donald James (D)
Peebles, Robert (R)
Petro, John William (R)
Phillips, Charles Eugene (R)
Phillips, Ralph Willard (D)
Pickering, Robert S. (R)
Pike, Charles Adams (R)
Pilot, Lynne Joyce (R)
Pinsky, Esther F. (D)
Plant, Mary Ann (D)
Pokorny, Frank R. (D)
Porter, Albert S. (D)
Pottenger, Thomas Alexander (R)
Price, Robert Ross (D)
Pulley, William W. (R)
Rankin, Martha Kelly (R)
Rath, Robert Karl (D)
Rausch, Eugene E. (D)
Reams, Frazier, Jr. (D)
Reckman, Robert Frederick (R)
Reed, Robert Gordon, Jr. (R)
Regula, Ralph S. (R)
Reichel, Richard Gene (R)
Reider, Robert W. (D)
Rekeweg, Wilmer D. (R)
Reno, Ottie Wayne (D)
Rentschler, Thomas Beckett (R)
Rhodes, James Allen (R)
Rice, Fred (R)
Rich, Carl W. (R)
Richard, Elmo (D)
Riffe, Vernal G, Jr. (D)
Robe, Edward Scott (R)
Rogers, Luther (R)
Romer, Harold William (D)
Rosemond, John Henry (D)
Ross, Raymond F. (D)
Rosselott, Herman John (D)
Rowe, Edmund (R)
Ruehlmann, Eugene P. (R)
Rutkowski, Walter Alexander (D)
Ryan, Margaret Mary (D)
Sark, Guy O. (R)
Sawyer, Charles (D)
Saxbe, William B. (R)
Scanlon, Leo John (D)
Schafer, Neal Edwin (R)
Schaufele, William Everett, Jr.
Schecter, Sheldon Dale (D)
Scherer, Gordon Harry (R)
Scherer, Gordon M. (R)
Schinnerer, Mark Christopher (R)
Schneider, Louis Jacob, Jr. (R)
Schneider, Russell Edward (D)
Schneider, William (R)
Schriver, Henry Haley (R)
Schrote, John E. (R)
Schwartzmiller, Fridolin (D)
Sealy, Albert Henry (R)
Secrest, Robert Thompson (D)
Seiter, Robert Franklin (D)
Sensenbrenner, Maynard E. (D)
Shackle, H. Gene (D)
Shaker, Mitchell Francis (D)
Shawan, Jacob Albright, III (R)
Shea, Joseph W, Jr. (D)
Shilts, William Winston (R)
Shocknessy, James White (D)
Shoemaker, Myrl Howard (D)
Shuman, Harold Eugene (R)
Sidwell, George C. (R)
Skipton, John Allen (R)
Slagle, Gene (D)
Smith, Larry Gilbert (D)
Snyder, Cecil Vernon (D)
Spafford, Enval Ainsworth (D)
Speeth, Henry William (D)
Spitler, Raymond Ruffner (D)
Spock, Benjamin (D)
Spraul, Thomas C. (D)
Stahl, Thomas Burton (R)
Stanhagen, John Franklin (R)
Stanton, John William (R)
Stanton, Ralph Calvin, Jr. (R)
Stephens, Carolyn Kay (R)
Stewart, Potter
Stillman, Saul G. (R)
Stockdale, Robert Edmonds (R)
Stocksdale, Vaughn Franklin (D)
Stokes, Carl Burton (D)
Stokes, Louis (D)
Stokes, Marian (R)
Stoldt, Robert James (R)
Strava, John F. (D)
Struna, Marjorie Conrad (D)
Sullivan, Francis Daniel (D)
Sutherland, James Frederick (R)
Sweeney, Patrick A. (D)
Sweeney, Robert Emmett (D)
Swiger, James Ephraim (R)
Taft, Charles P. (R)
Taft, Kingsley A. (R)
Taft, Robert, Jr. (R)
Taft, Seth Chase (R)
Taft, William W. (R)
Talisman, Mark Elliot (D)
Taylor, John (D)
Teagarden, Oscar Leslie (D)
Tetlow, Horace G. (D)
Thomas, Richard Joseph (D)
Thompson, Lockwood (D)
Thorpe, James (R)
Tidmore, Samuel Edward, IV (D)
Timmins, William Joseph, Jr. (D)
Tinge, Rolf Reid (D)
Tipps, Paul (D)
Tobias, Jean Frances (D)
Topper, Isadore (D)
Tracy, Roger Wahlquist, Jr. (R)
Tulley, Joseph P. (R)
Turk, Edmund John (D)
Turner, Ralph Franklin, Jr. (D)
Underwood, Mell G. (D)
Unger, Sherman Edward (R)
Van Heyde, Robert Lee (D)
Vanik, Charles Albert (D)
Vincent, Curtis Ralph (R)
Voinovich George V. (R)
Volkema, Russell H. (D)
Vukovich, George (D)
Wagner, Dale Earl (D)
Wagner, Jeannette Sechrist (R)
Walker, William O. (R)
Walter, Paul William, Jr. (R)
Walton, Joseph Maurice (D)
Ward, Robert Middleton (D)
Wareham, Levada E. (R)
Warner, Joan Fleenor (D)
Warner, Robert Edson (D)
Waters, Jean (R)
Watson, John L. (R)
Weaner, Karl Hull (R)
Weatherford, John William (D)
Weiker, Bryce Lamar (D)
Weil, Sidney, Jr. (D)
Weir, David Leroy (R)
Weis, John Harvey (R)
Weisenborn, Clara Elizabeth (R)
Weisenstine, Ernest Moore (D)
Weldishofer, James R. (R)
Welsh, Evelyn Margaret (D)
Wetzel, Darrel Ernest (D)
Whalen, Charles William, Jr. (R)
Wharton, Clyde Wilson (D)
Wheatcraft, Martha Clark (R)
Whitacre, James Marion (R)
White, Ray M. (D)
Williams, William Edward (R)
Willis, George Lewis (D)
Willis, Richard Robinson (R)
Willmarth, David Gerard (D)
Wilson, A. K. (R)
Wingett, Ernest A. (D)
Wise, Carl Francis (R)
Wise, John Norman (D)
Wiseman, Earl Leroy (R)
Wolf, Herbert Christian (D)
Wolf, Laurence Grambow (D)
Woodmansee, Donavin N. (D)
Wylie, Chalmers Pangburn (R)
Young, Frederick Nevin (R)
Young, Stephen M. (D)
Young, Thomas Franklin (R)
Zahn, Donald M. (R)
Zahorec, Joseph John (D)

OKLAHOMA

Abbott, Lonnie Lowell (D)
Albert, Carl Bert (D)
Allard, Lou Stockton (D)
Allen, Clinton D. (D)
Allen, Walt (D)
Ansley, Russell L. (R)
Arrington, James Hugh (D)
Baggett, Bryce A. (D)
Bamberger, Thomas A. (D)
Barker, Jim L. (D)
Barr, Robert Lincoln (D)
Barrett, James Luther (D)
Bartlett, Dewey Follett (R)
Beasley, Gerald LeRoy, Jr. (R)
Beauchamp, Donald Wayne (D)
Belcher, Page (R)
Bellmon, Henry L. (R)
Bengtson, L. H, Jr. (D)
Bennett, Bob E. (D)
Bennett, James Dean (R)
Bernard, Spencer Thomas (D)
Berrong, Ed (D)
Bird, Mary Louise (R)
Blankenship, George Tony (R)
Bode, Carl James (D)
Bonner, Merline (D)
Boren, David Lyle (D)
Boren, Lyle H. (D)
Bradley, Carter Wallace (D)
Brake, Betty Hess (R)
Brock, LeRoy (R)
Browers, Clyde Edward (D)
Brown, Stuart Barnett (R)
Brown, Tot Moffett (D)
Browne, James Broach (D)
Bullard, James Marvin (D)
Burns, John Howard
Burton, Edna Josephine (D)
Butler, Percy (R)
Calhoon, Ed Latta (R)
Cameron, Crawford Williams (D)
Camp, George (R)
Camp, John Newbold (R)
Carlton, Arthur Leroy (D)
Carmack, William Ross, Jr. (D)
Cartwright, Wilburn (D)
Cate, Byron Lee (D)
Clemons, A. J. (D)
Clowe, Charles Edward, Jr. (R)
Cobb, J. C. (D)
Coleman, Thomas William (R)
Collins, Charles C. (D)
Colvin, William Alvin (D)
Conaghan, Brian Francis (R)
Conaghan, Dorothy Dell (R)
Connor, James William (R)
Cook, H. Dale (R)
Cox, Barbour (D)
Cox, Frank Bernard (D)
Cox, James Burl (R)
Crawford, B. Hayden (R)
Criswell, John (D)
Crow, Herschal Hilliar, Jr. (D)
Crowder, Dale Farris (R)
Crume, Patricia Ann (R)
Cunningham, Clarence Marion (D)
Dale, Don (D)
Davis, Frank W. (R)
Davison, Denver N. (D)
Derryberry, Larry Dale (D)
Draper, Daniel David, II (D)
Eads, Felix (D)
Eberle, Ed J. (D)

Edmondson, Ed (D)
Edmondson, James Howard (D)
Elder, Charles (D)
Fair, Michael Edward (R)
Farmer, Earl Raymond (R)
Ferguson, Jo O. (R)
Ferguson, Leslie Guy (R)
Ferrell, Donald Forrest (R)
Field, Leon B. (D)
Filson, Gene H. (D)
Finch, Heber, Jr. (D)
Ford, Charles Reed (R)
Foreman, Eugene Harley (R)
Foshee, Katherine Almira (R)
Gambill, Bruce Warren (R)
Garrett, James Paul (D)
Garrison, Denzil Doss (R)
Gary, Raymond D. (D)
Gee, Robert S. (D)
Gockel, Gladys (R)
Gooden, William Josiah (R)
Goodfellow, Robert Lawson (D)
Goodwin, John William (D)
Gorman, Jimmie Edwin (D)
Grantham, Roy Emery (D)
Graves, Ralph Wayne (D)
Green, Warren Ernest (R)
Haley, Frances Shaller (R)
Halley, Harry Lee Stuart (D)
Ham, Glen (D)
Hancock, Richard E. (R)
Harber, W. Elmer (D)
Harris, Fred R. (D)
Harris, Thomas Jesse (R)
Hart, Walter Dean (D)
Hatchett, Texanna L. (R)
Hayes, Florence M. (R)
Heller, Frank John (R)
Hemphill, Joe Paul (D)
Henning, William Lewis (D)
Heskett, Bill Leon (D)
Hewgley, James Marion, Jr. (R)
Hill, Benjamin Harrison (D)
Hill, George Barker (D)
Hodge, Oliver (D)
Holaday, T. W. (R)
Hollomon, John Herbert (Independent)
Holmes, Herbert Hadley (D)
Hopkins, Robert E. (D)
Horn, Raymond Lee (D)
Howard, Gene C. (D)
Humphrey, Preston Adolph (D)
Hunt, Joe B. (D)
Hunt, McPherson Williss (R)
Hunter, Harold V. (R)
Hurst, Thurman Scott (D)
Hutchens, David Paul (D)
Inhofe, James Mountain (R)
Jarboe, John Bruce (D)
Jarman, John (D)
Johnson, Artis Visanio (D)
Johnson, Jed, Jr. (D)
Jones, Bobby S. (R)
Jones, Ray Charles (D)
Jones, Stephen (R)
Kamas, Lewis Melvin (R)
Kelly, Dorcas Burnumn (R)
Kennedy, J. C. (D)
Kerr, Robert Samuel, Jr. (D)
Kerr, William Graycen (D)
Key, Glen R. (D)
Kindle, Herbert (R)
King, Peter Cotterill (R)
Kreps, Leslie Ray (D)
Krumme, Roy Archibald (D)
Lane, Jim E. (D)
Lashley, F. J, Jr. (R)
Lavender, Robert Eugene (R)
Letcher, Isabelle Scott (R)
Likes, Henry L. (D)
Lindstrom, Jack Lewis Irvin (D)
Looper, Maxine Moody (D)
Lucas, Gerald Patrick (D)
Lyon, Robert Paul (D)
McCreary, Zora A. (R)
McCullough, George Dewey (R)
McCune, John W. (D)
McDonald, Joseph Paul (R)
McElroy, Bert (R)
McGraw, Joseph Robert, Jr. (R)
McNeill, Welton R. (D)
McSpadden, Clem Rogers (D)
Marcoux, Kathren Evelyn (D)
Martin, Ernest D. (D)
Marty, James Floyd (R)
Mason, Drew (R)
Massad, Anthony M. (D)
Massad, Ernest Louis (D)
Massey, John Lewis (D)
Maxwell, James Livingston (D)
Miller, George A. (D)
Miller, Mary Ellen (R)
Mitchell, Cecil Darrell (R)
Moore, Preston Jay (D)
Musgrave, Joe Edward (R)
Myers, Jack Fredondo (R)
Nance, Kenneth Robert (D)
Nelson, Jack W. (R)
Nesbitt, Charles R. (D)
Nigh, George Patterson (D)
Noreika, Louise A. (D)
North, Raymond D. (D)
Padgett, C. Ward (D)
Parrish, W. F, Jr. (R)
Patrick, Fred Laforest (D)
Patrick, Mary Louise (R)
Patterson, Frank Grover (D)
Patterson, Pat J. (R)
Patterson, Ruth M. (R)
Payne, Gary Edison (D)
Peterson, Jerry Burns (R)
Phelps, Edna Mae (D)
Phillips, Nancy Lee (D)
Phillips, W. Fred (D)
Pope, Charles Gerald (D)
Porter, E. Melvin (D)
Poulos, William Frederic (D)
Priebe, Milton W. (R)
Privett, Arnold Rex (D)
Rainbolt, John Vernon (D)
Rambo, G. Dan (D)
Reed, Michael Lee (D)
Rensvold, Roger Frederic (R)
Richardson, Truman (D)
Rizley, Ross (R)
Rizzuti, Theresa (R)
Roark, Wilson Eugene (R)
Robertson, (Anna) Carol (R)
Robinson, Carl (D)
Rogers, John (D)
Rogers, John Marvin (D)
Rogers, Will (D)
Romang, Richard Edward (R)
Roselle, Joe L. (D)
Ross, Hope Snider (D)
Ryan, Ella Marice (D)
Sandlin, Hugh Martin (D)
Sanguin, Wayne Curtis (D)
Sharp, Anthony Gray (R)
Shear, Daphfine (D)
Short, Jack Marwood (R)
Smalley, Phil (D)
Smisson, William Howard (R)
Smith, Bill (D)
Smith, James Vernon (R)
Smith, Norman A. (D)
Smith, Ray Allen (R)
Smith, Robert Gene (R)
Smith, Thomas G. (D)
Snipes, Al M. (R)
Snyder, F. Trigg, Jr. (R)
Spearman, Crawford Henry, Jr. (D)
Sponberg, Raymond Lindell (R)
Spradling, Sherman (D)
Stacy, John Raymond (R)
Stamps, Hal Burton (D)
Stanislaus, Dorothy Jeanne (R)
Stansberry, Richard Donald (R)
Steed, Tom (D)
Stephenson, Marguerite (D)
Steward, William Robert (D)
Stewart, E. L, Jr. (R)
Stickrod, Don Perry (R)
Stone, George William (D)
Sullivan, Jerome Cecil, Jr. (D)
Sullivan, Mike (D)
Sutton, Emmazette Collier (D)
Taber, John (William) (R)
Tabor, Pauline Edwards (D)
Tarwater, William Raymond (D)
Taylor, Owen Barney (D)
Terrill, Albert Lee (D)
Thain, Carl Ernest (R)
Thomas, John Pearce, Jr. (R)
Thompson, Ralph Gordon (R)
Thornhill, Lynn (R)
Townsend, James Baker (D)
Turner, Ethel Winborn (R)
Ungerman, Maynard Ivan (D)
Vincent, Robert Carr (R)
Ward, Lew O. (R)
Warner, Clarence E. (R)
Watkins, Ralph Austin (D)
Webb, James Edwin (D)
Weller, Chester E. (R)
Wheat, Vivian (R)
Whitson, Edmund Rayburn (D)
Whorton, J. D. (R)
Wickersham, Victor Eugene (D)
Wiedemann, Anna Belle (D)
Wiggins, Charles Delmar (R)
Wilkinson, Charles Burnham (R)
Williams, Granville Oliver (R)
Williams, Howard Dale (R)
Williamson, Allen (D)
Willis, William Pascal (D)
Wilson, George Howard (D)
Wilson, John Benjamin, Jr. (D)
Winters, Leo (D)
Wixson, Douglas Charles (R)
Wolfe, Stephen Charles (R)
Wright, Hildred Margaret (D)
Wyrick, Donald Norwood (D)
York, Joseph Ferrell (D)
Young, John Wallace (D)

OREGON

Adelsheim, Martha Ann Henderson (D)
Akeson, Harvey O. (D)
Allen, John Platt (D)
Appling, Howell Reedus, Jr. (R)
Asher, Janice Alora (D)
Baggs, Thomas Marshall (D)
Barry, Frank Joseph, Jr. (D)
Bateson, Cornelius Charles (D)
Bazett, Sidney (R)
Bedingfield, James B. (R)
Bell, Robert David (R)
Boe, Jason Douglas (D)
Boivin, Harry Dolan (D)
Bradley, William Edward (D)
Branchfield, Edward (R)
Browne, Elizabeth Wingreene (D)
Burns, John David (D)
Callahan, Everett Lawrence (D)
Camarot, Henry J. (D)
Campbell, Della B. (R)
Carson, Wallace P, Jr. (R)
Chapman, Richard F. (D)
Chuinard, Fritzi G. (R)
Clark, Donald E. (D)
Clawson, James Howard (R)
Conroy, Richard L. (R)
Cook, Ward H. (D)
Corbett, Alice Catherine (D)
Corbett, Orville Willard, Jr. (R)
Cornwall, Robert David (R)
Crothers, Morris King (R)
Crowhurst, Norman Herbert (R)
Day, L. B. (D)
Dellenback, John R. (R)
Dement, Sam (R)
Denman, Donald Kenneth (R)
Derrick, Harley Sidney (D)
Detering, Gerald W. (R)
Dielschneider, William Norwood (R)
Dole, Hollis M. (R)
Dugdale, Robert Earl (R)
Duncan, Robert Blackford (D)
Durno, Edwin Russell (R)
Eivers, George (R)
Elfstrom, Robert Lewis (R)
Elliott, Robert Amos (R)
Enna, Irving (R)
Fadeley, Edward Norman (D)
Fadeley, Nancie Peacocke (D)
Federici, Anthony Nicholas (D)
Feeney, Richard Edward (D)
Field, Shirley A. (R)
Flegel, Albert Gordon (D)
Ford, Lewis Franklin (R)
Frank, Gerald Wendel (R)
Frost, David Griffith (R)
Fuller, Dennis L. (D)
Garrigus, Forest Ora, Jr. (R)
Gilliam, Jean Marie (D)
Gillis, Jean W. (R)
Goldy, Daniel Louis (D)
Goodwin, Alfred Theodore (R)
Graham, Marva Frost (R)
Graham, Roger A. (D)
Grant, Virginia Anne (D)
Green, Edith S. (D)
Haas, Harl H. (D)
Hall, Amy Evelyn (R)
Hall, William O.
Hallock, Joseph Theodore (D)
Hand, Beulah Joan (D)
Hanneman, Paul A. (R)
Hansen, Marvin E. (D)
Harlan, Dale Morgan (D)
Hart, Floyd Henry (R)
Hartmann, Robert Trowbridge (R)
Hartung, Thomas Frederick (R)
Hatfield, Mark Odom (R)
Heard, Fred W. (D)
Hedges, Virginia Lee Mahon (R)
Hodel, Donald Paul (R)
Hoffman, Paul Jerome (D)
Howe, Carrol B. (R)
Hoyt, Charles Richard (R)
Huston, W. Glenn (D)
Inskeep, John Jerry (R)
Ireland, Arthur Pierce (R)
Kennedy, Richard Lee (D)
Lang, Philip David (D)
Lende, Russell Melvin (R)
Lent, Berkeley (D)
Lewis, Harold V. (D)
Linde, Hans Arthur (D)
Lusk, Hall S. (D)
Lynch, Jim C. (R)
McAllister, William Menzies
McCall, Tom Lawson (R)
McCoy, William, Jr. (D)
McCready, Connie (R)
McKenzie, Roderick Tulloch (R)
Macpherson, Gordon Leroy (R)
Mahoney, Thomas Randolph (D)
Markham, William Edwin (R)
Martin, Linden R. (D)
Martin, Roger Edward (R)
Mautz, Robert Theodore (R)
Mayer, William Hughes (R)
Meeker, Anthony (R)
Minear, Leon Pierson
Montgomery, F. F. (R)
Moore, Dorotha Huntley (R)
Moran, John Geary (D)
Morse, Wayne Lyman (D)
Moshofsky, William James (R)
Murphy, Peter C, Jr. (R)
Myers, Clay (R)
Nelson, Dixie Lee (R)
Neuberger, Maurine Brown (D)
O'Connell, Kenneth John (D)
O'Rourke, Robert Emmett (R)
Packwood, Robert William (R)
Parnell, Dale Paul (R)
Porter, Charles O. (D)
Priestley, Wallace Schuyler (D)
Pursell, Lucille (R)
Rademaker, Janice May (D)
Raymond, Raphael Royal (R)
Redden, James Anthony (D)
Reed, George Joseph (R)
Richardson, Eugene Allison (R)
Ridgley, Robert Louis (R)
Ripper, Jack Dorland (D)
Roberts, Betty R. (D)
Roberts, Frank Livezey (D)
Root, Mary (R)
Saslow, Michael George (D)
Schrunk, Terry Doyle (D)
Shay, Shirley Ann (R)
Skelton, Keith D. (D)
Stadelman, George Peter (R)
Stadelman, George Pierce (R)
Stadler, Glen M. (D)
Stathos, Donald L. (R)
Stevenson, Bill (D)
Stoll, Norman Adolph (D)
Stout, June Windle (R)
Straub, Robert W. (D)
Thornton, Leo Maze (R)
Thornton, Robert Y. (D)
Titus, Herbert William (D)
Ullman, Al (D)
Van Hoomissen, George A. (D)
Van Natta, Frederick William (R)
Van Patten, Cecil Robert (D)
Vargas, Sybil Rose Hunt (D)
Walsh, Wm. Edwin (R)
Warren, Douglas Stewart (R)
Weaver, James Howard (D)
Welty, Robert (D)
Whipple, Blaine (D)
Willner, Don S. (D)
Wilson, Donald James (R)
Wingard, George Frank (R)
Winkel, Morton Arnold (D)
Wood, Gordon Thompson (R)
Woodruff, Byron Edwin (D)
Wyatt, Wendell William (R)
Yturri, Anthony (R)
Zapp, John Shea (R)

PENNSYLVANIA

Abbott, Arnold Peter (D)
Afflerback, C. V. (R)
Alexander, George W. (R)
Alexander, Jane Marietta (D)
Alexander, Raymond Pace (D)

Allen, William Wilson (R)
Allison, Gilbert J. (D)
Anderson, John Hope (R)
Anderson, Sarah A. (D)
Annenberg, Walter H. (R)
Anspach, John Henry (D)
Appleton, William Maris (R)
Arlene, Herbert (D)
Armstrong, Joseph J. (D)
Ash, Richard A. (D)
Ashton, William H. (R)
Bachman, William T. (D)
Bailey, Daniel A. (R)
Baily, Thomas S. (R)
Bair, Donald O. (R)
Balaban, Thomas R. (D)
Barber, James David (D)
Barness, Herbert (R)
Barr, Harold A. (R)
Barr, Joseph M. (D)
Barrett, Thomas Edwin (D)
Barrett, William A. (D)
Bartoli, Sergio (D)
Baumunk, Lawrence Dale (R)
Bednarek, Stanley Michael (R)
Beers, Robert O. (R)
Bell, Clarence D. (R)
Bellomini, Robert E. (D)
Beloff, Leland M. (R)
Benner, Barbara Young (R)
Bennett, Reid L. (D)
Bennett, Verna Z. (R)
Beren, Daniel E. (R)
Berger, James Stanley (R)
Berkes, Milton (D)
Berman, Muriel M. (D)
Berman, Philip I. (D)
Berson, Norman S. (D)
Biester, Edward G, Jr. (R)
Bittle, R(ussell) Harry (R)
Bixler, Denny James (D)
Blair, John Ellis (R)
Blair, Russell Jenkins (D)
Blair, Stanley L. (R)
Blatt, Genevieve (D)
Bloom, George I. (R)
Bloom, Robert Kenneth (R)
Blystone, Rose A. L. (D)
Body, Ralph C. (D)
Bonetto, Joseph F. (D)
Bonsell, William Richard (R)
Bossert, Willard Max (R)
Bower, Adam T. (R)
Boyd, Thomas Hilary (D)
Boyle, Edward C. (D)
Braddock, LeRoy Ildefonze (D)
Bradley, Michael Joseph (D)
Branca, Ernest O. (D)
Brennan, Dorothy Teresa (D)
Broderick, Raymond Joseph (R)
Brouse, Robert O. (R)
Brown, William Hill, III (R)
Brugger, Jeanne De Bow (R)
Brumbaugh, D. Emmert (R)
Brunner, John L. (D)
Buchanan, William George (R)
Buckman, Ernest U. (R)
Burkardt, Robert F. (R)
Burlein, Lester F. (R)
Bush, Alvin C. (R)
Butera, Robert James (R)
Byrne, James Aloysius (D)
Caldwell, Thomas Dixon, Jr. (R)
Cameron, Martha E. (R)
Campbell, George W. (R)
Campbell, William Cowden (R)
Cantoni, Frank H. (D)
Carey, Ralph P. (R)
Carrigg, Joseph L. (R)
Casey, Robert P. (D)
Cavender, John C. (R)
Chapas, John William (D)
Chudoff, Earl (D)
Cianfrani, Henry J. (D)
Cioffi, Dominick E. (D)
Clark, Frank M. (D)
Clarke, James Francis (D)
Claypoole, William Harvey (R)
Cleeton, Alan Robert (D)
Cohen, David (D)
Coleman, Bruce Richard (D)
Coleman, Charles Bruce (D)
Coleman, William Matthew (D)
Comer, Harry R. J. (D)
Confair, Zehnder H. (R)
Cooke, Edward Francis (D)
Cooper, Douglas Winslow (R)
Corbett, Robert J. (R)
Corson, Philip Langdon (R)
Cosetti, Joseph L. (D)
Coughlin, R. Lawrence, Jr. (R)
Coveleskie, Stanley Robert (D)
Covey, John Knox (R)
Craley, N. Neiman, Jr. (D)
Crapo, Raymond F. (D)
Crawford, Patricia A. (R)
Crawford, Ruth Reed (R)
Creveling, Wilbur Curtis, Jr. (R)
Crow, William Josiah (R)
Crowley, Paul F. (D)
Csala, Lea Miner (D)
Culbertson, Stuart A. (D)
Culp, Carl Lester (D)
Curtin, Willard S. (R)
Curwood, William B. (D)
Cusimano, Fred (D)
Dague, Paul Bartram (R)
D'Arcy, James Andrew (D)
Dardanell, Edward L. (D)
Davis, Donald M. (D)
Davis, James Kepler (R)
Davis, Preston B. (R)
Davis, Robert Odgen (R)
Deardorff, John Howard (R)
Deibler, Adelaide Perrington (D)
Dende, Henry John (D)
Dengler, Clyde R. (R)
Dent, John H. (D)
Devlin, John H. (D)
Dickinson, Merle Eugene (R)
Diehl, Nancy Simons (R)
Dilworth, Richardson (D)
DiSilvestro, Anthony J. (D)
Dolan, Joseph Charles (D)
Donaldson, Lee A, Jr. (R)
Donnelly, Thomas J. (D)
Donolow, Benjamin R. (D)
Dorris, John L. (D)
Doud, J. Phil (D)
Drawbaugh, Robert Wayne (D)
Duff, James H. (R)
Duggan, Robert Ward (R)
Dumbauld, Peter Theodore (D)
Dunne, Isabelle Mary (D)
Dwyer, R. Budd (R)
Eckard, Hayes Woodrow (D)
Eckensberger, William H, Jr. (D)
Eilberg, Joshua (D)
Eilts, Hermann Frederick
Eisenhower, John Sheldon Doud (R)
Elish, Peter (D)
Ellenbogen, Henry (D)
Ellis, Edward Dale (D)
Elvey, Harry M. (R)
Emerson, Junius M. (D)
Englehart, Harry A, Jr. (D)
Eshback, J. Russell (R)
Eshleman, Edwin D. (R)
Ewing, Edwin C. (R)
Exler, John J. (D)
Faddis, Charles I. (D)
Fagan, Thomas Leo (D)
Falcone, Ernani Carlo (D)
Fels, Margaret Katherine (R)
Fenrich, Andrew T. (D)
Fetterolf, Carolyn Bauer (R)
Fiedler, Betty Mae (R)
Filo, Jules (D)
Fineman, Herbert (D)
Fink, Earl Barton (D)
Fischer, Donald Frederick (R)
Fischer, Roger M. (D)
Fischer, Roger Raymond (R)
Fisher, Ed Lamont (D)
Fitterer, B. P. (D)
Flack, Harold E. (R)
Fleming, Robert D. (R)
Fleming, Wilmot E. (R)
Flood, Daniel J. (D)
Foerster, Thomas Joseph (D)
Foglietta, Thomas M. (R)
Foor, Percy G. (R)
Fox, Donald William (R)
Fox, Harry M. (R)
Frame, Richard C. (R)
Frank, Samuel W. (D)
Frantz, Moulton Lewis Charles (R)
Frascella, Thomas A. (D)
Fry, Howard M. (R)
Fryer, Lester K. (D)
Fulmer, Eugene M. (R)
Fulton, James G. (R)
Gabreski, Max Paul (D)
Gailey, John R, Jr. (D)
Gallagher, James J. A. (D)
Gallen, James J. (R)
Garner, Marie G. (D)
Gartner, Fred Christian (R)
Gates, Robert David (D)
Gates, Thomas S. (R)
Gaydos, Joseph Matthew (D)
Geesey, Eugene Ronald (R)
Gekas, George William (R)
Gelfand, Eugene (D)
George, Lourene W. (R)
George, Samuel (R)
Gerber, Morris (D)
Gibb, Laurence V. (R)
Gibble, Harold McKinstry (D)
Giesey, Walter W. (D)
Gill, Alastair D. (R)
Gillette, Helen D. (D)
Glassmire, Daniel F. (D)
Gleason, Robert A. (R)
Gleim, Ira Kenny (D)
Goodling, George A. (R)
Goodman, James Anthony (D)
Goodrich, Ray C. (R)
Graham, Mortimer Elliott (R)
Grammes, Lloyd Edgar (R)
Granahan, Kathryn Elizabeth (D)
Green, James Allison (D)
Green, Richard J, Jr. (R)
Green, William Joseph (D)
Greenberg, Melvin J. (D)
Gremminger, John E. (D)
Gross, Bernard Morton (D)
Haenel, Loyola Theresa (R)
Hall, Edwin Arthur, Jr. (R)
Hall, Lyle Gillis (D)
Halverson, Kenneth Shafer (R)
Hamilton, John H, Jr. (R)
Hamilton, Robert K. (D)
Hammer, Edgar Thomas, Jr. (R)
Hankins, Freeman (D)
Hanna, Michael A. (D)
Hannum, Robert John (R)
Harkins, Bernard Joseph (D)
Harris, J. Mervyn (R)
Hartley, George B. (D)
Hawbaker, D. Elmer (R)
Hay, Malcolm (D)
Hayes, David Sayre (R)
Hearst, William Curtis (R)
Heffner, George W. (R)
Hegarty, Eugene D. (D)
Heinz, Henry John, III (R)
Helm, W. Stuart (R)
Hennessy, Arthur L, Jr. (D)
Hepford, H. Joseph (R)
Hershberger, Ross Edward (D)
Hess, Evelyn A. (D)
Hetrick, W. Brady (D)
Hill, Louis G. (D)
Hill, Sherman L. (R)
Hillman, Elsie Hilliard (R)
Hineman, Edwin S. (R)
Hobbs, Frederick Howard (R)
Hocker, Blaine C. (R)
Hoh, Paul Jacob (D)
Holl, Edwin G. (R)
Hollander, Thomas (D)
Holman, Allan W, Jr. (R)
Homer, Max H. (D)
Honaman, June N. (R)
Honnold, John Otis, Jr. (D)
Hoopes, Darlington (Socialist)
Horner, Jack B. (R)
Horting, Ruth Grigg (D)
Hose, Jacob W, Sr. (R)
Hostetler, H. Richard (D)
Huber, Ray Arlen (D)
Huber, William Irvin (D)
Huff, Sara Ellen (D)
Humes, Theodore Leon (R)
Ide, Raymond F. (R)
Ingram, John W. (R)
Irvis, K. Leroy (D)
Isaacs, Joseph W. (R)
Jacobs, Earl Bryan (R)
Jenkins, Frank Williamson (R)
Jirolanio, Justin Di (D)
Johanson, Louis Carl (D)
John, Louise Moses (D)
Johnson, Albert W. (R)
Johnson, George R. (R)
Johnson, Raymond Blair (R)
Johnson, Robert Anthony (D)
Johnson, Robert Livingston (R)
Johnson, Robert Peter (R)
Johnson, Theodore (D)
Jones, Frances R. (D)
Jordan, John C. (R)
Jordon, James Alonzo (D)
Joseph, William (D)
Kahle, Alvin (R)
Kalman, Thomas J. (D)
Kamyk, Walter Thomas (D)
Kaplan, Jerome (D)
Kaptik, Alexander, Jr. (R)
Kaufman, Gerald (D)
Kavulich, Stephen James (D)
Kearns, Carroll D. (R)
Kelchner, George Curry (R)
Keller, Marvin V. (R)
Kelley, Joseph John, Jr. (R)
Kelly, Anita Palermo (D)
Kelly, Audrey R. (R)
Kelly, John Brenden, Jr. (D)
Kennedy, Donald Patrick (R)
Kennedy, H. Francis (R)
Kernaghan, Mae W. (R)
Kessler, Harry A. (R)
Kester, Stanley R. (R)
Kistler, Guy A. (R)
Klein, H. Beryl (D)
Kline, Boyd Howard (R)
Kline, Ernest P. (D)
Klunk, Fred G. (D)
Knaur, Raymond Mowry (R)
Knox, James William (D)
Kolter, Joseph Paul (D)
Kooker, Margarette Fraley Sparver (R)
Kornick, Nicholas (D)
Kosco, John C. (R)
Kovach, Alexander Charles (D)
Kowalyshyn, Russell (D)
Kradel, John F. (D)
Kuhn, James Craighead, Jr. (D)
Kunkel, John Crain (R)
Kunzig, Robert Lowe (R)
Kurtz, Robert M, Jr. (R)
Kury, Franklin L. (D)
Kwitowski, Walter Anthony (D)
Lafore, John Armand, Jr. (R)
LaMarca, Russell J. (D)
Lamb, Thomas F. (D)
Lane, William J. (D)
Lark, Henry W. (R)
Laudadio, John F. (D)
Lawler, Joseph John (D)
Laws, William Charles (R)
Lawson, Paul M. (D)
Leach, Charles Parmley, Sr. (R)
Leader, George Michael (D)
Lederer, William J. (D)
Lee, Kenneth B. (R)
Lehr, Stanford Bud (R)
Lench, Ronald G. (D)
Lentz, Earl LeRoy, Jr. (R)
Lentz, William B. (R)
Leonard, Louis (D)
Lerch, Orville Harford (R)
Lichtenfeld, Samuel (D)
Liebermann, Shirley Correll (R)
Limper, William (D)
Lind, James Francis (D)
Lockard, Joseph Francis (D)
Logan, James Duval (R)
Lord, Lilias Montgomery (R)
Luger, Charles (R)
Lutty, Paul F. (D)
Lynch, Frank J. (R)
Maack, Herbert R. (R)
McAneny, Joseph John (D)
McArdle, William Thomas (D)
McCabe, Thomas Bayard (R)
McCloskey, Robert J.
McConnell, Samuel Kerns (R)
McCorkel, Franklin Myers (R)
McCormick, Robert John (D)
McCreesh, Thomas P. (D)
McDade, Joseph Michael (R)
McGinnis, Bernard B. (D)
McGlinchey, Herbert J. (D)
McGlinn, Frank C. P. (R)
McGraw, Andrew J. (D)
McGregor, Jack Edwin (R)
McKee, Richard Newcombe (R)
McLaughlin, William J, III (R)
McNally, Edward William (D)
McQuone, Gary Harding (R)
Madigan, Albert E. (R)
Magaw, Elden Samuel (D)
Mahady, Paul W. (D)
Mahany, Rowland B. (R)
Malady, Regis Rowland (D)
Malinzak, Frank Leonard (D)
Manbeck, Clarence F. (R)
Markle, John, Jr. (R)
Markley, Marian E. (R)
Markovitz, Harry (R)
Marshall, Howard W. (R)
Martz, John E (D)
Masloff, Sophie (D)
Mason, Louis, Jr. (D)
Masters, Richard Stearns (R)
Masters, Robert J. (D)

Mazur, John (D)
Mebus, Charles Fillmore (R)
Meehan, Andrew Martin (R)
Meholchick, Stanley A. (D)
Melton, Mitchell Wesley (D)
Meyer, Charles Appleton (R)
Mifflin, Edward B. (R)
Miller, Emma Guffey (D)
Miller, Marvin Eugene (R)
Mills, Charles J. (D)
Minehart, Thomas Zeno, II (D)
Monaghan, Thomas J. (D)
Moore, Frank Emerson (R)
Moorhead, William Singer, Jr. (D)
Moran, Cyril J. (D)
Moran, J. Anthony (D)
Morgan, Thomas Ellsworth (D)
Morley, Walter H. (D)
Morris, Brewster Hillard
Moyer, Glenn Roydon (D)
Mullen, Martin P. (D)
Munley, Marion L. (D)
Munley, Robert William (D)
Murphy, Austin J. (D)
Murray, Erwin L. (D)
Murray, Harvey P, Jr. (R)
Murtha, John Patrick (D)
Musto, James A. (D)
Myers, Robert Lee, III (D)
Needham, Michael J. (D)
Negley, Harry Hull, Jr. (R)
Newhall, David, III (R)
Newkirk, Rosa H. (D)
Nicholson, Charles Glanz (R)
Nix, Robert N. C. (D)
Normile, Paul Raymond (D)
Notherman, Joseph Paul (D)
O'Brien, Bernard F. (D)
O'Dell, Ford E. (R)
O'Donnell, James A. (D)
O'Donnell, James P. (D)
O'Donnell, John Joseph (D)
Odorisio, Rocco A. (R)
Oesterling, Donald Oswald (D)
Ogilvie, Robert S. (R)
O'Gorman, Francis Edmund (R)
Oliver, Covey Thomas (D)
O'Neil, Frank M. (D)
O'Pake, Michael Allen (D)
Otto, Henry P. (R)
Packroni, Telio (D)
Pancoast, G. Sieber (R)
Parker, H. Sheldon, Jr. (R)
Parlante, Alfonso (D)
Pashley, Kathryn Graham (D)
Pechan, Albert Raymond (R)
Pecsi, Andrew (D)
Penetar, Daniel Lawrence (D)
Perry, Peter E. (D)
Peters, Edward Emil, Jr. (R)
Pettibon, George T. (R)
Pezak, John (D)
Pickering, Grace Lippincott (R)
Piper, Robert Lewis (D)
Piper, William G. (R)
Pittenger, John Chapman (D)
Plowman, Francis Wilds (R)
Podcasy, Bernard John (D)
Polaski, Frank (D)
Polen, J. Dean (D)
Pott, George Frederick (R)
Prendergast, James Francis (D)
Price, Ethel A. (R)
Prosser, William Haydn (R)
Puchalla, Andrew Francis (D)
Pulakos, George Steve (D)
Purnell, Karl H. (R)
Pytko, Walter Stanley (D)
Randolph, Leonard Wray (D)
Rappaport, Samuel (D)
Reibman, Jeanette F. (D)
Renninger, John S. (R)
Renwick, William F. (D)
Reynolds, Benjamin J. (R)
Reynolds, Hobson Richman (R)
Rhodes, George Milton (D)
Rice, John S. (D)
Rider, Harry Durbin (D)
Rigby, Joseph P. (R)
Rinker, Donald Kirk (R)
Ritter, James Pierce (D)
Riviere, Ralph Louis (D)
Robie, Joseph Jerome (D)
Rooney, Fred B. (D)
Rose, Arthur (R)
Rosenfeld, Mitchell Allan (R)
Ross, James Eugene (D)
Roth, Gerald Irwin (D)
Rothrauff, Richard M. (D)
Royer, Baker (R)

Rozzi, Dolores Louise (D)
Ruane, Paul G. (R)
Rubel, Donald Clarke (R)
Rubin, Arthur (D)
Rubino, Theodore Salvatore A. (R)
Ruggiero, Philip S. (D)
Rush, Francis J. (D)
Russo, Marius Thomas (D)
Ruthrauff, William Edgar, Jr. (R)
Ryan, Matthew J. (R)
Rybak, William C. (D)
Sabol, Joseph, Jr. (R)
Sacks, Leon (D)
Saloom, Eugene George (R)
Satz, Arnold (R)
Saylor, John Phillips (R)
Saylor, John Thomas (D)
Saylor, Stanley Raymond (R)
Scanlon, Eugene Francis (D)
Scarcelli, Vincent F. (D)
Scheffner, Richard F. (D)
Schmidt, Adolph William (R)
Schmitt, C. L. (D)
Schneebeli, Herman Theodore (R)
Schucker, Albert Edwin (R)
Schwartz, George X. (D)
Schweiker, Richard Schultz (R)
Scott, Hugh (R)
Scott, William Z. (R)
Scranton, William Warren (R)
Seltzer, H. Jack (R)
Sennett, William C. (R)
Sesler, William G. (D)
Shafer, Raymond Philip (R)
Shapp, Milton J. (D)
Sharfsin, Joseph (D)
Shaughnessy, Edward Paul (D)
Shelhamer, Kent D. (D)
Shelton, Ulysses (D)
Sherman, Louis (D)
Shirk, Kenelm Lawrence, Jr. (R)
Shoemaker, Lewis Edgar (R)
Shoemaker, Philip Ray (D)
Shuman, William O. (D)
Shupnik, Fred Joseph (D)
Silvis, John Marshall (R)
Sinclair, Ivan Benjamin (R)
Sirianni, Carmel A. (R)
Sittler, Edward Lewis, Jr. (R)
Slack, C. Timothy (R)
Slattery, Frank (D)
Sloan, Grace McCalmont (D)
Sludden, Charles Joseph (D)
Smith, Glenn E. (D)
Smith, James K. K. (R)
Smith, L. Eugene (R)
Smith, Robert Fleck (R)
Snare, Orville E. (R)
Snyder, Elmer Andrew (R)
Snyder, Richard A. (R)
Specter, Arlen (R)
Spencer, Warren H. (R)
Sperat, Guy Joseph, Jr. (D)
Spingler, William Anthony (D)
Splain, Maurice Daniel, Jr. (D)
Springer, Eric W. (D)
Stader, Victor Bernard, Jr. (D)
Staisey, Leonard Clifton (D)
Stassen, Harold Edward (R)
Stauffer, John (R)
Stauffer, Sarah Ann (R)
Staves, Marion Cole (D)
Stefanelli, Joseph Charles (D)
Stemmler, Gust L. (D)
Stevens, Jean M. (R)
Stevenson, James W, Jr. (R)
Stokes, J. Emery (R)
Stone, Charles D. (D)
Strausz-Hupe, Robert
Stroup, Stanley G. (R)
Stuart, George B. (R)
Suchko, Paul (D)
Sullivan, Joseph A. (D)
Sullivan, Thomas F. (D)
Swartz, Edward Stover (R)
Tabor, John K. (R)
Tanzella, Septemio Vincent (D)
Tate, James Hugh Joseph (D)
Tayoun, James Joseph (D)
Templeton, Daniel Sheridan (R)
Thacik, Anne Smith (R)
Theodore, Nicholas Gerald (R)
Thomas, Reno Henry (R)
Thompson, Ronald L. (R)
Tiberi, Thomas J. (D)
Trimarchi, Eugene James (D)
Truax, Combs Craig (R)
Tullio, Louis Joseph (D)
Turner, Harry Woodruff (R)

Underwood, James Martin (R)
Ungerleider, Robert (D)
Vagley, Robert Everett (D)
Vann, Earl (D)
Van Sant, John T. (R)
Varallo, Mary A. (D)
Veitch, Agnes Bell (R)
Vessella, Peter Anthony (D)
Vigorito, Joseph Phillip (D)
Wade, George N. (R)
Walker, Earl Sidney (R)
Wall, Arthur J. (R)
Walsh, John T. (D)
Wansacz, John (D)
Ware, John H, III (R)
Wargo, Joseph G. (D)
Watkins, G. Robert (R)
Webster, Robert L. (R)
Weeks, Arthur DeWitte (D)
Weeks, Johanna Grieb (D)
Wegemer, Charles W. (D)
Weidner, Marvin Detweiler (R)
Weiner, Charles R. (D)
Weiss, Samuel Arthur (D)
Welsh, George A. (R)
Welsh, John T. (D)
Westerberg, Victor John (R)
Whalley, John Irving (R)
White, James Wilson (D)
Wideman, Edmund Charles, Jr. (D)
Willard, James E. (R)
Williams, Alan D, Jr. (R)
Williams, Evan S. (R)
Williams, Lawrence G. (R)
Wilson, Benj. H. (R)
Wilson, Laverne Blair (D)
Wilt, Raymond E. (R)
Wilt, William W. (R)
Winkelman, Robert Bernard, Jr. (D)
Wise, Robert C. (D)
Witman, William, II
Wolf, Charles William (R)
Wood, John Dudley (R)
Worley, Francis (R)
Worrilow, Thomas Henry, Sr. (R)
Wright, James L, Jr. (R)
Wynd, Elizabeth S. (R)
Yahner, Paul J. (D)
Yatron, Gus (D)
Yetter, Van D, Jr. (D)
Yohn, William H, Jr. (R)
Yoney, John F. (D)
Young, Richard Freeman (D)
Young, Robert Elmo (R)
Young, Thomas Harold (R)
Young, Wendell William (D)
Zearfoss, Herbert Keyser (R)
Zemprelli, Edward P. (D)
Zimmerman, Lester H. (R)
Zord, Joseph V, Jr. (R)
Zurick, William Philip (D)

RHODE ISLAND

Albro, John I, Jr. (R)
Allen, Charles Henry, III (D)
Allen, F. Monroe (R)
Allen, Kenneth Setzer (R)
Almond, Lincoln Carter (R)
Aquilotti, Samuel (D)
Arcaro, Harold Conrad, Jr. (D)
Arico, Anthony V, Jr. (D)
Audette, Marcel Gratien (R)
Babin, William Albert, Jr. (D)
Baccari, Vincent James (D)
Bagaglia, Alfred (D)
Baillargeon, Wilfred J. (D)
Balzano, Michael J, Jr. (R)
Barone, Anthony John (D)
Baronian, Leo P. (D)
Beaulieu, Ernest Robert (R)
Bechtold, Charles Harrison (R)
Belhumeur, Arthur A. (D)
Berg, Joseph M. (D)
Bevilacqua, Joseph A. (D)
Bianchini, Robert Vincent (D)
Bilgor, Irving J. (D)
Blaine, Richard Allan (R)
Bocchino, John (R)
Bonenfant, Gerald Leo (D)
Bonner, Donald R. (R)
Breslin, Robert Henry, Jr. (R)
Brosco, Anthony J. (D)
Brunero, Stephen (D)
Bruno, Joseph F. (D)
Campbell, Ambrose Leo (D)
Capaldi, John Fiore (D)

Capineri, Joseph A. (D)
Caranci, Anthony Benjamin, Jr. (R)
Carley, Robert Joseph (D)
Caswell, Richard W. (R)
Chafee, John Hubbard (R)
Chaharyn, Orist D. (D)
Champion, William J, Jr. (D)
Choquette, Paul J, Jr. (R)
Cobb, J. William, Jr. (R)
Cochran, Eugene F. (D)
Coelho, Peter J. (D)
Cofone, Charles Joseph (R)
Coman, E. Rex (R)
Cook, Kenneth R. (D)
Cornwell, Elmer Eckert, Jr. (D)
Corr, J. William, Jr. (R)
Costa, Francis R. (D)
Costello, Edward Denis (D)
Costello, James (D)
Cottrell, Arthur Maxson, Jr. (R)
Cottrell, George Carey (D)
Crooks, Samuel Coulter (D)
Cunningham, Matthew C. (D)
Cusson, Annette Forest (D)
D'Abate, William (D)
D'Attore, Harriet J. (R)
Davignon, Raymond Leo (D)
Del Giudice, Anthony Sabino (D)
Denomme, Ernest Francis (R)
DeSimone, Herbert Florie (R)
Desmarais, Raymond Wilfrid (R)
DeStefano, C. George (R)
Devany, Charles G. (D)
DiLorenzo, Amato P. (D)
DiLuglio, Thomas Ross (D)
DiPetrillo, Carmine R. (R)
Dolbashian, Edward Martin (R)
Doorley, Joseph Aloysius, Jr. (D)
Duffy, J. Howard (D)
Dunphy, Robert G. (D)
Durfee, Raymond M. (R)
Dwyer, Francis Gerard (R)
Dykeman, Calvin Carroll (R)
Edwards, Dorothy Beatrice (R)
Edwards, Tom (D)
Evans, David Vernon (D)
Ewing, Bayard (R)
Farmer, Malcolm, Jr. (R)
Fay, Thomas Frederic (D)
Fecteau, William C, Jr. (D)
Ferland, Roland O. (D)
Ferraro, Anthony Michael (D)
Folcarelli, Giovanni (D)
Fontaine, Paul Auray (D)
Forrest, Leonard Willis, Jr. (D)
Freda, Aldo (D)
Gallagher, James Augustine (D)
Gallagher, William F. (D)
Galvin, John Raymond (D)
Gardner, George W. (R)
Garrahy, J. Joseph (D)
Gencarelli, Francis A. (R)
Gendron, Joseph Saul (D)
Geoffroy, Fulda Emile (D)
George, Raymond David (D)
Giangiacomo, Anthony (D)
Giannini, Anthony Albert (D)
Gibbs, June Nesbitt (R)
Giguere, Noel A. (D)
Gladstone, Bernard C. (D)
Goodman, Jay S. (D)
Gorham, Bradford (R)
Greenwood, David Colbert (D)
Harlow, Allen S. (R)
Hawkins, Henry C. (R)
Hawksley, Raymond H. (D)
Hayden, Gerald C. (D)
Hayes, Patrick O'N. (D)
Hobbs, Horace Eastow (D)
Hogan, John J. (D)
Holmes, Herbert Underwood (R)
Horan, Michael Francis (D)
Huntoon, Maxwell C. (R)
Jackson, Mary Hillard (R)
Jacques, Norman Joseph (D)
Jamiel, Morphis A. (Independent)
Jendzejec, Stanley Michael (D)
Kagan, Samuel C. (D)
Kane, Walter J. (D)
Kelleher, Thomas (D)
Kelley, Charles P. (D)
Kennedy, Francis X. (D)
Kennedy, Fred J. (R)
Kiernan, James Henry (D)
Kiley, Richard B. (D)
Kirby, Patrick George (R)
Kiven, Arline Ruth (D)
Kobalinski, Stephen A. (D)
LaChapelle, Francis Joseph (D)

LaFrance, August P. (D)
Laliberte, Henry E. (D)
Lapointe, Agnes R. (R)
Lappin, William J. (D)
La Roche, Ulysses (D)
Lavallée, Gaston Harold (R)
Leary, Jeremiah R. (D)
Lech, Chester (D)
Lee, Arthur T. (R)
Leeds, Isabelle R. (D)
Levesque, Thomas Hughes (D)
Lewis, Ralph T. (R)
Licht, Frank (D)
Lippitt, Frederick (R)
Littlefield, Thomas C. (R)
Loiselle, Andrew J. (D)
Love, Lucille A. (R)
Low, Theodore F. (R)
Lucas, Lloyd M. (R)
Luckina, Howard Joseph (D)
Lussier, Arthur Edgar (D)
Lynch, Jeremiah C, Jr. (D)
Lynch, John Philip (D)
Lyons, John A. (D)
McBurney, John Francis, Jr. (D)
McCabe, Frances H. (D)
McDonald, George Francis (D)
McGowan, Leo Patrick (D)
Maggiacomo, Edward Louis (D)
Maher, James C. (D)
Mancini, Salvatore (D)
Mansi, Nicholas Anthony (D)
Marshall, James John (R)
Martin, Frank A, Jr. (D)
Massa, Salvatore (D)
Matheson, Gordon Cameron (R)
Maynard, Paul Joseph (R)
Michaelson, Julius Cooley (D)
Miska, Walter John (R)
Moan, Alfred R. (D)
Moran, John E. (D)
Morrone, Vero A.
Mott, Samuel D. (D)
Murphy, Robert T, Sr. (D)
Nathanson, Charles (R)
Needham, Thomas H. (R)
Nelson, Raymond (D)
Nero, Pat (D)
Newbury, George A. (D)
Noel, Philip William (D)
Notte, John Anthony, Jr. (D)
Nugent, John Joseph (D)
O'Brien, Joseph K. (D)
O'Brien, William W. (D)
O'Donnell, Joseph H, Jr. (R)
Pacheco, Henry W. (D)
Paquin, Henry L. (D)
Pasbach, Earl Francis (D)
Pastore, John O. (D)
Pederzani, Paul P, Jr. (D)
Pell, Claiborne (D)
Peloquin, J. Camille, Sr. (D)
Perry, Charles A, Jr. (R)
Perry, Joseph, Jr. (D)
Pisano, Paul J. (D)
Pratt, Oscar C. (D)
Price, Lenna Wroblinskee (R)
Prosser, Rufus K. (R)
Quattrocchi, Rocco Anthony (D)
Racewicz, William John (D)
Rawlings, Rob Roy (D)
Reid, William A. (R)
Revens, John Cosgrove, Jr. (D)
Ricci, Hugo L. (D)
Rivet, Eugene Edgar (D)
Rocha, Gelbert T. (D)
Rocha, James John (D)
Rodgers, Joseph F, Jr. (D)
Rosedale, Peter Klaus (D)
Russell, Howard Edwin, Jr. (R)
Russo, Joseph (R)
St. Germain, Fernand Joseph (D)
Santoro, Thomas D. (D)
Saobento, Augusto W. (D)
Saucier, Emily M. (D)
Sauté, Germain (R)
Savage, Joseph A. (D)
Scott, Henry (D)
Selya, Bruce Marshall (R)
Sepe, Michael (D)
Sgambato, Frank (D)
Shea, Donald F. (D)
Sheehan, John J, Jr. (D)
Skiffington, John Joseph, Jr. (D)
Slater, Eleanor Frances (D)
Smith, Francis P. (D)
Solomon, Anthony Joseph (D)
Stromberg, Vernon S. (R)
Sturges, Benjamin Rush (R)
Sundlun, Walter Irving (R)
Sweeney, David F, Jr. (D)
Sweet, Howard C. (R)
Taft, James L, Jr. (R)
Tarro, Richard Edward (D)
Taylor, Erich A. O'Driscoll (D)
Tessier, Eugene Joseph, Jr. (R)
Thibaudeau, Joseph P. (D)
Thibeault, Joseph A. (D)
Thibodeau, Eugene E. (D)
Thompson, Oliver L, Jr. (R)
Tiernan, Robert Owens (D)
Travers, Alfred, Jr. (D)
Tucker, Henry Harris (R)
Turnquist, Arnold G. (D)
Vaccaro, Vincent (R)
Varley, Joseph L. (D)
Vigeant, Agnes Martin (R)
Walsh, Joseph William (D)
Walsh, William L. (D)
Weaver, George Duncan, Jr. (D)
Wells, Guy Jackson (R)
Woodcock, Raymond Paul (D)
Wrenn, John Joseph (D)
Wyatt, Donald Walter (R)

SOUTH CAROLINA

Abercrombie, Marshall West (D)
Able, William F. (R)
Abrams, Pinckney N. (D)
Adams, Thurman Freddie (R)
Agnew, Anne A. (D)
Alford, Alexander (D)
Allen, Charles Guthrie (D)
Altman, J. Eugene (D)
Anderson, Jesse Thomas (D)
Armitage, Constance Dean (R)
Arrants, James Clator (D)
Ashmore, Robert Thomas (D)
Aycock, Robert James (D)
Ayers, Judson Freeman, Jr. (D)
Baggett, Julius Herbert (D)
Baggett, W. Tate (R)
Bailes, E. Lamar, Jr. (D)
Baker, Bennie Wade (D)
Baldwin, Frank Eugene, Jr. (D)
Ballard, Grady Cecil (D)
Beasley, Richard Lee (D)
Bell, Hoover Fay (D)
Bell, Lloyd B. (D)
Belser, Clinch Heyward (D)
Bethea, Alfred William (D)
Blatt, Solomon (D)
Bowen, Charles Benjamin (D)
Bowers, Grover Ford, Jr. (D)
Boyle, Rochelle (D)
Bradshaw, Charles Jackson (R)
Branham, Lester Province, Sr. (D)
Breazeale, Harold Delois (D)
Bristow, Walter James, Jr. (D)
Brockington, William John (D)
Brown, Ben Hill, Jr.
Brown, Edgar Allan (D)
Bull, Coralee Kitchings (D)
Burnett, Benjamin Oliver (D)
Buzhardt, J. Fred, Jr. (R)
Buzhardt, Joseph Fred (D)
Byrd, Waddell (D)
Byrnes, James Francis (D)
Cain, Charles Marshall (R)
Callison, Preston Harvey (D)
Carter, John Robert, Jr. (D)
Carter, Rex Lyle (D)
Carwile, Addison Brooks (D)
Chapman, Harry A, Jr. (D)
Chapman, Robert Foster (R)
Chestnut, Webster Robert (R)
Chick, John Frank (R)
Clark, Walter Hugh (D)
Cobb, Owens Taylor, Jr. (D)
Coker, Joseph Warren (D)
Collins, Purvis Wesley (D)
Comer, William Marshall (D)
Condon, James Mathewes (D)
Connor, Fred, Jr. (R)
Connor, James Manker (D)
Cook, Anne Milteer (D)
Cook, William A. (R)
Cottingham, Edward Benjamin (D)
Cox, Herman Elmer (D)
Cox, Toy Louis (D)
Cushman, Edward Charles, Jr. (D)
Cuttino, James, Jr. (D)
Dangerfield, Clyde Moultrie (D)
Davis, William Benbow (D)
Dennis, Rembert Coney (D)
Dent, Harry Shuler (R)
Des Champs, William Green, Jr. (D)
Doar, William Walter, Jr. (D)
Dobbins, William Camellus (D)
Dooley, Albert John (D)
Dorn, William Jennings Bryan (D)
Doyle, Clarence O'Dell (D)
Drummond, John (D)
Duffy, James Evan (R)
Duncan, Jason Charlie (D)
Edens, Henry Curtis (D)
Edens, J. Drake, Jr. (R)
Edwards, Tom W, Jr. (D)
Elliott, Thomas Edward (D)
Eubanks, Raymond Converse, Jr. (D)
Fendley, Furman Lester (D)
Fewell, Samuel Bruce, Jr. (D)
Fields, Richard Earl (D)
Finch, Hugh Edsel (D)
Floyd, Ervin Richard (R)
Floyd, Sidney Thomas (D)
Folk, Daniel Paul, II (D)
Fraser, Walter Samuel (D)
Frederick, Carolyn Essig (R)
Fuller, Fred Archie, Jr. (D)
Gaillard, John Palmer, Jr. (D)
Gardner, John Pickens (D)
Garrett, Charles G. (D)
Garrison, Thomas Edmond (D)
Gasque, J. Ralph (D)
Gettys, Thomas Smithwick (D)
Gibson, Charles MacDonald (D)
Godwin, Charles Edward (D)
Goodman, Carlyle Whittier, Sr. (D)
Graham, William Clyde (D)
Granger, Herbert Curry (D)
Grant, Edmund Griffin (D)
Grant, George Henry (D)
Graves, James Wilson (D)
Greene, Thomas Wesley (D)
Gregory, George Winfield, Jr. (D)
Gressette, Lawrence Marion (D)
Griffith, Eugene C. (R)
Grimball, John (D)
Grimes, Cecil Claymon, Jr. (D)
Guerard, Theodore Bogert (D)
Guerry, Henderson, Sr. (D)
Hager, H. William, Jr. (R)
Hammett, Robert A. (D)
Hanna, Niles Edwin (R)
Hare, William Ross (D)
Harper, C. Lem (D)
Harrelson, James P. (D)
Harrelson, William L. (D)
Harris, Raymond Alexander (R)
Hartnett, Thomas Forbes (D)
Harvey, William Brantley, Jr. (D)
Harwell, David Walker (D)
Hawkins, Jesse F. (D)
Hayes, Robert Wesley (D)
Haynsworth, Clement Furman, Jr.
Heller, Max M. (D)
Hemphill, Paul, Jr. (D)
Hemphill, Robert Witherspoon (D)
Henderson, James Marvin (R)
Hester, Lawrence Lamar (D)
Hinson, Caldwell Thomas (D)
Hodges, Charles Edward (D)
Hollings, Ernest Frederick (D)
Holman, George, Jr. (D)
Hooks, James C. (D)
Houck, Charles Weston (D)
Howell, Thomas Madison, Jr. (D)
Huff, Beattie Eugene (D)
Hughes, Jerry Miles, Jr. (R)
Hughes, Robert Earle (D)
Hunt, Lloyd Edward (D)
Hunter, William Harvey (R)
Hyatt, George Simpson (D)
Hyman, Peter DeWitt (D)
Jamison, Leslie D. (R)
Jenkins, Clyde David, Jr. (D)
Jenkins, William Green (R)
Jenrette, John Wilson, Jr. (D)
Jessen, Herbert Henry (D)
Johnson, Malcolm Kirkley (D)
Jolly, Henry Levi (D)
Jones, John Douglas (D)
Jones, William Townes (D)
Joy, Michael Bill (D)
Kelly, Bobby D. (D)
Kemp, Robert Watson (D)
Kirkland, Alma Walsh (R)
Kneece, Robert Edward (D)
Krawcheck, Leonard (D)
Lake, Robert Campbell, Jr. (D)
Lake, Walter Thomas (D)
Laney, Dan Foster, Jr. (D)
Laughlin, Michael Lukens (D,
Lawson, James Byrum (D)
Lawton, Marion R. (R)
League, James Christopher (D)
LeaMond, Frederick Julian (D)
Lee, Jamie Fletcher (D)
Legare, Allen T, Jr.
Leppard, Edward Melver (D)
Lever, Asbury Francis, Jr. (D)
Lewis, Ernest Crosby (D)
Lewis, Walter Woodward (D)
Lightsey, Hugh Tuten (D)
Lindsay, John Charles (D)
Long, John D, III (D)
Lourie, Isadore E. (D)
Love, Hugh J. (D)
Lowry, Samuel Earle (D)
McAlhany, Joseph Carlisle (D)
McClearen, Harber Addison (R)
McClellan, Joseph Marvin (R)
McDonald, Fred N. (D)
McDonald, Heyward Elliott (D)
McDonald, Milford Edgar (D)
McElveen, George Raymond (D)
McFadden, Robert Lawrence (D)
McGee, Joseph Halstead, Jr. (D)
McGowan, Edgar Leon (D)
Mack, Barron Bayles (D)
McKown, George Washington (D)
McLendon, James Malcolm (D)
McLeod, Daniel R. (D)
McLeod, William James (D)
McMaster, Fitz-John Creighton (D)
McMillan, Clara Gooding (D)
McMillan, John L. (D)
McNair, Robert Evander (D)
Mangum, Tom Gibson (D)
Mann, Fletcher Cullen (R)
Mann, James Robert (D)
Marett, Dan Thompson (D)
Martin, Jimmie Leewood (D)
Martin, John Alfred (D)
May, John Amasa (D)
Maybank, Burnet R. (D)
Medlock, Thomas Travis (D)
Mendenhall, Samuel Brooks (D)
Milliken, Roger (R)
Mishoe, W. Frank (D)
Mitchell, Carlton Adger (D)
Mitchell, Rudolph (D)
Mixson, William Edward (D)
Mobley, Garrett Judson (D)
Moore, Charles Carlisle (D)
Moore, Fred Thurman (D)
Moore, James Edward (D)
Morgan, Herbert Doyle (D)
Morphy, Ted L. (D)
Morrah, P. Bradley, Jr. (D)
Morris, Ann Barnett (R)
Morris, Earle E, Jr. (D)
Morris, James McCullum (D)
Mozingo, James Pierce, III (D)
Neisler, Robert Preston (R)
Nunnery, Jimmie Ernest (D)
Olmert, Joseph Phillip (R)
O'Shields, James Earl (D)
Owenby, William Emily (R)
Owens, Frank Capers (D)
Parker, Marshall Joyner (D)
Patterson, Grady Leslie, Jr. (D)
Patterson, Mac V. (R)
Pettit, Howard Gordon, Jr. (R)
Petty, George Beverly, Jr. (D)
Phinney, George Leon (D)
Pinckney, Francis Douglas (D)
Plaxico, Robert Lawrence (D)
Poston, Howard Henry, Jr. (R)
Powell, Charles Lewis (D)
Pracht, John Christopher, Jr. (D)
Pruitt, Bobby Maurice (D)
Pyle, Charles Victor, Jr. (D)
Raley, Robert A. (D)
Redfearn, Laurin Robert (D)
Reel, William Albert, Jr. (D)
Reynolds, Julian Alexander (D)
Rhodes, Eldridge C. (D)
Richardson, Henry Burchill (D)
Richardson, Jeff Roland, Jr. (R)
Riley, Edward Patterson (D)
Riley, Joseph Patrick, Jr. (D)
Riley, Richard Wilson (D)
Risher, William Rhett (R)
Rivers, L. Mendel (D)
Roddey, Frank Laney (D)
Roe, Thomas Anderson (R)
Rogers, Daniel Townsend (R)
Rogers, Joseph Oscar, Jr. (R)
Rosen, Meyer (D)
Ross, William G, Jr. (R)
Rouse, LeGrand Ariail, II (D)
Rowell, James Victor (R)
Rubin, Hyman (D)
Russell, Donald Stuart (D)

Saleeby, Thad Eli (D)
Sanders, Alexander Mullings, Jr. (D)
Sansbury, Paul Andrews (D)
Scarborough, Robert Bowman (D)
Schafer, Alan Heller (D)
Schumacher, Snead (D)
Schwartz, Ramon, Jr. (D)
Scott, Roger William (D)
Scurry, Frederick G. (D)
Seabrook, Cordes Gaillard, Jr. (R)
Sexton, Clarence D, Jr. (D)
Shealy, Wilson Otto (R)
Sheppard, Bazel Bunyan (D)
Shorey, Gregory Day, Jr. (R)
Shuler, Lewis Hayne (D)
Simons, Charles E, Jr. (D)
Sloan, Frank Keenan (D)
Smith, Abney Alexander (D)
Smith, Clary Hood (D)
Smith, Edward Jack (D)
Smith, Furman Beasley (D)
Smith, Harris Page (D)
Smith, Horace Carroll (D)
Smith, Thomas Earle, Jr. (D)
Smoak, Marion H. (R)
Spence, Floyd Davidson (R)
Stathakis, James John (D)
Stephen, James Barnett (D)
Stevens, James Price (D)
Strom, Clyde Franklin (D)
Stroud, William Hugh (R)
Stubbs, Archie Roy (R)
Stuckey, James Henry (D)
Suber, Martin Gay (R)
Sylvester, Barbara Thornton (D)
Talbert, S. Watson (D)
Taylor, David Surratt (D)
Theodore Nick Andrew (D)
Thornton, O. Frank (D)
Thurmond, James Strom (R)
Toole, Frampton Wyman, Jr. (D)
Townsend, Richard Taylor (D)
Trotter, Dan (R)
Turner, Robert Wilson
Turner, Roy R. (R)
Underwood, Camilla Knotts (R)
Van Exem, Elizabeth Hawley Gasque (D)
Venters, W. Odell (D)
Waddell, James Madison, Jr. (D)
Walker, Henry C. (D)
Wallace, Matthew Brevard, Jr. (R)
Wallace, Robert Buford (D)
Wallace, William Lewis (D)
Wannamaker, William Whetstone, Jr. (R)
Wannamaker, William Whetstone, III (R)
Watson, Albert W. (R)
Weatherford, Wade Stackhouse, Jr.
West, Harold Norman (D)
West, John Carl (D)
Whitaker, Charles James, Sr. (D)
Wienges, Othniel Henry, Jr. (D)
Wilder, Alice F. (R)
Williams, Audrey Patterson (D)
Williams, John Cornelius, Jr. (D)
Williams, Marshall Burns (D)
Wofford, James Mason
Worsham, George Frederick (R)
Wright, Elbridge Juette (D)
Wright, Luther Clark, Jr. (D)
Wyse, Jacob Frederick (R)
Yarborough, Foster Hall (D)
Yonce, Henry Grady (D)
Zeigler, Eugene Noel, Jr. (D)

SOUTH DAKOTA

Abdnor, James (R)
Abourezk, James G. (D)
Adams, H. G. (D)
Adams, John Gibbons (R)
Adelstein, Stanford Mark (R)
Allington, Thomas B. (D)
Anderson, Arthur Bennett (R)
Anderson, C. Marie Pingrey (R)
Anderson, Eunice (R)
Anderson, Nils Holger (R)
Anderson, Nora Tidball (R)
Anderson, Oscar L. (R)
Anderson, Sigurd (R)
Anderson, Virgil Ervin (R)
Assman, Joseph James (R)
Bader, Palmer Walter (D)
Baer, E. D. (R)
Baker, Ted R. (D)
Barnett, Joseph H. (R)
Bartron, G. Robert (R)
Behrens, E. Frederick (R)
Benda, Carol Joyce (R)
Bennett, Boyd (D)
Bennett, Donn (R)
Berry, E. Y. (R)
Bibby, John E. (R)
Biegelmeier, Frank (D)
Billion, David Henry (R)
Birkeland, Arthur C. (R)
Bliss, Ellen Elizabeth (R)
Blue, George (D)
Boe, Carl E. (D)
Boe, Nils A. (R)
Boehrs, C. E. (D)
Bottum, Joseph Henry (R)
Bratton, Richard Waldo (R)
Brown, H. Russell (R)
Brown, James Thomas (R)
Brown, Paul Eugene (R)
Buckingham, Harold D. (R)
Buehler, John (R)
Burges, Theodore Roosevelt (R)
Burgess, Carl T. (R)
Burke, Alfred J. (Independent)
Burns, Robert H. (R)
Bushfield, Vera Cahalan (R)
Cain, Elmo Virgil (D)
Campbell, E. J. (R)
Chamberlin, Robert Mather (D)
Chance, Simon W. (R)
Cheever, Gene G. (R)
Christensen, Nels P. (D)
Clark, Harland Calvin (R)
Clark, Raymond E. (D)
Clay, Charles E. (R)
Collingwood, Robert T. (D)
Collins, Claricie Visser (R)
Dahl, Oscar P. (R)
Dailey, Robert, Jr. (D)
Doherty, C. L. (R)
Dohmen, James Joseph (D)
Donley, Owen Joseph (D)
Dougherty, William Joseph (D)
Droz, Charles Clinton (R)
Dunmire, Joe R. (R)
Dupper, Ervin E. (R)
Dybvig, Clarence Adolph (R)
Ecker, Peder Kaloides (D)
Edlin, Ira (D)
Edwards, William Charles (R)
Eggers, Jean Ethalen (R)
Ellingson, Bertrum Edwin (D)
Elwood, Clell D. (R)
Engel, John A. (D)
Engelbrecht, Marlene Vivian (R)
Fairchild, Ruth (D)
Farrar, Frank L. (R)
Ferguson, Clifford Lindel (R)
Fillbach, George Wilson (R)
Fillmore, Lillian Garnet (R)
Fix, Jacob John (R)
Forell, Ora E. (R)
Frank, Helen Joyce (D)
Freiberg, Louis K. (R)
Galbraith, Francis J.
Gartland, Robert J. (D)
Geyerman, Peter Thomas (D)
Gibbs, Franklin Philip, Jr. (R)
Gibson, D(onald) Jack (R)
Gjesdal, Lars B, Jr. (R)
Gleich, Rudy J. (D)
Gruenwald, Max (R)
Gubbrud, Archie (R)
Guffey, Dorothy Anne (D)
Gullickson, Dale Dean (D)
Gunderson, Albert B. (R)
Gunderson, Dexter H. (R)
Gurney, Chan (John Chandler) (R)
Ham, Ernest Bollman (R)
Hamre, Al (R)
Hawley, W. Kermit (D)
Hawley, Wayne V. (D)
Heidepriem, Herbert A. (R)
Henderson, Frank E. (R)
Herbst, Ed (D)
Hilgemann, Calvin C. (R)
Hillgren, Ralph Oliver (R)
Hirsch, Robert William (R)
Hodson, Richard W. (D)
Hohn, Mayme R. (R)
Holland, William K. (D)
Hosmer, Larry F. (R)
Howard, Charles Allen, Jr. (R)
Huber, Oscar Edwin (R)
Humphrey, Louise B. (R)
Hurst, Glynn J. (D)
Hustead, D. W. (R)
Ingvalson, Elliott Louis (R)
Jelbert, James D. (R)
Jensen, William Martin (R)
Johnson, Charles Rick (R)
Johnson, Elton F. (R)
Johnson, John Dave (D)
Johnson, Louis L. (R)
Johnson, Melvin (D)
Johnson, Roy M. (D)
Johnson, Stanley Arthur (R)
Johnson, Walter Kirby (R)
Jones, Arthur Laurel (R)
Jones, Arthur W. (D)
Jones, David Lloyd (R)
Jones, Idwal (D)
Jones, Stephen Whitcomb (R)
Jorgensen, Harry V. (D)
Jorgensen, Leonard E. (R)
Jorgenson, Lloyd (R)
Juel, Orrin Perrine (R)
Justice, Clarence Wayne (D)
Kandaras, Homer Michael (D)
Katus, Thomas Michael (D)
Kime, Allan G. (R)
Klinkel, Thomas Edward (D)
Kneip, Richard Francis (D)
Knudsen, Henry I. (D)
Knudson, Loyd G. (R)
Koehn, Emil Alvin (R)
Kolkman, Lawrence Rick (D)
Kopecky, Bernie D. (D)
Krein, Reinhold (D)
Krog, Donald Richard (D)
Krull, Jacob Edward (D)
Kundert, Alice E. (R)
Kyle, Samuel William (R)
Lacey, (William) Charles (R)
Larkin, Charles Arthur (R)
Larson, Alma (R)
Leafstedt, Wendell Edward (R)
Lee, Wanda Karen (R)
Leighty, Ronald A. (D)
Lenker, William Fred (R)
Lerew, Theodore (D)
Levin, George Daniel (D)
Liljedahl, George H. (D)
Lindekugel, Fred (R)
Linn, Bernard (R)
Loen, Vernon Carroll (R)
Long, Winona Ruth (D)
Luckey, Mary Ellen (D)
Lyon, N. F. (R)
Lyons, Robert Emmet (D)
McCaughey, Robert L. (R)
McClellan, Joyce NaVonne (R)
McDaniel, Francis M, Jr. (D)
McGovern, George (D)
McKeever, Patrick James (D)
McKenzie, Frank (R)
MacLafferty, James Watson (R)
Magness, James M. (D)
March, Kathleen Olsen (R)
Marquardt, Lewis R. (D)
Matson, Maurice John (R)
Mees, Vearle Abbie (R)
Menning, C. J. (R)
Mentele, Edward Mathew (D)
Merkle, Chris A. (R)
Messner, George Donald (R)
Miles, Ethel Lola (R)
Millett, Harold (R)
Mills, Thomas Perry (R)
Moeller, Henry George (R)
Moore, Archie Ralph (D)
Moore, Roger R. (D)
Moran, Daniel Joseph (D)
Muenster, Theodore R. (D)
Mundt, Karl Earl (R)
Murphy, John Francis (D)
Mydland, Gordon J. (R)
Naddy, Donald William (D)
Nelson, H. Ivan (R)
Nelson, Ray O. (R)
Nichols, David Allen (D)
Novotny, Frank (D)
Olsen, Neva Argala (R)
Olson, Alex (R)
Olson, Kathleen W. (R)
Olson, Maurice Alan (D)
Opp, Norman (D)
Orr, Robert Dewey (D)
Osheim, Donald (R)
Oster, Henry J. (D)
Oster, Tony W. (D)
Overpeck, Lem Franklin (R)
Pashby, Fawn (D)
Paulson, Herman (R)
Peterson, June Rozelle (D)
Phillips, Margaret Louise (R)
Pieplow, E. C. (R)
Pommer, Merle Clausen (R)
Poppen, Henry Alvin (R)
Price, Garnet Ellen (R)
Prunty, Roger D. (D)
Pyle, Gladys (R)
Quam, Leslie James (R)
Raasch, Mary Elizabeth (R)
Raines, Thomas Lyle (R)
Ranney, Thomas Pollock (R)
Rasmussen, Donald Woodrow (D)
Reifel, Benjamin (R)
Renning, George (R)
Reppe, Lillian Lenora (R)
Rhian, Alvin J. (R)
Richardson, Lloyd Clifford, Jr. (R)
Ridley, Willard Clarence (D)
Risty, Albert R. (R)
Roberts, Godfrey Meyer, Jr. (R)
Roberts, Kenneth Lloyd (R)
Roesler, Alfred D. (R)
Rogers, Jack (R)
Rossiter, Michael Anthony (D)
Rossiter, Theodora Horn (D)
Rovang, John O. (D)
Rothstein, James L. (R)
Rubendall, Kay (R)
Sahr, William K. (R)
Samp, Rollyn H. (R)
Sande, Kermit Andrew (D)
Schrag, Lloyd (R)
Schroeder, William H. (D)
Schumacher, Anita M. A. (R)
Schumacher, Robert J. (R)
Schwader, Ferdinand (D)
Scribner, G. E. (Casey) (R)
Shaeffer, John Allen (R)
Smith, Edwin Steeves (R)
Smith, Eldon L. (R)
Smith, Henry A, Jr. (R)
Smith, Orville (D)
Snyder, Floyd Francis, Jr. (R)
Sorenson, Ed. C. (D)
Sperry, Allen R. (D)
Spiry, Arthur William (R)
Stalheim, Larry L. (R)
Stengel, James Lowell (R)
Stern, Otto (R)
Stickney, Harold Dean (R)
Stoia, Viorel G. (R)
Strand, Neal A. (R)
Stuelpnagel, Dan (R)
Sullivan, Agnes C. (R)
Sutton, John Edwin, Jr. (D)
Swenson, Duaine Vincent (D)
Swisher, Jay (R)
Temmey, Leo Albert (R)
Teske, Herb (D)
Thomas, Freda Katherine (D)
Tschetter, Menno (D)
Uecker, Wilmont M. (D)
Unzicker, Wayne (D)
Varilek, Elvern (D)
Voigt, Carl Emil (R)
Wagner, Colman H, Sr. (D)
Wallner, Mary (D)
Walsh, Daniel Clifford (D)
Walter, Merwyn H. (D)
Weisenberg, Webb (R)
Wernke, William D. (R)
White, Charles E. (R)
White, Doris Maude (R)
Whitehead, Emrey Lee (R)
Wiedenman, Walter V. (D)
Williams, Daisy Lee (D)
Williams, Joe (D)
Wood, Dorothy Mertis (R)
Wood, Royal James (R)
Wright, Donn Howard (D)
Wuger, Lavina Mardean (R)
Ylitalo, John Raymond
Young, Don (D)
Zimmer, John Herman (R)

TENNESSEE

Alexander, James H. (D)
Allen, Louis J. (D)
Allen, William Garrison (D)
Anderson, Charles Hill (R)
Anderson, Gordon LeRoy (R)
Anderson, Mary Mize (D)
Anderson, William Robert (D)
Armstrong, Jake Thomas (D)
Arnold, Edwin Harrison (R)
Ashe, Victor Henderson (R)
Atkins, Z. D. (D)
Atkisson, James Douglas (D)
Avery, John Buchanan, Jr. (D)
Avery, Thomas B(ouse) (R)

Bailey, Edward Riston (R)
Baird, Raymond Renfro (D)
Baker, E. Lamar (R)
Baker, Hayden Burnice (R)
Baker, Howard, Jr. (R)
Baker, Norval Sanders, Jr. (D)
Ballard, David George (D)
Barry, William Logan (D)
Bass, Ross (D)
Beasley, Thomas Woodrow (D)
Benton, George Oliver (D)
Berry, Fred Ogle, Sr. (R)
Berryhill, Grailey Hewitt (R)
Bible, Robert Joseph (R)
Black, John D. (D)
Blakemore, Murray G. (D)
Blanton, L. Ray (D)
Blue, Brantley (R)
Bomar, James La Fayette, Jr. (D)
Bowen, Maurice Richard, Jr. (D)
Boyd, Robert W. (R)
Bradley, Harold Whitman (D)
Bragg, John Thomas (D)
Briley, Clifton Beverly (D)
Briley, Melvin (D)
Brock, William Emerson III (R)
Brode, Freda Jean (D)
Brode, Marvin Jay (D)
Browder, Edward Carmack (D)
Brown, Aaron Clifton, Sr. (D)
Brown, James Monroe (D)
Bruce, William Roland, Jr. (D)
Burch, Charles Cowden (D)
Butcher, Jake F. (D)
Butler, G. Hilton (D)
Caldwell, James Carlton (D)
Callaway, Julia Bales Noe (R)
Callaway, Michael Engers (D)
Canaday, Travis (D)
Canale, Drew Justin (D)
Cannon, Calvin Lawrence (R)
Carbaugh, Harry Clarke (R)
Carr, Joe C. (D)
Carter, Allen H. (R)
Carter, Halbert L, Jr. (R)
Carter, James Reece (D)
Chambers, Louis (D)
Chapin, Edward Young, III (R)
Chattin, Chester Coles (D)
Chowning, James Paul (R)
Clement, Frank Goad (D)
Clements, Wallace DeWitt (D)
Coats, William Jean (R)
Cobb, John Bynum, II (D)
Cochran, Franklin Delano (D)
Collier, Woodrow Wilson (D)
Cook, Gayther Coleman, Jr. (R)
Cook, James Foster (D)
Cooper, Walter Claude (D)
Copeland, David Y, III (R)
Cowan, George Webb (D)
Creson, Thomas Kyle, Jr. (R)
Crutchfield, William Ward (D)
Cummings, James Harvey (D)
Daniel, Creed Allen (R)
Dann, Mimi Semmes (R)
Darnell, Alex Whitefield (D)
Davis, Ann M. (R)
Davis, James Carl (D)
Davis, Leon W, Jr. (D)
Denton, Herbert Jackson, Jr. (R)
Dickinson, Donald Warren (R)
Dilday, Jimmy B. (R)
Doane, J. N. (D)
Dodd, Wilma Neville Beardslee (D)
Donelson, Lewis R, III (R)
Dooley, John F. (D)
Drake, James Ellsworth (D)
Dudley, Guilford, Jr.
Dugger, John Frank (R)
Dunbar, Howard Raymond (R)
Duncan, John James (R)
Dyer, Ross Watkins (D)
Edens, Charles Joseph (R)
Elam, Clayton Paul (D)
Elder, James Bryan (D)
Ellington, Earl Buford (D)
Emerson, Ralph Waldo (D)
Evans, Buford (D)
Evins, Joe Landon (D)
Ewell, Milton Watkins, Jr. (D)
Eyerly, George Brown (R)
Fargarson, Robert Melvyn (D)
Felknor, Joe Hill (R)
Fisher, Richard Ashley (D)
Ford, Oron Russell (R)
Fowler, Hammond (D)
Frazier, James Beriah, Jr. (D)
Fritzsche, Lealand Carl (R)
Fulton, Richard Harmon (D)
Gaby, Gene Paul (D)
Galbreath, Charles (D)
Garland, Thomas Jack (R)
Garner, Thomas Franklin, Sr. (D)
Genette, Sidney Wilson, Jr. (D)
Gillock, Edgar Hardin (D)
Givens, David D. (D)
Goddard, Volta F. (R)
Gordon, S. Ralph (R)
Gore, Albert Arnold (D)
Gorrell, Frank (D)
Gray, Alexander Harbert (D)
Greene, Sarah Moore (R)
Grider, George William (D)
Halsell, Frank Ben (D)
Hamilton, Milton Hugh, Jr. (D)
Hampton, Keith (D)
Hargis, Gerroll (D)
Harris, Lyle (D)
Harris, Ruth Roberts (R)
Harris, Thomas Alan (D)
Hartman, Hervie Franklin (D)
Hassler, John David (D)
Hawks, Bob (D)
Henry, Joe W, Jr. (D)
Hicks, John Thomas, Sr. (D)
Hill, Donnelley Joseph (R)
Hill, George Lester, Jr. (R)
Hills, John Parker (R)
Hinton, Granville (R)
Hitchcox, Forrest L. (D)
Holcomb, S. Richard (D)
Hollar, Charles Hays (R)
Hudgens, Joe F. (D)
Huettel, William LePrince (R)
Hurst, Julius (R)
Hutcheson, R. H. (D)
Irwin, James Ellis (D)
Jackson, Mildred Kate C. (R)
Jenkins, R. David (R)
Jenkins, William Lewis (R)
Jennings, Lyndon Barger (D)
Jensen, Thomas Lee (R)
Johnson, Thomas A. (D)
Johnson, Zeake W, Jr.
Jones, Edward (D)
Jones, Gloria Lee (R)
Jones, John Martin (D)
Jordan, Hubert Bruce (D)
Jordan, Lois E. (D)
Keel, William Arnold, Jr. (D)
Kelley, Ralph Houston (D)
Kennedy, Frank William (R)
Kestner, Dolores Merville (R)
Kidwell, Allen V. (D)
Kimbrell, J. P.
King, Donald R. (D)
King, Leslie Henry (R)
Kinkead, Cecil Calvert (D)
Kissinger, Joseph Griffin (R)
Koella, Ernest, Jr. (R)
Kuykendall, Dan Heflin (R)
Lancaster, Robert Samuel (R)
Landers, William Lytle (D)
Law, James L. (R)
Law, Robert Eugene (R)
Lawson, William Vinton, Jr. (R)
Layne, Herbert Clayton (R)
Lee, John David (D)
Light, Frances H. (R)
Lillard, Robert Emmitt (D)
Loeb, Henry, III
Longley, Benjamin Lehmann (R)
Loser, Joseph Carlton (D)
Lucas, Maxwell Davis, Jr. (D)
McCaleb, Sammie Lee (R)
McCanless, George Folsom (D)
McDavid, Marion Foy (D)
McDonald, Jack (R)
McDowell, May Ross (R)
McInturff, Carl Emanuel (R)
McLean, Joseph Woodfen (D)
McSween, Donald M. (D)
McWherter, Ned R. (D)
Maddux, John Jared (D)
Magill, Joe Edward (R)
Majors, Joe Inman (D)
Martin, Leonard Watson (D)
Mathews, Harlan (D)
Matthews, William Joseph (R)
Mattox, Elmer Gooch (D)
Midyett, Thomas Earle, Sr. (D)
Miller, William Ernest (R)
Mobley, Ralph Carol (R)
Moore, Carl Randolph (D)
Moore, Carolyn Dabbs (D)
Moore, Don, Jr. (D)
Moore, James W. (D)
Morgan, Walter Henry (D)
Morris, William Harrell, Jr. (R)
Morton, Ambrose Gaines (R)
Moss, W. F. (D)
Motlow, Reagor (D)
Murphy, Ira H. (D)
Murray, Ronald J. (D)
Murray, Tom (D)
Nave, Marshall Toney (R)
Neal, Vernon (D)
Neal, William Henry, Jr. (R)
Nelson, Talmage L. (D)
Newman, Haggard Wright (D)
Nicks, Roy Sullivan (D)
Norman, Jack (D)
Norman, Seth Walker (D)
Northington, Arch Ewing (D)
Norvell, Richard (D)
Nowell, John C, Jr. (D)
Nunally, Van D, Jr.
Oakes, Roy Sidney (R)
Odem, Sue Edna (R)
Officer, Albert Fitzpatrick, Jr. (D)
Oldham, Edwin L. (D)
Oldham, Sarah Smith (D)
Oliver, Charles Preston (D)
Orr, Johnny Lynch (D)
Ousley, Roy Glenn (D)
Owens, Billy E. (D)
Pack, David M. (D)
Page, S. Rondall (R)
Patten, Zeboim Cartter (D)
Patterson, J. O, Jr. (D)
Peay, John H. (D)
Peeler, James Alfred, Jr. (D)
Penn, Marie Moore (D)
Pentecost, Cayce LaFon (D)
Perry, Jesse Laurence, Jr. (R)
Person, Curtis Standifer, Jr. (D)
Peters, Fornia Dungan (R)
Phillips, Dayton Edward (R)
Pickering, George Roscoe, Jr. (D)
Pitts, Knox (D)
Pope, James William, Jr. (D)
Pritchard, Howard Porter (R)
Qualls, James Franklin (R)
Quarles, W. Grundy (D)
Quillen, James Henry (R)
Quinn, Victor H. (R)
Rainey, Donald Glenn (D)
Randolph, Clarence Marvin, Jr. (D)
Redmond, Thomas Joseph (D)
Reece, Louis Goff (R)
Reed, Buford Leslie (D)
Reid, Will Carr (D)
Renner, Glenn Delmar (R)
Rhinehart, Shelby Aaron (D)
Roberts, John A. (D)
Roberts, Kenneth Lewis (R)
Runyon, Frank Jasper, II (D)
Russell, Ruth (D)
Sanders, Guynell R. (D)
Schoen, Kenneth Bernard (D)
Scholes, William Leon (D)
Scott, Mrs. C. Frank (D)
Senter, Harry Lee (D)
Shofner, Austin Williams (R)
Shoulders, Billy Joe (D)
Simpson, Paul Lee (D)
Smith, Doyle Jackson, Jr. (D)
Smith, Ewing, Jr. (D)
Smith, Frank E. (D)
Smith, John Elbert (R)
Smith, Quintin Miller (D)
Snodgrass, William R. (D)
Spurrier, Margaret Norvell (R)
Stafford, Edwin Samuel (D)
Stanton, Hugh W, Jr. (D)
Stapleton, Arley, Jr. (D)
Stegall, Whitney (D)
Steinhauer, John Mathias, Jr. (D)
Stephens, John Randol (D)
Swafford, Howard Graham (R)
Swan, Sara Victoria (D)
Taliaferro, Lewis (D)
Taylor, Lucas Parnell (R)
Taylor, Robert Campbell (D)
Terry, George Alvin (R)
Terry, W. Claude, Jr. (R)
Thorp, Mitchell Leon (D)
Threet, Ewing Jackson (D)
Timmons, William Evan (R)
Townsend, Hobart Lamar, Jr. (D)
Townsend, Wilburn Branson (D)
Trent, Delmus (R)
Tuck, Ann Litton Rowland (R)
Tuck, James Richard (R)
Upchurch, Ruble (R)
Wagner, Aubrey J. (Independent)
Wagner, Theodore Franklin (R)
Walker, William H, III (R)
Walters, Herbert Stanford (D)
Ward, Cleveland Ray (D)
Ward, Sara Elizabeth Little (D)
Ward, Wayman (D)
Warf, J. H.
Waters, John B, Jr. (R)
Watkins, James Paul (R)
Webber, Henry Earl III (D)
Webster, Ronald Arthur (R)
Webster, Warren Raymond (R)
Weldon, William Kimberly (R)
Wellford, Harry Walker (R)
White, Frank Louis (D)
White, James E. (R)
White, Ray D. (R)
Wilburn, Cordell Hull (D)
Wilde, Alma Lee (R)
Williams, Albert (D)
Williams, Avon Nyanza, Jr. (D)
Williams, John Taylor (R)
Williamson, Ernest Wilfert (D)
Wilson, Frank Wiley (D)
Wilson, George E, Jr. (R)
Wise, James Alan (D)
Witcher, Roger Kenneth (R)
Witt, Carter H. (D)
Worthington, Robert Fletcher, Jr. (D)
Wright, James Lee (D)

TEXAS

Abbott, S. L. (R)
Abraham, Malouf (R)
Adams, Donald Gilbert (D)
Adams, Gilbert Timbrell, Jr. (D)
Agnich, Fred Joseph (R)
Allen, John (D)
Allen, Lem B. (D)
Allison, James N, Jr. (R)
Allred, William David (D)
Anderson, Joe W. (D)
Anderson, John Richard (R)
Anderson, Marcellus Jack (D)
Anderson, Milton Jay (R)
Anderson, Thomas Dunaway (R)
Andujar, Elizabeth Richards (R)
Angly, Maurice, Jr. (R)
Archer, William Reynolds, Jr. (R)
Armstrong, Anne Legendre (R)
Armstrong, John Barclay (R)
Armstrong, Robert Landis (D)
Armstrong, Thomas DeBoy (D)
Atchison, James Wilbur (D)
Atkinson, Frances Hall (R)
Atlas, Morris (D)
Atwell, Ben Jumbo (D)
Aubrey, Mark Lee (R)
Baker, Charles Curtis (R)
Barber, Arthur Newell (D)
Barker, Thomas Wayne (D)
Barnes, Ben F. (D)
Barnes, Robert Field (R)
Barron, George Pinckney (D)
Barton, Jerry (D)
Bass, Bob (D)
Bass, Harvey Lee (D)
Bass, Thomas Hutcheson (D)
Baughman, Frank John (D)
Baum, Elmer Carl (D)
Beagle, Gail Joyce (D)
Beck, John Keitt (D)
Beckworth, Lindley (D)
Bell, E. R. (R)
Belzer, John Henry (R)
Bennett, John Mirza, Jr. (R)
Benson, Harry Eddie (R)
Bentsen, Beryl Ann (D)
Bentsen, Lloyd Millard, Jr. (D)
Bernal, Joe J. (D)
Berry, Mary Lucile (R)
Berry, V. E. (D)
Binkley, Marguerite Hall (R)
Blackmon, Jack Russell (D)
Blanchard, Horace J. (D)
Blaney, Walter Edwin (R)
Blanton, Jack (D)
Blanton, William Neal, Jr. (D)
Blessing, Elizabeth (D)
Boeckman, Duncan Eugene (R)
Boggus, Frank Nelson (R)
Bonilla, Tony (Independent)
Bonilla, William David (D)
Boyd, Nannette (D)
Boyd, Obie Dale (R)
Boyer, Max Wayne (D)
Braswell, Henry Gordon (D)
Braun, Rex (D)
Bray, James Houston (D)

Breitkreutz, Vernon Edgar (R)
Bridges, Ronald Wayne (D)
Bristol, George Lambert (D)
Brooks, Chet Edward (D)
Brooks, Jack (D)
Brooks, Marietta Moody (D)
Brown, Claude W. (D)
Brown, James Edward (R)
Brown, John Burns (D)
Brown, John Richard (D)
Brown, Kenneth Harold (R)
Browne, Maxine Gertrude (R)
Brownlee, Jerry L.
Bruce, Marion (D)
Brummett, Claudia Mae (D)
Buchanan, G. Sidney (R)
Buck, Raymond Elliot (D)
Buhler, Bette-Jo Simpson (R)
Bulgerin, Loretta (R)
Burdette, Lloyd Vernon (D)
Burleson, Omar (D)
Burnett, Robert Moore (D)
Burnett, Wayne Bart (D)
Burney, Cecil E. (D)
Bush, George (R)
Cabell, Earle (D)
Cahoon, Frank Kell (R)
Calder, N(orman) Bruce (R)
Caldwell, Neil (D)
Calhoun, Frank Wayne (D)
Campbell, Blake O. (D)
Cannon, Joseph Nathanial, Jr. (R)
Carpenter, Elizabeth Sutherland (D)
Carpenter, Robert Andy (D)
Carr, Waggoner (D)
Carrillo, Oscar, Sr. (D)
Casey, Robert Randolph (D)
Cassidy, Clifton Wilson, Jr. (D)
Cavness, Don W. (D)
Cayce, George L. (D)
Cervenka, William Joseph (R)
Chambers, Joe Reed (R)
Chambers, Robert Eugene (D)
Cherry, Dick (D)
Christian, George (D)
Christian, Tom Terrill (R)
Christie, Joe (D)
Clark, Edward A.
Clark, Thomas Campbell (D)
Clark, William Henry, III (D)
Clarkson, E. Milton (D)
Clayton, Bill W. (D)
Cleaveland, Bradford Ira (R)
Clemens, David Edward (D)
Clements, Richard Owen (R)
Clipson, James Hugh, Jr. (R)
Coates, Dennis Fleet, Jr. (D)
Cobb, Lawrence Dean (D)
Cockrum, Claudia O. (D)
Coffee, Tom Franklin (R)
Coffing, Thomas H. (R)
Coldwell, Colbert (D)
Coleman, Carobel Blair (D)
Coleman, Leonard Outlar (R)
Collins, Emmett Marvin (R)
Collins, James Mitchell (R)
Collins, Mary Ann Neuhoff (R)
Colson, Neveille H. (D)
Connally, Ben C. (D)
Connally, John Bowden (D)
Connell, Ted C. (D)
Cook, Clayton Henry (D)
Cook, Jack Randall, Sr. (R)
Cooke, Mary Swaney (D)
Cooper, Jesse Coyt (D)
Cornett, Leighton M. (D)
Cory, Richard Henry (D)
Cowden, George M. (D)
Cowden, Julianan (D)
Cowen, Joe N. (D)
Cox, Jack (R)
Craddick, Thomas Russell (R)
Craft, Jerry David (D)
Crawford, James Laird (R)
Crawford, Oliver Ray (D)
Creighton, Tom (D)
Crenshaw, Thomas William (R)
Crichton, Jack Alston (R)
Crockett, Kennedy McCampbell
Crooker, John H, Jr. (D)
Crowley, Frank Patrick (R)
Crutcher, Harry, III (D)
Cruz, Lauro (D)
Culver, Barbara Green (R)
Cunningham, Larry Jack (D)
Curlee, Clarence Lamar, Sr. (D)
Dailey, Herschel A. (R)
Daniel, Price (D)
Daniel, Price, Jr. (D)
Davis, Charles Russell (D)
Davis, Cletus Addison, Jr. (D)
Davis, Harold (D)
Davis, Will David (D)
Dawkins, Kirby Walls (D)
DeCluitt, Douglas Ronald (R)
De La Garza, Eligio (D)
Denius, Frank W. (D)
Densford, Charles Francis (R)
De Wetter, Herman Peter (D)
Diamond, Tom (D)
Dickie, Alexander, Sr. (D)
Dickson, Temple (D)
Dies, Martin, Jr. (D)
Doran, Hilary Brumley, Jr. (D)
Douthit, Jackson Sherrod (D)
Douthitt, Franklin Joseph (D)
Dowdy, John (D)
Doyle, Roy H. (D)
Drake, Robert Bert (D)
Dubuque, Louis Theodore (R)
Duggan, Fitzhugh Lee, Jr. (D)
Duncan, Norman E. (D)
Duran, Efrain A. (D)
Earthman, Jim (R)
Eastland, Anne Stacy (D)
Eckhardt, Robert Christian (D)
Edwards, Atticus Fitzgerald (D)
Eggers, Paul Walter (R)
Eidson, Wanda Carroll (R)
Elgin, George Kenneth (R)
Elliott, Ross Liles (D)
Ellis, Charles Edward (R)
Erwin, Frank Craig, Jr. (D)
Estes, Kate Reed (D)
Evans, Howard B. (D)
Evans, James Weldon (R)
Farenthold, Frances Tarlton (D)
Faulkner, James Eugene (R)
Fay, Albert Bel (R)
Field, John (D)
Finchum, Frank Dewayne (R)
Finnell, Charles Adkins (D)
Fisher, Norris (D)
Fisher, O. Clark (D)
Fletcher, Henry Arnold (D)
Flores, Angel A. (R)
Flores, Arturo Francisco (D)
Floyd, Jake Carlson (R)
Floyd, Paul (D)
Foerster, Alvin E, Jr. (R)
Ford, Tedroe Jay, Jr. (R)
Fore, Sam O, Jr. (D)
Foreman, Fred Wilson (D)
Fourmy, James C, Sr. (R)
Frandolig, Charles A. (D)
Friend, Harlan Dillman (D)
Fulks, Paul Moody (D)
Garcia, Joseph Alexander, Jr. (D)
Garcia, Zaragoza D, Jr. (D)
Garner, David Brown (D)
Garvey, James Sutherland (R)
George, Jesse Taylor (D)
George, Ralph Weir (R)
Gholson, Issac William (D)
Gillen, James Blake (D)
Gillespie, Charles B, Jr. (R)
Gilmore, Sibyl Irene (D)
Gish, David Hilton (R)
Glover, Donald Hair (D)
Godley, Gene Edwin (D)
Goldsum, John F. (D)
Golman, Joe H.
Gonzalez, Henry Barbosa (D)
Gordon, Virgil (R)
Gossett, Ed (D)
Gossett, James D. (R)
Gragg, Billy Hardin (R)
Graves, Curtis Matthew (D)
Green, Howard Lemuel (D)
Greenhill, Joe (D)
Griffin, Marvin Collins (D)
Groseclose, John Robert (R)
Grossenbacher, Jerome Francis (D)
Haag, George A. (R)
Haden, Charles McIntyre (R)
Hager, Ellen Hume Williams (R)
Haines, David Graves (D)
Hale, Louis Dewitt (D)
Hall, Billy (D)
Hall, Walter Gardner (D)
Hamilton, Robert William (D)
Hannah, John Henry, Jr. (D)
Hannay, Allen Burroughs (D)
Hardie, Thornton, Jr. (D)
Harding, Forrest Ashby (D)
Haring, Paul Byrne (D)
Harris, Orland Harold (R)
Harris, William Birch (R)
Harrison, John Ray (D)
Hart, Hugh Glen, Jr. (D)
Haven, Ivan Byron (D)
Hawkins, Jack Ross (D)
Hawn, Joe (D)
Haynes, Clyde, Jr. (D)
Haynes, Donald (D)
Hazlewood, Grady (D)
Heatly, William Stanford, Jr. (D)
Hefton, Don Warren (D)
Helms, Julian Dean (D)
Hendryx, Gene R. (D)
Henry, Forest Thomas (D)
Herndon, Chesley Coleman, Jr. (R)
Herring, Edgar Dale (R)
Herron, James Henry (R)
Hicks, Dick Walton (D)
Higgs, Rufus Franklin, Jr. (D)
Hightower, Cameron (D)
Hightower, Jack English (D)
Hill, Glenda (R)
Hill, John Luke (D)
Hobby, Oveta Culp (R)
Holland, W. Lamoine (D)
Holmes, Thomas Howard (D)
Holmes, Zan W, Jr. (D)
Houser, William Freeman (R)
Howard, Ed (D)
Howard, Rhea (D)
Howell, William Thomas (R)
Hoyt, Eugene R. (D)
Hubenak, Joe Adolph (D)
Hudson, James Aubrey (R)
Huffaker, Willie Calloway (D)
Hughes, Charles E. (D)
Hughes, Robert Higgins (D)
Hughes, Sarah Tilghman (D)
Hull, M. Cordell (D)
Hunsaker, Roger Clyde (R)
Hunt, Billy (R)
Hunt, Ocie (D)
Hurd, Howard (D)
Hutson, H. Keith (R)
Isaacks, Maud (D)
Jackson, Guy Cade, III (D)
Jackson, J. Rupert, Jr. (D)
Jackson, Randall Calvin (D)
Jacobson, Robert Lee (R)
Jacoby, William Roy (R)
Jindra, Roy I. (R)
Johnson, Frederic (D)
Johnson, Jacob Edgar (D)
Johnson, Jake (D)
Johnson, Louis Thomas (D)
Johnson, Lyndon Baines (D)
Jones, Delwin L. (D)
Jones, Edmund Eugene (R)
Jones, Grant (D)
Jones, James Paul (R)
Jones, Marvin (D)
Jones, Morton Edward (R)
Jones, Thomas Robert (R)
Jonsson, John Erik (R)
Juedeman, Rudolph F. (R)
Justice, William Wayne (D)
Kampmann, Flora Cameron (R)
Kazen, Abraham (D)
Kelleher, Herbert David (D)
Kelley, Oscar Lytle (D)
Kelly, Dee J. (D)
Kilgarlin, William Wayne (D)
Kilgore, Joe Madison (D)
Kilpatrick, Rufus Underwood (D)
Kimbrough, Lorraine M. (D)
King, Bill B. (R)
King, Mary Lois (R)
Kingsbery, John Russell (R)
Klattenhoff, William John (R)
Knaggs, John Ryan (R)
Knapp, Walter Lee, Jr. (D)
Knight, James Edward (R)
Kone, Sam L, Jr. (R)
Kothmann, Glenn Harold (D)
Krueger, Culp (D)
Kubiak, Dan (D)
Lavender, Robert M. (R)
Laxson, John H. (R)
Ledger, Lovett Lewis (D)
Lee, Bill H. (R)
Lee, Thomas J. (D)
Lee, William Ellsworth (R)
Leedom, John Nesbett (R)
Leissner, Martin William, Jr. (R)
Lemmon, Ray Allen (D)
Ligarde, Honore (D)
Little, Christopher Mark (D)
Locke, Eugene Murphy
Locke, Mrs. Eugene Murphy (D)
Logan, Bard A. (American Party)
Longoria, Raul L. (D)
Looney, James Cullen (D)
Lowe, Dorothy Erminie (R)
Luce, William Garrett (D)
Lynam, Marshall L. (D)
McAllen, Robert Ashley (D)
McAllister, Walter W, Sr.
McClaren, Howard Max (D)
McCrady, Bob (D)
McCready, Ellen Hausrath (R)
McCreary, Richard Edward, Jr. (R)
McCutchin, Pat Winston (R)
McDaniel, William Collin (D)
McDowell, Patrick Glenn, Jr. (D)
McFarlane, William D. (D)
McGee, William Sears (D)
McGuire, Marie Collins (D)
McIntosh, Carl Daniel (R)
McMullen, Mary Louise (D)
Mahon, George Herman (D)
Man, Barbara Smith (R)
Mann, Thomas Clifton (Independent)
Martin, Blanche Ruth (R)
Martin, Celia Hare (D)
Martin, Crawford Collins (D)
Martin, William Clyde (D)
Mask, William Glenn (R)
Mason, Clarence Edward (R)
Mauzy, Oscar Holcombe (D)
Mayborn, Frank Willis (D)
Mayer, Anita Engelking (D)
Mayor, James Miller (R)
Meinecke, Robert Lee (R)
Middleton, James Edward (D)
Milburn, Beryl Buckley (R)
Mills, Richard Coke, Jr. (D)
Mobley, John Allen (D)
Moffett, George Clarence (D)
Mogford, John L. (D)
Moon, Hiram A. (D)
Moore, Aubry Lee (D)
Moore, Jack Mitchell
Moore, Sydney Alton (R)
Moore, Thomas Griffith (D)
Moore, William Tyler (D)
Moorhead, Mrs. J. T. (R)
Morgan, Clyde Nathaniel (R)
Morgan, Jack Cochran (D)
Moss, Charles Holmes (D)
Moursund, Albert Wadel, III (D)
Mueller, Inez Lee (D)
Muniz, Raul (D)
Murphy, Ewell Edward, Sr. (D)
Murray, Menton Joseph (D)
Musgrove, Glenn Burke (D)
Musick, Virgil Lee (D)
Musslewhite, Charles Benton (D)
Mutscher, Gus Franklin (D)
Nabers, (Joseph) Lynn (D)
Napier, Donald Dudley, Jr. (R)
Negley, Nancy Brown (D)
Neumann, Frederick Sloan (R)
Nichols, Robert Cecil (D)
Nicolas, Toufic (D)
Nix, William Dale, Jr. (R)
Norsworthy, Isiah (D)
Norvell, James Rankin (D)
Nowlin, James Robertson (D)
O'Connor, Lawrence Joseph, Jr. (D)
O'Conor, Robert, Jr. (R)
O'Donnell, Peter, Jr. (R)
Ogg, Jack Clyde (D)
O'Hearn, Taylor Walters (R)
Orr, Freddie Ray (D)
Orr, James Weaver (R)
Orr, Roy Lee (D)
Outlaw, Nigle C. (D)
Palm, Nancy Dale (R)
Parker, Ben P. (D)
Parker, Carl Allen (D)
Parker, Harvie Allen (D)
Parker, L. L. Fox, Jr. (D)
Parker, Robert L. (R)
Parker, Walt E. (D)
Pate, Oscar Perry (D)
Patman, Wright (D)
Patterson, Charles Vaughan (D)
Patterson, Hugh Morris (D)
Pauken, Thomas Weir (R)
Paul, Herbert O. (D)
Pauly, Helen
Pearce, Paul Langston (R)
Pearson, Ray (D)
Penix, Chauncey Edward (D)
Pesek, Robert Joseph (D)
Phillips, Jimmy (D)
Phillips, Zeno Joseph (D)
Phinney, Carl L. (D)
Phinny, George Keil (R)
Pickard, Albert Marshall (R)

Pickens, Franklin Ace (D)
Pickle, J. J. (D)
Poage, William Robert (D)
Pope, Jack (D)
Porter, Albert (D)
Powell, Charles Caruth (D)
Powell, Edward Baker (R)
Presnal, Billy Charles (D)
Price, Robert Dale (R)
Price, (William) Rayford (D)
Purcell, Graham (D)
Putnam, Paul McQueen (R)
Quilliam, William Reed, Jr. (D)
Rather, Mary Alice (D)
Ratliff, David Wade (D)
Ray, Cread L, Jr. (D)
Ray, James R. (D)
Reavley, Thomas Morrow (D)
Rector, William Lee (R)
Reed, Ewell Richard (D)
Rees, Thomas L. (D)
Rhoden, Louis Allen (R)
Rhodes, George Fred (D)
Rich, Joe Lynn (D)
Richards, George Howe (D)
Richardson, Sam (D)
Roberts, Ray (D)
Roberts, Ronald E. (D)
Rodriguez, Antonio F. (R)
Roe, Charles G. (D)
Rogers, Andrew Jacob (D)
Rogers, Walter E. (D)
Rominger, James Corridon (R)
Rose, Howard Vance, Jr. (D)
Rosson, Renal B. (D)
Rostow, Walt Whitman (D)
Rozell, Franklin Russell (R)
Rummler, Joseph Manig (Constitution)
Salem, Joseph John (D)
Sammons, James Blaine (R)
Sanders, Harold Barefoot, Jr. (D)
Sandoval, Hilary Joseph, Jr. (R)
Sansom, Ernest Samuel (D)
Santiesteban, Humberto Tati (D)
Savage, Wallace Hamilton (D)
Sayers, Nancy J. (D)
Schiller, Milton Joe (D)
Schneider, Allan Ivan (R)
Schneider, Robert Allen (R)
Schreiber, John Paul (R)
Schroeder, Clarence Henry (R)
Schulz, Harry John (D)
Schumann, Merritt J. (R)
Schwartz, Aaron Robert (D)
Schwethelm, A. C. (D)
Scobee, Barry (D)
Scoggins, Ralph William (D)
Scott, Joseph Alexander (D)
Seale, Thomas Griswold (R)
Semos, Chris Victor (D)
Sessions, William Steele (R)
Shannon, Joe, Jr. (D)
Sharp, Dudley Crawford (R)
Shelton, Travis Duane (D)
Sheppard, L. E, Jr. (R)
Shivers, Allan (D)
Shollenbarger, Joseph Hiram (R)
Skelton, Byron George (D)
Smith, E. Arnold (D)
Smith, Forest Bowley (D)
Smith, Harry Clinton (D)
Smith, LeRoy Wilbur (D)
Smith, Lynn, Jr. (D)
Smith, Martha Aleene (R)
Smith, Perry Rowan (D)
Smith, Preston Earnest (D)
Smith, Will L. (D)
Smith, William Forrest (D)
Smith, Wini (R)
Snelson, W. E. (D)
Solis, Hilario Garcia (D)
Sowell, Polly Rollins (R)
Sparks, Sherman Paul (R)
Spears, Franklin Scott (D)
Steakley, Zollie Coffer, Jr. (D)
Steele, Newton J. (D)
Steger, William Merritt (R)
Stehling, Arthur (D)
Stewart, Richard Olin (R)
Stokes, John Myers (R)
Stovall, Reginald Morris (R)
Strauss, Robert S. (D)
Strauss, Teofil Nick (R)
Strong, Jack Boynton (D)
Stroud, James Ernest (R)
Stroud, James William (D)
Stumpf, Edward Adam, III (D)
Suits, Margaret Ann (R)
Tartt, Estelle Hurt (R)
Taylor, Sam Guthrie (D)
Teague, Olin E. (D)
Tedford, John Roy, Jr. (R)
Telles, Raymond
Thaxton, Richard Ray (R)
Thomason, Robert Ewing (D)
Thompson, Clark Wallace (D)
Thompson, Jimmy Eugene (D)
Thornberry, Jonathan Michael (D)
Thornberry, William Homer (D)
Thornton, Robert Ernest (D)
Tidwell, Jack Quinn (D)
Tinstman, Robert Mechling
Tittle, William Osborne (D)
Toft, Marjory Mayo (R)
Toler, James L. (D)
Tower, John Goodwin (R)
Towery, Roland Kenneth (R)
Townsend, James Terrell (D)
Traeger, John Andrew (D)
Traweek, Florence Irene (R)
Troxell, Richard Kimball (Constitution Party)
Truan, Carlos Flores (D)
Tunnell, Joe (D)
Tuttle, James (D)
Upham, Chester Robert, Jr. (R)
Vale, R. L. (D)
Valenti, Jack Joseph (D)
Varnon, Cliff Walter (D)
Vick, Gabe T. (D)
Vinson, Roy Furman (D)
Walker, Charles Ray (R)
Walker, Merle Royse, II (R)
Wallace, E. Howard (D)
Walton, Frank Edward (D)
Walton, James Neuman, Jr. (R)
Warren, John Fisken (R)
Watson, Ed Raymond (D)
Watson, Murray, Jr. (D)
Watson, William Marvin (D)
Wayne, Ralph E. (D)
Weber, Garry Allen (D)
Weber, O. J. (D)
Welch, Louie (D)
Weldon, Jimmie Dale (D)
West, Fowler Claud (D)
Westerholm, Leo Lyder (R)
Whatley, Willis (D)
Wheatley, Seagal V. (R)
White, Clarence Otho (D)
White, John Coyle (D)
White, Richard Crawford (D)
Whitfield, J. Charles, Jr. (D)
Wieting, Leroy James (D)
Wilkerson, Walter D, Jr. (R)
Willeford, George (R)
Williams, Floyd Bert (R)
Williams, Walter J. (D)
Willis, Doyle (D)
Wilson, Robert Izod (D)
Wingo, Cecil (D)
Witkowski, Leo Victor (D)
Wood, Clyde Norris (R)
Wood, Richard Glee (R)
Wooldridge, Harry Linn (D)
Word, James Powell (D)
Wright, James C. (D)
Wright, John Robert (D)
Wright, Sylvester Marilyn (D)
Wyly, Sam (R)
Wyman, Iris Juanita (D)
Wynn, Sproesser (R)
Yarborough, Ralph Webster (D)
Yarbrough, Joe Cone (D)
Young, John (D)
Young, Marion Webster (R)

UTAH

Abrams, Milton Charles (D)
Allen, C. Kay (D)
Allen, Golden L. (R)
Andersen, Hans Verlan (R)
Anderson, L. Robert (R)
Arbuckle, Robert M. (R) See Addenda
Astle, Orrin Wilford (R)
Atkin, Sidney Joseph (R)
Aycock, Kenneth R. (R)
Baker, Linn C. (D)
Barlow, Haven J. (R)
Barnett, Wilmer L. (R)
Bennett, Wallace Foster (R)
Benson, Ezra Taft (R)
Betenson, Glen (R)
Betenson, Scott Parker (D)
Bischoff, Douglas George (R)
Bittner, Frederick Warren (R)
Black, Wayne L. (D)
Bowden, Lawry J. (D)
Brady, Kenneth Anderson (R)
Bronson, Boyd Clinton (R)
Brough, Richard M. (R)
Brown, James Elmer (R)
Buckner, Elmer La Mar (R)
Buckway, Dallas Henry (D)
Buhler, Robert Earl (R)
Bullock, J. Robert (R)
Burton, Laurence Junior (R)
Call, Richard A. (R)
Callister, Louis H, Jr. (R)
Cannon, Ralph S. (R)
Cannon, T(homas) Quentin (R)
Carling, Richard Junius (R)
Clark, Ezra Thompson (R)
Clark, Nathaniel Douglas (D)
Cloward, McRay (D)
Clyde, George Dewey (R)
Collett, Byron Sylvester (R)
Conover, Eva W. (D)
Creer, John Preston (D)
Crockett, J. Allan
Dean, Ernest H. (D)
Dmitrich, Mike (D)
Duncan, David L. (D)
Ellett, Albert Hayden
Fairbanks, Madge H. (R)
Ferry, Miles Yeoman (R)
Finlinson, Fred Lyman (R)
Fisher, M. Byron (R)
Florence, Brian Rich (D)
Fonnesbeck, Verdun France (D)
Frandsen, Allen John (R)
Funk, Albert Gail (R)
Garff, Ken D. (R)
Gunnell, Franklin Wyatt (R)
Halverson, Ronald T. (R)
Hansen, Phil L. (D)
Harding, Ray Murray (R)
Harvey, David Christensen (D)
Harward, Royal Thomas (R)
Henderson, William H. (D)
Henriod, Frederic Henri (R)
Hill, James Dean (R)
Hinkins, Marilyn C. (D)
Hulbert, Gerald Erickson (D)
Humphrey, Isaac Bailey (D)
Inkley, Ronald Walter (R)
Ivins, Heber Grant (D)
Jiacoletti, Raymond N. (D)
Johnson, Minnie Bugg (D)
Jones, Lawrence Walter (R)
Judd, C. DeMont, Jr. (D)
Kaiser, Roland Glenn (R)
Klas, John Hall (D)
Knowlton, Franklin Whitesides (R)
Korologos, Tom Chris (R)
Lamb, Oliver Burnell (D)
Larsen, Sharp McCoy (D)
Leavitt, Dixie L. (R)
Lee, Joseph Bracken
Little, Madge Cram (D)
Lloyd, Sherman Parkinson (R)
Loveridge, Dilla Lisonbee (D)
Mace, Lee F. (D)
Mace, Shirley A. (D)
Macfarlane, M. James (D)
McKay, Koln Gunn (D)
Madsen, Alfred James (D)
Mangum, John Knight (R)
Marchant, Beatrice Alvaretta (D)
Maughan, Richard Johnson (D)
Mecham, Allan Elison (R)
Mecham, Leonidas Ralph (R)
Meikle, Kathleen Hurst (D)
Melich, Mitchell (R)
Midgley, Grant Winder (D)
Miller, Clyde L. (D)
Mitchell, J. Harold (R)
Monroe, Lamar Ralph (R)
Moss, Frank Edward (D)
Muhlestein, George (R)
Mulhall, Alla Nelson (D)
Nabors, Charles James, Jr. (D)
Nelson, Frank V. (R)
Nielson, Howard Curtis (R)
Oberhansley, Milly (D)
Olson, Kenneth C. (D)
Owens, Douglas Wayne (D)
Pace, Lorin Nelson (R)
Parry, John Waldo (D)
Peterson, M. Blaine (D)
Platt, James William (D)
Powell, Marion Lee (R)
Powell, Samuel Clarence (R)
Preece, Ralph Alma (R)
Rampton, Calvin Lewellyn (D)
Randall, Kenneth Alfred (R)
Rawlings, Calvin William (D)
Redd, John Packard (R)
Redd, Lucy (D)
Reece, Thomas Henry (D)
Regis, Larry, Jr. (D)
Renstrom, Darrell George (D)
Richards, Richard (R)
Romney, Janice Cahoon (R)
Romney, Vernon (R)
Sandack, A. Wally (D)
Savage, Leon H. (R)
Singleton, Samuel Morris (R)
Smith, John E. (D)
Sowards, Glade Milton (R)
Squire, Loren D. (D)
Stewart, Robert Potter (D)
Stockseth, Joseph O. (D)
Strike, John Louis (R)
Swenson, Jack Hughes (R)
Tebbs, Daniel A. (R)
Theurer, Gary Lloyd (R)
Thomas, Norma Giles (D)
Thomas, Robert C. (R)
Vance, Elizabeth Mary (D)
Waddingham, A. Thorpe (D)
Waldron, David Reeder (D)
Warnick, Robert William (R)
Watkins, Arthur Vivian (R)
Welch, Charles, Jr. (R)
Westwood, Jean Miles (D)
White, Beverly Jean (D)
Whiting, Harold Johnson (R)
Whittaker, Earl Horton (R)
Wilcox, Oma Ellison (R)
Wilde, Orvin Geral (D)
Wilkinson, Ernest LeRoy (R)
Willett, Douglas Warren (D)
Wirthlin, Madeline Bitner (R)
Wolbach, Robert Albert (D)
Wood, Freda B. (D)
Woodmansee, Gerald Louis (D)
Woolley, Naomi Rebecca (D)
Workman, Dale H. (R)
Wright, Fred Thornton (R)
Yardley, James Fredrick (R)
Zabriskie, Charles Vard (R)
Zupko, John Michael (D)

VERMONT

Adams, James H. (R)
Aiken, George David (R)
Alden, John Taylor (R)
Alexander, Doris Sears (R)
Anderson, Carl Alfred (R)
Angney, Allan B, Jr. (R)
Archambault, Lyle B. (D)
Arnold, Donald Speare (R)
Arthur, Allen Edward (D)
Babcock, Robert Shillingford
Bailey, Consuelo Northrop (R)
Baird, Rose D. (D)
Baker, Cleona Tatro (R)
Balke, Raymond E. (R)
Barnes, Ina F. (R)
Barry, Ray Henry, Sr. (D)
Bartholomew, Clyde (R)
Bates, Oren Warner (R)
Battles, George Herbert (R)
Battles, John Leo (D)
Bauer, Edith J. (R)
Bean, Candace M. E. (R)
Beaton, Franklyn George (R)
Beattie, Catherine M. (D)
Bedford, Henry Ward (R)
Bennett, Clinton Eugene (R)
Bentley, Charles Dyer, Jr. (R)
Bianchi, Carol Ann (R)
Billings, Franklin Swift, Jr. (R)
Billings, Harold Carlton (R)
Blachly, William (D)
Blake, Raymond (R)
Boardman, Robert Emmett (D)
Bongartz, Ferdinand A. (R)
Booth, Wallace Gordon (D)
Bove, Fiore Louis (D)
Boyce, Vaughan Field (R)
Brook, John Robert (R)
Brown, Earle V. (R)
Bryce, Olin S. (R)
Buckley, T. Garry (R)
Bullock, Elmer David (R)
Bunker, Ellsworth
Buraczynski, Anthony C. (D)
Burbank, Helen Elizabeth (R)
Burgess, John Stuart (R)
Burke, John Walter (R)
Burke, William J. (R)

Burnham, Dwight E, Sr. (R)
Burns, Brian Douglas (D)
Burns, William Thomas (R)
Cahoon, Paul Stacy (D)
Cain, Francis Joseph (D)
Cain, L. John (D)
Caracciola, Joseph John (R)
Carleton, William Henry (R)
Carlisle, Lilian Baker (D)
Carr, Harriet Louise (D)
Carrier, John T. (Independent R)
Carter, Harvey D, Jr. (R)
Chadwick, Otis Clifton (R)
Chadwick, Thomas Allen (R)
Choiniere, Ulric Emelien (D)
Christowe, Stoyan (R)
Cook, George Wallace Foster (R)
Cook, Henry Bushnell (R)
Cooke, Isabelle (D)
Cooley, Harry Hale (D)
Cooley, Reginald Gary (R)
Conlin, Edward Joseph (R)
Connarn, John Patrick (D)
Corbin, H. Ohmer (D)
Corley, Robert Townsend (R)
Costa, William Thomas, Jr. (D)
Coutermarsh, George Earl (D)
Coutts, Flora J. (R)
Crowe, Robert William (R)
Crowley, Arthur Edward, Jr. (R)
Crowley, Thomas M. (D)
Crowninshield, Hubert Brown (R)
Cutts, Royal Bartlett (R)
Dailey, Mildred Parker (D)
Daley, John J. (D)
Daniels, Robert Vincent (D)
Davis, Beth Olga (R)
Davis, Deane Chandler (R)
Davis, Frank H. (R)
Davis, Lee Murray (R)
DeBonis, Daniel Vincent, Jr. (D)
Delaney, Charles Lawrence (D)
Denny, Bradford Houston (R)
Desautels, Robert John (D)
Devereux, Reginald S. (D)
Doyle, Marjorie Poor (R)
Doyle, William Thompson (R)
Drake, Joan Edith (D)
Dubuque, Chester R. (D)
Dudley, L. Leland (R)
Dumas, J. Stewart (D)
Dunham, Marshall J. (D)
Eastman, Irving Willard (R)
Eastman, Lillian M. (R)
Eaton, Wendell Home (R)
Esposito, Francis James (D)
Eurich, Edward Richardson (R)
Evans, Henry Nelson (R)
Fair, Norman G. (D)
Farrington, Warren Arthur (R)
Field, Andrew Robert (R)
Field, James Arthur (R)
Fienberg, George Mitchel (D)
Finn, John Roderick (D)
Fisher, Josephine (D)
Fisher, Wilfred Joseph (D)
Fishman, Samuel William (D)
Fitzpatrick, Jerome M. (D)
Flanders, Ralph Edward (R)
Foley, Allen Richard (R)
Follett, Muriel (R)
Fontaine, Gerard Louis (R)
Foote, Ralph Albert (R)
Ford, Linwood Fred (R)
Foster, Bertha M. (R)
Foster, Howard Albert (R)
Foster, Roland Raymond (R)
Franco, Helen Morrie (D)
Franklin, Lawrence Elliot (R)
Free, Edwin Whitmore (R)
Fuller, Loren William (R)
Fuller, Wayne Clyde (R)
Gaiotti, Andrew John (Independent-D)
Gallagher, S. Renfrew (D)
Galli, Americo John (D)
Gauthier, Laurence William (R)
Gay, Olin Dow (R)
Gibb, Arthur (R)
Gibson, Charles Edward, Jr. (R)
Gibson, Ernest William (R)
Goodwin, Ernest E. (R)
Gordon, Jay H. (D)
Graf, Robert E. (R)
Graham, Lorraine Hunt (D)
Granai, Cornelius O. (R)
Gray, Carrie J. (R)
Greene, Charles Oland Haskell (D)
Greene, Merrill Kingsley (R)
Greenwood, Bernard (R)
Griffin, Frank J. (R)
Hackel, Donald H. (D)
Hackett, Luther Frederick (R)
Hamilton, George Henry (R)
Hammond, Margaret (R)
Harris, Merrill (R)
Harte, Helen C. (D)
Hartigan, Margaret (D)
Harwood, Madeline Bailey (R)
Hathorn, Byron C. (R)
Hayden, Mildred Mary (R)
Hayes, Thomas Lawlor (R)
Heaslip, George Joseph (R)
Heath, Ralph Lewis (R)
Hebard, Emory (R)
Heitman, Kathryn J. (R)
Hicks, Henry Nichols (Independent)
Hill, Arthur Ross (R)
Hinchey, Francis Nathaniel (D)
Hodgdon, S. Fox (R)
Hoff, Philip Henderson (D)
Hollister, William Hillman (D)
Houston, Neal J. (R)
Howe, Hugh Farnham (R)
Howrigan, James E. (D)
Hoyt, Herman E. (R)
Hunt, Arline Pat Brush (R)
Hunt, Lyman Curtis (R)
Hunter, William A. (D)
Hutchins, Frank A. (R)
Hutchinson, Warren Clark (R)
Hutt, Stanley Lowell (Independent)
Irish, Aaron D. (D)
Jackman, Lawrence McLam (R)
Janeway, Edward G. (R)
Jarvis, Arthur J. (R)
Jeffords, James Merrill (R)
Johnson, Constance Ada (R)
Johnson, Shirley Chase (R)
Jones, Arthur Henry (R)
Jones, Charlotte Thrall (R)
Jones, Elliott Vedder (R)
Jones, Lawrence Lawson (R)
Joseph, Peter Anthony (D)
Keenan, Madelyn Cahill (D)
Kehoe, Edward Franklin (D)
Kelley, Prescott C. (D)
Kellogg, Kenneth T. (R)
Kelton, Winifred Willena (R)
Kelty, John Edward (D)
Kennedy, James Norman (D)
Kennedy, Walter Lawrence (R)
Kenyon, Tracy Edmund, Jr. (R)
King, Robert Thomas (R)
Kingston, George J, Jr. (D)
Kitchel, Douglas Binney (R)
Ladeau, Christine Burbank (R)
Lafreniere, Bertha (R)
Landon, Alice Conant (R)
LaPlume, Loretta Graciella (D)
Lathrop, Clarence George (R)
Lawrence, George Roland (R)
Lawson, George (R)
Leavitt, Levi Dudley (R)
Loomis, Samuel R. (R)
Lounsbury, James William (D)
Lunderville, Howard P. (R)
McCandless, Clarence Hewitt (R)
McClaughry, John (R)
McCuin, Guy Luther (D)
McGregor, George R. J. (D)
McLam, Donald Clifford (R)
McMahon, Carlyle C. (D)
Mallary, Richard Walker (R)
Malloy, James Edward (D)
Mandigo, Melvin Harvey (R)
Mann, Daulton, Jr. (R)
Manning, Karl Raymond (D)
Manning, Madelyn C. (D)
Marcoux, Hector T. (D)
Marsh, Robert T, Sr. (R)
Martell, Arlene J. (D)
Masten, Leah Mae (R)
Maxham, Donald Howard (R)
May, Edgar
Mazan, Walter L. (R)
Mazza, Joseph M, Jr. (D)
Mehuron, Varnum R. (R)
Merola, Arthur Eugene (D)
Merriman, Russell Field (R)
Miller, Everett Howard (R)
Miner, Stanley Pingrey (R)
Montague, Harry Nichols (D)
Montague, Rupert James (R)
Mooney, Arthur Amos (R)
Morgan, Rufus Jay (R)
Morrison, Arthur Thomas (R)
Morse, George C. (R)
Morse, Muriel A. (D)
Mudgett, Galen Earl, Sr. (R)
Murphy, John Francis (D)
Murphy, Margaret Ansboro (D)
Myers, Daisy Loveland (R)
Nelson, T. Barden (R)
Newell, Graham Stiles (R)
Nolan, George Edward (D)
Oakes, James Lowell (R)
O'Brien, Daniel John (D)
O'Brien, John Joseph (D)
O'Brien, Leo, Jr. (D)
O'Dowd, George Edward (D)
Page, Sewell A. (D)
Page, Wayne Harold (R)
Parsons, Samuel A. (R)
Partch, Robert Frederick (R)
Partridge, Sanborn (R)
Paul, Edmund Laurence (D)
Paul, Madeline Rule (R)
Peet, Anson Walter (R)
Peisch, Francis Robert (R)
Pelkey, Frances Bailey (D)
Perry, Clarence Windfield (R)
Petit, Laurier Telesphore (R)
Pickard, Dwight A. (D)
Plante, Peter Paul (D)
Pratt, Levi B. (R)
Prouty, Winston L. (R)
Puffer, Erma E. (R)
Purdy, Ellery Redfield (R)
Putnam, Hollis James (R)
Quelch, Leslie H. (D)
Ranney, Zilpah Fay (R)
Raynolds, Harold, Jr. (D)
Rice, Doris Elizabeth (R)
Ridlon, Edgar M. (R)
Ridlon, George Henry (R)
Riley, John James (D)
Roberts, Grace Ester (R)
Robinson, Henry M. (R)
Roque, John B. (D)
Ross, Charles Robert
Rousse, Jeanne Laura (D)
Roy, Wendell P. (D)
Ruggles, Daniel B, III (R)
Russell, Harvey Potter (R)
Russell, Wallace Clayton, Sr. (R)
Ryan, William Joseph (D)
Sabens, Marshall T. (R)
Salmon, Thomas P. (D)
Sargeant, Marion Taylor (R)
Schmidt, Richard Huestis (D)
Schurman, Beatrice Redfield Parker (D)
Scott, Carl G. (D)
Selleck, Harold C. (R)
Seward, Roland Quincy (R)
Sharrow, Clement Charles (D)
Shattuck, Fay B. (R)
Shattuck, Paul Howard (R)
Shea, James D. (D)
Sholes, Russell George (R)
Silsby, Fannie J. (R)
Simpson, Wilder Arthur (R)
Smith, Cathleen Winsor (Independent)
Smith, Donald L. (R)
Smith, Edwin Angus (R)
Smith, Philip Lawrence (R)
Snelling, Richard Arkwright (R)
Spaulding, Emerson O. (R)
Stafford, Henry Alexander (R)
Stafford, Ralph E. (R)
Stafford, Robert T. (R)
Stahler, Herbert H. (R)
Starr, George Eddie (D)
Stebbins, Marguerite Ann (D)
Stiles, Frank O. (R)
Stone, Delbert James (R)
Stone, Floyd N. (R)
Stone, Harriet Reed (R)
Story, Clifton Martin (R)
Sykes, Mary Flanders (R)
Taylor, Howard Ezra (R)
Taylor, Myron Charles (R)
Thomas, Eustace Kirk (D)
Thomas, Richard Clark (R)
Thompson, Robert Moody (R)
Thurber, Mary D. (R)
Tomasi, Lawrence James (D)
Towne, Carroll Edmund (R)
Trepanier, Albert Edward (D)
Tuttle, Vivian Gilman (R)
Vaillancourt, Eugene (D)
Valsangiacomo, Oreste Victor (D)
Van Bree, Ivan (R)
Van Santvoord, George (D)
Veghte, Henry, Jr. (R)
Viens, Noel David (D)
Walsh, Basil Barry (R)
Ward, Aline Frances (R)
Ware, George Church (R)
Warner, Seth Willmarth (R)
Webb, Derick V. (R)
Webster, Roland H. (D)
Weed, Marion (R)
West, Robert Edward (R)
Wheatley, Walter Henry (R)
Wheeler, Alton Grover (R)
Whitaker, Harold W. (R)
Whitehill, Grace Elfreda (R)
Wilcock, Fred (R)
Williams, Arthur Foster (R)
Wilson, Frank G. (R)
Wilson, L. Earle (D)
Wilson, Robert Edward (R)
Wilson, Robert Mason (D)
Winslow, Eugene Clinton (D)
Wiquest, Walter William (D)
Woodward, Roy Smith (R)
Wright, William L. (D)
Yeaw, Earl Frank (R)
Zampieri, John James (D)

VIRGINIA

Abbitt, Watkins Moorman (D)
Aldhizer, George Statton, II (D)
Alexander, Joseph (D)
Allen, George Edward, Jr. (D)
Almond, James Lindsay, Jr. (D)
Ames, Edward Almer, Jr. (D)
Anderson, Bernard McNeil (D)
Anderson, George Banister (D)
Anderson, Howard Palmer (D)
Anderson, Matthew Garland (D)
Anderson, Willis Martin (D)
Andrews, Erin Webster (R)
Andrews, Hunter Booker (D)
Andrews, Thomas Coleman, Jr. (American Party)
Applegate, Albert Augustus (R)
Archer, Floy Evelyn (R)
Arey, Donald Lurton (R)
Arundel, Arthur Windsor (D)
Bacon, Edgar (D)
Bagley, Richard Marshall (D)
Bain, Carl Edgar (R)
Baker, Inez De Graw (D)
Baker, Keith Glosson (D)
Baker, Robert Donald (R)
Baldwin, Robert Frederick (D)
Barco, James William
Barger, Hazel Kathleen (R)
Barnes, George Francis (R)
Baroody, William J, Jr. (R)
Baroody, William Joseph (R)
Bateman, Fred W. (D)
Bateman, Herbert Harvell (D)
Battle, William Cullen (D)
Baxley, Henry L. (D)
Beasley, John Gerald (D)
Bedsaul, E. Clifford (R)
BeLieu, Kenneth Eugene
Bell, Corrie Lee (D)
Bemiss, Fitzgerald (D)
Bender, H. G. Tom (D)
Bendheim, Leroy S. (D)
Bergman, Patricia Zoe (D)
Bird, Daniel Woodrow (D)
Bird, Lloyd Campbell (D)
Birkhead, Kenneth Milton (D)
Bishop, Robert Granville (R)
Black, Hugo LaFayette
Blandford, John Russell (R)
Boehlert, Sherwood Louis (R)
Bolling, Brantley Lamberd (D)
Bolling, Cecil Winton (R)
Boothe, Armistead Lloyd (D)
Boren, James Harlan (D)
Bosone, Reva Beck (D)
Bradley, Wayne W. (R)
Bradshaw, Junie Leroy (D)
Brand, Edward Cabell (D)
Brault, Adelard Lionel (D)
Brawley, Hiram Wilks (D)
Breeden, Edward L, Jr. (D)
Brehm, William Keith
Brinkley, Arthur Sumner, Jr. (R)
Brown, Larry Robert (R)
Brown, Stuart Ellett, Jr. (D)
Broyhill, Joel T. (R)
Bryan, Stanley Gatewood (D)
Buford, Robert Pegram (R)
Burch, Katheryne Peregoy (D)
Burgess, Bradley Fleet (R)
Burkhardt, Dorothy Jean (R)
Burnett, Benifield (R)

Burruss, Robert S, Jr. (R)
Butler, Charles Frederick (R)
Butler, Manley Caldwell (R)
Button, Robert Young (D)
Butzner, John Decker, Jr.
Byrd, Harry Flood, Jr. (D)
Byroade, Henry A.
Callahan, Vincent Francis, Jr. (R)
Campbell, Archibald Algernon (D)
Campbell, Leslie Dunlop, Jr. (D)
Canaday, Alyce D.
Cantrell, Orby Lee (D)
Carlson, Jack Wilson
Carneal, George Upshur, Jr. (R)
Carneal, Russell Morris (D)
Carpenter, Samuel Emlen, III (R)
Carr, Delman R. (R)
Carter, Charles Hill, Jr. (D)
Caton, Edward T, III (Ned) (D)
Cephas, B. Addison, Jr. (D)
Charlton, Thomas Jackson (R)
Cherkasky, Shirley Evelyn (D)
Clapp, Norman Moses (D)
Clark, Kimball (D)
Clark, Robert Lybrook (D)
Cleaton, C. William (D)
Coakley, Richard Walker (R)
Coerr, Wymberley DeRenne (Independent)
Cohen, Bernard S. (D)
Cohen, Edwin Samuel (R)
Coleman, John Patrick (D)
Collins, Copp (R)
Collins, Michael McHale (D)
Conway, Martha Bell (D)
Cooke, John Warren (D)
Cooley, Raleigh Minor (D)
Coppedge, Cecil Robert (R)
Corber, Robert Jack (R)
Coulter, Raymond Curtis (R)
Counts, Thelma Evelyn (D)
Cowherd, Roderick Grymes (D)
Cox, Lawrence Morgan (Independent)
Crane, Robert Dickson (R)
Credle, Lola Fish (D)
Creel, George (R)
Cresswell, William Ephraim (D)
Croasdale, Carl Palmer (R)
Crowe, Morrill Martin
Culverhouse, Edgar Allen (D)
Curry, Richard Charles (R)
Dalton, Grady William (D)
Dalton, John Nichols (R)
Daniel, John Hannah (D)
Daniel, Wilbur Clarence (D)
Darden, Colgate Whitehead, Jr. (D)
Davis, Isaac Dabney (D)
Davis, James Woods (D)
Davis, Kenneth E. (R)
Davis, Russell Lewis (R)
Dawbarn, Henry Dunlop (R)
Day, James MacDonald (R)
DeBruhl, Garry Glenn (D)
Dell, Marie Hackney (D)
Dell, Robert Allen (R)
Dervishian, Harold H. (D)
Diamonstein, Alan Arnold (D)
Dickson, Wallace Gordon (D)
Dillard, Benton Oscar (D)
Disston, Harry (R)
Dobyns, Norman Lester (D)
Dollard, Louise Frederikke Charlotte (D)
Doolin, Dennis James (D)
Dotson, Bobby Joe (R)
Doumar, Robert George (R)
Downing, Thomas N. (D)
Driver, William Joseph (D)
Dudley, William McGarvey (D)
Durland, William R. (D)
DuVal, Clive, II (D)
Earman, Don E. (R)
Eastham, Thomas Granville (D)
Eastwood, James Randolph (D)
Echols, M. Patton, Jr. (R)
Eddins, Angus N. (R)
Edwards, Horace Hall (D)
Ehrlichman, John Daniel (R)
Elliott, Walter Carlton (D)
Emory, Samuel Thomas, Jr. (R)
Evans, John Marion (R)
Farley, Guy O, Jr. (D)
Fears, William Earl (D)
Fern, Benjamin R.
Fidler, Walther Balderson (D)
Field, John A, III (R)
Fine, Morris Heller (R)
Fisher, Joseph Lyman (Independent)

Fitzgerald, Robert Clayton (D)
Flemming, Harry S. (R)
Fletcher, James William (D)
Fletcher, W. Fred (D)
Forrester, E. Stewart (R)
Fowler, Henry Hamill (D)
Franzen, Richard S. (D)
Freburg, Charles Raymond (R)
Friedheim, Jerry Warden (R)
Fritter, Lindbergh Alexander (R)
Frost, Thomas Newton (D)
Fugate, James Boyd (D)
Funkhouser, Donald Kagey (R)
Galbraith, James Ronald (R)
Gallagher, Harold Milton (R)
Galland, Marion Gibbs (D)
Galleher, John (D)
Gambill, Walter Ray (R)
Garland, Ray Lucian (R)
Garrett, Ernest G, Jr. (D)
Gartner, David G. (D)
Gary, J. Vaughan (D)
Gehman, Earl W. (R)
Gehrig, James Joseph (D)
Geisler, Jerry Hubert (R)
Gentry, Richard Hayden (R)
Gibson, Donald Bancroft (D)
Gibson, Robert Edward (D)
Giesen, Arthur Rossa, Jr. (R)
Gifford, William Leo (R)
Gillilland, Whitney (R)
Gimer, Richard Harl (R)
Gladding, Harry Tilden, Jr. (R)
Glass, Thomas Reakirt (D)
Glenn, Robert Eastwood (R)
Godsey, Andrew Emmett (D)
Godwin, Mills Edwin, Jr. (D)
Goode, Virgil H. (D)
Graff, John Robert (R)
Graham, William M. (D)
Gray, Frederick Thomas (D)
Gray, Garland (D)
Gray, John David (D)
Green, Braxton (R)
Gregory, Howard Evans (R)
Gregson, Mary Poage (R)
Griffin, Oscar O'Neal, Jr. (R)
Guest, Raymond R. (D)
Gunn, Charles Wesley, Jr. (D)
Gurley, William Arthur, Jr. (D)
Gwathmey, Robert Ryland, III (D)
Gwyn, Rush Crockett, Jr. (D)
Habenicht, Robert Julius
Hagen, John William (R)
Haggerty, Kenneth M. (R)
Hall, Lewis Harvey, Jr. (D)
Hall, Virginia McDaniel (D)
Hamner, James L. (D)
Hancock, Clara C. (R)
Harding, Kenneth R. (D)
Harding, Margaret Katherine (D)
Hardy, Porter (D)
Harrison, Albertis Sydney, Jr. (D)
Harrison, Burr Powell (D)
Harrison, Gordon F. (D)
Harrison, Joseph Wylie (R)
Haywood, Isaac Henry (D)
Heartwell, Henry Lightfoot (D)
Hecht, Christine Sigrid (D)
Heflin, Dan Hugh, Jr. (R)
Helms, James Marvin, Jr. (R)
Henshaw, Edmund Lee, Jr. (D)
Heritage, John Maull (D)
Heslin, Helen Elaine (D)
Hess, James Douglas (R)
Heterick, Robert Cary, Jr. (R)
Hettrich, E. Daniel, Jr. (R)
Higgins, Mary Claire (R)
Hill, George Howard (D)
Hirst, Omer Lee (D)
Hodges, William Howard (D)
Holden, Dorothy Almond (D)
Holley, Thomas Phillip (R)
Hoover, Lawrence Harold (D)
Hopkins, William Benjamin (D)
Horne, Rufus Lee (R)
Howell, Henry Evans, Jr. (D)
Huddleston, George, Jr. (D)
Hudgins, Edward Morton (D)
Huffman, Donald Wise (R)
Hutchens, Charles Kunkle (D)
Hutcherson, Nathan B, Jr. (D)
Hutcheson, John Young (D)
Hyatt, Donald M. (D)
James, L. Eldon (D)
Jennings, William Pat (D)
Johnson, Augustus Clark (D)
Johnson, Joseph Pickett, Jr. (D)
Johnston, Ray S. (DFL)
Jones, James Ellyson (D)

Jones, Lewis (D)
Jones, Virgil Carrington (D)
Jurich, Anthony J. (R)
Kay, Thomas Oliver (R)
Kellam, Sidney Severn (D)
Kellam, William Page (D)
Kent, James Calvin (R)
Kincer, Rupert Neal (R)
Kinney, David B. (D)
Knott, Lawson B, Jr. (D)
Kostel, George James (D)
Kostopulos, Nick Peter (D)
Krout, Homer Lee (R)
Kuykendall, Jerome Kenneth (R)
Lambert, William Chesley (R)
Lane, Edward E. (D)
Langley, Lawrence Desales (D)
Lantz, Betty L. (R)
LaPlante, Bryan Franklin (R)
Largent, Flournoy Leonard, Jr. (D)
Leake, John Grey (D)
Leddy, John M (D)
Legate, A. B. Virkler (R)
Lehtonen, Alfred John (R)
LeKander, Gilbert (R)
Lemmon, Willard Lincoln (D)
Levin, Bernard (D)
Lewis, Roger Keith (D)
Lightsey, William Marion (D)
Lisk, David Kenneth (R)
Long, Macon Melville (D)
Loomis, Henry (Independent)
Loring, Murray (D)
Lowance, Carter Olin (D)
Ludden, Barbara Ann Harrison (R)
Lustig, Wayne (R)
Lykens, Ronald Everett (R)
Lynch, Alice Clarke (R)
Lyon, Carl Vernon (R)
McCall, John Robert (R)
McCormick, Robert L. L. (R)
McCoy, Rufus V, Sr. (Independent)
McCoy, Rufus V, Jr. (R)
McCue, Edward Overton, Jr. (D)
McCullough, Roland Alexander (R)
McCutcheon, Andrew H, Jr. (D)
McDiarmid, Dorothy Shoemaker (D)
McGhee, George Crews
McIvor, James Christopher (R)
McKee, William F.
McLucas, John L. (R)
McMath, George Nottingham (D)
McMurran, Lewis Archer, Jr. (D)
McReynolds, Leah Nielsen (R)
Mahoney, John Francis (D)
Manasco, Carter (D)
Mann, C. Harrison, Jr. (D)
Manns, Paul W. (D)
Marks, Charles Hardaway (D)
Marsh, John O. (D)
Marshall, Mary Aydelotte (D)
Marshall, Thurgood
Martin, Roy Butler, Jr. (D)
Marton, Larry Bruce (D)
Mason, Julien J. (D)
Mathisen, Chris (D)
Matus, Margaret Anna (D)
May, Clarence Edward (D)
Menaker, Edward Goward (D)
Mercuro, Tobia Gustave (R)
Michael, James Harry, Jr. (D)
Middleton, B. R. (D)
Middleton, Jack Lucas (R)
Middleton, Richard Hoxie (R)
Miller, Herbert Sidney (D)
Miller, Melvin M. (R)
Milstead, George L. (D)
Mogan, V. Devon (R)
Moncure, William Irby (D)
Montague, David Nicholls (R)
Moody, Willard James (D)
Moore, E. Blackburn (D)
Moore, Garnett St. Clair (D)
Moore, James Russell (R)
Moot, Robert C. (D)
Morris, Eugene, Jr. (R)
Morrison, Theodore V, Jr. (D)
Moss, Thomas Warren, Jr. (D)
Munsey, Everard (D)
Murphy, Rupert Leo
Murray, Thad S. (D)
Neblett, William Edwin (D)
New, Harry E. (R)
Newman, Cynthia Stair (R)
Newton, Blake Tyler (D)
Nicholas, Harry K. (R)
Nutter, G. Warren (R)
Obenshain, Richard Dudley (R)

Oberdorfer, Louis F. (D)
Olson, Donald Wayne (R)
Omohundro, Baxter Harrison (R)
O'Neal, Dudley Lee, Jr. (D)
Osborne, Julian Hanmer (D)
Owens, Stanley Albert (D)
Painter, James Medford (R)
Palmby, Clarence Donald (R)
Parker, Robert Elliott, Jr. (D)
Parkerson, William Francis, Jr. (D)
Patterson, Earl Edgar (R)
Pattisall, Richard Chapman (D)
Patton, Claude Herbert (R)
Paul, John Abbott (R)
Paxson, C. Armonde (D)
Payne, Nancy Kent (R)
Pearson, Henry Clyde (R)
Pendergraft, Phyllis M. (R)
Pendleton, Donald Grey (D)
Pendleton, Eugene Barbour, Jr. (D)
Pennington, William Alton (D)
Perry, Randolph Hope (D)
Phillips, Charles Franklin, Jr. (R)
Phillips, Lucas D. (D)
Philpott, Albert Lee (D)
Phipps, Alger Miller (R)
Pickens, John Kenneth (D)
Plante, Charles Larry (D)
Poff, Richard H. (R)
Poindexter, Gordon Wallace, Jr. (R)
Pointer, James Edgar, Jr. (D)
Pollard, Fred G. (D)
Pollard, Violet McDougall (D)
Pope, Samuel Eliba (D)
Porter, Annabelle Cunningham (R)
Potter, Irwin Lee (R)
Powell, Martha Brown (R)
Preece, Cecil H. (R)
Puhan, Alfred
Purcell, Harold Hidmore (D)
Puryear, Byron Nelson (D)
Putney, Lacey Edward (D)
Raines, Willie E. (D)
Ranson, Samuel Lee (R)
Rawlings, George Chancellor, Jr. (D)
Rawlings, William Vincent (D)
Rawls, John Lewis, Jr. (D)
Reede, William Saint Elmo (D)
Reiber, Paul (D)
Reid, Joseph Brackett (D)
Rettgers, Forrest Ithamar (D)
Reynolds, Julian Sargeant (D)
Rhodes, Fred Burnett (R)
Rice, Walter Lyman (R)
Richardson, Arthur Harris (D)
Richardson, John, Jr. (R)
Riddleberger, James W.
Roberts, James Walker (D)
Robertson, A. Willis (D)
Robertson, John Harte (R)
Robinson, James Kenneth (R)
Roller, O. Beverley (R)
Rose, Kathleen Blount (R)
Rosen, Judith Miriam (D)
Ross, William B.
Rowland, John Patrick (R)
Rustad, Elmer Lewis (R)
Sacks, Stanley Elliott (D)
Salvetti, Lloyd Donald (Independent)
Sanders, Donald Gilbert (D)
Santarelli, Donald Eugene (R)
Satterfield, David E, III (D)
Sayre, Robert Marion
Schleicker, James Gerard (D)
Scott, William L. (R)
Sears, John Raymond, Jr. (D)
Sharood, Richard Newell (R)
Sheppard, Eleanor Parker (D)
Shuey, Ruth Murphy (D)
Shufflebarger, Thomas Garnett (D)
Shultz, George P.
Shuman, Howard E. (D)
Sieminski, Alfred D. (D)
Simpson, Ray Chapman (D)
Singer, Ruth (D)
Slate, Harold Edwin (R)
Slaughter, Daniel French, Jr. (D)
Smalley, Robert Manning (R)
Smith, Claude Harman (R)
Smith, George Payne, Jr. (D)
Smith, Howard Worth (D)
Smith, Richard Maclin (D)
Smith, William Roy (D)
Smyth, John R. (R)

Speer, Keith Dempsey (D)
Spessard, Robert Woods (D)
Spivak, Alvin A. (D)
Spong, William Belser, Jr. (D)
Stafford, Chester Jefferson (D)
Stant, Frederick Thomas, Jr. (D)
Stephens, Vern (R)
Stokes, Diana Johnson (R)
Stoller, Murray Arthur (D)
Stone, William Francis (D)
Straughan, Nile (R)
Strauss, Lewis Lichtenstein (R)
Street, Tommy H. (D)
Stuart, Edward, Jr. (Conservative)
Stuckey, John M, Jr. (R)
Sullivan, Richard Joseph (D)
Sutton, Trible Dix (D)
Swiger, Joe Edward (R)
Switzer, Mary Elizabeth
Thomas, Alfred Victor (D)
Thomas, Nelson Edison (D)
Thomas, William Franklin, Jr. (D)
Thompson, John Roger (R)
Thompson, Lawrence Russell (D)
Thompson, R. Burnett, Jr. (R)
Thompson, William Carrington (D)
Thomson, James McIlhany (D)
Thweat, Theodore Oliver (D)
Tingler, Andrew Jackson (D)
Townes, Clarence Lee, Jr. (R)
Traylor, Lawrence Milton (R)
Tuck, Weldon Walter (R)
Tuck, William Munford (D)
Turk, James Clinton (R)
Tuten, James Russell (D)
Underwood, Malcolm Stanley, Jr. (R)
Urbanske, Leo, Jr. (D)
Van Clief, Daniel Good (D)
Vaughn, Jack Hood
Verkler, Jerry Thomas (D)
Walker, Stanley Clay (D)
Wall, H. Ewing (D)
Walters, Johnnie McKeiver (R)
Wampler, William Creed (R)
Ward, Charles Leland (D)
Warner, John William (R)
Warren, George Marvin, Jr. (D)
Warriner, D. Dortch (R)
Watkins, William Forbes, Jr. (D)
Watson, William Abner, Jr. (D)
Weaver, James D. (R)
Webber, Frederick Leroy (R)
Welsh, Edward Cristy (D)
Welsh, William Brownlee (D)
Wev, Oscar C. B. (R)
White, Joshua Warren, Jr. (D)
White, Pressley Byrne (D)
Whitehead, William Scholl (R)
Whitehurst, George William (R)
Wiggins, Warren William (D)
Willey, Edward Eugene (D)
Williams, Carrington (D)
Williams, Glen Morgan (R)
Williams, Henry Lee (R)
Wilson, Irl Donaker (D)
Wyatt, Landon Russell (D)
Yates, Glenn, Jr. (D)

WASHINGTON

Adams, Alfred O. (R)
Adams, Brockman (D)
Adams, Wayne Melvin (R)
Ahlquist, Hugo Maurice (R)
Albright, Albion D. (D)
Anderson, Eric O. (D)
Anderson, Gwen Adele (R)
Archer, Arden Frank, Jr. (R)
Armijo, Rosalio (D)
Atkinson, Dorothy Wright (D)
Atteberry, James R. (R)
Atwood, Roy Franklin, Jr. (R)
Austin, Russell Anderson, Jr. (R)
Avey, Art (D)
Backstrom, Henry (D)
Bagnariol, John A. (D)
Bailey, Robert C. (D)
Bansmer, Gustav (D)
Beck, Clifford Wallace (D)
Bedrossian, Robert Haig (R)
Benitz, Max Edward (R)
Berentson, Duane (R)
Bergh, Arnie (D)
Bledsoe, Stewart (R)
Bluechel, Alan J. (R)
Bottiger, R. Ted (D)
Bozarth, Horace W. (D)
Brachtenbach, Robert F. (R)
Braman, James D'orma (R)
Branch, Kenneth Gordon (D)
Brazier, Donald Hay, Jr. (R)
Brouillet, Frank B. (D)
Brown, Donald MacRae (D)
Bryan, Robert Jensen
Buckridge, Marilyn L. (D)
Burtch, Jack Lee (D)
Cafferty, Michael J. (D)
Campbell, Donald G. (R)
Canfield, Damon R. (R)
Ceccarelli, David Paul (D)
Chapin, Richard U. (R)
Charette, Robert L. (D)
Chase, Anthony Goodwin (R)
Chatalas, William (D)
Cherberg, John Andrew (D)
Christensen, William Patterson, Jr. (D)
Chytil, Joe (R)
Clark, Newman H. (R)
Clinton, Gordon Stanley (R)
Clocksin, Virginia Teitzel (R)
Cochrane, Gordon Swain (D)
Cochrane, James Gordon (D)
Cochrane, Pat (D)
Coffee, John Main (D)
Cole, Bert L. (D)
Cone, Charles W. (D)
Conner, Paul H. (D)
Connor, Frank Timothy (D)
Cooley, Florence H. (D)
Cooney, John L. (D)
Cooper, Frances Throckmorton (R)
Cooper, Frank E. (R)
Copeland, Thomas L. (R)
Cowen, David Charles (D)
Cox, Kenneth Allen (D)
Cunningham, Norwood (R)
Dahl, Allen W. (R)
Day, William S. (D)
De Jarnatt, Arlie U. (D)
DeLeo, James Anthony (D)
Derzai, Amy Ruth (D)
Dewitty, Thelma (D)
Dill, Clarence C. (D)
Donohue, Dewey C. (D)
Donohue, Hubert Francis (D)
Dootson, Jack (D)
Dore, Fred H. (D)
Douglas, William Orville (D)
Duffeck, Frank Gustav (R)
Durkan, Martin James (D)
Earley, Robert Gray (R)
Eberle, Robert Dean (R)
Edmondson, Betty Lavern (R)
Einhaus, Lyle L. (R)
Elder, Hayes (D)
Eldridge, Don D. (R)
Eliassen, Herb O. (R)
Elicker, Charles William (R)
Ellis, Dean D. (R)
England, Jack (R)
Epton, Kathryn (D)
Erickson, Wayne Curtis (R)
Evans, C. E.
Evans, Daniel Jackson (R)
Farr, Caswell James (R)
Faulk, Lawrence John (R)
Flaherty, Virginia Chatfield (R)
Flanagan, Sid (R)
Fletcher, Arthur Allen (R)
Foley, Frank W. (D)
Foley, Thomas Stephen (D)
Fortson, Eleanor Ann (D)
Fosseen, Neal Randolph (Independent)
Fowler, James Faulkner (R)
Francis, Peter David (D)
Freeman, LeRoy Homer (D)
Freise, Herbert H. (R)
Fullmer, Donald K. (R)
Funke, Diane Trew (R)
Gallagher, Michael J. (D)
Gallagher, P. J. (D)
Gardner, Lloyd H. (R)
Garrett, Avery (D)
Giersdorf, J. Robert (D)
Gissberg, William A. (D)
Gladder, Carlton Arthur (R)
Gluck, Joseph (D)
Goetz, Myra Gamburg (D)
Goetz, Robert Lynwood (R)
Goldsworthy, Robert F. (R)
Gorton, Slade (R)
Graham, Lloyd Kenneth (D)
Graham, Robert Vincent (D)
Grant, Gary S. (D)
Greive, R. R. (D)
Griffith, Robert R. (D)
Grinstein, Gerald Bates (D)
Guess, Sam C. (R)
Gunn, George, Jr. (R)
Hansen, Julia Butler (D)
Hansen, Reed Robert (D)
Harris, Edward F. (R)
Hawley, Dwight Spencer (R)
Haydon, John M.
Heater, Elliott Vermont, Jr. (R)
Henry, Al (D)
Herr, Gordon (D)
Herrmann, Karl V. (D)
Hicks, Floyd V. (D)
Hoggins, Dale Edwin (R)
Holt, W. Stull (D)
Hood, Jack C. (R)
Hughes, Robert E. (R)
Humiston, Homer (R)
Huntley, Elmer C. (R)
Hurley, Mrs. Joseph E. (D)
Jackson, Henry M. (D)
Jacobs, William Clyde (R)
Jansen, Leonard Francis (D)
Jastad, Elmer (D)
Johnson, C. Montgomery (R)
Johnson, Doris J. (D)
Johnson, Ernest Raymond (D)
Johnson, Marco (R)
Johnston, Elmer E. (R)
Jolly, Dan (D)
Jones, J. L. (D)
Jones, Lawrence Michael (New Party)
Judd, Walter Henry (R)
Jueling, Helmut L. (R)
Kalich, Hugh Edward (D)
Kearney, John Peters (D)
Keefe, James Edward (D)
Keller, Frank L. (D)
Kilbury, Charles Debriel (D)
King, Chet (D)
King, Marjorie Pitter (D)
King, Richard Arthur (D)
Kink, Dick J. (D)
Kirk, Gladys (R)
Klein, William C. (D)
Knievel, Anton John, III (R)
Knoblauch, Reuben A. (D)
Kramer, A. Ludlow, III (R)
Kuehnle, James Paul (R)
Kull, Robert R. (D)
Kupka, George (D)
Langen, Charles Edward (D)
Lapham, Harry Houston, Jr. (R)
Larsen, John J. (R)
Leland, Alfred E. (R)
Lewis, Brian John (R)
Lewis, Harry B. (R)
Lickar, John Ivan (D)
Lindjord, Haakon
Litchman, Mark, Jr. (D)
Livingston, Delila Elizabeth (R)
Lynch, Marjorie W. (R)
McCaffree, Mary Ellen (R)
McCarthy, Thomas Carrell (D)
McCormack, C. G. (D)
McCormick, W. L. (D)
McCutcheon, John T. (D)
McDougall, Robert Duncan (R)
McGregor, Nancy Rohwer (R)
McKenzie, William Irving (D)
Mackey, Ralph Earle (R)
McMillan, David E. (D)
McRae, John Hector (D)
Madden, Mary Ann (D)
Magnuson, Donald Hammer (D)
Magnuson, Warren G. (D)
Mahaffey, Audley F. (R)
Maloney, Thomas M. (D)
Mann, Ronald M. (R)
Mardesich, August P. (D)
Marsh, Daniel G. (D)
Martinis, John Anthony (D)
Marzano, Frank G. (D)
Mathews, Laurence Carroll (D)
May, Catherine Barnes (R)
May, William J. S. (D)
Meadowcroft, William Howarth (R)
Meeds, Lloyd (D)
Mentor, Joseph Perrine (R)
Metcalf, Jack Holace (R)
Mickelson, Bob J. (D)
Miller, Henry A. (R)
Miller, Weston Walters (R)
Mitchell, Hugh Burnton (D)
Moon, Charles (D)
Moore, C. Robert
Moos, Donald William (R)
Morgan, Frances Haddon (D)
Morgen, Gladys H. (D)
Moriarty, Charles Patrick, Jr. (R)
Morphis, Richard W. (R)
Morrison, Sid (R)
Morrison, Zelma Reeves (D)
Neill, Marshall A(llen)
Nelson, Helen M. (R)
Nelson, Norman Bernard (D)
Newhouse, Irving (R)
Newschwander, Charles E. (R)
Nuckolls, Kenneth Russell (R)
O'Brien, John L. (D)
O'Connell, John James (D)
Odegaard, Gary Martin (D)
Odell, Charles (R)
O'Dell, Robert W. (R)
Olsen, Ray (D)
Olson, Gary Miles (R)
Pelly, Thomas Minor (R)
Penfield, James Kedzie
Perry, Robert A. (D)
Peterson, Lowell (D)
Peterson, Ted G. (R)
Petrich, John A. (D)
Pithoud, Naida (R)
Pitt, Richard Lewis (D)
Pollard, William Donald (D)
Pranger, Robert John (Independent)
Prince, Eugene Augustus (R)
Pritchard, Joel M. (R)
Quast, Werner Carl (R)
Radcliffe, W. O. E. (D)
Rasmussen, A. L. (D)
Raugust, William C. (R)
Redmon, Fred G. (R)
Regan, Kathryn Delima (R)
Reynolds, Alma Ebright (R)
Richardson, Gordon W. (R)
Ridder, Robert Carl (D)
Riley, Edward Francis (D)
Ristuben, Peter J. (D)
Ritner, Roy R. (D)
Rodgers, David H. (R)
Rogers, Jack Henry (D)
Rosellini, Albert D. (D)
Rosellini, Evelyn Elizabeth (D)
Rowlands, David D.
Ruble, James D, Jr. (D)
Rustom, R. M. (R)
Ryder, John N. (R)
Ryherd, James Michael (D)
Saari, Ruth Desiree (D)
Saling, Gerald L. (R)
Sandison, Gordon (D)
Savage, Charles R. (D)
Sawyer, Leonard Alson (D)
Sax, Sarah Ellen (R)
Schaefer, Robert (D)
Schuchman, Winifred Guthrie (D)
Scott, George William (R)
Sheffield, William J. (D)
Shell, Roger Max (D)
Sheridan, George P. (D)
Shrum, William Paul (R)
Slagle, Frank (D)
Smith, Dean Conrad (R)
Smith, Samuel J. (D)
Snyder, Sidney R. (D)
Sparks, Donn Everett (R)
Spracher, Dwight (D)
Sprague, David Gorton (D)
Stender, John H. (R)
Stephens, Ronald LeMoyne (R)
Stevenson, Mary H. (R)
Stout, George R. (D)
Stripp, Jane Dearborn (R)
Sullivan, John Raymond (D)
Swayze, Frances G. (R)
Swayze, Thomas Allen, Jr. (R)
Swick, Frank H. (D)
Swift, Allan Byron (D)
Talley, Don L. (D)
Taplin, Ben F. (D)
Taylor, Richard (D)
Thompson, Alan (D)
Thompson, Albert C, Jr. (R)
Timm, Robert Dale (R)
Tollefson, Thor Carl (R)
Tracy, William Allan (D)
Trautmann, George Lambert (D)
Traylor, W. S. (D)
Uhlman, Wesley Carl (D)
Van Dyk, R. Daniel (D)
Venneberg, Bina Clarice (D)
Vernon, Manfred Claude (D)
Veroske, Frederick Anthony (R)
Wagner, George D, Jr. (D)
Walgren, Gordon Lee (D)
Walk, Ethel Edna (D)

Wanamaker, Floyd Allison (R)
Ware, Waymon Walter (Freedom Socialist Party)
Warnke, Frank J. (D)
Washington, Nat Willis (D)
Weatherly, Roy James (R)
Weber, Mary E. (D)
Whetzel, Jonathan (R)
Wilburn, Wesley Milton (D)
Wilets, Lawrence (D)
Williams, Jeanette K. (D)
Williams, Luke Gladstone, Jr. (R)
Williams, W. Walter (R)
Williams, Walter Baker (R)
Wilson, James (R)
Windsheimer, Walter W. (R)
Witherbee, C. G. (D)
Wolf, Harold E. (R)
Woodall, Perry B. (R)
Yuse, Frank T. (D)
Zepeda, Barbara Joyce (D)
Zimmerman, Harold Samuel (R)

WEST VIRGINIA

Adams, Jack R. (D)
Allen, Charles Edgar (D)
Allen, Elton Ellsworth (R)
Amos, John Ellis (D)
Anderson, W. N, Jr. (D)
Anderson, Wilson (R)
Armistead, Charles S. (D)
Ashley, Gene M. (R)
Auvil, Kenneth (D)
Ayers, J. Douglas (D)
Bailey, Gene W. (D)
Bailey, Harley Evan (D)
Bailey, Robert D. (D)
Bailey, Troy Samuel (D)
Baker, Betty H. (D)
Baker, David Martin (R)
Ballard, Wade Hampton, II (R)
Barker, Jesse S. (D)
Barker, Lawrence (D)
Barnes, Richard Wilson (D)
Barnett, Ralph Edward (D)
Bassett, Clement R. (D)
Beall, Russell G. (D)
Bedell, J(oel) F(erree) (D)
Beneke, George Frank (R)
Berry, Thornton Granville, Jr. (D)
Black, Thomas L. (D)
Blankenship, C. A. (D)
Bloch, Stuart Fulton (R)
Blue, Fred O, II (R)
Board, Pat, Jr. (D)
Bobbitt, John Maxwell (R)
Boiarsky, Ivor F. (D)
Bowers, Theodore Marker (R)
Bowling, John Harrison, Jr. (D)
Bowman, Richard Hatcher (D)
Brenda, Gust Gottlieb, Jr. (D)
Brotherton, W. T, Jr. (D)
Brown, Virginia Mae (D)
Browning, Chauncey H. (D)
Browning, Chauncey H, Jr. (D)
Buck, Forrest M. (R)
Burk, Robert William, Jr. (R)
Burke, Billy Brown (D)
Burke, Jerome A. (D)
Burke, Robert James (D)
Burton, Walter Weldon (D)
Byrd, Robert C. (D)
Cain, James Clement (D)
Calhoun, Harlan Mayberry (D)
Callaghan, David Courtney (D)
Canfield, John A. (D)
Cann, Carmine J. (D)
Carrigan, John E. (R)
Carson, Howard W. (D)
Casey, Mike (D)
Castleberry, Kelly L. (D)
Chapman, Alfred Francis (D)
Chilton, William Edwin, III (D)
Christian, Clarence Carr, Jr. (D)
Christian, Maud Truby (D)
Church, Corbett (D)
Clark, Andrew Lewis (D)
Coghill, Kenneth Lassiter (D)
Companion, James F. (R)
Corcoran, Howard V. (R)
Covey, H. Dale (D)
Crabtree, Paul Leonard (D)
Craig, Louis G. (D)
Crandall, Ethel Leanna (D)
Daugherty, David Black (R)
D'Aurora, Mino Rocco (D)
Davidson, Clayton C. (D)
Davidson, James Treaver, Jr. (D)
Davis, Clifford McKinley (R)
Davis, James Hornor, III (D)
Davisson, Russell Lee (R)
Dawson, Daniel Boone (R)
Dawson, Paul B. (D)
Dean, Betty Manown (D)
Deem, J. Frank (R)
Dickerson, Wilfred Lee (D)
DiTrapano, Rudolph Lidano (D)
Douglas, Guy (D)
Douglass, Gus R. (D)
Dunaway, Charles Clifford (D)
Dusci, Joseph Vincent (D)
Eagle, Harold Bentley (R)
Edgar, Thomas C. (D)
Eigenbrod, Wilbur F. (D)
Ellis, Galen Lane (D)
Elmore, Clarence C. (D)
Evans, William Dent, Jr. (D)
Everly, J. Donald (R)
Fanning, John Patton (D)
Fantasia, Nick (D)
Files, Wallace Lee (R)
Flanagan, Robert Kelleher (D)
Floyd, Noah Eugene (D)
Fox, David, Jr. (D)
Fox, Heisel Marion (R)
Frazer, D. R. (D)
Gainer, Carl E. (D)
Gainer, Denzil Lee (D)
Galbraith, Mrs. Carl (D)
Galperin, Simon Hirsch, Jr. (D)
Ghiz, Luther Harvey (D)
Gibson, Jarrett Dempsey (D)
Gibson, Joseph Richard (D)
Gill, Betty (D)
Given, D. P. (D)
Gladwell, Beatrice Howard (R)
Goe, William Robert (D)
Goodwin, Thomas G. (D)
Gore, Truman Earl (D)
Grewe, Fred A, Jr. (R)
Griffith, George G. (D)
Grimmett, Orville Bailey (R)
Hager, Earl B. (D)
Halbritter, Robert C. (R)
Hall, Thelma Noble (D)
Hamilton, Pat R. (D)
Harman, Charlton Newton (R)
Harman, Robert Dale (R)
Hawse, Thomas Jackson (D)
Haymond, Frank C. (D)
Hechler, Ken (D)
Hedrick, O. G. (D)
Henderson, Charles Robert (R)
Hey, John (D)
Hicks, Paul Edward (D)
Hill, Dennie Lee (D)
Hoard, Clifford Brooks (D)
Hogg, Robert Lynn (R)
Holden, Walter A. (D)
Holliday, Robert Kelvin (D)
Holroyd, Robert E. (D)
Hovermale, Ralph Ben (D)
Howell, Harry U. (D)
Howell, John E. (D)
Hubbard, Chester R. (R)
Huffman, Odell Hampton (D)
Humphreys, Priscilla Faith (R)
Humphreys, Raymond V. (R)
Hylton, Tracy W. (D)
Jackson, Lloyd George (D)
Jamison, John William (D)
Jasper, William N, Jr. (D)
Jennings, Rudolph Dillon (D)
Jennings, William Webb (D)
Jeter, James Clay (R)
Jones, Brereton Chandler (R)
Jones, Cleo Sattis (R)
Jones, James Roydice (R)
Jones, Jeniver James (R)
Jones, Orton Alan (R)
Jones, Ruth Thompson (D)
Kaufman, Paul Joseph (D)
Kee, Elizabeth (D)
Kee, James (D)
Kelly, John Henry (D)
Kessinger, James Edward (D)
Kidd, Paul H. (D)
Kilham, Dixie Donald (D)
Kincaid, Hugh Arthur (D)
Kinder, Lon Clark, Sr. (R)
Knapp, V. K. (R)
Knight, Thomas A. (D)
Knotts, Eugene A. (D)
Kopp, Donald Lee (D)
Kyer, Harry Franklin (R)
Kyle, John William (R)
Lambert, J. Kenton (R)
Lanham, F. Wayne (D)
Lantz, Marie (D)
Leonard, Charles Lee (D)
LePore, Ralph Frank (D)
Little, Henry Martin (D)
Lloyd, O. Winfield (D)
Lohr, Charles E. (D)
Long, Hilda Sheets (D)
Loop, James Whitcomb (D)
Love, Ronald L. (R)
Lowman, R. L. (R)
McCourt, E. Hansford (D)
McCoy, William, Jr. (D)
McDonough, Robert Paul (D)
McGraw, Warren Randolph (D)
McGuire, John Michael (D)
McKown, C. H. (D)
McManus, Lewis Nichols (D)
Madden, John Thomas (D)
Martin, Clarence E, Jr. (D)
Matthews, Virgil E(dison), Jr. (D)
Maxwell, Charles Brentley (R)
Mentz, W. Dewey (D)
Miller, Harlan Walter (D)
Miller, Jack Lee (R)
Mills, Okey Andrew (D)
Mitchell, Bryan Franklin (R)
Mollohan, Robert H. (D)
Montgomery, C. (D)
Moore, Arch A, Jr. (R)
Morasco, Samuel A. (D)
Moreland, William Alexander (D)
Moyers, Paul Shay (D)
Mullins, David Walker (D)
Myers, J. Howard (D)
Myles, Thomas Eberly (D)
Nelson, Robert R. (D)
Nicely, William Perry Amos (R)
Nogay, Walter William (D)
Ours, Larkin B. (R)
Palumbo, Mario Joseph (D)
Parker, O. Roy (D)
Parrish, Everett L. (D)
Paul, Freda Noble (D)
Pauley, Harry R. (D)
Pauley, Jack L. (D)
Payne, Edward M, III (D)
Perry, Roger J. (D)
Peyton, Angus E. (D)
Phillips, Willard L, Jr. (R)
Poffenbarger, John Tallman (R)
Poindexter, James Bernard (D)
Polen, Robert Caylor (R)
Poling, B. Noel (R)
Potter, Thomas Eugene (R)
Protan, John (D)
Pyles, John W. (D)
Queen, Kenneth E. (R)
Ragan, Martin (D)
Randolph, Jennings (D)
Revercomb, Chapman (R)
Revercomb, William C, Jr. (R)
Roberts, James Hazelton (R)
Robertson, C. Donald (D)
Rockefeller, John Davison, IV (D)
Rogers, John Isaac (R)
Rogerson, Roy Harold (R)
Romine, Charles Everett, Jr. (R)
Ross, William Robert (D)
Ruckman, Clarence Augustus (D)
Rutledge, Phyllis J. (D)
Sawyers, Ray Earl (D)
Schiffler, Andrew Charles (R)
Scott, Fred L. (D)
Shaffer, Charles Raymond (R)
Sharpe, William R, Jr. (D)
Shiflet, William Marion (D)
Shott, John Cary (R)
Seabright, John L. (D)
Seibert, George H. (R)
Simpkins, Robert Lee (D)
Slack, John M, Jr. (D)
Slonaker, William B. (D)
Smirl, Jody Guthrie (R)
Smith, Donald Albert (R)
Smith, Donald Edwin (D)
Smith, Hulett Carlson (D)
Smith, W. Murray (R)
Snedegar, Violet Cox (D)
Snyder, Melvin Claud (R)
Sparacino, Anthony Joseph (D)
Stacy, Ted Theodore (D)
Stafford, Jack Dwayne (R)
Staggers, Harley Orrin (D)
Stalnaker, Earl H. (D)
Stamp, Frederick P, Jr. (R)
Stanley, Miles Clark (D)
Steptoe, Robert M. (D)
Stewart, Earl C. (D)
Stewart, Robert F. (D)
Sweeney, Tom Bell, Jr. (R)
Taylor, Frank Lile, Jr. (D)
Taylor, Randall Alford (D)
Thomas, James Kay (D)
Thornhill, Lucille Wooten (D)
Tierney, Laurence E, Jr. (D)
Tokash, George Dermer (D)
Tompos, William (D)
Toney, Adam (D)
Tsapis, Callie (D)
Tsutras, Frank Gus (D)
Underwood, Cecil Harland (R)
Varney, T. I. (D)
Vest, Alton Harry (R)
Vickers, Earl M. (D)
Vincent, L. L. (D)
Wanstreet, Clarence Paul (D)
Watson, James Edwin (D)
Watson, William Edward (D)
Wells, John Marvin (R)
White, H. Laban (D)
White, Lawrence Clermont (R)
Wilson, Harlan Yates, Jr. (R)
Wilson, W. R. (D)
Wilt, Thornton W. (D)
Withrow, Mrs. W. W. (D)
Wolfe, Dallas (R)
Woo, George K. W. (D)
Wooten, Fred G. (D)
Wright, Ira Lloyd (D)
Yoak, Don (D)
Zagula, Edward Andrew (D)
Zakaib, Paul, Jr. (R)

WISCONSIN

Adams, Cameron (R)
Alberts, John Michael (R)
Alfonsi, Paul R. (R)
Allen, John Neville (R)
Altmeyer, Arthur Joseph (D)
Anderson, Gerald K. (R)
Anderson, Norman Carl (D)
Andresen, Karl Adolf (D)
Andringa, Cornelius George (R)
Anich, Thomas Matthew (D)
Aronin, Robert Mitchell (D)
Atkinson, William P. (D)
Azim, James N, Jr. (R)
Baldus, Alvin (D)
Barbee, Lloyd Augustus (D)
Barberg, William Warren (R)
Barland, Thomas Howard (Non-Partisan)
Baumann, Carol Edler (D)
Baumgartner, Stephen Eldon (D)
Becker, Anita M. (R)
Becker, Richard T. (R)
Beijer, Arthur (R)
Beilfuss, Bruce F.
Belting, George Bemis (R)
Benson, Taylor (D)
Berg, Mary Elizabeth DeBardeleben (D)
Berg, Oscar W. (D)
Beyer, William Henry
Bibby, John Franklin (R)
Bice, Raymond C. (R)
Bidwell, Everett V. (R)
Blanchard, Carolyn J. (R)
Blaska, Jerome Lyle (D)
Bleicher, Michael N. (D)
Bock, Gregor J. (R)
Boeckmann, Vernon R. (D)
Boileau, Gerald John (Non-Partisan)
Bolle, Everett E. (D)
Bolton, James Carroll (R)
Boltz, Richard Alan (R)
Bores, Jerome Clarence (D)
Borg, George M. (R)
Bosshard, John (R)
Bosshard, Rylla Jane (R)
Bradley, Gordon Roy (R)
Brotslaw, Irving (D)
Brown, Manny S. (D)
Browne, Jerome Fielding (D)
Brye, David L. (D)
Buchli, Milton S. (D)
Buckley, James P. (D)
Buehler, Paul Richard (D)
Bunn, George (D)
Burg, Mary Lou (D)
Busby, Allen Joseph (R)
Byers, Francis Robert (R)
Byrnes, Daniel Maurice (R)
Byrnes, John William (R)
Carley, David (D)

Carlson, Mary Ellen (R)
Ceci, Louis J. (R)
Chase, Theodore Willis (R)
Cherkasky, William Benjamin (D)
Chilsen, Walter John (R)
Christopherson, Frank W, Jr. (D)
Clemens, Harold W. (R)
Clossey, Christina (D)
Coad, Patricia M. (D)
Coleman, Eva Loretta (R)
Collins, Donald Eugene (D)
Conradt, Ervin W. (R)
Conway, John (R)
Copps, Lyman William (R)
Cormaney, Patricia K. (R)
Cormaney, Theodore Michael (R)
Cutrell, Fred Louis, Sr. (D)
Dahlstrom, Robert Victor (R)
Darr, Richard K. (D)
Davis, Glenn Robert (R)
Dawson, Stephen Vance (R)
Day, Laurence James (D)
Delveaux, Joseph Richard (D)
Dempsey, Chester E. (R)
Devitt, James C. (R)
Dorman, Henry (D)
Dorn, Robert Alan (D)
Doughty, Esther S. (R)
Draheim, William A. (R)
Dueholm, Harvey L. (D)
Duffy, F. Ryan (D)
Duffy, John Patrick (D)
Durning, Lawrence Warren (R)
Eakins, Arnold George (R)
Elfers, Earl H. (D)
Eliason, Al Burton (D)
Federer, Estelle Anastatia (D)
Ferrall, Grace Lois (D)
Ferrall, Russell Brown (D)
Festge, Otto (D)
Fink, Ralph William (R)
Finman, Susan F. (D)
Finman, Ted (D)
Fish, Ody J. (R)
Fitzgerald, Elaine Elizabeth (D)
Flaherty, Daniel T. (D)
Flynn, Gerald Thomas (D)
Foley, John Welden (R)
Fries, David John (Socialist)
Froehlich, Harold Vernon (R)
Fulwiler, Toby Edward (D)
Galazan, Jeanne K. (D)
Garrison, William L. (R)
Gee, Harvey F. (R)
Gefke, Caroline Lawrence (R)
Gehrmann, Bernard Eugene (R)
Gerber, Calvin Otto (D)
Gessert, Harry L. (R)
Gfall, Tom Karl (D)
Gleason, Leonard J. (R)
Gollberg, William Louis (R)
Gower, John Clark (R)
Greco, Angelo F. (D)
Green, Diana Biller (D)
Greenwald, James Lyon (D)
Grewe, Isabelle McNaughton (R)
Gronouski, John Austin (D)
Groshek, Leonard Anthony (D)
Grover, Herbert J.
Grubb, Kenneth Philip
Grunwaldt, David Carl (R)
Guenzl, Herbert Ferdinand (R)
Gundersen, Gunnar Adolf (D)
Guyant, George M. (D)
Haase, Robert Duane (R)
Haberman, Russell L, Jr. (D)
Hanna, Daniel D. (D)
Hansen, Connor Theodore
Hansen, James Magnus (D)
Hansen, William C. (D)
Hanson, Camilla Ruth (D)
Hanson, J. Louis (D)
Hanstedt, Augustus Ernest (R)
Harff, Helen G. (R)
Harff, James Warren (R)
Hartley, Fred D. (R)
Hartman, Roger L. (R)
Hawkes, Elizabeth (D)
Heffernan, Nathan Stewart (D)
Heinzen, Raymond Frank (R)
Held, James Edward (R)
Helgeson, Donald Keith (R)
Hicks, Harley Irving (R)
Hollander, Walter G. (R)
Hoskins, Robert Gerald (D)
Hough, John E. (R)
Howard, Florence C. (R)
Huber, Robert T. (D)
Huettl, Carl W. (R)
Huff, Richard Lee (R)
Huiras, Marvin Henry (D)

Hutchison, Carl Mahlon (R)
Hutnik, Willis J. (R)
Innes, George Barr (R)
Ipsen, Paul Martin (R)
Iverson, Donald L. (D)
Jacobson, Thomas Michael (D)
Jahnke, Franklin M. (R)
Jamison, Charles Hayden (D)
Jasper, Claude J. (R)
Johnson, Lawrence H. (R)
Johnson, Lester Rolland (D)
Johnson, Raymond C. (R)
Johnson, Robert Iver (R)
Johnson, William A. (D)
Jones, Joseph E. (D)
Jones, Lawrence F. (D)
Junghans, Robert William (D)
Jurgella, Richard Edward (D)
Kafka, Lawrence J. (R)
Kaiser, George Chapin (R)
Kastenmeier, Robert William (D)
Kaufman, Eugene S. (D)
Kealy, Robert Louis (D)
Kendziorski, Casimir (D)
Kenyon, Kyle (R)
Keppler, Ernest C. (R)
Kessler, Frederick Philip (D)
Kinnaman, Theodore Dwight (D)
Kleczka, Gerald Daniel (D)
Kloet, Alvin Robert (R)
Knowles, Robert Pierce (R)
Knowles, Warren P. (R)
Kohler, Walter Jodok, Jr. (R)
Kopp, W. Roy (R)
Kordus, Robert Paul (D)
Korpela, Ernest John (D)
Kraft, Ralph Glenn (R)
Kraus, William McCulloch (R)
Krautkramer, Ray George (D)
Krohn, Dorothy J. (R)
Krueger, Carl Edmund (R)
Krueger, Clifford W. (R)
Kunde, Kenneth (D)
LaFave, Reuben (R)
La Follette, Bronson Cutting (D)
Laird, Melvin Robert (R)
Lange, Martha Lund (R)
Laper, Oscar A. (R)
Larsen, John H. (D)
Lecy, Raymond Oscar (R)
LeFevre, Charles Frederic (R)
Leonard, Jerris (R)
Lerman, Philip E. (D)
Leverich, James Earl (R)
Lewis, Dean (D)
Lewison, Bernard (R)
Lipscomb, Mark G, Jr. (D)
Looby, Joseph Lawrence (D)
Lorge, Gerald D. (R)
Lotto, Myron Peter (R)
Lourigan, Joseph (D)
Lucey, Patrick Joseph (D)
Lungren, John Howard (R)
Lynch, Richard J. (D)
McCann, James A. (D)
McClain, Edward Ferrell (D)
McCormick, John E. (D)
McDougal, Milton (R)
McEssy, Earl F. (R)
MacIver, John Kenneth (R)
McKay, J. Curtis (R)
McLaughlin, James Joseph (R)
McParland, Leland S. (D)
McWilliams, John Cecil (D)
Maier, Henry W. (D)
Maiers, Jerald Edward (D)
Manders, Adrian J. (D)
Mares, John Keith (R)
Martin, David O. (R)
Martines, Mary-Alice Wallach (D)
Mathews, Vincent R. (D)
Mato, Louis V. (D)
Meier, Ervin A. (R)
Merkel, Kenneth J. (R)
Mertz, Edward F. (D)
Metzner, Carroll E. (R)
Meunier, Alex J. (R)
Michalski, Clemens Francis (D)
Miglautsch, Thomas John (D)
Miller, Edwina R. (D)
Miller, Lorna Marie (D)
Miller, Midge Leeper (D)
Miller, Robert Charles (R)
Miller, Victor A. (D)
Mittness, Lewis T, Jr. (D)
Molinaro, George (D)
Moser, Fred J. (D)
Mulrooney, Frank Leo (D)
Murch, Bertrand Loud (D)
Murray, Kenneth John (D)
Murray, Richard David (R)

Myhra Norman L. (D)
Nager, Edward (D)
Nash, Philleo (D)
Nelson, Gaylord Anton (D)
Nelson, Thomas Fowler (R)
Nickel, Dieter H. (R)
Nikolay, Frank Lawrence (D)
Nitschke, Elmer Clarence (R)
Nuttelman, Norbert (R)
Obey, David R. (D)
O'Konski, Alvin E. (R)
Olson, Jack R. (R)
O'Malley, David Donald (D)
Otte, Carl (D)
Parker, Nancy Bauhan (R)
Parkin, John Wilbur (R)
Parys, Ronald G. (D)
Pascavis, Glenn J. (D)
Patterson, John Francis (D)
Pauly, Gregory Emil (R)
Peloquin, Bruce Simon (D)
Pemble, Carl August (D)
Perala, Reino A. (D)
Perry, Mildred Mary (D)
Petersen, Lorraine Francis (R)
Peterson, Donald Oliver (D)
Peterson, Francis L. (R)
Pittle, Ronald David (D)
Pommerening, Glen E. (R)
Ponec, Gerald Robert (D)
Popkin, Samuel Lewis (D)
Potochnik, Stanley (D)
Potter, John Melvin (R)
Powers, Kieran Francis (R)
Proxmire, William (D)
Quinn, Jerome F. (R)
Quist, Kenneth Eugene (D)
Race, Howard Everett (R)
Race, John Abner (D)
Radcliffe, John (D)
Rasmusen, Holger B. (R)
Reuss, Henry S. (D)
Reynolds, John W. (D)
Reynolds, Robert Leonard, Jr. (D)
Rice, Robert Clifford (R)
Rice, William Gorham (D)
Riehle, Ben A. (D)
Riemer, Neal (D)
Rietz, Ken (R)
Risser, Andrew Warner (D)
Risser, Fred A. (D)
Robillard, Herbert Bernard (D)
Robinson, Donita Gail (R)
Rogers, William Joseph (D)
Romell, Louis C. (R)
Root, Harmer F. (R)
Rose, Clinton Ellsworth (D)
Roseleip, Gordon W. (R)
Rothwell, Angus Bernard
Sanasarian, Harout O. (D)
Schadeberg, Henry Carl (R)
Schaeffer, Frank E, Jr. (D)
Schaus, Thomas Martin (D)
Schilffarth, Richard Allen (R)
Schmidt, Robert (D)
Schmitt, John William (D)
Schneeberg, Ervin F. (R)
Schneider, Milton Edward (D)
Schowalter, Herbert Joseph (R)
Schreiber, Martin James (D)
Schroeder, Frederick Carl (R)
Schuck, Jarold Raymond (R)
Schuele, Wilfred (D)
Schultz, Waldemar Herbert (D)
Schwefel, William S. (R)
Seer, Edna Eleanor (D)
Sensenbrenner, Frank James, Jr. (R)
Serwer, Arnold (D)
Shabaz, John C. (R)
Shafer, Robert LeRoy (R)
Shaw, Robert Ernest (R)
Shipman, Gordon (D)
Shurbert, Floyd E. (R)
Sicula, Paul Edward (D)
Sigmund, Helen Nicolai (D)
Sindelar, Charles (D)
Smail, John Richard Wharton (D)
Smith, Charles F, Jr. (R)
Smith, Virgil Walter (D)
Soik, Nile Warren (R)
Sorrels, Cyril Pershing (R)
Spielman, Alois B. (R)
Spitzer, Robert R. (R)
Stalbaum, Lynn E. (D)
Stalbaum, Merrill (R)
Stauffacher, Madeline Jeanne (R)
Stauffer, Robert Edward (R)
Staum, Robert Marion (R)
Stearn, Sue Smith (R)
Steiger, William Albert (R)

Steinglass, Steven Henry (D)
Steinhilber, Jack Daniel (R)
Stevenson, Leslie R. (D)
Stevenson, William Henry (R)
Stock, Sherman Edward (D)
Stout, Carmen Lee (D)
Struebing, Wilmer Henry (R)
Stubenvoll, Kurt Hugo (R)
Swan, James D. (R)
Swed, Jeanette (D)
Sweda, Joseph (D)
Sweet, Lowell Elwin (R)
Sykes, James Thurman (D)
Sykes, Jay Gilbert (D)
Tadych, Albert R. (D)
Tamms, Erwin George (R)
Tanck, Marlin Lavern (D)
Tarr, Curtis William (R)
Tatley, Herbert Melvin (R)
Taylor, Don Lee (R)
Terry, Walter E. (R)
Tewes, Donald E. (R)
Thill, Lewis D. (R)
Thompson, Carl William (D)
Thompson, George (R)
Thompson, Tommy George (R)
Thomson, Vernon Wallace (R)
Thoresen, Walter Paul (D)
Tobiasz, Raymond Joseph (D)
Uehling, Robert O. (R)
Vanderperren, Cletus J. (D)
Van Hollen, John Carter (R)
Van Pelt, William K. (R)
Wackett, Byron F. (R)
Wallace, Carl S. (R)
Warren, Earl W. (D)
Warren, Robert Willis (R)
Warshafsky, Ted M. (D)
Wartinbee, D. Russell (R)
Wasielewski, Thaddeus Francis (D)
Weisensel, Russel R. (R)
Wetlaufer, Bruce Alvah (R)
Whittow, Wayne F. (D)
Wiesner, Susan Ann (D)
Wigderson, Maurice Brayton (R)
Wilbur, George Craig (D)
Wilcox, Jon Paul (R)
Wimmer, James William, Jr. (D)
Woodside, Howard Bush (R)
York, Stanley (R)
Zablocki, Clement John (D)
Zaborski, Richard J. (D)
Zien, Burt (D)
Zimmerman, Robert C. (R)

WYOMING

Adams, Robert (D)
Adams, Robert L. (D)
Acklin, Joseph Charles (D)
Anselmi, Donald Ray (D)
Anselmi, Rudolph Theodore (D)
Bagley, William D. (D)
Baldwin, Douglas Parks (R)
Barker, Harry C, Jr. (R)
Barrett, Frank A. (R)
Barrett, James E. (R)
Boal, LaVerne C. (R)
Bondi, Gene L. (D)
Boschetto, Louis (D)
Boyhan, Cynthia Anne (D)
Boyle, June (D)
Breece, Edward John (R)
Brimmer, Clarence Addison, Jr. (R)
Brown, Byron Terrell (D)
Brunk, James Don (R)
Buck, Arthur L. (D)
Budd, Joseph Lincoln (R)
Budd, William H, Jr. (R)
Bullock, Bob R. (D)
Bunnell, Orval E. (R)
Burke, Howard L. (D)
Burke, M. Joseph (R)
Burwell, Lina (D)
Butterfield, Alton (D)
Campbell, Allen E. (R)
Carroll, Howard Thomas (D)
Carroll, Thomas Jay (D)
Christensen, Earl (R)
Christian, Alvin E, Jr. (D)
Cole, Barney (D)
Cook, K. Richard (D)
Copenhaver, Everett Taylor (R)
Corbitt, Willa Wales (D)
Craft, William F. (R)
Curry, William Seeright (R)
Daily, O. R. (D)
Darrow, Robert O. (R)
Davis, C. H. (R)

Davis, Percy Terry (R)
Donley, Russ (R)
Economy, George P. (D)
Emrich, Marvin Earl (R)
Engen, Gerald B(ob) (R)
Escobedo, Joseph Herman (D)
Fagan, James W. (D)
Fausset, H. W. (D)
Field, Peter (D)
Flitner, Howard E. (R)
Forsgren, Richard Arvil (D)
Frisby, Robert W. (R)
Galicich, Marguerite Parker (R)
Geraud, Lawrence J. (R)
Gosman, Robert F. (R)
Graham, Alfred T. (D)
Greene, R. L. (R)
Gurney, Harry C, Jr. (R)
Hall, William Clarence (D)
Halseth, Elmer Johann (D)
Hansen, Clifford Peter (R)
Harrison, William Henry (R)
Hathaway, Stanley K. (R)
Hellbaum, Harold (R)
Herschler, Ed (D)
Hickey, John Joseph (D)
Hinkle, Joe Thomas (D)
Hooley, Quentin (R)
Hubbard, Donald (D)
Hufsmith, George W. (R)
Hutchinson, Esther Mau (R)
Irwin, Charles G. (R)
James, Verda I. (R)
Jensen, Leona Schroeder (R)
Jewett, Donald W. (R)
Johns, Merrill Blaine, Jr. (R)
Johnson, Robert Henry (D)
Jones, Richard R. (R)
Kaan, Nicolaas, Jr. (D)
Keith, Leon (R)
Kendig, A. Edward (D)
Kennedy, David Boyd (R)
Kidd, D. Thomas (R)
Kilfoy, Fred F. (D)
Kinnaman, Elmer D. (D)
Knobel, Arthur Robert (R)
Lawler, Violet M. (D)
Lee, John M. (R)
Lee, Theodore Robert (R)
Leimback, Harry Edward (D)
Leon, Claire Jensen (D)
Leon, Maurice (D)
Lonabaugh, E. E. (R)
Lubnau, Thomas E. (R)
McFadden, Wilmot Curnow (D)
McGee, Gale William (D)
McIlvain, Bill D. (R)
McIntyre, John Joseph (D)
McMaster, Andrew (R)
McMillan, Harry (R)
Macy, Richard James (D)
Madsen, Peter Edgar (R)
Majhanovich, Steve (D)
Manatos, Mike N. (D)
Mankus, Louis A. (D)
Marty, Lawrence A. (R)
Masters, Leonard E. (R)
Meenan, Patrick Henry (R)
Megeath, William A. (D)
Meier, Harold Ellswith (R)
Mickelson, Gordon Max (R)
Miller, Fremont W. (R)
Miller, Mayne Williams (D)
Mitchell, Minnie Alice (R)
Mockler, Franklin Henry (R)
Morrison, C. M. (D)
Morrison, Donald Edgar (R)
Morton, Warren Allen (R)
Mueller, Jack Frederick (R)
Murphy, Robert J. (D)
Murray, William McGarry (R)
Myers, J. W. (D)
Myers, Ward G. (R)
Nation, Bill (D)
Nicholas, W. J. (R)
Norris, William A, Jr. (D)
Northrup, L. Donald (R)
Otto, Carl J. (D)
Page, Leonard A, Jr. (R)
Parson, Elmer S, Jr. (R)
Patrick, Mary Veronica (D)
Patton, John W. (R)
Pease, Floyd H. (R)
Percival, Elizabeth Thompson (R)
Raper, John Frederick, Jr. (Non-Partisan)
Rector, William Gordon (D)
Reynolds, Adrian Wall (D)
Rhoads, Willard C. (D)
Robinson, Carl (D)
Rogers, Glenn K. (D)
Roncalio, Teno (D)
Rooney, John Joseph (D)
Rounds, Edwin Frederick (R)
Sadler, Richard Sherman (D)
Schaefer, Harry H. (D)
Schoeck, (Viola) Jean (D)
Schroeder, Martha K. (D)
Schwartz, Harry F. (D)
Scully, Leo P. (D)
Scully, Pat (D)
Searl, Tom (R)
Sidi, Jacques Albert (R)
Simons, John C. (D)
Simpson, Alan K. (R)
Simpson, Milward L. (R)
Sims, P. D. (D)
Smith, Christy Knut (R)
Smith, Clark A. (D)
Smith, Nels Jensen (R)
Smyth, John Richard (D)
Stack, Gerald Alphonsus (D)
Stacy, Estelle Mabry (R)
Stewart, Joe William (D)
Stierwalt, Lotus H. (R)
Stroock, Thomas F. (R)
Svilar, Daniel P. (D)
Swanton, William Francis (R)
Thatch, William R. (D)
Thompson, James L. (R)
Thomson, Thyra Godfrey (R)
Thorson, Harry T. (R)
Tobin, Dick (R)
Trowbridge, Elton (D)
Updike, Robert Elmer (R)
Urbigkit, Walter C, Jr. (D)
Vanderpoel, Wayne Gaylord (R)
Van Mark, Jack (R)
Van Velzor, James Daniel (R)
Wallop, Malcolm (R)
Ward, Gordon A. (D)
Wataha, Paul John (D)
Watson, Frank Rundell (R)
Watt, James Gaius (R)
Whitehead, Edwin H. (D)
Wilkins, Edness Kimball (D)
Williams, Jennie Winona (R)
Willox, James A. (R)
Wold, John S. (R)
Yonkee, Lawrence A. (R)
Youtz, Hewitt G. (R)
ZumBrunnen, Leslie Lee (R)

AMERICAN SAMOA

Amosa, Solofua
Eseroma, Ligoligo Kuresa (R)
Faamausili, Suiaunoa Talo (R)
Fia, Tofu T. (Am. Samoa Party)
Galea'i, Talimanu O. T. (D)
Meredith, Manutafea Edward (R)
Tuia, Muagututi'a Fa'atamala (Am. Samoa Party)
Tunoa, Tagoa'i Matagiese (D)
Valasi, John Siufaga

CANAL ZONE

Duisberg, Luella Annabelle (D)
Harris, Virginia Mary (D)
Joyce, Albert John, Jr. (D)
Koster, Richard M. (D)
Markun, Patricia Maloney (D)
Myer, Calvin Harley (D)
Young, GeDelle Brabham (D)

GUAM

Acfalle, Jose Manalisay (D)
Alger, James Pace (D)
Arriola, Joaquin Camacho (D)
Bordallo, Madeleine Mary (D)
Bordallo, Richard Jerome (D)
Camacho, Carlos Garcia (R)
Delfin, Oscar Liboon (D)
Flores, Alfred San Nicolas (D)
Guerrero, Manuel Flores Leon (D)
Larson, Margaret Ann (R)
Lujan, Francisco Guerrero (D)
Okiyama, Jesus Carbullido (D)
Paulino, Leonardo San Nicolas (D)
Perez, Joaquin Arriola (D)
Ramirez, Florencio Torres (D)
Sablan, James Taitano (D)
Salas, G. Ricardo (R)
Santos, Carlos Mesa (D)
Sgambelluri, Ralph Camacho (D)
Taitano, Richard Flores (D)
Terlaje, Edward Salas (D)
Torres, Jesus U. (D)
Won Pat, Antonio Borja (D)

MARIANA ISLANDS

Johnston, Edward Elliott (R)

PUERTO RICO

Alvarado, Arcilio (D)
Barbosa, Pedro Juan (New Progressive, P. R.)
Batlle, Josefina Ojeda (D)
Belaval Martinez, Eugenio S. (New Progressive, P. R.)
Bird, Jorge (Popular Dem, P.R.)
Bosco, Ruben Otero (R)
Capella, Antonio (New Progressive, P.R.)
Carrasguillo, Quiñones Ernesto (D)
Catalá, Luis Enrique (D)
Chardon, Fernando (New Progressive, P.R.)
Colberg, Severo E. (D)
Colón, Luis Alfredo (D)
Colon, Ramiro Luis (R)
Cordova, Jorge Luis (New Progressive, P.R.)
Cruz, Jimenez, Olga (Popular Dem, P.R.)
Dapena-Vidal, Ramon Enrique (P.R. Union Party)
de Gautier, Felisa Rincon (D)
Durham, Richard C. (D)
Ferre, Luis A. (R)
Garcia-Mendez, Miguel A. (R)
Garcia-Tanon, Jose (D)
Gautier, Augusto R. (D)
Gerena, Victor M. (R)
Hernandez, Edma Santiago de (Popular Dem, P.R.)
Hernandez, Sanchez Jesus Manuel (New Progressive, P.R.)
Hernandez, Colon, Miguel (Popular Dem, P.R.)
Hernandez-Colon, Rafael (Popular Dem, P.R.)
Ibanez, Francisco Barreras (R)
Julia, Gilda (R)
Lastra-Gonzalez, Carlos Juan
Lopez, Hilton L. (R)
Lopez, Soto Danny (New Progressive, P.R.)
Marcano, Hipolito (Popular Dem, P.R.)
Martinez Colon, Hector M. (New Progressive, P.R.)
Mendez, Justo A. (New Progressive, P.R.)
Mendez, Lionel Fernandez (D)
Menendez-Monroig, Jose M. (New Progressive, P.R.)
Miranda Jimenez, Maximino (New Progressive, P.R.)
Munoz-Marin, Luis (Popular D)
Muñoz, Padin Rene (Popular Dem, P.R.)
Munoz-Rivera, Luis (D)
Ortiz Stella, Cruz (Popular Dem, P.R.)
Ortiz-Toro, Arturo (R)
Padilla, Hernan (New Progressive, P.R.)
Picó, Rafael (D)
Pieras, Jaime, Jr. (R)
Pinero, Emilio R. (D)
Pizarro, Federico (Popular Dem, P.R.)
Polanco-Abreu, Santiago (D)
Pons, Victor Manuel, Jr. (Popular Dem, P.R.)
Quiñones, Samuel R. (D)
Ramos Yordan, Luis Ernesto (Popular Dem, P.R.)
Roldan, Israel Blas (R)
Sagardia Sanchez, Antonio (Popular Dem, P.R.)
Sanchez-Vilella, Roberto (People's Party, P.R.)
Serrano, Francisco Adrover (R)
Silva, Santiago Iglesias (R)
Soler-Favale, Santiago C. (New Progressive, P.R.)
Torres Santiago, Carlos Luis (Popular Dem, P.R.)
Trigo, Dennis (New Progressive, P.R.)
Urbina Urbina, David (New Progressive, P.R.)
Velázquez, Luis Magin (D)
Velez Ithier, Manuel (Popular Dem, P.R.)
Viera-Martinez, Angel (New Progressive, P.R.)
Virella, Jose Horacio Cora (R)

VIRGIN ISLANDS

Ambrose, Daniel Webster (D)
Anduze, Roy A. (D)
Brown, Omar (R)
Clark, Meredith P. (R)
Clark, Philip Cannady (R)
de Chabert, Ansetta (D)
Evans, Melvin H. (R)
Garcia, Santiago (D)
Golden, Arnold Mortimer (D)
Gottlieb, Roy A. (D)
Hamilton, David McGregor (D)
Hestres, Louis Phillippe (D)
Maduro, John Lawrence (D)
Moorehead, Theovald Eric (D)
Paiewonsky, Ralph (D)
Plantz, Donald James (R)
Puritz, Alfred David (D)
Rowe, Hortense C. Milligan (R)
Shaubah, Jose M. (R)
Thurland, Genevieve I. (D)
Williams, Bettie McLean Zacher (R)
Williams, Erle Rupert (R)
Williams, Patrick Nehemiah (D)
Wolfrey, Bernice (R)